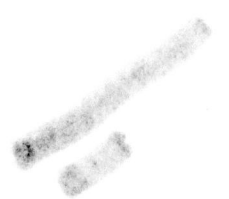

AN EXHAUSTIVE

CONCORDANCE

OF

THE MEANING

OF

QUR'AN

BASED UPON THE TRANSLATION OF ABDULLAH YUSUF ALI

COMPILED BY:
JOHN (YAHYA) CASON
1410-1415 A.H. ~ 1989-1994 C.E.

COMPUTER TECHNICAL SUPPORT BY:
KAMEL EL-FADL
1416-1418 A.H. ~ 1996-1997 C.E.

EDITED BY:
FREDRICK (FAREED) WALKER
1416-1421 A.H. ~ 1996-2000 C.E.

AN EXHAUSTIVE

CONCORDANCE

OF

THE MEANING

OF

QUR'AN

BASED UPON THE
TRANSLATION OF
ABDULLAH YUSUF ALI

COMPILED BY
JOHN (YAHYA) CASON
1410-1415 A.H. — 1989-1994 C.E.

COMPUTER TECHNICAL SUPPORT BY:
KAMEL EL-BADI
1416-1418 A.H. — 1996-1997 C.E.

EDITED BY:
FREDERICK (ALFRED) WALKER
1416-1421 A.H. — 1996-2000 C.E.

ACKNOWLEDGMENTS

I thank Allah (ﷻ) for all the assistance and support from the brothers and sisters in Islam who helped me through various means to produce this work. May Allah (ﷻ) reward them with the best of this life and the next, and may He grant them a place close to Him.

- Brother Mu'tazz Mujaahid Mutasir editing, and review.
- Brother Tarif Abdullah editing, and review.
- Brother Frederick "Fareed" Walker for typing, review, and consultation.
- Brother Kamel Ali El-Fadl for technical support, research, review, editing, typesetting, computer compilation, and consultation.
- Brother Muhammad A. Al-Akkas of I.C.C. for consultation and financial support.
- My wife Viola for typing, review, perseverance, and encouragement.
- My wife Intisar, (May Allah have Mercy on her) for typing, review, perseverance, and encouragement.

May Allah (ﷻ) increase these people in faith and make them among the best of His creation.

ISBN: 0-9700146-1-9
Library of Congress Card Number: 00-191629

PUBLISHER'S PREFACE

We thank Allah for allowing us the opportunity to be the publishers of this book. We believe it is a long overdue research component to the many millions of English speaking Muslims who rely on English translations of the Qur'an to enhance their understanding of Islam.

Although, Arabic is the original language of the Holy Qur'an, and best to be used for correct understanding, there is no dispute about the need to translate the meaning of the Holy Qur'an into many different languages.

English is the most spoken language of our time, it is not only the first language of many converts, it is also the most popular second language among most immigrant Muslims and the first language to their children who have been born, raised, and educated in the west.

Taking into consideration the above reasons, the existence of an exhaustive concordance is indispensable to the millions of English readers of the Qur'an in facilitating quick and easy access to its translated verses.

In this modern age where accessibility to information has become an indispensable phenomena, an English concordance of the translation of the meaning of the Holy Qur'an is a monumental step forward for the English readers of the Holy Qur'an.

The availability of an English concordance is not only a pressing need for all English speaking Muslims in the world, it is also an essential component for all reputable libraries, universities, colleges, and aid to professors of comparative religions, students of divinity, Muslim families and researchers.

The Islamic African Relief Agency (IARA) Eastern Regional Office is pleased to introduce this Exhaustive Concordance of the Yusef Ali translation of the meaning of the Holy Qur'an, to English speaking Muslims all over the world as a humble contribution in serving the deen of Allah ﷻ and promoting the Da'wah of Islam amongst English speaking people.

We pray that Allah will accept our efforts and make it a source of continuing benefit to all who have contributed to its development, production, and maintenance. May Allah reward us with good in this life as well as the next.

Seeking Allah's Mercy,
Mohamad Adam El-Sheikh, Ph.D.
Eastern Regional Director
IARA-USA

IN THE NAME OF ALLAH
THE MOST GRACIOUS, THE MOST MERCIFUL

PREFACE

All praise is due to Allah, the Lord of all the worlds, We praise Him, we seek His assistance and ask His forgiveness. We seek refuge in Allah from the evils of our selves and from our bad actions. Whomever Allah (ﷻ) guides, there is no misguidance for him and whomever Allah does not guide, there is no guidance for him. I testify that there is no god except Allah (ﷻ) alone, that He is unique and without any partners. I also testify that Muhammad (ﷺ) (the son of Abdullah) is His servant and His final Messenger. Allah bless him and give him peace, with his family and Companions.

May Allah (ﷻ) purify our hearts and make us of those who love what He loves and hate what He hates. May He make us love his prophet Muhammad (ﷺ) more than our own souls. And may He make us of those who adhere to the *Sunnah* (سُنَّة) of His last prophet and make us leaders among those who fear him.

It is a concordance that categorizes every word of the Yusuf Ali Translation. No words have been omitted. We hope that it will help those who use this translation to make easier reference.

We ask Allah to bless this work and make it useful to those who are in need of it. We ask for Allah's forgiveness and exemption from the Hell-Fire, and entrance into His Paradise.

John Yahya Cason

We invite your comments.

Islamic Education and Community Development Foundation of Baltimore, Maryland Inc.
3723 Gwynn Oak ave. Baltimore, Maryland 21207
atten: John Yahya Cason

Concordance
Reference

Concordance
Reference

Concordance Reference

Surat	No.	Ayat from ~ to	Place of Revelation
Al-Fatiha	001	001 ~ 007	Makkan
Al-Baqarah	002	000 ~ 286	Madinah
Al-i-'Imran	003	000 ~ 200	Madinah
An-Nisaa	004	000 ~ 176	Madinah
Al-Maidah	005	000 ~ 120	Madinah
Al-An'am	006	000 ~ 165	Makkan
Al-A'raf	007	000 ~ 206	Makkan
Al-Anfal	008	000 ~ 075	Madinah
At-Tauba	009	001 ~ 129	Madinah
Yunus	010	000 ~ 109	Makkan
Hud	011	000 ~ 123	Makkan
Yusuf	012	000 ~ 108	Makkan
Ar-Ra'd	013	000 ~ 043	Madinah
Ibrahim	014	000 ~ 052	Makkan
Al-Hijr	015	000 ~ 099	Makkan
An-Nahl	016	000 ~ 128	Makkan
Al-Israa	017	000 ~ 111	Makkan
Al-Kahf	018	000 ~ 110	Makkan
Maryam	019	000 ~ 098	Makkan
Ta-Ha	020	000 ~ 135	Makkan
Al-Anbiyaa	021	000 ~ 112	Makkan
Al-Hajj	022	000 ~ 078	Madinah
Al-Muminun	023	000 ~ 118	Makkan
An-Nur	024	000 ~ 064	Madinah
Al-Furqan	025	000 ~ 077	Makkan
Ash-Shu'araa	026	000 ~ 227	Makkan
An-Naml	027	000 ~ 093	Makkan
Al-Qasas	028	000 ~ 088	Makkan
Al-'Ankabut	029	000 ~ 069	Makkan
Ar-Rum	030	000 ~ 060	Makkan
Luqman	031	000 ~ 034	Makkan
As-Sajda	032	000 ~ 030	Makkan
Al-Ahzab	033	000 ~ 073	Madinah
Saba	034	000 ~ 054	Makkan
Fatir	035	000 ~ 045	Makkan
Ya-Sin	036	000 ~ 083	Makkan
As-Saffat	037	000 ~ 182	Makkan
Sad	038	000 ~ 088	Makkan

Concordance Reference

Surat	No.	Ayat from ~ to	Place of Revelation
Az-Zumar	039	000 ~ 075	Makkan
Gafir	040	000 ~ 085	Makkan
Fussilat	041	000 ~ 054	Makkan
Ash-Shura	042	000 ~ 053	Makkan
Az-Zukhruf	043	000 ~ 089	Makkan
Ad-Dukhan	044	000 ~ 059	Makkan
Al-Jathiya	045	000 ~ 037	Makkan
Al-Ahqaf	046	000 ~ 035	Makkan
Muhammad	047	000 ~ 038	Madinah
Al-Fat-h	048	000 ~ 029	Madinah
Al-Hujurat	049	000 ~ 018	Madinah
Qaf	050	000 ~ 045	Makkan
Az-Zariyat	051	000 ~ 060	Makkan
At-Tur	052	000 ~ 049	Makkan
An-Najm	053	000 ~ 062	Makkan
Al-Qamar	054	000 ~ 055	Makkan
Ar-Rahman	055	000 ~ 078	Madinah
Al-Waqi'a	056	000 ~ 096	Makkan
Al-Hadid	057	000 ~ 029	Madinah
Al-Mujadila	058	000 ~ 022	Madinah
Al-Hashr	059	000 ~ 024	Madinah
Al-Mumtahana	060	000 ~ 013	Madinah
As-Saff	061	000 ~ 014	Madinah
Al-Jumu'a	062	000 ~ 011	Madinah
Al-Munafiqun	063	000 ~ 011	Madinah
At-Tagabun	064	000 ~ 018	Madinah
At-Talaq	065	000 ~ 012	Madinah
At-Tahrim	066	000 ~ 012	Madinah
Al-Mulk	067	000 ~ 030	Makkan
Al-Qalam	068	000 ~ 052	Makkan
Al-Haqqa	069	000 ~ 052	Makkan
Al-Ma'arij	070	000 ~ 044	Makkan
Nuh	071	000 ~ 028	Makkan
Al-Jinn	072	000 ~ 028	Makkan
Al-Muzzammil	073	000 ~ 020	Makkan
Al-Muddaththir	074	000 ~ 056	Makkan
Al-Qiyamat	075	000 ~ 040	Makkan
Al-Insan	076	000 ~ 031	Madinah

Concordance Reference

Surat	No.	Ayat from ~ to	Place of Revelation
Al-Mursalat	077	000 ~ 050	Makkan
An-Nabaa	078	000 ~ 040	Makkan
An-Nazi'at	079	000 ~ 046	Makkan
'Abasa	080	000 ~ 042	Makkan
At-Takwir	081	000 ~ 029	Makkan
Al-Infitar	082	000 ~ 019	Makkan
Al-Mutaffifeen	083	000 ~ 036	Makkan
Al-Inshiqaq	084	000 ~ 025	Makkan
Al-Buruj	085	000 ~ 022	Makkan
At-Tariq	086	000 ~ 017	Makkan
Al-A'la	087	000 ~ 019	Makkan
Al-Gashiya	088	000 ~ 026	Makkan
Al-Fajr	089	000 ~ 030	Makkan
Al-Balad	090	000 ~ 020	Makkan
Ash-Shams	091	000 ~ 015	Makkan
Al-Lail	092	000 ~ 021	Makkan
Adh-Dhuha	093	000 ~ 011	Makkan
Al-Sharh	094	000 ~ 008	Makkan
At-Tin	095	000 ~ 008	Makkan
Al-'Alaq	096	000 ~ 019	Makkan
Al-Qadr	097	000 ~ 005	Makkan
Al-Baiyina	098	000 ~ 008	Madinah
Al-Zalzalah	099	000 ~ 008	Madinah
Al-'Adiyat	100	000 ~ 011	Makkan
Al-Qari'a	101	000 ~ 011	Makkan
At-Takathur	102	000 ~ 008	Makkan
Al-'Asr	103	000 ~ 003	Makkan
Al-Humaza	104	000 ~ 008	Makkan
Al-Fil	105	000 ~ 005	Makkan
Quraish	106	000 ~ 004	Makkan
Al-Ma'un	107	000 ~ 007	Makkan
Al-Kauthar	108	000 ~ 003	Makkan
Al-Kafirun	109	000 ~ 006	Makkan
Al-Nasr	110	000 ~ 003	Makkan
Al-Masad	111	000 ~ 005	Makkan
Al-Ikhlas	112	000 ~ 004	Makkan
Al-Falaq	113	000 ~ 005	Makkan
Al-Nas	114	000 ~ 006	Makkan

Concordance

Concordance

A (See Appendix)

A.L.M.
002:001 A.L.M.
003:001 A.L.M.
029:001 A.L.M.
030:001 A.L.M.
031:001 A.L.M.
032:001 A.L.M.

A.L.M.R.
013:001 A.L.M.R. These are the Verses of the

A.L.R.
010:001 A.L.R. These are the Ayats
011:001 A.L.R. (This is) a Book,
012:001 A.L.R. These are the Verses of the
014:001 A.L.R. A Book which We have revealed
015:001 A.L.R. These are the Ayats

AARON
002:248 the family of Moses and the family of **Aaron**,
004:163 to Jesus, Job, Jonah, **Aaron**, and Solomon, and to
006:084 Solomon, Jod, Joseph, Moses, and **Aaron**: thus do
007:122 "The Lord of Moses and **Aaron**."
007:142 his brother **Aaron** (before he went up): "Act for me
007:150 **Aaron** said: "Son of my mother! The people
010:075 Moses and **Aaron** to Pharaoh and his
010:089 (O Moses and **Aaron**)! So stand ye straight, and
019:028 "O sister of **Aaron**! thy father was not a man
019:053 his brother **Aaron**, (also) a prophet.
020:030 "**Aaron**, my brother;
020:045 They (Moses and **Aaron**) said: "Our Lord!
020:070 "We believe in the Lord of **Aaron** and Moses."
020:090 **Aaron** had already, before this said to them:
020:092 (Moses) said: "O **Aaron**! what kept thee back,
020:094 (**Aaron**) replied: "O son of my mother! Seize (me)
021:048 and **Aaron** the Criterion (for judgement). And a
023:045 his brother **Aaron**, with Our Signs and authority
025:035 his brother **Aaron** with him as Minister;
026:013 so send unto **Aaron**.
026:048 "The Lord of Moses and **Aaron**."
028:034 "And my brother **Aaron**-he is more
037:114 Our favour on Moses and **Aaron**,
037:120 "Peace and salutation to Moses and **Aaron**!"

ABANDON
007:127 and to **abandon** thee and thy gods?" He said;
071:023 '**Abandon** not your gods: **abandon** neither Wadd nor

ABANDONED
002:243 thy vision to those who **abandoned** their homes,
012:037 (I assure you) **abandoned** the ways of a people

ABASE
095:005 Then do We **abase** him (to be) the lowest of the low,

ABASED
040:060 to serve Me will surely enter Hell **abased**."

ABASEMENT
010:026 No darkness nor **abasement** shall cover

ABATED
011:044 And the water **abated**, and

ABATEMENT
011:109 their portion without (the least) **abatement**.
017:097 every time it shows **abatement**, We shall

ABHOR
049:012 Nay, ye would **abhor** it... But fear

ABIDE
002:025 and they **abide** therein (for ever).
002:039 they shall **abide** therein."
002:081 therein shall they **abide** (for ever).
002:082 therein shall they **abide** (for ever).
002:162 They will **abide** therein:
002:217 of the Fire and will **abide** therein.
002:275 they will **abide** therein (for ever).
004:013 to **abide** therein (for ever) and that
004:014 will be admitted to a Fire, to **abide** therein:
004:093 to **abide** therein (for ever): and
005:080 and in torment will they **abide**.

ABIDE (continued)
007:143 if it **abide** in its place, then shalt
010:026 they will **abide** therein (for aye)!
010:027 they will **abide** therein (for aye)!
014:014 to **abide** in the land, and succeed them.
020:101 They will **abide** in this (state): and grievous
021:099 But each one will **abide** therein.
023:103 their souls; in Hell will they **abide**.
043:071 and ye shall **abide** therein (for aye).
043:077 "Nay, but ye shall **abide**!"
055:027 But will **abide** (for ever) the Face of thy Lord,-

ABIDES
039:040 and on whom descends a Chastisement that **abides**."

ABIDING
020:073 compel us: for Allah is Best and Most **Abiding**."
054:038 an **abiding** Chastisement seized them:

ABJECT
042:045 to the (Penalty), **abject** in humbleness (and)

ABLE
002:264 They will be **able** to do nothing
004:003 be **able** to deal justly with the orphans,
004:003 be **able** to deal justly (with them),
004:129 Ye are never **able** to do justice between wives
005:003 unless ye are **able** to slaughter it (in due form);
005:031 "Was I not even **able** to be as this raven, and to
006:035 yet if thou wert **able** to seek a tunnel
011:033 ye will not be **able** to frustrate it!
014:034 never will ye be **able** to number them. Verily,
016:018 of Allah, never would ye be **able** to number them:
016:061 they would not be **able** to delay (the punishment)
016:061 just as they would not be **able** to anticipate
018:041 wilt never be **able** to find it."
018:043 against Allah, nor was he **able** to deliver himself.
018:067 be **able** to have patience with me!
021:039 (the time) when they will not be **able** to ward
022:040 (**Able** to enforce His Will).
023:018 and We certainly are **able** to drain
023:095 And We are certainly **able** to show thee
025:009 and never a way will they be **able** to find!
027:037 as they will never be **able** to meet: we shall
028:035 so they shall not be **able** to touch you: with Our
028:056 It is true thou wilt not be **able** to guide
028:066 will not be **able** (even) to question each other.
029:022 be **able** (fleeing) to frustrate (His Plan),
029:048 nor art thou (**able**) to transcribe it with

ABLE (continued)

029:048 And thou wast not (**able**) to recite a Book
033:060 be **able** to stay in it as thy neighbors for any
036:081 and the earth **able** to create the like thereof?"-
043:003 that ye may be **able** to understand.
043:013 for we could never be **able** to do it.
046:033 is **able** to give life to the dead? Yea, verily
055:033 authority shall ye be **able** to pass!
068:042 to prostrate, but they shall not be **able**,-
075:004 Nay, We are **able** to put together in perfect order
077:035 shall not be **able** to speak,
082:016 And they will not be **able** to keep away therefrom.
086:008 Surely (Allah) **able** to bring him back (to life)!

ABODE

003:151 their **abode** will be the Fire:
003:162 and whose **abode** is in Hell? A woeful refuse!
003:197 their Ultimate **abode** is Hell: what an evil
004:097 Such men will find their **abode** in Hell.
005:072 and the Fire will be his **abode**.
008:016 and his **abode** is Hell, an evil refuse (indeed)!
009:073 Their **abode** is hell, an evil refuge indeed.
010:008 Their **abode** is the Fire, because of
013:018 be terrible: their **abode** will be Hell,-what a
015:043 the promised **abode** for them all!
016:029 is the **abode** of the arrogant."
017:097 their **abode** will be Hell: every time
024:057 can escape in the earth their **abode** is the Fire,-
025:015 a reward as well as a final **abode**.
025:024 be well, that Day, in their **abode**, and have
025:066 "Evil indeed is it as an **abode**, and as
025:076 an **abode** and place of rest!
029:025 curse each other: and your **abode** will be the Fire,
032:020 and wicked, their **abode** will be the Fire:
039:032 an **abode** for the unbelievers?
039:060 is there not in Hell an **abode** for the Haughty?
039:072 (this) **abode** of the arrogant!"
040:076 is (this) **abode** of the arrogant!"
045:034 And your **abode** is the Fire, and no
047:012 and the Fire will be their **abode**.
053:015 Near it is the Garden of **Abode**.
054:055 In a sure **abode** with a Sovereign Omnipotent.
057:015 who rejected Allah. Your **abode** is the Fire:
066:009 Their **abode** is Hell,-an evil refuge (indeed).
079:039 The **Abode** will be Hell-Fire;
079:041 Their **abode** will be the Garden.

ABOMINABLE

004:022 an **abominable** custom indeed.

ABOMINATION

05:090 eschew such (**abomination**), that ye may prosper.
005:090 are an **abomination**,-of Satan's handiwork: eschew
006:125 thus doth Allah lay **abomination** on those
006:145 for it is an **abomination**,-or what is impious,
009:095 an **abomination**, and Hell is their dwelling-place,
010:100 and He will place **abomination** on those
022:030 but shun the **abomination** of idols, and shun
033:033 all **abomination** from you, ye Members
045:011 is a grievous Chastisement of **abomination**.
074:005 And all **abomination** shun

ABOMINATIONS

011:078 the habit of practicing **abominations**. He said:
021:074 the town which practiced **abominations**: truly they

ABOUND

011:003 on all who **abound** in merit! But if

ABOUNDING

002:105 for Allah is Lord of grace **abounding**.
011:003 and bestow His **abounding** grace on all
055:048 **Abounding** in branches;-
057:021 the Lord of Grace **abounding**.
057:029 He wills. For Allah is the Lord of Grace **abounding**.

ABOUT

002:076 in argument **about** it before your Lord?"
002:109 till Allah brings **about** His command;
002:134 ye shall not be asked **about** what they did.
002:139 Say: Will ye dispute with us **about** Allah,
002:141 **About** what they did!
002:182 And brings **about** a settlement among
002:204 whose speech **about** this world's life may
002:204 to witness **about** what is in his heart;
002:231 (are **about** to) fulfil the term of their ('Iddat),
002:258 to one who disputed with Abraham **about** his Lord,
002:273 And cannot move **about** in the land,
003:009 a Day **about** which there is no doubt;
003:025 against a Day **about** which there is no doubt,
003:065 Ye people of the Book! why dispute ye **about** Abraham,
003:120 for Allah compasseth round **about** all that they do.
003:152 and fell to disputing **about** the order,
003:152 His permission were **about** to annihilate your enemy,
003:159 they would have broken away from **about** thee:
003:188 who exult in what they have brought **about**,
003:196 Let not the strutting **about** of the Unbelievers
004:019 **about** through it a great deal of good.
004:025 and Allah hath full knowledge **about** your faith.
004:087 **about** which there is no doubt.
004:088 into two parties **about** the Hypocrites?
004:127 Say: Allah doth instruct you **about** them: and
004:141 (These are) the ones who wait and watch **about** you:
004:176 say: Allah directs (thus) **about** those who leave
005:052 they run **about** amongst them, saying:
005:101 **about** things which, if made plain to you, may
005:101 But if ye ask **about** things when the Qur'an
006:022 whom ye (invented and) talked **about**?"
006:068 in vain discourse **about** Our Signs, turn away
006:080 **about** Allah, when He (Himself) hath guided me? I
006:153 they will scatter you **about** from His (great) path:
007:022 So by deceit he brought **about** their fall: when
007:033 and saying things **about** Allah of which
007:038 Saith the last **about** the first: "Our Lord!
007:077 saying: "O Salih! bring **about** thy threats, if
007:098 while they played **about** (care-free)?
007:105 to say nothing but truth **about** Allah. Now have
007:119 and turned **about** humble.
007:187 They ask thee **about** the (final) Hour-when will
007:189 and carries it **about** (unnoticed). When she
009:024 then wait until Allah brings **about** His Decision:
009:064 should be sent down **about** them, showing them
009:101 round **about** you are Hypocrites, as well as
010:068 for this! Say ye **about** Allah what ye know not?
010:071 **about** your plan and among your Partners, so your
010:077 Said Moses: "Say ye (this) **about** the Truth when it
011:037 for they are **about** to be overwhelmed
011:078 and cover me not with shame **about** my guests!
012:032 the man **about** whom ye did blame me! I did
012:042 he considered **about** to be saved, he said:
012:054 to serve **about** my own person." Therefore when

ABOUT (continued)

012:087 **about** Joseph and his brother, and never
013:013 **about** Allah, He is Mighty in Power.
014:010 a doubt **about** Allah, the Creator of the heavens
015:028 "I am **about** to create man, from sounding
015:051 Tell them **about** the guests of Abraham.
017:060 round **about**: We granted the Vision which We
017:095 on earth, angels walking **about** in peace and quite,
018:019 and let him not inform anyone **about** you.
018:021 **about** them: those who prevailed over their
018:021 **about** the Hour of Judgement. Behold, they
018:022 nor consult any of them **about** (the affair
018:061 they forgot (**about**) their Fish, which took
018:063 to tell (you) **about** it: it took
018:063 I did indeed forget (**about**) the Fish: none but
018:068 **about** things which are beyond your knowledge?"
018:070 **about** anything until I myself speak to thee
018:076 **about** anything after this, keep me not
019:034 **about** which they (vainly) dispute.
019:068 on their knees round **about** Hell;
019:090 At it the skies are **about** to burst, the earth
020:053 has enabled you to go **about** therein by roads
022:003 as dispute **about** Allah, without knowledge,
022:004 **About** the (Satan) it is decreed that whoever
022:005 **about** the Resurrection, (consider) that
022:007 there can be no doubt **about** it, or **about**
022:007 or **about** (the fact) that Allah will raise up
022:008 as disputes **about** Allah, without knowledge,
022:019 each other **about** their Lord: but those
023:067 "In arrogance: talking nonsense **about** the (Qur'an),
024:037 will be turn **about**,-
024:058 to move **about** attending to each other: thus does
025:023 make such deeds as floating dust scattered **about**.
025:059 ask thou, then, **about** Him of any acquainted
026:043 "Throw ye-that which ye are **about** to throw!"
028:007 but when thou hast fears **about** him, cast him
028:019 Then, when he was **about** to lay his hands on their
028:020 are taking counsel together **about** thee, to slay
028:021 looking **about**, in a state of fear. He prayed:
031:020 who dispute **about** Allah, without knowledge
031:033 the Chief Deceiver deceive you **about** Allah.
033:008 **about** their truthfulness and He has prepared
033:010 (vain) thoughts **about** Allah!
033:020 **about** you (from a safe distance); and if
033:036 to have any option **about** their decision: if any
033:037 that which Allah was **about** to make manifest:
035:005 let the Chief Deceiver deceive you **about** Allah.
036:067 have been unable to move **about**, nor could
037:087 **about** the Lord of the Worlds?"
038:071 "I am **about** to create man from clay:
039:046 in those matters **about** which they have differed."
040:004 None can dispute **about** the Signs of Allah
040:004 Let not, then, their strutting **about** through the
040:035 "(Such) as dispute **about** the Signs of Allah,
040:056 Those who dispute **about** the Signs of Allah
042:035 who dispute **about** Our Signs, that there
043:061 therefore have no doubt **about** the (Hour),
044:009 Yet they play **about** in doubt.
045:026 for the Day of Judgement **about** which there is
045:029 "This Our Record speaks **about** you with truth:
045:032 there was no doubt **about** its (coming), ye used
046:027 **about** you; and We have shown the Signs in various
046:035 and be in no haste **about** the (Unbelievers).

ABOUT (continued)

047:019 for Allah knows how ye move **about** and how ye
049:016 Say: "What! Will ye tell Allah **about** your Religion?"
050:015 be in confused doubt **about** a new Creation?
052:024 Round **about** them will serve, (devoted) to
053:055 (O man), wilt thou dispute **about**?
054:036 violent Seizure but they disputed **about** the Warning.
056:017 Round **about** them will (serve) youths of
060:013 in despair **about** those (buried) in graves.
065:001 **about** thereafter some new situation.
068:011 A slanderer, going **about** with calumnies,
070:001 A questioner asked **about** a Chastisement to befall-
070:042 and play **about**, until they encounter that Day
071:020 That ye may go **about** therein, in spacious roads."
075:025 back-breaking calamity was **about** to be
076:019 And round **about** them will (serve) youths
077:032 "Indeed it throws **about** sparks (huge) as Forts,
078:003 **About** which they cannot agree.
079:042 They ask thee **about** the Hour,-'When will
084:013 Truly, did he go **about** among his people, rejoicing!
101:004 will be like moths Scattered **about**,
102:008 **about** the joy (ye indulged in)!

ABOVE

002:026 even of a gnat as well as anything **above** it.
002:063 and We raised **above** you the Mount (Sinai)
002:093 and We raised **above** you the mount (Sinai):
002:212 **above** them on the Day of Resurrection;
002:247 He said: "Allah hath chosen him **above** you.
002:253 with gifts, some **above** others:
003:033 and the family of 'Imran **above** all people,
003:042 chosen thee **above** the women of all nations.
004:034 for Allah is Most High, Great (**above** you all).
004:095 hath He distinguished **above** those who sit
004:171 (for Exalted is He) **above** having a son.
005:066 from **above** them and form below their feet.
006:065 send calamities on you, from **above** and below, or
006:086 and to all We gave favour **above** the nations:
006:100 (for He is) **above** what they attribute to Him!
006:165 some **above** others: that He may
007:041 and folds of covering **above**: such is
007:140 you with gifts **above** the nations?"
007:144 chosen thee **above** (other) men, by the
007:190 but Allah is exalted high **above** the partners
008:012 smite ye **above** their necks and smite
009:023 **above** faith: if any of you do so, they do wrong.
010:018 and far is He **above** the partners
011:027 (all) any merit **above** us: in fact
012:091 Allah preferred thee **above** us, and we
016:001 and far is He **above** having the partners
016:003 **above** having the partners they ascribe to Him!
016:026 fell down on them from **above**; and the Wrath
016:050 high **above** them, and they do all that
017:043 Glory to Him! He is high **above** all that they say!
017:062 one whom thou hast honoured **above** me! If Thou
017:070 **above** a great part of Our Creation.
020:114 High **above** all is Allah, the King, the Truth!
021:022 (high is He) **above** what they attribute to Him!
023:017 And We have made, **above** you, seven tracts;
024:040 one **above** another: if a man
027:015 Who has favoured us **above** many of His servants
027:063 High is Allah **above** what they associate with Him!
028:068 and far is He **above** the partners they ascribe
029:055 shall cover them from **above** them and from

ABOVE (continued)

030:040   Glory to Him! and High is He **above** the partners
033:010   **above** you and from below you, and behold,
039:004   (He is **above** such things). He is Allah,
039:016   **above** them, and Layers (of Fire) below them:
039:020   one **above** another have been built: beneath them
039:067   High is He **above** the Partners they attribute to Him!
041:010   **above** it, and bestowed blessings on the earth,
041:038   (nor feel themselves **above** it).
042:005   from **above** them (by His Glory): and the
043:032   of them **above** others in ranks, so that
044:032   **above** the nations, knowingly,
045:016   and We favoured them **above** the nations.
049:002   your voices **above** the voice of the Prophet,
050:006   **above** them?-How We have made it and adorned it,
052:043   Exalted is Allah far **above** the things
056:029   (or fruits) piled one **above** another,-
059:023   (high is He) **above** the partners
067:003   one **above** another: no want of proportion wilt thou
067:019   **above** them, spreading their wings and folding
069:017   bear the Throne of thy Lord **above** them.
071:015   the seven heavens one **above** another,
079:027   or the heaven (**above**)?

ABRAHAM

002:124   And remember that **Abraham** was tried
002:125   and We covenanted with **Abraham** and Isma'il,
002:125   the Station of **Abraham** as a place of prayer;
002:126   And remember **Abraham** said: "My Lord,
002:127   And remember **Abraham** and Isma'il raised
002:130   the religion of **Abraham** but such as debase
002:132   And **Abraham** enjoined upon his sons
002:133   of **Abraham**, Isma'il, and Isaac,
002:135   the Religion of **Abraham** the True,
002:136   and to **Abraham**, Isma'il, Isaac, Jacob,
002:140   **Abraham**, Isma'il, Isaac, Jacob
002:258   to one who disputed with **Abraham** about his Lord,
002:258   **Abraham** said: "My Lord is He Who Giveth
002:258   Said **Abraham**: "But it is Allah that causeth
002:260   Behold! **Abraham** said: "My Lord! show me how
003:033   the family of **Abraham**, and the family
003:065   Ye people of the Book! why dispute ye about **Abraham**,
003:067   **Abraham** was not a Jew nor yet a Christian;
003:068   nearest of kin to **Abraham**, are those
003:084   **Abraham**, Isma'il; Isaac, Jacob, and the Tribes,
003:095   follow the religion of **Abraham**, the sane in faith:
003:097   In it are Signs manifest; the Station of **Abraham**;
004:054   the people of **Abraham** the Book and Wisdom, and
004:125   For Allah did take **Abraham** for a friend.
004:125   way of **Abraham** the true in faith?
004:163   We sent inspiration to **Abraham**.
006:074   Lo! **Abraham** said to his father Azar: "Takest
006:075   So also did We show **Abraham** the kingdom
006:083   which We gave to **Abraham** (to use)
006:161   the Path (trod) by **Abraham** the true in faith, and
009:070   the people of **Abraham**, the men of Madyan, and the
009:114   And **Abraham** prayed for his father's forgiveness
009:114   for **Abraham** was most tender hearted, forbearing.
011:069   to **Abraham** with glad tidings. They said,
011:074   of) **Abraham** and the glad tidings had reached him,
011:075   For **Abraham** was, without doubt, forbearing
011:076   O **Abraham**! seek not this. The decree
012:006   thy fathers **Abraham** and Isaac aforetime! For thy
012:038   my fathers,-**Abraham**, Isaac, and Jacob; and never

ABRAHAM (continued)

014:035   Remember **Abraham** said: "O my Lord! make this
015:051   Tell them about the guests of **Abraham**.
015:057   **Abraham** said: "What then is the business
016:120   **Abraham** was indeed a model, devoutly obedient
016:123   "Follow the ways of **Abraham** the True in Faith,
019:041   (the story of) **Abraham**: he was a man of Truth,
019:046   O **Abraham**? If thou forbear not, I will
019:047   **Abraham** said: "Peace be on thee: I will
019:058   and of the posterity of **Abraham** and Israel-
021:051   We bestowed aforetime on **Abraham** his rectitude
021:060   talk of them: he is called **Abraham**."
021:062   did this with our gods, O **Abraham**?"
021:066   (**Abraham**) said, "Do ye then worship, besides Allah,
021:069   and (a means of)) safety for **Abraham**!"
022:026   Behold! We pointed the site, to **Abraham**, of the
022:043   And those of **Abraham** and Lut;
022:078   of your father **Abraham**. It is
029:016   And (We also saved) **Abraham**: behold, he said
029:027   And We gave (**Abraham**) Isaac and Jacob,
029:031   When Our Messengers came to **Abraham** with the
033:007   and from thee: from Noah, **Abraham**, Moses, and
037:083   Verily from his party was **Abraham**.
037:104   We called out to him, "O **Abraham**!
037:109   "Peace and salutation to **Abraham**!"
038:045   **Abraham**, Isaac, and Jacob, possessors of
042:013   on **Abraham**, Moses, and Jesus: namely, that
043:026   Behold! **Abraham** said to his father and his people:
051:024   of the honoured guest of **Abraham**?
051:031   (**Abraham**) said: "And what, O ye Messengers,
053:037   And of **Abraham** who fulfilled his (commandments)
057:026   And We sent Noah and **Abraham**, and established
060:004   (to follow) in **Abraham** and those with him,
060:004   and Him alone": but not when **Abraham** said to
087:019   The Books of **Abraham** and Moses.

ABRAHAM'S

026:069   (something of) **Abraham's** story.
029:024   (**Abraham's**) people except that they said: "Slay him

ABROAD

054:007   (torpid) like locusts scattered **abroad**,
056:006   Becoming dust scattered **abroad**,
077:005   Then spread **abroad** a Reminder,
100:009   is in the graves is Scattered **abroad**

ABROGATE

002:106   We **abrogate** or cause to be forgotten,

ABSENCE

002:051   and in his **absence** ye took the calf
004:034   and guard in (the husband's) **absence** what Allah
007:148   The people of Moses made, in his **absence**, out of
007:150   that ye have done in my place in my **absence**: did
012:052   to him in his **absence**, and that
020:085   in thy **absence**: the Samiri has led them astray."
027:021   me a clear reason (for **absence**)."

ABSENT

007:007   for We were never **absent** (at any time or place).

ABSENTEES

027:020   the Hoopoe? Or is he among the **absentees**?

ABSOLUTE

112:002   Allah, the Eternal, **Absolute**;

ABSOLVE

012:053   "Nor do I **absolve** my own self (of blame):

ABSORBS
018:045   the earth's vegetation **absorbs** it, but soon

ABSTAIN
005:091   and from prayer: will ye not then **abstain**?

ABSTENTION
002:226   an oath for **abstention** from their wives,

ABUNDANCE
002:212   His **abundance** without measures on whom He will.
002:247   gifted with wealth in **abundance**?"
004:100   And **abundance** should he die as a refugee
004:130   Allah will provide **abundance** for each of them
005:100   even though the **abundance** of the bad
006:006   rain from the skies in **abundance**, and gave
006:136   in **abundance** in tilth and in cattle, they
015:022   with water (in **abundance**), though ye
017:030   Verily thy Lord doth provide sustenance in **abundance**
023:055   granted them **abundance** of wealth and sons,
027:036   he said: "Will ye give me **abundance** in wealth?
038:051   for fruit in **abundance**, and (delicious) drink;
040:040   have **abundance** without measure.
043:073   Ye shall have therein **abundance** of fruit,
055:066   pouring forth water in continuous **abundance**:
056:032   And fruit in **abundance**.
071:011   "'He will send rain to you in **abundance**;
072:016   on them Rain in **abundance**.
074:012   To whom I granted resources in **abundance**,
076:006   do drink, making it flow in unstinted **abundance**.
078:014   the clouds water in **abundance**,
080:025   For that We pour forth water in **abundance**,
090:006   "Wealth have I squandered in **abundance**!"
108:001   To thee have We granted the **Abundance**.

ABUNDANT
004:094   with Allah are profits and spoils **abundant**.
011:052   the skies pouring **abundant** rain, and strength
012:049   have **abundant** water, and in which the will press
017:091   in their midst, carrying **abundant** water;
018:034   (**Abundant**) was the produce this man had: he said
022:040   is commemorated in **abundant** measure. Allah
023:019   in them have ye **abundant** fruits: and of them
069:010   with an **abundant** Penalty.

ABUNDANTLY
002:247   **abundantly** with knowledge and bodily prowess:
016:112   **abundantly** supplied with sustenance from every
085:005   Fire supplied (**abundantly**) with Fuel:

ACCEPT
002:127   "Our Lord! **accept** (this service) from us:
003:035   so **accept** this or me: for Thou hearest
003:037   Right graciously did her Lord **accept** her:
004:065   but **accept** them with the fullest conviction.
005:027   "Allah doth **accept** of the sacrifice
006:036   be sure, will **accept**: as to the dead, Allah
008:075   And those who **accept** Faith subsequently, and
009:104   **accept** repentance from His votaries and receives
011:017   Can they be (like) those who **accept** a Clear
011:028   Shall we compel you to **accept** it when ye
014:040   O our Lord! and **accept** Thou my Prayer.
018:057   even then will they never **accept** guidance.
027:092   and if any **accept** guidance, they do
043:049   for We shall truly **accept** guidance."
046:016   Such are they from whom We shall **accept** the best

ACCEPTABLE
019:055   **acceptable** in the sight of his Lord.

ACCEPTABLE (continued)
020:109   and whose word is **acceptable** to Him.
053:026   and that he is **acceptable** to Him.

ACCEPTED
002:048   nor shall intercession be **accepted** for her,
002:123   nor shall compensation be **accepted** from her
003:083   bowed to His Will (**accepted** Islam),
003:085   never will it be **accepted** of him;
003:086   who reject faith after they **accepted** it and bore
003:090   never will their repentance be **accepted**;
003:090   But those who reject faith after they **accepted** it.
003:091   never would be **accepted** from any such as much
003:195   And their Lord hath **accepted** of them, and
005:027   it was **accepted** from one, but not from the other.
005:036   it would never be **accepted** of them.
006:070   none will be **accepted**: such is (the end of)
009:053   will it be **accepted**: for ye are indeed a people
009:054   are not **accepted** are: that they reject Allah
009:066   rejected Faith after ye had **accepted** it. If We
010:089   Allah said: "**Accepted** is your prayer (O Moses
016:084   then will no excuse be **accepted** from Unbelievers,
042:016   after He has been **accepted**,-futile is
057:015   "This Day shall no ransom be **accepted** of you,
058:001   (and **accepted**) the statement of the woman
072:013   to the Guidance, we have **accepted** it: and any

ACCEPTETH
040:003   Who forgiveth Sin, **accepteth** Repentance, is Severe

ACCEPTING
003:106   "Did ye reject Faith after **accepting** it?
009:074   it after **accepting** Islam: and the meditated
016:106   Any one who, after **accepting** Faith in Allah,

ACCEPTS
004:017   Allah **accepts** the repentance of those who do evil
042:025   He is the One that **accepts** repentance from His

ACCESS
002:217   of Allah to prevent **access** to the path
002:217   to prevent **access** to the Sacred Mosque,
017:057   means of **access** to their Lord,-as to who
046:028   as a means of **access** (to Allah)? Nay, they

ACCOMPANYING
043:053   with him angels **accompanying** him in procession?"

ACCOMPLISH
003:040   "Doth Allah **accomplish** what He willeth."
008:042   that Allah might **accomplish** a matter already
008:044   That Allah might **accomplish** a matter
015:063   to thee to **accomplish** that of which they doubt.
065:003   **accomplish** His purpose: verily, for all things

ACCOMPLISHED
002:200   So when ye have **accomplished** your rites,
013:040   thy soul (before it is all **accomplished**), thy duty
019:071   a Decree which must be **accomplished**.
040:082   they **accomplished** was of no profit to them.
043:042   Or We shall show thee that (**accomplished**) which We
071:004   is **accomplished**, it cannot be put forward:
073:018   His Promise needs must be **accomplished**.

ACCOMPLISHER
011:107   **Accomplisher** of what He planneth.

ACCORD
010:015   of my own **accord**, to change it: I follow
018:082   I did it not of my own **accord**. Such is
023:071   If the Truth had been in **accord** with their
027:010   (of its own **accord**) as if it had been a snake,

ACCORD (continued)

028:031 But he saw it moving of (its own accord) as if it had

ACCORDANCE

004:064 in accordance with the leave of Allah.

ACCORDING

002:180 according to reasonable usage;
002:228 according to what is equitable;
002:236 the wealthy according to his means,
002:236 and the poor according to his means;
004:025 according to what is reasonable:
005:001 according to His Will and Plan.
006:132 (or ranks) according to their deeds: for thy
006:136 they say, according to their fancies: "This
006:160 be recompensed according to his evil: no wrong
007:135 from them according to a fixed term which they
008:007 to establish the Truth according to His words, and
009:079 who give according to their means,-and throw
013:017 each according to its measure: but the
014:051 each soul according to its deserts; and verily
016:096 their reward according to the best
016:097 their reward according to the best
017:084 Say: "Everyone acts according to his own
021:045 Say, "I do but warn you according to revelation":
023:018 the sky according to (due) measure, and We
024:038 That Allah may reward them according to the
029:007 them according to the best of their deeds.
035:045 according to what they deserve, He would
036:040 (its own) orbit (according to Law).
039:035 and give them their reward according to the
042:049 according to His Will,
043:049 invoke thy Lord for us according to his
045:014 or ill) each People according to what
046:019 according to the deeds which they (have done),
053:031 do evil, according to their deeds, and He
065:006 according to what is just and reasonable.
065:006 according to your means: annoy them not, so as
065:007 spend according to what Allah has given him.
065:007 Let the man of means spend according to his means:
076:016 thereof (according to their wishes).

ACCORDINGLY

004:123 whoever works evil, will be requited accordingly.

ACCOUNT

002:095 on account of the (sins) which their hands
002:202 and Allah is quick in account.
002:225 to account for thoughtlessness in your oaths,
002:233 treated unfairly on account of her child.
002:233 Nor father on account of his child,
002:284 Allah calleth you to account for it.
003:011 and Allah called them to account for their sins.
003:019 Allah is swift in calling to account.
003:062 This is the true account: there is no
003:199 and Allah is swift in account.
004:006 but all-sufficient is Allah in taking account.
004:086 Allah takes careful account of all things.
005:004 and fear Allah; for Allah is swift in taking account.
005:032 On that account: We ordained
005:089 to account for what is void in your oaths, but
005:089 to account for your deliberate oaths: for
005:102 and on that account lost their faith.
006:034 some account of those Messengers.
006:044 on a sudden, We called them to account, when lo!
006:062 and He is the Swiftest in taking account.

ACCOUNT (continued)

006:069 On their account no responsibility falls on
007:002 no more by any difficulty on that account,-that
007:095 Behold! We called them to account of a sudden,
007:137 considered weak (and of no account), inheritors
011:077 he was grieved on their account and felt himself
013:040 reach them: it is Our part to call them to account.
013:041 and He is swift in calling to account.
014:051 and verily Allah is Swift in calling account.
015:092 of a surety, call them to account,
016:046 Or that He may not call them to account in the
016:047 Or that He may not call them to account by a
016:056 to account for your false inventions.
016:093 to account for all your actions.
017:014 an account against thee."
018:049 or great, but takes account thereof! They will
018:058 (at once) to account for what they have earned,
019:094 He does take and account of them (all), and hath
020:066 so it seemed to him on account of their magic-
021:013 in order that ye may be called to account.
021:047 We will bring it (to account): and enough
021:047 and enough are We to take account.
022:027 lean (on account of journeys) through deep
023:113 but ask those who keep account."
023:115 brought back to Us (for account)"?
024:039 and Allah will pay him his account: and Allah
024:039 and Allah is swift in taking account.
026:113 "Their account is only with my Lord, if ye
028:078 called (immediately) to account for their sins.
029:013 they will be called to account for their falsehoods.
029:033 he was grieved on their account, and felt
033:039 to call (men) to account.
035:043 On account of their arrogance in the land
036:012 We taken account. In a clear Book (of evidence).
037:018 be humiliated (on account of your evil)."
038:016 our sentence (even) before the Day of Account!"
038:026 for that they forget the Day of Account.
038:039 no account will be asked."
038:053 to you for the Day of Account!
040:017 for Allah is Swift in taking account.
040:021 to account for their sins, and none
040:022 to account: for He is full of Strength,
040:027 one who believes not in the Day of Account!"
042:022 on account of what they have earned, and (the
042:048 to him, on account of the deeds which his hands
043:018 and unable to give a clear account in a dispute
043:019 and they will be called to account!
043:044 and soon shall ye (all) be brought to account.
048:025 trampling down and on whose account a guilt
050:004 with Us is a Record guarding (the full account).
051:039 But (Pharaoh) turned back on account of his might,
056:086 if you are exempt from (future) account,-
065:008 to severe account?-and We chastised them with
065:008 did We not then call to account,-to severe
066:010 on their account, but were told: "Enter ye
069:020 that my Account would (one Day) reach me!"
069:026 how my account (stood)!
072:013 has no fear, either of a short (account) or of
072:028 and takes account of every single thing."
078:027 for any account (for their deeds),
084:008 Soon will his account be taken by an easy reckoning,
088:026 Then it will be for Us to call them to account.

ACCOUNTABLE
006:052 In naught art thou **accountable** for them, and in
006:052 and in naught are they **accountable** for thee, that

ACCRUED
048:025 a guilt would have **accrued** to you without (your)

ACCURATELY
065:001 and count (**accurately**) their prescribed periods:

ACCURSED
. 005:064 be they **accursed** for the (blasphemy) they utter.
015:017 from every **accursed** Satan.
015:034 from here; for thou art rejected, **accursed**.
038:077 from here: for thou art rejected, **accursed**.
081:025 Nor is it the word of a Satan **accursed**.

ACCUSE
006:147 If they **accuse** thee of falsehood, say:
023:026 for that they **accuse** me of falsehood!
023:039 for that they **accuse** me of falsehood.”
028:034 for I fear that they may **accuse** me of falsehood.”

ACCUSED
023:044 they **accused** him of falsehood: so We

ACCUSER
024:009 on herself if (her **accuser**) is telling the truth.

ACHIEVE
009:020 They are the people who will **achieve** (salvation).
058:022 that will **achieve** Success.
059:009 they are the ones that **achieve** prosperity.
059:020 that will **achieve** Felicity.
064:016 they are the ones that **achieve** prosperity.

ACHIEVED
023:111 they are indeed the ones that have **achieved** Bliss.”

ACHIEVEMENT
004:013 and that will be the Supreme **achievement**.
009:111 that is the **achievement** supreme.
040:009 and that will be truly the highest **Achievement**.
044:057 That will be the supreme **achievement**!
078:031 there will be an **Achievement**,

ACKNOWLEDGE
009:029 nor **acknowledge** the religion of Truth, from among

ACKNOWLEDGED
009:102 have **acknowledged** their wrong-doings: they have
027:014 though their souls **acknowledged** them wrongfully

ACQUAINTED
002:095 **acquainted** with the wrong-doers.
002:231 well **acquainted** with all things.
002:234 And Allah is well **acquainted** with what ye do.
002:271 And Allah is well **acquainted** with what ye do.
002:282 And Allah is well **acquainted** with all things.
003:180 and Allah is well **acquainted** with all that ye do.
004:035 and is **acquainted** with all things.
005:097 and that Allah is well **acquainted** with all things.
006:018 and He is the Wise, **acquainted** with all things.”
006:073 well **acquainted** (with all things).
017:096 well **acquainted** with His servants, and He
021:051 and well were We **acquainted** with him.
023:096 We are well **acquainted** with the things they say.
024:030 and Allah is well **acquainted** with all that they do.
024:053 Allah is well **acquainted** with all that ye do.”
025:058 to be **acquainted** with the faults of His servants;-
025:059 of any **acquainted** (with such things).
027:088 for He is well **acquainted** with all that ye do.
031:029 is well **acquainted** with all that ye do?
031:034 is **acquainted** (with all things).

ACQUAINTED (continued)
033:002 for Allah is well **acquainted** with (all)
035:031 well **acquainted** and fully Observant.
048:011 **acquainted** with all that ye do.
049:013 and is well **acquainted** (with all things).
053:036 Nay, is he not **acquainted** with what is in
057:010 And Allah is well-**acquainted** with all that ye do.
064:008 And Allah is well-**acquainted** with all that ye do.
072:026 **acquainted** with His Secrets.-

ACQUIRE
008:041 that ye may **acquire** (in war), a fifth share
048:015 when ye set forth to **acquire** booty (in war):
048:019 **acquire** (besides): and Allah is Exalted in Power,
048:020 that ye shall **acquire**, and He

ACQUIRING
018:104 they were **acquiring** good by their works?”

ACROSS
007:138 (with safety) **across** the sea. They came
009:121 nor cut **across** a valley, but the deed
010:090 **across** the sea: Pharaoh and his hosts followed

ACT
002:223 But do some good **act** for your souls beforehand;
003:076 verily Allah loves those who **act** aright.
003:076 their plighted faith and **act** aright,
003:125 “Yea,-if ye remain firm, and **act** aright,
003:135 an **act** of indecency or wronged their own souls.
003:161 No prophet could (ever) **act** dishonestly
003:181 their word and (their **act**) of slaying the Prophets
005:045 it is an **act** of atonement for himself.
007:129 that so He may see how ye **act**.”
007:142 “**Act** for me amongst my people: do right,
008:017 it was not thy **act**, but Allah’s: in order
009:102 they have mixed an **act** that was good with another
014:022 I reject your former **act** in associating
015:071 (to marry), if ye must **act** (so).”
021:027 and they **act** (in all things) by His command.
021:094 Whoever works any **act** of righteousness and has
063:009 If any **act** thus, surely they are the losers.
069:018 not an **act** of yours that ye hide will be hidden.

ACTED
027:014 of those who **acted** corruptly!
028:076 of Moses; but he **acted** insolently towards them:

ACTING
002:224 or **acting** rightly, or making peace
012:079 we should be **acting** wrongfully.”
054:044 “We **acting** together can defend ourselves”?

ACTION
006:070 is caught in its own ruin by its own **action**: it
024:062 a matter requiring collective **action**, they do

ACTIONS
009:094 it is your **actions** that Allah and His Messenger
010:002 the good **actions** they have advanced (but) say
016:093 to account for all your **actions**.
016:096 the best of their **actions**.
016:097 the best of their **actions**.
016:111 (fully) for all its **actions**, and none
024:024 bear witness against them as to their **actions**.

ACTIVE
020:020 it was a snake, **active** in motion.
023:004 Who are **active** in giving zakat;

ACTS
002:271 If ye disclose (**acts** of) charity,

ACTS (continued)

003:161   If any person **acts** dishonestly he shall,
006:043   (sinful) **acts** seem alluring to them.
006:070   deliver themselves to ruin by their own **acts**: they
006:164   of its **acts** on none but itself: no bearer
008:048   (sinful) **acts** seem alluring to them, and said:
016:063   their own **acts** seem alluring: he is their
017:084   Say: "Everyone **acts** according to his own
021:023   He cannot be questioned for His **acts**, by they
037:142   and he had done **acts** worthy of blame.

ACTUALLY

004:066   what they were (**actually**) told, it would
010:051   when it **actually** cometh to pass? (It will
010:077   when it hath (**actually**) reached you? Is it
011:008   Ah! On the day it (**actually**) reaches them,
013:005   "When we are (**actually**) dust, shall we
016:085   When the wrong-doers (**actually**) see the
039:058   (**actually**) sees the Chastisement: 'If only
040:085   when they (**actually**) saw Our Punishment was not

'AD

007:065   To the '**Ad** people, (We sent) Hud, one of
007:074   inheritors after the '**Ad** people and gave
009:070   and '**Ad**, and Thamud; the people
011:050   To the '**Ad** People (We sent) Hud, one of
011:059   Such were the '**Ad** People: they rejected
011:060   Ah! behold! For the '**Ad** rejected their
011:060   Away with the '**Ad** the People of Hud!
014:009   and '**Ad**, and Thamud? And of those who (came)
022:042   and '**Ad**, and Thamud;
025:038   As also '**Ad** and Thamud, and the
026:123   The '**Ad** (people) rejected the messengers.
029:038   Remember also the '**Ad** and the Thamud
038:012   and '**Ad**, and Pharaoh the Lord of Stakes.
040:031   of Noah, the '**Ad**, and the Thamud, and those
041:013   like the thunderbolt of the '**Ad** and the Thamud!"
041:015   Now the '**Ad** behaved arrogantly through the land,
050:013   The '**Ad**, Pharaoh, the Brethren of Lut,
051:041   And in the '**Ad** (people) (was another
053:050   the (powerful) ancient '**Ad** (people),
054:018   The '**Ad** (people) (too) rejected (Truth): then how
069:004   The Thamud and the '**Ad** people disbelieved in
069:006   And the '**Ad**,-they were destroyed by a furious
089:006   Seest thou not how thy Lord dealt with the '**Ad** (people),-

'AD'S

046:021   Mention (Hud) one of '**Ad's** (own) brethren:

ADAM

002:031   And He taught **Adam** the names of all things;
002:033   He said: "O **Adam**! tell them their names."
002:034   "Bow down to **Adam**"; and they bowed down:
002:035   And We said: "O **Adam**! dwell thou and thy wife
002:037   Then learnt **Adam** from his Lord certain words
003:033   Allah did choose **Adam** and Noah,
003:059   Jesus before Allah is as that of **Adam**;
005:027   of the story of the two sons of **Adam**.
007:011   then We bade the angels prostrate to **Adam**,
007:019   O **Adam**! dwell thou and thy wife
007:026   O ye children of **Adam**! We have bestowed
007:027   O ye children of **Adam**! Let not
007:031   O children of **Adam**! wear your
007:035   O ye children of **Adam**! whenever there come to you
007:172   from the children of **Adam**-from their loins-
017:061   "Prostrate unto **Adam**": they prostrated

ADAM (continued)

017:070   We have honoured the sons of **Adam**; provided them
018:050   "Prostrate to **Adam**": they prostrated except Iblis.
019:058   of the posterity of **Adam**, and of those
020:115   taken the covenant of **Adam**, but he forgot: and We
020:116   "Prostrate yourselves to **Adam**," they prostrated
020:117   Then We said: "O **Adam**! verily, this is
020:120   he said, "O **Adam**! shall I lead thee to the Tree
020:121   the Garden: thus did **Adam** disobey His Lord,
036:060   of **Adam**, that ye should not worship Satan;

ADD

009:125   it will **add** doubt to their doubt, and they
011:052   and **add** strength to your strength: so turn ye
011:063   What then would ye **add** to my (portion)
011:101   nor did they **add** aught (to their
012:065   and **add** (at the same time) a full camel's load
014:007   "If ye are grateful, I will **add** more (favours)
016:088   will We **add** Chastisement to Chastisement; for that
019:079   and We Shall **add** and **add** to his punishment.
020:031   "**Add** to my strength through him,
024:038   and **add** even more for them out of His Grace:
031:027   with seven Oceans behind it to **add** to its (supply),
038:061   **add** to him a double Chastisement in the Fire!"
048:004   that they may **add** Faith to their Faith;-for to
074:015   Yet is he greedy-that I should **add** (yet more);

ADDED

009:047   they would not have **added** to your (strength)
018:109   my Lord, even if we **added** another ocean like it,
033:022   And it only **added** to their faith and their
038:024   ewe to be **added** to his (flock of) ewes:

ADDING

003:090   And then go on **adding** to their defiance of Faith,

ADDITION

009:037   prohibited month) is an **addition** to Unbelief:
009:101   and in **addition** shall they be sent
022:021   In **addition** there will be maces of iron

ADDITIONAL

017:079   a part of it as an **additional** prayer for thee:
021:072   as an **additional** gift, (a grandson), Jacob,

ADDRESS

002:174   Allah will not **address** them on the Day
011:037   and **address** Me no (further) on behalf
017:023   but **address** them in terms of honour.
021:058   that they might turn (and **address** themselves) to it.
023:027   and **address** Me not in favour of the wrong-doers:
025:063   and when the ignorant **address** them, they say,

ADDRESSED

007:143   and his Lord **addressed** him, he said: "O my lord!
040:010   The Unbelievers will be **addressed**: "Greater was

ADDS

035:001   He **adds** to Creation as He pleases: for Allah
035:039   but **adds** to the odium for the Unbelievers
035:039   their Lord: their disbelief but **adds** to (their

ADHERED

007:072   We saved him and those who **adhered** to him, by Our

ADHERENTS

015:059   "Excepting the **adherents** of Lut: them we
015:061   arrived among the **adherents** of Lut.
035:006   He only invites his **adherents**, that they
037:134   Behold, We delivered him and his **adherents**, all

ADHERES

006:146   except what **adheres** to their backs

ADJUDGED
005:095 As **adjudged** by two just men among you; or by

ADJURATION
056:076 And that is indeed a mighty **adjuration** if ye
089:005 Is there (not) in these an **adjuration** (or evidence)

ADMINISTER
009:060 and those employed to **administer** the (funds):

ADMIRATION
002:069 the **admiration** of beholders!"

ADMIT
003:192 "Our Lord! any whom Thou dost **admit** to the Fire,
003:195 and **admit** them into Gardens with rivers
004:031 and **admit** you to the Gate of great honor.
004:057 We shall soon **admit** to Gardens, with rivers
004:057 We shall **admit** them to shades, cool
004:122 We shall soon **admit** them to Gardens, with rivers
004:175 soon will He **admit** them to Mercy and Grace
005:012 and **admit** you to Gardens with rivers
005:084 to **admit** us to the company of the righteous?"
007:151 **Admit** us to Thy mercy! For Thou art
009:099 soon will Allah **admit** them to His Mercy: for Allah
018:110 **admit** no one as partner."
022:014 Verily Allah will **admit** those who believe
022:023 Allah will **admit** those who believe and work
022:059 Verily He will **admit** them to a place
027:019 and **admit** me, by Thy Grace, to the
029:009 righteous deeds,-them shall We **admit** to the
045:030 their Lord will **admit** them to His Mercy:
047:006 And **admit** them to the Garden which He has
047:012 Verily Allah will **admit** those who believe and do
048:005 That He may **admit** the men and women who believe,
048:017 and His Messenger,-(Allah) will **admit** him to
048:025 that He may **admit** to His mercy whom He will.
056:057 why will ye not **admit** the Truth?
058:022 And He will **admit** them to Gardens beneath which
061:012 and **admit** you to Gardens beneath which rivers
064:009 and He will **admit** them to gardens beneath which
065:011 and work righteousness, He will **admit** to Gardens
066:008 you your evil deeds, and **admit** you to Gardens
076:031 He will **admit** to His Mercy Whom He will; but the

ADMITS
042:008 but He **admits** whom He will to His Mercy; and the

ADMITTED
003:185 and **admitted** to the Garden will have succeeded:
004:013 will be **admitted** to Gardens with rivers flowing
004:014 will be **admitted** to a Fire, to abide therein:
005:065 and **admitted** them to Gardens of Bliss.
014:023 **admitted** to Gardens beneath which rivers flow,-
021:075 And We **admitted** him to Our Mercy: for he
021:086 We **admitted** them to Our Mercy: for they

ADMONISH
004:034 **admonish** them (first), (next), refuse to
006:063 so keep clear of them but **admonish** them,
006:070 But continue to **admonish** them with it (Al-Qur-an)
009:122 and **admonish** the people when they return to them,-
024:017 Allah doth **admonish** you, that ye
026:136 whether thou **admonish** us or be not
026:194 To thy heart and mind that thou mayest **admonish**
026:214 And **admonish** the nearest kinsmen,
032:003 that thou mayest **admonish** a people to whom
034:046 Say: "I do **admonish** you on one point: that ye
036:010 **admonish** them or thou do not **admonish** them:

ABMONISH (continued)
036:011 Thou canst but **admonish** such a one as follows
046:012 the Arabic tongue; to **admonish** the unjust, and as
050:045 So **admonish** with the Qur'an such as

ADMONISHED
006:080 Will ye not (yourselves) be **admonished**?
025:073 Those who, when they are **admonished** with the
026:173 on those who were **admonished** (but heeded not)!
027:058 on those who were **admonished** (but heeded not)!
036:019 an evil omen), if ye are **admonished**? Nay, but
037:013 And, when they are **admonished**, pay no heed,-
058:003 each other: this are ye **admonished** to perform:

ADMONISHERS
026:136 be not among (our) **Admonishers**!

ADMONISHING
031:013 **admonishing** him "O my son! join not in worship

ADMONITION
002:221 that they may receive **admonition**.
002:269 receive **admonition** but men of understanding.
002:275 **admonition** from their Lord, desist,
005:046 an **admonition** to those who fear Allah.
006:126 the Signs for those who receive **admonition**.
007:003 Little it is ye remember of **admonition**.
007:026 that they may receive **admonition**!
007:130 that they might receive **admonition**.
007:145 **Admonition** and explanation of all things,
010:003 will you not receive **admonition**?
010:057 to you an **admonition** from your Lord and a
013:019 with understanding that receive **admonition**;-
014:025 in order that they may receive **admonition**.
016:017 creates not? Will ye not receive **admonition**?
016:090 that ye may receive **admonition**.
017:041 receive **admonition**, but it only increases their
020:003 But only as an **admonition** to those
023:071 but they turn away from their **admonition**.
023:071 Nay, We have sent them their **admonition**, but they
023:085 Say: "Yet will ye not receive **admonition**?"
024:001 in order that ye may receive **admonition**.
024:034 and an **admonition** for those who fear (Allah).
025:001 that it may be an **admonition** to all creatures;-
025:007 to him to give **admonition** with him?
028:043 that they might receive **admonition**.
028:046 in order that they may receive **admonition**.
028:051 in order that they may receive **admonition**.
032:004 (for you): will lye not then receive **admonition**?
035:037 receive **admonition**? And (moreover) the warner
036:070 That it may give **admonition** to any (who are)
037:155 Will ye not then receive **admonition**?
038:001 of **Admonition**: (this is the Truth).
038:029 and that men of understanding may receive **admonition**.
038:049 This is a message (of **admonition**): and verily
039:009 endued with understanding that receive **admonition**.
039:027 in order that they may receive **admonition**.
040:013 receive **admonition** who turn (to Allah).
040:058 Little do ye learn by **admonition**!
041:004 Giving Good News and **Admonition**: yet most
045:023 Will ye not then receive **admonition**?
054:015 that will receive **admonition**?
054:017 then is there any that will receive **admonition**?
054:022 then is there any that will receive **admonition**?
054:032 then is there any that will receive **admonition**?
054:040 then is there any that will receive **admonition**?

ADMONITION (continued)

054:051 then is there any that will receive **admonition**?
065:002 Such is the **admonition** given to him who believes
069:042 of a soothsayer: little **admonition** it is ye receive.
073:019 Verily this is an **Admonition**: therefore, whoso
074:049 that they turn away from **admonition**?-
074:054 Nay, this surely is an **admonition**:
076:029 This is an **admonition**: whosoever will, let him
080:004 Or that he might receive **admonition**, and the
087:009 the **admonition** profits (the hearer).
087:009 Therefore give **admonition** in case the **admonition**

ADOPT

007:146 they will not **adopt** it as the Way; but if
007:146 that is the Way they will **adopt**. For they
012:021 much good, or we shall **adopt** him as a son."
015:096 Those who **adopt**, with Allah, another god:
028:009 or we may **adopt** him as a son." And they

ADOPTED

033:004 nor has He made your **adopted** sons your sons.
033:037 with the wives of their **adopted** sons, when the
059:009 had homes (in Madinah) and had **adopted** the Faith,-

ADORATION

003:113 and they prostrate themselves in **adoration**.
007:120 But the sorcerers fell down prostrate in **adoration**.
015:098 themselves in **adoration**.
019:058 in prostrate **adoration** and in tears.
025:064 in **adoration** of their Lord prostrate and standing;
026:046 prostrate in **adoration**,
032:015 fall down in **adoration**, and celebrate
039:009 (in **adoration**), who takes heed of the Hereafter,
055:006 both (alike) bow in **adoration**.
068:043 summoned aforetime to bow in **adoration**, while they
096:019 but prostrate down in **adoration**, and bring

ADORE

022:077 prostrate yourselves, and **adore** your Lord,
025:060 "**Adore** ye The Most Gracious!", they say,
025:060 Shall we **adore** that which thou commandest us?"
053:062 to Allah, and **adore** (Him)!

ADORNED

017:093 "Or thou have a house **adorned** with gold, or thou
018:031 be **adorned** therein with bracelets of gold,
022:023 they shall be **adorned** therein with bracelets
035:033 therein will they be **adorned** with bracelets
041:012 And We **adorned** the lower heaven with lights,
050:006 and **adorned** it, and there is not flaws in it?
067:005 **adorned** the lowest heaven with Lamps, and We
076:021 and they will be **adorned** with Bracelets of silver;

ADORNMENT

007:026 as well as to be an **adornment** to you, but the
016:008 an **adornment**; and He has created (other) things
057:020 and a pastime, **adornment** and mutual boasting and

ADORNMENTS

043:035 And also **adornments** of gold. But all this

ADULTERER

024:003 but an **adulterer** or an idolater; to the
024:003 The **adulterer** cannot have sexual relations

ADULTERESS

024:003 and the **adulteress**, none can have
024:003 an **adulteress** or idolatress, and the

ADULTERY

017:032 Nor come nigh to **adultery**: for it is
060:012 that they will not commit **adultery** (or fornication),

ADVANCE

007:034 nor (an hour) can they **advance** (it in anticipation).
010:049 can they **advance** (it in anticipation).
012:048 have laid by in **advance** for them,-(all except
020:083 in **advance** of thy people, O Moses?"
027:042 on us in **advance** of this, and we
050:028 I had already in **advance** sent you Warning.
052:025 They will **advance** to each other, engaging in

ADVANCED

002:250 When they **advanced** to meet Goliath
010:002 the good actions they have **advanced** (but) say
018:013 in their Lord, and We **advanced** them in guidance:

ADVANCING

046:024 **advancing** towards their valleys, they said,

ADVANTAGE

002:231 or to take undue **advantage**;
004:141 "Did we not gain an **advantage** over you.
007:039 "See then! no **advantage** have ye over us; so taste
009:008 seeing that if they get an **advantage** over you,
033:025 no **advantage** did they gain, and enough

ADVANTAGES

040:080 **advantages** in them for you (besides); that ye

ADVERSARIES

019:082 their worship, and become **adversaries** against them.

ADVERSARY

028:008 should be to them an **adversary** and a cause
036:077 Yet behold! he (stands forth) as an open **adversary**!

ADVERSITY

002:177 in pain (or suffering) and **adversity**,
002:214 They encountered suffering and **adversity**,
003:134 whether in prosperity, or in **adversity**;
006:042 with suffering and **adversity**, that they
007:094 in suffering and **adversity**, in order
007:168 with both prosperity and **adversity**: in order
010:021 of some mercy after **adversity** hath touched them,
011:010 (Our) favours after **adversity** hath touched him,
036:023 intend some **adversity** for me, of no
041:050 from Us, after some **adversity** has touched him,

ADVICE

007:062 Sincere is my **advice** to you, and I
012:067 against Allah (with my **advice**): none can
028:020 for I do give thee sincere **advice**."
027:032 **advise** me in (this) my affair: no affair

ADVISER

007:021 that he was their sincere **adviser**.
007:068 I am to you a sincere and trustworthy **adviser**".

ADVOCATE

004:105 so be not an **advocate** for those who

AFFAIR

003:154 Say thou: "Indeed, this **affair** is wholly Allah's."
003:154 "If we had had anything to do with this **affair**,
003:154 They said: "Have we any hand in the **affair**?
006:159 their **affair** is with Allah: He will
011:123 every **affair** (for decision): so worship Him,
012:015 this **affair** while they perceive not."
012:051 "What was your **affair** when ye
017:086 thy **affair** in that matter as against Us,-
018:010 and dispose of our **affair** for us in the right way!
018:016 of your **affair** towards comfort and ease."
018:021 over their **affair** said, "Let us
018:021 as to their **affair**. (Some) said,
018:022 (the **affair** of) the Sleepers.

AFFAIR (continued)

018:028   and his **affair** has become all excess.
020:062   over their **affair**, but they kept their talk secret.
021:093   their **affair** (of unity), one from another:
023:053   But people have cut off their **affair** (of unity),
024:012   the **affair**,-though well of their people and say,
024:014   glibly into this **affair**.
027:032   no **affair** have I decided except in your presence."
027:032   advise me in (this) my **affair**:
040:044   to you (now). My (own) **affair** I commit to Allah:
040:068   and when He decides upon an **affair**, He says
042:043   an **affair** of great resolution.
044:004   every **affair** of wisdom,
051:004   And those that distribute the **affair**;-
054:006   to a terrible **affair**,
059:011   to any one in your **affair**; And if

AFFAIRS

002:189   fixed periods of time in (the **affairs** of) men.
002:220   if ye mix their **affairs** with yours,
003:159   and consult them in **affairs** (of moment).
004:081   and enough is Allah as a disposer of **affairs**.
004:109   or who will carry their **affairs** through?
004:132   and enough is Allah to carry through all **affairs**.
004:171   And enough is Allah as a Disposer of **affairs**.
006:066   the responsibility for arranging your **affairs**;
006:094   whom ye thought to be partners in your **affairs**:
006:102   to dispose of all of all **affairs**.
006:107   to dispose of their **affairs**.
010:031   who is it that rules and regulates all **affairs**?"
010:108   over you to arrange your **affairs**."
011:012   It is Allah that arrangeth all **affairs**!
012:021   power and control over His **affairs**; but most
013:002   He doth regulate all **affairs**, explaining the
017:002   as Disposer of (your) **affairs**."
017:054   a disposer of their **affairs** for them.
017:065   for a Disposer of **affairs**.
022:041   the end (and decision) of (all) **affairs**.
022:076   and to Allah go back all **affairs** (for decision).
025:043   of **affairs** for him?
026:227   know what vicissitudes their **affairs** will take!
031:017   firmness (of purpose) in (the conduct of) **affairs**.
032:005   He directs the **affairs** from the heavens to the
033:003   and enough is Allah, as a Disposer of **affairs**.
033:048   as a disposer of **affairs**.
035:004   before thee: to Allah all **affairs** are returned.
036:050   by will, to dispose (of their **affairs**), nor to
039:062   and He is the Guardian and Disposer of all **affairs**.
042:006   the disposer of their **affairs**.
042:038   who (conduct) their **affairs** by mutual Consultation;
042:053   all **affairs** tend towards Allah!
045:017   in **affairs** (of Religion): it was
055:031   Soon shall We settle your **affairs**, O both
057:005   and all **affairs** go back to Allah.
073:009   take Him therefore for (thy) Disposer of **Affairs**.
088:022   Thou art not one to manage (their) **affairs**.

AFFECTETH

008:025   And fear the trial which **affecteth** not in

AFFECTION

004:073   ties of **affection** between you and them,
008:063   have produced that **affection**, but Allah
008:063   put **affection** between their hearts: not if
018:081   in purity (of conduct) and closer in **affection**.
059:009   the Faith,-show their **affection** to such as came

AFFECTIONS

016:078   and intelligence and **affections**:

AFFIRM

005:107   "We **affirm** that our witness is truer than that

AFFLICT

007:156   He said: "I **afflict** My punishment on whom
007:167   those who would **afflict** them with
019:045   a Chastisement **afflict** thee from (Allah) Most
020:047   and **afflict** them not: with a Sign, indeed, have

AFFLICTED

002:156   Who say, when **afflicted** with calamity:
006:042   and We **afflicted** the nations with suffering and
007:141   who **afflicted** you with the worst of punishment
024:061   nor in one **afflicted** with illness, nor in
034:008   or is he **afflicted** with madness." Nay, it is
038:041   "Satan has **afflicted** me with distress and suffering"!
068:006   Which of you is **afflicted** with madness.

AFFLICTION

006:017   "If Allah touch thee with **affliction**, none can
010:012   removed his **affliction**, he passeth on his way
010:012   for the **affliction** that touched him! Thus do
025:065   for its Wrath is indeed an **affliction** grievous,-
029:010   they suffer **affliction** in (the cause of) Allah,
039:038   some **affliction** for me, remove His
039:038   remove His **affliction** or if He wills some Mercy

AFFLICTIONS

022:035   over their **afflictions**, keep up

AFFLICTS

030:036   evil **afflicts** them become of what their (own)

AFFLUENCE

007:095   touched by suffering and **affluence**".. Behold!

AFFORD

002:196   but if he cannot **afford** it,
002:196   he must make an offering such as he can **afford**,
003:097   those who can **afford** the journey;

AFFORDING

023:050   on high ground, **affording** rest and security

AFFRIGHTED

074:050   As if they were **affrighted** asses,

AFORETIME

005:012   Allah did **aforetime** take a Covenant from
009:107   His Messenger **aforetime**. They will
010:051   and ye wanted (**aforetime**) to hasten it on!"
012:006   thy fathers Abraham and Isaac **aforetime**! For thy
012:064   you with his brother **aforetime**? But Allah
014:044   to swear **aforetime** that ye suffer no decline?
021:051   We bestowed **aforetime** on Abraham his rectitude
021:076   (to Us) **aforetime**: We listened to his (prayer)
027:045   We sent (**aforetime**), to the Thamud, their brother
032:023   We did indeed **aforetime** give the Book to Moses:
033:062   who lived **aforetime**: no change wilt thou find
034:010   We bestowed Grace **aforetime** on David
034:015   There was, for Saba', **aforetime**, a Sign
037:072   But We sent **aforetime**, among them, warners.
040:053   We did **aforetime** give Moses the Guidance,
040:078   We did **aforetime** send messengers before thee:
041:045   the book **aforetime**: but dispute arose therein.
041:048   to invoke **aforetime** will leave them in the lurch,
043:046   We did send Moses **aforetime**, with Our Signs,
044:030   We did deliver **aforetime** the Children of Israel
044:032   And We chose them **aforetime** above the
045:016   We did **aforetime** grant to the Children of Israel

AFORETIME (continued)

046:027 We destroyed **aforetime** towns round about you;
052:026 They will say: "**Aforetime**, We were not without
054:041 too, **aforetime**, came Warners (from Allah).
057:016 The Book **aforetime**, but long ages passed over
057:025 We sent **aforetime** our messengers with Clear
064:005 of those who rejected Faith **aforetime**? So they
068:043 summoned **aforetime** to bow in adoration, while they

AFRAID

003:175 be ye not **afraid** of them, but fear
005:054 and never **afraid** of the reproaches
008:026 and **afraid** that men might despoil and kidnap you;
009:056 yet they are **afraid** (of you).
009:064 The Hypocrites are **afraid** lest a Sura should be
015:052 "We feel **afraid** of you!"
033:072 to undertake it, being **afraid** thereof: but man
058:013 Is it that ye are **afraid** of spending sums

AFTER

002:027 Allah's Covenant **after** it is ratified,
002:056 Then We raised you up **after** your death;
002:075 knowingly **after** they understood it.
002:085 **After** this it is ye, the same people,
002:092 yet ye worshipped the Calf (even) **after** that,
002:109 back to infidelity **after** ye have believed,
002:109 **after** the truth hath become manifest
002:120 their desires **after** the knowledge
002:133 "What will ye worship **after** me?"
002:145 If thou **after** the knowledge hath reached thee,
002:159 **after** We have made it clear
002:178 **After** this whoever exceeds the limits
002:181 If anyone changes the bequest **after** hearing it,
002:209 If ye backslide **after** the clear (Signs)
002:211 **after** Allah's favour has come to him,
002:213 **after** the clear Signs came to them,
002:229 A divorce is only permissible twice: **after** that,
002:230 until **after** she has married another husband
002:230 he cannot, **after** that, re-marry her until
002:233 by mutual consent, and **after** due consultation.
002:237 but **after** the fixation of a dower for them,
002:246 Children of Israel **after** (the time of) Moses
002:253 **after** Clear (Signs) had come to them,
002:255 before or **after** or behind them.
002:259 **after** (this) its death?"
002:266 not strong (enough to look, **after** themselves)
002:275 Those who **after** receiving admonition
003:008 deviate now **after** Thou hast guided us,
003:019 **after** knowledge had come to them.
003:061 now **after** (full) knowledge hath come to thee,
003:065 were not revealed till **after** him?
003:080 **after** ye have bowed your will (to Allah in Islam)?
003:082 If any turn back **after** this, they are
003:086 who reject faith **after** they accepted it and bore
003:089 Except for those that repent (even) **after** that.
003:090 But those who reject faith **after** they accepted it.
003:094 If any, **after** this, invent a lie
003:100 render you apostates **after** ye have believed!
003:105 and fall into disputation **after** receiving Clear Signs:
003:106 "Did ye reject Faith **after** accepting it?
003:152 Among you are some that hanker **after** this world
003:152 and disobeyed it **after** He brought you in sight
003:153 one distress **after** another by way of requital,
003:154 **After** (the excitement) of the distress, He sent down
003:160 if He forsakes you, who is there, **after** that,

AFTER (continued)

003:172 even **after** being wounded,
004:011 **after** the payment of legacies and debts.
004:012 a fourth; **after** payment of legacies and debts.
004:012 a eighth; **after** payment of legacies and debts.
004:012 a third; **after** payment of legacies and debts;
004:024 but if, **after** a dower is prescribed, ye agree
004:043 until **after** washing your whole body if ye are ill,
004:115 even **after** guidance has been plainly conveyed
004:153 even **after** Clear Signs had come to them;
004:163 and the Messengers **after** him:
004:165 **after** (the coming) of the messengers,
005:012 but if any of you, **after** this, resisteth faith,
005:019 **after** the break in (the series of) Messengers,
005:032 yet, even **after** that, many of them continued
005:039 But if the thief repent **after** his crime, and amend
005:043 yet even **after** that, they would turn away.
005:050 Do they then seek **after** a judgement of
005:106 detain them both **after** prayer,
005:108 that other oaths would be taken **after** their oaths.
005:115 but if any of you **after** that resisteth faith, I
006:068 then **after** recollection, sit not thou
006:071 heels **after** receiving guidance from Allah?-
006:083 We raise whom We will, degree **after** degree: for
007:056 **after** it hath been set in order, but call
007:058 springs up produce, (rich) **after** its kind: but
007:069 He made you inheritors **after** the people
007:074 inheritors **after** the 'Ad people and gave
007:085 **after** it has been set in order: that will
007:089 **after** Allah hath rescued us therefrom; nor
007:103 Then **after** them We sent Moses with Our Signs
007:129 both before and **after** thou comest to us." He
007:169 **After** them succeeded an (evil) generation: they
007:173 but we are (their) descendants **after** them: wilt
007:185 In what message **after** this will they then believe?
008:006 the truth **after** it was made manifest, as if
008:042 might live **after** a Clear Sign (had been given).
008:042 who died might die **after** a clear Sign (had been
008:052 "(Deeds) **after** the manner of the people
008:054 "(Deeds) **after** the manner of the people
009:012 their oaths **after** their covenant, and taunt
009:027 Again will Allah, **after** this, turn (in mercy)
009:028 **after** this year of theirs, approach the
009:066 rejected Faith **after** ye had accepted it. If We
009:074 it **after** accepting Islam: and the meditated
009:113 **after** it is clear to them that they are
009:115 **after** He hath Guided them until He makes clear
009:117 **after** that the hearts of a part of them had
010:003 except **after** His leave (hath been obtained).
010:014 **after** them, to see how ye would behave!
010:021 of some mercy **after** adversity hath touched them,
010:074 Then **after** him We sent (many) messengers
010:075 Then **after** them sent We Moses and Aaron
010:092 a Sign to those who come **after** thee! But verily
010:093 of the best: it was **after** knowledge had been
011:007 **after** death, the Unbelievers would be sure to say,
011:010 (Our) favours **after** adversity hath touched him,
011:071 glad tidings of Isaac, and **after** him, of Jacob.
012:007 are Signs for Seekers (**after** Truth).
012:009 for you to be righteous **after** that!"
012:035 Then it occurred to them **after** they had seen
012:045 and who now remembered him **after** (so long)
012:048 "Then will come **after** that (period) seven

AFTER (continued)

012:049 "Then will come **after** that (period) a year
012:100 the desert, (even) **after** Satan had sown enmity
013:025 of Allah, **after** having plighted their word
013:037 their (vain) desires **after** the knowledge which
014:009 who (came) **after** them? None knows
015:023 remain Inheritors (**after** all else passes away).
016:041 **after** suffering oppression,-We will assuredly
016:065 to the earth **after** its death: verily in this
016:070 **after** having known (much): for Allah
016:091 and break not your oaths **after** ye have
016:092 **after** it has become strong. Using your oaths
016:094 may slip **after** it was firmly planted; and ye
016:106 Any one who, **after** accepting Faith in Allah,
016:110 **after** all this is Oft-Forgiving, Most Merciful.
016:110 leave their homes **after** trials and persecutions
016:119 and make amends,-thy Lord **after** all this, is
017:017 many generations have We destroyed **after** Noah?
017:076 have stayed (therein) **after** thee, except for
017:082 nothing but loss **after** loss.
018:006 **after** them, in grief, if they
018:064 seeking **after**": so they went back on their
018:076 about anything **after** this, keep me not
018:079 for there was **after** them a certain king who
019:005 (and colleagues) (will do) **after** me: but my
019:059 But **after** them there followed a posterity
019:059 and followed **after** lusts soon, then, will they
020:110 He knows what is before or **after** or behind them:
021:057 **after** ye go away and turn your backs"...
021:105 **after** the Message (given to Moses): My servants
022:005 **after** having known (much). And (further),
022:036 on their sides (**after** slaughter), eat ye
022:044 and (only) **after** that did I punish them:
023:015 **After** that, at length, ye will die.
023:031 Then We raised **after** them another generation.
023:042 Then We raised **after** them other generations.
023:101 nor will one ask **after** another!
024:004 and reject their evidence ever **after**: for such
024:033 yet, **after** such compulsion, is Allah
024:047 but even **after** that, some of them turn away:
024:055 If any do reject Faith **after** this, they are
024:055 **after** the fear in which they (lived), to one
024:058 and **after** the late-night prayer: these are
025:029 the Message (of Allah) **after** it had come to me!
026:227 and defend themselves **after** they are
028:043 **after** We had destroyed the earlier generations,
028:058 **after** them, are deserted,-all but
028:087 from Allah's revelations **after** they have been
029:063 **after** its death, they will
030:003 (even) **after** (this) defeat of theirs, will soon
030:019 to the earth **after** it is dead: and thus
030:024 **after** it is dead: verily in that are Signs
030:050 to the earth **after** its death: verily the
030:054 **after** weakness, then, **after** strength, gave you
033:005 Call them by **after** their fathers: that is
033:052 (to marry more) women **after** this, not to
033:053 **after** him at any time. Truly such
034:032 from Guidance **after** it reached you? Nay, rather,
035:009 the earth therewith **after** its death: even so
036:028 his People, **after** Him, any hosts from heaven,
036:045 will be **after** you, in order that ye may
036:067 nor could they have returned (**after** error).
038:035 will not belong to another **after** me: for Thou

AFTER (continued)

038:088 the truth of it (all) **after** a while."
039:006 one **after** another, in three veils of darkness.
039:054 comes on you: **after** that ye shall not be helped.
040:005 **after** them; and every People plotted against
040:031 and those who came **after** them: but Allah
040:034 send **after** him.' Thus doth Allah leave to stray
041:050 from Us, **after** some adversity has touched him,
042:014 who have inherited the Book **after** them are in
042:014 **after** knowledge reached them,-being insolent
042:016 **after** He has been accepted,-futile is
042:028 (even) **after** (men) have given up all hope,
042:041 defend themselves **after** a wrong (done) to him,
043:028 among those who came **after** him, that they
043:048 We showed them Sign **after** Sign, each greater
045:005 and revives therewith the earth **after** its death,
045:006 believe **after** Allah and His Signs?
045:017 it was only **after** knowledge had been granted to
045:023 **after** Allah (has withdrawn Guidance)? Will ye
046:021 Warners before him and **after** him: "Worship ye
046:030 **after** Moses, confirming what came before it:
047:025 **after** Guidance was clearly shown to them,-
047:032 **after** Guidance has been clearly shown to them,
048:011 in (looking **after**) our flocks and heads, and our
048:024 **after** that He gave you the victory over them.
049:011 (to be used of one) **after** he has believed:
050:040 and (so likewise) **after** the prostration.
053:024 (just) anything he hankers **after**?
053:026 will avail nothing except **after** Allah has given
057:017 life to the earth **after** its death! Already have
057:027 We sent **after** them Jesus the son of Mary,
059:010 And those who came **after** them say: "Our Lord!
061:006 **after** me, whose name shall be Ahmad. But when
065:007 has given him. **After** a difficulty, Allah will
070:010 And no friend will ask **after** a friend,
077:001 one **after** another (to man's profit);
077:050 Then what Message, **after** that, will they believe in?
095:007 What then, can **after** this make you
098:004 make schisms, until **after** there came to them
114:004 (of Evil), who withdraws (**after** his whisper),-

AFTER-ACHE

056:019 No **after-ache** will they receive therefrom, nor will

AFTERNOON

007:004 or while they slept for their **afternoon** rest.
030:018 and on earth; and in the late **afternoon** and when

AFTERWARDS

004:017 who do evil in ignorance and repent soon **afterwards**;
004:110 but **afterwards** seeks Allah's forgiveness, he
028:025 **Afterwards** one of the (damsels) came (back)
049:006 and **afterwards** become full of repentance
057:010 and fought **afterwards**. But to all has Allah

AGAIN

002:028 and **again** to Him will ye return.
002:028 and will **again** bring you to life;
002:196 and when ye are in peaceful conditions (**again**),
002:259 then raised him up (**again**).
003:041 of thy Lord **again** and **again**,
004:043 sins and forgive **again** and **again**.
004:099 and forgive **again** and **again**.
004:137 then believe (**again**) and (**again**) reject Faith, and
004:154 and (once **again**) We commanded them: "Transgress
005:071 yet **again** many of them became blind and deaf.

AGAIN (continued)

005:093　then **again**, guard themselves from evil and do good.
006:029　and never shall we be raised up **again**."
006:060　by day doth He raise you up **again**; that a term
006:093　or (**again**) who saith, "I can reveal the like of
007:169　came their way, they would (**again**) seize them.　Was
009:027　**Again** will Allah, after this, turn (in mercy)
009:077　and because they lied (**again** and **again**).
017:025　turn to Him **again** and **again** (in true penitence).
019:015　he will be raised up to life (**again**)!
019:033　I shall be raised up to life (**again**)!"
020:055　and from it shall We bring you out once **again**.
020:082　He that forgives **again** and **again**, to those
022:029　and (**again**) circumambulate the Ancient House."
022:060　out (sins) and forgives (**again** and **again**).
022:060　he received, and is **again** set upon inordinately.
022:066　and will **again** give you life: truly man
023:016　**Again**, on the Day of Judgement, will ye
023:035　ye shall be brought forth (**again**)?
023:037　But we shall never be raised up **again**!
023:082　could we really be raised up **again**?
024:036　(**again** and **again**),-
025:040　But they expect not to be raised **again**.
026:081　and then to live (**again**);
028:018　his help (**again**).　Moses said to him: "Thou art
030:040　to die; and **again** He will give you life.
033:020　the Confederates should come (**again**), they would
037:016　and bones, shall we (then) be raised up (**again**)?
037:114　**Again**, (of old).　We bestowed Our favour
039:005　He Who forgives **again** and **again**?
040:042　in Power, Who forgives **again** and **again**!
044:029　over them: nor were they given a respite (**again**).
044:035　and we shall not be raised **again**.
046:017　before me (without rising **again**)?"　And they
050:003　(shall we live **again**?)　That is
056:047　and bones, shall we then indeed be raised up **again**?-
056:061　creating you (**again**) in (Forms) that ye know not.
058:006　will raise them all up (**again**) and tell them
067:003　vision **again**: Seest thou any flaw?
067:004　**Again** turn thy vision a second time: (thy) vision
071:018　(**again** at the Resurrection)?
075:035　**Again**, woe to thee, (O man!), yea woe!
080:022　He will raise him up (**again**).
082:018　**Again**, what will explain to thee what the
102:004　**Again**, ye soon shall know!
102:007　**Again**, ye shall see it with certainty of sight!

AGAINST

002:048　Then guard yourselves **against** a day
002:085　assist (their enemies) **against** them,
002:089　prayed for victory **against** those
002:120　neither Protector nor Helper **against** Allah.
002:123　Then guard yourselves **against** a day
002:137　but Allah will suffice thee as **against** them,
002:150　of dispute **against** you among the people,
002:194　transgress ye likewise **against** him.
002:194　transgresses the prohibition **against** you,
002:224　an excuse in your oaths **against** doing good,
002:228　rights similar to the rights **against** them,
002:250　help us **against** those that reject faith."
003:009　gather mankind together **against** a Day about which
003:010　will avail them aught **against** Allah:
003:025　**against** a Day about which there is no doubt,
003:075　but they tell a lie **against** Allah,

AGAINST (continued)

003:078　it is they who tell a lie **against** Allah,
003:116　will avail them aught **against** Allah:
003:147　and help us **against** those that resist Faith."
003:173　"A great army is gathering **against** you,
003:186　persevere patiently, and guard **against** evil,
004:006　nor in haste **against** their growing up.
004:015　witnesses from amongst you **against** them;
004:019　forbidden to inherit women **against** their will.
004:024　Thus hath Allah ordained (prohibitions) **against** you:
004:034　seek not **against** them means (of annoyance):
004:041　a witness **against** these People!
004:050　Behold! how they invent a lie **against** Allah!
004:065　no resistance **against** thy decisions, but
004:076　so fight ye **against** the friends, of Satan:
004:090　no way for you (to war **against** them).
004:091　with a clear argument **against** them.
004:097　those who die in sin **against** their soul.
004:111　he earns it **against** his own soul: for Allah
004:135　and whether it be (**against**) rich or poor: for
004:135　even as **against** yourselves, or your parents, or
004:144　an open proof **against** yourselves?
004:156　that they uttered **against** Mary a grave false charge;
004:159　He will be a witness **against** them;
004:165　should have no plea **against** Allah: for Allah
005:011　the design to stretch out their hands **against** you,
005:017　**against** Allah, if His Will were to destroy
005:028　to stretch my hand **against** thee to slay thee: for
005:028　"If thou dost stretch thy hand **against** me, to slay
005:033　who wage war **against** Allah and His Messenger, and
005:041　for him **against** Allah.
005:054　mighty **against** the Rejecters, fighting in
005:103　who invent a lie **against** Allah, but most
006:021　who inventeth a lie **against** Allah or
006:024　Behold! how they lie **against** themselves but
006:051　that they may guard (**against** evil).
006:083　(to use) **against** his people: We raise
006:093　one who inventeth a lie **against** Allah, or saith,
006:093　for that ye used to tell lies **against** Allah, and
006:123　but they only plot **against** their own souls, and
006:130　"We bear witness **against** ourselves."　It was
006:130　So **against** themselves will they bear
006:138　forging a lie **against** Allah's name: soon will
006:140　inventing (lies) **against** Allah.　They have
006:144　than one who invents a lie **against** Allah, to lead
007:033　sins and trespasses **against** truth or reason;
007:037　and they will bear witness **against** themselves, that
007:037　who forges a lie **against** Allah or rejects
007:089　"We should indeed forge a lie **against** Allah, if
007:097　feel secure **against** the coming of Our wrath
007:098　**against** its coming in broad daylight while they
007:099　**against** Allah's devising but no one can fell
007:167　that He would send **against** them, to the
007:195　scheme (your worst) **against** me, and give
008:013　**against** Allah and His Messenger: if any contend
008:013　if any contend **against** Allah and His Messenger.
008:030　plotted **against** thee, to keep thee in bonds,
008:060　**Against** them make ready your strength to the
008:071　**against** Allah, and so hath He given thee
008:071　**against** thee, (O Messenger!), they have
008:072　except **against** a people with whom ye have
008:075　rights **against** each other in the Book
009:004　nor aided any one **against** you.　So fulfil

AGAINST (continued)

009:017 of Allah while they witness **against** their own
009:073 and be firm **against** them. Their abode
009:073 O Prophet! strive hard **against** the Unbelievers
009:091 be **against** such as do right: and Allah
009:093 The ground (of complaint) is only **against** such as
009:107 warred **against** Allah and His Messenger aforetime.
009:122 to guard themselves (**against** evil).
010:017 as forge a lie **against** Allah, or deny
010:021 to plotting **against** Our Signs! Say: "Swifter
010:023 O mankind! your insolence is **against** your own
010:033 proved true **against** those who rebel: verily they
010:036 can be of no avail **against** Truth. Verily Allah
010:060 **against** Allah, of the Day of Judgement? Verily
010:063 and (constantly) guard **against** evil;-
010:069 **against** Allah will never prosper."
010:096 Those **against** whom the Word of thy Lord
010:099 **against** their will, to believe!
011:018 those who forge a lie **against** Allah?
011:018 "These are the ones who lied **against** their Lord!
011:030 help me **against** Allah if I drove them away?
011:040 **against** whom the Word has already gone forth,-
011:055 So scheme (your worst) **against** me, all of you,
011:063 me **against** Allah if I were to disobey Him? What
011:070 been sent **against** the people of Lut."
012:005 lest they concoct a plot **against** thee: for Satan
012:018 **against** that which ye assert, it is
012:025 an evil design **against** thy wife, but prison
012:051 no evil know we **against** him!" Said the 'Aziz's
012:067 **against** Allah (with my advice): none can
012:068 in the least **against** (the Plan of) Allah: it served
012:081 and we could not well guard **against** the unseen!
012:107 the coming **against** them of the covering veil
012:107 Or of the coming **against** them of the (final)
013:034 and defender have they none **against** Allah.
013:037 protector nor defender **against** Allah.
014:021 **against** the wrath of Allah?" They will reply
014:042 He but giveth them respite **against** a Day when
015:095 unto thee **against** those who scoff.-
016:026 plot (**against** Allah' Way): but Allah
016:089 **against** these (thy people): and We
016:089 all peoples a witness **against** them, from amongst
017:005 came to pass, We sent **against** you Our servants
017:007 (ye did it) **against** yourselves. So when
017:014 an account **against** thee."
017:016 the word is proved true **against** them; then We
017:068 or that He will not send **against** you a violent
017:069 so that ye find no helper therein **against** Us?
017:069 and send **against** you a heavy gale to drown you
017:075 found none to help thee **against** Us!
017:086 thy affair in that matter as **against** Us,-
017:092 **against** us; or thou bring Allah and the angels
018:015 as invent a falsehood **against** Allah?
018:043 **against** Allah, nor was he able to deliver himself.
018:090 no covering protection **against** the sun.
019:044 for Satan is a rebel **against** (Allah) Most Gracious.
019:063 Our Servants who guard **against** evil.
019:069 **against** (Allah) Most Gracious.
019:072 **against** evil, and We shall leave the wrong-doers
019:082 their worship, and become adversaries **against** them.
019:083 set Satans on **against** the Unbelievers, to incite
019:084 So make no haste **against** them, for We
020:045 with insolence **against** us, or lest

AGAINST (continued)

020:061 forge not ye a lie **against** Allah, lest He
021:018 Nay, We hurl the Truth **against** falsehood, and it
021:057 plan **against** your idols-after ye
021:070 Then they planned **against** him: but We
021:077 We helped him **against** people who rejected
021:112 sought **against** the blasphemies ye utter!
022:039 To those **against** whom war is made, permission is
022:051 "But those who strive **against** Our Signs,
023:027 of them **against** whom the Word has already
023:038 **against** Allah, but we are not the ones to believe
023:093 they are warned **against**,-
023:095 **against** which they are warned.
024:004 a charge **against** chaste women, and produce
024:006 a charge **against** their wives, and have
024:022 by oath **against** helping their kinsmen, those in
024:024 bear witness **against** them as to their actions.
025:052 the Unbelievers, but strive **against** them with
025:055 is a helper (of Evil), **against** his own Lord!
026:014 of crime **against** me; and I fear they may slay me."
027:031 "'Be ye not arrogant **against** me, but come
027:082 **against** them (the unjust), We shall
027:085 **against** them, because of their wrong-doing,
028:015 **against** his foe, and Moses struck
028:032 to thy side (to guard) **against** fear. Those are
028:063 Those **against** whom the charge will be proved,
028:081 party to help him **against** Allah, nor could
029:030 me **against** people who do mischief!"
029:040 his crime: of them, **against** some We sent
029:068 who invents a lie **against** Allah or rejects
033:009 but We sent **against** them a hurricane and forces
033:060 **against** them: then will they not be able to
034:005 But those who strive **against** Our Signs,
034:008 "Has he invented a falsehood **against** Allah, or is
034:016 and We sent **against** them the flood (released)
034:028 and warning them (**against** sin), but most
034:038 Those who strive **against** Our Signs, to frustrate
036:007 The Word is proved true **against** the greater
036:028 And We sent not down **against** his People,
036:070 may be proved true **against** those who
037:007 **against** all obstinate rebellious Satans.
037:031 **against** us, the Word of our Lord that we
037:098 **against** him, but We made them the ones
038:006 a thing designed (**against** you)!
038:028 those who guard **against** evil, the same
039:019 Is, then, one **against** whom the decree of Punishment
039:022 hardened **against** the remembrance of Allah!
039:028 in order that they may guard **against** Evil.
039:053 transgressed **against** their souls! Despair not
039:060 see those who told lies **against** Allah;-their faces
039:071 has been proved true **against** the Unbelievers!"
040:005 plotted **against** their prophet, to seize
040:006 proved true **against** the Unbelievers; that truly
040:021 and none had they to defend them **against** Allah.
040:042 **against** Allah, and to join with Him partners of
040:045 that they plotted (**against** him), but the
041:015 the land, **against** (all) truth and reason, and said
041:016 So We sent **against** them a furious Wind
041:020 **against** them, as to (all) their deeds.
041:021 "Why bear ye witness **against** us?" They will
041:022 **against** you! But ye did think that Allah
041:025 **against** them; for they are utterly lost.
041:046 it is **against** his own soul: nor is

AGAINST (continued)

042:024 **against** Allah"? But is Allah willed, He could
042:041 to him, **against** such there is no cause of blame.
042:042 The blame is only **against** those who oppress men
043:033 that blasphemes **against** The Most Gracious,
043:054 truly were they a people rebellious (**against** Allah).
044:003 for We (ever) wish to warn (**against** Evil).
044:019 "And be not arrogant as **against** Allah: for I
044:020 my Lord and your Lord, **against** your injuring me.
045:015 if he does evil, it works **against** (His own soul).
046:008 **against** Allah. He knows best of that whereof ye
046:018 Such are they **against** whom is the word
047:036 and guard **against** evil, He will grant
048:016 (to fight) **against** a people given to vehement war
048:029 are strong **against** Unbelievers, (but) compassionate
049:009 transgresses beyond bounds **against** the other,
049:009 the other, then fight ye (all) **against** the one
051:041 **against** them the devastating Wind:
051:042 up **against**, but reduced it to ruin and rottenness.
052:042 (**against** thee)? But those who disbelieve
053:028 and conjecture avails nothing **against** Truth.
053:032 He knows best who it is that guards **against** evil.
054:019 For We sent **against** them a furious wind, on a
054:031 For We sent **against** them a single Mighty Blast,
054:034 We sent **against** them a violent tornado with
058:017 **against** Allah, will be their riches nor their
059:010 **against** those who have believed. Our Lord!
060:002 their hands and their tongues **against** you for evil;
061:007 who forges falsehood **against** Allah, even as
061:014 power to those who believed **against** their enemies,
063:004 **against** them. They are the enemies; so beware
066:004 each other **against** him, truly Allah
066:009 O Prophet! strive hard **against** the Unbelievers
067:017 is in Heaven will not send **against** you a violent
068:030 Then they turned, one **against** another, in reproach.
069:007 He made it rage **against** them seven nights
072:004 who used to utter extravagant lies **against** Allah;
072:005 is untrue **against** Allah.
073:017 deny (Allah), guard yourselves **against** a Day that
075:014 Nay, man will be evidence **against** himself,
077:031 and is of no use **against** the fierce Blaze.
077:039 (or plot), use it **against** Me!
079:022 striving hard (**against** Allah).
085:006 Behold! they sat over **against** the (fire),
085:007 doing **against** the Believers.
105:003 And He sent **against** them flights of Birds,
106:004 security **against** fear (of danger).
106:004 **against** hunger, and with security **against**

AGE

002:068 but of middling **age**;
002:259 they show no signs of **age**;
002:266 while he is stricken with old **age**,
004:002 their property (when they reach their **age**),
004:006 until they reach the **age** of marriage;
005:110 to the people in childhood and in old **age**. Behold!
006:152 until he attain the **age** of full strength; give
014:039 unto me in old **age** Isma'il and Isaac: for truly
015:054 glad tidings even though old **age** has seized me?
016:070 sent back to a feeble **age**, so that
017:023 old **age** in thy life, say not to them a word
017:034 until he attains the **age** of full strength;
018:082 attain their **age** of full strength and get out
019:008 and I have grown quite decrepit from old **age**?"

AGE (continued)

022:005 may reach your **age** of full strength; and some
022:005 old **age**, so that they know nothing after having
024:058 have not come of **age** ask your permission (before
024:059 come of **age**, let them (also) ask for permission,
028:014 When he reached full **age**, and was
037:102 (the **age** of) (serious) work with him, he said:
038:052 their glances, (companions) of equal **age**.
040:067 reach your **age** of full strength; then lets
046:015 the **age** of full strength and attains forty years,
056:037 Full of love (for their mates), equal in **age**,-
065:004 the **age** of monthly courses, for them
078:033 Maidens of Equal **Age**;

AGED

012:078 he has a father, **aged** and venerable, (who will

AGES

028:045 and long were the **ages** that passed over them;
043:056 and an Example to later **ages**.
057:016 The Book aforetime, but long **ages** passed over
078:023 They will dwell therein for **ages**.

AGGRESSIVE

044:022 (But they were **aggressive**): then he

AGITATION

079:008 Hearts that Day will be in **agitation**;

AGONIES

006:093 the wicked (do fare) in the **agonies** of death!-

AGONY

003:016 and save us from the **agony** of the Fire;"
068:048 when he cried out in **agony**.

AGREE

002:232 if they mutually **agree** on equitable terms.
003:081 They said: "We **agree**."
003:081 Allah said: "Do ye **agree**, and take My covenant
004:024 ye **agree** mutually (to vary it), there
009:037 in order to **agree** with the number of months
078:003 About which they cannot **agree**.

AGREEABLE

012:023 is my lord! He made my sojourn **agreeable**! Truly
016:066 pure and **agreeable** to those who drink it.

AGREED

012:015 and they all **agreed** to throw him down to the
037:141 He (**agreed** to) cast lots, and he

AGREEMENT

010:071 get ye then an **agreement** about your plan
028:028 He said: "Be that (the **agreement**) between me

AH

002:140 **Ah**! who is more unjust than those
002:175 **Ah**! what boldness (they show) for the Fire!
002:214 **Ah**! Verily, the help of Allah is (always) near!
003:066 **Ah**! Ye are those who fell to disputing (even)
003:119 **Ah**! ye are those who love them,
004:069 **Ah**! How beautiful is their Company.
004:109 **Ah**! these are the sort of men on whose behalf
005:052 **Ah**! perhaps Allah will give (thee) victory, or a
006:031 and they say: "**Ah**! woe unto us that we neglected;
007:060 "**Ah**! we see thee evident error."
007:066 "**Ah**! we see thou art in folly!" and "We think
010:051 (It will then be said): '**Ah**! now? And ye wanted
010:091 (It was said to him): "**Ah** now!-but a little
011:005 **Ah**! even when they cover themselves
011:008 **Ah**! On the day it (actually) reaches them,
011:060 **Ah**! behold! For the 'Ad rejected their

AH (continued)

011:068   **Ah**! Behold! For the Thamud
012:019   (into the well). He said: "**Ah** there! Good news
014:010   They said: "**Ah**! ye are no more then human,
016:059   **Ah**! what an evil (choice) they decide on!
018:049   "**Ah**! woe to us! what a book is this! It leaves
019:023   "**Ah**! would that I had died before this! would that
021:014   They said: "**Ah**! woe to us! we were
021:018   **Ah**! woe be to you for the (false) things
021:097   "**Ah**! woe to us! we were indeed heedless of this;
025:028   "**Ah**! woe is me! would that I had never taken
025:029   come to me! **Ah**! the Satan is but a traitor
028:082   us up! **Ah**! those who reject Allah will assuredly
028:082   the morrow: "**Ah**! It is indeed Allah Who enlarges
036:026   He said: "**Ah** me! would that my People knew
036:030   **Ah**! alas for (My) servants! There comes
036:052   They will say: "**Ah**! woe unto us! Who hath
037:020   They will say, "**Ah**! woe to us! this is
039:015   **Ah**! that is indeed the (real and) evident Loss!"
039:056   say: '**Ah**! woe is me!-in that
041:054   their Lord? **Ah** indeed! it is He that doth
041:054   **Ah** indeed! are they in doubt concerning
043:020   ("**Ah**!") they say, "If it had been the will
043:038   **Ah**! Evil is the companion (indeed)!
054:026   **Ah**! they will know on the morrow, which is
054:030   **Ah**! how (terrible) was My Chastisement and My
069:019   "**Ah** here! read ye my Record!
069:025   "**Ah**! would that my record had not been given to me!
069:027   "**Ah**! would that (Death) had made an end of me!
077:015   **Ah** woe, that Day, to the Rejecters of Truth!
077:019   **Ah** woe, that Day, to the Rejecters of Truth!
077:024   **Ah** woe, that Day, to the Rejecters of Truth!
077:028   **Ah** woe, that Day, to the Rejecters of Truth!
077:034   **Ah** woe, that Day, to the Rejecters of Truth!
077:037   **Ah** woe, that Day, to the Rejecters of Truth!
077:040   **Ah** woe, that Day, to the Rejecters of Truth!
077:045   **Ah** woe, that Day, to the Rejecters of Truth!
077:047   **Ah** woe, that Day, to the Rejecters of Truth!
077:049   **Ah** woe, that Day, to the Rejecters of Truth!
089:024   He will say: "**Ah**! would that I had sent forth

AHMAD

061:006   after me, whose name shall be **Ahmad**. But when

AID

001:005   Thee do we worship, and Thine **aid** we seek.
003:013   with His **aid** whom He pleaseth.
006:034   until Our **aid** did reach them: there is none
007:192   No **aid** can they give them, nor can
007:192   nor can they **aid** themselves!
008:026   strengthened you with His **aid**, and gave you
008:062   with His **aid** and with (the company of)
008:072   but if they seek your **aid** in religion, it is
008:072   who gave (them) asylum and **aid**,-these are
008:074   as well as those who give (them) asylum and **aid**,-
009:100   those who gave them **aid**, and (also) those who
010:038   and call (to your **aid**) anyone you can, besides
011:013   like unto it, and call (to your **aid**) whomsoever
017:080   and grant me from Thee an authority to **aid** (me)."
018:109   like it, for its **aid**."
021:043   to **aid** themselves, nor can they be defended
022:039   Allah is Most powerful for their **aid**;
022:040   Allah will certainly **aid** those who **aid** His (cause);-
030:047   to **aid** those who believed.
046:017   And they two seek Allah's **aid**, (and rebuke

AID (continued)

047:013   And there was none to **aid** them.

AIDED

033:026   who **aided** them-Allah did take them down from

AIDING

059:008   and **aiding** Allah and His Messenger: such are

AILMENT

002:196   or had an **ailment** in his scalp,

AIM

002:076   Do ye not understand (their **aim**)?
002:205   his **aim** everywhere is to spread mischief
002:267   and do not even **aim** at anything which is bad,
028:079   Said those whose **aim** is the Life of this World:

AIMS

002:203   if his **aims** is to do right.

'AIN

019:001   Kaf. Ha. Ya. '**Ain**. Sad.
042:002   '**Ain**. Sin. Qaf.

AIR

004:129   (as it were) hanging (in the **air**).
016:079   (the **air** and) the sky? Nothing holds
024:041   and the birds (of the **air**) with wings outspread?

AL-QUR-AN

006:070   with it (**Al-Qur-an**) lest a soul is caught in its

ALAS

006:128   but (**alas**!) we reached our term-which Thou
011:072   She said: "**Alas** for me! Shall I bear a child,
014:002   But **alas** for the Unbelievers for a
016:025   whom they misled. **Alas**, how grievous the burdens
028:080   (true) knowledge said: "**Alas** for you! The reward
036:030   Ah! **alas** for (My) servants! There comes
068:031   They said: "**Alas** for us! We have

ALIF

007:001   **Alif** Lam Mim Sad.

ALIKE

002:070   to us are all heifers **alike**:
002:118   Their hearts are **alike**.
003:113   Not all of them are **alike**: of the People
009:067   are **alike**: they enjoin evil, and forbid
021:109   to you all **alike** and in truth; but I
028:061   Are (these two) **alike**?-one to whom
035:012   Nor are the two seas **alike**,-the one
035:019   The blind and the seeing are not **alike**;
035:022   Nor are **alike** those that are living
041:010   **alike** for (all) who ask.
055:006   both (**alike**) bow in adoration.

ALIVE

007:127   (only) their females will we save **alive**; and
007:141   and saved **alive** your females: in that
019:066   shall I then be raised up **alive**?"
028:004   but he kept **alive** their females: for he
036:070   (who are) **alive**, and that the word may be
040:025   with him, and keep **alive** their females," but the
081:008   Buried **alive**, is questioned-

ALL

002:017   when it lighted **all** around him,
002:020   The lightning **all** but snatches away their sight:
002:020   for Allah hath power over **all** things.
002:029   for you **all** things that are on earth;
002:029   and of **all** things He hath perfect knowledge.
002:031   And He taught Adam the names of **all** things;
002:036   And We said: "Get ye down, (**all** you people),

ALL (continued)

002:038   We said: "Get ye down **all** from here;
002:047   and that I preferred you to **all** others.
002:070   to us are **all** heifers alike:
002:091   yet they reject **all** besides,
002:096   of **all** people, most greedy of life,
002:096   for Allah sees well **all** that they do.
002:106   Allah hath power over **all** things?
002:109   for Allah hath power over **all** things.
002:110   for Allah sees well **all** that ye do.
002:116   Nay, to Him belongs **all** that is in
002:122   and that I preferred you to **all** others.
002:136   (**all**) Prophets from their Lord:
002:143   For Allah is to **all** people most surely
002:145   **all** the Signs (together),
002:147   so be not at **all** in doubt.
002:148   (as in a race) towards **all** that is good.
002:148   For Allah hath power over **all** things.
002:161   and the curse of angels, and of **all** mankind;
002:164   in the beasts of **all** kinds
002:165   that to Allah belongs **all** power,
002:166   the Chastisement and **all** relations between
002:177   and throughout **all** periods of panic.
002:181   For Allah hears and knows (**all** things).
002:194   and so for **all** things prohibited,
002:196   making ten days in **all**.
002:210   **all** questions go back (for decision).
002:224   heareth and knoweth **all** things.
002:227   Allah heareth and knoweth **all** things.
002:231   well acquainted with **all** things.
002:232   This instruction is for **all** amongst you,
002:237   For Allah sees well **all** that ye do.
002:244   and know that Allah heareth and knoweth **all** things.
002:247   Allah is All-embracing, and He knoweth **all** things."
002:251   but Allah is full of bounty to **all** the worlds.
002:255   His are **all** things in the heavens and on earth.
002:255   the Self-subsisting, Supporter of **all**
002:256   And Allah heareth and knoweth **all** things.
002:259   **all** in ruins to its roofs.
002:259   Allah hath power over **all** things."
002:261   and He knoweth **all** things.
002:261   And Allah careth for **all** and He knoweth
002:263   Allah is free of **all** wants,
002:266   and **all** kinds of fruit,
002:267   and Worthy of **all** praise.
002:267   And know that Allah is free of **all** wants,
002:268   and Allah careth for **all** and He
002:268   and He knoweth **all** things.
002:270   be sure Allah knows it **all**.
002:273   they beg not importunately from **all** and sundry.
002:276   Allah will deprive usury of **all** blessing,
002:282   And Allah is well acquainted with **all** things.
002:283   And Allah knoweth **all** that ye do.
002:284   For Allah hath power over **all** things.
002:284   To Allah belongeth **all** that is in the heavens
002:285   and to Thee is the end of **all** journeys."
003:002   the Supporter of **all**.
003:015   For in Allah's sight are (**all**) His servants,
003:020   and in Allah's sight are (**all**) His servants.
003:026   in Thy hand is **all** Good.
003:026   Verily, over **all** things Thou hast power.
003:029   And Allah has power over **all** things.
003:029   in your hearts or reveal it, Allah knows it **all**:

ALL (continued)

003:030   be confronted with **all** the good it has done,
003:030   and **all** the evil it has done,
003:033   and the family of 'Imran above **all** people,
003:034   and Allah heareth and knoweth **all** things.
003:035   for Thou hearest and knoweth **all** things."
003:042   chosen thee above the women of **all** nations.
003:055   then shall ye **all** return to Me,
003:073   Say: "**All** bounties are in the hand of Allah:
003:073   and He knoweth **all** things."
003:073   and Allah careth for **all**,
003:079   Him (Who is truly the Cherisher of **all**)
003:083   While **all** creatures in the heavens and on earth have,
003:083   and to Him shall they **all** be brought back.
003:087   curse of Allah, of His angels, and of **all** mankind;
003:093   **All** food was lawful to the Children of Israel,
003:096   full of blessings and of guidance for **all** the worlds.
003:098   when Allah is Himself witness to **all** ye do?
003:099   But Allah is not unmindful of **all** that ye do."
003:103   And hold fast, **all** together, by the Rope
003:104   a band of people inviting to **all** that is good,
003:109   To Allah belongs **all** that is in the heavens
003:109   to Allah do **all** matters return.
003:113   Not **all** of them are alike: of the People
003:113   they rehearse the Signs of Allah **all** night long,
003:114   in (**all**) good works;
003:119   Allah knoweth well **all** the secrets of the heart."
003:120   for Allah compasseth round about **all** that they do.
003:121   and Allah heareth and knoweth **all** things.
003:129   To Allah belongeth **all** that is in the heavens
003:134   who restrain anger, and pardon (**all**) men;
003:147   **All** that they said was: "Our Lord forgive us
003:153   For Allah is well aware of **all** that ye do.
003:154   but (**all** this was) that Allah might test what
003:156   and Allah sees well **all** that ye do.
003:157   are far better than **all** they could amass.
003:163   and Allah sees well **all** that they do.
003:165   for Allah hath power over **all** things."
003:167   But Allah hath full knowledge of **all** they conceal.
003:180   and Allah is well acquainted with **all** that ye do.
003:189   and Allah hath power over **all** things.
003:191   not for naught hast Thou created (**all**) this!
004:011   (The distribution in **all** cases is) after
004:024   except for these, **all** others are lawful,
004:032   for Allah hath full knowledge of **all** things.
004:033   For truly Allah is witness to **all** things.
004:034   for Allah is Most High, Great (above you **all**).
004:035   and is acquainted with **all** things.
004:043   until ye can understand **all** that ye say,
004:047   fame of some (of you) beyond **all** recognition,
004:058   For Allah is He Who heareth and seeth **all** things.
004:065   judge in **all** disputes between them.
004:069   **All** who obey Allah and the Messenger are in the
004:070   and sufficient is it that Allah knoweth **all**.
004:071   or go forth **all** together.
004:078   Say: "**All** things are from Allah."
004:081   a section of them meditate **all** night on things
004:083   **all** but a few of you would have followed Satan.
004:085   and Allah hath power over **all** things.
004:086   Allah takes careful account of **all** things.
004:092   for Allah hath **all** knowledge and **all** wisdom.
004:094   for Allah is well aware of **all** that ye do.
004:095   Unto **all** (in Faith) hath Allah promised good: but

ALL (continued)

004:102   taking **all** precautions, and bearing arms: the
004:108   and Allah doth compass round **all** that they do.
004:126   But to Allah belong **all** things in the
004:126   and He it is that encompasseth **all** things.
004:128   Allah is well-acquainted with **all** that ye do.
004:130   for Allah is He that careth for **all** and is Wise.
004:131   belong **all** things in the heavens and on earth.
004:131   and Allah is free of **all** wants, worthy
004:131   To Allah belong **all** things in the
004:131   worthy of **all** praise.
004:132   and enough is Allah to carry through **all** affairs.
004:132   **all** things in the heavens and on earth, and
004:134   for Allah is He that heareth and seeth (**all** things).
004:135   verily Allah is well-acquainted with **all** that ye do.
004:139   Nay, **all** honor is with Allah.
004:140   and those who defy Faith-**all** in Hell;
004:147   and knoweth **all** things.
004:147   Nay, it is Allah that recogniseth (**all** good), and
004:148   for Allah is He who heareth and knoweth **all** things.
004:170   to Allah belong **all** things in the heavens
004:171   To Him belong **all** things in the
004:172   gather them **all** together unto Himself to (answer).
004:176   And Allah hath knowledge of **all** things.
005:001   O ye who believe! fulfil (**all**) obligations.
005:001   are **all** beasts of cattle with the exceptions
005:003   given up **all** hope of your religion: yet fear
005:004   Say: Lawful unto you are (**all**) things good and pure:
005:005   This day are (**all**) things good and pure
005:005   those who have lost (**all** spiritual good).
005:008   For Allah is well-acquainted with **all** that ye do.
005:011   And on Allah let Believers put (**all**) their trust.
005:016   Wherewith Allah guideth **all** who seek His good
005:017   and **all** that is between.
005:017   and **all**-every one that is on the earth?
005:017   For Allah hath power over **all** things."
005:018   and **all** that is between: and unto Him
005:018   and unto Him is the final goal (of **all**)."
005:019   and Allah hath power over **all** things.
005:040   and Allah hath power over **all** things.
005:048   The goal of you **all** is to Allah; it is He
005:048   so strive as in a race in **all** virtues.
005:053   **All** that they do will be in vain, and they
005:054   and He knoweth **all** things.
005:054   and Allah encompasseth **all**, and He
005:061   But Allah knoweth fully **all** that they hide.
005:066   the Gospel, and **all** the revelation that was
005:068   The Gospel, and **all** the revelation that has
005:071   But Allah sees well **all** that they do.
005:076   that heareth and knoweth **all** things."
005:097   and that Allah is well acquainted with **all** things.
005:099   but Allah knoweth **all** that ye reveal and ye conceal.
005:105   The return of you **all** is to Allah: it is
005:105   it is He that will inform you of **all** that ye do.
005:109   it is Thou who knowest in full **all** that is hidden.
005:115   on anyone among **all** the peoples.
005:116   For Thou knowest in full **all** that is hidden.
005:117   and Thou art a Witness to **all** things.
005:119   mighty Triumph (the fulfillment of **all** desires).
005:120   and **all** that is therein, and it is He
005:120   and it is He who hath power over **all** things.
006:012   Say: "To whom belongeth **all** that is in the
006:013   "To Him belongeth **all** that dwelleth (or lurketh)

ALL (continued)

006:013   Who heareth and knoweth **all** things.
006:017   He hath power over **all** things.
006:018   and He is the Wise, acquainted with **all** things."
006:019   that I may warn you and **all** whom it reaches.
006:022   On the day shall We gather them **all** together: We
006:038   and they (**all**) shall be gathered to
006:044   the gates of **all** (good) things, until, in the
006:060   then will He show you the truth of **all** that ye did.
006:060   **all** that ye have done by day: by day doth
006:064   from these and **all** (other) distresses: and yet
006:073   well acquainted (with **all** things).
006:078   this is the greatest (of **all**)." But when
006:080   my Lord comprehendeth in His knowledge **all** things.
006:084   **all** (three) We guided: and before
006:085   **all** in the ranks of the Righteous:
006:086   and to **all** We gave favour above the nations:
006:088   **all** that they did would be vain for them.
006:092   the Mother of Cities and **all** around her. Those
006:094   so now **all** relations between you
006:094   **all** (the favours) which We bestowed on you: We
006:099   with it We produce vegetation of **all** kinds: from
006:101   and He hath full knowledge of **all** things.
006:101   He created **all** things, and He hath
006:102   the Creator of **all** things: then worship
006:102   And He hath power to dispose of **all** affairs.
006:103   but His grasp is over **all** vision; He is
006:108   the truth of **all** that they did.
006:109   Say: "Certainly (**all**) Signs are in
006:111   **all** things before their very eyes, they are
006:115   for He is the one Who heareth and knoweth **all**.
006:120   Eschew **all** sin, open or secret: those who
006:124   and a severe chastisement, for **all** their plots.
006:128   gather them **all** together, (and say):
006:132   To **all** are degrees (or ranks)
006:134   **All** that hath been promised unto you
006:139   then **all** have shares therein. For their
006:141   and tilth with produce of **all** kinds, and olives
006:149   He could indeed have guided you **all**."
006:154   and explaining **all** things in detail,-and a
006:156   we remained unacquainted with **all** that they
006:159   the truth of **all** that they did.
006:162   my life and my death, are (**all**) for Allah, the
006:164   Cherisher of **all** things (that exist)?" Every
007:018   Hell will I fill with you **all**.
007:038   He will say: "Doubled for **all**": but this
007:038   until they follow each other, **all** into the Fire.
007:039   the Chastisement for **all** that ye did!"
007:052   a guide and a mercy to **all** who believe.
007:054   (**all**) are subservient by His Command. Verily,
007:089   Our Lord comprehends **all** things in His
007:096   to them (**all** kinds of) blessings from
007:107   plain (for **all** to see)!
007:108   and behold! it was white to **all** beholders!
007:112   And bring up to thee **all** (our) sorcerers well-versed."
007:117   **all** the falsehoods which they fake!
007:118   And **all** that they did was made of no effect.
007:124   and I will crucify you **all**."
007:145   Admonition and explanation of **all** things, (and
007:145   in the Tablets in **all** matters, Admonition
007:146   even if they see **all** the Signs, they will not
007:156   but My Mercy extendeth to **all** things. That
007:158   Say: "O men! I am sent unto you **all**, as the

ALL (continued)

007:166   they transgressed (**all**) prohibition, We said
007:185   and **all** that Allah hath created? (Do they
007:187   Only, **all** of a sudden, will it come to you." They
007:188   I should have multiplied **all** good, and no
007:200   for he heareth and knoweth (**all** things).
008:002   and put (**all**) their trust in their Lord;
008:012   and smite **all** their finger-tips off them."
008:017   He who heareth and knoweth (**all** things).
008:024   ye shall (**all**) be gathered.
008:029   remove from you (**all**) evil deeds and forgive you:
008:039   verily Allah doth see **all** that they do.
008:041   And know that out of **all** the booty that ye
008:041   For Allah hath power over **all** things.
008:042   is He Who heareth and knoweth (**all** things).
008:043   well the (secrets) of (**all**) hearts.
008:044   and unto Allah are **all** matters returned.
008:047   for Allah compasseth **all** that they do.
008:053   heareth and knoweth (**all** things)."
008:054   for they were **all** oppressors and wrong-doers.
008:061   the One that heareth and knoweth (**all** things).
008:063   not if thou hadst spent **all** that is in the earth,
008:072   and (remember) Allah seeth **all** that ye do.
008:072   these are (**all**) friends and protectors, one of
008:074   these are (**all**) in very truth the believers: for
008:075   Verily Allah is well-acquainted with **all** things.
009:010   It is they who have transgressed **all** bounds.
009:016   with (**all**) that ye do.
009:018   and fear none (at **all**) except Allah. It is
009:022   the greatest (of **all**).
009:025   For **all** that it is wide, did constrain
009:033   **all** religion, even though the Pagans
009:036   the Pagans **all** together as they fight
009:036   as they fight you **all** together. But know
009:039   hath power over **all** things.
009:042   they would (**all**) without doubt have followed thee,
009:049   Hell surrounds the Unbelievers (on **all** sides).
009:061   and say, "He is (**all**) ear." Say, "He listens
009:064   **all** that ye fear (should be revealed)."
009:078   well **all** things unseen?
009:088   for them are (**all**) good things: and it
009:094   He show you the truth of **all** that ye did."
009:098   that heareth and knoweth (**all** things).
009:100   those who follow them in (**all**) good deeds, well-
009:105   then will He show you the truth of **all** that ye did."
009:115   should avoid, for Allah hath knowledge of **all** things.
009:118   for **all** its speciousness, and their
010:003   regulating and governing **all** things. No
010:004   To Him will be your return-of **all** of you. The
010:006   and in **all** that Allah hath created, in the
010:012   he crieth unto Us (in **all** postures)-lying down
010:021   Verily, Our messengers record **all** the plots
010:022   and the waves come to them from **all** sides, and they
010:023   and We shall show you the truth of **all** that ye did.
010:024   it belongs think they have **all** powers of
010:028   One Day shall We gather them **all** together. Then
010:031   **all** affairs?" They will soon say: "Allah". Say,
010:036   Verily Allah is well aware of **all** that they do.
010:046   to **all** that they do.
010:054   if it possessed **all** that is on earth, would fain
010:056   and to Him shall ye **all** be brought back.
010:065   for **all** power and honour belong to Allah: it is
010:065   it is He Who heareth and knoweth (**all** things).

ALL (continued)

010:066   **all** creatures, in the heavens and on earth. What
010:068   His are **all** things in the heavens and on earth!
010:083   and one who transgressed **all** bounds.
010:099   they would **all** have believed,-**all** who
010:099   **all** who are on earth! Wilt thou
010:101   Say: "Behold **all** that is in the heavens
011:001   and Well-Acquainted (with **all** things):
011:003   on **all** who abound in merit! But if
011:004   and He hath power over **all** things."
011:006   **all** is in a clear Record.
011:010   "**All** evil has departed from me:" behold! he
011:012   It is Allah that arrangeth **all** affairs!
011:027   (**all**) any merit above us: in fact
011:031   will not grant them (**all**) that is good: Allah
011:055   **all** of you, and give me no respite.
011:057   For my Lord hath care and watch over **all** things."
011:073   For He is indeed Worthy of **all** praise, full of
011:073   full of **all** glory!"
011:084   that will compass (you) **all** round.
011:092   But verily my Lord encompasseth **all** that ye do!
011:111   For He knoweth well **all** that they do.
011:111   And, of a surety, to **all** will your Lord
011:112   (from the Path): for He seeth well **all** that ye do.
011:119   with jinns and men **all** together."
011:120   **All** that We relate to thee of the stories
012:015   and they **all** agreed to throw him down to the
012:019   But Allah knoweth well **all** that they do!
012:024   (**all**) evil and indecent deeds: for he
012:034   verily He heareth and knoweth (**all** things).
012:036   for we see thou art one that doth good (to **all**)."
012:048   (**all**) except a little which ye shall have
012:051   the truth manifest (to **all**): it was I
012:054   invested with **all** trust."
012:066   he said: "Over **all** that we say, be Allah
012:067   enter not **all** by one gate: enter ye
012:067   and let **all** that trust put their trust on Him."
012:076   whom We please: but over **all** endued with knowledge
012:083   them (back) **all** to me (in the end). For He
012:090   been gracious to us (**all**): behold, he that
012:093   together with **all** your family."
012:099   and said: "Enter ye Egypt (**all**) in safety
012:100   and brought you (**all** here) out of the desert,
012:100   in prostration (**all**) before him. He said:
012:104   than a Message for **all** creatures.
012:107   the (final) Hour **all** of a sudden while they
012:111   a detailed exposition of **all** things, and a
013:002   He doth regulate **all** affairs, explaining the
013:016   of **all** things: He is the One, the Supreme
013:018   are (**all**) good things. But those
013:018   even if they had **all** that is in the heavens
013:031   have guided **all** mankind (to the Right)?
013:031   the Command is with Allah in **all** things!
013:033   every soul (and knoweth) **all** that it doth,
013:040   thy soul (before it is **all** accomplished), thy duty
013:042   devise plots; but in **all** things Allah is the
014:001   in Power, Worthy of **all** Praise!-
014:002   Of Allah, to Whom do belong **all** things in the
014:008   ye and **all** on earth together,-yet
014:008   yet is Allah Free of **all** wants, Worthy of **all** praise.
014:011   And on Allah let **all** men of faith put their trust.
014:012   **all** the hurt you may cause us. For those
014:021   They will **all** be marshalled before Allah together:

ALL (continued)

014:021 can ye then avail us at **all** against the
014:025 It brings forth its fruit at **all** times, by the
014:034 And He giveth you of **all** that ye ask for. But if
014:041 my parents, and (**all**) Believers, on the
015:014 to continue (**all** day) ascending therein,
015:016 and made them fair-seeming to (**all**) beholders;
015:019 and produced therein **all** kinds of things in due balance.
015:023 remain Inheritors (after **all** else passes away).
015:030 prostrated themselves, **all** of them together:
015:039 and I will put them **all** in the wrong,-
015:043 the promised abode for them **all**!
015:059 to save (from Harm),-**all**-
015:070 (to speak) for **all** and sundry?"
015:084 And of no avail to them was **all** that they did
015:085 and **all** between them, but for just ends. And the
015:086 who is the All-Creator, knowing **all** things.
015:093 For **all** their deeds.
016:009 He could have guided **all** of you.
016:028 verily Allah knoweth **all** that ye did;
016:030 they say, "**All** that is good." To those
016:031 therein **all** that they wish: thus doth
016:049 And to Allah doth prostrate **all** that is in
016:050 They **all** fear their Lord, high above
016:050 **all** that they are commanded.
016:069 Then to eat of **all** the produce (of the
016:077 even quicker: for Allah hath power over **all** things.
016:084 from **all** Peoples a Witness: then will
016:087 and **all** their inventions shall leave them
016:089 **all** peoples a witness against them, from amongst
016:089 Book explaining **all** things, a guide a Mercy,
016:090 and He forbids **all** indecent deeds, and evil
016:091 for Allah knoweth **all** that ye do.
016:093 you **all** one People: but He leaves straying whom
016:093 to account for **all** your actions.
016:110 after **all** this is Oft-Forgiving, Most Merciful.
016:111 (fully) for **all** its actions, and none
016:119 **all** this, is Oft-Forgiving, Most Merciful.
016:125 Invite (**all**) to the Way of thy Lord with wisdom
017:001 Who heareth and seeth (**all** things).
017:007 **all** that fell into their power.
017:008 who reject (**all** Faith).
017:012 the years: **all** things have We explained in detail.
017:019 and strive therefor with **all** due striving,
017:020 We bestow freely on **all**-these as well as those:
017:030 for He doth know and regard **all** His servants.
017:036 **all** of those shall be questioned of.
017:038 Of **all** such things the evil is hateful
017:043 Glory to Him! He is high above **all** that they say!
017:044 and **all** beings therein, declare His
017:055 **all** beings that are in the heavens and on earth:
017:062 under my sway-**all** but a few!"
017:063 you (**all**)-an ample recompense.
017:071 **all** human beings with their (respective) Imams:
017:096 and He sees (**all** things)."
017:103 but We did drown him and **all** who were with him.
018:019 (At length) they (**all**) said, "Allah (alone)
018:028 and his affair has become **all** excess.
018:045 it is (only) Allah Who prevails over **all** things.
018:047 gather them, **all** together, nor shall
018:049 They will find **all** that they did, placed before
018:084 and We gave him the ways and the means to **all** ends.
018:099 and We shall collect them **all** together.

ALL (continued)

018:100 for Unbelievers to see, **all** spread out,-
019:013 And pity (for **all** creatures) as from Us,
019:017 and he appeared before her as a man in **all** respects.
019:040 and **all** beings thereon: to Us will
019:040 to Us will they **all** be returned.
019:048 "And I will turn away from you (**all**) and from
019:065 and of **all** that is between them: so worship
019:069 from every sect **all** those who were worst in
019:080 To Us shall return **all** that he talks of, and he
019:094 and hath numbered them (**all**) exactly.
019:094 He does take and account of them (**all**), and hath
020:006 and **all** between them, and **all** beneath the soil.
020:024 for he had indeed transgressed **all** bounds."
020:043 for he has indeed transgressed **all** bounds;
020:045 or lest he transgress **all** bounds."
020:047 And peace to **all** who follow guidance!
020:056 And We showed Pharaoh **all** Our Signs, but he
020:064 he wins (**all** along) to-day who gains
020:098 But the God of you **all** is Allah: there is
020:098 **all** things He comprehends in His Knowledge.
020:111 (**All**) faces shall be humbled before-the Living,
020:114 High above **all** is Allah, the King, the Truth!
020:123 **all** together, from the Garden, with enmity
020:133 of **all** that was in the former Books of revelation?
021:004 heareth and knoweth (**all** things)."
021:016 the heavens and the earth and **all** that is between!
021:019 To Him belong **all** (creatures) in the
021:027 and they act (in **all** things) by His command.
021:033 **All** (the celestial bodies) swim along, each in
021:040 Nay, it may come to them **all** of a sudden
021:058 (**all**) but the biggest of them, that they
021:068 your gods, if ye do (anything at **all**)!"
021:077 so We drowned them (in the Flood) **all** together.
021:079 with David: it was We Who did (**all** these things).
021:081 for We do know **all** things.
021:084 for **all** who serve Us.
021:085 and Zul-kifl, **all** (men) of constancy and patience;
021:091 and her son a Sign for **all** peoples.
021:093 from another: (yet) will they **all** return to Us.
021:107 We sent thee not, but as a mercy for **all** creatures.
21:109 to you **all** alike and in truth; but I
022:006 and it is He Who has power over **all** things.
022:007 raise up **all** who are in the graves.
022:014 for Allah carries out **all** that He desires.
022:017 for Allah is witness of **all** things.
022:018 **all** things that are in the heavens and on earth,-
022:018 for Allah carries out **all** that He wills.
022:024 to the path of Him Who is Worthy of (**all**) Praise.
022:025 to (**all**) men-equal is the dweller there and the
022:037 the Good News to **all** who do good.
022:041 the end (and decision) of (**all**) affairs.
022:048 punished them. To Me is the destination (of **all**).
022:061 Who hears and sees (**all** things).
022:064 For verily Allah, -He is free of **all** wants,
022:064 worthy of **all** praise.
022:064 To Him belongs **all** that is in the heavens
022:065 made subject to you (men) **all** that is on the
022:070 Indeed it is **all** in a record,
022:070 Allah knows **all** that is in heaven and on earth?
022:073 if they **all** met together for the purpose!
022:075 He Who hears and sees (**all** things).
022:076 and to Allah go back **all** affairs (for decision).

ALL (continued)

023:051   for I am well-acquainted with (**all**) that you do.
023:051   O ye messenger! enjoy (**all**) things good and pure,
023:071   and the earth, and **all** beings therein would
023:084   and **all** beings therein? (Say) if ye know!"
023:088   is the sovereignty of **all** things,-Who protects
023:088   Who protects (**all**), but is
024:021   hears and knows (**all** things).
024:025   that makes **all** things manifest.
024:025   (**all**) their just dues, and they
024:026   these are innocent of **all** what people say:
024:028   and Allah knows well **all** that ye do.
024:030   and Allah is well acquainted with **all** that they do.
024:031   **all** together towards Allah in repentance that ye
024:032   and He knoweth **all** things.
024:035   for men: and Allah doth know **all** things.
024:041   Whose praises **all** beings in the heavens and on
024:041   And Allah knows well **all** that they do.
024:045   for verily Allah has power over **all** things.
024:049   they come to him with **all** submission.
024:053   Allah is well acquainted with **all** that ye do."
024:060   and Allah is One Who sees and knows **all** things.
024:064   of what they did: for Allah doth know **all** things.
025:001   that it may be an admonition to **all** creatures;-
025:002   it is He Who created **all** things, and ordered
025:016   **all** that they wish for: they will
025:020   For Allah is One Who sees (**all** things).
025:020   before thee were **all** (men) who ate food
025:032   to him **all** at once?"
025:037   (**all**) wrong-doers a grievous Chastisement:
025:054   for thy Lord has power (over **all** things).
025:059   and the earth and **all** that is between, in six
026:007   how many noble things of **all** kinds we have
026:021   "So I fled from you (**all**) when I feared you;
026:024   and **all** between,- if ye had but sure belief."
026:028   and the West, and **all** between!
026:032   plain (for **all** to see)!
026:033   and behold, it was white to **all** beholders!
026:037   "And bring up to thee **all** (our) sorcerers
026:045   **all** the falsehoods which they fake!
026:049   and I will crucify you **all**"
026:053   Then Pharaoh sent heralds to (**all**) the Cities,
026:065   We delivered Moses and **all** who were with him;
026:119   in the Ark filled (with **all** creatures).
026:125   "I am to you a messenger worthy of **all** trust.
026:132   on you freely **all** that ye know.
026:143   I am to you a messenger worthy of **all** trust.
026:146   in (the enjoyment of) **all** that ye have here?-
026:162   "I am to you a messenger worthy of **all** trust.
026:165   "Of **all** the creatures in the world, will ye
026:166   Nay, ye are a people transgressing (**all** limits)!"
026:170   So We delivered him and his family,-**all**
026:178   "I am to you a messenger worthy of **all** trust.
026:220   For it is He Who heareth and knoweth **all** things.
027:017   and they were **all** kept in order and ranks.
027:040   truly my Lord is Free of **All** Needs, Supreme in
027:051   destroyed them and their people, **all** (of them).
027:074   as well as **all** that they reveal.
027:074   **all** that their hearts do hide, as well
027:087   and **all** shall come to Him in utter humility.
027:088   of Allah, Who disposes of **all** things in perfect
027:088   for He is well acquainted with **all** that ye do.
027:091   to Whom (belong) **all** things: and I

ALL (continued)

027:093   and thy Lord is not unmindful of **all** that ye do.
028:008   for Pharaoh and Haman and (**all**) their hosts
028:048   And they say: "For us, we reject **all** (such things)!"
028:057   fruits of **all** kinds,-a provision
028:058   **all** but a (miserable) few! and We
028:069   their hearts conceal and **all** that they reveal.
028:069   And thy Lord knows **all** that their hearts
028:070   and to Him shall ye (**all**) be brought back.
028:088   and to Him will ye (**all**) be brought back.
029:005   and He hears and knows (**all** things).
029:006   for Allah is free of **all** needs from **all** creation.
029:007   blot out **all** misdeeds that they have committed,
029:008   Ye have (**all**) to return to Me, and I will
029:008   and I will tell you (the truth) of **all** that ye did.
029:010   Does not Allah know **all** that is in
029:010   that is in the hearts of **all** Creation?
029:015   a Sign for **all** Peoples!
029:020   for Allah has power over **all** things.
029:060   and you: for He hears and knows (**all** things).
029:062   for Allah has full knowledge of **all** things.
029:067   from **all** around them? Then, do they
030:008   and **all** between them: yet are
030:014   that Day shall (**all** men) be sorted out.
030:026   **all** are devoutly obedient to Him.
030:050   for He has power over **all** things.
030:054   and it is He Who has **all** knowledge and power.
031:010   beasts of **all** kinds. We sent
031:012   verily Allah is free of **all** wants, worthy of
031:012   worthy of **all** praise.
031:015   in the End the return of you **all** is to Me,
031:015   is to Me, and I will tell you **all** that ye did."
031:020   to your (use) **all** things in the heavens and on
031:022   and to Allah shall **all** things return.
031:023   **all** that is in (men's) hearts.
031:026   To Allah belong **all** things in heaven and earth:
031:026   worthy of **all** praise.
031:026   (that is) free of **all** wants, worthy of
031:027   And if **all** the trees on earth were pens and the
031:028   for Allah is He Who hears and sees (**all** things).
031:029   is well acquainted with **all** that ye do?
031:031   Verily in this are Signs for **all** who constantly
031:034   is acquainted (with **all** things).
032:004   and the earth, and **all** between them, in six Days,
032:006   Such as He, the Knower of **all** things, hidden and
032:007   He Who has created **all** things in the best way
032:013   "I will fill Hell with Jinns and men **all** together."
033:002   with (**all**) that ye do.
033:009   but Allah sees (clearly) **all** that ye do.
033:025   for (**all**) their fury: no advantage
033:027   And Allah has power over **all** things.
033:033   **all** abomination from you, ye Members
033:040   and Allah has full knowledge of **all** things.
033:051   and Allah knows (**all**) that is in your hearts:
033:051   that of **all** of them-with that which thou hast
033:052   watch over **all** things.
033:054   has full knowledge of **all** things.
033:055   fear Allah; for Allah is Witness to **all** things.
033:056   and salute him with **all** respect.
034:001   **all** things in the heavens and on earth: to Him
034:002   and **all** that comes out thereof; **all** that
034:002   He knows **all** that goes into the earth,
034:002   and **all** that ascends thereto and He

ALL (continued)

034:002 all that comes down from the sky and all
034:006 of the Exalted (in Might), Worthy of all praise.
034:007 all scattered to pieces in disintegration, that ye
034:011 for be sure I see (clearly) all that ye do."
034:019 all in scattered fragments. Verily in this
034:020 all but a party that believed.
034:021 and thy Lord doth watch over all things.
034:026 the One Who knows all."
034:028 as a (Messenger) to all mankind, giving them
034:040 all together, and say to the angels, "Was it
034:047 from Allah: and He is Witness to all things."
034:048 of (all) that is hidden."
034:050 all things, and is (ever) near."
035:001 for Allah has power over all things.
035:004 before thee: to Allah all affairs are returned.
035:008 for Allah knows well all that they do!
035:010 To Him mount up (all) Words of Purity: it is
035:010 to Allah belong all glory and power.
035:011 a Book (ordained). All this is easy to Allah.
035:013 your Lord: to Him belongs all Dominion. And those
035:015 the One Free of all wants, worthy
035:015 worthy of all praise.
035:017 Nor is that (at all) difficult for Allah.
035:018 and the destination (of all) is to Allah.
035:034 Who has removed from us (all) sorrow: for our
035:038 full knowledge of all that is in (men's) hearts.
035:038 Verily Allah knows (all) the hidden things
035:045 in His sight all His servants.
036:012 leave behind, and of all things have We taken
036:019 Nay, but ye are a people transgressing all bounds!"
036:022 (all) be brought back.
036:025 of you (all): listen, then, to me!"
036:032 But each one of them all-will be
036:036 in pairs all things that the earth produces,
036:053 they will all be brought up before Us!
036:055 shall that Day have joy in all that they do;
036:065 bear witness, to all that they did.
036:079 For He fully knows all creation.
036:083 is the dominion of all things: and to Him
036:083 and to Him will ye be all brought back.
037:005 and all between them, and Lord
037:007 against all obstinate rebellious Satans.
037:033 (all) share in the Chastisement.
037:061 For the like of this let all strive, who wish
037:134 Behold, We delivered him and his adherents, all
038:005 "Has he made the gods (all) into one God?
038:008 to him-(of all persons) among us?." But they
038:010 and all between? If so, let them mount up
038:019 all with him did turn (to Allah).
038:027 all between! That were the thought of Unbelievers!
038:043 for all who have Understanding.
038:066 and all between-Exalted in Might, Ever-Forgiving.
038:073 all of them together;
038:082 I will lead them all astray.
038:087 a Reminder to (all) the Worlds.
038:088 the truth of it (all) after a while."
039:006 to Him belongs (all) dominion. There is
039:006 He created you (all) from a single person:
039:007 For He knoweth well all that is in (men's) hearts.
039:007 of all that ye did (in this life). For He
039:031 In the End will ye (all) dispute on
039:034 They shall have all that they wish for, in the

ALL (continued)

039:046 and the earth! Knower of all that is hidden
039:047 Even if the wrong-doers had all that there is
039:050 them say! But all that they did was of
039:053 for Allah forgives all sins: for He
039:062 Allah is the Creator of all things, and He
039:062 and He is the Guardian and Disposer of all affairs.
039:068 when all that are in the heavens and on
039:070 and (Allah) knoweth best all that they do.
039:075 (on all sides) will be, "Praise be to Allah,
039:075 on all sides, singing Glory and Praise to their
040:007 "Our Lord! Thou embracest all things, in Mercy
040:009 "And preserve them from (all) ills; and any
040:016 The Day whereon they will (all) come forth:
040:019 and all that hearts (of men) conceal.
040:020 Who hears and sees (all things).
040:020 will not (be in a position) to judge at all.
040:045 encompassed on all sides the People of Pharaoh.
040:048 "We are all in this (Fire)! Truly, Allah has
040:056 it is He Who hears and sees (all things).
040:062 the Creator of all things, there is
040:077 that they shall (all) return.
040:082 in the land: yet all that they accomplished was
041:009 He is the Lord of (all) the Worlds.
041:010 alike for (all) who ask.
041:015 the land, against (all) truth and reason, and said
041:020 against them, as to (all) their deeds.
041:029 so that they become the vilest."
041:031 therein shall ye have all that ye ask for!-
041:031 therein shall ye have all that you shall desire;
041:036 He is the One Who hears and knows all things.
041:039 who are dead. For He has power over all things.
041:040 seeth (clearly) all that ye do.
041:042 Worthy of all Praise.
041:043 (all) Forgiveness as well as a most
041:047 of the Hour (of Judgement: He knows all): no fruit
041:049 he gives up all hope (and) is lost in despair.
041:050 the Unbelievers the truth of all that they did,
041:053 enough that thy Lord doth witness all things?
041:054 that doth encompass all things!
042:004 To Him belongs all that is in the heavens
042:005 for (all) beings on earth: Behold! Verily
042:007 of Cities and all around her,-and warn
042:009 it is He Who has power over all things.
042:012 He will: for He knows full well all things.
042:022 before their Lord, all that they wish for.
042:024 For He knows well the secrets of all hearts.
042:025 and He knows all that ye do.
042:027 all bounds through the earth; but He
042:028 Worthy of all Praise.
042:028 all hope, and scatters His Mercy (far and wide).
042:053 all affairs tend towards Allah!
043:012 That has created pairs in all things, and has
043:033 And were it not that (all) men might become
043:035 But all this were nothing but enjoyment of the
043:044 and soon shall ye (all) be brought to account.
043:055 and We drowned them all.
043:066 that it should come on them all of a sudden,
043:071 there will be there all that the souls
043:071 all that the eyes could delight in: and ye
043:085 and the earth, and all between them: with Him
044:006 for He hears and knows (all things);
044:007 and all between them, if ye

ALL (continued)

044:018 I am to you a messenger worthy of **all** trust;
044:038 the earth, and **all** between them, merely in
044:040 is the time appointed for **all** of them,-
045:013 as from Him, **all** that is in the heavens and on
045:015 In the end will ye (**all**) be brought
045:028 ye be recompensed for **all** that ye did!
045:029 on record **all** that ye did."
045:036 the earth, Lord and Cherisher of **all** the worlds!
046:003 and **all** between them but for just ends, and for
046:019 And to **all** are (assigned) degrees according to
046:033 Yea, verily He has power over **all** things.
046:035 as did (**all**) messengers of firm resolution; and be
047:015 In it there are for them **all** kinds of fruits,
047:029 will not bring to light **all** their rancor?
047:030 And Allah knows **all** that ye do.
047:037 and He would bring out **all** your ill-feeling.
047:037 If He were to ask you for **all** of them,
047:038 of **all** wants, and it is ye that are needy.
048:011 Say: "Who then has any power at **all** (to intervene)
048:011 acquainted with **all** that ye do.
048:021 and Allah has power over **all** things.
048:024 over them. And Allah sees well **all** that ye do.
048:026 And Allah has full knowledge of **all** things.
048:028 to make it over **all** religion: and enough
049:001 for Allah is He who hears and knows **all** things.
049:009 the other, then fight ye (**all**) against the one
049:013 and is well acquainted (with **all** things).
049:016 He has full knowledge of **all** things.
049:016 But Allah knows **all** that is in
049:018 and Allah sees well **all** that ye do."
050:025 transgressed **all** bounds, cast doubts
050:035 **all** that they wish,-and there is more with Us.
050:038 and **all** between them in Six Days, nor did
050:039 Bear, then with patience, **all** that they say,
051:058 For Allah is He Who gives (**all**) Sustenance,-
053:031 Yea, to Allah belongs **all** that is in the heavens
053:052 for that they were (**all**) most unjust and most
054:015 (for **all** time): then is there any that will
054:025 of **all** people amongst us? Nay, he is
054:042 The (people) rejected **all** Our Signs; but We
054:049 Verily, **all** things have We created
054:052 **All** that they do is noted in (their)
055:026 **All** that is on earth will perish:
056:050 "**All** will certainly be gathered together for the
057:002 and He has Power over **all** things.
057:003 and He has full knowledge of **all** things.
057:004 may be. And Allah sees well **all** that ye do.
057:005 and **all** affairs go back to Allah.
057:006 of the secrets of (**all**) hearts.
057:010 But to **all** has Allah promised a goodly (reward).
057:010 And Allah is well acquainted with **all** that ye do.
057:013 and without it, **all** alongside, will be
057:016 in **all** humility should engage in the remembrance
057:017 Know ye (**all**) that Allah giveth life to the
057:020 Know ye (**all**), that the life of this world
057:024 verily Allah is free of **all** needs,
057:024 worthy of **all** praise.
058:001 for Allah hears and sees (**all** things).
058:003 well-acquainted with (**all**) that ye do.
058:006 for Allah is Witness to **all** things.
058:006 will raise them **all** up (again) and tell them
058:007 full knowledge of **all** things.

ALL (continued)

058:007 (**all**) that is in the heavens and on earth?
058:011 and Allah is well-acquainted with **all** ye do.
058:013 and Allah is well-acquainted with **all** that ye do.
058:018 **all** up (for Judgement): then will
059:006 and Allah has power over **all** things.
059:018 for Allah is well-acquainted with (**all**) that ye do.
059:022 no other god;-Who knows (**all** things) both secret
060:001 for I know full well **all** that ye conceal
060:001 ye conceal and **all** that ye reveal.
060:003 between you: for Allah sees well **all** that ye do.
060:006 Allah is free of **all** Wants,
060:006 Worthy, of **all** Praise.
060:007 For Allah has power (over **all** things); and Allah
061:009 **all** religion, even though the Pagans may detest
062:011 And Allah is the Best to provide (for **all** needs)."
063:011 acquainted with (**all**) that ye do.
064:001 and He has power over **all** things.
064:002 are Believers: and Allah see well **all** that ye do.
064:004 yes, Allah knows well the (secrets) of (**all**) hearts.
064:006 and Allah is free of **all** needs,
064:006 worthy of **all** praise.
064:007 (the truth) of **all** that ye did. And that
064:008 And Allah is well-acquainted with **all** that ye do.
064:009 The Day that He assembles you (**all**) for a day
064:011 for Allah knows **all** things.
065:003 for **all** things has Allah appointed a due proportion.
065:012 Allah comprehends **all** things in (His) Knowledge.
065:012 Allah has power over **all** things, and that
065:012 of them (**all**) descends His Command: that ye
066:005 It may be, if he divorced you (**all**), that Allah
066:007 Ye are being but requited for **all** that ye did!"
066:008 us Forgiveness: for Thou hast power over **all** things."
067:001 and He over **all** things Hath Power;-
067:013 (full) knowledge, of the secrets of (**all**) hearts.
067:019 truly it is He that watches over **all** things.
068:012 (**all**) good, transgressing beyond bounds, deep in
068:013 Violent (and cruel),-with **all** that, of a
068:019 (which swept away) **all** around, while they
068:052 a Message to **all** the worlds.
070:014 And **all**, **all** that is on earth,-so it
070:017 Inviting (**all**) such as turn their backs and turn
070:040 of **all** points in the East and the West that We
070:044 ignominy covering them (**all** over)! Such is
071:028 and (**all**) believing men and believing women:
071:028 **all** who enter my house in Faith,
072:028 and He encompasses **all** that is with them, and takes
073:002 Stand (to pray) by night, but not **all** night,-
074:005 And **all** abomination shun!
075:013 (**all**) that he put forward,
075:013 and **all** that he put back.
075:030 That Day the Drive will be (**all**) to thy Lord!
077:011 are (**all**) appointed a time (to collect);-
077:042 And (they shall have) fruits,-**all** they desire.
078:029 And **all** things have We preserved on record.
078:037 and the earth, and **all** between,-The Most
079:017 for he has indeed transgressed **all** bounds:
079:035 (**all**) that he strove for,
079:037 Then, for such as had transgressed **all** bounds,
081:027 a Message to (**all**) the Worlds:
082:012 They know **all** that ye do.
083:006 A Day when (**all**) mankind will stand before
083:023 a sight (of **all** things):

ALL (continued)

083:035   (a sight) (of **all** things).
085:007   And they witnessed (**all**) that they were doing
085:008   Exalted in Power, worthy of **all** Praise!
085:009   And Allah is Witness to **all** things.
085:015   Lord of the Throne full of **all** Glory,
085:016   Doer (without let) of **all** that He intends.
086:009   The Day that (**all**) things secret will be tested,
088:016   And rich carpets (**All**) spread out.
089:008   not produced in (**all**) the land?
089:011   (**All**) these transgressed beyond bounds in the lands.
089:019   And ye devour inheritance-**all** with greed,
090:020   On them will be Fire Vaulted over (**all** round).
092:006   And (in **all** sincerity) testifies to the Best,-
094:008   And to thy Lord turn (**all**) thy attention.
096:006   Nay, but man doth transgress **all** bounds,
096:008   Verily, to thy Lord is the return (of **all**).
098:008   **all** this for such as fear their Lord and Cherisher.
111:002   and **all** his gains!
111:002   No profit to him from **all** his wealth,

ALL-AWARE

022:063   All-Subtle, **All-Aware**.
033:034   for Allah is All-Subtle **All-Aware**.
034:001   and He is All-Wise, **All-Aware**.
035:014   like Him who is **All-Aware**.

ALL-BOUNTIFUL

040:003   and is **all-Bountiful**.

ALL-CREATOR

015:086   is the **All-Creator**, knowing all things.

ALL-EMBRACING

002:115   For Allah is **All-Embracing**, All-Knowing.
002:247   Allah is **All-Embracing**, and He knoweth all things."
006:147   say: "Your Lord is full of Mercy **All-Embracing**;

ALL-FORGIVING

058:002   but truly Allah is All-Pardoning, **All-Forgiving**.

ALL-HEARING

002:127   the **All-Hearing**, the All-Knowing.
002:137   and He is the **All-Hearing**, the All-Knowing.

ALL-KNOWING

002:115   For Allah is All-Embracing, **All-Knowing**.
002:127   the All-Hearing, the **All-Knowing**.
002:137   and He is the All-Hearing, the **All-Knowing**.
004:011   and Allah is **All-Knowing**, All-Wise.
004:012   and Allah is **All-Knowing**, Most Forbearing.
004:024   and Allah is **All-Knowing**, All-Wise.
004:026   and Allah is **All-Knowing**, All-Wise.
004:170   and Allah is **All-Knowing**, All-Wise.
009:028   His bounty, for Allah is **All-Knowing**, All-Wise.
009:097   but Allah is **All-Knowing**, All-Wise.
009:106   and Allah is **All-Knowing**, Wise.
009:110   And Allah is **All-Knowing**, Wise.
012:076   with knowledge is One, the **All-Knowing**.
016:070   for Allah is **All-Knowing**, All-Powerful.
022:059   **All-Knowing**, Most Forbearing.
027:006   from One Who All-Wise, **All-Knowing**.
027:078   and He is Exalted in Might, **All-Knowing**.
033:051   **All-Knowing**, Most Forbearing.
035:044   for He is **All-Knowing**, All-Powerful.
036:038   the Exalted in Might, the **All-Knowing**.
009:015   He will: and Allah is **All-Knowing**, All-Wise

ALL-PARDONING

058:002   but truly Allah is **All-Pardoning**, All-Forgiving.

ALL-POWERFUL

016:070   for Allah is All-Knowing, **All-Powerful**.
035:044   for He is All-Knowing, **All-Powerful.**

ALL-REACHING

004:130   for each of them form His **All-Reaching** bounty:

ALL-SUBTLE

022:063   **All-Subtle**, All-Aware.
033:034   for Allah is **All-Subtle** All-Aware.

ALL-SUFFICIENT

004:006   but **All-Sufficient** is Allah in taking account.

ALL-THANKFUL

064:017   for Allah is **All-Thankful**, Most Forbearing,-

ALL-WISE

004:011   and Allah is All-Knowing, **All-Wise**.
004:024   and Allah is All-Knowing, **All-Wise**.
004:026   and Allah is All-Knowing, **All-Wise**.
004:170   and Allah is All-Knowing, **All-Wise**.
009:015   He will: and Allah is All-Knowing, **All-Wise**
009:028   His bounty, for Allah is All-Knowing, **All-Wise**.
009:097   but Allah is All-Knowing, **All-Wise**.
027:006   from One Who **All-Wise**, All-Knowing.
034:001   and He is **All-Wise**, All-Aware.

ALLAH

001:001   In the name of **Allah**, Most Gracious, Most Merciful.
001:002   Praise be to **Allah**,
002:000   In the name of **Allah**, Most Gracious, Most Merciful.
002:002   to those who fear **Allah**;
002:007   **Allah** hath set a seal on their hearts
002:008   "We believe in **Allah** and the Last Day,"
002:009   Fain would they deceive **Allah**
002:010   and **Allah** has increased their disease,
002:015   **Allah** will throw back their mockery on them,
002:017   **Allah** took away their light
002:019   But **Allah** is ever round the rejecters of Faith!
002:020   And if **Allah** willed,
002:020   for **Allah** hath power over all things.
002:022   unto **Allah** when ye know (the truth).
002:023   (if there are any) besides **Allah**,
002:026   **Allah** disdains not to use
002:026   "What means **Allah** by this similitude?"
002:027   and who sunder what **Allah** has ordered
002:028   How can ye reject the faith in **Allah**?
002:033   **Allah** said: "Did I not tell you that
002:055   in thee until we see **Allah** manifestly,"
002:060   the sustenance provided by **Allah**,
002:061   they drew on themselves the wrath of **Allah**.
002:061   rejecting the Signs of **Allah** and slaying
002:062   and who believe in **Allah** and the last day,
002:063   perchance ye may fear **Allah**."
002:064   the Grace and Mercy of **Allah** to you
002:066   and a lesson to those who fear **Allah**.
002:067   "**Allah** commands that ye sacrifice a heifer."
002:067   He said: "**Allah** save me from being
002:070   we wish indeed for guidance if **Allah** wills."
002:072   but **Allah** was to bring forth what ye did hide.
002:073   Thus **Allah** bringeth the dead to life
002:074   and others which sink for fear of **Allah**.
002:074   And **Allah** is not unmindful of what ye do.
002:075   heard the Word of **Allah**,
002:076   what **Allah** hath revealed to you,
002:077   Know they not that **Allah** knoweth what
002:079   and then say: "This is from **Allah**,"

ALLAH (continued)

002:080 Say: "Have ye taken a promise from **Allah**,
002:080 ye say of **Allah** what ye do not know?"
002:083 worship none but **Allah**;
002:085 For **Allah** is not unmindful of what ye do.
002:089 a Book from **Allah**,
002:089 but the curse **Allah** is on those
002:090 (the revelation) which **Allah** has sent down,
002:090 **Allah** of His Grace should send it
002:091 "Believe in what **Allah** hath sent down,"
002:091 the prophets of **Allah** in times gone by,
002:094 Say: "If the last Home, with **Allah**,
002:095 And **Allah** is well acquainted with
002:096 for **Allah** sees well all that they do.
002:098 Whoever is an enemy to **Allah**
002:098 Lo! **Allah** is an enemy to those who
002:101 a Messenger from **Allah**,
002:101 Book of **Allah** behind their backs,
002:103 reward from **Allah** if they but knew!
002:105 for **Allah** is Lord of grace abounding.
002:105 But **Allah** will choose for His
002:106 **Allah** hath power over all things?
002:107 to **Allah** belongeth the dominion of the
002:109 for **Allah** hath power over all things.
002:109 till **Allah** brings about His command;
002:110 ye shall find it with **Allah**:
002:110 for **Allah** sees well all that ye do.
002:112 whole self to **Allah** and is a doer of good,
002:113 but **Allah** will judge between them
002:114 that in places for the worship of **Allah**,
002:115 To **Allah** belong the East and the West;
002:115 For **Allah** is All-Embracing, All-Knowing.
002:116 They say: "**Allah** hath begotten a son";
002:118 "Why speaketh not **Allah** unto Us?
002:120 neither Protector nor Helper against **Allah**.
002:120 Say: "The guidance of **Allah**,
002:126 believe in **Allah** and the Last Day."
002:132 "O my sons! **Allah** hath chosen the Faith for you;
002:135 and he joined not gods with **Allah**."
002:136 and we submit to **Allah**.
002:136 Say ye: "We believer in **Allah**,
002:137 but **Allah** will suffice thee as against them,
002:138 (Our religion) takes its hue from **Allah**
002:138 and who can give a better hue than **Allah**.
002:139 Say: Will ye dispute with us about **Allah**,
002:140 But **Allah** is not unmindful of what ye do!
002:140 Say: Do ye know better than **Allah**?
002:140 the testimony they have from **Allah**?
002:142 Say: To **Allah** belong both East and West:
002:143 except to those guided by **Allah**.
002:143 And never would **Allah** make your faith
002:143 For **Allah** is to all people most surely
002:144 nor is **Allah** unmindful of what they do.
002:148 **Allah** will bring you together.
002:148 To each is a goal to which **Allah** turns him;
002:148 For **Allah** hath power over all things.
002:149 And **Allah** is not unmindful of what ye do.
002:154 are slain in the way of **Allah**:
002:156 To **Allah** we belong,
002:158 be sure that **Allah** is He
002:158 are among the Symbols of **Allah**.
002:164 in the rain which **Allah** sends down
002:165 and **Allah** will strongly enforce the Punishment:

ALLAH (continued)

002:165 that to **Allah** belongs all power,
002:165 overflowing in their love for **Allah**.
002:165 they love them as they should love **Allah**.
002:165 as equal (with **Allah**):
002:165 (for worship) others besides **Allah**,
002:167 Thus will **Allah** show them (the fruits of)
002:169 of **Allah** that of which ye have no knowledge.
002:170 "Follow what **Allah** hath revealed,"
002:172 and be grateful to **Allah**,
002:173 For **Allah** is Oft-Forgiving, Most Merciful.
002:173 name hath been invoked besides that **Allah**,
002:174 **Allah** will not address them on the Day
002:176 (Their doom is) because **Allah** sent down the Book
002:177 believe in **Allah** and the Last Day,
002:181 For **Allah** hears and knows (all things).
002:182 for **Allah** is Oft-Forgiving, Most Merciful.
002:185 **Allah** intends every facility for you;
002:187 **Allah** knoweth what ye used to do secretly
002:187 and seek what **Allah** hath ordained for you,
002:187 Those are limits (set by) **Allah**:
002:187 Thus doth **Allah** make clear His Signs to men:
002:189 it is virtue if ye fear **Allah**.
002:189 and fear **Allah**: that ye may prosper.
002:190 for **Allah** loveth not transgressors.
002:190 Fight in the cause of **Allah** those who fight you
002:192 **Allah** is Oft-Forgiving, Most Merciful.
002:194 But fear **Allah**,
002:194 **Allah** is with those who restrain themselves
002:195 for **Allah** loveth those who do good.
002:195 your substance in the cause of **Allah**,
002:196 And fear **Allah**.
002:196 And know that **Allah**, is strict in punishment.
002:196 Hajj or 'Umra in the service of **Allah**,
002:197 (be sure) **Allah** knoweth it.
002:198 praises of **Allah** at the Sacred Monument,
002:199 For **Allah** is Oft-forgiving, Most Merciful.
002:200 celebrate the praises of **Allah**,
002:202 and **Allah** is quick in account.
002:203 Then fear **Allah**, and know that ye will surely
002:203 Remember **Allah** during the Appointed Days
002:204 and he calls **Allah** to witness
002:205 but **Allah** loveth not mischief.
002:206 When it is said to him, "Fear **Allah**,"
002:207 gives his life to earn the pleasure of **Allah**;
002:207 and **Allah** is full of kindness to (His) devotees.
002:209 then know that **Allah** is Exalted in Power, Wise.
002:210 But to **Allah** do all questions go back
002:210 **Allah** comes to them in canopies of clouds,
002:211 **Allah** is strict in punishment.
002:212 for **Allah** bestows His abundance
002:213 For **Allah** guides whom He will to a path
002:213 **Allah** by His Grace guided the Believers
002:213 And **Allah** sent Messengers with glad tidings
002:214 "When (will come) the help of **Allah**"
002:214 Ah! Verily, the help of **Allah** is (always) near!
002:215 **Allah** knoweth it well.
002:216 But **Allah** knoweth, and ye know not.
002:217 of **Allah** to prevent access to the path
002:217 to the path of **Allah** to deny Him,
002:218 in the path of **Allah**,
002:218 they have the hope of the Mercy of **Allah**;
002:218 and **Allah** is Oft-Forgiving, Most Merciful.

ALLAH (continued)

002:219   Thus doth **Allah** make clear to you His Signs:
002:220   but **Allah** knows the man who means mischief
002:220   And if **Allah** had wished,
002:221   But **Allah** beckons by His Grace to the Garden
002:222   For **Allah** loves those who turn to Him constantly
002:222   ordained for you by **Allah**
002:223   and fear **Allah**,
002:224   for **Allah** is one who heareth and knoweth
002:225   **Allah** will not call you to account
002:226   **Allah** is Oft-Forgiving, Most Merciful.
002:227   **Allah** heareth and knoweth all things.
002:228   if they have faith in **Allah** and the Last Day.
002:228   to hide what **Allah** hath created in their wombs,
002:228   and **Allah** is Exalted in Power, Wise.
002:229   unable to keep the limits ordained by **Allah**
002:229   if any do transgress the limits ordained by **Allah**,
002:229   these are the limits ordained by **Allah**;
002:229   be unable to keep the limits ordained by **Allah**,
002:230   keep the limits ordained by **Allah**.
002:230   Such are the limits ordained by **Allah**,
002:231   And fear **Allah**,
002:231   and know that **Allah** is well acquainted
002:232   who believe in **Allah** and the Last Day.
002:232   and **Allah** knows, and ye knows not.
002:233   know that **Allah** sees well what ye do.
002:233   But fear **Allah** and know that well
002:234   And **Allah** is well acquainted with what ye do.
002:235   **Allah** knows that ye cherish them in your hearts:
002:235   **Allah** knoweth what is in your hearts,
002:235   and know that **Allah** is Oft Forgiving, Most Forbearing.
002:237   For **Allah** sees well all that ye do.
002:238   **Allah** in a devout (frame of mind).
002:240   And **Allah** is Exalted in Power, Wise.
002:242   Thus doth **Allah** make clear His Signs to you:
002:243   **Allah** said to them: "Die:" Then He restored them
002:243   For **Allah** is full of bounty to mankind,
002:244   Then fight in the cause of **Allah**,
002:244   and know that **Allah** heareth and knoweth all things.
002:245   Who is he that will loan to **Allah** a beautiful loan,
002:245   which **Allah** will double unto his credit
002:245   It is **Allah** that giveth (you) want or Plenty,
002:246   we refuse to fight in the cause of **Allah**,
002:246   But **Allah** has full knowledge of those
002:246   that we may fight in the cause of **Allah**."
002:247   "**Allah** hath appointed Talut as king over you."
002:247   **Allah** is All-embracing, and He knoweth all things."
002:247   **Allah** granteth His authority to whom He pleaseth;
002:247   He said: "**Allah** hath chosen him above you.
002:249   he said: "**Allah** will test you at the stream;
002:249   **Allah** is with those who steadfastly persevere."
002:249   convinced that they must meet **Allah**,
002:251   And did not **Allah** check one set of people
002:251   but **Allah** is full of bounty to all the worlds.
002:251   and **Allah** gave him power and wisdom
002:252   These are the signs of **Allah**:
002:253   but **Allah** does what He wills.
002:253   to some of them **Allah** spoke;
002:253   If **Allah** had so willed, succeeding generations
002:253   If **Allah** had so willed, they would not have
002:255   **Allah**! There is no god but He, the living,
002:256   And **Allah** heareth and knoweth all things.
002:256   whoever rejects Tagut and believes in **Allah**

ALLAH (continued)

002:257   **Allah** is the Protector of those who have faith:
002:258   because **Allah** had granted Him Power?
002:258   **Allah** that causeth the sun to rise from the East,
002:258   Nor doth **Allah** give guidance to a people unjust.
002:259   But **Allah** caused him to die for a hundred years,
002:259   **Allah** hath power over all things."
002:259   shall **Allah** bring it (ever) to life,
002:260   Then know that **Allah** is Exalted in Power, Wise."
002:261   **Allah** giveth manifold increase to whom
002:261   And **Allah** careth for all and He knoweth
002:261   the way of **Allah** is that of a grain of corn:
002:262   their wealth in the cause of **Allah**,
002:263   **Allah** is free of all wants,
002:264   neither in **Allah** nor in the last day.
002:264   And **Allah** guideth not those who reject faith.
002:265   to please **Allah** and to strengthen their souls,
002:265   **Allah** seeth well whatever ye do.
002:266   Thus doth **Allah** make clear to you
002:267   And know that **Allah** is free of all wants,
002:268   And **Allah** careth for all and He knoweth
002:268   **Allah** promiseth you His forgiveness and bounties.
002:270   be sure **Allah** knows it all.
002:271   And **Allah** is well acquainted with what ye do.
002:272   But **Allah** guides to the right path
002:272   do so seeking the "Face" of **Allah**.
002:273   be assured **Allah** knoweth it well.
002:275   but **Allah** hath permitted trade
002:275   their case is for **Allah** (to judge);
002:276   **Allah** will deprive usury of all blessing,
002:278   O ye who believe! fear **Allah**,
002:279   notice of war from **Allah** and His Messenger:
002:281   when ye shall be brought back to **Allah**.
002:282   it is juster in the sight of **Allah**,
002:282   but let him fear **Allah** his Lord
002:282   And **Allah** is well acquainted with all things.
002:282   as **Allah** has taught him, so let him write.
002:282   for it is **Allah** that teaches you.
002:282   So fear **Allah**;
002:283   And **Allah** knoweth all that ye do.
002:283   and let him fear **Allah** his Lord.
002:284   **Allah** calleth you to account for it.
002:284   For **Allah** hath power over all things.
002:284   To **Allah** belongeth all that is in the heavens
002:285   each one (of them) believeth in **Allah**,
002:286   On no soul doth **Allah** place a burden
003:000   In the name of **Allah**, Most Gracious, Most Merciful.
003:002   **Allah**! there is no god but He,
003:004   and **Allah** is Exalted in Might, Lord of Retribution.
003:004   in the Signs of **Allah** will suffer
003:005   From **Allah**, verily nothing is hidden
003:007   but no one knows its true meanings except **Allah**.
003:009   for **Allah** never fails in His promise."
003:010   will avail them aught against **Allah**:
003:011   For **Allah** is strict in punishment.
003:011   and **Allah** called them to account for their sins.
003:013   the other resisting **Allah**;
003:013   one was fighting in the cause of **Allah**,
003:013   but **Allah** doth support with His aid
003:014   but with **Allah** is the best of the goals
003:015   the good pleasure of **Allah**.
003:017   who spend (in the way of **Allah**);
003:018   that is the witness of **Allah**, His angels,

ALLAH (continued)

003:019   But if any deny the Signs of **Allah**,
003:019   **Allah** is swift in calling to account.
003:019   The Religion before **Allah** is Islam
003:020   to **Allah** and so have those who follow me."
003:021   As to those who deny the Signs of **Allah**,
003:023   They are invited to the Book of **Allah**,
003:026   Say: "O **Allah**! Lord of Power (and Rule),
003:028   But **Allah** cautions you (to fear) Himself;
003:028   left with **Allah** except by way of precaution,
003:028   for the final goal is to **Allah**.
003:029   in your hearts or reveal it, **Allah** knows it all:
003:029   And **Allah** has power over all things.
003:030   But **Allah** cautions you (to fear) Him
003:030   and **Allah** is full of kindness to those
003:031   **Allah** will love you and forgive you your sins:
003:031   Say: "If ye do love **Allah**, follow me:
003:031   for **Allah** is Oft-Forgiving, Most Merciful.
003:032   **Allah** loveth not those who reject Faith.
003:032   Say: "Obey **Allah** and His Messenger": but if they
003:033   **Allah** did choose Adam and Noah,
003:034   and **Allah** heareth and knoweth all things.
003:036   And **Allah** knew best what she brought forth-
003:037   She said: "From **Allah**: for
003:037   for **Allah** provides sustenance to whom He pleases,
003:039   "**Allah** doth give thee glad tidings of Yahya,
003:039   confirming the truth of a Word from **Allah**,
003:040   "Doth **Allah** accomplish what He willeth."
003:042   "O Mary! **Allah** hath chosen thee and purified thee
003:045   "O Mary! **Allah** giveth thee glad tidings
003:045   and (of the company) of those nearest to **Allah**;
003:047   He said: "Even so; **Allah** createth what He willeth:
003:048   "And **Allah** will teach him the Book and Wisdom,
003:050   So fear **Allah**, and obey me.
003:051   "It is **Allah** who is my Lord and your Lord;
003:052   "We are Allah's helpers, We believe in **Allah**,
003:052   "Who will be my helpers to (the work of) **Allah**?"
003:054   and **Allah** too planned,
003:054   and the best of planners is **Allah**.
003:055   Behold! **Allah** said: "O Jesus! I will take thee
003:057   but **Allah** loveth not those who do wrong.
003:057   **Allah** will pay them (in full) their reward;
003:059   Jesus before **Allah** is as that of Adam;
003:061   And invoke the curse of **Allah** on those who lie!
003:062   there is no god except **Allah**;
003:062   and **Allah**-He is indeed the Exalted in Power,
003:063   **Allah** hath full knowledge of those who do mischief.
003:064   that we worship none but **Allah**;
003:064   lords and patrons other than **Allah**."
003:066   It is **Allah** Who knows, and ye who know not!
003:067   And he joined not gods with **Allah**.
003:068   and **Allah** is the Protector of those who have faith.
003:070   Why reject ye the Signs of **Allah**,
003:073   Say: "True guidance is the guidance of **Allah**:
003:073   Say: "All bounties are in the hand of **Allah**:
003:073   and **Allah** careth for all,
003:074   for **Allah** is the Lord of bounties unbounded.
003:075   but they tell a lie against **Allah**,
003:076   verily **Allah** loves those who act aright.
003:077   nor will **Allah** (deign to) speak to them
003:077   they owe to **Allah** and their own solemn plighted
003:078   but it is not from **Allah**:
003:078   it is they who tell a lie against **Allah**,

ALLAH (continued)

003:078   and they say "That is from **Allah**"
003:080   after ye have bowed your will (to **Allah** in Islam)?
003:081   **Allah** said: "Do ye agree, and take My covenant
003:081   Behold! **Allah** took the covenant of the Prophets,
003:083   Do they seek for other than the Religion of **Allah**?
003:084   and to **Allah** do we bow our will (in Islam)."
003:084   Say: "We believe in **Allah**, and in what
003:085   a religion other than Islam (submission to **Allah**)
003:086   But **Allah** guides not a people unjust.
003:086   How shall **Allah** guide those who reject faith
003:087   curse of **Allah**, of His angels, and of all mankind;
003:089   for verily **Allah** is Oft-Forgiving, Most Merciful.
003:092   and whatever ye give, **Allah** knoweth it well.
003:094   invent a lie and attribute it to **Allah**,
003:095   Say: "**Allah** speaketh the truth: follow the religion
003:097   pilgrimage thereto is a duty men owe to **Allah**,
003:097   **Allah** stands not in need of any of His creatures.
003:098   when **Allah** is Himself witness to all ye do?
003:098   why reject ye the Signs of **Allah**,
003:099   who believe, from the path of **Allah**,
003:099   But **Allah** is not unmindful of all that ye do."
003:101   while unto you are rehearsed the Signs of **Allah**,
003:101   Whoever holds firmly to **Allah** will be shown
003:102   O ye who believe! fear **Allah** as He should be feared,
003:103   by the Rope which **Allah** (stretches out for you),
003:103   Thus doth **Allah** make His Signs clear to you:
003:108   These are the Signs of **Allah**:
003:108   and **Allah** means no injustice to any
003:109   to **Allah** do all matters return.
003:109   To **Allah** belongs all that is in the heavens
003:110   and believing in **Allah**.
003:112   This because they rejected the Signs of **Allah**,
003:112   they draw on themselves wrath from **Allah**.
003:112   (of protection) from **Allah** and from men;
003:113   they rehearse the Signs of **Allah** all night long,
003:114   They believe in **Allah** and the Last Day;
003:115   for **Allah** knoweth well those that do right.
003:116   will avail them aught against **Allah**:
003:117   it is not **Allah** that hath wronged them,
003:119   **Allah** knoweth well all the secrets of the heart."
003:120   for **Allah** compasseth round about all that they do.
003:121   and **Allah** heareth and knoweth all things.
003:122   but **Allah** was their Protector,
003:122   and in **Allah** should the Faithful
003:123   **Allah** had helped you at Badr, when ye
003:123   then fear **Allah**; thus may ye show your gratitude.
003:124   Is it not enough for you that **Allah** should help
003:126   no victory except from **Allah**, the Exalted,
003:126   **Allah** made it but a message of hope for you,
003:128   Not for thee, (but for **Allah**), is the decision:
003:129   To **Allah** belongeth all that is in the heavens
003:129   but **Allah** is Oft-Forgiving, Most Merciful.
003:130   doubled and multiplied; but fear **Allah**;
003:132   And obey **Allah** and the Messenger;
003:134   for **Allah** loves those who do good:
003:135   and who can forgive sins except **Allah**?
003:135   Remember **Allah** and ask for forgiveness
003:138   a guidance and instruction to those who fear **Allah**!
003:140   that **Allah** may know those that believe,
003:140   And **Allah** loveth not those that do wrong.
003:142   enter Heaven without **Allah** testing those
003:144   not the least harm will he do to **Allah**;

ALLAH (continued)

003:144 but **Allah** (on the other hand) will swiftly
003:146 And **Allah** loves those who are firm and steadfast.
003:148 And **Allah** gave them a reward in this world,
003:148 For **Allah** loveth those who do good.
003:150 Nay, **Allah** is your Protector, and He
003:151 for that they joined partners with **Allah**,
003:152 for **Allah** is full of grace to those who believe.
003:152 **Allah** did indeed fulfil His promise to you
003:153 For **Allah** is well aware of all that ye do.
003:153 There did **Allah** give you one distress
003:154 wrong suspicions of **Allah**-suspicions due
003:154 for **Allah** knoweth well the secrets of your hearts.
003:154 but (all this was) that **Allah** might test what
003:155 for **Allah** is Oft-Forgiving, Most Forbearing.
003:155 But **Allah** has blotted out (their fault):
003:156 This that **Allah** may make it a cause of sighs
003:156 It is **Allah** that gives Life and Death,
003:156 and **Allah** sees well all that ye do.
003:157 And if ye are slain, or die, in the way of **Allah**,
003:157 forgiveness and mercy from **Allah** are far better
003:158 Lo! it is unto **Allah** that ye are brought together.
003:159 put thy trust in **Allah**.
003:159 For **Allah** loves those who put their trust (in Him).
003:159 It is part of the Mercy of **Allah** that thou
003:160 In **Allah**, then, let Believers put their trust.
003:160 If **Allah** helps you, none can overcome you:
003:162 the man who draws on Himself the wrath of **Allah**,
003:162 the good pleasure of **Allah** like the man who draws
003:163 They are in varying grades in the sight of **Allah**,
003:163 and **Allah** sees well all that they do.
003:164 rehearsing unto them the Signs of **Allah**,
003:164 **Allah** did confer a great favour on the Believers
003:165 for **Allah** hath power over all things."
003:166 was with the leave of **Allah**, in order
003:167 these were told: "Come, fight in the way of **Allah**
003:167 But **Allah** hath full knowledge of all they conceal.
003:170 They rejoice in the bounty provided by **Allah**:
003:171 and in the fact that **Allah** suffereth not
003:171 the Grace and the Bounty from **Allah**,
003:172 the call of **Allah** and the Messenger, even after
003:173 They said: "For us **Allah** sufficeth,
003:174 and **Allah** is the Lord of bounties unbounded.
003:174 And they returned with Grace and Bounty from **Allah**:
003:174 for they followed the good pleasure of **Allah**:
003:176 not the least harm will they do to **Allah**:
003:177 not the least harm will they do to **Allah**,
003:179 Nor will **Allah** disclose to you the secrets
003:179 **Allah** will not leave the Believers
003:179 So believe in **Allah** and His Messengers:
003:180 **Allah** hath given them of His Grace,
003:180 To **Allah** belongs the heritage of
003:180 and **Allah** is well acquainted with all that ye do.
003:181 **Allah** hath heard the taunt of those who say:
003:181 "Truly, **Allah** is indigent and we are rich!"
003:182 for **Allah** never do injustice those who serve Him."
003:183 They (also) said: "**Allah** took our promise
003:186 and from those who worship parties besides **Allah**.
003:187 And remember **Allah** took a Covenant from
003:189 and **Allah** hath power over all things.
003:189 To **Allah** belongeth the dominion of the heavens
003:191 Men who remember **Allah**, standing, sitting,
003:195 a reward from **Allah**, and from

ALLAH (continued)

003:195 and from **Allah** is the best of rewards.
003:198 an entertainment from **Allah**;
003:198 and that which is from **Allah** is the best (bliss)
003:199 the Signs of **Allah** for a miserable gain!
003:199 those who believe in **Allah**, in the revelation to you,
003:199 bowing in humility to **Allah**:
003:199 and **Allah** is swift in account.
003:200 and fear **Allah**; that ye may prosper.
004:000 In the name of **Allah**, Most Gracious, Most Merciful.
004:001 fear **Allah**, through Whom ye demand
004:001 for **Allah** ever watches over you.
004:005 which **Allah** has assigned to you to manage,
004:006 but all-sufficient is **Allah** in taking account.
004:009 let them fear **Allah**, and speak appropriate words.
004:011 **Allah** (thus) directs you as regards
004:011 and **Allah** is All-Knowing, All-Wise.
004:011 These are settled portions ordained by **Allah**:
004:012 and **Allah** is All-Knowing, Most Forbearing.
004:012 Thus is it ordained by **Allah**;
004:013 those who obey **Allah** and His Messenger will be
004:013 Those are limits set by **Allah**: those who
004:014 But those who disobey **Allah** and His Messenger
004:015 or **Allah** ordain for them some (other) way.
004:016 for **Allah** is Oft-returning, Most Merciful.
004:017 **Allah** accepts the repentance of those who do evil
004:017 to them will **Allah** turn in mercy;
004:017 for **Allah** is full of knowledge and wisdom.
004:019 and **Allah** brings about through it
004:023 for **Allah** is Oft-Forgiving, Most Merciful.
004:024 Thus hath **Allah** ordained (prohibitions) against you:
004:024 and **Allah** is All-Knowing, All-Wise.
004:025 And **Allah** is Oft-forgiving, Most Merciful.
004:025 and **Allah** hath full knowledge about your faith.
004:026 **Allah** doth wish to make clear to you and
004:026 and **Allah** is All-Knowing, All-Wise.
004:027 **Allah** doth wish to turn to you, but
004:028 **Allah** doth wish to lighten your (burdens):
004:029 for verily **Allah** hath been to you Most Merciful.
004:030 and easy it is for **Allah**.
004:032 in which **Allah** hath bestowed His gifts more
004:032 for **Allah** hath full knowledge of all things.
004:032 but ask **Allah** of His bounty: for **Allah**
004:033 For truly **Allah** is witness to all things.
004:034 what **Allah** would have them guard.
004:034 for **Allah** is Most High, Great (above you all).
004:034 because **Allah** has given the one more (strength)
004:035 **Allah** will cause their reconciliation:
004:035 for **Allah** hath full knowledge, and is
004:036 Serve **Allah**, and join not any partners with Him;
004:036 for **Allah** loveth not the arrogant, the
004:037 hide the bounties which **Allah** hath bestowed on them;
004:038 in **Allah** and the Last Day:
004:039 what **Allah** hath given them for sustenance?
004:039 if they had faith in **Allah** and in the Last Day,
004:039 For **Allah** hath full knowledge of them.
004:040 **Allah** is never unjust in the least degree:
004:042 but never will they hide a single fact from **Allah**!
004:043 For **Allah** doth blot out sins and forgive
004:045 and **Allah** is enough for a Helper.
004:045 **Allah** is enough for a Protector,
004:045 But **Allah** hath full knowledge of your enemies:
004:046 but **Allah** hath cursed them, for their Unbelief;

ALLAH (continued)

004:047 for the decision of **Allah** must be carries out.
004:048 **Allah** forgiveth not that partners
004:048 to set up partners with **Allah** is to devise a sin
004:049 Nay-but **Allah** doth purify whom He pleaseth.
004:050 Behold! how they invent a lie against **Allah**!
004:052 and those whom **Allah** hath cursed, thou wilt find,
004:052 They are (men) whom **Allah** hath cursed:
004:054 for what **Allah** hath given them of His bounty?
004:056 for **Allah** is Exalted in Power, Wise.
004:058 **Allah** doth command you to render back your trusts
004:058 For **Allah** is He Who heareth and seeth all things.
004:059 if ye do believe in **Allah** and the Last Day:
004:059 refer it to **Allah** and His Messenger, if ye
004:059 obey **Allah**, and obey the Messenger, and those
004:061 "Come to what **Allah** hath revealed. And
004:062 Then they come to thee, swearing by **Allah**: "We
004:063 Those men, **Allah** knows what is in their hearts;
004:064 found **Allah** indeed Oft-Returning, Most Merciful.
004:064 in accordance with the leave of **Allah**.
004:069 those on whom is the Grace of **Allah**, of the
004:069 All who obey **Allah** and the Messenger are in the
004:070 and sufficient is it that **Allah** knoweth all.
004:070 Such is the Bounty from **Allah**: and sufficient
004:072 They say: "**Allah** did favour us in that we
004:073 But if good fortune comes to you from **Allah**,
004:074 To him who fighteth in the cause of **Allah**, whether
004:074 Let those fight in the cause of **Allah** who sell
004:075 the cause of **Allah** and of those who, being
004:076 Those who believe fight in the cause of **Allah**,
004:077 or even more than, they should have feared **Allah**:
004:078 Say: "All things are from **Allah**."
004:078 they say, "This is from **Allah**"; but
004:079 and enough is **Allah** for a witness.
004:079 happens to thee, is from **Allah**: but
004:080 He who obeys the Messenger, obeys **Allah**: but
004:081 But **Allah** records their nightly (plots): so keep
004:081 so keep clear of them, and put thy trust in **Allah**,
004:081 and enough is **Allah** as a disposer of affairs.
004:082 Had it been from other than **Allah**, they
004:083 the Grace and Mercy of **Allah** unto you, all
004:084 It may be that **Allah** will restrain
004:084 for **Allah** is the strongest in might
004:085 and **Allah** hath power over all things.
004:086 **Allah** takes careful account of all things.
004:087 **Allah**! There is no god but He: of a surety
004:088 For those whom **Allah** hath thrown out of the Way,
004:088 guide those whom **Allah** hath thrown out of the Way?
004:088 **Allah** hath cast them for their (evil) deeds.
004:089 the way of **Allah** (from what is forbidden).
004:090 then **Allah** hath opened no way
004:090 If **Allah** had pleased, He could have
004:092 by way of repentance to **Allah**:
004:092 for **Allah** hath all knowledge and all wisdom.
004:093 and the wrath and the curse of **Allah** are upon him,
004:094 for **Allah** is well aware of all that ye do.
004:094 in the cause of **Allah**, investigate carefully,
004:094 till **Allah** conferred on you His favours:
004:094 with **Allah** are profits and spoils abundant.
004:095 in the cause of **Allah** with their goods
004:095 **Allah** hath granted a grade higher to those who
004:095 Unto all (in Faith) hath **Allah** promised good: but
004:096 For **Allah** is Oft-Forgiving. Most Merciful.

ALLAH (continued)

004:097 They say: "Was not the earth of **Allah** spacious
004:099 For these, there is hope that **Allah** will forgive:
004:099 for **Allah** doth blot out (sins) and
004:100 and **Allah** is Oft-Forgiving, Most Merciful.
004:100 his reward becomes due and sure with **Allah**:
004:100 for **Allah** and His Messenger,
004:100 He who forsakes his home in the cause of **Allah**,
004:102 **Allah** hath prepared a humiliating punishment.
004:103 remember **Allah**, standing, sitting down, or
004:104 but you hope from **Allah**, what they have not.
004:104 And **Allah** is full of knowledge and wisdom.
004:105 by that which **Allah** has shown thee; so be not
004:106 But seek the forgiveness of **Allah**;
004:106 for **Allah** is Oft-Forgiving, Most Merciful.
004:107 for **Allah** loveth not one given to perfidy and sin:
004:108 but they cannot hide from **Allah**, while
004:108 and **Allah** doth compass round all that they do.
004:109 but who will contend with **Allah** on their behalf
004:110 he will find **Allah** Oft-Forgiving, Most Merciful.
004:111 for **Allah** is full of knowledge and wisdom.
004:113 But for the Grace of **Allah** to thee and His Mercy,
004:113 For **Allah** hath sent down to thee the Book
004:113 and great is the Grace of **Allah** unto thee.
004:114 seeking the good pleasure of **Allah**, We
004:116 **Allah** forgiveth not (the sin of) joining
004:116 one who joins other gods with **Allah**, hath
004:118 **Allah** did curse him, but he said: "I will
004:119 and deface the (fair) nature created by **Allah**."
004:119 Whoever, forsaking **Allah**, takes Satan for a friend,
004:123 besides **Allah**, any protector or helper.
004:125 For **Allah** did take Abraham for a friend.
004:125 than one who submits his whole self to **Allah**,
004:126 But to **Allah** belong all things in the
004:127 but **Allah** is well-acquainted therewith.
004:127 Say: **Allah** doth instruct you about them: and
004:128 **Allah** is well-acquainted with all that ye do.
004:129 **Allah** is Oft-forgiving, Most Merciful.
004:130 **Allah** will provide abundance for each of them
004:130 for **Allah** is He that careth for all and is Wise.
004:131 and **Allah** is free of all wants, worthy
004:131 To **Allah** belong all things in the
004:131 But if ye deny Him, lo! unto **Allah** belong all
004:131 and you (O Muslims) to fear **Allah**, but if
004:132 and enough is **Allah** to carry through all affairs.
004:132 Yea, unto **Allah** belong all things
004:134 for **Allah** is He that heareth and seeth (all things).
004:135 as witnesses to **Allah**, even as against
004:135 for **Allah** can best protect both.
004:135 verily **Allah** is well-acquainted with all that ye do.
004:136 believe in **Allah** and His Messenger, and
004:136 And who denieth **Allah**, His angels, His Books,
004:137 **Allah** will not forgive them nor
004:139 Nay, all honor is with **Allah**.
004:140 For **Allah** will collect the Hypocrites and those
004:140 the Message of **Allah** held in defiance and ridicule,
004:141 And never will **Allah** grant to the Unbelievers
004:141 if ye do gain a victory from **Allah**, they say:
004:141 But **Allah** will judge betwixt you
004:142 The Hypocrites-they seek to deceive **Allah** but it
004:142 but it is **Allah** who deceive them.
004:142 but little do they hold **Allah** in remembrance;
004:143 Whom **Allah** leaves straying, never wilt

ALLAH (continued)

004:144	do ye wish to offer **Allah** an open
004:146	And soon will **Allah** grant to the Believers
004:146	religion devotion sincere to **Allah**: if so
004:146	mend (their life), hold fast to **Allah**, and
004:147	What can **Allah** gain by your punishment.
004:147	Nay, it is **Allah** that recogniseth (all good), and
004:148	**Allah** loveth not the shouting of evil
004:148	for **Allah** is He who heareth and knoweth all things.
004:149	surely **Allah** is ever pardoning Powerful.
004:150	between **Allah** and His Messengers, saying
004:150	Those who deny **Allah** and his Messenger, and
004:152	To those who believe in **Allah** and His messengers
004:152	for **Allah** is Oft-Forgiving, Most Merciful.
004:153	for they said: "Show us **Allah** in public," but
004:155	nay, **Allah** hath set the seal on their hearts
004:155	that they rejected the Signs of **Allah**; that they
004:157	the Messenger of **Allah**"; but
004:158	and **Allah** is Exalted in Power, Wise;
004:158	Nay, **Allah** raised him up unto Himself; and
004:162	and believe in **Allah** and in the Last Day: to them
004:164	and to Moses **Allah** spoke direct;
004:165	should have no plea against **Allah**:
004:165	for **Allah** is Exalted in Power, Wise.
004:166	but enough is **Allah** for a Witness.
004:166	But **Allah** beareth witness that what He hath
004:167	and keep off (men) from the way of **Allah**, have
004:168	**Allah** will not forgive them nor guide
004:169	and this to **Allah** is easy.
004:170	to **Allah** belong all things in the heavens
004:170	and **Allah** is All-Knowing, All-Wise.
004:170	to you in truth from **Allah**: believe in him:
004:171	was (no more than) an Messenger of **Allah**, and
004:171	so believe in **Allah** and His Messengers.
004:171	nor say of **Allah** aught but truth.
004:171	for **Allah** is One God: glory be to him:
004:171	And enough is **Allah** as a Disposer of affairs.
004:172	Christ disdaineth not to serve and worship **Allah**,
004:172	nor do the angels, those nearest (to **Allah**):
004:173	nor will they find, besides **Allah**, any to
004:175	Then those who believe in **Allah**, and hold
004:176	thus doth **Allah** make clear to you (His law),
004:176	And **Allah** hath knowledge of all things.
004:176	say: **Allah** directs (thus) about those who leave
005:000	In the name of **Allah**, Most Gracious, Most Merciful.
005:001	for **Allah** doth command according to His
005:002	the sanctity of the rites of **Allah**, nor of
005:002	in sin and rancour: fear **Allah**:
005:002	for **Allah** is strict in punishment.
005:003	**Allah** is indeed Oft-Forgiving, Most Merciful.
005:003	hath been invoked the name of other than **Allah**;
005:004	and fear **Allah**;
005:004	for **Allah** is swift in taking account.
005:004	but pronounce the name of **Allah** over it:
005:004	in the manner directed to you by **Allah**: eat
005:006	**Allah** doth not wish to place you in a difficulty,
005:007	"We hear and we obey": and fear **Allah**,
005:007	for **Allah** knoweth well the secrets of your hearts.
005:007	the favour of **Allah** unto you, and His Covenant,
005:008	For **Allah** is well-acquainted with all that ye do.
005:008	that is next to Piety: and fear **Allah**.
005:008	O ye who believe! stand out firmly for **Allah**, as
005:009	hath **Allah** promised forgiveness and a great reward.

ALLAH (continued)

005:011	call in remembrance the favour of **Allah** unto you
005:011	And on **Allah** let Believers put (all) their trust.
005:011	but (**Allah**) held back their hands from you: so
005:011	so fear **Allah**.
005:012	and **Allah** said: "I am with you: if ye (but)
005:012	and loan to **Allah** a beautiful loan, verily I will
005:012	**Allah** did aforetime take a Covenant from
005:013	for **Allah** loveth those who are kind.
005:014	And soon will **Allah** show them what
005:015	There hath come to you from **Allah** a (new)
005:016	Wherewith **Allah** guideth all who seek His good
005:017	For to **Allah** belongeth the dominion
005:017	against **Allah**, if His Will were to destroy
005:017	say that **Allah** is Christ the son of Mary.
005:017	For **Allah** hath power over all things."
005:018	"We are sons of **Allah**, and His beloved."
005:018	and to **Allah** belongeth the dominion of
005:019	and **Allah** hath power over all things.
005:020	the favour of **Allah** unto you, when He produced
005:021	which **Allah** hath assigned unto you, and turn
005:023	were two on whom **Allah** had bestowed His Grace:
005:023	But on **Allah** put your trust if ye have faith."
005:026	**Allah** said: "Therefore will the land
005:027	a sacrifice (to **Allah**): it was accepted
005:027	"**Allah** doth accept of the sacrifice
005:028	for I do fear **Allah**, the Cherisher of the worlds.
005:031	Then **Allah** sent a raven, who scratched
005:033	who wage war against **Allah** and His Messenger, and
005:034	know that **Allah** is Oft-Forgiving, Most Merciful.
005:035	O ye who believe! do your duty to **Allah**, seek
005:038	and **Allah** is Exalted in Power full of Wisdom.
005:038	and exemplary punishment from **Allah**,
005:039	for **Allah** is Oft-Forgiving, Most Merciful.
005:039	**Allah** turneth to him in forgiveness;
005:040	**Allah** (alone) belongeth the dominion of the
005:040	and **Allah** hath power over all things.
005:041	for him against **Allah**.
005:041	If any one's trial is intended by **Allah**, thou
005:042	For **Allah** loveth those who judge in equity.
005:043	Therein is the (plain) Command of **Allah**;
005:044	by what **Allah** hath revealed, they are Unbelievers.
005:045	by what **Allah** hath revealed, they are wrong-doers.
005:046	an admonition to those who fear **Allah**.
005:047	by what **Allah** hath revealed therein.
005:047	by what **Allah** hath revealed, they are indeed rebel.
005:048	If **Allah** had so willed, He would have
005:048	The goal of you all is to **Allah**; it is He
005:048	so judge between them by what **Allah** hath revealed,
005:049	(teaching) which **Allah** hath sent down to thee.
005:049	between them by what **Allah** hath revealed, and
005:050	can give better judgement than **Allah**?
005:051	Verily **Allah** guideth not a people unjust.
005:052	Ah! perhaps **Allah** will give (thee) victory, or a
005:053	who swore their strongest oaths by **Allah**, that
005:054	That is the Grace of **Allah**, which He will
005:054	and **Allah** encompasseth all, and He
005:054	soon will **Allah** produce a people whom He will
005:054	fighting in the way of **Allah**, and never afraid
005:055	Your (real) friends are (no less than) **Allah**, His
005:056	(for friendship) to **Allah**, His Messenger, and
005:056	the party of **Allah** that must certainly triumph.
005:057	but fear ye **Allah**, if ye have Faith (indeed).

ALLAH (continued)

005:059	no other reason than that we believer in **Allah**,
005:060	curse of **Allah** and His wrath, those of whom
005:060	by the treatment it received from **Allah**?
005:061	But **Allah** knoweth fully all that they hide.
005:064	from **Allah** increaseth in most of them their
005:064	And **Allah** loveth not those who do mischief.
005:064	**Allah** doth extinguish it; but they (ever)
005:067	And **Allah** will defend thee from men
005:067	For **Allah** guideth not those who reject Faith.
005:069	any who believe in **Allah** and the Last Day, and
005:071	But **Allah** sees well all that they do.
005:071	yet **Allah** (in mercy) turned to them: yet again
005:072	"O children of Israel! worship **Allah**, my Lord
005:072	Whoever joins other gods with **Allah**,-
005:072	"**Allah** is Christ the son of Mary." But said
005:072	**Allah** will forbid him the Garden, and the Fire
005:073	**Allah** is one of three in a Trinity: for there
005:074	Why turn they not to **Allah**, and seek
005:074	For **Allah** is Oft-forgiving, Most Merciful.
005:075	See how **Allah** doth makes His Signs
005:076	Say: Will ye worship, besides **Allah**, something
005:076	But **Allah**,-He it is that heareth
005:081	If only they had believed in **Allah**, in the
005:084	believe in **Allah** and the truth which has
005:085	hath **Allah** rewarded them with Gardens, with
005:087	for **Allah** loveth not those given to excess.
005:087	the good things which **Allah** hath made lawful
005:088	but fear **Allah**, in Whom ye believe.
005:088	which **Allah** hath provided for you, lawful
005:089	**Allah** will not call you to account for what is
005:089	Thus doth **Allah** make clear to you His Signs, that
005:091	and hinder you from the remembrance of **Allah**, and
005:092	Obey **Allah**, and obey the Messenger. And beware
005:093	For **Allah** loveth those who do good.
005:094	O ye who believe! **Allah** doth but make a trial
005:095	for repetition **Allah** will punish him
005:095	**Allah** forgives what is past:
005:095	for **Allah** is Exalted, and lord of Retribution.
005:096	and fear **Allah**, to Whom ye shall be gathered back.
005:097	that ye may know that **Allah** hath knowledge of what
005:097	**Allah** made the Ka'ba, the Sacred House, a means
005:097	and that **Allah** is well acquainted with all things.
005:098	Know ye that **Allah** is strict in punishment and
005:098	and that **Allah** is Oft-Forgiving, Most Merciful.
005:099	but **Allah** knoweth all that ye reveal and ye conceal.
005:100	so fear **Allah**, O ye that understand that;
005:101	for **Allah** is Oft-Forgiving, Most Forbearing
005:101	**Allah** will forgive those:
005:103	who invent a lie against **Allah**, but most
005:103	It was not **Allah** Who instituted
005:104	"Come to what **Allah** hath revealed; come to
005:105	The return of you all is to **Allah**: it is
005:106	we shall hide not the evidence we owe to **Allah**
005:106	and let them both swear by **Allah**:
005:107	let them swear by **Allah**: "We affirm that
005:108	for **Allah** guideth not a rebellious people.
005:108	But fear **Allah**, and listen (to His counsel): for
005:109	On the day when **Allah** will gather the
005:110	Then will **Allah** say: "O Jesus
005:111	we bow to **Allah** as Muslims'."
005:112	Said Jesus: "Fear **Allah**, if ye have faith."
005:114	"O **Allah** our Lord! send us from heaven a

ALLAH (continued)

005:115	**Allah** said: "I will send it down unto you: but
005:116	And behold! **Allah** will say "O Jesus
005:116	for two gods beside **Allah**'?" He will say:
005:117	to wit, 'Worship **Allah**, my Lord and your Lord':
005:119	and they with **Allah**: that is the mighty Triumph
005:119	**Allah** will say: "This is a day
005:119	**Allah** well-pleased with them, and they
005:120	To **Allah** doth belong the dominion of the
006:000	In the name of **Allah**, Most Gracious, Most Merciful.
006:001	Praise be to **Allah**, Who created the heavens
006:003	And He is **Allah** in the heavens and on earth.
006:012	Say: "To **Allah**. He hath inscribed for Himself
006:014	the first of those who bow to **Allah** (in Islam),
006:014	of those who join gods with **Allah**."
006:014	any other than **Allah**, the Maker of
006:017	"If **Allah** touch thee with affliction, none can
006:019	Say: "**Allah** is Witness between me and you: this
006:019	that besides **Allah** there is another gods?"
006:021	who inventeth a lie against **Allah** or
006:023	"By **Allah** Our Lord, we were not those
006:023	not those who joined gods with **Allah**."
006:031	as a falsehood that they must meet **Allah**,- until
006:033	it is the Signs of **Allah**, which the wicked deny.
006:034	the Words (and Decrees) of **Allah**. Already hast
006:036	**Allah** will raise them up: then will they
006:037	Say: "**Allah** hath certainly power to send
006:039	whom **Allah** willeth, He leaveth to wander: whom
006:040	would ye then call upon other than **Allah**?-
006:040	if there come upon you the Punishment of **Allah**,
006:042	that they call (**Allah**) in humility.
006:043	why then did they not call (**Allah**) in humility?
006:045	Praise be to **Allah**, the Cherisher of the Worlds.
006:046	Say: "Think ye, if **Allah** took away your hearing
006:046	who-a god other than **Allah**-could restore
006:047	if the Punishment of **Allah** comes to you, whether
006:050	with me are the treasures of **Allah**, nor do I
006:053	**Allah** hath favoured from amongst us?"
006:053	Doth not **Allah** know best those who are grateful?.
006:056	other than **Allah**, whom ye call upon." Say:
006:057	The Command rests with none but **Allah**: He
006:058	But **Allah** knoweth best those who do wrong."
006:062	Then are men returned unto **Allah**, their True
006:064	Say: "It is **Allah** that delivereth you from these
006:069	that they may (learn to) fear **Allah**.
006:070	for they persisted in rejecting **Allah**.
006:070	no protector or intercessor except **Allah**: if it
006:071	heels after receiving guidance from **Allah**?-
006:071	Say: "Shall we call on others besides **Allah**,-
006:072	and to fear **Allah**: for it is
006:078	from your (guilt) of giving partners to **Allah**.
006:079	I give partners to **Allah**."
006:080	about **Allah**, when He (Himself) hath guided me? I
006:080	I fear not (the beings) ye associate with **Allah**:
006:081	(the beings) ye associate with **Allah**, when ye
006:081	to give partners to **Allah** without any warrant
006:088	This is the Guidance of **Allah**: He giveth
006:091	"Nothing doth **Allah** send down to man
006:091	Say: "**Allah** (sent it down)": then leave
006:091	No just estimate of **Allah** do they
006:093	one who inventeth a lie against **Allah**, or saith,
006:093	reveal the like of what **Allah** hath revealed?"
006:093	for that ye used to tell lies against **Allah**, and

ALLAH (continued)

006:095	That is **Allah**: then how are ye
006:095	It is **Allah** Who causeth the seed-grain and the
006:100	Yet they make the Jinns equals with **Allah**,
006:100	though **Allah** did create the Jinns; And they
006:102	That is **Allah**, your Lord! There is no
006:106	those who join gods with **Allah**.
006:108	they out of spite revile **Allah** in their ignorance.
006:108	they call upon besides **Allah**, lest they
006:109	They swear their strongest oaths by **Allah**, that
006:109	are in the power of **Allah**: but what
006:114	Say: "Shall I seek for judge other than **Allah**?-
006:116	they will lead thee away from the Way of **Allah**.
006:124	be overtaken by humiliation before **Allah**, and
006:124	**Allah** knoweth best where to place His mission.
006:124	a Sign (from **Allah**), they say:" We shall
006:125	thus doth **Allah** lay abomination on those
006:125	Those whom **Allah** willeth to guide,- He openeth
006:128	except as **Allah** willeth." For the Lord
006:136	**Allah** reacheth their "partners"! Evil
006:136	reacheth not **Allah**, whilst the share
006:136	"This is for **Allah**, and this
006:136	Out of what **Allah** hath produced in abundance
006:137	If **Allah** had willed, they would
006:138	the name of **Allah** is not pronounced:-forging
006:139	attribution (of superstitions to **Allah**), He will
006:140	inventing (lies) against **Allah**. They have
006:140	and forbid food which **Allah** hath provided
006:141	for **Allah** loveth not the wasters.
006:142	eat what **Allah** hath provided for you, and
006:144	than one who invents a lie against **Allah**, to lead
006:144	**Allah** ordered you such a thing? But who
006:145	For **Allah** guideth not people who do wrong.
006:148	Those who give partners (to **Allah**) will say:
006:148	will say: "If **Allah** had wished, we should
006:149	Say: "With **Allah** is the argument
006:150	to prove that **Allah** did forbid so and so."
006:151	**Allah** hath (really) prohibited you from":
006:151	which **Allah** hath made sacred, except by
006:152	and fulfil the Covenant of **Allah**: thus doth
006:159	their affair is with **Allah**: He will
006:161	and he (certainly) joined not gods with **Allah**."
006:162	my life and my death, are (all) for **Allah**, the
006:164	Your return in the end is toward **Allah**: He will
006:164	for (my) Lord other than **Allah**. When
007:000	In the name of **Allah**, Most Gracious, Most Merciful.
007:012	(**Allah**) said: "What prevented thee from
007:013	(**Allah**) said: "Get thee down from it: it is not
007:015	(**Allah**) said: "Be thou among those
007:018	(**Allah**) said: "Get out from this, disgraced
007:024	(**Allah**) said: "Get ye down, with enmity
007:026	Such are among the Signs of **Allah**, that they
007:028	and "**Allah** commanded us thus": say: "Nay
007:028	say: "Nay **Allah** never commands what is Indecent:
007:028	do ye say of **Allah** what ye know not?"
007:030	the Satans in preference to **Allah**, for their
007:031	for **Allah** loveth not the wasters.
007:032	the beautiful (gifts) of **Allah**, which He
007:033	assigning of partners to **Allah**, for which
007:033	and saying things about **Allah** of which
007:037	that ye used to invoke besides **Allah**?" They will
007:037	that they had rejected **Allah**.
007:037	who forges a lie against **Allah** or rejects

ALLAH (continued)

007:043	had it not been for the guidance of **Allah**: indeed
007:043	and they shall say: "Praise be to **Allah**, Who
007:044	"The curse of **Allah** is on the wrong-doers;
007:045	from the path of **Allah** desiring to make
007:049	that **Allah** with His Mercy would never bless?
007:050	that **Allah** doth provide for your sustenance."
007:050	hath **Allah** forbidden to those who rejected Him;
007:054	Your Guardian Lord is **Allah**, Who created
007:054	and the Command, Blessed be **Allah**, the Cherisher
007:055	For **Allah** loveth not those who trespass
007:056	for the Mercy of **Allah** is (always)
007:059	worship **Allah**! ye have not other god but Him. I
007:062	and I know from **Allah** something that ye know not.
007:063	fear **Allah** and happily receive His Mercy?"
007:065	He said: "O my people! worship **Allah**! ye have
007:065	Will ye not fear (**Allah**)?"
007:069	the benefits (ye have received) from **Allah**: that
007:070	that we may worship **Allah** alone, and give up
007:071	without authority from **Allah**? Then wait:
007:073	This she-camel of **Allah** is a Sign unto you: so
007:073	he said: "O my people! worship **Allah**; ye have
007:074	the benefits (ye have received) from **Allah**, and
007:077	if thou art a Messenger (of **Allah**)!"
007:085	he said: "O my people! worship **Allah**; ye have
007:086	the path of **Allah** those who believe in Him, and
007:087	until **Allah** doth decide between us: for He
007:089	in the will of **Allah**, our Lord. Our Lord
007:089	in His knowledge in **Allah** is our trust.
007:089	"We should indeed forge a lie against **Allah**, if
007:089	after **Allah** hath rescued us therefrom; nor
007:096	had but believed and feared **Allah**, We should
007:099	can feel secure from the Plan of **Allah**, except
007:101	Thus doth **Allah** seal up the heart
007:105	to say nothing but truth about **Allah**. Now have
007:128	"Pray for help from **Allah**," and (wait)
007:140	a god other than **Allah**, when it is
007:143	**Allah** said: "By no means canst thou
007:144	(**Allah**) said: "O Moses! I have chosen thee
007:158	as the Messenger of **Allah**, to Whom
007:158	who believed in **Allah** and His Words:
007:158	So believe in **Allah** and His Messenger.
007:164	preach to a people whom **Allah** will destroy or
007:169	to **Allah** anything but the truth?
007:171	what is therein; perchance ye may fear **Allah**".
007:178	Whom **Allah** doth guide,-he is
007:180	The most beautiful names belong to **Allah**: so call
007:185	and all that **Allah** hath created? (Do they
007:186	To such as **Allah** rejects from His guidance, there
007:187	is with **Allah** (alone), but most men know not."
007:188	or harm to myself except as **Allah** willeth. If
007:189	they both pray to **Allah** their Lord (saying):
007:190	but **Allah** is exalted high above the partners
007:194	besides **Allah** are servants like unto you: call
007:196	"For my Protector is **Allah**, Who revealed
007:200	thy (mind), seek refuge with **Allah**; for He
007:201	Those who fear **Allah**, when a thought
007:201	bring **Allah** to remembrance when lo! they
008:000	In the name of **Allah**, Most Gracious, Most Merciful.
008:001	obey **Allah** and His Messenger,
008:001	at the disposal of **Allah** and the Messenger:
008:001	so fear **Allah**, and keep straight the relations
008:002	when **Allah** is mentioned, fell a tremor

ALLAH (continued)

008:007 Behold! **Allah** promised you one of the two
008:007 should be yours, but **Allah** willed to establish
008:010 **Allah** made it but a message of hope, and an
008:010 there is no help except from **Allah**:
008:010 and **Allah** is Exalted in Power,
008:013 against **Allah** and His Messenger:
008:013 if any contend against **Allah** and His Messenger.
008:013 **Allah** is strict in punishment.
008:016 he draws on himself the wrath of **Allah**, and his
008:017 it was **Allah**: when thou threwest (a handful)
008:017 from Himself: for **Allah** is He Who heareth
008:018 That, and also because **Allah** is He Who
008:019 for verily **Allah** is with those who believe!
008:020 O ye who believe! obey **Allah** and His Messenger,
008:022 the sight of **Allah** are the deaf and the dumb,-
008:023 If **Allah** had found in them any good, He would
008:024 give your response to **Allah** and His Messenger,
008:024 and know that **Allah** cometh in between
008:025 **Allah** is strict in punishment.
008:027 the trust of **Allah** and the Messenger, nor
008:028 and that it is **Allah** with whom lies
008:029 and forgive you: for **Allah** is the Lord
008:029 O ye who believe! if ye fear **Allah**, He will
008:030 but the best of planners is **Allah**.
008:030 They plot and plan, and **Allah** too plans, but the
008:032 Remember how they said: "O **Allah**! if this
008:033 But **Allah** was not going to send them
008:034 that **Allah** should not punish them, when they
008:035 Their prayer at the house (of **Allah**) is nothing
008:036 to hinder (men) from the path of **Allah**, and so
008:037 In order that **Allah** may separate the impure
008:039 verily **Allah** doth see all that they do.
008:040 be sure that **Allah** is your Protector-
008:041 a fifth share is assigned to **Allah**,-and to
008:041 if ye do believe in **Allah** and in the revelation
008:041 For **Allah** hath power over all things.
008:042 that **Allah** might accomplish a matter already
008:042 (had been given). And verily **Allah** is He who
008:043 but **Allah** saved (you): for He knoweth well the
008:043 Remember in thy dream **Allah** showed them
008:044 and unto **Allah** are all matters returned.
008:044 That **Allah** might accomplish a matter
008:045 and call **Allah** in remembrance much (and often);
008:046 for **Allah** is with those who patiently persevere.
008:046 And obey **Allah** and His Messenger; and fall
008:047 for **Allah** compasseth all that they do.
008:047 hinder (men) from the path of **Allah**:
008:048 Lo! I fear **Allah**;
008:048 for **Allah** is strict in punishment."
008:049 behold! **Allah** is Exalted in might, Wise.
008:049 But if any trust in **Allah**,
008:051 For **Allah** is never unjust to His servants."
008:052 for **Allah** is Strong, and Strict in punishment:
008:052 before them: they rejected the Signs of **Allah**, and
008:052 and **Allah** punished them for their crimes:
008:053 "Because **Allah** will never change the Grace
008:053 and verily **Allah** is He Who heareth and
008:055 sight of **Allah** are those who reject Him: they will
008:056 every time, and they have not the fear (of **Allah**).
008:058 for **Allah** loveth not the treacherous.
008:060 the cause of **Allah**, shall be repaid unto you,
008:060 but whom **Allah** doth know. Whatever ye

ALLAH (continued)

008:060 the enemies, of **Allah** and your enemies,
008:061 and trust in **Allah**: for He is the One
008:062 verily **Allah** sufficeth thee: He it is
008:063 but **Allah** hath done it: for He
008:064 is **Allah**,-and unto those who follow thee
008:066 for **Allah** is with those who patiently persevere.
008:066 two thousand, with the leave of **Allah**:
008:066 For the present, **Allah** hath lightened your
008:067 the Hereafter: and **Allah** is Exalted in might, Wise.
008:067 this world; but **Allah** looketh to the Hereafter:
008:068 a previous ordainment from **Allah**, a severe
008:069 for **Allah** is Oft-Forgiving, Most Merciful.
008:069 lawful and good: but fear **Allah**:
008:070 "If **Allah** findeth any good in your hearts, He will
008:070 for **Allah** Is Oft-Forgiving, Most Merciful."
008:071 And **Allah** is He who hath (full)
008:071 against **Allah**, and so hath He given thee
008:072 and (remember) **Allah** seeth all that ye do.
008:072 in the Cause of **Allah**, as well
008:074 in the Cause of **Allah**, as well
008:075 Verily **Allah** is well-acquainted with all things.
008:075 against each other in the Book of **Allah**.
009:001 from **Allah** and His Messenger, to those
009:002 but that **Allah** will cover with shame
009:002 frustrate **Allah** (by your falsehood), but that
009:003 frustrate **Allah**, and proclaim a grievous
009:003 that **Allah** and His Messenger dissolve (treaty)
009:003 And an announcement from **Allah** and His Messenger,
009:004 for **Allah** loveth the righteous.
009:005 for **Allah** is Oft-Forgiving, Most Merciful.
009:006 so that he may hear the Word of **Allah**; and then
009:007 for **Allah** doth love the righteous.
009:007 before **Allah** and His Messenger, with the
009:009 The Words of **Allah** have they sold
009:013 Nay, it is **Allah** whom ye should more justly fear,
009:014 Fight them, and **Allah** will punish them
009:015 For **Allah** will turn (in mercy) to whom He will:
009:015 He will: and **Allah** is All-Knowing, All-Wise
009:016 alone while **Allah** has not yet known those
009:016 and protectors except **Allah**, His Messenger, and
009:016 And **Allah** is well-acquainted with (all)
009:017 of **Allah** while they witness against their own
009:017 as join gods with **Allah**,
009:018 The mosques of **Allah** shall be visited and
009:018 and fear none (at all) except **Allah**.
009:018 as believe in **Allah** and the Last Day,
009:019 and **Allah** guides not those who do wrong.
009:019 They are not equal in the sight of **Allah**: and
009:019 believe in **Allah** and the Last Day, and strive
009:019 in the cause of **Allah**? They are
009:020 highest rank in the sight of **Allah**: they are
009:022 Verily with **Allah** is a reward, the greatest
009:024 His decision: and **Allah** guides not the rebellious.
009:024 then wait until **Allah** brings about His Decision:
009:024 than **Allah** or His Messenger, or the striving
009:025 Assuredly **Allah** did help you in many
009:026 But **Allah** did pour His calm on the Messenger
009:027 Again will **Allah**, after this, turn (in mercy)
009:027 for **Allah** is Oft-Forgiving, Most Merciful.
009:028 His bounty, for **Allah** is All-Knowing, All-Wise.
009:028 And if ye fear poverty, soon will **Allah** enrich you,
009:029 Fight those who believe not in **Allah** nor the

ALLAH (continued)

009:029	by **Allah** and His Messenger, nor acknowledge
009:030	Son of **Allah**. That is a saying from their mouth;
009:030	The Jews call 'Uzair a son of **Allah**, and the
009:031	beside **Allah**. And (they take as their Lord)
009:032	but **Allah** will not allow but that His light
009:034	and spend it not in the Way of **Allah**: announce
009:034	Way of **Allah**. And there are those who
009:036	sight of **Allah** is twelve (in a year)-so ordained
009:036	But know that **Allah** is with those
009:037	of months forbidden by **Allah** and make such
009:037	But **Allah** guideth not those who reject Faith.
009:038	forth in the Cause of **Allah**, ye cling
009:039	in the least. For **Allah** hath power
009:040	"Have no fear, for **Allah** is with us":
009:040	But the word of **Allah** is exalted to the heights:
009:040	then **Allah** sent down His peace upon him,
009:040	(it is no matter): for **Allah** did indeed help him,
009:040	to the heights: for **Allah** is Exalted in might
009:041	and your persons, in the cause of **Allah**.
009:042	for **Allah** doth know that they are lying.
009:042	They would indeed swear by **Allah**, "If we only
009:044	Those who believe in **Allah** and the Last Day
009:044	And **Allah** knoweth well those who do their duty.
009:045	who believe not in **Allah** and the Last Day,
009:046	some preparation therefor: but **Allah** was averse
009:047	But **Allah** knoweth well those who do wrong.
009:048	and the Decree of **Allah** became manifest, much to
009:051	except what **Allah** has decreed for us: He is
009:051	He is our Protector": and on **Allah** let the
009:052	that **Allah** will send His punishment from Him
009:054	they reject **Allah** and His Messenger; that they
009:055	may perish in their (very) denial of **Allah**.
009:056	They swear by **Allah** that they are indeed of you;
009:059	to **Allah** do we turn our hopes!" (That would
009:059	what **Allah** and His Messenger gave them, and had
009:059	"Sufficient onto us is **Allah**!
009:059	**Allah** and His Messenger will soon
009:060	(thus is it) ordained by **Allah**,
009:060	and **Allah** is full of knowledge and wisdom.
009:060	and in debt; in the cause of **Allah**; and for
009:061	for you; he believes in **Allah**, has faith
009:062	To you they swear by **Allah**. In order
009:062	should please **Allah** and His Messenger, if they
009:063	who oppose **Allah** and His Messenger, is the
009:064	But verily **Allah** will bring to light all that
009:065	Say: "Was it at **Allah**, and His Signs, and His
009:067	They have forgotten **Allah**; so He
009:068	**Allah** hath promised the Hypocrites, men and women,
009:068	for them is the curse of **Allah**. And an
009:070	with Clear Signs. It is not **Allah** Who wrongs
009:071	His mercy: for **Allah** is Exalted in power, Wise.
009:071	and His Messenger. On them will **Allah** pour His
009:071	regular prayers, pay Zakat and obey **Allah** and His
009:072	**Allah** hath promised to Believers, men and women,
009:072	Pleasure of **Allah**: that is the supreme triumph.
009:074	They swear by **Allah** that they said nothing (evil),
009:074	**Allah** and His Messenger had enriched them! If they
009:074	**Allah** will punish them with a grievous chastisement
009:075	a Covenant with **Allah**, that if He bestowed on them
009:077	their Covenant with **Allah**, and because
009:078	Know they not that **Allah** doth know their secret
009:078	secret counsels, And that **Allah** knoweth well all

ALLAH (continued)

009:079	**Allah** will throw back their ridicule on them: and
009:080	rejected **Allah** and His Messenger:
009:080	and **Allah** guideth not those who are
009:080	their forgiveness, **Allah** will not forgive them:
009:081	the Messenger of **Allah**: they hated
009:081	in the Cause of **Allah**: they said,
009:083	If, then, **Allah** bring thee back to any of them,
009:084	for they rejected **Allah** and His Messenger,
009:086	to believe in **Allah** and to strive and fight
009:089	**Allah** hath prepared for them Gardens under which
009:090	and those who were false to **Allah** and His Messenger
009:091	and **Allah** is Oft-Forgiving, Most Merciful.
009:091	(in duty) to **Allah** and His Messenger: no ground
009:093	**Allah** hath sealed their hearts: so they
009:094	it is your action that **Allah** and His Messenger
009:094	**Allah** hath already informed us of the true state
009:095	They will swear to you by **Allah**, when ye
009:096	**Allah** is not pleased with those who disobey.
009:097	but **Allah** is All-Knowing, All-Wise.
009:097	of the command which **Allah** hath sent down
009:098	for **Allah** is He that heareth
009:099	believe in **Allah** and The Last Day, and look
009:099	gifts bringing them nearer to **Allah** and obtaining
009:099	soon will **Allah** admit them to His Mercy:
009:099	for **Allah** is Oft-Forgiving, Most Merciful.
009:100	well-pleased is **Allah** with them, as are
009:102	for **Allah** is Oft-Forgiving, Most Merciful.
009:102	Perhaps **Allah** will turn unto them (in mercy): for
009:103	and **Allah** is one who heareth and knoweth.
009:104	and that **Allah** is verily He, the Oft-Returning,
009:104	Know they not that **Allah** doth accept repentance
009:105	soon will **Allah** observe your work, and His
009:106	and **Allah** is All-Knowing, Wise.
009:106	for the command of **Allah**, whether He will
009:107	but **Allah** doth declare that they
009:107	warred against **Allah** and His Messenger aforetime.
009:108	and **Allah** loveth those who make themselves pure.
009:109	his foundation on piety to **Allah** and His
009:109	And **Allah** guideth not people that do wrong.
009:110	And **Allah** is All-Knowing, Wise.
009:111	**Allah** hath purchased of the Believers their persons
009:111	faithful to his Covenant than **Allah**? Then rejoice
009:112	set by **Allah**;-(these do rejoice). So proclaim
009:112	to the Cause of **Allah**; that bow
009:112	Those that turn (to **Allah**) in repentance:
009:114	that he was an enemy to **Allah**, he dissociated
009:115	And **Allah** will not mislead a people after He
009:115	should avoid, for **Allah** hath knowledge of all things.
009:116	Unto **Allah** belongeth the dominion of the
009:117	**Allah** turned with favour to the Prophet,
009:118	no fleeing from **Allah** (and no refuge)
009:118	for **Allah** is Oft-Returning, Most Merciful.
009:119	O ye who Believe! Fear **Allah** and be
009:120	in the Cause of **Allah**, or trod paths
009:120	from an enemy: for **Allah** suffereth not the reward
009:121	their credit; that **Allah** may requite them
009:123	and know that **Allah** is with those who fear Him.
009:127	turn away: **Allah** hath turned their hearts
009:129	Say: "**Allah** sufficeth me: there is no god
010:000	In the name of **Allah**, Most Gracious, Most Merciful.
010:003	Verily your Lord is **Allah**, Who created
010:003	This is **Allah** your Lord; Him therefore serve ye:

ALLAH (continued)

010:004	The promise of **Allah** is true and sure.
010:005	Nowise did **Allah** create this but in truth
010:006	and in all that **Allah** hath created, in the
010:010	"Glory to Thee, O **Allah**!" and "Peace" will be
010:010	"Praise be to **Allah**, the Cherisher
010:011	If **Allah** were to hasten for men the ill
010:016	Say: "If **Allah** had so willed, I should
010:017	as forge a lie against **Allah**, or deny
010:018	intercessors with **Allah**." Say: "Do ye
010:018	Say: "Do ye indeed inform **Allah** of something
010:018	They serve, besides **Allah**, what can
010:020	**Allah** (to Know). Then wait ye: I too
010:021	Say: "Swifter to plan is **Allah**! Verily, Our
010:022	being overwhelmed: they pray unto **Allah**, sincerely
010:025	But **Allah** doth call to the Home of Peace: He doth
010:027	from (the wrath of) **Allah**: their faces
010:029	"Enough is **Allah** for a witness between us and you:
010:030	they will be brought back to **Allah** their rightful
010:031	They will soon say: "**Allah**". Say,
010:032	Such is **Allah**, your true Lord: apart from
010:034	Say: "It is **Allah** Who originates Creation
010:035	Say: "It is **Allah** Who gives guidance towards Truth.
010:036	Verily **Allah** is well aware of all that they do.
010:037	be produced by other than **Allah**; on the contrary
010:038	besides **Allah**, if it be ye speak the truth!"
010:044	Verily **Allah** will not deal unjustly with
010:045	who denied the meeting with **Allah** and refused
010:046	their return: ultimately **Allah** is witness to all
010:049	**Allah** willeth. To every People is a term appointed:
010:055	to **Allah** belongeth whatever is in the heavens
010:058	Say: "In the Bounty of **Allah**. And in His
010:059	Say: "Hath **Allah** indeed permitted you, or do
010:059	Say: "See ye what things **Allah** hath sent down
010:059	or do ye forge (things) to attribute to **Allah**?"
010:060	against **Allah**, of the Day of Judgement? Verily
010:060	Verily **Allah** is full of Bounty to mankind,
010:062	Behold! verily on the friends of **Allah** there is
010:064	in the Words of **Allah**. This is indeed
010:065	for all power and honour belong to **Allah**: it is
010:066	Behold! verily to **Allah** belong all creatures,
010:066	as His "partners" other than **Allah**? They follow
010:068	They say, "**Allah** hath begotten a son!"-Glory be
010:068	for this! Say ye about **Allah** what ye know not?
010:069	against **Allah** will never prosper."
010:071	and remind (you) the Signs of **Allah**,-
010:071	yet I put my trust in **Allah** get ye then
010:072	my reward is only due from **Allah**, and I
010:081	is sorcery: **Allah** will surely make it of no effect:
010:081	of no effect: for **Allah** prospereth not the work
010:082	"And **Allah** by His Words doth prove
010:084	if ye do (really) believe in **Allah**, then in Him
010:085	They said: "In **Allah** do we put our trust. Our Lord
010:089	**Allah** said: "Accepted is your prayer (O Moses
010:090	I am of those who submit (to **Allah** in Islam)."
010:093	Verily **Allah** will judge between them as to
010:095	Signs of **Allah**, or thou shalt be of those
010:100	except by the Will of **Allah**, and He
010:104	But I worship **Allah**-who will take your souls
010:104	ye worship other than **Allah**! But I
010:106	"Nor call on any, other than **Allah**,-such can
010:107	If **Allah** do touch thee with hurt, there is
010:109	till **Allah** doth decide: for He

ALLAH (continued)

011:000	In the name of **Allah**, Most Gracious, Most Merciful.
011:002	worship none but **Allah**. (Say:) "Verily I am
011:004	"To **Allah** is your return, and He
011:006	but its sustenance dependeth on **Allah**: He knoweth
011:012	It is **Allah** that arrangeth all affairs!
011:013	whomsoever ye can, other than **Allah**!-if ye
011:014	with the knowledge of **Allah**,
011:018	those who forge a lie against **Allah**? They will
011:018	their Lord! Behold! the Curse of **Allah** is on
011:019	path of **Allah** and wish it to be crooked:
011:020	nor have they protectors besides **Allah**!
011:026	"That ye serve none but **Allah**: verily I do
011:029	my reward is from none but **Allah**: but I
011:030	help me against **Allah** if I drove them away?
011:031	your eyes do despise that **Allah** will not
011:031	are the Treasures of **Allah**, nor do
011:031	**Allah** knoweth best what is in their souls:
011:033	He said: "Truly, **Allah** will bring it on you
011:034	(good) counsel, if it be that **Allah** willeth to
011:041	in the name of **Allah**, whether it move or be
011:043	of **Allah**, any but those on whom He hath mercy!"-
011:050	He said: "O my people! worship **Allah**! ye have
011:054	with evil." He said: "I call **Allah** to witness,
011:056	"I put my trust in **Allah**, my Lord and your Lord!
011:061	He said: "O my people! worship **Allah**: ye have
011:063	me against **Allah** if I were to disobey Him? What
011:064	of **Allah** is a sign to you: leave her
011:073	The grace of **Allah** and His blessings
011:078	for you (if ye marry)! Now fear **Allah**, and cover
011:084	he said: "O my people! worship **Allah**: ye have
011:086	'That which is left you by **Allah** is best for you,
011:088	(in my task) can only come from **Allah**. In Him I
011:092	of more consideration with you than **Allah**? For ye
011:101	the deities, other than **Allah**, whom they
011:112	(unto **Allah**); and transgress not (from the Path):
011:113	than **Allah**, nor shall ye be helped.
011:115	For verily **Allah** will not suffer the reward
011:123	To **Allah** do belong the unseen (secrets)
012:000	In the name of **Allah**, Most Gracious, Most Merciful.
012:018	it is **Allah** (alone) whose help can be sought."
012:019	But **Allah** knoweth well all that they do!
012:021	(and events). And **Allah** hath full power and
012:023	He said: "**Allah** forbid! truly (thy husband) is my
012:031	"**Allah** preserve us! no mortal is this! This is
012:037	of a people that believe not in **Allah** and that
012:038	that (comes) of the grace of **Allah** to us and to
012:038	any partners whatever to **Allah**: that comes
012:039	or **Allah** the One, Supreme and Irresistible?
012:040	ye and your fathers,-for which **Allah** hath sent
012:040	the Command is for none but **Allah**: He hath
012:051	The ladies said: "**Allah** preserve us! no evil
012:052	and that **Allah** will never guide the snare
012:064	But **Allah** is the best to take care (of him),
012:066	be **Allah** the Witness and Guardian!"
012:067	none can command except **Allah**: on Him
012:067	against **Allah** (with my advice): none can
012:068	in the least against (the Plan of) **Allah**: it served
012:073	(The brothers) said: "By **Allah**! well ye know that
012:076	except that **Allah** willed it (so). We raise
012:077	and **Allah** knoweth best the truth of what ye assert!"
012:079	He said: "**Allah** forbid that we take other than
012:080	or **Allah** judges for me; and He

ALLAH (continued)

012:083	May be **Allah** will bring them (back)
012:085	They said: "By **Allah**! (never) wilt thou cease
012:086	of my distraction and anguish to **Allah**, and I
012:086	and I know from **Allah** that which ye know not.
012:088	for **Allah** doth reward the charitable."
012:090	never will **Allah** suffer the reward to be lost,
012:090	my brother: **Allah** has indeed been gracious
012:091	**Allah** preferred thee above us, and we
012:091	They said: "By **Allah**! indeed has
012:092	be (cast) on you: **Allah** will forgive you, and He
012:095	They said: "By **Allah**! truly thou art in thine
012:096	to you, 'I know from **Allah** that which ye know not?'
012:099	in safety if it please **Allah**."
012:100	**Allah** hath made it come true! He was
012:106	not in **Allah** without associating (others as
012:107	covering veil of the wrath of **Allah**.
012:108	and never will I join gods with **Allah**!"
012:108	Glory to **Allah**! and never will I join gods with Allah!"
012:108	"This is my Way; I do invite unto **Allah**,-
013:000	In the name of **Allah**, Most Gracious, Most Merciful.
013:002	**Allah** is He Who raised the heavens without any
013:008	**Allah** doth know what every female (womb)
013:011	but when (once) **Allah** willeth a people's
013:011	they guard him by command of **Allah**. Verily
013:011	Verily never will **Allah** change the condition
013:013	about **Allah**, He is Mighty in Power.
013:015	do prostrate themselves to **Allah**-with good-will
013:016	Say: "(It is) **Allah**." Say: "Do ye then
013:016	to **Allah** partners who have created (anything)
013:016	them similar? Say: "**Allah** is the Creator of all
013:017	Thus doth **Allah** set forth parables.
013:017	Thus doth **Allah** (by parables) show forth
013:020	Those who fulfil the Covenant of **Allah** and fail
013:021	things which **Allah** hath commanded to be joined,
013:025	of **Allah**, after having plighted their word
013:025	those things which **Allah** has commanded to be
013:026	**Allah** doth enlarge, or grant by (strict) measure,
013:027	Say: "Truly **Allah** leaveth, to stray, whom He
013:028	of **Allah** do hearts find satisfaction.
013:028	the remembrance of **Allah**: for without
013:031	until the Promise of **Allah** come to pass,
013:031	the Believers know, that, had **Allah** (so) willed,
013:031	come to pass, for, verily, **Allah** will not fail
013:031	with **Allah** in things! Do not the Believers know,
013:033	they ascribe partners to **Allah**. Say: "But
013:033	**Allah** leaves to stray, no one can guide.
013:034	and defender have they none against **Allah**.
013:036	Say: "I am commanded to worship **Allah**, and not
013:037	protector nor defender against **Allah**.
013:038	except as **Allah** permitted (or commanded).
013:039	**Allah** doth blot out or confirm what He pleaseth:
013:041	(Where) **Allah** commands, there is none to put
013:042	**Allah** is the devising altogether. He knoweth
013:043	between me and you is **Allah**, and such
014:000	In the name of **Allah**, Most Gracious, Most Merciful.
014:002	Of **Allah**, to Whom do belong all things in the
014:003	**Allah** and seek to make it crooked: they are
014:004	to them. So **Allah** leads astray those whom He
014:005	the Days of **Allah**." Verily in this there are
014:006	"Call to mind the favour of **Allah** to you
014:008	yet is **Allah** Free of all wants, Worthy of
014:009	None knows them but **Allah**. To them came

ALLAH (continued)

014:010	a doubt about **Allah**, the Creator of the heavens
014:011	And on **Allah** let all men of faith put their trust.
014:011	an authority except as **Allah** permits.
014:011	but **Allah** doth grant His grace to such
014:012	should put their trust on **Allah**."
014:012	Why we should not put out trust on **Allah**.
014:019	Seest thou not that **Allah** created the
014:020	Nor is that for **Allah** any great matter.
014:021	before **Allah** together: then will the weak say to
014:021	against the wrath of **Allah**?" They will reply
014:021	received the guidance of **Allah**, we should
014:022	is decided: "It was **Allah** Who gave you a promise
014:022	in associating me with **Allah**. For wrong-doers
014:024	Seest thou not how **Allah** sets forth a parable?
014:025	So **Allah** sets forth parables for men, in order
014:027	the Hereafter; but **Allah** will leave, to stray,
014:027	**Allah** will establish in strength those who
014:027	**Allah** doeth what He willeth.
014:028	to those who exchanged the favour of **Allah**.
014:030	And they set up (idols) as equal to **Allah**,
014:032	It is **Allah** Who hath created the heavens
014:034	But if ye count the favours of **Allah**, never will
014:038	for nothing whatever is hidden from **Allah**,
014:039	"Praise be to **Allah**, who hath granted unto me
014:042	Think not that **Allah** doth not heed the deeds
014:046	(well) within the sight of **Allah**, even though
014:047	Never think that **Allah** would fail His messengers
014:047	for **Allah** is Exalted in power,-the Lord
014:048	marshalled forth, before **Allah**, the One,
014:051	That **Allah** may requite each soul
014:051	and verily **Allah** is Swift in calling account.
015:000	In the name of **Allah**, Most Gracious, Most Merciful.
015:032	(**Allah**) said: "O Iblis! what is your reason for
015:034	(**Allah**) said: "Then get thee out from here;
015:037	(**Allah**) said: "Respite is granted thee-
015:041	(**Allah**) said: "This is for me a straight path.
015:057	O ye messengers (of **Allah**)?"
015:069	"But fear **Allah**, and shame me not."
015:094	those who join false gods with **Allah**.
015:096	Those who adopt, with **Allah**, another god:
016:000	In the name of **Allah**, Most Gracious, Most Merciful.
016:001	the Command of **Allah**: seek ye not them to hasten
016:009	if **Allah** had willed, He could have guided
016:009	**Allah** alone can show the right path but there
016:014	seek (thus) of the bounty of **Allah** and that
016:018	number them: for **Allah** is Oft-Forgiving,
016:018	If ye would count up the favours of **Allah**,
016:019	And **Allah** doth know what ye conceal, and what
016:020	Those whom they invoke besides **Allah** create nothing
016:023	Undoubtedly **Allah** doth know what they conceal,
016:026	but **Allah** took their structures from their
016:028	verily **Allah** knoweth all that ye did;
016:031	thus doth **Allah** reward the righteous,-
016:033	But **Allah** wronged them not: nay, they wronged
016:035	"If **Allah** had so willed, we should not have
016:036	some whom **Allah** guided, and some
016:036	(with the Command), "Serve **Allah** and eschew Evil":
016:037	yet **Allah** guideth not such as He leaves to stray,
016:038	They swear their strongest oath by **Allah**,
016:038	that **Allah** will not raise up those who die:
016:041	in the cause of **Allah**, after suffering
016:045	(plots) feel secure that **Allah** will not cause

ALLAH (continued)

016:048 prostrating themselves to **Allah**,
016:049 And to **Allah** doth prostrate all that is in
016:051 **Allah** has said: "Take not (for worship) two gods:
016:052 then will ye fear other than **Allah**?
016:053 you have no good thing but is from **Allah**:
016:056 By **Allah**, ye shall certainly be called to account
016:057 And they assign daughters for **Allah**! - Glory be
016:060 of evil: to **Allah** applies the highest similitude:
016:061 It **Allah** were to punish men for their wrong-doing,
016:062 They attribute to **Allah** what they hate
016:063 By **Allah**, We (also) sent (our prophets) to
016:065 And **Allah** sends down rain from the skies,
016:070 It is **Allah** who creates you and takes
016:070 for **Allah** is All-Knowing, All-Powerful.
016:071 Will they then deny the favour of **Allah**?
016:071 **Allah** has bestowed His gifts of sustenance
016:072 And **Allah** has made for you mates of your own
016:073 And worship others than **Allah**,-such as
016:074 for **Allah** knoweth, and ye know not.
016:074 Invent not similitudes for **Allah**:
016:075 **Allah** sets forth the Parable (of two men):
016:075 (By no means); praise be to **Allah**.
016:076 **Allah** sets forth (another) Parable of two men:
016:077 To **Allah** belongeth the Unseen of the heavens
016:077 even quicker: for **Allah** hath power over all things.
016:078 that ye may give thanks (to **Allah**).
016:079 Nothing holds them up but (the power of) **Allah**.
016:080 It is **Allah** who made your habitations homes of
016:081 It is **Allah** who made, out of
016:083 They recognize the favours of **Allah**; then they
016:086 When those who gave partners to **Allah** will see
016:087 show (their) submission to **Allah**; and all
016:088 (men) from the Path of **Allah**-for them will We
016:088 Those who reject **Allah** and hinder (men) from
016:090 **Allah** commands justice, the doing of good,
016:091 for **Allah** knoweth all that ye do.
016:091 Fulfil the Covenant of **Allah** when ye have
016:091 indeed ye have made **Allah** your surety;
016:092 for **Allah** will test you by this; and on
016:093 If **Allah** so willed, He could make you all
016:094 (men) from the Path of **Allah**, and a
016:095 Nor sell the Covenant of **Allah** for a miserable
016:095 a miserable price: for with **Allah** is (a prize)
016:096 what is with **Allah** will endure. And We
016:100 who join partners with **Allah**.
016:101 for another,-and **Allah** knows best what He reveals
016:104 whose who believe in the Signs of **Allah**,-
016:104 **Allah** will not guide them, and theirs
016:105 the Signs of **Allah**, that forge falsehood: it is
016:106 Any one who, after accepting faith in **Allah**,
016:106 utters Unbelief,-on them is the Wrath from **Allah**,
016:107 and **Allah** will not guide those who reject Faith.
016:108 and eyes **Allah** has sealed up and they
016:112 **Allah** sets forth a parable: a city
016:112 so **Allah** made it taste of hunger and terror
016:112 for the favours of **Allah**:
016:114 for the favours of **Allah**, if it is He
016:114 which **Allah** has provided for you, lawful and good;
016:115 other than **Allah** has been invoked. But if
016:115 then **Allah** is Oft-Forgiving, Most Merciful.
016:116 so as to ascribe false things to **Allah**,
016:116 For those ascribe false things to **Allah**.

ALLAH (continued)

016:120 in faith, and he joined not gods with **Allah**.
016:120 devoutly obedient to **Allah**, (and) true in faith,
016:121 He showed his gratitude for the favours of **Allah**,
016:123 in Faith, and he joined not gods with **Allah**."
016:124 its observance); but **Allah** will judge between
016:127 the help from **Allah**; nor grieve over them:
016:128 For **Allah** is with those who restrain themselves,
017:000 In the name of **Allah**, Most Gracious, Most Merciful.
017:001 Glory to (**Allah**) Who did take His Servant
017:019 the ones whose striving will be thanked (by **Allah**).
017:022 Take not with **Allah** another god; or thou
017:033 Nor take life-which **Allah** has made sacred-
017:039 with **Allah**, another object of worship, lest thou
017:063 **Allah** said: "Go thy way; if any of them follow
017:092 against us; or thou bring **Allah** and the angels
017:094 "Has **Allah** sent a man (like us) to be (His)
017:096 Say: "Enough is **Allah** for a witness between me
017:097 It is he whom **Allah** guides, that is
017:099 See they not that **Allah**, Who created
017:110 Say: "Call upon **Allah**, or call
017:111 Say: "Praise be to **Allah** Who begets no son,
018:000 In the name of **Allah**, Most Gracious, Most Merciful.
018:001 Praise be to **Allah**, Who hath sent to His
018:004 who say, "**Allah** hath begotten a son":
018:015 as invent a falsehood against **Allah**?
018:016 they worship other than **Allah**,
018:017 but he whom **Allah** leaves to stray,-for him
018:017 he whom **Allah** guides is rightly guided; but he
018:017 Such are among the Signs of **Allah**: he whom
018:019 "**Allah** (alone) knows best how long ye have
018:021 that the promise of **Allah** it true, and that
018:024 Except "If **Allah** so wills" and remember
018:026 Say: "**Allah** knows best how long they stayed:
018:038 "But as for my part **Allah** is my Lord, and none
018:039 There is no power but from **Allah**!'
018:043 Nor had he numbers to help him against **Allah**,
018:044 There, the (only) protection comes from **Allah**,
018:045 it is (only) **Allah** Who prevails over all things.
018:069 if **Allah** so will, (truly) patient: nor shall
018:080 and ingratitude (to **Allah**).
019:000 In the name of **Allah**, Most Gracious, Most Merciful.
019:018 (come not near) if thou dost fear **Allah**."
019:018 "I seek refuge from thee to (**Allah**) Most Gracious:
019:026 'I have vowed a fast to (**Allah**) Most Gracious,
019:030 He said: "I am indeed a servant of **Allah**: He hath
019:035 (the majesty of) **Allah** that He should beget
019:036 Verily, **Allah** is my Lord and your Lord:
019:044 for Satan is a rebel against (**Allah**) Most Gracious.
019:045 a Chastisement afflict thee from (**Allah**)
019:048 those whom ye invoke besides **Allah**:
019:049 those whom they worshipped besides **Allah**,
019:058 (**Allah**) Most Gracious were rehearsed to them,
019:058 on whom **Allah** did bestow His Grace,-of the
019:061 (**Allah**) Most Gracious has promised to His
019:069 in obstinate rebellion against (**Allah**) Most Gracious.
019:075 (**Allah**) Most Gracious extends (the rope)
019:075 see the warning of **Allah** (being fulfilled)-
019:076 "And **Allah** doth increase in guidance those who
019:081 gods other than **Allah**, to give
019:085 shall gather the righteous to (**Allah**) Most Gracious,
019:087 (or promise) from (**Allah**) Most Gracious.
020:000 In the name of **Allah**, Most Gracious, Most Merciful.

ALLAH (continued)

020:003	to those who fear (**Allah**),
020:008	**Allah**! there is no god but He! To Him
020:014	"Verily, I am **Allah**: there is no god but I:
020:019	(**Allah**) said, "Throw it, O Moses!"
020:021	(**Allah**) said, "Seize it, and fear not: We shall
020:036	(**Allah**) said: "Granted is thy prayer, O Moses!"
020:044	perchance he may take warning or fear (**Allah**)."
020:061	forge not ye a lie against **Allah**, lest He
020:073	compel us: for **Allah** is Best and Most Abiding."
020:083	**Allah** said): "What made thee hasten in advance
020:085	(**Allah**) said: "We have tested thy people in thy
020:090	for verily your Lord is (**Allah**) Most Gracious:
020:098	But the God of you all is **Allah**: there is
020:113	in order that they may fear **Allah**, or that
020:114	High above all is **Allah**, the King, the Truth!
020:126	(**Allah**) will say: "Thus didst thou, when Our
021:000	In the name of **Allah**, Most Gracious, Most Merciful.
021:022	besides **Allah**, there would have been ruin in both!
021:022	in both! But glory to **Allah**, the Lord
021:057	"And by **Allah**, I will certainly plan against
021:066	"Do ye then worship, besides **Allah**, things that
021:067	that ye worship besides **Allah**! Have ye no sense?"
021:098	(false) gods that ye worship besides **Allah**, are (but)
021:106	for people who would (truly) worship **Allah**.
022:000	In the name of **Allah**, Most Gracious, Most Merciful.
022:002	but dreadful will be the Chastisement of **Allah**.
022:003	as dispute about **Allah**, without knowledge,
022:006	This is so, because **Allah** is the Reality: it is
022:007	or about (the fact) that **Allah** will raise up
022:008	as disputes about **Allah**, without knowledge,
022:009	from the Path of **Allah**: for him
022:010	for verily **Allah** is not unjust to His servants.
022:011	There are among men some who serve **Allah**,
022:012	They call on such deities, besides **Allah**, as can
022:014	Verily **Allah** will admit those who believe
022:014	for **Allah** carries out all that He desires.
022:015	If any think that **Allah** will not help him
022:016	and verily **Allah** doth guide whom He will!
022:017	for **Allah** is witness of all things.
022:017	**Allah** will judge between them on the Day of
022:018	Seest thou not that to **Allah** prostrate all things
022:018	for **Allah** carries out all that He wills.
022:018	And such as **Allah** shall disgrace,-none can
022:023	**Allah** will admit those who believe and work
022:025	As to those who have rejected (**Allah**), and would
022:025	from the Way of **Allah**, and from
022:028	and celebrate the name of **Allah**, through the
022:030	whoever honours the sacred Rites of **Allah**,
022:031	Being true in faith to **Allah**, and never
022:031	if anyone assigns partners to **Allah**, he is
022:032	whoever holds in honour the Rites of **Allah**,
022:034	celebrate the name of **Allah** over the sustenance
022:035	when **Allah** is mentioned, are filled
022:036	then pronounce the name of **Allah** over them
022:036	for you as among the Signs from **Allah**: in them
022:037	that reaches **Allah**: it is your
022:037	that ye may glorify **Allah** for His guidance to you:
022:038	verily, **Allah** loveth not any that is
022:038	Verily **Allah** will defend (from ill)
022:039	**Allah** is Most powerful for their aid;
022:040	Did not **Allah** check one set of people
022:040	in which the name of **Allah** is commemorated

ALLAH (continued)

022:040	that they say, "Our Lord is **Allah**." Did not
022:040	**Allah** will certainly aid those who aid His
022:040	aid His (cause);-for verily **Allah** is full of
022:041	and forbid wrong: with **Allah** rests the end
022:047	But **Allah** will not fail in His promise.
022:052	for **Allah** is full of knowledge and wisdom:
022:052	throws in, and **Allah** will confirm (and establish)
022:052	into his desire: but **Allah** will cancel anything
022:054	humbly (open) to it: for verily **Allah** is the
022:056	On that Day the Dominion will be that of **Allah**:
022:058	a goodly Provision: truly **Allah** is He Who
022:058	on them will **Allah** bestow verily a goodly
022:058	cause of **Allah**, and are slain or die,-on them
022:059	well pleased: for **Allah** is All-Knowing,
022:060	for **Allah** is One that blots out (sins)
022:060	**Allah** will help him: for
022:061	That is because **Allah** merges Night into Day,
022:061	and verily it is **Allah** Who hears
022:062	That is because **Allah**-He is the Reality; and those
022:062	vain Falsehood: verily **Allah** is He, Most High,
022:063	clothed with green? For **Allah** is All-subtle,
022:063	Seest thou not that **Allah** sends down
022:064	for verily **Allah**,-He is Free of all wants,
022:065	for **Allah** is Most Kind and Most Merciful to man.
022:065	Seest thou not that **Allah** has made subject
022:068	say, "**Allah** knows best what it is ye are doing."
022:069	"**Allah** will judge between you on the Day of Judgement
022:070	Knowest thou not that **Allah** knows all that is
022:070	and that is easy for **Allah**.
022:071	Yet they worship, besides **Allah**,
022:072	**Allah** has promised it to the Unbelievers!
022:073	Those on whom, besides **Allah** ye call,
022:074	No just estimate have they made of **Allah**:
022:074	for **Allah** is He Who is strong and able to carry
022:075	and from men: for **Allah** is He Who
022:075	**Allah** chooses Messengers from angels and from
022:076	and to **Allah** go back all affairs (for decision).
022:078	hold fast to **Allah**! He is
023:000	In the name of **Allah**, Most Gracious, Most Merciful.
023:014	another creature: so blessed be **Allah**, the Best
023:023	"O my people! worship **Allah**! Ye have
023:024	over you: if **Allah** had wished (to send
023:028	say: "Praise be to **Allah**, Who has
023:032	(saying), "Worship **Allah**! ye have no other god
023:038	against **Allah**, but we are not the ones to believe
023:040	(**Allah**) said: "In but a little while, they are
023:068	Do they not ponder over the Word (of **Allah**),
023:085	They will say, "To **Allah**!" Say: "Yet will
023:087	They will say, "(They belong) to **Allah**." Say:
023:089	They will say, "(It belongs) to **Allah**." Say:
023:091	Glory to **Allah** (He is free) from the (sort of)
023:091	No son did **Allah** beget, nor is
023:116	Therefore exalted be **Allah**, the King,
023:117	If anyone invokes, besides **Allah**, any other
024:000	In the name of **Allah**, Most Gracious, Most Merciful.
024:002	in a matter prescribed by **Allah**, if ye
024:002	if ye believe in **Allah** and the Last Day: and let
024:005	for **Allah** is Oft-Forgiving, Most Merciful.
024:006	testify four times by **Allah** that he is of those
024:007	invokes the curse of **Allah** on himself
024:008	four times (with an oath) by **Allah**, that (her
024:009	she solemnly invokes the wrath of **Allah** on herself

ALLAH (continued)

024:010	on you, and that **Allah** is Oft-Returning, Full of
024:013	in the sight of **Allah**, (stand forth)
024:014	and mercy of **Allah** on you, in this
024:015	while it was most serious in the sight of **Allah**.
024:017	**Allah** doth admonish you, that ye
024:018	for **Allah** is full of knowledge and wisdom.
024:018	And **Allah** makes the Signs plain to you:
024:019	**Allah** knows, and ye know not.
024:020	the grace and mercy of **Allah** on you,
024:020	and that **Allah** is full of kindness and mercy,
024:021	were it not for the grace and mercy of **Allah** on you,
024:021	but **Allah** doth purify whom He pleases:
024:021	and **Allah** is One Who hears and know
024:022	do you not wish that **Allah** should forgive you?
024:022	For **Allah** is Oft-Forgiving, Most Merciful.
024:025	and they will realize that **Allah** is the (very) truth
024:025	On that Day **Allah** will pay them back (all) their
024:028	and **Allah** knows well all that ye do.
024:029	for you: and **Allah** has knowledge of what ye
024:030	and **Allah** is well acquainted with all that they do.
024:031	all together towards **Allah** in repentance that ye
024:032	**Allah** will give them means out of His grace:
024:032	for **Allah** is Ample-giving, and He knoweth
024:033	out of the means which **Allah** has given to you.
024:033	is **Allah** Oft-Forgiving, Most Merciful (to them).
024:033	until **Allah** gives them means out of His grace.
024:034	and an admonition for those who fear (**Allah**).
024:035	**Allah** doth guide whom He will to His Light:
024:035	**Allah** is the Light of the heavens and the earth.
024:035	His Light: **Allah** doth set forth Parables for men:
024:035	and **Allah** doth know all things.
024:036	which **Allah** hath permitted to be raised to honour;
024:037	can divert from the Remembrance of **Allah**, nor from
024:038	His Grace: for **Allah** doth provide for those
024:038	That **Allah** may reward them according to the
024:039	but he finds **Allah** there,
024:039	and **Allah** is swift in taking account.
024:039	and **Allah** will pay him his account:
024:040	for any to whom **Allah** giveth not light,
024:041	Seest thou not that it is **Allah** Whose praises
024:041	And **Allah** knows well all that they do.
024:042	and to **Allah** is the return.
024:042	Yea, to **Allah** belongs the dominion of the
024:043	Seest thou not that **Allah** makes the clouds
024:044	It is **Allah** Who alternates the Night and the Day:
024:045	And **Allah** has created every animal from water:
024:045	for verily **Allah** has power over all things.
024:045	**Allah** creates what He wills; for verily
024:046	and **Allah** guides whom He wills to a way
024:047	They say, "We believe in **Allah** and in the
024:048	When they are summoned to **Allah** and His
024:050	that **Allah** and His Messenger will deal
024:051	when summoned to **Allah** and His Messenger,
024:052	It is such as obey **Allah** and His Messenger,
024:052	His Messenger, and fear **Allah** and do right,
024:053	**Allah** is well acquainted with all that ye do."
024:053	They swear their strongest oaths by **Allah** that,
024:054	Say: "Obey **Allah**, and obey the Messenger: but if
024:055	**Allah** has promised, to those among you who believe
024:058	thus does **Allah** make clear the Signs to you:
024:058	for **Allah** is full of knowledge and wisdom.
024:059	before them: thus does **Allah** make clear His

ALLAH (continued)

024:059	for **Allah** is full of knowledge and wisdom.
024:060	and **Allah** is One Who sees and knows all things.
024:061	blessing and purity as from **Allah**.
024:061	Thus does **Allah** make clear the Signs
024:062	are those who believe in **Allah** and His Messenger;
024:062	for **Allah** is Oft-Forgiving, Most Merciful.
024:062	who believe, in **Allah** and His Messenger:
024:062	thou wilt, and ask **Allah** for their forgiveness;
024:063	you to another: **Allah** doth know those of you
024:064	of what they did: for **Allah** doth know all things.
024:064	Be quite sure that to **Allah** doth belong
025:000	In the name of **Allah**, Most Gracious, Most Merciful.
025:017	those whom they worship besides **Allah**,
025:019	(**Allah** will say): "Now have
025:020	For **Allah** is One Who sees (all things).
025:029	the Message (of **Allah**) after it had come to me!
025:041	in mockery: "Is this the one whom **Allah** has sent
025:055	Yet do they worship, besides **Allah**, things that
025:059	on the Throne: **Allah** Most Gracious: ask thou
025:060	(**Allah**) Most Gracious? Shall we adore
025:063	(**Allah**) Most Gracious are those who walk on
025:068	nor slay such life as **Allah** has made sacred,
025:068	Those who invoke not, with **Allah**, any other
025:070	and **Allah** is Oft-Forgiving, Most Merciful,
025:070	for **Allah** will change the evil of such persons
025:071	has truly turned to **Allah** in repentance:
026:000	In the name of **Allah**, Most Gracious, Most Merciful.
026:011	"The people of Pharaoh: will they not fear **Allah**?"
026:015	**Allah** said: "By no means! proceed them, both of
026:089	that brings to **Allah** a sound heart;
026:093	"Besides **Allah**? Can they help you or help
026:097	"By **Allah**, we were truly in an error manifest,
026:106	"Will ye not fear (**Allah**)?
026:108	"So fear **Allah**, and obey me.
026:110	"So fear **Allah**, and obey me."
026:124	"Will ye not fear (**Allah**)?
026:126	"So fear **Allah**, and obey me.
026:131	"Now fear **Allah**, and obey me.
026:142	said to them: "Will you not fear (**Allah**)?
026:144	So fear **Allah**, and obey me.
026:150	"But fear **Allah**, and obey me;
026:161	"Will ye not fear (**Allah**)?
026:163	"So fear **Allah**, and obey me.
026:166	"And leave those whom **Allah** has created
026:177	"Will ye not fear (**Allah**)?
026:179	"So fear **Allah**, and obey me.
026:213	with **Allah**, or thou wilt be among those who
026:227	in the remembrance of **Allah**, and defend
027:000	In the name of **Allah**, Most Gracious, Most Merciful.
027:008	and those around: and Glory to **Allah**, the Lord
027:009	"O Moses! verily, I am **Allah**, the Exalted
027:015	and they both said: "Praise be to **Allah**, Who has
027:016	this is indeed Grace manifest (from **Allah**)."
027:024	worshipping the sun besides **Allah**: Satan has
027:025	So that they worship not **Allah** Who brings forth
027:026	"**Allah**!-there is no god but He!-Lord of
027:030	'In the name of **Allah**, Most Gracious, Most Merciful.
027:036	in wealth? But that which **Allah** has given me
027:042	and we have submitted to **Allah** (in Islam)."
027:043	the worship of others besides **Allah**: for she
027:045	"Serve **Allah**": but behold, they became
027:046	If only ye ask **Allah** for forgiveness, ye may

ALLAH (continued)

027:047   He said: "Your ill omen is with **Allah**; yea, ye
027:049   They said: "Swear a mutual oath by **Allah** that we
027:059   (Who) is better?- **Allah** or the
027:059   Say: Praise be to **Allah**, and Peace
027:060   (Can there be another) god besides **Allah**?
027:061   (Can there be another) god besides **Allah**? Nay,
027:062   (Can there be another) god besides **Allah**? Little
027:063   (Can the be another) god besides **Allah**?-
027:063   High is **Allah** above what they associate with Him!
027:064   (Can there be another) god besides **Allah**?
027:065   except **Allah**, knows what is hidden:
027:079   So put thy trust in **Allah**:
027:084   the Judgement-Seat), (**Allah**) will say; "Did ye
027:087   on earth, except such as **Allah** will please
027:088   of **Allah**, Who disposes of all things in perfect
027:093   And say: "Praise be to **Allah**, Who will
028:000   In the name of **Allah**, Most Gracious, Most Merciful.
028:013   the promise of **Allah** is true: but most
028:016   So (**Allah**) forgave him: for He
028:027   indeed, if **Allah** wills, one of the righteous."
028:028   Be **Allah** a witness to what we say."
028:030   Verily I am **Allah**, the Lord of the Worlds...
028:049   Say: "Then bring ye a Book from **Allah**, which is
028:050   For **Allah** guides not people given to wrong-doing.
028:050   devoid of guidance from **Allah**?
028:056   but **Allah** guides those whom He will and He
028:060   but that which is with **Allah** is better
028:062   That Day (**Allah**) will call to them, and say:
028:065   That Day (**Allah**) will call to them, and say:
028:068   (in the matter): Glory to **Allah**! and far
028:070   And He is **Allah**: there is no god but He. To Him
028:071   Say: See ye? If **Allah** were to make the night
028:071   what god is there other than **Allah**, who can
028:072   Say: see ye? If **Allah** were to make the Day
028:072   what god is there other than **Allah**, who can
028:075   the Truth is with **Allah** (alone), and the
028:076   "Exult not, for **Allah** loveth not those who
028:077   which **Allah** has bestowed on thee, the Home
028:077   but do thou good, as **Allah** has been good to thee,
028:077   for **Allah** loves not those who do mischief."
028:078   Did he not know that **Allah** had destroyed,
028:080   The reward of **Allah** (in the Hereafter) is best
028:081   party to help him against **Allah**, nor could
028:082   Ah! those who reject **Allah** will assuredly
028:082   **Allah** was gracious to us, He could
028:082   "Ah! It is indeed **Allah** Who enlarges
028:087   these who join gods with **Allah**.
028:088   And call not, besides **Allah**, on another
029:000   In the name of **Allah**, Most Gracious, Most Merciful.
029:003   and **Allah** will certainly know those who are
029:005   the Term (appointed) by **Allah** is surely coming:
029:005   in the meeting with **Allah**, the term
029:006   for **Allah** is free of all needs from all creation.
029:010   the Wrath of **Allah**! And if help comes (to them)
029:010   (the cause of) **Allah**, they treat men's oppression
029:010   with you!" Does not **Allah** know best all that
029:010   "We believe in **Allah**"; but when they suffer
029:011   And **Allah** most certainly knows those who believe,
029:016   "Serve **Allah** and fear Him: that will
029:017   The things that ye worship besides **Allah** have no
029:017   then seek ye sustenance from **Allah**, serve Him,
029:017   "For ye do worship idols besides **Allah**,

ALLAH (continued)

029:019   truly that is easy for **Allah**.
029:019   See they not how **Allah** originates creation,
029:020   for **Allah** has power over all things.
029:020   see how **Allah** did originate creation;
029:020   so will **Allah** produce a later creation:
029:022   beside **Allah**, any protector or helper."
029:023   Those who reject the Signs of **Allah** and the
029:024   But **Allah** did save him from the Fire.
029:025   (for worship) idols besides **Allah**,
029:029   "Bring us the Wrath of **Allah** if thou
029:036   serve **Allah**, and fear the last day: nor commit
029:040   it was not **Allah** Who wronged them: they wronged
029:041   take protectors other than **Allah** is that
029:042   Verily **Allah** doth know of (everything)
029:044   **Allah** created the heavens and the earth
029:045   And **Allah** knows the (deeds) that ye do.
029:045   and remembrance of **Allah** is the greatest
029:050   Say: "The Signs are indeed with **Allah**: and I
029:052   and reject **Allah**, that are losers.
029:052   Say: "Enough is **Allah** for a Witness
029:060   It is **Allah** Who feeds (both) them and you:
029:061   they will certainly reply, "**Allah**."
029:062   for **Allah** has full knowledge of all things.
029:062   **Allah** enlarges the sustenance
029:063   Say, "Praise be to **Allah**!" But most
029:063   they will certainly reply, "**Allah**!" Say, "Praise
029:065   they call on **Allah**, making their
029:067   and reject the Grace of **Allah**?
029:068   who invents a lie against **Allah** or rejects
029:069   to Our Paths: for verily **Allah** is with those
030:000   In the name of **Allah**, Most Gracious, Most Merciful.
030:004   with **Allah** is the Command in the Past and in
030:005   With the help of **Allah**. He gives
030:006   (It is) the promise of **Allah**.
030:006   Never does **Allah** fall from His promise: but most
030:008   a term appointed, did **Allah** create the heavens
030:009   it was not **Allah** Who wronged them, but they
030:010   the Signs of **Allah**, and held
030:011   It is **Allah** Who begins the creation; then repeats
030:017   So (give) glory to **Allah**, when ye
030:029   whom **Allah** leaves astray? to them
030:030   in the work (wrought) by **Allah**: that is
030:030   the nature in which **Allah** has made mankind:
030:031   and be not ye among those who join gods with **Allah**,-
030:037   See they not that **Allah** enlarges the provision
030:038   the Countenance, of **Allah**, and it
030:039   no increase with **Allah**: but that
030:039   seeking the Countenance of **Allah**, (will increase):
030:040   It is **Allah** Who has created you: further, He
030:041   that (**Allah**) may give them a taste of some
030:043   from **Allah** the Day which there is no chance
030:048   It is **Allah** Who sends the Winds,
030:054   It is **Allah** Who created you in a state
030:059   Thus does **Allah** seal up the hearts of those
030:060   for verily the promise of **Allah** is true:
031:000   In the name of **Allah**, Most Gracious, Most Merciful.
031:006   to mislead (men) from the Path of **Allah** and throw
031:009   To dwell therein. The promise of **Allah** is true:
031:011   Such is the Creation of **Allah**: now show Me
031:012   "Show (thy) gratitude to **Allah**."
031:012   verily **Allah** is free of all wants, worthy of
031:013   Join not in worship (others) with **Allah**:

ALLAH (continued)

031:016 or on earth, **Allah** will bring it forth:
031:016 for **Allah** is subtle and aware.
031:018 the earth: for **Allah** loveth not any
031:020 who dispute about **Allah**, without knowledge
031:020 Do ye not see that **Allah** has subjected to your
031:021 the (revelation) that **Allah** has sent down,
031:022 Whoever submits his whole self to **Allah**, and is
031:022 and to **Allah** shall all things return.
031:023 for **Allah** knows well all that is in (men's) hearts.
031:025 they will certainly say, "**Allah**."
031:025 Say: "Praise be to **Allah**!"
031:026 and earth: verily **Allah** is He (that is)
031:026 To **Allah** belong all things in heaven and earth:
031:027 of **Allah** be exhausted (in the writing):
031:027 for **Allah** is Exalted in power, Full of Wisdom.
031:028 for **Allah** is He Who hears and sees (all things).
031:029 Seest thou not that **Allah** merges Night into Day
031:029 a term appointed; and that **Allah** is well
031:030 That is because **Allah** is the Truth and because
031:030 and because **Allah**,-He is the Most High, Most Great.
031:031 the Ocean by the grace of **Allah**?-
031:032 they call upon **Allah**, offering Him
031:033 the Chief Deceiver deceive you about **Allah**.
031:033 Verily, the promise of **Allah** is true: let not
031:034 to die. Verily with **Allah** is full knowledge
031:034 is with **Allah** (alone). It is He
032:000 In the name of **Allah**, Most Gracious, Most Merciful.
032:004 It is **Allah** Who has created the heavens and the
033:000 In the name of **Allah**, Most Gracious, Most Merciful.
033:001 O Prophet! Fear **Allah**, and hearken
033:001 verily **Allah** is full of knowledge and wisdom.
033:002 for **Allah** is well acquainted with (all)
033:003 And put thy trust in **Allah**,
033:003 and enough is **Allah**, as a Disposer of affairs.
033:004 **Allah** has not made for any man two hearts
033:004 But **Allah** tells (you) the Truth, and He
033:005 Juster in the sight of **Allah**.
033:005 and **Allah** is Oft-Returning,
033:006 such is the writing in the Book (of **Allah**).
033:008 That (**Allah**) may question the Truthful about their
033:009 Remember the Grace of **Allah**, (bestowed) on
033:009 but **Allah** sees (clearly) all that ye do.
033:010 (vain) thoughts about **Allah**!
033:012 say: "**Allah** and His Messenger promised us nothing
033:015 with **Allah** not to turn their backs, and a
033:015 and a covenant with **Allah** must (surely)
033:017 for themselves, besides **Allah**, any protector
033:017 from **Allah** if it be His wish to give you
033:018 Verily **Allah** knows those among you who keep
033:019 and so **Allah** has made their deeds of none effect:
033:019 of none effect: and that is easy of **Allah**.
033:021 who hopes in **Allah** and the Final Day,
033:021 in the Messenger of **Allah** an excellent exemplar
033:021 and who remember **Allah** much.
033:022 "This is what **Allah** and His Messenger had promised
033:022 and **Allah** and His Messenger told us what was true."
033:023 been true to their Covenant with **Allah**: of them
033:024 That **Allah** may reward the men of Truth
033:024 for **Allah** is Oft-Forgiving, Most Merciful.
033:025 and enough is **Allah** for the Believers in their
033:025 And **Allah** turned back the Unbelievers for (all)
033:025 And **Allah** is full of Strength,

ALLAH (continued)

033:026 **Allah** did take them down from their strongholds
033:027 And **Allah** has power over all things.
033:029 verily **Allah** has prepared for the well-doers
033:029 But if ye seek **Allah** and His Messenger,
033:030 and that is easy for **Allah**.
033:031 in the service of **Allah** and His Messenger,
033:032 if ye do fear (**Allah**), be not
033:033 And **Allah** only wishes to remove all abomination
033:033 and obey **Allah** and His Messenger.
033:034 for **Allah** is All-Subtle All-Aware.
033:034 of the Signs of **Allah** and His Wisdom:
033:035 for them has **Allah** prepared forgiveness and
033:036 if any one disobeys **Allah** and His Messenger,
033:036 been decided by **Allah** and His Messenger,
033:037 (in wedlock) thy wife, and fear **Allah**."
033:037 had received the grace of **Allah** and thy favour:
033:037 that which **Allah** was about to make manifest:
033:037 more fitting that thou shouldst fear **Allah**.
033:038 to the Prophet in what **Allah** has indicated
033:038 of **Allah** amongst those of old that have
033:038 And the command of **Allah** is a decree determined.
033:039 And enough is **Allah** to call (men) to account.
033:039 who preach the Messages of **Allah**, and fear
033:039 and fear none but **Allah**.
033:040 and **Allah** has full knowledge of all things.
033:040 but (he is) the Messenger of **Allah**,
033:041 O ye who believe! remember **Allah**, with much
033:047 shall have from **Allah** a very great Bounty.
033:048 but put thy trust in **Allah**.
033:048 For enough is **Allah** as a Disposer of affairs.
033:050 And **Allah** is Oft-Forgiving, Most Merciful.
033:050 the captives of war whom **Allah** has assigned
033:051 and **Allah** is All-Knowing. Most Forbearing.
033:051 and **Allah** knows (all) that is in your hearts:
033:052 and **Allah** doth watch over all things.
033:053 but **Allah** is not shy (to tell you) the truth.
033:054 verily **Allah** has knowledge of all things.
033:055 and, (ladies), fear **Allah**;
033:055 for **Allah** is Witness to all things.
033:056 **Allah** and His Angels send blessings on the
033:057 and his Messenger-**Allah** has cursed them in this
033:057 Those who annoy **Allah** and his Messenger-
033:059 and **Allah** is Oft-Forgiving, Most Merciful.
033:062 (Such was) the practice (approved) of **Allah**
033:062 in the practice (approved) of **Allah.**
033:063 "The knowledge thereof is with **Allah** (alone)":
033:064 Verily **Allah** has cursed the Unbelievers
033:066 we had obeyed **Allah** and obeyed the Messenger!"
033:069 but **Allah** cleared him of the (calumnies) they
033:070 O ye who believe! fear **Allah**, and make
033:071 he that obeys **Allah** and His Messenger has already
033:073 and **Allah** turns in Mercy to the Believers,
033:073 (With the result) that **Allah** has to punish
033:073 for **Allah** is Oft-Forgiving, Most Merciful.
034:000 In the name of **Allah**, Most Gracious, Most Merciful.
034:001 Praise be to **Allah**, to Whom belong all things
034:008 "Has he invented a falsehood against **Allah**, or is
034:009 that turns to **Allah** (in repentance).
034:010 echo ye back the Praises of **Allah** with him!
034:016 But they turned away (from **Allah**), and We
034:022 whom ye fancy, besides **Allah**: they have
034:022 nor is any of them a helper to **Allah**.

ALLAH (continued)

034:024 Say: "It is **Allah**; and certain it is that
034:027 Nay, He is **Allah**, the Exalted in Power, the Wise."
034:033 to be ungrateful to **Allah** and to attribute
034:046 that ye do stand up before **Allah**,-(it may be)
034:047 my reward is only due from **Allah**:
035:000 In the name of **Allah**, Most Gracious, Most Merciful.
035:001 Praise be to **Allah**, the Originator
035:001 for **Allah** has power over all things.
035:002 What **Allah** out of His Mercy doth bestow
035:003 Is there a Creator, other than **Allah**,
035:003 O men! remember the grace of **Allah** unto you!
035:004 before thee: to **Allah** all affairs are returned.
035:005 O men! certainly the promise of **Allah** is true,
035:005 nor let the Chief Deceiver deceive you about **Allah**.
035:007 For those who reject **Allah**, is a
035:008 For **Allah** leaves to stray whom He wills,
035:008 for **Allah** knows well all that they do!
035:009 It is **Allah** Who sends forth the Winds, so that
035:010 to **Allah** belong all glory and power.
035:011 All this is easy to **Allah**.
035:011 And **Allah** did create you from dust;
035:012 the Bounty of **Allah** that ye may be grateful.
035:013 Such is **Allah** your Lord:
035:015 it is ye that have need of **Allah**:
035:015 but **Allah** is the One Free of all wants,
035:017 Nor is that (at all) difficult for **Allah**.
035:018 and the destination (of all) is to **Allah**.
035:022 **Allah** can make any that He wills to hear;
035:027 Seest thou not that **Allah** sends down
035:028 for **Allah** is Exalted in Might,
035:028 those truly fear **Allah**, among His Servants,
035:029 Those who rehearse the Book of **Allah**,
035:031 for **Allah** is assuredly-with respect to His servants-
035:034 And they will say: "Praise be to **Allah**, Who has
035:036 But those who reject (**Allah**)-for them
035:038 Verily **Allah** knows (all) the hidden things
035:040 `Partners' of yours whom you call on besides **Allah**?
035:041 It is **Allah** Who sustains the heavens and the
035:042 by **Allah** that if a warner came to them,
035:044 Nor is **Allah** to be frustrated by anything
035:045 If **Allah** were to punish men according to what
035:045 verily **Allah** has in His sight all His servants.
036:000 In the name of **Allah**, Most Gracious, Most Merciful.
036:006 therefore remain heedless (of the Signs of **Allah**).
036:036 Glory to **Allah**, Who created in pairs
036:047 if **Allah** had so willed, He could
036:047 (the bounties) which **Allah** has provided you,"
036:074 Yet they take (for worship) gods other than **Allah**,
037:000 In the name of **Allah**, Most Gracious, Most Merciful.
037:003 Those who thus proclaim the message (of **Allah**)!
037:023 "Besides **Allah**, and lead them to the Way
037:035 there is no god except **Allah**, would puff
037:040 But the chosen servants of **Allah**,-
037:056 He said: "By **Allah**! thou wast little short
037:074 Except the chosen servants of **Allah**.
037:086 gods other than **Allah** that ye desire?
037:096 "But **Allah** has created you and your handiwork!"
037:102 if **Allah** so wills one of the steadfast."
037:103 So when they had both submitted (to **Allah**),
037:124 "Will ye not fear (**Allah**)?
037:126 "**Allah**, your Lord and Cherisher and the
037:128 Except the chosen Servants of **Allah** (among them).

ALLAH (continued)

037:143 (repented and) glorified **Allah**,
037:152 "**Allah** has begotten children"? But they
037:159 Glory to **Allah**! (He is free) from the things
037:160 Not (so do) the servants of **Allah**, the chosen ones.
037:162 Can lead (any) into temptation concerning **Allah**,
037:169 Servants of **Allah**, sincere (and devoted)!"
037:182 And praise to **Allah**, the Lord and
038:000 In the name of **Allah**, Most Gracious, Most Merciful.
038:017 turned (in repentance to **Allah**).
038:019 all with him did turn (to **Allah**).
038:024 (in prostration), and turned (to **Allah** in repentance).
038:026 mislead thee from the Path of **Allah**:
038:026 for those who wander astray from the Path of **Allah**,
038:065 no god is there but **Allah**, the One
038:075 (**Allah**) said: "O Iblis! what prevents thee from
038:077 (**Allah**) said: "Then get thee out from here:
038:080 (**Allah**) said: "Respite then is granted thee-
038:084 (**Allah**) said: "This is the Truth, and the
039:000 In the name of **Allah**, Most Gracious, Most Merciful.
039:001 The revelation of this Book is from **Allah**,
039:003 take for protectors other than **Allah** (say):
039:003 Truly **Allah** will judge between them in that
039:003 Is it not to **Allah** that sincere devotion is due?
039:003 But **Allah** guides not such as are false and
039:003 they may bring us nearer to **Allah**."
039:004 Had **Allah** wished to take to Himself a son,
039:004 He is **Allah**, the One, the Overpowering.
039:006   Such is **Allah**, your Lord and Cherisher:
039:007 truly **Allah** hath no need of you;
039:007 If ye reject (**Allah**),
039:008 and he set up rivals unto **Allah**,
039:011 to serve **Allah** with sincere devotion;
039:012 of those who submit to **Allah** in Islam."
039:014 Say: "It is **Allah** I serve, with my
039:016 below them: with this doth **Allah** warn off
039:017 and turn to **Allah** (in repentance),-
039:018 those are the ones whom **Allah** has guided,
039:020 never doth **Allah** fail in (His) promise.
039:020 (such is) the promise of **Allah**:
039:021 Seest thou not that **Allah** sends down rain
039:022 so that he received light from **Allah**,
039:022 hardened against the remembrance of **Allah**!
039:022 Is one whose heart **Allah** has opened to Islam,
039:023 but such as **Allah** leaves to stray, can have
039:023 do soften to the remembrance of **Allah**.
039:023 Such is the guidance of **Allah**; He guides
039:023 **Allah** has revealed (from time to time) the most
039:026 So **Allah** gave them a taste of humiliation
039:029 Praise be to **Allah**! But most
039:029 **Allah** puts forth a Parable-a man belonging
039:032 one who utters a lie concerning **Allah** and rejects
039:035 So that **Allah** will remit from them (even) the
039:036 For such as **Allah** leaves to stray, there can
039:036 Is not **Allah** enough for His servant? But they
039:037 Is not **Allah** Exalted in Power, Lord of Retribution?
039:037 And such as **Allah** doth guide there can be
039:038 The things ye invoke besides **Allah**,-can they,
039:038 they would be sure to say, "**Allah**."
039:038 Say: "Sufficient is **Allah** for me!
039:038 can they, if **Allah** wills some affliction
039:042 It is **Allah** that takes the souls (of men)
039:043 intercessors others besides **Allah**?

ALLAH (continued)

039:044 Say: "To **Allah** belongs exclusively (the right
039:045 When **Allah**, Alone is mentioned, the hearts
039:046 Say: "O **Allah**! Creator of the heavens and the
039:047 but something will confront them from **Allah**,
039:052 Know they not that **Allah** enlarges the provision
039:053 Despair not of the Mercy of **Allah**: for
039:053 for **Allah** forgives all sins: for He
039:056 towards **Allah**, and was but among those who mocked!'
039:057 'If only **Allah** had guided me, I should
039:060 see those who told lies against **Allah**,-their faces
039:061 But **Allah** will deliver the righteous for they
039:062 **Allah** is the Creator of all things, and He
039:063 the Signs of **Allah**,-it is they
039:064 Say: "Is it someone other than **Allah** that ye
039:065 "If thou wert to join (gods with **Allah**), truly fruitless
039:066 Nay, but worship **Allah**, and be
039:067 No just estimate have they made of **Allah**,
039:068 except such as it will please **Allah** (to exempt).
039:070 and (**Allah**) knoweth best all that they do.
039:074 They will say: "Praise be to **Allah**, Who has
039:075 to **Allah**, the Lord of the Worlds!"
040:000 In the name of **Allah**, Most Gracious, Most Merciful.
040:002 The revelation of this Book is from **Allah**,
040:004 None can dispute about the Signs of **Allah** but the
040:007 Those who bear the Throne (of **Allah**) and those
040:010 "Greater was the aversion of **Allah** to you
040:012 "This is because, when **Allah** was invoked as the
040:012 ye believed! the Command is with **Allah**,
040:013 receive admonition who turn (to **Allah**).
040:014 Call ye, then, upon **Allah** with sincere devotion
040:016 not a single thing concerning them is hidden from **Allah**.
040:016 That of **Allah**, the One, the Overpowering!
040:017 for **Allah** is Swift in taking account.
040:019 (**Allah**) knows the treachery of the eyes, and all
040:020 Verily it is **Allah** (alone) Who hears
040:020 And **Allah** will judge with (Justice and) Truth:
040:021 in the land: but **Allah** did call them to account
040:021 and none had they to defend them against **Allah**.
040:022 rejected them: so **Allah** called them to account:
040:028 he says, 'My Lord is **Allah**'?-when he
040:028 he warns you: truly **Allah** guides not one
040:029 us from the Punishment of **Allah**, should it
040:031 but **Allah** never wishes injustice to His Servants.
040:033 no defender shall ye have from **Allah**:
040:033 any whom **Allah** leaves to stray,
040:034 Thus doth **Allah** leave to stray such as transgress
040:034 ye said: 'No messenger will **Allah** send after him.'
040:035 Thus doth **Allah** seal up every heart-
040:035 (is such conduct) in the sight of **Allah** and of
040:035 (such) as dispute about the Signs of **Allah**,
040:042 "Ye do call upon me to blaspheme against **Allah**,
040:043 our Return will be to **Allah**;
040:044 My (own) affair I commit to **Allah**:
040:044 for **Allah** (ever) watches over His Servants"
040:045 Then **Allah** saved him from (every) evil that they
040:048 Truly, **Allah** has judged between (His) Servants!"
040:055 for the Promise of **Allah** is true:
040:056 seek refuge, then, in **Allah**: it is He
040:056 of **Allah** without any authority bestowed on them,-
040:061 It is **Allah** Who has made the Night for you,
040:061 Verily **Allah** is Full of Grace and Bounty to men:
040:062 Such is **Allah**, your Lord, the Creator

ALLAH (continued)

040:063 to reject the Signs of **Allah**.
040:064 So Glory to **Allah**, the Lord of the Worlds!
040:064 such is **Allah** your Lord.
040:064 It is **Allah** Who has made for you the earth
040:065 Praise be to **Allah**, Lord of the Worlds!
040:066 those whom ye invoke besides **Allah**,-seeing that
040:069 those that dispute concerning the signs of **Allah**?
040:074 Thus does **Allah** leave the Unbelievers to stray.
040:074 "Besides **Allah**?" They will reply: "They have
040:077 For the Promise of **Allah** is true: and whether
040:078 by the leave of **Allah**: but when
040:078 but when the Command of **Allah** issued, the matter
040:079 It is **Allah** Who made cattle for you, that ye
040:081 then which of the Signs of **Allah** will ye deny?
040:084 they said: "We believe in **Allah**,-the One
040:085 the rejecters of **Allah** lose (utterly)!
041:000 In the name of **Allah**, Most Gracious, Most Merciful.
041:006 And woe to those who join gods with **Allah**,-
041:014 (preaching): "Serve none but **Allah**." They said,
041:015 that **Allah**, Who created them, was superior
041:019 The Day that the enemies of **Allah** will be
041:021 They will say: "**Allah** hath given us speech,-
041:022 that **Allah** knew not many of the things that ye
041:028 of **Allah**,-the Fire: therein will be for them
041:030 "Our Lord is **Allah**," and, further, stand straight
041:033 who calls (men) to **Allah**, work righteousness,
041:036 by the Satan, seek refuge in **Allah**.
041:037 but prostrate to **Allah**,
041:047 The Day that (**Allah**) will propound to them
041:052 is (really) from **Allah**, and yet do ye reject it?
042:000 In the name of **Allah**, Most Gracious, Most Merciful.
042:003 **Allah**, Exalted in Power, Full of Wisdom.
042:005 Behold! Verily **Allah** is He, the Oft-Forgiving,
042:006 others besides Him,-**Allah** doth watch over them;
042:008 If **Allah** had so willed, He could
042:009 But it is **Allah**,-He is the Protector, and it
042:010 the decision thereof is with **Allah**: such is
042:010 Such is **Allah** my Lord: in Him
042:013 worship other things than **Allah**, hard is
042:013 **Allah** chooses to Himself those whom he pleases,
042:015 **Allah** will bring us together, and to
042:015 **Allah** is Our Lord and your Lord! For us
042:015 "I believe in the Book which **Allah** has sent down;
042:016 But those who dispute concerning **Allah** after He
042:017 It is **Allah** Who has sent down the Book in truth,
042:019 Gracious is **Allah** to His servants: He gives
042:021 religion without the permission of **Allah**?
042:022 the magnificent Bounty (of **Allah**.
042:023 for **Allah** is Oft-Forgiving, Grateful.
042:023 That is (the Bounty) whereof **Allah** gives Glad
042:024 "He has forged a falsehood against **Allah**"?
042:024 And **Allah** blots out falsehood, and proves
042:024 But if **Allah** willed, He could
042:027 If **Allah** were to enlarge the provision
042:031 nor have ye, besides **Allah**, anyone to
042:036 but that which is with **Allah** is better
042:040 his reward is due from **Allah**:
042:040 for (**Allah**) loveth not those who do wrong.
042:044 For any whom **Allah** leaves astray, there is
042:046 to help them, other than **Allah**: and for
042:046 and for any whom **Allah** leaves to stray, there is
042:047 because of (the ordainment of) **Allah**! That Day

ALLAH (continued)

042:049 To **Allah** belongs the dominion of the heavens
042:051 that **Allah** should speak to him except by inspiration,
042:051 what **Allah** wills: for He is Most High, Most Wise.
042:053 all affairs tend towards **Allah**!
042:053 The Way of **Allah**, to whom belongs whatever is
043:000 In the name of **Allah**, Most Gracious, Most Merciful.
043:017 as a likeness to (**Allah**) Most Gracious, his face
043:018 in a dispute (to be associated with **Allah**)?
043:019 who themselves serve **Allah**.
043:028 that they may turn back (to **Allah**).
043:054 truly were they a people rebellious (against **Allah**).
043:063 ye dispute: therefore fear **Allah** and obey me.
043:064 "For **Allah**; He is my Lord and your Lord:
043:086 And those whom they invoke besides **Allah** have no
043:087 they will certainly say, **Allah**: how then
043:088 (**Allah** has knowledge) of the (Prophet's) cry,
044:000 In the name of **Allah**, Most Gracious, Most Merciful.
044:018 Saying: "Restore to me the servants of **Allah**: I am
044:019 "And be not arrogant as against **Allah**: for I
045:000 In the name of **Allah**, Most Gracious, Most Merciful.
045:002 is from **Allah** the Exalted in Power, Full of Wisdom.
045:005 and the fact that **Allah** sends down Sustenance
045:006 believe after **Allah** and His Signs?
045:006 Such are the Signs of **Allah**, which We
045:008 He hears the Signs of **Allah** rehearsed to him,
045:010 have taken to themselves besides **Allah**:
045:012 It is **Allah** Who has subjected the sea to you,
045:014 hope for the Days of **Allah**:
045:019 on use to thee in the sight of **Allah**:
045:019 but **Allah** is the Protector of the Righteous.
045:022 **Allah** created the heavens and the earth for just
045:023 **Allah** has, knowing (him as such),
045:023 after **Allah** (has withdrawn Guidance)?
045:026 Say: "It is **Allah** Who gives you life, then gives
045:027 To **Allah** belongs the dominion of the heavens
045:031 But as to those who reject **Allah**, (to them
045:032 the promise of **Allah** was true,
045:035 the Signs of **Allah** in jest, and the
045:036 Then Praise be to **Allah**, Lord of the
046:000 In the name of **Allah**, Most Gracious, Most Merciful.
046:002 is from **Allah** the Exalted in Power, Full of Wisdom.
046:004 what is ye invoke beside **Allah**?
046:005 who invokes, besides **Allah**, such as
046:008 no power to help me against **Allah**.
046:010 **Allah** guides not a people unjust."
046:010 from **Allah**, and ye reject it, and a
046:013 "Our Lord is **Allah**,"
046:017 For the promise of **Allah** is true."
046:019 (**Allah**) may recompense their deeds; and no
046:021 "Worship ye none other than **Allah**: truly I
046:023 will come) is only with **Allah**: I proclaim
046:026 when they went on rejecting the Signs of **Allah**:
046:028 as a means of access (to **Allah**)?
046:028 as gods, beside **Allah**, as a means
046:031 who invites (you) to **Allah**, and believe in him:
046:032 and no protectors can he have besides **Allah**:
046:032 the one who invites (Us) to **Allah**,
046:033 See they not that **Allah**, Who created
047:000 In the name of **Allah**, Most Gracious, Most Merciful.
047:001 Those who reject **Allah** and hinder (men) from the
047:001 from the Path of **Allah**,-
047:001 their deeds will **Allah** bring to naught.

ALLAH (continued)

047:003 This becaus those who reject **Allah** follow falsehood.
047:003 thus does **Allah** set forth for men their lessons
047:004 who are slain in the way of **Allah**,-
047:007 if ye will help (the cause of) **Allah**, He will
047:008 But those who reject (**Allah**),- for them
047:008 and (**Allah**) will bring their deeds to naught.
047:009 This is because they hate the Revelation of **Allah**;
047:010 **Allah** brought utter destruction on them,
047:010 and similar (fate await) those who reject **Allah**.
047:011 That is because **Allah** is the Protector of those
047:011 but those who reject **Allah** have no protector.
047:012 Verily **Allah** will admit those who believe and do
047:012 while those who reject **Allah** will enjoy (this
047:016 such are men whose hearts **Allah** has sealed,
047:019 that there is no god but **Allah**,
047:019 for **Allah** knows how ye move about and how ye
047:021 it were best for them if they were true to **Allah**.
047:023 Such are the men whom **Allah** has cursed
047:026 who hate what **Allah** has revealed, "We will
047:026 but **Allah** knows their (inner) secrets.
047:028 they followed that which displeased **Allah**,
047:029 think that **Allah** will not bring to light
047:030 And **Allah** knows all that ye do.
047:032 hinder (men) from the Path of **Allah**,
047:032 will not harm **Allah** in the least,
047:033 O ye who believe! obey **Allah**,
047:034 then die disbelieving,- **Allah** will not forgive them.
047:034 and hinder (men) from the Path of **Allah**,
047:035 for **Allah** is with you,
047:038 in the Way of **Allah**:
047:038 But **Allah** is free of all wants,
048:000 In the name of **Allah**, Most Gracious, Most Merciful.
048:002 That **Allah** may forgive thee thy faults of the
048:003 And that **Allah** may help thee with powerful help.
048:004 and **Allah** is full of Knowledge and Wisdom;-
048:004 for to **Allah** belong the Forces of the heavens
048:005 and that is, in the sight of **Allah**,
048:006 who think an evil thought of **Allah**.
048:006 the Wrath of **Allah** is on them: He has cursed
048:007 and **Allah** is Exalted in Power, Full of Wisdom.
048:007 For to **Allah** belong the Forces of the heavens
048:009 may believe in **Allah** and His Messenger, that ye
048:010 the Hand of **Allah** is over their hands:
048:010 **Allah** will soon grant him a great Reward.
048:010 their fealty in truth to **Allah**:
048:010 what he has covenanted with **Allah**,-
048:011 (to intervene) on your behalf with **Allah**,
048:011 But **Allah** is well acquainted with all that you do.
048:013 for those who reject **Allah**, a Blazing fire!
048:013 And if any believe not in **Allah** and His Messenger,
048:014 but **Allah** is Oft-Forgiving, Most Merciful.
048:014 To **Allah** belongs the dominion of the heavens
048:015 **Allah** has already declared (this) beforehand":
048:016 **Allah** will grant you a goodly reward,
048:017 (**Allah**) will punish him with a grievous Chastisement.
048:017 (**Allah**) will admit him to Gradens
048:017 but he that obeys **Allah** and His Messenger,-
048:019 acquire (besides): and **Allah** is Exalted in Power,
048:020 **Allah** has promised you many gains that ye
048:021 but which **Allah** has compassed:
048:021 and **Allah** has power over all things.
048:023 (Such has been) the practice of **Allah** already in

ALLAH (continued)

048:023	thou find in the practice of **Allah**.
048:024	over them. And **Allah** sees well all that ye do.
048:025	(**Allah** would have allowed you to force your way,
048:026	**Allah** sent down His tranquillity to His
048:026	And **Allah** has full knowledge of all things.
048:027	ye shall enter the Sacred Mosque, if **Allah** wills,
048:027	Truly did **Allah** fulfil the vision
048:028	and enough is **Allah** for a Witness.
048:029	**Allah** has promised those among them
048:029	(in prayer), seeking Grace from **Allah** and (His)
048:029	Muhammad is the Messenger of **Allah**;
049:000	In the name of **Allah**, Most Gracious, Most Merciful.
049:001	yourselves forward before **Allah** and His Messenger;
049:001	for **Allah** is He who hears and knows all things.
049:001	and His Messenger; but fear **Allah**:
049:003	their hearts has **Allah** tested of piety: for them
049:005	but **Allah** is Oft-Forgiving, Most Merciful.
049:007	certainly suffer: but **Allah** has endeared the
049:008	A grace and favour from **Allah**;
049:008	and **Allah** is full of Knowledge and Wisdom.
049:009	it complies with the command of **Allah**;
049:009	for **Allah** loves those who are fair (and just).
049:010	And fear **Allah**, that ye may receive Mercy.
049:012	But fear **Allah**:
049:012	for **Allah** is Oft-Returning,
049:013	And **Allah** has full knowledge and is well
049:013	in the sight of **Allah** is (he who is) the most
049:014	for **Allah** is Oft-Forgiving, Most Merciful."
049:014	But if ye obey **Allah** and His Messenger,
049:014	'We submitted our wills to **Allah**,'
049:015	in the Cause of **Allah**: such are
049:015	who have believed in **Allah** and His Messenger,
049:016	Say: "What! Will ye tell **Allah** about your Religion?"
049:016	But **Allah** knows all that is in the heavens
049:017	Nay, **Allah** has conferred a favour upon you
049:018	and **Allah** sees well all that ye do."
049:018	"Verily **Allah** knows the Unseen of the heavens
050:000	In the name of **Allah**, Most Gracious, Most Merciful.
050:008	and Reminder to every servant turning (to **Allah**).
050:024	every contumacious Rejector (of **Allah**)!
050:026	"Who set up another god besides **Allah**: throw him
051:000	In the name of **Allah**, Most Gracious, Most Merciful.
051:050	Therefore flee unto **Allah**: I am
051:051	make not another an object of worship with **Allah**:
051:058	For **Allah** is He Who gives (all) Sustenance,-
052:000	In the name of **Allah**, Most Gracious, Most Merciful.
052:027	"But **Allah** has been good to us, and has
052:043	Or have they a god other then **Allah**?
052:043	Exalted is **Allah** far above the things
053:000	In the name of **Allah**, Most Gracious, Most Merciful.
053:010	So did (**Allah**) convey the inspiration to His
053:023	for which **Allah** has sent down no authority
053:025	But to **Allah** belongeth the Hereafter and the
053:026	will avail nothing except after **Allah** has given
053:031	Yea, to **Allah** belongs all that is in the heavens
053:058	No one but **Allah** can disclose it.
053:062	fall ye down in prostration to **Allah** and adore (Him)!
054:000	In the name of **Allah**, Most Gracious, Most Merciful.
054:041	too, aforetime, came Warners (from **Allah**).
055:000	In the name of **Allah**, Most Gracious, Most Merciful.
056:000	In the name of **Allah**, Most Gracious, Most Merciful.
056:011	These will be those Nearest to **Allah**:

ALLAH (continued)

056:088	Thus, then, if he be of those Nearest to **Allah**,
057:000	In the name of **Allah**, Most Gracious, Most Merciful.
057:001	declares the Praises and Glory of **Allah**:
057:004	And **Allah** sees well all that ye do.
057:005	and all affairs go back to **Allah**.
057:007	Believe in **Allah** and His Messenger, and spend
057:008	that you believe not in **Allah**?
057:009	And verily, **Allah** is to you Most Kind and Merciful.
057:010	spend not in the cause of **Allah**?-
057:010	For to **Allah** belongs the heritage of the
057:010	And **Allah** is well acquainted with all that ye do.
057:010	has **Allah** promised a goodly (reward).
057:011	For (**Allah**) will increase it manifold to his credit,
057:011	Who is he that will loan to **Allah** a beautiful Loan?
057:014	And the Deceiver deceived you in respect of **Allah**.
057:014	until there issued the Command of **Allah**.
057:015	nor of those who rejected **Allah**.
057:016	the remembrance of **Allah** and of the Truth which
057:017	Know ye (all) that **Allah** giveth life to the
057:018	and loan to **Allah** a Beautiful Loan,
057:019	but those who reject **Allah** and deny Our Signs,-
057:019	And those who believe in **Allah** and His messengers-
057:020	Good Pleasure (for the devotees of **Allah**).
057:020	And Forgiveness from **Allah** and (His)
057:021	He pleases: and **Allah** is the Lord
057:021	that is the Grace of **Allah**, which He Bestows
057:021	prepared for those who believe in **Allah** and His
057:022	that is truly easy for **Allah**:
057:023	For **Allah** loveth not any vainglorious boaster,-
057:024	verily **Allah** is free of all needs,
057:025	that **Allah** may test who it is that will help,
057:025	His messengers: for **Allah** is Full of Strength,
057:027	seeking the Good pleasure of **Allah**;
057:028	O ye that believe! fear **Allah**, and believe
057:028	(your past): for **Allah** is Oft-Forgiving,
057:029	He wills. For **Allah** is the Lord of Grace abounding.
057:029	over the Grace of **Allah**, that (His)
058:000	In the name of **Allah**, Most Gracious, Most Merciful.
058:001	and **Allah** (always) hears the arguments
058:001	**Allah** has indeed heard (and accepted)
058:001	for **Allah** hears and sees (all things).
058:001	her complaint (in prayer) to **Allah**:
058:002	but truly **Allah** is All-Pardoning, All-Forgiving.
058:003	and **Allah** is well-acquainted with (all) that ye do.
058:004	Those limits (set by) **Allah**.
058:004	show your faith in **Allah** and His Messenger.
058:005	Those who oppose (the commands of) **Allah** and His
058:006	for **Allah** is Witness to all things.
058:006	On the Day that **Allah** will raise them all up (again)
058:006	**Allah** has reckoned and which they forgot,
058:007	Seest thou not that **Allah** doth know (all) that is
058:007	For **Allah** has full knowledge of all things.
058:008	they salute thee, not as **Allah** salutes thee,
058:008	"Why does not **Allah** Punish us for our words?
058:009	and fear **Allah**, to whom ye shall be brought back.
058:010	in the least, except as **Allah** permits; and on
058:010	and on **Allah** let the Believers put their trust.
058:011	(Ample) room will **Allah** provide for you.
058:011	**Allah** will raise up, to (suitable) ranks
058:011	and **Allah** is well-acquainted with all ye do.
058:012	**Allah** is Oft-Forgiving, Most Merciful.
058:013	and obey **Allah** and His Messenger.

ALLAH (continued)

058:013 If, then, ye do not so, and **Allah** forgives you,
058:013 And **Allah** is well-acquainted with all that ye do.
058:014 the Wrath of **Allah** upon them?
058:015 **Allah** has prepared for them a severe Chastisement:
058:016 obstruct (men) from the Path of **Allah**:
058:017 Of no profit whatever to them, against **Allah**,
058:018 The Day will **Allah** raise them all up
058:019 the remembrance of **Allah**.
058:020 Those who oppose (the Commands of) **Allah**
058:021 for **Allah** is Strong, Mighty.
058:021 **Allah** has decreed: "It is I and My Messenger
058:022 **Allah** will be well pleased with them, and they
058:022 who believe in **Allah** and the Last Day, loving those
058:022 loving those who oppose **Allah** and His Messenger,
058:022 Truly it is the Party of **Allah** that will
058:022 They are the Party of **Allah**. Truly it
059:000 In the name of **Allah**, Most Gracious, Most Merciful.
059:001 and Glory of **Allah**: for He
059:002 But the (wrath of) **Allah** came to them
059:002 fortresses would defend them from **Allah**! But the
059:003 And had it not been that **Allah** has decreed
059:004 that is because they resisted **Allah**, and His
059:004 and if any one resists **Allah**,
059:004 verily **Allah** is severe in Punishment.
059:005 it was by leave of **Allah**, and in
059:006 and **Allah** has power over all things.
059:006 but **Allah** gives power to His Messenger over any
059:006 What **Allah** has bestowed on His Messenger
059:007 the townships,-belongs to **Allah**,-
059:007 What **Allah** has bestowed on His Messenger
059:007 for **Allah** is strict in Punishment.
059:007 And fear **Allah**;
059:008 from **Allah** and (His) Good Pleasure, and aiding
059:008 and aiding **Allah** and His Messenger: such are
059:011 But **Allah** is witness that they are indeed liars.
059:013 greater fear in their hearts, than **Allah**.
059:016 I do fear **Allah**, the Lord of the Worlds!"
059:018 Yea, fear **Allah**:
059:018 for **Allah** is well-acquainted with (all) that ye do.
059:018 O ye who believe! Fear **Allah**, and let
059:019 And be ye not like those who forgot **Allah**; and He
059:021 and cleave asunder for the fear of **Allah**, such are
059:022 **Allah** is He, than Whom there is no other god;-
059:023 the justly Proud, Glory to **Allah**! (high is He)
059:023 **Allah** is He, than Whom there is no other god;-
059:024 He is **Allah**, the Creator, the Originator,
060:000 In the name of **Allah**, Most Gracious, Most Merciful.
060:001 (simply) because ye believe in **Allah** your Lord!
060:003 between you: for **Allah** sees well all that ye do.
060:004 no power (to get) aught on thy behalf from **Allah**."
060:004 ye worship besides **Allah**: we have
060:004 for ever,-unless ye believe in **Allah** and Him
060:006 for those whose hope is in **Allah** and in
060:006 But if any turn away, truly **Allah** is Free of all
060:007 and **Allah** is Oft-Forgiving, Most Merciful.
060:007 For **Allah** has power (over all things);
060:007 It may be that **Allah** will Establish friendship
060:008 **Allah** forbids you not, with regard to those who
060:008 for **Allah** loveth those who are just.
060:009 **Allah** only forbids you, with regard to those who
060:010 **Allah** knows best as to their Faith:
060:010 to you). Such is the command of **Allah**:

ALLAH (continued)

060:010 and **Allah** is Full Knowledge and Wisdom.
060:011 and fear **Allah**, in Whom ye believe.
060:012 any other thing whatever with **Allah**, that they
060:012 receive their fealty, and pray to **Allah** for the
060:012 for **Allah** is Oft-Forgiving, Most Merciful.
060:013 is the Wrath of **Allah**. Of the Hereafter
061:000 In the name of **Allah**, Most Gracious, Most Merciful.
061:001 declares the Praises and Glory of **Allah**.
061:003 Grievously hateful is it in the sight of **Allah**
061:004 Truly **Allah** loves those who fight in His Cause
061:005 For **Allah** guides not those who are rebellious
061:005 **Allah** let their hearts go wrong.
061:005 I am the messenger of **Allah** (sent) to you?"
061:006 I am the messenger of **Allah** (sent) to you,
061:007 who forges falsehood against **Allah**, even as
061:007 And **Allah** guides not those who do wrong.
061:008 their mouths: but **Allah** will complete His Light,
061:011 Cause of **Allah**, with your wealth and your persons:
061:011 That ye believe in **Allah** and His Messenger,
061:013 which ye do love,-help from **Allah** and a speedy
061:014 O ye who believe! be ye helpers of **Allah**:
061:014 "Who will be my helpers to (the work of) **Allah**?"
062:000 In the name of **Allah**, Most Gracious, Most Merciful.
062:001 and Glory of **Allah**,-the Sovereign, the Holy One,
062:004 and **Allah** is the Lord of the highest bounty.
062:004 Such is the Bounty of **Allah**, which He
062:005 and **Allah** guides not people who do wrong.
062:005 who falsify the Signs of **Allah**:
062:006 that ye are friends to **Allah**,
062:007 And **Allah** knows well those that do wrong!
062:009 hasten earnestly to the Remembrance of **Allah**,
062:010 and remember **Allah** frequently that ye may prosper.
062:010 and seek of the Bounty of **Allah**: and remember
062:011 And **Allah** is the Best to provide (for all needs)."
062:011 Say: "That which **Allah** has is better than any
063:000 In the name of **Allah**, Most Gracious, Most Merciful.
063:001 And **Allah** beareth witness that the Hypocrites
063:001 Yea, **Allah** knoweth that thou art
063:001 that thou art indeed the Messenger of **Allah**."
063:002 obstruct (men) from the Path of **Allah**:
063:004 The curse of **Allah** be on them! How are
063:005 "Come, the Messenger of **Allah** will pray for your
063:006 Truly **Allah** guides not rebellious transgressors.
063:006 **Allah** will not forgive them.
063:007 But to **Allah** belong the treasures of the
063:008 But honour belongs to **Allah** and His Messenger,
063:009 divert you from the remembrance of **Allah**.
063:011 But to no soul will **Allah** grant respite when the
063:011 has come; and **Allah** is well acquainted with (all)
064:000 In the name of **Allah**, Most Gracious, Most Merciful.
064:001 and Glory of **Allah**: to Him belongs Dominion, and
064:002 are Believers: and **Allah** see well all that ye do.
064:004 yes, **Allah** knows well the (secrets) of (all) hearts.
064:006 without (them): and **Allah** is free of all needs
064:006 and turned away. But **Allah** can do without (them):
064:007 And that is easy for **Allah**."
064:008 Believe, therefore, in **Allah** and His Messenger,
064:008 And **Allah** is well-acquainted with all that ye do.
064:009 those who believe in **Allah** and work righteousness,-
064:011 for **Allah** knows all things.
064:011 except by the leave of **Allah**:
064:011 and if anyone believes in **Allah**,

ALLAH (continued)

064:011 (**Allah**) guides his heart (aright):
064:012 So obey **Allah**, and obey His Messenger; but if
064:013 **Allah**! there is no god but He: and on
064:013 and on **Allah**, therefore, let the Believers
064:014 verily **Allah** is Oft-Forgiving, Most Merciful.
064:015 a trial: whereas **Allah**, with Him is the
064:016 So fear **Allah** as much as ye can; listen and
064:017 for **Allah** is All-Thankful, Most Forbearing,-
064:017 If ye loan to **Allah** a beautiful loan, He will
065:000 In the name of **Allah**, Most Gracious, Most Merciful.
065:001 perchance **Allah** will bring about thereafter
065:001 those are limits set by **Allah**: and any
065:001 and any who transgresses the limits of **Allah**,
065:001 prescribed periods: for fear **Allah** your Lord:
065:002 the evidence for the sake of **Allah**. Such is
065:002 who believes in **Allah** and the Last Day.
065:002 And for those who fear **Allah**,
065:003 For **Allah** will surely accomplish His purpose:
065:003 And if any one puts his trust in **Allah**,
065:003 sufficient is (**Allah**) for him.
065:003 for all things has **Allah** appointed a due proportion.
065:004 and for those who fear **Allah**, He will
065:005 That is the Command of **Allah**, which He
065:005 and if anyone fears **Allah**, He will
065:007 spend according to what **Allah** has given him.
065:007 **Allah** puts no burden on any person beyond what
065:007 **Allah** will soon grant relief.
065:010 Therefore fear **Allah**, O ye men of understanding-
065:010 **Allah** has prepared for them a severe Punishment
065:010 who have believed!-for **Allah** hath indeed sent
065:011 the Signs of **Allah** containing clear explanations,
065:011 **Allah** has indeed granted for them a most
065:011 And those who believe in **Allah** and work
065:012 **Allah** has power over all things, and that
065:012 and that **Allah** comprehends all things
065:012 **Allah** is He Who created seven Firmaments and of
066:000 In the name of **Allah**, Most Gracious, Most Merciful.
066:001 to be forbidden that which **Allah** has made
066:001 But **Allah** is Oft-Forgiving, Most Merciful.
066:002 **Allah** has already ordained for you, the expiation
066:002 (in some cases): and **Allah** is your Protector,
066:003 and **Allah** made it known to him, he confirmed
066:004 truly **Allah** is his Protector, and Gabriel,
066:005 who are devout; who turn to **Allah** in repentance,
066:005 that **Allah** will give him in exchange Consorts
066:006 the Commands they receive from **Allah**,
066:008 the Day that **Allah** will not permit to be
066:008 O ye who believe! turn to **Allah** with sincere
066:010 and they profited nothing before **Allah** on their
066:010 **Allah** sets forth, for an example to the
066:011 And **Allah** sets forth, as an example to those
067:000 In the name of **Allah**, Most Gracious, Most Merciful.
067:009 '**Allah** never sent down any (Message): ye are in
067:026 it is with **Allah** alone: I am a plain warner."
067:028 Say: "See ye?-if **Allah** were to destroy me,
068:000 In the name of **Allah**, Most Gracious, Most Merciful.
068:028 to you, 'Why not glorify (**Allah**)?'"
069:000 In the name of **Allah**, Most Gracious, Most Merciful.
069:033 would not believe in **Allah** Most High,
070:000 In the name of **Allah**, Most Gracious, Most Merciful.
070:003 (A Penalty) from **Allah**, Lord of the Ways of Ascent.
071:000 In the name of **Allah**, Most Gracious, Most Merciful.

ALLAH (continued)

071:003 "That ye should worship **Allah**, fear Him,
071:004 For when the Term given by **Allah** is accomplished,
071:015 "See ye not how **Allah** has created the seven
071:017 "And **Allah** has produced you from the earth,
071:019 "And **Allah** has made the earth for you as a carpet
071:025 and they found-in lieu of **Allah**-none to help them.
072:000 In the name of **Allah**, Most Gracious, Most Merciful.
072:004 who used to utter extravagant lies against **Allah**;
072:005 say aught that is untrue against **Allah**.
072:007 ye thought, that **Allah** would not raise up any one
072:012 by no means frustrate **Allah** throughout the earth,
072:014 their wills (to **Allah**), and some that swerve
072:018 "And the places of worship are for **Allah** (alone):
072:018 so invoke not any one along with **Allah**;
072:019 "Yet when the Devotee of **Allah** stands forth
072:022 Say: "No one can deliver me from **Allah** (if I
072:023 I receive from **Allah** and His Messages:
072:023 for any that disobey **Allah** and His Messenger,-
073:000 In the name of **Allah**, Most Gracious, Most Merciful.
073:017 if ye deny (**Allah**),
073:020 But **Allah** doth appoint Night and Day
073:020 and give zakat; and loan to **Allah** a Beautiful
073:020 ye shall find it with **Allah**.
073:020 and seek ye the Grace of **Allah**:
073:020 for **Allah** is Oft-Forgiving, Most Merciful.
074:000 In the name of **Allah**, Most Gracious, Most Merciful.
074:031 Thus doth **Allah** leave to stray whom He pleaseth,
074:031 "What doth **Allah** intend by this?"
074:056 in remembrance except as **Allah** wills:
075:000 In the name of **Allah**, Most Gracious, Most Merciful.
075:038 then did (**Allah**) make and fashion (him)
076:000 In the name of **Allah**, Most Gracious, Most Merciful.
076:006 A Fountain where the Devotees of **Allah** do drink,
076:008 And they feed, for the love of **Allah**, the indigent,
076:009 "We feed you for the sake of **Allah** alone:
076:011 But **Allah** will deliver them from the evil
076:030 But ye will not, except as **Allah** wills;
076:030 for **Allah** is full of Knowledge and Wisdom.
077:000 In the name of **Allah**, Most Gracious, Most Merciful.
078:000 In the name of **Allah**, Most Gracious, Most Merciful.
079:000 In the name of **Allah**, Most Gracious, Most Merciful.
079:022 he turned his back, striving hard (against **Allah**).
079:025 But **Allah** did punish him, (and made an)
079:026 for whosoever feareth (**Allah**).
079:027 (**Allah**) hath constructed it:
080:000 In the name of **Allah**, Most Gracious, Most Merciful.
080:017 Woe to man! what hath made him reject **Allah**?
080:023 fulfilled what **Allah** Hath commanded him.
080:042 Such will be the Rejecters of **Allah**, the Doers
081:000 In the name of **Allah**, Most Gracious, Most Merciful.
081:029 But ye shall not will except as **Allah** wills,
082:000 In the name of **Allah**, Most Gracious, Most Merciful.
082:019 will be (wholly) with **Allah**.
083:000 In the name of **Allah**, Most Gracious, Most Merciful.
083:021 To which bear witness those Nearest (to **Allah**).
083:028 whereof drink those Nearest to **Allah**.
084:000 In the name of **Allah**, Most Gracious, Most Merciful.
084:023 But **Allah** has full Knowledge of what they
085:000 In the name of **Allah**, Most Gracious, Most Merciful.
085:008 that they believed in **Allah**,
085:009 And **Allah** is Witness to all things.
085:020 But **Allah** doth encompass them from behind!

ALLAH (continued)

086:000   In the name of **Allah**, Most Gracious, Most Merciful.
086:008   Surely (**Allah**) able to bring him back (to life)!
087:000   In the name of **Allah**, Most Gracious, Most Merciful.
087:007   Except as **Allah** wills: for He knoweth
088:000   In the name of **Allah**, Most Gracious, Most Merciful.
088:024   **Allah** will chastise him with a mighty Chastisement.
089:000   In the name of **Allah**, Most Gracious, Most Merciful.
090:000   In the name of **Allah**, Most Gracious, Most Merciful.
091:000   In the name of **Allah**, Most Gracious, Most Merciful.
091:013   But the messenger of **Allah** said to them: "It is
091:013   "It is a She-camel of **Allah**! And (bar
092:000   In the name of **Allah**, Most Gracious, Most Merciful.
092:005   So he who gives (in charity) and fears (**Allah**),
092:017   But those most devoted to **Allah** shall be
093:000   In the name of **Allah**, Most Gracious, Most Merciful.
094:000   In the name of **Allah**, Most Gracious, Most Merciful.
095:000   In the name of **Allah**, Most Gracious, Most Merciful.
095:008   Is not **Allah** the wisest of Judges?
096:000   In the name of **Allah**, Most Gracious, Most Merciful.
096:014   Knoweth he not that **Allah** doth see?
096:019   and bring thyself the closer (to **Allah**)!
097:000   In the name of **Allah**, Most Gracious, Most Merciful.
098:000   In the name of **Allah**, Most Gracious, Most Merciful.
098:002   Messenger from **Allah**, rehearsing scriptures
098:005   than this: to worship **Allah**, offering Him
098:008   **Allah** well pleased with them, and them with Him:
098:008   Their reward is with **Allah**:
099:000   In the name of **Allah**, Most Gracious, Most Merciful.
100:000   In the name of **Allah**, Most Gracious, Most Merciful.
101:000   In the name of **Allah**, Most Gracious, Most Merciful.
102:000   In the name of **Allah**, Most Gracious, Most Merciful.
103:000   In the name of **Allah**, Most Gracious, Most Merciful.
104:000   In the name of **Allah**, Most Gracious, Most Merciful.
104:006   (It is) the Fire of **Allah** kindled (to a blaze),
105:000   In the name of **Allah**, Most Gracious, Most Merciful.
106:000   In the name of **Allah**, Most Gracious, Most Merciful.
107:000   In the name of **Allah**, Most Gracious, Most Merciful.
108:000   In the name of **Allah**, Most Gracious, Most Merciful.
109:000   In the name of **Allah**, Most Gracious, Most Merciful.
110:000   In the name of **Allah**, Most Gracious, Most Merciful.
110:001   When comes the Help of **Allah**, and Victory,
111:000   In the name of **Allah**, Most Gracious, Most Merciful.
112:000   In the name of **Allah**, Most Gracious, Most Merciful.
112:001   Say: He is **Allah**, the One;
112:002   **Allah**, the Eternal, Absolute;
113:000   In the name of **Allah**, Most Gracious, Most Merciful.
114:000   In the name of **Allah**, Most Gracious, Most Merciful.

ALLAH'S

002:027   **Allah's** Covenant after it is ratified,
002:045   Nay, seek (**Allah's**) help with
002:088   (which preserve **Allah's** word, we need no more)"
002:088   Nay, **Allah's** curse is on them
002:097   (revelation) to they heart by **Allah's** will,
002:102   anyone except by **Allah's** permission.
002:115   whithersoever ye turn, there is **Allah's** Face.
002:159   on them shall be **Allah's** curse,
002:161   on them is **Allah's** curse,
002:174   Those who conceal **Allah's** revelations in the Book,
002:193   and the religion becomes **Allah's**.
002:199   and ask for **Allah's** forgiveness.
002:211   after **Allah's** favour has come to him,
002:224   And make not **Allah's** (name) an excuse

ALLAH'S (continued)

002:231   but solemnly rehearse **Allah's** favours on you,
002:231   Do not treat **Allah's** Signs as a jest,
002:239   celebrate **Allah's** praises in the manner
002:249   "How oft, by **Allah's** will, hath a small force
002:251   By **Allah's** will they routed them:
002:273   in **Allah's** cause are restricted (from travel).
003:015   For in **Allah's** sight are (all) His servants,
003:020   and in **Allah's** sight are (all) His servants.
003:049   and it becomes a bird by **Allah's** leave:
003:049   and I bring the dead into life by **Allah's** leave;
003:052   "We are **Allah's** helpers, We believe in Allah,
003:064   are Muslims (bowing to **Allah's** Will)."
003:067   and bowed his will to **Allah's** (which is Islam).
003:079   "Be ye my worshippers rather than **Allah's**":
003:099   yourselves witnesses (to **Allah's** Covenant)?
003:103   and remember with gratitude **Allah's** favour on you;
003:107   they will be in (the light of) **Allah's** Mercy;
003:141   **Allah's** object also is to purge those
003:145   Nor can a soul die except by **Allah's** leave,
003:146   if they met with disaster in **Allah's** way,
003:146   How many of the Prophets fought (in **Allah's** way),
003:154   Say thou: "Indeed, this affair is wholly **Allah's**."
003:159   and ask for (**Allah's**) forgiveness for them;
003:169   who are slain in **Allah's** way as dead.
003:176   **Allah's** Plan is that He will give them no portion
004:064   come unto thee and asked **Allah's** forgiveness,
004:084   Then fight in **Allah's** cause, thou art held
004:087   And whose word can be truer than **Allah's**?
004:110   but afterwards seeks **Allah's** forgiveness, he
004:122   and whose word can be truer than **Allah's**?
004:122   **Allah's** promise is the truth, and whose
004:134   in **Allah's** (gift) is the reward (both) of
004:160   and that they hindered many from **Allah's** Way;
005:041   For such it is not **Allah's** will to purify their hearts.
005:044   the protection of **Allah's** Book,
005:044   who bowed (as in Islam) to **Allah's** will,
005:049   it is **Allah's** purpose to punish them.
005:064   The Jews say: "**Allah's** hand is tied up,"
005:080   that **Allah's** wrath is on them,
006:016   it is due to **Allah's** Mercy;
006:035   If it were **Allah's** will, He could gather
006:071   Say: "**Allah's** guidance is the (only)
006:090   who received **Allah's** guidance.
006:107   If it had been **Allah's** Will, they would
006:111   unless it is in **Allah's** Plan.
006:118   on which **Allah's** name hath been pronounced, if
006:119   on which **Allah's** name hath been pronounced, when
006:121   **Allah's** name hath not been pronounced: that
006:124   like those receive by **Allah's** messengers."
006:138   forging a lie against **Allah's** name: soon will
006:145   a name has been invoked, other than **Allah's**."
006:157   than one who rejecteth **Allah's** Signs,
007:073   so leave her to graze in **Allah's** earth, and
007:099   against **Allah's** devising but no one can fell
007:128   for the earth is **Allah's**,
007:131   the omens of evil are theirs in **Allah's** sight,
008:017   it was not thy act, but **Allah's**: in order
008:039   and religion becomes **Allah's** in its entirety
009:020   and main, in **Allah's** cause,
009:032   would extinguish **Allah's** light with their mouths,
009:055   in reality **Allah's** plan is to punish them
009:085   **Allah's** Wish is to punish them with these things

ALLAH'S (continued)

009:120   to say behind **Allah's** Messenger,
010:055   that **Allah's** promise is assuredly true?
010:072   of those who submit to **Allah's** Will (in Islam)."
011:064   leave her to feed on **Allah's** (free) earth,
011:073   "Dost thou wonder at **Allah's** decree?
012:066   to me, in **Allah's** name, that ye will be sure to
012:080   an oath from you in **Allah's** name, and how
012:087   of **Allah's** soothing Mercy, except those
012:087   and never give up hope of **Allah's** soothing Mercy:
016:026   did also plot (against **Allah's** Way):
016:048   Do they not look at **Allah's** creation.
016:072   and be ungrateful for **Allah's** favours?-
016:098   seek **Allah's** protection from Satan the Rejected one.
018:039   into thy garden, say: **Allah's** Will (be done)!
019:011   by signs to celebrate **Allah's** praises in the
024:010   If it were not for **Allah's** grace and mercy on you,
024:022   left their homes in **Allah's** cause:
027:091   who bow in Islam to **Allah's** Will,-
028:053   (bowing to **Allah's** Will) from before this."
028:086   in any way to those who reject (**Allah's** Message).
028:087   from **Allah's** revelations after they have been
030:050   the tokens of **Allah's** Mercy!-
030:056   **Allah's** Decree, to the Day of Resurrection,
033:035   who engage much in **Allah's** remembrance,
033:037   And **Allah's** command must be fulfilled.
033:046   to **Allah's** (Grace) by His leave,
033:053   that ye should annoy **Allah's** Messenger,
033:053   Truly such a thing is in **Allah's** sight an enormity.
033:069   and he was honorable in **Allah's** sight.
035:032   by **Allah's** leave, foremost in good deeds;
035:043   no change wilt thou find in **Allah's** way (of dealing).
035:043   turning off wit thou find in **Allah's** way (of dealing):
037:166   who declare (**Allah's**) glory!"
039:008   thus misleading others from **Allah's** Path.
039:010   Spacious is **Allah's** earth!
040:085   (Such has been) **Allah's** way of dealing with His
042:051   to reveal, with **Allah's** permission, what Allah
044:042   Except such as receive **Allah's** Mercy:
046:017   And they two seek **Allah's** aid, (and rebuke
047:004   but if it had been **Allah's** Will, He could
047:028   and they hated **Allah's** good pleasure;
048:015   They wish to change **Allah's** word: Say: "Not thus
048:018   **Allah's** Good Pleasure was on the Believers
049:003   in the presence of **Allah's** Messenger,-their hearts
049:007   **Allah's** Messenger: were he, in many matters,
050:001   (Thou art **Allah's** Messenger).
050:011   As sustenance for (**Allah's**) Servants; and We
057:014   ye doubted (**Allah's**) promise);
057:024   and if any turn back (from **Allah's** Way),
061:008   **Allah's** Light (by blowing) with their mouths:
061:014   "We are **Allah's** helpers!"
063:007   those who are with **Allah's** Messenger,
067:011   but far from **Allah's** mercy are the Companions
068:018   But made no reservation, ("If it be **Allah's** Will").
071:013   that ye are not conscious of **Allah's** majesty,-
072:016   (And **Allah's** Message is): "If they
073:020   the land, seeking of **Allah's** bounty;
073:020   yet others fighting in **Allah's** Cause.
097:004   and the Spirit by **Allah's** permission, on every
110:002   the People enter **Allah's** Religion in crowds,

ALLEGATIONS

024:004   (to support their **allegations**),-flog them

ALLIANCE

004:092   with whom ye have a treaty of mutual **alliance**,
008:072   ye have a treaty of mutual **alliance**.
009:004   ye have entered into **alliance** and who have not

ALLIANCES

009:001   ye have contracted mutual **alliances**:-

ALLIES

059:016   (Their **allies** deceived them), like Satan, when he

ALLOTTED

002:202   To these will be **allotted** what they have earned.
004:032   to men is **allotted** what they earn, and

ALLOW

009:032   but Allah will not **allow** but that His light

ALLOWED

016:084   be **allowed** to make amends.
018:001   and hath **allowed** therein no Crookedness:
030:057   nor will they be **allowed** to make amends.
033:016   a brief (respite) will ye be **allowed** to enjoy!"
048:025   (Allah would have **allowed** you to force your way,

ALLOWS

007:157   he **allows** them as lawful what is

ALLURE

002:221   even though she **allure** you.
002:221   even though he **allure** you.

ALLUREMENTS

018:046   Wealth and sons are **allurements** of the

ALLURING

002:212   is **alluring** to those who reject faith,
006:043   (sinful) acts seem **alluring** to them.
006:108   **alluring** to each people its own doings.
006:137   their "partners" made **alluring** the slaughter
008:048   (sinful) acts seem **alluring** to them, and said:
016:063   their own acts seem **alluring**: he is their
029:038   Satan made their deeds **alluring** to them,
035:008   of his conduct is made **alluring**, so that
040:037   Thus was made **alluring**, in Pharaoh's
041:025   who made **alluring** to them what was before them

ALMOST

020:015   I have **almost** kept it hidden-for every soul
028:010   she was going **almost** to disclose
042:005   The heavens are **almost** rent asunder from above
067:008   **Almost** bursting with fury:
068:051   And the Unbelievers would **almost** trip thee up

ALMS

009:058   of (the distribution of) the **alms**.
009:060   **Alms** are for the poor and the needy, and those
009:103   Of their goods take **alms**, that so

ALONE

002:014   but when they are **alone** with their evil ones,
002:041   and fear Me, and Me **alone**.
003:060   the truth (comes) from thy Lord **alone**;
003:119   but when they are **alone**,
004:016   If they repent and amend, leave them **alone**;
005:040   Allah (**alone**) belongeth the dominion of the
006:070   Leave **alone** those who take their religion
006:094   and **alone** as We created you for the first time:
006:137   but leave **alone** them and what they forged.
007:070   that we may worship Allah **alone**,
007:176   or if you leave him **alone**,
007:187   "The knowledge thereof is with my Lord (**alone**):
007:187   "The knowledge thereof is with Allah (**alone**),
009:016   **alone** while Allah has not yet known those

ALONE (continued)

009:095　that ye may leave them **alone**.
009:095　So leave them **alone**: for they are an abomination,
012:009　of your father may be given to you **alone**:
012:018　it is Allah (**alone**) whose help can be sought."
015:003　Leave them **alone**, to eat and enjoy and let
016:009　Allah **alone** can show the right path but there
016:051　then fear Me (and Me **alone**)."
017:046　and Him **alone**-in the Qur'an,
018:019　"Allah (**alone**) knows best how long ye have
019:080　and he shall appear before Us bare and **alone**.
024:055　'They will worship Me (**alone**) and not
028:075　the Truth is with Allah (**alone**), and the
029:002　men think that they be will left **alone** on saying,
029:056　therefore serve ye Me-(and Me **alone**)!
031:034　the knowledge of the Hour is with Allah (**alone**).
033:063　"The knowledge thereof is with Allah (**alone**)":
039:045　When Allah, **Alone** is mentioned, the hearts
040:020　Verily it is Allah (**alone**) Who hears
045:037　And unto Him (**alone**) belongeth Majesty in the
052:045　So leave them **alone** until they encounter
060:004　unless ye believe in Allah and Him **alone**":
067:026　the knowledge of the time, it is with Allah **alone**:
068:044　Then leave Me **alone** with such as reject
072:018　"And the places of worship for Allah (**alone**):
072:026　"He (**alone**) knows the Unseen,
073:011　And leave Me (**alone** to deal with) those in
074:011　Leave Me **alone**, (to deal) with the (creature)
074:011　the (creature) whom I created (bare and) **alone**!-
074:028　and naught doth it leave **alone**!-
075:012　Before thy Lord (**alone**), that Day
075:021　And leave **alone** the Hereafter.
076:009　"We feed you for the sake of Allah **alone**:

ALONG

007:105　so let the children of Israel depart **along** with me."
009:086　and fight **along** with His Messenger,
020:064　he wins (all **along**) to-day who gains
021:033　All (the celestial bodies) swim **along**, each in
023:091　nor is there any god **along** with Him:
029:013　and (other) burdens **along** with their own,
033:018　those who say to their brethren, "Come **along** to us,"
036:040　each (just) swims **along** in (its own) orbit
040:071　they shall be dragged **along**-
052:031　I too will wait **along** with you!"
066:010　"Enter ye the Fire **along** with (others)
072:018　so invoke not any one **along** with Allah;
079:003　And by those who glide **along** (on errands of mercy),

ALONGSIDE

057:013　and without it, all **alongside**, will be

ALONGWITH

062:003　**Alongwith** others of them, who have not already

ALOUD

017:110　Neither speak thy Prayer **aloud,** nor speak
020:007　If thou pronounce the word **aloud,** (it is
028:018　sought his help called **aloud** for his help (again).
035:037　Therein will they cry **aloud** (for assistance):
049:002　nor speak **aloud** to him in talk,
049:002　as ye may speak **aloud** to one another,
071:008　"So I have called to them **aloud**;

ALREADY

002:151　A similar (favour have ye **already** received)
003:013　"There has **already** been for you a Sign
003:118　rank hatred has **already** appeared from their mouths;

ALREADY (continued)

004:024　Also (prohibited are) women **already** married,
004:047　confirming what was (**already**) with you,
004:054　But We had **already** given the people of Abraham
004:140　**Already** has He sent you word in the Book,
004:164　Of some messengers We have **already** told thee
006:009　they have **already** covered with confusion.
006:034　**Already** hast thou received some account
007:071　have **already** come upon you from your Lord:
008:038　is **already** (a matter of warning for them).
008:042　Allah might accomplish a matter **already** decided;
008:044　accomplish a matter **already** decided
008:071　they have **already** been in treason against Allah,
009:049　Have they not fallen into trial **already**?
009:094　Allah hath **already** informed us of the true state
010:074　they had **already** rejected beforehand.
011:036　except those who have believed **already**!
011:040　against whom the Word has **already** gone forth,-
020:090　Aaron had **already**, before this said to them:
020:115　We had **already**, beforehand, taken the
023:027　against whom the Word has **already** gone forth:
024:034　We have **already** sent down to you verses making
033:015　And yet they had **already** covenanted with Allah
033:071　has **already** attained the great victory.
037:105　"Thou hast **already** fulfilled the dream!"-
037:171　**Already** has Our Word been passed before (this)
039:065　But it has **already** been revealed to thee,-
044:013　things clearly has (**already**) come to them,-
047:018　But **already** have come some tokens thereof,
048:015　Allah has **already** declared (this) beforehand":
048:023　the practice of Allah **already** in the past:
050:004　We **already** know how much of them the earth
050:028　I had **already** in advance sent you Warning.
053:023　Even though there has **already** come to them
054:004　There have **already** come to them such tidings
056:062　And ye certainly know **already** the first form
057:017　**Already** have We shown the Signs plainly to you,
058:005　for We have **already** sent down Clear Signs.
060:013　Of the Hereafter they are **already** in despair,
062:003　Who have not **already** joined them:
066:002　Allah has **already** ordained for you, the expiation
071:024　"They have **already** misled many;

ALSO

002:124　He pleaded: "And **also** (Imams) from my offspring!"
002:185　**also** clear (Signs) for guidance and judgment
002:186　let them **also**, with a will,
003:020　"Do ye (**also**) submit yourselves?"
003:068　as are **also** this Prophet and those who believe:
003:141　Allah's object **also** is to purge those
003:167　And the Hypocrites **also**,
003:183　They (**also**) said: "Allah took our promise
004:024　**Also** (prohibited are) women already married,
004:033　To those **also**, to whom your right hand was pledged,
004:127　as **also** concerning the children who
005:003　(forbidden) **also** is the division (of meat) by
005:097　as **also** the Sacred Months,
006:075　So **also** did We show Abraham the kingdom
007:044　have you **also** found your Lord's promises true?"
007:071　Then wait: I am amongst you, **also** waiting."
007:080　We **also** (sent) Lut: he said to his people:
007:167　but He is **also** Oft-Forgiving, Most Merciful.
008:018　That, and **also** because Allah is He Who
008:061　do thou (**also**) incline towards peace,

ALSO (continued)

009:090	among the desert Arabs (**also**), Men who
009:100	those who gave them aid, and (**also**) those who
009:117	but He turned to them (**also**): for He
009:118	(He turned in mercy **also**) to the three who were
013:006	and verily thy Lord is (**also**) strict in punishment.
013:042	Those before them did (**also**) devise plots;
014:032	and the rivers (**also**) hath He made subject to you.
014:033	hath He (**also**) made subject you.
014:040	and **also** (raise such) among my offspring,
015:078	of the Wood were **also** wrong-doers;
015:080	Rocky Tract **also** rejected the Messengers:
015:091	(So **also** on such) as have made Qur'an into
016:025	and **also** (something) of the burdens of
016:026	Those before them did **also** plot (against
016:044	unto thee (**also**) the Message; that thou
016:063	By Allah, We (**also**) sent (our prophets) to
016:063	he is **also** their patron to-day,
016:067	in this **also** is a Sign for those who are wise.
017:026	due rights, as (**also**) to those in want,
017:060	as **also** the Cursed Tree (mentioned) in
018:004	Further, that He may warn those (**also**) who say,
019:041	**Also** mention in the Book (the story of) Abraham:
019:051	**Also** mention in the Book (the story of) Moses:
019:053	his brother Aaron, (**also**) a prophet.
019:054	**Also** mention in the Book (the story
019:056	**Also** mention in the Book Idris: he was
019:068	and (**also**) Satans (with them);
020:082	"But, without doubt, I am (**also**) He that
021:007	Before thee, **also**, the messengers We sent
022:018	are (**also**) such as unto whom the chastisement
023:020	**Also** a tree springing out of Mount Sinai,
024:059	let them (**also**) ask for permission,
025:038	As **also** 'Ad and Thamud, and the
027:003	and **also** have sure faith in the Hereafter.
027:054	(We **also** sent) Lut (as a Messenger): behold, he
027:071	They **also** say: "When will this promise (come to
029:016	And (We **also** saved) Abraham: behold, he said
029:038	Remember **also** the 'Ad and the Thamud
029:039	(Remember **also**) Qarun, Pharaoh, and Haman:
029:047	believe therein, as **also** do some of these
034:010	with him! and ye birds (**also**)!
037:017	"And **also** our fathers of old?"
037:123	So **also** was Elias among those sent (by us).
037:133	So **also** was Lut among those sent (by us).
037:139	So **also** was Jonah among those sent (by Us).
038:037	As **also** the Satans, (including) every kind
038:038	As **also** others bound together in fetters.
039:025	Those before them (**also**) rejected (revelation),
043:031	**Also**, they say: "Why is not this Qur'an sent down
043:035	And **also** adornments of gold.
045:034	It will **also** be said: "This Day We will forget
050:040	(**also**), celebrate His praises, and (so likewise)
051:021	As **also** in your own selves: will ye not then see?
051:022	as (**also**) that which ye are promised.
052:049	And for part of the night **also** praise thou Him,-
054:023	The Thamud (**also**) rejected (their) Warners.
055:012	**Also** corn with (its) leaves and stalk for fodder,

ALTARS

005:003	that which is sacrificed on stone (**altars**);

ALTER

006:034	there is none that can **alter** the Words

ALTERNATES

024:044	It is Allah Who **alternates** the Night and the Day:

ALTERNATION

002:164	in the **alternation** of the Night and the Day;
003:190	and the **alternation** of Night and Day,
010:006	Verily, in the **alternation** of the Night
023:080	and to Him (is due) the **alternation** of Night
045:005	And in the **alternation** of Night and Day,

ALTHOUGH

002:089	**although** from of old they had prayed
003:165	**although** ye smote (your enemies)
005:032	Then **although** there came to them Our Messengers
019:010	**although** thou art not dumb."
062:002	**although** they had been, before, in

ALTOGETHER

004:129	but turn not away (from a woman) **altogether**,
013:042	but in all things Allah is the devising **altogether**.
025:022	"There is a barrier forbidden (to you) **altogether**!"
043:005	turn away the Reminder from you **altogether**,

ALWAYS

002:061	we cannot endure one kind of food (**always**);
002:214	Ah! Verily, the help of Allah is (**always**) near!
007:056	for the Mercy of Allah is (**always**) near to those
011:061	for my Lord is (**always**) near, ready to answer."
016:052	and to Him is the religion **always**:
029:010	to say, "We have (**always**) been with you!"
040:081	And He shows you (**always**) His Signs;
058:001	and Allah (**always**) hears the arguments

AM

002:160	for I **am** Oft-Returning, Most Merciful.
002:186	I **am** indeed close (to them):
003:036	I **am** delivered of a female child!"
003:040	seeing I **am** very old, and my wife is barren?"
003:081	and I **am** with you among the witnesses."
005:012	and Allah said: "I **am** with you: if ye (but)
006:014	Say: "Nay! but I **am** commanded to be the first
006:019	And I truly **am** innocent of (your blasphemy of)
006:050	Nor do I tell you I **am** an angel.
006:056	Say: "I **am** forbidden to worship those-other
006:057	Say: "For me, I **am** on a clear Sign
006:078	"O my people! I **am** indeed free from your (guilt)
006:104	I **am** not (here) to watch over your doings."
006:163	No partner hath He: this **am** I commanded,
006:163	and I **am** the first of those who
007:012	He said: "I **am** better than he:
007:061	on the contrary I **am** a messenger from the
007:067	but (I **am**) a Messenger from the Lord
007:068	I **am** to you a sincere and trustworthy adviser".
007:071	Then wait: I **am** amongst you, also waiting."
007:104	I **am** a messenger from the Lord of the worlds,-
007:143	and I **am** the first to believe."
007:158	Say: "O men! I **am** sent unto you all, as the
007:172	"**Am** I not your Lord (who cherishes
007:188	I **am** but a warner, and a bringer
008:012	"I **am** with you: give firmness to the Believers:
008:048	while I **am** near to you":
008:048	and said: "Lo! I **am** clear of you;
010:090	I **am** of those who submit (to Allah in Islam)."
010:104	I **am** commanded to be (in the ranks)
010:108	and I **am** not (set) over you
011:002	(Say:) "Verily I **am** (sent) unto you from Him
011:035	And I **am** free of the sins of which
011:054	that I **am** free from the sin of ascribing, to Him,

AM (continued)

011:072	seeing I **am** an old woman, and my husband
011:086	But I **am** not set over you to keep watch!"
011:093	for I too **am** watching with you!"
012:055	I **am** a good keeper, knowledgeable.
012:069	He said (to him): "Behold! I **am** thy (own) brother;
012:090	He said: "I **am** Joseph, and this is my brother:
013:036	Say: "I **am** commanded to worship Allah,
015:028	"I **am** about to create man, from sounding
015:033	(Iblis) said: "I **am** not one to prostrate
015:049	I **am** indeed the Oft-Forgiving, Most Merciful;
015:089	And say: "I **am** indeed he that warneth openly
017:093	"Glory to my Lord! **am** I aught but a man,-
018:036	even if I **am** brought back to my Lord.
018:110	Say: "I **am** but a man like yourselves,
019:004	But never **am** I unblest, O my Lord,
019:019	"Nay, I **am** only a messenger from thy Lord,
019:020	and I **am** not unchaste?"
019:030	He said: "I **am** indeed a servant of Allah:
019:066	Man says: "What! when I **am** dead, shall I
020:012	"Verily I **am** thy Lord!
020:014	"Verily, I **am** Allah: there is no god but I:
020:046	He said: "Fear not: for I **am** with you:
020:082	"But, without doubt, I **am** (also) He that
021:029	"I **am** a god besides Him," such a one
021:056	and I **am** a witness to this (truth).
021:092	and I **am** your Lord and Cherisher:
022:049	Say: "O men! I **am** (sent) to you only to give
023:051	for I **am** well-acquainted with (all) that you do.
023:052	and I **am** your Lord and Cherisher:
026:080	"And when I **am** ill, it is He Who cures me;
026:107	"I **am** to you a trustworthy messenger.
026:114	"I **am** not one to drive away those who believe.
026:115	"I **am** sent only as a plain warner."
026:125	"I **am** to you a messenger worthy of all trust.
026:143	"I **am** to you a messenger worthy of all trust.
026:162	"I **am** to you a messenger worthy of all trust.
026:178	"I **am** to you a messenger worthy of all trust.
026:216	"I **am** free (of responsibility) for what ye do!"
027:009	"O Moses! verily, I **am** Allah, the Exalted
027:011	I **am** Oft-Forgiving, Most Merciful.
027:035	But I **am** going to send him a present,
027:040	to test me whether I **am** grateful or ungrateful!
027:091	and I **am** commanded to be of those who bow
027:092	say: "I **am** only a Warner."
028:024	truly **am** I in (desperate) need of any good that
028:030	Verily I **am** Allah, the Lord of the Worlds...
028:038	but as far as I **am** concerned,
029:050	and I **am** indeed a clear Warner."
034:050	Say: "If I **am** astray, I only
037:089	And he said, "I **am** indeed sick (at heart)!"
038:065	Say: "Truly **am** I a Warner:
038:070	that I **am** to give warning plainly and publicly."
038:071	"I **am** about to create man from clay:
038:076	(Iblis) said: "I **am** better than he:
038:086	nor **am** I a pretender.
039:011	Say: "Verily, I **am** commanded to serve Allah
039:012	"And I **am** commanded to be the first of those
041:006	Say thou: "I **am** but a man like you:
041:033	"I **am** of those who bow in Islam"?
041:050	but if I **am** brought back to my Lord,
042:015	and I **am** commanded to judge justly
043:046	"I **am** a messenger of the Lord of the Worlds."

AM (continued)

043:052	"**Am** I not better than this (Moses), who is
044:018	I **am** to you a messenger worthy of all trust;
046:009	I **am** but a Warner open and clear."
046:009	Say: "I **am** not an innovation among the messengers,
051:050	I **am** from Him a Warner to you, clear and open!
051:051	I **am** from Him a Warner to you, clear and open!
054:010	"I **am** one overcome: do thou then help (me)!"
059:016	Satan says, "I **am** free of thee:
061:005	I **am** the messenger of Allah (sent) to you?"
061:006	I **am** the messenger of Allah (sent) to you,
067:026	I **am** a plain warner."
071:002	He said: "O my People! I **am** to you a Warner,
079:024	Saying, "I **am** your Lord, Most High."
086:016	And I **am** planning a scheme,

AMASS

003:157	are far better than all they could **amass**.
043:032	is better than the (wealth) which they **amass**.

AMAZEMENT

012:031	and (in their **amazement**) cut their hands:

AMBASSADORS

027:035	what (answer) return (my) **ambassadors**."

AMBIGUITY

015:089	warneth openly and without **ambiguity**,"-

AMBUSH

072:009	find a flaming fire watching him in **ambush**.
078:021	Truly Hell is as a place of **ambush**

AMEND

004:016	If they repent and **amend**, leave them alone;
005:039	after his crime, and **amend** his conduct,

AMENDED

006:054	and thereafter repented, and **amended** (his conduct),

AMENDS

002:160	Except those who repent and make **amends**
003:089	And make **amends**; for verily Allah
016:084	be allowed to make **amends**.
016:119	and make **amends**,-thy Lord after all this,
030:057	nor will they be allowed to make **amends**.
045:035	nor can they make **amends**.

AMICABLE

004:128	if they arrange an **amicable** settlement between

AMID

015:045	The righteous (will be) **amid** Gardens and fountains

AMIDST

077:041	they shall be **amidst** (cool) shades and springs

AMONG

002:064	ye had surely been **among** the lost.
002:072	a dispute **among** yourselves as to the crime:
002:074	For **among** rocks there are some
002:078	And there are **among** them illiterates,
002:083	then did ye turn back, except a few **among** you,
002:085	the same people, who slay **among** yourselves,
002:085	for those **among** you who behave like this
002:100	some party **among** them throw it aside?
002:105	without Faith **among** the people of the Book
002:142	The Fools **among** the people will say:
002:150	dispute against you **among** the people,
002:151	in that We have sent **among** you a Messenger
002:158	are **among** the Symbols of Allah.
002:182	settlement **among** (the parties concerned),
002:187	used to do secretly **among** yourselves:
002:188	your property **among** yourselves for vanities,

AMONG (continued)

002:213 did not differ **among** themselves,
002:246 They said to a Prophet (that was) **among** them:
002:246 they turned back except a small band **among** them.
002:253 would not have fought **among** each other,
002:282 to prevent doubts **among** yourselves
002:282 ye carry out on the spot **among** yourselves,
003:053 then write us down **among** those who bear witness."
003:064 that we erect not, from **among** ourselves,
003:068 Without doubt, **among** men, the nearest of kin
003:075 **Among** the People of the Book are some who,
003:078 There is **among** them a section who distort
003:081 and I am with you **among** the witnesses."
003:084 between one and another **among** them,
003:100 listen to a faction **among** the People of the Book,
003:101 and **among** you lives the Messenger?
003:103 and be not divided **among** yourselves;
003:110 **among** them are some who have faith,
003:152 **Among** you are some that hanker after this world
003:164 **among** them a Messenger from **among** themselves,
003:199 **among** the people of the Book, those who
004:016 If two persons **among** you are guilty of lewdness,
004:025 from **among** those whom your right hand possess:
004:025 for those **among** you who fear sin;
004:029 your property **among** yourselves in vanities:
004:059 If ye differ in anything **among** yourselves,
004:059 and those charged with authority **among** you.
004:072 There are certainly **among** you men who
004:072 in that we were not present **among** them."
004:083 or to those charged with authority **among** them,
004:139 is it honor they seek **among** them?
004:161 We have prepared for those **among** them who reject
004:162 But those **among** them who are well-grounded
005:005 but chaste women **among** the People of the Book,
005:012 and We appointed twelve chieftains **among** them,
005:020 when He produced prophets **among** you,
005:020 He had not given to any other **among** the peoples.
005:023 (But) **among** (their) God-fearing men were two
005:029 for thou wilt be **among** the companions of the Fire,
005:041 (whether it be) **among** those who say: "We believe"
005:041 or it be **among** the Jews, men who listen
005:048 To each **among** you have We prescribed
005:054 O ye who believe! if any from **among** you turn
005:057 or **among** those who reject Faith:
005:057 whether **among** those who have received
005:066 There is from **among** them a party
005:073 befall the blasphemers **among** them.
005:078 those **among** the Children of Israel who rejected
005:082 and nearest **among** them in love to the Believers
005:082 Strongest **among** men in enmity to the Believers
005:083 write us down **among** the witnesses.
005:095 As adjudged by two just men **among** you;
005:106 (take) witnesses **among** yourselves when making
005:107 nearest in kin from **among** those who claim
005:110 and the unbelievers **among** them said: 'This is
005:115 on anyone **among** all the peoples.
006:077 I shall surely be **among** those who go astray."
006:084 and **among** his progeny, David, Solomon,
006:112 satans **among** men and Jinns, inspiring each other
007:015 "Be thou **among** those who have respite."
007:026 Such are **among** the Signs of Allah,
007:066 **among** his people said: "Ah! we see
007:069 and give you a stature tall **among** the nations.

AMONG (continued)

007:075 those **among** them who believe: "Know ye
007:075 The leaders of the arrogant party **among** his people
007:087 "And if there is a party **among** you who believes
007:088 The leaders, the arrogant party **among** his people,
007:090 The leaders, the Unbelievers **among** his people,
007:149 we shall indeed be **among** the Losers.
007:155 for the deeds of the foolish ones **among** us?
007:162 But the transgressors **among** them changed the
007:168 There are **among** them some that are
008:005 even though a party **among** the Believers
008:048 and said: "No one **among** men can overcome
008:064 follow thee **among** the Believers.
009:016 known those **among** you who strive with
009:029 from **among** the People of the Book,
009:034 many **among** the priests and anchorites,
009:046 were told, "Sit ye **among** those who sit (inactive)."
009:047 some **among** you who would have listened to them.
009:047 midst and sowing sedition **among** you,
009:049 **Among** them is (many) a man who says: "Grant me
009:058 And **among** them are men who slander thee
009:061 **Among** them are men who molest the Prophet and say,
009:086 and influence **among** them ask thee for exemption,
009:090 seize the Unbelievers **among** them.
009:090 And there were, **among** the desert Arabs (also),
009:101 as well as **among** the Madinah folk: they are
010:002 Our inspiration to a man from **among** themselves?
010:042 **Among** them are some who (pretend to)
010:043 And **among** them are some who look at thee:
010:071 about your plan and **among** your Partners,
010:092 But verily, many **among** mankind are heedless
010:098 a single township (**among** those We warmed),
011:017 yet many **among** men do not believe!
011:027 Unbelievers **among** his people said: "We see
011:027 that any follow thee but the meanest **among** us,
011:043 and the son was **among** those who were drowned.
011:047 I should indeed be **among** the losers!"
011:078 Is there not **among** you a single right-minded man?"
011:091 For thou hast **among** us no great position!"
011:091 In fact **among** us we see that thou hast no strength!
011:116 (but there were none) except a few **among** them whom
012:003 thou too was **among** those who knew it not.
012:021 but most **among** mankind know it not.
012:021 "Make his stay (**among** us) honourable:
012:039 are many lords differing **among** themselves better,
012:080 The leader **among** them said: "Know ye not
013:023 the righteous **among** their fathers, their spouses,
013:036 but there are **among** the clans those who
014:036 the have indeed led astray many **among** mankind:
014:037 of some **among** men with love towards them,
014:040 and also (raise such) **among** my offspring,
015:031 he refused to be **among** those who prostrated
015:032 reason for not being **among** those who
015:040 "Except Thy chosen servants **among** them,
015:060 will be **among** those who will lag behind."
015:061 arrived **among** the adherents of Lut.
016:038 but most **among** mankind know it not.
016:048 **Among** things,-how their shadows turn round,
016:113 a Messenger from **among** themselves,
017:016 We command those **among** them who are given
017:039 These are **among** the (precepts of) wisdom,
017:040 for Himself daughters **among** the angels?
017:053 for Satan doth sow dissensions **among** them:

AMONG (continued)

017:064 And Arouse those whom thou canst **among** them,
018:009 the Inscription where wonders **among** Our Signs?
018:017 Such are **among** the Signs of Allah:
018:021 Behold they dispute **among** themselves as to
018:022 the dog being the fourth **among** them;
019:037 But the sects differ **among** themselves:
020:094 'Thou hast caused **among** the Children of Israel,
022:003 And yet **among** men there are such as dispute
022:008 Yet there is **among** men such a one as disputes
022:011 There are **among** men some who serve Allah,
022:018 and a great number **among** mankind?
022:027 "And proclaim the Pilgrimage **among** men:
022:036 for you as **among** the Signs from Allah:
023:024 The chiefs of the Unbelievers **among** his people
023:024   **among** our ancestors of old."
023:032 from **among** themselves, (saying), "Worship Allah!
024:011 who took on himself the lead **among** them,
024:011 the lie are a body **among** yourselves:
024:011 to every man **among** them (will come the punishment)
024:019 scandal circulate **among** the Believers,
024:022 Let not those **among** you who are endued with grace
024:032 Marry those **among** you who are single,
024:032 and the virtuous ones **among** your slaves,
024:055 Allah has promised, to those **among** you who believe
024:058 and the (children) **among** you who have not come
024:059 But when the children **among** you come of age,
024:063 of the Messenger **among** yourselves like the
025:019 And whoever **among** you does wrong,
025:031 for every prophet an enemy **among** the sinners:
026:018 "Did we not cherish thee as a child **among** us,
026:084 tongue of truth **among** the latest (generations);
026:086 for that he is **among** those astray;
026:136 be not **among** (our) Admonishers!
026:213 or thou wilt be **among** those who will be punished.
026:219 And thy movements **among** those who prostrate
027:012 (these are) **among** the nine Signs (thou wilt take)
027:020 Or is he **among** the absentees?
028:004 depressing a group **among** them:
028:033 I have slain a man **among** them,
028:036 hear the like **among** our fathers of old!"
028:042 be **among** the loathed (and despised).
028:045 a dweller **among** the people of Madyan,
028:061 is to be **among** those brought up (for punishment)?
028:079 So he went forth **among** his people in the
029:010 Then there are **among** men such as say, "We believe
029:014 and he tarried **among** them a thousand years
029:027 and Jacob, and ordained **among** his progeny
030:008 yet are there truly many **among** men who deny
030:013 No intercessor will they have **among** their "Partners,"
030:020 **Among** His Signs is this, that He
030:021 And **among** His Signs is this, that He created
030:021 created for you mates from **among** yourselves,
030:022 And **among** His Signs is the creation of the heavens
030:023 And **among** His Signs is the sleep that ye take
030:024 And **among** His Signs, He shows you the lightning,
030:025 And **among** His Signs is this, that heaven and earth
030:028 do ye have partners **among** those whom your
030:030 but most **among** mankind know not.
030:031 and be not ye **among** those who join gods with Allah,-
030:046 **Among** His Signs is this, that He sends the Winds,
031:006 But there are, **among** men, those who purchase idle
031:020 Yet there are **among** men those who dispute

AMONG (continued)

031:032 there are **among** them those that falter
032:024 And We appointed, from **among** them, Leaders,
032:025 matters wherein they differ (**among** themselves).
033:006 Blood-relations **among** each other have closer
033:013 Behold! A party **among** them said: "Ye men
033:018 Verily Allah knows those **among** you who keep
033:020 in the deserts (wandering) **among** the Bedouins,
033:023 **Among** the Believers are men who have been true
033:062 of Allah **among** those who lived aforetime:
034:034 the wealthy ones **among** them said: "We believe
035:024 a warner having lived **among** them (in the past).
035:028 **among** His Servants, who have knowledge:
035:032 **among** them some who wrong their own souls;
036:027 has enrolled me **among** those held in honour!"
036:046 to them from **among** the Signs of their Lord,
036:049 they are yet disputing **among** themselves!
036:071 **among** the things which Our hands have
037:057 have been **among** those brought (there)!
037:072 But We sent aforetime, **among** them, warners.
037:078 for him **among** generations to come in later times:
037:079 "Peace and salutation to Noah **among** the nations!"
037:108 And We left for him **among** generations (to come)
037:119 And We left for them **among** generations (to come)
037:123 So also was Elias **among** those sent (by us).
037:128 Except the chosen Servants of Allah (**among** them).
037:129 And We left for him **among** generations (to come)
037:133 So also was Lut **among** those sent (by us).
037:135 Except an old woman who was **among** those who
037:139 So also was Jonah **among** those sent (by Us).
038:004 a Warner has come to them from **among** themselves!
038:006 And the leaders **among** them go away (impatiently),
038:008 been sent to him-(of all persons) **among** us?."
038:062 who we used to number **among** the bad ones?
038:069 when they discuss (matters) **among** themselves.
039:056 and was but **among** those who mocked!'
039:057 I should certainly have been **among** the righteous!'
039:058 I should certainly be **among** those who do good!'
039:065 and thou wilt surely be **among** the losers.
039:071   messengers come to you from **among** yourselves,
040:008 and to the righteous **among** their fathers,
040:028 A Believer, a man from **among** the people of Pharaoh,
041:025 and the word **among** the previous generations of
041:029 Show us those **among** Jinns and men,
041:037 **Among** His Signs are the Night and the Day, and the
041:039 And **among** His Signs is this: thou seest
042:011 He has made for you pairs from **among** yourselves,
042:011 and pairs **among** cattle:
042:029 And **among** His Signs is the creation of the heavens
042:032 And **among** His Signs are the ships, smooth-running
043:018 Is then one brought up **among** trinkets,
043:023 the wealthy ones **among** them said: "We found
043:028 to endure **among** those who came after him,
043:051 And Pharaoh proclaimed **among** his people, saying:
043:065 But sects from **among** themselves fell into
043:079 Have they settled some Plan (**among** themselves)?
044:031 arrogant (even) **among** inordinate transgressors.
044:052 **Among** Gardens and Springs;
045:017 through insolent envy **among** themselves
046:009 Say: "I am not an innovation **among** the messengers,
046:010 and a witness from **among** the Children of Israel
046:016 (they shall be) **among** the Companions of the Garden:
046:018 the word proved true **among** the previous generations

AMONG (continued)

047:016 And **among** them are men who listen to thee,
047:031 until We test those **among** you who strive
047:038 but **among** you are some that are niggardly.
048:025 the Unbelievers **among** them with a grievous
048:029 Allah has promised those **among** them who believe
049:007 And know that **among** you is Allah's Messenger:
049:009 If two parties **among** the Believers fall into
049:011 Let not some men **among** you laugh at others:
050:002 has come to then a Warner from **among** themselves.
054:024 "What! A Man! a solitary one from **among** ourselves!
056:028 (They will be) **among** lote-trees without thorns,
056:029 **Among** Talh trees with flowers (or fruits)
057:010 Not equal **among** you are those who spent (freely)
057:016   For many **among** them are rebellious transgressors.
057:020 (in rivalry) **among** yourselves, riches and children.
057:027 Yet We bestowed, on those **among** them who believed,
058:002 If any men **among** you divorce their wives by Zihar
058:008 hold secret counsels **among** themselves for iniquity
058:020 will be **among** those most humiliated.
059:002 the Unbelievers **among** the People of the Book
059:007 make a circuit between the wealthy **among** you.
059:011 to their misbelieving brethren **among** the People of the
062:002 the Unlettered a messenger **among** themselves,
064:009 a day of mutual loss and gain (**among** you).
064:014 Truly, **among** your wives and your children are
065:002 for witness two persons from **among** you,
066:004 one **among** those who believe,-and furthermore,
067:010 be **among** the Companions of the Blazing Fire!"
068:007 which (**among** men) hath strayed from His Path:
072:004 'There were some foolish ones **among** us, who used
072:006 'True, there were persons **among** mankind who took
072:006 who took shelter with persons **among** the Jinns,
072:011 'There are **among** us some that are righteous,
073:020 may be (some) **among** you in ill-health;
076:024 to the sinner or the ingrate **among** them.
081:028 (With profit) to whoever **among** you wills to
084:013 Truly, did he go about **among** his people, rejoicing!
089:029 "Enter thou, then, **among** my Devotees!
091:012 behold, the most wicked man **among** them was
098:001 of the Book and **among** the Polytheists,
098:001 Those who disbelieve, **among** the People of the
098:006 Those who disbelieve, **among** the People of the
098:006 of the Book and **among** the Polytheists, will be
114:006 **Among** Jinns and **among** Men.

AMONGST

002:065 well ye knew those **amongst** you who transgressed
002:084 shed no blood **amongst** you,
002:129 "Our Lord! send **amongst** them a Messenger
002:232 most virtue and purity **amongst** you,
002:232 This instruction is for all **amongst** you,
003:105 Be not like those who are divided **amongst** themselves
004:015 witnesses from **amongst** you against them;
004:029 but let there be **amongst** you traffic
005:051 And he **amongst** you that turns to them
005:052 they run about **amongst** them, saying:
005:064 **Amongst** them We have placed enmity and hatred
005:082 because **amongst** these are men devoted to learning.
005:117 witness Over them whilst I dwelt **amongst** them;
006:027 but would be **amongst** those who believe!"
006:035 so be not thou **amongst** those who are swayed
006:053 Allah hath favoured from **amongst** us?"
006:122 and a Light whereby he can walk **amongst** men,

AMONGST (continued)

006:128 Their friends **amongst** men will say: "Our Lord!
006:130 unto you messengers from **amongst** you,
006:150 be not thou **amongst** them: nor follow
007:035 come to you messengers from **amongst** you,
007:071 Then wait: I am **amongst** you, also waiting."
007:142 "Act for me **amongst** my people: do right,
007:150 nor count thou me **amongst** the people of sin."
008:033 whilst thou wast **amongst** them;
008:065 If there are twenty **amongst** you, patient and
009:006 If one **amongst** the Pagans ask thee for asylum,
009:066 We will punish other **amongst** you, for that
009:075 and be truly **amongst** those who are righteous.
009:075 **Amongst** them are men who made a Covenant
009:128 a Messenger from **amongst** yourselves:
010:016 A whole life-time before this have I tarried **amongst** you:
010:093 between them as to the schisms **amongst** them,
013:030 Thus have We sent thee **amongst** a People
015:010 messengers before thee **amongst** the sects of old:
015:065 let no one **amongst** you look back,
016:036 For We assuredly sent **amongst** every People
016:089 a witness against them, from **amongst** themselves:
023:094 put me not **amongst** the people who do wrong!"
025:050 And We have distributed the (water) **amongst** them,
028:047 the Signs and been **amongst** those who believe!"
033:029 for the well-doers **amongst** you a great reward.
033:038 (approved) of Allah **amongst** those of old that have
035:028 And so **amongst** men and beasts and cattle,
038:083 "Except Thy Servants **amongst** them, sincere and
043:006 We sent **amongst** the peoples of old?
043:060 We could make angels from **amongst** you,
048:029 (but) compassionate **amongst** each other.
054:025 is sent to him, of all people **amongst** us?
059:014 Strong is their fighting (spirit) **amongst** themselves:
062:002 It is He Who has sent **amongst** the Unlettered
069:049 that there are **amongst** you those that reject (it).
072:014 '**Amongst** us are some that submit their wills
076:015 And **amongst** them will be passed round vessels

AMOUNT

002:236 a gift of a reasonable **amount** is due
028:078 in **amount** (of riches) they had collected?

AMPLE

017:063 you (all)-an **ample** recompense.
053:032 verily thy Lord is **ample** in forgiveness.
058:011 (**Ample**) room will Allah provide for you.

AMPLE-GIVING

024:032 His grace: for Allah is **Ample-giving**,

AMPLITUDE

024:022 with grace and **amplitude** of means resolve by oath

AMPLY

026:056 "But we are a multitude **amply** fore-warned."
078:036 Recompense from thy Lord, a Gift, (**amply**) sufficient,-

AMUSE

026:128 on every high place to **amuse** yourselves?

AMUSED

027:019 So he smiled, **amused** at her speech;

AMUSEMENT

006:032 the life of this world but play and **amusement**.
006:070 their religion to be mere play and **amusement**,
007:051 their religion to be mere **amusement** and play,
029:064 the life of this world but **amusement** and play?
047:036 the life of this world is but play and **amusement**:

AMUSEMENT (continued)

086:014   It is not a thing for **amusement**.

AN (See Appendix)

ANCESTORS

006:148   So did their **ancestors** argue falsely, until

023:024   among our **ancestors** of old."

044:008   and your earliest **ancestors**.

ANCHORITES

009:031   their **anchorites** to be their lords beside Allah.

009:034   many among the priests and **anchorites**, who in

ANCIENT

022:029   and (again) circumambulate the **Ancient** House."

022:033   place of sacrifice is near the **Ancient** House.

040:085   His Servants (from the most **ancient** times).

053:050   the (powerful) **ancient** 'Ad (people),

ANCIENTS

006:025   "These are nothing but tales of the **ancients**."

008:031   but tales of the **ancients**."

016:024   has revealed?" they say, "Tales of the **ancients**!"

018:055   the ways of the **ancients** to overtake them,

023:081   similar to what the **ancients** said.

023:083   They are nothing but tales of the **ancients**!"

025:005   And they say: "Tales of the **ancients**, which he

026:137   a customary device of the **ancients**,

027:068   these are nothing but tales of the **ancients**."

035:043   the way the **ancients** were dealt with?

037:071   many of the **ancients** went astray;-

046:017   "This is nothing but tales of the **ancients**!"

068:015   "Tales of the **Ancients**," he cries!

083:013   he says, "Tales of the **Ancients**!"

AND (See Appendix)

ANEW

017:099   has power to create the like of them (**anew**)?

ANGEL

006:008   They say: "Why is not an **angel** sent down to him?"

006:008   If We did send down an **angel**, the matter

006:009   If We had made it an **angel**, We should

006:050   Nor do I tell you I am an **angel**.

011:012   an **angel** come down with Him?

011:031   nor claim I to be an **angel**.

012:031   This is none other than a noble **angel**!"

017:095   an **angel** for a messenger."

019:017   then We sent to her Our **angel**, and he appeared

025:007   Why has not an **angel** been sent down to him

032:011   Say: "The **Angel** of Death, put in charge of you,

050:021   with each will be an (**angel**) to drive,

050:021   and an (**angel**) to bear witness.

ANGELS

002:030   Behold, thy Lord said to the **angels**:

002:031   then He placed them before the **angels**,

002:034   And behold, We said to the **angels**:

002:098   and His **angels** and prophets,

002:102   at Babylon to the **angels** Harut and Marut.

002:161   and the curse of **angels**, and of all mankind;

002:177   and the **Angels**, and the Book, and the Messengers;

002:210   with **angels** (in His train)

002:248   carried by **angels**.

002:285   His **Angels**, His books, and His Messengers.

003:018   that is the witness of Allah, His **angels**,

003:039   the **angels** called unto him: "Allah doth give thee

003:042   Behold! the **angels** said: "O Mary!

003:045   Behold! the **angels** said "O Mary!

ANGELS (continued)

003:080   to take **angels** and prophets for Lords and Patrons.

003:087   curse of Allah, of His **angels**, and of all mankind;

003:124   three thousand **angels** (specially) sent down?

003:125   with five thousand **angels** clearly marked.

004:097   When **angels** take the souls of those who die

004:136   And who denieth Allah, His **angels**, His Books,

004:166   and the **angels** bear witness: but enough

004:172   nor do the **angels**, those nearest (to Allah):

006:061   Our **angels** take his soul, and they never

006:093   the **angels** stretch forth their hands, (saying),

006:111   Even if We did send unto them **angels**, and the

006:158   if the **angels** come to them, or thy

007:011   then We bade the **angels** prostrate to Adam, and

007:020   lest ye should become **angels** or such

008:009   of the **angels**, ranks on ranks."

008:012   the **angels** (with the message): "I am with you:

008:050   when the **angels** take the souls of the

013:011   there are (**angels**) in succession, before and

013:013   and so do the **angels**, with awe:

013:023   and **angels** shall enter unto them from every

015:007   "Why bringest thou not **angels** to us if it be

015:008   We send not the **angels** down except for just cause:

015:028   Behold! thy Lord said to the **angels**: "I am about to

015:030   So the **angels** prostrated themselves,

016:002   He doth send down His **angels** with inspiration

016:028   "(Namely) those whose lives the **angels** take in

016:028   (The **angels** will reply), "Nay, but verily Allah

016:032   (Namely) those whose lives the **angels** take in

016:033   the **angels** to come to them, or there

016:049   whether moving creatures or the **angels**:

017:040   for Himself daughters among the **angels**?

017:061   Behold! We said to the **angels**: "Prostrate unto

017:092   and the **angels** before (us) face to face;

017:095   on earth, **angels** walking about in peace and quite,

018:050   Behold! We said to the **angels**, "Prostrate to Adam":

019:064   (The **angels** say:) "We descend not but by

020:116   When We said to the **angels**, "Prostrate yourselves

021:103   but the **angels** will meet them (with mutual greetings):

022:075   Allah chooses Messengers from **angels** and from

023:024   He could have sent down **angels**:

025:021   "Why are not the **angels** sent down to us,

025:022   the (**angels**) will say: "There is a barrier forbidden.

025:022   The Day they see the **angels**,-no joy

025:025   and **angels** shall be sent down, descending

033:043   Who sends blessings on you, as do His **angels**,

033:056   Allah and His **Angels** send blessings on the

034:040   and say to the **angels**, "Was it you that these men

035:001   the **angels** messengers with wings,-two, or three

037:150   Or that We created the **angels** female,

037:164   (The **angels**) "Not one of us but has a

038:071   Behold, thy Lord said to the **angels**: "I am

038:073   So the **angels** prostrated themselves, all of

039:075   And thou wilt see the **angels** surrounding the

041:014   He would certainly have sent down **angels**:

041:030   the **angels** descend on them (from time to time):

042:005   and the **angels** celebrate the Praises of their Lord,

043:019   And they make into females **angels** who themselves

043:053   with him **angels** accompanying him in procession?"

043:060   We could make **angels** from amongst you,

047:027   But how (will it be) when the **angels** take their

050:017   Behold, two (guardian **angels**) appointed to learn

053:026   How many-so-ever be the **angels** in the heavens,

ANGELS (continued)

053:027 the Hereafter, name the **angels** with female names.
066:004 and furthermore, the **angels**,-will back (him) up.
066:006 over which are (appointed) **angels** stern (and)
069:017 And the **angels** will be on its sides, and eight
070:004 The **angels** and the Spirit ascend unto Him
074:031 And We have set none but **angels** as guardians
078:038 The Day that the Spirit and the **angels** will stand
079:001 By the (**angels**) who tear out (the souls of the wicked)
082:010 (are appointed **angels**) to protect you,-
089:022 and His **angels**, rank upon rank,
096:018 We will call on the **angels** of punishment
097:004 Therein come down the **angels** and the Spirit

ANGER

003:134 who restrain **anger**, and pardon (all) men;
007:154 When the **anger** of Moses was appeased, he took
020:086 in state of **anger** and sorrow.

ANGRY

007:150 Moses came back to his people, **angry** and grieved,
042:037 when they are **angry** even then forgive;

ANGUISH

012:086 of my distraction and **anguish** to Allah, and I
019:023 she cried (in her **anguish**): "Ah! would
022:022 away therefrom, from **anguish**, they will

ANIMAL

005:003 (partly) eaten by a wild **animal**;
005:095 domestic **animal** equivalent to the one he killed.
006:038 There is not an **animal** (that lives)
006:146 We forbade every (**animal**) with undivided hoof,
024:045 And Allah has created every **animal** from water:

ANIMALS

005:001 but **animals** of the chase are forbidden while
005:002 nor the garlands that mark out such **animals**,
005:002 nor of the **animals** brought for sacrifice,
005:097 the **animals** for offerings, and the garlands
005:103 or idol sacrifices for twin-births in **animals**,
010:024 which provides food for men and **animals**:
016:080 out of the skins of **animals**, (tents for) dwellings,
022:018 the **animals**; and a great number among mankind?
022:032 honour the Rites of Allah, (in the sacrifice of **animals**),
022:034 He gave them from **animals** (fit for food).
022:036 thus have we made **animals** subject to you,
045:004 and the fact that **animals** are scattered
048:025 and the sacrificial **animals**, detained from

ANKLES

005:006 and (wash) your feet to the **ankles**.

ANNIHILATE

003:152 His permission were about to **annihilate** your enemy,

ANNIHILATION

025:039 to utter **annihilation** (for their sins).

ANNOUNCE

003:021 **announce** to them a grievous chastisement.
009:034 **announce** unto them a most grievous chastisement-
019:019 from thy Lord, (to **announce**) to thee the gift
031:007 **announce** to him a grievous Chastisement.
039:017 so **announce** the Good News to My Servants,-
045:008 then **announce** to him a Chastisement Grievous!
084:024 So **announce** to them a Chastisement Grievous,

ANNOUNCED

026:196 Without doubt it is (**announced**) in the revealed Books

ANNOUNCEMENT

009:003 And an **announcement** from Allah and His Messenger,

ANNOUNCEMENT (continued)

018:048 (with the **announcement**), "Now have ye come to Us

ANNOUNCETH

017:010 (it **announceth**) that We have prepared for them

ANNOY

033:053 ye should **annoy** Allah's Messenger, or that
033:057 Those who **annoy** Allah and his Messenger-
033:058 And those who **annoy** believing men and women
065:006 **annoy** them not, so as to restrict them.

ANNOYANCE

003:111 barring a trifling **annoyance**;
004:034 seek not against them means (of **annoyance**):

ANNOYS

033:053 Such (behavior) **annoys** the Prophet

ANOTHER

002:019 Or (**another** similitude) is that of
002:048 a day when one soul shall not avail **another**
002:123 a day when one soul shall not avail **another**,
002:136 between one and **another** of them:
002:230 until after she has married **another** husband
002:251 one set of people by means of **another**,
002:283 deposits a thing on trust with **another**,
002:285 between one and **another** of His Messengers."
003:084 between one and **another** among them,
003:153 one distress after **another** by way of requital,
003:154 while **another** band was stirred to anxiety
003:195 ye are members, one of **another**;
004:020 one wife in place of **another**, even if
004:025 Ye are one from **another**: wed them
004:133 O mankind, and create **another** race:
004:154 and (on **another** occasion) We said: "Enter
005:002 Help ye one **another** in righteousness and piety,
005:002 but help ye not one **another** in sin and rancor:
005:079 Nor did they forbid one **another** the iniquities
006:002 And there is with Him **another** determined term;
006:164 no bearer of burdens can bear the burden of **another**.
008:037 Put the impure, one on **another**, heap them
008:072 these are (all) friends and protectors, one of **another**.
008:073 The Unbelievers are protectors, one of **another**:
009:037 it lawful one year and forbidden **another** year,
009:071 men and women, are protectors, one of **another**:
009:102 mixed an act that was good with **another** that was evil.
011:057 make **another** People to succeed you, and you
012:017 we went racing with one **another**, and left
015:096 Those who adopt, with Allah, **another** god:
016:075 a slave under the dominion of **another**;
016:076 Allah sets forth (**another**) Parable of two men:
016:092 lest one party should be more numerous then **another**:
016:092 Using your oaths to deceive one **another**,
016:101 When We substitute one revelation for **another**,-
017:015 no bearer of burdens can bear the burden of **another**:
017:022 Take not with Allah **another** god;
017:039 with Allah, **another** object of worship, lest thou
018:089 Then followed he (**another**) way,
018:092 Then followed he (**another**) way,
018:099 to surge like waves on one **another**:
018:109 my Lord, even if we added **another** ocean like it,
020:022 (or stain)-as **another** Sign,-
020:037 on thee **another** time (before).
020:062 So they disputed, one with **another**, over their
020:123 with enmity one to **another**; but if, as is sure,
021:093 cut off their affair (of unity), one from **another**:
022:040 of people by means of **another**, there would

ANOTHER (continued)

023:014 then We developed out of it **another** creature:
023:031 Then We raised after them **another** generation.
023:101 nor will one ask after **another**!
024:040 depths of darkness one above **another**:
024:063 like the summons of one of you to **another**:
027:060 (Can there be **another**) god besides Allah?
027:061 the two seas (can there be **another**) god besides
027:062 (Can there be **another**) god besides Allah?
027:063 (Can there be **another**) god besides Allah?
027:064 (Can there be **another**) god besides Allah?
028:088 And call not, besides Allah, on **another** god.
034:031 throwing back the word (of blame) on one **another**!
035:018 heavily laden should call **another** to (bear)
037:027 And they will turn to one **another**, and question
037:027 and question one **another**.
037:050 Then they will turn to one **another** and question
037:050 and question one **another**.
038:035 will not belong to **another** after me: for Thou
039:006 one after **another**, in three veils of darkness.
039:007 No bearer of burdens can bear the burden of **another**.
039:020 one above **another** have been built:
039:058 'If only I had **another** chance I should
042:014 being insolent to one **another**.
043:067 Friends on that Day will be foes, one to **another**,
045:019 wrong-doers (that stand as) Protectors, one to **another**:
047:038 He will substitute in your stead **another** people;
049:002 as ye may speak aloud to one **another**,
050:010 with shoots of fruit-stalks, piled one over **another**;-
050:026 "Who set up **another** god besides Allah: throw him
051:038 And in Moses (was **another** Sign): behold, We sent
051:041 And in the 'Ad (people) (was **another** Sign):
051:043 And in the Thamud (was **another** Sign): behold,
051:051 And make not **another** an object of worship
051:053 Is this the legacy they have transmitted, one to **another**?
052:023 one with **another**, a cup free of frivolity,
052:047 there is **another** punishment besides this: but most
053:020 And **another**, the third (goddess), Manat?
053:038 that no bearer of burdens can bear the burden of **another**;
056:029 (or fruits) piled one above **another**,-
061:013 And **another** (favour will He bestow), which ye
065:006 let **another** woman suckle (the child)
066:003 and she then divulged it (to **another**), and Allah
067:003 He Who created the seven heavens one above **another**:
068:021 they called out, one to **another**,-
068:030 Then they turned, one against **another**, in reproach.
071:015 the seven heavens one above **another**,
075:029 And one leg will be joined with **another**:
077:001 one after **another** (to man's profit);
077:004 Then separate them, one from **another**,
082:019 shall have power (to do) aught for **another**:
089:018 Nor do ye encourage one **another** to feed the poor!-

ANOTHER'S

035:018 Nor can a bearer of burdens bear **another's** burden.

ANSAR

009:117 the Prophet, the Muhajirs, and the **Ansar**,-who

ANSWER

003:040 "Thus," was the **answer**, "Doth Allah accomplish
003:041 "Thy Sign," was the **answer**, "Shall be that thou
004:172 gather them all together unto Himself to (**answer**).
007:082 And his people gave no **answer** but this: they said,
008:035 (its only **answer** can be), "Taste ye the Chastisement
011:014 "If then they (your false gods) **answer** not your (call),

ANSWER (continued)

011:061 for my Lord is (always) near, ready to **answer**."
014:044 we will **answer** Thy Call, and follow
017:052 call you, and ye will **answer** (His call)
019:010 "Thy Sign," was the **answer**, "shall be
020:089 not return them a word (for **answer**), and that
024:051 The **answer** of the Believers, when summoned
027:028 and (wait to) see what **answer** they return"...
027:035 what (**answer**) return (my) ambassadors."
027:056 But his people gave no other **answer** but this:
028:065 and say: "What was the **answer** ye gave
029:024 So naught was the **answer** of (Abraham's) people
029:029 but his people gave no **answer** but this: they said:
035:014 they cannot **answer** your (prayer).
039:071 The **answer** will be: "True: but the Decree of
040:012 (The **answer** will be): "This is because,
040:060 I will **answer** your (Prayer): but those
046:005 such as will not **answer** him to the Day of Judgement,

ANSWERED

002:124 He **answered**: "But My Promise is not
003:172 Of those who **answered** the call of Allah
003:195 and **answered** them: "Never will I suffer
008:009 And He **answered** you: "I will assist
011:069 They said, "Peace!" He **answered**, "Peace!" and
018:072 He **answered**: "Did I not tell thee that thou canst
018:075 He **answered**: "Did I not tell thee that thou canst
018:078 He **answered**: "This is the parting between me
019:007 (His prayer was **answered**): "O Zakariya! We give
033:015 a covenant with Allah must (surely) be **answered** for.

ANTAGONISTS

022:019 These two **antagonists** dispute with each other

ANTICIPATE

015:005 Neither can a people **anticipate** its Term, nor delay it.
016:061 they would not be able to **anticipate** it (for a single hour).

ANTICIPATION

007:034 nor (an hour) can they advance (it in **anticipation**).
010:049 not (an hour) can they advance (it in **anticipation**).

ANTS

027:018 At, length, when they came to a valley of **ants**,
027:018 one of the **ants** said: "O ye **ants**, get into your

ANXIETY

003:154 stirred to **anxiety** by their own feelings,

ANXIOUS

009:128 should suffer, ardently **anxious** is he over you:
016:037 If thou art **anxious** for their guidance, yet Allah

ANY

002:023 (if there are **any**) besides Allah,
002:061 Go ye down to **any** town,
002:090 send it to **any** of His servants He pleases:
002:093 behests of your Faith if you have **any** faith!"
002:118 the Signs unto **any** people who hold
002:173 and that on which **any** other name
002:178 But if **any** remission is made by the brother
002:178 then grant **any** reasonable demand,
002:180 if he leave **any** goods,
002:180 when death approaches **any** of you,
002:184 but if **any** of you is ill, or on a journey,
002:185 but if **any** one is ill, or on a journey,
002:194 If then **any** one transgresses the prohibition
002:196 if **any** one wishes to continue
002:196 And if **any** of you is ill,
002:197 If **any** one undertakes that duty therein,

ANY (continued)

002:217 And if **any** of you turn back from their faith
002:229 if **any** do transgress the limits ordained by Allah,
002:229 to take back **any** of your gifts from (your wives),
002:234 If **any** of you die and leave widows behind;
002:249 if **any** drinks of its water,
002:266 Does **any** of you wish that he should have
002:276 for He loveth not **any** ungrateful Sinner.
003:019 But if **any** deny the Signs of Allah,
003:028 if **any** do that, shall have no relation left
003:061 If **any** one disputes in this manner with thee,
003:082 If **any** turn back after this, they are
003:091 never would be accepted from **any** such as much
003:094 If **any**, after this, invent a lie
003:097 Allah stands not in need of **any** of His creatures.
003:097 but if **any** deny faith, Allah stands not in need
003:108 no injustice to **any** of His creatures.
003:126 (in **any** case) there is no victory except
003:144 If **any** did turn back on his heels,
003:145 and if **any** do desire a reward in the Hereafter,
003:145 If **any** do desire a reward in this life,
003:154 They said: "Have we **any** hand in the affair?
003:161 If **any** person acts dishonestly he shall,
003:192 "Our Lord! **any** whom Thou dost admit to the Fire,
003:192 and never will wrong-doers find **any** helpers!
003:195 I suffer to be lost the work of **any** of you,
004:005 remit **any** part of it to you, take it
004:015 If **any** of your women are guilty of lewdness,
004:025 If **any** of you have not the means wherewith
004:030 If **any** do that in rancor and injustice,
004:036 Serve Allah, and join not **any** partners with Him;
004:038 if **any** take the Satan for their intimate,
004:040 if there is **any** good (done), He doubleth it,
004:080 but if **any** turn away, We have not
004:089 and (in **any** case) take no friends
004:123 besides Allah, **any** protector or helper.
004:124 If **any** do deeds of righteousness, be they
004:134 If **any** one desires a reward in this life,
004:152 make no distinction between **any** of the messengers,
004:168 Allah will not forgive them nor guide them to **any** way-
004:173 besides Allah, **any** to protect or help them.
005:003 But if **any** is forced by hunger, with no
005:005 If **any** one rejects faith, fruitless is his work,
005:012 but if **any** of you, after this, resisteht faith,
005:020 He had not given to **any** other among the peoples.
005:041 If **any** one's trial is intended by Allah,
005:041 men who will listen to **any** lie,-will listen even
005:044 If **any** do fail to judge by what Allah
005:045 And if **any** fail to judge by what
005:047 If **any** do fail to judge by what
005:049 beguile thee from **any** of that (teaching) which
005:054 O ye who believe! if **any** from among you turn
005:069 **any** who believe in Allah and the Last Day,
005:094 **any** who transgress thereafter will have
005:095 If **any** of you doth so intentionally,
005:106 when death approaches **any** of you, (take)
005:115 but if **any** of you after that resisteth faith,
005:115 I have not inflicted on **any** one among all the peoples.
006:014 for my protector **any** other than Allah,
006:016 if the penalty is averted from **any**, it is
006:047 will **any** be destroyed except those who do wrong?"
006:054 verily, if **any** of you did evil in ignorance,
006:081 without **any** warrant having been given to you?

ANY (continued)

006:104 if **any** will see, it will be
006:104 if **any** will be blind, it will be
006:145 **any** (meat) forbidden to be eaten by one
006:148 Say: "Have ye **any** (certain) Knowledge? If so,
006:148 nor should we have had **any** forbidden thing."
006:152 no burden do We place on **any** soul, but that
007:002 no more by **any** difficulty on that account,-that
007:007 for We were never absent (at **any** time or place).
007:018 If **any** of them follow thee,-Hell will
007:042 no burden do We place on **any** soul, but that
007:043 And We shall remove from their hearts **any** rancour;
007:089 nor could we by **any** manner of means return
007:188 Say: "I have no power over **any** good or harm
007:203 and Guidance, and Mercy, for **any** who have Faith."
008:010 (in **any** case) there is no help except from Allah:
008:013 if **any** contend against Allah and His Messenger.
008:016 If **any** do turn his back to them
008:023 If Allah had found in them **any** good, He would
008:049 But if **any** trust in Allah, behold! Allah
008:058 If thou fearest treachery from **any** group, throw
008:070 "If Allah findeth **any** good in your hearts, He will
009:004 nor aided **any** one against you.
009:023 if **any** of you do so, they do wrong.
009:052 Say: "Can you expect for us (**any** fate) other than
009:083 If, then, Allah bring thee back to **any** of them,
009:084 Nor do thou ever pray for **any** of them that dies,
009:120 or gain **any** gain from an enemy:
010:034 can **any** originate creation and repeat it?"
010:035 Say: "Of your 'partners' is there **any** that can give
010:035 that can give **any** guidance towards Truth?"
010:046 (before that),-in **any** case, to Us is their return:
010:049 Say: "I have no power over **any** harm or profit
010:102 Do they then expect (**any** thing) but (what happened in)
010:105 and never in **any** wise be of the Unbelievers;
010:106 "Nor call on **any**, other than Allah,-such can
011:027 nor do we see that **any** follow thee but the meanest
011:027 nor do we see in you (all) **any** merit above us: in fact
011:043 **any** but those on whom He hath mercy!"-
011:081 and let not **any** of you look back:
012:037 He said: "Before **any** food comes (in due course)
012:038 never could we attribute **any** partners whatever to Allah:
012:064 with **any** result other than when I trusted you with
012:109 (as Messengers) **any** but men, whom We did inspire,-
012:111 and a Guide and a Mercy to **any** such as believe.
013:002 without **any** pillars that ye can see; then He
013:010 It is the same (to Him) whether **any** of you
013:011 besides Him, **any** to protect.
013:014 **any** others that they call upon besides Him
013:033 soul (and knoweth) all that it doth, (like **any** others)?
014:020 Nor is that for Allah **any** great matter.
015:018 But **any** that gains a hearing by stealth,
015:047 remove from their hearts **any** lurking sense of injury:
015:085 So overlook (**any** human faults) with gracious
016:075 he has no power of **any** sort;
016:076 one of them dumb, with no power of **any** sort;
016:106 **Any** one who, after accepting Faith in Allah,
016:115 and **any** (food) over which the name of other than
016:116 But say not-for **any** false thing that your
017:018 If **any** do wish for the transitory things
017:051 "Or **any** created matter which, in your minds,
017:063 Allah said: "Go thy way; if **any** of them follow
017:111 nor (needs) He **any** to protect Him from humiliation:

ANY (continued)

018:014 upon **any** god other then Him: if we did;
018:022 nor consult **any** of them about (the affair of) the
018:026 He share His Command with **any** person whatsoever.
018:028 nor obey **any** whose heart We have permitted to
018:030 of **any** who do a (single) righteous deed.
018:047 nor shall We leave out **any** one of them.
018:105 on the Day of Judgement, give them **any** Weight.
019:026 And if thou dost see **any** man, say, 'I have
019:026 into no talk with **any** human being.'"
019:062 They will not there hear **any** vain discourse,
019:065 knowest thou of **any** who is worthy of the
020:077 and without (**any** other) fear."
020:100 If **any** do turn away therefrom, verily they
020:112 nor of **any** curtailment (of what is his due).
021:029 If **any** of them should say, "I am
021:034 We granted not to **any** man before thee
021:066 be of **any** good to you nor do you harm?
021:094 Whoever works **any** act of righteousness and has
021:095 But there is a ban on **any** population which We
022:015 If **any** think that Allah will not help him
022:025 and **any** whose purpose therein is profanity
022:038 verily, Allah loveth not **any** that is
023:088 but is not protected (of **any**)? (Say) if ye know."
023:091 nor is there **any** god along with Him:
023:117 If anyone invokes, besides Allah, **any** other god, he has
024:003 sexual relations with **any** but an adulteress
024:021 if **any** will follow the footsteps of Satan,
024:033 if ye know **any** good in them; yea, give
024:033 And if **any** of yours slaves ask for a deed in writing
024:040 for **any** to whom Allah giveth not light,
024:055 If **any** do reject Faith after this, they are
025:059 of **any** acquainted (with such things).
025:068 and **any** that does this (not only) meets punishment
025:068 Those who invoke not, with Allah, **any** other god,
026:029 (Pharaoh) said: "If thou takest **any** god other than me,
026:198 Had We revealed it to **any** of the non-Arabs,
026:213 So call not on **any** other god with Allah,
027:011 "But if **any** have done wrong and have
027:040 And if **any** is grateful, truly his gratitude is (a gain)
027:040 but if **any** is ungrateful, truly my Lord is Free of all Needs,
027:086 Verily in this are Signs for **any** people that believe!
027:089 If **any** do good, he will have better than it.
027:090 And if **any** do evil, their faces will be thrown
027:092 their own souls, and if **any** stray, say: "I
027:092 and if **any** accept guidance, they do
028:024 **any** good that Thou dost send me!"
028:067 But **any** that (in this life) had repented,
028:082 or restricts it, to **any** of His servants He pleases!
028:084 but if **any** does evil, the doers
028:084 If **any** does good, the reward to him is better
028:086 in **any** way to those who reject (Allah's Message).
029:006 And if **any** strive (with might and main), they do
029:022 beside Allah, **any** protector or helper."
029:035 for **any** people who (care to) understand.
030:040 who can do **any** single one of these things?
030:040 Are there **any** of your (false) "Partners"
030:058 but if thou bring to them **any** Sign, the Unbelievers
031:010 He created the heavens without **any** pillars that ye can
031:012 **Any** who is (so) grateful does so to the profit of his
031:012 but if **any** is ungrateful, verily Allah
031:018 not **any** arrogant boaster.
031:023 But if **any** reject Faith, let not

ANY (continued)

031:034 Nor does **any** one know what it is that he
033:004 Allah has not made for **any** man two hearts
033:017 **any** protector or helper.
033:030 O Consorts of the Prophet! if **any** of you were
033:031 But **any** of you that is devout in the service
033:032 ye are not like **any** of the (other) women:
033:036 to have **any** option about their decision:
033:036 if **any** one disobeys Allah and His Messenger,
033:040 Muhammad is not the father of **any** of your men,
033:050 and **any** believing woman who gives herself
033:051 defer (the turn of) **any** of them that thou pleasest,
033:051 and thou mayest receive **any** thou pleasest:
033:052 their beauty attract thee, except **any** thy right hand should
033:053 or that ye should marry his widows after him at **any** time.
033:060 to stay in it as thy neighbours for **any** length of time:
034:012 and if **any** of them turned aside from Our command,
034:022 nor is **any** of them a helper to Allah.
034:031 nor in (**any**) that (came) before it."
035:010 If **any** do seek for glory and power,-to Allah
035:022 Allah can make **any** that He wills to hear;
036:028 his People, after Him, **any** hosts from heaven,
036:068 If We grant long life to **any**, We cause
036:070 That it may give admonition to **any** (who are)
037:030 "Nor had we **any** authority over you.
037:162 Can lead (**any**) into temptation concerning Allah,
039:028 without **any** crookedness (therein):
039:052 enlarges the provision or restricts it, for **any** He pleases?
040:009 and **any** whom Thou dost preserve from ills
040:011 we recognized our sins: is there **any** way out (of this)?"
040:015 the spirit (of inspiration) to **any** of His servants
040:033 **any** whom Allah leaves to stray,
040:035 without **any** authority that hath reached them.
040:056 of Allah without **any** authority bestowed on them,-
040:077 (before that),-(in **any** case) it is to Us that they
040:078 for **any** messenger to bring a Sign except by the
040:080 to **any** need (there may be) in your hearts;
041:036 And if (at **any** time) an incitement to discord
041:052 who is in schism far (from **any** purpose)?"
042:020 To **any** that desires the tilth of the Hereafter,
042:020 and to **any** that desires the tilth of this world,
042:023 And if **any** one earns **any** good, We shall
042:031 besides Allah, **any** one to protect or to help.
042:041 But indeed if **any** do help and defend themselves
042:043 But indeed if **any** show patience and forgive,
042:044 say: "Is there **any** way (to effect) a return?"
042:044 For **any** whom Allah leaves astray, there is
042:046 and for **any** whom Allah leaves to stray, there is
042:047 will there be for you **any** room for denial (of your sins)!
043:023 a Warner before thee to **any** people, the wealthy
043:045 did We appoint **any** deities other than
045:010 nor **any** protectors they may have taken to
046:004 or **any** remnant of knowledge (ye may have), if ye
046:032 "If **any** does not hearken to the one who invites
046:035 but shall **any** be destroyed except those who transgress?
047:038 But **any** who are niggardly are so at the expense
048:010 then **any** one who violates His oath, does so to the harm
048:010 and **any** one who fulfils what he has covenanted
048:011 Say: "Who then has **any** power at all (to intervene)
048:013 And if **any** believe not in Allah and His Messenger,
049:006 comes to you with **any** news, ascertain the
049:012 Would **any** of you like to eat the flesh of his dead
050:030 It will say, "Are there **any** more (to come)?"

ANY (continued)

050:036	was there **any** place of escape (for them)?
050:037	Verily in this is a Message for **any** that has
050:038	nor did **any** sense of weariness touch Us.
051:036	But We found not there **any** except one
054:015	then is there **any** that will receive admonition?
054:017	then is there **any** that will receive admonition?
054:022	then is there **any** that will receive admonition?
054:032	then is there **any** that will receive admonition?
054:040	then is there **any** that will receive admonition?
054:051	then is there **any** that will receive admonition?
055:060	Is there **any** Reward for Good-other than Good?
056:020	And with fruits, **any** that they may select;
056:021	And the flesh of fowls, **any** that they may desire.
056:025	nor **any** mischief,-
057:023	not **any** vainglorious boaster,-
057:024	And if **any** turn back (from Allah's Way),
058:002	If **any** men among you divorce their wives by Zihar
058:004	And if **any** has not (the means), he should
058:004	touch each other, but if **any** is unable to do so,
058:022	Thou wilt not find **any** people who believe
059:004	and if **any** one resists Allah,
059:006	gives power to His messengers over **any** He pleases:
059:011	and we will never hearken to **any** one in your affair;
060:001	And **any** of you that does this has strayed
060:006	But if **any** turn away, truly Allah is Free of all
060:011	And if **any** of your wives deserts you to the
060:012	and that they will not disobey thee in **any** just matter,-
060:012	in worship **any** other thing whatever with Allah,
062:011	which Allah has in better than **any** pastime or bargain!
063:009	If **any** act thus, surely they are the losers.
063:010	before Death should come to **any** of you and he
065:001	and **any** who transgresses the limits of Allah,
065:004	if ye have **any** doubt, is three months, and those
065:007	on **any** person beyond what He has given him.
067:003	Seest thou **any** flaw?
067:009	'Allah never sent down **any** (Message): ye are in
069:008	Then seest thou **any** of them left surviving?
069:036	"Nor hath he **any** food except the foul pus
069:044	if the messenger were to invent **any** sayings in Our name,
069:047	Nor could **any** of you withhold him (from Our wrath).
071:027	"For, if Thou dost leave (**any** of) them, they will
072:002	we shall not join in (worship) **any** (gods) with our Lord,
072:007	Allah would not raise up **any** one (to Judgement).
072:009	but **any** who listens now will find a flaming fire
072:013	either of a short (account) or of **any** injustice.
072:013	and **any** who believes in his Lord has no fear,
072:017	But if **any** turns away from the remembrance
072:018	so invoke not **any** one along with Allah;
072:020	and I join not with Him **any** (false god)."
072:023	for **any** that disobey Allah and His Messenger,-
072:026	nor does He make **any** one acquainted with
074:006	Nor expect, in giving, **any** increase (for thyself)!
074:037	To **any** of you that chooses to press forward, or to
074:048	of (**any**) intercessors profit them.
074:055	Let **any** who will, keep it in remembrance!
078:024	taste therein, nor **any** drink,
078:027	for **any** account (for their deeds),
078:038	none shall speak except **any** who permitted by
088:023	But if **any** turn away and disbelieve,-

ANYONE

002:048	nor shall **anyone** be helped (from outside).
002:094	be for you specially, and not for **anyone** else,

ANYONE (continued)

002:102	**anyone** except by Allah's permission.
002:102	taught **anyone** (such things without saying:
002:123	nor shall **anyone** be helped (from outside)
002:158	And if **anyone** obeyeth his own impulse to Good,
002:181	If **anyone** changes the bequest after hearing it,
002:182	But if **anyone** fears partiality or wrong-doing
002:203	and if **anyone** stays on,
002:203	but if **anyone** hastens to leave in two days,
002:211	But if **anyone**,
002:231	if **anyone** does that, He wrongs his own soul.
003:022	nor will they have **anyone** to help.
003:056	nor will they have **anyone** to help.
003:085	If **anyone** desires a religion other than Islam
003:153	without even casting a side glance at **anyone**,
004:012	so that no loss is caused (to **anyone**).
004:094	and say not to **anyone** who offers you a salutation:
004:110	If **anyone** does evil or wrongs his own soul but
004:111	And if **anyone** earns sin, he earns it
004:112	But if **anyone** earns a fault or a sin and throws
004:115	If **anyone** contends with the Messenger even after
005:032	and if **anyone** saved a life, it would be as
005:032	that if **anyone** slew a person-unless it be for
005:045	But if **anyone** remits the retaliation by way of charity,
009:127	(saying), "Doth **anyone** see you?" then they turn away:
010:038	and call (to your aid) **anyone** you can, besides
017:020	the bounties of thy Lord are not closed (to **anyone**).
017:033	And if **anyone** is slain wrongfully, We have
018:019	and let him not inform **anyone** about you.
022:031	if **anyone** assigns partners to Allah, he is
023:117	If **anyone** invokes, besides Allah, any other
024:033	But if **anyone** compels them, yet, after
031:034	nor does **anyone** know in what land he is to die.
035:042	rightly guided than **anyone** of the nations:
043:036	If **anyone** withdraws himself from remembrance
045:015	If **anyone** does a righteous deed, it is
064:011	and if **anyone** believes in Allah, (Allah) guides
065:003	And if **anyone** puts his trust in Allah,
065:005	and if **anyone** fears Allah, He will
092:019	from **anyone** for which a reward is expected
099:007	Then shall **anyone** who has done an atom's weight
099:008	And **anyone** who has done an atom's weight

ANYTHING

002:026	even of a gnat as well as **anything** above it.
002:105	That **anything** good should come down
002:267	and do not even aim at **anything** which is bad,
003:147	and **anything** we may have done that transgressed
003:154	"If we had had thing to do with this affair,
004:048	but He forgiveth **anything** else, to whom
004:059	If ye differ in **anything** among yourselves,
005:042	of devouring **anything** forbidden.
006:059	nor **anything** fresh or dry (green or withered),
006:132	not unmindful of **anything** that they do.
006:151	join not **anything** with Him:
007:050	"Pour down to us water or **anything** that Allah
007:169	to Allah **anything** but the truth?
009:121	Nor could they spend **anything** (for the Cause),
013:016	partners who have created (**anything**) as He has created,
016:040	For to **anything** which We have willed, We but
016:073	with **anything** in heavens or earth, and cannot
018:023	Nor say of **anything**, "I shall be
018:070	about **anything** until I myself speak to thee
018:076	about **anything** after this, keep me not

ANYTHING (continued)

021:068   your gods, if ye do (**anything** at all)!"
022:026   "Associate not **anything** (in worship) with Me;
022:052   cancel **anything** (vain) that Satan throws in,
022:073   And if the fly should snatch away **anything** form them,
023:068   or has **anything** (new) come to them that did no come
029:008   **anything** of which thou hast no knowledge,
033:053   for **anything** ye want, ask them
033:054   Whether ye reveal **anything** or conceal it,
034:003   nor is there **anything** less than that, or greater,
035:044   to be frustrated by **anything** whatever in the
040:074   invoked not, of old, **anything** (that had real existence)."
045:010   and of no profit to them is **anything** they may
052:022   of fruit and meat, **anything** they shall desire.
053:024   (just) **anything** he hankers after?

ANYWHERE

031:016   in a rock, or (**anywhere**) in the heavens or on

APART

010:032   **apart** from the Truth, what (remains) but error?
012:040   Whatever ye worship **apart** from Him is nothing
035:002   none can grant, **apart** from Him:
036:059   And O ye in sin! get ye **apart** this Day!
048:025   If they had been **apart**, We should

APARTMENTS

049:004   from without the Inner **Apartments**-most of

APES

002:065   "Be ye **apes**, despised and rejected."
005:060   He transformed into **apes** and swine, those who
007:166   "Be ye **apes**, despised and rejected."

APPOINTMENT

013:038   For each period is an **appointment**.

APOSTATES

003:100   render you **apostates** after ye have believed!
047:025   Those who turn back as **apostates** after Guidance

APPAREL

007:031   wear your beautiful **apparel** at every time

APPARENTLY

011:027   **apparently** nor do we see in you (all) any

APPEALED

028:015   his own people **appealed** to him against his foe,

APPEAR

002:187   of dawn **appear** to you distinct from its black thread;
008:044   and He made you **appear** as contemptible in
015:062   He said: "Ye **appear** to be uncommon folk."
019:038   the Day that they will **appear** before Us!
019:080   and he shall **appear** before Us bare and alone.
024:031   what (ordinarily) **appear** thereof; that they
029:038   clearly will **appear** to you from (the traces) of their
033:055   no blame (on those ladies if they **appear**) before their
040:026   should cause mischief to **appear** in the land!"
045:033   Then will **appear** to them the evil (fruits)

APPEARED

002:133   when Death **appeared** before Jacob?
003:118   rank hatred has already **appeared** from their mouths;
019:017   and he **appeared** before her as a man in all respects.
020:121   and so their nakedness **appeared** to them:
030:041   Mischief has **appeared** on land and sea
053:006   For he **appeared** (in stately form)

APPEARETH

002:255   (**appeareth** to his creatures as) before or

APPEARS

002:187   then complete your fast till the night **appears**;
092:002   By the Day as it **appears** in glory;

APPEASED

007:154   When the anger of Moses was **appeased**, he took

APPLIES

016:060   in the Hereafter, **applies** the similitude of evil:
016:060   to Allah **applies** the highest similitude:

APPOINT

002:246   "**Appoint** for us a king,
003:049   "And (**appoint** him) a Messenger to the Children
004:035   **appoint** (two) arbiters, one from his family,
006:128   which Thou didst **appoint** for us."
006:133   and in your place **appoint** whom He will
019:021   and (We wish) to **appoint** him as a Sign unto men
022:034   To every people did We **appoint** rites (of sacrifice),
043:036   We **appoint** for him a Satan, to be
043:045   did We **appoint** any deities other than
072:025   or whether my Lord will **appoint** for it
073:020   But Allah doth **appoint** Night and Day

APPOINTED

002:051   And remember We **appointed** forty nights
002:143   and We **appointed** the Qiblah
002:203   Remember Allah during the **Appointed** Days
002:247   "Allah hath **appointed** Talut as king over you."
003:096   House (of worship) **appointed** for men was that at Bakka:
004:033   We have **appointed** sharers and heirs to property
005:012   and We **appointed** twelve chieftains among them,
006:060   that a term **appointed** be fulfilled; in the end
007:034   To every People is a term. **Appointed**:
007:037   For such, their portion **appointed** must reach
007:142   We **appointed** for Moses thirty nights,
007:143   When Moses came to the place **appointed** by Us,
007:187   when will be its **appointed** time?
010:049   To every People is a term **appointed**:
011:003   good (and true), for a term **appointed**, and bestow
011:081   Morning is their time **appointed**:
011:104   Nor shall We delay it but for a term **appointed**.
013:002   Each one runs (its course) for a term **appointed**.
013:038   and **appointed** for them wives and children:
014:010   and give you respite for a term **appointed**!"
015:038   "Till the Day of the Time **Appointed**."
017:099   a term **appointed**, of which there is no doubt.
018:058   but they have their **appointed** time, beyond which
018:059   but We fixed an **appointed** time for their
020:129   a term **appointed** (for respite).
022:005   to rest in the wombs for an **appointed** term,
022:028   through the Days **appointed**, over the
022:033   In them ye have benefits for a term **appointed**:
022:067   have We **appointed** rites which they must follow:
025:035   and **appointed** his brother Aaron with him as Minister,
026:021   and **appointed** me as one of the messengers.
026:155   (severally) on a day **appointed**.
029:005   the Term (**appointed**) by Allah is surely coming:
029:053   (of respite) **appointed**, the Punishment
030:008   a term **appointed**, did Allah create the heavens
031:029   each running its course for a term **appointed**;
032:024   And We **appointed**, from among them, Leaders, giving
033:050   We know what We have **appointed** for them
034:018   We had **appointed** stages of journey in due
035:013   each running its course for a term **appointed**.
037:164   "Not one of us but has a place **appointed**;
038:081   "Till the day of the Time **Appointed**."

APPOINTED (continued)

039:005 each one follows a course for a time **appointed**.
039:042 the rest He sends (to their bodies) for a term **appointed**.
040:067 and lets you reach a Term **appointed**: in order that ye
042:014 (tending) to a Term **appointed**, the matter
044:040 is the time **appointed** for all of them,-
046:003 but for just ends, and for a term **appointed**:
050:017 Behold, two (guardian angels) **appointed** to learn
054:003 but every matter has its **appointed** time.
056:050 for the meeting **appointed** for a Day Well-known.
063:011 when the time **appointed** (for it) has come;
065:002 Thus when they fulfil their term **appointed**, either take
065:003 for all things has Allah **appointed** a due proportion.
066:006 over which are (**appointed**) angels stern (and)
077:011 are (all) **appointed** a time (to collect);-
078:017 Verily the Day of Sorting Out is a thing **appointed**,-
079:042 'When will be its **appointed** time?'
082:010 (are **appointed** angels) to protect you,-

APPOINTMENT

008:042 ye would certainly have failed in the **appointment**:
008:042 Even if ye had made a mutual **appointment** to meet,
018:048 We shall not fulfil the **appointment** made to you
026:038 for the **appointment** of a day well-known,
034:030 Say: "The **appointment** to you is for a Day,

APPRECIATE

035:030 Oft-Forgiving, Most Ready to **appreciate** (service).
035:034 Ready to **appreciate** (service):

APPRECIATIVE

014:005 firmly patient and constant, grateful and **appreciative**.

APPREHEND

018:053 and **apprehend** that they have to fall therein;

APPROACH

002:035 but **approach** not this tree,
002:187 on the night of the fasts, is the **approach** to your wives.
002:187 are the limits (set by) Allah **approach** not night thereto.
002:222 and do not **approach** them until they are clean.
002:222 ye may **approach** them as ordained for you
002:223 so **approach** your tilth when or how ye will;
004:043 O ye who believe! **approach** not prayers in a state
004:090 or those who **approach** you with hearts restraining
005:035 seek the means of **approach** unto Him, and strive
007:019 but **approach** not this tree, lest you
009:028 after this year of theirs, **approach** the Sacred Mosque.
019:075 either in punishment or in (the **approach** of) the Hour,-
026:064 And We made the other party **approach** thither.
026:165 will ye **approach** males,
027:055 "Would ye really **approach** men in your
029:029 "Do ye indeed **approach** men, and cut
038:025 he enjoyed, indeed, a Near **Approach** to Us,
038:040 And he enjoyed, indeed, a Near **Approach** to Us,
041:042 No falsehood can **approach** it from before
047:020 of one in swoon at the **approach** of death.

APPROACHED

037:084 Behold, He **approached** his Lord with a sound heart.
053:008 Then he **approached** and came closer,

APPROACHES

002:180 when death **approaches** any of you,
005:106 when death **approaches** any of you, (take)
006:061 At length, when death **approaches** one of you.
011:114 of the day and at the **approaches** of the night:

APPROACHING

053:057 The (Hour) ever **approaching** draws nigh:

APPROPRIATE

004:009 let them fear Allah, and speak **appropriate** words.

APPROVE

004:108 In words that He cannot **approve**:
046:015 I may work righteousness such as Thou mayest **approve**;

APPROVED

033:038 It was the practice (**approved**) of Allah
033:062 wilt thou find in the practice (**approved**) of Allah.
033:062 (Such was) the practice (**approved**) of Allah among those

ARAB

041:044 What! a foreign (tongue) and (a Messenger) an **Arab** ?"

ARABIC

012:002 We have sent it down as an **Arabic** Qur'an, in order
013:037 We revealed it to be a judgment of authority in **Arabic**.
016:103 while this is **Arabic**, pure and clear.
020:113 an **Arabic** Qur'an-and explained therein in detail
026:195 In the perspicuous **Arabic** tongue.
039:028 (It is) a Qur'an in **Arabic**, without any
041:003 a Qur'an in **Arabic**, for people who understand,-
041:044 (in a language) other than **Arabic**, they would
042:007 We sent by inspiration to thee an **Arabic** Qur'an:
043:003 We have made it a Qur'an in **Arabic**, that ye
046:012 and this Book confirms (it) in the **Arabic** tongue;

ARABS

009:090 And there were, among the desert **Arabs** (also),
009:097 The Bedouin **Arabs** are the worst in unbelief
009:098 Some of the Bedouin **Arabs** look upon their payments
009:099 But some of the Bedouin **Arabs** believe in Allah
009:101 Certain of the desert **Arabs** round about you
009:120 and the Bedouin **Arabs** of the neighbourhood,
029:047 as also do some of these (pagan **Arabs**):
048:011 The desert **Arabs** who lagged behind will say
048:016 Say to the desert **Arabs** who lagged behind:
049:014 The desert **Arabs** say, "We believe." Say, "Ye

ARAFAT

002:198 Then when ye pour down from (Mount) '**Arafat,**

ARBITERS

004:035 appoint (two) **arbiters**, one from his family,

ARBITRARY

015:090 divided (Scripture into **arbitrary** parts),-

ARBITRATION

003:023 turn back and decline (the **arbitration**).

ARCHES

034:013 he desired, (making) **Arches**, Images, Basins as

ARDENT

004:129 between wives even if it is your **ardent** desire:

ARDENTLY

009:128 should suffer, **ardently** anxious is he over you:
012:103 mankind have, however **ardently** thou dost desire it.

ARE (See Appendix)

ARGUE

006:148 So did their ancestors **argue** falsely, until
016:125 and **argue** with them in ways that are best
078:037 none shall have power to **argue** with Him.

ARGUMENT

002:076 in **argument** about it before your Lord?"
003:073 should engage you in **argument** before your Lord?
004:091 with a clear **argument** against them.
006:083 That was Our **argument** which We gave
006:149 the **argument** that reaches home:
018:034 in the course of a mutual **argument**: "More wealth

ARGUMENT (continued)

018:037 in the course of the **argument** with him: "Dost thou
018:056 with vain **argument**, in order therewith to weaken
027:064 Say, "Bring forth your **argument**, if ye
038:023 and he overcame me in the **argument**."
042:016 futile is their dispute in the sight of their **argument**
045:025 to them, their **argument** is nothing but this:

ARGUMENTS

028:066 Then the **arguments** that day will be obscure
058:001 the **arguments** between both of you:

ARIGHT

002:053 there was a chance for you to be guided **aright**.
003:076 their plighted faith and act **aright**,
003:076 verily Allah loves those who act **aright**.
003:125 "Yea,-if ye remain firm, and act **aright**,
004:035 if they seek to set things **aright**, Allah
007:201 Allah to remembrance when lo! they see (**aright**)!
020:079 instead of leading them **aright**.
043:037 are being guided **aright**!
064:011 (Allah) guides his heart (**aright**):

ARISE

003:104 Let there **arise** out of you a band of people
074:002 **Arise** and deliver thy warning!

ARISEN

060:004 and there has **arisen** between us and you,

ARISES

010:024 by its mingling **arises** the produce of the earth-

ARK

002:248 shall come to you the **Ark** of the Covenant,
007:064 and those with him, in the **Ark**:
010:073 and those with him, in the **Ark**, and We made
011:037 "But construct an **Ark** under Our eyes
011:038 Forthwith he (starts) constructing the **Ark**:
011:041 So he said: "Embark ye on the **Ark**, in the
011:042 So the **Ark** floated with them on the waves
011:044 The **Ark** rested on Mount Judi, and the word went
011:048 (from the **Ark**) with Peace from Us, and Blessing
017:003 whom We carried (in the **Ark**) with Noah!
019:058 and of those whom We carried (in the **Ark**) with Noah,
023:027 "Construct the **Ark** within Our sight and under Our
023:028 on the **Ark**-thou and those with thee,-say: "Praise
026:119 in the **Ark** filled (with all creatures).
029:015 But We saved him and the Companions of the **Ark**,
029:015 and We made the (**Ark**) a Sign for all Peoples!
036:041 their race (through the flood) in the loaded **Ark**;
054:013 But We bore him on an (**Ark**) made of broad planks
069:011 carried you (mankind), in the floating (**Ark**).

ARM

028:035 "We will certainly strengthen thy **arm** through thy brother,

ARMIES

002:249 When Talut set forth with the **armies**,
003:013 a Sign in the two **armies** that met (in combat):
003:166 What ye suffered on the day the two **armies** met,

ARMOUR

034:011 balancing well the rings of chain **armour**,

ARMS

004:102 negligent of your **arms** and your baggage,
004:102 taking all precautions, and bearing **arms**:
004:102 put away your **arms** because of the inconvenience
004:102 Taking their **arms** with them:
005:006 and your hands (and **arms**) to the elbows;
019:027 brought the (babe) to her people, carrying (in her **arms**),

ARMY

002:249 he goes not with my **army**;
003:173 "A great **army** is gathering against you,
067:020 Nay, who is there that can help you (even as) an **army**,

AROSE

011:110 gave the Book to Moses, but differences **arose** therein:
041:045 Moses the Book aforetime: but disputes **arose** therein.

AROUND

002:017 when it lighted all **around** him,
006:092 the Mother of Cities and all **around** her.
026:025 (Pharaoh) said to those **around**: "Do ye not
026:034 (Pharaoh) said to the Chiefs **around** him: "This is
027:008 "Blessed are those in the Fire and those **around**:
029:067 men are being snatched away from all **around** them?
040:007 and those **around** it sing Glory and Praise
042:007 mayest warn the Mother of Cities and all **around** her,-
068:019 (which swept away) all **around**, while they

AROUSE

059:013 Of a truth ye **arouse** greater fear in their hearts,
017:064 And **arouse** those whom thou canst among them,

ARRANGE

004:128 if they **arrange** an amicable settlement between
010:108 over you to **arrange** your affairs."
079:005 Then **arrange** to do (the commands of their Lord),-

ARRANGED

052:020 on couches **arranged** in ranks, and We

ARRANGETH

011:012 It is Allah that **arrangeth** all affairs!

ARRANGING

006:066 the responsibility for **arranging** your affairs;

ARRAY

008:015 the Unbelievers in hostile **array**, never turn
061:004 in His Cause in battle **array**, as if

ARRIVE

007:037 Our messengers (of death) **arrive** and take their souls
039:071 until when they **arrive** there, its gates will be opened.
039:073 until behold, they **arrive** there; its gates
074:031 that the People of the Book may **arrive** at certainty,

ARRIVED

009:048 until the Truth **arrived**, and the Decree
015:061 the messengers **arrived** among the adherents of Lut.
017:081 And say: "Truth has (now) **arrived**, and Falsehood
026:041 So when the sorcerers **arrived**, they said
027:042 So when she **arrived**, she was asked, "Is this
028:023 And when he **arrived** at the watering (place)
034:049 Say: "The Truth has **arrived**, and Falsehood
057:016 Has not the time **arrived** for the Believers

ARRIVES

011:105 The day it **arrives**, no soul shall speak

ARROGANCE

002:206 he is led by **arrogance** to (more) crime.
002:258 who (in **arrogance**) rejected Faith.
007:036 and treat them with **arrogance**,-they are
007:040 and treat them with **arrogance**, no opening
007:133 but they were steeped in **arrogance**, a people
017:004 on the earth and be elated with mighty **arrogance**
023:067 "In **arrogance**: talking nonsense about the (Qur'an),
031:007 he turns away in **arrogance**, as if he heard them not,
035:043 On account of their **arrogance** in the land
063:005 see them turning away their faces in **arrogance**.
071:007 and given themselves up to **arrogance**.

ARROGANT

004:036	for Allah loveth not the **arrogant**,
004:172	those who disdain His worship and are **arrogant**,
004:173	but those who are disdainful and **arrogant**, He will
005:082	and they are not **arrogant**.
007:013	it is not for thee to be **arrogant** here: get out,
007:048	were your hoards and your **arrogant** ways?
007:075	The leaders of the **arrogant** party among his
007:076	The **arrogant** party said: "For our part, we
007:088	The leaders, the **arrogant** party among his people,
010:075	But they were **arrogant**: they were a wicked people.
014:021	the weak say to those who were **arrogant**, "For us
016:022	refuse to know and they are **arrogant**.
016:023	verily He loveth not the **arrogant**.
016:029	is the abode of the **arrogant**."
016:049	for none are **arrogant** (before their Lord).
023:046	they were an **arrogant** people.
025:021	an **arrogant** conceit of themselves, and mighty
027:031	"'Be ye not **arrogant** against me, but come
028:039	And he was **arrogant** and insolent in the land,
031:018	not any **arrogant** boaster.
034:031	who were deemed weak will say to the **arrogant** ones:
034:032	The **arrogant** ones will say to those who had
034:033	will say to the **arrogant** ones: Nay! it was
039:072	(this) abode of the **arrogant**!"
040:027	(for protection) from every **arrogant** one who
040:035	seal up every heart-of **arrogant** tyrinical."
040:047	will say to those who had been **arrogant**, "We but
040:048	Those who had been **arrogant** will say: "We are
040:060	but those who are too **arrogant** to serve Me
040:076	is (this) abode of the **arrogant**!"
041:038	But if the (Unbelievers) are **arrogant**, (no matter):
044:019	"And be not **arrogant** as against Allah:
044:031	he was **arrogant** (even) among inordinate transgressors.
045:031	But ye were **arrogant**, and were a people given to sin!
046:010	and has believed while ye are **arrogant**,
046:020	for that ye were **arrogant** on earth

ARROGANTLY

007:146	Those who behave **arrogantly** on the earth
041:015	Now the 'Ad behaved **arrogantly** through the land,

ARROWS

005:003	by raffling with **arrows**: that is impiety.
005:090	and (divination by) **arrows**, are an abomination,

ART

002:032	in truth it is Thou who **art** perfect
002:127	for thou **art** the All-Hearing,
002:128	for Thou **art** the Oft-Returning,
002:129	for Thou **art** the Exalted in Might, the Wise."
002:145	nor **art** thou going to follow their Qiblah;
002:252	verily thou **art** one of the Messengers.
002:286	Thou **art** our protector;
003:008	for Thou **art** the Grantor of bounties
003:009	"Our Lord! Thou **art** He that will gather mankind
003:038	for Thou **art** He that heareth prayer!
004:084	thou **art** held responsible only for thyself,
004:094	"Thou **art** none of a Believer!"
004:102	When thou (O Messenger) **art** with them,
005:114	for thou **art** the best Sustainer (of our needs)."
005:117	and Thou **art** a Witness to all things.
005:118	Thou **art** the Exalted, the Wise.
006:106	Follow what thou **art** taught by inspiration
006:107	nor **art** thou set over them to dispose
007:013	get out, for thou **art** of the meanest (of creatures)."

ART (continued)

007:066	and "We think thou **art** a liar!"
007:066	"Ah! we see thou **art** in folly!"
007:077	if thou **art** a Messenger (of Allah)!"
007:089	for thou **art** the best to decide."
007:151	For Thou **art** the Most Merciful of those
007:155	Thou **art** our Protector: so forgive us
007:155	for Thou **art** the best of those who forgive.
011:012	But thou **art** there only to warn! It is Allah
011:045	and Thou **art** the Justest of Judges!"
011:087	Truly, thou **art** the one that forbeareth with
011:112	stand firm (the straight path) as thou **art** commanded,-
012:036	for we see thou **art** one that doth good (to all)."
012:054	thou **art** of high standing with us, invested with
012:078	for we see that thou **art** (gracious) in doing good."
012:090	They said: "**Art** thou indeed, Joseph?"
012:095	They said: "By Allah! truly thou **art** in thine
012:101	Thou **art** my Protector in this world and in
013:007	But thou **art** truly a warner,
013:043	The Unbelievers say: "No messenger **art** thou."
014:036	but thou **art** indeed Oft-Forgiving, Most Merciful.
015:006	Truly thou **art** mad (or possessed)!
015:034	from here; for thou **art** rejected, accursed.
015:084	they did (with such **art** and care)!
015:094	Therefore expound openly what thou **art** commanded,
016:037	If thou **art** anxious for their guidance, yet Allah
016:101	they say, "Thou **art** but a forger" but most
019:006	one with whom Thou **art** well-pleased!"
019:010	although thou **art** not dumb."
019:046	"**Art** thou shrinking from my gods, O Abraham?
020:012	thou **art** in the sacred valley Tuwa.
020:035	For Thou **art** ever seeing."
020:117	the Garden, so that thou **art** landed in misery.
021:062	They said, "**Art** thou the one that did this
021:083	but Thou **art** the Most Merciful of those
021:089	though Thou **art** the best of inheritors."
022:067	for thou **art** assuredly on the right Way.
023:029	Thy blessing: for Thou **art** the Best to enable
023:118	for Thou **art** the Best of those who show mercy!"
026:019	and thou **art** an ungrateful!"
026:153	They said: "Thou **art** only the of those bewitched!
026:154	"Thou **art** no more than a mortal like us:
026:185	They said: "Thou **art** only one of those bewitched!
026:186	"Thou **art** no more than a mortal like us,
026:186	and indeed we think thou **art** a liar!
026:187	the sky to fall on us, if thou **art** truthful!"
027:079	for thou **art** on (the Path of) manifest Truth.
028:018	"Thou **art** truly, one erring manifestly."
028:031	and fear not: for thou **art** of those who are secure.
028:046	Yet (**art** thou sent) as a Mercy from thy Lord,
029:048	nor **art** thou (able) to transcribe it with
034:041	Thou **art** our protector-not them.
035:023	Thou **art** no other than a warner.
036:003	Thou **art** indeed one of the messengers,
037:102	"O my father! do as thou **art** commanded:
038:035	for Thou **art** the Grantor of Bounties
038:075	**Art** thou haughty? Or **art** thou one of the high
038:077	for thou **art** rejected, accursed.
039:008	verily thou **art** (one) of the Companions of the Fire!"
039:041	Nor **art** thou set a Custodian over them.
040:008	For Thou **art** (He), the Exalted in Might,
042:006	and thou **art** not the disposer of their affairs.
042:015	and stand fast as thou **art** commanded,

ART (continued)

043:043 verily thou **art** on a Straight Way.
044:049 Truly thou **art** Mighty, full of honour!
046:022 if thou **art** telling the truth!"
050:001 (Thou **art** Allah's Messenger).
050:030 "**Art** thou filled to the full?" It will say,
050:045 and thou **art** not one to compel them by force.
052:029 thou **art** no soothsayer nor possessed.
052:048 for verily thou **art** in Our eyes:
059:010 Our Lord! Thou **art** indeed Full of Kindness,
060:005 For Thou **art** the Exalted in Might
063:001 thou **art** indeed the Messenger of Allah."
063:001 that thou **art** indeed His Messenger.
068:002 Thou **art** not, by the grace of thy Lord, mad or
079:043 Wherein **art** thou (concerned) with the declaration
079:045 Thou **art** but a Warner for such as fear it.
084:006 O thou man! verily thou **art** ever toiling on
088:021 for thou **art** one to remind.
088:022 Thou **art** not one to manage (their) affairs.
090:002 And thou **art** an inhabitant of this City;-
094:004 (in which) thou (**art** held)?
094:007 when thou **art** free (from thine immediate task),

ARTERY

069:046 the **artery** of his heart:

ARTICLE

056:073 and an **article** of comfort and convenience for the

ARTICLES

016:080 their hair, rich stuff and **articles** of convenience

ARTISTRY

027:088 (such is) the **artistry** of Allah,
036:035 That they may enjoy the fruits of this (**artistry**):

AS   (See Appendix)

ASCEND

070:004 The angels and the Spirit **ascend** unto Him

ASCENDANTS

004:012 has left neither **ascendants** nor descendants, but
004:176 who leave no descendants or **ascendants** as heirs.

ASCENDING

015:014 to continue (all day) **ascending** therein,
077:030 (of smoke **ascending**) in three columns,

ASCENDS

032:005 then it **ascends** unto Him, on a Day the measure
034:002 and all that **ascends** thereto and He is the Most

ASCENT

070:003 (A Penalty) from Allah, Lord of the Ways of **Ascent**.

ASCERTAIN

049:006 **ascertain** the truth, lest ye harm people
060:010 as to their Faith: if ye **ascertain** that they

ASCERTAINABLE

015:021 thereof in due and **ascertainable** measures.

ASCERTAINED

015:060 his wife, who, we have **ascertained**, will be among

ASCRIBE

007:169 that they would not **ascribe** to Allah
007:190 they **ascribe** to others a share in the gift
007:190 exalted high above the partners they **ascribe** to Him.
007:191 Do they indeed **ascribe** to Him as partners
010:018 the partners they **ascribe** (to Him)!"
013:033 they **ascribe** partners to Allah.
016:001 the partners they **ascribe** unto Him!
016:003 above having the partners they **ascribe** to Him!

ASCRIBE (continued)

016:116 so as to **ascribe** false things to Allah.
016:116 For those who **ascribe** false things to Allah,
021:018 (false) things ye **ascribe** (to Us).
028:068 they **ascribe** (to Him)!
037:159 from the things they **ascribe** (to Him)!
037:180 from what they **ascribe** (to Him)!

ASCRIBED

006:022 who **ascribed** partners (to Us): "Where are
007:131 they **ascribed** it to evil omens connected with
018:042 Would I had never **ascribed** partners to my

ASCRIBING

011:054 that I am free from the sin of **ascribing**, to Him,

ASHES

014:018 as **ashes**, on which the wind blows furiously
021:015 is mown, as **ashes** silent and quenched.
036:029 (like **ashes**) quenched and silent.

ASIDE

002:100 some party among them throw it **aside**?
006:046 by various (symbols): Yet they turn **aside**.
006:106 and turn **aside** from those who join gods with Allah.
016:009 but there are ways that turn **aside**:
024:060 lay **aside** their (outer) garments, provided they
033:051 whose (turn) thou hadst set **aside**.
034:012 and if any of them turned **aside** from Our command,
038:028 the same as those who turn **aside** from the right?
046:022 to turn us **aside** from our gods?
063:005 they turn **aside** their heads, and though wouldst see

ASK

002:177 for the wayfarer, for those who **ask**,
002:186 When My servants **ask** thee concerning Me,
002:189 They **ask** thee concerning the New Moons.
002:199 and **ask** for Allah's forgiveness.
002:211 **Ask** the Children of Israel how many Clear (Signs)
002:215 They **ask** thee what they should spend (in charity).
002:217 They **ask** thee concerning fighting
002:219 They **ask** thee how much they are to spend;
002:219 They **ask** thee concerning wine and gambling.
002:220 They **ask** thee concerning orphans.
002:222 They **ask** thee concerning women's courses.
003:135 and **ask** for forgiveness for their sins,
003:159 and **ask** for (Allah's) forgiveness for them;
003:183 with Clear Signs and even with what ye **ask** for:
004:032 but **ask** Allah of His bounty:
004:127 They **ask** thy instruction concerning the Women.
004:153 The people of the Book **ask** thee to cause
004:176 They **ask** thee for a legal decision, say:
005:004 They **ask** thee what is lawful to them (as food).
005:101 O ye who believe! **ask** not questions about things
005:101 But if ye **ask** about things when the Qur'an
005:102 Some people before you did **ask** such questions,
005:109 and **ask**: "What was the response ye received
006:090 Say: "No reward for this do I **ask** of you:
007:163 **Ask** them concerning the town
007:187 They **ask** thee about the (final) Hour-when will
007:187 They **ask** thee as if thou wert eager
008:001 They **ask** thee concerning (things taken as)
008:033 whilst they could **ask** for pardon.
009:006 If one amongst the Pagans **ask** thee for asylum,
009:044 and the Last Day **ask** thee for no exemption from
009:045 Only those **ask** thee for exemption who believe
009:080 if thou **ask** seventy times for their forgiveness,

ASK (continued)

009:080 Whether thou **ask** for their forgiveness, or not,
009:083 and they **ask** thy permission to come (with thee),
009:086 among them **ask** thee for exemption, and say:
010:094 then **ask** those who have been reading the Book
011:029 I **ask** you for no wealth in return:
011:046 So **ask** not of Me that of which thou hast
011:051 "O my people! I **ask** of you no reward
011:052 "And O my people! **ask** forgiveness of your Lord,
011:061 then **ask** forgiveness of Him, and turn to Him
011:090 "But **ask** forgiveness of you Lord, and turn
012:029 (O wife), **ask** forgiveness for thy sin, for truly
012:039 "O my two companions of the prison! (I **ask** you):
012:050 thy lord, and **ask** him, 'What was the matter
012:082 **Ask** at the town where we have been and the
012:097 "O our father! **ask** for us forgiveness for our sins,
012:098 He said: "Soon will I **ask** my Lord for forgiveness
012:104 And no reward dost thou **ask** of them for this:
013:006 They **ask** thee to hasten on the evil
014:034 And He giveth you of all that ye **ask** for.
016:043 realize this not, **ask** of those who possess the Message.
017:085 They **ask** thee concerning the Spirit. Say: "The
017:101 We did give Nine Clear Signs: **ask** the Children of Israel:
018:070 follow me, **ask** me no questions about anything
018:076 (Moses) said: "If ever I **ask** thee about anything
018:083 They **ask** thee concerning Zul-Qarnain. Say, "I
020:105 They **ask** thee concerning the mountains: say, "My
020:132 We **ask** thee not to provide sustenance:
021:007 know this not, **ask** of those who possess the Message.
021:037 show you My Signs; so **ask** Me not to hasten them!
021:063 **Ask** them, if they can talk."
022:047 Yet they **ask** thee to hasten on the Punishment!
023:101 nor will one **ask** after another!
023:113 but **ask** those who keep account."
024:033 your slaves **ask** for a deed in writing (for emancipation)
024:058 you who have not come of age **ask** your permission
024:059 let them (also) **ask** for permission, as do those before
024:062 who **ask** for the leave are those who believe in Allah
024:062 so when they **ask** for thy leave, for some business of their,
024:062 whom thou wilt, and **ask** Allah for their forgiveness;
025:017 He will **ask**: "Was it ye who led these My servants astray.
025:057 Say: "No reward do I **ask** of you for it but this:
025:059 **ask** thou, then, about Him of any acquainted
026:109 "No reward do I **ask** of you for it: my reward
026:127 "No reward do I **ask** of you for it: my reward
026:145 "No reward do I **ask** of you for it: my reward
026:164 "No reward do I **ask** of you for it: my reward
026:180 "No reward do I **ask** of you for it: my reward
026:204 Do they then **ask** for Our Chastisement to be
027:046 If only ye **ask** Allah for forgiveness, ye may
027:046 He said: "O my people! why **ask** ye to hasten
029:053 They **ask** thee to hasten on the Punishment
029:054 They **ask** thee to hasten on the Punishment:
029:061 If indeed thou **ask** them who has created
029:063 And if indeed thou **ask** them who it is that sends
031:025 If thou **ask** them, who it that created the heavens
033:013 And a band of them **ask** for leave of the Prophet,
033:053 And when ye **ask** (his ladies) for anything
033:053 **ask** them from before a screen: that makes for greater
033:063 Men **ask** thee concerning the Hour: say, "The
034:047 Say: "Whatever reward do I **ask** of you:
036:021 "Obey those who **ask** no reward of you
037:011 Just **ask** their opinion: are they

ASK (continued)

037:149 Now **ask** them their opinion: is it
038:086 Say: "No reward do I **ask** of you
039:038 If indeed thou **ask** them who it is that created
040:055 and **ask** forgiveness for thy fault, and celebrate
041:006 the straight path unto Him and **ask** for His forgiveness."
041:010 alike for (all) who **ask**.
041:031 therein shall ye have all that ye **ask** for!-
042:023 Say: "No reward do I **ask** of you for this
043:087 If thou **ask** them, Who Created them, they will
047:019 and **ask** forgiveness for thy fault,
047:036 and will not **ask** you (to give up) your possession.
047:037 If He were to **ask** you for all of them,
048:011 do thou then **ask** forgiveness for us."
050:030 The Day We will **ask** Hell, "Art thou filled to the full?"
051:012 They **ask**, "When will be the Day of Judgment
051:014 this is what ye used to **ask** to be hastened!"
051:059 then let them not **ask** Me to hasten (that portion)!
052:040 Or is it that thou dost **ask** for a reward,
060:010 **ask** for what ye have spent on their dowers
060:010 and let the (Unbelievers) **ask** for what they have spent
067:008 its Keepers will **ask**, "Did no Warner come to you?"
067:025 They **ask**: When will this promise be (fulfilled)?
068:040 **Ask** thou of them, which of them will stand
068:046 Or is it that thou dost **ask** them for a reward,
070:010 And no friend will **ask** after a friend,
071:010 "Saying, `**Ask** forgiveness from your Lord, for He
074:041 And (**ask**) of the Sinners:
079:042 They **ask** thee about the Hour,-'When will

ASKED

002:119 be **asked** of Companions of the blazing fire.
002:134 ye shall not be **asked** about what they did.
002:141 Ye shall not be **asked**!
004:064 and the Messenger had **asked** forgiveness for them,
004:064 come unto thee and **asked** Allah's forgiveness,
004:153 indeed they **asked** Moses for an even greater (miracle),
007:160 when his (thirsty) people **asked** him for Water:
009:038 that when ye are **asked** to go forth in the Cause of Allah,
010:072 no reward have I **asked** of you: my reward
015:048 nor shall they (ever) be **asked** to leave.
018:077 they **asked** them for food, but they refused them
023:072 Or is it that thou **asked** them for some recompense?
024:027 until ye have **asked** permission and saluted
024:028 if ye are **asked** to go back, go back:
024:062 do not depart until they have **asked** for his leave;
027:042 So when she arrived, she was **asked**, "Is this
027:044 She was **asked** to enter the lofty Palace:
037:024 "But stop them, for they must be **asked**:
038:024 We had tried him: he **asked** forgiveness of his Lord,
038:039 no account will be **asked**."
046:034 (they will be **asked**), "Is this not the Truth?"
055:039 will be **asked** of man or Jinn as to his sin,
070:001 A questioner **asked** about a Chastisement to befall-

ASKING

011:047 from **asking** Thee for that of which i have no knowledge
041:049 Man does not weary of **asking** for good (things),
046:024 it is the (calamity) ye were **asking** to be hastened!-
070:025 is deprived (for some reason from **asking**);

ASKS

070:025 For the (needy) who **asks** and him who is deprived
093:010 Nor repulse him who **asks**;

ASLEEP
007:097 Our wrath by night while they were **asleep**?
018:018 have thought them awake, whilst they were **asleep**,
068:019 (which swept away) all around, while they were **asleep**.
ASPECTS
039:023 (yet) repeating (its teaching in various **aspects**):
ASPIRATIONS
083:026 and for this let those aspire, who have **aspirations**:
ASPIRE
083:026 and for this let those **aspire**, who have aspirations:
ASS
031:019 of sounds without doubt is the braying of the **ass**."
ASSAIL
007:200 If a suggestion from Satan **assail** thy (mind),
ASSAULT
004:102 to **assault** you in a single rush.
005:023 they said: "**Assault** them at the (proper) Gate:
007:017 "Then will I **assault** them from before them
ASSAULTS
007:201 when a thought of evil from Satan **assaults** them,
017:064 make **assaults** on them with thy cavalry and thy infantry;
ASSEMBLE
020:064 And then **assemble** in (serried) ranks:
075:003 Does man think that We cannot **assemble** his bones?
ASSEMBLED
009:003 people (**assembled**) on the day of the Great Pilgrimage,-
020:059 be **assembled** when the sun is well up."
026:039 "Are ye (now) **assembled**?"-
ASSEMBLES
064:009 The Day that He **assembles** you (all) for a day
ASSEMBLIES
038:019 And the birds gathered (in **assemblies**):
058:011 when you are told to make room in the **assemblies**,
ASSEMBLY
002:125 of **assembly** for men and a place of safety;
006:128 (and say): "O ye **assembly** of Jinns much (toll)
006:130 "O ye **assembly** of Jinns and men! came there
019:073 sides is best in point of position and fairer in **assembly**?"
037:008 in the direction of the Exalted **Assembly** and they
042:007 and warn (them) of the Day of **Assembly**, of which
055:033 O ye **assembly** of Jinns and men! If it be
062:009 proclaimed to prayer of Friday (the Day of **Assembly**),
064:009 Day that He assembles you (all) for a day of **Assembly**,-
ASSERT
012:018 against that which ye **assert**, it is
012:077 and Allah knoweth best the truth of what ye **assert**!"
016:062 and their tongues **assert** the falsehood that the
023:024 his wish is to **assert** his superiority over you:
ASSES
074:050 As if they were affrighted **asses**,
ASSIDUOUS
006:156 that they learned by **assiduous** study;"
ASSIDUOUSLY
021:052 to which ye are (so **assiduously**) devoted?"
ASSIGN
013:016 Or do the **assign** to Allah partners who have created
016:056 And they (even) **assign**, to things they do not know,
016:057 And they **assign** daughters for Allah!-
ASSIGNED
003:037 to the care of Zakariya was she **assigned**.
004:005 which Allah has **assigned** to you to manage,

ASSIGNED (continued)
005:021 which Allah hath **assigned** unto you, and turn
006:136 they **assigned** Him a share:
008:041 a fifth share is **assigned** to Allah,-
015:004 had not a term decreed and **assigned** beforehand.
015:044 is a (special) class (of sinners) **assigned**.
033:050 the captives of war whom Allah has **assigned** to thee;
041:012 and He **assigned** to each heaven its duty and command.
046:019 And to all are (**assigned**) degrees according to
ASSIGNING
007:033 **assigning** of partners to Allah, for which He hath given
022:031 and never **assigning** partners to Him:
ASSIGNS
022:031 if anyone **assigns** partners to Allah, he is
ASSIST
002:085 **assist** (their enemies) against them,
005:012 believe in Mu Messengers, honour and **assist** them,
008:009 "I will **assist** you with a thousand of the angels,
048:009 that ye may **assist** and honor him, and celebrate
ASSISTANCE
008:009 Remember ye implored the **assistance** of your Lord.
035:037 Therein will they cry aloud (for **assistance**): "Our Lord!
ASSISTED
037:172 That they would certainly be **assisted**,
ASSISTING
028:048 "Two kinds of sorcery, each **assisting** the other!"
ASSOCIATE
002:187 so now **associate** with them,
002:187 but do not **associate** with your wives while
003:064 that we **associate** no partners with Him;
006:080 I fear not (the beings) ye **associate** with Allah:
006:081 (the beings) ye **associate** with Allah, when ye
009:031 from having the partners they **associate** (with Him).
018:038 and none shall I **associate** with my Lord.
022:026 "**Associate** not anything (in worship) with Me;
024:055 and not **associate** aught with Me.'
027:059 or the false gods they **associate** (with Him)?
027:063 High is Allah above what they **associate** with Him!
052:043 the things they **associate** with Him!
060:012 not **associate** in worship any other thing
ASSOCIATED
043:018 in a dispute (to be **associated** with Allah)?
ASSOCIATES
036:056 They and their **associates** will be in pleasant
ASSOCIATING
012:106 not in Allah without **associating** (others as partners)
ASSOCIATING
014:022 I reject your former act in **associating** me with Allah.
ASSURANCE
002:004 have the **assurance** of the Hereafter.
002:248 with (an **assurance**) therein of security
003:126 and an **assurance** to your hearts:
008:010 and an **assurance** to your heart:
045:032 and we have no firm **assurance**.'
ASSURE
012:037 (I **assure** you) abandoned the ways of a people
041:047 "We do **assure** Thee not one of us can bear witness!"
ASSURED
002:273 be **assured** Allah knoweth it well.
005:049 And if they turn away, be **assured** that for some
005:050 But who, for a people whose faith is **assured**,

ASSURED (continued)

012:054 he said: "Be **assured** this day, thou art
044:007 if ye (but) have an **assured** faith.
045:004 are Signs for those of **assured** Faith.
045:020 and a Guidance and Mercy to those of **assured** Faith.
051:020 On the earth are Signs for those of **assured** Faith,
056:095 Verily, this is the very Truth of **assured** Certainty.
069:051 But verily it is Truth of **assured** certainty.

ASSUREDLY

009:025 **Assuredly** Allah did help you in many
010:045 **assuredly** those will be lost who denied the meeting
010:055 that Allah's promise is **assuredly** true?
015:009 and We will **assuredly** guard it (from corruption).
015:025 **Assuredly** it is thy Lord who will gather them
015:064 and **assuredly** we tell the truth.
016:036 For We **assuredly** sent amongst every People
016:041 We will **assuredly** give a goodly home in this
022:067 for thou art **assuredly** on the Right Way.
026:167 O Lut! thou wilt **assuredly** be cast out!"
028:082 those who reject Allah will **assuredly** never prosper."
035:031 for Allah is **assuredly**-with respect to His servants-
040:057 **Assuredly** the creation of the heavens and the
077:007 **Assuredly**, what ye are promised must come to pass.

ASTRAY

001:007 and who go not **astray**.
002:198 even though, before this, ye went **astray**.
003:069 But they shall lead **astray** (not you),
003:069 the People of the Book to lead you **astray**.
003:090 for they are those who have gone **astray**.
004:060 lead them **astray** far away (from the Right).
004:113 only lead their own souls **astray**,
004:113 have plotted to lead thee **astray**.
004:136 hath gone far, far **astray**.
005:060 and far more **astray** from the even Path!"
006:077 I shall surely be among those who go **astray**."
006:140 They have indeed gone **astray** and heeded
006:144 to lead **astray** men without knowledge?
007:175 so Satan followed him up, and he went **astray**.
011:034 if it be that Allah willeth to leave you **astray**:
012:030 we see she is evidently going **astray**."
014:003 they are **astray** by a long distance.
014:004 So Allah leads **astray** those whom He
014:036 led **astray** many among mankind:
015:056 the mercy of his Lord, but such as go **astray**?"
017:015 who goeth **astray** doth so to his own loss:
017:048 but they have gone **astray**, and never
017:072 and most **astray** from the Path.
017:097 but he whom He leaves **astray**-for such wilt thou
018:051 as helpers such as lead (men) **astray**!
019:075 Say: "Whoever goes **astray**, (Allah) Most
020:079 Pharaoh led his people **astray** instead of
020:085 the Samiri has led them **astray**."
022:004 for friendship, him will he lead **astray**, and he
022:009 in order to lead (men) **astray** from the
023:106 and we became a people **astray**!
025:009 But they have gone **astray**, and never
025:017 "Was it ye who led theses my servants **astray**,
025:029 "He did lead me **astray** from the Message
025:034 and, as to path, most **astray**.
025:044 they are farther **astray** from the way.
026:086 for that he is among those **astray**;
028:050 and who is more **astray** than one who follows his own
028:063 "Our Lord! These are the ones whom we led **astray**:

ASTRAY (continued)

028:063 we led them **astray**, as we were **astray** ourselves:
030:029 whom Allah leaves **astray**?
034:050 Say: "If I am **astray**, I only stray to the loss of my
036:062 "But he did lead **astray** a great multitude of you.
037:032 "We led you **astray**: for truly we were ourselves **astray**."
037:071 many of the ancients went **astray**;-
038:026 for those who wander **astray** from the Path
038:082 I will lead them all **astray**.
039:037 there can be none to lead **astray**.
041:052 Who is more **astray** than one who is in a schism far
042:018 dispute concerning the Hour are far **astray**.
042:044 For any whom Allah leaves **astray**, there is
045:023 Allah has, knowing (him as such), left him **astray**,
046:005 And who is more **astray** than one who invokes,
050:027 but he was (himself) far **astray**."
053:002 Your Companion is neither **astray** nor being misled,
083:032 "Behold! these are the people truly **astray**!"
105:002 Did He not make their treacherous plan go **astray**?

ASUNDER

002:074 when split **asunder** send fort water;
013:025 their word thereto and cut **asunder** those things
013:031 or the earth were cloven **asunder**, or the dead
017:037 rend the earth **asunder**, nor reach the mountains
019:090 the earth to split **asunder**, and the mountains to fall
021:030 before We clove them **asunder**?
025:025 rent **asunder** with clouds, and angels
042:005 The heavens are almost rent **asunder** from above
050:044 The Day when the Earth will be rent **asunder**,
054:001 and the moon was cleft **asunder**.
055:037 When the sky is rent **asunder**, and it becomes
059:021 and cleave **asunder** for the fear of Allah, such are
069:016 And the sky will be rent **asunder**, for it
073:018 Whereon the sky will be cleft **asunder**?
077:009 When the heaven is cleft **asunder**;
082:001 When the Sky is cleft **asunder**;
084:001 When the Sky is rent **asunder**,

ASYLUM

008:026 but He provided a safe **asylum** for you,
008:072 who gave (them) **asylum** and aid,-these are
008:074 as well as those who give (them) **asylum** and aid,-
009:006 If one amongst the Pagans ask thee for **asylum**,

AT

002:086 who buy the life of the world **at** the price of Hereafter:
002:102 as came down **at** Babylon to the angels Harut and Marut.
002:147 so be not **at** all in doubt.
002:158 the House in the Season or **at** other times,
002:185 So every one of you who is present (**at** his home)
002:191 but fight them not **at** the Sacred Mosque,
002:198 praises of Allah **at** the Sacred Monument,
002:212 and they scoff **at** those who believe.
002:249 he said: "Allah will test you **at** the stream;
002:259 but look **at** thy food and thy drink;
002:259 look further **at** the bones,
002:259 and look **at** thy donkey:
002:267 and do not even aim **at** anything which is bad,
003:064 say ye: "Bear witness that we (**at** least) are Muslims
003:072 but reject it **at** the end of the day:
003:077 or look **at** them on the Day of Judgement,
003:096 appointed for men was that **at** Bakka:
003:119 they bite off very tips of their fingers **at** you in their rage.
003:120 But if some misfortune overtakes you, they rejoice **at** it.
003:121 to post the Faithful **at** their stations for battler:

AT (continued)

003:123 Allah had helped you **at** Badr, when ye
003:153 without even casting a side glance **at** anyone,
003:167 or (**at** least) drive (the foe from your city)."
003:168 while they themselves sit (**at** ease):
003:177 Those who purchase Unbelief **at** the price of Faith,
004:008 But if **at** the time of division other relatives,
004:023 and two sisters in wedlock **at** one and the same time,
004:046 and "Do hear"; and "Do look **at** us":
004:077 When (**at** length) the order for fighting
004:086 more courteous, (**at** least) of equal courtesy.
004:092 to a people **at** war with you, and he was Believer,
004:095 Not equal are those Believers who sit (**at** home),
004:095 their goods and persons than those who sit (**at** home).
004:095 above those who sit **at** home by a great reward.
004:103 on Believers **at** stated times.
005:023 they said: "Assault them **at** the (proper) Gate:
006:005 the news of what they used to mock **at**.
006:008 the matter would be settled **at** once, and no
006:058 matter would be settled **at** once between you and me.
006:061 **At** length, when death approaches one of you.
006:138 and cattle on which (**at** slaughter) the name
007:007 for We were never absent (**at** any time or place).
007:025 but from it shall ye be taken out (**at** last)."
007:029 (to Him) **at** every time and place of prayer,
007:031 your beautiful apparel **at** every time and place of prayer:
007:198 looking **at** thee, but they see not.
008:001 Say: "(Such) spoils are **at** the disposal of
008:035 Their prayer **at** the house (of Allah) is nothing
008:036 regrets and sighs; **at** length they will be overcome:
008:050 of the Unbelievers (**at** death), (how) they
009:018 and fear none (**at** all) except Allah.
009:065 Say: "Was it **at** Allah, and His Signs, and His
009:084 that dies, nor stand **at** his grave;
009:086 we would be with those who sit (**at** home)."
009:087 who remain behind (**at** home):
009:127 they look **at** each other, (saying), "Doth anyone
010:011 then would their respite be settled **at** once.
010:043 And among them are some who look **at** thee:
010:051 "Would ye then believe in it **at** last, when it
010:052 "**At** length will be said to the wrong-doers:
010:090 **At** length, when overwhelmed with the flood, he said
010:104 Who will take your souls (**at** death):
011:008 which they used to mock **at**!
011:040 **At** length, behold! there came Our Command,
011:041 whether it move or be **at** rest!
011:057 "If ye turn away,-I (**at** least) have conveyed
011:073 They said: "Dost thou wonder **at** Allah's decree?
011:114 two ends of the day and **at** the approaches of the night:
011:114 And establish regular prayers **at** the two ends
012:028 he saw his shirt,-that it was torn **at** the back,
012:029 for truly thou hast been **at** fault!
012:065 and add (**at** the same time) a full camel's load
012:069 so grieve not **at** aught of their doings."
012:070 **At** length when he had furnished them forth
012:076 **at** length He brought it out of his brother's baggage.
012:082 Ask **at** the town where we have been and the
012:097 for we were truly **at** fault."
012:101 Take Thou my soul (**at** death) as one submitting
013:005 If thou dost marvel (**at** their want of faith),
013:036 rejoice **at** what hath been revealed unto thee:
014:021 can ye then avail us **at** all against the
014:025 It brings forth its fruit **at** all times, by the

AT (continued)

015:061 **At** length when the messengers arrived among
015:067 came in (mad) joy (**at** news of the young men).
015:073 overtook them **at** sunrise,
015:088 (Wistfully) **at** what We have bestowed on certain
015:097 is distressed **at** what they say.
016:034 (Wrath) **at** which they had scoffed hemmed them in.
016:048 Do they not look **at** Allah's creation.
016:070 and takes your souls **at** death;
016:079 Do they not look **at** the birds, held poised
016:086 throw back their word **at** them (and say): "Indeed ye are
017:067 When distress seizes you **at** sea, those that
017:078 Establish regular prayers-**at** the sun's decline
017:106 recite it to men **at** intervals:
018:012 best **at** calculating the term of years they had tarried!
018:018 if thou hadst looked **at** them, thou wouldst
018:019 (**At** length) they (all) said, "Allah (alone)
018:022 doubtfully guessing **at** the unknown;
018:058 (**at** once) to account for what they have earned,
018:062 suffered much fatigue **at** this (stage of) our journey."
018:096 **At** length, when he had filled up the space
019:027 **At** length she brought the (babe) to her people,
019:075 they will **at** length realize who is worst
019:090 **At** it the skies are about to burst, the earth
020:010 or find some guidance **at** the fire."
020:097 now look **at** thy god, of whom thou hast become a
020:130 of the night, and **at** the sides of the day;
021:036 And they blaspheme **at** the mention of the Most
021:068 your gods, if ye do (anything **at** all)!"
023:015 After that, **at** length, ye will die.
023:110 while ye were laughing **at** them!
025:004 and others have helped him **at** it."
025:027 will bite **at** his hands, he will say, "Oh! would
025:032 "Why is not the Qur'an revealed to him all **at** once?"
025:073 droop not down **at** them as if they were deaf
026:006 the truth of what they mocked **at**!
026:007 Do they not look **at** the earth,-how many
026:060 So they pursued them **at** sunrise.
026:206 Yet there comes to them **at** length the (Punishment)
027:018 **At** length, when they came to a valley of ants,
027:019 So he smiled, amused **at** her speech;
027:049 'We were not present **at** the slaughter of his
028:012 And We ordained that he refused suck **at** first,
028:015 And he entered the City **at** a time when its
028:023 And when he arrived **at** the watering (place)
028:046 Nor wast thou **at** the side of (the Mountain of) Tur
028:070 To him be praise, **at** the first and the last:
030:008 with their Lord (**at** the Resurrection)!
031:018 "And swell not thy check (for pride) **at** men.
033:050 and not for the Believers (**at** large);
033:053 ye should marry his windows after him **at** any time.
034:014 gnawing away **at** his staff:
034:019 **At** length We made them as a tale (that is told),
034:023 from their hearts (**at** the Day of Judgement, then)
035:017 Nor is that (**at** all) difficult for Allah.
036:078 and decomposed ones (**at** that)?"
037:005 and Lord of every point **at** the rising of the sun!
037:088 Then did he cast a glance **at** the Stars,
037:089 And he said, "I am indeed sick (**at** heart)!"
038:017 Have patience **at** what they say, and remember
038:018 Our Praises, **at** eventide and **at** break of day,
038:031 Behold! there were brought before him, **at** eventide,
038:051 Therein will they recline (**at** ease);

AT (continued)

038:051 therein can they call (**at** pleasure) for fruit
039:029 belonging to many partners **at** variance with each other,
039:042 It is Allah that takes the souls (of men) **at** death;
039:048 which they used to mock **at**!
039:075 between them (**at** Judgement) will be in (perfect)
040:020 will not (be in a position) to judge **at** all.
040:034 **at** length, when he died, ye said: 'No messenger will
040:049 us the Chastisement for a Day (**at** least)!"
040:083 but that very (Wrath) **at** which they were
041:020 **At** length, when they reach the (Fire),
041:026 this Qur'an, but talk **at** random in the midst
041:036 And if (**at** any time) an incitement to discord
041:043 surely thy Lord has **at** His command (all) Forgiveness
042:017 the Hour is close **at** hand?
042:021 would have been decided between them (**at** once):
043:038 **At** length, when (such a one) comes to Us,
043:047 behold, they laughed **at** them.
043:055 When **at** length they provoked Us, We exacted
044:021 believe me not, **at** least keep yourselves away from me."
045:033 by that which they used to mock **at**!
046:006 when mankind are gathered together (**at** the Resurrection),
046:015 **At** length, when he reaches the age of full strength
046:026 they used to mock **at**!
047:004 ye meet the Unbelievers (in fight), Smite **at** their necks,
047:004 **at** length, when ye have thoroughly subdued them,
047:020 of one in swoon **at** the approach of death.
047:020 is a disease looking **at** thee with a look of one
047:027 take their souls **at** death, and smite
047:038 are niggardly are so **at** the expense of their
048:011 Say: "Who then has any power **at** all (to intervene)
048:029 As a result, it fills the Unbelievers with rage **at** them..
049:011 let not some men among you laugh **at** others:
049:011 nor let some women laugh **at** others:
050:006 Do they not look **at** the sky above them?-
052:049 and **at** the setting of the stars!
053:009 And was **at** a distance of but two bow-lengths
053:013 For indeed he saw him **at** a second descent,
053:059 Do ye then wonder **at** this recital?
058:013 then (**at** least) establish regular prayer;
059:002 their homes **at** the first gathering (of the forces).
063:004 When thou lookest **at** them, their bodies
065:001 divorce them **at** their prescribed periods, and count
067:027 **At** length, when they see it close **at** hand, grieved will
069:014 and they are crushed **at** one stroke,-
071:018 and raise you forth (again **at** the Resurrection)?
072:024 **At** length, when they see (with their own eyes)
074:031 that the People of the Book may arrive **at** certainty,
075:007 **At** length, when the Sight is dazed,
079:046 or (**at** most till) the following morn!
080:024 Then let man look **at** his Food, (and how We provide it).
080:033 **At** length, when there comes the Deafening Noise,-
083:029 Those in sin used to laugh **at** those who believed,
083:030 used to wink **at** each other (in mockery);
083:034 will laugh **at** the Unbelievers:
088:017 Do they not look **at** the Camels, how they are made?-
088:018 And **at** the Sky, how it is raised high?-
088:019 And **at** the Mountains, how they are fixed firm?-
088:020 And **at** the Earth, how it is spread out?

ATE

005:093 there is no blame for what they **ate** (in the past),
020:121 In the result, they both **ate** of the tree, and so
021:008 Nor did We give them bodies that **ate** no food,

ATE (continued)

025:020 who **ate** food and walked through the markets.

ATOM

010:061 (so much as) the weight of an **atom** on the
034:003 the least little **atom** in the Heavens or on earth:
034:022 not the weight of an **atom**,-in the heavens or on earth:

ATOMS

056:005 And the mountains shall be crumbled to **atoms,**

ATOM'S

099:007 an **atom's** weight of good, see it!
099:008 an **atom's** weight of evil, shall see it.

ATONE

012:075 be held (as bondman) to **atone** for the (crime).

ATONEMENT

005:045 it is an act of **atonement** for himself.
005:095 or by way of **atonement**, the feeding

ATTACK

004:101 for fear the Unbelievers may **attack** you:
007:176 if you **attack** him, he lolls
008:019 if ye return (to the **attack**), so shall We.
009:012 and **attack** your Faith,- fight ye
022:072 They nearly **attack** with violence those who rehearse
027:049 that we shall make a secret night **attack** on him
033:013 Ye cannot stand (the **attack**)! Therefore go

ATTACKED

009:013 plotted to expel the Messenger, and **attacked** you first?
026:227 and defend themselves after they are unjustly **attacked**.
059:011 and if ye are **attacked** (in fight) we will help you."
059:012 and if they are **attacked** (in fight), they will never help

ATTAIN

003:092 By no means shall ye **attain** righteousness unless
003:104 they are the ones to **attain** felicity.
006:152 until he **attain** the age of full strength;
017:023 Whether one or both of them **attain** old age
018:020 and in that case ye would never **attain** prosperity."
018:082 Lord desired they should **attain** their age of full strength
028:080 but this none shall **attain**, save those who steadfastly
040:036 that I may **attain** the ways and means-
040:056 greatness, which they shall never **attain** to:
040:080 that ye may through them **attain** to any need
092:021 And soon will they **attain** (complete) satisfaction.

ATTAINED

012:022 When Joseph **attained** his full manhood, We gave
033:071 has already **attained** the great victory.

ATTAINMENT

013:022 the final **attainment** of the (Eternal) Home,-
053:030 That is their **attainment** of Knowledge.

ATTAINS

003:097 whoever enters it **attains** security;
017:034 until he **attains** the age of full strength;
046:015 the age of full strength and **attains** forty years,

ATTEND

012:013 devour him while ye **attend** no to him."
080:006 To him dost thou **attend**;

ATTENDANCE

026:071 and we remain constantly in **attendance** on them."

ATTENDANT

018:060 Behold, Moses said to his **attendant**, "I will
018:062 Moses said to his **attendant**: "Bring us

ATTENDANTS

024:031 or male **attendants** free of sexual desires.

ATTENDING
024:058 to move about **attending** to each other:

ATTENTION
007:204 listen to it with **attention,** and hold
024:031 their feet in order to draw **attention** to their
094:008 And to thy Lord turn (all) thy **attention**.

ATTEST
003:050 to **attest** the Torah which was before me.

ATTRACT
033:052 even though their beauty **attract** thee,

ATTRIBUTE
003:094 invent a lie and **attribute** it to Allah,
006:100 no knowledge, **attribute** to Him sons and daughters,
006:100 (for He is) above what they **attribute** to Him!
010:059 or do ye forge (things) to **attribute** to Allah?"
012:038 and never could we **attribute** any partners
016:062 They **attribute** to Allah what they hate
021:022 (high is He) above what they **attribute** to Him!
023:091 (sort of) things they **attribute** to Him!
023:092 for the partners they **attribute** to Him!
030:040 the partners they **attribute** (to Him)!
034:033 and to **attribute** equals to Him!"
039:067 High is He above the Partners they **attribute** to Him!
043:015 Yet they **attribute** to some of His servants
043:082 He is free from the things they **attribute** (to Him)!
059:023 the partners they **attribute** to Him.

ATTRIBUTED
019:091 That they **attributed** a son to The Most Gracious.
041:047 "Where are the partners (ye **attributed**) to Me?"

ATTRIBUTES
040:015 Exalted is he in His **attributes**.

ATTRIBUTION
006:139 For their (false) **attribution** (of superstitions to Allah),

AUDLTEROUS
004:025 not fornicators, nor taking **adulterous**:

AUGHT
002:255 nor shall they compass **aught** of his knowledge except
002:264 do nothing with **aught** they have earned.
002:282 and not diminish **aught** of what he owes.
003:010 will avail them **aught** against Allah:
003:116 will avail them **aught** against Allah:
003:120 If **aught** that is good befalls you, it grieves them;
004:171 nor say of Allah **aught** but truth.
005:117 "Never said I to them **aught** except what Thou
009:004 have not subsequently failed you in **aught,**
010:044 Allah will not deal unjustly with man in **aught**:
011:101 nor did they add **aught** (to their lot) but perdition!
011:123 and thy Lord is not unmindful of **aught** that ye do.
012:067 Not that I can profit you **aught** against Allah
012:069 so grieve not at **aught** of their doings."
014:018 no power have they over **aught** that they
016:035 not have worshipped **aught** but Him-neither we
017:093 am I **aught** but a man,-a messenger?"
018:069 nor shall I disobey thee in **aught**."
021:002 Never comes (**aught**) to them of a renewed Message
021:100 nor will they there hear (**aught** else).
024:055 and not associate **aught** with Me.'
025:050 most men are averse (to **aught**) but (rank) ingratitude.
031:033 when no father can avail **aught** for his son,
031:033 nor a son avail **aught** for his father.
036:049 They will not (have to) wait for **aught** but a single Blast:
044:041 The Day when no protector can avail his client in **aught,**

AUGHT (continued)
049:014 He will not belittle **aught** of your deeds:
052:021 (of the fruit) of **aught** of their works:
053:003 Nor does he say (**aught**) of (his own) Desire.
060:004 no power (to get) **aught** on thy behalf from Allah."
072:005 that no man or jinn should say **aught** that is untrue
082:019 shall have power (to do) **aught** for another: for the

AUGUR
027:047 They said: "Ill omen do we **augur** from thee
036:018 The (people) said: "For us, We **augur** an evil

AUNTS
033:050 and daughters of the paternal uncles and **aunts,**
033:050 and daughters of thy maternal uncles and **aunts,**

AUTHORITY
002:247 Allah granteth His **authority** to whom He pleaseth;
002:247 better fitted than he to exercise **authority,**
002:247 exercise **authority** over us when we are better fitted
002:248 "A sign of his **authority** is that there shall come
003:151 for which He had sent no **authority**:
004:059 and those charged with **authority** among you.
004:083 or to those charged with **authority** among them,
004:153 and gave Moses manifest proofs of **authority**.
005:041 thou hast no **authority** in the least for him
007:010 placed you with **authority** on earth, and provided
007:033 for which He hath given no **authority**;
007:071 without **authority** from Allah?
011:096 and an **authority** manifest,
012:040 hath sent down no **authority**:
013:037 to be a judgement of **authority** in Arabic.
014:010 then bring us some clear **authority**."
014:011 an **authority** except as Allah permits. And on
014:022 I had no **authority** over you except to call you,
015:042 "For over My servants no **authority** shalt thou have,
016:099 No **authority** has he over those who believe
016:100 His **authority** is over those only, who take
017:033 We have given his heir **authority** (to demand Qisas or
017:065 no **authority** shalt thou have over them."
017:080 and grant me from Thee an **authority** to aid (me)."
018:015 an **authority** clear (and convincing) for what
018:086 (thou hast **authority**), either to punish them,
022:071 things for which no **authority** has been sent down to them,
023:045 and **authority** manifest,
023:117 he has no **authority** thereof;
024:055 that He will establish in **authority** their religion
028:035 and invest you both with **authority,** so they
030:035 Or have We sent down **authority** to them,
034:021 But he had no **authority** over them,-except that
037:030 "Nor had we any **authority** over you.
037:156 Or have ye an **authority** manifest?
037:157 Then bring ye your Book (of **authority**) if ye be truthful!
040:023 with Our Signs and **Authority** manifest,
040:035 without any **authority** that hath reached them,
040:056 of Allah without any **authority** bestowed on them,-
044:019 for I come to you with **authority** manifest.
047:022 if ye were put in **authority,** that ye will do mischief
051:038 with **authority** manifest.
053:023 for which Allah has sent down no **authority** (whatever).
055:033 pass ye! not without **authority** shall ye be able to pass!
081:021 With **authority** there, (and) faithful of his trust.

AUTHORS
035:043 will hem in only the **authors** thereof.

AVAIL

002:048　a day when one soul shall not **avail** another
002:123　a day when one soul shall not **avail** another,
002:254　when no bargaining (will **avail**),
003:010　will **avail** them aught against Allah:
003:116　will **avail** them aught against Allah:
010:036　can be of no **avail** against Truth.
014:021　can ye then **avail** us at all against the
015:084　And of no **avail** to them was all that they did
020:109　On that Day shall no intercession **avail** except for
026:088　"The Day whereon neither wealth nor sons will **avail**,
030:057　that Day no excuse of theirs will **avail** the Transgressors,
031:033　when no father can **avail** aught for his son,
031:033　nor a son **avail** aught for his father. Verily, the
034:023　"No intercession can **avail** with Him, except for
043:039　it will **avail** you nothing, that day,
044:041　The Day when no protector can **avail** his client
052:046　The Day when their plotting will **avail** them nothing
053:026　will **avail** nothing except after Allah has given

AVAILED

009:025　great numbers elated you, but they **availed** you naught:

AVAILS

053:028　and conjecture **avails** nothing against Truth.

AVERAGE

005:089　on a scale of the **average** for the food

AVERSE

009:008　but their hearts are **averse** from you;
009:046　but Allah was **averse** to their being sent forth;
009:076　(from their Covenant), **averse** (from its fulfillment).
011:028　when ye are **averse** to it?
025:050　be mindful but most men are **averse** (to aught)

AVERSION

025:060　and it increases them in **aversion.**
035:042　to them, it has only increased their **aversion.**
040:010　"Greater was the **aversion** of Allah to you
040:010　to you than (is) your **aversion** to yourselves,

AVERT

003:168　Say: "**Avert** death from your own selves,
004:061　thou seest the Hypocrites **avert** their faces from thee
021:040　power will they have then to **avert** it,
024:008　But it would **avert** the punishment from the wife,
025:019　so ye cannot **avert** (your penalty) nor get help."
025:065　who say, "Our lord! **avert** from us the Wrath of Hell,
028:054　that they **avert** Evil with Good,
052:008　There is none can **avert** it;-

AVERTED

004:055　And some of them **averted** their faces from him:
006:016　if the penalty is **averted** from any, it is

AVERTING

030:043　the Day which there is no chance of **averting**:

AVOID

009:115　makes clear to them as to what they should **avoid**,
023:003　Who **avoid** vain talk;
042:037　Those who **avoid** the greater sins and indecencies
049:012　O ye who believe! **avoid** suspicion as much
053:032　Those who **avoid** great sins and indecent deeds,

AVOIDANCE

025:072　they pass by it with honourable (**avoidance**);

AVOIDED

087:011　But it will be **avoided** by the most

AVOWED

002:168　for he is to you an **avowed** enemy.

AVOWED (continued)

002:208　the Satan for he is to you an **avowed** enemy.
006:142　for he is to you an **avowed** enemy.
007:022　Satan was an **avowed** enemy unto you?"
012:005　for Satan is to man an **avowed** enemy!
017:053　for Satan is to man an **avowed** enemy.
036:060　for that he was to you an enemy **avowed**?-.
043:062　for he is to you an enemy **avowed**.

AWAIT

047:010　and similar (fates **await**) those who reject Allah.
052:030　Or do they say:-"A Poet! we **await** for him some
052:031　Say thou: "**Await** ye!-I too will wait along with you
052:048　Now **await** in patience the command of thy Lord:

AWAITS

020:048　that the Chastisement (**awaits**) those who

AWAKE

017:079　And as for the night keep **awake** a part of it
018:018　Thou wouldst have thought them **awake**, whilst they

AWARE

003:153　For Allah is well **aware** of all that ye do.
004:094　for Allah is well **aware** of all that ye do.
010:036　Verily Allah is well **aware** of all that they do.
012:050　well **aware** of their snare."
031:016　for Allah is subtle and **aware**.
067:014　And He is The Subtle The **Aware**.

AWAY

002:017　Allah took **away** their light
002:020　He could take **away** their faculty
002:020　The lightning all but snatches **away** their sight:
002:101　threw **away** the Book of Allah
002:130　And who turns **away** from the religion
002:134　That was a People that hath passed **away**.
002:141　That was a people that hath passed **away**.
002:214　came to those who passed **away** before you?
002:222　so keep **away** from women in their courses,
002:267　out of it ye may give **away** something,
003:137　that have passed **away** before you:
003:144　many were the Messengers that passed **away** before Him.
003:159　they would have broken **away** from about thee:
003:187　but they threw it **away** behind their backs,
004:019　that ye may take **away** part of the dower
004:027　ye should turn **away** (from Him), far, far **away**.
004:060　lead them astray far **away** (from the Right).
004:080　but if any turn **away**, We have not
004:097　to move yourselves **away** (form evil)?"
004:102　put **away** your arms because of the inconvenience
004:116　hath strayed far, far **away** (from the Right).
004:129　but turn not **away** (from a woman) altogether, so as
004:167　have verily strayed far, far **away** from the Path.
005:043　yet even after that, they would turn **away**.
005:049　And if they turn **away**, be assured that for some
005:075　they are deluded **away** from the truth!
005:075　that passed **away** before him.
006:004　but they turned **away** therefrom.
006:026　and themselves they keep **away**; but they
006:046　took **away** your hearing and your sight, and sealed
006:052　Send not **away** those who call on their Lord
006:052　that thou shouldst turn them **away**, and thus
006:068　turn **away** from them unless they turn
006:095　then how are ye deluded **away** from the truth?
006:116　they will lead thee **away** from the Way of Allah.
006:157　for their turning **away**.

AWAY (continued)

006:157   and turneth **away** therefrom?
006:157   those who turn **away** from Our Signs,
007:038   of the Peoples who passed **away** before you-men
007:134   and we shall send **away** the Children of Israel
007:146   them will I turn **away** from My Signs:
007:199   but turn **away** from the ignorant.
008:020   and turn not **away** from him when ye hear (him speak).
009:003   but if ye turn **away**, know ye
009:030   how they are deluded **away** from the Truth!
009:050   and they turn **away** rejoicing.
009:127   "Doth anyone see you?" Then they turn **away**:
009:129   But if they turn **away**, Say: "Allah sufficeth me:
010:032   How then are ye turned **away**?
010:034   then how are ye deluded **away** (from the truth)?"
010:078   to turn us **away** from the ways We found
010:102   of the men who passed **away** before them?
011:003   But if ye turn **away**, then I fear for you
011:008   nothing will turn it **away** from them,
011:029   but I will not drive **away** (in contempt)
011:030   who would help my against Allah if I drove them **away**?
011:044   the word went forth: "**Away** with those who do wrong!"
011:057   "If ye turn **away**,-I (at least) have conveyed
011:060   **Away** with the 'Ad the People of Hud!
011:068   So **away** with the Thamud!
011:092   For ye cast Him **away** behind your backs
011:095   So **away** with Madyan as were Thamud gone **away**.
012:013   that ye should take him **away**:
012:015   So they did take him **away**, and they
012:024   that We might turn **away** from him (all) evil
012:033   unless Thou turn **away** their snare
012:034   and turned **away** from him their snare:
012:084   And he turned **away** from them, and said: "How great
012:105   Yet they turn (their faces) **away** from them!
013:017   but the torrent bears **away** the foam that
013:030   have (other) Peoples (gone and) passed **away**;
014:010   Ye wish to turn us **away** from what our fathers
015:023   remain Inheritors (after all else passes **away**).
015:081   but they persisted in turning **away** from them.
015:094   and turn **away** from those who join false gods with Allah
016:082   But if they turn **away**, thy duty
017:028   And even if thou hast to turn **away** from them
017:067   He brings you back safe to land, ye turn **away** (from Him).
017:073   to tempt thee **away** from that which We had revealed
017:083   he turns **away** and becomes remote on his side
017:086   We could take **away** that which We have sent thee
018:016   "When ye turn **away** from them and the things
018:017   turning **away** from them to the left, while they
018:053   no means will they find to turn **away** therefrom.
018:057   but turns **away** from them, forgetting the
019:046   now get **away** from me for a good long while!"
019:048   "And I will turn **away** from you (all) and from
019:049   When he had turned **away** from them and from
020:048   those who reject and turn **away**.'"
020:063   and to do **away** with your most cherished way.
020:100   If any do turn **away** therefrom, verily they
020:124   "But whosoever turns **away** from My Message,
021:001   yet they heed not and they turn **away**.
021:024   but most of them know not the Truth, and so turn **away**.
021:032   Yet do they turn **away** from the Signs
021:042   Yet they turn **away** from the remembrance
021:057   after ye go **away** and turn your backs"...
022:022   Every time they wish to get **away** therefrom,

AWAY (continued)

022:073   And if the fly should snatch **away** anything form them,
023:041   So **away** with the people who do wrong!
023:044   so **away** with a people that will not believe!
023:071   but they turn **away** from their admonition.
023:091   each god would have taken **away** what he had created,
024:034   people who passed **away** before you,
024:043   and He turns it **away** from whom He pleases.
024:047   some of them turn **away**: they are not (really) Believers.
024:054   but if ye turn **away**, he is
024:063   doth know those of you who slip **away** under shelter
026:005   the Most Gracious, but they turn **away** therefrom.
026:114   "I am not one to drive **away** those who believe.
027:024   and has kept them **away** from the Path,-so they
027:088   but they shall pass **away** as the clouds pass **away**:
028:020   so get thee **away**, for I do give thee sincere advice."
028:021   He therefore got **away** therefrom, looking about,
028:055   they turn **away** therefrom and say: "To us our
028:057   we should be snatched **away** from our land."
028:087   Let no one turn you **away** from Allah's revelations
029:061   How are they then deluded **away** (from the truth)?
029:067   and that men are being snatched **away** from all
030:052   when they show their backs and turn **away**.
031:007   he turns **away** in arrogance, as if he heard them not,
032:020   every time they wish to get **away** therefrom, they will be
032:022   the Signs of his Lord, and who then **away** therefrom?
032:030   So turn **away** from them, and wait:
033:013   they intended nothing but to run **away**.
033:016   if ye are running **away** from death or slaughter;
033:016   Say: "Running **away** will not profit you if ye
033:038   amongst those of old that have passed **away**.
034:014   gnawing **away** at his staff:
034:016   But they turned **away** (from Allah), and We
036:046   but they turn **away** therefrom.
037:008   and they are cast **away** from every side,
037:010   Except such as snatch **away** something by stealth,
037:090   So they turned **away** from him, and departed.
037:140   When he ran **away** (like slave from captivity)
037:174   So turn thou **away** from them for a little while,
037:178   So turn thou **away** from them for a little while,
038:006   And the leaders among them go **away** (impatiently),
038:006   "Walk ye **away**, and remain constant to your gods!
038:068   "From which ye do turn **away**!
039:006   then how are ye turned **away** (from your true Lord)?
039:021   then He makes it dry up and crumble **away**.
040:062   then how ye are deluded **away** from the Truth!
040:069   How are they turned **away** (from Reality)?-
041:004   yet most of them turn **away**, and so
041:013   But if they turn **away**, say thou: "I have warned
041:025   who have passed **away**, is proved against them;
041:051   he turns **away**, and gets himself remote on his side
042:048   If then they turn **away**, We have not
043:005   Shall We then take **away** the Reminder from you
043:041   Even if We take thee **away**, We shall
043:087   how then are they deluded **away** (from the Truth)?
043:089   But turn **away** from them, and say "Peace!"
044:014   Yet they turn **away** from him and say: "Tutored (by
044:021   at least keep yourselves **away** from me."
046:003   turn **away** from that whereof they are warned.
046:018   generations of Jinns and men, that have passed **away**;
050:004   We already know how much of them the earth takes **away**:
051:002   And those that lift and bear **away** heavy weights;
051:009   Through which are deluded (**away** from the Truth)

AWAY (continued)

051:054 So turn **away** from them: not thine is the blame.
053:029 Therefore shun those who turn **away** from Our Message
054:002 But if they see a Sign, they turn **away**, and say,
054:006 Therefore, (O Prophet,) turn **away** from them.
054:037 snatch **away** his guests from him, but We
057:020 then it becomes dry and crumbles **away**.
059:006 bestowed on His Messenger (and taken **away**) from them
059:007 (and taken **away**) from the people of the townships,-
060:006 But if any turn **away**, truly Allah is Free of all
063:004 How are they deluded (**away** from the Truth)!
063:005 see them turning **away** their faces in arrogance.
064:006 So they rejected (The Message) and turned **away**.
067:005 made such (Lamps) (as) missiles to drive **away** Satans,
068:019 (which swept **away**) all around, while they
070:017 and turn **away** their faces (from the Right),
072:017 But if any turns **away** from the remembrance
074:049 that they turn **away** from admonition?-
075:032 He rejected Truth and turned **away**!
076:027 and put **away** behind them a Day (that will be) hard.
080:001 The (Prophet) frowned and turned **away**,
081:018 And the Dawn as it breathes **away** the darkness;-
082:016 And they will not be able to keep **away** therefrom.
088:023 But if any turn **away** and disbelieve,-
089:004 And by the Night when it passeth **away**;-
096:013 Seest thou if he denies (Truth) and turns **away**?

AWE

013:013 and so do the angels, with **awe**:
013:021 to be joined, hold their Lord in **awe**, and fear
021:028 well-pleased and they stand in **awe** and reverence
021:049 and who hold the Hour (of judgement) in **awe**.
021:090 they used to call on Us in yearning and **awe**.
023:057 Verily those who live in **awe** for fear
042:018 those who believe hold it in **awe**, and know

AWFUL

019:037 of the (coming) Judgement of an **awful** Day!

AYAT

002:099 manifest Signs (**ayat**);

AYATS

010:001 These are the **Ayats** of the Book of Wisdom.
015:001 These are the **Ayats** of Revelation,-of a Qur'an

AYE

009:099 **Aye**, indeed they bring them nearer (to Him):
010:026 they will abide therein (for **aye**)!
010:027 they will abide therein (for **aye**)!
010:053 "Is that true?" Say: "**Aye**! by my Lord! It is
011:023 to dwell therein for **aye**!
013:005 to dwell therein (for **aye**)!
014:023 to dwell therein for **aye** with the leave of their Lord.
018:048 **aye**, ye thought We shall not fulfil the appointment
018:108 Wherein they shall dwell (for **aye**):
020:076 they will dwell therein for **aye**:
025:016 they will dwell (there) for **aye**:
029:058 to dwell therein for **aye**;-an excellent
043:071 and ye shall abide therein (for **aye**).
043:074 of Hell, to dwell therein (for **aye**):
046:014 be Companion of the Garden, dwelling therein (for **aye**):
048:005 beneath which rivers flow, to dwell therein for **aye**,
057:012 To dwell therein for **aye**!
058:017 of the Fire, to swell therein (for **aye**)!
064:010 to dwell therein for **aye**:
098:006 to dwell therein (for **aye**).

AZAR

006:074 Lo! Abraham said to his father **Azar**: "Takest

'AZIZ

012:030 the (great) **'Aziz** is seeking to seduce her slave

'AZIZ'S

012:051 Said the **'Aziz's** wife: "Now is the truth manifest

B

BAAL
037:125 "Will ye call upon **Baal** and forsake

BABBLE
043:083 So leave them to **babble** and play (with vanities)

BABE
019:027 At length she brought the (**babe**) to her people,
019:029 But she pointed to the **babe**.

BABES
022:005 then do We bring you out as **babes**,

BABYLON
002:102 at **Babylon** to the angels Harut and Marut.

BACK
002:015 Allah will throw **back** their mockery on them,
002:064 But ye turned **back** thereafter:
002:083 Then did ye turn **back**,
002:109 you (people) **back** to infidelity after ye have believed,
002:137 but if they turn **back**,
002:189 ye enter your houses from the **back**:
002:205 When he turns his **back**,
002:210 all questions go **back** (for decision).
002:217 turn **back** from their faith and die in unbelief,
002:217 until they turn you **back** from your faith if they can.
002:228 better right to take them **back** in that period,
002:229 to take **back** any of your gifts from (your wives),
002:231 but do not take them **back** to injure them,
002:231 either take them **back** on equitable terms
002:246 they turned **back** except a small band among them.
002:272 shall be rendered **back** to you,
002:281 when ye shall be brought **back** to Allah.
003:020 but if they turn **back**, thy duty
003:023 turn **back** and decline (the arbitration).
003:032 but if they turn **back**, Allah loveth not
003:063 But if they turn **back**,
003:064 If then they turn **back**,
003:072 perchance they may (themselves) turn **back**;
003:075 will (readily) pay it **back**;
003:082 If any turn **back** after this, they are
003:083 and to Him shall they all be brought **back**.
003:127 and they should then be turned **back**,
003:144 If any did turn **back** on his heels,
003:144 will ye then turn **back** on your heels?
003:149 and ye will turn **back** (from Faith)
003:149 they will drive you **back** on your heels,
003:153 in your rear was calling you **back**.
003:155 Those of you who turned **back** on the day
004:020 take not the least bit of it **back**:
004:058 Allah doth command you to render **back** your trusts
004:077 to those who were told to hold **back** their hands
004:091 every time they are sent **back** to temptation, they
005:011 but (Allah) held **back** their hands from you:
005:021 and turn not **back** ignominiously, for then
005:054 you turn **back** from his Faith, soon will
005:096 and fear Allah, to Whom ye shall be gathered **back**.
006:027 "Would that we were but sent **back**!
006:147 never will His wrath be turned **back**.
007:053 Or could we be sent **back**?

BACK (continued)
007:125 "For us, we are but sent **back** unto our Lord."
007:150 When Moses came **back** to his people, angry and
008:016 If any do turn his **back** to them
008:023 turned **back** and declined (faith).
008:058 throw **back** (their covenant) to them,
009:025 did constrain you, and ye turned **back** in retreat.
009:074 but if they turn **back** (to their evil ways),
009:076 and turned **back** (from their Covenant),
009:079 Allah will throw **back** their ridicule on them:
009:081 in their sitting **back** behind the Messenger
009:083 If, then, Allah bring thee **back** to any of them,
009:092 they turned **back**, their eyes streaming with tears
009:094 in the end will ye be brought **back** to Him
009:105 soon will ye be brought **back** to the Knower of what
010:030 they will be brought **back** to Allah their rightful
010:056 and to Him shall ye all be brought **back**.
010:072 "But if ye turn **back**, (consider): no reward
010:107 there is none can keep **back** his favour:
011:008 they are sure to say, "What keeps it **back**?"
011:052 so turn ye not **back** in sin!"
011:076 that cannot be turned **back**!
011:081 and let not any of you look **back**:
011:109 pay them **back** (in full) their portion
011:111 your Lord pay **back** (in full the recompense)
011:123 and to Him goeth **back** every affair
012:025 and she tore his shirt from the **back**:
012:027 is torn from the **back**, then is she the liar,
012:028 that it was torn at the **back**, (her husband)
012:050 (Joseph) said: "Go thou **back** to thy lord,
012:062 in order that they might come **back**.
012:066 be sure to bring him **back** to me unless ye are
012:081 "Turn ye **back** to your father, and say,
012:083 Allah will bring them (**back**) all to me (in the end).
012:088 Then, when they came (**back**) into (Joseph's)
013:011 there can be no turning it **back**, nor will they find,
013:033 but they are kept **back** (thereby) from the Path.
013:041 there is none to put **back** His command:
015:065 let no one amongst you look **back**, but pass on
016:070 sent **back** to a feeble age, so that
016:071 are not going to throw **back** their gifts to those
016:086 But they will throw **back** their word at them
017:067 But when He brings you **back** safe to land, ye turn
017:069 not send you **back** a second time to sea and send
017:094 What kept men **back** from Belief when Guidance
017:100 behold, ye would keep them **back**, for fear
018:018 turned **back** from them in flight, and wouldst
018:036 even if I am brought **back** to my Lord.
018:055 And what is there to keep **back** men from believing,
018:064 so they went **back** on their footsteps, following
018:087 then shall he be sent **back** to his Lord;
020:040 So We brought thee **back** to thy mother, that her
020:060 his plan, and then came (**back**).
020:092 (Moses) said: "O Aaron! what keep thee **back**,
020:111 the man that carries iniquity (on his **back**).
021:109 But if they turn **back**, say: "I have
022:005 and some are sent **back** to the feeblest old age,
022:022 they will be forced **back** therein,
022:025 and would keep **back** (men) from the Way of Allah,
022:076 and to Allah go **back** all affairs (for decision).
023:066 but ye used to turn **back** on your heels-
023:079 and to Him shall ye be gathered **back**.
023:099 he says: "O my Lord! send me **back** to (life),-

BACK (continued)

023:115 brought **back** to Us (for account)"?
024:025 On that Day Allah will pay them **back** (all) their
024:028 to you: if ye are asked to go **back**, go **back**:
024:064 and one day they will be brought **back** to Him,
027:010 a snake, he turn **back** in retreat, and retraced
027:028 then draw **back** from them, and (wait to)
027:037 "Go **back** to them, and be sure we shall come
027:080 (especially) when they turn **back** in retreat.
028:023 until the shepherds take **back** (their flocks):
028:023 who were keeping **back** (their flocks).
028:024 then he turned **back** to the shade, and said:
028:025 came (**back**) to him, walking bashfully.
028:031 he turned **back** in retreat, and retraced
028:070 and to Him shall ye (all) be brought **back**.
028:085 will bring thee **back** to the Place of Return.
028:088 and to Him will ye (all) be brought **back**.
029:038 to them, and kept them **back** from the path,
029:057 in the end to Us shall ye be brought **back**.
030:011 ye be brought **back** to Him.
030:033 turning **back** to Him in repentance:
030:041 in order that they may turn **back** (from Evil).
030:053 Nor canst thou lead **back** the blind from their
032:011 then shall ye be brought **back** to your Lord."
032:012 now then send us **back** (to the world):
033:013 Therefore go **back**!" and a band of them ask for
033:018 who keep **back** (men) and those who say to their
033:025 And Allah turned **back** the Unbelievers for (all)
034:010 echo ye **back** the Praises of Allah with him!
034:030 for a Day, which ye cannot put **back** for an hour
034:031 throwing **back** the word (of blame) on one another!
034:032 "Was it we who kept you **back** from Guidance
035:045 He would not leave on the **back** of the (earth)
036:022 and to Whom ye shall (all) be brought **back**.
036:045 ye may receive Mercy," (they turn **back**).
038:033 "Bring them **back** to me."
038:043 And We gave him (**back**) his people and double
039:038 some Mercy for me, can they keep **back** His Mercy?"
039:042 He keeps **back** (from returning to life), but the
039:044 ye shall be brought **back**."
041:050 but if I am brought **back** to my Lord, I have
042:033 on the **back** of the (ocean).
042:047 will be no putting **back**, because of
043:014 "And to Our Lord, surely, Must We turn **back**!"
043:028 that they may turn **back** (to Allah).
043:085 And to Him shall ye be brought **back**.
044:036 "Then bring (**back**) our forefathers if what
045:015 be brought **back** to your Lord.
045:025 they say, "Bring (**back**) our forefathers,
047:025 Those who turn **back** as apostates after Guidance
047:038 If ye turn **back** (from the Path),
048:016 a goodly reward, but if ye turn **back** as ye
048:017 and he who turns **back**, (Allah) will
048:025 but He held **back** your hands) that He may admit
051:039 But (Pharaoh) turned **back** on account of his might,
053:033 Seest thou one who turns **back**,
056:087 Call **back** the soul, if ye are
057:005 and all affairs go **back** to Allah.
057:013 "Turn ye **back** to your rear!
057:024 And if any turn **back** (from Allah's Way),
058:003 to their wives then wish to go **back** on the words
058:009 and fear Allah, to whom ye shall be brought **back**.
060:010 then send them not **back** to the Unbelievers.

BACK (continued)

062:008 be sent **back** to the Knower of things
064:012 but if ye turn **back**, the duty of Our Messenger
065:002 either take them **back** on equitable terms or part with
066:004 but is ye **back** up each other against him,
066:004 and furthermore, the angels,-will **back** (him) up.
067:004 (thy) vision will come **back** to thee dull
074:023 Then he turned **back** and was haughty;
075:013 and all that he put **back**.
079:022 Further, he turned his **back**, striving hard
082:005 it hath sent forward and (what it hath) kept **back**.
083:036 paid **back** for what they did?
084:010 But he who is given his Record behind his **back**,-
086:008 Surely (Allah) able to bring him **back** (to life)!
089:028 "Come **back** thou to thy Lord,-well pleased
094:003 The which did gall thy **back**?-

BACK-BREAKING

075:025 In the thought that some **back-breaking** calamity was

BACKBITER

104:001 Woe to every (kind of) scandal-monger and **backbiter**,

BACKBONE

086:007 Proceeding from between the **backbone** and the ribs:

BACKED

017:088 even if they **backed** up each other

BACKS

002:101 Book of Allah behind their **backs**,
003:111 they will show you their **backs**, and no help
003:187 but they threw it away behind their **backs**,
006:031 for they bear their burdens on their **backs**;
006:146 except what adheres to their **backs** or their entrails,
008:015 never turn your **backs** to them.
008:050 (how) they smite their faces and their **backs** (saying):
009:035 branded their foreheads their flanks, and their **backs**,
011:092 For ye cast Him away behind your **backs** (with contempt).
017:046 they turn on their **backs**, fleeing (from the Truth).
021:039 the Fire from their faces, not yet from their **backs**,
021:057 after ye go away and turn your **backs**"...
030:052 when they show their **backs** and turn away.
033:015 with Allah not to turn their **backs**,
040:033 A day when ye shall turn your **backs** and flee:
043:013 and square on their **backs**,
047:027 and smite their faces and their **backs**?
048:022 they would certainly turn their **backs**;
049:012 nor speak ill of each other behind their **backs**.
054:045 to flight, and they will show their **backs**.
059:012 they will turn their **backs**;
070:017 Inviting (all) such as turn their **backs** and turn
092:016 Who give the lie to Truth and turn their **backs**.

BACKSLIDE

002:083 and ye **backslide** (even now).
002:209 If ye **backslide** after the clear (Signs)

BAD

002:216 and that ye love a thing which is **bad** for you.
002:267 and do not even aim at anything which is **bad**,
005:100 though the abundance of the **bad** may dazzle thee;
005:100 Say: "Not equal are things that are **bad** and things
007:058 but from the land that is **bad**, springs up
007:157 them from what is **bad** (and impure):
016:059 his people, because of the **bad** news he has had!
038:062 to number among the **bad** ones?

BADE

007:011 then We **bade** the angels prostrate to Adam,

BADR
003:123 Allah had helped you at **Badr**, when ye
BAGGAGE
004:102 negligent of your arms and your **baggage,**
012:065 Then when they opened their **baggage,** they found
012:076 he brought it out of his brother's **baggage.**
012:076 So he began (the search) with their **baggage,**
012:076 before (he came to) the **baggage** of his brother:
BAIT
002:188 nor use it as **bait** for the judges,
BAKE
028:038 light me a (kin to **bake** bricks) out of clay,
BAKED
011:082 **baked** clay, spread, layer on layer,-
015:074 on them brimstones hard as **baked** clay.
105:004 Striking them with stones of **baked** clay.
BAKKA
003:096 House (of worship) appointed for men was that at **Bakka:**
BALANCE
007:008 The **balance** that day will be true
015:019 of things in due **balance.**
017:035 and weigh with a **balance** that is straight:
023:102 Then those whose **balance** (of good deeds)
023:103 But those whose **balance** is light, will be
025:067 but hold a just (**balance**) between those (extremes);
042:017 and the **Balance** and what will make thee realize
055:007 and He has set up the **balance** (of Justice),
055:008 In order that ye may not transgress (due) **balance.**
055:009 and fall not short in the **balance.**
057:025 the book and the **Balance** (of Right and Wrong),
101:006 Then, he whose **balance** (of good deeds) will be
101:008 But he whose **balance** (of good deeds) will be
BALANCED
002:143 an Ummah justly **balanced.**
BALANCING
034:011 of mail, **balancing** well the rings of chain
BAN
021:095 But there is a **ban** on any population which We
BAND
002:246 they turned back except a small **band** among them.
003:104 a **band** of people inviting to all that is good,
003:154 while another **band** was stirred to anxiety
003:154 a **band** of you overcome with slumber,
008:026 Call to mind when ye were a small (**band**),
019:085 like a **band** (presented before a king for honours).
026:054 (Saying): "These (Israelites) are but a small **band**,
033:013 Therefore go back!" and a **band** of them ask for
072:027 and then He makes a **band** of watchers march before
BANDS
003:146 and with them (fought) large **bands** of godly men?
BANISH
002:085 not lawful for you to **banish** them.
002:085 and **banish** a party of you from their homes;
BANISHED
026:212 Indeed they are **banished** from hearing it.
BANISHMENT
059:003 has decreed **banishment** for them, He would
BANK
020:039 the river will cast him up on the **bank,** and he
028:030 he was called from the right **bank** of the valley,
BANQUET
012:031 she sent for them and prepared a **banquet** for them:

BAR
027:061 and made a separating **bar** between the two seas
036:009 And We have put a **bar** in front of them and a
036:009 and a **bar** behind them, and further, We have
091:013 And (**bar** her not from) having her drink!"
BARE
002:264 which leaves it (just) a **bare** stone.
006094 "And behold! ye come to Us **bare** and alone
018:048 come to Us (**bare**) as We created you first:
019:080 and he shall appear before Us **bare** and alone.
032:027 We do drive Rain to parched soil (**bare** of herbage),
033:013 "Truly our houses are **bare** and exposed,"
068:042 The Day that the Shin shall be laid **bare,**
074:011 the (creature) whom I created (**bare** and) alone!-
BARGAIN
003:187 And vile was the **bargain** they made!
009:111 Then rejoice in the **bargain** which ye have
061:010 to a **bargain** that will save you
062:011 But when they see some **bargain** or some pastime,
062:011 than any pastime or **bargain**!
BARGAINING
002:254 when no **bargaining** (will avail),
014:031 neither mutual **bargaining,** nor befriending.
BARREN
002:264 They are in Parable like a hard, **barren** rock,
003:040 seeing I am very old, and my wife is **barren**?"
019:005 but my wife is **barren:**
019:008 have a son, when my wife is **barren** and I have
022:005 thou seest the earth **barren** and lifeless,
022:055 the Chastisement of **a barren** day.
042:050 and He leaves **barren** whom He will:
051:029 "A **barren** old woman!"
BARRENNESS
021:090 We cured his wife's (**barrenness**) for him.
BARRIER
018:094 a **barrier** between us and them?
018:095 a strong **barrier** between you and them:
021:096 and Magog (people) are let through (their **barrier**),
025:022 "There is a **barrier** forbidden (to you)
025:053 yet has He made a **barrier** between them,
034:054 between them and their desires, is placed a **barrier,**
055:020 Between them is a **Barrier** which they
BARRING
003:111 They will do you no harm **barring** a trifling annoyance;
005:013 find them-**barring** a few-ever bent on (new) deceits:
BARTERED
002:016 have **bartered** guidance for error:
012:062 (with which they had **bartered**) into their saddle-bags,
BASE
070:039 out of the (**base** matter) they know!
BASED
007:052 had certainly sent them the Book, **based** on knowledge,
BASHFULLY
028:025 came (back) to him, walking **bashfully.**
BASIC
003:007 in it are verses **basic** or fundamental clear (in meaning);
BASINS
034:013 **Basins** as large as wells, and (cooking)
BATHE
005:006 **bathe** your whole body.
BATTLE
003:121 to post the Faithful at their stations for **battle:**
061:004 in His Cause in **battle** array, as if

BATTLE-FIELDS
009:025 in many **battle-fields** and on the day of Hunain:

BE
001:002 Praise **be** to Allah,
002:027 has ordered to **be** joined,
002:036 On earth will **be** your dwelling place
002:038 on them shall **be** no fear,
002:039 they shall **be** Companions of the Fire;
002:041 and **be** not the first to reject faith therein,
002:043 And **be** steadfast in prayer:
002:048 nor shall anyone **be** helped (from outside).
002:048 nor shall compensation **be** taken from her.
002:048 nor shall intercession **be** accepted for her,
002:052 there was a chance for you to **be** grateful.
002:053 there was a chance for you to **be** guided aright.
002:054 that will **be** better for you
002:056 ye had the chance to **be** grateful.
002:062 on them shall **be** no fear,
002:065 "**Be** ye apes, despised and rejected."
002:068 should **be** neither too old nor too young,
002:083 **be** steadfast in prayer; and Give Zakat.
002:085 they shall **be** consigned to the most
002:086 nor shall they **be** helped.
002:086 their chastisement shall not **be** lightened
002:091 even if it **be** Truth confirming
002:094 "If the last Home, with Allah, **be** for you specially,
002:096 he could **be** given a life of a thousand years:
002:106 We abrogate or cause to **be** forgotten,
002:110 And **be** steadfast in prayer
002:111 enter Paradise unless he **be** a Jew or a Christian."
002:112 on such shall **be** no fear,
002:114 His name should **be** celebrated?
002:116 Glory **be** to Him.
002:117 He saith to it: "**Be**," and it is.
002:119 shall **be** asked of Companions of the blazing fire.
002:120 Jews or the Christians **be** satisfied with thee unless
002:121 the Book study it as it should **be** studied:
002:123 nor shall anyone **be** helped (from outside)
002:123 nor shall compensation **be** accepted from her
002:130 and he will **be** in the Hereafter
002:134 ye shall not **be** asked about what they did.
002:135 if ye would **be** guided (to salvation)."
002:141 Ye shall not **be** asked!
002:143 That ye might **be** witnesses over the nations,
002:147 so **be** not at all in doubt.
002:150 that there **be** no ground of dispute
002:150 and ye may (consent to) **be** guided.
002:152 **Be** grateful to Me, and reject not Faith.
002:155 **Be** sure We shall test you with something
002:158 **be** sure that Allah is He Who recogniseth
002:159 on them shall **be** Allah's curse,
002:162 Their penalty will not **be** lightened,
002:162 nor will respite **be** their (lot).
002:166 relations between them would **be** cut off.
002:167 Nor will there **be** a way for them
002:172 and **be** grateful to Allah,
002:174 grievous will **be** their Chastisement.
002:177 and to **be** firm and patient,
002:177 to **be** steadfast in prayer,
002:178 the limits shall **be** in grave chastisement.
002:181 the guilt shall **be** on those who make the change.
002:184 (should **be** made up) from days later.
002:185 and perchance ye shall **be** grateful.

BE (continued)
002:185 (should **be** made up) by days later.
002:193 But if they cease, let there **be** no hostility
002:197 let there **be** no obscenity, nor wickedness,
002:197 (**be** sure) Allah knoweth it.
002:202 To these will **be** allotted what they have earned.
002:203 ye will surely **be** gathered unto Him.
002:212 But the righteous will **be** above them
002:217 they will **be** Companions of the Fire
002:229 fear that they would **be** unable to keep the limits
002:229 would **be** unable to keep the limits ordained by Allah,
002:233 No mother shall **be** treated unfairly
002:233 An heir shall **be** chargeable in the same way.
002:239 or riding, (as may **be** most convenient),
002:245 and to Him shall **be** your return.
002:251 the earth would indeed **be** full of mischief,
002:256 Let there **be** no compulsion in religion.
002:257 They will **be** Companions of the fire,
002:262 on them shall **be** no fear, nor shall they grieve.
002:264 They will **be** able to do nothing
002:264 spend their wealth to **be** seen of men,
002:266 with fire therein, and **be** burnt up?
002:266 that it should **be** caught in a whirlwind,
002:270 **be** sure Allah knows it all.
002:272 and ye shall not **be** dealt with unjustly.
002:272 shall **be** rendered back to you,
002:273 **be** assured Allah knoweth it well.
002:274 on them shall **be** no fear, nor shall they grieve.
002:275 shall **be** pardoned for the past;
002:277 on them shall **be** no fear,
002:279 and ye shall not **be** dealt with unjustly.
002:281 and none shall **be** dealt with unjustly.
002:281 Then shall every soul **be** paid what it earned,
002:281 when ye shall **be** brought back to Allah.
002:282 whether it **be** small or big:
002:282 it would **be** wickedness in you.
002:282 but if it **be** a transaction which ye carry out
003:011 (Their plight will **be**) no better than that
003:012 "Soon will ye **be** vanquished
003:025 and each soul will **be** paid out just what
003:030 "On the Day when every soul will **be** confronted
003:039 and (**be** besides) noble, chaste, and a Prophet,
003:041 "Shall **be** that thou shalt speak to no man for three
003:044 should **be** charged with the care of Mary:
003:045 his name will **be** Christ Jesus, the son of Mary,
003:046 And he shall **be** (of the company)
003:047 He but saith to it '**Be**,' and it is!
003:052 "Who will **be** my helpers to (the work of) Allah?"
003:059 then said to him: "**Be**": and he was.
003:060 so **be** not of those who doubt
003:073 revelation **be** sent to someone (else) like unto that
003:079 "**Be** ye my worshippers rather than Allah's":
003:079 "**Be** ye worshippers of Him (Who is truly The Cherisher
003:083 and to Him shall they all **be** brought back.
003:085 and in the Hereafter he will **be** in the ranks
003:085 never will it **be** accepted of him;
003:088 nor respite **be** their (lot);
003:088 nor will their punishment **be** lightened,
003:090 never will their repentance **be** accepted;
003:091 never would **be** accepted from any such as much
003:093 if ye **be** men of truth."
003:101 will **be** shown a way that is straight.
003:102 O ye who believe! fear Allah as He should **be** feared,

BE (continued)

003:103 that ye may **be** guided.
003:103 and **be** not divided among yourselves;
003:105 **Be** not like those who are divided amongst themselves
003:106 (will **be** said): "Did ye reject Faith
003:106 some faces will **be** (lit up with) white,
003:106 and some faces will **be** (in the gloom of) black:
003:106 to those whose faces will **be** black,
003:107 But those whose faces will **be** (lit with) white,
003:107 they will **be** in (the light of) Allah's Mercy;
003:115 nothing will **be** rejected of them;
003:116 they will **be** companions of the Fire,
003:117 life of this (material) world may **be** likened
003:127 and they should then **be** turned back,
003:133 **Be** quick in the race for forgiveness
003:140 **be** sure a similar wound hath touched the others.
003:151 their abode will **be** the Fire:
003:156 O ye who believe! **Be** not like the Unbelievers,
003:161 and none shall **be** dealt with unjustly.
003:167 They said: "Had we known there would **be** a fight,
003:171 the Faithful to **be** lost (in the Least).
003:175 **be** ye not afraid of them, but fear Me,
003:180 Nay, it will **be** the worse of them:
003:180 soon it will **be** tied to their necks
003:185 shall you **be** paid your full recompense.
003:186 Ye shall certainly **be** tried and tested
003:188 and love to **be** praised for what they have not done,
003:195 "Never will I suffer to **be** lost the work of any of you,
003:195 **be** he male or female: ye are members, one of another:
004:001 and **be** heedful of the wombs (that bore you):
004:003 ye shall not **be** able to deal justly (with them),
004:003 That will **be** more suitable, to prevent you
004:003 ye shall not **be** able to deal justly with the orphans,
004:007 whether the property **be** small or large,
004:010 they will soon **be** enduring a blazing Fire!
004:013 and that will **be** the Supreme achievement.
004:013 will **be** admitted to Gardens with rivers flowing
004:014 will **be** admitted to a Fire, to abide therein:
004:019 it may **be** that ye dislike a thing,
004:025 they should **be** chaste, not fornicators,
004:029 but let there **be** amongst you traffic and trade
004:038 those who spend of their substance, to **be** seen of men,
004:047 for the decision of Allah must **be** carries out.
004:048 that partners should **be** set up with him;
004:049 and they will not **be** wronged a whit.
004:064 We sent not a Messenger, but to **be** obeyed,
004:073 they would **be** sure to say-as it there had never
004:077 never will ye **be** dealt unjustly in the very least!
004:084 It may **be** that Allah will restrain
004:087 And whose word can **be** truer than Allah's?
004:088 Why should ye **be** divided into two parties
004:089 and thus **be** on the same footing (as they):
004:091 Others you will find that wish to **be** secure from
004:092 blood-money should **be** paid to his family,
004:092 and a believing slave **be** freed.
004:105 so **be** not an advocate for those who
004:122 and whose word can **be** truer than Allah's?
004:123 whoever works evil, will **be** requited accordingly.
004:124 and not the least injustice will **be** done to them.
004:124 **be** they male or female, and have faith,
004:125 Who can **be** better in religion than one
004:135 and whether it **be** (against) rich or poor:
004:140 if ye did, ye would **be** like them.

BE (continued)

004:142 they stand without earnestness, to **be** seen of men,
004:145 The hypocrites will **be** in the lowest of the Fire:
004:146 if so they will **be** (numbered) with the Believers.
004:159 He will **be** a witness against them;
004:171 Say not "Three": desist: it will **be** better for you:
004:171 for Allah is One God: glory **be** to him:
005:005 and in the Hereafter he will **be** in the ranks
005:006 that ye may **be** grateful.
005:008 **Be** just: that is next to Piety: and fear
005:010 will **be** Companions of Hell-fire.
005:021 for then will ye **be** overthrown, to your own ruin."
005:023 when once ye are in, victory will **be** yours;
005:026 the land **be** out of their reach for forty years:
005:027 Said the latter: "**Be** sure I will slay thee."
005:029 for thou wilt **be** among the companions of the Fire,
005:031 "Was I not even able to **be** as this raven, and to
005:032 it would **be** as if he slew the whole people:
005:032 unless it **be** for murder or for spreading
005:032 it would **be** as if he saved the life of the whole people.
005:036 Theirs would **be** a grievous Chastisement.
005:036 it would never **be** accepted of them.
005:037 Their wish will **be** to get out of the Fire,
005:037 their Chastisement will **be** one that endures.
005:041 (whether it **be**) among those who say: "We believe"
005:041 or it **be** among the Jews, men who listen to any lie,-
005:049 And if they turn away, **be** assured that for some
005:053 All that they do will **be** in vain, and they
005:064 **Be** their hands tied up and **be** they accursed for the
005:069 on them shall **be** no fear, nor shall they grieve.
005:071 They thought there would **be** no trial
005:072 There will for the wrong-doers **be** no one to help.
005:072 and the Fire will **be** his abode.
005:086 they shall **be** Companions of Hell-fire.
005:089 that ye may **be** grateful.
005:096 and fear Allah, to Whom ye shall **be** gathered back.
005:101 they will **be** made plain to you:
005:106 even though the (beneficiary) **be** our near relation:
005:106 if we do, then behold! we shall **be** sinners.
005:107 if we did, behold! we will **be** wrong-doers."
005:108 that other oaths would **be** taken after their oaths.
005:113 and that we ourselves may **be** witnesses to the miracle.
005:114 that there may **be** for us-for the first
006:001 Praise **be** to Allah, Who created the heavens
006:008 the matter would **be** settled at once,
006:008 and no respite would **be** granted them.
006:014 and **be** not thou of the company of those
006:014 Say: "Nay! but I am commanded to **be** the first
006:016 and that would **be** a Mighty Triumph.
006:023 There will then **be** (left) no excuse
006:027 when they shall **be** made to stand by the Fire!
006:027 but would **be** amongst those who believe!"
006:029 and never shall we **be** raised up again."
006:030 when they shall **be** made to stand before
006:035 so **be** not thou amongst those who are swayed
006:036 Those who listen (in truth), **be** sure, will accept:
006:036 then will they **be** turned unto Him.
006:038 and they (all) shall **be** gathered to
006:041 and if it **be** His Will, He would
006:045 Praise **be** to Allah, the Cherisher of the Worlds.
006:047 will any **be** destroyed except those who do wrong?"
006:048 upon them shall **be** no fear, nor shall they grieve.
006:050 Say: "Can the blind **be** held equal to the seeing?"

BE (continued)

006:051 that they will **be** brought (to judgment)
006:052 and thus **be** (one) of the unjust.
006:054 "Peace **be** on you: your Lord hath inscribed for
006:055 that the way of the sinners may **be** shown up.
006:056 and **be** not of the company of those who receive
006:058 the matter would **be** settled at once
006:060 in the end unto Him will **be** your return,
006:060 that a term appointed **be** fulfilled;
006:070 (or reparation), none will **be** accepted:
006:070 their religion to **be** mere play and amusement,
006:072 that we shall **be** gathered together."
006:073 the day He saith, "**Be**," Behold! it is.
006:073 His will **be** the dominion the day
006:073 the day the trumpet will **be** blown.
006:077 I shall surely **be** among those who go astray."
006:080 Will ye not (yourselves) **be** admonished?
006:088 all that they did would **be** vain for them.
006:093 Who can **be** more wicked than one who
006:094 whom ye thought to **be** partners in your affairs:
006:100 praise and glory **be** to Him! (for He is)
006:104 if any will **be** blind, it will **be** to his own (harm):
006:104 it will **be** for (the good of) his own soul:
006:114 Never **be** then of those who doubt.
006:121 ye would indeed **be** Pagans.
006:121 that would **be** impiety.
006:122 **be** like him who is in the depths of darkness,
006:124 the wicked **be** overtaken by humiliation before Allah,
006:127 For them will **be** a Home of Peace
006:127 He will **be** their Friend, because they
006:128 He will say: "The Fire **be** your dwelling-place:
006:135 whose end will **be** (best) in the Hereafter:
006:145 unless it **be** dead meat, or blood
006:145 any (meat) forbidden to **be** eaten by one
006:147 never will His wrath **be** turned back.
006:150 **be** not thou amongst them:
006:151 **be** good to your parents;
006:153 thus doth He command you, that ye may **be** righteous.
006:155 so follow it and **be** righteous, that ye
006:160 evil shall only **be** recompensed according to his evil:
006:160 No wrong shall **be** done unto them.
007:002 so let thy heart **be** oppressed no more
007:008 The balance that day will **be** true (to a nicety):
007:008 those whose scale (of good) will **be** heavy,
007:009 Those whose scale will **be** light, will find
007:011 he refused to **be** of those who prostrate.
007:013 it is not for thee to **be** arrogant here: get out,
007:015 (Allah) said: "**Be** thou among those
007:023 we shall certainly **be** lost."
007:024 On earth will **be** your dwelling-place and your
007:025 but from it shall ye **be** taken out (at last)."
007:026 as well as to **be** an adornment to you, but the
007:035 on them shall **be** no fear, nor shall they grieve.
007:040 no opening will there **be** of the gates
007:042 they will **be** Companions of the Garden, therein
007:043 and they shall say: "Praise **be** to Allah, Who
007:043 beneath them will **be** rivers flowing;-
007:046 Between them shall **be** a veil, and on
007:046 and on the Heights will **be** men who would
007:046 "Peace **be** upon you": they have not entered it,
007:047 When their eyes shall **be** turned towards
007:049 Enter ye the Garden: no fear shall **be** on you,
007:051 to **be** mere amusement and play,

BE (continued)

007:053 Or could we **be** sent back?
007:054 and the Command, Blessed **be** Allah, the Cherisher
007:070 if so **be** that thou tellest the truth!"
007:073 or ye shall **be** seized with a grievous punishment."
007:082 who want to **be** clean and pure!"
007:085 that will **be** best for you, if ye have Faith.
007:089 return thereto unless it **be** as in the will
007:090 said: "If ye follow Shu'aib, **be** sure then ye are ruined!"
007:114 for ye shall in that case **be** (raised to posts)
007:124 "**Be** sure I will cut off your hands and your
007:129 He said: "It may **be** that your Lord will destroy
007:132 "Whatever **be** the Signs thou bringest, to work
007:143 "Glory **be** to Thee! To Thee
007:144 and **be** of those who give thanks."
007:147 can they expect to **be** rewarded except
007:149 we shall indeed **be** among the Losers.
007:152 will indeed **be** overwhelmed with wrath
007:158 follow him that (so) ye may **be** guided."
007:166 "**Be** ye apes, despised and rejected."
007:169 "(Everything) will **be** forgiven us."
007:180 for what they do, they will soon **be** requited.
007:185 may well **be** that their term is nigh drawing
007:186 there can **be** no guide;
007:187 when will **be** its appointed time? Say: "The
007:189 we vow we shall (ever) **be** grateful."
007:205 and **be** not thou of those who are unheedful.
008:007 one of the two parties, that it should **be** yours:
008:007 ye wished that the one unarmed should **be** yours,
008:008 distasteful though it **be** to those in guilt.
008:014 Thus (will it **be** said): "Taste ye then
008:016 unless it **be** in a stratagem of war, or to
008:019 good will your forces **be** to you even if they
008:019 it will **be** best for you:
008:021 Nor **be** like those who say, "We hear,"
008:024 ye shall (all) **be** gathered.
008:026 that ye might **be** grateful.
008:034 No men can **be** its guardians except the righteous;
008:035 (its only answer can **be**), "Taste ye the Chastisement
008:036 and the Unbelievers will **be** gathered together
008:036 at length they will **be** overcome:
008:037 They will **be** the ones to have lost.
008:038 their past would **be** forgiven them;
008:040 **be** sure that Allah is your Protector-
008:045 when ye meet a force, **be** firm, and call
008:046 and **be** patient and persevering:
008:047 and to **be** seen of men, and to hinder (men) from
008:047 And **be** not like those who started from their homes
008:058 back (their Covenant) (so as to **be**) on equal terms:
008:060 and ye shall not **be** treated unjustly.
008:060 the cause of Allah, shall **be** repaid unto you,
008:073 (protect each other), there would **be** tumult and
009:006 and then escort him to where he can **be** secure,
009:007 How can there **be** a covenant before Allah
009:008 How (can there **be** such a league), seeing that
009:012 that thus they may **be** restrained.
009:016 Do you think that you would **be** left alone while
009:018 The mosques of Allah shall **be** visited and
009:018 It is they who are expected to **be** on true guidance.
009:024 Say: If it **be** that your fathers, your sons,
009:030 Allah's curse **be** on them:
009:031 their anchorites to **be** their lords beside Allah.
009:032 His light should **be** perfected, even though

BE (continued)

009:035 On the Day **when it will be** heated in the fire of Hell,
009:035 and with it will **be** branded their foreheads,
009:053 not from you will it **be** accepted:
009:064 all that ye fear (should **be** revealed)."
009:064 should **be** sent down about them, showing them
009:073 and **be** firm against them.
009:074 If they repent, it will **be** best for them:
009:075 and **be** truly amongst those who are righteous.
009:086 we would **be** with those who sit (at home)."
009:087 They prefer to **be** with (the women), who remain
009:091 (of complaint) can there **be** against such as do right:
009:092 came to thee to **be** provided with mount.
009:094 in the end will ye **be** brought back to Him
009:096 that ye may **be** pleased with them.
009:097 and most fitted to **be** in ignorance of the command
009:098 on them **be** the disaster of Evil:
009:101 addition shall they **be** sent to a grievous Chastisement.
009:105 soon will ye **be** brought back to the Knower of what
009:108 In it are men who love to **be** purified;
009:113 for forgiveness for Pagans, even though they **be** of kin,
009:119 and **be** with those who are truthful.
009:120 the reward to **be** lost of those who do good;-
010:004 To Him will **be** your return-of all of you.
010:005 It is He Who made the sun to **be** a shining glory
010:005 shining glory and the moon to **be** a light
010:010 (This will **be**) their prayer therein: "Glory to Thee,
010:010 And "Peace" will **be** their greeting therein
010:010 and the end of their prayer will **be**: "Praise **be** to Allah,
010:011 then would their respite **be** settled at once.
010:027 their faces will **be** covered, as it were,
010:030 they will **be** brought back to Allah their rightful
010:035 gives guidance to Truth more worthy to **be** followed,
010:036 truly conjecture can **be** of no avail against Truth.
010:037 is not such as can **be** produced by other than Allah;
010:038 besides Allah, if it **be** ye speak the truth!"
010:045 (it will **be**) as if they had tarried but an hour of a day;
010:045 assuredly those will **be** lost who denied the meeting
010:047 the matter will **be** judged between them with justice,
010:047 and they will not **be** wronged.
010:051 (It will then **be** said): 'Ah! now? and ye wanted
010:052 "At length will **be** said to the wrong-doers:
010:053 They seek to **be** informed by thee: "Is that true?"
010:054 but the judgment between them will **be** with justice,
010:054 and no wrong will **be** done unto them.
010:056 and to Him shall ye all **be** brought back.
010:061 In whatever business thou mayest **be**,
010:061 and whatever deed ye (mankind) may **be** doing,-
010:061 whatever portion thou mayest **be** reciting from the
010:064 no change can there **be** in the Words of Allah.
010:068 Glory **be** to Him! He is Self-Sufficient!
010:070 and, then, to Us will **be** their return.
010:071 "O my People, if it **be** hard on your (mind) that I
010:071 so your plan **be** not to you dark and dubious.
010:072 and I have been commanded to **be** of those who
010:092 that thou mayest **be** a Sign to those who come after
010:094 so **be** in no wise of those in doubt.
010:095 Nor **be** of those who reject the Signs of Allah,
010:095 or thou shalt **be** of those who perish.
010:104 to **be** (in the ranks) of the Believers,
010:105 and never in any wise **be** of the Unbelievers;
010:106 thou shalt certainly **be** of those who do wrong."
010:109 and **be** patient and constant, till Allah

BE (continued)

011:007 after death, the Unbelievers would **be** sure to say,
011:007 "Ye shall indeed **be** raised up after death,
011:008 and they will **be** completely encircled by that which
011:017 the Fire will **be** their promised meeting place.
011:017 **Be** not then in doubt thereon:
011:017 Can they **be** (like) those who accept a Clear
011:018 They will **be** brought before their Lord, and the
011:019 path of Allah and wish it to **be** crooked:
011:020 Their chastisement will **be** doubled!
011:023 they will **be** Companions of the Garden, to dwell
011:024 may **be** compared to the blind and deaf, and those
011:028 (it **be** that) I have a Clear Sign from my Lord
011:031 I should, if I did, indeed **be** a wrong-doer."
011:031 nor claim I to **be** an angel.
011:033 ye will not **be** able to frustrate it!
011:034 "Of no profit will **be** my counsel to you,
011:034 if it **be** that Allah willeth to leave you astray:
011:037 for they are about to **be** overwhelmed
011:039 on whom will **be** unloosed a Chastisement lasting."
011:041 in the name of Allah, whether it move or **be** at rest!
011:041 For my Lord is, **be** sure, Oft-Forgiving, Most Merciful!"
011:042 and **be** not with the Unbelievers!"
011:043 The son replied: "I will **be** take myself to some
011:047 I should indeed **be** among the losers!"
011:048 (there will **be** other) Peoples to whom We shall grant
011:065 (behold) there is a promise not to **be** belied!"
011:065 in your homes for three days,: (then will **be** your ruin):
011:072 That would indeed **be** a wonderful thing!"
011:076 that cannot **be** turned back!
011:098 woeful indeed will **be** the place to which they are led!
011:099 which shall **be** given (unto them)!
011:103 that will **be** a Day of Testimony.
011:103 is a Day for which mankind will **be** gathered together:
011:105 some will **be** wretched and some will **be** blessed.
011:106 Those who are wretched shall **be** in the Fire:
011:106 will **be** for them therein (nothing but) the heaving
011:108 And those who are blessed shall **be** in the Garden:
011:109 **Be** not then in doubt as to what these men worship.
011:113 protectors other than Allah, nor shall ye **be** helped.
011:115 And **be** steadfast in patience; for verily
011:117 Nor would thy Lord **be** the One to destroy
011:119 and the Word of thy Lord shall **be** fulfilled:
012:009 the favour of your father may **be** given to you alone:
012:009 (there will **be** time enough) for you to **be** righteous after
012:010 he will **be** picked up by some caravan of travellers."
012:014 we are (so large) a party, then should we **be** the losers!
012:018 it is Allah (alone) whose help can **be** sought."
012:026 (thus)-" If it **be** that his shirt is rent
012:027 "But if it **be** that his shirt is torn
012:032 he shall certainly **be** cast into prison,
012:032 and (what is more) **be** in the company of the vilest!"
012:042 he considered about to **be** saved, he said:
012:043 if it **be** that ye can interpret visions."
012:054 he said: "**Be** assured this day, thou art
012:056 and We suffer not, to **be** lost, the reward
012:060 nor shall ye (even) come near me."
012:066 ye will **be** sure to bring him back to me unless ye are
012:066 **be** Allah the Witness and Guardian!"
012:072 I will **be** bound by it."
012:074 shall **be** the penalty of this, if ye are
012:075 should **be** held (as bondman) to atone
012:075 They said: "The penalty should **be** that he in whose

BE (continued)

012:079 we should **be** acting wrongfully."
012:090 never will Allah suffer the reward to **be** lost,
012:092 "This day let no reproach **be** (cast) on you:
012:110 (Respite will **be** granted) until, when the
012:110 But never will **be** warded off Our punishment from
013:005 shall we indeed then **be** in a creation renewed?"
013:005 those round whose neck will **be** yokes (of servitude):
013:005 they will **be** Companions of the Fire,
013:011 a people's punishment, there can **be** no turning it back
013:018 For them will the reckoning **be** terrible:
013:018 their abode will **be** Hell,-what a bed of misery!
013:021 things which Allah hath commanded to **be** joined,
013:025 those things which Allah has commanded to **be** joined,
013:031 or the dead were made to speak, (this would **be** the one!)
013:037 to **be** a judgment of authority in Arabic.
014:007 your Lord caused to **be** declared (publicly):
014:013 "**Be** sure we shall drive you out of our land,
014:017 will **be** a chastisement unrelenting.
014:017 but never well he **be** near swallowing it
014:021 They will all **be** marshalled before Allah together:
014:022 For wrong-doers there must **be** a grievous Chastisement."
014:023 work righteousness will **be** admitted to Gardens beneath
014:023 their greeting therein will **be**: "Peace!"
014:031 of a Day in which there will **be** neither mutual
014:034 never will ye **be** able to number them.
014:039 "Praise **be** to Allah, who hath granted unto me
014:041 on the Day that the Reckoning will **be** established!"
014:048 the Heavens, and (men) will **be** marshalled forth,
014:048 One day the Earth will **be** changed to a
014:048 to a different Earth, and so will **be** the Heavens,
015:007 if it **be** that thou hast the Truth?"
015:031 Not so Iblis: he refused to **be** among those
015:035 "And the Curse shall **be** on thee
015:045 The righteous (will **be**) amid Gardens and fountains
015:046 (Their greeting will **be**): "Enter ye here
015:047 (they will **be**) brothers (joyfully) facing
015:048 nor shall they (ever) **be** asked to leave.
015:050 will **be** indeed the most grievous Chastisement.
015:055 in truth; **be** not then in despair!"
015:060 will **be** among those who will lag behind."
015:062 He said: "Ye appear to **be** uncommon folk."
015:066 those (sinners) should **be** cut off by the morning.
015:085 the Hour is surely coming (when this will **be** manifest).
015:098 and **be** of those who prostrate themselves in
016:014 and that ye may **be** grateful.
016:018 of Allah, never would ye **be** able to number them:
016:021 nor do thy know when they will **be** raised up.
016:032 saying (to them), "Peace **be** on you; enter ye
016:039 (They must **be** raised up), in order that He may
016:040 We but say the Word, "**Be**," and it is.
016:041 of the Hereafter will **be** greater, if they
016:056 By Allah, ye shall certainly **be** called to account
016:057 Glory **be** to Him!-and for themselves what they desire!
016:061 they would not **be** able to delay (the punishment)
016:061 just as they would not **be** able to anticipate
016:062 and they will **be** the first to **be** hastened on into it!
016:064 and that it should **be** a guide a mercy to those who
016:071 so as to **be** equal in that respect.
016:072 and **be** ungrateful for Allah's favours?-
016:075 (By no means); praise **be** to Allah.
016:084 Then will no excuse **be** accepted from Unbelievers,
016:084 nor will they **be** allowed to make amends.

BE (continued)

016:085 the Chastisement then will it in no way **be** mitigated,
016:092 lest one party should **be** more numerous
016:092 And **be** not like a woman who breaks
016:093 but ye shall certainly **be** called to account
016:104 and theirs will **be** a grievous Chastisement.
016:106 and theirs will **be** a dreadful Chastisement.
016:109 they will **be** the losers.
016:111 and none will **be** unjustly dealt with.
016:111 and every soul will **be** recompensed (fully) for
016:114 and **be** grateful for the favours of Allah,
016:122 and he will **be**, in the Hereafter, in the ranks
016:126 let your punishment **be** proportionate to the
016:127 And do thou **be** patient, for thy
017:004 on the earth and **be** elated with mighty arrogance
017:004 (and twice would they **be** punished)!
017:008 It may **be** that your Lord may (yet) show Mercy
017:014 (It will **be** said to him:) "Read thine
017:016 (to **be** obedient) but they continued to
017:019 the ones whose striving will **be** thanked (by Allah).
017:023 and that ye **be** kind to parents.
017:034 will **be** enquired into (on the Day of Reckoning).
017:036 all of those shall **be** questioned of.
017:039 lest thou shouldst **be** thrown into Hell,
017:049 should we really **be** raised up (to **be**) a new creation?"
017:050 Say: "(Nay!) **be** ye stones or iron,
017:051 Say, "Maybe it will **be** quite soon!
017:051 is hardest (to **be** raised up),-(yet shall ye **be** raised up)!"
017:051 and say, "When will that **be**?"
017:051 Say, "May **be** it will be quite soon!
017:052 "It will **be** on a Day when He will call you,
017:054 We have not sent thee to **be** a disposer
017:063 Verily Hell will **be** the recompense of you (all)-
017:068 not cause you to **be** swallowed up beneath the
017:071 will not **be** dealt with unjustly in the least.
017:072 will **be** blind in the Hereafter, and most
017:080 Say: "O my Lord! let my entry **be** by the Gate
017:094 "Has Allah sent a man (like us) to **be** (His) Messenger?"
017:097 their abode will **be** Hell:
017:098 really **be** raised up (to **be**) a new Creation?"
017:102 O Pharaoh, to **be** one doomed to destruction!"
017:111 Say: "Praise **be** to Allah Who begets no son,
018:001 Praise **be** to Allah, Who hath sent to His
018:019 best food (to **be** had) and bring some to you,
018:021 and that there can **be** no doubt about the
018:023 "I shall **be** sure to do so and so to-morrow"
018:029 relief they will **be** granted water like melted
018:031 For them will **be** Gardens of Eternity;
018:031 they will **be** adorned therein with bracelets of gold,
018:039 (**be** done)! There is no power but from Allah!'
018:040 "It may **be** that my Lord will give me something
018:041 wilt never **be** able to find it."
018:048 And they will **be** marshalled before thy Lord
018:049 And the Book (of Deeds) will **be** placed (before you);
018:050 Evil would **be** the exchange for the wrong-doers!
018:052 "Call on those whom ye thought to **be** My partners,"
018:055 or the Wrath **be** brought to them face to face?
018:067 thou will not **be** able to have patience with me!
018:087 then shall he **be** sent back to his Lord;
018:088 and easy will **be** his task as We order it
018:099 the trumpet will **be** blown, and We
018:105 vain will **be** their works, nor shall We,
018:109 ocean **be** exhausted than would the words of my Lord,

019:007 his name shall **be** Yahya: on none by that name
019:009 He said: "So (it will **be**): thy Lord saith,
019:010 "shall **be** that thou shalt speak to no man
019:015 he will **be** raised up to life (again)!
019:021 He said: "So (it will **be**): thy Lord saith,
019:031 wheresoever I **be**, and hath enjoined on me Prayer
019:033 I shall **be** raised up to life (again)!"
019:035 Glory **be** to Him! When He determines a matter,
019:035 He only says to it, "**Be**," and it is.
019:039 when the matter will **be** determined: for (behold),
019:040 to Us will they all **be** returned.
019:047 Abraham said: "Peace **be** on thee: I will
019:048 I shall **be** not unblest."!
019:060 and will not **be** wronged in the least,-
019:065 so worship Him, and **be** constant and patient
019:066 shall I then **be** raised up alive?"
019:071 a Decree which must **be** accomplished.
019:077 "I shall certainly **be** given wealth and children"?
020:002 to **be** (an occasion) for thy distress,
020:039 mayest **be** reared under Mine eye.
020:039 and he will **be** taken up by one who is an enemy
020:040 that her eye might **be** cooled and she
020:059 the people **be** assembled when the sun is well up."
020:065 thou throw (first) or that we **be** the first
020:066 of their magic-began to **be** in lively motion!
020:071 Surely this must **be** your leader.
020:071 **Be** sure I will cut off your hands and feet
020:097 in this life will **be** that thou wilt say, 'Touch me not';
020:101 and grievous will the burden **be** to them on that Day,-
020:102 The Day when the Trumpet will **be** sounded: that Day,
020:108 and the voices will **be** hushed to The Most Gracious:
020:111 The Sustainer, helpless indeed will **be** the man
020:111 (All) faces shall **be** humbled before-the Living,
020:114 **Be** not in haste with the Qur'an
020:126 forgot them: so wilt thou, this day, **be** forgotten.
020:130 of the day: that thou may **be** pleased.
020:130 Therefore **be** patient with what they say,
020:132 Enjoin prayer on they people, and **be** constant therein.
021:013 in order that ye may **be** called to account.
021:018 Ah! woe **be** to you for the (false) things
021:023 but they will **be** questioned (for theirs).
021:023 He cannot **be** questioned for His acts, by they
021:039 (the time) when they will not **be** able to ward
021:043 nor can they **be** defended from Us.
021:047 And if there **be** (no more than) the weight
021:047 so that not a soul will **be** dealt with unjustly
021:059 He must indeed **be** one of the unjust one.
021:066 can neither **be** of any good to you nor do you harm?
021:069 We said, "O Fire! **be** thou cool, and, (a means of)
021:080 will ye then **be** grateful?
021:094 his endeavour will not **be** rejected:
021:100 There, sobbing will **be** their lot, nor will
021:101 will **be** removed far therefrom.
021:111 "I know not but that it may **be** a trial for you,
021:112 the One Whose assistance should **be** sought against
022:001 (of judgment) will **be** a thing terrible!
022:002 but dreadful will **be** the Chastisement of Allah.
022:007 there can **be** no doubt about it, or about
022:010 (It will **be** said): "This is because of the deeds
022:019 for them will **be** cut out a garment of Fire:
022:019 over their heads will **be** poured out boiling water.
022:020 With it will **be** melted what is within their

022:021 In addition there will **be** maces of iron
022:022 from anguish, they will **be** forced back therein,
022:022 and (it will **be** said), "Taste ye the chastisement
022:023 and their garments there will **be** of silk.
022:023 they shall **be** adorned therein with bracelets
022:036 to you, that ye may **be** grateful.
022:051 they will **be** Companions of the Fire."
022:054 and their hearts may **be** made humbly (open)
022:055 to **be** in doubt concerning (Revelation) until the
022:056 On that Day the Dominion will **be** that of Allah:
022:056 righteous deeds will **be** in Gardens of Delight.
022:057 there will **be** a humiliating Punishment.
022:059 to a place with which they shall **be** well pleased:
022:078 and ye **be** witnesses for mankind!
022:078 that the Messenger may **be** a witness for you,
023:010 Those will **be** the heirs,
023:014 so blessed **be** Allah, the Best to create!
023:016 Again, on the Day of Judgment, will ye **be** raised up.
023:027 for they shall **be** drowned (in the Flood).
023:028 say: "Praise **be** to Allah, Who has
023:034 behold, it is certain ye will **be** lost.
023:035 ye shall **be** brought forth (again)?
023:037 But we shall never **be** raised up again!
023:040 they are sure to **be** sorry!"
023:062 They will never **be** wronged.
023:065 for ye shall certainly not **be** helped by Us.
023:065 (It will **be** said): "Groan not
023:066 "My Signs used to **be** rehearsed to you, but ye
023:077 then Lo! they will **be** plunged in despair therein!
023:079 and to Him shall ye **be** gathered back.
023:082 could we really **be** raised up again?
023:101 there will **be** no more relationships between
023:103 will **be** those who have lost their souls;
023:107 then shall we **be** wrong-doers indeed!"
023:108 He will say: "**Be** ye driven into it
023:115 and that ye would not **be** brought back
023:116 Therefore exalted **be** Allah, the King,
023:117 and his reckoning will **be** only with his Lord!
024:007 And the fifth (oath) (should **be**) that he
024:009 And the fifth (oath) should **be** that she solemnly
024:010 Full of Wisdom,-(ye would **be** ruined indeed).
024:011 think it not to **be** an evil to you;
024:011 among them, will **be** a Chastisement grievous.
024:015 and ye thought it to **be** a light matter, while it
024:020 (ye would **be** ruined indeed).
024:031 that ye may **be** successful.
024:036 which Allah hath permitted to **be** raised to honour;
024:037 the Day when hearts and eyes will **be** turn about,-
024:039 until when he comes up to it, he finds it to **be** nothing:
024:054 If ye obey him, ye shall **be** on right guidance.
024:060 but it is best for them to **be** modest:
024:063 or a grievous Chastisement **be** inflicted on them.
024:064 **Be** quite sure that to Allah doth belong
024:064 and one day they will **be** brought back to Him,
025:001 that it may **be** an admonition to all creatures;-
025:005 which he has caused to **be** written:
025:009 and never a way will they **be** able to find!
025:016 "For them there will **be** therein all that
025:022 no joy will there **be** to the sinners that Day:
025:024 The Companions of the Garden will **be** well, that Day,
025:025 The Day the heaven shall **be** rent asunder
025:025 and angels shall **be** sent down, descending

025:026 shall **be** (wholly) for The Most Gracious:
025:026 it will **be** a Day of dire difficulty for the
025:034 Those who will **be** gathered to Hell
025:034 they will **be** in an evil plight, and, as
025:040 But they expect not to **be** raised again.
025:043 Could thou **be** a disposer of affairs
025:050 in order that they may **be** mindful but most men are
025:053 a partition that is not to **be** passed.
025:058 to **be** acquainted with the faults of His servants;-
025:062 for such as desire to **be** mindful or to show
025:069 the Day of Judgment will **be** doubled to him, and he
025:074 and offspring who will **be** the comfort of our
025:075 **be** rewarded with the highest place in heaven,
025:075 **be** met with salutations and peace,
026:003 It may **be** thou will kill thy self with grief,
026:013 "My breast will **be** straitened. And my
026:042 for ye shall in that case **be** (raised to posts)
026:049 **Be** sure I will cut off your hands and your
026:052 for surely ye shall **be** pursued."
026:061 "We are sure to **be** overtaken."
026:087 on the Day when (men) will **be** raised up;-
026:087 "And let me not **be** in disgrace on the Day
026:090 the Garden will **be** brought near,
026:091 the Fire will **be** placed in full view;
026:092 "And it shall **be** said to them: `Where are
026:094 "Then they will **be** thrown headlong into
026:102 we shall truly **be** of those who believe!'"
026:116 O Noah! thou shalt **be** stone (to death)."
026:136 thou admonish us or **be** not among (our) Admonishers!
026:146 "Will ye **be** left secure, in (the enjoyment of) all that ye
026:166 has created for you to **be** your mates?
026:167 O Lut! thou wilt assuredly **be** cast out!"
026:203 Then they will say: "Shall we **be** respited?"
026:204 then ask for Our Chastisement to **be** hastened on?
026:213 or thou wilt **be** among those who will **be** punished.
027:005 and in the Hereafter theirs will **be** the greatest loss.
027:015 and they both said: "Praise **be** to Allah, Who has
027:019 so order me that I may **be** grateful for Thy favours,
027:031 "'**Be** ye not arrogant against me, but come
027:037 "Go back to them, and **be** sure we shall come
027:037 with such hosts as they will never **be** able to meet:
027:039 the purpose, and may **be** trusted."
027:056 men who want to **be** clean and pure!"
027:057 to **be** of those who lagged behind.
027:059 Say: Praise **be** to Allah, and Peace
027:060 (Can there **be** another) god besides Allah?
027:061 the two seas (can there **be** another) god besides
027:062 (Can there **be** another) god besides Allah?
027:063 (Can there **be** another) god besides Allah?-
027:064 (Can there **be** another) god besides Allah?
027:065 shall **be** raised up (for Judgment).
027:067 shall we really **be** raised (from the dead)?
027:072 hasten on may **be** (close) in your pursuit!
027:072 Say: "It may **be** that some of the events
027:081 Nor canst thou **be** a guide to the Blind,
027:083 and they shall **be** kept in ranks,-
027:085 And the Word will **be** fulfilled against them,
027:085 and they will **be** unable to speak (in plea).
027:087 will **be** sounded-then will **be** smitten with terror
027:089 And they will **be** secure from terror that Day.
027:090 their faces will **be** thrown headlong into the Fire:
027:091 and I am commanded to **be** of those who bow

027:093 And say: "Praise **be** to Allah, Who will
028:005 And We wished to **be** gracious to those who
028:008 should **be** to them an adversary and a cause
028:009 It may **be** that he will **be** of use to us, or we
028:013 that her eye might **be** comforted, that she
028:017 never shall I **be** a help to those who sin!"
028:019 and not to **be** one who sets things right!"
028:027 thou complete ten years, it will **be** (grace) from thee.
028:028 He said: "**Be** that (the agreement) between me
028:028 let there **be** no injustice to me.
028:028 **Be** Allah a witness to what we say."
028:035 so they shall not **be** able to touch you:
028:037 from Him and whose End will **be** best in the
028:042 Day of Judgment they will **be** among the
028:054 Twice will they **be** given their reward, for that
028:055 peace **be** to you: we seek not the ignorant."
028:056 It is true thou wilt not **be** able to guide
028:057 we should **be** snatched away from our land."
028:060 will ye not then **be** wise?
028:061 is to **be** among those brought up (for punishment)?
028:062 whom ye imagined (to **be** such)?"
028:063 Those against whom the charge will **be** proved,
028:064 It will **be** said (to them): "Call upon
028:066 will not **be** able (even) to question each other.
028:067 haply he shall **be** one of the successful.
028:070 To him **be** praise, at the first and the last:
028:070 and to Him shall ye (all) **be** brought back.
028:073 and in order that ye may **be** grateful.
028:074 whom ye imagined (to **be** such)?"
028:086 that the Book would **be** sent to thee except as
028:087 and **be** not of the company of these who
028:088 and to Him will ye (all) **be** brought back.
029:002 Do men think that they will **be** left alone
029:002 and that they will not **be** tested?
029:013 they will **be** called to account for their falsehoods.
029:016 that will **be** best for you-if ye understand!
029:017 serve Him, and **be** grateful to Him:
029:017 to Him will **be** your return.
029:022 will ye **be** able (fleeing) to frustrate (His Plan),
029:025 curse each other: and your abode will **be** the Fire,
029:027 in this life; and he will **be** in the Hereafter
029:046 unless it **be** with those of them who do wrong
029:057 in the end to Us shall ye **be** brought back.
029:063 Say, "Praise **be** to Allah!" But most
030:003 after (this) defeat of theirs, will soon **be** victorious-
030:010 In the long run evil will **be** the End of those
030:011 then shall ye **be** brought back to Him.
030:012 the guilty will **be** struck dumb with despair.
030:014 that Day shall (all men) **be** sorted out.
030:015 shall **be** made happy in a Mead (of Delight).
030:016 such shall **be** brought forth to Punishment.
030:017 So glory **be** to Allah, when ye reach eventide
030:018 Yea, To Him **be** praise, in the heavens and on
030:019 and thus shall ye **be** brought out (from the dead).
030:029 To them there will **be** no helpers.
030:031 and **be** not ye among those who join gods with Allah,-
030:043 on that Day shall men **be** divided (in two).
030:046 in order that ye may **be** grateful.
030:055 the Day that the Hour (or reckoning) **be** established,
030:057 nor will they **be** allowed to make amends.
031:006 for such there will **be** a humiliating Chastisement.
031:008 there will **be** Gardens of Bliss,-

031:014 (to **be** good) to his parents:
031:016 "If there **be** (but) the weight of a mustard-seed
031:019 "And **be** moderate in thy pace, and lower
031:025 Say: "Praise **be** to Allah!"
031:027 of Allah **be** exhausted (in the writing):
032:003 in order that they may **be** rightly guided.
032:010 shall we indeed **be** in a Creation renewed?"
032:011 then shall ye **be** brought back to your Lord."
032:020 rebellious and wicked, their abode will **be** the Fire:
032:020 to get away therefrom, they will **be** forced thereinto,
032:020 and it will **be** said to them: "Taste ye the Chastisement
032:023 **be** not then in doubt of its reaching (thee):
032:028 They say: "When will this decision **be**, if ye
032:029 Nor will they **be** granted a respite."
032:029 no profit will it **be** to Unbelievers if they
033:015 must (surely) **be** answered for.
033:016 a brief (respite) will ye **be** allowed to enjoy!"
033:017 from Allàh if it **be** His wish to give you
033:024 and punish the Hypocrites if that **be** His Will,
033:028 "If it **be** that ye desire the life of this world,
033:030 the Punishment would **be** doubled to her,
033:032 **be** not too complaisant of speech,
033:032 whose heart is a disease should **be** moved with desire:
033:037 (in future) there may **be** no difficulty to the Believers
033:037 And Allah's command must **be** fulfilled.
033:038 There can **be** no difficulty to the Prophet
033:044 salutation on the Day they meet Him will **be** "peace!";
033:050 in order that there should **be** no difficulty for thee.
033:059 that they should **be** known (as such) and not molested.
033:060 then will they not **be** able to stay in it as thy neighbors
033:061 they shall **be** seized and slain.
033:066 The Day that their faces will **be** turned over
033:069 O ye who believe! **be** ye not like those who
034:001 Praise **be** to Allah, to Whom belong all things
034:001 to Him **be** Praise in the Hereafter:
034:005 for such will **be** a Chastisement of Painful wrath.
034:007 that ye shall (then **be** raised) in a New Creation?
034:011 for **be** sure I see (clearly) all that ye do."
034:015 by your Lord, and **be** grateful to Him:
034:025 Say: "Ye shall not **be** questioned as to our sins,
034:025 nor shall we **be** questioned as to what ye do."
034:031 the wrong-doers will **be** made to stand before
034:033 ye (constantly) ordered us to **be** ungrateful to Allah
034:033 it would only **be** a requital for their (ill) Deeds.
034:035 in wealth and in sons, and we cannot **be** chastised."
034:038 to frustrate them, will **be** given over into Chastisement,
034:046 (it may **be**) in pairs, or (it may **be**) singly,-and reflect
034:051 but then there will **be** no escape (for them),
034:051 and they will **be** seized from a position (quite) near.
035:001 Praise **be** to Allah, the Originator
035:008 So let not thy soul **be** vested in regret
035:009 even so (will **be**) the Resurrection!
035:010 and the plotting of such will **be** void (of result).
035:012 of Allah that ye may **be** grateful.
035:018 not the least portion of it can **be** carried (by the other),
035:018 even though he **be** nearly related.
035:033 therein will they **be** adorned with bracelets
035:033 and their garments there will **be** of silk.
035:034 And they will say: "Praise **be** to Allah, Who has
035:036 no term shall **be** determined for them, so they
035:036 for them will **be** the Fire of Hell:
035:036 nor shall its Chastisement **be** lightened for them.

035:039 his disbelief **be** on his own self their disbelief:
035:042 they would **be** more rightly guided than anyone
035:044 to **be** frustrated by anything whatever in the
036:018 indeed will **be** inflicted on you by us."
036:022 (all) **be** brought back.
036:023 of no use whatever will **be** their intercession
036:024 "I would indeed, then **be** in manifest Error.
036:032 will **be** brought before Us (for judgment).
036:043 then would there **be** no helper (to hear their cry),
036:043 nor could they **be** delivered,
036:045 will **be** after you, in order that ye may
036:051 The trumpet shall **be** sounded, when behold!
036:053 It will **be** no more than a single Blast,
036:053 they will all **be** brought up before Us!
036:054 on that Day, not a sol will **be** wronged in the least,
036:054 ye shall but **be** repaid the meeds of your past Deeds.
036:056 They and their associates will **be** in pleasant shade,
036:057 (Every) fruit will **be** there for them; they shall
036:068 We cause him to **be** reversed in nature:
036:070 may **be** proved true against those who
036:073 Will they not then **be** grateful?
036:074 than Allah, (hoping) that they might **be** helped!
036:082 His command is, "**Be**," and it is!
036:083 and to Him will ye **be** all brought back.
037:016 and bones, shall we (then) **be** raised up (again)?
037:018 ye shall then **be** humiliated (on account of your evil)."
037:019 Then it will **be** a single (compelling) cry;
037:022 "Bring ye up," it shall **be** said, "The wrong-doers
037:024 "But stop them, for they must **be** asked:
037:045 Round will **be** passed to them a Cup from a
037:048 And beside them will **be** chaste women;
037:059 and that we shall not **be** punished?"
037:067 they will **be** given a mixture made of boiling water.
037:068 Then shall their return **be** to the (Blazing) Fire.
037:127 and they will certainly **be** called up (for punishment),
037:157 (of authority) if ye **be** truthful!
037:158 that they will **be** brought before Him.
037:172 That they would certainly **be** assisted,
037:177 Evil will **be** the morning for those who were
038:011 and they will **be** put to flight.
038:024 ewe to **be** added to his (flock of) ewes:
038:039 no account will **be** asked."
038:050 will (ever) **be** open to them;
038:052 And beside them will **be** chaste women
038:054 Truly such will **be** Our Bounty (to you); it will
038:055 will **be** an evil place of (final) Return!-
038:078 "And My Curse shall **be** on thee till the
039:004 but Glory **be** to Him! (He is above such things).
039:012 "And I am commanded to **be** the first of those
039:024 It will **be** said to the wrong-doers: "Taste ye
039:029 Praise **be** to Allah! But most of them have no
039:036 there can **be** no guide.
039:037 there can **be** none to lead astray.
039:038 they would **be** sure to say, "Allah."
039:044 ye shall **be** brought back."
039:048 and they will **be** (completely) encircled by that which
039:054 comes on you: after that ye shall not **be** helped.
039:058 I should certainly **be** among those who do good!'
039:059 "(The reply will be) `Nay, but there came to thee
039:060 their faces will **be** turned black;
039:063 it is they who will **be** in loss.
039:065 truly fruitless will **be** thy work (in life),

BE (continued)

039:065 and thou wilt surely **be** among the losers.

039:066 and **be** of those who give thanks.

039:067 of the earth will **be** but His handful, and the

039:067 and the heavens will **be** rolled up in his

039:068 The Trumpet will (just) **be** sounded, when all

039:068 Then will a second **one be** sounded, when, behold,

039:068 they will **be** standing and looking on!

039:069 the Record (of Deeds) will **be** placed (open);

039:069 prophets and the witnesses will **be** brought forward;

039:069 and they will not **be** wronged (in the least).

039:070 And to every soul will **be** paid in full

039:071 The Unbelievers will **be** led to Hell in groups;

039:071 when they arrive there, its gates will **be** opened.

039:071 The answer will **be**: "True: but the Decree

039:072 (To them) will **be** said: "Enter ye the gates of Hell,

039:073 feared their Lord will **be** led to the Garden in groups:

039:073 they arrive there; its gates will **be** opened;

039:073 and its Keepers will say: "Peace **be** upon you!

039:074 They will say: "Praise **be** to Allah, Who has

039:075 between them (at Judgment) will **be** in (perfect)

039:075 and the cry (on all sides) will **be**, "Praise **be** to Allah,

040:009 and that will **be** truly the highest Achievement.

040:010 The Unbelievers will **be** addressed: "Greater was

040:012 (The answer will **be**): "This is because,

040:016 Whose will **be** the Dominion that Day?

040:017 That Day will every soul **be** requited for what

040:017 no injustice will there **be** that Day, for Allah

040:018 wrong-doers have, who could **be** listened to.

040:020 will not (**be** in a position) to judge at all.

040:028 And if he **be** a liar, on him is

040:032 a Day when there will **be** mutual calling

040:040 "He that works evil will not **be** requited but by

040:043 will **be** Companions of the Fire!

040:043 or the Hereafter; our Return will **be** to Allah;

040:043 one who has no claim to **be** called to, whether in

040:046 In front of the Fire will they **be** brought, morning and

040:046 and (the Sentence will **be**) on the Day when the

040:052 The Day when no profit will it **be** to Wrong-doers

040:065 Praise **be** to Allah, Lord of the Worlds!

040:068 He says to it, "**Be**," and it is.

040:071 When the yokes (shall **be**) round their necks,

040:071 they shall **be** dragged along-

040:072 then in the Fire shall they **be** burned;

040:073 Then shall it **be** said to them: "Where are

040:075 the Truth, and that ye were wont to **be** insolent.

040:080 to any need (there may **be**) in your hearts;

041:016 of the Hereafter will **be** more humiliating still:

041:019 they will **be** marched in ranks.

041:019 will **be** gathered together to the Fire,

041:024 the Fire will **be** a Home for them!

041:024 their suit shall not **be** granted.

041:028 therein will **be** for them the Eternal Home:

041:034 Nor can Goodness and Evil **be** equal.

041:035 And no one will **be** granted such goodness except

041:050 (of Judgment) will (ever) **be** established;

042:007 (when) some will **be** in the Garden, and some

042:010 Whatever it **be** wherein ye differ, the decision

042:016 and for them will **be** a Chastisement Terrible.

042:022 That will indeed **be** the magnificent Bounty (of Allah).

042:022 righteous deeds will **be** in the Meadows of the Gardens:

042:033 If it **be** His Will, He can

042:042 for such there will **be** a Chastisement grievous.

042:043 that would truly **be** an affair of great resolution.

042:047 come a Day which there will **be** no putting back,

042:047 That Day there will **be** for you no place of refuge

042:047 nor will there **be** for you any room for denial

043:003 that ye may **be** able to understand.

043:009 They would **be** sure to reply, 'They were created

043:011 even so will ye **be** raised (from the dead);-

043:013 for we could never **be** able to do it.

043:018 in a dispute (to **be** associated with Allah)?

043:019 and they will **be** called to account!

043:019 Their evidence will **be** recorded, and they

043:036 to **be** an intimate companion to him.

043:039 that day, that ye shall **be** partners in punishment!

043:041 We shall **be** sure to exact retribution from them,

043:044 and soon shall ye (all) **be** brought to account.

043:045 other than The Most Gracious, to **be** worshipped?

043:061 And (Jesus) shall **be** a Sign (for the coming of)

043:067 Friends on that Day will **be** foes, one to

043:068 My devotees! no fear shall **be** on you today,

043:071 To them will **be** passed round, dishes and

043:071 there will **be** there all that the souls

043:072 Such will **be** the Garden of which ye are made

043:074 The Sinners will **be** in the Punishment of Hell,

043:075 Nowise will the (punishment) **be** lightened for them,

043:075 will they **be** there overwhelmed.

043:076 Nowise shall We **be** unjust to them:

043:081 I would **be** the first to worship."

043:085 And to Him shall ye **be** brought back.

044:011 this will **be** a Chastisement Grievous.

044:019 "And **be** not arrogant as against Allah:

044:023 for ye are sure to **be** pursued.

044:024 For they are a host (destined) to **be** drowned."

044:035 and we shall not **be** raised again.

044:044 Will **be** the food of the Sinful,-

044:051 As to the Righteous (they will **be**) in a

044:057 That will **be** the supreme achievement!

045:009 for such there will **be** a humiliating Chastisement.

045:012 of His Bounty, and that ye may **be** grateful.

045:015 in the end will ye (all) **be** brought back to your Lord.

045:019 They will **be** of no use to thee in the sight

045:021 righteous deeds,-that equal will **be** their Life

045:022 it has earned, and none of them shall **be** wronged.

045:028 ye **be** recompensed for all that ye did!

045:028 every nation will **be** called to its Record:

045:030 that will **be** the manifest triumph.

045:031 (to them will **be** said): "Were not Our

045:033 and they will **be** completely encircled by that

045:034 It will also **be** said: "This Day We will forget

045:035 therefore, they shall not **be** taken out thence,

045:036 Then Praise **be** to Allah, Lord of the

046:006 they will **be** hostile to them and deny that (men) had

046:009 nor do I know what will **be** done with me or with you.

046:010 Say: "See ye? If (this teaching) **be** from Allah,

046:013 (on that Path),-on them shall **be** no fear,

046:014 Such shall **be** Companions of the Garden,

046:015 grant me that I may **be** grateful for Thy favour

046:015 and **be** gracious to me in my issue.

046:016 (they shall **be**) among the Companions of the Garden:

046:017 I shall **be** raised up, even though

046:018 for they will **be** (utterly) lost.

046:019 and no injustice will **be** done to them.

046:020 Day that the Unbelievers will **be** placed before the Fire,

BE (continued)

046:020 (it will **be** said to them): "Ye squandered your good
046:020 but to-day shall ye **be** recompensed with a Chastisement
046:024 ye were asking to **be** hastened!-a wind
046:025 nothing was to **be** seen but (the ruins of)
046:034 the Unbelievers will **be** placed before the Fire,
046:034 (they will **be** asked), "Is this not the Truth?"
046:035 and **be** in no haste about the (Unbelievers).
046:035 (it will **be**) as if they had not tarried more than an
046:035 but shall any **be** destroyed except those who
047:004 He will never let their deeds **be** lost.
047:012 and the Fire will **be** their abode.
047:015 (can those in such Bliss) **be** compared to such as shall
047:015 and **be** given, to drink, boiling water, so that
047:022 Then, is it to **be** expected of you, if ye
047:027 But how (will it **be**) when the angels take their
047:035 **Be** not weary and faint-hearted crying for peace,
047:038 then they would not **be** like you!
048:016 "Ye shall **be** summoned (to fight)
048:020 that is may **be** a Sign for the Believers,
049:005 come out to them, it would **be** best for them:
049:009 make peace between them with justice, and **be** fair:
049:011 it may **be** that the (latter) are better than the (former):
049:011 laugh at others: it may **be** that the (latter) is better
049:011 nor defame nor **be** sarcastic to each other,
049:011 (to **be** used of one) after he has believed:
049:017 if ye **be** true and sincere.
050:011 thus will **be** the Resurrection.
050:015 they should **be** in confused doubt about a new Creation?
050:020 that will **be** the Day whereof warning
050:020 And the Trumpet shall **be** blown:
050:021 with each will **be** an (angel) to drive, and an
050:022 (It will **be** said:) "Thou wast heedless of this;
050:024 (The sentence will **be**:) "Throw, both of
050:031 And the Garden will **be** brought nigh to the
050:035 There will **be** for them therein all that
050:042 that will **be** the day of Resurrection.
050:044 that will **be** a gathering together,-quite easy
050:044 The Day when the Earth will **be** rent asunder,
051:009 (away from the Truth) such as would **be** deluded.
051:010 Cursed **be** the conjecturers.
051:012 They ask, "When will **be** the Day of Judgement
051:013 (It will **be**) a Day when they will **be** tried (and tested)
051:014 this is what ye used to ask to **be** hastened!"
051:015 they will **be** in the midst of Gardens and Springs,
052:009 when the firmament will **be** in dreadful commotion.
052:013 That Day shall they **be** thrust down to the
052:014 "This," it will **be** said, "Is the Fire,-
052:017 they will **be** in Gardens, and in Happiness,-
052:019 (To them will **be** said:) "Eat and drink ye,
052:034 like unto it,-if (it **be**) they speak the Truth!
052:045 wherein they shall **be** thunderstruck.
052:046 avail them nothing and no help shall **be** given them.
053:022 Behold, such would **be** indeed a division
053:026 How many-so-ever **be** the angels in the heavens,
053:041 Then will he **be** rewarded with a reward complete;
054:024 Truly should we then **be** in error and madness.
054:028 And tell them that the water is to **be** divided between
054:045 Soon will their multitude **be** put to flight,
054:046 and that Hour will **be** most grievous and most bitter.
054:048 The Day they will **be** dragged through the Fire
054:054 they will **be** in the midst of Gardens and Rivers.
055:033 If it **be** ye can pass beyond the zones

BE (continued)

055:033 authority shall ye **be** able to pass!
055:035 On you will **be** sent (O ye evil ones twain)!
055:039 will **be** asked of man or Jinn as to his sin,
055:041 (For) the sinners will **be** known by their Marks:
055:041 and they will **be** seized by their forelocks and their feet.
055:046 there will **be** two Gardens-
055:050 In them (each) will **be** two Springs flowing (free);
055:052 In them will **be** Fruits of every kind, two and two.
055:054 will **be** Near (and easy of reach).
055:054 whose inner linings will **be** of rich brocade:
055:056 In them will **be** (Maidens), Chaste, restraining
055:066 In them (each) will **be** two springs pouring forth
055:068 In them will **be** Fruits, and dates and pomegranates:
055:070 In them will **be** fair (Maidens), good, beautiful;-
055:078 Blessed **be** the name of thy Lord, full of
056:004 When the earth shall **be** shaken to its depths,
056:005 And the mountains shall **be** crumbled to atoms,
056:007 And ye shall **be** sorted out into three classes.
056:008 Then (there will **be**) the Companions
056:008 what will **be** the Companions of the Right Hand?
056:009 what will **be** the Companions of the Left Hand?
056:010 will **be** Foremost (in the Hereafter).
056:011 These will **be** those Nearest to Allah:
056:015 (They will **be**) on couches encrusted (with gold
056:022 And (there will **be**) Companions with beautiful,
056:027 what will **be** the Companions of the Right Hand!
056:028 (They will **be**) among lote-trees without thorns,
056:041 what will **be** the Companions of the Left Hand!
056:042 (They will **be**) in the midst of a fierce
056:045 to **be** indulged, before that, in sinful luxury,
056:047 and bones, shall we then indeed **be** raised up again?-
056:050 "All will certainly **be** gathered together for the
056:056 Such will **be** their entertainment on the Day
056:060 We have decreed Death to **be** your common lot,
056:060 and We are not to **be** frustrated
056:065 And ye would **be** left in wonderment,
056:088 Thus, then, if he **be** of those Nearest to Allah,
056:090 And if he **be** of the Companions of the Right Hand,
056:091 "Peace **be** unto thee," from the Companions
056:092 And if he **be** of those who deny (the truth)
057:004 And He is with you wheresoever ye may **be**.
057:012 (their greeting will **be**): "Good News for you this Day!
057:013 It will **be** said: "Turn Ye back to your rear!
057:013 So a wall will **be** put up betwixt them,
057:013 Within it will **be** Mercy throughout, and without it,
057:013 all alongside, will **be** (wrath and) Punishment!
057:015 "This Day shall no ransom **be** accepted of you,
057:018 a Beautiful Loan, it shall **be** increased manifold
057:021 **Be** ye foremost (in seeking) forgiveness from your
058:002 none can **be** their mothers except those
058:002 they cannot **be** their mothers:
058:005 and His Messenger will **be** humbled to dust,
058:007 but He is with them, wheresoever they **be**:
058:009 and fear Allah, to whom ye shall **be** brought back.
058:012 That will **be** best for you, and most
058:017 against Allah, will **be** their riches nor their sons:
058:017 they will **be** Companions of the Fire,
058:020 Allah and His Messenger will **be** among those
058:022 Allah will **be** well pleased with them, and they
059:017 The end of both will **be** that they
059:019 And **be** ye not like those who forgot Allah;
060:003 Of no profit to you will **be** your relatives

BE (continued)

060:007 It may **be** that Allah will Establish friendship
060:010 And there will **be** no blame on you if ye marry
061:006 after me, whose name shall **be** Ahmad.
061:011 and your persons: that will **be** best for you,
061:014 O ye who believe! **be** ye helpers of Allah:
061:014 "Who will **be** my helpers to (the work of) Allah?"
062:008 then will ye **be** sent back to the Knower of things
063:004 The curse of Allah **be** on them!
064:007 then shall ye **be** told (the truth)
064:007 will not **be** raised up (for Judgment).
064:007 ye shall surely **be** raised up:
064:009 that will **be** the Supreme Triumph.
064:009 for a day of Assembly,-that will **be** a day
064:010 they will **be** Companions of the Fire, to dwell
064:015 Your riches and your children may **be** but a trial:
066:001 to **be** forbidden that which Allah has made
066:005 It may **be**, if he divorced you (all), that Allah
066:007 (It will **be** said), "O ye Unbelievers! make no
066:008 to **be** humiliated the Prophet and those who
066:009 and **be** harsh with them.
067:001 Blessed **be** He in Whose hands is Dominion;
067:010 not (now) **be** among the Companions of the Blazing Fire!"
067:016 to **be** swallowed up by the earth when it shakes
067:024 and to Him shall ye **be** gathered together."
067:025 When will this promise **be** (fulfilled)?
067:027 grieved will **be** the faces of the of the Unbelievers,
067:027 it will **be** said (to them): "This is (the promise fulfilled)
067:030 Say: "See ye?-if your stream **be** some morning lost
068:009 Their desire is that thou shouldst **be** pliant:
068:009 so would thy **be** pliant.
068:018 But made no reservation, ("If it **be** Allah's Will").
068:032 "It may **be** that our Lord will give us in exchange
068:042 The Day that the Shin shall **be** laid bare,
068:042 and they shall **be** summoned to prostrate,
068:042 to prostrate, but they shall not **be** able,-
068:043 Their eyes will **be** cast down,-ignominy will
068:048 and **be** not like the Companion of the Fish,-
069:016 for it will that Day **be** flimsy,
069:016 And the sky will **be** rent asunder, for it
069:017 And the angels will **be** on its sides, and eight
069:018 That Day shall ye **be** brought to Judgment:
069:018 not an act of yours that ye hide will **be** hidden.
069:019 Then He that will **be** given his Record in his
069:021 And he will **be** in a life of Bliss,
069:025 And he that will **be** given his Record in his
070:008 The Day that the sky will **be** like molten brass,
070:009 And the mountains will **be** like wool,
070:011 each other,-the sinner's desire will **be**:
070:011 Though they will **be** put in sight of each other,-
070:015 By no means! for it would **be** the Blazing Fire-
070:030 hands possess,-for (then) they are not to **be** blamed,
070:035 Such will **be** the honoured ones in the
070:041 to **be** defeated (in Our Plan).
071:004 is accomplished, it cannot **be** put forward:
073:014 earth and the mountains will **be** in violent commotion.
073:014 And the mountains will **be** as a heap of sand
073:015 a Messenger, to **be** a witness concerning you,
073:018 Whereon the sky will **be** cleft asunder?
073:018 His Promise needs must **be** accomplished.
073:020 of the Qur'an as much as may **be** easy for you.
073:020 as may **be** easy (for you); and establish
073:020 may **be** (some) among you in ill-health;

BE (continued)

074:007 for thy Lord's (Cause) **be** patient and constant!
074:009 That will **be**-that Day-a Day of Distress,-
074:013 And sons to **be** by his side!-
074:031 and that no doubts may **be** left for the People
074:038 Every soul will **be** (held) in pledge for its deeds.
074:040 (They will **be**) in Gardens (of Delight); they will
074:052 to **be** given scrolls (of revelation) spread out!
075:012 that Day will **be** the place of rest.
075:013 That Day will Man **be** told (all) that
075:014 Nay, man will **be** evidence against himself,
075:024 And some faces, that Day, will **be** sad and dismal,
075:025 calamity was about to **be** inflicted on them;
075:027 And there will **be** a cry, "Who is a magician
075:029 And one leg will **be** joined with another:
075:030 That Day the Drive will **be** (all) to thy Lord!
075:036 Does man think that he will **be** left uncontrolled,
076:003 whether he **be** grateful or ungrateful.
076:015 And amongst them will **be** passed round vessels of
076:017 And they will **be** given to drink there of a Cup
076:021 and they will **be** adorned with Bracelets of silver;
076:021 Upon them will **be** green Garments of fine silk
076:024 Therefore **be** patient with constancy to the
076:027 behind them a Day (that will **be**) hard.
077:029 (It will **be** said:) "Depart ye to that which ye
077:035 shall not **be** able to speak,
077:035 That will **be** a Day when they shall not
077:036 Nor will it **be** open to them to put forth pleas.
077:038 That will **be** a Day of Sorting out!
077:041 they shall **be** amidst (cool) shades and springs
078:018 The Day that the Trumpet shall **be** sounded, and ye
078:019 And the heavens shall **be** opened as if
078:031 there will **be** an Achievement,
079:006 in commotion will **be** in violent commotion,
079:006 One Day everything that can **be** in commotion
079:008 Hearts that Day will **be** in agitation;
079:009 Cast down will **be** (their owners') eyes.
079:010 shall we indeed **be** returned to (our) former state?-
079:012 "It would, in that case, **be** a return with loss!"
079:013 But verily, it will **be** but a single
079:018 thou shouldst **be** purified (from sin)?-
079:036 And Hell-Fire shall **be** placed in full view
079:039 The Abode will **be** Hell-Fire;
079:041 Their abode will **be** the Garden.
079:042 'When will **be** its appointed time?'
079:046 (it will **be**) as if they had tarried but a single
080:011 By no means (should it **be** so)!
080:038 Some Faces that Day will **be** beaming.
080:040 And other faces that Day will **be** dust-stained;
080:042 Such will **be** the Rejecters of Allah, the Doers
082:013 As for the Righteous, they will **be** in Bliss;
082:014 And the Wicked-they will **be** in the Fire,
082:016 And they will not **be** able to keep away therefrom.
082:019 will **be** (wholly) with Allah.
082:019 (It will **be**) the Day when no soul shall have
083:004 Do they not think that they will **be** raised up?-
083:015 that Day, will they **be** veiled.
083:017 Further, it will **be** said to them: "This is the
083:022 Truly the Righteous will **be** in Bliss:
083:025 Their thirst will **be** slaked with Pure Wine sealed;
083:026 The seal thereof will **be** Musk: and for this
083:027 With it will **be** (given) a mixture of Tasnim:
084:008 Soon will his account **be** taken by an easy reckoning,

BE (continued)

085:011 who believe and do righteous deeds, will **be** Gardens.
086:009 The Day that (all) things secret will **be** tested,
087:011 But it will **be** avoided by the most
088:002 Some faces, that Day, will **be** humiliated,
088:006 No food will there **be** for them but a bitter Dhari
088:008 (Other) faces that Day will **be** joyful,
088:012 Therein will **be** a bubbling spring:
088:013 Therein will **be** couches (of dignity),
088:025 For to Us will **be** their Return;
088:026 Then it will **be** for Us to call them to account.
089:025 For, that Day, His Chastisement will **be** such as
089:026 And His bonds will **be** such as none (other) can bind.
089:027 (To the righteous soul will **be** said:) "O (thou)
090:017 Then will he **be** of those who believe, and enjoin
090:020 On them will **be** Fire Vaulted over (all round).
092:017 shall **be** removed far from it,-
093:004 And verily the hereafter will **be** better for thee
093:005 thou shalt **be** well-pleased.
095:005 Then do We abase him (to **be**) the lowest of the low,
098:006 will **be** in hell-fire, to dwell
099:006 sorted out, to **be** shown the Deeds that they
101:004 will **be** like moths Scattered about,
101:005 And the mountains will **be** like carded wool.
101:006 whose balance (of good deeds) will **be** (found) heavy,
101:007 Will **be** in a life of good pleasure and satisfaction.
101:008 whose balance (of good deeds) will **be** (found) light,-
102:008 Then, shall ye **be** Questioned that Day about the
104:004 to **be** thrown into that which Breaks to Pieces.
104:004 By no means! He will **be** sure to **be** thrown
104:008 It shall **be** made into a vault over them,
107:006 Those who (want but) to **be** seen,
108:003 he will **be** cut off (from Future Hope).
109:006 To you **be** your Way, and to me mine.
111:003 Burnt soon will he **be** in a Fire of blazing Flame!

BEACONS
006:097 the stars (as **beacons**) for you, that ye

BEAKER
012:072 They said: "We miss the great **beaker** of the king;

BEAKERS
056:018 With goblets, (shining) **beakers**, and cups

BEAM
075:022 will **beam** (in brightness and beauty);-

BEAMING
080:038 Some Faces that Day will be **beaming**.
083:024 the **beaming** brightness of Bliss.

BEAR
002:046 Who **bear** in mind the certainty
002:217 their works will **bear** no fruit in this life
002:233 But he shall **bear** the cost of their food
002:233 laid on it greater than it can **bear**.
002:286 than we have the strength to **bear**.
002:286 place a burden greater than it can **bear**.
003:022 They are those whose works will **bear** no fruit
003:052 and do thou **bear** witness that we are Muslims.
003:053 then write us down among those who **bear** witness."
003:064 say ye: "**Bear** witness that we (at least) are Muslims
003:081 He said: "Then **bear** witness, and I am with you
004:166 and the angels **bear** witness:
005:111 and do thou **bear** witness that we bow to Allah
006:019 Say: "Nay! I cannot **bear** witness!"
006:019 Can ye possibly **bear** witness that besides
006:031 and evil indeed are the burdens that they **bear**!

BEAR (continued)
006:031 for they **bear** their burdens on their backs;
006:099 when they begin to **bear** fruit, feast your
006:130 they **bear** witness that they rejected Faith.
006:130 "We **bear** witness against ourselves."
006:152 but that which it can **bear**;-whenever ye speak
006:164 can **bear** the burden of another.
007:037 and they will **bear** witness against themselves,
007:042 but that which it can **bear**,-they will be
009:017 The works of such **bear** no fruit:
011:054 to witness, and do ye **bear** witness, that I am
011:072 She said: "Alas for me! Shall I **bear** a child,
012:081 we **bear** witness only to what we know, and we
013:008 every female (womb) doth **bear**, by how
014:012 We shall certainly **bear** with patience all the
014:021 (now) whether we rage, or **bear** (these torments)
016:025 That they may **bear**, on the Day of Judgment,
016:025 the burdens they will **bear**!
017:015 can **bear** the burden of another:
020:100 verily they will **bear** a burden on the
021:061 that they may **bear** witness:"
023:062 greater than it can **bear**:
024:024 **bear** witness against them as to their actions.
029:012 and we will **bear** (the consequences) of your
029:012 will they **bear** their faults:
029:013 They will **bear** their own burdens, and other
031:014 in travail upon travail did his mother **bear** him.
031:015 obey them not; yet **bear** them company in this
031:017 and **bear** with patient constancy whatever betide
033:058 and women undeservedly, **bear** (on themselves)
035:018 Nor can a bearer of burdens **bear** another's burden.
035:018 heavily laden should call another to (**bear**) his load,
036:065 and their feet **bear** witness, to all that they did.
039:007 No bearer of burdens can **bear** the burden
040:007 Those who **bear** the Throne (of Allah) and those
041:020 and their skins will **bear** witness against them,
041:021 "Why **bear** ye witness against us?"
041:022 and your skins should **bear** witness against you!
041:047 "We do assure Thee not one of us can **bear** witness!"
046:015 in pain did his mother **bear** him,
050:021 and an (angel) to **bear** witness.
050:039 **Bear**, then with patience, all that they say,
051:002 And those that lift and **bear** away heavy weights;
052:016 to you whether ye **bear** it with patience, or not:
053:038 can **bear** the burden of another;
063:001 they say, "We **bear** witness that thou art
069:012 should **bear** its (lessons) in remembrance.
069:017 that Day, **bear** the Throne of thy Lord above them.
073:011 and **bear** with them for a little while.
083:021 To which **bear** witness those Nearest (to Allah).

BEARD
020:094 Seize (me) not by my **beard** nor by

BEARER
002:119 in truth as a **bearer** of glad tidings
006:164 no **bearer** of burdens can bear the burdens
012:096 Then when the **bearer** of the good news came,
017:015 no **bearer** of burdens can bear the burdens
033:045 as a Witness, a **Bearer** of Glad Tidings, and a
035:018 Nor can a **bearer** of burdens bear another's
035:024 as a **bearer** of glad tidings, and as a warner:
039:007 No **bearer** of burdens can bear the burden
053:038 Namely, that no **bearer** of burdens can bear

BEARETH
004:166 But Allah **beareth** witness that what He hath
063:001 And Allah **beareth** witness that the Hypocrites
BEARING
004:102 taking all precautions, and **bearing** arms:
BEARINGS
002:220 (Their **bearings**) on this life and the Hereafter.
BEARS
007:189 she **bears** a light burden and carries
013:017 but the torrent **bears** away the foam that
024:008 the wife, if she **bears** witness four times
043:086 only he who **bears** witness to the Truth,
100:007 And to that (fact) he **bears** witness (by his deeds);
BEAST
005:004 the **beasts** and birds of prey, training them
027:082 a **beast** to speak unto them because mankind had
068:016 Soon shall We brand (the **beast**) on the snout!
BEASTS
002:164 in the **beasts** of all kinds
005:001 are all **beasts** of cattle with the exceptions
008:022 For the worst of **beasts** in the sight
008:055 For the worst of **beasts** in the sight of Allah
031:010 and He scattered through it **beasts** of all kinds.
035:028 And so amongst men and **beasts** and cattle,
081:005 When the wild **beasts** are herded together
BEAT
004:034 (and last) **beat** them (lightly);
020:018 with it I **beat** down fodder for my flocks;
BEAUTIFUL
002:245 Who is he that will loan to Allah a **beautiful** loan,
004:069 Ah! How **beautiful** is their Company.
005:012 and loan to Allah a **beautiful** loan, verily I will
007:031 wear your **beautiful** apparel at every time
007:032 the **beautiful** (gifts) of Allah, which He
007:180 The most **beautiful** names belong to Allah: so call
009:072 and **beautiful** mansions in Gardens of everlasting
012:003 the most **beautiful** of stories, in that
013:029 and a **beautiful** place of (final) return."
016:125 with wisdom and **beautiful** preaching; and argue
017:110 the Most **Beautiful** Names.
018:031 How **beautiful** a couch to recline on!
020:008 To Him belong the Most **Beautiful** Names.
022:005 forth every kind of **beautiful** growth (in pairs).
025:076 Dwelling therein;-how **beautiful** an abode
038:025 and a **beautiful** place of (final) Return.
038:040 to Us, and a **beautiful** Place of (final) Return.
038:049 is a **beautiful** place of (final) Return,-
039:023 the most **beautiful** message in the form of a Book,
040:064 and made your shapes **beautiful**,-and has
044:054 to maidens with **beautiful**, big, and lustrous eyes.
049:007 and has made it **beautiful** in your hearts, and He
050:007 every kind of **beautiful** growth (in pairs)-
052:020 with **beautiful**, big and lustrous eyes.
055:070 In them will be fair (Maidens), good, **beautiful**;-
056:022 with **beautiful**, big, and lustrous eyes,-
057:011 Who is he that will loan to Allah a **beautiful** Loan?
057:018 a **Beautiful** Loan, it shall be increased manifold
059:024 to Him belong the Most **Beautiful** Names:
061:012 which rivers flow, and to **beautiful** mansions in
064:003 and made your shapes **beautiful**:
064:017 If ye loan to Allah a **beautiful** loan, He will
070:005 a Patience of **beautiful** (contentment).
073:020 and loan to Allah a **Beautiful** Loan.

BEAUTY
003:037 He made her grow in purity and **beauty**:
010:005 a shining glory and the moon to be a light (of **beauty**),
010:024 its golden ornaments and is decked out (in **beauty**):
016:006 And ye have a sense of pride and **beauty** in them
024:031 their **beauty** except to their husbands,
024:031 their **beauty** and ornaments except what (ordinarily)
024:060 they make not a wanton display of their **beauty**:
027:060 well-planted orchards full of **beauty** and delight:
033:052 even though their **beauty** attract thee,
037:006 the lower heaven with **beauty** (in) the stars,-
037:007 (For **beauty**) and for guard against all
037:048 with big eyes (of wonder and **beauty**).
043:070 ye and your wives, in (**beauty** and) rejoicing.
055:076 and rich Carpets of **beauty**.
075:022 will beam (in brightness and **beauty**);-
BECAME
002:074 they **became** like a rock
003:103 so that by His Grace, Ye **became** brethren;
005:030 and **became** (himself) one of the lost ones.
005:031 Then he **became** full of regrets.
005:071 so they **became** blind and deaf; yet Allah
005:071 yet again many of them **became** blind and deaf.
006:043 On the contrary their hearts **became** hardened,
007:022 their shameful parts **became** manifest to them,
007:092 The men who rejected Shu'aib **became** as if they had
009:048 and the Decree of Allah **became** manifest, much to
009:076 they **became** covetous, and turned
009:114 But when it **became** clear to him that he was
012:084 And his eyes **became** white with sorrow, and he
016:036 and some on whom Error **became** inevitably (established).
023:048 So they rejected them and they **became** of those
026:063 part **became** like the huge, firm mass of a mountain.
023:106 and we **became** a people astray!
027:045 they **became** two factions quarreling with each other.
028:010 And the heart of the mother of Moses **became** void:
038:074 and **became** one of those who reject Faith.
039:059 and **became** one of those who reject Faith!'"
042:014 And they **became** divided only after knowledge
054:031 Mighty Blast, and they **became** like the dry
057:026 but many of them **became** rebellious transgressors.
061:014 and they **became** the ones that prevailed.
068:020 So the (garden) **became**, by the morning, like a dark
BECAUSE
002:010 they (incur), **because** they lie (to themselves).
002:061 This **because** they went on rejecting the Signs of Allah.
002:061 This **because** they rebelled and went on transgressing.
002:093 (with the love of the Calf **because** of their Faithlessness.
002:176 (Their doom is) **because** Allah sent down the Book
002:258 **because** Allah had granted Him Power?
002:273 **because** of their modesty,
002:275 That is **because** they say: "Trade
003:024 This **because** they say: "The Fire shall not touch us
003:075 **because**, they say, "There is no way over us
003:112 this **because** they rebelled and transgressed
003:112 This **because** they rejected the Signs of Allah,
003:155 **because** of some (evil) they had done.
003:182 "This is **because** of the (unrighteous deeds) which
004:034 and **because** they support them from their means.
004:034 **because** Allah has given the one more (strength)
004:062 **Because** of the deeds which their hands
004:102 the inconvenience of rain or **because** ye are ill;
004:102 put away your arms **because** of the inconvenience

BECAUSE (continued)

005:013 But **because** of their breach of their Covenant, We
005:058 that is **because** they are a people
005:078 **because** they disobeyed and persisted in Excesses.
005:082 **because** amongst these are men devoted to learning.
006:030 the Chastisement, **because** ye rejected Faith."
006:127 **because** they practiced (righteousness).
006:129 turn to each other, **because** of what they earn.
007:016 He said: "**Because** Thou hast thrown me
007:126 on us simply **because** we believed in the Signs
007:136 **because** they rejected Our Signs, and failed
007:137 **because** they had patience and constancy, and We
007:165 **because** they were given to transgression.
007:173 wilt Thou then destroy us **because** of the deeds
008:013 This **because** they contended against Allah
008:018 That, and also **because** Allah is He Who
008:035 "Taste ye the Chastisement **because** ye blasphemed."
008:051 This is "**Because** of (the deeds) which your
008:053 "**Because** Allah will never change the Grace
009:006 that is **because** they are men without knowledge.
009:077 **because** they broke their Covenant
009:077 and **because** they lied (again and again).
009:080 **because** they have rejected Allah
009:114 only **because** of a promise he had made to him.
009:120 **because** nothing could they suffer or do,
010:004 Chastisement grievous, **because** they did reject Him.
010:008 **because** of the (evil) they earned.
010:009 will guide them **because** of their Faith:
010:083 **because** of the fear of Pharaoh and his chiefs,
011:012 **because** they say, "Why is not a treasure sent down
015:039 **because** Thou hast put me in the wrong, I will
016:032 enter ye the Garden, **because** of (the good)
016:059 his people, **because** of the bad news he has had!
016:107 This **because** they love the life of this world
016:112 **because** of the (evil) which (its people) wrought.
016:127 and distress not thyself **because** of their plots.
017:059 only **because** the men of former generations treated
017:069 to drown you **because** of your ingratitude, so that
017:098 **because** they rejected Our Signs, and said,
018:049 in great terror **because** of what is (recorded)
018:106 **because** they rejected Faith, and took
019:037 and woe to the Unbelievers **because** of the
021:011 We utterly destroyed **because** of their iniquities,
022:006 This is so, **because** Allah is the Reality:
022:010 (It will be said): "This is **because** of the deeds
022:039 **because** they are wronged;-and verily, Allah is
022:061 That is **because** Allah merges Night into Day,
022:062 That is **because** Allah-He is the Reality; and those
023:055 Do they think that **because** We have granted them
023:060 **because** they will return to their Lord;-
025:075 place in heaven, **because** of their patient
027:052 in utter ruin,-**because** they practised wrong-doing.
027:070 nor distress thyself **because** of their plots.
027:082 **because** mankind had no faith in Our Signs.
027:085 against them, **because** of their wrong-doing,
028:078 **because** of a certain knowledge which I have."
029:034 **because** they have been wickedly rebellious."
030:036 evil afflicts them **because** of what their (own)
030:041 and sea **because** of (the meed) that the hands
031:030 That is **because** Allah is the Truth
031:030 and **because** whatever else they invoke besides Him
031:030 and **because** Allah,-He is the Most High, Most Great.
034:017 them **because** they ungratefully rejected Faith:

BECAUSE (continued)

034:050 it is **because** of the inspiration of my
038:027 the Unbelievers **because** of the Fire (of Hell)!
039:049 **because** of a certain knowledge (I have)!"
040:012 "This is **because**, when Allah was invoked as the
040:022 That was **because** there came to them
040:028 said: "Will ye slay a man **because** he says,
040:075 "That was **because** ye were wont to rejoice on the
041:017 seized them, **because** of what they had earned.
042:030 is **because** of the things your hands have wrought,
042:034 Or He can cause them to perish **because** of the
042:047 **because** of (the ordainment of) Allah!
044:037 We destroyed them **because** they were
045:035 "This, **because** ye used to take the Signs
047:003 This **because** those who reject Allah
047:009 That is **because** they hate the Revelation of Allah;
047:011 That is **because** Allah is the Protector of those
047:026 This, **because** they said to those who hate
047:028 This **because** they followed that which displeased
051:016 **because**, before then, they had done good deeds
052:019 and health, **because** of your (good) deeds."
059:004 That is **because** they resisted Allah and His
059:013 This is **because** they are men devoid
059:014 that is **because** they are a people devoid of wisdom.
060:001 (from your homes), (simply) **because** ye believe
062:007 **because** of the (deeds) their hands have sent
063:003 That is **because** they believed, then they
064:006 That was **because** there came to them messengers
068:014 **Because** he possesses wealth and (numerous) sons.
069:024 **because** of the (good) that ye sent before you,
071:025 **Because** of their sins they were drowned
076:012 And **because** they were patient and constant, He will
080:002 **Because** there came to him the blind

BECKON

002:221 Unbelievers do (but) **beckon** you to the Fire.

BECKONING

031:021 What! even if it is Satan **beckoning** them to the

BECKONS

002:221 But Allah **beckons** by His Grace to the Garden

BECOME

002:021 that ye may **become** righteous,
002:109 **become** manifest unto them:
002:135 They say: "**Become** Jews or Christians
006:028 will **become** manifest what before they concealed.
007:019 lest you **become** of the unjust."
007:020 lest ye should **become** angels or such
011:046 lest thou **become** one of the ignorants!"
016:092 after it has **become** strong.
017:029 **become** blameworthy and destitute.
018:028 and his affair has **become** all excess.
019:045 so that thou **become** to Satan a friend."
019:082 their worship, and **become** adversaries against them.
020:097 of whom thou hast **become** a devoted worshipper:
023:035 and **become** dust and bones, ye shall
023:082 and **become** dust and bones, could we
026:003 with grief, that they do not **become** Believers.
026:157 then did they **become** full of regrets.
027:067 "What! when we **become** dust,-we and our fathers,
028:019 to **become** a tyrant in the land, and not
030:032 and **become** (mere) Sects,-each party
030:051 they **become**, thereafter, ungrateful (Unbelievers)!
035:006 that they may **become** Companions of the Blazing Fire.
037:016 "What! when we die, and **become** dust and bones,

BECOME (continued)

037:053 "'When we die and **become** dust and bones,
040:067 then lets you **become** old,-through of you there are
041:023 and (now) have ye **become** of those utterly lost!"
041:029 so that they **become** the vilest."
041:034 and thee was hatred **become** as it were thy
042:033 then would they **become** motionless on the back
043:033 might **become** of one community We would provide,
049:002 lest your deeds **become** vain and ye perceive not.
049:006 and afterwards **become** full of repentance
050:003 "What! when we die and **become** dust,
056:047 "What! when we die and **become** dust and bones,
057:016 not **become** like those to whom was given The Book
075:038 Then did he **become** a leech-like clot;
077:008 Then when the stars **become** dim;
079:011 "What!-when we shall have **become** rotten bones?"

BECOMES

002:193 and the religion **becomes** Allah's.
003:049 and it **becomes** a bird by Allah's leave:
004:085 intercedes in a good cause **becomes** a partner therein:
004:100 his reward **becomes** due and sure with Allah:
008:039 and religion **becomes** Allah's in its entirety
016:004 and behold this same (man) **becomes** an open disputer!
017:083 he turns away and **becomes** remote on his side
018:045 but soon it **becomes** dry stubble, which the
022:063 and forthwith the earth **becomes** clothed with
041:053 until it **becomes** manifest to them that this
048:029 it then **becomes** thick, and it stands
055:037 and it **becomes** red like ointment:
057:020 then it **becomes** dry and crumbles away.
084:004 and **becomes** (clean) empty,

BECOMETH

005:110 and it **becometh** a bird by My leave.

BECOMING

004:115 a path other than that **becoming** to men of Faith,
056:006 **Becoming** dust scattered abroad,

BED

002:206 an evil **bed** indeed (to lie on)!
003:012 an evil **bed** indeed (to lie on)!
003:197 what an evil **bed** (to lie on)!
013:018 what a **bed** of misery!
038:056 an evil **bed** (indeed, to lie on)!-

BEDOUIN

009:097 The **Bedouin** Arabs are the worst in unbelief
009:098 Some of the **Bedouin** Arabs look upon their payments
009:099 But some of the **Bedouin** Arabs believe in Allah
009:120 of Madinah and the **Bedouin** Arabs of the

BEDOUINS

033:020 the **Bedouins**, and seeking news about you

BEDS

004:034 (next), refuse to share their **beds**,
032:016 They forsake their **beds** of sleep, the while
036:052 Who hath raised us up from our **beds** of repose?...

BEE

016:068 And thy Lord taught the **Bee** to build

BEEN

002:036 the state (of felicity) in which they had **been**.
002:059 the word from that which had **been** given them;
002:064 had it not **been** for the Grace
002:064 ye had surely **been** among the lost.
002:101 as if (it had **been** something)
002:103 far better had **been** the reward from Allah
002:173 name hath **been** invoked besides that Allah,

BEEN (continued)

002:285 hath **been** revealed to him from his Lord,
003:013 "There has already **been** for you a Sign
003:023 those who have **been** given a portion of the Book?
003:084 and in what has **been** revealed to us and what
003:137 There have **been** examples that have passed
003:154 we should not have **been** in the slaughter here."
003:156 they would not have died, or **been** slain."
003:164 while, before that, they had **been** in manifest error.
003:168 they would not have **been** slain."
004:019 except where they have **been** guilty of open lewdness;
004:023 (those who have **been**) wives of your son
004:029 for verily Allah hath **been** to you Most Merciful.
004:043 or ye have **been** in contact with women,
004:046 it would have **been** better for them, and more proper;
004:066 it would have **been** best for them, and would
004:073 as if there had never **been** ties of affection
004:073 "Oh! I wish I had **been** with them:
004:082 Had it **been** from other than Allah, they
004:115 even after guidance has **been** plainly conveyed
004:127 what hath **been** rehearsed unto you in the Book,
004:148 except by one who has **been** wronged, for Allah
004:160 which had **been** lawful for them; in that
004:162 believe in what hath **been** revealed to thee and
005:003 hath **been** invoked the name of other than Allah;
005:003 that which hath **been** (partly) eaten
005:003 that which hath **been** killed by strangling, or by
005:006 or ye have **been** in contact with women, and you
005:044 By its standard have **been** judged the Jews, by the
005:065 had believed and **been** righteous.
005:067 which hath **been** sent to thee from thy Lord.
005:081 hath **been** revealed to him, never would they
006:007 the Unbelievers would have **been** sure to say: "This
006:019 this Qur'an hath **been** revealed to me
006:071 and we have **been** directed to submit ourselves
006:081 without any warrant having **been** given to you?
006:094 between you have **been** cut off, and your
006:107 If it had **been** Allah's Will, they would
006:114 that it hath **been** sent down from thy
006:118 on which Allah's name hath **been** pronounced,
006:119 on which Allah's name hath **been** pronounced,
006:121 Allah's name hath not **been** pronounced:
006:134 All that hath **been** promised unto you
006:145 (meat) on which a name has **been** invoked, other
006:149 if it had **been** His Will. He could
006:157 "If the Book had only **been** sent down to us,
007:043 had it not **been** for the guidance of Allah:
007:043 Ye have **been** made its inheritors, for your
007:056 after it hath **been** set in order, but call
007:075 in the revelation which hath **been** sent through him."
007:085 after it has **been** set in order:
007:087 with which I have **been** sent, and a party
007:092 became as if they had never **been** in the homes
007:155 he prayed: "O my Lord! if it had **been** Thy will
007:162 which had **been** given them, so We sent
007:165 that had **been** given them, We rescued
007:171 as if it had **been** a canopy, and they
007:176 If it had **been** Our Will, We should
008:042 who died might die after a Clear Sign (had **been** given),
008:042 who lived might live after a Clear Sign (had **been** given).
008:043 ye would surely have **been** discouraged, and ye
008:068 Had it not **been** for a previous ordainment
008:070 than what has **been** taken from you, and He

BEEN (continued)

008:071 they have already **been** in treason against Allah,
009:029 forbidden which hath **been** forbidden by Allah
009:042 If there had **been** immediate gain (in sight),
009:047 and there would have **been** some among you
009:059 If only they had **been** content with what Allah
009:059 (That would **been** the right course).
009:060 have **been** (recently) reconciled (to Truth);
010:003 except after His leave (hath **been** obtained).
010:019 Had it not **been** for a Word that went forth before
010:019 their differences would have **been** settled between them.
010:072 and I have **been** commanded to be of those who
010:093 had **been** granted to them, that they
010:094 then ask those who have **been** reading the Book
010:096 of thy Lord hath **been** verified would not believe-
010:098 If only there had **been** a single township
010:099 If it had **been** the Lord's Will, they would
011:028 hath **been** obscured from your sight?
011:062 They said: "O Salih! thou hast **been** of us!-
011:070 We have **been** sent against the people of Lut."
011:078 and they had **been** long in the habit
011:100 and some have **been** mown down (by the sickle of time).
011:110 the matter would have **been** decided between them:
011:110 had it not **been** that a Word had gone forth
011:116 If only there had **been** of the generations
012:029 for truly thou hast **been** at fault!
012:041 (So) hath **been** decreed that matter whereof ye
012:045 one of the two (who had **been** in prison) and who
012:045 But the man who had **been** released, one of
012:052 may know that I have never **been** false to him
012:065 their stock-in-trade had **been** returned to them.
012:065 This our stock-in-trade has **been** returned to us:
012:082 Ask at the town where we have **been** and the
012:090 Allah has indeed **been** gracious to us (all):
012:091 and we certainly have **been** guilty of sin!"
013:001 that which hath **been** revealed unto thee
013:019 that which hath **been** revealed unto thee from
013:036 rejoice at what hath **been** revealed unto thee:
014:009 ye have **been** sent, and we are really in suspicious
015:002 wish that they had **been** Muslims.
015:013 in the Message, such has **been** the way of those
015:015 "Our eyes have **been** intoxicated:
015:015 nay, we have **been** bewitched by sorcery."
015:058 They said: "We have **been** sent to a people
016:115 other than Allah has **been** invoked.
016:126 to the wrong that has **been** done to you:
017:042 Say: if there had **been** (other) gods with Him,-
017:101 to have **been** worked upon by sorcery!"
017:102 these things have **been** sent down by none
017:108 Truly has the promise of our Lord **been** fulfilled!"
018:018 and wouldst certainly have **been** filled with
018:027 what has **been** revealed to thee of the Book of thy Lord:
018:066 which thou hast **been** taught?"
018:082 their father had **been** a righteous man:
018:101 and who had **been** unable even to hear.
018:101 (Unbelievers) whose eyes had **been** under a veil
018:104 "Those whose efforts have **been** wasted in this life,
019:009 when thou hadst **been** nothing!'"
019:023 would that I had **been** a thing forgotten."
020:048 'Verily it has **been** revealed to us that the
020:109 has **been** granted by The Most Gracious and whose
020:129 Had it not **been** for a Word that went forth
021:017 If it had **been** Our wish to take (just) a pastime,

BEEN (continued)

021:022 besides Allah, there would have **been** ruin in both!
021:054 He said, "Indeed ye have **been** in manifest error-
021:099 If these had **been** gods, they would
022:024 they have **been** guided to the Path
022:024 For they have **been** guided (in this life)
022:031 and **been** snatched up by birds, or the
022:040 there would surely have **been** pulled down
022:040 (They are) those who have **been** expelled from
022:054 has **been** bestowed may learn that the (Qur'an)
022:071 things for which no authority has **been** sent down to them,
023:071 therein would have **been** in ruin.
023:071 If the Truth had **been** in accord with their desires,
023:083 "Such things have **been** promised to us and to
024:021 not one of you would ever have **been** pure:
025:007 Why has not an angel **been** sent down to him
025:008 "Or (why) has not a treasure **been** bestowed on him,
025:042 had it not **been** that we were constant to them!"-
025:051 Had it **been** Our Will, We could
026:016 to Pharaoh, and say: 'We have **been** sent by the
026:027 who has **been** sent to you is a veritable madman!"
026:075 whom ye have **been** worshipping,-
027:010 (of its own accord) as if it had **been** a snake,
027:016 we have **been** taught the speech of Birds,
027:016 and we have **been** given of everything, this is
027:069 what has **been** the end of those guilty (of sin)."
027:091 For me, I have **been** commanded to serve the Lord
028:031 moving (of its own accord) as if it had **been** a snake,
028:047 followed the Signs and **been** amongst those
028:053 indeed we have **been** Muslims (bowing to
028:064 If only they had **been** open to guidance!'
028:076 that their very keys would have **been** a burden
028:077 but do thou good, as Allah has **been** good to thee,
028:078 He said: "This has **been** given to me because of
028:080 But those who had **been** granted (true) knowledge
028:082 Had it not **been** that Allah was gracious to us,
028:087 after they have **been** revealed to thee:
029:010 to say, "We have (always) **been** with you!"
029:034 because they have **been** wickedly rebellious."
029:053 had it not **been** for a term (of respite)
030:002 The Roman Empire has **been** defeated-
033:014 And if an entry had **been** effected to them
033:014 and they had **been** incited to sedition.
033:023 men who have **been** true to their Covenant with Allah:
033:036 when a matter has **been** decided by Allah and His
034:031 we should certainly have **been** believers!"
034:031 the arrogant ones: "Had it not **been** for you,
034:032 who had **been** deemed weak: "Was it we
034:033 Those who had **been** deemed weak will say to
034:034 with which ye have **been** sent."
036:014 they said, "Truly, we have **been** sent on a
036:016 we have **been** sent on a mission to you:
036:066 If it had **been** Our Will, We could
036:067 And if it had **been** Our Will, We could
036:067 Then should they have **been** unable to move about,
037:031 "So now has **been** proved true, against us,
037:057 "Had it not **been** for the Grace of my Lord,
037:057 I should certainly have **been** among those brought (there)!
037:143 Had it not **been** that he (repented and)
037:169 "We should certainly have **been** Servants of Allah,
037:171 Already has Our Word **been** passed before (this)
038:008 "What! Has the Message **been** sent to him-
038:070 "Only this has **been** revealed to me: that I

BEEN (continued)

039:020 one above another have **been** built:
039:049 he says, "This has **been** given to me because of
039:057 I should certainly have **been** among the righteous!'
039:065 But it has already **been** revealed to thee,-as it
039:071 has **been** proved true against the Unbelievers!"
040:047 will say to those who had **been** arrogant, "We but
040:048 Those who had **been** arrogant will say: "We are
040:066 Say: "I have **been** forbidden to invoke those whom
040:066 and I have **been** commanded to submit (in Islam)
040:085 (Such has **been**) Allah's way of dealing with His
041:011 and it had **been** (as) smoke:
041:045 Had it not **been** for a Word that went forth before
041:045 (their differences) would have **been** settled between them:
042:014 Had it not **been** for a Word that went forth before
042:014 the matter would have **been** settled between them:
042:016 after He has **been** accepted,-futile is
042:021 Had it not **been** for the Decree
042:021 the matter would have **been** decided between them
043:020 ("Ah!") they say, "If it had **been** the will of The Most
043:076 but it is they who have **been** unjust themselves.
043:083 that Day of theirs, which they have **been** promised.
045:017 it was only after knowledge had **been** granted to
046:021 but there have **been** Warners before
046:023 to you the mission on which I have **been** sent:
047:004 but if it had **been** Allah's Will, He could
047:032 after Guidance has **been** clearly shown to them,
048:023 (Such has **been**) the practice of Allah already in
048:025 If they had **been** apart, We should
048:025 Had there not **been** believing men
050:020 whereof warning (had **been** given).
051:032 They said, "We have **been** sent to a people
051:060 they have **been** promised!
052:027 "But Allah has **been** good to us, and has
054:014 recompense to one who had **been** rejected (with scorn)!
057:016 the Truth which has **been** revealed (to them),
058:011 and who have **been** granted Knowledge:
059:003 And had it not **been** that Allah has decreed
062:002 and Wisdom,-although they had **been**, before,
063:010 and I should have **been** one of the doers of good."
068:020 dark and desolate stop, (whose fruit had **been** gathered).
068:029 Verily we have **been** doing wrong!"
068:043 seeing that they had **been** summoned aforetime
068:049 he would indeed have **been** cast off on the
069:007 in its (path), as if they had **been** roots of
069:025 "Ah! would that my record had not **been** given to me!
069:028 "Of no profit to me has **been** my wealth!
070:042 that Day of theirs which they have **been** promised!
072:001 Say: It has **been** revealed to me that a company
074:016 for to Our Signs he has **been** refractory!
076:001 Has there not **been** over Man a long period of Time,
083:033 But they had not **been** sent as Keepers over them!
083:036 Will not the Unbelievers have **been** paid back
098:005 And they have **been** commanded no more than this:
100:011 That their Lord had **been** well-acquainted
105:005 and straw (of which the corn) has **been** eaten up.
109:004 that which ye have **been** wont to worship,

BEFALL

005:073 chastisement will **befall** the blasphemers among them.
012:037 and meaning of this err it **befall** you.
024:063 lest some trial **befall** them,
040:029 the Punishment of Allah, should it **befall** us?"
070:001 A questioner asked about a Chastisement to **befall**-

BEFALLEN

003:153 and for (the ill) that had **befallen** you.

BEFALLS

003:120 If aught that is good **befalls** you, it grieves them;
004:072 if a misfortune **befalls** you, they say: "Allah
004:078 If some good **befalls** them, they say, "This
005:106 and the chance of death **befalls** you (thus).
009:050 If good **befalls** thee, it grieves them;
009:050 but if a misfortune **befalls** thee, they say
022:011 if good **befalls** them, they are, therewith,

BEFITTING

019:035 It is not **befitting** to (the majesty of) Allah

BEFORE

002:004 and sent **before** thy time,
002:021 who created you and those who came **before** you
002:025 we were fed with **before**,"
002:031 then He placed them **before** the angles,
002:076 in argument about it **before** your Lord?"
002:095 their hands have sent on **before** them.
002:097 a confirmation of what went **before**,
002:110 send forth for your souls **before** you,
002:118 the people **before** them words of similar import.
002:133 when Death appeared **before** Jacob?
002:183 as it was prescribed to those **before** you,
002:198 even though, **before** this, ye went astray.
002:214 came to those who passed away **before** you?
002:236 ye divorce women **before** consummation
002:237 And if ye divorce them **before** consummation,
002:238 and stand **before** Allah in a devout
002:239 which ye knew not (**before**).
002:254 **before** the Day comes when no bargaining (will avail),
002:255 (appeareth to His creatures as) **before** or after or behind
002:286 like that which Thou didst lay on those **before** us;
003:003 confirming what went **before** it;
003:003 **Before** this, as a guide to mankind,
003:019 The Religion **before** Allah is Islam
003:050 to attest the Torah which was **before** me.
003:050 part of what was (**before**) forbidden to you;
003:059 Jesus **before** Allah is as that of Adam;
003:073 should engage you in argument **before** your Lord?
003:093 for himself **before** the Torah was revealed.
003:137 that have passed away **before** you:
003:143 for death **before** ye encountered it:
003:144 many were the Messengers that passed away **before** Him.
003:164 while, **before** that, they had been in manifest error.
003:182 which your hands sent on **before** ye:
003:183 Say: "There came to you Messengers **before** me,
003:184 so were rejected messengers **before** thee,
003:186 from those who received the Book **before** you
004:026 and to guide you into the ways of those **before** you;
004:047 **before** We change the face and fame of some (of you)
004:060 that have come to thee and to those **before** thee?
004:094 Even thus were ye yourselves **before**, till Allah
004:113 taught thee what thou knewest not (**before**):
004:131 the people of the Book **before** you, and you
004:136 and the scripture which He sent to those **before** (him).
004:159 but must believe in Him **before** his death;
004:162 and what was revealed **before** thee:
005:005 revealed **before** your time, when you
005:034 those who repent **before** they fall into your power:
005:043 when they have (their own) Torah **before** them?
005:046 confirming the Torah that had come **before** him:
005:046 that had come **before** him:

BEFORE (continued)

005:048 confirming the scripture that came **before** it,
005:057 those who received the Scripture **before** you,
005:059 come to us and that which came **before** (us),
005:075 that passed away **before** him.
005:080 forward **before** them (with the result), that Allah's
005:102 Some people **before** you did ask such questions,
006:006 how many of those **before** them We did destroy?
006:010 Mocked were (many) Messengers **before** thee;
006:028 will become manifest what **before** they concealed.
006:030 to stand **before** their Lord!
006:034 Rejected were the Messengers **before** thee:
006:042 **Before** thee We sent (Messengers)
006:051 brought (to judgment) **before** their Lord:
006:084 and **before** him, We guided Noah, and among
006:092 (the revelations) which came **before** it:
006:111 all things **before** their very eyes, they are
006:124 be overtaken by humiliation **before** Allah,
006:148 If so, produce it **before** us.
006:156 sent down to two Peoples **before** us, and for
006:158 if it believed not **before** nor earned righteousness
007:017 I assault them from **before** them and behind them
007:020 their shame that was hidden from them (**before**):
007:038 of the Peoples who passed away **before** you-men
007:038 it curses its sister-People (that went **before**),
007:043 "Behold! the Garden **before** you! Ye have
007:053 those who have forgotten it **before** will say: "The
007:057 of glad tidings, going **before** His Mercy:
007:080 no people in creation (ever) committed **before** you?
007:091 in their homes **before** the morning!
007:101 what they had rejected **before**.
007:123 "Believe ye in Him **before** I give you permission?
007:129 both **before** and after thou comest to us."
007:142 his brother Aaron (**before** he went up):
007:155 long **before**, both them and me:
007:173 "Our fathers **before** us took false gods, but we
007:206 they glorify Him and prostrate **before** Him.
008:031 they say: "We have heard this (**before**):
008:038 the punishment of those **before** them is already
008:052 of the People of Pharaoh and of those **before** them:
008:054 of the People of Pharaoh and of those **before** them":
009:007 there be a covenant **before** Allah and His Messenger,
009:048 Indeed they had plotted sedition **before**, and upset
009:069 As in the case of those **before** you:
009:069 and ye have yours, as did those **before** you;
009:070 Hath not the story reached them of those **before** them?
010:002 that they have **before** their Lord the good
010:013 Generations **before** you We destroyed when they
010:016 A whole lifetime **before** this have I tarried
010:019 for a word that went forth **before** from thy Lord,
010:024 as if it had not flourished the day **before**!
010:030 (the fruits of) the deeds it sent **before**:
010:037 it is a confirmation of (revelations) that went **before** it,
010:039 even **before** the interpretation thereof hath reached them:
010:039 thus did those **before** them make charges of falsehood:
010:046 or We take thy soul (**before** that)-in any case,
010:047 when their messenger comes (**before** them),
010:091 but a little while **before**, wast thou in rebellion!-
010:094 who have been reading the Book from **before** thee:
010:102 of the men who passed away **before** them?
011:017 and **before** him is the Book of Moses-a guide
011:018 They will be brought **before** their Lord, and the
011:023 and humble themselves **before** their Lord-they will

BEFORE (continued)

011:049 **before** this, neither thou nor thy People knew them.
011:067 prostrate in their homes **before** the morning,-
011:098 He will go **before** his people on the
011:109 but what their fathers worshipped **before** (them):
011:110 had gone forth **before** from thy Lord the matter
011:116 If only thee had been of the generations **before** you,
012:003 **before** this,thou too was among those who knew not.
012:031 and she said (to Joseph) "Come out **before** them."
012:032 She said: "There **before** you is the man
012:037 He said: "**Before** any food comes (in due course)
012:076 **before** (he came to) the baggage of his brother:
012:077 there was a brother of his who did steal **before** (him)."
012:080 and how, **before** this, ye did fail in your duty
012:100 in prostration (all) **before** him.
012:109 the end of those **before** them?
012:109 Nor did We send **before** thee (as Messengers)
012:111 of what went **before** it,-a detailed
013:006 to pass, **before** them, (many) exemplary punishments!
013:011 there are (angels) in succession, **before** and behind him;
013:030 a People **before** whom (long since) have (other)
013:032 Mocked were (many) messengers **before** thee:
013:038 We did send messengers **before** thee, and appointed
013:040 thy soul (**before** it is all accomplished), thy duty
013:042 Those **before** them did (also) devise plots;
014:009 (O people!), of those who (went) **before** you?
014:014 when they shall stand **before** My tribunal,-
014:021 They will all be marshalled **before** Allah together:
014:031 secretly and openly, **before** the coming of a Day
014:048 marshalled forth, **before** Allah, the One,
015:010 We did send messengers **before** thee amongst
015:013 the way of those who went **before** them.
015:027 And the Jinn race, We had created **before**, from the
016:026 Those **before** them did also plot (against Allah's 'Way):
016:033 So did those who went **before** them.
016:035 So did those who went **before** them.
016:043 And **before** thee We sent were but men, to whom
016:049 for none are arrogant (**before** their Lord).
016:063 (our prophets) to Peoples **before** thee; but Satan
016:118 as We have mentioned to thee **before**:
017:007 as they had entered it **before**, and to
017:058 We shall destroy it **before** the Day
017:077 with the messengers We sent **before** thee:
017:092 and the angels **before** (us) face to face;
018:048 And they will be marshalled **before** thy Lord in ranks,
018:049 And the Book (of deeds) will be placed (**before** you);
018:049 They will find all that they did, placed **before** them;
018:087 him with a punishment unheard-of (**before**).
018:091 We completely understood what was **before** him.
019:007 that name have We conferred distinction **before**."
019:009 I did indeed create thee **before**, when thou
019:017 and he appeared **before** her as a man in all respects.
019:023 "Ah! would that I had died **before** this! would that
019:038 the Day that they will appear **before** Us!
019:064 to Him belongeth what is **before** us and what
019:067 that We created him **before** out of nothing?
019:074 (countless) generations **before** them have We destroyed,
019:080 and he shall appear **before** Us bare and alone.
019:085 like a band (presented **before** a king for honours).
019:098 generation **before** them have We destroyed?
020:037 We conferred a favour on thee another time (**before**).
020:071 "Believe ye in Him **before** I give you permission?
020:088 out (of the fire) **before** the (people) the image of a calf:

BEFORE (continued)

020:090 Aaron had already, **before** this said to them:
020:099 some stories of what happened **before**:
020:110 He knows what is **before** or after or behind them:
020:111 (All) faces shall be humbled **before**-the Living,
020:114 the Qur'an **before** its revelation to thee
020:125 while I had sight (**before**)?"
020:128 generations **before** them We destroyed, in whose
020:129 that went forth **before** from thy Lord,
020:130 **before** the rising of the sun, and **before** its setting;
020:134 Had We destroyed them with a punishment **before** this,
020:134 should certainly have followed Thy Signs **before** we were
021:006 (As to those) **before** them, not one of the towns
021:007 **Before** thee, also, the messengers We sent
021:024 and the Message of those **before** me."
021:025 Not a messenger did We send **before** thee without this
021:027 They speak not **before** He speaks, and they
021:028 He knows what is **before** them, and what
021:030 (as one unit of Creation) **before** We clove them asunder?
021:034 granted not to any man **before** thee permanent life (here):
021:041 Mocked were (many) messengers **before** thee;
021:061 They said, "Then bring him **before** the eyes
021:090 And humble themselves **before** Us.
021:101 Those for whom the Good from Us has gone **before**,
021:105 **Before** this We wrote in the Psalms, after the
022:042 the Peoples **before** them (with their prophets),-
022:052 Never did We send a messenger or a prophet **before** thee,
022:076 He knows what is **before** them and what
022:078 both **before** and in this (Revelation);
023:062 **before** Us is a record which clearly speaks
023:083 been promised to us and to our fathers **before**!
023:100 **Before** them is a Partition till the Day they are raised up,
024:034 people who passed away **before** you,
024:055 as He granted it to those **before** them; that He
024:058 ask your permission (**before** they come to your presence),
024:058 on three occasions: **before** morning prayer; the while ye
024:059 them (also) ask for permission, as do those **before** them:
025:005 and they are dictated **before** him morning and evening."
025:020 the messengers whom We sent **before** thee were all (men)
025:035 (**Before** this), We sent Moses the Book,
025:048 going **before** His Mercy, and We send down pure water
026:049 Said (Pharaoh): "Believe ye in Him **before** I give
026:076 "Ye and your fathers **before** you?-
026:184 and (Who created) the generations **before** (you)."
027:017 And **before** Solomon were marshalled his hosts,-
027:038 can bring me her throne **before** they come to me
027:039 "I will bring it to thee **before** thou rise
027:040 placed firmly **before** him, he said: "This is
027:040 "I will bring it to thee **before** even thy glance
027:046 to hasten on the evil **before** the good?
027:063 of glad tidings, going **before** His Mercy?
027:068 we were promised this,-we and our fathers **before** (us):
027:084 Until, when they come (**before** the Judgment-Seat),
028:018 the man who had, the day **before**, sought his
028:046 no warner had come **before** thee:
028:052 Those to whom We sent the Book **before** this,-
028:053 (bowing to Allah's Will) from **before** this."
028:064 and they will see the Chastisement (**before** them);
028:078 had destroyed, **before** him, (whole) generations,-
028:082 the day **before** began to say on the morrow:
029:003 We did test those **before** them, and Allah
029:018 so did generations **before** you:
029:028 in Creation (ever) committed **before** you.

BEFORE (continued)

029:048 not (able) to recite a Book, **before** this (Book came),
030:009 and see what was the End of those **before** them?
030:042 and see what was the End of those **before** (you):
030:043 the right Religion, **before** there come from Allah
030:047 We did indeed send, **before** thee, messengers to
030:049 Even though, **before** they received (the rain)-
030:049 just **before** this-they were dumb with despair!
032:003 to whom no warner has come **before** thee:
032:012 their heads **before** their Lord, (saying): "Our Lord!
032:021 of the lighter Chastisement **before** the greater
032:026 how many generations We destroyed **before** them,
033:027 and of a land which ye had not frequented (**before**).
033:049 and then divorce them **before** ye have touched them,
033:053 ask them from **before** a screen:
033:055 (on those ladies if they appear) **before** their fathers
034:009 See they not what is **before** them and behind
034:031 nor in (any) that (came) **before** it."
034:031 to stand **before** their Lord, throwing back
034:044 nor sent messengers to them **before** thee as Warners.
034:046 that ye do stand up **before** Allah,-(it may be)
034:053 Seeing that they did reject faith (entirely) **before**,
035:004 so were messengers rejected **before** thee:
035:031 is the Truth,-confirming what was (revealed) **before** it:
035:044 and see what was the End of those **before** them,-
036:012 sent **before** and that which they leave behind,
036:031 how many generations **before** them We destroyed?
036:032 will be brought **before** Us (for judgment).
036:045 which is **before** you and that which will be
036:053 they will all be brought up **before** Us!
036:075 and they are a host brought up **before** them.
037:037 (the Message of) the messengers (**before** him).
037:071 And truly **before** them, many of the ancients went astray;-
037:091 "Will ye not eat (of the offerings **before** you)?
037:158 that they will be brought **before** Him.
037:168 "If only we had had **before** us a message
037:171 Our Word been passed **before** (this) to Our Servants sent
037:177 But when it descends upon their courtyards **before** them,
038:003 How many generations **before** them did We destroy?
038:012 **Before** them (were many who) rejected messengers,-
038:016 our sentence (even) **before** the Day of Account!"
038:031 Behold, there were brought **before** him, at eventide,
039:008 (man) doth forget what he cried and prayed for **before**,
039:025 Those **before** them (also) rejected (revelation),
039:050 Thus did the (generations) **before** them say!
039:054 and submit to Him, **before** the Chastisement come on
039:055 **before** the Chastisement comes on you-of a sudden,
039:065 as it was to those **before** thee,-
040:005 But (there were people) **before** them, who denied
040:021 and see what was the End of those **before** them?
040:067 though of you there are some die **before**;-
040:077 or We take thy soul (to Our Mercy) (**before** that),-
040:078 We did aforetime send messengers **before** thee:
040:082 and see what was the End of those **before** them?
041:014 from **before** them and behind them, (preaching):
041:025 was **before** them and behind them;
041:042 No falsehood can approach it from **before** or behind it:
041:043 to the messengers **before** thee:
041:045 for a Word that went forth **before** from thy Lord,
042:003 to thee as (He did) to those **before** thee,-Allah,
042:014 not been for a Word that went forth **before** from thy Lord,
042:022 they shall have **before** their Lord, all that they wish for.
042:047 **before** there come a Day which there will be no putting

BEFORE (continued)

042:052 thou knewest not (**before**) what was Revelation,
043:021 What! have We given them a Book **before** this,
043:023 a Warner **before** thee to any people, the wealthy
043:045 question thou our messengers whom We sent **before** thee;
044:017 We did, **before** them, try the people of Pharaoh:
044:037 people of Tubba and those who were **before** them?
046:004 Bring me a Book (revealed) **before** this, or any
046:011 (such men) would not have gone to it first, **before** us!"
046:012 And **before** this, was the Book of Moses as a
046:017 have passed **before** me (without rising again)?"
046:020 Day that the Unbelievers will be placed **before** the Fire,
046:021 Warners **before** him and after him:
046:030 revealed after Moses, confirming what came **before** it:
046:034 the Unbelievers will be placed **before** the Fire,
047:010 what was the End of those **before** them (who did evil)?
048:016 but if ye turn back as ye did **before**, He will punish you
049:001 yourselves forward **before** Allah and His Messenger;
050:012 **Before** them was denied (the Hereafter) by the
050:036 But how many generations **before** them did We
050:039 **before** the rising of the sun and **before** (its) setting,
051:016 because, **before** then, they had done good deeds
051:027 And placed it **before** them...
051:046 So were the people of Noah **before** them:
051:052 no messenger came to the Peoples **before** them,
053:052 And **before** them, the people of Noah,
054:009 **Before** them the People of Noah rejected
055:046 they will stand **before** (the Judgment Seat of)
055:056 whom no man or Jinn **before** them has touched;-
055:074 Whom no man or Jinn **before** them has touched;-
056:045 to be indulged, **before** that, in sinful luxury,
057:010 those who spent (freely) and fought **before** the Victory,
057:012 how their Light runs forward **before** their right hands:
057:022 is recorded in a Book **before** We bring it into existence:
058:003 should free a slave **before** they touch each other:
058:004 two months consecutively **before** they touch each
058:005 as were those **before** them:
058:012 spend something in charity **before** your private
058:013 spending sums in charity **before** your private
059:009 And those who **before** them, had homes
059:010 who came **before** us into the Faith and leave not,
061:006 (which came) **before** me, and giving glad Tidings
062:002 although they had been, **before**, in manifest error;-
062:007 the (deeds) their hands have sent on **before** them!
063:010 **before** Death should come to any of you and he
066:008 Their Light will run forward **before** them and by
066:010 and they profited nothing **before** Allah on their
067:018 But indeed men **before** them rejected (My warning):
069:009 And Pharaoh, and those **before** him, and the
069:024 that ye sent **before** you, in the days
070:036 the Unbelievers that they rush madly **before** thee-
071:001 thy People **before** there comes to them
072:027 march **before** him and behind him,
075:012 **Before** thy Lord (alone), that Day
077:038 We shall Gather you together and those **before** (you)!
079:040 the fear of standing **before** their Lord's (tribunal)
083:006 will stand **before** the Lord of the Worlds?

BEFOREHAND

002:223 But do some good act for your souls **beforehand**;
009:050 "We took indeed our precautions **beforehand**,"
010:074 they had already rejected **beforehand**.
015:004 had not a term decreed and assigned **beforehand**.
017:107 given knowledge **beforehand**, when it

BEFOREHAND (continued)

020:115 We had already, **beforehand**, taken the
048:015 Allah has already declared (this) **beforehand**":
048:020 and He has given you these **beforehand**; and He

BEFRIEND

007:196 and He will **befriend** the righteous.

BEFRIENDING

014:031 neither mutual bargaining, nor **befriending**.

BEG

002:273 they **beg** not importunately from all and sundry.
022:036 and feed such as (**beg** not but) live in contentment,
022:036 and such as **beg** with due humility:
041:024 And if they **beg** for pardon, their suit

BEGAN

007:020 Then **began** Satan to whisper
007:022 and they **began** to sew together the leaves
007:095 until they grew and multiplied, and **began** to say:
011:074 he **began** to plead with Us for Lut's people.
012:076 So he **began** (the search) with their baggage,
020:066 of their magic-**began** to be in lively motion!
020:121 they **began** to sew together, for their covering,
028:082 the day before **began** to say on the morrow:
032:007 the best way and He **began** the creation of man
038:033 Then **began** he to pass his hand over (their)

BEGET

019:035 to (the majesty of) Allah that He should **beget** a son.
019:092 that He should **beget** a son.
023:091 No son did Allah **beget**, nor is

BEGETS

017:111 Say: "Praise be to Allah Who **begets** no son,

BEGETTER

090:003 And the **begetter** and that he begot;-

BEGETTETH

112:003 He **begetteth** not, nor is He begotten;

BEGGAR

051:019 a due share for the **beggar** and the deprived.

BEGIN

006:099 when they **begin** to bear fruit, feast your
037:019 they will **begin** to see!

BEGINNETH

010:004 It is He Who **beginneth** the process of Creation,

BEGINNING

007:029 such as He created you in the **beginning**,
026:026 of your fathers from the **beginning**!"
085:013 from the very **beginning**, and He
092:013 the End and the **Beginning**.

BEGINS

030:011 It is Allah Who **begins** the creation; then repeats
030:018 and when the day **begins** to decline.
030:027 It is He Who **begins** (the process of) creation;

BEGOT

090:003 And the begetter and that he **begot**;-

BEGOTTEN

002:116 They say: "Allah hath **begotten** a son";
010:068 They say, "Allah hath **begotten** a son!"-Glory be
018:004 who say, "Allah hath **begotten** a son":
019:088 They say: "The Most Gracious has **begotten** a son!"
025:002 no son has He **begotten**, nor has He
037:152 "Allah has **begotten** children"?
112:003 He begetteth not, nor is He **begotten**;

BEGUILE

005:049 beware of them lest they **beguile** thee from any of that

BEHALF
002:068 They said: "Beseech on our **behalf** thy Lord
002:069 They said: "Beseech on our **behalf** thy Lord
002:070 They said, "Beseech on our **behalf** thy Lord
004:107 Contend not on **behalf** of such as
004:109 on their **behalf** on the Day of Judgment,
004:109 whose **behalf** ye may contend in this world;
007:053 now to intercede on our **behalf**?
007:134 they said: "O Moses! on our **behalf** call on
009:103 sanctify them; and pray on their **behalf**.
011:037 on **behalf** of those who are in sin: for they
048:011 (to intervene) on your **behalf** with Allah,
060:004 no power (to get) aught on thy **behalf** from Allah."
065:006 (the child) on the (father's) **behalf**.

BEHAVE
002:085 you who **behave** like this but disgrace in this life?
002:092 and ye did **behave** wrongfully.
007:053 Then should we **behave** differently from our
007:146 Those who **behave** arrogantly on the earth
010:014 after them, to see how ye would **behave**!
018:019 and let him **behave** with care and courtesy,
027:034 of its people its meanest thus do they **behave**.
060:002 If they overcome you they would **behave** to you

BEHAVED
023:046 these **behaved** insolently: they were an arrogant people.
029:039 but they **behaved** with insolence on the earth;
041:015 Now the 'Ad **behaved** arrogantly through the land,

BEHAVIOR
007:053 we behave differently from our **behavior** in the past."
033:053 Such (**behavior**) annoys the Prophet

BEHESTS
002:093 "Vile indeed are the **behests** of your Faith if you have
033:048 And obey not (the **behests**) of the Unbelievers

BEHIND
002:101 Book of Allah **behind** their backs,
002:234 If any of you die and leave widows **behind**;
002:255 before or after or **behind** them.
003:170 and with regard to those left **behind**, who have
003:187 but they threw it away **behind** their backs,
004:009 if they had left a helpless family **behind**:
004:072 men who would tarry **behind**:
006:094 Ye have left **behind** you all (the favours)
007:017 before them and **behind** them from their right
007:083 she was of those who lagged **behind**.
009:046 so He made them lag **behind** and they were told,
009:081 Those who were left **behind** (in the Tabuk expedition)
009:081 rejoiced in their sitting back **behind** the Messenger
009:083 then sit ye (now) with those who stay **behind**."
009:086 ask thee for exemption, and say: "Leave us (**behind**):
009:087 who remain **behind** (at home):
009:090 and His Messenger (Merely) sat **behind**:
009:093 the (women) who remain **behind**:
009:118 to the three who were left **Behind**; (they felt guilty)
009:120 the neighbourhood, to stay **behind** Allah's Messenger,
011:081 but thy wife (will remain **behind**):
011:092 For ye cast Him away **behind** your backs
013:011 there are (angels) in succession, before and **behind** him;
015:024 who hasten forward, and those who lag **behind**.
015:060 those who will lag **behind**."
015:065 and do thou go **behind** them:
019:064 Him belongeth what is before us and what is **behind** us,
020:110 He knows what is before or after or **behind** them:
021:028 He knows what is before and what is **behind** them,

BEHIND (continued)
022:076 He knows what is before then and what is **behind** them:
026:120 Thereafter We drowned those who remained **behind**.
026:171 Except an old woman who lingered **behind**.
027:057 to be of those who lagged **behind**.
029:032 she is of those who lag **behind**!"
029:033 she is of those who lag **behind**.
031:027 with seven Oceans **behind** it to add to its (supply),
034:009 See they not what is before them and **behind** them,
036:009 have put a bar in front of them and a bar **behind** them,
036:012 they send before and that which they leave **behind**,
037:135 those who lagged **behind**:
041:014 from before them and **behind** them, (preaching):
041:025 was before them and **behind** them;
041:042 No falsehood can approach it from before or **behind** it:
042:051 by inspiration, or from **behind** a veil,
044:025 and springs they left **behind**.
048:011 The desert Arabs who lagged **behind** will say
048:015 Those who lagged **behind** (will say), when ye
048:016 Say to the desert Arabs who lagged **behind**: "Ye shall be
049:012 nor speak ill of each other **behind** their backs.
059:014 except in fortified townships, or from **behind** walls.
072:027 march before him and **behind** him,
074:037 you that chooses to press forward, or to follow **behind**;-
076:027 and put away **behind** them a Day (that will be) hard.
084:010 But he who is given his Record **behind** his back,-
085:020 But Allah doth encompass them from **behind**!

BEHOLD
002:030 **Behold**, thy Lord said to the angels:
002:034 And **behold**, We said to the angels:
002:076 **Behold**! when they meet the men of Faith,
002:131 **Behold**! his Lord said to him: "Submit
002:133 **Behold**, he said to his sons: "What
002:158 **Behold**! Safa and Marwa are among
002:164 **Behold**! In the creation of the heavens
002:165 **Behold**, they would see the Punishment:
002:260 **Behold**! Abraham said: "My Lord! show me how
003:035 **Behold**! wife of 'Imran said: "O my Lord!
003:036 "O my Lord! **behold**! I am delivered
003:042 **Behold**! the angels said: "O Mary!
003:045 **Behold**! the angels said "O Mary!
003:055 **Behold**! Allah said: "O Jesus! I will take thee
003:081 **Behold**! Allah took the covenant of the Prophets,
003:153 **Behold**! ye were climbing up the high ground,
003:190 **Behold**! In the creation of the heavens
004:050 **Behold**! how they invent a lie against Allah!
004:053 **Behold**, they give not a farthing to
004:077 **behold**! a section of them feared men as, or even
005:027 **Behold**! they each presented a sacrifice (to Allah):
005:106 if we do, then **behold**! we shall be sinners.
005:107 if we did, **behold**! we will be wrong-doers."
005:110 **Behold**! I taught thee the Book and Wisdom,
005:110 **Behold**! I strengthened thee with the Holy Spirit.
005:110 And **behold**! thou makest out of clay, as it
005:110 And **behold**! thou bringest forth the dead
005:110 And **behold**! I did restrain the Children of Israel
005:111 "And **behold**! I inspired the Disciples to have
005:112 **Behold**! the Disciples said: "O Jesus the son of Mary!
005:116 And **behold**! Allah will say "O Jesus the son of Mary!
006:024 **Behold**! how they lie against themselves but
006:073 the day He saith, "Be," **Behold**! it is.
006:089 **behold**! We shall entrust their charge to a new
006:094 "And **behold**! ye come to Us bare and alone

BEHOLD (continued)

006:099 Behold! in these things there are Signs
007:043 "Behold! the Garden before you! Ye have
007:049 "Behold! are these not the men whom
007:095 Behold! We called them to account of a sudden,
007:107 and behold! it was a serpent, plain
007:108 and behold! it was white to all beholders!
007:117 and behold! it swallows up all the
007:131 Behold! in truth the omens of evil are theirs
007:135 Behold! they broke their word!
007:163 Behold! they transgressed in the matter
007:167 Behold! thy Lord did declare that He
008:007 Behold! Allah promised you one of the two
008:049 behold! Allah is Exalted in might, Wise.
009:025 behold! your great numbers elated you, but they availed
009:058 behold! they are indignant!
010:021 behold! they take to plotting against Our Signs!
010:023 behold! they transgress insolently through the
010:062 Behold! verily on the friends of Allah there is
010:066 Behold! verily to Allah belong all creatures,
010:071 Behold! he said to his People: "O my People,
010:101 Say: "Behold all that is in the heavens
010:104 (behold!) I worship not what ye worship
010:106 behold! thou shalt certainly be of those who do wrong."
011:005 Behold! they fold up their hearts, that they
011:009 behold! he is in despair and (falls into) ingratitude,
011:010 behold! he falls into exultation and pride.
011:018 Behold! the Curse of Allah is on those who do wrong!-
011:040 At length, behold! there came Our Command,
011:060 Ah! behold! For the 'Ad rejected their
011:065 (behold) there is a promise not to be belied!"
011:068 Ah! Behold! For the Thamud rejected their Lord
012:004 Behold, Joseph said to his father: "O my father!
012:028 (her husband) said: "Behold! it is a snare
012:069 He said (to him): "Behold! I am thy (own) brother;
012:070 "O ye (in) the Caravan! Behold! ye are thieves,
012:078 They said: "O exalted one! Behold! he has a father,
012:081 and say, 'O our father! behold! thy son committed
012:090 behold, he that is righteous and patient,-
013:003 Behold, verily in these things there are Signs for those
013:004 Behold, verily in these things there are Signs
015:008 (to the ungodly), behold! no respite would they have!
015:028 Behold! thy Lord said to the angels: "I am about to create
015:075 Behold! in this are Signs for those
015:077 Behold! in this is a Sign for those who believe!
016:004 and behold this same (man) becomes an
016:054 behold! some of you turn to other gods
016:067 behold, in this also is a Sign for those who are wise.
017:042 behold, they would certainly have sought out a way in
017:047 behold, the wicked say, "Ye follow none other than
017:060 Behold! We told thee that thy Lord doth
017:061 Behold! We said to the angels: "Prostrate unto
017:073 behold! they would certainly have made thee (their)
017:100 behold, ye would keep them back, for fear
018:010 Behold, the youths betook themselves to the
018:014 Behold, they stood up and said: "Our Lord
018:021 Behold they dispute among themselves as to
018:050 Behold! We said to the angels, "Prostrate to Adam":
018:060 Behold, Moses said to his attendant, "I will
019:003 Behold! he cried to his Lord in secret.
019:039 for (behold), they are negligent and they
019:042 Behold, he said to his father: "O my father!
020:010 Behold, he saw a fire: so he said

BEHOLD (continued)

020:020 He threw it, and behold! it was a snake,
020:038 "Behold! We sent to thy mother, by inspiration,
020:040 "Behold! thy sister goeth forth and saith,
020:066 Then behold their ropes and their rods-so it
020:084 He replied: "Behold, they are close on my footsteps:
021:012 Our Punishment (coming), behold, they (tried to)
021:018 and behold, falsehood doth perish!
021:052 Behold! he said to his father and his people,
021:097 then behold! the eyes of the Unbelievers will fixedly stare
022:026 Behold! We pointed the site, to Abraham, of the
023:034 behold, it is certain ye will be lost.
023:064 behold, they will groan in supplication!
023:091 (if there were many gods), behold, each god
024:015 Behold, ye received it on your tongues, and said
024:048 behold, some of them decline (to come).
026:010 Behold, thy Lord called Moses: "Go to the
026:032 and behold, it was a serpent, plain (for all to see)!
026:033 and behold, it was white to all beholders!
026:045 when behold, it straightway swallows up all the
026:070 Behold, he said to his father and his people:
026:106 Behold, their brother Noah said to them: "Will ye not
026:124 Behold, their brother Hud said to them: "Will ye not fear
026:142 Behold, their brother Salih said to them: "Will ye not
026:161 Behold, their brother Lut said to them: "Will ye not fear
026:177 Behold, Shu'aib said to them: "Will ye not fear Allah
027:007 Behold! Moses said to his family: "I perceive
027:045 but behold, they became two factions quarreling
027:054 behold, he said to his people, "Do ye do what is
028:018 fearful and vigilant when behold, the man
028:040 now behold what was the End of those
028:076 Behold, his people said to him: "Exult not,
029:016 behold, he said to his people, "Serve Allah and fear
029:028 And (remember) Lut: behold, he said to his people:
029:065 them safely to (dry) land, behold, they give
030:020 behold, ye are men scattered (far and wide)!
030:025 behold, ye (straightway) come forth.
030:033 behold, some of them pay part-worship to other gods
030:036 behold, they are in despair!
030:048 them in the shy as He wills, behold, they do rejoice!-
030:050 Then behold (O man!) the tokens of Allah's Mercy!-
030:051 they see (their) tilth) turn yellow,-behold, they become,
031:013 Behold, Luqman said to his son admonishing him
033:010 and behold, the eyes swerved and the hearts
033:010 Behold! they came on you from above you
033:012 And behold! The Hypocrites and those in whose
033:013 Behold! A party among them said: "Ye men
033:037 Behold! thou didst say to one who had received
034:033 Behold! ye (constantly) ordered us to be
036:013 Behold, there came messengers to it.
036:029 a single mighty Blast, and behold! they were (like ashes)
036:037 and behold they are plunged in darkness;
036:051 when behold! from the sepulchers (men) will
036:077 Yet behold! he (stands forth) as an open adversary!
036:080 when behold! ye kindle therewith (your own fires)!
037:019 (compelling) cry; and behold, they will begin to see!
037:084 Behold, He approached his Lord with a sound heart.
037:085 Behold, he said to his father and to his people,
037:124 Behold, he said to his people, "Will ye
037:134 Behold, We delivered him and his adherents,
037:151 Behold they say, out of their own invention,
038:021 Behold, they climbed over the wall of the private
038:031 Behold, there were brought before him, at eventide,

BEHOLD (continued)

038:041 **behold** he cried to his Lord: "Satan has afflicted me
038:071 **Behold**, thy Lord said to the angels: "I am
039:045 than He are mentioned, **behold**, they are
039:068 be sounded, when, **behold**, they will
039:073 until **behold**, they arrive there; its gates
040:047 **Behold**, they will dispute with each other
041:014 **Behold**, the messengers came to them, from before
042:005 **Behold**! Verily Allah is He, the Oft-Forgiving,
042:018 **Behold**, verily those that dispute concerning
042:045 **Behold**! Truly the wrong-doers are in a
042:053 **Behold** (how) all affairs tend towards Allah!
043:026 **Behold**! Abraham said to his father and his people:
043:047 **behold**, they laughed at them.
043:050 from them, **behold**, they broke their word.
043:057 as an example, **behold** thy people raise a clamour
045:013 **behold**, in that are Signs indeed for those who reflect
046:021 **behold**, he wanted his people beside the winding Sand
046:029 **Behold**, We turned towards thee a company of Jinns
047:038 **Behold**, ye are those invited to spend (of your substance)
050:017 **Behold**, two (guardian angels) appointed to learn
051:025 **Behold**, they entered His presence, and said:
051:038 **Behold**, We sent him to Pharaoh, with authority
051:041 **behold**, We sent against them the devastating Wind:
051:043 **Behold**, they were told "Enjoy (your brief day) for a little
053:016 **Behold**, the Lote-tree was shrouded with
053:022 **Behold**, such would be indeed a division
066:011 **behold**, she said: "O my Lord! build for me,
079:014 When, **behold**, they will be brought out to the open.
079:016 **Behold**, thy Lord did call to him in the sacred
083:032 "**Behold**! these are the people truly astray!"
085:006 **Behold**! they sat over against the (fire),
086:013 **Behold** this is the Word that distinguishes
087:016 Nay (**behold**), ye prefer the life of this world;
091:012 **Behold**, the most wicked man among them

BEHOLDERS

002:069 the admiration of **beholders**!"
007:108 and behold! it was white to all **beholders**!
015:016 and made them fair-seeming to (all) **beholders**;
026:033 and behold, it was white to all **beholders**!

BEHOLDETH

090:007 Thinketh he that none **beholdeth** him?

BEHOOF

014:045 (many) Parables in your **behoof**!"

BEING

002:067 from **being** an ignorant (fool)!"
003:145 the term **being** fixed as by writing.
003:172 even after **being** wounded,
004:075 those who, **being** weak, are ill-treated (and oppressed)?
005:003 or by **being** gored to death; that which
005:101 when the Qur'an is **being** revealed, they will
006:038 nor a **being** that flies on its wings,
008:006 as if they were **being** driven to death
009:040 **being** the second of the two they two were in the Cave,
009:046 but Allah was averse to their **being** sent forth; so He
010:022 and they think they are **being** overwhelmed:
015:006 "O thou to whom the Message is **being** revealed!
015:032 "O Iblis! what is your reason for not **being** among those
018:019 Such (**being** their state), We raised
018:022 the dog **being** the eighth.
018:022 the dog **being** the fourth among them; (others) say
018:022 the dog **being** the sixth,-doubtfully guessing
019:026 into no talk with any human **being**.'"

BEING (continued)

019:070 are most worthy of **being** burned therein.
019:075 warning of Allah (**being** fulfilled)-either in punishment
020:077 without fear of **being** overtaken (by Pharaoh) and with
020:090 "O my people! ye are **being** tested in this:
022:031 **Being** true in faith to Allah, and never
028:005 those who were **being** depressed in the land,
029:067 and that men are **being** snatched away from all
030:026 To Him belongs every **being** that is in the
030:029 fellow their own desires **being** devoid of
030:030 to the religion **being** upright, the nature
030:055 thus were they used to **being** deluded!
033:072 but they refused to undertake it, **being** afraid thereof:
038:003 no longer time for **being** save!
041:044 they are (as it were) **being** called from
042:014 knowledge reached them,-**being** insolent to one another.
043:037 But they think that they are **being** guided aright!
048:029 and their marks, (**being**) the traces of their prostration.
053:002 Your Companion is neither astray nor **being** misled,
054:028 each one's right to drink **being** brought forward
061:007 even as he is **being** invited to Islam?
066:007 Ye are **being** but requited for all that ye did!"
070:016 Plucking out (his **being**) right to the skull!-
081:007 the souls are sorted out, (**Being** joined, like with like);
098:005 offering Him sincere devotion, **being** True (in faith);

BEINGS

006:080 I fear not (the **beings**) ye associate with Allah:
006:081 "How should I fear (the **beings**) ye associate with Allah,
007:020 or such **beings** as live for ever."
013:015 Whatever **beings** there are in the heavens
017:044 and all **beings** therein, declare His
017:055 all **beings** that are in the heavens and on earth:
017:071 all human **beings** with their (respective) Imams:
019:040 We Who will inherit the earth, and all **beings** thereon:
019:093 Not one of the **beings** in the heavens and the
023:071 and all **beings** therein would have been in ruin
023:084 Say: "To whom belong the earth, and all **beings** therein?
024:041 Whose praises all **beings** in the heavens and on earth
037:011 or the (other) **beings** We have created?
042:005 and pray for forgiveness for (all) **beings** on earth:
064:006 "Shall (mere) human **beings** direct us?"

BELEAGUER

009:005 and seize them **beleaguer** them, and lie in wait for them

BELIE

002:039 reject Faith and **belie** Our Signs,
005:086 and **belie** Our Signs, they shall be

BELIED

011:065 (behold) there is a promise not to be **belied**!"

BELIEF

017:094 What kept men back from **Belief** when Guidance
026:024 and all between,- if ye had but sure **belief**."
052:036 Nay, they have no firm **belief**.

BELIEFS

006:082 and mix not their **beliefs** with wrong-that are

BELIEVE

002:003 Who **believe** in the Unseen,
002:004 And who **believe** in the Revelation
002:006 or do not warn them; they will not **believe**.
002:008 but they do not (really) **believe**.
002:008 "We **believe** in Allah and the Last Day,"
002:009 deceive Allah and those who **believe**,
002:013 "**Believe** as the others **believe**"
002:013 **believe** as the fools **believe**?"

BELIEVE (continued)

002:014 When they meet those who **believe**.
002:014 they say: "We **believe**," but when they are alone
002:025 who **believe** and work righteousness,
002:026 Those who **believe** know that it is the truth
002:041 And **believe** in what I reveal,
002:055 "O Moses! we shall never **believe** in thee
002:062 and who **believe** in Allah and the last day,
002:062 Those who **believe** (in the Qur'an)
002:075 they will **believe** in you?
002:076 they say: "We **believe**":
002:085 a part of the Book that ye **believe** in,
002:088 little is it they **believe**.
002:089 they refused to **believe** in it
002:091 "**Believe** in what Allah hath sent down,"
002:091 they say, "We **believe** in what was sent
002:091 if ye did indeed **believe**?"
002:097 glad tidings for those who **believe**,
002:121 they are the ones that **believe** therein:
002:126 **believe** in Allah and the Last Day."
002:136 Say ye: "We **believe**r in Allah,
002:137 So if they **believe** as ye **believe**,
002:153 O ye who **believe**! seek help with
002:172 O ye who **believe**! eat of the good things
002:177 **believe** in Allah and the Last Day,
002:178 O ye who **believe**! the law of equality
002:183 O ye who **believe**! fasting is prescribed to you
002:186 listen to My call, and **believe** in Me:
002:208 O ye who **believe**! enter into Islam
002:212 and they scoff at those who **believe**.
002:221 Do not marry unbelieving women until they **believe**;
002:221 Nor marry (your girls) to unbelievers until they **believe**;
002:223 good tidings to those who **believe**.
002:232 who **believe** in Allah and the Last Day.
002:254 O ye who **believe**! spend out of (the bounties)
002:260 He said: "Dost thou not then **believe**?"
002:264 O ye who **believe**! cancel not your charity
002:264 but **believe** neither in Allah
002:267 O ye who **believe**! give of the good things
002:277 Those who **believe**, and do deeds
002:278 O ye who **believe**! fear Allah,
002:282 O ye who **believe**! when ye deal with each other,
003:007 in knowledge say: "We **believe** in it;
003:049 Surely therein is a Sign for you if ye did **believe**.
003:052 "We are Allah's helpers, We **believe** in Allah,
003:053 "Our Lord! we **believe** in what thou hast revealed,
003:057 "As to those who **believe** and work righteousness,
003:068 as are also this Prophet and those who **believe**:
003:072 "**Believe** in the morning what is revealed
003:073 "And **believe** no one unless he follows your religion."
003:081 do ye **believe** him and render him help."
003:084 Say: "We **believe** in Allah, and in what
003:099 obstruct ye those who **believe**, from the path of Allah,
003:100 O ye who **believe**! if ye listen to a faction
003:102 O ye who **believe**! fear Allah as He should be feared,
003:114 They **believe** in Allah and the Last Day;
003:118 O ye who **believe**! take not into your intimacy
003:119 though ye **believe** in the whole of the Book,
003:119 when they meet you, they say, "We **believe**";
003:130 O ye who **believe**! devour not usury,
003:140 that Allah may know those that **believe**,
003:149 O ye who **believe**! If ye obey the Un**believe**rs,
003:152 for Allah is full of grace to those who **believe**.

BELIEVE (continued)

003:156 O ye who **believe**! Be not like the Un**believe**rs,
003:179 and if ye **believe** and do right, ye have
003:179 So **believe** in Allah and His Messengers:
003:183 our promise not to **believe** in a messenger unless he
003:193 '**Believe** ye in the Lord', and we have **believe**d.
003:199 those who **believe** in Allah, in the revelation to you,
003:200 O ye who **believe**! Persevere in patience
004:019 O ye who **believe**! ye are forbidden to inherit
004:029 O ye who **believe**! eat not up your property
004:043 O ye who **believe**! approach not prayers in a state
004:046 and but few of them will **believe**.
004:047 **believe** in what We have (now) revealed, confirming
004:051 They **believe** in sorcery and Tagut and say to the
004:057 But those who **believe** and do
004:059 O ye who **believe**! obey Allah, and obey
004:059 if ye do **believe** in Allah and the Last Day:
004:060 they **believe** in the revelations that have come
004:071 O ye who **believe**! take your precautions.
004:076 Those who **believe** fight in the cause of Allah,
004:094 O ye who **believe**! when ye go out in the cause
004:122 But those who **believe** and do deeds
004:135 O ye who **believe**! stand out firmly for justice,
004:136 O ye who **believe**! **believe** in Allah and His Messenger,
004:137 Those who **believe**, then reject Faith,
004:137 then **believe** (again) and (again) reject Faith,
004:144 O ye who **believe**! take not for friends
004:147 If ye are grateful and ye **believe**?
004:150 saying: "We **believe** in some but reject others":
004:152 To those who **believe** in Allah and His messengers
004:155 and little is it they **believe**;
004:159 but must **believe** in Him before his death;
004:162 **believe** in what hath been revealed to thee and
004:162 and **believe** in Allah and in the Last Day: to them
004:170 in truth from Allah: **believe** in him: it is best for you.
004:171 so **believe** in Allah and His Messengers.
004:173 But those who **believe** and do deeds
004:175 Then those who **believe** in Allah, and hold
005:001 O ye who **believe**! fulfill (all) obligations.
005:002 O ye who **believe**! violate not the sanctity
005:006 O ye who **believe**! when ye prepare for prayer, wash
005:008 O ye who **believe**! stand out firmly for Allah,
005:009 To those who **believe** and do deeds of righteousness
005:011 O ye who **believe**! call in remembrance
005:012 pay Zakat **believe** in My Messengers, honour and
005:035 O ye who **believe**! do your duty to Allah, seek
005:041 "We **believe**" with their lips but whose
005:051 O ye who **believe**! take not the Jews and the
005:053 And those who **believe** will say: "Are these
005:054 O ye who **believe**! if any from among you turn
005:057 O ye who **believe**! take not for friends
005:059 no other reason than that we **believe**r in Allah,
005:061 "We **believe**": but in fact they enter
005:069 any who **believe** in Allah and the Last Day,
005:069 Those who **believe** (in the Qur'an).
005:083 they pray: "Our Lord! we **believe**; write us
005:084 **believe** in Allah and the truth which has
005:087 O ye who **believe**! make not unlawful the good
005:088 but fear Allah, in Whom ye **believe**.
005:090 O ye who **believe**! intoxicants and gambling
005:093 guard themselves from evil and **believe**,
005:093 On those who **believe** and do deeds
005:094 O ye who **believe**! Allah doth but make a trial

BELIEVE (continued)

005:095 O ye who **believe**! kill not game, while in
005:101 O ye who **believe**! ask not questions about things
005:105 O ye who **believe**! guard your own souls:
005:106 O ye who **believe**! when death approaches any of you,
006:012 who have lost their own souls, that will not **believe**.
006:020 who have lost their own souls refuse therefore to **believe**.
006:025 they will not **believe** in them;
006:027 but would be amongst those who **believe**!"
006:048 so those who **believe** and mend (their lives),-
006:054 who **believe** in Our Signs, say: "Peace be on you:
006:082 "It is those who **believe** and mix not
006:092 Those who **believe** in the Hereafter **believe** in this (Book),
006:099 are Signs for people who **believe**.
006:109 a (special) Sign came to them, by it they would **believe**.
006:109 if (special) Signs came, they will not **believe**."?
006:110 even as they refused to **believe** in this
006:111 they are not the ones to **believe**, unless it
006:124 "We shall not **believe** until we receive
006:125 lay abomination on those who refuse to **believe**.
006:150 and such as **believe** not in the Hereafter:
006:154 that they might **believe** in the meeting with their Lord
006:158 no good will it do to a soul to **believe** then,
007:032 They are, in the life of this world, for those who **believe**,
007:042 But those who **believe** and work righteousness,-
007:052 a guide and a mercy to all who **believe**.
007:072 of those who rejected Our Signs and did not **believe**.
007:075 They said: "We do indeed **believe** in the revelation
007:076 we reject what ye **believe** in."
007:086 the path of Allah those who **believe** in Him,
007:087 and a party which does not **believe**,
007:088 (thee) and those who **believe** with thee;
007:093 a people who refuse to **believe**!"
007:101 but they would not **believe** what they
007:121 Saying: "We **believe** in the Lord of the Worlds.
007:123 Said Pharaoh: "**Believe** ye in him before I
007:132 we shall never **believe** in thee."
007:134 we shall truly **believe** in thee, and we
007:143 and I am the first to **believe**."
007:146 they will not **believe** in them;
007:153 but repent thereafter and (truly) **believe**,-
007:156 and pay Zakat and those who **believe** in Our Signs;
007:157 So it is those who **believe** in him, honor him,
007:158 So **believe** in Allah and His Messenger.
007:185 In what message after this will they then **believe**?
008:001 obey Allah and His Messenger, it ye do **believe**."
008:015 O ye who **believe**! when ye meet the Unbelievers
008:019 for verily Allah is with those who **believe**!
008:020 O ye who **believe**! obey Allah and His Messenger,
008:024 O ye who **believe**! give your response
008:027 O ye that **believe**! betray not the trust
008:029 O ye who **believe**! if ye fear Allah, He will
008:041 if ye do **believe** in Allah and in the revelation
008:045 O ye who **believe**! when ye meet a force, be firm,
008:055 are those who reject Him: they will not **believe**.
008:074 Those who **believe**, and emigrate, and fight
009:013 justly fear, if ye **believe**!
009:018 as **believe** in Allah and the Last Day,
009:019 **believe** in Allah and the Last Day, and strive
009:020 Those who **believe**, and emigrate and strive
009:023 O ye who **believe**! Take not for protectors
009:028 O ye who **believe**! Truly the Pagans are unclean;
009:029 Fight those who **believe** not in Allah nor the

BELIEVE (continued)

009:034 O ye who **believe**! There are indeed many among
009:038 O ye who **believe**! what is the matter with you,
009:044 Those who **believe** in Allah and the Last Day
009:045 who **believe** not in Allah and the Last Day,
009:061 and is a Mercy to those of you who **believe**."
009:086 to **believe** in Allah and to strive and fight
009:088 who **believe** with him, strive and fight with
009:094 we shall not **believe** you:
009:099 **believe** in Allah and The Last Day,
009:113 and those who **believe**, that they
009:119 O ye who **Believe**! Fear Allah and be
009:123 O ye who **believe**! Fight the Un**believe**rs who are
009:124 Yea, those who **believe**, their faith is increased,
010:004 those who **believe** and work righteousness, but those
010:009 Those who **believe**, and work righteousness,
010:013 to them with Clear Signs, but they would not **believe**!
010:033 verily they will not **believe**.
010:040 **Of them there are some who believe** therein, and some
010:051 "Would ye then **believe** in it at last, when it
010:057 and for those who **believe**, a Guidance and a Mercy.
010:063 Those who **believe** and (constantly) guard against evil;-
010:074 but they would not **believe** what they had
010:078 But not we shall **believe** in you!"
010:084 if ye do (really) **believe** in Allah, then in Him
010:087 and give Glad Tidings to those who **believe**!"
010:088 so they will not **believe** until they see
010:090 he said: "I **believe** that there is no god except
010:090 the Children of Israel **believe** in:
010:096 of thy Lord hath been verified would not **believe**-
010:099 thou then compel mankind, against their will, to **believe**!
010:100 No soul can **believe**, except by
010:101 profit those who **believe** not.
010:103 that We should deliver those who **believe**!
010:103 Our messengers and those who **believe**:
011:017 They **believe** therein; but those of the Sects
011:017 yet many among men do not **believe**!
011:023 But those who **believe** and work righteousness,
011:029 I will not drive away (in contempt) those who **believe**:
011:036 "None of thy People will **believe** except those
011:053 Nor shall we **believe** in thee!
011:120 a message of remembrance to those who **believe**.
011:121 Say to those who do not **believe**: "Do whatever
012:017 But thou wilt never **believe** us even though
012:037 of a people that **believe** not in Allah and that
012:057 who **believe**, and are constant in righteousness.
012:106 And most of them **believe** not in Allah
012:111 and a Guide and a Mercy to any such as **believe**.
013:001 but most men **believe** not.
013:002 that ye may **believe** with certainty in the
013:028 "Those who **believe**, and whose hearts find
013:029 "For those who **believe** and work righteousness,
013:033 Nay! to those who **believe** not, their devising
014:023 But those who **believe** and work righteousness
014:027 those who **believe**, with the Word that stands firm,
015:013 That they not **believe** in the Message,
015:077 Behold! in this is a Sign for those who **believe**!
016:022 as to those who **believe** not in the Hereafter,
016:060 To those who **believe** not in the Hereafter,
016:064 a guide and a mercy to those who **believe**.
016:072 will they then **believe** in vain things, and be
016:079 are Signs for those who **believe**.
016:099 who **believe** and put their trust in their Lord.

BELIEVE (continued)

016:102 in order to strengthen those who **believe**,
016:104 Those who **believe** not in the Signs of Allah,-
016:105 It is those who **believe** not in the Signs of
017:010 And to those who **believe** not in the Hereafter,
017:045 **believe** not in the Hereafter, a veil invisible:
017:082 and a mercy to those who **believe**:
017:090 They say: "We shall not **believe** in thee,
017:093 even **believe** in thy mounting until thou
017:107 Say: "Whether ye **believe** in it or not, it is
018:006 if they **believe** not in this Message.
018:029 let him who will, **believe**, and let
018:030 As to those who **believe** and work righteousness,
018:107 As to those who **believe** and work righteous deeds,
019:039 and they do not **believe**!
019:060 Except those who repent and **believe**, and work
019:073 the Unbelievers say to those who **believe**, "Which of the
019:096 On those who **believe** and work deeds
020:016 "Therefore let not such as **believe** not therein
020:070 "We **believe** in the Lord of Aaron and Moses."
020:071 (Pharaoh) said: "**Believe** ye in Him before I
020:082 to those who repent, **believe**, and do right,-
021:006 will these **believe**?
021:030 Will they not then **believe**?
022:014 who **believe** and work righteous deeds, to Gardens,
022:017 Those who **believe** (in the Qur'an), those who
022:023 Allah will admit those who **believe** and work
022:038 Verily Allah will defend (from ill) those who **believe**:
022:050 "Those who **believe** and work righteousness,
022:054 and that they may **believe** therein, and their
022:054 is the Guide of those who **believe**, to the
022:056 so those who **believe** and work righteous deeds
022:077 O ye who **believe**! bow down, prostrate yourselves,
023:038 but we are not ones to **believe** in him!"
023:044 so away with a people that will not **believe**!
023:047 They said: "Shall we **believe** in two men
023:058 Those who **believe** in the Signs of their Lord;
023:074 And verily those who **believe** not in the Hereafter
023:109 'Our Lord! we **believe**; then do Thou forgive us,
024:002 if ye **believe** in Allah and the Last Day:
024:021 O ye who **believe**! follow not Satan's footsteps:
024:027 O ye who **believe**! enter not houses
024:047 They say, "We **believe** in Allah and in the
024:055 who **believe** and work righteous deeds, that He
024:058 O ye who **believe**! let those whom your right
024:062 Only those are Believers who **believe** in Allah
024:062 are those who **believe** in Allah and His Messenger;
026:008 but most of them do not **believe**.
026:047 Saying: "We **believe** in the Lord of the Worlds.
026:049 Said (Pharaoh): "**Believe** ye in Him before I give
026:051 since we are the first to **believe**."
026:067 but most of them do not **believe**.
026:102 we shall truly be of those who **believe**!'"
026:103 but most of them do not **believe**.
026:111 They said: "Shall we **believe** in thee when it
026:114 "I am not one to drive away those who **believe**.
026:121 but most of them do not **believe**.
026:139 but most of them do not **believe**.
026:158 but most of them do not **believe**.
026:174 but most of them do not **believe**.
026:190 but most of them do not **believe**.
026:201 They will not **believe** in it until they see
026:227 Except those who **believe**, work righteousness,

BELIEVE (continued)

027:004 As to those who **believe** not in the Hereafter,
027:015 of His servants who **believe**!"
027:077 and a Mercy to those who **believe**.
027:081 to listen who **believe** in Our Signs, so they
027:086 for any people that **believe**!
028:003 in Truth, for people who **believe**.
028:047 amongst those who **believe**!"
028:052 before this,-they do **believe** in this (Revelation);
028:053 they say: "We **believe** therein, for it is
028:080 is best for those who **believe** and work
029:002 left alone on saying, "We **believe**", and that
029:007 Those who **believe** and work righteous deeds,-
029:009 And those who **believe** and work righteous deeds,-
029:010 "We **believe** in Allah"; but when they suffer
029:011 And Allah most certainly knows those who **believe**,
029:012 the Unbelievers say to those who **believe**: "Follow our
029:024 Verily in this are Signs for people who **believe**.
029:044 verily in that is a Sign for those who **believe**.
029:046 "We **believe** in the Revelation which has
029:047 So the People of the Book **believe** therein,
029:051 in it is Mercy and a Reminder to those who **believe**.
029:052 those who **believe** in vanities and reject Allah,
029:056 O My servants who **believe**! truly, spacious
029:058 But those who **believe** and work deeds
029:067 Then, do they **believe** in that which is vain,
030:037 are Signs for those who **believe**.
030:045 That He may reward those who **believe** and work
030:053 thou make to hear, who **believe** in Our Signs
031:008 For those who **believe** and work righteous deeds,
032:012 for we do indeed (now) **believe**."
032:015 Only those **believe** in Our Signs who, when they
032:019 For those who **believe** and do righteous deeds,
032:029 no profit will it be to Unbelievers if they (then) **Believe**!
033:009 O ye who **believe**! Remember the Grace of Allah,
033:041 O ye who **believe**! remember Allah, with much
033:049 O ye who **believe**! when ye marry believing women,
033:053 O ye who **Believe**! enter not the Prophet's houses,-
033:056 O ye that **believe**! send ye blessings on him,
033:069 O ye who **believe**! be ye not like those who
033:070 O ye who **believe**! fear Allah, and make
034:004 That He may reward those who **believe** and work
034:008 Nay, it is those who **believe** not in the Hereafter,
034:031 neither **believe** in this scripture nor in (any)
034:034 "We **believe** not in the (message) with which
034:037 but only those who **believe** and work
034:052 "We do **believe** (now) in the (truth)";
035:007 but for those who **believe** and work righteous deeds,
036:007 for they do not **believe**.
036:010 admonish them: they will not **believe**.
036:047 the Unbelievers say to those who **believe**: "Shall we then
037:052 "Who used to say, Do you really **believe**?
038:024 who **believe** and work deeds of righteousness,
038:028 Shall We treat those who **believe** and work
039:010 Say: "O ye my servants who **believe**! Fear your
039:045 the hearts of those who **believe** not in the Hereafter
039:052 Verily, in this are Signs for those who **believe**!
040:007 sing Glory and Praise to their Lord; **believe** in Him;
040:007 and implore forgiveness for those who **believe**:
040:025 "Slay the sons of those who **believe** with him,
040:051 help Our messengers and those who **believe**,
040:058 nor are (equal) those who **believe** and work
040:059 therein is no doubt: yet most men **believe** not.

BELIEVE (continued)

040:084 they said: "We **believe** in Allah,-the One
041:008 For those who **believe** and work deeds of
041:044 "It is a guide and a healing to those who **believe**;
041:044 and for those who **believe** not, there is a deafness
042:015 "I **believe** in the Book which Allah has sent down;
042:018 Only those wish to hasten it who **believe** not in it:
042:018 those who **believe** hold it in awe, and know that it is
042:022 But those who **believe** and work righteous deeds
042:023 Allah gives Glad Tidings to His Servants who **believe**
042:026 And He listens to those who **believe** and do
042:036 (it is) for those who **believe** and put their trust
043:088 Truly these are a people who **believe** not!"
044:012 for We do really **believe**!"
044:021 "If ye **believe** me not, at least keep
045:003 are Signs for those who **believe**.
045:006 exposition will they **believe** after Allah and His Signs?
045:014 Tell those who **believe**, to forgive
045:021 with those who **believe** and do righteous deeds,-
046:011 The Unbelievers will say of those who **believe**:
046:031 who invites (you) to Allah, and **believe** in him:
047:002 and **believe** in the (Revelation) sent down
047:002 But those who **believe** and work deeds
047:003 While those who **believe** follow the Truth
047:007 O ye who **believe**! if ye will
047:011 of those who **believe**, but those who
047:012 Verily Allah will admit those who **believe** and do
047:019 and for the men and women who **believe**:
047:020 Those who **believe** say, "Why is not a Sura sent down
047:033 O ye who **believe**! obey Allah, and obey
047:036 and if ye **believe** and guard against evil,
048:005 that He may admit the men and women who **believe**,
048:009 may **believe** in Allah and His Messenger, that ye
048:013 And if any **believe** not in Allah and His Messenger,
048:029 among them who **believe** and do righteous
049:001 O ye who **believe**! put not yourselves forward
049:002 O ye who **believe**! raise not your voices
049:006 O ye who **believe**! if a sinner comes to you
049:011 O ye who **believe**! let not some men among you
049:012 O ye who **believe**! avoid suspicion as much
049:014 The desert Arabs say, "We **believe**." Say, "Ye
052:021 And those who **believe** and whose seeds
053:027 Those who **believe** not in the Hereafter,
057:007 who **believe** and spend (in charity),-for them
057:007 **Believe** in Allah and His Messenger, and spend
057:008 How is it with you that you not **believe** in Allah?-
057:008 you to **believe** in your Lord and has indeed taken
057:019 And those who **believe** in Allah and His messengers-
057:021 prepared for those who **believe** in Allah and His
057:028 O ye that **believe**! fear Allah,
057:028 and **believe** in His Messenger, and He will bestow on
058:009 O ye who **believe**! when ye hold secret counsel,
058:011 O ye who **believe**! When ye are told to make room
058:011 those of you who **believe** and who have been granted
058:012 O ye who **believe**! When ye consult the Messenger
058:022 who **believe** in Allah and the Last Day, loving those
059:018 O ye who **believe**! Fear Allah, and let every soul look
060:001 O ye who **believe**! take not My enemies and yours
060:001 (simply) because ye **believe** in Allah your Lord!
060:004 for ever,-unless ye **believe** in Allah and Him
060:010 O ye who **believe**! when there come to you
060:011 and fear Allah, in Whom ye **believe**.
060:013 O ye who **believe**! turn not (for friendship)

BELIEVE (continued)

061:002 O ye who **believe**! why say ye that which
061:010 O ye who **believe**! shall I lead you to a bargain
061:011 That ye **believe** in Allah and His Messenger,
061:014 O ye who **believe**! be ye helpers of Allah:
062:009 O ye who **believe**! when the call is proclaimed
063:009 O ye who **believe**! let not your riches or your
064:008 **Believe**, therefore, in Allah and His Messenger,
064:009 And those who **believe** in Allah and work righteousness,-
064:014 O ye who **believe**! truly, among your wives
065:011 lead forth those who **believe** and do
065:011 And those who **believe** in Allah and work
066:004 one among those who **believe**,-and furthermore,
066:005 who submit (their wills), who **believe**, who are
066:006 O ye who **believe**! save yourselves and your
066:008 O ye who **believe**! turn to Allah with sincere
066:008 and those who **believe** with him.
066:011 to those who **believe**, the wife of Pharaoh: behold
069:033 "This was he that would not **believe** in Allah Most High,
069:041 little it is ye **believe**!
077:050 Then what Message, after that, will they **believe** in?
084:020 What then is the matter with them, that they **believe** not?-
084:025 Except to those who **believe** and work
085:011 For those who **believe** and do righteous deeds,
090:017 Then will he be of those who **believe**, and enjoin
095:006 Except such as **believe** and do righteous deeds:

BELIEVED

002:109 back to infidelity after ye have **believed** from selfish envy,
002:218 Those who **believed** and those who suffered
003:016 "Our Lord! we have indeed **believed**:
003:100 render you apostates after ye have **believed**!
003:193 'Believe ye in the Lord', and we have **believed**.
004:055 Some of them **believed**.
005:065 the People of the Book had **believed** and been righteous.
005:081 If only they had **believed** in Allah,
006:158 if it **believed** not before nor earned righteousness
007:096 had but **believed** and feared Allah, We should
007:126 on us simply because we **believed** in the Signs
007:158 who **believed** in Allah and His Words:
008:072 who **believed** but did not emigrate ye owe
008:072 Those who **believed**, and emigrated and fought
010:083 But none **believed** in Moses except some
010:098 township (among those We warned), which **believed**,
010:098 When they **believed**, We removed from them
010:099 they would all have **believed**,-all who
011:036 except those who have **believed** already!
011:040 But only a few **believed** with him.
011:058 We saved Hud and those who **believed** with him,
011:066 We saved Salih and those who **believed** with him,
011:086 left you by Allah is best for you, if ye (but) **believed**!
011:094 We saved Shu'aib and those who **believed** with him,
014:031 Speak to My servants who have **believed**, that they
018:013 they were youths who **believed** in their Lord,
020:073 For us, we have **believed** in our Lord:
021:006 the towns which We destroyed **believed**:
026:199 they would not have **believed** in it.
027:053 And We saved those who **believed** and practiced
028:067 had repented, **believed**, and worked righteousness,
029:026 But Lut **believed** Him: he said: "I will
030:015 Then those who have **believed** and worked
030:047 to aid those who **believed**.
034:020 all but a party that **believed**.
034:041 most of them **believed** in them."

BELIEVED (continued)

037:148 And they **believed**; so We permitted them to enjoy
040:012 but when partners were joined to Him, ye **believed**!
040:030 Then said the man who **believed**: "O my People!
040:038 The man who **believed** said further: "O my People!
041:018 But We delivered those who **believed** and practiced
043:069 Those who have **believed** in Our Signs and submitted
045:030 Then, as to those who **believed** and did
046:010 and has **believed** while ye are arrogant,
049:011 (to be used of one) after he has **believed**:
049:015 who have **believed** in Allah and His Messenger,
057:027 Yet We bestowed, on those who **believed**, their (due)
059:010 (or sense of injury) against those who have **believed**.
061:014 Then a portion of the Children of Israel **believed**,
061:014 gave power to those who **believed** against their enemies,
063:003 That is because they **believed**, then they rejected Faith:
065:010 O ye men of understanding-who have **believed**!-
067:029 we have **believed** in Him, and on Him
072:002 gives guidance to the Right, and we have **believed** therein:
083:029 Those in sin used to laugh at those who **believed**,
085:008 them for no other reason than they **believed** in Allah,

BELIEVER

004:092 Never should a **Believer** kill a **Believer**; except by
004:092 and whoever kills a **Believer** by mistake it is ordained
004:092 to a people at war with you, and he was **Believer**,
004:093 If a man kills a **Believer** intentionally, his recompense is
004:094 "Thou art none of a **Believer**!"
009:010 In a **Believer** they respect not the ties either of kinship
028:010 so that she might remain a (firm) **believer**.
033:036 It is not fitting for a **Believer**, man or woman,
040:028 A **Believer**, a man from among the people of Pharaoh,
040:040 whether man or woman-and is a **believer**-such will

BELIEVERS

002:213 guided the **Believers** to the Truth,
002:278 if ye are indeed **believers**.
003:028 Let not the **Believers** take for friends
003:028 **Unbelievers** rather than **Believers**:
003:072 what is revealed to the **Believers**,
003:160 In Allah, then, let **Believers** put their trust.
003:164 on the **Believers** when He sent among them
003:166 in order that He might test the **Believers**,
003:179 the **Believers** in the state in which ye are now,
004:051 in the (right) way than the **Believers**!
004:084 and rouse the **Believers**.
004:095 Not equal are those **Believers** who sit (at home),
004:103 on **Believers** at stated times.
004:139 who take for friends Unbelievers rather than **believers**:
004:141 And did we not guard you from the **Believers**?"
004:141 the Unbelievers a way (to triumph) over the **Believers**.
004:144 for friends Unbelievers rather than **Believers**:
004:146 if so they will be (numbered) with the **Believers**.
004:146 to the **Believers** a reward of immense value.
004:162 well-grounded in knowledge, and the **Believers**,
005:005 are (not only) chaste women who are **believers**,
005:011 And on Allah let **Believers** put (all) their trust.
005:054 lowly with the **Believers**, mighty against the Rejecters,
005:055 and the **Believers**,-those who establish regular prayers
005:056 His Messenger, and the **Believers**,-it is the party of
005:082 to the **Believers** wilt thou find the Jews and
005:082 to the **Believers** wilt thou find those who say,
007:002 warn (the erring) and a reminder the **Believers**.
008:002 For, **Believers** are those who, when Allah
008:004 Such in truth are the **Believers**:

BELIEVERS (continued)

008:005 even though a party among the **Believers** disliked it.
008:012 "I am with you: give firmness to the **Believers**:
008:017 the **Believers** a gracious benefit from Himself:
008:062 (the company of) the **Believers**,
008:064 follow thee among the **Believers**.
008:065 O Prophet! rouse the **Believers** to the fight.
008:074 these are (all) in very truth the **believers**:
009:014 heal the breasts of **Believers**.
009:016 and the (community of) **Believers**?
009:026 the Messenger and on the **Believers**, and sent
009:051 let the **believers** put their trust.
009:061 has faith in the **Believers**, and is
009:062 if they are **Believers**.
009:071 The **Believers**, men and women, are protectors,
009:072 Allah hath promised to **Believers**, men and women,
009:079 Those who slander such of the **Believers** as give
009:105 and His Messenger, and the **Believers**:
009:107 to disunite the **Believers**-and in preparation
009:111 Allah hath purchased of the **Believers** their persons
009:112 So proclaim the glad tidings to the **Believers**.
009:122 It is not for the **Believers** to go forth together:
009:128 to the **Believers** is he most kind and merciful.
010:002 and give the good news to the **Believers** that they
010:104 to be (in the ranks) of the **Believers**,
011:040 the Word has already gone forth,-and the **Believers**."
013:031 the **Believers** know, that, had Allah (so) willed,
014:041 my parents, and (all) **Believers**, on the
015:088 (in gentleness) to the **Believers**.
017:009 to the **Believers** who work deeds of righteousness,
018:002 to the **Believers** who work righteous deeds,
020:075 But such as comes to Him as **Believers** who have
023:001 Successful indeed are the **Believers**,-
024:002 the **Believers** witness their punishment.
024:003 to the **Believers** such a thing is forbidden.
024:012 Why did not the **Believers**-men and women-
024:017 if ye are (true) **Believers**.
024:019 scandal circulate among the **Believers**, will have
024:031 And O ye **Believers**! turn ye all together towards
024:047 some of them turn away: they are not (really) **Believers**.
024:051 The answer of the **Believers**, when summoned
024:062 Only those are **Believers** who believe in Allah
026:003 with grief, that they do not become **Believers**.
026:118 the **Believers** who are with me."
026:215 And lower thy wing to the **Believers** who follow thee.
027:002 A Guide; and Glad Tidings for the **Believers**,
030:004 on that Day shall the **Believers** rejoice-
033:006 than (the Brotherhood of) **Believers** and Muhajirs:
033:006 the **Believers** than their own selves, and his
033:011 In that situation were the **Believers** tried:
033:022 When the **Believers** saw the Confederate forces,
033:023 Among the **Believers** are men who have been true
033:025 and enough is Allah for the **Believers** in their
033:037 be no difficulty to the **Believers** in (the matter of)
033:043 and He is Full of Mercy to the **Believers**.
033:047 Then give the glad tidings to the **Believers**,
033:050 and not for the **Believers** (at large); We know
033:073 Allah turns in Mercy to the **Believers**, men and women:
034:031 we should certainly have been **believers**!"
040:035 in the sight of Allah and of the **Believers**.
042:045 And the **Believers** will say: "Those are indeed in lose
048:004 sent down Tranquillity into the hearts of the **Believers**,
048:012 and the **Believers** would never return to their

BELIEVERS (continued)

048:018 The **Believers** when they swore Fealty to thee
048:020 that it may be a Sign for the **Believers**,
048:026 His Tranquillity to His Messenger and to the **Believers**,
049:009 If two parties among the **Believers** fall into
049:010 The **Believers** are but a single Brotherhood:
049:015 Only those are **Believers** who have
051:035 the **Believers** who were there,
051:055 But remind: for reminding benefits the **Believers**.
057:013 say to the **Believers**: "Wait for us! Let us
057:016 the **Believers** that their hearts in all humility
058:010 in order that he may cause grief to the **Believers**;
058:010 and on Allah let the **Believers** put their trust.
059:002 by their own hands and the hands of the **Believers**.
060:010 that they are **Believers**, then send
061:013 the Glad Tidings to the **Believers**.
063:008 and His Messenger, and to the **Believers**;
064:002 and some that are **Believers**:
064:013 let the **Believers** put their trust.
074:031 and the **Believers**, and that those in whose heart
074:031 and the **Believers** may increase in Faith,-and that
083:034 But on this Day the **Believers** will laugh
085:007 (all) that they were doing against the **Believers**.
085:010 Those who persecute the **Believers**, men and women,

BELIEVES

002:221 a slave woman who **believes** is better
002:221 a man slave who **believes** is better
002:256 whoever rejects Tagut and **believes** in Allah
007:087 who **believes** in the message with which
009:061 he **believes** in Allah, has faith in the Believers,
018:088 "But whoever **believes**, and works righteousness
020:127 and **believes** not in the Signs of his Lord:
025:070 Unless he repents, **believes**, and works righteous deeds,
032:018 Is then the man who **believes** no better than the
034:021 We might test the man who **believes** in the Hereafter,
040:027 one who **believes** not in the Day of Account!"
064:011 and if anyone **believes** in Allah, (Allah) guides
065:002 who **believes** in Allah and the Last Day.
072:013 and any who **believes** in his Lord has no fear,

BELIEVETH

002:285 The Messenger **believeth** in what hath been
002:285 each one (of them) **believeth** in Allah,

BELIEVING

002:253 some **believing** and others rejecting.
003:110 and **believing** in Allah.
004:025 they may wed **believing** girls from among those
004:025 the means wherewith to wed free **believing** women,
004:092 he should free a **believing** slave.
004:092 and a **believing** slave be freed.
004:092 the freeing of a **believing** slave (is enough).
018:055 from **believing**, now that guidance has come to them,
024:023 indiscreet and **believing** women are cursed
024:030 Say to the **believing** men that they should lower
024:031 And say to the **believing** women that they should
033:035 for **believing** men and women, for devour
033:049 O ye who believe! when ye marry **believing** women,
033:050 and any **believing** woman who gives herself
033:058 And those who annoy **believing** men and women
033:059 and the **believing** women, that they
037:081 For he was one of Our **believing** Servants.
037:111 For he was one of Our **believing** Servants.
037:122 For they were two of Our **believing** Servants.
037:132 For He was one of Our **believing** Servants.

BELIEVING (continued)

048:025 Had there been **believing** men and **believing** women
057:012 and the **believing** women-how their Light
057:012 The Day shalt thou see the **believing** men and the
060:010 when there come to you **believing** women refugees,
060:012 O Prophet! when **believing** women come to thee
071:028 and (all) **believing** men and **believing** women:

BELITTLE

049:014 He will not **belittle** aught of your deeds:

BELLIES

024:045 that creep on their **bellies**;
037:066 and fill their **bellies** therewith.

BELLOWS

018:096 "Blow (with your **bellows**)" then, when he

BELONG

002:115 To Allah **belong** the East and the West;
002:142 Say: To Allah **belong** both East and West:
002:156 To Allah we **belong**,
004:126 But to Allah **belong** all things in the
004:131 To Allah **belong** all things in the heavens and on earth
004:131 unto Allah **belong** all things in the heavens and on earth.
004:132 Yea, unto Allah **belong** all things
004:170 to Allah **belong** all things in the heavens
004:171 To Him **belong** all things in the
005:120 To Allah doth **belong** the dominion of the
007:180 The most beautiful names **belong** to Allah: so call
010:065 for all power and honour **belong** to Allah:
010:066 Behold! verily to Allah **belong** all creatures,
011:123 To Allah do **belong** the unseen (secrets)
014:002 Of Allah, to Whom do **belong** all things in the
017:110 for to Him **belong** the Most Beautiful Names.
020:008 To Him **belong** the Most Beautiful Names.
021:019 To Him **belong** all (creatures) in the
023:084 Say: "To whom **belong** the earth and all beings therein?
023:087 They will say, "(They **belong**) to Allah."
024:064 to Allah doth **belong** whatever is in the heavens and on
027:091 to Whom (**belong**) all things:
031:026 To Allah **belong** all things in heaven and earth:
034:001 Praise be to Allah, to Whom **belong** all things
035:010 to Allah **belong** all glory and power.
038:035 will not **belong** to another after me:
039:063 To Him **belong** the keys of the heavens and the
042:012 To Him **belong** the keys of the heavens and the
043:051 the dominion of Egypt **belong** to me, (witness)
048:004 for to Allah **belong** the Forces of the heavens
048:007 For to Allah **belong** the Forces of the heavens
059:024 to Him **belong** the Most Beautiful Names:
063:007 But to Allah **belong** the treasures of the
092:013 And verily unto Us (**belong**) the End

BELONGED

004:092 If he **belonged** to a people with whom
004:092 If the deceased **belonged** to a people
018:079 As for the boat, it **belonged** to certain men
018:082 "As for the wall, it **belonged** to two youths,

BELONGETH

002:107 to Allah **belongeth** the dominion of the
002:284 To Allah **belongeth** all that is in the heavens
003:129 To Allah **belongeth** all that is in the heavens
003:189 To Allah **belongeth** the dominion of the heavens
005:017 For to Allah **belongeth** the dominion
005:018 and to Allah **belongeth** the dominion of
005:040 Allah (alone) **belongeth** the dominion of the
006:012 Say: "To whom **belongeth** all that is in the

BELONGETH (continued)

006:013 "To Him **belongeth** all that dwelleth (or lurketh)
007:158 to Whom **belongeth** the dominion of the
009:116 Unto Allah **belongeth** the dominion of the
010:055 to Allah **belongeth** whatever is in the heavens
016:077 To Allah **belongeth** the Unseen of the heavens
019:064 to Him **belongeth** what is before us and what
045:037 And unto Him (alone) **belongeth** Majesty in the
053:025 But to Allah **belongeth** the Hereafter and the

BELONGING

004:143 **belonging** neither to these nor those whom Allah
039:029 and a man **belonging** entirely to one master:
039:029 a man **belonging** to many partners at variance

BELONGINGS

049:015 with their **belongings** and their persons in the

BELONGS

002:116 Nay, to Him **belongs** all that is in
002:165 that to Allah **belongs** all power,
003:109 To Allah **belongs** all that is in the heavens
003:180 To Allah **belongs** the heritage of the heavens
010:024 people to whom it **belongs** think they have all powers
016:052 To Him **belongs** whatever is in the heavens
020:006 To Him **belongs** what is in the heavens
022:064 To Him **belongs** all that is in the heavens
023:089 They will say, "(It **belongs**) to Allah."
024:042 Yea, to Allah **belongs** the dominion of the
025:002 He to Whom **belongs** the dominion of the heavens
028:088 To Him **belongs** the Command, and to Him
030:026 To Him **belongs** every being that is in the
030:027 To Him **belongs** the loftiest similitude (We can think of)
035:013 your Lord: to Him **belongs** all Dominion.
039:006 to Him **belongs** (all) dominion.
039:044 Say: "To Allah **belongs** exclusively (the right to grant)
039:044 to Him **belongs** the dominion of the heavens
042:004 To Him **belongs** all that is in the heavens
042:049 To Allah **belongs** the dominion of the heavens
042:053 The Way of Allah, to whom **belongs** whatever is
043:085 And blessed is He to Whom **belongs** the dominion
045:027 To Allah **belongs** the dominion of the heavens
048:014 To Allah **belongs** the dominion of the heavens
053:031 Yea, to Allah **belongs** all that is in the heavens
057:002 To Him **belongs** the dominion of the heavens
057:005 To Him **belongs** the dominion of the heavens
057:010 For to Allah **belongs** the heritage of the
059:007 the townships,-**belongs** to Allah,-to His Messenger,
063:008 But honour **belongs** to Allah and His Messenger,
064:001 to Him **belongs** Dominion, and to Him **belongs** Praise:
085:009 Him to Whom **belongs** the dominion of the heavens

BELOVED

005:018 "We are sons of Allah, and His **beloved**."

BELOW

005:066 from above them and from **below** their feet.
006:065 send calamities on you, from above and **below**,
007:041 as a couch (**below**) and folds and folds
029:055 and from **below** them, and (a Voice)
033:010 above you and from **below** you, and behold,
039:016 and layers (of Fire) **below** them:

BEND

026:004 to which they would **bend** their necks in humility.
032:012 the guilty ones will **bend** low their heads before

BENDING

022:009 (Disdainfully) **bending** his side, in order

BENEATH

002:025 **beneath** which rivers flow.
003:015 nearness to their Lord with rivers flowing **beneath**;
003:195 into Gardens with rivers flowing **beneath**;
003:198 are Gardens, with rivers flowing **beneath**;
004:013 rivers flowing **beneath**, to abide therein
004:057 with rivers flowing **beneath**, their eternal home:
004:122 with rivers flowing **beneath**, to dwell
005:012 with rivers flowing **beneath**; but if any
005:119 with rivers flowing **beneath**, their eternal home:
006:006 and gave streams flowing **beneath** their (feet):
007:043 **beneath** them will be rivers flowing;-and they
010:009 **beneath** them will flow rivers in Gardens of Bliss.
013:035 the righteous are promised!-**beneath** if flow rivers:
014:023 admitted to Gardens **beneath** which rivers flow,-
016:031 **beneath** them flow (pleasant) rivers:
017:068 **beneath** the earth when ye are on land,
018:031 Gardens of Eternity; **beneath** them rivers will
018:082 there was, **beneath** it, a buried treasure, to which
018:093 **beneath** them, a people who scarcely
019:024 But (a voice) cried to her from **beneath** the (palm-tree):
019:024 for thy Lord hath provided a rivulet **beneath** thee;
020:006 and all between them, and all **beneath** the soil.
020:076 Gardens of Eternity, **beneath** which flow rivers:
022:014 to Gardens, **beneath** which rivers flow:
022:023 to Gardens **beneath** which rivers flow:
025:010 Gardens **beneath** which rivers flow; and He
029:058 Lofty mansions **beneath** which flow rivers,-
039:020 have been built: **beneath** them flow rivers:
041:029 we shall crush them **beneath** our feet, so that
047:012 to Gardens **beneath** which rivers flow; while those
048:005 who believe, to Gardens **beneath** which rivers flow,
048:017 him to Gardens **beneath** which rivers flow; and he
057:012 Gardens **beneath** which flow rivers!
058:022 will admit them to Gardens **beneath** which Rivers flow,
061:012 and admit you to Gardens **beneath** which rivers
064:009 will admit them to Gardens **beneath** which rivers flow,
065:011 to Gardens **beneath** which rivers flow, to dwell
066:008 to Gardens **beneath** which rivers flow,-the Day
085:011 **Beneath** which Rivers flow:
098:008 Gardens of Eternity, **Beneath** which rivers flow;

BENEFICENT

052:028 the **Beneficent**, the Merciful!"
082:006 from thy Lord Most **Beneficent**?-

BENEFICIARY

005:106 even though the (**beneficiary**) be our near relation:

BENEFIT

002:269 granted receiveth indeed a **benefit** overflowing;
004:011 or your children are nearest to you in **benefit**.
004:033 To (**benefit**) everyone, We have appointed
005:076 no power either to harm or **benefit** you?
005:096 for the **benefit** of yourselves and those who
008:017 the Believers a gracious **benefit** from Himself:
010:107 if He do design some **benefit** for thee, there is
017:015 receiveth it for his own **benefit**:
018:054 for the **benefit** of mankind, every kind
021:080 for your **benefit**, to guard you from each other's
035:018 for the **benefit** of his own soul; and the
045:015 it is to his own **benefit**; if he
064:016 for the **benefit** of your own souls:

BENEFITS

002:272 ye give **benefits** your own souls,
007:069 the **benefits** (ye have received) from Allah:

BENEFITS (continued)

007:074 the **benefits** (ye have received) from Allah,
016:005 and numerous **benefits**, and of their (meat) ye eat.
022:028 the **benefits** (provided) for them, and celebrate
022:033 In them ye have **benefits** for a term appointed:
023:021 numerous (other) **benefits** for you;
039:041 He, then, that receives guidance **benefits** his own soul:
041:046 Whoever works righteousness **benefits** his own soul;
051:055 But remind: for reminding **benefits** the Believers.
057:025 as well as many **benefits** for mankind, that Allah

BENT

002:150 that are **bent** on wickedness;
005:013 barring a few-ever **bent** on (new) deceits:

BEQUEATH

002:240 should **bequeath** for their widows a year's

BEQUEST

002:180 that he make a **bequest** to parents
002:181 If anyone changes the **bequest** after hearing it,
005:106 when making **bequest**,-two just men of your own

BESEECH

002:061 so **beseech** thy Lord for us to produce for us
002:068 They said: "**Beseech** on our behalf thy Lord
002:069 They said: "**Beseech** on our behalf thy Lord
002:070 They said, "**Beseech** on our behalf thy Lord

BESIDE

005:116 'Take me and my mother for two gods **beside** Allah'?"
009:031 and their anchorites to be their lords **beside** Allah.
037:048 And **beside** them will be chaste women;
038:052 And **beside** them will be chaste women
046:021 his people **beside** the winding Sand-tracts:

BESIDES

002:023 (if there are any) **besides** Allah,
002:091 yet they reject all **besides**,
002:107 And **besides** Him ye have neither
002:165 (for worship) others **besides** Allah,
002:173 name hath been invoked **besides** that Allah,
003:039 and (be **besides**) noble, chaste, and a Prophet,
003:186 and from those who worship parties **besides** Allah.
004:091 you (guarantees) of peace **besides** restraining their hands,
004:123 Nor will he find, **besides** Allah, any protector or helper.
004:173 nor will they find, **besides** Allah, any to protector or help
005:076 Say: Will ye worship, **besides** Allah, something
006:019 that **besides** Allah there is another gods?"
006:071 Say: "Shall we call on others **besides** Allah,-
006:108 they call upon **besides** Allah, lest they
007:037 that ye used to invoke **besides** Allah?"
007:194 ye call upon **besides** Allah are servants like unto you:
007:197 "But those ye call upon **besides** Him, are unable
008:060 and others **besides**, whom ye may not know, but
010:018 They serve, **besides** Allah, what can
010:038 and call (to your aid) anyone you can, **besides** Allah,"
011:020 nor have they protectors **besides** Allah!
013:011 nor will they find, **besides** Him, any to protect.
013:014 others that they call **besides** Him hear them no more than
016:020 Those whom they invoke **besides** Allah create nothing
016:086 those whom we used to invoke **besides** Thee."
017:056 Say: "Call on those-**besides** Him-whom ye fancy:
017:067 those that ye call upon-**besides** Himself-leave you
017:097 wilt thou find no protector **besides** Him.
018:102 that they can take My servants as protectors **besides** Me?
019:048 you (all) and from those whom ye invoke **besides** Allah:
019:049 and from those whom ye worshipped **besides** Allah,
021:022 in the heavens and the earth, other gods **besides** Allah,

BESIDES (continued)

021:024 (other) gods **besides** Him? Say, "Bring
021:029 If any of them should say, "I am a god **besides** Him,"
021:066 (Abraham) said, "Do ye then worship, **besides** Allah,
021:067 that ye worship **besides** Allah! Have ye no sense?"
021:082 for him, and did other work **besides**;
021:098 gods that ye worship **besides** Allah, are (but) fuel for
022:012 They call on such deities, **besides** Allah, as can neither
022:062 and those **besides** Him whom they invoke,-
022:071 Yet they worship, **besides** Allah,
022:073 Those on whom, **besides** Allah ye call,
023:021 there are, in them, (**besides**), numerous other
023:063 and there are, **besides** that, deeds of theirs,
023:117 If anyone invokes, **besides** Allah, any other
025:003 Yet have they taken, **besides** Him, gods that
025:017 those whom they worship **besides** Allah, He will ask:
025:018 that we should take for protectors other **besides** Thee:
025:055 Yet do they worship, **besides** Allah, things that
026:093 "`**Besides** Allah? Can they help you or help themselves?'"
027:024 worshipping the sun **besides** Allah:
027:043 the worship of others **besides** Allah:
027:060 (Can there be another) god **besides** Allah? Nay, they
027:061 (Can there be another) god **besides** Allah? Nay, most of
027:062 (Can there be another) god **besides** Allah? Little it is
027:063 (Can there be another) god **besides** Allah?-High is Allah
027:064 (Can there be another) god **besides** Allah? Say,
028:023 and **besides** them he found two women who were
028:088 And call not, **besides** Allah, on another
029:017 "For ye do worship idols **besides** Allah, and ye
029:017 The things that ye worship **besides** Allah have no
029:022 nor have ye, **besides** Allah, any protector or helper."
029:025 (for worship) idols **besides** Allah, out of
029:042 what ever they call upon **besides** Him:
030:033 pay part-worship to other gods **besides** their Lord,-
031:011 that others **besides** Him have created:
031:030 invoke **besides** Him is Falsehood; and because
032:004 ye have none **besides** Him, to protect or intercede
033:017 for themselves, **besides** Allah, any protector
034:022 whom ye fancy, **besides** Allah:
035:013 And those whom ye invoke **besides** Him own not a straw.
035:040 'Partners' of yours whom ye call upon **besides** Allah?
036:023 "Shall I take (other) gods **besides** Him?
036:073 and they have (other) profits from them (**besides**),
037:023 "**Besides** Allah, and lead them to the Way
039:015 "Serve ye what ye will **besides** Him."
039:036 with other (gods) **besides** Him!
039:038 The things ye invoke **besides** Allah,-can they,
039:043 intercessors others **besides** Allah? Say:
040:020 but those whom (men) invoke **besides** Him, will not
040:066 those whom ye invoke **besides** Allah,-seeing that
040:074 "**Besides** Allah?" They will reply: "They have left us
040:080 advantages in them for you (**besides**); that ye
042:006 And those who take as protectors others **besides** Him,-
042:009 (for worship) protectors **besides** Him?
042:031 nor have ye, **besides** Allah, anyone to protect or to help.
043:086 And those whom they invoke **besides** Allah have no
045:010 they may have taken to themselves **besides** Allah:
046:004 Say: "Do ye see what it is ye invoke **besides** Allah?
046:005 who is more astray than one who invokes, **besides** Allah,
046:028 whom they worshipped as gods, **besides** Allah, as a means
046:032 and no protectors can he have **besides** Allah:
048:019 And many gains will they acquire (**besides**):
048:027 and He granted, **besides** this, a speedy victory.

BESIDES (continued)

050:026 "Who set up another god **besides** Allah:
052:047 there is another punishment **besides** this:
055:062 And **besides** these two, there are two other Gardens,-
057:011 and he will have (**besides**) a generous reward.
057:018 and they shall have (**besides**) a generous reward.
060:004 clear of you and if whatever ye worship **besides** Allah:
067:020 help you (even as) an army, **besides** The Most Merciful?

BEST

002:197 but the **best** of provisions is right conduct.
002:220 Say: "The **best** thing to do
002:271 that is **best** for you:
002:280 that is **best** for you if ye only knew.
003:014 the **best** of the goals (to return to).
003:036 And Allah knew **best** what she brought forth-
003:054 and the **best** of planners is Allah.
003:110 it were **best** for them:
003:110 Ye are the **best** of Peoples, evolved for mankind.
003:150 and He is the **best** of helpers.
003:173 and He is the **best** Guardian."
003:195 and from Allah is the **best** of rewards.
003:198 is the **best** (bliss) for the righteous.
004:059 that is **best**, and most suitable
004:066 it would have been **best** for them, and would
004:077 the Hereafter is the **best** for those who do right:
004:128 and such settlement is **best**; even though
004:135 for Allah can **best** protect both.
004:170 believe in him: it is **best** for you.
005:114 for thou art the **best** Sustainer (of our needs)."
006:032 But **best** is the Home in the Hereafter,
006:053 Doth not Allah know **best** those who are grateful?.
006:057 and He is the **best** of Judges."
006:058 But Allah knoweth **best** those who do wrong."
006:117 He knoweth **best** those who are rightly guided.
006:117 Thy Lord knoweth **best** who strayeth
006:119 Thy Lord knoweth **best** those who transgress.
006:124 Allah knoweth **best** where to place His mission.
006:135 whose end will be (**best**) in the Hereafter:
007:026 but the raiment of righteousness-that is the **best**.
007:085 that will be **best** for you, if ye have Faith.
007:087 for He is the **best** to decide."
007:089 for thou art the **best** to decide."
007:128 and the end is (**best**) for the righteous.
007:145 they people to hold fast by the **best** in the precepts:
007:155 for Thou art the **best** of those who forgive.
007:169 But **best** for the righteous is the Home
008:019 if ye desist (from wrong), it will be **best** for you:
008:030 but the **best** of planners is Allah.
008:040 the **Best** to protect and the **Best** to help.
009:003 If, then, ye repent, it were **best** for you; but if
009:041 That is **best** for you, if ye (but) knew.
009:061 Say, "He listens to what is **best** for you;
009:074 If they repent, it will be **best** for them:
009:109 Which then is **best**?-he that layeth his foundation
009:121 requite them with the **best** (possible reward).
010:040 and thy Lord knoweth **best** those who
010:093 and provided for them sustenance of the **best**:
010:109 for He is the **Best** to decide.
011:007 which of you is **best** in conduct.
011:031 Allah knoweth **best** what is in their souls:
011:086 'That which is left you by Allah is **best** for you,
011:088 I only desire (your) betterment to the **best** of my power;
012:035 (that it was **best**) to imprison him for a time.

BEST (continued)

012:057 the Hereafter is the **best**, for those who believe,
012:059 and that I do provide the **best** hospitality?
012:064 But Allah is the **best** to take care (of him),
012:077 and Allah knoweth **best** the truth of what ye assert!"
012:080 and He is the **best** to judge.
012:109 But the home of the Hereafter is **best**, for those
016:072 and provided for you sustenance of the **best**:
016:096 the **best** of their actions.
016:097 the **best** of their actions.
016:101 and Allah knows **best** what He reveals
016:125 for thy Lord knoweth **best**, who have strayed from the
016:125 argue with them in ways that are **best** and most gracious:
016:126 that is indeed the **best** (course) for those
017:025 Your Lord knoweth **best** what is in your hearts:
017:047 We know **best** what it is they listen, when they
017:053 (only) say those things that are **best**:
017:054 It is your Lord that knoweth you **best**:
017:055 And it is your Lord that knoweth **best** all beings
017:084 but your Lord knows **best** who it is that is **best** guided
018:007 as to which of them are **best** in conduct.
018:012 which of the two parties was **best** at calculating
018:019 "Allah (alone) knows **best** how long ye have stayed
018:019 let him find out which is the **best** food (to be had)
018:021 their Lord knows **best** about them:
018:022 Say thou: "My Lord knoweth **best** their number;
018:026 Say: "Allah knows **best** how long they stayed:
018:044 He is the **Best** to reward, and the **Best** to give success.
018:046 and **best** as (the foundation for) hopes.
018:046 Good Deeds, are **best** in the sight of thy Lord,
019:070 And certainly We know **best** those who are most
019:073 "Which of the two sides is **best** in point of position
019:076 Good Deeds, are **best** in the sight of thy Lord,
019:076 and **best** in respect of (their) eventual returns."
020:073 for Allah is **Best** and Most Abiding."
020:104 We know **best** what they will say, when the
020:104 when the **best** of them in judgment will say:
021:089 the **best** of inheritors."
022:058 He Who **best**ows the **best** Provision.
022:068 say, "Allah knows **best** what it is ye are doing."
022:078 the **Best** to protect and the **Best** to help!
023:014 So blessed be Allah the **Best** to create!
023:029 for Thou art the **Best** to enable (us) to disembark."
023:072 He is the **Best** of those who give sustenance.
023:072 But the recompense of thy Lord is **best**:
023:096 Repel evil with that which is **best**:
023:109 for Thou art the **best** of those Who show mercy!'
023:118 for Thou art the **Best** of those who show mercy!"
024:027 that is **best** for you, in order
024:038 to the **best** of their deeds, and add
024:060 but it is **best** for them to be modest:
025:015 Say: "Is that **best**, or the eternal Garden,
025:033 and **best** explanation (thereof).
026:188 He said: "My Lord knows **best** what ye do."
028:026 truly the **best** of men for thee to employ
028:037 Moses said: "My Lord knows **best** who it is
028:037 from Him and whose End will be **best** in the
028:056 and He knows **best** those who receive guidance.
028:080 The reward of Allah (in the Hereafter) is **best** for those
028:083 and the End is (**best**) for the righteous.
028:085 Say: "My Lord knows **best** who it is that brings
029:007 them according to the **best** of their deeds.
029:010 Does not Allah know **best** all that is the hearts

BEST (continued)

029:016 that will be **best** for you-if ye understand!
029:046 of the Book, except in the **best** way, unless it
030:038 that is **best** for those who seek the Countenance,
032:007 the **best** way and He began the creation of man
034:039 for He is the **Best** of those Who grant Sustenance.
037:075 and We are the **Best** to hear prayer.
037:125 and forsake the **Best** of Creators,-
039:018 Those who listen to the Word, and follow the **best** of it:
039:035 to the **best** of what they have done.
039:055 "And follow the **Best** that which revealed to you
039:070 and (Allah) knoweth **best** all that they do.
043:058 And they say, " Are Our gods **best**, or He?"
046:008 He knows **best** of that whereof ye talk (so glibly)!
046:016 the **best** of their deeds and pass by
047:021 it were **best** for them if they were true to Allah.
049:005 it would be **best** for them:
050:045 We know **best** what they say; and thou
053:030 and He knoweth **best** those who receive guidance.
053:030 Verily thy Lord knoweth **best** those who
053:031 He rewards those who do good, with what is **best**.
053:032 He knows **best** who it is that guards against evil.
058:012 That will be **best** for you, and most
060:010 Allah knows **best** as to their Faith:
061:011 that will be **best** for you,
062:009 that is **best** for you if ye but knew!
062:011 And Allah is the **Best** to provide (for all needs)."
067:002 that He may try which of you is **best** in deed:
068:007 Verily it is thy Lord that knoweth **best**,
068:007 and He knoweth **best** those who receive (true) Guidance.
077:023 for We are the **Best** to determine (things).
092:006 And (in all sincerity) testifies to the **Best**,-
092:009 And gives the lie to the **Best**,-
095:004 We have indeed created man in the **best** of molds,
098:007 do righteous deeds,-they are the **best** of creatures.

BESTOW

002:236 but **bestow** on them (a suitable gift),
005:054 which He will **bestow** on whom He pleaseth.
007:023 and **bestow** not upon us Thy Mercy, we shall
009:076 But when He did **bestow** of His bounty, they became
011:003 and **bestow** His abounding grace on all
012:053 unless my Lord do **bestow** His Mercy:
012:056 We **bestow** of Our mercy on whom We please,
016:096 And We will certainly **bestow**, on those
016:097 and We will **bestow** on such their reward
017:020 We **bestow** freely on all-these as well as those:
017:024 "My Lord! **bestow** on them Thy Mercy even as they
017:083 Yet when We **bestow** Our favours on man, he turns
018:010 "Our Lord! **bestow** on us Mercy from Thyself,
019:058 on whom Allah did **bestow** His Grace,-
019:096 will The Most Gracious **bestow** Love.
022:058 on them will Allah **bestow** verily a goodly
025:018 but Thou didst **bestow**, on them and their fathers,
026:083 "O my Lord! **bestow** wisdom on me, and join
035:002 doth **bestow** on mankind none can withhold:
038:039 whether thou **bestow** them (on others)
039:049 but when We **bestow** a favour upon him as from Us,
041:051 When We **bestow** favours on man, he turns
042:038 of what We **bestow** on them for Sustenance;
052:022 And We shall **bestow** on them, of fruit
057:028 and He will **bestow** on you a double portion
057:029 His Hand, to **bestow** it on whomsoever He Wills.
061:013 And another (favour will He **bestow**), which ye

BESTOW (continued)

071:012 and **bestow** on you Gardens and **bestow** on you Rivers

BESTOWED

001:007 The way of those on whom Thou has **bestowed** Thy Grace,
002:040 favour which I **bestowed** upon you,
002:047 favour which I **bestowed** upon you,
002:122 the special favour which I **bestowed** upon you,
004:032 in which Allah hath **bestowed** His gifts more
004:037 hide the bounties which Allah hath **bestowed** on them;
004:096 Ranks specially **bestowed** by Him,
004:171 and His Word, which He **bestowed** on Mary,
005:023 were two on whom Allah had **bestowed** His Grace:
006:094 all (the favours) which We **bestowed** on you:
007:026 We have **bestowed** raiment upon you to
008:053 the Grace which He hath **bestowed** on a people
009:075 a Covenant with Allah, that if He **bestowed** on them
010:088 "Our Lord! Thou hast indeed **bestowed** on Pharaoh
011:119 Except those on whom thy Lord hath **bestowed** His Mercy:
012:101 "O my Lord! Thou hast **bestowed** on me some power,
013:022 We have **bestowed** for their sustenance, secretly
015:087 And We have **bestowed** upon thee the Seven Oft-
015:088 (Wistfully) at what We have **bestowed** on certain
016:055 the favours We have **bestowed** on them!
016:056 We have **bestowed** for their sustenance!
016:071 Allah has **bestowed** His gifts of sustenance
016:075 on whom We have **bestowed** goodly favours from
017:021 See how We have **bestowed** more on some than on
018:065 On whom We had **bestowed** Mercy from Ourselves
019:049 We **bestowed** on him Isaac and Jacob,
019:050 And We **bestowed** of Our Mercy on them,
021:051 We **bestowed** aforetime on Abraham his rectitude
021:072 And We **bestowed** on him Isaac and, as an
022:035 We have **bestowed** upon them.
022:054 has been **bestowed** may learn that the (Qur'an)
023:033 had **bestowed** the good things of this life,
025:008 been **bestowed** on him, or why
026:132 "Yea, fear Him Who has **bestowed** on you
026:133 "Freely has He **bestowed** on you cattle and sons,-
027:019 for Thy favours, which Thou has **bestowed** on me
027:042 And knowledge was **bestowed** on us
028:014 We **bestowed** on him wisdom and knowledge:
028:017 Thou hast **bestowed** Thy Grace on me, never shall
028:076 We had **bestowed** on him, that their
028:077 which Allah has **bestowed** on thee, the Home
030:028 We have **bestowed** on you?
030:034 for the (favours) We have **bestowed** on them!
031:012 We **bestowed** (in the past) wisdom on Luqman:
032:016 We have **bestowed** on them.
033:009 remember the Grace of Allah, (**bestowed**) on you,
034:010 We **bestowed** Grace aforetime on David
037:114 We **bestowed** Our favour on Moses and Aaron,
038:030 To David We **bestowed** Solomon (for a son),-
040:009 Thou have **bestowed** Mercy indeed:
040:056 of Allah without any authority **bestowed** on them,-
041:010 above it, and **bestowed** blessings on the earth,
043:053 "Then why are not gold bracelets **bestowed** on him,
046:015 Thy favour which Thou hast **bestowed** upon me,
052:018 their Lord hath **bestowed** on them, and their
057:023 nor exult over favours **bestowed** upon you.
057:027 Yet We **bestowed**, on those among them who believed,
057:027 son of Mary, and **bestowed** on him the Gospel;
059:006 What Allah has **bestowed** on His Messenger
059:007 What Allah has **bestowed** on His Messenger

BESTOWED (continued)
063:010 We have **bestowed** on you, before Death
072:016 We should certainly have **bestowed** on them Rain
BESTOWETH
039:008 but when He **bestoweth** a favour upon him
BESTOWS
002:212 for Allah **bestows** His abundance
022:058 He Who **bestows** the best Provision.
042:049 He **bestows** (children) male or female according to
042:050 Or He **bestows** both males and females, and He
047:017 He increases their Guidance, and **bestows** on them
057:021 Grace of Allah, which He **bestows** on whom He pleases:
062:004 the Bounty of Allah which He **bestows** on whom He will:
067:028 or if He **bestows** His Mercy on us,-yet who
BETAKE
011:080 to suppress you or that I could **betake** myself to
018:016 than Allah, **betake** yourself to the Cave:
BETIDE
031:017 and bear with patient constancy whatever **betide** thee;
BETIMES
068:022 "Go ye to your tilth (**betimes**) in the morning,
BETOOK
018:010 Behold, the youths **betook** themselves to the Cave
018:063 when we **betook** ourselves to the rock?
BETRAY
004:105 those who **betray** their trust;
004:107 such as **betray** their own souls; for Allah
008:027 O ye that believe! **betray** not the trust
BETRAYED
066:010 they **betrayed** their (husbands), and they
BETROTHAL
002:235 an indirect offer of **betrothal** or hold it in your hearts.
BETTER
002:054 that will be **better** for you
002:061 exchange the **better** for the worse?
002:103 far **better** had been the reward from Allah
002:106 something **better** or similar:
002:138 and who can give a **better** hue than Allah.
002:140 Say: Do ye know **better** than Allah?
002:184 And it is **better** for you that ye fast,
002:184 of his own free will,-it is **better** for him.
002:221 who believes is **better** than an unbelieving woman,
002:221 man slave who believes is **better** than an unbeliever,
002:228 have a **better** right to take them back in that period,
002:247 when we are **better** fitted than he to exercise authority,
002:263 covering of faults are **better** than charity
003:011 no **better** than that of the people of Pharaoh,
003:015 glad tidings of things far **better** than those?
003:157 are far **better** than all they could amass:
004:025 but it is **better** for you that ye
004:046 it would have been **better** for them, and more proper;
004:051 they are **better** guided in the (right) way
004:125 Who can be **better** in religion than one
004:171 Say not "Three": desist: it will be **better** for you:
005:050 can give **better** judgment than Allah?
006:157 its guidance **better** than they."
007:012 He said: "I am **better** than he: thou didst
008:070 He will give you something **better** than what
010:058 that is **better** than the (wealth) they hoard.
012:039 differing among themselves **better**, or Allah
016:030 the Hereafter is even **better** and excellent indeed
016:095 (a prize) far **better** for you, if ye only knew.
016:107 they love the life of this world **better** than the Hereafter:

BETTER (continued)
017:035 that is **better** and fairer in the final determination.
018:036 something **better** in exchange."
018:040 me something **better** than thy garden, and that
018:081 give them in exchange (a son) **better** in purity
018:095 My Lord has established me is **better** (than tribute):
019:074 who were even **better** in equipment and in glitter to the
020:131 but the provision of thy Lord is **better** and more enduring.
025:010 His Will, could give thee **better** (things) than
027:036 has given me is **better** than that which He has
027:059 (Who) is **better**?- Allah or the false gods they associate
027:089 If any do good, he will have **better** than it.
028:049 which is a **better** Guide than either of them,
028:060 is **better** and more enduring:
028:084 is **better** than his deed; but if
032:018 Is then the man who believes no **better** than the
037:062 Is that the **better** entertainment or the
038:076 (Iblis) said: "I am **better** than he:
039:022 light from Allah, (no **better** than one hard-hearted)?
041:033 Who is **better** in speech than one who calls
041:034 Repel (Evil) with what is **better**:
041:040 Which is **better**?-he that is cast into the Fire,
042:036 but that which is with Allah is **better** and more lasting:
043:024 you **better** guidance than that which ye found
043:032 is **better** than the (wealth) which they amass.
043:052 "Am I not **better** than this (Moses), who is
044:037 What! are they **better** than the people of Tubba
047:014 no **better** than one to whom the evil of his conduct seems
049:011 the (latter) are **better** than the (former):
049:011 it may be that the (latter) are **better** than the
054:043 Are your Unbelievers, (O Quraish), **better** than they?
058:019 Satan has got the **better** of them:
062:011 Say: "That which Allah has is **better** than any
066:005 in exchange Consorts **better** than you,-who submit
067:022 with his face grovelling, **better** guided,-or one
068:032 in exchange a **better** (garden) than this:
070:041 Substitute for them **better** (men) than they;
073:020 Yea, **better** and greater, in Reward, and seek ye
087:017 But the Hereafter is **better** and more enduring.
093:004 And verily the Hereafter will be **better** for thee
097:003 The Night of Power is **better** than a thousand Months.
BETTERMENT
011:088 I only desire (your) **betterment** to the best of my power;
BETWEEN
002:036 with enmity **between** yourselves.
002:053 and the criterion (**between** right and wrong),
002:102 the means to sow discord **between** man and wife.
002:113 but Allah will judge **between** them
002:136 we make on difference **between** one and another of them:
002:164 trail like their slaves **between** the sky and the earth;
002:166 relations **between** them would be cut off.
002:185 guidance and judgment (**between** right and wrong).
002:213 to judge **between** people in matters
002:224 or making peace **between** persons;
002:237 And do not forget liberality **between** yourselves.
002:282 write down faithfully as **between** the parties:
002:285 (they say) **between** one and another of His Messengers."
003:003 Criterion (of judgement **between** right and wrong).
003:030 a great distance **between** it and its evil.
003:055 will judge **between** you of the matters wherein ye dispute.
003:064 no distinction **between** one and another among them,
004:035 If ye fear a breach **between** them twain, appoint
004:058 and when ye judge **between** people that ye

BETWEEN (continued)

004:065 judge in all disputes **between** them.
004:073 ties of affection **between** you and them,
004:090 a group **between** whom and you there is a treaty
004:105 that thou mightest judge **between** people by that
004:114 or conciliation **between** people (secrecy is permissible):
004:128 they arrange an amicable settlement **between** themselves;
004:129 do justice **between** wives even if it is your ardent desire:
004:143 (They are) wavering **between** this and that belonging
004:150 wish to separate **between** Allah and His Messengers,
004:152 make no distinction **between** any of the messengers,
004:176 of the inheritance (**between** them):
005:014 enmity and hatred **between** the one and the other,
005:017 the heavens and the earth, and all that is **between**.
005:018 the heavens and the earth, and all that is **between**:
005:042 If thou judge, judge in equity **between** them.
005:042 either judge **between** them, or decline to interfere.
005:048 so judge **between** them by what Allah hath revealed,
005:049 judge thou **between** them by what Allah hath revealed,
005:091 to excite enmity and hatred **between** you,
006:019 Say: "Allah is Witness **between** me and you:
006:058 the matter would be settled at once **between** you and me.
006:094 so now all relations **between** you have been cut off,
007:024 with enmity **between** yourselves.
007:044 but a Crier shall proclaim **between** them: "The curse
007:046 **Between** them shall be a veil,
007:087 until Allah doth decide **between** us:
007:089 Our Lord! Decide thou **between** us and our
008:001 and keep straight the relations **between** yourselves:
008:024 know that Allah cometh in **between** a man and his heart,
008:029 grant you a Criterion (to judge **between** right and wrong),
008:063 put affection **between** their hearts:
010:019 have been settled **between** them.
010:029 "Enough is Allah for a witness **between** us and you:
010:047 judged **between** them with justice, and they
010:054 but the judgment **between** them will be
010:093 Verily Allah will judge **between** them as to
011:043 the waves came **between** them, and the son was among
011:110 the matter would have been decided **between** them:
012:100 sown enmity **between** me and my brothers.
013:043 "Enough for a witness **between** me and you is Allah,
015:085 created not the heavens and the earth and all **between**
016:066 what is within their bodies, **between** excretions and blood,
016:080 their soft fibres (**between** wool and hair), and their hair,
016:094 to practice deception **between** yourselves.
016:124 judge **between** them on the Day of Judgment as to
017:045 We put, **between** thee and those who believe not
017:096 "Enough is Allah for a witness **between** me and you:
017:110 but seek a middle course **between**."
018:032 with date-palms; in **between** the two We placed tillage.
018:078 He answered: "This is the parting **between** me and thee:
018:093 Until, when he reached (a tract) **between** two mountains,
018:094 thou mightest erect a barrier **between** us and them?
018:095 I will erect a strong barrier **between** you and them:
018:096 the space **between** the two steep mountain-sides,
019:064 and what is behind us, and what is **between**:
019:065 and of all that is **between** them:
020:006 and all **between** them, and all beneath the soil.
020:058 So make a tryst **between** us and thee, which we shall not
021:016 the heavens and the earth and all that is **between**!
021:031 broad highways (**between** mountains) for them
022:017 Allah will judge **between** them on the Day of
022:056 He will judge **between** them:

BETWEEN (continued)

022:069 "Allah will judge **between** you on the Day of Judgment
023:053 have cut off their affair (of unity), **between** them,
023:101 relationships **between** them that day, nor will
024:048 in order that He may judge **between** them, behold,
024:051 He may judge **between** them, is no
025:038 and many a generation **between** them.
025:053 yet has He made a barrier **between** them, a partition that
025:059 and the earth and all that is **between**, in six days,
025:067 but hold a just (balance) **between** those (extremes);
026:024 Cherisher of the heavens and the earth and all **between**,-
026:028 "Lord of the East and the West, and all **between**!
026:118 "Judge thou, then, **between** me and them openly,
027:061 and made a separating bar **between** the two seas
027:078 Verily thy Lord will decide **between** them by His
028:028 "Be that (the agreement) **between** me and thee:
029:025 mutual love and regard **between** yourselves in this life;
029:052 a Witness **between** me and you:
030:008 create the heavens and the earth and all **between** them:
030:021 and mercy **between** your (hearts):
031:032 those that falter **between** (right and wrong).
032:004 and the earth, and all **between** them, in six Days,
032:025 Verily thy Lord will judge **between** them on the
034:018 **Between** them and the Cities on which We had
034:018 in prominent positions, and **between** them We had
034:019 place longer distances **between** our journey-stages":
034:026 the matter **between** us (and you) in truth
034:054 And **between** them and their desires, is placed
037:005 the heavens and the earth, and all **between** them,
037:158 they have invented a kinship **between** Him and the Jinns:
038:010 of the heavens and the earth, and all **between**?
038:022 the other: decide now **between** us with truth,
038:026 so judge thou **between** men in truth (and justice):
038:027 did We create the heaven and earth and all **between**!
038:066 and all **between**-Exalted in Might, Ever-Forgiving.
039:003 Truly Allah will judge **between** them in that
039:046 wilt judge **between** Thy Servants in those matters
039:069 and a just decision pronounced **between** them;
039:075 The Decision **between** them (at Judgment) will be in
040:048 Truly, Allah has judged **between** (His) Servants!"
041:005 and **between** us and thee is a screen:
041:034 then will he **between** whom and thee was hatred
041:045 would have been settled **between** them: but they
042:014 the matter would have been settled **between** them:
042:015 There is no contention **between** us and you.
042:015 to judge justly **between** you.
042:021 the matter would have been decided **between** them
043:032 It is We Who portion out **between** them their
043:038 "Would that **between** me and thee were the distance
043:085 of the heavens and the earth, and all **between** them:
044:007 Lord of the heavens and the earth and all **between** them,
044:038 and all **between** them, merely in (idle) sport:
045:017 Verily thy Lord will judge **between** them on the
046:003 and all **between** them but for just ends, and for
046:008 Enough is He for a witness **between** me and you!
049:009 Believers fall into a fight, make ye peace **between** them;
049:009 then make peace **between** them with justice, and be fair:
049:010 peace and reconciliation **between** your two
050:038 and all **between** them in Six Days, nor did
054:028 tell them that the water is to be divided **between** them:
055:020 **Between** them is a Barrier which they
058:001 the arguments **between** both of you:
058:007 There is not a secret consultation **between** three,

BETWEEN (continued)
058:007 nor **between** five but He makes the sixth,-
058:007 nor **between** fewer not more, but He is with them.
059:007 make a circuit **between** the wealth among you.
060:003 He will judge **between** you: for Allah sees well all that
060:004 and there has arisen **between** us and you,
060:007 Establish friendship **between** you and those whom
060:010 He judges (with justice) **between** you.
078:037 the Lord of the heavens and the earth, and all **between**,-
086:007 Proceeding from **between** the backbone and the ribs:

BETWIXT
004:141 **betwixt** you on the Day of Judgment.
057:013 So a wall will be put up **betwixt** them, with a

BEWARE
005:041 but if not, **beware**!”
005:049 but **beware** of them lest they beguile thee from
005:092 and obey the Messenger. And **beware** (of evil):
024:063 then let those **beware** who withstand the Messenger's '
063:004 They are the enemies; so **beware** of them.
064:014 (some that are) enemies to yourselves: so **beware** of them!
096:015 Let him **beware**! If he desist not, We will
102:005 with certainty of mind, (ye would **beware**)!

BEWILDERED
006:071 wandering **bewildered** through the earth,

BEWITCHED
007:116 they **bewitched** the eyes of the people,
015:015 Nay, we have been **bewitched** by sorcery.”
017:047 “Ye follow none other than a man **bewitched**!”
025:008 “Ye follow none other than a man **bewitched**.”
026:153 They said: “Thou art only the of those **bewitched**!
026:185 They said: “Thou art only one of those **bewitched**!

BEYOND
002:219 say: “What is **beyond** your needs.”
003:112 and transgressed **beyond** bounds.
004:047 fame of some (of you) **beyond** all recognition,
004:092 For those who find this **beyond** their means,
005:077 trespassing **beyond** the truth, nor follow
005:089 If that is **beyond** your means, fast for three days.
005:107 trespassed (**beyond** the truth):
007:055 those who trespass **beyond** bounds.
007:081 ye are indeed a people transgressing **beyond** bounds.”
017:043 they say! Exalted and Great (**beyond** measure)!
018:028 and let not thine eyes pass **beyond** them,
018:058 appointed time, **beyond** which they will find no refuge.
018:068 about things which are **beyond** your knowledge?”
020:127 him who transgresses **beyond** bounds and believes
021:009 those who transgressed **beyond** bounds.
028:039 he was arrogant and insolent in the land, **beyond** reason,-
042:027 they would indeed transgress **beyond** all bounds
042:042 and insolently transgress **beyond** bounds through the land,
043:005 a people transgressing **beyond** bounds?
044:035 “There is nothing **beyond** our first death, and we
049:009 transgresses **beyond** bounds against the other,
051:034 who trespass **beyond** bounds.”
051:053 themselves a people transgressing **beyond** bounds!
052:032 a people transgressing **beyond** bounds?
055:033 If it be ye can pass **beyond** the zones
065:007 on any person **beyond** what He has given him.
068:012 (all) good, transgressing **beyond** bounds, deep in
069:011 the water (of Noah’s flood) overflowed **beyond** its limits,
070:031 But those who trespass **beyond** this are transgressors;-
083:012 the Transgressor **beyond** bounds, the Sinner!
089:011 (All) these transgressed **beyond** bounds in the lands.

BIAS
082:007 and gave thee a just **bias**;

BICKERINGS
026:096 “They will say there in their mutual **bickerings**:

BID
003:080 What! would he **bid** you to unbelief after ye have

BIDDING
012:032 And now, if he doth not my **bidding**, he shall
026:151 “And follow not the **bidding** of those

BIDS
002:268 and **bids** you to conduct unseemly.

BIG
002:249 hath a small force vanquished a **big** one?
002:282 whether it be small or **big**:
037:048 with **big** eyes (of wonder and beauty).
037:142 Then the **big** Fish did swallow him, and he
044:054 to maidens with beautiful, **big**, and lustrous eyes.
052:020 with beautiful, **big** and lustrous eyes.
056:022 with beautiful, **big**, and lustrous eyes,-

BIGGEST
021:058 (all) but the **biggest** of them, that they
021:063 "nay, this was done by this the **biggest** one!

BILLOW
024:040 overwhelmed with **billow** topped by **billow**,

BIND
047:004 subdued them, **bind** (the captives) firmly:
069:030 “Seize ye him, and **bind** ye him,
073:012 With Us are Fetters (to **bind** them), and a Fire
089:026 And His bonds will be such as none (other) can **bind**.

BINDING
003:081 and take My covenant as **binding** on you?”
009:111 a promise **binding** on Him in Truth, through the
016:038 a promise (**binding**) on Him in truth:
025:016 a promise **binding** upon thy Lord.”

BIRD
003:049 the figure of a **bird**, and breathe into it,
003:049 and it becomes a **bird** by Allah’s leave:
005:110 as it were, the figure of a **bird**, by My leave.
005:110 and it becometh a **bird** by My leave.
022:031 or the wind had swooped (like a **bird** on its prey)

BIRDS
002:260 He said: “Take four **birds**;
005:004 the beasts and **birds** of prey, training them
012:036 and **birds** are eating thereof.”
012:041 the cross, and the **birds** will eat from off his
016:079 Do they not look at the **birds**, held poised
021:079 and the **birds** celebrate Our praises, with David:
022:031 and been snatched up by **birds**, or the
024:041 and the **birds** (of the air) with wings outspread?
027:016 been taught the speech of **Birds**, and we
027:017 his hosts,-of Jinns and men and **birds**, and they
027:020 And he took a muster of the **Birds**; and he
034:010 with him! and ye **birds** (also)!
038:019 And the **birds** gathered (in assemblies):
067:019 Do they not observe the **birds** above them,
105:003 And He sent against them flights of **Birds**,

BIRTH
016:058 of (the **birth** of) a female (child), his face
043:017 them of (the **birth** of) what he sets up as a
046:015 and in pain did she give him **birth**.
058:002 except those who gave them **birth**.
068:013 of a doubtful **birth**,-

BIT

004:020 take not the least **bit** of it back:

006:134 nor can ye frustrate it (in the least **bit**).

BITE

003:119 they **bite** off the very tips of their fingers

025:027 will **bite** at his hands, he will say, "Oh! would

BITTER

025:053 and the other salt and **bitter**; yet has

034:016 two garden (rows) into "gardens producing **bitter** fruit,

035:012 and the other, salt and **bitter**.

054:019 on a Day of **bitter** ill-luck,

054:046 be most grievous and most **bitter**.

088:006 No food will there be for them but a **bitter** Dhari

BLACK

002:187 appear to you distinct from its **black** thread;

003:106 and some faces will be (in the gloom of) **black**:

003:106 to those whose faces will be **black**,

035:027 and **black** intense in hue.

039:060 their faces will be turned **black**;

056:043 And in the shades of **Black** Smoke:

BLADE

048:029 like a seed which sends forth its **blade**,

BLAME

002:203 to leave in two days, there is no **blame** on him,

002:203 and if any one stays on, there is no **blame** on him,

002:229 there is no **blame** on either of them id she gave something

002:230 no **blame** on either of them if they re-unite,

002:233 There is no **blame** on them,

002:233 for your offspring there is no **blame** on you,

002:234 there is no **blame** on you if they dispose

002:235 There is no **blame** on you if ye make an indirect

002:236 There is no **blame** on you if ye divorce women

002:240 there is no **blame** on you for what they do

002:282 there is no **blame** on you if ye reduce it

004:024 there is no **blame** on you, and Allah

004:101 there is no **blame** on you if ye shorten

004:102 But there is no **blame** on you if ye put away

004:128 there is no **blame** on them if they arrange

005:093 there is no **blame** for what they ate

009:091 There is no **blame** on those who are infirm, or ill,

009:092 Nor (is there **blame**) on those who came to thee

012:032 the man about whom ye did **blame** me!

012:053 "Yet I don not absolve myself (of **blame**):

023:006 they are free from **blame**,

024:060 there is no **blame** on them if they lay aside

024:061 friend of yours: there is no **blame** on you,

033:005 But there is no **blame** on you if ye make a mistake

033:051 and there is no **blame** on thee if thou invite one whose

033:055 There is no **blame** (on those ladies if they appear)

034:031 throwing back the word (of **blame**) on one another!

037:142 and he had done acts worthy of **blame**.

042:041 to him, against such there is no cause of **blame**.

042:042 The **blame** is only against those who oppress men

048:017 No **blame** is there on the blind,

048:017 nor is there **blame** on the lame,

051:040 and threw them into the sea: and his was the **blame**.

051:054 So turn away from them: not thine is the **blame**.

060:010 And there will be no **blame** on you if ye marry

080:007 Though it is no **blame** to thee if he grow

BLAMED

070:030 hands possess,-for (then) they are not to be **blamed**,

BLAMEWORTHY

017:029 become **blameworthy** and destitute.

BLAMEWORTHY (continued)

017:039 into Hell, **blameworthy** and rejected.

BLASPHEME

002:102 so do not **blaspheme**."

003:055 (of the falsehoods) of those who **blaspheme**;

021:036 And they **blaspheme** at the mention of

040:042 "Ye do call upon me to **blaspheme** against Allah,

BLASPHEMED

008:035 "Taste ye the Chastisement because ye **blasphemed**."

BLASPHEMES

043:033 that **blasphemes** against The Most Gracious,

BLASPHEMIES

021:112 sought against the **blasphemies** ye utter!

BLASPHEMY

002:088 is on them for their **blasphemy**;

004:155 on their hearts for their **blasphemy**,

005:064 them their obstinate rebellion and **blasphemy**.

005:064 be they accursed for the (**blasphemy**) they utter.

005:068 them their obstinate rebellion and **blasphemy**.

005:073 If they desist not from their word (of **blasphemy**),

006:019 And I truly an innocent (your **blasphemy** of) joining others

009:074 but indeed they uttered **blasphemy**, and they uttered it

BLAST

011:067 The (mighty) **Blast** overtook the wrong-doers,

011:094 but the (mighty) **Blast** did seize the wrong-doers,

015:073 But the (mighty) **Blast** overtook

015:083 But the (mighty) **Blast** seized them of a morning,

023:041 Then the **Blast** overtook them with justice,

029:037 then the mighty **Blast** seized them, and they

029:040 some were caught by a (mighty) **Blast**; some We

036:029 It was on more than a single mighty **Blast**,

036:049 They will not (have to) wait for aught but a single **Blast**:

036:053 It will be no more than a single **Blast**, when lo!

038:015 These (to-day) only wait for a single mighty **Blast**,

050:042 a (mighty) **Blast** in (very) truth):

054:031 Mighty **Blast**, and they became like the dry

056:042 of a fierce **Blast** of Fire and in Boiling Water,

069:013 Then, when one **Blast** is sounded on the Trumpet,

BLAZE

077:031 and is of no use against the fierce **Blaze**.

104:006 (It is) the Fire of Allah kindled (to a **blaze**),

BLAZES

067:007 of its breath even as it **blazes** forth.

BLAZING

002:119 be asked of Companions of the **blazing** fire.

004:010 they will soon be enduring a **blazing** Fire!

008:050 "Taste the chastisement of the **blazing** Fire-

020:097 a **blazing** fire and scatter it broadcast in the sea!

025:011 a **Blazing** Fire for such as deny the Hour:

031:021 to the Chastisement of the (**Blazing**) Fire!

033:064 for them a **Blazing** Fire,-

034:012 of the Chastisement of the **Blazing** Fire.

035:006 that they may become Companions of the **Blazing** Fire.

037:068 Then shall their return be to the (**Blazing**) Fire.

037:097 and throw him into the **blazing** fire!"

037:163 going to the **blazing** Fire!

040:007 of the **Blazing** Fire!

042:007 and some in the **Blazing** Fire.

044:047 and drag him into the midst of the **Blazing** Fire!

044:056 the Chastisement of the **Blazing** Fire,-

048:013 for those who reject Allah, a **Blazing** fire!

067:005 the Chastisement of the **Blazing** Fire.

067:010 be among the Companions of the **Blazing** Fire!"

BLAZING (continued)

067:011 are the Companions of the **Blazing** Fire!
069:031 "And burn ye him in the **Blazing** Fire.
070:015 By no means! for it would be the **Blazing** Fire-
076:004 prepared Chains, Yokes, and a **Blazing** Fire.
078:013 And placed (therein) a **blazing** lamp.
081:012 When the **Blazing** Fire is kindled to fierce heat;
084:012 And he will enter a **Blazing** Fire.
088:004 The while they enter the **Blazing** Fire,-
092:014 Therefore do I warn you of a Fire **blazing** fiercely;
101:011 (It is) a Fire **Blazing** fiercely!
111:003 Burnt soon will he be in a Fire of **blazing** Flame!

BLEAR-EYED

020:102 We shall gather the sinful, **blear-eyed** (with terror).

BLEMISH

002:071 sound and without **blemish**."

BLESS

007:049 that Allah with His Mercy would never **bless**?
017:001 We did **Bless**,-in order that We might show him

BLESSED

007:054 and the Command, **Blessed** be Allah, the Cherisher
011:105 be wretched and some will be **blessed**.
011:108 And those who are **blessed** shall be in the Garden:
019:031 "And He hath made me **Blessed** wheresoever I be,
021:050 And this is a **blessed** Message which We
021:071 to the land which We have **blessed** for the nations.
021:081 to the land which We had **blessed**: for We
023:014 so **blessed** be Allah, the Best to create!
024:035 lit from a **blessed** Tree, an Olive, neither of
025:001 **Blessed** is He Who sent down the Criterion
025:010 **Blessed** is He Who, if that were His Will,
025:061 **Blessed** is He Who made Constellations in the skies,
027:008 "**Blessed** are those in the Fire and those around:
037:113 We **blessed** him and Isaac: but of their
043:085 And **blessed** is He to Whom belongs the dominion
044:003 We sent it down during a **blessed** night: for We
055:078 **Blessed** be the name of thy Lord, full of
067:001 **Blessed** be He in Whose hands is Dominion; and He
079:002 (the souls of the **blessed**);

BLESSEDNESS

013:029 work righteousness, is (ever) **blessedness**, and a

BLESSING

002:276 Allah will deprive usury of all **blessing**,
003:096 full of **blessing**s and of guidance for all the worlds.
003:141 of **blessing**s those that resist Faith.
006:155 which We have revealed as a **blessing**: so follow
011:048 and **Blessing** on thee and on some of the Peoples
023:029 "O my Lord! enable me to disembark with Thy **blessing**:
024:061 a greeting or **blessing** and purity as from Allah.
037:078 And We left (this **blessing**) for him
050:009 Rain charged with **blessing**, and We

BLESSINGS

002:157 (descend) **blessings** from their Lord, and Mercy.
006:092 a Book Which We sent down, bringing **blessings**,
007:096 indeed have opened out to them (all Kinds of) **blessings**
007:137 lands whereon We sent down our **blessings**.
011:073 and His **blessings** on you, O ye people
033:043 He it is Who sends **blessings** on you, as do
033:056 send ye **blessings** on him, and salute
033:056 Allah and His Angels send **blessings** on the
034:018 We had poured Our **blessings**, We had
038:029 sent down unto thee, full of **blessings**, that they
041:010 above it, and bestowed **blessings** on the earth,

BLIND

002:015 like **blind** ones (to and fro).
002:018 Deaf, dumb, and **blind**,
002:171 deaf, dumb, and **blind**,
003:049 and I heal those born **blind**, and the lepers,
005:071 so they became **blind** and deaf;
005:071 yet again many of them became **blind** and deaf.
005:110 and thou healest those born **blind**, and the
006:050 Say: "Can the **blind** be held equal to the seeing?"
006:104 if any will be **blind**, it will be
007:064 they were indeed a **blind** people!
010:043 the **blind**,-even though they will not see?
011:024 may be compared to the **blind** and deaf, and those
013:016 Say: "Are the **blind** equal with those who see?
013:019 like one who is **blind**?
017:072 But those who were **blind** in this world,
017:072 will be **blind** in the Hereafter, and most
017:097 prone on their faces, **blind**, dumb, and deaf:
020:124 him up **blind** on the Day of Judgment."
020:125 why hast thou raised me up **blind**, while I
022:046 Truly it is not the eyes that are **blind**,
024:061 It is no fault in the **blind** nor in one born lame
025:073 they were deaf or **blind**;
027:066 nay, they are **blind** thereunto!
027:081 to the **Blind**, (to prevent them) from straying:
030:053 Nor canst thou lead back the **blind** from their
035:019 The **blind** and the seeing are not alike;
040:058 Not equal are the **blind** and those who
043:040 or give direction to the **blind** or to such
048:017 No blame is there on the **blind**, nor is
080:002 the **blind** man (interrupting).

BLINDED

047:023 and **blinded** their sight.
054:037 but We **blinded** their eyes. (They heard):

BLINDLY

006:110 to (stumble **blindly**).
010:011 wandering in distraction **blindly**.
027:004 and so they wander **blindly**.

BLINDNESS

041:017 but they preferred **blindness** (of heart) to Guidance:
041:044 and it is **blindness** in their (eyes):

BLINDS

024:043 well-nigh **blinds** the sight.

BLISS

002:214 ye shall enter the Garden (of **Bliss**)
002:221 to the Garden (of **Bliss**) and forgiveness,
003:170 who have not yet joined them (in their **bliss**),
003:198 is the best (**bliss**) for the righteous.
005:065 and admitted them to Gardens of **Bliss**.
009:072 greatest **bliss** in the Good Pleasure of Allah:
010:009 beneath them will flow rivers in Gardens of **Bliss**.
013:023 Gardens of perpetual **bliss**:
023:111 they are indeed the ones that have achieved **Bliss**."
026:085 of the Garden of **Bliss**;
031:008 there will be Gardens of **Bliss**,-
040:040 such will enter the Garden (of **Bliss**):
041:030 But receive the Glad Tidings of the Garden (of **Bliss**),
047:015 (can those in such **Bliss**) be compared
052:018 Enjoying the (**Bliss**) which their Lord
056:012 In Gardens of **Bliss**:
057:021 from your Lord, and a Garden (of **Bliss**), the width
069:021 And he will be in a life of **Bliss**,
070:035 in the Gardens of (**Bliss**).

BLISS (continued)
070:038 to enter the Garden of **Bliss**?
076:020 see a **Bliss** and a Realm Magnificent.
082:013 As for the Righteous, they will be in **Bliss**;
083:022 Truly the Righteous will be in **Bliss**:
083:024 the beaming brightness of **Bliss**.

BLISSFUL
076:011 and a (**blissful**) Joy.

BLOCKS
018:096 "Bring me **blocks** of iron."

BLOOD
002:030 make mischief therein and shed **blood**?
002:084 shed no **blood** amongst you,
002:173 dead meat, and **blood**, and the flesh of swine,
003:014 horses branded (for **blood** and excellence);
005:003 dead meat, **blood**, the flesh of swine, and that
006:145 or **blood** poured forth, or the
007:133 Wholesale Death, Locusts, Lice, Frogs, and **Blood**:
008:075 But kindred by **blood** have prior rights against
012:018 They stained his shirt with false **blood**.
016:066 between excretions and **blood**, We produce,
016:115 dead meat, and **blood**, and the flesh of swine,
022:037 It is not their meat nor their **blood**, that reaches
023:014 a clot of congealed **blood**;

BLOOD-MONEY
004:092 **blood-money** should be paid to his family,
004:092 And pay **blood-money** to the deceased's family,

BLOOD-RELATIONS
033:006 **Blood-relations** among each other have closer

BLOT
002:286 **Blot** out our Signs.
003:193 forgive us our sins, **blot** out from us our iniquities,
003:195 verily, I will **blot** out from them their iniquities,
004:043 For Allah doth **blot** out sins and forgive
004:099 for Allah doth **blot** out (sins) and
013:039 Allah doth **blot** out or confirm what He pleaseth:
029:007 righteous deeds,-from them shall We **blot** out
035:016 If He so pleased, He could **blot** you out

BLOTS
022:060 for Allah is One that **blots** out (sins)
042:024 And Allah **blots** out falsehood, and proves

BLOTTED
003:155 But Allah has **blotted** out (their fault):
005:065 We should indeed have **blotted** out their iniquities
036:066 We could surely have **blotted** out their eyes;

BLOW
005:003 or by a violent **blow**, or a headlong fall, or by
018:096 "**Blow** (with your bellows)" then, when he
077:002 Which then **blow** violently in tempestuous Gusts,
113:004 From the mischief of those who **blow** on knots;

BLOWING
061:008 Allah's Light (by **blowing**) with their mouths:

BLOWN
006:073 the day the trumpet will be **blown**.
018:099 the trumpet will be **blown**, and We
023:101 Then when the Trumpet is **blown**, there will
050:020 And the Trumpet shall be **blown**:

BLOWS
014:018 which the wind **blows** furiously on a tempestuous day:

BOARD
010:022 till when ye even **board** ships;-they sail
023:027 take thou on **board** pairs of every species,

BOAST
004:157 That they said (in **boast**), "We killed Christ Jesus

BOASTER
031:018 not any arrogant **boaster**.
057:023 not any vainglorious **boaster**,-

BOASTFULLY
090:006 He may say (**boastfully**): "Wealth have I

BOASTING
057:020 adornment and mutual **boasting** and multiplying,

BOAT
018:071 when they were in the **boat**, he scuttled it.
018:079 king who seized on every **boat** by force.
018:079 As for the **boat**, it belonged to certain men
029:065 Now, if they embark on a **boat**, they call

BODIES
004:010 eat up a fire into their own **bodies**:
007:022 the leaves of the Garden over their **bodies**.
016:066 From what is within their **bodies**, between
016:069 from within their **bodies** a drink of varying
021:008 Nor did We give them **bodies** that ate no food,
021:033 All (the celestial **bodies**) swim along, each in
022:020 within their **bodies**, as well as (their) skins.
023:021 from within their **bodies** We produce (milk)
025:053 the two **bodies** of flowing water:
026:061 And when the two **bodies** saw each other,
039:042 (to their **bodies**) for a term appointed.
063:004 their **bodies** please thee;

BODILY
002:247 abundantly with knowledge and **bodily** prowess:

BODY
002:073 "Strike the (**body**) with a piece of the (heifer)."
004:043 until after washing your whole **body** if ye are ill,
005:006 bathe your whole **body**.
005:031 the naked **body** of his brother.
005:031 and to hide the naked **body** of my brother?"
007:148 the **body** of a calf, (for worship):
010:092 "This day shall We save thee in thy **body**,
012:008 but we are a goodly **body**!
024:011 a **body** among yourselves:
028:076 a burden to a **body** of strong men.
038:034 We placed on his throne a **body** but he
066:012 and We breathed into her (**body**) of Our spirit;

BOIL
044:045 Like molten brass; it will **boil** in their insides,
081:006 When the oceans **boil** over with a swell;

BOILING
006:070 they will have for drink (only) **boiling** water,
010:004 but draughts of **boiling** fluids,
014:016 and he is given, for drink, **boiling** fetid water.
022:019 over their heads will be poured out **boiling** water.
037:067 be given a mixture made of **boiling** water.
038:057 a **boiling** fluid, and a fluid dark,
040:072 In the **boiling** fetid fluid; then in
044:046 Like the **boiling** of scalding water.
044:048 the Chastisement of **Boiling** Water;
047:015 and be given, to drink, **boiling** water, so that
055:044 of **boiling** hot water will they wander round!
056:042 of a fierce Blast of Fire and in **Boiling** Water,
056:054 "And drink **Boiling** Water on top of it:
056:093 For him is Entertainment with **Boiling** Water,
078:025 Save a **boiling** fluid and a fluid, dark, murky,
088:005 to drink, of a **boiling** hot spring,

BOLDNESS

002:175 Ah! what **boldness** (they show) for the Fire!

BOND

023:006 Except with those joined to them in the marriage **bond**,

BONDAGE

009:060 for those in **bondage** and in debt;

BONDMAN

012:075 should be held (as **bondman**) to atone

090:013 (It is:) freeing the **bondman**;

BONDS

008:030 to keep thee in **bonds**, or slay thee, or get thee out

089:026 And His **bonds** will be such as none (other) can bind.

BONE

006:146 or is mixed up with a **bone**:

BONES

002:259 look further at the **bones**,

017:049 to **bones** and dust, should we really be raised up

017:098 to **bones** and broken dust, should we really be

019:004 Praying "O my Lord! infirm indeed are my **bones**,

023:014 We made out of that lump **bones** and clothed the **bones**

023:014 and clothed the **bones** with flesh;

023:035 and become dust and **bones**, ye shall

023:082 and become dust and **bones**, could we

036:078 "Who can give life to (dry) **bones** and decomposed

037:016 and **bones**, shall we (then) be raised up (again)?

037:053 and **bones**, shall we indeed receive rewards

056:047 and **bones**, shall we then indeed be raised up again?-

075:003 Does man think that We cannot assemble his **bones**?

079:011 "What!-when we shall have become rotten **bones**?"

BOOK

002:002 This is the **Book**;

002:078 who know not the **Book**,

002:079 the **Book** with their own hands,

002:085 a part of the **Book** that ye believe in,

002:087 We gave Moses the **Book**

002:089 a **Book** from Allah,

002:101 threw away the **Book** of Allah behind their backs,

002:101 a party of the people of the **Book**

002:105 without Faith among the people of the **Book**

002:109 Quite a number of the people of the **Book**

002:113 Yet they (profess) to study the (same) **Book**.

002:121 the **Book** study it as it should be studied:

002:144 The people of the **book** know well that

002:145 the people of the **Book** all the Signs

002:146 The people of the **Book** know this

002:159 clear for the People in the **Book**,

002:174 Those who conceal Allah's revelations in the **Book**,

002:176 the **Book** in truth but those who seek causes

002:176 the **Book** are in a schism far (from the purpose).

002:177 and the Angels, and the **Book**, and the Messengers;

002:213 and with them He sent the **Book** in truth,

002:213 but the People of the **Book**,

002:231 the **Book** and Wisdom, for your instruction.

003:003 (step by step), in truth, the **Book**,

003:007 He it is Who has sent down to thee the **Book**:

003:007 they are the foundation of the **Book**:

003:019 the **Book** dissent therefrom except through

003:020 the **Book** and to those who are unlearned:

003:023 those who have been given a portion of the **Book**?

003:023 They are invited to the **Book** of Allah,

003:048 the **Book** and Wisdom, the Torah and the Gospel.

003:064 Say: "O people of the **Book**!

003:065 Ye people of the **Book**! why dispute ye about Abraham,

BOOK (continued)

003:069 the People of the **Book** to lead you astray.

003:070 Ye People of the **Book**!

003:071 Ye People of the **Book**!

003:072 A section of the People of the **Book** say: "Believe

003:075 Among the People of the **Book** are some who,

003:078 but it is no part of the **Book**;

003:078 you would think it is a part of the **Book**,

003:078 a section who distort the **Book** with their tongues;

003:079 for ye have taught the **Book** and ye have

003:079 that a man, to whom is given the **Book**, and Wisdom.

003:081 saying: "I give you a **Book** and Wisdom:

003:098 Say: "O people of the **Book**!

003:099 Say: "O ye People of the **Book**!

003:100 listen to a faction among the People of the **Book**,

003:110 If only the People of the **Book** had faith,

003:113 of the People of the **book** are a portion that stand

003:119 though ye believe in the whole of the **Book**,

003:184 And the **Book** of Enlightenment.

003:186 from those who received the **Book** before you

003:187 a Covenant from the People of the **Book**,

003:199 among the people of the **Book**, those who

004:044 to those who were given a portion of the **Book**?

004:047 O ye people of the **Book**! believe in what

004:051 to those who were given a portion of the **Book**?

004:054 the people of Abraham the **Book** and Wisdom,

004:105 We have sent down to thee the **Book** in truth,

004:113 the **Book** and wisdom and taught thee what

004:123 nor those of the people of the **Book** (can prevail):

004:127 been rehearsed unto you in the **Book**, concerning

004:131 the people of the **Book** before you, and you

004:140 Already has He sent you word in the **Book**,

004:153 The people of the **Book** ask thee to cause

004:153 to cause a **book** to descend to them from heaven:

004:159 And there is none of the People of the **Book**

004:171 O people of the **Book**! commit no excesses

005:005 The food of the People of the **Book** is lawful

005:005 but chaste women among the People of the **Book**,

005:015 a (new) Light and a perspicuous **Book**,

005:015 O People of the **Book**! there hath come

005:015 that ye used to hide in the **Book**,

005:019 O people of the **Book**! now hath come

005:044 the protection of Allah's **Book**, and the were

005:059 Say: "O People of the **Book**! do ye disapprove

005:065 If only the people of the **Book** had believed

005:068 Say: "O People of the **Book**! ye have

005:077 Say: "O people of the **Book**! exceed not

005:110 Behold! I taught thee the **Book** and Wisdom,

006:020 Those to whom We have given the **Book** know this

006:038 Nothing have We omitted from the **Book**, and they

006:089 These were the men to whom We gave the **Book**,

006:091 the **Book** which Moses brought?-A light

006:092 believe in this (**Book**), and they

006:092 And this is a **Book** which We

006:114 to whom We have given the **Book**, that it

006:114 Who hath sent unto you the **Book**, explained

006:154 Moreover, We gave Moses the **Book**, completing

006:155 And this is a **Book** which We have

006:156 Lest ye should say: "The **Book** was sent down

006:157 "If the **Book** had only been sent down to us, we

007:002 A **Book** revealed unto thee,- so let

007:037 must reach them from the **Book** (of Decrees):

007:052 For We had certainly sent unto them a **Book**, based

BOOK (continued)

007:096 and We brought them to **book** for their misdeeds.
007:169 of the **Book** taken from them, that they
007:169 And they study what is in the **Book**. But best
007:169 they inherited the **Book**, but they
007:170 by the **Book** and establish regular prayer,-never
007:196 Who revealed the **Book**, (from time to time), and He
008:075 prior rights against each other in the **Book** of Allah.
009:029 from among the People of the **Book**, until they
010:001 These are the Ayats of the **Book** of Wisdom.
010:037 and a fuller explanation of the **Book**-wherein
010:094 who have been reading the **Book** from before thee:
011:001 Alif Lam Ra. (This is) a **Book**, with verse
011:017 and before him is the **Book** of Moses-a guide
011:110 We certainly gave the **Book** to Moses,
012:001 of the Perspicuous **Book**.
013:001 These are the Verses of the **Book**: that which
013:036 Those to whom We have given the **Book** rejoice at
013:039 He pleaseth: with Him is the Mother of the **Book**.
013:043 and such as have knowledge of the **Book**."
014:001 A **Book** which We have revealed unto thee, in order
016:064 And We sent down the **Book** to thee so that
016:089 **Book** explaining all things, a Guide a Mercy,
017:002 We gave Moses the **Book**, and made
017:004 the Children of Israel in the **Book**, that twice
017:093 until thou send down to us a **book** that we could read."
018:001 to His Servant the **Book**, and hath
018:027 been revealed to thee of the **Book** of thy Lord:
018:049 "Ah! woe to us! what a **book** is this! It leaves
018:049 And the **Book** (of Deeds) will be
019:012 "O Yahya! take hold of the **Book** with might":
019:016 Relate in the **Book** (the story of) Mary, when she
019:041 Also mention in the **Book** (the story of) Abraham:
019:051 Also mention in the **Book** (the story of) Moses:
019:054 Also mention in the **Book** (the story of) Isma'il:
019:056 Also mention in the **Book** Idris
021:010 a **book** which We give you eminence.
022:008 and without a **Book** of Enlightenment,-
023:049 And We gave Moses the **Book**, in order
025:035 (Before this), We sent Moses the **Book**,
026:002 These are Verses of the **Book** that makes
027:001 a **Book** that makes (things) clear;
027:040 Said one who had knowledge of the **Book**: "I will
028:002 These are Verses of the **Book** that makes
028:043 We did reveal to Moses the **Book** after We
028:049 Say: "Then bring ye a **Book** from Allah, which is
028:052 Those to whom We sent the **Book** before this,-
028:086 that the **Book** would be sent to thee except as
029:045 Recite what is sent of the **Book** by inspiration
029:046 And dispute ye not with the People of the **Book**,
029:047 thus (it is) that We have sent down the **Book** to thee.
029:047 So the People of the **Book** believe therein,
029:048 wast not (able) to recite a **Book**, before this (**Book** came),
029:051 the **Book** which is rehearsed to them?
031:002 These are Verses of the Wise **Book**,-
031:020 a **Book** to enlighten them!
032:002 (This is) the revelation of the **Book** in which
032:023 We did indeed aforetime give the **Book** to Moses:
033:006 each other have closer personal ties, in the **Book** of Allah,
033:006 such is the writing in the **Book** (of Allah).
033:026 And those of the people of the **Book** who aided
035:011 a part cut off from his life, but is in a **Book** (ordained).
035:025 Scriptures and the illuminating **Book**.

BOOK (continued)

035:029 Those who rehearse the **Book** of Allah,
035:031 of the **Book** is the Truth,-confirming what
035:032 Then We have given the **Book** for inheritance
035:040 Or have We given them a **Book** from which
036:012 We taken account. In a clear **Book** (of evidence).
037:117 And We gave them the **Book** which helps
037:157 Then bring ye your **Book** (of authority)
038:029 (Here is) a **Book** which We have sent down
039:001 The revelation of this **Book** is from Allah,
039:002 We who have revealed the **Book** to thee in Truth:
039:023 the most beautiful Message in the form of a **Book**,
039:041 Verily We have revealed the **Book** to thee in Truth,
040:002 The revelation of this **Book** is from Allah,
040:053 the Guidance, and We gave the **Book** in inheritance
040:070 Those who reject the **Book** and the
041:003 A **Book**, whereof the verses are explained in detail;
041:041 and indeed it is a **Book** of exalted power.
041:045 We certainly gave Moses the **book** aforetime:
042:014 who have inherited the **Book** after them are in
042:015 "I believe in the **Book** which Allah has sent down;
042:017 It is Allah Who has sent down the **Book** in truth,
043:002 By the **Book** that makes things clear,-
043:004 of the **Book**, with Us, high (in dignity),
043:021 What! have We given them a **Book** before this,
044:002 By the **Book** that makes things clear;-
045:002 The revelation of the **book** is from Allah
045:016 Children of Israel the **Book**, the Power
046:002 The revelation of the **Book** is from Allah
046:004 Bring me a **Book** (revealed) before this, or any
046:012 And before this, was the **Book** of Moses as a
046:012 and this **Book** confirms it in the Arabic tongue;
046:030 We have heard a **Book** revealed after Moses,
052:002 By a **Book** Inscribed
056:078 In a **Book** well-guarded,
057:016 The **Book** aforetime, but long ages passed over
057:022 a **Book** before We bring it into existence:
057:025 the **book** and the Balance (of Right and Wrong),
057:029 That the People of the **Book** may know that they
059:002 among the People of the **Book** from their homes
059:011 misbelieving brethren among the People of the **Book**?-
062:002 and to instruct them in the **Book** and Wisdom,-
068:037 Or have ye a **Book** through which ye learn-
074:031 for the People of the **book** and the Believers,
074:031 in order that the People of the **Book** may arrive
098:001 of the **Book** and among the Polytheists, were not
098:004 Nor did the people of the **Book** make schisms,
098:006 of the **Book** and among the Polytheists, will be

BOOKS

002:285 His Angles, His **books**, and His Messengers.
003:084 and in (the **Books**) given to Moses, Jesus,
004:136 His **Books**, His Messenger, and the Day
020:133 of all that was in the former **Books** of revelation?
021:104 the heavens like a scroll rolled up for **books** (completed);-
026:196 in the revealed **Books** of former peoples.
034:044 But We had not given them **Books** which they
053:036 is he not acquainted with what is in the **books** of Moses-
054:043 Or have ye an immunity in the Sacred **Books**?
054:052 in (their) **Books** (of Deeds):
080:013 (It is) in **Books** held (greatly) in honor.
087:018 And this is in the **Books** of the earliest (Revelations),-
087:019 The **Books** of Abraham and Moses.
098:003 Wherein are **books** right and straight.

BOOTY
003:153 (the **booty**) that had escaped you and for (the ill)
008:041 And know that out of all the **booty** that ye
048:015 when ye set forth to acquire **booty** (in war):

BORDERS
013:041 We gradually reduce the land from its outlying **borders**?
021:044 the land (in their control) from its outlying **borders**?

BORE
003:086 and **bore** witness that the Messenger was true
004:001 and be heedful the wombs (that **bore** you):
006:034 with patience and constancy they **bore** their rejection
012:026 saw (this) and **bore** witness, (thus):-
036:041 And a Sign for them is that We **bore** their race
054:013 But We **bore** him on an (Ark) made of

BORN
003:049 and I heal those **born** blind, and the lepers,
004:023 **born** of your wives to whom ye have gone in,-
005:110 and thou healest those **born** blind, and the
019:015 So Peace on him the day he was **born**, the day
019:033 "So Peace is on me the day I was **born**, the day
024:061 nor in one **born** lame, nor in one

BORROW
057:013 Let us **borrow** (a light) from your Light!"

BOSOM
027:012 "Now put thy hand into thy **bosom**, and it
028:032 "Thrust thy hand into thy **bosom**, and it

BOSOMS
024:031 over their **bosoms** and not display their beauty

BOTH
002:142 Say: To Allah belong **both** East and West:
002:229 except when **both** parties fear that
002:233 If they **both** decide on weaning,
004:016 among you are guilty of lewdness, punish them **both**.
004:112 he carries (on himself) (**both**) a false charge and a flagrant
004:134 Allah's (gift) is the reward (**both**) of this life and of the
004:135 for Allah can best protect **both**.
005:018 (**Both**) the Jews and the Christians say: "We are
005:064 Nay, **both** His hands are widely outstretched:
005:066 they would have eaten **both** from above them
005:075 They had **both** to eat their (daily) food.
005:106 and let them **both** swear by Allah: "We will not
005:106 detain them **both** after prayer, and let
007:021 And he swore to them **both**, that he
007:050 They will say: "**Both** these things hath Allah
007:129 (nothing but) trouble, **both** before and after thou comest
007:137 inheritors of lands in **both** East and West,-
007:155 couldst have destroyed long before, **both** them and me:
007:158 it is He that giveth **both** life and death.
007:168 with **both** prosperity and adversity:
007:189 they **both** pray to Allah their Lord (saying):
012:025 So they **both** raced each other to the door, and she
012:025 they **both** found her lord near the door.
013:012 by way **both** of fear and of hope: it is
014:033 sun and the moon, **both** diligently pursuing their courses:
015:079 They were **both** on an open highway, plain to see.
017:023 Whether one or **both** of them attain old age
018:071 So they **both** proceeded: until, when they
020:043 "Go, **both** of you, to Pharaoh, for he
020:047 "So go ye **both** to him, and say, `Verily we
020:058 in a place where **both** shall have even chances."
020:117 so let him not get you **both** out of the Garden,
020:121 In the result, they **both** ate of the tree, and so
020:123 He said: "Get ye down, **both** of you,-all together,

BOTH (continued)
021:022 there would have been ruin in **both**!
022:011 they lose **both** this world and the Hereafter:
022:078 named you Muslims, **both** before and in this (Revelation);
023:050 We gave them **both** shelter on high ground,
025:036 And We commanded: "Go ye **both**, to the
026:015 "By no means! proceed then, **both** of you, with Our Signs;
026:016 "So go forth, **both** of you, to Pharaoh,
027:015 and they **both** said: "Praise be to Allah, Who has
028:035 and invest you **both** with authority, so they
029:060 It is Allah Who feeds (**both**) them and you:
030:024 by way **both** of fear and of hope, and He
031:007 as if there were deafness in **both** his ears:
031:020 in exceeding measure, (**both**) seen and unseen?
037:103 So when they had **both** submitted (to Allah),
040:051 who believe, (**both**) in this world's life and on
042:050 Or He bestows **both** males and females, and He
046:015 upon me, and upon **both** my parents, and that
050:024 "Throw, **both** of you, into Hell every contumacious
055:006 And the herbs and the trees-**both** (alike) bow in adoration.
055:031 O **both** ye worlds!
058:001 the arguments between **both** of you: for Allah
058:002 And in fact they use words (**both**) iniquitous and false:
059:017 The end of **both** will be that they will go into the Fire,
059:022 Who knows (all things) **both** secret and open;

BOTTOM
012:010 throw him down to the **bottom** of the well: he will
012:015 to the **bottom** of the well: and We
037:064 out of the **bottom** of Hell-fire:

BOTTOMLESS
101:009 Will have his home in a (**bottomless**) pit.

BOUGHT
012:021 The man in Egypt who **bought** him, said to his wife:

BOUND
007:139 the cult they are in is **bound** to destruction,
012:072 I will be **bound** by it."
014:049 that day **bound** together in fetters:-
017:081 for Falsehood is (by its nature) **bound** to perish."
025:013 And when they are cast, **bound** together, into a
038:038 As also others **bound** together in fetters.

BOUNDARY
053:014 Near the Lote-tree of the utmost **boundary**.

BOUNDS
003:112 and transgressed beyond **bounds**.
005:077 the **bounds** (of what is proper), trespassing
007:055 those who trespass beyond **bounds**.
007:081 ye are indeed a people transgressing beyond **bounds**."
009:010 It is they who have transgressed all **bounds**.
010:083 and one who transgressed all **bounds**.
017:033 but let him not exceed **bounds** in the matter
020:024 for he had indeed transgressed all **bounds**."
020:043 for he has indeed transgressed all **bounds**;
020:045 or lest he transgress all **bounds**."
020:127 him who transgresses beyond **bounds** and believes
021:009 those who transgressed beyond **bounds**.
036:019 Nay, but ye are a people transgressing all **bounds**!"
042:027 all **bounds** through the earth; but He
042:042 beyond **bounds** through the land, defying right
043:005 a people transgressing beyond **bounds**?
049:009 transgresses beyond **bounds** against the other,
050:025 transgressed all **bounds**, cast doubts
051:034 who trespass beyond **bounds**."
051:053 themselves a people transgressing beyond **bounds**!

BOUNDS (continued)

052:032 a people transgressing beyond **bounds**?
068:012 (all) good, transgressing beyond **bounds**, deep in
079:017 for he has indeed transgressed all **bounds**:
079:037 Then, for such as had transgressed all **bounds**,
083:012 the Transgressor beyond **bounds**, the Sinner!
089:011 (All) these transgressed beyond **bounds** in the lands.
096:006 Nay, but man doth transgress all **bounds**,

BOUNTIES

002:200 "Our Lord! Give us (thy **bounties**) in this world!"
002:254 (the **bounties**) We have provided for you,
002:268 Allah promiseth you His forgiveness and **bounties**.
003:008 Grantor of **bounties** without measure.
003:073 Say: "All **bounties** are in the hand of Allah:
003:074 for Allah is the Lord of **bounties** unbounded.
003:174 and Allah is the Lord of **bounties** unbounded.
004:037 hide the **bounties** which Allah hath bestowed on them;
017:020 Of the **bounties** of thy Lord We bestow freely on all-
017:020 the **bounties** of thy Lord are not closed (to anyone).
031:020 has made His **bounties** flow to you in exceeding measure,
036:047 "Spend ye of (the **bounties**) with which Allah
038:009 the Grantor of **Bounties** without measure?
038:035 for Thou art the Grantor of **Bounties** (without measure)."
038:039 "Such are Our **Bounties**: whether thou

BOUNTIFUL

002:035 and eat of the **bountiful** things therein
096:003 Proclaim! And thy Lord is Most **Bountiful**,-

BOUNTY

002:198 the **bounty** of your Lord (during pilgrimage).
002:243 For Allah is full of **bounty** to mankind,
002:251 but Allah is full of **bounty** to all the worlds.
003:170 They rejoice in the **bounty** provided by Allah:
003:171 the Grace and the **Bounty** from Allah,
003:174 And they returned with Grace and **Bounty** from Allah:
004:032 but ask Allah of His **bounty**: for Allah
004:054 for what Allah hath given them of His **bounty**?
004:070 Such is the **Bounty** from Allah: and sufficient
004:130 for each of them from His all-reaching **bounty**:
004:173 and more, out of His **bounty**:
005:002 seeking of the **bounty** and good pleasure
005:064 He giveth and spendeth (of His **Bounty**) as He pleaseth.
009:028 soon will Allah enrich you, if He wills, out of His **bounty**,
009:059 will soon give us of His **bounty**:
009:074 only return for the **bounty** with which Allah and
009:075 that if He bestowed on them of His **bounty**; they would
009:076 But when He did bestow of His **bounty**, they became
010:058 Say: "In the **Bounty** of Allah. And in His
010:060 Verily Allah is full of **Bounty** to mankind,
016:014 seek (thus) of the **bounty** of Allah and that
017:012 **Bounty** from your Lord and that ye may know
017:066 in order that ye may seek of His **Bounty**.
017:087 for His **Bounty** is to thee (indeed) great.
030:023 (make for livelihood) out of His **Bounty**:
030:045 and work righteous deeds, out of His **Bounty**,
030:046 and that ye may seek of His **Bounty**:
033:047 shall have from Allah a very great **Bounty**.
035:012 that ye may seek (thus) of the **Bounty** of Allah
035:030 He will give them (even) more out of His **Bounty**;
035:035 "Who has, out of His **bounty**, settled us
038:054 Truly such will be Our **Bounty** (to you);
040:061 Verily Allah is Full of Grace and **Bounty** to men:
042:022 that will indeed be the magnificent **Bounty** (of Allah).
042:023 That is (the **Bounty**) whereof Allah gives Glad

BOUNTY (continued)

042:026 gives them increase of His **bounty**:
044:057 As a **Bounty** from thy Lord! That will
045:012 ye may seek of His **Bounty**, and that ye may be grateful.
055:027 thy Lord,-full of Majesty, **Bounty** and Honour.
055:078 full of Majesty, **Bounty** and Honour.
062:004 Such is the **Bounty** of Allah, which He
062:004 and Allah is the Lord of the highest **bounty**.
062:010 and seek of the **Bounty** of Allah: and remember
073:020 the land, seeking of Allah's **bounty**; yet others
093:011 But the **Bounty** of thy Lord-rehearse and proclaim!

BOW

002:034 "**Bow** down to Adam"; and they **bowed** down:
002:043 and **bow** down your heads with those who **bow** down
002:125 or use it as a retreat, or **bow**,
003:043 (in prayer) with those who **bow** down."
003:043 prostrate thyself, and **bow** down (in prayer)
003:084 and to Allah do we **bow** our will (in Islam)."
005:055 they **bow** down humbly (in worship).
005:111 we **bow** to Allah as Muslims'."
006:014 the first of those who **bow** to Allah (in Islam),
007:126 as Muslims (who **bow** to Thy Will)"!
009:112 that **bow** down and prostrate themselves in prayer;
021:108 will ye therefore **bow** to His Will (in Islam)?"
022:026 or stand up, or **bow**, or prostrate
022:077 O ye who believe! **bow** down, prostrate yourselves,
027:091 who **bow** in Islam to Allah's Will,-
036:008 so that they cannot **bow** their heads.
041:033 "I am of those who **bow** in Islam"?
048:029 Thou wilt see them **bow** and prostrate themselves
055:006 both (alike) **bow** in adoration.
068:043 summoned aforetime to **bow** in adoration, while they

BOW-LENGTHS

053:009 two **bow-lengths** or (even) nearer;

BOWED

002:034 "Bow down to Adam"; and they **bowed** down:
003:067 and **bowed** his will to Allah's (which is Islam).
003:080 after ye have **bowed** your will (to Allah in Islam)?
003:083 willing or unwilling, **bowed** to His Will (accepted Islam),
005:044 by the Prophets who **bowed** (as in Islam)

BOWELS

047:015 so that it cuts up their **bowels** (to pieces)?

BOWING

002:128 "Our Lord! make us Muslims, **bowing** to Thy (Will),
002:128 of our progeny a people Muslim, **bowing** to Thy (Will),
003:064 are Muslims (**bowing** to Allah's Will)."
003:199 **bowing** in humility to Allah:
028:053 (**bowing** to Allah's Will) from before this."
038:024 fell down, **bowing** (in prostration),
045:028 And thou wilt see every nation **bowing** the knee:

BOY

018:074 when they met a young **boy**, he slew

BRACELETS

018:031 be adorned therein with **bracelets** of gold,
022:023 with **bracelets** of gold and pearls; and their
035:033 with **bracelets** of gold and pearls; and their
043:053 "Then why are not gold **bracelets** bestowed on him,
076:021 and they will be adorned with **Bracelets** of silver;

BRAIN

021:018 and it knocks out its **brain,** and behold,

BRANCHES

014:024 and its **branches** (reach) to the heavens,-
055:048 Abounding in **branches**;-

BRAND

020:010 burning **brand** therefrom or find some

027:007 a burning **brand** (to light our fuel), that ye

068:016 Soon shall We **brand** (the beast) on the snout!

BRANDED

003:014 horses **branded** (for blood and excellence);

009:035 and with it will be **branded** their foreheads,

BRASS

018:029 like melted **brass**, that will scald their

034:012 a Font of molten **brass** to flow for him; and there

044:045 Like molten **brass**; it will boil in their insides,

055:035 A flame of fire (to burn) and a (flash of) molten **brass**,

070:008 The Day that the sky will be like molten **brass**,

BRAYING

031:019 is the **braying** of the ass."

BREACH

004:035 If ye fear a **breach** between them twain, appoint

005:013 But because of their **breach** of their Covenant, We

BREAD

012:036 (in a dream) carrying **bread** on my head, and birds

BREAK

002:027 Those who **break** Allah's Covenant

005:019 after the **break** in (the series of) Messengers,

006:159 and **break** up into sects, thou hast

008:056 but they **break** their covenant every time,

011:108 thy Lord willeth: a gift without **break**.

013:025 But those who **break** the Covenant of Allah,

016:091 and **break** not your oaths after ye have

030:048 as He wills, and **break** them into fragments,

038:018 at eventide and at **break** of day,

038:044 and strike therewith: and **break** not (thy oath)."

047:022 and **break** your ties of kith and kin?

068:024 "Let not a single indigent person **break** in upon

BREAKEST

003:194 for thou never **breakest** Thy promise."

BREAKING

026:148 with spathes near **breaking** (with the weight of fruit)?

BREAKS

002:080 for He never **breaks** His promise?

002:256 the most trustworthy hand-hold that never **breaks**.

016:092 who **breaks** into untwisted strands the yarn

104:004 to be thrown into that which **Breaks** to Pieces.

104:005 That which **Breaks** to Pieces?

BREAST

006:125 He maketh their **breast** close and constricted,

006:125 He openeth their **breast** to Islam; those whom

016:106 but such as open their **breast** to Unbelief,-

020:025 (Moses) said: "O my Lord! expand me my **breast**;"

026:013 "My **breast** will be straitened. And my

033:004 two hearts in his **breast**: nor has

094:001 Have We not expanded thee thy **breast**?-

BREASTS

003:154 test what is in your **breasts** and purge

009:014 heal the **breasts** of Believers.

022:046 but the hearts which are in their **breasts**.

040:056 there is nothing in their **breasts** but (the quest of)

084:023 of what they secrete (in their **breasts**).

100:010 in (human) **breasts** is made manifest-

BREATH

021:046 If but a **breath** of the Wrath of thy Lord

067:007 of its **breath** even as it blazes forth.

100:001 By the (Steeds) that run, with panting (**breath**),

BREATHE

003:049 the figure of a bird, and **breathe** into it,

BREATHED

015:029 (in due proportion) and **breathed** into him

021:091 We **breathed** into her from Our spirit,

032:009 and **breathed** into him of His spirit.

038:072 and **breathed** into him of My spirit, fall ye

066:012 and We **breathed** into her (body) of Our spirit;

BREATHES

081:018 And the Dawn as it **breathes** away the darkness;-

BREATHEST

005:110 And thou **breathest** into it, and it becometh

BREATHING

007:086 "And squat not on every road, **breathing** threats,

BREED

071:027 and they will **breed** none but wicked

BREEDING

038:031 coursers of the highest **breeding**; and swift of foot;

BRETHREN

002:220 they are your **brethren**;

003:103 so that by His Grace, Ye became **brethren**;

003:156 who say of their **brethren**, when they

003:168 (of their **brethren** slain), while they themselves

006:087 (To them) and to their fathers, and progeny and **brethren**:

007:065 one of their (own) **brethren**: he said: "O my

007:073 one of their own **brethren**: he said: "O my

007:085 one of their own **brethren**: he said:

007:202 But their **brethren** (the evil ones) plunge them

009:011 they are your **brethren** in Faith:

011:050 one of their own **brethren**. He said: "O my

011:061 one of their own **brethren**. He said: "O my

011:084 one of their own **brethren**: he said: "O my people!

012:007 Verily in Joseph and his **brethren** are Signs

012:020 The (**Brethren**) sold him for a miserable price,-

012:058 Then came Joseph's **brethren**: they entered

033:018 those who say to their **brethren**, "Come along to us,"

046:021 Mention (Hud) one of 'Ad's (own) **brethren**:

050:013 The 'Ad, Pharaoh, the **Brethren** of Lut,

059:010 "Our Lord! Forgive us, and our **brethren** who came

059:011 say to their misbelieving **brethren** among the

BRICKS

028:038 O Haman! light me a (kiln to bake **bricks**) out of clay,

BRIEF

014:030 Say: "Enjoy (your **brief** power)! But verily

016:055 Then enjoy (your **brief** day); but soon

030:034 Then enjoy (your **brief** day); but soon

033:014 with none but a **brief** delay!

033:016 a **brief** (respite) will ye be allowed to enjoy!"

051:043 "Enjoy (your **brief** day) for a little while!"

BRIGHT

015:018 a fiery comet, **bright** (to see).

017:012 We have made **bright** that ye may seek bounty from

BRIGHTNESS

037:010 by a flaming fire, of piercing **brightness**.

075:022 will beam (in **brightness** and beauty);-

076:011 and will shed over them **brightness** and a

083:024 the beaming **brightness** of Bliss.

086:003 (It is) the tar of piercing **brightness**;-

BRILLIANT

024:035 the glass as it were a **brilliant** star:

BRIM

078:034 And a Cup full (to the **Brim**).

BRIMSTONE

007:084 on them a shower (of **brimstone**):
026:173 We rained down on them a shower (of **brimstone**):
027:058 We rained down on them a shower (of **brimstone**):
051:033 stones of clay (**brimstone**),
011:082 down on them **brimstones** hard as baked clay,
015:074 on them **brimstones** hard as baked clay.

BRING

002:028 and will again **bring** you to life;
002:063 We have given you and **bring** (ever) to
002:072 but Allah was to **bring** forth what ye did hide.
002:145 Even if thou wert to **bring** to the people
002:148 Allah will **bring** you together.
002:259 shall Allah **bring** it (ever) to life,
002:259 how We **bring** them together and clothe them
003:049 and I **bring** the dead into life by Allah's leave;
003:093 ay: "**Bring** ye the Torah and study it,
005:052 a change of fortune **bring** us disaster."
006:035 and **bring** them a Sign,-(what good?).
006:150 If they **bring** such witnesses, be not
006:150 Say: "**Bring** forward your witnesses to prove
007:053 did indeed **bring** true (tidings).
007:070 **Bring** us what thou threatenest us with, if so
007:074 so **bring** to remembrance the benefits (ye have received)
007:077 saying: "O Salih! **bring** about thy threats,
007:112 And **bring** up to thee all (our) sorcerers well-versed."
007:150 did ye make haste to **bring** on the judgment
007:171 and **bring** (even) to remembrance what is therein;
007:201 from Satan assaults them, **bring** Allah to remembrance
007:203 If thou **bring** them not a revelation, they say:
007:205 And so thou (O reader!) **bring** thy Lord to remembrance
009:064 But verily Allah will **bring** to light all that
009:083 If, then, Allah **bring** thee back to any of them,
009:099 Aye, indeed they **bring** them nearer (to Him):
010:015 say: "**Bring** us a Qur'an other than this,
010:038 Say: "**Bring** then a Sura like unto it, and call
010:079 aid Pharaoh: "**Bring** me every sorcerer well versed."
011:002 from Him to warn and to **bring** glad tidings:
011:013 Say. "**Bring** ye then ten Suras forged, like unto
011:032 now **bring** upon us what thou threatenest us with,
011:033 He said: "Truly, Allah will **bring** it on you
012:021 may be he will **bring** us much good,
012:050 So the king said: "**Bring** ye him unto me." But when
012:054 So the king said: "**Bring** him unto me; I will take
012:059 he said: "**Bring** unto me a brother ye have,
012:060 "Now if ye **bring** him not to me, ye shall
012:066 be sure to **bring** him back to me unless ye are
012:083 May be Allah will **bring** them (back)
013:038 a messenger to **bring** a Sign except as Allah
014:002 (their Unfaith will **bring** them)!-
014:005 "**Bring** out thy people from the depths of darkness
014:010 then **bring** us some clear authority."
014:011 It is not for us to **bring** you an authority
016:089 and We shall **bring** thee as a witness against these
017:013 We shall **bring** out for him a scroll, which he
017:062 I will surely **bring** his descendants under my sway-
017:092 thou **bring** Allah and the angels
018:015 why do they not **bring** forward an authority
018:019 best food (to be had) and **bring** some to you,
018:062 "**Bring** us our early meal; truly we have
018:096 he said: "**Bring** me, that I may pour over it,
018:096 "**Bring** me blocks of iron." At length,
019:068 then shall We **bring** them forth on their

BRING (continued)

020:010 perhaps I can **bring** you some burning brand
020:055 and from it shall We **bring** you out once again.
020:133 They say: "Why does he not **bring** us a Sign
021:005 Let him then **bring** us a Sign like the ones
021:024 "**Bring** your convincing proof: this is
021:047 We will **bring** it (to account): and enough
021:061 They said, "Then **bring** him before the eyes
021:103 The Great Terror will **bring** them no grief:
022:005 appointed term, then do We **bring** you out as babes,
023:107 "Our Lord! **bring** us out of this:
024:013 Why did they not **bring** four witnesses to prove it?
025:033 And no question do they **bring** to thee but We
026:037 "And **bring** up to thee all (our) sorcerers
026:154 then **bring** us a Sign, if thou
026:210 The Satans did not **bring** it down:
027:007 or I will **bring** you a burning brand (to light our fuel,)
027:007 soon will I **bring** you from there some information,
027:021 or execute him, unless he **bring** me a clear
027:038 which of you can **bring** me her throne before they
027:039 "I will **bring** it to thee before thou rise
027:040 "I will **bring** it to thee before even thy glance
027:064 Say, "**Bring** forth your argument, if ye
027:082 We shall **bring** forth from the earth a beast
028:012 and **bring** him up for you and take care of him."
028:029 I hope to **bring** you from there some information,
028:049 Say: "Then **bring** ye a Book from Allah, which is
028:085 will **bring** thee back to the Place of Return.
029:029 "**Bring** us the Wrath of Allah if thou
029:034 "For we are going to **bring** down on the
030:058 but if thou **bring** to them any Sign, the Unbelievers
031:016 in the heavens or on earth, Allah will **bring** it forth:
033:043 that He may **bring** you out from the depths
034:037 that will **bring** you nearer to Us in degree:
035:016 He could blot you out and **bring** in a New Creation:
035:027 With it We then **bring** out produce of various
035:037 **Bring** us out: we shall work righteousness,
037:022 "**Bring** ye up," it shall be said, "The wrong-doers
037:157 Then **bring** ye your Book (of authority)
038:033 "**Bring** them back to me."
039:003 in order that they may **bring** us nearer to Allah."
040:078 for any messenger to **bring** a Sign except by the
041:047 (within her womb) nor **bring** forth (young), but by
042:015 Allah will **bring** us together, and to
044:010 that the sky will **bring** forth a kind of smoke
044:036 "Then **bring** (back) our forefathers if what
045:025 they say, "**Bring** (back) our forefathers,
046:004 **Bring** me a Book (revealed) before this, or any
046:022 Then **bring** upon us the (calamity) with which
047:001 their deeds will Allah **bring** to naught.
047:008 and (Allah) will **bring** their deeds to naught.
047:029 will not **bring** to light all their rancor?
047:037 and He would **bring** out all your ill-feeling.
051:033 "To **bring** on, on them (a shower of) stones of
056:003 (Many) will it **bring** low; (many) will it exalt;
056:069 Do ye **bring** it Down (in rain) from the Cloud,
057:022 a Book before We **bring** it into existence:
065:001 perchance Allah will **bring** about thereafter
072:021 or to **bring** you to right conduct."
079:029 and its splendor doth He **bring** out (with light).
086:008 Surely (Allah) is able to **bring** him back (to life)!
096:019 and **bring** thyself the closer (to Allah)!

BRINGER

005:019 unto us no **bringer** of glad tidings and no warner.
005:019 a **bringer** of glad tidings and a warner.
007:188 and a **bringer** of glad tidings to those who have faith."
048:008 as a **bringer** of Glad Tidings, and as a Warner:

BRINGEST

003:026 and thou **bringest** low whom Thou pleasest:
003:027 and Thou **bringest** the dead out of the living;
003:027 Thou **bringest** the Living out of the dead,
005:110 And behold! thou **bringest** forth the dead
007:132 "Whatever be the Signs thou **bringest**, to work
015:007 "Why **bringest** thou not angels to us if it be

BRINGETH

002:073 Thus Allah **bringeth** the dead to life
014:032 and with it **bringeth** out fruits wherewith
087:004 And Who **bringeth** out the (green and luscious) pasture,

BRINGING

006:092 **bringing** blessings, and confirming (the revelations)
009:099 gifts **bringing** them nearer to Allah and obtaining
037:056 little short of **bringing** me to perdition!

BRINGS

002:097 for he **brings** down the (revelation)
002:109 till Allah **brings** about His command;
002:182 And **brings** about a settlement among
003:117 likened to a Wind which **brings** a nipping frost:
004:019 and Allah **brings** about through it a great deal of good.
009:024 then wait until Allah **brings** about His Decision:
010:031 And who is it that **brings** out the living from the dead
014:025 It **brings** forth its fruit at all times, by the
016:076 whichever way he directs him, he **brings** no good:
017:067 But when He **brings** you back safe to land, ye turn
026:089 that **brings** to Allah a sound heart;
027:025 "So that they worship no Allah who **brings** forth what is
028:085 "My Lord knows best who it is that **brings** true guidance,
030:019 It is He Who **brings** out the living from the dead,
030:019 and **brings** out the dead for the living,
039:033 And he who **brings** the Truth and he
053:032 He knows you well when He **brings** you out
057:020 how rain and the growth which it **brings** forth,

BRINK

003:103 and ye were on the **brink** of the Pit of Fire,

BROAD

007:098 against its coming in **broad** daylight while they
021:031 And We have made therein **broad** highways
054:013 made of **broad** planks and caulked with palm-fibre:

BROADCAST

020:097 a blazing fire and scatter it **broadcast** in the sea!
051:001 By the (Winds) that scatter **broadcast**;

BROCADE

018:031 will wear green garments of fine silk and heavy **brocade**;
044:053 Dressed in fine silk and in rich **brocade**,
055:054 whose inner linings will be of rich **brocade**:
076:021 of fine silk and heavy **brocade**, and they

BROKE

004:155 in that they **broke** their Covenant; that they
007:135 Behold! they **broke** their word!
007:168 We **broke** them up into sections
009:077 because they **broke** their Covenant with Allah,
018:050 and he **broke** the Command of his Lord.
020:086 and so ye **broke** your promise to me?"
020:087 They said: "We **broke** not the promise to thee,
021:058 So he **broke** them to pieces, (all) but the biggest
025:039 and each one We **broke** to utter annihilation (for the sins).

BROKE (continued)

043:050 behold, they **broke** their word.
068:021 As the morning **broke**, they called out, one to

BROKEN

003:159 they would have **broken** away from about thee:
017:098 to bones and **broken** dust, should we really be
056:065 we could make it **broken** orts.

BROOK

038:015 will **brook** no delay.

BROTHER

002:178 by the **brother** of the slain,
004:012 but has left a **brother** or a sister, each one
004:176 her **brother** takes her inheritance:
005:025 I have power only over myself and my **brother**:
005:030 led him to the murder of his **brother**:
005:031 and to hide the naked body of my **brother**?"
005:031 the naked body of his **brother**.
007:111 They said: "Keep him and his **brother** in suspense
007:142 had charged his **brother** Aaron (before he went up):
007:150 seized his **brother** by (the hair of) his head,
007:151 forgive me and my **brother**!
010:078 in order that thou and thy **brother** may have
010:087 We inspired Moses and his **brother** with this
012:008 They said: "Truly Joseph and his **brother** are loved
012:059 a **brother** ye have, of the same father
012:063 so send our **brother** with us, that we
012:063 of grain shall we get (unless we take our **brother**):
012:064 when I trusted you with his **brother** aforetime?
012:065 take care of our **brother**; and add
012:069 he received his (full) **brother** to stay with him.
012:069 "Behold! I am thy (own) **brother**;
012:076 before (he came to) the baggage of his **brother**:
012:076 He could not take his **brother** by the law
012:077 a **brother** of his who did steal before (him)."
012:087 about Joseph and his **brother**, and never
012:089 with Joseph, and his **brother**, not knowing
012:090 "I am Joseph, and this is my **brother**:
019:053 his **brother** Aaron, (also) a prophet.
020:030 "Aaron, my **brother**;
020:042 "Go, thou and thy **brother**, with My
023:045 Then We sent Moses and his **brother** Aaron,
025:035 his **brother** Aaron with him as Minister;
026:036 They said: "Keep him and his **brother** in suspense
026:106 Behold, their **brother** Noah said to them: "Will ye
026:124 Behold, their **brother** Hud said to them: "Will ye
026:142 Behold, their **brother** Salih said to them:
026:161 Behold, their **brother** Lut said to them: "Will ye
027:045 their **brother** Salih, saying, "Serve Allah":
028:034 "And my **brother** Aaron-he is more
028:035 will certainly strengthen thy arm through thy **brother**,
029:036 (We sent) their **brother** Shu'aib.
038:023 "This man is my **brother**; he has
049:012 to eat the flesh of his dead **brother**?
070:012 His wife and his **brother**,
080:034 That Day shall a man flee from his own **brother**,

BROTHER'S

004:023 mother's sisters; **brother's** daughters,
012:070 cup into his **brother's** saddle-bag.
012:076 out of his **brother's** baggage.

BROTHERHOOD

005:106 of your own (**brotherhood**) or others from outside
033:006 than (the **Brotherhood** of) Believers and Muhajirs:
049:010 a single **Brotherhood**:

BROTHERS

004:011 if the deceased left **brothers** (or sisters),
004:176 if there are **brothers** and sisters, (they share),
009:023 your **brothers** if they love infidelity above Faith:
009:024 your sons, your **brothers**, your mates, or your
012:005 relate not thy vision to thy brother, lest they
012:073 (The **brothers**) said: "By Allah! well ye know that
012:100 sown enmity between me and my **brothers**.
015:047 (they will be) **brothers** (joyfully) facing
017:027 Verily spendthrifts are **brothers** of the Satans.
024:031 their husbands' sons, their **brothers** or their
024:031 or their **brothers'** sons, or their sisters'
024:061 or your mothers, or your **brothers**, or your sisters
024:061 or your father's **brothers**, or your father's sisters
024:061 or your mother's **brothers**, or your mother's sister
033:005 (then they are) your **Brothers** in faith,
033:055 or their sons, their **brothers**, or their
049:010 your two (contending) **brothers**; and fear
058:022 or their **brothers**, or their kindred.

BROTHERS'

033:055 or their **brothers'** sons, or their sisters' sons,

BROUGHT

002:022 and **brought** forth therewith fruits
002:071 They said: "Now hast thou **brought** the truth."
002:281 when ye shall be **brought** back to Allah.
003:036 And Allah knew best what she **brought** forth-
003:083 and to Him shall they all be **brought** back.
003:152 and disobeyed it after He **brought** you in sight
003:158 Lo! it is unto Allah that ye are **brought** together.
003:188 who exult in what they have **brought** about,
004:041 and We **brought** thee as a witness
004:041 How then if We **brought** from each People a witness,
005:002 nor of the animals **brought** for sacrifice, nor the
005:095 an offering, **brought** to the Ka'ba, of a domestic animal
006:051 they will be **brought** (to judgment) before their Lord:
006:091 the Book which Moses **brought**?-A light
007:022 So by deceit he **brought** about their fall:
007:043 the Messengers of our Lord **brought** unto us."
007:096 and We **brought** them to book for their misdeeds.
009:094 in the end will ye be **brought** back to Him
009:105 soon will ye be **brought** back to the Knower of what
010:030 they will be **brought** back to Allah their rightful
010:056 and to Him shall ye all be **brought** back.
010:074 they **brought** them Clear Signs, but they
010:081 Moses said: "What ye have **brought** is sorcery:
010:097 Even if every Sign was **brought** unto them,-until
011:018 They will be **brought** before their Lord, and the
011:053 "O Hud! no Clear (Sign) hast thou **brought** us,
012:076 at length He **brought** it out of his brother's baggage.
012:088 we have (now) **brought** but scanty capital:
012:100 and **brought** you (all here) out of the desert,
016:058 When news is **brought** to one of them,
016:078 It is He Who **brought** you forth from the wombs
016:102 Say, the Holy Spirit has **brought** the revelation
018:033 Each of those gardens **brought** forth its produce,
018:036 even if I am **brought** back to my Lord.
018:055 or the Wrath be **brought** to them face to face?
019:027 "O Mary! truly a strange thing hast thou **brought**!
019:027 At length she **brought** the (babe) to her people,
020:040 So We **brought** thee back to thy mother, that her
020:088 "Then he **brought** out (of the fire) before the
021:055 They said, "Have you **brought** us the Truth, or are
023:035 ye shall be **brought** forth (again)?

BROUGHT (continued)

023:070 Nay, he has **brought** them the Truth, but most
023:115 that ye would not be **brought** back to Us (for account)"?
024:011 Those who **brought** forward the lie are a body
024:013 When they have not **brought** the witnesses, such men,
024:064 and one day they will be **brought** back to Him,
026:090 the Garden will be **brought** near,
028:051 Now have We **brought** them the word in order
028:057 to which are **brought** as tribute fruits of all kinds,-
028:061 is to be among those **brought** up (for punishment)?
028:070 and to Him shall ye (all) be **brought** back.
028:088 and to Him will ye (all) be **brought** back.
029:057 in the end to Us shall ye be **brought** back.
030:011 then shall ye be **brought** back to Him.
030:016 such shall be **brought** forth to Punishment.
030:019 and thus shall ye be **brought** out (from the dead).
032:011 then shall ye be **brought** back to your Lord."
032:013 We could certainly have **brought** every soul
033:014 They would certainly have **brought** it to pass,
036:022 and to Whom ye shall (all) be **brought** back.
036:032 will be **brought** before Us (for judgment).
036:053 they will all be **brought** up before Us!
036:075 and they are a host **brought** up before them.
036:083 and to Him will ye be all **brought** back.
037:057 been among those **brought** (there)!
037:158 that they will be **brought** before Him.
038:031 Behold, there were **brought** before him, at eventide,
038:060 It is ye who have **brought** this upon us!
038:061 Whoever **brought** this upon us,-add to
039:044 ye shall be **brought** back."
039:069 and the witnesses will be **brought** forward;
040:025 Now, when he **brought** them the Truth, from Us,
040:046 In front of the Fire will they be **brought**,
041:023 hath **brought** you to destruction,
041:050 but if I am **brought** back to my Lord, I have
042:045 And thou wilt see them **brought** forward to the
043:017 When news is **brought** to one of them of
043:018 Is then one **brought** up among trinkets, and unable
043:024 He said: "What! even if I **brought** you better
043:044 and soon shall ye (all) be **brought** to account.
043:078 Verily We have **brought** the truth to you: but most
043:085 And to Him shall ye be **brought** back.
045:015 In the end will ye (all) be **brought** back to your Lord.
047:010 Allah **brought** utter destruction on them,
050:031 And the Garden will be **brought** nigh to the
050:033 and **brought** a heart turned in devotion (to Him):
051:026 quickly to his household, **brought** out a fatted calf.
054:028 right to drink being **brought** forward (by suitable turns).
058:009 and fear Allah, to whom ye shall be **brought** back.
069:018 That Day shall ye be **brought** to Judgment:
072:028 (truly) **brought** and delivered the Messages
079:014 When, behold, they will be **brought** out to the open.
081:013 And when the Garden is **brought** near;-
089:023 And Hell, that Day, is **brought** (face to face),-

BRUNT

039:024 the **brunt** of the Chastisement on the Day of
040:045 but the **brunt** of the Chastisement encompassed on

BUBBLING

088:012 Therein will be a **bubbling** spring:

BUCKET

012:019 and he let down his **bucket** (into the well).

BUILD

007:074 ye **build** for yourselves palaces and castles in (open)

BUILD (continued)

009:110 The foundation of those who so **build** is never
016:068 to **build** its cells in hills, on trees, and in
018:021 "Let us surely **build** a place of worship over them."
026:128 "Do ye **build** a landmark on every high place
028:038 and **build** me a lofty palace, that I
037:097 They said: "**Build** him a furnace, and throw
040:036 Pharaoh said: "O Haman! **Build** me a lofty palace,
066:011 "O my Lord! **build** for me, in nearness to Thee,

BUILDER

038:037 every kind of **builder** and diver,-

BUILDING

018:021 (Some) said, "Construct a **building** over them":
007:137 the great works and fine **Buildings** which Pharaoh
026:129 ye get for yourselves fine **buildings** in the hope
029:038 from (the traces) of their **buildings** (their fate):
044:026 And corn-fields and noble **buildings**,

BUILDS

029:041 of the Spider, who **builds** (to itself) a house;

BUILT

004:078 even if ye are in towers **built** up strong and high!"
039:020 one above another have been **built**:
051:047 We have **built** the Firmament with might:
078:012 And (have We not) **built** over you the seven

BUNCHES

069:023 The Fruits whereof (will hang in **bunches**) low and near.
076:014 and the **bunches** (of fruit), there, will hang

BUOYED

047:025 and **buoyed** them up with false hopes.

BURDEN

002:233 No soul shall have a **burden** laid on it greater than it
002:286 doth Allah place a **burden** greater than it can bear.
002:286 our Lord! Lay not on us a **burden** like that which Thou
002:286 not on us a **burden** greater than we have the strength
004:039 And what **burden** were it on them if they had faith
004:085 helps an evil cause, shares in its **burden**:
006:138 forbidden to yoke or **burden**, and cattle
006:142 Of the cattle are some for **burden** and some for meat:
006:152 no **burden** do We place on any soul, but that
006:164 no bearer of burdens can bear the **burden** of another.
007:042 no **burden** do We place on any soul, but that
007:187 Heavy were its **burden** through the heavens
007:189 she bears a light **burden** and carries
008:066 For the present, Allah hath lightened your (**burden**),
016:076 a wearisome **burden** is he to his master;
017:015 no bearer of burdens can bear the **burden** of another:
020:100 verily they will bear a **burden** on the Day of Judgment;
020:101 and grievous will the **burden** be to them on that Day,-
023:062 On no soul do We place a **burden** greater than
028:076 keys would have been a **burden** to a body of strong men.
035:018 Nor can a bearer of burdens bear another's **burden**.
039:007 No bearer of burdens can bear the **burden** of another.
042:022 and (the **burden** of) that must (necessarily) fall on them.
053:038 can bear the **burden** of another;
065:006 until they deliver their **burden**:
065:007 Allah puts no **burden** on any person beyond what He has
094:002 And removed from thee thy **burden**

BURDENED

052:040 are **burdened** with a load of debt?-
068:046 so that they are **burdened** with a load

BURDENS

004:028 Allah doth wish to lighten your (**burdens**):
006:031 and evil indeed are the **burdens** that they bear!

BURDENS (continued)

006:031 for they bear their **burdens** on their backs;
006:164 no bearer of **burdens** can bear
007:157 He releases them from their heavy **burdens** and from
016:025 Day of Judgment, their own **burdens** in full,
016:025 also (something) **burdens** of those without knowledge,
016:025 the **burdens** they will bear!
017:015 no bearer of **burdens** can bear
029:013 and (other) **burdens** along with their own,
029:013 They will bear their own **burdens**,
035:018 Nor can a bearer of **burdens** bear another's
039:007 No bearer of **burdens** can bear the burden
047:004 until the war lays down its **burdens**.
053:038 Namely, that no bearer of **burdens** can bear
065:004 their period is until they deliver their **burdens**:
099:002 And the Earth throws up her **burdens** (from within),

BURIED

018:082 there was, beneath it, a **buried** treasure, to which
035:022 to hear who are (**buried**) in graves.
060:013 in despair about those (**buried**) in graves.
075:008 And the moon is **buried** in darkness.
081:008 When the female (infant), **buried** alive, is questioned-

BURN

014:029 Into Hell? They will **burn** therein,-an evil
017:018 they will **burn** therein, disgraced and rejected.
020:097 we will certainly **burn** it in a blazing fire
021:068 They said, "**Burn** him and protect your gods,
023:104 The Fire will **burn** their faces, and they
029:024 "Slay him or **burn** him." But Allah
038:056 Hell!-they will **burn** therein-an evil
038:059 Truly, they shall **burn** in the Fire!
052:016 "**Burn** ye therein: the same is it to you whether ye bear
055:035 A flame of fire (to **burn**) and a (flash of) molten brass
058:008 in it will they **burn**, and evil is that destination!
069:031 "And **burn** ye him in the Blazing Fire.
073:012 and a Fire (to **burn** them),
092:015 None shall **burn** therein but those most unfortunate ones.

BURNED

019:070 are most worthy of being **burned** therein.
040:072 then in the Fire shall they be **burned**;

BURNING

004:055 and enough is Hell for a **burning** fire.
020:010 perhaps I can bring you some **burning** brand therefrom
022:009 make him taste the chastisement of **burning** (Fire).
022:022 "Taste ye the Chastisement of **Burning**!"
027:007 a **burning** brand (to light our fuel), that ye
028:029 **burning** firebrand, that ye may warm yourselves."
056:094 And **burning** in Hell-Fire.
085:010 They will have the Chastisement of the **Burning** Fire.

BURNT

002:266 with fire therein, and be **burnt** up?
111:003 **Burnt** soon will he be in a Fire of blazing Flame!

BURROW

006:123 to plot (and **burrow**) therein:

BURST

019:090 At it the skies are about to **burst**, the earth
082:003 When the Oceans are suffered to **burst** forth;

BURSTING

067:008 Almost **bursting** with fury: every time

BURY

016:059 or **bury** it in the dust?

BUSINESS

010:061 In whatever **business** thou mayest be, and whatever

BUSINESS (continued)

015:057 the **business** on which ye (Have come), O ye
024:062 for some **business** of theirs, give leave
038:024 the Partners (in **business**) who wrong each other:
062:009 and leave off **business** (and traffic):

BUT

002:008 **but** they do not (really) believe.
002:009 **but** they only deceive themselves
002:012 **but** they realize (it) not.
002:013 they are the fools **but** they do not know.
002:014 **but** when they are alone with their evil ones,
002:016 **but** their traffic is profitless,
002:019 **But** Allah is ever round the rejecters of Faith!
002:020 The lightning all **but** snatches away their sight:
002:024 **But** if ye cannot-and of a surety ye cannot
002:025 **But** give glad tidings to those who believe
002:026 **but** those who reject Faith say:
002:026 **but** He causes not to stray,
002:035 **but** approach not this tree,
002:039 "**But** those who reject Faith and belie Our Signs,
002:040 and fear none **but** Me.
002:057 (**but** they rebelled); to Us they did no harm,
002:057 **but** they harmed their own selves.
002:059 **But** the transgressors changed the word
002:064 **But** ye turned back thereafter:
002:068 nor too young, **but** of middling age;
002:072 **but** Allah was to bring forth what ye did hide.
002:076 **but** when they meet each other in private,
002:078 and they do nothing **but** conjecture.
002:078 **but** (see therein their own) desires,
002:080 not touch us **but** for few numbered days:"
002:082 **But** those who have faith and work righteousness,
002:083 worship none **but** Allah;
002:085 **but** disgrace in this life?
002:085 **But** what is the reward for those among you who
002:089 **but** the curse Allah is on those
002:095 **But** they will never seek for death,
002:096 **but** the grant of such life will not
002:099 and none reject them **but** those who are perverse.
002:102 Solomon did not disbelieve **but** Satans disbelieved,
002:102 **But** neither of these taught anyone (such things)
002:102 **But** they could not thus harm anyone except by Allah's
002:102 they did sell their souls, if they **but** knew!
002:103 better had been the reward from Allah if they **but** knew!
002:104 **but** say, 'Unzurna and hearken (to him):
002:105 **But** Allah will choose for His Mercy whom He will-
002:106 **but** We substitute something better or similar:
002:108 **But** whoever changeth from Faith to Unbelief,
002:109 **but** forgive and overlook,
002:113 **but** Allah will judge between them
002:114 **but** disgrace in this world,
002:119 **but** of thee no question shall be asked
002:124 He answered: "**But** My Promise is not within the reach
002:126 **but** will soon drive them to the torment of fire,-
002:130 the religion of Abraham **but** such as debase
002:137 **but** Allah will suffice thee as against them,
002:137 **but** if they turn back,
002:140 **But** Allah is not unmindful of what ye do!
002:146 **but** some of them conceal the truth
002:150 so fear them not, **but** fear Me;
002:155 **but** give glad tidings to those who patiently persevere,-
002:163 there is no god **but** He,
002:165 **But** those of Faith are overflowing

BUT (continued)

002:167 (the fruits of) their deeds as (nothing **but**) regrets.
002:171 listen to nothing **but** calls and cries:
002:173 **but** if one is forced by necessity,
002:174 they swallow into themselves naught **but** Fire;
002:176 the Book in truth **but** those who seek causes
002:177 **but** it is righteousness-to believe in Allah
002:178 **But** if any remission is made by the brother
002:182 **But** if anyone fears partiality or wrong-doing
002:184 **But** he that will give more, of his own free will,
002:184 **but** if any of you is ill, or on a journey,
002:185 **but** if any one is ill, or on a journey,
002:187 **but** He turned to you and forgave you:
002:187 **but** do not associate with your wives while
002:189 Say: They are **but** Signs to mark fixed periods
002:190 those who fight you **but** do not transgress limits;
002:191 **but** fight them not at the Sacred Mosque,
002:191 **but** if they fight you, slay them.
002:192 **But** if they cease, Allah is Oft-Forgiving,
002:193 **But** if they cease, let there be no hostility
002:194 **But** fear Allah,
002:195 contribute to (your) destruction; **but** do good:
002:196 **but** if ye are prevented (from completing it),
002:196 **but** if he cannot afford it,
002:197 **but** the best of provisions is right conduct.
002:200 **But** they will have no portion in the Hereafter.
002:203 **but** if anyone hastens to leave in two days,
002:205 **but** Allah loveth not mischief.
002:210 **But** to Allah do all questions go back
002:211 **But** if anyone, after Allah's favour has come to him,
002:212 **But** the righteous will be above them
002:213 **but** the People of the Book,
002:216 **But** it is possible that ye dislike a thing
002:216 **But** Allah knoweth, and ye know not.
002:217 **but** graver is it in the sight of Allah
002:219 **but** the sin is greater than the profit."
002:220 **but** Allah knows the man who means mischief
002:221 Unbelievers do (**but**) beckon you to the Fire.
002:221 **But** Allah beckons by His Grace to the Garden
002:222 **But** when they have purified themselves,
002:223 **But** do some good act for your souls beforehand;
002:225 **but** for the intention in your hearts;
002:227 **But** if their intention is firm for divorce,
002:228 **but** men have a degree over them
002:231 **but** solemnly rehearse Allah's favours on you,
002:231 **but** do not take them back to injure them,
002:233 **But** he shall bear the cost of their food
002:233 **But** fear Allah and know that Allah sees well
002:235 **but** do not make a secret contract with them
002:236 **but** bestow on them (a suitable gift),
002:237 **but** after the fixation of a dower for them,
002:239 **but** when ye are in security,
002:240 **but** if they leave (the residence),
002:243 **but** most of them are ungrateful.
002:246 **But** when they were commanded to fight,
002:246 **But** Allah has full knowledge of those
002:249 "**But** they drank of it, except a few.
002:249 **But** those who were convinced that they must meet
002:251 **but** Allah is full of bounty to all the worlds.
002:253 **but** they (chose) to wrangle,
002:253 **but** Allah does what He wills.
002:255 Allah! There is no god **but** He, the living,
002:258 "**But** it is Allah that causeth the sun to rise from the

BUT (continued)

002:259 **but** look at thy food and thy drink;
002:259 **But** Allah caused him to die for a hundred years,
002:260 He said: "Yea! **but** to satisfy my own heart."
002:264 **but** believe neither in Allah nor in the Last Day.
002:265 **but** makes it yield a double increase of harvest,
002:269 **but** none will receive admonition **but** men of
002:270 **But** the wrong-doers have no helpers.
002:271 **but** if ye conceal them,
002:272 **But** Allah guides to the right path
002:275 **but** those who repeat (the offense)
002:275 **but** Allah hath permitted trade and forbidden usury.
002:276 **but** will give increase for deeds of charity:
002:279 **but** if ye repent ye shall have your capital sums:
002:280 **But** if ye remit it by way of charity,
002:282 **but** let him fear Allah his Lord and not diminish aught
002:282 **but** if it be a transaction which ye carry out on the spot
002:282 **But** take witnesses whenever ye make a commercial
003:002 Allah! there is no god **but** He,
003:006 There is no god **but** He,
003:007 **but** no one knows its true meanings except Allah.
003:007 **But** those in whose hearts is perversity follow
003:008 **but** grant us mercy from Thee:
003:010 they are themselves **but** fuel for the Fire.
003:013 **But** Allah doth support with His aid whom He pleaseth.
003:014 **but** with Allah is the best of the goals
003:018 There is no god **but** He the Exalted in Power,
003:018 There is no god **but** He:
003:019 **But** if any deny the Signs of Allah,
003:020 **but** if they turn back, thy duty
003:023 **but** a party of them turn back
003:024 not touch us **but** for a few numbered days":
003:025 **But** how (will they fare) when We gather them
003:028 **But** Allah cautions you (to fear) Himself;
003:030 **But** Allah cautions you (to fear) Him
003:032 **but** if they turn back, Allah loveth not
003:041 shalt speak to no man for three days **but** with signals.
003:047 He **but** saith to it 'Be,' and it is!
003:057 **but** Allah loveth not those who do wrong.
003:063 **But** if they turn back,
003:064 that we worship none **but** Allah;
003:066 **but** why dispute ye in matters of which ye have no
003:067 **but** he was Upright.
003:069 **But** they shall lead astray (not you),
003:069 **but** themselves, and they do not perceive!
003:072 **but** reject it at the end of the day:
003:075 **but** they tell a lie against Allah,
003:078 **but** it is no part of the Book;
003:078 **but** it is not from Allah:
003:086 **But** Allah guides not a people unjust.
003:090 **But** those who reject faith after they accepted it.
003:097 **but** if any deny faith, Allah stands not in need
003:099 **But** Allah is not unmindful of all that ye do."
003:107 **But** those whose faces will be (lit with) white,
003:110 **but** most of them are perverted transgressors.
003:117 **but** they wrong themselves.
003:119 **but** they love you not,
003:119 **but** when they are alone,
003:120 **but** if some misfortune overtakes you,
003:120 **But** if ye are patient and do right,
003:122 **but** Allah was their Protector,
003:126 Allah made it **but** a message of hope for you,
003:128 Not for thee, (**but** for Allah), is the decision:

BUT (continued)

003:129 **but** Allah is Oft-Forgiving, Most Merciful.
003:130 **but** fear Allah; that ye may (really) prosper.
003:144 **but** Allah (on the other hand) will swiftly reward those
003:146 **But** they never lost heart if they met with disaster
003:152 **But** He forgave you:
003:154 **but** (all this was) that Allah might test what
003:155 **But** Allah has blotted out (their fault):
003:167 **But** Allah hath full knowledge of all they conceal.
003:173 **but** it only increased their Faith:
003:175 **but** fear Me, if ye have Faith.
003:176 no portion in the Hereafter, **but** a severe punishment.
003:177 **but** they will have a grievous punishment.
003:178 **but** they will have a shameful punishment.
003:179 **but** He chooses of his Messengers whom He pleases.
003:185 is **but** goods and chattels of deception.
003:186 **But** if ye persevere patiently,
003:187 **but** they threw it away behind their backs,
004:003 **but** if ye fear that ye shall not be able to deal justly
004:004 **but** if they, of their own good pleasure, remit any part
004:005 **but** feed and clothe them therewith, and speak to them
004:006 **but** consume it not wastefully, nor in haste
004:006 **but** all-sufficient is Allah in taking account.
004:006 **but** if he is poor, let him have for himself
004:008 **But** if at the time of division other relatives,
004:012 **but** if they leave a child, ye get a fourth;
004:012 **but** if ye leave a child, they get an eighth;
004:012 **but** has left a brother or a sister, each one
004:012 **but** if more than two, they share in a third;
004:014 **But** those who disobey Allah and His Messenger
004:020 **But** if ye decide to take one wife
004:024 **but** if, after a dower is prescribed, ye agree
004:025 **but** it is better for you that ye practise self-restraint.
004:027 **but** the wish of those who follow their lusts is that ye
004:029 **but** let there be amongst you traffic
004:031 If ye (**but**) eschew the most heinous of the things
004:032 **but** ask Allah of His bounty: for Allah
004:034 **but** if they return to obedience, seek not
004:042 **but** never will they hide a single fact from Allah!
004:045 **But** Allah hath full knowledge of your enemies:
004:046 and **but** few of them will believe.
004:046 **but** Allah hath cursed them, for their Unbelief;
004:048 **but** He forgiveth anything else, to whom
004:049 Nay-**but** Allah doth purify whom He pleaseth.
004:050 **but** that by itself is a manifest sin!
004:054 **But** We had already given the people of Abraham
004:057 **But** those who believe and do deeds of righteousness,
004:060 **But** Satan's wish is to lead them astray
004:063 so keep clear of them **but** admonish them,
004:064 We sent not a Messenger, **but** to be obeyed,
004:065 **but** accept them with the fullest conviction.
004:065 **But** no, by thy Lord, they can have no (real) Faith.
004:066 **but** if they had done what they were (actually) told,
004:073 **But** if good fortune comes to you from Allah,
004:077 **but** establish regular prayers and spend
004:078 **but** if evil, they say, "This is from thee"
004:078 **But** what hath come to these people.
004:079 **but** whatever evil happens to thee, is from
004:080 **but** if any turn away, We have not
004:081 **but** when they leave thee, a section of them meditate
004:081 **But** Allah records their nightly (plots):
004:083 all **but** a few of you would have followed Satan.
004:087 Allah! There is no god **but** He:

BUT (continued)

004:089 They **but** wish that ye should reject Faith.
004:089 **But** if they turn renegades, seize them
004:090 withdraw from you **but** fight you not,
004:095 **but** those who strive and fight hath He distinguished
004:102 **But** there is no blame on you if ye put away your arms
004:102 **but** take (every) precaution for yourselves.
004:103 **but** when ye are free from danger, set up
004:104 **but** you hope from Allah, what they have not.
004:106 **But** seek the forgiveness of Allah; for Allah
004:108 **but** they cannot hide from Allah, while
004:109 **but** who will contend with Allah on their behalf
004:110 **but** afterwards seeks Allah's forgiveness,
004:112 **But** if anyone earns a fault or a sin and throws
004:113 **But** (in fact) they will only lead their own souls astray.
004:113 **But** for the Grace of Allah to thee and His Mercy,
004:114 **but** if one exhorts to a deed of charity
004:116 **but** He forgiveth whom He pleaseth
004:117 (The Pagans), leaving Him, call **but** upon female deities:
004:117 they call **but** upon Satan the persistent rebel!
004:118 Allah did curse him, **but** he said: "I will take of Thy
004:120 **but** Satan's promises are nothing **but** deception.
004:122 **But** those who believe and do deeds
004:126 **But** to Allah belong all things in the
004:127 **but** Allah is well-acquainted therewith.
004:128 **But** if ye do good and practice self-restraint,
004:129 **but** turn not away (from a woman) altogether, so as
004:130 **But** if they separate Allah will provide
004:131 **But** if ye deny Him, lo! unto Allah belong all
004:141 **But** if the Unbelievers gain a success, they say
004:141 **But** Allah will judge betwixt you
004:142 seek to deceive Allah **but** it is Allah who deceive them.
004:142 **but** little do they hold Allah in remembrance;
004:150 saying: "We believe in some **but** reject others":
004:153 **but** they were seized for their presumption,
004:157 **but** they killed him not, nor crucified him.
004:157 **But** only conjecture to follow, for of a surety
004:159 **but** must believe in Him before his death;
004:162 **But** those among them who are well-grounded
004:166 **But** Allah beareth witness that what He hath
004:166 **but** enough is Allah for a Witness.
004:170 **But** if ye reject Faith, to Allah belong
004:171 nor say of Allah aught **but** truth.
004:173 **But** those who believe and do deeds of righteousness,
004:173 **but** those who are disdainful and arrogant, He will
004:176 That dies, leaving a sister **but** no child, she
005:001 **but** animals of the chase are forbidden while ye are in
005:002 **but** help ye not one another in sin and rancor:
005:002 **But** when ye are clear of the Sacred Precincts
005:003 **But** if any is forced by hunger, with no
005:003 yet fear them not **but** fear Me.
005:004 **but** pronounce the name of Allah over it:
005:005 **but** chaste women among the People of the Book,
005:006 **But** if ye are ill, or on a journey, or one of you cometh
005:006 **but** to make you clean, and to complete His favour
005:011 **but** (Allah) held back their hands from you:
005:012 if ye (**but**) establish regular Prayers, pay Zakat
005:012 **but** if any of you, after this, resisteht faith,
005:013 **But** because of their breach of their Covenant,
005:013 **but** forgive them and overlook (their misdeeds):
005:014 We did take a Covenant, **but** they forgot a good
005:018 Nay, ye are **but** men, of the men He hath created:
005:019 **but** now hath come unto you a bringer

BUT (continued)

005:023 (**But**) among (their) God-fearing men were two on whom
005:023 **but** on Allah put your trust if ye have faith."
005:026 **but** sorrow thou not over these rebellious people.
005:027 it was accepted from one, **but** not from the other.
005:037 **but** never will they get out therefrom:
005:039 **But** if the thief repent after his crime, and amend
005:041 "We believe" with their lips **but** whose hearts have no
005:041 "If ye are given this, take it, **but** if not, beware!"
005:043 **But** why do they come to thee for decision, when
005:044 therefore fear not men, **but** fear Me, and sell not
005:045 **But** if anyone remits the retaliation by way of charity,
005:048 **but** (His Plan is) to test you in what He
005:049 **but** beware of them lest they beguile thee from
005:050 **But** who, for a people whose faith is assured, can
005:051 they are **but** friends and protectors to each other.
005:053 and they will fall into (nothing **but**) ruin.
005:057 **but** fear ye Allah, if ye have Faith (indeed).
005:058 they take it (**but**) as mockery and sport;
005:061 "We believe": **but** in fact they enter with a disbelief,
005:061 **But** Allah knoweth fully all that they hide.
005:064 **But** the revelation that cometh to thee from Allah
005:064 **but** they (ever) strive to do mischief on earth.
005:066 **but** many of them follow a course that is evil.
005:068 **But** sorrow thou not over (these) people without Faith.
005:071 **But** Allah sees well all that they do.
005:072 **But** said Christ: "O children of Israel!
005:076 **But** Allah,-He it is that heareth
005:081 **but** most of them are rebellious wrong-doers.
005:086 **But** those who reject Faith and belie
005:087 made lawful for you, **but** commit no excess:
005:088 **but** fear Allah, in Whom ye believe.
005:089 **but** He will call you to account for your deliberate oaths:
005:089 **But** keep to your oaths. Thus doth Allah make clear
005:091 Satan's plan is (**but**) to excite enmity and hatred between
005:094 O ye who believe! Allah doth **but** make a trial
005:096 **but** forbidden is the pursuit of land-game:
005:099 The Messenger's duty is **but** to proclaim (the message).
005:099 **But** Allah knoweth all that ye reveal and ye conceal.
005:101 **But** if ye ask about things when the Qur'an
005:103 **but** most of them lack wisdom.
005:107 **But** if it gets known that these two were guilty
005:108 **But** fear Allah, and listen (to His counsel):
005:110 'This is nothing **but** evident magic'.
005:115 **but** if any of you after that resisteth faith, I
006:004 **But** never did a single one of the Signs of their Lord
006:004 **but** they turned away therefrom.
006:005 **but** soon shall come to them the news
006:007 "This is nothing **but** obvious magic!"
006:010 **but** the scoffers were hemmed in by the thing
006:014 And He is that feedeth **but** is not fed."
006:014 Say: "Nay! **but** I am commanded to be the first of those
006:017 touch thee with affliction, none can remove it **but** He;
006:019 Say: "**But** in truth He is the One God.
006:021 **But** verily the wrong-doers never shall prosper.
006:023 no excuse for them **but** to say: "By Allah
006:024 **but** the (lie) which they invented will leave
006:025 **but** We have thrown veils on their hearts,
006:025 when they come to thee, they (**but**) dispute with thee;
006:025 "These are nothing **but** tales of the ancients."
006:026 **but** they only destroy themselves and they
006:027 If thou couldst **but** see when they shall be made to stand
006:027 they will say: "Would that we were **but** sent back!

BUT (continued)

006:027 **but** would be amongst those who believe!"
006:028 **But** if they were returned, they would
006:030 If thou couldst **but** see when they shall be made to stand
006:032 Nothing is the life of this world **but** play and amusement.
006:032 **But** best is the Home in the Hereafter, for those who are
006:037 **but** most of them understand not."
006:038 **but** (forms part of) communities like you.
006:044 **But** when they forget the warning
006:049 **But** those who reject Our Signs,-them shall
006:050 I **but** follow what is revealed to me."
006:057 I am on a clear Sign from my Lord, **but** ye reject Him.
006:057 The Command rests with none **but** Allah:
006:058 **But** Allah knoweth best those who do wrong."
006:059 of the Unseen, the treasures that none knoweth **but** He.
006:059 Not a leaf doth fall **but** with His knowledge:
006:059 **but** is (inscribed) in a Record Clear
006:066 **But** thy people reject this, though it is the Truth.
006:069 **but** (their duty) is to remind them, that they
006:070 **But** continue to admonish them with it (Al-Qur-an)
006:076 **But** when it set, he said: "I love not
006:077 **But** when the moon set, he said: "Unless my
006:078 **But** when the sun set, he said: "O my people!
006:090 this is **but** a Reminder to the nations."
006:091 **but** ye make it into (separate) sheets for show,
006:093 If thou couldst **but** see how the wicked
006:102 There is no god **but** He, the Creator
006:103 **but** His grasp is over all vision;
006:106 there is no god **but** He:
006:107 **but** We made thee not one to watch over their doings,
006:109 **but** what will make you (Muslims) realize
006:111 **But** most of them ignore (the truth).
006:116 they do nothing **but** lie.
006:116 They follow nothing **but** conjecture:
006:119 **But** many do mislead (men) by low desires without
006:121 **But** the satans ever inspire their friends
006:123 **but** they only plot against their own souls,
006:128 **but** (alas!) we reached our term-which Thou
006:136 **But** the share of their "partners" reacheth
006:137 **but** leave alone them and what they forged.
006:139 **but** if it is still-born, then all have shares therein.
006:141 **But** waste not by excess: for Allah
006:141 **but** render the dues that are proper on the
006:144 **But** who doth more wrong than one who invents a lie
006:145 **But** (even so), if a person is forced be necessity,
006:147 **but** from people in guilt never will His wrath be turned
006:148 Ye follow nothing **but** conjecture:
006:148 Ye do nothing **but** lie."
006:152 **but** that which it can bear;-whenever ye speak
006:164 Every soul draws the meed of its acts on none **but** itself:
007:005 no cry did they utter **but** this: "Indeed we did wrong."
007:019 **but** approach not this tree, lest you become of the unjust."
007:025 **but** from it shall ye be taken out (at last)."
007:026 **but** the raiment of righteousness-that is the best.
007:031 eat and drink: **but** waste not by excess, for Allah loveth
007:036 **But** those who reject Our Sings and treat
007:038 **but** this ye do not understand.
007:042 **But** those who believe and work righteousness,-
007:042 **but** that which it can bear,-they will be
007:044 **but** a Crier shall proclaim between them: "The curse
007:046 **but** they still hoped. To (enter it).
007:056 **but** call on Him with fear and longing
007:058 springs up nothing **but** that which is scanty, thus

BUT (continued)

007:058 **but** from the land that is bad, springs up
007:059 worship Allah! ye have not other god **but** Him.
007:062 "I **but** I convey to you" the Message
007:064 **But** they rejected him, and We
007:064 **But** We overwhelmed in the flood those who
007:065 ye have no other god **but** Him.
007:067 **but** (I am) a Messenger from the Lord
007:068 "I **but** convey to you the messages of my Lord:
007:073 ye have no other god **but** Him.
007:079 **but** ye love not good counsellors!"
007:082 And his people gave no answer **but** this: they said,
007:083 **But** We saved him and his family, except
007:085 ye have no other god **but** Him.
007:086 **but** remember how ye were little, and He
007:091 **But** the earthquake took them unawares, and they
007:093 **but** how shall I lament over a people
007:096 had **but** believed and feared Allah, We should
007:096 **but** they rejected (the truth), and We
007:099 **but** no one can feel secure from the Plan of Allah,
007:101 **but** they would not believe what they had rejected before.
007:102 **but** most of them We found rebellious and disobedient.
007:103 **But** they wrongfully rejected them:
007:105 to say nothing **but** truth about Allah.
007:120 **But** the sorcerers fell down prostrate in adoration.
007:123 **but** soon shall ye know (the consequences).
007:125 "For us, we are **but** sent back unto our Lord."
007:126 "**But** thou dost wreak thy vengeance on us
007:129 They said: "We have had (nothing **but**) trouble,
007:131 **But** when good (times) came, they said,
007:131 **but** most of them do not understand!
007:133 **but** they were steeped in arrogance, a people
007:135 **But** when We removed the Plague from them
007:143 **but** look upon the mount; if it abide
007:146 **but** if they see the way of error, that is
007:153 **But** those who do wrong **but** repent thereafter and (truly)
007:156 **but** My Mercy extendeth to all things.
007:158 there is no god **but** He: it is He
007:160 (**but** they rebelled); to Us they did no harm,
007:160 **but** they harmed their own souls.
007:161 **but** say forgive (us) and enter the gate in a posture of
007:162 **But** the transgressors among them changed the
007:163 **but** on the day they had no Sabbath, they came
007:165 **but** We visited the wrong-doers with a grievous
007:167 **but** He is also Oft-Forgiving, Most Merciful.
007:169 **but** they chose (for themselves) the vanities of this world,
007:169 that they would no ascribe to Allah anything **but** the truth?
007:169 **But** best for the righteous is the Home in the Hereafter.
007:173 **but** we are (their) descendants after them:
007:175 to whom We sent Our Signs, **but** he passed them by:
007:176 **but** he inclined to the earth, and followed
007:180 **but** shun such men as distort His names:
007:184 he is **but** a perspicuous warner.
007:187 none **but** He can reveal as to when it will occur.
007:187 **but** most men know not."
007:188 I am **but** a warner, and a bringer
007:190 **but** Allah is exalted high above the partners
007:190 **But** when He giveth them a goodly child, they
007:191 **but** are themselves created?
007:197 "**But** those ye call upon besides Him, are unable
007:198 looking at thee, **but** they see not.
007:199 **but** turn away from the ignorant.
007:202 **But** their brethren (the evil ones) plunge them

BUT (continued)

007:203 Say: "I **but** follow what is revealed to me from my Lord:
007:203 This is (nothing **but**) lights from your Lord,
008:007 **but** Allah willed to establish the Truth according to His
008:010 Allah made it **but** a message of hope, and an assurance
008:017 threwest (a handful of dust), it was not thy act, **but** Allah's:
008:021 "We hear," **but** listen not:
008:023 they would **but** have turned back and declined (faith).
008:026 **but** He provided a safe asylum for you, strengthened you
008:028 that your possession and your progeny are **but** a trial:
008:030 **but** the best of planners is Allah.
008:031 these are nothing **but** tales of the ancients."
008:033 **But** Allah was not going to send them a Chastisement:
008:034 **but** most of them do not understand.
008:034 **But** what plea have they that Allah should not punish
008:035 is nothing **but** whistling and clapping of hands:
008:036 **but** in the end they will have (only) regrets and sighs;
008:038 **but** if they persist, the punishment of those before them
008:039 religion becomes Allah's in its entirety **but** if they cease,
008:042 **but** (thus ye met), that Allah might accomplish a matter
008:043 **but** Allah saved (you): for He knoweth well the (secrets)
008:048 **but** when the two forces came in sight of each other,
008:049 **But** if any trust in Allah, behold! Allah
008:056 **but** they break their covenant every time,
008:060 whom ye may not know, **but** whom Allah doth know.
008:061 **But** if the enemy incline towards peace, do thou
008:063 have produced that affection, **but** Allah hath done it:
008:066 **but** (even so), if there are a hundred of you,
008:067 **but** Allah looketh to the Hereafter:
008:069 **But** (now) enjoy what ye took in war, lawful and good:
008:069 **but** fear Allah: for Allah is Oft-forgiving, Most Merciful.
008:071 **But** if they have treacherous designs against thee,
008:072 who believed **but** did not emigrate ye owe no duty
008:072 **but** if they seek your aid in religion, it is
008:075 **But** kindred by blood have prior rights against
009:002 **but** that Allah will cover with shame
009:002 **but** know ye that ye cannot frustrate Allah
009:003 **but** if ye turn away, know ye that ye cannot frustrate Allah,
009:004 (**But** the treaties are) not dissolved with those
009:005 **but** if they repent, and establish regular prayers.
009:005 **But** when the forbidden months are past, then fight
009:008 **but** their hearts are averse from you;
009:011 **But** (even so), if they repent, establish regular
009:012 **But** if they violate their oaths
009:025 great numbers elated you, **but** they availed you naught:
009:026 **But** Allah did pour His calm on the Messenger
009:030 they **but** imitate what the Unbelievers of old
009:031 yet they were commanded to worship **but** One God:
009:031 there is no god **but** He.
009:032 **but** Allah will not allow **but** that His light should be
009:036 **But** know that Allah is with those restrain themselves.
009:037 **But** Allah guideth not those who reject Faith.
009:038 **But** little is the comfort of this life, as compared to the
009:039 **but** Him ye would not harm in the least,
009:040 **But** the word of Allah is exalted to the heights:
009:041 That is best for you, if ye (**but**) knew.
009:042 **but** the distance was long, (and weighed) on them.
009:046 **but** Allah was averse to their being sent forth;
009:047 have added your (strength) **but** only (made for) disorder,
009:047 **But** Allah knoweth well those who do wrong.
009:050 **but** if a misfortune befalls thee, they say
009:052 **But** we can expect for you either that Allah
009:056 that they are indeed of you; **but** they are not of you:

BUT (continued)

009:058 they are pleased, **but** if not, behold!
009:061 **But** those who molest the Prophet will have
009:062 **but** it is more fitting that they should please
009:064 **But** verily Allah will bring to light all that
009:070 Who wrongs them, **but** they wrong their own souls.
009:072 of everlasting stay **but** the greatest bliss
009:074 **but** indeed they uttered blasphemy,
009:074 **but** if they turn back (to their evil ways), Allah
009:076 **But** when He did bestow of His bounty, they became
009:088 **But** the Messenger, and those who believe
009:096 **But** if ye are pleased with them.
009:097 **but** Allah is All-Knowing, All-Wise.
009:099 **But** some of the Bedouin Arabs believe in Allah
009:107 will indeed swear that their intention is nothing **but** good;
009:107 **but** Allah doth declare that they are certainly liars.
009:114 **But** when it became clear to him that he was
009:117 **but** He turned to them (also):
009:118 no fleeing from Allah (and no refuge) **but** to Himself.
009:120 **but** was reckoned to their credit as a deed
009:121 **but** the deed is inscribed to their credit;
009:125 **But** those in whose hearts is a disease,-it will
009:129 **But** if they turn away, say: "Allah sufficeth me:
009:129 there is no god **but** He: On him is my trust,-
010:002 (**but**) say the Unbelievers: "This is indeed an evident
010:004 **but** those who reject Him will have draughts of boiling
010:005 Nowise did Allah create this **but** in truth and
010:007 **but** are pleased and satisfied with the life
010:011 **But** We leave those who rest not their hope
010:012 **But** when We have removed his affliction,
010:013 with Clear Sings, **but** they would not believe!
010:015 I follow naught **but** what is revealed unto me:
010:015 **But** when Our Clear Sings are rehearsed unto them,
010:017 **But** never will prosper those who sin.
010:019 Mankind was **but** one nation, **but** differed (later).
010:023 **But** when He delivereth them, behold! they
010:025 **But** Allah doth call to the Home of Peace:
010:027 **But** those who have earned evil will have
010:032 apart from the Truth, what (remains) **but** error?
010:036 **But** most of them follow nothing **but** conjecture:
010:039 **but** see what was the end of those who did wrong!
010:042 **but** canst thou make the deaf to hear,-even though
010:043 **but** canst thou guide the blind,-
010:045 (It will be) as if they had tarried **but** an hour of a day:
010:052 Ye get **but** the recompense of what ye earned!' "
010:054 **but** the judgment between them will be with justice,
010:060 Bounty to mankind, **but** most of them are ungrateful.
010:061 the greatest of these things **but** are recorded
010:066 and they do nothing **but** lie.
010:066 They follow nothing **but** conjecture, and they
010:072 "**But** if ye turn back, (consider): no reward
010:073 They rejected him, **but** We delivered him, and those
010:073 those who were warned (**but** heeded not)!
010:074 **but** they would not believe what they had already rejected
010:075 **But** they were arrogant: they were a wicked people.
010:077 **But** sorcerers will not prosper."
010:078 **But** not we shall believe in you!"
010:083 **But** none believed in Moses except some children
010:091 **but** a little while before, wast thou in rebellion!-
010:092 **But** verily, many among mankind are heedless
010:101 **but** neither Sings nor Warners profit those
010:102 **but** (what happened in) the days of the men who
010:104 **But** I worship Allah-who will take your souls

BUT (continued)

010:107 there is none can remove it **but** He: if He
011:002 (It teacheth) that ye should worship none **but** Allah.
011:003 **But** if ye turn away, then I fear for you
011:006 creature on earth **but** its sustenance dependeth on Allah:
011:007 **But** if thou wert to say to them, "Ye shall indeed be raised
011:007 be sure to say, "This is nothing **but** obvious sorcery!"
011:010 **But** if We give him a taste of (Our) favours
011:012 **But** thou art there only to warn!
011:014 and that there is no god **but** He! Will ye even then submit
011:016 for whom there is nothing in the Hereafter **but** the Fire:
011:017 They believe therein; **but** those of the Sects that reject it,
011:023 **But** those who believe and work righteousness,
011:026 "That ye serve none **but** Allah: verily I do
011:027 **But** the Chiefs of the Unbelievers among his People said:
011:027 "'We see (in) thee nothing **but** a man like ourselves:
011:027 we see that any follow thee **but** the meanest among us,
011:028 **but** that the Mercy hath been obscured from your sight?
011:029 **but** I will not drive away (in contempt) those who believe:
011:029 my reward is from none **but** Allah:
011:037 "**But** construct an Ark under Our eyes
011:039 "**But** soon will ye know who it is on whom
011:040 **But** only a few believed with him.
011:043 any **but** those on whom He hath mercy!"-
011:048 **but** (there will be other) Peoples to whom We shall grant
011:048 **but** in the end will a grievous Chastisement
011:050 ye have no other god **but** Him.
011:051 My reward is from none **but** Him Who created Me:
011:054 "We say nothing **but** that (perhaps) some of our gods
011:056 not a moving creature, **but** He hath grasp of its fore-lock.
011:061 ye have not other god **but** Him.
011:062 **But** we are really in suspicious (disquieting) doubt
011:063 then would ye add to my (portion) **but** perdition?
011:065 **But** they did ham-string her.
011:070 **But** when he saw their hands not reaching towards the
011:071 **but** We gave her Glad tidings of Isaac, and after him,
011:081 **but** thy wife (will remain behind):
011:084 ye have no other god **but** Him.
011:084 I see you in prosperity, **but** I fear for you
011:086 left you by Allah is best for you, if ye (**but**) believed!
011:086 **But** I am not set over you to keep watch!"
011:090 "**But** ask forgiveness of you Lord, and turn
011:092 **But** verily my Lord encompasseth all that ye do!
011:094 **but** the (mighty) Blast did seize the wrong-doers,
011:097 **but** they followed the command of Pharaoh,
011:098 **but** woeful indeed will be the place to which they are
011:101 nor did they add aught (to their lot) **but** perdition!
011:104 Nor shall We delay it **but** for a term appointed.
011:106 therein (nothing **but**) the heaving of sighs and sobs:
011:109 They worship nothing **but** what their fathers worshipped
011:109 **but** verily We shall pay them back (in full) their portion
011:110 gave the Book to Moses, **but** differences arose therein:
011:110 **but** they are in suspicious doubt concerning it.
011:116 **But** the wrong-doers pursued the enjoyment of the
011:116 (**but** there were none) except a few among them whom
011:118 **but** they will not cease to differ,
012:008 **but** we are a goodly body!
012:010 "Slay not Joseph, **but** if ye must do something,
012:017 **But** thou wilt never believe us even though we tell the
012:018 He said: "Nay, **but** your minds have made up a tale
012:019 **But** Allah knoweth well all that they do!
012:021 **but** most among mankind know it not.
012:023 **But** she, in whose house he was, sought to

BUT (continued)

012:024 **but** that he saw the evidence of his Lord:
012:025 **but** prison or a grievous chastisement?"
012:027 "**But** if it be that his shirt is torn from the back,
012:032 from his (true) self **but** he did firmly save himself
012:040 apart from Him is nothing **but** names which ye have
012:040 the Command is for none **but** Allah:
012:040 He hath commanded that ye worship none **but** Him:
012:040 that is the right religion, **but** Most men understand not.
012:042 **But** Satan made him forget to mention him to his lord:
012:045 **But** the man who had been released, one of the two
012:050 **But** when the messenger came to him, (Joseph) said:
012:053 **but** surely certainly my Lord is Oft-Forgiving,
012:057 **But** verily the reward of the Hereafter is the best,
012:058 and he knew them, **but** they knew him not.
012:059 of the same father as yourselves, (**but** a different mother):
012:064 **But** Allah is the best to take care (of him),
012:065 This is **but** a small quantity.
012:068 **but** most men know not.
012:076 **but** over all endued with knowledge is One,
012:077 **But** these things did Joseph keep locked in his heart,
012:083 Jacob said: "Nay, **but** ye have yourselves contrived
012:088 we have (now) brought **but** scanty capital:
012:109 did We send before thee (as Messengers) any **but** men,
012:109 **But** the home of the Hereafter is best, for those
012:110 **But** never will be warded off Our punishment for those
012:111 **but** a confirmation of what went before it.
013:001 **but** most men believe not.
013:006 **But** verily thy Lord is full of forgiveness
013:007 **But** thou art truly a warner, and to
013:011 **but** when (once) Allah willeth a people's punishment,
013:014 for water to reach their mouths **but** it reaches them not:
013:014 prayer of those without Faith is nothing **but** vain prayer.
013:017 **but** the torrent bears away the foam that mounts up
013:018 **But** those who respond not to Him,-even if they had all
013:025 **But** those who break the Covenant of Allah,
013:026 **but** the life of this world is **but** little comfort compared
013:027 **but** He guideth to Himself those who turn to Him
013:030 there is no God **but** He! On Him is my trust,
013:031 **But**, truly, the Command is with Allah in all things!
013:031 **But** the Unbelievers,-never will disaster cease to seize
013:032 **but** I granted respite to the Unbelievers,
013:033 Say: "**But** name them! is it that ye will inform
013:033 **but** they are kept back (thereby) from the Path.
013:034 **but** harder, truly is the Chastisement of the Hereafter:
013:036 **but** there are among the clans those who reject a part
013:042 **but** in all things Allah is the devising altogether.
014:002 **But** alas for the Unbelievers for a terrible Chastisement
014:007 **but** if ye show ingratitude, truly My punishment
014:009 None knows them **but** Allah.
014:009 **but** they put their hands up to their mouths,
014:011 **but** Allah doth grant His grace to such of His servants
014:013 **But** their Lord inspired (this Message) to them:
014:015 **But** they sought victory and decision
014:017 **but** never well he be near swallowing it
014:021 "For us, we **but** followed you;
014:022 **but** I failed in my promise to you.
014:022 over you except to call you, **but** ye listened to me;
014:022 then reproach not me, **but** reproach your own souls.
014:023 **But** those who believe and work righteousness
014:027 **but** Allah will leave, to stray, those who do wrong:
014:030 **But** verily ye are making straightway for Hell!"
014:034 **But** if ye count the favours of Allah, never will

BUT (continued)

014:036 **but** thou art indeed Oft-Forgiving, Most Merciful.
014:042 He **but** giveth them respite against a Day when
014:046 **but** their plots were (well) within the sight of Allah,
015:011 **But** never came a messenger to them **but** they mocked
015:018 **But** any that gains a hearing by stealth,
015:021 And there is not a thing **but** its (sources and)
015:021 **but** We only send down thereof in due and ascertainable
015:056 despairs of the mercy of his Lord, **but** such as go astray?"
015:065 **but** pass on whither ye are ordered."
015:069 "**But** fear Allah, and shame me not."
015:073 **But** the (mighty) Blast overtook them at sunrise,
015:081 **but** they persisted in turning away from them.
015:083 **But** the (mighty) Blast seized them of a morning,
015:085 and all between them, **but** for just ends.
015:088 **but** lower thy wing (in gentleness) to the Believers.
015:096 **but** soon will they come to know.
015:098 **But** celebrate the praises of thy Lord and be
016:002 "Warn (Man) that there is No God **but** I:
016:009 the right path **but** there are ways that turn aside:
016:026 **but** Allah took their structures from their foundations,
016:028 (The angels will reply), "Nay, **but** verily Allah knoweth
016:033 Do the (ungodly) wait **but** for the angels to come to them,
016:033 **But** Allah wronged them not: nay, they wronged
016:034 **But** the evil results of their deeds overtook them,
016:035 we should not have worshipped aught **but** Him-
016:035 **But** what is the mission of messengers **but** to preach
016:038 nay, **but** it is a promise (binding) on Him in truth:
016:038 **but** most among mankind know it not.
016:040 We **but** say the Word, "Be," and it is.
016:041 **but** truly the reward of the Hereafter will be greater.
016:043 And before thee We sent were none **but** men, to whom
016:053 And ye have no good thing **but** is from Allah:
016:055 **but** soon will ye know (your folly)!
016:061 **but** He gives them respite for a stated Term:
016:063 **but** Satan made, (to the wicked), their own acts seem
016:063 so **but** they shall have a most grievous chastisement.
016:075 **But** most of them understand not.
016:079 Nothing holds them up **but** (the power of) Allah.
016:082 **But** if they turn away, thy duty
016:086 **But** they will throw back their word at them
016:093 **but** He leaves straying whom He pleases and He guides
016:093 **but** ye shall certainly be called to account for all your
016:101 they say, "Thou art **but** a forger"
016:101 **but** most of them understand not.
016:106 **but** such as open their breast to Unbelief,-
016:110 **But** verily thy Lord,-to those who leave their
016:113 **but** they falsely rejected him;
016:115 **But** if one is forced by necessity, without wilful
016:116 **But** say not-for any false thing that your tongues may
016:117 In such falsehood is **but** a paltry profit;
016:117 **but** they will have a most grievous Chastisement.
016:118 **but** they were used to doing wrong to themselves.
016:119 **But** verily thy Lord, to those who do wrong in ignorance,
016:119 **but** who thereafter repent and make amends,-
016:124 **but** Allah will judge between them on the Day of
016:126 **but** if ye show patience, that is indeed
016:127 for thy patience is **but** with the help
017:008 **but** it ye revert (to your sins), We shall revert
017:016 (to be obedient) **but** they continued to transgress;
017:021 **but** verily the Hereafter is more in rank and gradation
017:023 Thy Lord hath decreed that ye worship none **but** Him,
017:023 nor repel them **but** address them in terms of honour.

BUT (continued)

017:026 **but** squander not (your wealth) in the manner
017:033 **but** let him not exceed bounds in the matter
017:041 **but** it only increases their flight (from the Truth)!
017:044 there is not a thing **but** celebrates His praise;
017:048 **but** they have gone astray, and never
017:052 ye tarried **but** a little while!"
017:058 There is not a population **but** We shall destroy
017:059 **but** they treated her wrongfully:
017:060 which We showed thee, **but** as a trail for men,-
017:060 **but** it only increases their inordinate
017:062 under my sway-all **but** a few!"
017:062 If Thou wilt **but** respite me to the Day
017:064 **But** Satan promises them nothing **but** deceit.
017:067 **But** when He brings you back safe to land, ye turn
017:072 **But** those who were blind in this world, will be
017:076 **but** in that case they would not have stayed
017:082 to the unjust it causes nothing **but** loss after loss.
017:084 **but** your Lord knows best who it is that is best guided
017:093 am I aught **but** a man,-a messenger?"
017:094 was nothing **but** this: they said, "Has Allah sent a man
017:097 **but** he whom He leaves astray-for such wilt thou
017:099 **But** the unjust refuse (to receive it) except with
017:102 by none **but** the Lord of the heavens and the earth
017:103 **but** We did drown him and all who were with him.
017:104 **but** when the second of the warnings came to pass,
017:105 and We sent thee **but** to give Glad Tidings
017:110 **but** seek a middle course between."
018:005 What they say in nothing **but** falsehood!
018:007 is on earth We have made **but** as a glittering show for it,
018:008 what is on earth We shall make **but** as dust and dry soil
018:017 **but** he whom Allah leaves to stray,-for him wilt thou find
018:022 it is **but** few that know their (real case)."
018:038 "**But** as for my part Allah is my Lord, and none shall I
018:039 There is no power **but** from Allah!'
018:040 making it (**but**) slippery sand!
018:045 **but** soon it becomes dry stubble, which the
018:046 **but** the things that endure, Good Deeds,
018:049 nothing small or great, **but** takes account thereof!
018:052 **but** they will not listen to them;
018:054 **but** man is, in most things, contentious.
018:055 **but** that (they wait for) the ways of the ancients
018:056 **but** the Unbelievers dispute with vain argument,
018:057 **but** turns away from them, forgetting the
018:058 **but** they have their appointed time, beyond which
018:058 **But** your Lord is Most Forgiving, Full of Mercy.
018:059 **but** We fixed an appointed time for their destruction.
018:061 **But** when they reached the Junction, they forgot
018:063 none **but** Satan made me forget to tell (you)
018:077 **but** they refused them hospitality.
018:077 wall on the point of falling down, **but** he set it up straight.
018:079 I **but** wished to render it unserviceable,
018:088 "**But** whoever believes, and works righteousness
018:098 **but** when the promise of my Lord comes to pass,
018:110 Say: "I am **but** a man like yourselves,
018:110 (**but**) the inspiration has come to me, that your God
019:004 **but** never am I unblest, O my Lord! in my prayer
019:005 **but** my wife is barren: so give me an heir as from Thyself,-
019:024 **But** (a voice) cried to her from beneath
019:029 **But** she pointed to the babe.
019:037 **But** the sects differ among themselves:
019:038 **But** the unjust to-day are in error manifest!.
019:039 **But** warn them of the Day of Distress, when the

BUT (continued)

019:059 **But** after them there followed a posterity
019:062 vain discourse, **but** only salutations of Peace:
019:064 "We descend not **but** by command of thy Lord:
019:067 **But** does not man call to mind that We created him
019:071 Not one of you **but** will pass over it: this is,
019:072 **But** We shall save those who guarded against evil,
019:074 **But** how many (countless) generations before them
019:084 for We **but** count out to them a (limited)
019:087 **but** such a one as has received permission
019:093 and the earth **but** must come to The Most Gracious
019:098 **But** how many (countless) generation before
020:003 **But** only as an admonition to those
020:008 Allah! there is no god **but** He!
020:011 **But** when he came to the fire, he was called "O Moses!
020:014 "Verily, I am Allah: there is no god **but** I:
020:016 not such as believe not therein **but** follow their own lust,
020:039 **but** I endued thee with love from Me:
020:040 **but** We saved thee from trouble, and We
020:044 "**But** speak to him mildly; perchance he
020:056 **but** he did reject and refuse.
020:058 "**But** we can surely produce magic to match thine!
020:062 over their affair, **but** they kept their talk secret.
020:069 What they have faked is **but** a magician's trick:
020:075 **But** such as comes to Him as Believers who have
020:078 **but** the waters completely overwhelmed them
020:081 **but** commit no excess therein, lest My Wrath
020:082 "**But**, without doubt, I am (also) He that forgives
020:087 **but** we were made to carry the weight of the ornaments
020:088 and the god of Moses, **but** (Moses) has forgotten!"
020:097 **but** thy (punishment) in this life will be that thou wilt
020:098 **But** the God of you all is Allah: there is no god **but** He:
020:108 so that thou hearest not **but** murmuring.
020:110 **but** they shall comprehend Him not.
020:112 **But** he who works deeds of righteousness, and has
020:114 **but** say, "O my lord! increase me in knowledge."
020:115 beforehand, taken the covenant of Adam, **but** he forgot:
020:116 **but** not Iblis: he refused.
020:120 **But** Satan whispered evil to him:
020:122 **But** his Lord chose him (for His Grace):
020:123 **but** if, as is sure, there comes to you guidance from Me,
020:124 "**But** whosoever turns away from My Message,
020:129 **but** there is a term appointed (for respite).
020:131 **but** the provision of thy Lord is better and more
020:132 **But** the (fruit of) the Hereafter is for Righteousness.
021:002 **but** they listen to it as in jest,-
021:005 Nay, He is (**but**) a poet!" Let him
021:007 the messengers We sent were **but** men, to whom We
021:009 **but** We destroyed those who transgressed beyond bounds.
021:013 Flee not, **but** return to the good things of this
021:022 **But** glory to Allah, the Lord
021:023 **but** they will be questioned (for theirs).
021:024 **But** most of them know not the Truth, and so
021:025 that there is no god **but** I; therefore worship
021:026 They are (**but**) servants raised to honour.
021:041 **but** their scoffers were hemmed in by the thing that
021:045 Say, "I do **but** warn you according to revelation":
021:045 **but** the deaf will not hear the call,
021:046 If **but** a breath of the Wrath of thy Lord
021:058 (all) **but** the biggest of them, that they
021:070 **but** We made them the Greater losers.
021:071 **But** We delivered him and (his nephew)
021:083 **but** Thou art the Most Merciful of those that are merciful."

BUT (continued)

021:087 "There is no god **but** Thou: Glory to
021:087 **But** he cried through the depths of darkness,
021:093 **But** (later generations) cut off their affair
021:095 **But** there is a ban on any population which We
021:098 that ye worship besides Allah, are (**but**) fuel for Hell!
021:099 **But** each one will abide therein.
021:103 **but** the angels will meet them (with mutual greetings):
021:107 We sent thee not, **but** as a mercy for all creatures.
021:109 **but** I know not whether that which ye are
021:109 **But** if they turn back, say: "I have
021:111 "I know not **but** that it may be a trial for you,
022:002 **but** dreadful will be the Chastisement of Allah.
022:005 barren and lifeless, **but** when We pour down rain
022:011 **but** if a trial comes to them, they turn
022:018 **But** a great number are (also) such as unto whom
022:019 **but** those who deny (their Lord),-for them
022:034 **But** your God is One God: submit then your wills
022:036 and feed such as (beg not **but**) live in contentment,
022:044 **But** I granted respite to the Unbelievers,
022:044 **but** how (terrible) was My punishment (of them)!
022:046 **but** the hearts which are in their breasts.
022:047 **But** Allah will not fail in His promise.
022:051 "**But** those who strive against Our Signs,
022:052 **but**, when he framed a desire, Satan threw some (vanity)
022:052 **but** Allah will cancel anything (vain) that Satan throws
022:053 **but** a trial for those in whose hearts is a disease
022:062 whom they invoke,-they are **but** vain Falsehood:
022:067 **but** do thou invite (them) to thy Lord:
023:007 **But** those whose desires exceed those limits
023:023 Ye have no other god **but** Him.
023:032 no other god **but** Him. Will ye not fear (Him)?"
023:037 "There is nothing **but** our life in this world!
023:037 **But** we shall never be raised up again!
023:038 **but** we are not the ones to believe in him!
023:040 (Allah) said: "In **but** a little while, they are sure to
023:046 **but** these behaved insolently:
023:053 **But** people have cut off their affair (of unity),
023:054 **But** leave them in their confused ignorance
023:063 **But** their hearts are in confused ignorance
023:066 **but** ye used to turn back on your heels-
023:070 **but** most of them hate the Truth.
023:071 **but** they turn away from their admonition.
023:072 **But** the recompense of thy Lord is best:
023:073 **But** verily thou callest them to the Straight Way;
023:076 **but** they humbled not themselves to their Lord,
023:083 They are nothing **but** tales of the ancients!"
023:088 Who protects (all), **but** is not protected (of any)?
023:090 **but** they indeed are liars.
023:100 "By no means! it is **but** a word he says."-
023:103 **But** those whose balance is light, will be
023:105 and ye did **but** treat them as falsehoods?"
023:110 "**But** ye treated them with ridicule, so much
023:113 **but** ask those who keep account."
023:114 He will say: "Ye stayed not **but** a little,-
023:116 there is no god **but** He, the Lord of the Throne
024:003 can have sexual relations with any **but** an adulteress
024:003 sexual relations with her **but** an adulterer or an idolater;
024:006 and have (in support) no evidence **but** their own,-
024:008 **But** it would avert the punishment from the wife,
024:021 **but** Allah doth purify whom He pleases:
024:021 he will (**but**) command what is indecent and wrong:
024:033 **But** force not your maids to prostitution

BUT (continued)

024:033 **But** if anyone compels them, yet, after such compulsion,
024:039 **But** the Unbelievers,-their deeds are like a mirage
024:039 **but** he finds Allah there, and Allah will pay him his
024:047 **but** even after that, some of them turn away:
024:049 **But** if the right is on their side, they come
024:054 **but** if ye turn away, he is only responsible for the duty
024:059 **But** when the children among you come of age,
024:060 **but** it is best for them to be modest:
024:061 **But** if ye enter houses, salute each other-
025:003 gods that can create nothing **but** are themselves created;
025:004 **But** the Misbelievers say: "Naught is this **but** a lie which
025:009 **But** they have gone astray, and never a way will they
025:011 **but** We have prepared a Blazing Fire for such as deny
025:018 **but** Thou didst bestow, on them and on their fathers,
025:029 Ah! the Satan is **but** a traitor to man!
025:031 **but** enough is the Lord to guide and to help.
025:033 **but** We reveal to thee the truth and the best
025:040 **But** they expect not to be raised again.
025:050 men are averse (to aught) **but** (rank) ingratitude.
025:050 in order that they may be mindful **but** most men are averse
025:052 **but** strive against them with the utmost strenuousness,
025:056 **But** thee We only sent to give glad tidings and warnings.
025:057 Say: "No reward do I ask of you for it **but** this:
025:067 **but** hold a just (balance) between those (extremes);
025:069 **(But)** the Chastisement on the Day of Judgment
025:077 not concern Himself with you **but** for your call on Him:
025:077 **but** ye have indeed rejected (Him), and soon will come
026:005 **But** there comes not to them a newly-revealed message
026:005 from the Most Gracious, **but** they turn away therefrom.
026:008 **but** most of them do not believe.
026:021 I feared you; **but** my Lord has (since) invested me
026:024 and all between,- if ye had **but** sure belief."
026:049 **But** soon shall ye know! Be sure
026:050 we shall **but** return to our Lord!
026:054 (Saying): "These (Israelites) are **but** a small band,
026:059 Thus it was, **but** We made the Children of Israel inheritors
026:066 **But** We drowned the others.
026:067 **but** most of them do not believe.
026:074 They said: "Nay, **but** we found our fathers doing thus
026:089 "**But** only he (will prosper) that brings to Allah
026:103 **but** most of them do not believe.
026:113 if ye could **(but)** understand.
026:121 **but** most of them do not believe.
026:139 **but** most of them do not believe.
026:150 "**But** fear Allah, and obey me;
026:157 **But** they ham-strung her:
026:158 **but** most of them do not believe.
026:158 **But** the Chastisement seized them.
026:173 on those who were admonished (**but** heeded not)!
026:174 **but** most of them do not believe.
026:189 **But** they rejected him.
026:190 **but** most of them do not believe.
026:202 **But** the (Penalty) will come to them of a sudden,
026:208 Never did We destroy a town **but** had its warners-
027:008 **But** when he came to the (Fire), a voice
027:010 **But** when he saw it moving (of its own accord)
027:011 "**But** if any have done wrong and have
027:013 **But** when Our Signs came to them, visibly they
027:022 **But** the Hoopoe tarried not far:
027:026 "Allah!-there is no god **but** He!-Lord of
027:031 **but** come to me in submission (to the true Religion)."'
027:033 **but** the command is with thee; so consider

BUT (continued)

027:035 **But** I am going to send him a present, and wait
027:036 **But** that which Allah has given me is better
027:040 **but** if any is ungrateful, truly my Lord is Free of all
027:044 **but** when she saw it, she thought it was a lake of water
027:044 He said: "This is **but** a palace paved smooth with slabs
027:045 **but** behold, they became two factions quarreling
027:050 They platted and planned, **but** We too planned,
027:056 **But** his people gave no other answer **but** this: they said,
027:057 **But** We saved him and his family, except his
027:058 on those who were admonished (**but** heeded not)!
027:066 Nay, **but** their knowledge fails as to the Hereafter,
027:068 these are nothing **but** tales of the ancients."
027:070 **But** grieve not over them, nor distress
027:073 **But** verily thy Lord is full of grace to mankind:
027:075 **but** is (recorded) in a clear record.
027:088 **but** they shall pass away as the clouds pass away:
028:004 **but** he kept alive their females:
028:007 **but** when thou hast fears about him, cast him
028:007 **but** fear not nor grieve: for We
028:013 **but** most of them do not know.
028:027 **But** I intend not to place thee under a difficulty:
028:027 for eight years, **but** if thou complete ten years,
028:030 **But** when he came to the (Fire), he was
028:031 **But** when he saw it moving (of its own accord)
028:036 "This is nothing **but** sorcery faked up:
028:038 "O Chiefs! no god do I know for you **but** myself:
028:038 **but** as far as I am concerned, I think (Moses) is a liar!"
028:041 And We made them (**but**) leaders inviting
028:045 **But** We raised up (new) generations, and long
028:045 **but** thou wast not a dweller among the people of Madyan,
028:045 **but** it is We Who send messengers (with inspiration).
028:048 **But** (now), when the Truth has come to them
028:050 **But** if they hearken not to thee, know that
028:056 **but** Allah guides those whom He will and He
028:057 **But** most of them understand not.
028:058 after them, are deserted,-all **but** a (miserable) few!
028:060 ye are given are **but** the conveniences of this life
028:060 **but** that which is with Allah is better
028:061 the good things of this life, **but** who, on the
028:064 **but** they will not listen to them; and they
028:067 **But** any that (in this life) had repented,
028:070 And He is Allah: there is no god **but** He. To Him
028:076 of Moses; **but** he acted insolently towards them:
028:077 **but** do thou good, as Allah has been good to thee,
028:077 "**But** seek, with the (wealth) which Allah
028:078 **But** the wicked are not called (immediately)
028:080 **but** this none shall attain, save those
028:080 **But** those who had been granted (true) knowledge
028:084 **but** if any does evil, the doers of evil are only punished
028:088 There is no god **but** He.
029:008 **but** if they (either of them) strive (to force) thee to join
029:010 "We believe in Allah"; **but** when they suffer
029:014 **but** the Deluge overwhelmed them while they
029:015 **But** We saved him and the Companions of the Ark,
029:024 **But** Allah did save him from the Fire.
029:025 **but** on the Day of Judgement ye shall
029:026 **But** Lut believed Him: he said: "I will
029:029 **But** his people gave no answer **but** this: they said:
029:032 He said: "**But** there is Lut there." They said:
029:033 **but** they said: "Fear thou not, nor grieve:
029:037 **But** they rejected him:
029:039 **but** they behaved with insolence on the earth;

BUT (continued)

029:041   **but** truly the flimsiest of houses is the Spider's house;-
029:041   if they **but** knew.
029:043   **but** only those understand them who have Knowledge.
029:046   who do wrong **but** say, "We believe
029:047   and none **but** Unbelievers reject Our Signs.
029:049   and none **but** the unjust reject Our Signs.
029:054   **but**, of a surety, Hell will encompass the rejecters
029:058   **But** those who believe and work deeds
029:063   **But** most of them understand not.
029:064   What is the life of this world **but** amusement and play?
029:064   **But** verily the Home in the Hereafter,-
029:064   that is life indeed, if they **but** knew.
029:065   **but** when He had delivered them safely
029:066   **But** soon will they know.
030:003   In a land close by: **but** they, (even) after
030:006   **but** most men understand not.
030:007   They know **but** the outer (things) in the life of this
030:007   **but** of the Hereafter they are heedless.
030:008   Not **but** in truth and for a term appointed,
030:009   **but** they wronged their own souls.
030:029   **But** who will guide those whom Allah
030:030   **but** most among mankind know not.
030:033   **but** when He gives them a taste of Mercy
030:034   **but** soon will ye know (your folly).
030:039   **but** that which you give for charity, seeking the
030:043   **But** set thou thy face to the right Religion,
030:051   And if We (**but**) send a Wind from which they see
030:055   swear that they tarried not **but** an hour:
030:056   **But** those endued with knowledge and faith
030:056   the Day of Resurrection: **but** ye-ye did not know!"
030:058   **but** if thou bring to them any Sign, the Unbelievers
030:058   "Ye do nothing **but** talk vanities."
031:006   **But** there are, among men, those who
031:011   nay, **but** the Transgressors are in manifest error.
031:012   **but** if any is ungrateful, verily Allah
031:015   "**But** if they strive to make thee join in
031:016   "If there be (**but**) the weight of a mustard-seed
031:023   **But** if any reject Faith, let not
031:025   **But** most of them know not.
031:028   is in no wise **but** as an individual soul:
031:032   **But** when He has delivered them safely to land,
031:032   **But** none reject Our Signs except only a perfidious
032:009   **But** He fashioned him in due proportion,
032:013   **but** the Word from Me will come true, "I Will
033:002   **But** follow that which comes to thee by inspiration
033:004   **But** Allah tells (you) the Truth, and He
033:005   **But** if ye know not their father's names (then they are)
033:005   **But** there is no blame on you if ye make a mistake therein:
033:009   **but** We sent against them a hurricane and forces
033:009   **but** Allah sees (clearly) all that ye do.
033:012   and His Messenger promised us nothing **but** delusion!"
033:013   they intended nothing **but** to run away.
033:014   with none **but** a brief delay!
033:018   **but** come not to the fight except for just a little while,
033:019   **but** when the fear is past, they will
033:020   they would fight **but** little.
033:023   **but** they have never changed (their determination) in
033:029   **But** if ye seek Allah and His Messenger,
033:031   **But** any of you that is devout in the service
033:032   **but** speak ye a speech (that is) just.
033:037   **But** thou didst hide in thy heart that which Allah was
033:037   **but** it is more fitting that thou shouldst, Fear Allah.

033:039   and fear Him, and fear none **but** Allah.
033:040   **but** (he is) the Messenger of Allah,
033:048   and disregard their insolence **but** put thy trust in Allah.
033:053   **but** Allah is not shy (to tell you) the truth.
033:053   **but** when ye are invited, enter; and when
033:069   **but** Allah cleared him of the (calumnies) they had
033:072   **but** they refused to undertake it, being afraid thereof:
033:072   **but** man undertook it: he was indeed unjust and foolish;-
034:003   **but** is in the Record Perspicuous:
034:003   say, "Nay! **but** most surely, by my Lord, it will
034:005   **But** those who strive against Our Signs,
034:013   sons of David, **but** few of My servants
034:016   **But** they turned away (from Allah), and We
034:019   **but** they wronged themselves (therein).
034:019   **But** they said: "Our Lord! place longer distances
034:020   all **but** a party that believed.
034:021   **But** he had no authority over them,-except that
034:028   **but** most men understand not.
034:028   We have not sent thee **but** as a (Messenger)
034:031   Couldst thou **but** see when the wrong-doers
034:034   to a population, **but** the wealthy ones among
034:036   to whom He pleases, **but** most men know not."
034:037   **but** only those who believe and work
034:039   do ye send in the least (in His Cause) **but** He replaces it:
034:041   Nay, **but** they worshipped the Jinns:
034:043   "This is nothing **but** evident magic!
034:044   **But** We had not given them Books which they
034:050   **but** if I receive guidance, it is
034:051   **but** then there will be no escape (for them),
034:051   If thou couldst **but** see when they will quake
034:052   **but** how could they receive (Faith) from a
035:003   There is no god **but** He: how then
035:007   **but** for those who believe and work righteous deeds,
035:011   or lays down (her lord), **but** with His knowledge.
035:011   a part cut off from his life, **but** is in a Book (ordained).
035:015   **but** Allah is the One Free of all wants,
035:018   Thou canst **but** warn such as fear their Lord
035:022   **but** thou canst not make those to hear who are (buried)
035:032   **but** there are among them some who wrong their own
035:036   **But** those who reject (Allah)-for them
035:039   **but** adds to the odium for the Unbelievers
035:039   their disbelief **but** adds to (their own) loss.
035:040   wrong-doers promise each other nothing **but** delusions.
035:042   **but** when a warner came to them,
035:043   **But** the plotting of Evil will hem in only the authors
035:043   Now are they **but** looking for the way
035:043   **But** no change wilt thou find in Allah's way
035:045   **but** he gives them respite for a stated Term:
036:011   Thou canst **but** admonish such a one as follows
036:014   **but** We strengthened them with a third:
036:015   Ye do nothing **but** lie."
036:019   Nay, **but** ye are a people transgressing all bounds!"
036:030   comes not a messenger to them **but** they mock Him!
036:032   **But** each one of them all-will be brought before Us
036:046   **but** they turn away therefrom.
036:047   Ye are in nothing **but** manifest error."
036:049   They will not (have to) wait for aught **but** a single Blast:
036:054   **but** be repaid the meeds of your past Deeds.
036:062   "**But** he did lead astray a great multitude of you.
036:065   **But** their hands will speak to Us,
036:066   **but** how could they have seen?
037:015   And say, "This is nothing **but** evident sorcery!

BUT (continued)

037:024 "**But** stop them, for they must be asked:
037:026 Nay, **but** that day they shall submit (to Judgment);
037:040 **But** the chosen servants of Allah,-
037:072 **But** We sent aforetime, among them, warners.
037:096 "**But** Allah has created you and your handiwork!"
037:098 **but** We made them the ones most humiliated!
037:113 **but** of their progeny are (some) that do right,
037:127 **But** they rejected him, and they
037:145 **But** We cast him forth on the naked shore
037:152 **But** they are liars!
037:158 **but** the Jinns know (quite well) that they
037:164 **but** has a place appointed;
037:170 they reject it: **but** soon will they know!
037:170 **But** (now that the Qur'an has come), they reject
037:177 **But** when it descends upon their courtyards
038:002 **But** the Unbelievers (are steeped) in Self-glory
038:007 this is nothing **but** a made-up tale!
038:008 **But** they are in doubt concerning My (own)
038:011 They are **but** a host of confederates and they
038:014 **but** My Punishment came justly and inevitably (on them).
038:014 Not one (of them) **but** rejected the messengers,
038:022 **but** guide us to the even Path.
038:023 he has nine and ninety ewes, and I have (**but**) one:
038:027 **But** woe to the Unbelievers because of the Fire (of Hell)!
038:034 **but** he did turn (to Us in true devotion):
038:055 Yea, such! **But**-for the wrong-doers will be
038:065 no god is there **but** Allah, the One
039:003 **But** those who take for protectors others than Allah
039:003 **But** Allah guides not such as are false and ungrateful.
039:004 **but** Glory be to Him! (He is above such things).
039:006 There is no god **but** He: then how
039:007 **but** He liketh not ingratitude from His servants:
039:008 **but** when He bestoweth a favour upon him
039:020 **But** it is for those who fear their Lord,
039:023 **but** such as Allah leaves to stray, can have
039:026 **but** greater is the Punishment of the Hereafter,
039:029 **But** most of them have no knowledge.
039:036 **But** they try to frighten thee with other
039:039 I will do (my part): **but** soon will ye know-
039:041 **but** he that strays injures his own soul.
039:042 **but** the rest He sends (to their bodies) for a term
039:045 **but** when (gods) other than He are mentioned, behold,
039:047 **but** something will confront them from Allah,
039:049 Nay, **but** this is **but** a trial, **but** most of them understand
039:049 **but** when We bestow a favour upon him
039:050 **But** all that they did was of no profit to them.
039:056 and was **but** among those who mocked!'
039:059 "(The reply will be) `Nay, **but** there came to thee
039:061 **But** Allah will deliver the righteous for they
039:065 **But** it has already been revealed to thee,-as it
039:066 Nay, **but** worship Allah, and be
039:067 the whole of the earth will be **but** His handful,
039:071 **but** the Decree of Chastisement has been proved
040:003 There is no god **but** He: to Him is the Final Goal.
040:004 can dispute about the Sings of Allah **but** the Unbelievers.
040:005 **But** (there were people) before them, who denied
040:005 **but** it was I that seized them!
040:012 **but** when partners were joined to Him,
040:013 **but** only those receive admonition who turn (to Allah).
040:020 **but** those whom (men) invoke besides Him,
040:021 **but** Allah did call them to account
040:022 with Clear (Signs), **but** they rejected them:

BUT (continued)

040:024 **but** they called (him) "a sorcerer telling lies!"...
040:025 in nothing **but** errors (and delusions)!...
040:025 **but** the plots of Unbelievers (end) in nothing
040:028 **but**, if he is telling the Truth, then will
040:029 **but** who will help us from the Punishment of Allah,
040:029 "I **but** point out to you that which I see (myself);
040:029 **but** to the Path of Right!"
040:031 **but** Allah never wishes injustice to His Servants.
040:034 **but** ye ceased not to doubt of the (mission)
040:037 **but** surely, I think (Moses) is a liar!"
040:037 to nothing **but** perdition (for him).
040:039 the present is nothing **but** (temporary) enjoyment:
040:040 will not be requited **but** by the like thereof:
040:045 **but** the brunt of the Chastisement encompassed on
040:047 "We **but** followed you: can ye
040:050 **But** the Prayer of those without Faith is nothing
040:050 is nothing **but** (futile wandering) in (mazes of) error!"
040:052 **but** they will (only) have the Curse and the Home
040:056 is nothing in their breasts **but** (the quest of) greatness,
040:060 **but** those who are too arrogant to serve Me
040:062 there is no god **but** He: then how
040:065 There is no god **but** He: call upon
040:070 **but** soon shall they know,-
040:078 **but** when the Command of Allah issued, the matter
040:083 **but** that very (Wrath) at which they were
040:084 **But** when they saw Our Might, they said
040:085 **But** their professing the Faith when they
041:006 Say thou: "I am **but** a man like you:
041:013 **But** if they turn away, say thou: "I have warned
041:014 (preaching): "Serve none **but** Allah."
041:015 **But** they continued to reject Our Signs!
041:016 **but** the Penalty of the Hereafter will be more humiliating
041:017 **but** they preferred blindness (of heart) to Guidance:
041:018 **But** We delivered those who believed
041:022 **But** ye did think that Allah knew not many of the things
041:023 "**But** this thought of yours which ye did entertain
041:026 **but** talk at random in the midst of its (reading),
041:027 **But** We will certainly give the Unbelievers a taste
041:030 **But** receive the Glad Tidings of the
041:035 none **but** persons of the greatest good fortune.
041:037 and the moon, **but** prostrate to Allah,
041:038 **But** if they (Unbelievers) are arrogant,
041:039 **but** when We send down rain to it, it is
041:045 the book aforetime: **but** dispute arose therein.
041:045 **but** they remained in suspicious disquieting doubt
041:047 nor bring forth (young), **but** by His Knowledge.
041:049 **but** if ill touches him, he gives up all hope (and) is lost
041:050 **but** if I am brought back to my Lord, I have
041:050 **But** We will show the Unbelievers the truth of all that
042:008 **but** He admits whom He will to His Mercy;
042:009 **But** it is Allah,-He is the Protector,
042:014 **but** truly those who have inherited the Book after them
042:015 nor follow thou their vain desires; **but** say: "I believe in
042:016 **But** those who dispute concerning Allah after He
042:020 **but** he has no share or lot in the Hereafter.
042:021 **but** verily the wrong-doers will have a grievous
042:022 **But** those who believe and work righteous deeds
042:024 **But** is Allah willed, He could seal up thy heart.
042:026 **but** for the Unbelievers there is a terrible Chastisement.
042:027 **but** He sends (it) down in due measure
042:034 **but** much doth He forgive.
042:035 **But** let those know, who dispute about Our Signs,

BUT (continued)

042:036 ye are given (here) is (**but**) the enjoyment of this Life:
042:036 **but** that which is with Allah is better
042:039 (are not cowed **but**) help and defend themselves.
042:040 **but** if a person forgives and makes reconciliation,
042:041 **But** indeed if any do help and defend themselves
042:043 **But** indeed if any show patience and forgive,
042:048 Thy duty is **but** to convey (the Message).
042:048 **but** when some ill happens to him,
042:052 **but** We have made the (Qur'an) a Light, wherewith
043:006 **But** how many were the prophets We sent
043:007 never came there a prophet to them **but** they mocked
043:020 They do nothing **but** lie!
043:030 **But** when the Truth came to them, they said:
043:032 **But** the Mercy of thy Lord in better
043:035 **But** all this were nothing **but** enjoyment of the present
043:037 **but** they think that they are being guided aright!
043:047 **But** when he came to them with Our Signs, behold,
043:050 **But** when We removed the Chastisement from them,
043:061 a Sign (for the coming of) the (Hour), **but** follow ye Me:
043:065 **But** sects from among themselves fell into disagreement:
043:076 **but** it is they who have been unjust to themselves.
043:077 "Nay, **but** ye shall abide!"
043:078 **but** most of you have a hatred for Truth.
043:079 **But** it is We Who settle things.
043:089 **But** turn away from them, and say "Peace!"
043:089 **but** soon shall they know!
044:007 if ye (**but**) have an assured faith.
044:008 There is no god **but** He:
044:015 (**but**) truly ye will revert (to your ways).
044:022 (**But** they were aggressive):
044:039 **but** most of them do not know.
045:019 **but** Allah is the Protector of the Righteous.
045:024 "What is there **but** our life in this world?
045:024 **But** of that they have no knowledge:
045:024 and nothing **but** Time can destroy us."
045:025 their argument is nothing **but** this: they say, "Bring (back)
045:026 **but** most men not know.
045:031 **But** as to those who reject Allah, (to them will be said):
045:031 **But** ye were arrogant, and were a people given to sin!
042:048 Thy duty is **but** to convey (the Message).
046:003 and all between them **but** for just ends, and for
046:003 **but** those who reject Faith turn away
046:009 I am **but** a Warner open and clear."
046:009 I follow **but** that which is revealed to me
046:017 **But** (there is one) who says to his parents, "'Fie on you!
046:017 **But** he says, "This is nothing **but** tales of the ancients!"
046:020 **but** to-day shall ye be recompensed with a Chastisement
046:021 **but** there have been Warners before
046:023 **but** I see that ye are a people in ignorance!"...
046:025 nothing was to be seen **but** (the ruins of)
046:026 **but** of no profit to them were their (faculties of)
046:028 **but** that was their Falsehood and their invention.
046:035 (Thine **but**) to deliver the Message:
046:035 **but** shall any be destroyed except those who transgress?
047:002 **But** those who believe and work deeds
047:004 **but** if it had been Allah's Will, He could certainly have
047:004 **But** those who are slain in the way of Allah,
047:004 **but** (He lets you fight) in order to test you,
047:008 **But** those who reject (Allah),- for them
047:011 **but** those who reject Allah have no protector.
047:017 **But** to those who receive Guidance, He increases
047:018 **But** already have come some tokens thereof,

BUT (continued)

047:019 Know, therefore, that there is no god **but** Allah,
047:020 **But** when a Sura of decisive meaning is revealed,
047:020 **But** more fitting for them-
047:026 **but** Allah knows their (inner) secrets.
047:027 **But** how (will it be) when the angels take their souls
047:030 **but** surely thou wilt know them by the tome of their
047:032 **but** He will make their deeds of no effect.
047:036 The life of this world is **but** play and amusement:
047:038 **But** Allah is free of all wants,
047:038 **but** among you are some that are niggardly.
047:038 **But** any who are niggardly are so at the expense of their
048:011 **But** Allah is well acquainted with all that ye do.
048:014 **but** Allah is Oft-Forgiving, Most Merciful.
048:015 "**But** ye are jealous of us."
048:015 Nay, **but** little do they understand (such things).
048:016 **but** if ye turn back as ye did before,
048:017 **but** he that obeys Allah and His Messenger,-
048:021 are not within your power, **but** which Allah has
048:025 **but** He held back your hands) that He may admit to His
048:029 (**but**) compassionate amongst each other.
049:001 forward before Allah and His Messenger; **but** fear Allah:
049:005 **but** Allah is Oft-Forgiving, Most Merciful.
049:007 **but** Allah has endeared the Faith to you,
049:009 **but** if one them transgresses beyond against the other,
049:009 **but** if it complies, then make peace between them with
049:010 The believers are **but** a single Brotherhood:
049:012 **But** fear Allah: for Allah is Oft-Returning,
049:014 **But** if ye obey Allah and His Messenger, He will
049:014 **but** ye (only) say, 'We have submitted our wills
049:015 **but** have striven with their belongings and their persons
049:016 **But** Allah knows all that is in the heavens and on earth.
050:002 **But** they wonder that there has come to them
050:005 **But** they deny the truth when it comes to them:
050:018 Not a word does he utter **but** there is a vigilant Guardian.
050:027 **but** he was (himself) far astray."
050:036 **But** how many generations before them did We
051:017 They were in the habit of sleeping **but** little by night,
051:029 **But** his wife came forward clamouring: she smote
051:036 **But** We found not there any except one Muslim
051:039 **But** (Pharaoh) turned back on account of his might,
051:042 **but** reduced it to ruin and rottenness.
051:044 **But** they insolently defied the command of their
051:052 **but** they said (of him) in like manner, ""A sorcerer,
051:055 **But** remind: for reminding benefits the Believers.
052:016 ye **but** receive the recompense of your (own) deeds."
052:027 "**But** Allah has been good to us, and has
052:032 or are they **but** a people transgressing beyond bounds?
052:042 **But** those who disbelieve are themselves ensnared in
052:047 **but** most of them know not.
053:009 And was at a distance of **but** two bow-lengths
053:023 These are nothing **but** names which ye have devised,-
053:023 They follow nothings **but** conjecture and what the souls
053:025 **But** to Allah belongeth the Hereafter and the
053:028 They follow nothing **but** conjecture;
053:028 **But** they have no knowledge therein.
053:029 and desire nothing **but** the life of this world.
053:039 That man can have nothing **but** what he strives for;
053:058 No one **but** Allah can disclose it.
053:062 **But** fall ye down in prostration to Allah,
054:002 and say, "This is (**but**) continuous magic."
054:002 **But** if they see a Sign, they turn away,
054:003 **but** every matter has its appointed time.

BUT (continued)

054:005 **but** (the preaching of) Warners profits them not.
054:013 **But** We bore him on an (Ark) made of
054:016 **But** how (terrible) was My Chastisement and My
054:022 **But** We have indeed made the Qur'an easy to
054:029 **But** they called to their companion, and he
054:036 violent Seizure **but** they disputed about the Warning.
054:037 **but** We blinded their eyes. (They heard):
054:042 **but** We seized them with the Seizure of a Mighty,
054:050 And Our Command is **but** a single Word,-like the
055:027 **But** will abide (for ever) the Face of thy Lord,-
055:046 **But** for such as fear the time when they will
056:076 And that is indeed a mighty adjuration if ye **but** knew,-
056:079 Which none shall touch **but** those who are clean:
056:085 **But** We are nearer to him than ye, and yet see not,-
057:010 and fought afterwards. **But** to all has Allah
057:014 will reply, "True! **but** ye led yourselves into
057:016 The Book aforetime, **but** long ages passed over
057:019 **but** those who reject Allah and deny Our Signs,-
057:020 that the life of this world is **but** play and a pastime,
057:020 **But** in the Hereafter is a Chastisement severe
057:020 life of this world, **but** goods and chattels of deception?
057:022 or in your souls **but** is recorded in a Book before
057:026 **but** many of them became rebellious transgressors.
057:027 **But** the Monasticism which they invented for themselves.
057:027 **but** that they did not foster as they should have done.
057:027 **but** many of them are rebellious transgressors.
058:002 **but** truly Allah is All-Pardoning, All-Forgiving.
058:003 **But** those who pronounce the word "Zihar" to their
058:004 **but** if any is unable to do so, he should feed sixty indigent
058:007 **but** He is with them, wheresoever they be:
058:007 **but** He is the fourth among them,
058:007 nor between five **but** He makes the sixth,-
058:008 salutes thee, (**but** in crooked ways):
058:009 **but** do it for righteousness and self-restraint;
058:010 **but** he cannot harm them in the least,
058:012 **But** if ye find not (the wherewithal), Allah is
058:018 No, indeed! they are **but** liars!
059:002 **But** the (wrath of) Allah came to them
059:006 **but** Allah gives power to His Messenger over any
059:009 **but** give them preference over themselves,
059:011 **But** Allah is witness that they are indeed liars.
059:014 **but** their hearts are divided:
059:016 **but** when (man) disbelieves, Satan says,
060:004 **but** not when Abraham said to his father: "I will pray
060:005 **but** forgive us, our Lord! for Thou art the Exalted
060:006 **But** if any turn away, truly Allah is Free of all
060:010 **But** pay the Unbelievers what they have spent
060:010 **But** hold not to the ties (marriage contract) of Unbelieving
061:006 **But** when he came to them with Clear Signs,
061:008 **but** Allah will complete His Light,
061:011 that will be best for you, if ye **but** knew!
061:014 **but** We gave power to those who believed against
062:005 **but** who subsequently failed in those (obligations),
062:005 which carries huge tomes (**but** understands them not).
062:007 **But** never will they express their desire for Death,
062:009 that is best for you if ye **but** knew!
062:011 **But** when they see some bargain or some pastime,
063:007 **but** the Hypocrites understand not.
063:007 **But** to Allah belong the treasures of the
063:008 **But** honour belongs to Allah and His Messenger,
063:008 **but** the Hypocrites know not.
063:011 **But** to no soul will Allah grant respite when the

BUT (continued)

064:006 **but** they said: "Shall (mere) human beings direct us?"
064:006 **But** Allah can do without (them):
064:010 **But** those who reject Faith and treat Our Signs as
064:012 and obey His Messenger: **but** if ye turn back, the duty
064:012 the duty of Our Messenger is **but** to deliver (the Message)
064:013 Allah! there is no god **but** He:
064:014 **But** if ye forgive and overlook, and cover
064:015 Your riches and your children may be **but** a trial:
066:001 **But** Allah is Oft-Forgiving, Most Merciful.
066:004 **but** is ye back up each other against him,
066:006 **but** do (precisely) what they are commanded.
066:007 Ye are being **but** requited for all that ye did!"
066:010 righteous servants **but** they betrayed their (husbands),
066:010 **but** were told: "Enter ye the Fire along with (others)
067:009 **but** we rejected him and said, 'Allah never sent
067:009 ye are in nothing **but** a grave error!'"
067:010 "Had we **but** listened or used our intelligence,
067:011 **but** far from Allah's mercy are the Companions
067:015 **but** unto Him is the Resurrection.
067:018 **But** indeed men before them rejected (My warning):
067:020 In nothing **but** delusion are the Unbelievers.
068:018 **But** made no reservation, ("If it be Allah's Will").
068:026 **But** when they saw the (garden), they said:
068:033 **but** greater is the Punishment in the Hereafter,-
068:042 be summoned to prostrate, **but** they shall not be able,-
068:052 **But** it is nothing less than a Message
069:005 **But** the Thamud,-they were destroyed by a terrible
069:037 "Which none do eat **but** those in sin."
069:048 **But** verily this is a Message for the God-fearing.
069:050 **But** truly (Revelation) is a cause of sorrow
069:051 **But** verily it is Truth of assured certainty.
070:007 **But** We see it (quite) near.
070:031 **But** those who trespass beyond this
071:006 "**But** my call only increases (their) flight
071:021 **but** they follow (men) whose wealth and children
071:021 and children give them no Increase **but** only Loss.
071:024 the wrong-doers **but** in straying (from their mark)."
071:027 if thou dost leave (any of) them, they will **but** mislead
071:027 and they will breed none **but** wicked ungrateful ones.
071:028 wrong-doers grant Thou on increase **but** in Perdition!"
072:005 'But we do think that no man or Jinn should say aught
072:006 **but** they increased them into further error.
072:008 **but** we found it filled with stern guards and flaming fires.
072:009 **but** any who listens now will find a flaming fire watching
072:012 'But we think that we can by no means frustrate Allah
072:015 'But those who swerve,-they are (**but**) fuel for Hell Fire'-
072:017 **But** if any turns away from the remembrance
073:002 Stand (to pray) by night, **but** not all night,-
073:008 **But** keep in remembrance the name of the Lord,
073:009 there is no god **but** He: take Him
073:016 **But** Pharaoh disobeyed the messenger; so We
073:020 **But** Allah doth appoint Night and Day
074:007 **But**, for thy Lord's (Cause), be patient
074:024 "This is nothing **but** magic, derived from of old;"
074:025 "This is nothing **but** the word of a mortal!"
074:031 And We have set none **but** angels as guardians
074:035 This is **but** one of the mighty (Portents),
074:045 "**But** we used to talk vanities with vain talkers;
074:053 By no means! **But** they fear not the Hereafter.
074:056 **But** none will keep it in remembrance except as
075:005 **But** man wishes to do wrong (even) in the
075:018 **But** when We have recited it, follow thou

BUT (continued)

075:020 Nay, (ye men!) **but** ye love the fleeting life,
075:032 **But** on the contrary, He rejected
076:011 **But** Allah will deliver them from the evil
076:028 **but**, when We will, We shall exchange their likes.
076:030 **But** ye will not, except as Allah wills; for Allah
076:031 **but** the wrong-doers,-for them has He prepared
077:046 enjoy yourselves (**but**) a little while, for that
078:028 **But** they (impudently) treated Our Signs as false
079:013 **But** verily, it will be **but** a single (compelling) Cry,
079:021 **But** (Pharaoh) rejected it and disobeyed (guidance);
079:025 **But** Allah did punish him, (and made an)
079:045 Thou art **but** a Warner for such as fear it.
079:046 (it will be) as if they had tarried **but** a single evening,
080:003 **But** what could tell thee **but** that perchance he might
080:008 **But** as to him who came to thee striving earnestly,
081:029 **But** ye shall not will Except as Allah wills,-
082:009 Nay! **but** ye do Reject The Judgment!
082:010 **But** verily over you (are appointed angels)
083:003 **But** when they have to give by measure or weight
083:012 And none can deny it **but** the Transgressor
083:014 By no means! **but** on their hearts is the stain of the (ill)
083:033 **But** they had not been sent as Keepers over them!
083:034 **But** on this Day the Believers will laugh
084:006 painfully toiling, **but** thou shalt meet Him.
084:010 **But** he who is given his Record behind his back,-
084:022 **But** on the contrary the Unbelievers reject (it).
084:023 **But** Allah has full Knowledge of what they
085:020 **But** Allah doth encompass them from behind!
086:004 There is no soul **but** has a protector over it.
086:005 Now let man **but** think from what he is created!
086:015 As for them, they are **but** plotting a scheme,
087:005 And then doth make it (**but**) swarthy stubble.
087:011 **But** it will be avoided by the most unfortunate one.
087:014 **But** he will prosper who purify himself.
087:017 **But** the Hereafter is better and more enduring.
088:006 No food will there be for them **but** a bitter Dhari
088:023 **But** if any turn away and disbelieve,-
089:016 **But** when He trieth him, restricting his
089:017 Nay, nay! **But** ye honour not the orphans!
089:023 man remember, **but** how will that remembrance
090:011 **But** he hath made not haste on the path that is steep.
090:019 **But** those who reject Our Signs, they are
091:013 **But** the messenger of Allah said to them: "It is a
092:008 **But** he who is a greedy miser and thinks
092:015 None shall reach it **but** those most unfortunate ones
092:017 **But** those most devoted to Allah shall be
092:020 **But** only the desire to seek for the countenance
093:011 **But** the Bounty of thy Lord-rehearse and proclaim!
096:006 Nay, **but** man doth transgress all bounds,
096:019 Nay, heed him not: **but** prostrate down in adoration,
101:008 **But** he whose balance (of good deeds) will be
102:003 **But** nay, ye soon shall know (the reality).
107:006 Those who (want **but**) to be seen,
107:007 **But** refuse (to supply) (even) neighborly needs.

BUY

002:086 the people who **buy** the life of this world at the price
002:175 They are the ones who **buy** Error in place of Guidance

BUYERS

002:102 And they knew that the **buyers** of (magic)

BY

002:026 "What means Allah **by** this similitude?"
002:026 **By** it He causes many to stray,

BY (continued)

002:054 wronged yourselves **by** your worship of the calf:
002:060 the sustenance provided **by** Allah,
002:081 and are girt round **by** their sins,
002:091 the prophets of Allah in times gone **by**,
002:097 (revelation) to they heart **by** Allah's will,
002:102 anyone except **by** Allah's permission.
002:124 was tried **by** his lord with certain Commands,
002:143 except to those guided **by** Allah.
002:173 but if one is forced **by** necessity,
002:178 But if any remission is made **by** the brother of the slain,
002:185 the prescribed period (should be made up) **by** days later.
002:187 Those are limits (set **by**) Allah:
002:206 he is led **by** arrogance to (more) crime.
002:213 Allah **by** His Grace guided the Believers
002:221 But Allah beckons **by** His Grace to the Garden
002:222 ye may approach them as ordained for you **by** Allah;
002:229 they would be unable to keep the limits ordained **by** Allah
002:229 these are the limits ordained **by** Allah;
002:229 if any do transgress the limits ordained **by** Allah,
002:229 be unable to keep the limits ordained **by** Allah,
002:230 keep the limits ordained **by** Allah.
002:230 Such are the limits ordained **by** Allah,
002:233 If they both decide on weaning, **by** mutual consent,
002:237 is remitted **by** him in whose hands is the marriage tie;
002:248 and the relics left **by** the family of Moses
002:248 and the family of Aaron, carried **by** angles.
002:249 they must meet Allah said: "How oft, **by** Allah's will,
002:251 one set of people **by** means of another,
002:251 **By** Allah's will they routed them:
002:259 the similitude of one who passed **by** a hamlet,
002:263 than charity followed **by** injury.
002:264 cancel not your charity **by** reminders of your generosity
002:264 or **by** injury-like those who spend their wealth to be seen
002:273 Thou shalt know them **by** their (unfailing) mark:
002:274 spend of their goods **by** night and **by** day,
002:275 the Satan **by** his touch hath driven to madness.
002:280 But if ye remit it **by** way of charity,
003:003 He Who sent down to thee (step **by** step), in truth,
003:028 left with Allah except **by** way of precaution,
003:044 which We reveal unto thee (O Prophet!) **by** inspiration:
003:049 and I bring the dead into life **by** Allah's leave;
003:049 and it becomes a bird **by** Allah's leave:
003:092 **By** no means shall ye attain righteousness unless
003:103 so that **by** His Grace, Ye became brethren;
003:103 **by** the Rope which Allah (stretches out for you),
003:140 We give to men and men **by** turns:
003:145 the term being fixed as **by** writing.
003:145 Nor can a soul die except **by** Allah's leave,
003:153 one distress after another **by** way of requital,
003:154 stirred to anxiety **by** their own feelings,
003:154 moved **by** wrong suspicions of Allah-
003:170 They rejoice in the bounty provided **by** Allah:
003:183 consumed **by** fire (from heaven)."
004:002 their substance (**by** mixing it up) with your own.
004:007 From what is left **by** parents and those nearest
004:011 These are settled portions ordained **by** Allah:
004:012 Thus is it ordained **by** Allah;
004:013 Those are limits set **by** Allah:
004:020 would ye take it **by** slander and a manifest sin?
004:029 you traffic and trade **by** mutual good-will:
004:033 to property left **by** parents and relatives.
004:036 the Companion **by** your side, the way-farer (ye meet),

004:043 except when you are passing **by** (through the mosque),
004:050 but that **by** itself is a manifest sin!
004:062 Then they come to thee, swearing **by** Allah:
004:062 How then, when they are seized **by** misfortune.
004:065 But no, **by** thy Lord, they can have no (real) Faith.
004:092 should a Believer kill a Believer; except **by** mistake,
004:092 and whoever kills a Believer **by** mistake it is ordained
004:092 **by** way of repentance to Allah: for Allah
004:095 those who sit at home **by** a great reward.
004:096 Ranks specially bestowed **by** Him,
004:105 judge between people **by** that which Allah has shown
004:108 while He is with them when they plot **by** night.
004:119 and deface the (fair) nature created **by** Allah."
004:128 even though men's souls are swayed **by** greed.
004:147 What can Allah gain **by** your punishment.
004:148 except **by** one who has been wronged, for Allah
004:153 **by** thunder and lightning.
004:175 and guide them to Himself **by** a straight Way.
005:003 that which hath been killed **by** strangling,
005:003 or **by** a violent blow, or a headlong fall,
005:003 or **by** being gored to death;
005:003 that which hath been (partly) eaten **by** a wild animal;
005:003 division (of meat) **by** raffling with arrows: that is impiety.
005:003 But if any is forced **by** hunger, with no inclination
005:004 in the manner directed to you **by** Allah:
005:016 **by** His Will, unto the light, guideth them
005:041 If any one's trial is intended **by** Allah, thou
005:044 **By** its standard have been judged the Jews,
005:044 **by** the Prophets who bowed (as in Islam)
005:044 **by** the Rabbis and the Doctors of Law:
005:044 **by** what Allah hath revealed, they are Unbelievers.
005:045 But if any one remits the retaliation **by** way of charity,
005:045 And if any fail to judge **by** what Allah hath revealed,
005:047 **by** what Allah hath revealed, they are indeed rebel.
005:047 **by** what Allah hath revealed therein.
005:048 so judge between them **by** what Allah hath revealed,
005:049 judge thou between them **by** what Allah hath revealed,
005:053 who swore their strongest oaths **by** Allah,
005:060 (as judged) **by** the treatment it received from Allah?
005:066 If only they had stood fast **by** the Torah,
005:068 unless ye stand fast **by** the Torah.
005:077 of people who went wrong in times gone **by**,
005:078 **by** the tongue of David and of Jesus son of Mary:
005:083 the revelation received **by** the Messenger,
005:090 and (divination **by**) arrows, are an abomination,
005:095 As adjudged **by** two just men among you;
005:095 or **by** way of atonement, the feeding
005:106 and let them both swear **by** Allah: "We will not
005:107 let them swear **by** Allah: "We affirm that
005:110 as it were, the figure of a bird, **by** My leave.
005:110 and it becometh a bird **by** My leave.
005:110 thou healest those born blind, and the lepers **by** My leave.
005:110 And behold! thou bringest from the dead **by** My leave.
006:003 the (recompense) which ye earn (**by** your deeds).
006:010 scoffers were hemmed in **by** the thing that they mocked.
006:019 this Qur'an hath been revealed to me **by** inspiration.
006:023 "**By** Allah Our Lord, we were not those
006:027 when they shall be made to stand **by** the Fire!
006:030 They will say: "Yea, **by** our Lord!" He will say:
006:035 who are swayed **by** ignorance (and impatience)!
006:046 See how We explain the Signs **by** various (symbols):
006:053 Thus did We test some of them **by** other, that

006:060 It is He Who doth take your souls **by** night,
006:060 and hath knowledge of all that ye have done **by** day:
006:060 **by** day doth He raise you up again;
006:070 a soul is caught in its own ruin **by** its own action:
006:070 deliver themselves to ruin **by** their own acts:
006:070 and are deceived **by** the life of this world.
006:091 send down to man (**by** way of revelation)":
006:105 the Signs **by** various (ways) that they may say,
006:106 Follow what thou art taught **by** inspiration from thy Lord:
006:109 They swear their strongest oaths **by** Allah,
006:109 if a (special) Sign came to them, **by** it they would believe.
006:112 each other with flowery discourses **by** way of deception.
006:119 do mislead (men) **by** low desires without knowledge.
006:124 be overtaken **by** humiliation before Allah,
006:124 like those receive **by** Allah's messengers."
006:141 But waste not **by** excess:
006:145 "I find not in the Message received **by** me **by** inspiration
006:145 **by** inspiration any (meat) forbidden to be eaten
006:145 to be eaten **by** one who wishes to eat it, unless it be dead
006:145 if a person is forced **by** necessity, without wilful
006:151 except **by** way of justice and law:
006:156 that they learned **by** assiduous study;"
006:161 the Path (trod) **by** Abraham the true in faith,
007:002 no more **by** any difficulty on that account,-that
007:004 Our punishment took them on a sudden **by** night or
007:006 and those **by** whom We sent it.
007:022 So **by** deceit he brought about their fall:
007:031 eat and drink: but waste not **by** excess,
007:046 who would know every one **by** his marks:
007:051 and were deceived **by** the life of the world."
007:054 (all) are subservient **by** His Command.
007:058 **by** the Will of its Cherisher, springs up produce,
007:058 We explain the Signs **by** various (symbols) to those
007:072 **by** Our Mercy and We cut off the roots of those who
007:079 the message for which I was sent **by** my Lord:
007:089 nor could we **by** any manner of means return
007:093 the Message for which I was sent **by** my Lord:
007:095 (too) were touched **by** suffering and affluence"
007:097 Our wrath **by** night while they were asleep?
007:131 when gripped **by** calamity, they ascribed it
007:143 When Moses came to the place appointed **by** Us,
007:143 Allah said: "**By** no means canst thou see Me (direct):
007:144 **by** the messages I (have given thee) and the words
007:145 thy people to hold fast **by** the best in the precepts:
007:150 seized his brother **by** (the hair of) his head,
007:155 **by** it Thou causest whom Thou wilt to stray,
007:160 We directed Moses **by** inspiration, when his
007:163 the town standing close **by** the sea.
007:170 who hold fast **by** the Book and establish regular prayer,-
007:175 man to whom We sent Our Signs, but he passed them **by**:
007:180 beautiful names belong to Allah: so call on Him **by** them;
007:182 We will lead them step **by** step to ruin
008:075 But kindred **by** blood have prior rights against
009:002 that ye cannot frustrate Allah (**by** your falsehood),
009:014 Fight them, and Allah will punish them **by** your hands,
009:018 visited and maintained **by** such as believe in Allah
009:029 which hath been forbidden **by** Allah and His Messenger,
009:036 so ordained **by** Him the day He created
009:037 of months forbidden **by** Allah and make such
009:042 They would indeed swear **by** Allah, "If we only
009:043 who told the truth were seen **by** thee in a clear
009:052 will send His punishment from Him, or **by** our hands.

BY (continued)

009:056 They swear **by** Allah that they are indeed of you;
009:060 (thus is it) ordained **by** Allah,
009:062 To you they swear **by** Allah.
009:074 They swear **by** Allah that they said nothing (evil),
009:095 They will swear to you **by** Allah, when ye
009:107 who put up a mosque **by** way of mischief and infidelity-
009:112 and observe the limits set **by** Allah;-(there do rejoice).
009:124 "Which of you has had his faith increased **by** it?"
010:024 **by** its mingling arises the produce of the earth-
010:024 there reaches it Our command **by** night or **by** day,
010:037 is not such as can be produced **by** other than Allah;
010:050 His punishment should come to you **by** night or **by** day,-
010:053 They seek to be informed **by** thee: "Is that true?"
010:053 Say: "Aye! **by** my Lord! It is the very truth!
010:082 "And Allah **by** His Words doth prove and establish the
010:086 "And deliver us **by** Thy Mercy from those who reject
010:100 except **by** the Will of Allah, and He
011:008 completely encircled **by** that which they used to mock at!
011:017 followed **by** a witness from Him and before is the Book
011:038 every time that the Chiefs of his People passed **by** him,
011:058 those who believed with him, **by** (special) Grace from
011:060 And they were pursued **by** a Curse in this Life,-
011:066 those who believed with him, **by** (special) Grace from
011:081 **By** no means shall they reach thee!
011:086 'That which is left you **by** Allah is best for you,
011:094 and they lay prostrate in their homes **by** the morning,-
011:094 who believed with him, **by** (special) Mercy from Us:
011:099 And they are followed **by** a curse in this (life)
011:100 some have been mown down (**by** the sickle of time).
011:105 no soul shall speak except **by** His leave:
012:008 are loved more **by** our father than we:
012:010 he will be picked up **by** some caravan of travellers."
012:048 devour what ye shall have laid **by** in advance for them,-
012:067 enter not all **by** one gate: enter ye **by** different gates.
012:068 For he was, **by** Our instruction, full of knowledge
012:072 I will be bound **by** it."
012:073 (The brothers) said: "**By** Allah! well ye know that
012:076 He could not take his brother **by** the law of the king
012:085 They said: "**By** Allah! (never) wilt thou cease to remember
012:091 They said: "**By** Allah! indeed has Allah preferred thee
012:095 They said: "**By** Allah! truly thou art in thine old wandering
012:102 which We reveal **by** inspiration unto thee:
012:105 many Signs in the heavens and the earth do they pass **by**?
013:008 **by** how much the wombs fall short (of their time or
013:010 whether he lie hid **by** night or walk freely **by** day.
013:011 they guard him **by** command of Allah.
013:012 show you the lightning, **by** way both of fear and of hope:
013:017 Thus doth Allah (**by** parables) show forth Truth
013:026 Allah doth enlarge, or grant **by** (strict) measure,
013:030 We send down unto thee **by** inspiration; yet do
014:001 of the depths of darkness into light-**by** the leave of their
014:003 they are astray **by** a long distance.
014:025 It brings forth its fruit at all times **by** the leave of its
014:026 It is torn up **by** the root from the surface of the earth:
014:032 that they may sail through the sea **by** His Command;
014:037 **by** Thy Sacred House; in order, O our Lord,
015:015 nay, we have been bewitched **by** sorcery."
015:018 But any that gains a hearing **by** stealth,
015:018 is pursued **by** a fiery comet, bright (to see).
015:065 "Then travel **by** night with thy household, when a
015:066 those (sinners) should be cut off **by** the morning.
015:072 Verily, **by** thy life (O Prophet), in their

BY (continued)

015:075 for those who **by** tokens do understand.
015:092 Therefore, **by** the Lord, We will, of a surety
016:012 and the Stars are in subjection **by** His Command:
016:016 and **by** the stars (men) guide themselves.
016:038 They swear their strongest oath **by** Allah,
016:047 call them to account **by** a process of slow wastage-
016:053 when ye are touched **by** distress,
016:056 **By** Allah, ye shall certainly be called to account
016:063 **By** Allah, We (also) sent (our prophets) to Peoples
016:075 (**By** no means); praise be to Allah.
016:092 for Allah will test you **by** this;
016:115 But if one is forced **by** necessity, without wilful
017:001 His Servant for a Journey **by** night from the Sacred
017:019 the ones whose striving will be thanked (**by** Allah).
017:033 for he is helped (**by** the Law).
017:059 We only sent the Signs **by** way of frightening
017:080 and likewise my exit **by** the Gate of Truth and Honor,
017:081 for Falsehood is (**by** its nature) bound to perish."
017:082 We send down (stage **by** stage) of the Qur'an
017:086 We have sent thee **by** inspiration:
017:101 indeed, to have been worked upon **by** sorcery!"
017:102 these things have been sent down **by** none but the Lord
017:106 We have revealed it **by** stages.
017:110 **by** whatever name ye call upon Him, (it is well):
018:040 garden thunderbolts (**by** way of reckoning) from heaven,
018:073 nor grieve me **by** raising difficulties in my case."
018:079 king who seized on every boat **by** force.
018:080 we feared that he would grieve them **by** obstinate rebellion
018:088 as We order it **by** our command."
018:104 they were acquiring good **by** their works?"
018:106 and took My Signs and My Messengers **by** way of jest.
019:007 on none **by** that name have We conferred distinction
019:011 he told them **by** Signs to celebrate Allah's praises
019:048 my Lord perhaps, **by** my prayer to my Lord, I shall
019:064 "We descend not but **by** command of thy Lord:
019:068 So, **by** thy Lord, without doubt, We shall gather them
020:015 soul to receive its reward **by** the measure of its Endeavour.
020:038 We sent to thy mother **by** inspiration, the message:
020:039 and he will be taken up **by** one who is an enemy
020:047 'Verily we are Messengers sent **by** thy Lord:
020:053 enabled you to go about therein **by** roads (and channels);
020:061 lest He destroy you (at once) utterly **by** chastisement:
020:077 "Travel **by** night with my servants, and strike
020:077 of being overtaken (**by** Pharaoh) and without
020:094 Seize (me) not **by** my beard nor **by** (the hair of) my head!
020:109 has been granted **by** The Most Gracious and whose
021:025 before thee without this inspiration sent **by** Us to him:
021:027 and they act (in all things) **by** His command.
021:035 and We test you **by** evil and **by** good **by** way of trial.
021:041 hemmed in **by** the thing that they mocked.
021:042 Say, "Who can keep you safe **by** night and **by** day
021:057 "And **by** Allah, I will certainly plan against your idols-
021:063 "Nay, this was done **by** this the biggest one!
021:073 We made them leaders guiding (men) **by** Our Command,
021:078 which the sheep of certain people had strayed **by** night:
021:108 "What has come to me **by** inspiration is that your God
022:031 had fallen from heaven and been snatched up **by** birds,
022:040 Did not Allah check one set of people **by** means of another,
022:053 That He may make the suggestions thrown in **by** Satan,
022:065 and the ships that sail through the sea **by** His command?
022:065 the sky from falling on the earth except **by** His leave:
023:065 for ye shall certainly not be helped **by** Us.

BY (continued)

023:067 the (Qur'an), like one telling fables **by** night,"
023:100 "**By** no means! it is but a word be says."-
024:002 in a matter prescribed **by** Allah,
024:006 let one of them testify four times **by** Allah that he is
024:008 she bears witness four times (with an oath) **by** Allah,
024:022 of means resolve **by** oath against helping their kinsmen,
024:037 **By** men whom neither trade nor sale can divert
024:040 with topped **by** billow, topped **by** (dark) clouds:
024:053 They swear their strongest oaths **by** Allah that,
025:006 sent down **by** Him Who knows the secret (that is) in the
025:026 That Day, the dominion right **by** shall be (wholly) for
025:040 have passed **by** the town on which was rained
025:046 towards Ourselves,- a contraction **by** easy stages.
025:072 if they pass **by** futility, they pass **by** it with honourable
026:015 Allah said: "**By** no means! proceed then, both of you,
026:016 'We have been sent **by** the Lord and Cherisher of all the
026:035 "His plan is to get you out of your land **by** his sorcery;
026:044 "**By** the might of Pharaoh, it is
026:052 **By** inspiration We told Moses: "Travel **by** night with My
026:062 (Moses) said: "**By** no means! my Lord is with me!
026:063 Then We told Moses **by** inspiration: "Strike the sea
026:097 '**By** Allah, we were truly in an error manifest,
026:181 "'Give just measure, and cause no loss (to others **by** fraud).
026:209 **By** way of reminder; and We never are unjust.
027:019 and admit me, **by** Thy Grace, to the ranks of Thy righteous
027:040 "This is **by** the grace of my Lord!-to test
027:049 They said: "Swear a mutual oath **by** Allah that we
027:078 Verily they Lord will decide between them **by** His Decree:
027:090 that which ye have earned **by** your deeds?"
029:005 the Term (appointed) **by** Allah is surely coming:
029:037 and they lay prostrate in their homes in the morning.
029:040 some were caught **by** a (mighty) Blast; some We
029:045 Recite what is sent of the Book **by** inspiration to thee,
029:062 He (similarly) grants **by** (strict) measure, (as He pleases):
030:003 In a land close **by**: but they, (even) after
030:023 His Signs is the sleep that ye take **by** night and **by** day,
030:024 **by** way both of fear and of hope, and He sends
030:025 that heaven and earth stand **by** His command:
030:025 then when He calls you, **by** a single call, from the earth,
030:030 no change (there is) in the work (wrought) **by** Allah:
030:046 that the ships may sail **by** His Command and that
031:031 the ships sail through the Ocean **by** the grace of Allah?
033:002 that which comes to thee **by** inspiration from thy Lord:
033:004 ye divorce **by** Zihar your mothers:
033:004 (manner of) speech **by** your mouths.
033:005 Call them **by** after their fathers:
033:011 they were shaken as **by** a tremendous shaking.
033:036 been decided **by** Allah and His Messenger, to have
033:046 And as one who invites to Allah's (Grace) **by** His leave,
034:003 say, "Nay! but most surely, **by** my Lord, it will come
034:003 it will come upon you;-**by** Him Who knows the unseen,
034:012 Jinns that worked in front of him, **by** the leave of his
034:015 "Eat of the Sustenance (provided) **by** your Lord,
034:018 "Travel therein, secure, **by** night and **by** day."
034:027 have joined with Him as partners: **by** no means (can ye).
034:033 "Nay! it was a plot (of yours) **by** day and **by** night:
035:018 not the least portion of it can be carried (**by** the other),
035:032 who are **by** Allah's leave, foremost in good deeds;
035:042 their strongest oaths, **by** Allah that if a warner came
035:044 Nor is Allah to be frustrated **by** anything whatever in the
036:002 **By** the Qur'an, full of Wisdom,-
036:005 (It is a Revelation) sent down **by** (Him), the Exalted in

BY (continued)

036:013 Set forth to them, **by** way of a parable,
036:018 punishment indeed will be inflicted on you **by** us."
036:044 Except **by** way of Mercy from Us, and **by** way of (worldly)
036:050 No (chance) will they then have, **by** will, to dispose
037:001 **By** those who range themselves in ranks,
037:010 Except such as snatch away something **by** stealth,
037:010 and they are pursued **by** a flaming of piercing brightness.
037:056 He said: "**By** Allah! thou wast little short
037:123 So also was Elias among those sent (**by** us).
037:133 So also was Lut among those sent (**by** us).
037:137 Verily, ye pass **by** their (sites), **by** day-
037:138 And **by** night: will ye not understand?
037:139 So also was Jonah among those sent (**by** Us).
037:171 been passed before (this) to Our Servants sent (**by** Us),
038:001 Sad: **By** the Qur'an, full of Admonition:
038:082 (Iblis) said: "Then, **by** Thy Power, I will lead them all
038:083 amongst them, sincere and purified (**by** Thy grace)."
039:024 on the Day of Judgment (and receive it) **by** his face,
039:048 be (completely) encircled **by** that which they
040:005 to seize him, and disputed **by** means of vanities,
040:015 **by** His Command doth He send the spirit (of inspiration)
040:034 "And to you there came Joseph in times gone **by**,
040:040 that works evil will not be requited but **by** the like thereof:
040:058 Little do ye learn **by** admonition!
040:078 messenger to bring a Sign except **by** the leave of Allah:
041:006 it is revealed to me **by** inspiration,
041:036 And if (at any time) an incitement to discord **by** the Satan,
041:038 who celebrate His praises **by** night and **by** day.
041:042 it is sent down **by** One Full of Wisdom, Worthy of
041:047 nor bring forth (young), but **by** His Knowledge.
042:005 are almost rent asunder from above them (**by** His Glory):
042:007 Thus have We sent **by** inspiration to thee
042:011 **by** this means does He multiply you:
042:013 the which We have sent **by** inspiration to thee-
042:024 and proves the Truth **by** His Words.
042:038 who (conduct) their affairs **by** mutual Consultation;
042:051 that Allah should speak to him except **by** inspiration,
042:051 or **by** the sending of a Messenger to reveal,
042:052 And thus have We, **by** Our command, sent inspiration
043:002 **By** the Book that makes things clear,-
043:009 'They were created **by** (Him), the Exalted in Power,
043:022 and we do guide ourselves **by** their footsteps."
043:058 This they set forth to thee, only **by** way of disputation:
043:080 and Our Messengers are **by** them, to record.
044:002 **By** the Book that makes things clear;-
044:005 **By** command, from Us. For We
044:014 "Tutored (**by** others), a man possessed!"
044:023 "March forth with My servants **by** night:
044:031 Inflicted **by** Pharaoh, for he was arrogant (even)
045:012 that ships may sail through it **by** His command,
045:033 encircled **by** that which they used to mock at!
046:009 I follow but that which is revealed to me **by** inspiration;
046:016 the best of their deeds and pass **by** their ill deeds:
046:025 "Everything will it destroy **by** the command of its Lord!"
046:025 Then **by** the morning they-nothing was to be seen but
046:026 encircled **by** that which they used to mock at!
046:034 They will say, "Yea, **by** our Lord!"
047:003 Allah set forth for men their lessons **by** similitudes.
047:030 know them **by** the tone of their speech!
047:030 and thou shouldst known them **by** their marks:
049:011 nor call each other **by** (offensive) nicknames:
050:001 **By** the Glorious Qur'an (Thou art Allah's Messenger).

BY (continued)

050:012 was denied (the Hereafter) **by** the people of Noah,
050:045 and thou art not one to compel them **by** force
051:001 **By** the (Winds) that scatter broadcast;
051:007 **By** the Sky with (its) numerous Paths,
051:017 They were in the habit of sleeping but little **by** night,
051:023 Then, **by** the Lord of heaven and earth, this is
052:001 **By** the Mount (of Revelation);
052:002 **By** a Book Inscribed
052:004 **By** the much-frequented House;
052:005 **By** the Canopy Raised High;
052:006 And **by** the Ocean filled with Swell;-
052:029 Therefore Remind for **by** the Grace of thy Lord,
052:030 for him some calamity (hatched) **by** Time!"
052:038 **by** which they can (climb up to heaven and) listen
053:001 **By** the Star when it goes down,-
053:005 He was taught **by** one Mighty in Power,
054:027 For We will send the she-camel **by** way of trial for them.
054:028 brought forward (**by** suitable turns).
054:031 the dry stubble used **by** one who pens cattle.
054:034 Lut's household: them We delivered **by** early Dawn,-
055:041 (For) the sinners will be known **by** their Marks:
055:041 and they will be seized **by** their forelocks and their feet.
056:031 **By** water flowing constantly,
056:075 Furthermore I swear **by** the setting of the Stars,-
057:012 Light runs forward before them and **by** their right hands:
057:023 over matters that pass you **by**, nor exult
057:028 **by** which ye shall walk (straight in your path),
058:002 If any men divorce their wives **by** Zihar
058:004 Those are limits (set **by**) Allah.
058:010 Secret counsels are only (inspired) **by** Satan,
059:002 **by** their own hands and the hands of the Believers.
059:005 it was **by** leave of Allah, and in order that He might
060:011 (**by** the coming over of a woman from the other side).
061:008 Allah's Light (**by** blowing) with their mouths:
064:007 Say: "Yea, **by** my Lord, ye shall surely be raised up:
064:011 No kind of calamity can occur, except **by** the leave of
065:001 those are limits set **by** Allah:
066:008 and **by** their right hands, while they say,
067:016 to be swallowed up **by** the earth when it shakes
068:001 Nun. **By** the Pen and **by** the (Record) which (men)
068:002 Thou art not, **by** the grace of thy Lord, mad or
068:020 So the (garden) became, **by** the morning, like a
068:044 **by** degrees shall We draw them on little **by** little from
069:005 destroyed **by** a terrible storm of thunder and lightning!
069:006 And the 'Ad,- they were destroyed **by** a furious wind,
069:045 We should certainly seize him **by** his right hand
070:011 from the Chastisement of that Day **by** his children,
070:015 **By** no means! for it would be the Blazing Fire-
070:039 **By** no means! for We have created them out of
071:004 For when the Term given **by** Allah is accomplished,
072:012 we can **by** no means frustrate Allah throughout the earth,
072:012 nor can we escape Him **by** flight.
072:017 "That We might try them **by** that (means).
073:002 Stand (to pray) **by** night, but not all night,-
073:006 Truly the rising **by** night is a time
073:007 True, there is for thee **by** day prolonged occupation
074:013 And sons to be **by** his side!-
074:016 **By** no means! For to Our Signs he has
074:031 "What doth Allah intend **by** this?"
074:032 Nay, verily: **by** the Moon,
074:033 And **by** the Night as it retreateth,
074:034 And **by** the Dawn as it shineth forth,-

BY (continued)

074:053 **By** no means! But they fear not the Hereafter.
075:001 I do swear **by** the Resurrection Day;
075:002 And I do swear **by** the self-reproaching soul.
075:011 **By** no means! No place of safety!
076:023 We Who have sent down the Qur'an to thee **by** stages.
077:001 **By** the (Winds) Sent Forth one after another
078:038 speak except any who is permitted **by** The Most Gracious,
079:001 **By** the (angels) who tear out (the souls of the wicked)
079:002 **By** those who gently draw out (the souls of the blessed);
079:003 And **by** those who glide along (on errands of mercy),
079:007 Followed **by** oft-repeated (commotions):
080:011 **By** no means (should it be so)!
080:015 (Written) **by** the hands of scribes-
080:023 **By** no means hath he fulfilled what Allah
081:020 held in honour **by** the Lord of the Throne,
083:002 when they have to receive **by** measure from men,
083:003 But when they have to give **by** measure or weight
083:014 **By** no means! but on their hearts is the
083:030 And whenever they passed **by** them, used to
084:008 Soon will his account be taken **by** an easy reckoning,
085:001 **By** the Sky, with its constellations;
085:002 **By** the promised Day (of Judgment);
085:003 **By** one that witnesses, and the
086:001 **By** the Sky and the Night-Visitant (therein);
086:011 **By** the Firmament which giveth returns rain,
086:012 And **by** the Earth which opens out
087:006 **By** degrees shall We teach thee (the Message),
087:011 But it will be avoided **by** the most unfortunate one,
089:001 **By** the Dawn;
089:002 **By** the ten Nights;
089:003 **By** the Even and Odd (contrasted);
089:004 And **by** the Night when it passeth away;-
090:001 Nay I do swear **by** this City;-
091:001 **By** the Sun and his (glorious) splendor;
091:002 **By** the Moon as she follow him;
091:003 **By** the Day as it shows up (the Sun's) glory;
091:004 **By** the Night as it conceals it;
091:005 **By** the Firmament and its (wonderful) structure;
091:006 **By** the Earth and its (wide) expanse;
091:007 **By** the Soul, and the proportion and order
092:001 **By** the Night as it conceals (the light);
092:002 **By** the Day as it appears in glory;
092:003 **By** the creation of male and female;-
093:001 **By** the Glorious Morning Light.
093:002 And **by** the Night when it is still,-
095:001 **By** the Fig and the Olive,
096:015 We will drag him **by** the forelock,-
097:004 the angels and the Spirit **by** Allah's permission,
100:001 **By** the (Steeds) that run, with panting (breath),
100:007 And to that (fact) he bears witness (**by** his deeds);
103:001 **By** the time,
104:002 Who pileth up wealth and layeth it **by**,
104:004 **By** no means! He will be sure to be thrown
106:002 journeys **by** winter and summer,-

C

CALAMITIES
006:065 send **calamities** on you, from above and below, or
074:017 Soon will I visit him with a mount of **calamities**!

CALAMITY
002:156 Who say, when afflicted with **calamity**:
007:131 when gripped by **calamity**, they ascribed it
028:047 in case a **calamity** should seize them for (the deeds)
037:076 from the Great **Calamity**.
040:028 of the (**calamity**) of which he warns you:
046:022 Then bring upon us the (**calamity**) with which
046:024 "Nay, it is the (**calamity**) ye were asking to be
052:030 for him some **calamity** (hatched) by Time!"
064:011 No kind of **calamity** can occur, except by
075:025 back-breaking **calamity** was about to be

CALCULATING
018:012 at **calculating** the term of years they had tarried!

CALF
002:051 ye took the **calf** (for worship),
002:054 wronged yourselves by your worship of the **calf**:
002:092 yet ye worshipped the **Calf** (even) after that,
002:093 filled (with the love) of the **Calf**
004:153 Yet they worshipped the **calf** even after
007:148 the body of a **calf**, (for worship):
007:152 Those who took the **calf** (for worship) will
011:069 and hastened to entertain them with roasted **calf**.
020:088 before the (people) the image of a **calf**:
020:096 and threw it (into the **calf**):
051:026 to his household, brought out a fatted **calf**.

CALL
002:023 and **call** your witnesses or helpers
002:040 O children of Israel! **call** to mind the (special) favour
002:047 O children of Israel! **call** to mind the (special) favour
002:122 O children of Israel! **call** to mind the special favour
002:186 listen to My **call**, and believe in Me:
002:225 Allah will not **call** you to account
002:260 on every hill, and **call** to them:
003:172 the **call** of Allah and the Messenger, even after
003:193 the **call** of one calling (us) to Faith,
004:117 (The Pagans), leaving Him, **call** but upon female deities:
004:117 they **call** but upon Satan the persistent rebel!
005:007 And **call** in remembrance the favour of Allah
005:011 O ye who Believe! **call** in remembrance the favour of
005:014 From those, too, who **call** themselves Christians,
005:020 "O my people! **call** in remembrance the favour
005:058 When ye proclaim your **call** to prayer, they take
005:089 Allah will not **call** you to account
005:089 but He will **call** you to account
006:040 would ye then **call** upon other than Allah?-
006:041 which occasioned your **call** upon Him, and ye
006:041 "Nay,-On Him would ye **call**, and if
006:042 that they **call** (Allah) in humility.
006:043 why then did they not **call** (Allah) in humility?
006:052 Send not away those who **call** on their Lord
006:056 other than Allah, whom ye **call** upon."
006:063 when ye **call** upon Him in humility
006:071 Say: "Shall we **call** on others besides Allah,-

CALL (continued)
006:108 they **call** upon besides Allah, lest they
007:029 and **call** upon Him, making your devotion
007:044 will **call** out to the Companions of the Fire: "We
007:046 they will **call** out to the Companions of the Garden,
007:048 will **call** to certain men whom they will
007:050 will **call** to the Companions of the Garden: "Pour
007:055 **Call** on your Lord with humility and in private:
007:056 but **call** on Him with fear and longing
007:069 **Call** in remembrance that He made you
007:069 **Call** in remembrance the benefits
007:094 in order that they might **call** in humility.
007:134 "O Moses! on our behalf **call** on thy Lord in virtue
007:180 so **call** on Him by them; but shun
007:193 ye **call** them or ye keep silent.
007:193 If ye **call** them to guidance, they will
007:194 Verily those whom ye **call** upon besides Allah
007:194 **call** upon them, and let them listen to your prayer,
007:195 Say: "**Call** your `god-partners', scheme
007:197 "But those ye **call** upon besides Him, are unable
008:026 **Call** to mind when ye were a small (band),
008:045 and **call** Allah in remembrance much (and often);
009:030 The Jews **call** 'Uzair a son of Allah, and the
009:030 and the Christians **call** Christ the Son of Allah.
010:025 But Allah doth **call** to the Home of Peace:
010:038 and **call** (to your aid) anyone you can, besides
010:106 "Nor **call** on any, other than Allah,-such can
011:013 and **call** (to your aid) whomsoever ye can,
011:014 "If then they (your false gods) answer not your (**call**),
011:054 He said: "I **call** Allah to witness,
013:014 any others that they **call** upon besides Him
013:036 Unto Him do I **call**, and unto Him is my return."
013:040 it is Our part to **call** them to account.
014:006 "**Call** to mind the favour of Allah to you
014:022 I had no authority over you except to **call** you,
014:044 we will answer Thy **Call**, and follow
015:092 by thy Lord, We will, of a surety, **call** them to account,
016:046 Or that He may not **call** them to account in the
016:047 Or that He may not **call** them to account by a
017:052 "It will be on the Day when He will **call** you,
017:052 and ye will answer (His **call**) with (words of) His praise,
017:056 Say: "**Call** on those-besides Him-whom ye fancy:
017:057 Those whom they **call** upon do seek (for themselves)
017:067 those that ye **call** upon-besides Himself-leave you
017:071 On the day We shall **call** together all human
017:110 Say: "**Call** upon Allah, or **call** upon Rahman:
017:110 by whatever name ye **call** upon Him, (it is well):
018:014 never shall we **call** upon any god other than Him:
018:028 who **call** on their Lord morning and evening,
018:052 "**Call** on those whom ye thought to be My partners,"
018:052 and they will **call** on them, but they will not listen
018:058 If He were to **call** them (at once)
019:048 I will **call** on my Lord perhaps,
019:067 But does not man **call** to mind that We
020:128 (to **call** to mind) how many generations before
021:045 not hear the **call**, (even) when they are warned!
021:090 they used to **call** on Us in yearning and awe.
022:012 They **call** on such deities, besides Allah,
022:013 (Perhaps) they **call** on one whose hurt is nearer
022:073 Those on whom, besides Allah ye **call**,
025:077 with you but for your **call** on Him:
026:015 We are with you, and will listen (to your **call**).
026:072 when ye **call** (on them),

CALL (continued)

026:213 So **call** not on any other god with Allah,
027:080 the Deaf to hear the **call**, (especially) when
028:062 That Day (Allah) will **call** to them, and say:
028:064 "**Call** upon your `partners' (for help)":
028:064 they will **call** upon them, but they will not listen
028:065 That Day (Allah) will **call** to them, and say:
028:074 The Day that He will **call** on them, He will
028:088 And **call** not, besides Allah, on another
029:042 whatever that they **call** upon besides Him:
029:065 they **call** on Allah, making their
030:025 by a single **call**, from the earth, behold, ye
030:052 the deaf to hear the **call**, when they
031:032 they **call** upon Allah, offering Him
032:016 the while they **call** on their Lord, in Fear
033:005 **Call** them by after their fathers:
033:039 to **call** (men) to account.
034:022 Say: "**Call** upon other (gods) whom ye fancy,
035:014 they will not listen to your **call**, and if
035:018 heavily laden should **call** another to (bear)
035:040 of yours whom ye **call** upon besides Allah?
036:057 they shall have whatever they **call** for;
037:125 "Will ye **call** upon Baal and forsake
038:051 therein can they **call** (at pleasure) for fruit
040:014 **Call** ye, then, upon Allah with sincere devotion
040:021 but Allah did **call** them to account
040:026 and let him **Call** on his Lord!
040:041 for me to **call** you to Salvation while ye **call** me to
040:042 "Ye do **call** upon me to blaspheme against Allah,
040:042 and I **call** you to the Exalted in Power,
040:043 "Without doubt ye do **call** me to one who
040:060 And your Lord says: "**Call** on Me; I will
040:065 **call** upon Him, giving Him sincere devotion.
042:015 **call** (them to the Faith), and stand steadfast
044:055 There can they **call** for every kind of fruit
046:005 are unconscious of their **call** (to them)?
049:011 nor **call** each other by (offensive) nicknames:
050:041 will **call** out from a place quite near,-
052:028 "Truly we did **call** unto Him from of old:
054:006 the Day that the Caller will **call** (them) to a terrible
056:087 **Call** back the soul, if ye are
057:014 (Those without) will **call** out, "Were we
062:009 O ye who believe! when the **call** is proclaimed
065:008 did We not then **call** to account,-to severe
069:038 So I do **call** to witness what ye see
070:040 Now I do **call** to witness the Lord of all points
071:006 "But my **call** only increases (their) flight
079:016 Behold, thy Lord did **call** to him in the sacred
081:015 So verily I **call** to witness the Planets-that recede,
084:016 So I do **call** to witness the ruddy glow of Sunset;
088:026 Then it will be for Us to **call** them to account.
096:017 Then, let him **call** (for help) to his
096:018 We will **call** on the angels of punishment

CALLED

002:087 Some ye **called** impostors,
002:282 refuse when they are **called** on (for evidence).
003:011 and Allah **called** them to account for their sins.
003:039 the angels **called** unto him: "Allah doth give thee
005:070 they **called** impostors, and some they slay.
006:044 on a sudden, We **called** them to account, when lo!
007:022 And their Lord **called** unto them: "Did I not
011:042 and Noah **called** out to his son, who had
011:045 And Noah **called** upon his Lord and said: "O my

CALLED (continued)

016:056 By Allah, ye shall certainly be **called** to account
016:093 but ye shall certainly be **called** to account
018:051 I **called** them not to witness the creation
019:052 And We **called** him from the right side
020:011 he was **called** "O Moses!
021:013 in order that ye may be **called** to account.
021:060 talk of them: he is **called** Abraham."
022:005 and some of you are **called** to die, and some
026:010 Behold, thy Lord **called** Moses: "Go to the
027:010 those **called** as messengers have no fear,-
028:018 sought his help **called** aloud for his help (again).
028:030 he was **called** from the right bank of the valley,
028:046 (the Mountain of) Tur when We **called** (to Moses).
028:078 But the wicked are not **called** (immediately) to account
029:013 they will be **called** to account for their falsehoods.
037:104 We **called** out to him, "O Abraham!
037:127 and they will certainly be **called** up (for punishment),
040:010 seeing that ye were **called** to the to the Faith
040:022 so Allah **called** them to account:
040:024 but they **called** (him) "a sorcerer telling lies!"...
040:027 Moses said: "I have indeed **called** upon my Lord
040:043 one who has no claim to be **called** to, whether in
041:044 are (as it were) being **called** from a place far distant!"
043:019 and they will be **called** to account!
045:028 every nation will be **called** to its Record: "This Day shall
054:010 Then he **called** on his Lord: "I am one
054:029 But they **called** to their companion, and he
068:021 As the morning broke, they **called** out, one to
071:005 He said: "O my Lord! I have **called** to my People
071:007 "And every time I have **called** to them, that thou
071:008 "So I have **called** to them aloud;
076:018 A fountain there, **called** Salsabil.

CALLER

020:108 On that Day will they follower the **Caller** (straight):
050:041 And listen the Day when the **Caller** will call
054:006 that the **Caller** will call (them) to a terrible affair,
054:008 Hastening, with eyes transfixed towards the **Caller**!-

CALLEST

007:198 If thou **callest** them to guidance, they hear
018:057 If thou **callest** them to guidance, even then
023:073 But verily thou **callest** them to the Straight Way;
042:013 hard is the (way) to which thou **callest** them.

CALLETH

002:186 of every suppliant when he **calleth** on Me:
002:284 Allah **calleth** you to account for it.
008:024 and His Messenger, when He **calleth** you to that

CALLING

003:019 Allah is swift in **calling** to account.
003:153 in your rear was **calling** you back.
003:193 the call of one **calling** (us) to Faith,
006:071 his friends **calling** 'Come to us', (vainly)
013:041 and He is swift in **calling** to account.
014:051 and verily Allah is Swift in **calling** account.
040:032 mutual **calling** (and wiling),-
058:002 by Zihar (**calling** them mothers), they cannot
067:027 is (the promise fulfilled), which ye were **calling** for!"

CALLS

002:171 listen to nothing but **calls** and cries:
002:204 and he **calls** Allah to witness
027:062 when it **calls** on Him, and Who
030:025 then when He **calls** you, by a single call, from the earth,
041:033 who **calls** (men) to Allah, work righteousness,

CALM

003:154 He sent down **calm** on a band of you
008:011 to give you **calm** as from Himself, and He
009:026 But Allah did pour His **calm** on the Messenger

CALUMNIES

033:069 cleared him of the (**calumnies**) they had uttered:
068:011 A slanderer, going about with **calumnies**,

CALUMNY

033:058 (on themselves) a **calumny** and a glaring sin.

CAME

002:021 who created you and those who **came** before you
002:092 There **came** to you Moses with clear (Signs);
002:101 And when **came** to them a Messenger
002:102 and such things as **came** down at Babylon
002:213 after the clear Signs **came** to them,
002:214 (trials) as **came** to those who passed away before you?
003:183 Say: "There **came** to you Messengers before me,
003:184 who **came** with Clear Signs, and the Scriptures.
005:019 lest ye should say: "There **came** unto us no bringer
005:032 Then although there **came** to them Our Messengers
005:048 confirming the scripture that **came** before it,
005:059 come to us and that which **came** before (us),
005:070 Every time there **came** to them a Messenger
006:092 (the revelations) which **came** before it:
006:109 that if a (special) Sign **came** to them, by it
006:109 realize that even if a (special) Sign **came**,
006:130 **came** there not unto you messengers from amongst you,
007:101 there **came** indeed to them their Messengers
007:113 So there **came** the sorcerers to Pharaoh: they said:
007:131 But when good (times) **came**, they said,
007:138 They **came** upon a people devoted entirely
007:143 When Moses **came** to the place appointed by Us,
007:150 When Moses **came** back to his people, angry and
007:163 but on the day they had no Sabbath, they **came** not:
007:169 if similar vanities **came** their way, they would (again)
008:048 but when the two forces **came** in sight of each other,
009:070 To them **came** their Messenger with Clear Signs.
009:090 men who made excuses and **came** to claim exemption;
009:092 Nor (is there blame) on those who **came** to thee
010:013 their Messengers **came** to them with Clear Signs,
010:080 When the sorcerers **came**, Moses said
011:040 At length, behold! there **came** Our Command,
011:043 He hath mercy!"-And the waves **came** between them,
011:048 The word **came**: "O Noah! come down (from the
011:069 There **came** Our Messengers to Abraham
011:077 When Our Messengers **came** to Lut, he was
011:078 And his people **came** rushing towards him, and they
012:016 Then they **came** to their father in the
012:019 Then there **came** a caravan of travellers: they sent
012:036 Now with him there **came** into the prison
012:050 But when the messenger **came** to him, (Joseph) said:
012:058 Then **came** Joseph's brethren: they entered
012:069 Now when they **came** into Joseph's presence,
012:073 know that we **came** not to make mischief in the land,
012:076 before (he **came** to) the baggage of his brother:
012:088 Then, when they **came** (back) into (Joseph's)
012:096 Then when the bearer of the good news **came**, he cast
014:009 To them **came** Messengers with Clear (Signs);
014:009 and Thamud?-and of those who (**came**) after them?
015:008 if they **came** (to the ungodly),
015:011 But never **came** a messenger to them
015:067 The inhabitants of the City **came** in (mad) joy
016:113 And there **came** to them a Messenger from among

CAME (continued)

017:005 When the first warnings **came** to pass, We sent
017:007 So when the second of the warnings **came** to pass,
017:094 when Guidance **came** to them, was nothing
017:101 when he **came** to them, Pharaoh said
017:104 but when the second to the warnings **came** to pass,
018:077 when they **came** to the inhabitants of a town,
018:090 Until, when he **came** to the rising of the sun,
019:011 So Zakariya **came** out to his people from his
019:012 (To his son **came** the command): "O Yahya!
020:011 But when he **came** to the fire, he was call
020:060 He concerted his plan, and then **came** (back).
020:126 when Our Signs **came** unto thee, forgot them:
023:044 every time there **came** to a people their messenger,
026:193 With it **came** down the Truthful spirit
027:008 But when he **came** to the (Fire), a voice
027:013 But when Our Signs **came** to them, visibly they
027:018 At length, when they **came** to a valley of ants,
027:022 he (**came** up and) said: "I have compassed
027:036 Now when (the embassy) **came** to Solomon, he said:
028:012 until (his sister **came** up and) said: "Shall I point out
028:020 And there **came** a man, running, from the
028:025 Afterwards one of the (damsels) **came** (back) to him,
028:025 So when he **came** to him and narrated the story,
028:030 But when he **came** to the (Fire), he was
028:036 When Moses **came** to them with Our Clear Signs,
029:031 When Our Messengers **came** to Abraham with the
029:033 And when Our Messengers **came** to Lut, he was
029:039 there **came** to them Moses with Clear Signs,
029:046 and in that which **came** do to you; Our God
029:048 a Book, before this (Book **came**), nor art
030:009 there **came** to them their messengers with Clear
030:047 and they **came** to them with Clear Signs:
033:009 when there **came** down on you hosts
033:010 Behold! they **came** on you from above you
034:031 nor in (any) that (**came**) before it."
035:025 to whom **came** their messengers with Clear Signs,
035:037 And (moreover) the warner **came** to you.
035:042 by Allah that if a warner **came** to them,
035:042 but when a warner **came** to them,
036:013 Behold, there **came** messengers to it.
036:020 Then there **came** running, from the farthest part of
037:094 Then **came** (the worshippers) with hurried
038:014 but My Punishment **came** justly and inevitably (on them).
039:025 the Punishment **came** to them from directions
039:059 "(The reply will be) `Nay, but there **came** to thee
040:022 That was because there **came** to them
040:031 and those who **came** after them:
040:034 "And to you there **came** Joseph in times gone by,
040:083 For when their messengers **came** to them
041:014 Behold, the messengers **came** to them, from before
043:007 And never **came** there a prophet to them
043:028 among those who **came** after him, that they
043:030 But when the Truth **came** to them, they said:
043:047 But when he **came** to them with Our Signs, behold,
043:063 When Jesus **came** with Clear Signs, he said:
044:017 there **came** to them a messenger most honourable,
044:023 (The reply **came**): "March forth with my servants by night:
046:030 after Moses, confirming what **came** before it:
051:029 But his wife **came** forward clamouring:
051:042 It left nothing whatever that it **came** up against,
051:052 Similarly, no messenger **came** to the Peoples
053:008 Then he approached and **came** closer,

CAME (continued)

054:041 aforetime, **came** Warners (from Allah).
059:002 the (Wrath of) **came** to them from quarters from which
059:009 as **came** to them for refuge, and entertain
059:010 And those who **came** after them say: "Our Lord!
059:010 who **came** before us into the Faith and leave not,
061:006 (which **came**) before me, and giving glad Tidings
061:006 But when he **came** to them with Clear Signs,
064:006 That was because there **came** to them messengers
068:019 Then there **came**, on the (garden) a visitation
072:007 'And they (**came** to) think as ye thought,
074:047 "Until there **came** to us (the Hour) that is certain."
080:002 Because there **came** to him the blind
080:008 But as to him who **came** to thee striving earnestly,
098:004 until after there **came** to them Clear Evidence.

CAMEL

007:040 until the **camel** can pass through the eye of the needle:
012:072 Is (the reward of) a **camel**-load; I will be bound by it."
022:027 to thee on foot and (mounted) on every kind of **camel**,

CAMEL'S

012:065 a full **camel's** load (of grain to our provisions).

CAMELRY

059:006 with either cavalry or **camelry**:

CAMELS

006:144 Of **camels** a pair, and of oxen a pair; say,
022:036 The sacrificial **camels** We have made for you
056:055 diseased **camels** raging with thirst!
077:033 yellow **camels** (marching swiftly)."
088:017 Do they not look at the **Camels**, how they are made?-

CAN

002:028 How **can** ye reject the faith in Allah?
002:075 **Can** ye (O ye men of Faith) entertain
002:138 and who **can** give a better hue than Allah.
002:184 For those who **can** do it (with hardship),
002:196 he must make an offering such as he **can** afford,
002:217 back from your faith if they **can**.
002:230 provided they feel that they **can** keep the limits
002:233 laid on it greater than it **can** bear.
002:247 They say: "How **can** he exercise authority
002:255 No slumber **can** seize Him nor sleep.
002:255 Who is thee **can** intercede in His presence
002:282 The other **can** remind her.
002:286 place a burden greater than it **can** bear.
003:097 those who **can** afford the journey;
003:135 and who **can** forgive sins except Allah?
003:145 Nor **can** a soul die except by Allah's leave,
003:160 If Allah helps you, none **can** overcome you:
003:160 Who is there, after that, that **can** help you?
003:188 think not that they **can** escape the Chastisement.
004:043 until ye **can** understand all that ye say,
004:065 But no, by thy Lord, they **can** have no (real) Faith.
004:087 And whose word **can** be truer than Allah's?
004:098 nor **can** they find a way (to escape).
004:113 and to thee they **can** do no harm in the least.
004:122 and whose word **can** be truer than Allah's?
004:123 nor those of the people of the Book (**can** prevail):
004:125 Who **can** be better in religion than one
004:135 for Allah **can** best protect both.
004:147 What **can** Allah gain by your punishment.
005:050 faith is assured, **can** give better judgment than Allah?
005:084 "What cause **can** we have not to believe in Allah
005:105 no hurt **can** come to you from those who stray.
005:112 **Can** thy Lord send down to us a Table set

CAN (continued)

006:017 none **can** remove it but He; if He
006:019 **Can** ye possibly bear witness that besides
006:034 there is none that **can** alter the Words
006:050 Say: "**Can** the blind be held equal to the seeing?"
006:059 a Record Clear (to those who **can** read).
006:071 things that **can** do us neither good nor harm,
006:080 unless my Lord willeth, (nothing **can** happen),
006:093 or (again) who saith, "I **can** reveal the like of
006:093 Who **can** be more wicked than one who
006:101 how **can** He have a son when He
006:103 No vision **can** grasp Him, but His grasp
006:115 none **can** change His Words:
006:122 **Can** he who was dead, to whom We gave life,
006:122 and a Light whereby he **can** walk amongst men,
006:122 depths of darkness, from which he **can** never come out?
006:134 nor **can** ye frustrate it (in the least bit).
006:135 Say: "O my people! do whatever ye **can**: I will
006:152 but that which it **can** bear;-whenever ye speak
006:164 no bearer of burdens **can** bear the burden of another.
007:034 nor (an hour) **can** they advance (it in anticipation).
007:034 not an hour **can** they cause delay, nor (an hour)
007:040 until the camel **can** pass through the eye of the needle:
007:042 We place on any soul, but that which it **can** bear,
007:099 but on one **can** feel secure from the Plan of Allah,
007:147 **can** they expect to be rewarded except as they have
007:186 as Allah rejects from His guidance, there **can** be no guide;
007:187 none but He **can** reveal as to when it will occur.
007:191 as partners things that **can** create nothing,
007:192 No aid **can** they give them, nor **can** they aid themselves!
008:034 No men **can** be its guardians
008:035 (its only answer **can** be), "Taste ye
008:048 "No one among men **can** overcome you this day, while I
009:006 and then escort him to where he **can** be secure,
009:007 How **can** there be a covenant before Allah
009:008 How (**can** there be such a league), seeing that
009:052 Say: "**Can** you expect for us (any fate) other than
009:052 But we **can** expect for you either that Allah
009:091 no ground (of complaint) **can** there be against
009:092 "I **can** find no mounts for you," they turned
010:003 No intercessor (**can** plead with Him) except after
010:018 besides Allah, what **can** hurt them not nor profit them,
010:034 your 'partners', **can** any originate creation and repeat it?"
010:035 is there any that **can** give guidance towards Truth?"
010:036 truly conjecture **can** be of no avail against Truth.
010:037 This Qur'an is not such as **can** be produced by
010:038 and call (to your aid) anyone you **can**, besides
010:049 not an hour **can** they cause delay,
010:049 nor (an hour) **can** they advance (it in anticipation).
010:064 no change **can** there be in the Words of Allah.
010:100 No soul **can** believe, except by
010:107 there is none **can** remove it but He:
010:107 there is none **can** keep back his favour:
011:013 whomsoever ye **can**, other than Allah!-if ye
011:017 **Can** they be (like) those who accept a Clear
011:024 and those who **can** see and hear well.
011:038 we (in our turn) **can** look down on you with
011:043 nothing **can** save, from the Command of Allah,
011:063 who then **can** help me against Allah if I were to disobey
011:088 (in my task) **can** only come from Allah.
011:093 "And O my people! do whatever ye **can**: I will
011:121 "Do whatever ye **can**: we shall do our part;
012:018 it is Allah (alone) whose help **can** be sought."

CAN (continued)

012:043 if it be that ye **can** interpret visions."
012:065 What (more) **can** we desire?
012:067 none **can** command except Allah:
012:067 Not that I **can** profit you aught against Allah
013:002 without any pillars that ye **can** see; then He
013:011 willeth a people's punishment, there **can** be no turning
013:033 Allah leaves to stray, no one **can** guide.
014:019 If He so will, He **can** remove you
014:021 **can** ye then avail us at all against the Wrath of Allah"
014:022 I cannot listen to your cries, nor **can** ye listen to mine.
015:005 Neither **can** a people anticipate its Term,
016:009 Allah alone **can** show the right path but there
017:015 no bearer of burdens **can** bear the burden of another:
017:048 and never **can** they find a way.
018:021 and that there **can** be no doubt about the Hour
018:027 none **can** change His Words, and none
018:102 that they **can** take my servants as protectors besides Me?
019:029 They said: "How **can** we talk to one who is
019:042 and **can** profit thee nothing?
020:010 perhaps I **can** bring you some burning brand
020:058 "But we **can** surely produce magic to match thine!
020:071 which of us **can** give the more severe and the
021:021 gods from the earth who **can** raise (the dead)?
021:039 and (when) no help **can** reach them!
021:042 Say, "Who **can** keep you safe by night and by day
021:043 Or have they gods that **can** guard them from Us?
021:043 to aid themselves, nor **can** they be defended from Us.
021:063 Ask them, if they **can** talk."
021:066 things that **can** neither be of any good to you
022:007 there **can** be no doubt about it, or about
022:012 besides Allah, as **can** neither hurt nor profit them:
022:018 none **can** rise to honor:
023:043 No people **can** hasten their term, nor **can** they delay (it).
023:062 no soul do We place a burden greater than it **can** bear:
024:003 none **can** have sexual relations with her but an
024:037 nor sale **can** divert from the Remembrance of Allah,
024:040 he **can** hardly see it!
024:057 Unbelievers **can** escape in the earth their abode is the
025:003 gods that **can** create nothing but are themselves created;
025:003 nor **can** they control Death nor life nor Resurrection.
025:055 things that **can** neither profit them nor harm them:
026:093 "'Besides Allah? **Can** they help you or help themselves?'"
027:038 which of you **can** bring me her throne before they
027:060 (**Can** there be another) god besides Allah?
027:061 between the two seas (**can** there be another) god besides
027:062 (**Can** there be another) god besides Allah?
027:063 (**Can** there be another) god besides Allah?-
027:064 (**Can** there be another) god besides Allah?
027:065 nor **can** they perceive when they shall be
028:071 who **can** give you light?
028:072 who **can** give you a Night in which ye **can** rest?
030:027 (We **can** think of) in the heavens and the earth:
030:040 your (false) "Partners" who **can** do any single
031:010 any pillars that ye **can** see; He set
031:033 when no father **can** avail aught for his son,
033:017 Say: "Who is it that **can** screen you from Allah
033:038 There **can** be no difficulty to the Prophet
034:023 "No intercession **can** avail with Him, except for
034:027 with Him ye have as partners: by no means (**can** ye).
035:002 His Mercy doth bestow on mankind none **can** withhold:
035:002 what He doth withhold, none **can** grant, apart from Him:
035:014 And none, (O man!) **can** inform you like Him

CAN (continued)

035:018 not the least portion of it **can** be carried
035:018 Nor **can** a bearer of burdens bear another's
035:022 Allah **can** make any that He wills to hear;
035:040 from which they (**can** derive) clear (evidence)?-
035:041 There is none-not one-**can** sustain them thereafter:
036:023 nor **can** they deliver me.
036:040 nor **can** the Night outstrip the Day:
036:078 "Who **can** give life to (dry) bones and decomposed
037:162 **Can** lead (any) into temptation concerning Allah,
038:051 therein **can** they call (at pleasure) for fruit
039:007 No bearer of burdens **can** bear the burden
039:023 but such as Allah leaves to stray, **can** have none to guide.
039:036 For such as Allah leaves to stray, there **can** be no guide.
039:037 there **can** be none to lead astray.
039:038 **can** they, if Allah wills some affliction for me, remove
039:038 some Mercy for me, **can** they keep back His Mercy?"
039:039 Say: "O my people! Do whatever ye **can**: I will
039:074 We **can** dwell in the Garden as we will:
040:004 None **can** dispute about the Signs of Allah
040:047 **can** ye then take (on yourselves) from us some share of
041:034 Nor **can** Goodness and Evil be equal.
041:039 to the (dead) earth **can** surely give life to (men) who are
041:042 No falsehood **can** approach it from before
041:047 "We do assure Thee not one of us **can** bear witness!"
042:031 Nor **can** ye escape through the earth;
042:033 He **can** still the Wind:
042:034 Or He **can** cause them to perish because of the
043:052 and **can** scarcely express himself clearly?
044:041 his client in aught, and no help **can** they receive,
044:041 The Day when no protector **can** avail his client
044:055 There **can** they call for every kind of fruit
045:024 and nothing but Time **can** destroy us."
045:035 shall not be taken out thence, nor **can** they make amends.
046:032 and no protectors **can** he have besides Allah:
047:015 (**can** those in such Bliss) be compared to such as shall
051:023 ye **can** speak intelligently to each other.
052:008 There is none **can** avert it;-
052:038 by which they **can** (climb up to heaven and) listen
053:035 Has he knowledge of the unseen so that he **can** see?
053:038 that no bearer of burdens **can** bear the burden of another;
053:039 That man **can** have nothing but what he strives for;
053:058 No one but Allah **can** disclose it.
054:044 "We acting together **can** defend ourselves"?
055:033 If it be ye **can** pass beyond the zones
057:013 Then seek a light (where ye **can**)!"
057:022 No misfortune **can** happen on earth or in your
058:002 none **can** be their mothers except those
064:006 But Allah **can** do without (them):
064:011 No kind of calamity **can** occur, except by
064:016 So fear Allah as much as ye **can**; listen and obey;
067:019 None **can** uphold them except the Most Gracious:
067:020 Nay, who is there that **can** help you, (even as) an army,
067:021 Or who is there that **can** provide you with Sustenance
067:028 yet who **can** deliver the Unbelievers from a grievous
067:030 who then **can** supply you with clear-flowing
068:047 so that they **can** write it down?
070:040 a;; points in the East and the West that We **can** certainly-
072:012 'But we think that we **can** by no means frustrate Allah
072:012 nor **can** we escape Him by flight.
072:022 Say: "No one **can** deliver me from Allah
074:031 and none **can** know the forces of thy Lord,
079:006 One Day everything that **can** be in commotion

CAN (continued)
083:012 And none **can** deny it but the Transgressor
085:013 and He **can** restore (life).
089:025 such as none (else) **can** inflict,
089:026 And His bonds will be such as none (other) **can** bind.
095:007 What then, **can** after this make you deny the last

CANCEL
002:264 O ye who believe! **cancel** not your charity
022:052 but Allah will **cancel** anything (vain) that Satan throws

CANNOT
002:024 But if ye **cannot**-and of a surety ye **cannot**-then fear the
002:061 we **cannot** endure one kind of food (always);
002:196 but if he **cannot** afford it,
002:230 he **cannot**, after that, re-marry her until
002:249 "This day we **cannot** cope with Goliath and his forces."
002:273 And **cannot** move about in the land,
002:283 and **cannot** find a scribe,
004:108 but they **cannot** hide from Allah,
004:108 In words that He **cannot** approve:
005:042 If thou decline, they **cannot** hurt thee in the least.
006:019 Say: "Nay! I **cannot** bear witness!"
007:027 from a position where ye **cannot** see them:
009:002 but know ye that ye **cannot** frustrate Allah
009:003 know ye that ye **cannot** frustrate Allah,
010:039 falsehood that whose knowledge they **cannot** compass,
010:053 And ye **cannot** frustrate it!"
011:076 cometh a Chastisement that **cannot** be turned back!
014:022 I **cannot** listen to your cries, nor can
016:073 and **cannot** possibly have such power?
021:023 He **cannot** be questioned for His acts,
022:073 besides Allah, ye call, **cannot** create (even) a fly,
024:003 The adulterer **cannot** have sexual relations
025:019 so ye **cannot** avert (your penalty) nor get) help."
028:023 They said: "We **cannot** water (our flocks) until the
033:013 Ye **cannot** stand (the attack)!
034:030 for a Day, which ye **cannot** put back for an hour
034:035 and in sons, and we **cannot** be chastised."
035:014 they **cannot** answer your (prayer).
036:008 so that they **cannot** bow their heads.
036:009 so that they **cannot** see.
046:032 he **cannot** escape in the earth,
058:002 they **cannot** be their mothers:
058:010 but he **cannot** harm them in the least, except as Allah
071:004 is accomplished, it **cannot** be put forward:
075:003 Does man think that We **cannot** assemble his bones?
078:003 About which they **cannot** agree.

CANOPIES
002:210 Allah comes to them in **canopies** of clouds,

CANOPY
002:022 and the heaven your **canopy**;
007:171 as if it had been a **canopy**, and they
021:032 as a **canopy** well guarded:
031:032 When a wave covers them like the **canopy** (of clouds),
040:064 and the sky as a **canopy**, and has given
052:005 By the **Canopy** Raised High;
079:028 On high hath He raised its **canopy**, and He

CANST
007:143 Allah said: "By no means **canst** thou see Me (direct);
010:042 but **canst** thou make the deaf to hear,-even though
010:043 but **canst** thou guide the blind,-
017:037 for thou **canst** not rend the earth asunder,
017:064 And Arouse those whom thou **canst** among them,
018:068 "For how **canst** thou have patience about things

CANST (continued)
018:072 thou **canst** have no patience with me?"
018:075 thou **canst** have no patience with me?"
019:098 **Canst** thou find a single one of them (now) or hear
020:072 for thou **canst** only decree (touching)
027:080 Truly thou **canst** not cause the Dead to listen,
027:080 to listen, nor **canst** thou cause the Deaf
027:081 Nor **canst** thou be a guide to the Blind,
030:052 So verily thou **canst** not make the dead to hear,
030:052 nor **canst** thou make the deaf to hear the call,
030:053 Nor **canst** thou lead back the blind from their
035:018 Thou **canst** but warn such as fear their Lord
035:022 but thou **canst** not make those to hear who are (burred)
036:011 Thou **canst** but admonish such a one as follows
043:040 **Canst** thou then make the deaf to hear, or give

CANT
048:026 the Unbelievers got up in their hearts heat and **cant**-
048:026 the heat and **cant** of Ignorance,-Allah sent down

CAPITAL
002:279 ye shall have your **capital** sums:
012:088 we have (now) brought but scanty **capital**:

CAPTIVE
076:008 the indigent, the orphan, and the **captive**,-

CAPTIVES
002:085 and if they come to you as **captives**,
008:070 who are **captives** in your hands:
023:006 or (the **captives**) whom their right hands
033:026 and some ye made **captives**.
033:050 the **captives** of war whom Allah has assigned
033:050 the **captives** whom their right hands possess;-
047:004 blind (the **captives**) firmly:
070:030 and the (**captives**) whom their right hands possess,-

CAPTIVITY
037:140 (like a slave from **captivity**) to the ship (fully) laden,

CARAVAN
008:042 and the **caravan** on lower ground than ye.
012:010 he will be picked up by some **caravan** of travellers."
012:019 Then there came a **caravan** of travellers:
012:070 (in) the **Caravan**! Behold! ye are thieves,
012:082 and the **caravan** in which we returned,
012:094 When the **Caravan** left (Egypt), their father

CARDED
101:005 And the mountains will be like **carded** wool.

CARE
003:037 to the **care** of Zakariya was she assigned.
003:044 should be charged with the **care** of Mary:
011:057 For my Lord hath **care** and watch over all things."
012:012 and we shall take every **care** of him."
012:063 and we will indeed take every **care** of him."
012:064 But Allah is the best to take **care** (of him),
012:065 take **care** of our brother; and add
015:084 they did (with such art and **care**)!
018:019 behave with **care** and courtesy, and let
028:012 and take **care** of him."
029:035 for any people who (**care** to) understand.
038:023 'Commit her to my **care**,' and he
054:014 She floats under Our eyes (and **care**):
093:006 and give thee shelter (and **care**)?

CARE-FREE
007:098 while they played about (**care-free**)?

CAREFUL
004:086 Allah takes **careful** account of all things.

CAREFULLY
004:094 therefore **carefully** investigate, for Allah
004:094 in the cause of Allah, investigate **carefully,**
CARETH
002:261 And Allah **careth** for all and He knoweth
002:268 And Allah **careth** for all and He knoweth
003:073 and Allah **careth** for all,
004:130 for Allah is He that **careth** for all and is Wise.
CARNAL
024:031 who have no **carnal** knowledge of women; and that
CARPET
015:019 And the earth We have spread out (like a **carpet**);
020:053 the earth like a **carpet** spread out; has enabled
071:019 as a **carpet** (spread out),
CARPETS
055:054 They will recline on **Carpets,** whose inner
055:076 and rich **Carpets** of beauty.
088:016 And rich **carpets** (All) spread out.
CARRIED
002:248 of Moses, and the family of Aaron, **carried** by angles.
004:047 for the decision of Allah must be **carries** out.
007:057 when they have **carried** the heavy-laden clouds.
017:003 whom We **carried** (in the Ark) with Noah!
019:058 and of those whom We **carried** (in the Ark)
035:018 not the least portion of it can be **carried** (by the other),
040:080 and on them and on ships ye are **carried.**
069:011 **carried** you (mankind), in the floating (Ark),
CARRIES
004:112 He **carries** (on himself) (both) a false charge
007:189 and **carries** it about (unnoticed).
020:111 the man that **carries** iniquity (on his back).
022:014 for Allah **carries** out all that He desires.
022:018 for Allah **carries** out all that He wills.
058:001 concerning her husband and **carries** her complaint
062:005 of a donkey which **carries** huge tomes
CARRY
002:282 ye **carry** out on the spot among yourselves,
004:109 or who will **carry** their affairs through?
004:132 and enough is Allah to **carry** through all affairs.
009:074 which they were enable to **carry** out:
016:007 And they **carry** your heavy loads to lands that ye
020:087 but we were made to **carry** the weight of the
029:060 that **carry** not their own sustenance?
036:072 Of them some do **carry** them and some they eat:
111:004 His wife shall **carry** the (crackling) wood-as fuel!
CARRYING
012:036 (in a dream) **carrying** bread on my head, and birds
017:091 in their midst, **carrying** abundant water;
019:027 to her people, **carrying** him (in her arms),
046:015 The **carrying** of the (child) to his weaning is
CARVE
007:074 and **carve** out homes in the mountains;
026:149 "And ye **carve** house out of (rocky) mountains
CARVED
037:095 ye have (yourselves) **carved**?
CASE
002:100 Is it not (the **case**) that every time
002:230 In that **case** there is no blame
002:275 their **case** is for Allah (to judge);
003:126 (in any **case**) there is no victory except
004:089 and (in any **case**) take no friends
004:091 in their **case** We have provided you with a clear
005:034 in that **case,** know that Allah

CASE (continued)
007:114 for ye shall in that **case** be (raised to posts)
008:010 (in any **case**) there is no help except from Allah:
009:069 As in the **case** of those before you: they were
010:046 (before that)-in any **case,** to Us is their return:
010:055 Is it not (the **case**) that Allah's promise
010:055 Is it not (the **case**) that to Allah belongeth
017:073 (in that **case**), behold! they would
017:075 In that **case** We should have made thee taste
017:076 but in that **case** they would not have stayed
018:020 and in that **case** ye would never attain prosperity."
018:021 Thus did We make their **case** known to the people,
018:022 it is but few that know their (real **case**)."
018:073 by raising difficulties in my **case.**"
020:095 (Moses) said: "What then is thy **case,** O Samiri?"
023:006 for (in their **case**) they are free form blame,
024:002 let not compassion move you in their **case,**
026:042 for ye shall in that **case** be (raised to posts) nearest
028:010 she was going almost to disclose his (**case**),
028:047 in **case** a calamity should seize for the (deeds) that their
029:048 in that **case,** indeed, would the talkers of vanities have
034:023 So far (is this the **case**) that, when terror
037:058 "Is it (the **case**) that we shall not die,
040:077 (in any **case**) it is to Us that they shall (all) return.
041:030 In the **case** of those who say, "Our Lord is Allah",
065:001 except in **case** they are guilty of some open lewdness,
079:012 They say: "It would, in that **case,** be a return with loss!"
087:009 Therefore give admonition in **case** the admonition
CASES
002:178 prescribed to you in **cases** of murder:
004:011 (The distribution in all **cases** is) after the payment
049:012 for suspicion in some **cases** is a sin:
066:002 the expiation of your oaths (in some **cases**):
CAST
003:044 when they **cast** lots with pens,
003:151 Soon shall We **cast** terror into the hearts
004:030 soon shall We **cast** them into the Fire:
004:056 We shall soon **cast** into the Fire:
004:088 Allah hath **cast** them for their (evil) deeds.
008:037 heap them together, and **cast** them into Hell.
011:092 For ye **cast** Him away behind your backs
012:009 "Slay ye Joseph or **cast** him out to some
012:032 he shall certainly be **cast** into prison, and (what
012:092 "This day let no reproach be (**cast**) on you:
012:093 and **cast** it over the face of my father:
012:096 news came, he **cast** (the shirt) over his face,
013:017 For the scum disappears like froth **cast** out;
020:039 the river will **cast** him up on the bank, and he
025:013 And when they are **cast,** bound together, into a
026:167 O Lut! thou wilt assuredly be **cast** out!"
028:007 thou hast fears about him, **cast** him into the river,
033:026 from their strongholds and **cast** terror into their hearts,
033:059 that they should **cast** their outer garments
034:048 Say: "Verily my Lord doth **cast** the Truth,-
034:053 and that they **cast** (conjectures) with regard
037:008 and they are **cast** away from every side,
037:088 Then did he **cast** a glance at the Stars,
037:141 He (agreed to) **cast** lots, and he
037:145 But We **cast** him forth on the naked shore
040:046 "**Cast** ye the People of Pharaoh into the
041:040 he that is **cast** into the Fire,
050:025 transgressed all bounds, **cast** doubts and suspicions;
059:002 and **cast** terror into their hearts, so that

CAST (continued)

067:007 When they are **cast** therein, they will
067:008 every time a Group is **cast** therein, its Keepers
068:043 Their eyes will be **cast** down,-ignominy will
068:049 he would indeed have been **cast** off on the
074:026 Soon will **cast** him into Hell-Fire!
079:009 **Cast** down will be (their owners') eyes.

CASTING

003:153 without even **casting** a side glance at anyone,

CASTLES

007:074 palaces and **castles** in (open) plains,
022:045 and **castles** lofty and well-built?

CASTS

084:004 And **casts** forth what is within it and becomes

CATCH

002:191 And slay them wherever ye **catch** them,
005:004 eat what they **catch** for you, but pronounce
036:040 It is not permitted to the Sun to **catch** up the Moon,

CATTLE

003:014 and (wealth of) **cattle** and well-tilled land.
004:119 I will order them to slit the ears of **cattle**,
005:001 are all beasts of **cattle** with the exceptions
006:136 in abundance in tilth and in **cattle**,
006:138 say that such and such **cattle** and crops are forbidden,
006:138 there are **cattle** forbidden to yoke or burden,
006:138 and **cattle** on which (at slaughter) the name of Allah
006:139 the wombs of such and such **cattle** is specially
006:142 Of the **cattle** are some for burden
006:143 (Take) eight (head of **cattle**) in (four) pairs:
007:179 They are like **cattle**,- nay more
016:005 And **cattle** He has created for you (men):
016:010 the vegetation on which ye feed your **cattle**.
016:066 And verily in **cattle** (too) will ye find an
019:086 to Hell, (like thirsty **cattle** driven down to water,-)
020:054 Eat (for yourselves) and pasture your **cattle**:
022:028 over the **cattle** which He has provided for
022:030 are **cattle** except those mentioned to you
023:021 And in **cattle** (too) ye have an instructive example:
025:044 They are only like **cattle**;-nay, they are
025:049 We have created,-**cattle** and men in great numbers.
026:133 "Freely has He bestowed on you **cattle** and sons,-
032:027 providing food for their **cattle** and themselves?
035:028 And so amongst men and beasts and **cattle**, are they of
036:071 Which our hands have fashioned-**cattle**, which are under
039:006 eight head of **cattle** in pairs:
040:079 It is Allah Who made **cattle** for you, that ye
042:011 and pairs among **cattle**:
043:012 and **cattle** on which ye ride,
047:012 enjoy (this world) and eat as **cattle** eat;
054:031 the dry stubble used by one who pens **cattle**.
079:033 A provision for you and your **cattle**.
080:032 A provision for you and your **cattle**.

CAUGHT

002:266 that it should be **caught** in a whirlwind,
006:070 is **caught** in its own ruin by its own action:
029:040 some were **caught** by a (mighty) Blast;

CAULDRONS

034:013 and (cooking) **Cauldrons** fixed (in their places):

CAULKED

054:013 made of broad planks and **caulked** with palm-fibre:

CAUSE

002:027 These **cause** loss (only) to themselves.
002:028 then will He **cause** you to die,

CAUSE (continued)

002:061 and slaying His Messengers without just **cause**.
002:106 We abrogate or **cause** to be forgotten,
002:190 Fight in the **cause** of Allah those who fight you
002:195 your substance in the **cause** of Allah,
002:244 Then fight in the **cause** of Allah,
002:246 that we may fight in the **cause** of Allah."
002:246 we refuse to fight in the **cause** of Allah,
002:258 do thou then **cause** it to rise from the West."
002:262 their wealth in the **cause** of Allah,
002:273 in Allah's **cause** are restricted (from travel).
003:013 one was fighting in the **cause** of Allah,
003:142 (in His **cause**) and remained steadfast?
003:156 a **cause** of sighs and regrets in their hearts.
003:170 nor have they (**cause** to) grieve.
003:195 or suffered harm in My **cause**, and fought
004:035 Allah will **cause** their reconciliation:
004:074 To him who fighteth in the **cause** of Allah, whether
004:074 Let those fight in the **cause** of Allah who sell
004:075 the **cause** of Allah and of those who, being
004:076 Those who believe fight in the **cause** of Allah,
004:076 fight in the **cause** of Evil (Tagut):
004:084 Then fight in Allah's **cause**, thou art held
004:085 and whoever recommends and helps an evil **cause**,
004:085 Whoever intercedes in a good **cause** becomes
004:094 in the **cause** of Allah, investigate carefully,
004:095 in the **cause** of Allah with their goods
004:100 He who forsakes his home in the **cause** of Allah,
004:153 to **cause** a book to descend to them from heaven:
005:035 and strive (with might and main) in His **cause**:
005:084 "What **cause** can we have not to believe in Allah
005:101 if made plain to you, may **cause** you trouble.
006:033 which their words do **cause** thee:
006:095 And He is the One to **cause** the dead to issue from the
006:137 and **cause** confusion in their religion.
007:034 not an hour can they **cause** delay, nor (an hour)
008:060 the **cause** of Allah, shall be repaid unto you,
008:072 in the **Cause** of Allah, as well
008:074 in the **Cause** of Allah, as well
009:019 and strive with might and main in the **cause** of Allah?
009:020 in Allah's **cause**, with their goods and their
009:024 or the striving in His **cause**;-then wait
009:033 to **cause** it to prevail over all religion,
009:038 forth in the **Cause** of Allah, ye cling
009:041 and your persons, in the **cause** of Allah.
009:053 Say: "Spend (for the **cause**) willingly
009:060 for those in bondage and in debt; in the **cause** of Allah;
009:081 their goods and their persons, in the **Cause** of Allah:
009:091 or who find no resources to spend (on the **Cause**),
009:111 they fight in His **Cause**, and slay and are slain:
009:112 that wander in devotion to the **Cause** of Allah;
009:120 or fatigue, or hunger, in the **Cause** of Allah,
009:121 Nor could they spend anything (for the **Cause**)-
010:049 not an hour can they **cause** delay, nor (an hour)
011:089 (from you) **cause** you to sin, lest ye suffer
014:012 all the hurt you may **cause** us.
014:013 "Verily We shall **cause** the wrong-doers to perish!
014:014 "And verily We shall **cause** you to abide
015:008 We send not the angels down except for just **cause**:
015:022 then **cause** the rain to descend from the shy,
016:041 in the **cause** of Allah, after suffering
016:045 will not **cause** the earth to swallow them up,
017:033 made sacred-except for just **cause**.

CAUSE (continued)

017:051   Then will they say: "Who will **cause** us to return?"
017:068   not **cause** you to be swallowed up beneath the
017:090   until thou **cause** a spring to gush forth for us from
017:091   and **cause** rivers to gush forth in their midst,
017:092   "Or thou **cause** the sky to fall in pieces, as thou
020:113   or that it may **cause** their remembrance (of Him).
022:005   and We **cause** whom We will to rest in
022:025   We **cause** to taste of a most grievous chastisement.
022:040   (for no **cause**) except that they say, "Our Lord is Allah".
022:040   Allah will certainly aid those who aid His (**cause**);-
022:058   Those who leave their home in the **cause** of Allah,
022:066   It is He Who gave you life, will **cause** you to die,
022:078   And strive in His **cause** as ye ought to strive,
023:018   and We **caused** it to soak in the soil;
024:022   left their homes in Allah's **cause**:
025:019   him shall We **cause** to taste of a grievous Chastisement.
025:068   such life as Allah has made sacred, except for just **cause**,
026:081   "Who will **cause** me to die, and then
026:181   Give just measure, and **cause** not loss (to others by fraud).
026:187   "Now **cause** a piece of the sky to fall on us,
027:060   Yea, with it We **cause** to grow well-planted
027:060   to **cause** the growth of the trees in them.
027:080   Truly thou canst not **cause** the Dead to listen,
027:080   nor canst thou **cause** the Deaf to hear the call,
028:008   should be to them an adversary and a **cause** of sorrow:
029:010   but when they suffer affliction in (the **cause** of) Allah,
029:069   And those who strive in Our (**Cause**),-We will
030:040   then He will **cause** you to die; and again He will give you
034:009   or **cause** a piece of the sky to fall
034:009   We could **cause** the earth to swallow them up,
034:039   ye spend in the least (in His **Cause**) but He replaces it:
036:034   and We **cause** springs to gush forth therein.
036:068   We **cause** him to be reversed in nature:
040:026   should **cause** mischief to appear in the land!"
042:034   Or He can **cause** them to perish because of the
042:041   to him, against such there is no **cause** of blame.
046:020   for that ye were arrogant on earth without just **cause**,
047:007   if ye will help (the **cause** of) Allah, He will
049:015   their belongings and their persons in the **Cause** of Allah:
056:064   Is it ye that **cause** it to grow, or are We the **Cause**?
057:010   is it with you that you spend not in the **cause** of Allah?-
058:010   in order that he may **cause** grief to the Believers;
061:004   Allah loves those who fight in His **Cause** in battle array,
061:011   and that ye strive (your utmost) in the **Cause** of Allah,
067:016   is in heaven will not **cause** you to be swallowed
069:050   But truly (Revelation) is a **cause** of sorrow
072:017   He will **cause** him to undergo ever-growing
072:021   Say: "It is not in my power to **cause** you harm,
073:020   yet others fighting in Allah's **Cause**.
074:007   But, for thy Lord's (**Cause**), be patient

CAUSED

002:259   But Allah **caused** him to die for a hundred years,
003:155   it was Satan who **caused** them to fail,
004:012   so that no loss is **caused** (to anyone).
006:009   And We should certainly have **caused** them confusion
008:011   and He **caused** rain to descend on you from heaven,
014:007   And remember! your Lord **caused** to be declared
014:028   with ingratitude and **caused** their people to descend to
018:033   We **caused** a river to flow.
020:094   'Thou hast **caused** a division among the Children of Israel,
025:005   "Tales of the ancients, which he has **caused** to be written:
026:200   Thus have We **caused** it to enter the hearts

CAUSED (continued)

028:081   Then We **caused** the earth to swallow up him
028:082   He could have **caused** the earth to swallow us up!
029:040   some We **caused** the earth to swallow up; and some
037:146   And We **caused** to grow over him, a spreading
054:012   And We **caused** the earth to gush forth with springs,

CAUSES

002:026   but He **causes** not to stray,
002:026   By it He **causes** many to stray,
002:176   seek **causes** of dispute in the Book
017:082   to the unjust it **causes** nothing but loss after loss.
039:021   Then He **causes** to grow, therewith,

CAUSEST

003:027   And Thou **causest** the Day to gain on the Night;
003:027   "Thou **causest** the Night to gain on the Day.
007:155   by it Thou **causest** whom Thou wilt to stray,

CAUSETH

002:258   Allah that **causeth** the sun to rise from the East,
006:095   He **causeth** the living to issue from the dead.
006:095   It is Allah Who **causeth** the seed-grain and the
010:107   He **causeth** it to reach whomsoever of His servants
080:021   Then He **causeth** him to die, and putteth

CAUTIONS

003:028   But Allah **cautions** you (to fear) Himself;
003:030   But Allah **cautions** you (to fear) Him

CAVALRY

017:064   them with thy **cavalry** and thy infantry;
059:006   with either **cavalry** or camelry:

CAVE

009:040   the two they were in the **Cave**, and he
018:009   the Companions of the **Cave** and of the Inscription
018:010   Behold, the youths betook themselves to the **Cave**:
018:011   for a number of years, in the **cave**,
018:016   betake yourselves to the **Cave**:
018:017   when it rose, declining to the fight from their **Cave**,
018:017   while they lay in the open space in the midst of the **Cave**.
018:025   So they stayed in their **Cave** three hundred years,

CAVES

009:057   If they could find a place to flee to, or **caves**,

CEASE

002:192   But if they **cease**,
002:193   But if they **cease**, let there be no hostility
002:217   Nor will they **cease** fighting you until they turn you
005:013   nor wilt thou **cease** to find them-barring a few,
008:039   religion becomes Allah's in its entirety but if they **cease**,
011:118   but they will not **cease** to differ,
012:085   thou **cease** to remember Joseph until though reach
013:031   never will disaster **cease** to seize them for their (ill) deeds,
020:091   They had said: "We will not **cease** to worship it,
022:055   Those who reject Faith will not **cease** to be
035:041   and the earth, lest they **cease** (to function):

CEASED

006:049   for that they **ceased** not from transgressing.
021:015   And that cry of theirs **ceased** not, till We
040:034   but ye **ceased** not to doubt of the (mission)

CEILING

022:015   a rope to the **ceiling** and cut (himself) off:

CELEBRATE

002:030   Whilst we do **celebrate** Thy praises
002:198   **celebrate** the praises of Allah at the Sacred Monument
002:198   and **celebrate** His praises as He has directed you,
002:200   accomplished your rites, **celebrate** the praises of Allah,
002:200   as ye used to **celebrate** the praises of your fathers

CELEBRATE (continued)

002:239   **celebrate** Allah's praises in the manner He has taught
003:041   Then **celebrate** the praises of thy Lord
015:098   But **celebrate** the praises of thy Lord and be
019:011   by signs to **celebrate** Allah's praises in the
020:033   "That we may **celebrate** Thy praise without stint,
020:130   they say, and **celebrate** (constantly) the praises of thy
020:130   **celebrate** them for part of the hours of the night,
021:020   They **celebrate** His praises night and day, nor do
021:079   and the birds **celebrate** Our praises, with David:
022:028   and **celebrate** the name of Allah, through the
022:034   that they might **celebrate** the name of Allah
024:041   all beings in the heavens and on earth do **celebrate**,
025:058   Him Who lives and dies not; and **celebrate** His praise;
032:015   and **celebrate** the praises of their Lord,
040:055   and **celebrate** the Praises of thy Lord in the
041:038   who **celebrate** His praises by night and by day.
042:005   and the angels **celebrate** the Praises of their Lord,
048:009   and **celebrate** His praises morning and evening.
050:039   they say, and **celebrate** the praises of they Lord,
050:040   (also), **celebrate** His praises, and (so likewise)
052:048   and **celebrate** the praises of thy Lord the while thou
076:025   And **celebrate** the name of thy Lord
110:003   **Celebrate** the Praises of thy Lord, and pray

CELEBRATED

002:114   His name should be **celebrated**?

CELEBRATES

017:044   there is not a thing but **celebrates** His praise;

CELEBRATION

002:128   for the **celebration** of (due) rites;
024:036   to honour; for the **celebration**, in them, of His

CELESTIAL

021:033   All (the **celestial** bodies) swim along, each in

CELLS

016:068   to build its **cells** in hills, on trees, and in

CEMENTED

061:004   as if they were a solid **cemented** structure.

CENTER

011:062   thou hast been of us!-a **center** of our hopes hitherto!
028:059   to its **Center** a messenger, rehearsing to

CEREMONIAL

004:043   nor in a state of **ceremonial** impurity except
005:006   If ye are in a state of **ceremonial** impurity, bathe

CERTAIN

002:037   Then learnt Adam from his Lord **certain** words
002:124   was tried by his lord with **certain** Commands,
004:157   are full of doubts, with no (**certain**) knowledge.
004:160   We made unlawful for them **certain** (foods)
005:011   unto you when **certain** men formed the design to
006:135   **certain** it is that the wrong-doers will not prosper."
006:148   Say: "Have ye any (**certain**) Knowledge? If so,
006:158   or **certain** of the Signs of thy Lord!
006:158   The day that **certain** of the Signs of thy
007:048   will call to **certain** men whom they will
009:101   **Certain** of the desert Arabs round about you
012:108   with a **certain** knowledge I and whoever follow me.
015:088   on **certain** classes of them, nor grieve over them:
015:099   come unto thee the Hour that is **Certain**.
018:079   "As for the boat, it belonged to **certain** men in dire want:
018:079   for there was after them a **certain** king who
020:071   So shall ye know for **certain**, which of
021:078   of **certain** people had strayed by night:
023:034   behold, it is **certain** ye will be lost.

CERTAIN (continued)

028:037   **certain** it is that the wrong-doers will not prosper.
028:078   because of a **certain** knowledge which I have."
034:024   Say: "It is Allah; and **certain** it is that
039:049   because of a **certain** knowledge (I have)!"
043:022   fathers following a **certain** religion, and we
043:023   "We found our fathers following a **certain** religion,
073:006   and speech more **certain**.
074:047   "Until there came to us (the Hour) that is **certain**."

CERTAINLY

003:154   would **certainly** have gone forth to the place
003:167   we should **certainly** have followed you."
003:181   We shall **certainly** record their word
003:186   shall **certainly** be tried and tested in your possessions
003:186   and ye shall **certainly** hear much that will grieve you,
003:199   And there are, **certainly**, among the people
004:072   There are **certainly** among you men who
004:113   a party of them would **certainly** have plotted
005:056   the party of Allah that must **certainly** triumph.
005:072   **Certainly** they disbelieve who say: "Allah is
006:009   and We should **certainly** have caused them confusion
006:028   they would **certainly** relapse to the things
006:037   Say: "Allah hath **certainly** power to send
006:109   Say: "**Certainly** (all) Signs are in
006:161   and he (**certainly**) joined not gods with Allah."
007:023   we shall **certainly** be lost."
007:052   For We had **certainly** sent unto them a Book, based
007:088   said: "O Shu'aib! we shall **certainly** drive thee
008:042   ye would **certainly** have failed in the appointment:
009:042   for Allah doth know that they are **certainly** lying.
009:042   "If we only could, we should **certainly** have come
009:046   they would **certainly** have made some preparation
009:107   that they are **certainly** liars.
010:029   we **certainly** knew nothing of your worship of us!"
010:083   and **certainly** Pharaoh was mighty on earth and one who
010:106   thou shalt **certainly** be of those who do wrong."
011:091   we should **certainly** have stoned thee!
011:110   We **certainly** gave the Book to Moses,
012:032   he shall **certainly** be cast into prison,
012:050   For my Lord is **certainly** well aware of their snare."
012:053   but surely **certainly** my Lord is Oft-Forgiving,
012:053   the (human) soul **certainly** incites evil,
012:091   and we **certainly** have been guilty of sin!"
014:012   We shall **certainly** bear with patience all the
015:059   them we are **certainly** (charged) to save
016:056   By Allah, ye shall **certainly** be called to account
016:092   will **certainly** make clear to you (the truth of) that
016:093   but ye shall **certainly** be called to account
016:096   And We will **certainly** bestow, on those
017:042   behold, they would **certainly** have sought out
017:073   they would **certainly** have made thee (their) friend!
017:095   We should **certainly** have sent them down from the
018:018   and wouldst **certainly** have been filled with terror
018:018   thou wouldst have **certainly** turned back
019:069   Then shall We **certainly** drag out from every
019:070   And **certainly** We know best those who are most
019:077   "I shall **certainly** be given wealth and children"?
020:063   They said: "'These two are **certainly** (expert) magicians:
020:097   we will **certainly** burn it in a blazing fire
020:134   we should **certainly** have followed the Signs before we
021:057   "And by Allah, I will **certainly** plan against
022:040   Allah will **certainly** aid those who aid His
023:018   and We **certainly** are able to drain

CERTAINLY (continued)

023:023 and **certainly** We sent Noah to his people:
023:065 for ye shall **certainly** not be helped by Us.
023:095 And We are **certainly** able to show thee
026:029 I will **certainly** put thee in prison!"
026:044 it is we who will **certainly** win!"
027:021 "I will **certainly** punish him with a
027:077 And it **certainly** is a Guide and Mercy
028:035 He said: "We will **certainly** strengthen thy arm
029:003 and Allah will **certainly** know those who are
029:011 And Allah most **certainly** knows those who believe,
029:011 and as **certainly** those who are Hypocrites.
029:032 we will **certainly** save him and his following,-
029:053 and it will **certainly** reach them,-
029:053 the Punishment would **certainly** have come to them:
029:061 they will **certainly** reply, "Allah." How are
029:063 they will **certainly** reply, "Allah!" Say, "Praise
029:069 We will **certainly** guide them to Our Paths:
031:025 They will **certainly** say, "Allah." Say: "Praise be to
032:013 We could **certainly** have brought every soul
033:014 They would **certainly** have brought it to pass,
033:060 We shall **certainly** stir thee up against them:
034:031 we should **certainly** have been believers!"
035:005 O men! **certainly** the promise of Allah is true,
036:018 desist not, we will **certainly** stone you,
037:057 I should **certainly** have been among those brought (there)!
037:127 and they will **certainly** be called up (for punishment),
037:144 He would **certainly** have remained inside the
037:169 "We should **certainly** have been Servants of Allah,
037:172 That they would **certainly** be assisted,
038:085 "That I will **certainly** fill Hell with thee
038:088 "And ye shall **certainly** know the truth
039:057 I should **certainly** have been among the righteous!'
039:058 I should **certainly** be among those who do good!'
040:059 The Hour will **certainly** come: therein is
041:014 He would **certainly** have sent down angels:
041:027 But We will **certainly** give the Unbelievers a taste
041:045 We **certainly** gave Moses the book aforetime:
043:023 will **certainly** follow in their footsteps."
043:027 and He will **certainly** guide me."
043:087 they will **certainly** say, Allah:
047:004 He could **certainly** have exacted retribution
048:022 they would **certainly** turn their backs;
048:025 We should **certainly** have punished the Unbelievers
049:007 to follow your (wishes) ye would **certainly** suffer:
056:050 "All will **certainly** be gathered together for the
056:062 And ye **certainly** know already the first form
059:003 He would **certainly** have punished them in this
059:003 they shall (**certainly**) have the Punishment
067:013 or make it known, He **certainly** has (full) knowledge,
069:045 We should **certainly** seize him by his right hand
069:046 And We should **certainly** then cut off the artery
069:049 And We **certainly** know that there are amongst you
070:040 in the East and the West that We can **certainly**-
072:016 We should **certainly** have bestowed on them
077:044 Thus do We **certainly** reward the Doers of Good.
102:006 Ye shall **certainly** see Hell-fire!

CERTAINTY

002:046 Who bear in mind the **certainty** that they are to meet
013:002 that ye may believe with **certainty** in the meeting with
030:060 who have (themselves) no **certainty** of faith.
056:095 Verily, this is the very Truth of assured **Certainty**.
069:051 But verily it is Truth of assured **certainty**.

CERTAINTY (continued)

074:031 that the People of the Book may arrive at **certainty**,
102:005 with **certainty** of mind, (ye would beware)!
102:007 Again, ye shall see it with **certainty** of sight!

CERTITUDE

006:075 that he might have **certitude**.

CHAIN

034:011 balancing well the rings of **chain** armour,
069:032 "Further, insert him in a **chain**, whereof the

CHAINS

040:071 their necks, and the **chains**; they shall
076:004 prepared **Chains**, Yokes, and a Blazing Fire.

CHAMBER

003:037 Every time that he entered her **chamber** to see her,
003:039 While he was standing in prayer in the **chamber**,
019:011 So Zakrya came out to his people from his **chamber**:
038:021 over the wall of the private **chamber**;

CHANCE

002:052 there was a **chance** for you to be grateful.
002:053 there was a **chance** for you to be guided aright.
002:056 ye had the **chance** to be grateful.
002:167 "If only we had one more **chance**,
005:106 and the **chance** of death befalls you (thus).
016:046 to and fro, without a **chance** of their frustrating Him?
026:102 "'Now if we only had a **chance** of return, we shall
030:043 the Day which there is no **chance** of averting:
036:050 No (**chance**) will they then have, by will,
039:058 'If only I had another **chance** I should

CHANCES

020:058 in a place where both shall have even **chances**."

CHANGE

002:143 Indeed it was (a **change**) momentous,
002:164 in the **change** of the winds,
002:181 the guilt shall be on those who make the **change**.
004:047 before We **change** the face and fame of some
004:056 We shall **change** them for fresh skins, that they
005:013 they **change** the words from their (right) places
005:041 They **change** the words from their (right) places;
005:052 a **change** of fortune bring us disaster."
006:115 none can **change** His Words:
008:053 "Because Allah will never **change** the Grace
008:053 on a people until they **change** what is in their
010:015 of my own accord, to **change** it:
010:015 "'Bring us a Qur'an other than this, or **change** this."
010:064 no **change** can there be in the Words of Allah.
013:011 until they **change** what is in themselves but when
013:011 Verily never will Allah **change** the condition
017:056 to remove your troubles from you nor to **change** them."
017:077 thou wilt find no **change** in Our ways.
018:027 none can **change** His Words, and none
018:108 no **change** will they wish for from them.
024:055 and that He will **change** (their state), after the
025:070 for Allah will **change** the evil of such persons
030:030 no **change** (there is) in the work (wrought) by Allah:
033:052 nor to **change** them for (other) wives, even though
033:062 no **change** wilt thou find in the practice (approved)
035:043 But no **change** wilt thou find in Allah's way
040:026 What I fear is lest he should **change** your religion,
045:005 and in the **change** of the winds,-
048:015 They wish to **change** Allah's word: Say: "Not thus
048:023 no **change** wilt thou find in the practice of Allah.

CHANGED

002:059 But the transgressors **changed** the word

CHANGED (continued)
007:095 Then We **changed** their suffering
007:162 But the transgressors among them **changed** the word from
014:048 One day the Earth will be **changed** to a
033:023 but they have never **changed** (their determination) in the

CHANGES
002:181 If anyone **changes** the bequest after hearing it,
047:015 rivers of milk of which the taste never **changes**
050:029 "The Word **changes** not before Me, and I

CHANGETH
002:108 But whoever **changeth** from Faith to Unbelief,

CHANGING
056:061 From **changing** your Forms and creating you
074:029 Darkening and **changing** the colour of man!

CHANNELS
013:017 and the **channels** flow, each according
020:053 enabled you to go about therein by roads (and **channels**);
043:010 and has made for you roads (and **channels**) therein,

CHARGE
004:156 that they uttered against Mary a grave false **charge**;
006:089 behold! We shall entrust their **charge** to a new
010:039 Nay, they **charge** with falsehood that whose
010:041 If they **charge** thee with falsehood, say: "My work
024:004 a **charge** against chaste women, and produce
024:006 a **charge** against their wives, and have
024:012 and say, "This (**charge**) is an obvious lie?"
026:012 I do fear that they will **charge** me with falsehood:
026:014 "And (further), they have a **charge** of crime
028:063 Those against whom the **charge** will be proved,
032:011 Say: "The Angel of Death, put in **charge** of you,
100:003 And push home the **charge** in the morning,

CHARGEABLE
002:233 An heir shall be **chargeable** in the same way.

CHARGED
003:044 should be **charged** with the care of Mary:
004:059 and those **charged** with authority among you.
004:083 or to those **charged** with authority among them,
007:142 And Moses had **charged** his brother Aaron
015:059 them we are certainly (**charged**) to save
050:009 Rain **charged** with blessing, and We

CHARGES
010:039 thus did those before them make **charges** of falsehood:

CHARITABLE
012:088 for Allah doth reward the **charitable**."

CHARITY
002:215 They ask thee what they should spend (in **charity**).
002:263 than **charity** followed by injury.
002:264 your **charity** by reminders of your generosity
002:270 And whatever ye spend in **charity** or whatever
002:271 If ye disclose (acts of) **charity**,
002:273 (**Charity** is) for those in need, who,
002:274 Those who (in **charity**) spend of their goods
002:276 but will give increase for deeds of **charity**:
002:280 But if ye remit it by way of **charity**,
004:114 but if one exhorts to a deed of **charity** or
005:045 by way of **charity**, it is an act
009:075 they would give (largely) in **charity**, and be
009:079 as give themselves freely to (deeds of) **charity**,
009:104 and receives their gifts of **charity**,
012:088 and treat it as **charity** to us;
014:031 and spend (in **charity**) out of the Sustenance
022:035 and spend (in **charity**) out of what We have
023:060 And those who dispense their **charity** with their

CHARITY (continued)
028:054 and that they spend (in **charity**) out of
030:039 but that which you give for **charity**, seeking the
032:016 (in **charity**) out of the sustenance which We have
033:035 who give in **charity**, for men and women who fast,
035:029 and spend (in **Charity**) out of what We have
057:007 who believe and spend (in **charity**),-for them
057:007 and spend (in **charity**) out of the (substance)
057:018 For those who give in **Charity**, men and women,
058:012 spend something in **charity** before your private
058:013 spending sums in **charity** before your private
063:010 And spend something (in **charity**) out of substance
063:010 I should then have given (largely) in **charity**,
064:016 and spend in **charity** for the benefit of your own souls:
075:031 So he gave nothing in **charity**, nor did he pray!-
092:005 So he who gives (in **charity**) and fears (Allah),

CHASE
005:001 but animals of the **chase** are forbidden while

CHASTE
003:039 and (be besides) noble, **chaste**, and a Prophet,
004:025 they should be **chaste**, not fornicators,
005:005 are (not only) **chaste** women who are believers,
005:005 but **chaste** women among the People of the Book,
024:004 a charge against **chaste** women, and produce
024:023 Those who slander **chaste** women, indiscreet
024:033 keep themselves **chaste**, until Allah
037:048 And besides them will be **chaste** women; restraining their
038:052 And besides them will be **chaste** women restraining their
055:056 will be (Maidens), **chaste**, restraining their glances,

CHASTISED
034:035 and in sons, and we cannot be **chastised**."

CHASTISEMENT
002:007 great is the **chastisement** they (incur).
002:010 and grievous is the **chastisement** they (incur),
002:049 they set you hard tasks and **chastisement**,
002:085 the most grievous **chastisement**
002:086 their **chastisement** shall not be lightened
002:090 **Chastisement** of those who reject Faith.
002:096 will not save him from (due) **chastisement**
002:166 the **Chastisement** and all relations between
002:174 grievous will be their **Chastisement**.
002:178 the limits shall be in grave **chastisement**.
003:004 will suffer the severest **chastisement**
003:021 announce to them a grievous **chastisement**.
003:056 severe **chastisement** in this world and the Hereafter
003:077 they shall have a grievous **Chastisement**.
003:091 For such is (in store) a **chastisement** grievous,
003:105 for them is a dreadful **Chastisement**,
003:106 Taste then the **Chastisement** for rejecting Faith.
003:181 "Taste ye the **Chastisement** of the scorching Fire!
003:188 think not that they can escape the **Chastisement**.
003:188 For them is a **Chastisement** grievous indeed.
003:191 salvation from the **Chastisement** of the Fire.
004:018 a **chastisement** most grievous.
004:056 that they may taste the **Chastisement**:
004:093 and a dreadful **chastisement** is prepared for him.
004:138 that there is for them a grievous **Chastisement**.
004:161 who reject faith a grievous **chastisement**.
004:173 He will punish with a grievous **chastisement**:
005:036 for the **Chastisement** of the Day of Judgment,
005:036 Theirs would be a grievous **Chastisement**.
005:037 their **Chastisement** will be one that endures.
005:073 a grievous **chastisement** will befall the

CHASTISEMENT (continued)

005:094 will have a grievous **chastisement**.
005:115 I will punish him with a **chastisement** such as I
006:015 the **Chastisement** of a Mighty Day.
006:030 the **Chastisement**, because ye rejected Faith."
006:093 a **chastisement** of disgrace, for that
006:124 and a severe **chastisement**, for all their plots.
006:157 with a dreadful **chastisement** for their
007:039 the **Chastisement** for all that ye did!"
007:167 those who would afflict hem with grievous **Chastisement**.
008:014 is the **chastisement** of the Fire."
008:032 from the sky, or send us a grievous **chastisement**."
008:033 But Allah was not going to send them a **Chastisement**:
008:035 "Taste ye the **Chastisement** because ye blasphemed."
008:050 "Taste the **chastisement** of the blazing Fire-
009:003 a grievous **chastisement** to those who reject Faith.
009:034 announce unto them a most grievous **chastisement**-
009:061 molest the Prophet will have a grievous **chastisement**.
009:074 a grievous **chastisement** in this life and in
009:079 and they shall have a grievous **chastisement**.
009:090 Soon will a grievous **chastisement** seize the
009:101 be sent to a grievous **Chastisement**.
010:004 and a **Chastisement** grievous, because they
010:015 the **Chastisement** of a Great Day (to come)."
010:054 when they see the **Chastisement**:
010:070 the severest **Chastisement** for their disbelief.
010:088 until they see the grievous **Chastisement**."
010:097 (for themselves) the **Chastisement** Grievous.
010:098 from them the **Chastisement** of Ignominy in the
011:003 for you the **Chastisement** of a Great Day:
011:008 If We delay the **chastisement** for them
011:020 Their **chastisement** will be doubled!
011:039 on whom will descend a **Chastisement** that will
011:039 on whom will be unloosed a **Chastisement** lasting."
011:048 a grievous **Chastisement** reach them from Us."
011:058 We saved them from a severe **chastisement**.
011:076 for them there cometh a **Chastisement** that cannot
011:084 for you the **Chastisement** of a Day that will
011:093 the **Chastisement** of ignominy, and who
011:102 indeed, and severe is His **chastisement**.
011:102 Such is the **chastisement** of thy Lord when He
011:103 who fear the **Chastisement** of the Hereafter:
012:025 but prison or a grievous **chastisement**?"
013:034 the **Chastisement** of the Hereafter:
014:002 a terrible **Chastisement** (their Unfaith will bring them)!
014:017 will be a **chastisement** unrelenting.
014:022 the wrong-doers there must be a grievous **Chastisement**."
015:050 And that My **Chastisement** will be indeed
015:050 will be indeed the most grievous **Chastisement**.
016:063 a most grievous **chastisement**.
016:085 see the **Chastisement** then will it in no way
016:088 will We add **Chastisement** to **Chastisement**; for that
016:104 and theirs will be a grievous **Chastisement**.
016:106 and theirs will be a dreadful **Chastisement**.
016:117 but they will have a most grievous **Chastisement**.
017:010 prepared for them a **Chastisement** grievous (indeed).
017:058 a dreadful **Chastisement**.
019:045 a **Chastisement** afflict thee from (Allah) Most
020:048 that the **Chastisement** (awaits) those who
020:061 lest He destroy you (at once) utterly by **chastisement**:
020:127 and the **Chastisement** of the Hereafter
022:002 but dreadful will be the **Chastisement** of Allah.
022:004 to the **Chastisement** of the Fire.

CHASTISEMENT (continued)

022:009 make him taste the **chastisement** of burning (Fire).
022:018 the **chastisement** is justly due.
022:022 "Taste ye the **Chastisement** of Burning!"
022:025 We cause to taste of a most grievous **chastisement**.
022:055 the **Chastisement** of a barren day.
024:011 among them, will be a **Chastisement** grievous.
024:014 a grievous **chastisement** would have seized you
024:019 will have a grievous **Chastisement** in this life
024:023 for them is a grievous **Chastisement**-
024:063 or a grievous **Chastisement** be inflicted on them.
025:019 him shall We cause to taste of a grievous **Chastisement**.
025:037 (all) wrong-doers a grievous **Chastisement**:
025:042 when they see the **Chastisement**,
025:069 (But) the **Chastisement** on the Day of Judgment
026:135 the **Chastisement** of a Great Day."
026:138 to receive Pains and **Chastisement**!"
026:156 lest the **Chastisement** of a Great Day seize you."
026:158 But the **Chastisement** seized them.
026:189 and that was the **Chastisement** of a Great Day.
026:201 they see the grievous **Chastisement**
026:204 Do they then ask for Our **Chastisement** to be
027:005 a grievous **Chastisement** is (waiting):
028:064 and they will see the **Chastisement** (before them);
029:023 they who will (suffer) a most grievous **Chastisement**.
031:006 for such there will be a humiliating **Chastisement**.
031:007 announce to him a grievous **Chastisement**.
031:021 to the **Chastisement** of the (Blazing) Fire!
031:024 drive them to a **chastisement** unrelenting.
032:014 taste ye the **Chastisement** of Eternity for your
032:020 "Taste ye the **Chastisement** of the Fire,
032:021 the greater **Chastisement** in order that they may
032:021 of the lighter **Chastisement** before the greater
033:008 prepared for the Unbelievers a grievous **Chastisement**.
033:068 Double **Chastisement** and curse them with a very
034:005 for such will be a **Chastisement** of Painful wrath.
034:008 that are in (real) **Chastisement**, and in farthest Error.
034:012 of the **Chastisement** of the Blazing Fire.
034:014 in the humiliating **Chastisement** (of their Task).
034:033 When they see the **Chastisement**: We shall
034:038 will be given over into **Chastisement**.
034:042 "Taste ye the **Chastisement** of the Fire,-the which
034:046 in face of a terrible **Chastisement**."
035:007 For those who reject Allah, is a terrible **Chastisement**
035:010 lay Plots of Evil, for them is a **Chastisement** terrible;
035:036 nor shall its **Chastisement** be lightened for them.
037:009 is a perpetual **chastisement**,
037:033 (all) share in the **Chastisement**.
037:038 Ye shall indeed taste of the Grievous **Chastisement**;-
038:026 from the Path of Allah, is a **Chastisement** Grievous,
038:061 add to him a double **Chastisement** in the Fire!"
039:013 the **Chastisement** of a Mighty Day."
039:024 the brunt of the **Chastisement** on the Day of
039:040 "'Who it is to whom comes a **Chastisement** of ignominy,
039:040 and on whom descends a **Chastisement** that abides."
039:047 from the pain of the **Chastisement** on the
039:054 and submit to Him, before the **Chastisement** come on
039:055 before the **Chastisement** comes on you-of a
039:058 it should say when it (actually) sees the **Chastisement**:
039:071 but the Decree of **Chastisement** has been proved
040:007 and preserve them from the **Chastisement** of the
040:045 but the brunt of the **Chastisement** encompassed on
040:049 us the **Chastisement** for a Day (at least)!"

CHASTISEMENT (continued)

041:016   of a **Chastisement** of humiliation in this life;
041:017   of the **Chastisement** of humiliation seized them,
041:027   a taste of a severe **Chastisement**, and We
041:043   Forgiveness as well as a most Grievous **Chastisement**.
041:050   the taste of a severe **Chastisement**.
042:016   and for them will be a **Chastisement** Terrible.
042:021   the wrong-doers will have a grievous **Chastisement**.
042:026   but for the Unbelievers there is a terrible **Chastisement**.
042:042   for such there will be a **Chastisement** grievous.
042:044   when in sight of the **Chastisement**, say: "Is there
042:045   Truly the wrong-doers are in a lasting **Chastisement**!"
043:050   But when We removed the **Chastisement** from them,
043:065   from the **Chastisement** of a Grievous Day!
044:011   this will be a **Chastisement** Grievous.
044:012   remove the **Chastisement** from us for We
044:015   We shall indeed remove the **Chastisement** for a
044:048   the **Chastisement** of Boiling Water;
044:056   the **Chastisement** of the Blazing Fire,-
045:008   then announce to him a **Chastisement** Grievous!
045:009   for such there will be a humiliating **Chastisement**.
045:010   for them is a tremendous **Chastisement**.
045:011   is a grievous **Chastisement** of abomination.
046:020   with a **Chastisement** of humiliation:
046:021   the **Chastisement** of a Mighty Day."
046:024   a wind wherein is a Grievous **Chastisement**!
046:031   and deliver you from a **Chastisement** Grievous.
046:034   "Then taste ye the **Chastisement**, for that
048:016   He will punish you with a grievous **Chastisement**."
048:017   (Allah) will punish him with a grievous **Chastisement**.
050:026   throw him into a severe **Chastisement**."
051:037   as fear the Grievous **Chastisement**.
052:007   Verily, the **Chastisement** of thy Lord will indeed
052:018   them from the **Chastisement** of the Fire.
052:027   the **Chastisement** of the Scorching Wind.
054:016   But how (terrible) was My **Chastisement** and My
054:018   then how terrible was my **Chastisement** and My
054:021   Yea, how (terrible) was my **Chastisement** and my
054:030   Ah! how (terrible) was My **Chastisement** and My
054:038   an abiding **Chastisement** seized them:
054:039   "So taste ye My **Chastisement** and My Warning."
057:020   a **Chastisement** severe (for the devotees of wrong).
058:004   Reject (Him), there is a grievous **Chastisement**.
058:005   (will have) a humiliating **Chastisement**,
058:015   Allah has prepared for them severe **Chastisement**:
058:016   they have a humiliating **Chastisement**.
059:015   the Hereafter there is) for them a grievous **Chastisement**;-
061:010   save you from a grievous **Chastisement**?-
064:005   their conduct; and they had a grievous **Chastisement**.
065:008   and We chastised them with a horrible **Chastisement**.
067:005   the **Chastisement** of the Blazing Fire.
067:006   (and Cherisher) is the **Chastisement** of Hell:
067:028   deliver the Unbelievers from a grievous **Chastisement**?
070:001   A questioner asked about a **Chastisement** to befall-
070:011   from the **Chastisement** of that Day by his children,
071:001   before there comes to them a grievous **Chastisement**."
072:017   will cause him to undergo ever-growing **Chastisement**.
073:013   And Food that chokes, and a **Chastisement** Grievous.
076:031   He prepared a grievous **Chastisement**.
078:030   on increase shall We grant you, except in **Chastisement**.
078:040   of a **Chastisement** near,-the Day when man will see
084:024   So announce to them a **Chastisement** Grievous,
085:010   turn in repentance, will have the **Chastisement** of Hell:

CHASTISEMENT (continued)

085:010   will have the **Chastisement** of the of the Burning Fire.
088:024   Allah will chastise him with a mighty **Chastisement**.
089:025   For, that Day, His **Chastisement** will be such as

CHASTISEMENTS

089:013   a scourge of diverse **chastisements**:

CHASTISES

011:102   when He **chastises** communities in the midst of

CHASTITY

004:024   desiring **chastity**, not fornication.
005:005   and desire **chastity**, not lewdness.
021:091   And (remember) her who guarded her **chastity**:
024:033   desire **chastity**, in order that ye may make a gain
033:035   who guard their **chastity**,
066:012   who guarded her **chastity**;
070:029   And those who guard their **chastity**,

CHATTELS

003:185   is but goods and **chattels** of deception.
057:020   of this world, but goods and **chattels** of deception?

CHECK

002:251   And did not Allah **check** one set of people
022:040   Did not Allah **check** one set of people

CHEEK

031:018   "And swell not thy **cheek** (for pride) at men.

CHEER

004:005   take it and enjoy it with right good **cheer**.

CHERISH

002:235   Allah knows that ye **cherish** them in your hearts:
026:018   (Pharaoh) said: "Did we not **cherish** thee as a

CHERISHED

017:024   even as they **cherished** me in childhood."
020:063   and to do away with your most **cherished** way.

CHERISHER

001:002   the **Cherisher** and Sustainer of the Worlds:
002:131   to the Lord and **Cherisher** of the Universe."
003:079   Him (Who is truly the **Cherisher** of all)
005:028   for I do fear Allah, the **Cherisher** of the worlds.
006:045   Praise be to Allah, the **Cherisher** of the Worlds.
006:162   the **Cherisher** of the Worlds:
006:164   When He is the **Cherisher** of all things (that exist)?"
007:054   the **Cherisher** and Sustainer of the Worlds!
007:058   by the Will of its **Cherisher**, springs up
007:061   from the Lord and **Cherisher** of the Worlds!"
007:067   from the Lord and **Cherisher** of the Worlds!
010:010   the **Cherisher** and Sustainer of the Worlds!"
011:059   their Lord and **Cherisher**; disobeyed His
011:060   rejected their Lord and **Cherisher**! Away with
011:068   For the Thamud rejected their Lord and **Cherisher**!
018:042   to my Lord and **Cherisher**!"
021:092   Your Lord and **Cherisher**: therefore serve
023:052   and I am your Lord and **Cherisher**: therefore fear Me
026:016   by the Lord and **Cherisher** of all the Worlds;
026:023   and **Cherisher** of the Worlds?"
026:024   (Moses) said: "The Lord and **Cherisher** of the
026:077   not so the Lord and **Cherisher** of the Worlds;
029:059   and put their trust in their Lord and **Cherisher**.
037:126   and the Lord and **Cherisher** of your fathers of old?"
037:126   "Allah, your Lord and **Cherisher** and the
037:182   the Lord and **Cherisher** of the Worlds.
039:006   your Lord and **Cherisher**: to Him belongs
044:008   the Lord and **Cherisher** to you and your
045:036   Lord and **Cherisher** of all the worlds!
067:006   (and **Cherisher**) is the Chastisement of Hell:

CHERISHER (continued)
081:029   as Allah wills, The **Cherisher** of the Worlds.
096:001   of thy Lord and **Cherisher**, Who created-
098:008   all this for such as fear their Lord and **Cherisher**.
114:001   the Lord and **Cherisher** of Mankind,

CHERISHES
007:172   "Am I not Your Lord (who **cherishes** and sustains you)?"-

CHEST
020:039   "`Throw (the child) into the **chest**, and throw (the **chest**)

CHIEF
031:033   the **Chief** Deceiver deceive you about Allah.
035:005   let the **Chief** Deceiver deceive you about Allah.
043:031   in either of the two (**Chief**) cities?"

CHIEFS
002:246   thy vision to the **chiefs** of the Children of Israel after
007:103   with Our Signs to Pharaoh and his **chiefs**.
007:109   Said the **Chiefs** of the people of Pharaoh: "This
007:127   Said the **Chiefs** of Pharaoh's people: "Wilt
009:012   fight ye the **chiefs** of Unfaith:
010:075   and his **Chiefs** with Our Signs.
010:083   and his **Chiefs**, lest they should persecute them:
010:088   and his **Chiefs** splendor and wealth in the life
011:027   But the **Chiefs** of the Unbelievers among his
011:038   every time that the **Chiefs** of his People
011:097   Unto Pharaoh and his **Chiefs**: but they
012:043   O ye **Chiefs**! expound to me my vision if it be
023:024   The **Chiefs** of the Unbelievers among his people
023:033   And the **chiefs** of his people, who disbelieved
023:046   To Pharaoh and his **Chiefs**:
026:034   (Pharaoh) said to the **Chiefs** around him:
027:029   (The Queen) said: "Ye **Chiefs**! here is-
027:032   She said: "Ye **Chiefs**! advise me
027:038   He said (to his own men): "Ye **Chiefs**! which of
028:020   He said: "O Moses! the **Chiefs** are taking counsel
028:032   from thy Lord to Pharaoh and his **Chiefs**:
028:038   Pharaoh said: "O **Chiefs**! no god do I know
033:067   We obeyed our **chiefs** and our great ones, and they
038:069   Exalted **Chiefs**, when they discuss (matters)
043:046   with Our Signs, to Pharaoh and his **Chiefs**:

CHIEFTAINS
005:012   and We appointed twelve **chieftains** among them,

CHILD
002:233   treated unfairly on account of her **child**.
002:233   Nor father on account of his **child**,
003:036   I am delivered of a female **child**!"
004:012   their share is a fourth, if ye leave no **child**;
004:012   but if ye leave a **child**, they get an eighth;
004:012   but if they leave a **child**, ye get a fourth;
004:012   your share is a half, if they leave no **child**;
004:176   if (such deceased was) a woman, who left no **child**,
004:176   That dies, leaving a sister but no **child**,
007:189   (saying): "If Thou givest us a goodly **child**, we
007:190   But when He giveth them a goodly **child**, they
011:072   shall I bear a **child**, seeing I am an old woman,
016:058   of (the birth of) a female (**child**),
019:029   who is a **child** in the cradle?"
020:039   "`Throw (the **child**) into the chest, and throw
020:040   who will nurse and rear the (**child**)?'
026:018   as a **child** among us, and didst
028:007   mother of Moses: "Suckle (thy **child**), but when
040:067   then does He get you out (into the light) as a **child**:
046:015   The carrying of the (**child**) to his weaning is (a period of)
065:006   let another woman suckle (the **child**) on the (father's)

CHILDBIRTH
019:023   And the pains of **childbirth** drove her to the

CHILDHOOD
003:046   in **childhood** and in maturity.
005:110   to the people in **childhood** and in old age. Behold!
017:024   even as they cherished me in **childhood**."

CHILDREN
002:040   O **children** of Israel! call to mind
002:047   O **children** of Israel! call to mind
002:083   the **children** of Israel (to this effect):
002:122   O **Children** of Israel! call to mind
002:211   Ask the **Children** of Israel how many
002:246   Chiefs of the **Children** of Israel after (the time of) Moses
002:266   and his **children** are not strong
003:049   the **Children** of Israel, (with this message):
003:093   All food was lawful to the **Children** of Israel,
004:011   the inheritance to each, if the deceased left **children**;
004:011   if no **children**, and the parents are the (only) heirs,
004:011   or your **children** are nearest to you in benefit.
004:075   Men, women, and **children**, whose cry is: "Our Lord!
004:098   and **children** who have no means in their power,
004:127   the **children** who are weak and oppressed:
005:012   a Covenant from the **Children** of Israel, and We
005:032   We ordained for the **Children** of Israel that if
005:070   the **Children** of Israel and sent them Messengers.
005:072   "O **children** of Israel! worship Allah, my Lord
005:078   those among the **Children** of Israel who rejected
005:110   the **Children** of Israel from (violence to) thee
006:137   the slaughter of their **children**, in order
006:140   Lost are those who slay their **children**,
006:151   kill not your **children** on a plea of want;-
007:026   O ye **children** of Adam! We have bestowed
007:027   O ye **children** of Adam! Let not
007:031   O **children** of Adam! wear your
007:035   O ye **children** of Adam! whenever there come to you
007:105   so let the **children** of Israel depart along with me."
007:127   He said: "Their male **children** will we slay;
007:134   and we shall send away the **Children** of Israel with thee."
007:137   was fulfilled for the **Children** of Israel, because
007:138   We took the **Children** of Israel (with safety)
007:141   of punishment who slew your male **children** and
007:172   from the **children** of Adam-from their loins-
009:055   nor their **children** dazzle thee:
009:069   and more flourishing in wealth and **children**.
009:085   nor their **children** dazzle thee:
010:083   except some **children** of his People, because of
010:090   We took the **Children** of Israel across the sea:
010:090   the **Children** of Israel believe in:
010:093   We settled the **Children** of Israel in a
013:038   and appointed for them wives and **children**:
017:002   made it a Guide to the **Children** of Israel, (Commanding):
017:004   the **Children** of Israel in the Book, that twice
017:031   Kill not your **children** for fear of want:
017:064   mutually share with them wealth and **children**;
017:101   We did give Nine Clear Signs: ask the **Children** of Israel:
017:104   And We said thereafter to the **Children** of Israel, "Dwell
019:077   "I shall certainly be given wealth and **children**"?
020:047   send forth, therefore, the **Children** of Israel with us,
020:080   O ye **Children** of Israel! We delivered
020:094   Thou hast caused a division among the **Children** of Israel,
024:031   Or small **children** who have no carnal knowledge of
024:058   and the (**children**) among you who have not come
024:059   But when the **children** among you come of age,

CHILDREN (continued)

026:017 "'Send thou with us the **Children** of Israel.'"
026:022 that you hast enslaved the **Children** of Israel!"
026:059 the **Children** of Israel inheritors of such things.
026:197 the learned of the **Children** of Israel knew it
027:076 to the **Children** of Israel most of the matters
032:023 and We made it a guide to the **Children** of Israel.
036:060 "Did I not enjoin on you, O ye **children** of Adam,
037:152 "Allah has begotten **children**"?
040:053 in inheritance to the **Children** of Israel,-
042:049 He bestows (**children**) male or female according to
043:059 We made him an example to the **Children** of Israel.
044:030 We did deliver aforetime the **Children** of Israel
045:016 We did aforetime grant to the **Children** of Israel the Book,
046:010 and a witness from among the **Children** of Israel
057:020 (in rivalry) among yourselves, riches and **children**.
060:003 your relatives and your **children** on the Day
060:012 that they will not kill their **children**,
061:006 said: "O **Children** of Israel! I am the messenger
061:014 of the **Children** of Israel believed, and a
063:009 or your **children** divert you from the
064:014 among your wives and your **children** are (some
064:015 Your riches and your **children** may be but a trial:
070:011 from the Chastisement of that Day by his **children**,
071:021 whose wealth and **children** give them no Increase
073:017 a Day that will make **children** hoary-headed?-
080:036 And from his wife and his **children**.

CHILDREN'S

004:011 as regards your **children's** (inheritance):

CHILLY

035:021 Nor are the (**chilly**) shade and the (genial)

CHINS

036:008 right up to their **chins**, so that

CHOICE

004:003 marry women of your **choice**, two, or three, or four;
016:059 Ah! what an evil (**choice**) they decide on!
028:068 no **choice** have they (in the matter):
043:016 and granted to you sons for **choice**?

CHOKE

040:018 Hearts will (come) right up to the Throats to **choke** (them);

CHOKES

073:013 And Food that **chokes**, and a Chastisement Grievous.

CHOOSE

002:105 But Allah will **choose** for His special Mercy whom He
002:282 such as ye **choose**, for witnesses,
003:033 Allah did **choose** Adam and Noah,
012:006 "Thus will thy Lord **choose** thee and teach thee
028:068 Thy Lord does create and **choose** as He pleases:
037:153 Did He (then) **choose** daughters rather than sons?
068:038 That ye shall have, through it whatever ye **choose**?
068:050 Thus did his Lord **choose** him and make him

CHOOSES

003:179 but He **chooses** of his Messengers whom He pleases.
022:075 Allah **chooses** Messengers from angels and from
042:013 Allah **chooses** to Himself those whom He pleases,
074:037 To any of you that **chooses** to press forward, or to

CHOOSETH

003:074 specially **chooseth** whom He pleaseth:

CHOSE

002:130 Him We **chose** and rendered pure in this world:
002:253 but they (**chose**) to wrangle,
006:087 We **chose** them, and We guided them to a straight Way.
007:155 And Moses **chose** seventy of his people

CHOSE (continued)

007:169 but they **chose** (for themselves) the vanities
016:121 Who **chose** him, and guided him to a Straight Way.
019:058 of those whom We guided and **chose**.
020:122 But his Lord **chose** him (for His Grace):
038:046 Verily We did **chose** them for a special (purpose)-
044:032 We **chose** them aforetime above the nations, knowingly,

CHOSEN

002:132 "O my sons! Allah hath **chosen** the Faith for you;
002:247 He said: "Allah hath **chosen** him above you.
003:042 "O Mary! Allah hath **chosen** thee and purified thee
003:042 **chosen** thee above the women of all nations.
004:115 We shall leave him in the path he has **chosen**,
005:003 and have **chosen** for you Islam as your religion.
007:144 "O Moses! I have **chosen** thee above (other) men,
012:024 for he was one of Our servants **chosen**.
015:040 "Except Thy **chosen** servants among them,
019:051 for he was specially **chosen**.
020:013 "I have **chosen** thee: listen, then to the
022:078 He has **chosen** you, and has imposed no difficulties
024:055 their religion-the one which He has **chosen** for them
027:059 He has **chosen** (for his Message).
035:032 inheritance to such of Our servants as We have **chosen**:
037:040 But the **chosen** servants of Allah,-
037:074 Except the **chosen** servants of Allah.
037:128 Except the **chosen** Servants of Allah (among them).
037:160 Not (so do) the servants of Allah, the **chosen** ones.
039:004 He could have **chosen** whom He pleased
072:027 "Except an apostle whom He has **chosen**:

CHRIST

003:045 his name will be **Christ** Jesus, the son of Mary,
004:157 "We killed **Christ** Jesus the son of Mary,
004:171 **Christ** Jesus the son of Mary was (no more than)
004:172 **Christ** disdaineth not to serve and worship Allah,
005:017 those that say that Allah is **Christ** the son of Mary.
005:017 if His Will were to destroy **Christ** the son of Mary,
005:072 "Allah is **Christ** the son of Mary."
005:072 But said **Christ**: "O children of Israel!
005:075 **Christ** the son of Mary was no more than a Messenger;
009:030 and the Christians call **Christ** the Son of Allah.
009:031 And (they take as their Lord) **Christ** the son of Mary;

CHRISTIAN

002:111 Paradise unless he be a Jew or a **Christian**."
003:067 Abraham was not a Jew nor yet a **Christian**;

CHRISTIANS

002:062 and the **Christians** and the Sabians,
002:113 and the **Christians** say: "The Jews
002:113 "The **Christians** have naught (to stand) upon";
002:120 Never will the Jews or the **Christians**
002:135 They say: "Become Jews or **Christians**
002:140 and the Tribes were Jews or **Christians**?
005:014 From those, too, who call themselves **Christians**,
005:018 (Both) the Jews and the **Christians** say: "We are
005:051 and the **Christians** for your friends and protectors:
005:069 and the Sabians and the **Christians**,-any who
005:082 who say, "We are **Christians**:" because amongst
009:030 and the **Christians** call Christ the Son of Allah.
022:017 and the Sabians, **Christians**, Magians, and

CHURCHES

022:040 pulled down Monasteries, **churches**, synagogues,

CIRCUIT

059:007 make a **circuit** between the wealth among you.

CIRCULATE
024:019 scandal **circulate** among the Believers, will have

CIRCUMAMBULATE
022:029 and (again) **circumambulate** the Ancient House."

CIRCUMSTANCES
060:009 It is such as turn to them (in these **circumstances**),

CITIES
006:092 the Mother of **Cities** and all around her.
007:111 and send to the **cities** men to collect-
009:070 the men of Midian, and the **cities** overthrown.
011:082 Our decree issued, We turned (the **cities**) upside down,
015:074 And We turned (the **Cities**) upside down,
015:076 And the (**cities** were) right on the high-road.
026:036 and dispatch to the **Cities** heralds to collect-
026:053 Then Pharaoh sent heralds to (all) the **Cities**,
034:018 We had placed **Cities** in prominent positions,
034:018 Between them and the **Cities** on which We had
042:007 warn the Mother of **Cities** and all around her,
043:031 in either of the two (Chief) **cities**?"
047:013 And how many **cities**, with more power them the city
053:053 the Overthrown **Cities** (of Sodom and Gomorrah),
069:009 and the **Cities** Overthrown, committed habitual Sin,

CITY
002:126 make this a **City** of Peace,
003:167 or (at least) drive (the foe from your **city**)."
007:082 they said, "Drive them out of your **city**:
007:088 we shall certainly drive thee out of our **city**-(thee)
007:123 which ye have planned in the **city** to drive out its people:
012:030 Ladies said in the **City**: "The wife of the great
014:035 make this **city** one of peace and security:
015:067 The inhabitants of the **City** came in (mad)
016:112 a **city** enjoying security and quiet, abundantly supplied
027:048 There were in the **City** nine men, who made
027:056 from your **city**: these are indeed men who
027:091 the Lord of this **City**, Him Who has
028:015 And he entered the **City** at a time when its
028:018 In the morning, he was in the **city**, fearful and
028:020 from the furthest end of the **City**.
033:014 to them from the sides of the (**City**), and they
033:060 and those who stir up sedition in the **City**,
036:013 the (story of) the Companions of the **City**.
036:020 from the farthest part of the **City**, a man,
047:013 with more power than thy **city** which has driven
089:007 Of the (**city** of) Iram, with lofty pillars,
090:001 Nay I do swear by this **City**;-
090:002 And thou art an inhabitant of this **City**;-
095:003 And this **City** of Security,-

CLAD
010:024 (it grows) till the earth is **clad** with its golden

CLAIM
004:006 let him **claim** no remuneration,
004:015 to houses until death do **claim** them,
004:049 to those who **claim** purity for themselves?
005:107 nearest in kin from among those who **claim** a lawful right:
009:090 men who made excuses and came to **claim** exemption;
009:093 such as **claim** exemption while they are rich.
011:031 nor **claim** I to be an angel.
040:043 one who has no **claim** to be called to, whether in
056:087 if ye are true (in your **claim** of Independence)?
057:015 abode is the Fire: that is the proper place to **claim** you:

CLAIMS
090:015 To the orphan with **claims** of relationship,

CLAMOR
043:057 a **clamor** thereat (in ridicule)!

CLAMOUR
001:001 The (Day) of Noise and **Clamour**:
101:002 What is the (Day) of **Clamour**?
101:003 what the (Day) of Noise and **Clamour** is?
069:004 disbelieved in the day of Noise and **Clamour**!

CLAMOURING
051:029 But his wife came forward **clamouring**: she smote

CLANS
013:036 but there are among the **clans** those who reject a part

CLAPPING
008:035 is nothing but whistling and **clapping** of hands:

CLASS
015:044 is a (special) **class** (of sinners) assigned.

CLASSES
015:088 on certain **classes** of them, nor grieve over them:
056:007 And ye shall be sorted out into three **classes**.

CLAY
003:049 in that I make for you out of **clay**, as it were,
005:110 And behold! thou makest out of **clay**, as it were,
006:002 He it is Who created you from **clay**, and then
007:012 thou didst create me from fire and him from **clay**."
011:082 baked **clay**, spread, layer on layer,-
015:026 We created man from sounding **clay**, from mud moulded
015:028 "I am about to create man from sounding **clay**,
015:033 Whom Thou didst create sounding **clay**, from mud
015:074 on them brimstones hard as baked **clay**.
017:061 whom Thou didst create from **clay**?"
023:012 Man We did create from a quintessence (of **clay**);
028:038 O Haman! light me a (kiln to bake bricks) out of **clay**,
032:007 the creation of man from **clay**,
037:011 Them have We created out of a sticky **clay**!
038:071 "I am about to create man from **clay**:
038:076 and him Thou createdst from **clay**."
051:033 stones of **clay** (brimstone),
055:014 sounding **clay** like unto pottery.
105:004 Striking them with stones of baked **clay**.

CLEAN
002:222 who keep themselves pure and **clean**.
002:222 and do not approach them until they are **clean**.
004:043 then take for yourselves **clean** sand (or earth),
005:006 then take for yourselves **clean** sand or earth,
005:006 but to make you **clean**, and to complete his favour
007:032 and the things, **clean** and pure, (which He
007:058 From the land that is **clean** and good, by the
007:082 who want to be **clean** and pure!"
008:011 descend on you from heaven, to **clean** you therewith,
027:056 men who want to be **clean** and pure!"
056:079 Which none shall touch but those who are **clean**:
084:004 and becomes (**clean**) empty,

CLEAN-MOWN
010:024 and We make it like a harvest **clean-mown**,

CLEANSE
003:077 nor will He **cleanse** them (of sin):

CLEAR
002:087 We gave Jesus the son of Mary **clear** (Signs)
002:092 There came to you Moses with **clear** (Signs);
002:118 We have indeed made **clear** the Signs
002:159 **clear** for the People in the Book,
002:159 Those who conceal the **clear** (Signs)
002:166 are followed **clear** themselves of those who follow (them):
002:167 we would **clear** ourselves of them,

CLEAR (continued)

002:185	also **clear** (Signs) for guidance and judgment
002:187	Thus doth Allah make **clear** His Signs to men:
002:209	the **clear** (signs) have come to you,
002:211	how many **Clear** (Signs) We have sent them.
002:213	after the **clear** Signs came to them,
002:219	Thus doth Allah make **clear** to you His Signs:
002:221	and makes His Signs **clear** to mankind:
002:242	Thus doth Allah make **clear** His Signs to you:
002:253	to Jesus the son of Mary, We gave **Clear** (Signs),
002:253	after **Clear** (Signs) had come to them,
002:256	Truth stands out **clear** from Error;
002:266	Thus doth Allah make **clear** to you (His) Signs;
003:007	basic or fundamental **clear** (in meaning);
003:007	others are not entirely **clear**.
003:007	that is not entirely **clear**.
003:055	and **clear** thee (of the falsehoods)
003:086	and that **Clear** Signs had come unto them?
003:103	Thus doth Allah make His Signs **clear** to you:
003:105	and fall into disputation after receiving **Clear** Signs:
003:183	with **Clear** Signs and even with what ye ask for:
003:184	who came with **Clear** Signs, and the Scriptures.
003:187	to make it known and **clear** to mankind and not
004:026	Allah doth wish to make **clear** to you and
004:063	so keep **clear** of them but admonish them,
004:081	so keep **clear** of them, and put thy trust in Allah,
004:091	with a **clear** argument against them.
004:153	even after **Clear** Signs had come to them;
004:176	thus doth Allah make **clear** to you (His law),
005:002	But when ye are **clear** of the Sacred Precincts
005:019	making (things) **clear** unto you, Our Messenger,
005:032	Our Messengers with **Clear** Signs, yet, even after
005:075	makes His Signs **clear** to them;
005:089	Thus doth Allah make **clear** to you His Signs
005:110	show them the **Clear** Signs, and the unbelievers
006:057	"For me, I am on a **clear** Sign from my Lord,
006:059	a Record **Clear** (to those who can read).
006:105	We may make the matter **clear** to those who know.
006:157	then hath come unto you a **Clear** (Sign) from your Lord,-
007:073	Now hath come unto you a **clear** (Sign) from your Lord!
007:085	Now hath come unto you a **clear** (Sign) from your Lord!
007:101	came indeed to them their Messengers with **clear** (Signs);
007:105	from your Lord with a **clear** (Sign):
008:042	who lived might live after a **Clear** Sign (had been given).
008:042	who died might die after a **clear** Sign (had been given),
008:048	and said: "Lo! I am **clear** of you;
009:043	who told the truth were seen by thee in a **clear** light,
009:070	To them came their Messengers with **Clear** Signs.
009:113	after it is **clear** to them that they are
009:114	But when it became **clear** to him that he was
009:115	makes **clear** to them as to what they should avoid,
010:013	with **Clear** Signs, but they would not believe!
010:015	But when Our **Clear** Signs are rehearsed unto them,
010:061	are recorded in a **clear** Record.
010:074	they brought them **Clear** Signs, but they
011:006	all is in a **clear** Record.
011:017	a **Clear** (Sign) from their Lord, and followed
011:025	as a **clear** warner.
011:028	(it be that) I have a **Clear** Sign from my Lord
011:053	They said: "O Hud! no **Clear** (Sign) hast thou
011:063	If I have a **Clear** (Sign) from my Lord and He
011:088	I have a **Clear** (Sign) from my Lord, and He
011:096	And We sent Moses, with Our **Clear** (Signs) and an

CLEAR (continued)

012:096	and he forthwith regained **clear** sight.
014:004	in order to make (things) **clear** to them.
014:009	To them came messengers **Clear** (Signs);
014:010	then bring us some **clear** authority."
015:001	of a Qur'an that makes things **clear**.
016:035	but to preach the **Clear** Message?
016:044	(We sent them) with **Clear** Signs and Scriptures
016:064	so that thou shouldst make **clear** to them
016:082	thy duty is only to preach the **Clear** Message.
016:092	He will certainly make **clear** to you (the truth of) that
016:103	while this is Arabic, pure and **clear**.
017:101	To Moses We did give nine **Clear** Signs:
018:002	(He hath made it) Straight (and **Clear**) in order
018:015	an authority **clear** (and convincing) for what
018:022	except on a matter that is **clear**, nor consult
019:073	When Our **Clear** Signs are rehearsed to them,
020:072	what has come to us of **Clear** Signs Him Who created us!
020:133	Has not a **Clear** Sign come to them of all
022:016	Thus have We sent down **Clear** Signs; and verily
022:049	to give a **clear** warning:
022:072	When Our **Clear** Signs are rehearsed to them,
024:001	in it have We sent down **Clear** Signs, in order
024:034	verses making things **clear**, an illustration
024:054	is only to preach the **clear** (Message)".
024:058	thus does Allah make **clear** the Signs to you:
024:059	make **clear** His Signs to you:
024:061	make **clear** the Signs to you: that you
026:002	that makes (things) **clear**.
026:030	you something **clear** (and) convincing?"
027:001	a Book that makes (things) **clear**;
027:021	unless he bring me a **clear** reason (for absence)."
027:075	in heaven or earth, but is (recorded) in a **clear** record.
028:002	that makes (things) **clear**.
028:036	When Moses came to them with Our **Clear** Signs,
029:039	there came Moses with **Clear** Signs, but they behaved
029:050	and I am indeed a **clear** Warner."
030:009	there came to them their messengers with **Clear** (Signs),
030:047	and they came to them with **Clear** Signs:
034:043	When Our **Clear** Signs are rehearsed to them,
035:025	to whom came their messengers **Clear** Signs,
035:040	a Book from which they (can derive) **clear** (evidence)?-
036:012	In a **clear** Book (of evidence).
036:017	to deliver the **clear** Messenger."
036:069	and a Qur'an making things **clear**:
037:106	For this was a **clear** trial-
037:117	which helps to make things **clear**;
040:022	with **Clear** (Signs), but they rejected them:
040:028	with **Clear** (Signs) from your Lord?
040:034	gone by, with **Clear** Signs, but ye
040:050	there came Joseph in times gone by, **Clear** Signs?"
040:066	seeing that the **Clear** Signs have come to me
040:083	to them with **Clear** Signs, they exulted
043:002	By the Book that makes things **clear**,-
043:018	and unable to give a **clear** account in a dispute
043:026	"I do indeed **clear** myself of what ye worship:
043:029	and a Messenger making things **clear**.
043:063	with Wisdom, and in order to make **clear** to you
043:063	When Jesus came with **Clear** Signs, he said:
044:002	By the Book that makes things **clear**;-
045:017	And We granted them **clear** Signs in affairs
045:020	These are **clear** evidences to men, and a
045:025	And when Our **Clear** Signs are rehearsed to them,

CLEAR (continued)

046:007 When Our **Clear** Signs are rehearsed to them,
046:009 I am but a Warner open and **clear**."
047:014 Is then one who is on a **clear** (Path) from his Lord,
047:015 and rivers of honey pure and **clear**.
051:050 I am from Him a Warner to you, **clear** and open!
051:051 I am from Him a Warner to you, **clear** and open!
056:018 and cups (filled) out of **clear**-flowing fountains:
057:025 with **Clear** Signs and sent down with them the Book
058:005 for We have already sent down **Clear** Signs.
060:004 "We are **clear** of you and of whatever ye worship
061:006 But when he came to them with **Clear** Signs, they said,
064:006 to them messengers with **Clear** Signs, but they
065:011 to you the Signs of Allah containing **clear** explanations,
071:002 a Warner, **clear** and open:
075:019 to explain it (and make it **clear**):
081:023 And without doubt he saw him in the **clear** horizon.
098:001 come to them **Clear** Evidence,-
098:004 came to them **Clear** Evidence.

CLEAR-FLOWING

015:045 and fountains (of **clear-flowing** water).
037:045 from a **clear-flowing** fountain,
067:030 you with **clear-flowing** water?"

CLEARED

002:167 as they have **cleared** themselves of us."
033:069 but Allah **cleared** him of the (calumnies) they had

CLEAREST

005:095 (the Message) in the **clearest** manner.

CLEARLY

002:145 then wert thou indeed (**clearly**) in the wrong.
002:259 When this was shown **clearly** to him,
003:125 with five thousand angels **clearly** marked.
012:093 he will come to see (**clearly**).
014:045 ye were **clearly** shown how We dealt with them;
016:044 that thou mayest explain **clearly** to men
018:026 how **clearly** He sees, how finely He hears
023:062 before Us is a record which **clearly** speaks the truth.
029:018 is only to preach publicly (and **clearly**)."
029:038 **clearly** will appear to you from (the traces) of their
033:009 but Allah sees (**clearly**) all that ye do.
033:036 on a **clearly** wrong Path.
034:011 for be sure I see (**clearly**) all that ye do."
040:058 and those who (**clearly**) see:
041:040 seeth (**clearly**) all that ye do.
043:015 Truly is man **clearly** unthankful.
043:052 and can scarcely express himself **clearly**?
044:013 things **clearly** has (already) come to them,-
047:025 after Guidance was **clearly** shown to them,-
047:032 after Guidance has been **clearly** shown to them,
064:012 to deliver (the Message) **clearly** and openly.

CLEAVE

059:021 and **cleave** asunder for the fear of Allah,

CLEAVETH

006:096 He it is that **cleaveth** the daybreak

CLEFT

054:001 and the moon was **cleft** asunder.
073:018 Whereon the sky will be **cleft** asunder?
077:009 When the heaven is **cleft** asunder;
082:001 When the Sky is **cleft** asunder;

CLIENT

044:041 The day when no protector can avail his **client** in aught,

CLIMB

006:125 as if they had to **climb** up to the skies:

CLIMB (continued)

052:038 by which they can (**climb** up to heaven and) listen

CLIMBED

038:021 they **climbed** over the wall of the private chamber;

CLIMBING

003:153 Behold! ye were **climbing** up the high ground,

CLING

009:038 ye **cling** heavily to the earth?

CLOSE

002:186 I am indeed **close** (to them):
006:125 He maketh their breast **close** and constricted,
007:163 the town standing **close** by the sea.
013:031 or to settle **close** to their homes, until the
020:022 Now draw thy hand **close** to thy side:
020:084 He replied: "Behold, they are **close** on my footsteps:
027:072 hasten on may be (**close**) in your pursuit!
028:032 and draw thy hand **close** to thy side
030:003 In a land **close** by: but they, (even) after
042:017 the Hour is **close** at hand?
048:026 and made them stick **close** to the command
067:027 At length, when they see it **close** at hand,

CLOSE-COMPOUNDED

006:099 **close-compounded** grain out of the date-palm and its

CLOSED

002:267 receive it except with **closed** eyes.
017:020 are not **closed** (to anyone).

CLOSELY

037:049 As if they were (delicate) eggs **closely** guarded.

CLOSER

018:024 ever **closer** (even) than this to the right course."
018:081 in purity (of conduct) and **closer** in affection.
021:001 **Closer** and **closer** to mankind comes their Reckoning:
033:006 The Prophet is **closer** to the Believers than their own
033:006 Blood-relations among each other have **closer** personal
053:008 Then he approached and came **closer**,
096:019 and bring thyself the **closer** (to Allah)!

CLOSEST

033:006 nevertheless do ye what is just to your **closest** friends:

CLOSING

016:112 and terror (in extremes) (**closing** in on it) like

CLOT

022:005 then out of a leech-like **clot**,
023:014 a **clot** of congealed blood;
023:014 then of that **clot** We made a (foetus) lump;
040:067 then from a leech-like **clot**;
075:038 Then did he become a leech-like **clot**;
096:002 Created man, out of a leech-like **clot**:

CLOTHE

002:259 and **clothe** them with flesh."
003:071 Why do ye **clothe** truth with falsehood,
004:005 but feed and **clothe** them therewith, and speak
005:089 or **clothe** them; or give a slave his freedom.

CLOTHED

022:063 and forthwith the earth becomes **clothed** with green?
023:014 of that lump bones and **clothed** the bones

CLOTHES

024:058 the while ye doff your **clothes** for the

CLOTHING

002:233 of their food and **clothing** on equitable terms.

CLOUD

002:019 is that of a rain-laden **cloud** from the sky:
046:024 they said, "This **cloud** will give us rain!"
046:024 Then, when they saw a **cloud** advancing towards

CLOUD (continued)
056:069 Do ye bring it Down (in rain) from the **Cloud**, or do We?

CLOUDS
002:057 And We gave You the shade of **clouds**
002:164 and the **clouds** which they trail
002:210 Allah comes to them in canopies of **clouds**,
007:057 when they have carried the heavy-laden **clouds**.
007:160 We gave them the shade of **clouds**, and sent
013:012 the **clouds**, heavy with (fertilizing) rain!
024:040 topped by (dark) **clouds**:
024:043 mountain masses (of **clouds**) wherein is hail:
024:043 the **clouds** move gently, then joins
025:025 rent asunder with **clouds**, and angels
027:088 but they shall pass away as the **clouds** pass away:
030:048 and they raise the **Clouds**:
031:032 When a wave covers them like the canopy (of **clouds**),
035:009 so that they raise up the **Clouds**, and We
052:044 they would (only) say: "**Clouds** gathered in heaps!"
078:014 And do We not send down from the **clouds** water in
100:004 And raise the dust in **clouds** the while,

CLOVE
021:030 before We **clove** them asunder?

CLOVEN
013:031 or the earth were **cloven** asunder, or the dead

CLUSTERS
006:099 (come) **clusters** of dates hanging low and near:

COATS
016:081 and **coats** of mail to protect you from your
021:080 the making of **coats** of mail for your benefit,
034:011 (Commanding), "Make thou **coats** of mail,

COIN
003:075 others, who, if entrusted with a single silver **coin**,

COLD
038:057 a fluid dark, murky, intensely **cold**!-
076:013 (excessive heat) nor excessive **cold**.
078:025 dark, murky, intensely **cold**,-

COLLAR
003:180 tied to their necks like a twisted **collar**,

COLLAR-BONE
075:026 when (the soul) reaches to the **collar-bone** (in its exit),

COLLEAGUES
019:005 "Now I fear (what) my relatives (and **colleagues**)

COLLECT
004:140 For Allah will **collect** the Hypocrites and those
007:111 and send to the cities men to **collect**-
018:099 and We shall **collect** them all together.
026:036 and dispatch to the Cities heralds to **collect**-
070:018 And **collect** (wealth) and hide it (from use)!
075:017 It is for Us to **collect** it and to recite it:
077:011 are (all) appointed a time (to **collect**);-

COLLECTED
028:078 in amount (of riches) they had **collected**?
079:023 Then he **collected** (his men) and made a proclamation,

COLLECTIVE
024:062 a matter requiring **collective** action, they do

COLOUR
002:069 to make plain to us her **colour**."
035:027 and red, of various shades of **colour**, and black
055:064 Dark green in **colour** (from plentiful watering).
074:029 Darkening and changing the **colour** of man!

COLOURED
002:069 He said: "He says, a fawn-**coloured** heifer,

COLOURS
016:013 which He has multiplied in **colours** (and qualities);
016:069 issues from within their bodies a drink of varying **colours**,
030:022 and the variations on your languages and your **colours**:
035:027 With it We then bring out produce of various **colours**.
035:028 and beasts and cattle, are they of various **colours**.
039:021 He causes to grow therewith, produce of various **colours**:

COLUMNS
077:030 (of smoke ascending) in three **columns**,
104:009 In **columns** outstretched.

COMBAT
003:013 a Sign in the two armies that met (in **combat**):

COME
002:085 and if they **come** to you as captives,
002:105 That anything good should **come** down to you from
002:114 and in the world to **come**,
002:209 the clear (signs) have **come** to you,
002:211 after Allah's favour has **come** to him,
002:214 "When (will **come**) the help of Allah"
002:248 shall **come** to you the Ark of the Covenant,
002:253 after Clear (Signs) had **come** to them,
002:260 they will **come** to thee (flying) with speed.
003:019 after knowledge had **come** to them.
003:049 I have **come** to you, with a Sign from your Lord,
003:050 "(I have **come** to you), to attest the Torah
003:050 I have **come** to you with a Sign from your Lord.
003:061 now after (full) knowledge hath **come** to thee,
003:061 say: "**Come**! let us gather together,
003:064 **come** to common terms as between us and you:
003:086 and that Clear Signs had **come** unto them?
003:111 if they **come** out to fight you, they will show
003:167 these were told: "**Come**, fight in the way of Allah
004:060 that have **come** to thee and to those before thee?
004:061 "**Come** to what Allah hath revealed.
004:062 Then they **come** to thee, swearing by Allah:
004:064 **come** unto thee and asked Allah's forgiveness,
004:078 But what hath **come** to these people.
004:102 And let the other party **come** up which hath
004:129 If ye **come** to a friendly understanding,
004:153 even after Clear Signs had **come** to them;
004:170 O mankind! the Messengers hath **come** to you
004:174 Verily there hath **come** to you a convincing proof from
005:015 There hath **come** to you from Allah a (new)
005:015 there hath **come** to you Our Messenger, revealing
005:019 now hath **come** unto you, making (things) clear
005:019 but now hath **come** unto you a bringer
005:041 who have never so much as **come** to thee.
005:042 If they do **come** to thee, either judge
005:043 But why do they **come** to thee for decision,
005:046 confirming the Torah that had **come** before him:
005:046 And confirmation of the Torah that had **come** before him:
005:048 diverging from the truth that hath **come** to thee.
005:059 that hath **come** to us and that which came before (us),
005:061 When they **come** to thee, they say: "We believe":
005:068 that has **come** to you from your Lord."
005:084 which has **come** to us, seeing that we long for
005:104 "**Come** to what Allah hath revealed; **come** to the
005:105 no hurt can **come** to you from those who stray.
006:005 but soon shall **come** to them the news
006:025 in so much that when they **come** to thee,
006:040 if there **come** upon you the Punishment of Allah,
006:054 When those **come** to thee who believe
006:071 his friends calling '**Come** to us', (vainly)

COME (continued)

006:080   He said: "(**Come**) ye to dispute with me, about

006:094   "And behold! ye **come** to Us bare and alone

006:099   (or spathes) (**come**) clusters of dates

006:104   "Now have **come** to you, from your Lord

006:122   from which he can never **come** out?

006:134   unto you will **come** to pass:

006:151   Say: "**Come**, I will rehearse what Allah hath (really)

006:151   **come** not nigh to indecent deeds,

006:152   And **come** not nigh to the orphan's property,

006:157   Now then hath **come** unto you a Clear (Sign)

006:158   are they waiting to see if the angels **come** to them,

006:158   The day that certain of the Signs of thy Lord do **come**,

007:035   Whenever there **come** to you messengers from amongst

007:063   "Do ye wonder that there hath **come** to you a reminder

007:069   hath **come** to you a message from your Lord

007:071   have already **come** upon you from your Lord:

007:073   Now hath **come** unto you a clear

007:073   and let her **come** to no harm, or ye shall

007:085   Now hath **come** unto you a clear

007:105   Now have I **come** unto you (people), from your

007:106   "If indeed thou hast **come** with a Sign,

007:163   their fish did **come** to them, openly

007:187   Only, all of a sudden, will it **come** to you."

008:019   now hath the judgment **come** to you:

009:042   have **come** out with you," they would destroy their

009:046   If they had intended to **come** out, they would

009:047   If they had **come** out with you, they would

009:054   that they **come** not to prayer save lazily and that

009:083   and they ask thy permission to **come** out (with thee),

009:083   say: "Never shall ye **come** out with me, nor fight

009:128   Now hath **come** unto you a Messenger

010:015   the Chastisement of a Great Day (to **come**)."

010:022   and the waves **come** to them from all sides, and they

010:048   They say: "When will this promise **come** to pass-

010:050   should **come** to you by night or by day,-

010:057   O mankind! there hath **come** to you

010:076   When the Truth did **come** to them from Us, they said:

010:078   They said: "Hast thou **come** to us to turn us

010:092   a Sign to those who **come** after thee!

010:094   the Truth hath indeed **come** to thee from thy Lord:

011:012   an angel **come** down with Him?

011:025   "I have **come** to you as a clear warner.

011:048   The word came: "O Noah! **come** down (from the Ark)

011:088   (in my task) can only **come** from Allah.

012:023   and she fastened the doors, and said: "Now **come**,"

012:023   Truly to no good **come** those who do wrong!"

012:031   and she said (to Joseph), "**Come** out before them."

012:048   "Then will **come** after that (period) seven

012:049   "Then will **come** after that (period) a year

012:060   nor shall ye (even) **come** near me."

012:062   in order that they might **come** back.

012:093   he will **come** to see (clearly).

012:093   Then **come** ye (here) to me together with

012:100   Allah hath made it **come** true! He was

012:110   (of their people) and (**come** to) think that they

013:006   the evil is preference to good yet have **come** to pass,

013:031   until the promise of Allah **come** to pass,

014:017   death will **come** to him from every quarter,

015:057   the business on which ye (Have **come**), O ye

015:063   They said: "Yea, we have **come** to thee

015:064   "We have **come** to thee with the Truth and assuredly

015:096   but soon will they **come** to know.

COME (continued)

015:099   until there **come** unto thee the Hour that is Certain.

016:033   the angels to **come** to them, or there

016:111   On the Day every soul will **come** up pleading

017:032   Nor **come** nigh to adultery:

017:034   **Come** not nigh to the orphan's property,

018:020   "For if thy should **come** upon you, they would

018:036   do I deem that the Hour (of Judgment) will (ever) **come**:

018:048   "Now have ye **come** to Us (bare) as We created you first:

018:055   now that guidance has **come** to them,

018:064   on their footsteps, following (the path they had **come**).

018:110   (but) the inspiration has **come** to me, that your

019:018   (**come** not near) if thou dost fear Allah."

019:043   "O my father! to me hath **come** knowledge which

019:061   for His promise must (necessarily) **come** to pass.

019:093   and the earth but must **come** to The Most Gracious

019:095   And every one of them will **come** to him singly

020:022   it shall **come** forth white (and shining),

020:040   Then didst thou **come** hither as ordained, O Moses!

020:047   indeed, have we **come** from thy Lord!

020:057   He said: "Hast thou **come** to drive us out

020:072   to what has **come** to us of the Clear Signs

020:129   (their punishment) must necessarily have **come**;

020:133   Has not a Clear Sign **come** to them of all

021:038   "When will this promise **come** to pass, if ye are telling

021:040   Nay, it may **come** to them all of a sudden

021:098   To it will ye (surely) **come**!

021:108   Say: "What has **come** to me by inspiration

022:007   And verily the Hour will **come**: there can

022:027   they will **come** to thee on foot and (mounted)

022:032   such (honour) should **come** truly from piety of heart.

023:068   has anything (new) **come** to them that did not **come** to

023:098   O my Lord! lest they should **come** near me."

024:011   to every man among them (will **come** the punishment)

024:048   behold, some of them decline (to **come**).

024:049   they **come** to him with all submission.

024:058   ask your permission (before they **come** to your presence),

024:058   (children) among you who have not **come** of age ask your

024:059   But when the children among you **come** of age, let them

025:011   Nay, then deny the Hour (of the Judgment to **come**):

025:029   from the Message (of Allah) after it had **come** to me!

025:077   and soon will **come** the inevitable (punishment)!"

026:202   But the (Penalty) will **come** to them of a sudden,

027:012   and it will **come** forth white without stain

027:022   and I have **come** to thee from Saba

027:031   but **come** to me in submission (to the true Religion).' "

027:037   we shall **come** to them with such hosts as they

027:038   before they **come** to me in submission?"

027:071   They also say "When will this promise (**come** to pass)?

027:084   Until, when they **come** (before the Judgment-Seat),

027:087   and all shall **come** to Him in utter humility.

028:032   and it will **come** forth white without stain

028:046   no warner had **come** before thee:

028:048   But (now), when the Truth has **come** to them

029:046   which has **come** down to us and in that

029:053   the Punishment would certainly have **come** to them:

030:012   On the Day that the Hour will **come**, the guilty

030:014   On the Day that the Hour will **come**, that Day

030:025   behold, ye (straightway) **come** forth.

030:043   the right Religion, before there **come** from Allah

032:003   to whom no warner has **come** before thee:

032:013   but the Word from Me will **come** true, "I Will

033:018   to their brethren, "**Come** along to us,"

COME (continued)

033:018	but **come** not to the fight except for just
033:020	the Confederates should **come** (again), they would
033:028	then **come**! I will provide for your enjoyment and set
034:003	"Never to us will **come** the Hour": say, "Nay!
034:003	it will **come** upon you;-by Him Who knows the unseen,
034:006	And those to whom knowledge has **come** see that the
034:029	"When will this promise (**come** to pass) if ye are telling
036:048	this promise (**come** to pass), if what
037:028	to **come** to us from the right hand."
037:037	Nay! he has **come** with the (very) Truth,
037:078	for him among generations to **come** in later times:
037:108	for him among generations (to **come**) in later times:
037:119	for him among generations (to **come**) in later times:
037:129	for him among generations (to **come**) in later times:
037:170	But (now that the Qur'an has **come**), they reject
038:004	So they wonder that a Warner has **come** to them
039:040	"Who it is to whom **come**s a Chastisement
039:071	"Did not messengers **come** to you from among
040:016	The day whereon they will (all) **come** forth:
040:018	will (**come**) right up to the Throats to choke
040:028	when he has indeed **come** to you with Clear (Signs)
040:034	not to doubt of the (mission) for which he had **come**:
040:050	"Did there not **come** to you your messengers with Clear
040:059	The Hour will certainly **come**:
040:066	seeing that the Clear Signs have **come** to me
041:011	"**Come** ye together, willingly or unwillingly."
041:011	"We do **come** (together), in willing obedience."
042:047	before there **come** a Day which there will be
043:029	until the Truth has **come** to them, and a Messenger
043:053	or (why) **come** (not) with him angels accompanying
043:063	he said: "Now have I **come** to you with Wisdom,
043:066	that it should **come** on them all of a sudden,
044:013	things clearly has (already) **come** to them,-
044:019	for I **come** to you with authority manifest.
046:022	They said: "Hast thou **come** in order to turn
046:023	"The Knowledge (of when it will **come**) is only with
047:018	that it should **come** on them of a sudden?
047:018	But already have **come** some tokens thereof,
049:005	until thou couldst **come** out to them, it would
050:002	But they wonder that there has **come** to them
050:021	And there will **come** forth every soul:
050:030	It will say, "Are there any more (to **come**)?"
051:006	will surely **come** to pass.
052:007	will indeed **come** to pass;-
053:023	Even though there has already **come** to them
053:040	will soon **come** in sight;
054:004	There have already **come** to them such tidings
054:007	They will **come** forth,-their eyes humbled-from
055:022	Out of them **come** Pearls and Coral:
058:008	And when they **come** to thee, they salute thee,
060:001	If ye have **come** out to strive in My Way and seek
060:001	the truth that has **come** to you, and have
060:010	(on their dowers of women who came over to you).
060:010	O ye who believe! when there **come** to you
060:012	O Prophet! when believing women **come** to thee
061:006	glad Tidings of a messenger to **come** after me,
063:001	When the Hypocrites **come** to thee, they say,
063:005	"**Come**, the Messenger of Allah will pray for your
063:010	before Death should **come** to any of you and he
063:011	grant respite when the time appointed (for it) has **come**;
067:004	(thy) vision will **come** back to thee dull
067:008	its Keepers will ask, "Did no Warner **come** to you?"

COME (continued)

067:009	a Warner did **come** to us, but we
069:015	On that Day shall the (Great) Event **come** to pass,
076:014	will **come** low over them, and the bunches
077:007	Assuredly, what ye are promised must **come** to pass.
078:004	Verily, they shall soon (**come** to) know!
078:005	Verily, verily they shall soon (**come** to) know!
078:018	and ye shall **come** forth in crowds;
084:005	(then will **come** Home the full Reality).
089:028	"**Come** back thou to thy Lord,-well pleased
097:004	Therein **come** down the angels and the Spirit
098:001	until there should **come** to them Clear Evidence,-
107:001	Seest thou one who denies the Judgment (to **come**)?

COMES

002:038	there **comes** to you guidance from Me,
002:087	Is it that whenever there **comes** to you an Messenger
002:089	And when there **comes** to them a Book
002:089	when there **comes** to them that which they (should) have
002:210	Allah **comes** to them in canopies of clouds,
002:254	before the Day **comes** when no bargaining
003:037	He said: "O Mary! whence (**comes**) this to you?"
003:060	the truth (**comes**) from thy Lord alone;
003:081	then **comes** to you an Messenger, confirming
004:073	But if good fortune **comes** to you from Allah,
004:083	When there **comes** to them some matter
006:047	if the Punishment of Allah **comes** to you,
006:124	When there **comes** to them a Sign
009:086	When a Sura **comes** down, enjoining them to believe
010:022	then **comes** a stormy wind and the waves
010:047	when their Messenger **comes** (before them),
012:037	He said: "Before any food **comes** (in due course)
012:038	that (**comes**) of the grace of Allah to us and to
016:033	or there **comes** the Command of thy Lord
018:044	There, the (only) protection **comes** from Allah,
018:098	but when the promise of my Lord **comes** to pass,
020:074	Verily he who **comes** to his Lord as a sinner
020:075	But such as **comes** to Him as Believers who have
020:123	as is sure, there **comes** to you guidance from Me,
021:001	Closer and closer to mankind **comes** their Reckoning:
021:002	Never **comes** (aught) to them of a renewed Message
022:011	but if a trial **comes** to them, they turn
022:055	until the Hour (of Judgment) **comes** suddenly upon them,
022:055	or there **comes** to them the Chastisement of a barren day.
023:027	then when **comes** Our command, and the
023:099	Until, when death **comes** to one of them, he says:
024:039	mistakes for water; until when he **comes** up to it,
026:005	But there **comes** not to them a newly-revealed
026:206	Yet there **comes** to them at length the (Punishment)
028:037	who it is that **comes** with guidance from Him
029:010	And if help **comes** (to thee) from thy Lord,
033:002	But follow that which **comes** to thee by inspiration
033:019	Then when fear **comes**, thou wilt
034:002	that goes into the earth and all that **comes** out thereof;
034:002	all that **comes** down from the sky and all that ascends
034:043	And the Unbelievers say of Truth when it **comes** to them,
036:030	There **comes** not a messenger to them
036:046	Not a Sign **comes** to them from among
038:015	mighty Blast, which (when it **comes**) will brook
039:032	and rejects the Truth when it **comes** to him!
039:054	before the Chastisement **comes** on you:
039:055	before the Chastisement **comes** on you-of a
040:046	when the Hour **comes** to pass:
041:040	or he that **comes** safe through, on the

COMES (continued)

041:041 Those who reject the Message when it **comes** to them
041:047 no fruit **comes** out of its sheath, nor does
041:051 (he **comes**) full of prolonged prayer!
043:038 At length, when (such a one) **comes** to Us, he says
046:007 of the Truth when it **comes** to them:
047:018 and when it **comes** to them, how shall they have their
049:006 if a sinner **comes** to you with any news,
050:005 But they deny the truth when it **comes** to them:
050:019 And the stupor of death **comes** in truth.
057:004 what **comes** down from heaven and what mounts up to it.
057:004 within the earth and what **comes** forth out of it,
071:001 thy People before there **comes** to them
079:034 Therefore, when there **comes** the great,
080:033 At length, when there **comes** the Deafening Noise,-
110:001 When **comes** the Help of Allah, and Victory,

COMEST

007:070 They said: "**Comest** thou to us, that we
007:129 both before and after thou **comest** to us."

COMET

015:018 a fiery **comet**, bright (to see).

COMETH

002:118 Or why **cometh** not Us a Sign?"
004:043 you **cometh** from the privy, or ye have been
005:006 or one of you **cometh** from the privy or ye have
005:064 But the revelation that **cometh** to thee from Allah
005:068 that **cometh** to thee from thy Lord,
008:024 and know that Allah **cometh** in between
009:124 Whenever there **cometh** down a Sura, some of
009:127 Whenever there **cometh** down a Sura, they look
010:051 when it actually **cometh** to pass?
011:076 for them there **cometh** a Chastisement that cannot
011:120 in them there **cometh** to thee the Truth, as well
016:001 (Inevitable) **cometh** (to pass) the Command
056:001 When the Event Inevitable **cometh** to pass,
089:022 And thy Lord **cometh**, and His angels,

COMFORT

009:038 But little is the **comfort** of this life, as compared
013:026 is but little **comfort** compared to the Hereafter.
018:016 of your affair towards **comfort** and ease."
025:074 and offspring who will be the **comfort** of our
056:073 and an article of **comfort** and convenience for the

COMFORTABLE

074:014 To whom I made (life) smooth and **comfortable**!

COMFORTED

028:013 that her eye might be **comforted**, that she

COMING

004:165 after (the **coming**) of the messengers,
007:097 feel secure against the **coming** of Our wrath
007:098 against its **coming** in broad daylight while they
012:107 Or of the **coming** against them of the (final)
012:107 the **coming** against them of the covering veil
014:031 secretly and openly, before the **coming** of a Day
015:085 the Hour is surely **coming** (when this will be manifest).
017:083 become remote on his side (instead of **coming** to Us),
019:037 of the (**coming**) Judgment of an awful Day!
020:015 "Verily the Hour is **coming**-I have almost
020:086 Did then the promise seem to you long (in **coming**)?
021:012 when they felt Our Punishment (**coming**), behold, they
029:005 the Term (appointed) by Allah is surely **coming**:
031:033 and fear (the **coming** of) a Day when no father
041:051 himself remote on his side (instead of **coming** to Us);
043:061 And (Jesus) shall be a Sign (for the **coming** of) the Hour

COMING (continued)

045:032 there was no doubt about its (**coming**), ye used
056:002 Then will no (soul) deny its **coming**.
060:011 (by the **coming** over of a woman from the other side).

COMMAND

002:059 infringed (Our **command**) repeatedly.
002:109 till Allah brings about His **command**;
004:058 Allah doth **command** you to render back your trusts
005:001 for Allah doth **command** according to His
005:043 Therein is the (plain) **command** of Allah;
005:117 except what Thou didst **command** me to say, to wit,
006:057 The **Command** rests with none but Allah:
006:062 surely His is the **Command**, and He
006:151 thus doth He **command** you, that ye may learn wisdom.
006:152 thus doth He **command** you, that ye may remember.
006:153 thus doth He **command** you, that ye may be righteous.
007:054 His are the creation and the **Command**,
007:054 (all) are subservient by His **Command**.
007:199 Hold to forgiveness; **command** what is right;
009:097 of the **command** which Allah hath sent down
009:106 for the **command** of Allah, whether He will
010:024 there reaches it Our **command** by night or by day,
011:040 At length, behold! there came Our **Command**,
011:043 nothing can save, from the **Command** of Allah,
011:059 and followed the **command** of every powerful,
011:087 Does thy prayer **command** thee that we leave off
011:097 but they followed the **command** of Pharaoh,
011:097 and the **command** of Pharaoh was no rightly (guide).
012:040 the **Command** is for none but Allah: He hath
012:067 none can **command** except Allah:
013:011 they guard him by **command** of Allah.
013:031 But, truly, the **Command** is with Allah
013:041 there is none to put back His **command**:
014:005 We sent Moses with Our Signs (and the **command**).
014:032 that they may sail through the sea by His **Command**;
016:001 (Inevitable) cometh (to pass) the **Command** of Allah:
016:002 with inspiration of His **Command**, to such
016:012 and the Stars are in subjection by His **Command**:
016:033 or there comes the **Command** of thy Lord
016:036 (with the **Command**), "Serve Allah and eschew Evil":
017:016 We **command** those among them who are given
017:085 Say: "The Spirit is of the **command** of my Lord
018:026 nor does He share His **Command** with any
018:050 and he broke the **Command** of his Lord.
018:088 as We order it by our **command**."
019:012 (To his son came the **command**): "O Yahya!
019:064 but by **command** of thy Lord: to Him belongeth
020:090 so follow me and obey my **command**."
021:027 and they act (in all things) by His **command**.
021:073 guiding (men) by Our **Command**, and We
022:065 sail through the sea by His **command**?
023:027 then when comes Our **command**, and the
024:021 he will (but) **command** what is indecent and wrong:
024:053 if only thou wouldst **command** them,
027:033 so consider what thou wilt **command**."
027:033 but the **command** is with thee;
028:070 for Him is the **Command**, and to Him shall ye (all) be
028:088 To Him belongs the **Command**, and to Him
030:004 with Allah is the **Command** in the Past and in
030:025 thta heaven and earth stand by His **command**:
030:046 that the ships may sail by His **Command** and that
031:014 (hear the **Command**), "Show gratitude to Me and to thy
032:024 Leaders, giving guidance under Our **command**, so long

COMMAND (continued)

033:037   And Allah's **command** must be fulfilled.
033:038   And the **command** of Allah is a decree determined.
034:012   from Our **command**, We made him taste of the
036:082   His **command** is, "Be," and it is!
040:012   The **Command** is with Allah,
040:015   by His **Command** doth He send the spirit
040:078   but when the **Command** of Allah issued, the matter
041:012   to each heaven its duty and **command**.
041:043   surely thy Lord has at His **command** (all) Forgiveness
042:052   by Our **command**, sent inspiration to thee:
043:032   so that some may **command** work from others.
044:005   By **command**, from Us. For We
045:012   it by His **command**, that ye may seek of His Bounty,
045:016   the Power of **Command**, and Prophethood;
046:025   by the **command** of its Lord!"
048:026   to the **command** of self-restraint; and well
049:009   it complies with the **command** of Allah;
051:044   But they insolently defied the **command** of their
052:048   Now await in patience the **command** of thy Lord:
054:050   And Our **Command** is but a single Word,-like the
057:014   until there issued the **Command** of Allah.
060:010   Such is the **command** of Allah: He judges
065:005   That is the **Command** of Allah, which He
065:008   insolently opposed the **command** of their Lord
065:012   through the midst of them (all) descends His **Command**:
068:048   So wait with patience for the **command** of thy Lord,
069:030   (The stern **command** will say): "Seize ye him,
071:001   (with the **Command**): "Do thou warn thy People
076:024   to the **Command** of thy Lord, and obey
082:019   for the **Command**, that Day, will be
083:023   On raised couches will they **command** a sight
083:035   On raised couches they will **command** (a sight)
084:002   And hearkens to (the **Command** of) its Lord,-and it
084:005   And hearkens to (the **Command** of) its Lord,-and it

COMMANDED

002:068   now do what ye are **commanded**!"
002:246   But when they were **commanded** to fight,
002:246   if ye were **commanded** to fight,
004:154   and (once again) We **commanded** them: "Transgress
006:014   Say: "Nay! but I am **commanded** to be the first
006:163   No partner hath He: this am I **commanded**, and
007:012   thee from prostrating when I **commanded** thee?"
007:028   and "Allah **commanded** us thus": say: "Nay
007:029   Say: "My Lord hath **commanded** justice; and that
009:031   yet they were **commanded** to worship but One God:
010:072   and I have been **commanded** to be of those who
010:104   I am **commanded** to be (in the ranks) of the Believers;
011:112   stand firm (in the straight path) as thou art **commanded**,
012:040   He hath **commanded** that ye worship none but Him:
013:021   things which Allah hath **commanded** to be joined,
013:025   those things which Allah has **commanded** to be
013:036   Say: "I am **commanded** to worship Allah, and not
013:038   bring a Sign except as Allah Permitted (or **commanded**).
015:094   Therefore expound openly what thou art **commanded**,
016:050   all that they are **commanded**.
025:036   And We **commanded**: "Go ye both, to the
027:091   For me, I have been **commanded** to serve the Lord
027:091   and I am **commanded** to be of those who bow
034:023   will they say, 'What is it that your Lord **commanded**?'
037:102   "O my father! do as thou art **commanded**:
039:011   Say: "Verily, I am **commanded** to serve Allah
039:012   "And I am **commanded** to be the first of those

COMMANDED (continued)

040:066   and I have been **commanded** to submit (in Islam)
042:015   and I am **commanded** to judge justly
042:015   and stand steadfast as thou art **commanded**,
047:004   Thus (are ye **commanded**):
057:027   (We **commanded**) only the seeking for the Good
066:006   but do (precisely) what they are **commanded**.
080:023   what Allah Hath **commanded** him.
098:005   And they have been **commanded** no more than this:

COMMANDEST

025:060   Shall we adore that which thou **commandest** us?"

COMMANDING

017:002   Children of Israel, (**Commanding**): "Take not other
034:011   (**Commanding**), "Make thou coats of mail,

COMMANDMENTS

053:037   And of Abraham who fulfilled his (**commandments**)

COMMANDS

002:067   "Allah **commands** that ye sacrifice a heifer.
002:124   was tried by his lord with certain **Commands**,
002:169   For he **commands** you what is evil and shameful,
005:049   And this (He **commands**): Judge thou between them
007:028   say: "Nay Allah never **commands** what is Indecent:
007:157   for he **commands** them what is just and forbids
013:041   (Where) Allah **commands**, there is none to put
016:076   who **commands** justice, and is on the Straight Way?
016:090   Allah **commands** justice, the doing of good,
058:005   Those who oppose (the **commands** of) Allah and His
058:020   Those who oppose (the **commands** of) Allah and
066:006   not (from executing) the **Commands** they receive
079:005   Then arrange to do (the **commands** of their Lord),-

COMMEMORATE

038:041   **Commemorate** Our servant Job, behold he
038:045   And **commemorate** Our Servants Abraham, Isaac,
038:048   And **commemorate** Isma'il, Elisha, and Zul-Kifl:

COMMEMORATED

022:040   is **commemorated** in abundant measure.

COMMEMORATION

021:084   and a thing for **commemoration**, for all who serve Us.
038:043   and a thing for **commemoration**, for all

COMMEND

003:036   and I **commend** her and her offspring to Thy
057:024   and **commend** covetousness to men.

COMMERCE

009:024   the **commerce** in which ye fear a decline:
035:029   a **Commerce** that will never fail:

COMMERCIAL

002:282   whenever ye make a **commercial** contract;

COMMISSION

028:044   when We decreed the **commission** to Moses, nor wast

COMMIT

004:025   if they **commit** indecency their punishment is
004:171   People of the Book! **commit** no excesses in your religion:
005:032   continued to **commit** excesses in the land.
005:087   made lawful for you, but **commit** no excess:
007:028   When they **commit** an indecency, they say: "We
007:080   "Do ye **commit** lewdness such as no people
011:085   **commit** not evil in the land with intent to do mischief.
020:081   but **commit** no excess therein, lest My Wrath
025:068   except for just cause, not **commit** fornication;-
029:028   "Ye do **commit** lewdness, such as no people in Creation
029:036   nor **commit** evil on the earth, with intent
038:023   '**Commit** her to my care,' and he
040:044   My (own) affair I **commit** to Allah:

COMMIT (continued)
060:012 that they will not **commit** adultery (or fornication),

COMMITTED
005:079 the iniquities which they **committed**:
007:080 no people in creation (ever) **committed** before you?
012:081 thy son **committed** theft! we bear witness
018:059 when they **committed** iniquities;
029:007 We blot out all misdeeds that they have **committed**,
029:028 as no people in Creation (ever) **committed** before you.
069:009 and the Cities Overthrown, **committed** habitual Sin,

COMMON
003:064 come to **common** terms as between us and you:
006:116 the **common** run of those on earth, they will
018:052 a place of **common** perdition.
056:060 We have decreed Death to be your **common** lot,

COMMOTION
052:009 will be in dreadful **commotion**.
073:014 will be in violent **commotion**.
079:006 that can be in **commotion** will be in violent **commotion**,

COMMOTIONS
079:007 Followed by oft-repeated (**commotions**):

COMMUNICATED
017:085 a little that is **communicated** to you, (O men!)"

COMMUNITIES
006:038 but (forms part of) **communities** like you.
011:100 of **communities** which We relate unto thee:
011:102 when He chastises **communities** in the midst of

COMMUNITY
009:016 and the (**community** of) Believers?
043:033 might become of one **community** We would provide,

COMPANION
004:036 the **Companion** by your side, the way-farer (ye meet),
007:184 Their **Companion** is not seized with madness:
009:040 and he said to his **companion**, "Have no fear,
018:034 he said to his **companion**, in the course
018:037 His **companion** said to him, in the course
022:013 is the patron, and evil the **companion** (for help)!
034:046 your **Companion** is not possessed:
037:051 "I had an intimate **companion** (on the earth),
043:036 to be an intimate **companion** to him.
043:038 he says (to his evil-**companion**): 'Would that
043:038 Ah! Evil is the **companion** (indeed)!
050:023 And his **companion** will say: "Here is
050:027 His **companion** will say: "Our Lord!
053:002 Your **Companion** is neither astray nor being misled,
054:029 But they called to their **companion**, and he
068:048 the **Companion** of the Fish,-when he
081:022 And (O people!) your **Companion** is not one possessed;

COMPANIONS
002:039 they shall be **Companions** of the Fire;
002:081 they are **Companions** of the Fire,
002:082 they are **companions** of the Garden,
002:119 be asked of **Companions** of the blazing fire.
002:217 they will be **Companions** of the Fire
002:257 They will be **Companions** of the fire,
002:275 (the offense) are Companion of the Fire:
003:116 they will be **companions** of the Fire,
005:010 will be **Companions** of Hell-fire.
005:029 for thou wilt be among the **companions** of the Fire,
005:086 they shall be **Companions** of Hell-fire.
007:036 they are **Companions** of the Fire, to dwell
007:042 they will be **Companions** of the Garden, therein
007:044 will call out to the **Companions** of the Fire: "We

COMPANIONS (continued)
007:044 The **Companions** of the Garden will call out
007:046 to the **Companions** of the Garden, "Peace be
007:047 turned towards the **Companions** of the Fire, they
007:050 will call to the **Companions** of the Garden: "Pour
007:050 The **Companions** of the Fire will call
009:113 that they are **companions** of the Fire.
010:026 They are **Companions** of the Garden; they will
011:023 they will be **Companions** of the Garden, to dwell
012:039 "O my two **companions** of the prison! (I ask you):
012:041 "O my two **companions** of the prison! As to
013:005 they will be **Companions** of the Fire, to dwell
015:078 And the **Companions** of the Wood
015:080 The **Companions** of the Rocky Tract
018:009 the **Companions** of the Cave and of the
022:044 And the **Companions** of the Madyan people;
022:051 they will be **Companions** of the Fire."
025:024 The **Companions** of the Garden will be well,
025:038 and the **Companions** of the Rass, and many
026:176 The **Companions** of the Wood rejected the
029:015 But We saved him and the **Companions** of the Ark,
035:006 that they may become **Companions** of the Blazing Fire.
036:013 the (story of) the **Companions** of the City,
036:055 Verily the **Companions** of the Garden shall that Day
038:013 and the **Companions**! of the Wood;-such were
038:052 restraining their glances, (**companions**) of equal age.
039:008 of the **Companions** of the Fire!"
040:006 that truly they are **Companions** of Fire!
040:043 will be **Companions** of the Fire!
041:025 intimate **companions** (of like nature), who made
046:014 Such shall be **Companions** of the Garden,
046:016 (they shall be) among the **Companions** of the Garden:
050:012 the **Companions** of the Rass, the Thamud,
050:014 The **Companions** of the Wood, and the
056:008 what will be the **Companions** of the Right Hand?
056:008 Then (there will be) the **Companions** of the Right Hand;-
056:009 what will be the **Companions** of the Left Hand?
056:009 And the **Companions** of the Left Hand,-
056:022 And (there will be) **Companions** with beautiful,
056:027 The **Companions** of the Right Hand,-
056:027 what will be the **Companions** of the Right Hand!
056:038 For the **Companions** of the Right Hand.
056:041 what will be the **Companions** of the Left Hand!
056:041 The **Companions** of the Left Hand,-
056:090 And if he be of the **Companions** of the Right Hand,
056:091 from the **Companions** of the Right Hand.
057:019 Our Signs,-they are the **Companions** of Hell-Fire.
058:017 they will be **Companions** of the Fire,
059:020 and the **Companions** of the Garden:
059:020 it is the **Companions** of the Garden, that will
059:020 Not equal are the **Companions** of the Fire and the
064:010 they will be **Companions** of the Fire, to dwell
067:010 be among the **Companions** of the Blazing Fire!"
067:011 are the **Companions** of the Blazing Fire!
074:039 Except the **Companions** of the Right Hand.
090:018 Such are the **Companions** of the Right Hand.
090:019 they are the (unhappy) **Companions** of the Left Hand.
105:001 with the **Companions** of the Elephant?

COMPANY
003:039 of the (goodly) **company** of the righteous."
003:045 and (of the **company**) of those nearest to Allah;
003:046 (of the **company**) of the righteous."
003:193 in the **company** of the righteous.

COMPANY (continued)
004:069 are in the **Company** of those on whom is the Grace
005:084 to admit us to the **company** of the righteous?"
006:014 and be not thou of the **company** of those who joins
006:056 the **company** of those who receive guidance."
006:068 sit not thou in the **company** of those who do wrong.
007:038 He will say: "Enter ye in the **company** of the
007:047 send us not to the **company** of the wrong-doers."
008:062 (the **company** of) the Believers,
008:075 in your **company**,-they are of you.
012:032 and (what is more) be in the **company** of the vilest!"
018:076 keep me not in thy **company**:
024:061 whether ye eat in **company** or separately.
028:087 and be not of the **company** of these who joins gods
029:009 to the **company** of the Righteous.
031:015 yet bear them **company** in this life with justice
038:047 of the **company** of the Elect and the Good.
038:048 of the **company** of the Good.
046:029 Behold, We turned towards thee a **company** of Jinns
068:050 and make him of the **company** of the Righteous.
072:001 a **company** of Jinns listened (to the Qur'an).

COMPARED
009:038 as **compared** with the Hereafter.
011:024 may be **compared** to the blind and deaf, and those
011:024 Are they equal when **compared**? Will ye
013:026 is but little comfort **compared** to the Hereafter.
047:015 be **compared** to such as shall dwell for ever

COMPARISON
039:029 are those two equal in **comparison**?

COMPARISONS
025:009 See what kinds of **companions** they make for thee!
036:078 And he makes **comparisons** for Us, and forgets

COMPASS
002:125 My House for those who **compass** it round,
002:158 in the Season or at times should **compass** them round,
002:255 Nor shall they **compass** aught of his knowledge
004:108 and Allah doth **compass** round all that they do.
010:039 falsehood that whose knowledge they cannot **compass**,
011:084 that will **compass** (you) all round.
022:026 for those who **compass** it round, or stand up,

COMPASSED
027:022 "I have **compassed** which thou hast not **compassed**,
048:021 but which Allah has **compassed**:

COMPASSETH
003:120 for Allah **compasseth** round about all that they do.
008:047 for Allah **compasseth** all that they do.

COMPASSION
024:002 let not **compassion** move you in their case,
057:027 of those who followed him **Compassion** and Mercy.
090:017 of kindness and **compassion**.

COMPASSIONATE
011:075 forbearing (of faults), **compassionate**, and given
048:029 (but) **compassionate** amongst each other.

COMPEL
010:099 Wilt thou then **compel** mankind, against their
011:028 Shall we **compel** you to accept it when ye
020:073 and the magic to which thou didst **compel** us:
050:045 and thou art not one to **compel** them by force.

COMPELLING
037:019 Then it will be a single (**compelling**) cry;
079:013 a single (**compelling**) Cry.

COMPELS
024:033 But if anyone **compels** them, yet, after

COMPENSATE
002:178 and **compensate** him with handsome gratitude.

COMPENSATION
002:048 nor shall **compensation** be taken from her.
002:123 nor shall **compensation** be accepted from her
002:196 (he should) in **compensation** either fast,
005:095 the **compensation** is an offering, brought to

COMPLAIN
012:086 He said: "I only **complain** of my distraction

COMPLAINT
009:091 no ground (of **complaint**) can there be against
009:093 The ground (of **complaint**) is only against such as
058:001 her **complaint** (in prayer) to Allah:

COMPLAISANT
033:032 be not too **complaisant** of speech, lest one

COMPLETE
002:150 and that I may **complete** My favours on you,
002:185 (He wants you) to **complete** the prescribed period,
002:187 then **complete** your fast till the night appears;
002:196 And **complete** the Hajj or 'Umra
002:233 for him who desires to **complete** the term.
005:006 and to **complete** His favour to you, that ye
016:081 Thus does He **complete** his favours on you,
022:029 "Then let them **complete** the rites prescribed
028:027 for eight years, but if thou **complete** ten years,
053:041 Then will he be rewarded with a reward **complete**;
061:008 but Allah will **complete** His Light,
089:027 "O (thou) soul, in (**complete**) rest and satisfaction!
092:021 And soon will they attain (**complete**) satisfaction.

COMPLETED
005:003 **completed** my favour upon you,
007:142 and **completed** (the period) with ten (more):
007:142 thus was **completed** the term with his Lord, forty
020:114 the Qur'an before its revelation to thee is **completed**,
021:104 the heavens like a scroll rolled up for books (**completed**);-
041:012 So He **completed** them as seven firmaments in two

COMPLETELY
011:008 and they will be **completely** encircled by that which
017:005 and it was a warning (**completely**) fulfilled.
018:091 We **completely** understood what was before him.
020:078 **completely** overwhelmed them and covered them up.
039:048 be (**completely**) encircled by that which they
045:033 and they will be **completely** encircled by that
046:026 and they were (**completely**) encircled by that which they

COMPLETING
002:196 but if ye are prevented (from **completing** it),
006:154 gave Moses the Book, **completing** (Our favour) to those

COMPLIES
049:009 transgresses until it **complies** with the command of Allah;
049:009 but if it **complies**, then make peace between them with

COMPREHEND
020:110 but they shall **comprehend** Him not.

COMPREHENDED
027:084 though ye **comprehended** them not in knowledge,

COMPREHENDETH
006:080 my Lord **comprehendeth** in His knowledge all things.

COMPREHENDS
007:089 Our Lord **comprehends** all things in His
020:098 all things He **comprehends** in His Knowledge.
065:012 and that Allah **comprehends** all things

COMPULSION
002:256 Let there be no **compulsion** in religion.
006:119 except under **compulsion** of necessity?

COMPULSION (continued)

016:106 except under **compulsion**, his heart remaining firm
024:033 yet, after such **compulsion**, is Allah

COMPUTED

055:005 follow courses (exactly) **computed**;

COMRADES

096:017 to his council (of **comrades**):

CONCEAL

002:033 and I know what ye reveal and what ye **conceal**?"
002:042 nor **conceal** the Truth when ye know
002:077 what they **conceal** and what they reveal?
002:140 those who **conceal** the testimony
002:146 but some of them **conceal** the truth
002:159 Those who **conceal** the clear (Signs)
002:174 Those who **conceal** Allah's revelations in the Book,
002:271 even so it is well, but if ye **conceal** them,
002:283 **Conceal** not evidence; for whoever conceals it,
002:284 Whether ye show what is in your minds or **conceal** it,
003:071 and **conceal** the Truth, while you have knowledge?
003:118 what their hearts **conceal** is far worse.
003:167 But Allah hath full knowledge of all they **conceal**.
004:149 or **conceal** it or cover evil with pardon, surely
005:099 but Allah knoweth all that ye reveal and ye **conceal**.
006:091 while ye **conceal** much (of its contents):
011:005 He knoweth what they **conceal**, and what
013:010 any of you **conceal** his speech or declare it openly;
014:038 what we **conceal** and what we reveal:
016:019 And Allah doth know what ye **conceal**, and what
016:023 Allah doth know what they **conceal**, and what they
021:003 The wrong-doers **conceal** their private counsels,
024:029 of what ye reveal and what ye **conceal**.
028:069 their hearts **conceal** and all that they reveal.
033:054 Whether ye reveal anything or **conceal** it, verily Allah
040:019 and all that hearts (of men) **conceal**.
060:001 for I know full well all that ye **conceal** and all that ye
064:004 what ye **conceal** and what ye reveal:

CONCEALED

006:028 will become manifest what before they **concealed**.
012:019 So they **concealed** him as a treasure!
040:028 from the people of Pharaoh, who had **concealed** his faith,
041:005 "Our hearts are under veils, (**concealed**) from that to

CONCEALMENT

009:057 or caves, or a place of **concealment**, they would

CONCEALS

002:283 **Conceal** not evidence; for whoever **conceals** it,
091:004 By the Night as it **conceals** it;
092:001 By the Night as it **conceals** (the light);

CONCEIT

025:021 an arrogant **conceit** of themselves, and mighty
075:033 Then did he stalk to his family in full **conceit**!

CONCEIVE

041:047 nor does a female **conceive** (within her womb)

CONCEIVED

011:070 and **conceived** a fear of them.
019:022 So she **conceived** him, and she retired with him
020:067 So Moses **conceived** in his mind a (sort of) fear.
048:012 in your hearts, and ye **conceived** an evil thought,
051:028 He **conceived** a fear of them.

CONCEIVES

035:011 And no female **conceives**, or lays down

CONCERN

025:077 "My Lord would not **concern** Himself with you
080:037 will have enough **concern** (of his own) to make

CONCERNED

002:182 settlement among (the parties **concerned**),
006:152 even if a near relative is **concerned**;
028:038 but as far I am **concerned**, I think
070:043 Wherein art thou (**concerned**) with the

CONCERNING

002:186 When My servants ask thee **concerning** Me,
002:189 They ask thee **concerning** the New Moons.
002:213 to the Truth, **concerning** that wherein they differed.
002:217 They ask thee **concerning** fighting in the Prohibited
002:219 They ask thee **concerning** wine and gambling.
002:220 They ask thee **concerning** orphans.
002:222 They ask thee **concerning** women's courses.
002:228 women shall wait **concerning** themselves for three
002:234 they shall wait **concerning** themselves four months and
004:127 as also **concerning** the children who are weak and
004:127 They ask thy instruction **concerning** the Women.
004:127 **concerning** the orphaned women to whom ye give not
007:163 Ask them **concerning** the town standing by the sea.
007:172 and made them testify **concerning** themselves, (saying):
008:001 They ask thee **concerning** (things taken as)
008:006 Disputing with thee **concerning** the truth
009:094 the true state of matters **concerning** you: it is
011:110 is suspicious doubt **concerning** it.
016:027 "Where are My 'partners' **concerning** whom ye used
017:085 They ask thee **concerning** the Spirit. Say: "The
018:022 into controversies **concerning** them, except on
018:070 anything until I myself speak to thee **concerning** it."
018:083 They ask thee **concerning** Zul-Qarnain. Say, "I
020:105 They ask thee **concerning** the mountains: say, "My
022:055 to be in doubt **concerning** (Revelation) until the
022:069 on the Day of Judgment **concerning** the matter
033:063 Men ask thee **concerning** the Hour: say, "The
034:021 from him who is in doubt **concerning** it:
037:162 Can lead (any) into temptation **concerning** Allah,
038:008 But they are in doubt **concerning** My (own)
039:032 one who utters a lie **concerning** Allah and rejects
040:016 not a single thing **concerning** them is hidden from Allah.
040:069 dispute **concerning** the signs of Allah?
041:023 which ye did entertain **concerning** your Lord,
041:054 doubt **concerning** the Meeting with their Lord?
042:014 are in suspicious (disquieting) doubt **concerning** it.
042:016 But those who dispute **concerning** Allah after He
042:018 dispute **concerning** the Hour are far astray.
053:012 with him **concerning** what he saw?
058:001 the woman who pleads with thee **concerning** her husband
073:015 (O men!) a Messenger, to be a witness **concerning** you,
075:016 Move not thy tongue **concerning** the (Qur'an)
078:001 **Concerning** what are they disputing?
078:002 **Concerning** the Great News,

CONCERT

020:064 "Therefore **concert** your plan, and then

CONCERTED

012:102 when they **concerted** their plans together in the
020:060 So Pharaoh withdrew: he **concerted** his plan,

CONCESSION

002:178 This is a **concession** and a Mercy from your Lord.

CONCILIATION

004:062 "We meant no more than good-will and **conciliation**!"
004:114 or goodness or **conciliation** between people

CONCLUDED

009:111 then rejoice in the bargain which ye have **concluded**:

CONCOCT
012:005　lest they **concoct** a plot against thee:
CONDEMN
002:286　(Pray:) "Our Lord! **Condemn** us not if we
CONDITION
013:011　never will Allah change the **condition** of a people until
020:021　We shall return it at once to its former **condition**"...
020:051　"What then is the **condition** of previous generations?"
028:027　on **condition** that thou serve me for eight years,
047:002　from them their ills and improve their **condition**.
047:005　Soon will He guide them and improve their **condition**,
CONDITIONS
002:196　and when ye are in peaceful **conditions** (again),
CONDUCIVE
058:012　and most **conducive** to purity (of conduct).
CONDUCT
002:044　Do ye enjoin right **conduct** on the people,
002:197　but the best of provisions is right **conduct**.
002:268　and bids you to **conduct** unseemly.
005:039　and amend his **conduct**, Allah turneth
006:054　and amended (his **conduct**), lo! He is
007:146　and if they see the way of right **conduct**, they
011:007　which of you is best in **conduct**.
011:046　for his **conduct** is unrighteous.
018:007　as to which of them are best in **conduct**.
018:081　in purity (of **conduct**) and closer in affection.
021:051　bestowed aforetime on Abraham his rectitude of **conduct**,
024:005　and mend (their **conduct**):
024:017　that ye may never repeat such (**conduct**), if ye
031:017　firmness (of purpose) in (the **conduct** of) affairs.
033:030　if any of you were guilty of evident unseemly **conduct**,
033:071　That He may make your **conduct** whole and sound
035:008　to whom the evil of his **conduct** is made alluring,
040:035　very hateful (is such **conduct**) in the sight of Allah
042:038　who (**conduct**) their affairs by mutual Consultation;
047:014　to whom the evil of his **conduct** seems pleasing,
058:012　and most conducive to purity (of **conduct**).
059:015　they have tasted the evil result of their **conduct**;
064:005　So they have tasted the evil result their **conduct**;
065:009　Then did they taste the evil result of their **conduct**,
065:009　and the End of their **conduct** was Perdition.
072:010　to guide them to right **conduct**.
072:014　they have sought out (the path) of right **conduct**:
072:021　or to bring you to right **conduct**."
CONFEDERATE
033:022　the **Confederate** forces, they said: "This is what Allah
CONFEDERATES
033:020　the **Confederates** should come (again), they would
033:020　They think that the **Confederates** have not
038:011　They are but a host of **confederates** and they
038:013　such were the **Confederates**.
040:005　of Noah, and the **Confederates** after them;
040:030　(of disaster) of the **Confederates** (in sin)!-
CONFER
003:164　Allah did **confer** a great favour on the Believers
008:017　in order the He might **confer** on the Believers
CONFERENCE
012:080　they held a **conference** in private.
CONFERRED
004:054　and **conferred** upon them a great kingdom.
004:094　till Allah **conferred** on you His favours:
017:070　and **conferred** on them special favours, above a
019:007　that name have We **conferred** distinction before."

CONFERRED (continued)
020:037　"And indeed We **conferred** a favour on thee
049:017　Nay, Allah has **conferred** a favour upon you
CONFESS
067:011　They will then **confess** their sins:
CONFIDENCE
066:003　in **confidence** to one of his consorts, and she
CONFINE
004:015　and if they testify, **confine** them to houses
CONFIRM
013:039　Allah doth blot out or **confirm** what He pleaseth:
022:052　and Allah will **confirm** (and establish) His Signs:
028:034　to **confirm** (and strengthen) me:
CONFIRMATION
002:097　a **confirmation** of what went before,
005:046　And **confirmation** of the Torah that had
010:037　a **confirmation** of (revelations) that went before
012:111　but a **confirmation** of what went before it,-
CONFIRMED
007:118　Thus truth was **confirmed**. And all that
016:091　and break not your oaths after ye have **confirmed** them;
066:003　he **confirmed** part thereof and passed over a part.
CONFIRMING
002:041　**confirming** the revelation which is with you,
002:089　**confirming** what is with them,
002:091　even if it be Truth **confirming** what is with them.
002:101　**confirming** what was with them,
003:003　**confirming** what went before it;
003:039　**confirming** the truth of a Word from Allah,
003:081　**confirming** what is with you;
004:047　**confirming** what was (already) with you,
005:046　**confirming** the Torah that had come before him:
005:048　**confirming** the scripture that came before it,
006:092　and **confirming** (the revelations) which cam before it
035:031　**confirming** what was (revealed) before it:
046:030　after Moses, **confirming** what came before it:
061:006　to you **confirming** the Taurat (which came)
CONFIRMS
037:037　and he **confirms** (the Message of) the messengers
039:033　and he who **confirms** (and supports) it-such are
046:012　and this Book **confirms** it in the Arabic tongue;
CONFOUND
021:040　come to them all of a sudden and **confound** them:
CONFOUNDED
002:258　Thus was he **confounded** who (in arrogance)
021:065　Then were they **confounded** with shame: (they said),
CONFRONT
039:047　but something will **confront** them from Allah,
039:048　For the evils of their Deeds will **confront** them,
CONFRONTED
003:030　be **confronted** with all the good it has done,
CONFUSED
012:044　They said: "A **confused** medley of dreams:
023:054　But leave them in their **confused** ignorance for a time.
023:063　But their hearts are in **confused** ignorance of this;
050:005　so they are in a **confused** state.
050:015　they should be in **confused** doubt about a new Creation?
CONFUSION
006:009　they have already covered with **confusion**.
006:009　caused them **confusion** in a matter which they have
006:065　or to cover you with **confusion** in party strife,
006:110　We (too) shall turn to (**confusion**) their hearts
006:137　and cause **confusion** in their religion.

CONFUSION (continued)
051:011 in a flood of **confusion:**
CONGEALED
023:014 a clot of **congealed** blood;
CONJECTURE
002:078 and they do nothing but **conjecture.**
004:157 But only **conjecture** to follow, for of a surety
006:116 They follow nothing but **conjecture:**
006:148 Ye follow nothing but **conjecture:**
010:036 But most of them follow nothing but **conjecture:**
010:036 truly **conjecture** can be of no avail against Truth.
010:066 They follow nothing but **conjecture**, and they
045:024 of that they have no knowledge: they merely **conjecture:**
045:032 know not what is the Hour: we only think it a **conjecture,**
053:023 They follow nothings but **conjecture** and what
053:028 They follow nothing but **conjecture;**
053:028 and **conjecture** avails nothing against Truth.
CONJECTURERS
051:010 Cursed be the **conjecturers.**
034:053 and that they cast (**conjectures**) with regard
CONNECTED
007:131 to evil omens **connected** with Moses and those with Him!
CONNOTING
049:011 is a name **connoting** wickedness,
CONQUER
037:173 And that Our forces,-they surely must **conquer.**
CONSCIOUS
071:013 that ye are not **conscious** of Allah's majesty,-
CONSECUTIVELY
058:004 two months **consecutively** before they touch each
CONSENT
002:150 and ye may (**consent** to) be guided.
002:233 by mutual **consent**, and after due consultation.
CONSEQUENCE
009:077 So He hath put as a **consequence** hypocrisy into
CONSEQUENCES
007:123 but soon shall ye know (the **consequences**).
016:094 evil (**consequences**) of having hindered (men) from
029:012 and we will bear (the **consequences**) of your
091:015 And for Him is no fear of its **consequences.**
CONSIDER
002:219 clear to you His Signs: in order that ye may **consider-**
002:266 clear to you (His) Signs; that ye may **consider.**
006:050 Will ye then **consider** not?
009:019 Do ye **consider** the giving of drink to pilgrims,
010:072 "But if ye turn back, (**consider**): no reward
013:003 in these things are Signs for those who **consider!**
017:101 "O Moses! I **consider** thee, indeed, to have
017:102 and I **consider** thee, indeed, O Pharaoh,
022:005 (**consider**) that We created you out of dust,
027:033 so **consider** what thou wilt command."
CONSIDERATION
011:092 of more **consideration** with you than Allah? For ye
031:015 company in this life with justice (and **consideration**),
CONSIDERED
007:137 We made a people, **considered** weak (and of no account),
012:042 to that one whom he **considered** about to be saved,
CONSIGNED
002:085 they shall be **consigned** to the most grievous chastisement
CONSISTENT
039:023 of a Book, **consistent** with itself, (yet) repeating
CONSONANT
019:092 For it is not **consonant** with the majesty

CONSORT
006:101 when He hath no **consort**?
CONSORTS
033:028 O Prophet! say to thy **Consorts:** "If it be that ye desire
033:030 O **Consorts** of the Prophet! if any of you were
033:032 O **Consorts** of the Prophet! ye are not like any
066:001 thou seekest to please thy **consorts**?
066:003 in confidence to one of his **consorts**, and she
066:005 in exchange **Consorts** better than you,-who submit
CONSTANCY
002:250 they prayed: "Our Lord! Pour out **constancy** on us
003:200 Persevere in patience and **constancy:**
006:034 with patience and **constancy** they bore their
007:126 Our Lord! pour out on us patience and **constancy,**
007:128 and (wait) in patience and **constancy:**
007:137 because they had patience and **constancy**, and We
011:011 Not so do those who show patience and **constancy,**
021:085 and Zul-kifl, all (men) of **constancy** and patience;
023:111 for their patience and **constancy:**
025:075 place in heaven, because of their patient **constancy;**
031:017 and bear with patient **constancy** whatever betide
038:044 Truly We found him full of patience and **constancy.**
076:024 Therefore be patient with **constancy** to the Command
090:017 and enjoin patience, (**constancy**, and self-restraint),
103:003 enjoining of Truth, and of Patience and **Constancy.**
CONSTANT
006:092 and they are **constant** in guarding their Prayers.
010:109 and be patient and **constant**, till Allah
012:057 who believe, and are **constant** in righteousness.
014:005 firmly patient and **constant**,-grateful and
019:065 so worship Him, and be **constant** and patient
020:132 Enjoin prayer on thy people, and be **constant** therein.
025:042 had it not been that we were **constant** to them!"-
033:035 for men and women who are patient and **constant,**
034:019 (soul that is) patiently **constant** and grateful.
038:006 "Walk ye away, and remain **constant** to your gods!
074:007 But, for they Lord's (Cause) be patient and **constant!**
076:012 And because they were patient and **constant**, He will
CONSTANTLY
002:222 For Allah loves those who turn to Him **constantly**
003:075 unless thou **constantly** stoodest demanding,
010:063 and (**constantly**) guard against evil;-
020:130 they say, and celebrate (**constantly**) the praises
021:073 they **constantly** served Us (and Us only).
026:071 and we remain **constantly** in attendance on them."
031:031 who **constantly** persevere and give thanks.
034:033 Behold! ye (**constantly**) ordered us to be
056:031 By water flowing **constantly,**
CONSTELLATIONS
015:016 It is We Who have set out **constellations** in the heavens
025:061 Blessed is He Who made **Constellations** in the skies,
085:001 By the Sky, with its **constellations;**
CONSTRAIN
009:025 did **constrain** you, and ye turned back in retreat.
CONSTRAINED
009:118 that the earth seemed **constrained** to them,
CONSTRICTED
006:125 He maketh their breast close and **constricted,**
025:013 into a **constricted** place therein, they will
CONSTRUCT
011:037 "But **construct** an Ark under Our eyes
018:021 (Some) said, "**Construct** a building over them":
023:027 "**Construct** the Ark within Our sight and under Our

CONSTRUCTED
079:027 (Allah) hath **constructed** it:

CONSTRUCTING
011:038 Forthwith he starts **constructing** the Ark:

CONSULT
003:159 and **consult** them in affairs (of moment).
018:022 nor **consult** any of them about (the affair of) the
020:103 In whispers will they **consult** each other:
058:012 O ye who believe! When ye **consult** the Messenger

CONSULTATION
002:233 by mutual consent, and after due **consultation**.
042:038 who (conduct) their affairs by mutual **Consultation**;
058:007 a secret **consultation** between three, but He is
058:012 something in charity before your private **consultation**.
058:013 in charity before your private **consultation** (with him)?

CONSUME
004:006 but **consume** it not wastefully, nor in haste

CONSUMED
003:183 showed us a sacrifice **consumed** by fire (from heaven)."

CONSUMMATION
002:236 ye divorce women before **consummation**
002:237 And if ye divorce them before **consummation**,

CONTACT
004:043 or ye have been in **contact** with women,
005:006 or ye have been in **contact** with women, and you

CONTAIN
054:004 such tidings as **contain** a deterrent,

CONTAINING
065:011 the Signs of Allah **containing** clear explanations,

CONTAINS
003:091 as much gold as the earth **contains**,

CONTEMPLATE
003:191 and **contemplate** the (wonders of) creation

CONTEMPT
004:037 a Punishment that steeps them in **contempt**;
011:029 I will not drive away (in **contempt**) those who believe:
011:092 ye cast Him away behind your backs (with **contempt**)
016:059 Shall he retain it on (sufferance and) **Contempt**,
017:023 say not to them a word of **contempt**,

CONTEMPTIBLE
008:044 and He made you appear as **contemptible** in their eyes:
043:052 who is a **contemptible** wretch and can scarcely express

CONTEND
004:107 **Contend** not on behalf of such as betray their own soul;
004:109 whose behalf ye may **contend** in this world;
004:109 but who will **contend** with Allah on their behalf
006:121 their friends to **contend** with you if ye
008:013 if any **contend** against Allah and His Messenger.

CONTENDED
008:013 This because they **contended** against Allah

CONTENDING
049:010 your two (**contending**) brothers;

CONTENDS
004:115 If anyone **contends** with the Messenger even after

CONTENT
009:059 If only they had been **content** with what Allah
018:028 And keep yourself **content** with those who call
022:011 it good befalls them, they are therewith, well **content**;
077:043 "Eat ye and drink ye to heart's **content**:

CONTENTION
019:097 and warnings to people given to **contention**.
042:015 There is no **contention** between us and you.

CONTENTIOUS
002:204 yet is he the most **contentious** of enemies.
018:054 in most things, **contentious**.
043:058 they are a **contentious** people.

CONTENTMENT
022:036 (beg not but) live in **contentment**,
070:005 a Patience of beautiful (**contentment**).

CONTENTS
006:091 while ye conceal much (of its **contents**):

CONTINGENT
009:122 if a **contingent** from every expedition go forth to devote

CONTINUE
002:196 to **continue** the 'Umra on to the Hajj.
004:018 of those who **continue** to do evil, until death
006:070 But **continue** to admonish them with it (Al-Qur-an)
008:036 and so will they **continue** to spend;
015:014 to **continue** (all day) ascending therein,
023:063 deeds of theirs, which they will (**continue**) to do,-

CONTINUED
005:032 many of them **continued** to commit excesses in the land.
017:016 (to be obedient) but they **continued** to transgress;
032:024 with patience and **continued** to have faith
041:015 But they **continued** to reject Our Signs!

CONTINUOUS
054:002 and say, "This is (but) **continuous** magic."
055:066 pouring forth water in **continuous** abundance:

CONTRACT
002:235 but do not make a secret **contract** with them
002:282 whenever ye make a commercial **contract**;
002:282 to writing (your **contract**) for a future period,
060:010 the ties (marriage **contract**) of Unbelieving women:

CONTRACTED
009:001 ye have **contracted** mutual alliances:-

CONTRACTION
025:046 towards Ourselves,-a **contraction** by easy stages.

CONTRACTS
002:177 to fulfil the **contracts** which ye have made;

CONTRARY
003:079 on the **contrary** (he would say): "Be ye worshippers
004:019 on the **contrary** live with them on a footing of kindness
006:043 On the **contrary** their hearts became hardened,
007:061 on the **contrary** I am a messenger from the
010:037 on the **contrary** it is a confirmation of (revelations)
023:081 On the **contrary** they say things similar to what the
024:011 on the **contrary** it is good for you:
060:001 and have (on the **contrary**) driven out the Messenger
072:011 are righteous, and some the **contrary**:
075:032 But on the **contrary**, He rejected
084:022 But on the **contrary** the Unbelievers reject (it).

CONTRASTED
089:003 By the Even and Odd (**contrasted**);

CONTRIBUTE
002:195 not your own hands **contribute** to (your) destruction;

CONTRIBUTIONS
009:054 The only reasons why their **contributions** are not
009:054 and that they offer **contributions** unwillingly.

CONTRIVED
012:083 yourselves **contrived** a story (good enough) for you.

CONTROL
012:021 power and **control** over His affairs;
017:100 Say: "If ye had **control** of the Treasures
021:044 the land (in their **control**) from its outlying
025:003 they **control** Death nor Life nor Resurrection.

CONTROL (continued)
025:003 that have no **control** of hurt or good
052:037 or have they **control** over them.
CONTROVERSIES
018:022 into **controversies** concerning them, except on
CONTUMACIOUS
050:024 every **contumacious** Rejector (of Allah)!
CONTUMACY
002:213 except through selfish **contumacy**.
CONVENIENCE
016:080 of **convenience** (to serve you) for a time.
036:044 and by way of (worldly) **convenience** (to serve them)
056:073 and an article of comfort and **convenience** for the
CONVENIENCES
028:060 are but the **conveniences** of this life and the
CONVENIENT
002:239 pray on foot, or riding, (as may be most **convenient**),
002:282 and more **convenient** to prevent doubts
033:059 over their persons (when out of doors): most **convenient**,
CONVERSE
019:052 for **converse** in secret.
CONVERSING
068:023 So they departed, **conversing** in secret low tones,
CONVERTED
034:016 and We **converted** their two Garden (rows) into
CONVEY
003:020 thy duty is to **convey** the Message;
007:062 "I but I **convey** to you" the Message
007:068 "I but **convey** to you the messages of my Lord:
007:079 I did indeed **convey** to you the message for which I
007:093 I did indeed **convey** to you the Messages for which I
042:048 Thy duty is but to **convey** (the Message).
053:010 to His Servant-(conveyed) what He (meant) to **convey**.
053:010 So did (Allah) **convey** the inspiration to His Servant-
CONVEYED
004:115 plainly **conveyed** to him, and follows a path
011:057 have **conveyed** the Message with which I was
053:010 to His Servant-(**conveyed**) what He (meant) to convey.
CONVICTION
004:065 but accept them with the fullest **conviction**.
CONVINCED
002:249 But those who are **convinced** that they must meet Allah,
CONVINCING
004:174 come to you a **convincing** proof from your Lord
018:015 an authority clear (and **convincing**) for what
021:024 "Bring your **convincing** proof:
026:030 "Even if I showed you something clear (and) **convincing**?"
CONVULSION
022:001 For the **convulsion** of the Hour (of judgment)
099:001 to her (utmost) **convulsion**,
COOKING
034:013 and (**cooking**) Cauldrons fixed (in their places):
COOL
004:057 we shall admit them to shades, **cool** and ever deepening.
019:026 "So eat and drink and **cool** (thine) eye.
021:069 We said, "O Fire! be thou **cool**, and (a means of) safety
038:042 here is (water) wherein to wash, **cool** and refreshing,
056:044 Neither **cool** nor refreshing:
077:041 they shall be amidst (**cool**) shades and springs
078:024 Nothing **cool** shall they taste therein,
COOLED
020:040 that her eye might be **cooled** and she

COOLING
033:051 This were nigher to the **cooling** of their eyes,
COOLNESS
077:031 "(Which yields) no shade of **coolness**, and is
COPE
002:249 cannot **cope** with Goliath and his forces."
CORAL
055:022 Out of them come Pearls and **Coral**:
055:058 Like unto rubies and **coral**.
CORN
002:261 the way of Allah is that of a grain of **corn**:
012:043 and seven green ears of **corn**, and seven
012:046 and of seven green ears of **corn** and (seven) others
012:060 ye shall have no measure (of **corn**) from me,
013:004 and gardens of vines and fields sown with **corn,**
016:011 With it He produces for you **corn**, olives, date-
055:012 Also **corn** with (its) leaves and stalk for fodder,
105:005 and straw (of which the **corn**) has been eaten up.
CORN-FIELDS
026:148 "And **corn-fields** and date-palms with spathes
044:026 And **corn-fields** and noble buildings,
CORRUPT
003:118 they will not fail to **corrupt** you.
CORRUPTION
015:009 assuredly guard it (from **corruption**).
CORRUPTLY
027:014 of those who acted **corruptly**!
CORRUPTS
091:010 And he fails that **corrupts** it!
COST
002:233 But he shall bear the **cost** of their food
COUCH
002:022 who has made the earth your **couch**,
007:041 as a **couch** (below) and folds and folds
018:029 How uncomfortable a **couch** to recline on!
018:031 How beautiful a **couch** to recline on!
COUCHES
015:047 (joyfully) facing each other on raised **couches**.
036:056 be in pleasant shade, reclining on raised **couches**;
037:044 Facing each other on raised **couches**.
043:034 and **couches** (of silver) on which they could recline,
052:020 on **couches** arranged in ranks, and We
056:015 on **couches** encrusted (with gold and precious stones),
056:034 And on **couches** raised high.
076:013 on raised **couches**, they will see there neither
083:023 On raised **couches** will they command a sight
083:035 On raised **couches** they will command (a sight)
088:013 Therein will be **couches** (of dignity),
COULD
002:017 so they **could** not see.
002:020 He **could** take away their faculty
002:096 each one of them wishes he **could** be given a life
002:102 But they **could** not thus harm anyone except
002:109 wish they **could** turn you (people) back to infidelity
002:165 If only the unrighteous **could** see,
002:220 He **could** have put you into difficulties:
002:246 They said: "How **could** we refuse to fight
003:157 are far better than all they **could** amass.
003:161 No prophet **could** (ever) dishonestly
004:021 And how **could** ye take it when ye
004:090 He **could** have given them power over you,
004:133 If it were His will, He **could** destroy you, O
005:116 never **could** I say what I had no right (to say).

COULD (continued)

006:007 so that they **could** touch it with their hands,
006:035 He **could** gather them together unto true guidance:
006:046 who-a god other then Allah **could** restore them to you?"
006:133 if it were His Will, He **could** destroy you,
006:149 He **could** indeed have guided you all."
006:157 then who **could** do more wrong than one
007:043 never **could** we have found guidance, had it not
007:053 Or **could** we be sent back?
007:089 nor **could** we by any manner of means return
007:100 so that they **could** not hear?
007:100 We **could** punish them (too) for their sins,
007:148 that it **could** neither speak to them, nor show
008:031 if we wished, we **could** say (words) like these:
008:033 whilst they **could** ask for pardon.
009:042 "If we only **could**, we should certainly have come
009:057 If they **could** find a place to flee to, or caves,
009:081 If only they **could** understand!
009:120 because nothing **could** they suffer or do, but was
009:121 Nor **could** they spend anything (for the Cause),
011:020 They **could** not hear, nor **could** they see!
011:080 to suppress you or that I **could** betake myself to
011:118 He **could** have made mankind one People:
012:038 and never **could** we attribute any partners
012:076 He **could** not take his brother by the law
012:081 and we **could** not well guard against the unseen!
013:031 He **could** have guided all mankind (to the Right)?
016:007 that ye **could** not (otherwise) reach except with
016:009 He **could** have guided all of you.
016:093 If Allah so willed, He **could** make you all
017:086 We **could** take away that which We have sent thee
017:088 they **could** not produce the like thereof, even if
017:093 until thou send down to us a book that we **could** read."
018:042 and he **could** only say, "Woe is me! Would I had
020:089 **Could** they not see that it **could** not return
023:024 He **could** have sent down angels:
023:082 dust and bones, **could** we really be raised up again?
025:010 were His Will **could** give thee better (things) than those,-
025:010 and He **could** give thee Palaces (secure to dwell in).
025:045 If He willed, He **could** make it stationary!
025:051 We **could** have sent a warner to every town.
026:004 We **could** send down to them from the sky a Sign,
026:113 if ye **could** (but) understand.
028:081 nor **could** he defend himself.
028:082 He **could** have caused the earth to swallow us up!
029:039 yet they **could** not overreach (Us).
032:013 We **could** certainly have brought every soul
034:009 We **could** cause the earth to swallow them up,
034:044 We had not given them Books which they **could** study,
034:052 but how **could** they receive (Faith) from a position (so)
035:016 If He so pleased, He **could** blot you out
036:043 nor **could** they be delivered,
036:043 If it were Our Will, We **could** drown them;
036:066 but how **could** they have seen?
036:066 We **could** surely have blotted out their eyes;
036:067 We **could** have transformed them in their places;
036:067 nor **could** they have returned (after error).
039:004 He **could** have chosen whom He pleased
039:047 which they **could** never have counted upon!
040:018 wrong-doers have, who **could** be listened to.
042:008 He **could** have made them a single people;
042:024 He **could** seal up thy heart.
043:013 for we **could** never be able to do it.

COULD (continued)

043:034 and couches (of silver) on which they **could** recline,
043:060 We **could** make angels from amongst you,
043:071 all that the eyes **could** delight in:
043:071 there will be there all that the souls **could** desire,
047:004 He **could** certainly have exacted retribution
047:030 We **could** have shown them up to thee, and thou
051:045 nor **could** they help themselves.
051:045 Then they **could** not even stand (on their feet),
056:065 Were it Our Will, we **could** make it broken orts.
056:070 Were it Our Will, We **could** make it saltish
065:003 provides for him from (sources) he never **could** expect.
069:047 Nor **could** any of you withhold him (from Our wrath).
070:011 would that he **could** redeem himself from the
070:014 so it **could** deliver him:
080:003 But what **could** tell thee but that perchance

COULDST

006:027 If thou **couldst** but see when they shall be made to stand
006:030 If thou **couldst** but see when they shall be made to stand
006:093 If thou **couldst** but see how the wicked
007:155 Thy will thou **couldst** have destroyed,
008:050 If thou **couldst** see, when the angels take the souls
008:063 **couldst** thou have produced that affection
018:077 surely thou **couldst** have exacted some
025:043 **Couldst** thou be a disposer of affairs
032:012 If only thou **couldst** see when the guilty ones
034:031 **Couldst** thou but see when the wrong-doers
034:051 If thou **couldst** but see when they will quake
049:005 until thou **couldst** come out to them, it would
069:007 so that thou **couldst** see the (whole) people

COUNCIL

027:039 thou rise from thy **Council**:
096:017 to his **council** (of comrades):

COUNCILS

029:029 and practise wickedness (even) in your **councils**?"

COUNSEL

005:108 But fear Allah, and listen (to His **counsel**):
007:079 I gave you good **counsel**, but ye love
007:093 I gave you good **counsel**, but how
007:110 then what is it ye **counsel**?"
011:034 much as I desire to give you (good) **counsel**,
011:034 "Of no profit will be my **counsel** to you,
011:046 I give thee **counsel**, lest thou become one of the
026:035 then what is it ye **counsel**?"
028:020 are taking **counsel** together about thee, to slay
058:009 O ye who believe! when ye hold secret **counsel**,
065:006 and take mutual **counsel** together, according to

COUNSELLORS

007:079 but ye love not good **counsellors**!"

COUNSELS

009:078 their secret (thoughts) and their secret **counsels**,
021:003 The wrong-doers conceal their private **counsels**,
043:080 their secrets and their private **counsels**?
058:008 And they hold **counsels** among themselves for iniquity
058:008 forbidden secret **counsels** yet revert to that which
058:010 Secret **counsels** are only (inspired) by Satan,

COUNT

007:150 nor **count** thou me amongst the people of sin."
010:005 might know the number of years and the **count** (of time).
014:034 But if ye **count** the favours of Allah, never will
016:018 If ye would **count** up the favours of Allah,
017:012 may know the number and **count** of the years:
019:084 for We but **count** out to them a (limited)

COUNT (continued)
033:049 no period of 'Iddat have ye to **count** in respect
049:017 Say, "**Count** not your Islam as a favour upon me:
065:001 and **count** (accurately) their prescribed periods:
073:020 He knoweth that ye are unable to keep **count** thereof.
COUNTED
012:020 for a few dirhams **counted** out:
039:047 which they could never have **counted** upon!
COUNTENANCE
013:022 seeking the **countenance** their Lord;
030:038 that is best for those who seek the **Countenance**,
030:039 seeking the **Countenance** of Allah, (will increase):
092:020 for the **countenance** of their Lord Most High;
COUNTLESS
004:001 scattered (like seeds) **countless** men and women;
019:074 But how many (**countless**) generations before them
019:098 But how many (**countless**) generation before
COUNTRY
022:025 and the visitor from the **country**-and any
027:034 She said: "Kings, when they enter a **country**, despoil it,
COUNTS
033:005 (what **counts** is) the intention of your hearts:
COURSE
002:232 That is (the **course** making for) most virtue
004:150 and wish to take a **course** midway,
005:066 but many of them follow a **course** that is evil.
005:066 a party on the right **course**:
007:113 they said, "Of **course** we shall have a (suitable)
009:037 The evil of their **course** seems pleasing to them.
009:059 (That would been the right **course**).
012:037 (in due **course**) to feed either of you I will
013:002 each one runs (its **course**) for a term appointed.
016:126 that is indeed the best (**course**) for those
017:110 but seek a middle **course** between."
018:024 ever closer (even) than this to the right **course**."
018:034 in the **course** of a mutual argument:
018:037 in the **course** of the argument with him:
018:061 which took its **course** through the sea
018:063 it took its **course** through the sea
021:033 each in its rounded **course**.
026:041 they said to Pharaoh: "Of **course**-shall we
031:029 each running its **course** for a term appointed;
035:013 each one runs its **course** for a term appointed.
035:032 some who follow a middle **course**; and some who are,
039:005 (to His law) each one follow a **course** for a time
COURSES
038:031 at eventide, **courses** of the highest breeding,
002:222 They ask thee concerning women's **courses**.
002:222 so keep away from women in their **courses**,
014:033 both diligently pursuing their **courses**:
055:005 follow **courses** (exactly) computed;
065:004 and for those who have no **courses** (it is the same):
065:004 the age of monthly **courses**, for them
COURTEOUS
004:086 meet it with a greeting still more **courteous**,
004:086 When a (**courteous**) greeting is offered you,
COURTESY
004:086 still more **courteous**, (at least) of equal **courtesy**.
018:019 behave with care and **courtesy**, and let
COURTYARDS
037:177 their **courtyards** before them, Evil will
COVENANT
002:027 Allah's **Covenant** after it is ratified,

COVENANT (continued)
002:040 and I shall fulfil My **Covenant** with you,
002:040 and fulfil your **Covenant** with Me
002:063 And remember We took your **Covenant**
002:083 a **covenant** from the children of Israel
002:084 your **Covenant** (to this effect):
002:093 And remember We took your **Covenant**
002:100 every time they make a **Covenant**,
002:248 shall come to you the Ark of the **Covenant**,
003:081 Behold! Allah took the **covenant** of the Prophets,
003:081 and take My **covenant** as binding on you?"
003:099 yourselves witnesses (to Allah's **Covenant**)?
003:112 except when under a **covenant** (of protection)
003:187 a **Covenant** from the People of the Book,
004:021 and they have taken from you a solemn **covenant**?
004:154 And for their **Covenant** We raised over them
004:154 And We took from them a solemn **Covenant**.
004:155 in that they broke their **Covenant**; that they
005:007 and His **Covenant**, which He ratified with you,
005:012 a **Covenant** from the Children of Israel, and We
005:013 But because of their breach of their **Covenant**, We
005:014 We did take a **Covenant**, but they forgot a good
005:070 We took the **Covenant** of the Children of Israel
006:152 and fulfil the **Covenant** of Allah:
007:102 not men (true) to their **covenant**:
007:169 Was not the **Covenant** of the Book
008:056 They are those with whom thou didst make a **covenant**,
008:056 but they break their **covenant** every time,
008:058 throw back (their **covenant**) to them,
009:007 How can there be a **covenant** before Allah
009:008 not in you the ties either of kinship or of **covenant**?
009:008 How (can there be such a **covenant**), seeing that
009:010 the ties either of kinship or of **covenant**!
009:012 But if they violate their oaths after their **covenant**,
009:075 a **Covenant** with Allah, that if He bestowed on them
009:076 and turned back (from their **Covenant**),
009:077 because they broke their **Covenant** with Allah,
009:111 and who is more faithful to his **Covenant** than Allah?
013:020 Those who fulfil the **Covenant** of Allah and fail
013:025 But those who break the **Covenant** of Allah,
016:091 Fulfil the **Covenant** of Allah when ye have
016:095 Nor sell the **Covenant** of Allah for a miserable
020:080 and We made a **Covenant** with you on the
020:115 taken the **covenant** of Adam, but he forgot:
033:007 the Prophets their **Covenant**:
033:007 We took from them a solemn **Covenant**:
033:015 and a **covenant** with Allah must (surely)
033:023 been true to their **Covenant** with Allah:
043:049 thy Lord for us according to his **covenant** with thee;
057:008 in your Lord and has indeed taken your **Covenant**,
COVENANTED
002:125 and We **covenanted** with Abraham and Isma'il,
033:015 And yet they had already **covenanted** with Allah
048:010 what he has **covenanted** with Allah,-Allah will
COVENANTS
023:008 their trust and their **covenants**;
068:039 Or have ye **Covenants** with Us on oath,
070:032 And those who respect their trusts and **covenants**;
COVER
002:042 And **cover** not Truth with falsehood,
004:149 or conceal it or **cover** evil with pardon, surely
006:065 or to **cover** you with confusion
007:026 upon you to **cover** your shame, as well as

COVER (continued)

009:002 but that Allah will **cover** with shame
010:026 No darkness nor abasement shall **cover** their faces!
010:027 ignominy will **cover** their (faces):
011:005 **cover** themselves with their garments, He knoweth
011:039 a Chastisement that will **cover** them with shame,-
011:078 and **cover** me not with shame about my guests!
014:041 "O our Lord! **cover** (us) with Thy Forgiveness-me,
016:027 He will **cover** them with shame, and say:
029:055 shall **cover** them from above them and from
045:023 and put a **cover** on his sight.
059:005 and in order that He might **cover** with shame
064:014 and **cover** up (their faults), verily Allah
068:043 Their eyes will be cast down,-ignominy will **cover** them;
080:041 Blackness will **cover** them:

COVERED

002:061 They were **covered** with humiliation and misery:
006:009 they have already **covered** with confusion.
006:076 When the night **covered** him over, he saw
008:011 Remember He **covered** you with drowsiness, to give
010:027 their faces will be **covered**, as it were,
014:050 and their faces **covered** with Fire;
016:027 are the Unbelievers **covered** with Shame and Misery,-
020:078 completely overwhelmed them and **covered** them up.
036:009 We have **covered** them up:
053:054 So that there **covered** it that which **covered**.
071:007 **covered** themselves up with their garments,

COVEREST

003:192 truly Thou **coverest** with shame,

COVERING

002:263 kind words and **covering** of faults are better than charity
007:041 and folds of **covering** above:
012:107 against them of **covering** veil of the wrath of Allah.
018:090 no **covering** protection against the sun.
020:121 for their **covering**, leaves from the Garden:
070:044 ignominy **covering** them (all over)!
078:010 And made the night as a **covering**,

COVERINGS

017:046 And We put **coverings** over their hearts

COVERS

031:032 When a wave **covers** them like the canopy

COVET

003:014 the love of things they **covet**: women and sons;
003:152 in sight (of the Victory) which ye **covet**.
004:032 And in no wise **covet** those things in which

COVETING

004:094 **Coveting** the perishable goods of this life:

COVETOUS

033:019 **Covetous** over you.
033:019 sharp tongues, **covetous** of goods.
057:024 Such persons as are **covetous** and commend

COVETOUSLY

003:180 And let not those who **covetously** withhold of the
047:037 ye would **covetously** withhold, and He

COVETOUSNESS

057:024 and commend **covetousness** to men.
059:009 And those saved from the **covetousness** of their
064:016 and those saved from the **covetousness** of their

COWARDICE

003:122 Remember two of your parties meditated **cowardice**;

COWED

042:039 (are not **cowed** but) help and defend themselves.

CRACKLING

111:004 His wife shall carry the (**crackling**) wood-as fuel!

CRADLE

019:029 who is a child in the **cradle**?"

CREATE

002:030 "I will **create** a vicegerent on earth."
004:119 and I will **create** in them false desires;
004:133 O mankind, and **create** another race:
006:100 though Allah did **create** the Jinns; And they
007:012 thou didst **create** me from fire and him from clay."
007:191 as partners things that can **create** nothing,
010:005 Nowise did Allah **create** this but in truth
011:119 and for this did He **create** them:
015:028 "I am about to **create** man, from sounding
015:033 Whom Thou didst **create** from sounding clay,
016:020 invoke besides Allah **create** nothing and are themselves
017:061 whom Thou didst **create** from clay?"
017:099 has power to **create** the like of them (anew)?
019:009 I did indeed **create** thee before, when thou
020:055 From the (earth) did We **create** you, and into
021:016 Not for (idle) sport did We **create** the heavens
022:073 cannot **create** (even) a fly,
023:012 Man We did **create** from a quintessence (of clay);
023:014 the Best to **create**!
025:003 gods that can **create** nothing but are
028:068 Thy Lord does **create** and choose as He pleases:
030:008 did Allah **create** the heavens and the earth,
035:011 And Allah did **create** you from dust;
036:081 and the earth able to **create** the like thereof?"-
037:011 are they the more difficult to **create**, or the
038:027 We **create** heaven and earth and all between!
038:071 "I am about to **create** man from clay:
039:004 whom He pleased out of those whom He doth **create**:
052:036 Or did they **create** the heavens and the earth?
053:045 That He did **create** in pairs-male and female,
056:059 Is it ye who **create** it, or are We the Creators?
079:027 What! Are ye the more difficult to **create** or the

CREATED

002:021 who **created** you and those who came before you
002:029 It is He who hath **created** for you
002:228 to hide what Allah hath **created** in their wombs,
003:059 He **created** him from dust,
003:191 not for naught hast Thou **created** (all) this!
004:001 **created**, out of it, his mate, and from them
004:001 Who **created** you from a single person,
004:028 for man was **created** weak in (resolution).
004:119 and deface the (fair) nature **created** by Allah."
005:018 of the men He hath **created**:
006:001 Praise be to Allah, Who **created** the heavens
006:002 He it is Who **created** you from clay, and then
006:073 It is He Who **created** the heavens and
006:079 toward Him Who **created** the heavens and the
006:094 and alone as We **created** you for the first time:
006:101 He **created** all things, and He hath
007:011 It is We who **created** you and gave
007:029 such as He **created** you in the beginning,
007:054 Who **created** the heavens and the earth
007:181 Of those We have **created** are people who direct
007:185 and all that Allah hath **created**?
007:189 It is He Who **created** you from a single person,
007:191 but are themselves **created**?
009:036 He **created** the heavens and the earth;
010:003 Who **created** the heavens and the earth in six

CREATED (continued)

010:006 and in all that Allah hath **created**,
011:007 He it is Who **created** the heavens and the earth
011:051 My reward is from none But Him who **created** Me:
013:016 partners who have **created** (anything) as He has **created**,
014:019 that Allah **created** the Heavens and the earth in Truth?
014:032 It is Allah Who hath **created** the heavens
015:026 We **created** man from sounding clay, from mud
015:027 And the Jinn race, We had **created** before, from the
015:085 We **created** not the heavens, the earth, and all
016:003 He has **created** the heavens and the earth
016:004 He has **created** man from a sperm-drop and behold
016:005 And cattle He has **created** for you (men):
016:008 And (He has **created**) horses, mules, and donkeys,
016:008 and He has **created** (other) things of which ye have
016:020 create nothing and are themselves **created**.
016:081 out of the things He **created**, some things
017:051 Say: "He Who **created** you first!"
017:051 "Or any **created** matter which, in your minds,
017:099 Who **created** the heavens and the earth, has power
018:037 "Dost thou deny Him Who **created** thee out of dust,
018:048 "Now have ye come to Us (bare) as We **created** you first:
019:067 that We **created** him before out of nothing?
020:004 A revelation from Him Who **created** the earth
020:050 to each (**created**) thing its form, then, gave (it)
020:072 Clear Signs Him Who **created** us!
021:033 It is He Who **created** the Night and the
021:056 He Who **created** them (from nothing):
022:005 (consider) that We **created** you out of dust,
023:078 It is He Who has **created** for you (the faculties
023:091 each god would have taken away what he had **created**
023:115 "Did ye then think that We had **created** you in jest,
024:045 And Allah has **created** every animal from water:
025:002 it is He Who **created** all things, and ordered
025:003 but are themselves **created**;
025:049 of things We have **created**,-cattle and
025:054 It is He Who has **created** man from water:
025:059 He Who **created** the heavens and the earth
026:078 "Who **created** me, and it is He Who guides me;
026:166 has **created** for you to be your mates?
026:184 "And fear Him Who **created** you and (Who **created**)
027:060 Or, who has **created** the heaven and the earth,
029:044 Allah **created** the heavens and the earth
029:061 who has **created** the heavens and the earth
030:020 that He **created** you from dust; and then,-behold,
030:021 that He **created** for you mates from among
030:040 It is Allah Who has **created** you: further, He
030:054 It is Allah Who **created** you in a state
031:010 He **created** the heavens without any pillars
031:011 that others besides Him have **created**:
031:025 who it is that **created** the heavens and the earth.
032:004 It is Allah Who has **created** the heavens and the
032:007 He Who has **created** all things in the best way
035:040 they have **created** in the (wide) earth.
036:022 Who **created** me, and to Whom ye shall (all) be
036:036 Glory to Allah, Who **created** in pairs
036:042 And We have **created** for them similar (vessels
036:071 have **created** for them-among the things
036:077 We Who **created** Him from sperm? Yet behold!
036:079 Who **created** them for the first time! For He
036:081 "Is not He Who **created** the heavens and the
037:011 or the (other) beings We have **created**?
037:011 Them have We **created** out of sticky clay!

CREATED (continued)

037:096 "But Allah has **created** you and your handiwork!"
037:150 Or that We **created** the angels female, and they
038:075 whom I have **created** with My hands?
039:005 He **created** the heavens and the earth in true
039:006 then **created**, of like nature, his mate;
039:006 He **created** you (all) from a single person:
039:038 that **created** the heavens and the earth, they would
040:067 It is He Who has **created** you from dust, then from
041:009 Say: Is it that ye Deny Him Who **created** the earth
041:015 What! did they not see that Allah, Who **created** them,
041:021 He **created** you for the first time,
041:037 but prostrate to Allah, Who **created** them,
043:009 'Who **created** the heavens and the earth?'
043:009 to reply, 'They were **created** by (Him),
043:012 That has **created** pairs in all things, and has
043:087 If thou ask them, Who **Created** them, they will
044:038 We **created** not the heavens, the earth,
044:039 We **created** them not except for just ends:
045:022 Allah **created** the heavens and the earth for just
046:003 We **created** not the heavens and the earth and all
046:004 they have **created** on earth, or have
046:033 Who **created** the heavens and the earth, and never
049:013 O mankind! We **created** you from a single (pair)
050:016 It was We who **created** man, and We
050:038 We **created** the heavens and the earth and all
051:049 And of every thing We have **created** pairs:
051:056 I have only **created** Jinns and men, that they
052:035 Were they **created** of nothing, or were
054:049 We **created** in proportion and measure.
055:003 He has **created** man:
055:014 He **created** man from sounding clay
055:015 And He **created** Jinns from fire free of smoke:
056:035 We have **created** them of special creation.
056:057 It is We Who have **created** you:
057:004 He it is Who **created** the heavens and the earth
064:002 It is He Who has **created** you; and of you
064:003 He has **created** the heavens and the earth
065:012 Allah is He Who **created** seven Firmaments and of
067:002 He Who **created** Death and Life, that He
067:003 He Who **created** the seven heavens one above another:
067:014 Should He not know,-He that **created**?
067:023 Say: "It is He Who has **created** you, and made
070:019 Truly man was **created** very impatient;
070:039 By no means! for We have **created** them out of
071:014 "'Seeing that it is He that has **created** you in diverse
071:015 "'See ye not how Allah has **created** the seven
074:011 the (creature) whom I **created** (bare and) alone!-
076:002 Verily We **created** Man from a drop of mingled sperm,
076:028 It is We Who **created** them, and We have
077:020 Have We not **created** you from a fluid
078:008 And (have We not) **created** you in pairs,
080:018 From what stuff hath He **created** him?
080:019 From a sperm-drop: He hath **created** him, and then
082:007 Him Who **created** thee, fashioned thee
086:005 Now let man but think from what he is **created**!
086:006 He is **created** from a drop emitted-
087:002 Who hath **created**, and further, given order
090:004 Verily We have **created** Man into toil and struggle.
095:004 We have indeed **created** man in the best of molds,
096:001 in the name of thy Lord and Cherisher, Who **created**-
096:002 **Created** man, out of a leech-like clot:
113:002 From the mischief of **created** things;

CREATEDST
038:076 Thou **createdst** me from fire, and him **createdst** from
CREATES
004:120 and **creates** in them false hopes,
016:017 Is then He Who **creates** like one that **creates** not?
016:070 It is Allah who **creates** you and takes
024:045 Allah **creates** what He wills; for verily
030:054 He **creates** whatever He wills, and it
039:006 He **creates** you, in the wombs of your mothers,
042:049 He **creates** what He wills.
043:016 what He Himself **creates**, and granted
085:013 It is He Who **Creates** from the very beginning,
CREATETH
003:047 He said: "Even so; Allah **createth** what He willeth:
005:017 He **createth** what He pleaseth.
CREATING
056:061 and **creating** you (again) in (Forms) that ye know not.
CREATION
002:164 Behold! In the **creation** of the heavens
003:190 Behold! In the **creation** of the heavens
003:191 the (wonders of) **creation** in the heavens and the earth,
007:054 Verily, His are the **Creation** and the Command,
007:080 no people in **creation** (ever) committed before you?
010:004 It is He who beginneth the process of **Creation**,
010:034 originates **Creation** and repeats it:
010:034 can any originate **creation** and repeat it?"
013:005 shall we indeed then be in a **creation** renewed?"
013:016 so that the **creation** seemed to them similar?
014:019 (in your place) a new **Creation**?
016:048 Do they not look at Allah's **creation**.
017:049 be raised up (to be) a new **creation**?"
017:070 above a great part of Our **Creation**.
017:098 really be raised up (to be) a new **Creation**?"
018:051 not (even) their own **creation**:
018:051 witness the **creation** of the heavens and the earth,
021:030 joined together (as one unit of **Creation**),
021:104 We produced the first **Creation**, shall We
023:017 unmindful of (Our) **Creation**.
027:064 Or, Who originates **Creation**, then repeats
029:006 for Allah is free of all needs from all **creation**.
029:010 all that is in the hearts of all **Creation**?
029:019 originates **creation**, then repeats it:
029:020 so will Allah produce a later **creation**:
029:020 see how Allah did originate **creation**;
029:028 in **Creation** (ever) committed before you.
030:011 It is Allah Who begins the **creation**; then repeats
030:022 And among His Signs is the **creation** of the
030:027 It is He Who begins the **creation**; then repeats it;
031:011 Such is the **Creation** of Allah: now show Me
031:028 And your **creation** or your resurrection is in no
032:007 the **creation** of man from clay,
032:010 shall we indeed be in a **Creation** renewed?"
034:007 that ye shall (then be raised) in a New **Creation**?
035:001 He adds to **Creation** as He pleases:
035:016 He could blot you out and bring in a New **Creation**:
036:078 and forgets his own (origin and) **Creation**:
036:079 For He fully knows all **creation**.
040:057 Assuredly the **creation** of the heavens and the earth
040:057 is a greater (matter) than the **creation** of men:
042:029 And among His Signs is the **creation** of the heaven
043:019 Did they witness their **creation**?
045:004 And in the **creation** of yourselves and the fact
046:033 and never wearied with their **creation**,

CREATION (continued)
050:015 be in confused doubt about a new **Creation**?
050:015 Were We then weary with the first **Creation**,
053:047 a Second **Creation** (raising of the Dead);
056:035 We have created them of special **creation**.
056:062 And ye certainly know already the first form of **creation**:
067:003 wilt thou see in the **Creation** of The Most Gracious.
092:003 By the **creation** of male and female;-
CREATOR
006:102 the **Creator** of all things:
012:101 O Thou **Creator** of the heavens and the earth!
013:016 Say: "Allah is the **Creator** of all things:
014:010 a doubt about Allah, the **Creator** of the heavens
035:003 Is there a **Creator**, other than
036:081 He is the **Creator** Supreme, of skill
039:046 Say: "O Allah! **Creator** of the heavens and the
039:062 Allah is the **Creator** of all things, and He
040:062 the **Creator** of all things, there is
042:011 (He is) the **Creator** of the heavens and the earth:
059:024 He is Allah, the **Creator**, the Originator,
CREATORS
037:125 and forsake the Best of **Creators**,-
052:035 or were they themselves the **creators**?
056:059 Is it ye who create it, or are We the **Creators**?
CREATURE
011:006 There is no moving **creature** on earth but its
011:056 there is not a moving **creature**, but He hath grasp of
016:061 would not leave, on the (earth), a single living **creature**:
021:037 Man is a **creature** of haste:
022:066 truly man is a most ungrateful **creature**!
023:014 then We developed out of it another **creature**:
031:010 every kind of noble **creature**, in pairs.
035:045 of the (earth) a single living **creature**:
055:029 every **creature** in the heavens and on earth:
074:011 the (**creature**) whom I created (bare and) alone!-
CREATURES
002:255 (appeareth to his **creatures** as) before or
003:083 While all **creatures** in the heavens and on earth have,
003:097 Allah stands not in need of any of His **creatures**.
003:108 no injustice to any of His **creatures**.
007:013 the meanest (of **creatures**)."
010:066 Behold! verily to Allah belong all **creatures**,
012:104 than a Message for all **creatures**.
016:049 whether moving **creatures** or the angels:
016:083 and most of them are (**creatures**) ungrateful.
019:013 And pity (for all **creatures**) as from Us,
021:019 To Him belong all (**creatures**) in the
021:107 We sent thee not, but as a mercy for all **creatures**.
025:001 that it may be an admonition to all **creatures**;-
026:119 in the Ark filled (with all **creatures**).
026:165 "Of all the **creatures** in the world, will ye
029:060 How many are the **creatures** that carry
042:029 and the living **creatures** that He has scattered
055:010 the earth for (His) **creatures**:
098:006 They are the worst of **creatures**.
098:007 do righteous deeds,-they are the best of **creatures**.
CREDENTIALS
028:032 Those are the two **credentials** from thy Lord
CREDIT
002:245 unto his **credit** and multiply many times?
006:160 ten times as much to his **credit**:
009:120 but was reckoned to their **credit** as a deed
009:121 but the deed is inscribed to their **credit**;

CREDIT (continued)
057:011 increase it manifold to his **credit**, and he
057:018 increased manifold (to their **credit**), and they
064:017 He will double it to your (**credit**), and He

CREEP
015:012 so do We let it **creep** into the hearts of the sinners-
024:045 of them there are some that **creep** on their bellies;

CRIED
002:214 those of faith who were with him **cried**:
010:012 on his way as if he had never **cried** to Us for the
019:003 Behold! he **cried** to his Lord in secret.
019:023 she **cried** (in her anguish): "Ah! would
019:024 But (a voice) **cried** to her from beneath
021:076 (Remember) Noah, when he **cried** (to Us) aforetime:
021:083 And (remember) Job, when he **cried** to his Lord
021:087 But he **cried** through the depths of darkness,
021:089 when he **cried** to his Lord: "O my Lord! leave me
037:075 (In the days of old), Noah **cried** to Us, and We
038:003 In the end they **cried** (for mercy)
038:041 behold he **cried** to his Lord: "Satan has
039:008 (man) doth forget what he **cried** and prayed
044:022 then he **cried** to his Lord: "These are
068:048 when he **cried** out in agony.

CRIER
007:044 but a **Crier** shall proclaim between them: "The curse
012:070 Then shouted out a **Crier**: "O ye (in) the

CRIES
002:171 listen to nothing but calls and **cries**:
014:022 I cannot listen to your **cries**, nor can
039:049 Now, when trouble touches man, he **cries** to Us;
068:015 "Tales of the Ancients," he **cries**!
099:003 And man **cries** (distressed): 'What is the

CRIETH
010:012 he **crieth** unto Us (in all postures)-lying down
039:008 he **crieth** unto his Lord, turning to Him

CRIME
002:072 a dispute among yourselves as to the **crime**:
002:198 It is no **crime** in you if ye seek of the bounty
002:206 he is led by arrogance to (more) **crime**.
005:039 But if the thief repent after his **crime**, and amend
007:084 those who indulged in sin and **crime**!
012:075 to atone for the (**crime**).
026:014 they have a charge of **crime** against me;
029:040 Each one of them We sized for his **crime**:
081:009 For what **crime** she was killed;

CRIMES
005:049 that for some of their **crimes** it is Allah's
008:052 and Allah punished them for their **crimes**:
008:054 destroyed them for their **crimes**, and We

CRITERION
002:053 and the **criterion** (between right and wrong),
003:003 **Criterion** (of judgement between right and wrong).
008:029 He will grant you a **Criterion** (to judge between right
021:048 and Aaron the **Criterion** (for judgment).
025:001 Blessed is He Who sent down the **Criterion** to His

CROOKED
003:099 seeking to make it **crooked**,
007:045 desiring to make something **crooked**:
007:086 and seeking in it something **crooked**;
011:019 path of Allah and wish it to be **crooked**:
014:003 Allah and seek to make it **crooked**:
020:107 Nothing **crooked** or curved wilt thou see
058:008 salutes thee, (but in **crooked** ways):

CROOKEDNESS
018:001 and hath allowed therein no **Crookedness**:
020:108 the Caller (straight): no **crookedness** in him:
039:028 without any **crookedness** (therein):

CROPS
002:205 and destroy **crops** and progeny
006:099 from some We produce green (**crops**), out of
006:138 such and such cattle and **crops** are forbidden,
007:130 with years (of drought) and shortness of **crops**;
032:027 and produce therewith **crops**, providing food for their

CROSS
012:041 as for the other, he will hang from the **cross**,

CROSSED
002:249 When they **crossed** the river,

CROWD
017:104 in a mingled **crowd**.
072:019 they just make round him a dense **crowd**."

CROWDS
070:037 From the right and from the left, in **crowds**?
078:018 and ye shall come forth in **crowds**;
110:002 enter Allah's Religion in **crowds**,

CRUCIFIED
004:157 but they killed him not, nor **crucified** him.
020:071 and I will have you **crucified** on trunks

CRUCIFIXION
005:033 execution or **crucifixion**, or the cutting

CRUCIFY
007:124 and I will **crucify** you all."
026:049 and I will **crucify** you all"

CRUEL
068:013 Violent (and **cruel**),-with all that,

CRUELTY
004:128 If a wife fears **cruelty** or desertion

CRUMBLE
009:109 And it doth **crumble** to pieces with him,
009:109 sand-cliff ready to **crumble** to pieces?
039:021 then He makes it dry up and **crumble** away.

CRUMBLED
056:005 And the mountains shall be **crumbled** to atoms,

CRUMBLES
057:020 then it becomes dry and **crumbles** away.

CRUSH
027:018 and his host **crush** you (under foot)
041:029 we shall **crush** them beneath our feet, so that

CRUSHED
069:014 and they are **crushed** at one stroke,-
091:014 **crushed** them for their sin and levelled them.

CRY
004:075 Men, women, and children, whose **cry** is: "Our Lord!
007:005 no **cry** did they utter but this: "Indeed
007:043 And they shall hear the **cry**: "Behold!
016:053 unto Him ye **cry** with groans;
021:015 And that **cry** of theirs ceased not, till We
030:033 they **cry** to their Lord, turning back
035:037 Therein will they **cry** aloud (for assistance):
036:043 no helper (to hear their **cry**), nor could
037:019 Then it will be a single (compelling) **cry**;
038:060 (The followers shall **cry** to the misleaders:)
039:075 and the **cry** (on all sides) will be, "Praise be to Allah.
043:077 They will **cry**: "O Malik! would that thy Lord
043:088 (Prophet's) **cry**, "O my Lord! Truly these
044:047 (A voice will **cry**:) "Seize ye him and drag him
063:004 They think that every **cry** is against them.

CRY (continued)
075:027 And there will be a **cry**, "Who is a magician
079:013 a single (compelling) **Cry**.
084:011 Soon will he **cry** for Perdition,
CRYING
047:035 Be not weary and faint-hearted **crying** for peace,
CRYSTAL
076:015 vessels of silver and goblets of **crystal**,-
CRYSTAL-CLEAR
076:016 **Crystal-clear**, made of silver:
CRYSTAL-WHITE
037:046 **Crystal-white**, of a taste delicious to those
CUBITS
069:032 whereof the length is seventy **cubits**!
CUCUMBERS
002:061 its pot-herbs, and **cucumbers**,
CULT
007:139 the **cult** they are in is bound to destruction,
CULTIVATION
014:037 in a valley without **cultivation**, but Thy
CUNNING
003:120 not the least harm will their **cunning** do to you;
004:076 feeble indeed is the **cunning** of Satan.
CUP
012:070 he put the drinking **cup** into his brother's saddle-bag.
037:045 Round will be passed to them a **Cup** from a clear-
052:023 one with another, a **cup** free of frivolity,
076:005 of a **Cup** (of Wine) mixed with Kafur,-
076:017 of a **Cup** mixed with Zanjabil,-
078:034 And a **Cup** full (to the Brim).
CUPS
056:018 and **cups** (filled) out of clear-flowing fountains:
CURED
021:090 We **cured** his wife's (barrenness) for him.
CURES
026:080 "And when I am ill, it is He Who **cures** me;
CURSE
002:088 Nay, Allah's **curse** is on them
002:089 but the **curse** Allah is on those
002:159 and the **curse** of those entitled to **curse**.
002:159 on them shall be Allah's **curse**,
002:161 and the **curse** of angels, and of all mankind;
002:161 on them is Allah's **curse**,
003:061 And invoke the **curse** of Allah on those who lie!
003:087 the reward is that on them (rests) the **curse** of Allah,
004:047 or **curse** them as We cursed the Sabbath-breakers,
004:093 and the wrath and the **curse** of Allah are upon him,
004:118 Allah did **curse** him, but he said: "I will
005:060 Those who incurred the **curse** of Allah and His wrath,
007:044 "The **curse** of Allah is on the wrong-doers;
009:030 Allah's **curse** be on them: how are they deluded
009:068 for them is the **curse** of Allah.
011:018 Behold! the **Curse** of Allah is on those who do wrong!-
011:060 And they were pursued by a **Curse** in this Life,-
011:099 And they are followed by a **curse** in this (life)
013:025 and work mischief in the land;-on them is the **Curse**;
015:035 "And the **Curse** shall be on thee
024:007 that he solemnly invokes the **curse** of Allah
028:042 In this world We made a **Curse** to follow them:
029:025 ye shall disown each other and **curse** each other:
033:061 They shall have a **curse** on them: wherever they
033:068 Double Chastisement and **curse** them with a very
033:068 with a very great **Curse**!"

CURSE (continued)
038:078 "And My **Curse** shall be on thee till the
040:052 but they will (only) have the **Curse** and the Home
063:004 The **curse** of Allah be on them!
CURSED
004:046 but Allah hath **cursed** them, for their Unbelief;
004:047 as We **cursed** the Sabbath-breakers:
004:052 and those whom Allah hath **cursed**, thou wilt find,
004:052 They are (men) whom Allah hath **cursed**:
005:013 We **cursed** them, and made their hearts grow hard:
017:060 as also the **Cursed** Tree (mentioned) in the Qur-an:
024:023 are **cursed** in this life and in the Hereafter:
033:057 Allah has **cursed** them in this world and in the Hereafter,
033:064 Verily Allah has **cursed** the Unbelievers
047:023 has **cursed** for He has made them deaf and blinded
048:006 He has **cursed** them and got Hell ready for them:
051:010 **Cursed** be the conjecturers.
CURSES
005:078 **Curses** were pronounced on those among
007:038 it **curses** its sister-People (that went before),
CURTAILMENT
020:112 nor of any **curtailment** (of what is his due).
CURVED
020:107 Nothing crooked or **curved** wilt thou see
CUSHIONS
055:076 Reclining on green **Cushions** and rich
088:015 And **Cushions** set in rows,
CUSTODIAN
039:041 a **Custodian** over them.
CUSTOM
004:022 an abominable **custom** indeed.
CUSTOMARY
026:137 a **customary** device of the ancients,
CUT
002:166 relations between them would be **cut** off.
002:260 tie them (**cut** them into pieces),
003:127 That He might **cut** off a fringe of the Unbelievers
005:038 As to the thief, male or female, **cut** off his or her hands:
006:045 the last remnant was **cut** off.
006:094 so now all relations between you have been **cut** off,
007:072 by Our Mercy and We **cut** off the roots
007:124 "Be sure I will **cut** off your hands and your
008:007 and to **cut** off the roots of the Unbelievers;-
009:110 until their hearts are **cut** to pieces.
009:121 nor **cut** across a valley, but the deed
012:031 and (in their amazement) **cut** their hands:
012:050 the matter with the ladies who **cut** their hands?'
013:025 their word thereto and **cut** asunder those things
015:066 those (sinners) should be **cut** off by the morning.
020:071 Be sure I will **cut** off your hands and feet
021:093 But (later generations) **cut** off their affair
022:015 a rope to the ceiling and **cut** (himself) off:
022:019 for them will be **cut** out a garment of Fire:
023:053 But people have **cut** off their affair (of unity),
026:049 Be sure I will **cut** off your hands and your
029:029 and **cut** off the highway?-And practise
035:011 nor is a part **cut** off from his life,
048:027 heads shaved, hair **cut** short, and without fear.
059:005 Whether ye **cut** down (O ye Muslims!) of the tender
069:046 And We should certainly then **cut** off the artery
089:009 who **cut** out (huge) rocks in the valley?-
108:003 he will be **cut** off (from Future Hope).

CUTS

047:015 so that it **cuts** up their bowels (to pieces)?

CUTTING

005:033 or the **cutting** off of hands and feet from opposite

D

DAILY
005:075   They had both to eat their (**daily**) food.

DAMS
034:016   the flood (released) from the **Dams**, and We

DAMSELS
028:025   Afterwards one of the (**damsels**) came (back)
028:026   Said one of the (**damsels**): "O my (dear) father!

DANGER
004:103   but when ye are free from **danger**, set up
010:002   That he should warn mankind (of their **danger**),
106:004   security against fear (of **danger**).

DANGERS
006:063   'If He only delivers us from these (**dangers**),

DARE
003:154   what they **dare** not reveal to thee.

DARK
006:063   the **dark** recesses of land and sea, when ye call
006:096   the daybreak (from the **dark**):
006:097   through the **dark** spaces of land and sea:
010:071   so your plan be not to you **dark** and dubious.
017:012   made **dark** while the Sign of the Day We have
024:040   topped by (**dark**) clouds:
038:057   a fluid **dark**, murky, intensely cold!-
055:064   **Dark** green in colour (from plentiful watering).
068:020   like a **dark** and desolate spot,
078:025   and a fluid, **dark**, murky, intensely cold,-

DARKENING
074:029   **Darkening** and changing the colour of man!

DARKENS
016:058   his face **darkens**, and he is filled with
043:017   his face **darkens**, and he is filled

DARKNESS
002:017   and left them in utter **darkness**,
002:019   in it are zones of **darkness**,
002:020   and when the **darkness** grows on them,
002:257   lead them forth into the depths of **darkness**.
002:257   from the depths of **darkness** he leads them
005:016   and leadeth them out of **darkness**, by His Will,
006:001   and made the **Darkness** and the Light.
006:039   in the midst of **darkness** profound:
006:059   the **darkness** (or depths) of the earth,
006:122   the depths of **darkness**, from which he
010:026   No **darkness** nor abasement shall cover
010:027   with pieces form the depth of the **darkness** of Night:
013:016   Or the depths of **darkness** equal with
014:001   out of the depths of **darkness** into light-by
014:005   thy people from the depths of **darkness** into light,
017:078   sun's decline till the **darkness** of the night,
021:087   But he cried through the of **darkness**, "There is no god
024:040   depths of **darkness**, one above another:
024:040   the depths of **darkness** in a vast deep ocean,
027:063   the depths of **darkness** on land and sea, and Who
033:043   the depths of **Darkness** into Light:
035:020   Nor are the depths of **Darkness** and the Light;
036:037   and behold they are plunged in **darkness**;

DARKNESS (continued)
039:006   in three veils of **darkness**.
057:009   the depths of **Darkness** into the Light.
065:011   righteous deeds from the depths of **Darkness** into Light.
075:008   And the moon is buried in **darkness**.
079:029   Its night doth He endow with **darkness**, and its
080:041   **Darkness** will cover them:
081:018   And the Dawn as it breathes away the **darkness**;-
113:003   From the mischief of **Darkness** as it overspreads;

DATE
017:091   of **date** trees and vines, and cause rivers

DATE-PALM
006:099   the **date-palm** and its sheaths (or spathes)
016:067   And from the fruit of the **date-palm** and the vine,

DATE-PALMS
002:266   should have a garden with **date-palms**
016:011   olives, **date-palms**, grapes, and every kind of
018:032   with **date-palms**; in between the two
023:019   of **date-palms** and vines:
026:148   "And corn-fields and **date-palms** with spathes
036:034   with **date-palms** and Vines, and We
055:011   Therein is fruit and **date-palms**, producing spathes

DATE-STALK
036:039   (and withered) lower part of **date-stalk**.

DATE-STONE
006:095   and the **date-stone** to split and sprout.

DATES
006:099   clusters of **dates** hanging low and near:
006:141   with trellises and without, and **dates**, and tilth
019:025   it will let fall fresh ripe **dates** upon thee.
055:011   producing spathes (enclosing **dates**);
055:068   In them will be Fruits, and **dates** and pomegranates:
080:029   And Olives and **Dates**,

DAUGHTER
066:012   And Mary the **daughter** of 'Imran, who guarded

DAUGHTERS
004:011   if only **daughters**, two or more, their share
004:023   sister's **daughters**; foster-mothers
004:023   mother's sisters; brother's **daughters**,
004:023   your mother, **daughters**, sisters, father's sisters,
006:100   attribute to Him sons and **daughters**, praise and
011:078   He said: "O my people! Here are my **daughters**:
011:079   "Well dost thou know we have no need of thy **daughters**:
015:071   He said: "There are my **daughters** (to marry),
016:057   And they assign **daughters** for Allah! - Glory be
016:072   out of them, sons and **daughters** and grandchildren,
017:040   for Himself **daughters** among the angels?
028:027   one of these my **daughters** to thee, on condition
033:050   and **daughters** of thy maternal uncles
033:050   and **daughters** of thy paternal uncles and aunts,
033:059   O prophet! Tell thy wives and **daughters**, and the
037:149   is it that thy Lord has (only) **daughters**, and they have
037:153   Did He (then) choose **daughters** rather than sons?
043:016   What! Has He taken **Daughters** out of what He
052:039   Or has He only **daughters** and ye have sons?

DAVID
002:251   and **David** slew Goliath;
004:163   and to **David** We gave the Psalms.
005:078   by the tongue of **David** and of Jesus
006:084   and among his progeny, **David**, Solomon,
017:055   and We gave to **David** the Psalms.
021:078   And remember **David** and Solomon, when they

DAVID (continued)

021:079 the hills and the birds celebrate Our praises, with **David**:
027:015 We gave knowledge to **David** and Solomon:
034:010 We bestowed Grace aforetime on **David** from Us:
034:013 "Exercise thanks sons of **David**,
038:017 and remember Our Servant **David**, the man
038:022 When they entered the presence of **David**, and he
038:024 (**David**) said: "He has undoubtedly wronged thee
038:024 And **David** gathered that We had tried him:
038:026 O **David**! We did indeed make thee a vicegerent
038:030 To **David** We gave Solomon (for a son),-

DAVID'S

027:016 And Solomon was **David's** heir.

DAWN

002:187 until the white thread of **dawn** appear to you
017:078 in morning prayer for the recital of **dawn** is witnessed.
051:018 And in the hours of early **dawn**,
054:034 Lut's household: them We delivered by early **Dawn**,-
074:034 And by the **Dawn** as it shineth forth,-
081:018 And the **Dawn** as it breathes away the darkness;-
089:001 By the **Dawn**;
113:001 Say: I seek refuge with the Lord of the **Dawn**,

DAY

001:004 Master of the **Day** of Judgment.
002:008 "We believe in Allah and the Last **Day**,"
002:048 a **day** when one soul shall not avail another
002:062 and who believe in Allah and the last **day**,
002:085 and on the **Day** of Judgment
002:113 in their quarrel on the **Day** of Judgment.
002:123 a **day** when one soul shall not avail another,
002:126 believe in Allah and the Last **Day**."
002:164 in the alternation of the Night and the **Day**;
002:174 on the **Day** of Resurrection,
002:177 believe in Allah and the Last **Day**,
002:212 above them on the **Day** of Resurrection;
002:228 if they have faith in Allah and the Last **Day**.
002:232 who believe in Allah and the Last **Day**.
002:249 they said: "This **day** we cannot cope
002:254 before the **Day** comes when no bargaining
002:259 He said: "(Perhaps) a **day** or part of a **day**."
002:264 neither in Allah nor in the last **day**.
002:274 spend of their goods by night and by **day**,
002:281 And fear the **Day** when ye shall be
003:009 a **Day** about which there in no doubt;
003:025 against a **Day** about which there is no doubt,
003:027 And Thou causest the **Day** to gain on the Night;
003:027 "Thou causest the Night to gain on the **Day**.
003:030 "On the **day** when every soul will be confronted
003:055 to the **Day** of Resurrection:
003:072 but reject it at the end of the **day**:
003:077 or look at them on the **Day** of Judgment,
003:106 On the **day** when some faces will be
003:114 They believe in Allah and the Last **Day**;
003:155 on the **day** the two hosts met, it was Satan
003:161 he shall, on the **Day** of Judgment, restore
003:166 What ye suffered on the **day** the two armies met,
003:167 They were that **day** nearer to Unbelief than of Faith,
003:180 on the **Day** of Judgment.
003:185 and only on the **Day** of Judgment shall you
003:190 and the alternation of Night and **Day**,
003:194 and save us from shame on the **Day** of Judgment:
004:038 in Allah and the Last **Day**:
004:039 if they had faith in Allah and in the Last **Day**,

DAY (continued)

004:042 On that **day** those who reject Faith and
004:059 if ye do believe in Allah and the Last **Day**:
004:087 gather you together on the **Day** of Judgement,
004:109 on their behalf on the **Day** of Judgment,
004:136 and the **Day** of Judgment
004:141 betwixt you on the **Day** of Judgment.
004:159 and on the **Day** of Judgment He will be
004:162 and believe in Allah and in the Last **Day**:
005:003 This **day** have I perfected your religion for you,
005:003 This **day** have those who reject Faith given up
005:005 This **day** are (all) things good and pure
005:014 the one and the other, to the **Day** of Judgement.
005:036 for the Chastisement of the **Day** of Judgment,
005:064 enmity and hatred till the **Day** of Judgment.
005:069 any who believe in Allah and the Last **Day**,
005:109 On the **day** when Allah will gather the
005:119 "This is a **day** on which the truthful will profit
006:012 for the **Day** of Judgment, there is
006:013 (or lurketh) in the Night and the **Day**.
006:015 the Chastisement of a Mighty **Day**.
006:016 "On that **day**, if the penalty
006:022 On the **day** shall We gather them all together:
006:060 by **day** doth He raise you up again;
006:060 all that ye have done by **day**: by **day** doth
006:073 the **day** He saith, "Be," Behold! it is.
006:073 the **day** the trumpet will be blown.
006:093 This **day** shall ye receive your reward,-
006:128 On the **day** when He will gather them
006:130 and warning you of the meeting of this **day** of yours?"
006:141 on the **day** that the harvest is gathered.
006:158 The **day** that certain of the Signs of thy
007:008 The balance that **day** will be true
007:014 respite till the **day** they are raised up."
007:032 (and) purely for them on the **Day** of Judgment.
007:051 That **day** shall We forget them as they
007:051 as they forgot the meeting of this **day** of theirs,
007:053 On the **day** when it is fulfilled those who
007:054 He draweth the night as a veil O'er the **day**,
007:059 I fear for you the Punishment of a dreadful **Day**!"
007:163 for on the **day** of their Sabbath their fish
007:163 but on the **day** they had no Sabbath, they came
007:167 to the **Day** of Judgment, those who
007:172 lest ye should say on the **Day** of Judgment:
008:016 to them on such a **day**-unless it
008:041 to our Servant on the **Day** of Discrimination-
008:041 the **Day** of the meeting of the two forces.
008:048 can overcome you this **day**, while I
009:003 on the **day** of the Great Pilgrimage,-that Allah
009:018 as believe in Allah and the Last **Day**, establish
009:019 believe in Allah and the Last **Day**, and strive
009:025 in many battle-fields and on the **day** of Hunain:
009:029 nor the Last **Day**, nor hold that forbidden which
009:035 On the **Day** when it will be heated
009:036 so ordained by Him the **day** He created
009:044 and the Last **Day** ask thee for no exemption from
009:045 and the Last **Day**, and whose hearts are in doubt,
009:077 (to last) till the **day** whereon they shall meet Him:
009:099 believe in Allah and The Last **Day**, and look
009:108 was laid from the first **day** on piety;
010:006 Verily, in the alternation of the Night and the **Day**,
010:015 the Chastisement of a Great **Day** (to come)."
010:024 as if it had not flourished only the **day** before!

DAY (continued)

010:024 there reaches it Our command by night or by **day**,
010:028 One **Day** shall We gather them all together.
010:045 had tarried but an hour of a **day**:
010:045 And on the **day** when He will gather them together:
010:050 His punishment should come to you by night or by **day**,-
010:060 against Allah, of the **Day** of Judgment?
010:067 and the **Day** to make things visible (to you).
010:092 "This **day** shall We save thee in thy body,
010:093 on the **Day** of Judgment.
011:003 for you the Chastisement of a Great **Day**:
011:008 Ah! On the **day** it (actually) reaches them,
011:026 the punishment of a Grievous **Day**."
011:043 Noah said: "This **day** nothing can save,
011:060 in this Life,-and on the **Day** of Judgment.
011:066 and from the Ignominy of that **Day**.
011:077 He said: "This is a distressful **day**."
011:084 for you the Chastisement of a **Day** that will
011:098 on the **Day** of Judgment, and lead
011:099 this (life) and on the **Day** of Judgment:
011:103 that is a **Day** for which mankind will be
011:103 that will be a **Day** of Testimony.
011:105 The **day** it arrives, no soul shall speak
011:114 two ends of the **day** and at the approaches
012:015 (one **day**) tell them the truth of this affair
012:054 he said: "Be assured this **day**, thou art
012:092 He said: "This **day** let no reproach be (cast)
013:003 He draweth the Night as a veil o'er the **Day**.
013:010 by night or walk freely by **day**.
014:018 blows furiously on a tempestuous **day**:
014:031 of a **Day** in which there will be neither mutual
014:033 and the Night and the **Day** hath He (also)
014:041 on the **Day** that the Reckoning will be established!"
014:042 a **Day** when the eyes will fixedly stare in horror,-
014:044 So warn mankind of the **Day** when the Wrath
014:048 One **day** the Earth will be changed to a
014:049 that **day** bound together in fetters:-
015:014 to continue (all **day**) ascending therein,
015:035 on thee till the **Day** of Judgment."
015:036 then respite till the **Day** the (dead) are raised."
015:038 "Till the **Day** of the Time Appointed."
016:012 He has made subject to you the Night and the **Day**;
016:025 That they may bear, on the **Day** of Judgment,
016:027 Then, on the **Day** of Judgment, He will
016:027 with knowledge will say: "This **Day**, indeed, are
016:055 Then enjoy (your brief **day**); but soon
016:084 On the **Day** We shall raise from all Peoples
016:087 That **day** shall they (openly) show (their)
016:089 On the **day** We shall raise from all peoples
016:092 and on the **Day** of Judgment He will certainly
016:111 On the **Day** every soul will come up pleading
016:124 judge between them on the **Day** of Judgment as to
017:012 We have made the Night and the **Day** as two
017:012 made dark while the Sign of the **Day** We have
017:013 On the **Day** of Judgment We shall bring out an account
017:014 thy soul this **day** to make out an account
017:034 will be enquired into (on the **Day** of Reckoning).
017:052 "It will be on a **Day** when He will call you,
017:058 the **Day** of Judgment or punish it with a dreadful
017:062 to the **Day** of Judgment, I will surely
017:071 On the **day** We shall call together all human
017:097 On the **Day** of Judgment We shall gather them
018:019 "We have stayed (perhaps) a **day**, or part of a **day**."

DAY (continued)

018:047 On the **Day** We shall remove the mountains, and thou
018:052 On the **Day** He will say, "Call on
018:099 On that **day** We shall leave them to surge
018:100 And We shall present Hell that **day** for Unbelievers
018:105 on the **Day** of Judgment, give them any Weight.
019:015 the **day** that he dies, and the **day** that he will
019:015 So Peace on him the **day** he was born,
019:026 and this **day** will I enter into no talk with any human
019:033 the **day** that I die, and the **day** that I shall
019:033 "So Peace is on me the **day** I was born,
019:037 of the (coming) Judgment of an awful **Day**!
019:038 the **Day** that they will appear before Us!
019:039 But warn them of the **Day** of Distress, when the
019:085 The **day** We shall gather the righteous to (Allah)
019:095 to him singly on the **Day** of Judgment.
020:059 Moses said: "Your tryst is the **Day** of the Festival,
020:100 on the **Day** of Judgement;
020:101 and grievous will the burden be to them on that **Day**,-
020:102 that **Day**, We shall gather the sinful, blear-eyed
020:102 The **Day** when the Trumpet will be sounded:
020:104 will say: "Ye tarried not longer than a **day**!"
020:108 On that **Day** will they follow the caller
020:109 On that **Day** shall no intercession avail except for
020:124 We shall raise him up blind on the **Day** of Judgment."
020:126 so wilt thou, this **day**, be forgotten.
020:130 and at the sides of the **day**:
021:020 They celebrate His praises night and **day**, nor do
021:033 and the **Day**, and the sun and the moon:
021:042 and by **day** from (the Wrath of) The Most Gracious?"
021:047 for the **Day** of Judgment, so that
021:103 "This is your **Day**,-(the **day**) that ye were promised."
021:104 The **Day** that we roll up the heavens like a
022:002 The **Day** ye shall see it, every mother
022:009 and on the **Day** of Judgment We shall make him
022:017 Allah will judge between them on the **Day** of Judgment:
022:047 Verily a **Day** in the sight of thy Lord is like a thousand
022:055 the Chastisement of a barren **day**.
022:056 On that **Day** the Dominion will be that of Allah:
022:061 That is because Allah merges Night into **Day**,
022:061 and He merges **Day** in Night, and verily
022:069 "Allah will judge between you on the **Day** of Judgment
023:016 Again, on the **Day** of Judgment, will ye
023:065 "Groan not in supplication this **day**; for ye
023:080 and to Him (is due) the alternation of Night and **Day**:
023:100 the **Day** they are raised up.
023:101 relationships between them that **day**, nor will
023:111 "I have rewarded them this **day** for their
023:113 They will say: "We stayed a **day** or part of a **day**:
024:002 if ye believe in Allah and the Last **Day**:
024:024 On the **Day** when their tongues, their hands,
024:025 On that **Day** Allah will pay them back (all) their
024:037 is for the **Day** when hearts and eyes will be
024:044 It is Allah Who alternates the Night and the **Day**:
024:064 and one **day** they will be brought back to Him,
025:014 "This **day** plead not for a single destruction:
025:017 The **Day** He will gather them together as well
025:022 The **Day** they see the angels,-
025:022 no joy will there be to the sinners that **Day**:
025:024 The Companions of the Garden be well, that **Day**,
025:025 The **Day** the heaven shall be rent asunder
025:026 it will be a **Day** of dire difficulty for the
025:026 That **Day**, the dominion right by shall be

DAY (continued)

025:027 The **Day** that the wrong-doer will bite
025:047 and makes the **Day** (as it were) a Resurrection.
025:062 and the **Day** to follow each other:
025:069 the **Day** of Judgment will be doubled to him, and he
026:038 for the appointment of a **day** well-known,
026:082 will forgive me my faults on the **Day** of Judgment.
026:087 on the **Day** when (men) will be raised up;-
026:088 "The **Day** whereon neither wealth nor sons will avail,
026:135 the Chastisement of a Great **Day**."
026:155 (severally) on a **day** appointed.
026:156 lest the Chastisement of a Great **Day** seize you."
026:189 and that was the Chastisement of a Great **Day**.
026:189 Then the punishment of a **day** of overshadowing
027:083 The **Day** We shall gather together from every
027:086 and the **Day** to give them light?
027:087 And the **Day** that the Trumpet will be sounded
027:089 be secure from terror that **Day**.
028:018 the man who had, the **day** before, sought his
028:041 and on the **Day** of Judgment no help
028:042 **Day** of Judgment they will be among the
028:061 but who, on the **Day** of Judgment, is to be among
028:062 That **Day** (Allah) will call to them, and say:
028:065 That **Day** (Allah) will call to them, and say:
028:066 Then the arguments that **day** will be obscure
028:071 the Night perpetual over you to the **Day** of Judgment,
028:072 the **Day** perpetual over you to the **Day** of Judgment,
028:073 has made for you Night and **Day**,-that ye
028:074 The **Day** that He will call on them, He will
028:082 the **day** before began to say on the morrow:
029:013 and on the **Day** of Judgement they will
029:025 but on the **Day** of Judgement ye shall
029:036 serve Allah, and fear the last **day**:
029:055 On the **Day** that the Punishment shall cover
030:004 on that **Day** shall the Believers rejoice-
030:012 On the **Day** that the Hour will come, the guilty
030:014 On the **Day** that the Hour will come,
030:014 that **Day** shall (all men) be sorted out.
030:018 and when the **day** begins to decline.
030:023 that ye take by night and by **day**,
030:034 Then enjoy (your brief **day**); but soon
030:043 on that **Day** shall men be divided (in two).
030:043 from Allah the **Day** which there is no chance
030:055 On the **Day** that the Hour (of reckoning)
030:056 the **Day** of Resurrection: but ye-ye did not know!"
030:056 Allah's Decree, to the **Day** of Resurrection,
030:057 So on that **Day** no excuse of theirs will avail
031:029 Allah merges into **Day** and He merges **Day** into Night;
031:033 and fear (the coming of) a **Day** when no father
032:005 on a **Day**, the measure of which is a thousand
032:014 for ye forgot the Meeting of this **day** of yours,
032:025 on the **Day** of Judgement, in the matters wherein
032:029 Say: "On the **Day** of Decision, no profit
033:021 who hope in Allah and the Final **Day**, and who
033:044 Their salutation on the **Day** they meet
033:066 The **Day** that their faces will be turned over
034:018 secure, by night and by **day**."
034:023 (at the **Day** of Judgment, then) will they
034:030 for a **Day**, which ye cannot put back for an hour
034:033 by **day** and by night: behold! ye
034:040 On the **day** He will gather them all together,
034:042 So on that **Day** no power shall they have
035:013 He merges Night into **Day**, and He

DAY (continued)

035:013 and He merges **Day** into Night,
035:014 On the **Day** of Judgement they will
036:037 We withdraw therefrom the **Day**, and behold
036:040 nor can the Night outstrip the **Day**:
036:054 Then, on that **Day**, not a soul will be wronged
036:055 shall that **Day** have joy in all that they do;
036:059 And O ye in sin! get ye apart this **Day**!
036:064 "Embrace ye the (Fire) this **Day**, for that
036:065 That **Day** shall We set a seal on their mouths.
037:020 This is the **Day** of Judgement!"
037:021 "This is the **Day** of Sorting Out, whose truth
037:026 Nay, but that **day** they shall submit (to Judgment);
037:033 Truly, that **day**, they will (all) share
037:137 Verily, ye pass by their (sites), by **day**-
037:144 inside the Fish till the **Day** of Resurrection.
038:016 our sentence (even) before the **Day** of Account!"
038:018 at eventide and at break of **day**,
038:026 for that they forget the **Day** of Account.
038:053 to you for the **Day** of Account!
038:078 till the **Day** of Judgement."
038:079 then respite till the **Day** the (dead) are raised."
038:081 "Till the **day** of the Time Appointed."
039:005 He makes the Night overlap the **Day**,
039:005 and the **Day** overlap the Night:
039:013 the Chastisement of a Mighty **Day**."
039:015 on the **Day** of Judgement: Ah! that is
039:024 on the **Day** of Judgment (and receive it) by his face,
039:030 Truly thou wilt die (one **day**) and truly
039:030 and truly they (too) will die (one **day**).
039:031 dispute on the **Day** of Judgment,
039:047 pain of the Chastisement on the **Day** of Judgement:
039:060 On the **Day** of Judgement wilt thou see those
039:067 on the **Day** of Judgement the whole of the earth
039:071 and warning you of the Meeting of this **Day** of yours?"
040:009 "And any whom Thou dost preserve from ills that **Day**,-
040:015 of the **Day** of Mutual Meeting,-
040:016 Whose will be the Dominion that **Day**?
040:016 The **Day** whereon they will (all) come forth:
040:017 That **Day** will every soul be requited for what
040:017 no injustice will there be that **Day**, for Allah
040:018 Warn them of the **Day** that is (ever) drawing near,
040:027 one who believes not in the **Day** of Account!"
040:029 this **day**: ye have the upper hand in the land:
040:030 for you something like the **Day** (of disaster)
040:032 a **Day** when there will be mutual calling
040:033 A **day** when ye shall turn your backs and flee:
040:046 and (the Sentence will be) on the **Day** when the
040:049 us the Chastisement for a **Day** (at least)!"
040:051 and on the **Day** when the Witnesses will stand forth,-
040:052 The **Day** when no profit will it be to Wrong-doers
040:061 and the **Day**, as to give you light.
041:019 The **Day** that the enemies of Allah will be
041:037 Among His Signs are the Night and the **Day**,
041:038 are those who celebrate His praises by night and by **day**.
041:040 or he that comes safe through on the **Day** of Judgement?
041:047 The **Day** that (Allah) will propound to them
042:007 and warn (them) of the **Day** of Assembly, of which
042:045 On the **Day** of Judgement. Behold! Truly
042:047 That **Day** there will be for you no place of refuge
042:047 before there come a **Day** which there will be no putting
043:039 that **day**, that ye shall be partners in punishment!
043:065 from the Chastisement of a Grievous **Day**!

DAY (continued)

043:067   Friends on that **Day** will be foes, one to
043:083   (with vanities) until they meet that **Day** of theirs,
044:010   Then watch thou for the **Day** that the sky will bring
044:016   The **day** We shall seize you with a mighty onslaught:
044:040   Verily the **Day** of Sorting Out is the
044:041   The **Day** when no protector can avail his client
045:005   And in the alternation of Night and **Day**, and the
045:017   on the **Day** of Judgement as to those matters in
045:026   for the **Day** of Judgement about which there is
045:027   that **Day** will the followers of Falsehood perish!
045:027   and the **Day** that the Hour of Judgement
045:028   "This **Day** shall ye be recompensed for all that ye did!
045:034   the meeting of this **day** of yours!
045:034   It will also be said: "This **Day** We will forget
045:035   (From) that **Day**, therefore, they shall not be taken out
046:005   such as will not answer him to the **Day** of Judgment,
046:020   And on the **Day** that the Unbelievers will be
046:021   the Chastisement of a Mighty **Day**."
046:034   And on the **Day** that the Unbelievers will be
046:035   they had not tarried more than an hour in a single **day**.
046:035   the **Day** that they see the (Punishment) promised them,
050:020   that will be the **Day** whereof warning
050:022   and sharp is thy sight this **Day**!"
050:030   The **Day** We will ask Hell, "Art thou filled to the full?"
050:034   this is a **Day** of Eternal Life!"
050:041   And listen the **Day** when the Caller will call
050:042   that will be the **day** of Resurrection.
050:042   The **Day** when they will hear a (mighty) Blast
050:044   The **Day** when the Earth will be rent asunder,
051:012   **Day** of Judgment and Justice?"
051:013   (It will be) a **Day** when they will be tried
051:043   "Enjoy (your brief **day**) for a little while!"
051:060   from the **Day** of theirs which they have
052:009   On the **Day** when the firmament will be
052:011   Then woe that **Day** to the rejecters (of Truth);-
052:013   That **Day** shall they be thrust down to the
052:045   they encounter that **Day** of theirs, wherein they
052:046   The **Day** when their plotting will avail them
054:006   (And wait for) the **Day** that the Caller will call (them)
054:008   eyes transfixed towards the Caller!-"Hard is this **Day**!"
054:019   on a **Day** of bitter ill-luck,
054:048   The **Day** they will be dragged through the Fire
055:029   every **day** in (new) Splendour doth He (shine)!
055:039   On that **Day** no question will be asked
056:050   for the meeting appointed for a **Day** Well-known.
056:056   on the **Day** of Requital!
057:006   and He merges **Day** into Night; and He
057:006   He merges Night into **Day**,
057:012   The **Day** shalt thou see the believing men and the
057:012   (there greeting will be) "Good News for you this **Day**!
057:013   The **day** will the Hypocrites-men and women-say to
057:015   "This **Day** shall no ransom be accepted of you,
058:006   On the **Day** that Allah will raise
058:007   will He them what they did on the **Day** of Judgment.
058:018   The **Day** will Allah raise them all up
058:022   who believe in Allah and the Last **Day**, loving those
060:003   on the **Day** of Judgment: He will judge between you:
060:006   for those whose hope is in Allah and in the Last **Day**.
062:009   is proclaimed to prayer on Friday (the **Day** of Assembly),
064:009   that will be a **day** of mutual loss and gain (among you).
064:009   The **Day** that He assembles you (all) for a **day** of
065:002   the Last **Day**. And for those who fear Allah,

DAY (continued)

066:007   make no excuses this **Day**!
066:008   the **Day** that Allah will not permit to be
068:024   in upon you into the (garden) this **day**."
068:039   on oath, reaching to the **Day** of Judgment,
068:042   The **Day** that the Shin shall be laid bare,
069:004   disbelieved in the **day** of Noise and Clamour!
069:015   On that **Day** shall the (Great) Event come to pass,
069:016   for it will that **Day** be flimsy,
069:017   and eight will, that **Day**, bear the Throne
069:018   That **Day** shall ye be brought to Judgment:
069:020   that my Account would (one **Day**) reach me!"
069:035   "So no friend hath he here this **Day**.
070:004   unto Him in a **Day** the measure whereof is (as)
070:006   They see the (**Day**) indeed as a far-off (event):
070:008   The **Day** that the sky will be like molten brass,
070:011   from the Chastisement of that **Day** by his children,
070:026   those who hold to the Truth of the **Day** of Judgment;
070:042   that **Day** of theirs which they have been promised!
070:043   The **Day** whereon they will issue from their sepulchres
070:044   Such is the **Day** the which they are promised!
071:005   to my People night and **day**:
073:007   True, there is for thee by **day** prolonged occupation
073:014   The **Day** the earth and the mountains will be
073:017   a **Day** that will make children hoary-headed?-
073:020   But Allah doth appoint Night and **Day** in due measure.
074:009   That will be-that **Day**-a **Day** of Distress,-
074:046   "And we used to deny the **Day** of Judgment,
075:001   I do swear by the Resurrection **Day**;
075:006   He questions: "When is the **Day** of Resurrection?"
075:010   That **Day** will Man say "Where is the refuge?"
075:012   that **Day** will be the place of rest.
075:013   That **Day** will Man be told (all) that
075:022   Some faces that **Day**, will beam
075:024   And some faces, that **Day**, will be sad and dismal,
075:030   That **Day** the Drive will be (all) to thy Lord!
076:007   and they fear a **Day** whose evil flies far and wide.
076:010   "We only fear a **Day** of frowning and distress
076:011   from the evil of that **Day**, and will
076:027   behind them a **Day** (that will be) hard.
077:012   For what **Day** are these (Portents) deferred?
077:013   For the **Day** of Sorting out.
077:014   what is the **Day** of Sorting out?
077:015   Ah woe, that **Day**, to the Rejecters of Truth!
077:019   Ah woe, that **Day**, to the Rejecters of Truth!
077:024   Ah woe, that **Day**, to the Rejecters of Truth!
077:028   Ah woe, that **Day**, to the Rejecters of Truth!
077:034   Ah woe, that **Day**, to the Rejecters of Truth!
077:035   That will be a **Day** when they shall not
077:037   Ah woe, that **Day**, to the Rejecters of Truth!
077:038   That will be a **Day** of Sorting out
077:040   Ah woe, that **Day**, to the Rejecters of Truth!
077:045   Ah woe, that **Day**, to the Rejecters of Truth!
077:047   Ah woe, that **Day**, to the Rejecters of Truth!
077:049   Ah woe, that **Day**, to the Rejecters of Truth!
078:011   And made the **day** as a means of subsistence?
078:017   Verily the **Day** of Sorting Out is a thing appointed,-
078:018   The **Day** that the Trumpet shall be sounded, and ye
078:038   The **Day** that the Spirit and the angels will stand
078:039   That is the True **Day**: therefore, whoso will,
078:040   of a Chastisement near,-the **Day** when man will see
079:006   One **Day** everything that can be in commotion
079:008   Hearts that **Day** will be in agitation;

DAY (continued)

079:035	The **Day** when Man shall remember (all) that
079:046	The **Day** they see it, (it will be)
080:034	That **Day** shall a man flee from his own brother,
080:037	Each one of them, that **Day**, will have enough concern
080:038	Some Faces that **Day** will be beaming.
080:040	And other faces that **Day** will be dust-stained;
082:015	Which they will enter on the **Day** of Judgment,
082:017	what the **Day** of Judgment is?
082:018	what the **Day** of Judgment is?
082:019	(It will be) the **Day** when no soul shall have power
082:019	for the Command, that **Day**, will be (wholly) with Allah.
083:005	On a Mighty **Day**,
083:006	A **Day** when (all) mankind will stand before
083:010	Woe, that **Day**, to those that deny-
083:011	Those that deny the **Day** of Judgment.
083:015	that **Day**, will they be veiled.
083:034	But on this **Day** the Believers will laugh
085:002	By the promised **Day** (of Judgment);
086:009	The **Day** that (all) things secret will be tested,
088:002	Some faces, that **Day**, will be humiliated,
088:008	(Other) faces that **Day** will be joyful,
089:023	And Hell, that **Day**, is brought (face to face),-
089:023	(face to face),-on that **Day** will man remember,
089:025	For, that **Day**, His Chastisement will be such as
090:014	Or the giving of food in a **day** of privation
091:003	By the **Day** as it shows up (the Sun's) glory;
092:002	By the **Day** as it appears in glory;
099:004	On that **Day** will she declare her tidings:
099:006	On that **Day** will men proceed in groups sorted out,
100:011	well-acquainted with them, (Even to) that **Day**?
101:001	The (**Day**) of Noise and Clamour:
101:002	What is the (**Day**) of Clamour?
101:003	what the (**Day**) of Noise and Clamour is?
101:004	(It is) a **Day** whereon Men will be like
102:008	Then, shall ye be Questioned that **Day** about the

DAY-BREAK

006:096	He it is that cleaveth the **day-break** (from the dark):

DAYLIGHT

007:098	against its coming in broad **daylight** while they

DAYS

002:080	not touch us but for few numbered **days**:"
002:184	(Fasting) for a fixed number of **days**;
002:184	(should be made up) from **days** later.
002:185	(should be made up) by **days** later.
002:196	And seven **days** on his return,
002:196	he should fast three **days** during the Hajj.
002:196	making ten **days** in all.
002:203	but if anyone hastens to leave in two **days**,
002:203	Remember Allah during the Appointed **Days**
002:234	concerning themselves four months and ten **days**
003:024	not touch us but for a few numbered **days**":
003:041	no man for three **days** but with signals.
003:140	Such **days** (of varying fortunes) We give to men
005:050	a judgment of (the **Days** of) Ignorance?
005:089	If that is beyond your means, fast for three **days**.
007:054	Who created the heavens and the earth in six **days**,
010:003	Who created the heavens and the earth in six **Days**,
010:102	but (what happened in) the **days** of the men who
011:007	and the earth in six **Days**-and His Throne
011:065	in your homes for three **days**:
014:005	and remind them of the **Days** of Allah."
019:084	a (limited) number (of **days**).

DAYS (continued)

020:103	"Ye tarried not longer than ten (**days**);"
022:028	through the **Days** appointed, over the
025:059	and the earth and all that is between, in six **days**,
032:004	heavens and the earth and all between them, in six **Days**,
035:011	Nor is a man long-lived granted length of **days**,
037:075	(In the **days** of old), Noah cried to Us, and We
041:009	that ye deny Him Who created the earth in two **Days**?
041:010	and measured therein its sustenance in four **Days**,
041:012	So He completed them as seven firmaments in two **Days**,
041:016	a furious Wind through **days** of disaster, that We
045:014	hope for the **Days** of Allah:
050:038	and all between them in Six **Days**,
057:004	and the earth in six **Days**, then He
069:007	seven nights and eight **days** in succession:
069:024	in the **days** that are gone!"

DAZED

075:007	At length, when the Sight is **dazed**,

DAZZLE

002:204	life may **dazzle** thee,
005:100	of the bad may **dazzle** thee; So fear
009:055	nor their children **dazzle** thee: in reality
009:085	nor their children **dazzle** thee: Allah's Wish

DAZZLING

033:033	and make not a **dazzling** display, like that

DEAD

002:073	Thus Allah bringeth the **dead** to life
002:154	"They are **dead**."
002:164	gives therewith to an earth that is **dead**;
002:173	He hath only forbidden you **dead** meat,
002:260	"My Lord! show me how thou givest life to the **dead**.
003:027	and Thou bringest the **dead** out of the living;
003:027	Thou bringest the Living out of the **dead**,
003:049	and I bring the **dead** into life by Allah's leave;
003:169	who are slain in Allah's way as **dead**.
005:003	Forbidden to you (for food) are: **dead** meat, blood,
005:110	thou bringest forth the **dead** by My leave.!
006:036	be sure, will accept: as to the **dead**, Allah
006:095	He causeth the living to issue from the **dead**.
006:095	cause the **dead** to issue from the living.
006:111	and the **dead** did speak unto them, and We
006:122	Can he who was **dead**, to whom
006:145	unless it be **dead** meat, or blood
007:057	We drive them to a land that is **dead**, make rain
007:057	thus shall We raise up the **dead**:
010:031	and the **dead** from the living?
010:031	brings out the living from the **dead** and the
013:031	or the **dead** were made to speak,
015:036	then respite till the Day the (**dead**) are raised."
016:021	(They are things) **dead**, lifeless: nor do thy
016:115	He has only forbidden you **dead** meat, and blood,
019:066	Man says: "What! when I am **dead**, shall I
021:021	gods from the earth who can raise (the **dead**)?
022:006	it is He Who gives life to the **dead**,
023:041	as rubbish of **dead** leaves.
025:049	That with it We may give life to a **dead** land,
027:067	shall we really be raised (from the **dead**)?
027:080	Truly thou canst not cause the **Dead** to listen,
030:019	and thus shall ye be brought out (from the **dead**).
030:019	It is He Who brings out the living from the **dead**,
030:019	and brings out the **dead** for the living,
030:019	and Who gives life to the earth after it is **dead**:
030:024	and with it gives life to the earth after it is **dead**:

DEAD (continued)

030:050 verily the Same will give life to the men who are **dead**:
030:052 So verily thou canst not make the **dead** to hear,
035:009 and We drive them to a land that is **dead**,
035:022 are living and those that are **dead**.
036:012 Verily We shall give life to the **dead**, And We
036:033 A Sign for them is the earth that is **dead**;
038:079 then respite till the Day the (**dead**) are raised."
041:039 He Who gives life to the (**dead**) earth can surely
041:039· can surely give life to (men) who are **dead**.
042:009 and it is He Who gives life to the **dead**:
043:011 and We raise to life therewith a land that is **dead**;
043:011 even so will ye be raised (from the **dead**);-
046:033 is able to give life to the **dead**?
049:012 to eat the flesh of his **dead** brother?
050:011 and We give (new) life therewith to a land that is **dead**:
053:047 a Second Creation (raising of the **Dead**);
075:040 the power to give life to the **dead**?
077:026 The living and the **dead**,

DEAF

002:018 **Deaf**, dumb, and blind,
002:171 to nothing but calls and cries: **deaf**, dumb, and blind,
005:071 yet again many of them became blind and **deaf**.
005:071 so they became blind and **deaf**; yet Allah
006:039 Those who reject Our Signs are **deaf** and dumb,-
008:022 the sight of Allah are the **deaf** and the dumb,-
010:042 but canst thou make the **deaf** to hear,-even though
011:024 may be compared to the blind and **deaf**, and those
017:097 their faces, blind, dumb, and **deaf**:
021:045 but the **deaf** will not hear the call,
025:073 they were **deaf** or blind;
027:080 the **Deaf** to hear the call, (especially) when
030:052 the **deaf** to hear the call, when they
043:040 Canst thou then make the **deaf** to hear, or give
047:023 has cursed for He has made them **deaf** and blinded

DEAFENING

080:033 At length, when there comes the **Deafening** Noise,-

DEAFNESS

006:025 and **deafness** believe in them;
017:046 and **deafness** into their ears:
018:057 and over their ears, **deafness**.
031:007 as if there were **deafness** in both his ears:
041:005 and in our ears is a **deafness**,
041:044 there is a **deafness** in their ears,

DEAL

002:279 ye shall have your capital sums: **deal** not unjustly,
002:282 O ye who believe! when ye **deal** with each other,
003:159 that thou dost **deal** gently with them.
004:003 be able to **deal** justly with the orphans,
004:003 be able to **deal** justly (with them),
004:019 about through it a great **deal** of good.
010:044 Verily Allah will not **deal** unjustly with man in aught:
024:050 Allah and His Messenger will **deal** unjustly with them?
037:034 Verily that is how We shall **deal** with Sinners.
073:011 And leave Me (alone to **deal** with) those in
074:011 Leave Me alone, (to **deal**) with the (creature)
077:018 Thus do We **deal** with men of sin.
083:001 Woe to those that **deal** in fraud,-
096:018 call on the angels of punishment (to **deal** with him)!

DEALING

003:021 and slay those who teach just **dealing** with mankind,
005:008 as witnesses to fair **dealing**, and let not
035:043 in Allah's way (of **dealing**).

DEALING (continued)

035:043 in Allah's way (of **dealing**): no turning
040:085 (Such has been) Allah's way of **dealing** with His
060:008 from **dealing** kindly and justly with them:

DEALT

002:272 and ye shall not be **dealt** with unjustly.
002:279 and ye shall no be **dealt** with unjustly.
002:281 and none shall be **dealt** with unjustly.
003:161 and none shall be **dealt** with unjustly.
004:077 never will ye be **dealt** unjustly in the very least!
012:089 He said: "Know ye how ye **dealt** with Joseph,
014:045 ye were clearly shown how We **dealt** with them;
016:111 and none will be unjustly **dealt** with.
017:071 will not be **dealt** with unjustly in the least.
021:047 that not a soul will be **dealt** with unjustly in the least.
035:043 the way the ancients were **dealt** with?
089:006 Seest thou not how thy Lord **dealt** with the 'Ad
105:001 Seest thou not how thy Lord **dealt** with the

DEAR

012:005 Said (the father): "My (**dear**) little son! relate
028:026 "O my (**dear**) father! engage him on wages:

DEARER

009:024 in which ye delight-are **dearer** to you than Allah
012:033 He said: "O my Lord! the prison is **dearer** to my

DEATH

002:019 the while they are in terror of **death**.
002:056 Then We raised you up after your **death**;
002:094 then seek ye for **death**,
002:095 But they will never seek for **death**,
002:133 when **Death** appeared before Jacob?
002:180 when **death** approaches any of you,
002:243 for fear of **death**?
002:258 "My Lord is He Who Giveth life and **death**."
002:258 He said: "I give life and **death**."
002:259 after (this) its **death**?"
003:143 Ye did indeed wish for **death** before ye encountered it:
003:154 to the place of their **death**":
003:154 those for whom **death** was decreed would certainly
003:156 It is Allah that gives Life and **Death**,
003:168 Say: "Avert **death** from your own selves,
003:185 Every soul shall have a taste of **death**:
004:015 to houses until **death** do claim them,
004:018 until **death** faces one of them, and he says,
004:078 "Wherever ye are, **death** will find you out,
004:159 but must believe in Him before his **death**;
005:003 or by being gored to **death**; that which
005:106 and the chance of **death** befalls you (thus)
005:106 when **death** approaches any of you,
006:061 At length, when **death** approaches one of you.
006:093 the wicked (do fare) in the agonies of **death**!-
006:162 my life and my **death**, are (all) for Allah,
007:037 until, when Our messengers (of **death**) arrive
007:133 Wholesale **Death**, Locusts, lice, Frogs,
007:158 it is He that giveth both life and **death**.
008:006 as if they were being driven to **death** and they saw it.
008:050 angels take the soul of the Unbelievers (at **death**),
010:104 Who will take your souls (at **death**):
011:007 "Ye shall indeed be raised up after **death**, the Unbelievers
012:101 Take Thou my soul (at **death**) as one submitting
014:017 **death** will come to him from every quarter,
015:023 it is We Who give life, and Who give **death**:
016:065 to the earth after its **death**:
016:070 and takes your souls at **death**;

DEATH (continued)

017:075   and an equal portion in **death**:
018:006   fret thyself to **death**, following after them,
021:035   Every soul shall have a taste of **death**:
023:080   It is He Who gives life and **death**,
023:099   Until, when **death** comes to one of them,
025:003   they control **Death** nor Life nor Resurrection.
026:116   O Noah! thou shalt be stone (to **death**)."
029:057   Every soul shall have a taste of **death**:
029:063   and gives life therewith after its **death**,
030:050   how He gives life to the earth after its **death**:
032:011   Say: "The Angel of **Death**, put in charge of you,
033:016   if ye are running away from **death** or slaughter;
033:019   like one who faints from **death**:
034:014   nothing showed them his **death** except a little worm
034:014   Then, when We decreed (Solomon's) **death**,
035:009   the earth therewith after its **death**:
037:059   "Except our first **death**, and that
039:042   It is Allah that takes the souls (of men) at **death**;
039:042   those on whom He has passed the decree of **death**,
040:068   It is He Who gives Life and **Death**;
044:008   it is He Who gives life and gives **death**,-the Lord
044:035   "There is nothing beyond our first **death**, and we
044:056   Nor will they there taste **Death**,
044:056   except the first **Death**;
045:005   and revives therewith the earth after its **death**,
045:021   their Life and their **death**?
045:026   then gives you **death**;
047:020   with a look of one in swoon at the approach of **death**.
047:027   take their souls at **death**, and smite
050:019   And the stupor of **death** comes in truth.
050:043   Verily it is We Who give Life and **Death**;
053:044   That it is He who Granteth **Death** and Life;
056:060   We have decreed **Death** to be your common lot,
057:002   it is He Who gives life and **Death**;
057:017   life to the earth after its **death**!
062:006   then express your desire for **Death**, if ye
062:007   their desire (for **Death**), because of
062:008   Say "The **Death** from which ye flee will truly
063:010   before **Death** should come to any of you and he
067:002   He Who created **Death** and Life, that He
069:027   "Ah! would that (**Death**) had made an end of me!

DEBASE

002:130   as **debase** their souls with folly?

DEBT

009:060   for those in bondage and in **debt**; in the cause
052:040   are burdened with a load of **debt**?-
068:046   with a load of **debt**?-

DEBTOR

002:280   If the **debtor** is in a difficulty,

DEBTS

004:011   after the payment of legacies and **debts**.
004:012   after payment of legacies and **debts**.
056:066   with **debts** (for nothing):

DECAYS

020:120   and to a kingdom that never **decays**?"

DECEASED

004:011   if the **deceased** left brothers (or sisters),
004:011   if the **deceased** left children; if no children
004:092   If the **deceased** belonged to a people
004:176   if (such a **deceased** was) a woman, who left no child,

DECEASED'S

004:092   And pay blood-money to the **deceased's** family,

DECEIT

006:113   To such (**deceit**) let the hearts
007:022   So by **deceit** he brought about their fall:
017:064   But Satan promises them nothing but **deceit**.

DECEITS

005:013   barring a few-ever bent on (new) **deceits**:

DECEIVE

002:009   Fain would they **deceive** Allah
002:009   but they only **deceive** themselves
003:024   for their forgeries **deceive** them as to their own religion.
003:196   of the unbelievers through the land **deceive** thee:
004:142   The Hypocrites-they seek to **deceive** Allah but it
004:142   but it is Allah who **deceive** them.
008:062   Should they intend to **deceive** thee,- verily
016:092   Using your oaths to **deceive** one another, lest one
031:033   the Chief **Deceiver** deceive you about Allah.
031:033   **deceive** you, nor let the Chief **Deceiver**
035:005   let the Chief **Deceiver** deceive you about Allah.
035:005   life **deceive** you, nor let the Chief **Deceiver**
040:004   through the land **deceive** thee!

DECEIVED

006:070   and are **deceived** by the life of this world.
006:130   It was the life of this world that **deceived** them.
007:051   and were **deceived** by the life of the world."
045:035   and the life of the world **deceived** you."
057:014   And the Deceiver **deceived** you in respect of Allah.
057:014   and (your false) desires **deceived** you; until there
059:016   (Their allies **deceived** them), like Satan, when he

DECEIVER

031:033   the Chief **Deceiver** deceive you about Allah.
035:005   let the Chief **Deceiver** deceive you about Allah.
057:014   And the **Deceiver** deceived you in respect of Allah.

DECEPTION

003:185   is but goods and chattels of **deception**.
004:120   but Satan's promises are nothing but **deception**.
006:112   flowery discourses by way of **deception**.
016:094   to practice **deception** between yourselves.
057:020   of this world, but goods and chattels of **deception**?

DECIDE

002:233   If they both **decide** on weaning,
002:233   if ye **decide** on a foster-mother for your offspring
004:020   But if ye **decide** to take one wife
007:087   until Allah doth **decide** between us:
007:087   for He is the best to **decide**."
007:089   Our Lord! **Decide** thou between us and our
007:089   for thou art the best to **decide**."
010:109   for He is the Best to **decide**.
010:109   till Allah doth **decide**:
016:059   Ah! what an evil (choice) they **decide** on!
017:016   When We **decide** to destroy a town, We command
027:078   Verily thy Lord will **decide** between them
034:026   and He is the One to **decide**, the One
034:026   and will in the end **decide** the matter
038:022   **decide** now between us with truth,

DECIDED

008:042   a matter already **decided**; that those who died
008:044   a matter already **decided** and unto
011:110   the matter would have been **decided** between them:
014:022   And Satan will say when the matter is **decided**: "It was
027:032   no affair have I **decided** except in your presence."

DECIDED (continued)

033:036   been **decided** by Allah and His Messenger, to have
040:078   the matter was **decided** in truth and justice,
042:021   the matter would have been **decided** between them

DECIDES

040:068   and when He **decides** upon an affair, He says

DECISION

002:210   all questions go back (for **decision**).
003:128   Not for thee, (but for Allah), is the **decision**:
003:159   Then, when thou hast taken a **decision**,
004:047   for the **decision** of Allah must be carries out.
004:176   They ask thee for a legal **decision**, say:
005:043   But why do they come to thee for **decision**,
005:052   or a **decision** from Him then will they regret of
008:043   and ye would surely have disputed in (your) **decision**:
009:024   then wait until Allah brings about His **decision**:
011:123   and to Him goeth back every affair (for **decision**):
014:015   But they sought victory and **decision** (there and then)
022:041   the end (and **decision**) of (all) affairs.
022:076   and to Allah go back all affairs (for **decision**).
032:028   They say: "When will this **decision** be, if ye
032:029   Say: "On the Day of **Decision**, no profit
033:036   to have any option about their **decision**:
038:020   and sound judgment in speech and **decision**.
039:069   and a just **decision** pronounced between them;
039:075   The **Decision** between them (at Judgment) will be in
042:010   the **decision** thereof is with Allah:

DECISIONS

004:065   no resistance against thy **decisions**,

DECISIVE

047:020   of **decisive** meaning is revealed, and fighting

DECKED

010:024   its golden ornaments and is **decked** out (in beauty):
037:006   We have indeed **decked** the lower heaven

DECLARATION

009:001   A (**declaration**) of immunity from Allah
079:043   with the **declaration** thereof?

DECLARE

002:160   make amends and openly **declare** (the Truth):
003:049   and I **declare** to you what ye eat,
004:060   to those who **declare** that they believe in
007:167   Behold! thy Lord did **declare** that He
009:065   they **declare** (with emphasis): "We were only
009:107   but Allah doth **declare** that they
010:054   they would **declare** (their) repentance when they
013:010   of you conceal his speech or **declare** it openly;
017:044   And yet ye understand not how they **declare** His glory!
017:044   and all beings therein, **declare** His glory:
037:166   who **declare** (Allah's) glory!"
038:018   It was We that made the hills **declare**, in unison
056:082   that ye should **declare** it false?
059:024   and on earth, doth **declare** His Praises and Glory:
062:001   and on earth, doth **declare** the Praises and Glory
064:001   and on earth, doth **declare** the Praises and Glory
099:004   On that Day will she **declare** her tidings:

DECLARED

014:007   to be **declared** (publicly): "If ye are grateful,
048:015   Allah has already **declared** (this) beforehand":

DECLARES

006:057   He **declares** the Truth, and He is
057:001   and on earth,-**declares** the Praises and Glory
059:001   and on earth, **declares** the Praises and Glory

DECLARES (continued)

061:001   and on earth, **declares** the Praises and Glory

DECLINE

003:023   turn back and **decline** (the arbitration).
004:135   or **decline** to do justice, verily Allah
005:042   either judge between them, or **decline** to interfere.
005:042   If thou **decline**, they cannot hurt thee in the least.
009:024   the commerce in which ye fear a **decline**:
014:044   to swear aforetime that ye suffer no **decline**?
017:078   sun's **decline** till the darkness of the night,
024:048   behold, some of them **decline** (to come).
030:018   and when the day begins to **decline**.

DECLINED

008:023   turned back and **declined** (faith).

DECLINING

018:017   when it rose, **declining** to the right from their

DECOMPOSED

036:078   and **decomposed** ones (at that)?"

DECREE

009:048   and the **Decree** of Allah became manifest, much to
011:058   So when Our **decree** issued, We saved Hud
011:066   When Our **Decree** issued, We saved Salih
011:073   They said: "Dost thou wonder at Allah's **decree**?
011:076   The **decree** of thy Lord hath gone forth:
011:082   When Our **decree** issued, We turned (the cities)
011:094   When Our **decree** issued, We saved Shu'aib
011:101   when there issued the **decree** of thy Lord:
015:066   And We made known this **decree** to him, that the
019:071   a **Decree** which must be accomplished.
020:072   So **decree** whatever thou desirest to degree:
020:072   for thou canst only **decree** (touching) the life of this
027:078   Verily thy Lord will decide between them by His **Decree**:
030:056   Allah's **Decree**, to the Day of Resurrection,
033:038   And the command of Allah is a **decree** determined.
036:038   that is the **decree** of (Him), the Exalted
039:019   Is, then, one against whom the **decree** of Punishment
039:042   has passed the **decree** of death, He keeps
039:071   but the **Decree** of Chastisement has been proved
041:012   Such is the **Decree** of (Him) the Exalted in Might,
042:021   Had it not been for the **Decree** of Judgement, the matter

DECREED

003:047   when He hath **decreed** a matter,
003:154   those for whom death was **decreed** would certainly
006:002   and then **decreed** a stated term (for you).
009:051   except what Allah has **decreed** for us:
012:041   (So) hath been **decreed** that matter whereof ye
015:004   had not a term **decreed** and assigned beforehand.
017:004   And We **decreed** for the Children of Israel
017:023   Thy Lord hath **decreed** that ye worship none but Him,
017:099   Only He has **decreed** a term appointed,
019:021   it is a matter (so) **decreed**."
022:004   About the (Satan) it is **decreed** that whoever
028:044   when We **decreed** the commission to Moses,
034:014   Then, when We **decreed** (Solomon's) death,
054:012   (and rose) to the extent **decreed**.
056:060   We have **decreed** Death to be your common lot,
058:021   Allah has **decreed**: "It is I and My messengers
059:003   has **decreed** banishment for them, He would

DECREES

006:034   the Words (and **Decrees**) of Allah.
007:037   must reach them from the Book (of **Decrees**):

DECREETH
002:117 when He **decreeth** a matter He saith to it:

DECREPIT
019:008 and I have grown quite **decrepit** from old age?"

DEDICATE
003:035 "O my Lord! I do **dedicate** unto thee what is in

DEED
003:017 who are true (in word and **deed**);
004:114 but if one exhorts to a **deed** of charity or
004:127 There is not a good **deed** which ye do, but
004:149 Whether you do openly a good **deed** or conceal
005:038 a retribution for their **deed**s and exemplary
005:095 that he may taste of the penalty of his **deed**.
009:120 was reckoned to their credit as a **deed** of righteousness,-
009:121 but the **deed** is inscribed to their credit;
010:061 and whatever **deed** ye (mankind) may be doing,-
017:032 for it is an indecent (**deed**) and an way.
018:030 of any who do a (single) righteous **deed**.
024:033 your slaves ask for a **deed** in writing (for emancipation)
024:033 give them such a **deed** if ye know any good in them;
026:019 "And thou didst a **deed** of thine which (thou knowest)
028:084 If any does good the reward to him is better than his **deed**;
035:010 it is He Who exalts each **Deed** of Righteousness.
040:040 and he that works a righteous **deed**-whether man
045:015 If anyone does a righteous **deed**, it is
067:002 that He may try which of you is best in **deed**:

DEEDS
002:167 (the fruits of) their **deeds** as (nothing but)
002:276 but will give increase for **deeds** of charity:
002:277 and do **deeds** of righteousness,
003:182 "This is because of the (unrighteous **deeds**) which
004:031 We shall remit your evil **deeds**, and admit
004:057 and do **deeds** of righteousness, We shall
004:062 Because of the **deeds** which their hands
004:088 Allah hath cast them for their (evil) **deeds**.
004:122 and do **deeds** of righteousness, We shall soon
004:124 If any do **deeds** of righteousness, be they
004:173 and do **deeds** of righteousness, He will
005:009 and do **deeds** of righteousness hath Allah promised
005:079 evil indeed were the **deeds** which they did.
005:093 and do **deeds** of righteousness there is no
005:093 and do **deeds** of righteousness,-then again
006:003 the (recompense) which ye earn (by your **deeds**).
006:122 their own **deeds** seem pleasing.
006:132 (or ranks) according to their **deeds**:
006:151 come not nigh to indecent **deeds**, whether
007:033 indecent **deeds**, whether open or secret;
007:043 for your **deeds** (of righteousness)."
007:147 vain are their **deeds**:
007:155 wouldst Thou destroy us for the **deeds** of the
007:173 the **deeds** of men who followed falsehood?"
008:029 remove from you (all) evil **deeds** and forgive you:
008:051 This is "Because of (the **deeds**) which your
008:052 "(**Deeds**) after the manner of the people
008:054 "(**Deeds**) after the manner of the people
009:009 evil indeed are the **deeds** thy have done.
009:079 of the Believers as give themselves (**deeds** of) charity,
009:100 those who follow them in (all) good **deeds**,
010:012 Thus do the **deeds** of transgressors seem fair
010:030 (the fruits of) the **deeds** it sent before:
011:015 their **deeds** therein,-without diminution.
011:016 and of no effect are the **deeds** that they do!
011:036 So grieve no longer over their (evil) **deeds**.

011:111 (in full the recompense) of their **deeds**:
012:024 (all) evil and indecent **deeds**:
013:031 cease to seize them for their (ill) **deeds**, or to
014:042 the **deeds** of those who do wrong.
015:093 For all their **deeds**.
016:034 But the evil results of their **deeds** overtook them,
016:090 and He forbids all indecent **deeds**, and evil
017:009 to the Believers who work **deeds** of righteousness,
017:025 in your hearts: if ye do **deeds** of righteousness,
018:002 Glad Tidings to the Believers who work righteous **deeds**,
018:046 Good **Deeds**, are best in the sight of thy Lord,
018:049 And the Book (of **Deeds**) will be
018:057 forgetting the (**deeds**) which his hands have sent
018:103 lose most in respect of their **deeds**?
018:107 As to those who believe and work righteous **deeds**,
019:076 Good **Deeds**, are best in the sight of thy Lord,
019:096 and work **deeds** of righteousness, will The
020:075 who have worked righteous **deeds**,-for them
020:112 But he who works **deeds** of righteousness, and has
021:073 and We inspired them to do good **deeds**,
022:010 of the **deeds** which thy hands sent forth, for verily
022:014 who believe and work righteous **deeds**, to Gardens,
022:023 and work righteous **deeds**, to Gardens
022:056 righteous **deeds** will be in Gardens of Delight.
023:063 and there are, besides that **deeds** of theirs, which they
023:102 Then those whose balance (of good **deeds**) is heavy,-
024:038 to the best of their **deeds**, and add
024:039 their **deeds** are like a mirage in sandy
024:055 who believe and work righteous **deeds**, that He
025:023 make such **deeds** as floating dust scattered about.
025:023 And We shall turn to whatever **deeds** they did
025:070 and works righteous **deeds**, for Allah
027:004 We have made their **deeds** pleasing in their eyes;
027:024 Satan has made their **deeds** seem pleasing
027:090 that which ye have earned by your **deeds**?"
028:047 should seize them for (the **deeds**) that their
028:055 "To us our **deeds**, and to you yours; peace be
028:084 punished (to the extent) of their **deeds**.
029:007 Those who believe and work righteous **deeds**,-
029:007 them according to the best of their **deeds**.
029:009 And those who believe and work righteous **deeds**,-
029:038 Satan made their **deeds** alluring to them,
029:045 the (**deeds**) that ye do.
029:045 for Prayer restrains from shameful and evil **deeds**;
029:055 "Taste ye (the fruits) of your **deeds**!"
029:058 and work **deeds** of righteousness-to them
030:015 and worked righteous **deeds**, shall be
030:041 may give them a taste of some of their **deeds**:
030:045 and work righteous **deeds**, out of His Bounty.
031:008 For those who believe and work righteous **deeds**,
031:023 and We shall tell them the truth of their **deeds**:
032:014 for your (evil) **deeds**!"
032:017 for them-as a reward for their (good) **Deeds**.
032:019 Gardens as hospitable homes, for their (good) **deeds**.
032:019 For those who believe and do righteous **deeds**,
033:019 and so Allah has made their **deeds** of none effect:
034:004 and work **deeds** of righteousness:
034:033 be a requital for their (ill) **Deeds**.
034:037 whom there is a multiplied Reward for their **deeds**,
035:007 who believe and work righteous **deeds**, is Forgiveness,
035:032 by Allah's leave, foremost in good **deeds**;
035:037 So taste ye (the fruit of your **deeds**):

DEEDS (continued)

035:037 not the (**deeds**) we used to do!"-"Did we not
036:054 but be repaid the meeds of your past **Deeds**.
038:024 who believe and work **deeds** of righteousness,
038:028 and work **deeds** of righteousness, the same
039:035 (even) the worst in their **deeds** and give
039:048 For the evils of their **Deeds** will confront them,
039:051 Nay, the evil results of their **deeds** overtook them.
039:051 evil results of their **deeds** will soon overtake them (too),
039:069 the Record (of **Deeds**) will be placed (open);
039:070 in full (the fruit) of its **deeds**;
040:037 in Pharaoh's eyes, the evil of his **deeds**,
040:058 and work **deeds** of righteousness, and those
041:008 and work **deeds** of righteousness is a reward that will
041:020 against them, as to (all) their **deeds**.
041:027 for the worst of their **deeds**.
042:015 Our **deeds**, and for you for your **deeds**.
042:022 righteous **deeds** will be in the Meadows of the
042:023 who believe and do righteous **deeds**.
042:026 and do **deeds** of righteousness, and gives
042:048 to him, on account of the **deeds** which his hands
043:072 ye are made heirs for your (good) **deeds** (in life).
045:021 those who believe and do righteous **deeds**,-that equal
045:021 What! do those who do evil **deeds** think that
045:030 and did righteous **deeds**, their Lord
046:014 recompense for their (good) **deeds**.
046:016 the best of their **deeds** and pass by
046:016 and pass by their ill **deeds**: (they shall
046:019 according to the **deeds** which they (have done),
046:019 (Allah) may recompense their **deeds**;
047:001 their **deeds** will Allah bring to naught.
047:002 work **deeds** of righteousness, and believe
047:004 He will never let their **deeds** be lost.
047:008 and (Allah) will bring their **deeds** to naught.
047:009 so He has made their **deeds** fruitless.
047:012 and do righteous **deeds**, to Gardens
047:028 so He made their **deeds** of no effect.
047:032 their **deeds** of no effect.
047:033 and make not vain your **deeds**!
047:035 in loss for your (good) **deeds**.
048:029 and do righteous **deeds** Forgiveness, and a
049:002 lest your **deeds** become vain
049:014 He will not belittle aught of your **deeds**:
051:016 because, before then, they had done good **deeds**
052:016 ye but receive the recompense of your (own) **deeds**."
052:019 and health, because of your (good) **deeds**."
052:021 (Yet) is each individual in pledge for his **deeds**.
053:031 do evil, according to their **deeds**, and He
053:032 Those who avoid great sins indecent **deeds**,
054:052 in (their) Books (of **Deeds**):
056:024 A Reward for the **Deeds** of their past (Life).
058:006 and tell them of their **deeds** (which) Allah has
058:015 evil indeed are their **deeds**.
062:007 because of the (**deeds**) their hands have sent
063:002 of Allah: truly evil are their **deeds**.
065:005 He will remove his evil **deeds** from him
065:011 and do righteous **deeds** from the depths of Darkness
066:008 you your evil **deeds**, and admit you to Gardens
074:038 Every soul will be (held) in pledge for its **deeds**.
078:027 for any account (for their **deeds**),
078:030 "So taste ye (the fruits of your **deeds**);
078:040 man will see (the **Deeds**) which his hands have sent
082:011 Kind and honorable, writing down (your **deeds**):

DEEDS (continued)

084:025 and work righteous **deeds**:
085:011 righteous **deeds**, will be Gardens.
089:024 sent forth (Good **Deeds**) for (this) my (Future) Life."
090:017 and enjoin **deeds** of kindness and compassion.
095:006 Except such as believe and do righteous **deeds**:
098:007 do righteous **deeds**,-they are the best of creatures.
099:006 to be shown the **Deeds** that they (had done).
100:007 And to that (fact) he bears witness (by his **deeds**);
101:006 Then, he whose balance (of good **deeds**) will be
101:008 But he whose balance (of good **deeds**) will be
103:003 do righteous **deeds**, and (join together) in the

DEEM

018:035 "I **deem** not that this will ever perish,"
018:036 "Nor do I **deem** that the Hour (of Judgment)
024:063 **Deem** not the summons of the Messenger
036:019 (**deem** ye this an evil omen),

DEEMED

008:026 a small (band), **deemed** weak through the land,
034:031 Those who were **deemed** weak will say to the arrogant
034:032 will say to those who had been **deemed** weak:
034:033 Those who had been **deemed** weak will say to

DEEP

015:058 to a people (**deep**) in sin,
022:027 through **deep** and distant mountain highways;
024:040 is like the depths of darkness in a vast **deep** ocean,
051:032 a people (**deep**) in sin;-
068:012 transgressing beyond bounds, **deep** in sin.

DEEPENING

004:057 cool and ever **deepening**.

DEEPER

007:202 plunge them **deeper** into error, and never

DEEPLY

010:061 when ye are **deeply** engrossed therein.

DEFACE

004:119 and **deface** the (fair) nature created by Allah."
010:088 **Deface** our Lord the features of their wealth,

DEFAME

049:011 nor **defame** nor be sarcastic to each,

DEFEAT

030:003 (even) after (this) **defeat** of theirs,

DEFEATED

030:002 The Roman Empire has been **defeated**-
070:041 to be **defeated** (in Our Plan).

DEFENCE

055:035 No **defense** will ye have:

DEFEND

005:067 And Allah will **defend** thee from men
022:038 Verily Allah will **defend** (from ill)
026:227 and **defend** themselves after they are
028:081 nor could he **defend** himself.
040:021 and none had they to **defend** them against Allah.
042:039 (are not cowed but) help and **defend** themselves.
042:041 and **defend** themselves after a wrong (done) to him,
054:044 "We acting together can **defend** ourselves"?
059:002 fortresses would **defend** them from Allah!

DEFENDED

021:043 be **defended** from Us.

DEFENDER

010:027 no **defender** will they have from (the wrath of)
013:034 and **defender** have they none against Allah.
013:037 protector nor **defender** against Allah.

DEFENDER (continued)

040:033 no **defender** shall ye have from Allah:

DEFER

033:051 Thou mayest **defer** (the turn of) any of them

DEFERRED

077:012 For what Day are these (Portents) **deferred**?

DEFIANCE

003:021 and in **defiance** of right, slay the prophets,
003:090 And then go on adding to their **defiance** of Faith,
003:112 and slew the Prophets in **defiance** of right:
003:181 of slaying the Prophets in **defiance** of right,
004:140 the Message of Allah held in **defiance** and ridicule,
004:155 that they slew the Messengers in **defiance** of right;
007:146 on the earth in **defiance** of right-them will I
010:023 through the earth in **defiance** of right!
022:040 expelled from their homes in **defiance** of right,-

DEFICIENT

002:282 If the party liable is mentally **deficient**,

DEFIED

007:077 and insolently **defied** the order of their Lord,
051:044 But they insolently **defied** the command of their

DEFINITE

011:008 for them for a **definite** term, they are

DEFY

004:140 and those who **defy** Faith-all in Hell;

DEFYING

042:042 **defying** right and justice:

DEGREE

002:228 but men have a **degree** over them
004:040 Allah is never unjust in the least **degree**:
006:083 We raise whom We will, **degree** after **degree**:
009:118 (they felt guilty) to such a **degree** that the earth
034:037 that will bring you nearer to Us in **degree**:
042:040 is an injury equal thereto (in **degree**):

DEGREES

002:253 others He raised to **degrees** (of honor);
006:132 To all are **degrees** (or ranks)
012:076 We raise to **degrees** (of wisdom) whom We please:
046:019 And to all are (assigned) **degrees** according to
058:011 to (suitable) ranks (and **degrees**),
068:044 by **degrees** shall We draw them on little be little
087:006 By **degrees** shall We teach thee (the Message),

DEIGN

003:077 nor will Allah (**deign** to) speak to them

DEITIES

004:117 call but upon female **deities**:
011:101 the **deities**, other than Allah, whom they
022:012 They call on such **deities**, besides Allah,
040:073 "Where are the (**deities**) to which ye gave
041:048 The (**deities**) they used to invoke aforetime
043:020 we should not have worshipped such (**deities**)!"
043:045 did We appoint any **deities** other than

DEJECTION

070:044 Their eyes lowered in **dejection**,-ignominy covering

DELAY

007:034 not an hour can they cause **delay**, nor (an hour)
010:049 not an hour can they cause **delay**, nor (an hour)
011:008 If We **delay** the chastisement for them
011:104 Nor shall We **delay** it but for a term appointed.
015:005 anticipate its Term, nor **delay** it.
016:061 they would not be able to **delay** (the punishment)
023:043 nor can they **delay** (it).

DELAY (continued)

033:014 with none but a brief **delay**!
038:015 will brook no **delay**.
086:017 Therefore grant a **delay** to the unbelievers:

DELIBERATE

005:089 to account for your **deliberate** oaths:

DELICATE

037:049 As if they were (**delicate**) eggs closely guarded.

DELICIOUS

037:046 Crystal-white, of a taste **delicious** to those
038:051 for fruit in abundance, and (**delicious**) drink;

DELIGHT

006:113 and let them **delight** in it, and let
009:024 in which ye **delight**-are dearer to you than Allah
022:056 righteous deeds will be in Gardens of **Delight**.
027:060 to grow well-planted orchards full of beauty and **delight**:
030:015 shall be made happy in a Mead (of **Delight**).
037:043 In Gardens of **delight**.
043:071 all that the eyes could **delight** in:
044:027 they had taken such **delight**!
048:029 (filling) the sowers with wonder and **delight**.
057:020 brings forth, **delight** (the hearts of) the tillers;
068:034 Verily for the Righteous, are Gardens of **Delight**,
074:040 (They will be) in Gardens (of **Delight**);

DELIGHTS

009:021 for them, wherein are **delights** that endure:
032:017 Now no person knows what **delights** of the eye
056:089 and a Garden of **Delights**.

DELIVER

006:070 those who **deliver** themselves to ruin by their own acts:
010:022 saying, "If Thou dost **deliver** us from this,
010:086 "And **deliver** us by Thy Mercy from those
010:103 In the end We **deliver** Our messengers
010:103 that We should **deliver** those who believe!
018:043 against Allah, nor was he able to **deliver** himself.
021:088 and thus do We **deliver** those who have faith.
026:118 and **deliver** me and those of the Believers
026:169 "O my Lord! **deliver** me and my family
027:028 with this letter of mine, and **deliver** it to them:
036:017 to **deliver** the clear Messenger."
036:023 nor can they **deliver** me.
039:019 Wouldst thou, then, **deliver** one (who is)
039:061 But Allah will **deliver** the righteous for they
044:030 We did **deliver** aforetime the Children of Israel
046:031 your faults, and **deliver** you from a Chastisement
046:035 (Thine but) to **deliver** the Message:
052:018 and their Lord shall **deliver** them from
064:012 to **deliver** (the Message) clearly and openly.
065:004 they **deliver** their burdens:
065:006 until they **deliver** their burden:
067:028 yet who can **deliver** the Unbelievers from a
070:014 all that is on earth,-so it could **deliver** him:
072:022 Say: "No one can **deliver** me from Allah
072:023 "Unless I **deliver** what I receive from Allah
074:002 Arise and **deliver** thy warning!
076:011 But Allah will **deliver** them from the evil

DELIVERED

002:049 We **delivered** you from the people of Pharaoh:
003:036 I am **delivered** of a female child!"
003:036 When she was **delivered**, she said: "O my Lord!
007:064 and We **delivered** him, and those
010:073 They rejected him, but We **delivered** him, and those

DELIVERED (continued)

012:110 and those whom We will are **delivered** into safety.
014:006 to you when He **delivered** you from the people
020:049 (When this message was **delivered**), (Pharaoh) said:
020:080 We **delivered** you from your enemy, and We
021:071 But We **delivered** him and (his nephew)
021:076 to his (prayer) and **delivered** him and his
021:088 and **delivered** him from distress:
026:065 We **delivered** Moses and all who were with him;
026:119 'So we **delivered** him and those with him.
026:170 So We **delivered** him and his family,-
027:029 here is-**delivered** to me-a letter
029:065 but when He had **delivered** them safely
031:032 But when He has **delivered** them safely to land,
036:043 nor could they be **delivered**,
037:076 And We **delivered** him and his people from the
037:115 And We **delivered** them and their people
037:134 Behold, We **delivered** him and his adherents,
041:018 But We **delivered** those who believed
052:027 and has **delivered** us from the Chastisement
054:034 Lut's household: them We **delivered** by early Dawn,-
072:028 (truly) brought and **delivered** the Messages

DELIVERETH

006:063 Say: "Who is it that **delivereth** you from the dark
006:064 Say: "It is Allah that **delivereth** you from these
010:023 But when He **delivereth** them, behold! they

DELIVERS

006:063 'If He only **delivers** us from these (dangers),

DELUDED

005:075 they are **deluded** away from the truth!
006:095 then how are ye **deluded** away from the truth?
009:030 how they are **deluded** away from the Truth!
010:034 then how are ye **deluded** away (from the truth)?"
023:089 Say: "Then how are ye **deluded**?"
029:061 How are they then **deluded** away (from the truth)?
030:055 thus were they used to being **deluded**!
040:062 then how ye are **deluded** away from the Truth!
040:063 Thus are **deluded** those who are wont to reject
043:087 how then are they **deluded** away (from the Truth)?
051:009 (away from the Truth) such as would be **deluded**.
051:009 Through which are **deluded** (away from the Truth)
063:004 How are they **deluded** (away from the Truth)!

DELUGE

029:014 but the **Deluge** overwhelmed them while they

DELUSION

067:020 In nothing but **delusion** are the Unbelievers.

DELUSIONS

033:012 and His Messenger promised us nothing but **delusions**!"
035:040 wrong-doers promise each other nothing but **delusions**.
040:025 in nothing but errors (and **delusions**)!...

DEMAND

002:178 then grant any reasonable **demand**,
002:278 remains of your **demand** for usury,
004:001 through Whom ye **demand** your mutual (rights),
017:033 given his heir authority (to **demand** Qisas or to forgive):
068:039 shall have whatever ye shall **demand**?

DEMANDING

003:075 unless thou constantly stoodest **demanding**,
038:024 wronged thee in **demanding** thy (single) ewe to be

DENIAL

009:055 may perish in their (very) **denial** of Allah.
022:072 thou wilt notice a **denial** on the faces of the Unbelievers!

DENIED

042:047 any room for **denial** (of your sins)!
003:011 they **denied** Our Signs, and Allah called them
007:045 they were those who **denied** the Hereafter."
010:045 who **denied** the meeting with Allah and refused
011:019 "These were they who **denied** the Hereafter!"
016:036 what was the end of those who **denied** (the Truth).
023:033 who disbelieved and **denied** the Meeting in the
027:014 And they **denied** them, though their
030:016 and falsely **denied** Our Signs and the meeting
037:021 whose truth ye (once) **denied**!"
040:005 who **denied** (the Signs),-the People of Noah,
050:012 Before them was **denied** (the Hereafter) by the

DENIES

096:013 Seest thou if he **denies** (Truth) and turns away?
107:001 Seest thou one who **denies** the Judgment (to come)?

DENIETH

004:136 And who **denieth** Allah, His angels, His Books,

DENIZENS

056:073 for the **denizens** of deserts.

DENSE

072:019 they just make round him a **dense** crowd."
080:030 And enclosed Gardens, **dense** with lofty trees,

DENY

002:090 in that they **deny** (the revelation)
002:217 to the path of Allah to **deny** Him,
003:019 But if any **deny** the Signs of Allah,
003:021 As to those who **deny** the Signs of Allah,
003:097 but if any **deny** faith, Allah stands not in need
003:101 And how would ye **deny** Faith while unto you
004:131 But if ye **deny** Him, lo! unto Allah belong all
004:150 Those who **deny** Allah and his Messenger,
005:010 Those who reject faith and **deny** Our Signs will be
006:033 it is the Signs of Allah, which the wicked **deny**.
010:017 such as forge a lie against Allah, or **deny** His Signs?
012:037 and that (even) **deny** the Hereafter.
013:005 those who **deny** their Lord!
014:009 "We do **deny** (the mission) on which ye have
016:071 Will they then **deny** the favour of Allah?
016:083 they recognize the favours of Allah; then they **deny** them;
018:037 "Dost thou **deny** Him Who created thee out of dust,
018:105 They are those who **deny** the Signs of their Lord
022:019 but those who **deny** (their Lord),-for them
022:057 And for those who reject Faith and **deny** Our Signs,
023:069 they not recognize their Messenger, that they **deny** him?
025:011 a Blazing Fire for such as **deny** the Hour:
025:011 Nay, they **deny** the Hour (of the Judgment to come):
030:008 who **deny** the meeting with their Lord
032:010 Nay, they **deny** the meeting with their Lord!
034:042 the which ye were wont to **deny**!"
040:081 then which of the Signs of Allah will ye **deny**?
041:007 and who even **deny** the Hereafter.
041:009 Say: Is it that ye **Deny** Him Who created the earth
043:024 They said: "For us, We **deny** that ye (prophets)
046:006 be hostile to them and **deny** that (men) had
046:034 for that ye were wont to **deny** (Truth)!"
050:005 But they **deny** the truth when it comes to them:
052:014 "Is the Fire,-which ye were wont to **deny**!
055:013 Then which of the favours of your Lord will ye **deny**?
055:016 Then which of the favours of your Lord will ye **deny**?
055:018 Then which of the favours of your Lord will ye **deny**?
055:021 Then which of the favours of your Lord will ye **deny**?
055:023 Then which of the favours of your Lord will ye **deny**?

DENY (continued)

055:028 Then which of the favours of your Lord will ye **deny**?
055:030 Then which of the favours of your Lord will ye **deny**?
055:032 Then which of the favours of your Lord will ye **deny**?
055:034 Then which of the favours of your Lord will ye **deny**?
055:036 Then which of the favours of your Lord will ye **deny**?
055:038 Then which of the favours of your Lord will ye **deny**?
055:040 Then which of the favours of your Lord will ye **deny**?
055:042 Then which of the favours of your Lord will ye **deny**?
055:043 This is the Hell which the Sinners **deny**:
055:045 Then which of the favours of your Lord will ye **deny**?
055:047 Then which of the favours of your Lord will ye **deny**?-
055:049 Then which of the favours of your Lord will ye **deny**?-
055:051 Then which of the favours of your Lord will ye **deny**?-
055:053 Then which of the favours of your Lord will ye **deny**?
055:055 Then which of the favours of your Lord will ye **deny**?
055:057 Then which of the favours of your Lord will ye **deny**?
055:059 Then which of the favours of your Lord will ye **deny**?
055:061 Then which of the favours of your Lord will ye **deny**?
055:063 Then which of the favours of your Lord will ye **deny**?
055:065 Then which of the favours of your Lord will ye **deny**?
055:067 Then which of the favours of your Lord will ye **deny**?
055:069 Then which of the favours of your Lord will ye **deny**?
055:071 Then which of the favours of your Lord will ye **deny**?
055:073 Then which of the favours of your Lord will ye **deny**?
055:075 Then which of the favours of your Lord will ye **deny**?
055:077 Then which of the favours of your Lord will ye **deny**?
056:002 Then will no (soul) **deny** its coming.
056:051 go wrong, and **deny** (the truth);
056:092 And if he be of those who **deny** (the truth)
057:019 but those who reject Allah and **deny** Our Signs,-
068:008 So obey not to those who **deny** (the Truth).
073:011 (who yet) **deny** the Truth); and bear
073:017 Then how shall ye, if ye **deny** (Allah), guard yourselves
074:046 "And we used to **deny** the Day of Judgment,
083:010 Woe, that Day, to those that **deny**-
083:011 Those that **deny** the Day of Judgment.
083:012 And none can **deny** it but the Transgressor
095:007 make you **deny** the Last Judgment?

DEPART

005:008 and **depart** from justice.
007:105 so let the children of Israel **depart** along with me."
008:046 lest ye lose heart and your power **depart**; and be
009:085 and that their souls may **depart** while they
024:062 they do not **depart** until they have asked
077:029 (It will be said:) "**Depart** ye to that which ye
077:030 "**Depart** ye to a Shadow (of smoke ascending)
098:001 were not going to **depart** (from their ways)

DEPARTED

011:010 "All evil has **departed** from me:" Behold! he falls into
021:087 And remember Zun-nun, when he **departed** in wrath:
037:090 So they turned away from him, and **departed**.
068:023 So they **departed**, conversing in secret low tones,

DEPENDETH

011:006 but its sustenance **dependeth** on Allah:

DEPOSIT

011:006 and its temporary **deposit**:

DEPOSITS

002:283 And it one of you **deposits** a thing on trust with another,

DEPRESSED

028:005 those who were being **depressed** in the land,

DEPRESSING

028:004 into sections, **depressing** a group among them:

DEPRIVE

002:276 Allah will **deprive** usury of all blessing,
003:141 in Faith and to **deprive** of blessings those that resist Faith.
052:021 nor shall We **deprive** them (of the fruit)

DEPRIVED

051:019 a due share for the beggar and the **deprived**.
056:067 "Indeed we are **deprived**."
068:027 "Indeed we are **deprived** (of the fruits of our labour)!"
070:025 and him who is **deprived** (for some reason from asking);

DEPTH

010:027 as it were, with pieces from the **depth** of the darkness

DEPTHS

002:257 lead them forth into the **depths** of darkness.
002:257 from the **depths** of darkness he leads them
004:145 the lowest **depths** of the Fire:
006:059 the darkness (or **depths**) of the earth,
006:122 the **depths** of darkness, from which he
009:040 and humbled to the **depths** the word
013:016 Or the **depths** of darkness equal with
014:001 out of the **depths** of darkness into light-by
014:005 thy people from the **depths** of darkness into light,
021:087 But he cried through the **depths** of darkness,
024:040 (dark) clouds: **depths** of darkness, one above
024:040 the **depths** of darkness in a vast deep ocean,
027:063 the **depths** of darkness on land and sea, and Who
033:043 the **depths** of Darkness into Light:
035:020 Nor are the **depths** of Darkness and the Light;
056:004 When the earth shall be shaken to its **depths**,
057:009 the **depths** of Darkness into the Light.
065:011 and do righteous deeds from the **depths** of Darkness

DEPUTED

091:012 among them was **deputed** (for impiety).

DERIVE

016:005 from them ye **derive** warmth, and numerous
035:040 from which they (can **derive**) clear (evidence)?-

DERIVED

074:024 but magic **derived** from of old;"

DESCEND

002:157 are those on whom (**descend**) blessings from their Lord,
004:153 to cause a book to **descend** to them from heaven:
007:057 make rain to **descend** thereon, and produce
008:011 and He caused rain to **descend** on you from heaven,
011:039 on whom will **descend** a Chastisement that will
014:028 and caused their people to **descend** to the
015:022 then cause the rain to **descend** from the shy,
016:094 and a mighty Wrath **descend** on you.
019:064 (The angels say:) "We **descend** not but by
020:081 lest My Wrath should **descend** on you: and those
020:086 that Wrath should **descend** from your Lord on you,
026:221 on whom it is that the Satans **descend**?
026:222 They **descend** on every lying, wicked person
041:030 the angels **descend** on them (from time to time):

DESCENDANTS

004:012 has left neither ascendants nor **descendants**,
004:176 those who leave no **descendants** or ascendants
006:089 if these (their **descendants**) reject them, behold!
007:172 from their loins-their **descendants**, and made
007:173 but we are (their) **descendants** after them:
017:062 I will surely bring his **descendants** under my sway-

DESCENDED
017:105   and in Truth has it **descended**:

DESCENDING
025:025   and angels shall be sent down, **descending** (in ranks),-

DESCENDS
011:093   soon will ye know who it is on whom **descends** the
020:081   and those on whom **descends** My Wrath
037:177   But when it **descends** upon their courtyards
039:040   and on whom **descends** a Chastisement that abides."
065:012   through the midst of them (all) **descends** His Command:

DESCENT
053:013   For indeed he saw him at a second **descent**,

DESCRIPTION
047:015   (Here is) the **description** of the Garden which the

DESERT
009:090   **And there were, among the desert** Arabs (also),
009:101   Certain of the **desert** Arabs round about you
011:053   the ones to **desert** our gods on thy word!
012:100   and brought you (all here) out of the **desert**,
048:011   The **desert** Arabs who lagged behind will say
048:016   Say to the **desert** Arabs who lagged behind:
049:014   The **desert** Arabs say, "We believe." Say, "Ye

DESERTED
028:058   after them, are **deserted**,-all but
060:011   have **deserted** the equivalent of what they had

DESERTION
004:128   or **desertion** on her husband's part,

DESERTS
014:051   each soul according to its **deserts**; and verily
024:039   in sandy **deserts**, which the man parched with
033:020   in the **deserts** (wandering) among the Bedouins,
056:073   for the denizens of **deserts**.
060:011   And if any of your wives **deserts** you to the

DESERVE
035:045   according to what they **deserve**, He would

DESERVED
007:030   others have **deserved** the loss of their way,

DESIGN
005:011   the **design** to stretch out their hands against you,
010:107   if He do **design** some benefit for thee, there is
012:025   an evil **design** against thy wife, but prison

DESIGNED
038:006   a thing **designed** (against you)!

DESIGNS
008:071   But if they have treacherous **designs** against thee,
011:016   vain are the **designs** they frame therein, and of

DESIRE
002:087   with what ye yourselves **desire** not,
003:118   They only **desire** for you to suffer:
003:145   If any do **desire** a reward in this life,
003:145   and if any do **desire** a reward in the Hereafter,
003:152   and some that **desire** the Hereafter.
004:127   and yet whom ye **desire** to marry, as also
004:129   between wives even if it is your ardent **desire**:
005:005   and **desire** chastity, not lewdness.
011:015   Those who **desire** the life of the Present
011:034   much as I **desire** to give you (good) counsel,
011:088   I only **desire** (your) betterment to the
012:024   And (with passion) did she **desire** him, and he
012:065   What (more) can we **desire**?
012:068   Jacob's heartfelt **desire**.
012:103   mankind have, however ardently thou dost **desire** it.

DESIRE (continued)
016:057   Glory be to Him!-and for themselves what they **desire**!
020:086   Or did ye **desire** that Wrath should
022:052   or a prophet before thee, but, when he framed a **desire**,
022:052   Satan threw some (vanity) into his **desire**:
024:033   your maids to prostitution when they **desire** chastity,
025:062   for such as **desire** to be mindful or to show
026:051   "Only, our **desire** is that our Lord will
028:019   Thou only **desire** to become a tyrant in the land,
033:028   "If it be that ye **desire** the life of this world,
033:032   should be moved with **desire**: but speak
037:086   "Is it a Falsehood- gods other than Allah that ye **desire**?
041:031   your souls shall **desire**; therein shall
043:071   the souls could **desire**, all that
045:023   as his god his own vain **desire**?
052:022   of fruit and meat, anything they shall **desire**.
053:003   Nor does he say (aught) of (his own) **Desire**.
053:023   and what their own souls **desire**!-Even though
053:029   away from Our Message and **desire** nothing but
056:021   And the flesh of fowls, any that they may **desire**.
059:009   and entertain no **desire**, in their hearts
060:002   and they **desire** that ye should reject the Truth.
062:006   then express your **desire** for Death, if ye
062:007   their **desire** (for Death), because of
068:009   Their **desire** is that thou shouldst be pliant:
070:011   each other,-the sinner's **desire** will be:
076:009   no reward do we **desire** from you,
077:042   And (they shall have) fruits,-all they **desire**.
092:020   But only the **desire** to seek for the countenance

DESIRED
005:070   to them a Messengers with what they **desired** not-
012:024   and he would have **desired** her, but that
018:081   "So we **desired** that their Lord would give them
018:082   so thy Lord **desired** that they should attain their
021:102   what their souls **desired**, in that will they dwell.
034:013   They worked for him as he **desired**, (making) Arches,

DESIRES
002:078   but (see therein their own) **desires**,
002:111   Those are their (vain) **desires**.
002:120   Wert thou to follow their **desires** after the knowledge
002:145   wert to follow their (vain) **desires**,
002:233   for him who **desires** to complete the term.
003:085   If anyone **desires** a religion other than Islam
004:119   and I will create in them false **desires**;
004:123   Not your **desires**, nor those of the People of the Book
004:134   If any one **desires** a reward in this life,
005:048   and follow not their vain **desires**, diverging
005:049   and follow not their vain **desires**, but beware
005:077   nor follow the vain desire of people who went
005:119   mighty Triumph (the fulfillment of all **desires**).
006:056   Say: "I will not follow your vain **desires**:
006:119   by low **desires** without knowledge.
006:150   nor follow thou the vain **desires** of such
007:176   and followed his own vain **desires**.
013:037   their (vain) **desires** after the knowledge which
018:028   one who follows his own **desires**, and his
022:014   for Allah carries out all that He **desires**.
023:007   But those whose **desires** exceed those limits
023:071   If the Truth had been in accord with their **desires**,
024:031   or male attendants free of sexual **desires**.
030:029   fellow their own **desires** being devoid of
034:054   And between them and their **desires**, is placed
042:015   nor follow thou their vain **desires**; but say: "I believe

DESIRES (continued)

042:020 and to any that **desires** the tilth of this world,
042:020 To any that **desires** the tilth of the Hereafter,
045:018 and follow not the **desires** of those who know not.
057:014 and (your false) **desires** deceived you;
079:040 restrained (their) soul from lower **Desires,**

DESIREST

020:072 So decree whatever thou **desirest** to degree:

DESIRING

004:024 **desiring** chastity, not fornication.
007:045 **desiring** to make something crooked: they were

DESIST

002:275 who after receiving admonition from their Lord, **desist,**
004:171 Say not "Three": **desist:** it will be better for you:
005:073 If they **desist** not from their word (of blasphemy),
008:019 if ye **desist** (from wrong), it will
008:038 if (now) they **desist** (from Unbelief),
026:116 They said: "If thou **desist** not, O Noah!
026:167 They said: "If thou **desist** not, O Lut!
033:060 in the City, **desist** not, We shall
036:018 if ye **desist** not, we will certainly stone you,
049:011 and those who do not **desist** are (indeed) doing wrong.
096:015 Let him beware! If he **desist** not, We will

DESOLATE

007:145 homes of the wicked, (how they lie **desolate**)."
068:020 like a dark and **desolate** spot,

DESPAIR

003:139 So lose not heart, nor fall into **despair:**
006:044 when lo! they were plunged in **despair!**
011:009 behold! he is in **despair** and (falls into) ingratitude,
015:055 give thee glad tidings in truth; be not then in **despair!"**
017:083 he gives himself up to **despair!**
023:077 then Lo! they will be plunged in **despair** therein!
029:023 it is they who shall **despair** of My mercy:
030:012 the guilty will be struck dumb with **despair.**
030:036 behold, they are in **despair!**
030:049 they were dumb with **despair!**
039:053 **Despair** not of the Mercy of Allah:
041:049 he gives up all hope (and) is lost in **despair.**
043:075 and in **despair** will they be there overwhelmed.
057:023 In order that ye may not **despair** over matters
060:013 of the Hereafter they are already in **despair,**
060:013 as the Unbelievers are in **despair** about those (buried)
089:016 saith he (in **despair**), "My Lord hath humiliated me!"

DESPAIRS

012:087 truly no one **despairs** of Allah's Soothing Mercy,
015:056 He said: "And who **despairs** of the mercy of his Lord,

DESPERATE

028:024 truly am I in (**desperate**) need of any good that

DESPICABLE

077:020 a fluid (held) **despicable?**-

DESPISE

011:031 your eyes do **despise** that Allah will not
049:013 know each other (not that ye may **despise** each other).

DESPISED

002:065 "Be ye apes, **despised** and rejected."
007:018 (Allah) said: "Get out form this, **despised** and expelled.
007:166 "Be ye apes, **despised** and rejected."
028:042 be among the loathed (and **despised**).
032:008 a quintessence of **despised** fluid.

DESPOIL

008:026 and afraid that men might **despoil** and kidnap you;

DESPOIL (continued)

027:034 She said: "Kings, when they enter a country, **despoil** it,

DESTINATION

002:126 an evil **destination** (indeed)!"
022:048 To Me is the **destination** (of all).
022:072 And evil is that **destination!**
035:018 and the **destination** (of all) is to Allah.
048:006 and evil is it for a **destination.**
058:008 and evil is that **destination!**
067:006 and evil is (such) **destination.**
078:022 For the transgressors a place of **destination:**

DESTINED

027:057 her We **destined** to be of those who lagged behind.
041:025 And We have **destined** for them intimate companions
044:024 For they are a host (**destined**) to be drowned."

DESTITUTE

017:029 become blameworthy and **destitute.**

DESTITUTION

003:112 And pitched over them is (the tent of) **destitution.**
017:022 in disgrace and **destitution.**

DESTROY

002:205 and **destroy** crops and progeny
004:029 nor kill (or **destroy**) yourselves:
004:133 If it were His will, He could **destroy** you,
005:017 to **destroy** Christ the son of Mary, his mother,
006:006 how many of those before them We did **destroy?**-
006:026 but they only **destroy** themselves and they
006:131 for thy Lord would not **destroy** the towns
006:133 if it were His Will, He could **destroy** you,
007:129 will **destroy** your enemy and make you
007:155 wouldst Thou **destroy** us for the deeds of the
007:164 whom Allah **destroy** or visit with a terrible punishment?"-
007:173 wilt Thou then **destroy** us because of the deeds
009:042 they would **destroy** their own souls;
011:117 to **destroy** the towns unjustly while their people
015:004 Never did We **destroy** a population that had not
017:016 When We decide to **destroy** a town, We command
017:016 then We **destroy** them utterly.
017:058 We shall **destroy** it before the Day of Judgment
020:061 lest He **destroy** you (at once) utterly by
026:208 Never did We **destroy** a town but had its warners-
028:059 Nor was thy Lord the one to **destroy** a town
028:059 nor are We going to **destroy** a population except
029:031 "We are indeed going to **destroy** the people
038:003 How many generations before them did We **destroy?**
045:024 and nothing but Time can **destroy** us."
046:025 "Everything will it **destroy** by the command
050:036 generations before them did We **destroy** (for their Sins),-
067:028 Say: "See ye?- if Allah to **destroy** me, and those with me,
077:016 Did We not **destroy** the men of old (for their evil)?

DESTROYED

006:006 yet for their sins We **destroyed** them, and raised
006:047 will any be **destroyed** except those who do wrong?"
007:004 How many towns have We **destroyed** (for their sins)?
007:155 Thy will thou couldst have **destroyed,**
008:054 so We **destroyed** them for their crimes,
010:013 Generations before you We **destroyed** when they
017:017 How many generations have We **destroyed** after Noah?
018:059 Such were the towns We **destroyed** when they
019:074 before them have We **destroyed,** who were
019:098 (countless) generations before them have We **destroyed?**
020:128 generations before them We **destroyed,** in whose

DESTROYED (continued)

020:134 Had We **destroyed** them a punishment before this,
021:006 the towns which We **destroyed** believed:
021:009 but We **destroyed** those who transgressed beyond bounds.
021:011 We utterly **destroyed** because of their iniquities,
021:095 which We have **destroyed**:
022:045 How many populations have We **destroyed**, which were
023:048 of those who were **destroyed**.
025:018 for they were a people **destroyed**."
025:036 We **destroyed** with utter destruction.
026:139 So they rejected him, and We **destroyed** them.
026:172 Then the rest We **destroyed** utterly.
027:051 that We **destroyed** them and their people,
028:043 after We had **destroyed** the earlier generations,
028:058 And how many towns We **destroyed**, which exulted
028:078 Did he not know that Allah had **destroyed**, before him,
032:026 how many generations We **destroyed** before them,
036:031 how many generations before them We **destroyed**?
037:136 Then We **destroyed** the rest.
043:008 So We **destroyed** men-stronger in power than these;-
044:037 We **destroyed** them because they were
046:027 We **destroyed** aforetime towns round about you;
046:035 but shall any be **destroyed** except those who transgress?
047:013 have We **destroyed** (for their sins)?
053:050 And that it is He Who **destroyed** the (powerful)
053:053 And He **destroyed** the Overthrown Cities
054:034 (which **destroyed** them), except Lut's household:
054:051 have We **destroyed** gangs like unto you:
059:002 so that they **destroyed** their dwellings by their
069:005 But the Thamud,-they were **destroyed** by a terrible
069:006 And the 'Ad,-they were **destroyed** by a furious

DESTROYS

003:117 it strikes and **destroys** the harvest of men

DESTRUCTION

002:195 not your own hands contribute to (your) **destruction**;
006:137 in order to lead them to their own **destruction**,
007:139 the cult they are in is bound to **destruction**,
017:007 and to visit with **destruction** all that
017:102 O Pharaoh, to be one doomed to **destruction**!"
018:059 but We fixed an appointed time for their **destruction**.
019:059 soon, then, will they face **Destruction**,-
025:013 they will plead for **destruction** there and then!
025:014 plead for **destruction** oft-repeated!"
025:014 "This day plead not for a single **destruction**:
025:036 We destroyed with utter **destruction**.
030:009 (Signs), (which they rejected, to their own **destruction**):
041:023 hath brought you to **destruction**, and (now) you have
047:008 But those who reject (Allah),-for them is **destruction**,
047:010 Allah brought utter **destruction** on them,

DETAIL

006:055 Thus do We explain the Signs in **detail**:
006:097 We **detail** Our Signs for people who know.
006:098 We **detail** Our signs for people who understand.
006:114 Who hath sent unto you the Book, explained in **detail**."
006:119 in **detail** what is forbidden to you-except
006:154 and explaining all things in **detail**,-and a
007:032 in **detail** for those who know.
007:052 based on knowledge, Which We explained in **detail**,-
007:174 Thus do We explain the Signs in **detail**;
009:011 (thus) do We explain Signs in **detail**, for those
010:005 He explain His Signs in **detail**, for those who know.
010:024 the Signs in **detail** for those who reflect.
011:001 further explained in **detail**, from One Who is Wise

DETAIL (continued)

013:002 explaining the Signs in **detail**, that ye
017:012 tall things have We explained in **detail**.
018:054 We have explained in **detail** in this Qur'an, for the
020:113 and explained therein in **detail** some of the warnings,
030:028 Thus do We explain the Signs in **detail** to a
041:003 A Book, whereof the verses are explained in **detail**;-
041:044 "Why are not its verses explained in **detail**?

DETAILED

006:126 We have **detailed** the Signs for those who receive
012:111 a **detailed** exposition of all things,

DETAIN

005:106 If ye doubt (their truth), **detain** them both after prayer,

DETAINED

048:025 **detained** from reaching their place of sacrifice.

DETERMINATE

004:007 a **determinate** share.

DETERMINATION

004:059 most suitable for final **determination**.
017:035 in the final **determination**.
033:023 changed (their **determination**) in the least:

DETERMINE

076:016 they will **determine** the measure thereof
077:023 For We do **determine** for We are the Best
077:023 We are the Best to **determine** (things).

DETERMINED

006:002 And there is with Him another **determined** term;
019:039 when the matter will be **determined**:
033:038 And the command of Allah is a decree **determined**.
035:036 no term shall be **determined** for them, so they
037:041 For them is a Sustenance **determined**,
074:018 For he thought and he **determined**;-
074:019 And woe to him! How he **determined**!-
074:020 Yea, woe to him: how he **determined**!-
077:022 For a period (of gestation), **determined**?

DETERMINES

019:035 When He **determines** a matter, He only says

DETERRENT

054:004 such tidings as contain a **deterrent**,

DETEST

007:088 He said: "What! even though we do **detest** (them)?
009:032 even though the Unbelievers may **detest** (it).
009:033 the Pagans may **detest** (it).
026:168 He said: "I do **detest** your doings."
040:014 even though the Unbelievers may **detest** it.
061:008 even though the Unbelievers may **detest** (it).
061:009 even though the Pagans may **detest** (it).

DEVASTATING

051:041 against them the **devastating** Wind:

DEVELOPED

023:014 then We **developed** out of it another creature:

DEVIATE

003:008 "Let not our hearts **deviate** now after Thou hast guided

DEVIATING

023:074 in the Hereafter are **deviating** from that Way.

DEVICE

026:137 a customary **device** of the ancients,

DEVILS

037:065 are like the heads of **devils**:

DEVISE

004:048 to set up partners with Allah is to **devise** a sin

DEVISE (continued)
013:042   Those before them did (also) **devise** plots;
016:045   Do then those who **devise** evil (plots) feel

DEVISED
007:071   over names which ye have **devised**-ye and
053:023   which ye have **devised**,-ye and
071:022   "And they have **devised** a tremendous Plot.

DEVISING
007:099   against Allah's **devising** but no one can fell
013:033   their **devising** seems pleasing, but they
013:042   Allah is the **devising** altogether.

DEVOID
028:050   who follows his own lusts, **devoid** of guidance from Allah?
030:029   follow their own desires being **devoid** of knowledge.
059:013   men **devoid** of understanding.
059:014   that is because they are a people **devoid** of wisdom.

DEVOTE
009:122   to **devote** themselves to studies in religion,
020:091   to worship it, will **devote** ourselves to it
073:008   the Lord and **devote** thyself to Him wholeheartedly.

DEVOTED
005:082   because amongst these are men **devoted** to learning.
007:138   they came upon a people **devoted** entirely to some idols
020:097   become a **devoted** worshipper:
021:052   to which ye are (so assiduously) **devoted**?"
037:169   Servants of Allah, sincere (and **devoted**)!"
052:024   Round about them will serve, (**devoted**) to them, youths
070:022   Not so those **devoted** to Prayer:-
092:017   But those most **devoted** to Allah shall be

DEVOTEE
017:003   Verily he was a **devotee** most grateful.
034:009   is a Sign for every **devotee** that turns
072:019   "Yet when the **Devotee** of Allah stands forth

DEVOTEES
002:207   and Allah is full of kindness to (His) **devotees**.
043:068   My **devotees**! no fear shall be on you today,
057:020   and (His) Good Pleasure (for the **devotees** of Allah).
057:020   a Chastisement severe (for the **devotees** of wrong).
071:027   they will but mislead Thy **devotees**, and they
076:006   A Fountain where the **Devotees** of Allah do drink,
089:029   "Enter thou, then, among my **Devotees**!

DEVOTION
004:146   and make their religion **devotion** sincere to Allah:
007:029   making your **devotion** sincere such as He created
009:112   that wander in **devotion** to the Cause of Allah;
029:065   making their **devotion** sincerely (and exclusively)
031:032   offering Him sincere **devotion**.
038:034   but he did turn (to Us in true **devotion**):
039:002   so serve Allah, offering Him sincere **devotion**.
039:003   Is it not to Allah that sincere **devotion** is due?
039:011   to serve Allah with sincere **devotion**;
039:014   with my sincere (and exclusive) **devotion**:
040:014   sincere **devotion** to Him, even though
040:065   call upon Him, giving Him sincere **devotion**.
050:033   and brought a heart turned in **devotion** (to Him):
098:005   offering Him sincere **devotion**, being True

DEVOUR
002:275   Those who **devour** usury will not stand
003:130   O ye who believe! **devour** not usury,
004:002   and **devour** not their substance (by mixing it up)
009:034   who in falsehood **devour** the wealth of men
012:013   the wolf should **devour** him while ye attend not to him."

DEVOUR (continued)
012:014   the wolf were to **devour** him while we are (so large)
012:043   whom seven lean ones **devour**,-and seven
012:046   of seven fat kine whom seven lean ones **devour**,
012:048   which will **devour** what ye shall have laid
089:019   And ye **devour** inheritance-all with greed,

DEVOURED
004:161   and that they **devoured** men's wealth wrongfully;
012:017   and the wolf **devoured** him.

DEVOURING
005:042   of **devouring** anything forbidden.

DEVOUT
002:238   Allah in a **devout** (frame of mind).
019:013   as from Us, and purity: he was **devout**,
033:031   But any of you that is **devout** in the service
033:035   for **devout** men and women, for true
066:005   who are **devout**; who turn to Allah in repentance,
066:012   and was one of the **devout** (Servants).

DEVOUTLY
003:017   who worship **devoutly**:
003:043   "O Mary! worship thy Lord **devoutly**;
004:034   are **devoutly** obedient, and guard
016:120   Abraham was indeed a model, **devoutly** obedient to Allah,
030:026   all are **devoutly** obedient to Him.
039:009   Is one who worships **devoutly** during the hours

DHARI
088:006   No food will there be for them but a bitter **Dhari**

DICTATE
002:282   or weak, or unable himself to **dictate**,
002:282   Let him who incurs the liability **dictate**,
002:282   let his guardian **dictate** faithfully.

DICTATED
025:005   and they are **dictated** before him

DID
002:033   Allah said: "**Did** I not tell you that I know the secrets
002:036   Then **did** Satan make them slip from the (garden),
002:051   and ye **did** grievous wrong.
002:052   Even then We **did** forgive you,
002:057   to Us they **did** no harm,
002:071   and they scarcely **did** it.
002:072   but Allah was to bring forth what ye **did** hide.
002:083   Then **did** ye turn back,
002:091   if ye **did** indeed believe?"
002:092   and ye **did** behave wrongfully.
002:101   as it (it had been something) they **did** not know!
002:102   which they **did** sell their souls,
002:102   Solomon **did** not disbelieve but Satans
002:132   upon his sons and so **did** Jacob;
002:134   ye shall not be asked about what they **did**.
002:134   They shall reap the fruit of what they **did**,
002:141   About what they **did**!
002:141   They shall reap the fruit of what they **did**,
002:213   Signs came to them, **did** not differ among themselves,
002:251   And **did** not Allah check one set of people
003:019   nor **did** the People of the Book
003:033   Allah **did** choose Adam and Noah,
003:037   Right graciously **did** her Lord accept her:
003:038   There **did** Zakariya pray to his Lord, saying:
003:049   Surely therein is a Sign for you if ye **did** believe.
003:106   "**Did** ye reject Faith after accepting it?
003:142   **Did** ye think that ye would enter Heaven
003:143   Ye **did** indeed wish for Death before ye

DID (continued)

003:144	If any **did** turn back on his heels,
003:146	nor **did** they weaken (in will) nor give in.
003:152	Allah **did** indeed fulfil His promise to you
003:152	Then **did** He divert you from your foes
003:153	There **did** Allah give you one distress
003:164	Allah **did** confer a great favour on the Believers
003:183	why then **did** ye slay them, if ye speak the truth?.
004:072	They say: "Allah **did** favour us in that we
004:118	Allah **did** curse him, but he said: "I will
004:125	For Allah **did** take Abraham for a friend.
004:140	if ye **did**, ye would be like them.
004:141	"**Did** we not gain an advantage over you.
004:141	And **did** we not guard you from the Believers?"
005:012	Allah **did** aforetime take a Covenant from
005:014	We **did** take a Covenant, but they forgot a good
005:079	evil indeed were the deeds which they **did**.
005:079	Nor **did** they forbid one another the iniquities
005:102	Some people before you **did** ask such questions, and
005:107	if we **did**, behold! we will be wrong-doers."
005:110	And behold! I **did** restrain the Children of Israel
006:004	But never **did** a single one of the Signs
006:006	before them We **did** destroy?-
006:008	If We **did** send down an angel, the matter
006:034	until Our aid **did** reach them:
006:043	why then **did** they not call (Allah) in humility?
006:053	Thus **did** We test some of them by other,
006:054	verily, if any of you **did** evil in ignorance,
006:056	if I **did**, I would stray from the path, and be
006:060	then will He show you the truth of all that ye **did**.
006:075	So also **did** We show Abraham the kingdom
006:088	all that they **did** would be vain for them.
006:100	though Allah **did** create the Jinns;
006:108	the truth of all that they **did**.
006:111	and the dead **did** speak unto them, and We
006:111	Even if We **did** send unto them angels, and the
006:112	Likewise **did** We make for every Messenger
006:128	much (toll) **did** ye take of men."
006:148	So **did** their ancestors argue falsely, until
006:150	to prove that Allah **did** forbid so and so."
006:159	the truth of all that they **did**.
007:005	"Indeed we **did** wrong."
007:005	no cry **did** they utter but this: "Indeed
007:022	"**Did** I not forbid you that tree, and tell
007:039	the Chastisement for all that ye **did**!"
007:053	"The Messengers of our Lord **did** indeed bring true
007:072	of those who rejected Our Sings and **did** not believe.
007:079	saying: "O my people! I **did** indeed convey to you
007:086	And see what was the end of those who **did** mischief.
007:093	saying: "O my people! I **did** indeed convey to
007:097	**Did** the people of the towns feel secure
007:098	Or else **did** they feel secure against its
007:099	**Did** they then fell secure against Allah's
007:118	And all that they **did** was made of no effect.
007:148	having lowing sound **did** they not see that it could
007:148	They took it for worship and they **did** wrong.
007:150	**did** ye make haste to bring on the judgment
007:150	The people **did** indeed reckon me as naught,
007:160	to Us they **did** no harm,
007:163	thus **did** We make a trial of them,
007:163	the day of their Sabbath their fish **did** come to them,
007:167	Behold! thy Lord **did** declare that He
008:072	who believed but **did** not emigrate ye owe

DID (continued)

009:025	Assuredly Allah **did** help you in many battle-fields
009:025	For all that it is wide, **did** constrain and ye turned back
009:026	But Allah **did** pour His calm on the Messenger
009:040	for Allah **did** indeed help him,
009:069	and ye have of yours, as **did** those before you;
009:069	in idle talk as they **did**.
009:076	But when He **did** bestow of His bounty, they became
009:094	He show you the truth of all that ye **did**."
009:095	recompense for the (evil) that they **did**.
009:105	then will He show you the truth of all that ye **did**."
010:004	because they **did** reject Him.
010:005	Nowise **did** Allah create this but in truth
010:013	before you We destroyed when they **did** wrong:
010:023	and We shall show you the truth of all that ye **did**.
010:039	but see what was the end of those who **did** wrong!
010:039	thus **did** those before them make charges of falsehood:
010:076	When the Truth **did** come to them from Us, they said:
011:031	I should, if I **did**, indeed be a wrong-doer."
011:065	But they **did** ham-string her.
011:094	but the (mighty) Blast **did** seize the wrong-doers,
011:101	nor **did** they add aught (to their lot) but perdition!
011:119	and for this **did** He create them:
012:004	"O my father! I **did** see eleven stars and the
012:015	So they **did** take him away, and they
012:020	in such low estimation **did** they hold him!
012:021	Thus **did** We establish Joseph in the land, that We
012:024	And (with passion) **did** she desire him, and he
012:024	thus (**did** We order) that We might
012:031	they **did** extol him, and (in their amazement)
012:032	I **did** seek to seduce him from his (true) self
012:032	(true) self but he **did** firmly save himself guiltless!...
012:032	the man about whom ye **did** blame me!
012:051	when ye **did** seek to seduce Joseph"?
012:056	Thus **did** We give established power to Joseph
012:068	it **did** not profit them in the least
012:076	Thus **did** We plan for Joseph.
012:077	a brother of his who **did** steal before (him)."
012:077	But these things **did** Joseph keep locked in his heart,
012:079	indeed (if we **did** so), we should be acting wrongfully.
012:080	"Know ye not that your father **did** take an oath
012:080	and how, before this, ye **did** fail in your duty
012:096	He said: "**Did** I not say to you,
012:109	any but men, whom We **did** inspire,-
012:109	Nor **did** We send before thee (as Messengers)
013:038	We **did** send messengers before thee, and appointed
013:042	Those before them **did** (also) devise plots;
015:004	Never **did** We destroy a population that had not
015:010	We **did** send messengers before thee amongst
015:070	They said: "**Did** we not forbid thee (to speak)
015:082	Out of the mountains **did** they hew (their) edifices,
015:084	they **did** (with such art and care)!
016:026	Those before them **did** also plot (against Allah's Way):
016:026	from directions they **did** not perceive.
016:028	verily Allah knoweth all that ye **did**;
016:028	"We **did** no evil (knowingly)."
016:032	(the good) which ye **did** (in the world)."
016:033	So **did** those who went before them.
016:035	So **did** those who went before them.
016:118	We **did** them no wrong, but they
017:001	Glory to (Allah) Who **did** take His Servant
017:001	We **did** Bless,-in order that We might show him
017:006	Then **did** We grant you victory over them:

DID (continued)

017:007 if ye **did** evil (ye **did** it) against yourselves.
017:007 If ye **did** well, ye **did** well for yourselves;
017:101 To Moses We **did** give nine Clear Signs:
017:103 but We **did** drown him and all who were with him.
018:014 if we **did**; we should indeed have uttered
018:021 Thus **did** We make their case known to the people,
018:049 They will find all that they **did**, placed before
018:063 I **did** indeed forget (about) the Fish:
018:072 He answered: "**Did** I not tell thee that thou canst
018:075 He answered: "**Did** I not tell thee that thou canst
018:082 I **did** it not of my own accord.
019:009 I **did** indeed create thee before, when thou
019:058 on whom Allah **did** bestow His Grace,-of the
020:055 From the (earth) **did** We create you, and into
020:056 but he **did** reject and refuse.
020:086 **Did** then the promise seem to you long (in coming)?
020:086 He said: "O my people! **did** not your Lord make a
020:086 Or **did** ye desire that Wrath should
020:096 thus **did** my soul suggest to me."
020:121 thus **did** Adam disobey His Lord,
021:008 Nor **did** We give them bodies that ate no food,
021:016 Not for (idle) sport **did** We create the heavens
021:025 Not a messenger **did** We send before thee
021:046 we **did** wrong indeed!"
021:062 the one that **did** this with our gods, O Abraham?"
021:078 We **did** witness their judgment.
021:079 with David: it was We Who **did** (all these things).
021:082 for him, and **did** other work besides;
021:097 of this; nay, we truly **did** wrong!"
022:034 To every people **did** We appoint rites (of sacrifice),
022:040 **Did** not Allah check one set of people
022:042 If they disbelieve you so **did** the Peoples
022:044 and (only) after that **did** I punish them:
022:048 And to how many populations **did** I give respite,
022:052 Never **did** We send a messenger or a prophet
023:012 Man We **did** create from a quintessence (of clay);
023:024 never **did** we hear such a thing (as he says),
023:068 come to them that **did** not come to their
023:091 No son **did** Allah beget, nor is
023:105 and ye **did** but treat them as falsehoods?"
023:112 "What number of years **did** ye stay on earth?"
023:115 "**Did** ye then think that We had created you
024:012 Why **did** not the Believers-men and women-
024:013 Why **did** they not bring four witnesses to prove it?
024:016 And why **did** ye not, when ye heard
024:064 He will tell them the truth of what they **did**:
025:017 or **did** they stray from the Path themselves?"
025:023 We shall turn to whatever deeds they **did** (in this life),
025:029 "He **did** lead me astray from the Message
025:040 **did** they not then see it (with their own eyes)?
026:018 (Pharaoh) said: "**Did** we not cherish thee as a
026:020 Moses: "I **did** it then, when I was in error.
026:046 Then **did** the sorcerers fall down, prostrate in
026:157 then **did** they become full of regrets.
026:208 Never **did** We destroy a town but had its warners-
026:210 The Satans **did** not bring it down:
027:084 not in knowledge, or what was it ye **did**?"
027:084 "**Did** ye reject My signs, though ye
028:013 Thus **did** We restore him to his mother, that her
028:036 never **did** we hear the like among our
028:040 of those who **did** wrong!
028:043 We **did** reveal to Moses the Book after We

DID (continued)

028:078 **Did** he not know that Allah had destroyed,
029:003 We **did** test those before them, and Allah
029:008 and I will tell you (the truth) of all that ye **did**.
029:014 We **did** sent Noah to his people, and he
029:018 so **did** generations before you:
029:020 see how Allah **did** originate creation;
029:024 But Allah **did** save him from the Fire.
030:008 **did** Allah create the heavens and the earth,
030:047 We **did** indeed send, before thee, messengers to
030:056 "Indeed ye **did** tarry, within Allah's Decree,
030:056 the Day of Resurrection: but ye-ye **did** not know!"
031:014 in travail upon travail **did** his mother bear him.
031:015 is to Me, and I will tell you all that ye **did**."
032:023 We **did** indeed aforetime give the Book to Moses:
033:025 no advantage **did** they gain, and enough
033:026 who aided them-Allah **did** take them down from
033:072 We **did** indeed offer the Trust to the Heavens
034:020 And on them **did** Satan prove true his idea,
034:034 Never **did** We send a Warner to a population,
034:053 Seeing that they **did** reject faith (entirely)
035:011 And Allah **did** create you from dust; then from
035:025 so **did** their predecessors, to whom
035:026 In the end **did** I punish those who rejected Faith:
035:037 **Did** we not give you long enough life so that
036:060 "**Did** I not enjoin on you, O ye children of Adam,
036:062 "But he **did** lead astray a great multitude of you.
036:062 **Did** ye not, then understand?
036:065 bear witness, to all that they **did**.
037:039 And you are requited naught save what ye **did**.
037:088 Then **did** he cast a glance at the Stars,
037:091 Then **did** he turn to their gods and said,
037:093 Then **did** he turn upon them, striking (them)
037:142 Then the big Fish **did** swallow him, and he
037:153 **Did** He (then) choose daughters rather than sons?
038:003 How many generations before them **did** We destroy?
038:019 all with him **did** turn (to Allah).
038:026 O David! We **did** indeed make thee a vicegerent
038:027 Not without purpose **did** We create
038:030 the Servant! Ever **did** he turn (to Us in repentance)!
038:034 but he **did** turn (to Us in true devotion):
038:034 And We **did** try Solomon: We placed
038:044 Ever **did** he turn (to Us)!
038:046 Verily We **did** chose them for a special (purpose)-
038:063 "**Did** we treat them (as such) in ridicule, or have
039:007 of all that ye **did** (in this life).
039:025 from directions they **did** not perceive.
039:050 But all that they **did** was of no profit to them.
039:050 Thus **did** the (generations) before them say!
039:071 "**Did** not messengers come to you from among
040:012 ye **did** reject Faith, but when partners were
040:021 but Allah **did** call them to account
040:050 They will say: "**Did** there not come to you
040:053 We **did** aforetime give Moses the Guidance,
040:078 We **did** aforetime send messengers before thee:
040:085 And even thus **did** the rejecters of Allah lose (utterly)!
041:015 What! **did** they not see that Allah,
041:022 "Ye **did** not seek to hide yourselves, lest your
041:022 But ye **did** think that Allah
041:023 thought of yours which ye **did** entertain concerning your
041:050 will show the Unbelievers the truth of all that they **did**,
042:003 to thee as (He **did**) to those before thee,-Allah,
043:019 **Did** they witness their creation?

DID (continued)

043:045   **did** We appoint any deities other than The Most
043:046   We **did** send Moses aforetime, with Our Signs,
043:054   Thus **did** he make fools of his people, and they
044:017   We **did**, before them, try the people of Pharaoh:
044:030   We **did** deliver aforetime the Children of Israel
045:016   We **did** aforetime grant to the Children of Israel
045:028   ye be recompensed for all that ye **did**!
045:029   on record all that ye **did**."
045:030   and **did** righteous deeds, their Lord
045:033   the evil (fruits) of what they **did**, and they
046:015   in pain **did** his mother bear him,
046:015   and in pain **did** she give him birth.
046:035   as **did** (all) messengers of firm resolution; and be
047:010   before them (who **did** evil)?
048:016   but if ye turn back as ye **did** before, He will punish
048:025   ye **did** not know that ye were trampling down
048:026   Truly **did** Allah fulfil the vision
050:027   "Our Lord! I **did** not make him transgress, but he
050:036   how many generations **did** We destroy (for their Sins),-
050:036   Then **did** they wander through the land:
050:038   nor **did** any sense of weariness touch Us.
051:028   (When they **did** not eat), He conceived
052:028   "Truly we **did** call unto Him from of old:
052:036   Or **did** they create the heavens and the earth?
053:010   So **did** (Allah) convey the inspiration to His
053:017   (His) sight never swerved, nor **did** it go wrong!
053:018   For truly **did** he see, of the Signs
053:045   That He **did** create in pairs-male and female,
054:036   And (Lut) **did** warn them of Our violent Seizure
057:010   before the Victory, (with those who **did** so later).
057:027   but that they **did** not foster as they should have
057:027   We **did** not prescribe for them:
058:007   them what they **did** on the Day of Judgment.
059:002   (of the forces). Little **did** ye think that they
062:008   and He will tell you the things that ye **did**!"
064:007   (the truth) of all that ye **did**.
065:008   **did** We not then call to account,-
065:009   Then **did** they taste the evil result of their
066:007   Ye are being but requited for all that ye **did**!"
067:008   its Keepers will ask, "**Did** no Warner come to you?"
067:009   "Yes indeed; a Warner **did** come to us, but we
068:028   "**Did** I not say to you,
068:050   Thus **did** his Lord choose him and make him
069:020   "I **did** really understand that my Account
075:031   So he gave nothing in charity, nor **did** he pray!-
075:033   Then **did** he stalk to his family in full conceit!
075:038   then **did** (Allah) make and fashion (him)
075:038   Then **did** he become a leech-like clot;
077:016   **Did** We not destroy the men of old (for their evil)?
079:016   Behold, thy Lord **did** call to him in the sacred
079:020   Then **did** (Moses) show him the Great Sign.
079:025   But Allah **did** punish him, (and made an)
083:036   paid back for what they **did**?
084:013   Truly, **did** he go about among his people, rejoicing!
084:014   Truly, **did** he think that he would not
089:013   Therefore **did** thy Lord pour on them a scourge
093:006   **Did** He not find thee an orphan and give
094:003   The which **did** gall thy back?-
098:004   Nor **did** the people of the Book make schisms,
105:002   **Did** He not make their treacherous plan go astray?
105:005   Then **did** He make them like an empty field

DIDST

002:243   **Didst** thou not turn thy vision
002:259   He said: "How long **didst** thou tarry (thus)?"
002:286   like that which Thou **didst** lay on those
003:121   thou **didst** leave the household (early)
003:194   Thou **didst** promise unto us through Thy Messengers,
005:067   If thou **didst** not, thou wouldst not
005:110   So that thou **didst** speak to the people
005:110   (violence to) thee when thou **didst** show them
005:116   "O Jesus the son of Mary! **didst** thou say unto men,
005:117   except what Thou **didst** command me to say, to wit,
005:117   when Thou **didst** take me up, thou wast
006:128   which Thou **didst** appoint for us."
007:012   thou **didst** create me from fire and him from clay."
008:056   thou **didst** make a covenant, but they
009:043   God give thee grace! Why **didst** thou grant them
010:091   and thou **didst** mischief (and violence)!
015:033   Whom Thou **didst** create from sounding clay,
017:061   whom Thou **didst** create from clay?"
018:039   "Why **didst** thou not, as thou wentest into thy
020:040   Then thou **didst** slay a man, but We
020:040   Then **didst** thou come hither as ordained, O Moses!
020:040   Then **didst** thou tarry a number of years with the
020:073   and the magic to which thou **didst** compel us:
020:093   **Didst** thou then disobey my order?"
020:094   and thou **didst** not observe my word!'"
020:126   (Allah) will say: "Thus **didst** thou, when Our
025:018   but Thou **didst** bestow, on them
026:018   and **didst** thou not stay in our midst many years
026:019   "And thou **didst** a deed of thine which (thou knowest)
026:019   which (thou knowest) thou **didst**, and thou art an
028:047   why **didst** Thou not send us a messenger?
033:037   But thou **didst** hide in thy heart that which
033:037   Behold! thou **didst** say to one who had received
033:037   thou **didst** fear the people,
039:059   to thee My Signs, and thou **didst** reject them:
063:010   Why **didst** thou not give me respite for a little while?

DIE

002:028   then will He cause you to **die**,
002:132   then **die** not except in the state of submission
002:161   Those who reject Faith, and **die** rejecting,
002:217   turn back from their faith and **die** in unbelief,
002:234   If any of you **die** and leave widows behind;
002:240   Those of you who **die** and leave widows
002:243   for fear of death? Allah said to them: "**Die**."
002:259   But Allah caused him to **die** for a hundred years,
003:091   As to those who reject faith, and **die** rejecting,
003:102   and **die** not except in a state of Islam.
003:145   Nor can a soul **die** except by Allah's leave,
003:157   And if ye are slain, or **die**, in the way of Allah,
003:158   And if ye **die**, or are slain,
004:018   nor of those who **die** rejecting faith:
004:097   those who **die** in sin against their soul.
004:100   And abundance should he **die** as a refugee
007:025   and therein shall ye **die**: but from it
008:042   who died might **die** after a clear Sign (had been given),
009:125   and they will **die** in a state of Unbelief.
012:085   of illness, or until thou **die**!"
014:017   yet will he not **die**:
016:038   raise up those who **die**:
019:033   the day that I **die**, and the day that I shall
020:074   therein shall he neither **die** or live.
021:034   if then thou shouldst **die**, would they

DIE (continued)

022:005 and some of you are called to **die**, and some
022:058 cause of Allah, and are slain or **die**,-on them
022:066 will cause you to **die**, and will
023:015 After that, at length, ye will **die**.
023:035 "Does he promise that when ye **die** and become
023:037 We shall **die** and we live!
023:082 They say: "What! when we **die** and become
026:081 "Who will cause me to **die**, and then
030:040 then He will cause you to **die**; and again He will give
031:034 Nor does any one know in what land he is to **die**.
035:036 so they should **die**, nor shall
037:016 "What! when we **die**, and become dust and bones,
037:053 "'When we **die** and become dust and bones,
037:058 "Is it (the case) that we shall not **die**,
039:030 and truly they (too) will **die** (one day).
039:030 Truly thou wilt **die** (one day) and truly
039:042 and those that **die** not (He takes) during their
040:011 made us to **die**, and twice hast Thou given us Life!
040:067 though of you there are some who **die** before;-
045:024 We shall **die** and we live, and nothing
047:034 (men) from the Path of Allah, then **die** disbelieving,-
050:003 "What! when we **die** and become dust,
056:047 "What! when we **die** and become dust and bones,
080:021 Then He causeth him to **die**, and putteth
087:013 In which he will then neither **die** nor live.

DIED

003:144 If he **died** or were slain,
003:156 they would not have **died**, or been slain."
008:042 who **died** might die after a clear Sign (had been given).
009:084 and **died** in a state of perverse rebellion.
019:023 "Ah! would that I had **died** before this! would that
033:023 of them some have **died** and some (still) wait:
040:034 at length, when he **died**, ye said:

DIES

004:176 That **dies**, leaving a sister but no child,
009:084 Nor do thou ever pray for any of them that **dies**,
019:015 the day that he **dies**, and the day that he will
025:058 And put thy trust in Him Who lives and **dies** not;

DIFFER

002:213 did not **differ** among themselves,
004:059 If ye **differ** in anything among yourselves,
004:157 And those who **differ** therein are full of doubts,
011:118 but they will not cease to **differ**,
016:039 of that wherein they **differ**, and that
016:064 make clear to them those things in which they **differ**,
019:037 But the sects **differ** among themselves:
022:069 concerning the matter in which ye **differ**."
032:025 matters wherein they **differ** (among themselves).
039:003 in that wherein they **differ**.
042:010 Whatever it be wherein ye **differ**, the decision

DIFFERED

002:213 concerning that wherein they **differed**.
002:213 in matters wherein they **differed**;
010:019 Mankind was but one nation, but **differed** (later).
039:046 in those matters about which they have **differed**."

DIFFERENCE

002:136 we make no **difference** between one
014:021 to us it makes no **difference** (now) whether

DIFFERENCES

010:019 their **differences** would have been settled between them.
011:110 to Moses, but **differences** arose therein:

DIFFERENCES (continued)

016:124 as to their **differences**.
041:045 (their **differences**) would have been settled between them:
045:017 matters in which they set up **differences**.

DIFFERENT

004:081 on things very **different** from what
004:140 unless they turn to a **different** Theme:
006:068 they turn to a **different** theme.
006:099 each similar (in kind) yet **different** (in variety):
006:141 similar (in kind) and **different** (in variety):
012:059 of the same father as yourselves, (but a **different** mother):
012:067 enter ye by **different** gates.
014:048 to a **different** Earth, and so will be the Heavens,
017:073 Our name something quite **different**:

DIFFERENTLY

007:053 Then should we behave **differently** from our

DIFFERING

012:039 are many lords **differing** among themselves better,

DIFFICULT

035:017 Nor is that (at all) **difficult** for Allah.
037:011 are they the more **difficult** to create, or the
079:027 What! Are ye the more **difficult** to create or the

DIFFICULTIES

002:185 He does not want to put you to **difficulties**.
002:220 He could have put you into **difficulties**:
018:073 by raising **difficulties** in my case."
022:078 and has imposed no **difficulties** on you
065:006 find yourselves in **difficulties**,

DIFFICULTY

002:280 If the debtor is in a **difficulty**,
005:006 Allah doth not wish to place you in a **difficulty**,
007:002 no more by any **difficulty** on that account,-
025:026 it will be a Day of dire **difficulty** for the
028:027 But I intend not to place thee under a **difficulty**:
033:037 be no **difficulty** to the Believers in (the matter of)
033:038 There can be no **difficulty** to the Prophet
033:050 in order that there should be no **difficulty** for thee.
065:007 After a **difficulty**, Allah will soon grant relief.
094:005 So, verily, with every **difficulty**, there is relief:
094:006 Verily, with every **difficulty** there is relief.

DIG

018:097 to scale it or to **dig** through it.

DIGNITY

008:004 they have grades of **dignity** with their Lord,
037:042 Fruits, and they (shall enjoy) honour and **dignity**,
043:004 high (in **dignity**), full of wisdom.
073:010 and leave them with noble (**dignity**).
080:014 Exalted (in **dignity**), kept pure and holy,
088:013 therein will be couches (of **dignity**), raised on high,

DILIGENTLY

012:047 shall ye **diligently** sow as is your wont:
014:033 both **diligently** pursuing their courses:

DIM

077:008 Then when the stars become **dim**;

DIMINISH

002:282 and not **diminish** aught of what he owes.

DIMINUTION

011:015 their deeds therein,-without **diminution**.

DIRE

018:079 certain men in **dire** want:
025:026 it will be a Day of **dire** difficulty for the

DIRECT

004:083 would have known it from them (**direct**).
004:164 and to Moses Allah spoke **direct**;
007:143 canst thou see Me (**direct**); but look
007:181 who **direct** (others) with truth, and dispense
064:006 "Shall (mere) human beings **direct** us?"

DIRECTED

002:198 as He has **directed** you,
004:131 Verily We have **directed** the people
005:004 in the manner **directed** to you by Allah:
006:071 and we have been **directed** to submit ourselves
007:160 We **directed** Moses by inspiration, when his
021:071 and (his nephew) Lut (and **directed** them) to the

DIRECTION

002:016 and they have lost true **direction**.
002:144 turn your faces in that **direction**.
002:144 in the **direction** of the Sacred Mosque:
002:149 in the **direction** of the Sacred Mosque;
002:150 in the **direction** of the Sacred Mosque;
028:029 he perceived a fire in the **direction** of Mount Tur.
037:008 in the **direction** of the Exalted Assembly and they
043:040 or give **direction** to the blind or to such

DIRECTIONS

016:026 from **directions** they did not perceive.
016:045 seize them from **directions** they little perceive?
039:025 from **directions** they did not perceive.
068:044 from **directions** they perceive not.

DIRECTS

004:011 Allah (thus) **directs** you as regards
004:176 say: Allah **directs** (thus) about those who leave
016:076 whichever way he **directs** him, he brings no good:
032:005 He **directs** the affairs from the heavens to the

DIRHAMS

012:020 a miserable price,-for a few **dirhams** counted out:

DISABLED

004:095 except those who are **disabled**.

DISAGREE

016:092 (the truth of) that wherein ye **disagree**.
027:076 the matters in which they **disagree**.

DISAGREED

016:124 for those who **disagreed** (as to its observance);

DISAGREEMENT

043:065 fell into **disagreement**:

DISAPPEARS

013:017 For the scum **disappears** like froth cast out;

DISAPPROVE

005:059 do ye **disapprove** of us for no other reason

DISASTER

003:146 if they met with **disaster** in Allah's way,
003:165 What! when a single **disaster** smites you,
005:052 a change of fortune bring us **disaster**."
009:098 on them be the **disaster** of Evil:
013:031 But the Unbelievers,-never will **disaster** cease to
040:030 (of **disaster**) of the Confederates (in sin)!-
041:016 a furious Wind through days of **disaster**, that We

DISASTERS

009:098 and watch for **disasters** for you:

DISBELIEF

005:061 they enter with a **disbelief**, and they go out
010:070 the severest Chastisement for their **disbelief**.
035:039 their **disbelief** but adds to (their own) loss.
035:039 so, he who disbelieves his **disbelief** be on

DISBELIEF (continued)

035:039 be on his own self their **disbelief**:
039:008 Say "Enjoy thy **disbelief** for a little while:

DISBELIEVE

002:102 Solomon did not **disbelieve** but Satans
005:072 Certainly they **disbelieve** who say: "Allah is
005:073 They **disbelieve** who say: Allah is one
015:002 Often will those who **disbelieve**, wish that
022:042 If they **disbelieve** you so did the Peoples
041:014 so we **disbelieve** in the Message you were sent with.
047:032 Those who **disbelieve**, hinder (men) from the
047:034 Those who **disbelieve**, and hinder (men) from the
052:042 who **disbelieve** are themselves ensnared in a Plot.
059:016 when he says to man, "**Disbelieve**":
088:023 But if any turn away and **disbelieve**,-
098:001 Those who **disbelieve**, among the People of the
098:006 Those who **disbelieve**, among the People of the

DISBELIEVED

002:102 but Satans **disbelieved**,
005:017 They **disbelieved** indeed those that say that Allah
023:033 who **disbelieved** and denied the Meeting in the
048:025 They are the ones who **disbelieved** and hindered
061:014 and a portion **disbelieved**:
069:004 'Ad people **disbelieved** in the day of Noise and Clamour!

DISBELIEVERS

005:073 chastisement will befall the **disbelievers** among them.
005:103 it is the **disbelievers** who invent a lie

DISBELIEVES

035:039 so, he who **disbelieves** his disbelief be on
059:016 but when (man) **disbelieves**, Satan says,

DISBELIEVING

047:034 then die **disbelieving**,- Allah will not forgive them.

DISCHARGE

002:283 let the trustee (faithfully) **discharge** his trust,
007:164 Said the preachers: "To **discharge** our duty

DISCIPLES

003:052 Said the **Disciples**: "We are Allah's helpers
005:111 "And behold! I inspired the **Disciples** to have
005:112 Behold! the **Disciples** said: "O Jesus
061:014 son of Mary to the **Disciples**, "Who will be my helpers
061:014 Said the **Disciples**, "We are Allah's helpers!"

DISCIPLINE

022:078 ye ought to strive, (with sincerity and under **discipline**):

DISCLOSE

002:271 If ye **disclose** (acts of) charity,
003:179 Nor will He **disclose** to you the secrets
028:010 she was going almost to **disclose** his (case),
036:076 what they hide as well as what they **disclose**.
053:058 No one but Allah can **disclose** it.

DISCLOSED

066:003 When the Prophet **disclosed** a matter in confidence

DISCOMFITED

067:004 to thee dull and **discomfited**, in a state worn out.

DISCORD

002:102 the means to sow **discord** between man and wife.
003:007 Seeking **discord**, and searching for interpretation,
041:036 an incitement to **discord** is made to thee by the Satan,

DISCOURAGED

008:043 ye would surely have been **discouraged**, and ye

DISCOURSE

006:068 in vain **discourse** about Our Signs, turn away
006:091 in vain **discourse** and trifling.

DISCOURSE (continued)
019:062　They will not there hear any vain **discourse**,

DISCOURSES
006:112　flowery **discourses** by way of deception.

DISCREPANCY
004:082　found therein much **discrepancy**.

DISCRIMINATION
008:041　to our Servant on the Day of **Discrimination**-

DISCUSS
038:069　when they **discuss** (matters) among themselves.

DISDAIN
002:282　**Disdain** not to reduce to writing (your contract)
004:172　those who **disdain** His worship and are arrogant,
007:206　who are near to thy Lord, **disdain** not to worship Him:

DISDAINETH
004:172　Christ **disdaineth** not to serve and worship Allah,

DISDAINFUL
004:173　but those who are **disdainful** and arrogant, He will

DISDAINFULLY
022:009　(**Disdainfully**) bending his side, in order to lead (men)

DISDAINING
029:066　**Disdaining** ungratefully Our gifts and giving

DISDAINS
002:026　Allah **disdains** not to use the similitude of things,

DISEASE
002:010　In their hearts is a **disease**;
002:010　and Allah has increased their **disease**,
005:052　Those in whose heart is a **disease**-thou seest how
008:049　in whose hearts is a **disease**: say:
009:125　But those in whose hearts is a **disease**,-it will
022:053　is a **disease** and who are hardened of heart:
024:050　Is it that there is a **disease** in their hearts?
033:012　in whose hearts is a **disease** say: "Allah
033:032　lest one in whose heart is a **disease** should be
033:060　in whose hearts is a **disease**, and those
047:020　is a **disease** looking at thee with a look of one
047:029　Or do those in whose hearts is a **disease**,
074:031　in whose hearts is a **disease** and the Unbelievers

DISEASED
056:055　ye shall drink like **diseased** camels raging with thirst!

DISEASES
010:057　and a healing for the (**diseases**) in your hearts,-

DISEMBARK
023:029　to enable us to **disembark**."
023:029　enable me to **disembark** with Thy blessing:

DISFIGURE
017:007　(We permitted your enemies) to **disfigure** your faces,

DISGRACE
002:085　but **disgrace** in this life?
002:114　but **disgrace** in this world,
005:033　that is their **disgrace** in this world, and a heavy
005:041　For them there is **disgrace** in this world, and in
006:093　a chastisement of **disgrace**, for that
009:014　and **disgrace** them, help you (to victory) over them,
009:063　That is the supreme **disgrace**.
015:068　Lut said: "These are my guests: **disgrace** me not:
017:022　in **disgrace** and destitution.
022:009　for him there is **disgrace** in this life, and on
022:018　And such as Allah shall **disgrace**,-none can
026:087　"And let me not be in **disgrace** on the Day
027:037　We shall expel them from there in **disgrace**,

DISGRACE (continued)
068:049　on the naked shore, in **disgrace**.

DISGRACED
017:018　burn therein, **disgraced** and rejected.

DISGUISE
027:041　He said: "**Disguise** her throne, let us

DISGUST
004:061　avert their faces from thee in **disgust**.
009:048　much to their **disgust**.
039:045　who believe not in the Hereafter are filled with **disgust**,

DISHES
043:071　To them will be passed round, **dishes** and goblets of gold:

DISHONESTLY
003:161　If any person acts **dishonestly** he shall,
003:161　No prophet could (ever) **dishonestly** if any

DISINTEGRATION
034:007　all scattered to pieces in **disintegration**, that ye

DISLIKE
002:216　ye **dislike** a thing which is good for you,
002:216　and ye **dislike** it.
004:019　and equity if ye take a **dislike** to them it may
004:019　it may be that ye **dislike** a thing,

DISLIKED
008:005　the Believers **disliked** it.

DISLOYALTY
004:034　whose part ye fear **disloyalty** and ill-conduct,

DISMAL
075:024　And some faces, that Day, will be sad and **dismal**,

DISMISS
033:053　the Prophet: he is shy to **dismiss** you, but Allah

DISOBEDIENCE
002:173　without wilful **disobedience**,
006:145　without wilful **disobedience**, nor transgressing
006:146　this in recompense for their wilful **disobedience**:
016:115　without wilful **disobedience**, nor transgressing
058:008　and **disobedience** to the Messenger.
058:009　and **disobedience** to the Messenger;

DISOBEDIENT
005:059　are rebellious and **disobedient**?"
007:102　We found rebellious and **disobedient**.

DISOBEY
002:093　they said: "We hear, and we **disobey**":
004:014　But those who **disobey** Allah and His Messenger
004:042　and **disobey** the Messenger will wish that
004:046　and say: "We hear and we **disobey**";
009:096　Allah is not pleased with those who **disobey**.
010:015　if I were to **disobey** my Lord, I should myself
011:063　me against Allah if I were to **disobey** Him?
018:069　nor shall I **disobey** thee in aught."
020:093　Didst thou then **disobey** my order?"
020:121　thus did Adam **disobey** His Lord,
026:216　Then if they **disobey** thee, say: "I am free
060:012　and that they will not **disobey** thee in any
072:022　one can deliver me from Allah (if I were to **disobey** Him),
072:023　for any that **disobey** Allah and His Messenger,-

DISOBEYED
003:152　and **disobeyed** it after He brought you in sight
005:078　because they **disobeyed** and persisted in Excesses.
006:015　Say: "I would, if I **disobeyed** my Lord, indeed
011:059　their Lord and Cherisher; **disobeyed** His Messengers;
039:013　Say: "I would, if I **disobeyed** my Lord,

DISOBEYED (continued)

069:010 And **disobeyed** (each) the messenger of their Lord;
071:021 Noah said: "O my Lord they have **disobeyed** me,
073:016 But Pharaoh **disobeyed** the messenger; so We
079:021 But (Pharaoh) rejected it and **disobeyed** (guidance);

DISOBEYS

014:036 and he that **disobeys** me,-but thou
033:036 if any one **disobeys** Allah and His Messenger,

DISORDER

009:047 added to your (strength) but only (made for) **disorder**,

DISOWN

029:025 ye shall **disown** each other and curse each other:

DISPATCH

026:036 and **dispatch** to the Cities heralds to collect-

DISPENSE

007:181 and **dispense** justice therewith.
023:060 And those who **dispense** their charity with their

DISPERSE

008:057 them in war, **disperse**, with them, those who
033:053 and when ye have taken your meal, **disperse**,
062:010 then may ye **disperse** through the land, and seek
062:011 or some pastime, they **disperse** headlong to it,
063:007 till they **disperse** (and quit Madinah).

DISPERSED

034:019 and We **dispersed** them all in scattered fragments.

DISPLACE

004:046 those who **displace** words from their (right) places,

DISPLACED

023:104 with their lips **displaced**.

DISPLAY

024:031 that they should not **display** their beauty
024:031 over their bosoms and not **display** their beauty
024:060 provided they make not wanton **display** of their
033:033 and make not a dazzling **display**, like that

DISPLEASED

047:028 which **displeased** Allah, and they hated Allah's
093:003 nor is He **displeased**.

DISPLEASURE

004:155 (They have incurred divine **displeasure**):

DISPOSAL

008:001 the **disposal** of Allah and the Messenger:
010:024 powers of **disposal** over it:

DISPOSE

002:234 no blame on you if they **dispose** of themselves in a just
006:102 to **dispose** of all of all affairs.
006:107 to **dispose** of their affairs.
018:010 and **dispose** of our affair for us in the right way!
018:016 His mercies on you and **dispose** of your affair
036:050 to **dispose** (of their affairs), nor to

DISPOSER

004:081 and enough is Allah as a **disposer** of affairs.
004:171 And enough is Allah as a **Disposer** of affairs.
017:002 as **Disposer** of (your) affairs."
017:054 a **disposer** of their affairs for them.
017:065 for a **Disposer** of affairs.
025:043 Could thou be a **disposer** of affairs
033:003 and enough is Allah, as a **Disposer** of affairs.
033:048 as a **disposer** of affairs.
039:062 and He is the Guardian and **Disposer** of all affairs.
042:006 the **disposer** of their affairs.
073:009 take Him therefore for (thy) **Disposer** of Affairs.

DISPOSES

027:088 Who **disposes** of all things in perfect order:

DISPOSING

004:009 Let those (**disposing** of an estate) have

DISPOSITION

017:084 Say: "'Everyone acts according to his own **disposition**:

DISPUTANTS

038:021 Has the Story of the **Disputants** reached thee?
038:022 two **disputants**, one of whom has wronged the other:

DISPUTATION

043:058 only by way of **disputation**:

DISPUTATIONS

003:105 and fall into **disputations** after receiving Clear Signs:

DISPUTE

002:072 a **dispute** among yourselves as to the crime:
002:139 Say: Will ye **dispute** with us about Allah,
002:150 of **dispute** against you among the people,
002:176 seek causes of **dispute** in the Book
003:020 So if they **dispute** with thee,
003:023 to settle their **dispute**,
003:055 between you of the matters wherein ye **dispute**.
003:065 Ye people of the Book! why **dispute** ye about Abraham,
003:066 but why **dispute** ye in matters of which
005:048 the truth of the matters in which ye **dispute**;
006:025 they (but) **dispute** with thee; the Unbelievers
006:080 He said: "(Come) ye to **dispute** with me, about
007:071 **dispute** ye with me over names which ye have devised-
011:032 prolonged the **dispute** with us:
016:027 concerning whom ye used to **dispute** (with the godly)
018:021 Behold they **dispute** among themselves as to
018:056 but the Unbelievers **dispute** with vain argument,
019:034 about which they (vainly) **dispute**.
022:003 as **dispute** about Allah, without knowledge,
022:019 These two antagonists **dispute** with each other
022:067 let them not then **dispute** with thee on the matter,
029:046 And **dispute** ye not with the People of the Book,
031:020 who **dispute** about Allah, without knowledge
039:031 In the End will ye (all) **dispute** on the Day of Judgment,
040:004 None can **dispute** about the Signs of Allah
040:035 "(Such) as **dispute** about the Signs of Allah,
040:047 Behold, they will **dispute** with each other
040:056 Those who **dispute** about the Signs of Allah
040:069 not those that **dispute** concerning the signs of Allah?
042:016 But those who **dispute** concerning Allah after He
042:018 those that **dispute** concerning the Hour are far astray.
042:035 who **dispute** about Our Signs, that there
043:018 in a **dispute** (to be associated with Allah)?
043:063 clear to you some of the (points) on which ye **dispute**:
050:028 He will say: "Dispute not with each other
053:012 Will ye then **dispute** with him
053:055 (O man), wilt thou **dispute** about?

DISPUTED

002:258 to one who **disputed** with Abraham about his Lord,
003:044 when they dispute (the point).
006:080 His people **disputed** with him.
006:164 of things wherein ye **disputed**."
008:043 have **disputed** in (your) decision:
011:032 They said: "O Noah! thou hast **disputed** with us,
020:062 So they **disputed**, one with another, over their
040:005 and **disputed** by means of vanities,
054:036 violent Seizure but they **disputed** about the Warning.

DISPUTER
016:004 becomes an open **disputer**!

DISPUTES
003:061 If any one **disputes** in this manner with thee,
004:060 together for judgment (in their **disputes**) to the Evil
004:065 judge in all **disputes** between them.
008:046 and fall into no **disputes**, lest ye
022:008 as **disputes** about Allah, without knowledge,
041:045 the book aforetime: but **disputes** arose therein.

DISPUTING
003:066 to **disputing** (even) in matters of which ye had
003:152 and fell to **disputing** about the order,
008:006 **Disputing** with thee concerning the truth
013:013 the while they are **disputing** about Allah,
036:049 yet **disputing** among themselves!
078:001 Concerning what are they **disputing**?

DISQUIETING
011:062 suspicious (**disquieting**) doubt as to that
014:009 in suspicious (**disquieting**) doubt as to that
034:054 in suspicious (**disquieting**) doubt.
041:045 they remained in suspicious **disquieting** doubt thereon.
042:014 are in suspicious (**disquieting**) doubt concerning it.

DISREGARD
033:048 and **disregard** their insolence but pit thy trust in Allah.

DISREGARDED
007:165 When they **disregarded** the warnings that had

DISSENSIONS
017:053 for Satan doth sow **dissensions** among them:

DISSENT
003:019 the Book **dissent** therefrom except through
011:089 "And O my people! let not my **dissent** (from you)

DISSIPATES
081:017 And the Night as it **dissipates**;

DISSOCIATED
009:114 he **dissociated** himself from him:

DISSOLVE
009:003 and His Messenger **dissolve** (treaty) obligations with the

DISSOLVED
009:004 (But the treaties are) not **dissolved** with those
033:037 when the latter have **dissolved** (their marriage)
033:037 Then when Zaid had **dissolved** (his marriage)

DISTANCE
003:030 a great **distance** between it and its evil.
009:042 followed thee, but the **distance** was long,
014:003 they are astray by a long **distance**.
018:062 When they had passed on (some **distance**), Moses said
028:011 from a **distance** and they perceived not.
033:020 about you (from a safe **distance**); and if
043:038 the **distance** of East and West!"
053:009 And was at a **distance** of but two bow-lengths

DISTANCES
034:019 place longer **distances** between our journey-stages":

DISTANT
022:027 through deep and **distant** mountain highways;
041:044 called from a place far **distant**!"
050:031 nigh to the righteous,-no more a thing **distant**.
072:025 for it a **distant** term.

DISTASTEFUL
008:008 and prove Falsehood false, **distasteful** though

DISTINCT
002:187 appear to you **distinct** from its black thread;

DISTINCT (continued)
044:004 In that (night) is made **distinct** every affair

DISTINCTION
002:285 "We make no **distinction** (they say) between
003:084 we make no **distinction** between one and another
004:152 make no **distinction** between any of the messengers,
019:007 that name have We conferred **distinction** before."

DISTINGUISHED
004:095 hath He **distinguished** above those who sit

DISTINGUISHES
086:013 that **distinguishes** (Good from Evil):

DISTORT
003:078 a section who **distort** the Book with their tongues;
004:135 and if ye **distort** (Justice) or decline to do justice,
007:180 but shun such men as **distort** His names:

DISTRACT
015:003 and let (false) Hope **distract** them:

DISTRACTED
026:225 wander **distracted** in every valley?-

DISTRACTION
005:026 in **distraction** will they wander through the land:
007:186 wandering in **distraction**.
010:011 wandering in **distraction** blindly.
012:086 of my **distraction** and anguish to Allah,
015:072 they wander in **distraction**, to and fro.
023:075 wandering in **distraction** to and fro.

DISTRESS
003:153 one **distress** after another by way of requital,
003:154 After (the excitement) of the **distress**, He sent down calm
006:041 He would remove (the **distress**) which occasioned
009:117 who followed Him in a time of **distress**, after
012:088 "O exalted one! **distress** has seized us
016:053 are touched by **distress**, unto Him
016:054 Yet, when He removes the **distress** from you,
016:127 and **distress** not thyself because of their plots.
017:067 When **distress** seizes you at sea, those that
019:039 But warn them of the Day of **Distress,** when the
020:002 to be (an occasion) for thy **distress**,
021:076 and his family from great **distress**.
021:083 when he cried to his Lord "Truly **distress** has seized me,
021:084 We removed the **distress** that was on him, and We
021:088 and delivered him form **distress**:
023:075 and removed the **distress** which is on them,
027:070 nor **distress** thyself because of their plots.
037:115 and their people from (their) Great **distress**.
038:041 "Satan has afflicted me with **distress** and suffering"!
074:009 That will be-that Day-a Day of **Distress**,-
076:010 and **distress** from the side of our Lord."

DISTRESSED
015:097 is **distressed** at what they say.
016:007 except with souls **distressed**:
022:028 the **distressed** ones in want.
027:062 Or, Who listens to the **distressed** when he calls
099:003 And man cries (**distressed**): 'What is the

DISTRESSES
006:064 from these and all (other) **distresses**:

DISTRESSFUL
011:077 He said: "This is a **distressful** day."

DISTRIBUTE
051:004 And those that **distribute** the affair;-

DISTRIBUTED
025:050 And We have **distributed** the (water) amongst them,
DISTRIBUTION
004:011 (The **distribution** in all cases is) after the payment
009:058 thee in the matter of (the **distribution** of) the alms.
DISUNITE
009:107 to **disunite** the Believers-and in preparation
DIVED'
021:082 And of Satans were some who **dived** for him,
DIVER
038:037 every kind of builder and **diver**,-
DIVERGENT
072:011 we follow **divergent** paths.
DIVERGING
005:048 and follow not their vain desires, **diverging** from the truth
DIVERS
020:053 With it have We produced **divers** pairs of plants
DIVERSE
006:065 See how We explain the Signs in **diverse** ways;
013:004 And in the earth are tracts (**diverse** though) neighboring,
071:014 created you in **diverse** stages?
089:013 a scourge of **diverse** chastisement:
092:004 Verily, (the ends) ye strive for are **diverse**.
DIVERT
003:152 Then did He **divert** you from your foes
020:016 but follow their one lusts, **divert** thee therefrom,
024:037 can **divert** from the Remembrance of Allah,
063:009 or your children **divert** you from the remembrance
DIVERTED
027:043 And he **diverted** her from the worship
DIVERTS
102:001 (the good things of this world) **diverts** you
DIVIDE
006:159 As for those who **divide** their religion and
DIVIDED
002:050 And remember We **divided** the sea for you
003:103 and be not **divided** among yourselves;
003:105 Be not like those who are **divided** amongst themselves
004:088 Why should ye be **divided** into two parties
007:160 We **divided** them into twelve tribes or nations.
015:090 on those who **divided** (Scripture into arbitrary parts),-
017:106 (It is) a Qur'an which We have **divided** (into parts
026:063 So it **divided**, and each separate part became like
028:004 in the land and **divided** its people into sections,
030:043 on that Day shall men be **divided** (in two).
042:014 And they became **divided** only after knowledge
044:024 "And leave the sea as a furrow (**divided**):
054:028 tell them that the water is to be **divided** between them:
059:014 but their hearts are **divided**:
DIVINATION
005:090 and (**divination** by) arrows, are an abomination,
DIVINE
004:155 (They have incurred **divine** displeasure):
039:075 surrounding the Throne (**Divine**) on all sides,
DIVISION
004:008 But if at the time of **division** other relatives,
005:003 (forbidden) also is the **division** (of meat) by
020:094 'Thou hast caused a **division** among the
053:022 a **division** most unfair!
DIVISIONS
042:013 and make no **divisions** therein:

DIVORCE
002:227 But if their intention is firm for **divorce**,
002:229 A **divorce** is only permissible twice: after that,
002:231 When ye **divorce** women, and they (are about to)
002:232 When ye **divorce** women,
002:236 ye **divorce** women before consummation
002:237 And if ye **divorce** them before consummation,
033:004 ye **divorce** by Zihar your mothers:
033:049 believing women, and then **divorce** them before
058:002 If any men among you **divorce** their wives by Zihar
065:001 O Prophet! when ye do **divorce** women, **divorce** them
DIVORCED
002:228 **Divorced** women shall wait concerning themselves
002:230 and he has **divorced** her.
002:241 For **divorced** women is a suitable Gift
066:005 It may be, if he **divorce**d you (all), that Allah
DIVORCES
002:230 So if a husband **divorces** his wife (irrevocably),
DIVULGE
004:083 safety or fear, they **divulge** it.
DIVULGED
066:003 and she then **divulged** it (to another), and Allah
DO
001:005 Thee **do** we worship, and Thine aid we seek.
002:006 whether thou warn them or **do** not warn them;
002:008 but they **do** not (really) believe.
002:013 they are the fools but they **do** not know.
002:027 and **do** mischief on earth:
002:030 Whilst we **do** celebrate Thy praises
002:044 **Do** ye enjoin right conduct on the people,
002:058 (the portion of) those who **do** good."
002:060 and **do** no evil nor mischief
002:068 now **do** what ye are commanded!"
002:074 And Allah is not unmindful of what ye **do**.
002:076 **Do** ye not understand (their aim)?
002:078 and they **do** nothing but conjecture.
002:079 Woe to them for what their hands **do** write,
002:080 ye say of Allah what ye **do** not know?"
002:085 and **do** ye reject the rest?
002:085 For Allah is not unmindful of what ye **do**.
002:096 for Allah sees well all that they **do**.
002:102 so **do** not blaspheme."
002:106 None of Our revelations **do** We abrogate
002:110 for Allah sees well all that ye **do**.
002:134 and ye of what ye **do**!
002:140 Say: **Do** ye know better than Allah?
002:140 But Allah is not unmindful of what ye **do**!
002:140 Or **do** ye say that Abraham,
002:141 and ye of what ye **do**!
002:144 nor is Allah unmindful of what they **do**.
002:149 And Allah is not unmindful of what ye **do**.
002:152 Then **do** ye remember Me; I will remember you.
002:168 and **do** not follow the footsteps of Satan for he
002:184 For those who can **do** it (with hardship),
002:187 but **do** not associate with your wives while
002:187 used to **do** secretly among yourselves:
002:188 And **do** not eat up your property
002:190 those who fight you but **do** not transgress limits;
002:195 for Allah loveth those who **do** good.
002:195 contribute to (your) destruction; but **do** good:
002:196 and **do** not shave your heads until
002:197 And whatever good ye **do**,
002:199 it is usual for the multitude so to **do**,

DO (continued)

002:203   if his aims is to **do** right.
002:210   But to Allah **do** all questions go back
002:214   Or **do** ye think that ye shall enter
002:215   And whatever ye **do** that is good,
002:220   to **do** is what is for their good;
002:221   **Do** not marry unbelieving women (idolaters),
002:221   Unbelievers **do** (but) beckon you to the Fire.
002:222   and **do** not approach them until they are clean.
002:223   But **do** some good act for your souls beforehand;
002:229   so **do** not transgress them
002:229   If ye (judges) **do** indeed fear that they would be
002:229   if any **do** transgress the limits ordained by Allah,
002:231   but **do** not take them back to injure them,
002:231   **Do** not treat Allah's Signs as a jest,
002:232   **do** not prevent them from marrying their (former)
002:233   that Allah sees well what ye **do**.
002:234   And Allah is well acquainted with what ye **do**.
002:235   but **do** not make a secret contract with them
002:236   is due from those who wish to **do** the right thing.
002:237   And **do** not forget liberality between yourselves.
002:237   For Allah sees well all that ye **do**.
002:240   for what they **do** with themselves,
002:246   knowledge of those who **do** wrong.
002:258   **do** thou then cause it to rise from the West."
002:264   will be able to **do** nothing with aught they have earned.
002:265   Allah seeth well whatever ye **do**.
002:267   and **do** not even aim at anything which is bad,
002:271   And Allah is well acquainted with what ye **do**.
002:272   and ye shall only **do** so seeking the "Face" of Allah.
002:277   and **do** deeds of righteousness,
002:279   If ye **do** it not, take notice of war
002:282   If ye **do** (such harm), it would be
002:283   And Allah knoweth all that ye **do**.
002:285   as **do** the men of faith,
003:020   If they **do**, they are in right guidance,
003:020   "**Do** ye (also) submit yourselves?"
003:028   if any **do** that, shall have no relation left with Allah
003:031   Say: "If ye **do** love Allah, follow me:
003:035   "O my Lord! I **do** dedicate unto thee what is in
003:052   and **do** thou bear witness that we are Muslims.
003:057   but Allah loveth not those who **do** wrong.
003:063   Allah hath full knowledge of those who **do** mischief.
003:069   but themselves, and they **do** not perceive!
003:071   Why **do** ye clothe truth with falsehood,
003:081   **do** ye believe him and render him help."
003:081   Allah said: "**Do** ye agree, and take My covenant
003:083   **Do** they seek for other than the Religion of Allah?
003:084   and to Allah **do** we bow our will (in Islam)."
003:098   when Allah is Himself witness to all ye **do**?
003:099   But Allah is not unmindful of all that ye **do**."
003:109   to Allah **do** all matters return.
003:111   They will **do** you no harm, barring a trifling
003:115   Of the good that they **do**, nothing
003:115   for Allah knoweth well those that **do** right.
003:120   for Allah compasseth round about all that they **do**.
003:120   not the least harm will their cunning **do** to you;
003:120   But if ye are patient and **do** right,
003:134   for Allah loves those who **do** good:
003:140   And Allah loveth not those that **do** wrong.
003:144   not the least harm will he **do** to Allah;
003:145   If any **do** desire a reward in this life,
003:145   and if any **do** desire a reward in the Hereafter,

DO (continued)

003:148   For Allah loveth those who **do** good.
003:153   For Allah is well aware of all that ye **do**.
003:154   "If we had had thing to **do** with this affair,
003:156   and Allah sees well all that ye **do**.
003:163   and Allah sees well all that they **do**.
003:165   **do** ye say? "Whence is this?"
003:172   those who **do** right and refrain from wrong
003:176   not the least harm will they **do** to Allah:
003:177   not the least harm will they **do** to Allah,
003:179   and if ye believe and **do** right, ye have
003:180   and Allah is well acquainted with all that ye **do**.
003:182   for Allah never **do** injustice those who serve Him."
004:015   to houses until death **do** claim them, or
004:017   who **do** evil in ignorance and repent soon afterwards;
004:018   of those who continue to **do** evil, until death
004:030   If any **do** that in rancor and injustice, soon
004:031   of the things which ye are forbidden to **do**,
004:036   and **do** good to parents, kinsfolk, orphans, those
004:046   and "**Do** hear"; and "**Do** look at us":
004:054   Or **do** they envy mankind for what
004:057   and **do** deeds of righteousness, We shall
004:059   if ye **do** believe in Allah and the Last Day:
004:069   the martyres, and the Righteous (who **do** good):
004:077   the Hereafter is the best for those who **do** right:
004:082   **Do** they not ponder on the Qur'an?
004:089   As they **do**, and thus be
004:094   for Allah is well aware of all that ye **do**.
004:108   and Allah **do**th compass round all that they **do**.
004:113   and to thee they can **do** no harm in the least.
004:122   and **do** deeds of righteousness, We shall soon
004:124   If any **do** deeds of righteousness, be they
004:127   There is not a good deed which ye **do**, but
004:128   Allah is well-acquainted with all that ye **do**.
004:128   But if ye **do** good and practice self-restraint,
004:129   Ye are never able to **do** justice between wives
004:133   for He hath power this to **do**.
004:135   verily Allah is well-acquainted with all that ye **do**.
004:135   or decline to **do** justice, verily Allah
004:141   if ye **do** gain a victory from Allah, they say:
004:142   but little **do** they hold Allah in remembrance;
004:144   **do** ye wish to offer Allah an open proof against
004:149   Whether you **do** openly a good deed or conceal
004:168   Those who reject Faith and **do** wrong,-Allah will
004:172   nor **do** the angels, those nearest (to Allah):
004:173   and **do** deeds of righteousness, He will
005:008   For Allah is well-acquainted with all that ye **do**.
005:009   To those who believe and **do** deeds of righteousness
005:028   for I **do** fear Allah, the Cherisher of the worlds.
005:029   and that is the reward of those who **do** wrong."
005:035   O ye who believe! **do** your duty to Allah, seek
005:042   If they **do** come to thee, either judge
005:043   But why **do** they come to thee for decision, when
005:044   If any **do** fail to judge by what Allah
005:047   If any **do** fail to judge by what
005:050   **Do** they then seek after a judgment of
005:052   saying: "We **do** fear lest a change of fortune bring us
005:053   All that they **do** will be in vain, and they
005:059   **do** ye disapprove of us for no other reason than that we
005:062   Evil indeed are the things that they **do**.
005:063   Why **do** not the Rabbis and the **do**ctors of laws
005:064   but they (ever) strive to **do** mischief on earth.
005:064   And Allah loveth not those who **do** mischief.

DO (continued)

005:071 But Allah sees well all that they **do**.
005:085 Such is the recompense of those who **do** good.
005:093 and **do** deeds of righteousness,-
005:093 then again, guard themselves from evil and **do** good.
005:093 and **do** deeds of righteousness there is no
005:093 For Allah loveth those who **do** good.
005:095 and beware (of evil): if ye **do** turn back, know
005:105 it is He that will inform you of all that ye **do**.
005:106 if we **do**, then behold! we shall be sinners.
005:111 and **do** thou bear witness that we bow to Allah
006:033 which their words **do** cause thee:
006:047 will any be destroyed except those who **do** wrong?"
006:050 Nor **do** I tell you I am an angel. I but follow
006:050 nor **do** I know what is hidden.
006:055 Thus **do** We explain the Signs in detail:
006:058 But Allah knoweth best those who **do** wrong."
006:068 sit not thou in the company of those who **do** wrong.
006:071 things that can **do** us neither good nor harm,
006:084 thus **do** We reward those who **do** good:
006:090 Say: "No reward for this **do** I ask of you:
006:091 No just estimate of Allah **do** they make when they say:
006:093 the wicked (**do** fare) in the agonies of death!-
006:105 Thus **do** We explain the Signs
006:116 they **do** nothing but lie.
006:119 But many **do** mislead (men) by low
006:129 Thus **do** We make the wrong-**do**ers turn to
006:132 not unmindful of anything that they **do**.
006:135 I will **do** (my part): soon will ye know
006:135 Say: "O my people! **do** whatever ye can:
006:145 For Allah guideth not people who **do** wrong.
006:148 Ye **do** nothing but lie."
006:152 no burden **do** We place on any soul, but that
006:154 completing (Our favour) to those who would **do** right,
006:157 then who could **do** more wrong than one
006:158 The day that certain of the Signs of thy Lord **do** come,
006:158 no good will it **do** to a soul to believe them,
007:028 **do** ye say of Allah what ye know not?"
007:032 Thus **do** We explain the Signs in detail
007:038 but this ye **do** not understand.
007:041 such is Our requital of those who **do** wrong.
007:042 no burden **do** We place on any soul, but that
007:056 **Do** no mischief on the earth, after it
007:056 is (always) near to those who **do** good.
007:058 thus **do** We explain the Signs by various
007:063 "**Do** ye wonder that there hath come to you
007:069 "**Do** ye wonder that there hath come
007:075 They said: "We **do** indeed believe in the
007:080 "**Do** ye commit lewdness such as no people
007:085 and **do** no mischief on the earth after it
007:088 He said: "What! even though we **do** detest (them)?
007:131 but most of them **do** not understand!
007:142 and follow not the way of those who **do** mischief."
007:142 "Act for me amongst my people: **do** right,
007:152 thus **do** We recompense those who invent
007:153 But those who **do** wrong but repent
007:156 for those who **do** right, and pay
007:159 and **do** justice in the light of truth.
007:161 (the portion of) those who **do** good."
007:164 When some of them said: "Why **do** ye preach to a
007:172 They said: "Yea! we **do** testify! (This), lest ye
007:174 Thus **do** We explain the Signs in detail; and
007:180 for what they **do**, they will soon be requited.

DO (continued)

007:184 **Do** they not reflect? Their Companion
007:185 (**Do** they not see) that it may well be
007:185 **Do** they see nothing in the king**do**m of the
007:191 **Do** they indeed ascribe to Him as partners
007:205 And **do** thou (O reader!) bring thy
008:001 obey Allah and His Messenger,, it ye **do** believe."
008:016 If any **do** turn his back to them
008:025 in particular (only) on those of you who **do** wrong:
008:034 but most of them **do** not understand.
008:039 verily Allah **do**th see all that they **do**.
008:041 if ye **do** believe in Allah and in the revelation
008:047 for Allah compasseth all that they **do**.
008:061 towards peace, **do** thou (also) incline towards peace,
008:072 and (remember) Allah seeth all that ye **do**.
008:073 unless ye **do** this. (Protect each other) there would be
009:011 (thus) **do** We explain Signs in detail, for those
009:013 **Do** ye fear them? Nay, it is Allah Whom ye should more
009:016 And Allah is well-acquainted with (all) that ye **do**.
009:016 **Do** you think that you would be left alone while
009:019 **Do** ye make the giving of drink to pilgrims,
009:019 and Allah guides not those who **do** wrong.
009:023 if any of you **do** so, they **do** wrong.
009:038 **Do** ye prefer the life of this world to the
009:044 And Allah knoweth well those who **do** their duty.
009:047 But Allah knoweth well those who **do** wrong.
009:059 to Allah **do** we turn our hopes!"
009:082 the (evil) that they **do**.
009:084 Nor **do** thou ever pray for any of them that dies,
009:091 be against such as **do** right:
009:109 And Allah guideth not people that **do** wrong.
009:112 and observe the limits set by Allah;-(these **do** rejoice).
009:120 the reward to be lost of those who **do** good;-
009:120 because nothing could they suffer or **do**, but was
009:124 their faith is increased, and they **do** rejoice.
010:012 Thus **do** the deeds of transgressors seem fair
010:013 Thus **do** We requite those who sin!
010:018 Say: "**Do** ye indeed inform Allah of something
010:024 Thus **do** We explain the Signs
010:026 To those who **do** right is a goodly (reward)-yea,
010:036 Verily Allah is well aware of all that they **do**.
010:038 Or **do** they say, "He forged it"? Say: "Bring
010:040 some who believe therein, and some who **do** not:
010:041 from responsibility for what I **do**, and I for what ye **do**!"
010:046 ultimately Allah is witness to all that they **do**.
010:050 Say: "**Do** ye see-if His punishment should come
010:055 Yet most of them **do** not understand.
010:059 or **do** ye forge (things) to attribute to Allah?"
010:066 What **do** they follow who worship as His "partners"
010:066 and they **do** nothing but lie.
010:074 Thus **do** We seal the hearts of the transgressors.
010:084 if ye **do** (really) believe in Allah, then in Him
010:085 They said: "In Allah **do** we put our trust.
010:102 **Do** they then expect (anything) but (what happened in)
010:106 thou shalt certainly be of those who **do** wrong."
010:107 if He **do** design some benefit for thee, there is
010:107 If Allah **do** touch thee with hurt, there is
010:108 receive guidance, **do** so for the good of their own souls;
010:108 those who stray, **do** so to their own loss:
010:109 and be patient and constant, till Allah, **do** decide:
011:011 Not so **do** those who show patience and constancy,
011:016 and of no effect are the deeds that they **do**!
011:017 yet many among men **do** not believe!

DO (continued)

011:018   is on those who **do** wrong!-
011:026   Verily I **do** fear for you the punishment
011:027   nor **do** we see that any follow thee but the
011:027   apparently nor **do** we see in you (all) any
011:031   your eyes **do** despise that Allah will not
011:031   Nor yet **do** I say, of those whom your eyes
011:031   nor **do** I know what is hidden, nor claim
011:035   Or **do** they say, "He has forged it?" Say:
011:044   "Away with those who **do** wrong!"
011:047   Noah said: "O my Lord! I **do** seek refuge with Thee,
011:054   and **do** ye bear witness, that I am free from the sin of
011:063   He said: "O my people! **Do** ye see?-If I have
011:083   ever far from those who **do** wrong!
011:085   with intent to **do** mischief.
011:088   to **do** that which I forbid you to **do**.
011:091   thou sayest we **do** not understand! In fact
011:092   But verily my Lord encompasseth all that ye **do**!
011:093   I will **do** (my part): soon will ye
011:093   "And O my people! **do** whatever ye can:
011:111   For He knoweth well all that they **do**.
011:112   for He seeth well all that ye **do**.
011:113   And incline not to those who **do** wrong, or the
011:121   Say to those who **do** not believe: "**Do** whatever
011:121   "**Do** whatever ye can: we shall **do** our part;
011:123   and thy Lord is not unmindful of aught that ye **do**.
011:123   To Allah **do** belong the unseen (secrets)
012:003   We **do** relate unto thee the most beautiful
012:010   but if ye must **do** something, throw him
012:019   But Allah knoweth well all that they **do**!
012:022   thus **do** We reward those who **do** right.
012:023   Truly to no good come those who **do** wrong!"
012:041   whereof ye twain **do** enquire."
012:043   The king (of Egypt) said: "I **do** see (in a vision)
012:053   "Nor **do** I absolve my own self (of blame):
012:053   unless my Lord **do** bestow His Mercy:
012:056   the reward of those who **do** good.
012:059   and that I **do** provide the best hospitality?
012:061   win him from his father: indeed we shall **do** it."
012:067   on Him **do** I put my trust:
012:090   to be lost, of those who **do** right."
012:094   their father said: "I **do** indeed scent the presence
012:105   and the earth **do** they pass by?
012:107   **Do** they then feel secure from the coming against
012:108   Say thou: "This my Way; I **do** invite unto Allah,-
012:109   **Do** they not travel through the earth, and see what was
012:109   the Hereafter is best, for those who **do** right.
013:008   (of their time or number) or **do** exceed.
013:013   and so **do** the angels, with awe:
013:015   so **do** their shadows in the mornings and evenings.
013:015   and the earth **do** prostrate themselves to Allah-with good-
013:016   Or **do** they assign to Allah partners who have created
013:016   Say: "**Do** ye then take (for worship) protectors
013:028   in the remembrance of Allah **do** hearts find satisfaction.
013:030   On Him is my trust, and to Him **do** I turn!"
013:030   yet **do** they reject (Him), the Most Gracious!
013:031   **Do** not the Believers know,
013:036   Unto Him **do** I call, and unto Him is my return."
014:002   to Whom **do** belong all things in the heavens and on
014:009   "We **do** deny (the mission) on which ye have
014:027   but Allah will leave, to stray, those who **do** wrong:
014:042   the deeds of those who **do** wrong.
015:012   Even so **do** We let it creep into the

DO (continued)

015:013   They **do** not believe in the Message,
015:054   He said: "**Do** ye give me such glad tidings
015:065   and **do** thou go behind them:
015:075   for those who by tokens **do** understand.
015:097   We **do** indeed know how thy heart is distressed
016:002   so **do** your duty unto Me."
016:021   nor **do** thy know when they will be raised up.
016:030   To those who **do** good, there is good in this world,
016:033   **Do** the (ungodly) wait but for the angels
016:045   **Do** then those who devise evil (plots) feel
016:048   **Do** they not look at Allah's creation.
016:050   and they **do** all that they are commanded.
016:056   And they (even) assign, to things they **do** not know,
016:079   **Do** they not look at the birds, held poised
016:091   for Allah knoweth all that ye **do**.
016:119   to those who **do** wrong in ignorance, but who
016:127   And **do** thou be patient, for thy
016:128   restrain themselves, and those who **do** good.
017:004   that twice would they **do** mischief on the earth
017:018   If any **do** wish for the transitory things
017:019   Those who **do** wish for the (things of)
017:025   in your hearts: if ye **do** deeds of righteousness,
017:057   Those whom they call upon **do** seek (for themselves)
017:068   **Do** ye then feel secure that He will not cause
017:069   Or **do** ye feel secure that He will not send
018:015   why **do** they not bring forward an authority
018:015   an authority clear (and convincing) for what they **do**?
018:023   "I shall be sure to **do** so and so to-morrow"
018:030   of any who **do** a (single) righteous deed.
018:036   "Nor **do** I deem that the Hour (of Judgment)
018:045   which the winds **do** scatter:
018:094   the Gog and Magog (people) **do** great mischief on earth:
018:102   **Do** the Unbelievers think that they can take
019:005   (and colleagues) (will **do**) after me:
019:039   and they **do** not believe!
020:063   and to **do** away with your most cherished way.
020:081   My Wrath **do** perish indeed!
020:082   and **do** right,-who, in fine, are no true guidance."
020:089   to harm them or to **do** them good?
020:099   Thus **do** We relate to thee some stories
020:100   If any **do** turn away therefrom, verily they
020:127   And thus **do** We recompense him who transgresses
021:017   if We would **do** (such a thing)!
021:020   nor **do** they ever flag or intermit.
021:029   thus **do** We reward those who **do** wrong.
021:030   **Do** not the Unbelievers see that the heavens
021:032   Yet **do** they turn away from the Signs
021:045   Say, "I **do** but warn you according to revelation":
021:046   If but a breath of the Wrath of thy Lord **do** touch them,
021:048   for those who would **do** right,-
021:065   that these (idols) **do** not speak!"
021:066   be of any good to you nor **do** you harm?
021:066   (Abraham) said, "**Do** ye then worship, besides Allah,
021:068   your gods, if ye **do** (anything at all)!"
021:073   and We sent them inspiration to **do** good deeds,
021:081   for We **do** know all things.
021:088   and thus **do** We deliver those who have faith.
022:005   then **do** We bring you out as babes,
022:037   the Good News to all who **do** good.
022:046   **Do** they not travel through the land, so that
022:067   but **do** thou invite (them) to thy Lord:
022:068   If they **do** wrangle with thee,

DO (continued)

022:071	for those that **do** wrong there is no helper.
022:074	They **do** not have right estimate of Allah,
022:077	and adore your Lord; and **do** good; that ye may prosper.
023:028	Who has saved us from the people who **do** wrong."
023:041	So away with the people who **do** wrong!
023:051	for I am well-acquainted with (all) that you **do**.
023:055	**Do** they think that because We have granted them
023:056	Nay, they **do** not perceive.
023:062	On no soul **do** We place a burden greater than
023:063	deeds of theirs, which they will (continue) to **do**,-
023:068	**Do** they not ponder over the Word (of Allah),
023:069	Or **do** they not recognize their Messenger,
023:070	Or **do** they say, "He is possessed"? Nay, he
023:076	nor **do** they submissively entreat (Him)!-
023:094	amongst the people who **do** wrong!"
023:109	'Our Lord! we believe; then **do** Thou forgive us,
024:022	**do** you not wish that Allah should forgive you?
024:028	and Allah knows well all that ye **do**.
024:030	and Allah is well acquainted with all that they **do**.
024:041	And Allah knows well all that they **do**.
024:041	all beings in the heavens and on earth **do** celebrate,
024:050	Nay, it is they themselves who **do** wrong.
024:050	Or **do** they doubt, or are they in fear,
024:052	and **do** right, that will triumph.
024:053	Allah is well acquainted with all that ye **do**."
024:055	If any **do** reject Faith after this, they are
024:059	ask for permission, as **do** those before them:
024:062	they **do** not depart until they have asked
025:021	Those who **do** not hope to meet Us (for Judgment)
025:021	or (why) **do** we not see Our Lord?"
025:033	And no question **do** they bring to thee but We
025:045	Then **do** We make the sun its guide;
025:055	Yet **do** they worship, besides Allah, things that
025:057	Say: "No reward **do** I ask of you for it but this:
026:003	thy self with grief, that they **do** not become Believers.
026:007	**Do** they not look at the earth,-how many
026:008	but most of them **do** not believe.
026:012	I **do** fear that they will charge me with falsehood:
026:025	"**Do** ye not listen (to what he says)?"
026:067	but most of them **do** not believe.
026:072	He said: "**Do** they listen to you when ye
026:073	"Or **do** you good or harm?"
026:074	our fathers **doing** thus (what we **do**)."
026:075	He said: "**Do** ye then see whom ye have been
026:103	but most of them **do** not believe.
026:109	"No reward **do** I ask of you for it:
026:112	He said: "And what **do** I know as to what they **do**?
026:121	but most of them **do** not believe.
026:127	"No reward **do** I ask of you for it: my reward
026:128	"**Do** ye build a landmark on every high place
026:129	"And **do** ye get for yourselves fine buildings
026:139	but most of them **do** not believe.
026:145	No reward **do** I ask of you for it: my reward
026:158	but most of them **do** not believe.
026:164	"No reward **do** I ask of you for it: my reward
026:168	He said: "I **do** detest your doings."
026:169	and my family from such things as they **do**!"
026:174	but most of them **do** not believe.
026:180	"No reward **do** I ask of you for it: my reward
026:183	due to men, nor **do** evil in the land,
026:188	He said: "My Lord knows best what ye **do**."
026:190	but most of them **do** not believe.

DO (continued)

026:204	**Do** they then ask for Our Chastisement to be
026:205	Seest thou? If we **do** let them enjoy (this life)
026:216	"I am free (of responsibility) for what ye **do**!"
027:010	"Now **do** thou throw thy rod!" But when
027:034	thus **do** they behave.
027:044	I **do** (now) submit (in Islam), with Solomon,
027:047	They said: "Ill omen **do** we augur from thee
027:054	"**Do** ye **do** what is indecent though ye see
027:074	all that their hearts **do** hide, as well
027:088	for He is well acquainted with all that ye **do**.
027:089	If any **do** good, he will have better than it.
027:090	And if any **do** evil, their faces will be thrown
027:090	"**Do** ye receive a reward other than that which
027:092	they **do** it for the good of their own souls,
027:093	and thy Lord is not unmindful of all that ye **do**.
028:013	but most of them **do** not know.
028:014	for thus **do** We reward those who **do** good.
028:016	**Do** Thou then forgive me!"
028:020	for I **do** give thee sincere advice."
028:022	"I **do** hope that my Lord will show me
028:031	"Now **do** thou throw thy rod!" But when
028:038	Pharaoh said: "O Chiefs! no god **do** I know
028:048	**Do** they not then reject (the Signs) which were
028:049	(**Do**), if ye are truthful!"
028:052	before this,-they **do** believe in this (Revelation);
028:077	for Allah loves not those who **do** mischief."
028:077	but **do** thou good, as Allah has been good to thee,
029:002	**Do** men think that they will be left alone
029:004	**Do** those who practice evil think that they
029:006	they **do** so for their own soul:
029:017	"For ye **do** worship idols besides Allah, and ye
029:028	he said to his people: "Ye **do** commit lewdness,
029:029	"**Do** ye indeed approach men, and cut
029:030	Help Thou me against people who **do** mischief!"
029:036	with intent to **do** mischief."
029:045	the (deeds) that ye **do**.
029:046	who **do** wrong but say, "We believe
029:047	believe therein, as also **do** some of these
029:058	an excellent reward for those who **do** (good)!-
029:067	Then, **do** they believe in that which is vain,
029:067	**Do** they not then see that We have made
029:069	is with those who **do** right.
030:008	**Do** they not reflect in their own minds?
030:009	**Do** they not travel through the earth, and see
030:010	In the long run will be the End of those who **do** evil;
030:028	Thus **do** We explain the Signs in detail
030:028	**Do** ye fear them as ye fear each other?
030:028	**do** ye have partners among those whom your
030:040	your (false) "Partners" who can **do** any single
030:048	as He wills, behold, they **do** rejoice!-
030:058	"Ye **do** nothing but talk vanities."
031:020	**Do** ye not see that Allah has subjected to your
031:029	is well acquainted with all that ye **do**?
031:033	O mankind! **do** your duty to your Lord and fear
032:003	Or **do** they say, "He has forged it"? Nay, it
032:009	little thanks **do** ye give!
032:012	for we **do** indeed (now) believe."
032:019	For those who believe and **do** righteous deeds,
032:026	Verily in that are Signs: **do** they not then listen?
032:027	And **do** they not see that We **do** drive Rain to parched
033:002	with (all) that ye **do**.
033:006	nevertheless **do** ye what is just to your

DO (continued)

033:009 but Allah sees (clearly) all that ye **do**.
033:016 and even if (ye **do** escape), no more than a brief (respite)
033:032 if ye **do** fear (Allah), be not too complaisant
033:043 He it is Who sends blessings on you, as **do** His angels,
034:011 for be sure I see (clearly) all that ye **do**."
034:017 and never **do** We give (such) requital except to such
034:025 nor shall we be questioned as to what ye **do**."
034:039 and nothing **do** ye spend in the least (in His Cause)
034:046 Say: "I **do** admonish you on one point: that ye
034:046 that ye **do** stand up before Allah,-(it may be)
034:047 Say: "Whatever reward **do** I ask of you: it is
034:052 "We **do** believe (now) in the (truth)"; but how
035:008 for Allah knows well all that they **do**!
035:010 If any **do** seek for glory and power,-to Allah
035:012 (kind of water) **do** ye eat flesh fresh and tender,
035:036 Thus **do** We reward every ungrateful one!
035:037 shall work righteousness, not the (deeds) we used to **do**!"-
035:044 **Do** they not travel through the earth, and see
036:007 for they **do** not believe.
036:010 admonish them or thou **do** not admonish them:
036:015 Ye **do** nothing but lie."
036:028 from heaven, nor was it needful for Us so to **do**.
036:033 We **do** give it life, and produce
036:033 and produce grain therefrom, of which ye **do** eat.
036:055 shall that Day have joy in all that they **do**;
036:072 Of them some **do** carry them and osme they eat:
037:052 "Who used to say, **Do** you really believe?
037:080 Thus indeed **do** We reward those who **do** right.
037:102 "O my father! **do** as thou art commanded: thou will
037:105 thus indeed **do** We reward those who **do** right
037:110 Thus indeed **do** We reward those who **do** right.
037:113 and (some) that obviously **do** wrong, to themselves.
037:113 but of their progeny are (some) tha**t do** right,
037:121 Thus indeed **do** We reward those who **do** right.
037:131 Thus indeed **do** We reward those who **do** right.
037:160 Not (so **do**) the servants of Allah, the chosen ones.
037:176 **Do** they wish (indeed) to hurry on Our Punishment?
038:024 not so **do** those who believe and work deeds
038:028 the same as those who **do** mischief on earth?
038:032 And he said, "Truly **do** I prefer wealth to the
038:068 "From which ye **do** turn away!
038:086 Say: "No reward **do** I ask of you
039:009 those who know and those who **do** not know?
039:010 for those who **do** good in this world.
039:023 and their hearts **do** soften to the remembrance of Allah.
039:033 such are the men who **do** right.
039:034 such is the reward of those who **do** good:
039:039 Say: "O my people! **Do** whatever ye can: I will
039:039 I will **do** (my part): but soon will ye know-
039:043 What! **Do** they take for intercessors others
039:058 I should certainly be among those who **do** good!'
039:070 and (Allah) knoweth best all that they **do**.
040:021 **Do** they not travel through the earth and see
040:029 I see (myself); nor **do** I guide you but to
040:030 "O my People! truly I **do** fear for you something
040:042 "Ye **do** call upon me to blaspheme against Allah,
040:043 "Without doubt ye **do** call me to one who
040:058 Little **do** ye learn by admonition!
040:058 and those who **do** evil.
040:082 **Do** they not travel through the earth and see
041:005 so **do** thou (what thou wilt); for us,
041:005 for us, we shall **do** (what we will!)"

DO (continued)

041:009 And **do** ye join equals with Him?
041:011 "We **do** come (together), in willing obedience."
041:022 Allah knew not many of the things that ye used to **do**!
041:040 **Do** what ye will: Verily He seeth (clearly) all that ye **do**.
041:047 "We **do** assure Thee not one of us can bear witness!"
041:052 is (really) from Allah, and yet **do** ye reject it?
042:023 who believe and **do** righteous deeds.
042:023 Say: "No reward **do** I ask of you for this
042:024 What! **Do** they say, "He has forged
042:025 and He knows all that ye **do**.
042:026 and **do** deeds of righteousness, and gives
042:040 those who **do** wrong.
042:041 But indeed if any **do** help and defend themselves
043:013 for we could never be able to **do** it.
043:020 They **do** nothing but lie!
043:022 and we **do** guide ourselves by their footsteps."
043:026 "I **do** indeed clear myself of what ye worship:
043:030 they said: "This is sorcery, and we **do** reject it."
043:066 **Do** they only wait for the Hour-that it
043:080 Indeed (We **do**), and Our Messengers are by them,
043:080 Or **do** they think that We hear not their secrets
044:012 for We **do** really believe!"
044:039 but most of them **do** not know.
045:014 to forgive those who **do** not hope for
045:021 What! **do** those who **do** evil deeds think that
045:021 with those who believe and **do** righteous deeds,-
045:026 there is no doubt": but most men not know.
046:004 Say: "**Do** ye see what it is ye invoke beside Allah?
046:008 Or **do** they say, "He has forged it"? Say:
046:009 nor **do** I know what will be   with me or with you.
046:012 and as Glad Tidings to those who **do** right.
046:015 and truly **do** I submit (to Thee) in Islam."
046:017 **Do** ye hold out the promise to me that I shall
046:025 Thus **do** We recompense those given to sin!
047:010 **Do** they not travel through the earth, and see
047:012 and **do** righteous deeds, to Gardens
047:018 **Do** they then only wait for the Hour,-that it
047:022 that ye will **do** mischief in the land, and break
047:024 **Do** they not then earnestly seek to understand
047:029 Or **do** those in whose hearts is a disease,
047:030 And Allah knows all that ye **do**.
048:011 But Allah is well acquainted with all that ye **do**.
048:011 **do** thou then ask forgiveness for us."
048:015 Nay, but little **do** they understand (such things).
048:024 And Allah sees well all that ye **do**.
048:029 who believe and **do** righteous deeds Forgiveness,
049:011 and those who **do** not desist are (indeed) doing wrong.
049:018 and Allah sees well all that ye **do**."
050:006 **Do** they not look at the sky above them?-
050:029 and I **do** not the least injustice to My Servants."
051:048 how excellently We **do** spread out!
051:057 nor **do** I require that they should feed Me.
051:057 No sustenance **do** I require of them,
052:015 "Is this then a magic, or is it ye that **do** not see?
052:030 Or **do** they say:-"A Poet! we await for him some
052:033 Or **do** they say, "He fabricated the (Message)?"
052:042 Or **do** they intend a plot (against thee)?
052:047 And verily, for those who **do** wrong, there is
053:031 so that He rewards those who **do** evil, according to their
053:031 and He rewards those who **do** good, with what
053:059 **Do** ye then wonder at this recital?
054:010 "I am one overcome: **do** thou then help (me)!"

DO (continued)

054:035 Thus **do** We reward those who give thanks.
054:044 Or **do** they say: "We acting together
054:052 All that they **do** is noted in (their)
055:020 which they **do** not transgress:
056:058 **Do** ye then see? The (human Seed) that ye emit,-
056:062 why then **do** ye not take heed?
056:069 **Do** ye bring it **Down** (in rain) from the Cloud,
056:069 from the Cloud, or **do** We?
056:070 then why **do** ye not give thanks?
056:072 which feeds the fire, or **do** We grow it?
056:083 Then why **do** ye not (intervene) when
056:086 Then why **do** you not,-if you are
057:004 And Allah sees well all that ye **do**.
057:010 And Allah is well acquainted with all that ye **do**.
058:003 well-acquainted with (all) that ye **do**.
058:004 but if any is unable to **do** so, he should feed sixty
058:008 yet revert to that which they were forbidden (to **do**)?
058:009 but **do** it for righteousness and self-restraint;
058:009 hold secret counsel, **do** it not for iniquity and hostility,
058:011 and Allah is well-acquainted with all ye **do**.
058:013 and Allah is well-acquainted with all that ye **do**.
058:013 If, then, ye **do** not so, and Allah forgives you,
059:012 and if they **do** help them, they will
059:016 I **do** fear Allah, the Lord of the Worlds!"
059:018 for Allah is well-acquainted with (all) that ye **do**.
060:003 for Allah sees well all that ye **do**.
060:004 "Our Lord! in Thee **do** we trust, and to Thee
060:004 and to Thee **do** we turn in repentance:
060:009 (in these circumstances), that **do** wrong.
060:012 then **do** thou receive their fealty,
061:002 O ye who believe! why say ye that which ye **do** not?
061:003 of Allah that ye say that which ye **do** not.
061:005 "O my people! why **do** ye vex and insult me,
061:007 And Allah guides not those who **do** wrong.
061:013 which ye **do** love,-help from Allah and a speedy
062:005 and Allah guides not people who **do** wrong.
062:007 And Allah knows well those that **do** wrong!
063:011 acquainted with (all) that ye **do**.
064:002 and Allah see well all that ye **do**.
064:006 But Allah can **do** without (them):
064:008 And Allah is well-acquainted with all that ye **do**.
065:001 O Prophet! when ye **do** divorce women, divorce them
065:011 and **do** righteous deeds from the depths of Darkness
066:006 but **do** (precisely) what they are commanded.
066:011 and save me from those that **do** wrong";
067:016 **Do** ye feel secure that He Who is in heaven
067:017 Or **do** ye feel secure that He Who is in
067:019 **Do** they not observe the birds above them,
068:032 for we **do** turn to Him (in repentance)!"
069:037 "Which none **do** eat but those in sin."
069:038 So I **do** call to witness what ye see
070:005 Therefore **do** thou hold Patience,-a Patience
070:040 Now I **do** call to witness the Lord of all points
071:001 (with the Command): "**Do** thou warn thy People
072:005 'But we **do** think that no man or Jinn
072:020 Say: "I **do** no more than invoke my Lord, and I
074:003 And thy Lord **do** thou magnify!
075:001 I **do** swear by the Resurrection Day;
075:002 And I **do** swear by the self-reproaching soul.
075:005 But man wishes to **do** wrong (even) in the
076:006 A Fountain where the Devotees of Allah **do** drink,
076:009 no reward **do** we desire from you,

DO (continued)

077:018 Thus **do** We deal with men of sin.
077:023 For We **do** determine for We are the Best
077:044 Thus **do** We certainly reward the Doers of Good.
077:048 "Prostrate yourselves!" They **do** not so.
078:014 And **do** We not send down from the clouds
079:005 Then arrange to **do** (the commands of their Lord),-
082:009 Nay! but ye **do** Reject The Judgment!
082:012 They know all that ye **do**.
082:019 shall have power (to **do**) aught for another:
083:004 **Do** they not think that they will be raised up?-
083:014 is the stain of the (ill) which they **do**!
084:002 (the Command of) its Lord, and it must needs (**do** so);-
084:005 (the Command of) its Lord, and it must needs (**do** so);-
084:016 So I **do** call to witness the ruddy glow of Sunset;
085:010 men and women, and **do** not turn in repentance,
085:011 For those who believe and **do** righteous deeds,
088:017 **Do** they not look at the Camels, how they are made?-
088:021 Therefore **do** thou remind, for thou
089:018 Nor **do** ye encourage one another to feed the poor!-
090:001 Nay I **do** swear by this City;-
092:014 Therefore **do** I warn you of a Fire blazing fiercely;
095:005 Then **do** We abase him (to be) the lowest of the low,
095:006 Except such as believe and **do** righteous deeds:
098:007 Those who have faith and **do** righteous deeds,-
103:003 Except such as have Faith and **do** righteous deeds,

DOCTORS

005:044 by the Rabbis and the **Doctors** of Law:
005:063 the **doctors** of laws forbid them from their

DOER

002:112 whole self to Allah and is a **doer** of good,
031:022 and is a **doer** of good, has grasped indeed the firmest
085:016 **Doer** (without let) of all that He intends.

DOERS

028:084 the **doers** of evil are only punished (to the extent)
031:003 A Guide and a Mercy to the **Doers** of Good,-
063:010 and I should have been one of the **doers** of good."
077:044 Thus do We certainly reward the **Doers** of Good.
080:042 the **Doers** of Iniquity.

DOES

002:185 He **does** not want to put you to difficulties.
002:231 if anyone **does** that, He wrongs his own soul.
002:253 but Allah **does** what He wills.
002:266 **Does** any of you wish that he should have
004:110 If anyone **does** evil or wrongs his own soul but
004:114 to him who **does** this, seeking
004:125 who submits his whole self to Allah, **does** good,
007:087 and a party which **does** not believe,
011:012 or why **does** not an angel come down with him?"
011:087 **Does** thy prayer command thee that we leave off
016:059 With shame **does** he hide himself from his people,
016:081 Thus **does** He complete his favours on you,
018:026 nor **does** He share His Command with any
019:067 But **does** not man call to mind that We
019:094 He **does** take and account of them (all), and hath
020:133 They say: "Why **does** he not bring us a Sign
023:035 "**Does** he promise that when ye die and become
024:058 thus **does** Allah make clear the Signs to you:
024:059 thus **does** Allah make clear His Signs to you:
024:061 Thus **does** Allah make clear His Signs to you:
025:019 And whoever among you **does** wrong, him shall
025:068 and any that **does** this (not only) meets punishment

DOES (continued)

025:071   And whoever repents and **does** good has truly
028:068   Thy Lord **does** create and choose as He pleases:
028:084   If any **does** good, the reward to him is better
028:084   but if any **does** evil, the doers
029:010   **Does** not Allah know best all that
029:068   And who **does** more wrong than he who invents
030:006   Never **does** Allah fail from His promise:
030:028   He **does** propound to you a similitude from
030:048   then **does** He spread them in the sky as He wills,
030:059   Thus **does** Allah seal up the hearts of those
031:012   Any who is (so) grateful **does** so to the profit of his
031:034   nor **does** anyone know in what land he is to die.
031:034   Nor **does** any one know what it is that he
032:022   And who **does** more wrong than one to whom
032:026   **Does** it not teach them a lesson, how many
035:018   And whoever purifies himself **does** so for the
039:009   hope in the Mercy of his Lord-(like one who **does** Not)?
040:067   then **does** He get you out (into the light) as a
040:074   Thus **does** Allah leave the Unbelievers to stray.
041:047   nor **does** a female conceive (within her womb)
041:049   Man **does** not weary of asking for good (things),
042:011   by this means **does** He multiply you:
043:051   saying: "O my people! **Does** not the dominion
045:015   If anyone **does** a righteous deed, it is
045:015   if he **does** evil, it works against (His own soul).
046:032   "If any **does** not hearken to the one who invites
047:003   thus **does** Allah set forth for men their lessons
048:010   His oath, **does** so to the harm of his own soul,
050:018   Not a word **does** he utter but there is a
053:003   Nor **does** he say (aught) of (his own) Desire.
058:008   "Why **does** not Allah Punish us for our words?
060:001   And any of you that **does** this has strayed
065:001   transgresses the limits of Allah, **does** verily wrong his
070:038   **Does** every man of them long to enter
072:026   nor **does** He make any one acquainted with
075:003   **Does** man think that We cannot assemble his bones?
075:036   **Does** Man think that he will be left uncontrolled,
082:008   In whatever Form He wills, **does** He put thee together.
100:009   **Does** he not know,-when that which is in the

DOETH

006:160   he that **doeth** evil shall only be recompensed
006:160   He that **doeth** good shall have ten times
014:027   Allah **doeth** what He willeth.

DOFF

024:058   the while ye **doff** your clothes for the

DOG

007:176   His similitude is that of a **dog**:
018:018   their **dog** stretching forth his two fore-legs
018:022   the **dog** being the sixth,-doubtfully guessing
018:022   the **dog** being the fourth among them;
018:022   the **dog** being the eighth.

DOING

002:224   an excuse in your oaths against **doing** good,
004:003   to prevent you from **doing** injustice.
007:028   they say: "We found our fathers **doing** so";
010:061   and whatever deed ye (mankind) may be **doing**,-
011:087   or that we leave off **doing** what we like with our property?
012:078   for we see that thou art (gracious) in **doing** good."
012:089   not knowing (what ye were **doing**)?"
016:090   Allah commands justice, the **doing** of good,
016:118   but they were used to **doing** wrong to themselves.
021:090   These (three) were ever quick in **doing** in good works:

DOING (continued)

022:068   say, "Allah knows best what it is ye are **doing**."
026:074   our fathers **doing** thus (what we do)."
028:009   And they perceived not (what they were **doing**)!
049:011   desist are (indeed) **doing** wrong.
068:029   Verily we have been **doing** wrong!"
085:007   witnessed (all) that they were **doing** against the Believers.

DOINGS

002:139   for our **doings** and ye for yours;
006:104   I am not (here) to watch over your **doings**."
006:107   not one to watch over their **doings**, nor art
006:108   alluring to each people its own **doings**.
012:069   at aught of their **doings**."
013:042   He knoweth the **doings** of every soul:
026:168   He said: "I do detest your **doings**."
050:017   to learn (his **doings**) learn (and note them),
066:011   and save me from Pharaoh and his **doings**, and save

DOMESTIC

005:095   of a **domestic** animal equivalent to the one he killed.

DOMINION

002:107   to Allah belongeth the **dominion** of the
003:189   the **dominion** of the heavens and the earth;
004:053   Have they a share in **dominion** or power?
005:017   the **dominion** of the heavens and the earth, and
005:018   the **dominion** of the heavens and the earth, and all
005:040   the **dominion** of the heavens and the earth?
005:120   To Allah doth belong the **dominion** of the
006:073   His will be the **dominion** the day
007:158   to Whom belongeth the **dominion** of the
009:116   Unto Allah belongeth the **dominion** of the
016:075   a slave under the **dominion** of another;
017:111   and has no partner in (His) **dominion**:
022:056   On that Day the **Dominion** will be that of Allah:
024:042   Yea, to Allah belongs the **dominion** of the
025:002   nor has He a partner in His **dominion**:
025:002   He to Whom belongs the **dominion** of the heavens
025:026   That Day, the **dominion** right by shall be
035:013   to Him belongs all **Dominion**.
036:071   which are under their **dominion**?-
036:083   is the **dominion** of all things:
038:010   Or have they the **dominion** of the heavens
039:006   to Him belongs (all) **dominion**.
039:044   to Him belongs the **dominion** of the heavens
040:016   Whose will be the **Dominion** that Day?
040:029   "O my people! yours is the **dominion** this day:
042:049   To Allah belongs the **dominion** of the heavens
043:051   the **dominion** of Egypt belong to me, (witness)
043:085   the **dominion** of the heavens and the earth,
045:027   To Allah belongs the **dominion** of the heavens
048:014   To Allah belongs the **dominion** of the heavens
057:002   To Him belongs the **dominion** of the heavens
057:005   To Him belongs the **dominion** of the heavens
064:001   and Glory of Allah: to Him belongs **Dominion**,
067:001   Blessed be He in Whose hands is **Dominion**;
085:009   Him to Whom belongs the **dominion** of the heavens

DONE

003:030   be confronted with all the good it has **done**,
003:030   and all the evil it has **done**,
003:135   persisting knowingly in (the wrong) they have **done**.
003:135   And those who, having **done** an act of indecency
003:147   and anything we may have **done** that transgressed
003:155   because of some (evil) they had **done**.
003:188   and love to be praised for what they have not **done**,

DONE (continued)

004:040 if there is any good (**done**), He doubleth it,
004:066 very few of them would have **done** it:
004:066 but if they had **done** what they
004:124 and not the least injustice will be **done** to them.
005:014 show them what it is they have **done**.
006:060 all that ye have **done** by day: by day doth
006:112 they would not have **done** it: so leave
006:137 they would not have **done** so: but leave
006:160 No wrong shall be **done** unto them.
007:150 that ye have **done** in my place in my absence:
008:063 but Allah hath **done** it: for He
009:009 evil indeed are the deeds thy have **done**.
010:054 and no wrong will be **done** unto them.
016:126 to the wrong that has been **done** to you:
018:039 say: 'Allah's Will (be **done**)!
018:071 Truly a strange thing hast thou **done**!"
018:074 Truly a foul (unheard-of) thing hast thou **done**!"
021:059 They said, "Who has **done** this to our gods?
021:063 He said: "Nay, this was **done** by this the biggest one!
027:011 "But if any have **done** wrong and have
030:009 populated it in greater numbers than these have **done**:
034:054 as was **done** in the past with their partisans:
037:142 and he had **done** acts worthy of blame.
039:035 to the best of what they have **done**.
039:073 Well have ye **done**! Enter ye
042:041 defend themselves after a wrong (**done**) to him,
043:039 When ye have **done** wrong, it will
046:009 nor do I know what will be **done** with me or with you.
046:019 and no injustice will be **done** to them.
046:019 degrees according to the deeds which they (have **done**),
049:006 of repentance for what ye have **done**.
051:016 because, before then, they had **done** good deeds
057:027 but that they did not foster as they should have **done**.
099:006 to be shown the Deeds that they (had **done**).
099:007 Then shall anyone who has **done** an atom's weight
099:008 And anyone who has **done** an atom's weight

DONKEY

002:259 and look at thy **donkey**:
062:005 of a **donkey** which carries huge tomes

DONKEYS

016:008 And (He has created) horses, mules, and **donkeys**,

DOOM

002:176 (Their **doom** is) because Allah sent down the Book
016:033 of thy Lord (for their **doom**)?

DOOMED

007:099 except those (**doomed**) to ruin!
017:102 O Pharaoh, to be one **doomed** to destruction!"
048:012 for ye are a people **doomed** to perish."

DOOR

012:025 So they both raced each other to the **door**, and she
012:025 they both found her lord near the **door**. She said:

DOORS

002:189 Enter houses through the proper **doors**:
012:023 and she fastened the **doors**, and said: "Now come,"
033:059 outer garments over their person (when out of **doors**):
038:050 Gardens of Eternity, whose **doors** will (ever) be open
043:034 And (silver) **doors** to their houses, and couches
078:019 as if there were **doors**,

DOST

002:260 He said: "**Dost** thou not then believe?"
003:159 that thou **dost** deal gently with them.

DOST (continued)

003:192 "Our Lord! any whom Thou **dost** admit to the Fire,
005:028 "If thou **dost** stretch thy hand against me, to slay
005:062 Many of them **dost** thou see, racing each
005:118 "If Thou **dost** punish them, they are
005:118 if Thou **dost** forgive them, Thou art
007:126 "But thou **dost** wreak thy vengeance on us
009:065 If thou **dost** question them, they declare
010:022 saying, "If Thou **dost** deliver us from this,
010:106 nor hurt thee: if thou **dost**, behold! thou shalt
011:062 **Dost** thou (now) forbid us the worship of what
011:073 They said: "**Dost** thou wonder at Allah's decree?
011:079 They said: "Well **dost** thou know we have no need
012:011 why **dost** thou not trust us with Joseph,-seeing we
012:103 mankind have, however ardently thou **dost** desire it.
012:104 And no reward **dost** thou ask of them for this:
013:005 If thou **dost** marvel (at their want of faith),
014:038 "O our Lord! truly Thou **dost** know what we
016:098 When thou **dost** read the Qur'an, seek Allah's
017:028 from thy Lord which thou **dost** expect, yet speak
017:045 When thou **dost** recite the Qur'an, We put,
017:046 when thou **dost** mention thy Lord-and Him
018:009 Or **dost** thou reflect that the Companions
018:037 "**Dost** thou deny Him Who created thee out of dust,
018:039 If thou **dost** see me less than thee in wealth and sons,
019:018 (come not near) if thou **dost** fear Allah."
019:026 And if thou **dost** see any man, say, 'I have
026:022 thou **dost** reproach me,-that you
028:024 any good that Thou **dost** send me!"
037:012 Truly **dost** thou marvel, while they ridicule,
040:009 and any whom Thou **dost** preserve from ills
041:005 (concealed) from that to which thou **dost** invite us,
042:052 and verily thou **dost** guide (men) to the Straight Way,-
046:022 with which thou **dost** threaten us, if thou
052:040 Or is it that thou **dost** ask for a reward,
068:046 Or is it that thou **dost** ask them for a reward,
071:027 "For, if Thou **dost** leave (any of) them, they will
080:006 To him **dost** thou attend;
110:002 And thou **dost** see the People enter Allah's

DOTARD

012:094 nay, think me not a **dotard**."

DOTH

002:187 Thus **doth** Allah make clear His Signs to men:
002:219 Thus **doth** Allah make clear to you His Signs:
002:242 Thus **doth** Allah make clear His Signs to you:
002:255 His throne **doth** extend over the heavens
002:258 Nor **doth** Allah give guidance to a people unjust.
002:266 Thus **doth** Allah make clear to you
002:286 On no soul **doth** Allah place a burden
003:013 but Allah **doth** support with His aid
003:039 "Allah **doth** give thee glad tidings of Yahya,
003:040 "**Doth** Allah accomplish what He willeth."
003:103 Thus **doth** Allah make His Signs clear to you:
004:026 and (He **doth** wish to) turn to you (in Mercy):
004:026 Allah **doth** wish to make clear to you and
004:027 Allah **doth** wish to turn to you,
004:028 Allah **doth** wish to lighten your (burdens):
004:043 For Allah **doth** blot out sins and forgive
004:049 Nay-but Allah **doth** purify whom He pleaseth.
004:058 Allah **doth** command you to render back your trusts
004:099 for Allah **doth** blot out (sins) and
004:108 and Allah **doth** compass round all that they do.
004:127 Say: Allah **doth** instruct you about them:

DOTH (continued)

004:176	thus **doth** Allah make clear to you (His law),
005:001	for Allah **doth** command according to His
005:006	Allah **doth** not wish to place you in a difficulty,
005:018	Say: "Why then **doth** He punish you for your sins?
005:027	"Allah **doth** accept of the sacrifice
005:064	Allah **doth** extinguish it; but they (ever)
005:075	See how Allah **doth** makes His Signs
005:089	Thus **doth** Allah make clear to you His Signs, that
005:094	O ye who believe! Allah **doth** but make a trial
005:095	If any of you **doth** so intentionally, the
005:120	To Allah **doth** belong the dominion of the
006:021	Who **doth** more wrong than he who inventeth
006:053	**Doth** not Allah know best those who are grateful?.
006:059	Not a leaf **doth** fall but with His knowledge:
006:060	by day **doth** He raise you up again;
006:060	It is He Who **doth** take your souls by night,
006:091	"Nothing **doth** Allah send down to man
006:115	The Word of thy Lord **doth** find its fulfillment
006:125	thus **doth** Allah lay abomination on those
006:144	But who **doth** more wrong than one
006:151	thus **doth** He command you, that ye may learn wisdom.
006:152	thus **doth** He command you, that ye may remember.
006:153	thus **doth** He command you, that ye may be righteous.
007:050	that Allah **doth** provide for your sustenance."
007:087	until Allah **doth** decide between us:
007:101	Thus **doth** Allah seal up the heart
007:178	Whom Allah **doth** guide,-he is
008:039	verily Allah **doth** see all that they do.
008:060	but whom Allah **doth** know.
009:007	for Allah **doth** love the righteous.
009:021	Their Lord **doth** give them glad tidings of a
009:026	thus **doth** He reward those without Faith.
009:042	for Allah **doth** know that they are lying.
009:078	Know they not that Allah **doth** know their secret
009:104	Know they not that Allah **doth** accept repentance
009:107	but Allah **doth** declare that they
009:109	And it **doth** crumble to pieces with him, into the
009:127	(saying), "**Doth** anyone see you?" then they turn away:
010:005	(Thus) **doth** He explain His Signs in detail,
010:017	Who **doth** more wrong than such as forge
010:025	He **doth** guide whom He pleaseth to a way
010:025	But Allah **doth** call to the Home of Peace:
010:082	"And Allah by His Words **doth** prove and establish
011:018	Who **doth** more wrong than those who
012:032	And now, if he **doth** not my bidding, he shall
012:036	for we see thou art one that **doth** good (to all)."
012:088	for Allah **doth** reward the charitable."
013:002	He **doth** regulate all affairs, explaining the
013:008	Allah **doth** know what every female (womb) **doth** bear,
013:012	it is He Who **doth** raise up the clouds,
013:012	It is He Who **doth** show you the lightning, by way
013:017	Thus **doth** Allah set forth parables.
013:017	Thus **doth** Allah (by parables) show forth
013:019	Is then one who **doth** know that that which
013:026	Allah **doth** enlarge, or grant by (strict) measure,
013:033	standeth over every soul (and knoweth) all that it **doth**,
013:039	Allah **doth** blot out or confirm what He pleaseth:
014:011	but Allah **doth** grant His grace to such
014:042	Think not that Allah **doth** not heed the deeds
016:002	He **doth** send down His angels with inspiration
016:019	And Allah **doth** know what ye conceal, and what
016:023	Undoubtedly Allah **doth** know what they conceal,

DOTH (continued)

016:031	thus **doth** Allah reward the righteous,-
016:049	And to Allah **doth** prostrate all that is in
017:009	Verily this Qur'an **doth** guide to that which
017:015	who goeth astray **doth** so to his own loss:
017:030	Verily thy Lord **doth** provide sustenance in
017:030	for He **doth** know and regard all His servants.
017:053	for Satan **doth** sow dissensions among them:
017:060	thy Lord **doth** encompass mankind round about:
018:015	Who **doth** more wrong than such as invent
018:057	And who **doth** more wrong than one who is reminded
018:087	He said: "Whoever **doth** wrong, him shall we punish;
019:004	and the hair of my head **doth** glisten with grey:
019:064	and thy Lord never **doth** forget,-
019:076	"And Allah **doth** increase in guidance those who
021:018	and behold, falsehood **doth** perish!
022:016	and verily Allah **doth** guide whom He will!
024:017	Allah **doth** admonish you, that ye
024:021	but Allah **doth** purify whom He pleases:
024:035	and Allah **doth** know all things.
024:035	Allah **doth** set forth Parables for men:
024:035	Allah **doth** guide whom He will to His Light:
024:038	for Allah **doth** provide for those
024:063	Allah **doth** know those of you
024:064	for Allah **doth** know all things.
024:064	that to Allah **doth** belong whatever is in the heavens
024:064	Well **doth** He know what ye are intent upon:
025:045	thou not see how thy Lord?-**doth** prolong the Shadow!
027:076	Verily this Qur'an **doth** explain to the
029:042	Verily Allah **doth** know of (everything)
033:052	and Allah **doth** watch over all things.
034:021	and thy Lord **doth** watch over all things.
034:048	Say: "Verily my Lord **doth** cast the Truth,-
035:002	What Allah out of His Mercy **doth** bestow on mankind
035:002	what He **doth** withhold, none can grant, apart from Him
036:016	They said: "Our Lord **doth** know that we have been
036:077	**Doth** not man see that it is We Who created
039:004	whom He pleased out of those whom He **doth** create:
039:008	(man) **doth** forget what he cried and prayed
039:008	and he **doth** set up rivals unto Allah,
039:016	with this **doth** Allah warn off His servants:
039:020	never **doth** Allah fail in (His) promise.
039:032	Who, then, **doth** more wrong than one who
039:037	And such as Allah **doth** guide there can be
040:015	by His Command **doth** He send the spirit
040:034	Thus **doth** Allah leave to stray
040:035	Thus **doth** Allah seal up
041:053	enough that thy Lord **doth** witness all things?
041:054	that **doth** encompass all things!
042:003	Thus **doth** (He) send Inspiration to thee
042:006	others besides Him,-Allah **doth** watch over them;
042:034	but much **doth** He forgive.
042:048	of Mercy from Us, he **doth** exult thereat,
055:029	(new) Splendor **doth** He (shine)!
058:007	Seest thou not that Allah **doth** know (all) that is
059:024	and on earth, **doth** declare His Praises and Glory:
061:007	Who **doth** greater wrong than one who forges
062:001	and on earth, **doth** declare the Praises and Glory
064:001	and on earth, **doth** declare the Praises and Glory
073:020	The Lord **doth** know that thou standest forth
073:020	and so **doth** a party of those with thee.
073:020	But Allah **doth** appoint Night and Day
074:028	and naught **doth** it leave alone!-

DOTH (continued)

074:028 Naught **doth** it permit to endure, and naught
074:031 "What **doth** Allah intend by this?"
074:031 Thus **doth** Allah leave to stray whom He pleaseth,
079:029 and its splendor **doth** He bring out (with light).
079:029 Its night **doth** He endow with darkness,
080:020 Then **doth** He make His path smooth for him;
081:024 Neither **doth** he withhold Grudgingly a knowledge
085:020 But Allah **doth** encompass them from behind!
087:005 And then **doth** make it (but) swarthy stubble.
096:006 Nay, but man **doth** transgress all bounds,
096:014 Knoweth he not that Allah **doth** see?
104:007 The which **doth** mount (Right) to the Hearts:

DOUBLE

002:245 which Allah will **double** unto his credit
002:265 but makes it yield a **double** increase of harvest,
007:038 so give them a **double** punishment in the Fire."
017:075 thee taste **double** portion (of punishment)
033:068 **Double** Chastisement and curse them with a very
038:061 add to him a **double** Chastisement in the Fire!"
057:028 a **double** portion of His Mercy:
064:017 He will **double** it to your (credit), and He

DOUBLED

003:130 devour not Usury, **doubled** and multiplied; but fear Allah;
007:038 He will say: "**Doubled** for all": but this
011:020 Their chastisement will be **doubled**!
021:084 and **doubled** their number,-as a Grace
025:069 the Day of Judgment will be **doubled** to him, and he
033:030 would be **doubled** to her, and that
038:043 and **doubled** their number,-as a Grace from Us,

DOUBLETH

004:040 if there is any good (done), He **doubleth** it, and

DOUBT

002:002 in it is guidance sure; without **doubt**,
002:023 in **doubt** as to what We have revealed
002:108 hath strayed without **doubt** from the even way.
002:147 so be not at all in **doubt**.
003:009 a Day about which there in no **doubt**;
003:025 against a Day about which there is no **doubt**,
003:060 so be not of those who **doubt**
003:068 Without **doubt**, among men, the nearest of kin
004:087 about which there is no **doubt**.
005:106 If ye **doubt** (their truth), detain them
006:002 yet ye **doubt** within yourselves!
006:012 there is no **doubt** whatever, it is they
006:114 Never be then of those who **doubt**.
009:042 they would (all) without **doubt** have followed thee,
009:045 and whose hearts are in **doubt**,
009:125 it will add **doubt** to their **doubt**, and they
010:037 wherein there is no **doubt**-from the
010:094 so be in no wise of those in **doubt**.
010:094 If thou wert in **doubt** as to what We have
010:104 in **doubt** as to my religion, (behold!) I
011:017 Be not then in **doubt** thereon:
011:022 Without a **doubt**, these are the very ones who
011:062 suspicious (disquieting) **doubt** as to that
011:075 For Abraham was, without **doubt**, forbearing
011:109 Be not then in **doubt** as to what these men worship.
011:110 is suspicious **doubt** concerning it.
012:070 ye are thieves, without **doubt**!"
013:028 for without **doubt** in the remembrance of Allah
014:009 in suspicious (disquieting) **doubt** as to that
014:010 a **doubt** about Allah, the Creator of the heavens

DOUBT (continued)

015:009 We have, without **doubt**, sent down the Message;
015:063 to thee to accomplish that of which they **doubt**.
016:062 without **doubt** for them is the Fire,
016:109 Without **doubt**, in the Hereafter they will
017:099 degreed a term appointed, of which there is no **doubt**.
018:021 and that there can be no **doubt** about the
019:068 So, by thy Lord, without **doubt**, We shall
020:082 "But, without **doubt**, I am (also) He that
022:005 O mankind! if ye have a **doubt** about the
022:007 there can be no **doubt** about it, or about
022:055 to be in **doubt** concerning (Revelation) until the
024:050 Or do they **doubt**, or are they in fear,
026:196 Without **doubt** it is (announced) in the
027:066 they are in **doubt** and uncertainty thereanent;
029:045 Allah is the greatest (thing in life) without **doubt**.
031:019 for the harshest of sounds without **doubt** is the
032:002 in which there is no **doubt**,-from the
032:023 be not then in **doubt** of its reaching (thee):
034:021 from him who is in **doubt** concerning it:
034:054 in suspicious (disquieting) **doubt**.
038:008 But they are in **doubt** concerning My (own)
040:034 and live in **doubt**,-
040:034 but ye ceased not to **doubt** of the (mission)
040:043 "Without **doubt** ye do call me to one who
040:051 We will, without **doubt**, help Our mesengers
040:059 The Hour will certainly come: therein is no **doubt**:
041:045 disquieting **doubt** thereon.
041:054 they in **doubt** concerning the Meeting with their Lord?
042:007 the Day of Assembly, of which there is no **doubt**.
042:014 are in suspicious (disquieting) **doubt** concerning it.
043:061 therefore have no **doubt** about the (Hour),
044:009 Yet they play about in **doubt**.
044:050 "Truly this is what ye used to **doubt**!"
045:026 for the Day of Judgment about which there is no **doubt**":
045:032 there was no **doubt** about its (coming), ye used
050:015 be in confused **doubt** about a new Creation?
065:004 if ye have any **doubt**, is three months, and those
081:023 And without **doubt** he saw him in the clear horizon.

DOUBTED

029:048 indeed, would the talkers of vanities have **doubted**.
049:015 and have since **doubted**, but have striven with their
057:014 ye **doubted** (Allah's promise);

DOUBTFUL

068:013 of a **doubtful** birth,-

DOUBTFULLY

018:022 being the sixth,-**doubtfully** guessing at the unknown;

DOUBTLESS

028:076 Qarun was **doubtless**, of the people of Moses;

DOUBTS

002:282 to prevent **doubts** among yourselves
004:157 are full of **doubts**, with no (certain) knowledge.
009:045 in their **doubts** to and fro.
050:025 cast **doubts** and suspicions;
074:031 and that no **doubts** may be left for the People

DOWER

002:236 or the fixation of their **dower**;
002:237 then the half of the **dower** (is due to them),
002:237 but after the fixation of a **dower** for them,
004:005 (on marriage) their **dower** as an obligation;
004:019 of the **dower** ye have given them, except
004:020 the latter a whole treasure for **dower**, take not

DOWER (continued)

004:024   but if, after a **dower** is prescribed, ye agree
060:010   what they have spent (on their **dower**).
060:010   if ye marry them on payment of their **dower** to them.
060:011   they had spent (on their **dower**).

DOWERS

004:025   and give them their **dowers**, according
005:005   when ye give them their due **dowers**, and desire
033:050   thy wives to whom thou hast paid their **dowers**;
060:010   have spent on their **dowers**, and let
060:010   (on their **dowers** of women who came over to you).

DOWERY

004:024   Give them their **dowery** for the enjoyment

DOWN

002:022   and sent **down** rain from the heavens;
002:034   "Bow **down** to Adam"; and they bowed **down**:
002:036   And We said: "Get ye **down**, (all you people),
002:038   We said: "Get ye **down** all from here;
002:043   with those who bow **down** (in worship).
002:043   and bow **down** your heads with those
002:057   and sent **down** to you manna and quails,
002:061   Go ye **down** to any town,
002:090   (the revelation) which Allah has sent **down**,
002:091   what was sent **down** to us":
002:091   "Believe in what Allah hath sent **down**,"
002:097   for he brings **down** the (revelation)
002:099   We have sent **down** to thee manifest Signs
002:102   and such things as came **down** at Babylon
002:105   come **down** to you from your Lord.
002:159   (Signs) We have sent **down**, and the Guidance,
002:164   in the rain which Allah sends **down** from the skies,
002:176   (Their doom is) because Allah sent **down** the Book
002:185   in which was sent **down** the Qur'an,
002:198   Then when ye pour **down** from (Mount) 'Arafat,
002:231   He sent **down** to you the Book and Wisdom,
002:282   write **down** faithfully as between the parties:
003:003   It is He Who sent **down** to thee (step by step),
003:003   and He sent **down** the Criterion
003:003   and He sent **down** the Torah (of Moses)
003:007   He it is Who has sent **down** to thee the Book:
003:043   and bow **down** (in prayer) with those who bow **down**."
003:053   then write us **down** among those who bear witness."
003:124   three thousand angels (specially) sent **down**?
003:154   He sent **down** calm on a band of you
003:191   and lying **down** on their sides, and contemplate
004:103   or lying **down** on your sides;
004:103   remember Allah, standing, sitting **down**, or
004:105   We have sent **down** to thee the Book in truth,
004:113   For Allah hath sent **down** to thee the Book
005:049   (teaching) which Allah hath sent **down** to thee.
005:055   they bow **down** humbly (in worship).
005:083   write us **down** among the witnesses.
005:112   Can thy Lord send **down** to us a Table set
005:115   Allah said: "I will send it **down** unto you:
006:008   If We did send **down** an angel, the matter
006:008   They say: "Why is not an angel sent **down** to him?"
006:037   a Sign sent **down** to him from his Lord?"
006:037   power to send **down** a Sign:
006:091   Say: "Allah (sent it **down**)": then leave
006:091   send **down** to man (by way of revelation)":
006:091   Say: "Who then sent **down** the Book
006:092   which We have sent **down**, bringing
006:099   sendeth **down** rain from the skies:

DOWN (continued)

006:114   that it hath been sent **down** from thy Lord in truth.
006:156   sent **down** to two Peoples before us, and for
006:157   "If the Book had only been sent **down** to us, we
007:013   (Allah) said: "Get thee **down** from it: it is not
007:024   (Allah) said: "Get ye **down**, with enmity
007:050   "Pour **down** to us water or anything that Allah
007:084   And We rained **down** on them
007:120   But the sorcerers fell **down** prostrate in adoration.
007:137   lands whereon We sent **down** our blessings.
007:143   He made it as dust and Moses fell **down** in a swoon.
007:150   He put **down** the Tablets, seized his brother
007:157   the Light which is sent **down** with him,-it is
007:160   and sent **down** to them manna and quails, (saying):
008:032   rain **down** on us a shower of stones from the sky,
008:041   the revelation We sent **down** to our Servant
009:026   and sent **down** forces which ye saw not: He punished
009:040   then Allah sent **down** His peace upon him,
009:064   should be sent **down** about them, showing them
009:086   When a Sura comes **down**, enjoining them to believe
009:097   sent **down** to His Messenger:
009:112   that bow **down** and prostrate themselves in prayer;
009:124   Whenever there cometh **down** a Sura, some of
009:127   Whenever there cometh **down** a Sura, they look
010:012   lying **down** on his side, or sitting, or standing.
010:020   sent **down** to him from his Lord?"
010:024   is as the rain which We send **down** from the skies:
010:059   sent **down** to you for sustenance?
011:012   an angel come **down** with Him?
011:012   sent **down** unto him, or why does not an angel
011:014   sent **down** (replete) with the knowledge of Allah,
011:038   we (in our turn) can look **down** on you with
011:048   The word came: "O Noah! come **down** (from the Ark)
011:082   We turned (the cities) upside **down**,
011:082   and rained **down** on them brimstones hard as baked clay,
011:100   and some have been mown **down** (by the
012:002   We have sent it **down** as an Arabic Qur'an, in order
012:010   throw him **down** to the bottom of the well:
012:015   and they all agreed to throw him **down** to the
012:019   and he let **down** his bucket (into the well).
012:040   hath sent **down** no authority:
012:100   the throne and they fell **down** in prostration,
013:007   a Sign sent **down** to him from his Lord?"
013:017   He sends **down** water from the skies, and the
013:027   a Sign sent **down** to him from his Lord?"
013:030   We send **down** unto thee by inspiration; yet do
014:017   swallowing it **down** his throat; death will come
014:032   and sendeth **down** rain from the skies, and with it
015:008   We send not the angels **down** except for just cause:
015:009   We have, without doubt, sent **down** the Message;
015:021   but We only send **down** thereof in due and ascertainable
015:029   fall ye **down** in obeisance unto him."
015:074   And We turned (the cities) upside **down**,
015:074   and rained **down** on them brimstones hard as baked clay.
015:090   as We sent **down** on those who divided
016:002   He doth send **down** His angels with inspiration
016:010   It is He Who sends **down** rain from the sky:
016:026   fell **down** on them from above; and the Wrath
016:044   and Scriptures and We have sent **down** unto thee
016:064   And We sent **down** the Book to thee so that
016:065   And Allah sends **down** rain from the skies,
016:089   and We have sent **down** to thee the Book explaining
017:082   We send **down** (stage by stage) of the Qur'an

DOWN (continued)

017:093 until thou send **down** to us a book that we
017:095 sent them **down** from the heavens an angel
017:102 these things have been sent **down** by none
017:105 We sent **down** the (Qur'an) in Truth, and in
017:107 fall **down** on their faces in humble prostration,
017:109 They fall **down** on their faces in tears, and it
018:045 We send **down** from the skies: the earth's
018:077 on the point of falling **down**, but he
019:058 they would fall **down** in prostrate adoration and in tears.
019:086 (like thirsty cattle driven **down** to water),-
019:090 and the mountains to fall **down** in utter ruin.
020:002 We have not sent **down** the Qur'an to thee to be
020:018 with it I beat **down** fodder for my flocks;
020:053 and has sent **down** water from the sky."
020:070 So the magicians were thrown **down** to prostration:
020:080 and We sent **down** to you Manna and quails:
020:113 Thus have we sent this **down**-an Arabic Qur'an-
020:123 He said: "Get ye **down**, both of you,-all together,
020:124 a life narrowed **down**, and We shall raise him up
021:050 this is a blessed message which We have sent **down**:
022:005 but when We pour **down** rain on it, it is stirred (to life),
022:016 Thus have We sent **down** Clear Signs; and verily
022:036 (for sacrifice): when they are **down** on their
022:040 pulled **down** monasteries, churches, synagogues,
022:045 They tumbled **down** on their roofs.
022:063 sends **down** rain from the sky, and forthwith
022:071 things for which no authority has been sent **down** to them,
022:077 O ye who believe! bow **down**, prostrate yourselves,
023:018 And We send **down** water from the sky according
023:024 He could have sent **down** angels:
024:001 A Sura which We have sent **down** and which
024:001 in it have We sent **down** Clear Signs, in order
024:034 We have already sent **down** to you verses making
024:043 And He sends **down** from the sky mountain masses
024:046 We have indeed sent **down** Signs that make
025:001 Blessed is He Who sent **down** the Criterion
025:006 Say: "The (Qur'an) was sent **down** by Him
025:007 Why has not an angel been sent **down** to him
025:021 "Why are not the angels sent **down** to us,
025:025 and angels shall be sent **down**,
025:048 and We send **down** pure water from the sky,-
025:073 droop not **down** at them as if they were deaf
026:004 We could send **down** to them from the sky a Sign,
026:046 Then did the sorcerers fall **down**, prostrate in
026:173 We rained **down** on them a shower (of brimstone):
026:193 With it came **down** the Truthful spirit
026:210 The Satans did not bring it **down**:
027:058 And We rained **down** on them a shower (of brimstone):
027:060 and the earth, and who sends you **down** rain from
029:034 "For we are going to bring **down** on the
029:046 and in that which came do to you; Our God
029:046 which has come **down** to us and in that
029:047 that We have sent **down** the Book to thee.
029:050 "Why are not Signs sent **down** to him from his Lord?"
029:051 We have sent **down** to thee the Book
029:063 that sends **down** rain from the sky, and gives
030:024 and He sends **down** rain from the sky and with
030:035 Or have We sent **down** authority to them,
031:010 We send **down** rain from the sky, and produce
031:021 to follow the (Revelation) that Allah has sent **down**,
031:034 It is He Who sends **down** rain, and He
032:015 when they are recited to them fall **down** in adoration,

DOWN (continued)

033:009 (bestowed) on you, when there came **down** on you
033:026 Allah did take them **down** from their strongholds
034:002 all that comes **down** from the sky and all
034:006 see that the (Revelation) sent **down** to thee
034:014 so when he fell **down**, the Jinns
035:011 or lays **down** (her load), but with
035:027 sends **down** rain from the sky?
036:005 (It is a Revelation) sent **down** by (Him),
036:028 And We sent not **down** against his People,
037:054 He said: "Would ye like to look **down**?"
037:055 He looked **down** and saw him in the midst
037:070 So they (too) were rushed **down** on their footsteps!
038:024 of his Lord, fell **down**, bowing (in prostration),
038:029 (Here is) a Book which We have sent **down** unto thee,
038:072 fall ye **down** in prostrated unto him."
039:006 and He sent **down** for you eight head
039:021 Seest thou not that Allah sends **down** rain from the sky,
040:013 and sendeth **down** sustenance for you from the sky:
041:014 He would certainly have sent **down** angels: so we
041:039 but when We send **down** rain to it, it is
041:042 it is sent **down** by One Full of Wisdom, Worthy of
042:015 "I believe in whatever Book Allah has sent **down**;
042:017 It is Allah Who has sent **down** the Book in truth,
042:027 but He sends (it) **down** in due measure
042:028 He is the One that sends **down** rain (even) after
043:011 That sends **down** (from time to time) rain from
043:031 sent **down** to some leading man in either of
043:043 So hold thou fast to the Revelation sent **down** to thee:
044:003 We sent it **down** during a blessed night: for We
045:005 the fact that Allah sends **down** Sustenance from the shy,
047:002 sent **down** to Muhammad-for is the Truth from their
047:004 until the war lays **down** its burdens.
047:020 "Why is not a Sura sent **down** (for us)?"
048:004 It is He who sent **down** Tranquillity into the
048:018 and He sent **down** tranquillity to them, and He
048:025 trampling **down** and on whose account a guilt
048:026 Allah sent **down** His tranquillity to His
050:009 And We send **down** from the sky Rain charged
052:013 That Day shall they be thrust **down** to the
052:041 and they write it **down**?
053:001 By the Star when it goes **down**,-
053:004 It is no less than inspiration sent **down** to him:
053:023 for which Allah has sent **down** no authority
053:062 But fall ye **down** in prostration to Allah,
056:069 Do ye bring it **Down** (in rain) from the Cloud,
057:004 out of it, what comes **down** from heaven and what
057:025 and We sent **down** Iron, in which
057:025 with Clear Signs and sent **down** with them the Book
058:005 for We have already sent **down** Clear Signs.
059:005 Whether ye cut **down** (O ye Muslims!) of the tender
059:021 Had We sent **down** this Qur'an on a mountain,
064:008 and the Light which We have sent **down**.
065:005 which He has sent **down** to you:
065:010 sent **down** to you a Message,-
067:009 'Allah never sent **down** any (Message): ye are in
068:043 Their eyes will be cast **down**,-ignominy will
068:047 so that they can write it **down**?
069:007 roots of hollow palm-trees tumbled **down**!
069:043 (This is) a Message sent **down** from the
073:005 Soon shall We send **down** to thee a weighty Word.
073:014 a heap of sand poured out and flowing **down**.
076:023 It is We Who have sent **down** the Qur'an

DOWN (continued)

078:014 And do We not send **down** from the clouds
079:009 Cast **down** will be (their owners') eyes.
082:004 And when the Graves are turned upside **down**;-
082:011 Kind and honorable, writing **down** (your deeds):
090:016 Or to the indigent (**down**) in the dust.
097:004 Therein come **down** the angels and the Spirit

DRAG

019:069 Then shall We certainly **drag** out from every
044:047 and **drag** him into the midst of the Blazing Fire!
096:015 We will **drag** him by the forelock,-

DRAGGED

007:150 and **dragged** him to him.
040:071 they shall be **dragged** along-
054:048 The Day they will be **dragged** through the Fire

DRAIN

023:018 to **drain** it off (with ease).

DRANK

002:249 "But they **drank** of it, except a few.

DRAUGHTS

010:004 but **draughts** of boiling fluids, and a

DRAW

003:112 they **draw** on themselves wrath from Allah.
005:029 thee **draw** on thyself my sin as well as thine,
009:049 "Grant me exemption and **draw** me not into trial."
019:052 and made him **draw** near to Us, for converse
020:022 Now **draw** thy hand close to thy side:
021:097 Then will the true Promise **draw** nigh (of fulfillment):
024:031 their feet in order to **draw** attention to their
024:031 that they should **draw** their veils over their
025:046 Then We **draw** it in towards Ourselves,-
027:028 then **draw** back from them, and (wait to)
028:031 "O Moses!" (It was said), "**Draw** near, and fear
028:032 and **draw** thy hand close to thy side
028:075 And from each people shall We **draw** a witness,
068:044 We **draw** them on little by little from directions
077:025 (as a place) to **draw** together
079:002 By those who gently **draw** out (the souls of the blessed);

DRAWETH

007:054 He **draweth** the night as a veil O'er the day,
013:003 He **draweth** the Night as a veil o'er the Day.
079:031 He **draweth** out therefrom its water and its pasture,

DRAWING

007:185 it may be that their term is nigh **drawing** to an end?
040:018 Warn them of the Day that is (ever) **drawing** near,
067:007 they will hear the (terrible) **drawing** in of its

DRAWN

002:090 thus have they **drawn** on themselves

DRAWS

003:162 the man who **draws** on Himself the wrath of Allah,
006:164 Every soul **draws** the meed of its
008:016 he **draws** on himself the wrath of Allah,
053:057 The (Hour) ever approaching **draws** nigh:

DREAD

006:040 or the Hour (that ye **dread**), would ye then

DREADFUL

003:105 for them is a **dreadful** Chastisement,
004:038 what a **dreadful** intimate he is!
004:093 and a **dreadful** chastisement is prepared for him.
006:157 with a **dreadful** chastisement for their
007:059 I fear for you the Punishment of a **dreadful** Day!"
012:048 (period) seven **dreadful** (years), which will

DREADFUL (continued)

016:106 a **dreadful** Chastisement.
017:040 Truly ye utter a most **dreadful** saying!
017:058 a **dreadful** Chastisement.
018:029 scald their faces, how **dreadful** the drink!
022:002 but **dreadful** will be the Chastisement of Allah.
052:009 will be in **dreadful** commotion.

DREADING

028:006 what they were **dreading** from them.

DREAM

008:043 Remember in thy **dream** Allah showed them
012:036 (in a **dream**) pressing wine."
012:036 (in a **dream**) carrying bread on my head, and birds
012:046 Expound to us (the **dream**) of seven
037:102 in a **dream** that I offer thee in sacrifice:
037:105 "Thou hast already fulfilled the **dream**!"-

DREAMS

012:044 in the interpretation of **dreams**."
012:044 They said: "A confused medley of **dreams**:
012:101 of the interpretation of **dreams**,-O Thou
021:005 "Nay," they say, "(these are) medleys of **dreams**!-

DRESSED

044:053 **Dressed** in fine silk and in rich brocade,

DREW

002:061 they **drew** on themselves the wrath of Allah.
007:108 And he **drew** out his hand, and behold!
007:172 When thy Lord **drew** forth from the
018:011 Then We **drew** (a veil) over their ears, for a
026:033 And he **drew** out his hand, and behold

DRINK

002:060 So eat and **drink** of the sustenance
002:187 and eat and **drink**, until the white thread of dawn
002:259 but look at thy food and thy **drink**;
006:070 they will have for **drink** (only) boiling water,
007:031 eat and **drink**: but waste not by excess,
009:019 Do ye make the giving of **drink** to pilgrims,
012:041 out the wine for his lord to **drink**:
014:016 and he is given, for **drink**, boiling fetid water.
016:010 from it ye **drink**, and out (grows) the vegetation
016:066 We produce, for your **drink**, milk, pure and
016:066 pure and agreeable to those who **drink** it.
016:067 strong **drink**, and wholesome food:
016:069 from within their bodies a **drink** of varying
018:029 how dreadful the **drink**!
019:026 "So eat and **drink** and cool (thine) eye.
023:021 We produce (milk) for you to **drink**;
023:033 he eats and drinks of what ye **drink**.
026:079 "Who gives me food and **drink**,
035:012 sweet, and pleasant to **drink**, and the other,
036:073 get (milk) to **drink**.
037:046 to those who **drink** (thereof),
038:042 cool and refreshing, and (water) to **drink**."
038:051 for fruit in abundance, and (delicious) **drink**;
047:015 a joy to those who **drink**; and rivers
047:015 and be given, to **drink**, boiling water, so that
052:019 "Eat and **drink** ye, with profit and health,
054:028 each one's right to **drink** being brought forward
056:054 "And **drink** Boiling Water on top of it:
056:055 "Indeed ye shall **drink** like diseased camels
056:068 See ye the water which ye **drink**?
069:024 "Eat ye and **drink** ye, with full satisfaction;
076:005 As to the Righteous, they shall **drink** of a Cup

DRINK (continued)

076:006 A fountain where the Devotees of Allah do **drink**,
076:017 And they will be given to **drink** there of a Cup
076:021 And their Lord will give to them to **drink** a pure **drink**.
077:043 "Eat ye and **drink** ye to your heart's content:
078:024 taste therein, nor any **drink**,
083:028 whereof **drink** those Nearest to Allah.
088:005 The while they are given, to **drink**, of a boiling hot spring,
091:013· And (bar her not from) having her **drink**!"

DRINKING

012:070 (suitable) for them, he put the **drinking** cup into

DRINKS

002:249 if any **drinks** of its water,
023:033 he eats and **drinks** of what ye drink.

DRIVE

002:126 but will soon **drive** them to the torment
002:217 and **drive** out its members.
003:149˙ they will **drive** you back on your heels,
003:167 or (at least) **drive** (the foe from your city)."
007:057 We **drive** them to a land that is dead, make rain
007:082 they said, "**Drive** them out of your city: these are
007:088 "O Shu'aib! we shall certainly **drive** thee out of our city-
007:123 to **drive** out its people:
011:029 but I will not **drive** away (in contempt)
014:013 "Be sure we shall **drive** you out of our land,
016:006 in them as ye **drive** them home in the evening,
019:086 And We shall **drive** the sinners to Hell,
020:057 He said: "Hast thou come to **drive** us out
020:063 their object is to **drive** you out from your land
026:114 "I am not one to **drive** away those who believe.
027:056 "**Drive** out the followers of Lut from your city:
031:024 in the end shall We **drive** them to a chastisement
032:027 that We do **drive** Rain to parched soil (bare of herbage),
035:009 and We **drive** them to a land that is dead,
050:021 with each will be an (angel) to **drive**, and an
060:008 (your) Faith nor **drive** you out of your homes,
060:009 and **drive** you out of your homes, and support
067:005 (as) missiles to **drive** away Satans, and have
075:030 That Day the **Drive** will be (all) to thy Lord!

DRIVEN

002:275 the Satan by his touch hath **driven** to madness.
003:195 and were drive out therefrom, or suffered harm
008:006 as if they were being **driven** to death
019:086 (like thirsty cattle **driven** down to water),-
023:108 He will say: "Be ye **driven** into it
047:013 which has **driven** thee out, have We
054:009 "Here is one possessed!", and he was **driven** out.
060:001 and have (on the contrary) **driven** out the Messenger

DRIVING

060:009 and support (others) in **driving** you out,

DROOP

025:073 Signs of their Lord, **droop** not down at them as if they

DROP

022:002 shall **drop** her load (unformed):
023:013 Then We placed him as (a **drop** of) sperm in a
075:037 Was he not a **drop** of sperm emitted (in lowly form)?
076:002 Verily We created Man from a **drop** of mingled sperm,
086:006 He is created from a **drop** emitted-

DROUGHT

007:130 with years (of **drought**) and shortness

DROVE

009:040 help him, when the Unbelievers **drove** him out:

DROVE (continued)

011:030 help me against Allah if I **drove** them away?
019:023 And the pains of childbirth **drove** her to the

DROWN

017:069 to **drown** you because of your ingratitude, so that
017:103 but We did **drown** him and all who were with him.
018:071 to **drown** those in it?
036:043 If it were Our Will, We could **drown** them;

DROWNED

002:050 and saved you and **drowned** Pharaoh's people
007:136 We **drowned** them in the sea, because they
008:054 and We **drowned** the people of Pharaoh:
010:073 while We **drowned** in the Flood those who
011:043 those who were **drowned**.
021:077 so We **drowned** them (in the Flood) all together.
023:027 be **drowned** (in the Flood).
025:037 We **drowned** them, and We made them as a Sign
026:066 But We **drowned** the others.
026:120 Thereafter We **drowned** those who remained behind.
029:040 and some We **drowned** (in the waters):
043:055 and We **drowned** them all.
044:024 For they are a host (destined) to be **drowned**."
071:025 were **drowned** (in the flood), and were

DROWSINESS

008:011 Remember He covered you with **drowsiness**, to give

DRUNK

022:002 a drunken riot, yet not **drunk**:

DRUNKEN

022:002 a **drunken** riot, yet not drunk:

DRY

006:059 nor anything fresh or **dry** (green or withered),
018:008 but as dust and **dry** soil (without growth or herbage).
018:045 but soon it becomes **dry** stubble, which the
020:077 and strike a **dry** path for them through the sea,
029:065 them safely to (**dry**) land, behold, they give
036:078 "Who can give life to (**dry**) bones and decomposed
039:021 then He makes it **dry** up and crumble away.
054:031 the **dry** stubble used by one who pens cattle.
057:020 then it becomes **dry** and crumbles away.

DUBIOUS

010:071 so your plan be not to you dark and **dubious**.

DUE

002:096 will not save him from (**due**) chastisement
002:128 for the celebration of (**due**) rites;
002:173 nor transgressing **due** limits,
002:180 this is **due** from the God-fearing.
002:233 by mutual consent, and after **due** consultation.
002:236 is **due** from those who wish to do the right thing.
002:237 then the half of the dower (is **due** to them),
003:154 suspicions **due** to Ignorance.
003:161 receive its **due** whatever it earned,
004:033 give their **due** portion.
004:058 your trusts to those to whom they are **due**;
004:100 his reward becomes **due** and sure with Allah:
004:152 We shall soon give their (**due**) rewards:
004:173 He will give their (**due**) rewards,-and more,
005:003 unless ye are able to slaughter it (in **due** form);
005:005 when ye give them their **due** dowers, and desire
006:016 it is **due** to Allah's Mercy;
006:120 those who earn is will get **due** recompense for their
006:145 nor transgressing **due** limits,-thy Lord
007:085 the things that are their **due**; and do

DUE (continued)

007:131   they said, "This is **due** to us"; when gripped
010:072   my reward is only **due** from Allah, and I
011:085   nor withhold from the people the thing that are their **due**:
012:037   (in **due** course) to feed either of you I will
013:008   every single thing is with Him in (**due**) proportion.
013:014   To Him is **due** the true prayer any others
015:019   of things in **due** balance.
015:021   thereof in **due** and ascertainable measures.
015:029   (in **due** proportion) and breathed into him
016:115   nor transgressing **due** limits,-then Allah
017:019   and strive therefor with all **due** striving, and Faith,-
017:026   And render to the kindred their **due** rights,
020:112   nor of any curtailment (of what is his **due**).
022:018   the chastisement is justly **due**.
022:036   and such as beg with **due** humility:
023:018   the sky according to (**due**) measure, and We
023:080   and to Him (is **due**) the alternation of Night
025:002   and ordered them in **due** proportions.
026:183   "And withhold not things justly **due** to men,
030:038   So give what is **due** to kindred, the needy
032:009   But He fashioned him in **due** proportion,
032:022   who transgress We shall exact (**Due**) Retribution.
034:018   We had appointed stages of journey in **due** proportion:
034:047   my reward is only **due** from Allah:
039:003   Is it not to Allah that sincere devotion is **due**?
039:019   Punishment is justly **due** (equal to one who eschews evil?)
039:067   estimate have they made of Allah, such as is **due** to Him:
041:050   "This is **due** to my (merit): I think
042:027   in **due** measure as He pleases:
042:040   makes reconciliation, his reward is **due** from Allah:
043:011   rain from the sky in **due** measure;-
051:019   a **due** share for the beggar and the deprived.
055:008   In order that ye may not transgress (**due**) balance.
057:027   who believed, their (**due**) reward, but many
059:008   (Some part is **due**) to the indigent Muhajirs,
065:003   for all things has Allah appointed a **due** proportion.
073:020   and Day in **due** measure.
075:038   and fashion (him) in **due** proportion.
080:019   and then mouldeth him in **due** Proportions;
082:007   fashioned thee in **due** proportion, and gave
083:003   or weight to men, give less than **due**.

DUES

006:141   but render the **dues** that are proper on the
024:025   that Day Allah will pay them back (all) their just **dues**,

DULL

067:004   to thee **dull** and discomfited, in a state worn out.

DULY

020:052   is with my Lord, **duly** recorded:
032:011   will (**duly**) take your souls:
050:014   and My warning was **duly** fulfilled (in them).

DUMB

002:018   Deaf, **dumb**, and blind,
002:171   deaf, **dumb**, and blind,
006:039   Those who reject Our Signs are deaf and **dumb**,-
008:022   and the **dumb**,-those who understand not.
016:076   Parable of two men: one of them **dumb**, with no power
017:097   their faces, blind, **dumb**, and deaf:
019:010   although thou art not **dumb**."
030:012   the guilty will be struck **dumb** with despair.
030:049   they were **dumb** with despair!

DUPES

004:121   They (his **dupes**) will have their dwelling in hell,

DURING

002:185   (at his home) **during** that month should spent it in fasting,
002:196   he should fast three days **during** the hajj.
002:198   the bounty of your Lord (**during** pilgrimage).
002:203   Remember Allah **during** the Appointed Days
039:009   Is one who worships devoutly **during** the hours
039:042   and those that die not (He takes) **during** their sleep:
044:003   We sent it down **during** a blessed night: for We
050:040   And **during** part of the night, (also), celebrate

DUST

003:059   He created him from **dust**,
007:143   He made it as **dust** and Moses fell down in a swoon.
008:017   when thou threwest (a handful) of **dust**, it was not
013:005   "When we are (actually) **dust**, shall we
016:059   or bury it in the **dust**?
017:049   to bones and **dust**, should we really be raised up
017:098   to bones and broken **dust**, should we really be
018:008   but as **dust** and dry soil (without growth
018:037   "Dost thou deny Him Who created thee out of **dust**,
018:098   comes to pass, He will make it into **dust**;
020:096   so I took a handful (of **dust**) from the
020:105   and scatter them as **dust**;
022:005   out of **dust**, then out of sperm, then out
023:035   and become **dust** and bones, ye shall
023:082   and become **dust** and bones, could we
025:023   make such deeds as floating **dust** scattered about.
027:067   become **dust**,-we and our fathers,-shall we
030:020   that He created you from **dust**; and then,-behold,
035:011   And Allah did create you from **dust**; then from
037:016   "What! when we die, and become **dust** and bones,
037:053   "'When we die and become **dust** and bones,
040:067   It is He Who has created you from **dust**, then from
050:003   when we die and become **dust**, (shall we live again?)
056:006   Becoming **dust** scattered abroad,
056:047   "What! when we die and become **dust** and bones,
058:005   and His Messenger will be humbled to **dust**,
077:010   (to the winds) as **dust**;
078:040   "Woe unto me! Would that I were (mere) **dust**!"
090:016   Or to the indigent (down) in the **dust**.
100:004   And raise the **dust** in clouds the while,

DUST-STAINED

080:040   And other faces that Day will be **dust-stained**;

DUTIES

073:007   prolonged occupation with ordinary **duties**:

DUTY

002:197   If any one undertakes that **duty** therein,
002:241   suitable Gift this is **duty** on the righteous.
003:020   thy **duty** is to convey the Message;
003:097   pilgrimage thereto is a **duty** men owe to Allah,
003:147   that transgressed our **duty**:
004:024   dowery for the enjoyment you have of them as **duty**;
005:035   O ye who believe! do your **duty** to Allah, seek
005:092   it is Our Messenger's **duty** to proclaim (the Message)
005:099   The Messenger's **duty** is but to proclaim
006:061   and they never fail in their **duty**.
006:069   but (their **duty**) is to remind them, that they
007:164   our **duty** to your Lord and perchance
008:072   it is your **duty** to help them, except against
008:072   ye owe no **duty** of protection to them
009:044   And Allah knoweth well those who do their **duty**.
009:091   (in **duty**) to Allah and His Messenger:

DUTY (continued)

009:117 of them had nearly swerved (from **duty**), but He
010:022 sincerely offering (their) **duty** unto Him, saying:
012:037 That is part of the (**Duty**) which my
012:080 in your **duty** with Joseph?
013:040 thy **duty** is to (make the Message) reach them:
016:002 so do your **duty** unto Me."
016:082 thy **duty** is only to preach the Clear Message.
024:054 The Messenger's **duty** is only
024:054 the **duty** placed on him and ye
029:018 and the **duty** of the messenger is only
030:047 and it was a **duty** incumbent upon Us to aid
031:033 O mankind! do your **duty** to your Lord and fear
033:038 has indicated to him as a **duty**.
036:017 "And Our **duty** is only to deliver
039:056 in that I neglected (my **duty**) towards Allah,
041:012 to each heaven its **duty** and command.
042:048 Thy **duty** is but to convey
064:012 the **duty** of Our Messenger is but to deliver

DWELL

002:035 "O Adam! **dwell** thou and thy wife in the Garden;
002:257 to **dwell** therein (for ever).
003:088 In that will they **dwell**; nor will their punishment
003:107 therein to **dwell** (for ever).
003:198 therein are they to **dwell** (for ever),
004:122 to **dwell** therein for ever.
004:169 to **dwell** therein for ever: and this
006:128 you will **dwell** therein for ever, except as
007:019 O Adam! **dwell** thou and thy wife
007:036 to **dwell** therein (for ever).
007:042 therein to **dwell** (for ever).
007:161 "**Dwell** in this town and eat therein as ye wish,
007:189 in order that he might **dwell** with her
009:017 in Fire shall they **dwell**.
009:022 They will **dwell** therein for ever.
009:063 Wherein they shall **dwell**.
009:068 therein shall they **dwell**:
009:072 Gardens under which rivers flow, to **dwell** therein,
009:089 under which rivers flow, to **dwell** therein:
009:100 rivers flow, to **dwell** therein for ever:
011:023 to **dwell** therein for aye!
011:107 They will **dwell** therein so long as the heavens
011:108 they will **dwell** therein so long as
013:005 to **dwell** therein (for aye)!
014:023 to **dwell** therein for aye with the leave of their Lord.
014:037 of my offspring to **dwell** in a valley without
016:029 "So enter the gates of Hell, to **dwell** therein.
017:104 Children of Israel, "**Dwell** securely in the land
018:108 Wherein they shall **dwell** (for aye): no change
020:076 they will **dwell** therein for aye:
021:102 in that will they **dwell**.
023:011 they will **dwell** therein (for ever).
025:010 (secure to **dwell** in).
025:016 they will **dwell** (there) for aye: a promise
025:069 and he will **dwell** therein in ignominy,-
029:058 to **dwell** therein for aye;-an excellent
030:021 that ye may **dwell** in tranquillity with them,
031:009 To **dwell** therein. The promise of Allah is true:
033:065 To **dwell** therein for ever: no protector
039:072 "Enter ye the gates of Hell, to **dwell** therein:
039:073 Enter ye here, to **dwell** therein."
039:074 We can **dwell** in the Garden as we will:
040:076 "Enter ye the gates of Hell, to **dwell** therein:

DWELL (continued)

043:074 in the Punishment of Hell, to **dwell** therein (for aye):
047:015 be compared to such as **dwell** for ever in the Fire,
047:019 and how ye **dwell** in your homes.
048:005 beneath which rivers flow, to **dwell** therein for aye,
057:012 To **dwell** therein for aye! This is
058:017 of the Fire, to swell therein (for aye)!
058:022 to **dwell** therein (for ever).
064:009 to **dwell** therein for ever: that will
064:010 to **dwell** therein for aye: and evil
065:011 to **dwell** therein for ever: Allah has
072:023 they shall **dwell** therein for ever."
078:023 They will **dwell** therein for ages.
098:006 to **dwell** therein (for aye).
098:008 They will **dwell** therein for ever; Allah well

DWELLER

022:025 to (all) men-equal is the **dweller** there and the
028:045 a **dweller** among the people of Madyan,

DWELLETH

006:013 "To Him belongeth all that **dwelleth** (or lurketh)

DWELLING

002:036 On earth will be your **dwelling** place
003:116 Companions of the Fire,-**dwelling** therein (for ever).
003:136 an eternal **dwelling**:
004:121 They (his dupes) will have their **dwelling** in hell,
025:076 **Dwelling** therein;-how beautiful an abode
046:014 of the Garden, **dwelling** Therein (for aye):
059:017 that they will go into the Fire, **dwelling** therein for ever.

DWELLING-PLACE

006:128 "The Fire be your **dwelling-place**:
007:024 On earth will be your **dwelling-place** and your
009:095 their **dwelling-place**, a fitting recompense for
010:093 in a honourable **dwelling-place**, and provided

DWELLINGS

009:024 or the **dwellings** in which delight-
010:087 with this message: "Provide **dwellings** for your
010:087 make your **dwellings** into places of worship,
014:045 "And ye dwelt in the **dwellings** of men
016:080 of animals, (tents for) **dwellings**, which ye
032:026 before them, in whose **dwellings** they (now) go
034:037 in the **dwellings** on high!
059:002 so that they destroyed their **dwellings** by their

DWELT

005:117 whilst I **dwelt** amongst them; when thou
011:068 As if they had never **dwelt** and flourished there.
011:095 As if they had never **dwelt** and flourished there!
014:045 "And ye **dwelt** in the dwellings of men

DYING

056:083 when (the soul of the **dying** man) reaches the throat,

E

EACH

002:060	**Each** group knew its own place for water.
002:076	but when they meet **each** other in private,
002:096	**each** one of them wishes he could be given a life for
002:145	they follow **each** other's Qiblah.
002:148	To **each** is a goal to which Allah turns him;
002:253	have fought among **each** other,
002:253	they would not have fought **each** other;
002:261	and **each** ear hath a hundred grains.
002:282	O ye who believe! when ye deal with **each** other,
002:285	**each** one (of them) believeth in Allah,
003:019	except through envy of **each** other,
003:025	and **each** soul will be paid out just what
003:200	vie in such perseverance: strengthen **each** other;
004:011	a sixth share of the inheritance to **each**,
004:012	**each** one of the two gets a sixth;
004:021	when ye have gone in unto **each** other,
004:041	How then if We brought from **each** People a witness,
004:130	for **each** of them from His all-reaching bounty:
005:027	Behold! they **each** presented a sacrifice (to Allah):
005:041	who race **each** other into Unbelief: (whether it be)
005:048	To **each** among you have We prescribed
005:051	they are but friends and protectors to **each** other.
005:062	racing **each** other in sin and transgression and
006:065	mutual vengeance-**each** from the other."
006:099	**each** similar (in kind) yet different
006:108	alluring to **each** people its own doings.
006:112	inspiring **each** other with flowery discourses
006:128	"Our Lord! we made profit from **each** other:
006:129	turn to **each** other, because of what they earn.
007:038	until they follow **each** other, all into the Fire.
007:054	**each** seeking the other in rapid succession:
007:160	**each** group knew its own place for water.
008:048	came in sight of **each** other, he turned
008:073	Unless you do this. (Protect **each** other), there would
008:075	rights against **each** other in the Book
009:127	they look at **each** other, (saying), "Doth anyone
010:045	they will recognize **each** other: assuredly those
011:040	We said: "Embark therein, of **each** kind two,
012:025	So they both raced **each** other to the door, and she
012:031	she gave **each** of them a knife: and she
013:002	**each** one runs (its course) for a term appointed.
013:011	For **each** (such person) there are (angels)
013:017	**each** according to its measure:
013:038	For **each** period is an appointment.
014:051	That Allah may requite **each** soul according to its deserts;
015:044	for **each** of those Gates is a (special) class
015:047	(joyfully) facing **each** other on raised couches.
017:088	even it they backed up **each** other with help and support.
018:019	that they might question **each** other.
018:033	**Each** of those gardens brought forth its produce,
019:049	Isaac and Jacob, and **each** one of them We made
020:050	to **each** (created) thing its form, then, gave (it)
020:053	of plants **each** separate from the others.
020:103	In whispers will they consult **each** other:
020:135	Say: "**Each** one (of us), is waiting: wait ye,

EACH (continued)

021:033	**each** in its rounded course.
021:079	to **each** (of them) We gave Judgment and Knowledge;
021:080	to guard you from **each** other's violence:
021:099	But **each** one will abide therein.
022:019	These two antagonists dispute with **each** other about
023:044	so We made them follow **each** other (in punishment):
023:053	**each** party rejoices in that which is with itself.
023:091	**each** god would have taken away what he had created,
024:002	of fornication,-flog **each** of them with a hundred
024:041	**Each** one knows its own (mode of) prayer and praise.
024:058	to move about attending to **each** other: thus does
024:061	salute **each** other-a greeting of blessing and purity
025:039	To **each** one We set forth parables and examples;
025:039	and **each** one We broke to utter annihilation
025:057	that **each** one who will may take a (straight) Path
025:062	and the Day to follow **each** other:
026:061	And when the two bodies saw **each** other, the people
026:063	So it divided, and **each** separate part became like
027:045	they became two factions quarreling with **each** other.
028:048	"Two kinds of sorcery, **each** assisting the other!"
028:066	will not be able (even) to question **each** other.
028:075	And from **each** people shall We draw a witness,
029:025	ye shall disown **each** other and curse **each** other:
029:040	**Each** one of them We seized for his crime:
030:028	Do ye fear them as ye fear **each** other?
030:032	**each** party rejoicing in that which is with itself!
031:029	**each** running its course for a term appointed;
033:006	Blood-relations among **each** other have closer
034:042	they have over **each** other, for profit
035:010	it is He Who exalts **each** Deed of Righteousness.
035:012	Yet from **each** (kind of water) do ye eat flesh fresh
035:013	**each** one runs its course for a term appointed.
035:040	the wrong-doers promise **each** other nothing but
036:032	But **each** one of them all-will be
036:040	**each** (just) swims along in (its own) orbit
037:025	that ye help not **each** other?'"
037:044	Facing **each** other on raised couches.
038:024	are the Partners (in business) who wrong **each** other:
038:048	**each** of them was of the company of the Good.
039:005	(to His law) **each** one follow a course for a
039:029	at variance with **each** other, and a man
040:047	Behold, they will dispute with **each** other in the Fire!
041:012	to **each** heaven its duty and command.
043:048	We showed them Sign after Sign, **each** greater then its
043:060	amongst you, succeeding **each** other on the earth.
044:053	rich brocade, they will face **each** other;
045:007	Woe to **each** sinful imposter.
045:014	(for good or ill) **each** People according to what they
045:022	and in order that **each** soul my find the recompense of
048:029	(but) compassionate amongst **each** other.
049:011	nor defame nor be sarcastic to **each** other,
049:011	nor call **each** other by (offensive) nicknames:
049:012	and spy not on **each** other, nor speak ill of **each** other
049:013	into nations and tribes, that ye may know **each** other
049:013	(not that ye may despise **each** other).
050:014	**each** one (of them) rejected the messengers,
050:021	with **each** will be an (angel) to drive, and an
050:028	with **each** other in My Presence:
051:023	ye can speak intelligently to **each** other.
052:021	(Yet) is **each** individual in pledge for his deeds.
052:025	They will advance to **each** other, engaging in
054:028	**each** one's right to drink being brought forward

EACH (continued)

055:050 In them (**each**) will be two Springs flowing (free);
055:066 In them (**each**) will be two springs pouring forth
056:016 Reclining on them, facing **each** other.
058:003 should free a slave before they touch **each** other:
058:004 touch **each** other, but if any is unable to do so,
066:004 but if ye back up each other against him, truly Allah
069:010 And disobeyed (**each**) the messenger of their Lord;
070:011 Though they will be put in sight **each** other,-
071:023 "And they have said (to **each** other), `Abandon not
074:040 they will question **each** other,
074:052 Forsooth, **each** one of them wants to be given
080:037 **Each** one of them, that Day, will have
081:014 (Then) shall **each** soul know what it has put forward.
082:005 (Then) shall **each** soul know what it hath sent
083:030 used to wink at **each** other (in mockery);

EAGER

007:187 They ask thee as if thou wert **eager** in search thereof:

EAGERLY

005:052 thou seest how **eagerly** they run about
026:223 They listen **eagerly** and most of them are liars.

EAR

002:261 and each **ear** hath a hundred grains.
005:045 nose for nose, **ear** for **ear**, tooth for tooth, and
009:061 men who molest the Prophet and say, "He is (all) **ear**."
012:047 ye shall leave them in the **ear**,-except a
050:037 or who gives **ear** and earnestly witnesses.

EARLIER

028:043 the Book after We had destroyed the **earlier** generations,
046:010 of Israel testifies to its similarity (with **earlier** scriptures),
051:059 unto the portion of their fellows (of **earlier** generations):

EARLIEST

044:008 and your **earliest** ancestors.
087:018 of the **earliest** (Revelations),-

EARLY

003:017 forgiveness in the **early** hours of the morning
003:121 thou didst leave the household (**early**)
012:016 in the **early** part of the night, weeping.
018:062 "Bring us our **early** meal; truly we have
033:053 (and then) not (so **early** as) to wait
034:012 the Wind (obedient): its **early** morning (stride)
051:018 And in the hours of **early** dawn, they (were found)
054:034 Lut's household: them We delivered by **early** Dawn,-
054:038 **Early** on the morrow an abiding Chastisement

EARN

002:207 gives his life to **earn** the pleasure of Allah;
004:032 and to women what they **earn**:
004:032 to men is allotted what they **earn**,
006:003 the (recompense) which ye **earn** (by your deeds).
006:113 and let them **earn** from it what they may.
006:120 those who **earn** sin will get due recompense
006:129 turn to each other, because of what they **earn**.
031:034 that he will **earn** on the morrow:

EARNED

002:202 To these will be allotted what they have **earned**.
002:264 do nothing with aught they have **earned**.
002:267 good things which ye have (honorably) **earned**,
002:281 Then shall every soul be paid what it **earned**,
003:025 just what it has **earned**, without
003:161 receive its due whatever it **earned**,
006:158 nor **earned** righteousness through its Faith.
010:008 because of the (evil) they **earned**.

EARNED (continued)

010:011 the ill (they have **earned**) as they
010:027 But those who have **earned** evil will have
010:052 the recompense of what ye **earned**!'"
014:018 no power have they over aught that they have **earned**:
018:058 call them (at once) to account for what they have **earned**,
024:011 (will come the punishment) of the sin that he **earned**,
027:090 that which ye have **earned** by your deeds?"
030:041 the hands of men have **earned**, that (Allah)
039:024 "Taste ye (the fruits of) what ye **earned**!"
039:061 for they have **earned** salvation:
040:017 That Day will every soul be requited for what it **earned**;
041:017 seized them, because of what they had **earned**.
042:022 on account of what they have **earned**,
042:034 because of the (evil) which (the men) have **earned**:
045:010 no profit to them is anything they may have **earned**,
045:014 each People according to what they have **earned**.
045:022 each soul may find the recompense of what it has **earned**,

EARNEST

017:109 and it increases their (**earnest**) humility.

EARNESTLY

003:061 then let us **earnestly** pray.
003:079 and ye have studied it **earnestly**."
047:024 Do they not then **earnestly** seek to understand
062:009 (the Day of Assembly), hasten **earnestly** to the
080:008 But as to him who came to thee striving **earnestly**,

EARNESTNESS

004:142 they stand without **earnestness**, to be seen

EARNINGS

006:120 due recompense for their "**earnings**."

EARNS

002:286 and it suffers every ill that it **earns**.
002:286 It gets every good that it **earns**,
004:111 if anyone **earns** sin, he **earns** it against his own soul:
004:112 But if anyone earns a fault or a sin and throws
042:023 And if anyone **earns** any good, We shall

EARS

002:019 in their **ears** to keep out the stunning
002:261 it groweth seven **ears**,
004:119 I will order them to slit the **ears** of cattle,
006:025 and deafness in their **ears**; if they
007:179 and **ears** wherewith they hear not.
007:195 Or **ears** to hear with? Say: "Call your
012:043 and seven green **ears** of corn, and seven
012:046 ones devour, and of seven green **ears** of corn and
016:108 Those are they whose hearts, **ears**, and eyes
017:046 and deafness into their **ears**:
018:011 Then We drew (a veil) over their **ears**, for a
018:057 and over their **ears**, deafness.
022:046 thus learn wisdom and their **ears** may thus
031:007 as if there were deafness in both his **ears**:
037:008 (So) they should not strain their **ears** in the direction
041:005 invite us, and in our **ears** is a deadness,
041:044 there is a deafness in their **ears**, and it
069:012 and that **ears** (that should hear the tale and) retain its
071:007 they have (only) thrust their fingers into their **ears**,

EARTH

002:011 "Make not mischief on the **earth**,"
002:022 who has made the **earth** your couch,
002:027 and do mischief on **earth**:
002:029 for you all things that are on **earth**;
002:030 "I will create a vicegerent on **earth**."

EARTH (continued)

002:033	that I know the secrets of the heaven and **earth**,
002:036	On **earth** will be your dwelling place
002:060	evil nor mischief on the (face of the) **earth**.
002:061	to produce for us of what the **earth** groweth,
002:107	of the heavens and the **earth**?
002:116	that is in the heavens and the **earth**:
002:117	the heavens and the **earth**:
002:164	of the heavens and the **earth**;
002:164	between the sky and the **earth**;
002:164	kinds that He scatters through the **earth**;
002:164	gives therewith to an **earth** that is dead;
002:168	O ye people! eat of what is on **earth**,
002:205	to spread mischief through the **earth**
002:251	the **earth** would indeed be full of mischief,
002:255	His are all things in the heavens and on **earth**.
002:255	over the heavens and the **earth**,
002:267	and of the fruits of the **earth** which We
002:284	that is in the heavens and on **earth**.
003:005	is hidden on **earth** or in the heavens.
003:029	in the heavens, and what is on **earth**.
003:083	While all creatures in the heavens and on **earth** have,
003:091	as much gold as the **earth** contains,
003:109	that is in the heavens and **earth**:
003:129	that is in the heavens and on **earth**.
003:133	(of the whole) of the heavens and of the **earth**,
003:137	travel through the **earth**, and see what was the end
003:156	through the **earth** or engaged in fighting:
003:180	the heritage of the heavens and the **earth**;
003:189	the dominion of the heavens and the **earth**;
003:190	the heavens and the **earth**, and the
003:191	creation in the heavens and the **earth**,
004:042	wish that the **earth** were made one with them:
004:043	then take for yourselves clean sand (or **earth**),
004:097	"Weak and oppressed were we in the **earth**."
004:097	They say: "Was not the **earth** of Allah spacious
004:100	finds in the **earth** many a refuge.
004:101	When ye travel through the **earth**, there is
004:126	in the heavens and on **earth**: and He
004:131	belong all things in the heavens and on **earth**.
004:131	in the heavens and on **earth**.
004:132	all things in the heavens and on **earth**,
004:170	in the heavens and on **earth**: and Allah
004:171	in the heavens and on **earth**.
005:006	then take for yourselves clean sand or **earth**,
005:017	the dominion of the heavens and the **earth**,
005:017	and all-every one that is on the **earth**?
005:018	the dominion of the heavens and the **earth**, and all
005:036	if they had everything on **earth**, and twice
005:040	the dominion of the heavens and the **earth**?
005:064	but they (ever) strive to do mischief on **earth**.
005:097	of what is in the heavens and on **earth** and that
005:106	journeying through the **earth**, and the chance
005:120	of the heavens and the **earth**, and all
006:001	the heavens and the **earth**, and made the
006:003	And He is Allah in the heavens and on **earth**.
006:006	Generations We had established on the **earth**,
006:011	Say: "Travel through the **earth** and see what was
006:012	is in the heavens and on **earth**?"
006:014	the Maker of the heavens and the **earth**?
006:029	"There is nothing except our life on this **earth**,
006:038	(that lives) on the **earth**, nor a being
006:059	on the **earth** and in the sea.

EARTH (continued)

006:059	the darkness (or depths) of the **earth**,
006:071	wandering bewildered through the **earth**,
006:073	and the **earth** with truth:
006:075	the kingdom of the heavens and the **earth**,
006:079	towards Him Who created the heavens and the **earth**,
006:101	of the heavens and the **earth**: how can
006:116	the common run of those on **earth**, they will
006:165	the inheritors of the **earth**:
007:010	placed you with authority on **earth**, and provided
007:024	On **earth** will be your dwelling-place and your
007:054	and the **earth** in six days, then He
007:056	Do no mischief on the **earth**, after it
007:073	so leave her to graze in Allah's **earth**,
007:074	and refrain from evil and mischief on the **earth**."
007:085	and do no mischief on the **earth** after it
007:096	blessings from heaven and **earth**; but they
007:100	To those who inherit the **earth** in succession
007:128	for the **earth** is Allah's, to give as
007:129	and make you inheritors in the **earth**; that so
007:146	on the **earth** in defiance of right-them will I
007:158	of the heavens and the **earth**: there is
007:168	into sections on this **earth**.
007:176	but he inclined to the **earth**, and followed
007:185	of the heavens and the **earth** and all
007:187	the heavens and the **earth**.
008:063	in the **earth**, couldst thou have produced that
008:073	tumult and oppression on **earth**, and great
009:036	He created the heavens and the **earth**; of them
009:038	ye cling heavily to the **earth**?
009:074	none on **earth** to protect or help them.
009:116	of the heavens and the **earth**.
009:118	that the **earth** seemed constrained to them, for all
010:003	Who created the heavens and the **earth** in six
010:006	in the heavens and the **earth**, are Signs
010:018	in the heaven or on **earth**?-Glory to Him! and far
010:023	through the **earth** in defiance of right!
010:024	arises the produce of the **earth**-which provides
010:024	(it grows) till the **earth** is clad with its golden
010:031	(in life) from the sky and from the **earth**?
010:054	if it possessed all that is on **earth**, would fain
010:055	the heavens and on **earth**?
010:061	on the **earth** or in heaven.
010:066	all creatures, in the heavens and on **earth**.
010:068	His are all things in the heavens and on **earth**!
010:073	and We made them inherit (the **earth**), while We
010:083	was mighty on the **earth** and one who
010:099	all who are on **earth**!
010:101	in the heavens and on **earth**"; but neither
011:006	There is no moving creature on **earth** but its
011:007	and the **earth** in six Days-and His Throne
011:020	They will not escape in **earth**, nor have
011:040	and the fountains of the **earth** gushed forth!
011:044	Then the word went forth: "O **earth**! swallow up
011:061	the **earth** and settled you therein:
011:064	leave her to feed On Allah's (free) **earth**,
011:107	the heavens and the **earth** endure, except as
011:108	the **earth** endure, except as the Lord willeth:
011:116	men from mischief in the **earth** (but there were none)
011:123	belong the unseen (secrets) of the heavens and the **earth**,
012:101	O Thou Creator of the heavens and the **earth**!
012:105	and the **earth** do they pass by?
012:109	through the **earth**, and see what was the end of

EARTH (continued)

013:003   And it is He Who spread out the **earth**, and set
013:004   And in the **earth** are tracts (diverse though)
013:015   in the heavens and the **earth** do prostrate
013:016   the Lord and Sustainer of the heavens and the **earth**?"
013:017   the good of mankind remains on the **earth**.
013:018   in the heavens and on **earth**, and as much
013:031   or the **earth** were cloven asunder, or the dead
013:033 '   inform Him of something He knoweth not on **earth**,
014:002   in the heavens and on **earth**! But alas
014:008   ye and all on **earth** together,-yet is Allah
014:010   of the heavens and the **earth**? It is He
014:019   created the Heavens and the **earth** in Truth?
014:026   from the surface of the **earth**:
014:032   the heavens and the **earth** and sendeth down
014:038   from Allah, whether on **earth** or in heaven.
014:048   to a different **Earth**, and so will be the Heavens,
014:048 ·   One day the **Earth** will be changed to a
015:019   And the **earth** We have spread out (like a carpet);
015:039   to them on the **earth**, and I will
015:085   We created not the heavens, the **earth**, and all
016:003   and the **earth** with truth far is He above having
016:013   And the things on this **earth** which He has
016:015   And He has set up on the **earth** mountains standing
016:036   So travel through the **earth**, and see what was
016:045   will not cause the **earth** to swallow them up,
016:049   is in the heavens and on **earth**, whether moving
016:052   the heavens and on **earth**, and to Him
016:061   on the (**earth**), a single living creature: but He
016:065   to the **earth** after its death: verily in this
016:069   Then to eat of all the produce (of the **earth**),
016:073   with anything in heavens or **earth**, and cannot
016:077   of the heavens and the **earth**.
017:004   on the **earth** and be elated with mighty arrogance
017:037   Nor walk on the **earth** with insolence: for thou
017:037   rend the **earth** asunder, nor reach the mountains
017:044   The seven heavens and the **earth**, and all
017:055   all beings that are in the heavens and on **earth**:
017:068   beneath the **earth** when ye are on land, or that
017:090   to gush forth for us from the **earth**,
017:095   on **earth**, angels walking about in peace and quite,
017:099   Who created the heavens and the **earth**, has power
017:102   and the **earth** as eye-opening evidence:
017:103   from the face of the **earth**: but We
018:007   That which is on **earth** We have made but as
018:008   Verily what is on **earth** We shall make but as
018:014   "Our Lord is the Lord of the heavens and of the **earth**:
018:026   the heavens and the **earth**: how clearly
018:047   and thou wilt see the **earth** as a level stretch,
018:051   and the **earth**, nor (even) their own creation:
018:084   Verily We established his power on **earth**, and We
018:094   do great mischief on **earth**:
019:040   It is We Who will inherit the **earth**, and all
019:065   Lord of the heavens and of the **earth**, and of
019:090   the **earth** to split asunder, and the
019:093   and the **earth** but must come to The Most Gracious
020:004   the **earth** and the heavens on high.
020:006   in the heavens and on **earth**, and all
020:053   the **earth** like a carpet spread out; has enabled
020:055   From the (**earth**) did We create you, and into
021:004   (every) word (spoken) in the heavens and on **earth**:
021:016   the heavens and the **earth** and all that is between!
021:019   in the heavens and on **earth**: even those

EARTH (continued)

021:021   gods from the **earth** who can raise (the dead)?
021:022   and the **earth**, other gods besides Allah,
021:030   the heavens and the **earth** were joined together
021:031   And We have set on the **earth** mountains standing
021:056   of the heavens and the **earth**, He Who
021:105   shall inherit the **earth**."
022:005   And (further), thou seest the **earth** barren and
022:018   and on **earth**,-the sun, the moon, the stars;
022:063   and forthwith the **earth** becomes clothed with
022:064   the heavens and on **earth**: for verily
022:065   on the **earth** except by His leave: for Allah
022:065   on the **earth**, and the ships that sail through
022:070   Allah knows all that is in heaven and on **earth**?
023:071   and the **earth**, and all beings therein would
023:079   And He Has multiplied you through the **earth**,
023:084   Say: "To whom belong the **earth** and all
023:112   did ye stay on **earth**?"
024:035   Allah is the Light of the heavens and the **earth**.
024:041   and on **earth** do celebrate, and the
024:042   of the heavens and the **earth**; and to
024:057   can escape in the **earth** their abode is the Fire,-
024:064   doth belong whatever is in the heavens and on **earth**.
025:002   of the heavens and the **earth**: no son
025:006   in the heavens and the **earth**: verily He
025:059   and the **earth** and all that is between, in six
025:063   who walk on the **earth** in humility, and when
026:007   Do they not look at the **earth**,-how many
026:024   of the heavens and the **earth**, and all
027:025   in the heavens and the **earth**, and knows
027:060   and the **earth**, and who sends you down rain from
027:061   Or, who has made the **earth** firm to live in;
027:062   and makes you (mankind) inheritors of the **earth**?
027:064   you sustenance from heaven and **earth**?
027:065   Say: None in the heavens or on **earth**, except
027:069   Say: "Go ye through the **earth** and see what has
027:075   And there is nothing hidden in heaven or **earth**,
027:082   We shall bring forth from the **earth** a beast
027:087   and those who are on **earth**, except such as Allah will
028:081   Then We caused the **earth** to swallow up him
028:082   He could have caused the **earth** to swallow us up!
028:083   high-handedness or mischief on **earth**:
029:020   Say: "Travel through the **earth** and see how
029:022   "Not on **earth** nor in heaven will ye be able
029:036   nor commit evil on the **earth**, with intent
029:039   on the **earth**; yet they cold not overreach (Us).
029:040   some We caused the **earth** to swallow up; and some
029:044   Allah created the heavens and the **earth** in truth:
029:052   He knows what is in the heavens and on **earth**."
029:056   truly, spacious is My **Earth**: therefore serve
029:061   and the **earth** and subjected the sun and the moon
029:063   and gives life therewith to the **earth** after its
030:008   the heavens and the **earth**, and all
030:009   Do they not travel through the **earth**, and see
030:018   Yea, to Him be praise, in the heavens and on **earth**;
030:019   and Who gives life to the **earth** after it is dead:
030:022   of the heavens and the **earth**, and the
030:024   and with it gives life to the **earth** after it
030:025   by a single call, from the **earth**, behold, ye
030:025   that heaven and **earth** stand by His command:
030:026   is in the heavens and on **earth**: all are
030:027   and the **earth**: for He is
030:042   Say: "Travel through the **earth** and see

EARTH (continued)

030:050	How He gives life to the **earth** after its death:
031:010	and produce on the **earth** every kind
031:010	He set on the **earth** mountains standing firm,
031:016	or on **earth**, Allah will bring it forth: for Allah
031:018	Nor walk in insolence through the **earth**:
031:020	and on **earth**, and has made His bounties flow to
031:025	who it is that created the heavens and the **earth**.
031:026	To Allah belong all things in heaven and **earth**:
031:027	And if all the trees on **earth** were pens and the
032:004	and the **earth**, and all between them, in six Days,
032:005	He directs the affairs from the heavens to the **earth**:
032:010	hidden and lost, in the **earth**, shall we
033:072	to the Heavens and the **Earth** and the Mountains:
034:001	all things in the heavens and on **earth**: to Him
034:002	He knows all that goes into the **earth**, and all
034:003	hidden the least little atom in the Heavens or on **earth**:
034:009	We could cause the **earth** to swallow them up,
034:009	of the sky and the **earth**?
034:014	of the **earth**, which kept (slowly) gnawing away
034:022	of an atom,-in the heavens or on **earth**:
034:024	from the heavens and the **earth**?"
035:001	and the **earth**, Who made the angels messengers
035:003	you Sustenance from heaven or **earth**?
035:009	the **earth** therewith after its death:
035:038	(all) the hidden things of the heavens and the **earth**:
035:039	you inheritors in the **earth**: so, he who
035:040	they have created in the (wide) **earth**.
035:041	and the **earth**, lest they cease (to function):
035:044	Do they not travel through the **earth**, and see
035:044	in the heavens or on **earth**: for He
035:045	of the (**earth**) a single living creature: but He
036:033	A Sign for them is the **earth** that is dead;
036:036	the **earth** produces, as well as their own (human)
036:081	and the **earth** able to create the like thereof?"-
037:005	Lord of the heavens and of the **earth**, and all
037:051	"I had an intimate companion (on the **earth**),
037:077	And made his progeny to endure (on this **earth**);
038:010	of the heavens and the **earth** and all between?
038:026	a vicegerent on **earth**: so judge
038:027	We create heaven and **earth** and all between!
038:028	the same as those who do mischief on **earth**?
038:066	"The Lord of the heavens and the **earth**, and all
039:005	He created the heavens and the **earth** in true
039:010	Spacious is Allah's **earth**!
039:021	and leads it through springs in the **earth**?
039:038	that created the heavens and the **earth**, they would
039:044	of the heavens and the **earth**: in the end,
039:046	Say: "O Allah! Creator of the heavens and the **earth**!
039:047	there is on **earth**, and as much more, (in vain)
039:063	and the **earth**: and those who reject the Signs
039:067	of the **earth** will be but His handful, and the
039:068	and on **earth** will swoon, except such
039:069	And the **Earth** will shine with the light
040:021	Do they not travel through the **earth** and see
040:057	and the **earth** is a greater (matter) than the
040:064	the **earth** as a resting place, and the
040:075	on the **earth** in things other than the Truth,
040:082	Do they not travel through the **earth** and see
041:009	deny Him Who created the **earth** in two Days?
041:010	and bestowed blessing on the **earth**, and measured
041:010	He set on the (**earth**), mountains standing firm,
041:011	He said to it and to the **earth**: "Come ye

EARTH (continued)

041:039	gives life to the (dead) **earth** can surely
041:039	thou seest the **earth** humble; but when
041:053	in the (furthest) regions (of the **earth**), and in
042:004	in the heavens and on **earth**: and He is
042:005	for (all) beings on **earth**: Behold! Verily
042:011	and the **earth**: He had made for you pairs from
042:012	and the **earth**: He enlarges and restricts
042:027	all bounds through the **earth**; but He
042:029	of the heavens and the **earth**, and the living
042:031	Nor can ye escape through the **earth**; nor have
042:049	belongs the dominion of the heavens and the **earth**.
042:053	whatever is in the heavens and whatever is on **earth**.
043:009	'Who created the heavens and the **earth**?'
043:010	the **earth** spread out, and has
043:060	amongst you, succeeding each other on the **earth**.
043:082	and the **earth**, the Lord of the Throne! He is
043:084	and God on **earth**; and He is Full of Wisdom
043:085	and the **earth**, and all between them: with Him
044:007	The Lord of the heavens and the **earth** and all
044:029	And neither heaven nor **earth** shed a tear over them:
044:038	the **earth**, and all between them, merely in
045:003	Verily in the heavens and the **earth**, are Signs
045:004	are scattered (through the **earth**), are Signs
045:005	and revives therewith the **earth** after its death,
045:013	and on **earth**: behold, in that are Signs
045:022	Allah created the heavens and the **earth** for just
045:027	of the heavens and the **earth**, and the
045:036	the **earth**, Lord and Cherisher of all the worlds!
045:037	in the heavens and the **earth**: and He
046:003	We created not the heavens and the **earth** and all
046:004	they have created on **earth**, or have
046:020	on **earth** without just cause, and that
046:032	he cannot escape in the **earth**, and no
046:033	Who created the heavens and the **earth**, and never
047:010	Do they not travel through the **earth**, and see
048:004	of the heavens and the **earth**; and Allah
048:007	of the heavens and the **earth**; and Allah
048:014	of the heavens and the **earth**: He forgives
049:016	is in the heavens and on **earth**: He has
049:018	of the heavens and the **earth**: and Allah
050:004	already know how much of them the **earth** takes away:
050:007	And the **earth**-We have spread it out, and set
050:038	We created the heavens and the **earth** and all
050:044	The Day when the **Earth** will be rent asunder,
051:020	On the **earth** are Signs for those of assured Faith,
051:023	Then, by the Lord of heaven and **earth**, this is
051:048	(spacious) **earth**: how excellently We do spread out!
052:036	Or did they create the heavens and the **earth**?
053:031	in the heavens and on **earth**: so that
053:032	you out of the **earth**, and when
054:012	And We caused the **earth** to gush forth with springs,
055:010	the **earth** for (His) creatures:
055:026	All that is on **earth** will perish:
055:029	and on **earth**: every day in (new) Splendour
055:033	the zones of the heavens and the **earth**, pass ye!
056:004	When the **earth** shall be shaken to its depths,
057:001	and on **earth**,-declares the Praises and Glory
057:002	of the heavens and the **earth**: it is He
057:004	within the **earth** and what comes forth out of it,
057:004	and the **earth** in six Days, then He
057:005	of the heavens and the **earth**: and all
057:010	of the heavens and the **earth**. Not equal

EARTH (continued)

057:017 life to the **earth** after its death! Already have
057:021 of heaven and **earth**, prepared for those
057:022 No misfortune can happen on **earth** or in your
058:007 (all) that is in the heavens and on **earth**?
059:001 and on **earth**, declares the Praises and Glory
059:024 and on **earth**, doth declare His Praises and Glory:
061:001 and on **earth**, declares the Praises and Glory
062:001 and on **earth**, doth declare the Praises and Glory
063:007 of the heavens and the **earth**; but the Hypocrites
064:001 and on **earth**, doth declare the Praises and Glory
064:003 and the **earth** with the truth, and has
064:004 and on **earth**: and He knows what ye conceal
065:012 and of the **earth** a similar number, through the
067:015 It is He Who has made the **earth** manageable for you,
067:016 to be swallowed up by the **earth** when it shakes
067:024 you through the **earth**, and to
067:030 be some morning lost (in the underground **earth**),
069:014 And the **earth** is moved, and its mountains,
070:014 And all, all that is on **earth**,-so it
071:017 from the **earth**, growing (gradually),
071:018 "'And in the End He will return you into the (**earth**),
071:019 "'And Allah has made the **earth** for you as a carpet
071:026 a single one on **earth**!
072:010 is intended to those on **earth**, or whether
072:012 can by no means frustrate Allah throughout the **earth**,
073:014 The Day the **earth** and the mountains will be
077:025 Have We not made the **earth** (as a place)
078:006 Have We not made the **earth** as a wide expanse,
078:037 and the **earth**, and all between,-The Most
079:030 And the **earth**, moreover; hath He
080:026 And We split the **earth** in fragments,
084:003 And when the **Earth** is flattened out,
085:009 of the heavens and the **earth**! And Allah
086:012 And by the **Earth** which opens out
088:020 And at the **Earth**, how it is spread out?
089:021 Nay! When the **earth** is pounded to powder,
091:006 By the **Earth** and its (wide) expanse;
099:001 When the **Earth** is shaken to her
099:002 And the **Earth** throws up her burden (from within),

EARTH'S

018:045 the **earth's** vegetation absorbs it, but soon

EARTHQUAKE

007:078 So the **earthquake** took them unawares, and they
007:091 But the **earthquake** took them unawares, and they
067:016 when it shakes (as in an **earthquake**)?

EASE

003:168 while they themselves sit (at **ease**):
018:016 of your affair towards comfort and **ease**."
020:026 "**Ease** my task for me;
023:018 to drain it off (with **ease**).
028:058 which exulted in their life (of **ease** and plenty)!
038:051 Therein will they recline (at **ease**); therein can
051:003 And those that flow with **ease** and gentleness;
052:020 They will recline (with **ease**) on couches
092:007 for him the path to **Ease**.

EAST

002:115 To Allah belong the **East** and the West;
002:142 Say: To Allah belong both **East** and West:
002:177 ye turn your faces toward **East** or West;
002:258 Allah that causeth the sun to rise from the **East**,
007:137 inheritors of lands in both **East** and West,-
019:016 to a place in the **East**.

EAST (continued)

024:035 neither of the **East** nor of the West, whose Oil
026:028 (Moses) said: "Lord of the **East** and the West,
043:038 the distance of **East** and West!" Ah! Evil
070:040 of all points in the **East** and the West that We
073:009 (He is) Lord of the **East** and the West: there is

EASTS

055:017 (He is) Lord of the two **Easts** and Lord

EASY

002:280 grant him time till it is **easy** for him to repay.
004:030 and **easy** it is for Allah.
004:169 and this to Allah is **easy**.
009:042 (in sight), and the journey **easy**, they would
017:028 yet speak to them a word of **easy** kindness.
018:088 a goodly reward, and **easy** will be his task as We
019:009 thy Lord saith, "That is **easy** for Me: I did
019:021 thy Lord saith, 'That is **easy** for Me:
019:097 So have We made the (Qur'an) **easy** in thine
022:070 and that is **easy** for Allah.
025:046 towards Ourselves,- a contraction by **easy** stages.
029:019 truly that is **easy** for Allah.
030:027 and for Him it is most **easy**.
033:019 of none effect: and that is **easy** of Allah.
033:030 and that is **easy** for Allah.
035:011 All this is **easy** to Allah.
044:058 Verily, We have made this (Qur'an) **easy**, in thy
050:044 that will be a gathering together,-quite **easy** for Us.
054:017 made the Qur'an **easy** to understand and remember:
054:022 made the Qur'an **easy** to understand and remember:
054:032 made the Qur'an **easy** to understand and remember:
054:040 made the Qur'an **easy** to understand and remember:
055:054 will be Near (and **easy** of reach).
057:022 that is truly **easy** for Allah:
064:007 And that is **easy** for Allah."
065:004 He will make things **easy** for them.
073:020 of the Qur'an as much as may be **easy** for you.
073:020 as may be **easy** (for you); and establish
074:010 Far from **easy** for those without Faith.
076:014 will hang low **easy** to reach.
084:008 Soon will his account be taken by an **easy** reckoning,
087:008 And We will make it **easy** for thee (to follow)

EAT

002:035 and **eat** of the bountiful things therein
002:057 saying: "**Eat** of the good things
002:058 and **eat** of the plenty therein as ye wish;
002:060 So **eat** and drink of the sustenance
002:168 O ye people! **eat** of what is on earth,
002:172 O ye who believe! **eat** of the good things
002:187 and **eat** and drink,
002:188 And do not **eat** up your property
002:188 with intent that ye may **eat** up wrongfully
003:049 and I declare to you what ye **eat**,
004:010 Those who unjustly **eat** up the property of orphans,
004:010 **eat** up a fire into their own bodies:
004:029 O ye who believe! **eat** not up your property
005:004 **eat** what they catch for you, but pronounce the name
005:075 They had both to **eat** their (daily) food.
005:088 **Eat** of the things which Allah hath
005:113 to **eat** thereof and satisfy our hearts, and to know
006:118 So **eat** of (meats) on which Allah's name
006:119 Why should ye not **eat** of (meats) on which
006:121 **Eat** not of (meats) on which Allah's name
006:138 and none should **eat** of them except those

EAT (continued)

006:141 eat of their fruit in their season, but render
006:142 eat what Allah hath provided for you,
006:145 by one who wishes to eat it, unless it
007:031 eat and drink: but waste not by excess,
007:160 (saying): "Eat of the good things We have
007:161 "Dwell in this town and eat therein as ye wish,
012:041 and the birds will eat from off his
012:047 except a little, of which ye shall eat.
013:004 more excellent than others to eat.
015:003 Leave them alone, to eat and enjoy and let
016:005 and numerous benefits, and of their (meat) ye eat.
016:014 that ye may eat thereof flesh that is
016:069 Then to eat of all the produce (of the earth),
016:114 So eat of the sustenance which Allah
019:026 "So eat and drink and cool (thine) eye.
020:054 Eat (for yourselves) and pasture your cattle:
020:081 (Saying): "Eat of the good things We have
022:028 then eat ye thereof and feed the distressed
022:036 eat ye thereof, and feed such as (beg not but)
023:019 and of them ye eat (and have enjoyment),-
023:021 and of their (meat) ye eat;
024:061 on you, whether ye eat in company or separately.
024:061 that ye should eat in your own houses, or those
034:015 "Eat of the Sustenance (provided) by your Lord,
035:012 (kind of water) do ye eat flesh fresh and tender,
036:033 and produce grain therefrom, of which ye do eat.
036:072 carry them and some they eat:
037:066 Truly they will eat thereof and fill
037:091 and said, "Will ye not eat (of the offerings before you)?
043:073 of fruit, from which ye shall eat.
047:012 enjoy (this world) and eat as cattle eat; and the
049:012 to eat the flesh of his dead brother?
051:027 He said, "Will ye not eat?"
051:028 (When they did not eat), He conceived
052:019 "Eat and drink ye, with profit and health,
069:024 "Eat ye and drink ye, with full satisfaction;
069:037 "Which none do eat but those in sin."
077:043 "Eat ye and drink ye to your heart's content:
077:046 (O ye Unjust!) Eat ye and enjoy yourselves (but)

EATEN

005:003 (partly) eaten by a wild animal;
005:066 they would have eaten both from above them
006:145 any (meat) forbidden to be eaten by one
105:005 and straw (of which the corn) has been eaten up.

EATING

005:062 transgression and their eating of things forbidden.
005:063 sinful words and eating things forbidden?
012:036 and birds are eating thereof."

EATS

023:033 he eats and drinks of what ye drink.
025:007 is this, who eats food, and walks

ECHO

034:010 "O ye Mountains! echo ye back the Praises of Allah

EDIFICES

015:082 (their) edifices, (feeling themselves) secure.

EFFECT

002:083 the children of Israel (to this effect):
002:084 your Covenant (to this effect):
002:143 make your faith of no effect.
004:018 Of no effect is the repentance of those
007:118 And all that they did was made of no effect.

EFFECT (continued)

010:081 of no effect: for Allah prospereth not the work
011:016 and of no effect are the deeds that they do!
033:019 and so Allah has made their deeds of none effect:
042:044 say: "Is there any way (to effect) a return?"
047:028 so He made their deeds of no effect.
047:032 their deeds of no effect.

EFFECTED

033:014 And if an entry had been effected to them

EFFORTS

007:202 and never relax (their efforts).
018:104 "Those whose efforts have been wasted in this life,

EGGS

037:049 As if they were (delicate) eggs closely guarded.

EGYPT

010:087 for your People in Egypt, make your dewllings
012:021 The man in Egypt who bought him, said to his wife:
012:043 The king (of Egypt) said: "I do see (in a vision)
012:094 When the Caravan left (Egypt), their father
012:099 and said: "Enter ye Egypt (all) in safety
043:051 the dominion of Egypt belong to me, (witness)

EGYPTIANS

012:074 (The Egyptians) said: "What then shall be

EIGHT

006:143 (Take) eight (head of cattle) in (four) pairs:
028:027 on condition that thou serve me for eight years,
039:006 and He sent down for you eight head of cattle in pairs:
069:007 seven nights and eight days in succession:
069:017 and eight will, that Day, bear the Throne

EIGHTH

004:012 but if ye leave a child, they get an eighth;
018:022 the dog being the eighth.

EIGHTY

024:004 flog them with eighty stripes; and reject

EITHER

002:196 (he should) in compensation either fast,
002:229 the parties should either hold together
002:229 there is no blame on either of them
002:230 no blame on either of them if they re-unite,
002:231 either take them back on equitable terms
004:071 And either go forth in parties or go
005:042 either judge between them, or decline to interfere.
005:076 no power either to harm or benefit you?
009:008 the ties either of kinship or of covenant?
009:010 the ties either of kinship or of covenant!
009:052 But we can expect for you either that Allah
012:037 (in due course) to feed either of you I will
013:016 such as have no power either for good or for
018:086 (thou hast authority), either to punish them,
019:075 (being fulfilled)-either in punishment or in
020:042 and slacken not, either of you, in keeping Me in
020:089 and that it had no power either to harm
028:049 which is a better Guide than either of them,
029:008 but if they (either of them) strive (to force) thee to
034:024 it is that either we or ye are on right
043:031 in either of the two (Chief) cities?"
047:004 therefore (is the time for) either generosity or ransom:
059:006 with either cavalry or camelry:
065:002 either take them back on equitable
072:013 has no fear, either of a short (account) or of

ELATED

009:025 your great numbers elated you, but they

ELATED (continued)
017:004 on the earth and be **elated** with mighty arrogance
028:004 Truly Pharaoh **elated** himself in the land
ELBOWS
005:006 (and arms) to the **elbows**; rub your heads
ELDERLY
024:060 Such **elderly** women as are past the prospect
ELECT
038:047 of the company of the **Elect** and the Good.
ELEMENT
063:008 surely the more honourable (**element**) will expel
ELEPHANT
105:001 with the Companions of the **Elephant**?
ELEVATED
007:176 We should have **elevated** him with Our Signs; but he
ELEVEN
012:004 "O my father! I did see **eleven** stars and the
ELIAS
006:085 And Zakariya and John, and Jesus and **Elias**:
037:123 So also was **Elias** among those sent (by us).
037:130 "Peace and salutation to such as **Elias**!"
ELISHA
006:086 And Isma'il and **Elisha**, and Jonas, and Lot:
038:048 And commemorate Isma'il, **Elisha**, and Zul-Kifl:
ELOQUENT
028:034 he is more **eloquent** in speech than I: so send
ELSE
002:094 and not for anyone **else**,
002:211 substitutes (something **else**),
002:251 and taught him whatever (**else**) He willed.
003:073 revelation be sent to someone (**else**) like unto that
004:048 but He forgiveth anything **else**, to whom
005:108 or **else** they would fear that other oaths
007:088 or **else** ye (thou and they) shall have
007:098 Or **else** did they feel secure against its
015:023 remain Inheritors (after all **else** passes away).
021:100 nor will they there hear (aught **else**).
031:030 and because whatever **else** they invoke besides
089:025 such as none (**else**) can inflict,
EMANCIPATION
024:033 (for **emancipation**) give them such a deed if you
EMBARK
011:040 We said: "**Embark** therein, of each kind two,
011:041 So he said: "**Embark** ye on the Ark, in the
011:042 "O my son! **embark** with us, and be
029:065 Now, if they **embark** on a boat, they call
EMBARKED
023:028 And when thou hast **embarked** on the Ark-
EMBASSY
027:036 Now when (the **embassy**) came to Solomon, he said:
EMBRACE
036:064 "**Embrace** ye the (Fire) this Day, for that
EMBRACED
049:017 that they have **embraced** Islam.
EMBRACEST
040:007 "Our Lord! Thou **embracest** all things, in Mercy
EMIGRATE
008:072 who believed but did not **emigrate** ye owe
008:072 to them until they **emigrate**; but if
008:074 Those who believe, and **emigrate**, and fight
008:075 and **emigrate**, and fight for the Faith in your

EMIGRATE (continued)
009:020 Those who believe, and **emigrate** and strive
EMIGRATED
008:072 Those who believed, and **emigrated** and fought
EMINENCE
021:010 a book which We give you **eminence**.
EMIT
056:058 Do ye then see? The (human Seed) that ye **emit**,-
EMITTED
075:037 Was he not a drop of sperm **emitted** (in lowly form)?
086:006 He is created from a drop **emitted**-
EMPHASIS
009:065 they declare (with **emphasis**): "We were only
EMPLOY
028:026 to **employ** is the (man) who is strong and trusty."
EMPLOYED
009:060 and those **employed** to administer the (funds):
EMPTY
084:004 and becomes (clean) **empty**,
105:005 an **empty** field of stalks and straw,
EMULATION
003:114 and they (hasten in **emulation**) in (all)
EN MASSE
100:005 the midst (of the foe) **en masse**;-
ENABLE
023:029 for Thou art the Best to **enable** us to disembark."
023:029 "O my Lord! **enable** me to disembark with Thy blessing:
ENABLED
020:053 has **enabled** you to go about therein by roads
ENABLETH
010:022 He it is Who **enableth** you to traverse through
ENCHANTER
075:027 "Who is a **enchanter** (to restore him)?"
ENCIRCLED
011:008 completely **encircled** by that which they
039:048 be (completely) **encircled** by that which they
045:033 and they will be completely **encircled** by that
046:026 (completely) **encircled** by that which they used
ENCLOSE
006:143 which the wombs of the two females **enclose**?
006:144 which the wombs of the two females **enclose**?-
ENCLOSED
024:035 a Lamp: the Lamp **enclosed** in Glass: the glass
078:032 Gardens **enclosed**, and Grapevines;
080:030 And **enclosed** Gardens, dense with lofty trees,
ENCLOSING
055:011 producing spathes (**enclosing** dates);
ENCOMPASS
017:060 thy Lord doth **encompass** mankind round about:
029:054 Hell will **encompass** the rejecters of Faith!-
041:054 that doth **encompass** all things!
085:020 But Allah doth **encompass** them from behind!
ENCOMPASSED
018:042 So his fruits were **encompassed** (with ruin),
040:045 the Chastisement **encompassed** on all sides the People
ENCOMPASSES
072:028 and He **encompasses** all that is with them, and takes
ENCOMPASSETH
004:126 and He it is that **encompasseth** all things.
005:054 and Allah **encompasseth** all, and He
011:092 But verily my Lord **encompasseth** all that ye do!

ENCOUNTER
052:045 they **encounter** that Day of theirs, wherein they
070:042 and play about, until they **encounter** that Day

ENCOUNTERED
002:214 They **encountered** suffering and adversity,
003:143 for death before ye **encountered** it:

ENCOURAGE
069:034 "And would not **encourage** the feeding
089:018 Nor do ye **encourage** one another to feed the poor!-

ENCOURAGES
107:003 And **encourages** not the feeding of the indigent.

ENCRUSTED
056:015 (They will be) on couches **encrusted** (with gold and

END
002:285 and to Thee is the **end** of all journeys."
003:072 but reject it at the **end** of the day:
003:137 what was the **end** of those who rejected Truth.
006:011 what was the **end** of those who rejected Truth."
006:038 gathered to their Lord in the **end**.
006:060 in the **end** unto Him will be your return,
006:070 such is (the **end** of) those who deliver themselves
006:108 In the **end** will they return to their Lord and He
006:135 whose **end** will be (best) in the Hereafter:
006:159 He will in the **end** tell them the truth
006:164 Your return in the **end** is toward Allah: He will
007:084 then see what was the **end** of those who
007:086 And see what was the **end** of those who did mischief.
007:103 so see what was the **end** of those
007:128 and the **end** is (best) for the righteous.
007:185 nigh drawing to an **end**?
008:036 but in the **end** they will have (only)
009:004 to the **end** of their term: for Allah
009:094 in the **end** will ye be brought back to Him
010:010 and the **end** of their prayer will be: "Praise be to
010:023 in the **end**, to Us your return,
010:039 but see what was the **end** of those who did wrong!
010:073 Then see what was the **end** of those who
010:103 In the **end** We deliver Our messengers
011:048 but in the **end** will a grievous Chastisement
011:049 for the **End** is for those who are righteous.
012:083 them (back) all to me (in the **end**).
012:109 the **end** of those before them?
013:035 and the **End** of Unbelievers is the Fire.
013:035 such is the **End** of the Righteous;
013:042 who gets home in the **End**.
016:036 what was the **end** of those who denied (the Truth).
017:018 in the **end** have We provided Hell for them:
022:033 in the **end** their place of sacrifice is near the Ancient
022:041 the **end** (and decision) of (all) affairs.
022:048 In the **end** I punished them.
027:014 so see what was the **end** of those who
027:051 Then see what was the **end** of their plot!-
027:069 what has been the **end** of those guilty (of sin)."
028:020 from the furthest **end** of the City. He said:
028:037 from Him and whose **End** will be best in the
028:040 now behold what was the **End** of those
028:083 and the **End** is (best) for the righteous.
029:057 in the **end** to Us shall ye be brought back.
030:009 and see what was the **End** of those before them?
030:010 In the long run evil will be the **End** of those
030:042 and see what was the **End** of those before (you):
031:015 in the **End** the return of you all is to Me,
031:024 in the **end** shall We drive them

END (continued)
034:026 and will in the **end** decide the matter
035:026 In the **end** did I punish those who rejected Faith:
035:044 and see what was the **End** of those before them,-
037:073 Then see what was the **end** of those
038:003 In the **end** they cried (for mercy)
038:010 and means (to reach that **end**)!
039:007 In the **End**, to your Lord is your return, when He
039:031 In the **End** will ye (all) dispute on
039:044 in the **End**, it is to Him that ye shall
040:021 and see what was the **End** of those before them?
040:025 but the plots of Unbelievers (**end**) in nothing
040:082 and see what was the **end** of those before them?
043:025 now see what was the **end** of those who
043:077 thy Lord put and **end** to us!" He will say, "Nay,
044:028 Thus (was their **end**)! And We
045:015 In the **end** will ye (all) be brought
047:010 and see what was the **End** of those before them
058:007 they be: in the **end** will He tell them what
059:017 The **end** of both will be that they
065:009 and the **End** of their conduct was Perdition.
069:027 "Ah! would that (Death) had made an **end** of me!
071:018 "And in the **End** He will return you into the
079:044 With they Lord is the final **end** of it.
092:013 the **End** and the Beginning.

ENDEARED
049:007 but Allah has **endeared** the Faith to you, and has

ENDEAVOUR
020:015 by the measure of its **Endeavour**.
021:094 and has Faith,-his **endeavour** will not be rejected:
076:022 and your **Endeavour** is accepted and recognized."

ENDED
011:044 and the water abated, and the matter was **ended**.

ENDOW
079:029 Its night doth He **endow** with darkness, and its

ENDOWED
002:253 Those Messengers We **endowed** with gifts,
007:140 when it is He who hath **endowed** you with
015:053 glad tidings of a son **endowed** with knowledge."
029:049 in the hearts of those **endowed** with knowledge:
046:026 and We had **endowed** them with (faculties of)
051:028 a son **endowed** with knowledge.

ENDS
011:114 two **ends** of the day and at the approaches
015:085 and all between them, but for just **ends**.
018:084 and We gave him the ways and the means to all **ends**.
044:039 We created them not except for just **ends**:
045:022 Allah created the heavens and the earth for just **ends**,
046:003 and all between them but for just **ends**, and for
092:004 Verily, (the **ends**) ye strive for are diverse.

ENDUED
003:018 and those **endued** with knowledge,
012:076 whom We please: but over all **endued** with knowledge
012:111 instruction for men **endued** with understanding.
013:019 It is those who are **endued** with understanding
016:027 Those **endued** with knowledge
020:039 but I **endued** thee with love from Me:
020:054 Signs for men **endued** with understanding.
020:128 for men **endued** with understanding.
024:022 Let not those among you who are **endued** with grace
027:033 They said: "We are **endued** with strength,
030:056 But those **endued** with knowledge and faith

ENDUED (continued)
039:009   those who are **endued** with understanding that receive
039:018   ones **endued** with understanding.
053:006   **Endued** with Wisdom: For he appeared
065:002   two persons from among you, **endued** with justice,
081:020   **Endued** with Power, held in honour by the Lord

ENDUEST
003:026   Thou **enduest** with honour whom Thou pleasest,

ENDURE
002:061   we cannot **endure** one kind of food (always);
009:021   for them, wherein are delights that **endure**:
011:107   the heavens and the earth **endure**, except as
011:108   the earth **endure**, except as the Lord willeth:
016:096   what is with Allah will **endure**.
018:046   but the things that **endure**, Good Deeds,
019:076   and the things that **endure**, Good Deeds,
037:077   And made his progeny to **endure** (on this earth);
043:028   And he left it as a Word to **endure** among those
074:028   Naught doth it permit to **endure**, and naught

ENDURES
005:037   their Chastisement will be one that **endures**.

ENDURING
004:010   they will soon be **enduring** a blazing Fire!
009:068   And an **enduring** punishment,-
010:052   the wrong-doers: 'Taste ye the **enduring** punishment!
020:127   more grievous and more **enduring**.
020:131   is better and more **enduring**.
028:060   is better and more **enduring**: will ye
087:017   But the Hereafter is better and more **enduring.**

ENEMIES
002:085   assist (their **enemies**) against them,
002:204   yet is he the most contentious of **enemies**.
003:103   for ye were **enemies** and He joined your hearts
003:165   smote (your **enemies**) with one twice as great,
004:045   But Allah hath full knowledge of your **enemies**:
004:101   for the Unbelievers are unto you open **enemies**.
007:150   Make not the **enemies** rejoice over my misfortune,
008:060   the **enemies**, of Allah and your **enemies**, and others
017:007   (We permitted your **enemies**) to disfigure your faces,
018:050   And they are **enemies** to you!
026:077   "For they are **enemies** to me; not so
041:019   The Day that the **enemies** of Allah will be
041:028   Such is the requital of the **enemies** of Allah,-
060:001   O ye who believe! take not My **enemies** and yours
060:002   to you as **enemies**, and stretch forth their hands
060:007   those whom ye (now) hold as **enemies**.
061:014   power to those who believed against their **enemies**,
063:004   They are the **enemies**; so beware
064:014   are (some that are) **enemies** to yourselves:

ENEMY
002:097   Say: Whoever is an **enemy** to Gabriel
002:098   Lo! Allah is an **enemy** to those who
002:098   Whoever is an **enemy** to Allah
002:168   for he is to you an avowed **enemy**.
002:208   the Satan for he is to you an avowed **enemy**.
002:239   If ye fear (an **enemy**), pray on foot,
003:125   even if the **enemy** should rush here
003:152   His permission were about to annihilate your **enemy**,
004:104   And slacken not in following up the **enemy**:
006:112   for every Messenger an **enemy**,-Satans among
006:142   for he is to you an avowed **enemy**.
007:022   Satan was an avowed **enemy** unto you?"

ENEMY (continued)
007:129   will destroy your **enemy** and make you
008:061   But if the **enemy** incline towards peace, do thou
009:083   nor fight an **enemy** with me:
009:114   that he was an **enemy** to Allah, he dissociated
009:120   or gain any gain from an **enemy**:
012:005   for Satan is to man an avowed **enemy**!
017:053   for Satan is to man an avowed **enemy**.
020:039   by one who is an **enemy** to Me and an **enemy** to him':
020:080   We delivered you from your **enemy**, and We
020:117   this is an **enemy** to thee and thy wife:
025:031   an **enemy** among the sinners:
028:015   for he is an **enemy** that manifestly misleads!"
028:019   Then, when he was about to lay his hand on their **enemy**,
035:006   Verily Satan is an **enemy** to you:
035:006   so treat him as an **enemy**.
036:060   to you an **enemy** avowed?-.
043:062   for he is to you an **enemy** avowed.

ENFORCE
002:165   and Allah will strongly **enforce** the Punishment:
022:040   (Able to **enforce** His Will).

ENGAGE
002:076   that they may **engage** you in argument
003:073   should **engage** you in argument before your Lord?
028:026   (dear) father! **engage** him on wages: truly the
033:035   who **engage** much in Allah's remembrance, for them
057:016   in all humility should **engage** in the remembrance

ENGAGED
003:156   through the earth or **engaged** in fighting:
006:068   When thou seest men **engaged** in vain
026:227   **engaged** much in the remembrance of Allah,
048:011   will say to thee: "We were **engaged** in (looking

ENGAGEMENT
017:034   and fulfil (every) **engagement**,
017:034   for every **engagement** will be enquired into

ENGAGEMENTS
009:004   So fulfil your **engagements** with them to the

ENGAGING
052:025   will advance to each other, **engaging** in mutual enquiry.

ENGROSSED
010:061   when ye are deeply **engrossed** therein.

ENJOIN
002:044   Do ye **enjoin** right conduct on the people,
003:114   they **enjoin** what is right, and forbid
004:037   those who are niggardly **enjoin** niggardliness on others,
007:145   and **enjoin** the people to hold fast by the
009:067   they **enjoin** evil, and forbid
009:071   they **enjoin** what is just, and forbid what is evil:
009:112   that **enjoin** good and forbid evil;
019:055   He used to **enjoin** on his people Prayer and Zakat
020:132   **Enjoin** prayer on thy people, and be
022:041   and give zakat, **enjoin** the right and forbid
031:017   **enjoin** what is just, and forbid what is wrong:
036:060   "Did I not **enjoin** on you, O ye children of Adam,
090:017   and **enjoin** patience, (constancy, and self-restraint),
090:017   and **enjoin** deeds of kindness and compassion.

ENJOINED
002:132   And Abraham **enjoined** upon his sons
004:103   for such prayers are **enjoined** on Believers
012:068   in the manner their father had **enjoined**, it did
019:031   wheresoever I be, and hath **enjoined** on me Prayer
029:008   We have **enjoined** on man kindness to parents:

ENJOINED (continued)
031:014 And We have **enjoined** on man (to be good) to his
042:013 to thee-and that which We **enjoined** on Abraham,
042:013 for you as that which He **enjoined** on Noah-the which
046:015 We have **enjoined** on man kindness to his parents:

ENJOINING
003:104 **enjoining** what is right, and forbidding what is wrong:
003:110 **Enjoining** what is right, forbidding what is wrong,
009:086 When a Sura comes down, **enjoining** them to believe
103:003 and (join together) in the mutual **enjoining** of Truth,

ENJOINS
096:012 Or **enjoins** Righteousness?

ENJOY
004:005 take it and **enjoy** it with right good cheer.
007:019 and **enjoy** (its good things) as ye wish:
008:069 But (now) **enjoy** what ye took in war, lawful
010:098 and permitted them to **enjoy** (their life) for a while.
011:065 So he said: "**Enjoy** yourselves in your homes
012:012 "Send him with us to-morrow to **enjoy** himself and play,
014:030 Say: "**Enjoy** (your brief power)! But verily
015:003 Leave them alone, to eat and **enjoy** and let
016:055 Then **enjoy** (your brief day); but soon
023:051 O ye messenger! **enjoy** (all) things good and pure,
026:205 Seest thou? If we do let them **enjoy** (this life)
030:034 Then **enjoy** (your brief day); but soon
033:016 a brief (respite) will ye be allowed to **enjoy**!"
036:035 That they may **enjoy** the fruits of this
037:042 Fruits, and they (shall **enjoy**) honour and dignity,
037:148 to **enjoy** (their life) for a while.
039:008 Say "**Enjoy** thy disbelief for a little while:
047:012 reject Allah will **enjoy** (this world) and eat as cattle eat;
051:043 "**Enjoy** (your brief day) for a little while!"
067:015 its tracts and **enjoy** of the Sustenance which He
077:046 eat ye and **enjoy** yourselves (but) a little while,

ENJOYED
038:025 he **enjoyed**, indeed, a Near Approach to Us, and a
038:040 And he **enjoyed**, indeed, a Near Approach to Us,

ENJOYING
016:112 a city **enjoying** security and quiet, abundantly
052:018 **Enjoying** the (Bliss) which their Lord

ENJOYMENT
003:197 Little is it for **enjoyment**; their Ultimate
004:024 the **enjoyment** you have of them as a duty; but if,
004:077 Say: "Short is the **enjoyment** of this world:
006:044 in the midst of their **enjoyment** of Our gifts,
009:069 They had their **enjoyment** of their portion:
010:023 an **enjoyment** of the life of the Present:
010:070 A little **enjoyment** in this world!-and the,
011:003 that He may grant you **enjoyment**,
011:116 But the wrong-doers pursued the **enjoyment** of the
020:131 for **enjoyment** to parties of them, the splendour
023:019 and of them ye eat (and have **enjoyment**),-
025:008 or why has he (not) a garden for **enjoyment**?"
026:146 in (the **enjoyment** of) all that ye have here?-
026:207 It will profit them not the **enjoyment** they were given.
029:066 and giving themselves up to (worldly) **enjoyment**!
033:028 your **enjoyment** and set you free in a
040:039 is nothing but (temporary) **enjoyment**:
042:036 is (but) the **enjoyment** of this Life:
043:035 But all this were nothing but **enjoyment** of the

ENLARGE
013:026 Allah doth **enlarge**, or grant by (strict) measure,

ENLARGE (continued)
042:027 If Allah were to **enlarge** the provision
065:005 from him and will **enlarge** his reward.

ENLARGES
028:082 Who **enlarges** the provision or restricts it,
029:062 Allah **enlarges** the sustenance (which He gives)
030:037 See they not that Allah **enlarges** the provision
034:036 Say: "Verily my Lord **enlarges** and restricts
034:039 Say: "Verily my Lord **enlarges** and restricts
039:052 Know they not that Allah **enlarges** the provision
042:012 He **enlarges** and restricts the Sustenance to whom

ENLIGHTEN
031:020 a Book to **enlighten** them!

ENLIGHTENMENT
003:184 And the Book of **Enlightenment**.
022:008 and without a Book of **Enlightenment**,-

ENMITY
002:036 with **enmity** between yourselves.
005:014 so We stirred up **enmity** and hatred between the one
005:064 We have placed **enmity** and hatred till the Day of
005:082 Strongest among men in **enmity** to the Believers
005:091 to excite **enmity** and hatred between you,
007:024 with **enmity** between yourselves.
012:100 sown **enmity** between me and my brothers.
020:123 with **enmity** one to another; but if, as is sure,
060:004 us and you, **enmity** and hatred for ever,-

ENORMITY
018:014 have uttered an **enormity**!"
033:053 Truly such a thing is in Allah's sight an **enormity**.

ENOUGH
002:206 **Enough** for him is Hell;
002:266 not strong (**enough** to look, after themselves)
003:124 Is it not **enough** for you that Allah should help
004:045 and Allah is **enough** for a Helper.
004:045 Allah is **enough** for a Protector,
004:055 and **enough** is Hell for a burning fire.
004:077 to our (natural) term, near (**enough**)?
004:079 and **enough** is Allah for a witness.
004:081 and **enough** is Allah as a disposer of affairs.
004:092 the freeing of a believing slave (is **enough**).
004:097 spacious **enough** for you to move yourselves
004:132 and **enough** is Allah to carry through all affairs.
004:166 but **enough** is Allah for a Witness.
004:171 And **enough** is Allah as a Disposer of affairs.
005:104 they say: "**Enough** for us are the ways
010:029 "**Enough** is Allah for a witness between us and you:
012:009 (there will be time **enough**) for you
012:083 yourselves contrived a story (good **enough**) for you.
013:043 Say "**Enough** for a witness between me
017:017 And **enough** is thy Lord to note
017:065 **Enough** is thy Lord for a disposer
017:096 Say: "**Enough** is Allah for a witness between me
020:118 "There is therein (**enough** provision) for thee
021:037 soon (**enough**) will I show you My Signs; so ask
021:047 and **enough** are We to take account.
025:031 but **enough** is the Lord to guide and to help.
025:058 and **enough** is He to be acquainted
026:006 so they will know soon (**enough**) the truth
029:051 And is it not **enough** for them that We have
029:052 Say: "**Enough** is Allah for a Witness
033:003 and **enough** is Allah, as a Disposer of affairs.
033:025 and **enough** is Allah for the Believers in their

ENOUGH (continued)

033:039 And **enough** is Allah to call
033:048 For **enough** is Allah as a Disposer
035:037 Did we not give you long **enough** life so that
039:036 Is not Allah **enough** for His servant? But they
041:053 Is it not **enough** that thy Lord doth witness all things?
046:008 **Enough** is He for a witness between me and you!
048:028 and **enough** is Allah for a Witness.
058:008 **Enough** for them is Hell:
080:037 will have **enough** concern (of his own) to make

ENQUIRE

012:041 whereof ye twain do **enquire**."
012:087 "O my sons! go ye and **enquire** about Joseph

ENQUIRED

017:034 will be **enquired** into (on the Day of Reckoning).

ENQUIRY

052:025 engaging in mutual **enquiry**.

ENRAGED

026:055 "And they have surely **enraged** us;

ENRAGES

022:015 his plan will remove that which **enrages** (him)!

ENRICH

009:028 soon will Allah **enrich** you, if He wills, out of His

ENRICHED

009:074 Allah and His Messenger had **enriched** them!

ENROLLED

036:027 me Forgiveness and has **enrolled** me among

ENSLAVED

026:022 that you hast **enslaved** the Children of Israel!"

ENSNARED

052:042 who disbelieve are themselves **ensnared** in a Plot.

ENTER

002:058 And remember We said: "**Enter** this town,
002:058 and **enter** the gate prostrating,
002:111 And they say: "None shall **enter** Paradise
002:114 should themselves **enter** them except in fear.
002:189 **Enter** houses through the proper doors:
002:189 ye **enter** your houses from the back:
002:208 O ye who Believe! **enter** into Islam whole-heartedly;
002:214 ye shall **enter** the Garden (of Bliss)
003:142 that ye would **enter** Heaven without Allah testing
004:124 they will **enter** Heaven and not the least
004:154 We said: "**Enter** the gate with humility";
005:021 "O my people! **enter** the holy land which Allah
005:022 never shall we **enter** it until they leave it:
005:022 (once) they leave, then shall we **enter**."
005:024 never **enter** it as long as they are in it.
005:061 they **enter** with a disbelief, and they go out
007:038 He will say: "**Enter** ye in the company of the
007:040 nor will they **enter** the Garden, until the
007:046 but they still hoped. To (**enter** it).
007:049 **Enter** ye the Garden: no fear shall be on you,
007:161 and **enter** the gate in a posture of humility:
012:067 "O my sons! **enter** not all by one gate:
012:067 **enter** ye by different gates.
012:099 and said: "**Enter** ye Egypt (all) in safety
013:023 they shall **enter** there, as well as the righteous
013:023 and angels shall **enter** unto them from every
015:046 "**Enter** ye here in Peace and Security."
016:029 "So **enter** the gates of Hell, to dwell therein.
016:031 Gardens of Eternity which they will **enter**:
016:032 "Peace be on you; **enter** ye the Garden, because of

ENTER (continued)

017:007 and to **enter** your Temple as they had
018:022 **Enter** not, therefore, into controversies
019:026 Most Gracious, and this day will I **enter** into no
019:060 for these will **enter** the Garden and will
024:027 O ye who believe! **enter** not houses other than your own,
024:028 **enter** not until permission is given to you:
024:029 to **enter** houses not used for living in,
024:061 But if ye **enter** houses, salute each other-a greeting of
026:200 Thus have We caused it to **enter** the hearts
027:034 She said: "Kings, when they **enter** a country,
027:044 She was asked to **enter** the lofty Palace:
033:053 O ye who Believe! **enter** not the Prophet's houses,-
033:053 but when ye are invited, **enter**; and when
035:033 Gardens of Eternity will they **enter**:
036:026 It was said: "**Enter** thou the Garden."
039:072 "**Enter** ye the gates of Hell, to dwell
039:073 **Enter** ye here, to dwell therein."
040:008 "And grant, our Lord! that they **enter** the Gardens of
040:040 such will **enter** the Garden (of Bliss):
040:060 to serve Me will surely **enter** Hell abased."
040:076 "**Enter** ye the gates of Hell, to dwell
043:070 **Enter** ye the Garden, ye and
048:027 ye shall **enter** the Sacred Mosque, if Allah
050:034 "**Enter** ye therein in Peace and Security; this Day
066:010 "**Enter** ye the Fire along with (others)
066:010 with (others) that **enter**!"
070:038 to **enter** the Garden of Bliss?
071:025 and were made to **enter** the Fire and they found-
071:028 all who **enter** my house in Faith, and (all)
082:015 Which they will **enter** on the Day of Judgment,
083:016 Further, they will **enter** the Fire of Hell.
084:012 And he will **enter** a Blazing Fire.
087:012 Who will **enter** the Great Fire,
088:004 The while they **enter** the Blazing Fire,-
089:029 "**Enter** thou, then, among my Devotees!
089:030 "Yea, **enter** thou my Heaven!"
110:002 dost see the People **enter** Allah's Religion in crowds,

ENTERED

003:037 Every time that he **entered** her chamber to see her,
007:046 "Peace be upon you": they have not **entered** it, but
009:004 ye have **entered** into alliance and who have not
012:058 they **entered** his presence, and he knew them,
012:068 And when they **entered** in the manner
012:099 Then when they **entered** the presence of Joseph,
015:052 When they **entered** his presence and said,
016:091 ye have **entered** into it, and break
017:005 they **entered** the very inmost parts of your homes;
017:007 as they had **entered** it before, and to
028:015 And he **entered** the City at a time when its
038:022 When they **entered** the presence of David, and he
049:014 has Faith **entered** your hearts.
051:025 Behold, they **entered** His presence, and said:

ENTERS

003:097 whoever **enters** it attains security;
007:038 Every time a new People **enters**, it curses
057:004 He knows what **enters** within the earth

ENTERTAIN

002:075 (O ye men of Faith) **entertain** the hope that they will
011:069 "Peace!" and hastened to **entertain** them with
041:023 did **entertain** concerning your Lord, hath brought
059:009 and **entertain** no desire, in their hearts

ENTERTAINED
079:040 And for such as had **entertained** the fear

ENTERTAINMENT
003:198 an **entertainment** from Allah;
018:102 for the Unbelievers for (their) **entertainment**.
018:107 for their **entertainment**, the Gardens of Paradise,
037:062 Is that the better **entertainment** or the
056:056 Such will be their **entertainment** on the Day
056:093 For him is **Entertainment** with Boiling Water,

ENTIRELY
003:007 others are not **entirely** clear.
003:007 that is not **entirely** clear.
007:138 devoted **entirely** to some idols they had.
034:053 Seeing that they did reject faith (**entirely**) before,
039:029 and a man belonging **entirely** to one master:
057:029 that (His) Grace is (**entirely**) in His Hand,

ENTIRETY
008:039 in its **entirety** but if they cease, verily Allah

ENTITLED
002:159 and the curse of those **entitled** to curse.
018:082 to which they were **entitled**; their father
048:026 and well were they **entitled** to it

ENTRAILS
006:146 except what adheres to their backs or their **entrails**,

ENTREAT
023:076 submissively **entreat** (Him)!

ENTRUST
006:089 behold! We shall **entrust** their charge to a new

ENTRUSTED
003:075 others, who, if **entrusted** with a single silver coin,
003:075 if **entrusted** with a hoard of gold,
005:044 for to them was **entrusted** the protection
008:027 things **entrusted** to you.
062:005 those who **entrusted** with the (obligations of) Taurat,

ENTRY
017:080 Say: "O my Lord! let my **entry** be by the Gate
033:014 And if an **entry** had been effected to them

ENVELOPING
044:011 **Enveloping** the people: this will

ENVIED
028:082 And those who had **envied** his position the day

ENVIOUS
113:005 the **envious** one as he practices envy.

ENVY
002:090 in insolent **envy** that Allah of His grace
002:109 have believed from selfish **envy**,
003:019 except through **envy** of each other,
004:054 Or do they **envy** mankind for what
045:017 through insolent **envy** among themselves.
113:005 the envious one as he practices **envy**.

EQUAL
002:165 as **equal** (with Allah):
004:011 to the male, a portion **equal** to that of two females:
004:086 more courteous, (at least) of **equal** courtesy.
004:095 Not **equal** are those Believers who sit (at home),
005:045 tooth for tooth, and wounds **equal** for **equal**."
005:100 Say: "Not **equal** are things that are bad and
006:001 (others) as **equal** with their Guardian Lord.
006:050 Say: "Can the blind be held **equal** to the seeing?"
006:150 as **equal** with their Guardian Lord.
008:058 (so as to be) on **equal** terms:

EQUAL (continued)
009:019 **equal** to (the pious service of) those who believe in Allah
009:019 They are not **equal** in the sight of Allah:
011:024 Are they **equal** when compared?
013:016 Say: "Are the blind **equal** with those who see?
013:016 Or the depths of darkness **equal** with Light?"
014:030 And they set up (idols) as **equal** to Allah,
016:071 so as to be **equal** in that respect.
016:075 and publicly: are the two **equal**? (By no means);
016:076 is such a man **equal** with one who commands justice,
017:075 and an **equal** portion in death: and moreover
022:025 to (all) men-**equal** is the dweller there and the
032:018 Not **equal** are they.
035:008 upon it as good, (**equal** to one who is rightly guided)?
038:052 their glances, (companions) of **equal** age.
039:009 Say: "Are those **equal**, those who
039:019 is justly due (**equal** to one who eschews evil)?
039:029 to one master: are these two **equal** in comparison?
040:058 nor are (**equal**) those who believe and work
040:058 Not **equal** are the blind and those who
041:034 Nor can Goodness and Evil be **equal**. Repel (Evil)
042:040 is an injury **equal** thereto (in degree): but if
045:021 righteous deeds,-that **equal** will be their Life
045:021 think that We shall hold them as **equal** with those
056:037 Full of love (for their mates), **equal** in age,-
057:010 Not **equal** among you are those who spent (freely)
059:020 Not **equal** are the Companions of the Fire and the
063:006 It is **equal** to them whether thou pray for their
078:033 Maidens of **Equal** Age;

EQUALITY
002:178 the law of **equality** is prescribed to you
002:179 In the Law of **Equality** there is (saving of)
002:194 there is the law of **equality**.

EQUALS
006:100 the Jinns **equals** with Allah, though Allah
026:098 "When we held you as **equals** with the
030:028 to share as **equals** in the wealth We have
034:033 and to attribute **equals** to Him!"
041:009 And do ye join **equals** with Him?

EQUIPMENT
019:074 who were even better in **equipment** and in

EQUIPPED
009:041 Go ye forth, (whether **equipped**) lightly

EQUITABLE
002:228 according to what is **equitable**;
002:229 hold together on **equitable** terms,
002:231 either take them back on **equitable** terms
002:231 or set them free on **equitable** terms;
002:232 if they mutually agree on **equitable** terms.
002:233 on **equitable** terms.
002:233 of their food and clothing on **equitable** terms.
065:002 or part with them on **equitable** terms;
065:002 either take them back on **equitable** terms or part

EQUITY
004:019 and **equity** if ye take a dislike to them it may
005:042 For Allah loveth those who judge in **equity**.
005:042 If thou judge, judge in **equity** between them.

EQUIVALENT
005:095 domestic animal **equivalent** to the one he killed.
005:095 or its **equivalent** in fasts: that he
060:011 have deserted the **equivalent** of what they had

ERE

012:037 and meaning of this **ere** it befall you.

ERECT

003:064 that we **erect** not, from among ourselves,
018:094 in order that thou mightest **erect** a barrier
018:095 I will **erect** a strong barrier

ERECTED

007:137 which Pharaoh and his people **erected** (with such pride).

ERR

004:176 lest ye **err**.

ERRAND

051:031 O ye Messengers, is your **errand** (now)?"
097:004 on every **errand**:

ERRANDS

079:003 And by those who glide along (on **errands** of mercy),

ERRED

007:149 and saw that they had **erred**, they said:

ERRING

007:002 warn (the **erring**) and a reminder the Believers.
028:018 "Thou art truly, one **erring** manifestly."

ERROR

002:016 have bartered guidance for **error**:
002:175 buy **error** in place of Guidance and Torment
002:256 Truth stands out clear from **Error**;
002:286 if we forget or fall into **error**;
003:164 while, before that, they had been in manifest **error**.
004:044 They traffic in **error**, and wish
006:074 For I see thee and thy people in manifest **error**."
007:060 "Ah! we see thee in evident **error**."
007:061 He said: "O my people! there is no **error** in me:
007:146 but if they see the way of **error**, that is
007:202 plunge them deeper into **error**, and never
010:032 apart from the Truth, what (remains) but **error**?
012:008 Really our father is obviously in **error**!
016:036 and some on whom **Error** became inevitably
019:038 are in **error** manifest!
020:121 His Lord, and fell into **error**.
021:054 in manifest **error**-ye and your fathers."
026:020 Moses: "I did it then, when I was in **error**.
026:097 "By Allah, we were truly in an **error** manifest,
028:085 and who is in manifest **error**."
031:011 nay, but the Transgressors are in manifest **error**.
034:008 (real) Chastisement, and in farthest **Error**.
034:024 on right guidance or in manifest **error**!"
036:024 "I would indeed, then be in manifest **Error**.
036:047 Ye are in nothing but manifest **error**."
036:067 nor could they have returned (after **error**).
039:022 they are manifestly wandering (in **error**)!
040:050 in (mazes of) **error**!"
043:040 or to such as (wander) in manifest **error**?
046:032 besides Allah: such are in manifest **error**."
054:024 Truly should we then be in **error** and madness.
054:047 the ones in **error** and madness.
062:002 before, in manifest **error**;-
067:009 ye are in nothing but a grave **error**!'"
067:029 (of us) it is that is in manifest **error**."
072:006 into further **error**.

ERRORS

040:025 in nothing but **errors** (and delusions)!...

ERRS

002:282 so that if one of them **errs**.
020:052 my Lord never **errs**, nor forgets,-

ESCAPE

003:188 think not that they can **escape** the Chastisement.
004:098 nor can they find a way (to **escape**).
004:121 and from it they will find no way of **escape**.
011:020 They will not **escape** in earth, nor have
014:021 for ourselves there is no way of **escape**."
024:057 can **escape** in the earth their abode is the Fire,-
033:016 and even if (ye do **escape**),
034:051 but then there will be no **escape** (for them),
039:051 them (too), and they shall not **escape**!
041:048 that they have no way of **escape**.
042:031 Nor can ye **escape** through the earth; nor have
042:035 that there is for them no way of **escape**.
046:032 he cannot **escape** in the earth, and no
050:019 thou wast trying to **escape**!"
050:036 was there any place of **escape** (for them)?
072:012 nor can we **escape** Him by flight.

ESCAPED

003:153 (the booty) that had **escaped** you and for (the ill)
008:059 that they have **escaped**, they will
028:025 (well) hast thou **escaped** from unjust people."

ESCHEW

004:031 If ye (but) **eschew** the most heinous of the things
005:090 **eschew** such (abomination), that ye may prosper.
006:120 **Eschew** all sin, open or secret: those who
016:036 "Serve Allah, and **eschew** Evil":
039:017 Those who **eschew** Taghut and fall not into

ESCHEWS

039:019 Punishment is justly due (equal to one who **eschews** evil)?

ESCORT

009:006 and then **escort** him to where he can be secure,

ESPECIALLY

002:238 **Especially** the Middle Prayer;
004:162 and (**especially**) those who establish regular prayer
027:080 (**especially**) when they turn back in retreat.

ESTABLISH

002:277 and **establish** regular prayers and give Zakat,
003:147 **establish** our feet firmly, and help us
004:077 but **establish** regular prayers and spend
004:162 and (especially) those who **establish** regular prayer
005:012 if ye (but) **establish** regular Prayers, pay Zakat
005:055 those who **establish** regular prayers and pay
006:072 "To **establish** regular prayers and
007:170 by the Book and **establish** regular prayer,-never
008:003 Who **establish** regular prayers and spend
008:007 to **establish** the Truth according to His words,
008:008 That He might **establish** Truth and prove
009:005 but if they repent, and **establish** regular prayers.
009:011 **establish** regular prayers, and pay Zakat they are
009:018 **establish** regular prayers, and pay Zakat, and fear
010:082 doth prove and **establish** the Truth, however much
010:087 of worship, and **establish** regular prayers: and give
011:114 And **establish** regular prayers at the two ends
012:021 Thus did We **establish** Joseph in the land, that We
013:022 **establish** regular prayers; spend, out of
014:027 Allah will **establish** in strength those who
014:031 that they may **establish** regular prayers, and spend
014:037 may **establish** regular prayer:
017:078 **Establish** regular prayers-at the sun's decline
020:014 and **establish** regular prayer for My remembrance.
021:073 good deeds, to **establish** regular prayers, and to
022:041 if We **establish** them in the land,

ESTABLISH (continued)

022:041	establish regular prayer and give zakat,
022:052	and Allah will confirm (and establish) His Signs:
022:078	So establish regular Prayer,
024:055	that He will establish in authority their religion
024:056	So establish regular Prayer and give zakat
027:003	Those who establish regular prayers and give
028:006	To establish a firm place for them in the land,
029:045	and establish Regular Prayer: for Prayer
030:031	and fear Him: establish regular prayers, and be
031:004	Those who establish regular Prayer, and give
031:017	"O my son! establish regular prayer, enjoin what
033:033	of Ignorance; and establish regular Prayer,
035:018	as fear their Lord unseen and establish regular Prayer.
035:029	establish regular Prayer, and spend
042:038	and establish regular prayer; who (conduct)
055:009	So establish weight with justice and fall
058:013	establish regular prayer; give zakat and obey
060:007	Establish friendship between you and those whom
065:002	endued with justice, and establish the evidence
073:020	and establish regular Prayer and give zakat;
098:005	to establish regular Prayer; and to

ESTABLISHED

006:006	Generations We had established on the earth, in
010:003	in six Days, then He established Himself on the
011:001	with verses fundamental (of established meaning),
012:056	Thus did We give established power to Joseph
013:002	then He established Himself on the Throne.
014:041	on the Day that the Reckoning will be established!"
016:036	became inevitably (established).
018:084	Verily We established his power on earth, and We
018:095	my Lord has established me is better (than tribute).
020:005	is firmly established on the throne.
025:054	then has He established relationships of lineage
025:059	in six days, then He established Himself on the
028:014	and was firmly established (in life), We bestowed
028:057	Have We not established for them a secure sanctuary,
030:055	the Day that the Hour (of reckoning) will be established,
032:004	in six Days, then He established Himself on the
041:050	(of Judgment) will (ever) be established; but if
042:013	The same religion has He established for you
042:021	who have established for them some religion
045:027	Hour of Judgement is established,-that Day
046:026	And We had firmly established them in a
057:004	then He established Himself on the Throne.
057:026	and established in their line Prophethood and

ESTABLISHES

014:040	who establishes regular Prayer, and also

ESTATE

004:009	Let those (disposing of an estate) have

ESTEEM

056:081	ye would hold in light esteem?
094:004	And raised high the esteem (in which)

ESTIMATE

006:091	No just estimate of Allah do they
022:074	No just estimate have they made of Allah:
039:067	No just estimate have they made of Allah,

ESTIMATION

012:020	counted out: in such low estimation did they

ETERNAL

003:015	therein is their eternal home;
003:136	an eternal dwelling:

ETERNAL (continued)

004:057	with rivers flowing beneath, their eternal home:
005:085	with rivers flowing underneath, their eternal home.
005:119	with rivers flowing beneath, their eternal home:
013:022	the final attainment of the (Eternal) Home,-
017:058	That is written in the (eternal) Record.
025:015	Say: "Is that best, or the eternal Garden, promised to
041:028	for them the Eternal Home:
050:034	this is a Day of Eternal Life!"
112:002	Allah, the Eternal, Absolute;

ETERNITY

016:031	Gardens of Eternity which they will enter:
018:031	Gardens of Eternity; beneath them rivers will
019:061	Gardens of Eternity, those which (Allah) Most
020:076	Gardens of Eternity, beneath which flow rivers:
020:120	to the Tree of Eternity and to a kingdom
032:014	taste ye the Chastisement of Eternity for your
035:033	Gardens of Eternity will they enter: therein will
038:050	Gardens of Eternity, whose doors will (ever)
040:008	enter the Gardens of Eternity, which Thou
061:012	mansions in Gardens of Eternity: that is
098:008	Gardens of Eternity, Beneath which rivers flow;

EVACUATED

051:035	Then We evacuated those of the Believers

EVEN

002:026	even of a gnat as well as anything above it.
002:052	Even then We did forgive you,
002:074	and even worse in hardness.
002:083	and ye backslide (even now).
002:091	even if it be Truth confirming
002:092	yet ye worshipped the Calf (even) after that,
002:096	even more than the idolaters:
002:108	hath strayed without doubt from the even way.
002:145	Even if thou wert to bring to the people
002:170	What! even though their fathers were
002:198	even though, before this, ye went astray.
002:214	that even the Messenger and those of faith
002:221	even though she allure you.
002:221	even though he allure you.
002:247	and he is not even gifted with wealth
002:271	even so it is well,
003:047	He said: "Even so; Allah createth what He willeth:
003:066	to disputing (even) in matters of which ye had
003:089	Except for those that repent (even) after that.
003:125	even if the enemy should rush here
003:153	without even casting a side glance at anyone,
003:154	Say: "Even if you had remained in your homes,
003:172	even after being wounded,
003:183	with Clear Signs and even with what ye ask for:
004:020	even if ye had given the latter
004:077	death will find you out, even if ye are in towers built
004:094	Even thus were ye yourselves before, till Allah
004:115	even after guidance has been plainly conveyed
004:128	even though men's souls are swayed by greed.
004:129	between wives even if it is your ardent desire:
004:135	even as against yourselves, or your parents,
004:153	for an even greater (miracle), for they said:
004:153	even after Clear Signs had come to them;
004:153	even so We forgave them; and gave Moses
005:031	"Was I not even able to be as this raven, and to
005:032	yet, even after that, many of them continued
005:041	will listen even to others who have never so much
005:043	yet even after that, they would turn away.

EVEN (continued)

005:060   and far more astray from the **even** Path!"
005:077   and strayed themselves from the **even** Way.
005:100   **even** though the abundance of the bad
005:104   What! **even** though their fathers were void
005:106   **even** though the (beneficiary) be our near relation:
006:109   realize that **even** if a (special) Sign came, they
006:110   **even** as they refused to believe in this
006:111   **Even** if We did send unto them angels, and the
006:133   **even** as He raised you up
006:137   **Even** so, in the eyes of most
006:145   But (**even** so), if a person
006:152   **even** if a near relative is concerned; and fulfil
007:088   He said: "What! **even** though we do detest (them)?
007:146   **even** if they see all the Signs, they will not
007:169   (**Even** so), if similar vanities came their way,
008:005   **even** though a party among the Believers
008:019   **even** if they were multiplied:
008:042   **Even** if ye had made a mutual appointment to meet,
008:066   spot in you: but (**even** so), if there
009:011   But (**even** so), if they repent, establish regular
009:032   **even** though the Unbelievers may detest (it).
009:033   **even** though the Pagans may detest (it).
009:113   for Pagans, **even** though they be of kin, after it
010:022   till when ye **even** board ships;-they sail
010:039   cannot compass, **even** before the interpretation
010:042   **even** though they are without understanding.
010:043   the blind,-**even** though they will not see?
010:097   **Even** if every Sign was brought unto them,-until
011:005   Ah! **even** when they cover themselves
011:014   Will ye **even** then submit (to Islam)?"
012:006   of Jacob-**even** as He perfected it to thy fathers
012:017   **even** though we tell the truth."
012:037   and that (**even**) deny the Hereafter.
012:060   from me, nor shall ye (**even**) come near me."
012:100   the desert, (**even**) after Satan had sown enmity
013:017   **Even** so, from that (ore) which
013:018   **even** if they had all that is in the heavens
014:046   **even** though they were such as to shake the hills!
015:012   **Even** so do We let it creep into the
015:014   **Even** if We opened out to them a gate
015:054   glad tidings **even** though old age has seized me?
016:030   the Hereafter is **even** better and excellent indeed
016:056   And they (**even**) assign, to things they do not know,
016:077   the twinkling of an eye, or **even** quicker:
016:113   seized them **even** in the midst of their iniquities.
017:024   thy Mercy **even** as they cherished me in childhood."
017:028   And **even** if thou hast to turn away from them
017:088   **even** if they backed up each other
017:093   No, we shall not **even** believe in thy mounting until
018:024   ever closer (**even**) than this to the right course."
018:036   **even** if I am brought back to my Lord.
018:051   and the earth, nor (**even**) their own creation:
018:057   **even** then will they never accept guidance.
018:101   and who had been unable **even** to hear.
018:109   **even** if we added another ocean like it,
019:012   and We gave him Wisdom **even** as a youth,
019:043   a Way that is **even** and straight.
019:074   who were **even** better in equipment and in
020:058   in a place where both shall have **even** chances."
020:135   the straight and **even** way, and who
021:019   **even** those who are with Him are not
021:045   not hear the call, (**even**) when they are warned!

EVEN (continued)

021:104   **even** as We produced the first Creation,
022:073   cannot create (**even**) a fly,
024:038   and add **even** more for them out of His Grace:
024:047   but **even** after that, some of them turn away:
026:030   (Moses) said: "**Even** if I showed you something
027:050   **even** while they perceived it not.
028:066   will not be able (**even**) to question each other.
029:029   And practice wickedness (**even**) in your councils?"
030:003   (**even**) after (this) defeat of theirs, will soon
030:049   **Even** though, before they received (the rain)-
031:021   What! **even** if it is Satan beckoning them to the
033:016   or slaughter; and **even** if (ye do escape),
033:052   **even** though their beauty attract thee,
035:009   **even** so (will be) the Resurrection!
035:018   **even** though he be nearly related.
035:030   nay, He will give them (**even**) more out of
038:016   our sentence (**even**) before the Day of Account!"
038:022   with injustice, but guide us to the **even** Path.
039:035   remit form them (**even**) the worst in their deeds and give
039:043   Say: "**Even** if they have no power whatever
039:047   **Even** if the wrong-doers had all that there is
040:014   **even** though the Unbelievers may detest it.
040:021   They were **even** superior to them
040:085   And **even** thou did the rejecters of Allah lose
041:007   and who **even** deny the Hereafter.
042:028   down rain (**even**) after (men) have given up all hope,
042:037   are angry **even** then forgive;
043:011   **even** so will ye be raised (form the dead),-
043:024   He said: "What! **even** if I brought you better
043:041   **Even** if We take thee away, We shall
044:031   arrogant (**even**) among inordinate transgressors.
046:017   **even** though generations have passed before me
051:030   They said, "**Even** so has thy Lord spoken:
051:044   seized them, **even** while they were looking on.
051:045   Then they could not **even** stand (on their feet),
053:009   two bow-lengths or (**even**) nearer;
053:023   **Even** though there has already come to them
054:037   And they **even** sought to snatch away
058:022   and His Messenger, **even** though they were their
059:009   **even** though poverty was their (own lot).
059:014   They will not fight you (**even**) together, except in
060:001   **even** though they have rejected the truth
061:007   **even** as he is being invited to Islam?
061:008   His Light, **even** though the Unbelievers may detest
061:009   all religion, **even** though the Pagans may detest
067:007   of its breath **even** as it blazes forth.
067:020   nay, who is there that can help you, (**even** as) an army,
073:015   concerning you, **even** as We sent a messenger
075:005   man wishes to do wrong (**even**) in the time in front of
075:015   **Even** though he were to put up his excuses.
076:001   when he was nothing-(not **even**) mentioned?
089:003   By the **Even** and Odd (contrasted);
100:011   well-acquainted with them, (**Even** to) that Day?
107:007   But refuse (to supply) (**even**) neighborly needs.

EVENING

003:041   and glorify Him in the **evening** and in the morning."
006:052   on their Lord morning and **evening**, seeking
016:006   in the **evening**, and as ye lead them froth
018:028   those who call on their Lord morning and **evening**,
019:011   in the morning and in the **evening**.
019:062   their sustenance, morning and **evening**.
025:005   before him morning and **evening**."

EVENING (continued)

033:042 And glorify Him morning and **evening**.
034:012 and its **evening** (stride) was a month's (journey);
040:046 be brought, morning and **evening**:
040:055 in the **evening** and in the morning.
048:009 and celebrate His praises morning and **evening**.
076:025 of thy Lord morning and **evening**,
079:046 (it will be) as if they had tarried but a single **evening**,

EVENINGS

007:205 in the mornings and **evenings**; and be not
013:015 so do their shadows in the mornings and **evenings**.
024:036 in the mornings and in the **evenings**,

EVENLY

067:022 or one who walks **evenly** on a Straight Way?

EVENT

056:001 When the **Event** Inevitable cometh to pass,
069:015 On that Day shall the (Great) **Event** come to pass,
070:006 They see the (Day) indeed as a far-off (**event**):
079:034 the great, overwhelming (**Event**),-
088:001 of the Overwhelming (**Event**)?

EVENTIDE

030:017 when ye reach **eventide** and when ye rise
038:018 Our Praises, at **eventide** and at break of day,
038:031 Behold, there were brought before him, at **eventide**,

EVENTS

012:006 of stories (and **events**) and perfect His favour
012:021 might teach him the interpretation of stories (and **events**).
027:072 the **events** which ye wish to hasten on
028:044 nor wast thou a witness (of those **events**).

EVENTUAL

019:076 respect of (their) **eventual** returns."

EVER

002:019 But Allah is **ever** round the rejecters of Faith!
002:025 and they abide therein (for **ever**).
002:063 and bring (**ever**) to remembrance what is therein,
002:081 therein shall they abide (for **ever**).
002:082 therein shall they abide (for **ever**).
002:257 to dwell therein (for **ever**).
002:259 shall Allah bring it (**ever**) to life,
002:275 they will abide therein (for **ever**).
003:107 therein to dwell (for **ever**).
003:116 dwelling therein (for **ever**).
003:122 the Faithful (**ever**) put their trust.
003:161 No prophet could (**ever**) dishonestly
003:174 no harm **ever** touched them: for they followed
003:198 therein are they to dwell (for **ever**),
004:001 for Allah **ever** watches over you.
004:013 to abide therein (for **ever**) and that
004:057 cool and **ever** deepening.
004:093 to abide therein (for **ever**):
004:122 to dwell therein for **ever**.
004:149 surely Allah is **ever** pardoning Powerful.
004:169 to dwell therein for **ever**:
005:013 barring a few-**ever** bent on (new) deceits:
005:064 but they (**ever**) strive to do mischief on earth.
006:068 If Satan **ever** makes thee forget, then after
006:121 But the satans **ever** inspire their friends
006:128 you will dwell therein for **ever**, except as
007:020 or such beings as live for **ever**."
007:036 to dwell therein (for **ever**).
007:042 therein to dwell (for **ever**).
007:080 no people in creation (**ever**) committed before you?

EVER (continued)

007:171 and bring (**ever**) to remembrance what is
007:189 we vow we shall (**ever**) be grateful."
009:022 They will dwell therein for **ever**.
009:084 Nor do thou **ever** pray for any of them that dies,
009:100 rivers flow, to dwell therein for **ever**:
011:083 nor are they **ever** far from those who do wrong!
012:051 he is indeed of those who are (**ever**) true (and virtuous).
015:048 nor shall they (**ever**) be asked to leave.
017:100 for man is (**ever**) niggardly!"
018:024 guide me **ever** closer (even) than this to the right course."
018:035 "I deem not that this will **ever** perish,"
018:036 (of Judgment) will (**ever**) come:
018:076 (Moses) said: "If **ever** I ask thee about anything
020:035 For Thou art **ever** seeing."
021:019 nor are they (**ever**) weary (of His service):
021:020 nor do they **ever** flag or intermit.
023:011 they will dwell therein (for **ever**).
023:107 if **ever** we return (to evil), then shall
024:004 and reject their evidence **ever** after:
024:021 not one of you would **ever** have been pure:
026:129 of living therein (for **ever**)?
027:040 "I will bring it to thee before **ever** thy glance returns
029:028 in Creation (**ever**) committed before you.
032:015 nor are they (**ever**) puffed up with pride.
033:065 To dwell therein for **ever**: no protector
034:050 all things, and is (**ever**) near."
038:017 for he **ever** turned (in repentance to Allah).
038:030 **Ever** did he turn (to Us in repentance)!
038:044 **Ever** did he turn (to Us)!
038:050 will (**ever**) be open to them;
040:018 Warn them of the Day that is (**ever**) drawing near,
040:044 for Allah (**ever**) watches over
041:046 nor is thy Lord **ever** unjust (in the least)
041:050 (of Judgment) will (**ever**) be established;
044:003 for We (**ever**) wish to warn (against Evil).
044:005 For We (**ever**) send (revelations),
046:020 and that ye (**ever**) transgressed."
047:015 dwell for **ever** in the Fire, and be
051:058 Lord of Power,-Steadfast (for **ever**).
053:057 The (Hour) **ever** approaching draws nigh:
055:027 But will abide (for **ever**) the Face of thy Lord,-
058:022 to dwell therein (for **ever**).
059:017 dwelling therein for **ever**.
060:004 between us and you, enmity and hatred for **ever**,-
064:009 to dwell therein for **ever**:
065:002 fear Allah, He (**ever**) prepares a way out,
065:011 to dwell therein for **ever**:
072:023 they shall dwell therein for **ever**."
084:006 verily thou art **ever** toiling on towards the Lord-
084:015 Nay, nay! for his Lord was (**ever**) watchful of him!
098:008 They will dwell therein for **ever**;
104:003 would make him last for **ever**!

EVER-FORGIVING

038:066 and all between-Exalted in Might, **Ever-Forgiving**.

EVER-GROWING

072:017 will cause him to undergo **ever-growing** Chastisement.

EVERLASTING

009:072 in Gardens of **everlasting** stay but the greatest bliss

EVERY

002:020 **every** time the light (helps) them,
002:025 **Every** time they are fed with fruits
002:100 **every** time they make a Covenant,

EVERY (continued)

002:185   So **every** one of you who is present (at his home)
002:185   Allah intends **every** facility for you;
002:186   of **every** suppliant when he calleth on Me:
002:260   on **every** hill, and call to them:
002:281   Then shall **every** soul be paid what it earned,
002:286   and it suffers **every** ill that it earns.
002:286   It gets **every** good that it earns,
003:030   "On the day when **every** soul will be confronted
003:037   **Every** time that he entered her chamber to see her,
003:161   then shall **every** soul receive its due
003:185   **Every** soul shall have a taste of death:
004:091   **every** time they are sent back to temptation,
004:102   but take (**every**) precaution for yourselves.
005:064   **Every** time they kindle the fire of war,
005:070   **Every** time there came to them a Messenger
006:025   if they saw **every** one of the Signs, they will
006:067   "For **every** Prophecy is a limit of time, and soon
006:070   if it offered **every** ransom (or reparation),
006:112   for **every** Messenger an enemy,-satans among
006:123   Thus have We placed leaders in **every** town,
006:146   We forbade **every** (animal) with undivided hoof,
006:164   **Every** soul draws the meed of its
007:029   (to Him) at **every** time and place of prayer,
007:031   at **every** time and place of prayer:
007:034   To **every** People is a term, appointed:
007:038   **Every** time a new People enters, it curses
007:057   and produce **every** kind of harvest therewith:
007:086   "And squat not on **every** road, breathing
008:056   but they break their covenant **every** time,
009:005   for them in **every** stratagem (of war); but if
009:122   from **every** expedition go forth to devote
009:126   are tried **every** year once or twice?
010:030   There will **every** soul see (the fruits of)
010:047   To **every** people (was sent) an Messenger:
010:049   To **every** People is a term appointed:
010:054   **Every** soul that hath sinned, if it
010:079   Said Pharaoh: "Bring me **every** sorcerer well versed."
010:097   Even if **every** Sign was brought unto them,-until
011:038   **every** time that the Chiefs of his People
011:059   and followed the command of **every** powerful, obstinate
011:123   and to Him goeth back **every** affair (for decision):
012:012   and we shall take **every** care of him."
012:063   and we will indeed take **every** care of him."
013:003   and fruit of **every** kind He made in pairs,
013:007   and to **every** people a guide.
013:008   Allah doth know what **every** female (womb) doth bear,
013:008   **Every** single thing is with Him in (due)
013:023   from **every** gate (with the salutation)
013:029   work righteousness, is (**every**) blessedness, and a
013:033   He Who standeth over **every** soul (and knoweth) all that
013:042   He knoweth the doings of **every** soul: and soon
014:015   the lot of **every** powerful obstinate transgressor.
014:017   death will come to him from **every** quarter, yet will he
015:017   (moreover) We have guarded from **every** accursed Satan.
016:011   olives, date-palms, grapes, and **every** kind of fruit:
016:036   We assuredly sent amongst **every** People a messenger,
016:111   and **every** soul will be recompensed (fully) for
016:111   On the Day **every** soul will come up pleading
016:112   abundantly supplied with sustenance from **every** place:
016:112   (closing in on it) like a garment (from **every** side),
017:013   **Every** man's fate We have fastened on his
017:034   and fulfil (**every**) engagement, for **every** engagement will

EVERY (continued)

017:089   in this Qur'an, **every** kind of similitude:
017:097   their abode will be Hell: **every** time it shows abatement,
018:054   for the benefit of mankind, **every** kind of similitude:
018:079   king who seized on **every** boat by force.
019:069   from **every** sect all those who were worst in
019:095   And **every** one of them will come to him singly
020:015   for **every** soul to receiver its reward by the
021:004   Say: "My Lord knoweth (**every**) word (spoken)
021:030   We made from water **every** living thing.
021:035   **Every** soul shall have a taste of death:
021:072   and We made righteous men of **every** one (of them).
021:096   and they swiftly swarm from **every** hill.
022:002   **every** mother giving suck shall forget her suckling-
022:002   and **every** pregnant female shall drop her load
022:003   and follow **every** Satan obstinate in rebellion!
022:005   forth **every** kind of beautiful growth (in pairs).
022:022   **Every** time they wish to get away therefrom,
022:027   and (mounted) on **every** kind of camel,
022:034   To **every** people did We appoint rites (of sacrifice),
022:067   To **every** People have We appointed rites
023:027   of **every** species, male and female, and thy
023:044   **every** time there came to a people
023:056   We would hasten them on in **every** good?
023:061   It is these who hasten in **every** good work,
024:011   to **every** man among them (will come the punishment)
024:045   And Allah has created **every** animal from water:
025:031   Thus have We made for **every** prophet an enemy
025:051   We could have sent a warner to **every** town.
026:058   Treasures, and **every** kind of honorable position;
026:128   "Do ye build a landmark on **every** high place
026:222   They descend on **every** lying, wicked person
026:225   wander distracted in **every** valley?-
027:023   ruling over them and provided with **every** requisite;
027:083   from **every** people a troop of those who reject
029:057   **Every** soul shall have a taste of death:
030:026   To Him belongs **every** being that is in the
030:058   in this Qur'an. **Every** kind of Parable:
031:010   and produce on the earth **every** kind of noble creature,
032:013   We could certainly have brought **every** soul its true
032:020   **every** time they wish to get away
034:009   is a Sign for **every** devotee that turns
034:019   Verily in this are Signs for **every** (soul that is)
035:036   Thus do We reward **every** ungrateful one!
036:057   (**Every**) fruit will be there for them; they shall
037:005   and Lord of **every** point at the rising of the sun!
037:008   and they are cast away from **every** side,
038:037   (including) **every** kind of builder and diver,-
038:085   with thee and those that follow thee,-**every** one."
039:027   in this Qur'an **every** kind of Parable, in order
039:070   And to **every** soul will be paid in full
040:005   and **every** People plotted against
040:017   That Day will **every** soul be requited for what
040:027   (for protection) from **every** arrogant one who
040:035   seal up **every** heart-of arrogant tyrinical."
040:045   Then Allah saved him from (**every**) evil that they
044:004   In that (night) is made distinct **every** affair of wisdom,
044:055   There can they call for **every** kind of fruit
045:028   **every** nation will be called to its
045:028   And thou wilt see **every** nation bowing the knee:
050:007   therein **every** kind of beautiful growth (in pairs)-
050:008   to **every** servant turning (to Allah).
050:021   And there will come forth **every** soul: with each

EVERY (continued)

050:024   into Hell **every** contumacious Rejector (of Allah)!
051:049   And of **every** thing We have created pairs:
054:003   but **every** matter has its appointed time.
054:053   **Every** matter, small and great, is on record.
055:029   (its need) **every** creature in the heavens and on earth:
055:029   **every** day in (new) Splendour
055:052   In them will be Fruits of **every** kind, two and two.
059:018   and let **every** soul look to what (provision) he has
063:004   They think that **every** cry is against them.
066:004   and Gabriel, and (**every**) righteous one among
067:008   **every** time a Group is cast therein, its Keepers
068:010   Obey not **every** mean,-swearer,
070:038   Does **every** man of them long to enter
071:007   "And **every** time I have called to them, that thou
072:028   and takes account of **every** single thing."
074:038   **Every** soul will be (held) in pledge for its deeds.
094:005   So, verily, with **every** difficulty, there is relief:
094:006   Verily, with **every** difficulty there is relief.
097:004   and the Spirit by Allah's permission, on **every** errand:
104:001   Woe to **every** (kind of) scandal-monger and backbiter,

EVERYONE

004:033   To (benefit) **everyone**, We have appointed
005:017   and all-**everyone** that is on the earth?
007:046   who would know **everyone** by his marks:
017:084   Say: "**Everyone** acts according to his own
028:056   to guide **everyone** whom thou lovest:
042:033   for **everyone** who patiently perseveres and is grateful.
043:033   for **everyone** that blasphemes against The Most Gracious,
050:032   for **everyone** penitent heedful one,

EVERYTHING

002:116   **everything** renders worship to Him.
005:036   if they had **everything** on earth, and twice
007:169   "(**Everything**) will be forgiven us." (Even so),
018:026   He hears (**everything**)!
020:046   I hear and see (**everything**).
027:016   and we have been given of **everything**, this is
028:088   **Everything** (that exists) will perish
029:042   of (**everything**) whatever that they call upon
041:021   (He) Who giveth speech to **everything**:
046:025   "**Everything** will it destroy by the command
079:006   One Day **everything** that can be in commotion

EVERYWHERE

002:205   his aim **everywhere** is to spread mischief

EVIDENCE

002:282   refuse when they are called on (for **evidence**).
002:282   more suitable as **evidence**,
002:283   Conceal not **evidence**; for whoever conceals it,
004:015   take the **evidence** of four (reliable) witnesses
005:106   we shall hide not the **evidence** we owe to Allah if
005:108   that they may give the **evidence** in its true
006:019   Say: "What thing is most weighty in **evidence**?"
012:024   but that he saw the **evidence** of his Lord:
017:102   and the earth as eye-opening **evidence**:
024:004   and reject their **evidence** ever after:
024:006   and have (in support) no **evidence** but their own,-
035:040   a Book from which they (can derive) clear (**evidence**)?-
036:012   In a clear Book (of **evidence**).
043:019   Their **evidence** will be recorded, and they
065:002   and establish the **evidence** for the sake of Allah.
075:014   Nay, man will be **evidence** against himself,
089:005   an adjuration (or **evidence**) for those who understand?

EVIDENCE (continued)

098:001   come to them Clear **Evidence**,-
098:004   came to them Clear **Evidence**.

EVIDENCES

045:020   These are clear **evidences** to men, and a

EVIDENT

005:110   'This is nothing but **evident** magic'.
007:060   "Ah! we see thee **evident** error."
010:002   "This is indeed a **evident** sorcerer!"
010:076   they said: "This is indeed **evident** sorcery!"
029:035   an **evident** Sign, for any
033:030   of you were guilty of **evident** unseemly conduct,
034:043   "This is nothing but **evident** magic!
037:015   And say, "This is nothing but **evident** sorcery!
039:015   Ah! that is indeed the (real and) **evident** Loss!"
046:007   "This is **evident** sorcery!"
057:003   the **Evident** and the Hidden:
061:006   Clear Signs, they said, "This is **evident** sorcery!"

EVIDENTLY

012:030   we see she is **evidently** going astray."

EVIL

002:014   but when they are alone with their **evil** ones,
002:060   and do no **evil** nor mischief on the (face of the) earth.
002:081   Nay, those who seek gain in **Evil**,
002:103   and guarded themselves from **evil**,
002:126   an **evil** destination (indeed)!"
002:169   For he commands you what is **evil** and shameful,
002:206   an **evil** bed indeed (to lie on)!
002:271   some of your (stains of) **evil**.
003:012   an **evil** bed indeed (to lie on)!
003:030   and all the **evil** it has done,
003:030   a great distance between it and its **evil**.
003:151   and **evil** is the home of the wrong-doers!
003:155   because of some (**evil**) they had done.
003:179   until He separates what is **evil** from what is good.
003:186   persevere patiently, and guard against **evil**,
003:197   what an **evil** bed (to lie on)!
004:017   who do **evil** in ignorance and repent soon afterwards;
004:018   of those who continue to do **evil**, until death
004:031   We shall remit your **evil** deeds, and admit
004:060   To the **Evil** (Tagut), though they were ordered
004:076   fight in the cause of **Evil** (Tagut):
004:078   but if **evil**, they say, "This is from
004:079   but whatever **evil** happens to thee, is from
004:085   helps an **evil** cause, shares in its burden:
004:088   Allah hath cast them off for their (**evil**) deeds.
004:097   What an **evil** refuge!
004:097   for you to move yourselves away (from **evil**)?"
004:110   If anyone does **evil** or wrongs his own soul but
004:115   and land him in Hell, what an **evil** refuge!
004:123   whoever works **evil**, will be requited accordingly.
004:148   shouting of **evil** words in public speech, except
004:149   or conceal it or cover **evil** with pardon, surely
005:060   those who worshipped **Evil** (Tagut)-these are
005:062   **Evil** indeed are the things that they do.
005:063   **Evil** indeed are their works.
005:066   but many of them follow a course that is **evil**.
005:079   **evil** indeed were the deeds which they did.
005:080   **Evil** indeed are (the works) which their souls
005:092   and beware (of **evil**):
005:093   guard themselves from **evil** and believe,
005:093   then again, guard themselves from **evil** and do good.

EVIL (continued)

006:031 and **evil** indeed are the burdens that they bear!
006:051 that they may guard (against **evil**).
006:054 verily, if any of you did **evil** in ignorance,
006:136 **Evil** (and unjust) is their judgment.
006:160 he that doeth **evil** shall only be recompensed
006:160 be recompensed according to his **evil**: no wrong
007:074 and refrain from **evil** and mischief on the earth."
007:131 they ascribed it to **evil** omens connected with
007:131 Behold! in truth the omens of **evil** are theirs
007:150 angry and grieved, he said: "**Evil** it is that ye
007:157 and forbids them what is **evil**:
007:165 We rescued those who forbade **evil**; but We
007:169 After them succeeded an (**evil**) generation:
007:177 **Evil** as an example are people who reject
007:188 and no **evil** should have touched me:
007:201 when a thought of **evil** from Satan
007:202 But their brethren (the **evil** ones) plunge them
008:016 and his abode is Hell, an **evil** refuse (indeed)!
008:029 remove from you (all) **evil** deeds and forgive you:
009:009 **evil** indeed are the deeds thy have done.
009:037 The **evil** of their course seems pleasing to them.
009:067 they enjoin **evil**, and forbid
009:071 they enjoin what is just and forbid what is **evil**:
009:073 Their abode is hell, an **evil** refuge indeed.
009:074 They swear by Allah that they said nothing (**evil**),
009:074 but if they turn back (to their **evil** ways), Allah
009:082 the (**evil**) that they do.
009:095 recompense for the (**evil**) that they did.
009:098 on them be the disaster of **Evil**:
009:102 and act that was good with another that was **evil**.
009:112 forbid **evil**; and observe the limits set by Allah;-
009:122 to guard themselves (against **evil**).
010:008 because of the (**evil**) they earned.
010:027 But those who have earned **evil** will have
010:027 will have a reward of like **evil**:
010:063 and (constantly) guard against **evil**;-
011:010 "All **evil** has departed from me:" behold! he falls
011:036 So grieve no longer over their (**evil**) deeds.
011:054 some of our gods may have seize thee with **evil**."
011:085 commit not **evil** in the land with intent
011:114 remove those that are **evil**: that is a
012:024 (all) **evil** and indecent deeds:
012:025 an **evil** design against thy wife, but prison
012:051 no **evil** know we against him!" Said the 'Aziz's
012:053 certainly incites **evil**, unless my Lord do bestow
013:006 the **evil** in preference to the good yet have
013:022 **Evil** with good: for such there is the final
014:026 is that of an **evil** tree:
014:026 And the parable of an **evil** Word is that
014:029 an **evil** place to stay in!
016:028 "We did no **evil** (knowingly)."
016:029 Thus **evil** indeed is the abode
016:034 But the **evil** results of their deeds overtook them,
016:036 "Serve Allah, and eschew **Evil**":
016:045 Do then those who devise **evil** (plots) feel
016:059 Ah! what an **evil** (choice) they decide on!
016:060 applies the similitude of **evil**:
016:090 He forbids all indecent deeds, and **evil** and rebellion:
016:094 taste the **evil** (consequences) of having hindered (men)
016:112 because of the (**evil**) which (its people) wrought.
017:007 if ye did **evil** (ye did it) against yourselves.
017:011 Man prays for **evil** as fervently as he prays

EVIL (continued)

017:032 for it is an indecent (deed) and an **evil** way.
017:038 Of all such things the **evil** is hateful
017:059 of frightening (and warning from **evil**).
017:083 and when **Evil** seizes him he gives himself
018:050 **Evil** would be the exchange for the
019:028 a man of **evil**, nor thy mother a woman unchaste!"
019:063 Our Servants who guard against **evil**.
019:072 But We shall save those who guarded against **evil**,
020:076 who purify themselves (from **evil**).
020:120 But Satan whispered **evil** to him:
021:035 and We test you by **evil** and by good
021:074 given to **Evil**, a rebellious people.
021:077 truly they were a people given to **Evil**: so We
022:013 and **evil** the companion (for help)!
022:013 **evil**, indeed, is the is the patron,
022:072 And **evil** is that destination!"
023:096 Repel **evil** with that which is best: We are
023:107 if ever we return (to **evil**), then shall
024:011 think it not to be an **evil** to you; on the
024:057 is the Fire,-and it is indeed an **evil** refuge!
025:034 they will be in an **evil** plight, and, as
025:040 by the town on which was rained a shower of **evil**:
025:055 is a helper (of **Evil**), against his own Lord!
025:066 "**Evil** indeed is it as an abode, and as
025:070 for Allah will change the **evil** of such persons
026:091 "And to those straying in **evil**, the Fire
026:094 they and those straying in **evil**,
026:173 and **evil** was the shower on those who were admonished
026:183 due to men, nor do **evil** in the land,
026:224 straying in **Evil**, who follow them:
027:011 to take the place of **evil**, truly, I am
027:046 to hasten on the **evil** before the good?
027:058 and **evil** was the shower on those
027:090 And if any do **evil**, their faces will be thrown
028:054 that they avert **Evil** with Good, and that
028:084 but if any does **evil**, the doers of **evil** are only punished
029:004 **Evil** is their judgment!
029:004 Do those who practice **evil** think that they
029:036 nor commit **evil** on the earth, with intent
029:045 for Prayer restrains from shameful and **evil** deeds;
030:010 of those who do **evil**; for that
030:010 In the long run **evil** will be the End of those who do **evil**;
030:036 when some **evil** afflicts them become of what their (own)
030:041 in order that they may turn back (from **Evil**).
032:014 for your (**evil**) deeds!"
035:008 Is he, then, to whom the **evil** of his conduct
035:010 Those that lay Plots of **Evil**,-for them is a Chastisement
035:043 their arrogance in the land and their plotting of **Evil**.
035:043 the plotting of **Evil** will hem in only the authors thereof.
036:018 an **evil** omen from you:
036:019 They said: "Your **evil** omens are with yourselves:
036:019 (deem ye this an **evil** omen), if ye are admonished?
037:002 Those who are strong in repelling (**evil**),
037:018 be humiliated (on account of your **evil**)."
037:177 **Evil** will be the morning for those who were
038:028 those who guard against **evil**, the same
038:055 will be an **evil** place of (final) Return!-
038:056 an **evil** bed (indeed, to lie on)!-
038:060 Now **evil** is (this) place to stay in!"
039:019 is justly due (equal to one who eschews **evil**)?
039:028 in order that they may guard against **Evil**.
039:051 Nay, the **evil** results of their deeds overtook them.

EVIL (continued)

039:051 of this (generation)-the **evil** results of their
039:061 no **evil** shall touch them, nor shall they grieve.
039:072 and **evil** is (this) abode of the arrogant!
040:037 in Pharaoh's eyes, the **evil** of his deeds, and he
040:040 "He that works **evil** will not be requited but by
040:045 Then Allah saved him from (every) **evil** that they
040:058 and those who do **evil**.
040:076 to dwell therein: and **evil** is (this) abode
041:034 Repel (**Evil**) with what is better:
041:034 Nor can Goodness and **Evil** be equal.
041:046 whoever works **evil**, it is against his own soul:
041:051 and when **Evil** seizes him, (he comes) full
042:034 of the (**evil**) which (the men) have earned:
043:038 he says (to his **evil**-companion): 'Would that
043:038 Ah! **Evil** is the companion (indeed)!
044:003 for We (ever) wish to warn (against **Evil**).
045:015 if he does **evil**, it works against (His own soul).
045:021 What! do those who do **evil** deeds think that
045:033 the **evil** (fruits) of what they did, and they
047:010 before them (who did **evil**)?
047:014 the **evil** of his conduct seems pleasing, and such
047:017 on them their Piety and Restraint (from **evil**).
047:036 and guard against **evil**, He will grant
048:006 On them is a round of **Evil**: the Wrath of
048:006 who think an **evil** thought of Allah.
048:006 and **evil** is it for a destination.
048:012 and ye conceived an **evil** thought,
053:031 so that he rewards those who do **evil**, according to their
053:032 He knows best who it is that guards against **evil**.
055:035 On you will be sent (O ye **evil** ones twain)!
057:015 is the proper place to claim you: and an **evil** refuge it is!"
058:008 and **evil** is that destination!
058:015 severe Chastisement: **evil** indeed are their deeds.
059:015 they have tasted the **evil** result of their conduct;
060:002 forth their hands and their tongues against you for **evil**;
062:005 **Evil** is the similitude of people who falsify
063:002 truly **evil** are their deeds.
064:005 So they tasted the **evil** result of their conduct;
064:010 and **evil** is that Goal.
065:005 He will remove his **evil** deeds from him
065:009 Then did they taste the **evil** result of their
066:008 hope that your Lord will remove from you your **evil** deeds,
066:009 Their abode is Hell,-an **evil** refuge (indeed).
067:006 and **evil** is (such) destination.
070:020 Fretful when **evil** touches him;
076:007 and they fear a Day whose **evil** flies far and wide.
076:011 from the **evil** of that Day, and will
077:016 Did We not destroy the men of old (for their **evil**)?
086:013 that distinguishes (Good from **Evil**):
099:008 an atom's weight of **evil**, shall see it.
114:004 From the mischief of the Whisperer (of **Evil**),-

EVIL-DOER

028:004 for he was indeed an **evil-doer.**

EVIL-DOERS

002:124 is not within the reach of **evil-doers**."

EVILS

005:012 verily I will wipe out from you your **evils**,
039:048 For the **evils** of their Deeds will confront them,

EVOLVED

003:110 Ye are the best of Peoples, **evolved** for mankind.

EWE

038:024 thy (single) **ewe** to be added to his (flock of) ewes:

EWES

038:023 he has nine and ninety **ewes**, and I
038:024 thy (single) ewe to be added to his (flock of) **ewes**:

EXACT

032:022 who transgress We shall **exact** (Due) Retribution.
043:041 We shall be sure to **exact** retribution from them,
044:016 (then) **exact** retribution!
083:002 by measure from men, **exact** full measure,

EXACTED

007:136 So We **exacted** retribution from them: We drowned
015:079 So We **exacted** retribution from them.
018:077 thou couldst have **exacted** some recompense for it!"
043:025 So We **exacted** retribution from them: now see
043:055 We **exacted** retribution from them, and We
047:004 could have **exacted** retribution from them (Himself);

EXACTLY

006:124 we receive one (**exactly**) like those
019:094 and hath numbered them (all) **exactly**.
055:005 follow courses (**exactly**) computed;

EXALT

056:003 (Many) will it bring low; (many) will it **exalt**;

EXALTED

002:129 for Thou art the **Exalted** in Might, the Wise."
002:209 then know that Allah is **Exalted** in Power, Wise.
002:220 He is indeed **Exalted** in Power, Wise."
002:228 and Allah is **Exalted** in Power, Wise.
002:240 And Allah is **Exalted** in Power, Wise.
002:260 Then know that Allah is **Exalted** in Power, Wise."
003:004 and Allah is **Exalted** in Might, Lord of Retribution.
003:006 the **Exalted** and Might, the Wise.
003:018 the **Exalted** in Power, the Wise.
003:062 the **Exalted** in Power, the Wise.
003:126 the **Exalted**, the Wise:
004:056 for Allah is **Exalted** in Power, Wise.
004:158 and Allah is **Exalted** in Power, Wise;
004:165 for Allah is **Exalted** in Power, Wise.
004:171 (for **Exalted** is He) above having a son.
005:038 and Allah is **Exalted** in Power full of Wisdom.
005:095 for Allah is **Exalted**, and lord of Retribution.
005:118 Thou art the **Exalted**, the Wise.
006:096 the **Exalted** in Power, the Omniscient.
007:190 but Allah is **exalted** high above the partners
008:010 **Exalted** in Power, Wise.
008:049 behold! Allah is **Exalted** in might, Wise.
008:063 for He is **Exalted** in might, Wise.
008:067 and Allah is **Exalted** in might, Wise.
009:040 But the word of Allah is **exalted** to the heights:
009:040 **Exalted** in might, Wise.
009:071 for Allah is **Exalted** in power, Wise.
012:078 They said: "O **exalted** one! Behold! he has
012:088 "O **exalted** one! distress has seized us
014:001 to the Way of (Him) the **Exalted** in Power,
014:004 is **Exalted** in power, Full of Wisdom.
014:047 for Allah is **Exalted** in power,-the Lord
016:060 for He is the **Exalted** in Power, Full of Wisdom.
017:043 they say! **Exalted** and Great (beyond measure)!
020:075 for them are ranks **exalted**,-
022:040 is Full of Strength, **Exalted** in Might, (able to
023:116 Therefore **exalted** be Allah, the King,
026:009 the **Exalted** in Might, Most Merciful.

EXALTED (continued)

026:068   the **Exalted** in Might, Most Merciful.
026:104   the **Exalted** in Might, Most Merciful.
026:122   the **Exalted** in Might, Most Merciful.
026:140   the **Exalted** in Might, Most Merciful.
026:159   the **Exalted** in Might, Most Merciful.
026:175   the **Exalted** in Might, Most Merciful.
026:191   The **Exalted** in Might, Most Merciful
026:217   on the **Exalted** in Might, the Merciful,-
027:009   the **Exalted** in Might, the Wise!...
027:078   and He is **Exalted** in Might, All-knowing.
029:026   for He is **Exalted** in Might, and Wise."
029:042   and He is **Exalted** (in power), Wise.
030:005   and He is **Exalted** in Might, Most Merciful.
030:027   for He is **Exalted** in Might, Full of Wisdom.
031:009   and He is **Exalted** in power, Wise.
031:027   for Allah is **Exalted** in power, Full of Wisdom.
032:006   the **Exalted** (in power), the Merciful;-
033:025   full of Strength, **Exalted** in might.
034:006   of the **Exalted** (in Might), Worthy of all praise.
034:027   Nay, He is Allah, the **Exalted** in Power, the Wise."
035:002   and He is the **Exalted** in Power, Full of Wisdom.
035:028   **Exalted** in Might, Oft-Forgiving.
036:005   by (Him), the **Exalted** in Might, Most Merciful.
036:038   the **Exalted** in Might, the All-Knowing.
037:008   in the direction of the **Exalted** Assembly and they
038:009   the **Exalted** in Power, the Grantor
038:066   and all between-**Exalted** in Might, Ever-Forgiving.
038:069   **Exalted** Chiefs, when they discuss (matters)
039:001   from Allah, the **Exalted** in Power, Full of Wisdom.
039:005   Is not He the **Exalted** in Power-He Who
039:037   Is not Allah **Exalted** in Power, Lord of Retribution?
040:002   is from Allah, **Exalted** in Power, Full of Knowledge,-
040:008   the **Exalted** in Might, Full of Wisdom.
040:015   **Exalted** is he in His attributes.
040:042   and I call you to the **Exalted** in Power,
041:012   of (Him) the **Exalted** in Might, Full of knowledge.
041:041   and indeed it is a Book of **exalted** power.
042:003   Allah, **Exalted** in Power, Full of Wisdom.
043:009   by (Him), the **Exalted** in Power, Full of Knowledge';
044:042   for He is **exalted** in Might, Most Merciful.
045:002   is from Allah the **Exalted** in Power, Full of Wisdom.
045:037   and He is **Exalted** in Power, Full of Wisdom!
046:002   is from Allah the **Exalted** in Power, Full of Wisdom.
048:007   and Allah is **Exalted** in Power, Full of Wisdom.
048:019   **Exalted** in Power, Full of Wisdom.
052:043   **Exalted** is Allah far above the things
057:001   for He is the **Exalted** in Might, the Wise.
057:025   Full of Strength, **Exalted** in Might.
059:001   for He is the **Exalted** in Might, the Wise.
059:023   the **Exalted** in Might, the Irresistible, the justly
059:024   and He is the **Exalted** in Might,
060:005   the **Exalted** in Might, the Wise."
061:001   the **Exalted** in Might, the Wise.
062:001   the Holy One, the **Exalted** in Might, the Wise.
062:003   is **Exalted** in Might, Wise.
064:018   is open, **Exalted** in Might, Full of Wisdom.
067:002   the **Exalted** in Might, Oft-Forgiving;
072:003   'And **exalted** is the Majesty of our Lord: He has
080:014   **Exalted** (in dignity), kept pure and holy,
085:008   **Exalted** in Power, worthy of all Praise!

EXALTS

035:010   it is He Who **exalts** each Deed of Righteousness.

EXAMINE

060:010   believing women refugees, **examine** (and test) them:

EXAMPLE

002:066   So We made it an **example** to their own time,
007:177   Evil as an **example** are people who reject
023:021   And in cattle (too) ye have an instructive **example**:
024:044   is an instructive **example** for those who
043:008   the **example** of the peoples of old.
043:056   and an **Example** to later ages.
043:057   as an **example**, behold thy people raise a clamour
043:059   and We made him an **example** to the
060:004   There is for you an excellent **example** (to follow)
060:006   an excellent **example** for you to follow,-for those
066:010   Allah sets forth, for an **example** to the
066:011   And Allah sets forth, as an **example** to those
079:025   (and made an) **example** of him,-in the Hereafter,

EXAMPLES

003:137   There have been **examples** that have passed
025:039   To each one We set forth parables and **examples**;

EXCEED

005:077   **exceed** not in your religion the bounds
013:008   (of their time or number) or do **exceed.**
017:033   but let him not **exceed** bounds in the matter
023:007   But those whose desires **exceed** those limits

EXCEEDING

002:114   an **exceeding** torment.
005:022   are a people of **exceeding** strength: never shall
031:020   flow to you in **exceeding** measure, (both) seen

EXCEEDINGLY

069:006   by a furious wind, **exceedingly** violent;

EXCEEDS

002:178   After this whoever **exceeds** the limits

EXCEL

017:055   of the Prophets to **excel** others and We gave

EXCELLENCE

003:014   horses branded (for blood and **excellence**);
017:021   and more in **excellence**.

EXCELLENT

003:136   how excellent a recompense for those who work
003:148   and the excellent reward of the Hereafter.
004:058   verily how excellent is the teaching
013:004   more **excellent** than others to eat.
013:024   Now how **excellent** is the final Home!"
016:030   and **excellent** indeed is the Home of the righteous,-
029:058   an **excellent** reward for those who do (good)!-
033:021   of Allah an **excellent** exemplar for him who hopes
038:030   (for a son),-how **excellent** is the Servant!
038:044   how **excellent** is the servant!
039:074   how **excellent** a reward for those who
060:004   There is for you an **excellent** example (to follow)
060:006   an **excellent** example for you to follow,-for those
065:011   a most **excellent** provision.

EXCELLENTLY

051:048   how **excellently** We do spread out!

EXCEPT

002:026   **except** those who forsake (the path),
002:045   **except** to those who are humble.
002:083   **except** a few among you,
002:102   anyone **except** by Allah's permission.
002:114   should themselves enter them **except** in fear.
002:132   then die not **except** in the state
002:143   **except** to those guided by Allah.

EXCEPT (continued)

002:150	**except** those of them that are bent
002:160	**Except** those who repent and make amends
002:193	**except** to those who practice oppression.
002:213	**except** through selfish contumacy.
002:229	**except** when both parties fear that
002:235	with them **except** that you speak to them
002:246	they turned back **except** a small band among them.
002:249	"But they drank of it, **except** a few.
002:255	in His presence **except** as He permitteth?
002:255	aught of his knowledge **except** as He willeth.
002:267	receive it **except** with closed eyes.
002:275	not stand **except** as stands one whom the Satan
003:007	but no one knows its true meanings **except** Allah.
003:007	the Message **except** men of understanding.
003:019	**except** through envy of each other,
003:028	left with Allah **except** by way of precaution,
003:062	there is no god **except** Allah;
003:089	**Except** for those that repent (even) after that.
003:093	**except** what Israel made unlawful for himself
003:102	and die not **except** in a state of Islam.
003:112	**except** when under a covenant (of protection)
003:126	no victory **except** from Allah, the Exalted,
003:135	and who can forgive sins **except** Allah?
003:145	Nor can a soul die **except** by Allah's leave,
004:019	**except** where they have been guilty of open lewdness;
004:022	your fathers married, **except** what is past:
004:023	**except** for what is past;
004:024	**except** for these, all others are lawful,
004:024	Also (prohibited are) women already married,
004:043	**except** when you are passing by (through the mosque),
004:090	**Except** those who join a group between whom
004:092	**except** by mistake, and whoever kills
004:095	**except** those who are disabled.
004:098	**Except** those who are (really) weak and oppressed,
004:146	**Except** for those who repent, mend (their life),
004:148	**except** by one who has been wronged, for Allah
004:169	**Except** the way of Hell, to dwell
005:034	**Except** for those who repent before they
005:073	for there is no god **except** One God.
005:117	**except** what Thou didst command me to say, to wit,
006:029	"There is nothing **except** our life on this earth,
006:047	will any be destroyed **except** those who do wrong?"
006:051	**except** from Him they will have no protector
006:070	no protector or intercessor **except** Allah:
006:119	**except** under compulsion of necessity?
006:128	**except** as Allah willeth." For thy Lord
006:138	none should eat of them **except** those whom-so they say-
006:146	**except** what adheres to their backs or their entrails,
006:151	**except** by way of justice and law:
006:152	**except** to improve it, until he
007:083	**except** His wife: she was of those who
007:099	**except** those (doomed) to ruin!
007:147	rewarded **except** as they have wrought?
007:188	or harm to myself **except** as Allah willeth.
008:010	(in any case) there is no help **except** from Allah:
008:034	its guardians **except** the righteous; but most
008:072	**except** against a people with whom ye have
009:007	with the Pagans, **except** those with whom ye
009:016	and protectors **except** Allah, His Messenger,
009:018	and fear none (at all) **except** Allah. It is
009:051	**except** what Allah has decreed for us:
009:116	**Except** for Him ye have no protector nor helper.

EXCEPT (continued)

010:003	**except** after His leave (hath been obtained).
010:049	or profit to myself **except** as Allah willeth.
010:083	**except** some children of his People, because of
010:090	no god **except** Him Who the Children
010:098	**except** the people of Jonah?
010:100	**except** by the Will of Allah, and He
011:036	**except** those who have believed already!
011:040	and your family-**except** those against whom
011:105	shall speak **except** by His leave:
011:107	**except** as thy Lord willeth: for thy Lord
011:108	the earth endure, **except** as the Lord willeth:
011:116	(but there were none) **except** a few among them whom
011:119	**Except** those on whom thy Lord hath bestowed
012:047	**except** a little, of which ye shall eat.
012:048	(all) **except** a little which ye shall have
012:067	none can command **except** Allah:
012:076	**except** that Allah willed it (so).
012:087	**except** those who have no faith."
013:038	**except** as Allah permitted (or commanded).
014:004	We sent not a messenger **except** (to teach) in the
014:011	an authority **except** as Allah permits.
014:022	I had no authority over you **except** to call you,
015:008	We send not the angels down **except** for just cause:
015:040	"**Except** Thy chosen servants among them,
015:042	**except** such as put themselves in the wrong and follow
015:060	"**Except** his wife, who, we have ascertained,
016:007	could not (otherwise) reach **except** with souls distressed:
016:106	**except** under compulsion, his heart remaining firm
017:033	made sacred-**except** for just cause.
017:034	orphan's property **except** to improve it, until he
017:061	they prostrated **except** Iblis:
017:076	would not have stayed (therein) **except** for a little while.
017:087	**Except** for Mercy from thy Lord; for His
017:089	men refuse (to receive it) **except** with ingratitude!
017:099	(to receive it) **except** with ingratitude.
018:022	**except** on a matter that is clear, nor consult
018:024	**Except** "If Allah so wills" and remember
018:050	they prostrated **except** Iblis.
019:060	**Except** those who repent and believe, and work
020:109	**except** for those for whom permission has been
021:028	**except** for those who with whom He is well-pleased
021:036	they treat thee not **except** with ridicule.
022:030	are cattle **except** those mentioned to you
022:040	(for no cause) **except** that they say, "Our Lord is Allah".
022:065	the sky from falling on the earth **except** by His leave:
023:006	**Except** with those joined to them in the
023:027	and thy family-**except** those of them against whom
024:005	**Except** those who repent thereafter and mend
024:031	their beauty **except** to their husbands,
024:031	their beauty and ornaments **except** what (ordinarily)
025:068	**except** for just cause, nor commit fornication,-
026:171	**Except** an old woman who lingered behind.
026:227	**Except** those who believe, work righteousness,
027:032	no affair have I decided **except** in your presence."
027:057	But We saved him and his family **except** his wife:
027:065	or in the earth, **except** Allah, knows what is hidden:
027:087	**except** such as Allah will please (to exempt):
028:059	a population **except** when its members practice
028:086	**except** as a Mercy from thy Lord:
028:088	will perish **except** His Face.
029:024	(Abraham's) people **except** that they said: "Slay him
029:032	and his following,-**except** his wife: she is

EXCEPT (continued)

029:033   and thy following, **except** thy wife: she is
029:046   of the Book, **except** in the best way, unless it
031:032   **except** only a perfidious ungrateful (wretch)!
033:018   but come not to the fight **except** for just
033:052   attract thee, **except** any thy right hand should
034:014   his death **except** a little worm of the earth,
034:017   give (such) requital **except** to such as are
034:021   **except** that We might test the man who believes
034:023   **except** for those for whom He has granted
036:044   **Except** by way of Mercy from Us, and by
037:010   **Except** such as snatch away something by stealth,
037:035   there is no god **except** Allah, would puff
037:059   "**Except** our first death, and that
037:074   **Except** the chosen servants of Allah.
037:128   **Except** the chosen Servants of Allah (among them).
037:135   **Except** an old woman who was among those who
037:163   **Except** such as are (themselves) going to
038:083   "**Except** Thy Servants amongst them, sincere and
039:068   **except** such as it will please Allah (to exempt).
040:078   for any messenger to bring a Sign **except** by the
041:035   goodness **except** those who exercise patience
042:023   for this **except** the love of those near of kin."
042:051   that Allah should speak to him **except** by inspiration,
043:067   one to another,-**except** the Righteous
044:039   We created them not **except** for just ends:
044:042   **Except** such as receive Allah's Mercy: for He
044:056   Nor will they there taste Death, **except** the first Death;
046:035   destroyed **except** those who transgress?
051:036   We found not there any **except** one (Muslim) household:
053:026   will avail nothing **except** after Allah has given
054:034   (which destroyed them), **except** Lut's household:
058:002   None can be their mothers **except** those who gave them
058:010   he cannot harm them in the least, **except** as Allah permits;
059:014   **except** in fortified townships, or from behind walls.
064:011   No kind of calamity can occur, **except** by the leave of
065:001   **except** in case they are guilty of some open lewdness,
067:019   uphold them **except** The Most Gracious:
069:036   "Nor hath he any food **except** the foul pus
070:030   **Except** with their wives and the (captives)
072:022   nor should I find refuge **except** in Him.
072:027   "**Except** an apostle whom He has chosen:
074:031   the forces of the Lord, **except** He, and this
074:039   **Except** the Companions of the Right Hand.
074:056   **except** as Allah wills: He is
076:030   But ye will not, **except** as Allah wills; for Allah
078:030   no increase shall We grant you, **except** in Chastisement.
078:038   none shall speak **except** any who permitted by
081:029   But ye shall not will **Except** as Allah wills,-
084:025   **Except** to those who believe and work
087:007   **Except** as Allah wills: for He knoweth
095:006   **Except** such as believe and do righteous deeds:
103:003   **Except** such as have Faith, and do righteous deeds,

EXCEPTING

015:059   "**Excepting** the adherents of Lut:

EXCEPTIONS

005:001   with the **exceptions** named:
022:030   except those mentioned to you (as **exceptions**):

EXCESS

005:087   for Allah loveth not those given to **excess**.
005:087   made lawful for you, but commit no **excess**:
006:141   But waste not by **excess**: for Allah
007:031   eat and drink: but waste not by **excess**,

EXCESS (continued)

018:028   and his affair has become all **excess**.
020:081   but commit no **excess** therein, lest My Wrath

EXCESSES

004:171   commit no **excesses** in your religion: nor say
005:032   continued to commit **excesses** in the land.
005:078   because they disobeyed and persisted in **Excesses**.

EXCESSIVE

076:013   neither the sun's (**excessive** heat) nor **excessive** cold.

EXCHANGE

002:061   "Will ye **exchange** the better for the worse?
018:036   something better in **exchange**."
018:050   Evil would be the **exchange** for the
018:081   give them in **exchange** (a son) better in purity
052:023   They shall there **exchange**, one with
066:005   in **exchange** Consorts better than you,-who submit
068:032   in **exchange** a better (garden) than this:
076:028   but, when We will, We shall **exchange** their likes.

EXCHANGED

014:028   to those who have **exchanged** the favour of Allah.

EXCITE

005:091   to **excite** enmity and hatred between you, with
030:060   nor let those **excite** thee, who have

EXCITEMENT

003:154   After (the **excitement**) of the distress,

EXCLUSION

062:006   to the **exclusion** of (other) men, then express

EXCLUSIVE

039:014   with my sincere (and **exclusive**) devotion:

EXCLUSIVELY

029:065   their devotion sincerely (and **exclusively**) to Him;
039:044   Say: "To Allah belongs **exclusively** (the right to grant)

EXCRETIONS

016:066   between **excretions** and blood, We produce,

EXCUSE

002:224   an **excuse** in your oaths against doing good,
006:023   no **excuse** for them but to say: "By Allah
007:169   saying (for **excuse**): "(Everything) will be forgiven us."
016:084   then will no **excuse** be accepted from Unbelievers,
018:076   received (full) **excuse** from my side."
024:063   under shelter of some **excuse**:
030:057   So on that Day no **excuse** of theirs will avail

EXCUSED

002:249   a mere sip out of the hand is **excused**."

EXCUSES

009:066   Make ye no **excuses**: ye have rejected Faith
009:090   men who made **excuses** and came to claim exemption;
009:094   They will present their **excuses** to you when ye
009:094   Say thou: "Present no **excuses**: we shall
040:052   to Wrong-doers to present their **excuses**, but they
066:007   make no **excuses** this Day!
075:015   Even though he were to put up his **excuses**.

EXECUTE

027:021   or **execute** him, unless he bring me a clear

EXECUTING

066:006   not (from **executing**) the Commands they receive

EXECUTION

005:033   mischief through the land is: **execution** or crucifixion, or

EXEMPLARY

005:038   and **exemplary** punishment from Allah, and Allah
013:006   before them, (many) **exemplary** punishments!

EXEMPLAR
033:021 of Allah an excellent **exemplar** for him who hopes
EXEMPT
027:087 except such as Allah will please (to **exempt**):
039:068 except such as it will please Allah (to **exempt**).
056:086 if you are **exempt** from (future) account,-
EXEMPTION
009:043 grant them **exemption** until those who told
009:044 no **exemption** from fighting with their goods
009:045 Only those ask thee for **exemption** who believe
009:049 "Grant me **exemption** and draw me not into trial."
009:086 among them ask thee for **exemption**, and say:
009:090 excuses and came to claim **exemption**; and those
009:093 such as claim **exemption** while they are rich.
EXERCISE
002:247 They say: "How can he **exercise** authority
002:247 better fitted than he to **exercise** authority,
034:013 "**Exercise** thanks sons of David, but few of My servants
041:035 except those who **exercise** patience and self-restraint,-
EXHAUSTED
018:109 be **exhausted** than would the words of my Lord,
031:027 of Allah be **exhausted** (in the writing): for Allah
EXHORTATION
011:120 as well as an **exhortation** and a message of
EXHORTS
004:114 but if one **exhorts** to a deed of charity or
EXILE
002:218 who suffered **exile** and fought
005:033 from opposite sides, or **exile** from the land:
EXIST
006:164 Cherisher of all things (that **exist**)?"
EXISTENCE
040:074 anything (that had real **existence**)."
057:022 a Book before We bring it into **existence**:
EXISTS
028:088 Everything (that **exists**) will perish
EXIT
017:080 and likewise my **exit** by the Gate
075:026 the collar-bone (in its **exit**),
EXPAND
020:025 (Moses) said: "O my Lord! **expand** me my breast;"
EXPANDED
094:001 Have We not **expanded** thee thy breast?-
EXPANSE
078:006 Have We not made the earth as a wide **expanse**,
079:030 hath He extended (to a wide **expanse**);
091:006 By the Earth and its (wide) **expanse**;
EXPECT
007:147 can they **expect** to be rewarded except
009:052 But we can **expect** for you either that Allah
009:052 Say: "Can you **expect** for us (any fate) other than
010:102 Do they then **expect** (any thing) but the like of
017:028 from thy Lord which thou dost **expect**, yet speak
065:003 provides for him from (sources) he never could **expect**.
074:006 Nor **expect**, in giving, any increase (for thyself)!
EXPECTANT
009:052 So wait (**expectant**); we too will wait with you."
EXPECTED
009:018 It is they who are **expected** to be on true guidance.
025:040 But they **expected** not to be raised again.
028:086 And thou hadst not **expected** that the Book

EXPECTED (continued)
047:022 Then, is it to be **expected** of you, if ye
059:002 they little **expected** (it), and cast
092:019 from anyone for which is a reward is **expected** in return,
EXPECTS
018:110 whoever **expects** to meet his Lord, let him
EXPEDITION
009:081 (in the Tabuk **expedition**) rejoiced in their
009:122 from every **expedition** go forth to devote
059:006 for this ye made no **expedition** with either
EXPEL
009:013 plotted to **expel** the Messenger, and attack
017:076 was to scare thee off the land, in order to **expel** thee;
027:037 we shall **expel** them from there in disgrace,
063:008 will **expel** therefrom the meaner."
EXPELLED
007:018 (Allah) said: "Get out from this disgraced and **expelled**.
022:040 have been **expelled** from their homes in defiance of right,-
026:057 So We **expelled** them from gardens, springs,
059:008 **expelled** from their homes and their property,
059:011 "If ye are **expelled**, We too will go out with you,
059:012 If they are **expelled**, never will they go out
EXPENSE
047:038 are niggardly are so at the **expense** of their
EXPENSES
009:092 no resources wherewith to provide the **expenses**.
EXPERIENCE
012:068 full of knowledge (and **experience**): but most
EXPERT
020:063 certainly (**expert**) magicians: their object
EXPIATION
005:089 for **expiation**, feed then indigent persons,
005:089 That is the **expiation** for the oaths ye have sworn.
066:002 the **expiration** of your oaths (in some cases):
EXPIRES
016:061 when their Term **expires**, they would
035:045 Term **expires**, verily Allah has in His sight
EXPLAIN
006:046 See how We **explain** the Signs by various
006:055 Thus do We **explain** the Signs in detail:
006:065 See how We **explain** the Signs in diverse ways;
006:105 Thus do We **explain** the Signs
007:032 Thus do We **explain** the Signs in detail
007:058 thus do We **explain** the Signs by various
007:174 Thus do We **explain** the Signs in detail;
009:011 (thus) do We **explain** Signs in detail, for those
010:005 (Thus) doth He **explain** His Signs in detail,
010:024 Thus do We **explain** the Signs
016:044 that thou mayest **explain** clearly to men
027:076 Verily this Qur'an doth **explain** to the
030:028 Thus do We **explain** the Signs in detail to a
074:027 And what will **explain** to thee what Hell-Fire is?
075:019 it is for Us to to **explain** it (and make it clear):
077:014 And what will **explain** to thee what is
082:017 And what will **explain** to thee what the
082:018 Again, what will **explain** to thee what the
083:008 And what will **explain** to thee what Sijjin is?
083:019 And what will **explain** to thee what 'Illiyin is?
086:002 And what will **explain** to thee
090:012 And what will **explain** to thee
097:002 And what will **explain** to thee what the
101:003 And what will **explain** to thee what the

EXPLAIN (continued)

101:010 And what will **explain** to Thee what this is?
104:005 And what will **explain** to thee That which

EXPLAINED

006:114 Who hath sent unto you the Book, **explained** in detail."
006:119 when He hath **explained** to you in detail
007:052 based on knowledge, Which We **explained** in detail,-
011:001 (of established meaning), further **explained** in detail,-
017:012 all things have We **explained** in detail.
017:041 We have **explained** (things) in various (ways)
017:089 And We have **explained** to man, in this Qur'an,
018:054 We have **explained** in detail in this Qur'an, for the
020:113 an Arabic Qur'an-and **explained** therein in detail
041:003 A Book, whereof the verses are **explained** in detail;
041:044 "Why are not its verses **explained** in detail?

EXPLAINING

006:154 and **explaining** all things in detail,-
013:002 doth regulate all affairs, **explaining** the Signs in detail,
016:089 Book **explaining** all things, a guide a Mercy,
044:013 Seeing that a Messenger **explaining** things clearly

EXPLANATION

007:145 Admonition and **explanation** of all things,
010:037 and a fuller **explanation** of the Book-wherein
025:033 and best **explanation** (thereof).

EXPLANATIONS

065:011 clear **explanations**, that he may lead forth those

EXPOSE

003:127 of the Unbelievers or **expose** them to infamy,
007:027 to **expose** their shame:

EXPOSED

033:013 Saying, "Truly our houses are bare and **exposed**,"
033:013 though they were not **exposed**:

EXPOSITION

012:111 a detailed **exposition** of all things,
045:006 then in what **exposition** will they believe after

EXPOUND

012:043 O ye chiefs! **expound** to me my vision if it be
012:046 **Expound** to us (the dream) of seven
015:094 Therefore **expound** openly what thou art commanded,

EXPRESS

043:052 and can scarcely **express** himself clearly?
062:006 then **express** your desire for Death, if ye
062:007 But never will they **express** their desire

EXPULSION

002:240 a year's maintenance without **expulsion**;

EXTEND

002:255 His throne doth **extend** over the heavens

EXTENDED

079:030 hath He **extended** (to a wide expanse);

EXTENDETH

007:156 but My Mercy **extendeth** to all things.

EXTENDS

019:075 (Allah) Most Gracious **extends** (the rope)

EXTENT

022:060 to no greater **extent** than the injury he received,
028:084 punished (to the **extent**) of their deeds.
054:012 (and rose) to the **extent** decreed.

EXTINGUISH

005:064 Allah doth **extinguish** it; but they (ever)
009:032 Fain would they **extinguish** Allah's light
061:008 Their intention is to **extinguish** Allah's Light

EXTOL

012:031 they did **extol** him, and (in their amazement)

EXTRACT

016:014 and that ye may **extract** therefrom ornaments
035:012 and tender, and ye **extract** ornaments to wear;

EXTRAVAGANT

025:067 are not **extravagant** and not niggardly, but hold
026:151 of those who are **extravagant**,-
072:004 who used to utter **extravagant** lies against Allah;

EXTREMES

016:112 and terror (in **extremes**) (closing in on it) like

EXTREMES

025:067 but hold a just (balance) between those (**extremes**);

EXTREMITY

012:085 though reach the last **extremity** of illness,

EXULT

003:188 who **exult** in what they have brought about,
028:076 those who **exult** (in riches).
028:076 "**Exult** not, for Allah loveth not those who
030:036 We sent down a taste of Mercy, they **exult** thereat:
042:048 a taste of a Mercy from Us, he doth **exult** thereat,
057:023 nor **exult** over favours bestowed upon you.

EXULTATION

011:010 behold! he falls into **exultation** and pride.

EXULTED

028:058 which **exulted** in their life (of ease and plenty)!
040:083 they **exulted** in such knowledge (and skill)

EYE

005:045 "Life for life, **eye** for **eye**, nose for nose,
007:040 pass through the **eye** of the needle: such is
016:077 is as the twinkling of an **eye**, or even quicker:
019:026 "So eat and drink and cool (thine) **eye**.
019:074 and in glitter to the **eye**?
020:039 mayest be reared under Mine **eye**.
020:040 that her **eye** might be cooled and she
028:009 "(Here is) a joy of the **eye**, for me
028:013 that her **eye** might be comforted, that she
032:017 of the **eye** are kept hidden (in reserve) for them-
054:050 like the twinkling of an **eye**.
057:019 and the martyrs, in the **eye** of their Lord:

EYE-OPENING

017:102 and the earth as **eye-opening** evidence:

EYES

002:007 and on their **eyes** is a veil;
002:267 receive it except with closed **eyes**.
003:013 these saw with their own **eyes** twice their number.
003:013 In this is a lesson for such as have **eyes** to see."
003:014 Fair in the **eyes** of men is the love of things
003:143 with your own **eyes** (and flinch!).
005:083 thou wilt see their **eyes** overflowing with tears,
006:028 Yea, in their own (**eyes**) will become
006:099 feast your **eyes** with the fruit and the
006:104 from your Lord proofs (to open your **eyes**):
006:110 their hearts and their **eyes**, even as
006:111 all things before their very **eyes**, they are
006:137 Even so, in the **eyes** of most
007:047 When their **eyes** shall be turned towards
007:116 they bewitched the **eyes** of the people,
007:179 **eyes** wherewith they see not, and ears wherewith they
007:195 Or **eyes** to see with? Or ears
008:044 as contemptible in their **eyes**: that Allah
008:044 He showed them to you as few in your **eyes**,

EYES (continued)

009:092 they turned back, their **eyes** streaming with tears
010:012 seem fair in their **eyes**!
011:031 your **eyes** do despise that Allah will not
011:037 Our **eyes** and Our inspiration, and address Me
012:084 And his **eyes** became white with sorrow, and he
014:042 a Day when the **eyes** will fixedly stare in horror,-
015:015 They would only say: "Our **eyes** have been
015:088 Strain not thine **eyes**. (Wistfully) at what We have
016:108 and **eyes** Allah has sealed up and they
018:028 and let not thine **eyes** pass beyond them,
018:101 (Unbelievers) whose **eyes** had been under a veil
020:131 Nor strain thine **eyes** in longing for the
021:003 to witchcraft with your **eyes** open?"
021:061 the **eyes** of the people, that they
021:097 the **eyes** of the Unbelievers will fixedly
022:046 Truly it is not the **eyes** that are blind, but the
024:037 is for the Day when hearts and **eyes** will be
025:040 did they not then see it (with their own **eyes**)?
025:074 wives and offspring who will be the comfort of our **eyes**,
027:004 We have made their deeds pleasing in their **eyes**;
027:024 seem pleasing in their **eyes**, and has
033:010 and behold, the **eyes** swerved and the hearts
033:019 their **eyes** revolving, like one
033:051 This were nigher to the cooling of their **eyes**,
036:066 We could surely have blotted out their **eyes**;
037:048 with big **eyes** (of wonder and beauty).
038:063 or have (our) **eyes** failed to perceive them?"
040:019 (Allah) knows the treachery of the **eyes**, and all
040:037 in Pharaoh's **eyes**, the evil of his deeds, and he
041:044 and it is blindness in their (**eyes**): they are
043:071 all that the **eyes** could delight in: and ye
044:054 to maidens with beautiful, big, and lustrous **eyes**.
052:020 with beautiful, big and lustrous **eyes**.
052:048 for verily thou art in Our **eyes**:
054:007 They will come forth,-their **eyes** humbled-from
054:008 Hastening, with **eyes** transfixed, towards the
054:014 She floats under Our **eyes** (and care):
054:037 but We blinded their **eyes**.
056:022 with beautiful, big, and lustrous **eyes**,-
059:002 O ye with **eyes** (to see)!
068:043 Their **eyes** will be cast down,-ignominy will
068:051 thee up with their **eyes** when they hear the Message;
070:044 Their **eyes** lowered in dejection,-ignominy covering
072:024 (with their own **eyes**) that which they are promised,-
079:009 Cast down will be (their owners') **eyes**.
090:008 Have We not made for him a pair of **eyes**?-

F

FABLES
023:067 the (Qur'an), like one telling **fables** by night,"
FABRICATED
052:033 Or do they say, "He **fabricated** the (Message)?"
FACE
002:060 evil nor mischief on the (**face** of the) earth.
002:115 there is Allah **Face**.
002:144 Turn then thy **face** in the direction
002:144 thy **face** (for guidance) to the heavens:
002:149 turn thy **face** in the direction of the
002:150 turn your **face** thither:
002:150 turn thy **face** in the direction
002:272 do so seeking the "**Face**" of Allah.
004:047 before We change the **face** and fame of some
006:052 seeking His **Face**.
006:079 "For me, I have set my **face**, firmly
010:105 set thy **face** towards Religion with true piety,
012:093 and cast it over the **face** of my father:
012:096 he cast (the shirt) over his **face**,
016:058 his **face** darkens, and he is filled with
017:092 and the angels before (us) **face** to **face**;
017:103 from the **face** of the earth:
018:028 and evening, seeking his **Face**; and let
018:055 or the Wrath be brought to them **face** to **face**?
019:059 will they **face** Destruction,-
028:022 Then when he turned his **face** towards (the land of)
028:088 will perish except His **Face**.
030:030 So set thou thy **face** truly to the religion
030:043 But set thou thy **face** to the right Religion,
034:046 in **face** of a terrible Chastisement."
034:049 and Falsehood showeth not its **face** and will
039:024 on the Day of Judgment (and receive it) on his **face**,
043:017 his **face** darkens, and he is filled
044:053 rich brocade, they will **face** each other;
055:027 But will abide (for ever) the **Face** of thy Lord,-
067:022 with his **face** grovelling, better guided,-
089:023 And Hell that Day, is brought (**face** to **face**),-
FACES
002:144 turn your **faces** in that direction.
002:177 ye turn your **faces** toward East or West;
003:106 some **faces** will be (lit up with) white,
003:106 to those whose **faces** will be black,
003:106 and some **faces** will be (in the gloom of) black:
003:107 But those whose **faces** will be (lit with) white,
004:018 until death **faces** one of them, and he says,
004:043 and rub therewith your **faces** and hands.
004:055 And some of them averted their **faces** from him:
004:061 avert their **faces** from thee in disgust.
005:006 and rub therewith your **faces** and hands.
005:006 wash your **faces**, and your hands (and arms)
008:050 (how) they smite their **faces** and their backs
010:026 No darkness nor abasement shall cover their **faces**!
010:027 their **faces** will be covered, as it were,
010:027 ignominy will cover their (**faces**): no defender
012:105 Yet they turn (their **faces**) away from them!
014:050 and their **faces** covered with Fire;

FACES (continued)
017:007 (We permitted your enemies) to disfigure your **faces**,
017:097 prone on their **faces**, blind, dumb, and deaf:
017:107 fall down on their **faces** in humble prostration,
017:109 They fall down on their **faces** in tears, and it
018:029 that will scald their **faces**, how dreadful the drink!
020:111 (All) **faces** shall be humbled before-the Living,
021:039 to ward off the Fire from their **faces**, not yet
022:011 a trial comes to them, they turn on their **faces**:
022:072 thou wilt notice a denial on the **faces** of the Unbelievers!
023:104 The Fire will burn their **faces**, and they
025:034 to Hell (prone) on their **faces**,-they will
027:090 And if any do evil, their **faces** will be thrown
033:066 The Day that their **faces** will be turned over
039:060 their **faces** will be turned black; is there
047:027 and smite their **faces** and their backs?
048:029 On their **faces** are their marks, (being) the
054:048 through the Fire on their **faces**, (they will hear):
063:005 see them turning away their **faces** in arrogance.
067:027 grieved will be the **faces** of the Unbelievers,
070:017 and turn away their **faces** (from the Right),
075:022 Some **faces** that Day, will beam
075:024 And some **faces**, that Day, will be sad and dismal,
080:038 Some **Faces** that Day will be beaming.
080:040 And other **faces** that Day will be dust-stained;
083:024 Thou wilt recognize in their **Faces** the beaming
088:002 Some **faces**, that Day, will be humiliated,
088:008 (Other) **faces** that Day will be joyful,
FACILITY
002:185 Allah intends every **facility** for you;
FACING
015:047 (joyfully) **facing** each other on raised couches.
037:044 **Facing** each other on raised couches.
056:016 Reclining on them, **facing** each other.
FACT
002:114 whose zeal is (in **fact**) to ruin them?
002:231 and the **fact** that He sent down to you
003:170 the **fact** that on them is no fear,
003:171 and in the **fact** that Allah suffereth not
004:042 but never will they hide a single **fact** from Allah!
004:078 that they fail to understand a single **fact**?.
004:113 But (in **fact**) they will only lead
005:061 "We believe": but in **fact** they enter
007:053 In **fact** they will have lost their souls, and the
011:027 in **fact** we think ye are liars!"
011:091 In **fact** among us we see that thou hast no strength!
018:105 of their Lord and the **fact** of their having to
022:007 or about (the **fact**) that Allah will raise up
029:012 in **fact** they are liars!
045:004 and the **fact** that animals are scattered
045:005 and the **fact** that Allah sends down Sustenance
046:005 and who (in **fact**) are unconscious of their call
051:023 as much as the **fact** that ye can speak
058:002 And in **fact** they use words (both) iniquitous
100:007 And to that (**fact**) he bears witness (by his deeds);
FACTION
003:100 listen to a **faction** among the People of the Book,
FACTIONS
027:045 they became two **factions** quarreling with each other.
FACULTIES
023:078 (the **faculties** of) hearing, sight, feeling and
032:009 (the **faculties** of) hearing and sight

FACULTIES (continued)
046:026 them were their (**faculties** of) hearing, seeing,
046:026 to them were there (**faculties** of) hearing, sight,
067:023 and made for you the **faculties** of hearing

FACULTY
002:020 their **faculty** of hearing and seeing;

FAIL
003:118 they will not **fail** to corrupt you.
003:155 it was Satan who caused them to **fail**,
004:078 that they **fail** to understand a single fact?.
005:044 If any do **fail** to judge by what Allah
005:045 And if any **fail** to judge by what
005:047 If any do **fail** to judge by what
006:061 and they never **fail** in their duty.
012:080 and how, before this, ye did **fail** in your duty
013:020 and **fail** not in their plighted word;
013:031 not **fail** in His promise.
014:047 Never think that Allah would **fail** His messengers
020:058 not **fail** to keep-neither we nor thou-in a place
020:097 a promise that will not **fail**:
022:047 But Allah will not **fail** in His promise.
030:006 Never does Allah **fail** from His promise: but most
035:029 a Commerce that will never **fail**:
035:041 and if they should **fail**.
038:054 such will be Our Bounty (to you); it will never **fail**;-
039:020 never doth Allah **fail** in (His) promise.
041:008 of righteousness is a reward that will never **fail**.
084:025 for them is a Reward that will never **fail**.

FAILED
007:136 and **failed** to take warning from them.
007:146 and **failed** to take warning from them.
008:042 ye would certainly have **failed** in the
009:004 have not subsequently **failed** you in aught,
014:022 but I **failed** in my promise to you. I had no
018:033 its produce, and **failed** not in the least therein:
038:063 or have (our) eyes **failed** to perceive them?"
062:005 but who subsequently **failed** in those (obligations),

FAILING
037:098 (This **failing**), they then plotted against him,

FAILS
003:009 for Allah never **fails** in His promise."
027:066 Nay, but their knowledge **fails** as to the Hereafter,
091:010 And he **fails** that corrupts it!

FAILURE
020:061 the forger must suffer **failure**!

FAIN
002:009 **Fain** would they deceive Allah
009:032 **Fain** would they extinguish Allah's light
010:011 as they would **fain** hasten on the good,-then would
010:054 would **fain** give it in ransom:

FAINT-HEARTED
047:035 Be not weary and **faint-hearted** crying for peace,

FAINTS
033:019 like one who **faints** from death:

FAIR
002:083 speak **fair** to the people;
003:014 **Fair** in the eyes of men is the love of things
004:119 and deface the (**fair**) nature created by Allah."
005:008 as witnesses to **fair** dealing, and let not
007:137 The **fair** promise of the Lord was fulfilled
009:008 With (**fair** words from) their mouths they please
010:012 seem **fair** in their eyes!

FAIR (continued)
016:062 that the reward most **fair** is for themselves:
034:015 a territory **fair** and happy, and a Lord
049:009 for Allah loves those who are **fair** (and just).
049:009 make peace between them with justice, and be **fair**:
055:070 In them will be **fair** (Maidens), good, beautiful;-

FAIR-SEEMING
015:016 and made them **fair-seeming** to (all) beholders;
015:039 I will make (wrong) **fair-seeming** to them on

FAIRER
017:035 that is better and **fairer** in the final determination.
019:073 and **fairer** in assembly?"

FAIREST
025:024 and have the **fairest** of places for repose.

FAITH
027:082 because mankind had no **faith** in Our Signs.
002:006 As to those who reject **Faith**,
002:019 But Allah is ever round the rejecters of **Faith**!
002:024 which is prepared for those who reject **faith**.
002:026 but those who reject **Faith** say:
002:028 How can ye reject the **faith** in Allah?
002:034 he was of those who reject **Faith**.
002:039 reject **Faith** and belie Our Signs,
002:041 and be not the first to reject **faith** therein,
002:075 Can ye (O ye men of **Faith**) entertain
002:076 Behold! when they meet the men of **Faith**,
002:082 have **faith** and work righteousness,
002:089 is on those without **Faith**.
002:089 those without **Faith**,
002:090 Chastisement of those who reject **Faith**.
002:093 behests of your **Faith** if you have any **faith**!"
002:098 those who reject **Faith**.
002:103 If they had kept their **Faith**
002:104 to those without **Faith** is a grievous punishment.
002:104 O ye of **Faith**! say not (to the Prophet) Ra'ina,
002:105 without **Faith** among the people of the Book
002:108 But whoever changeth from **Faith** to Unbelief,
002:118 who hold firmly to **Faith** (in their hearts).
002:121 those who reject **faith** therein,
002:126 He said: "(Yea), and such as reject **Faith**,
002:132 "O my sons! Allah hath chosen the **Faith** for you;
002:139 sincere (in our **faith**) in Him?
002:143 who would turn on their heels (from the **Faith**).
002:143 make your **faith** of no effect.
002:152 Be grateful to Me, and reject not **Faith**.
002:161 Those who reject **Faith**, and die rejecting,
002:165 But those of **Faith** are overflowing
002:171 The parable of those who reject **Faith**
002:191 Such is the reward of those who reject **faith**.
002:212 is alluring to those who reject **faith**,
002:214 those of **faith** who were with him cried:
002:217 back from your **faith** if they can.
002:217 turn back from their **faith** and die in unbelief,
002:228 if they have **faith** in Allah and the Last Day.
002:248 Symbol for you if ye indeed have **faith**."
002:250 help us against those that reject **faith**."
002:254 Those who reject **Faith**-they are the wrong-doers
002:257 Allah is the Protector of those who have **faith**:
002:257 Of those who reject **faith** the patrons
002:258 who (in arrogance) rejected **Faith**.
002:264 And Allah guideth not those who reject **faith**.
002:285 as do the men of **faith**,
003:004 Then those who reject **Faith** in the Signs

FAITH (continued)

003:010 Those who reject **faith**,
003:012 Say to those who reject **Faith**: "Soon
003:032 Allah loveth not those who reject **Faith**.
003:055 who follow thee superior to those who reject **faith**,
003:056 "As to those who reject **faith**,
003:068 and Allah is the Protector of those who have **faith**.
003:076 their plighted **faith** and act aright,
003:077 As for those who sell the **faith** they owe to Allah
003:086 who reject **faith** after they accepted it and bore
003:090 But those who reject **faith** after they accepted it.
003:090 And then go on adding to their defiance of **Faith**,
003:091 As to those who reject **faith**, and die rejecting,
003:095 follow the religion of Abraham, the sane in **faith**:
003:097 but if any deny **faith**, Allah stands not in need
003:101 And how would ye deny **Faith** while unto you
003:106 "Did ye reject **Faith** after accepting it?
003:106 Taste then the Chastisement for rejecting **Faith**.
003:110 If only the People of the Book had **faith**,
003:110 among them are some who have **faith**,
003:116 Those who reject **faith**, neither their
003:131 prepared for those who reject **Faith**.
003:139 for ye must gain mastery if ye are true in **Faith**.
003:141 of blessings those that resist **Faith**.
003:141 true in **faith** and deprive of blessings
003:147 and help us against those that resist **Faith**."
003:149 (from **Faith**) to your own loss.
003:167 They were that day nearer to Unbelief than of **Faith**,
003:173 but it only increased their **Faith**:
003:175 but fear Me, if ye have **Faith**.
003:177 Those who purchase Unbelief at the price of **Faith**,
003:193 the call of one calling (us) to **Faith**,
004:018 nor of those who die rejecting **faith**:
004:025 and Allah hath full knowledge about your **faith**.
004:037 for We have prepared, for those who resist **Faith**,
004:038 to be seen of men, and have no **faith** in Allah
004:039 if they had **faith** in Allah and in the Last Day,
004:042 On that day those who reject **Faith** and
004:046 their tongues and a slander to **Faith**.
004:065 But no, by thy Lord, they can have no (real) **Faith**.
004:066 to strengthen their (**faith**).
004:076 and those who reject **Faith** fight in the cause
004:089 They but wish that ye should reject **Faith**.
004:095 Unto all (in **Faith**) hath Allah promised good:
004:115 a path other than that becoming to men of **Faith**,
004:124 be they male or female, and have **faith**, they
004:125 way of Abraham the true in **faith**?
004:137 then believe (again) and (again) reject **Faith**, and
004:137 Those who believe, then reject **Faith**, then
004:140 and those who defy **Faith**-all in Hell;
004:156 That they rejected **Faith**: that they uttered
004:161 who reject **faith** a grievous chastisement.
004:167 Those who reject **Faith** and keep off
004:168 Those who reject **Faith** and do wrong,-Allah will
004:170 But if ye reject **Faith**, to Allah belong
005:003 This day have those who reject **Faith** given up
005:005 If anyone rejects **faith**, fruitless is his work,
005:010 Those who reject **faith** and deny Our Signs will be
005:012 but if any of you, after this, resisteth **faith**, he hath
005:023 But on Allah put your trust if ye have **faith**."
005:036 As to those who reject **Faith**,-if they had
005:041 but whose hearts have no **faith**; or it be
005:043 For they are not (really) people of **Faith**.

FAITH (continued)

005:050 But who, for a people whose **faith** is assured,
005:054 you turn back from his **Faith**, soon will
005:057 but fear ye Allah, if ye have **Faith** (indeed).
005:057 or among those who reject **Faith**:
005:067 For Allah guideth not those who reject **Faith**.
005:068 over (these) people without **Faith**.
005:078 who rejected **Faith**, by the tongue
005:086 But those who reject **Faith** and belie
005:102 and on that account lost their **faith**.
005:111 they said, 'We have **faith**, and do thou
005:111 to have **faith** in Me and Mine Messenger:
005:112 Said Jesus: "Fear Allah, if ye have **faith**."
005:115 but if any of you after that resisteth **faith**, I
006:001 Yet those who reject **Faith** hold (others)
006:030 the Chastisement, because ye rejected **Faith**."
006:113 who have no **faith** in the Hereafter:
006:118 if ye have **faith** in His Signs.
006:122 Thus to those without **Faith** their own
006:130 they bear witness that they rejected **Faith**.
006:158 nor earned righteousness through its **Faith**.
006:161 the Path (trod) by Abraham the true in **faith**,
007:027 (only) to those without **Faith**.
007:085 that will be best for you, if ye have **Faith**.
007:101 the heart of those who reject **Faith**.
007:188 to those who have **faith**."
007:203 and Guidance, and Mercy, for any who have **Faith**."
008:002 find their **faith** strengthened, and put (all)
008:023 turned back and declined (**faith**).
008:072 and fought for the **Faith**, with their
008:074 and fight for the **Faith**, in the Cause
008:075 And those who accept **Faith** subsequently,
008:075 and emigrate, and fight for the **Faith** in your
009:003 a grievous chastisement to those who reject **Faith**.
009:011 they are your brethren in **Faith**: (thus) do
009:012 and attack your **Faith**,- fight ye
009:023 and your brothers if they love infidelity above **faith**:
009:026 thus doth He reward those without **Faith**.
009:037 not those who reject **Faith**.
009:061 has **faith** in the Believers, and is
009:066 rejected **Faith** after ye had accepted it.
009:068 men and women, and the rejecters of **Faith**, the fire
009:124 had his **faith** increased by it?"
009:124 Yea, those who believe, their **faith** is increased,
010:009 will guide them because of their **Faith**:
010:098 so its **Faith** should have should have profited it,-
012:087 except those who have no **faith**."
012:103 Yet no **faith** will the greater part of mankind have,
013:005 If thou dost marvel (at their want of **faith**),
013:014 for the prayer of those without **Faith** is nothing
014:011 And on Allah let all men of **faith** put their trust.
016:097 man or woman, and has **Faith**, verily, to him
016:106 his heart remaining firm in **Faith**,-
016:106 Any one who, after accepting **Faith** in Allah,
016:107 and Allah will not guide those who reject **Faith**.
016:110 strive and fight for the **Faith** and patiently
016:120 devoutly obedient to Allah, (and) true in **faith**,
016:123 "Follow the ways of Abraham The True in **Faith**,
017:008 have made Hell a prison for those who reject (all **Faith**).
017:019 due striving, and **Faith**,-they are the ones
018:080 his parents were people of **Faith**, and we
018:106 because they rejected **Faith**, and took
020:112 and has **faith**, will have no fear of harm nor of

FAITH (continued)

021:088 and thus do We deliver those who have **faith**.
021:094 and has **Faith**,-his endeavour will not be rejected:
022:031 Being true in **faith** to Allah, and never
022:055 Those who reject **Faith** will not cease to be
022:057 And for those who reject **Faith** and deny
024:055 If any do reject **Faith** after this, they are
025:032 Those who reject **Faith** say: "Why is not
027:003 and also have sure **faith** in the Hereafter.
027:043 for she was (sprung) of a people that had no **faith**.
028:005 to make them leaders (in **faith**) and make them heirs,
028:010 had We not strengthened her heart (with **faith**),
029:054 Hell will encompass the rejecters of **Faith**!-
029:068 a home in Hell for those who reject **Faith**?
030:016 And those who have rejected **Faith** and falsely
030:044 Those who reject **Faith** will suffer from that
030:045 those who reject **Faith**.
030:056 But those endued with knowledge and **faith** will say:
030:060 who have (themselves) no certainty of **faith**.
031:004 sure **faith** in the Hereafter.
031:023 But if any reject **Faith**, let not
032:024 have **faith** in Our Signs.
033:005 father's names, (then they are) your Brothers in **faith**,
033:019 Such men have no **faith**, and so
033:022 And it only added to their **faith** and their
034:017 We gave them because they ungrateful rejected **Faith**:
034:052 but how could they receive (**Faith**) from a position (so)
034:053 Seeing that they did reject **faith** (entirely) before,
035:026 In the end did I punish those who rejected **Faith**:
036:025 "For me, I have **faith** in the Lord of you (all):
037:029 They will reply: "Nay, ye yourselves had no **Faith**!
038:074 and became one of those who reject **Faith**.
039:059 and became one of those who reject **Faith**!'"
040:010 to the **Faith** and ye used to refuse."
040:012 ye did reject **Faith**, but when partners were
040:028 of Pharaoh, who had concealed his **faith**, said:
040:050 But the Prayer of those without **Faith** is nothing
040:085 But their professing the **Faith** when they
042:015 call (them to the **Faith**), and stand
042:052 what was revelation, and what was **Faith**; but We
044:007 if ye (but) have an assured **faith**.
045:004 are Signs for those of assured **Faith**.
045:020 and a Guidance and Mercy to those of assured **Faith**.
046:003 but those who reject **Faith** turn away
046:017 "Woe to thee! Have **Faith**! For the promise of Allah
048:004 that they may add **Faith** to their **Faith**;-for to
049:007 endeared the **Faith** to you, and has
049:014 for not yet has **Faith** entered your hearts.
049:014 Say, "Ye have no **faith**; but ye (only) say, We have
049:017 guided you to the **Faith**, if ye
051:020 On the earth are Signs for those of assured **Faith**,
052:021 and whose seeds follow them in **Faith**,-to them
052:033 Nay, they have no **faith**!
056:010 And those Foremost (in **Faith**) will be
057:008 if ye are men of **faith**.
058:004 show your **faith** in Allah and His Messenger.
058:022 For such He has written **Faith** in their hearts,
059:009 had homes (In Madinah) and had adopted the **Faith**,-
059:010 who came before us into the **Faith** and leave not,
059:023 The Guardian of **Faith**, the Preserver of Safety,
060:008 with regard those who fight you not for (your) **Faith**
060:009 to those who fight you for (your) **Faith**,
060:010 Allah knows best as to their **Faith**:

FAITH (continued)

063:003 then they rejected **Faith**: so a seal
064:005 of those who rejected **Faith** aforetime?
064:010 But those who reject **Faith** and treat
068:035 then treat the People of **Faith** like the People of Sin?
071:028 all who enter my house in **Faith**, and (all)
074:010 Far from easy for those without **Faith**.
074:031 and the Believers may increase in **Faith**,-and that
098:005 being True (in **faith**); to establish
098:007 Those who have **faith** and do righteous deeds,-
103:003 Except such as have **Faith**, and do righteous deeds,
109:001 Say: O ye that reject **Faith**!

FAITHFUL

002:249 he and the **faithful** ones with him,
003:121 to post the **Faithful** at their stations for battle:
003:122 the **Faithful** (ever) put their trust.
003:124 Remember thou saidst to the **faithful**: "Is it not
003:171 the **Faithful** to be lost (in the Least).
009:111 and who is more **faithful** to his Covenant than Allah?
081:021 With authority there, (and) **faithful** of his trust.

FAITHFULLY

002:282 let his guardian dictate **faithfully**.
002:282 write down **faithfully** as between the parties:
002:283 let the trustee (**faithfully**) discharge his trust,
023:008 Those who **faithfully** observe their trust

FAITHLESS

002:100 Nay, most of them are **faithless**.

FAITHLESSNESS

002:093 because of their **Faithlessness**.

FAKE

007:117 all the falsehoods which the **fake**!
026:045 all the falsehoods which they **fake**!

FAKED

020:069 that which they have **faked**:
020:069 What they have **faked** is but a magician's trick:
028:036 "This is nothing but sorcery **faked** up: never did

FALL

002:286 if we forget or **fall** into error;
003:105 and **fall** into disputation after receiving Clear Signs:
003:139 So lose not heart, nor **fall** into despair:
005:003 or by a violent blow, or a headlong **fall**, or by
005:034 before they **fall** into your power:
005:053 and they will **fall** into (nothing but) ruin.
006:059 Not a leaf doth **fall** but with His knowledge:
007:022 So by deceit he brought about their **fall**:
007:171 it was going to **fall** on them (We said): "Hold firmly
008:046 and **fall** into no disputes, lest ye
013:008 much the wombs **fall** short (of their time or number)
015:029 **fall** ye down in obeisance unto him."
017:092 "Or thou cause the sky to **fall** in pieces, as thou
017:107 **fall** down on their faces in humble prostration,
017:109 They **fall** down on their faces in tears,
018:053 see the and apprehend that they have to **fall** therein;
019:025 it will let **fall** fresh ripe dates upon thee.
019:058 to them, they would **fall** down in prostrate
019:090 and the mountains to **fall** down in utter ruin.
020:123 will not lose his way, nor **fall** into misery.
026:046 Then did the sorcerers **fall** down, prostrate in
026:187 to **fall** on us, if thou art truthful!"
032:015 when they are recited to they **fall** down in adoration,
034:009 or cause a piece of the sky to **fall** upon them.
038:072 **fall** ye down in prostrated unto him."

FALL (continued)

039:017 Those who eschew Taghut and **fall** not into
040:028 then will **fall** on you something of the (calamity)
042:022 (the burden of) that must (necessarily) **fall** on them.
049:009 If two parties among the Believers **fall** into a fight,
053:062 But **fall** ye down in prostration to Allah,
055:009 and **fall** not short in the balance.
081:002 When the stars **fall**, losing their lustre;
084:021 the Qur'an is read to them they **fall** not prostrate.

FALLEN

009:049 Have they not **fallen** into trial
022:031 he is as if he had **fallen** from heaven and been

FALLING

018:077 on the point of **falling** down, but he
022:065 He withholds the sky from **falling** on the earth
052:044 of the sky **falling** (on them), they would

FALLS

002:264 on it **falls** a heavy rain,
002:265 heavy rain **falls** on it but makes it yield
006:069 their account no responsibility **falls** on the righteous,
011:009 behold! he is in despair and (**falls** into) ingratitude,
011:010 behold! he **falls** into exultation and pride.
092:011 when he **falls** headlong (into the Pit).

FALSE

004:112 (both) a **false** charge and a flagrant sin.
004:119 and I will create in them **false** desires;
004:120 and creates in them **false** hopes, but
004:156 that they uttered against Mary a grave **false** charge;
006:041 (the **false** gods) which ye join with Him!"
006:064 and yet ye worship **false** gods!"
006:107 they would not have taken **false** gods: but We
006:139 For their (**false**) attribution
007:173 "Our fathers before us took **false** gods, but we
008:008 and prove Falsehood **false**, distasteful though
008:054 they treated as **false** the Signs of their Lord so We
009:090 and those who were **false** to Allah and His Messenger
011:014 "If then they (your **false** gods) answer not
012:018 They stained his shirt with **false** blood.
012:052 may know that I have never been **false** to him
012:052 the snare of the **false** ones.
015:003 and let (**false**) Hope distract them:
015:094 those who join **false** gods with Allah.
016:035 The worshippers of **false** gods say: "If Allah
016:056 to account for your **false** inventions.
016:116 so as to ascribe **false** things to Allah.
016:116 For those who ascribe **false** things to Allah,
016:116 But say not-for any **false** thing that your
017:059 the men of former generations treated them as **false**:
021:018 woe be to you for the (**false**) things ye ascribe (to Us).
021:098 and the (**false**) gods that ye worship besides Allah,
022:030 and shun the word that is **false**,-
027:059 or the **false** gods they associate (with Him)?
029:003 who are true from those who are **false**.
030:040 Are there any of your (**false**) "Partners" who can do
031:013 for **false** worship is indeed the highest
032:020 the which ye were wont to reject as **false**."
039:003 But Allah guides not such as are **false** and ungrateful.
047:025 and buoyed them up with **false** hopes.
056:082 that ye should declare it **false**?
057:014 and (your **false**) desires deceived you; until there
058:002 (both) iniquitous and **false**:
072:020 and I join not with Him any (**false** god)."
077:029 which ye used to reject as **false**!

FALSE (continued)

078:028 But they (impudently) treated Our Signs as **false**
083:017 "This is the (reality) which ye rejected as **false**!"
091:014 Then they rejected him (as a **false** prophet),

FALSEHOOD

002:042 And cover not Truth with **falsehood**,
003:071 Why do ye clothe truth with **falsehood**,
005:042 (They are fond of) listening to **falsehood**,
006:031 as a **falsehood** that they must meet Allah,-
006:147 If they accuse thee of **falsehood**, say:
007:173 the deeds of men who followed **falsehood**?"
008:008 and prove **Falsehood** false, distasteful though
009:002 frustrate Allah (by your **falsehood**), but that
009:034 who in **falsehood** devour the wealth of men
010:039 did those before them make charges of **falsehood**:
010:039 Nay, they charge with **falsehood** that whose knowledge
010:041 If they charge thee with **falsehood**, say: "My work
013:017 show forth Truth and **falsehood**.
016:062 and their tongues assert the **falsehood** that the
016:105 the Signs of Allah, that forge **falsehood**:
016:117 In such **falsehood** is but a paltry profit;
017:081 for **Falsehood** is (by its nature) bound to perish."
017:081 "Truth has (now) arrived, and **Falsehood** perished:
018:005 What they say in nothing but **falsehood**!
018:015 as invent a **falsehood** against Allah?
021:018 Nay, We hurl the Truth against **falsehood**, and it
021:018 and behold, **falsehood** doth perish!
022:062 they are but vain **Falsehood**:
023:026 for that they accuse me of **falsehood**!
023:039 for that they accuse me of **falsehood**."
023:044 they accused him of **falsehood**: so We
025:004 put forward an iniquity and a **falsehood**.
025:072 Those who witness no **falsehood**, and, if
026:012 I do fear that they will charge me with **falsehood**:
028:034 for I fear that they may accuse me of **falsehood**."
029:017 worship idols besides Allah, and ye invent **falsehood**.
031:030 invoke besides Him is **Falsehood**; and because
034:008 "Has he invented a **falsehood** against Allah, or is
034:043 "This is only a **falsehood** invented!"
034:049 and **Falsehood** showeth not its face and will
037:086 "Is it a **Falsehood**-gods other than Allah
041:042 No **falsehood** can approach it from before
042:024 "He has forged a **falsehood** against Allah"?
042:024 And Allah blots out **falsehood**, and proves
045:027 that Day will the followers of **Falsehood** perish!
046:011 "This is an (old), old **falsehood**!"
046:028 but that was their **Falsehood** and their invention.
047:003 reject Allah follow **falsehood**.
058:014 and they swear to **falsehood** knowingly.
060:012 intentionally forging **falsehood**, and that they
061:007 who forges **falsehood** against Allah, even as

FALSEHOODS

003:055 (of the **falsehoods**) of those who blaspheme;
006:150 of such as treat Our Signs as **falsehoods**,
007:117 all the **falsehoods** which the fake!
007:152 those who invent (**falsehoods**).
010:030 invented **falsehoods** will leave them in the lurch.
023:105 and ye did but treat them as **falsehoods**?"
026:045 all the **falsehoods** which they fake!
029:013 they will be called to account for their **falsehoods**.
040:078 there and then, those who stood on **Falsehoods**.
064:010 and treat Our Signs as **falsehoods**, they will

FALSELY
006:100 and they **falsely**, having no knowledge, attribute
006:148 So did their ancestors argue **falsely**, until
016:113 but they **falsely** rejected him;
030:016 and **falsely** denied Our Signs and the meeting

FALSIFIED
053:011 in no way **falsified** that which he saw.

FALSIFY
062:005 who **falsify** the Signs of Allah:

FALTER
031:032 those that **falter** between (right and wrong).

FAME
004:047 face and **fame** of some (of you) beyond all recognition,

FAMILIAR
033:053 disperse, without seeking **familiar** talk.

FAMILIARITY
106:001 For the **familiarity** of the Quraish,
106:002 Their **familiarity** with the journeys by

FAMILIES
002:246 turned out of our homes and our **families**?"
005:089 for the food of your **families**; or clothe
042:045 who lose themselves and their **families**.
048:011 (looking after) our flocks and herds, and our **families**:
048:012 and the Believers would never return to their **families**;
052:021 to them shall We join their **families**:
066:006 save yourselves and your **families** from a Fire whose fuel

FAMILY
002:248 the **family** of Moses and the **family** of Aaron,
003:033 did choose Adam and Noah, the **family** of Abraham,
003:033 and the **family** of 'Imran above all people,
004:009 if they had left a helpless **family** behind:
004:035 appoint (two) arbiters, one from his **family**,
004:092 And pay blood-money to the deceased's **family**,
004:092 blood-money should be paid to his **family**,
007:083 But We saved him and his **family**, except
011:040 of each two, male and female, and your **family**-
011:045 "O my Lord! surely my son is of my **family** and Thy
011:046 He said: "O Noah! he is not of thy **family**:
011:081 Now travel with thy **family** while yet a part
011:091 Were it not for thy **family**, we should
011:092 He said: "O my people! is then my **family** of more
012:065 so we shall get (more) food for our **family**;
012:088 seized us and our **family**:
012:093 together with all your **family**."
019:016 when she withdrew from her **family** to a place
020:010 so he said to his **family**, "Tarry ye;
020:029 "And give me a Minister from my **family**,
021:076 and his **family** from great distress.
023:027 pairs of every species, male and female, and thy **family**-
026:169 and my **family** from such things as they do!"
026:170 So We delivered him and his **family**,-
027:007 Behold! Moses said to his **family**: "I perceive
027:057 But We saved him and his **family**, except his
028:029 and was travelling with his **family**, he perceived
028:029 He said to his **family**: "Tarry ye; I perceive a fire;
033:033 ye Members of the **Family**, and to make
075:033 Then did he stalk to his **family** in full conceit!

FANCIES
006:094 and your (pet) **fancies** have left you in the lurch!"
006:136 they say, according to their **fancies**: "This
011:021 and the (**fancies**) they forged have left them in the lurch!

FANCY
017:056 Say: "'Call on those-besides Him-whom ye **fancy**:
034:022 whom ye **fancy**, besides Allah: they have

FAR
002:103 **far** better had been the reward from Allah if they but
002:176 the Book are in a schism **far** (from the purpose).
002:200 yea, with **far** more heart and soul.
003:015 glad tidings of things **far** better than those?
003:118 what their hearts conceal is **far** worse.
003:157 are **far** better than all they could amass:
003:185 Only he who is saved **far** from the fire and
004:027 ye should turn away (from Him), **far**, **far** away.
004:060 lead them astray **far** away (from the Right).
004:116 hath strayed **far**, **far** away (from the Right).
004:136 hath gone **far**, **far** astray.
004:167 have verily strayed **far**, **far** away from the Path.
004:171 glory be to him (**far** Exalted is He) above having a son.
005:060 and **far** more astray from the even Path!"
009:031 Praise and glory to Him: (**far** is He) from having
010:018 and **far** is He above the partners
011:083 ever **far** from those who do wrong!
011:089 the people of Lut **far** off from you!
014:018 that is the straying **far**, **far** (from the goal).
016:001 and **far** is He above having the partners
016:003 and the earth with truth **far** is He above having
016:095 (a prize) **far** better for you, if ye only knew.
020:087 the promise to thee, as **far** as lay in our power:
020:127 of the Hereafter is **far** more grievous
021:101 will be removed **far** therefrom.
021:109 ye are promised is near or **far**.
022:012 that is straying **far** indeed (from the Way)!
022:053 in a schism **far** (from the Truth):
022:072 Say, "Shall I tell you of something (**far**) worse than
023:036 "**Far**, very **far** is that which ye are promised!
025:012 When it sees them from a place **far** off, they will
027:022 But the Hoopoe tarried not **far**:
028:038 but as **far** as I am concerned, I think
028:068 and **far** is He above the partners they ascribe
030:020 behold, ye are men scattered (**far** and wide)!
034:023 So **far** (is this the case) that, when terror
034:052 from a position (so) **far** off,-
034:053 with regard to the Unseen from a position **far** off?
041:044 called from a place **far** distant!"
041:052 who is in schism **far** (from any purpose)?"
042:018 dispute concerning the Hour are **far** astray.
042:028 all hope, and scatters His Mercy (**far** and wide).
050:003 Return **far** (from our understanding)."
050:027 but he was (himself) **far** astray."
052:043 Exalted is Allah **far** above the things
067:011 but **far** from Allah's mercy are the Companions
074:010 **Far** from easy for those without Faith.
076:007 and they fear a Day whose evil flies **far** and wide.
077:003 And scatter (things) **far** and wide;
092:017 shall be removed **far** from it,-

FAR-DISTANT
022:031 and thrown him into a **far-distant** place.

FAR-OFF
070:006 They see the (Day) indeed as a **far-off** (event):

FAR-REACHING
054:005 A wisdom **far-reaching**:-

FARE
003:025 But how (will they **fare**) when We gather them

FARE (continued)

006:093 the wicked (do **fare**) in the agonies of death!-
037:175 And watch them (how they **fare**), and they
037:179 And watch (how they **fare**) and they

FAREST

037:175 and they soon shall see (how thou **farest**)!
037:179 and they soon shall see (how thou **farest**)!

FARTHER

008:042 the valley, and they on the **farther** side, and the
025:044 they are **farther** astray from the way.

FARTHEST

004:066 and would have gone **farthest** to strengthen
017:001 **Farthest** Mosque whose precincts We did Bless,-
034:008 (real) Chastisement, and in **farthest** Error.
036:020 from the **farthest** part of the City, a man,

FARTHING

004:053 behold, they give not a **farthing** to their fellow-men!

FASHION

007:138 They said: "O Moses! **fashion** for us a god
075:038 and **fashion** (him) in due proportion.

FASHIONED

015:029 "When I have **fashioned** him (in due proportion)
018:037 a sperm-drop, then **fashioned** thee into a man?
032:009 But He **fashioned** him in due proportion,
036:071 hands have **fashioned**-cattle, which are
038:072 "When I have **fashioned** him and breathed
082:007 Who created thee, **fashioned** thee in due proportion,

FASHIONER

059:024 the Originator, the **Fashioner**, to Him belong

FAST

002:184 And it is better for you that ye **fast**,
002:187 then complete your **fast** till the night appears;
002:196 he should **fast** three days during the Hajj.
002:196 (he should) in compensation either **fast**,
003:103 And hold **fast**, all together, by the Rope
004:092 (is prescribed) a **fast** for two months running:
004:146 mend (their life), hold **fast** to Allah,
004:175 and hold **fast** to Him,-soon will He admit
005:066 If only they had stood **fast** by the Torah,
005:068 unless ye stand **fast** by the Torah.
005:089 If that is beyond your means, **fast** for three days.
007:145 and enjoin the people to hold **fast** by the
007:170 As to those who hold **fast** by the Book
019:026 'I have vowed a **fast** to (Allah) Most Gracious,
022:078 hold **fast** to Allah!
033:035 for men and women who **fast**,
043:021 before this, to which they are holding **fast**?
043:043 So hold thou **fast** to the Revelation sent down
058:004 he should **fast** for two months consecutively
066:005 who worship (in humility), who **fast**,-

FASTENED

012:023 sought to seduce him and she **fastened** the doors,
017:013 Every man's fate We have **fastened** on his

FASTING

002:183 O ye who believe! **fasting** is prescribed to you
002:184 O ye who believe! (**Fasting**) for a fixed number of days;
002:185 during that month should spent it in **fasting**,

FASTS

002:187 Permitted to you on the night of the **fasts**,
005:095 or its equivalent in **fasts**:

FAT

006:146 and We forbade them the **fat** of the ox
012:043 (in a vision) seven **fat** kine, whom seven
012:046 of seven **fat** kine whom seven lean ones devour,

FATE

009:052 Say: "Can you expect for us (any **fate**) other than
011:089 lest ye suffer a **fate** similar to that of the
017:013 Every man's **fate** We have fastened on his
029:038 to you from the (traces) of their buildings (their **fate**):
040:031 "Something like the **fate** of the people of Noah,

FATES

047:010 and similar (**fates** await) those who reject Allah.

FATHER

002:233 Nor **father** on account of his child,
006:074 Lo! Abraham said to his **father** Azar: "Takest
012:004 Behold, Joseph said to his **father**: "O my **father**!
012:004 "O my **father**! I did see eleven stars and the
012:005 Said (the **father**): "My (dear) little son! relate
012:008 are loved more by our **father** than we: but we
012:008 Really our **father** is obviously in error!
012:009 of your **father** may be given to you alone:
012:011 They said: "O our **father**! why dost
012:016 Then they came to their **father** in the
012:017 They said: "Oh our **father**! we went
012:059 the same **father** as yourselves,
012:061 win him from his **father**: indeed we shall do it."
012:063 they said: "O our **father**! No more measure
012:063 Now when they returned to their **father**, they said:
012:065 They said: "O our **father**! What (more)
012:068 in the manner their **father** had enjoined, it did
012:078 he has a **father**, aged and venerable,
012:080 until my **father** permits me, or Allah
012:080 "Know ye not that your **father** did take an oath
012:081 and say, 'O our **father**! behold! thy son
012:081 "Turn ye back to your **father**, and say,
012:093 and cast it over the face of my **father**: he will
012:094 their **father** said: "I do indeed scent the presence
012:097 They said: "O our **father**! ask for
012:100 He said: "O my **father**! this is the fulfillment
018:082 their **father** had been a righteous man:
019:028 "O sister of Aaron! thy **father** was not a man
019:042 "O my **father**! why worship that which heareth not
019:042 Behold, he said to his **father**: "O my **father**! why worship
019:043 "O my **father**! to me hath come knowledge which
019:044 "O my **father**! serve not Satan: for Satan
019:045 "O my **father**! I fear lest a Chastisement afflict
019:046 (The **father**) replied: "Art thou shrinking
021:052 Behold! he said to his **father** and his people,
022:078 it is the religion of your **father** Abraham.
026:070 Behold, he said to his **father** and his people:
026:086 "Forgive my **father**, for that
028:023 and our **father** is a very old man."
028:025 She said: "My **father** invites thee that he may
028:026 (dear) **father**! engage him on wages:
031:033 when no **father** can avail aught for his son,
031:033 nor a son avail aught for his **father**.
033:040 Muhammad is not the **father** of any of your men,
037:085 Behold, he said to his **father** and to his people,
037:102 "O my **father**! do as thou art commanded: thou will
043:026 Behold! Abraham said to his **father** and his people:
060:004 said to his **father**: "I will pray for forgiveness
080:035 And from his mother, and his **father**,
111:001 Perish the hands of the **Father** of Flame! Perish he!

FATHER'S
004:023 your mother, daughters, sisters, **father's** sisters,
009:114 And Abraham prayed for his **father's** forgiveness only
024:061 or your **father's's** sisters, or your
024:061 or your **father's** brothers, or your
033:005 But if ye know not their **father's** names, (then they are)
065:006 (the child) on the (**father's**) behalf.

FATHERS
002:133 worship thy God and the God of thy **fathers**,
002:170 they say: "Nay! we shall follow the ways of our **fathers**."
002:170 even though their **fathers** were void of wisdom and
002:200 the praises of your **fathers**,
004:022 your **fathers** married, except what is past:
005:104 the ways we found our **fathers** following."
005:104 What! even though their **fathers** were void
006:087 (To them) and to their **fathers**, and progeny
006:091 which ye knew not-neither ye nor your **fathers**."
006:148 nor would our **fathers**; nor should
007:028 they say: "We found our **fathers** doing so";
007:070 which our **fathers** used to worship.
007:071 over names which ye-have devised-ye and your **fathers**,
007:095 "Our **fathers** (too) were touched by suffering
007:173 "Our **fathers** before us took false gods, but we
009:023 for protectors your **fathers** and your brothers
009:024 Say: If it be that your **fathers**, your sons,
010:078 We found our **fathers** following,-in order
011:062 of what our **fathers** worshipped?
011:087 that we leave off the worship which our **fathers** practiced,
011:109 but what their **fathers** worshipped before (them):
012:006 thy **fathers** Abraham and Isaac aforetime!
012:038 "'And I follow the ways of my **fathers**,-Abraham, Isaac,
012:040 but names which ye have named, ye and your **fathers**,-
013:023 the righteous among their **fathers**, their spouses,
014:010 our **fathers** used to worship; then bring
016:035 neither we nor our **fathers**,-nor should
018:005 aught but Him-neither we nor had their **fathers**.
021:044 and their **fathers** until the period grew long for
021:053 They said, "We found our father worshipping them."
021:054 in manifest error-ye and your **fathers**."
023:068 to their **fathers** of old?
023:083 and to our **fathers** before!
024:031 their **fathers**, their husbands' **fathers**, their sons,
024:061 or those of your **fathers**, or your
025:018 on them and their **fathers**, good things
026:026 of your **fathers** from the beginning!"
026:074 our **fathers** doing thus (what we do)."
026:076 "Ye and your **fathers** before you?-
027:067 become dust,-we and our **fathers**,-shall we
027:068 we and our **fathers** before (us): these are
028:036 among our **fathers** of old!"
031:021 we found our **fathers** (following)."
033:005 Call them by after their **fathers**: that is
033:055 (on those ladies if they appear) before their **fathers**
034:043 you from the (worship) which your **fathers** practiced."
036:006 warn a people, whose **fathers** were not warned,
037:017 "And also our **fathers** of old?"
037:069 Truly they found their **fathers** on the wrong Path;
037:126 and the Lord and Cherisher of your **fathers** of old?"
040:008 their **fathers**, their wives, and their posterity!
043:022 "We found our **fathers** following a certain religion,
043:023 "We found Our **fathers** following a certain
043:024 ye found your **fathers** following?"
043:029 good things of this life to these (men) and their **fathers**,

FATHERS (continued)
053:023 but names which ye have devised,-ye and your **fathers**,-
056:048 "(We) and our **fathers** of old?"
058:022 even though they were their **fathers** or their sons,

FATIGUE
002:255 and He feeleth no **fatigue** in guarding and preserving
009:120 whether they suffer thirst, or **fatigue**, or hunger,
015:048 There no sense of **fatigue** shall touch them,
018:062 truly we have suffered much **fatigue** at this

FATTED
051:026 to his household, brought out a **fatted** calf.

FAULT
003:155 But Allah has blotted out (their **fault**):
004:112 But if anyone earns a **fault** or a sin and throws
005:054 the reproaches of such as find **fault**.
012:029 for truly thou hast been at **fault**!
012:097 for we were truly at **fault**."
024:029 It is no **fault** on your part to enter houses
024:061 It is no **fault** in the blind nor in
040:055 and ask forgiveness for thy **fault**, and celebrate
047:019 and ask forgiveness for thy **fault**,

FAULTS
002:058 forgive you your **faults** and increase
002:263 covering of **faults** are better than charity
003:159 so pass over (their **faults**), and ask for (Allah's)
007:161 We shall forgive you your **faults**; We shall
011:075 forbearing (of **faults**), compassionate, and given
011:087 forbeareth with **faults** and is right-minded!
015:085 So overlook (any human **faults**) with gracious
020:073 may He forgive us our **faults**, and the
025:058 to be acquainted with the **faults** of His servants;-
026:051 our Lord will forgive us our **faults**, since we
026:082 will forgive me my **faults** on the Day of Judgment.
029:012 and we will bear (the consequences) of your **faults**."
029:012 Never in the least will they bear their **faults**:
046:031 He will forgive you your **faults**, and deliver you from a
048:002 That Allah may forgive thee thy **faults** of the
064:014 and cover up (their **faults**), verily Allah

FAVOUR
002:040 call to mind the (special) **favour** which I bestowed upon
002:047 call to mind the (special) **favour** which I bestowed upon
002:122 the special **favour** which I bestowed upon you,
002:151 A similar (**favour** have ye already received)
002:211 after Allah's **favour** has come to him,
003:025 without (**favour** or) injustice?
003:103 and remember with gratitude Allah's **favour** on you;
003:164 Allah did confer a great **favour** on the Believers
004:072 They say: "Allah did **favour** us in that we
005:003 completed my **favour** upon you, and have chosen
005:006 and to complete His **favour** to you, that ye
005:007 the **favour** of Allah unto you, and His Covenant,
005:011 call in remembrance the **favour** of Allah unto you
005:020 the **favour** of Allah unto you, when He produced
005:110 recount my **favour** to thee and to thy mother.
006:086 and to all We gave **favour** above the nations:
006:154 completing (Our **favour**) to those who
009:117 Allah turned with **favour** to the Prophet,
010:107 there is none can keep back his **favour**: He causeth
012:006 His **favour** to thee and to the posterity of Jacob-
012:009 to some (unknown) land, that so the **favour** of your
014:006 "Call to mind the **favour** of Allah to you
014:028 to those who have exchanged the **favour** of Allah.

FAVOUR (continued)

018:082 a mercy (and **favour**) from thy Lord.
020:037 "And indeed We conferred a **favour** on thee
021:094 We shall record it in his **favour**.
023:027 and address Me not in **favour** of the wrong-doers:
026:022 "And this is the **favour** with which thou dost
033:037 one who had received the grace of Allah and thy **favour**:
037:114 Our **favour** on Moses and Aaron,
039:008 but when He bestoweth a **favour** upon him
039:049 but when We bestow a **favour** upon him
043:013 ye may remember the (kind) **favour** of your Lord,
043:059 We granted Our **favour** to him, and We
046:015 Thy **favour** which Thou hast bestowed upon me,
048:002 fulfil His **favour** to thee; and guide
049:008 A grace and **favour** from Allah; and Allah
049:017 They impress on thee as **favour** that they
049:017 a **favour** upon you that He has guided you
049:017 Say, "Count not your Islam as a **favour** upon me:
061:013 And another (**favour** will He bestow), which ye
092:019 And have in their minds no **favour** from anyone

FAVOURABLE

010:022 they sail with them with a **favourable** wind,

FAVOURED

006:053 Allah hath **favoured** from amongst us?"
016:071 those more **favoured** are not going to throw back their
027:015 Who has **favoured** us above many of His servants
045:016 and We **favoured** them above the nations.

FAVOURS

002:150 and that I may complete My **favours** on you,
002:231 but solemnly rehearse Allah's **favours** on you,
004:094 till Allah conferred on you His **favours**:
006:094 all (the **favours**) which We bestowed on you:
011:010 (Our) **favours** after adversity hath touched him,
014:007 more (**favours**) unto you; but if ye
014:034 But if ye count the **favours** of Allah, never will
016:018 If ye would count up the **favours** of Allah,
016:055 the **favours** We have bestowed on them!
016:071 Will they then deny the **favours** of Allah?
016:072 and be ungrateful for Allah's **favours**?-
016:075 whom We have bestowed goodly **favours** from Ourselves,
016:081 Thus does He complete his **favours** on you,
016:083 They recognize the **favours** of Allah; then they
016:112 for the **favours** of Allah: so Allah
016:114 for the **favours** of Allah, if it is He
016:121 He showed his gratitude for the **favours** of Allah,
017:070 and conferred on them special **favours**, above a
017:083 Yet when We bestow Our **favours** on man, he turns
027:019 for Thy **favours**, which Thou has bestowed on me
030:034 for the (**favours**) We have bestowed on them!
041:051 When We bestow **favours** on man, he turns
053:055 Then which of the **favours** of thy Lord, (O man),
055:013 Then which of the **favours** of your Lord
055:016 Then which of the **favours** of your Lord
055:018 Then which of the **favours** of your Lord
055:021 Then which of the **favours** of your Lord
055:023 Then which of the **favours** of your Lord
055:025 Then which of the **favours** of your Lord
055:028 Then which of the **favours** of your Lord
055:030 Then which of the **favours** of your Lord
055:032 Then which of the **favours** of your Lord
055:034 Then which of the **favours** of your Lord
055:036 Then which of the **favours** of your Lord
055:038 Then which of the **favours** of your Lord

FAVOURS (continued)

055:040 Then which of the **favours** of your Lord
055:042 Then which of the **favours** of your Lord
055:045 Then which of the **favours** of your Lord
055:047 Then which of the **favours** of your Lord
055:049 Then which of the **favours** of your Lord
055:051 Then which of the **favours** of your Lord
055:053 Then which of the **favours** of your Lord
055:055 Then which of the **favours** of your Lord
055:057 Then which of the **favours** of your Lord
055:059 Then which of the **favours** of your Lord
055:061 Then which of the **favours** of your Lord
055:063 Then which of the **favours** of your Lord
055:065 Then which of the **favours** of your Lord
055:067 Then which of the **favours** of your Lord
055:069 Then which of the **favours** of your Lord
055:071 Then which of the **favours** of your Lord
055:073 Then which of the **favours** of your Lord
055:075 Then which of the **favours** of your Lord
055:077 Then which of the **favours** of your Lord
057:023 nor exult over **favours** bestowed upon you.

FAWN

002:069 He said: "He says, a **fawn**-coloured heifer,

FEALTY

048:010 Verily those who plight their **fealty** to thee
048:010 to thee plight their **fealty** in truth to Allah:
048:018 The Believers when they swore **Fealty** to thee
060:012 receive their **fealty**, and pray to Allah for the
060:012 then do thou receive their **fealty** to thee, that they will

FEAR

002:002 to those who **fear** Allah;
002:024 then **fear** the fire whose fuel
002:038 on them shall be no **fear**,
002:040 and **fear** none but Me.
002:041 and **fear** Me, and Me alone.
002:062 on them shall be no **fear**,
002:063 perchance ye may **fear** Allah."
002:066 and a lesson to those who **fear** Allah.
002:074 and others which sink for **fear** of Allah.
002:112 on such shall be no **fear**,
002:114 should themselves enter them except in **fear**.
002:150 so **fear** them not, but **fear** Me;
002:155 something of **fear** and hunger,
002:189 and **fear** Allah: that ye may prosper.
002:189 it is virtue if ye **fear** Allah.
002:194 But **fear** Allah,
002:196 And **fear** Allah.
002:197 So **fear** Me, O ye that are wise.
002:203 Then **fear** Allah, and know that ye will surely
002:206 When it is said to him, "**Fear** God,"
002:223 and **fear** Allah, and know that ye are to meet Him
002:229 If ye (judges) do indeed **fear** that they would be unable
002:229 except when both parties **fear** that they would be unable
002:231 And **fear** Allah,
002:233 But **fear** Allah and know that Allah sees well
002:239 If ye **fear** (an enemy), pray on foot,
002:243 they were thousands (in number), for **fear** of death?
002:262 on them shall be no **fear**, nor shall they grieve.
002:274 on them shall be no **fear**, nor shall they grieve.
002:277 on them shall be no **fear**,
002:278 O ye who believe! **fear** Allah,
002:281 And **fear** the Day when ye shall be
002:282 but let him **fear** Allah his Lord

FEAR (continued)

002:282 So **fear** Allah; for it is Allah
002:283 and let him **fear** Allah his Lord.
003:028 But Allah cautions you (to **fear**) Himself;
003:030 But Allah cautions you (to **fear**) Him
003:050 So **fear** Allah, and obey me.
003:073 (**fear** ye) lest a revelation be sent to someone
003:102 O ye who believe! **fear** Allah as He should be feared,
003:123 then **fear** Allah; thus may ye show your gratitude.
003:130 doubled and multiplied; but **fear** Allah;
003:131 **Fear** the fire, which is prepared for those
003:138 a guidance and instruction to those who **fear** Allah!
003:170 the fact that on them is no **fear**,
003:173 so **fear** them": but it only increased their Faith:
003:175 but **fear** Me, if ye have Faith.
003:175 suggests to you the **fear** of his votaries:
003:198 On the other hand, for those who **fear** their Lord,
003:200 and **fear** Allah; that ye may prosper.
004:001 **fear** Allah, through Whom ye demand
004:001 O mankind! **fear** your Guardian Lord, Who created
004:003 If ye **fear** that ye shall not be able
004:003 but if ye **fear** that ye shall not be able
004:009 have the same **fear** in their minds as they would
004:009 let them **fear** Allah, and speak appropriate words.
004:025 for those among you who **fear** sin;
004:034 whose part ye **fear** disloyalty and ill-conduct,
004:035 If ye **fear** a breach between them twain, appoint
004:083 safety or **fear**, they divulge it.
004:101 for **fear** the Unbelievers may attack you:
004:131 and you (O Muslims) to **fear** Allah, but if
005:002 **fear** Allah: for Allah is strict in punishment.
005:003 yet **fear** them not but **fear** Me.
005:004 and **fear** Allah; for Allah is swift in taking account.
005:007 and **fear** Allah, for Allah knoweth well
005:008 and **fear** Allah.
005:011 so **fear** Allah.
005:028 for I do **fear** Allah, the Cherisher of the worlds.
005:044 therefore **fear** not men, but **fear** Me, and sell not
005:046 an admonition to those who **fear** Allah.
005:052 saying: "We do **fear** lest a change
005:057 but **fear** ye Allah, if ye have Faith (indeed).
005:069 on them shall be no **fear**, nor shall they grieve.
005:088 but **fear** Allah, in Whom ye believe.
005:096 and **fear** Allah, to Whom ye shall be gathered back.
005:100 so **fear** Allah, O ye that understand that;
005:108 But **fear** Allah, and listen (to His counsel):
005:108 or else they would **fear** that other oaths
005:112 Said Jesus: "**Fear** Allah, if ye have faith."
006:015 indeed have **fear** of the Chastisement
006:048 upon them shall be no **fear**, nor shall they grieve.
006:051 in whose (hearts) is the **fear** that they will
006:069 that they may (learn to) **fear** Allah.
006:072 and to **fear** Allah: for it is
006:080 I **fear** not (the beings) ye associate with Allah:
006:081 "How should I **fear** (the beings) ye
006:081 when ye **fear** not to give partners
007:035 on them shall be no **fear**, nor shall they grieve.
007:049 Enter ye the Garden: no **fear** shall be on you,
007:056 but call on Him with **fear** and longing
007:059 I **fear** for you the Punishment of a dreadful Day!"
007:063 so that ye may **fear** Allah and haply receive His Mercy?"
007:065 Will ye not **fear** (Allah)?"

FEAR (continued)

007:154 Guidance and Mercy for such as **fear** their Lord.
007:164 and perchance they may **fear** Him."
007:171 what is therein; perchance ye may **fear** Allah".
007:201 Those who **fear** Allah, when a thought
008:001 so **fear** Allah, and keep straight the relations
008:025 And **fear** the trial which affecteth not in
008:029 O ye who believe! if ye **fear** Allah, He will
008:048 lo! I **fear** Allah; for Allah
008:056 every time, and they have not the **fear** (of Allah).
008:069 lawful and good: but **fear** Allah: for Allah
009:013 Do ye **fear** them?
009:013 Nay, it is Allah whom ye should more justly **fear**,
009:018 and **fear** none (at all) except Allah.
009:024 the commerce in which ye **fear** a decline:
009:028 And if ye **fear** poverty, soon will Allah enrich you,
009:040 "Have no **fear**, for Allah is with us": then Allah
009:064 all that ye **fear** (should be revealed)."
009:119 O ye who Believe! **Fear** Allah and be
009:123 and know that Allah is with those who **fear** Him.
010:006 are Signs for those who **fear** Him.
010:015 I should myself **fear** the Chastisement
010:062 there is no **fear**, nor shall they grieve;
010:083 because of the **fear** of Pharaoh and his chiefs,
011:003 But if ye turn away, then I **fear** for you
011:026 Verily I do **fear** for you the punishment
011:070 and conceived a **fear** of them.
011:070 They said: "**Fear** not: we have been sent
011:074 When **fear** had passed from (the mind of) Abraham
011:078 Now **fear** Allah, and cover me not with disgrace
011:084 I see you in prosperity, but I **fear** for you
011:103 who **fear** the Chastisement of the Hereafter:
012:013 I **fear** lest the wolf should devour him
013:012 by way both of **fear** and of hope:
013:021 and **fear** the terrible reckoning;
014:014 This for such as **fear** the Time when they
014:014 My tribunal,-such as **fear** My Punishment."
015:053 They said: "**Fear** not! we give thee glad tidings
015:069 "But **fear** Allah, and shame me not."
016:050 They all **fear** their Lord, high above
016:051 then **fear** Me (and Me alone)."
016:052 then will ye **fear** other than Allah?
017:031 Kill not your children for **fear** of want:
017:057 they hope for His Mercy and **fear** His Wrath:
017:060 We put **fear** (and warning) into them, but it
017:100 ye would keep them back, for **fear** or spending them:
019:005 "Now I **fear** (what) my relatives (and colleagues)
019:018 (come not near) if thou dost **fear** Allah."
019:045 "O my father! I **fear** lest a Chastisement afflict
020:003 to those who **fear** (Allah),
020:021 (Allah) said, "Seize it, and **fear** not: We shall
020:044 perchance he may take warning or **fear** (Allah)."
020:045 "Our Lord! we **fear** lest He hasten with insolence
020:046 He said: "**Fear** not: for I am with you: I hear
020:067 So Moses conceived in his mind a (sort of) **fear**.
020:068 We said: "**Fear** not! for thou hast indeed
020:077 through the sea, without **fear** of being overtaken
020:077 and without (any other) **fear**."
020:112 and has faith, will have no **fear** of harm nor of
020:113 in order that they may **fear** Allah, or that
021:049 Those who **fear** their Lord in their
022:001 O mankind! **Fear** your Lord! For the convulsion
022:035 are filled with **fear**, who show

FEAR (continued)

023:023	will ye not **fear** (Him)?"
023:032	Will ye not **fear** (Him)?"
023:052	therefore **fear** Me (and no other).
023:057	for **fear** of their Lord;
023:060	with their hearts full of **fear**, because they
023:087	Say: "Will ye not then **fear**?"
024:034	and an admonition for those who **fear** (Allah).
024:037	nor from paying zakat their (only) **fear** is for
024:050	or are they in **fear**, that Allah
024:052	His Messenger, and **fear** Allah and do right,
024:055	after the **fear** in which they (lived), to one
026:011	"The people of Pharaoh: will they not **fear** Allah?"
026:012	I do **fear** that they will charge me with falsehood:
026:014	of crime against me; and I **fear** they may slay me."
026:106	"Will ye not **fear** (Allah)?
026:108	"So **fear** Allah, and obey me.
026:110	"So **fear** Allah, and obey me."
026:124	"Will ye not **fear** (Allah)?
026:126	"So **fear** Allah, and obey me.
026:131	"Now **fear** Allah, and obey me.
026:132	"Yea, **fear** Him Who has bestowed on you
026:135	"Truly I **fear** for you the Chastisement
026:142	said to them: "Will you not **fear** (Allah)?
026:144	So **fear** Allah, and obey me.
026:150	"But **fear** Allah, and obey me;
026:161	"Will ye not **fear** (Allah)?
026:163	"So **fear** Allah, and obey me.
026:177	"Will ye not **fear** (Allah)?
026:179	"So **fear** Allah, and obey me.
026:184	"And **fear** Him Who created you and (Who created)
027:010	those called as messengers have no **fear**,-
027:010	"O Moses!" (it was said), "**fear** not: truly, in My presence,
028:007	but **fear** not nor grieve: for We
028:021	looking about, in a state of **fear**.
028:025	he said: "**Fear** thou not: (well) hast
028:031	and **fear** not: for thou art of those who are secure.
028:032	to thy side (to guard) against **fear**.
028:033	among them, and I **fear** lest they slay me.
028:034	for I **fear** that they may accuse me of falsehood."
029:016	"Serve Allah and **fear** Him: that will
029:033	"**Fear** thou not, nor grieve: we are
029:036	serve Allah, and **fear** the last day: nor commit
030:024	by way both of **fear** and of hope, and He
030:028	Do ye **fear** them as ye **fear** each other?
030:031	Turn ye in repentance to Him, and **fear** Him:
031:033	and **fear** (the coming of) a Day when no father
032:016	the while they call on their Lord, in **Fear** and Hope:
033:001	O Prophet! **Fear** Allah, and hearken
033:019	but when the **fear** is past, they will
033:019	Then when **fear** comes, thou wilt
033:032	if ye do **fear** (Allah), be not
033:037	thou didst **fear** the people,
033:037	but it is more fitting that thou shouldst, **fear** Allah.
033:037	"Retain thou (in wedlock) thy wife, and **fear** Allah."
033:039	and **fear** Him, and **fear** none but Allah.
033:055	And, (ladies), **fear** Allah; for Allah is Witness to all things.
033:070	O ye who believe! **fear** Allah, and make
035:018	Thou canst but warm such as **fear** their Lord unseen
035:028	Those truly **fear** Allah, among His Servants, who have
036:045	When they are told, "**Fear** ye that which is
037:124	"Will ye not **fear** (Allah)?
038:022	they said: "**Fear** not: We are two disputants,

FEAR (continued)

039:010	**Fear** your Lord: good is (the reward) for those
039:013	my Lord, indeed have **fear** of the Chastisement
039:016	"O my servants! Then **fear** ye Me!"
039:020	But it is for those who **fear** their Lord,
039:023	who **fear** their Lord tremble thereat; then their
040:026	What I **fear** is lest he should change your
040:030	"O my People! truly I do **fear** for you something
040:032	"And, O my People! I **fear** for you a Day
041:030	"**Fear** ye not!" (they suggest),
042:022	Thou wilt see the wrong-doers in **fear** on account
043:063	therefore **fear** Allah and obey me.
043:068	My devotees! no **fear** shall be on you today,
046:013	no **fear**, nor shall they grieve.
046:021	truly I **fear** for you the Chastisement
048:027	heads shaved, hair cut short, and without **fear**.
049:001	before Allah and His Messenger; but **fear** Allah:
049:010	And **fear** Allah, that ye may receive Mercy.
049:012	But **fear** Allah: for Allah is Oft-Returning,
050:045	such as **fear** My Warning!
051:028	He conceived a **fear** of them. They said, "**Fear** not,"
051:037	as **fear** the Grievous Chastisement.
052:026	not without **fear** for the sake of our people.
055:046	But for such as **fear** the time when they will
057:028	O ye that believe! **fear** Allah, and believe
058:009	and **fear** Allah, to whom ye shall be brought back.
059:007	And **fear** Allah; for Allah is strict in Punishment.
059:013	Of a truth ye arouse greater **fear** in their hearts,
059:016	I do **fear** Allah, the Lord of the Worlds!"
059:018	O ye who believe! **Fear** Allah, and let
059:018	Yea, **fear** Allah: for Allah
059:021	and cleave asunder for the **fear** of Allah, such are
060:011	and **fear** Allah, in Whom ye believe.
064:016	So **fear** Allah as much as ye can; listen and
065:001	their prescribed periods: and **fear** Allah your Lord:
065:002	for those who **fear** Allah, He (ever) prepares a way out,
065:004	and for those who **fear** Allah, He will
065:010	Therefore **fear** Allah, O ye men of understanding-
067:012	As for those who **fear** their Lord unseen, for them
070:027	And those who **fear** the punishment of their Lord,-
071:003	"That ye should worship Allah, **fear** Him, and obey me:
072:013	has no **fear**, either of a short (account) or of
074:053	By no means! But they **fear** not the Hereafter.
076:007	and they **fear** a Day whose evil flies far and wide.
076:010	"We only **fear** a Day of frowning and distress
079:019	so thou shouldst **fear** Him?'"
079:040	the **fear** of standing before their Lord's (tribunal)
079:045	Thou art but a Warner for such as **fear** it.
080:009	And with **fear** (in his heart),
091:015	And for Him is no **fear** of its consequences.
098:008	all this for such as **fear** their Lord and Cherisher.
106:004	security against **fear** (of danger).

FEARED

003:102	O ye who believe! fear Allah as He should be **feared**,
004:077	or even more than, they should have **feared** Allah:
004:077	behold! a section of them **feared** men as, or even
007:096	had but believed and **feared** Allah, We should
018:080	and we **feared** that he would grieve them by
020:094	Truly I **feared** lest thou shouldst say, 'Thou hast
026:021	I **feared** you; but my Lord has (since) invested me
039:073	And those who **feared** their Lord will be led
050:033	"Who **feared** The Most Gracious unseen, and brought

FEAREST
008:058 If thou **fearest** treachery from any group,

FEARETH
005:094 that He may test who **feareth** Him unseen:
079:026 for whosoever **feareth** (Allah).

FEARFUL
028:018 he was in the city, **fearful** and vigilant when behold,

FEARS
002:182 But if anyone **fears** partiality or wrong-doing
004:128 If a wife **fears** cruelty or desertion
028:007 but when thou hast **fears** about him, cast him
036:011 as follows the Message and **fears** the Most
065:005 and if anyone **fears** Allah, He will
087:010 He will heed who **fears**:
092:005 So he who gives (in charity) and **fears** (Allah),

FEAST
006:099 they begin to bear fruit, **feast** your eyes with the fruit

FEAT
007:116 and they showed a great (**feat** of) magic.

FEATURES
010:088 the **features** of their wealth, and send

FECUNDATING
015:022 And We send the **fecundating** winds, then cause

FED
002:025 Every time they are **fed** with fruits
002:025 we were **fed** with before,"
006:014 And He is that feedeth but is not **fed**."
036:047 He would have **fed**, (himself)?- Ye are
074:044 "Nor were we of those who **fed** the indigent;

FEEBLE
004:076 **feeble** indeed is the cunning of Satan.
008:018 He Who makes **feeble** the Plans and stratagems
016:070 sent back to a **feeble** age, so that
022:073 **Feeble** are those who petition and those whom they

FEEBLEST
022:005 and some are sent back to the **feeblest** old age,

FEED
002:126 and **feed** its People with fruits,
002:196 or **feed** the poor, or offer sacrifice;
004:005 but **feed** and clothe them therewith, and speak
005:089 for expiation, **feed** then indigent persons,
011:064 leave her to **feed** on Allah's (free) earth,
012:037 (in due course) to **feed** either of you I will
014:032 fruits wherewith to **feed** you; is He
014:037 and **feed** them with Fruits: so that
016:010 the vegetation on which ye **feed** your cattle.
022:028 then eat ye thereof and **feed** the distressed
022:036 eat ye thereof, and **feed** such as (beg not but)
036:047 who believe: "Shall we then **feed** those whom,
051:057 nor do I require that they should **feed** Me.
058:004 to do so, he should **feed** sixty indigent ones.
076:008 And they **feed**, for the love of Allah, the indigent,
076:009 (Saying), "We **feed** you for the sake of Allah alone:
089:018 Nor do ye encourage one another to **feed** the poor!-

FEEDETH
006:014 And He is that **feedeth** but is not fed."

FEEDING
002:184 the **feeding** of one that is indigent.
005:095 the **feeding** of the indigent; or its
069:034 the **feeding** of the indigent!
107:003 And encourages not the **feeding** of the indigent.

FEEDS
029:060 It is Allah Who **feeds** (both) them and you:
056:072 which **feeds** the fire, or do We grow it?

FEEL
002:230 provided they **feel** that they can keep the limits
007:097 Did the people of the towns **feel** secure against the coming
007:098 Or else did they **feel** secure against its
007:099 can **feel** secure from the Plan of Allah, except
007:099 Did they then **fell** secure against Allah's
008:002 when Allah it mentioned, **feel** a tremor in their hearts,
009:029 willing submission, and **feel** themselves subdued.
011:012 Perchance thou mayest (**feel** the inclination)
012:033 their snare from me, I should **feel** inclined towards
012:107 Do they then **feel** secure from the coming against
015:052 "We **feel** afraid of you!"
016:045 (plots) **feel** secure that Allah will not cause
017:068 Do ye then **feel** secure that He will not cause
017:069 Or do ye **feel** secure that He will not send
027:037 in disgrace, and they will **feel** humbled (indeed)."
041:038 And they never flag (nor **feel** themselves above it).
067:016 Do ye **feel** secure that He Who is in heaven
067:017 Or do ye **feel** secure that He Who is in
070:028 a thing to **feel** secure from:-

FEELETH
002:255 and He **feeleth** no fatigue in guarding
011:012 and thy heart **feeleth** straitened lest they say,

FEELING
015:082 (their) edifices, (**feeling** themselves) secure.
023:078 (the faculties of) hearing, sight, **feeling** and

FEELINGS
003:154 stirred to anxiety by their own **feelings**,

FEET
003:147 establish our **feet** firmly, and help us
005:006 and (wash) your **feet** to the ankles.
005:033 or the cutting off of hands and **feet** from opposite
005:066 from above them and from below their **feet**.
006:006 and gave streams flowing beneath their (**feet**):
007:124 and your **feet** on opposite sides, and I
007:195 Have they **feet** to walk with?
008:011 and to plant your **feet** firmly therewith.
020:071 and **feet** on opposite sides, and I
024:024 their hands, and their **feet** will bear witness
024:031 their **feet** in order to draw attention to their
026:049 and your **feet** on opposite sides, and I
036:065 will speak to Us, and their **feet** bear witness,
041:029 we shall crush them beneath our **feet**, so that
047:007 He will help you, and plant your **feet** firmly.
051:045 Then they could not even stand (on their **feet**),
055:041 be seized by their forelocks and their **feet**.

FELICITY
002:036 the state (of **felicity**) in which they had been.
003:104 they are the ones to attain **felicity**.
007:043 Who hath guided us to this (**felicity**):
059:020 that will achieve **Felicity**.

FELL
002:072 Remember ye slew a man and **fell** into a dispute
003:066 Ah! Ye are those who **fell** to disputing (even)
003:152 and **fell** to disputing about the order,
007:120 But the sorcerers **fell** down prostrate in adoration.
007:134 And when the Plague **fell** on them, they said:
007:143 He made it as dust and Moses **fell** down in a swoon.
010:093 that they **fell** into schisms.

FELL (continued)
012:100 the throne and they **fell** down in prostration,
016:026 and the roof **fell** down on them from above;
017:007 all that **fell** into their power.
020:121 His Lord, and **fell** into error.
034:014 so when he **fell** down, the Jinns
038:024 of his Lord, **fell** down, bowing (in prostration),
043:065 But sects from among themselves **fell** into disagreement:
045:017 granted to them that they **fell** into schisms,

FELLOW
043:048 them Sign after Sign, each greater then its **fellow**,

FELLOW-MEN
004:053 farthing to their **fellow-men**!

FELLOWS
051:059 their **fellows** (of earlier generations):

FELT
009:118 (they **felt** guilty) to such a degree that the earth
011:070 he **felt** some mistrust of them, and conceived
011:077 and **felt** himself powerless (to protect) them.
021:012 Yet, when they **felt** Our Punishment (coming),
029:033 and **felt** himself powerless (to protect) them:

FEMALE
003:036 "And is not the male like the **female**.
003:036 I am delivered of a **female** child!"
003:195 be he male or **female**: ye are members,
004:117 call but upon **female** deities:
004:124 be they male or **female**, and have faith, they
004:176 the male having twice the share of the **female**,
005:038 As to the thief, male or **female**, cut off
011:040 kind two, male and **female**, and your family-
013:008 every **female** (womb) doth bear, by how
016:058 of (the birth of) a **female** (child), his face
022:002 and every pregnant **female** shall drop her
023:027 of every species, male and **female**, and thy
024:032 your slaves, male or **female**:
035:011 And no **female** conceives, or lays down
037:150 Or that We created the angels **female**, and they
041:047 nor does a **female** conceive (within her womb)
042:049 He bestows (children) male or **female** according to
049:013 a single (pair) of a male and a **female**, and made
053:021 and for Him, the **female**?
053:027 name the angels with **female** names.
053:045 That He did create in pairs-male and **female**,
075:039 And of him He made two sexes, male and **female**.
081:008 When the **female** (infant), Buried alive,
092:003 By the creation of male and **female**;-

FEMALES
004:011 to the male, a portion equal to that of two **females**:
006:143 which the wombs of the two **females** enclose?
006:143 or the two **females**, or, (the young) which the
006:144 or the two **females**, or, (the young) which the
006:144 which the wombs of the two **females** enclose?-
007:127 (only) their **females** will we save alive;
007:141 and saved alive your **females**: in that
028:004 but he kept alive their **females**: for he
040:025 with him, and keep alive their **females**," but the
042:050 Or He bestows both males and **females**, and He
043:019 And they make into **females** angels who themselves

FERTILE
002:265 is as a garden, high and **fertile**:

FERTILIZING
013:012 the clouds, heavy with (**fertilizing**) rain!

FERVENTLY
017:011 Man prays for evil as **fervently** as he prays

FESTIVAL
005:114 a solemn **festival** and a Sign from Thee;
020:059 Moses said: "Your tryst is the Day of the **Festival**,

FETID
014:016 and he is given, for drink, boiling **fetid** water.
040:072 In the boiling **fetid** fluid; then in

FETTERS
014:049 that day bound together in **fetters**:-
038:038 As also others bound together in **fetters**.
073:012 With Us are **Fetters** (to bind them), and a Fire

FEW
002:080 not touch us but for **few** numbered days:"
002:083 except a **few** among you,
002:249 "But they drank of it, except a **few**.
003:024 not touch us but for a **few** numbered days":
004:046 and but **few** of them will believe.
004:066 very **few** of them would have done it:
004:083 all but a **few** of you would have followed Satan.
005:013 barring a **few**-ever bent on (new) deceits:
008:043 showed them to thee as **few**:
008:044 He showed them to you as **few** in your eyes,
011:040 But only a **few** believed with him.
011:116 (but there were none) except a **few** among them whom
012:020 a miserable price,-for a **few** dirhams counted out:
012:042 and (Joseph) lingered in prison a **few** (more) years.
017:062 under my sway-all but a **few**!"
018:022 it is but **few** that know their (real case)."
026:205 (this life) for a **few** years,
028:058 all but a (miserable) **few**! and We
030:004 Within a **few** years, with Allah
034:013 sons of David, but **few** of My servants
034:016 and some **few** (stunted) Lote-trees.
038:024 of righteousness, and how **few** are they?"
056:014 And a **few** from those of later times.

FEWER
058:007 the sixth,-nor between **fewer** not more, but He

FIBRE
111:005 A twisted rope of palm-leaf **fibre** round her

FIBRES
016:080 their wool, and their soft **fibres** (between wool and hair),

FIE
021:067 "**Fie** upon you, and upon the things that ye
046:017 But (there is one) who says to his parents, "**Fie** on you!

FIELD
021:015 till We made them as a **field** that is mown,
021:078 of the **field** into which the sheep of certain
105:005 an empty **field** of stalks and straw,

FIELDS
002:071 to till the soil or water the **fields**;
013:004 and gardens of vines and **fields** sown with corn,

FIERCE
037:023 the Way to the (**Fierce**) Fire!
056:042 of a **fierce** Blast of Fire and in Boiling Water,
077:031 and is of no use against the **fierce** Blaze.
081:012 When the Blazing Fire is kindled to **fierce** heat;

FIERCELY
092:014 Therefore do I warn you of a Fire blazing **fiercely**;
101:011 (It is) a Fire Blazing **fiercely**!

FIERCENESS
017:097   the **fierceness** of the Fire.

FIERCER
009:081   Say, "The fire of Hell is **fiercer** in heat."

FIERY
015:018   a **fiery** comet, bright (to see).

FIFTH
008:041   a **fifth** share is assigned to Allah,-and to
024:007   And the **fifth** (oath) (should be) that he
024:009   And the **fifth** (oath) should be that she solemnly

FIFTY
029:014   a thousand years less **fifty**:
070:004   is (as) **fifty** thousand years:

FIG
095:001   By the **Fig** and the Olive,

FIGHT
002:190   **Fight** in the cause of Allah those who **fight** you
002:191   unless they (first) **fight** you there;
002:191   but if they **fight** you, slay them.
002:191   but **fight** them not at the Sacred Mosque,
002:193   And **fight** them on until there is no more
002:244   Then **fight** in the cause of Allah,
002:246   But when they were commanded to **fight**,
002:246   that we may **fight** in the cause of Allah."
002:246   if ye were commanded to **fight**,
002:246   that ye will not **fight**?"
002:246   we refuse to **fight** in the cause of Allah,
003:111   if they come out to **fight** you, they will show
003:167   They said: "Had we known there would be a **fight**,
003:167   these were told: "Come, **fight** in the way of Allah,
004:074   Let those **fight** in the cause of Allah who sell
004:075   And why should ye not **fight** in the cause
004:076   those who reject Faith **fight** in the cause of Evil (Tagut):
004:076   so **fight** ye against the friends, of Satan:
004:076   Those who believe **fight** in the cause of Allah,
004:077   why hast Thou ordered us to **fight**?
004:077   their hands (from **fight**) but establish regular
004:084   Then **fight** in Allah's cause, thou art held
004:090   withdraw from you but **fight** you not,
004:095   And those who strive and **fight** in the cause
004:095   to those who strive and **fight** with their goods
004:095   but those who strive and **fight** hath He
005:024   and **fight** ye two, while we sit here.
008:039   And **fight** them on until there is no
008:065   O Prophet! rouse the Believers to the **fight**.
008:074   and **fight** for the Faith, in the Cause
008:075   and emigrate, and **fight** for the Faith in your
009:005   then **fight** and slay the Pagans wherever ye
009:012   and attack your Faith, **fight** ye the chiefs of Unfaith:
009:013   Will ye not **fight** people who violated
009:014   **Fight** them, and Allah will punish them.
009:029   **Fight** those who believe not in Allah nor the
009:036   and **fight** the Pagans all together as they **fight** you all
009:081   they hated to strive and **fight**, with their
009:083   nor **fight** an enemy with me:
009:086   and **fight** along with His Messenger, those with
009:088   strive and **fight** with their wealth and their persons:
009:111   they **fight** in His Cause, and slay and are slain:
009:123   O ye who believe! **Fight** the Unbelievers who are
016:110   strive and **fight** for the Faith and patiently
022:039   permission is given (to **fight**), because they
033:018   but come not to the **fight** except for just

FIGHT (continued)
033:020   they would **fight** but little.
033:025   and enough is Allah for the Believers in their **fight**.
047:004   Therefore, when ye meet the Unbelievers (in **fight**),
047:004   but (He lets you **fight**) in order to test you,
048:016   then shall ye **fight**, or they shall submit.
048:016   (to **fight**) against a people given to vehement war
048:022   If the Unbelievers should **fight** you, they would
049:009   If two parties among the Believers fall into a **fight**,
049:009   then **fight** ye (all) against the one that transgresses
059:011   and if ye are attacked (in **fight**) we will help you."
059:012   are attacked (in **fight**), they will never help them;
059:014   They will not **fight** you (even) together, except in
060:008   to those who **fight** you not for (your) Faith
060:009   to those who **fight** you for (your) Faith, and drive
061:004   Truly Allah loves those who **fight** in His Cause

FIGHTETH
004:074   To him who **fighteth** in the cause of Allah, whether

FIGHTING
002:216   **Fighting** is prescribed for you,
002:217   concerning **fighting** in the Prohibited Month.
002:217   Say: "**Fighting** therein is a grave (offense);
002:217   Nor will they cease **fighting** you until
003:013   one was **fighting** in the cause of Allah,
003:156   through the earth or engaged in **fighting**:
004:077   the order for **fighting** was issued to them, behold!
004:090   you or **fighting** their own people.
004:090   hearts restraining them from **fighting** you or
005:054   mighty against the Rejecters, **fighting** in the way of Allah,
009:044   no exemption from **fighting** with their goods
028:015   and he found there two men **fighting**,-one of
047:020   and **fighting** is mentioned therein, thou wilt
059:014   Strong is their **fighting** (spirit) amongst
073:020   yet others **fighting** in Allah's Cause.

FIGURE
003:049   the **figure** of a bird, and breathe into it,
005:110   as it were, the **figure** of a bird, by My leave.

FILL
007:018   Hell will I **fill** with you all.
011:119   "I will **fill** Hell with Jinns and men all together."
014:037   so **fill** the hearts of some among men with love towards
032:013   "I will **fill** Hell with Jinns and men all together."
037:066   and **fill** their bellies therewith.
038:085   "That I will certainly **fill** Hell with thee
056:053   "Then will ye **fill** your insides therewith,

FILLED
002:093   and their hearts were **filled** (with the love) of the Calf
016:058   his face darkens, and he is **filled** with inward grief!
018:018   and wouldst certainly have been **filled** with terror of them.
018:096   At length, when he had **filled** up the space
022:035   are **filled** with fear, who show
026:119   in the Ark **filled** (with all creatures).
034:033   They are **filled** with remorse.
039:045   in the Hereafter are **filled** with disgust,
039:045   they are **filled** with joy!
043:017   is **filled** with inward grief!
050:030   "Art thou **filled** to the full?" It will say,
052:006   And by the Ocean **filled** with Swell;-
056:018   and cups (**filled**) out of clear-flowing fountains:
072:008   but we found it **filled** with stern guards and flaming fires.

FILLING
048:029   its own stem, (**filling**) the sowers with wonder and delight.

FILLS
048:029 it **fills** the Unbelievers with rage at him.

FINAL
003:028 for the **final** goal is to Allah.
004:059 most suitable for **final** determination.
005:018 and unto Him is the **final** goal (of all)."
007:187 They ask thee about the (**final**) Hour-when will
012:107 the (**final**) Hour all of a sudden while they
013:022 the **final** attainment of the (Eternal) Home,-
013:024 Now how excellent is the **final** Home!"
013:029 and a beautiful place of (**final**) return."
017:035 in the **final** determination.
025:015 a reward as well as a **final** abode.
031:014 to Me is (thy **final**) Goal.
033:021 who hope in Allah and the **Final** Day, and who
038:025 and a beautiful place of (**final**) Return.
038:040 to Us, and a beautiful Place of (**final**) Return.
038:049 is a beautiful place of (**final**) Return,-
038:055 will be an evil place of (**final**) Return!-
040:003 There is no god but He: to Him is the **Final** Goal.
042:015 and to Him is (Our) **final** goal.
050:043 and to Us is the **Final** Return-
053:042 That to thy Lord is the **final** Goal;
060:004 to Thee is (our) **final** Return.
064:003 and to Him is the **final** Return.
079:044 With they Lord is the **final** end of it.

FINALLY
013:032 the Unbelievers, and **finally** I punished them:
074:008 **Finally** when the Trumpet is sounded,

FIND
002:061 and ye shall **find** what ye want!"
002:096 Thou wilt indeed **find** them,
002:110 ye shall **find** it with Allah:
002:120 then wouldst thou **find** neither Protector
002:196 such as ye may **find**,
002:283 and cannot **find** a scribe,
003:091 and they will **find** on helpers.
003:192 and never will wrong-doers **find** any helpers!
004:006 if then ye **find** sound judgment in them, release
004:043 and ye **find** no water, then take
004:052 thou wilt **find**, have no one to help.
004:065 And **find** in their souls no resistance
004:078 "Wherever ye are, death will **find** you out, even
004:088 never shalt thou **find** the Way.
004:089 seize them and slay them wherever ye **find** them;
004:091 Others you will **find** that wish to be secure from
004:092 For those who **find** this beyond their means,
004:097 Such men will **find** their abode in Hell.
004:098 nor can they **find** a way (to escape).
004:110 he will **find** Allah Oft-Forgiving, Most Merciful.
004:121 and from it they will **find** no way of escape.
004:123 Nor will he **find**, besides Allah,
004:143 never wilt thou **find** for him the Way.
004:145 no helper wilt thou **find** for them;
004:173 nor will they **find**, besides Allah, any to
005:006 and you **find** no water, then take
005:013 nor wilt thou cease to **find** them-barring a few,
005:054 the reproaches of such as **find** fault.
005:082 to the Believers wilt thou **find** the Jews and
005:082 to the Believers wilt thou **find** those who say,
006:070 it will **find** for itself no protector
006:115 The Word of thy Lord doth **find** its fulfillment
006:145 Say: "I **find** not in the Message received by

FIND (continued)
007:009 will **find** their souls in perdition, for that
007:017 nor wilt Thou **find**, in most of them, gratitude
007:157 whom they **find** mentioned in their own (Scriptures),-
008:002 **find** their faith strengthened, and pit (all) their trust
009:005 wherever ye **find** them, and seize them, beleaguer
009:057 If they could **find** a place to flee to, or caves,
009:091 or who **find** no resources to spend (on the Cause),
009:092 "I can **find** no mounts for you," they turned
009:123 and let them **find** harshness in you: and know
012:082 and (you will **find**) we are indeed telling the truth."
013:011 no turning it back, nor will they **find**, besides
013:028 hearts **find** satisfaction in the remembrance
013:028 of Allah do hearts **find** satisfaction.
013:037 then wouldst thou **find** neither protector nor
016:066 And verily in cattle (too) will ye **find** an instructive Sign.
016:080 which ye **find** so light (and handy) when ye
017:048 and never can they **find** a way.
017:068 so that ye shall **find** no protector?
017:069 so that ye **find** no helper therein against Us?
017:077 thou wilt **find** no change in Our ways.
017:086 then wouldst thou **find** none to plead thy affair
017:097 wilt thou **find** no protector besides Him.
018:017 for him wilt thou **find** no protector to lead
018:019 let him **find** out which is the best food
018:027 and none wilt thou **find** as a refuge
018:036 I shall surely **find** (there) something better
018:041 wilt never be able to **find** it."
018:049 They will **find** all that they did, placed before
018:053 no means will they **find** to turn away therefrom.
018:058 beyond which they will **find** no refuge.
018:069 Moses said: "Thou wilt **find** me, if Allah
019:098 Canst thou **find** a single one of them (now) or hear
020:010 or **find** some guidance at the fire."
020:018 and in it I **find** other uses."
021:031 that they may **find** their way.
024:028 If ye **find** no one in the house, enter not
024:033 Let those who **find** not the wherewithal for
025:009 and never a way will they be able to **find**!
028:027 thou wilt **find** me, indeed, if Allah wills, one of the
028:041 no help shall they **find**.
033:017 Nor will they **find** for themselves,
033:062 wilt thou **find** in the practice (approved) of
033:065 no protector will they **find**, nor helper.
035:043 But no change wilt thou **find** in Allah's way
035:043 no turning off wilt thou **find** in Allah's way
037:102 thou will **find** me, if Allah
041:016 more humiliating still: and they will **find** no help.
043:010 in order that ye may **find** guidance (on the way);
045:022 soul may **find** the recompense of what it has earned,
048:022 then would they **find** neither protector nor helper.
048:023 on change wilt thou **find** in the practice of Allah.
058:012 But if ye **find** not (the wherewithal),
058:022 Thou wilt not **find** any people who believe
065:006 and if ye **find** yourselves in difficulties, let another
072:009 but any who listen now will **find** a flaming fire watching
072:022 nor should I **find** refuge except in Him.
073:020 ye shall **find** it with Allah.
093:006 Did He not **find** thee an orphan and give

FINDETH
008:070 "If Allah **findeth** any good in your hearts, He will

FINDING
003:169 Nay, they live, **finding** their sustenance from their Lord.

FINDS

004:100 in the cause of Allah, **finds** in the earth many a refuge.
010:035 to be followed, or he who **finds** not guidance
024:039 but he **finds** Allah there, and Allah
024:039 to it, he **finds** it to be nothing:

FINE

004:073 a **fine** thing should I then have made of it!"
007:137 the great works and **fine** Buildings which Pharaoh
009:098 their payments as a **fine**, and watch
012:019 Good news! Here is a (**fine**) young man!
018:031 green garments of **fine** silk and heavy brocade;
020:082 and do right,-who, in **fine**, are no true guidance."
026:129 "And so ye get for yourselves **fine** buildings in the
044:053 Dressed in **fine** silk and in rich brocade,
076:021 of **fine** silk and heavy brocade, and they

FINELY

018:026 how clearly He sees, how **finely** He hears

FINGER-TIPS

008:012 and smite all their **finger-tips** off them."

FINGERS

002:019 they press their **fingers** in their ears
003:119 of their **fingers** at you in their rage.
071:007 they have (only) thrust their **fingers** into their
075:004 in perfect order the very tips of his **fingers**.

FINISH

004:102 when they **finish** their prostrations, let them

FINISHED

046:029 (reading) was **finished**, they returned to their
062:010 And when the Prayer is **finished**, then may

FIRE

002:017 a man who kindled a **fire**;
002:024 then fear the **fire** whose fuel
002:039 they shall be Companions of the **Fire**;
002:080 And they say: "The **fire** shall not touch us
002:081 they are Companions of the **Fire**,
002:119 be asked of Companions of the blazing **fire**.
002:126 to the torment of **Fire**,
002:167 a way for them out of the **Fire**.
002:174 they swallow into themselves naught but **Fire**;
002:175 Ah! what boldness (they show) for the **Fire**!
002:201 and save us from the torment on the **Fire**!"
002:217 of the **Fire** and will abide therein.
002:221 Unbelievers do (but) beckon you to the **Fire**.
002:257 They will be Companions of the **fire**,
002:266 in a whirlwind, with **fire** therein, and be burnt up?
002:275 (the offense) are Companion of the **Fire**:
003:010 they are themselves but fuel for the **Fire**.
003:016 and save us from the agony of the **Fire**;"
003:024 This because they say: "The **Fire** shall not touch us
003:103 and ye were on the brink of the Pit of **Fire**,
003:116 they will be companions of the **Fire**,
003:131 Fear the **fire**, which is prepared for those
003:151 their abode will be the **Fire**:
003:181 "Taste ye the Chastisement of the scorching **Fire**!
003:183 consumed by **fire** (from heaven)."
003:185 Only he who is saved far from the **fire** and
003:191 salvation from the Chastisement of the **Fire**.
003:192 "Our Lord! any whom Thou dost admit to the **Fire**,
004:010 eat up a **fire** into their own bodies:
004:010 they will soon be enduring a blazing **Fire**!
004:014 will be admitted to a **Fire**, to abide therein:
004:030 soon shall We cast them into the **Fire**:

FIRE (continued)

004:055 and enough is Hell for a burning **fire**.
004:056 We shall soon cast into the **Fire**:
004:145 the lowest depths of the **Fire**: no helper
005:029 for thou wilt be among the companions of the **Fire**,
005:037 Their wish will be to get out of the **Fire**,
005:064 Every time they kindle the **fire** of war, Allah
005:072 and the **Fire** will be his abode.
006:027 when they shall be made to stand by the **Fire**!
006:128 He will say: "The **Fire** be your dwelling-place:
007:012 thou didst create me from **fire** and him from clay."
007:036 they are Companions of the **Fire**, to dwell
007:038 so give them a double punishment in the **Fire**."
007:038 until they follow each other, all into the **Fire**.
007:038 men and Jinns,-into the **Fire**.
007:044 will call out to the Companions of the **Fire**: "We
007:047 turned towards the Companions of the **Fire**,
007:050 The Companions of the **Fire** will call
008:014 is the chastisement of the **Fire**."
008:050 "Taste the chastisement of the blazing **Fire**-
009:017 in **Fire** shall they dwell.
009:035 be heated in the **fire** of Hell, and with it
009:063 oppose Allah and His Messenger, is the **Fire** of Hell?
009:068 and the rejecters of Faith, the **fire** of Hell:
009:081 Say, "The **fire** of Hell is fiercer in heat."
009:109 it doth crumble to pieces with him, into the **fire** of Hell.
009:113 that they are companions of the **Fire**.
010:008 Their abode is the **Fire**, because of
010:027 they are Inhabitants of the **Fire**: they will
011:016 is nothing in the Hereafter but the **Fire**:
011:017 the **Fire** will be their promised meeting place.
011:098 and lead them into the **Fire**, but woeful
011:106 Those who are wretched shall be in the **Fire**:
011:113 or the **Fire** will touch you; and ye have
013:005 they will be Companions of the **Fire**, to dwell
013:017 (ore) which they heat in the **fire**, to make
013:035 and the End of Unbelievers is the **Fire**.
014:050 and their faces covered with **Fire**;
015:027 from the **fire** of a scorching wind.
016:062 without doubt for them is the **Fire**, and they will be
017:097 the fierceness of the **Fire**.
018:029 a **Fire** whose (smoke and flames), like the
018:053 And the Sinful shall see the **Fire** and apprehend
018:096 when he had made it (red) as **fire**, he said:
020:010 "Tarry ye; I perceive a **fire**; perhaps I can
020:010 or find some guidance at the **fire**."
020:010 Behold, he saw a **fire**: so he said
020:011 But when he came to the **fire**, he was call
020:087 and we threw them (into the **fire**), and that
020:088 "Then he brought out (of the **fire**) before the
020:097 a blazing **fire** and scatter it broadcast in the sea!
021:039 to ward off the **Fire** from their faces, not yet
021:069 We said, "O **Fire**! be thou cool, and (a means of)
022:004 to the Chastisement of the **Fire**.
022:009 make him taste the chastisement of burning (**Fire**).
022:019 for them will be cut out a garment of **Fire**:
022:051 they will be Companions of the **Fire**."
022:072 It is the **fire** (of Hell)!
023:104 The **Fire** will burn their faces, and they
024:035 though **fire** scarce touched it:
024:057 is the **Fire**,-and it is indeed an evil refuge!
025:011 a Blazing **Fire** for such as deny the Hour:
026:091 the **Fire** will be placed in full view;

FIRE (continued)

026:094 '"Then they will be thrown headlong into the (Fire),-
027:007 "I perceive a fire; soon will
027:008 But when he came to the (Fire), a voice
027:008 "Blessed are those in the Fire and those around:
027:090 will be thrown headlong into the Fire:
028:029 "Tarry ye; I perceive a fire; I hope
028:029 he perceived a fire in the direction of Mount Tur.
028:030 But when he came to the (Fire), he was
028:041 leaders inviting to the Fire;
029:024 But Allah did save him from the Fire.
029:025 and your abode will the Fire, and ye shall have none
031:021 to the Chastisement of the (Blazing) Fire!
032:020 of the Fire, the which ye were wont to reject
032:020 their abode will be the Fire:
033:064 for them a Blazing Fire,-
033:066 turned over in the Fire, they will say:
034:012 of the Chastisement of the Blazing Fire.
034:042 "Taste ye the Chastisement of the Fire,-the which
035:006 that they may become Companions of the Blazing Fire.
035:036 for them will be the Fire of Hell:
036:064 "Embrace ye the (Fire) this Day, for that
036:080 "The same Who produces for you fire out of
037:010 by a flaming fire, of piercing brightness.
037:023 the Way to the (Fierce) Fire!
037:055 in the midst of the Fire.
037:068 Then shall their return be to the (Blazing) Fire.
037:097 and throw him into the blazing fire!"
037:163 going to the blazing Fire!
038:027 the Unbelievers because of the Fire (of Hell)!
038:059 Truly, they shall burn in the Fire!
038:061 add to him a double Chastisement in the Fire!"
038:064 of the People of the Fire!
038:076 Thou createdst me from fire, and him
039:008 of the Companions of the Fire!"
039:016 above them, and Layers (of Fire) below them:
039:016 They shall have Layers of Fire above them,
039:019 (who is) in the Fire?
040:006 that truly they are Companions of Fire!
040:007 of the Blazing Fire!
040:041 while ye call me to the Fire!
040:043 will be Companions of the Fire!
040:046 In front of the Fire will they be brought,
040:047 from us some share of the Fire?"
040:047 Behold!, they will dispute with each other in the Fire!
040:048 "We are all in this (Fire)! Truly, Allah has
040:049 Those in the Fire will say to the Keepers of Hell:
040:072 then in the Fire shall they be burned;
041:019 will be gathered together to the Fire, they will
041:020 At length, when they reach the (Fire),
041:024 the Fire will be a Home for them!
041:028 such is the requital of the enemies of Allah,-the Fire:
041:040 he that is cast into the Fire, or he
042:007 and some in the Blazing Fire.
044:047 and drag him into the midst of the Blazing Fire!
044:056 the Chastisement of the Blazing Fire,-
045:034 And your abode is the Fire, and no
046:020 the Unbelievers will be placed before the Fire,
046:034 the Unbelievers will be placed before the Fire,
047:012 and the Fire will be their abode.
047:015 dwell for ever in the Fire, and be
048:013 for those who reject Allah, a Blazing fire!
051:013 be tried (and tested) over the Fire!

FIRE (continued)

052:013 to the Fire of Hell, irresistibly.
052:014 "Is the Fire,-which ye were wont to deny!
052:018 them from the Chastisement of the Fire.
054:048 through the Fire on their faces, (they will hear):
055:015 And He created Jinns from fire free of smoke:
055:035 a flame of fire (to burn) and a (flash of) molten brass
056:042 of a fierce Blast of Fire and in Boiling Water,
056:071 See ye the Fire which ye kindle?
056:072 which feeds the fire, or do We grow it?
057:015 Your abode is the Fire:
058:017 they will be Companions of the Fire, to dwell therein
059:003 the Punishment of the Fire,
059:017 that they will go into the Fire, dwelling therein
059:020 Not equal are the Companions of the Fire and the
064:010 they will be Companions of the Fire, to dwell
066:006 and your families from a Fire whose fuel
066:010 "Enter ye the Fire along with (others)
067:005 the Chastisement of the Blazing Fire.
067:010 be among the Companions of the Blazing Fire!"
067:011 are the Companions of the Blazing Fire!
069:031 "And burn ye him in the Blazing Fire.
070:015 By no means! for it would be the Blazing Fire-
071:025 and were made to enter the Fire and they found-
072:009 find a flaming fire watching him in ambush.
073:012 and a Fire (to burn them),
074:031 as guardians of the Fire; and We
076:004 prepared Chains, Yokes, and a Blazing Fire.
081:012 When the Blazing Fire is kindled to fierce heat;
082:014 And the Wicked-they will be in the Fire,
083:016 Further, they will enter the Fire of Hell.
084:012 And he will enter a Blazing Fire.
085:004 Woe to the makers of the pit (of Fire),
085:005 Fire supplied (abundantly) with Fuel:
085:006 Behold! they sat over against the (fire),
085:010 they will have the Chastisement of the Burning Fire.
087:012 Who will enter the Great Fire,
088:004 The while they enter the Blazing Fire,-
090:020 On them will be Fire Vaulted over (all round).
092:014 Therefore do I warn you of a Fire blazing fiercely;
100:002 And strike sparks of fire,
101:011 (It is) a Fire Blazing fiercely!
104:006 (It is) the Fire of Allah kindled (to a blaze),
111:003 Burnt soon will he be in a Fire of blazing Flame!

FIREBRAND

028:029 burning firebrand, that ye may warm yourselves."

FIRES

036:080 when behold! ye kindle therewith (your own fires)!
072:008 filled with stern guards and flaming fires.

FIRM

002:177 and to be firm and patient,
002:227 But if their intention is firm for divorce,
002:250 on us and make our steps firm:
003:018 standing firm on justice.
003:125 "Yea,-if ye remain firm, and act aright,
003:146 And Allah loves those who are firm and steadfast.
004:127 that ye stand firm for justice to orphans.
008:045 when ye meet a force, be firm, and call
009:073 and be firm against them.
011:112 Therefore stand firm (in the straight path)
011:120 with it We make firm they heart:
013:003 and set thereon Mountains standing firm,
014:027 with the Word that stands firm, in this world and in the

FIRM (continued)

015:019 set thereon mountains **firm** and immovable;
016:015 mountains standing **firm**, lest it should shake
016:106 remaining **firm** in Faith,-but such
020:115 and We found on his part no **firm** resolve.
021:031 mountains standing **firm**, lest it should
026:063 became like the huge, **firm** mass of a mountain.
027:061 Or, who has made the earth **firm** to live in;
028:006 To establish a **firm** place for them in the land,
028:010 a (**firm**) believer.
031:010 standing **firm**, lest it should shake with you;
041:010 mountains standing **firm**, high above it,
043:013 In order that ye may sit **firm** and square
045:032 and we have no **firm** assurance.'"
046:013 "Our Lord is Allah," and remain **firm** (on that Path),-
046:035 as did (all) messengers of **firm** resolution;
050:007 and set thereon standing **firm**, and produced therein
052:036 Nay, they have no **firm** belief.
070:033 And those who stand **firm** in their testimonies;
077:027 And made therein mountains standing **firm**,
088:019 And at the Mountains, how they are fixed **firm**?-

FIRMAMENT

051:047 We have built the **Firmament** with might: and We
052:009 On the Day when the **firmament** will be
055:007 And the **Firmament** has He raised high, and He
086:011 By the **Firmament** which giveth returns rain,
091:005 By the **Firmament** and its (wonderful) structure;

FIRMAMENTS

002:029 and made them into seven **firmaments**;
041:012 So He completed them as seven **firmaments** in two
065:012 Allah is He Who created seven **Firmaments** and of
078:012 over you the seven **firmaments**,

FIRMLY

002:063 (saying): "Hold **firmly** to what We have
002:093 (saying): "Hold **firmly** to what We given you,
002:118 who hold **firmly** to Faith (in their hearts).
003:007 And those who are **firmly** grounded in knowledge
003:101 Whoever holds **firmly** to Allah will be shown
003:147 establish our feet **firmly**, and help us
004:135 O ye who believe! stand out **firmly** for justice,
005:008 O ye who believe! stand out **firmly** for Allah,
006:079 "For me, I have set my face, **firmly** and truly,
007:171 "Hold **firmly** to what We have given you, and bring
008:011 and to plant your feet **firmly** therewith.
012:032 his (true) self but he did **firmly** save himself guiltless!
014:005 are Signs for such as are **firmly** patient and constant,-
014:024 a goodly tree, whose root is **firmly** fixed, and its
016:094 may slip after it was **firmly** planted;
020:005 is **firmly** established on the throne.
023:013 in a place of rest, **firmly** fixed;
027:040 placed **firmly** before him, he said: "This is
027:088 thinkest them **firmly** fixed:
028:014 and was **firmly** established (in life), We bestowed
046:026 And We had **firmly** established them in a
047:004 bind (the captives) **firmly**:
047:007 He will help you, and plant your feet **firmly**.
077:021 The which We placed in a place of rest, **firmly** fixed,
079:032 And the mountains hath He **firmly** fixed;-

FIRMNESS

003:017 Those who show patience, (**firmness** and self-control);
007:145 (and said): "Take and hold these with **firmness**,
008:012 "I am with you: give **firmness** to the Believers:
031:017 for this is **firmness** (of purpose) in (the conduct of) affairs.

FIRST

002:041 and be not the **first** to reject faith therein,
002:191 unless they (**first**) fight you there;
003:096 The **first** House (of worship) appointed for men
004:034 admonish them (**first**), (next), refuse to
005:114 for the **first** and the last of us-a solemn
006:014 the **first** of those who bow to Allah (in Islam),
006:094 and alone as We created you for the **first** time:
006:110 they refused to believer in this in the **first** instance:
006:163 and I am the **first** of those who submit to His Will.
007:038 Saith the last about the **first**: "Our Lord!
007:039 Then the **first** will say to the last: "See then!
007:115 or shall we have the (**first**) throw?"
007:115 They said: "O Moses! wilt thou throw (**first**),
007:116 Said Moses: "Throw ye (**first**)." So when
007:143 and I am the **first** to believe."
009:013 plotted to expel the Messenger, and attack you **first**?
009:083 for ye preferred to sit inactive on the **first** occasion:
009:100 The vanguard (of Islam)-the **first** of those who
009:108 was laid from the **first** day on piety; it is
016:062 and they will be the **first** to be hastened on into it!
017:005 When the **first** of the warnings came to pass,
017:051 Say: "He Who created you **first**!"
018:048 "Now have ye come to Us (bare) as We created you **first**:
020:065 thou throw (**first**) or that we be the **first** to throw?"
020:066 He said, "Nay, throw ye **first**!" Then behold
021:104 We produced the **first** Creation, shall We
026:051 since we are the **first** to believe."
028:012 And We ordained that he refused suck at **first**,
028:070 To him be praise, at the **first** and the last:
036:014 When We (**first**) sent to them two messengers,
036:079 Who created them for the **first** time!
037:059 "Except our **first** death, and that
039:012 "And I am commanded to be the **first** of those
041:021 He created you for the **first** time, and unto Him were
043:081 I would be the **first** to worship."
044:035 "There is nothing beyond our **first** death, and we
044:056 except the **first** Death; and He
046:011 (such men) would not have gone to it **first**, before us!"
050:015 Were We then weary with the **first** Creation,
056:062 And ye certainly know already the **first** form of creation:
057:003 He is the **First** and the Last, the Evident
059:002 from their homes at the **first** gathering (of the forces).

FISH

007:163 their **fish** did come to them, openly
018:061 they forgot (about) their **Fish**, which took
018:063 I did indeed forget (about) the **Fish**:
037:142 Then the big **Fish** did swallow him, and he
037:144 inside the **Fish** till the Day of Resurrection.
068:048 the Companion of the **Fish**,-when he

FIST

028:015 and Moses struck him with his **fist** and killed

FIT

022:034 He gave them from animals (**fit** for food).
041:028 a (**fit**) requital, for that they were wont to reject Our

FITTED

002:247 better **fitted** than he to exercise authority,
009:097 and most **fitted** to be in ignorance of the command

FITTING

002:114 It was not **fitting** that such should
008:067 It is not **fitting** for a Prophet that he
009:062 but it is more **fitting** that they should please
009:095 their dwelling-place, a **fitting** recompense for

FITTING (continued)

009:113   It is not **fitting**, for the Prophet and those
009:120   It was not **fitting** for the people of Madinah
010:103   thus is it **fitting** on Our part that We
012:018   (For me) patience is most **fitting**:
012:025   She said: "What is the (**fitting**) punishment for
012:083   So patience is most **fitting** (for me).
033:036   It is not **fitting** for a Believer, man or woman,
033:037   but it is more **fitting** that thou shouldst. Fear Allah.
042:051   It is not **fitting** for a man that Allah
047:020   But more **fitting** for them-
078:026   A **fitting** recompense (for them).

FIVE

003:125   with **five** thousand angels clearly marked.
018:022   (others) say they were **five**, the dog
058:007   nor between **five** but He makes the sixth,-

FIXATION

002:236   or the **fixation** of their dower;
002:237   but after the **fixation** of a dower for them,

FIXED

002:184   (Fasting) for a **fixed** number of days;
002:189   to mark **fixed** periods of time in (the affairs of) men.
002:282   future obligations in a **fixed** period of time,
003:145   the term being **fixed** as by writing.
007:135   from them according to a **fixed** term which they
014:024   a goodly tree, whose root is firmly **fixed**, and its
018:059   but We **fixed** an appointed time for their
023:013   in a place of rest, firmly **fixed**;
027:088   Thus seest the mountains and thinkest them firmly **fixed**:
034:013   and (cooking) Cauldrons **fixed** (in their places):
070:043   a goal-post (**fixed** for them),-
074:031   and We have **fixed** their number only as trial
077:021   The which We placed in a place of rest, firmly **fixed**,
079:032   And the mountains hath He firmly **fixed**;-
088:019   And at the Mountains, how they are **fixed** firm?-

FIXEDLY

014:042   a Day when the eyes will **fixedly** stare in horror,-
021:097   will **fixedly** stare in horror: "Ah! woe to us!

FLAG

021:020   nor do they ever **flag** or intermit.
041:038   And they never **flag** (nor feel themselves above it).

FLAGRANT

004:112   (both) a false charge and a **flagrant** sin.

FLAME

055:035   a **flame** of fire (to burn) and a (flash of) molten brass
111:001   Perish the hands of the Father of **Flame**! Perish he!
111:003   Burnt soon will he be in a Fire of blazing **Flame**!

FLAMES

018:029   a Fire whose (smoke and **flames**), like the

FLAMING

037:010   by a **flaming** fire, of piercing brightness.
072:008   filled with stern guards and **flaming** fires.
072:009   find a **flaming** fire watching him in ambush.

FLANKS

009:035   their foreheads, their **flanks**, and their backs,-

FLASH

024:043   The vivid **flash** of His lightning well-nigh
055:035   (to burn) and a (**flash** of) molten brass

FLATTENED

084:003   And when the Earth is **flattened** out,

FLAW

067:003   So turn thy vision again: Seest thou any **flaw**?

FLAWS

050:006   and adorned it, and there is not **flaws** in it?

FLED

026:021   "So I **fled** from you (all) when I feared you;

FLEE

004:089   until they **flee** in the way of Allah
009:057   If they could find a place to **flee** to, or caves,
021:012   they (tried to) **flee** from it.
021:013   **Flee** not, but return to the good things of this
040:033   "'A Day when ye shall turn your backs and **flee**:
051:050   Therefore **flee** unto Allah: I am
062:008   Say "The Death from which ye **flee** will truly
080:034   That Day shall a man **flee** from his own brother,

FLEEING

009:118   no **fleeing** from Allah (and no refuge)
017:046   they turn on their backs, **fleeing** (from the Truth).
029:022   be able (**fleeing**) to frustrate (His Plan),
074:051   **Fleeing** from a lion!

FLEETING

075:020   Nay, (ye men!) but ye love the **fleeting** life,
076:027   the **fleeting** life, and put away behind them

FLESH

002:173   and blood, and the **flesh** of swine,
002:259   and clothe them with **flesh**."
005:003   dead meat, blood, the **flesh** of swine, and that
006:145   or the **flesh** of swine,-for it is
016:014   that ye may eat thereof **flesh** that is
016:115   and blood, and the **flesh** of swine, and any
022:005   then out a morsel of **flesh**, partly formed
023:014   the bones with **flesh**; then We developed
035:012   (kind of water) do ye eat **flesh** fresh and tender,
049:012   to eat the **flesh** of his dead brother? Nay, ye
056:021   And the **flesh** of fowls, any that they may desire.

FLIES

006:038   nor a being that **flies** on its wings,
076:007   and they fear a Day whose evil **flies** far and wide.

FLIGHT

017:041   increases their **flight** (from the Truth)!
018:018   turned back from them in **flight**, and wouldst
038:011   and they will be put to **flight**.
054:045   Soon will their multitude be put to **flight**,
067:021   in insolent impiety and **flight** (from the Truth).
071:006   (their) **flight** (from the Right)."
072:012   nor can we escape Him by **flight**.

FLIGHTS

105:003   And He sent against them **flights** of Birds,

FLIMSIEST

029:041   but truly the **flimsiest** of houses is the

FLIMSY

069:016   for it will that Day be **flimsy**,

FLINCH

003:143   with your own eyes (and **flinch**!).
066:006   stern (and) severe, who **flinch** not (from executing)

FLINCHED

003:152   until ye **flinched** and fell to disputing

FLINGETH

013:013   He **flingeth** the loud-voiced thunder-bolts,

FLOATING

025:023   make such deeds as **floating** dust scattered about.
069:011   in the **floating** (Ark).

FLOATS

054:014 She **floats** under Our eyes (and care):

FLOCK

038:024 thy (single) ewe to be added to his (**flock** of) ewes:

FLOCKS

020:018 with it I beat down fodder for my **flocks**;

028:023 men watering (their **flocks**), and besides

028:023 who were keeping back (their **flocks**).

028:023 They said: "We cannot water (our **flocks**) until the

028:023 two women who were keeping back (their **flocks**):

028:024 So he watered (their **flocks**) for them; then he

028:025 watered (our **flocks**) for us."

048:011 in (looking after) our **flocks** and heads, and our

FLOG

024:002 of fornication,-**flog** each of them with a hundred

024:004 **flog** them with eighty stripes;

FLOOD

007:064 But We overwhelmed in the **flood** those who

010:073 while We drowned in the **Flood** those who

010:090 At length, when overwhelmed with the **flood**, he said

011:037 overwhelmed (in the **flood**)."

021:077 so We drowned them (in the **Flood**) all together.

023:027 be drowned (in the **Flood**).

034:016 the **flood** (released) from the Dams, and We

036:041 their race (through the **flood**) in the loaded Ark;

037:082 Then the rest We overwhelmed in the **Flood**.

051:011 in a **flood** of confusion:

069:011 the water (of Noah's **flood**) overflowed beyond its limits,

071:025 were drowned (in the **flood**), and were

FLOUNDER

051:011 Those who (**flounder**) heedless in a

FLOURISHED

007:092 in the homes where they had **flourished** the men

010:024 as if it had not **flourished** only the day before!

011:068 As if they had never dwelt and **flourished** there.

011:095 As if they had never dwelt and **flourished** there!

FLOURISHING

009:069 and more **flourishing** in wealth and children.

FLOW

002:025 beneath which rivers **flow**.

009:072 Gardens under which rivers **flow**, to dwell therein,

009:089 gardens under which rivers **flow**, to dwell therein:

009:100 gardens under which rivers **flow**, to dwell therein for ever:

010:009 beneath them will **flow** rivers in Gardens of Bliss.

013:017 and the channels **flow**, each according

013:035 beneath it **flow** rivers: perpetual is the fruits thereof

014:023 Gardens beneath which rivers **flow**,-to dwell therein

016:031 beneath them **flow** (pleasant) rivers:

018:031 rivers will **flow**; they will be adorned therein

018:033 We caused a river to **flow**.

020:076 Gardens of Eternity, beneath which **flow** rivers:

021:081 the violent (unruly) wind **flow** (tamely) for

022:014 to Gardens, beneath which rivers **flow**: for Allah

022:023 to Gardens beneath which rivers **flow**: they shall

025:010 Gardens beneath which rivers **flow**; and He

029:058 beneath which **flow** rivers,-to dwell therein

031:020 made His bounties **flow** to you in exceeding measure,

034:012 a Font of molten brass to **flow** for him;

038:036 to **flow** gently to his order, whithersoever he

039:020 beneath them **flow** rivers:

047:012 to Gardens beneath which rivers **flow**; while those

048:005 to Gardens beneath which rivers **flow**, to dwell therein

FLOW (continued)

048:017 him to Gardens beneath which rivers **flow**; and he

051:003 And those that **flow** with ease and gentleness;

057:012 Gardens beneath which **flow** rivers!

058:022 beneath which Rivers **flow**, to dwell

061:012 which rivers **flow**, and to beautiful mansions in

064:009 beneath which rivers **flow**, to dwell therein

065:011 to Gardens beneath which rivers **flow**, to dwell

066:008 to Gardens beneath which rivers **flow**,-the Day

076:006 do drink, making it **flow** in unstinted abundance.

085:011 Beneath which Rivers **flow**: that is

098:008 Gardens of Eternity, Beneath which rivers **flow**;

FLOWERS

056:029 Among Talh trees with **flowers** (or fruits)

FLOWERY

006:112 inspiring each other with **flowery** discourses by way

FLOWING

002:266 and vines and streams **flowing** underneath,

003:015 nearness to their Lord with rivers **flowing** beneath;

003:136 and Gardens with rivers **flowing** underneath,

003:195 into Gardens with rivers **flowing** beneath;

003:198 are Gardens, with rivers **flowing** beneath;

004:013 rivers **flowing** beneath, to abide therein

004:057 with rivers **flowing** beneath, their eternal home:

004:122 with rivers **flowing** beneath, to dwell

005:012 with rivers **flowing** beneath; but if any

005:085 with rivers **flowing** underneath, their eternal home.

005:119 with rivers **flowing** beneath, their eternal home:

006:006 and gave streams **flowing** beneath their (feet):

007:043 beneath them will be rivers **flowing**;-and they

013:003 standing firm, and (**flowing**) rivers:

025:053 the two bodies of **flowing** water: one palatable

043:051 (witness) these streams **flowing** underneath my

055:050 In them (each) will be two Springs **flowing** (free);

056:031 By water **flowing** constantly,

071:012 and bestow on you Rivers (of **flowing** water).

073:014 a heap of sand poured out and **flowing** down.

056:018 and cups (filled) out of clear-**flowing** fountains:

FLUID

032:008 a quintessence of despised **fluid**.

038:057 a boiling **fluid**, and a **fluid** dark, murky, intensely cold!-

040:072 In the boiling fetid **fluid**; then in

077:020 a **fluid** (held) despicable?-

078:025 Save a boiling **fluid** and a **fluid**, dark, murky,

FLUIDS

010:004 but draughts of boiling **fluids**, and a

FLUNG

028:040 and We **flung** them into the sea: now behold

FLY

022:073 they would have no power to release it from the **fly:**

022:073 And if the **fly** should snatch away anything from them,

022:073 cannot create (even) a **fly**,

FLYING

002:260 they will come to thee (**flying**) with speed.

FOAM

013:017 the **foam** that mounts up to the surface.

FODDER

020:018 with it I beat down **fodder** for my flocks;

055:012 Also corn, with (it's) leaves and stalk for **fodder**,

080:031 And Fruits and **Fodder**,-

FOE

003:167 or (at least) drive (the **foe** from your city)."

FOE (continued)

028:015   man of his own people appealed to him against his **foe**,
100:005   the midst (of the **foe**) en masse;-

FOES

003:152   from your **foes** in order to test you.
028:015   one of his own people, and the other , of his **foes**.
043:067   Friends on that Day will be **foes**, one to

FOETUS

023:014   then of that clot We made a (**foetus**) lump;

FOLD

011:005   Behold! they **fold** up their hearts, that they

FOLDED

073:001   O thou **folded** in garments!
081:001   When the sun (with its spacious light) is **folded** up;

FOLDING

067:019   spreading their wings and **folding** them in?

FOLDS

007:041   a couch (below) and **folds** and **folds** of covering above:

FOLK

007:139   "As to these **folk**,-the cult
009:101   as well as among the Madinah **folk**: they are
015:062   He said: "Ye appear to be uncommon **folk**."

FOLLOW

002:062   and those who **follow** the Jewish (Scriptures),
002:120   unless thou **follow** their form of religion.
002:120   Wert thou to **follow** their desires
002:145   nor art thou going to **follow** their Qiblah;
002:145   they **follow** each other's Qiblah.
002:145   they would not **follow** thy Qiblah;
002:145   wert to **follow** their (vain) desires,
002:166   clear themselves of those who **follow** (them):
002:168   and do not **follow** the footsteps of Satan for he
002:170   shall **follow** the ways of our fathers."
002:170   "**Follow** what Allah hath revealed,"
002:208   and **follow** not the footsteps of the Satan
002:262   and **follow** not up their gifts with reminders
003:007   perversity **follow** the part thereof that is not
003:020   to Allah and so l have those who **follow** me."
003:031   Say: "If ye do love Allah, **follow** me:
003:053   and we **follow** the Messenger;
003:055   who **follow** thee superior to those who reject faith,
003:068   are those who **follow** him,
003:095   **follow** the religion of Abraham, the sane in faith:
004:027   who **follow** their lusts is that ye should turn
004:135   **Follow** not the lusts (of your hearts), lest
004:157   But only conjecture to **follow**, for of a surety
005:048   and **follow** not their vain desires, diverging
005:049   and **follow** not their vain desires, but beware
005:066   but many of them **follow** a course that is evil.
005:069   Those who **follow** the Jewish (Scriptures), and
005:077   nor **follow** the vain desire of people who went
005:105   if ye **follow** (right) guidance. No hurt
006:050   I but **follow** what is revealed to me." Say:
006:056   Say: "I will not **follow** your vain desires: if I
006:090   **Follow** the guidance they received; say: "No
006:106   **Follow** what thou art taught by inspiration
006:116   Wert thou to **follow** the common run
006:116   They **follow** nothing but conjecture: they do
006:142   and **follow** not the footsteps of Satan: for he
006:148   Ye **follow** nothing but conjecture: Ye do
006:150   nor **follow** thou the vain desires of such
006:153   Verily, this is My Way leading straight: **follow** it:

FOLLOW (continued)

006:153   **follow** not (other) paths: they will
006:155   so **follow** it and be righteous, that ye
007:003   **Follow** (O men!) the revelation given unto
007:003   and **follow** not, as friends
007:018   If any of them **follow** thee,-Hell will
007:038   until they **follow** each other, all into the Fire.
007:090   said: "If ye **follow** Shu'aib, be sure
007:142   and **follow** not the way of those who do mischief.
007:157   "Those who **follow** the Messenger, the unlettered
007:157   honor him, Help him, and **follow** the Light which
007:158   **follow** him that (so) ye may be guided."
007:203   Say: "I but **follow** what is revealed
008:057   those who **follow** them, that they may remember.
008:064   and unto those who **follow** thee among the Believers.
009:100   those who **follow** them in (all) good deeds,
010:015   I **follow** naught but what is revealed unto me: if I
010:036   But most of them **follow** nothing but conjecture:
010:066   They **follow** nothing but conjecture, and they
010:066   What do they **follow** who worship as His "partners"
010:089   and **follow** not the path of those who know not."
010:109   **Follow** thou the inspiration sent unto thee, and be
011:027   nor do we see that any **follow** thee but the
012:038   "And I **follow** the ways of my fathers,-Abraham,
013:037   Wert thou to **follow** their (vain) desires after the
014:012   to the Ways we (**follow**).
014:044   and **follow** the messengers!"
015:042   put themselves in the wrong and **follow** thee."
016:069   (of the earth), and **follow** the ways of Thy Lord
016:123   "**Follow** the ways of Abraham the True in Faith,
017:047   "Ye **follow** none other than a man bewitched!"
017:063   "Go thy way; if any of them **follow** thee,
018:066   Moses said to him: "May I **follow** thee, on the
018:070   "If then thou wouldst **follow** me, ask me no questions
019:043   so **follow** me: I will guide thee to a Way that
020:016   not therein but **follow** their own lust, divert thee
020:047   And peace to all who **follow** guidance!
020:090   so **follow** me and obey my command."
020:108   On that Day will they **follow** the caller
022:003   without knowledge, and **follow** every Satan
022:017   those who **follow** the Jewish (scriptures), and the
022:067   appointed rites which they must **follow**:
023:044   so We made them **follow** each other (in punishment):
024:021   if any will **follow** the footsteps of Satan, he will (but)
024:021   O ye who believe! **follow** not Satan's footsteps:
025:008   "Ye **follow** none other than a man bewitched."
025:062   and the Day to **follow** each other:
026:040   "That we may **follow** the sorcerers if they win?"
026:111   when it is the meanest that **follow** thee?"
026:151   "And **follow** not the bidding of those
026:215   And lower thy wing to the Believers who **follow** thee.
026:224   straying in Evil, who **follow** them:
028:035   you two as well as those who **follow** you."
028:042   In this world We mad a Curse to **follow** them:
028:049   better Guide than either of them, that I may **follow** it!
028:050   know that they only **follow** their own lusts:
028:057   They say: "If we were to **follow** the guidance
029:012   "**Follow** our path, and we will bear (the consequences)
030:029   the wrong-doers (merely) **follow** their own desires being
031:015   and **follow** the way of those who turn to me:
031:021   When they are told to **follow** the (revelation)
031:021   "Nay, we shall **follow** the ways that we found
033:002   But **follow** that which comes to thee by

FOLLOW (continued)

035:032 some who **follow** a middle course
038:026 nor **follow** thou the lust (of thy heart),
038:085 with thee and those that **follow** thee,-every one."
039:018 Those who listen to the Word, and **follow** the best of it:
039:055 "And **follow** the Best that which revealed to you
040:007 in repentance, and **follow** Thy Path; and preserve
040:038 "O my People! **follow** me: I will
042:015 thou art commanded, nor **follow** thou their vain desires;
043:023 will certainly **follow** in their footsteps."
043:061 have no doubt about the (Hour), but **follow** ye Me:
045:018 so **follow** thou that (Way),
045:018 and **follow** not the desires of those who know not.
046:009 I **follow** but that which is revealed to me
047:003 While those who believe **follow** the Truth
047:003 This because those who reject Allah **follow** falsehood.
047:014 and such as **follow** their own lusts?
047:016 Allah has sealed, and who **follow** their own lusts.
048:002 of the past and those to **follow**; fulfil His
048:015 Say: "Not thus will ye **follow** us: Allah has
048:015 "Permit us to **follow** you."
049:007 in many matters, to **follow** your (wishes),
052:021 and whose seeds **follow** them in Faith,-to them
053:023 They **follow** nothings but conjecture and what
053:028 They **follow** nothing but conjecture; and conjecture
054:003 and **follow** their (own) lusts but every matter
054:024 Shall we **follow** such a one?
055:005 The sun and the moon **follow** courses (exactly) computed;
060:004 (to **follow**) in Abraham and those with him,
060:006 an excellent example for you to **follow**,-for those
071:021 but they **follow** (men) whose wealth and children
072:011 we **follow** divergent paths.
074:037 you that chooses to press forward or to **follow** behind;-
075:018 We have recited it, **follow** thou its recital (as promulgated):
077:017 So shall We make later (generations) **follow** them.
087:008 (to **follow**) the simple (Path).
091:002 By the Moon as she **follow** him;

FOLLOWED

002:087 and **followed** him up with a succession
002:102 They **followed** what the Satans recited
002:143 who **followed** the Messenger from those who
002:166 Then would those who are **followed** clear
002:167 And those who **followed** would say: "If only
002:263 than charity **followed** by injury.
003:167 we should certainly have **followed** you."
003:174 for they **followed** the good pleasure of Allah:
004:083 all but a few of you would have **followed** Satan.
006:146 For those who **followed** the Jewish Law, We
006:157 we should have **followed** its guidance
007:173 the deeds of men who **followed** falsehood?"
007:175 so Satan **followed** him up, and he went astray.
007:176 and **followed** his own vain desires.
009:042 they would (all) without doubt have **followed** thee,
009:117 who **followed** Him in a time of distress,
010:035 Who gives guidance to Truth more worthy to be **followed**,
010:090 hosts **followed** them in insolence and spite.
011:017 and **followed** by a witness from Him and before
011:059 and **followed** the command of every powerful,
011:097 but they **followed** the command of Pharaoh, and the
011:099 And they are **followed** by a curse in this (life)
014:021 "For us, we but **followed** you; can ye
018:085 One (such) way he **followed**,
018:089 Then **followed** he (another) way,

FOLLOWED (continued)

018:092 Then **followed** he (another) way,
019:059 and **followed** after lusts soon, then, will they
019:059 But after them there **followed** a posterity
020:134 have **followed** Thy Signs before we were
028:047 We should then have **followed** the Signs and been
034:020 his idea, and they **followed** him, all but
040:047 "We but **followed** you: can ye
040:047 The weak ones (who **followed**) will say to those
047:028 This because they **followed** that which displeased
057:027 Then, in their wake, We **followed** them up with
057:027 of those who **followed** him Compassion and Mercy.
079:007 **Followed** by oft-repeated (commotions):

FOLLOWERS

027:056 "Drive out the **followers** of Lut from your city:
038:060 (The **followers** shall cry to the misleaders:)
045:027 that Day will the **followers** of Falsehood perish!

FOLLOWING

004:104 And slacken not in **following** up the enemy:
005:104 the ways we found our fathers **following**."
010:078 We found our fathers **following**,-in order
018:006 fret thyself to death, **following** after them,
018:034 more honour and power in (my **following** of) men."
018:064 on their footsteps, **following** (the path they had come).
020:093 "From **following** me?
029:032 we will certainly save him and his **following**,-
029:033 we are (here) to save thee and thy **following**,
031:021 we found our fathers (**following**)."
043:022 fathers **following** a certain religion, and we
043:023 "We found Our fathers **following** a certain
043:024 ye found your fathers **following**?"
079:046 or (at most till) the **following** morn!

FOLLOWS

002:038 whosoever **follows** My guidance,
003:073 "And believe no one unless he **follows** your religion."
003:162 Is the man who **follows** the good pleasure of Allah
004:115 plainly conveyed to him, and **follows** a path
004:125 does good, and **follows** the way of Abraham
012:108 I and whoever **follows** me. Glory to Allah!
014:036 he then who **follows** my (ways) is of me, and he
018:028 of Us, one who **follows** his own desires, and his
020:123 from Me, whosoever **follows** My guidance, will not
027:030 and is (as **follows**): 'In name of Allah,
028:050 one who **follows** his own lusts, devoid of
036:011 as **follows** the Message and fears the Most
039:005 (to His law) each one **follows** a course for a

FOLLY

002:130 as debase their souls with **folly**?
006:140 Lost are those who slay their children, from **folly**,
007:066 "Ah! we see thou art in **folly**!" and "We think
007:067 there is no **folly** in me" but (I am)
016:055 but soon will ye know (your **folly**)!
030:034 but soon will ye know (your **folly**).

FOND

005:042 (They are **fond** of) listening to falsehood,

FONT

034:012 a **Font** of molten brass to flow for him; and there

FOOD

002:061 we cannot endure one kind of **food** (always);
002:233 of their **food** and clothing on equitable terms.
002:259 but look at thy **food** and thy drink;
003:093 All **food** was lawful to the Children of Israel,

FOOD (continued)

005:001 Lawful unto you (for **food**) are all
005:003 Forbidden to you (for **food**) are: dead meat, blood,
005:004 They ask thee what is lawful to them (as **food**).
005:005 The **food** of the People of the Book is lawful
005:075 They had both to eat their (daily) **food**.
005:089 for the **food** of your families; or clothe
005:096 and its use for **food**,-for the
006:139 is specially reserved (for **food**) for our men,
006:140 and forbid **food** which Allah hath provided
010:024 which provides **food** for men and animals:
012:037 He said: "Before any **food** comes (in due course)
012:065 so we shall get (more) **food** for our family;
016:067 ye get out strong drink, and wholesome **food**:
016:115 and any (**food**) over which the name of other than
018:019 best **food** (to be had) and bring some to you,
018:077 they asked them for **food**, but they refused them
021:008 ate no **food**, nor were they immortals.
022:030 Lawful to you (for **food** in pilgrimage) are cattle
022:034 the sustenance He gave them from animals (fit for **food**).
023:020 and relish for those who use it for **food**.
025:007 "What sort of a messenger is this, who eats **food**,
025:020 who ate **food** and walked through the markets.
026:079 "Who gives me **food** and drink,
032:027 therewith crops, providing **food** for their cattle
040:079 that ye may use some for riding and some for **food**;
044:044 Will be the **food** of the Sinful,-
069:036 "Nor hath he any **food** except the foul pus
073:013 And **Food** that chokes, and a Chastisement Grievous.
080:024 Then let man look at his **Food**, (and how We provide it):
088:006 No **food** will there be for them but a bitter Dhari
090:014 Or the giving of **food** in a day of privation
106:004 Who provides them with **food** against hunger,

FOODS

004:160 We made unlawful for them certain (**foods**) good and

FOOL

002:067 from being an ignorant (**fool**)!"
006:071 like one whom the Satans have made into a **fool**,

FOOLISH

007:155 of the **foolish** ones among us?
033:072 he was indeed unjust and **foolish**;-
072:004 'There were some **foolish** ones among us, who used

FOOLS

002:013 Nay of a surety they are the **fools**,
002:013 "Shall we believe as the **fools** believe?"
002:142 The **Fools** among the people will say:
043:054 Thus did he make **fools** of his people, and they

FOOT

002:239 If ye fear (an enemy), pray on **foot**,
016:094 With the result that someone's **foot** may slip
022:027 they will come to thee on **foot** and (mounted)
027:018 (under **foot**) without knowing it."
038:031 highest breeding; and swift of **foot**;
038:042 "Strike with thy **foot**: here is (water)

FOOTING

004:019 with them on a **footing** of kindness and equity
004:089 and thus be on the same **footing** (as they):
018:066 on the **footing** that thou teach me something

FOOTPRINT

020:096 from the **footprint** of the Messenger, and threw

FOOTSTEPS

002:168 and do not the **footsteps** of Satan for he is to you

FOOTSTEPS (continued)

002:208 and follow not the **footsteps** of the Satan
005:046 And in their **footsteps** We sent Jesus
006:142 and follow not the **footsteps** of Satan: for he
018:064 so they went back on their **footsteps**,
020:084 He replied: "Behold, they are close on my **footsteps**:
024:021 O ye who believe! follow not Satan's **footsteps**:
024:021 if any will follow **footsteps** of Satan, he will (but)
037:070 So they (too) were rushed down on their **footsteps**!
043:022 and we do guide ourselves by their **footsteps**."
043:023 will certainly follow in their **footsteps**."

FOR See Appendix

FORBADE

006:146 We **forbade** every (animal) with undivided hoof,
006:146 and We **forbade** them the fat of the ox
007:020 "Your Lord only **forbade** you this tree,
007:165 We rescued those who **forbade** evil; but We
050:025 "Who **forbade** what was good, transgressed all

FORBEAR

019:046 O Abraham? If thou **forbear** not, I will

FORBEARETH

011:087 the one that **forbeareth** with faults and is right-minded!

FORBEARING

002:225 and He is Oft-Forgiving, Most **Forbearing**.
002:235 and know that Allah is Oft Forgiving, Most **Forbearing**.
002:263 and he is Most **Forbearing**.
003:155 for Allah is Oft-Forgiving, Most **Forbearing**.
004:012 and Allah is All-Knowing, Most **Forbearing**.
005:101 for Allah is Oft-Forgiving, Most **Forbearing**
009:114 for Abraham was most tender hearted, **forbearing**.
011:075 For Abraham was, without doubt, **forbearing** (of faults),
022:059 All-Knowing, Most **Forbearing**.
033:051 All-knowing, Most **Forbearing**.
035:041 verily He is Most **Forbearing**, Oft-Forgiving.
037:101 So We gave him the good news of a **forbearing** son.
064:017 for Allah is All-Thankful, Most **Forbearing**,-

FORBID

003:114 and **forbid** what is wrong;
005:063 the doctors of laws **forbid** them from their
005:072 Allah will **forbid** him the Garden, and the Fire
005:079 Nor did they **forbid** one another the iniquities
006:026 Others they **forbid** it and themselves
006:140 and **forbid** food which Allah hath provided
006:150 to prove that Allah did **forbid** so and so."
007:022 "Did I not **forbid** you that tree, and tell
009:067 and **forbid** what in just, and tighten
009:071 they enjoin what is just, and **forbid** what is evil:
009:112 that enjoin good and **forbid** evil; and observe the limits
011:062 Dost thou (now) **forbid** us the worship of what
011:088 to do that which I **forbid** you to do.
012:023 He said: "Allah **forbid**! truly (thy husband) is my
012:079 He said: "Allah **forbid** that we take other than
015:070 They said: "Did we not **forbid** thee (to speak)
022:041 enjoin the right and **forbid** wrong:
031:017 and **forbid** what is wrong: and bear

FORBIDDEN

002:173 He hath only **forbidden** you dead meat,
002:275 permitted trade and **forbidden** usury.
003:050 part of what was (before) **forbidden** to you;
004:019 Ye are **forbidden** to inherit women against their will.
004:031 of the things which ye are **forbidden** to do,
004:089 the way of Allah (from what is **forbidden**).

FORBIDDEN (continued)

004:161 That they took usury, though they were **forbidden**;
005:001 are **forbidden** while ye are in the Sacred Precincts
005:003 **Forbidden** to you (for food) are: dead meat, blood,
005:003 (**forbidden**) also is the division (of meat) by raffling with
005:042 of devouring anything **forbidden**.
005:062 transgression and their eating of things **forbidden**.
005:063 sinful words and eating things **forbidden**?
005:096 but **forbidden** is the pursuit of land-game: as long
006:028 to the things they were **forbidden**, for they
006:056 Say: "I am **forbidden** to worship those-other
006:119 in detail what is **forbidden** to you-except
006:138 such and such cattle and crops are **forbidden**,
006:138 there are cattle **forbidden** to yoke or burden, and cattle
006:139 and **forbidden** to our women; but if it is still-born
006:143 say, hath He **forbidden** the two males, or the
006:144 say, hath He **forbidden** the two males, or the
006:145 any (meat) **forbidden** to be eaten by one
006:148 nor should we have had any **forbidden** thing."
007:032 Say: Who hath **forbidden** the beautiful
007:033 my Lord hath indeed **forbidden** are: indecent deeds,
007:050 hath Allah **forbidden** to those who rejected Him;
009:005 But when the **forbidden** months are past, then fight
009:029 hold that **forbidden** which hath been **forbidden** by Allah
009:037 and make such **forbidden** ones lawful.
009:037 and **forbidden** another year, in order
009:037 of months **forbidden** by Allah and make such
010:059 Yet ye hold **forbidden** some things thereof and
016:115 He has only **forbidden** you dead meat, and blood,
016:116 "This is lawful, and this is **forbidden**," so as
024:003 to the Believers such a thing is **forbidden**.
025:022 "There is a barrier **forbidden** (to you)
040:066 Say: "I have been **forbidden** to invoke those whom
056:033 Whose season is not limited, nor (supply) **forbidden**,
058:008 to that which they were **forbidden** (to do)?
058:008 Seest thou not those who were **forbidden** secret counsels
066:001 Why holdest thou to be **forbidden** that which Allah has

FORBIDDING

003:104 and **forbidding** what is wrong:
003:110 Enjoining what is right, **forbidding** what is wrong,

FORBIDS

002:114 And who is more unjust than he who **forbids**
007:157 and **forbids** them what is evil:
016:090 and He **forbids** all indecent deeds, and evil
060:008 Allah **forbids** you not, with regard to those who
060:009 Allah only **forbids** you, with regard to those who
096:009 Seest thou one who **forbids**-

FORCE

002:249 hath a small **force** vanquished a big one?
008:045 when ye meet a **force**, be firm, and call
018:020 they would stone you or **force** you to return
018:079 king who seized on every boat by **force**.
024:033 But **force** not your maids to prostitution when they
029:008 (either of them) strive (to **force**) to join
048:025 (Allah would have allowed you to **force** your way,
050:045 and thou art not one to compel them by **force**.

FORCED

002:173 but if one is **forced** by necessity,
005:003 But if any is **forced** by hunger, with no
006:145 if a person is **forced** by necessity, without
016:115 But if one is **forced** by necessity, without wilful
022:022 they will be **forced** back therein,
032:020 they will be **forced** thereinto, and it will be said to them:

FORCES

002:249 cannot cope with Goliath and his **forces**."
002:250 meet Goliath and his **forces**,
008:019 good will your **forces** be to you even if they
008:041 the Day of the meeting of the two **forces**.
008:048 but when the two **forces** came in sight
009:026 and sent down **forces** which ye saw not: He punished
009:040 with **forces** which ye saw not, and humbled
019:075 and (who) weakest in **forces**!
020:078 Then Pharaoh pursued them with his **forces**,
033:009 and **forces** that ye saw not: but Allah
033:022 the Confederate **forces**, they said: "This is
037:173 And that Our **forces**,-they surely must conquer.
048:004 for to Allah belong the **Forces** of the heavens
048:007 For to Allah belong the **Forces** of the heavens
051:040 So We took him and his **forces**, and threw
059:002 from their homes at the first gathering (of the **forces**).
074:031 none can know the **forces** of the Lord, except He,
085:017 Has the story reached thee, of the **Forces**-

FORE-LEGS

018:018 two **fore-legs** on the threshold: if thou

FORE-LOCK

011:056 but He hath grasp of its **fore-lock**.

FORE-WARNED

026:056 "But we are a multitude amply **fore-warned**."

FOREFATHERS

044:036 "Then bring (back) our **forefathers** if what
045:025 "Bring (back) our **forefathers**, if what ye say is true!"

FOREHEAD

037:103 prostrate on his **forehead** (for sacrifice),
051:029 she smote her **forehead** and said: "A barren

FOREHEADS

009:035 their **foreheads**, their flanks, and their backs,-

FOREIGN

016:103 point to is notable **foreign**, while this
041:044 What! a **foreign** (tongue) and (a Messenger) an Arab?

FORELOCK

096:015 We will drag him by the **forelock**,-
096:016 A lying, sinful **forelock**!

FORELOCKS

055:041 be seized by their **forelocks** and their feet.

FOREMOST

023:061 good work, and these who are **foremost** in them.
035:032 by Allah's leave, **foremost** in good deeds; that is
056:010 will be **Foremost** (in the Hereafter).
056:010 And those **Foremost** (in Faith) will be
057:021 Be ye **foremost** (in seeking) forgiveness from your

FOREVER

018:003 Wherein they shall remain **forever**:

FORGAVE

002:187 but He turned to you and **forgave** you:
003:152 But He **forgave** you:
004:153 even so We **forgave** them; and gave Moses
028:016 So (Allah) **forgave** him: for He
038:025 So We **forgave** him this (lapse): he enjoyed,

FORGE

006:112 so leave them and they **forge**.
007:089 "We should indeed **forge** a lie against Allah,
010:017 as **forge** a lie against Allah, or deny
010:059 or do ye **forge** (things) to attribute to Allah?"
010:060 And what think those who **forge** lies against Allah,
010:069 Say: "Those who **forge** a lie against Allah

FORGE (continued)

011:018 those who **forge** a lie against Allah?
016:105 the Signs of Allah, that **forge** falsehood:
020:061 "Woe to you! **Forge** not ye a lie against Allah,

FORGED

006:137 but leave alone them and what they **forged**.
006:138 soon will He requite them for what they **forged**.
007:053 and the things they **forged** will leave
010:038 Or do they say, "He **forged** it"? Say: "Bring
011:013 Or they may say, "He **forged** it."
011:013 Say, "Bring ye then ten Suras **forged**, like unto
011:021 and the (fancies) they **forged** have left them in the lurch!
011:035 Say: "If I had **forged** it, on me were my sin!
011:035 Or do they say, "He has **forged** it?" Say:
021:005 Nay, He **forged** it!-Nay, He is (but) a poet!
025:004 "Naught is this but a lie which he has **forged**,
032:003 Or do they say, "He has **forged** it"?
042:024 "He has **forged** a falsehood against Allah"?
046:008 Say: "Had I **forged** it, then ye
046:008 Or do they say, "He has **forged** it"?

FORGER

016:101 they say, "Thou art but a **forger**" but most
020:061 the **forger** must suffer failure!

FORGERIES

003:024 for their **forgeries** deceive them

FORGERS

011:050 You are only **forgers**.

FORGES

007:037 who **forges** a lie against Allah or rejects
061:007 who **forges** falsehood against Allah, even as

FORGET

002:044 and **forget** to practice it yourselves,
002:237 And do not **forget** liberality between yourselves.
002:286 if we **forget** or fall into error;
005:013 (right) places and **forget** a good part of the
006:041 and ye would **forget** (the false gods)
006:068 If Satan ever makes thee **forget**, then after
007:051 That day shall We **forget** them as they
012:042 But Satan made him **forget** to mention him
018:063 none but Satan made me **forget** to tell (you)
018:063 I did indeed **forget** (about) the Fish:
019:064 and thy Lord never doth **forget**,-
022:002 shall **forget** her suckling-babe, and every
023:110 made you **forget** My Message while ye
028:077 nor **forget** thy portion in this world:
032:014 and We too will **forget** you-taste ye
038:026 for that they **forget** the Day of Account.
039:008 (man) doth **forget** what he cried and prayed
045:034 We will **forget** you as ye forgot the meeting
059:019 and He made them **forget** themselves!
087:006 (the Message), so thou shalt not **forget**,

FORGETS

020:052 my Lord never errs, nor **forgets**,-
036:078 and **forgets** his own (Origin and) Creation:

FORGETTEST

018:024 thou **forgettest**, and say, "I hope

FORGETTING

018:057 **forgetting** the (deeds) which his hands have sent
018:073 Moses said: Rebuke me not for **forgetting**,

FORGING

006:138 **forging** a lie against Allah's name:
060:012 intentionally **forging** falsehood, and that they

FORGIVE

002:052 Even then We did **forgive** you,
002:058 and say: Forgive (us) We shall **forgive** you your
002:109 but **forgive** and overlook,
003:016 **forgive** us, then, our sins, and save us from the agony
003:031 Allah will love you and **forgive** you your sins:
003:135 and who can **forgive** sins except Allah?
003:147 "Our Lord **forgive** us our sins and anything
003:193 Our Lord! **Forgive** us our sins, blot out
004:043 sins and **forgive** again and again.
004:099 and **forgive** again and again.
004:099 For these, there is hope that Allah will **forgive**:
004:137 Allah will not **forgive** them nor
004:168 Allah will not **forgive** them nor guide
005:013 but **forgive** them and overlook (their misdeeds):
005:101 Allah will **forgive** those: for Allah
005:118 if Thou dost **forgive** them, Thou art
007:023 if Thou **forgive** us not and bestow not
007:149 upon us and **forgive** us, we shall indeed
007:151 "O my Lord! **Forgive** me and my brother!
007:155 for Thou art the best of those who **forgive**.
007:155 so **forgive** us and give us Thy mercy; for Thou
007:161 We shall **forgive** you your faults; We shall
007:161 but say **forgive** (us) and enter the gate in a posture
008:029 remove from you (all) evil deeds and **forgive** you:
008:070 and He will **forgive** you:
009:080 Allah will not **forgive** them:
011:047 and unless Thou **forgive** me and have
012:092 Allah will **forgive** you, and He is the Most Merciful
014:010 in order that He may **forgive** you your sins
017:033 his heir authority (to demand Qisas or to **forgive**):
020:073 may He **forgive** us our faults,
023:109 'Our Lord! we believe; then do Thou **forgive** us,
024:022 let them **forgive** and overlook:
024:022 do you not wish that Allah should **forgive** you?
026:051 our Lord will **forgive** us our faults, since we
026:082 will **forgive** me my faults on the Day of Judgment.
026:086 "**Forgive** my father, for that
028:016 Do Thou then **forgive** me!"
033:071 and sound and **forgive** you your sins:
038:035 He said, "O my Lord! **Forgive** me, and grant me
040:007 **Forgive**, then, those who turn in repentance,
042:034 but much doth He **forgive**.
042:037 are angry even then **forgive**;
042:043 But indeed if any show patience and **forgive**,
045:014 to **forgive** those who do not hope for
046:031 He will **forgive** you your faults.
047:034 then die disbelieving,- Allah will not **forgive** them.
048:002 That Allah may **forgive** thee thy faults of the
057:028 and He will **forgive** you (your past):
059:010 "Our Lord! **Forgive** us, and our brethren who came
060:005 trial for the Unbelievers, but **forgive** us, our Lord!
061:012 He will **forgive** you your sins, and admit
063:006 Allah will not **forgive** them.
064:014 But if ye **forgive** and overlook, and cover
071:004 "So He may **forgive** you your sins and give you
071:007 that thou mightest **forgive** them, they have
071:028 "O my Lord! **Forgive** me, my parents, all who

FORGIVEN

007:169 "(Everything) will be **forgiven** us."
008:038 their past would be **forgiven** them; but if

FORGIVENESS

002:054 Then He turned towards you (in **forgiveness**):

FORGIVENESS (continued)

002:175	and Torment in place of **Forgiveness**.
002:199	and ask for Allah's **forgiveness**.
002:221	to the Garden (of Bliss) and **forgiveness**,
002:268	Allah promiseth you His **forgiveness** and bounties.
002:285	(We seek) Thy **forgiveness**, our Lord,
002:286	And grant us **forgiveness**.
003:017	and who pray for **forgiveness** in the early hours of the
003:133	for **forgiveness** from your Lord and for a Garden
003:135	and ask for **forgiveness** for their sins,
003:136	is **forgiveness** from their Lord, and Gardens
003:157	**forgiveness** and mercy from Allah are far better
003:159	and ask for (Allah's) **forgiveness** for them;
004:064	come unto thee and asked Allah's **forgiveness**,
004:064	and the Messenger had asked **forgiveness** for them,
004:096	and **Forgiveness** and Mercy.
004:106	But seek the **forgiveness** of Allah; for Allah
004:110	but afterwards seeks Allah's **forgiveness**,
005:009	hath Allah promised **forgiveness** and a great reward.
005:039	Allah turneth to him in **forgiveness**; for Allah
005:074	and seek His **forgiveness**?
007:199	Hold to **forgiveness**; command what is right;
008:004	they have grades of dignity their Lord, and **forgiveness**,
008:074	for them is the **forgiveness** of sins and a provision
009:080	Whether thou ask for their **forgiveness**, or not,
009:080	if thou ask seventy times for their **forgiveness**,
009:113	that they should pray for **forgiveness** for Pagans,
009:114	father's **forgiveness** only because of a promise
011:003	"Seek ye the **forgiveness** of your Lord, and turn
011:011	for them is **forgiveness** (of sins)
011:052	"And O my people! ask **forgiveness** of your Lord,
011:061	then ask **forgiveness** of Him, and turn
011:090	"But ask **forgiveness** of you Lord, and turn
012:029	(O wife), ask **forgiveness** for thy sin, for truly
012:097	ask for us **forgiveness** for our sins, for we
012:098	"Soon will I ask my Lord for **forgiveness** for you:
013:006	full of **forgiveness** for mankind for their
014:041	"O our Lord! cover (us) with Thy **Forgiveness**-
015:085	with gracious **forgiveness**.
018:055	for **forgiveness** from their Lord but that
019:047	I will pray to my Lord for thy **forgiveness**: for He
022:050	is **forgiveness** and a sustenance most generous.
023:118	grant thou **forgiveness** and mercy!
024:026	people say: for them there is **forgiveness**,
024:062	and ask Allah for their **forgiveness**:
027:046	If only ye ask Allah for **forgiveness**, ye may
033:035	for them has Allah prepared **forgiveness** and great
034:004	for such is **Forgiveness** and a Sustenance
035:007	is **Forgiveness**, and a magnificent Reward.
036:011	of **Forgiveness** and a Reward most generous.
036:027	me **Forgiveness** and has enrolled me among
038:024	We had tried him: he asked **forgiveness** of his Lord,
040:007	believe in Him; and implore **forgiveness** for those
040:055	and ask **forgiveness** for thy fault, and celebrate
041:006	and ask for His **forgiveness**."
041:043	thy Lord has at His command (all) **Forgiveness** as well
042:005	and pray for **forgiveness** for all beings on earth:
042:030	(a sin) He grants **forgiveness**.
047:015	of fruits, and **forgiveness** from their Lord,
047:019	and ask **forgiveness** for thy fault,
048:011	ask **forgiveness** for us."
048:029	who believe and do righteous deeds **forgiveness**,
049:003	for them is **Forgiveness** and a great Reward.

FORGIVENESS (continued)

051:018	they (were found) praying for **Forgiveness**;
053:032	verily thy Lord is ample in **forgiveness**.
057:020	And **Forgiveness** from Allah and (His)
057:021	Be ye foremost (in seeking) **forgiveness** from your
060:004	for **forgiveness** for thee, though I have no power
060:012	for the **forgiveness** (of their sins): for Allah
063:005	the Messenger of Allah will pray for your **forgiveness**,"
063:006	for their **forgiveness** or not.
064:017	and He will grant you **Forgiveness**: for Allah
066:008	and grant us **Forgiveness**:
067:012	for them is **Forgiveness** and a great Reward.
071:010	"Saying, `Ask **forgiveness** from your Lord, for He
074:056	and the Lord of **Forgiveness**.
110:003	and pray for His **Forgiveness**:

FORGIVES

005:095	Allah **forgives** what is past:
020:082	He that **forgives** again and again, to those
022:060	out (sins) and **forgives** (again and again).
039:005	He Who **forgives** again and again?
039:053	for Allah **forgives** all sins:
040:042	the Exalted in Power, Who **forgives** again and again!
042:025	from His Servants and **forgives** sins:
042:040	but if a person **forgives** and makes reconciliation,
048:014	He **forgives** whom He wills, and He punishes
058:013	**If, then, ye do not so, and Allah forgives you,**

FORGIVETH

002:284	He **forgiveth** whom He pleaseth,
003:129	He **forgiveth** whom He pleaseth and punisheth
004:048	but He **forgiveth** anything else, to whom
004:048	Allah **forgiveth** not that partners
004:116	but He **forgiveth** whom He pleaseth
004:116	Allah **forgiveth** not (the sin of) joining
005:018	He **forgiveth** whom He pleaseth, and He
005:040	and He **forgiveth** whom he pleaseth:
040:003	Who **forgiveth** Sin, accepteth Repentance, is Severe

FORGIVING

008:070	for Allah Is Oft-**Forgiving**, Most Merciful."
017:025	Most **Forgiving** to those who turn to Him
017:044	Verily He is Oft-Forbearing, Most **Forgiving**!
018:058	But your Lord is Most **Forgiving**, Full of Mercy.

FORGIVENESS

110:003	for He is Oft-Returning (in **forgiveness**).

FORGOT

005:014	but they **forgot** a good part of the Message that was
006:044	But when they **forgot** the warning they had received,
007:051	as they **forgot** the meeting of this day of theirs,
018:061	they **forgot** (about) their Fish, which took
020:115	taken the covenant of Adam, but he **forgot**:
020:126	when Our Signs came unto thee, **forgot** them:
025:018	until they **forgot** the Message: for they
032:014	"Taste ye then-for ye **forgot** the Meeting of this
045:034	We will forget you as ye **forgot** the meeting
058:006	Allah has reckoned and which they **forgot**, For Allah
058:019	so he has made them **forgot** the remembrance
059:019	And be ye not like those who **forgot** Allah; and He

FORGOTTEN

002:106	We abrogate or cause to be **forgotten**,
007:053	those who have **forgotten** it before will say: "The
009:067	so He hath **forgotten** them.
009:067	They have **forgotten** Allah; so He
019:023	would that I had been a thing **forgotten**."

FORGOTTEN (continued)

020:088   god of Moses, but (Moses) has **forgotten**!"
020:126   so wilt thou, this day, be **forgotten**.

FORM

002:120   unless thou follow their **form** of religion.
005:003   unless ye are able to slaughter it (in due **form**);
020:050   to each (created) thing its **form**, then, gave (it)
039:023   the most beautiful message in the **form** of a Book,
053:006   For he appeared (in stately **form**)
056:062   the first **form** of creation:
075:037   Was he not a drop of sperm emitted (in lowly **form**)?
082:008   In whatever **Form** He wills, does He

FORMED

005:011   unto you when certain men **formed** the design to
012:025   punishment for one who **formed** an evil
022:005   partly **formed** and partly unformed, in order

FORMER

002:232   from marrying their (**former**) husbands,
005:027   "Surely," said the **former**, "Allah doth accept
014:022   I reject your **former** act in associating
017:059   of **former** generations treated them as false:
020:021   to its **former** condition"...
020:133   of all that was in the **former** Books of revelation?
026:196   in the revealed Books of **former** peoples.
033:033   like that of the **former** Times of Ignorance;
049:011   it may be that the (latter) are better than the (**former**):
049:011   it may be that the (latter) are better than the (**former**):
053:025   and the **Former** life.
079:010   be returned to (our) **former** state?-

FORMERLY

028:048   which were **formerly** sent to Moses?

FORMS

006:038   but (**forms** part of) communities like you.
056:061   From changing your **Forms** and creating you
056:061   creating you (again) in (**Forms**) that ye know not.

FORNICATION

004:024   desiring chastity, not **fornication**.
024:002   The woman and the man guilty of **fornication**,-
025:068   except for just cause, not commit **fornication**;-
060:012   that they will not commit adultery (or **fornication**),

FORNICATORS

004:025   they should be chaste, not **fornicators**,

FORSAKE

002:026   except those who **forsake** (the path),
032:016   They **forsake** their beds of sleep, the while
037:125   and **forsake** the Best of Creators,-

FORSAKEN

093:003   Thy Guardian-Lord Hath not **forsaken** thee, nor is

FORSAKES

003:160   if He **forsakes** you, who is there, after that,
004:100   He who **forsakes** his home in the cause of Allah,

FORSAKING

004:119   Whoever, **forsaking** Allah, takes Satan for a friend,

FORSOOK

009:100   those who **forsook** (their homes) and of those who

FORSOOTH

044:034   As to these (Quraish), they say **forsooth**:
074:052   **Forsooth**, each one of them wants to be given

FORTH

002:022   and brought **forth** therewith fruits
002:060   Then gushed **forth** therefrom twelve springs.

FORTH (continued)

002:072   but Allah was to bring **forth** what ye did hide.
002:074   others there are when split asunder send **forth** water;
002:074   there are some from which rivers gush **forth**;
002:110   send **forth** for your souls before you,
002:149   From whencesoever thou startest **forth**,
002:150   So from whencesoever thou startest **forth**,
002:249   When Talut set **forth** with the armies,
002:257   he leads them **forth** into light.
002:257   lead them **forth** into the depths of darkness.
003:036   And Allah knew best what she brought **forth**-
003:154   would certainly have gone **forth** to the place
004:062   their hands have sent **forth**?
004:071   or go **forth** all together.
004:071   And either go **forth** in parties or go
005:107   Let two others stand **forth** in their places,-
005:110   And behold! thou bringest **forth** the dead
006:093   the angels stretch **forth** their hands, (saying),
006:130   setting **forth** unto you My Signs and warning
006:145   or blood poured **forth**, or the
007:106   show it **forth**,-if thou tellest the truth."
007:160   out of it there gushed **forth** twelve springs:
007:172   When thy Lord drew **forth** from the
008:051   which your (own) hands sent **forth**.
009:038   when ye are asked to go **forth** in the Cause of Allah,
009:039   Unless ye go **forth**, He will punish you with a grievous
009:041   Go ye **forth**, (whether equipped) lightly
009:046   was averse to their being sent **forth**;
009:081   they said, "Go not **forth** in the heat."
009:108   standing **forth** (for prayer) therein.
009:108   Never stand thou **forth** therein.
009:122   from every expedition go **forth** to devote
009:122   it is not for the believers to go **forth** together:
010:019   for a word that went **forth** before from thy Lord,
011:040   those against whom the Word has already gone **forth**,-
011:040   and the fountains of the earth gushed **forth**!
011:044   Then the word went **forth**: "O earth! swallow up
011:044   rested on Mount Judi and the word went **forth**:
011:076   The decree of thy Lord hath gone **forth**:
011:110   had gone **forth** before from thy Lord the matter
012:059   them **forth** with provisions (suitable) for them,
012:070   them **forth** with provisions (suitable) for them,
013:014   if they were to stretch **forth** their hands
013:017   Thus doth Allah set **forth** parables.
013:017   show **forth** Truth and falsehood.
014:024   Seest thou not how Allah sets **forth** a parable?
014:025   So Allah sets **forth** parables for men, in order
014:025   It brings **forth** its fruit at all times, by the
014:045   and We put **forth** (many) Parables
014:048   marshalled **forth**, before Allah, the One,
016:006   lead them **forth** to pasture in the morning.
016:075   Allah sets **forth** the Parable (of two men):
016:076   Allah sets **forth** (another) Parable of two men:
016:078   It is He Who brought you **forth** from the wombs
016:112   Allah sets **forth** a parable: a city
016:116   that your tongues may put **forth**, "This is
017:029   nor stretch it **forth** to its utmost reach,
017:090   to gush **forth** for us from the earth,
017:091   and cause rivers to gush **forth** in their midst,
018:018   their dog stretching **forth** his two fore-legs
018:032   Set **forth** to them the parable of two men:
018:033   Each of those gardens brought **forth** its produce,
018:045   Set **forth** to them the similitude of the life of the world:

FORTH (continued)

018:057 forgetting the (deeds) which his hands have sent **forth**?
019:068 then shall We bring them **forth** on their
019:089 Indeed ye have put **forth** a thing most monstrous!
020:022 it shall come **forth** white (and shining),
020:040 "Behold! thy sister goeth **forth** and saith,
020:047 send **forth**, therefore, the Children
020:129 that went **forth** before from thy Lord,
022:005 it puts **forth** every kind of beautiful growth (in pairs).
022:010 of the deeds which thy hands sent **forth**, for verily
022:073 O men! Here is a parable set **forth**!
023:027 and the oven gushes **forth**, take thou on board
023:027 when comes Our command, has already gone **forth**:
023:035 ye shall be brought **forth** (again)?
024:013 (stand **forth**) themselves as liars!
024:035 Allah doth set **forth** Parables for men:
024:043 issue **forth** from their midst.
025:039 To teach one We set **forth** parables and examples;
026:016 "So go **forth**, both of you, to Pharaoh,
026:218 Who seeth thee standing **forth** (in prayer),
027:012 and it will come **forth** white without stain
027:025 brings **forth** what is hidden in the heavens
027:064 Say, "Bring **forth** your argument, if ye
027:082 We shall bring **forth** from the earth a beast
028:032 and it will come **forth** white without stain
028:047 that their hands have sent **forth**, they might
028:079 So he went **forth** among his people in the
029:043 And such are the Parables We set **forth** for mankind,
030:016 such shall be brought **forth** to Punishment.
030:025 behold, ye (straightway) come **forth**.
030:036 their (own) hands have sent **forth**, behold,
031:016 or on earth, Allah will bring it **forth**:
035:009 It is Allah Who sends **forth** the Winds, so that
036:013 Set **forth** to them, by way of a parable,
036:034 and We cause springs to gush **forth** therein.
036:051 (men) will rush **forth** to their Lord!
036:077 Yet behold! he (stands **forth**) as an open adversary!
037:145 But We cast him **forth** on the naked shore
039:027 We have put **forth** for men, in the
039:029 Allah puts **forth** a Parable-a man belonging
040:016 The Day whereon they will (all) come **forth**:
040:051 and on the Day when the Witnesses will stand **forth**,-
041:045 for a Word that went **forth** before from thy Lord,
041:047 (within her womb) nor bring **forth** (young), but by
042:014 not been for a Word that went **forth** before from thy Lord,
042:048 his hands have sent **forth**, truly then
043:058 This they set **forth** to thee, only by
044:010 that the sky will bring **forth** a kind of smoke
044:023 "March **forth** with My servants by night:
047:003 thus does Allah set **forth** for men their lessons
048:015 when ye set **forth** to acquire booty (in war):
048:029 like a seed which sends **forth** its blade,
050:021 And there will come **forth** every soul:
052:048 of thy Lord the while thou standest **forth**,
054:007 They will come **forth**,-their eyes humbled-from
054:011 with water pouring **forth**.
054:012 And We caused the earth to gush **forth** with springs,
055:066 pouring **forth** water in continuous abundance:
057:004 within the earth and what comes **forth** out of it,
057:020 how rain and the growth which it brings **forth**,
057:025 that men may stand **forth** in justice;
059:018 he has sent **forth** for the morrow.
060:002 to you as enemies, and stretch **forth** their hands

FORTH (continued)

065:011 lead **forth** those who believe and do
066:010 Allah sets **forth**, for an example to the
066:011 And Allah sets **forth**, as an example to those
067:007 of its breath even as it blazes **forth**.
071:018 and raise you **forth** (again at the Resurrection)?
073:020 that thou standest **forth** (to prayer) nigh two-thirds
073:020 And whatever good ye send **forth** for yourselves,
074:034 And by the Dawn as it shineth **forth**,-
077:001 By the (Winds) Sent **Forth** one after another
077:036 Nor will it be open to them to put **forth** pleas.
078:018 and ye shall come **forth** in crowds;
078:038 will stand **forth** in ranks, none shall
078:040 man will see (the Deeds) which his hands have sent **forth**,,
080:025 For that We pour **forth** water in abundance,
082:003 When the Oceans are suffered to burst **forth**;
084:004 And casts **forth** what is within it and becomes
089:024 sent **forth** (Good Deeds) for (this) my (Future) Life."

FORTHCOMING

046:028 Why then was no help **forthcoming** to them

FORTHWITH

011:038 **Forthwith** he starts constructing the Ark:
012:096 and he **forthwith** regained clear sight.
022:063 and **forthwith** the earth becomes clothed with
100:005 And penetrate **forthwith** into the midst

FORTIFIED

059:014 except in **fortified** townships,

FORTRESSES

059:002 that their **fortresses** would defend them from Allah!

FORTS

077:032 "Indeed it throws about sparks (huge) as **Forts**,

FORTUNE

004:073 But if good **fortune** comes to you from Allah,
005:052 a change of **fortune** bring us disaster."
028:079 For he is truly a lord of mighty good **fortune**."
041:035 none but persons of the greatest good **fortune**.

FORTUNES

003:140 Such days (of varying **fortunes**) We give to men

FORTY

002:051 appointed **forty** nights for Moses,
005:026 the land be out of their reach for **forty** years:
007:142 thus was completed them term with his Lord, **forty** nights.
046:015 he reaches the age of full strength and attains **forty** years,

FORWARD

005:080 souls have sent **forward** before them (with the result),
006:150 Say: "Bring **forward** your witnesses to prove
014:043 They running **forward** with necks outstretched,
015:024 who hasten **forward**, and those who lag behind.
018:015 why do they not bring **forward** an authority
024:011 Those who brought **forward** the lie are a body
025:004 put **forward** an iniquity and a falsehood.
033:070 and make your utterance straight **forward**:
034:030 for an hour nor put **forward**."
039:069 and the witnesses will be brought **forward**;
042:045 And thou wilt see them brought **forward** to the
049:001 yourselves **forward** before Allah and His Messenger;
051:029 But his wife came **forward** clamouring:
054:028 brought **forward** (by suitable turns).
057:012 how their Light runs **forward** before their
066:008 Their Light will run **forward** before them and by
071:004 it cannot be put **forward**: if ye only knew."
074:037 To any of you that chooses to press **forward**,

FORWARD (continued)

075:013 (all) that he put **forward**, and all
079:004 Then press **forward** as in a race,
081:014 (Then) shall each soul know what it has put **forward**.
082:005 it hath sent **forward** and (what it hath) kept back.

FOSTER

002:233 (the **foster** mother) what ye offered,
022:005 as babes, then (**foster** you) that ye may reach
057:027 but that they did not **foster** as they

FOSTER-MOTHER

002:233 if ye decide on a **foster-mother** for your offspring

FOSTER-MOTHERS

004:023 **foster-mothers** (who gave you suck),

FOSTER-SISTERS

004:023 **foster-sisters**; your wives, mothers;

FOUGHT

002:218 and **fought** (and strove and struggled)
002:253 they would not have **fought** each other;
002:253 generations would not have fought among each other,
003:142 who **fought** hard (in His Cause)
003:146 How many of the Prophets **fought** (in Allah's way),
003:146 and with them (**fought**) large bands of godly men?
003:195 and **fought** and were slain, verily,
004:090 and they would have **fought** you:
008:072 and **fought** for the Faith, with their
057:010 among you are those who spent (freely) and **fought**,
057:010 those who spent (freely) and **fought** afterwards.

FOUL

018:074 Truly a **foul** (unheard-of) thing hast thou done!"
069:036 the **foul** pus from the washing of wounds,

FOUND

003:037 he **found** her supplied with sustenance.
003:052 When Jesus **found** unbelief on their part
003:112 (like a tent) wherever they are **found**,
004:064 they would have **found** Allah indeed Oft-Returning,
004:082 they would surely have **found** therein much discrepancy.
005:104 the ways we **found** our fathers following."
007:028 they say: "We **found** our fathers doing so";
007:043 never could we have **found** guidance, had it not
007:044 "We have indeed **found** the promises
007:044 have you also **found** your Lord's promises true?"
007:102 We **found** rebellious and disobedient.
007:102 Most of them We **found** not men (true)
008:023 If Allah had **found** in them any good, He would
010:078 We **found** our fathers following,-in order
012:025 they both **found** her lord near the door.
012:065 they **found** their stock-in-trade had been
012:075 in whose saddle-bag it is **found**, should be
012:079 other than him with whom we **found** our property:
017:075 thou wouldst have **found** none to help thee against Us!
018:065 So they **found** one of Our servants. On whom
018:077 They **found** there a wall on the point
018:086 near it he **found** a People:
018:086 he **found** it set in a spring of murky water:
018:090 he **found** it rising on a people for whom We had provided
018:093 between two mountains, he **found**, beneath them,
020:115 and We **found** on his part no firm resolve.
021:053 They said, "We **found** our father worshipping them."
026:074 They said: "Nay, but we **found** our fathers
027:023 "I **found** (there) a woman ruling over them
027:024 "I **found** her and her people worshipping the
028:015 and he **found** there two men fighting,-one of

FOUND (continued)

028:023 he **found** there a group of men watering
028:023 and besides them he **found** two women who were
031:021 we **found** our fathers (following)."
033:061 wherever they are **found**, they shall
037:069 Truly they **found** their fathers on the wrong Path;
038:044 Truly We **found** him full of patience
043:022 Nay! they say: "We **found** Our fathers following
043:023 "We **found** Our fathers following a certain
043:024 ye **found** your fathers following?"
051:018 they (were **found**) praying for Forgiveness;
051:036 But We **found** not there any except one
071:025 and they **found**-in lieu of Allah-none to help them.
072:008 (secrets of) heaven; but we **found** it filled with
093:007 And He **found** thee wandering, and He
093:008 And He **found** thee in need, and made
101:006 will be (**found**) heavy,
101:008 will be (**found**) light,-

FOUNDATION

003:007 they are the **foundation** of the Book:
009:108 There is a mosque whose **foundation** was laid
009:109 layeth his **foundation** on an undermined sand-cliff
009:109 his **foundation** on piety to Allah and His
009:110 The **foundation** of those who so build is never
018:046 and best as (the **foundation** for) hopes.

FOUNDATIONS

002:127 raised the **foundations** of the House
016:026 from their **foundations**, and the roof fell down
018:042 to pieces to its very **foundations**, and he

FOUNTAIN

037:045 from a clear-flowing **fountain**,
076:006 A **Fountain** where the Devotees of Allah do drink,
076:018 A **fountain** there, called Salsabil.

FOUNTAINS

011:040 and the **fountains** of the earth gushed forth!
015:045 and **fountains** (of clear-flowing water).

FOUR

002:226 a waiting for **four** months is ordained;
002:234 concerning themselves **four** months and ten days
002:260 He said: "Take **four** birds;
004:003 marry women of your choice, two, or three, or **four**;
004:015 take the evidence of **four** (reliable) witnesses
006:143 (Take) eight (head of cattle) in (**four**) pairs:
009:002 Go ye, then, for **four** months, (as you will),
009:036 of them **four** are sacred;
024:004 and produce not **four** witnesses,
024:006 testify **four** times by Allah that he is of those
024:008 if she bears witness **four** times (with an oath) by Allah,
024:013 Why did they not bring **four** witnesses to prove it?
024:045 and some that walk on **four**.
035:001 two, or three, or **four** (Pairs):
041:010 its sustenance in **four** Days, alike for

FOURTH

004:012 but if they leave a child, ye get a **fourth**;
004:012 their share is a **fourth**, if ye leave no child;
018:022 the dog being the **fourth** among them; (others) say
058:007 but He is the **fourth** among them,-nor between

FOWLS

056:021 And the flesh of **fowls**, any that they may desire.

FRAGMENTS

030:048 break them into **fragments**, until thou seest rain-drops
034:019 and We dispersed them all in scattered **fragments**.

FRAGMENTS (continued)
080:026 And We split the earth in **fragments,**

FRAME
002:238 Allah in a devout (**frame of** mind).
011:016 vain are the designs they **frame** therein,
076:028 and We have made their **frame** strong; but, when

FRAMED
022:052 when he **framed** a desire, Satan threw

FRAUD
026:181 and cause on loss (to others by **fraud**).
083:001 Woe to those that deal in **fraud,**-

FREE
002:178 the **free** for the **free,**
002:184 But he that will give more, of his own **free** will,
002:231 or set them **free** on equitable terms;
002:263 Allah is **free** of all wants,
002:267 And know that Allah is **free** of all wants,
002:273 that they are **free** from want.
004:025 the means wherewith to wed **free** believing women,
004:025 their punishment is half that for **free** women.
004:092 he should **free** a believing slave.
004:103 but when ye are **free** from danger, set up
004:131 and Allah is **free** of all wants, worthy
005:103 or a she-camel let loose for **free** pasture,
006:078 "O my people! I am indeed **free** from your (guilt)
009:110 is never **free** from suspicion and shakiness
010:041 Ye are **free** from responsibility for what I do,
011:035 And I am **free** of the sins of which
011:054 that I am **free** from the sin of ascribing, to Him,
011:064 leave her to feed on Allah's (**free**) earth,
014:008 yet is Allah **Free** of all wants, Worthy of
022:064 for verily Allah,-He is **Free** of all wants,
023:006 they are **free** from blame,
023:091 Glory to Allah (He is **free**) from the (sort of)
024:031 or male attendants **free** of sexual desires.
025:053 It is He Who has let **free** the two bodies
026:216 "I am **free** (of responsibility) for what ye do!"
027:040 truly my Lord is **Free** of All Needs, Supreme in
028:063 we **free** ourselves (from them) to you.
029:006 for Allah is **free** of all needs from all creation.
031:012 verily Allah is **free** of all wants, worthy of
031:026 (that is) **free** of all wants, worthy of
033:028 your enjoyment and set you **free** in a
035:015 the One **Free** of all wants, worthy of all praise.
037:047 **Free** from headiness; nor will
037:159 Glory to Allah! (He is **free**) from the things
037:180 (He is **free**) from what they ascribe (to Him)!
043:082 He is **free** from the things they attribute (to Him)!
047:038 But Allah is **free** of all wants,
052:023 one with another, a cup **free** of frivolity, **free** from sin.
055:015 And He created Jinns from fire **free** of smoke:
055:019 He has let **free** the two Seas meeting together:
055:050 In them (each) will be two Springs flowing (**free**);
057:024 verily Allah is **free** of all needs, worthy of all praise.
058:003 should **free** a slave before they touch each other:
059:016 Satan says, "I am **free** of thee: I do
060:006 But if any turn away, truly Allah is **Free** of all
064:006 and Allah is **free** of all needs worthy of all praise.
074:004 And thy garments keep **free** from stain!
094:007 when thou art **free** (from thine immediate task),

FREED
004:092 and a believing slave be **freed.**
005:103 or stallion-camels **freed** from work:

FREEDOM
002:229 if she give something for her **freedom**
005:089 or clothe them; or give a slave his **freedom.**

FREEING
004:092 the **freeing** of a believing slave (is enough).
090:013 (It is:) **freeing** the bondman;

FREELY
003:092 unless ye give (**freely**) of that which ye love:
003:134 Those who spend (**freely**), whether in prosperity,
004:032 gifts more **freely** on some of you than on others:
004:092 unless they remit it **freely.**
008:003 and spend (**freely**) out of the gifts We have
009:079 as give themselves **freely** to (deeds of) charity,
013:010 by night or walk **freely** by day.
016:071 of sustenance more **freely** on some of you than
016:075 spends thereof (**freely**), privately and publicly:
017:020 We bestow **freely** on all-these as well as those:
026:132 on you **freely** all that ye know.
026:133 "**Freely** has He bestowed on you cattle and sons,-
057:010 equal among you are those who spent (**freely**) and fought,
057:010 than those who spent (**freely**) and fought afterwards.

FREQUENTED
033:027 ye had not **frequented** (before).

FREQUENTLY
062:010 and remember Allah **frequently** that ye may prosper.

FRESH
004:056 We shall change them for **fresh** skins, that they
006:006 raised in their wake **fresh** generations (to succeed them).
006:059 nor anything **fresh** or dry (green or withered),
016:014 that is **fresh** and tender, and that
019:025 it will let fall **fresh** ripe dates upon thee.
035:012 (kind of water) do ye eat flesh **fresh** and tender,
080:028 And Grapes and the **fresh** vegetation,

FRESHNESS
056:017 youths of perpetual (**freshness**),
076:019 (serve) youths of perpetual (**freshness**):

FRET
018:006 Thou would only, perchance, **fret** thyself to death,

FRETFUL
070:020 **Fretful** when evil touches him;

FRIDAY
062:009 is proclaimed to prayer on **Friday** (the Day of Assembly),

FRIEND
004:119 Whoever, forsaking Allah, takes Satan for a **friend,**
004:125 For Allah did take Abraham for a **friend.**
006:127 He will be their **Friend,** because they
017:073 they would certainly have made thee (their) **friend!**
019:045 so that thou become to Satan a **friend.**"
024:061 or in the house of a sincere **friend** of yours:
025:028 never taken such a one for a **friend!**
026:101 "Nor a single intimate **friend.**
040:018 to choke (them); no intimate **friend** nor intercessors
041:034 were thy **friend** and intimate!
069:035 "So no **friend** hath he here this Day.
070:010 And no **friend** will ask after a **friend,**

FRIENDLY
004:129 If ye come to a **friendly** understanding,

FRIENDS
003:028 take for **friends** or helpers Unbelievers rather
004:076 so fight ye against the **friends,** of Satan:
004:089 take no **friends** or helpers from their ranks:
004:089 so take not **friends** from their ranks until

FRIENDS (continued)

004:139 Those who take for **friends** Unbelievers rather
004:144 for **friends** Unbelievers rather than Believers:
005:051 and the Christians for your **friends** and protectors:
005:051 they are but **friends** and protectors to each other.
005:055 Your (real) **friends** are (no less than) Allah,
005:057 take not for **friends** and protectors those who
005:081 would they have taken them for **friends** and protectors,
006:071 his **friends** calling 'Come to us', (vainly)
006:121 their **friends** to contend with you if ye
006:128 Their **friends** amongst men will say: "Our Lord!
007:003 as **friends** or protectors, other than Him.
007:027 We made the Satans **friends** (only) to
007:030 for their **friends** and protectors, and think
008:072 these are (all) **friends** and protectors, one of
009:016 and take none for **friends** and protectors
010:062 Behold! verily on the **friends** of Allah there is
033:005 (then they are) your Brothers in faith, or your **friends**.
033:006 nevertheless do ye what is just to your closest **friends**:
043:067 **Friends** on that Day will be foes, one to
060:001 take not My enemies and yours as **friends** (or protectors),-
062:006 that ye are **friends** to Allah,

FRIENDSHIP

002:254 nor **friendship** nor intercession.
005:051 to them (for **friendship**) is of them.
005:056 As to those who turn (for **friendship**) to Allah,
005:080 in **friendship** to the Unbelievers.
022:004 it is decreed that whoever turns to him for **friendship**,
058:014 (in **friendship**) to such as have the Wrath of
060:001 showing **friendship** unto them in secret:
060:007 Establish **friendship** between you and those whom
060:009 form turning to them (for **friendship** and protection).
060:013 O ye who believe! (for **friendship**) to people on whom

FRIGHTEN

039:036 But they try to **frighten** thee with other

FRIGHTENING

017:059 of **frightening** (and warning from evil).

FRINGE

003:127 That He might cut off a **fringe** of the Unbelievers

FRIVOLITY

052:023 a cup free of **frivolity**, free from sin.
056:025 No **frivolity** will they hear therein, nor any

FRO

002:015 like blind ones (to and **fro**).
009:045 in their doubts to and **fro**.
009:047 disorder, hurrying to and **fro** in your midst and
015:072 they wander in distraction, to and **fro**.
016:046 them to account in the midst of their goings to and **fro**,
023:075 wandering in distraction to and **fro**.
032:026 in whose dwellings they (now) go to and **fro**?

FROGS

007:133 Wholesale Death, Locusts, lice, **Frogs**, and

FROM

002:005 They are on (true guidance), **from** their Lord,
002:019 is that of a rain-laden cloud **from** the sky:
002:022 and sent down rain **from** the heavens;
002:023 revealed **from** time to our servants
002:026 that it is the truth **from** their Lord;
002:036 Then did Satan make them slip **from** the (garden),
002:037 Then learnt Adam **from** his Lord certain words
002:038 We said: "Get ye down all **from** here;
002:038 there comes to you guidance **from** Me,

FROM (continued)

002:048 nor shall anyone be helped (**from** outside).
002:048 nor shall compensation be taken **from** her.
002:049 therein was a tremendous trial **from** your Lord.
002:049 delivered you **from** the people of Pharaoh:
002:059 the transgressors a plague **from** heaven,
002:059 the word **from** that which had been given them;
002:067 "Allah save me **from** being an ignorant (fool)!"
002:074 some **from** which rivers gush forth;
002:079 and then say: "This is **from** Allah,"
002:080 Say: "Have ye taken a promise **from** Allah,
002:083 a covenant **from** the Children of Israel
002:084 your own people **from** your homes:
002:085 and banish a party of you **from** their homes;
002:089 a Book **from** Allah,
002:089 although **from** of old they had prayed
002:096 will not save him **from** (due) chastisement
002:101 a Messenger **from** Allah,
002:102 They learned **from** them the means
002:103 reward **from** Allah if they but knew!
002:103 and guarded themselves **from** evil,
002:105 come down to you **from** your Lord.
002:108 hath strayed without doubt **from** the even way.
002:108 But whoever changeth **from** Faith to Unbelief,
002:109 have believed **from** selfish envy,
002:123 nor shall compensation be accepted **from** her
002:123 nor shall anyone be helped (**from** outside)
002:124 He pleaded: "And also (Imams) **from** my offspring!"
002:127 "Our Lord! accept (this service) **from** us:
002:130 And who turns away **from** the religion
002:136 (all) Prophets **from** their Lord:
002:138 (Our religion) takes its hue **from** Allah
002:140 the testimony they have **from** Allah?
002:142 "What hath turned them **from** the Qiblah
002:143 who followed the Messenger **from** those who
002:143 who would turn on their heels (**from** the Faith).
002:144 that is the truth **from** their Lord,
002:147 The truth is **from** thy Lord,
002:149 **From** whencesoever thou startest forth,
002:149 that is indeed the truth **from** thy Lord.
002:150 So **from** whencesoever thou startest forth,
002:157 (descend) blessings **from** their Lord, and Mercy.
002:164 sends down **from** the skies,
002:176 the Book are in a schism far (**from** the purpose).
002:178 This is a concession and a Mercy **from** your Lord.
002:180 this is due **from** the God-fearing.
002:184 (should be made up) **from** days later.
002:187 appear to you distinct **from** its black thread;
002:189 ye enter your houses **from** the back:
002:191 and turn them out **from** where they have turned you out;
002:196 but if ye are prevented (**from** completing it),
002:198 Then when ye pour down **from** (Mount) 'Arafat,
002:199 Then return **from** the place whence it is usual
002:201 and save us **from** the torment on the Fire!"
002:217 back **from** your faith if they can.
002:217 turn back **from** their faith and die in unbelief,
002:220 means mischief **from** the man who means good.
002:222 so keep away **from** women in their courses,
002:226 an oath for abstention **from** their wives,
002:229 to take back any of your gifts **from** (your wives),
002:232 do not prevent them **from** marrying their (former)
002:236 is due **from** those who wish to do the right thing.
002:248 of security **from** your Lord,

FROM (continued)

002:256 Truth stands out clear **from** Error;
002:257 **from** the depths of darkness he leads them forth into light.
002:257 are the Tagut **from** light they will lead them forth
002:258 Allah that causeth the sun to rise **from** the East,
002:258 do thou then cause it to rise **from** the West."
002:271 it will remove **from** you some of
002:273 that they are free **from** want.
002:273 in Allah's cause are restricted (**from** travel).
002:273 they beg not importunately **from** all and sundry.
002:275 admonition **from** their Lord, desist,
002:279 notice of war **from** Allah and His Messenger:
002:285 hath been revealed to him **from** his Lord,
003:005 **From** Allah, verily nothing is hidden
003:007 the whole of it is **from** our Lord:"
003:008 but grant us mercy **from** Thee:
003:016 and save us **from** the agony of the Fire;"
003:026 and Thou strippest off Power **from** whom Thou pleasest:
003:028 that ye may guard yourselves **from** them.
003:036 to Thy protection **from** Satan the Rejected."
003:037 She said: "**From** Allah: for Allah provides
003:038 Grant unto me **from** Thee a progeny that is pure:
003:039 confirming the truth of a Word **from** Allah,
003:045 glad tidings of a Word **from** Him:
003:049 I have come to you, with a Sign **from** your Lord,
003:050 I have come to you with a Sign **from** your Lord.
003:059 He created him **from** dust,
003:060 the truth (comes) **from** thy Lord alone;
003:064 that we erect not, **from** among ourselves,
003:078 but it is not **from** Allah:
003:078 and they say "That is **from** Allah"
003:084 and the Prophets, **from** their Lord;
003:091 never would be accepted **from** any such as much
003:099 who believe, **from** the path of Allah,
003:103 and He saved you **from** it.
003:112 (of protection) **from** Allah and **from** men;
003:112 they draw on themselves wrath **from** Allah.
003:118 rank hatred has already appeared **from** their mouths;
003:126 no victory except **from** Allah, the Exalted,
003:133 for forgiveness **from** your Lord and for a Garden
003:136 is forgiveness **from** their Lord, and Gardens
003:140 may take to Himself **from** your ranks Martyr-witnesses
003:149 and ye will turn back (**from** Faith) to your own loss.
003:152 did He divert you **from** your foes in order to test you.
003:157 forgiveness and mercy **from** Allah are far better
003:159 they would have broken away **from** about thee:
003:164 among them a Messenger **from** among themselves,
003:165 Say (to them): "It is **from** yourselves:
003:167 or (at least) drive (the foe **from** your city)."
003:168 Say: "Avert death **from** your own selves,
003:169 finding their sustenance **from** their Lord.
003:171 the Grace and the Bounty **from** Allah,
003:172 and refrain **from** wrong have a great reward;
003:174 And they returned with Grace and Bounty **from** Allah:
003:179 until He separates what is evil **from** what is good.
003:183 consumed by fire (**from** heaven)."
003:185 Only he who is saved far **from** the fire and
003:186 and **from** those who worship parties besides Allah.
003:186 **from** those who received the Book before you
003:187 a Covenant **from** the People of the Book,
003:191 salvation **from** the Chastisement of the Fire.
003:193 blot out **from** us our iniquities, and take
003:194 and save us **from** shame on the Day of Judgment:

FROM (continued)

003:195 verily, I will blot out **from** them their iniquities,
003:195 a reward **from** Allah, and **from** Allah is the best of
003:198 an entertainment **from** Allah;
003:198 and that which is **from** Allah is the best (bliss)
004:001 Who created you **from** a single person,
004:001 and **from** them twain scattered (like seeds)
004:003 to prevent you **from** doing injustice.
004:007 **From** what is left by parents and those nearest
004:015 witnesses **from** amongst you against them;
004:021 and they have taken **from** you a solemn covenant?
004:023 your son proceeding **from** your loins;
004:024 with gifts **from** your property, desiring
004:025 believing girls **from** among those whom your right hand
004:025 Ye are one **from** another: wed them with the leave of
004:027 ye should turn away (**from** Him), far, far away.
004:034 and because they support them **from** their means.
004:035 and the other **from** hers; if they seek
004:035 appoint (two) arbiters, one **from** his family,
004:040 and giveth **from** His Own self a great reward.
004:041 How then if We brought **from** each People a witness,
004:042 but never will they hide a single fact **from** Allah!
004:043 you cometh **from** the privy, or ye have been
004:046 those who displace words **from** their (right) places,
004:055 And some of them averted their faces **from** him:
004:060 lead them astray far away (**from** the Right).
004:061 avert their faces **from** thee in disgust.
004:067 given them **from** Ourselves a great reward;
004:070 Such is the Bounty **from** Allah: and sufficient
004:073 But if good fortune comes to you **from** Allah,
004:075 and raise for us **from** Thee one who will help!"
004:075 and raise for us **from** Thee one who will protect;
004:075 "Our Lord! rescue us **from** this town.
004:077 hold their hands (**from** fight) but establish regular
004:078 Say: "All things are **from** Allah."
004:078 they say, "This is **from** Allah"; but
004:078 "This is **from** thee" (O Prophet).
004:079 happens to thee, is **from** Allah:
004:079 is **from** thyself and We have sent thee as
004:081 on things very different **from** what thou tellest them.
004:082 Had it been **from** other than Allah, they
004:083 would have known it **from** them (direct).
004:089 the way of Allah (**from** what is forbidden).
004:089 so take not friends **from** their ranks until
004:089 take no friends or helpers **from** their ranks:
004:090 hearts restraining them **from** fighting you or
004:090 withdraw **from** you but fight you not,
004:091 secure **from** you as well as that of their people:
004:091 if they withdraw not **from** you nor give you
004:097 to move yourselves away (**from** evil)?"
004:100 as a refugee **from** home for Allah and
004:103 but when ye are free **from** danger, set up
004:104 but you hope **from** Allah, what they have not.
004:108 They seek to hide themselves **from** the people but
004:108 but they cannot hide **from** Allah,
004:116 hath strayed far, far away (**from** the Right).
004:121 and **from** it they will find no way of escape.
004:129 but turn not away (**from** a woman) altogether,
004:130 for each of them **from** His all-reaching bounty:
004:141 And did we not guard you **from** the Believers?"
004:141 if ye do gain a victory **from** Allah, they say:
004:153 to cause a book to descend to them **from** heaven:
004:154 And We took **from** them a solemn Covenant.

FROM (continued)

004:160 and that they hindered many **from** Allah's Way;
004:167 have verily strayed far, far away **from** the Path.
004:167 and keep off (men) **from** the way of Allah,
004:170 to you in truth **from** Allah: believe in him:
004:171 and a Spirit proceeding **from** Him: so believe
004:174 there hath come to you a convincing proof **from** your Lord
004:175 to Mercy and Grace **from** Himself, and guide
005:006 or one of you cometh **from** the privy or ye have
005:008 and depart **from** justice.
005:011 but (Allah) held back their hands **from** you:
005:012 verily I will wipe out **from** you your evils,
005:012 a Covenant **from** the Children of Israel, and We
005:012 truly wandered **from** the path of rectitude."
005:013 they change the words **from** their (right) places
005:014 **From** those, too, who call themselves Christians,
005:015 There hath come to you **from** Allah a (new)
005:025 so separate us **from** this rebellious people!"
005:027 it was accepted **from** one, but not **from** the other.
005:033 or the cutting off of hands and feet **from** opposite sides,
005:033 or exile **from** the land:
005:038 and exemplary punishment **from** Allah, and Allah
005:041 They change the words **from** their (right) places;
005:048 diverging **from** the truth that hath come to thee.
005:049 beguile thee **from** any of that (teaching) which
005:052 or a decision **from** Him then will they regret of
005:054 you turn back **from** his Faith, soon will
005:054 O ye who believe! if any **from** among you turn
005:060 by the treatment it received **from** Allah?
005:060 and far more astray **from** the even Path!"
005:063 law forbid them **from** their (habit of) uttering sinful words
005:064 cometh to thee **from** Allah increaseth in most of them
005:066 There is **from** among them a party of the right course:
005:066 have eating **from** above them and **from** below their feet.
005:066 all the revelation that was sent to them **from** their Lord,
005:067 Allah will defend thee **from** men (who mean mischief).
005:067 the (Message) which hath been sent to thee **from** thy
005:068 that cometh to thee **from** thy Lord,
005:068 that has come to you **from** your Lord."
005:073 If they desist not **from** their word (of blasphemy),
005:075 they are deluded away **from** the truth!
005:077 and strayed themselves **from** the even Way.
005:091 you **from** the remembrance of Allah, and **from** prayer:
005:093 then again, guard themselves **from** evil and do good.
005:093 guard themselves **from** evil and believe,
005:103 or stallion-camels freed **from** work:
005:105 no hurt can come to you **from** those who stray.
005:106 or others **from** outside if ye are journeying through
005:107 nearest in kin **from** among those who claim
005:109 ye received (**from** men to your teaching)?"
005:110 the Children of Israel **from** (violence to) thee
005:112 a Table set (with viands) **from** heaven?"
005:114 a solemn festival and a Sign **from** Thee;
005:114 "O Allah our Lord! send us **from** heaven a table
005:119 will profit **from** their truth:
006:002 He it is Who created you **from** clay, and then
006:006 rain **from** the skies in abundance, and gave
006:016 if the penalty is averted **from** any, it is
006:037 a Sign sent down to him **from** his Lord?"
006:038 Nothing have We omitted **from** the Book, and they
006:043 When the suffering reached them **from** Us,
006:049 for that they ceased not **from** transgressing.
006:053 Allah hath favoured **from** amongst us?"

FROM (continued)

006:056 if I did, I would stray **from** the path, and be
006:057 a clear Sign **from** my Lord, but ye
006:063 Say: "Who is it that delivereth you **from** the dark
006:063 'If He only delivers us **from** these (dangers),
006:064 that delivereth you **from** these and all (other) distresses:
006:065 mutual vengeance-each **from** the other."
006:065 send calamities on you, **from** above and below,
006:068 turn away **from** them unless they turn
006:071 heels after receiving guidance **from** Allah?-
006:078 I am indeed free **from** your (guilt) of giving partners to
006:095 cause the dead to issue **from** the living.
006:095 He causeth the living to issue **from** the dead.
006:095 then how are ye deluded away **from** the truth?
006:096 the daybreak (**from** the dark):
006:098 produced you **from** a single soul:
006:099 It is He Who sendeth down rain **from** the skies:
006:099 **from** some We produce green (crops),
006:104 come to you, **from** your Lord proofs (to open your eyes):
006:105 "Thou hast learnt this (**from** somebody), and that We
006:106 and turn aside **from** those who
006:106 by inspiration **from** thy Lord: there is
006:113 and let them earn **from** it what they may.
006:114 that it hath been sent down **from** thy Lord in truth.
006:116 they will lead thee away **from** the Way of Allah.
006:117 who strayeth **from** His Way:
006:122 depths of darkness, **from** which he can never come out?
006:124 a Sign (**from** Allah), they say:" We shall
006:128 "Our Lord! we made profit **from** each other:
006:130 messengers **from** amongst you, setting forth
006:133 you up **from** the posterity of other people.
006:140 Lost are those who slay their children **from** folly,
006:147 but **from** people in guilt never will
006:151 Allah hath (really) prohibited you **from**":
006:153 they will scatter you about **from** His (great) path:
006:157 a Clear (Sign) **from** your Lord,-and a
006:157 those who turn away **from** Our Signs,
007:003 given unto you **from** your Lord, and follow
007:012 thee **from** prostrating when I commanded thee?"
007:012 thou didst create me **from** fire and him **from** clay."
007:013 (Allah) said: "Get thee down **from** it: it is not
007:017 **from** their right and their left:
007:017 "Then will I assault them **from** before them and behind
007:018 (Allah) said: "Get out **from** this, disgraced
007:020 their shame that was hidden **from** them (before):
007:025 but **from** it shall ye be taken out (at last)."
007:027 see you **from** a position where ye cannot see them:
007:035 come to you messengers **from** amongst you, rehearsing
007:037 must reach them **from** the Book (of Decrees):
007:043 And We shall remove **from** their hearts any rancour;
007:045 "Those who would hinder (men) **from** the path of Allah
007:048 they will know **from** their marks, saying:
007:053 Then should we behave differently **from** our behavior in
007:058 **From** the land that is clean and good, by the
007:058 but **from** the land that is bad, springs up
007:061 on the contrary I am a messenger **from** the Lord and
007:062 and I know **from** Allah something that ye know not.
007:063 come to you a reminder **from** your Lord, through
007:067 but (I am) a messenger **from** the Lord and Cherisher of
007:069 the benefits (ye have received) **from** Allah: that
007:069 to you a message **from** your Lord through a man of your
007:071 without authority **from** Allah?
007:071 have already come upon you **from** your Lord:

FROM (continued)

007:073　a clear (Sign) **from** your Lord!
007:074　the benefits (ye have received) **from** Allah,
007:074　and refrain **from** evil and mischief on the earth."
007:075　is a messenger **from** his Lord?"
007:085　a clear (Sign) **from** your Lord!
007:085　nor withhold **from** the people the things
007:086　breathing threats, hindering **from** the path of Allah
007:096　blessings **from** heaven and earth; but they
007:099　can feel secure **from** the Plan of Allah, except
007:104　I am a messenger **from** the Lord of the worlds,-
007:105　unto you (people), **from** your Lord with a clear (Sign):
007:128　"Pray for help **from** Allah," and (wait)
007:134　if thou wilt remove the Plague **from** us,
007:135　remove the Plague **from** them according to a fixed term
007:136　So We exacted retribution **from** them: We drowned
007:136　and failed to take warning **from** them.
007:141　in that was a momentous trial **from** your Lord.
007:141　We rescued you **from** Pharaoh's people, who afflicted
007:146　them will I turn away **from** My Signs:
007:146　and failed to take warning **from** them.
007:152　with wrath **from** their Lord, and with
007:157　them **from** what is bad (and impure):
007:157　and **from** the yokes that are upon them.
007:157　He releases them **from** their heavy burdens and
007:162　so We sent on them a plague **from** heaven.
007:162　changed the word **from** that which had
007:169　of the Book taken **from** them, that they
007:172　**from** their loins-their descendants,
007:172　When thy Lord drew forth **from** the children of Adam-
007:178　whom He rejects **from** His guidance.
007:186　To such as Allah rejects **from** His guidance,
007:189　created you **from** a single person, and made
007:196　Who revealed the Book, (**from** time to time), and He
007:199　but turn away **from** the ignorant.
007:200　If a suggestion **from** Satan assail thy (mind),
007:201　when a thought of evil **from** Satan assaults them,
007:203　is revealed to me **from** my Lord:
007:203　This is (nothing but) lights **from** your Lord,
008:010　(in any case) there is no help except **from** Allah:
008:011　to give you calm as **from** Himself,
008:011　to remove **from** you the stain of Satan,
008:011　and He caused rain to descend on you **from** heaven,
008:017　confer on the Believers a gracious benefit **from** Himself:
008:019　if ye desist (**from** wrong), it will
008:020　and turn not away **from** him when ye hear (him speak).
008:029　remove **from** you (all) evil deeds and forgive you:
008:032　rain down on us a shower of stones **from** the sky,
008:032　"O Allah! if this is indeed the truth **from** Thee,
008:034　when they keep out (men) **from** the Sacred Mosque-
008:036　to hinder (men) **from** the path of Allah,
008:037　the impure **from** the pure.
008:038　if (now) they desist (**from** Unbelief),
008:047　And be not like those who started **from** their homes
008:047　hinder (men) **from** the path of Allah:
008:058　If thou fearest treachery **from** any group,
008:068　a previous ordainment **from** Allah, a severe
008:070　than what has been taken **from** you, and He
009:001　A (declaration) of immunity **from** Allah and His
009:003　And an announcement **from** Allah and His Messenger,
009:008　but their hearts are averse **from** you;
009:008　With (fair words **from**) their mouths they please
009:009　and (many) have they hindered **from** His Way:

FROM (continued)

009:021　of a Mercy **from** Himself, of His good pleasure.
009:029　the Religion of Truth, **from** among the People of the Book,
009:030　That is a saying **from** their mouths; (in this) they but
009:030　how they are deluded away **from** the Truth!
009:031　(Far is He) **from** having the partners they associate
009:031　of men and hinder (them) **from** the Way of Allah.
009:034　no exemption **from** fighting with their goods
009:044　either that Allah will send His punishment **from** Him
009:052　not **from** you will it be accepted:
009:053　and turned back (**from** their Covenant),
009:076　averse (**from** its fulfillment).
009:076　accept repentance **from** His votaries and receives
009:104　was laid **from** the first day on piety;
009:108　is never free **from** suspicion and shakiness
009:110　he dissociated himself **from** him: for Abraham was most
009:114　of them had nearly swerved (**from** duty), but He
009:117　no fleeing **from** Allah (and no refuge)
009:118　or gain any gain **from** an enemy:
009:120　if a contingent **from** every expedition go forth to devote
009:122　their hearts (**from** the light); for they
009:127　a Messenger **from** amongst yourselves:
009:128　to a man **from** among themselves?
010:002　been for a Word that went forth before **from** thy Lord,
010:019　sent down to him **from** his Lord?"
010:020　"If Thou dost deliver us **from** this, we shall truly show
010:022　and the waves come to them **from** all sides, and they
010:022　as the rain which We send down **from** the skies:
010:024　no defender will the have **from** (the wrath of) Allah:
010:027　as it were, with pieces **from** the depth of the darkness
010:027　(in life) **from** the sky and **from** the earth?
010:031　brings out the living **from** the dead and the
010:031　and the dead **from** the living?
010:031　apart **from** the Truth, what (remains) but error?
010:032　then how are ye deluded away (**from** the truth)?"
010:034　wherein there is no doubt-**from** the Lord of the Worlds.
010:037　Ye are free **from** responsibility for what I do,
010:041　to you an admonition **from** your Lord and a
010:057　be reciting **from** the Qur'an,-and whatever
010:061　Nor is hidden **from** thy Lord (so much as)
010:061　my reward is only due **from** Allah, and I
010:072　When the Truth did come to them **from** Us, they said:
010:076　to turn us away **from** the ways We found
010:078　delivers us by thy Mercy **from** those who reject (Thee)."
010:086　our Lord they mislead (men) **from** Thy Path.
010:088　the Book **from** before thee: the Truth
010:094　the Truth hath indeed come to thee **from** thy Lord:
010:094　We remove **from** them the Chastisement of Ignominy
010:098　reached you **from** your Lord!
010:108　in detail, **from** One Who is Wise and Well-
011:001　unto you **from** Him to warn and to bring glad tidings:
011:002　that they may lie hid **from** Him!
011:005　nothing will turn it away **from** them, and they will be
011:008　and then withdraw it **from** him, behold! he is in despair
011:009　If We give man a taste of mercy **from** Ourselves,
011:009　"All evil has departed **from** me:" behold! he
011:010　for it is the Truth **from** thy Lord:
011:017　those who accept a Clear (Sign) **from** their Lord,
011:017　and followed by a witness **from** Him and before
011:017　"Those who would hinder (men) **from** the path of
011:019　but that the Mercy hath been obscured **from** your sight?
011:028　and that He hath sent Mercy unto me **from** Him,
011:028　see ye if (it be that) I have a Clear Sign **from** my Lord

FROM (continued)

011:029 my reward is **from** none but Allah:
011:042 who had separated himself (**from** the rest):
011:043 nothing can save, **from** the Command of Allah,
011:043 to some mountain: it will save me **from** the water."
011:047 with Thee, **from** asking Thee for that of which
011:048 a grievous Chastisement reach them **from** Us."
011:048 the Peoples (who will spring) **from** those with thee:
011:048 come down (**from** the Ark) with Peace **from** Us,
011:051 My reward is **from** none but Him Who created Me:
011:054 that I am free **from** the sin of ascribing, to Him,
011:058 with him, by (special) Grace **from** Us:
011:058 We saved them **from** a severe chastisement.
011:061 It is He Who hath produced you **from** the earth
011:063 sent mercy unto me **from** Himself,-who then can help
011:063 If I have a Clear (Sign) **from** my Lord and He have sent
011:066 and **from** the Ignominy of that Day.
011:066 with him, by (special) Grace **from** Us-
011:074 When fear had passed **from** (the mind of) Abraham
011:081 we are Messengers **from** thy Lord!
011:083 ever far **from** those who do wrong!
011:083 Marked **from** thy Lord; nor are they ever far
011:085 nor withhold **from** the people the things that are their
011:088 I have a Clear (Sign) **from** my Lord, and He
011:088 (pure and) good as **from** Himself?
011:088 (in my task) can only come **from** Allah.
011:089 the people of Lut far off **from** you!
011:089 "And O my people! let not my dissent (**from** you) cause
011:094 by (special) Mercy **from** Us:
011:110 had gone forth before **from** thy Lord the matter
011:112 and transgress not (**from** the Path):
011:116 who prohibited men **from** mischief in the earth
011:116 them whom We saved (**from** harm)?
012:024 that We might turn away **from** him (all) evil
012:025 and she tore his shirt **from** the back:
012:026 she that sought to seduce me-**from** my (true) self."
012:027 is torn **from** the back, then is she the liar,
012:032 I did seek to seduce him **from** his (true) self but he did
012:033 their snare **from** me, I should feel inclined towards
012:034 (in his prayer) and turned away **from** him their snare:
012:040 Whatever ye worship apart **from** Him is nothing
012:041 and the birds will eat **from** off his head.
012:041 as for the other, he will hang **from** the cross,
012:060 ye shall have no measure (of corn) **from** me,
012:061 win him **from** his father: indeed we shall do it."
012:080 an oath **from** you in Allah's name, and how
012:084 And he turned away **from** them, and said: "How great
012:086 and I know **from** Allah that which ye know not.
012:096 'I know **from** Allah that which ye know not?'
012:105 Yet they turn (their faces) away **from** them!
012:107 Do they then feel secure **from** the coming against
012:109 did inspire,-(men) **from** the people of the towns.
012:110 Our punishment **from** those who are in sin.
013:001 unto thee **from** thy Lord is the Truth; but most
013:007 a Sign sent down to him **from** his Lord?"
013:017 He sends down water **from** the skies, and the
013:017 Even so, **from** that (ore) which
013:019 unto thee **from** thy Lord is the Truth, like one
013:023 enter unto them **from** every gate (with the salutation)
013:027 a Sign sent down to him **from** his Lord?"
013:033 but they are kept back (thereby) **from** the Path.
013:041 the land **from** its outlying borders?
014:003 who hinder (men) **from** the Path of Allah and seek

FROM (continued)

014:005 thy people **from** the depths of darkness into light,
014:006 to you when He delivered you **from** the people
014:006 a tremendous trial **from** your Lord."
014:010 Ye wish to turn us away **from** what our fathers
014:017 death will come to him **from** every quarter, yet will he
014:018 that is the straying far, far (**from** the goal).
014:026 it is torn up by the root **from** the surface of the earth:
014:030 to mislead (men) **from** the Path!
014:032 and sendeth down rain **from** the skies, and with it
014:035 sons **from** worshipping idols.
014:038 for nothing whatever is hidden **from** Allah,
015:009 assuredly guard it (**from** corruption).
015:014 a gate **from** heaven, and they were to continue
015:017 We have guarded them **from** every accursed Satan.
015:022 then cause the rain to descend **from** the shy,
015:026 We created man **from** sounding clay, **from** mud molded
015:027 had created before, **from** the fire of a scorching wind.
015:028 "I am bout to create man, **from** sounding clay,
015:028 **from** mud molded into shape;
015:033 **from** mud moulded into shape."
015:033 Whom Thou didst create **from** sounding clay,
015:034 "Then get thee out **from** here; for thou art rejected,
015:047 And We shall remove **from** their hearts any lurking
015:059 them we are certainly (charged) to save (**from** Harm),-
015:079 So We exacted retribution **from** them.
015:081 but they persisted in turning away **from** them.
015:094 and turn away **from** those who join false gods with Allah.
016:004 He has created man **from** a sperm-drop and behold
016:005 **from** them ye derive warmth, and numerous benefits,
016:010 It is He Who sends down rain **from** the sky:
016:010 **from** it ye drink, and out (grows) the vegetation
016:026 but Allah took their structures **from** their foundations,
016:026 and the roof fell down on them **from** above;
016:026 Wrath seized them **from** directions they did not perceive.
016:045 seize them **from** directions they little perceive?
016:048 turn round, **from** the right and the left,
016:053 And ye have no good thing but is **from** Allah:
016:054 Yet, when He removes the distress **from** you, behold!
016:059 With shame does he hide himself **from** his people,
016:065 And Allah sends down rain **from** the skies,
016:066 **From** what is within their bodies, between excretions
016:067 And **from** the fruit of the date-palm and the vine,
016:069 there issues **from** within their bodies a drink of varying
016:075 favours **from** Ourselves, and he spends thereof
016:078 It is He Who brought you forth **from** the wombs of your
016:081 coats of mail to protect you **from** your (mutual) violence.
016:081 He made you garments to protect you **from** heat,
016:084 then will no excuse be accepted **from** Unbelievers,
016:084 On the day We shall raise **from** all Peoples a Witness:
016:088 (men) **from** the Path of Allah-for them will We
016:089 On the day We shall raise **from** all peoples a witness
016:089 a witness against them, **from** amongst themselves:
016:094 (men) **from** the Path of Allah, and a
016:098 seek Allah's protection **from** Satan the Rejected one.
016:102 the revelation **from** thy Lord in Truth, in order
016:106 on them is Wrath **from** Allah, and theirs will be a
016:112 abundantly supplied with sustenance **from** every place:
016:112 (closing on it) like a garment (**from** every side),
016:113 came to them a Messenger **from** among themselves,
016:125 who have strayed **from** His Path, and who
016:127 for the patience is but with the help **from** Allah;
017:001 for a Journey by night **from** the Sacred Mosque

FROM (continued)

017:003 O ye that are sprung **from** those whom We
017:012 Bounty **from** your Lord and that ye may know
017:028 Mercy **from** thy Lord which thou dost expect,
017:028 thou hast to turn away **from** them in pursuit of the
017:041 increases their flight (**from** the Truth)!
017:046 they turn on their backs, fleeing (**from** the Truth).
017:056 to remove your troubles **from** you nor to change them."
017:059' And We refrain **from** sending the Signs,
017:059 of frightening (and warning **from** evil).
017:061 whom Thou didst create **from** clay?"
017:067 ye turn away (**from** Him). Most ungrateful is man!
017:072 and most astray **from** the Path.
017:073 away **from** that which We had revealed unto thee,
017:080 and grant me **from** Thee an authority to aid (me)."
017:087 Except for Mercy **from** thy Lord; for His
017:090 to gush forth for us **from** the earth,
017:094 What kept men back **from** Belief when Guidance
017:095 sent them down **from** the heavens an angel
017:103 So he resolved to remove them **from** the face of the
017:106 which We have divided (into parts **from** time to time),
017:111 to protect Him **from** humiliation: yea, magnify
018:002 of a terrible Punishment **from** Him, and that
018:005 grievous thing that issues **from** their mouths as a saying.
018:010 bestow on us Mercy **from** Thyself, and dispose
018:016 "When ye turn away **from** them and the things
018:017 turning away **from** them to the left, while they
018:017 declining to the right **from** their Cave, and when it set,
018:018 turned back **from** them in flight, and wouldst
018:019 We raised them up (**from** sleep), that they
018:029 Say, "The Truth is **from** your Lord"
018:040 garden thunderbolts (by way of reckoning) **from** heaven,
018:044 There, the (only) protection comes **from** Allah,
018:045 We send down **from** the skies:
018:055 And what is there to keep back men **from** believing,
018:055 nor **from** praying for forgiveness **from** their Lord but that
018:057 of the Signs of his Lord but turns away **from** them,
018:065 On whom We had bestowed Mercy **from** Ourselves
018:065 whom We had taught knowledge **from** Our own presence.
018:076 received (full) excuse **from** my side."
018:082 a mercy (and favour) **from** thy Lord.
018:098 He said: "This is a mercy **from** my Lord: but when
018:101 a veil **from** Remembrance of Me, and who
018:108 no change will they wish for **from** them.
019:005 so give me an heir as **from** Thyself,-
019:008 and I have grown quite decrepit **from** old age?"
019:011 So Zakriya came out to his people **from** his chamber:
019:013 And pity (for all creatures) as **from** Us, and purity:
019:016 when she withdrew **from** her family to a place
019:017 She placed a screen (to screen herself) **from** them:
019:018 She said: "I seek refuge **from** thee to (Allah)
019:019 He said: "Nay, I am only a messenger **from** thy Lord,
019:021 unto men and a Mercy **from** Us':
019:024 But (a voice) cried to her **from** beneath the (palm-tree):
019:045 I fear lest a Chastisement afflict thee **from** (Allah)
019:046 now get away **from** me for a good long while!"
019:046 "Art thou shrinking **from** my gods, O Abraham?
019:048 "And I will turn away **from** you (all) and **from** those
019:049 When he had turned away **from** them and **from** those
019:052 And We called him **from** the right side
019:069 drag out **from** every sect all those who were worst in
019:087 permission (or promise) **from** (Allah) Most Gracious.
020:004 A revelation **from** Him Who created the earth

FROM (continued)

020:027 "And remove the impediment **from** my speech.
020:029 "And give me a Minister **from** my family,
020:039 but I endued thee with love **from** Me:
020:040 but We saved thee **from** trouble, and We
020:047 indeed, have we come **from** thy Lord!
020:053 and has sent down water **from** the sky."
020:053 of plants each separate **from** the others.
020:055 and **from** it shall We bring you out once again.
020:055 **From** the (earth) did We create you, and into
020:063 their object is to drive you out **from** your land
020:076 who purify themselves (**from** evil).
020:080 We delivered you **from** your enemy, and We
020:086 that Wrath should descend **from** your Lord on you,
020:093 "**From** following me? Didst thou them disobey my
020:096 a handful (of dust) **from** the footprint of the Messenger,
020:099 for We have sent thee a reminder **from** Us.
020:119 "Nor to suffer **from** thirst, nor **from** the sun's heat."
020:121 for their covering, leaves **from** the Garden:
020:123 both of you,-all together, **from** the Garden, with enmity
020:123 but if, as is sure, there comes to you guidance **from** Me,
020:124 "But whosoever turns away **from** My Message,
020:129 that went forth before **from** thy Lord,
020:133 a Sign **from** His Lord?"
021:002 a renewed Message **from** their Lord, but they
021:012 they (tried to) flee **from** it.
021:017 it **from** the things nearest to Us, if We
021:021 gods **from** the earth who can raise (the dead)?
021:030 We made **from** water every living thing.
021:032 Yet do they turn away **from** the Signs
021:039 to ward off the Fire **from** their faces,
021:039 not yet **from** their backs, and (when)
021:042 and by day **from** (the Wrath of) The Most Gracious?"
021:042 Yet they turn away **from** the remembrance
021:043 nor can they be defended **from** Us.
021:043 Or have they gods that can guard them **from** Us?
021:044 the land (in their control) **from** its outlying
021:056 He Who created them (**from** nothing):
021:074 and We saved him **from** the town which
021:076 and his family **from** great distress.
021:080 to guard you **from** each other's violence:
021:084 as a Grace **from** Ourselves, and a thing
021:088 and delivered him **from** distress:
021:091 We breathed into her **from** Our spirit,
021:093 cut off their affair (of unity), **from** another:
021:096 and they swiftly swarm **from** every hill.
021:101 Those for whom the Good (Record) **from** Us
022:009 in order to lead (men) astray **from** the Path of Allah:
022:012 that is straying far indeed (**from** the Way)!
022:022 they wish to get away therefrom, **from** anguish,
022:025 and the visitor **from** the country-and any
022:025 and would keep back (men) **from** the Way of Allah,
022:025 and **from** the Sacred Mosque, which We have made
022:031 he is as if he had fallen **from** heaven and been
022:032 come truly **from** piety of heart.
022:034 He gave them **from** animals (fit for food).
022:036 for you as among the Signs **from** Allah:
022:038 Verily Allah will defend (**from** ill) those who believe:
022:040 expelled **from** their homes in defiance of right,-
022:053 in a schism far (**from** the Truth):
022:054 the (Qur'an) is the Truth **from** the Lord, and that
022:063 sends down rain **from** the sky, and forthwith
022:065 He withholds the sky **from** falling on the earth

FROM (continued)

022:073   they would have no power to release it **from** the fly:

022:073   And if the fly should snatch away anything **from** them,

022:075   Allah chooses Messengers **from** angels and **from** men:

023:006   they are free **from** blame,

023:012   Man We did create **from** a quintessence (of clay);

023:018   And We send down water **from** the sky according

023:021   **from** within their bodies We produce (milk)

023:028   Who has saved us **from** the people who do wrong."

023:032   We sent to them a messenger **from** among themselves,

023:071   but they turn away **from** their admonition.

023:074   in the Hereafter are deviating **from** that Way.

023:091   Glory to Allah (He is free) **from** the (sort of)

023:097   with Thee **from** the suggestions of the Satans.

024:008   But it would avert the punishment **from** the wife,

024:034   an illustration **from** (the story of) people who

024:035   lit **from** a blessed Tree, an Olive, neither of

024:037   nor **from** regular Prayer, nor **from** paying zakat

024:037   nor sale can divert **from** the Remembrance of Allah,

024:043   then wilt thou see rain issue forth **from** their midst.

024:043   And He sends down **from** the sky mountain masses

024:043   and He turns it away **from** whom He pleases.

024:045   And Allah has created every animal **from** water:

024:061   a greeting of blessing and purity as **from** Allah.

025:012   When it sees them **from** a place far off, they will

025:017   or did they stray **from** the Path themselves?"

025:029   "He did lead me astray **from** the Message

025:042   indeed would well-nigh have misled us **from** our gods,

025:044   they are farther astray **from** the way.

025:048   and We send down pure water **from** the sky,-

025:054   It is He Who has created man **from** water:

025:065   avert **from** us the Wrath of Hell, for its

026:004   We could send down to them **from** the sky a Sign,

026:005   a newly-revealed message **from** the Most Gracious,

026:021   "So I fled **from** you (all) when I feared you;

026:026   of your fathers **from** the beginning!"

026:057   So We expelled them **from** gardens, springs,

026:109   my reward is only **from** the Lord of the Worlds:

026:127   my reward is only **from** the Lord of the Worlds.

026:145   my reward is only **from** the Lord of the Worlds.

026:164   my reward is only **from** the Lord of the Worlds.

026:169   and my family **from** such things as they do!"

026:180   my reward is only **from** the Lord of the Worlds.

026:192   Verily this is a Revelation **from** the Lord of the Worlds:

026:212   Indeed they are banished **from** hearing it.

026:216   "I am free (of responsibility) **from** what ye do!"

027:006   thou receivest the Qur'an **from** One All-Wise,

027:007   soon will I bring you **from** there some information,

027:016   this is indeed Grace manifest (**from** Allah)."

027:022   and I have come to thee **from** Saba with tidings true.

027:024   and has kept them away **from** the Path,-so they

027:028   then draw back **from** them, and (wait to)

027:030   It is **from** Solomon, and is (as follows):

027:037   we shall expel them **from** there in disgrace,

027:039   thou rise **from** thy Council:

027:043   And he diverted her **from** the worship

027:047   "Ill omen do we augur **from** thee and those that are

027:056   "Drive out the followers of Lut **from** your city:

027:060   and Who sends you down rain **from** the sky?

027:060   Nay, they are a people who swerve **from** justice.

027:064   you sustenance **from** heaven and earth?

027:067   shall we really be raised (**from** the dead)?

027:081   (to prevent them) **from** straying:

FROM (continued)

027:082   We shall bring forth **from** the earth a beast

027:083   gather together **from** every people a troop of those

027:089   be secure **from** terror that Day.

028:006   what they were dreading **from** them.

028:008   picked him up (**from** the river):

028:011   watched him **from** a distance and they perceived not.

028:020   came a man, running, **from** the furthest end of the City.

028:021   save me **from** people given to wrong-doing."

028:025   (well) hast thou escaped **from** unjust people."

028:027   ten years, it will be (grace) **from** thee.

028:029   I hope to bring you **from** there some information,

028:030   he was called **from** the right bank of the valley,

028:030   of the valley, **from** a tree in hallowed ground:

028:032   Those are two credentials **from** thy Lord to Pharaoh

028:037   with guidance **from** Him and whose End will be best

028:046   as a Mercy **from** thy Lord, to give

028:048   to them **from** Ourselves, they say, "Why are

028:049   Say: "Then bring ye a Book **from** Allah, which is

028:050   devoid of guidance **from** Allah?

028:053   for it is the Truth **from** our Lord:

028:053   (bowing to Allah's Will) **from** before this."

028:057   a provision **from** Ourselves?

028:057   We should be snatched away **from** our land."

028:063   we free ourselves (**from** them) to you.

028:075   And **from** each people shall We draw a witness,

028:086   except as a Mercy **from** thy Lord: therefore lend

028:087   Let no one turn you away **from** Allah's revelations after

029:003   who are true **from** those who are false.

029:006   for Allah is free of all needs **from** all creation.

029:007   righteous deeds,-**from** them shall We blot out

029:010   (to thee) **from** thy lord, they are sure to say,

029:017   then seek ye sustenance **from** Allah, serve Him,

029:024   But Allah did save him **from** the Fire.

029:034   a Punishment **from** heaven, because they

029:038   and kept them back **from** the Path, though they were

029:038   will appear to you **from** (the traces) of their buildings

029:045   for Prayer restrains **from** shameful and evil

029:050   sent down to him **from** his Lord?"

029:055   shall cover them **from** above them and **from** below them,

029:061   How are they then deluded away (**from** the truth)?

029:063   that sends down rain **from** the sky, and gives

029:067   men are being snatched **away from** all around them?

030:006   Never does Allah fall **from** His promise: but most

030:019   It is He Who brings out the living **from** the dead,

030:019   and thus shall ye be brought out (**from** the dead).

030:019   and brings out the dead **from** the living,

030:020   that He created you **from** dust; and then,-behold,

030:021   that He created for you mates **from** among yourselves,

030:024   and He sends down rain **from** the sky and with

030:025   by a single call, **from** the earth, behold, ye

030:028   He does propound to you a similitude **from** yourselves:

030:033   but when He gives them a taste of Mercy **from** Himself,

030:041   in order that they may turn back (**from** Evil).

030:043   before there come **from** Allah the Day which there is no

030:044   Those who reject Faith will suffer **from** that rejection:

030:048   seest rain-drops issue **from** the midst thereof:

030:051   And if We (but) send a Wind **from** which they see

030:053   Nor canst thou lead back the blind **from** their straying:

031:005   These are on (true) guidance **from** their Lord;

031:006   to mislead (men) **from** the Path of Allah and throw

031:010   We send down rain **from** the sky, and produce

032:002   in which there is no doubt,-**from** the Lord of the Worlds.

FROM (continued)

032:003 Nay, it is the Truth **from** thy Lord, that thou
032:005 He directs the affairs **from** the heavens to the
032:007 the creation of man **from** clay,
032:008 And made his progeny **from** a quintessence
032:013 but the Word **from** Me will come true, "I Will
032:022 Verily **from** those who transgress
032:024 And We appointed, **from** among them, Leaders, giving
032:030 So turn away **from** them, and wait: they too
033:002 to thee by inspiration **from** thy Lord: for Allah
033:007 and **from** thee: **from** Noah, Abraham, Moses,
033:007 We took **from** them a solemn Covenant:
033:007 And remember We took **from** the Prophets their
033:010 they came on you **from** above you and **from** below you,
033:014 to them **from** the sides of the (City), and they
033:016 if ye are running away **from** death or slaughter;
033:017 that can screen you **from** Allah if it be His wish to give
033:019 like one who faints **from** death:
033:020 and seeking news about you (**from** a safe distance);
033:026 down **from** their strongholds and cast terror
033:033 Allah only wishes to remove all abomination **from** you,
033:043 that He may bring you out **from** the depths
033:047 shall have **from** Allah a very great Bounty.
033:053 ask them **from** before a screen: that makes
034:002 all that comes down **from** the sky and all
034:003 **from** Whom is not hidden the least little atom
034:006 to thee **from** thy Lord-that is the Truth, and that
034:010 We bestowed Grace aforetime on David **from** Us:
034:012 and if any of them turned aside **from** Our command,
034:016 But they turned away (**from** Allah), and We
034:016 the flood (released) **from** the Dams, and We
034:021 in the Hereafter **from** him who is in doubt concerning it:
034:023 when terror is removed **from** their hearts
034:024 gives you sustenance, **from** the heavens and the earth?"
034:032 who kept you back **from** Guidance after it reached you?
034:043 you **from** the (worship) which your fathers practiced."
034:047 my reward is only due **from** Allah:"
034:051 and they will be seized **from** a position (quite) near.
034:052 could they receive (Faith) **from** a position (so) far off,-
034:053 with regard to the Unseen **from** a position far off?
035:002 none can grant, apart **from** Him:
035:003 you Sustenance **from** heaven or earth?
035:011 then **from** a sperm-drop; then He made you in pairs.
035:011 nor is a part cut off **from** his life, but is in a Book
035:011 And Allah did create you **from** dust;
035:012 Yet **from** each (kind of water) do ye eat flesh fresh and
035:027 sends down rain **from** the sky?
035:034 Who has removed **from** us (all) sorrow:
035:040 a Book **from** which they (can derive) clear (evidence)?-
036:018 an evil omen **from** you: if ye desist not,
036:020 came running, **from** the farthest part of the City, a man,
036:028 after him, any hosts **from** heaven,
036:044 Except by way of Mercy **from** Us, and by
036:046 Not a Sign comes to them **from** among the Signs of their
036:051 when behold! **from** the sepulchers (men) will
036:052 Who hath raised us up **from** our beds of repose?...
036:058 "Peace!"-a Word (of salutation) **from** a Lord Most
036:073 And they have (other) profits **from** them (besides),
036:077 not man see that it is We Who created him **from** sperm?
037:008 and they are cast away **from** every side,
037:028 to come to us **from** the right hand."
037:045 be passed to them a Cup **from** a clear-flowing fountain,
037:047 Free **from** headiness; nor will they suffer intoxication

FROM (continued)

037:076 We delivered him and his people **from** the Great Calamity.
037:083 Verily **from** his party was Abraham.
037:090 So they turned away **from** him, and departed.
037:115 and their people **from** (their) Great distress.
037:140 away (like a slave **from** captivity) to the ship (fully) laden,
037:159 (He is free) **from** the things they ascribe (to Him)!
037:168 a message **from** those of old,
037:174 So turn thou away **from** them for a little while,
037:178 So turn thou away **from** them for a little while,
037:180 and Power! (He is free) **from** what they ascribe (to Him)!
038:004 that a Warner has come to them **from** among themselves!
038:026 for those who wander astray **from** the Path
038:026 for it will mislead thee **from** the Path of Allah:
038:028 the same as those who turn aside **from** the right?
038:043 as a Grace **from** Us, and a thing for commemoration,
038:068 "**From** which ye do turn away!
038:071 "I am about to create man **from** clay:
038:075 what prevents thee **from** prostrating thyself to one whom
038:076 Thou createdst me **from** fire, and him
038:076 and him Thou createdst **from** clay."
038:077 "Then get thee out **from** here: for thou art rejected,
039:001 The revelation of this Book is **from** Allah,
039:006 then how are ye turned away (**from** your true Lord)?
039:006 He created you (all) **from** a single person:
039:007 but He liketh not ingratitude **from** His servants:
039:008 thus misleading others **from** Allah's Path.
039:008 He bestoweth a favour upon him as **from** Himself,
039:021 Seest thou not that Allah sends down rain **from** the sky,
039:022 so that he has received light **from** Allah,
039:023 Allah has revealed (**from** time to time) the most
039:025 came to them **from** directions they did not perceive.
039:035 So that Allah will remit **from** them (even) the
039:042 He keeps back (**from** returning to life), but the
039:047 offer it for ransom **from** the pain of the Chastisement
039:047 but something will confront them **from** Allah,
039:049 but when We bestow a favour upon him as **from** Us,
039:055 the best that which was revealed to you **from** your Lord,
039:071 "Did not messengers come to you **from** among yourselves,
040:002 The revelation of this Book is **from** Allah, Exalted in
040:007 and preserve them **from** the Chastisement of the
040:009 "And preserve them **from** (all) ills;
040:009 and any whom Thou dost preserve **from** ills that Day,-
040:013 and sendeth down Sustenance for you **from** the sky:
040:016 not a single thing concerning them is hidden **from** Allah.
040:025 Now, when he brought them the Truth, **from** Us,
040:027 (for protection) **from** every arrogant one who
040:028 A Believer, a man **from** among the people of Pharaoh,
040:028 with Clear (Signs) **from** your Lord?
040:029 but who will help us **from** the Punishment of Allah,
040:033 no defender shall ye have **from** Allah:
040:037 and he was hindered **from** the Path; and the
040:045 Then Allah saved him **from** (every) evil that they
040:047 take (on yourselves) **from** us some share of the Fire?"
040:062 then how ye are deluded away **from** the Truth!
040:066 that the Clear Sings have come to me **from** my Lord;
040:067 It is He Who has created you **from** dust,
040:067 then **from** a sperm-drop, then **from** leech-like clot;
040:069 How are they turned away (**from** Reality)?-
040:085 with His servants (**from** the most ancient times).
041:002 A revelation **from** The Most Gracious, Most Merciful;-
041:005 (concealed) **from** that to which thou dost invite us,
041:014 messengers came to them, **from** before them and behind

FROM (continued)

041:030 the angels descend on them (**from** time to time):
041:032 "A hospitable gift **from** One Oft-Forgiving,
041:040 the Truth in Our Signs are not hidden **from** Us.
041:041 to them (are not hidden **from** Us).
041:042 No falsehood can approach it **from** before or behind it:
041:044 called **from** a place far distant!"
041:045 not been for a Word that went forth before **from** thy Lord,
041:050 When We give him a taste of some mercy **from** Us,
041:052 is (really) **from** Allah, and yet do ye reject it?
041:052 who is in schism far (**from** any purpose)?"
042:005 heavens are almost rent asunder **from** above them
042:011 pairs **from** among yourselves, and pairs
042:014 forth before **from** thy Lord, (tending) to a
042:025 He is the One that accepts repentance **from** His Servants
042:040 and makes reconciliation, his reward is due **from** Allah:
042:048 of Mercy **from** Us, he doth exult thereat,
042:051 by inspiration, or **from** behind a veil, or by
043:005 Shall We then turn away Reminder **from** you altogether,
043:011 even so will ye be raised (**from** the dead);-
043:011 That sends down (**from** time to time) rain **from** the sky
043:025 So We exacted retribution **from** them:
043:032 so that some may command work **from** others.
043:036 If anyone withdraws himself **from** remembrance of the
043:037 Such (Satans) really hinder them **from** the Path,
043:041 We shall be sure to exact retribution **from** them,
043:050 But when We removed the Chastisement **from** them,
043:055 We exacted retribution **from** them, and We
043:060 We could make angels **from** amongst you,
043:065 But sects **from** among themselves fell into
043:065 **from** the Chastisement of a Grievous Day!
043:073 of fruit, **from** which ye shall eat.
043:082 He is free **from** the things they attribute (to Him)!
043:087 how then are they deluded away (**from** the Truth)?
043:089 But turn away **from** them, and say "Peace!"
044:005 By command, **from** Us.
044:006 As a Mercy **from** thy Lord: for He
044:012 remove the Chastisement **from** us for We
044:014 Yet they turn away **from** him and say: "Tutored
044:021 at least keep yourselves away **from** me."
044:030 of Israel **from** humiliating Punishment,
044:056 and He will preserve them **from** the Chastisement
044:057 As a Bounty **from** thy Lord!
045:002 The revelation of the Book is **from** Allah the Exalted
045:005 down Sustenance **from** the sky, and revives
045:013 And He has subjected to you, as **from** Him, all that is
045:035 (**From**) that Day, therefore, they shall not be taken out
046:002 The revelation of the Book is **from** Allah the Exalted
046:003 turn away **from** that whereof they are warned.
046:010 and a witness **from** among the Children of Israel
046:010 "See ye? If (this reaching) be **from** Allah, and ye reject
046:016 Such are they **from** whom We shall accept the best
046:022 to turn us aside **from** our gods?
046:028 to them **from** those whom they worshipped as gods,
046:031 and deliver you **from** a Chastisement Grievous.
047:001 Those who reject Allah and hinder (men) **from** the Path
047:002 for it is the Truth **from** their Lord,-
047:002 **from** them their ills and improve their condition.
047:003 those who believe follow the Truth **from** their Lord:
047:004 exacted retribution **from** them (Himself); but He
047:014 Is then one who is on a clear (Path) **from** his Lord,
047:015 of fruits, and forgiveness **from** their Lord,
047:016 till when they go out **from** thee,

FROM (continued)

047:017 on them their Piety and Restraint (**from** evil).
047:032 who disbelieve, hinder (men) **from** the Path of Allah,
047:034 who disbelieve, and hinder (men) **from** the Path of Allah,
047:038 If ye turn back (**from** the Path),
048:005 and remove their sins **from** them; and that
048:020 and He has restrained the hands of men **from** you;
048:024 and your hand **from** them in the valley of Makkah,
048:024 He Who has restrained their hands **from** you and your
048:025 detained **from** reaching their place of sacrifice.
048:025 and hindered you **from** the Sacred Mosque and the
048:029 seeking Grace **from** Allah and (His) Good Pleasure.
049:004 shout out to thee **from** without the Inner Apartments-
049:008 A grace and favour **from** Allah; and Allah
049:013 O mankind! We created you **from** a single (pair)
050:002 to them a Warner **from** among themselves.
050:003 Return far (**from** our understanding)."
050:009 And We send down **from** the sky Rain charged
050:041 will call out **from** a place quite near,-
051:009 Through which are deluded (away **from** the Truth)
051:034 "Marked as **from** thy Lord for those who trespass
051:050 I am **from** Him a Warner to you, clear and open!
051:051 I am **from** Him a Warner to you, clear and open!
051:054 So turn away **from** them: not thine is the blame.
051:060 to the Unbelievers, **from** the Day of theirs which they
052:018 them **from** the Chastisement of the Fire.
052:027 and has delivered us **from** the Chastisement
052:028 "Truly we did call unto Him **from** of old:
053:023 to them Guidance **from** their Lord!
053:029 away **from** Our Message and desire nothing but
053:030 those who stray **from** His path, and He
053:046 **From** a seed when lodged (in its place);
054:006 Therefore, (O Prophet), turn away **from** them.
054:007 humbled-**from** (their) graves, (torpid) like
054:020 roots of palm-trees torn up (**from** the ground).
054:024 a solitary one **from** among ourselves!
054:035 As a Grace **from** Us: Thus do We
054:037 snatch away his guests **from** him, but We
054:041 aforetime, came Warners (**from** Allah).
055:014 He created man **from** sounding clay
055:015 And He created Jinns **from** fire free of smoke:
055:064 Dark green in colour (**from** plentiful watering).
056:013 A number of people **from** those of old,
056:014 And a few **from** those of later times.
056:039 A (goodly) number **from** those of old,
056:040 And a (goodly) number **from** those of later times.
056:061 **From** changing your Forms and creating you
056:069 Do ye bring it Down (in rain) **from** the Cloud, or do We?
056:080 A Revelation **from** the Lord of the Worlds.
056:086 if you are exempt **from** (future) account,-
056:091 "Peace be unto thee, **from** the Companions of the Right
057:004 out of it, what comes down **from** heaven and what
057:009 that He may lead you **from** the depths
057:013 Let us borrow (a light) **from** your Light!"
057:020 And Forgiveness **from** Allah and (His)
057:021 Be ye foremost (in seeking) forgiveness **from** your Lord,
057:024 And if any turn back (**from** Allah's Way), verily Allah
058:016 thus they obstruct (men) **from** the Path of Allah:
058:022 them with a spirit **from** Himself.
059:002 came to them **from** quarters **from** which they little
059:002 fortresses would defend them **from** Allah!
059:002 among the People of the Book **from** their homes
059:006 (and taken away) **from** them-for this

FROM (continued)

059:007 gives you, and refrain **from** what He prohibits you.
059:007 (and taken away) **from** the people of the townships,-
059:008 while seeking Grace **from** Allah and (His) Good Pleasure,
059:008 who were expelled **from** their homes and their property,
059:009 And those saved **from** the covetousness of their
059:014 except in fortified townships, or **from** behind walls.
060:001 out the Messenger and yourselves (**from** your homes),
060:001 has strayed **from** the Straight Path.
060:004 I have no power (to get) aught on thy behalf **from** Allah."
060:008 **from** dealing kindly and justly with them:
060:009 **from** turning to them (for friendship and protection).
060:011 (by the coming over of a woman **from** the other side).
061:010 save you **from** a grievous Chastisement?-
061:013 which ye do love,-help **from** Allah and a speedy
062:002 the Unlettered a messenger **from** among themselves,
062:008 Say "The Death **from** which ye flee will truly
063:002 thus they obstruct (men) **from** the path of Allah:
063:004 How are they deluded (away **from** the Truth)!
063:009 or your children divert you **from** the remembrance of
064:009 He will remove **from** them their ills, and He
064:016 and those saved **from** the covetousness of their
065:002 for witness two persons **from** among you, endued with
065:003 And He provides for him **from** (sources) he never
065:005 He will remove his evil deeds **from** him, and will
065:011 and do righteous deeds **from** the depths of Darkness
066:006 they receive **from** Allah, but do
066:006 not (**from** executing) the Commands they receive
066:006 and your families **from** a Fire whose fuel
066:008 that your Lord will remove **from** you your
066:011 and save me **from** Pharaoh and his doings,
066:011 and save me **from** those that do wrong";
067:005 And We have, (**from** of old), adorned the
067:011 but far **from** Allah's mercy are the Companions
067:021 in insolent impiety and flight (**from** the Truth).
067:028 deliver the Unbelievers **from** a grievous Chastisement?
068:007 which (among men) hath strayed **from** His Path:
068:019 there came on the (garden) a visitation **from** thy Lord,
068:044 them on little by little **from** directions they perceive not.
068:049 Had not Grace **from** His Lord reached him, he would
069:029 "My power has perished **from** me!"...
069:036 the foul pus **from** the washing of wounds,
069:043 a Message sent down **from** the Lord of the Worlds.
069:047 Nor could any of you withhold him (**from** Our wrath).
070:003 (A Penalty) **from** Allah, Lord of the Ways of Ascent.
070:011 could redeem himself **from** the Chastisement of that Day
070:017 and turn away their faces (**from** the Right),
070:018 And collect (wealth) and hide it (**from** use)!
070:025 is deprived (for some reason **from** asking);
070:028 a thing to feel secure **from**:-
070:037 **From** the right and **from** the left, in crowds?
070:043 they will issue **from** their sepulchers in sudden hast
071:006 (their) flight (**from** the Right)."
071:010 "Saying, `Ask forgiveness **from** your Lord, for He
071:017 "'And Allah has produced you **from** the earth, growing
071:024 the wrong-doers but in straying (**from** their mark)."
072:014 that swerve **from** justice.
072:017 But if any turns away **from** the remembrance
072:022 Say: "No one can deliver me **from** Allah
072:023 "Unless I deliver what I receive **from** Allah and His
074:004 And thy garments keep free **from** stain!
074:010 Far **from** easy for those without Faith.
074:024 but magic derived **from** of old;"

FROM (continued)

074:049 that they turn away **from** admonition?-
074:051 Fleeing **from** a lion!
076:002 Verily We created Man **from** a drop of mingled sperm,
076:009 no reward do we desire **from** you, nor thanks.
076:010 and distress **from** the side of our Lord."
076:011 But Allah will deliver them **from** the evil of that Day,
077:004 Then separate them, one **from** another,
077:020 Have We not created you **from** a fluid
078:014 And do We not send down **from** the clouds
078:036 Recompense **from** thy Lord, a Gift,
078:037 (**From**) the Lord of the heavens and the earth,
079:018 thou shouldst be purified (**from** sin)?-
079:040 restrained (their) soul **from** lower Desires,
080:018 **From** what stuff Hath He created him?
080:019 **From** a sperm-drop: He hath created him, and then
080:034 That Day shall a man flee **from** his own brother,
080:035 And **from** his mother, and his father,
080:036 And **from** his wife and his children.
082:006 O man! what has seduced thee **from** thy Lord Most
083:002 by measure **from** men, exact full measure,
083:015 Verily, **from** (the Light of) their Lord, that Day,
083:028 A spring, **from** (the waters) whereof drink
084:019 Ye shall surely travel **from** stage to stage.
085:013 It is He Who Creates **from** the very beginning, and He
085:020 But Allah doth encompass them **from** behind!
086:005 Now let man but think **from** what he is created!
086:006 He is created **from** a drop emitted-
086:007 Proceeding **from** between the backbone and the ribs:
086:013 that distinguishes (Good **from** Evil):
091:013 And (bar her not **from**) having her drink!"
092:017 shall be removed far **from** it,-
092:019 And have in their minds no favour **from** anyone for
094:002 And removed **from** thee thy burden
094:007 when thou art free (**from** thine immediate task),
098:001 to depart (**from** their ways) until there should come to
098:002 Messenger **from** Allah, rehearsing scriptures
099:002 And the Earth throws up her burden (**from** within),
102:001 diverts you (**from** the more serious things),
108:003 he will be cut off (**from** Future Hope).
111:002 No profit to him **from** all his wealth, and all
113:002 **From** the mischief of created things;
113:003 **From** the mischief of Darkness as it overspreads;
113:004 **From** the mischief of those who blow on knots;
113:005 And **from** the mischief of the envious one
114:004 **From** the mischief of the Whisperer (of Evil),

FRONT

012:026 is rent from the **front**, then is her tale true,
014:016 In **front** of such a one is Hell, and he
014:017 and in **front** of him will be a
034:012 in **front** of him, by the leave of his Lord, and if
036:009 And We have put a bar in **front** of them and a
040:046 In **front** of the Fire will they be brought,
045:010 In **front** of them is Hell: and of no
075:005 (even) in the time in **front** of him.

FROST

003:117 likened to a Wind which brings a nipping **frost**:

FROTH

013:017 For the scum disappears like **froth** cast out;

FROWNED

074:022 Then he **frowned** and he scowled;
080:001 The (Prophet) **frowned** and turned away,

FROWNING

076:010 "We only fear a Day of **frowning** and distress

FRUIT

002:134 They shall reap the **fruit** of what they did,
002:141 They shall reap the **fruit** of what they did,
002:217 no **fruit** in this life and in the Hereafter;
002:266 and all kinds of **fruit**,
003:022 no **fruit** in this world and in the Hereafter,
006:099 when they begin to bear **fruit**, feast your
006:099 feast your eyes with the **fruit** and the
006:141 eat of their **fruit** in their season, but render
009:017 The works of such bear no **fruit**:
013:003 and **fruit** of every kind He made in pairs,
014:025 It brings forth its **fruit** at all times, by the
016:011 and every kind of **fruit**:
016:067 And from the **fruit** of the date-palm and the vine,
020:132 But the (**fruit** of) the Hereafter
026:148 with spathes near breaking (with the weight of **fruit**)?
034:016 two garden (rows) into "gardens" producing bitter **fruit**,
035:037 So taste ye (the **fruit** of your deeds):
036:057 (Every) **fruit** will be there for them; they shall
038:051 for **fruit** in abundance, and, (delicious) drink;
039:070 in full (the **fruit**) of its deeds; and Allah
041:047 no **fruit** comes out of its sheath, nor does
043:073 Ye shall have therein abundance of **fruit**, from which
044:055 they call for every kind of **fruit** in peace and security;
052:021 We deprive them (of the **fruit**) of aught of their works:
052:022 And We shall bestow on them, of **fruit** and meat,
053:040 That (the **fruit** of) his striving will soon
055:011 Therein is **fruit** and date-palms, producing spathes
055:054 the **Fruit** of the Gardens will be
056:032 And **fruit** in abundance.
068:020 and desolate spot,(whose **fruit** had been gathered).
076:014 and the bunches (of **fruit**), there, will hang

FRUIT-STALKS

037:065 The shoots of its **fruit-stalks** are like
050:010 with shoots of **fruit-stalks**, piled one

FRUITLESS

005:005 If anyone rejects faith, **fruitless** is his work,
009:069 They!-their works are **fruitless** in this world
039:065 truly **fruitless** will be thy work
047:009 so He has made their deeds **fruitless**.

FRUITS

002:022 and brought forth therewith **fruits** for your sustenance;
002:025 every time they are fed with **fruits** therefrom,
002:126 and feed its People with **fruits**,
002:155 lives and the **fruits** (of your toil),
002:167 (the **fruits** of) their deeds as (nothing but)
002:267 and of the **fruits** of the earth which We
010:030 (the **fruits** of) the deeds it sent before:
013:035 perpetual is the **fruits** thereof and the
014:032 and with it bringeth our **fruits** wherewith to feed you;
014:037 and feed them with **Fruits**: so that they may give
018:042 So his **fruits** were encompassed (with ruin),
023:019 in them have ye abundant **fruits**: and of them
028:057 to which are brought as tribute **fruits** of all kinds,-
029:055 "Taste ye (the **fruits**) of your deeds!"
036:035 That they may enjoy the **fruits** of this
037:042 **Fruits**, and they (shall enjoy) honour and dignity,
039:024 "Taste ye (the **fruits** of) what ye earned!"
045:033 the evil (**fruits**) of what they did, and they
047:015 In it there are for them all kinds of **fruits**,

FRUITS (continued)

055:052 In them will be **Fruits** of every kind, two and two.
055:068 In them will be **Fruits**, and dates and pomegranates:
056:020 And with **fruits**, any that they may select;
056:029 with flowers (or **fruits**) piled one above another,-
068:017 when they resolved to gather the **fruits** of the
068:022 in the morning, if ye would gather the **fruits**."
068:027 "Indeed we are deprived (of the **fruits** of our labor)!"
069:023 The **Fruits** whereof (will hang in bunches)
077:042 And (they shall have) **fruits**,-all they desire.
078:030 "So taste ye (the **fruits** of your deeds);
080:031 And **Fruits** and Fodder,-

FRUSTRATE

006:134 nor can ye **frustrate** it (in the least bit).
008:059 they will never **frustrate** (them).
009:002 that ye cannot **frustrate** Allah (by your falsehood),
009:003 know ye that ye cannot **frustrate** Allah,
010:053 And ye cannot **frustrate** it!"
011:033 ye will not be able to **frustrate** it!
022:051 Our Signs, to **frustrate** them,-they will
029:022 be able (fleeing) to **frustrate** (His Plan),
034:005 Our Signs, to **frustrate** them,-for such
034:038 Those who strive against Our Signs, to **frustrate** them,
072:012 by no means **frustrate** Allah throughout the earth,

FRUSTRATED

003:127 should then be turned back **frustrated** of their purpose.
035:044 to be **frustrated** by anything whatever in the
056:060 your common lot, and We are not to be **frustrated**

FRUSTRATING

016:046 of their **frustrating** Him?-

FRUSTRATION

014:015 and **frustration** was the lot of every powerful obstinate

FUEL

002:024 whose **fuel** is Men and Stones,
003:010 they are themselves but **fuel** for the Fire.
021:098 besides Allah, are (but) **fuel** for Hell!
027:007 a burning brand (to light our **fuel**), that ye
066:006 whose **fuel** is Men and Stones, over which
072:015 they are (but) **fuel** for Hell Fire'-
085:005 Fire supplied (abundantly) with **Fuel**:
111:004 His wife shall carry the (crackling) wood-as **fuel**!

FULFIL

002:040 and I shall **fulfil** My Covenant with you,
002:040 and **fulfil** your Covenant with Me
002:177 to **fulfil** the contracts which ye have made;
002:231 (are about to) **fulfil** the term of their ('Iddat),
002:232 and they **fulfil** the term of their ('Iddat),
003:152 Allah did indeed **fulfil** His promise to you
005:001 O ye who believe! **fulfil** (all) obligations.
006:152 and **fulfil** the Covenant of Allah: thus doth
007:135 which they had to **fulfil**,-Behold!
009:004 So **fulfil** your engagements with them to the
013:020 Those who **fulfil** the Covenant of Allah and fail
016:091 **Fulfil** the Covenant of Allah when ye have
017:034 full strength; and **fulfil** (every) engagement,
018:048 We shall not **fulfil** the appointment made to you
021:104 truly shall We **fulfil** it.
022:029 the rites prescribed for them, **fulfil** their vows,
028:028 whichever of the two terms I **fulfil**, let there
048:002 **fulfil** His favour to thee; and guide thee on
048:027 Truly did Allah **fulfil** the vision
065:002 Thus when they **fulfil** their term appointed,

FULFILLED

002:124 which he **fulfilled**:
002:234 when they have **fulfilled** their term,
002:235 marriage till the term prescribed is **fulfilled**.
005:067 thou wouldst not have **fulfilled** and proclaimed
006:060 that a term appointed be **fulfilled**; in the end
007:053 On the day when it is **fulfilled** those who
007:137 was **fulfilled** for the Children of Israel, because
011:119 and the Word of they Lord shall be **fulfilled**:
017:005 and it was a warning (completely) **fulfilled**.
017:108 Truly has the promise of our Lord been **fulfilled**!"
019:075 when they see the warning of Allah (being **fulfilled**)-
021:009 Then We **fulfilled** to them Our promise, and We
027:082 And when the Word is **fulfilled** against them
027:085 And the Word will be **fulfilled** against them,
028:029 Now when Moses had **fulfilled** the term, and was
033:037 And Allah's command must be **fulfilled**.
037:105 "Thou hast already **fulfilled** the dream!"-
039:074 Who has truly **fulfilled** His promise to us,
050:014 and My warning was duly **fulfilled** (in them).
053:037 And of Abraham who **fulfilled** his (commandments)?
067:025 They ask: When will this promise be (**fulfilled**)?
067:027 "This is (the promise **fulfilled**), which ye were calling
080:023 By no means hath he **fulfilled** what Allah

FULFILLMENT

005:119 mighty Triumph (the **fulfillment** of all desires).
006:115 its **fulfillment** in truth and in justice:
007:010 for the **fulfillment** of your life:
007:053 Are they waiting for its **fulfillment**?
009:076 averse (from its **fulfillment**).
012:100 the **fulfillment** of my vision of old!
021:097 draw nigh (of **fulfillment**): then behold! the eyes
023:095 show thee (in **fulfillment**) that against which
028:061 to reach its (**fulfillment**), and one

FULFILLS

048:010 his own soul, and any one who **fulfills** what he

FULL

002:143 most surely **full** of kindness, Most Merciful.
002:207 and Allah is **full** of kindness to (His) devotees.
002:243 For Allah is **full** of bounty to mankind,
002:246 But Allah has **full** knowledge of those
002:251 the earth would indeed be **full** of mischief,
002:251 but Allah is **full** of bounty to all the worlds.
003:030 and Allah is **full** of kindness to those
003:057 Allah will pay them (in **full**) their reward;
003:061 now after (**full**) knowledge hath come to thee,
003:063 Allah hath **full** knowledge of those who do mischief.
003:096 **full** of blessings and of guidance for all the worlds.
003:152 for Allah is **full** of grace to those who believe.
003:167 But Allah hath **full** knowledge of all they conceal.
003:185 shall you be paid your **full** recompense.
004:017 for Allah is **full** of knowledge and wisdom.
004:025 and Allah hath **full** knowledge about your faith.
004:032 for Allah hath **full** knowledge of all things.
004:035 for Allah hath **full** knowledge, and is
004:039 For Allah hath **full** knowledge of them.
004:045 But Allah hath **full** knowledge of your enemies:
004:104 And Allah is **full** of knowledge and wisdom.
004:111 for Allah is **full** of knowledge and wisdom.
004:157 And those who differ therein are **full** of doubts,
005:031 Then he became **full** of regrets.
005:038 and Allah is Exalted in Power **full** of Wisdom.

FULL (continued)

005:109 it is Thou who knowest in **full** all that is hidden.
005:116 For Thou knowest in **full** all that is hidden.
006:083 for thy Lord is **full** of wisdom and knowledge.
006:101 and He hath **full** knowledge of all things.
006:114 They know **full** well, to whom
006:128 For thy Lord is **full** of wisdom and knowledge.
006:133 Thy Lord is Self-sufficient, **full** of Mercy:
006:139 for He is **full** of Wisdom and Knowledge.
006:147 say: "Your Lord is **full** of Mercy All-embracing;
006:152 give measure and weight with (**full**) justice;-
006:152 until he attain the age of **full** strength;
008:071 who hath (**full**) knowledge and wisdom.
009:060 and Allah is **full** of knowledge and wisdom.
010:060 Verily Allah is **full** of Bounty to mankind,
011:073 all praise, **full** of all glory!"
011:090 for my Lord is indeed **Full** of mercy
011:109 pay them back (in **full**) their portion
011:111 your Lord pay back (in **full** the recompense)
012:006 For thy Lord is **full** of knowledge and wisdom."
012:021 And Allah hath **full** power and
012:022 When Joseph attained his **full** manhood, We gave
012:059 I pay out **full** measure, and that
012:065 and add (at the same time) a **full** camel's load
012:068 by Our instruction, **full** of knowledge (and experience):
012:069 he received (**full**) brother to stay with him.
012:083 For He is indeed **full** of knowledge and wisdom."
012:088 so pay us **full** measure, (we pray thee), and treat
012:100 He is **full** of knowledge and wisdom.
013:006 But verily thy Lord is **full** of forgiveness for mankind
014:004 is Exalted in power, **Full** of Wisdom.
016:025 on the Day of Judgment, their own burdens in **full**,
016:047 for thy Lord is indeed **full** of kindness and mercy.
016:060 for He is the Exalted in Power, **Full** of Wisdom.
017:034 until he attains the age of **full** strength;
017:035 Give **full** measure when ye measure, and weigh
018:058 But your Lord is Most Forgiving, **Full** of Mercy.
018:076 received (**full**) excuse from my side."
018:082 attain their age of **full** strength and get out
021:065 (they said), "Thou knowest **full** well that these
022:005 may reach your age of **full** strength; and some
022:040 is **Full** of Strength, Exalted in Might,
022:052 for Allah is **full** of knowledge and wisdom:
023:060 with their hearts **full** of fear, because they
024:010 and that Allah is Oft-Returning, **Full** of Wisdom,-
024:018 for Allah is **full** of knowledge and wisdom.
024:020 is **full** of kindness and mercy,
024:058 for Allah is **full** of knowledge and wisdom.
024:059 for Allah is **full** of knowledge and wisdom.
026:091 the Fire will be placed in **full** view;
026:157 then did they become **full** of regrets.
027:039 indeed I have **full** strength for the purpose,
027:060 well-planted orchards **full** of beauty and delight:
027:073 **But verily thy Lord is full** of grace to mankind:
028:014 When he reached **full** age, and was
029:062 for Allah has **full** knowledge of all things.
030:027 for He is Exalted in Might, **Full** of Wisdom.
031:027 for Allah is Exalted in power, **Full** of Wisdom.
031:034 is **full** knowledge and He is acquainted
033:001 verily Allah is **full** of knowledge and wisdom.
033:025 And Allah is **full** of Strength, Exalted in might.
033:040 and Allah has **full** knowledge of all things.
033:043 and He is **Full** of Mercy to the Believers.

FULL (continued)

033:054   has **full** knowledge of all things.
034:048   He that has **full** knowledge of (all)
035:002   and He is the Exalted in Power, **Full** of Wisdom.
035:038   verily He has **full** knowledge of all that is in (men's)
036:002   By the Qur'an, **full** of Wisdom,-
038:001   Sad: By the Qur'an, **full** of Admonition:
038:029   sent down unto thee, **full** of blessings, that they
038:044   Truly We found him **full** of patience
039:001   from Allah, the Exalted in Power, **Full** of Wisdom.
039:070   in **full** (the fruit) of its deeds; and Allah
040:002   is from Allah, Exalted in Power, **Full** of Knowledge,-
040:008   the Exalted in Might, **Full** of Wisdom.
040:022   for He is **full** of Strength, Severe Punishment.
040:061   Verily Allah is **Full** of Grace and Bounty to men:
040:067   reach your age of **full** strength; then lets
041:012   of (Him) the Exalted in Might, **Full** of knowledge.
041:042   it is sent down by One **Full** of Wisdom, Worthy of
041:051   (he comes) **full** of prolonged prayer!
042:003   Allah, Exalted in Power, **Full** of Wisdom.
042:012   for He knows **full** well all things.
042:050   for He is **full** of knowledge and power.
043:004   high (in dignity), **full** of wisdom.
043:009   by (Him), the Exalted in Power, **Full** of Knowledge';
043:084   **Full** of Wisdom and Knowledge.
043:086   to the Truth, and with **full** knowledge.
044:049   Truly thou art Mighty, **full** of honour!
045:002   is from Allah the Exalted in Power, **Full** of Wisdom.
045:037   and He is Exalted in Power, **Full** of Wisdom!
046:002   is from Allah the Exalted in Power, **Full** of Wisdom.
046:015   the age of **full** strength and attains forty years,
048:004   and Allah is **full** of Knowledge and Wisdom;-
048:007   and Allah is Exalted in Power, **Full** of Wisdom.
048:019   Exalted in Power, **Full** of Wisdom.
048:026   And Allah has **full** knowledge of all things.
049:006   and afterwards become **full** of repentance
049:008   and Allah is **full** of Knowledge and Wisdom.
049:013   And Allah has **full** knowledge and is well
049:016   He has **full** knowledge of all things.
050:004   with Us is a Record guarding (the **full** account).
050:030   "Art thou filled to the **full**?" It will say,
051:030   and He is **full** of Wisdom and Knowledge."
054:046   is the time promised them (for their **full** recompense):
055:027   thy Lord,-**full** of Majesty, Bounty and Honour.
055:078   **full** of Majesty, Bounty and Honour.
056:037   **Full** of love (for their mates), equal in age,-
057:003   and He has **full** knowledge of all things.
057:006   and He has **full** knowledge of the secrets
057:025   **Full** of Strength, Exalted in Might.
058:007   For Allah has **full** knowledge of all things.
059:010   Thou art indeed **Full** of Kindness, Most Merciful."
060:001   for I know **full** well all that ye conceal
060:010   and Allah is **Full** Knowledge and Wisdom.
064:018   Exalted in Might, **Full** of Wisdom.
066:002   and He is **Full** of Knowledge and Wisdom.
067:013   He certainly has (**full**) knowledge, of the secrets of
069:024   "Eat ye and drink ye, with **full** satisfaction;
075:033   Then did he stalk to his family in **full** conceit!
076:030   for Allah is **full** of Knowledge and Wisdom.
078:034   And a Cup **full** (to the Brim).
079:036   in **full** view for him who sees.-
083:002   by measure from men, exact **full** measure,
084:005   (then will come Home the **full** Reality).

FULL (continued)

084:023   But Allah has **full** Knowledge of what they
085:014   **Full** of loving-kindness,
085:015   Lord of the Throne **full** of all Glory,

FULLER

010:037   and a **fuller** explanation of the Book-wherein

FULLEST

004:065   but accept them with the **fullest** conviction.

FULLNESS

084:018   And the Moon in her **Fullness**:

FULLY

005:061   But Allah knoweth **fully** all that they hide.
016:111   every soul will be recompensed (**fully**) for all its actions,
035:031   well acquainted and **fully** Observant.
036:079   For He **fully** knows all creation.
037:140   (like a slave from captivity) to the ship (**fully**) laden,
083:009   (There is) a Register (**fully**) inscribed.
083:020   (There is) a Register (**fully**) inscribed.

FUNCTION

035:041   lest they cease (to **function**):

FUNDAMENTAL

003:007   basic or **fundamental** clear (in meaning);
011:001   with verses **fundamental** (of established meaning),

FUNDS

009:060   and those employed to administer the (**funds**):

FURIOUS

041:016   a **furious** Wind through days of disaster, that We
054:019   For We sent against them a **furious** wind, on a
069:006   by a **furious** wind, exceedingly violent;

FURIOUSLY

014:018   blows **furiously** on a tempestuous day: no power

FURNACE

037:097   They said: "Build him a **furnace**, and throw

FURNISHED

012:059   And when he had **furnished** them forth
012:070   At length when he had **furnished** them forth
023:050   and security and **furnished** with springs.

FURNISHES

067:015   which He **furnishes**: but unto Him is the Resurrection.

FURROW

044:024   "And leave the sea as a **furrow** (divided): for they

FURTHER

002:248   And (**further**) their Prophet said to them: "A Sign
002:259   look **further** at the bones,
006:138   we wish; **further**, there are cattle forbidden to yoke or
010:105   "And **further** (thus): set thy face towards
011:001   (of established meaning), **further** explained in detail,-
011:037   and address Me no (**further**) on behalf
012:067   **Further** he said; "O my sons! enter not
018:004   **Further**, that He may warn those (also) who say,
022:005   And (**further**), thou seest the earth barren and
026:014   "And (**further**), they have a charge of crime
030:040   **further**, He has provided for your sustenance;
036:009   and a bar behind them, and **further**, We have
036:048   **Further**, they say, "When will this promise
040:038   The man who believed said **further**: "O my People!
041:030   "Our Lord is Allah," and, **further**, stand straight
067:010   They will **further** say: "Had we but
069:032   "**Further**, insert him in a chain, whereof the
071:009   "**Further** I have spoken to them in public
072:006   but they increased them into **further** error.

FURTHER (continued)

079:022 **Further**, he turned his back, striving hard
083:016 **Further**, they will enter the Fire of Hell.
083:017 **Further**, it will be said to them: "This is the
087:002 Who hath created, and **further**, given order

FURTHERMORE

056:075 **Furthermore** I swear by the setting of the Stars,-
066:004 and **furthermore**, the angels,-will back (him) up.

FURTHEST

028:020 from the **furthest** end of the City.
041:053 in the (**furthest**) regions (of the earth), and in

FURY

004:084 will restrain the **fury** of the Unbelievers;
019:083 to incite them with **fury**?
025:012 they will hear its **fury** and its raging sigh.
033:025 Allah turned back the Unbelievers for (all) their **fury**:
067:008 Almost bursting with **fury**: every time

FUTILE

040:050 is nothing but (**futile** wandering) in (mazes of) error!"
042:016 **futile** is their dispute in the sight of their Lord:

FUTILITY

025:072 and, if they pass by **futility**, they pass

FUTURE

002:282 to writing (your contract) for a **future** period,
002:282 involving **future** obligations in a fixed period of time,
020:097 (for a **future** penalty) thou hast a promise that
030:004 is the Command is the Past and in the **Future**:
033:037 in order that (in **future**) there may be no
056:086 if you are exempt from (**future**) account,-
089:024 sent forth (Good Deeds) for (this) my (**Future**) Life."
108:003 he will be cut off (from **Future** Hope).

G

GABRIEL
002:097 Say: Whoever is an enemy to **Gabriel**
002:098 to **Gabriel** and Michael,
066:004 and **Gabriel**, and (every) righteous one among

GAIN
002:079 and for the **gain** they make thereby.
002:081 Nay, those who seek **gain** in Evil,
003:027 "Thou causest the Night to **gain** on the Day.
003:027 And Thou causest the Day to **gain** on the Night;
003:139 for ye must **gain** mastery if ye are true in Faith.
003:187 and purchased with it some miserable **gain**!
003:199 the Signs of Allah for a miserable **gain**!
004:141 if ye do **gain** a victory from Allah, they say:
004:141 "Did we not **gain** an advantage over you.
004:141 But if the Unbelievers **gain** a success, they say
004:147 What can Allah **gain** by your punishment.
008:057 If ye **gain** the mastery over them in war,
009:042 If there had been immediate **gain** (in sight),
009:120 or **gain** any **gain** from an enemy:
024:033 a **gain** in the goods of this life.
027:040 truly his gratitude is (a **gain**) for his own soul;
033:025 no advantage did they **gain**, and enough
041:026 that ye may **gain** the upper hand!"
064:009 a day of mutual loss and **gain** (among you).

GAINED
009:024 the wealth that ye have **gained**;

GAINS
015:018 But any that **gains** a hearing by stealth,
020:064 who **gains** the upper hand."
048:019 And many **gains** will they acquire (besides):
048:020 Allah has promised you many **gains** that ye
048:021 And other **gains** (there are), which are
111:002 and all his **gains**!

GALE
017:069 and send against you a heavy **gale** to drown you

GALL
094:003 The which did **gall** thy back?-

GAMBLING
002:219 They ask thee concerning wine and **gambling**.
005:090 intoxicants and **gambling**, sacrificing to stones,
005:091 with intoxicants and **gambling**, and hinder you

GAME
005:094 of **game** well within reach of your hands and
005:095 O ye who believe! kill not **game**, while in

GANGS
054:051 have We destroyed **gangs** like unto you:

GAPED
033:010 and the hearts **gaped** up to the throats, and ye

GAPING
014:043 and their hearts a (**gaping**) void!

GARDEN
002:035 dwell thou and thy wife in the **Garden**;
002:036 Then did Satan make them slip from the (**garden**),
002:082 they are companions of the **Garden**,
002:214 ye shall enter the **Garden** (of Bliss)

GARDEN (continued)
002:221 to the **Garden** (of Bliss) and forgiveness,
002:265 is as a **garden**, high and fertile:
002:266 should have a **garden** with date-palms
003:133 and for a **Garden** whose width is that (of the whole)
003:185 and admitted to the **Garden** will have succeeded:
005:072 Allah will forbid him the **Garden**, and the Fire
007:019 and thy wife in the **Garden**, and enjoy
007:022 the leaves of the **Garden** over their bodies.
007:027 he got your parents out of the **Garden**, stripping
007:040 nor will they enter the **Garden**, until the
007:042 they will be Companions of the **Garden**, therein
007:043 "Behold! the **Garden** before you! Ye have
007:044 The Companions of the **Garden** will call out
007:046 to the Companions of the **Garden**, "Peace be
007:049 Enter ye the **Garden**: no fear shall be on you, nor
007:050 will call to the Companions of the **Garden**: "Pour
009:111 for theirs (in return) is the **Garden** (of Paradise):
010:026 They are Companions of the **Garden**; they will
011:023 they will be Companions of the **Garden**, to dwell
011:108 And those who are blessed shall be in the **Garden**:
013:035 The parable of the **Garden** which the righteous
016:032 enter ye the **Garden**, because of (the good)
017:091 "Or (until) thou have a **garden** of date trees
018:035 He went into his **garden** while he wronged himself:
018:039 "Why didst thou not, as thou wentest into thy **garden**,
018:040 my Lord will give me something better than thy **garden**,
018:040 and that He will send On thy **garden** thunderbolts
018:041 "Or the water of the **garden** will run off
019:060 for these will enter the **Garden** and will
019:063 Such is the **Garden** which We give as an
020:117 so let him not get you both out of the **Garden**,
020:121 for their covering, leaves from the **Garden**:
020:123 all together, from the **Garden**, with enmity
025:008 or why has he (not) a **garden** for enjoyment?"
025:015 eternal **Garden**, promised to the righteous?
025:024 The Companions of the **Garden** will be well,
026:085 of the **Garden** of Bliss;
026:090 the **Garden** will be brought near,
034:016 and We converted their two **Garden** (rows) into
036:026 It was said: "Enter thou the **Garden**."
036:055 Verily the Companions of the **Garden** shall that day
039:073 will be led to the **Garden** in groups: until behold,
039:074 We can dwell in the **Garden** as we will:
040:040 such will enter the **Garden** (of Bliss):
041:030 of the **Garden** (of Bliss), the which
042:007 (when) some will be in the **Garden**, and some
043:070 Enter ye the **Garden**, ye and
043:072 Such will be the **Garden** of which ye are made
046:014 Such shall be Companion of the **Garden**, dwelling
046:016 (they shall be) among the Companions of the **Garden**:
047:006 And admit them to the **Garden** which He has
047:015 (Here is) the description of the **Garden** which the
050:031 And the **Garden** will be brought nigh to the
053:015 Near it is the **Garden** of Abode.
056:089 and a **Garden** of Delights.
057:021 from your Lord, and a **Garden** (of Bliss), the width
059:020 and the Companions of the **Garden**:
059:020 it is the Companions of the **Garden**, that will
066:011 a mansion in the **Garden**, and save
068:017 of the (**garden**) in the morning.
068:017 the People of the **Garden**, when they
068:019 Then there came, on the (**garden**) a visitation

GARDEN (continued)

068:020 So the (**garden**) became, by the morning, like a
068:024 in upon you into the (**garden**) this day."
068:026 But when they saw the (**garden**), they said:
068:032 in exchange a better (**garden**) than this: for we
069:022 In a **Garden** on high,
070:038 to enter the **Garden** of Bliss?
076:012 He will reward them with a **Garden** and (garments of)
076:013 Reclining in the (**Garden**) on raised couches,
076:014 And the shades of the (**Garden**) will come
079:041 Their abode will be the **Garden**.
081:013 And when the **Garden** is brought near;-
088:010 In a **Garden** on high,

GARDENS

002:025 that their portion is **Gardens**,
003:015 For the righteous are **Gardens** in nearness to
003:136 and **Gardens** with rivers flowing underneath,
003:195 into **Gardens** with rivers flowing beneath;
003:198 for those who fear their Lord, are **Gardens**, with rivers
004:013 will be admitted to **Gardens** with rivers flowing
004:057 We shall soon admit to **Gardens**, with rivers
004:122 We shall soon admit them to **Gardens**, with rivers
005:012 and admit you to **Gardens** with rivers
005:065 and admitted them to **Gardens** of Bliss.
005:085 hath Allah rewarded them with **Gardens**,
005:119 theirs are **Gardens**, with rivers flowing beneath,-
006:099 and (then there are) **gardens** of grapes,
006:141 It is He who produceth **gardens**,
009:021 And of **Gardens** for them,
009:072 men and women, **Gardens** under which rivers flow,
009:072 and beautiful mansions in **Gardens** of everlasting
009:089 Allah hath prepared for them **Gardens** under which
009:100 hath He prepared **Gardens** under which rivers flow,
010:009 beneath them will flow rivers in **Gardens** of Bliss.
013:004 and **gardens** of vines and fields sown with corn,
013:023 **Gardens** of perpetual bliss: they shall enter there,
014:023 admitted to **Gardens** beneath which rivers flow,-
015:045 The righteous (will be) amid **Gardens** and fountains
016:031 **Gardens** of Eternity which they will enter:
018:031 For them will be **Gardens** of Eternity; beneath them rivers
018:032 We provided two **gardens** of grape-vines and
018:033 Each of those **gardens** brought forth its produce,
018:107 for their entertainment, the **Gardens** of Paradise,
019:061 **Gardens** of Eternity, those which (Allah) Most
020:076 **Gardens** of Eternity, beneath which flow rivers:
022:014 who believe and work righteous deeds, to **Gardens**,
022:023 and work righteous deeds, to **Gardens** beneath which
022:056 righteous deeds will be in **Gardens** of Delight.
023:019 With it We grow for you **gardens** of date-palms
025:010 **Gardens** beneath which rives flow;
026:057 So We expelled them from **gardens**, springs,
026:134 "And **Gardens** and Springs.
026:147 "**Gardens** and Springs,
031:008 there will be **Gardens** of Bliss,-
032:019 do righteous deeds, are **Gardens** as hospitable
034:015 a Sign in their homeland-two **Gardens** to the
034:016 (rows) into "**gardens**" producing bitter fruit,
035:033 **Gardens** of Eternity will they enter: therein will
037:043 In **Gardens** of delight.
038:050 **Gardens** of Eternity, whose doors will (ever)
040:008 enter the **Gardens** of Eternity, which Thou
042:022 righteous deeds will be in the Meadows of the **Gardens**:
044:025 How many were the **gardens** and springs

GARDEN (continued)

044:052 Among **Gardens** and Springs;
047:012 to **Gardens** beneath which rivers flow; while those
048:005 who believe, to **Gardens** beneath which rivers flow,
048:017 him to **Gardens** beneath which rivers flow; and he
050:009 and We produce therewith **Gardens** and Grain
051:015 they will be in the midst of **Gardens** and Springs,
052:017 they will be in **Gardens**, and in Happiness,-
054:054 they will be in the midst of **Gardens** and Rivers.
055:046 there will be two **Gardens**-
055:054 the Fruit of the **Gardens** will be near (and easy of reach).
055:062 there are two other **Gardens**,-
056:012 In **Gardens** of Bliss:
057:012 **Gardens** beneath which flow rivers!
058:022 And He will admit them to **Gardens** beneath which
061:012 mansions in **Gardens** of Eternity: that is
061:012 and admit you to **Gardens** beneath which rivers
064:009 and He will admit them to **gardens** beneath which
065:011 to **Gardens** beneath which rivers flow, to dwell
066:008 to **Gardens** beneath which rivers flow,-the Day
068:034 Verily, for the righteous are **Gardens** of Delight,
070:035 in the **Gardens** of (Bliss).
071:012 and sons; and bestow on you **Gardens** and bestow
074:040 (They will be) in **Gardens** (of Delight); they will
078:016 And **gardens** of luxurious growth?
078:032 **Gardens** enclosed, and Grapevines;
080:030 And enclosed **Gardens**, dense with lofty trees,
085:011 and do righteous deeds, will be **Gardens**.
098:008 **Gardens** of Eternity, Beneath which rivers flow;

GARLANDS

005:002 nor the **garlands** that mark out such animals,
005:097 and the **garlands** that mark them:

GARLIC

002:061 its **garlic**, lentils, and onions."

GARMENT

016:112 (closing in on it) like a **garment** (from every side),
022:019 for them will be cut out a **garment** of Fire:

GARMENTS

002:187 They are your **garments** and ye are their **garments**.
011:005 cover themselves with their **garments**, He knoweth
014:050 Their **garments** of liquid pitch, and their
016:081 He made you **garments** to protect you
018:031 green **garments** of fine silk and heavy brocade;
022:023 and their **garments** there will be of silk.
024:060 lay aside their (outer) **garments**, provided they
033:059 outer **garments** over their persons (when out of doors):
035:033 and their **garments** there will be of silk.
071:007 with their **garments**, grown obstinate, and given
073:001 O thou folded in **garments**!
074:004 And thy **garments** keep free from stain!
076:012 and (**garments** of) silk.
076:021 Upon them will be green **Garments** of fine silk

GATE

002:058 and enter the **gate** prostrating,
004:031 and admit you to the **Gate** of great honor.
004:154 We said: "Enter the **gate** with humility";
005:023 they said: "Assault them at the (proper) **Gate**:
007:161 and enter the **gate** in a posture of humility:
012:067 enter not all by one **gate**: enter ye
013:023 from every **gate** (with the salutation)
015:014 a **gate** from heaven, and they were to continue
017:080 by the **Gate** of Truth and Honor, and likewise
017:080 the **Gate** of Truth and Honor; and grant

GATE (continued)

023:077 Until We open on them a **gate** leading to
057:013 will be put up betwixt them, with a **gate** therein.

GATES

006:044 the **gates** of all (good) things, until, in the
007:040 the **gates** of heaven, nor will
012:067 enter ye by different **gates**.
015:044 for each of those **Gates** is a (special) class
015:044 To it are seven **Gates**: for each
016:029 "So enter the **gates** of Hell, to dwell therein.
039:071 arrive there, its **gates** will be opened.
039:072 "Enter ye the **gates** of Hell, to dwell
039:073 its **gates** will be opened; and its Keepers
040:076 "Enter ye the **gates** of Hell, to dwell
054:011 So We opened the **gates** of heaven, with water

GATHER

003:009 "Our Lord! Thou art He that will **gather** mankind together
003:025 We **gather** them together against a Day
003:061 say: "Come! let us **gather** together,
004:087 of a surety He will **gather** you together on the Day of
004:172 He will **gather** them all together unto Himself to (answer).
005:109 the day when Allah will **gather** the Messengers together,
006:012 That He will **gather** you together for
006:022 On the day shall We **gather** them all together:
006:035 He could **gather** them together unto true guidance:
006:128 On the day when He will **gather** them all together,
010:028 One Day shall We **gather** them all together.
010:045 And on the day when He will **gather** them together:
015:025 Assuredly it is thy Lord Who will **gather** them together:
017:088 were to **gather** together to produce the like
017:097 On the Day of Judgment We shall **gather** them together,,
018:047 and We shall **gather** them, all together, nor shall
019:068 We shall **gather** them together, and (also)
019:085 The day We shall **gather** the righteous to (Allah)
020:102 that Day, We shall **gather** the sinful, blear-eyed
025:017 The Day He will **gather** them together as well
027:083 The Day We shall **gather** together from every
034:026 Say: "Our Lord will **gather** us together and will
034:040 On the day He will **gather** them all together,
042:029 and He has power to **gather** them together
045:026 then He will **gather** you together for the Day
068:017 when they resolved to **gather** the fruits of the
068:022 in the morning, if ye would **gather** the fruits."
077:038 We shall **Gather** you together and those before (you)!

GATHERED

002:203 ye will surely be **gathered** unto Him.
003:012 vanquished and **gathered** together to Hell,
005:096 and fear Allah, to Whom ye shall be **gathered** back.
006:038 and they (all) shall be **gathered** to their Lord in the end.
006:072 that we shall be **gathered** together."
006:111 and We **gathered** together all things
006:141 on the day that the harvest is **gathered**.
008:024 ye shall (all) be **gathered**.
008:036 and the Unbelieers will be **gathered** together to Hell;-
011:103 that is a Day for which mankind will be **gathered** together:
011:105 of those (**gathered**) some will be wretched
017:104 We **gathered** you together in a mingled crowd.
023:079 and to Him shall ye be **gathered** back.
025:034 Those who will be **gathered** to Hell
038:019 And the birds **gathered** (in assemblies): all with
038:024 And David **gathered** that We had tried him:
041:019 will be **gathered** together to the Fire, they will
046:006 And when mankind are **gathered** together

GATHERED (continued)

052:044 they would (only) say: "Clouds **gathered** in heaps!"
056:050 "All will certainly be **gathered** together for the
067:024 and to Him shall ye be **gathered** together."
068:020 a dark and desolate spot, (whose fruit had been **gathered**).

GATHERING

003:173 "A great army is **gathering** against you,
050:044 that will be a **gathering** together,-quite easy
059:002 their homes at the first **gathering** (of the forces).

GUARDIAN

003:173 and He is the best **Guardian**."

GAVE

002:028 and He **gave** you life;
002:053 And remember We **gave** Moses the Scripture
002:057 And We **gave** You the shade of clouds
002:087 We **gave** Jesus the son of Mary clear (Signs)
002:087 We **gave** Moses the Book
002:251 and Allah **gave** him power and wisdom
002:253 to Jesus the son of Mary, We **gave** Clear (Signs),
003:148 And Allah **gave** them a reward in this world,
004:023 foster-mothers (who **gave** you suck),
004:153 and **gave** Moses manifest proofs of authority.
004:163 and to David We **gave** the Psalms.
004:165 Messengers who **gave** good news as well
005:020 made you kings, and **gave** you what He had not
006:006 and **gave** streams flowing beneath their (feet):
006:084 We **gave** him Isaac and Jacob: all (three)
006:086 and to all We **gave** favour above the nations:
006:089 These were the men to whom We **gave** the Book,
006:122 to whom We **gave** life, and a light
006:154 Moreover, We **gave** Moses the Book, completing
007:011 and **gave** you shape; then We bade
007:069 and **gave** you a stature tall among
007:074 and **gave** you habitations in the land:
007:079 I **gave** you good counsel, but ye love
007:082 And his people **gave** no answer but this: they said,
007:086 and He **gave** you increase.
007:093 I **gave** you good counsel, but how
007:160 We **gave** them the shade of clouds, and sent
008:026 and **gave** you good things for sustenance: that ye
008:072 who **gave** (them) asylum and aid,-these are
009:059 what Allah and His Messenger **gave** them, and had
009:100 those who **gave** them aid, and (also) those who
011:071 and she laughed: but We **gave** her Glad tidings
011:110 We certainly **gave** the Book to Moses,
012:022 We **gave** him power and knowledge: thus do
012:031 she **gave** each of them a knife: and she
014:022 "It was Allah Who **gave** you a promise
016:078 when ye knew nothing; and He **gave** you hearing
016:086 When those who **gave** partners to Allah will see
016:122 And We **gave** him Good in this world, and he
017:002 We **gave** Moses the Book, and made
017:006 We **gave** you increase in resources
017:055 and We **gave** to David the Psalms.
018:014 We **gave** strength to their hearts: behold, they
018:084 and We **gave** him the ways and the means to all ends.
019:012 and We **gave** him Wisdom even as
019:053 And, out of Our Mercy, We **gave** him his brother
020:050 each (created) thing its form then, **gave** (it) guidance."
020:050 He said: "Our Lord is He Who **gave** to each (created)
020:122 He turned to him, and **gave** him guidance.
021:044 Nay, We **gave** the good things of this life
021:074 We **gave** Judgment and Knowledge, and We

GAVE (continued)

021:078 when they **gave** judgment in the matter of the
021:079 to each (of them) We **gave** Judgment and Knowledge;
022:034 He **gave** them from animals (fit for food).
022:066 It is He Who **gave** you life, will cause
023:049 And We **gave** Moses the Book, in order
023:050 We **gave** them both shelter on high ground,
027:015 We **gave** knowledge to David and Solomon: and they
027:056 But his people **gave** no other answer but this:
028:065 "What was the answer ye **gave** to the messengers?"
029:027 And We **gave** (Abraham) Isaac and Jacob,
029:029 But his people **gave** no answer but this: they said: "Bring
030:054 then **gave** (you) strength after weakness,
032:009 And He **gave** you (the faculties of) hearing and sight and
034:017 That was the Requital We **gave** them because
037:101 So We **gave** him the good news of a forbearing son.
037:112 And We **gave** him the good news of Isaac-
037:117 And We **gave** them the Book which helps
038:020 and **gave** him wisdom and sound judgment
038:043 And We **gave** him (back) his people and double
039:026 So Allah **gave** them a taste of humiliation
040:053 and We **gave** the Book in inheritance to the Children of
040:073 "Where are the (deities) to which ye **gave** part-worship-
041:017 As to the Thamud, We **gave** them guidance, but they
041:045 We certainly **gave** Moses the book aforetime:
045:016 We **gave** them, for Sustenance, things good and pure;
048:024 after that He **gave** you the victory over them.
051:028 and they **gave** him glad tidings of a son endowed with
058:002 except those who **gave** them birth.
061:014 but We **gave** power to those who believed against their
075:031 So he **gave** nothing in charity, nor did he pray!-
076:002 so We **gave** him (the gifts), of Hearing and Sight.
082:007 and **gave** thee a just bias;
093:007 and He **gave** thee guidance.

GAZE

014:043 their **gaze** returning not towards them, and their
024:030 should lower their **gaze** and guard their modesty:
024:031 they should lower their **gaze** and guard

GENERATION

007:169 After them succeeded an (evil) **generation**:
019:098 But how many (countless) **generation** before them have
023:031 Then We raised after them another **generation**.
025:038 and many a **generation** between them.
039:051 of this (**generation**)-the evil results of their

GENERATIONS

002:253 succeeding **generations** would not have fought
006:006 **Generations** We had established on the earth,
006:006 fresh **generations** (to succeed them).
010:013 **Generations** before you We destroyed when they
011:116 the **generations** before you, men of righteousness
017:017 How many **generations** have We destroyed after Noah?
017:059 of former **generations** treated them as false:
019:074 But how many (countless) **generations** before them
020:051 condition of previous **generations**?"
020:128 how many **generations** before them We destroyed,
021:093 But (later **generations**) cut off their affair
023:042 Then We raised after them other **generations**.
026:084 among the latest (**generations**);
026:184 and (Who created) the **generations** before (you)."
028:043 destroyed earlier **generations**, (to give) Insight to men,
028:045 But We raised up (new) **generations**, and long
028:078 Allah had destroyed before, him, (whole) **generations**,-
029:018 so did **generations** before you:

GENERATIONS (continued)

032:026 how many **generations** We destroyed before them,
036:031 See they not how many **generations** before them
037:078 for him among **generations** to come in later times:
037:108 And We left for him among **generations** (to come)
037:119 And We left for them among **generations** (to come)
037:129 And We left for him among **generations** (to come)
038:003 How many **generations** before them did We destroy?
039:050 Thus did the (**generations**) before them say!
041:025 word among the previous **generations** of Jinns and men,
046:017 even though **generations** have passed before me
046:018 previous **generations** of Jinns and men, that have
050:036 But how many **generations** before them did We
051:059 their fellows (of earlier **generations**):
077:017 So shall We make later (**generations**) follow them.

GENEROSITY

002:262 with reminders of their **generosity** or with injury,
002:264 your **generosity** or by injury-like those
047:004 time for) either **generosity** or ransom: until the

GENEROUS

008:004 and **generous** sustenance:
008:074 and a provision most **generous**.
022:050 is forgiveness and a sustenance most **generous**.
033:031 for her a **generous** Sustenance.
033:044 and He has prepared for them a **generous** Reward.
034:004 and a Sustenance Most **Generous**."
036:011 of Forgiveness and a Reward most **generous**.
057:011 and he will have (besides) a **generous** reward.
057:018 and they shall have (besides) a **generous** reward.

GENIAL

035:021 and the (**genial**) heat of the sun:

GENTLENESS

015:088 (in **gentleness**) to the Believers.
051:003 And those that flow with ease and **gentleness**;

GENTLY

003:159 that thou dost deal **gently** with them.
024:043 the clouds move **gently**, then joins
038:036 to flow **gently** to his order, whithersoever he
079:002 By those who **gently** draw out (the souls of the blessed);
086:017 give respite to them **gently** (for a while).

GESTATION

077:022 For a period (of **gestation**), determined?

GET

002:036 and **get** them out of the state (of felicity)
002:036 And We said: "**Get** ye down, (all you people),
002:038 We said: "**Get** ye down all from here;
002:112 he will **get** his reward with his Lord;
002:282 And **get** two witnesses, out of your own men.
003:111 and no help shall they **get**.
004:012 but if ye leave a child, they **get** an eighth;
004:012 but if they leave a child, ye **get** a fourth;
004:091 seize them and slay them wherever ye **get** them:
005:037 but never will they **get** out therefrom:
005:037 Their wish will be to **get** out of the Fire,
006:120 those who earn sin will **get** due recompense
007:013 **get** out, for thou art of the meanest (of creatures)."
007:013 (Allah) said: "**Get** thee down from it: it is not for thee
007:018 (Allah) said: "**Get** out from this, disgraced
007:024 (Allah) said: "**Get** ye down, with enmity
007:110 "His plan is to **get** you out of your land:
008:030 or slay thee, or **get** thee out (of they home).
009:008 seeing that if they **get** an advantage over you,

GET (continued)

010:052 Ye **get** but the recompense of what ye earned!'"
010:071 yet I put my trust in Allah **get** ye then an agreement about
012:063 No more measure of grain shall we **get** (unless we take
012:063 our brother with us, that we may **get** our measure;
012:065 so we shall **get** (more) for our family; we shall take care
015:034 (Allah) said: "Then **get** thee out from here;
016:067 and the vine, ye **get** out strong drink,
018:082 and **get** out their treasure-a mercy
019:046 now **get** away from me for a good long while!"
020:097 (Moses) said: "**Get** thee gone! but thy (punishment)
020:117 so let him not **get** you both out of the Garden,
020:123 He said: "**Get** ye down, both of you,-all to**get**her,
021:040 to avert it, nor will they (then) **get** respite.
022:022 Every time they wish to **get** away therefrom,
025:019 so ye cannot avert (your penalty) nor (**get**) help."
026:035 "His plan is to **get** you out of your land
026:129 "And do ye **get** for yourselves fine buildings
027:018 "O ye ants, **get** into your habitations,
027:081 only those wilt thou **get** to listen who believe in Our
028:020 so **get** thee away, for I do give thee sincere advice."
030:039 who will **get** a recompense multiplied.
032:020 every time they wish to **get** away therefrom, they will be
036:059 And O ye in sin! **get** ye apart this Day!
036:073 profits from them (besides), and they **get** (milk) to drink.
038:077 (Allah) said: "Then **get** thee out from here:
040:067 then does He **get** you out (into the light) as a
059:002 Little did ye think that they would **get** out:
060:004 no power (to **get**) aught on thy behalf from Allah."

GETS

002:286 It **gets** every good that it earns,
004:012 each one of the two **gets** a sixth;
004:074 whether he is slain or **gets** victory, soon shall
005:107 But if it **gets** known that these two were guilty
013:042 who **gets** home in the End.
041:051 he turns away, and **gets** himself remote on his side

GIFT

002:236 a **gift** of a reasonable amount is due
002:236 but bestow on them (a suitable **gift**),
002:241 suitable **Gift** this is duty on the righteous.
004:134 in Allah's (**gift**) is the reward (both) of
007:190 in the **gift** they have received:
011:099 and woeful is the **gift** which shall
011:108 thy Lord willeth: a **gift** without break.
019:019 the **gift** of a pure son."
021:072 as an additional **gift**, (a grandson), Jacob,
027:036 Nay it is ye who rejoice in your **gift**!
041:032 "A hospitable **gift** from One Oft-Forgiving,
078:036 a **Gift**, (amply) sufficient,-

GIFTED

002:247 and he is not even **gifted,** with wealth in abundance?"
002:247 and hath **gifted** him abundantly with knowledge

GIFTS

002:229 to take back any of your **gifts** from (your wives),
002:253 Those Messengers We endowed with **gifts**,
002:262 and follow not up their **gifts** with reminders
003:180 withhold of the **gifts** which Allah hath given them
004:024 with **gifts** from your property, desiring
004:032 Allah hath bestowed His **gifts** more freely on some of
006:044 in the midst of their enjoyment of Our **gifts**,
006:165 in the **gifts** He hath given you: for thy
007:032 the beautiful (**gifts**) of Allah, which He
007:140 you with **gifts** above the nations?"

GIFTS (continued)

008:003 and spend (freely) out of the **gifts** We have
009:099 as pious **gifts** bringing them nearer to Allah and obtaining
009:104 and receives their **gifts** of charity, and that
013:022 spend, out of (the **gifts**) We have bestowed
016:071 are not going to throw back their **gifts** to those
016:071 Allah has bestowed His **gifts** of sustenance
029:066 Disdaining ungratefully Our **gifts** and giving
076:002 so We gave him (the **gifts**), of Hearing and Sight.
089:015 giving him honour and **gifts**, then saith he, (puffed up),

GIRLS

002:221 Nor marry (your **girls**) to unbelievers
004:025 they may wed believing **girls** from among those

GIRT

002:081 and are **girt** round by their sins,

GIVE

002:015 and **give** them rope in their trespasses;
002:025 But **give** glad tidings to those who believe
002:043 And be steadfast in prayer: **give** Zakat,
002:083 be steadfast in prayer; and **Give** Zakat.
002:110 prayer and **give** Zakat:
002:138 and who can **give** a better hue than Allah.
002:155 but **give** glad tidings to those
002:177 and **give** regular Zakat,
002:184 But he that will **give** more, of his own free will,
002:200 "Our Lord! **Give** us (thy bounties) in this world!"
002:201 "Our Lord! **give** us good in this world
002:223 and **give** (these) good tidings
002:229 if she **give** something for her freedom
002:233 The mothers shall **give** suck to their offspring
002:258 He said: "I **give** life and death."
002:258 Nor doth Allah **give** guidance to a people unjust.
002:267 out of it ye may **give** away something,
002:267 O ye who believe! **give** of the good things
002:272 ye **give** benefits your own souls,
002:272 Whatever good ye **give**, shall be
002:273 And whatever of good ye **give**,
002:276 but will **give** increase for deeds of charity:
002:277 and establish regular prayers and **give** Zakat,
002:278 and **give** up what remains of your demand
003:015 Say: shall I **give** you glad tidings of things
003:039 "Allah doth **give** thee glad tidings of Yahya,
003:041 He said: "O my Lord! **Give** me a Sign!"
003:081 saying: "I **give** you a Book and Wisdom:
003:092 and whatever ye **give**, Allah knoweth it well.
003:092 unless ye **give** (freely) of that which ye love:
003:140 We **give** to men and men by turns:
003:145 We shall **give** it to him.
003:145 We shall **give** it to him;
003:146 nor did they weaken (in will) nor **give** in.
003:153 There did Allah **give** you one distress
003:176 Allah's Plan is that He will **give** them no portion
003:191 Glory to thee! **Give** us salvation from
004:005 To those weak of understanding **give** not your property
004:005 And **give** the women (on marriage) their dower
004:008 are present, **give** them out of the (property),
004:024 **Give** them their dowery for the enjoyment
004:025 and **give** them their dowers, according
004:033 whom your right hand was pledged, **give** their due portion.
004:053 Behold, they **give** not a farthing to
004:074 soon shall We **give** him a reward of great (value).
004:091 nor **give** you guarantees of peace besides
004:114 We shall soon **give** a reward of the highest (value).

GIVE (continued)

004:127 to whom ye **give** not the portions prescribed,
004:138 To the Hypocrites **give** the glad tidings that
004:152 We shall soon **give** their (due) rewards: for Allah
004:162 to them shall We soon **give** a great reward.
004:173 He will **give** their (due) rewards,-and more,
005:005 when ye **give** them their due dowers, and desire
005:036 and twice repeated, to **give** as ransom for the
005:050 can **give** better judgment than Allah?
005:052 Ah! perhaps Allah will **give** (thee) victory, or a
005:089 or clothe them; or **give** a slave his freedom.
005:108 that they may **give** the evidence in its true
006:048 only to **give** good news and to warn: so those
006:051 **Give** this warning to those in whose (hearts)
006:079 I **give** partners to Allah."
006:081 to **give** partners to Allah without any warrant
006:148 Those who **give** partners (to Allah) will say:
006:152 **give** measure and weight with (full) justice;-
007:010 small are the thanks that ye **give**!
007:014 He said: "**Give** me respite till the day
007:038 so **give** them a double punishment in the Fire."
007:070 and **give** up that which our fathers
007:085 **Give** just measure and weight, nor withhold
007:123 before I **give** you permission?
007:128 to **give** as a heritage to such of His
007:144 and be of those who **give** thanks."
007:144 take then the (revelation) which I **give** thee,
007:155 so for**give** us and **give** us Thy mercy; for Thou
007:192 No aid can they **give** them, nor can
007:195 and **give** me no respite!
008:011 to **give** you calm as from Himself, and He
008:012 "I am with you: **give** firmness to the Believers:
008:024 to that which will **give** you life; and know
008:024 O ye who believe! **give** your response to Allah and His
008:070 He will **give** you something better than what
008:074 as well as those who **give** (them) asylum and aid,-
009:021 Their Lord doth **give** them glad tidings of a
009:043 God **give** thee grace! Why didst thou grant them
009:059 will soon **give** us of His bounty:
009:075 they would **give** (largely) in charity, and be
009:079 who **give** according to their means,-and throw
009:079 as **give** themselves freely to (deeds of) charity,
010:002 and **give** the good news to the Believers that they
010:035 any that can **give** guidance towards Truth?"
010:054 all that is on earth, would fain **give** it in ransom:
010:071 then pass your sentence on me, and **give** me no respite.
010:087 and **give** Glad Tidings to those who believe!"
011:009 If We **give** man a taste of mercy from Ourselves,
011:010 But if We **give** him a taste of (Our) favours
011:012 (feel the inclination) to **give** up a part of what is revealed
011:034 much as I desire to **give** you (good) counsel,
011:046 I **give** thee counsel, lest thou become one of the ignorants!"
011:055 all of you, and **give** me no respite.
011:084 And **give** not short measure or weight: I see you
011:085 "And O my people! **give** just measure and weight,
012:056 Thus did We **give** established power to Joseph
012:087 and never **give** up hope of Allah's soothing Mercy:
012:110 when the messengers **give** up hope (of their people)
014:010 your sins and **give** you respite for a term
014:037 so that they may **give** thanks.
015:023 And verily, it is We Who **give** life, and Who **give** death:
015:036 (Iblis) said: "O my Lord! **give** me then respite
015:053 They said: "Fear not! we **give** thee glad tidings

GIVE (continued)

015:054 He said: "Do ye **give** me such glad tidings
015:055 They said: "We **give** thee glad tidings in truth;
016:011 is a Sign for those who **give** thought.
016:041 We will assuredly **give** a goodly home in this
016:044 and that they may **give** thought.
016:069 for those who **give** thought.
016:078 that ye may **give** thanks (to Allah).
016:081 some things to **give** you shade; of the
016:097 to him will We **give** a life that is
017:015 We had sent a messenger (to **give** warning).
017:035 **Give** full measure when ye measure, and weigh
017:101 To Moses We did **give** nine Clear Signs:
017:105 and We sent thee but to **give** Glad Tidings
018:002 and that He may **give** Glad Tidings to the
018:040 "It may be that my Lord will **give** me something
018:044 and the Best to **give** success.
018:056 glad tidings and to **give** warnings: but the
018:056 We only send the Messengers to **give** glad tidings
018:060 "I will not **give** up until I reach the junction
018:081 their Lord would **give** them in exchange (a son) better in
018:105 on the Day of Judgment, **give** them any Weight.
019:005 so **give** me an heir as from Thyself,-
019:007 We **give** thee good news of a son: his name
019:010 (Zakariya) said "O my Lord! **give** me a Sign,"
019:063 Such is the Garden which We **give** as an
019:081 to **give** them power and glory!
019:097 that with it thou mayest **give** glad tidings
020:029 "And **give** me a Minister from my family,
020:071 before I **give** you permission? Surely this
020:071 which of us can **give** the more severe and the
021:008 Nor did We **give** them bodies that ate no food,
021:010 a book which We **give** you eminence.
021:073 and to **Give** zakat and they constantly served
022:034 and **give** thou the good news to those who humble
022:041 and **give** zakat, enjoin the right and forbid
022:048 And to how many populations **did I give** respite,
022:049 to **give** a clear warning:
022:066 and will again **give** you life: truly man
022:078 regular Prayer, **give** zakat and hold fast
023:072 He is the Best of those who **give** sustenance.
023:078 little thanks it is ye **give**!
024:032 Allah will **give** them means out of His grace:
024:033 yea, **give** them something yourselves out of
024:033 (for emancipation) **give** them such a deed if you
024:056 and **give** zakat and obey the Messenger; that ye
024:062 **give** leave to those of them whom thou wilt,
025:007 to him to **give** admonition with him?
025:010 and He could **give** thee Palaces (secure to dwell in).
025:010 His Will, could **give** thee better (things) than those,-
025:049 That with it We may **give** life to a dead land,
025:056 to **give** glad tidings and warnings.
025:074 and **give** us (the grace) to lead the righteous."
026:049 "Believe ye in Him before I **give** you permission?
026:181 **Give** just measure, and cause not loss (to others by fraud).
027:003 Those who establish regular prayers and **give** zakat,
027:036 he said: "Will ye **give** me abundance in wealth?
027:086 and the Day to **give** them light?
028:020 for I do **give** thee sincere advice."
028:043 earlier generations, (to **give**) Insight to men,
028:046 to **give** warning to a people to whom no warner
028:071 who can **give** you light?
028:072 who can **give** you a Night in which ye can rest?

GIVE (continued)

028:083 Home of the Hereafter We shall **give** to those who intend
029:017 have no power to **give** you sustenance: then seek
029:058 to them shall We **give** a Home in Heaven,-
029:065 they **give** a share (of their worship to others)!-
030:036 When We **give** men a taste of Mercy, they exult
030:038 So **give** what is due to kindred, the needy
030:039 That which you **give** in usury for increase
030:039 but that which you **give** for charity, seeking the
030:040 to die; and again He will **give** you life.
030:041 that (Allah) may **give** them a taste of some
030:050 verily the Same will **give** life to the men
031:004 and **give** zakat and have sure faith
031:031 who constantly persevere and **give** thanks.
032:009 little thanks do ye **give**!
032:023 We did indeed aforetime **give** the Book to Moses:
033:017 to **give** you punishment or to **give** you Mercy?"
033:033 regular Prayer and **give** zakat and obey
033:035 who **give** in charity, for men and women who fast,
033:047 Then **give** the glad tidings to the Believers,
033:049 so **give** them a present, and release
033:051 with that which thou hast to **give** them:
033:068 "Our Lord! **give** them Double Chastisement
034:017 and never do We **give** (such) requital except to such as
035:003 other than Allah, to **give** you sustenance
035:030 nay, He will **give** them (even) more out of
035:037 Did we not **give** you long enough life so that
036:011 **give** such a one, therefore, good things, or Forgiveness
036:012 Verily We shall **give** life to the dead, And We
036:033 We do **give** it life, and produce
036:035 will they not then **give** thanks?
036:070 That it may **give** admonition to any (who are)
036:078 "Who can **give** life to (dry) bones and decomposed
036:079 Say, "He will **give** them life Who created
037:036 And say: "What! Shall we **give** up our gods
038:070 that I am to **give** warning plainly and publicly."
038:079 (Iblis) said: "O my Lord! **give** me then respite
039:035 and **give** them their reward according to the
039:066 and be of those who **give** thanks.
040:053 We did aforetime **give** Moses the Guidance,
040:061 and the Day, as to **give** you light.
040:061 yet most men **give** no thanks.
041:016 that We might **give** them a taste of a Chastisement
041:027 But We will certainly **give** the Unbelievers a taste
041:039 can surely **give** life to (men) who are dead.
041:050 We shall **give** them the taste of a severe Chastisement.
041:050 When We **give** him a taste of some mercy from Us,
042:020 of the Hereafter, We **give** increase in his tilth;
042:023 We shall **give** Him an increase of good
042:048 And truly, when We **give** man a taste of Mercy
043:018 and unable to **give** a clear account in a dispute
043:040 or **give** direction to the blind or to such
044:058 in thy tongue, in order that they may **give** heed.
046:015 bear him, and in pain did she **give** him birth.
046:024 they said, "This cloud will **give** us rain!"
046:033 is able to **give** life to the dead?
047:036 and will not ask you (to **give** up) your possession.
048:011 if His Will is to **give** you some loss or to **give** you some
050:011 and We **give** (new) life therewith to land
050:043 Verily it is We Who **give** Life and Death;
054:035 Thus do We reward those who **give** thanks.
056:070 then why do ye not **give** thanks?
057:018 For those who **give** in Charity, men and women,

GIVE (continued)

058:013 establish regular prayer; **give** zakat and obey
059:009 but **give** them preference over themselves,
061:013 So **give** the Glad Tidings
063:010 Why didst thou not **give** me respite for a
065:006 suckle your (offspring), **give** them their recompense:
066:005 that Allah will **give** him in exchange Consorts
067:023 and understanding: little thanks it is ye **give**.
068:032 "It may be that our Lord will **give** us in exchange
071:004 and **give** you respite for a stated Term:
071:012 "`**Give** you increase in wealth and sons;
071:021 whose wealth and children **give** them no Increase
073:020 and establish regular Prayer and **give** zakat;
075:040 the power to **give** life to the dead?
076:021 and their Lord will **give** to them to drink a pure drink.
083:003 or weight to men, **give** less than due.
083:003 But when they have to **give** by measure or weight
086:017 **give** respite to them gently (for a while).
087:009 Therefore **give** admonition in case the admonition
092:016 Who **give** the lie to Truth and turn their backs.
093:005 will thy Guardian-Lord **give** thee (that wherewith)
093:006 and **give** thee shelter (and care)?
098:005 and to **give** zakat; and that

GIVEN

002:025 for they are **given** things in similitude;
002:059 the word from that which had been **given** them;
002:063 We have **given** you and bring (ever) to
002:093 (saying): "Hold firmly to what We **given** you,
002:096 be **given** a life of a thousand years:
002:121 Those to whom We have **given** the Book
002:136 and that **given** to (all) Prophets
002:136 and that **given** to Moses and Jesus,
002:136 and the revelation **given** to us,
003:023 those who have been **given** a portion of the Book?
003:079 that a man, to whom is **given** the Book, and Wisdom.
003:084 and in (the books) **given** to Moses, Jesus, and the
003:180 Allah hath **given** them of His Grace,
004:019 of the dower ye have **given** them, except
004:020 even if ye had **given** the latter
004:034 because Allah has **given** the one more (strength)
004:039 what Allah hath **given** them for sustenance?
004:044 to those who were **given** a portion of the Book?
004:051 to those who were **given** a portion of the Book?
004:054 But We had already **given** the people of Abraham
004:054 for what Allah hath **given** them of His bounty?
004:067 And We should then have **given** them from Ourselves a
004:090 He could have **given** them power over you,
004:107 for Allah loveth not one **given** to perfidy and sin:
005:003 who reject Faith **given** up all hope of your religion:
005:020 He had not **given** to any other among the peoples.
005:041 they say, "If ye are **given** this, take it, but if
005:048 in what He hath **given** you: so strive
005:087 for Allah loveth not those **given** to excess.
006:006 in strength such as We have not **given** to you-
006:020 Those to whom We have **given** the Book know this
006:081 without any warrant having been **given** to you?
006:114 to whom We have **given** the Book, that it
006:148 we should not have **given** partners to Him,
006:165 in the gifts He hath **given** you: for thy
007:003 Follow (O men!) the revelation **given** unto you from
007:033 for which He hath **given** no authority; and saying
007:133 a people **given** to sin.
007:144 by the messages I (have **given** thee) and the

GIVEN (continued)

007:162 which had been **given** them, so We sent
007:163 for they were **given** to transgression.
007:165 that had been **given** them, We rescued
007:165 because they were **given** to transgression.
007:171 "Hold firmly to what We have **given** you, and bring
008:003 We have **given** them for sustenance:
008:042 who live might live after a Clear Sign (had been **given**).
008:042 who died might die after a Clear Sign (had been **given**),
008:071 and so hath He **given** (thee) power over them.
009:058 If they are **given** part thereof, they are pleased,
011:075 and **given** to penitence.
011:088 and He hath **given** me sustenance (pure and)
011:099 which shall be **given** (unto them)!
011:116 the good things of life which were **given** them,
012:009 of your father may be **given** to you alone:
013:036 Those to whom We have **given** the Book rejoice at
014:016 and he is **given**, for drink, boiling fetid water.
014:021 we should have **given** it to you:
014:031 the Sustenance We have **given** them, secretly and
014:034 Verily, man is **given** up to injustice
017:005 Our servants **given** to terrible warfare:
017:011 as he prays for good for man is **given** to haste.
017:016 are **given** the good things of this life (to be obedient)
017:033 We have **given** his heir authority (to demand Qisas or to
017:070 **given** them for sustenance things good and pure;
017:071 those who are **given** their record in their right hand will
017:074 And had We not **given** thee strength, thou wouldst
017:107 that those who were **given** knowledge beforehand,
019:030 He hath **given** me revelation and made me a prophet:
019:077 "I shall certainly be **given** wealth and children"?
019:097 and warnings to people **given** to contention.
020:013 then to the inspiration (**given** to thee).
020:131 for the things We have **given** for enjoyment
021:013 of this life which were **given** you, and to
021:074 truly they were a people **given** to Evil, a rebellious
021:077 truly they were a people **given** to Evil: so We
021:105 after the Message (**given** to Moses): My servants
022:039 permission is **given** (to fight), because they
022:045 which were **given** to wrong-doing?
022:048 give respite, which were **given** to wrong-doing?
024:028 enter not until permission is **given** to you:
024:033 out of the means which Allah has **given** to you.
026:207 It will profit them not the enjoyment they were **given.**
027:016 and we have been **given** of everything, this is
027:033 with strength, and **given** to vehement war:
027:036 He has **given** you! Nay it is
027:036 has **given** me is better than that which He has
028:021 save me from people **given** to wrong-doing."
028:050 For Allah guides not people **given** to wrong-doing.
028:054 Twice will they be **given** their reward, for that
028:054 out of what We have **given** them.
028:060 The (material) things which ye are **given** are but
028:061 and one to whom We have **given** the good
028:078 He said: "This has been **given** to me because of
033:053 is **given** you,- for a meal, (and then)
034:038 to frustrate them, will be **given** over into
034:044 But We had not **given** them Books which they
035:032 Then We have **given** the Book for inheritance
035:040 Or have We **given** them a Book from which
037:067 be **given** a mixture made of boiling water.
039:049 he says, "This has been **given** to me because of
039:074 and has **given** us (this) land in heritage:

GIVEN (continued)

040:011 made us to die, and twice hast Thou **given** us Life!
040:064 and has **given** you shape-and made
041:021 They will say: "Allah hath **given** us speech,-
042:028 (even) after (men) have **given** up all hope,
042:036 Whatever ye are **given** (here) is (but)
043:021 What! have We **given** them a Book before this,
043:029 Yea, I have **given** the good things of this life
044:022 "These are indeed a people **given** to sin."
044:029 nor were they **given** a respite (again).
045:031 and were a people **given** to sin!
046:025 Thus do We recompense those **given** to sin!
046:026 We have not **given** to you (ye Quraish)! and We
047:015 and be **given**, to drink, boiling water, so that
048:016 (to fight) against a people **given** to vehement war
048:020 and He has **given** you these beforehand; and He
050:020 whereof warning (had been **given**).
052:046 avail them nothing and no help shall be **given** them.
053:026 has **given** leave for whom He pleases and that
057:016 not become like those to whom was **given** The Book
059:009 in their hearts for things **given** to the (latter),
063:010 have **given** (largely) in charity, and I
064:003 and has **given** you shape, and made
065:002 Such is the admonition **given** to him who believes
065:007 let him spend according to what Allah has **given** him.
065:007 no burden o any person beyond what He has **given** him.
069:019 Then He that will be **given** his Record in his
069:025 And he that will be **given** his Record in his
069:025 "Ah! would that my record had not been **given** to me!
071:004 For when the Term **given** by Allah is accomplished,
071:007 and **given** themselves up to arrogance.
074:052 to be **given** scrolls (of revelation) spread out!
076:017 And they will be **given** to drink there of a Cup
079:028 and He hath **given** it order and perfection.
083:027 With it will be (**given**) a mixture of Tasnim:
084:007 Then he who is **given** his Record in his Right hand,
084:010 But he who is **given** his Record behind his back,-
087:002 Who hath created and further, **given** order and proportion;
088:005 The while they are **given**, to drink,
091:007 and order **given** to it;
099:005 For that thy Lord will have **given** her inspiration.

GIVES

002:164 the life which He **gives** therewith to an earth that is dead;
002:207 type of man who **gives** his life to earn the pleasure of
003:156 It is Allah that **gives** Life and Death,
010:035 Say: "It is Allah Who **gives** guidance towards Truth.
010:035 Is then He Who **gives** guidance to Truth more worthy to
016:061 but He **gives** them respite for a stated Term:
016:065 the skies, and **gives** therewith life to the earth
017:083 he **gives** himself up to despair!
022:006 it is He Who **gives** life to the dead, and it
023:080 It is He Who **gives** life and death, and to
024:033 until Allah **gives** them means out of His grace.
026:079 "Who **gives** me food and drink,
027:064 then repeats it, and Who **gives** you sustenance
029:062 (which He **gives**) to whichever of His servants
029:063 and **gives** life therewith to the earth after its
030:005 He **gives** victory to whom He will, and He
030:019 and Who **gives** life to the earth after it is dead:
030:024 and with it **gives** life to the earth after it
030:033 but when He **gives** them a taste of Mercy
030:050 Allah's Mercy!-how He **gives** life to the earth
033:050 any believing woman who **gives** herself to the Prophet

GIVES (continued)

034:024   Say: "Who **gives** you sustenance, from the
035:045   but he **gives** them respite for a stated Term:
040:068   It is He Who **gives** Life and Death; and when
041:039   He Who **gives** life to the (dead) earth can surely
041:049   he **gives** up all hope (and) is lost in despair.
042:009   and it is He Who **gives** life to the dead:
042:019   He **gives** Sustenance to whom He pleases: and He
042:023   Allah **gives** Glad Tidings to His Servants who believe
042:026   and **gives** them increase of His bounty:
044:008   it is He Who **gives** life and **gives** death,-the Lord
045:026   then **gives** you death; then He
045:026   Say: "It is Allah Who **gives** you life,
050:037   or who **gives** ear and earnestly witnesses.
051:016   which their Lord **gives** them, because, before
051:058   For Allah is He Who **gives** (all) Sustenance,-
053:034   **Gives** a little, then hardens (his heart)?
057:002   it is He Who **gives** life and Death; and He
059:006   but Allah **gives** power to His Messenger over any
059:007   So take what the Messenger **gives** you, and refrain from
072:002   'It **gives** guidance to the Right, and we
092:005   So he who **gives** (in charity) and fears (Allah),
092:009   And **gives** the lie to the Best,-

GIVEST

002:260   "My Lord! show me how thou **givest** life to the dead.
003:026   thou **givest** power to whom Thou pleasest,
003:027   and Thou **givest** sustenance to whom Thou pleasest,
007:189   (saying): "If Thou **givest** us a goodly child, we

GIVETH

002:245   It is Allah that **giveth** (you) want or Plenty,
002:258   "My Lord is He Who **Giveth** life and death."
002:261   Allah **giveth** manifold increase to whom
003:045   "O Mary! Allah **giveth** thee glad tidings
004:040   and **giveth** from His Own self a great reward.
004:058   the teaching which He **giveth** you!
005:064   He **giveth** and spendeth (of His Bounty)
006:088   He **giveth** that guidance to whom He pleaseth,
007:158   it is He that **giveth** both life and death.
007:190   But when He **giveth** them a goodly child, they
009:116   He **giveth** life and He taketh it.
010:056   Is it He who **giveth** life and who taketh it, and to
013:026   (which He **giveth**) to whom so He pleaseth.
014:034   And He **giveth** you of all that ye ask for.
014:042   He but **giveth** them respite against a Day when
017:009   and **giveth** the glad tidings to the Believers who work
024:040   for any to whom Allah **giveth** not light,
041:021   us speech,-(He) Who **giveth** speech to everything:
053:048   That it is He Who **giveth** wealth and satisfaction,
057:017   Know ye (all) that Allah **giveth** life to the
086:011   By the Firmament which **giveth** returns rain,

GIVING

006:065   **giving** you a taste of mutual vengeance-
006:078   from your (guilt) of **giving** partners to Allah.
009:019   Do ye make the **giving** of drink to pilgrims,
016:090   of good, and **giving** to kith and kin, and He
022:002   every mother **giving** suck shall forget
025:061   a lamp and a Moon **giving** light;
029:066   and **giving** themselves up to (worldly) enjoyment!
030:046   **giving** you a taste of His Mercy,-
032:024   Leaders, **giving** guidance under Our command, so long
034:028   **giving** them glad tidings, and warning them (against sin),
040:065   call upon Him, **giving** Him sincere devotion.
041:004   **Giving** Good News and Admonition:

GIVING (continued)

061:006   (which came) before me, and **giving** glad Tidings
074:006   Nor expect, in **giving**, any increase (for thyself)!
089:015   trieth him, **giving** him honour and gifts,
090:014   Or the **giving** of food in a day of privation

GLAD

002:025   But give **glad** tidings to those who believe
002:097   and guidance and **glad** tidings for those who believe,
002:119   in truth as a bearer of **glad** tidings and a warner:
002:155   but give **glad** tidings to those
002:213   with **glad** tidings and warnings;
003:015   Shall I give you **glad** tidings of things far better than
003:039   "Allah doth give thee **glad** tidings of Yahya,
003:045   Allah giveth thee **glad** tidings of a Word from Him:
005:019   unto us no bringer of **glad** tidings and no warner.
005:019   a bringer of **glad** tidings and a warner.
007:057   the Winds like heralds of **glad** tidings, going
007:188   and a bringer of **glad** tidings to those
009:021   Their Lord doth give them **glad** tidings of a
009:112   So proclaim the **glad** tidings to the Believers.
010:064   For them are **Glad** Tidings, in the life
010:087   and give **Glad** Tidings to those who believe!"
011:002   from Him to warn and to bring **glad** tidings:
011:069   to Abraham with **glad** tidings.
011:071   but We gave her **glad** tidings of Isaac, and after him
011:074   (the mind of) Abraham and the **glad** tidings had reached
015:053   "Fear not! We give thee **glad** tidings of a son endowed
015:054   give me such **glad** tidings even though old age has seized
015:055   They said: "We give thee **glad** tidings in truth;
016:089   a Mercy, and **Glad** Tidings to Muslims.
016:102   and as a Guide and **Glad** tidings to Muslims.
017:009   and giveth the **glad** tidings to the Believers who work
017:105   **Glad** Tidings and to warn (sinners).
018:002   and that He may give **Glad** Tidings to the
018:056   Messengers to give **glad** tidings and to give warnings:
019:097   that with it thou mayest give **glad** tidings to the righteous,
025:048   as heralds of **glad** tidings, going before
025:056   to give **glad** tidings and warnings.
027:002   A Guide; and **Glad** Tidings for the Believers,
027:063   of **glad** tidings, going before His Mercy?
030:046   as heralds go **Glad** Tidings, giving you
033:045   as a Witness, a Bearer of **Glad** Tidings, and a
033:047   Then give the **glad** tidings to the Believers,
034:028   giving them **glad** tidings, and warning
035:024   as a bearer of **glad** tidings, and as a warner:
041:030   But receive the **Glad** Tidings of the
042:023   gives **Glad** Tidings to His Servants who believe
046:012   and as **Glad** Tidings to those who do right.
048:008   as a bringer of **Glad** Tidings, and as a Warner:
051:028   gave him **glad** tidings of a son endowed
061:006   giving **glad** Tidings of a messenger to come after me,
001:013   the **Glad** Tidings to the Believers.

GLANCE

003:153   without even casting a side **glance** at anyone,
027:040   bring it to thee before ever thy **glance** returns to thee.
037:088   Then did he cast a **glance** at the Stars,
042:045   abject in humbleness (and) looking with a stealthy **glance**.

GLANCES

037:048   chaste women; restraining their **glances**, with big
038:052   will be chaste women restraining their **glances**,
055:056   Chaste, restraining their **glances**, whom no
055:072   maidens restrained (as to their **glances**), in (goodly)

GLARING
033:058 (on themselves) a calumny and a **glaring** sin.

GLASS
024:035 the Lamp enclosed in **Glass**:
024:035 the **glass** as it were a brilliant star: lit from
027:044 paved smooth with slabs of **glass**."

GLIBLY
024:014 seized you in that ye rushed **glibly** into this affair.
046:008 whereof ye talk (so **glibly**)!

GLIDE
079:003 And by those who **glide** along (on errands of mercy),

GLISTEN
019:004 and the hair of my head doth **glisten** with grey:

GLITTER
011:015 the Present and its **glitter**,-to them
018:028 and **glitter** of this Life; nor obey
019:074 in enjoyment and in **glitter** to the eye?
028:060 and the **glitter** thereof; but that
028:079 in the (pride of his worldly) **glitter**.
033:028 of this world, and its **glitter**,-then come!

GLITTERING
018:007 but as a **glittering** show for it, in order

GLOOM
003:106 and some faces will be (in the **gloom** of) black:
026:189 of overshadowing **gloom** seized them, and that

GLORIFIED
024:036 in them is He **glorified** in the in the mornings
037:143 (repented and) **glorified** Allah,

GLORIFY
002:030 Thy praises and **glorify** Thy Holy (name)?"
002:185 and to **glorify** Him in that He has guide you;
003:041 and **glorify** Him in the evening and in the morning."
007:206 they **glorify** Him and prostrate before Him.
022:037 that ye may **glorify** Allah for His guidance to you:
033:042 And **glorify** Him morning and evening.
056:074 Then **glorify** the name of the Lord, the Supreme!
056:096 So **glorify** the name of thy Lord, the Supreme.
068:028 "Did I not say to you, 'Why not **glorify** (Allah)?'"
069:052 So **glorify** the name of thy Lord Most High.
076:026 and **glorify** Him a long night through.
087:001 **Glorify** the name of thy Guardian-Lord, Most High,

GLORIOUS
009:052 other than one of two **glorious** things-
050:001 Qaf. By the **Glorious** Qur'an (Thou art
071:016 as a (**Glorious**) Lamp?
085:021 Nay, this is a **Glorious** Qur'an,
091:001 By the Sun and his (**glorious**) splendor;
093:001 By the **Glorious** Morning Light.

GLORY
002:032 They said: "**Glory** to Thee,
002:116 **Glory** be to Him.-
002:255 For He is the Most High, the Supreme (in **glory**).
003:170 the (Martyrs) **glory** in the fact
003:191 **Glory** to thee! Give us salvation from
004:171 for Allah is One God: **glory** be to him:
005:116 He will say: "**Glory** to Thee! never could
006:100 praise and **glory** be to Him! (for He is)
007:143 "**Glory** be to Thee! To Thee
009:031 Praise and **glory** to Him: (far is He) from having
010:005 shining **glory** and the moon to be a light
010:010 "**Glory** to Thee, O Allah!" and "Peace" will be
010:018 in the heaven or on earth?-**Glory** to Him! and far

GLORY (continued)
010:068 **Glory** be to Him! He is Self-Sufficient!
011:073 all praise, full of all **glory**!"
012:108 **Glory** to Allah! and never will I join gods
016:001 **glory** to Him, and far is he above having the partners
016:057 **Glory** be to Him!-and for themselves what they desire!
017:001 **Glory** to (Allah) Who did take His Servant
017:043 **Glory** to Him! He is high above all that they say!
017:044 and all beings therein, declare His **glory**:
017:044 ye understand not how they declare His **glory**!
017:079 raise thee to a Station of Praise and **Glory**!
017:093 Say: "**Glory** to my Lord! am I aught
017:108 And they say: "**Glory** to our Lord! Truly has
017:111 Yea, magnify Him for His greatness and **glory**!"
019:035 **Glory** to Him! When He determines a matter,
019:081 to give them power and **glory**!
021:022 But **glory** to Allah, the Lord
021:026 **Glory** to Him! They are (but) servants raised to honour.
021:028 and reverence of His (**glory**).
021:087 **Glory** to Thee: I was indeed wrong!"
023:091 **Glory** to Allah (He is free) from the (sort of)
024:016 **glory** to Thee (our Lord) this is
025:018 They will say: "**Glory** to Thee! not meant
027:008 and those around: and **Glory** to Allah, the Lord
028:068 **Glory** to Allah! and far is He above the partners
030:017 So (give) **glory** to Allah, when ye
030:040 **Glory** to Him! and High is He above the partners
034:041 They will say, "**Glory** to thee! Thou art
035:010 to Allah belong all **glory** and power.
035:010 If any do seek for **glory** and power,-to Allah
036:036 **Glory** to Allah, Who created in pairs
036:083 So **glory** to Him in Whose hands is the
037:159 **Glory** to Allah! (He is free) from the things
037:166 who declare (Allah's) **glory**!"
037:180 **Glory** to thy Lord, the Lord of Honour and Power!
039:004 but **Glory** be to Him! (He is above such things).
039:067 **Glory** to Him! High is He above the Partners they
039:075 on all sides, singing **Glory** and Praise to their
040:007 and those around it sing **Glory** and Praise
040:064 So **Glory** to Allah, the Lord of the Worlds!
042:005 from above them (by His **Glory**): and the
043:013 of your Lord, and say, "**Glory** to Him Who has
043:082 **Glory** to the Lord of the heavens and the earth,
057:001 and **Glory** of Allah: for He is
059:001 and **Glory** of Allah: for He
059:023 the justly Proud, **Glory** to Allah! (high is He)
059:024 doth declare His Praises and **Glory**:
061:001 declares the Praises and **Glory** of Allah:
062:001 and **Glory** of Allah,-the Sovereign, the Holy One,
064:001 and **Glory** of Allah: to Him belongs Dominion,
068:029 They said: "**Glory** to our Lord! Verily we
085:015 Lord of the Throne full of all **Glory**,
091:003 By the Day as it shows up (the Sun's) **glory**;
092:002 By the Day as it appears in **glory**;

GLOW
084:016 So I do call to witness the ruddy **glow** of Sunset;

GNAT
002:026 even of a **gnat** as well as anything above it.

GNAWING
034:014 which kept (slowly) **gnawing** away at his staff:

GO
001:007 and who **go** not astray.
002:061 **Go** ye down to any town,

GO (continued)

002:210   all questions **go** back (for decision).
002:249   only those who taste not of it **go** with me;
003:090   And then **go** on adding to their defiance of Faith,
004:071   And either **go** forth in parties or **go** forth all together.
004:094   O ye who believe! when ye **go** out in the cause
004:137   and **go** on increasing in Unbelief, Allah will
005:024   **Go** thou, and thy Lord, and fight
005:061   and they **go** out with the same.
006:077   I shall surely be among those who **go** astray."
009:002   **Go** ye, then, for four months, (as you will),
009:038   that when ye are asked to **go** forth in
009:039   Unless ye **go** forth, He will
009:041   **Go** ye forth, (whether equipped) lightly
009:081   they said, "**Go** not forth in the heat."
009:122   It is not for the Believers to **go** forth together:
009:122   from every expedition **go** forth to devote
011:098   He will **go** before his people on the
012:050   (Joseph) said: "**Go** thou back to thy lord,
012:087   "O my sons! **go** ye and enquire about Joseph
012:093   "**Go** with this my shirt, and cast it
015:056   the mercy of his Lord, but such as **go** astray?"
015:065   and do thou **go** behind them: let no one
017:063   Allah said: "**Go** thy way; if any of them follow
017:066   maketh the Ship **go** smoothly for you through the sea,
019:075   Say: "Whoever **goes** astray, (Allah) Most
020:024   "**Go** thou to Pharaoh, for he
020:042   "**Go**, thou and thy brother, with My
020:043   "**Go**, both of you, to Pharaoh, for he
020:047   "So **go** ye both to him, and say, `Verily we
020:053   has enabled you to **go** about therein by roads
020:118   for thee not to **go** hungry nor to **go** naked,
021:003   Will ye **go** to witchcraft with
021:057   after ye **go** away and turn your backs"...
022:076   and to Allah **go** back all affairs (for decision).
024:028   if ye are asked to **go** back, **go** back:
025:036   And We commanded: "**Go** ye both, to the
026:010   "**Go** to the people of iniquity,-
026:016   "So **go** forth, both of you, to Pharaoh,
027:028   **Go** thou, with this letter of mine, and deliver
027:037   "**Go** back to them, and be sure we shall come
027:069   Say: "**Go** ye through the earth and see what has
032:026   in whose dwellings they (now) **go** to and fro?
033:013   Therefore **go** back!" and a band of them ask for
037:099   He said: "I will **go** to my Lord! He will
038:006   And the leaders among them **go** away (impatiently),
043:033   and (silver) stair-ways on which to **go** up,
047:016   till when they **go** out from thee,
053:017   (His) sight never swerved, nor did it **go** wrong!
056:051   "Then will ye truly,-**go** wrong, and deny (the truth);
056:092   if he be of those who deny (the truth) who **go** wrong,
057:005   and all affairs **go** back to Allah.
058:003   to their wives then wish to **go** back on the words
059:011   "If ye are expelled, We too will **go** out with you,
059:012   If they are expelled, never will they **go** out with them;
059:017   that they will **go** into the Fire, dwelling therein
061:005   Allah let their hearts **go** wrong.
068:022   "**Go** ye to your tilth (betimes) in the morning,
071:020   That ye may **go** about therein, in spacious roads."
079:017   "**Go** thou to Pharaoh, for he has
081:016   **Go** straight, or hide;
081:026   Then whither **go** ye?
081:028   wills to **go** straight:

GO (continued)

084:013   Truly, did he **go** about among his people, rejoicing!
105:002   Did He not make their treacherous plan **go** astray?

GOAL

002:148   To each is a **goal** to which Allah turns him;
003:028   for the final **goal** is to Allah.
005:018   and unto Him is the final **goal** (of all)."
005:048   The **goal** of you all is to Allah; it is He
014:018   that is the straying far, far (from the **goal**).
031:014   to Me is (thy final) **Goal**.
040:003   There is no god but He: to Him is the Final **Goal**.
042:015   and to Him is (Our) final **goal**.
042:046   there is no way (to the **Goal**).
053:042   That to thy Lord is the final **Goal**;
064:010   and evil is that **Goal**.

GOAL-POST

070:043   a **goal-post** (fixed for them),-

GOALS

003:014   the best of the **goals** (to return to).

GOAT-HERD

002:171   is as if one were to shout like a **goat-herd**,

GOATS

006:143   of sheep a pair, and of **goats** a pair, say,

GOBLETS

043:071   dishes and **goblets** of gold:
056:018   With **goblets**, (shining) beakers, and cups
076:015   vessels of silver and **goblets** of crystal,-
088:014   **Goblets** placed (ready),

GOD

002:133   worship thy **God** and the **God** of thy fathers,
002:133   the one (True) **God**;
002:153   for **God** is with those who patiently persevere.
002:163   And your **God** is One **God**:
002:163   there is no **god** but He,
002:255   Allah! There is no **god** but He, the living,
003:002   Allah! there is no **god** but He,
003:006   There is no **god** but He,
003:018   There is no **god** but He:
003:018   There is no **god** but He the Exalted in Power,
003:062   there is no **god** except Allah;
004:171   for Allah is One **God**: glory be to him:
005:073   for there is no **god** except One **God**.
006:019   Say: "But in truth He is the One **God**.
006:046   who-a **god** other than Allah-could restore
006:102   There is no **god** but He, the Creator
006:106   there is no **god** but He: and turn
007:059   worship Allah! ye have not other **god** but Him.
007:065   ye have no other **god** but Him.
007:073   ye have no other **god** but Him.
007:085   ye have no other **god** but Him.
007:138   a **god** like unto the **god**s they have."
007:140   a **god** other than Allah, when it is
007:158   there is no **god** but He: it is He
009:031   to worship but One **God**: there is no **god** but He.
009:043   **God** give thee grace! Why didst thou grant them
009:129   there is no **god** but He: On him is my trust,-He the
010:090   no **god** except Him Who the Children
011:084   ye have no other **god** but Him.
013:030   Say: "He is my Lord! There is no **god** but He!
014:052   and may know that He is One **God**: let men
015:096   Those who adopt, with Allah, another **god**:
016:002   (saying): "Warn (Man) that there is no **god** but I:

GOD (continued)

016:022 Your **God** is One **God**: as to those
016:051 for He is just one **God**: then fear Me
017:022 Take not with Allah another **god**; or thou
018:110 that your **God** is one **God**: whoever expects
020:008 Allah! there is no **god** but He!
020:014 "Verily, I am Allah: there is no **god** but I:
020:088 "This is your **god**, and the **god** of Moses, but (Moses)
020:097 now look at thy **god**, of whom thou hast become a
020:098 But the **God** of you all is Allah: there is no **god** but He:
021:025 that there is no **god** but I; therefore worship
021:029 "I am a **god** besides Him," such a one
021:087 "There is no **god** but Thou: Glory to
022:034 But your **God** is One **God**: submit then
023:023 Ye have no other **god** but Him.
023:032 no other **god** but Him. Will ye not fear (Him)?"
023:091 each **god** would have taken away what he had created,
023:091 nor is there any **god** along with Him:
023:116 there is no **god** but He, the Lord
023:117 If anyone invokes, besides Allah, any other **god**, he has
025:043 for his **god** his own passion (or impulse)?
025:068 Those who invoke not, with Allah, any other **god**,
026:029 "If thou takest any **god** other than me, I will
026:213 So call not on any other **god** with Allah,
027:026 "Allah!-there is no **god** but He!-Lord of
027:060 (Can there be another) **god** besides Allah? Nay, they
027:061 (can there be another) **god** besides Allah? Nay, most
027:062 (Can there be another) **god** besides Allah?
027:063 (Can there be another) **god** besides Allah?-High is Allah
027:064 (Can there be another) **god** besides Allah? Say, "Bring
028:038 that I may mount up to the **god** of Moses:
028:038 Pharaoh said: "O Chiefs! no **god** do I know
028:070 And He is Allah: there is no **god** but He. To Him
028:071 what **god** is there other than Allah, who can
028:072 what **god** is there other than Allah, who can
028:088 And call not, besides Allah, on another **god**.
028:088 There is no **god** but He.
029:046 Our **God** and your **God** is one; and it
035:003 There is no **god** but He: how then
037:004 Verily, verily, your **God** is One!-
037:035 there is no **god** except Allah, would puff
038:005 "Has he made gods (all) into one **God**?
038:065 no **god** is there but Allah, the One
039:006 There is no **god** but He: then how
040:003 There is no **god** but He: to Him is the Final Goal.
040:037 to the **God** of Moses; but surely
040:062 there is no **god** but He: then how
040:065 There is no **god** but He: call upon
040:084 the One **God**-and we reject the partners we used
041:006 that your **God** is One **God**: so take
043:084 It is He Who is **God** in heaven and **God** on earth;
044:008 There is no **god** but He: it is He
045:023 as his **god** his own vain desire?
047:019 Know, therefore, that there is no **god** but Allah,
050:026 "Who set up another **god** besides Allah: throw him
052:043 Or have they a **god** other then Allah?
059:022 Allah is He, than Whom there is no other **god**;-
059:023 Allah is He, than Whom there is no other **god**;-
064:013 Allah! there is no **god** but He: and on
072:020 and I join not with Him any (false **god**)."
073:009 there is no **god** but He: take Him
114:003 The **God** (or Judge) of Mankind,-

GOD-FEARING

002:177 Such are the people of truth, the **God-fearing**.
002:180 this is due from the **God-fearing**.
005:023 (But) among (their) **God-fearing** men were two
069:048 But verily this is a Message for the **God-fearing**.

GOD-PARTNERS

007:195 Say: "Call your '**god-partner**s', scheme

GODDESS

053:020 And another, the third (**goddess**), Manat?

GODHEAD

042:021 What! have they partners (in **godhead**), who have
068:041 Or have they some "Partners" (in **Godhead**)?

GODLESS

018:002 in order that He may warn (the **godless**) of a

GODLY

003:146 and with them (fought) large bands of **godly** men?
016:027 concerning whom ye used to dispute (with the **godly**)?"

GODS

002:135 and he joined not **gods** with Allah."
003:067 And he joined not **gods** with Allah.
004:116 (the sin of) joining other **gods** with Him:
004:116 one who joins other **gods** with Allah, hath
005:072 Whoever joins other **gods** with Allah,-Allah will
005:116 for two **gods** beside Allah'?" He will say:
006:014 of those who join **gods** with Allah."
006:019 that besides Allah there is another **gods**?"
006:023 not those who joined **gods** with Allah."
006:041 (the false **gods**) which ye join with Him!"
006:064 and yet ye worship false **gods**!"
006:074 "Takest thou idols for **gods**?
006:088 If they were to join other **gods** with Him,
006:106 those who join **gods** with Allah.
006:107 they would not have taken false **gods**: but We
006:161 and he (certainly) joined not **gods** with Allah."
007:127 and to abandon thee and thy **gods**?"
007:138 a god like unto the **gods** they have."
007:173 "Our fathers before us took false **gods**, but we
009:017 It is not for such as join **gods** with Allah,
010:028 Then shall We say to those who joined **gods** (with Us):
011:014 "If then they (your false **gods**) answer not
011:053 the ones to desert our **gods** on thy word!
011:054 some of our **gods** may have seized thee with evil."
011:055 "Other **gods** as partners! So scheme
012:108 I join **gods** with Allah!"
015:094 those who join false **gods** with Allah.
016:035 The worshippers of false **gods** say: "If Allah
016:051 Allah has said: "Take not (for worship) two **gods**:
016:054 to other **gods** to join with their Lord-
016:120 and he joined not **gods** with Allah.
016:123 and he joined not **gods** with Allah."
017:042 Say: if there had been (other) **gods** with Him,-
018:015 for worship **gods** other than Him:
019:046 "Art thou shrinking from my **gods**, O Abraham?
019:081 And they have taken (for worship) **gods** other than Allah,
021:021 Or have they taken (for worship) **gods** from the earth
021:022 and the earth, other **gods** besides Allah,
021:024 Or have they taken for worship (other) **gods** besides Him?
021:036 "The one who talks of your **gods**?"
021:043 Or have they **gods** that can guard them from Us?
021:059 They said, "Who has done this to our **gods**?
021:062 "Art thou the one that did this with our **gods**,
021:068 "Burn him and protect your **gods**, if ye do

GODS (continued)

021:098 and the (false) **gods** that ye worship besides Allah,
021:099 If these had been **gods**, they would
023:091 (if there were many **gods**), behold, each god
025:003 **gods** that can create nothing but are themselves
025:042 misled us from our **gods**, had it
026:092 'Where are the (**gods**) ye worshipped-
027:059 or the false **gods** they associate (with Him)?
028:087 these who join **gods** with Allah.
030:031 and be not ye among those who join **gods** with Allah,-
030:033 other **gods** besides their Lord,-
034:022 Say: "Call upon other (**gods**) whom ye fancy,
036:023 "Shall I take (other) **gods** besides Him?
036:074 Yet they take (for worship) **gods** other than Allah,
037:036 our **gods** for the sake of a Poet possessed?"
037:086 "Is it a Falsehood-**gods** other than Allah
037:091 Then did he turn to their **gods** and said,
038:005 "Has he made the **gods** (all) into one God?
038:006 "Walk ye away, and remain constant to your **gods**!
039:036 with other (**gods**) besides Him!
039:045 but when (**gods**) other than He are mentioned,
039:065 "If thou wert to join (**gods** with Allah),
041:006 And woe to those who join **gods** with Allah,-
043:058 And they say, " Are Our **gods** best, or He?"
046:022 to turn us aside from our **gods**?
046:028 to them from those whom they worshipped as **gods**,
071:023 'Abandon not your **gods**: abandon neither Wadd nor
072:002 We shall not join (in worship) any (**gods**) with our Lord,

GOES

002:249 he **goes** not with my army;
034:002 He knows all that **goes** into the earth, and all
053:001 By the Star when it **goes** down,-

GOETH

011:123 and to Him **goeth** back every affair
017:015 who **goeth** astray doth so to his own loss:
020:040 "Behold! thy sister **goeth** forth and saith,

GOG

018:094 the **Gog** and Magog (people) do great mischief
021:096 Until the **Gog** and Magog (people) are let

GOING

002:145 nor art thou **going** to follow their Qiblah;
007:057 like heralds of glad tidings, **going** before His mercy:
007:171 and they thought it was **going** to fall
008:033 nor was He **going** to send it whilst they
008:033 But Allah was not **going** to send them
012:030 we see she is evidently **going** astray."
016:071 are not **going** to throw back their gifts to those
020:092 what kept thee back, when thou sawest them **going** wrong.
025:048 winds as heralds of glad tidings **going** before His Mercy,
027:035 But I am **going** to send him a present, and wait
027:063 of glad tidings, **going** before His Mercy?
028:010 she was **going** almost to disclose his (case),
028:059 nor are We **going** to destroy a population except
028:061 a goodly promise, and who is **going** to reach
029:031 "We are indeed **going** to destroy the people
029:034 "For we are **going** to bring down on the
037:163 Except such as are (themselves) **going** to the blazing Fire!
040:085 was not **going** to profit them.
068:011 A slanderer, **going** about with calumnies,
098:001 were not **going** to depart (from their ways)

GOINGS

016:046 in the midst of their **goings** to and fro,

GOLD

003:014 heaped-up hoards of **gold** and silver;
003:075 if entrusted with a hoard of **gold**,
003:091 as much **gold** as the earth contains,
009:034 those who hoard **gold** and silver and spend
017:093 "Or thou have a house adorned with **gold**, or thou
018:031 they will be adorned therein with bracelets of **gold**,
022:023 with bracelets of **gold** and pearls; and their
035:033 with bracelets of **gold** and pearls; and their
043:035 And also adornments of **gold**.
043:053 "Then why are not **gold** bracelets bestowed on him,
043:071 dishes and goblets of **gold**: there will
056:015 on couches encrusted (with **gold** and precious stones),

GOLDEN

010:024 its **golden** ornaments and is decked out (in beauty):

GOLIATH

002:249 cannot cope with **Goliath** and his forces."
002:250 meet **Goliath** and his forces,
002:251 and David slew **Goliath**;

GOMORRAH

053:053 the Overthrown Cities (of Sodom and **Gomorrah**),

GONE

002:091 the prophets of Allah in times **gone** by,
003:090 for they are those who have **gone** astray.
003:154 would certainly have **gone** forth to the place
004:021 when ye have **gone** in unto each other,
004:023 no prohibition if ye have not **gone** in;
004:023 born of your wives to whom ye have **gone** in,
004:066 and would have **gone** farthest to strengthen
004:136 hath **gone** far, far astray.
005:077 of people who went wrong in times **gone** by,-who
006:140 They have indeed **gone** astray and heeded
011:040 those against whom the Word has already **gone** forth,-
011:076 The decree of thy Lord hath **gone** forth:
011:095 as were Thamud **gone** away.
011:110 had **gone** forth before from thy Lord the matter
013:030 have (other) Peoples (**gone** and) passed away;
017:048 but they have **gone** astray, and never
020:097 (Moses) said: "Get thee **gone**! but thy (punishment)
021:101 from Us has **gone** before, will be
023:027 has already **gone** forth: and address
025:009 But they have **gone** astray, and never
040:034 "And to you there came Joseph in times **gone** by,
046:011 (such men) would not have **gone** to it first,
069:024 that ye sent before you, in the days that are **gone**!"

GOOD

002:057 the **good** things We have provided for you:"
002:058 (the portion of) those who do **good**."
002:105 That anything **good** should come down
002:110 and whatever **good** ye send forth
002:112 whole self to Allah and is a doer of **good**,
002:148 (as in a race) towards all that is **good**.
002:158 his own impulse to **Good**,
002:168 lawful and **good**;
002:172 the **good** things that We have provided for you.
002:195 contribute to (your) destruction; but do **good**:
002:195 for Allah loveth those who do **good**.
002:197 And whatever **good** ye do,
002:201 "Our Lord! give us **good** in this world and **good** in the
002:215 Say: Whatever wealth ye spend that is **good**,
002:215 And whatever ye do that is **good**,
002:216 ye dislike a thing which is **good** for you,
002:220 man who means mischief from the man who means **good**.

GOOD (continued)

002:220   "The best thing to do is what is for their **good**;
002:223   and give (these) **good** tidings to those who believe.
002:223   But do some **good** act for your souls beforehand;
002:224   an excuse in your oaths against doing **good**,
002:267   give of the **good** things which ye have (honorably) earned,
002:272   Whatever of **good** ye give benefits
002:272   Whatever **good** ye give, shall be
002:273   And whatever of **good** ye give,
002:286   It gets every **good** that it earns,
003:015   the **good** pleasure of Allah.
003:026   in Thy hand is all **Good**.
003:030   be confronted with all the **good** it has done,
003:104   a band of people inviting to all that is **good**,
003:114   in (all) **good** works;
003:115   Of the **good** that they do, nothing
003:120   If aught that is **good** befalls you, it grieves them;
003:134   for Allah loves those who do **good**:
003:148   For Allah loveth those who do **good**.
003:162   the **good** pleasure of Allah like the man who draws
003:174   for they followed the **good** pleasure of Allah:
003:178   our respite to them is **good** for themselves:
003:179   until He separates what is evil from what is **good**.
003:180   think that it is **good** for them:
004:002   worthless things for (their) **good** ones;
004:005   but if they, of their own **good** pleasure, remit
004:005   take it and enjoy it with right **good** cheer.
004:019   about through it a great deal of **good**.
004:036   and do **good** to parents, kinsfolk, orphans,
004:040   if there is any **good** (done), He doubleth it,
004:069   the martyres, and the Righteous (who do **good**):
004:073   But if **good** fortune comes to you from Allah,
004:078   If some **good** befalls them, they say, "This
004:079   Whatever **good**, (O man!) happens to thee,
004:085   Whoever intercedes in a **good** cause becomes
004:095   Unto all (in Faith) hath Allah promised **good**:
004:114   seeking the **good** pleasure of Allah,
004:114   In most of their secret talks there is no **good**:
004:125   who submits his whole self to Allah, does **good**,
004:127   There is not a **good** deed which ye do,
004:128   But if ye do **good** and practice self-restraint,
004:138   To the Hypocrites give the **good** tidings that
004:147   Nay, it is Allah that recognizeth (all **good**),
004:149   Whether you do openly a **good** deed or conceal
004:160   (foods) **good** and wholesome which had been lawful
004:165   Messengers who gave **good** news as well
005:002   and **good** pleasure of their Lord.
005:004   Say: Lawful unto you are (all) things **good** and pure:
005:005   those who have lost (all spiritual **good**).
005:005   things **good** and pure made lawful unto you.
005:013   (right) places and forget a **good** part of the
005:014   forgot a **good** part of the Message that was
005:016   His **good** pleasure to ways of peace and safety,
005:085   Such is the recompense of those who do **good**.
005:087   the **good** things which Allah hath made lawful
005:088   lawful and **good**: but fear Allah,
005:093   For Allah loveth those who do **good**.
005:093   then again, guard themselves from evil and do **good**,
005:100   and things that are **good**, even though
006:035   and bring them a Sign,-(what **good**?).
006:044   the gates of all (**good**) things, until, in the
006:048   only to give **good** news and to warn: so those
006:071   things that can do us neither **good** nor harm,

006:084   thus do We reward those who do **good**:
006:104   it will be for (the **good** of) his own soul:
006:151   be **good** to your parents; kill not
006:157   In **good** time shall We requite those who
006:158   no **good** will it do to a soul
006:160   He that doeth **good** shall have ten times
007:008   those whose scale (of **good**) will be
007:019   and enjoy (its **good** things) as ye wish:
007:056   is (always) near to those who do **good**.
007:058   From the land that is clean and **good**, by the
007:079   I gave you **good** counsel, but ye love
007:079   but ye love not **good** counsellors!"
007:093   I gave you **good** counsel, but how
007:131   But when **good** (times) came, they said,
007:156   "And ordain for us that which is **good**, in this
007:157   what is **good** (and pure) and prohibits them from
007:160   (saying): "Eat of the **good** things We have
007:161   (the portion of) those who do **good**."
007:188   I should have multiplied all **good**, and no
007:188   Say: "I have no power over any **good** or harm
008:019   Not the least **good** will your forces be to you even if they
008:023   If Allah had found in them any **good**, He would
008:026   and gave you **good** things for sustenance:
008:069   But (now) enjoy what ye took in war, lawful and **good**:
008:070   "If Allah findeth any **good** in your hearts, He will
009:021   glad tidings of a Mercy from Himself, His **good** pleasure.
009:050   If **good** befalls thee, it grieves them; but if
009:072   greatest bliss in the **Good** Pleasure of Allah:
009:088   for them are (all) **good** things:
009:100   those who follow them in (all) **good** deeds, well-
009:102   they have mixed an act that was **good** with another
009:107   their intention is nothing but **good**; but Allah
009:109   on piety to Allah and His **good** pleasure?-
009:112   that enjoin **good** and forbid evil;
009:120   the reward to be lost of those who do **good**;-
010:002   the **good** actions they have advanced (but) say
010:002   and give the **good** news to the Believers that they
010:011   as they would fain hasten on the **good**,-then would
010:108   do so for the **good** of their own souls;
011:003   that he may grant you enjoyment, **good** (and true),
011:031   will not grant them (all) that is **good**:
011:034   much as i desire to give you (**good**) counsel,
011:088   (pure and) **good** as from Himself?
011:114   for those things that are **good** remove those
011:116   of the **good** things of life which were given them,
012:019   **Good** news! Here is a (fine) young man!" So they
012:021   may be he will bring us much **good**, or we shall adopt
012:023   Truly to no **good** come those who do wrong!"
012:036   for we see thou art one that doth **good** (to all)."
012:055   I am a **good** keeper, knowledgeable.
012:056   the reward of those who do **good**.
012:078   for we see that thou art (gracious) in doing **good**."
012:083   yourselves contrived a story (**good** enough) for you.
012:096   Then when the bearer of the **good** news came,
012:100   He was indeed **good** to me when He took
013:006   the evil in preference to the **good** yet have
013:016   such as have no power either for **good** or for
013:017   the **good** of mankind remains on the earth.
013:018   who respond to their Lord, are (all) **good** things.
013:022   secretly and openly; and turn off Evil with **good**:
015:054   Of what, then, is your **good** news?"
016:030   To those who do **good**, there is **good** in this world,

GOOD (continued)

016:030   they say, "All that is **good**."
016:032   (the **good**) which ye did (in the world)."
016:053   And ye have no **good** thing but is from Allah:
016:076   whichever way he directs him, he brings no **good**:
016:090   Allah commands justice, the doing of **good**, and giving
016:097   that is **good** and pure, and We
016:114   lawful and **good**; and be grateful for the
016:122   And We gave him **Good** in this world, and he
016:128   restrain themselves, and those who do **good**.
017:011   as he prays for **good** for man is given to haste.
017:016   are given the **good** things of this life (to be obedient)
017:070   things **good** and pure; and conferred
018:031   How **good** the recompense! How beautiful
018:046   **Good** Deeds, are best in the sight of thy Lord,
018:104   they were acquiring **good** by their works?"
019:007   We give thee **good** news of a son: his name
019:046   now get away from me for a **good** long while!"
019:076   **Good** Deeds, are best in the sight of thy Lord,
020:081   (Saying): "Eat of the **good** things We have
020:089   to harm them or to do them **good**?
021:013   Flee not, but return to the **good** things of this
021:035   and by **good** by way of trial.
021:044   Nay, We gave the **good** things of this life
021:066   be of any **good** to you nor do you harm?
021:073   and We inspired them to do **good** deeds,
021:090   These (three) were ever quick in doing in **good** works:
021:101   Those for whom the **Good** (Record) from Us
022:011   if **good** befalls them, they are, therewith, well content;
022:030   for him it is **good** in the sight
022:034   the **Good** News to those who humble themselves,
022:036   in them is (much) **good** for you: then pronounce
022:037   the **Good** News to all who do **good**.
022:077   your Lord; and do **good**; that ye may prosper.
023:033   had bestowed the **good** things of this life,
023:051   O ye messengers! enjoy (all) things **good** and pure,
023:056   We would hasten them on in every **good**?
023:061   It is these who hasten in every **good** work, and these who
023:064   the **good** things of this world, behold, they
023:102   (of **good** deeds) is heavy,-they will be successful.
024:011   on the contrary it is **good** for you:
024:033   if ye know any **good** in them; yea, give
025:003   or **good** to themselves; nor can they control
025:018   on them and their fathers **good** things (in life), until they
025:070   of such persons into **good**, and Allah
025:071   And whoever repents and does **good** has truly
026:073   "Or do you **good** or harm?"
027:011   and have thereafter substituted **good** to take
027:046   to hasten on the evil before the **good**?
027:089   If any do **good**, he will have better than it.
027:092   they do it for the **good** of their own souls,
028:014   for thus do We reward those who do **good**.
028:024   any **good** that Thou dost send me!"
028:054   that they avert Evil with **Good**, and that
028:061   the **good** things of this life, but who, on the
028:077   but do thou **good**, as Allah has been **good** to thee,
028:079   For he is truly a lord of mighty **good** fortune."
028:080   save those who steadfastly persevere (in **good**)."
028:084   If any does **good**, the reward to him is better
029:031   with the **good** news, they said: "We are
029:058   an excellent reward for those who do (**good**)!-
031:003   A Guide and a Mercy to the Doers of **Good**,-
031:014   (to be **good**) to his parents:

GOOD (continued)

031:022   and is a doer of **good**, has grasped
032:017   for them-as a reward for their (**good**) Deeds.
032:019   as hospitable homes, for their (**good**) deeds.
035:008   so that he looks upon it as **good**,
035:032   by Allah's leave, foremost in **good** deeds;
036:011   therefore, **good** tidings, of Forgiveness
037:101   So We gave him the **good** news of a forbearing son.
037:112   And We gave him the **good** news of Isaac-
038:047   of the company of the Elect and the **Good**.
038:048   of the company of the **Good**.
039:010   for those who do **good** in this world.
039:010   Fear your Lord: **good** is (the reward) for those
039:017   for them is **Good** News:
039:017   so announce the **Good** News to My Servants,-
039:034   such is the reward of those who do **good**:
039:058   I should certainly be among those who do **good**!'
040:064   of things pure and **good**;-such is Allah
041:004   Giving **Good** News and Admonition: yet most
041:035   none but persons of the greatest **good** fortune.
041:049   Man does not weary of asking for **good** (things),
041:050   I have (much) **good** (stored) in His sight!"
042:023   And it anyone earns any **good**, We shall
042:023   We shall give him an increase of **good** in respect thereof:
043:029   Yea, I have given the **good** things of this life
043:072   ye are made heirs for your (**good**) deeds (in life).
045:014   it is for Him to recompense (for **good** or ill)
045:016   for Sustenance things **good** and pure; and We
046:011   "If (this Message) were a **good** thing, (such men) would
046:014   recompense for their (**good**) deeds.
046:020   "Ye squandered your **good** things in the life
047:028   hated Allah's **good** pleasure; so He
047:035   in loss for your (**good**) deeds.
048:018   Allah's **Good** Pleasure was on the Believers
048:029   seeking Grace from Allah and (His) **Good** Pleasure.
050:025   "Who forbade what was **good**, transgressed all
051:016   because, before then, they had done **good** deeds
052:019   and health, because of your (**good**) deeds."
052:027   "But Allah has been **good** to us, and has
053:031   and He rewards those who do **good**, with what
055:060   Is there any Reward for **Good**-other than **Good**?
055:070   In them will be fair (Maidens), **good**, beautiful;-
057:012   "**Good** News for you this Day!
057:020   and (His) **Good** Pleasure (for the devotees of Allah).
057:027   the **Good** pleasure of Allah; but that
059:008   from Allah and (His) **Good** Pleasure, and aiding
060:001   and to seek My **Good** Pleasure, showing friendship
063:010   and I should have been one of the doers of **good**."
068:012   (Habitually) hindering (all) **good**, transgressing beyond
069:024   full satisfaction; because of the (**good**) that ye
070:021   And niggardly when **good** reaches him;-
073:011   those in possession of the **good** things of life,
073:020   a Beautiful Loan. And whatever **good** ye send forth
077:044   Thus do We certainly reward the Doers of **Good**.
086:013   that distinguishes (**Good** from Evil):
089:024   sent forth (**Good** Deeds) for (this) my (Future) Life."
099:007   an atom's weight of **good**, see it!
101:006   Then, he whose balance (of **good** deeds) will be
101:007   Will be in a life of **good** pleasure and satisfaction.
101:008   But he whose balance (of **good** deeds) will be
102:001   (the **good** things of this world) diverts you

GOOD-WILL

004:029   you traffic and trade by mutual **good-will**:

GOOD-WILL (continued)
004:062 "We meant no more than **good-will** and conciliation!"
013:015 with **good-will** or in spite of themselves:

GOODLY
003:039 of the (**goodly**) company of the righteous."
007:189 (saying): "If Thou givest us a **goodly** child, we
007:190 But when He giveth them a **goodly** child, they
010:026 To those who do right is a **goodly** (reward)-yea,
012:008 but we are a **goodly** body!
014:024 a **goodly** tree, whose root is firmly fixed, and its
014:024 a parable?-a **goodly** Word like a **goodly** tree,
016:041 We will assuredly give a **goodly** home in this
016:075 on whom We have bestowed **goodly** favours from
018:002 shall have a **goodly** Reward.
018:088 he shall have a **goodly** reward, and easy will be his task
022:058 on them will Allah bestow verily a **goodly** Provision:
028:061 one to whom We have made a **goodly** promise,
048:016 a **goodly** reward, but if ye turn back as ye
055:072 restrained (as to their glances), in (**goodly**) pavilions:-
056:039 A (**goodly**) number from those of old,
056:040 And a (**goodly**) number from those of later times.
057:010 has Allah promised a **goodly** (reward).

GOODNESS
004:114 or **goodness** or conciliation between people
041:034 Nor can **Goodness** and Evil be equal.
041:035 And no one will be granted such **goodness** except those

GOODS
002:155 some loss in **goods**,
002:180 if he leave any **goods**,
002:274 spend of their **goods** by night and by day,
003:185 is but **goods** and chattels of deception.
004:094 Coveting the perishable **goods** of this life:
004:095 with their **goods** and their persons.
004:095 with their **goods** and persons than to those who
008:067 Ye look for the temporal **goods** of this world;
009:020 in Allah's cause, with their **goods** and their
009:041 and struggle, with your **goods** and your person,
009:044 with their **goods** and persons.
009:081 with their **goods** and their persons, in the
009:111 their persons and their good; for theirs
024:033 a gain in the **goods** of this life.
033:019 sharp tongues, covetous of **goods**.
033:027 and their **goods**, and of a land which ye had
057:020 of this world, but **goods** and chattels of deception?

GORED
005:003 or by being **gored** to death; that which

GOSPEL
003:003 Torah (of Moses) and the **Gospel** (of Jesus).
003:048 the Book and Wisdom, the Torah and the **Gospel**.
003:065 when the Torah and the **Gospel** were not revealed
005:046 We sent him the **Gospel**: therein was
005:047 Let the people of the **Gospel** Judge by what
005:066 the **Gospel**, and all the revelation that was
005:068 The **Gospel**, and all the revelation that has
005:110 the Torah and the **Gospel**.
007:157 in the Taurat and the **Gospel**; for he
009:111 through the Torah, the **Gospel**, and the Qur'an:
048:029 and their similitude in the **Gospel** is: like a seed
057:027 and bestowed on him the **Gospel**;

GOT
007:027 he **got** your parents out of the Garden, stripping
007:203 they say: "Why hast thou not **got** it together?"

GOT (continued)
021:099 they would not have **got** there!
026:038 So the sorcerers were **got** together for the
028:021 He therefore **got** away therefrom, looking about,
028:079 of what Qarun has **got**! For he is
048:006 He has cursed them and **got** Hell ready for them:
048:026 While the Unbelievers **got** up in their hearts
058:019 Satan has **got** the better of them: so he
059:002 It is He who **got** out the Unbelievers among the

GOURD
037:146 a spreading plant of the **Gourd** kind.

GOVERNING
010:003 regulating and **governing** all things.

GRACE
001:007 hast bestowed Thy **Grace**,
002:064 the **Grace** and Mercy of Allah to you
002:090 Allah of His **Grace** should send it
002:105 for Allah is Lord of **grace** abounding.
002:213 Allah by His **Grace** guided the Believers
002:221 But Allah beckons by His **Grace** to the Garden
003:103 so that by His **Grace**, Ye became brethren;
003:152 for Allah is full of **grace** to those who believe.
003:171 the **Grace** and the Bounty from Allah,
003:174 And they returned with **Grace** and Bounty from Allah:
003:180 Allah hath given them of His **Grace**,
004:069 those on whom is the **Grace** of Allah,
004:083 the **Grace** and Mercy of Allah unto you,
004:113 and great is the **Grace** of Allah unto thee.
004:113 But for the **Grace** of Allah to thee and His Mercy,
004:175 to Mercy and **Grace** from Himself, and guide
005:023 were two on whom Allah had bestowed His **Grace**:
005:054 That is the **Grace** of Allah, which He will
008:029 is the Lord of **grace** unbounded.
008:053 the **Grace** which He hath bestowed on a people
009:043 God give thee **grace**!
011:003 and bestow His abounding **grace** on all
011:058 with him, by (special) **Grace** from Us: We saved
011:066 with him, by (special) **Grace** from Us-and from
011:073 The **grace** of Allah and His
012:038 that (comes) of the **grace** of Allah to us and to
014:011 but Allah doth grant His **grace** to such
019:058 on whom Allah did bestow His **Grace**,-of the
020:122 But his Lord chose him (for His **Grace**):
021:084 as a **Grace** from Ourselves, and a thing
024:010 If it were not for God's **grace** and mercy on you,
024:014 Were it not for the **grace** and mercy
024:020 Were it not for the **grace** and mercy of Allah
024:021 for the **grace** and mercy of Allah on you, not one
024:022 with **grace** and amplitude of means resolve by oath
024:032 Allah will give them means out of His **grace**:
024:033 Allah will give them means out of His **grace**.
024:038 and add even more for them out of His **Grace**:
025:074 of our eyes, and give us (the **grace**) to lead
027:016 this is indeed **Grace** manifest (from Allah)."
027:019 and admit me, by Thy **Grace**, to the
027:040 "This is by the **grace** of my Lord!-to test
027:073 full of **grace** to mankind: yet most
028:017 Thou hast bestowed Thy **Grace** on me, never shall
028:027 ten years, it will be (**grace**) from thee.
028:073 and that ye may seek of His **Grace**;-and in
029:067 is vain, and reject the **Grace** of Allah?
031:031 the Ocean by the **grace** of Allah?-that He
033:009 Remember the **Grace** of Allah, (bestowed) on

GRACE (continued)

033:037 had received the **grace** of Allah and thy favour:
033:046 to Allah's (**Grace**) by His leave, and as
034:010 We bestowed **Grace** aforetime on David
035:003 O men! remember the **grace** of Allah unto you!
035:032 that is the highest **Grace**.
037:057 "Had it not been for the **Grace** of my Lord,
038:043 and doubled their number,-as a **Grace** from Us,
038:083 sincere and purified (by Thy **grace**)."
040:061 Verily Allah is Full of **Grace** and Bounty to men:
048:029 (in prayer), seeking **Grace** from Allah and (His)
049:008 A **grace** and favour from Allah; and Allah
052:029 Therefore Remind for by the **Grace** of thy Lord,
054:035 As a **Grace** from Us: Thus do We
057:021 the Lord of **Grace** abounding.
057:021 and His messengers: that is the **Grace** of Allah,
057:029 For Allah is the Lord of **Grace** abounding.
057:029 they have no power whatever over the **Grace** of Allah,
057:029 that (His) **Grace** is (entirely) in His Hand,
059:008 their property, while seeking **Grace** from Allah
068:002 Thou art not, by the **grace** of thy Lord, mad or
068:049 Had not **Grace** from His Lord reached him, he would
073:020 and seek ye the **Grace** of Allah: for Allah

GRACIOUS

001:001 In the name of Allah, Most **Gracious**, Most Merciful.
001:003 Most **Gracious**, Most Merciful.
002:000 In the name of Allah, Most **Gracious**, Most Merciful.
002:163 Most **Gracious**, Most Merciful.
003:000 In the name of Allah, Most **Gracious**, Most Merciful.
004:000 In the name of Allah, Most **Gracious**, Most Merciful.
005:000 In the name of Allah, Most **Gracious**, Most Merciful.
006:000 In the name of Allah, Most **Gracious**, Most Merciful.
007:000 In the name of Allah, Most **Gracious**, Most Merciful.
008:000 In the name of Allah, Most **Gracious**, Most Merciful.
008:017 the Believers a **gracious** benefit from Himself:
010:000 In the name of Allah, Most **Gracious**, Most Merciful.
011:000 In the name of Allah, Most **Gracious**, Most Merciful.
012:000 In the name of Allah, Most **Gracious**, Most Merciful.
012:078 for we see that thou art (**gracious**) in doing good."
012:090 been **gracious** to us (all): behold, he that
012:100 Verily my Lord is **gracious** to whom He wills
013:000 In the name of Allah, Most **Gracious**, Most Merciful.
013:030 yet do they reject (Him), the Most **Gracious**!
014:000 In the name of Allah, Most **Gracious**, Most Merciful.
015:000 In the name of Allah, Most **Gracious**, Most Merciful.
015:085 with **gracious** forgiveness.
016:000 In the name of Allah, Most **Gracious**, Most Merciful.
016:125 are best and most **gracious**: for thy
017:000 In the name of Allah, Most **Gracious**, Most Merciful.
018:000 In the name of Allah, Most **Gracious**, Most Merciful.
019:000 In the name of Allah, Most **Gracious**, Most Merciful.
019:018 to (Allah) Most **Gracious**: (come not near) if
019:026 Most **Gracious**, and this day will I enter into no
019:044 for Satan is a rebel against (Allah) Most **Gracious**.
019:045 from (Allah) Most **Gracious**, so that
019:047 for He is to me Most **Gracious**.
019:058 (Allah) Most **Gracious** were rehearsed to them,
019:061 (Allah) Most **Gracious** has promised to His
019:069 against (Allah) Most **Gracious**.
019:075 (Allah) Most **Gracious** extends (the rope)
019:078 or has he taken a promise with the Most **Gracious**?
019:085 to (Allah) Most **Gracious**, like a band
019:087 from (Allah) Most **Gracious**.

GRACIOUS (continued)

019:088 They say: "The Most **Gracious** has begotten a son!"
019:091 That they attributed a son to The Most **Gracious**.
019:092 the majesty of The Most **Gracious** that He
019:093 to The Most **Gracious** as a servant.
019:096 will The Most **Gracious** bestow Love.
020:000 In the name of Allah, Most **Gracious**, Most Merciful.
020:005 The Most **Gracious** is firmly established
020:090 Most **Gracious**: so follow me and obey my command."
020:108 to The Most **Gracious**: so that
020:109 has been granted by The Most **Gracious** and whose
021:000 In the name of Allah, Most **Gracious**, Most Merciful.
021:026 And they say: "The Most **Gracious** has taken a son."
021:036 the mention of The Most **Gracious**!
021:042 and by day from (the Wrath of) The Most **Gracious**?"
021:112 "Our Lord Most **Gracious** is the One Whose
022:000 In the name of Allah, Most **Gracious**, Most Merciful.
023:000 In the name of Allah, Most **Gracious**, Most Merciful.
024:000 In the name of Allah, Most **Gracious**, Most Merciful.
025:000 In the name of Allah, Most **Gracious**, Most Merciful.
025:026 shall be (wholly) for The Most **Gracious**: it will
025:059 on the Throne: Allah Most **Gracious**: ask thou
025:060 "Adore ye The Most **Gracious**!", they say,
025:060 (Allah) Most **Gracious**? Shall we adore
025:063 (Allah) Most **Gracious** are those who walk on
026:000 In the name of Allah, Most **Gracious**, Most Merciful.
026:005 the Most **Gracious**, but they turn away therefrom.
027:000 In the name of Allah, Most **Gracious**, Most Merciful.
027:030 Most **Gracious**, Most Merciful:
028:000 In the name of Allah, Most **Gracious**, Most Merciful.
028:005 And We wished to be **gracious** to those who
028:082 Allah was **gracious** to us, He could
029:000 In the name of Allah, Most **Gracious**, Most Merciful.
030:000 In the name of Allah, Most **Gracious**, Most Merciful.
031:000 In the name of Allah, Most **Gracious**, Most Merciful.
032:000 In the name of Allah, Most **Gracious**, Most Merciful.
033:000 In the name of Allah, Most **Gracious**, Most Merciful.
034:000 In the name of Allah, Most **Gracious**, Most Merciful.
035:000 In the name of Allah, Most **Gracious**, Most Merciful.
036:000 In the name of Allah, Most **Gracious**, Most Merciful.
036:011 the Most **Gracious**, unseen: given such a one,
036:015 like ourselves; and the Most **Gracious** sends no
036:023 If The Most **Gracious** should intend some
036:052 "This is what The Most **Gracious** had promised.
037:000 In the name of Allah, Most **Gracious**, Most Merciful.
038:000 In the name of Allah, Most **Gracious**, Most Merciful.
039:000 In the name of Allah, Most **Gracious**, Most Merciful.
040:000 In the name of Allah, Most **Gracious**, Most Merciful.
041:000 In the name of Allah, Most **Gracious**, Most Merciful.
041:002 A revelation from The Most **Gracious**, Most Merciful;-
042:000 In the name of Allah, Most **Gracious**, Most Merciful.
042:019 **Gracious** is Allah to His servants: He gives
043:000 In the name of Allah, Most **Gracious**, Most Merciful.
043:017 as a likeness to (Allah) Most **Gracious**, his face
043:020 the will of (Allah) Most **Gracious**, we should
043:033 Most **Gracious**, silver roofs for their houses,
043:036 from remembrance of the Most **Gracious**, We appoint
043:045 other than The Most **Gracious**, to be worshipped?
043:081 Say: "If The Most **Gracious** had a son, I would
044:000 In the name of Allah, Most **Gracious**, Most Merciful.
045:000 In the name of Allah, Most **Gracious**, Most Merciful.
046:000 In the name of Allah, Most **Gracious**, Most Merciful.
046:015 and be **gracious** to me in my issue.

GRACIOUS (continued)

047:000 In the name of Allah, Most **Gracious**, Most Merciful.
048:000 In the name of Allah, Most **Gracious**, Most Merciful.
049:000 In the name of Allah, Most **Gracious**, Most Merciful.
050:000 In the name of Allah, Most **Gracious**, Most Merciful.
050:033 "Who feared The Most **Gracious** unseen, and brought
051:000 In the name of Allah, Most **Gracious**, Most Merciful.
052:000 In the name of Allah, Most **Gracious**, Most Merciful.
053:000 In the name of Allah, Most **Gracious**, Most Merciful.
054:000 In the name of Allah, Most **Gracious**, Most Merciful.
055:000 In the name of Allah, Most **Gracious**, Most Merciful.
055:001 The Most **Gracious**!
056:000 In the name of Allah, Most **Gracious**, Most Merciful.
057:000 In the name of Allah, Most **Gracious**, Most Merciful.
058:000 In the name of Allah, Most **Gracious**, Most Merciful.
059:000 In the name of Allah, Most **Gracious**, Most Merciful.
059:022 He, Most **Gracious**, Most Merciful.
060:000 In the name of Allah, Most **Gracious**, Most Merciful.
061:000 In the name of Allah, Most **Gracious**, Most Merciful.
062:000 In the name of Allah, Most **Gracious**, Most Merciful.
063:000 In the name of Allah, Most **Gracious**, Most Merciful.
064:000 In the name of Allah, Most **Gracious**, Most Merciful.
065:000 In the name of Allah, Most **Gracious**, Most Merciful.
066:000 In the name of Allah, Most **Gracious**, Most Merciful.
067:000 In the name of Allah, Most **Gracious**, Most Merciful.
067:003 The Most **Gracious**. So turn thy vision again:
067:019 uphold them except The Most **Gracious**: truly it
067:029 Say: "He is The Most **Gracious**: we have
068:000 In the name of Allah, Most **Gracious**, Most Merciful.
069:000 In the name of Allah, Most **Gracious**, Most Merciful.
070:000 In the name of Allah, Most **Gracious**, Most Merciful.
071:000 In the name of Allah, Most **Gracious**, Most Merciful.
072:000 In the name of Allah, Most **Gracious**, Most Merciful.
073:000 In the name of Allah, Most **Gracious**, Most Merciful.
074:000 In the name of Allah, Most **Gracious**, Most Merciful.
075:000 In the name of Allah, Most **Gracious**, Most Merciful.
076:000 In the name of Allah, Most **Gracious**, Most Merciful.
077:000 In the name of Allah, Most **Gracious**, Most Merciful.
078:000 In the name of Allah, Most **Gracious**, Most Merciful.
078:037 The Most **Gracious**: none shall have power to argue
078:038 permitted by The Most **Gracious**, and he
079:000 In the name of Allah, Most **Gracious**, Most Merciful.
080:000 In the name of Allah, Most **Gracious**, Most Merciful.
081:000 In the name of Allah, Most **Gracious**, Most Merciful.
082:000 In the name of Allah, Most **Gracious**, Most Merciful.
083:000 In the name of Allah, Most **Gracious**, Most Merciful.
084:000 In the name of Allah, Most **Gracious**, Most Merciful.
085:000 In the name of Allah, Most **Gracious**, Most Merciful.
086:000 In the name of Allah, Most **Gracious**, Most Merciful.
087:000 In the name of Allah, Most **Gracious**, Most Merciful.
088:000 In the name of Allah, Most **Gracious**, Most Merciful.
089:000 In the name of Allah, Most **Gracious**, Most Merciful.
090:000 In the name of Allah, Most **Gracious**, Most Merciful.
091:000 In the name of Allah, Most **Gracious**, Most Merciful.
092:000 In the name of Allah, Most **Gracious**, Most Merciful.
093:000 In the name of Allah, Most **Gracious**, Most Merciful.
094:000 In the name of Allah, Most **Gracious**, Most Merciful.
095:000 In the name of Allah, Most **Gracious**, Most Merciful.
096:000 In the name of Allah, Most **Gracious**, Most Merciful.
097:000 In the name of Allah, Most **Gracious**, Most Merciful.
098:000 In the name of Allah, Most **Gracious**, Most Merciful.
099:000 In the name of Allah, Most **Gracious**, Most Merciful.
100:000 In the name of Allah, Most **Gracious**, Most Merciful.

GRACIOUS (continued)

101:000 In the name of Allah, Most **Gracious**, Most Merciful.
102:000 In the name of Allah, Most **Gracious**, Most Merciful.
103:000 In the name of Allah, Most **Gracious**, Most Merciful.
104:000 In the name of Allah, Most **Gracious**, Most Merciful.
105:000 In the name of Allah, Most **Gracious**, Most Merciful.
106:000 In the name of Allah, Most **Gracious**, Most Merciful.
107:000 In the name of Allah, Most **Gracious**, Most Merciful.
108:000 In the name of Allah, Most **Gracious**, Most Merciful.
109:000 In the name of Allah, Most **Gracious**, Most Merciful.
110:000 In the name of Allah, Most **Gracious**, Most Merciful.
111:000 In the name of Allah, Most **Gracious**, Most Merciful.
112:000 In the name of Allah, Most **Gracious**, Most Merciful.
113:000 In the name of Allah, Most **Gracious**, Most Merciful.
114:000 In the name of Allah, Most **Gracious**, Most Merciful.

GRACIOUSLY

003:037 Right **graciously** did her Lord accept her:

GRADATION

017:021 is more in rank and **gradation** and more

GRADE

004:095 Allah hath granted a **grade** higher to those who

GRADES

003:163 They are in varying **grades** in the sight of Allah,
008:004 they have **grades** of dignity with their Lord,

GRADUALLY

013:041 See they not that We **gradually** reduce the land
021:044 see they not that We **gradually** reduce the land
025:032 well-arranged stages, **gradually**.
071:017 from the earth, growing (**gradually**),

GRAIN

002:261 the way of Allah is that of a **grain** of corn:
006:059 there is not a **grain** in the darkness
006:099 close-compounded **grain** out of the date-palm
012:063 No more measure of **grain** shall we get
012:065 camel's load (of **grain** to our provisions).
036:033 and produce **grain** therefrom, of which ye do eat.
050:009 and **Grain** for harvests;
078:015 That We may produce therewith **grain** and vegetables,
080:027 And produce therein **grain**,

GRAINS

002:261 and each ear hath a hundred **grains**.

GRAND

015:087 Seven Oft-Repeated (verses) and the **Grand** Qur'an.
048:005 the **grand** triumph,

GRANDCHILDREN

016:072 make out of them sons and daughters and **grandchildren**,

GRANDSON

021:072 as an additional gift, (a **grandson**), Jacob,

GRANT

002:096 but the **grant** of such life will not
002:126 for a while will I **grant** them their pleasure,
002:178 then **grant** any reasonable demand,
002:280 **grant** him time till it is easy for him to repay.
002:286 And **grant** us forgiveness.
002:286 **grant** us victory over the unbelievers.
003:008 but **grant** us mercy from Thee:
003:038 **Grant** unto me from Thee a progeny that is pure:
003:178 We **grant** them respite that they may grow
003:194 "Our Lord! **grant** us what Thou didst promise
004:077 Wouldst Thou not **grant** us respite to our
004:141 And never will Allah **grant** to the Unbelievers
004:146 And soon will Allah **grant** to the Believers

GRANT (continued)

007:183 Respite will I **grant** unto them: for My
008:029 He will **grant** you a Criterion
009:006 for asylum, **grant** it to him, so that
009:043 Why didst thou **grant** them exemption until those who
009:049 "**Grant** me exemption and draw me not into trial."
011:003 that He may **grant** you enjoyment, good (and true),
011:031 will not **grant** them (all) that is good:
011:048 to whom We shall **grant** their pleasures (for a time),
013:026 Allah doth enlarge, or **grant** by (strict) measure,
014:011 but Allah doth **grant** His grace to such
017:006 Then did We **grant** you victory over them:
017:018 We readily **grant** them-such things as We will,
017:080 and **grant** me from Thee an authority to aid (me)."
021:111 and a **grant** of (worldly) livelihood (to you) for a time."
023:118 So say: "O my Lord! **grant** thou forgiveness and mercy!
024:055 Will, of a surety, **grant** them in the land, inheritance
025:074 "Our Lord! **Grant** unto us wives and offspring
026:084 "**Grant** me honorable mention on the tongue
031:024 We **grant** them their pleasure for a little while:
033:031 to her shall We **grant** her reward twice: and We
034:039 for He is the Best of those Who **grant** Sustenance.
035:002 none can **grant**, apart from Him: and He
036:068 If We **grant** long life to any, We cause
037:100 "O my Lord! **grant** me a righteous (son)!"
038:035 and **grant** me a Kingdom, which, will not
039:044 (the right to **grant**) Intercession: to Him
040:008 "And **grant**, our Lord! That they enter the
042:020 We **grant** somewhat thereof, but he
045:016 We did aforetime **grant** to the Children of Israel
046:015 "O my Lord! **grant** me that I may be grateful for Thy
047:036 He will **grant** you your recompense, and will
048:010 Allah will soon **grant** him a great Reward.
048:016 show obedience, Allah will **grant** you a goodly
063:011 But to no soul will Allah **grant** respite when the
064:017 and He will **grant** you Forgiveness: for Allah
065:007 Allah will soon **grant** relief.
066:008 perfect our light for us and **grant** us Forgiveness:
068:045 A (long) respite will I **grant** them: truly powerful
071:024 and **grant** Thou no increase to the wrong-doers
071:028 wrong-doers **grant** Thou no increase but in
078:030 for no increase shall We **grant** you, except in
086:017 Therefore **grant** a delay to the unbelievers:

GRANTED

002:258 because Allah had **granted** Him Power?
002:269 wisdom **granted** receiveth indeed a benefit overflowing;
004:095 Allah hath **granted** a grade higher to those who
006:008 and no respite would be **granted** them.
010:093 had been **granted** to them, that they
012:110 (Respite will be **granted**) until, when the
013:032 but I **granted** respite to the Unbelievers,
014:039 "Praise be to Allah, who hath **granted** unto me
015:037 (Allah) said: "Respite is **granted** thee-
016:043 to whom We **granted** inspiration: if ye
017:060 We **granted** the Vision which We
018:029 relief they will be **granted** water like melted
019:050 and We **granted** them lofty honour on the tongue
020:036 (Allah) said: "**Granted** is thy prayer, O Moses!"
020:109 has been **granted** by The Most Gracious and whose
021:007 to whom We **granted** inspiration: if ye
021:034 We **granted** not to any man before thee
021:048 In the past We **granted** to Moses and Aaron
021:090 So We listened to him: and We **granted** him Yahya:

GRANTED (continued)

022:044 But I **granted** respite to the Unbelievers,
023:055 We have **granted** them abundance of wealth and sons,
024:055 as He **granted** it to those before them; that He
028:080 But those who had been **granted** (true) knowledge
029:027 and We **granted** him his reward in this life;
032:029 Nor will they be **granted** a respite."
034:023 except for those for whom He has **granted** permission.
034:045 a tenth of what We had **granted** to those: yet when
035:011 Nor is a man long-lived **granted** length of days,
036:027 "For that my Lord has **granted** me Forgiveness
038:080 (Allah) said: "Respite then is **granted** thee-
041:024 their suit shall not be **granted**.
041:035 And no one will be **granted** such goodness except
043:016 and **granted** to you sons for choice?
043:059 We **granted** Our favour to him, and We
044:033 And **granted** them Signs in which
045:017 had been **granted** to them that they fell into schisms,
045:017 And We **granted** them clear Signs in affairs
048:001 Verily We have **granted** thee a manifest Victory:
048:027 ye knew not, and He **granted**, besides this,
058:011 and who have been **granted** Knowledge: and Allah
065:011 Allah has indeed **granted** for them a most
074:012 To whom I **granted** resources in abundance,
087:003 And **granted** guidance;
108:001 To thee have We **granted** the Abundance.

GRANTETH

002:247 Allah **granteth** His authority to whom He pleaseth;
002:269 He **granteth** wisdom to whom He pleaseth;
003:073 He **granteth** them to whom He pleaseth:
017:054 if He please, He **granteth** you mercy, or if
053:043 That it is He who **Granteth** Laughter and Tears;
053:044 That it is He who **Granteth** Death and Life;

GRANTOR

003:008 **Grantor** of bounties without measure.
038:009 the **Grantor** of Bounties without measure?
038:035 for Thou art the **Grantor** of Bounties

GRANTS

029:021 and He **grants** mercy to whom He pleases,
029:062 and He (similarly) **grants** by (strict) measure,
042:030 (a sin) He **grants** forgiveness.

GRAPE-VINES

018:032 **grape-vines** and surrounded the with date-palms;

GRAPES

006:099 and (then there are) gardens of **grapes**,
016:011 olives, date-palms, **grapes**, and every kind of
080:028 And **Grapes** and the fresh vegetation,

GRAPEVINES

078:032 Gardens enclosed, and **Grapevines**;

GRASP

003:007 and none will **grasp** the Message
006:103 No vision can **grasp** Him, but His **grasp** is over all
011:056 but He hath **grasp** of its forelock.

GRASPED

002:256 hath **grasped** the most trustworthy hand-hold,
031:022 has **grasped** indeed the firmest hand-hold: and to

GRASS

038:044 "And take in thy hand a little **grass**, and strike

GRATEFUL

002:052 there was a chance for you to be **grateful**.
002:056 ye had the chance to be **grateful**.
002:152 Be **grateful** to Me, and reject not Faith.

GRATEFUL (continued)

002:172 and be **grateful** to Allah,
002:185 and perchance ye shall be **grateful**.
004:147 If ye are **grateful** and ye believe?
005:006 that ye may be **grateful**.
005:089 that ye may be **grateful**.
006:053 Doth not Allah know best those who are **grateful**?.
007:058 by various (symbols) to those who are **grateful**.
007:189 we vow we shall (ever) be **grateful**."
008:026 that ye might be **grateful**.
012:038 and to mankind: yet most men are not **grateful**.
014:005 firmly patient and constant,-**grateful** and appreciative.
014:007 "If ye are **grateful**, I will add more (favours)
016:014 and that ye may be **grateful**.
016:114 lawful and good; and be **grateful** for the
017:003 Verily he was a devotee most **grateful**.
021:080 will ye then be **grateful**?
022:036 to you, that ye may be **grateful**.
027:019 so order me that I may be **grateful** for Thy favours,
027:040 to test me whether I am **grateful** or ungrateful!
027:040 And if any is **grateful**, truly his
028:073 and in order that ye may be **grateful**.
029:017 serve Him, and be **grateful** to Him: to Him
030:046 in order that ye may be **grateful**.
031:012 Any who is (so) **grateful** does so
034:013 of My servants are **grateful**!"
034:015 by your Lord, and be **grateful** to Him: a territory
034:019 (soul that is) patiently constant and **grateful**.
035:012 of Allah that ye may be **grateful**.
036:073 Will they not then be **grateful**?
039:007 if ye are **grateful**, He is pleased with you.
042:023 for Allah is Oft-Forgiving, **Grateful**.
042:033 everyone who patiently perseveres and is **grateful**.
045:012 of His Bounty, and that ye may be **grateful**.
046:015 grant me that I may be **grateful** for Thy favour
076:003 whether he be **grateful** or ungrateful.

GRATITUDE

002:178 and compensate him with handsome **gratitude**.
003:103 and remember with **gratitude** Allah's favour on you;
003:123 then fear Allah; thus may ye show your **gratitude**.
003:144 those who (serve him) with **gratitude**.
003:145 those that (serve us with) **gratitude**.
006:063 (we vow) we shall truly show our **gratitude**.'?"
007:017 in most of them, **gratitude** (for Thy mercies)."
010:022 from this, we shall truly show our **gratitude**!
016:121 He showed his **gratitude** for the favours of Allah,
025:062 or to show their **gratitude**.
027:040 truly his **gratitude** is (a gain) for his own soul;
031:012 wisdom on Luqman: "Show (thy) **gratitude** to Allah."
031:014 "Show **gratitude** to Me and to thy parents: to Me

GRAVE

002:178 the limits shall be in **grave** chastisement.
002:217 Say: "Fighting therein is a **grave** (offense);
004:156 that they uttered against Mary a **grave** false charge;
009:084 that dies, nor stand at his **grave**; for they
067:009 ye are in nothing but a **grave** error!'"
080:021 and putteth him in his **Grave**;

GRAVER

002:217 but **graver** is it in the sight of Allah

GRAVES

022:007 raise up all who are in the **graves**.
035:022 to hear who are (buried) in **graves**.
054:007 humbled-from (their) **graves**, (torpid) like

GRAVES (continued)

060:013 in despair about those (buried) in **graves**.
082:004 And when the **Graves** are turned upside down;-
100:009 is in the **graves** is Scattered abroad
102:002 Until ye visit the **graves**.

GRAZE

007:073 so leave her to **graze** in Allah's earth, and

GREAT

002:007 **great** is the chastisement they (incur).
002:219 Say: "In them is **great** sin,
003:030 a **great** distance between it and its evil.
003:164 Allah did confer a **great** favour on the Believers
003:165 smote (your enemies) with one twice as **great**,
003:172 and refrain from wrong have a **great** reward;
003:173 "A **great** army is gathering against you,
003:179 ye have a reward **great** without measure.
004:002 For this is indeed a **great** sin.
004:019 about through it a **great** deal of good.
004:031 and admit you to the Gate of **great** honor.
004:034 for Allah is Most High, **Great** (above you all).
004:040 and giveth from His Own self a **great** reward.
004:054 and conferred upon them a **great** kingdom.
004:067 given them from Ourselves a **great** reward;
004:074 soon shall We give him a reward of **great** (value).
004:095 those who sit at home by a **great** reward.
004:113 and **great** is the Grace of Allah unto thee.
004:162 to them shall We soon give a **great** reward.
005:009 hath Allah promised forgiveness and a **great** reward.
007:116 and they showed a **great** (feat of) magic.
007:137 the **great** works and fine Buildings which Pharaoh
008:073 and **great** mischief.
009:003 on the day of the **Great** Pilgrimage,-that Allah
009:025 your **great** numbers elated you, but they
009:121 (for the Cause)-small or **great**-nor cut
010:015 the Chastisement of a **Great** Day (to come)."
011:003 for you the Chastisement of a **Great** Day:
011:011 (of sins) and a **great** reward.
011:091 For thou hast among us no **great** position!"
012:030 the (**great**) 'Aziz is seeking to seduce her slave
012:072 They said: "We miss the **great** beaker of the king;
012:084 "How **great** is my grief for Joseph!"
013:009 which is open: He is the **Great**, the Most High.
014:020 Nor is that for Allah any **great** matter.
017:031 Verily the killing of them is a **great** sin.
017:043 they say! Exalted and **Great** (beyond measure)!
017:070 above a **great** part of Our Creation.
017:087 for His Bounty is to thee (indeed) **great**.
018:049 What a book is this! it leaves out nothing small or **great**,
018:049 see the sinful in **great** terror because of what is (recorded)
018:094 do **great** mischief on earth:
021:076 and his family from **great** distress.
021:103 The **Great** Terror will bring them no grief:
022:018 But a **great** number are (also) such as unto whom the
022:018 the animals; and a **great** number among mankind?
022:062 Most High, Most **Great**.
025:049 cattle and men in **great** numbers.
026:135 the Chastisement of a **Great** Day."
026:149 carve houses out of (rocky) mountains with **great** skill.
026:156 lest the Chastisement of a **Great** Day seize you."
026:189 and that was the Chastisement of a **Great** Day.
031:030 and because Allah,-He is the Most High, Most **Great**.
033:029 amongst you a **great** reward.
033:035 forgiveness and **great** reward.

GREAT (continued)

033:047 shall have from Allah a very **great** Bounty.
033:067 We obeyed our chiefs and our **great** ones, and they
033:068 with a very **great** Curse!"
033:071 has already attained the **great** victory.
034:023 and He is the Most High, Most **Great**.'"
036:062 "But he did lead astray a **great** multitude of you.
037:076 from the **Great** Calamity.
037:115 and their people from (their) **Great** distress.
040:012 with Allah, Most High, Most **Great**!"
042:004 and He is Most High, Most **Great**.
042:043 an affair of **great** resolution.
048:010 Allah will soon grant him a **great** Reward.
048:029 and a **great** Reward.
049:003 for them is Forgiveness and a **great** Reward.
053:032 Those who avoid **great** sins and indecent deeds,
054:053 Every matter, small and **great**, is on record.
057:007 for them is a **great** Reward.
057:025 in which is **great** might, as well as
067:012 for them is Forgiveness and a **great** Reward.
069:015 On that Day shall the (**Great**) Event come to pass,
078:002 Concerning the **Great** News,
079:020 Then did (Moses) show him the **Great** Sign.
079:034 the **great**, overwhelming (Event),-
085:011 that is the **great** Triumph.
087:012 Who will enter the **Great** Fire,

GREATER

002:219 but the sin is **greater** than the profit."
002:233 laid on it **greater** than it can bear.
002:286 a burden **greater** than we have the strength
002:286 place a burden **greater** than it can bear.
004:153 for an even **greater** (miracle), for they said:
012:103 Yet no faith will the **greater** part of mankind have,
016:041 of the Hereafter will be **greater**, if they
017:089 yet the **greater** part of men refuse
020:023 show thee of Our **Greater** Signs.
021:070 but We made them the **Greater** losers.
022:060 to no **greater** extent than the injury he received,
023:062 On no soul do We place a burden **greater** than it can
024:028 that makes for **greater** purity for
024:030 that will make for **greater** purity for them:
028:078 to him in strength and **greater** in amount
030:009 and populated it in **greater** numbers than these
032:021 the **greater** Chastisement in order that they may
033:053 that makes for **greater** purity for your
034:003 less than that, or **greater**, but is
036:007 the **greater** part of them; for they
039:026 but **greater** is the Punishment of the Hereafter,
040:010 "**Greater** was the aversion of Allah to you
040:057 and the earth is a **greater** (matter) than the
042:037 Those who avoid the **greater** sins and indecencies
043:048 each **greater** then its fellow, and We
059:013 Of a truth ye arouse **greater** fear in their hearts,
061:007 Who doth **greater** wrong than one who forges
068:033 but **greater** is the Punishment in the Hereafter,-
073:020 Yea, better and **greater**, in Reward, and seek ye

GREATEST

006:078 this is the **greatest** (of all)."
009:022 the **greatest** (of all).
009:072 but the **greatest** bliss in the Good Pleasure of Allah:
010:061 the **greatest** of these things but are recorded
027:005 will be the **greatest** loss.
029:045 is the **greatest** (thing in life) without doubt.

GREATEST (continued)

041:035 none but persons of the **greatest** good fortune.
053:018 of the Signs of his Lord, the **Greatest**!

GREATLY

080:013 (It is) in Books held (**greatly**) in honor.

GREATNESS

010:078 may have **greatness** in the land?
017:111 Yea, magnify Him for His **greatness** and glory!"
040:056 but (the quest of) **greatness**, which they

GREED

004:128 even though men's souls are swayed by **greed**.
089:019 And ye devour inheritance-all with **greed**,

GREEDY

002:096 of all people, most **greedy** of life,
074:015 Yet is he **greedy**-that I should add (yet more);
092:008 But he who is a **greedy** miser and thinks

GREEN

006:059 nor anything fresh or dry (**green** or withered),
006:099 from some We produce **green** (crops), out of
012:043 and seven **green** ears of corn, and seven
012:046 ones devour, and of seven **green** ears of corn and
018:031 will wear **green** garments of fine silk and heavy brocade;
022:063 and forthwith the earth becomes clothed with **green**?
036:080 out of the **green** tree, when behold!
055:064 Dark **green** in colour (from plentiful watering).
055:076 Reclining on **green** Cushions and rich
076:021 Upon them will be **green** Garments of fine silk
087:004 And Who bringeth out the (**green** and luscious) pasture,

GREETING

004:086 meet it with a **greeting** still more courteous,
004:086 When a (courteous) **greeting** is offered you,
010:010 will be their **greeting** therein and the end
014:023 their **greeting** therein will be: "Peace!"
015:046 (Their **greeting** will be): "Enter ye here
024:061 a **greeting** or blessing and purity as from Allah.
057:012 before their right hands: (their **greeting** will be)

GREETINGS

021:103 meet them (with mutual **greetings**): "This is

GREW

007:095 until they **grew** and multiplied, and began
021:044 and their fathers until the period **grew** long for them;
057:016 long ages passed over them and their hearts **grew** hard?

GREY

019:004 and the hair of my head doth glisten with **grey**:

GRIEF

006:033 We know indeed the **grief** which their words
009:092 with tears of **grief** that they had no resources
012:084 "How great is my **grief** for Joseph!"
016:058 filled with inward **grief**!
018:006 after them, in **grief**, if they
021:103 The Great Terror will bring them no **grief**:
026:003 with **grief**, that they do not become Believers.
033:051 of their **grief**, and their satisfaction-that of
043:017 is filled with inward **grief**!
058:010 by Satan, in order that he may cause **grief** to the

GRIEVE

002:038 nor shall they **grieve**.
002:062 nor shall they **grieve**.
002:112 nor shall they **grieve**.
002:262 on them shall be no fear, nor shall they **grieve**.
002:274 on them shall be no fear, nor shall they **grieve**.
002:277 nor shall they **grieve**.

GRIEVE (continued)

003:153   to teach you not to **grieve** for (the booty)
003:170   nor have they (cause to) **grieve**.
003:176   Let not those **grieve** thee who rush headlong
003:186   certainly hear much that will **grieve** you,
005:041   O Messenger! let not those **grieve** thee, who race
005:069   on them shall be no fear, nor shall they **grieve**.
006:048   upon them shall be no fear, nor shall they **grieve**.
007:035   on them shall be no fear, nor shall they **grieve**.
007:049   nor shall ye **grieve**."
010:062   there is no fear, nor shall they **grieve**;
010:065   Let not their speech **grieve** thee: for all
011:036   So **grieve** no longer over their (evil) deeds.
012:069   (own) brother; so **grieve** not at aught
012:078   a father, aged and venerable, (who will **grieve** for him):
015:088   on certain classes of them, nor **grieve** over them:
016:127   the help from Allah; nor **grieve** over them:
018:073   for forgetting, nor **grieve** me by raising
018:080   and we feared that he would **grieve** them by
019:024   "**Grieve** not! for thy Lord hath provided
020:040   and she should not **grieve**.
027:070   But **grieve** not over them, nor distress
028:007   but fear not nor **grieve**: for We
028:013   that she might not **grieve**, and that
029:033   "Fear thou not, nor **grieve**: we are
031:023   let not his rejection **grieve** thee: to Us
036:076   let not their speech, then, **grieve** thee.
039:061   no evil shall touch them, nor shall they **grieve**.
041:030   (they suggest), "Nor **grieve**! But receive
043:068   you today, nor shall ye **grieve**,-
046:013   no fear, nor shall they **grieve**.

GRIEVED

007:150   angry and **grieved**, he said: "Evil it is that ye
011:077   he was **grieved** on their account and felt himself
029:033   he was **grieved** on their account, and felt
067:027   at hand, **grieved** will be the faces of the

GRIEVES

003:120   If aught that is good befalls you, it **grieves** them;
009:050   If good befalls thee, it **grieves** them; but if
009:128   it **grieves** him that ye should suffer, ardently

GRIEVOUS

002:010   and **grievous** is the chastisement they (incur),
002:051   and ye did **grievous** wrong.
002:085   the most **grievous** chastisement
002:104   Faith is a **grievous** punishment.
002:174   nor purify them: **grievous** will be their Chastisement.
003:021   announce to them a **grievous** chastisement.
003:077   they shall have a **grievous** Chastisement.
003:091   For such is (in store) a chastisement **grievous**,
003:177   but they will have a **grievous** punishment.
003:188   For them is a Chastisement **grievous** indeed.
004:018   a chastisement most **grievous**.
004:138   that there is for them a **grievous** Chastisement.
004:161   who reject faith a **grievous** chastisement.
004:173   He will punish with a **grievous** chastisement:
005:036   Theirs would be a **grievous** Chastisement.
005:073   a **grievous** chastisement will befall the
005:094   will have a **grievous** chastisement.
006:070   and for punishment, one most **grievous**: for they
007:073   or ye shall be seized with a **grievous** punishment."
007:165   with a **grievous** punishment, because they
007:167   them with **grievous** Chastisement.
008:032   from the sky, or send us a **grievous** chastisement."

GRIEVOUS (continued)

009:003   a **grievous** chastisement to those who reject Faith.
009:034   announce unto them a most **grievous** chastisement-
009:039   he will punish you with a **grievous** penalty, and put
009:061   will have a **grievous** chastisement.
009:074   a **grievous** chastisement in this life and in
009:079   and they shall have a **grievous** chastisement.
009:090   Soon will a **grievous** chastisement seize the
009:101   be sent to a **grievous** Chastisement.
010:004   and a Chastisement **grievous**, because they
010:088   until they see the **grievous** Chastisement."
010:097   (for themselves) the Chastisement **Grievous**.
011:026   the punishment of a **Grievous** Day."
011:048   a **grievous** Chastisement reach them from Us."
011:102   the midst of their wrong: **grievous**, indeed,
012:025   but prison or a **grievous** chastisement?"
014:022   be a **grievous** Chastisement."
015:050   will be indeed the most **grievous** Chastisement.
016:025   Alas, how **grievous** the burdens
016:063   a most **grievous** chastisement.
016:104   and theirs will be a **grievous** Chastisement.
016:117   a most **grievous** Chastisement.
017:010   a Chastisement **grievous** (indeed).
018:005   It is a **grievous** thing that issues from their
020:101   and **grievous** will the burden be to
020:127   more **grievous** and more enduring.
022:025   We cause to taste of a most **grievous** chastisement.
024:011   among them, will be a Chastisement **grievous**.
024:014   a **grievous** chastisement would have seized you
024:019   will have a **grievous** Chastisement in this life
024:023   for them is a **grievous** Chastisement-
024:063   or a **grievous** Chastisement be inflicted on them.
025:019   of a **grievous** Chastisement.
025:037   (all) wrong-doers a **grievous** Chastisement:
025:065   for its Wrath is indeed an affliction **grievous**,-
026:201   they see the **grievous** Chastisement
027:005   a **grievous** Chastisement is (waiting):
029:023   they who will (suffer) a most **grievous** Chastisement.
031:007   announce to him a **grievous** Chastisement.
033:008   a **grievous** Chastisement.
036:018   stone you, and a **grievous** punishment indeed will
037:038   Ye shall indeed taste of the **Grievous** Chastisement;-
038:026   is a Chastisement **Grievous**, for that
041:043   a most **Grievous** Chastisement.
042:021   the wrong-doers will have a **grievous** Chastisement.
042:042   for such there will be a Chastisement **grievous**.
043:065   from the Chastisement of a **Grievous** Day!
044:011   this will be a Chastisement **Grievous**.
045:008   then announce to him a Chastisement **Grievous**!
045:011   is a **grievous** Chastisement of abomination.
046:024   a wind wherein is a **Grievous** Chastisement!
046:031   from a Chastisement **Grievous**.
048:016   He will punish you with a **grievous** Chastisement."
048:017   (Allah) will punish him with a **grievous** Chastisement.
048:025   with a **grievous** punishment.
051:037   as fear the **Grievous** Chastisement.
054:046   be most **grievous** and most bitter.
058:004   Reject (Him), there is a **grievous** Chastisement.
059:015   the hereafter there is) for them a **grievous** Chastisement;-
061:010   save you from a **grievous** Chastisement?-
064:005   their conduct; and they had a **grievous** Chastisement.
067:028   from a **grievous** Chastisement?
071:001   to them a **grievous** Chastisement."

GRIEVOUS (continued)
073:013 And Food that chokes, and a Chastisement **Grievous**.
076:031 He prepared a **grievous** Chastisement.
084:024 So announce to them a Chastisement **Grievous**,

GRIEVOUSLY
061:003 **Grievously** hateful is it in the sight of Allah

GRIN
023:104 and they will therein **grin**, with their

GRIP
085:012 Truly strong is the **Grip** of thy Lord.

GRIPPED
007:131 when **gripped** by calamity, they ascribed it

GROAN
023:064 behold, they will **groan** in supplication!
023:065 "**Groan** not in supplication this day; for ye

GROANS
016:053 unto Him ye cry with **groans**;

GROSSLY
027:055 Nay, ye are a people (**grossly**) ignorant!"

GROUND
002:150 that there be no **ground** of dispute
003:153 Behold! ye were climbing up the high **ground**,
005:031 who scratched the **ground**, to show him how
005:068 ye have no **ground** to stand upon unless ye stand
006:035 a tunnel in the **ground** or a ladder
007:137 and We levelled to the **ground** the great
008:042 and the caravan on lower **ground** than ye.
009:091 no **ground** (of complaint) can there be against
009:093 The **ground** (of complaint) is only against such as
023:050 on high **ground**, affording rest and security
028:030 from a tree in hallowed **ground**: "O Moses! Verily I am
054:020 roots of palm-trees torn up (from the **ground**).
056:063 See ye the seed that ye sow in the **ground**?

GROUNDED
003:007 And those who are firmly **grounded** in knowledge

GROUP
002:060 Each **group** knew its own place for water.
004:090 Except those who join a **group** between whom
007:160 each **group** knew its own place for water.
008:058 If thou fearest treachery from any **group**, throw
028:004 into sections, depressing a **group** among them:
028:023 he found there a **group** of men watering
067:008 every time a **Group** is cast therein, its Keepers

GROUPS
039:071 in **groups**; until, when they arrive there,
039:073 will be led to the Garden in **groups**: until behold,
099:006 On that Day will men proceed in **groups** sorted out,

GROVELLING
067:022 with his face **grovelling**, better guided,-or one

GROW
003:037 He made her **grow** in purity and beauty:
003:178 that they may **grow** in their iniquity:
005:013 We cursed them, and made their hearts **grow** hard:
023:019 With it We **grow** for you gardens of date-palms
027:060 Yea, with it We cause to **grow** well-planted
037:146 And We caused to **grow** over him, a spreading
039:021 thou wilt see it **grow** yellow; then He makes it dry up
039:021 Then He causes to **grow**, therewith, produce of various
040:067 as a child: then lets you (**grow** and) reach your
056:064 Is it ye that cause it to **grow**, or are We the Cause?
056:072 Is it ye who **grow** the tree which feeds the fire,
056:072 which feeds the fire, or do We **grow** it?

GROW (continued)
057:020 thou wilt see it **grow** yellow; then it becomes
080:003 but that perchance he might **Grow** in purity?
080:007 if he **grow** not in purity.

GROWETH
002:061 to produce for us of what the earth **groweth**,
002:261 it **groweth** seven ears,

GROWING
004:006 nor in haste against their **growing** up.
071:017 from the earth, **growing** (gradually),

GROWN
019:008 and I have **grown** quite decrepit from old age?"
071:007 with their garments, **grown** obstinate, and given

GROWS
002:020 and when the darkness **grows** on them,
007:189 When she **grows** heavy, they both
010:024 (it **grows**) till the earth is clad with its golden
016:010 and out of it (**grows**) the vegetation on which ye feed

GROWTH
018:008 but as dust and dry soil (without **growth** or herbage).
022:005 forth every kind of beautiful **growth** (in pairs).
027:060 to cause the **growth** of the trees in them.
050:007 every kind of beautiful **growth** (in pairs)-
057:020 and the **growth** which it brings forth,
078:016 And gardens of luxurious **growth**?

GRUDGINGLY
081:024 Neither doth he withhold **Grudgingly** a knowledge

GUARANTEES
004:090 and (instead) send you (**guarantees** of) peace, then
004:091 nor give you **guarantees** of peace besides

GUARD
002:048 Then **guard** yourselves against a day
002:123 Then **guard** yourselves against a day
002:238 **Guard** strictly your (habit of) prayers.
003:028 that ye may **guard** yourselves from them.
003:186 persevere patiently, and **guard** against evil,
004:034 what Allah would have them **guard**.
004:034 and **guard** in (the husband's) absence what Allah
004:141 And did we not **guard** you from the Believers?"
005:093 then again, **guard** themselves from evil and do good.
005:093 when they **guard** themselves from evil and believe,
005:105 O ye who believe! **guard** your own souls: if ye
006:051 that they may **guard** (against evil).
009:122 to **guard** themselves (against evil).
010:063 and (constantly) **guard** against evil;-
012:081 and we could not well **guard** against the unseen!
013:011 they **guard** him by command of Allah.
015:009 assuredly **guard** it (from corruption).
019:063 Our Servants who **guard** against evil.
021:043 Or have they gods that can **guard** them from Us?
021:080 for your benefit, to **guard** you from each other's
023:005 Who **guard** their modesty,
023:009 And who (strictly) **guard** their prayer;-
024:030 should lower their gaze and **guard** their modesty:
024:031 and **guard** their modesty; that they
028:032 to thy side (to **guard**) against fear.
033:035 who **guard** their chastity, and for
037:007 (For beauty) and for **guard** against all
038:028 those who **guard** against evil, the same
039:028 in order that they may **guard** against Evil.
041:012 and (provided it) with **guard**.
042:048 We have not sent thee as a **guard** over them.

GUARD (continued)

047:036   and **guard** against evil, He will grant
070:029   And those who **guard** their chastity,
070:034   And those who (strictly) **guard** their worship;-
073:017   deny (Allah), **guard** yourselves against a Day that

GUARDED

002:103   and **guarded** themselves from evil,
012:048   shall have (specially) **guarded**.
015:017   And (moreover) we have **guarded** them from every
019:072   But We shall save those who **guarded** against evil,
021:032   as a canopy well **guarded**: yet do
021:082   and it was We Who **guarded** them.
021:091   And (remember) her who **guarded** her chastity:
037:049   As if they were (delicate) eggs closely **guarded**.
039:024   (and receive it) by his face, (like one **guarded** therefrom)?
066:012   who **guarded** her chastity; and We

GUARDIAN

002:282   let his **guardian** dictate faithfully.
004:001   O mankind! fear your **Guardian** Lord, Who created
004:006   If the **guardian** is well-off, let him
006:001   (others) as equal with their **Guardian** Lord.
006:150   as equal with their **Guardian** Lord.
007:054   Your **Guardian** Lord is Allah, Who created
012:066   be Allah the Witness and **Guardian**!"
039:062   and He is the **Guardian** and Disposer of all affairs.
050:017   Behold, two (**guardian** angels) appointed to learn
050:018   is a vigilant **Guardian**.
059:023   The **Guardian** of Faith,

GUARDIAN-LORD

002:021   O ye people! worship your **Guardian-Lord**,
087:001   Glorify the name of thy **Guardian-Lord**, Most High,
087:015   their **Guardian-Lord**, and prays.
093:003   Thy **Guardian-Lord** Hath not forsaken thee, nor is
093:005   And soon will thy **Guardian-Lord** give thee

GUARDIANS

006:061   and He sets **guardians** over you.
008:034   No men can be its **guardians** except the righteous;
008:034   and they are not its **guardians**?
015:022   though ye are not the **guardians** of its stores.
074:031   as **guardians** of the Fire; and We

GUARDIANSHIP

004:023   your step-daughters under your **guardianship**, born

GUARDING

002:255   fatigue in **guarding** and preserving them
005:048   and **guarding** it in safety: so judge
006:092   and they are constant in **guarding** their Prayers.
050:004   with Us is a Record **guarding** (the full account).

GUARDS

053:032   He knows best who it is that **guards** against evil.
072:008   filled with stern **guards** and flaming fires.

GUESSING

018:022   doubtfully **guessing** at the unknown; (yet others)

GUESTS

011:078   and cover me not with disgrace about my **guests**!
015:051   Tell them about the **guests** of Abraham.
015:068   Lut said: "These are my **guests**: disgrace me not:
051:024   of the honoured **guest** of Abraham?
054:037   snatch away his **guests** from him, but We

GUIDANCE

002:002   in it is **guidance** sure; without doubt,
002:005   They are on (true) **guidance**,
002:016   have bartered **guidance** for error:

GUIDANCE (continued)

002:038   there comes to you **guidance** from Me,
002:038   whosoever follows My **guidance**,
002:070   we wish indeed for **guidance** if Allah wills."
002:097   and **guidance** and glad tidings
002:120   Say: "The **guidance** of Allah,
002:120   that is the (only) **guidance**."
002:144   thy face (for **guidance**) to the heavens:
002:157   and they are the ones that receive **guidance**.
002:159   (Signs) We have sent down, and the **Guidance**,
002:170   fathers were void of wisdom and **guidance**?.
002:175   buy error in place of **Guidance** and Torment
002:185   for **guidance** and judgment (between right and wrong).
002:258   Nor doth Allah give **guidance** to a people unjust.
003:020   If they do, they are in right **guidance**,
003:073   Say: "True **guidance** is the **guidance** of Allah:
003:096   full of blessings and of **guidance** for all the worlds.
003:138   a **guidance** and instruction to those who fear Allah!
004:115   even after **guidance** has been plainly conveyed
005:044   therein was **guidance** and light.
005:046   a **guidance** and an admonition
005:046   therein was **guidance** and light.
005:104   were void of knowledge and **guidance**?.
005:105   if ye follow (right) **guidance**.
006:035   He could gather them together unto true **guidance**:
006:056   the company of those who receive **guidance**."
006:071   Say: "Allah's **guidance** is the (only) **guidance**, and we
006:071   heels after receiving **guidance** from Allah?-
006:082   for they are on (right) **guidance**."
006:088   This is the **Guidance** of Allah: He giveth
006:088   He giveth that **guidance** to whom He pleaseth,
006:090   Follow the **guidance** they received; say: "No
006:090   were the (prophets) who received Allah's **guidance**.
006:091   A light and **guidance** to man: but ye make it into
006:140   and heeded no **guidance**.
006:157   its **guidance** better than they."
007:030   and think that they receive **guidance**.
007:043   never could we have found **guidance**, had it not
007:043   had it not been for the **guidance** of Allah:
007:154   **Guidance** and Mercy for such as fear their Lord.
007:178   whom He rejects from His **guidance**.
007:186   To such as Allah rejects from His **guidance**, there
007:193   If ye call them to **guidance**, they will
007:198   If thou callest them to **guidance**, they hear
007:203   and **Guidance**, and Mercy, for any who have Faith."
009:018   It is they who are expected to be on true **guidance**.
009:033   His Messenger with **Guidance** and the
010:035   not **guidance** (himself) unless he is guided?
010:035   Say: "It is Allah Who gives **guidance** towards Truth."
010:035   gives **guidance** to Truth more worthy to be followed,
010:035   any that can give **guidance** towards Truth?"
010:045   and refused to receive true **guidance**.
010:057   who believe, a **Guidance** and a Mercy.
010:108   Those, who receive **guidance**, do so for
014:021   received the **guidance** of Allah, we should
016:037   If thou art anxious for their **guidance**, yet Allah
016:125   and who receive **guidance**.
017:015   Who receiveth **guidance**, receiveth it
017:094   when **Guidance** came to them, was nothing
017:097   that is on true **guidance**; but he
018:013   in their Lord, and We increased them in **guidance**:
018:055   from believing, now that **guidance** has come to them,
018:057   even then will they never accept **guidance**.

GUIDANCE (continued)

018:057   If thou callest them to **guidance**, even then
019:076   "And Allah doth increase in **guidance** those who
019:076   those who seek **guidance**: and the good things that
020:010   or find some **guidance** at the fire."
020:047   And peace to all who follow **guidance**!
020:050   then, gave (it) **guidance**."
020:082   and do right,-who, in fine, are no true **guidance**."
020:122   and gave him **guidance**.
020:123   as is sure, there comes to you **guidance** from Me,
020:123   whosoever follows My **guidance**, will not
020:128   Is it not a **guidance** to such men (to call to mind)
020:135   and who it is that has received **guidance**."
022:008   without knowledge, without **guidance**, and without
022:037   that ye may glorify Allah for His **guidance** to you:
023:027   within Our sight and under Our **guidance**:
023:049   in order that they might receive **guidance**.
024:054   If ye obey him, ye shall be on right **guidance**.
027:024   so they receive no **guidance**,-
027:092   and if any accept **guidance**, they do
028:037   who it is that comes with **guidance** from Him
028:043   Insight to men and **Guidance** and Mercy, that they
028:050   devoid of **guidance** from Allah?
028:056   and He knows best those who receive **guidance**.
028:057   the **guidance** with thee, we should
028:064   If only they had been open to **guidance**!'
028:085   that brings true **guidance**, and who
031:005   These are on (true) **guidance** from their Lord;
031:020   without **guidance**, and without a Book
032:013   every soul its true **guidance**:
032:024   Leaders, giving **guidance** under Our command, so long
034:024   on right **guidance** or in manifest error!"
034:032   from **Guidance** after it reached you?
034:050   but if I receive **guidance**, it is
039:023   Such is the **guidance** of Allah; He guides
039:041   He, then, that receives **guidance** benefits his
040:053   We did aforetime give Moses the **Guidance**, and We
041:017   but they preferred blindness (of heart) to **Guidance**:
041:017   As to the Thamud, We gave them **guidance**,
043:010   in order that ye may find **guidance** (on the way);
043:024   you better **guidance** than that which ye found
043:049   for We shall truly accept **guidance**."
045:011   This is (true) **Guidance**: and for those who reject
045:020   and a **Guidance** and Mercy to those of assured Faith.
045:023   after Allah (has withdrawn **Guidance**)?
047:017   But to those who receive **Guidance**, He increases
047:017   He increases their **Guidance**, and bestows on them
047:025   after **Guidance** was clearly shown to them,-
047:032   after **Guidance** has been clearly shown to them,
048:028   His Messenger with **Guidance** and the Religion
053:023   to them **Guidance** from their Lord!
053:030   and He knoweth best those who receive **guidance**.
057:026   and some of them were on right **guidance**, but many
061:009   with **Guidance** and the Religion of Truth.
068:007   who receive (True) **Guidance**.
072:002   'It gives **guidance** to the Right, and we
072:013   to the **Guidance**, we have accepted it:
079:021   But (Pharaoh) rejected it and disobeyed (**guidance**);
087:003   And granted **guidance**;
093:007   and He gave thee **guidance**.
096:011   Seest thou if He is on (the road of) **Guidance**?-

GUIDE

002:185   as a **guide** to mankind,

GUIDE (continued)

002:272   It is not for you to **guide** them to the right path.
003:003   Before this, as a **guide** to mankind,
003:086   How shall Allah **guide** those who reject faith
004:026   and to **guide** you into the ways of those before you;
004:088   Would ye **guide** those whom Allah
004:137   nor **guide** them on the Way.
004:168   nor **guide** them to any way-
004:175   and **guide** them to Himself by a straight Way.
006:077   "Unless my Lord **guide** me, I shall
006:097   that ye may **guide** yourselves, with their
006:125   Those whom Allah willeth to **guide**,- He openeth
006:154   and a **guide** and a mercy, that they
006:157   and a **guide** and a mercy: then who
007:052   a **guide** and a mercy to all who believe.
007:159   there is a section who **guide** and do justice
007:178   Whom Allah doth **guide**,-he is
007:186   there can be no **guide**; He will
010:009   will **guide** them because of their Faith:
010:025   He doth **guide** whom He pleaseth to a way
010:043   but canst thou **guide** the blind,-
011:017   is the Book of Moses-a **guide** and a mercy?
012:052   and that Allah will never **guide** the snare
012:111   and a **Guide** and a Mercy to any such as believe.
013:007   and to every people a **guide**.
013:033   Allah leaves to stray, no one can **guide**.
016:015   that ye may **guide** yourselves;
016:016   and by the stars (men) **guide** themselves.
016:064   a **guide** and a mercy to those who believe.
016:089   Book explaining all things, a **guide** a Mercy,
016:102   and as a **Guide** and Glad tidings to Muslims.
016:104   Allah will not **guide** them, and theirs
016:107   and Allah will not **guide** those who reject Faith.
017:002   and made it a **Guide** to the Children of Israel,
017:009   Verily this Qur'an doth **guide** to that which
018:024   "I hope that my Lord will **guide** me ever closer
019:043   so follow me: I will **guide** thee to a Way that
022:004   and he will **guide** him to the Chastisement
022:016   and verily Allah doth **guide** whom He will!
022:054   is the **Guide** of those who believe, to the
024:035   Allah doth **guide** whom He will to His Light:
025:031   but enough is the Lord to **guide** and to help.
025:045   Then do We make the sun its **guide**;
026:062   Soon will He **guide** me!
027:002   A **Guide**; and Glad Tidings for the Believers,
027:077   And it certainly is a **Guide** and Mercy
027:081   Nor canst thou be a **guide** to the Blind,
028:049   which is a better **Guide** than either of them,
028:056   to **guide** everyone whom thou lovest: but Allah
029:069   We will certainly **guide** them to Our Paths:
030:029   But who will **guide** those whom Allah
031:003   A **Guide** and a Mercy to the Doers of Good,-
032:023   and We made it a **guide** to the Children of Israel.
037:099   He will surely **guide** me!
038:022   with injustice, but **guide** us to the even Path.
039:023   can have none to **guide**.
039:036   there can be no **guide**.
039:037   And such as Allah doth **guide** there can be
040:029   I see (myself); nor do I **guide** you but to
040:033   to stray, there is none to **guide**...
040:054   A **Guide** and a Message to men of understanding.
041:044   Say: "It is a **guide** and a healing to those
042:052   wherewith We **guide** such of Our servants as We will;

GUIDE (continued)

042:052 and verily thou dost **guide** (men) to the Straight Way,-
043:022 and we do **guide** ourselves by their footsteps."
043:027 and He will certainly **guide** me."
045:023 Who, then, will **guide** him after Allah
046:011 and seeing that they **guide** not themselves thereby,
046:012 as a **guide** and a mercy; and this Book
047:005 Soon will He **guide** them and improve their condition,
048:002 and **guide** thee on the Straight Way;
048:020 the Believers, and that He may **guide** you to a
072:010 to **guide** them to right conduct.
074:031 whom He pleaseth, and **guide** whom He pleaseth;
079:019 "And that I **guide** thee to thy Lord, so thou
092:012 Verily We take upon Us to **guide**,

GUIDED

002:053 there was a chance for you to be **guided** aright.
002:135 if ye would be **guided** (to salvation)."
002:143 except to those **guided** by Allah.
002:150 and ye may (consent to) be **guided**.
002:185 and to glorify Him in that He has **guided** you;
002:213 Allah by His Grace **guided** the Believers to the Truth,
003:008 deviate now after Thou hast **guided** us,
003:103 that ye may be **guided**.
004:051 they are better **guided** in the (right) way
006:080 about Allah, when He (Himself) hath **guided** me?
006:084 and before him, We **guided** Noah, and among
006:084 We gave him Isaac and Jacob: all (three) We **guided**:
006:087 and We **guided** them to a straight Way.
006:117 He knoweth best those who are rightly **guided**.
006:149 He could indeed have **guided** you all."
006:161 my Lord hath **guided** me to a way that is straight,-
007:030 Some He hath **guided**: others have
007:043 Who hath **guided** us to this (felicity):
007:158 follow him that (so) ye may be **guided**."
009:115 after He hath **Guided** them until He makes clear
010:035 not guidance (himself) unless he is **guided**?
011:097 and the command of Pharaoh was not rightly **guided**.
013:031 (so) willed, He could have **guided** all mankind
014:012 Indeed He has **guided** us to the Ways
016:009 He could have **guided** all of you.
016:036 some whom Allah **guided**, and some
016:121 and **guided** him to a Straight Way.
017:084 is best **guided** on the Way."
018:017 he whom Allah guides is rightly **guided**; but he
019:058 and Israel-of those whom We **guided** and chose.
022:024 they have been **guided** to the Path
022:024 For they have been **guided** (in this life)
027:041 let us see whether she is **guided** (to the truth)
027:041 those who are not rightly **guided**."
032:003 in order that they may be rightly **guided**.
035:008 (equal to one who is rightly **guided**)?
035:042 rightly **guided** than anyone of the nations:
036:021 and who are themselves **guided**.
037:118 And We **guided** them to the Straight Way.
039:018 those are the ones who Allah has **guided**, and those are
039:057 'If only Allah had **guided** me, I should
043:037 are being **guided** aright!
049:017 a favour upon you that He has **guided** you to the Faith,
067:022 with his face grovelling, better **guided**,-or one

GUIDES

002:213 For Allah **guides** whom He will to a path
002:272 But Allah **guides** to the right path
003:086 But Allah **guides** not a people unjust.

GUIDES (continued)

009:019 and Allah **guides** not those who do wrong.
009:024 and Allah **guides** not the rebellious.
014:004 those whom He pleases and **guides** whom He pleases
016:093 and He **guides** whom He pleases: but ye
017:097 It is he whom Allah **guides**, that is
018:017 he whom Allah **guides** is rightly guided; but he
024:046 and Allah **guides** whom He wills to a way
026:078 "Who created me, and it is He Who **guides** me;
027:063 Or, Who **guides** you through the depths of
028:050 For Allah **guides** not people given to wrong-doing.
028:056 but Allah **guides** those whom He will and He
034:006 and that it **guides** to the path of the
035:008 whom He wills, and **guides** whom He wills.
039:003 But Allah **guides** not such as are
039:023 He **guides** therewith whom He pleases, but such
040:028 truly Allah **guides** not one who transgresses and lies!
042:013 and **guides** to Himself those who turn (to Him).
046:010 Allah **guides** not a people unjust."
046:030 it **guides** to the Truth and to a Straight Path.
061:005 For Allah **guides** not those who are rebellious
061:007 And Allah **guides** not those who do wrong.
062:005 and Allah **guides** not people who do wrong.
063:006 Truly Allah **guides** not rebellious transgressors.
064:011 (Allah) **guides** his heart (aright): for Allah

GUIDETH

002:142 He **guideth** whom He will to a Way
002:264 And Allah **guideth** not those who reject faith.
005:016 Unto the light,-**guideth** them to a Path that is Straight.
005:016 Wherewith Allah **guideth** all who seek His good
005:051 Verily Allah **guideth** not a people unjust.
005:067 For Allah **guideth** not those who reject Faith.
005:108 for Allah **guideth** not a rebellious people.
006:145 For Allah **guideth** not people who do wrong.
009:037 But Allah **guideth** not those who reject Faith.
009:080 and Allah **guideth** not those who are
009:109 And Allah **guideth** not people that do wrong.
013:027 but He **guideth** to Himself those turn to Him
016:037 yet Allah **guideth** not such as He leaves to stray,

GUIDING

006:071 (vainly) **guiding** him to the Path."
007:100 is it not a **guiding** (lesson) that, if We
021:073 made them leaders, **guiding** (men) by Our Command,

GUILT

002:085 in **guilt** and transgression;
002:181 the **guilt** shall be on those who make the change.
006:078 from your (**guilt**) of giving partners to Allah.
006:147 but from people in **guilt** never will
008:008 distasteful though it be to those in **guilt**.
026:099 who were steeped in **guilt**.
048:025 a **guilt** would have accrued to you without (your)

GUILTLESS

002:173 then is he **guiltless**.
012:032 firmly save himself **guiltless**!

GUILTY

004:015 If any of your women are **guilty** of lewdness,
004:016 If two persons among you are **guilty** of lewdness,
004:019 except where they have been **guilty** of open lewdness;
005:107 were **guilty** of the sin (of perjury), let two
009:118 (they felt **guilty**) to such a degree that the earth
011:035 of which ye are **guilty**!
012:091 and we certainly have been **guilty** of sin!"
024:002 The woman and the man **guilty** of fornication,-

GUILTY (continued)

027:069 what has been the end of those **guilty** (of sin)."
030:012 the **guilty** will be struck dumb with despair.
032:012 the **guilty** ones will bend low their heads before
033:030 of you were **guilty** of evident unseemly conduct,
044:037 they were **guilty** of sin.
065:001 they are **guilty** of some open lewdness, those are

GULPS

014:017 In **gulps** will he sip it, but never

GUSH

002:074 some from which rivers **gush** forth;
017:090 to **gush** forth for us from the earth,
017:091 and cause rivers to **gush** forth in their midst,
036:034 and We cause springs to **gush** forth therein.
054:012 And We caused the earth to **gush** forth with springs,

GUSHED

002:060 Then **gushed** forth therefrom twelve springs.
007:160 out of it there **gushed** forth twelve springs:
011:040 and the fountains of the earth **gushed** forth!

GUSHES

023:027 and the oven **gushes** forth, take thou

GUSHING

086:012 (for the **gushing** of springs or the sprouting of vegetation)-

GUSTS

077:002 Which then blow violently in tempestuous **Gusts**,

H

HA

019:001 Kaf. **Ha**. Ya. 'Ain. Sad.
020:001 Ta-**Ha**.
040:001 **Ha**-Mim.
041:001 **Ha**-Mim.
042:001 **Ha**-Mim;
043:001 **Ha**-Mim.
044:001 **Ha** Mim.
045:001 **Ha**-Mim.
046:001 **Ha**-Mim.

HABIT

002:238 Guard strictly your (**habit** of) prayers.
005:063 from their (**habit** of) uttering sinful words
011:078 the **habit** of practicing abominations.
051:017 They were in the **habit** of sleeping but little

HABITATIONS

007:074 and gave you **habitations** in the land: ye build
016:068 and in (men's) **habitations**;
016:080 It is Allah who made your **habitations** homes of
027:018 "O ye ants, get into your **habitations**, lest Solomon
028:058 Now those **habitations** of theirs, after them,
081:005 herded together (in human **habitations**);

HABITUAL

069:009 and the Cities Overthrown, committed **habitual** Sin,

HABITUALLY

068:012 (**Habitually**) hindering (all) good,

HAD

002:033 "When he **had** told them their names,
002:036 the state (of felicity) in which they **had** been.
002:056 ye **had** the chance to be grateful.
002:059 the word from that which **had** been given them;
002:064 Mercy of Allah to you ye **had** surely been among the lost.
002:064 ye turned back thereafter: **had** it not been for the Grace
002:089 although from of old they **had** prayed
002:101 as if (it **had** been something) they did not know!
002:103 If they **had** kept their Faith
002:103 far better **had** been the reward from Allah
002:167 "If only we **had** one more chance,
002:220 And if Allah **had** wished,
002:253 If Allah **had** so willed, they would not have
002:253 after Clear (Signs) **had** come to them,
002:253 If Allah **had** so willed, succeeding generations
002:258 because Allah **had** granted Him Power?
003:019 after knowledge **had** come to them.
003:066 which ye **had** some Knowledge!
003:086 and that Clear Signs **had** come unto them?
003:110 If only the People of the Book **had** faith,
003:123 Allah **had** helped you at Badr, when ye
003:151 for which He **had** sent no authority:
003:153 and for (the ill) that **had** befallen you.
003:153 (the booty) that **had** escaped you and for (the ill)
003:154 "If we **had** had thing to do with this affair,
003:154 Say: "Even if you **had** remained in your homes,
003:155 because of some (evil) they **had** done.
003:156 "If they **had** stayed with us, they would
003:164 while, before that, they **had** been in manifest error.
003:167 They said: "**Had** we known there would be a fight,
003:168 "If only they **had** listened to us,

HAD (continued)

004:009 if they **had** left a helpless family behind:
004:020 even if ye **had** given the latter
004:039 if they **had** faith in Allah and in the Last Day,
004:046 If only they **had** said: "We hear and we obey";
004:054 But We **had** already given the people of Abraham
004:064 and the Messenger **had** asked forgiveness for them,
004:064 If they **had** only, when they were unjust
004:066 If We **had** ordered them to sacrifice their lives
004:066 but if they **had** done what they
004:073 "Oh! I wish I **had** been with them:
004:073 as if there **had** never been ties of affection
004:082 **Had** it been from other than Allah, they
004:083 If they **had** only referred it to the Messenger
004:090 If Allah **had** pleased, He could have
004:153 even after Clear Signs **had** come to them; even
004:160 which **had** been lawful for them; in that
005:020 He **had** not given to any other among the peoples.
005:023 were two on whom Allah **had** bestowed His Grace:
005:036 if they **had** everything on earth, and twice
005:046 that **had** come before him: a guidance and
005:046 confirming the Torah that **had** come before him: We
005:048 If Allah **had** so willed, He would have
005:065 **had** believed and been righteous. We
005:066 If only they **had** stood fast by the Torah, the
005:075 They **had** both to eat their (daily) food.
005:081 If only they **had** believed in Allah, in the
005:116 **Had** I said such a thing. Thou wouldst indeed have
005:116 never could I say what I **had** no right (to say).
006:006 Generations We **had** established on the earth,
006:007 If We **had** sent unto thee a written (Message)
006:009 If We **had** made it an angel, We should
006:044 the warning they **had** received, We opened
006:107 If it **had** been Allah's Will, they would
006:112 If thy Lord **had** so willed, they would
006:125 as if they **had** to climb up to the skies:
006:137 If Allah **had** willed, they would
006:148 nor should we have **had** any forbidden thing."
006:148 will say: "If Allah **had** wished, we should
006:149 the argument taht reaches home: if it **had** been His Will.
006:157 "If the Book **had** only been sent down to us, we
007:037 that they **had** rejected Allah.
007:043 **had** it not been for the guidance of Allah:
007:052 For We **had** certainly sent unto them a Book, based
007:092 became as if they **had** never been in the homes
007:092 in the homes where they **had** flourished: the men
007:096 the people of the towns **had** but believed and feared Allah,
007:101 what they **had** rejected before.
007:129 They said: "We have **had** (nothing but) trouble,
007:135 which they **had** to fulfil,-Behold!
007:137 because they **had** patience and constancy, and We
007:138 devoted entirely to some idols they **had**.
007:142 And Moses **had** charged his brother
007:149 and saw that they **had** erred, they said:
007:155 he prayed: "O my Lord! if it **had** been Thy will
007:162 which **had** been given them, so We sent
007:163 but on the day they **had** no Sabbath, they came
007:165 that **had** been given them, We rescued
007:171 as if it **had** been a canopy, and they
007:176 If it **had** been Our Will, We should
007:188 If I **had** knowledge of the unseen, I should
008:023 If Allah **had** found in them any good, He would
008:023 if He **had** made them listen, they would

HAD (continued)

008:042 who died might die after a clear sign (**had** been given),
008:042 who lived might live after a Clear Sign (**had** been given).
008:042 Even if ye **had** made a mutual appointment to meet,
008:043 if He **had** shown them to thee as many, ye would
008:068 **Had** it not been for a previous ordainment
009:042 If there **had** been immediate gain (in sight),
009:046 If they **had** intended to come out, they would
009:047 If they **had** come out with you, they would
009:048 Indeed they **had** plotted sedition before, and upset
009:059 and **had** said, "Sufficient unto us is Allah!
009:059 If only they **had** been content with what Allah
009:066 rejected Faith after ye **had** accepted it.
009:069 They **had** their enjoyment of their portion: and ye
009:074 Allah and His Messenger **had** enriched them!
009:092 with tears of grief that they **had** no resources
009:114 a promise he **had** made to him.
009:117 hearts of a part of them **had** nearly swerved (from duty),
009:124 "Which of you has **had** his faith increased by it?"
010:012 on his way as if he **had** never cried to Us for the
010:016 Say: "If Allah **had** so willed, I should
010:019 **Had** it not been for a Word that went forth before
010:024 as if it **had** not flourished only the day before!
010:045 (it will be) as if they **had** tarried but an hour of a day:
010:074 they **had** already rejected beforehand.
010:081 When they **had had** their throw, Moses said:
010:093 it was after knowledge **had** been granted to them,
010:098 If only there **had** been a single township
010:099 If it **had** been the Lord's Will, they would
011:035 Say: "If I **had** forged it, on me were my sin!
011:042 who **had** separated himself (from the rest):
011:068 As if they **had** never dwelt and flourished there.
011:074 When fear **had** passed from (the mind of) Abraham
011:074 Abraham and the glad tidings **had** reached him,
011:078 and they **had** been long in the habit
011:080 He said: "Would that I **had** power to suppress you
011:095 As if they **had** never dwelt and flourished there!
011:110 **had** it not been that a Word **had** gone forth before from
011:116 If only there **had** been of the generations
011:118 If thy Lord **had** so willed, He could
012:035 they **had** seen the Signs, (that it was best)
012:045 one of the two (who **had** been in prison) and who
012:045 But the man who **had** been released, one of
012:054 Therefore when he **had** spoken to him, he said:
012:059 And when he **had** furnished them forth
012:062 (with which they **had** bartered) into their saddle-bags,
012:065 found their stock-in-trade **had** been returned to them.
012:066 they **had** sworn their solemn oath, he said:
012:068 in the manner their father **had** enjoined, it did
012:070 At length when he **had** furnished them forth
012:100 the desert, (even) after Satan **had** sown enmity
013:018 even if they **had** all that is in the heavens
013:031 the Believers know, that, **had** Allah (so) willed,
014:021 They will reply, "If we **had** received the
014:022 I **had** no authority over you except to call you,
015:002 wish that they **had** been Muslims.
015:004 did We destroy a population that **had** not a term decreed
015:027 And the Jinn race, We **had** created before, from the
016:009 if Allah **had** willed, He could
016:034 at which they **had** scoffed hemmed them in.
016:035 "If Allah **had** so willed, we should not have
016:059 because of the bad news he has **had**!
017:007 as they **had** entered it before, and to

HAD (continued)

017:015 We **had** sent a messenger (to give warning).
017:042 Say: if there **had** been (other) gods with Him,-
017:073 away from that which We **had** revealed unto thee,
017:074 And **had** We not given thee strength, thou wouldst
017:100 Say: "If ye **had** control of the Treasures
018:005 have they of such a thing, nor **had** their fathers.
018:012 at calculating the term of years they **had** tarried!
018:019 best food (to be **had**) and bring some to you,
018:034 (Abundant) was the produce this man **had**:
018:042 turning his hands over what he **had** spent on his property,
018:042 "Woe is me! Would I **had** never ascribed partners to my
018:042 which **had** (now) tumbled to pieces to its very foundations,
018:043 Nor **had** he numbers to help him against Allah,
018:062 When they **had** passed on (some distance), Moses said
018:064 following (the path they **had** come).
018:065 from Ourselves and whom We **had** taught knowledge
018:065 On whom We **had** bestowed Mercy from Ourselves
018:074 thou slain an innocent person who **had** slain none?
018:082 their father **had** been a righteous man:
018:090 for whom We **had** provided no covering protection
018:096 when he **had** made it (red) as fire, he said:
018:096 At length, when he **had** filled up the space
018:101 and who **had** been unable even to hear.
018:101 (Unbelievers) whose eyes **had** been under a veil
019:023 "Ah! would that I **had** died before this! would that
019:023 would that I **had** been a thing forgotten."
019:049 When he **had** turned away from them and from
020:024 for he **had** indeed transgressed all bounds."
020:089 and that it **had** no power either to harm
020:090 Aaron **had** already, before this said to them:
020:091 They **had** said: "We will not cease to worship it,
020:115 We **had** already, beforehand, taken the
020:125 while I **had** sight (before)?"
020:129 **Had** it not been for a Word that went forth
020:134 **Had** We destroyed them with a punishment before this,
021:017 If it **had** been Our wish to take (just) a pastime,
021:078 of certain people **had** strayed by night:
021:081 to the land which We **had** blessed: for We
021:087 he imagined that We **had** no power
021:099 If these **had** been gods, they would
022:031 he is as if he **had** fallen from heaven and been
022:031 or the wind **had** swooped (like a bird on its prey)
023:024 if Allah **had** wished (to send messengers),
023:033 whom We **had** bestowed the good things of this life,
023:071 If the Truth **had** been in accord with their
023:075 If We **had** mercy on them and removed
023:091 each god would have taken away what he **had** created,
023:114 a little,-if ye **had** only known!
023:115 "Did ye then think that We **had** created you
024:015 of which ye **had** no knowledge; and ye
025:027 "Oh! would that I **had** taken a (straight) path
025:028 "Ah! woe is me! would that I **had** never taken
025:029 the Message (of Allah) after it **had** come to me!
025:042 **had** it not been that we were constant to them!"-
025:051 **Had** it been Our Will, We could
026:024 and all between,- if ye **had** but sure belief."
026:028 If ye only **had** sense!"
026:102 "Now if we only **had** a chance of return, we shall
026:198 **Had** We revealed it to any of the non-Arabs,
026:199 And **had** he recited it to them, they would
026:208 Never did We destroy a town but **had** its warners-
027:010 (of its own accord) as if it **had** been a snake,

HAD (continued)

027:040 Said one who **had** knowledge of the Book: "I will
027:043 for she was (sprung) of a people that **had** no faith.
027:082 because mankind **had** no faith in Our Signs.
028:010 **had** We not strengthened her heart (with faith),
028:018 the man who **had**, the day before, sought his
028:029 Now when Moses **had** fulfilled the term, and was
028:031 moving (of its own accord) as if it **had** been a snake,
028:043 after We **had** destroyed the earlier generations,
028:046 no warner **had** come before thee:
028:047 If (We **had**) not (sent thee to the Quraish),
028:059 a town until He **had** sent to its Centre
028:064 If only they **had** been open to guidance!'
028:067 But any that (in this life) **had** repented, believed,
028:076 We **had** bestowed on him, that their
028:078 in amount (of riches) they **had** collected?
028:078 Allah **had** destroyed, before him, (whole) generations,-
028:079 "Oh! that we **had** the like of what Qarun has got!"
028:080 But those who **had** been granted (true) knowledge
028:081 and he **had** not (the least little) party to
028:082 **Had** it not been that Allah was gracious to us,
028:082 And those who **had** envied his position the day
029:053 **had** it not been for a term (of respite) appointed,
029:065 but when He **had** delivered them safely
032:013 If We **had** so willed, We could
033:014 and they **had** been incited to sedition.
033:014 And if an entry **had** been effected to them
033:015 And yet they **had** already covenanted with Allah
033:022 what Allah and His Messenger **had** promised us,
033:027 ye **had** not frequented (before).
033:037 Then when Zaid **had** dissolved (his marriage)
033:037 to one who **had** received the grace of Allah and thy favour:
033:066 we **had** obeyed Allah and obeyed the Messenger!"
033:069 but Allah cleared him of the (calumnies) they **had** uttered:
034:014 the Jinns saw plainly that if they **had** known the unseen,
034:018 between them We **had** appointed stages of journey in
034:018 and the Cities on which We **had** poured Our blessings,
034:018 We **had** placed Cities in prominent positions,
034:021 But he **had** no authority over them,-except that
034:031 the arrogant ones: "**Had** it not been for you,
034:032 who **had** been deemed weak: "Was it we
034:033 Those who **had** been deemed weak will say to
034:044 But We **had** not given them Books which they
034:045 a tenth of what We **had** granted to those: yet when
036:047 those whom, if Allah **had** so willed, He could
036:052 "This is what The Most Gracious **had** promised."
036:066 If it **had** been Our Will, We could
036:067 And if it **had** been Our Will, We could
037:029 They will reply: "Nay, ye yourselves **had** no Faith!
037:030 "Nor **had** we any authority over you.
037:051 "I **had** an intimate companion (on the earth),
037:057 "**Had** it not been for the Grace of my Lord,
037:103 So when they **had** both submitted (to Allah),
037:103 he **had** laid him prostrate on his forehead (for sacrifice)
037:142 and he **had** done acts worthy of blame.
037:143 **Had** it not been that he (repented and)
037:168 "If only we **had had** before us a message
038:024 We **had** tried him: he asked forgiveness of his Lord,
039:004 **Had** Allah wished to take to Himself a son,
039:047 Even if the wrong-doers **had** all that there is
039:057 'If only Allah **had** guided me, I should
039:058 'If only I **had** another chance I should
040:021 and none **had** they to defend them against Allah.

HAD (continued)

040:028 of Pharaoh, who **had** concealed his faith, said:
040:034 not to doubt of the (mission) for which he **had** come:
040:047 will say to those who **had** been arrogant, "We but
040:048 Those who **had** been arrogant will say: "We are
040:074 anything (that **had** real existence)."
040:083 (and skill) as they **had**; but that
041:011 and it **had** been (as) smoke: He said
041:014 They said, "If our Lord **had** so pleased, He would
041:017 seized them, because of what they **had** earned.
041:044 **Had** We sent this as a Qur'an (in a language)
041:045 **Had** it not been for a Word
042:008 If Allah **had** so willed, He could
042:014 **Had** it not been for a Word that went forth before
042:021 **Had** it not been for the Decree
043:020 ("Ah!") they say, "If it **had** been the will
043:081 Say: "If The Most Gracious **had** a son, I would
044:027 they **had** taken such delight!
045:008 as if he **had** not heard them: then announce
045:017 it was only after knowledge **had** been granted to
046:006 (men) **had** worshipped them.
046:008 Say: "**Had** I forged it, then ye
046:026 And We **had** firmly established them in a
046:026 and We **had** endowed them with (faculties of)
046:035 (it will be) as if they **had** not tarried more
047:004 but if it **had** been Allah's Will, He could
047:030 **Had** We so willed, We could have
048:025 If they **had** been apart, We should
048:025 **Had** there not been believing men
049:005 If only they **had** patience until thou
050:020 whereof warning (**had** been given).
050:028 I **had** already in advance sent you Warning.
054:014 a recompense to one who **had** been rejected (with scorn)!
059:003 And **had** it not been that Allah **had** decreed banishment
059:009 **had** homes (in Madinah) and **had** adopted the Faith,-
059:021 **Had** We sent down this Qur'an on a mountain,
060:011 they **had** spent (on their dower).
062:002 and Wisdom,-although they **had** been, before, in
064:005 their conduct; and they **had** a grievous Chastisement.
067:010 "**Had** we but listened or used our intelligence,
068:020 a dark and desplate spot, (whose fruit **had** been gathered).
068:043 seeing that they **had** been summoned aforetime
068:043 while they were whole, (and **had** refused).
068:049 **Had** not Grace from His Lord reached him, he would
069:007 in its (path), as if they **had** been roots of
069:025 "Ah! would that my record **had** not been given to me!
069:026 "And that I **had** never realized how my
069:027 "Ah! would that (Death) **had** made an end of me!
072:016 "If they (the pagans) **had** (only) remained on the
079:037 Then, for such as **had** transgressed all bounds,
079:038 And **had** preferred the life of this world,
079:040 their Lord's (tribunal) and **had** restrained (their)
079:040 And for such as **had** entertained the fear
079:046 (it will be) as if they **had** tarried but a single
083:033 But they **had** not been sent as Keepers over them!
089:024 He will say: "Ah! would that I **had** sent forth
099:006 that they (**had** done).
100:011 That their Lord **had** been well-acquainted

HADST

008:063 not if thou **hadst** spent all that is in the earth,
009:043 and thou **hadst** proved the liars?
018:018 if thou **hadst** looked at them, thou wouldst
018:077 (Moses) said: "If thou **hadst** wished, surely thou

HADST (continued)
019:009   when thou **hadst** been nothing!'"
020:134   "Our Lord! if only Thou **hadst** sent us a messenger,
028:086   And thou **hadst** not expected that the Book
033:051   whose (turn) thou **hadst** set aside.

HAIL
024:043   from the shy mountain masses (of clouds) wherein is **hail**:

HAIR
007:150   seized his brother by (the **hair** of) his head,
016:080   their soft fibres (between wool and **hair**), and their **hair**,
019:004   my bones, and the **hair** of my head doth glisten
020:094   nor by (the **hair** of) my head!
048:027   heads shaved, **hair** cut short, and without fear.

HAJJ
002:196   if any onw wishes to continue the 'umra on to the **hajj**.
002:196   And complete the **Hajj** or 'Umra in the service of Allah,
002:196   he should fast three days during the **Hajj**.
002:197   For **Hajj** are the months well known.
002:197   nor wrangling in the **Hajj**.

HALF
002:237   Or (the man's **half**) is remitted by him
002:237   and the remission (of the man's **half**)
002:237   then the **half** of the dower (is due to them),
004:011   if only one, her share is a **half**.
004:012   your share is a **half**, if they leave no child;
004:025   their punishment is **half** that for free women.
004:176   she shall have **half** the inheritance:
073:003   **Half** of it,-or a little less,
073:020   or **half** the night, or a third of the night, so do

HALLOWED
028:030   from a tree in **hallowed** ground: "O Moses! Verily I am

HAM-STRING
011:065   But they did **ham-string** her.:

HAM-STRUNG
007:077   Then they **ham-strung** the she-camel,
026:157   But they **ham-strung** her: then did

HAMAN
028:006   and to show Pharaoh, **Haman**, and their hosts, what they
028:008   for Pharaoh and **Haman** and (all) their hosts
028:038   therefore, O **Haman**! light me a (kiln to bake
029:039   (Remember also) Qarun, Pharaoh, and **Haman**:
040:024   To Pharaoh, **Haman**, and Qarun; but they
040:036   Pharaoh said: "O **Haman**! Build me a lofty palace,

HAMLET
002:259   of one who passed by a **hamlet**,

HAMSTRUNG
054:029   and he took a sword in hand, and **hamstrung** (her).
091:014   and they **hamstrung** her so their Lord,

HAND
002:249   a mere sip out of the **hand** is excused."
003:026   in Thy **hand** is all Good.
003:073   Say: "All bounties are in the **hand** of Allah:
003:144   but Allah (on the other **hand**) will swiftly
003:154   They said: "Have we any **hand** in the affair?
003:198   On the other **hand**, for those who fear their Lord,
004:033   To those also, to whom your right **hand** was pledged,
005:028   "If thou dost stretch thy **hand** against me, to slay
005:028   to stretch my **hand** against thee to slay thee:
005:064   The Jews say: "Allah's **hand** is tied up," Be
007:108   And he drew out his **hand**, and behold!
017:029   Make not thy **hand** tied (like a niggard's)
017:071   given their record in their right **hand** will read

HAND (continued)
020:017   And what is that in thy right **hand**, O Moses?"
020:022   Now draw thy **hand** close to thy side: it shall
020:064   who gains the upper **hand**."
020:068   hast indeed the upper **hand**:
020:069   "Throw that which is in thy right **hand**:
024:040   if a man stretches out his **hand**, he can
026:033   And he drew out his **hand**, and behold
027:012   "Now put thy **hand** into thy bosom, and it
028:032   "Thrust thy **hand** into thy bosom, and it
028:032   and draw thy **hand** close to thy side
029:048   nor art thou (able) to transcribe it with thy right **hand**:
033:050   thy right **hand** possesses out of the captives
033:052   right **hand** should possess (as **hand**maidens):
037:028   to come to us from the right **hand**."
037:093   striking (them) with the right **hand**.
038:033   Then began he to pass his **hand** over (their)
038:044   "And take in thy **hand** a little grass, and strike
039:067   and the heavens will be rolled up in his right **hand**:
040:029   this day: ye have the upper **hand** in the land:
041:026   that ye may gain the upper **hand**!"
042:017   the Hour is close at **hand**?
048:010   the **Hand** of Allah is over their hands:
048:024   their hands from you and your **hand** from them
054:029   and he took a sword in **hand**, and hamstrung (her).
056:008   the Companions of the Right **Hand**;-what will be
056:008   what will be the Companions of the Right **Hand**?
056:009   And the Companions of the Left **Hand**,-what will be
056:009   what will be the Companions of the Left **Hand**?
056:027   The Companions of the Right **Hand**,-what will be
056:027   what will be the Companions of the Right **Hand**!
056:038   For the Companions of the Right **Hand**.
056:041   The Companions of the Left **Hand**,-what will be
056:041   what will be the Companions of the Left **Hand**!
056:090   And if he be of the Companions of the Right **Hand**,
056:091   from the Companions of the Right **Hand**.
057:029   that (His) grace is (entirely) in His **Hand**, to bestow it on
067:027   At lenght, when they see it close at **hand**, grieved will be
069:019   that will be given his Record in his right **hand** will say:
069:025   that will be given his Record in his left **hand**, will say:
069:045   We should certainly seize him by his right **hand**
074:039   Except the Companions of the Right **Hand**.
084:007   Then he who is given his Record in his Right **hand**,
090:018   Such are the Companions of the Right **Hand**.
090:019   they are the (unhappy) Companions of the Left **Hand**.

HAND-HOLD
002:256   hath grasped the most trustworthy **hand-hold**,
031:022   has grasped indeed the firmest **hand-hold**:

HANDFUL
008:017   (a **handful**) of dust, it was not
020:096   so I took a **handful** (of dust) from the
039:067   of the earth will be but His **handful**, and the

HANDIWORK
005:090   are an abomination,-of Satan's **handiwork**:
037:096   "But Allah has created you and your **handiwork**!"

HANDMAIDENS
033:052   except any thy hand should possess (as **handmaidens**):

HANDS
002:079   Woe to them for what their **hands** do write,
002:079   the Book with their own **hands**,
002:095   their **hands** have sent on before them.
002:195   and make not your own **hands** contribute
002:237   by him in whose **hands** is the marriage tie;

HANDS (continued)

003:182 which your **hands** sent on before ye:
004:003 or that which your right **hands** possess.
004:024 except those whom your right **hands** possess:
004:025 from among those whom your right hand possess:
004:036 and what your right **hands** possess:
004:043 and rub therewith your faces and **hands**.
004:062. their **hands** have sent forth?
004:077 their **hands** (from fight) but establish regular
004:091 besides restraining their **hands**, seize them
005:006 and rub therewith your faces and **hands**.
005:006 wash your faces, and your **hands** (and arms)
005:011 but (Allah) held back their **hands** from you:
005:011 the design to stretch out their **hands** against you,
005:033 or the cutting off of **hands** and feet from opposite
005:038 cut off his or her **hands**: a retribution
005:064 Nay, both His **hands** are widely outstretched:
005:064 Be their **hands** tied up and be they
005:094 of your **hands** and your lances, that he
006:007 so that they could touch it with their **hands**,
006:093 the angels stretch forth their **hands**, (saying),
007:124 "Be sure I will cut off your **hands** and your
007:195 Or **hands** to lay hold with? Or eyes
008:035 is nothing but whislting and clapping of **hands**:
008:051 which your (own) **hands** sent forth.
008:070 who are captives in your **hands**: "If Allah
009:014 punish them by your **hands**, and disgrace
009:052 from Him, or by our **hands**.
011:070 But when he saw their **hands** not reaching
012:031 and (in their amazement) cut their **hands**: they said,
012:050 the matter with the ladies who cut their **hands**?'
013:014 their **hands** for water to reach their mouths
014:009 Clear (Signs); but they put their **hands** up to
016:071 to those whom their right **hands** possess, so as
018:042 twisting and turning his **hands** over what
018:057 forgetting the (deeds) which his **hands** have sent
020:071 Be sure I will cut off your **hands** and feet
022:010 of the deeds which thy **hands** sent forth, for verily
023:006 right **hands** possess,-for (in their case) they are
023:088 Say: "Who is it in whose **hands** is the
024:024 their **hands**, and their feet will bear witness
024:031 right **hands** possess, or male attendants free
024:058 whom your right **hands** possess, and the
025:027 will bite at his **hands**, he will say, "Oh! would
026:049 Be sure I will cut off your **hands** and your
028:019 Then, when he was about to lay his **hands** on their
028:047 that their **hands** have sent forth, they might
030:028 whom your right **hands** possess, to share
030:036 their (own) **hands** have sent forth, behold,
030:041 the **hands** of men have earned, that (Allah)
033:050 the captives whom their right **hands** possess;-
033:055 or the (slaves) whom their right **hands** possess.
036:035 it was not their **hands** that made this:
036:065 But their **hands** will speak
036:071 among the things which our **hands** have fashioned-
036:083 So glory to Him in Whose **hands** is the
038:075 whom I have created with My **hands**?
042:030 is because of the things your **hands** have wrought,
042:048 his **hands** have sent forth, truly then
048:010 the Hand of Allah is over their **hands**:
048:020 and He has restrained the **hands** of men from you;
048:024 their **hands** from you and your hand from them
048:025 you to force your way, but He held back your **hands**)

HANDS (continued)

052:041 Or that the Unseen is in their **hands**, and they
057:012 forward before them and by their right **hands**:
059:002 by their own **hands** and the **hands** of the Believers.
060:002 their **hands** and their tongues against you for evil;
062:007 because of the (deeds) their **hands** have sent
066:008 and by their right **hands**, while they say,
067:001 Blessed be He in Whose **hands** is Dominion; and He
068:047 Or that the Unseen is in their **hands**, so that
070:030 their wives and the (captives) whom their **hands** possess,-
078:040 man will see (the Deeds) which his **hands** have sent
080:015 (Written) by the **hands** of scribes-
111:001 Perish the **hands** of the Father of Flame! Perish he!

HANDSOME

002:178 and compensate him with **handsome** gratitude.
020:086 make a **handsome** promise to you?
033:028 in a **handsome** manner."
033:049 and release them in a **handsome** manner.
052:024 (devoted) to them, youths (**handsome**) as Pearls

HANDY

016:080 which ye find so light (and **handy**) when ye

HANG

012:041 as for the other, he will **hang** from the cross,
069:023 The Fruits whereof (will **hang** in bunches)
076:014 will **hang** low easy to reach.

HANGING

004:129 (as it were) **hanging** (in the air).
006:099 clusters of dates **hanging** low and near:

HANKER

003:152 Among you are some that **hanker** after this world

HANKERS

053:024 (just) anything he **hankers** after?

HAPLY

007:063 fear Allah and **haply** receive His Mercy?"
028:067 and worked righteousness, **haply** he shall be one

HAPPEN

006:080 unless my Lord willeth, (nothing can **happen**),
009:051 Say: "Nothing will **happen** to us except what
011:081 to her will **happen** what happens to the people.
017:092 as thou sayest (will **happen**), against us;
057:022 No misfortune can **happen** on earth or in your

HAPPENED

010:102 but (what **happened** in) the days of the men who
012:102 Such is one of the stories of what **happened** unseen,
018:063 He replied: "Sawest thou (what **happened**) when we
020:099 some stories of what **happened** before: for We

HAPPENS

004:079 Whatever good, (O man!) **happens** to thee, is from Allah;
004:079 but whatever evil **happens** to thee, is from thyself
011:081 to her will happen what **happens** to the people.
042:030 Whatever misfortune **happens** to you, is because
042:048 exult thereat, but when some ill **happens** to him,

HAPPINESS

002:102 the **happiness** of the Hereafter.
006:017 if He touch thee with **happiness**, He hath
052:017 they will be in Gardens, and in **Happiness**,-

HAPPY

030:015 shall be made **happy** in a Mead (of Delight).
034:015 a territory fair and **happy**, and a Lord

HARBOURED

005:052 which they secretly **harboured** in their hearts.

HARD

002:045   it is indeed **hard**,
002:049   they set you **hard** tasks and chastisement,
002:264   They are in Parable like a **hard**, barren rock,
003:142   who fought **hard** (in His Cause)
005:013   We cursed them, and made their hearts grow **hard**:
006:035   If their spurning is **hard** on thee, yet if
009:073   O Prophet! strive **hard** against the Unbelievers
010:071   "O my People, if it be **hard** on your (mind) that I
011:082   down on them brimstones **hard** as baked clay,
014:006   they set you **hard** tasks and punishments, slaughtered
015:074   on them brimstones **hard** as baked clay.
042:013   **hard** is the (way) to which thou callest them.
054:008   towards the Caller!-"**Hard** is this Day!"
057:016   long ages passed over them and their hearts grew **hard**?
066:009   O Prophet! strive **hard** against the Unbelievers
076:027   behind them a Day (that will be) **hard**.
079:022   striving **hard** (against Allah).
088:003   Laboring (**hard**), weary,-
094:007   (from thine immediate task), still labor **hard**,

HARD-HEARTED

039:022   Light from Allah, (no better than one **hard-hearted**)?

HARDENED

002:074   Thenceforth were your hearts **hardened**:
006:043   On the contrary their hearts became **hardened**,
022:053   is a disease and who are **hardened** of heart:
039:022   hearts are **hardened** against the remembrance of Allah!

HARDENS

053:034   Gives a little, then **hardens** (his heart)?

HARDER

013:034   this world, but **harder**, truly, is the Chastisement of the

HARDEST

017:051   in your minds, is **hardest** (to be raised up),-

HARDLY

024:040   if a man stretches out his hnad, he can **hardly** see it!

HARDNESS

002:074   and even worse in **hardness**.
010:088   and send **hardness** to their hearts, so they

HARDSHIP

002:184   For those who can do it (with **hardship**),

HARDSHIPS

004:104   if ye are suffering **hardships**, they are
004:104   they are suffering similar **hardships**;

HARM

002:035   or ye run into **harm** and transgression."
002:057   (but they rebelled); to Us they did no **harm**,
002:102   But they could not thus **harm** anyone except
002:282   If ye do (such **harm**), it would be
002:282   and let neither scribe nor witness suffer **harm**.
003:111   They will do you no **harm**, barring a trifling
003:120   not the least **harm** will their cunning do to you;
003:144   not the least **harm** will he do to Allah;
003:174   no **harm** ever touched them: for they followed
003:176   not the least **harm** will they do to Allah:
003:177   not the least **harm** will they do to Allah,
003:195   or suffered **harm** in My cause, and fought
004:113   and to thee they can do no **harm** in the least.
005:076   no power either to **harm** or benefit you?
006:071   things that can do us neither good nor **harm**,
006:104   it will be to his own (**harm**): I am not
007:073   and let her come to no **harm**, or ye shall
007:160   (but they rebelled): to Us they did no **harm**,

HARM (continued)

007:188   or **harm** to myself except as Allah willeth.
009:039   but Him ye would not **harm** in the least,
010:049   Say: "I have no power over any **harm** or profit
011:057   and you will not **harm** Him in the least.
011:064   (free) earth, and inflict no **harm** on her, or a
011:116   them whom We saved (from **harm**)?
013:016   or for **harm** to themselves?"
015:059   to save (from **harm**),-all-
020:022   (and shining), without **harm** (or stain),-
020:089   to **harm** them or to do them good?
020:112   and has faith, will have no fear of **harm** nor of
021:066   be of any good to you nor do you **harm**?
025:055   things that can neither profit them nor **harm** them:
026:073   "Or do you good or **harm**?"
026:156   "Touch her not with **harm**, lest the
027:012   without stain (or **harm**):
028:032   without stain (or **harm**), and draw
034:042   for profit or **harm**: and We
047:032   will not **harm** Allah in the least,
048:010   His oath, does so to the **harm** of his own soul,
049:006   lest ye **harm** people unwittingly, and afterwards
058:010   to the Believers; but he cannot **harm** them in the
072:021   Say: "It is not in my power to cause you **harm**,

HARMED

002:057   but they **harmed** their own selves.
002:102   And they learned what **harmed** them,
007:160   but they **harmed** their own souls.

HARSH

066:009   and be **harsh** with them.

HARSH-HEARTED

003:159   Wert thou severe or **harsh-hearted**, they would

HARSHEST

031:019   for the **harshest** of sounds without doubt is the

HARSHNESS

004:019   Nor should ye treat them with **harshness**,
009:123   and let them find **harshness** in you: and know
093:009   Therefore, treat not the orphan with **harshness**,

HARUT

002:102   at Babylon to the angels **Harut** and Marut.

HARVEST

002:265   but makes it yield a double increase of **harvest**,
003:117   the **harvest** of men who have wronged their own souls:
006:141   on the day that the **harvest** is gathered.
007:057   and produce every kind of **harvest** therewith:
010:024   a **harvest** clean-mown, as if it

HARVESTS

012:047   and the **harvests** that ye reap, ye shall
050:009   and Grain for **harvests**;

HAS

002:010   and Allah **has** increased their disease,
002:022   who **has** made the earth your couch,
002:027   and who sunder what Allah **has** ordered to be joined,
002:090   (the revelation) which Allah **has** sent down,
002:185   and to glorify Him in that He **has** guide you;
002:196   or **has** an ailment in his scalp,
002:198   as He **has** directed you,
002:211   after Allah's favour **has** come to him,
002:230   and he **has** divorced her.
002:230   until after she **has** married another husband
002:239   in the manner He **has** taught you,
002:246   **Has** thou not turned thy vision to the chiefs

HAS (continued)

002:246   But Allah **has** full knowledge of those
002:282   as Allah **has** taught him, so let him write.
003:007   He it is Who **has** sent down to thee the Book:
003:013   "There **has** already been for you a Sign
003:025   just what it **has** earned, without
003:029   And Allah **has** power over all things.
003:030   and all the evil it **has** done,
003:030   be confronted with all the good it **has** done,
003:084   and in what **has** been revealed to us and what
003:118   rank hatred **has** already appeared from their mouths;
003:155   But Allah **has** blotted out (their fault):
004:005   which Allah **has** assigned to you to manage,
004:011   brothers (or sisters), the mother **has** a sixth.
004:011   the mother **has** a third:
004:012   but **has** left a brother or a sister, each one
004:012   **has** left neither ascendants nor descendants,
004:034   because Allah **has** given the one more (strength)
004:115   We shall leave him in the path he **has** chosen,
004:115   even after guidance **has** been plainly conveyed
004:140   Already **has** He sent you word in the Book, that
004:148   except by one who **has** been wronged, for Allah
005:068   that **has** come to you from your Lord."
005:084   which **has** come to us, seeing that we long for
006:145   (meat) on which a name **has** been invoked, other than
007:085   after it **has** been set in order: that will
008:049   their religion **has** misled them."
008:070   than what **has** been taken from you, and He
009:016   alone while Allah **has** not yet known those
009:051   except what Allah **has** decreed for us: He is
009:061   he believes in Allah, **has** faith in the Believers,
009:124   some of them say: "Which of you **has** had his faith
010:031   Or who is it that **has** power over hearing and sight?
011:010   "All evil **has** departed from me:" behold! he
011:035   Or do they say, "He **has** forged it?"
011:040   against whom the Word **has** already gone forth,-
012:065   this our stock-in-trade **has** been returned to us:
012:078   he **has** a father, aged and venerable,
012:088   "O exalted one! distress **has** seized us
012:090   Allah **has** indeed been gracious to us (all):
012:091   They said: "By Allah! indeed **has** Allah preferred
013:002   He **has** subjected the sun and the moon! each one
013:016   created (anything) as He **has** created, so that
013:025   those things which Allah **has** commanded to be
014:009   **Has** not the story reached you, (O people!),
014:012   Indeed He **has** guided us to the Ways
014:026   it **has** no stability.
015:013   in the Message, such **has** been the way of those
015:054   glad tidings even though old age **has** seized me?
016:003   He **has** created the heavens and the earth
016:004   He **has** created man from a sperm-drop and behold
016:005   And cattle He **has** created for you (men): from them
016:008   an adornment; and He **has** created (other) things
016:008   And (He **has** created) horses, mules, and donkeys,
016:012   He **has** made subject to you the Night and the Day;
016:013   He **has** multiplied in varying colours (and qualities);
016:014   It is He Who **has** made the sea subject, that ye
016:015   And He **has** set up on the earth mountains standing
016:024   "What is it that your Lord **has** revealed?"
016:030   "What is it that your Lord **has** revealed?"
016:051   Allah **has** said: "Take not (for worship) two gods:
016:059   because of the bad news he **has** had!
016:071   Allah **has** bestowed His gifts of sustenance

HAS (continued)

016:072   And Allah **has** made for you mates of your own
016:075   the dominion of another; he **has** no power of any
016:092   after it **has** become strong.
016:092   the yarn which she **has** spun, after it
016:097   man or woman, and **has** Faith, verily, to him
016:099   No authority **has** he over those who believe
016:102   Say, the Holy Spirit **has** brought the revelation
016:108   and eyes Allah **has** sealed up and they
016:114   which Allah **has** provided for you, lawful and good;
016:115   He **has** only forbidden you dead meat, and blood,
016:115   other than Allah **has** been invoked.
016:126   to the wrong that **has** been done to you: but if
017:033   Nor take life-which Allah **has** made sacred-
017:039   which thy Lord **has** revealed to thee.
017:040   **Has** then your Lord, (O Pagans!) preferred for
017:081   And say: "Truth **has** (now) arrived, and Falsehood
017:094   "**Has** Allah sent a man (like us) to be (His)
017:099   **has** power to create the like of them (anew)?
017:099   Only He **has** decreed a term appointed,
017:105   and in Truth **has** it descended: and We sent
017:108   Truly **has** the promise of our Lord been fulfilled!"
017:111   no son, and **has** no partner in (His) dominion:
018:027   And recite (and teach) what **has** been revealed
018:028   and his affair **has** become all excess.
018:055   from believing, now that guidance **has** come to them,
018:095   my Lord **has** established me is better (than tribute):
018:110   (but) the inspiration **has** come to me, that your
019:020   seeing that no man **has** touched me, and I am
019:061   (Allah) Most Gracious **has** promised to His
019:078   or **has** he taken a promise with the Most Gracious?
019:078   **Has** he penetrated to the Unseen,
019:087   one as **has** received permission (or promise) from
019:088   They say: "The Most Gracious **has** begotten a son!"
020:009   **Has** the story of Moses reached thee?
020:043   for he **has** indeed transgressed all bounds;
020:048   'Verily it **has** been revealed to us that the
020:053   "He Who **has** made for you the earth
020:053   **has** enabled you to go about therein by roads
020:053   and **has** sent down water from the sky."
020:071   Who **has** taught you magic!
020:072   to what **has** come to us of the Clear Signs
020:085   in thy absence: the Samiri **has** led them astray."
020:088   god of Moses, but (Moses) **has** forgotten!"
020:109   whom permission **has** been granted by The Most Gracious
020:112   But he who works deeds of righteousness, and **has** faith,
020:133   **Has** not a Clear Sign come to them of all
020:135   and who it is that **has** received guidance."
021:026   And they say: "The Most Gracious **has** taken a son."
021:059   They said, "Who **has** done this to our gods?
021:083   to his Lord "Truly distress **has** seized me,
021:094   and **has** Faith,-his endeavour will not be rejected:
021:101   from Us **has** gone before, will be
021:108   Say: "What **has** come to me by inspiration
022:006   and it is He Who **has** power over all things.
022:028   over the cattle which He **has** provided for
022:037   He **has** thus made them subject to you, that ye
022:054   And that those on whom knowledge **has** been bestowed
022:060   That (is so)..And if one **has** retaliated to no greater extent
022:065   Seest thou not that Allah **has** made subject
022:071   things for which no authority **has** been sent down to them,
022:072   Allah **has** promised it to the Unbelievers!
022:078   It is He Who **has** named you Muslims, both before

HAS (continued)

022:078   He **has** chosen you, and **has** imposed no difficulties on
023:027   of them against whom the Word **has** already gone forth:
023:028   Who **has** saved us from the people who do wrong."
023:068   or **has** anything (new) come to them
023:070   Nay, he **has** brought them the Truth, but most
023:078   It is He Who **has** created for you (the faculties of) hearing,
023:079   And He **has** multiplied you through the earth,
023:117   he **has** no authority thereof; and his
024:029   and Allah **has** knowledge of what ye
024:033   out of the means which Allah **has** given to you.
024:045   And Allah **has** created every animal from water:
024:045   for verily Allah **has** power over all things.
024:055   He **has** chosen for them; and that
024:055   Allah **has** promised, to those among you who believe
025:002   no son **has** He begotten, nor **has** He a partner in His
025:004   "Naught is this but a lie which he **has** forged,
025:005   which he **has** caused to be written:
025:007   Why **has** not an angel been sent down to him
025:008   "Or (why) **has** not a treasure been bestowed
025:008   or why **has** he (not) a garden for enjoyment?"
025:041   "Is this the one whom Allah **has** sent as a messenger?"
025:053   yet **has** He made a barrier between them,
025:053   It is He Who **has** let free the two bodies
025:054   for thy Lord **has** power (over all things).
025:054   It is He Who **has** created man from water:
025:054   then **has** He established relationships of lineage
025:068   nor slay such life as Allah **has** made sacred, except for
025:071   whoever repents and does good **has** truly turned to Allah
026:021   I feared you; but my Lord **has** (since) invested me
026:027   who **has** been sent to you is a veritable madman!"
026:049   who **has** taught you sorcery!
026:132   "Yea, fear Him Who **has** bestowed on you
026:133   "Freely **has** He bestowed on you cattle and sons,-
026:155   she **has** a right of watering, and ye
026:166   "And leave those whom Allah **has** created for you to be
027:015   Who **has** favoured us above many of His servants
027:023   every requisite; and she **has** a magnificent throne.
027:024   Satan **has** made their deeds seem pleasing
027:024   and **has** kept them away from the Path,-so they
027:036   But that which Allah **has** given me is better than that
027:036   that which He **has** given you!
027:059   He **has** chosen (for his Message).
027:060   Or, who **has** created the heaven and the earth,
027:061   Or, who **has** made the earth firm to live in;
027:069   what **has** been the end of those guilty (of sin)."
027:091   Him Who **has** sanctified it and to Whom
028:048   But (now), when the Truth **has** come to them
028:073   His Mercy that He **has** made for you Night and Day,-
028:077   which Allah **has** bestowed on thee, the Home
028:077   but do thou good, as Allah **has** been good to thee,
028:078   He said: "This **has** been given to me because of
028:079   of what Qarun **has** got!
029:020   for Allah **has** power over all things.
029:046   which **has** come down to us and in that
029:061   who **has** created the heavens and the earth
029:062   for Allah **has** full knowledge of all things.
030:021   and He **has** put love and mercy between your (hearts):
030:030   the nature in which Allah **has** made mankind:
030:040   It is Allah Who **has** created you:
030:040   further, He **has** provided for your sustenance;
030:041   Mischief **has** appeared on land and sea
030:048   then when He **has** made them reach such of His servants

HAS (continued)

030:050   for He **has** power over all things.
030:054   and it is He Who **has** all knowledge and power.
031:020   Do ye not see that Allah **has** subjected to your
031:020   and on earth, and **has** made His bounties flow to
031:021   the (revelation) that Allah **has** sent down,
031:022   a doer of good, **has** grasped indeed the firmest hand-hold:
031:029   that He **has** subjected the sun and the moon
031:032   But when He **has** delivered them safely to land,
032:003   Or do they say, "He **has** forged it"? Nay, it
032:003   to whom no warner **has** come before thee: in order
032:004   It is Allah Who **has** created the heavens and the
033:004   nor **has** He made your wives whom ye divorce
033:004   Allah **has** not made for any man two hearts
033:004   nor **has** He made your adopted sons your sons.
033:008   and He **has** prepared for the Unbelievers a grievous
033:019   and so Allah **has** made their deeds of none effect:
033:027   And Allah **has** power over all things.
033:029   verily Allah **has** prepared for the well-doers amongst you
033:035   for them **has** Allah prepared forgiveness and
033:036   man or woman, when a matter **has** been decided
033:038   in what Allah **has** indicated to him as a duty.
033:040   and Allah **has** full knowledge of all things.
033:044   and He **has** prepared for them a generous Reward.
033:050   the captives of war whom Allah **has** assigned to thee;
033:054   verily Allah **has** full knowledge of all things.
033:057   and **has** prepared for them a humiliating Punishment.
033:057   and his Messenger-Allah **has** cursed them in this
033:064   Verily Allah **has** cursed the Unbelievers
033:071   and His Messenger, **has** already attained the great victory.
033:073   (With the result) that Allah **has** to punish the Hypocrites,
034:006   And those to whom knowledge **has** come see that
034:008   "**Has** he invented a falsehood against Allah, or is
034:023   except for those for whom He **has** granted permission.
034:048   He that **has** full knowledge of (all) that is hidden."
034:049   Say: "The Truth **has** arrived, and Falsehood
035:001   for Allah **has** power over all things.
035:013   and He **has** subjected the sun and the moon
035:034   Who **has** removed from us (all) sorrow: for our
035:035   "Who **has**, out of His bounty, settled us
035:038   He **has** full knowledge of all that is in (men's) hearts.
035:039   He it is that **has** made you inheritors
035:042   to them, it **has** only increased their aversion.
035:045   Term expires, verily Allah **has** in His sight
036:027   "For that my Lord **has** granted me Forgiveness
036:027   me Forgiveness and **has** enrolled me among
036:047   which Allah **has** provided you," the Unbelievers
037:031   "So now **has** been proved true, against us,
037:037   Nay! he **has** come with the (very) Truth,
037:096   "But Allah **has** created you and your handiwork!"
037:149   is it that thy Lord **has** (only) daughters,
037:152   "Allah **has** begotten children"?
037:164   but **has** a place appointed;
037:170   But (now that the Qur'an **has** come), they reject
037:171   Already **has** Our Word been passed before (this)
038:004   So they wonder that a Warner **has** come to them
038:005   "**Has** he made the gods (all) into one God?
038:008   "What! **Has** the Message been sent to him-
038:021   **Has** the Story of the Disputants reached thee?
038:022   two disputants, one of whom **has** wronged the other:
038:023   he **has** nine and ninety ewes, and I
038:024   (David) said: "He **has** undoubtedly wronged thee
038:041   "Satan **has** afflicted me with distress and suffering"!

HAS (continued)

038:070   "Only this **has** been revealed to me: that I
039:005   He **has** subjected the sun and the moon (to His law):
039:018   those are the ones who Allah **has** guided, and those are
039:022   Is one whose heart Allah **has** opened to Islam,
039:022   so that he **has** received light from Allah,
039:023   Allah **has** revealed (from time to time) the most
039:024   Is, then, one who **has** to ward off the brunt
039:042   those on whom He **has** passed the decree of death,
039:049   he says, "This **has** been given to me because of
039:065   But it **has** already been revealed to thee,-as it
039:071   Decree of Chastisement **has** been proved true against
039:074   to us, and **has** given us (this) land in heritage:
039:074   Who **has** truly fulfilled His promise to us,
040:028   when he **has** indeed come to you with Clear (Signs)
040:043   one who **has** no claim to be called to, whether in
040:048   Truly, Allah **has** judged between (His) Servants!"
040:061   It is Allah Who **has** made the Night for you,
040:064   and **has** provided for you Sustenance, of things
040:064   and **has** given you shape-and made
040:064   It is Allah Who **has** made for you the earth
040:067   It is He Who **has** created you from dust, then from
040:085   (Such **has** been) Allah's way of dealing with His
041:039   For He **has** power over all things.
041:043   surely thy Lord **has** at His command (all) Forgiveness
041:050   after some adversity **has** touched him, he is sure to say,
042:009   it is He Who **has** power over all things.
042:011   He **has** made for you pairs from among yourselves,
042:013   The same religion **has** He established for you
042:015   "I believe in the Book which Allah **has** sent down;
042:016   after He **has** been accepted,-futile is
042:017   It is Allah Who **has** sent down the Book in truth,
042:020   but he **has** no share or lot in the Hereafter.
042:024   "He **has** forged a falsehood against Allah"?
042:029   and He **has** power to gather them together
042:029   the living creatures that **He has** scattered through them:
043:008   and (thus) **has** passed on the example of the peoples
043:010   (Yea, the same that) **has** made for you the earth
043:010   and **has** made for you roads (and channels)
043:012   and **has** made for you ships and cattle
043:012   That **has** created pairs in all things,
043:013   Who **has** subjected these to Our (use), for we
043:016   What! **Has** He taken Daughters out of what He
043:029   until the Truth **has** come to them, and a Messenger
043:088   (Allah **has** knowledge) of the (Prophet's) cry,
044:013   things clearly **has** (already) come to them,-
045:012   It is Allah Who **has** subjected the sea to you,
045:013   And He **has** subjected to you, as from
045:022   it **has** earned, and none of them shall be wronged.
045:023   after Allah (**has** withdrawn Guidance)?
045:023   Allah **has**, knowing (him as such), left him
046:008   Or do they say, "He **has** forged it"? Say:
046:010   (with earlier scriptures), and **has** believed while
046:033   Yea, verily He **has** power over all things.
047:006   He **has** made known for them.
047:009   so He **has** made their deeds fruitless.
047:013   which **has** driven thee out, have We
047:016   Allah **has** sealed, and who follow their own lusts.
047:023   whom Allah **has** cursed for He **has** made them deaf and
047:025   Satan **has** instigated them and buoyed
047:026   who hate what Allah **has** revealed, "We will
047:032   after Guidance **has** been clearly shown to them,
048:006   He **has** cursed them and got Hell ready for them:

HAS (continued)

048:010   what he **has** covenanted with Allah,-Allah will
048:011   Say: "Who then **has** any power at all (to intervene)
048:015   Allah **has** already declared (this) beforehand":
048:020   and He **has** restrained the hands of men from you;
048:020   Allah **has** promised you many gains that ye
048:020   and He **has** given you these beforehand; and He
048:021   but which Allah **has** compassed:
048:021   and Allah **has** power over all things.
048:023   (Such **has** been) the practice of Allah already in
048:024   And it is He who **has** restrained their hands
048:026   And Allah **has** full knowledge of all things.
048:028   It is He who **has** sent His Messenger
048:029   Allah **has** promised those among them who believe
049:003   their hearts **has** Allah tested of piety: for them
049:007   but Allah **has** endeared the Faith to you,
049:007   and He **has** made hateful to you unbelief,
049:007   and **has** made it beautiful in your hearts,
049:011   (to be used of one) after he **has** believed:
049:013   And Allah **has** full knowledge and is well
049:014   for not yet **has** Faith entered your hearts.
049:016   He **has** full knowledge of all things.
049:017   Nay, Allah **has** conferred a favour upon you
049:017   that He **has** guided you to the Faith,
050:002   But they wonder that there **has** come to them
050:037   that **has** a heart and understanding or who
051:024   **Has** the story reached thee, of the honoured
051:030   They said, "Even so **has** thy Lord spoken:
052:027   "But Allah **has** been good to us, and **has** delivered us
052:039   Or **has** He only daughters and ye have sons?
053:023   Even though there **has** already come to them
053:023   for which Allah **has** sent down no authority
053:026   avail nothing except after Allah **has** given leave for whom
053:035   What! **Has** he knowledge of the Unseen so that
054:003   but every matter **has** its appointed time.
055:002   It is He Who **has** taught the Qur'an.
055:003   He **has** created man:
055:004   He **has** taught him an intelligent speech.
055:007   and He **has** set up the balance (of Justice),
055:007   And the Firmament **has** He raised high,
055:010   It is He Who **has** spread out the earth
055:019   He **has** let free the two Seas meeting together:
055:056   whom no man or Jinn before them **has** touched;-
055:074   Whom no man or Jinn before them **has** touched;-
057:002   and He **has** Power over all things.
057:003   and He **has** full knowledge of all things.
057:006   and He **has** full knowledge of the secrets
057:007   of the (substance) whereof He **has** made you heirs.
057:008   you to believe in your Lord and **has** indeed taken
057:010   **has** Allah promised a goodly (reward).
057:016   **Has** not the time arrived for the Believers
057:016   the Truth which **has** been revealed (to them),
058:001   Allah **has** indeed heard (and accepted)
058:004   And if any **has** not (the means), he should
058:006   Allah **has** reckoned and which they forgot, For Allah
058:007   For Allah **has** full knowledge of all things.
058:015   Allah **has** prepared for them a severe Chastisement:
058:019   Satan **has** got the better of them:
058:019   so he **has** made them forgot the remembrance
058:021   Allah **has** decreed: "It is I and My messengers who must
058:022   For such He **has** written Faith in their hearts,
059:006   and Allah **has** power over all things.
059:006   What Allah **has** bestowed on His Messenger

HAS (continued)

059:007   What Allah **has** bestowed on His Messenger
059:018   he **has** sent forth for the morrow.
060:001   they have rejected the Truth that **has** come to you,
060:001   of you that does this **has** strayed from the Straight Path.
060:004   and there **has** arisen between us and you,
060:007   For Allah **has** power (over all things); and Allah
061:009   It is He Who **has** sent His Messenger with Guidance
062:002   It is He Who **has** sent amongst the Unlettered
062:011   Say: "That which Allah **has** is better than any
063:011   grant respite when the time appointed (for it) **has** come;
064:001   and He **has** power over all things.
064:002   It is He Who **has** created you; and of you
064:003   He **has** created the heavens and the earth
064:003   and **has** given you shape, and made
064:005   **Has** not the story reached you, of those
065:003   for all things **has** Allah appointed a due proportion.
065:005   which He **has** sent down to you: and if
065:007   let him spend according to what Allah **has** given him.
065:007   burden on any person beyond what He **has** given him.
065:010   Allah **has** prepared for them a severe Punishment
065:011   Allah **has** indeed granted for them a most
065:012   Allah **has** power over all things, and that
066:001   forbidden that which Allah **has** made lawful to thee,
066:002   Allah **has** already ordained for you, the expiation
067:013   or make it known, He certainly **has** (full) knowledge,
067:015   It is He Who **has** made the earth manageable for you,
067:023   Say: "It is He Who **has** created you, and made
067:024   Say: "It is He Who **has** multiplied you through
069:028   "Of no profit to me **has** been my wealth!
069:029   "My power **has** perished from me!"...
071:014   "Seeing that it is He that **has** created you
071:015   "See ye not how Allah **has** created the seven
071:017   "And Allah **has** produced you from the earth,
071:019   "And Allah **has** made the earth for you as a carpet
072:001   Say: It **has** been revealed to me that a company
072:003   He **has** taken neither a wife nor a son.
072:013   and any who believes in his Lord **has** no fear,
072:027   "Except an apostle whom He **has** chosen: and then
074:016   he **has** been refractory!
075:040   **Has** not He, (the same), the power
076:001   **Has** there not been over Man a long period of Time,
076:031   but the wrong-doers,-for them **has** He prepared
079:015   **Has** the story of Moses reached thee?
079:017   for he **has** indeed transgressed all bounds:
081:014   (Then) shall each soul know what it **has** put forward.
082:006   O man! what **has** seduced thee from thy Lord
084:023   But Allah **has** full Knowledge of what they
085:017   **Has** the story reached thee, of the Forces-
086:004   There is no soul but **has** a protector over it.
088:001   **Has** the story reached thee, of the
099:007   Then shall anyone who **has** done an atom's weight
099:008   And anyone who **has** done an atom's weight
105:005   and straw (of which the corn) **has** been eaten up.

HAST

001:007   way of those on whom Thou **hast** bestowed Thy Grace,
002:032   save what Thou **hast** taught Us:
002:071   They said: "Now **hast** thou brought the truth."
002:258   **Hast** thou not turned thy thought to one
002:259   "Nay, thou **hast** tarried thus a hundred years:
003:008   deviate now after Thou **hast** guided us,
003:023   **Hast** thou not turned thy thought to those who
003:026   Verily, over all things Thou **hast** power.

HAST (continued)

003:053   "Our Lord! we believe in what thou **hast** revealed,
003:159   Then, when thou **hast** taken a decision,
003:191   not for naught **hast** Thou created (all) this!
004:044   **Hast** thou not turned thy thought to those who
004:049   **Hast** thou not turned thy thought to those
004:051   **Hast** thou not turned thy thought to those who
004:060   **Hast** thou not turned thy thought to those who
004:077   why **hast** Thou ordered us to fight?
004:077   **Hast** thou not turned thy thought to those who
005:041   thou **hast** no authority in the least for him
005:113   and to know that thou **hast** indeed told us
006:034   Already **hast** thou received some account
006:105   may say, "Thou **hast** learnt this (from somebody),
006:159   thou **hast** no part in them in the least:
007:016   He said: "Because Thou **hast** thrown me
007:106   thou **hast** come with a Sign, show it
007:203   they say: "Why **hast** thou not got it together?"
010:078   They said: "**Hast** thou come to us to turn us
010:088   Moses prayed: "Our Lord! Thou **hast** indeed bestowed
011:032   with us, and (much) **hast** thou prolonged the
011:032   They said: "O Noah! thou **hast** disputed with us,
011:046   So ask not of Me that of which thou **hast** no knowledge!
011:053   They said: " Hud! no Clear (Sign) **hast** thou brought us,
011:062   They said: "O Salih! thou **hast** been of us!-
011:091   In fact among us we see that thou **hast** no strength!
011:091   For thou **hast** among us no great position!"
012:029   for truly thou **hast** been at fault!
012:101   "O my Lord! Thou **hast** indeed bestowed on me
014:028   **Hast** thou not turned thy thought to those
015:007   if it be that thou **hast** the Truth?"
015:039   because Thou **hast** put me in the wrong, I will
017:028   And even if thou **hast** to turn away from them
017:036   thou **hast** no knowledge; for surely the hearing,
017:062   one whom thou **hast** honoured above me!
018:066   which thou **hast** been taught?"
018:071   "**Hast** thou scuttled it in order to drown
018:071   Truly a strange thing **hast** thou done!"
018:074   "**Hast** thou slain an innocent person who had
018:074   Truly a foul (unheard-of) thing **hast** thou done!"
018:086   (thou **hast** authority), either to punish them,
019:027   "O Mary! truly a strange thing **hast** thou brought!
019:077   **Hast** thou then seen the (sort of) man who
020:057   He said: "**Hast** thou come to drive us out
020:068   We said: "Fear not! for thou **hast** indeed the upper hand:
020:094   'Thou **hast** caused a division among the
020:097   (for a future penalty) thou **hast** a promise that
020:097   now look at thy god, of whom thou **hast** become a
020:125   why **hast** thou raised me up blind, while I
023:028   And when thou **hast** embarked on the Ark-
025:045   **Hast** thou not seen how thy Lord?-doth prolong
026:022   that you **hast** enslaved the Children of Israel!"
027:019   for Thy favours, which Thou **has** bestowed on me
027:022   "I have compassed which thou **hast** not compassed,
027:027   whether thou **hast** told the truth or lied!
028:007   but when thou **hast** fears about him, cast him
028:017   Thou **hast** bestowed Thy Grace on me, never shall
028:025   (well) **hast** thou escaped from unjust people."
029:008   anything of which thou **hast** no knowledge,
031:015   of which thou **hast** no knowledge, obey them not;
033:050   to thee thy wives to whom thou **hast** paid their
033:051   thou **hast** to give them: and Allah
037:105   "Thou **hast** already fulfilled the dream!"-

HAST (continued)

040:008 which Thou **hast** promised to them, and to
040:011 made us to die, and twice **hast** Thou given us Life!
040:011 They will say:" Our Lord! twice **hast** Thou made us
046:015 Thy favour which Thou **hast** bestowed upon me,
046:022 They said: "**Hast** thou come in order to turn
059:011 **Hast** thou not observed the Hypocrites say to
066:008 us Forgiveness: for Thou **hast** power over all things."
068:004 And surely thou **hast** sublime morals.
070:043 from their sepulchers in sudden **hast** as if they

HASTE

003:125 rush here on you in hot **haste**,
004:006 nor in **haste** against their growing up.
007:150 did ye make **haste** to bring on the
017:011 as he prays for good for man is given to **haste**.
019:084 So make no **haste** against them, for We
020:114 Be not in **haste** with the Qur'an
021:037 Man is a creature of **haste**: soon (enough)
046:035 and be in no **haste** about the (Unbelievers).
075:016 the (Qur'an) to make **haste** therewith.
090:011 But he hath made not **haste** on the

HASTEN

003:114 and they (**hasten** in emulation) in (all)
010:011 as they would fain **hasten** on the good,-then would
010:011 If Allah were to **hasten** for men the ill
010:050 would the Sinners wish to **hasten**?
010:051 and ye wanted (aforetime) to **hasten** it on!"
013:006 They ask thee to **hasten** on the evil
015:024 who **hasten** forward, and those who lag behind.
016:001 seek ye not then to **hasten** it: glory to Him,
020:045 "Our Lord! we fear lest He **hasten** with insolence
020:083 "What made thee **hasten** in advance of thy people,
021:037 so ask Me not to **hasten** them!
022:047 Yet they ask thee to **hasten** on the Punishment!
023:043 No people can **hasten** their term, nor can
023:056 We would **hasten** them on in every good? Nay, they
023:061 It is these who **hasten** in every good work,
027:046 to **hasten** on the evil before the good?
027:072 the events which ye wish to **hasten** on
029:053 They ask thee to **hasten** on the Punishment
029:054 They ask thee to **hasten** on the Punishment:
038:016 They say: "Our Lord! **Hasten** to us our sentence
042:018 Only those wish to **hasten** it who believe
051:059 then let them not ask Me to **hasten** (that portion)!
062:009 (the Day of Assembly), **hasten** earnestly to the

HASTENED

006:057 What ye would see **hastened** is not in my power.
006:058 "If what ye would see **hastened** were in my power,
011:069 "Peace!" and **hastened** to entertain them with
016:062 to be **hastened** on into it!
018:058 have **hastened** their Punishment: but they
020:084 on my footsteps: I **hastened** to Thee, O my Lord
026:204 to be **hastened** on?
046:024 ye were asking to be **hastened**!-a wind
051:014 this is what ye used to ask to be **hastened**!"

HASTENING

054:008 **Hastening**, with eyes transfixed, towards the

HASTENS

002:203 but if anyone **hastens** to leave in two days,

HATCHED

052:030 for him some calamity (**hatched**) by Time!"

HATE

010:082 however much the Sinners may **hate** it!"
016:062 they **hate** (for themselves), and their
023:070 but most of them **hate** the Truth.
047:009 That is because they **hate** the Revelation of Allah;
047:026 who **hate** what Allah has revealed, "We will

HATED

009:081 they **hated** to strive and fight, with their
047:028 and they **hated** Allah's good pleasure; so He

HATEFUL

017:038 is **hateful** in the sight of thy Lord.
040:035 very **hateful** (is such conduct) in the sight of Allah
049:007 and He has made **hateful** to you unbelief,
061:003 Grievously **hateful** is it in the sight of Allah

HATETH

108:003 For he who **hateth** thee,-he will

HATH

002:007 Allah **hath** set a seal on their hearts
002:020 for Allah **hath** power over all things.
002:029 and of all things He **hath** perfect knowledge.
002:029 It is He who **hath** created for you
002:076 what Allah **hath** revealed to you,
002:091 "Believe in what Allah **hath** sent down,"
002:106 Allah **hath** power over all things?
002:108 **hath** strayed without doubt from the even way.
002:109 after the truth **hath** become manifest
002:109 for Allah **hath** power over all things.
002:116 They say: "Allah **hath** begotten a son";
002:120 the knowledge which **hath** reached thee,
002:132 "O my sons! Allah **hath** chosen the Faith for you;
002:134 That was a People that **hath** passed away.
002:141 That was a people that **hath** passed away.
002:142 "What **hath** turned them from the Qiblah
002:145 If thou after the knowledge **hath** reached thee,
002:148 For Allah **hath** power over all things.
002:170 "Follow what Allah **hath** revealed,"
002:173 He **hath** only forbidden you dead meat, and blood,
002:173 any other name **hath** been invoked besides that Allah,
002:187 and seek what Allah **hath** ordained for you,
002:228 to hide what Allah **hath** created in their wombs,
002:247 "Allah **hath** appointed Talut as king over you."
002:247 and **hath** gifted him abundantly with knowledge
002:247 He said: "Allah **hath** chosen him above you.
002:249 by Allah's will, **hath** a small force vanquished a big one?
002:256 in Allah **hath** grasped the most trustworthy hand-hold,
002:259 Allah **hath** power over all things."
002:261 and each ear **hath** a hundred grains.
002:275 but Allah **hath** permitted trade
002:275 the Satan by his touch **hath** driven to madness.
002:284 For Allah **hath** power over all things.
002:285 in what **hath** been revealed to him from his Lord,
003:042 "O Mary! Allah **hath** chosen thee and purified thee
003:047 how shall I have a son when no man **hath** touched Me?"
003:047 when He **hath** decreed a matter,
003:061 now after (full) knowledge **hath** come to thee,
003:063 Allah **hath** full knowledge of those who do mischief.
003:117 it is not Allah that **hath** wronged them,
003:140 If a wound **hath** touched you, be sure a similar
003:140 be sure a similar wound **hath** touched the others.
003:165 for Allah **hath** power over all things."
003:167 But Allah **hath** full knowledge of all they conceal.
003:180 Allah **hath** given them of His Grace,
003:181 Allah **hath** heard the taunt of those who say:

HATH (continued)

003:189   and Allah **hath** power over all things.
003:195   And their Lord **hath** accepted of them,
004:024   Thus **hath** Allah ordained (prohibitions) against you:
004:025   and Allah **hath** full knowledge about your faith.
004:029   for verily Allah **hath** been to you Most Merciful.
004:032   in which Allah **hath** bestowed His gifts more
004:032   for Allah **hath** full knowledge of all things.
004:035   for Allah **hath** full knowledge, and is
004:037   hide the bounties which Allah **hath** bestowed on them;
004:039   For Allah **hath** full knowledge of them.
004:039   what Allah **hath** given them for sustenance?
004:045   But Allah **hath** full knowledge of your enemies:
004:046   but Allah **hath** cursed them, for their Unbelief;
004:052   and those whom Allah **hath** cursed, thou wilt find,
004:052   They are (men) whom Allah **hath** cursed:
004:054   for what Allah **hath** given them of His bounty?
004:061   "Come to what Allah **hath** revealed.
004:078   But what **hath** come to these people.
004:085   and Allah **hath** power over all things.
004:088   whom Allah **hath** thrown out of the Way?
004:088   For those whom Allah **hath** thrown out of the Way,
004:088   Allah **hath** cast them for their (evil) deeds.
004:090   then Allah **hath** opened no way
004:092   for Allah **hath** all knowledge and all wisdom.
004:095   Allah **hath** granted a grade higher to those who strive
004:095   all (in Faith) **hath** He distinguished above those who sit
004:095   Unto all (in Faith) **hath** Allah promised good:
004:102   which **hath** not yet prayed and let them
004:102   Allah **hath** prepared a humiliating punishment.
004:113   For Allah **hath** sent down to thee the Book
004:116   joins other gods with Allah, **hath** strayed far, far away
004:119   a friend, **hath** of a surety suffered a loss that is manifest.
004:127   and (remember) what **hath** been rehearsed unto you
004:133   for He **hath** power this to do.
004:136   He **hath** sent to His Messenger and the scripture
004:136   and the Day of Judgment, **hath** gone far, far astray.
004:155   nay, Allah **hath** set the seal on their hearts
004:162   believe in what **hath** been revealed to thee and
004:166   He **hath** sent unto thee He **hath** sent from His (Own)
004:170   O mankind! the Messengers **hath** come to you
004:174   O mankind! verily there **hath** come to you
004:176   And Allah **hath** knowledge of all things.
005:003   that which **hath** been killed by strangling, or by
005:003   which **hath** been invoked the name of other than Allah;
005:003   that which **hath** been (partly) eaten
005:009   deeds of righteousness **hath** Allah promised
005:012   resisteth faith, he **hath** truly wandered from
005:015   There **hath** come to you from Allah a (new)
005:015   there **hath** come to you Our Messenger, revealing
005:017   Say: "Who then **hath** the least power against Allah,
005:017   For Allah **hath** power over all things."
005:018   of the men He **hath** created: He forgiveth
005:019   now **hath** come unto you, making (things) clear
005:019   but now **hath** come unto you a bringer
005:019   and Allah **hath** power over all things.
005:021   which Allah **hath** assigned unto you, and turn
005:040   and Allah **hath** power over all things.
005:044   by what Allah **hath** revealed, they are Unbelievers.
005:045   by what Allah **hath** revealed, they are wrong-doers.
005:047   judge by what Allah **hath** revealed therein.
005:047   If any do fail to judge by what Allah **hath** revealed,
005:048   so judge between them by what Allah **hath** revealed,

005:048   diverging from the truth that **hath** come to thee.
005:048   in what He **hath** given you: so strive
005:049   between them by what Allah **hath** revealed,
005:049   (teaching) which Allah **hath** sent down to thee.
005:059   and the revelation that **hath** come to us
005:067   which **hath** been sent to thee from thy Lord.
005:076   something which **hath** no power either
005:081   in the Prophet, and in what **hath** been revealed to him,
005:085   this their prayer **hath** Allah rewarded them with Gardens,
005:087   the good things which Allah **hath** made lawful
005:088   which Allah **hath** provided for you, lawful
005:097   that ye may know that Allah **hath** knowledge of what
005:104   "Come to what Allah **hath** revealed; come to
005:120   and it is He who **hath** power over all things.
006:012   Say: "To Allah. He **hath** inscribed for Himself
006:017   He **hath** power over all things.
006:019   this Qur'an **hath** been revealed to me
006:037   Say: "Allah **hath** certainly power to send
006:053   Allah **hath** favoured from amongst us?"
006:054   "Peace be on you: your Lord **hath** inscribed for
006:060   and **hath** knowledge of all that
006:065   Say: "He **hath** power to send calamities
006:080   about Allah, when He (Himself) **hath** guided me?
006:081   Which of (us) two parties **hath** more right to security?
006:093   reveal the like of what Allah **hath** revealed?"
006:093   when he **hath** received none, or (again)
006:098   It is He who **hath** produced you
006:101   and He **hath** full knowledge of all things.
006:101   when He **hath** no consort?
006:102   and He **hath** power to dispose
006:114   Who **hath** sent unto you the Book, explained
006:114   that it **hath** been sent down from thy
006:118   on which Allah's name **hath** been pronounced,
006:119   when He **hath** explained to you in detail
006:119   on which Allah's name **hath** been pronounced,
006:121   Allah's name **hath** not been pronounced:
006:134   All that **hath** been promised unto you
006:136   Out of what Allah **hath** produced in abundance
006:140   and forbid food which Allah **hath** provided for them,
006:142   eat what Allah **hath** provided for you,
006:143   say, **hath** He forbidden the two males, or the
006:144   say, **hath** He forbidden the two males, or the
006:151   Allah **hath** (really) prohibited you from":
006:151   which Allah **hath** made sacred, except by
006:157   Now then **hath** come unto you a Clear (Sign)
006:161   Say: "Verily, my Lord **hath** guided me
006:163   No partner **hath** He: this am I commanded, and
006:165   It is He Who **hath** made you the inheritors
006:165   He **hath** raised you in ranks, some above
006:165   in the gifts He **hath** given you: for thy
007:029   Say: "My Lord **hath** commanded justice; and that
007:030   Some He **hath** guided: others have
007:032   Say: Who **hath** forbidden the beautiful
007:032   (which He **hath** provided) for sustenance?
007:032   which He **hath** produced for His servants,
007:033   my Lord **hath** indeed forbidden are: indecent
007:033   for which He **hath** given no authority; and saying
007:043   Who **hath** guided us to this (felicity): never
007:050   "Both these things **hath** Allah forbidden to those who
007:056   after it **hath** been set in order, but call
007:063   "Do ye wonder that there **hath** come to you
007:069   "Do ye wonder that there **hath** come to you a message

HATH (continued)

007:073   Now **hath** come unto you a clear
007:075   in the revelation which **hath** been sent
007:085   Now **hath** come unto you a clear
007:089   after Allah **hath** rescued us therefrom;
007:140   when it is He who **hath** endowed you with
007:185   and all that Allah **hath** created?
008:019   now **hath** the judgment come to you: if you
008:041   For Allah **hath** power over all things.
008:053   the Grace which He **hath** bestowed on a people
008:062   He it is that **hath** strengthened thee with His
008:063   And (moreover) He **hath** put affection
008:063   but Allah **hath** done it: for He
008:066   For the present, Allah **hath** lightened your
008:067   until he **hath** thoroughly subdued the land.
008:071   and so **hath** He given (thee) power over them.
008:071   Allah is He who **hath** (full) knowledge and wisdom.
009:029   forbidden which **hath** been forbidden by Allah
009:033   It is He who **hath** sent His Messenger
009:039   for Allah **hath** power over all things.
009:067   so He **hath** forgotten them.
009:068   Allah **hath** promised the Hypocrites, men and women,
009:070   **Hath** not the story reached them of those
009:072   Allah **hath** promised to Believers, men and women,
009:077   So He **hath** put as a consequence hypocrisy into
009:089   Allah **hath** prepared for them Gardens under which
009:093   Allah **hath** sealed their hearts: so they
009:094   Allah **hath** already informed us of the true state
009:097   of the command which Allah **hath** sent down
009:100   for them **hath** He prepared Gardens under which rivers
009:111   Allah **hath** purchased of the Believers their persons
009:115   should avoid, for Allah **hath** knowledge of all things.
009:115   after He **hath** Guided them until He makes clear
009:127   Allah **hath** turned their hearts (form the light);
009:128   Now **hath** come unto you a Messenger
010:003   except after His leave (**hath** been obtained).
010:006   and in all that Allah **hath** created, in the
010:021   of some mercy after adversity **hath** touched them,
010:039   the interpretation thereof **hath** reached them:
010:054   Every soul that **hath** sinned, if it
010:057   O mankind! there **hath** come to you
010:059   Say: "**Hath** Allah indeed permitted you, or do
010:059   Say: "See ye what things Allah **hath** sent down
010:067   He it is that **hath** made for you the Night
010:068   They say, "Allah **hath** begotten a son!"-Glory be
010:077   when it **hath** (actually) reached you?
010:094   the Truth **hath** indeed come to thee from thy Lord:
010:096   of thy Lord **hath** been verified would not believe-
010:108   Say: "O ye men! now Truth **hath** reached you
011:004   and He **hath** power over all things."
011:010   (Our) favours after adversity **hath** touched him,
011:028   from my Lord and that He **hath** sent Mercy unto me
011:028   but that the Mercy **hath** been obscured from your sight?
011:043   any but those on whom He **hath** mercy!"-
011:056   a moving creature, but He **hath** grasp of its fore-lock.
011:057   For my Lord **hath** care and watch over all things."
011:061   It is He Who **hath** produced you from the earth
011:063   and He **hath** sent Mercy unto me from Himself,-
011:076   The decree of thy Lord **hath** gone forth: for them
011:088   and He **hath** given me sustenance (pure and)
011:119   Except hose on whom thy Lord **hath** bestowed His Mercy:
012:021   And Allah **hath** full power and control over His affairs;
012:030   her slave truly **hath** he inspired her with violent

HATH (continued)

012:037   which my Lord **hath** taught me I have (I assure you)
012:040   He **hath** commanded that ye worship none but Him:
012:040   for which Allah **hath** sent down no authority:
012:041   (So) **hath** been decreed that matter whereof ye
012:100   Allah **hath** made it come true!
013:001   that which **hath** been revealed unto thee
013:019   that which **hath** been revealed unto thee from
013:021   things which Allah **hath** commanded to be joined,
013:036   rejoice at what **hath** been revealed unto thee:
013:037   the knowledge which **hath** reached thee, then wouldst
014:032   and the rivers (also) **hath** He made subject to you.
014:032   It is Allah Who **hath** created the heavens
014:032   it is He Who **hath** made the ships subject to you,
014:033   And He **hath** made subject to you the sun
014:033   Night and the Day **hath** He (also) made subject you.
014:039   "Praise be to Allah, who **hath** granted unto me
016:077   even quicker: for Allah **hath** power over all things.
017:023   Thy Lord **hath** decreed that ye worship none but Him,
018:001   and **hath** allowed therein no Crookedness:
018:001   Praise be to Allah, Who **hath** sent to His
018:002   (He **hath** made it) Straight (and Clear) in order
018:004   who say, "Allah **hath** begotten a son":
019:024   for they Lord **hath** provided a rivulet beneath thee;
019:030   He **hath** given me revelation and made me a prophet:
019:031   wheresoever I be, and **hath** enjoined on me Prayer
019:031   "And He **hath** made me Blessed wheresoever I be,
019:032   "(He) **hath** made me kind to my mother, and not
019:043   "O my father! to me **hath** come knowledge which
019:043   knowledge which **hath** not reached thee: so follow
019:094   and **hath** numbered them (all) exactly.
024:036   which Allah **hath** permitted to be raised to honour;
036:052   Who **hath** raised us up from our beds of repose?...
039:007   truly Allah **hath** no need of you; but He
040:035   without any authority that **hath** reached them,
041:021   They will say: "Allah **hath** given us speech,-
041:023   concering your Lord, **hath** brought you to destruction,
052:018   their Lord **hath** bestowed on them, and their
053:047   That He **hath** promised a Second Creation
065:010   who have believed!-for Allah **hath** indeed sent
067:001   and He over all things **Hath** Power;-
068:007   which (among men) **hath** strayed from His Path:
069:035   "So no friend **hath** he here this Day.
069:036   "Nor **hath** he any food except the foul pus
073:020   So He **hath** turned to you (in mercy):
079:027   (Allah) **hath** constructed it:
079:028   and He **hath** given it order and perfection.
079:028   On high **hath** He raised its canopy, and He
079:030   moreover, **hath** He extended (to a wide expanse);
079:032   And the mountains **hath** He firmly fixed;-
080:017   Woe to man! what **hath** made him reject Allah?
080:018   From what stuff **Hath** He created him?
080:019   From a sperm-drop: He **hath** created him, and then
080:023   what Allah **Hath** commanded him.
080:023   By no means **hath** he fulfilled what Allah
082:005   what it **hath** sent forward and (what it **hath**) kept back.
087:002   Who **hath** created, and further, given order
087:003   Who **hath** measured. And granted guidance;
089:015   "My Lord **hath** honoured me."
089:016   "My Lord **hath** humiliated me!"
090:005   Thinketh he, that none **hath** power over him?
090:011   But he **hath** made not haste on the
093:003   Thy Guardian-Lord **Hath** not forsaken thee, nor is

HATRED

003:118   rank **hatred** has already appeared from their mouths;
005:002   and let not the **hatred** of some people
005:008   and let not the **hatred** of others to you
005:014   enmity and **hatred** between the one and the other,
005:064   enmity and **hatred** till the Day of Judgment.
005:091   to excite enmity and **hatred** between you, with
041:034   and thee was **hatred** become as it were thy
043:078   but most of you have a **hatred** for Truth.
060:004   us and you, enmity and **hatred** for ever,-

HAUGHTY

002:034   not so Iblis, he refused and was **haughty**:
038:074   Not so Iblis: he was **haughty**, and became
038:075   Art thou **haughty**? Or art thou one of the high
039:059   thou wast **haughty**, and became one of those who reject
039:060   is there not in Hell an abode for the **Haughty**?
074:023   Then he turned back and was **haughty**;

HAUNTS

020:128   in whose **haunts** they (now) move?

HAVE

002:003   We **have** provided for them.
002:004   and (in their hearts) **have** the assurance of the Hereafter.
002:016   These are they who **have** bartered guidance for error:
002:016   and they **have** lost true direction.
002:023   in doubt as to what We **have** revealed
002:025   and they **have** therein spouses (purified);
002:032   of knowledge we **have** none,
002:054   "O my people! Ye **have** indeed wronged yourselves
002:057   the good things We **have** provided for you:"
002:062   shall **have** their reward with their Lord
002:063   We **have** given you and bring (ever) to
002:080   Say: "**Have** ye taken a promise from Allah,
002:082   But those who **have** faith and work righteousness,
002:089   that which they (should) **have** recognized,
002:090   thus **have** they drawn on themselves
002:090   for which they **have** sold their souls,
002:091   Say: Why then **have** ye slain the prophets
002:093   (saying): "Hold firmly to what We **have** given you,
002:093   behests of your Faith if you **have** any faith!"
002:095   their hands **have** sent on before them.
002:099   We **have** sent down to thee manifest Signs
002:102   would **have** no share in the happiness
002:107   And besides Him ye **have** neither patron nor helper.
002:109   to infidelity after ye **have** believed, from selfish envy,
002:113   "The Jews **have** naught (to stand) upon";
002:113   "The Christians **have** naught (to stand) upon";
002:118   We **have** indeed made clear the Signs
002:119   Verily We **have** sent thee in truth
002:121   Those to whom We **have** given the Book
002:140   the testimony they **have** from Allah?
002:143   Thus **have** We made of you an Ummah
002:151   A similar (favour **have** ye already received)
002:151   in that We **have** sent among you a Messenger
002:159   after We **have** made it clear
002:159   (Signs) We **have** sent down, and the Guidance,
002:167   as they **have** cleared themselves of us."
002:169   of Allah that of which ye **have** no knowledge.
002:172   the good things that We **have** provided for you.
002:177   to fulfil the contracts which ye **have** made;
002:191   from where they **have** turned you out;
002:200   But they will **have** no portion in the Hereafter.
002:200   So when ye **have** accomplished your rites,
002:202   To these will be allotted what they **have** earned.

HAVE (continued)

002:209   the clear (signs) **have** come to you,
002:211   how many Clear (Signs) We **have** sent them.
002:218   they **have** the hope of the Mercy of Allah;
002:220   He could **have** put you into difficulties:
002:222   But when they **have** purified themselves,
002:228   And their husbands **have** the better right
002:228   if they **have** faith in Allah and the Last Day.
002:228   but men **have** a degree over them
002:228   And women shall **have** rights similar
002:233   No soul shall **have** a burden laid on it
002:234   when they **have** fulfilled their term,
002:248   Symbol for you if ye indeed **have** faith."
002:253   generations would not **have** fought among each other,
002:253   they would not **have** fought each other;
002:254   (the bounties) We **have** provided for you,
002:257   Allah is the Protector of those who **have** faith:
002:264   do nothing with aught they **have** earned.
002:266   should **have** a garden with date-palms
002:267   good things which ye **have** (honorably) earned,
002:267   the fruits of the earth which We **have** produced for you,
002:270   But the wrong-doers **have** no helpers.
002:274   and in public, **have** their reward with their Lord:
002:277   will **have** their reward with their Lord:
002:279   ye shall **have** your capital sums:
002:286   than we **have** the strength to bear.
002:286   **Have** mercy on us.
003:013   In this is a lesson for such as **have** eyes to see."
003:016   "Our Lord! we **have** indeed believed:
003:020   say: "I **have** submitted my whole self to Allah
003:020   to Allah and so l **have** those who follow me."
003:022   nor will they **have** anyone to help.
003:023   those who **have** been given a portion of the Book?
003:028   if any do that, shall **have** no relation left
003:036   I **have** named her Mary,
003:040   He said: "O my Lord! how shall I **have** a son,
003:047   how shall I **have** a son when man hath touched Me?"
003:049   I **have** come to you, with a Sign from your Lord,
003:050   "(I **have** come to you), to attest the Torah
003:050   I **have** come to you with a Sign from your Lord.
003:056   nor will they **have** anyone to help.
003:065   **Have** ye no understanding?
003:066   in matters of which ye **have** no knowledge?
003:068   and Allah is the Protector of those who **have** faith.
003:071   while ye **have** knowledge?
003:077   they shall **have** no portion in the Hereafter:
003:077   they shall **have** a grievous Chastisement.
003:079   for ye **have** taught the Book and ye **have** studied it
003:080   after ye **have** bowed your will (to Allah in Islam)?
003:083   While all creatures in the heavens and on earth **have**,
003:085   in the ranks of those who **have** lost.
003:090   for they are those who **have** gone astray.
003:100   render you apostates after ye **have** believed!
003:110   among them are some who **have** faith,
003:117   harvest of men who **have** wronged their own souls:
003:118   the Signs, if ye **have** wisdom.
003:118   We **have** made plain to you the Signs,
003:135   persisting knowingly in (the wrong) they **have** done.
003:137   There **have** been examples that **have** passed away before
003:143   now ye **have** seen it with your own eyes
003:147   and anything we may **have** done that transgressed
003:154   we should not **have** been in the slaughter here."
003:154   would certainly **have** gone forth to the place

HAVE (continued)

003:154   They said: "**Have** we any hand in the affair?
003:156   they would not **have** died, or been slain."
003:159   they would **have** broken away from about thee:
003:167   we should certainly **have** followed you."
003:168   they would not **have** been slain."
003:170   who **have** not yet joined them (in their bliss),
003:170   nor **have** they (cause to) grieve.
003:172   and refrain from wrong **have** a great reward;
003:175   but fear Me, if ye **have** Faith.
003:177   but they will **have** a grievous punishment.
003:178   but they will **have** a shameful punishment.
003:179   ye **have** a reward great without measure.
003:185   Every soul shall **have** a taste of death:
003:185   and admitted to the Garden will **have** succeeded:
003:188   and love to be praised for what they **have** not done,
003:188   who exult in what they **have** brought about,
003:193   'Believe ye in the Lord', and we **have** believed.
003:193   "Our Lord! We **have** heard the call
003:195   those who **have** left their homes, and were driven
004:006   let him **have** for himself what is just and reasonable.
004:009   (disposing of an estate) **have** the same fear in their minds
004:009   as they would **have** for their own if they had left
004:014   and they shall **have** a humiliating punishment.
004:018   and he says, "Now **have** I repented indeed";
004:018   for them **have** We prepared a chastisement
004:019   of the dower ye **have** given them, except
004:019   except where they **have** been guilty of open lewdness;
004:021   and they **have** taken from you a solemn covenant?
004:021   when ye **have** gone in unto each other,
004:023   (those who **have** been) wives of your son
004:023   no prohibition if ye **have** not gone in;
004:023   born of your wives to whom ye **have** gone in,
004:024   the enjoyment you **have** of them as a duty; but if,
004:025   If any of you **have** not the means wherewith
004:033   We **have** appointed sharers and heirs to property
004:034   what Allah would **have** them guard.
004:037   for We **have** prepared, for those who resist Faith,
004:038   to be seen of men, and **have** no faith in Allah
004:043   or ye **have** been in contact with women, and
004:046   it would **have** been better for them, and more proper;
004:047   believe in what We **have** (now) revealed, confirming
004:052   thou wilt find, **have** no one to help.
004:053   **Have** they a share in dominion or power?
004:057   therein shall they **have** spouses purified
004:060   that **have** come to thee and to those before thee?
004:062   their hands **have** sent forth?
004:064   they would **have** found Allah indeed
004:065   But no, by thy Lord, they can **have** no (real) Faith.
004:066   it would **have** been best for them, and would
004:066   very few of them would **have** done it: but if
004:066   and would **have** gone farthest to strengthen
004:067   And We should then **have** given them from
004:068   And We should **have** shown them the Straight Way.
004:073   a fine thing should I then **have** made of it!"
004:077   or even more than, they should **have** feared Allah:
004:079   is from thyself and We **have** sent thee as
004:080   We **have** not sent thee to watch over them.
004:081   They **have** "Obedience" on their lips; but
004:082   they would surely **have** found therein
004:083   all but a few of you would **have** followed Satan.
004:083   would **have** known it from them (direct).
004:090   He could **have** given them power over you,

HAVE (continued)

004:090   and they would **have** fought you: therefore
004:091   in their case We **have** provided you with a clear
004:092   with whom ye **have** a treaty of mutual alliance,
004:098   and children who **have** no means in their power,
004:103   When ye **have** performed the prayers, remember
004:104   but you hope from Allah, what they **have** not.
004:105   We **have** sent down to thee the Book in truth, that
004:105   by that which Allah has shown thee; so be not
004:113   would certainly **have** plotted to lead thee astray.
004:121   They (his dupes) will **have** their dwelling in hell,
004:124   be they male or female, and **have** faith, they
004:131   Verily We **have** directed the people
004:151   and We **have** prepared for Unbelievers
004:155   (They **have** incurred divine displeasure): in that
004:161   We **have** prepared for those among them who reject
004:163   We **have** sent thee inspiration, as We sent
004:164   told thee the story; of others We **have** not;
004:164   Of some messengers We **have** already told thee the story;
004:165   should **have** no plea against Allah: for Allah
004:167   from the Way of Allah, **have** verily strayed far, far away
004:174   from your Lord for We **have** sent unto you
004:176   they shall **have** two-thirds of the inheritance
004:176   she shall **have** half the inheritance:
005:003   This day **have** I perfected your religion for you,
005:003   This day **have** those who reject Faith given up
005:003   and **have** chosen for you Islam as your religion.
005:004   and what ye **have** taught the beasts
005:005   those who **have** lost (all spiritual good).
005:006   or ye **have** been in contact with women, and you
005:014   show them what it is they **have** done.
005:023   But on Allah put your trust if ye **have** faith."
005:025   I **have** power only over myself and my bother:
005:041   but whose hearts **have** no faith; or it be
005:041   who **have** never so much as come to thee.
005:043   when they **have** (their own) Torah before them?
005:044   By its standard **have** been judged the Jews, by the
005:048   To each among you **have** We prescribed a Law and an
005:048   He would **have** made you a single People, but
005:057   but fear ye Allah, if ye **have** Faith (indeed).
005:064   Amongst them We **have** placed enmity and hatred
005:065   We should indeed **have** blotted out their
005:066   they would **have** eaten both from above them
005:067   thou wouldst not **have** fulfilled and proclaimed
005:068   ye **have** no ground to stand upon unless ye stand
005:080   which their souls **have** sent forward before
005:081   never would they **have** taken them for friends
005:082   And men who **have** renounced the world, and they
005:084   "What cause can we **have** not to believe in Allah
005:089   That is the expiation for the oaths ye **have** sworn.
005:094   will **have** a grievous chastisement.
005:107   and that we **have** not trespassed (beyond the truth):
005:109   They will say: "We **have** no knowledge: it is
005:111   they said, 'We **have** faith, and do thou
005:111   to **have** faith in Me and Mine Messenger:
005:112   Said Jesus: "Fear Allah, if ye **have** faith."
005:115   such as I **have** not inflicted on anyone
005:116   Thou wouldst indeed **have** known it. Thou knowest
006:006   in strength such as We **have** not given to you-for
006:007   the Unbelievers would **have** been sure to say: "This
006:009   We should **have** sent him as a man.
006:009   and We should certainly **have** caused them confusion
006:009   they **have** already covered with confusion.

HAVE (continued)

006:012 It is they who **have** lost their own souls,
006:015 indeed **have** fear of the Chastisement
006:020 Those who **have** lost their own souls refuse
006:020 Those to whom We **have** given the Book know this
006:025 but We **have** thrown veils on their hearts,
006:038 Nothing **have** We omitted from the Book, and they
006:051 except from Him they will **have** no protector
006:060 all that ye **have** done by day: by day doth
006:070 they will **have** for drink (only) boiling water,
006:071 we **have** been directed to submit ourselves to the Lord
006:071 like one whom the Satans **have** made into a fool,
006:075 that he might **have** certitude.
006:079 "For me, I **have** set my face, firmly
006:092 which We **have** sent down, bringing
006:093 or saith, "I **have** received inspiration," when
006:094 and your (pet) fancies **have** left you in the lurch!"
006:094 between you **have** been cut off, and your
006:094 Ye **have** left behind you all (the favours)
006:101 how can He **have** a son when He
006:104 "Now **have** come to you, from your Lord
006:107 they would not **have** taken false gods: but We
006:108 Thus **have** We made alluring to each
006:112 they would not **have** done it: so leave
006:113 who **have** no faith in the Hereafter:
006:114 to whom We **have** given the Book, that it
006:118 if ye **have** faith in His Signs.
006:123 Thus **have** We placed leaders in every town,
006:126 We **have** detailed the Signs
006:137 they would not **have** done so:
006:139 then all **have** shares therein.
006:140 They **have** indeed gone astray and heeded
006:148 Say: "**Have** ye any (certain) Knowledge?
006:148 we should not **have** given partners to Him,
006:148 nor should we **have** had any forbidden thing."
006:149 He could indeed **have** guided you all."
006:155 which We **have** revealed as a blessing: so follow
006:157 we should **have** followed its guidance
006:160 He that doeth good shall **have** ten times
007:004 How many towns **have** We destroyed
007:010 It is We who **have** placed you
007:015 "Be thou among those who **have** respite."
007:023 we **have** wronged our own souls: if Thou
007:026 We **have** bestowed raiment upon you to
007:030 others **have** deserved the loss of their way,
007:033 of which ye **have** no knowledge.
007:037 They will reply, "They **have** left us in the lurch,"
007:039 "See then! no advantage **have** ye over us; so taste
007:043 Ye **have** been made its inheritors, for your
007:043 never could we **have** found guidance, had it not
007:044 **have** you also found your Lord's promises true?"
007:044 "We **have** indeed found the promises of our Lord to us
007:046 "Peace be upon you": they **have** not entered it, but
007:053 In fact they will **have** lost their souls, and the
007:053 **Have** we no intercessors now to
007:053 those who **have** forgotten it before will say: "The
007:057 when they **have** carried the heavy-laden clouds.
007:059 worship Allah! ye **have** not other god but Him.
007:065 ye **have** no other god but Him. Will ye
007:069 the benefits (ye **have** received) from Allah:
007:071 over names which ye **have** devised-ye and
007:071 "Punishment and wrath **have** already come upon you
007:073 ye **have** no other god but Him. Now hath

HAVE (continued)

007:074 the benefits (ye **have** received) from Allah,
007:085 that will be best for you, if ye **have** Faith.
007:085 ye **have** no other god but Him. Now hath come
007:087 with which I **have** been sent, and a party
007:088 shall **have** to return to our religion."
007:096 We should indeed **have** opened out to them
007:105 Now **have** I come unto you (people), from your
007:113 they said, "Of course we shall **have** a (suitable)
007:115 or shall we **have** the (first) throw?"
007:123 a trick which ye **have** planned in the city to drive out
007:127 and we **have** over them (power) irresistible.
007:129 They said: "We **have** had (nothing but) trouble,
007:138 a god like unto the gods they **have**."
007:144 (Allah) said: "O Moses! I **have** chosen thee
007:144 by the messages I (**have** given thee) and the
007:144 and the words I (**have** spoken to thee); take then
007:146 For they **have** rejected Our Signs, and failed
007:147 rewarded except as they **have** wrought?
007:149 they said: "If our Lord **have** not mercy upon us
007:150 that ye **have** done in my place in my absence:
007:155 Thy will thou couldst **have** destroyed,
007:156 for we **have** turned unto Thee."
007:160 We **have** provided for you": (but they rebelled);
007:168 We **have** tried them with both prosperity
007:171 "Hold firmly to what We **have** given you, and bring
007:176 We should **have** elevated him with Our Signs; but he
007:179 They **have** hearts wherewith they understand not,
007:179 Many are the Jinns and men We **have** made for Hell:
007:181 Of those We **have** created are people who direct
007:188 I should **have** multiplied all good, and no
007:188 to those who **have** faith."
007:188 Say: "I **have** no power over any good or harm
007:188 and no evil should **have** touched me: I am
007:190 in the gift they **have** received: but Allah
007:195 **Have** they feet to walk with? Or hands
007:203 and Guidance, and Mercy, for any who **have** Faith."
008:003 We **have** given them for sustenance:
008:004 they **have** grades of dignity with their Lord,
008:023 they would but **have** turned back
008:023 He would indeed **have** made them listen:
008:031 they say: "We **have** heard this (before): if we
008:034 But what plea **have** they that Allah
008:036 but in the end they will **have** (only) regrets and sighs;
008:037 They will be the ones to **have** lost.
008:042 ye would certainly **have** failed in the appointment:
008:043 ye would surely **have** been discouraged,
008:043 and ye would surely **have** disputed in (your) decision:
008:056 every time, and they **have** not the fear (of Allah).
008:059 that they **have** escaped, they will
008:063 couldst thou **have** produced that affection, but Allah
008:067 that he should **have** prisoners of war until he
008:068 a severe punishment would **have** reached you
008:071 But if they **have** treacherous designs against thee,
008:071 they **have** already been in treason against Allah,
008:072 ye **have** a treaty of mutual alliance.
008:075 But kindred by blood **have** prior rights against
009:001 ye **have** contracted mutual alliances:-
009:004 those Pagans with whom ye **have** entered into alliance
009:004 and who **have** not subsequently failed you in aught,
009:009 evil indeed are the deeds thy **have** done.
009:009 and (many) **have** they hindered from His Way:
009:009 The Words of Allah **have** they sold

HAVE (continued)

009:010   It is they who **have** transgressed all bounds.
009:020   and their persons, **have** the highest rank in
009:024   the wealth that ye **have** gained;
009:040   "**Have** no fear, for Allah is with us": then Allah
009:042   they would (all) without doubt **have** followed thee,
009:042   We should certainly **have** come out with you,"
009:046   they would certainly **have** made some preparation
009:047   and there would **have** been some among you
009:047   they would not **have** added to your (strength)
009:047   among you who would **have** listened to them.
009:049   **Have** they not fallen into trial
009:059   (That would **have** been the right course).
009:060   whose hearts **have** been (recently) reconciled (to Truth);
009:061   will **have** a grievous chastisement.
009:066   Make ye no excuses: ye **have** rejected Faith
009:067   They **have** forgotten Allah; so He
009:069   and ye **have** of yours, as did those before you;
009:074   they shall **have** none on earth to protect or help them.
009:079   and they shall **have** a grievous chastisement.
009:080   forgive them: because they **have** rejected Allah
009:102   they **have** mixed an act that was good with another
009:102   (there are who) **have** acknowledged their wrong-doings:
009:111   Then rejoice in the bargain which ye **have** concluded:
009:116   Except for Him ye **have** no protector nor helper.
010:002   that they **have** before their Lord the good
010:002   that We **have** set Our inspiration to a man
010:002   the good actions they **have** advanced (but) say
010:004   but those who reject Him will **have** draughts of
010:011   the ill (they **have** earned) as they would fain hasten
010:012   But when We **have** removed his affliction,
010:016   A whole lifetime before this **have** I tarried
010:016   I should not **have** rehearsed it to you, nor should
010:016   nor should He **have** made it known to you.
010:019   their differences would **have** been settled between them.
010:024   it belongs think they **have** all powers of
010:027   But those who **have** earned evil will **have** a reward of
010:027   no defender will they **have** from (the wrath of) Allah:
010:049   Say: "I **have** no power over any harm or profit
010:068   No warrant **have** ye for this!
010:072   no reward **have** I asked of you: my reward
010:072   and I **have** been commanded to be of those who
010:078   may **have** greatness in the land?
010:081   Moses said: "What ye **have** brought is sorcery:
010:094   We **have** revealed unto thee, then ask
010:094   then ask those who **have** been reading the Book
010:098   should **have** profited it,-except the people
010:099   they would all **have** believed,-all who
011:020   nor **have** they protectors besides Allah!
011:021   they forged **have** left them in the lurch!
011:021   They are the ones who **have** lost their own souls:
011:025   (with a mission): "I **have** come to you as a
011:028   (it be that) I **have** a Clear Sign from my Lord
011:036   except those who **have** believed already!
011:047   and **have** Mercy on me, I should indeed
011:047   of which I **have** no knowledge and unless Thou
011:049   of the Unseen, which We **have** revealed unto thee:
011:050   ye **have** no other god but Him.
011:054   some of our gods may **have** seized thee with evil."
011:057   I (at least) **have** conveyed the Message with which I was
011:061   ye **have** not other god but Him. It is He Who
011:063   If I **have** a Clear (Sign) from my Lord and He
011:070   They said: "Fear not: we **have** been sent

HAVE (continued)

011:079   They said: "Well dost thou know we **have** no need
011:084   ye **have** no other god but Him.
011:088   I **have** a Clear (Sign) from my Lord, and He
011:091   we should certainly **have** stoned thee!
011:100   and some **have** been mown down (by the sickle of time).
011:110   the matter would **have** been decided between them:
011:113   and ye **have** no protectors other than Allah,
011:118   He could **have** made mankind one People: but they
012:002   We **have** sent it down as an Arabic Qur'an, in order
012:018   He said: "Nay, but your minds **have** made up
012:024   and he would **have** desired her, but that
012:037   which my Lord hath taught me I **have** (I assure you)
012:040   is nothing but names which ye **have** named, ye and
012:048   except a little which ye shall **have** (specially) guarded.
012:048   devour what ye shall **have** laid by in advance for them,-
012:049   a year in which the people will **have** abundant water,
012:052   may know that I **have** never been false to him
012:059   a brother ye **have**, of the same father
012:060   ye shall **have** no measure (of corn) from me,
012:074   if ye are (proved) to **have** lied?"
012:082   Ask at the town where we **have** been and the
012:083   Jacob said: "Nay, but ye **have** yourselves contrived
012:087   except those who **have** no faith."
012:088   we **have** (now) brought but scanty capital: so pay
012:091   and we certainly **have** been guilty of sin!"
012:103   mankind **have**, however ardently thou dost desire it.
013:006   yet **have** come to pass, before them,
013:016   such as **have** no power either for good or for
013:016   to Allah partners who **have** created (anything)
013:022   We **have** bestowed for their sustenance, secretly
013:030   (long since) **have** (other) Peoples (gone and) passed away;
013:030   Thus **have** We sent thee amongst a Peoplebefore whom
013:031   (so) willed, He could **have** guided all mankind
013:034   and defender **have** they none against Allah.
013:036   Those to whom We **have** given the Book rejoice at
013:037   Thus **have** We revealed it to be a judgment
013:043   and such as **have** knowledge of the Book."
014:001   A Book which We **have** revealed unto thee, in order
014:009   ye **have** been sent, and we are really in suspicious
014:018   no power **have** they over aught that they **have** earned:
014:021   we should **have** given it to you:
014:031   Speak to My servants who **have** believed, that they
014:031   the Sustenance We **have** given them, secretly and
014:036   "O my Lord! they **have** indeed led astray
014:037   "O our Lord! I **have** made some of my offspring
015:008   behold! no respite would they **have**!
015:009   We **have**, without doubt, sent down the Message;
015:015   They would only say: "Our eyes **have** been intoxicated:
015:015   nay, we **have** been bewitched by sorcery."
015:016   It is We who **have** set out constellations in
015:017   And (moreover) we **have** guarded them from every
015:019   And the earth We **have** spread out (like a carpet);
015:020   And We **have** provided therein means of subsistence,-
015:029   "When I **have** fashioned him (in due proportion)
015:042   shalt thou **have**, except such as put themselves
015:057   the business on which ye (**Have** come), O ye
015:058   They said: "We **have** been sent to a people
015:060   we **have** ascertained, will be among those who
015:063   They said: "Yea, we **have** come to thee
015:064   "We **have** come to thee with the Truth and assuredly
015:087   And We **have** bestowed upon thee the Seven Oft-
015:088   (Wistfully) at what We **have** bestowed on certain

HAVE (continued)

015:091 (So also on such) as **have** made Qur'an into
016:006 And ye **have** a sense of pride and beauty in them
016:008 (other) things of which ye **have** no knowledge.
016:009 He could **have** guided all of you.
016:031 they will **have** therein all that they wish:
016:035 nor should we **have** prescribed prohibitions other
016:035 not **have** worshipped aught but Him-neither we
016:040 For to anything which We **have** willed, We but
016:044 and Scriptures and We **have** sent down unto thee
016:053 And ye **have** no good thing but is from Allah:
016:055 the favours We **have** bestowed on them!
016:056 We **have** bestowed for their sustenance!
016:063 so but they shall **have** a most grievous
016:073 such as **have** no power of providing them,
016:073 and cannot possibly **have** such power?
016:075 on whom We **have** bestowed goodly favours from
016:089 and We **have** sent down to thee the Book explaining
016:091 Fulfil the Covenant of Allah when ye **have** entered into
016:091 and break not your oaths after ye **have** confirmed them;
016:091 indeed ye **have** made Allah your surety; for Allah
016:094 and ye may **have** to taste the evil (consequences)
016:117 a paltry profit; but they will **have** a most
016:118 as We **have** mentioned to thee before:
016:125 who **have** strayed from His Path, and who
017:008 (to Our punishments): and We **have** made Hell
017:009 that they shall **have** a magnificent reward;
017:010 that We **have** prepared for them a Chastisement
017:012 We **have** made the Night and the Day as two
017:012 all things **have** We explained in detail.
017:012 We **have** made bright that ye may seek bounty from
017:012 the Sign of the Night **have** We made dark
017:013 Every man's fate We **have** fastened on his
017:017 How many generations **have** We destroyed after Noah?
017:018 in the end **have** We provided Hell for them:
017:019 and strive therefor with all due striving, and have Faith,-
017:021 See how We **have** bestowed more on some than on
017:033 We **have** given his heir authority (to demand Qisas or to
017:041 We **have** explained (things) in various (ways)
017:042 behold, they would certainly **have** sought out
017:048 but they **have** gone astray, and never
017:054 We **have** not sent thee to be a disposer
017:056 whom ye fancy: they **have** neither the power
017:065 no authority shalt thou **have** over them."
017:070 We **have** honoured the sons of Adam; provided them
017:073 they would certainly **have** made thee (their) friend!
017:074 thou wouldst nearly **have** inclined to them a little.
017:075 and moreover thou wouldst **have** found none
017:075 In that case We should **have** made thee taste
017:076 but in that case they would not **have** stayed (therein)
017:086 We **have** sent thee by inspiration: then wouldst
017:089 And We **have** explained to man, in this Qur'an,
017:091 "Or (until) thou **have** a garden of date trees
017:093 "Or thou **have** a house adorned with gold, or thou
017:095 and quiet, We should certainly **have** sent them
017:101 to **have** been worked upon by sorcery!"
017:102 these things **have** been sent down by none
017:106 We **have** revealed it by stages.
017:106 (It is) a Qur'an which We **have** divided (into parts from
018:002 shall **have** a goodly Reward.
018:005 No knowledge **have** they of such a thing, nor had
018:007 That which is on earth We **have** made but as
018:014 we should indeed **have** uttered an enormity!"

HAVE (continued)

018:015 "These our people **have** taken for worship
018:017 Thou wouldst **have** seen the sun, when it rose,
018:018 thou wouldst **have** certainly turned back
018:018 Thou wouldst **have** thought awake, whilst they
018:018 and wouldst certainly **have** been filled with
018:019 "How long **have** ye stayed (here)?"
018:019 "Allah (alone) knows best how long ye **have** stayed here...
018:019 They said, "We **have** stayed (perhaps) a day,
018:026 They **have** no protector other than Him; nor does
018:028 nor obey any whose heart We **have** permitted to
018:029 for the wrong-doers We **have** prepared a Fire
018:034 "More wealth **have** I than you, and more honour
018:048 (with the announcement), "Now **have** ye come to Us
018:053 and apprehend that they **have** to fall therein;
018:054 We **have** explained in detail in this Qur'an, for the
018:057 forgetting the (deeds) which his hands **have** sent forth?
018:057 Verily We **have** set veils over their hearts
018:058 to call them (at once) to account for what they **have** earned,
018:058 then surely He would **have** hastened their Punishment:
018:058 but they **have** their appointed time, beyond which
018:062 truly we **have** suffered much fatigue at this
018:067 be able to **have** patience with me!
018:068 "For how canst thou **have** patience about things
018:072 thou canst **have** no patience with me?"
018:075 thou canst **have** no patience with me?"
018:076 then wouldst thou **have** received (full)
018:077 surely thou couldst **have** exacted some
018:088 works righteousness-he shall **have** a goodly reward,
018:102 Verily We **have** prepared Hell for the
018:104 "Those whose efforts **have** been wasted in this life,
018:107 work righteous deeds, they **have**, for their
019:007 that name **have** We conferred distinction before."
019:008 is barren and I **have** grown quite decrepit from old age?"
019:008 "O my Lord how shall I **have** a son, when my wife is
019:020 She said: "How shall I **have** a son, seeing that
019:026 'I **have** vowed a fast to (Allah) Most Gracious,
019:062 and they will **have** therein their sustenance,
019:074 before them **have** We destroyed, who were
019:081 And they **have** taken (for worship) gods other
019:083 Seest thou not that We **have** set Satans
019:087 None shall **have** the power of intercession,
019:089 Indeed ye **have** put forth a thing most monstrous!
019:097 So **have** We made the (Qur'an) easy in thine
019:098 generation before them **have** We destroyed?
020:002 We **have** not sent down the Qur'an to thee to be
020:013 "I **have** chosen thee: listen, then to the
020:015 I **have** almost kept it hidden-for every soul
020:041 "And I **have** prepared thee for Myself (for service)."
020:047 indeed, **have** we come from thy Lord!
020:053 With it **have** We produced divers pairs of plants
020:058 in a place where both shall **have** even chances."
020:069 that which they **have** faked:
020:069 What they **have** faked is but a magician's trick:
020:071 and I will **have** you crucified on trunks
020:073 For us, we **have** believed in our Lord: may He
020:075 who **have** worked righteous deeds,-for them
020:081 We **have** provided for your sustenance, but commit
020:085 (Allah) said: "We **have** tested thy people in thy
020:099 for We **have** sent thee a reminder from Us.
020:112 and has faith, will **have** no fear of harm nor of
020:113 Thus **have** we sent this down-an Arabic Qur'an-
020:129 (their punishment) must necessarily **have** come;

HAVE (continued)

020:131 for the things We **have** given for enjoyment
020:134 they would **have** said: "Our Lord! If only thou hadst sent
020:134 We should certainly **have** followed Thy Signs before we
021:010 We **have** revealed for you (O men!) a book
021:017 take (just) a pastime, We should surely **have** taken it from
021:021 Or **have** they taken (for worship) gods from
021:022 besides Allah, there would **have** been ruin in both!
021:024 Or **have** they taken for worship (other) gods
021:031 And We **have** set on the earth mountains standing
021:031 and We **have** made therein broad highways
021:032 And We **have** made the heavens as a
021:035 Every soul shall **have** a taste of death: and We
021:040 no power will they **have** then to avert it,
021:043 They **have** no power to aid themselves,
021:043 Or **have** they gods that can guard them from Us?
021:050 And this is a blessed message which We **have** sent down:
021:054 He said, "Indeed ye **have** been in manifest error-
021:055 They said, "**Have** you brought us the Truth, or are
021:067 that ye worship besides Allah! **Have** ye no sense?"
021:071 to the land which We **have** blessed for the nations.
021:088 and thus do We deliver those who **have** faith.
021:095 which We **have** destroyed: that they
021:099 they would not **have** got there!
021:104 a promise We **have** undertaken: truly shall
021:109 say: "I **have** proclaimed the Message to you all
022:005 O mankind! if ye **have** a doubt about the
022:016 Thus **have** We sent down Clear Signs; and verily
022:024 of speeches; they **have** been guided to the Path
022:024 For they **have** been guided (in this life)
022:025 As to those who **have** rejected (Allah), and would
022:025 which We **have** made (open) to (all) men-
022:033 In them ye **have** benefits for a term appointed:
022:035 We **have** bestowed upon them.
022:036 The sacrificial camels We **have** made for you
022:036 thus **have** we made animals subject to you,
022:040 there would surely **have** been pulled down
022:040 (They are) those who **have** been expelled from
022:045 How many populations **have** We destroyed, which were
022:067 To every People **have** We appointed rites
022:071 and of which they **have** (really) no knowledge:
022:073 they would **have** no power to release it from the fly:
022:074 No just estimate **have** they made of Allah:
023:017 And We **have** made, above you, seven tracts;
023:019 and of them ye eat (and **have** enjoyment),-
023:019 in them **have** ye abundant fruits: and of them
023:021 And in cattle (too) ye **have** an instructive example:
023:023 Ye **have** no other god but Him.
023:024 (to send messenger), He could **have** sent down angels:
023:025 wait (and **have** patience) with him for a time."
023:032 (saying), "Worship Allah! ye **have** no other god
023:053 But people **have** cut off their affair (of unity),
023:055 Do they think that because We **have** granted them
023:071 and all beings therein would **have** been in ruin.
023:071 Nay, We **have** sent them their admonition, but they
023:083 "Such things **have** been promised to us and to
023:090 We **have** sent them the Truth: but they
023:091 had created, and some would **have** lorded it over
023:091 each god would **have** taken away what he had created,
023:103 will be those who **have** lost their souls;
023:109 forgive us, and **have** mercy upon us: for Thou
023:111 they are indeed the ones that **have** achieved Bliss."
023:111 "I **have** rewarded them this day for their

HAVE (continued)

024:001 and which We **have** ordained:
024:001 in it **have** We sent down Clear Signs, in order
024:001 A Sura which We **have** sent down and which
024:003 The adulterer cannot **have** sexual relations
024:003 none can **have** sexual relations with her but an
024:006 and **have** (in support) no evidence but their own,-
024:013 When they **have** not brought the witness, such men,
024:014 a grievous chastisement would **have** seized you
024:019 will **have** a grievous Chastisement in this life
024:021 not one of you would ever **have** been pure:
024:022 those in want, and those who **have** left their
024:027 until ye **have** asked permission and saluted
024:031 who **have** no carnal knowledge of women; and that
024:034 We **have** already sent down to you verses making
024:044 those who **have** vision!
024:046 We **have** indeed sent down Signs that make
024:058 among you who **have** not come of age ask your permission
024:062 they do not depart until they **have** asked for his leave;
025:003 that **have** no control of hurt or good
025:003 Yet **have** they taken, besides Him, gods that
025:004 In truth it is they who **have** put forward
025:004 has forged, and others **have** helped him at it."
025:009 But they **have** gone astray, and never
025:011 but We **have** prepared a Blazing Fire for such as deny the
025:019 "Now **have** they proved you liars in what ye say:
025:020 will ye **have** patience? For Allah is One Who sees
025:020 We **have** made some of you as a trial for others:
025:021 Indeed they **have** an arrogant conceit of themselves,
025:024 and **have** the fairest of places for repose.
025:031 Thus **have** We made for every prophet an enemy
025:032 thy heart thereby, and We **have** rehearsed it
025:036 to the people who **have** rejected Our Signs":
025:037 and We **have** prepared for (all) wrong-doers
025:040 the (Unbelievers) must indeed **have** passed by the town
025:042 "He indeed would well-nigh **have** misled us
025:049 of things We **have** created,-cattle and
025:050 And We **have** distributed the (water) amongst them,
025:051 We could **have** sent a warner to every town.
025:077 but ye **have** indeed rejected (Him), and soon
026:006 They **have** indeed rejected (the Message): so they
026:007 we **have** produced therein?
026:014 "And (further), they **have** a charge of crime
026:016 to Pharaoh, and say: 'We **have** been sent by the
026:041 shall we **have** a (suitable) reward if we win?"
026:055 "And they are raging furiously against us;
026:075 whom ye **have** been worshipping,-
026:100 "Now, then, we **have** none to intercede (for us),
026:117 truly my people **have** rejected me.
026:146 in (the enjoyment of) all that ye **have** here?-
026:155 and ye **have** a right of watering, (severally) on
026:199 they would not **have** believed in it.
026:200 Thus **have** We caused it to enter the hearts
027:003 and also **have** sure faith in the Hereafter.
027:004 We **have** made their deeds pleasing in their eyes;
027:010 those called as messengers **have** no fear,-
027:011 "But if any **have** done wrong and **have** thereafter
027:016 and we **have** been given of everything, this is
027:016 He said: "O ye people! we **have** been taught
027:022 and I **have** come to thee from Saba
027:022 "I **have** compassed which thou hast not compassed,
027:032 no affair **have** I decided except in your presence."
027:039 indeed I **have** full strength for the purpose,

HAVE (continued)

027:042 and we **have** submitted to Allah (in Islam)."
027:044 I **have** indeed wronged my soul: I do
027:086 See they not that We **have** made the Night
027:089 If any do good, he will **have** better than it.
027:090 that which ye **have** earned by your deeds?"
027:091 For me, I **have** been commanded to serve the Lord
028:016 I **have** indeed wronged by soul!
028:033 He said: "O my Lord! I **have** slain a man among them,
028:039 they would not **have** to return to Us!"
028:047 seize them for (the deeds) that their hands **have** sent forth,
028:047 We should then **have** followed the Signs and been amongst
028:051 Now **have** We brought them the word in order
028:053 indeed we **have** been Muslims (bowing to Allah's Will)
028:054 out of what We **have** given them.
028:054 for that they **have** persevered, that they
028:057 **Have** We not established for them a secure sanctuary,
028:061 one to whom We **have** made a goodly promise,
028:061 and one to whom We **have** given the good
028:068 no choice **have** they (in the matter):
028:076 that their very keys would **have** been a burden
028:078 given to me because of a certain knowledge which I **have**."
028:082 He could **have** caused the earth to swallow us up!
028:087 away from Allah's revelations after **have** been revealed
029:007 shall We blot out all misdeeds that they **have** committed,
029:008 Ye **have** (all) to return to Me, and I will
029:008 We **have** enjoined on man kindness to parents:
029:010 to say, "We **have** (always) been with you!"
029:017 besides Allah **have** no power to give you sustenance:
029:022 (His Plan), nor **have** ye, beside Allah,
029:025 the Fire, and ye shall **have** none to help."
029:025 And He said: "For you, ye **have** taken (for worship)
029:034 because they **have** been wickedly rebellious."
029:035 And We **have** left thereof an evident Sign,
029:043 those understand them who **have** Knowledge.
029:047 And thus (it is) that We **have** sent down
029:048 indeed, would the talkers of vanities **have** doubt.
029:051 We **have** sent down to thee the Book
029:053 the Punishment would certainly **have** come to them:
029:057 Every soul shall **have** a taste of death:
029:067 We **have** made a Sanctuary secure, and that
030:002 The Roman Empire **have** been defeated-
030:009 and populated it in greater numbers than these **have** done:
030:013 No intercessor will they **have** among their
030:015 Then those who **have** believed and worked
030:016 And those who **have** rejected Faith and falsely
030:028 We **have** bestowed on you?
030:028 do ye **have** partners among those whom your
030:034 for the (favours) We **have** bestowed on them!
030:035 Or **have** We sent down authority to them,
030:036 their (own) hands **have** sent forth, behold,
030:039 of (other) people, will **have** no increase with
030:041 the hands of men **have** earned, that (Allah)
030:058 Verily We **have** propounded for men, in this
030:060 who **have** (themselves) no certainty of faith.
031:004 and give zakat and **have** sure faith
031:011 that others besides Him **have** created: nay, but
031:014 And We **have** enjoined on man (to be good) to his
032:004 on the Throne: ye **have** none, besides Him,
032:012 "Our Lord! We **have** seen and we **have** heard:
032:013 We could certainly **have** brought every soul
032:016 We **have** bestowed on them.
032:024 with patience and contnued to **have** faith in Our Signs.

HAVE (continued)

032:027 **Have** they not the vision?
033:006 Blood-relations among each **have** closer personal ties,
033:014 They would certainly **have** brought it to pass, with none
033:019 Such men **have** no faith, and so
033:020 They think that the Confederates **have** not withdrawn;
033:021 Ye **have** indeed in the Messenger of Allah
033:023 Among the Believers are men who **have** been true
033:023 of them some **have** died and some (still) wait:
033:023 but they **have** never changed (their determination) in the
033:031 and We **have** prepared for her a generous Sustenance.
033:036 to **have** any option about their decision:
033:037 when the latter **have** dissolved (their marriage)
033:038 amongst those of all that **have** passed away.
033:045 O Prophet! Truly We **have** sent thee as a Witness,
033:047 shall **have** from Allah a very great Bounty.
033:049 no period of 'Iddat **have** ye to count in respect
033:049 and then divorce them before ye **have** touched them,
033:050 O prophet! We **have** made lawful to thee
033:050 We know what We **have** appointed for them
033:053 and when ye **have** taken your meal, disperse,
033:061 They shall **have** a curse on them: wherever they
034:014 they would not **have** tarried in the humiliating
034:022 they **have** no power,-not the weight of an atom,-
034:022 no (sort of) share **have** they therein, nor is
034:027 Say: "Show me those whom ye **have** joined with
034:028 We **have** not sent thee but as a (Messenger)
034:031 for you, we should certainly **have** been believers!"
034:034 with which ye **have** been sent."
034:035 They said: "We **have** more in wealth and in sons,
034:042 they **have** over each other, for profit
034:045 (the Truth); these **have** not received a tenth
035:015 O ye men! it is ye that **have** need of Allah:
035:024 Verily We **have** sent thee with truth, as a
035:028 who **have** knowledge: for Allah is Exalted in
035:029 We **have** provided for them, secretly and
035:031 That which We **have** revealed to thee of the Book
035:032 Then We **have** given the Book for inheritance
035:032 as We **have** chosen: but there are among them
035:040 they **have** created in the (wide) earth.
035:040 Or **have** We given them a Book from which
035:040 Say: "**Have** ye seen (these) `partners' of yours
035:040 Or **have** they a share in the heavens?
036:008 We **have** put yokes round their necks right up
036:009 And We **have** put a bar in front of them and a
036:009 We **have** covered them up: so that
036:012 and of all things **have** We taken account.
036:014 they said, "Truly, we **have** been sent on a
036:016 we **have** been sent on a mission to you:
036:025 "For me, I **have** faith in the Lord of you (all):
036:036 of which they **have** no knowledge.
036:039 And the Moon,-We **have** measured for her stations
036:042 And We **have** created for them similar (vessels)
036:047 He would **have** fed, (himself)?-Ye are
036:049 They will not (**have** to) wait for aught but a
036:050 No (chance) will they then **have**, by will,
036:055 shall that Day **have** joy in all that they do;
036:057 they shall **have** whatever they call for;
036:066 We could surely **have** blotted out their eyes;
036:066 then they should **have** raced to the Path,
036:066 but how could they **have** seen?
036:067 nor could they **have** returned (after error).
036:067 then should they **have** been unable to move about,

HAVE (continued)

036:067	We could **have** transformed them in their places;
036:069	We **have** not instructed the (Prophet) in Poetry,
036:071	See they not that it is We Who **have** created for them-
036:071	among the things which our hands **have** fashioned-cattle,
036:072	And that We **have** subjected them to their (use)?
036:073	And they **have** (other) profits from them
036:075	They **have** not the power to help them: and they
037:006	We **have** indeed decked the lower heaven
037:011	or the (other) beings We **have** created?
037:011	Them **have** We created out of a sticky clay!
037:031	that we shall indeed (**have** to) taste (the punishment of
037:057	my Lord, I should certainly **have** been among
037:063	For We **have** truly made it (as) a trial
037:095	ye **have** (yourselves) carved?
037:102	he said: "O my son! I **have** seen in a dream
037:144	He would certainly **have** remained inside the
037:149	(only) daughters, and they **have** sons?-
037:156	Or **have** ye an authority manifest?
037:158	And they **have** invented a kinship between Him
037:169	"We should certainly **have** been Servants of Allah,
038:008	Nay, they **have** not yet tasted My Punishment!
038:009	Or **have** they the Treasures of the Mercy
038:010	Or **have** they the dominion of the heavens
038:017	**Have** patience at what they say, and remember
038:023	and I **have** (but) one: ye he says, 'Commit her
038:029	(Here is) a Book which We **have** sent down
038:043	for all who **have** Understanding.
038:060	It is ye who **have** brought this upon us!
038:063	or **have** (our) eyes failed to perceive them?"
038:069	"No knowledge **have** I of the Exalted Chiefs,
038:072	"When I **have** fashioned him and breathed
038:075	whom I **have** created with My hands?
039:002	Verily it is We Who **have** revealed the Book
039:004	a son, He could **have** chosen whom He pleased
039:013	indeed **have** fear of the Chastisement
039:016	They shall **have** Layers of Fire above them,
039:020	one above another **have** been built: beneath them
039:023	can **have** none to guide.
039:027	We **have** put forth for men, in the
039:029	But most of them **have** no knowledge.
039:034	They shall **have** all that they wish for, in the
039:035	to the best of what they **have** done.
039:041	Verily We **have** revealed the Book to thee in Truth,
039:043	"Evn if they **have** no power whatever and no intelligence?"
039:046	in those matters about which they **have** differed."
039:047	which they could never **have** counted upon!
039:049	given to me because of a certain knowledge (I **have**)!"
039:053	Say: "O my Servants who **have** transgressed against
039:057	I should certainly **have** been among the righteous!'
039:061	for they **have** earned salvation: no evil
039:067	No just estimate **have** they made of Allah,
039:073	Well **have** ye done! Enter ye
040:009	Thou **have** bestowed Mercy indeed: and that
040:011	Now **have** we recognized our sins:
040:018	wrong-doers **have**, who could be listened to.
040:021	and in the traces (they **have** left) in the land:
040:027	Moses said: "I **have** indeed called upon my Lord
040:029	this day: ye **have** the upper hand in the land:
040:033	and flee: no defender shall ye **have** from Allah:
040:040	therein will they **have** abundance without measure.
040:042	partners of whom I **have** no knowledge; and I
040:052	but they will (only) **have** the Curse and the Home

HAVE (continued)

040:066	seeing that the Clear Signs **have** come to me
040:066	and I **have** been commanded to submit (in Islam)
040:066	Say: "I **have** been forbidden to invoke those whom
040:074	"They **have** left us in the lurch: nay, we
040:078	and some whose story We **have** not related to thee.
040:078	whose story We **have** related to thee, and some
040:082	and in the traces (they **have** left) in the land:
041:013	"I **have** warned you of a thunderbolt like the
041:014	He would certainly **have** sent down angels: so we
041:023	and (now) **have** ye become of those utterly lost!"
041:024	If, then, they **have** patience, the Fire
041:025	who **have** passed away, is proved against them;
041:025	And We **have** destined for them intimate companions
041:031	therein shall ye **have** all that your souls
041:031	therein shall ye **have** all that ye ask for!-
041:044	they would **have** said: "Why are not
041:045	would **have** been settled between them: but they
041:048	that they **have** no way of escape.
041:050	I **have** (much) good (stored) in His sight!"
042:007	Thus **have** We sent by inspiration to thee
042:008	He could **have** made them a single people; but He
042:008	and the wrong-doers will **have** no protector
042:009	What! **Have** they taken (for worship)
042:013	the which We **have** sent by inspiration to thee-
042:014	who **have** inherited the Book after them are in
042:014	the matter would **have** been settled between them:
042:021	the wrong-doers will **have** a grievous Chastisement.
042:021	What! **have** they partners (in godhead),
042:021	who **have** established for them some religion
042:021	the matter would **have** been decided between them
042:022	wrong-doers in fear on account of what they **have** earned,
042:022	they shall **have**, before their Lord, all that they wish for.
042:028	(even) after (men) **have** given up all hope,
042:030	is because of the things your hands **have** wrought,
042:031	nor **have** ye, besides Allah, anyone to
042:034	because of the (evil) which (the men) **have** earned:
042:046	And no protectors **have** they to help them,
042:048	his hands **have** sent forth, truly then
042:048	We **have** not sent thee as a guard over them.
042:052	but We **have** made the (Qur'an) a Light, wherewith
042:052	And thus **have** We, by Our
043:003	We **have** made it a Qur'an in Arabic, that ye
043:020	Of that they **have** no knowledge!
043:020	we should not **have** worshipped such (deities)!"
043:021	What! **have** We given them a Book before this,
043:029	Yea, I **have** given the good things of this life
043:039	When ye **have** done wrong, it will
043:042	for verily We **have** power over them.
043:042	thee that (accomplished) which We **have** promised them:
043:061	therefore **have** no doubt about the (Hour),
043:063	he said: "Now **have** I come to you with Wisdom,
043:069	Those who **have** believed in Our Signs and submitted
043:073	Ye shall **have** therein abundance of fruit,
043:076	but it is they who **have** been unjust themselves.
043:078	Verily We **have** brought the truth to you: but most
043:078	but most of you **have** a hatred for Truth.
043:079	What! **have** they settled some Plan
043:083	meet that Day of theirs, which they **have** been promised.
043:086	And those whom they invoke besides Allah **have** no
044:007	if ye (but) **have** an assured faith.
044:013	How shall they **have** the Reminder. Seeing that
044:020	"For me, I **have** sought Safety with my Lord

HAVE (continued)

044:058 Verily, We **have** made this (Qur'an) easy, in thy
045:010 nor any protectors they may **have** taken to
045:010 no profit to them is anything they may **have** earned,
045:014 to what they **have** earned.
045:024 But of that they **have** no knowledge: they merely
045:032 and we **have** no firm assurance.'"
045:034 and no helpers **have** ye!
046:004 Show me what it is they **have** created on earth,
046:004 or any remnant of knowledge (ye may **have**), if ye
046:004 or **have** they a share in the heavens?
046:008 then can ye **have** no power to help me against Allah.
046:011 good thing, (such men) would not **have** gone to it
046:015 Truly **have** I turned to Thee and truly do I
046:015 We **have** enjoined on man kindness to his parents:
046:017 "Woe to thee! **Have** Faith! For the promise of Allah is
046:017 even though generations **have** passed before me
046:018 enerations of Jinns and men, that **have** passed away;
046:019 degrees according to the deeds which they (**have** done),
046:021 but there **have** been Warners before
046:023 I proclaim to yout the mission on which I **have** been sent:
046:026 We **have** not given to you (ye Quraish)! and We
046:027 and We **have** shown the Signs in various
046:030 We **have** heard a Book revealed after Moses,
046:032 and no protectors can he **have** besides Allah:
047:004 at length, when ye **have** thoroughly subdued them,
047:004 He could certainly **have** exacted retribution
047:011 but those who reject Allah **have** no protector.
047:013 has driven thee out, **have** We destroyed (for their sins)?
047:016 from thee, they say to those who **have** received
047:018 to them, how shall they **have** their Reminder?
047:018 But already **have** come some tokens
047:030 We could **have** shown them up to thee, and thou
047:030 and thou shouldst **have** known them by their marks:
048:001 Verily We **have** granted thee a manifest Victory:
048:008 We **have** truly sent thee as a witness, as a
048:013 His Messenger, We **have** prepared, for those
048:025 We should certainly **have** punished the Unbelievers
048:025 (Allah would **have** allowed you to force your way,
048:025 a guilt would **have** accrued to you without (your)
049:006 of repentance for what ye **have** done.
049:014 but ye (only) say, 'We **have** submitted our wills
049:014 Say, "Ye **have** no faith; but ye
049:015 and **have** never since doubted, but **have** striven with their
049:015 who **have** believed in Allah and His Messenger,
049:017 that they **have** embraced Islam.
050:006 How We **have** made it and adorned it,
050:007 And the earth-We **have** spread it out, and set
050:022 now **have** We removed thy veil, and sharp
051:016 because, before then, they **have** done good deeds
051:032 They said, "We **have** been sent to a people
051:047 and We indeed **have** vast power.
051:047 We **have** built the Firmament with might:
051:048 And We **have** spread out the (spacious) earth:
051:049 And of every thing We **have** created pairs: that ye
051:053 Is this the legacy they **have** transmitted, one to
051:056 I **have** only created Jinns and men, that they
051:060 they **have** been promised!
052:033 Nay, they **have** no faith!
052:036 Nay, they **have** no firm belief.
052:037 with them, or **have** they control over them.
052:038 Or **have** they a ladder, by which
052:039 Or has He only daughters and ye **have** sons?

HAVE (continued)

052:043 Or **have** they a god other then Allah?
053:019 **Have** ye seen Lat, an 'Uzza,
053:023 which ye **have** devised,-ye and
053:024 Nay, shall man **have** (just) anything
053:028 But they **have** no knowledge therein. They follow
053:039 That man can **have** nothing but what he strives for;
054:004 There **have** already come to them such tidings
054:015 And We **have** left this as a Sign (for all time):
054:017 And We **have** indeed made the Qur'an easy to
054:022 But We **have** indeed made the Qur'an easy to
054:032 And We **have** indeed made the Qur'an easy to
054:040 And We **have** indeed made the Qur'an easy to
054:043 Or **have** ye an immunity in the Sacred Books?
054:049 Verily, all things **have** We created
054:051 (oft) in the past, **have** We destroyed gangs like unto you:
055:035 No defense will ye **have**:
056:035 We **have** created them of special creation.
056:057 It is We Who **have** created you: why will
056:060 We **have** decreed Death to be your common lot,
056:073 We **have** made it a reminder and an article
056:082 And **have** ye made it your livelihood that ye
057:011 and he will **have** (besides) a generous reward.
057:017 Already **have** We shown the Signs plainly to you,
057:018 and they shall **have** (besides) a generous reward.
057:019 of their Lord: they shall **have** their Reward
057:027 but that they did not foster as they should **have** done.
057:029 that they **have** no power whatever over the Grace
058:005 (will **have**) a humiliating Chastisement,
058:005 for We **have** already sent down Clear Signs.
058:011 and who **have** been granted Knowledge: and Allah
058:014 (in friendship) to such as **have** the Wrath of
058:016 They **have** made their oaths a screen
058:016 they **have** a humiliating Chastisement.
058:018 they **have** something (to stand upon). No, indeed!
059:003 they shall (certainly) **have** the Punishment
059:003 He would certainly **have** punished them in this
059:010 against those who **have** believed.
059:015 they **have** tasted the evil result of their conduct;
059:021 **have** seen it humble itself and cleave
060:001 If ye **have** come out to strive in My Way and seek
060:001 and **have** (on the contrary) driven out
060:001 even though they **have** rejected the truth
060:004 we **have** rejected you, and there
060:004 for forgiveness for thee, though I **have** no power
060:010 what they **have** spent on their dowers, and let
060:010 Unvelievers what they **have** spent (on their dower).
060:010 ask for what ye **have** spent on their dowers,
060:011 and ye **have** your turn (by the coming over of a woman
060:011 whose wives **have** deserted the equivalent of what they
062:003 Along with others of them, who **have** not already
062:007 of the (deeds) their hands **have** sent on before them!
063:002 They **have** made their oaths a screen
063:010 out of the substance which We **have** bestowed on you,
063:010 and I should **have** been one of the doers of good."
063:010 I should then **have** given (largely) in charity,
064:008 and in the Light which which We **have** sent down.
065:004 Such of your women as **have** passed the age
065:004 and for those who **have** no courses (it is the same):
065:004 if ye **have** any doubt, is three months, and those
065:010 who **have** believed!-for Allah hath indeed sent
067:005 And We **have**, (from of old), adorned the
067:005 and We **have** made such (Lamps) (as) missiles

HAVE (continued)

067:005 and **have** prepared for them the Chastisement
067:029 and on Him **have** we put our trust: so, soon
067:029 we **have** believed in Him, and on Him
068:017 Verily We **have** tried them as We tried the People
068:026 they said: "We **have** surely lost our way:
068:029 Verily we **have** been doing wrong!"
068:031 We **have** indeed transgressed!
068:037 Or **have** ye a Book through which ye learn-
068:038 That ye shall **have**, through it whatever ye choose?
068:039 Or **have** ye Covenants with Us on oath,
068:039 shall **have** whatever ye shall demand?
068:041 Or **have** they some "Partners" (in Godhead)?
068:049 he would indeed **have** been cast off on the
070:039 By no means! for We **have** created them out of
070:042 that Day of theirs which they **have** been promised!
071:005 He said: "O my Lord! I **have** called to my People
071:007 they **have** (only) thrust their fingers into their
071:007 "And every time I **have** called to them, that thou
071:008 "So I **have** called to them aloud;
071:009 "Further I **have** spoken to them in public
071:021 Noah said: "O my Lord! they **have** disobeyed me,
071:022 "And they **have** devised a tremendous Plot.
071:023 "And they **have** said (to each other), `Abandon not
071:024 "They **have** already misled many; and grant
072:001 'We **have** really heard a wonderful Recital!
072:002 and we **have** believed therein: we shall
072:013 to the Guidance, we **have** accepted it: and any
072:013 'And as for us, since we **have** listened to the
072:014 they **have** sought out (the path) of right conduct:
072:016 We should certainly **have** bestowed on them
072:028 "That he may know that they **have** (truly) brought
073:010 And **have** patience with what they say, and leave
073:015 We **have** sent to you, (O men!) a Messenger,
074:031 and We **have** fixed their number only as trial
074:031 And We **have** set none but angels as guardians
075:018 But when We **have** recited it, follow thou
076:004 For the Rejecters We **have** prepared Chains, Yokes,
076:023 It is We Who **have** sent down the Qur'an
076:028 and We **have** made their frame strong; but, when
077:020 **Have** We not created you from a fluid
077:025 **Have** We not made the earth (as a place)
077:039 Now, if ye **have** a trick (or plot),
077:042 And (they shall **have**) fruits,-all they desire.
078:006 **Have** We not made the earth as a wide expanse,
078:008 And (**have** We not) created you in pairs,
078:012 And (**have** We not) built over you
078:029 And all things **have** We preserved on record.
078:037 The Most Gracious: none shall **have** power to argue
078:040 Verily, We **have** warned you of a Chastisement near,-
078:040 man will see(the deeds) which his hands **have** sent forth,
079:011 "What!-when we shall **have** become rotten bones?"
080:037 will **have** enough concern (of his own) to make
082:019 shall **have** power (to do) aught for another: for the
083:002 Those who, when they **have** to receive by measure
083:003 But when they **have** to give by measure or weight
083:026 who **have** aspirations:
083:036 Will not the Unbelievers **have** been paid back
084:014 would not **have** to return (to Us)!
085:010 turn in repentance, will **have** the Chastisement
085:010 they will **have** the Chastisement of the
086:010 (Man) will **have** no power, and no helper.
090:004 Verily We **have** created Man into toil and struggle.

HAVE (continued)

090:006 "Wealth **have** I squandered in abundance!"
090:008 **Have** We not made for him a pair of eyes?-
092:019 And **have** in their minds no favour from anyone
094:001 **Have** We not expanded thee thy breast?-
095:004 We **have** indeed created man in the best of molds,
095:006 for they shall **have** a reward unfailing.
097:001 We **have** indeed revealed this (Message)
098:005 And they **have** been commanded no more than this:
098:007 Those who **have** faith and do righteous deeds,-
099:005 For that thy Lord will **have** given her inspiration.
101:009 Will **have** his home in a (bottomless) pit.
103:003 Except such as **have** Faith, and do righteous deeds,
108:001 To thee **have** We granted the Abundance.
109:004 that which ye **have** been wont to worship,

HAVING

003:135 And those who, **having** done an act of indecency
004:171 (for Exalted is He) above **having** a son.
004:176 the male **having** twice the share of the female,
006:081 without any warrant **having** been given to you?
006:100 and they falsely, **having** no knowledge, attribute
007:148 the body of a calf, (for worship): **having** lowing sound
009:031 from **having** the partners they associate (with Him).
013:025 after **having** plighted their word thereto,
016:001 and far is He above **having** the partners
016:003 above **having** the partners they ascribe to Him!
016:070 after **having** known (much): for Allah
016:094 evil (consequences) of **having** hindered (men) from
018:105 and the fact of their **having** to meet Him (in the Hereafter):
022:005 so that they know nothing after **having** known (much).
028:025 may reward thee for **having** watered (our flocks) for us."
035:024 a people, without a warner **having** lived among
091:013 And (bar her not from) **having** her drink!"

HE

002:020 **He** could take away their faculty
002:026 but **He** causes not to stray,
002:026 By it **He** causes many to stray,
002:026 and many **He** leads into the right path,
002:028 and **He** gave you life;
002:028 then will **He** cause you to die,
002:029 It is **He** who hath created for you
002:029 then **He** turned to the heaven and made them
002:029 and of all things **He** hath perfect knowledge.
002:030 **He** said: "I know what ye know not."
002:031 And **He** taught Adam the names of all things;
002:031 then **He** placed them before the angles,
002:033 **He** said: "O Adam! tell them their names."
002:033 "When **he** had told them their names,
002:034 not so Iblis, **he** refused and was haughty:
002:034 **he** was of those who reject Faith.
002:037 for **He** is Oft-Returning, Most Merciful.
002:054 Then **He** turned towards you (in forgiveness):
002:054 for **He** is Oft-returning, Most Merciful.
002:061 **He** said: "Will ye exchange the better
002:067 **He** said: "Allah save me from being
002:068 **He** said: "**He** says: The heifer should be neither too old
002:069 **He** said: "**He** says, a fawn-coloured heifer,
002:071 **He** said: "**He** says, a heifer not trained
002:080 for **He** never breaks His promise?
002:090 send it to any of His servants **He** pleases:
002:096 each one of them wishes **he** could be
002:097 for **he** brings down the (revelation)
002:105 for His special Mercy whom **He** will

HE (continued)

002:111 Paradise unless **he** be a Jew or a Christian."
002:112 **he** will get his reward with his Lord;
002:114 And who is more unjust than **he** who forbids
002:117 when **He** decreeth a matter **He** saith to it: "Be," and it
002:124 **He** pleaded: "And also (Imams) from my offspring!"
002:124 **He** said: "I will make thee an Imam
002:124 **He** answered: "But My Promise is not
002:124 which **he** fulfilled:
002:126 **He** said: "(Yea), and such as reject Faith,
002:130 and **he** will be in the Hereafter
002:131 **He** said: "I submit (my will) to the Lord
002:133 Behold, **he** said to his sons: "What
002:135 and **he** joined not gods with Allah."
002:137 and **He** is the All-Hearing, the All-Knowing.
002:138 and it is **He**. Whom we worship.
002:139 seeing that **He** is our Lord and your Lord;
002:142 **He** guideth whom **He** will to a Way
002:158 **He** Who recognizeth and knoweth.
002:163 there is no god but **He**,
002:164 kinds that **He** scatters through the earth;
002:164 and the life which **He** gives therewith
002:168 for **he** is to you an avowed enemy.
002:169 For **he** commands you what is evil and shameful,
002:173 then is **he** guiltless.
002:173 **He** hath only forbidden you dead meat,
002:180 that **he** make a bequest to parents
002:180 if **he** leave any goods,
002:184 But **he** that will give more, of his own free will,
002:185 and to glorify Him in that **He** has guide you;
002:185 **He** does not want to put you to difficulties.
002:185 (**He** wants you) to complete the prescribed period,
002:186 of every suppliant when **he** calleth on Me:
002:187 but **He** turned to you and forgave you:
002:196 but if **he** cannot afford it,
002:196 **he** must make an offering such as **he** can afford,
002:196 (**he** should) in compensation either fast, or feed the poor,
002:196 **he** should fast three days during the Hajj.
002:198 as **He** has directed you,
002:204 yet is **he** the most contentious of enemies.
002:204 and **he** calls Allah to witness
002:205 When **he** turns his back,
002:206 **"Fear Allah," he** is led by arrogance to (more) crime.
002:208 the Satan for **he** is to you an avowed enemy.
002:212 His abundance without measures on whom **He** will.
002:213 For Allah guides whom **He** will to a path
002:213 and with them **He** sent the Book in truth,
002:220 **He** could have put you into difficulties:
002:220 **He** is indeed Exalted in Power, Wise."
002:221 even though **he** allure you.
002:222 and **He** loves those who keep themselves pure
002:225 and **He** is Oft-Forgiving, Most Forbearing.
002:230 which **He** makes plain to those who know.
002:230 she married anohter husband and **he** has divorced her.
002:230 if a husband divorces his wife (irrevocably), **he** cannot,
002:231 if anyone does that, **He** wrongs his own soul.
002:231 **He** sent down to you the Book and Wisdom,
002:233 But **he** shall bear the cost of their food
002:239 in the manner **He** has taught you,
002:243 "Die." Then **He** restored them to life.
002:245 Who is **he** that will loan to Allah a beautiful loan,
002:246 **He** said: "Is it not possible if ye were
002:247 Allah granteth His authority to whom **He** pleaseth;

HE (continued)

002:247 better fitted than **he** to exercise authority,
002:247 **He** said: "Allah hath chosen him above you.
002:247 and **he** is not even gifted with wealth
002:247 They say: "How can **he** exercise authority
002:247 Allah is All-embracing, and **He** knoweth all things."
002:249 they crossed the river,-**he** and the faithful ones with him,
002:249 **he** said: "Allah will test you at the stream;
002:249 if any drinks of its water, **he** goes not with my army;
002:251 and taught him whatever (else) **He** willed.
002:253 others **He** raised to degrees (of honor);
002:253 but Allah does what **He** wills.
002:255 Allah! There is no god but **He**, the living,
002:255 aught of his knowledge except as **He** willeth.
002:255 For **He** is the Most High, the Supreme (in glory).
002:255 and **He** feeleth no fatigue in guarding
002:255 **He** knoweth what (appeareth to his creatures as)
002:255 in His presence except as **He** permitteth?
002:257 from thedepths of darkness **he** leads them forth into light.
002:258 **He** said: "I give life and death."
002:258 Thus was **he** confounded who (in arrogance)
002:258 "My Lord is **He** Who Giveth life and death."
002:259 **He** said: "How long didst thou tarry (thus)?"
002:259 **He** said: "(Perhaps) a day or part of a day."
002:259 **He** said: "Oh! how shall Allah bring it
002:259 **he** said: "I know that Allah hath power
002:259 **He** said "Nay, thou hast tarried
002:260 **He** said: "Dost thou not then believe?"
002:260 **He** said: "Take four birds;
002:260 **He** said: "Yea! but to satisfy my own heart."
002:261 and **He** knoweth all things.
002:261 manifold increase to whom **He** pleaseth:
002:263 and **he** is Most Forbearing.
002:266 Does any of you wish that **he** should have
002:266 while **he** is stricken with old age,
002:268 and **He** knoweth all things.
002:269 **He** granteth wisdom to whom **He** pleaseth;
002:269 and **he** to whom wisdom is granted receiveth
002:272 the right path whom **He** pleaseth.
002:276 for **He** loveth not any ungrateful Sinner.
002:282 and not diminish aught of what **he** owes.
002:284 **He** forgiveth whom **He** pleaseth,
002:284 and punisheth whom **He** pleaseth.
003:002 Allah! there is no god but **He**,
003:003 and **He** sent down the Torah (of Moses)
003:003 and **He** sent down the Criterion
003:003 It is **He** Who sent down to thee (step by step),
003:006 There is no god but **He**,
003:006 **He** it is Who shapes you in the wombs as **He** pleases.
003:007 **He** it is Who has sent down to thee the Book:
003:009 "Our Lord! Thou art **He** that will gather mankind
003:013 with His aid whom **He** pleaseth.
003:018 There is no god but **He** the Exalted in Power,
003:018 There is no god but **He**:
003:029 **He** knows what is in the heavens,
003:037 **He** made her grow in purity and beauty:
003:037 **He** said: "O Mary! Whence (comes) this to you?"
003:037 for Allah provides sustenance to whom **He** pleases,
003:037 **he** found her supplied with sustenance.
003:037 Every time that **he** entered her chamber to see her,
003:038 for Thou art **He** that heareth prayer!
003:039 While **he** was standing in prayer in the chamber,
003:040 "Doth Allah accomplish what **He** willeth."

HE (continued)

003:040   He said: "O my Lord! how shall I have a son,
003:041   He said: "O my Lord! Give me a Sign!"
003:046   And he shall be (of the company)
003:046   "He shall speak to the people in childhood
003:047   when He hath decreed a matter,
003:047   He said: "Even so; Allah createth what He willeth:
003:047   He but saith to it 'Be,' and it is!
003:052   unbelief on their part he said: "Who will be
003:059   He created him from dust,
003:059   then said to him: "Be": and he was.
003:062   and Allah-He is indeed the Exalted in Power,
003:067   but he was Upright.
003:067   And he joined not gods with Allah.
003:073   He granteth them to whom He pleaseth:
003:073   "And believe no one unless he follows your religion."
003:073   and He knoweth all things."
003:073   He granteth them to whom He pleaseth:
003:074   For His Mercy He specially chooseth
003:074   specially chooseth whom He pleaseth:
003:077   nor will He cleanse them (of sin):
003:079   on the contrary (he would say): "Be ye worshippers
003:080   What! would he bid you to unbelief after ye have
003:080   Nor would he instruct you to take angels
003:081   He said: "Then bear witness, and I am with you
003:085   and in the Hereafter he will be in the ranks
003:095   the sane in faith: he was not of the Pagans."
003:102   O ye who believe! fear Allah as He should be feared,
003:103   and He saved you from it.
003:103   He joined your hearts in love,
003:127   That He might cut off a fringe of the Unbelievers
003:128   whether He turn in mercy to them, or punish them;
003:129   and punisheth whom He pleaseth;
003:129   He forgiveth whom He pleaseth and punisheth
003:140   and that He may take to Himself from your ranks
003:144   not the least harm will he do to Allah;
003:144   If he died or were slain,
003:150   and He is the best of helpers.
003:151   for which He had sent no authority:
003:152   and disobeyed it after He brought you in sight
003:152   Then did He divert you from your foes
003:152   But He forgave you:
003:154   He sent down calm on a band of you
003:160   if He forsakes you, who is there, after that,
003:161   restore what he misappropriated;
003:161   he shall, on the Day of Judgment, restore
003:164   on the Believers when He sent among them
003:166   in order that He might test the Believers,
003:173   and He is the best Guardian."
003:176   Allah's Plan is that He will give them no portion
003:179   but He chooses of his Messengers whom He pleases.
003:179   until He separates what is evil from what is good.
003:183   unless he showed us a sacrifice consumed by fire
003:185   Only he who is saved far from the fire and
003:195   be he male or female: ye are members,
004:006   but if he is poor, let him have for himself
004:018   and he says, "Now have I repented indeed";
004:026   and (He doth wish to) turn to you (in Mercy):
004:038   what a dreadful intimate he is!
004:040   if there is any good (done), He doubleth it,
004:048   but He forgiveth anything else, to whom He pleaseth;
004:049   Nay-but Allah doth purify whom He pleaseth.
004:058   the teaching which He giveth you!

HE (continued)

004:058   For Allah is He Who heareth and seeth all things.
004:074   whether he is slain or gets victory, soon shall
004:080   He who obeys the Messenger, obeys Allah:
004:087   of a surety He will gather you together
004:087   Allah! There is no god but He: of a surety
004:090   He could have given them power over you,
004:092   If he belonged to a people with whom
004:092   it is ordained that he should free a believing slave.
004:092   to a people at war with you, and he was Believer,
004:095   hath He distinguished above those who sit
004:100   And abundance should he die as a refugee
004:100   He who forsakes his home in the cause of Allah,
004:108   In words that He cannot approve: and Allah
004:108   while He is with them when they plot by night.
004:110   he will find Allah Oft-Forgiving, Most Merciful.
004:111   And if any one sins, he earns it against his own soul:
004:112   He carries (on himself) (both)
004:115   We shall leave him in the path he has chosen,
004:116   but He forgiveth whom He pleaseth other sins than this:
004:118   Allah did curse him, but he said: "I will
004:123   Nor will he find, besides Allah,
004:126   and He it is that encompasseth all things.
004:130   for Allah is He that careth for all and is Wise.
004:133   for He hath power this to do.
004:133   If it were His will, He could destroy you, O mankind,
004:134   for Allah is He that heareth and seeth (all things).
004:136   the scripture which He hath sent to His Messenger and
004:136   and the scripture which He sent to those before (him).
004:140   Already has He sent you word in the Book,
004:148   for Allah is He who heareth and knoweth all things.
004:159   Day of Judgment He will be a witness against them;
004:166   Allah beareth witness that what He hath sent unto thee
004:166   He hath sent from His (Own) knowledge,
004:171   (for Exalted is He) above having a son.
004:171   and His Word, which He bestowed on Mary,
004:172   are arrogant, He will gather them all together
004:173   He will give their (due) rewards,-and more,
004:173   He will punish with a grievous chastisement:
004:175   soon will He admit them to Mercy and Grace
005:005   and in the Hereafter he will be in the ranks
005:007   and His Covenant, which He ratified with you,
005:012   resisteth faith, he hath truly wandered from
005:017   He createth what He pleaseth.
005:018   He forgiveth whom He pleaseth,
005:018   ye are but men,-of the men He hath created:
005:018   Say: "Why then doth He punish you for your sins?
005:018   and He punisheth whom He Pleaseth:
005:020   He had not given to any other among the peoples.
005:020   when He produced prophets among you, made you
005:025   He said: "O my Lord! I have power
005:030   he murdered him, and became (himself) one of the lost
005:031   "Woe is me!" said he: "Was I not even able
005:031   Then he became full of regrets.
005:032   it would be as if he slew the whole people:
005:032   It would be as if he saved the life of the whole people.
005:040   and He forgiveth whom He pleaseth:
005:040   He punisheth whom He pleaseth,
005:048   in what He hath given you: so strive
005:048   it is He that will show you the truth
005:048   He would have made you a single People, but
005:049   And this (He commands): Judge thou between them
005:051   And he amongst you that turns to them

HE (continued)

005:054 which **He** will bestow on whom **He** pleaseth.
005:054 whom **He** will love as they will love him,
005:054 and **He** knoweth all things.
005:060 **He** transformed into apes and swine, those who
005:064 **He** giveth and spendeth (of His Bounty)
005:064 (of His Bounty) as **He** pleaseth.
005:076 But Allah,-**He** it is that heareth
005:089 but **He** will call you to account
005:094 that **He** may test who feareth Him unseen:
005:095 that **he** may taste of the penalty of his deed.
005:095 domestic animal equivalent to the one **he** killed.
005:105 it is **He** that will inform you of all that ye do.
005:116 **He** will say: "Glory to Thee! never could
005:120 and it is **He** who hath power over all things.
006:002 **He** it is Who created you from clay, and then
006:003 And **He** is Allah in the heavens and on earth.
006:003 **He** knoweth what ye hide, and what ye reveal,
006:003 and **He** knoweth the (recompense) which
006:012 Say: "To Allah. **He** hath inscribed for Himself
006:012 That **He** will gather you together for
006:013 For **He** is the One Who heareth
006:014 And **He** is that feedeth but is not fed."
006:017 if **He** touch thee with happiness, **He** hath power over all
006:017 touch thee with affliction, none can remove it but **He**;
006:018 "**He** is Irresistibly Supreme
006:018 and **He** is the Wise, acquainted with all things."
006:019 Say: "But in truth **He** is the One God.
006:021 Who doth more wrong than **he** who inventeth
006:030 **He** will say: "Is not this the truth?" They will
006:030 **He** will say: "Taste ye then the Chastisement,
006:035 **He** could gather them together unto true guidance:
006:039 whom Allah willeth, **He** leaveth to wander:
006:039 whom **He** willeth, **He** placeth on the Way that is Straight.
006:041 **He** would remove (the distress) which occasioned
006:054 lo! **He** is Oft-Forgiving, Most Merciful.
006:057 **He** declares the Truth, and **He** is the best of Judges."
006:059 **He** knoweth whatever there is on the earth and in the
006:059 the treasures that none knoweth but **He**.
006:060 by day doth **He** raise you up again; that a term
006:060 It is **He** Who doth take your souls by night,
006:060 then will **He** show you the truth of all that ye did.
006:061 and **He** sets guardians over you.
006:061 **He** is the Irresistible, Supreme over
006:062 and **He** is the Swiftest in taking account.
006:063 'If **He** only delivers us from these (dangers),
006:065 Say: "**He** hath power to send calamities
006:073 For **He** is the Wise, well acquainted
006:073 **He** knoweth the Unseen as well
006:073 the day **He** saith, "Be," Behold! it is.
006:073 It is **He** Who created the heavens and
006:075 that **he** might have certitude.
006:076 **he** saw a star: **he** said: "This is my Lord."
006:076 But when it set, **he** said: "I love not
006:077 When **he** saw the moon rising in splendor,
006:077 **He** said: "This is my Lord."
006:077 But when the moon set, **he** said: "Unless my Lord guide
006:078 But when the sun set, **he** said: "O my people!
006:078 When **he** saw the sun rising (in splendor),
006:078 **he** said: "This is my Lord; this is
006:080 about Allah, when **He** (Himself) hath guided me?
006:080 **He** said: "(Come) ye to dispute with me, about
006:088 **He** giveth that guidance to whom **He** pleaseth,

HE (continued)

006:093 when **he** hath received none, or (again)
006:095 **He** causeth the living to issue from the dead.
006:095 And **He** is the one to cause the dead
006:096 **He** makes the night for rest and tranquillity,
006:096 **He** it is that cleaveth the daybreak
006:097 It is **He** Who maketh the stars
006:098 It is **He** who hath produced you
006:099 It is **He** who sendeth down
006:100 (for **He** is) above what they attribute to Him!
006:101 **He** created all things, and **He** hath full knowledge
006:101 how can **He** have a son when **He** hath no consort?
006:102 and **He** hath power to dispose of all affairs.
006:102 There is no god but **He**, the Creator of all things:
006:103 But His grasp is over all vision; **He** is subtle well-aware.
006:106 there is no god but **He**: and turn
006:114 When **He** it is Who hath sent
006:115 for **He** is the one Who heareth and knoweth all.
006:117 **He** knoweth best those who are rightly guided.
006:119 when **He** hath explained to you in detail
006:122 Can **he** who was dead, to whom We gave life,
006:122 from which **he** can never come out?
006:122 and a Light whereby **he** can walk amongst men,
006:125 those whom **He** willeth to leave straying,
006:125 **He** maketh their breast close and constricted,
006:125 **He** openeth their breast to Islam; those whom
006:127 **He** will be their Friend, because they
006:128 **He** will say: "The Fire be your dwelling-place:
006:128 On the day when **He** will gather them
006:133 if it were His Will, **He** could destroy you,
006:133 even as **He** raised you up
006:133 whom **He** will as your successors,
006:138 soon will **He** requite them for what they forged.
006:139 **He** will soon punish them: for **He** is full of Wisdom
006:141 It is **He** who produceth gardens, with
006:142 for **he** is to you an avowed enemy.
006:143 say, hath **He** forbidden the two males, or the
006:144 say, hath **He** forbidden the two males, or the
006:149 **He** could indeed have guided you all."
006:151 thus doth **He** command you, that ye may learn wisdom.
006:152 thus doth **He** command you, that ye may remember.
006:152 until **he** attain the age of full strength; give
006:153 thus doth **He** command you, that ye may be righteous.
006:159 **He** will in the end tell them the truth
006:160 **he** that doeth evil shall only be recompensed
006:160 **He** that doeth good shall have ten times as much
006:161 and **he** (certainly) joined not gods with Allah."
006:163 No partner hath **He**: this am I commanded, and
006:164 **He** will tell you the truth of things
006:164 When **He** is the Cherisher of all
006:165 **He** hath raised you in ranks, some above
006:165 It is **He** Who hath made you the inheritors of the earth:
006:165 that **He** may try you in the gifts **He** hath given you:
006:165 yet **He** is indeed Oft-Forgiving, Most Merciful.
007:011 not so Iblis; **he** refused to be of those who prostrate.
007:012 **He** said: "I am better than **he**: thou didst
007:014 **He** said: "Give me respite till the day
007:016 **He** said: "Because Thou hast thrown me
007:020 **he** said: "Your Lord only forbade you this tree,
007:021 And **he** swore to them both, that **he** was their sincere
007:022 So by deceit **he** brought about their fall: when
007:025 **He** said: "Therein shall ye live, and therein
007:027 for **he** and his tribe see you from a position where ye

HE (continued)

007:027 same manner as **he** got your parents out of the Garden,
007:029 such as **He** created you in the beginning,
007:030 Some **He** hath guided: others have deserved the loss
007:032 (which **He** hath provided) for sustenance?
007:032 which **He** hath produced for His servants,
007:033 for which **He** hath given no authority; and saying
007:038 **He** will say: "Doubled for all": but this
007:038 **He** will say: "Enter ye in the company of the
007:054 then **He** settled Himself on the Throne:
007:054 **He** draweth the night as a veil O'er the day,
007:057 It is **He** Who sendeth the Winds
007:059 **He** said: "O my people! worship Allah!
007:061 **He** said: "O my people! there is no error in me:
007:065 **He** said: "O my people! worship Allah! ye have
007:067 **He** said: "O my people! there is no folly in me"
007:069 **He** made you inheritors after the people of Noah,
007:071 **He** said: "Punishment and wrath have already
007:073 **he** said: "O my people! worship Allah; ye have
007:074 "And remember how **He** made you inheritors
007:080 We also (sent) Lut: **he** said to his people: "Do
007:085 **he** said: "O my people! worship Allah; ye have
007:086 and **He** gave you increase.
007:087 for **He** is the best to decide."
007:088 **He** said: "What! even though we do detest (them)?
007:108 And **he** drew out his hand, and behold!
007:114 **He** said: "Yea, (and more),-for ye shall
007:127 **He** said: "Their male children will we slay;
007:128 such of His servants as **He** pleaseth; and the
007:129 that so **He** may see how ye act."
007:129 **He** said: "It may be that your Lord will destroy
007:138 **He** said: "Surely ye are a people without knowledge."
007:140 when it is **He** who hath endowed you with
007:140 **He** said: "Shall I seek for you a god
007:142 his brother Aaron (before **he** went up): "Act for me
007:143 **He** said: "O my Lord! show (Thyself) to me,
007:143 When **he** recovered his senses **he** said: "Glory be
007:143 **He** made it as dust and Moses fell down in a swoon.
007:150 angry and grieved, **he** said: "Evil it is that ye
007:150 **He** put down the Tablets, seized his brother
007:154 anger of Moses was appeased, **he** took up the tablets:
007:155 **he** prayed: "O my Lord! if it had been Thy will
007:156 **He** said: "I afflict My punishment on whom
007:157 **He** releases them from their heavy burdens and from
007:157 **he** allows them as lawful what is
007:157 for **he** commands them what is just and forbids them
007:158 there is no god but **He**:
007:158 it is **He** that giveth both life and death.
007:167 but **He** is also Oft-Forgiving, Most Merciful.
007:167 that **He** would send against them, to the
007:175 so Satan followed him up, and **he** went astray.
007:175 to whom We sent Our Signs, but **he** passed them by:
007:176 or if you leave him alone, **he** (still) lolls out his tongue.
007:176 if you attack him, **he** lolls out his tongue,
007:176 but **he** inclined to the earth, and followed his own vain
007:178 Whom Allah doth guide,-**he** is on the right path:
007:178 whom **He** rejects from His guidance. Such are the persons
007:184 is not seized with madness: **he** is but a perspicuous warner.
007:186 **He** will leave them in their trespasses, wandering
007:187 none but **He** can reveal as to
007:189 in order that **he** might dwell with her
007:189 It is **He** Who created you
007:190 But when **He** giveth them a goodly child, they

HE (continued)

007:196 and **He** will befriend the righteous.
007:200 for **he** heareth and knoweth (all things).
008:008 That **He** might establish Truth and prove
008:009 And **He** answered you: "I will assist
008:011 Remember **He** covered you with drowsiness, to give
008:011 and **He** caused rain to descend on you from heaven,
008:016 **he** draws on himself the wrath of Allah, and his abode
008:017 **He** Who heareth and knoweth (all things).
008:017 in order that **He** might confer on the Believers
008:018 **He** Who makes feeble the Plans and stratagems
008:023 if **He** had made them listen, they would
008:023 **He** would indeed have made them listen:
008:024 and that it is **He** to Whom ye shall
008:024 and His Messenger, when **He** calleth you to that
008:026 and kidnap you; but **He** provided a safe asylum
008:029 **He** will grant you a Criterion (to judge between right and
008:033 nor was **He** going to send it whilst they
008:042 is **He** Who heareth and knoweth (all things).
008:043 but Allah saved (you): for **He** knoweth well the
008:043 if **He** had shown them to thee as many, ye would
008:044 **He** showed them to you as few in your eyes,
008:044 and **He** made you appear as contemptible in
008:048 **he** turned on his heels, and said: "Lo! I am clear of you;
008:053 the Grace which **He** hath bestowed on a people
008:053 and verily Allah is **He** Who heareth and
008:061 and trust in Allah: for **He** is the One
008:062 **He** it is that hath strengthened thee with His
008:063 And (moreover) **He** hath put affection
008:063 for **He** is Exalted in might, Wise.
008:066 for **He** knoweth that there is a weak spot in you:
008:067 of war until **he** hath thoroughly subdued the land.
008:067 not fitting for a Prophet tthat **he** should have prisoners
008:070 and **He** will forgive you: for Allah
008:070 **He** will give you something better than what
008:071 And Allah is **He** who hath (full) knowledge and wisdom.
008:071 and so hath **He** given (thee) power over them.
009:006 so that **he** may hear the Word of Allah; and then
009:006 and then escort him to where **he** can be secure,
009:015 For Allah will turn (in mercy) to whom **He** will:
009:026 thus doth **He** reward those without Faith.
009:026 forces which ye saw not: **He** punished the Unbelievers:
009:027 turn (in mercy) to whom **He** will: for Allah
009:028 enrich you, if **He** wills, out of His bounty,
009:031 Praise and glory to Him: (far is **He**) from having
009:031 to worship but One God: there is no god but **He**.
009:033 It is **He** who hath sent His Messenger
009:036 **He** created the heavens and the earth; of them
009:039 **He** will punish you with a grievous penalty,
009:040 and **he** said to his companion, "Have no fear,
009:046 so **He** made them lag behind and they were told,
009:051 **He** is our Protector": and on Allah let the
009:061 men who molest the Prophet and say, "**He** is (all) ear."
009:061 Say, "**He** listens to what is best for you;
009:061 **he** believes in Allah, has faith in the Believers,
009:067 so **He** hath forgotten them.
009:075 a Covenant with Allah, that if **He** bestowed on them
009:076 But when **He** did bestow of His bounty, they became
009:077 So **He** hath put as a consequence hypocrisy into
009:094 **He** show you the truth of all that ye did."
009:098 for Allah is **He** that heareth
009:100 hath **He** prepared Gardens under which rivers flow,
009:104 and that Allah is verily **He**, the Oft-Returning,

HE (continued)

009:105   then will **He** show you the truth of all that ye did."
009:106   whether **He** will punish them, or turn in mercy
009:109   and His good pleasure?-or **he** that layeth his
009:109   Which then is best?-**he** that layeth his foundation
009:114   it became clear to him that **he** was an enemy to Allah,
009:114   forgiveness only because a promise **he** had made to him.
009:114   **he** dissociated himself from him:
009:115   after **He** hath Guided them until **He** makes clear
009:116   **He** giveth life and **He** taketh it.
009:117   swerved (from duty); but **He** turned to them (also):
009:117   for **He** is unto them Most Kind, Most Merciful.
009:118   (**He** turned in mercy also) to the three who were
009:118   Then **He** turned to them, that they
009:128   should suffer, ardently anxious is **he** over you:
009:128   to the Believers is **he** most kind and merciful.
009:129   **He** the Lord of the Throne Supreme!"
009:129   there is no god but **He**: On him is my trust,-
010:002   That **he** should warn mankind (of their danger),
010:003   in six Days, then **He** established Himself on the
010:004   that **He** may reward with justice those who
010:004   It is **He** Who beginneth the process of Creation,
010:005   It is **He** Who made the sun to be a shining glory
010:005   (Thus) doth **He** explain His Signs in detail,
010:012   trouble toucheth a man **he** crieth unto Us (in all postures)-
010:012   **he** passeth on his way as if **he** had never cried to Us
010:016   nor should **He** have made it known to you.
010:018   and far is **He** above the partners
010:018   of something **He** knows not, in the
010:022   **He** it is Who enableth you to traverse through
010:023   But when **He** delivereth them, behold! they
010:025   **He** doth guide whom **He** pleaseth to a way
010:035   Is then **He** Who gives guidance to Truth more worthy
010:035   or **he** who finds not guidance (himself) unless **he** is
010:038   Or do they say, "**He** forged it"? Say: "Bring
010:045   And on the day when **He** will gather them together:
010:056   Is it **He** who giveth life and who taketh it, and to
010:065   it is **He** Who heareth and knoweth (all things).
010:067   **He** it is that hath made you the Night
010:068   Glory be to Him! **He** is Self-Sufficient! His are
010:071   Behold! **he** said to his People: "O my People,
010:090   **he** said: "I believe that there is no god except Him Whom
010:100   and **He** will place abomination on those
010:107   whomsoever of His servants **He** pleaseth.
010:107   if **He** do design some benefit for thee, there is none can
010:107   And **He** is the Oft-Forgiving, Most Merciful.
010:107   touch thee with hurt, here is none can remove it but **He**:
010:107   **He** causeth it to reach whomsoever
010:109   for **He** is the Best to decide.
011:003   that **He** may grant you enjoyment,
011:004   and **He** hath power over all things."
011:005   for **He** knoweth well the (innermost secrets) of the
011:005   **He** knoweth what they conceal, and what they reveal:
011:006   **He** knoweth its resting place and its
011:007   **He** it is Who created the heavens and the earth
011:007   that **He** might try you, which of you
011:009   behold! **he** is in despair and (falls inot) ingratitude,
011:010   behold! **he** falls into exultation and pride.
011:010   touched him, **he** is sure to say, "All evil has
011:013   Or they may say, "**He** forged it." Say, "Bring ye
011:014   the knowledge of Allah, and that there is no god but **He**!
011:028   from my Lord and that **He** hath sent Mercy unto me
011:028   **He** said: "O my people! see ye if (it be that)

HE (continued)

011:033   on you if **He** wills-and then, ye will
011:033   **He** said: "Truly, Allah will bring it on you
011:034   **He** is your Lord! and to Him will ye return!
011:035   Or do they say, "**He** has forged it?" Say:
011:038   **He** said: "If ye ridicule us now, we (in our turn)
011:038   Forthwith **he** starts constructing the Ark:
011:041   So **he** said: "Embark ye on the Ark, in the
011:043   any but those on whom **He** hath mercy!"-
011:046   **He** said: "O Noah! **he** is not of thy family:
011:050   **He** said: "O my people! worship Allah! ye have
011:052   **He** will send you the skies pouring abuntdant rain,
011:054   **He** said: "I call Allah to witness,
011:056   a moving creature, but **He** hath grasp of
011:061   **He** said: "O my people! worship Allah: ye have
011:061   It is **He** Who hath produced you from the earth
011:063   and **He** hath sent Mercy unto me from Himself,-
011:063   **He** said: "O my people! Do ye see?-If I have
011:065   So **he** said: "Enjoy yourselves in your homes
011:066   For thy Lord-**He** is the Strong One, and the Mighty.
011:069   They said, "Peace!" **He** answered, "Peace!"
011:070   But when **he** saw their hands not reaching towards
011:070   **he** felt some mistrust of them, and conceived
011:073   For **He** is indeed worthy of all praise,
011:074   **he** began to plead with Us for Lut's people.
011:077   **he** was grieved on their account and felt himself
011:077   **He** said: "This is a distressful day."
011:078   **He** said: "O my people! here are my daughters:
011:080   **He** said: "Would that I had power to suppress you
011:084   **he** said: "O my people! worship Allah: ye have
011:088   **He** said: "O my people! see ye whether I have
011:088   and **He** hath given me sustenance (pure and)
011:092   **He** said: "O my people! is then my family of more
011:098   **He** will go before his people on the
011:102   when **He** chastises communities in the midst of
011:107   Accomplisher of what **He** planneth.
011:111   For **He** knoweth well all that they do.
011:112   (from the Path): for **He** seeth well all that ye do.
011:118   **He** could have made mankind one People: but they
011:119   and for this did **He** create them: and the Word
012:006   of Jacob-even as **He** perfected it to thy fathers
012:010   **he** will be picked up by some caravan of travellers."
012:018   **He** said: "Nay, but your minds have made up
012:019   and **he** let down his bucket (into the well).
012:019   **He** said: "Ah there! Good news
012:021   may be **he** will bring us much good,
012:023   **He** made my sojourn agreeable! Truly
012:023   But she, in whose house **he** was, sought to
012:023   **He** said: "Allah forbid! truly (thy husband) is my
012:024   for **he** was one of Our servants chosen.
012:024   but that **he** saw the evidence of his Lord:
012:024   and **he** would have desired her,
012:026   **He** said: "It was she that sought to seduce me-
012:026   her tale true, and **he** is a liar!
012:027   she the liar, and **he** is telling the truth!"
012:028   So when **he** saw his shirt,-that it
012:030   her slave truly hath **he** inspired her with violent
012:032   And now, if **he** doth not my bidding,
012:032   **he** shall certainly be cast into prison,
012:032   from his (true) self but **he** did firmly save
012:033   **He** said: "O my Lord! the prison is dearer to my
012:034   verily **He** heareth and knoweth (all things).
012:037   **He** said: "Before any food comes (in due course)

HE (continued)

012:040	**He** hath commanded that ye worship none but Him:
012:041	As to one of you, **he** will pour out the wine
012:041	as for the other, **he** will hang from the cross,
012:042	to that one whom **he** considered about to be saved,
012:042	**he** said: "Mention me to thy lord." But Satan
012:046	"O Joseph!" (**he** said), "O man of truth! Expound
012:051	to seduce him **he** is indeed of those who are (ever) true
012:052	"This (say I), in order that **he** may know
012:054	Therefore when **he** had spoken to him,
012:054	**he** said: "Be assured this day, thou art
012:056	to take possession therein as, when, or where **he** pleased.
012:058	they entered his presence, and **he** knew them,
012:059	for them, **he** said: "Bring unto me a brother
012:059	And when **he** had furnished them forth
012:064	and **He** is the Most Merciful of those
012:064	**He** said: "Shall I trust you with him with any
012:066	**he** said: "Over all that we say, be Allah the Witness
012:067	Further **he** said; "O my sons! enter not
012:068	For **he** was, by Our instruction, full of
012:069	**He** said (to him): "Behold! I am thy (own) brother;
012:069	Joseph's presence, **he** received his (full) brother
012:070	(suitable) for them, **he** put the drinking cup into
012:070	At length when **he** had furnished them forth
012:075	They said: "The penalty should be that **he** in whose
012:076	**He** could not take his brother by the law
012:076	before (**he** came to) the baggage
012:076	So **he** began (the search) with their baggage,
012:076	at length **He** brought it out of
012:077	They said: "If **he** steals, there was a brother
012:077	**He** (simply) said (to himself): "Ye are
012:078	behold! **he** has a father, aged and venerable,
012:079	**He** said: "Allah forbid that we take other than
012:080	and **He** is the best to judge.
012:083	For **He** is indeed full of knowledge and wisdom."
012:084	and **he** was suppressed with silent sorrow.
012:084	And **he** turned away from them, and said: "How great
012:086	**He** said: "I only complain of my distraction
012:089	**He** said: "Know ye how ye dealt with Joseph,
012:090	behold, **he** that is righteous and patient,-
012:090	**He** said: "I am Joseph, and this is my brother:
012:092	and **He** is the Most Merciful of those
012:092	**He** said: "This day let no reproach be (cast)
012:093	over the face of my father, **he** will come to see (clearly).
012:096	his face, and **he** forthwith regained clear sight.
012:096	**He** said: "Did I not say to you,
012:096	news came, **he** cast (the shirt) over his face,
012:098	**He** said: "Soon will I ask my Lord for forgiveness
012:098	for **He** is indeed Oft-Forgiving, Merciful."
012:099	the presence of Joseph, **he** provided a home for
012:100	**He** said: "O my father! this is the fulfillment of my
012:100	Verily my Lord is gracious to whom **He** wills for verily
012:100	for verily **He** is full of knowledge and wisdom.
012:100	**He** was indeed good to me when **He** took me out of
012:100	And **he** raised his parents high on the throne
013:002	then **He** established Himself on the Throne.
013:002	Allah is **He** Who raised the heavens without any
013:002	**He** doth regulate all affairs, explaining the
013:002	**He** has subjected the sun and the moon! each one
013:003	and fruit of every kind **He** made in pairs,
013:003	And it is **He** Who spread out the earth, and set
013:003	**He** draweth the Night as a veil o'er the Day.
013:009	**He** is the Great, the Most High.

HE (continued)

013:009	**He** knoweth the Unseen and that which is open:
013:010	it openly; whether **he** lie hid by night
013:012	it is **He** Who doth raise up the clouds,
013:012	It is **He** Who doth show you the lightning, by way
013:013	**He** flingeth the loud-voiced thunder-bolts,
013:013	and therewith **He** striketh whomsoever **He** will.
013:013	about Allah, **He** is Mighty in Power.
013:016	of all things: **He** is the One, the Supreme
013:016	created (anything) as **He** has created, so that
013:017	**He** sends down water from the skies, and the
013:026	sustenance (which **He** giveth) to whom so **He** pleaseth.
013:027	"Truly Allah leaveth, to stray, whom **He** will;
013:027	but **He** guideth to Himself those who turn to Him in
013:030	Say: "**He** is my Lord! There is no god but **He**!
013:031	(so) willed, **He** could have guided all mankind
013:033	inform Him of something **He** knoweth not on earth,
013:033	Is then **He** Who standeth over every soul
013:039	Allah doth bolt out or comfirm what **He** pleaseth:
013:041	and **He** is swift in calling to account.
013:042	**He** knoweth the doings of every soul: and soon
014:004	and guides whom **He** pleases and **He** is Exalted in
014:004	So Allah leads to astray those whom **He** pleases
014:006	to you when **He** delivered you from the people
014:010	It is **He** Who invites you, in order
014:010	in order that **He** may forgive you your sins
014:011	to such of His servants as **He** pleases.
014:012	Indeed **He** has guided us to the Ways
014:016	and **he** is given, for drink, boiling fetid water.
014:017	In gulps will **he** sip it,
014:017	but never well **he** be near swallowing it down his throat;
014:017	will come to him from every quarter, yet will **he** not die;
014:019	If **He** so will, **He** can remove you
014:027	Allah doeth what **He** willeth.
014:032	it is **He** Who hath made the ships subject to you,
014:032	and the rivers (also) hath **He** made subject to you.
014:033	And **He** hath made subject to you the sun
014:033	hath **He** (also) made subject you.
014:034	And **He** giveth you of all that ye ask for.
014:036	**he** then who follows my (ways) is of me,
014:036	and **he** that disobeys me,-but thou
014:039	for truly my Lord is **He**, the Hearer of Prayer!
014:042	**He** but giveth them respite against a Day when
014:052	and may know that **He** is One God: let men
015:025	for **He** is Perfect in Wisdom and Knowledge.
015:031	Not so Iblis: **he** refused to be among those
015:052	and said, "Peace!" **He** said, "We feel
015:054	**He** said: "Do ye give me such glad tidings
015:056	**He** said: "And who despairs of the mercy
015:062	**He** said: "Ye appear to be uncommon folk."
015:071	**He** said: "There are my daughters (to marry),
015:089	And say: "I am indeed **he** that warneth openly
016:001	and far is **He** above having the partners
016:002	to such of His servants as **He** pleaseth, (saying):
016:002	**He** doth send down His angels with inspiration
016:003	and the earth with truth far is **He** above having
016:003	**He** has created the heavens and the earth
016:004	**He** has created man from a sperm-drop and behold
016:005	And cattle **He** has created for you (men): from them
016:008	an adornment; and **He** has created (other) things
016:008	And (**He** has created) horses, mules, and donkeys,
016:009	**He** could have guided all of you.
016:010	It is **He** Who sends down rain from the sky: from it

HE (continued)

016:011 With it **He** produces for you corn, olives, date-
016:012 **He** has made subject to you the Night and the Day;
016:013 on this earth which **He** has multiplied in varying colours
016:014 It is **He** Who has made the sea subject, that ye
016:015 And **He** has set up on the earth mountains standing
016:017 Is then **He** Who creates like one that creates not?
016:023 verily **He** loveth not the arrogant.
016:027 **He** will cover them with shame, and say:
016:037 yet Allah guideth not such as **He** leaves to stray,
016:039 **He** may manifest to them the truth of that
016:046 Or that **He** may not call them to account in the
016:047 Or that **He** may not call them to account by a
016:051 for **He** is just One God: then fear Me
016:054 Yet, when **He** removes the distress from you,
016:058 his face darkens, and **he** is filled with
016:059 because of the bad news **he** has had!
016:059 Shall **he** retain it on (sufferance and) Contempt,
016:059 With shame does **he** hide himself from his people,
016:060 for **He** is the Exalted in Power, Full of Wisdom.
016:061 but **He** gives them respite for a stated Term:
016:061 their wrong-doing, **He** would not leave, on the
016:063 **he** is also their patron to-day, so but they shall have
016:075 favours from Ourselves, and **he** spends thereof
016:075 the dominion of another; **he** has no power of any
016:076 whichever way **he** directs him, **he** brings no good:
016:076 a wearisome burden is **he** to his master;
016:078 It is **He** Who brought you forth from the wombs
016:078 when ye knew nothing; and **He** gave you hearing
016:081 Thus does **He** complete his favours on you,
016:081 out of the things **He** created, some things
016:081 **He** made you garments to protect you
016:081 of the hills **He** made some for your shelter;
016:090 **He** instructs you, that ye may receive admonition.
016:090 and **He** forbids all indecent deeds, and evil and rebellion:
016:092 and on the Day of Judgment **He** will certainly
016:093 and **He** guides whom **He** pleases: but ye
016:093 If Allah so willed, **He** could make you all one People:
016:093 but **He** leaves straying whom **He** pleases,
016:099 No authority has **he** over those who believe
016:101 **He** reveals (in stages),-they say, "Thou art
016:114 if it is **He** whom ye serve.
016:115 **He** has only forbidden you dead meat, and blood,
016:120 in faith, and **he** joined not gods with Allah.
016:121 **He** showed his gratitude for the favours of Allah,
016:122 and **he** will be, in the Hereafter, in the ranks
016:123 in Faith, and **he** joined not gods with Allah."
017:001 for **He** is the One Who heareth
017:003 Verily **he** was a devotee most grateful.
017:011 as **he** prays for good for man is given to haste.
017:013 which **he** will see spread open.
017:025 of righteousness, verily **He** is Most Forgiving
017:030 provide sustenance in abundance for whom **He** pleaseth,
017:030 and **He** straiten it for **He** doth know and regard all His
017:033 for **he** is helped (by the Law).
017:034 until **he** attains the age of full strength;
017:043 Glory to Him! **He** is high above all that they say!
017:044 Verily **He** is Oft-Forbearing, Most Forgiving!
017:051 Say: "**He** Who created you first!"
017:052 "It will be on a Day when **He** will call you,
017:054 if **He** please, **He** granteth you mercy,
017:054 or if **He** please, punishment: We have not
017:061 **he** said, "Shall I prostrate to one whom Thou

HE (continued)

017:062 **He** said, "Seest Thou? This is the one whom
017:066 For **He** is unto you Most Merciful.
017:066 Your Lord is **He** that maketh the Ship go smoothly
017:067 But when **He** brings you back safe to land, ye turn
017:068 or that **He** will not send against you a violent
017:068 Do ye then feel secure that **He** will not cause
017:069 Or do ye feel secure that **He** will not send
017:083 when evil seizes him **he** gives himself up to despair!
017:083 **he** turns away and becomes remote on his side
017:096 between me and you: for **He** is well acquainted
017:096 and **He** sees (all things)."
017:097 but **he** whom **He** leaves astray-for such wilt thou
017:097 It is **he** whom Allah guides, that is
017:099 Only **He** has decreed a term
017:101 when **he** came to them, Pharaoh said
017:103 So **he** resolved to remove them from the
017:111 nor (needs) **He** any to protect
018:002 and that **He** may give Glad Tidings to the
018:002 (**He** hath made it) Straight (and Clear) in order
018:002 in order that **He** may warn (the godless) of a
018:004 Further, that **He** may warn those (also) who say,
018:017 but **he** whom Allah leaves to stray,-for him
018:017 **he** whom Allah guides is rightly guided;
018:026 nor does **He** share His Command with any
018:026 how clearly **He** sees, how finely **He** hears (everything)!
018:034 **he** said to his companion, in the course of a mutual
018:035 **he** said, "I deem not that this will ever perish,"
018:035 **He** went into his garden while **he** wronged himself:
018:040 and that **He** will send on thy garden thunderbolts
018:042 his hands over what **he** had spent on his property,
018:042 and **he** could only say, "Woe is me! Would I had
018:042 and **he** remained twisting and turning his hands
018:043 Nor had **he** numbers to help him against Allah,
018:043 against Allah, nor was **he** able to deliver himself.
018:044 **He** is the Best to reward, and the Best
018:050 **He** was one of the Jinns, and **he** broke the Command of
018:052 On the Day **He** will say, "Call on
018:058 If **He** were to call them (at once) to account for what they
018:058 then surely **He** would have hastened their Punishment:
018:063 **He** replied: "Sawest thou (what happened) when we
018:071 when they were in the boat, **he** scuttled it.
018:072 **He** answered: "Did I not tell thee that thou canst
018:074 when they met a young boy, **he** slew him.
018:075 **He** answered: "Did I not tell thee that thou canst
018:077 wall on the point of falling down, but **he** set it up straight.
018:078 **He** answered: "This is the parting between me and thee:
018:080 and we feared that **he** would grieve them by
018:085 One (such) way **he** followed,
018:086 the sun, **he** found it set in a spring of murky water:
018:086 Until, when **he** reached the setting of the sun,
018:086 near it **he** found a People: We said:
018:087 **He** said: "Whoever doth wrong, him shall we punish;
018:087 and **He** will punish him with a punishment unheard-of
018:087 then shall **he** be sent back to his Lord;
018:088 works righteousness-**he** shall have a goodly reward,
018:089 Then followed **he** (another) way,
018:090 Until, when **he** came to the rising of the sun,
018:090 the sun, **he** found it rising on a people for whom
018:091 (**He** left them) as they were: We completely
018:092 Then followed **he** (another) way,
018:093 **he** found, beneath them, a people who scarcely
018:093 Until, when **he** reached (a tract) between two mountains,

HE (continued)

018:095 **He** said: "(The power) in which my Lord has
018:096 **he** said, "Blow (with your bellows)"
018:096 **he** said: "Bring me, that I may pour over it, molten lead."
018:096 then, when **he** had made it (red) as fire,
018:096 At length, when **he** had filled up the space bewteen the o
018:098 **He** said: "This is a mercy from my Lord: but when
018:098 my Lord comes to pass, **He** will make it into dust;
019:003 Behold! **he** cried to his Lord in secret.
019:008 **He** said: "O my Lord! how shall I have a son,
019:009 **He** said: "So (it will be): thy Lord saith,
019:011 from his chamber: **he** told them by signs to
019:013 as from Us, and purity: **he** was devout,
019:014 and **he** was not overbearing or rebellious.
019:015 Peace on him the day **he** was born, the day that **he** dies,
019:015 and the day that **he** will be raised up to life (again)!
019:017 and **he** appeared before her as a man in all respects.
019:019 **He** said: "Nay, I am only a messenger from thy Lord,
019:021 **He** said: "So (it will be): thy Lord saith,
019:030 **He** said: "I am indeed a servant of Allah:
019:030 **He** hath given me revelation and made me a prophet:
019:031 "And **He** hath made me Blessed wheresoever I be,
019:032 "(**He**) hath made me kind to my mother, and not
019:035 (the majesty of) Allah that **He** should beget
019:035 When **He** determines a matter, **He** only says to it, "Be,"
019:041 (the story of) Abraham: **he** was a man of Truth,
019:042 Behold, **he** said to his father: "O my father!
019:047 for **He** is to me Most Gracious.
019:049 When **he** had turned away from them and from
019:051 (the story of) Moses: for **he** was specially chosen.
019:051 And **He** was a messenger and a prophet.
019:054 **he** was (strictly) true to what **he** promised,
019:054 and **he** was a messenger (and) a prophet.
019:055 Prayer and Zakat and **he** was most acceptable in
019:055 **He** used to enjoin on his people Prayer and Zakat
019:056 **he** was a man of truth (and sincerity),
019:065 of the same Name as **He**?
019:078 Has **he** penetrated to the Unseen,
019:078 or has **he** taken a promise with the Most Gracious?
019:079 Nay! We shall record what **he** says, and We
019:080 To Us shall return all that **he** talks of,
019:080 and **he** shall appear before Us bare and alone.
019:092 that **He** should beget a son.
019:094 **He** does take and account of them (all), and hath
020:007 for verily **He** knoweth what secret and what is yet more
020:008 Allah! there is no god but **He**!
020:010 Behold, **he** saw a fire: so **he** said to his family, "Tarry ye;
020:011 But when **he** came to the fire, **he** was called "O Moses!
020:018 **He** said, "It is my rod: on it I lean; with it
020:020 **He** threw it, and behold! it was a snake,
020:024 for **he** had indeed transgressed all bounds."
020:039 and **he** will be taken up by one who is an enemy
020:043 for **he** has indeed transgressed all bounds;
020:044 perchance **he** may take warning or fear (Allah)."
020:045 or lest **he** transgress all bounds."
020:045 "Our Lord! we fear lest **He** hasten with insolence
020:046 **He** said: "Fear not: for I am with you: I hear
020:050 **He** said: "Our Lord is **He** Who gave to each (created)
020:052 **He** replied: "The knowledge of that is with
020:053 "**He** Who has made for you the earth
020:056 but **he** did reject and refuse.
020:057 **He** said: "Hast thou come to drive us out
020:060 So Pharaoh withdrew: **he** concerted his plan,

HE (continued)

020:061 lest **He** destroy you (at once) utterly by
020:064 **he** wins (all along) to-day who gains the upper hand."
020:066 **He** said, "Nay, throw ye first!" Then behold
020:073 may **He** forgive us our faults, and the
020:074 Verily **he** who comes to his Lord as a sinner (at Judgment)
020:074 for him is Hell: therein shall **he** neither die or live.
020:082 **He** that forgives again and again, to those
020:084 **He** replied: "Behold, they are close on my footsteps:
020:086 **He** said: "O my people! did not your Lord make a
020:088 "Then **he** brought out (of the fire) before the
020:096 **He** replied: "I saw what they saw not: so I
020:098 all things **He** comprehends in His Knowledge.
020:098 there is no god but **He**:
020:106 "**He** will leave them as plains smooth and level;
020:110 **He** knows what is before or after or behind them:
020:112 But **he** who works deeds of righteousness, and has
020:115 taken the covenant of Adam, but **he** forgot: and We
020:116 but not Iblis: **he** refused.
020:120 **he** said, "O Adam! shall I lead thee to the Tree
020:122 **He** turned to him, and gave him guidance.
020:123 **He** said: "Get ye down, both of you,-all together,
020:125 **He** will say: "O my Lord! why hast
020:133 They say: "Why does **he** not bring us a Sign
021:004 **He** is the One that heareth and knoweth (all things)."
021:005 Nay, **He** forged it!-Nay, **He** is (but) a poet!"
021:022 (high is **He**) above what they attribute to Him!
021:023 **He** cannot be questioned for His acts, but they
021:027 They speak not before **He** speaks, and they
021:028 except for those who with whom **He** is well-pleased
021:028 **He** knows what is before them, and what
021:033 It is **He** Who created the Night and the
021:052 Behold! **he** said to his father and his people,
021:054 **He** said, "Indeed ye have been in manifest error-
021:056 **He** Who created them (from nothing):
021:056 **He** said, "Nay, your Lord is the Lord of the
021:058 So **he** broke them to pieces, (all) but
021:059 **He** must indeed be one of the unjust one.
021:060 talk of them: **he** is called Abraham."
021:063 **He** said: "Nay, this was done by this
021:075 for **he** was one of the Righteous.
021:076 (Remember) Noah, when **he** cried (to Us) aforetime:
021:083 And (remember) Job, when **he** cried to his Lord
021:087 But **he** cried through the depths of darkness,
021:087 **he** imagined that We had no power
021:087 And remember Zun-nun, when **he** departed in wrath:
021:089 when **he** cried ti his Lord: "O my Lord! leave me
021:110 "It is **He** Who knows what is open in speech
022:004 for friendship, him will **he** lead astray,
022:004 and **he** will guide him to the Chastisement
022:006 it is **He** Who gives life to the dead,
022:006 and it is **He** Who has power over all things.
022:014 for Allah carries out all that **He** desires.
022:016 and verily Allah doth guide whom **He** will!
022:018 for Allah carries out all that **He** wills.
022:028 over the cattle which **He** has provided for
022:031 anyone assigns partners to Allah, **he** is as if **he** had fallen
022:034 **He** gave them from animals (fit for food).
022:037 **He** has thus made them subject to you, that ye
022:052 when **he** framed a desire, Satan threw
022:053 That **He** may make the suggestions thrown in
022:056 **He** will judge between them: so those
022:058 **He** Who bestows the best Provision.

HE (continued)

022:059 Verily **He** will admit them to a place
022:060 to no greater extent than the injury **he** received,
022:061 and **He** merges Day in Night, and verily
022:062 are but vain Falsehood: verily Allah is **He**, Most High,
022:062 That is because Allah-**He** is the Reality; and those
022:064 for verily Allah,-**He** is Free of all wants,
022:065 **He** withholds the sky from falling on the earth
022:066 It is **He** Who gave you life, will cause
022:075 **He** Who hears and sees (all things).
022:076 **He** knows what is before them and what
022:078 **He** is your Protector-the best to protect and the Best
022:078 **He** has chosen you, and has and has imposed no
022:078 It is **He** Who has named you Muslims, both before
023:023 We sent Noah to his people: **he** said, "O my people!
023:024 his people said: "**He** is no more than a man
023:024 (to send messengers), **He** could have sent down
023:024 such a thing (as **he** says), among our
023:025 (And some said:) "**He** is only a man possessed:
023:033 **he** eats and drinks of what ye drink.
023:033 said "**He** is no more than a man like yourselves,
023:035 "Does **he** promise that when ye die and become
023:038 "**He** is only a man who invents a lie against Allah,
023:070 Nay, **he** has brought them the Truth, but most
023:070 Or do they say, "**He** is possessed"?
023:072 **He** is the Best of those who give sustenance.
023:078 It is **He** Who has created for you (the faculties of) hearing
023:079 And **He** has multiplied you through the earth,
023:080 It is **He** Who gives life and death, and to
023:091 each god would have taken away what **he** had created,
023:091 Glory to Allah (**He** is free) from the (sort of)
023:092 **He** knows what is hidden and what is open:
023:092 too high is **He** for the partners
023:099 **he** says: "O my Lord! send me back to (life),-
023:100 it is but a word **he** says."-Before them
023:108 **He** will say: "Be ye driven into it
023:112 **He** will say: "What number of years did ye
023:114 **He** will say: "Ye stayed not but a little,-
023:116 there is no god but **He**, the Lord
023:117 besides Allah, any other god, **he** has no authority thereof;
024:006 testify four times by Allah that **he** is of those
024:011 the punishment) of the sin that **he** earned, and to
024:021 **he** will (but) command what is indecent and wrong:
024:021 but Allah doth purify whom **He** pleases:
024:032 and **He** knoweth all things.
024:035 Allah doth guide whom **He** will to His Light:
024:036 in them is **He** glorified in the morning and in the evenings,
024:038 for those whom **He** will, without measure.
024:039 until when **he** comes up to it, **he** finds it to be nothing:
024:039 but **he** finds Allah there, and Allah will pay him his
024:040 if a man stretches out his hand, **he** can hardly see it!
024:043 and **He** turns it away from whom **He** pleases.
024:043 **He** strikes therewith whom **He** pleases
024:043 And **He** sends down from the sky mountain masses
024:045 Allah creates what **He** wills; for verily
024:046 and Allah guides whom **He** wills to a way
024:048 in order that **He** may judge between them, behold,
024:051 His Messenger, in order that **He** may judge
024:054 **he** is only responsible for the duty placed on him
024:055 that **He** will establish in authority their religion-
024:055 that **He** will, of a surety, grant them in the land,
024:055 and that **He** will change (their state), after the
024:055 their religion-the one which **He** has chosen

HE (continued)

024:055 as **He** granted it to those before them;
024:064 **He** will tell them the truth of what they did:
024:064 Well doth **He** know what ye are intent upon:
025:001 Blessed is **He** Who sent down the Criterion
025:002 **He** to Whom belongs the dominion of the heavens
025:002 it is **He** Who created all things, and ordered
025:002 no son has **He** begotten,
025:002 nor has **He** a partner in His dominion: it is
025:004 "Naught is this but a lie which **he** has forged,
025:005 which **he** has caused to be written: and they
025:006 verily **He** is Oft-Forgiving, Most Merciful."
025:008 or why has **he** (not) a garden for enjoyment?"
025:010 Blessed is **He** Who, if that were His Will,
025:010 and **He** could give thee Palaces (secure to dwell in).
025:017 **He** will ask: "Was it ye who led these My servants astray,
025:017 The Day **He** will gather them together as well
025:027 will bite at his hands, **he** will say, "Oh! would
025:029 "**He** did lead me astray from the Message
025:042 "**He** indeed would well-nigh have misled us
025:045 If **He** willed, **He** could make it stationary!
025:047 And **He** it is Who makes the Night as a Robe
025:048 And **He** it is Who sends the Winds as heralds
025:053 yet has **He** made a barrier between them,
025:053 It is **He** Who has let free the two bodies
025:054 then has **He** established relationships of lineage
025:054 It is **He** Who has created man from water: then has
025:058 and enough is **He** to be acquainted with the faults of His
025:059 **He** Who created the heavens and the earth
025:059 in six days, then **He** established Himself on the
025:061 Blessed is **He** Who made Constellations in the skies,
025:062 And it is **He** Who made the Night and the Day
025:069 and **he** will dwell therein in ignominy,-
025:070 Unless **he** repents, believes, and works righteous
026:009 And verily, thy Lord is **He**, the Exalted
026:012 **He** said: "O my Lord! I do fear
026:025 "Do ye not listen (to what **he** says)?"
026:033 And **he** drew out his hand, and behold
026:042 **He** said: "Yea, (and more),-for ye
026:049 Surely **he** is your leader, who has
026:062 Soon will **He** guide me!
026:068 And verily thy Lord is **He**, the Exalted
026:070 Behold, **he** said to his father and his people:
026:072 **He** said: "Do they listen to you when ye
026:075 **He** said: "Do ye then see whom ye
026:078 "Who created me, and it is **He** Who guides me;
026:080 "And when I am ill, it is **He** Who cures me;
026:086 for that **he** is among those astray;
026:089 "But only **he** (will prosper) that brings
026:104 And verily the Lord is **He**, the Exalted
026:112 **He** said: "And what do I know as to what they do?
026:117 **He** said: "O my Lord! truly my
026:122 And verily thy Lord is **He**, the Exalted
026:133 "Freely has **He** bestowed on you cattle and sons,-
026:140 And verily thy Lord is **He**, the Exalted
026:155 **He** said: "Here is a she-camel: she has
026:159 And verily thy Lord is **He**, the Exalted
026:168 **He** said: "I do detest your doings."
026:175 And verily thy Lord is **He**, the Exalted
026:188 **He** said: "My Lord knows best what ye do."
026:191 And verily thy Lord is **He**, the Exalted
026:199 And had **he** recited it to them, they would
026:220 For it is **He** Who heareth and knoweth all things.

HE (continued)

027:008 But when **he** came to the (Fire), a voice
027:010 But when **he** saw it moving (of its own accord)
027:010 a snake, **he** turn back in retreat, and retraced
027:016 **He** said: "O ye people! we have been taught
027:019 So **he** smiled, amused at her speech; and she
027:019 and **he** said: "O my Lord! so order
027:020 And **he** took a muster of the Birds;
027:020 and **he** said: "Why is it I see not the Hoopoe?
027:020 Or is **he** among the absentees?
027:021 or execute him, unless **he** bring me a clear
027:022 **he** (came up and) said: "I have compassed which thou
027:026 "Allah!-there is no god but **He**!-Lord of of the Throne
027:036 **he** said: "Will ye give me abundance in wealth?
027:036 has given me is better than that which **He** has given you!
027:038 **He** said (to his own men): "Ye Chiefs! which of
027:040 firmly before him, **he** said: "This is by the grace of my
027:041 **He** said: "Disguise her throne, let us
027:043 And **he** diverted her from the worship
027:044 **He** said: "This is but a palace paved smooth
027:046 **He** said: "O my people! why ask ye to hasten
027:047 **He** said: "Your ill omen is with Allah; yea, ye
027:049 (when **he** seeks vengeance): 'We were not present at
027:054 behold, **he** said to his people, "Do ye do what is indecent
027:059 His servants whom **He** has chosen (for his Message).
027:062 Or, who listens to the distressedwhen **he** calls on Him,
027:078 and **He** is Exalted in Might, All-knowing.
027:088 for **He** is well acquainted with all that ye do.
027:089 If any do good, **he** will have better than it.
028:004 for **he** was indeed an evil-doer.
028:004 their sons **he** slew, but **he** kept alive their females:
028:009 It may be that **he** will be of use to us, or we
028:012 And We ordained that **he** refused suck at first,
028:014 When **he** reached full age, and was
028:015 **He** said: "This is a work of Satan: for **he** is an enemy that
028:015 and **he** found there two men fighting,-one of
028:015 And **he** entered the City at a time when its
028:016 **He** prayed: "O my Lord! I have
028:016 for **He** is the Oft-Forgiving, Most Merciful.
028:017 **He** said: "O my Lord! for that Thou hast bestowed
028:018 In the morning, **he** was in the city, fearful and
028:019 Then, when **he** was about to lay his hands on their
028:020 **He** said: "O Moses! the Chiefs are taking counsel
028:021 **He** prayed: "O my Lord! save me
028:021 **He** therefore got away therefrom, looking about,
028:022 **he** said: "I do hope that my Lord will show me the smooth
028:022 when **he** turned his face towards (the land of) Madyan,
028:023 **He** said: "What is the matter with you?"
028:023 **he** found there a group of men watering (their flocks),
028:023 besides them **he** found two women who were keeping
028:023 And when **he** arrived at the watering (place) in Madyan,
028:024 So **he** watered (their flocks) for them;
028:024 then **he** turned back to the shade,
028:025 **he** said: "Fear thou not: (well) hast escaped from unjust
028:025 So when **he** came to him and narrated the story,
028:025 that **he** may reward thee for having watered (our flocks)
028:027 **He** said: "I intended to wed one of these
028:028 **He** said: "Be that (the agreement) between me
028:029 **He** said to his family: "Tarry ye; i perceive a fire;
028:029 **he** perceived a fire in the direction of Mount Tur.
028:030 But when **he** came to the (Fire),
028:030 **he** was called from the right bank of the valley,
028:031 **he** turned back in retreat, and retraced not his steps:

HE (continued)

028:031 But when **he** saw it moving (of its own accord)
028:033 **He** said: "O my Lord! I have slain a man among them,
028:034 "And my brther Aaron-**he** is more eloquent in speech than
028:035 **He** said: "We will certainly strengthen thy arm
028:039 And **he** was arrogant and insolent in the land,
028:039 and insolent in the land, beyond reason,-**he** and his hosts:
028:056 but Allah guides those whom **He** will and **He** knows best
028:059 a town until **He** had sent to its Center a messenger,
028:067 haply **he** shall be one of the successful.
028:068 and far is **He** above the partners they ascribe
028:068 Thy Lord does create and chosse as **He** pleases:
028:070 And **He** is Allah: there is no god but **He**.
028:073 It is out of His Mercy that **He** has made
028:074 **He** will say: "Where are My `partners' whom ye
028:074 The Day that **He** will call on them,
028:076 but **he** acted insolently towards them:
028:078 Did **he** not know that Allah had destroyed,
028:078 **He** said: "This has been given to me because of
028:079 For **he** is truly a lord of mighty good fortune."
028:079 So **he** went forth among his people in the
028:081 nor could **he** defend himself.
028:081 and **he** had not (the least little) party to
028:082 or restricts it, to any of His servants **He** pleases!
028:082 **He** could have caused the earth to swallow us up!
028:085 Verily **He** Who ordained the Qur'an for thee,
028:088 There is no god but **He**.
029:005 and **He** hears and knows (all things).
029:014 and **he** tarried among them a thousand years
029:016 **he** said to his people, "Serve Allah and fear Him:
029:021 and **He** grants mercy to whom **He** pleases,
029:021 "**He** punishes whom **He** pleases,
029:025 And **He** said: "For you, ye have taken (for worship)
029:026 for **He** is Exalted in Might, and Wise."
029:026 **he** said: "I will leave home for the sake of my Lord:
029:027 and **he** will be in the Hereafter of the Righteous.
029:028 **he** said to his people: "Ye do commit lewdness,
029:030 **He** said: "O my Lord! help Thou me against
029:032 **He** said: "But there is Lut there." They said:
029:033 **he** was grieved on their account, and felt himself
029:036 Then **he** said: "O my people! serve Allah,
029:042 and **He** is Exalted (in power), Wise.
029:052 **He** knows what is in the heavens and on earth.
029:060 and you: for **He** hears and knows (all things).
029:062 Allah enlarges the sustenance (which **He** gives)
029:062 to whichever of His servants **He** pleases;
029:062 **He** (similarly) grants by (strict) measure, (as **He** pleases):
029:065 but when **He** had delivered them safely
029:068 And who does more wrong than **he** who invents
030:005 **He** gives victory to whom **He** will,
030:005 and **He** is Exalted in Might, Most Merciful.
030:019 It is **He** Who brings out the living from the dead,
030:020 that **He** created you from dust; and then,-behold,
030:021 that **He** created for you mates from among yourselves,
030:021 and **He** has put love and mercy between your (hearts):
030:024 **He** shows you the lightning, by way
030:024 and **He** sends down rain from the sky and with
030:025 then when **He** calls you, by a single call,
030:027 It is **He** Who begins (the process of) creation;
030:027 for **He** is Exalted in Might, Full of Wisdom.
030:028 **He** does propound to you a similitude from
030:033 but when **He** gives them a taste of Mercy
030:037 the provision and restricts it to whomsoever **He** pleases?

HE (continued)

030:040 further, **He** has provided for your sustenance;
030:040 Glory to Him! and High is **He** above the partners
030:040 then **He** will cause you to die; and again **He** will give you
030:045 That **He** may reward those who believe and work
030:045 For **He** loves not those who reject Faith.
030:046 that **He** sends the Winds, as heralds
030:048 **He** has made them reach such of His servants as **He** wills,
030:048 then does **He** spread them in the sky as **He** wills,
030:050 for **He** has power over all things.
030:050 Allah's Mercy!-how **He** gives life to the earth
030:054 and it is **He** Who has all knowledge and power.
030:054 **He** creates whatever **He** wills, and it
031:007 are rehearsed to such a one, **he** turns away in arrogance,
031:007 as if **he** heard them not, as if there were deafness
031:009 and **He** is Exalted in power, Wise.
031:010 and **He** scattered through it beast of
031:010 **He** set on the earth mountains standing firm,
031:010 **He** created the heavens without any pillars
031:026 verily Allah is **He** (that is) free of all wants,
031:028 for Allah is **He** Who hears and sees (all things).
031:029 that **He** has subjected the sun and the moon
031:029 into Day and **He** merges Day into Night;
031:030 and because Allah,-**He** is the Most High, Most Great.
031:031 that **He** may show you of His Signs?
031:032 But when **He** has delivered them safely to land,
031:034 is full knowledge and **He** is acquainted
031:034 It is **He** Who sends down rain,
031:034 and **He** Who knows what is in the wombs.
031:034 nor does anyone know in what land **he** is to die.
031:034 anyone know what it is that **he** will earn on the morrow:
032:003 Or do they say, "**He** has forged it"? Nay, it
032:004 in six Days, then **He** established Himself on the
032:005 **He** directs the affairs from the heavens to the
032:006 Such as **He**, the knower of all things, hidden and
032:007 the best way and **He** began the creation of man
032:007 **He** Who has created all things in the best way
032:009 But **He** fashioned him in due proportion,
032:009 And **He** gave you (the faculties of) hearing and sight
033:004 nor has **He** made your adopted sons your sons.
033:004 and **He** shows the (right) Way.
033:004 nor has **He** made your wives whom ye divorce
033:008 about their truthfulness and **He** has prepared
033:027 And **He** made you heirs of their lands,
033:036 and His Messenger, **he** is indeed on a clearly
033:040 any of your men, but (**he** is) the Messenger of Allah,
033:043 and **He** is Full of Mercy to the Believers.
033:043 that **He** may bring you out from the depths
033:043 **He** it is Who sends blessings on you, as do
033:044 and **He** has prepared for them a generous Reward.
033:053 **he** is shy to dismiss you, but Allah
033:069 and **he** was honourable in Allah's sight.
033:071 That **He** may make your conduct whole and sound
033:071 **he** that obeys Allah and His Messenger has already
033:072 **he** was indeed unjust and foolish;-
034:001 and **He** is All-Wise, All-Aware.
034:002 **He** knows all that goes into the earth, and all
034:002 and **He** is the Most Merciful, the Oft-Forgiving.
034:004 That **He** may reward those who believe and work
034:008 or is **he** afflicted with madness."
034:008 "Has **he** invented a falsehood against Allah,
034:013 They worked for him as **he** desired, (making) Arches,
034:014 so when **he** fell down, the Jinns

HE (continued)

034:021 But **he** had no authority over them,-except that
034:023 except for those for whom **He** has granted
034:023 and **He** is the Most High, Most Great.'"
034:026 and **He** is the One to decide, the One
034:027 Nay, **He** is Allah, the Exalted in Power, the Wise."
034:036 to whom **He** pleases, but most men know not."
034:039 for **He** is the Best of those Who grant Sustenance.
034:039 the Sustenance to such of His servants as **He** pleases:
034:039 you spend in the least (in His Cause) but **He** replaces it:
034:040 On the day **He** will gather them all together,
034:046 **he** is no less than a Warner to you, in face of a terrible
034:047 and **He** is Witness to all things."
034:048 the Truth,-**He** that has full knowledge of (all)
034:050 it is **He** Who hears all things,
035:001 **He** adds to Creation as **He** pleases:
035:002 and **He** is the Exalted in Power, Full of Wisdom.
035:002 what **He** doth withhold, none can grant, apart from Him:
035:003 There is no god but **He**: how then
035:006 **He** only invites his adherents, that they
035:008 Is **he**, then, to whom the evil of his conduct is made
035:008 is made alluring, so that **he** looks upon it as good,
035:008 For Allah leaves to stray whom **He** wills,
035:008 and guides whom **He** wills.
035:010 it is **He** Who exalts each Deed of Righteousness.
035:011 then **He** made you in pairs.
035:013 **He** merges Night into Day,
035:013 and **He** merges Day into Night,
035:013 and **He** has subjected the sun and the moon
035:016 If **He** so pleased, **He** could blot you out
035:018 even though **he** be nearly related.
035:022 Allah can make any that **He** wills to hear;
035:030 For **He** will pay them their meed,
035:030 out of His Bounty; for **He** is Oft-Forgiving,
035:030 nay, **He** will give them (even) more out of
035:037 so that **he** that would should receive admonition?
035:038 verily **He** has full knowledge of all that is in (men's)
035:039 **He** it is that has made you inheritors
035:039 so, **he** who disbelieves his disbelief be on
035:041 verily **He** is Most Forbearing, Oft-Forgiving.
035:044 for **He** is All-Knowing, All-Powerful.
035:045 but **he** gives them respite for a stated Term:
035:045 **He** would not leave on the back of the (earth)
036:026 **He** said: "Ah me! would that my People knew
036:047 **He** would have fed, (himself)?-Ye are
036:060 for that **he** was to you an enemy avowed?-
036:062 "But **he** did lead astray a great multitude of you.
036:077 Yet behold! **he** (stands forth) as an open adversary!
036:078 **he** says, "Who can give life to (dry) bones
036:078 And **he** makes comparisons for Us, and forgets his own
036:079 Say, "**He** will give them life Who created
036:079 For **He** fully knows all creation.
036:081 **He** is the Creator Supreme, of skill
036:081 "Is not **He** Who created the heavens and the
036:082 Verily, when **He** intends a thing, His Command
037:037 and **he** confirms (the Message of) the messengers
037:037 Nay! **he** has come with the (very) Truth,
037:054 **He** said: "Would ye like to look down?"
037:055 **He** looked down and saw him in the midst
037:056 **He** said: "By Allah! thou wast little short
037:081 For **he** was one of Our believing Servants.
037:084 Behold, **He** approached his Lord with a sound heart.
037:085 Behold, **he** said to his father and to his people,

HE (continued)

037:088   Then did **he** cast a glance at the Stars,
037:089   And **he** said, "I am indeed sick (at heart)!"
037:091   Then did **he** turn to their gods and said,
037:093   Then did **he** turn upon them, striking (them)
037:095   **He** said: "Worship ye that which ye have
037:099   **He** said: "I will go to my Lord! **He** will surely guide me!
037:102   **he** said: "O my son! I have seen in a dream
037:103   and **he** had laid him prostrate on his forehead
037:111   For **he** was one of Our believing Servants.
037:124   Behold, **he** said to his people, "Will ye
037:132   For **He** was one of Our believing Servants.
037:140   When **he** ran away (like a slave from captivity)
037:141   **He** (agreed to) cast lots, and **he** was of the rebutted:
037:142   and **he** had done acts worthy of blame.
037:143   Had it not been that **he** (repented and)
037:144   **He** would certainly have remained inside the
037:153   Did **He** (then) choose daughters rather than sons?
037:159   Glory to Allah! (**He** is free) from the things
037:180   Honour and Power! (**He** is free) from what
038:005   "Has **he** made the gods (all) into one God?
038:017   for **he** ever turned (in repentance to Allah).
038:022   and **he** was terrified of them, they said:
038:023   yet **he** says, 'Commit her to my care',
038:023   **he** has nine and ninety ewes, and I (but) one:
038:023   and **he** overcame me in the argument."
038:024   (David) said: "**He** has undoubtedly wronged thee
038:024   We had tried him: **he** asked forgiveness of his Lord,
038:025   **he** enjoyed, indeed, a Near Approach to Us, and a
038:030   Ever did **he** turn (to Us in repentance)!
038:032   And **he** said, "Truly do I prefer wealth to the
038:033   Then began **he** to pass his hand over (their)
038:034   but **he** did turn (to Us in true devotion):
038:035   **He** said, "O my Lord! Forgive me, and grant me
038:036   whithersoever **he** willed,-
038:040   And **he** enjoyed, indeed, a Near Approach to Us,
038:041   behold **he** cried to his Lord: "Satan has
038:044   Ever did **he** turn (to Us)!
038:074   Not so Iblis: **he** was haughty, and became
038:076   (Iblis) said: "I am better than **he**: Thou createdst me from
039:004   **He** is Allah, the One, the Overpowering.
039:004   to take to Himself a son, **He** could have chosen
039:004   whom **He** pleased out of those whom **He** doth create:
039:004   but Glory be to Him! (**He** is above such things).
039:005   **He** has subjected the sun and the moon (to His law):
039:005   **He** created the heavens and the earth in true (proportions)
039:005   Is not **He** the Exalted in Power-
039:005   **He** Who forgives again and again?
039:005   **He** makes the Night overlap the Day, and the Day overlap
039:006   **He** creates you, in the wombs of your mothers,
039:006   There is no god but **He**: then how
039:006   **He** created you (all) from a single person:
039:006   and **He** sent down for you eight head
039:007   For **He** knoweth well all that is in (men's) hearts.
039:007   if ye are grateful, **He** is pleased with you.
039:007   but **He** liketh not ingratitude from His servants:
039:007   when **He** will tell you the truth of all
039:008   but when **He** bestoweth a favour upon him
039:008   When some trouble toucheth man **he** crieth unto his Lord,
039:008   and **he** doth set up rivals unto Allah,
039:008   (man) doth forget what **he** cried and prayed
039:021   grow yellow; then **He** makes it dry up and crumble
039:021   Then **He** causes to grow, therewith,

HE (continued)

039:022   to Islam, so that **he** has received light
039:023   **He** guides therewith whom **He** pleases, but such
039:033   And **he** who brings the Truth and **he** who confirms
039:038   remove His affliction or if **He** wills some Mercy
039:041   **He**, then, that receives guidance benefits his
039:041   but **he** that strays injures his own soul.
039:042   but the rest **He** sends (to their bodies) for a term
039:042   **He** keeps back (from returning to life),
039:042   and those that die not (**He** takes) during their sleep:
039:042   those on whom **He** has passed the decree of death,
039:045   but when (gods) other than **He** are mentioned, behold,
039:049   **he** says, "This has been given to me because of
039:049   Now, when trouble touches man, **he** cries to Us;
039:052   enlarges the provision or srstricts it, for any **He** pleases?
039:053   for **He** is Oft-Forgiving, Most Merciful.
039:062   and **He** is the Guardian and Disposer of all affairs.
039:067   High is **He** above the Partners they attribute to Him!
040:003   There is no god but **He**: to Him is the Final Goal.
040:008   For Thou art (**He**), the Exalted
040:013   **He** it is Who showeth you His Signs, and sendeth
040:015   spirit (of inspiration) to any of His servants **He** pleases,
040:015   (**He** is) the Lord of the Throne:
040:015   by His Command doth **He** send the spirit (of inspiration)
040:015   Exalted is **he** in His attributes.
040:022   so Allah called them to account: for **He** is full of Strength,
040:025   Now, when **he** brought them the Truth, from Us,
040:026   or lest **he** should cause mischief to appear in the land!"
040:026   What I fear is lest **he** should change your religion,
040:028   but, if **he** is telling the Truth, then will
040:028   "Will ye slay a man because **he** says, 'My Lord is Allah'?-
040:028   when **he** has indeed come to you with Clear (Signs)
040:028   on you something the (calamity) of which **he** warns you:
040:028   And if **he** be a liar, on him is (the sin of) this lie:
040:034   of the (mission) for which **he** had come:
040:034   at length, when **he** died, ye said: 'No messenger will Allah
040:037   and **he** was hindered from the Path; and the
040:040   "**He** that works evil will not be requited but by
040:040   and **he** that works a righteous deed-whether man
040:056   it is **He** Who hears and sees (all things).
040:062   there is no god but **He**: then how
040:065   **He** is the living (One): There is no god but **He**: call upon
040:067   then does **He** get you out (into the light) as a
040:067   It is **He** Who has created you from dust, then from
040:068   and when **He** decides upon an affair, **He** says to it, "Be,"
040:068   It is **He** Who gives Life and Death; and when
040:081   And **He** shows you (always) His Signs; then which
041:009   **He** is the Lord of (all) the Worlds.
041:010   **He** set on the (earth), mountains standing
041:011   Then **He** turned to the sky, and it
041:011   **He** said to it and to the earth: "Come ye
041:012   and **He** assigned to each heaven its duty and command.
041:012   So **He** completed them as seven firmaments in two Days,
041:014   **He** would certainly have sent down angels:
041:021   (**He**) Who giveth speech to everything:
041:021   **He** created you for the first time,
041:034   then will **he** between whom and thee was
041:036   **He** is the One Who hears and knows all things.
041:039   Truly, **He** Who gives life to the dead earth can surely
041:039   For **He** has power over all things.
041:040   Which is better?-**he** that is cast into the Fire,
041:040   Do what ye will: Verily **He** seeth (clearly) all that ye do.
041:040   or **he** that comes safe through, on the Day of Judgment?

HE (continued)

041:047 touches him, he gives up all hope (and) is lost in despair.
041:050 he is sure to say, "This is due to my (merit):
041:051 he turns away, and gets himself remote on his side
041:051 when evil seizes him, (he comes) full of prolonged prayer!
041:054 Ah indeed! it is He that doth encompass all things!
042:003 to thee as (He did) to those before thee,-Allah,
042:003 Thus doth (He) send Inspiration to thee
042:004 and He is Most High, Most Great.
042:005 Behold! Verily Allah is He, the Oft-Forgiving,
042:008 He could have made them a single people;
042:008 but He admits whom He will to His Mercy;e
042:009 it is He Who has power over all things.
042:009 and it is He Who gives life to the dead:
042:009 But it is Allah,-He is the Protector, and it
042:011 by this means does He multiply you: there is
042:011 and He is the One that hears and sees.
042:011 He had made for you pairs from among yourselves,
042:011 (He is) the Creator of the heavens and the earth:
042:012 to whom He will: for He knows full well all things.
042:012 He enlarges and restricts the Sustenance to whom He
042:013 Allah chooses to Himself those whom He pleases,
042:013 for you as that which He enjoined on Noah-
042:013 The same religion has He established for you as that
042:016 dispute concerning Allah after He has been accepted,-
042:019 He gives Sustenance to whom He pleases:
042:019 and He is the Strong, the Mighty.
042:020 but he has no share or lot in the Hereafter.
042:024 For He knows well the secrets of all hearts.
042:024 "He has forged a falsehood against Allah"?
042:024 But if Allah Willed, He could seal up thy heart.
042:025 and He knows all that ye do.
042:025 He is the One that accepts repentance from His
042:026 And He listens to those who believe and do
042:027 but He sends (it) down in due measureas He pleases:
042:027 for He is with His Servants well-acquainted,
0042:028 He is the One that sends down rain (even) after
042:028 And He is the Protector, Worthy of
042:029 and He has power to gather them together when He wills.
042:029 and the living creatures that He has scattered through
042:030 and for many (a sin) He grants forgiveness.
042:033 If it be His Will, He can still the Wind
042:034 which (the men) have earned: but much doth He forgive.
042:034 Or He can cause them to perish because of the (evil)
042:048 give man a teast of Mercy from Us, he doth exult thereat,
042:049 He creates what He wills.
042:049 He bestows (children) male or female according to His
042:050 and He leaves barren whom He will:
042:050 for He is full of knowledge and power.
042:050 Or He bestows both males and females,
042:051 what Allah wills: for He is Most High, Most Wise.
043:016 What! Has He taken Daughters out of what
043:016 out of what He Himself creates, and granted to you sons
043:017 his face darkens, and he is filled with inward grief!
043:017 of (the birth of) what he sets up as a likeness to (Allah)
043:024 He said: "What! even if I brought you better
043:027 and He will certainly guide me."
043:028 And he left it as a Word to endure among those
043:038 he says (to his evil-companion): 'Would that between
043:046 to Pharaoh and his Chiefs: he said, "I am a messenger
043:047 But when he came to them with Our Signs, behold,
043:054 Thus did he make fools of his people, and they
043:058 And they say, "Are our god best or He?"

HE (continued)

043:059 He was no more than a servant: We granted
043:062 for he is to you an enemy avowed.
043:063 he said: "Now have I come to you with Wisdom,
043:064 "For Allah; He is my Lord and your Lord:
043:077 He will say, "Nay, but ye shal abide!"
043:082 He is free from the things they attribute (to Him)!
043:084 It is He Who is God in heaven and God on earth;
043:084 and He is Full of Wisdom and Knowledge.
043:085 And blessed is He to Whom belongs the dominion
043:086 only he who bears witness to the Truth,
044:006 for He hears and knows (all things);
044:008 There is no god but He:
044:008 it is He Who gives life and gives death,-the Lord
044:022 then he cried to his Lord: "These are indeed a people
044:031 Inflicted by Pharaoh, for he was arrogant (even)
044:042 for He is exalted in Might, Most Merciful.
044:056 and He will preserve them from the Chastisement
045:008 as if he had not heard them: then announce
045:008 He hears the Signs of Allah rehearsed to him,
045:009 And when he learns something of Our Signs,
045:009 of Our Signs, he takes them in jest: for such
045:013 And He has subjected to you, as from
045:015 if he does evil, it works against (His own soul).
045:026 then He will gather you together for the Day
045:037 and He is Exalted in Power, Full of Wisdom!
046:008 He knows best of that whereof ye talk (so glibly)
046:008 Enough is He for a witness between me and you!
046:008 And He is Oft-Forgiving, Most Merciful."
046:008 Or do they say, "He has forged it"?
046:015 At length, when he reaches the age of full strenght
046:015 He says, "O my Lord! grant me that I may be grateful
046:017 But he says, "This is nothing but tales of the ancients!"
046:021 behold, he wanted his people beside the wnding Snad-
046:023 He said: "The Knowledge (of when it will come)
046:031 He will forgive you your faults.
046:032 he cannot escape in the earth,
046:032 and no protectors can he have besides Allah:
046:033 Yea, verily He has power over all things.
046:034 "Yea, by our Lord!" (He will say): "Then taste
047:002 He will remove from them their ills and improve their
047:004 He could certainly have exacted retribution
047:004 but (He lets you fight) in order to test you,
047:004 way of Allah,-He will never let their deeds be lost.
047:005 Soon will He guide them and improve their condition,
047:006 He has made known for them.
047:007 He will help you, and plant your feet firmly.
047:009 so He has made their deeds fruitless.
047:016 received Knowledge: "What is it he said just then?"
047:017 He increases their Guidance, and bestows on them
047:023 has cursed for He has made them deaf and blinded
047:028 so He made their deeds of no effect.
047:032 but He will make their deeds of no effect.
047:036 He will grant you your recompense, and will
047:037 If He were to ask you for all of them,
047:037 and He would bring out all your ill-feeling.
047:038 He will substitute in your stead another people;
048:004 It is He who sent down Tranquillity into the
048:005 That He may admit the men and women who believe,
048:006 And that He may punish the Hypocrites,
048:006 He has cursed them and got Hell ready for them:
048:010 any one who fulfils what he has covenanted with Allah,
048:014 He forgives whom He wills,

HE (continued)

048:014	and He punishes whom He wills:
048:016	He will punish you with a grievous Chastisement."
048:017	and he who turns back, (Allah) will punish him
048:017	but he that obeys Allah and His Messenger,-
048:017	nor on one ill (if he joins not the war):
048:018	He knew what was in their hearts,
048:018	and He sent down tranquillity to them,
048:018	and He rewarded them with a speedy Victory;
048:020	and He has given you these beforehand;
048:020	and He has restrained the hands of men from you;
048:020	and that He may guide you to a Straight Path;
048:024	after that He gave you the victory over them.
048:024	And it is He who has restrained their hands
048:025	you to force your way, but He held back your hands)
048:025	that He may admit to His mercy whom He will.
048:027	and He granted, besides this, a speedy victory.
048:027	For He knew what ye knew ye knew not,
048:028	It is He who has sent His Messenger
049:001	for Allah is He who hears and knows all things.
049:007	and He has made hateful to you unbelief,
049:007	Allah's Messenger: were he, in many matters,
049:011	(to be used of one) after he has believed:
049:013	in the sight of Allah is (he who is) the most
049:014	He will not belittle aught of your deeds:
049:016	He has full knowledge of all things.
049:017	a favour upon you that He has guided you
050:018	Not a word does he utter but there is a
050:027	but he was (himself) far astray."
050:028	He will say: "Dispute not with each other
051:025	and said: "Peace!" He said, "Peace!"
051:026	Then he turned quickly to his household,
051:027	He said, "Will ye not eat?"
051:028	He conceived a fear of them
051:030	and He is full of Wisdom and Knowledge."
051:058	For Allah is He Who gives (all) Sustenance,-
052:028	truly it is He, the Beneficent, the Merciful!"
052:033	Or do they say, "He fabricated the (Message)?"
052:039	Or has He only daughters and ye have sons?
053:003	Nor does he say (aught) of (his own) Desire.
053:005	He was taught by one Mighty in Power,
053:006	For he appeared (in stately form)
053:007	While he was in the highest part of the horizon:
053:008	Then he approached and came closer,
053:010	to His Servant-(conveyed) what He (meant) to convey.
053:011	in no way falsified that which he saw.
053:012	with him concerning what he saw?
053:013	For indeed he saw him at a second descent,
053:018	For truly did he see, of the Signs
053:024	(just) anything he hankers after?
053:026	has given leave for whom He pleases and that
053:026	and that he is acceptable to Him.
053:030	and He knoweth best those who receive guidance.
053:031	so that He rewards those who do evil,
053:031	and He rewards those who do good, with what
053:032	He knows you well when He brings you out
053:032	He knows best who it is that guards against evil.
053:035	What! Has he knowledge of the Unseen so that
053:035	so that he can see?
053:036	Nay, is he not acquainted with what is in
053:039	That man can have nothing but what he strives for;
053:041	Then will he be rewarded with a reward complete;
053:043	That it is He who Granteth Laughter and Tears;

HE (continued)

053:044	That it is He who Granteth Death and Life;
053:045	That He did create in pairs-male and female,
053:047	That He hath promised a Second Creation
053:048	That it is He Who giveth wealth and satisfaction,
053:049	That He is the Lord of Sirius (the Mighty Star);
053:050	And that it is He Who destroyed the (powerful)
053:051	And the Thamud, He left no trace of them.
053:053	And He destroyed the Overthrown Cities
054:009	"Here is one possessed!", and he was driven out.
054:010	Then he called on his Lord: "I am one overcome:
054:025	Nay, he is a liar an insolent one!
054:029	and he took a sword in hand, and hamstrung (her).
055:002	It is He Who has taught the Qur'an.
055:003	He has created man:
055:004	He has taught him an intelligent speech.
055:007	and He has set up the balance (of Justice),
055:007	And the Firmament has He raised high,
055:010	It is He Who has spread out the earth
055:014	He created man from sounding clay
055:015	And He created Jinns from fire free of smoke:
055:017	(He is) Lord of the two Easts and Lord
055:019	He has let free the two Seas meeting together:
055:029	(new) Splendor doth He (shine)!
056:088	Thus, then, if he be of those Nearest to Allah,
056:090	And if he be of the Companions of the Right Hand,
056:092	And if he be of those who deny (the truth)
057:001	for He is the Exalted in Might, the Wise.
057:002	and He has Power over all things.
057:002	it is He Who gives life and Death;
057:003	He is the First and the Last, the Evident
057:003	and He has full knowledge of all things.
057:004	He knows what enters within the earth ans what comes
057:004	then He established Himself on the Throne.
057:004	He it is Who created the heavens and the earth
057:004	And He is with you wheresoever ye may be.
057:006	and He has full knowledge of the secrets of (all) hearts.
057:006	He merges Night into Day, and He merges Day into Night;
057:007	of the (substance) whereof He has made you heirs.
057:009	He is the One Who Sends to His Servants
057:009	that He may lead you from the depths
057:011	and he will have (besides) a generous reward.
057:011	Who is he that will loan to Allah a beautiful Loan?
057:021	Grace of Allah, which He bestows on whom He pleases:
057:028	and He will bestow on you a double portion
057:028	and He will forgive you (your past):
057:028	He will provide for you a light by which
057:029	to bestow it on whomsoever He wills.
058:004	he should fast for two months consecutively
058:004	to do so, he should feed sixty indigent ones.
058:007	but He is the fourth among them,-
058:007	but He is with them, wheresoever they be:
058:007	nor between five but He makes the sixth,-
058:007	in the end will He tell them what
058:010	to the Believers; but he cannot harm them in the
058:010	by Satan, in order that he may cause grief to the
058:019	so he has made them forgot the remembrance
058:022	For such He has written Faith in their hearts,
058:022	And He will admit them to Gardens beneath which
059:001	for He is the Exalted in Might, the Wise.
059:002	It is He who got out the Unbelievers among the
059:003	He would certainly have punished them in this
059:005	and in order that He might cover with shame

HE (continued)

059:006	Allah gives power to His messengers over any **He** pleases:
059:007	gives you, and refrain from what **He** prohibits you.
059:016	when **he** says to man, "Disbelieve": but when
059:018	look to what (provision) **he** has sent forth for the morrow.
059:019	and **He** made them forget themselves!
059:022	**He**, Most Gracious, Most Merciful.
059:022	Allah is **He**, than Whom there is no other god;-
059:023	(high is **He**) above the partners
059:023	Allah is **He**, than Whom there is no other god;-
059:024	and Glory: and **He** is the Exalted in Might,
059:024	**He** is Allah, the Creator, the Originator,
060:003	on the Day of Judgment: **He** will judge between you:
060:010	**He** judges (with justice) between you.
061:001	and Glory of Allah: for **He** is the Exalted
061:006	But when **he** came to them with Clear Signs,
061:007	even as **he** is being invited to Islam?
061:009	That **He** make it prevail over all religion,
061:009	It is **He** Who has sent His Messenger with Guidance
061:012	**He** will forgive you your sins, and admit
061:013	And another (favour will **He** bestow), which ye
062:002	It is **He** Who has sent amongst the Unlettered
062:003	not already joined them: and **He** is Exalted
062:004	which **He** bestows on whom **He** will: and Allah
062:008	and **He** will tell you the things that ye did!"
063:010	and **he** should say, "O my Lord! Why didst
064:001	and **He** has power over all things.
064:002	It is **He** Who has created you; and of you
064:003	**He** has created the heavens and the earth
064:004	**He** knows what is in the heavens and on earth;
064:004	and **He** knows what ye conceal and what ye reveal:
064:009	and **He** will admit them to gardens beneath which rivers
064:009	**He** will remove from them their ills,
064:009	Day that **He** assembles you (all) for a day of Assembly,-
064:013	Allah! there is no god but **He**:
064:017	**He** will double it to your (credit),
064:017	and **He** will grant you Forgiveness: for Allah
065:002	fear Allah, **He** (ever) prepares a way out,
065:003	**He** provides for him from (sources) **he** never could expect.
065:004	**He** will make things easy for them.
065:005	which **He** has sent down to you: and if
065:005	**He** will remove his evil deeds from him
065:007	on any person beyond what **He** has given him.
065:011	and work righteousness, **He** will admit to Gardens
065:011	clear explanations, that **he** may lead forth those
065:012	Allah is **He** Who created seven Firmaments and of
066:002	is your Protector, and **He** is Full of Knowledge
066:003	**He** said, "**He** told me Who is the Knower, The Aware."
066:003	**he** confirmed part thereof and passed over a part.
066:003	Then when **he** told her thereof, she said,
066:005	It may be, if **he** divorced you (all), that Allah
067:001	and **He** over all things Hath Power;-
067:001	Blessed be **He** in Whose hands is Dominion;
067:002	**He** Who created Death and Life,
067:002	and **He** is the Exalted in Might, Oft-Forgiving.
067:002	that **He** may try which of you is best in deed:
067:003	**He** Who created the seven heavens one above another:
067:013	or make it known, **He** certainly has (full) knowledge,
067:014	Should **He** not know,-**He** that created?
067:014	And **He** is The Subtle The Aware.
067:015	It is **He** Who has made the earth manageable for you,
067:015	which **He** furnishes: but unto Him is the Resurrection.
067:016	Do ye feel secure that **He** Who is in heaven

HE (continued)

067:017	Or do ye feel secure that **He** Who is in
067:019	truly it is **He** that watches over all things.
067:021	provide you with Sustenance if **He** were to
067:023	Say: "It is **He** Who has created you, and made
067:024	Say: "It is **He** Who has multiplied you through
067:028	or if **He** bestows His Mercy on us,-yet who
067:029	Say: "**He** is The Most Gracious: we have
068:007	and **He** knoweth best those who receive
068:014	Because **he** possesses wealth and (numerous) sons.
068:015	"Tales of the Ancients," **he** cries!
068:048	when **he** cried out in agony.
068:049	**he** would indeed have been cast off on the naked shore,
068:051	Surely **he** is possessed!"
069:007	**He** made it rage against them seven nights
069:010	of their Lord; so **He** punished them with an
069:019	Then **He** that will be given his Record in his
069:021	And **he** will be in a life of Bliss,
069:025	And **he** that will be given his Record in his
069:033	"This was **he** that would not believe
069:035	"So no friend hath **he** here this Day.
069:036	"Nor hath **he** any food except the foul pus
070:011	would that **he** could redeem himself from the
071:002	**He** said: "O my People! I am to you a Warner,
071:004	"So **He** may forgive you your sins and give you
071:005	**He** said: "O my Lord! I have called to my People
071:010	for **He** is Oft-Forgiving;
071:011	"'He** will send rain to you in abundance;
071:014	"'Seeing that it is **He** that has created you
071:018	"'And in the End **He** will return you into the
072:003	**He** has taken neither a wife nor a son.
072:017	**He** will cause him to undergo ever-growing
072:026	"**He** (alone) knows the Unseen, nor does
072:026	nor does **He** make any one acquainted with
072:027	"Except an apostle whom **He** has chosen:
072:027	and then **He** makes a band of watchers march before
072:028	"That **he** may know that they have (truly) brought
072:028	and **He** encompasses all that is with them, and takes
073:009	there is no god but **He**: take Him
073:009	(**He** is) Lord of the East and the West: there is
073:020	So **He** hath turned to you (in mercy):
073:020	**He** knoweth that there may be (some) among you in ill-
073:020	**He** knoweth that ye are unable to keep count thereof.
074:015	Yet is **he** greedy-that I should add (yet more);
074:016	By no means! for to Our Signs **he** has been refractory!
074:018	For **he** thought and **he** determined;-
074:019	And woe to him! How **he** determined!-
074:020	Yea, woe to him: how **he** determined!-
074:021	Then **he** reflected;
074:022	Then **he** frowned and **he** scowled;
074:023	Then **he** turned back and was haughty;
074:024	Then said **he**: "This is nothing but magic
074:031	and guide whom **He** pleaseth; and none can know the
074:031	Thus doth Allah leaves to stray whom **He** pleaseth,
074:031	the forces of the Lord, except **He**,
074:056	**He** is the Lord of Righteousness, and the
075:006	**He** questions: "When is the Day of Resurrection?"
075:013	(all) that **he** put forward, and all that **he** put back.
075:015	Even though **he** were to put up his excuses.
075:028	And **he** will think that it was (the Time)
075:031	So **he** gave nothing in charity, nor did **he** pray!-
075:032	**He** rejected Truth and turned away!
075:033	Then did **he** stalk to his family in full conceit!

HE (continued)

075:036 Does Man think that **he** will be left uncontrolled,
075:037 Was **he** not a drop of sperm emitted (in lowly form)?
075:038 Then did **he** become a leech-like clot; then did
075:039 And of him **He** made two sexes, male and female.
075:040 Has not **He**, (the same), the power
076:001 when **he** was nothing-(not even) mentioned?
076:003 whether **he** be grateful or ungrateful.
076:012 **He** will reward them with a Garden and (garments of)
076:031 **He** will admit to His Mercy Whom **He** will;
076:031 **He** prepared a grievous Chastisement.
078:038 and **he** will say what is right.
079:017 for **he** has indeed transgressed all bounds:
079:022 Further, **he** turned his back, striving hard
079:023 Then **he** collected (his men) and made a proclamation,
079:028 and **He** hath given it order and perfection.
079:028 On high hath **He** raised its canopy,
079:029 and its splendor doth **He** bring out (with light).
079:029 Its night doth **He** endow with darkness, and its
079:030 hath **He** extended (to a wide expanse);
079:031 **He** draweth out therefrom its water and its pasture,
079:032 And the mountains hath **He** firmly fixed;-
079:035 (all) that **he** strove for,
080:003 but that perchance **he** might Grow purity?
080:004 Or that **he** might receive admonition, and the
080:007 if **he** grow not in purity.
080:018 From what stuff hath **He** created him?
080:019 From a sperm-drop: **He** hath created him, and then
080:020 Then doth **He** make his path smooth for him;
080:021 Then **He** causeth him to die, and putteth
080:022 **He** will raise him up (again).
080:023 By no means hath **he** fulfilled what Allah
081:023 And without doubt **he** saw him in the clear horizon.
081:024 Neither doth **he** withhold Grudgingly a knowledge
082:008 In whatever Form **He** wills, does **He** put thee together.
083:013 Signs rehearsed to him, **he** says, "Tales of the Ancients!"
084:007 Then **he** who is given his Record in his Right hand,
084:009 And **he** will turn to his people, rejoicing!
084:010 But **he** who is given his Record behind his back,-
084:011 Soon will **he** cry for Perdition,
084:012 And **he** will enter a Blazing Fire.
084:013 Truly, did **he** go about among his people, rejoicing!
084:014 Truly, did **he** think that **he** would not
085:013 It is **He** Who Creates from the very beginning,
085:013 and **He** can restore (life).
085:014 And **He** is the Oft-Forgiving, Full of
085:016 Doer (without let) of all that **He** intends.
086:005 Now let man but think from what **he** is created!
086:006 **He** is created from a drop emitted-
087:007 for **He** knoweth what is manifest and what is hidden.
087:010 **He** will heed who fears:
087:013 In which **he** will then neither die nor live.
087:014 But **he** will prosper who purify himself.
089:015 then saith **he**, (puffed up), "My Lord hath honoured me."
089:016 But when **He** trieth him, restricting his
089:016 then saith **he** (in despair), "My Lord
089:024 **He** will say: "Ah! would that I had sent forth
090:003 And the begetter and that **he** begot;-
090:005 Thinketh **he**, that none hath power over him?
090:006 **He** may say (boastfully): "Wealth have I
090:007 Thinketh **he** that none beholdeth him?
090:011 But **he** hath made not haste on the
090:017 Then will **he** be of those who believe, and enjoin

HE (continued)

091:009 Truly **he** succeeds that purifies it,
091:010 And **he** fails that corrupts it!
092:005 So **he** who gives (in charity) and fears (Allah),
092:008 But **he** who is a greedy miser and thinks
092:011 when **he** falls headlong (into the Pit).
093:003 nor is **He** displeased.
093:006 Did **He** not find thee an orphan and give
093:007 And **He** found thee wandering,
093:007 and **He** gave thee guidance.
093:008 And **He** found thee in need, and made
096:004 **He** Who taught (the use of) the Pen,-
096:005 Taught man that which **he** knew not.
096:007 In that **he** looketh upon himself as self-sufficient.
096:010 A votary when **he** (turns) to pray?
096:011 Seest thou if **He** is on (the road of) Guidance?-
096:013 Seest thou if **he** denies (Truth) and turns away?
096:014 Knoweth **he** not that Allah doth see?
096:015 Let him beware! If **he** desist not, We will
100:007 And to that (fact) **he** bears witness (by his deeds);
100:008 And violent is **he** in his love of wealth.
100:009 Does **he** not know,-when that which is in the
101:006 Then, **he** whose balance (of good deeds) will be
101:008 But **he** whose balance (of good deeds) will be
104:004 By no means! **He** will be sure to be thrown
105:002 Did **He** not make their treacherous plan go astray?
105:003 And **He** sent against them flights of Birds,
105:005 Then did **He** make them like an empty field
108:003 **he** will be cut off (from Future Hope).
108:003 For **he** who hateth thee,-
110:003 for **He** is Oft-Returning (in forgiveness).
111:001 Perish the hands of the Father of Flame! Perish **he**!
111:003 Burnt soon will **he** be in a Fire of blazing Flame!
112:001 Say: **He** is Allah, the One;
112:003 **He** begetteth not, nor is **He** begotten;
113:005 the envious one as **he** practices envy.

HEAD

006:143 (Take) eight (**head** of cattle) in (four) pairs:
007:150 seized his brother by (the hair of) his **head**,
012:036 (in a dream) carrying bread on my **head**, and birds
012:041 and birds will eat from off his **head**.
019:004 and the hair of my **head** doth glisten
020:094 nor by (the hair of) my **head**!
030:054 give (you) weakness and a hoary **head**:
039:006 eight **head** of cattle in pairs:
044:048 "Then pour over his **head** the Chastisement

HEADINESS

037:047 Free from **headiness**; nor will

HEADLONG

003:176 who rush **headlong** into Unbelief:
005:003 or by a violent blow, or a **headlong** fall, or by
026:094 "Then they will be thrown **headlong** into the (Fire),-
027:090 will be thrown **headlong** into the Fire:
038:059 Here is a troop rushing **headlong** with you!
062:011 or some pastime, they disperse **headlong** to it,
067:022 Is then one who walks **headlong**, with his
092:011 when he falls **headlong** (into the Pit).

HEADS

002:043 and bow down your **heads** with those
002:196 and do not shave your **heads** until
005:006 rub your **heads** (with water); and wash your
007:163 fish did come to them, openly (holding up their **heads**),
014:043 necks outstretched, their **heads** uplifted,

HEADS (continued)

017:051 their **heads** towards thee, and say, "When will
022:019 over their **heads** will be poured out
032:012 their **heads** before their Lord, (saying): "Our Lord!
036:008 so that they cannot bow their **heads**.
037:065 are like the **heads** of devils:
048:027 if Allah wills, with minds secure, **heads** shaved, hair cut
063:005 they aside their **heads**, and though wouldst see them

HEAL

003:049 and I **heal** those born blind, and the lepers,
009:014 **heal** the breasts of Believers.

HEALEST

005:110 and thou **healest** those born blind, and the

HEALING

010:057 and a **healing** for the (diseases) in your hearts,-
016:069 of varying colours, wherein is **healing** for men:
017:082 of the Qur'an that which is a **healing** and a mercy
041:044 Say: "It is a guide and a **healing** to those

HEALTH

052:019 "Eat and drink ye, with profit and **health**,

HEAP

008:037 Put the impure, one on another, **heap** them together,
024:043 then makes them into a **heap**?
073:014 a **heap** of sand poured out and flowing down.

HEAPED

089:012 And **heaped** therein mischief (on mischief).

HEAPED-UP

003:014 women and sons, **heaped-up** hoards of gold and silver;

HEAPS

052:044 they would (only) say: "Clouds gathered in **heaps**!"

HEAR

002:093 they said: "We **hear**, and we disobey":
002:285 And they say: "We **hear**, and we obey:
003:186 certainly **hear** much that will grieve you,
004:046 If only they had said: "We **hear** and we obey";
004:046 and "Do **hear**"; and "Do look at us":
004:046 and "**Hear** what is not heard"; and "Ra'ina"
004:046 and say: "We **hear** and we disobey"; and
004:140 that when ye **hear** the Message of Allah
005:007 when ye said: "We **hear** and we obey":
007:043 And they shall **hear** the cry: "Behold!
007:100 so that they could not **hear**?
007:179 and ears wherewith they **hear** not.
007:195 Or ears to **hear** with? Say: "Call your 'god-partners',
007:198 If thou callest them to guidance, they **hear** not.
008:002 and when they **hear** His revelations rehearsed,
008:020 from him when ye **hear** (him speak).
008:021 "We **hear**," but listen not:
009:006 so that he may **hear** the Word of Allah; and then
010:042 but canst thou make the deaf to **hear**,-even though
011:020 They could not **hear**, nor could they see!
011:024 and those who can see and **hear** well.
013:014 call upon besides Him **hear** them no more than if they
018:101 and who had been unable even to **hear**.
019:038 How plainly will they see and **hear**, the Day
019:062 They will not there **hear** any vain discourse,
019:098 or **hear** (so much as) a whisper of them?
020:046 I **hear** and see (everything).
021:045 not **hear** the call, (even) when they are warned!
021:100 nor will they there **hear** (aught else).
021:102 Not the slightest sound will they **hear** of Hell:
022:046 may thus learn to **hear**?

HEAR (continued)

023:024 never did we **hear** such a thing
024:051 "We **hear** and we obey": it is
025:012 they will **hear** its fury and its raging sigh.
027:080 the Deaf to **hear** the call, (especially) when
028:036 never did we **hear** the like among our
028:055 And when they **hear** vain talk, they turn
030:052 the dead to **hear**, nor canst thou make the deaf
030:052 the deaf to **hear** the call, when they
030:053 thou make to **hear**, who believe in Our Signs
031:014 (**hear** the Command), "Show gratitude to Me and to
035:022 Allah can make any that He wills to **hear**;
035:022 canst not make those to **hear** who are (buried) in graves.
036:043 no helper (to **hear** their cry), nor could
037:075 and We are the Best to **hear** prayer.
041:004 and so they **hear** not.
043:040 Canst thou then make the deaf to **hear**, or give
043:080 Or do they think that We **hear** not their secrets
050:042 The Day when they will **hear** a (mighty) Blast
054:048 (they will **hear**): "Taste ye the touch of Hell!"
056:025 No frivolity will they **hear** therein, nor any
067:007 they will **hear** the (terrible) drawing in of its
068:051 thee up with their eyes when they **hear** the Message;
069:012 and that ears (that should **hear** the tale and) retain its
078:035 No Vanity shall they **hear** therein, nor Untruth;-
088:011 Where they shall **hear** no (word) of vanity:

HEARD

002:075 seeing that a party of them **heard** the Word of Allah,
003:181 Allah hath **heard** the taunt of those who say:
003:193 "Our Lord! We have **heard** the call
008:031 they say: "We have **heard** this (before): if we
012:031 When she **heard** of their malicious talk, she sent
018:011 (so that they **heard** not):
021:060 They said, "We **heard** a youth talk of them:
024:012 men and women-when ye **heard** of the affair,-
024:016 when ye **heard** it, say? "It is not right of us to speak
027:008 a voice was **heard**: "Blessed are those in the Fire
031:007 he turns away in arrogance, as if he **heard** them not,
032:012 (saying): "Our Lord! we have seen and we have **heard**:
038:007 "We never **heard** (the like) of this in the
045:008 as if he had not **heard** them: then announce
046:030 We have **heard** a Book revealed after Moses,
054:037 (They **heard**): "Now taste ye My Wrath
058:001 Allah has indeed **heard** (and accepted)
072:001 'We have really **heard** a wonderful Recital!

HEARER

014:039 for truly my Lord is He, the **Hearer** of Prayer!
087:009 the admonition profits (the **hearer**).

HEAREST

003:035 for Thou **hearest** and knoweth all things."
020:108 so that thou **hearest** not but murmuring.

HEARETH

002:224 for Allah is One Who **heareth** and knoweth all things.
002:227 Allah **heareth** and knoweth all things.
002:244 and know that Allah **heareth** and knoweth all things.
002:256 And Allah **heareth** and knoweth all things.
003:034 and Allah **heareth** and knoweth all things.
003:038 for Thou art He that **heareth** prayer!
003:121 and Allah **heareth** and knoweth all things.
004:058 For Allah is He Who **heareth** and seeth all things.
004:134 for Allah is He that **heareth** and seeth (all things).
004:148 for Allah is He who **heareth** and knoweth all things.
005:076 that **heareth** and knoweth all things."

HEARETH (continued)

006:013   Who **heareth** and knoweth all things.
006:115   for He is the one Who **heareth** and knoweth all.
007:200   for he **heareth** and knoweth (all things).
008:017   He who **heareth** and knoweth (all things).
008:042   is He Who **heareth** and knoweth (all things).
008:053   Allah is He Who **heareth** and knoweth (all things)."
008:061   the One that **heareth** and knoweth (all things).
009:098   that **heareth** and knoweth (all things).
009:103   and Allah is one who **heareth** and knoweth.
010:065   it is He Who **heareth** and knoweth (all things).
012:034   verily He **heareth** and knoweth (all things).
017:001   Who **heareth** and seeth (all things).
019:042   which **heareth** not and seeth not, and can
021:004   He is the One that **heareth** and knoweth (all things)."
026:220   For it is He Who **heareth** and knoweth all things.

HEARING

002:007   seal on their hearts and on their **hearing**,
002:020   their faculty of **hearing** and seeing;
002:181   If anyone changes the bequest after **hearing** it,
006:046   took away your **hearing** and your sight, and sealed
010:031   **hearing** and sight? And who is it that brings out
015:018   But any that gains a **hearing** by stealth,
016:078   you **hearing** and sight and intelligence
017:036   the **hearing**, the seeing, the heart all of those
023:078   (the faculties of) **hearing**, sight, feeling and
026:212   Indeed they are banished from **hearing** it.
032:009   (the faculties of) **hearing** and sight
041:020   the (Fire), their **hearing**, their sight, and their
041:022   lest your **hearing**, your sight, and your skins
045:023   left him astray, and sealed his **hearing** and his
046:026   and We had endowed them with (faculties of) **hearing**,
046:026   but of no profit to them were their (faculties of) **hearing**,
067:023   and made for you the faculties of **hearing**, seeing,
072:009   to sit there in (hidden) stations, to (steal) a **hearing**;
076:002   so We gave him (the gifts), of **Hearing** and Sight.

HEARKEN

002:093   and **hearken** (to the law)"
002:104   but say, 'Unzurna and **hearken** (to him):
028:050   But if they **hearken** not to thee, know that
028:071   Will ye not then **hearken**?
030:023   verily in that are Signs for those who **hearken**.
033:001   and **hearken** not to the Unbelievers and the
046:031   "O our people, **hearken** to the one who invites
046:032   "If any does not **hearken** to the one who invites
059:011   and we will never **hearken** to any one

HEARKENED

012:034   So his Lord **hearkened** to him (in his paryer)

HEARKENS

084:002   And **hearkens** to (the Command of) its Lord,-and it
084:005   And **hearkens** to (the Command of) its Lord,-and it

HEARS

002:181   For Allah **hears** and knows (all things).
018:026   He **hears** (everything)!
022:061   Who **hears** and sees (all things).
022:075   He Who **hears** and sees (all things).
024:021   and Allah is One Who **hears** and knows (all things).
029:005   and He **hears** and knows (all things).
029:060   for He **hears** and knows (all things).
031:028   for Allah is He Who **hears** and sees (all things).
034:050   it is He Who **hears** all things,
040:020   Who **hears** and sees (all things).
040:056   it is He Who **hears** and sees (all things).

HEARS (continued)

041:036   He is the One Who **hears** and knows all things.
042:011   and He is the One that **hears** and sees.
044:006   for He **hears** and knows (all things);
045:008   He **hears** the Signs of Allah rehearsed to him,
049:001   for Allah is He who **hears** and knows all things.
058:001   and Allah (always) **hears** the arguments
058:001   for Allah **hears** and sees (all things).

HEART

002:097   (revelation) to they **heart** by Allah's will,
002:200   yea, with far more **heart** and soul.
002:204   to witness about what is in his **heart**;
002:260   He said: "Yea! but to satisfy my own **heart**."
002:283   his **heart** is tainted with sin.
003:119   Allah knoweth well all the secrets of the **heart**."
003:139   So lose not **heart**, nor fall into despair:
003:146   But they never lost **heart** if they met
005:052   Those in whose **heart** is a disease-thou seest how
005:116   Thou knowest what is in my **heart**, though I
007:002   so let thy **heart** be oppressed no more
007:101   the **heart** of those who reject Faith.
008:024   in between a man and his **heart**, and that
008:046   lest ye lose **heart** and your power depart; and be
011:012   and thy **heart** feeleth straitened lest they say,
011:120   with it We make firm they **heart**: in them
012:015   and We put into his **heart** (this Message):
012:077   Joseph keep locked in his **heart**, revealing not
015:097   We do indeed know how thy **heart** is distressed
016:106   except under compulsion, his **heart** remaining firm
017:036   the hearing, the seeing, the **heart** all of those
018:028   nor obey any whose **heart** We have permitted to
022:032   come truly from piety of **heart**.
022:053   hearts is a disease and who are hardend of **heart**:
025:032   that We may strenghten thy **heart** thereby,
026:089   that brings to Allah a sound **heart**;
026:194   To thy **heart** and mind that thou mayest admonish
028:010   And the **heart** of the mother of Moses became void:
028:010   had We not strengthened her **heart** (with faith),
033:032   lest one in whose **heart** is a disease should be
033:037   But thou didst hide in thy **heart** that which
037:084   Behold, He approached his Lord with a sound **heart**.
037:089   And he said, "I am indeed sick (at **heart**)!"
038:026   (of thy **heart**), for it will mislead thee from
039:022   Is one whose **heart** Allah has opened to Islam,
040:035   seal up every **heart**-of arrogant tyrant."
041:017   but they preferred blindness (of **heart**) to Guidance:
042:024   He could seal up thy **heart**.
045:023   and his **heart** (and understanding), and put
046:026   hearing, sight, and **heart** and intellect, when they
046:026   with (faculties of) hearing, sight, **heart** and intellect:
050:033   and brought a **heart** turned in devotion (to Him):
050:037   that has a **heart** and understanding or who
053:011   The (Prophet's) (mind and) **heart** in no way
053:034   Gives a little, then hardens (his **heart**)?
064:011   (Allah) guides his **heart** (aright): for Allah
069:046   the artery of his **heart**:
080:009   And with fear (in his **heart**),

HEART'S

077:043   "Eat ye and drink ye to your **heart's** content:

HEARTED

009:114   for Abraham was most tender **hearted**, forbearing.

HEARTFELT
012:068   Jacob's **heartfelt** desire.

HEARTS
002:004   and (in their **hearts**) have the assurance
002:007   Allah hath set a seal on their **hearts** and on their hearing.
002:010   In their **hearts** is a disease;
002:074   Thenceforth were your **hearts** hardened:
002:088   They say, "Our **hearts** are the wrappings
002:093   and their **hearts** were filled
002:118   Their **hearts** are alike.
002:118   who hold firmly to Faith (in their **hearts**).
002:225   but for the intention in your **hearts**;
002:235   betrothal or hold it in your **hearts**.
002:235   Allah knows that ye cherish them in your **hearts**:
002:235   Allah knoweth what is in your **hearts**,
003:007   But those in whose **hearts** is perversity follow
003:008   "let not our **hearts** deviate now after Thou
003:029   in your **hearts** or reveal it, Allah knows it all:
003:103   He joined your **hearts** in love,
003:118   what their **hearts** conceal is far worse.
003:126   and an assurance to your **hearts**:
003:151   terror into the **hearts** of the Unbelievers,
003:154   for Allah knoweth well the secrets of your **hearts**.
003:154   and purge what is in your **hearts**.
003:156   a cause of sighs and regrets in their **hearts**.
003:167   saying with their lips what was not in their **hearts**.
004:063   Those men, Allah knows what is in their **hearts**;
004:090   **hearts** restraining them from fighting you or
004:135   Follow not the lusts (of your **hearts**), lest
004:155   that they said, "Our **hearts** are the Wrappings; nay,
004:155   on their **hearts** for their blasphemy,
005:007   for Allah knoweth well the secrets of your **hearts**.
005:013   We cursed them, and made their **hearts** grow hard:
005:041   Allah's will to purify their **hearts**.
005:041   but whose **hearts** have no faith; or it be
005:052   which they secretly harboured in their **hearts**.
005:113   to eat thereof and satisfy our **hearts**, and to know
006:025   but We have thrown veils on their **hearts**,
006:043   On the contrary their **hearts** became hardened,
006:046   and sealed up your **hearts**, who-a god
006:051   in whose (**hearts**) is the fear that they will
006:110   their **hearts** and their eyes, even as
006:113   the **hearts** of those incline, who have
007:043   from their **hearts** any rancour; beneath
007:056   and longing (in your **hearts**): for the
007:100   and seal up their **hearts** so that they
007:179   They have **hearts** wherewith they understand not,
008:002   fell a tremor in their **hearts**, and when
008:010   a message of hope, and an assurance to your **hearts**:
008:011   to strengthen your **hearts**, and to plant
008:012   into the **hearts** of the Unbelievers:
008:043   well the (secrets) of (all) **hearts**.
008:049   in whose **hearts** is a disease: say:
008:060   to strike terror into (the **hearts** of) the enemies,
008:063   He hath put affection between their **hearts**:
008:070   "If Allah findeth any good in your **hearts**, He will
009:008   they please you, but their **hearts** are averse
009:015   And still the indignation of their heart.
009:045   and the Last Day, and whose **hearts** are in doubt,
009:060   for those whose **hearts** have been (recently) reconciled
009:064   showing them what is (really passing) in their **hearts**.
009:077   hypocrisy into their **hearts**, (to last)
009:087   their **hearts** are sealed and so they understand not.

HEARTS (continued)
009:093   Allah hath sealed their **hearts**: so they
009:110   and shakiness in their **hearts**, until their
009:110   until their **hearts** are cut to pieces.
009:117   after that the **hearts** of a part of them had
009:125   But those in whose **hearts** is a disease,-it will
009:127   their **hearts** (from the light); for they
010:057   in your **hearts**,-and for those who believe,
010:074   Thus do We seal the **hearts** of the transgressors.
010:088   and send hardness to their **hearts**, so they
011:005   Behold! they fold up their **hearts**, that they
011:005   knoweth well the (inmost secrets) of the **hearts**.
013:028   and whose **hearts** find satisfaction in the remembrance
013:028   of Allah do **hearts** find satisfaction.
014:037   so fill the **hearts** of some among men
014:043   and their **hearts** a (gaping) void!
015:012   into the **hearts** of the sinners-
015:047   And We shall remove from their **hearts** any lurking
016:022   in the Hereafter, their **hearts** refuse to know,
016:108   Those are they whose **hearts**, ears, and eyes
017:025   Your Lord knoweth best what is in your **hearts**:
017:046   And We put coverings over their **hearts** (and minds)
018:014   We gave strength to their **hearts**: behold, they
018:057   veils over their **hearts** so that they should
021:003   Their **hearts** toying as with trifles.
021:110   in speech and what ye hide (in your **hearts**).
022:035   To those whose **hearts**, when Allah
022:046   so that their **hearts** (and mind) may thus learn
022:046   but the **hearts** which are in their breasts.
022:053   but a trial for those in whose **hearts** is a
022:054   and their **hearts** may be made humbly (open)
023:060   with their **hearts** full of fear, because they
023:063   But their **hearts** are in confused ignorance
024:037   is for the Day when **hearts** and eyes will be
024:050   Is it that there is a disease in their **hearts**?
026:200   the **hearts** of the Sinners.
027:074   all that their **hearts** do hide, as well
028:069   their **hearts** conceal and all that they reveal.
029:010   all that is in the **hearts** of all Creation?
029:049   in the **hearts** of those endowed with knowledge:
030:021   and mercy between your (**hearts**): verily in
030:059   Thus does Allah seal up the **hearts** of those
031:023   all that is in (men's) **hearts**.
033:004   two **hearts** in his breast: nor has
033:005   (what counts is) the intention of your **hearts**:
033:010   and the **hearts** gaped up to the throats, and ye
033:012   in whose **hearts** is a disease say: "Allah
033:026   cast terror into their **hearts**, (so that)
033:051   and Allah knows (all) that is in your **hearts**:
033:053   makes for greater purity for your **hearts** and for theirs.
033:060   in whose **hearts** is a disease, and those
034:023   when terror is removed from their **hearts**
035:038   full knowledge of all that is in (men's) **hearts**.
039:007   For He knoweth well all that is in (men's) **hearts**.
039:022   Woe to those whose **hearts** are hardened against
039:023   then their skins and their **hearts** do soften
039:045   the **hearts** of those who believe not in the
040:018   drawing near, when the **Hearts** will (come)
040:019   and all that **hearts** (of men) conceal.
040:080   to any need (there may be) in your **hearts**; and on
041:005   They say: "Our **hearts** are under veils, (concealed)
042:024   For He knows well the secrets of all **hearts**.
047:016   Such are men whose **hearts** Allah has sealed,

HEARTS (continued)

047:020   thou wilt see those in whose **hearts** is a disease
047:024   or is that there are locks upon their **hearts**?
047:029   Or do those in whose **hearts** is a disease,
048:004   into the **hearts** of the Believers, that they
048:011   They say with their tongues what is not in their **hearts**.
048:012   this seemed pleasing in your **hearts**, and ye conceived
048:018   He knew what was in their **hearts**, and He
048:026   the Unbelievers got up in their **hearts** heat and cant-
049:003   their **hearts** has Allah tested of piety:
049:007   and has made it beautiful in your **hearts**, and He
049:014   for not yet has Faith entered your **hearts**.
057:006   of the secrets of (all) **hearts**.
057:016   the Believers that their **hearts** in all humility
057:016   passed over them and their **hearts** grew hard?
057:020   brings forth, delight (the **hearts** of) the tillers;
057:027   and We ordained in the **hearts** of those who followed
058:022   For such He has written Faith in their **hearts**,
059:002   and cast terror into their **hearts**, so that
059:009   in their **hearts** for things given to the (latter),
059:010   and leave not, in our **hearts**, rancor (or sense of injury)
059:013   Of a truth ye arouse greater fear in their **hearts**,
059:014   but their **hearts** are divided:
061:005   Allah let their **hearts** go wrong.
063:003   so a seal was set on their **hearts**: therefore
064:004   yes, Allah knows well the (secrets) of (all) **hearts**.
066:004   to Allah, your **hearts** are indeed so inclined;
067:013   (full) knowledge, of the secrets of (all) **hearts**.
074:031   in whose **hearts** is a disease and the Unbelievers
079:008   **Hearts** that Day will be in agitation;
083:014   By no means! but on their **hearts** is the
104:007   The which doth mount (Right) to the **Hearts**:
114:005   Who whispers into the **hearts** of Mankind,-

HEAT

009:081   Say, "The fire of Hell is fiercer in **heat**."
009:081   they said, "Go not forth in the **heat**."
013:017   (ore) which they **heat** in the fire, to make
016:081   to protect you from **heat**, and coats
020:119   nor from the sun's **heat**."
024:058   for the noonday **heat**; and after
035:021   and the (genial) **heat** of the sun:
048:026   their hearts **heat** and cant-the **heat** and cant
076:013   neither the sun's (excessive **heat**) nor excessive cold.
081:012   When the Blazing Fire is kindled to fierce **heat**;

HEATED

009:035   be **heated** in the fire of Hell, and with it

HEAVEN

002:022   and the **heaven** your canopy;
002:029   then He turned to the **heaven** and made them
002:033   that I know the secrets of the **heaven** and earth,
002:059   the transgressors a plague from **heaven**,
003:142   enter **Heaven** without Allah testing those
003:183   consumed by fire (from **heaven**)."
004:124   they will enter **Heaven** and not the least
004:153   to cause a book to descend to them from **heaven**:
005:112   a Table set (with viands) from **heaven**?"
005:114   "O Allah our Lord! send us from **heaven** a table
007:040   the gates of **heaven**, nor will
007:096   blessings from **heaven** and earth; but they
007:162   so We sent on them a plague from **heaven**.
008:011   from **heaven**, to clean you therewith, to remove
010:061   on the earth or in **heaven**.
014:038   from Allah, whether on earth or in **heaven**.

HEAVEN (continued)

015:014   a gate from **heaven**, and they were to continue
018:040   thunderbolts (by way of reckoning) from **heaven**,
022:031   he is as if he had fallen from **heaven** and been
022:070   Allah knows all that is in **heaven** and on earth?
025:025   The Day the **heaven** shall be rent asunder
025:075   place in **heaven**, because of their patient
027:060   Or, who has created the **heaven** and the earth,
027:064   you sustenance from **heaven** and earth?
027:075   And there is nothing hidden in **heaven** or earth,
029:022   "Not on earth nor in **heaven** will ye be able
029:034   a Punishment from **heaven**, because they
029:058   a Home in **Heaven**,-lofty mansions beneath which
030:025   that **heaven** and earth stand by His command:
030:044   will make provision for themselves (in **heaven**):
031:026   To Allah belong all things in **heaven** and earth:
035:003   you Sustenance from **heaven** or earth?
036:028   after him, any hosts from **heaven**, nor was it needful
037:006   the lower **heaven** with beauty (in) the stars,-
038:027   We create **heaven** and earth and all between!
041:012   And We adorned the lower **heaven** with lights,
041:012   to each **heaven** its duty and command.
043:084   It is He Who is God in **heaven** and God
044:029   And neither **heaven** nor earth shed a tear over them:
051:022   And in **heaven** is your Sustenance, as (also)
051:023   Then, by the Lord of **heaven** and earth, this is
052:038   by which they can (climb up to **heaven** and) listen
054:011   So We opened the gates of **heaven**, with water
057:004   out of it, what comes down from **heaven** and what
057:021   of **heaven** and earth, prepared for those
067:005   adorned the lowest **heaven** with Lamps, and We
067:016   is in **heaven** will not cause you to be swallowed
067:017   is in **Heaven** will not send against you a violent
072:008   'And we pried into the (secrets of) **heaven**;
077:009   When the **heaven** is cleft asunder;
079:027   Are ye the more difricult to create or the **heaven** (above)?
089:030   "Yea, enter thou my **Heaven**!"

HEAVENS

002:022   and sent down rain from the **heavens**;
002:107   of the **heavens** and the earth?
002:116   that is in the **heavens** and the earth:
002:117   the **heavens** and the earth:
002:144   thy face (for guidance) to the **heavens**:
002:164   of the **heavens** and the earth;
002:255   His are all things in the **heavens** and on earth.
002:255   over the **heavens** and the earth,
002:284   that is in the **heavens** and on earth.
003:005   is hidden on earth or in the **heavens**.
003:029   in the **heavens**, and what is on earth.
003:083   While all creatures in the **heavens** and on earth have,
003:109   that is in the **heavens** and earth:
003:129   that is in the **heavens** and on earth.
003:133   (of the whole) of the **heavens** and of the earth,
003:180   the heritage of the **heavens** and the earth;
003:189   the dominion of the **heavens** and the earth;
003:190   the **heavens** and the earth, and the
003:191   creation in the **heavens** and the earth,
004:126   in the **heavens** and on earth: and He
004:131   in the **heavens** and on earth.
004:131   belong all things in the **heavens** and on earth.
004:132   all things in the **heavens** and on earth,
004:170   in the **heavens** and on earth: and Allah
004:171   in the **heavens** and on earth.

HEAVENS (continued)

005:017   the dominion of the **heavens** and the earth,
005:018   the dominion of the **heavens** and the earth, and all
005:040   the dominion of the **heavens** and the earth?
005:097   of what is in the **heavens** and on earth and that
005:120   of the **heavens** and the earth, and all
006:001   the **heavens** and the earth, and made the
006:003   And He is Allah in the **heavens** and on earth.
006:012   is in the **heavens** and on earth?"
006:014   the Maker of the **heavens** and the earth?
006:073   It is He Who created the **heavens** and
006:075   the kingdom of the **heavens** and the earth,
006:079   toward Him Who created the **heavens** and the
006:101   of the **heavens** and the earth: how can
007:054   Who created the **heavens** and the earth
007:158   of the **heavens** and the earth: there is
007:185   of the **heavens** and the earth and all
007:187   the **heavens** and the earth.
009:036   He created the **heavens** and the earth; of them
009:116   of the **heavens** and the earth.
010:003   Who created the **heavens** and the earth in six
010:006   in the **heavens** and the earth, are Signs
010:018   in the heaven or on earth?-Glory to Him! and far
010:055   the **heavens** and on earth?
010:066   all creatures, in the **heavens** and on earth.
010:068   His are all things in the **heavens** and on earth!
010:101   in the **heavens** and on earth"; but neither
011:007   He it is Who created the **heavens** and the earth
011:107   the **heavens** and the earth endure, except as
011:108   so long as the **heavens** and the earth endure,
011:123   unseen (secrets) of the **heavens** and the earth,
012:101   O Thou Creator of the **heavens** and the earth!
012:105   And how many Signs in the **heavens** and the earth
013:002   Allah is He Who raised the **heavens** without any
013:015   in the **heavens** and the earth do prostrate
013:016   of the **heavens** and the earth?" Say: "(It is)
013:018   in the **heavens** and on earth, and as much
014:002   in the **heavens** and on earth! But alas
014:010   of the **heavens** and the earth? It is He
014:019   created the **Heavens** and the earth in Truth?
014:024   and its branches (reach) to the **heavens**,-
014:032   the **heavens** and the earth and sendeth down
014:048   and so will be the **Heavens**, and (men) will be
015:016   constellations in the **heavens** and made
015:085   We created not the **heavens**, the earth, and all
016:003   He has created the **heavens** and the earth
016:049   is in the **heavens** and on earth, whether moving
016:052   the **heavens** and on earth, and to Him
016:073   with anything in **heavens** or earth, and cannot
016:077   of the **heavens** and the earth.
017:044   The seven **heavens** and the earth, and all
017:055   all beings that are in the **heavens** and on earth:
017:095   sent them down from the **heavens** an angel
017:099   Who created the **heavens** and the earth, has power
017:102   by none but the Lord of the **heavens** and the earth
018:014   "Our Lord is the Lord of the **heavens** and of
018:026   the **heavens** and the earth: how clearly
018:051   the creation of the **heavens** and the earth,
019:065   Lord of the **heavens** and of the earth, and of
019:093   Not one of the beings in the **heavens** and the
020:004   the earth and the **heavens** on high.
020:006   in the **heavens** and on earth, and all
021:004   word (spoken) in the **heavens** and the earth:

HEAVENS (continued)

021:016   the **heavens** and the earth and all that is between!
021:019   in the **heavens** and on earth: even those
021:022   If there were, in the **heavens** and the earth,
021:030   the **heavens** and the earth were joined together
021:032   And We have made the **heavens** as a
021:056   of the **heavens** and the earth, He Who
021:104   The Day that we roll up the **heavens** like a
022:018   all things that are in the **heavens** and on earth,-
022:064   the **heavens** and on earth: for verily
023:071   with their desires, truly the **heavens** and the
023:086   seven **heavens**, and the Lord of the Mighty Throne?"
024:035   Allah is the Light of the **heavens** and the earth.
024:041   Whose praises all beings in the **heavens** and on
024:042   of the **heavens** and the earth; and to
024:064   doth belong whatever is in the **heavens** and on
025:002   of the **heavens** and the earth: no son
025:006   in the **heavens** and the earth: verily He
025:059   He Who created the **heavens** and the earth
026:024   of the **heavens** and the earth, and all
027:025   in the **heavens** and the earth, and knows
027:065   Say: None in the **heavens** or on earth, except
027:087   in the **heavens**, and those who are on earth,
029:044   Allah created the **heavens** and the earth
029:052   He knows what is in the **heavens** and on earth.
029:061   who has created the **heavens** and the earth
030:008   the **heavens** and the earth, and all
030:018   Yea, To Him be praise, in the **heavens** and on
030:022   of the **heavens** and the earth, and the
030:026   is in the **heavens** and on earth: all are
030:027   (We can think of) in the **heavens** and the earth:
031:010   He created the **heavens** without any pillars
031:016   in a rock, or (anywhere) in the **heavens** or on
031:020   to your (use) all things in the **heavens** and on
031:025   who it is that created the **heavens** and the earth.
032:004   It is Allah Who has created the **heavens** and the
032:005   He directs the affairs from the **heavens** to the
033:072   to the **Heavens** and the Earth and the Mountains:
034:001   all things in the **heavens** and on earth: to Him
034:003   the least little atom in the **Heavens** or on earth:
034:022   of an atom,-in the **heavens** or on earth:
034:024   from the **heavens** and the earth?"
035:001   the Originator of the **heavens** and the earth,
035:038   the hidden things of the **heavens** and the earth:
035:040   Or have they a share in the **heavens**?
035:041   It is Allah Who sustains the **heavens** and the
035:044   in the **heavens** or on earth: for He
036:081   "Is not He Who created the **heavens** and the
037:005   Lord of the **heavens** and of the earth, and all
038:010   of the **heavens** and the earth and all between?
038:066   "The Lord of the **heavens** and the earth, and all
039:005   He created the **heavens** and the earth in true
039:038   that created the **heavens** and the earth, they would
039:044   of the **heavens** and the earth: in the end,
039:046   Say: "O Allah! Creator of the **heavens** and the
039:063   To Him belong the keys of the **heavens** and the
039:067   and the **heavens** will be rolled up in his
039:068   when all that are in the **heavens** and on
040:037   "The ways and means of (reachng) the **heavens**,
040:057   Assuredly the creation of the **heavens** and the
042:004   in the **heavens** and on earth: and He is
042:005   The **heavens** are almost rent asunder from above
042:011   (He is) the Creator of the **heavens** and the earth:

HEAVENS (continued)

042:012 To Him belong the keys of the **heavens** and the
042:029 of the **heavens** and the earth, and the living
042:049 of the **heavens** and the earth.
042:053 whatever is in the **heavens** and whatever is on earth.
043:009 'Who created the **heavens** and the earth?'
043:082 Glory to the Lord of the **heavens** and the earth,
043:085 the dominion of the **heavens** and the earth,
044:007 The Lord of the **heavens** and the earth and all
044:038 We created not the **heavens**, the earth,
045:003 Verily in the **heavens** and the earth, are Signs
045:013 as from Him, all that is in the **heavens** and on
045:022 Allah created the **heavens** and the earth for just
045:027 of the **heavens** and the earth, and the
045:036 Lord of the **heavens** and Lord of the earth,
045:037 in the **heavens** and the earth: and He
046:003 We created not the **heavens** and the earth and all
046:004 or have they a share in the **heavens**?
046:033 Who created the **heavens** and the earth, and never
048:004 of the **heavens** and the earth; and Allah
048:007 of the **heavens** and the earth; and Allah
048:014 of the **heavens** and the earth: He forgives
049:016 is in the **heavens** and on earth: He has
049:018 of the **heavens** and the earth: and Allah
050:038 We created the **heavens** and the earth and all
052:036 Or did they create the **heavens** and the earth?
053:026 in the **heavens**, their intercession will avail
053:031 in the **heavens** and on earth: so that
055:029 every creature in the **heavens** and on earth:
055:033 the zones of the **heavens** and the earth, pass ye!
057:001 Whatever is in the **heavens** and on earth,-
057:002 of the **heavens** and the earth: it is He
057:004 He it is Who created the **heavens** and the earth
057:005 of the **heavens** and the earth: and all
057:010 of the **heavens** and the earth.
058:007 (all) that is in the **heavens** and on earth?
059:001 Whatever is in the **heavens** and on earth,
059:024 whatever is in the **heavens** and on earth,
061:001 Whatever is in the **heavens** and on earth,
062:001 Whatever is in the **heavens** and on earth,
063:007 of the **heavens** and the earth; but the Hypocrites
064:001 Whatever is in the **heavens** and on earth,
064:003 He has created the **heavens** and the earth
064:004 He knows what is in the **heavens** and on earth;
067:003 He Who created the seven **heavens** one above another:
071:015 the seven **heavens** one above another,
078:019 And the **heavens** shall be opened as if
078:037 (From) the Lord of the **heavens** and the earth,
085:009 of the **heavens** and the earth!

HEAVILY

009:038 ye cling **heavily** to the earth?
009:041 lightly or **heavily**, and strive and struggle,
035:018 If one **heavily** laden should call another to (bear)

HEAVING

011:106 therein (nothing but) the **heaving** of sighs and sobs:

HEAVY

002:264 on it falls a **heavy** rain,
002:265 and if it receives not **heavy** rain,
002:265 high and fertile: **heavy** rain falls on it but makes it yield
005:033 and a **heavy** punishment is theirs in the Hereafter;
005:041 and in the Hereafter a **heavy** punishment.
007:008 those whose scale (of good) will be **heavy**, will prosper:
007:157 He releases them from their **heavy** burdens and from

HEAVY (continued)

007:187 **Heavy** were its burden through the heavens
007:189 When she grows **heavy**, they both
013:012 the clouds, **heavy** with (fertilizing) rain!
016:007 And they carry your **heavy** loads to lands that ye
017:069 and send against you a **heavy** gale to drown you
018:031 will wear green garments of fine silk and **heavy** brocade;
023:102 Then those whose balance (of good deeds) is **heavy**,-
051:002 And those that lift and bear away **heavy** weights;
073:016 so We seized him with a **heavy** Punishment.
076:021 of fine silk and **heavy** brocade, and they
101:006 will be (found) **heavy**,

HEAVY-LADEN

007:057 when they have carried the **heavy-laden** clouds.

HEED

002:235 and take **heed** of Him;
009:126 and they take no **heed**.
010:007 and those who **heed** not Our Signs,-
011:024 Will ye not then take **heed**?
011:030 Will ye not then take **heed**?
014:042 Think not that Allah doth not **heed** the deeds
014:052 let men of understanding take **heed**.
016:108 and they take no **heed**.
017:057 is something to take **heed** of.
021:001 yet they **heed** not and they turn away.
024:027 in order that ye may **heed** (what is seemly).
027:062 Little it is that ye **heed**!
037:013 And, when they are admonished, pay no **heed**,-
039:009 (in adoration), who takes **heed** of the Hereafter,
044:058 in thy tongue, in order that they may give **heed**.
056:062 why then do ye not take **heed**?
087:010 He will **heed** who fears:
096:019 Nay, **heed** him not: but prostrate

HEEDED

006:140 and **heeded** no guidance.
010:073 those who were warned (but **heeded** not)!
026:173 on those who were admonished (but **heeded** not)!
027:058 on those who were admonished (but **heeded** not)!
037:177 who were warned (and **heeded** not)!

HEEDFUL

004:001 and be **heedful** the wombs (that bore you):

HEEDLESS

007:179 for they are **heedless** (of warning).
010:092 are **heedless** of Our Signs!
021:097 "Ah! woe to us! we were indeed **heedless** of this;
030:007 but of the Hereafter they are **heedless**.
036:006 therefore remain **heedless** (of the Signs of Allah).
050:022 (It will be said:) "Thou wast **heedless** of this;
051:011 Those who (flounder) **heedless** in a

HEEDFUL

050:032 for everyone penitent **heedful** one,

HEELS

002:143 who would turn on their **heels** (from the Faith).
003:144 will ye then turn back on your **heels**?
003:144 If any did turn back on his **heels**,
003:149 they will drive you back on your **heels**,
006:071 turn on our **heels** after receiving guidance from Allah?-
008:048 he turned on his **heels**, and said: "Lo! I am clear of you;
023:066 but ye used to turn back on your **heels**-

HEIFER

002:067 "Allah commands that ye sacrifice a **heifer**.
002:068 He said: "He says: The **heifer** should be

HEIFER (continued)

002:068 to make plain to us what **heifer** it is!"
002:069 He said: "He says, a fawn-coloured **heifer**,
002:071 He said: "He says, a **heifer** not trained
002:073 "Strike the (body) with a piece of the (**heifer**)."

HEIFERS

002:070 to us are all **heifers** alike:

HEIGHT

017:037 the mountains in **height**.

HEIGHTS

007:046 and on the **Heights** will be men who would
007:048 The men on the **Heights** will call
009:040 But the word of Allah is exalted to the **heights**:

HEINOUS

004:031 If ye (but) eschew the most **heinous** of the things
004:048 a sin most **heinous** indeed.

HEIR

002:233 An **heir** shall be chargeable in the same way.
017:033 We have given his **heir** authority (to demand Qisas
019:005 so give me an **heir** as from Thyself,-
027:016 And Solomon was David's **heir**.
027:049 we shall then say to his **heir** (when he seeks vengeance):

HEIRS

004:011 and the parents are the (only) **heirs**,
004:033 We have appointed sharers and **heirs** to property
004:176 or ascendants as **heirs**.

HEIRS (continued)

010:014 Then We made you **heirs** in the land after them,
023:010 Those will be the **heirs**,
028:005 (in faith) and make them **heirs**,
028:058 and We are their **heirs**!
033:027 And He made you **heirs** of their lands,
043:072 ye are made **heirs** for your (good) deeds (in life).
057:007 of the (substance) whereof He has made you **heirs**.

HELD

003:045 the son of Mary, **held** in honour in this world and the
004:084 thou art **held** responsible only for thyself,
004:140 the Message of Allah **held** in defiance and ridicule,
005:011 but (Allah) **held** back their hands from you:
006:050 Say: "Can the blind be **held** equal to the seeing?"
009:106 There are (yet) others, **held** in suspense for the
012:075 should be **held** (as bondman) to atone
012:080 they **held** a conference in private.
016:079 Do they not look at the birds, **held** poised in the midst
026:098 "'When we **held** you as equals with the
030:010 and **held** them up to ridicule.
036:027 me among those **held** in honour!"
043:057 When (Jesus) the son of Mary is **held** up as an
048:025 your way, but He **held** back your hands) that He
074:038 Every soul will be (**held**) in pledge for its deeds.
077:020 a fluid (**held**) despicable?-
080:013 (It is) in Books **held** (greatly) in honor.
081:020 Endued with Power, **held** in honour by the Lord
094:004 (in which) thou (art **held**)?

HELL

002:206 Enough for him is **Hell**;
003:012 vanquished and gathered together to **Hell**,
003:162 and whose abode is in **Hell**? A woeful refuse!
003:197 their Ultimate abode is **Hell**: what an evil
004:055 and enough is **Hell** for a burning fire.
004:093 his recompense is **Hell**, to abide
004:097 Such men will find their abode in **Hell**.

HELL (continued)

004:115 and land him in **Hell**, what an evil refuge!
004:121 They (his dupes) will have their dwelling in **hell**,
004:140 and those who defy Faith-all in **Hell**;
004:169 Except the way of **Hell**, to dwell
007:018 **Hell** will I fill with you all.
007:041 For them there is **hell**, as a couch
007:179 Mawny are the Jinns and men We have made for **Hell**:
008:016 and his abode is **Hell**, an evil refuse (indeed)!
008:036 gathered together to **Hell**;-
008:037 heap them together, and cast them into **Hell**.
009:035 be heated in the fire of **Hell**, and with it
009:049 **Hell** surrounds the Unbelievers (on all sides).
009:063 oppose Allah and His Messenger, is the Fire of **Hell**?
009:068 and the rejecters of Faith, the fire of **Hell**:
009:073 Their abode is **hell**, an evil refuge indeed.
009:081 Say, "The fire of **Hell** is fiercer in heat."
009:095 an abomination, and **Hell** is their dwelling-place,
009:109 crumble to pieces with him, into the fire of **Hell**.
011:119 "I will fill **Hell** with jinns and men all together."
013:018 their abode will be **Hell**,-what a bed of misery!
014:016 In front of such a one is **Hell**, and he
014:029 Into **Hell**? They will burn therein,-an evil place to stay
014:030 But verily ye are making straightway for **Hell**!"
015:043 And verily, **Hell** is the promised
016:029 "So enter the gates of **Hell**, to dwell therein.
017:008 made **Hell** a prison for those who reject
017:018 in the end have We provided **Hell** for them:
017:039 be thrown into **Hell**, blameworthy and rejected.
017:063 verily **Hell** will be the recpmpense of you (all)-
017:097 their abode will be **Hell**: every time
018:100 And We shall present **Hell** that day for Unbelievers
018:102 Verily We have prepared **Hell** for the Unbelievers
018:106 That is their reward, **Hell**; because they
019:068 on their knees round about **Hell**;
019:086 And We shall drive the sinners to **Hell**,
020:074 for him is **Hell**: therein shall he neither die or live.
021:029 such a one We should reward with **Hell**: thus do
021:098 besides Allah, are (but) fuel for **Hell**!
021:102 Not the slightest sound will they hear of **Hell**:
022:072 It is the fire (of **Hell**)!
023:103 their souls; in **Hell** will they abide.
025:034 to **Hell** (prone) on their faces,-they will
025:065 avert from us the Wrath of **Hell**, for its
029:054 **Hell** will encompass the rejecters of Faith!-
029:068 a home in **Hell** for those who reject Faith?
032:013 "I will fill **Hell** with Jinns and men all together."
035:036 for them will be the Fire of **Hell**: no term
036:063 "This is the **Hell** of which ye were promised!
038:027 the Unbelievers because of the Fire (of **Hell**)!
038:056 **Hell**!-they will burn therein-an evil bed
038:085 "That I will certainly fill **Hell** with thee
039:032 Is there not in **Hell** an abode
039:060 is there not in **Hell** an abode for the Haughty?
039:071 The Unbelievers will be led to **Hell** in groups;
039:072 "Enter ye the gates of **Hell**, to dwell
040:049 Those in the Fire will say to the Keepers of **Hell**,
040:060 to serve Me will surely enter **Hell** abased."
040:076 "Enter ye the gates of **Hell**, to dwell therein:
043:074 The Sinners will be in the Punishment of **Hell**,
045:010 In front of them is **Hell**: and of no
048:006 He has cursed them and got **Hell** ready for them:
050:024 "Throw, both of you, into **Hell** every contumacious

HELL (continued)

050:030   The Day We will ask **Hell**, "Art thou filled to the full?"
052:013   to the Fire of **Hell**, irresistibly.
054:048   (they will hear): "Tastes ye the touch of **Hell**!"
055:043   This is the **Hell** which the Sinners deny:
058:008   Enough for them is **Hell**: in it
066:009   Their abode is **Hell**,-an evil refuge (indeed).
067:006   their Lord (and Cherisher) is the Chastisement of **Hell**:
072:023   that disobey Allah and His Messenger,-for them is **Hell**:
078:021   Truly **Hell** is as a place of ambush
083:016   Further, they will enter the Fire of **Hell**.
085:010   will have the Chastisement of **Hell**: they will
089:023   And **Hell**, that Day, is brought (face to face),-

HELL-FIRE

005:010   will be Companions of **Hell-fire**.
005:086   they shall be Companions of **Hell-fire**.
037:064   out of the bottom of **Hell-fire**:
056:094   And burning in **Hell-Fire**.
057:019   Our Signs,-they are the Companions of **Hell-Fire**.
072:015   they are (but) fuel for **Hell-Fire**'-
074:026   Soon will cast him into **Hell-Fire**!
074:027   And what will explain to thee what **Hell-Fire** is?
074:042   "What led you into **Hell-Fire**?"
079:036   And **Hell-Fire** shall be placed in full view
079:039   The Abode will be **Hell-Fire**;
098:006   will be in **hell-fire**, to dwell
102:006   Ye shall certainly see **Hell-fire**!

HELP

002:045   Nay, seek (Allah's) **help** with
002:153   O ye who believe! seek **help** with
002:214   "When (will come) the **help** of Allah"
002:214   Ah! Verily, the **help** of Allah is (always) near!
002:250   **help** us against those that reject faith."
003:022   nor will they have anyone to **help**.
003:056   nor will they have anyone to **help**.
003:081   do ye believe him and render him **help**."
003:111   and no **help** shall they get.
003:124   should **help** you with three thousand angels
003:125   your Lord would **help** you with five thousand angels
003:147   and **help** us against those that resist Faith."
003:160   who is there, after that, that can **help** you?
004:052   thou wilt find, have no one to **help**.
004:075   and raise for us from Thee one who will **help**!"
004:173   any to protect or **help** them.
005:002   **Help** ye one another in righteousness and piety,
005:002   but **help** ye not one another in sin and rancor:
005:072   There will for the wrong-doers be no one to **help**.
006:097   with their **help**, through the dark
007:128   "Pray for **help** from Allah," and (wait)
007:157   honor him, **help** him, and follow the Light which
007:197   are unable to **help** you, and indeed
007:197   and indeed to **help** themselves."
008:010   (in any case) there is no **help** except from Allah:
008:040   the Best to protect and the Best to **help**.
008:072   it is your duty to **help** them, except against
009:014   and disgrace them, **help** you (to victory)
009:025   Assuredly Allah did **help** you in many
009:040   If ye **help** not (the Prophet), (it is no matter):
009:040   for Allah did indeed **help** him, when the Unbelievers
009:074   none on earth to protect or **help** them.
011:030   who would **help** me against Allah if I drove them away?
011:063   who then can **help** me against Allah if I were to disobey
012:018   it is Allah (alone) whose **help** can be sought."

HELP (continued)

012:110   there reaches them Our **help**, and those
016:037   to stray, and there is none to **help** them.
016:127   for thy patience is but with the **help** from Allah;
017:075   found none to **help** thee against Us!
017:088   each other with **help** and support.
018:043   Nor had he numbers to **help** him against Allah,
018:095   **help** me therefore with strength (and labour):
021:039   and (when) no **help** can reach them!
022:013   is the patron, and evil the companion (for **help**)!
022:015   **help** him (His Messenger) in this world and the
022:060   Allah will **help** him: for Allah
022:078   the Best to protect and the Best to **help**!
023:026   (Noah) said: "O my Lord! **help** me: for that
023:039   (The prophet) said: "O my Lord! **help** me: for that
025:019   so ye cannot avert (your penalty) nor (get) **help**."
025:031   but enough is the Lord to guide and to **help**.
026:093   Can they **help** you or **help** themselves?'"
028:017   never shall I be a **help** to those who sin!"
028:018   sought his **help** called aloud for his **help** (again).
028:041   no **help** shall they find.
028:064   "Call upon your `partners' (for **help**)": they will
028:081   party to **help** him against Allah, nor could
029:010   the Wrath of Allah! And if **help** comes (to them)
029:025   the Fire, and ye shall have none to **help**."
029:030   He said: "O my Lord! **help** Thou me against
030:005   With the **help** of Allah.
036:075   They have not the power to **help** them: and they
037:025   that ye **help** not each other?'"
040:029   but who will **help** us from the Punishment of Allah,
040:051   without doubt, **help** Our messengers and those who
041:016   more humiliating still: and they will find no **help**.
042:031   anyone to protect or to **help**.
042:039   (are not cowed but) **help** and defend themselves.
042:041   But indeed if any do **help** and defend themselves
042:046   to **help** them, other than Allah:
044:041   his client in aught, and no **help** can they receive,
046:008   then can ye have no power to **help** me against Allah.
046:028   Why then was no **help** forthcoming to them
047:007   He will **help** you, and plant your feet firmly.
047:007   if ye will **help** (the cause of) Allah, He will
048:003   And that Allah may **help** thee with powerful **help**.
051:045   stand (on their feet), nor could they **help** themselves.
052:046   avail them nothing and no **help** shall be given them.
054:010   "I am one overcome: do thou then **help** (me)!"
057:025   that Allah may test who is that will **help**, unseen Him
059:011   (in fight) we will **help** you."
059:012   so they will receive no **help**.
059:012   they will never **help** them; and if they do **help** them,
061:013   which ye do love,-**help** from Allah and a speedy
067:020   Nay, who is there that can **help** you, (even as)
071:025   and they found-in lieu of Allah-none to **help** them.
096:017   Then, let him call (for **help**) to his
110:001   When comes the **Help** of Allah, and Victory,

HELPED

002:048   nor shall anyone be **helped** (from outside).
002:086   nor shall they be **helped**.
002:123   nor shall anyone be **helped** (from outside)
003:123   Allah had **helped** you at Badr, when ye
011:113   than Allah, nor shall ye be **helped**.
017:033   for he is **helped** (by the Law).
021:077   We **helped** him against people who rejected
023:065   for ye shall certainly not be **helped** by Us.

HELPED (continued)

025:004   has forged, and others have **helped** him at it."
036:074   than Allah, (hoping) that they might be **helped**!
037:116   And We **helped** them, so they were victorious;
039:054   comes on you: after that ye shall not be **helped**.

HELPER

002:107   have neither patron nor **helper**.
002:120   neither Protector nor **Helper** against Allah.
004:045   and Allah is enough for a **Helper**.
004:123   besides Allah, any protector or **helper**.
004:145   no **helper** wilt thou find for them;
009:116   Except for Him ye have no protector nor **helper**.
017:069   so that ye find no **helper** therein against Us?
022:071   for those that do wrong there is no **helper**.
025:055   is a **helper** (of Evil), against his own Lord!
028:034   so send him with me as a **helper**, to confirm
029:022   beside Allah, any protector or **helper**."
033:017   any protector or **helper**.
033:065   no protector will they find, nor **helper**.
034:022   nor is any of them a **helper** to Allah.
035:037   for the Wrong-doers there is no **helper**."
036:043   no **helper** (to hear their cry), nor could
042:008   no protector nor **helper**.
048:022   find neither protector nor **helper**.
072:024   in (his) **helper** and least important in point
086:010   (Man) will have no power, and no **helper**.

HELPERS

002:023   and call your witnesses or **helpers**
002:270   But the wrong-doers have no **helpers**.
003:028   take for friends or **helpers** Unbelievers rather
003:052   "Who will be my **helpers** to (the work of) Allah?"
003:052   "We are Allah's **helpers**, We believe in Allah,
003:091   and they will find on **helpers**.
003:150   and He is the best of **helpers**.
003:192   and never will wrong-doers find any **helpers**!
004:089   take no friends or **helpers** from their ranks:
018:051   for Me to take as **helpers** such as lead (men) astray!
030:029   To them there will be no **helpers**.
045:034   and no **helpers** have ye!
061:014   Said the Disciples, "We are Allah's **helpers**!"
061:014   "Who will be my h**elpers** to (the work of) Allah?"
061:014   O ye who believe! be ye **helpers** of Allah:

HELPING

024:022   by oath against **helping** their kinsmen, those in

HELPLESS

003:123   when ye were **helpless**:
004:009   if they had left a **helpless** family behind:
030:054   in a state of (**helpless**) weakness, then gave

HELPS

002:020   every time the light (**helps**) them,
003:160   If Allah **helps** you, none can overcome you:
004:085   and whoever recommends and **helps** an evil cause,
037:117   which **helps** to make things clear;

HEM

018:029   like the walls and roof of a tent, will **hem** them in:
035:043   will **hem** in only the authors thereof.

HEMMED

006:010   but the scoffers were **hemmed** in by the thing
012:066   him back to me unless ye are yourselves **hemmed** in
016:034   at which they had scoffed **hemmed** them in.
021:041   scoffers were **hemmed** in by the thing that they mocked.
040:083   they were wont to scoff **hemmed** them in.

HER

002:048   nor shall intercession be accepted for **her**,
002:048   nor shall compensation be taken from **her**.
002:069   to make plain to us **her** colour."
002:071   Then they offered **her** in sacrifice,
002:123   nor shall compensation be accepted from **her**
002:123   nor shall intercession profit **her**
002:229   if she give something for **her** freedom
002:230   and he has divorced **her**.
002:230   he cannot, after that, re-marry **her** until
002:233   treated unfairly on account of **her** child.
002:282   The other can remind **her**.
003:036   I have named **her** Mary,
003:036   and I commend **her** and **her** offspring to Thy
003:037   Every time that he entered **her** chamber to see **her**,
003:037   Right graciously did **her** Lord accept **her**:
003:037   he found **her** supplied with sustenance.
003:037   He made **her** grow in purity and beauty:
004:011   if only one, **her** share is a half.
004:128   or desertion on **her** husband's part, there
004:129   so as to leave **her** (as it were)
004:176   who left no child, **her** brother takes **her** inheritance:
005:038   cut off his or **her** hands: a retribution
006:092   the Mother of Cities and all around **her**.
007:073   and let **her** come to no harm, or ye shall
007:073   so leave **her** to graze in Allah's earth, and
007:189   in order that he might dwell with **her** (in love).
011:064   leave **her** to feed on Allah's (free) earth,
011:064   and inflict no harm on **her**, or a
011:065   But they did ham-string **her**. So he said:
011:071   and she laughed: but We gave **her** Glad tidings
011:081   to **her** will happen what happens to the people.
012:024   and he would have desired **her**, but that
012:025   they both found **her** lord near the door.
012:026   And one of **her** household saw (this) and bore witness,
012:026   then **her** tale true, and he is a liar!
012:028   (**her** husband) said: "Behold! it is a snare of you women!
012:030   wife of the (great) 'Aziz is seeking to seduce **her** slave
012:030   truly hath he inspired **her** with violent love:
017:059   but they treated **her** wrongfully: We only
019:016   when she withdrew from **her** family to a place
019:017   then We sent to **her** Our angel, and he
019:017   and he appeared before **her** as a man in all respects.
019:023   And the pains of childbirth drove **her** to the trunk
019:023   she cried (in **her** anguish): "Ah! would that I had
019:024   But (a voice) cried to **her** from beneath the (palm-tree):
019:027   carrying him (in **her** arms), they said: "O Mary! truly
019:027   At length she brought the (babe) to **her** people,
020:040   that **her** eye might be cooled and she
021:091   We breathed into **her** from Our spirit,
021:091   And (remember) **her** who guarded **her** chastity:
021:091   and We made **her** and **her** son a Sign for all peoples.
022:002   every mother giving suck shall forget **her** suckling-babe,
022:002   every pregnatnt female shall drop **her** load (unformed):
024:003   none can have sexual relations with **her** but an
024:008   that (**her** husband) is telling a lie;
024:009   on herself if (**her** accuser) is telling the truth.
026:156   "Touch **her** not with harm, lest the
026:157   But they ham-strung **her**: then did
027:019   So he smiled, amused at **her** speech; and she
027:024   "I found **her** and **her** people worshipping the
027:038   which of you can bring me **her** throne before they
027:041   He said: "Disguise **her** throne, let us see whether she

HER (continued)

027:043 And he diverted **her** from the worship
027:044 and she (tucked up **her** skirts), uncovering **her** legs.
027:057 except his wife: **her** We destined to be of those who lagged
028:010 had We not strengthened **her** heart (with faith),
028:013 that **her** eye might be comforted, that she
033:030 would be doubled to **her**, and that
033:031 for **her** a generous Sustenance.
033:031 to **her** shall We grant **her** reward twice: and We
033:037 We joined **her** in marriage to thee: in order
033:037 Then when Zaid had dissolved (his marriage) with **her**,
033:050 the Prophet wishes to wed **her**;-this only
035:011 or lays down (**her** load), but with
036:039 for **her** stations (to traverse) till she returns
038:023 'Commit **her** to my care,' and he
041:047 (within **her** womb) nor bring forth (young), but by
042:007 of Cities and all around **her**,-and warn
051:029 she smote **her** forehead and said: "A barren
054:029 and he took a sword in hand, and hamstrung (**her**).
058:001 and carries **her** complaint (in prayer) to Allah:
058:001 woman who pleads with thee concerning **her** husband
066:003 Then when he told **her** thereof, she said,
066:012 to the truth of the words of **her** Lord and of is
066:012 who guarded **her** chastity; and We
066:012 and We breathed into **her** (body) of Our spirit;
084:018 And the Moon in **her** Fullness:
091:013 And (bar **her** not from) having **her** drink!"
091:014 and they hamstrung **her**.
099:001 When the Earth is shaken to **her** (utmost) convulsion,
099:002 And the Earth throws up **her** burden (from within),
099:003 'What is the matter with **her**?'-
099:004 On that Day will she declare **her** tidings:
099:005 For that thy Lord will have given **her** inspiration.
111:005 round **her** (own) neck!

HERALDS

007:057 the Winds like **heralds** of glad tidings, going
025:048 as **heralds** of glad tidings, going before
026:036 and dispatch to the Cities **heralds** to collect-
026:053 Then Pharaoh sent **heralds** to (all) the Cities,
027:063 and who sends the winds as **heralds** of glad tidings,
030:046 as **heralds** go Glad Tidings, giving you

HERBAGE

018:008 dust and dry soil (without growth or **herbage**).
032:027 that We do drive Rain to parched soil (bare of **herbage**),

HERBS

002:061 its pot-**herbs**, and cucumbers,
055:006 And the **herbs** and the trees-both (alike)

HERDED

081:005 wild beasts are **herded** together (in human habitations);

HERDS

048:011 in (looking after) our flocks and **herds**, and our

HERE

002:038 We said: "Get ye down all from **here**;
002:164 (**here**) indeed are Signs for a people that are wise.
003:125 rush **here** on you in hot haste,
003:138 **Here** is a plain statement to men,
003:154 we should not have been in the slaughter **here**."
004:046 and "**Here**, may you not hear"; and "Ra'ina"
005:024 and fight ye two, while we sit **here**.
006:104 I am not (**here**) to watch over your doings."
007:013 it is not for thee to be arrogant **here**: get out,
011:072 and my husband **here** is an old man?

HERE (continued)

011:078 He said: "O my people! **here** are my daughters:
012:019 Good news! **Here** is a (fine) young man! So they
012:093 Then come ye (**here**) to me together with
012:100 and brought you (all **here**) out of the desert,
014:052 **Here** is a Message for mankind: that they
015:034 (Allah) said: "Then get thee out from **here**;
015:046 "Enter ye **here** in Peace and Security."
018:019 "How long have ye stayed (**here**)?"
018:019 (alone) know best how long ye have stayed **here**...
021:034 before thee permanent life (**here**):
022:073 O men! **Here** is a parable set forth!
026:146 in (the enjoyment of) all that ye have **here**?-
026:155 He said: "**Here** is a she-camel: she has
027:029 "Ye chiefs! **here** is-delivered to me-a letter
028:009 "(**Here** is) a joy of the eye, for me
029:033 we are (**here**) to save thee and thy following,
029:049 Nay, **here** are Signs self-evident in the hearts
038:029 (**Here** is) a Book which We have sent down
038:042 "Strike with the foot: **here** is (water) wherein to wash,
038:059 **Here** is a troop rushing headlong with you!
038:077 (Allah) said: "Then get thee out from **here**:
039:073 Enter ye **here**, to dwell therein."
042:036 Whatever ye are given (**here**) is (but)
047:015 (**Here** is) the description of the Garden which the
050:023 "**Here** is (his record) ready with me!"
054:009 "**Here** is one possessed!", and he was driven out.
057:020 **Here** is a similitude: how rain and the growth
069:019 "Ah **here**! read ye my Record!
069:035 "So no friend hath he **here** this Day.

HEREAFTER

002:004 have the assurance of the **Hereafter**.
002:086 at the price of **Hereafter**:
002:102 the happiness of the **Hereafter**.
002:130 the **Hereafter** in the ranks of the Righteous.
002:200 But they will have no portion in the **Hereafter**.
002:201 in this world and good in the **Hereafter**.
002:217 no fruit in this life and in the **Hereafter**;
002:220 (Their bearings) on this life and the **Hereafter**.
002:223 to meet Him (in the **Hereafter**),
003:022 no fruit in this world and in the **Hereafter**,
003:045 held in honour in this world and the **Hereafter**
003:056 severe chastisement in this world and the **Hereafter**
003:077 they shall have no portion in the **Hereafter**:
003:085 and in the **Hereafter** he will be in the ranks
003:145 and if any do desire a reward in the **Hereafter**,
003:148 and the excellent reward of the **Hereafter**.
003:152 and some that desire the **Hereafter**.
003:176 no portion in the **Hereafter**, but a severe punishment.
004:074 who sell the life of this world for the **Hereafter**.
004:077 the **Hereafter** is the best for those who do right:
004:134 (both) of this life and of the **Hereafter**:
005:005 and in the **Hereafter** he will be in the ranks
005:033 and a heavy punishment is theirs in the **Hereafter**;
005:041 and in the **Hereafter** a heavy punishment.
006:032 But best is the Home in the **Hereafter**,
006:092 Those who believe in the **Hereafter** believe in
006:113 who have no faith in the **Hereafter**: and let
006:135 whose end will be (best) in the **Hereafter**:
006:150 and such as believe not in the **Hereafter**:
007:045 they were those who denied the **Hereafter**."
007:147 and the Meeting in the **Hereafter**,-vain are
007:156 in this life and in the **Hereafter**: for we

HEREAFTER (continued)

007:169 is the home in the **hereafter**.
008:067 but Allah looketh to the **Hereafter**:
009:038 comfort of this life, as compared with the **Hereafter**.
009:038 Do ye prefer the life of this world to the **Hereafter**?
009:069 in this world and in the **Hereafter**, and they
009:074 grievous chastisement in this life and in the **Hereafter**:
010:064 in the life of the Present and in the **Hereafter**:
011:016 is nothing in the **Hereafter** but the Fire:
011:019 "These were they who denied the **Hereafter**!"
011:022 ones who will lose most in the **Hereafter**!
011:103 who fear the Chastisement of the **Hereafter**:
012:037 and that (even) deny the **Hereafter**.
012:057 the **Hereafter** is the best, for those who believe,
012:101 art my Protector in this world and in the **Hereafter**.
012:109 But the home of the **Hereafter** is best, for those
013:026 is but little comfort compared to the **Hereafter**.
013:034 the Chastisement of the **Hereafter**: and defender
014:003 of this world to the **Hereafter**, who hinder
014:027 that stands firm, in this world and in the **Hereafter**;
016:022 in the **Hereafter**, their hearts refuse to know,
016:030 the **Hereafter** is even better and excellent indeed
016:041 of the **Hereafter** will be greater, if they
016:060 in the **Hereafter**, applies the similitude of evil:
016:107 this world better than the **Hereafter**: and Allah
016:109 Without doubt, in the **Hereafter** they will
016:122 and he will be, in the **Hereafter**, in the ranks
017:010 in the **Hereafter**, (it announceth) that We
017:019 (things of) the **Hereafter**, and strive therefor
017:021 than on others; but verily the **Hereafter** is more
017:045 believe not in the **Hereafter**, a veil invisible:
017:072 will be blind in the **Hereafter**, and most
018:105 having to meet Him (in the **Hereafter**): vain will
020:127 of the **Hereafter** is far more grievous
020:132 the **Hereafter** is for righteousness.
022:011 they lose both this world and the **Hereafter**:
022:015 him (His Messenger) in this world and the **Hereafter**,
023:033 in the **Hereafter**, and on whom We had bestowed
023:074 in the **Hereafter** are deviating from that Way.
024:014 in this world and the **Hereafter**, a grievous
024:019 in this life and in the **Hereafter**: Allah knows,
024:023 the **Hereafter**: for them is a grievous Chastisement-
027:003 and also have sure faith in the **Hereafter**.
027:004 As to those who believe not in the **Hereafter**,
027:005 and in the **Hereafter** theirs will be
027:066 Nay, but their knowledge fails as to the **Hereafter**,
028:037 form Him and whose End will be best in the **Hereafter**:
028:077 the Home of the **Hereafter**, nor forget
028:080 The reward of Allah (in the **Hereafter**) is best
028:083 That Home of the **Hereafter** We shall give to
029:023 (in the **Hereafter**),-it is they who shall despair
029:027 in the **Hereafter** of the Righteous.
029:064 But verily the Home in the **Hereafter**,-that is
030:007 but of the **Hereafter** they are heedless.
030:016 and the meeting of the **Hereafter**,-such shall
031:004 sure faith in the **Hereafter**.
033:029 the **Hereafter**, verily Allah has prepared for
033:057 in this world and in the **Hereafter**, and has
034:001 to Him be Praise in the **Hereafter**: and He
034:008 in the **Hereafter**, that are in (real) Chastisement,
034:021 who believes in the **Hereafter**, from him
038:046 the remembrance of the **Hereafter**.
039:009 who takes heed of the **Hereafter**, and who places his

HEREAFTER (continued)

039:026 but greater is the Punishment of the **Hereafter**,
039:045 in the **Hereafter** are filled with disgust,
040:039 it is the **Hereafter** that is the Home that will last.
040:043 or the **Hereafter**; our Return will be to Allah;
041:007 and who even deny the **Hereafter**.
041:016 of the **Hereafter** will be more humiliating still:
041:031 and in the **Hereafter**: therein shall
042:020 of the **Hereafter**, We give increase in his tilth;
042:020 but he has no share or lot in the **Hereafter**.
043:035 of the present life: the **Hereafter**, in the sight
050:012 Before them was denied (the **Hereafter**) by the people
053:025 But to Allah belongeth the **Hereafter** and the
053:027 Those who believe not in the **Hereafter**,
056:010 will be Foremost (in the **Hereafter**).
057:020 But in the **Hereafter** is a Chastisement severe
059:003 in this world: and in the **Hereafter** they shall
059:015 of their conduct; and (in the **Hereafter** there is)
060:013 Of the **Hereafter** they are already in despair,
065:010 for them a severe Punishment (in the **Hereafter**).
068:033 in the **Hereafter**,-if only they knew!
074:053 By no means! But they fear not the **Hereafter**.
075:021 And leave alone the **Hereafter**.
079:025 in the **Hereafter**, as in this life.
087:017 But the **Hereafter** is better and more enduring.
093:004 And verily the **hereafter** will be better for thee

HERITAGE

003:180 the **heritage** of the heavens and the earth;
007:128 to give as a **heritage** to such of His
039:074 and has given us (this) land in **heritage**:
057:010 For to Allah belongs the **heritage** of the

HERS

004:035 and the other from **hers**; if they seek

HERSELF

019:017 She placed a screen (to screen **herself**) from them:
024:009 on **herself** if (her accuser) is telling the truth.
033:050 gives **herself** to the Prophet if the Prophet

HEW

015:082 Out of the mountains did they **hew** (their) edifices,

HID

011:005 that they may lie **hid** from Him!
013:010 whether he lie **hid** by night

HIDDEN

003:005 is **hidden** on earth or in the heavens.
005:109 it is Thou who knowest in full all that is **hidden**.
005:116 For Thou knowest in full all that is **hidden**.
006:050 nor do I know what is **hidden**.
007:020 their shame that was **hidden** from them (before):
009:094 to Him Who knoweth what is **hidden** and what
009:105 of what is **hidden** and what is open: then will He
010:061 Nor is **hidden** from thy Lord (so much as)
011:031 nor do I know what is **hidden**, nor claim
014:038 for nothing whatever is **hidden** from Allah,
020:007 knoweth what is secret and what is yet more **hidden**.
020:015 I have almost kept it **hidden**-for every soul
023:092 He knows what is **hidden** and what is open:
024:031 in order to draw attention to their **hidden** ornaments.
027:025 brings forth what is **hidden** in the heavens
027:065 except Allah, knows what is **hidden**:
027:075 And there is nothing **hidden** in heaven or earth,
031:016 a mustard-seed and it were (**hidden**) in a rock,
032:006 the Knower of all things, **hidden** and open,

HIDDEN (continued)

032:010 "What! when we lie, **hidden** and lost, in the earth,
032:017 of the eye are kept **hidden** (in reserve) for them-
034:003 the unseen,-from Whom is not **hidden** the least
034:048 of (all) that is **hidden**."
035:038 the **hidden** things of the heavens and the earth:
038:032 Until (the sun) was **hidden** in the veil (of Night):
039:046 Knower of all thai is **hidden** and open!
040:016 concerning them is **hidden** from Allah.
041:040 the Truth in Our Signs are not **hidden** from Us.
041:041 when is comes to them (are not **hidden** from Us).
053:032 and when ye are **hidden** in your mother's wombs.
057:003 the Evident and the **Hidden**: and He has
064:018 Knower of what is **hidden** and what is open,
069:018 not an act of yours that ye hide will be **hidden**.
072:009 in (**hidden**) stations, to (steal) a hearing;
087:007 for He knoweth what is manifest and what is **hidden**.

HIDE

002:072 but Allah was to bring forth what ye did **hide**.
002:228 to **hide** what Allah hath created in their wombs,
003:029 Say: "Whether ye **hide** what is in your hearts
003:154 They **hide** in their minds what they
003:187 and not to **hide** it; but they threw
004:037 **hide** the bounties which Allah hath bestowed on them;
004:042 but never will they **hide** a single fact from Allah!
004:108 but they cannot **hide** from Allah,
004:108 They seek to **hide** themselves from the people but
005:015 that ye used to **hide** in the Book,
005:031 to show him how to **hide** the naked body
005:031 and to **hide** the naked body of my brother?"
005:061 But Allah knoweth fully all that they **hide**.
005:106 we shall **hide** not the evidence we owe to Allah if
006:003 He knoweth what ye **hide**, and what ye reveal,
016:059 With shame does he **hide** himself from his people,
021:110 in speech and what ye **hide** (in your hearts).
027:025 and knows what ye **hide** and what ye reveal.
027:074 all that their hearts do **hide**, as well
033:037 But thou didst **hide** in thy heart that which
036:076 what they **hide** as well as what they disclose.
041:022 "Ye did not seek to **hide** yourselves, lest your
067:013 And whether ye **hide** your word or make it
069:018 not an act of yours that ye **hide** will be hidden.
070:018 And collect (wealth) and **hide** it (from use)!
081:016 Go straight, or **hide**;

HIGH

002:255 For He is the Most **High**, the Supreme (in glory).
002:265 is as a garden, **high** and fertile:
003:153 Behold! ye were climbing up the **high** ground,
004:034 for Allah is Most **High**, Great (above you all).
004:078 even if ye are in towers built up strong and **high**!"
007:190 but Allah is exalted **high** above the partners
012:054 thou art of **high** standing with us, invested with
012:100 And he raised his parents **high** on the throne
013:009 He is the Great, the Most **High**.
016:050 They all fear their Lord, **high** above them,
017:043 Glory to Him! He is **high** above all that they say!
020:004 the earth and the heavens on **high**.
020:114 **High** above all is Allah, the King, the Truth!
021:022 (**high** is He) above what they attribute to Him!
022:062 Most **High**, Most Great.
023:050 on **high** ground, affording rest and security
023:092 too **high** is He for the partners
026:128 ye build a landmark on every **high** place to amuse

HIGH (continued)

027:063 **High** is Allah above what they associate with Him!
030:040 Glory to Him! and **High** is He above the partners
031:030 and because Allah,-He is the Most **High**, Most Great.
034:023 and He is the Most **High**, Most Great.'"
034:037 in the dwellings on **high**!
038:075 the **high** (and mighty) ones?"
039:067 **High** is He above the Partners they attribute to Him!
040:012 with Allah, Most **High**, Most Great!"
041:010 mountains standing firm, **high** above it,
042:004 and He is Most **High**, Most Great.
042:051 what Allah wills: for He is Most **High**, Most Wise.
043:004 the Mother of the Book, with Us, **high** (in dignity),
052:005 By the Canopy Raised **High**;
055:007 And the Firmament has He raised **high**, and He
056:034 And on couches raised **high**.
059:023 (**high** is He) above the partners they attribute to Him.
069:022 In a Garden on **high**,
069:033 not believe in Allah Most **High**,
069:052 So glorify the name of thy Lord Most **High**.
079:024 Saying, "I am your Lord, Most **High**."
079:028 On **high** hath He raised its canopy, and He
087:001 Glorify the name of thy Guardian-Lord, Most **High**,
088:010 In a Garden on **high**,
088:013 (of dignity), raised on **high**,
088:018 And at the Sky, how it is raised **high**?-
092:020 for the countenance of their Lord Most **High**;
094:004 And raised **high** the esteem (in which)

HIGH-HANDEDNESS

028:083 who intend not **high-handedness** or mischief on earth:

HIGH-ROAD

015:076 And the (cities were) right on the **high-road**.

HIGHER

004:095 Allah hath granted a grade **higher** to those who
018:066 me something of the (**Higher**) Truth which thou
057:010 Those are **higher** in rank than those

HIGHEST

004:114 We shall soon give a reward of the **highest** (value).
008:028 whom lies your **highest** reward.
009:020 have the **highest** rank in the sight of Allah:
016:060 to Allah applies the **highest** similitude:
025:075 be rewarded with the **highest** place in heaven,
031:013 the **highest** wrong-doing."
035:032 that is the **highest** Grace.
038:031 **highest** breeding; and swift of foot;
040:009 and that will be truly the **highest** Achievement.
053:007 While he was in the **highest** part of the horizon:
057:012 This is indeed the **highest** Triumph.
062:004 and Allah is the Lord of the **highest** bounty.
064:015 with Him is the **highest** Reward.

HIGHWAY

015:079 They were both on an open **highway**, plain to see.
029:029 and cut off the **highway**?-And practise

HIGHWAYS

021:031 broad **highways** (between mountains) for them
022:027 through deep and distant mountain **highways**;
090:010 And shown him the two **highways**?

HILL

002:260 on every **hill**, and call to them:
021:096 and they swiftly swarm from every **hill**.

HILLS

014:046 even though they were such as to shake the **hills**!

HILLS (continued)

016:068   to build its cells in **hills**, on trees, and in
016:081   of the **hills** He made some for your shelter;
021:079   that made the **hills** and the birds
022:018   the stars; the **hills**, the trees, the animals;
038:018   It was We that made the **hills** declare, in unison

HIM

002:017   when it lighted all around **him**,
002:028   and again to **Him** will ye return.
002:037   and his Lord turned towards **him**;
002:046   and that they are to return to **Him**.
002:087   and strengthened **him** with the holy spirit.
002:087   and followed **him** up with a succession
002:096   will not save **him** from (due) chastisement
002:104   but say, 'Unzurna and hearken (to **him**):
002:107   And besides **Him** ye have neither
002:116   Glory be to **Him**.
002:116   Nay, to **Him** belongs all that is in
002:116   everything renders worship to **Him**.
002:130   **Him** We chose and rendered pure in this world:
002:131   Behold! his Lord said to **him**: "Submit
002:133   to **Him** do we submit."
002:139   sincere (in our faith) in **Him**?
002:148   To each is a goal to which Allah turns **him**;
002:156   and to **Him** is our return":
002:172   if it is **Him** ye worship.
002:177   out of love for **Him**,
002:178   and compensate **him** with handsome gratitude.
002:182   there is no wrong in **Him**;
002:184   it is better for **him**.
002:185   and to glorify **Him** in that He has guide you;
002:194   transgress ye likewise against **him**.
002:203   there is no blame on **him**,
002:203   ye will surely be gathered unto **Him**.
002:203   there is no blame on **him**,
002:206   Enough for **him** is Hell;
002:206   When it is said to **him**, "Fear God,"
002:211   after Allah's favour has come to **him**,
002:214   those of faith who were with **him** cried:
002:217   to the path of Allah to deny **Him**,
002:222   For Allah loves those who turn to **Him** constantly
002:223   to meet **Him** (in the Hereafter),
002:233   for **him** who desires to complete the term.
002:235   and take heed of **Him**;
002:237   is remitted by **him** in whose hands is the marriage tie;
002:245   and to **Him** shall be your return.
002:247   He said: "Allah hath chosen **him** above you.
002:247   and hath gifted **him** abundantly with knowledge
002:249   he and the faithful ones with **him**,
002:251   and Allah gave **him** power and wisdom
002:251   and taught **him** whatever (else) He willed.
002:253   and strengthened **him** with the Holy Spirit.
002:255   No slumber can seize **Him** nor sleep.
002:258   because Allah had granted **Him** Power?
002:259   When this was shown clearly to **him**,
002:259   then raised **him** up (again).
002:259   But Allah caused **him** to die for a hundred years,
002:280   grant **him** time till it is easy for **him** to repay.
002:282   but let **him** fear Allah his Lord and not dminsh aught
002:282   Let **him** who incurs the liability dictate,
002:282   as Allah has taught **him**, so let **him** write.
002:283   and let **him** fear Allah his Lord.
002:285   hath been revealed to **him** from his Lord,

HIM (continued)

003:030   kindness to those that serve **Him**."
003:030   But Allah cautions you (to fear) **Him**
003:039   the angels called unto **him**: "Allah doth give thee
003:041   and glorify **Him** in the evening and in the morning."
003:045   glad tidings of a Word from **Him**:
003:048   "And Allah will teach **him** the Book and Wisdom,
003:049   "And (appoint **him**) a Messenger to the Children
003:051   then worship **Him**.
003:059   He created **him** from dust,
003:059   then said to **him**: "Be": and he was.
003:064   that we associate no partners with **Him**;
003:065   were not revealed till after **him**?
003:068   are those who follow **him**,
003:079   **Him** (Who is truly the Cherisher of all)
003:081   do ye believe **him** and render **him** help."
003:083   and to **Him** shall they all be brought back.
003:085   never will it be accepted of **him**;
003:144   many were the Messengers that passed away before **Him**,
003:144   those who (serve **him**) with gratitude.
003:145   We shall give it to **him**;
003:159   For Allah loves those who put their trust (in **Him**).
003:182   for Allah never do injustice those who serve **Him**."
004:006   If the guardian is well-off, let **him** claim no remuneration,
004:006   let **him** have for himself what is just and reasonable.
004:027   ye should turn away (from **Him**), far, far away.
004:036   Serve Allah, and join not any partners with **Him**;
004:048   that partners should be set up with **him**;
004:055   And some of them averted their faces from **him**:
004:060   though they were ordered to reject **him**.
004:074   soon shall We give **him** a reward of great (value).
004:074   To **him** who fighteth in the cause of Allah, whether
004:093   and the wrath and the curse of Allah are upon **him**,
004:093   and a dreadful chastisement is prepared for **him**.
004:096   Ranks specially bestowed by **Him**,
004:114   to **him** who does this, seeking
004:115   and land **him** in Hell, what an evil refuge!
004:115   plainly conveyed to **him**, and follows a path
004:115   We shall leave **him** in the path he has chosen,
004:116   (the sin of) joining other gods with **Him**:
004:117   (The pagans), leaving **Him**, call but
004:118   Allah did curse **him**, but he said: "I will
004:131   But if ye deny **Him**, lo! unto Allah belong all
004:136   and the scripture which He sent to those before (**him**).
004:143   never wilt thou find for **him** the Way.
004:157   for of a surety they killed **him** not:
004:157   but they killed **him** not, nor crucified **him**.
004:158   Nay, Allah raised **him** up unto Himself;
004:159   but must believe in **Him** before his death;
004:163   and the Messengers after **him**: We sent
004:170   believe in **him**: it is best for you.
004:171   To **Him** belong all things in the
004:171   for Allah is One God: glory be to **him**:
004:171   and a Spirit proceeding from **Him**: so believe
004:175   and hold fast to **Him**,-soon will He admit
005:018   and unto **Him** is the final goal (of all)."
005:030   he murdered **him**, and became (himself)
005:030   led **him** to the murder of his brother:
005:031   to show **him** how to hide the naked body
005:035   seek the means of approach unto **Him**, and strive
005:039   Allah turneth to **him** in forgiveness; for Allah
005:041   thou hast no authority in the least for **him** against Allah.
005:046   comfirmation of the Torah that had come before **him**:

HIM (continued)

005:046 confirming the Torah that had come before **him**:
005:046 We sent **him** the Gospel: therein was guidance and light.
005:052 or a decision from **Him** then will they regret of
005:054 whom He will love as they will love **him**, lowly
005:072 Allah will forbid **him** the Garden, and the Fire
005:075 many were the Messengers that passed away before **him**.
005:081 hath been revealed to **him**, never would they
005:094 that He may test who feareth **Him** unseen:
005:095 for repetition Allah will punish **him** for Allah
005:115 I will punish **him** with a chastisement such as I
006:002 And there is with **Him** another determined term;
006:008 They say: "Why is not an angel sent down to **him**?"
006:009 We should have sent **him** as a man.
006:013 "To **Him** belongeth all that dwelleth (or lurketh)
006:019 (your blasphemy of) joining others with **Him**."
006:036 then will they be turned unto **Him**.
006:037 a Sign sent down to **him** from his Lord?"
006:041 which occasioned your call upon **Him**, and ye
006:041 "Nay,-On **Him** would ye call, and if
006:041 (the false gods) which ye join with **Him**!"
006:051 except from **Him** they will have no protector
006:057 but ye reject **Him**.
006:059 With **Him** are the keys of the Unseen,
006:060 in the end unto **Him** will be your return,
006:063 when ye call upon **Him** in humility
006:071 (vainly) guiding **him** to the Path."
006:072 for it is to **Him** that we
006:076 When the night covered **him** over, he saw
006:079 toward **Him** Who created the heavens and the
006:080 His people disputed with **him**.
006:084 and before **him**, We guided Noah, and among
006:084 We gave **him** Isaac and Jacob: all (three)
006:088 If they were to join other gods with **Him**,
006:096 such is the judgment and ordering of (**Him**),
006:100 attribute to **Him** sons and daughters,
006:100 praise and glory be to **Him**!
006:100 (for He is) above what they attribute to **Him**!
006:102 then worship ye **Him**: and He hath
006:103 No vision can grasp **Him**, but His grasp
006:122 be like **him** who is in the depths
006:136 they assigned **Him** a share: They say,
006:148 we should not have given partners to **Him**,
006:151 join not anything with **Him**: be good
007:003 as friends or protectors, other than **Him**.
007:012 thou didst create me from fire and **him** from clay."
007:029 and call upon **Him**, making your devotion
007:029 (to **Him**) at every time and place of prayer,
007:050 hath Allah forbidden to those who rejected **Him**;
007:056 but call on **Him** with fear and longing
007:059 worship Allah! ye have not other god but **Him**.
007:064 and those with **him**, in the Ark: but We
007:064 But they rejected **him**, and We
007:064 and We delivered **him**, and those
007:065 ye have no other god but **Him**.
007:072 We saved **him** and those who adhered to **him**, by Our
007:073 ye have no other god but **Him**.
007:075 been sent through **him**."
007:083 But We saved **him** and his family, except
007:085 ye have no other god but **Him**.
007:086 the path of Allah those who believe in **Him**,
007:111 They said: "Keep **him** and his brother in suspense
007:123 Said Pharaoh: "Believe ye in **him** before I

HIM (continued)

007:131 connected with Moses and those with **Him**! Behold!
007:143 and his Lord addressed **him**, he said: "O my lord!
007:145 And We ordained for **him** in the Tablets in all matters,
007:150 by (the hair of) his head, and dragged **him** to **him**.
007:157 So it is those who believe in **him**, honor **him**,
007:157 honor **him**, Help **him**, and follow the Light which
007:157 the Light which is sent down with **him**,-it is
007:158 follow **him** that (so) ye may be guided."
007:160 when his (thirsty) people asked **him** for Water:
007:164 and perchance they may fear **Him**."
007:175 so Satan followed **him** up, and he went astray.
007:176 We should have elevated **him** with Our Signs; but he
007:176 if you attack **him**, he lolls
007:176 or if you leave **him** alone, he (still)
007:180 so call on **Him** by them; but shun
007:190 the partners the ascribe to **Him**.
007:191 Do they indeed ascribe to **Him** as partners
007:197 "But those ye call upon besides **Him**, are unable
007:206 they glorify **Him** and prostrate before **Him**.
007:206 disdain not to worship **Him**:
008:020 from **him** when ye hear (**him** speak).
008:055 sight of Allah are those who reject **Him**: they will
009:002 with shame those who reject **Him**.
009:006 and then escort **him** to where he can be secure,
009:006 for asylum, grant it to **him**, so that
009:031 Praise and glory to **Him**: (far is He) from having
009:031 from having the partners they associate (with **Him**).
009:036 so ordained by **Him** the day He created
009:039 but **Him** ye would not harm in the least,
009:040 for Allah did indeed help **him**,
009:040 when the Unbelievers drove **him** out:
009:040 then Allah sent down His peace upon **him**,
009:040 and strengthened **him** with forces which ye saw not,
009:052 either that Allah will send His punishment from **Him**,
009:077 (to last) till the day whereon they shall meet **Him**:
009:088 who believe with **him**, strive and fight with
009:094 to **Him** Who knoweth what is hidden and what
009:099 Aye, indeed they bring them nearer (to **Him**):
009:100 as are they with **him**: for them hath He prepared
009:109 And it doth crumble to pieces with **him**, into the
009:111 a promise binding on **Him** in Truth, through the
009:112 in repentance: that serve **Him**, and praise **Him**;
009:114 But when it became clear to **him** that he was
009:114 a promise he had made to **him**.
009:114 he dissociated himself from **him**: for Abraham
009:116 Except for **Him** ye have no protector nor helper.
009:117 who followed **Him** in a time of distress,
009:123 and know that Allah is with those who fear **Him**.
009:128 it grieves **him** that ye should suffer,
009:129 there is no god but He: On **him** is my trust,-He the
010:003 This is Allah your Lord; **Him** therefore serve ye:
010:003 No intercessor (can plead with **Him**) except after
010:004 but those who reject **Him** will have draughts of
010:004 because they did reject **Him**.
010:004 To **Him** will be your return-of all of you.
010:006 are Signs for those who fear **Him**.
010:012 for the affliction that touched **him**!
010:018 the partners they ascribe (to **Him**)!"
010:018 in the heaven or on earth?-Glory to **Him**! and far
010:020 sent down to **him** from his Lord?"
010:022 sincerely offering (their) duty unto **Him**, saying:
010:031 Say, "Will ye not then show piety (to **Him**)?"

HIM (continued)

010:056 and to **Him** shall ye all be brought back.
010:068 Glory be to **Him**! He is Self-Sufficient!
010:073 They rejected **him**, but We delivered **him**,
010:073 and those with **him**, in the Ark, and We made
010:074 Then after **him** We sent (many) messengers
010:084 then in **Him** put your trust if ye
010:090 no god except **Him** Who the Children
010:091 (It was said to **him**): "Ah now!-but a little
011:002 I am (sent) unto you from **Him** to warn and to bring
011:003 and turn to **Him** in repentance; that He
011:005 that they may lie hid from **Him**!
011:009 and then withdraw it from **him**, behold! he is in despair
011:010 after adversity hath touched **him**, he is sure to say,
011:010 But if We give **him** a taste of (Our) favours after
011:012 or why does not an angel come down with **Him**?
011:012 "Why is not a treasure sent down unto **him**,
011:017 and before **him** is the Book of Moses-a guide
011:017 and followed by a witness from **Him** and before
011:028 unto me from **Him**, but that the Mercy hath been
011:034 He is your Lord! and to **Him** will ye return!
011:038 his People passed by **him**, they threw ridicule on **him**.
011:040 But only a few believed with **him**.
011:050 ye have no other god but **Him**.
011:051 My reward is from none but **Him** Who created Me:
011:052 your Lord, and turn to **Him** (in repentance):
011:054 that I am free from the sin of ascribing, to **Him**,
011:057 and you will not harm **Him** in the least.
011:058 We saved hud and those who believed with **him**,
011:061 then ask forgiveness of **Him**, and turn
011:061 and turn to **Him** (in repentance):
011:061 ye have not other god but **Him**.
011:063 me against Allah if I were to disobey **Him**?
011:066 We saved Salih and those who believed with **him**,
011:071 glad tidings of Isaac, and after **him**, of Jacob.
011:074 (the mind of) Abraham and the glad tidings reached **him**,
011:078 And his people came rushing towards **him**, and they
011:084 ye have no other god but **Him**.
011:088 In **Him** I trust, and unto **Him** I turn.
011:090 and turn unto **Him** (in repentance): for my Lord
011:092 For ye cast **Him** away behind your backs
011:094 believed with **him**, by (special) Mercy from Us:
011:123 so worship **Him**, and put thy trust in **Him**: and thy
011:123 and the earth, and to **Him** goeth back every affair
012:009 "Slay ye Joseph or cast **him** out to some
012:010 throw **him** down to the bottom of the well: he will
012:012 "Send **him** with us to-morrow to enjoy himself
012:012 and we shall take every care of **him**."
012:013 lest the wolf devour **him** while ye attend no to **him**."
012:013 "Really it saddens me that ye should take **him** away:
012:014 wolf were to devour **him** while we are (so large) a party,
012:015 and they all agreed to throw **him** down to the
012:015 So they did take **him** away, and they
012:017 and the wolf devoured **him**.
012:019 So they concealed **him** as a treasure!
012:020 The (Brethren) sold **him** for a miserable price,-
012:020 in such low estimation did they hold **him**!
012:021 much good, or we shall adopt **him** as a son."
012:021 The man in Egypt who bought **him**, said to his wife:
012:021 that We might teach **him** the interpretation
012:022 We gave **him** power and knowledge: thus do
012:023 sought to seduce **him** and she fastened the doors,
012:024 And (with passion) did she desire **him**, and he

HIM (continued)

012:024 that We might turn away from **him** (all) evil
012:031 When they saw **him**, they did extol **him**,
012:032 I did seek to seduce **him** from his
012:034 So his Lord hearkened to **him** (in his prayer)
012:034 and turned away from **him** their snare:
012:035 (that it was best) to imprison **him** for a time.
012:036 Now with **him** there came into the prison
012:040 Whatever ye worship apart from **Him** is nothing
012:040 he hath commanded that ye worship none but **Him**:
012:042 But Satan made **him** forget to mention **him** to his lord:
012:045 and who now remembered **him** after (so long)
012:050 So the king said: "Bring ye **him** unto me."
012:050 But when the messenger came to **him**, (Joseph) said:
012:050 thy lord, and ask **him**, 'What was the matter
012:051 it was I who sought to seduce **him** he is indeed
012:051 no evil know we against **him**!" Said the 'Aziz's
012:052 to **him** in his absence, and that
012:054 I will take **him** specially to serve about
012:054 So the king said: "Bring **him** unto me; I will take
012:054 Therefore when he had spoken to **him**, he said:
012:058 knew them, but they knew **him** not.
012:060 "Now if ye bring **him** not to me, ye shall
012:061 win **him** from his father: indeed we shall do it."
012:063 and we will indeed take every care of **him**."
012:064 But Allah is the best to take care (of **him**),
012:064 He said: "Shall I trust you with **him** with any result
012:066 be sure to bring **him** back to me unless ye are
012:066 (Jacob) said: "Never will I send **him** with you
012:067 on **Him** do I put my trust:
012:067 and let all that trust put their trust on **Him**."
012:069 he received his (full) brother to stay with **him**.
012:069 He said (to **him**): "Behold! I am thy (own) brother;
012:072 the great beaker of the king; for **him** who produces it.
012:077 there was a brother of his who did steal before (**him**)."
012:078 a father, aged and venerable, (who will grieve for **him**):
012:079 other than **him** with whom we found our property:
012:100 and they fell down in prostration (all) before **him**.
012:106 Allah without associating (others as partners) with **Him**!
013:007 a Sign sent down to **him** from his Lord?"
013:008 Every single thing is with **Him** in (due) proportion.
013:010 It is the same (to **Him**) whether any of you
013:011 they guard **him** by command of Allah.
013:011 before and behind **him**; they guard
013:011 besides **Him**, any to protect.
013:014 besides **Him** hear them no more than if they
013:014 To **Him** is due the true prayer any others
013:016 (for worship) protectors other than **Him**, such as
013:018 But those who respond no to **Him**,-even if
013:027 to himself those who turn to **Him** in penitence,-
013:027 a Sign sent down to **him** from his Lord?"
013:030 yet do they reject (**Him**), the Most Gracious!
013:030 On **Him** is my trust, and to **Him** I turn!"
013:033 will inform **Him** of something He knoweth not
013:036 and not to join partners with **Him**.
013:036 Unto **Him** do I call, and unto **Him** is my return."
013:039 with **Him** is the Mother of the Book.
014:001 to the Way of (**Him**) the Exalted in Power,
014:017 death will come to **him** from every quarter,
014:017 and in front of **him** will be a chastisement unrelenting.
015:011 to them but they mocked **him**.
015:029 and breathed into **him** of My spirit,
015:029 fall ye down in obeisance unto **him**."

HIM (continued)

015:029 "When I have fashioned **him** (in due proportion)
015:066 And We made known this decree to **him**, that the
016:001 and far is He above the partners they ascribe unto **Him**!
016:001 seek ye not then to hasten it: glory to **Him**,
016:003 above having the partners they ascribe to **Him**!
016:035 not have worshipped aught but **Him**-neither we
016:038 a promise (binding) on **Him** in truth: but most
016:046 of their frustrating **Him**?-
016:052 To **Him** belongs whatever is in the heavens
016:052 and to **Him** is the religion always: then will
016:053 unto **Him** ye cry with groans;
016:057 Glory be to **Him**!-and for themselves what they desire!
016:076 whichever way he directs **him**, he brings no good:
016:097 to **him** will We give a life that is
016:100 who take **him** as patron and who join
016:103 "It is a man that teaches **him**."
016:103 The tongue of **him** they wickedly point to
016:113 falsely rejected **him**; so the Wrath seized them
016:121 and guided **him** to a Straight Way.
016:121 his gratitude for the favours of Allah, Who chose **him**,
016:122 And We gave **him** Good in this world, and he
017:001 show **him** some of Our Signs: for he
017:013 We shall bring out for **him** a scroll, which he
017:014 (It will be said to **him**:) "Read thine (own) record:
017:023 Thy Lord hath decreed that ye worship none but **Him**,.
017:025 turn to **Him** again and again (in true penitence).
017:033 but let **him** not exceed bounds in the matter
017:042 Say: if there had been (other) gods with **Him**,-
017:043 Glory to **Him**! He is high above all that they say!
017:046 and **Him** alone-in the Qur'an, they turn
017:056 Say: "Call on those-besides **Him**-whom ye fancy:
017:067 He brings you back to safe land, ye turn away (from **Him**).
017:083 and when Evil seizes **him** he gives himself
017:097 wilt thou find no protector besides **Him**.
017:101 Pharaoh said to **him**: "O Moses! I consider thee,
017:103 but We did drown **him** and all who were with **him**.
017:110 for to **Him** belong the Most Beautiful Names.
017:110 by whatever name ye call upon **Him**, (it is well):
017:111 to protect **Him** from humiliation:
017:111 Yea, magnify **Him** for His greatness and glory!"
018:002 of a terrible Punishment from **Him**, and that
018:014 upon any god other then **Him**: if we did;
018:015 for worship gods other than **Him**: why do
018:017 protector to lead to lead **him** to the Right Way.
018:017 whom Allah leaves to stray,-for **him** wilt thou find no
018:019 and let **him** behave with care and courtesy,
018:019 and let **him** not inform anyone about you.
018:019 let **him** find out which is the best food
018:026 They have no protector other than **Him**; nor does
018:026 with **Him** is (the knowledge of) the secrets of the
018:027 as a refuge other than **Him**.
018:029 "the Truth is from your Lord" let **him** who will, believe,
018:029 and let **him** who will, reject (it):
018:037 His companion said to **him**, in the course
018:037 "Dost thou deny **Him** Who created thee out of dust,
018:037 in the course of the argument with **him**:
018:043 Nor had he numbers to help **him** against Allah,
018:050 Will ye then take **him** and his progeny
018:066 Moses said to **him**: "May I follow thee, on the
018:074 when they meet a young boy, he slew **him**.
018:084 and We gave **him** the ways and the means to all ends.
018:087 He said: "Whoever doth wrong, **him** shall we punish;

HIM (continued)

018:087 and He will punish **him** with a punishment unheard-
018:091 We completely understood what was before **him**.
018:105 having to meet **Him** (in the Hereafter): vain will
018:110 let **him** work righteousness, and in the
019:006 and make **him**, O my Lord! one with
019:012 and We gave **him** Wisdom even as
019:015 So Peace on **him** the day he was born, the day
019:021 and (We wish) to appoint **him** as a Sign unto men
019:022 with **him** to a remote place.
019:022 So she conceived **him**, and she retired with **him**
019:027 to her people, carrying **him** (in her arms),
019:035 Glory to **Him**! When He determines a matter,
019:036 Allah is my Lord and your Lord: **Him** therefore serve ye:
019:049 We bestowed on **him** Isaac and Jacob,
019:052 and made **him** draw near to Us, for converse
019:052 And We called **him** from the right side
019:053 And, out of Our Mercy, We gave **him** his brother
019:057 And We raised **him** to a lofty station.
019:064 to **Him** belongeth what is before us and what
019:065 so worship **Him**, and be constant and patient
019:067 that We created **him** before out of nothing?
019:095 to **him** singly on the Day of Judgment.
020:004 A revelation from **Him** Who created the earth
020:006 To **Him** belongs what is in the heavens
020:008 To **Him** belong the Most Beautiful Names.
020:031 "Add to my strength through **him**,
020:032 "And make **him** share my task:
020:039 is an enemy to Me and an enemy to **him**': but I
020:039 the river will cast **him** up on the bank, and he
020:044 "But speak to **him** mildly; perchance he
020:047 "So go ye both to **him**, and say, `Verily we
020:061 Moses said to them: "Woe to you! Forge
020:066 so it seemed to **him** on account of their magic-
020:071 (Pharaoh) said: "Believe ye in **Him** before I
020:072 Clear Signs **Him** Who created us! So decree
020:074 as a sinner (at judgment),-for **him** is Hell:
020:075 But such as comes to **Him** as Believers who have
020:108 will follow the caller (straight): no crookedness in **him**:
020:109 and whose word is acceptable to **Him**.
020:110 or behind them: but they shall comprehend **Him** not.
020:113 or that it may cause their remembrance (of **Him**).
020:117 so let **him** not get you both out of the Garden,
020:120 But Satan whispered evil to **him**: he said,
020:122 But his Lord chose **him** (for His Grace):
020:122 He turned to **him**, and gave **him** guidance.
020:124 and We shall raise **him** up blind on the Day of Judgment."
020:124 My Message, verily for **him** is a life narrowed
020:127 We recompense **him** who transgresses beyond
021:005 Let **him** then bring us a Sign like the ones
021:019 are not too proud to serve **Him**, nor are
021:019 To **Him** belong all (creatures) in the
021:019 even those who are with **Him** are not
021:022 (high is He) above what they attribute to **Him**!
021:024 have they taken for worship (other) gods besides **Him**?
021:025 before thee without this inspriation sent by Us to **him**:
021:026 Glory to **Him**! They are (but) servants raised to honour.
021:029 If any of them should say, "I am a god besides **Him**,"
021:051 and well were We acquainted with **him**.
021:061 They said, "Then bring **him** before the eyes
021:068 They said, "Burn **him** and protect your gods,
021:070 Then they planned against **him**: but We
021:071 But We delivered **him** and (his nephew)

HIM (continued)

021:072　And We bestowed on **him** Isaac and, as an
021:074　and We saved **him** from the town which
021:075　And We admitted **him** to Our Mercy: for he
021:076　to his (prayer) and delivered **him** and his
021:077　We helped **him** against people who rejected
021:080　It was We Who taught **him** the making of
021:082　And of Satans were some who dived for **him**,
021:084　We removed the distress that was on **him**,
021:084　and We restored his people to **him**, and doubled
021:087　he imagined that We had no power over **him**!
021:088　and delivered **him** from distress: and thus
021:088　So We listened to **him**: and delivered
021:090　So We listened to **him**: and We granted **him** Yahya:
021:090　We cured his wife's (barrenness) for **him**.
022:004　and he will guide **him** to the Chastisement
022:004　**him** will he lead astray,
022:004　that whoever turns to **him** for friendship,
022:009　make **him** taste the chastisement of burning (Fire).
022:009　for **him** there is disgrace in this life, and on
022:015　let **him** stretch out a rope to the ceiling and cut
022:015　then let **him** see whether his plan will remove that
022:015　Allah will not help **him** (His Messenger) in this world
022:015　will remove that which enrages (**him**)!
022:024　to the path of **Him** Who is Worthy of (all) Praise.
022:030　for **him** it is good in the sight of his Lord,
022:031　and thrown **him** into a far-distant place.
022:031　and never assigning partners to **Him**:
022:034　submit then your wills to **Him** (in Islam):
022:037　it is your piety that reaches **Him**: He has
022:060　Allah will help **him**: for Allah
022:062　and those besides **Him** whom they invoke,-
022:064　To **Him** belongs all that is in the heavens
023:013　Then We placed **him** as (a drop of) sperm
023:023　Ye have no other god but **Him**.
023:023　will ye not fear (**Him**)?"
023:025　wait (and have patience) with **him** for a time."
023:027　So We inspired **him** (with this message);
023:032　"Worship Allah! ye have no other god but **Him**.
023:032　Will ye not fear (**Him**)?"
023:038　but we are not the ones to believe in **him**!"
023:044　they accused **him** of falsehood: so We
023:069　their Messenger, that they deny **him**?
023:076　submissively entreat (**Him**)!
023:079　and to **Him** shall ye be gathered back.
023:080　and to **Him** (is due) the alternation of Night
023:091　nor is there any god along with **Him**:
023:091　(sort of) things they attribute to **Him**!
023:092　for the partners they attribute to **Him**!
024:011　and to **him** who took on himself the lead among them,
024:039　and Allah will pay **him** his account: and Allah
024:049　they come to **him** with all submission.
024:054　If ye obey **him**, ye shall be on right guidance.
024:054　the duty placed on **him** and ye for that placed on you.
024:062　when they are with **him** on a matter requiring
024:064　and the day they will be brought back to **Him**,
025:003　Yet have they taken, besides **Him**, gods that
025:004　has forged, and others have helped **him** at it."
025:005　before **him** morning and evening."
025:006　by **Him** Who knows the secret (that is) in the
025:007　to **him** to give admonition with **him**?
025:008　been bestowed on **him**, or why
025:019　**him** shall We cause to taste of a greivous chastisement.

HIM (continued)

025:032　"Why is not the Qur'an revealed to **him** all at once?"
025:035　his brother Aaron with **him** as Minister;
025:043　Couldst thou be a disposer of affairs for **him**?
025:058　And put thy trust in **Him** Who lives and dies not;
025:059　ask thou, then, about **Him** of any acquainted
025:069　the Day of Judgment will be doubled to **him**, and he
025:077　but ye have indeed rejected (**Him**), and soon
025:077　with you but for your call on **Him**: but ye
026:034　(Pharaoh) said to the Chiefs around **him**: "This is indeed
026:036　They said: "Keep **him** and his brother in suspense
026:049　Said (Pharaoh): "Believe ye in **Him** before I give
026:065　We delivered Moses and all who were with **him**;
026:119　So we delivered **him** and those with **him**.
026:132　"Yea, fear **Him** Who has bestowed on you
026:139　So they rejected **him**, and We
026:170　So We delivered **him** and his family,-all
026:184　"And fear **Him** Who created you and (Who created)
026:189　But they rejected **him**.
027:021　or execute **him**, unless he bring me a clear
027:021　"I will certainly punish **him** with a
027:035　But I am going to send **him** a present, and wait
027:040　placed firmly before **him**, he said: "This is
027:049　shall make a secret night attack on **him** and his people,
027:057　But We saved **him** and his family, except his
027:059　or the false gods they associate (with **Him**)?
027:062　who listens to the distressed when he calls on **Him**,
027:063　High is Allah above what they associate with **Him**!
027:087　and all shall come to **Him** in utter humility.
027:091　**Him** Who has sanctified it and to Whom
028:007　"Suckle (thy child), but when thou hast fears about **him**,
028:007　and We shall make **him** one of Our messengers."
028:007　cast **him** into the river, but fear not nor grieve:
028:007　for We shall restore **him** to thee,
028:008　picked **him** up (from the river):
028:009　for me and for thee: slay **him** not.
028:009　or we may adopt **him** as a son."
028:011　So she (the sister) watched **him** from a distance
028:011　And she said to the sister of (Moses), "Trace **him**."
028:012　and bring **him** up for you and take care of **him**."
028:013　Thus did We restore **him** to his mother, that her
028:014　We bestowed on **him** wisdom and knowledge:
028:015　his own people appealed to **him** against his foe,
028:015　and Moses struck **him** with his fist and killed **him**.
028:016　So (Allah) forgave **him**: for He
028:018　Moses said to **him**: "Thou art truly, one erring manifestly."
028:025　So when he came to **him** and narrated the story,
028:025　came (back) to **him**, walking bashfully.
028:026　(dear) father! engage **him** on wages: truly the
028:034　so send **him** with me as a helper, to confirm
028:037　from **Him** and whose End will be best in the
028:040　So We seized **him** and his hosts, and We
028:048　"Why are not (Signs) sent to **him**, like those
028:068　they ascribe (to **Him**)!
028:070　for **Him** is the Command, and to **Him** shall ye (all) be.
028:070　To **him** be praise, at the first and the last:
028:076　We had bestowed on **him**, that their
028:076　Behold, his people said to **him**: "Exult not,
028:078　had destroyed, before **him**, (whole) generations,-
028:078　to **him** in strength and greater in amount
028:081　party to help **him** against Allah, nor could
028:081　We caused the earth to swallow up **him** and his house;
028:084　If any does good, the reward to **him** is better

HIM (continued)

028:088 To **Him** belongs the Command, and to **Him** will ye (all)
029:015 But We saved **him** and the Companions of the Ark,
029:016 "Serve Allah and fear **Him**: that will
029:017 then seek ye sustenance from Allah, serve **Him**,
029:017 and be grateful to **Him**: to **Him** will be your return.
029:021 and towards **Him** are ye turned.
029:023 and the Meeting, with **Him** (in the Hereafter),-
029:024 "Slay **him** or burn **him**."
029:024 But Allah did save **him** from the Fire.
029:026 But Lut believed **Him**: he said: "I will
029:027 and We granted **him** his reward in this life;
029:032 we will certainly save **him** and his following,-
029:037 But they rejected **him**: then the
029:042 call upon besides **Him**: and He
029:046 and it is to **Him** we submit (in Islam)."
029:050 sent down to **him** from his Lord?"
029:065 making their devotion sincerely (and exclusively) to **Him**;
029:068 or rejects the Truth when it reaches **him**?
030:011 ye be brought back to **Him**.
030:018 Yea, To **Him** be praise, in the heavens and on
030:026 all are devoutly obedient to **Him**.
030:026 To **Him** belongs every being that is in the
030:027 and for **Him** it is most easy.
030:027 To **Him** belongs the loftiest similitude
030:031 Turn ye in repentance to **Him**, and fear **Him**
030:033 turning back to **Him** in repentance: but when
030:040 the partners they attribute (to **Him**)!
030:040 Glory to **Him**! and High is He above the partners
031:007 announce to **him** a grievous Chastisement.
031:011 that others besides **Him** have created: nay, but
031:013 admonishing **him** "O my son! join not in worship
031:014 in travial upon travail did his mother bear **him**.
031:030 invoke besides **Him** is Falsehood; and because
031:032 offering **Him** sincere devotion.
032:004 besides **Him**, to protect or intercede (for you):
032:005 then it ascends unto **Him**, on a Day the measure
032:009 and breathed into **him** of His spirit.
032:009 But He fashioned **him** in due proportion,
033:021 of Allah an excellent exemplar for **him** who hopes
033:038 has indicated to **him** as a duty.
033:039 and fear **Him**, and fear none but Allah.
033:042 And glorify **Him** morning and evening.
033:044 they meet **Him** will be "peace!"; and He
033:053 ye should marry his widows after **him** at any time.
033:056 and salute **him** with all respect.
033:056 send ye blessings on **him**, and salute
033:069 cleared **him** of the (calumnies) they had uttered:
034:001 to **Him** be Praise in the Hereafter: and He
034:003 it will come upon you;-by **Him** Who knows the unseen,
034:010 back the Praisses of Allah with **him**! and ye birds (also)!
034:010 and We made the iron soft for **Him**;-
034:012 from Our command, We made **him** taste of the
034:012 in front of **him**, by the leave of his Lord, and if
034:012 a Font of molten brass to flow for **him**; and there
034:013 They worked for **him** as he desired,
034:015 by your Lord, and be grateful to **Him**:
034:020 his idea, and they followed **him**, all but
034:021 from **him** who is in doubt concerning it:
034:023 "No intercession can avail with **Him**, except for
034:027 joined with **Him** as partners: by no means
034:033 and to attribute equals to **Him**!"
035:002 none can grant, apart from **Him**: and He

HIM (continued)

035:006 so treat **him** as an enemy.
035:010 To **Him** mount up (all) Words of Purity:
035:013 to **Him** belongs all Dominion.
035:013 besides **Him** own not a straw.
035:014 like **Him** who is All-Aware.
036:005 (It is a Revealtion) sent down by (**Him**),
036:022 "Why should not I serve **Him** Who created me,
036:023 "Shall I take (other) gods besides **Him**?
036:028 his People, after **Him**, any hosts from heaven,
036:030 to them but they mock **Him**!
036:038 And the Sun runs unto a resting place, for **Him**:
036:038 that is the decree of (**Him**), the Exalted
036:068 We cause **him** to be reversed in nature: will they
036:069 in Poetry, nor is it meant for **him**: this is
036:077 We Who created **Him** from sperm? Yet behold!
036:083 So glory to **Him** in Whose hands is the
036:083 and to **Him** will ye be all brought back.
037:037 (the Message of) the messengers (before **him**).
037:055 He looked down and saw **him** in the midst
037:076 And We delivered **him** and his people from the
037:078 for **him** among generations to come in later times:
037:090 So they turned away from **him**, and departed.
037:094 with hurried steps, to **him**.
037:097 and throw **him** into the blazing fire!"
037:097 They said: "Build **him** a furnace, and throw
037:098 (This failing), they then plotted against **him**,
037:101 So We gave **him** the good news of a forbearing son.
037:102 (the age of) (serious) work with **him**, he said:
037:103 and he had laid **him** prostrate on his forehead
037:104 We called out to **him**, "O Abraham!
037:107 And We ransomed **him** with a momentous sacrifice:
037:108 And We left for **him** among generations (to come)
037:112 And We gave **him** the good news of Isaac-
037:113 We blessed **him** and Isaac: but of their
037:127 But they rejected **him**, and they
037:129 And We left for **him** among generations (to come)
037:134 Behold, We delivered **him** and his adherents,
037:142 Then the big Fish did swallow **him**, and he
037:145 But We cast **him** forth on the naked shore
037:146 And We caused to grow over **him**, a spreading
037:147 And We sent **him** (on a mission) to a
037:158 that they will be brought before **Him**.
037:158 between **Him** and the Jinns: but the
037:159 from the things they ascribe (to **Him**)!
037:180 from what they ascribe (to **Him**)!
038:008 "What! Has the Message been sent to **him**-
038:018 in unison with **him**, Our Praises, at eventide
038:019 all with **him** did turn (to Allah).
038:020 and gave **him** wisdom and sound judgment
038:024 We had tried **him**: he asked forgiveness of his Lord,
038:025 So We forgave **him** this (lapse): he enjoyed,
038:031 Behold, there were brought before **him**, at eventide,
038:043 And We gave **him** (back) his people and double
038:044 Truly We found **him** full of patience
038:061 add to **him** a double Chastisement in the Fire!"
038:072 "When I have fashioned **him** and breathed
038:072 and breathed into **him** of My spirit, fall ye
038:072 fall ye down in prostrated unto **him**."
038:076 and **him** Thou createdst from clay."
039:002 so serve Allah, offering **Him** sincere devotion.
039:004 but Glory be to **Him**! (He is above such things).
039:006 to **Him** belongs (all) dominion.

HIM (continued)

039:008 upon **him** as from Himself, (man) doth
039:008 turning to **Him** in repentance: but when
039:015 "Serve ye·what ye will besides **Him**."
039:032 and rejects the truth when it comes to **him**!
039:036 with other (gods) besides **Him**! For such
039:038 In **Him** trust those who put their trust."
039:044 in the End, it is to **Him** that ye shall
039:044 to **Him** belongs the dominion of the heavens
039:049 but when We bestow a favour upon **him** as from Us,
039:054 and submit to **Him**, before the Chastisement come on
039:063 To **Him** belong the keys of the heavens and the
039:067 have they made of Allah, such as is due to **Him**:
039:067 High is He above the Partners they attribute to **Him**!
039:067 heavens will be rolled up in his right hand: Glory to **Him**!
040:003 There is no god but He: to **Him** is the Final Goal.
040:005 to seize **him**, and disputed by means of vanities,
040:007 believe in **Him**; and implore forgiveness for those
040:012 partners were joined to **Him**, ye believed!
040:014 sincere devotion to **Him**, even though
040:020 invoke besides **Him**, will not
040:024 but they called (**him**) "a sorcerer telling lies!"...
040:025 "Slay the sons of those who believe with **him**,
040:026 and let **him** Call on his Lord!
040:028 on **him** is (the sin of) his lie; but, if he
040:034 "No messenger will Alah send after **him**.'
040:037 to nothing but perdition (for **him**).
040:042 and to join with **Him** partners of whom I have no
040:045 that they plotted (against **him**), but the
040:045 Then Allah saved **him** from (every) evil that they
040:065 call upon **Him**, giving **Him** sincere devotion.
040:084 we used to join with **Him**."
041:006 so take the straight path unto **Him** and ask for
041:009 Say: Is it that ye Deny **Him** Who created the earth
041:009 And do ye join equals with **Him**?
041:012 of (**Him**) the Exalted in Might, Full of knowledge.
041:021 the first time, and unto **Him** were ye to return.
041:037 if it is **Him** ye wish to serve.
041:047 To **Him** is referred the Knowledge of the Hour
041:049 but if ill touches **him**, he gives up all hope
041:050 after some adversity has touched **him**, he is sure to say,
041:050 When We give **him** a taste of some mercy from Us,
041:051 and when Evil seizes **him**, (he comes) full
042:004 To **Him** belongs all that is in the heavens
042:006 others besides **Him**,-Allah doth watch over them;
042:009 (for worship) protectors besides **Him**?
042:010 in **Him** I trust, and to **Him** I turn.
042:011 there is nothing whatever like unto **Him**, and He
042:012 To **Him** belong the keys of the heavens and the
042:013 and guides to Himself those who turn (to **Him**).
042:015 and to **Him** is (Our) final goal.
042:023 We shall give **Him** an increase of good
042:041 and defend himself after a wrong (done) to **him**,
042:048 but when some ill happens to **him**,
042:051 that Allah should speak to **him** except by inspiration,
043:007 to them but they mocked **him**.
043:009 'They were created by (**Him**),
043:013 and say, "Glory to **Him** Who has subjected these to our
043:015 of His servants a share with **Him**.
043:027 "(I worship) only **Him** Who made me, and He
043:028 among those who came after **him**, that they
043:036 to be an intimate companion to **him**.
043:036 We appoint for **him** a Satan, to be

HIM (continued)

043:053 or (why) come (not) with **him** angels accompanying **him**
043:053 "Then why are not gold bracelets bestowed on **him**,
043:054 and they obeyed **him**: truly were
043:059 and We made **him** an example to the
043:059 We granted Our favour to **him**, and We
043:064 and your Lord: so worship ye **Him**: this is
043:082 He is free from the things they attribute (to **Him**)!
043:085 And to **Him** shall ye be brought back.
043:085 with **Him** is the knowledge of the Hour
044:014 Yet they turn away from **him** and say: "Tutored (by
044:047 and drag **him** into the midst of the Blazing Fire!
044:047 (A voice will cry:) "Seize ye **him** and drag **him**
045:008 then announce to **him** a Chastisement Grievous!
045:008 He hears the Signs of Allah rehearsed to **him**,
045:013 And He has subjected to you, as from **Him**, all that is in
045:014 it is for **Him** to recompense (for good or ill)
045:023 Allah has, knowing (**him** as such), left **him** astray,
045:023 Who, then, will guide **him** after Allah
045:037 And unto **Him** (alone) belongeth Majesty in the
046:005 such as will not answer **him** to the Day of Judgment,
046:015 in pain did his mother bear **him**,
046:015 and in pain did she give **him** birth.
046:021 Warners before **him** and after **him**: "Worship ye
046:031 and believe in **him**: He will forgive you your faults.
048:009 that ye may assist and honor **him**, and celebrate
048:010 Allah will soon grant **him** a great Reward.
048:017 (Allah) will admit **him** to Gardens beneath which rivers
048:017 (Allah) will punish **him** with a grievous Chastisement.
048:029 and those who are with **him** are strong
049:002 of the Prophet, nor speak aloud to **him** in talk,
050:016 and We know what suggestions hissoul makes to **him**:
050:016   for We are nearer to **him** than (his) jugular vein.
050:026 throw **him** into a severe Chastisement."
050:027 "Our Lord! I did not make **him** transgress,
050:033 and brought a heart turned in devotion (to **Him**):
051:028 gave **him** glad tidings of a son endowed
051:038 Behold, We sent **him** to Pharaoh, with authority
051:040 So We took **him** and his forces, and threw
051:050 I am from **Him** a Warner to you, clear and open!
051:052 but they said (of **him**) in like manner, "A sorcerer,
052:028 "Truly we did call unto **Him** from of old:
052:030 for **him** some calamity (hatched) by Time!"
052:043 the things they associate with **Him**!
052:049 And for part of the night also praise thou **Him**,-
053:004 It is no less than inspiration sent down to **him**:
053:012 with **him** concerning what he saw?
053:013 For indeed he saw **him** at a second descent,
053:021 and for **Him**, the female?
053:026 and that he is acceptable to **Him**.
053:062 to Allah, and adore (**Him**)!
054:013 But We bore **him** on an (Ark) made of
054:025 "Is It that the Message is sent to **him**, of all
054:037 snatch away his guests from **him**, but We
055:004 He has taught **him** an intelligent speech.
055:029 Of **Him** seeks (its need) every creature
056:085 But We are nearer to **him** than ye, and yet see not,-
056:089 (There is for **him**) Rest and Satisfaction, and a
056:091 (For **him** is the salutation), "Peace be
056:093 For **him** is Entertainment with Boiling Water,
057:002 To **Him** belongs the dominion of the heavens
057:005 To **Him** belongs the dominion of the heavens
057:025 will help, unseen **Him** and His messengers:

HIM (continued)

057:027 of those who followed **him** Compassion and Mercy.
057:027 son of Mary, and bestowed on **him** the Gospel;
058:004 Reject (**Him**), there is a grievous Chastisement.
058:013 your private consultation (with **him**)?
058:018 then will they swear to **Him** as they swear to you:
058:022 Allah will be well pleased with them, and they with **Him**.
059:023 the partners they attribute to **Him**.
059:024 to **Him** belong the Most Beautiful Names:
060:004 example (to follow) in Abraham and those with **him**,
060:004 unles you believe in Allah and **Him** alone":
064:001 and to **Him** belongs Praise: and He
064:001 and Glory of Allah: to **Him** belongs Dominion,
064:003 and to **Him** is the final Return.
064:015 with **Him** is the highest Reward.
065:002 Such is the admonition given to **him** who believes
065:003 And He provides for **him** from (sources) he never
065:003 sufficient is (Allah) for **him**.
065:005 He will remove his evil deeds from **him**,
065:007 no bruden on any person beyond what He has given **him**.
065:007 let **him** spend according to what Allah has given **him**.
066:003 and Allah made it known to **him**, he confirmed
066:004 to Allah, your hearts are indeed so inclined;
066:004 and furthermore, the angels,-will back (**him**) up.
066:004 each other against **him**, truly Allah
066:005 that Allah will give **him** in exchange Consorts
066:008 and those who believe with **him**.
067:009 but we rejected **him** and said, 'Allah never sent
067:015 which He furnishes: but unto **Him** is the Resurrection.
067:024 and to **Him** shall ye be gathered together."
067:029 we have believed in **Him**,
067:029 and on **Him** have we put our trust: so, soon
068:015 When to **him** are rehearsed Our Signs, "Tales of
068:032 for we do turn to **Him** (in repentance)!"
068:049 Had not Grace from His Lord reached **him**, he would
068:050 Thus did his Lord choose **him** and make **him** of the
069:009 And Pharaoh, and those before **him**, and the
069:030 "Seize ye **him**, and bind ye **him**,
069:031 "And burn ye **him** in the Blazing Fire.
069:032 "Further, insert **him** in a chain, whereof the
069:045 We should certainly seize **him** by his right hand
069:047 Nor could any of you withhold **him** (from Our wrath).
070:004 unto **Him** in a Day the measure whereof is (as)
070:013 His kindred who sheltered **him**.
070:014 so it could deliver **him**:
070:020 Fretful when evil touches **him**;
070:021 And niggardly when good reaches **him**;-
070:025 For the (needy) who asks and **him** who is deprived
071:003 fear **Him**, and obey me:
072:009 find a flaming fire watching **him** in ambush.
072:012 nor can we escape **Him** by flight.
072:017 He will cause **him** to undergo ever-growing
072:019 they just make round **him** a dense crowd."
072:019 stands forth to invoke **Him**,
072:020 and I join not with **Him** any (false god)."
072:022 deliver me form Allah (if I were to disobey **Him**),
072:022 nor should I find refuge except in **Him**.
072:027 march before **him** and behind **him**,
073:008 the Lord and devote thyself to **Him** wholeheartedly.
073:009 take **Him** therefore for (thy) Disposer of Affairs.
073:016 so We seized **him** with a heavy Punishment.
073:019 Therefore, whoso will, let **him** take a (straight)
074:017 Soon will I visit **him** with a mount of calamities!
074:019 And woe to **him**! How he determined!-

HIM (continued)

074:020 Yea, woe to **him**: how he determined!-
074:026 Soon will cast **him** into Hell-Fire!
075:005 (even) in the time in front of **him**.
075:027 "Who is a magician (to restore **him**)?"
075:038 and fashion (**him**) in due proportion.
075:039 And of **him** He made two sexes, male and female.
076:002 of mingled sperm, in order to try **him**:
076:002 so We gave **him** (the gifts), of Hearing and Sight.
076:003 We showed **him** the Way: whether he
076:026 And part of the night, prostrate thyself to **Him**;
076:026 and glorify **Him** a long night through.
076:029 let **him** take a (straight) Path to his Lord.
078:037 to argue with **Him**.
078:039 whoso will, let **him** take a (straight) Return
079:016 Behold, thy Lord did call to **him** in the sacred
079:018 "And say to **him**, `Wouldst thou that thou shouldst
079:019 so thou shouldst fear **Him**?'"
079:020 Then did (Moses) show **him** the Great Sign.
079:025 (and made an) example of **him**,-in the Hereafter,
079:025 But Allah did punish **him**, (and made an)
079:036 in full view for **him** who sees.-
080:002 Because there came to **him** the blind
080:004 and the Reminder might profit **him**?
080:006 To **him** dost thou attend;
080:008 But as to **him** who came to thee striving earnestly,
080:010 Of **him** wast thou unmindful.
080:017 Woe to man! what hath made **him** reject Allah?
080:018 From what stuff Hath He created **him**?
080:019 From a sperm-drop: He hath created **him**, and then
080:019 and then mouldeth **him** in due Proportions;
080:020 Then doth He make His path smooth for **him**;
080:021 and putteth **him** in his Grave;
080:021 Then He causeth **him** to die, and putteth
080:022 He will raise **him** up (again).
080:023 what Allah Hath commanded **him**.
080:037 to make **him** indifferent to the others.
081:023 And without doubt he saw **him** in the clear horizon.
082:007 **Him** Who created thee, fashioned thee
083:013 When Our Signs are rehearsed to **him**, he says,
084:006 painfully toiling, but thou shalt meet **Him**.
084:015 Nay, nay! for his Lord was (ever) watchful of **him**!
085:009 **Him** to Whom belongs the dominion of the heavens
086:008 Surely (Allah) able to bring **him** back (to life)!
088:024 Allah will chastise **him** with a mighty Chastisement.
089:015 trieth **him**, giving **him** honour and gifts,
089:016 restricting his subsistence for **him**, then saith
089:016 But when He trieth **him**, restricting his
089:023 that remembrance profit **him**?
089:028 well pleased (thyself), and well-pleasing unto **Him**!
090:005 Thinketh he, that none hath power over **him**?
090:007 Thinketh he that none beholdeth **him**?
090:008 Have We not made for **him** a pair of eyes?-
090:010 And shown **him** the two highways?
091:002 By the Moon as she follow **him**;
091:014 Then they rejected **him** (as a false prophet),
091:015 And for **Him** is no fear of its consequences.
092:007 for **him** the path to Ease.
092:010 for **him** the Path to Misery;
092:011 Nor will his wealth profit **him** when he falls
093:010 Nor repulse **him** who asks;
095:005 Then do We abase **him** (to be) the lowest of the low,
096:015 We will drag **him** by the forelock,-

HIM (continued)

096:015 Let **him** beware! If he desist not, We will
096:017 Then, let **him** call (for help) to his
096:018 of punishment (to deal with **him**)!
096:019 Nay, heed **him** not: but prostrate
098:005 offering **Him** sincere devotion, being True
098:008 Allah well pleased with them, and they with **Him**:
104:003 would make **him** last for ever!
111:002 No profit to **him** from all his wealth, and all
112:004 And there is none like unto **Him**.

HIMSELF

002:282 or weak, or unable **himself** to dictate,
003:028 But Allah cautions you (to fear) **Himself**;
003:093 for **himself** before the Torah was revealed.
003:098 when Allah is **Himself** witness to all ye do?
003:140 and that He may take to **Himself** from your ranks
003:162 the man who draws on **Himself** the wrath of Allah,
004:006 let him have for **himself** what is just and reasonable.
004:112 He carries (on **himself**) (both)
004:158 Nay, Allah raised him up unto **Himself**;
004:172 gather them all together unto **Himself** to (answer).
004:175 and guide them to **Himself** by a straight Way.
004:175 to Mercy and Grace from **Himself**, and guide
005:030 and became (**himself**) one of the lost ones.
005:045 it is an act of atonement for **himself**.
006:012 inscribed for **Himself** (the rule of) Mercy.
006:054 inscribed for **Himself** (the rule of) Mercy: verily,
006:080 about Allah, when He (**Himself**) hath guided me?
006:158 or thy Lord (**Himself**), or certain
007:054 then He settled **Himself** on the Throne: He draweth
008:011 to give you calm as from **Himself**, and He
008:016 he draws on **himself** the wrath of Allah, and his
008:017 confer on the Believers a gracious benefit from **Himself**:
009:021 of a Mercy from **Himself**, of His good pleasure.
009:114 he dissociated **himself** from him: for Abraham
009:118 (and no refuge) but to **Himself**.
010:003 in six Days, then He established **Himself** on the
010:035 not guidance (**himself**) unless he is guided?
011:042 who had separated **himself** (from the rest):
011:063 and He hath sent Mercy unto me from **Himself**,-
011:077 and felt **himself** powerless (to protect) them.
011:088 (pure and) good as from **Himself**? I wish not,
012:012 enjoy **himself** and play, and we
012:032 firmly save **himself** guiltless!
012:077 He (simply) said (to **himself**): "Ye are the worse situated;
012:099 a home for his parents with **himself**, and said:
013:027 to **himself** those who turn to Him in penitence,-
016:059 With shame does he hide **himself** from his people,
017:027 his Lord (**Himself**) ungrateful.
017:040 for **Himself** daughters among the angels?
017:067 those that ye call upon-besides **Himself**-leave you
017:083 he gives **himself** up to despair!
018:035 He went inot his garden while he wronged **himself**:
018:043 against Allah, nor was he able to deliver **himself**.
022:015 stretch out a rope to the ceiling and cut (**himself**) off:
024:007 of Allah on **himself** if he tells a lie.
024:011 and to him who took on **himself** the lead among them,
025:059 in six days, then He established **Himself** on the
025:077 "My Lord would not concern **Himself** with you
028:004 Truly Pharaoh elated **himself** in the land
028:081 nor could he defend **himself**.
029:033 and felt **himself** powerless (to protect) them:
030:033 of Mercy from **Himself**, behold, some of

HIMSELF (continued)

032:004 in six Days, then He established **Himself** on the
035:018 And whoever purifies **himself** does so for the
036:047 He would have fed, (**himself**)?-Ye are
039:004 Had Allah wished to take to **Himself** a son,
039:008 upon him as from **Himself**, (man) doth
039:009 prostrating **himself** or standing (in adoration),
041:051 he turns away, and gets **himself** remote on his side
042:013 Allah chooses to **Himself** those whom
042:013 and guides to **Himself** those who turn (to Him).
042:041 defend themselves after a wrong (done) to him,
043:016 what He **Himself** creates, and granted
043:036 If anyone withdraws **himself** from remembrance
043:052 and can scarcely express **himself** clearly?
047:004 exacted retribution from them (**Himself**); but He
050:027 but he was (**himself**) far astray."
057:004 then He established **Himself** on the Throne.
058:022 them with a spirit from **Himself**.
070:011 would that he could redeem **himself** from the
075:014 Nay, man will be evidence against **himself**,
080:005 As to one who regards **himself** as self-sufficient,
092:008 and thinks **himself** self-sufficient.
096:007 In that he looketh upon **himself** as self-sufficient.

HINDER

005:091 and **hinder** you from the remembrance of Allah,
007:045 "Those who would **hinder** (men) from the
008:036 to **hinder** (men) from the path of Allah, and so
008:047 and to **hinder** (men) from the path of Allah:
009:034 of men and **hinder** (them) from the Way of Allah.
011:019 "Those who would **hinder** (men) from the path of
014:003 who **hinder** (men) from the Path of Allah and seek
016:088 Those who reject Allah and **hinder** (men) from
034:043 a man who wishes to **hinder** you from the
043:037 Such (Satans) really **hinder** them from the Path,
043:062 Let not the Satan **hinder** you: for he
047:001 Those who reject Allah and **hinder** (men) from the
047:032 Those who disbelieve, **hinder** (men) from the
047:034 Those who disbelieve, and **hinder** (men) from the

HINDERED

004:160 and that they **hindered** many from Allah's Way;
009:009 and (many) have they **hindered** from His Way:
016:094 evil (consequences) of having **hindered** (men) from
040:037 and he was **hindered** from the Path; and the
048:025 and **hindered** you from the Sacred Mosque and the

HINDERING

007:086 breathing threats, **hindering** from the path of Allah
068:012 (Habitually) **hindering** (all) good,

HINDWARDS

004:047 and turn them **hindwards**, or curse them as We

HIS

002:037 and **his** Lord turned towards him;
002:037 Then learnt Adam from **his** Lord certain words
002:051 and in **his** absence ye took the calf
002:054 And remember Moses said to **his** people:
002:060 for water for **his** people;
002:061 and slaying **His** Messengers without just cause.
002:067 And remember Moses said to **his** people:
002:073 and showeth you **His** Signs,
002:080 for He never breaks **His** promise?
002:090 send it to any of **His** servants He pleases:
002:090 Allah of **His** Grace should send it
002:098 and **His** angels and prophets,
002:105 for **His** special Mercy whom He will

HIS (continued)

002:109	till Allah brings about **His** command;
002:112	he will get **his** reward with **his** Lord;
002:112	Nay, whoever submits **his** whole self
002:114	**His** name should be celebrated?
002:124	was tried by **his** lord with certain Commands,
002:131	Behold! **his** Lord said to him: "Submit
002:132	upon **his** sons and so did Jacob;
002:133	Behold, he said to **his** sons: "What
002:158	And if any one obeyeth **his** own impulse to Good,
002:184	But he that will give more, of **his** own free will,
002:185	So every one of you who is present (at **his** home)
002:187	Thus doth Allah make clear **His** Signs to men:
002:196	or has an ailment in **his** scalp, (necessitating shaving),
002:196	And seven days on **his** return,
002:198	and celebrate **His** praises as He
002:203	if **his** aims is to do right.
002:204	to witness about what is in **his** heart;
002:205	When he turns **his** back,
002:205	**his** aim everywhere is to spread mischief through the
002:207	and Allah is full of kindness to (**His**) devotees.
002:207	gives **his** life to earn the pleasure of Allah;
002:210	with angels (in **His** train)
002:212	**His** abundance without measures on whom He will.
002:213	Allah by **His** Grace guided the Believers
002:219	Thus doth Allah make clear to you **His** Signs:
002:221	But Allah beckons by **His** Grace to the Garden
002:221	and makes **His** Signs clear to mankind:
002:230	So if a husband divorces **his** wife (irrevocably),
002:231	if anyone does that, He wrongs **his** own soul.
002:233	Nor father on account of **his** child,
002:236	and the poor according to **his** means;
002:236	the wealthy according to **his** means,
002:242	Thus doth Allah make clear **His** Signs to you:
002:245	unto **his** credit and multiply many times?
002:247	Allah granteth **His** authority to whom He pleaseth;
002:248	"A sign of **his** authority is that there shall come
002:249	cannot cope with Goliath and **his** forces."
002:250	meet Goliath and **his** forces,
002:255	He knoweth what (appeareth to **his** creatures as) before
002:255	aught of **his** knowledge except as He willeth.
002:255	in **His** presence except as He permitteth?
002:255	**His** throne doth extend over the heavens
002:255	**His** are all things in the heavens and on earth.
002:258	to one who disputed with Abraham about **his** Lord,
002:266	clear to you (**His**) Signs; that ye may consider.
002:266	and **his** children are not strong
002:268	Allah promiseth you **His** forgiveness and bounties.
002:275	the Satan by **his** touch hath driven to madness.
002:279	notice of war from Allah and **His** Messenger:
002:282	but let him fear Allah **his** Lord
002:282	let **his** guardian dictate faithfully.
002:283	let the trustee (faithfully) discharge **his** trust,
002:283	and let him fear Allah **his** Lord.
002:283	for whoever conceals it,-**his** heart is tainted with sin.
002:285	**His** Angles, **His** books, and **His** Messengers.
002:285	between one and another of **His** Messengers."
002:285	hath been revealed to him from **his** Lord,
003:009	for Allah never fails in **His** promise."
003:013	with **His** aid whom He pleaseth.
003:015	For in Allah's sight are (all) **His** servants,
003:018	that is the witness of Allah, **His** angels,
003:019	Allah is Islam (submission to **His** Will):

HIS (continued)

003:020	and in Allah's sight are (all) **His** servants.
003:032	Say: "Obey Allah and **His** Messenger": but if they
003:038	There did Zakariya pray to **his** Lord, saying:
003:045	**his** name will be Christ Jesus, the son of Mary,
003:067	and bowed **his** will to Allah's (which is Islam).
003:074	For **His** Mercy He specially chooseth
003:083	bowed to **His** Will (accepted Islam),
003:087	curse of Allah, of **His** angels, and of all mankind;
003:097	Allah stands not in need of any of **His** creatures.
003:103	so that by **His** Grace, Ye became brethren;
003:103	Thus doth Allah make **His** Signs clear to you:
003:108	no injustice to any of **His** creatures.
003:142	who fought hard (in **His** cause) and remained steadfast?
003:144	If any did turn back on **his** heels,
003:152	Allah sis indeed fulfil **His** promise to you when we with
003:152	with **His** permission were about to annihilate your enemy,
003:175	suggests to you the fear of **his** votaries:
003:179	but He chooses of **his** Messengers whom He pleases.
003:179	So believe in Allah and **His** Messengers:
003:180	Allah hath given them of **His** Grace,
004:001	created, out of it, **his** mate, and from them
004:013	those who obey Allah and **His** Messenger will be
004:014	But those who disobey Allah and **His** Messenger
004:014	and transgress **His** limits will be admitted
004:032	in which Allah hath bestowed **His** gifts more
004:032	but ask Allah of **His** bounty: for Allah
004:035	appoint (two) arbiters, one from **his** family,
004:040	and giveth from **His** Own self a great reward.
004:054	for what Allah hath given them of **His** bounty?
004:059	refer it to Allah and **His** Messenger, if ye
004:092	blood-money should be paid to **his** family,
004:093	man kills a believer intentionally, **his** recompense is Hell,
004:094	till Allah conferred on you **His** favours:
004:100	He who forsakes **his** home in the cause of Allah,
004:100	**his** reward becomes due and sure with Allah:
004:100	as a refugee from home for Allah and **His** Messenger,
004:110	If anyone does evil or wrongs **his** own soul but
004:111	he earns it against **his** own soul: for Allah
004:113	But for the Grace of Allah to thee and **His** Mercy,
004:121	They (**his** dupes) will have their dwelling in hell,
004:125	than one who submits **his** whole self to Allah,
004:130	for each of them from **His** all-reaching bounty:
004:133	If it were **His** will, He could destroy you,
004:136	believe in Allah and **His** Messenger,
004:136	denieth Allah, **His** angels, **His** Books, **His** Messenger,
004:136	He hath sent to **His** Messenger and the scripture
004:150	between Allah and **His** Messengers, saying
004:150	Those who deny Allah and **his** Messenger,
004:152	and **His** messengers and make no distinction
004:159	but must believe in Him before **his** death;
004:166	He hath sent from **His** (Own) knowledge,
004:171	and **His** Word, which He bestowed on Mary,
004:171	so believe in Allah and **His** Messengers.
004:172	those who disdain **His** worship and are arrogant,
004:173	and more, out of **His** bounty:
004:176	thus doth Allah make clear to you (**His** law),
005:001	according to **His** Will and Plan.
005:005	If anyone rejects faith, fruitless is **his** work,
005:006	and to complete **His** favour to you, that ye
005:007	and **His** Covenant, which He ratified with you,
005:016	by **His** Will, unto the light, guideth them
005:016	**His** good pleasure to ways of peace and safety,

HIS (continued)

005:017 to destroy Christ the son of Mary, **his** mother,
005:017 against Allah, if **His** Will were to destroy
005:018 "We are sons of Allah, and **His** beloved."
005:020 Remember Moses said to **his** people: "O my people!
005:023 were two on whom Allah had bestowed **His** Grace:
005:030 led him to the murder of **his** brother: he murdered
005:031 the naked body of **his** brother.
005:033 who wage war against Allah and **His** Messenger,
005:035 and main in **His** cause: that ye may prosper.
005:038 cut off **his** or her hands: a retribution
005:039 and amend **his** conduct, Allah turneth
005:039 But if the thief repent after **his** crime, and amend
005:048 but (**His** Plan is) to test you in what He
005:054 you turn back from **his** Faith, soon will
005:055 **His** Messenger, and the Believers,-those who
005:056 (for friendship) to Allah, **His** Messenger,
005:060 curse of Allah and **His** wrath, those of whom
005:064 Nay, both **His** hands are widely outstretched:
005:064 He giveth and spendeth (of **His** Bounty) as He pleaseth.
005:067 and proclaimed **His** Mission.
005:072 and the Fire will be **his** abode.
005:074 and seek **His** forgiveness?
005:075 **His** mother was a woman of truth.
005:075 makes **His** Signs clear to them; yet see
005:089 Thus doth Allah make clear to you **His** Signs,
005:089 or clothe them; or give a slave **his** freedom.
005:095 that he may taste of the penalty of **his** deed.
005:108 But fear Allah, and listen (to **His** counsel):
006:018 Irresistibly Supreme over **His** servants.
006:021 or rejecteth **his** Signs?
006:037 a Sign sent down to him from **his** Lord?"
006:041 and if it be **His** Will, He would remove (the distress)
006:052 their Lord morning and evening, seeking **His** Face.
006:054 and amended (**his** conduct), lo! He is
006:059 Not a leaf doth fall but with **His** knowledge:
006:061 Supreme over **His** servants and He sets guardians
006:061 Our angels take **his** soul, and they never
006:062 surely **His** is the Command, and He
006:071 through the earth, **his** friends calling 'Come to us',
006:073 **His** will be the dominion the day the trumpet will be
006:073 **His** Word is the Truth.
006:074 Lo! Abraham said to **his** father Azar: "Takest thou idols
006:080 **His** people disputed with him.
006:080 my Lord comprehendeth in **His** knowledge all things.
006:083 which We gave to Abraham (to use) against **his** people:
006:084 and among **his** progeny, David, Solomon,
006:088 of **His** servants, if they were to join other gods with Him,
006:093 and scornfully to reject of **His** Signs!"
006:103 but **His** grasp is over all vision; He is
006:104 it will be to **his** own (harm): I am not
006:104 it will be for (the good of) **his** own soul:
006:115 none can change **His** Words: for He
006:117 who strayeth from **His** Way: He knoweth
006:118 if ye have faith in **His** Signs.
006:124 Allah knoweth best where to place **His** mission.
006:133 if it were **His** Will, He could destroy you,
006:147 never will **His** wrath be turned back.
006:149 if it had been **His** Will.
006:153 they will scatter you about from **His** (great) path:
006:160 be recompensed according to **his** evil: no wrong
006:160 ten times as much to **his** credit: he that
006:163 those who submit to **His** Will.

HIS (continued)

007:027 for he and **his** tribe see you from a position
007:032 which He hath produced for **His** servants,
007:037 or rejects **His** Signs?
007:046 who would know every one by **his** marks: they will
007:049 that Allah with **His** Mercy would never bless?
007:054 (all) are subservient by **His** Command.
007:054 Verily, **His** are the Creation and the Command,
007:057 going before **His** mercy: when they
007:059 We sent Noah to **his** people. He said: "O
007:060 The leaders of **his** people said: "Ah! we see
007:063 fear Allah and haply receive **His** Mercy?"
007:066 among **his** people said: "Ah! we see
007:075 is a messenger from **his** Lord?"
007:075 among **his** people said to those who were
007:080 We also (sent) Lut: he said to **his** people: "Do ye
007:082 And **his** people gave no answer but this: they said,
007:083 But We saved him and **his** family,except **His** wife:
007:088 The leaders, the arrogant party among **his** people,
007:089 Our Lord comprehends all things in **His** knowledge.
007:090 The leaders, the Unbelievers among **his** people,
007:103 with Our Signs to Pharaoh and **his** chiefs.
007:107 Then (Moses) threw **his** rod, and behold!
007:108 And he drew out **his** hand, and behold!
007:110 "**His** plan is to get you out of your land:
007:111 They said: "Keep him and **his** brother in suspense
007:127 "Wilt thou leave Moses and **his** people,
007:128 such of **His** servants as He pleaseth; and the
007:128 Said Moses to **his** people: "Pray for help
007:134 in virtue of **his** promise to thee: if thou
007:137 which Pharaoh and **his** people erected
007:142 had charged **his** brother Aaron (before he went up):
007:142 thus was completed the term with **his** Lord, forty nights.
007:143 When he recovered **his** senses he said: "Glory be
007:143 When **his** Lord manifested Himself to the mount,
007:143 and **his** Lord addressed him, he said: "O my lord!
007:148 The people of Moses made, in **his** absence, out of
007:150 seized **his** brother by (the hair of) **his** head,
007:150 When Moses came back to **his** people, angry and
007:155 chose seventy of **his** people for Our place of meeting:
007:158 So believe in Allah and **His** Messenger.
007:158 who believed in Allah and **His** Words: follow him
007:160 when **his** (thirsty) people asked him for Water:
007:176 **His** similitude is that of a dog: if you attack him,
007:176 and followed **his** own vain desires.
007:176 he lolls out **his** tongue, or if you leave him alone,
007:176 he (still) lolls out **his** tongue.
007:178 whom He rejects from **His** guidance.
007:180 but shun such men as distort **His** names: for what
007:186 To such as Allah rejects from **His** guidance, there
007:189 and made **his** mate of like nature, in order
008:001 obey Allah and **His** Allah, if ye do believe."
008:002 and when they hear **His** revelations rehearsed, find their
008:007 to establish the Truth according to **His** words,
008:013 against Allah and **His** Messenger: if any contend
008:013 if any contend against Allah and **His** Messenger.
008:016 or to retreat to a troop (of **his** own)-he draws
008:016 and **his** abode is Hell, an evil refuse (indeed)!
008:016 If any do turn **his** back to them
008:020 and **His** Messenger, and turn not away from him
008:024 and **His** Messenger, when He calleth you to that
008:024 in between a man and **his** heart, and that
008:026 strengthened you with **His** aid, and gave you

HIS (continued)

008:046 And obey Allah and **His** Messenger; and fall
008:048 he turned on **his** heels, and said:
008:051 For Allah is never unjust to **His** servants."
008:062 with **His** aid and with (the company of)
009:001 from Allah and **His** Messenger, to those
009:003 And an announcement from Allah and **His** Messenger,
009:003 that Allah and **His** Messenger dissolve (treaty)
009:007 before Allah and **His** Messenger, with the
009:009 and (many) have they hindered from **His** Way:
009:016 and protectors except Allah, **His** Messenger,
009:021 glad tidings of a Mercy from Himself, **His** good pleasure.
009:024 then wait until Allah brings about **His** decision:
009:024 are dearer to you than Allah or **His** Messenger,
009:024 or the striving in **His** cause;-
009:026 But Allah did pour **His** calm on the Messenger
009:028 out of **His** bounty, for Allah is All-Knowing, All-Wise.
009:029 by Allah and **His** Messenger, nor acknowledge
009:032 Allah will not allow but that **His** light should be perfected,
009:033 It is He Who hath sent **His** Messenger with Guidance
009:040 and he said to **his** companion, "Have no fear,
009:040 then Allah sent down **His** peace upon him,
009:052 that Allah will send **His** punishment from Him
009:054 they reject Allah and **His** Messenger; that they
009:059 Allah and **His** Messenger will soon give us of **His** bounty:
009:059 what Allah and **His** Messenger gave them,
009:062 should please Allah and **His** Messenger, if they
009:063 who oppose Allah and **His** Messenger, is the
009:065 Say: "Was it at Allah, and **His** Signs, and **His** Messenger,
009:071 and obey Allah and **His** Messenger.
009:071 On them will Allah pour **His** mercy: for Allah is Exalted
009:074 Allah and **His** Messenger had enriched them!
009:075 on them of **His** bounty; they would
009:076 But when He did bestow of **His** bounty, they became
009:080 rejected Allah and **His** Messenger: and Allah
009:084 for they rejected Allah and **His** Messenger,
009:084 pray for any of them that dies, nor stand at **his** grave;
009:086 and fight along with **His** Messenger, those with
009:090 and **His** Messenger (Merely) sat behind:
009:091 (in duty) to Allah and **His** Messenger: no ground
009:094 and **His** Messenger will observe: in the end
009:097 sent down to **His** Messenger: but Allah
009:099 soon will Allah admit them to **His** Mercy: for Allah
009:104 accept repentance from **His** votaries and receives
009:105 and **His** Messenger, and the Believers: soon will
009:107 who warred against Allah and **His** Messenger aforetime.
009:109 that layeth **his** foundation on an undermined sand-cliff
009:109 that layeth **his** foundation on piety to Allah
009:109 to Allah and **His** good pleasure?-
009:111 they fight in **His** Cause, and slay and are slain:
009:111 and who is more faithful to **his** Covenant than Allah?
009:114 And Abraham prayed for **his** father's forgiveness
009:120 nor to prefer their own lives to **his**:
009:124 "Which of you has had **his** faith increased by it?"
010:003 except after **His** leave (hath been obtained).
010:005 (Thus) doth He explain **His** Signs in detail,
010:012 lying down on **his** side, or sitting, or standing.
010:012 But when We removed **his** affliction,
010:012 he passeth on **his** way as if he had never cried to Us
010:017 than such as forge a lie against or deny **His** Signs?
010:020 sent down to him from **his** Lord?"
010:044 it is man that wrongs **his** own soul.
010:050 Say: "Do ye see-if **His** punishment should come

010:058 And in **His** Mercy,-in that let them rejoice":
010:066 who worship as **His** "partners" other than Allah?
010:067 for those who listen (to **His** Message).
010:068 **His** are all things in the heavens and on earth!
010:071 Behold! he said to **his** People: "O my People,
010:075 and Aaron to Pharaoh and **his** chiefs with Our Signs.
010:082 "And Allah by **His** Words doth prove and establish
010:083 believed in Moses except some children of **his** People,
010:083 because of the fear of Pharaoh and **his** chiefs,
010:084 if ye submit (your will to **His**)."
010:087 We inspired Moses and **his** brother with this
010:088 and **his** Chiefs splendor and wealth in the life
010:090 Pharaoh and **his** hosts followed them in insolence
010:107 whomsoever of **His** servants He pleaseth.
010:107 there is none can keep back **his** favour:
011:003 and bestow **His** abounding grace on all
011:007 and **His** Throne was over the Waters-that He
011:025 We sent Noah to **his** People (with a mission)
011:027 among **his** people said: "We see (in) thee
011:038 that the Chiefs **his** People passed by him, they threw
011:042 and Noah called out to **his** son, who had separated
011:045 And Noah called upon **his** Lord and said: "O my Lord
011:046 for **his** conduct is unrighteous.
011:059 disobeyed **His** Messengers; and followed
011:071 And **his** wife was standing (there), and she
011:073 and **His** blessings on you, O ye people
011:078 And **his** people came rushing towards him, and they
011:097 Unto Pharaoh and **his** Chiefs: but they
011:098 He will go before **his** people on the
011:102 indeed, and severe is **His** chastisement.
011:105 shall speak except by **His** leave: of those
011:119 hath bestowed **His** Mercy:
012:004 Behold, Joseph said to **his** father: "O my father!
012:006 **His** favour to thee and to the posterity of Jacob-
012:007 Verily in Joseph and **his** brethren are Signs
012:008 They said: "Truly Joseph and **his** brother are loved
012:011 seeing we are indeed **his** sincere well-wishers?
012:015 and We put into **his** heart (this Message):
012:018 They stained **his** shirt with false blood.
012:019 and he let down **his** bucket (into the well).
012:021 said to **his** wife: "Make **his** stay (among us) honourable:
012:021 power and control over **His** affairs;
012:022 When Joseph attained **his** full manhood, We gave
012:024 but that he saw the evidence **his** Lord:
012:025 and she tore **his** shirt from the back: they both
012:026 (thus)-"If it be that **his** shirt is rent
012:027 "But if it be that **his** shirt is torn
012:028 So when he saw **his** shirt,-that it
012:032 from **his** (true) self but he did firmly save
012:034 So **his** Lord hearkened to him (in **his** prayer),
012:041 and the birds will eat from off **his** head.
012:041 he will pour out the wine for **his** lord to drink:
012:042 but Satan made him forget to mention him to **his** lord:
012:052 to him in **his** absence, and that
012:053 do bestow **His** Mercy: but surely certainly my Lord is
012:058 they entered **his** presence, and he knew them,
012:061 win him from **his** father: indeed we shall do it."
012:062 And (Joseph) told **his** servants to put their stock-
012:064 you with **his** brother aforetime?
012:069 Joseph's presence, he received **his** (full) brother
012:070 cup into **his** brother's saddle-bag.
012:076 out of **his** brother's baggage.

HIS (continued)

012:076	the baggage of **his** brother: at length
012:076	He could not take **his** brother by the law
012:077	Joseph keep locked in **his** heart, revealing not
012:077	a brother of **his** who did steal before (him)."
012:078	so take one of us in **his** place: for we
012:080	Now when they saw no hope of **his** (yielding),
012:084	And **his** eyes became white with sorrow, and he
012:087	about Joseph and **his** brother, and never
012:089	with Joseph, and **his** brother, not knowing
012:096	he cast (the shirt) over **his** face, and he forthwith
012:099	a home for **his** parents with himself, and said:
012:100	And he raised **his** parents high on the throne
013:007	a Sign sent down to him from **his** Lord?"
013:010	of you conceal **his** speech or declare it openly;
013:013	Nay, thunder repeateth **His** praises, and so
013:027	a Sign sent down to him from **his** Lord?"
013:031	not fail in **His** promise.
013:041	to put back **His** command: and He
014:004	in the language of **his** (own) people, in order
014:006	Remember! Moses said to **his** people: "Call to mind
014:011	but Allah doth grant **His** grace to such
014:011	to such of **His** servants as He pleases.
014:017	swallowing it down **his** throat; death will come
014:030	to Allah, to mislead (men) from the Path!
014:032	through the sea by **His** Command; and the
014:047	that Allah wold fail **His** messengers in **His** promise:
015:052	When they entered **his** presence and said,
015:056	the mercy of **his** Lord, but such as go astray?"
015:060	"Except **his** wife, who, we have ascertained,
016:002	He doth send down **His** angels with inspiration
016:002	with inspiration of **His** Command,
016:002	to such of **His** servants as He pleaseth, (saying):
016:012	and the Stars are in subjection by **His** Command:
016:035	prohibitions other than **His**."
016:058	of (the birth of) a female (child),**his** face darkens,
016:059	With shame does he hide himself from **his** people,
016:071	Allah has bestowed **His** gifts of sustenance
016:076	a wearisome butden is he to **his** master;
016:081	Thus does He complete **his** favours on you,
016:081	that ye may surrender to **His** will (in Islam).
016:100	**His** authority is over those only, who take his as patron
016:106	except under compulsion, **his** heart remaining firm
016:121	He showed **his** gratitude for the favours of Allah,
016:125	who have strayed from **His** Path, and who
017:001	Who did that **His** Servant for a Journey by night from the
017:013	Every man's fate We have fastened on **his** own neck:
017:015	who goeth astray doth so to **his** own loss:
017:015	receiveth it for **his** own benefit:
017:017	to note and see the sins of **His** servants.
017:027	**his** Lord (Himself) ungrateful.
017:030	for He doth know and regard all **His** servants.
017:033	We have given **his** heir authority (to demand Qisas
017:044	there is not a thing but celebrates **His** praise;
017:044	and all beings therein, declare **His** glory:
017:044	yet ye understand not how they declare **His** glory!
017:052	(**His** call) with (words of) **His** praise, and ye
017:057	they hope for **His** Mercy and fear **His** Wrath:
017:062	I will surely bring **his** descendants under my sway-
017:066	in order that ye may seek of **His** Bounty.
017:083	becomes remote on **his** side (instead of coming to Us),
017:084	Say: "Everyone acts according to **his** own disposition:
017:087	for **His** Bounty is to thee (indeed) great.

HIS (continued)

017:094	"Has Allah sent a man (like us) to be (**His**) Messenger?"
017:096	well acquainted with **His** servants, and He
017:111	Yea, magnify Him for **His** greatness and glory!"
017:111	and has no partner in (**His**) dominion:
018:001	Who hath sent to **His** Servant the Book, and hath
018:016	shower **His** mercies on you and dispose of your affair
018:018	their dog stretching forth **his** two fore-legs
018:026	nor does He share **His** Command with any
018:027	none can change **His** Words, and none
018:028	and **his** affair has become all excess.
018:028	call on thie Lord morning and evening, seeking **his** Face;
018:028	one who follows **his** own desires,
018:034	he said to **his** companion, in the course
018:035	He went into **his** garden while he wronged himself:
018:037	**His** companion said to him, in the course of the
018:042	So **his** fruits were encompassed (with ruin),
018:042	turning his hands over what he had spent **his** property,
018:050	and **his** progeny as protectors rather than Me?
018:050	and he broke the Command of **his** Lord.
018:057	forgetting the (deeds) which **his** hands have sent
018:057	who is reminded of the Signs of **his** Lord but turns
018:060	Behold, Moses said to **his** attendant, "I will
018:062	Moses said to **his** attendant: "Bring us
018:080	"As for the youht, **his** parents were people of Faith,
018:083	"I will rehearse to you something of **his** story."
018:084	Verily We established **his** power on earth, and We
018:087	then shall be sent back to **his** Lord; and He will punish
018:088	a goodly reward, and easy will be **his** task as We
018:110	whoever expects to meet **his** Lord, let him
018:110	and in the worship of **his** Lord, admit no one
019:002	of thy Lord to **His** Servant Zakariya.
019:003	Behold! he cried to **his** Lord in secret.
019:007	**his** name shall be Yahya: on none by that name
019:007	(**His** prayer was answered): "O Zakariya! We give thee
019:011	So Zakariya came out to **his** people from **his** chamber:
019:012	(To **his** son came the command): "O Yahya!
019:014	And kind to **his** parents, and he
019:042	Behold, he said to **his** father: "O my father!
019:053	We gave him **his** brother Aaron, (also) a prophet.
019:055	acceptable in the sight of **his** Lord.
019:055	He used to enjoin on **his** people Prayer and Zakat
019:058	on whom Allah did bestow **His** Grace,-of the
019:061	for **His** promise must (necessarily) come to pass.
019:061	has promised to **His** servants in the Unseen:
019:065	and patient in **His** worship: knowest thou
019:079	and We Shall add and add to **his** punishment.
020:010	so he said to **his** family, "Tarry ye;
020:060	So Pharaoh withdrew: he concerted **his** plan,
020:067	So Moses conceived in **his** mind a (sort of) fear.
020:074	Verily he who comes to **his** Lord as a sinner
020:078	Then Pharaoh pursued htm with **his** forces,
020:079	Pharaoh led **his** people astray instead of
020:086	So Moses returned to **his** people in state
020:098	all things He comprehends in **His** Knowledge.
020:111	the man that carries iniquity (on **his** back).
020:112	nor of any curtailment (of what is **his** due).
020:115	and We found on **his** part no firm resolve.
020:121	thus did Adam disobey **His** Lord, and fell into error.
020:122	But **his** Lord chose him (for **His** Grace):
020:123	will not lose **his** way, nor fall into misery.
020:127	and believes not in the Signs of **his** Lord:
020:133	"Why does he not bring us a Sign from **His** Lord?"

HIS (continued)

021:019	nor are they (ever) weary of **His** service):
021:020	They celebrate **His** praises night and day, nor do
021:023	He cannot be questioned for **His** acts, by they
021:027	and they act (in all things) by **His** command.
021:028	and reverence of **His** (glory).
021:051	bestowed aforetime on Abraham **his** rectitude of conduct,
021:052	he said to **his** father and **his** people, "What are these
021:071	and (**his** nephew) Lut (and directed them) to the
021:076	listened to **his** (prayer) and delivered him and **his** family
021:081	flow (tamely) for Solomon, to **his** order, to the land
021:083	when he cried to **his** Lord "Truly distress has seized me,
021:084	and We restored **his** people to him, and doubled
021:089	when he cried to **his** Lord: "O my Lord! leave me
021:090	We cured **his** wife's (barrenness) for him.
021:094	We shall record it in **his** favour.
021:094	and has Faith,-**his** endeavour will not be rejected:
021:108	bow to **His** Will (in Islam)?"
022:009	(Disdainfully) bending **his** side, in order
022:010	for verily Allah is not unjust to **His** servants.
022:013	is nearer than **his** profit: evil, indeed, is the
022:015	Allah will not help him (**His** Messenger) in this world
022:015	whether **his** plan will remove that which enrages (him)!
022:030	in the sight of **his** Lord, Lawful to
022:032	Such (is **his** state): and whoever
022:037	that ye may glorify Allah for **His** guidance to you:
022:040	(Able to enforce **His** Will).
022:040	Allah will certainly aid those who aid **His** (cause);-
022:047	But Allah will not fail in **His** promise.
022:052	Satan threw some (vanity) into **his** desire:
022:052	and Allah will confirm (and establish) **His** Signs:
022:065	sail through the sea by **His** command?
022:065	on the earth except by **His** leave: for Allah
022:078	And strive in **His** cause as ye ought to strive,
023:023	And certainly We sent Noah to **his** people: he said,
023:024	The Chiefs of the Unbelievers among **his** people said:
023:024	**his** wish is to assert **his** superiority over you:
023:033	And the chiefs of **his** people, who disbelieved
023:045	Then We sent Moses and **his** brother Aaron, with Our
023:046	To Pharaoh and **his** Chiefs: but these
023:050	and **his** mother as a Sign: We gave
023:117	and **his** reckoning will be only with **his** Lord!
024:032	Allah will give them means out of **His** grace:
024:033	until Allah gives them means out of **His** grace.
024:035	Allah doth guide whom He will to **His** Light:
024:035	The parable of **His** Light is as if there were a Niche
024:036	for the celebration in them, of **His** name:
024:038	and add even more for them out of **His** Grace:
024:039	and Allah will pay him **his** account:
024:040	if a man stretches out **his** hand, he can
024:043	The vivid flash of **His** lightning well-nigh
024:048	Whey they are summoned to Allah and **His** Messenger,
024:050	that Allah and **His** Messenger will deal unjustly
024:051	when summoned to Allah and **His** Messenger,
024:052	It is such as obey Allah and **His** Messenger,
024:059	make clear **His** Signs to you: for Allah
024:062	have asked for **his** leave; those who ask
024:062	and **His** Messenger; so when
024:062	who believe in Allah and **His** Messenger: when they
025:001	the Criterion to **His** servant, that it
025:002	nor has He a partner in **His** dominion:
025:010	Blessed is He Who if that were **His** Will, could give thee
025:027	will bite at **his** hands, he will say, "Oh! would

HIS (continued)

025:035	appointed **his** brother Aaron with him as Minister;
025:043	on as taketh for **his** god **his** own passion (or impulse)?
025:048	going before **His** Mercy, and We
025:055	is a helper (of Evil), against **his** own Lord!
025:057	may take a (straight) Path to **his** Lord."
025:058	Him Who lives and dies not, and cecbrte **His** praise;
025:058	to be acquainted with the faults of **His** servants;-
026:032	So (Moses) threw **his** rod, and behold,
026:033	And he drew out **his** hand, and behold
026:035	"**His** plan is to get you out of your land by **his** sorcery;
026:036	They said: "Keep him and **his** brother in suspense
026:045	Then Moses threw **his** rod, when, behold,
026:070	he said to **his** father and **his** people: "What worship
026:170	So We delivered him and **his** family,-
027:007	Behold! Moses said to **his** family: "I perceive
027:010	and retraced not **his** steps: "O Moses!"
027:012	nine Signs (thou will take) to Pharaoh and **his** people:
027:015	has favoured us above many of **His** servants who believe!"
027:017	And before Solomon were marshalled **his** hosts,-
027:018	and **his** host crush you (under foot)
027:038	He said (to **his** own men): "Ye Chiefs! which of
027:040	truly **his** gratitude is (a gain) for **his** own soul;
027:049	"We were not present at the slaughter of **his** people,
027:049	we shall then say to **his** heir (when he seeks vengeance):
027:049	we shall make a secret night attack on him and **his** people,
027:054	behold, he said to **his** people, "Do ye do what is indecent
027:056	But **his** people gave no other answer but this:
027:057	But We saved him and **his** family, except **his** wife:
027:059	He has chosen (for **his** Message).
027:059	and Peace on **His** servants whom He has chosen
027:062	and Who relieves **his** suffering, and makes
027:063	winds as herarlds of glad tidings, going before **His** Mercy?
027:078	between them by **His** Decree:
027:093	Who will soon show you **His** Signs, so that
028:010	to disclose **his** (case), had We
028:012	at first, until (**his** sister came up and) said:
028:013	Thus did We restore him to **his** mother, that her
028:015	one of **his** own people, and the other, of **his** foes.
028:015	Now the man of **his** own people appealed to him against
028:015	to him against **his** foe, and Moses struck him
028:015	and Moses struck him with **his** fist and killed
028:018	sought **his** help called aloud for **his** help (again).
028:019	Then, when he was about to lay **his** hands on their
028:022	Then when he turned **his** face towards (the land of)
028:029	and was travelling with **his** family, he perceived
028:029	He said to **his** family: "Tarry ye;
028:031	and retraced not **his** steps: "O Moses
028:032	from thy Lord to Pharaoh and **his** Chiefs: for truly
028:039	insolent in the land beyond reason,- he and **his** hosts:
028:040	So We seized him and **his** hosts, and We
028:050	one who follows **his** own lusts, devoid of
028:073	and that ye may seek of **His** Grace;-and in
028:073	It is out of **His** Mercy that He has made
028:076	Behold, **his** people said to him: "Exult not,
028:079	So he went forth among **his** people in the
028:079	in the (pride of **his** worldly) glitter.
028:081	caused the earth to swallow up him and **his** house;
028:082	or restricts it, to any of **His** servants He pleases!
028:082	And those who had envied **his** position the day
028:084	is better than **his** deed; but if
028:088	will perish except **His** Face.
029:014	We did sent Noah to **his** people, and he

HIS (continued)

029:016 he said to **his** people, "Serve Allah
029:022 will ye be able (fleeing) to frustrate (**His** Plan),
029:027 and ordained among **his** progeny Prophethood and
029:027 and We granted him **his** reward in this life;
029:028 he said to **his** people: "Ye do commit lewdness,
029:029 But **his** people gave no answer but this:
029:032 certainly save him and **his** following,-except **his** wife:
029:040 Each one of them We seized for **his** crime:
029:050 sent down to him from **his** Lord?"
029:061 and the moon (to **His** Law), they will
029:062 to whichever of **His** servants He pleases;
030:006 Never does Allah fail from **His** promise:
030:020 Among **His** Signs is this, that He
030:021 And among **His** Signs is this, that He
030:022 And among **His** Signs is the creation of the
030:023 And among **His** Signs is the sleep that ye take
030:023 (make for livelihood) out of **His** Bounty:
030:024 And among **His** Signs, He shows
030:025 And among **His** Signs is this, that heaven
030:025 that the heaven and earth stand by **His** command:
030:045 beleive and work righteous deeds, out of **His** Bounty.
030:046 and that ye may seek of **His** Bounty:
030:046 giving you a taste of **His** Mercy,-
030:046 Among **His** Signs is this, that He the Winds
030:046 that the ships may sail by **His** Command and that
030:048 made them reach such of **his** servants as He wills,
031:007 as if there were deafness in both **his** ears:
031:012 does so to the profit of **his** own soul:
031:013 Behold, Luqman said to **his** son admonishing him
031:014 have enjoined on man (to be good) to **his** parents:
031:014 in travail upon travail did **his** mother bear him.
031:014 And in years twain was **his** weaning:
031:020 and has made **His** bounties flow to you in exceeding
031:022 Whoever submits **his** whole self to Allah, and is
031:023 let not **his** rejection grieve thee:
031:029 that He has sunjected the sun and the moon (to **His** Law),
031:031 that He may show you of **His** Signs?
031:033 nor a son avail aught for **his** father.
031:033 when no father can avail aught for **his** son, nor a
032:008 And made **his** progeny from a quintessence
032:009 and breathed into him of **His** spirit.
032:022 than one to whom are recited the Signs of **his** Lord,
033:004 two hearts in **his** breast: nor has
033:006 and **his** wives are their mothers.
033:012 say: "Allah and **His** Messenger promised us nothing
033:017 from Allah if it be **His** wish to give you
033:022 and **His** Messenger told us what was true."
033:022 "This is what Allah and **His** Messenger had promised
033:024 and punish the Hypocrited if that be **His** Will,
033:029 But is ye seek Allah and **His** Messenger, and the Home
033:031 that is devout in the service of Allah and **His** Messenger,
033:033 and obey Allah and **His** Messenger.
033:034 of the Signs of Allah and **His** Wisdom:
033:036 been decided by Allah and **His** Messenger, to have
033:036 and **His** Messenger, he is indeed on a clearly
033:037 then when Zaid had dissolved (**his** marriage) with her,
033:043 He it is Who sends blessing on you, as do **His** angels,
033:046 to Allah's (Grace) by **His** leave, and as
033:053 And when ye ask (**his** ladies) for anything
033:053 or that ye should marry **his** widows after him
033:056 Allah and **His** Angels send blessings on the
033:057 Those who annoy Allah and **his** Messenger-Allah has

HIS (continued)

033:071 he that obeys Allah and **His** Messenger has already
034:012 in front of him, by the leave of **his** Lord, and if
034:014 nothing showed them **his** death except a little worm
034:014 which kept (slowly) gnawing away at **his** staff:
034:020 And on them did Satan prove true **his** idea,
034:039 the Sustenance to such of **His** servants as He pleases:
034:039 (in **His** Cause) but He replaces it:
035:002 What Allah out of **His** Mercy doth bestow
035:006 He only invites **his** adherents, that they
035:008 the evil of **his** conduct is made alluring,
035:011 nor is a part cut off from **his** life, but is in a Book
035:011 or lays down (her load), but with **His** knowledge.
035:013 and the moon (to **His** Law): each one
035:018 heavily laden should call another to (bear) **his** load,
035:018 does so for the benefit of **his** own soul;
035:028 among **His** Servants, who have knowledge:
035:030 out of **His** Bounty; for He is Oft-Forgiving,
035:031 with respect to **his** servants-well acquainted
035:035 "Who has, out of **His** bounty, settled us
035:039 so, he who disbelieves **his** disbelief be on
035:039 be on **his** own self their disbelief:
035:045 verily has in **His** sight all **His** servants.
036:028 And We sent not down against **his** People, after Him,
036:078 and forgets **his** own (Origin and) Creation:
036:082 Verily when He intends a thing, **His** command is, "Be,"
037:076 And We delivered him and **his** people from the
037:077 And made **his** progeny to endure (on this earth);
037:083 Verily from **his** party was Abraham.
037:084 Behold, He approached **his** Lord with a sound heart.
037:085 Behold, he said to **his** father and to **his** people, "What is
037:103 prostrate on **his** forehead (for sacrifice),
037:124 Behold, he said to **his** people, "Will ye not fear (Allah)?
037:134 Behold, We delivered him and **his** adherents,
038:020 We strengthened **his** kingdom, and gave
038:024 ewe to be added to **his** (flock of) ewes:
038:024 he aksed forgiveness of **his** Lord, fell down, bowing
038:033 Then began he to pass **his** hand over (their)
038:034 We placed on **his** throne a body but he
038:036 Then We subjected the Wind to **his** power,
038:036 to flow gently to **his** order, whithersoever he
038:041 behold he cried to **his** Lord: "Satan has
038:043 And We gave him (back) **his** people and double
039:005 he has subjected the sun and the moon (to **His** law)
039:006 then created, of like nature, **his** mate;
039:007 but He liketh not ingratitude from **His** servants:
039:008 he crieth unto **his** Lord, turning to Him
039:009 and who places **his** hope in the Mercy of **his** Lord-
039:016 warn off **His** servants: "O My Servants!
039:020 never doth Allah fail in (**His**) promise.
039:024 on the Day of Judgment (and receive it) on **his** face,
039:036 Is not Allah enough for **His** servant?
039:038 can they keep back **His** Mercy?"
039:038 remove **His** affliction or if He wills some Mercy for me
039:041 that receives guidance benefits **his** own soul:
039:041 but he that strays injures **his** own soul.
039:067 the whole of the earth will be but **His** handful,
039:067 and the heavens will be rolled up in **his** right hand:
039:074 Who has truly fulfilled **His** promise to us,
040:013 He it is Who showeth you **His** Signs, and sendeth
040:015 to any of **His** servants He pleases, that it may warn (men)
040:015 by **His** Command doth He send the spirit (of inspiration)
040:015 Exalted is he in **His** attributes.

HIS (continued)

040:026 and let him Call on **his** Lord!
040:028 of Pharaoh, who had concealed **his** faith, said:
040:028 on him is (the sin of) **his** lie; but, if he
040:031 but Allah never wishes injustice to **His** Servants.
040:037 in Pharaoh's eyes, the evil of **his** deeds, and he
040:044 watches over **His** Servants."
040:048 Truly, Allah has judged between (**His**) Servants!"
040:081 And He shows you (always) **His** Signs; then which
040:085 with **His** servants (from the most ancient times).
041:006 and ask for **His** forgiveness."
041:037 Among **His** Signs are the Night and the Day, and the
041:038 who celebrate **His** praises by night and by day.
041:039 And among **His** Signs is this: thou seest
041:043 surely thy Lord has at **His** command (all) Forgiveness
041:046 Whoever works righteousness benefits **his** own soul;
041:046 nor is thy Lord ever unjust (in the least) to **His** servants.
041:046 whoever works evil, it is against **his** own soul:
041:047 not brign forth (young), but by **His** Knowledge.
041:050 I have (much) good (stored) in **His** sight!"
041:051 himself remote on **his** side (instead of coming to Us);
042:005 from above them (by **His** Glory):
042:008 but He admits whom He will to **His** Mercy; and the
042:019 Gracious is Allah to **His** servants: He gives
042:020 We give increease in **his** tilth; and to any that desires
042:023 gives Glad Tidings to **His** Servants who believe
042:024 and proves the Truth by **His** Words.
042:025 from **His** Servants and forgives sins:
042:026 gives them increase of **His** bounty: but for
042:027 for He is with **His** Servants well-acquainted,
042:027 the provision for **His** Servants, they would
042:028 all hope, and scatters **His** Mercy (far and wide).
042:029 And among **His** Signs is the creation of the
042:032 And among **His** Signs are the ships, smooth-running
042:033 If it be **His** Will, He can
042:040 makes reconciliation, **his** reward is due from Allah:
042:048 on account of the deeds which **his** hands have sent forth,
042:049 according to **His** Will,
043:015 attribute to some of **His** servants a share with Him.
043:017 **his** face darkens, and he is filled with inward grief!
043:026 Abraham said to **his** father and **his** people: "I do indeed
043:038 he says (to **his** evil-companion): 'Would that between
043:046 to Pharaoh and **his** Chiefs: he said, "I am a messenger
043:049 thy Lord foe us according to **his** covenant with thee;
043:051 And Pharaoh proclaimed among **his** people, saying:
043:054 Thus did he make fools of **his** people, and they
044:022 then he cried to **his** Lord: "These are indeed a people
044:041 The Day when no protector can avail **his** client in aught,
044:048 "Then pour over **his** head the Chastisement
045:006 believe after Allah and **His** Signs?
045:012 it by **His** command, that ye may seek of **His** Bounty,
045:015 any one does a righteous deed, it is to **his** own benefit;
045:015 if he does evil, it works against (**His** own soul).
045:023 such a one as takes as **his** god **his** own vain desire?
045:023 and put a cover on **his** sight.
045:023 and sealed **his** hearing and **his** heart (and understanding)
045:030 their Lord admit them to **His** Mercy:
046:015 the (child) to **his** weaning is (a period of) thirty months.
046:015 We have enjoined on man kindness to **his** parents:
046:015 in pain did **his** mother bear him,
046:017 (there is one) who says to **his** parents, "Fie on you!
046:021 he warned **his** people beside the winding Sand-tracts:
047:014 one to whom the evil of **his** conduct seems pleasing,

HIS (continued)

047:014 Is then one who is on a clear (Path) from **his** Lord,
048:002 fulfil **His** favour to thee; and guide
048:009 may believe in Allah and **His** Messenger, that ye
048:009 and celebrate **His** praises morning and evening.
048:010 violates **His** oath, does so to the harm of **his** own soul,
048:011 if **His** Will is to give you some loss or to give you some
048:013 And if any believe not in Allah **His** Messenger, We have
048:017 But he that obeys Allah and **His** Messenger,-(Allah) will
048:025 that He may admit to **His** mercy whom He will.
048:026 Allah sent down **His** tranquillity to **His** Messenger
048:027 the vision for **His** Messenger: ye shall
048:028 It is He Who sent **His** Messenger with Guidance and the
048:029 seeking Grace from Allah and (**His**) Good Pleasure.
049:001 not yourself forward before Allah and **His** Messenger;
049:012 any of you like to eat the flesh of **his** dead brother?
049:014 But if ye obey Allah and **His** Messenger, He will
049:015 believers who have believed in and **His** Messenger,
050:016 and We know what suggestions **his** soul makes to him:
050:016 to him than (**his**) jugular vein.
050:017 to learn (**his** doings) learn (and note them),
050:023 And **his** companion will say: "Here is (**his** record) ready
050:027 **His** companion will say: "Our Lord! I did not make him
050:040 (also), celebrate **His** praises, and (so likewise)
051:025 Behold, they entered **His** presence, and said:
051:026 Then he turned quickly to **his** household,
051:029 But **his** wife came forward clamouring: she smote
051:039 But (pharaoh turned back on account of **his** might,
051:040 So We took him and **his** forces, and threw
051:040 and threw them into the sea: and **his** was the blame.
052:021 (Yet) is each individual in pledge for **his** deeds.
053:003 Nor does he say (aught) of (**his** own) Desire.
053:010 to **His** Servant-(conveyed) what He (meant) to convey.
053:017 (**His**) sight never swerved, nor did it go wrong!
053:018 of the Signs of **his** Lord, the Greatest!
053:030 those who stray from **His** path, and He
053:034 Gives a little, then hardens (**his** heart)?
053:037 And of Abraham who fulfilled **his** (commandments)
053:040 That (the fruit of) **his** striving will soon
054:010 Then he called on **his** Lord: "I am one overcome:
054:033 The People of Lut rejected (**his**) Warning.
054:037 snatch away **his** guests from him, but We
055:010 the earth for (**His**) creatures:
055:024 And **His** are the Ships sailing smoothly through
055:039 will be asked of man or Jinn as to **his** sin,
057:007 Believe in Allah and **His** Messenger, and spend
057:009 to **His** Servants manifest Signs, that He
057:011 increase it manifold to **his** credit, and he
057:019 and **His** messengers-they are the Truthful and the
057:020 and (**His**) Good Pleasure (for the devotees of Allah).
057:021 for those who believe in Allah and **His** messengers:
057:025 who it is the will help unseen, Him and **His** messengers:
057:028 He will bestow on you a double portion of **His** Mercy:
057:028 fear Allah,and believe in **His** Messenger,
057:029 that (**His**) Grace is (entirely) in **His** Hand,
058:004 that ye may show your faith in Allah and **His** Messenger.
058:005 and **His** Messenger will be humbled to dust,
058:013 and obey Allah and **His** Messenger.
058:020 Allah and **His** Messenger will be among those
058:022 loving those who oppose Allah and **His** Messenger,
059:004 That is because they resisted Allah and **His** Messenger:
059:006 but Allah gives power to **His** Messenger over any
059:006 What Allah has bestowed on **His** Messenger (and taken

HIS (continued)

059:007   to **His** Messenger, and to kindred and orphans,
059:007   What Allah has bestowed on **His** Messenger (and taken
059:008   and aiding Allah and **His** Messenger: such are
059:008   from Allah and (**His**) Good Pleasure,
059:024   and on earth, doth declare **His** Praises and Glory:
060:004   Abraham said to **his** father: "I will pray for forgiveness
061:004   in **His** Cause in battle array, as if
061:005   And remember, Moses said to **his** people: "O my
061:008   Their intention is to extinguish Allah's **His** Light,
061:009   It is He Who has sent **His** Messenger with Guidance
061:011   Tah ye believer in Allah and **His** Messenger, and that ye
062:002   to rehearse to them **His** Signs, to purify them,
063:001   that thou art indeed **His** Messenger.
063:008   and **His** Messenger, and to the Believers; but the
064:008   and **His** Messenger, and in the Light which We
064:011   (Allah) guides **his** heart (aright): for Allah
064:012   So obey Allah, and obey **His** Messenger; but if
065:001   does verily wrong **his** (own) soul:
065:003   And if anyone puts **his** trust in Allah,
065:003   For Allah will surely accomplish **His** purpose:
065:005   He will remove **his** evil deeds from him
065:005   from him and will enlarge **his** reward.
065:007   Let the man of means spend according to **his** means:
065:008   of their Lord and of **His** messengers, did We
065:012   (all) descends **His** Command: that ye
065:012   all things in (**His**) Knowledge.
066:003   in confidence to one of **his** consorts, and she
066:004   truly Allah is **his** Protector, and Gabriel,
066:011   and save me from Pharaoh and **his** doings, and save
066:012   the truth of the words of her Lord and of **His** Revelations,
067:021   were to withhold **His** provision?
067:022   with **his** face grovelling, better guided,-or one
067:028   or if He bestows **His** Mercy on us,-yet who
068:007   hath strayed from **His** Path: and He
068:049   Had not Grace from **His** Lord reached him, he would
068:050   Thus did **his** Lord choose him and make him
069:019   Then he that will be given **his** Record in **his** right hand
069:025   And he that will be given **his** Record in **his** left hand,
069:045   We should certainly seize him by **his** right hand
069:046   the artery of **his** heart:
070:011   from the Chastisement of that Day by **his** children,
070:012   **His** wife and **his** brother,
070:013   **His** kindred who sheltered him.
070:016   Plucking out (**his** being) right to the skull!-
071:001   We sent Noah to **his** People (with the Command):
072:013   and any who believes in **his** Lord has no fear,
072:017   the remembrance of **his** Lord, He will
072:023   from Allah and **His** Messages: for any
072:023   and **His** Messenger,-for them is Hell: they shall
072:024   in (**his**) helper and least important in point
072:026   acquainted with **His** Secrets.-
073:018   **His** Promise needs must be accomplished.
073:019   a (straight) path to **his** Lord!
074:013   And sons to be by **his** side!-
075:003   Does man think that We cannot assemble **his** bones?
075:004   in perfect order the very tips of **his** fingers.
075:015   Even though he were to put up **his** excuses.
075:033   Then did he stalk to **his** family in full conceit!
076:029   let him take a (straight) Path to **his** Lord.
076:031   He will admit to **His** Mercy Whom He will; but the
078:039   a (straight) Return to **his** Lord!
078:040   man will see (the Deeds) which **his** hands have sent

HIS (continued)

079:022   Further, he turned **his** back, striving hard
079:023   Then he collected (**his** men) and made a proclamation,
080:009   And with fear (in **his** heart),
080:020   Then doth He make **His** path smooth for him;
080:021   and putteth him in **his** Grave;
080:022   Then, when it is **His** will, He will
080:024   Then let man look at **his** Food, (and how We provide it):
080:034   That Day shall a man flee from **his** own brother,
080:035   And from **his** mother, and **his** father,
080:036   And from **his** wife and **his** children.
080:037   will have enough concern (of **his** own) to make
081:021   With authority there, (and) faithful of **his** trust.
084:007   Then he who is given **his** Record in **his** Right hand,
084:008   Soon will **his** account be taken by an easy reckoning,
084:009   And he will turn to **his** people, rejoicing!
084:010   But he who is given **his** Record behind **his** back,-
084:013   Truly, did he go about among **his** people, rejoicing!
084:015   Nay, nay! for **his** Lord was (ever) watchful of him!
089:015   Now, as for man, when **his** Lord trieth him,
089:016   restricting **his** subsistence for him, then saith
089:022   and **His** angels, rank upon rank,
089:025   For, that Day, **His** Chastisement will be such as
089:026   And **His** bonds will be such as none (other) can bind.
091:001   By the Sun and **his** (glorious) splendor;
092:011   Nor will **his** wealth profit him when he falls
096:017   to **his** council (of comrades):
100:006   Truly Man is to **his** Lord, ungrateful;
100:007   And to that (fact) he bears witness (by **his** deeds);
100:008   And violent is he in **his** love of wealth.
101:009   Will have **his** home in a (bottomless) pit.
104:003   Thinking that **his** wealth would make him
110:003   and pray for **His** Forgiveness: for he
111:002   No profit to him from all **his** wealth, and all **his** gains!
111:004   **His** wife shall carry the (crackling) wood-as fuel!
114:004   (of Evil), who withdraws (after **his** whisper),-

HITHER

008:042   Remember ye were on the **hither** side of the valley,
020:040   Then didst thou come **hither** as ordained, O Moses!

HITHERTO

011:062   a center of our hopes **hitherto**!

HOARD

003:075   if entrusted with a **hoard** of gold,
009:034   those who **hoard** gold and silver and spend
010:058   the (wealth) they **hoard**.

HOARDED

009:035   taste ye, then, the (treasures) ye **hoarded**!"
009:035   (treasure) which ye **hoarded** for yourselves:

HOARDS

003:014   heaped-up **hoards** of gold and silver;
007:048   were your **hoards** and your arrogant ways?

HOARY

030:054   give (you) weakness and a **hoary** head:

HOARY-HEADED

073:017   a Day that will make children **hoary-headed**?-

HOLD

002:063   (saying): "**Hold** firmly to what We have
002:093   (saying): "**Hold** firmly to what We given you,
002:118   who **hold** firmly to Faith (in their hearts).
002:229   parties should either **hold** together on equitable terms,
002:235   betrothal or **hold** it in your hearts.
003:103   And **hold** fast, all together, by the Rope

HOLD (continued)

004:077 to those who were told to **hold** back their hands
004:142 but little do they **hold** Allah in remembrance;
004:146 mend (their life), **hold** fast to Allah, and
004:175 and **hold** fast to Him,-soon will He admit
006:001 Faith **hold** (others) as equal with their Guardian Lord.
006:150 for they **hold** others as equal
007:087 **hold** yourselves in patience until Allah
007:145 and enjoin the people to **hold** fast by the
007:145 (and said): "Take and **hold** these with firmness,
007:170 As to those who **hold** fast by the Book
007:171 "**Hold** firmly to what We have given you, and bring
007:195 Or hands to lay **hold** with?
007:199 **Hold** to forgiveness; command what is right; but
007:204 and **hold** your peace: that ye may receive Mercy.
009:029 nor the Last Day, nor **hold** that forbidden which
010:059 Yet ye **hold** forbidden some things thereof and
012:020 did they **hold** him!
013:021 to be joined, **hold** their Lord in awe, and fear
018:078 wast unable to **hold** patience.
018:082 thou wast unable to **hold** patience."
019:012 "O Yahya! take **hold** of the Book with might":
021:049 and who **hold** the Hour (of judgment) in awe.
022:078 give zakat and **hold** fast to Allah!
025:067 but **hold** a just (balance) between those (extremes);
042:018 those who believe **hold** it in awe, and know
043:043 So **hold** thou fast to the Revelation sent down
046:017 Do ye **hold** out the promise to me that I shall
053:032 Therefore **hold** not yourselves purified:
056:081 ye would **hold** in light esteem?
058:008 And they **hold** secret counsels among
058:009 O ye who believe! when ye **hold** secret counsel,
060:007 those whom ye (now) **hold** as enemies.
060:010 But **hold** not to the ties (marriage contract) of
070:005 Therefore do thou **hold** Patience,-a Patience
070:026 And those who **hold** to the truth of the

HOLDEST

066:001 O Prophet! why **holdest** thou to be forbidden

HOLDING

007:163 openly (**holding** up their heads,) but on
043:021 before this, to which they are **holding** fast?

HOLDS

003:101 Whoever **holds** firmly to Allah will be shown
016:079 Nothing **holds** them up but (the power of) Allah.
022:032 and whoever **holds** in honour the Rites of Allah,

HOLLOW

063:004 They are as (worthless as **hollow**) pieces of
069:007 roots of **hollow** palm-trees tumbled down!

HOLY

002:030 Thy praises and glorify Thy **Holy** (name)?"
002:087 and strengthened him with the **holy** spirit.
002:253 and strengthened him with the **Holy** Spirit.
005:021 "O my people! enter the **holy** land which Allah
005:110 Behold! I strengthened thee with the **Holy** Spirit.
016:102 Say, the **Holy** Spirit has brought the revelation
059:023 the **Holy** One, the Source of Peace (and Perfection).
062:001 the **Holy** One, the Exalted in Might, the Wise.
080:014 Exalted (in dignity), kept pure and **holy**,
098:002 rehearsing scriptures kept pure and **holy**:

HOME

002:094 Say: "If the last **Home**, with Allah,
002:185 So every one of you who is present (at his **home**)

HOME (continued)

003:015 therein is their eternal **home**;
003:151 and evil is the **home** of the wrong-doers!
004:057 with rivers flowing beneath, their eternal **home**:
004:095 their goods and persons than those who sit (at **home**).
004:095 Not equal are those Believers who sit (at **home**),
004:095 those who sit at **home** by a great reward.
004:100 as a refugee from **home** for Allah and
004:100 He who forsakes his **home** in the cause of Allah,
005:085 with rivers flowing underneath, their eternal **home**.
005:119 with rivers flowing beneath, their eternal **home**:
006:032 But best is the **Home** in the Hereafter,
006:127 a **Home** of Peace with their Lord: He will
006:149 the argument that reaches **home**: if it had
007:169 is the **home** in the hereafter.
008:030 or get thee out (of thy **home**).
009:086 we would be with those who sit (at **home**)."
009:087 who remain behind (at **home**): their hearts
010:025 But Allah doth call to the **Home** of Peace: He doth
012:099 a **home** for his parents with himself, and said:
012:109 But the **home** of the Hereafter is best, for those
013:022 the final attainment of the (Eternal) **Home**,-
013:024 Now how excellent is the final **Home**!"
013:025 for them is the terrible **Home**!
013:042 who gets **home** in the End.
016:006 in them as ye drive them **home** in the evening,
016:030 and excellent indeed is the **Home** of the righteous,-
016:030 and the **Home** of the Hereafter is even better
016:041 We will assuredly give a goodly **home** in this
028:077 the **Home** of the Hereafter, nor forget
028:083 That **Home** of the Hereafter We shall give to
029:026 "I will leave **home** for the sake of my Lord:
029:058 a **Home** in Heaven,-lofty mansions beneath which
029:064 But verily the **Home** in the Hereafter,-that is
029:068 a **home** in Hell for those who reject Faith?
033:029 His Messenger, and the **Home** of the Hereafter,
035:035 settled us in a **Home** that will last: no toil
040:039 it is the Hereafter that is the **Home** that will last.
040:052 and the **Home** of Misery.
041:024 the Fire will be a **Home** for them!
041:028 for them the Eternal **Home**: a (fit)
084:005 (then will come **Home** the full Reality).
100:003 And push **home** the charge in the morning,
101:009 Will have his **home** in a (bottomless) pit.

HOME-LAND

034:015 a Sign in their **homeland**-two Gardens to the

HOMES

002:084 your own people from your **homes**:
002:085 and banish a party of you from their **homes**;
002:243 thy vision to those who abandoned their **homes**,
002:246 turned out of our **homes** and our families?"
003:154 Say: "Even if you had remained in your **homes**,
003:195 those who have left their **homes**, and were driven
004:066 sacrifice their lives or to leave their **homes**,
007:074 and carve out **homes** in the mountains; so bring
007:078 in their **homes** in the morning!
007:091 in their **homes** before the morning!
007:092 in the **homes** where they had flourished: the men
007:145 soon shall I show you the **homes** of the wicked,
008:047 from their **homes** insolently and to be seen of men,
009:100 those who forsook (their **homes**) and of those who
011:065 "Enjoy yourselves in your **homes** for three days:
011:067 prostrate in their **homes** before the morning,-

HOMES (continued)

011:094 in their **homes** by the morning,-
013:031 or to settle close to their **homes**, until the
016:041 To those who leave their **homes** in the cause
016:080 your habitaions **homes** of rest and quiet for you;
016:110 leave their **homes** after trials and persecutions
017:005 very inmost parts of your **homes**; and it
021:013 and to your **homes**, in order
022:040 expelled from their **homes** in defiance of right,-
022:058 Those who leave their **homes** in the cause of
024:022 left their **homes** in Allah's cause: let them
024:053 they would leave (their **homes**).
029:037 in their **homes** in the morning.
032:019 as hospitable **homes**, for their (good) deeds.
033:034 to you in your **homes**, of the Signs
047:019 and how ye dwell in your **homes**.
059:002 their **homes** at the first gathering (of the forces).
059:008 expelled from their **homes** and their property,
059:009 had **homes** (in Madinah) and had adopted the Faith,-
060:001 (from your **homes**), (simply) because ye believe
060:008 of your **homes**, from dealing kindly and justly
060:009 and drive you out of your **homes**, and support

HOMING

084:017 The Night and its **Homing**;

HONEY

047:015 and rivers of **honey** pure and clear.

HONOUR

002:253 others He raised to degrees (of **honour**);
003:026 Thou enduest with **honour** whom Thou pleasest,
003:045 held in **honour** in this world and the Hereafter
004:031 and admit you to the Gate of great **honour**.
004:139 Nay, all **honour** is with Allah.
004:139 is it **honour** they seek among them?
005:012 believe in My Messengers, **honour** and assist them,
007:157 So it is those who believe in him, **honour** him, Help him,
010:065 for all power and **honour** belong to Allah:
017:023 but address them in terms of **honour**.
017:080 the Gate of Truth and **Honour**; and grant
017:080 by the Gate of Truth and **Honour**, and likewise
018:034 more **honour** and power in (my following of) men."
019:050 and We granted them lofty **honour** on the tongue
021:026 They are (but) servants raised to **honour**.
022:018 none can rise to **honour**: for Allah
022:032 and whoever holds in **honour** the Rites of Allah,
022:032 such (**honour**) should come truly from piety of heart.
024:036 which Allah hath permitted to be raised to **honour**;
027:040 Supreme in **Honour**!"
023:116 the Lord of the Throne of **Honour**!
036:027 me among those held in **honour**!"
037:042 Fruits, and they (shall enjoy) **honour** and dignity,
037:180 Glory to thy Lord, the Lord of **Honour** and Power!
044:049 Truly thou art Mighty, full of **honour**!
048:009 that ye may assist and **honour** him, and celebrate
055:027 thy Lord,-full of Majesty, Bounty and **Honour**.
055:078 full of Majesty, Bounty and **Honour**.
063:008 But **honour** belongs to Allah and His Messenger,
080:013 (It is) in Books held (greatly) in **honour**.
081:020 Endued with Power, held in **honour** by the Lord
089:015 trieth him, giving him **honour** and gifts,
089:017 Nay, nay! But ye **honour** not the orphans!

HONOURABLE

002:235 speak to them in terms **honourable**,
010:093 in a **honourable** dwelling-place, and provided

HONOURABLE (continued)

012:021 "Make his stay (among us) **hononrable**:
024:026 and a provision **honourable**.
025:072 they pass by it with **honourable** (avoidance);
026:058 Treasures, and every kind of **honourable** position;
026:084 "Grant me **honourable** mention on the tongue
033:069 was **honourable** in Allah's sight.
044:017 a Messenger most **honourable**,
056:077 That this is indeed a Qur'an most **honourable**,
063:008 surely the more **honourable** (element) will expel
080:016 **Honourable** and Pious and Just.
081:019 of a most **honourable** Messenger,
082:011 Kind and **honourable**, writing down (your deeds):

HONOURABLY

002:267 good things which ye have (**honourably**) earned,

HONOURED

070:035 Such will be the **honoured** ones in the
017:062 one whom thou hast **honoured** above me! If Thou
017:070 We have **honoured** the sons of Adam; provided them
049:013 Verily the most **honoured** of you in the sight
051:024 of the **honoured** guest of Abraham?
069:040 of a **honoured** messenger;
089:015 "My Lord hath honoured me."

HONOURS

019:085 like a band (presented before a king for **honours**).
022:030 whoever **honours** the sacred rites of Allah,

HOOF

006:146 We forbade every (animal) with undivided **hoof**,

HOOPOE

027:020 "Why is it I see not the **Hoopoe**?
027:022 But the **Hoopoe** tarried not far:

HOPE

002:075 entertain the **hope** that they will believe
002:218 they have the **hope** of the Mercy of Allah;
003:126 Allah made it but a message of **hope** for you,
004:099 For these, there is **hope** that Allah will forgive:
004:104 but you **hope** from Allah, what they have not.
005:003 given up all **hope** of your religion: yet fear
008:010 Allah made it but a message of **hope**, and an
010:007 Those who rest not their **hope** on their
010:011 their **hope** of their meeting with Us, in their
010:015 unto them, those who rest not their **hope** on their
012:080 Now when they saw no **hope** of his (yielding),
012:087 and never give up **hope** of Allah's soothing Mercy:
012:110 when the messengers give up **hope** (of their people)
013:012 by way both of fear and of **hope**:
015:003 and let (false) **Hope** distract them:
017:057 they **hope** for His Mercy and fear His Wrath:
018:024 "I **hope** that my Lord will guide me ever closer
025:021 Those who do not **hope** to meet Us (for Judgment)
026:082 "And Who, I **hope**, will forgive
026:129 fine buildings in the **hope** of living
027:046 ye may **hope** to receive mercy."
028:022 "I do **hope** that my Lord will show me
028:029 I **hope** to bring you from there some information,
030:024 by way both of fear and of **hope**, and He
032:016 the while they call on their Lord, in Fear and **Hope**:
035:029 secretly and openly, **hope** for a Commerce
039:009 the Hereafter, and who places his **hope** in the
041:049 he gives up all **hope** (and) is lost in despair.
042:028 down rain (even) after (men) have given up all **hope**,

HOPE (continued)

045:014 to forgive those who do not **hope** for the Days of Allah:
060:006 for those whose **hope** is in Allah and in
066:008 with sincere repentance: in the **hope** that your
108:003 he will be cut off (from Future **Hope**).

HOPED

007:046 but they still **hoped**. To (enter it).

HOPELESS

020:111 The Sustainer, **hopeless** indeed will be the man

HOPES

004:120 and creates in them false **hopes**,
009:059 to Allah do we turn our **hopes**!"
011:062 of us!-a center of our **hopes** hitherto!
018:046 and best as (the foundation for) **hopes**.
029:005 For those whose **hopes** are in the meeting
033:021 who **hopes** in Allah and the Final Day, and who
047:025 and buoyed them up with false **hopes**.

HOPING

036:074 than Allah, (**hoping**) that they might be helped!

HORIZON

053:007 While he was in the highest part of the **horizon**:
081:023 And without doubt he saw him in the clear **horizon**.

HORRIBLE

065:008 them with a **horrible** Chastisement.

HORROR

014:042 a Day when the eyes will fixedly stare in **horror**,-
021:097 will fixedly stare in **horror**: "Ah! woe to us!

HORSES

003:014 **horses** branded (for blood and excellence);
016:008 And (He has created) **horses**, mules, and donkeys,

HOSPITABLE

032:019 as **hospitable** homes, for their (good) deeds.
041:032 "A **hospitable** gift from One Oft-Forgiving,

HOSPITALITY

012:059 and that I do provide the best **hospitality**?
018:077 but they refused them **hospitality**.

HOST

036:075 and they are a **host** brought up before them.
038:011 They are but a **host** of confederates and they
044:024 For they are a **host** (destined) to be drowned."

HOSTILE

008:015 the Unbelievers in **hostile** array, never turn
046:006 be **hostile** to them and deny that (men) had

HOSTILITY

002:193 But if they cease, let there be no **hostility**
005:002 transgression (and **hostility** on your part).
058:008 for iniquity and **hostility**, and disobedience
058:009 iniquity and **hostility**, and disobedience to the

HOSTS

003:155 on the day the two **hosts** met, it was Satan
010:090 Pharaoh and his **hosts** followed them in insolence
026:095 "And the whole **hosts** of Iblis together.
027:017 his **hosts**,-of Jinns and men and birds, and they
027:018 and his **hosts** crush you (under foot)
027:037 we shall come to them with such **hosts** as they
028:006 Haman, and their **hosts**, what they
028:008 their **hosts** were men of sin.
028:039 in the land beyond reeason, he and his **hosts**:
028:040 So We seized him and his **hosts**, and We
033:009 on you **hosts** (to overwhelm you): but We
036:028 his People, after Him, any **hosts** from heaven,

HOT

003:125 rush here on you in **hot** haste,
055:044 of boiling **hot** water will they wander round!
088:005 to drink, of a boiling **hot** spring,

HOUR

006:031 until on a sudden the **hour** is on them, and they
006:040 or the **Hour** (that ye dread), would ye then
007:034 nor (an **hour**) can they advance (it in anticipation).
007:034 not an **hour** can they cause delay,
007:187 They ask thee about the (final) **Hour**-when will
010:045 had tarried but an **hour** of a day: they will
010:049 nor (an **hour**) can they advance
010:049 not an **hour** can they cause delay,
012:107 the (final) **Hour** all of a sudden while they
015:085 And the **Hour** is surely coming (when this will be
015:099 come unto thee the **Hour** that is Certain.
016:061 to anticipate it (for a single **hour**).
016:061 (the punishment) for a single **hour**, just as
016:077 And the matter of the **Hour** (of Judgment) is as
018:021 there can be no doubt about the **Hour** of Judgment.
018:036 "Nor do I deem that the **Hour** (of Judgment)
019:075 or in (the approach of) the **Hour**,-they will
020:015 "Verily the **Hour** is coming-I have almost
021:049 and who hold the **Hour** (of judgment) in awe.
022:001 For the convulsion of the **Hour** (of judgment)
022:007 And verily the **Hour** will come: there can
022:055 until the **Hour** (of Judgment) comes suddenly
025:011 a Blazing Fire for such as deny the **Hour**:
025:011 Nay, they deny the **Hour** (of the Judgment to come):
030:012 On the Day that the **Hour** will come, the guilty
030:014 On the Day that the **Hour** will come, that Day
030:055 will swear that they tarried not but an **hour**:
030:055 On the Day that the **Hour** (of reckoning) will be
031:034 Verily the knowledge of the **Hour** is with Allah
033:063 make thee understand?-perchance the **Hour** is nigh!
033:063 Men ask thee concerning the **Hour**: say, "The
034:003 "Never to us will come the **Hour**": say, "Nay!
034:030 for an **hour** nor put forward."
040:046 when the **Hour** comes to pass: "Cast ye
040:059 The **Hour** will certainly come: therein is
041:047 of the **Hour** (of Judgment: He knows all): no fruit
041:050 I think not that the **Hour** (of Judgment)
042:017 the **Hour** is close at hand?
042:018 dispute concerning the **Hour** are far astray.
043:061 therefore have no doubt about the (**Hour**),
043:061 (Jesus) shall be a Sign (for the coming of) the **Hour**
043:066 Do they only wait for the **Hour**-
043:085 with Him is the knowledge of the **Hour** (of Judgment):
045:027 and the Day that the **Hour** of Judgement is established,-
045:032 "We know not wht is the **Hour**:
045:032 and that the **Hour**-there was no doubt about its (coming),
046:035 tarried more than an **hour** in a single day.
047:018 Do they then only wait for the **Hour**,-that it
053:057 The (**Hour**) ever approaching draws nigh:
054:001 The **Hour** (of Judgment) is nigh, and the
054:046 and that **Hour** will be most grievous and most bitter.
054:046 Nay, the **Hour** (of Judgment) is the time promised
074:047 "Until there came to us (the **Hour**) that is certain."
079:042 They ask thee about the **Hour**,- 'When will

HOURS

003:017 forgiveness in the early **hours** of the morning
020:130 celebrate them for part of the **hours** of the night,
039:009 the **hours** of the night prostrating himself

HOURS (continued)

051:018 And in the **hours** of early dawn,

HOUSE

002:125 Remember We made the **house** a place of assembly
002:125 My **House** for those who compass it round,
002:127 the **House** (with this prayer):
002:158 the **House** in the Season or at other times,
003:096 The first **House** (of worship) appointed for men
005:002 nor the people resorting to the Sacred **House**,
005:097 Allah made the Ka'ba, the Sacred **House**, a means
008:005 out of the **house** in truth, even though
008:035 Their prayer at the **house** (of Allah) is nothing
011:073 O ye people of the **house**! For He is indeed
012:023 But she, in whose **house** he was, sought to
014:028 to the **House** of perdition?-
014:037 by Thy Sacred **House**; in order, O our Lord,
017:093 "Or thou have a **house** adorned with gold, or thou
022:026 of the (Sacred) **House**, (saying): "Associate not
022:026 and sanctify My **House** for those who
022:029 and (again) circumambulate the Ancient **House**."
022:033 place of sacrifice is near the Ancient **House**.
024:028 If ye find no one in the **house**, enter not
024:061 or in the **house** of a sincere friend of yours:
026:149 "And ye carve **house** out of (rocky) mountains
028:012 the people of a **house** that will nourish and bring
028:081 caused the earth to swallow up him and his **house**;
029:041 is the Spider's **house**;-if they but knew.
029:041 who builds (to itself) a **house**; but truly
052:004 By the much-frequented **House**;
071:028 all who enter my **house** in Faith, and (all)
106:003 Let them worship the Lord of this **House**,

HOUSEHOLD

002:196 This is for those whose **household** is not
003:121 thou didst leave the **household** (early)
012:026 And one of her **household** saw (this)
015:065 "Then travel by night with thy **household**, when a
051:026 to his **household**, brought out a fatted calf.
051:036 except one (Muslim) **household**:
054:034 Lut's **household**: them We delivered by early Dawn,-

HOUSES

002:189 Enter **houses** through the proper doors:
002:189 ye enter your **houses** from the back:
003:049 and what ye store in your **houses**.
004:015 confine them to **houses** until death do claim them,
024:027 enter not **houses** other than your own, until ye
024:029 to enter **houses** not used for living in,
024:036 (Lit is such a Light) in **houses**, which Allah
024:061 But if ye enter **houses**, salute each other-
024:061 or in **houses** of which the keys are in your
024:061 that ye should eat in your own **houses**,
027:052 Now such were their **houses**,-in utter
029:041 but truly the flimsiest of **houses** is the
033:013 "Truly our **houses** are bare and exposed,"
033:027 of their lands, their **houses**, and their
033:033 And stay quietly in your **houses**,
033:053 the Prophet's **houses**,-until leave is given you,-
043:033 silver roofs for their **houses**, and (silver) stair-ways
043:034 And (silver) doors to their **houses**, and couches
046:025 nothing was to be seen but (the ruins of) their **houses**!
065:001 and turn them not out of their **houses**,

HOW

002:028 **How** can ye reject the faith in Allah?
002:211 Ask the children of Israel **how** many Clear (Signs)

HOW (continued)

002:219 They ask thee **how** much they are to spend;
002:223 so approach your tilth when or **how** ye will;
002:246 They said: "**How** could we refuse to fight
002:247 They say: "**How** can he exercise authority
002:249 said: "**How** oft, by Allah's will,
002:259 Look further at the bones, **how** We bring them together
002:259 He said: "Oh! **how** shall Allah bring it (ever) to life,
002:259 He said: "**How** long didst thou tarry (thus)?"
002:260 "My Lord! show me **how** thou givest life to the dead.
003:025 But **how** (will they fare) when We gather them
003:040 He said: "O my Lord! **how** shall I have a son,
003:047 **how** shall I have a son when man hath touched Me?"
003:086 **How** shall Allah guide those who reject faith
003:101 And **how** would ye deny Faith while unto you
003:136 **how** excellent a recompense for those who work
003:146 **How** many of the Prophets fought (in Allah's way),
004:021 And **how** could ye take it when ye
004:041 **How** then if We brought from each People a witness,
004:050 Behold! **how** they invent a lie against Allah!
004:058 verily **how** excellent is the teaching
004:062 **How** then, when they are seized by misfortune.
004:069 Ah! **How** beautiful is their Company.
005:031 to show him **how** to hide the naked body
005:052 thou seest **how** eagerly they run about
005:075 See **how** Allah doth makes His Signs
006:006 See they not **how** many of those before them
006:024 Behold! **how** they lie against themselves but
006:046 See **how** We explain the Signs by various
006:065 See **how** We explain the Signs in diverse ways;
006:081 "**How** should I fear (the beings) ye
006:093 If thou couldst but see **how** the wicked
006:095 then **how** are ye deluded away from the truth?
006:101 **how** can He have a son when He hath no consort?
007:004 **How** many towns have We destroyed
007:074 "And remember **how** He made you inheritors
007:086 but remember **how** ye were little, and He
007:093 but **how** shall I lament over a people
007:129 that so He may see **how** ye act."
007:145 homes of the wicked, (**how** they lie desolate)."
008:030 Remember **how** the Unbelievers plotted against
008:032 Remember **how** they said: "O Allah! if this
008:050 (**how**) they smite their faces and their backs
009:007 **How** can there be a covenant before Allah
009:008 **How** (can there be such a league), seeing that
009:030 **how** they are deluded away from the Truth!
010:014 after them, to see **how** ye would behave!
010:032 **How** then are ye turned away?
010:034 then **how** are ye deluded away (from the truth)?"
010:035 What then is the matter with you? **How** judge ye?
012:080 and, **how**, before this, ye did fail in your duty
012:084 "**How** great is my grief for Joseph!" And his eyes
012:089 He said: "Know ye **how** ye dealt with Joseph,
012:105 And **how** many Signs in the heavens and the earth
013:008 by **how** much the wombs fall short (of their time and
013:024 Now **how** excellent is the final Home!"
013:032 I punished them: then **how** (terrible) was My
014:024 Seest thou not **how** Allah sets forth a parable?
014:045 ye were clearly shown **how** We dealt with them;
015:097 We do indeed know **how** thy heart is distressed
016:025 Alas, **how** grievous the burdens
016:048 Among things,-**how** their shadows turn round,
017:017 **How** many generations have We destroyed after Noah?

HOW (continued)

017:021 See **how** We have bestowed more on some than on
017:044 and yet ye understand not **how** they declare
018:019 "Allah (alone) knows best **how** long ye have
018:019 "**How** long have ye stayed (here)?" They said,
018:026 **how** clearly He sees, **how** finely He hears (everything)!
018:026 Say: "Allah knows best **how** long they stayed:
018:029 **How** uncomfortable a couch to recline on!
018:029 scald their faces, **how** dreadful the drink!
018:031 **How** good the recompense!
018:031 **How** beautiful a couch to recline on!
018:068 "For **how** canst thou have patience about things
019:008 He said: "O my Lord! **how** shall I have a son,
019:020 She said: "**How** shall I have a son, seeing that
019:029 They said: "**How** can we talk to one who is
019:038 **How** plainly will they see and hear, the Day
019:074 But **how** many (countless) generations before them
019:098 But **how** many (countless) generation before
020:128 (to call to mind) **how** many generations before
021:011 **How** many were the towns. We utterly destroyed
022:044 but **how** (terrible) was My punishment
022:045 **How** many populations have We destroyed, which were
022:045 And **how** many wells are lying idle and neglected,
022:048 And to **how** many populations did I give respite,
023:089 Say: "Then **how** are ye deluded?"
025:045 Hast thou not seen **how** thy Lord?-doth prolong
025:076 Dwelling therein;-**how** beautiful an abode
026:007 **how** many noble things of all kinds we have produced
028:058 And **how** many towns We destroyed, which exulted
028:064 (before them); (**how** they wish) 'If only
029:019 See they not **how** Allah originates creation,
029:020 see **how** Allah did originate creation; so will
029:060 **How** many are the creatures that carry
029:061 **How** are they then deluded away (from the truth)?
030:050 Allah's Mercy!-**how** He gives life to the earth
032:026 **how** many generations We destroyed before them,
034:045 My messengers, **how** (terrible) was My punishment!
034:052 but **how** could they receive (Faith) from a
035:003 **how** then are ye perverted?
035:026 who rejected Faith: and **how** (terrible) was My
036:031 See they not **how** many generations before them
036:066 but **how** could they have seen?
037:034 Verily that is **how** We shall deal with Sinners.
037:154 What is the matter with you? **How** judge ye?
037:175 And watch them (**how** they fare), and they
037:175 and they soon shall see (**how** thou farest)!
037:179 and they soon shall see (**how** thou farest)!
037:179 And watch (**how** they fare) and they
038:003 **How** many generations before them did We destroy?
038:024 of righteousness, and **how** few are they?"
038:030 (for a son),-**how** excellent is the Servant!
038:044 **how** excellent is the servant!
038:062 And they will say: "**How** is it with us that we
039:006 then **how** are ye turned away (from your true Lord)?
039:074 **how** excellent a reward for those who
040:005 And **how** (terrible), was My Requital!
040:041 "And O my People! **how** (strange) it is for me
040:062 then **how** ye are deluded away from the Truth!
040:069 **How** are they turned away (from Reality)?-
042:053 Behold (**how**) all affairs tend towards Allah!
043:006 But **how** many were the prophets We sent
043:087 **how** then are they deluded away (from the Truth)?
044:013 **How** shall they have the Reminder.

HOW (continued)

044:025 **How** many were the gardens and springs
046:010 (**how** unjust ye are!) truly, Allah guides not a people
047:013 And **how** many cities, with more
047:018 to them, **how** shall they have their Reminder?
047:019 for Allah knows **how** ye move about
047:019 and **how** ye dwell in your homes.
047:027 But **how** (will it be) when the angels take their
050:004 We already know **how** much of them the earth
050:006 **How** We have made it and adorned it,
050:036 But **how** many generations before them did We
051:048 **how** excellently We do spread out!
053:026 **How** many-so-ever be the angels in the heavens,
054:016 But **how** (terrible) was My Chastisement and My
054:018 then **how** terrible was my Chastisement and My
054:021 Yea, **how** (terrible) was my Chastisement and my
054:030 Ah! **how** (terrible) was My Chastisement and My
057:008 **How** is it with you that you not believe in Allah?-
057:010 **How** is it with you that you spend not in the cause
057:012 **how** their Light runs forward before them
057:020 Here is a similitude: **how** rain and the growth
063:004 **How** are they deluded (away from the Truth)!
065:008 **How** many populations that insolently opposed
067:017 so that ye shall know **how** (terrible) was My warning?
067:018 (My warning): then **how** (terrible) was My
068:036 What is the matter with you? **How** judge ye?
069:026 "And that I had never realised **how** my account (stood)!
071:015 "'See ye not **how** Allah has created the seven
073:017 Then **how** shall ye, if ye deny (Allah),
074:019 And woe to him! **How** he determined!-
074:020 Yea, woe to him: **how** he determined!-
080:024 (Then let men look at his food, (and **how** We provide it):
088:017 Do they not look at the Camels, **how** they are made?-
088:018 And at the Sky, **how** it is raised high?-
088:019 And at the Mountains, **how** they are fixed firm?-
088:020 And at the Earth, **how** it is spread out?
089:006 Seest thou not **how** thy Lord dealt with
089:023 but **how** will that remembrance that remembrance profit
105:001 Seest thou not **how** thy Lord dealt with the

HOWEVER

010:082 the Truth, **however** much the Sinners may hate it!"
012:103 mankind have, **however** ardently thou dost desire it.

HUD

007:065 To the 'Ad people, (We sent) **Hud**, one of
011:050 To the 'Ad People (We sent) **Hud**, one of
011:053 They said: "O **Hud**! no Clear (Sign) hast thou
011:058 We saved **Hud** and those who believed with him,
011:060 Away with the 'Ad the People of **Hud**!
011:089 of the people of Noah or of **Hud** or of Salih,
026:124 Behold, their brother **Hud** said to them: "Will ye
046:021 Mention (**Hud**) one of 'Ad's (own) brethren:

HUE

002:138 (Our religion) takes its **hue** from Allah
002:138 and who can give a better **hue** than Allah.
035:027 and black intense in **hue**.

HUGE

026:063 became like the **huge**, firm mass of a mountain.
062:005 of a donkey which carries **huge** tomes
077:032 "Indeed it throws about sparks (**huge**) as Forts,
089:009 who cut out (**huge**) rocks in the valley?-

HUMAN

012:053 the (**human**) soul certainly incites
014:010 "Ah! ye are no more than **human**, like ourselves!

HUMAN (continued)

014:011 "True, we are **human** like yourselves, but Allah
015:085 So overlook (any **human** faults) with gracious
017:071 all **human** beings with their (respective) Imams:
019:026 into no talk with any **human** being.'"
036:036 own (**human**) kind and (other) things of which
056:058 Do ye then see? The (**human** Seed) that ye emit,-
064:006 "Shall (mere) **human** beings direct us?"
081:005 herded together (in **human** habitations);
100:010 (locked up) in (**human**) breasts is made manifest-

HUMBLE

002:045 except to those who are **humble**.
011:023 and **humble** themselves before their Lord-they will
017:107 fall down on their faces in **humble** prostration,
021:090 And **humble** themselves before Us.
022:034 the Good News to those who **humble** themselves,
023:002 Those who **humble** themselves in their prayers;
033:035 who **humble** themselves, for men and women who give
041:039 thou seest the earth **humble**; but when
059:021 have seen it **humble** itself and cleave

HUMBLED

007:119 and turned about **humbled**.
009:040 and **humbled** to the depths the word
019:072 the wrong-doers therein, (**humbled**) to their knees.
020:111 (All) faces shall be **humbled** before-the Living,
020:134 we were **humbled** and put to shame."
023:076 but they **humbled** not themselves to their Lord,
027:037 in disgrace, and they will feel **humbled** (indeed)."
054:007 their eyes **humbled**-from (their) graves,
058:005 and His Messenger will be **humbled** to dust, as were

HUMBLENESS

042:045 in **humbleness** (and) looking with a stealthy glance.

HUMBLEST

016:048 to Allah, and all that in the **humblest** manner?

HUMBLY

005:055 they bow down **humbly** (in worship).
022:054 and their hearts may be made **humbly** (open) to it:

HUMILIATED

037:018 be **humiliated** (on account of your evil)."
037:098 the ones most **humiliated**!
058:020 among those most **humiliated**.
066:008 to be **humiliated** the Prophet and those who
088:002 Some faces, that Day, will be **humiliated**,
089:016 "My Lord hath **humiliated** me!"

HUMILIATING

002:090 And **humiliating** is the Chastisement
004:014 and they shall have a **humiliating** punishment.
004:102 Allah hath prepared a **humiliating** punishment.
004:151 for Unbelievers a **humiliating** punishment.
022:057 there will be a **humiliating** Punishment.
031:006 for such there will be a **humiliating** Chastisement.
033:057 and has prepared for them a **humiliating** Punishment.
034:014 in the **humiliating** Chastisement (of their Task).
041:016 more **humiliating** still: and they will find no help.
044:030 of Israel from **humiliating** Punishment,
045:009 for such there will be a **humiliating** Chastisement.
058:005 (will have) a **humiliating** Chastisement,
058:016 they have a **humiliating** Chastisement.

HUMILIATION

002:061 They were covered with **humiliation** and misery:
006:124 be overtaken by **humiliation** before Allah,
017:111 to protect Him from **humiliation**: yea, magnify

HUMILIATION (continued)

039:026 of **humiliation** in the present life, but greater
041:016 of a Chastisement of **humiliation** in this life;
041:017 of the Chastisement of **humiliation** seized them,
046:020 with a Chastisement of **humiliation**: for that

HUMILITY

003:199 bowing in **humility** to Allah:
004:154 We said: "Enter the gate with **humility**";
006:042 that they call (Allah) in **humility**.
006:043 why then did they not call (Allah) in **humility**?
006:063 when ye call upon Him in **humility** and in secret:
007:055 Call on your Lord with **humility** and in private:
007:094 in order that they might call in **humility**.
007:161 and enter the gate in a posture of **humility**:
007:205 in thy (very) soul, with **humility** and remember
017:024 the wing of **humility**, and say: "My Lord!
017:109 and it increases their (earnest) **humility**.
022:036 and such as beg with due **humility**: thus have
025:063 who walk on the earth in **humility**, and when
026:004 bend their necks in **humility**.
027:087 and all shall come to Him in utter **humility**.
057:016 in all **humility** should engage in the remembrance
066:005 who worshio (in **humility**), who fast,-

HUNAIN

009:025 the day of **Hunain**: behold! your great numbers

HUNDRED

002:259 But Allah caused him to die for a **hundred** years,
002:259 hast tarried thus a **hundred** years:
002:261 and each ear hath a **hundred** grains.
008:065 and persevering, they will vanquish two **hundred**:
008:065 if a **hundred**. They will vanquish a thousand
008:066 they will vanquish two **hundred**, and if a thousand,
008:066 if there are a **hundred** of you, patient
018:025 three **hundred** years, and nine (more).
024:002 flog each of them with a **hundred** stripes:
037:147 to a **hundred** thousand (men) or more.

HUNGER

002:155 something of fear and **hunger**,
005:003 But if any is forced by **hunger**, with no
009:120 or fatigue, or **hunger**, in the Cause of Allah,
016:112 so Allah made it taste of **hunger** and terror
018:019 (that ye may satisfy your **hunger** therewith)
088:007 Which will neither nourish nor satisfy **hunger**.
106:004 Who provides them with food against **hunger**,

HUNGRY

020:118 for thee not to go **hungry** nor to go naked,

HUNT

005:002 the state of pilgrimage, ye may **hunt**, and let not
005:004 training them to **hunt** in the manner directed

HURL

021:018 Nay, We **hurl** the Truth against falsehood, and it

HURRICANE

033:009 but We sent against them a **hurricane** and forces

HURRIED

037:094 with **hurried** steps, to him.

HURRY

037:176 Do they wish (indeed) to **hurry** on Our Punishment?

HURRYING

009:047 disorder, **hurrying** to and fro in your midst and
050:044 rent asunder, from (men) **hurrying** out: that will

HURT

002:222   Say: They are a **hurt** and a pollution:
005:042   If thou decline, they cannot **hurt** thee in the least.
005:105   no **hurt** can come to you from those who stray.
010:018   what can **hurt** them not nor profit them, and they
010:106   such can neither profit thee nor **hurt** thee:
010:107   If Allah do touch thee with **hurt**, there is
014:012   all the **hurt** you may cause us.
022:012   besides Allah, as can neither **hurt** nor profit
022:013   (Perhaps) they call on one whose **hurt** is nearer
025:003   that have no control of **hurt** or good
033:069   those who **hurt** Moses, but Allah cleared him

HUSBAND

002:230   until after she has married another **husband**
002:230   So if a **husband** divorces his wife (irrevocably),
011:072   and my **husband** here is an old man?
012:023   He said: "Allah forbid! truly (thy **husband**) is my
012:028   (her **husband**) said: "Behold! it is a snare
024:008   that (her **husband**) is telling a lie;
058:001   concerning her **husband** and carries her complaint

HUSBAND'S

004:034   and guard in (the **husband's**) absence what Allah
004:128   or desertion on her **husband's** part, there

HUSBANDS

002:228   And their **husbands** have the better right
002:232   from marrying their (former) **husbands**,
024:031   their sons, their **husbands'** sons
024:031   to their **husbands**, their fathers, their **husbands'** fathers,
060:010   the (Unbelievers) lawful (**husbands**) for them.
066:010   they betrayed their (**husbands**), and they

HUSHED

020:108   in him: and the voices will be **hushed** to The

HYPOCRISY

009:077   put as a consequence **hypocrisy** into their hearts,
009:097   in unbelief and **hypocrisy**, and most fitted
009:101   they are obstinate in **hypocrisy**: thou knowest

HYPOCRITES

003:167   And the **Hypocrites** also,
004:061   thou seest the **Hypocrites** avert their faces
004:088   into two parties about the **Hypocrites**?
004:138   To the **Hypocrites** give the glad tidings that
004:140   For Allah will collect the **Hypocrites** and those
004:142   The **Hypocrites**-they seek to deceive Allah but it
004:145   The **hypocrites** will be in the lowest
008:049   Lo! the **Hypocrites** and those in whose heart
009:064   The **Hypocrites** are afraid lest a Sura should be
009:067   Verily the **Hypocrites** are rebellious and perverse.
009:067   The **Hypocrites**, men and women, are alike:
009:068   Allah hath promised the **Hypocrites**, men and women,
009:073   the Unbelievers and the **Hypocrites**, and be
009:101   round about you are **Hypocrites**, as well as
029:011   those who are **Hypocrites**.
033:001   and hearken not the the Unbelievers and the **Hypocrites**:
033:012   And behold! The **Hypocrites** and those in whose
033:024   and punish the **Hypocrites** if that be His Will,
033:048   (the behests) of the Unbelievers and the **Hypocrites**,
033:060   Truly, if the **Hypocrites**, and those in whose
033:073   has to punish the **Hypocrites**, men and women,
048:006   And that He may punish the **Hypocrites**,
057:013   The day will the **Hypocrites**-men and women-say to
059:011   Hast thou not observed the **Hypocrites** say to
063:001   When the **Hypocrites** come to thee, they say,

HYPOCRITES (continued)

063:001   the **Hypocrites** are indeed liars.
063:007   but the **Hypocrites** understand not.
063:008   but the **Hypocrites** know not.
066:009   the Unbelievers and the **Hypocrites**, and be

I

002:030 He said: "**I** know what ye know not."
002:030 "**I** will create a vicegerent on earth."
002:033 that **I** know the secrets of the heaven and earth,
002:033 Allah said: "Did **I** not tell you that
002:033 and **I** know what ye reveal and what ye conceal?"
002:040 and **I** shall fulfil My Covenant with you,
002:040 favour which **I** bestowed upon you,
002:041 And believe in what **I** reveal,
002:047 and that **I** preferred you to all others.
002:047 favour which **I** bestowed upon you,
002:122 the special favour which **I** bestowed upon you,
002:122 and that **I** preferred you to all others.
002:124 He said: "**I** will make thee an Imam
002:126 for a while will **I** grant them their pleasure,
002:131 He said: "**I** submit (my will) to the Lord
002:135 Say thou: "Nay! (**I** would rather) the Religion
002:150 and that **I** may complete My favours on you,
002:152 Then do ye remember Me; **I** will remember you.
002:160 to them **I** turn;
002:160 for **I** am Oft-Returning, Most Merciful.
002:186 **I** am indeed close (to them):
002:186 **I** respond to every prayer of every suppliant
002:258 He said: "**I** give life and death."
002:259 he said: "**I** know that Allah hath power
003:015 Say: shall **I** give you glad tidings of things
003:020 say: "**I** have submitted my whole self to Allah
003:035 "O my Lord! **I** do dedicate unto thee what is in
003:036 and **I** commend her and her offspring to Thy
003:036 **I** am delivered of a female child!"
003:036 **I** have named her Mary,
003:040 seeing **I** am very old, and my wife is barren?"
003:040 He said: "O my Lord! how shall **I** have a son,
003:047 how shall **I** have a son when man hath touched Me?"
003:049 and **I** declare to you what ye eat,
003:049 in that **I** make for you out of clay, as it were,
003:049 **I** have come to you, with a Sign from your Lord,
003:049 and **I** heal those born blind, and the lepers,
003:049 and **I** bring the dead into life by Allah's leave;
003:050 "(**I** have come to you), to attest the Torah
003:050 **I** have come to you with a Sign from your Lord.
003:055 **I** will make those who follow thee superior
003:055 "O Jesus! **I** will take thee and raise thee to Myself
003:055 and **I** will judge between you
003:056 **I** will punish them with severe chastisement
003:081 saying: "**I** give you a Book and Wisdom:
003:081 and **I** am with you among the witnesses."
003:195 verily, **I** will blot out from them their iniquities,
003:195 **I** suffer to be lost the work of any of you,
004:018 and he says, "Now have **I** repented indeed";
004:073 a fine thing should **I** then have made of it!"
004:073 "Oh! **I** wish **I** had been with them: a fine
004:118 "**I** will take of Thy servants a portion marked off:
004:119 "**I** will mislead them, and **I** will create
004:119 and **I** will create in them false desires;
004:119 **I** will order them to slit the ears of cattle,

I (continued)

005:003 This day have **I** perfected your religion for you,
005:012 verily **I** will wipe out from you your evils,
005:012 and Allah said: "**I** am with you: if ye (but)
005:025 **I** have power only over myself and my bother:
005:027 Said the latter: "Be sure **I** will slay thee."
005:028 for **I** do fear Allah, the Cherisher of the worlds.
005:029 "For me, **I** intend to let thee draw on thyself
005:031 "Was **I** not even able to be as this raven, and to
005:060 Say: "Shall **I** point out to you something
005:110 Behold! **I** strengthened thee with the Holy Spirit.
005:110 Behold! **I** taught thee the Book and Wisdom, the
005:110 And behold! **I** did restrain the Children of Israel
005:111 "And behold! **I** inspired the Disciples to have
005:115 **I** will punish him with a chastisement such as **I**
005:115 Allah said: "**I** will send it down unto you:
005:115 such as **I** have not inflicted on anyone
005:116 never could **I** say what **I** had no right (to say).
005:116 Had **I** said such a thing. Thou wouldst
005:116 though **I** know not what is in Thine.
005:116 never could **I** say what **I** had no right (to say).
005:117 whilst **I** dwelt amongst them; when thou
005:117 and **I** was a witness over them whilst **I**
005:117 "Never said **I** to them aught except what Thou
006:014 Say: "Nay! but **I** am commanded to be the first
006:014 Say: "Shall **I** take for my protector any other
006:015 Say: "**I** would, if **I** disobeyed my Lord, indeed
006:019 And **I** truly am innocent of (your blasphemy of)
006:019 that **I** may warn you and all whom it reaches.
006:019 Say: "Nay! **I** cannot bear witness!"
006:050 **I** but follow what is revealed to me."
006:050 Nor do **I** tell you **I** am an angel.
006:050 nor do **I** know what is hidden.
006:050 Say: "**I** tell you not that with me
006:056 Say: "**I** will not follow your vain desires:
006:056 Say: "**I** am forbidden to worship those-other
006:056 if **I** did, **I** would stray from the path, and be
006:057 Say: "For me, **I** (work) on a clear Sign
006:074 For **I** see thee and thy people in manifest error."
006:076 "**I** love not those that set."
006:077 **I** shall surely be among those who go astray."
006:078 "O my people! **I** am indeed free from your (guilt)
006:079 "For me, **I** have set my face, firmly
006:079 and never shall **I** give partners to Allah
006:080 **I** fear not (the beings) ye associate with Allah:
006:081 "How should **I** fear (the beings) ye
006:090 Say: "No reward for this do **I** ask of you:
006:093 or saith, "**I** have received inspiration," when
006:093 or (again) who saith, "**I** can reveal the like of
006:104 **I** am not (here) to watch over your doings."
006:114 Say: "Shall **I** seek for judge other than Allah?-
006:135 **I** will do (my part): soon will ye know
006:145 Say: "**I** find not in the Message received by
006:151 Say: "Come, **I** will rehearse what Allah hath
006:163 No partner hath He: this am **I** commanded,
006:163 and **I** am the first of those who
006:164 Say: "Shall **I** seek for (my) Lord
007:012 He said: "**I** am better than he: thou didst
007:012 thee from prostrating when **I** commanded thee?"
007:016 lo! **I** will lie in wait for them on Thy
007:017 "Then will **I** assault them from before them
007:018 Hell will **I** fill with you all.
007:022 "Did **I** not forbid you that tree, and tell

I (continued)

037:099 He said: "I will go to my Lord! He will
037:102 he said: "O my son! I have seen in a dream
037:102 in a dream that I offer thee in sacrifice:
038:023 and I have (but) one: ye he says, 'Commit her
038:032 And he said, "Truly do I prefer wealth to the
038:065 Say: "Truly am I a Warner: no god
038:069 "No knowledge have I of the Exalted Chiefs,
038:070 that I am to give warning plainly and publicly."
038:071 "I am about to create man from clay:
038:072 "When I have fashioned him and breathed
038:075 whom I have created with My hands?
038:076 (Iblis) said: "I am better than he:
038:082 I will lead them all astray.
038:084 and the Truth I say.
038:085 "That I will certainly fill Hell with thee
038:086 Say: "No reward do I ask of you
038:086 of you for this (Qur'an), nor am I a pretender.
039:011 Say: "Verily, I am commanded to serve Allah
039:012 "And I am commanded to be the first of those
039:013 Say: "I would, if I disobeyed my Lord,
039:014 Say: "It is Allah I serve, with my
039:039 I will do (my part): but soon will ye know-
039:049 given to me because of a certain knowledge (I have)!"
039:056 in that I neglected (my duty) towards Allah,
039:057 I should certainly have been among the righteous!'
039:058 'If only I had another chance I should certainly be among
040:005 but it was I that seized them!
040:026 What I fear is lest he should change your
040:027 Moses said: "I have indeed called upon my Lord
040:029 "I but point out to you that which I see (myself);
040:029 nor do I guide you but to the Path of Right?"
040:030 "O my People! truly I do fear for you something
040:032 "And, O my People! I fear for you a Day
040:036 a lofty palace, that I may attain the ways
040:037 the heavens, and that I may look up to the God
040:037 but surely, I think (Moses) is a liar!"
040:038 I will lead you to the Path of Right.
040:042 partners of whom I have no knowledge;
040:042 and I call you to the Exalted in Power,
040:044 "Soon will ye remember what I say to you (now).
040:044 My (own) affair I commit to Allah:
040:060 I will answer your (Prayer): but those
040:066 Say: "I have been forbidden to invoke those whom
040:066 and I have been commanded to submit (in Islam)
041:006 Say thou: "I am but a man like you: it is
041:013 "I have warned you of a thunderbolt like the
041:033 "I am of those who bow in Islam"?
041:050 but if I am brought back to my Lord,
041:050 I have (much) good (stored) in His sight!"
041:050 I think not that the Hour (of Judgment)
042:010 in Him I trust, and to Him I turn.
042:015 "I believe in the Book which Allah has sent down;
042:015 and I am commanded to judge justly
042:023 Say: "No reward do I ask of you for this
043:024 He said: "What! even if I brought you better
043:026 "I do indeed clear myself of what
043:027 "(I worship) only Him Who made me, and He
043:029 Yea, I have given the good things of this life
043:046 "I am a messenger of the Lord of the Worlds."
043:052 "Am I not better than this (Moses), who is
043:063 he said: "Now have I come to you with Wisdom,
043:081 I would be the first to worship."

I (continued)

044:018 I am to you a messenger worthy of all trust;
044:019 for I come to you with authority manifest.
044:020 "For me, I have sought Safety with my Lord
046:008 Say: "Had I forged it, then ye
046:009 Say: "I am not an innovation among the messengers,
046:009 I am but a Warner open and clear."
046:009 nor do I know what will be done
046:009 I follow but that which is revealed to me
046:015 and that I may work righteousness such as Thou
046:015 grant me that I may be grateful for Thy favour
046:015 Truly have I turned to Thee and truly do I submit
046:017 Do ye hold out the promise to me that I shall be raised
046:021 truly I fear for you the Chastisement
046:023 but I see that ye are a people in ignorance!"...
046:023 I proclaim to you the mission on which I have been sent:
050:027 "Our Lord! I did not make him transgress, but he
050:028 I had already in advance sent you Warning.
050:029 and I do not the least injustice to My Servants."
051:051 I am from Him a Warner to you, clear and open!
051:056 I have only created jinns and men, that they
051:057 nor do I require that they should feed Me
051:057 No sustenance do I require of them,
052:031 I too will wait along with you!"
054:010 "I am one overcome: do thou then help (me)!"
056:075 Furthermore I swear by the setting of the Stars,-
058:021 "It is I and My messenger who must prevail":
059:016 Satan says, "I am free of thee: I do fear Allah,
060:001 for I know full well all that ye conceal
060:004 Abraham said to his father: "I will pray for forgiveness
060:004 though I have no power (to get) aught on the behalf
061:006 I am the messenger of Allah (sent) to you,
061:010 O ye who believe! shall I lead you to a bargain
063:010 I should then have given (largely) in charity,
063:010 and I should have been one of the doers of good."
067:026 it is with Allah alone: I am a plain warner."
068:028 "Did I not say to you, 'why not glorify (Allah)?'"
068:045 A (long) respite will I grant them: truly powerful
069:020 "I did really understand that my Account
069:026 "And that I had never realized how my
069:038 So I do call to witness what ye see
070:040 Now I do call to witness the Lord of all points
071:002 He said: "O my People! I am to you a Warner,
071:005 He said: "O my Lord! I have called to my People
071:007 "And every time I have called to them, that thou
071:008 "So I have called to them aloud;
071:009 "Further I have spoken to them in public
072:020 and I join not with Him any (false god)."
072:022 can deliver me from Allah (if I were to disobey Him),
072:022 nor should I find refuge except in Him.
072:023 "Unless I deliver what I receive from Allah
072:025 Say: "I know not whether the (Punishment) which ye
074:011 the (creature) whom I created (bare and) alone!-
074:012 To whom I granted resources in abundance,
074:014 To whom I made (life) smooth and comfortable!
074:015 Yet is he greedy-that I should add (yet more);
074:017 Soon will I visit him with a mount of calamities!
075:001 I do swear by the Resurrection Day;
075:002 And I do swear by the self-reproaching soul.
078:040 "Woe unto me! Would that I were (mere) dust!"
079:019 "And that I guide thee to thy Lord, so thou
079:024 Saying, "I am your Lord, Most High."
081:015 So verily I call to witness the Planets-that recede,

I (continued)

084:016 So **I** do call to witness the ruddy glow of Sunset;
086:016 And **I** am planning a scheme,
089:024 He will say: "Ah! would that **I** had sent forth
090:001 Nay **I** do swear by this City;-
090:006 "Wealth have **I** squandered in abundance!"
092:014 Therefore do **I** warn you of a Fire blazing fiercely;
109:002 **I** worship not that which ye worship,
109:003 Nor will ye worship that which **I** worship.
109:004 And **I** will not worship that which
109:005 Nor will ye worship that which **I** worship.
113:001 Say: **I** seek refuge with the Lord of the Dawn,
114:001 Say: **I** seek refuge with the Lord

IBLIS

002:034 not so **Iblis**, he refused and was haughty:
007:011 and they prostrated, not so **Iblis**; he refused
015:031 Not so **Iblis**: he refused to be among those
015:032 (Allah) said: "O **Iblis**! what is your reason for
015:033 (**Iblis**) said: "I am not one to prostrate
015:036 (**Iblis**) said: "O my Lord! give me then respite
015:039 (**Iblis**) said: "O my Lord! because Thou hast
017:061 they prostrated except   : he said,
018:050 they prostrated except **Iblis**. He was one of the Jinns,
020:116 but not **Iblis**: he refused.
026:095 "And the whole hosts of **Iblis** together.
038:074 Not so **Iblis**: he was haughty, and became
038:075 (Allah) said: "O **Iblis**! what prevents thee from
038:076 (**Iblis**) said: "I am better than he:
038:079 (**Iblis**) said: "O my Lord! give me then respite
038:082 (**Iblis**) said: "Then, by Thy Power, I will

IDDAT

002:231 (are about to) fulfil the term of their ('**Iddat**),
002:232 and they fulfil the term of their ('**Iddat**),
033:049 no period of '**Iddat** have ye to count in respect
065:006 Let the women live (in '**iddat**) in the same

IDEA

034:020 And on them did Satan prove true his **idea**,
037:087 "Then what is your **idea** about the

IDLE

009:069 and ye indulge in **idle** talk as they did.
021:016 Not for (**idle**) sport did We create the heavens
022:045 And how many wells are lying **idle** and neglected,
031:006 those who purchase **idle** tales, without knowledge
044:038 merely in (**idle**) sport:

IDLY

009:065 "We were only talking **idly** and in play."

IDOL

005:103 or **idol** sacrifices for twin-births in animals,

IDOLATER

024:003 but an adulterer or an **idolater**; to the

IDOLATERS

002:096 even more than the **idolaters**:
030:042 before (you): most of them were **idolaters**.

IDOLATRESS

024:003 an adulteress or **idolatress**, and the

IDOLS

006:074 "Takest thou **idols** for gods?
007:138 devoted entirely to some **idols** they had.
014:030 And they set up (**idols**) as equal to Allah,
014:035 sons from worshipping **idols**.
021:057 plan against your **idols**-after ye
021:065 that these (**idols**) do not speak!"

IDOLS (continued)

022:030 but shun the abomination of **idols**, and shun
026:071 They said: "We worship **idols**, and we
029:017 "For ye do worship **idols** besides Allah, and ye
029:025 (for worship) **idols** besides Allah, out of

IDRIS

019:056 Also mention in the Book **Idris**: he was
021:085 And (remember) Isma'il, **Idris**, and Zul-kifl,

IF

002:020 And **if** Allah willed,
002:023 And **if** ye are in doubt
002:023 **if** ye are truthful.
002:023 (**if** there are any) besides Allah,
002:024 But **if** ye cannot-and of a surety ye cannot
002:031 names of these **if** ye are right."
002:038 and **if**, as is sure,
002:070 we wish indeed for guidance **if** Allah wills."
002:085 and **if** they come to you as captives,
002:091 **if** ye did indeed believe?"
002:091 even **if** it be Truth confirming what is with them.
002:093 behests of your Faith **if** you have any faith!"
002:094 Say: "**If** the last Home, with Allah,
002:094 then seek ye for death, **if** ye are sincere."
002:101 as **if** (it had been something)
002:102 **if** they but knew!
002:103 **If** they had kept their Faith
002:103 reward from Allah **if** they but knew!
002:111 Say: "Produce your proof **if** ye are truthful."
002:135 or Christians **if** ye would be guided (to salvation)."
002:137 but **if** they turn back,
002:137 So **if** they believe as ye believe,
002:145 Even **if** thou wert to bring to the people
002:145 **If** thou after the knowledge hath reached thee,
002:158 So **if** those who visit the House
002:158 And **if** anyone obeyeth his own
002:165 **If** only the unrighteous could see,
002:167 "**If** only we had one more chance,
002:171 is as **if** one were to shout like a goat-herd,
002:172 **if** it is Him ye worship.
002:173 but **if** one is forced by necessity,
002:178 But **if** any remission is made by the brother
002:180 **if** he leave any goods,
002:181 **If** anyone changes the bequest after hearing it,
002:182 But **if** anyone fears partiality or wrong-doing
002:184 but **if** any of you is ill, or on a journey,
002:184 **if** ye only knew.
002:185 but **if** any one is ill, or on a journey,
002:189 It is no virtue **if** ye enter your houses
002:189 it is virtue **if** ye fear Allah.
002:191 but **if** they fight you, slay them.
002:192 But **if** they cease,
002:193 But **if** they cease, let there be no hostility
002:194 **If** then any one transgresses the prohibition
002:196 but **if** he cannot afford it,
002:196 And **if** any of you is ill,
002:196 but **if** ye are prevented (from completing it),
002:196 **if** any one wishes to continue the 'umra
002:197 **If** any one undertakes that duty therein,
002:198 It is no crime in you **if** ye seek of the bounty
002:203 and **if** anyone stays on,
002:203 but **if** anyone hastens to leave in two days,
002:203 **if** his aims is to do right.
002:209 **If** ye backslide after the clear (Signs)

IF (continued)

002:211   But **if** anyone,
002:217   back from your faith **if** they can.
002:217   And **if** any of you turn back from their faith
002:220   And **if** Allah had wished,
002:220   **if** ye mix their affairs with yours,
002:226   **if** then they return,
002:227   But **if** their intention is firm for divorce,
002:228   **if** they have faith in Allah and the Last Day.
002:228   **if** they wish for reconciliation.
002:229   them **if** any do transgress the limits ordained by Allah,
002:229   either of them **if** she give something for her freedom
002:229   by Allah **if** ye (judges) do indeed fear that they would be
002:230   So **if** a husband divorces his wife (irrevocably),
002:230   no blame on either of them **if** they re-unite,
002:231   **if** anyone does that, He wrongs his own soul.
002:232   **if** they mutually agree on equitable terms.
002:233   **if** ye decide on a foster-mother for your offspring
002:233   **If** they both decide on weaning,
002:234   **If** any of you die and leave widows behind;
002:234   there is no blame on you **if** they dispose
002:235   There is no blame on you **if** ye make an indirect
002:236   There is no blame on you **if** ye divorce women
002:237   And **if** ye divorce them before consummation,
002:237   (of the man's half) **if** the nearest to righteousness.
002:239   **If** ye fear (an enemy), pray on foot,
002:240   but **if** they leave (the residence),
002:246   **if** ye were commanded to fight,
002:248   Symbol for you **if** ye indeed have faith."
002:249   **if** any drinks of its water,
002:253   **If** Allah had so willed, they would not have
002:253   **If** Allah had so willed, succeeding generations
002:265   and **if** it receives not heavy rain,
002:271   **If** ye disclose (acts of) charity,
002:271   but **if** ye conceal them,
002:278   **if** ye are indeed believers.
002:279   but **if** ye repent ye shall have
002:279   **If** ye do it not, take notice of war
002:280   But **if** ye remit it by way of charity,
002:280   **If** the debtor is in a difficulty,
002:280   that is best for you **if** ye only knew.
002:282   And **if** there are not two men,
002:282   no blame on you **if** ye reduce it not to writing.
002:282   **If** the party liable is mentally deficient,
002:282   **If** ye do (such harm), it would be
002:282   so that **if** one of them errs.
002:282   but **if** it be a transaction which ye carry out
002:283   And **if** one of you deposits a thing
002:283   **If** ye are on a journey, and cannot find a scribe,
002:286   condemn us not **if** we forget or fall into error;
003:019   But **if** any deny the Signs of Allah,
003:020   **If** they do, they are in right guidance,
003:020   but **if** they turn back, thy duty
003:020   So **if** they dispute with thee,
003:028   **if** any do that, shall have no relation left
003:031   Say: "**If** ye do love Allah, follow me:
003:032   but **if** they turn back, Allah loveth not
003:049   Surely therein is a Sign for you **if** ye did believe.
003:061   **If** any one disputes in this manner with thee,
003:063   But **if** they turn back,
003:064   **If** then they turn back,
003:075   others, who, **if** entrusted with a single silver coin,
003:075   **if** entrusted with a hoard of gold,

IF (continued)

003:082   **If** any turn back after this, they are
003:085   **If** anyone desires a religion other than Islam
003:093   **if** ye be men of truth."
003:094   **If** any, after this, invent a lie
003:097   but **if** any deny faith, Allah stands not in need
003:100   O ye who believe! **if** ye listen to a faction
003:110   **If** only the People of the Book had faith,
003:111   **if** they come out to fight you, they will show
003:118   the Signs, **if** ye have wisdom.
003:120   But **if** ye are patient and do right,
003:120   **If** aught that is good befalls you, it grieves them;
003:120   but **if** some misfortune overtakes you,
003:125   "Yea,-**if** ye remain firm, and act aright,
003:125   even **if** the enemy should rush here
003:139   for ye must gain mastery **if** ye are true in Faith.
003:140   **If** a wound hath touched you, be sure a similar
003:144   **If** he died or were slain,
003:144   **If** any did turn back on his heels,
003:145   and **if** any do desire a reward in the Hereafter,
003:145   **If** any do desire a reward in this life,
003:146   never lost heart **if** they met with disaster in Allah's way,
003:149   O ye who believe! **If** ye obey the Unbelievers,
003:154   "**If** we had had anything to do with this affair,
003:154   Say: "Even **if** you had remained in your homes,
003:156   "**If** they had stayed with us, they would
003:157   And **if** ye are slain, or die, in the way of Allah,
003:158   And **if** ye die, or are slain,
003:160   **if** He forsakes you, who is there, after that,
003:160   **If** Allah helps you, none can overcome you:
003:161   **If** any person acts dishonestly he shall,
003:168   **if** ye speak the truth."
003:168   "**If** only they had listened to us,
003:175   but fear Me, **if** ye have Faith.
003:179   and **if** ye believe and do right, ye have
003:183   why then did ye slay them, **if** ye speak the truth?.
003:184   Then **if** they reject thee, so were rejected
003:186   But **if** ye persevere patiently,
004:003   **If** ye fear that ye shall not be able
004:003   but **if** ye fear that ye shall not be able
004:005   but **if** they, of their own good pleasure, remit
004:006   **If** the guardian is well-off, let him
004:006   but **if** he is poor, let him have for himself
004:006   **if** then ye find sound judgment in them, release
004:008   But **if** at the time of division other relatives,
004:009   for their own **if** they had left a helpless family behind:
004:011   **if** the deceased left children; **if** no children, and the parents
004:011   **if** only one, her share is a half.
004:011   **if** the deceased left brothers (or sisters),
004:011   **if** only daughters, two or more, their share
004:012   your share is a half, **if** they leave no child;
004:012   but **if** more than two, they share in a third;
004:012   **If** the man or woman whose inheritance
004:012   their share is a fourth, **if** ye leave no child;
004:012   but **if** ye leave a child, they get an eighth;
004:012   but **if** they leave a child, ye get a fourth;
004:015   and **if** they testify, confine them to houses
004:015   **If** any of your women are guilty of lewdness,
004:016   **If** two persons among you are guilty of lewdness,
004:016   **If** they repent and amend, leave them alone;
004:019   and equity **if** ye take a dislike to them it may
004:020   even **if** ye had given the latter
004:020   But **if** ye decide to take one wife

IF (continued)

004:023 no prohibition **if** ye have not gone in;
004:024 but **if**, after a dower is prescribed, ye agree
004:025 **If** any of you have not the means wherewith
004:025 **if** they commit indecency their punishment is
004:030 **If** any do that in rancor and injustice, soon
004:031 **If** ye (but) eschew the most heinous of the things
004:034 but **if** they return to obedience, seek not
004:035 **if** they seek to set things aright, Allah
004:035 **If** ye fear a breach between them twain, appoint
004:038 **if** any take the Satan for their intimate,
004:039 on them **if** they had faith in Allah and in the Last Day,
004:040 **if** there is any good (done), He doubleth it,
004:041 How then **if** We brought from each People a witness,
004:043 until after washing your whole body **if** ye are ill,
004:046 **If** only they had said: "We hear and we obey";
004:059 **If** ye differ in anything among yourselves,
004:059 **if** ye do believe in Allah and the Last Day:
004:064 **If** they had only, when they were unjust
004:066 **If** We had ordered them to sacrifice their lives
004:066 but **if** they had done what they
004:072 **if** a misfortune befalls you, they say: "Allah did favour
004:073 as **if** there had never been ties of affection
004:073 But **if** good fortune comes to you from Allah,
004:078 but **if** evil, they say, "This is from
004:078 even **if** ye are in towers built up strong and high!"
004:078 **If** some good befalls them, they say, "This
004:080 but **if** any turn away, We have not
004:083 **If** they had only referred it to the Messenger
004:089 But **if** they turn renegades, seize them
004:090 **If** Allah had pleased, He could have
004:090 therefore **if** they withdraw from you
004:091 **if** they withdraw not from you nor give you
004:092 **If** he belonged to a people with whom
004:092 **If** the deceased belonged to a people
004:093 **If** a man kills a Believer intentionally,
004:101 no blame on you **if** ye shorten your prayers, for fear
004:102 the Unbelievers wish, **if** ye were negligent of
004:102 But there is no blame on you **if** ye put away
004:104 **if** ye are suffering hardships, they are suffering
004:110 **If** anyone does evil or wrongs his own soul but
004:111 And **if** anyone earns sin, he earns it
004:112 But **if** anyone earns a fault or a sin and throws
004:114 but **if** one exhorts to a deed of charity or
004:115 **If** anyone contends with the Messenger even after
004:124 **If** any do deeds of righteousness, be they
004:128 **If** a wife fears cruelty or desertion
004:128 there is no blame on them **if** they arrange an amicable
004:128 But **if** ye do good and practice self-restraint,
004:129 **If** ye come to a friendly understanding,
004:129 between wives even **if** it is your ardent desire:
004:130 But **if** they separate Allah will provide
004:131 But **if** ye deny Him, lo! unto Allah belong all
004:133 **If** it were His will, He could destroy you,
004:134 **If** any one desires a reward in this life,
004:135 and **if** ye distort (Justice) or decline to do justice,
004:140 **if** ye did, ye would be like them.
004:141 But **if** the Unbelievers gain a success, they say
004:141 **if** ye do gain a victory from Allah, they say:
004:146 **if** so they will be (numbered) with the Believers.
004:147 **If** ye are grateful and ye believe?
004:170 But **if** ye reject Faith, to Allah belong
004:176 **If** it is a man. That dies,

IF (continued)

004:176 **if** there are brothers and sisters, (they share),
004:176 **if** there are two sisters, they shall
004:176 **if** (such a deceased was) a woman, who left no child,
005:003 But **if** any is forced by hunger, with no
005:005 **If** anyone rejects faith, fruitless is his work,
005:006 But **if** ye are ill, or on a journey, or one
005:006 **If** ye are in a state of ceremonial impurity, bathe
005:012 **if** ye (but) establish regular Prayers, pay Zakat
005:012 but **if** any of you, after this, resisteth faith,
005:017 against Allah, **if** His Will were to destroy
005:022 **If** (once) they leave, then shall we enter."
005:023 But on Allah put your trust **if** ye have faith."
005:028 "**If** thou dost stretch thy hand against me, to slay
005:032 it would be as **if** he slew the whole people:
005:032 and **if** anyone saved a life, it would be as **if** he saved
005:032 that **if** anyone slew a person-unless it be for
005:036 **if** they had everything on earth, and twice
005:039 But **if** the thief repent after his crime, and amend
005:041 they say, "**If** ye are given this, take it, but **if** not, beware!"
005:041 **If** any one's trial is intended by Allah,
005:042 **If** they do come to thee, either judge
005:042 **If** thou decline, they cannot hurt thee in the least.
005:042 **If** thou judge, judge in equity between them.
005:044 **If** any do fail to judge by what Allah
005:045 But **if** anyone remits the retaliation by way of charity,
005:045 And **if** any fail to judge by what
005:047 **If** any do fail to judge by what
005:048 **If** Allah had so willed, He would have
005:049 And **if** they turn away, be assured that for some
005:054 O ye who believe! **if** any from among you turn
005:057 but fear ye Allah, **if** ye have Faith (indeed).
005:065 **If** only the people of the Book had believed
005:066 **If** only they had stood fast by the Torah,
005:067 **If** thou didst not, thou wouldst not
005:073 **If** they desist not from their word (of blasphemy),
005:081 **If** only they had believed in Allah, in the
005:089 **If** that is beyond your means, fast for three days.
005:092 and beware (of evil): **if** ye do turn back, know
005:095 **If** any of you doth so intentionally,
005:101 But **if** ye ask about things when the Qur'an
005:101 about things which, **if** made plain to you, may
005:105 **if** ye follow (right) guidance.
005:106 **if** we do, then behold! we shall be sinners.
005:106 from outside **if** ye are journeying through
005:106 **If** ye doubt (their truth), detain them
005:107 But **if** it gets known that these two were guilty
005:107 **if** we did, behold! we will be wrong-doers."
005:112 Said Jesus: "Fear Allah, **if** ye have faith."
005:115 but **if** any of you after that resisteth faith,
005:118 **if** Thou dost forgive them, Thou art
005:118 "**If** Thou dost punish them, they are
006:007 **If** We had sent unto thee a written (Message)
006:008 **If** We did send down an angel, the matter
006:009 **If** We had made it an angel, We should
006:015 Say: "I would, **if** I disobeyed my Lord, indeed
006:016 **if** the penalty is averted from any, it is due to Allah's
006:017 **if** He touch thee with happiness, He hath
006:017 "**If** Allah touch thee with affliction, none can
006:025 **if** they saw every one of the Signs, they will
006:027 **If** thou couldst but see when they
006:028 But **if** they were returned, they would
006:030 **If** thou couldst but see when they

IF (continued)

006:035	yet **if** thou wert able to seek a tunnel
006:035	**If** their spurning is hard on thee,
006:035	**If** it were Allah's will, He could gather
006:040	**if** there come upon you the Punishment of Allah,
006:040	(Reply) **if** ye are truthful!
006:041	and **if** it be His Will, He would
006:046	Say: "Think ye, **if** Allah took away your hearing
006:047	"Think ye, **if** the Punishment of Allah comes to you,
006:054	verily, **if** any of you did evil in ignorance,
006:056	**if** I did, I would stray from the path,
006:058	Say: "**If** what ye would see hastened
006:063	'If He only delivers us from these (dangers),
006:068	**If** Satan ever makes thee forget, then after
006:070	**if** it offered every ransom (or reparation),
006:081	(Tell me) **if** you know.
006:088	**If** they were to join other gods with Him,
006:089	**if** these (their descendants) reject them, behold!
006:093	**If** thou couldst but see how the wicked
006:104	**if** any will be blind, it will be to his own (harm):
006:104	**if** any will see, it will be for (the good of) his own soul:
006:107	**If** it had been Allah's Will, they would
006:109	that **if** a (special) Sign came to them,
006:109	realize that even **if** a (special) Sign came,
006:111	Even **if** We did send unto them angels, and the
006:112	**If** thy Lord had so willed, they would
006:118	**if** ye have faith in His Signs.
006:121	to contend with you **if** ye were to obey them,
006:125	as **if** they had to climb up to the skies:
006:133	**if** it were His Will, He could destroy you,
006:137	**If** Allah had willed, they would
006:139	but **if** it is still-born then all
006:143	Tell me with knowledge **if** ye are truthful:
006:145	**if** a person is forced by necessity, without
006:147	**If** they accuse thee of falsehood, say:
006:148	**If** so, produce it before us.
006:148	will say: "**If** Allah had wished, we should
006:149	**if** it had been His Will.
006:150	**If** they bring such witnesses, be not
006:152	even **if** a near relative is concerned; and fulfil
006:157	"**If** the Book had only been sent down to us, we
006:158	Are they waiting to see **if** the angels come to them,
006:158	**if** it believed not before nor earned
007:018	**If** any of them follow thee,-Hell will
007:023	**if** Thou forgive us not and bestow not
007:070	**if** so be that thou tellest the truth!"
007:077	**if** thou art a Messenger (of Allah)!"
007:085	that will be best for you, **if** ye have Faith.
007:087	"And **if** there is a party among you who believes
007:089	**if** we returned to your religion after Allah
007:090	said: "**If** ye follow Shu'aib, be sure
007:092	became as **if** they had never been in the homes
007:096	**If** the people of the towns had but
007:100	**if** We so willed, We could
007:106	show it forth,-**if** thou tellest the truth."
007:106	(Pharaoh) said: "**If** indeed thou hast
007:113	a (suitable) reward **if** we win!"
007:134	**if** thou wilt remove the Plague from us,
007:143	**if** it abide in its place, then shalt
007:146	but **if** they see the way of error, that is
007:146	even **if** they see all the Signs, they will not
007:146	and **if** they see the way of right conduct, they
007:149	they said: "**If** our Lord have not mercy upon us

IF (continued)

007:155	he prayed: "O my Lord! **if** it had been Thy will
007:169	(Even so), **if** similar vanities came their way,
007:171	as **if** it had been a canopy, and they
007:176	or **if** you leave him alone, he (still) lolls out his tongue,
007:176	**If** it had been Our Will, We should
007:176	**if** you attack him, he lolls out his tongue
007:187	They ask thee as **if** thou wert eager
007:188	**If** I had knowledge of the unseen, I should
007:189	(saying): "**If** Thou givest us a goodly child,
007:193	**If** ye call them to guidance, they will
007:194	**if** ye are (indeed) truthful!
007:198	**If** thou callest them to guidance, they hear
007:200	**If** a suggestion from Satan assail thy (mind),
007:203	**If** thou bring them not a revelation, they say:
008:001	obey Allah and His Allah, **if** ye do believe."
008:006	as **if** they were being driven to death
008:013	**if** any contend against Allah and His Messenger.
008:016	**If** any do turn his back to them
008:019	**if** ye return (to the attack), so shall We.
008:019	(O Unbelievers!) **if** ye prayed for victory
008:019	**if** ye desist (from wrong), it will be best for you:
008:019	your forces be to you even **if** they were multiplied:
008:023	**If** Allah had found in them any good, He would
008:023	**if** He had made them listen, they would
008:029	O ye who believe! **if** ye fear Allah, He will
008:031	**if** we wished, we could say (words) like these:
008:032	"O Allah! **if** this is indeed the truth from Thee,
008:038	**if** (now) they desist (from Unbelief),
008:038	but **if** they persist, the punishment
008:039	in its entirety but **if** they cease, verily Allah
008:040	**If** they refuse, be sure
008:041	**if** ye do believe in Allah and in the revelation
008:042	Even **if** ye had made a mutual appointment to meet,
008:043	**if** He had shown them to thee as many, ye would
008:049	But **if** any trust in Allah, behold! Allah
008:050	**If** thou couldst see, when the
008:057	**If** ye gain the mastery over them in war,
008:058	**If** thou fearest treachery from any group,
008:061	But **if** the enemy incline towards peace, do thou
008:063	not **if** thou hadst spent all that is in the earth,
008:065	**if** a hundred. They will vanquish a thousand
008:065	**If** there are twenty amongst you,
008:066	and **if** a thousand, they will vanquish two thousand,
008:066	**if** there are a hundred of you, patient
008:070	"**If** Allah findeth any good in your hearts, He will
008:071	But **if** they have treacherous designs against thee,
009:003	**If**, then, ye repent, it were best for you;
009:003	but **if** ye turn away, know ye
009:005	but **if** they repent, and establish regular prayers.
009:006	**If** one amongst the Pagans ask thee for asylum,
009:008	seeing that **if** they get an advantage over you,
009:011	But (even so), **if** they repent, establish regular
009:012	But **if** they violate their oaths
009:013	justly fear, **if** ye believe!
009:023	**if** any of you do so, they do wrong.
009:023	your brothers **if** they love infidelity above Faith:
009:024	Say: **If** it be that your fathers, your sons,
009:028	And **if** ye fear poverty, soon will Allah enrich you,
009:028	enrich you, **if** He wills, out of His bounty,
009:040	**If** ye help not (the Prophet), (it is no matter):
009:041	That is best for you, **if** ye (but) knew.
009:042	**If** there had been immediate gain (in sight),

IF (continued)

009:042 "If we only could, we should certainly have come
009:046 If they had intended to come out, they would
009:047 If they had come out with you, they would
009:050 If good befalls thee, it grieves them;
009:050 but if a misfortune befalls thee, they say
009:057 If they could find a place to flee to, or caves,
009:058 If they are given part thereof, they are pleased,
009:058 they are pleased, but if not, behold!
009:059 If only they had been content with what Allah
009:062 if they are Believers.
009:065 If thou dost question them, they declare
009:066 If We pardon some of you, We will
009:074 but if they turn back (to their evil ways), Allah
009:074 If they repent, it will be best for them:
009:075 a Covenant with Allah, that if He bestowed on them
009:080 if thou ask seventy times for their forgiveness,
009:081 If only they could understand!
009:083 If, then, Allah bring thee back to any of them,
009:091 (on the Cause), if they are sincere (in duty)
009:096 But if ye are pleased with them. Allah is not
009:122 if a contingent from every expedition go forth
009:129 But if they turn away, Say: "Allah sufficeth me:
010:011 If Allah were to hasten for men the ill
010:012 on his way as if he had never cried to Us for the
010:015 if I were to disobey my Lord, I should myself
010:016 Say: "If Allah had so willed, I should
010:022 saying, "If Thou dost deliver us from this,
010:024 as if it had not flourished only the day before!
010:038 besides Allah, if it be ye speak the truth!"
010:041 If they charge thee with falsehood, say: "My work
010:045 (it will be) as if they had tarried
010:048 "will this promise come to pass-if ye speak the truth?"
010:050 Say: "Do ye see-if His punishment should come
010:054 if it possessed all that is on earth,
010:071 "O my People, if it be hard on your (mind) that I
010:072 "But if ye turn back, (consider): no reward
010:084 put your trust if ye submit (your will to His)."
010:084 if ye do (really) believe in Allah, then in Him
010:094 If thou wert in doubt as to what We have
010:097 Even if every Sign was brought unto them,-until
010:098 If only there had been a single township
010:099 If it had been the Lord's Will, they would
010:104 Say: "O ye men! if ye are in doubt
010:106 nor hurt thee: if thou dost, behold! thou shalt
010:107 if He do design some benefit for thee, there is
010:107 If Allah do touch thee with hurt, there is
011:003 But if ye turn away, then I fear for you
011:007 But if thou wert to say to them, "Ye shall
011:008 If We delay the chastisement for them
011:009 If We give man a taste of mercy from Ourselves,
011:010 But if We give him a taste of (Our) favours
011:013 if ye speak the truth!
011:014 "If then they (your false gods) answer not
011:028 He said: "O my people! see ye if (it be that)
011:030 help me against Allah if I drove them away?
011:031 I should, if I did, indeed be a wrong-doer."
011:032 us with, if thou speakest the truth!"
011:033 on you if He wills-and then, ye will
011:034 if it be that Allah willeth to leave you astray:
011:035 Say: "If I had forged it, on me were my sin!
011:038 He said: "If ye ridicule us now, we (in our turn)
011:057 "If ye turn away,-I (at least) have conveyed

IF (continued)

011:063 If I have a Clear (Sign) from my Lord and He
011:063 me against Allah if I were to disobey Him?
011:068 As if they had never dwelt and flourished there.
011:078 they are purer for you (if ye marry)!
011:086 left you by Allah is best for you, if ye (but) believed!
011:095 As if they had never dwelt and flourished there!
011:116 If only there had been of the generations
011:118 If thy Lord had so willed, He could
012:010 but if ye must do something, throw him
012:014 They said: "If the wolf were to devour him
012:026 (thus)-" If it be that his shirt is rent
012:027 "But if it be that his shirt is torn
012:032 And now, if he doth not my bidding, he shall
012:043 to me my vision if it be that ye can interpret visions."
012:060 "Now if ye bring him not to me, ye shall
012:074 if ye are (proved) to have lied?"
012:077 They said: "If he steals, there was a brother
012:079 indeed (if we did so), we should
012:099 in safety if it please Allah."
013:005 If thou dost marvel (at their want of faith),
013:014 no more than if they were to stretch forth their hands
013:018 even if they had all that is in the heavens
013:031 If there were a Qur'an with which mountains
014:007 but if ye show ingratitude, truly My punishment
014:007 "If ye are grateful, I will add more (favours)
014:008 And Moses said: "If ye show ingratitude, ye and
014:019 If He so will, He can remove you
014:021 They will reply, "If we had received the
014:034 But if ye count the favours of Allah, never will
014:044 "Our Lord! respite us (if only) for a short Term:
015:007 bringest thou not Angels if it be that thou hast the Truth?"
015:008 if they came (to the ungodly)
015:014 Even if We opened out to them a gate
015:071 my daughters (to marry), if ye must act (so)."
016:009 if Allah had willed, He could have
016:018 If ye would count up the favours of Allah,
016:035 "If Allah had so willed, we should not have
016:037 If thou art anxious for their guidance, yet Allah
016:041 if they only realize (this)!
016:043 if ye realize this not, ask of those
016:061 If Allah were to punish men for their wrong-doing,
016:082 But if they turn away, thy duty
016:093 If Allah so willed, He could make you all
016:095 (a prize) far better for you, if ye only knew.
016:114 if it is He whom ye serve.
016:115 But if one is forced by necessity, without wilful
016:126 but if ye show patience, that is indeed
016:126 And if ye punish, let your
017:007 if ye did evil (ye did it) against yourselves.
017:007 If ye did well, ye did well for yourselves;
017:008 show Mercy unto you; but if ye revert (to your sins),
017:018 If any do wish for the transitory things
017:025 if ye do deeds of righteousness,
017:028 And even if thou hast to turn away from them
017:033 And if anyone is slain wrongfully, We have
017:042 Say: if there had been (other) gods with Him,-
017:054 if He please, He granteth you mercy, or if He please,
017:062 If Thou wilt but respite me to the Day
017:063 Allah said: "Go thy way; if any of them follow
017:086 If it were Our Will, We could
017:088 even if they backed up each other
017:088 Say: "If the whole of mankind and Jinns were to

IF (continued)

017:095 Say, "If there were settled, on earth,
017:100 Say: "If ye had control of the Treasures
018:006 if they believe not in this Message.
018:014 if we did; we should indeed have uttered
018:018 if thou hadst looked at them, thou wouldst
018:020 "For if thy should come upon you, they would
018:024 Except "If Allah so wills" and remember
018:029 if they implore relief they will be granted water like
018:036 even if I am brought back to my Lord.
018:039 If thou dost see me less than
018:057 If thou callest them to guidance, even then
018:058 If He were to call them (at once)
018:069 if Allah so will, (truly) patient:
018:070 The other said: "If then thou wouldst follow me,
018:076 (Moses) said: "If ever I ask thee about anything
018:077 (Moses) said: "If thou hadst wished, surely thou
018:109 even if we added another ocean like it,
018:109 Say: "If the ocean were ink (wherewith to write out)
019:018 (come not near) if thou dost fear Allah."
019:026 And if thou dost see any man, say, 'I have
019:046 If thou forbear not, I will indeed stone thee:
020:007 If thou pronounce the word aloud, (it is no matter):
020:100 If any do turn away therefrom, verily they
020:123 with enmity one to another; but if, as is sure,
020:134 "Our Lord! if only Thou hadst sent us a messenger,
021:007 if ye know this not, ask of those
021:017 if We would do (such a thing)!
021:017 If it had been Our wish to take (just) a pastime,
021:022 If there were, in the heavens and the earth,
021:029 If any of them should say, "I am
021:034 if then thou shouldst die, would they live permanently?
021:038 come to pass, if ye are telling the truth?"
021:039 If only the Unbelievers knew (the time)
021:046 If but a breath of the Wrath of thy Lord
021:047 And if there be (no more than) the weight
021:063 Ask them, if they can talk."
021:068 and protect your gods, if ye do (anything at all)!"
021:099 If these had been gods, they would
021:109 But if they turn back, say: "I have
022:005 O mankind! if ye have a doubt about the
022:011 if good befalls them, they are, therewith, well content:
022:011 but if a trial comes to them, they turn
022:015 If any think that Allah will not help him
022:031 he is as if he had fallen from heaven and been
022:031 if anyone assigns partners to Allah, he is as if he had
022:041 if We establish them in the land,
022:042 If they disbelieve you so did the Peoples
022:060 And if one has retaliated to no greater
022:068 If they do wrangle with thee,
022:073 if they all met together for the purpose!
022:073 And if the fly should snatch away anything from them,
023:024 if Allah had wished (to send messengers),
023:034 "If ye obey a man like yourselves, behold, it is
023:071 If the Truth had been in accord with their
023:075 If We had mercy on them and removed
023:084 the earth and all beings therein? (Say) if ye know!"
023:088 but is not protected (of any)? (Say) if ye know."
023:091 (if there were many gods), behold, each god
023:093 Say: "O my Lord! if Thou wilt show me (in my lifetime)
023:107 if ever we return (to evil), then shall be wrong-doers
023:114 "Ye stayed not but a little,-if ye had only known!
023:117 If anyone invokes, besides Allah, any other

IF (continued)

024:002 if ye believe in Allah and the Last Day:
024:007 of Allah on himself if he tells a lie.
024:008 the wife, if she bears witness four times
024:009 on herself if (her accuser) is telling the truth.
024:010 If it were not for God's grace and mercy on you,
024:017 if ye are (true) Believers.
024:021 if any will follow the footsteps of Satan,
024:028 if ye are asked to go back, go back
024:028 If ye find no one in the house, enter not
024:032 if they are in poverty, Allah will give them
024:033 But if anyone compels them, yet, after
024:033 And if any of yours slaves ask for a deed
024:033 give them such a deed if ye know any good in them;
024:035 is as if there were a Niche and within it a Lamp:
024:040 if a man stretches out his hand, he can hardly see it!
024:049 But if the right is on their side, they come
024:053 by Allah that, if only thou wouldst command
024:054 but if ye turn away, he is
024:054 If ye obey him, ye shall be on right guidance.
024:055 If any do reject Faith after this, they are
024:060 there is no blame on them if they lay aside
024:061 But if ye enter houses,
025:010 Blessed is He Who, if that were His Will,
025:045 If He willed, He could make it stationary!
025:072 and, if they pass by futility, they pass
025:073 droop not down at them as if they were deaf
026:004 If (such) were Our Will, We could
026:024 and all between,- if ye had but sure belief."
026:028 If ye only had sense!"
026:029 (Pharaoh) said: "If thou takest any god other
026:030 (Moses) said: "Even if I showed you something
026:031 (Pharaoh) said: "Show it then, if thou tellest the truth!"
026:040 "That we may follow the sorcerers if they win?"
026:041 shall we have a (suitable) reward if we win?"
026:102 "Now if we only had a chance of return, we shall
026:113 account is only with my Lord, if ye could (but) understand.
026:116 They said: "If thou desist not, O Noah!
026:154 then bring us a Sign, if thou tellest the truth!"
026:167 They said: "If thou desist not, O Lut!
026:187 to fall on us, if thou art truthful!"
026:205 If we do let them enjoy (this life)
026:216 Then if they disobey thee, say: "I am free
027:010 (of its own accord) as if it had been a snake,
027:011 "But if any have done wrong and have
027:040 but if any is ungrateful, truly my
027:040 And if any is grateful, truly his
027:046 If only ye ask Allah for forgiveness, ye may
027:064 "Bring forth your argument, if ye are telling the truth!"
027:071 (come to pass)? If ye are truthful."
027:089 If any do good, he will have better than it.
027:090 And if any do evil, their faces will be thrown
027:092 and if any stray, say: "I am only a Warner."
027:092 and if any accept guidance, they do
028:027 indeed, if Allah wills, one of the righteous."
028:027 for eight years, but if thou complete ten years,
028:031 moving (of its own accord) as if it had been a snake,
028:047 If (We had) not (sent thee to the Quraish),
028:049 (Do), if ye are truthful!"
028:050 But if they hearken not to thee, know that
028:057 They say: "If we were to follow the guidance
028:064 If only they had been open to guidance!'
028:071 Say: See ye? If Allah were to make the night

IF (continued)

045:008   as **if** he had not heard them: then announce
045:015   **if** he does evil, it works against (His own soul).
045:015   **If** anyone does a righteous deed, it is
045:025   our forefathers, **if** what ye say is true!"
046:004   of knowledge (ye may have), **if** ye are telling the truth!"
046:010   Say: "See ye? **If** (this teaching) be from Allah,
046:011   who believe: "**If** (this Message) were a good thing,
046:022   **if** thou art telling the truth!"
046:032   "**If** any does not hearken to the one who invites
046:035   (it will be) as **if** they had not tarried more
047:004   but **if** it had been Allah's Will, He could
047:007   O ye who believe! **if** ye will help (the cause of) Allah,
047:021   it were best for them **if** they were true to Allah.
047:022   to be expected of you, **if** ye were put in authority,
047:036   and **if** ye believe and guard against evil,
047:037   **If** He were to ask you for all of them,
047:038   **If** ye turn back (from the Path),
048:011   with Allah, **if** His Will is to give you some
048:013   And **if** any believe not in Allah and His Messenger,
048:016   a goodly reward, but **if** ye turn back as ye
048:016   Then **if** ye show obedience,
048:017   nor on one ill (**if** he joins not the war): but he
048:022   **If** the Unbelievers should fight you, they would
048:025   **If** they had been apart, We should
048:027   **if** Allah wills, with minds secure, heads shaved,
049:005   **If** only they had patience until thou
049:006   O ye who believe! **if** a sinner comes to you
049:009   **If** two parties among the Believers fall into
049:009   but **if** one them transgresses beyond against the other,
049:009   but **if** it complies, then make peace between them
049:014   But **if** ye obey Allah and His Messenger, He will
049:017   He has guided you to the Faith, **if** ye be true and sincere.
052:034   like unto it,-**if** (it be) they speak the Truth!
054:002   But **if** they see a Sign, they turn away, and say,
054:020   Plucking out men as **if** they were roots of
055:033   **If** it be ye can pass beyond the zones
056:076   a mighty adjuration, **if** ye but knew,-
056:086   **if** you are exempt from (future) account,-
056:087   **if** ye are true (in your claim of Independence)?
056:088   Thus, then, **if** he be of those Nearest to Allah,
056:090   And **if** he be of the Companions of the Right Hand,
056:092   And **if** he be of those who deny (the truth)
057:008   **if** ye are men of faith.
057:024   And **if** any turn back (from Allah's Way),
058:002   **If** any men among you divorce their wives by Zihar
058:004   And **if** any has not (the means), he should
058:004   touch each other, but **if** any is unable to do so,
058:012   But **if** ye find not (the wherewithal),
058:013   **If**, then, ye do not so, and Allah forgives you,
059:004   and **if** any one resists Allah,
059:011   "**If** ye are expelled, We too will go out with you,
059:011   and **if** ye are attacked (in fight) we will help you."
059:012   and **if** they are attacked (in fight),
059:012   and **if** they do help them, they will
059:012   **If** they are expelled, never will they go out with you,
060:001   **If** ye have come out to strive in My Way and seek
060:002   **If** they overcome you they would behave to you
060:006   But **if** any turn away, truly Allah is Free of all
060:010   as to their Faith: **if** ye ascertain that they
060:010   **if** ye marry them on payment of their dower to them.
060:011   And **if** any of your wives deserts you to the
061:004   as **if** they were a solid cemented structure.

IF (continued)

061:011   that will be best for you, **if** ye but knew!
062:006   Say: "O ye of Jewry! **if** ye think that ye are friends
062:006   then express your desire for Death, **if** ye are truthful!
062:009   that is best for you **if** ye but knew!
063:008   They say, "**If** we return to Madinah, surely the
063:009   **If** any act thus, surely they are the losers.
064:011   and **if** anyone believes in Allah, (Allah) guides
064:012   but **if** ye turn back, the duty
064:014   But **if** ye forgive and overlook, and cover
064:017   **If** ye loan to Allah a beautiful loan, He will
065:001   thou knowest not **if** perchance Allah
065:003   And **if** anyone puts his trust in Allah,
065:004   **if** ye have any doubt, is three months,
065:005   and **if** anyone fears Allah, He will
065:006   And **if** they are pregnant, then spend
065:006   And **if** ye find yourselves in difficulties,
065:006   and **if** they suckle your (offspring), give them
066:004   but **if** ye back up each other against him,
066:004   **If** ye two turn in repentance to Allah,
066:005   It may be, **if** he divorced you (all), that Allah
067:021   provide you with Sustenance **if** He were to
067:025   **If** ye are telling the truth.
067:028   Say: "See ye?-**if** Allah were to destroy me,
067:028   or **if** He bestows His Mercy on us,-yet who
067:030   Say: "See ye?-**if** your stream be some morning lost
068:018   But made no reservation, ("**If** it be Allah's Will").
068:022   in the morning, **if** ye would gather the fruits."
068:033   in the Hereafter,-**if** only they knew!
068:041   produce their "partners," **if** they are truthful!
069:007   in its (path), as **if** they had been roots of
069:044   And **if** the messenger were to invent any sayings
070:043   as **if** they were rushing to a goal-post
071:004   it cannot be put forward: **if** ye only knew."
071:027   "For, **if** Thou dost leave (any of) them, they will
072:016   "**If** they (the pagans) had (only) remained on the
072:017   But **if** any turns away from the remembrance
072:022   can deliver me form Allah (**if** I were to disobey Him),
073:017   Then how shall ye, **if** ye deny (Allah),
074:050   As **if** they were affrighted asses,
076:019   **if** thou seest them, thou wouldst think
077:033   "As **if** there were (a string of) yellow camels
077:039   Now, **if** ye have a trick (or plot),
078:019   as **if** there were doors,
078:020   as **if** they were a mirage.
079:046   (it will be) as **if** they had tarried but a single
080:007   Though it is no blame to thee **if** he grow not in purity.
088:023   But **if** any turn away and disbelieve,-
096:011   Seest thou **if** He is on (the road of) Guidance?-
096:013   Seest thou **if** he denies (Truth) and turns away?
096:015   Let him beware! **If** he desist not, We will

IGNOMINIOUSLY

005:021   and turn not back **ignominiously**, for then

IGNOMINY

010:027   a reward of like evil: **ignominy** will cover their (faces):
010:098   from them the Chastisement of **Ignominy** in the
011:066   and from the **Ignominy** of that Day.
011:093   the Chastisement of **ignominy**, and who
023:108   into it (with **ignominy**)! and speak
025:069   and he will dwell therein in **ignominy**,-
039:040   a Chastisement of **ignominy**, and on whom
068:043   Their eyes will be cast down,-**ignominy** will cover them;
070:044   lowered in dejection,-**ignominy** covering them (all over)!

IGNORANCE
003:154   suspicions due to **Ignorance**.
004:017   who do evil in **ignorance** and repent soon afterwards;
005:050   a judgment of (the Days of) **Ignorance**?
006:035   who are swayed by **ignorance** (and impatience)!
006:054   verily, if any of you did evil in **ignorance**,
006:108   revile Allah in their **ignorance**.
009:097   and most fitted to be in **ignorance** of the command
016:119   to those who do wrong in **ignorance**, but who
023:054   confused **ignorance** for a time.
023:063   in confused **ignorance** of this; and there
033:033   like that of the former Times of **Ignorance**;
046:023   but I see that ye are a people in **ignorance**!"...
048:026   and cant of **Ignorance**,-Allah sent down

IGNORANT
002:067   from being an **ignorant** (fool)!"
002:273   the **ignorant** man thinks, because of
007:199   but turn away from the **ignorant**.
011:029   and ye I see are the **ignorant** ones!
012:033   and join the ranks of the **ignorant**."
025:063   and when the **ignorant** address them, they say,
027:055   Nay, ye are a people (grossly) **ignorant**!"
028:055   peace be to you: we seek not the **ignorant**."
039:064   O ye **ignorant** ones?"

IGNORANTS
011:046   one of the **ignorants**!"

IGNORE
006:111   But most of them **ignore** (the truth).

ILL
002:184   but if any of you is **ill**, or on a journey,
002:185   but if any one is **ill**, or on a journey,
002:196   And if any of you is **ill**,
002:286   and it suffers every **ill** that it earns.
003:153   and for (the **ill**) that had befallen you.
004:043   until after washing your whole body if ye are **ill**,
004:102   the inconvenience of rain or because ye are **ill**;
005:006   But if ye are **ill**, or on a journey, or one
009:091   There is no blame on those who are infirm, or **ill**,
010:011   the **ill** (they have earned) as they
013:031   cease to seize them for their (**ill**) deeds, or to
022:038   Verily Allah will defend (from **ill**) those who believe:
026:080   "And when I am **ill**, it is He Who cures me;
027:047   They said: "**Ill** omen do we augur from thee
027:047   He said: "Your **ill** omen is with Allah; yea, ye
034:033   be a requital for their (**ill**) Deeds.
041:049   but if **ill** touches him, he gives
042:048   exult thereat, but when some **ill** happens to him,
045:014   for Him to recompense (for good or **ill**) each People
045:021   **Ill** is the judgment that they make.
046:016   and pass by their **ill** deeds:
048:017   nor on one **ill** (if he joins not the war):
049:012   nor speak **ill** of each other behind their backs.
072:010   'And we understand not whether **ill** is intended
083:014   is the stain of the (**ill**) which they do!

ILL-CONDUCT
004:034   whose part ye fear disloyalty and **ill-conduct**,

ILL-FEELING
047:037   and He would bring out all your **ill-feeling**.

ILL-HEALTH
073:020   that there may be (some) among you in **ill-health**;

ILL-LUCK
054:019   on a Day of bitter **ill-luck**,

ILL-SEEMING
049:011   by (offensive) nicknames: **ill-seeming** is a name

ILL-TREATED
004:075   being weak, are **ill-treated** (and oppressed)?
085:008   And they **ill-treated** them for no other reason

ILLITERATES
002:078   And there are among them **illiterates**,

ILLIYIN
083:018   the Righteous is (preserved) in '**Illiyin**.
083:019   And what will explain to thee what '**Illiyin** is?

ILLNESS
012:085   until thou reach the last extremity of **illness**,
024:061   nor in one afflicted with **illness**, nor in

ILLS
040:009   "And preserve them from (all) **ills**; and any
040:009   from **ills** that Day,-on them wilt Thou have
047:002   from them their **ills** and improve their condition.
064:009   He will remove from them their **ills**, and He

ILLUMINATING
035:025   the **illuminating** Book.

ILLUSION
012:095   in thine old wandering **illusion**."

ILLUSTRATION
024:034   an **illustration** from (the story of) people who

IMAGE
020:088   before the (people) the **image** of a calf: it seemed

IMAGES
021:052   and his people, "What are these **images**, to which
034:013   he desired, (making) Arches, **Images**, Basins as

IMAGINED
021:087   he **imagined** that We had no power
028:062   whom ye **imagined** (to be such)?"
028:074   whom ye **imagined** (to be such)?"
033:010   and ye **imagined** various (vain) thoughts

IMAM
002:124   an **Imam** to the people."

IMAMS
002:124   He pleaded: "And also (**Imams**) from my offspring!"
017:071   together all human beings with their (respective) **Imams**:

IMITATE
009:030   they but **imitate** what the Unbelievers of old

IMMEDIATE
009:042   If there had been **immediate** gain (in sight),
094:007   (from thine **immediate** task), still labor hard,

IMMEDIATELY
028:078   called (**immediately**) to account for their sins.

IMMENSE
004:146   to the Believers a reward of **immense** value.

IMMOVABLE
015:019   mountains firm and **immovable**; and produced
027:061   set thereon mountains **immovable**; and made

IMMUNITY
009:001   A (declaration) of **immunity** from Allah
054:043   Or have ye an **immunity** in the Sacred Books?

IMMORTALS
021:008   ate no food, nor were they **immortals**.

IMPATIENCE
006:035   who are swayed by ignorance (and **impatience**)!

IMPATIENT
070:019   Truly man was created very **impatient**;

IMPATIENTLY
038:006 And the leaders among them go away (**impatiently**),
IMPEDIMENT
020:027 "And remove the **impediment** from my speech.
IMPIETY
005:003 by raffling with arrows: that is **impiety**.
006:121 that would be **impiety**.
025:021 and mighty is the insolence of their **impiety**!
067:021 in insolent **impiety** and flight (from the Truth).
091:012 among them was deputed (for **impiety**).
IMPIOUS
006:145 for it is an abomination,-or what is **impious**,
IMPLORE
018:029 if they **implore** relief they will be granted water like
040:007 believe in Him; and **implore** forgiveness for those
IMPLORED
008:009 Remember ye **implored** the assistance
IMPORT
002:118 before them words of similar **import**.
IMPORTANT
072:024 in (his) helper and least **important** in point
IMPORTUNATELY
002:273 they beg not **importunately** from all and sundry.
IMPOSED
022:078 and has **imposed** no difficulties on you
IMPOSTER
045:007 Woe to each sinful **imposter**.
IMPOSTORS
002:087 Some ye called **impostors**,
005:070 they called **impostors**, and some they slay.
IMPRESS
049:017 They **impress** on thee as favour that they
IMPRESSION
073:006 is a time when **impression** is more keen and speech
IMPRISON
012:035 (that it was best) to **imprison** him for a time.
IMPROVE
006:152 except to **improve** it, until he
017:034 orphan's property except to **improve** it, until he
047:002 from them their ills and **improve** their condition.
047:005 Soon will He guide them and **improve** their condition,
IMPUDENTLY
078:028 But they (**impudently**) treated Our Signs as false
IMPULSE
002:158 his own **impulse** to Good,
025:043 as taketh for his god his won passion (or **impulse**)?
IMPURE
007:157 them from what is bad (and **impure**):
008:037 Allah may separate the **impure** from the pure.
008:037 Put the **impure**, one on another, heap them
024:026 Women **impure** are for men **impure**, and men
024:026 and men **impure** are for women **impure**, and women
IMPURITY
004:043 nor in a state of ceremonial **impurity** except
005:006 If ye are in a state of ceremonial **impurity**, bathe
IMRAN
003:033 and the family of '**Imran** above all people,
003:035 Behold! wife of '**Imran** said: "O my Lord!
066:012 And Mary the daughter of '**Imran**, who guarded

IN (See Appendix)
INACTIVE
009:046 were told, "Sit ye among those who sit (**inactive**)."
009:083 for ye preferred to sit **inactive** on the
INCITE
019:083 to **incite** them with fury?
INCITED
033:014 and they had been **incited** to sedition.
INCITEMENT
041:036 And if (at any time) an **incitement** to discord
INCITES
012:053 certainly **incites** evil, unless my Lord do bestow
INCLINATION
005:003 with no **inclination** to transgression,
011:012 mayest (feel the **inclination**) to give up a part of what
INCLINE
006:113 the hearts of those **incline**, who have
008:061 do thou (also) **incline** towards peace, and trust
008:061 But if the enemy **incline** towards peace, do thou
011:113 And **incline** not to those who do wrong, or the
INCLINED
007:176 but he **inclined** to the earth, and followed
012:033 I should feel **inclined** towards them and join the
017:074 thou wouldst nearly have **inclined** to them a little.
066:004 your hearts are indeed so **inclined**; but if ye back up each
INCLUDING
008:060 to the upmost of your power, **including** steeds of war,
038:037 As also the Satans, (**including**) every kind
INCONVENIENCE
004:102 the **inconvenience** of rain or because ye are ill;
INCREASE
002:058 forgive you your faults and **increase**
002:261 manifold **increase** to whom He pleaseth:
002:265 but makes it yield a double **increase** of harvest,
002:276 but will give **increase** for deeds of charity:
007:086 and He gave you **increase**.
007:161 We shall **increase** (the portion of)
017:006 We gave you **increase** in resources
017:097 We shall **increase** for them the fierceness
019:076 "And Allah doth **increase** in guidance those who
020:114 "O my Lord! **increase** me in knowledge."
030:039 you give in ususry for **increase** through the property
030:039 seeking the Countenance of Allah, (will **increase**):
030:039 will have no **increase** with Allah:
041:039 it is stirred to life and yields **increase**.
042:020 of the Hereafter, We give **increase** in his tilth;
042:023 We shall give Him an **increase** of good
042:026 gives them **increase** of His bounty:
057:011 For (Allah) will **increase** it manifold to his credit,
071:012 "'Give you **increase** in wealth and sons;
071:021 no **Increase** but only Loss.
071:024 and grant Thou no **increase** to the wrong-doers
071:028 wrong-doers grant Thou no **increase** but in Perdition!
074:006 Nor expect, in giving, any **increase** (for thyself)!
074:031 and the Believers may **increase** in Faith,-and that
078:030 for no **increase** shall We grant you, except in
092:018 for **increase** in self-purification,
INCREASED
002:010 and Allah has **increased** their disease,
003:173 so fear them": but it only **increased** their Faith:
009:124 "Which of you has had his faith **increased** by it?"

INCREASED (continued)

009:124 their faith is **increased**, and they do rejoice.
035:042 it has only **increased** their aversion.
057:018 it shall be **increased** manifold (to their credit),
072:006 the Jinns, but they **increased** them into further

INCREASES

017:041 but it only **increases** their flight (from the Truth)!
017:060 but it only **increases** their inordinate
017:109 and it **increases** their (earnest) humility.
025:060 commandest us?" and it **increases** them in aversion.
047:017 He **increases** their Guidance, and bestows on them
071:006 "But my call only **increases** (their) flight

INCREASETH

005:064 from Allah **increaseth** in most of them their
005:068 that **increaseth** in most of them their

INCREASING

004:137 and go on **increasing** in Unbelief, Allah will

INCUMBENT

030:047 and it was a duty **incumbent** upon Us to aid

INCUR

002:007 great is the chastisement they (**incur**).
002:010 and grievous is the chastisement they (**incur**),

INCURRED

004:155 (They have **incurred** divine displeasure):
005:060 Those who **incurred** the curse of Allah

INCURS

002:282 Let him who **incurs** the liability dictate,

INDECENCIES

042:037 Those who avoid the greater sins and **indecencies** and,

INDECENCY

004:025 if they commit **indecency** their punishment is
007:028 When they commit an **indecency**, they say: "We found
003:135 an act of **indecency** or wronged their own souls.

INDECENT

006:151 come not nigh to **indecent** deeds, whether
007:028 say: "Nay Allah never commands what is **Indecent**:
007:033 that my Lord hath indeed forbidden are: **indecent** deeds,
012:024 (all) evil and **indecent** deeds:
016:090 and He forbids all **indecent** deeds, and evil
017:032 for it is an **indecent** (deed) and an way.
024:021 he will (but) command what is **indecent** and wrong:
027:054 "Do ye do what is **indecent** though ye see
053:032 Those who avoid great sins and **indecent** deeds,

INDEED

002:045 it is **indeed** hard,
002:054 "O my people! Ye have **indeed** wronged yourselves
002:070 we wish **indeed** for guidance if Allah wills."
002:091 if ye did **indeed** believe?"
002:093 Say: "Vile **indeed** are the behests
002:096 Thou wilt **indeed** find them,
002:118 We have **indeed** made clear the Signs
002:126 an evil destination (**indeed**)!"
002:137 they are **indeed** on the right path;
002:143 **Indeed** it was (a change) momentous,
002:145 then wert thou **indeed** (clearly) in the wrong.
002:145 nor **indeed** will they follow
002:149 that is **indeed** the truth from thy Lord.
002:164 (here) **indeed** are Signs
002:186 I am **indeed** close (to them):
002:206 an evil bed **indeed** (to lie on)!
002:220 He is **indeed** Exalted in Power, Wise."
002:229 If ye (judges) do **indeed** fear that they would be

INDEED (continued)

002:248 Symbol for you if ye **indeed** have faith."
002:251 the earth would **indeed** be full of mischief,
002:269 granted receiveth **indeed** a benefit overflowing;
002:278 if ye are **indeed** believers.
003:012 an evil bed **indeed** (to lie on)!
003:016 "Our Lord! we have **indeed** believed:
003:062 and Allah-He is **indeed** the Exalted in Power,
003:094 they are **indeed** unjust wrong-doers.
003:100 they would (**indeed**) render you apostates
003:128 for they are **indeed** wrong-doers.
003:143 Ye did **indeed** wish for Death before ye
003:152 Allah did **indeed** fulfil His promise to you
003:154 Say thou: "**Indeed**, this affair is wholly Allah's."
003:186 then that **indeed** is a matter of great Resolution.
003:188 For them is a Chastisement grievous **indeed**.
003:190 there are **indeed** Signs for men of understanding,
004:002 For this is **indeed** a great sin.
004:018 and he says, "Now have I repented **indeed**";
004:022 an abominable custom **indeed**.
004:048 a sin most heinous **indeed**.
004:064 found Allah **indeed** Oft-Returning, Most Merciful.
004:076 feeble **indeed** is the cunning of Satan
004:153 **indeed** they asked Moses for an even greater (miracle),
005:003 Allah is **indeed** Oft-Forgiving, Most Merciful.
005:017 They disbelieved **indeed** those that say that Allah
005:057 but fear ye Allah, if ye have Faith (**indeed**).
005:062 Evil **indeed** are the things that they do.
005:063 Evil **indeed** are their works.
005:065 We should **indeed** have blotted out their
005:079 evil **indeed** were the deeds which they did.
005:080 Evil **indeed** are (the works) which their souls
005:113 and to know that thou hast **indeed** told us
005:116 Thou wouldst **indeed** have known it.
006:015 **indeed** have fear of the Chastisement of a Mighty Day,
006:028 for they are **indeed** liars.
006:031 Lost **indeed** are they who treat it as a falsehood
006:031 and evil **indeed** are the burdens that they bear!
006:033 We know **indeed** the grief which their words
006:078 "O my people! I am **indeed** free from your (guilt)
006:121 ye would **indeed** be Pagans.
006:140 They have **indeed** gone astray and heeded
006:149 He could **indeed** have guided you all."
006:165 yet He is **indeed** Oft-Forgiving, Most Merciful.
007:005 "**Indeed** we did wrong."
007:033 my Lord hath **indeed** forbidden are:
007:043 **indeed** it was the truth that the Messengers
007:044 "We have **indeed** found the promises
007:053 did **indeed** bring true (tidings).
007:064 they were **indeed** a blind people!
007:075 They said: "We do **indeed** believe in the
007:075 "Know ye **indeed** that Salih is a messenger
007:079 saying: "O my people! I **indeed** convey to you
007:081 ye are **indeed** a people transgressing beyond bounds."
007:082 these are **indeed** men who want
007:089 "We should **indeed** forge a lie against Allah,
007:093 saying: "O my people! I did **indeed** convey to
007:096 We should **indeed** have opened out to them
007:101 there came **indeed** to them their Messengers
007:106 (Pharaoh) said: "If **indeed** thou hast
007:109 "This is **indeed** a sorcerer well-versed.
007:149 we shall **indeed** be among the Losers.
007:150 The people did **indeed** reckon me as naught,

INDEED (continued)

007:152 will **indeed** be overwhelmed with wrath
007:191 Do they **indeed** ascribe to Him as partners
007:194 if ye are (**indeed**) truthful!
007:197 and **indeed** to help themselves."
008:016 and his abode is Hell, an evil refuse (**indeed**)!
008:023 He would **indeed** have made them listen:
008:032 if this is **indeed** the truth from Thee, rain down
009:009 evil **indeed** are the deeds thy have done.
009:034 O ye who believe! There are **indeed** many among
009:040 (it is no matter): for Allah did **indeed** help him,
009:042 They would **indeed** swear by Allah, "If we only
009:048 **Indeed** they had plotted sedition before, and upset
009:049 And **indeed** Hell surrounds the Unbelievers
009:050 they say, "We took **indeed** our precautions
009:053 for ye are **indeed** a people rebellious and wicked."
009:056 They swear by Allah that they are **indeed** of you;
009:073 Their abode is hell, an evil refuge **indeed**.
009:074 nothing (evil), but **indeed** they uttered blasphemy,
009:099 Aye, **indeed** they bring them nearer (to Him):
009:107 They will **indeed** swear that their intention
010:002 "This is **indeed** a evident sorcerer!"
010:018 Say: "Do ye **indeed** inform Allah of something
010:059 Say: "Hath Allah **indeed** permitted you, or do
010:064 This is **indeed** the supreme Triumph.
010:076 they said: "This is **indeed** evident sorcery!"
010:088 "Our Lord Thou hast **indeed** bestowed on Pharaoh and
010:094 the Truth hath **indeed** come to thee from thy Lord:
011:007 "Ye shall **indeed** be raised up after death,
011:031 I should, if I did, **indeed** be a wrong-doer."
011:047 I should **indeed** be among the losers!"
011:072 That would **indeed** be a wonderful thing!"
011:073 For He is **indeed** worthy of all praise,
011:079 **indeed** thou knowest quite well what we want!"
011:090 for my Lord is **indeed** Full of mercy
011:098 but woeful **indeed** will be the place
011:102 grievous, **indeed**, and severe is His chastisement.
012:011 seeing we are **indeed** his sincere well-wishers?
012:051 he is **indeed** of those who are (ever) true
012:061 win him from his father: **indeed** we shall do it."
012:063 and we will **indeed** take every care of him."
012:079 **indeed** (if we did so), we should be acting wrongfully.
012:082 and (you will find) we are **indeed** telling the truth."
012:083 For He is **indeed** full of knowledge and wisdom."
012:090 They said: "Art thou **indeed**, Joseph?" He said
012:090 Allah has **indeed** been gracious
012:091 They said: "By Allah! **indeed** has Allah preferred
012:094 their father said: "I do **indeed** scent the presence
012:098 for He is **indeed** Oft-Forgiving, Merciful."
012:100 He was **indeed** good to me when He took
012:101 "O my Lord! Thou hast **indeed** bestowed on me
013:005 shall we **indeed** then be in a creation renewed?"
014:007 truly My punishment is terrible **indeed**."
014:012 **Indeed** He has guided us to the Ways
014:036 "O my Lord! they have **indeed** led astray
014:036 but thou art **indeed** Oft-Forgiving, Most Merciful.
014:046 Mighty **indeed** were the plots which they made,
015:049 I am **indeed** the Oft-Forgiving, Most Merciful;
015:050 will be **indeed** the most grievous Chastisement.
015:089 And say: "I am **indeed** he that warneth openly
015:097 We do **indeed** know how thy heart is distressed
016:007 for your Lord is **indeed** Most Kind, Most Merciful.
016:027 "This Day, **indeed**, are the Unbelievers covered with

INDEED (continued)

016:029 Thus evil **indeed** is the abode
016:030 excellent **indeed** is the Home of the righteous,-
016:047 for thy Lord is **indeed** full of kindness and mercy.
016:086 back their word at them (and say): "**Indeed** ye are liars!"
016:091 **indeed** ye have made Allah your surety;
016:103 We know **indeed** that they say, "It is a man that teaches
016:120 Abraham was **indeed** a model, devoutly obedient
016:126 that is **indeed** the best (course) for those
017:010 a Chastisement grievous (**indeed**).
017:087 for His Bounty is to thee (**indeed**) great.
017:101 "O Moses! I consider thee, **indeed**, to have
017:102 and I consider thee, **indeed**, O Pharaoh,
018:014 if we did; we should **indeed** have uttered
018:063 I did **indeed** forget (about) the Fish:
019:004 Praying: "O my Lord! infirm **indeed** are my bones,
019:009 I did **indeed** create thee before, when thou
019:030 He said: "I am **indeed** a servant of Allah: He hath
019:046 I will **indeed** stone thee: now get
019:089 **Indeed** ye have put forth a thing most monstrous!
020:024 for he had **indeed** transgressed all bounds."
020:037 "And **indeed** We conferred a favour on thee
020:043 for he has **indeed** transgressed all bounds;
020:047 with a Sign, **indeed**, have we come from thy Lord!
020:068 hast **indeed** the upper hand:
020:081 My Wrath do perish **indeed**!
020:111 The Sustainer, helpless **indeed** will be the man
021:014 we were **indeed** wrong-doers!"
021:046 we did wrong **indeed**!"
021:054 He said, "**Indeed** ye have been in manifest error-
021:059 he must **indeed** be one of the unjust one.
021:087 Glory to Thee: I was **indeed** wrong!"
021:097 "Ah! woe to us! we were **indeed** heedless of this;
022:011 that is **indeed** the manifest loss,
022:012 far **indeed** (from the Way)!
022:013 evil, **indeed**, is the patron, and evil the companion
022:070 **Indeed** it is all in a record,
023:001 Successful **indeed** are the Believers,-
023:090 but they **indeed** are liars.
023:107 then shall we be wrong-doers **indeed**!"
023:111 they are **indeed** the ones that have achieved Bliss."
024:010 Full of Wisdom,-(ye would be ruined **indeed**).
024:020 (ye would be ruined **indeed**).
024:046 We have **indeed** sent down Signs that make
024:057 is the Fire,-and it is **indeed** an evil refuge!
025:021 **Indeed** they have an arrogant
025:040 And the (Unbelievers) must **indeed** have passed
025:042 "He **indeed** would well-nigh have misled us
025:065 for its Wrath is **indeed** an affliction grievous,-
025:066 "Evil **indeed** is it as an abode, and as
025:077 but ye have **indeed** rejected (Him), and soon
026:006 They have **indeed** rejected (the Message): so they
026:034 "This is **indeed** a sorcerer well-versed:
026:186 like us, and **indeed** we think thou art a liar!
026:212 **Indeed** they are banished from hearing it.
027:016 this is **indeed** Grace manifest (from Allah)."
027:037 in disgrace, and they will feel humbled (**indeed**)."
027:039 **indeed** I have full strength for the purpose,
027:044 I have **indeed** wronged my soul: I do
027:056 these are **indeed** men who want to be clean and pure!"
028:004 for he was **indeed** an evil-doer.
028:016 I have **indeed** wronged by soul!
028:027 wilt find me, **indeed**, if Allah wills, one of the righteous."

INDEED (continued)

028:053   **indeed** we have been Muslims (bowing to Allah's Will)
028:082   "Ah! It is **indeed** Allah Who enlarges
029:029   "Do ye **indeed** approach men, and cut
029:031   "We are **indeed** going to destroy the people
029:048   **indeed**, would the talkers of vanities have doubt.
029:050   and I am **indeed** a clear Warner."
029:050   Say: "The Signs are **indeed** with Allah: and I
029:061   If **indeed** thou ask them who has created
029:063   And if **indeed** thou ask them who it is that sends
029:064   that is life **indeed**, if they but knew.
030:047   We did **indeed** send, before thee, messengers to
030:056   "**Indeed** ye did tarry, within Allah's Decree,
031:013   for false worship is **indeed** the highest
031:022   has grasped **indeed** the firmest hand-hold:
032:010   shall we **indeed** be in a Creation renewed?"
032:012   work righteousness: for we do **indeed** (now) believe."
032:021   And **indeed** We will make them taste of the
032:023   We did **indeed** aforetime give the Book to Moses:
033:021   Ye have **indeed** in the Messenger of Allah
033:036   and His Messenger, he is **indeed** on a clearly
033:072   We did **indeed** offer the Trust to the Heavens
033:072   he was **indeed** unjust and foolish;-
034:054   for they were **indeed** in suspicious
035:034   for Our Lord is **indeed** Oft-Forgiving ready to
036:003   Thou art **indeed** one of the messengers,
036:018   a grievous punishment **indeed** will be inflicted on you
036:024   "I would **indeed**, then be in manifest Error.
036:081   Yea, **indeed**! for He is the Creator Supreme,
037:006   We have **indeed** decked the lower heaven
037:031   that we shall **indeed** (have to) taste (the punishment
037:038   Ye shall **indeed** taste of the Grievous Chastisement;-
037:053   and bones, shall we **indeed** receive rewards
037:080   Thus **indeed** do We reward those who do right.
037:089   And he said, "I am **indeed** sick (at heart)!"
037:105   thus **indeed** do We reward those who
037:110   Thus **indeed** do We reward those who do right.
037:121   Thus **indeed** do We reward those who do right.
037:131   Thus **indeed** do We reward those who do right.
037:176   Do they wish (**indeed**) to hurry on Our Punishment?
038:025   he enjoyed, **indeed**, a Near Approach to Us, and a
038:026   O David! We did **indeed** make thee a vicegerent
038:040   And he enjoyed, **indeed**, a Near Approach to Us,
038:056   an evil bed (**indeed**, to lie on)!-
039:013   my Lord, **indeed** have fear of the Chastisement
039:015   Ah! that is **indeed** the (real and) evident Loss!"
039:038   If **indeed** thou ask them who it is that created
040:009   Thou have bestowed Mercy **indeed**: and that
040:027   Moses said: "I have **indeed** called upon my Lord
040:028   when he has **indeed** come to you with Clear (Signs)
041:041   and **indeed** it is a Book of exalted power.
041:054   Ah **indeed**! are they in doubt concerning the Meeting
041:054   Ah **indeed**! it is He that doth encompass all things!
042:022   That will **indeed** be the magnificent
042:027   they would **indeed** transgress beyond all bounds
042:041   But **indeed** if any do help and defend themselves
042:043   But **indeed** if any show patience and forgive,
042:045   will say: "Those are **indeed** in loss who lose
043:026   and his people: "I do **indeed** clear myself of what
043:038   Ah! Evil is the companion (**indeed**)!
043:044   The (Qur'an) is **indeed** a Reminder for thee
043:080   **Indeed** (We do), and Our Messengers are by them,
044:015   We shall **indeed** remove the Chastisement for a

INDEED (continued)

044:016   We will **indeed** (then) exact Retribution!
044:022   "These are **indeed** a people given to sin."
045:013   are Signs **indeed** for those who reflect.
049:007   such **indeed** are those who walk in righteousness;-
049:011   desist are (**indeed**) doing wrong.
051:047   and We **indeed** have vast power.
052:007   will **indeed** come to pass;-
053:013   For **indeed** he saw him at a second descent,
053:022   Behold, such would be **indeed** a division
054:017   And We have **indeed** made the Qur'an easy to
054:022   But We have **indeed** made the Qur'an easy to
054:032   And We have **indeed** made the Qur'an easy to
054:040   And We have **indeed** made the Qur'an easy to
056:047   and bones, shall we then **indeed** be raised up again?-
056:055   "**Indeed** ye shall drink like diseased camels
056:066   (Saying), "We are **indeed** left with debts
056:067   "**Indeed** we are deprived."
056:076   And that is **indeed** a mighty adjuration if ye
056:077   That this is **indeed** a Qur'an most honourable,
057:008   your Lord and has **indeed** taken your Convenant,
057:012   This is **indeed** the highest Triumph.
058:001   Allah has **indeed** heard (and accepted)
058:015   severe Chastisement: evil **indeed** are their deeds.
058:018   No, **indeed**! they are but liars!
059:008   such are **indeed** the truthful;-
059:010   Our Lord! Thou art **indeed** Full of Kindness,
059:011   But Allah is witness that they are **indeed** liars.
060:006   There was **indeed** in them an excellent example
061:012   that is **indeed** the supreme Triumph.
063:001   thou art **indeed** the Messenger of Allah."
063:001   that thou art **indeed** His Messenger.
063:001   the Hypocrites are **indeed** liars.
065:010   sent down to you a Message,-
065:011   Allah has **indeed** granted for them a most
066:004   to Allah, your hearts are **indeed** so inclined;
066:009   Their abode is Hell,-an evil refuge (**indeed**).
067:009   They will say: "Yes **indeed**: a Warner
067:018   But **indeed** men before them rejected (My warning):
068:027   "**Indeed** we are deprived (of the fruits of our labour)!"
068:031   We have **indeed** transgressed!
068:049   he would **indeed** have been cast off on the
070:006   They see the (Day) **indeed** as a far-off (event):
072:009   'We used, **indeed**, to sit there in (hidden)
077:032   "**Indeed** it throws about sparks (huge) as Forts,
079:010   They say (now): "What! shall we **indeed** be returned
079:017   for he has **indeed** transgressed all bounds:
080:011   For it is **indeed** a Message of remembrance.
092:007   We will **indeed** make smooth for him
092:010   We will **indeed** make smooth for him
095:004   We have **indeed** created man in the best of molds,
097:001   We have **indeed** revealed this (Message)

INDEPENDENCE

056:087   if ye are true (in your claim of **Independence**)?

INDEPENDENT

093:008   and made thee **independent**.

INDICATED

033:038   has **indicated** to him as a duty.

INDIFFERENT

080:037   to make him **indifferent** to the others.

INDIGENT

002:184   the feeding of one that is **indigent**.

INDIGENT (continued)

003:181   "Truly, Allah is **indigent** and we are rich!"
005:089   for expiation, feed then **indigent** persons,
005:095   the feeding of the **indigent**;
058:004   he should feed sixty **indigent** ones.
059:008   (Some part is due) to the **indigent** Muhajirs,
068:024   "Let not a single **indigent** person break in upon
069:034   the feeding of the **indigent**!
074:044   "Nor were we of those who fed the **indigent**;
076:008   the **indigent**, the orphan, and the captive,-
090:016   Or to the **indigent** (down) in the dust.
107:003   And encourages not the feeding of the **indigent**.

INDIGNANT

009:058   behold! they are **indignant**!

INDIGNATION

009:015   And still the **indignation** of their heart.

INDIRECT

002:235   an **indirect** offer of betrothal or hold it

INDISCREET

024:023   who slander chaste, **indiscreet** and believing women are

INDIVIDUAL

031:028   is in no wise but as an **individual** soul:
052:021   (Yet) is each **individual** in pledge for his deeds.

INDULGE

009:069   and ye **indulge** in idle talk as they did.

INDULGED

007:084   those who **indulged** in sin and crime!
056:045   For that they were wont to be **indulged**,
102:008   about the joy (ye **indulged** in)!

INEVITABLE

016:001   (**Inevitable**) cometh (to pass) the Command of Allah:
025:077   and soon will come the **inevitable** (punishment)!"
056:001   When the Event **Inevitable** cometh to pass,

INEVITABLY

016:036   became **inevitably** (established).
038:014   came justly and **inevitably** (on them).

INEXHAUSTIBLE

015:021   (sources and) treasures (**inexhaustible**) are with

INFAMY

003:127   of the Unbelievers or expose them to **infamy**,

INFANT

081:008   When the female (**infant**), Buried alive,

INFANTRY

017:064   assaults on them with thy cavalry and thy **infantry**;

INFIDELITY

002:109   back to **infidelity** after ye have believed,
009:017   their own souls to **infidelity**.
009:023   your brothers if they love **infidelity** above Faith:
009:107   by way of mischief and **infidelity**-to disunite

INFINITE

036:081   of skill and knowledge (**infinite**)!

INFIRM

009:091   There is no blame on those who are **infirm**, or ill,
019:004   Praying: "O my Lord! **infirm** indeed are my bones,

INFLICT

011:064   (free) earth, and **inflict** no harm on her,
089:025   such as none (else) can **inflict**,

INFLICTED

005:115   such as I have not **inflicted** on anyone
023:076   We **inflicted** Punishment on them, but they
024:063   or a grievous Chastisement be **inflicted** on them.

INFLICTED (continued)

036:018   indeed will be **inflicted** on you by us."
042:039   oppressive wrong is **inflicted** on them,
044:031   **Inflicted** by Pharaoh, for he was arrogant (even)
075:025   to be **inflicted** on them;

INFLUENCE

009:086   those with wealth and **influence** among them

INFORM

005:105   it is He that will **inform** you of all that ye do.
010:018   Say: "Do ye indeed **inform** Allah of something
013:033   will **inform** Him of something He knoweth not
018:019   and let him not **inform** anyone about you.
026:221   Shall I **inform** you, (O people!), on whom
035:014   And none, (O man!) can **inform** you like Him

INFORMATION

027:007   soon will I bring you from there some **information**,
028:029   I hope to bring from thee some **information**,

INFORMED

009:094   Allah hath already **informed** us of the true state
010:053   They seek to be **informed** by thee: "Is that true?"

INFRINGED

002:059   for that they **infringed** (Our command) repeatedly.

INGRATE

076:024   or the **ingrate** among them.

INGRATITUDE

011:009   and (falls into) **ingratitude**,
014:007   but if ye show **ingratitude**, truly My punishment
014:008   And Moses said: "If ye show **ingratitude**, ye and
014:028   With **ingratitude** and caused their people to descend
014:034   up to injustice and **ingratitude**.
016:055   To show their **ingratitude** for the favours
017:069   to drown you because of your **ingratitude**, so that
017:089   men refuse (to receive it) except with **ingratitude**!
017:099   (to receive it) except with **ingratitude**.
018:080   and **ingratitude** (to Allah).
025:050   (to aught) but (rank) **ingratitude**.
030:034   (As if) to show their **ingratitude** for the
039:007   but He liketh not **ingratitude** from His servants:

INHABITANT

090:002   And thou art an **inhabitant** of this City;-

INHABITANTS

010:027   they are **Inhabitants** of the Fire: they will
015:067   The **inhabitants** of the City came in (mad)
018:077   when they came to the **inhabitants** of a town,

INHERIT

004:019   forbidden to **inherit** women against their will.
007:100   To those who **inherit** the earth in succession
010:073   and We made them **inherit** (the earth), while We
019:006   and **inherit** the posterity of Jacob; and make
019:006   "(One that) will (truly) **inherit** me,
019:040   It is We Who will **inherit** the earth, and all
021:105   shall **inherit** the earth."
023:011   Who will **inherit** Paradise: they will
044:028   And We made other people **inherit** (those things)!

INHERITANCE

004:011   as regards your children's (**inheritance**):
004:011   a sixth share of the **inheritance** to each,
004:011   their share is two-thirds of the **inheritance**;
004:012   whose **inheritance** is in question, has left
004:176   she shall have half the **inheritance**:
004:176   of the **inheritance** (between them): if there

INHERITANCE (continued)

004:176   her brother takes her **inheritance**: if there
019:063   as an **inheritance** to those of Our Servants
024:055   grant them in the land, **inheritance** (of power),
035:032   for **inheritance** to such of Our servants as We
040:053   in **inheritance** to the Children of Israel,-
089:019   And ye devour **inheritance**-all with greed,

INHERITED

007:169   they **inherited** the Book, but they
042:014   who have **inherited** the Book after them are in

INHERITORS

006:165   the **inheritors** of the earth:
007:043   Ye have been made its **inheritors**, for your
007:069   He made you **inheritors** after the people
007:074   how He made you **inheritors** after the 'Ad people
007:129   and make you **inheritors** in the earth; that so
007:137   **inheritors** of lands in both East and West,-
015:023   remain **Inheritors** (after all else passes away).
021:089   the best of **inheritors**."
026:059   the Children of Israel **inheritors** of such things.
026:085   "Make me one of the **inheritors** of the
027:062   and makes you (mankind) **inheritors** of the earth?
035:039   you **inheritors** in the earth: so, he who

INIQUITIES

003:193   blot out from us our **iniquities**, and take
003:195   verily, I will blot out from them their **iniquities**,
005:065   blotted out their **iniquities** and admitted
005:079   the **iniquities** which they committed: evil indeed
016:113   seized them even in the midst of their **iniquities**.
018:059   when they committed **iniquities**; but We
021:011   We utterly destroyed because of their **iniquities**,

INIQUITOUS

058:002   (both) **iniquitous** and false:

INIQUITY

003:178   that they may grow in their **iniquity**:
004:160   For the **iniquity** of the Jews We made
020:111   the man that carries **iniquity** (on his back).
025:004   put forward an **iniquity** and a falsehood.
026:010   "Go to the people of **iniquity**,-
027:054   though ye see (its **iniquity**)?
028:059   members practice **iniquity**.
058:008   for **iniquity** and hostility, and disobedience
058:009   do it not for **iniquity** and hostility, and disobedience
080:042   the Doers of **Iniquity**.

INJURE

002:231   but do not take them back to **injure** them,

INJURES

039:041   but he that strays **injures** his own soul.

INJURING

044:020   my Lord and your Lord, against your **injuring** me.

INJURY

002:262   with reminders of their generosity or with **injury**,
002:263   than charity followed by **injury**.
002:264   your generosity or by **injury**-like those
015:047   any lurking sense of **injury**:
022:060   to no greater extent than the **injury** he received,
042:040   The recompense for an **injury** is an **injury** equal thereto
059:010   rancor (or sense of **injury**) against those

INJUSTICE

003:025   without (favour or) **injustice**?
003:108   no **injustice** to any of His creatures.
003:182   for Allah never do **injustice** those who serve Him."

INJUSTICE (continued)

004:003   to prevent you from doing **injustice**.
004:030   If any do that in rancor and **injustice**, soon
004:124   and not the least **injustice** will be done to them.
014:034   up to **injustice** and ingratitude.
018:049   thy Lord treat with **injustice**.
028:028   let there be no **injustice** to me.
038:022   and treat us not with **injustice**, but guide us to the
040:017   no **injustice** will there be that Day, for Allah
040:031   but Allah never wishes **injustice** to His Servants.
046:019   and no **injustice** will be done to them.
050:029   and I do not the least **injustice** to My Servants."
072:013   or of any **injustice**.

INK

018:109   Say: "If the ocean were **ink** (wherewith to write
031:027   and the Ocean (were **ink**), with seven

INMOST

011:005   knoweth well the (**inmost** secrets) of the hearts.
017:005   very **inmost** parts of your homes;

INNER

047:026   their (**inner**) secrets.
049:004   from without the **Inner** Apartments-most of
055:054   whose **inner** linings will be of rich brocade:

INNOCENT

004:112   and throws it on to one that is **innocent**,
006:019   And I truly am **innocent** of (your blasphemy of)
018:074   "Hast thou slain an **innocent** person who had
024:026   these are **innocent** of all what people say:

INNOVATION

046:009   Say: "I am not an **innovation** among the messengers,

INORDINATE

017:060   their **inordinate** transgression!
044:031   arrogant (even) among **inordinate** transgressors.
089:020   And ye love wealth with **inordinate** love!
091:011   (their prophet) through their **inordinate** wrong-doing.

INORDINATELY

022:060   and is again set upon **inordinately**.

INSCRIBED

006:012   He hath **inscribed** for Himself (the rule of) Mercy.
006:054   your Lord hath **inscribed** for Himself (the rule of) Mercy:
006:059   but is (**inscribed**) in a Record Clear
009:121   but the deed is **inscribed** to their credit;
052:002   By a Book **Inscribed**
083:009   (There is) a Register (fully) **inscribed**.
083:020   (There is) a Register (fully) **inscribed**.
085:022   (**Inscribed**) in a Tablet Preserved!

INSCRIPTION

018:009   and of the **Inscription** were wonders among

INSERT

069:032   "Further, **insert** him in a chain, whereof the

INSIDE

037:144   He would certainly have remained **inside** the Fish till

INSIDES

044:045   Like molten brass; it will boil in their **insides**,
056:053   "Then will ye fill your **insides** therewith,

INSIGHT

028:043   **Insight** to men and Guidance and Mercy, that they
050:008   For an **insight** and Reminder to every

INSOLENCE

007:166   When in their **insolence** they transgressed

INSOLENCE (continued)

010:023 O mankind! your **insolence** is against your own
010:090 hosts followed them in **insolence** and spite.
017:037 Nor walk on the earth with **insolence**: for thou
020:045 with **insolence** against us,
025:021 and mighty is the **insolence** of their impiety!
029:039 but they behaved with **insolence** on the earth;
031:018 Nor walk in **insolence** through the earth:
033:048 their **insolence** but put thy trust in Allah.

INSOLENT

002:090 in **insolent** envy that Allah of His grace
028:039 And he was arrogant and **insolent** in the land,
040:075 the Truth, and that ye were wont to be **insolent**.
042:014 being **insolent** to one another.
045:017 into schisms, though **insolent** envy among
053:052 and most **insolent** transgressors,
054:025 Nay, he is a liar an **insolent** one!
054:026 which is the liar the **insolent** one!
067:021 in **insolent** impiety and flight (from the Truth).

INSOLENTLY

007:077 and **insolently** defied the order of
008:047 from their homes **insolently** and to
010:023 behold! they transgress **insolently** through the
023:046 but these behaved **insolently**: they were
028:076 but he acted **insolently** towards them:
042:042 and **insolently** transgress beyond bounds
051:044 But they **insolently** defied the command of their
065:008 How many populations that **insolently** opposed the

INSPIRATION

003:044 (O Prophet!) by **inspiration**:
004:163 We have sent thee **inspiration**, as We sent it to Noah
004:163 We sent **inspiration** to Abraham.
006:019 revealed to me by **inspiration** that I may
006:093 or saith, "I have received **inspiration**,"
006:106 by **inspiration** from thy Lord: there is
006:145 received by me by **inspiration** any (meat)
007:160 We directed Moses by **inspiration**, when his
010:002 that We have set Our **inspiration** to a man
010:109 Follow thou the **inspiration** sent unto thee, and be
011:037 Our eyes and Our **inspiration**, and address Me
012:102 which We by **inspiration** unto thee:
013:030 We send down unto thee by **inspiration**; yet do
016:002 with **inspiration** of His Command, to such
016:043 to whom We granted **inspiration**:
017:086 We have sent thee by **inspiration**: then wouldst
018:110 (but) the **inspiration** has come to me, that your
020:013 then to the **inspiration** (given to thee).
020:038 by **inspiration**, the message:
020:077 We sent an **inspiration** to Moses: "Travel by
021:007 to whom We granted **inspiration**: if ye
021:025 before thee without this **inspiration** sent by
021:108 by **inspiration** is that your God is one God:
026:052 By **inspiration** We told Moses: "Travel by
026:063 Then We told Moses by **inspiration**: "Strike the
028:007 So We sent this **inspiration** to the mother of Moses:
028:045 Who send messengers (with **inspiration**).
029:045 by **inspiration** to thee, and establish
033:002 to thee by **inspiration** from thy Lord:
034:050 it is because of the **inspiration** of my
040:015 the spirit (of **inspiration**) to any of His servants
041:006 it is revealed to me by **inspiration**, that your
042:003 Thus doth (He) send **Inspiration** to thee
042:007 Thus have We sent by **inspiration** to thee

INSPIRATION (continued)

042:013 the which We have sent by **inspiration** to thee-
042:051 that Allah should speak to him except by **inspiration**,
042:052 by Our command, sent **inspiration** to thee:
046:009 to me by **inspiration**; I am
053:004 It is no less than **inspiration** sent down to him:
053:010 So did (Allah) convey the **inspiration** to His
091:008 And its **inspiration** as to its wrong and its right;
099:005 For that thy Lord will have given her **inspiration**.

INSPIRE

006:121 But the satans ever **inspire** their friends
012:109 did **inspire**,-(men) from the people of the towns.

INSPIRED

005:111 "And behold! I **inspired** the Disciples to have
008:012 Remember the Lord **inspired** the angels
010:087 We **inspired** Moses and his brother with this
012:030 her slave truly hath he **inspired** her with violent
014:013 But their Lord **inspired** (this Message) to them:
021:073 and We **inspired** them to do good deeds,
021:079 To Solomon We **inspired** the (right)
023:027 So We **inspired** him (with this message);
058:010 Secret counsels are only (**inspired**) by Satan,

INSPIRING

006:112 **inspiring** each other with flowery discourses

INSTANCE

006:110 refused to believe in this in the first **instance**:

INSTEAD

004:090 and (**instead**) send you (guarantees of) peace,
017:083 his side (**instead** of coming to Us), and when
019:082 **Instead**, they shall reject their worship,
020:079 Pharaoh led his people astray **instead** of leading them
041:051 on his side (**instead** of coming to Us); and when

INSTIGATED

047:025 Satan has **instigated** them and buoyed

INSTILL

008:012 I will **instill** terror into the hearts of the Unbelievers:

INSTITUTED

005:103 not Allah Who **instituted** (superstitions like those of)

INSTRUCT

002:129 and **instruct** them in Scripture and Wisdom,
003:080 Nor would he **instruct** you to take angels
004:079 sent thee as a Messenger to (**instruct**) mankind.
004:127 Say: Allah doth **instruct** you about them:
062:002 and to **instruct** them in the Book and Wisdom,-

INSTRUCTED

036:069 We have not **instructed** the (Prophet) in Poetry,

INSTRUCTING

002:151 and **instructing** you in Scripture and Wisdom,
003:164 and **instructing** them in Scripture and Wisdom,
039:041 in Truth, for (**instructing**) mankind.

INSTRUCTION

002:231 the Book and Wisdom, for your **instruction**.
002:232 This **instruction** is for all amongst you,
003:138 a guidance and **instruction** to those who fear Allah!
004:127 They ask thy **instruction** concerning the Women.
012:068 For he was, by Our **instruction**, full of
012:111 **instruction** for men endued with understanding.

INSTRUCTIVE

016:066 cattle (too) will ye find an **instructive** Sign.
023:021 And in cattle (too) ye have an **instructive** example:
024:044 is an **instructive** example for those who

INSTRUCTS
016:090 He **instructs** you, that ye may receive admonition.
INSULT
061:005 and **insult** me, though ye know that I am
INTELLECT
046:026 with (faculties of) hearing, sight, heart and **intellect**:
046:026 hearing, sight, and heart and **intellect**, when they
INTELLECTS
052:032 Is it that their **intellects** urges them to this,
INTELLIGENCE
016:078 and **intelligence** and affections:
039:043 no power whatever and no **intelligence**?"
067:010 'Had we but listened or used our **intelligence**, we should
INTELLIGENT
055:004 He has taught him an **intelligent** speech.
INTELLIGENTLY
051:023 ye can speak **intelligently** to each other.
INTEND
005:029 "For me, I **intend** to let thee draw on thyself
008:062 Should they **intend** to deceive thee,-
028:027 He said: "I **intend**ed to wed one of these
028:027 But I **intend** not to place thee under a difficulty:
028:083 give to those who **intend** not high-handedness
036:023 If the Most Gracious should **intend** some adversity for
052:042 Or do they **intend** a plot (against thee)?
074:031 "What doth Allah **intend** by this?"
INTENDED
005:041 If any one's trial is **intended** by Allah,
009:046 If they had **intended** to come out, they would
028:008 (it was **intended**) that (Moses) should be
033:013 they **intended** nothing but to run away.
072:010 'And we understand not whether ill is **intended** to those
INTENDS
002:185 Allah **intends** every facility for you;
036:082 Verily, when He **intends** a thing, His Command
072:010 or whether their Lord (really) **intends** to guide
085:016 Doer (without let) of all that He **intends**.
INTENSE
035:027 and black **intense** in hue.
INTENSELY
038:057 a fluid dark, murky, **intensely** cold!-
078:025 dark, murky, **intensely** cold,-
INTENT
002:188 with **intent** that ye may eat up wrongfully
011:085 with **intent** to do mischief.
024:064 what ye are **intent** upon:
029:036 with **intent** to do mischief."
INTENTION
002:225 but for the **intention** in your hearts;
002:227 But if their **intention** is firm for divorce,
009:107 their **intention** is nothing but good;
028:019 "O Moses! is it thy **intention** to slay me
033:005 (what counts is) the **intention** of your hearts:
061:008 Their **intention** is to extinguish Allah's Light
INTENTIONALLY
004:093 If a man kills a Believer **intentionally**,
005:095 If any of you doth so **intentionally**,
060:012 will not utter slander, **intentionally** forging falsehood,
INTERCEDE
002:255 Who is thee can **intercede** in His presence
007:053 now to **intercede** on our behalf?

INTERCEDE (continued)
026:100 "Now, then, we have none to **intercede** (for us),
032:004 besides Him, to protect or **intercede** (for you):
INTERCEDES
004:085 Whoever **intercedes** in a good cause becomes
INTERCESSION
002:048 nor shall **intercession** be accepted for her,
002:123 nor shall **intercession** profit her
002:254 nor friendship nor **intercession**.
019:087 None shall have the power of **intercession**,
020:109 On that Day shall no **intercession** avail except for
021:028 and they offer no **intercession** except for
034:023 "No **intercession** can avail with Him, except for
036:023 of no use whatever will be their **intercession** for me,
039:044 (the right to grant) **Intercession**:
043:086 no power of **intercession**;-only he
053:026 in the heavens, their **intercession** will avail
074:048 Then will no **intercession** of (any)
INTERCESSOR
006:051 no protector nor **intercessor**: that they
006:070 no protector or **intercessor** except Allah:
010:003 No **intercessor** (can plead with Him) except after
030:013 No **intercessor** will they have among their
INTERCESSORS
040:018 nor **intercessors** will the wrong-doers have,
006:094 We see not with you your **intercessors** whom ye
007:053 Have we no **intercessors** now to intercede on our behalf
010:018 "These are our **intercessors** with Allah."
039:043 What! Do they take for **intercessors** others besides Allah?
074:048 of (any) **intercessors** profit them.
INTERFERE
005:042 either judge between them, or decline to **interfere**.
INTERMIT
021:020 nor do they ever flag or **intermit**.
INTERPRET
012:043 if it be that ye can **interpret** visions."
INTERPRETATION
003:007 seeking discord, and searching for **interpretation**,
010:039 the **interpretation** thereof hath reached them:
012:006 and teach thee the **interpretation** of stories
012:021 the **interpretation** of stories (and events).
012:044 in the **interpretation** of dreams."
012:045 of its **interpretation**: send ye me (therefore)."
012:101 of the **interpretation** of dreams,-O Thou
018:078 thee the **interpretation** of (those things)
018:082 Such is the **interpretation** of (those things)
INTERRUPTING
080:002 the blind man (**interrupting**).
INTERVALS
017:106 recite it to men at **intervals**:
INTERVENE
048:011 (to **intervene**) on your behalf with Allah,
056:083 Then why do ye not (**intervene**) when (the soul of the
INTIMACY
003:118 into your **intimacy** those outside your ranks:
INTIMATE
004:038 what a dreadful **intimate** he is!
004:038 if any take the Satan for their **intimate**,
026:101 "Nor a single **intimate** friend.
037:051 "I had an **intimate** companion (on the earth),
040:018 no **intimate** friend nor intercessors will the wrong-doers

INTIMATE (continued)

041:025 And We have destined for them **intimate** companions
041:034 were thy friend and **intimate**!
043:036 to be an **intimate** companion to him.

INTO

002:026 and many He leads **into** the right path,
002:029 and made them **into** seven firmaments.
002:035 or ye run **into** harm and transgression."
002:072 Remember ye slew a man and fell **into** a dispute
002:174 they swallow **into** themselves naught but Fire;
002:208 enter **into** Islam whole-heartedly;
002:220 He could have put you **into** difficulties:
002:257 he leads them forth **into** light.
002:257 lead them forth **into** the depths of darkness.
002:260 tie them (cut them **into** pieces),
002:286 if we forget or fall **into** error;
003:035 "O my Lord! I do dedicate **into** thee what is in
003:049 the figure of a bird, and breathe **into** it,
003:049 and I bring the dead **into** life by Allah's leave;
003:105 and fall **into** disputation after receiving Clear Signs:
003:118 take not **into** your intimacy those outside your ranks:
003:139 So lose not heart, nor fall **into** despair:
003:151 terror **into** the hearts of the Unbelievers,
003:176 who rush headlong **into** Unbelief:
003:195 and admit them **into** Gardens with rivers flowing beneath;
004:010 eat up a fire **into** their own bodies:
004:026 and to guide you **into** the ways of those before you;
004:030 soon shall We cast them **into** the Fire:
004:056 We shall soon cast **into** the Fire:
004:088 ye be divided **into** two parties about the Hypocrites?
005:034 before they fall **into** your power:
005:041 who race each other **into** Unbelief:
005:053 and they will fall **into** (nothing but) ruin.
005:060 He transformed **into** apes and swine, those who
005:110 And thou breathest **into** it, and it becometh
006:071 have made **into** a fool, wandering bewildered
006:091 but ye make it **into** (separate) sheets for show,
006:159 and break up **into** sects, thou hast
007:038 until they follow each other, all **into** the Fire.
007:038 men and Jinns,-**into** the Fire.
007:095 their suffering **into** prosperity, until they
007:116 and struck terror **into** them:
007:155 Thou wilt **into** the right path.
007:160 We divided them **into** twelve tribes or nations.
007:168 We broke them up **into** sections on this earth.
007:202 plunge them deeper **into** error, and never
008:012 I will instill terror **into** the hearts of the Unbelievers:
008:037 and cast them **into** Hell.
008:046 and fall **into** no disputes, lest ye
008:060 to strike terror **into** (the hearts of) the enemies,
009:004 ye have entered **into** alliance and who have not
009:049 Have they not fallen **into** trial already?
009:049 "grant me exemption and draw me not **into** trial."
009:077 hypocrisy **into** their hearts, (to last)
009:109 it doth crumble to pieces with him, **into** the fire of Hell.
010:087 make your dwellings **into** places of worship,
010:093 that they fell **into** schisms.
011:009 and (falls **into**) ingratitude,
011:010 behold! he falls **into** exultation and pride.
011:098 and lead them **into** the Fire, but woeful
012:015 and We put **into** his heart (this Message):
012:019 and he let down his bucket (**into** the well).
012:032 he shall certainly be cast **into** prison,

INTO (continued)

012:036 Now with him there came **into** the prison two young men.
012:062 (with which they had bartered) **into** their saddle-bags,
012:069 Now when they came **into** Joseph's presence,
012:070 he put the drinking cup **into** his brother's saddle-bag.
012:088 Then, when they came (back) **into** (Joseph's) presence
012:110 and those whom We will are delivered **into** safety.
014:001 out of the depths of darkness **into** light-by the leave of
014:005 out thy people from the depths of darkness **into** light,
014:029 **Into** Hell? They will burn therein,-an evil place to stay
015:012 Even so do We let it creep **into** the hearts of the sinners-
015:026 from mud molded **into** shape;
015:028 from sounding clay, from mud molded **into** shape;
015:029 and breathed **into** him of My spirit, fall ye down
015:033 sounding clay, from mud moulded **into** shape."
015:090 divided (Scripture **into** arbitrary parts),-
015:091 Qur'an **into** shreds (as they please).
016:062 to be hastened on **into** it!
016:091 ye have entered **into** it, and break
016:092 who breaks **into** untwisted strands the yarn
017:007 all that fell **into** their power.
017:034 will be enquired **into** (on the Day of Reckoning).
017:039 lest thou shouldst be thrown **into** Hell, blameworthy
017:046 and deafness **into** their ears:
017:060 We put fear (and warning) **into** them,
017:093 or thou mount a ladder right **into** the skies.
017:106 Which we have divided (**into** parts from time to time),
018:022 Enter not, therefore, **into** controversies concerning them,
018:035 He went **into** his garden while he wronged himself:
018:037 a sperm-drop, then fashioned thee **into** a man?
018:039 "Why didst thou not, as thou wentest **into** thy garden,
018:098 comes to pass, He will make it **into** dust;
019:026 this day will I enter **into** no talk with any human being.'"
020:039 and throw (the chest) **into** the river:
020:039 "`Throw (the child) **into** the chest, and throw
020:055 and **into** it shall We return you, and from
020:087 and we threw them (**into** the fire),
020:096 and threw it (**into** the calf):
020:121 thus did Adam disobey His Lord, and fell **into** error.
020:123 will not lose his way, nor fall **into** misery.
021:078 of the field **into** which the sheep of certain
021:091 We breathed **into** her from Our Spirit,
022:031 and thrown him **into** a far-distant place.
022:052 Satan threw some (vanity) **into** his desire:
022:061 and He merges Night **into** Day,
022:061 and He merges Day **into** Night,
023:014 Then We made the sperm **into** a clot of
023:053 cut off their affair (of unity), between them, **into** sects:
023:108 "Be ye driven **into** it (with ignominy)!
024:014 glibly **into** this affair.
024:043 then makes them **into** a heap?
025:013 bound together, **into** a constricted place therein,
025:070 for Allah will change the evil of such persons **into** good,
026:094 "Then they will be thrown headlong **into** the (Fire),-
027:012 "Now put thy hand **into** thy bosom, and it
027:018 "O ye ants, get **into** your habitations,
027:090 will be thrown headlong **into** the Fire: "Do ye receive
028:004 elated himself in the land and divided **into** sections,
028:007 cast him **into** the river, but fear
028:032 "Thrust thy hand **into** thy bosom, and it
028:040 and We flung them **into** the sea: now behold
030:048 and break them **into** fragments,
031:029 He merges Night **into** Day and He merges Day **into** Night;

INTO (continued)

032:009 and breathed **into** him of His spirit.
033:026 cast terror **into** their hearts, (so that)
033:043 the depths of Darkness **into** Light:
034:002 He knows all that goes **into** the earth, and all
034:016 (rows) **into** "gardens" producing bitter fruit,
034:038 over **into** Chastisement.
035:013 He merges Night **into** Day, and He merges Day **into** Night,
037:097 and throw him **into** the blazing fire!"
037:162 Can lead (any) **into** temptation concerning Allah,
038:005 "Has he made goods (all) **into** one God?
038:072 and breathed **into** him of My spirit, fall ye
039:017 Those who eschew Taghut and fall not **into** its worship,-
040:046 "Cast ye the People of Pharaoh **into** the severest Penalty"
040:067 then does He get you out (**into** the light) as a child:
041:040 he that is cast **into** the Fire, or he
043:019 And they make **into** females angels who themselves
043:065 But sects from among themselves fell **into** disagreement:
044:047 and drag him **into** the midst of the Blazing Fire!
045:017 had been granted to them that they fell **into** schisms,
048:004 sent down Tranquillity **into** the hearts of the Believers,
049:009 If two parties among the believers fall **into** a fight,
049:013 and made you **into** nations and tribes, that ye
050:024 "Throw, both of you, **into** Hell every contumacious
050:026 throw him **into** a severe Chastisement."
051:040 and threw them **into** the sea:
056:007 And ye shall be sorted out **into** three classes.
057:006 merges Night **into** Day, and He merges Day **into** Night;
057:009 the depths of Darkness **into** the Light.
057:014 "True! but ye led yourselves **into** temptation;
057:022 a Book before We bring it **into** existence:
059:002 and cast terror **into** their hearts, so that
059:010 who came before us **into** the Faith and leave not,
059:017 that they will go **into** the Fire, dwelling therein
065:011 from the depths of Darkness **into** Light.
066:012 and We breathed **into** her (body) of Our spirit;
068:024 in upon you **into** the (garden) this day."
071:007 they have (only) thrust their fingers **into** their ears,
071:018 "'And in the End He will return you **into** the (earth),
072:006 but they increased them **into** further error.
072:008 'And we pried **into** the (secrets of) heaven;
074:026 Soon will cast him **into** Hell-Fire!
074:042 "What led you **into** Hell-Fire?"
090:004 Verily We have created Man **into** toil and struggle.
092:011 when he falls headlong (**into** the Pit).
100:005 And penetrate forthwith **into** the midst
104:004 to be thrown **into** that which Breaks to Pieces.
104:008 It shall be made **into** a vault over them,
114:005 Who whispers **into** the hearts of Mankind,-

INTOXICANTS

005:090 O ye who believe! **intoxicants** and gambling,
005:091 with **intoxicants** and gambling, and hinder you

INTOXICATED

015:015 "Our eyes have been **intoxicated**:

INTOXICATION

004:043 in a state of **intoxication**, until
015:072 in their wild **intoxication**, they wander
037:047 nor will they suffer **intoxication** therefrom.
056:019 nor will they suffer **intoxication**:

INVENT

003:094 If any, after this, **invent** a lie and attribute it to Allah,
004:050 Behold! how they **invent** a lie against Allah!

INVENT (continued)

005:103 who **invent** a lie against Allah, but most
007:152 those who **invent** (falsehoods).
016:074 **Invent** not similitudes for Allah: for Allah
018:015 as **invent** a falsehood against Allah?
029:017 and ye **invent** falsehood.
069:044 And if the messenger were to **invent** any sayings

INVENTED

006:022 whom ye (**invented** and) talked about?"
006:024 but the (lie) which they **invented** will leave
010:030 and their **invented** falsehoods will leave them in the lurch.
012:111 It is not a tale **invented**,
028:075 and the (lies) which they **invented** will leave
034:008 "Has he **invented** a falsehood against Allah,
034:043 "This is only a falsehood **invented**!"
037:158 And they have **invented** a kinship between Him
057:027 which they **invented** for themselves, We did not

INVENTETH

006:021 who **inventeth** a lie against Allah or
006:093 one who **inventeth** a lie against Allah, or saith,

INVENTION

037:151 Behold they say, out of their own **invention**,
046:028 but that was their Falsehood and their **invention**.

INVENTIONS

016:056 to account for your false **inventions**.
016:087 and all their **inventions** shall leave them

INVENTS

006:144 than one who **invents** a lie against Allah, to lead
023:038 "He is only a man who **invents** a lie against Allah,
029:068 who **invents** a lie against Allah or rejects

INVEST

028:035 and **invest** you both with authority, so they

INVESTED

012:054 **invested** with all trust."
026:021 **invested** me with judgment (and wisdom) and

INVESTIGATE

004:094 in the cause of Allah, **investigate** carefully,
004:094 therefore carefully **investigate**, for Allah

INVESTIGATORS

004:083 the proper **investigators** would have known

INVISIBLE

017:045 believe not in the Hereafter, a veil **invisible**:

INVITE

012:033 to my liking than that to which they **invite** me:
012:108 Say thou: "This my Way; I do **invite** unto Allah,-
014:009 as to that to which ye **invite** us."
016:125 **Invite** (all) to the Way of thy Lord with wisdom
022:067 but do thou **invite** (them) to thy Lord:
028:087 and **invite** (men) to thy Lord and be not
033:051 on thee if thou **invite** one whose (turn)
041:005 (concealed) from that to which thou dost **invite** us,

INVITED

003:023 They are **invited** to the Book of Allah,
033:053 but when ye are **invited**, enter; and when
047:038 Behold, ye are those **invited** to spend
061:007 even as he is being **invited** to Islam?

INVITES

014:010 It is He Who **invites** you, in order
028:025 She said: "My father **invites** thee that he may
033:046 And as one who **invites** to Allah's (Grace)

INVITES (continued)

035:006 He only **invites** his adherents, that they
046:031 who **invites** (you) to Allah, and believe in him:
046:032 who **invites** (Us) to Allah, he cannot
057:008 And the Messenger **invites** you to believe

INVITEST

011:062 to that to which thou **invitest** us."

INVITING

003:104 a band of people **inviting** to all that is good,
028:041 leaders **inviting** to the Fire;
070:017 **Inviting** (all) such as turn their backs and turn

INVOKE

003:061 And **invoke** the curse of Allah on those who lie!
007:037 that ye used to **invoke** besides Allah?"
016:020 Those whom they **invoke** besides Allah create nothing
016:086 those whom we used to **invoke** besides Thee."
019:048 and from those whom ye **invoke** besides Allah:
022:062 and those besides Him whom they **invoke**,-
024:007 that he solemnly **invokes** the curse of Allah
025:068 Those who **invoke** not, with Allah, any other
031:030 and because whatever else they **invoke** besides Him
035:013 And those whom ye **invoke** besides Him
035:014 If ye **invoke** them, they will
039:038 The things ye **invoke** besides Allah,-can they,
040:020 But those whom (men) **invoke** besides Him,
040:066 Say: "I have been forbidden to **invoke** those whom
040:066 those whom ye **invoke** besides Allah,-seeing that
041:048 to **invoke** aforetime will leave them in the lurch,
043:049 **invoke** thy Lord for us according to his
043:086 And those whom they **invoke** besides Allah have no
046:004 Say: "Do ye see what it is ye **invoke** beside Allah?
072:018 so **invoke** not any one along with Allah;
072:019 stands forth to **invoke** Him, they just
072:020 Say: "I do no more than **invoke** my Lord, and I

INVOKED

002:173 name hath been **invoked** besides that Allah,
005:003 hath been **invoked** the name of other than Allah;
006:145 (meat) on which a name has been **invoked**,
011:101 whom they **invoked**, profited them no whit when there
016:115 other than Allah has been **invoked**.
040:012 "This is because, when Allah was **invoked** as the
040:074 nay, we **invoked** not, of old, anything

INVOKES

023:117 If anyone **invokes**, besides Allah, any other
024:009 she solemnly **invokes** the wrath of Allah on herself
046:005 who **invokes**, besides Allah, such as

INVOLVING

002:282 in transactions **involving** future obligations

INWARD

016:058 filled with **inward** grief!
043:017 is filled with **inward** grief!

IRAM

089:007 Of the (city of) **Iram**, with lofty pillars,

IRE

009:120 or trod paths to raise the **ire** of the Unbelievers,

IRON

017:050 Say: "(Nay!) be ye stones or **iron**,
018:096 "Bring me blocks of **iron**."
022:021 In addition there will be maces of **iron** (to punish) them.
034:010 and We made the **iron** soft for Him;-
057:025 and We sent down **Iron**, in which

IRRESISTIBLE

007:127 and we have over them (power) **irresistible**.
012:039 or Allah the One, Supreme and **Irresistible**?
013:016 the Supreme and **Irresistible**."
014:048 the One, the **Irresistible**;
038:065 the One, Supreme and **Irresistible**,-
059:023 the Exalted in Might, the **Irresistible**, the justly

IRRESISTIBLY

006:018 **Irresistibly** Supreme over His servants.
006:061 He is the **Irresistibly**, Supreme over
052:013 to the Fire of Hell, **irresistibly**.

IRREVOCABLY

002:230 So if a husband divorces his wife (**irrevocably**),

IS (See Appendix)

ISAAC

002:133 of Abraham, Isma'il, and **Isaac**,
002:136 and to Abraham, Isma'il, **Isaac**, Jacob,
002:140 Abraham, Isma'il, **Isaac**, Jacob
003:084 Abraham, Isma'il; **Isaac**, Jacob, and the Tribes,
004:163 Isma'il, **Isaac**, Jacob and the Tribes, to Jesus,
006:084 We gave him **Isaac** and Jacob: all (three)
011:071 glad tidings of **Isaac**, and after him, of Jacob.
012:006 thy fathers Abraham and **Isaac** aforetime!
012:038 my fathers,-Abraham, **Isaac**, and Jacob; and never
014:039 unto me in old age Isma'il and **Isaac**: for truly
019:049 We bestowed on him **Isaac** and Jacob,
021:072 And We bestowed on him **Isaac** and, as an
029:027 And We gave (Abraham) **Isaac** and Jacob,
037:112 of **Isaac**-a prophet,-one of the Righteous.
037:113 We blessed him and **Isaac**: but of their
038:045 Abraham, **Isaac**, and Jacob, possessors of

ISLAM

002:208 enter into **Islam** whole-heartedly;
003:019 Religion before Allah is **Islam** (submission to His Will):
003:067 and bowed his will to Allah's (which is **Islam**).
003:080 after ye have bowed your will (to Allah in **Islam**)?
003:083 bowed to His Will (accepted **Islam**),
003:084 and to Allah do we bow our will (in **Islam**)."
003:085 a religion other than **Islam** (submission to Allah)
003:102 and die not except in a state of **Islam**.
005:003 and have chosen for you **Islam** as your religion.
005:044 (as in **Islam**) to Allah's will, by the
006:014 the first of those who bow to Allah (in **Islam**),
006:125 He openeth their breast to **Islam**; those whom
009:074 and they uttered it after accepting **Islam**:
009:100 The vanguard (of **Islam**)-the first of those who
010:072 of those who submit to Allah's Will (in **Islam**)."
010:090 I am of those who submit (to Allah in **Islam**)."
011:014 Will ye even then submit (to **Islam**)?"
016:081 to His will (in **Islam**).
021:108 bow to His Will (in **Islam**)?"
022:034 submit then your wills to Him (in **Islam**):
027:042 and we have submitted to Allah (in **Islam**)."
027:044 I do (now) submit (in **Islam**), with Solomon,
027:091 who bow in **Islam** to Allah's Will,-
029:046 and it is to Him we submit (in **Islam**)."
030:053 in Our Signs and submit (their wills in **Islam**).
039:012 of those who submit to Allah in **Islam**."
039:022 Is one whose heart Allah has opened to **Islam**,
040:066 I have been commanded to submit (in **Islam**) to the Lord
041:033 "I am of those who bow in **Islam**"?
046:015 do I submit (to Thee) in **Islam**."

ISLAM (continued)

049:017 Say, "Count not your **Islam** as a favour upon me:
049:017 that they have embraced **Islam**.
061:007 even as he is being invited to **Islam**?

ISMA'IL

002:125 and We covenanted with Abraham and **Isma'il,**
002:127 And remember Abraham and **Isma'il** raised
002:133 of Abraham, **Isma'il**, and Isaac,
002:136 and to Abraham, **Isma'il**, Isaac, Jacob,
002:140 Abraham, **Isma'il**, Isaac, Jacob
003:084 Abraham, **Isma'il'**; Isaac, Jacob, and the Tribes,
004:163 **Isma'il**, Isaac, Jacob and the Tribes, to Jesus,
006:086 And **Isma'il** and Elisha, and Jonah, and Lot:
014:039 unto me in old age **Isma'il** and Isaac: for truly
019:054 (the story of) **Isma'il**: he was (strictly) true
021:085 And (remember) **Isma'il**, Idris, and Zul-kifl,
038:048 And commemorate **Isma'il**, Elisha, and Zul-Kifl:

ISRAEL

002:040 O children of **Israel**! call to mind
002:047 O children of **Israel**! call to mind
002:083 the children of **Israel** (to this effect):
002:122 O Children of **Israel**! call to mind
002:211 Ask the Children of **Israel** how many
002:246 Children of **Israel** after (the time of) Moses
003:049 the Children of **Israel**, (with this message):
003:093 All food was lawful to the Children of **Israel**,
003:093 except what **Israel** made unlawful for himself
005:012 a Covenant from the Children of **Israel**, and We
005:032 We ordained for the Children of **Israel** that if
005:070 the Children of **Israel** and sent them Messengers.
005:072 "O children of **Israel**! worship Allah, my Lord
005:078 those among the Children of **Israel** who rejected
005:110 the Children of **Israel** from (violence to) thee
007:105 so let the children of **Israel** depart along with me."
007:134 the Children of **Israel** with thee."
007:137 was fulfilled for the Children of **Israel**, because
007:138 We took the Children of **Israel** (with safety)
010:090 the Children of **Israel** believe in: I am
010:090 We took the Children of **Israel** across the sea:
010:093 We settled the Children of **Israel** in an honourable
017:002 Children of **Israel**, (Commanding): "Take not other
017:004 the Children of **Israel** in the Book, that twice
017:101 ask the Children of **Israel**: when he
017:104 Children of **Israel**, "Dwell securely in the land
019:058 and **Israel**-of those whom We guided and chose.
020:047 the Children of **Israel** with us, and afflict
020:080 O ye Children of **Israel**! We delivered
020:094 among the Children of **Israel**, and thou
026:017 "'Send thou with us the Children of **Israel**.'"
026:022 that you hast enslaved the Children of **Israel**!"
026:059 the Children of **Israel** inheritors of such things.
026:197 the learned of the Children of **Israel** knew it
027:076 to the Children of **Israel** most of the matters
032:023 and We made it a guide to the Children of **Israel**.
040:053 in inheritance to the Children of **Israel**,-
043:059 to the Children of **Israel**.
044:030 deliver aforetime the Children of **Israel** from humiliating,
045:016 Children of **Israel** the Book, the Power
046:010 and a witness from among the Children of **Israel** testifies
061:006 said: "O Children of **Israel**! I am the messenger
061:014 of the Children of **Israel** believed,

ISRAELITES

026:054 (Saying): "These (**Israelites**) are but a small band,

ISSUE

006:095 He causeth the living to **issue** from the dead.
006:095 cause the dead to **issue** from the living.
024:043 then wilt thou see rain **issue** forth from their midst.
030:048 seest rain-drops **issue** from the midst thereof:
046:015 and be gracious to me in my **issue**.
070:043 The Day whereon they will **issue** from their

ISSUED

004:077 the order for fighting was **issued** to them, behold!
011:058 So when Our decree **issued**, We saved Hud
011:066 When Our Decree **issued**, We saved Salih
011:082 When Our decree **issued**, We turned (the cities)
011:094 When Our decree **issued**, We saved Shu'aib
011:101 when there **issued** the decree of thy Lord:
040:078 but when the Command of Allah **issued**, the matter
057:014 until there **issued** the Command of Allah.

ISSUES

016:069 Thy Lord made smooth: there **issues** from within
018:005 It is a grievous thing that **issues** from their

IT

002:002 in **it** is guidance sure; without doubt,
002:005 and **it** is these who will prosper.
002:006 **It** is the same to them whether thou warn them
002:009 themselves and realize (**it**) not!
002:011 When **it** is said to them: "Make not mischief
002:012 but they realize (**it**) not.
002:013 When **it** is said to them: "Believe
002:017 when **it** lighted all around him,
002:019 in **it** are zones of darkness,
002:026 By **it** He causes many to stray,
002:026 that **it** is the truth from their Lord;
002:026 even of a gnat as well as anything above **it**.
002:027 Allah's Covenant after **it** is ratified,
002:029 **It** is He who hath created for you
002:032 in truth **it** is Thou who art perfect
002:042 when ye know (what **it** is).
002:044 and forget to practice **it** yourselves,
002:045 with patient perseverance and prayer: **it** is indeed hard,
002:064 had **it** not been for the Grace
002:066 So We made **it** an example to their own time,
002:068 to make plain to us what heifer **it** is!"
002:071 and they scarcely did **it**.
002:075 knowingly after they understood **it**.
002:075 and perverted **it** knowingly
002:076 in argument about **it** before your Lord?"
002:079 to traffic with **it** for a miserable price!
002:080 Or is **it** that ye say of Allah
002:085 Then is **it** only a part of the Book
002:085 After this **it** is ye, the same people,
002:085 though **it** was not lawful for you
002:087 Is **it** that whenever there comes to you
002:088 little is **it** they believe.
002:089 they refused to believe in **it**
002:090 send **it** to any of His servants He pleases:
002:091 When **it** is said to them,
002:091 even if **it** be Truth confirming
002:100 Is **it** not (the case) that every time
002:100 some party among them throw **it** aside?
002:101 as if (**it** had been something)
002:105 **It** is never the wish of those without
002:110 ye shall find **it** with Allah:
002:114 **It** was not fitting that such should
002:117 He saith to **it**: "Be," and **it** is.

IT (continued)

002:121	the Book study **it** as **it** should be studied:
002:125	My House for those who compass **it** round,
002:125	or use **it** as a retreat, or bow,
002:137	but if they turn back, **it** is they who are in schism;
002:138	**It** is He. Whom we worship.
002:143	Indeed **it** was (a change) momentous,
002:154	though ye perceive (**it**) not.
002:158	should compass them round, **it** is no sin in them.
002:159	after We have made **it** clear
002:170	When **it** is said to them: "Follow what Allah
002:172	be grateful to Allah if **it** is Him ye worship.
002:177	**It** is not righteousness that ye turn your faces
002:177	but **it** is righteousness-to believe in Allah
002:180	**It** is prescribed, when death approaches
002:181	If anyone changes the bequest after hearing **it**,
002:183	as **it** was prescribed to those before you,
002:184	For those who can do **it** (with hardship),
002:184	And **it** is better for you that ye fast,
002:184	of his own free will,- **it** is better for him.
002:185	during that month should spent **it** in fasting,
002:188	nor use **it** as bait for the judges,
002:189	**It** is no virtue if ye enter your houses
002:189	**it** is virtue if ye fear Allah.
002:196	but if ye are prevented (from completing **it**),
002:196	but if he cannot afford **it**,
002:197	(be sure) Allah knoweth **it**.
002:198	**It** is no crime in you if ye seek of the bounty
002:199	the place whence **it** is usual for the multitude so to do,
002:206	When **it** is said to him, "Fear God,"
002:215	Allah knoweth **it** well.
002:216	fighting is prescribed upon you, and ye dislike **it**.
002:216	But **it** is possible that ye dislike a thing
002:217	but graver is **it** in the sight of Allah
002:228	and **it** is not lawful for them to hide
002:229	**It** is not lawful for you, (men),
002:233	laid on **it** greater than **it** can bear.
002:235	betrothal or hold **it** in your hearts.
002:237	unless they remit **it**.
002:240	provided **it** is reasonable.
002:245	**It** is Allah that giveth (you) want or Plenty,
002:246	He said: "Is **it** not possible if ye were
002:249	"But they drank of **it**, except a few.
002:249	only those who taste not of **it** go with me;
002:258	Said Abraham: "But **it** is Allah that causeth
002:258	do thou then cause **it** to rise from the West."
002:259	shall Allah bring **it** (ever) to life,
002:261	of a grain of corn: **it** groweth seven ears,
002:264	on **it** falls a heavy rain,
002:264	which leaves **it** (just) a bare stone.
002:265	light moisture suffice **it**.
002:265	but makes **it** yield a double increase of harvest,
002:265	heavy rain falls on **it** but makes **it** yield
002:265	and if **it** receives not heavy rain,
002:266	that **it** should be caught in a whirlwind,
002:267	out of **it** ye may give away something,
002:267	receive **it** except with closed eyes.
002:270	be sure Allah knows **it** all.
002:271	**it** will remove from you some of your (stains of)
002:271	If ye disclose (acts of) charity, even so **it** is well,
002:272	**It** is not for you to guide them
002:273	be assured Allah knoweth **it** well.
002:279	If ye do **it** not, take notice of war

IT (continued)

002:280	But if ye remit **it** by way of charity,
002:280	grant him time till **it** is easy for him
002:281	Then shall every soul be paid what **it** earned,
002:282	but if **it** be a transaction which ye carry out
002:282	**it** is juster in the sight of Allah,
002:282	**it** would be wickedness in you.
002:282	for **it** is Allah that teaches you.
002:282	if ye reduce **it** no to writing.
002:282	whether **it** be small or big:
002:283	Conceal not evidence; for whoever conceals **it**,
002:284	Allah calleth you to account for **it**.
002:284	your minds or conceal **it**,
002:286	**It** gets every good that **it** earns,
002:286	place a burden greater than **it** can bear.
002:286	and **it** suffers every ill that **it** earns.
003:003	confirming what went before **it**;
003:003	**It** is He Who sent down to thee (step by step),
003:006	He **it** is Who shapes you in the wombs
003:007	in knowledge say: "We believe in **it**;
003:007	the whole of **it** is from our Lord:"
003:007	in **it** are verses basic or fundamental
003:007	He **it** is Who has sent down to thee the Book:
003:025	each soul will be paid out just what **it** has earned,
003:029	in your hearts or reveal **it**, Allah knows **it** all:
003:030	and all the evil **it** has done,
003:030	**it** will wish there were a great distance between
003:030	be confronted with all the good **it** has done,
003:030	a great distance between **it** and **its** evil.
003:047	He but saith to **it** 'Be,' and **it** is!
003:049	and **it** becomes a bird by Allah's leave:
003:049	in that I make for you out of clay, as **it** were,
003:049	the figure of a bird, and breathe into **it**,
003:051	"**It** is Allah who is my Lord and your Lord;
003:066	**It** is Allah Who knows, and ye who know not!
003:069	**It** is the wish of a section of the People
003:072	but reject **it** at the end of the day:
003:075	will not repay **it** unless thou constantly
003:075	will (readily) pay **it** back;
003:075	and (well) they know **it**.
003:078	**it** is they who tell a lie against Allah,
003:078	but **it** is no part of the Book;
003:078	but **it** is not from Allah:
003:078	and (well) they know **it**!
003:078	you would think **it** is a part of the Book,
003:079	and ye have studied **it** earnestly."
003:079	**It** is not (possible) that a man,
003:085	never will **it** be accepted of him;
003:086	who reject faith after they accepted **it** and bore
003:090	But those who reject faith after they accepted **it**.
003:091	though they should offer **it** for ransom.
003:092	and whatever ye give, Allah knoweth **it** well.
003:093	Say: "Bring ye the Torah and study **it**,
003:094	invent a lie and attribute **it** to Allah,
003:097	In **it** are Signs manifest; the Station of Abraham;
003:097	whoever enters **it** attains security;
003:099	seeking to make **it** crooked,
003:103	and He saved you from **it**.
003:106	"Did ye reject Faith after accepting **it**?
003:110	the People of the book had faith, **it** were best for them:
003:117	**it** is not Allah that hath wronged them, but they
003:117	**it** strikes and destroys the harvest of men who wronged
003:120	If aught that is good befalls you, **it** grieves them;

IT (continued)

003:120	they rejoice at **it**.
003:124	Is **it** not enough for you that Allah should help
003:126	Allah made **it** but a message of hope for you,
003:143	for death before ye encountered **it**:
003:143	now ye have seen **it** with your own eyes
003:145	We shall give **it** to him.
003:152	and disobeyed **it** after He brought you in sight
003:155	**it** was Satan who caused them to fail,
003:156	This that Allah may make **it** a cause of sighs
003:156	**It** is Allah that gives Life and Death,
003:158	Lo! **it** is unto Allah that ye are brought together.
003:159	**It** is part of the Mercy of Allah that thou
003:161	receive **its** due whatever **it** earned,
003:165	Say (to them): "**It** is from yourselves:
003:173	so fear them": but **it** only increased their Faith:
003:175	**It** is only the Satan that suggests to you
003:180	Nay, **it** will be the worse of them:
003:180	soon **it** will be tied to their necks
003:180	think that **it** is good for them:
003:187	and purchased with **it** some miserable gain!
003:187	but they threw **it** away behind their backs,
003:187	and not to hide **it**; but they threw
003:187	to make **it** known and clear to mankind
003:197	Little is **it** for enjoyment; their Ultimate
004:001	created, out of **it**, his mate, and from them
004:002	(by mixing **it** up) with your own.
004:004	remit any part of **it** to you,
004:004	take **it** and enjoy **it** with right good cheer.
004:006	but consume **it** not wastefully, nor in haste
004:012	Thus is **it** ordained by Allah;
004:019	a dislike to them **it** may be that ye dislike a thing,
004:019	about through **it** a great deal of good.
004:020	would ye take **it** by slander and a manifest sin?
004:020	take not the least bit of **it** back:
004:021	And how could ye take **it** when ye
004:022	**it** was shameful and odious, an abominable
004:024	ye agree mutually (to vary **it**),
004:025	but **it** is better for you that ye
004:030	and easy **it** is for Allah.
004:039	And what burden were **it** on them if they had faith
004:040	if there is any good (done), He doubleth **it**,
004:046	**it** would have been better for them, and more proper;
004:059	refer **it** to Allah and His Messenger,
004:061	When **it** is said to them: "Come to what
004:066	**it** would have been best for them,
004:066	very few of them would have done **it**:
004:070	and sufficient is **it** that Allah knoweth all.
004:073	a fine thing should I then have made of **it**!"
004:082	Had **it** been from other than Allah,
004:083	safety or fear, they divulge **it**.
004:083	Were **it** not for the Grace
004:083	would have known **it** from them (direct).
004:083	If they had only referred **it** to the Messenger
004:084	**It** may be that Allah will restrain
004:086	meet **it** with a greeting still more courteous,
004:092	kills a believers by mistake **it** is ordained that he
004:092	unless they remit **it** freely.
004:111	he earns **it** against his own soul: for Allah
004:112	and throws **it** on to one that is innocent,
004:121	and from **it** they will find no way of escape.
004:126	and He **it** is that encompasseth all things.
004:129	(as **it** were) hanging (in the air).

IT (continued)

004:129	between wives even if **it** is your ardent desire:
004:133	If **it** were His will, He could destroy you,
004:135	and whether **it** be (against) rich or poor:
004:139	is **it** honor they seek among them?
004:142	but **it** is Allah who deceive them.
004:147	Nay, **it** is Allah that recognizeth (all good),
004:149	or conceal **it** or cover evil with pardon, surely
004:155	and little is **it** they believe;
004:163	as We sent **it** to Noah and the Messengers after
004:170	believe in him: **it** is best for you.
004:171	desist: **it** will be better for you:
004:176	If **it** is a man. That dies,
005:003	unless ye are able to slaughter **it** (in due form);
005:004	but pronounce the name of Allah over **it**: and fear
005:014	show them what **it** is they have done.
005:022	never shall we enter **it** until they leave **it**:
005:024	never enter **it** as long as they are in **it**.
005:027	**it** was accepted from one, but not from the other.
005:028	to slay me, **it** is not for me to stretch my hand
005:032	unless **it** be for murder or for spreading
005:032	**it** would be as if he slew the whole people:
005:032	**it** would be as if he saved the life of the whole people.
005:036	**it** would never be accepted of them.
005:041	For such **it** is not Allah's will
005:041	they say, "If ye are given this, take **it**, but if
005:041	(whether **it** be) among those who say: "We believe"
005:041	or **it** be among the Jews, men who listen
005:044	**It** was We who revealed the Torah (to Moses):
005:045	**it** is an act of atonement for himself.
005:048	and guarding **it** in safety: so judge
005:048	**it** is He that will show you the truth of the matters
005:048	confirming the scripture that came before **it**, and
005:049	of their crimes **it** is Allah's purpose to punish them.
005:056	and the Believers,-**it** is the party of Allah
005:058	they take **it** (but) as mockery and sport;
005:060	by the treatment **it** received from Allah?
005:064	Allah doth extinguish **it**; but they (ever)
005:068	**It** is the revelation that cometh to thee
005:076	But Allah,-He **it** is that heareth
005:095	know ye that **it** is Our Messenger's duty to
005:103	**It** was not Allah Who instituted (superstitions like
005:103	**it** is the disbelievers who invent a lie against Allah;
005:104	When **it** is said to them: "Come to what Allah
005:105	**it** is He that will inform you of all that ye do.
005:106	"We will not take for **it** a price even though
005:107	But if **it** gets known that these two were guilty
005:109	**it** is Thou who knowest in full all that is hidden.
005:110	thou makest out of clay, as **it** were, the figure of a bird,
005:110	And thou breathest into **it**, and **it** becometh a bird by My
005:115	Allah said: "I will send **it** down unto you:
005:116	Thou wouldst indeed have known **it**. Thou knowest
005:120	and **it** is He who hath power over all things.
006:002	He **it** is Who created you from clay, and then
006:005	the truth when **it** reaches them: but soon
006:007	so that they could touch **it** with their hands,
006:009	If We had made **it** an angel, We should
006:012	**It** is they who have lost their own souls,
006:016	Penalty is averted from any, **it** is due to Allah's Mercy;
006:017	none can remove **it** but He; if He
006:019	that I may warn you and all whom **it** reaches.
006:025	so they understand **it** not, and deafness
006:026	and they perceive **it** not.

IT (continued)

006:026   Others they forbid **it** and themselves
006:031   Lost indeed are they who treat **it** as a falsehood
006:033   **it** is not thee they reject: **it** is the Signs of Allah,
006:035   If **it** were Allah's will, He could gather
006:041   and if **it** be His Will, He would
006:053   Is **it** these then that Allah hath favoured
006:060   **It** is He Who doth take your souls by night,
006:063   Say: "Who is **it** that delivereth you from the dark
006:064   Say: "**It** is Allah that delivereth you from these
006:066   But thy people reject this, though **it** is the Truth.
006:067   and soon shall ye know **it**."
006:070   if **it** offered every ransom (or reparation), none
006:070   **it** will find for itself no protector or intercessor except
006:070   with **it** (Al-Qur-an) lest a soul is caught in its own ruin
006:072   for **it** is to Him that we
006:073   **It** is He Who created the heavens and
006:073   the day He saith, "Be," Behold! **it** is.
006:076   But when **it** set, he said: "I love not
006:082   "**It** is those who believe and mix not
006:091   but ye make **it** into (separate)
006:091   Say: "Allah (sent **it** down)": then leave
006:092   (the revelations) which came before **it**:
006:095   **It** is Allah Who causeth the seed-grain and the
006:096   He **it** is that cleaveth the daybreak
006:097   **It** is He Who maketh the stars
006:098   **It** is He who hath produced you
006:099   **It** is He who sendeth down
006:099   with **it** We produce vegetation of all kinds:
006:104   any will see, **it** will be for (the good of) his own soul:
006:104   if any will be blind, **it** will be to his own (harm):
006:107   If **it** had been Allah's Will, they would
006:109   by **it** they would believe.
006:111   unless **it** is in Allah's Plan.
006:112   they would not have done **it**: so leave
006:113   and let them delight in **it**, and let
006:113   and let them earn from **it** what they may.
006:114   that **it** hath been sent down from thy
006:114   When He **it** is Who hath sent
006:123   and they perceive **it** not.
006:130   **It** was the life of this world that deceived them.
006:133   if **it** were His Will, He could destroy you,
006:134   nor can ye frustrate **it** (in the least bit).
006:135   certain **it** is that the wrong-doers
006:135   soon will ye know who **it** is whose end
006:139   but if **it** is still-born then all
006:141   **It** is He who produceth gardens,
006:145   by one who wishes to eat **it**, unless **it** be dead meat,
006:145   for **it** is an abomination,-or what is impious,
006:148   If so, produce **it** before us.
006:149   if **it** had been His Will. He could indeed have granted
006:152   but that which **it** can bear;-whenever ye speak
006:152   except to improve **it**, until he
006:153   follow **it**: follow not (other) paths:
006:155   so follow **it** and be righteous, that ye
006:158   if **it** believed not before nor earned
006:158   no good will **it** do to a soul to believe then,
006:165   **It** is He Who hath made you the inheritors
007:002   that with **it** thou mightest warn
007:003   Little **it** is ye remember of admonition.
007:006   and those by whom We sent **it**.
007:010   **It** is We who have placed you
007:011   **It** is We who created you and gave

007:013   (Allah) said: "Get thee down from **it**:
007:013   **it** is not for thee to be arrogant here:
007:025   but from **it** shall ye be taken out (at last)."
007:034   nor (an hour) can they advance (**it** in anticipation).
007:038   "Our Lord! **it** is these that misled us: so give
007:038   **it** curses its sister-People (that went before),
007:042   but that which **it** can bear,-they will be
007:043   had **it** not been for the guidance of Allah: indeed
007:043   indeed **it** was the truth that the Messengers
007:046   "Peace be upon you": they have not entered **it**,
007:046   but they still hoped. To (enter **it**).
007:053   those who have forgotten **it** before will say: "The
007:053   On the day when **it** is fulfilled those who
007:056   after **it** hath been set in order, but call
007:057   **It** is He Who sendeth the Winds
007:085   after **it** has been set in order: that will
007:086   and seeking in **it** something crooked;
007:089   return thereto unless **it** be as in the will
007:092   who rejected Shu'aib- **it** was they who were ruined!
007:100   is **it** not a guiding (lesson) that, if We
007:105   One for whom **it** is right to say nothing
007:106   show **it** forth,-if thou tellest the truth."
007:107   and behold! **it** was a serpent, plain
007:108   and behold! **it** was white to all beholders!
007:110   then what is **it** ye counsel?"
007:117   and behold! **it** swallows up all the
007:129   He said: "**It** may be that your Lord will destroy
007:131   they ascribed **it** to evil omens connected with
007:140   when **it** is He who hath endowed you with
007:143   if **it** abide in its place, then shalt
007:143   He made **it** as dust and Moses fell down in a swoon.
007:146   they will not adopt **it** as the Way; but if
007:148   that **it** could neither speak to them, nor show
007:148   They took **it** for worship and they did wrong.
007:150   angry and grieved, he said: "Evil **it** is that ye
007:155   he prayed: "O my Lord! if **it** had been Thy will
007:155   by **it** Thou causest whom Thou wilt to stray,
007:157   So **it** is those who believe in him, honor him,
007:157   **it** is they who will prosper."
007:158   **it** is He that giveth both life and death.
007:160   out of **it** there gushed forth twelve springs:
007:161   And remember **it** was said to them: "Dwell in
007:171   as if **it** had been a canopy, and they
007:171   and they thought **it** was going to fall
007:176   If **it** had been Our Will, We should
007:185   (Do they not see) that **it** may well be
007:187   Only, all of a sudden, will **it** come to you."
007:187   as to when **it** will occur.
007:189   and carries **it** about (unnoticed).
007:189   **It** is He Who created you
007:193   for you **it** is the same whether ye call
007:203   they say: "Why hast thou not got **it** together?"
007:204   listen to **it** with attention, and hold
008:005   the Believers disliked **it**.
008:006   to death and they saw **it**.
008:006   the truth after **it** was made manifest, as if
008:007   the two parties, that **it** should be yours: ye wished
008:008   distasteful though **it** be to those in guilt.
008:010   Allah made **it** but a message of hope, and an
008:014   Thus (will **it** be said): "Taste ye then
008:016   unless **it** be in a stratagem of war,
008:017   **It** is not ye who slew them; **it** was Allah:

IT (continued)

008:017 **it** was not thy act, but Allah's:
008:019 if ye desist (from wrong), **it** will be best for you:
008:023 made them listen: (as **it** is), if He had
008:024 and that **it** is He to Whom ye shall
008:028 and that **it** is Allah with whom lies
008:033 nor was He going to send **it** whilst they
008:062 He **it** is that hath strengthened thee with His
008:063 but Allah hath done **it**: for He
008:067 **It** is not fitting for a Prophet that he
008:068 Had **it** not been for a previous ordainment
008:072 seek your aid in religion, **it** is your duty to help them,
009:003 If, then, ye repent, **it** were best for you;
009:006 for asylum, grant **it** to him, so that
009:010 **It** is they who have transgressed all bounds.
009:013 Nay, **it** is Allah whom ye should more justly fear,
009:017 **It** is not for such as join gods with Allah,
009:018 **It** is they who are expected to be on true guidance.
009:024 Say: If **it** be that your fathers, your sons,
009:025 For all that **it** is wide, did constrain
009:032 even though the Unbelievers may detest (**it**).
009:033 **It** is He who hath sent His Messenger
009:033 the Pagans may detest (**it**).
009:033 to cause **it** to prevail over all religion,
009:034 and spend **it** not in the Way of Allah: announce
009:035 and with **it** will be branded their foreheads,
009:035 On the Day when **it** will be heated
009:037 for they make **it** lawful one year, and forbidden
009:040 If ye help not (the Prophet), (**it** is no matter):
009:050 If good befalls thee, **it** grieves them; but if
009:053 will **it** be accepted: for ye are indeed a people
009:060 (thus is **it**) ordained by Allah, and Allah
009:062 but **it** is more fitting that they should please
009:065 Say: "Was **it** at Allah, and His Signs, and His
009:066 rejected Faith after ye had accepted **it**.
009:068 they dwell: sufficient is **it** for them:
009:070 **It** is not Allah Who wrongs
009:074 and they uttered **it** after accepting Islam:
009:074 If they repent, **it** will be best for them:
009:088 and **it** is they who will prosper.
009:094 **it** is your action that Allah and His Messenger will
009:108 In **it** are men who love to be purified; and Allah
009:108 **it** is more worthy of thy standing forth (for prayer)
009:109 And **it** doth crumble to pieces with him, into the
009:113 **It** is not fitting, for the Prophet and those
009:113 after **it** is clear to them that they are
009:114 But when **it** became clear to him that he was
009:116 He giveth life and He taketh **it**.
009:120 **It** was not fitting for the people of Madinah
009:122 **It** is not for the Believers to go forth together:
009:124 had his faith increased by **it**?"
009:125 hearts is a disease,-**it** will add doubt to their doubt,
009:128 **it** grieves him that ye should suffer,
010:002 Is **it** a matter of wonderment to men that We
010:004 **It** is He Who beginneth the process of Creation,
010:004 of Creation, and repeateth **it**, that He
010:005 and measured out stages for **it**, that ye might
010:005 **It** is He Who made the sun to be a shining glory
010:015 of my own accord, to change **it**: I follow
010:015 Say: "**It** is not for me, of my own
010:016 nor should He have made **it** known to you.
010:016 I should not have rehearsed **it** to you, nor should
010:019 Had **it** not been for a Word

IT (continued)

010:022 He **it** is Who enableth you to traverse through
010:024 as if **it** had not flourished only the day before!
010:024 there reaches **it** Our command by night or by day,
010:024 (**it** grows) till the earth is clad with its golden ornaments
010:024 the people to whom **it** belongs think they have all
010:024 have all powers of disposal over **it**: there reaches
010:024 and We make **it** like a harvest clean-mown,
010:027 as **it** were, with pieces from the depth of the
010:028 "**It** was not us that ye worshipped!"
010:030 (the fruits of) the deeds **it** sent before: they will
010:031 And who is **it** that rules and regulates all affairs?"
010:031 Or who is **it** that has power over hearing and sight?
010:031 And who is **it** that brings out the living from the dead
010:031 Say: "Who is **it** that sustains you (in life)
010:034 Say: "**It** is Allah Who originates Creation
010:034 can any originate creation and repeat **it**?"
010:034 originates Creation and repeats **it**: then how
010:035 Say: "**It** is Allah Who gives guidance towards Truth.
010:037 on the contrary **it** is a confirmation of
010:037 that went before **it**, and a fuller
010:038 Or do they say, "He forged **it**"? Say: "Bring
010:038 besides Allah, if **it** be ye speak the truth!"
010:038 Say: "Bring then a Sura like unto **it**, and call
010:044 **it** is man that wrongs his own soul.
010:045 (**it** will be) as if they had tarried
010:049 can they advance (**it** in anticipation).
010:050 what portion of **it** would the Sinners
010:051 and ye wanted (aforetime) to hasten **it** on!"
010:051 "Would ye then believe in **it** at last,
010:051 (**It** will then be said): 'Ah! now? and ye wanted
010:051 when **it** actually cometh to pass?
010:053 **It** is the very truth! And ye cannot frustrate **it**!"
010:054 would fain give **it** in ransom: they would
010:054 if **it** possessed all that is on earth, would fain
010:055 Is **it** not (the case) that Allah's promise
010:055 Is **it** not (the case) that to Allah belongeth
010:056 Is **it** He who giveth life and who taketh **it**,
010:065 **it** is He Who heareth and knoweth (all things).
010:067 He **it** is that hath made you the Night
010:071 "O my People, if **it** be hard on your (mind) that I
010:077 when **it** hath (actually) reached you?
010:077 Is **it** sorcery (like) this? But sorcerers
010:081 Allah will surely make **it** of no effect:
010:082 however much the Sinners may hate **it**!"
010:091 (**It** was said to him): "Ah now!-but a little
010:093 **it** was after knowledge had been
010:098 should have profited **it**,-except the people
010:099 If **it** had been the Lord's Will, they would
010:103 thus is **it** fitting on Our part that We
010:107 He causeth **it** to reach whomsoever of His
010:107 there is none can remove **it** but He: if He
011:002 (**It** teacheth) that ye should worship none
011:007 He **it** is Who created the heavens and the earth
011:008 they are sure to say, "What keeps **it** back?"
011:008 Ah! On the day **it** (actually) reaches them,
011:008 reaches them, nothing will turn **it** away from them,
011:009 from Ourselves, and then withdraw **it** from him,
011:012 **It** is Allah that arrangeth all affairs!
011:013 Or they may say, "He forged **it**."
011:013 Say. "Bring ye then ten Suras forged, like unto **it**,
011:017 the Sects that reject **it**,-the Fire
011:017 doubt thereon: for **it** is the Truth from thy Lord:

011:019   path of Allah and wish **it** to be crooked:
011:028   when ye are averse to **it**?
011:028   see ye if (**it** be that) I have a Clear Sign from my Lord
011:028   Shall we compel you to accept **it** when ye
011:033   He said: "Truly, Allah will bring **it** on you
011:033   ye will not be able to frustrate **it**!
011:034   (good) counsel, if **it** be that Allah willeth to
011:035   Say: "If I had forged **it**, on me were my sin!
011:035   Or do they say, "He has forged **it**?"
011:036   **It** was revealed to Noah: "None of thy People
011:039   "But soon will ye know who **it** is on whom
011:041   in the name of Allah, whether **it** move or be
011:043   to some mountain: **it** will save me from the water."
011:056   Verily, **it** is my Lord that is on a Straight Path.
011:061   **It** is He Who hath produced you from the earth
011:091   Were **it** not for thy family, we should
011:093   soon will ye know who **it** is on whom descends the
011:101   **It** was not We that wronged them: they wronged
011:104   Nor shall We delay **it** but for a term appointed.
011:105   The day **it** arrives, no soul shall speak
011:110   is suspicious doubt concerning **it**.
011:110   had **it** not been that a Word had gone forth
011:120   with **it** We make firm they heart: in them
012:002   We have sent **it** down as an Arabic Qur'an, in order
012:003   among those who knew **it** not.
012:006   of Jacob-even as He perfected **it** to thy fathers
012:013   (Jacob) said: "Really **it** saddens me that ye
012:018   **it** is Allah (alone) whose help can be sought."
012:021   but most among mankind know **it** not.
012:026   He said: "**It** was she that sought to seduce me-
012:026   (thus)-" If **it** be that his shirt is rent
012:027   "But if **it** be that his shirt is torn
012:028   (her husband) said: "Behold! **it** is a snare
012:028   that **it** was torn at the back, (her husband)
012:035   (that **it** was best) to imprison him for a time.
012:035   Then **it** occurred to them after they had seen
012:037   and meaning of this ere **it** befall you.
012:043   if **it** be that ye can interpret visions."
012:051   **it** was I who sought to seduce him he is indeed
012:061   win him from his father: indeed we shall do **it**."
012:062   so they should know **it** only when they
012:068   **it** did not profit them in the least
012:068   **it** served only to satisfy Jacob's heartfelt desire.
012:071   "What is **it** that ye miss?"
012:072   I will be bound by **it**."
012:072   the king; for him who produces **it**.
012:075   Thus **it** is We punish the wrong-doers!
012:075   in whose saddle-bag **it** is found, should be
012:076   except that Allah willed **it** (so).
012:076   at length He brought **it** out of
012:088   and treat **it** as charity to us; for Allah
012:093   and cast **it** over the face of my father: he will
012:099   in safety if **it** please Allah."
012:100   Allah hath made **it** come true!
012:103   mankind have, however ardently thou dost desire **it**.
012:104   for this: **it** is no lest than a Message
012:111   but a confirmation of what went before **it**,-
012:111   **It** is not a tale invented, but a confirmation
013:003   And **it** is He Who spread out the earth,
013:010   **It** is the same (to Him) whether any of you
013:010   any of you conceal his speech or declare **it** openly;
013:011   there can be no turning **it** back, nor will they find,

013:012   **it** is He Who doth raise up the clouds,
013:012   **It** is He Who doth show you the lightning, by way
013:014   their mouths but **it** reaches them not:
013:016   Say: "(**It** is) Allah." Say: "Do ye then
013:018   would they offer **it** for ransom.
013:019   **It** is those who are endued with understanding
013:033   over every soul (and knoweth) **it** doth, (like any others)?
013:033   or is **it** (just) a show of words?"
013:033   Say: "But name them! is **it** that ye will inform
013:035   beneath **it** flow rivers: perpetual is the fruits thereof
013:037   Thus have We revealed **it** to be a judgment
013:038   and **it** was never the part of a messenger
013:040   **it** is Our part to call them to account.
013:040   thy soul (before **it** is all accomplished), thy duty
014:003   Allah and seek to make **it** crooked: they are
014:010   **It** is He Who invites you, in order
014:011   **It** is not for us to bring you an authority
014:017   swallowing **it** down his throat; death will come
014:017   In gulps will he sip **it**, but never
014:021   to us **it** makes no difference (now) whether
014:021   we should have given **it** to you:
014:022   "**It** was Allah Who gave you a promise
014:025   **It** brings forth its fruit at all times, by the
014:026   **It** is torn up by the root from the surface of the earth:
014:026   surface of the earth: **it** has no stability.
014:032   and with **it** bringeth out fruits wherewith
014:032   **it** is He Who hath made the ships subject to you,
014:032   **It** is Allah Who hath created the heavens
015:005   anticipate its Term, nor delay **it**.
015:007   if **it** be that thou hast the Truth?"
015:009   assuredly guard **it** (from corruption).
015:012   Even so do We let **it** creep into the
015:016   **It** is We who have set out constellations in
015:023   And verily, **it** is We Who give life, and Who
015:023   **it** is We Who remain Inheritors (after all else passes
015:025   Assuredly **it** is thy Lord who will gather them
015:044   To **it** are seven Gates: for each
015:086   For verily **it** is thy Lord Who is the All-Creator,
016:001   seek ye not then to hasten **it**: glory to Him,
016:010   **It** is He Who sends down rain from the sky:
016:010   from **it** ye drink, and out (grows) the vegetation
016:011   With **it** He produces for you corn, olives, date-
016:014   **It** is He Who has made the sea subject, that ye
016:015   mountains standing firm, lest **it** should shake
016:024   When **it** is said to them, "What is **it** that your Lord has
016:030   To the righteous (when) **it** is said, "What is **it** that your
016:038   but most among mankind know **it** not.
016:038   nay, but **it** is a promise (binding) on Him in truth:
016:040   We but say the Word, "Be," and **it** is.
016:059   or bury **it** in the dust?
016:059   Shall he retain **it** on (sufferance and) Contempt,
016:061   to anticipate **it** (for a single hour).
016:062   to be hastened on into **it**!
016:064   they differ, and that **it** should be a guide
016:066   pure and agreeable to those who drink **it**.
016:070   **It** is Allah who creates you and takes
016:078   **It** is He Who brought you forth from the wombs
016:080   **It** is Allah who made your habitations homes of
016:081   **It** is Allah who made, out of
016:085   see the Chastisement then will **it** in no way
016:091   ye have entered into **it**, and break
016:092   after **it** has become strong.

IT (continued)

016:094 may slip after it was firmly planted; and ye
016:103 "It is a man that teaches him."
016:104 It is those who believe not in the Signs of Allah,
016:105 that forge falsehood: it is they who lie!
016:112 yet was it ungrateful for the favours of Allah:
016:112 so Allah made it taste of hunger and terror
016:112 (closing in on it) like a garment (from every side),
016:114 if it is He whom ye serve.
017:002 and made it a Guide to the Children of Israel,
017:005 and it was a warning (completely) fulfilled.
017:007 as they had entered it before, and to
017:007 (ye did it) against yourselves.
017:008 It may be that your Lord may (yet) show Mercy
017:010 in the Hereafter, (it announceth) that We
017:014 (It will be said to him:) "Read thine (own) record:
017:015 receiveth it for his own benefit: who goeth
017:029 nor stretch it forth to its utmost reach,
017:030 He pleaseth, and He straiten it for He doth
017:032 for it is an indecent (deed) and an way.
017:034 orphan's property except to improve it, until he
017:041 receive admonition, but it only increases their
017:047 We know best what it is they listen, when they
017:051 Say, "Maybe it will be quite soon!
017:052 "It will be on a Day when He will call you,
017:054 It is your Lord that knoweth you best: if He
017:055 And it is your Lord that knoweth best all beings
017:058 the Day of Judgment or punish it with a dreadful
017:058 We shall destroy it before the Day
017:060 but it only increases their inordinate
017:071 will read it (with pleasure), and they will not
017:079 a part of it as an additional prayer for thee:
017:082 to the unjust it causes nothing but
017:084 knows best who it is that is best
017:085 of my Lord of Knowledge it is only a little
017:086 If it were Our Will, We could
017:089 men refuse (to receive it) except with ingratitude!
017:097 every time it shows abatement, We shall
017:097 It is he whom Allah guides, that is
017:099 (to receive it) except with ingratitude.
017:105 and in Truth has it descended: and We sent
017:106 (It is) a Qur'an which We have divided
017:106 recite it to men at intervals:
017:106 We have revealed it by stages.
017:107 it is true that those who were given knowledge
017:107 when it is recited to them, fall down
017:107 Say: "Whether ye believe in it or not,
017:109 and it increases their (earnest) humility.
017:110 by whatever name ye call upon Him, (it is well):
017:110 nor speak it in a low tone, but seek
018:002 (He hath made it) Straight (and Clear) in order
018:005 It is a grievous thing that issues from their
018:007 but as a glittering show for it, in order
018:017 Thou wouldst have seen the sun when it rose,
018:017 and when it set, turning away from them to the left,
018:022 it is but few that know their (real case)."
018:029 and let him who will, reject (it):
018:040 "It may be that my Lord will give me something
018:040 making it (but) slippery sand!
018:041 wilt never be able to find it."
018:045 it is like the rain which We send down
018:045 it is (only) Allah Who prevails over all things.
018:045 but soon it becomes dry stubble, which the

IT (continued)

018:045 the earth's vegetation absorbs it, but soon
018:049 It leaves out nothing small or great,
018:051 own creation: nor is it for Me to take as helpers
018:063 to tell (you) about it: it took its course through the sea
018:070 speak to thee concerning it."
018:071 "Hast thou scuttled it in order to drown those in it?
018:071 when they were in the boat, he scuttled it.
018:077 exacted some recompense for it!"
018:077 the point of falling down but he set it up straight.
018:079 I but wished to render it unserviceable, for there
018:079 As for the boat, it belonged to certain men
018:082 there was, beneath it, a buried treasure, to which
018:082 "As for the wall, it belonged to two youths,
018:082 I did it not of my own accord.
018:086 near it he found a People: We said: O Zul-qarnain!
018:086 the sun, he found it set in a spring of murky
018:088 as We order it by our command."
018:090 the sun, he found it rising on a people for whom
018:096 when he had made it (red) as fire,
018:096 "Bring me, that I may pour over it, molten lead."
018:097 to scale it or to dig through it.
018:098 comes to pass, He will make it into dust;
018:109 even it we added another ocean like it, for its aid."
019:009 He said: "So (it will be): thy Lord saith,
019:021 He said: "So (it will be): thy Lord saith,
019:021 it is a matter (so) decreed."
019:025 it will let fall fresh ripe dates upon thee.
019:034 (it is) a statement of truth, about which
019:035 It is not befitting to (the majesty of) Allah
019:035 He only says to it, "Be," and it is.
019:040 It is We Who will inherit the earth, and all
019:071 Not one of you but will pass over it: this is,
019:090 At it the skies are about to burst, the earth
019:092 For it is not consonant with the majesty
019:097 that with it thou mayest give glad tidings
020:007 If thou pronounce the word aloud, (it is no matter):
020:015 I have almost kept it hidden-for every soul
020:018 and in it I find other uses."
020:018 He said, "It is my rod: on it I lean;
020:018 with it I beat down fodder for my flocks;
020:019 (Allah) said, "Throw it, O Moses!"
020:020 He threw it, and behold! it was a sneak, active in motion.
020:021 (Allah) said, "Seize it, and fear not: We shall
020:021 We shall return it at once to its former condition"...
020:022 it shall come forth white (and shining),
020:048 'Verily it has been revealed to us that the
020:050 then, gave (it) guidance."
020:053 With it have We produced divers pairs of plants
020:055 and from it shall We bring you out once again.
020:055 and into it shall We return you, and from
020:066 so it seemed to him on account of their magic-
020:069 quickly will it swallow up that which
020:088 the image of a calf: it seemed to low: so they said: "This
020:089 and that it had no power either to harm
020:089 Could they not see that it could not return
020:091 will devote ourselves to it until Moses returns to us."
020:091 They had said: "We will not cease to worship it,
020:096 and threw it (into the calf):
020:097 we will certainly burn it in a blazing fire
020:097 a blazing fire and scatter it broadcast in the sea!
020:113 or that it may cause their remembrance (of Him).
020:128 Is it not a guidance to such men (to call to mind)

IT (continued)

020:129 Had **it** not been for a Word that went forth
020:132 We provide **it** for thee.
020:135 ye know who **it** is that is on the straight
020:135 and who **it** is that has received guidance."
021:002 but they listen to **it** as in jest,-
021:005 Nay, He forged **it**!-Nay, He
021:012 they (tried to) flee from **it**.
021:017 should surely have taken **it** from the things nearest to Us,
021:017 If **it** had been Our wish to take (just) a pastime,
021:018 and **it** knocks out its brain, and behold,
021:031 lest **it** should shake with them, and We
021:033 **It** is He Who created the Night and the
021:040 Nay, **it** may come to them all of a sudden
021:040 no power will they have then to avert **it**,
021:044 Is **it** then they who will win?
021:047 We will bring **it** (to account): and enough
021:050 will ye then reject **it**?
021:058 that they might turn (and address themselves) to **it**.
021:079 and Knowledge; **it** was Our power that made the
021:079 with David: **it** was We Who did (all these things).
021:080 **It** was We Who taught him the making of
021:081 (**It** was Our power that made) the violent
021:082 and **it** was We Who guarded them.
021:094 We shall record **it** in his favour.
021:098 To **it** will ye (surely) come!
021:104 truly shall We fulfil **it**.
021:110 "**It** is He Who knows what is open in speech
021:111 "I know not but that **it** may be a trial for you,
022:002 The Day ye shall see **it**, every mother
022:004 About the (Satan) **it** is decreed that whoever
022:005 **it** swells, and **it** puts forth every
022:005 down rain on **it**, **it** is stirred (to life),
022:006 and **it** is He Who has power over all things.
022:006 **it** is He Who gives life to the dead,
022:007 there can be no doubt about **it**, or about   -
022:010 (**It** will be said): "This is because of the deeds
022:011 as **it** were, on the verge:
022:020 With **it** will be melted what is within their
022:022 and (**it** will be said), "Taste ye the chastisement of
022:026 for those who compass **it** round, or stand up,
022:030 for him **it** is good in the sight of his Lord,
022:037 **It** is not their meat nor their blood, that reaches
022:037 **it** is your piety that reaches Him:
022:046 Truly **it** is not the eyes that are blind, but the
022:054 and their hearts may be made humbly (open) to **it**:
022:061 and verily **it** is Allah Who hears
022:066 **It** is He Who gave you life, will cause
022:068 say, "Allah knows best what **it** is ye are doing."
022:070 Indeed **it** is all in a record,
022:072 Allah has promised **it** to the Unbelievers!
022:072 **It** is the fire (of Hell)!
022:073 they would have no power to release **it** from the fly:
022:073 Listen to **it**!
022:078 **It** is He Who has named you Muslims, both before
022:078 on you in religion; **it** is the religion of your
023:014 then We developed out of **it** another creature:
023:018 to drain **it** off (with ease).
023:018 and We caused **it** to soak in the soil; and We
023:019 With **it** We grow for you gardens of date-palms
023:020 and relish for those who use **it** for food.
023:034 behold, **it** is certain ye will be lost.
023:043 nor can they delay (**it**).

IT (continued)

023:061 **It** is these who hasten in every good work,
023:062 On no soul do We place a burden greater than **it** can bear:
023:065 (**It** will be said): "Groan not in supplication this day;
023:072 Or is **it** that thou asked them for some recompense?
023:078 little thanks **it** is ye give!
023:078 **It** is He Who has created for you (the faculties
023:080 **It** is He Who gives life and death,
023:088 Say: "Who is **it** in whose hands is the
023:089 They will say, "(**It** belongs) to Allah."
023:091 and some would have lorded **it** over others!
023:100 "By no means! **it** is but a word he says."-
023:108 into **it** (with ignominy)! and speak
024:001 in **it** have We sent down Clear Signs, in order
024:008 But **it** would avert the punishment from the wife,
024:010 If **it** were not for Allah's grace and mercy on you,
024:011 think **it** not to be an evil to you;
024:011 on the contrary **it** is good for you: to every
024:013 Why did they not bring four witnesses to prove **it**?
024:014 Were **it** not for the grace and mercy
024:015 and ye thought **it** to be a light matter,
024:015 while **it** was most serious in the sight of Allah.
024:015 Behold, ye received **it** on your tongues, and said
024:016 "**It** is not right of us to speak of this:
024:016 And why did ye not, when ye heard **it**, say?-
024:020 Were **it** not for the grace and mercy of Allah
024:021 and were **it** not for the grace
024:029 **It** is no fault on your part to enter houses
024:035 is as if there were a Niche and within **it** a Lamp:
024:035 though fire scarce touched **it**: Light upon
024:035 the glass as **it** were a brilliant star: lit from
024:039 until when he comes up to **it**, he finds **it** to be nothing:
024:040 he can hardly see **it**!
024:041 Seest thou not that **it** is Allah Whose praises
024:043 He pleases and He turns **it** away from whom
024:044 **It** is Allah Who alternates the Night and the Day:
024:050 Nay, **it** is they themselves who do wrong.
024:050 Is **it** that there is a disease in their hearts?
024:051 **it** is such as these that will prosper.
024:052 **It** is such as obey Allah and His Messenger,
024:055 as He granted **it** to those before them; that He
024:057 is the Fire,-and **it** is indeed an evil refuge!
024:058 outside those times **it** is not wrong for you or for them
024:060 but **it** is best for them to be modest:
024:061 **It** is no fault in the blind nor in
025:001 that **it** may be an admonition to all creatures;-
025:002 **it** is He Who created all things, and ordered
025:004 and others have help him at **it**."
025:004 In truth **it** is they who have put forward
025:012 When **it** sees them from a place far off, they will
025:017 "Was **it** ye who led these my servants astray,
025:018 not meant was **it** for us that we should take
025:026 **it** will be a Day of dire difficulty for the Misbelievers.
025:029 the Message (of Allah) after **it** had come to me!
025:032 Thus (is **it** revealed), that We may
025:032 rehearsed **it** to thee in slow, well-arranged
025:040 did they not then see **it** (with their own eyes)?
025:042 who **it** is that is most misled in Path!
025:042 had **it** not been that we were constant to them!"-
025:045 If He willed, He could make **it** stationary!
025:046 Then We draw **it** in towards Ourselves,-
025:047 And He **it** is Who makes the Night as a Robe
025:047 and makes the Day (as **it** were) a Resurrection.

IT (continued)

025:048 And He it is Who sends the Winds as heralds
025:049 That with it We may give life to a dead land,
025:051 Had it been Our Will, We could
025:053 It is He Who has let free the two bodies
025:054 It is He Who has created man from water: then has
025:057 Say: "No reward do I ask of you for it but this:
025:060 commandest us?" and it increases them in aversion.
025:060 When it is said to them, "Adore ye The Most Gracious!",
025:062 And it is He Who made the Night and the Day
025:066 "Evil indeed is it as an abode, and as
025:072 they pass by it with honourable (avoidance);
026:003 It may be thou will kill thy self with grief,
026:020 Moses: "I did it then, when I was in error.
026:031 (Pharaoh) said: "Show it then, if thou
026:032 and behold, it was a serpent, plain (for all to see)!
026:033 and behold, it was white to all beholders!
026:035 then what is it ye counsel?"
026:044 the might of Pharaoh, it is we who will certainly win!"
026:045 when behold, it straightway swallows up all the
026:059 Thus it was, but We made the Children of
026:063 So it divided, and each separate part became like
026:078 "Who created me, and it is He Who guides me;
026:080 "And when I am ill, it is He Who cures me;
026:092 "And it shall be said to them: `Where are the (gods) ye
026:109 "No reward do I ask of you for it: my reward
026:111 when it is the meanest that follow thee?"
026:127 "No reward do I ask of you for it: my reward
026:136 They said: "It is the same to us whether thou
026:145 No reward do I ask of you for it: my reward
026:164 "No reward do I ask of you for it: my reward
026:180 "No reward do I ask of you for it: my reward
026:193 With it came down the Truthful spirit
026:196 Without doubt it is (announced) in the
026:197 Is it not a Sign to them that the learned
026:197 knew it (as true)?
026:198 Had We revealed it to any of the non-Arabs,
026:199 they would not have believed in it.
026:199 And had he recited it to them, they would
026:200 Thus have We caused it to enter the hearts
026:201 They will not believe in it until they see
026:202 of a sudden, while they perceive it not;
026:207 It will profit them not the enjoyment
026:210 The Satans did not bring it down:
026:211 It is not meant for them, nor is
026:212 Indeed they are banished from hearing it.
026:220 For it is He Who heareth and knoweth all things.
026:221 on whom it is that the Satans descend?
026:224 And the Poets,- it is those straying in Evil,
027:010 (of its own accord) as if it had been a snake,
027:010 "O Moses!" (it was said), fear not:
027:010 But when he saw it moving (of its own accord)
027:012 and it will come forth white without stain
027:018 (under foot) without knowing it."
027:020 and he said: "Why is it I see not the Hoopoe?
027:028 and deliver it to them: then draw
027:030 It is from Solomon, and is (as follows):
027:034 She said: "Kings, when they enter a country, despoil it,
027:036 Nay it is ye who rejoice in your gift!
027:039 "I will bring it to thee before thou rise
027:040 Then when (Solomon) saw it placed firmly
027:040 "I will bring it to thee before even thy glance
027:042 "It seems the same. And knowledge

027:044 she saw it, she thought it was a lake of water,
027:050 even while they perceived it not.
027:060 it is not in your power to cause
027:060 Yea, with it We cause to grow well-planted
027:062 Little it is that ye heed!
027:064 then repeats it, and Who gives you sustenance
027:068 "It is true we were promised this,-we and
027:072 Say: "It may be that some of the events
027:077 And it certainly is a Guide and Mercy
027:084 not in knowledge, or what was it ye did?"
027:089 If any do good, he will have better than it.
027:091 Him Who has sanctified it and to Whom
027:092 they do it for the good of their own souls,
028:008 (it was intended) that (Moses) should be
028:009 It may be that he will be of use to us, or we
028:019 "O Moses! is it thy intention to slay me
028:027 ten years, it will be (grace) from thee.
028:031 But when he saw it moving (of its own accord)
028:031 "O Moses!" (It was said), "Draw near, and fear
028:031 (of its own accord) as if it had been a snake,
028:032 and it will come forth white without stain
028:037 certain it is that the wrong-doers will not prosper.
028:037 who it is that comes with guidance from Him
028:045 but it is We Who send Messengers (with inspiration)
028:049 than either of them, that I may follow it!
028:053 And when it is recited to them, they say:
028:053 for it is the Truth from our Lord: indeed we
028:056 It is true thou wilt not be able to guide
028:063 It was not us they worshipped."
028:064 It will be said (to them): "Call upon your 'partners'
028:073 It is out of His Mercy that He has made
028:082 or restricts it, to any of His servants He pleases!
028:082 Had it not been that Allah was
028:082 "Ah! It is indeed Allah Who enlarges
028:085 Say: "My Lord knows best who it is that brings
029:010 men's oppression as if it were the Wrath of Allah!
029:019 originates creation, then repeats it: truly that
029:023 it is they who shall despair of My mercy:
029:023 it is they who will (suffer) a most grievous Chastisement.
029:040 it was not Allah Who wronged them: they wronged
029:046 unless it be with those of them who do wrong
029:046 and it is to Him we submit (in Islam)."
029:047 And thus (it is) that We have sent down
029:048 nor art thou (able) to transcribe it with thy right hand:
029:051 And is it not enough for them that We have
029:051 Verily, in it is Mercy and Reminder to those
029:052 And it is those who believe
029:053 had it not been for a term (of respite)
029:053 and it will certainly reach them,-
029:060 It is Allah Who feeds (both) them and you:
029:063 And if indeed thou ask them who it is that sends
029:068 or rejects the Truth when it reaches him?
030:006 (It is) the promise of Allah.
030:009 it was not Allah Who wronged them, but they wronged
030:009 and populated it in greater numbers than these
030:011 It is Allah Who begins the creation; then repeats it;
030:019 It is He Who brings out the living from the dead,
030:019 and Who gives life to the earth after it is dead:
030:024 and with it gives life to the earth after it is dead:
030:027 It is He Who begins (the process of) creation;
030:027 then repeats it; and for Him it is most easy.
030:037 the provision and restricts it, to whomsoever

IT (continued)

030:038   and **it** is they who will prosper.
030:039   **it** is these who will get a recompense multiplied.
030:040   **It** is Allah Who has created you: further,
030:047   and **it** was a duty incumbent upon Us to aid
030:048   **It** is Allah Who sends the Winds, and they
030:054   **It** is Allah Who created you in a state
030:054   and **it** is He Who has all knowledge and power.
031:010   standing firm, lest **it** should shake with you;
031:010   and He scattered through **it** beast of all kinds.
031:016   a mustard-seed and **it** were (hidden) in a rock,
031:016   or on earth, Allah will bring **it** forth: for Allah
031:021   What! even if **it** is Satan beckoning them to the
031:025   who **it** is that created the heavens and the earth.
031:027   with seven Oceans behind **it** to add to its (supply),
031:034   **It** is He Who sends down rain, and He
031:034   Nor does any one know what **it** is that he
032:003   Or do they say, "He has forged **it**"?
032:003   Nay, **it** is the Truth from thy Lord, that thou
032:004   **It** is Allah Who has created the heavens and the
032:005   then **it** ascends unto Him, on a day the measure of which
032:020   be forced thereinto, and **it** will be said to them:
032:023   and We made **it** a guide to the Children of Israel.
032:026   Does **it** not teach them a lesson, how many
032:029   no profit will **it** be to Unbelievers if they
033:014   have brought **it** to pass, with none
033:017   from Allah if **it** be His wish to give you
033:017   Say: "Who is **it** that can screen you from Allah
033:022   And **it** only added to their faith and their
033:028   "If **it** be that ye desire the life of this world,
033:036   **It** is not fitting for a Believer, man or woman,
033:037   but **it** is more fitting that thou shouldst, fear Allah.
033:038   **It** was the practice (approved) of Allah
033:039   (**It** is the practice of those) who preach
033:043   He **it** is Who sends blessings on you, as do
033:052   **It** is not lawful for thee (to marry more)
033:053   Nor is **it** right for you that ye should
033:054   Whether ye reveal anything or conceal **it**,
033:060   be able to stay in **it** as thy neighbors for any
033:072   but they refused to undertake **it**, being afraid thereof:
033:072   but man undertook **it**:- he was indeed unjust and foolish;-
034:003   Nay! but most surely, by my Lord, **it** will come upon you;-
034:006   and that **it** guides to the path of the
034:008   Nay, **it** is those who believe not in the Hereafter,
034:021   from him who is in doubt concerning **it**: and thy
034:023   will they say, 'What is **it** that your Lord
034:024   Say: "**It** is Allah; and certain **it** is that either we or ye are
034:031   nor in (any) that (came) before **it**."
034:031   "Had **it** not been for you,
034:032   from Guidance after **it** reached you?
034:032   Nay, rather **it** was ye who transgressed."
034:032   "Was **it** we who kept you back from Guidance
034:033   **it** would only be a requital for their (ill) Deeds.
034:033   "Nay! **it** was a plot (of yours) by day
034:037   **It** is not your wealth nor your sons, that will
034:039   (in His Cause) but He replaces **it**: for He
034:040   "Was **it** you that these men used to worship?"
034:043   when **it** comes to them, "This is nothing
034:046   (**it** may be) in pairs, or (**it** may be) singly,
034:047   Say" Whatever reward do I ask of you: **it** is yours:
034:050   **it** is because of the inspiration of my of my Lord to me:
034:050   **it** is He Who hears all things,
035:008   so that he looks upon **it** as good,

IT (continued)

035:009   **It** is Allah Who sends forth the Winds, so that
035:010   **it** is He Who exalts each Deed of Righteousness.
035:015   O ye men! **it** is ye that have need of Allah:
035:018   not the least portion of **it** can be carried
035:027   With **it** We then bring out produce of various
035:031   confirming what was (revealed) before **it**:
035:039   He **it** is that has made you inheritors
035:040   Show me what **it** is they have
035:041   **It** is Allah Who sustains the heavens and the
035:042   to them, **it** has only increased their aversion.
036:005   (**It** is a Revelation) sent down by (Him),
036:013   Behold, there came messengers to **it**.
036:026   **It** was said: "Enter thou the Garden."
036:028   from heaven, nor was **it** needful for Us so to do.
036:029   **It** was no more than a single mighty Blast,
036:033   We do give **it** life, and produce
036:035   of this (artistry): **it** was not their hands
036:040   **It** is not permitted to the Sun to catch
036:043   If **it** were Our Will, We could drown them;
036:049   **it** will seize them while they are yet disputing among
036:053   **It** will be no more than a single Blast,
036:066   If **it** had been Our Will, We could
036:067   And if **it** had been Our Will, We could
036:069   in Poetry, nor is **it** meant for him:
036:070   That **it** may give admonition to any (who are)
036:071   See they not that **it** is We Who have created
036:077   Doth not man see that **it** is We Who created
036:082   His command is, "Be," and **it** is!
037:014   And, when they see a Sign, turn **it** to mockery,
037:019   Then **it** will be a single (compelling) cry;
037:022   "Bring ye up," **it** shall be said, "The wrong-doers
037:028   They will say: "**It** was ye who used to come
037:030   Nay, **it** was ye who were a people in
037:057   "Had **it** not been for the Grace of my Lord,
037:058   "Is **it** (the case) that we shall not die,
037:063   For We have truly made **it** (as) a trial
037:064   For **it** is a tree that springs out of
037:086   "Is **it** a Falsehood-gods other than Allah
037:143   Had **it** not been that he (repented and)
037:149   is **it** that thy Lord has (only) daughters,
037:170   they reject **it**: but soon will they know!
037:177   But when **it** descends upon their courtyards
038:015   which (when **it** comes) will brook no delay.
038:018   **It** was We that made the hills declare, in unison
038:026   for **it** will mislead thee from the Path of Allah:
038:054   Truly such will be Our bounty (to you): **it** will never fail;-
038:057   Yea, such!-Then shall they taste **it**,-a boiling
038:060   **It** is ye who have brought this upon us!
038:062   And they will say: "How is **it** with us that we
038:088   the truth of **it** (all) after a while."
039:002   Verily **it** is We Who have revealed the Book
039:003   Is **it** not to Allah that sincere devotion is due?
039:009   **It** is those who are endued with
039:014   Say: "**It** is Allah I serve, with my
039:018   and follow the best of **it**: those are
039:020   But **it** is for those who fear their Lord,
039:021   then He makes **it** dry up and crumble
039:021   then **it** withers; thou wilt see **it** grow yellow;
039:021   and leads **it** through springs in the earth?
039:024   on the Day of Judgment (and receive **it**) on his face,
039:024   **It** will be said to the wrong-doers: "Taste ye
039:028   (**It** is) a Qur'an in Arabic, without any

IT (continued)

039:032 and rejects the Truth when **it** comes to him!
039:033 and he who confirms (and supports) **it**-such are
039:038 If indeed thou ask them who **it** is that created
039:040 "Who **it** is to whom comes a Chastisement
039:042 **It** is Allah that takes the souls (of men)
039:044 in the End, **it** is to Him that ye shall
039:046 **It** is Thou that wilt judge
039:047 (in vain) would they offer **it** for ransom from the
039:052 the provision or restricts **it**, for any
039:057 "Or (lest) **it** should say: `If only Allah had guided me,
039:058 "Or (lest) **it** should say when **it** (actually) sees
039:063 reject the Signs of Allah, **it** is they who will be in loss.
039:064 Say: "Is **it** someone other than Allah that ye
039:065 as **it** was to those before thee,-" If thou
039:065 But **it** has already been revealed to thee,-
039:068 except such as **it** will please Allah (to exempt).
040:005 the Truth; but **it** was I that seized them!
040:007 and those around **it** sing Glory and Praise
040:013 He **it** is Who showeth you His Signs, and sendeth
040:014 even though the Unbelievers may detest **it**.
040:015 that **it** may warn (men) of the Day
040:017 That Day will every soul be requited for what **it** earned;
040:020 Verily **it** is Allah (alone) Who hears
040:029 us form the Punishment of Allah, should **it** befall us?"
040:039 **it** is the Hereafter that is the Home that will last.
040:041 "And O my People! how (strange) **it** is for me
040:052 The Day when no profit will **it** be to Wrong-doers
040:056 **it** is He Who hears and sees (all things).
040:061 **It** is Allah Who has made the Night for you,
040:064 **It** is Allah Who has made for you the earth
040:067 **It** is He Who has created you from dust, then from
040:068 **It** is He Who gives Life and Death; and when
040:068 He says to **it**, "Be," and **it** is.
040:073 Then shall **it** be said to them: "Where are the (deities)
040:077 (in any case) **it** is to Us that they shall (all) return.
040:078 **It** was not (possible) for any messenger to bring a Sign
040:079 **It** is Allah Who made cattle for you, that ye
041:006 **it** is revealed to me by inspiration, that your God
041:009 Say: Is **it** that ye Deny Him Who created the earth
041:010 on the (earth), mountains standing firm, high above **it**,
041:011 He said to **it** and to the earth: "Come ye together,
041:011 Then He turned to the sky, and **it** had been (as) smoke:
041:012 with lights, and (provided **it**) with guard.
041:034 and thee was hatred become as **it** were thy
041:037 if **it** is Him ye wish to serve.
041:038 (nor feel themselves above **it**).
041:039 but when We send down rain to **it**, **it** is stirred to life
041:041 Those who reject the Message when **it** comes to them
041:041 and indeed **it** is a Book of exalted power.
041:042 **it** is sent down by One Full of Wisdom, Worthy of
041:042 No falsehood can approach **it** from before or behind **it**:
041:044 Say: "**It** is a guide and a healing to those
041:044 they are (as **it** were) being called from
041:044 and **it** is blindness in their (eyes): they are
041:045 Had **it** not been for a Word
041:046 whoever works evil, **it** is against his own soul:
041:052 is (really) from Allah, and yet do ye reject **it**?
041:053 until **it** becomes manifest to them that this is the Truth.
041:053 Is **it** not enough that thy Lord doth witness all things?
041:054 Ah indeed! **it** is He that doth encompass all things!
042:009 **it** is He Who has power over all things.
042:009 and **it** is He Who gives life to the dead:

IT (continued)

042:009 But **it** is Allah,-He is the Protector,
042:010 Whatever **it** be wherein ye differ, the decision
042:014 are in suspicious (disquieting) doubt concerning **it**.
042:014 Had **it** not been for a Word that went forth before
042:017 **It** is Allah Who has sent down the Book in truth,
042:018 Only those wish to hasten **it** who believe not in **it**:
042:018 those who believe hold **it** in awe,
042:018 and know that **it** is the Truth.
042:021 Had **it** not been for the Decree
042:027 but He sends (**it**) down in due measure
042:033 If **it** be His Will, He can
042:036 (**it** is) for those who believe and put their trust
043:003 We have made **it** a Qur'an in Arabic, that ye
043:004 And verily, **it** is in the Mother of the Book,
043:013 for we could never be able to do **it**.
043:020 ("Ah!") they say, "If **it** had been the will
043:028 And he left **it** as a Word to endure among those
043:030 they said: "This is sorcery, and we do reject **it**."
043:032 **It** is We Who portion out between them their
043:032 Is **it** they who would portion out the Mercy
043:033 And were **it** not that (all) men might become
043:039 When ye have done wrong, **it** will avail you nothing,
043:060 And if **it** were Our Will, We could
043:066 that **it** should come on them all of a sudden,
043:076 but **it** is they who have been unjust themselves.
043:079 But **it** is We Who settle things.
043:084 **It** is He Who is God in heaven and God
044:003 We sent **it** down during a blessed night: for We
044:008 **it** is He Who gives life and gives death,-
044:045 Like molten brass; **it** will boil in their insides,
045:012 **It** is Allah Who has subjected the sea to you,
045:012 that ships may sail through **it** by His command,
045:014 **it** is for Him to recompense (for good or ill)
045:015 if he does evil, **it** works against (His own soul).
045:015 If any one does a righteous deed, **it** is to his own benefit;
045:017 **it** was only after knowledge had been granted to
045:019 **it** is only wrong-doers (that stand as) Protectors,
045:022 each soul may find the recompense of what **it** has earned,
045:026 Say: "**It** is Allah Who gives you life, then gives
045:032 the Hour: we only think **it** a conjecture, and we
045:032 "And when **it** was said that the promise of Allah
045:034 **It** will also be said: "This Day We will forget
046:004 Show me what **it** is they have created on earth,
046:004 Say: "Do ye see what **it** is ye invoke beside Allah?
046:007 of the Truth when **it** comes to them:
046:008 Or do they say, "He has forged **it**"? Say: "Had I forged **it**,
046:010 from Allah, and ye reject **it**,
046:011 (such men) would not have gone to **it** first, before us!"
046:012 and this Book confirms **it** in the Arabic tongue;
046:020 (**it** will be said to them): "Ye squandered
046:023 He said: "The Knowledge (of when **it** will come)
046:024 "Nay, **it** is the (calamity) ye were
046:025 "Everything will **it** destroy by the command
046:030 revealed after Moses, confirming what came before **it**:
046:030 **it** guides to the Truth and to a Straight Path.
046:035 (**it** will be) as if they had not tarried more than an hour
047:002 sent down to Muhammad-for **it** the Truth from their
047:004 but if **it** had been Allah's Will, He could
047:015 In **it** there are for them all kinds of fruits,
047:015 so that **it** cuts up their bowels (to pieces)?
047:015 in **it** are rivers of water installing;
047:016 received Knowledge: "What is **it** he said just then?"

IT (continued)

047:018   that **it** should come on them of a sudden?
047:018   some tokens thereof, and when **it** comes to them
047:021   Were **it** to obey and say what is just, and when
047:021   **it** were best for them if they were true to Allah.
047:022   Then, is **it** to be expected of you, if ye
047:027   But how (will **it** be) when the angels take their
047:038   of all wants, and **it** is ye that are needy.
048:004   **It** is He who sent down Tranquillity into the
048:006   and evil is **it** for a destination.
048:020   that **it** may be a Sign for the Believers,
048:024   And **it** is He who has restrained their hands
048:026   and well were they entitled to **it** and worthy of **it**.
048:028   **It** is He who has sent His Messenger with Guidance
048:028   and the Religion of Truth, to make **it** over all religion:
048:029   As a result, **it** fills the Unbelievers with rage at him.
048:029   and **it** stands on **its** own stem, (filling) the sowers with
048:029   then makes **it** strong; **it** then becomes thick,
049:005   thou couldst come out to them, **it** would be best for them:
049:007   and has made **it** beautiful in your hearts, and He
049:009   transgresses until **it** complies with the command of Allah;
049:009   but if **it** complies, then make peace between them
049:011   **it** may be that the (latter) are better than the (former):
049:011   **it** may be that the (latter) are better than the (former):
049:012   Nay, ye would abhor **it**... But fear
050:005   But they deny the truth when **it** comes to them:
050:006   and adorned **it**, and there is not flaws in **it**?
050:006   How We have made **it** and adorned **it**,
050:007   And the earth-We have spread **it** out, and set
050:016   **It** was We who created man, and We
050:022   (**It** will be said:) "Thou wast heedless of this;
050:030   **It** will say, "Are there any more (to come)?"
050:043   Verily **it** is We Who give Life and Death;
051:013   (**It** will be) a Day when they will be tried
051:027   And placed **it** before them... He said,
051:042   **It** left nothing whatever that **it** came up against,
051:042   but reduced **it** to ruin and rottenness.
052:008   There is none can avert **it**;-
052:014   "This," **it** will be said, "Is the Fire,-
052:015   "Is this then a magic, or is **it** ye that do not see?
052:016   the same is **it** to you whether ye bear it with patience,
052:028   truly **it** is He, the Beneficent
052:032   Is **it** that their intellects urges them to this,
052:034   like unto **it**,-if (**it** be) they speak the Truth!
052:040   Or is **it** that thou dost ask for a reward,
052:041   and they write **it** down?
053:001   By the Star when **it** goes down,-
053:004   **It** is no less than inspiration sent down to him:
053:015   Near **it** is the Garden of Abode.
053:017   (His) sight never swerved, nor did **it** go wrong!
053:032   He knows best who **it** is that guards against evil.
053:043   That **it** is He who Granteth Laughter and Tears;
053:044   That **it** is He who Granteth Death and Life;
053:048   That **it** is He Who giveth wealth and satisfaction,
053:050   And that **it** is He Who destroyed the (powerful)
053:054   So that there covered **it** that which covered.
053:058   No one but Allah can disclose **it**.
054:025   "Is **It** that the Message is sent to him, of all
055:002   **It** is He Who has taught the Qur'an.
055:010   **It** is He Who has spread out the earth
055:033   If **it** be ye can pass beyond the zones
055:037   and **it** becomes red like ointment:
056:003   (Many) will **it** bring low; (many) will **it** exalt;

056:054   "And drink Boiling Water on top of **it**:
056:057   **It** is We Who have created you: why will
056:059   Is **it** ye who create **it**, or are We the Creators?
056:064   Is **it** ye that cause **it** to grow, or are We the Cause?
056:065   Were **it** Our Will, we could make **it** broken orts.
056:069   Do ye bring **it** Down (in rain) from the Cloud,
056:070   Were **it** Our Will, We could make **it** saltish
056:072   Is **it** ye who grow the tree which feeds the fire,
056:072   which feeds the fire, or do We grow **it**?
056:073   We have made **it** a reminder and an article
056:081   Is **it** such a Message that ye would hold
056:082   that ye should declare **it** false?
056:082   And have ye made **it** your livelihood that ye
057:002   **it** is He Who gives life and Death; and He has power
057:004   enters within the earth and what comes out of **it**,
057:004   He **it** is Who created the heavens and the earth
057:004   what comes down from heaven and what mounts up to **it**.
057:008   How is **it** with you that you not believe in Allah?-
057:010   And is **it** with you that you spend not
057:011   increase **it** manifold to his credit,
057:013   Within **it** will be Mercy throughout, and without **it**,
057:013   **It** will be said: "Turn ye back to your rear!
057:015   to claim you: and an evil refuge **it** is!"
057:018   a Beautiful Loan, **it** shall be increased manifold
057:020   How rain and he growth which **it** brings forth,
057:020   delight (the hearts of) the tillers; soon **it** withers;
057:020   thou wilt see **it** grow yellow; then **it** becomes dry and
057:022   a Book before We bring **it** into existence:
057:025   that Allah may test who **it** is that will help,
057:029   His Hand, to bestow **it** on whomsoever He wills.
058:003   (**it** is ordained that such a one) should free
058:008   in **it** will they burn, and evil
058:009   do **it** not for iniquity and hostility, disobedience
058:009   but do **it** for righteousness and self-restraint,
058:013   Is **it** that ye are afraid of spending sums
058:019   Truly, **it** is the Party of Satan that will lose.
058:021   "**It** is I and My messenger who must prevail":
058:022   Truly **it** is the Party of Allah that will
059:002   **It** is He who got out the Unbelievers among the
059:002   they little expected (**it**), and cast
059:003   And had **it** not been that Allah has decreed
059:005   left them standing on their roots, **it** was by leave of Allah,
059:007   in order that **it** may not (Merely) make a circuit
059:020   **it** is the Companions of the Garden,
059:021   have seen **it** humble itself and cleave
060:007   **It** may be that Allah will Establish friendship
060:009   **It** is such as turn to them (in these circumstances),
061:003   Grievously hateful is **it** in the sight of Allah
061:008   may detest (**it**).
061:009   That He make **it** prevail over all religion,
061:009   may detest (**it**).
061:009   **It** is He Who has sent His Messenger with Guidance
062:002   **It** is He Who has sent amongst the Unlettered
062:011   they disperse headlong to **it**, and leave thee standing.
063:005   And when **it** is said to them, "Come, the Messenger
063:006   **It** is equal to them whether thou pray for their
063:011   when the time appointed (for **it**) has come;
064:002   **It** is He Who has created you; and of you
064:017   He will double **it** to your (credit), and He
065:004   (**it** is the same): for those who are pregnant,
066:003   and she then divulged **it** (to another), and Allah
066:003   and Allah made **it** known to him, he confirmed

IT (continued)

066:005 It may be, if he divorced you (all), that Allah
066:007 (It will be said), "O ye Unbelievers! make no
067:007 of its breath even as it blazes forth.
067:013 or make it known, He certainly has (full) knowledge,
067:015 It is He Who has made the earth manageable for you,
067:016 when it shakes (as in an earthquake)?
067:019 truly it is He that watches over all things.
067:023 and understanding: little thanks it is ye give.
067:023 Say: "It is He Who has created you, and made
067:024 Say: "It is He Who has multiplied you through
067:026 "As to the knowledge of the time, it is with Allah alone:
067:027 of the Unbelievers, and it will be said (to them):
067:027 At length, when they see it close at hand,
067:029 (of us) it is that is in manifest error."
068:007 Verily it is thy Lord that knoweth best,
068:018 But made no reservation, ("If it be Allah's Will").
068:032 "It may be that our Lord will give us in exchange
068:038 That ye shall have, through it whatever ye choose?
068:046 Or is it that thou dost ask them for a reward,
068:047 so that they can write it down?
068:052 But it is nothing less than a Message
069:007 He made it rage against them seven nights
069:012 That We might make it a Reminder unto you,
069:016 for it will that Day be flimsy,
069:041 It is not the word of a poet: little it is ye believe!
069:042 of a soothsayer: little admonition it is ye receive.
069:042 Nor is it the word of a soothsayer:
069:049 amongst you those that reject (it).
069:051 But verily it is Truth of assured certainty.
070:007 But We see it (quite) near.
070:014 so it could deliver him:
070:015 By no means! for it would be the Blazing Fire-
070:018 And collect (wealth) and hide it (from use)!
071:004 is accomplished, it cannot be put forward:
071:014 "`Seeing that it is He that has created you
072:001 Say: It has been revealed to me that a company
072:002 'It gives guidance to the Right, and we
072:008 but we found it filled with stern guards and flaming
072:013 to the Guidance, we have accepted it:
072:021 Say: "It is not in my power to cause you harm,
072:024 who it is that is weakest in (his) helper
072:025 for it a distant term.
073:003 Half of it,-or a little less,
073:020 ye shall find it with Allah.
074:028 and naught doth it leave alone!-
074:028 Naught doth it permit to endure, and naught
074:030 Over it are Nineteen.
074:033 And by the Night as it retreateth,
074:034 And by the Dawn as it shineth forth,-
074:055 Let any who will, keep it in remembrance!
074:056 But none will keep it in remembrance except as
075:017 It is for Us to collect it and to recite it:
075:018 But when We have recited it, follow thou
075:019 Nay more, it is for Us to explain it (and make it clear):
075:028 And he will think that it was (the Time)
076:006 do drink, making it flow in unstinted abundance.
076:020 And when thou lookest, it is there thou wilt see a
076:023 It is We Who have sent down the Qur'an
076:028 It is We Who created them, and We have
077:029 (It will be said:) "Depart ye to that which ye
077:032 "Indeed it throws about sparks (huge) as Forts,
077:036 Nor will it be open to them to put forth pleas.

IT (continued)

077:039 (or plot), use it against Me!
077:048 And when it is said to them, "Prostrate yourselves!"
079:012 They say: "It would, in that case, be a
079:013 But verily, it will be but a single
079:021 But (Pharaoh) rejected it and disobeyed (guidance);
079:027 (Allah) hath constructed it:
079:028 and He hath given it order and perfection.
079:044 With they Lord is the final end of it.
079:045 Thou art but a Warner for such as fear it.
079:046 The Day they see it, (it will be) as if they had tarried
080:007 Though it is no blame to thee if he grow
080:011 By no means (should it be so)!
080:011 For it is indeed a Message of remembrance.
080:012 Therefore let whose will, keep it in remembrance.
080:013 (It is) in Books held (greatly) in honor.
080:022 Then, when it is His will, He will
080:024 Then let man look at his food, (and how We provide it):
081:014 (Then) shall each soul know what it has put forward.
081:017 And the Night as it dissipates;
081:018 And the Dawn as it breathes away the darkness;-
081:025 Nor is it the word of a Satan accursed.
082:005 what it hath sent forward and (what it hath) kept back.
082:019 (It will be) the Day when no soul shall have
083:012 And none can deny it but the Transgressor
083:017 Further, it will be said to them: "This is the
083:027 With it will be (given) a mixture of Tasnim:
084:002 and it must needs (do so);-
084:004 And casts forth what is within it and becomes
084:005 and it must needs (do so);-(then will
084:022 But on the contrary the Unbelievers reject (it).
085:013 It is He Who Creates from the very beginning,
086:003 (It is) the Star of piercing brightness;-
086:004 There is no soul but has a protector over it.
086:014 It is not a thing for amusement.
087:005 And then doth make it (but) swarthy stubble.
087:008 And We will make it easy for thee (to follow)
087:011 But it will be avoided by the most
088:018 And at the Sky, how it is raised high?-
088:020 And at the Earth, how it is spread out?
088:026 Then it will be for Us to call them to account.
089:004 And by the Night when it passeth away;-
090:013 (It is:) freeing the bondman;
091:003 By the Day as it shows up (the Sun's) glory;
091:004 By the Night as it conceals it;
091:007 and order given to it;
091:009 Truly he succeeds that purifies it,
091:010 And he fails that corrupts it!
091:013 "It is a She-camel of Allah!
092:001 By the Night as it conceals (the light);
092:002 By the Day as it appears in glory;
092:017 shall be removed far from it,-
093:002 And by the Night when it is still,-
099:007 anyone who has done an atom's weight of good, see it!
099:008 who has done an atom's weight of evil, shall see it.
101:004 (It is) a Day whereon Men will be like
101:011 (It is) a Fire Blazing fiercely!
102:007 Again, ye shall see it with certainty of sight!
104:002 Who pileth up wealth and layeth it by,
104:006 (It is) the Fire of Allah kindled (to a blaze),
104:008 It shall be made into a vault over them,
113:003 From the mischief of Darkness as it overspreads;

ITS

002:060	Each group knew **its** own place for water.
002:061	**its** pot-herbs, and cucumbers, **its** garlic, lentils,
002:126	and feed **its** People with fruits,
002:138	(Our religion) takes **its** hue from Allah
002:187	appear to you distinct from **its** black thread;
002:217	and drive out **its** members.
002:249	if any drinks of **its** water,
002:259	after (this) **its** death?"
002:259	all in ruins to **its** roofs.
003:007	but no one knows **its** true meanings except Allah.
003:007	seeking discord, and searching for **its** interpretation,
003:030	a great distance between it and **its** evil.
003:161	receive **its** due whatever it earned,
004:085	helps an evil cause, shares in **its** burden:
005:044	By **its** standard have been judged the Jews, by the
005:095	or **its** equivalent in fasts: that he
005:096	and **its** use for food,-for the
005:108	in **its** true nature and shape, or else
006:038	nor a being that flies on **its** wings,
006:070	is caught in **its** own ruin by **its** own action:
006:091	while ye conceal much (of **its** contents):
006:099	the date-palm and **its** sheaths (or spathes)
006:108	alluring to each people **its** own doings.
006:115	thy Lord doth find **its** fulfillment in truth and in justice:
006:123	We placed leaders in every town, **its** wicked men,
006:157	We should have followed **its** guidance better than they."
006:158	nor earned righteousness through **its** Faith.
006:164	every soul draws the meed of **its** acts on none but itself:
007:019	and enjoy (**its** good things) as ye wish:
007:038	it curses **its** sister-People (that went before),
007:043	Ye have been made **its** inheritors, for your
007:053	Are they waiting for **its** fulfillment?
007:058	by the Will of **its** Cherisher, springs up
007:058	springs up produce, (rich) after **its** kind:
007:094	We took up **its** people in suffering
007:098	against **its** coming in broad daylight while they
007:100	in succession to **its** (previous) possessors,
007:123	to drive out **its** people: but soon
007:143	if it abide in **its** place, then shalt
007:160	each group knew **its** own place for water.
007:187	when will be **its** appointed time?
007:187	Heavy were **its** burden through the heavens
008:034	and they are not **its** guardians?
008:034	No men can be **its** guardians except the righteous;
008:035	(**its** only answer can be), "Taste ye the Chastisement
008:039	in **its** entirety but if they cease, verily Allah
009:076	averse (from **its** fulfillment).
009:118	for all **its** speciousness, and their
010:024	by **its** mingling arises the produce of the earth-
010:024	the earth is clad with **its** golden ornaments and is
010:098	so **its** Faith should have profited it,-
011:006	but **its** sustenance dependeth on Allah:
011:006	He knoweth **its** resting place and **its** temporary deposit:
011:015	who desire the life of the Present and **its** glitter,-
011:056	but He hath grasp of **its** forelock.
012:045	said: "I will tell you the truth of **its** interpretation:
013:002	each one runs (**its** course) for a term appointed.
013:017	each according to **its** measure: but the
013:041	the land from **its** outlying borders?
014:024	and **its** branches (reach) to the heavens,-
014:025	brings forth **its** fruit at all times, by the leave of **its** Lord.
014:051	each soul according to **its** deserts; and verily

ITS (continued)

015:005	anticipate **its** Term, nor delay it.
015:021	And there is not a thing but **its** (sources and)
015:022	though ye are not the guardians of **its** stores.
016:065	to the earth after **its** death: verily in this
016:068	to build **its** cells in hills, on trees, and in
016:111	(fully) for all **its** actions, and none
016:112	because of the (evil) which (**its** people) wrought.
016:124	for those who disagreed (as to **its** observance);
017:029	nor stretch it forth to **its** utmost reach,
017:081	for Falsehood is (by **its** nature) bound to perish."
018:033	Each of those gardens brought forth **its** produce,
018:042	to pieces to **its** very foundations, and he
018:061	which took **its** course through the sea
018:063	it took **its** course through the sea
018:109	even it we added another ocean like it, for **its** aid."
020:015	for every soul to receiver **its** reward by the
020:015	by the measure of **its** Endeavour.
020:021	to **its** former condition"...
020:050	to each (created) thing **its** form, then, gave (it)
020:114	the Qur'an before **its** revelation to thee
020:130	and before **its** setting; yea, celebrate them
021:018	and it knocks out **its** brain, and behold,
021:033	each in **its** rounded course.
021:044	the land (in their control) from **its** outlying borders?
022:031	(like a bird on **its** prey) and thrown him into a far-
024:041	Each one knows **its** own (mode of) prayer and praise.
025:012	they will hear **its** fury and **its** raging sigh.
025:045	Then do We make the sun **its** guide;
025:065	for **its** Wrath is indeed an affliction grievous,-
026:208	Never did We destroy a town but had **its** warners-
027:010	(of **its** own accord) as if it had been a snake,
027:034	make the noblest of **its** people meanest thus do
027:054	though ye see (**its** iniquity)?
027:061	to live in; made rivers in **its** midst; set thereon
028:004	in the land and divided **its** people into sections,
028:015	when **its** people were not watching: and he
028:031	But when he saw it moving (of **its** own accord)
028:059	a population except when **its** members practice
028:059	to **its** Centre a messenger, rehearsing to
028:061	to reach **its** (fulfillment), and one
029:063	and gives life therewith to the earth after **its** death,
030:050	to the earth after **its** death:
031:027	with seven Oceans behind it to add to **its** (supply),
031:029	each running **its** course for a term appointed;
032:013	certainly have brought every soul **its** true guidance:
032:023	be not then in doubt of **its** reaching (thee):
033:028	that ye desire the life of this world, and **its** glitter,-
033:053	to wait for **its** preparation:
034:012	the Wind (obedient): **its** early morning (stride)
034:012	and **its** evening (stride) was a month's (journey);
034:049	and Falsehood showeth not **its** face and will
035:009	the earth therewith after **its** death:
035:013	each one runs **its** course for a term appointed.
035:036	nor shall **its** Chastisement be lightened for them.
036:040	(just) swims along in (**its** own) orbit (according to Law).
037:065	The shoots of **its** fruit-stalks are like
038:029	that they may meditate on **its** Signs, and that
039:017	not into **its** worship,-and turn to Allah
039:023	(yet) repeating (**its** teaching in various aspects):
039:069	with the light of **its** Lord: the Record
039:070	in full (the fruit) of **its** deeds;
039:071	when they arrive there, **its** gates will be opened.

ITS (continued)

039:071	And its Keepers will say, "Did not messengers
039:073	and its Keepers will say: "Peace be upon you!
039:073	they arrive there; its gates will be opened;
041:010	and measured therein its sustenance in four Days,
041:012	to each heaven its duty and command.
041:026	in the midst of its (reading), that ye
041:044	"Why are not its verses explained in detail?
041:047	no fruit comes out of its sheath, nor does
043:048	each greater then its fellow, and We
045:005	and revives therewith the earth after its death,
045:028	called to its Record: "This Day shall ye be
045:032	there was no doubt about its (coming), ye used
046:010	Israel testifies to its similarity (with earlier scripture),
046:025	by the command of its Lord!"
047:004	until the war lays down its burdens.
048:029	and it stands on its own stem, (filling) the
048:029	like a seed which sends forth its blade,
050:039	of the sun and before (its) setting,
051:007	By the Sky with (its) numerous Paths,
052:038	(climb up to heaven and) listen (to its secrets)?
053:046	From a seed when lodged (in its place);
054:003	but every matter has its appointed time.
055:012	Also corn with (its) leaves and stalk for fodder,
055:029	Of Him seeks (its need) every creature
055:044	In its midst and in the midst of boiling hot
056:002	Then will no (soul) deny its coming.
056:004	When the earth shall be shaken to its depths,
057:017	life to the earth after its death!
067:007	of its breath even as it blazes forth.
067:008	its Keepers will ask, "Did no Warner come to you?"
067:015	so traverse ye through its tracts and enjoy of the
069:007	see the (whole) people lying overthrown in its (path),
069:011	the water (of Noah's Flood) overflowed beyond its limits,
069:012	should bear its (lessons) in remembrance.
069:012	(that should hear the tale and) retain its memory should
069:014	And the earth in moved, and its mountains,
069:017	And the angels will be on its sides, and eight
074:038	Every soul will be (held) in pledge for its deeds.
075:018	follow thou its recital (as promulgated):
075:026	the collar-bone (in its exit),
079:028	On high hath He raised its canopy, and He
079:029	and its splendor doth He bring out (with light).
079:029	Its night doth He endow with darkness,
079:031	He draweth out therefrom its water and its pasture,
079:042	'When will be its appointed time?'
081:001	When the sun (with its spacious light) is folded up;
084:002	And hearkens to (the Command of) its Lord,-and it
084:005	And hearkens to (the Command of) its Lord,-and it
084:017	The Night and its Homing;
085:001	By the Sky, with its constellations;
091:005	By the Firmament and its (wonderful) structure;
091:006	By the Earth and its (wide) expanse;
091:008	And its inspiration as to its wrong and its right;
091:015	And for Him is no fear of its consequences.

ITSELF

004:050	but that by itself is a manifest sin!
006:070	it will find for itself no protector
006:164	of its acts on none but itself: no bearer
016:111	up pleading for itself, and every
023:053	each party rejoices in that which is with itself.
029:041	who builds (to itself) a house; but truly
030:032	each party rejoicing in that which is with itself!

ITSELF (continued)

039:023	of a Book, consistent with itself, (yet) repeating
059:021	have seen it humble itself and cleave

J

JACOB
002:132 upon his sons and so did **Jacob**;
002:133 when Death appeared before **Jacob**?
002:136 and to Abraham, Isma'il, Isaac, **Jacob**,
002:140 Abraham, Isma'il, Isaac, **Jacob**
003:084 Abraham, Isma'il; Isaac, **Jacob**, and the Tribes,
004:163 Isma'il, Isaac, **Jacob** and the Tribes, to Jesus,
006:084 We gave him Isaac and **Jacob**: all (three)
011:071 glad tidings of Isaac, and after him, of **Jacob**.
012:006 perfect His favour to thee and to the posterity of **Jacob**-
012:013 (**Jacob**) said: "Really it saddens me that ye
012:038 my fathers,-Abraham, Isaac, and **Jacob**; and never
012:066 (**Jacob**) said: "Never will I send him with you
012:083 **Jacob** said: "Nay, but ye have yourselves contrived
019:006 and inherit the posterity of **Jacob**; and make
019:049 Isaac and **Jacob**, and each one of them We made
021:072 as an additional gift, (a grandson) „**Jacob**,
029:027 and **Jacob**, and ordained among his progeny
038:045 Abraham, Isaac, and **Jacob**, possessors of

JACOB'S
012:068 it served only to satisfy **Jacob's** heartfelt desire.

JEALOUS
048:015 "But ye are **jealous** of us." Nay, but little

JEST
002:231 Do not treat Allah's Signs as a **jest**,
018:056 My Signs and warnings as a **jest**.
018:106 and took My Signs and My Messengers by way of **jest**.
021:002 but they listen to it as in **jest**,-
021:055 or are you one of those who **jest**?"
023:115 created you in **jest**, and that
045:009 of Our Signs, he takes them in **jest**: for such
045:035 the Signs of Allah in **jest**, and the

JESTING
002:014 we (were) only **jesting**."
083:031 to their own people, they would return **jesting**;

JESUS
002:087 We gave **Jesus** the son of Mary clear (Signs)
002:136 and that given to Moses and **Jesus**,
002:253 to **Jesus** the son of Mary, We gave Clear (Signs),
003:003 Torah (of Moses) and the Gospel (of **Jesus**).
003:045 his name will be Christ **Jesus**, the son of Mary,
003:052 When **Jesus** found unbelief on their part
003:055 "O **Jesus**! I will take thee and raise thee to Myself
003:059 **Jesus** before Allah is as that of Adam;
003:084 given to Moses, **Jesus**, and the Prophets
004:157 "We killed Christ **Jesus** the son of Mary,
004:163 to **Jesus**, Job, Jonah, Aaron, and Solomon, and to
004:171 Christ **Jesus** the son of Mary was (no more than)
005:046 We sent **Jesus** the son of Mary, confirming the Torah
005:078 and of **Jesus** the son of Mary: because they
005:110 "O **Jesus** the son of Mary! recount my favour
005:112 "O **Jesus** the son of Mary! Can thy Lord
005:112 Said **Jesus**: "Fear Allah, if ye have faith."
005:114 Said **Jesus** the son of Mary: "O Allah
005:116 "O **Jesus** the son of Mary! didst thou say unto men,

JESUS (continued)
006:085 And Zakariya and John, and **Jesus** and Elias:
019:034 Such (was) **Jesus** the son of Mary: (it is)
033:007 Moses, and **Jesus** the son of Mary: We took
042:013 on Abraham, Moses, and **Jesus**: namely, that
043:057 When (**Jesus**) the son of Mary is held up as an
043:061 And (**Jesus**) shall be a Sign (for the coming of)
043:063 When **Jesus** came with Clear Signs, he said:
057:027 We sent after them **Jesus** the son of Mary,
061:006 And remember, **Jesus**, the son of Mary, said:
061:014 as said **Jesus**, the son of Mary, to the

JEW
002:111 Paradise unless he be a **Jew** or a Christian."
003:067 Abraham was not a **Jew** nor yet a Christian;

JEWISH
002:062 and those who follow the **Jewish** (Scriptures),
005:069 Those who follow the **Jewish** (Scriptures),
006:146 For those who followed the **Jewish** Law,
022:017 those who follow the **Jewish** (scriptures), and the

JEWRY
062:006 Say: "O ye of **Jewry**! if ye think that ye are

JEWS
002:113 The **Jews** say: "The Christians have
002:113 "The **Jews** have naught (to stand) upon";
002:120 Never will the **Jews** or the Christians
002:135 They say: "Become **Jews** or Christians
002:140 and the Tribes were **Jews** or Christians?
004:046 Of the **Jews** there are those who displace words
004:160 For the iniquity of the **Jews** We made
005:018 (Both) the **Jews** and the Christians say: "We are
005:041 or it be among the **Jews**, men who listen
005:044 By its standard have been judged the **Jews**, by the
005:051 O ye who believe! take not the **Jews** and the
005:064 The **Jews** say: "Allah's hand is tied up," Be
005:082 the **Jews** and Pagans; and nearest among them
009:030 The **Jews** call 'Uzair a son of Allah, and the
016:118 To the **Jews** We prohibited such things as We

JINN
015:027 And the **Jinn** race, We had created before, from the
027:039 A stalwart of the **Jinn** said: "I will bring thou rise from
055:039 will be asked of man or **Jinn** as to his sin,
055:056 whom no man or **Jinn** before them has touched;-
055:074 Whom no man or **Jinn** before them has touched;-
072:005 or **Jinn** should say aught that is untrue

JINNS
006:100 though Allah did create the **Jinns**; And they
006:100 the **Jinns** equals with Allah, though Allah
006:112 satans among men and **Jinns**, inspiring each other
006:128 (and say): "O ye assembly of **Jinns** much (toll)
006:130 "O ye assembly of **Jinns** and men! came there not
007:038 men and **Jinns**,-into the Fire.
007:179 Many are the **Jinns** and men, We have
011:119 with **Jinns** and men all together."
017:088 Say: "If the whole of mankind and **Jinns** were to
018:050 He was one of the **Jinns**, and he
027:017 his hosts,-of **Jinns** and men and birds, and they
032:013 "I will fill Hell with **Jinns** and men all together."
034:012 and there were **Jinns** that worked in front of him,
034:014 the **Jinns** saw plainly that if they had known
034:041 Nay, but they worshipped the **Jinns**:
037:158 but the **Jinns** know (quite well) that they
037:158 between Him and the **Jinns**: but the

JINNS (continued)

041:025   generations of **Jinns** and men, who have
041:029   among **Jinns** and men, who misled us: we shall
046:018   previous generations of **Jinns** and men, that have
046:029   of **Jinns** (quietly) listening to the Qur'an:
051:056   I have only created **Jinns** and men, that they
055:015   And He created **Jinns** from fire free of smoke:
055:033   O ye assembly of **Jinns** and men! If it be
072:001   a company of **Jinns** listened (to the Qur'an).
072:006   the **Jinns**, but they increased them into further
114:006   Among **Jinns** and among Men.

JIZYA

009:029   until they pay **Jizya** with willing submission,

JOB

004:163   to Jesus, **Job**, Jonah, Aaron, and Solomon, and to
006:084   Solomon, **Job**, Joseph, Moses, and Aaron: thus do
021:083   And (remember) **Job**, when he cried to his Lord
038:041   Commemorate Our servant **Job**, behold he

JOHN

006:085   And Zakariya and **John,** and Jesus and Elias:

JOIN

004:036   Serve Allah, and **join** not any partners with Him;
004:090   Except those who **join** a group between whom
006:014   of those who **join** gods with Allah."
006:041   (the false gods) which ye **join** with Him!"
006:088   If they were to **join** other gods with Him,
006:106   those who **join** gods with Allah.
006:151   **join** not anything with Him:
009:017   It is not for such as **join** gods with Allah,
012:033   and **join** the ranks of the ignorant."
012:108   I **join** gods with Allah!"
013:021   Those who **join** together those things which
013:036   and not to **join** partners with Him.
015:094   those who **join** false gods with Allah.
016:054   to other gods to **join** with their Lord-
016:100   who **join** partners with Allah.
023:059   Those who **join** not (in worship) partners with
026:083   and **join** me with the righteous;
028:087   these who **join** gods with Allah.
029:008   to **join** with Me (in worship) anything of which
030:031   and be not ye among those who **join** gods with Allah,-
031:013   admonishing him "O my son! **join** not in worship
031:015   to make thee **join** in worship with Me things of which
039:065   "If thou wert to **join** (gods with Allah),
040:042   against Allah, and to **join** with Him partners of
040:084   we used to **join** with Him."
041:006   And woe to those who **join** gods with Allah,-
041:009   And do ye **join** equals with Him?
052:021   to them shall We **join** their families: nor shall
072:002   We shall not **join** (in worship) any (gods)
072:020   and I **join** not with Him any (false god)."
103:003   do righteous deeds, and (**join** together) in the

JOINED

002:027   has ordered to be **joined,**
002:135   and he **joined** not gods with Allah."
003:067   And he **joined** not gods with Allah.
003:103   He **joined** your hearts in love,
003:151   for that they **joined** partners with Allah,
003:170   who have not yet **joined** them (in their bliss),
006:023   not those who **joined** gods with Allah.
006:161   and he (certainly) **joined** not gods with Allah."
010:028   Then shall We say to those who **joined** gods (with Us):
010:028   ye and those ye **joined** as 'partners'."

JOINED (continued)

013:021   to be **joined**, hold their Lord in awe, and fear
013:025   to be **joined**, and work mischief in the land;
016:120   in faith, and he **joined** not gods with Allah.
016:123   in Faith, and he **joined** not gods with Allah."
021:030   the earth were **joined** together (as one unit of Creation),
023:006   Except with those **joined** to them in the
033:037   We **joined** her in marriage to thee: in order
034:027   me those whom ye have **joined** with Him as partners:
040:012   partners were **joined** to Him, ye believed!
062:003   not already **joined** them: and He is Exalted
075:009   And the sun and moon are **joined** together,-
075:029   And one leg will be **joined** with another:
081:007   (Being **joined**, like with like);

JOINING

004:116   (the sin of) **joining** other gods with Him:
006:019   (your blasphemy of) **joining** others with Him."

JOINS

004:116   one who **joins** other gods with Allah, hath
005:072   Whoever **joins** other gods with Allah,-Allah will
024:043   then **joins** them together, then makes
048:017   nor on one ill (if he **joins** not the war): but he

JONAH

004:163   to Jesus, Job, **Jonah**, Aaron, and Solomon, and to
010:098   except the people of **Jonah**?
037:139   So also was **Jonah** among those sent (by Us).
006:086   And Isma'il and Elisha, and **Jonah**, and Lot:

JOSEPH

006:084   Solomon, Job, **Joseph**, Moses, and Aaron: thus do
012:004   Behold, **Joseph** said to his father: "O my father!
012:007   Verily in **Joseph** and his brethren are Signs
012:008   They said: "Truly **Joseph** and his brother are loved
012:009   "Slay ye **Joseph** or cast him out to some
012:010   Said one of them: "Slay not **Joseph**, but if
012:011   why dost thou not trust us with **Joseph**,-seeing we
012:017   and left **Joseph** with our things: and the wolf
012:021   Thus did We establish **Joseph** in the land, that We
012:022   When **Joseph** attained his full manhood, We gave
012:029   "O **Joseph**, pass this over! (O wife),
012:031   and she said (to **Joseph**), "Come out before them."
012:042   and (**Joseph**) lingered in prison a few (more) years.
012:046   "O **Joseph**!" (he said), "O man of truth! Expound
012:047   (**Joseph**) said: "For seven years shall ye
012:050   (**Joseph**) said: "Go thou back to thy lord,
012:051   when ye did seek to seduce **Joseph**"?
012:055   (**Joseph**) said: "Set me over the store-houses
012:056   power to **Joseph** in the land, to take
012:062   And (**Joseph**) told his servants to put their stock-
012:076   Thus did We plan for **Joseph**. He could not
012:077   **Joseph** keep locked in his heart, revealing not
012:080   in your duty with **Joseph**? Therefore will I
012:084   "How great is my grief for **Joseph**!"
012:085   thou cease to remember **Joseph** until though reach
012:087   about **Joseph** and his brother, and never
012:089   with **Joseph**, and his brother, not knowing
012:090   He said: "I am **Joseph**, and this is my brother:
012:090   They said: "Art thou indeed, **Joseph**?" He said
012:094   scent the presence of **Joseph**:
012:099   the presence of **Joseph**, he provided a home for
040:034   "And to you there came **Joseph** in times gone by,

JOSEPH'S

012:058   Then came **Joseph's** brethren: they entered

JOSEPH'S (continued)
012:069   **Joseph's** presence, he received his (full) brother
012:088   into (**Joseph's**) presence they said: "O exalted

JOURNEY
002:184   but if any of you is ill, or on a **journey**,
002:185   but if any one is ill, or on a **journey**,
002:197   And take a provision (with you) for the **journey**,
002:283   If ye are on a **journey**, and cannot find a scribe,
003:097   those who can afford the **journey**;
004:043   or on a **journey**, or one of you cometh from
005:006   But if ye are ill, or on a **journey**, or one
009:042   and the **journey** easy, they would
017:001   His Servant for a **Journey** by night from the
018:062   at this (stage of) our **journey**."
034:012   morning (stride) was a month's (**journey**), and its
034:012   a month's (**journey**); and We made a Font of
034:018   We had appointed stages of **journey** in due

JOURNEY-STAGES
034:019   place longer distances between our **journey-stages**":

JOURNEYING
005:106   others from outside if ye are **journeying** through the earth,

JOURNEYS
002:285   and to Thee is the end of all **journeys**."
022:027   lean (on account of **journeys**) through deep
106:002   familiarity with the **journeys** by winter and summer,-

JOY
015:067   came in (mad) **joy** (at news of the young men).
025:022   no **joy** will there be to the sinners that Day:
028:009   "(Here is) a **joy** of the eye, for me
036:055   shall that Day have **joy** in all that they do;
039:045   they are filled with **joy**!
047:015   a **joy** to those who drink; and rivers
051:016   Taking **joy** in the things which their
076:011   and a (blissful) **Joy**.
102:008   about the **joy** (ye indulged in)!

JOYFUL
088:008   (Other) faces that Day will be **joyful**,

JOYFULLY
015:047   brothers (**joyfully**) facing each other on raised couches.

JUDGE
002:113   but Allah will **judge** between them
002:213   to **judge** between people in matters
002:275   their case is for Allah (to **judge**);
003:055   and I will **judge** between you
004:058   that ye **judge** with justice:
004:058   and when ye **judge** between people that ye
004:065   until they make thee **judge** in all disputes between them.
004:105   that thou mightest **judge** between people by that
004:141   But Allah will **judge** betwixt you
005:042   If thou **judge**, **judge** in equity between them.
005:042   either **judge** between them, or decline to interfere.
005:042   If thou **judge**, **judge** in equity between them.
005:042   For Allah loveth those who **judge** in equity.
005:044   If any do fail to **judge** by what Allah
005:045   And if any fail to **judge** by what
005:047   If any do fail to **judge** by what
005:047   Let the people of the Gospel **Judge** by what
005:048   so **judge** between them by what Allah hath revealed,
005:049   And this (He commands): **Judge** thou between them
006:114   Say: "Shall I seek for **judge** other than Allah?-
008:029   (to **judge** between right and wrong), remove from
010:035   What then is the matter with you? How **judge** ye?

JUDGE (continued)
010:093   Verily Allah will **judge** between them as to
012:080   and He is the best to **judge**.
016:124   but Allah will **judge** between them on the Day of
021:112   Say: "O my Lord! **judge** Thou in truth!"
022:017   Allah will **judge** between them on the Day of
022:056   He will **judge** between them: so those
022:069   "Allah will **judge** between you on the Day of Judgment
024:048   in order that He may **judge** between them, behold,
024:051   He may **judge** between them, is no
026:118   "**Judge** thou, then, between me
032:025   Verily thy Lord will **judge** between them on the
037:154   What is the matter with you? How **judge** ye?
038:026   so **judge** thou between men in truth (and justice):
039:003   Truly Allah will **judge** between them in that
039:046   wilt **judge** between Thy Servants in those matters
040:020   And Allah will **judge** with (Justice and) Truth:
040:020   will not (be in a position) to **judge** at all.
042:015   to **judge** justly between you.
045:017   Verily thy Lord will **judge** between them on the
060:003   on the Day of Judgment: He will **judge** between you:
068:036   What is the matter with you? How **judge** ye?
114:003   The God (or **Judge**) of Mankind,-

JUDGED
005:044   By its standard have been **judged** the Jews, by the
005:060   (as **judged**) by the treatment
010:047   the matter will be **judged** between them with justice,
040:048   Truly, Allah has **judged** between (His) Servants!"

JUDGEMENT
001:004   Master of the Day of **Judgement**.
002:085   and on the Day of **Judgement**
002:113   in their quarrel on the Day of **Judgement**.
002:185   guidance and **judgement** (between right and wrong).
003:003   Criterion (of **judgement** between right and wrong).
003:077   or look at them on the Day of **Judgement**,
003:161   he shall, on the Day of **Judgement**, restore
003:180   on the Day of **Judgement**.
003:185   and only on the Day of **Judgement** shall you
003:194   and save us from shame on the Day of **Judgement**:
004:006   if then ye find sound **judgement** in them, release
004:060   together for **judgement** (in their disputes) to the Evil
004:087   gather you together on the Day of **Judgement**,
004:109   on their behalf on the Day of **Judgement**,
004:136   and the Day of **Judgement**, hath
004:141   betwixt you on the Day of **Judgement**.
004:159   and on the Day of **Judgement** He will be
005:014   the one and the other, to the Day of **Judgement**.
005:036   for the Chastisement of the Day of **Judgement**,
005:050   can give better **judgement** than Allah?
005:050   a **judgement** of (the Days of) Ignorance?
005:064   enmity and hatred till the Day of **Judgement**.
006:012   for the Day of **Judgement**, there is
006:051   brought (to **judgement**) before their Lord:
006:089   and **Judgement**, and Prophethood:
006:096   such is the **judgement** and ordering of (Him),
006:136   Evil (and unjust) is their **judgement**.
007:032   (and) purely for them on the Day of **Judgement**.
007:150   on the **judgement** of your Lord?"
007:167   to the Day of **Judgement**, those who
007:172   lest ye should say on the Day of **Judgement**:
008:019   for victory and **judgement**, now hath
008:019   now hath the **judgement** come to you: if you
010:054   but the **judgement** between them will be

JUDGEMENT (continued)

010:060 against Allah, of the Day of **Judgement**?
010:093 on the Day of **Judgement**.
011:060 in this Life,-and on the Day of **Judgement**.
011:098 on the Day of **Judgement**, and lead
011:099 this (life) and on the Day of **Judgement**: and woeful
013:037 to be a **judgement** of authority in Arabic.
015:035 on thee till the Day of **Judgement**."
016:025 Day of **Judgement**, their own burdens in full,
016:027 Then, on the Day of **Judgement**, He will
016:077 And the matter of the Hour (of **Judgement**) is as
016:092 and on the Day of **Judgement** He will certainly
016:124 judge between them on the Day of **Judgement** as to
017:013 On the Day of **Judgement** We shall
017:058 the Day of **Judgement** or punish it with a dreadful
017:062 to the Day of **Judgement**, I will surely
017:097 On the Day of **Judgement** We shall gather them
018:021 about the Hour of **Judgement**. Behold, they
018:036 (of **Judgement**) will (ever) come: even if
018:105 on the Day of **Judgement**, give them any Weight.
019:037 of the (coming) **Judgement** of an awful Day!
019:095 to him singly on the Day of **Judgement**.
020:074 as a sinner (at **judgement**),-for him is Hell:
020:100 on the Day of **Judgement**;
020:104 when the best of them in **judgement** will say:
020:124 him up blind on the Day of **Judgement**."
021:047 for the Day of **Judgement**, so that
021:048 and Aaron the Criterion (for **judgement**).
021:049 and who hold the Hour (of **judgement**) in awe.
021:074 We gave **Judgement** and Knowledge, and We
021:078 when they gave **judgement** in the matter of the
021:078 We did witness their **judgement**.
021:079 to each (of them) We gave **Judgement** and Knowledge;
022:001 (of **judgement**) will be a thing terrible!
022:009 and on the Day of **Judgement** We shall make him
022:017 the Day of **Judgement**: for Allah
022:055 until the Hour (of **Judgement**) comes suddenly
022:069 "Allah will judge between you on the Day of **Judgement**
023:016 Again, on the Day of **Judgement**, will ye
025:011 Nay, they deny the Hour (of the **Judgement** to come):
025:021 (for **Judgement**) say: "Why are not
025:069 the Day of **Judgement** will be doubled to him, and he
026:021 invested me with **judgement** (and wisdom) and
026:082 will forgive me my faults on the Day of **Judgement**.
027:065 shall be raised up (for **Judgement**).
028:041 and on the Day of **Judgement** no help
028:042 Day of **Judgement** they will be among the
028:061 on the Day of **Judgement**, is to be
028:071 to the Day of **Judgement**, what god
028:072 to the Day of **Judgement**, what god
029:004 Evil is their **judgement**!
029:013 and on the Day of **Judgement** they will
029:025 but on the Day of **Judgement** ye shall
032:025 on the Day of **Judgement**, in the matters wherein
034:023 (at the Day of **Judgement**, then) will they
035:014 On the Day of **Judgement** they will
036:032 will be brought before Us (for **judgement**).
037:020 This is the Day of **Judgement**!"
037:026 Nay, but that day they shall submit (to **Judgement**);
038:078 till the Day of **Judgement**."
038:020 and sound **judgement** in speech and decision.
039:015 and their people on the Day of **Judgement**:
039:024 on the Day of **Judgement** (and receive it) by his face,

JUDGEMENT (continued)

039:031 dispute on the Day of **Judgement**, in the
039:047 on the Day of **Judgement**: but something
039:060 On the Day of **Judgement** wilt thou see those
039:067 on the Day of **Judgement** the whole of the earth
039:075 between them (at **Judgement**) will be in (perfect)
041:040 on the Day of **Judgement**?
041:047 of the Hour (of **Judgement**: He knows all): no fruit
041:050 (of **Judgement**) will (ever) be established; but if
042:021 the Decree of **Judgement**, the matter
042:045 On the Day of **Judgement**. Behold! Truly
043:061 a Sign (for the coming of) the Hour (of **Judgement**):
043:085 with Him is the knowledge of the Hour (of **Judgement**):
045:017 on the Day of **Judgement** as to those matters in
045:021 Ill is the **judgement** that they make.
045:026 for the Day of **Judgement** about which there is
045:027 Hour of **Judgement** is established,-that Day
046:005 will not answer him to the Day of **Judgement**,
051:006 And verily **Judgement** and Justice will surely come
051:012 Day of **Judgement** and Justice?"
054:001 The Hour (of **Judgement**) is nigh, and the
054:046 Nay, the Hour (of **Judgement**) is the time promised
055:046 they will stand before (the **Judgement** Seat of)
058:007 He tell them what they did on the Day of **Judgement**.
058:018 The Day will Allah raise them all up (for **Judgement**):
060:003 on the Day of **Judgement**: He will judge between you:
064:007 will not be raised up (for **Judgement**).
068:039 reaching to the Day of **Judgement**,
069:018 That Day shall ye be brought to **Judgement**:
070:026 of the Day of **Judgement**;
072:007 any one (to **Judgement**).
074:046 "And we used to deny the Day of **Judgement**,
082:009 Nay! but ye do Reject The **Judgement**!
082:015 Which they will enter on the Day of **Judgement**,
082:017 what the Day of **Judgement** is?
082:018 what the Day of **Judgement** is?
083:011 Those that deny the Day of **Judgement**.
085:002 By the promised Day (of **Judgement**);
095:007 make you deny the Last **Judgement**?
107:001 Seest thou one who denies the **Judgement** (to come)?

JUDGES

002:188 nor use it as bait for the **judges**,
002:229 If ye (**judges**) do indeed fear that they would be
006:057 and He is the best of **Judges**."
011:045 and Thou art the Justest of **Judges**!"
012:080 or Allah **judges** for me; and He
060:010 He **judges** (with justice) between you.
095:008 Is not Allah the wisest of **Judges**?

JUDGEMENT-SEAT

027:084 Until, when they come (before the **Judgement-Seat**),

JUDI

011:044 rested on Mount **Judi** and the word went forth:

JUGULAR

050:016 for We are nearer to him than (his) **jugular** vein.

JUNCTION

018:060 the **junction** of the two seas or (until)
018:061 But when they reached the **Junction**, they forgot

JUST

002:061 and slaying His Messengers without **just** cause.
002:234 dispose of themselves in a **just** and reasonable manner.
002:264 which leaves it (**just**) a bare stone.
003:021 and slay those who teach **just** dealing with mankind,

JUST (continued)

003:025 and each soul will be paid out **just** what it has earned,
004:006 let him have for himself what is **just** and reasonable.
005:008 Be **just**: that is next to Piety: and fear
005:095 As adjudged by two **just** men among you; or by
005:106 when making bequests,-two **just** men of your own
006:091 No **just** estimate of Allah do they
007:085 Give **just** measure and weight, nor withhold
007:157 for he commands them what is **just** and forbids
008:005 **Just** as thy Lord ordered thee out of
009:067 and forbid what in **just**, and tighten
009:071 they enjoin what is **just**, and forbid what is evil:
011:085 "And O my people! give **just** measure and weight,
013:033 or is it (**just**) a show of words?"
015:008 We send not the angels down except for **just** cause:
015:085 and all between them, but for **just** ends.
015:090 (Of **just** such wrath) as We sent down
016:051 for He is **just** one God: then fear Me
016:061 **just** as they would not be able to anticipate
017:033 made sacred-except for **just** cause.
021:017 If it had been Our wish to take (**just**) a pastime,
024:025 (all) their **just** dues, and they
025:067 but hold a **just** (balance) between those (extremes);
025:068 except for **just** cause, nor commit
026:181 Give **just** measure, and cause not loss (to others by
030:049 (the rain)-**just** before this-they were
031:017 enjoin what is **just**, and forbid
033:006 nevertheless do ye what is **just** to your
033:018 for **just** a little while,
033:032 but speak ye a speech (that is) **just**.
034:023 'That which is true and **just**; and He
036:040 each (**just**) swims along in (its own) orbit
037:011 **Just** ask their opinion: are they
039:067 No **just** estimate have they made of Allah,
039:068 The Trumpet will (**just**) be sounded, when all
039:069 and a **just** decision pronounced between them;
043:023 **Just** in the same way, whenever We sent a Warner
044:039 We created them not except for **just** ends:
045:022 Allah created the heavens and the earth for **just** ends,
046:003 and all between them but for **just** ends,
046:020 on earth without **just** cause, and that
047:016 "What is it he said **just** then?"
047:021 Were it to obey and say what is **just**, and when
049:009 for Allah loves those who are fair (and **just**).
053:024 Nay, shall man have (**just**) anything he hankers after?
060:008 for Allah loveth those who are **just**.
060:012 in any **just** matter,-then so thou receive their
060:013 in despair, **just** as the Unbelievers are in despair
065:006 according to what is **just** and reasonable.
068:028 Said one of them, more **just** (than the rest):
072:019 they **just** make round him a dense crowd."
080:016 Honorable and Pious and **Just**.
082:007 and gave thee a **just** bias;

JUSTER

002:282 it is **juster** in the sight of Allah,
033:005 that is **juster** in the sight of Allah.

JUSTEST

011:045 and Thou art the **Justest** of Judges!"

JUSTICE

003:018 standing firm on **justice**.
004:005 and speak to them words of kindness and **justice**.
004:008 and speak to them words of kindness and **justice**.
004:058 that ye judge with **justice**:

JUSTICE (continued)

004:127 that ye stand firm for **justice** to orphans.
004:129 Ye are never able to do **justice** between wives
004:135 or decline to do **justice**, verily Allah
004:135 O ye who believe! stand out firmly for **justice**,
004:135 lest ye swerve, and if ye distort (**Justice**) or
005:008 and depart from **justice**.
006:115 its fulfillment in truth and in **justice**:
006:151 except by way of **justice** and law: thus doth
006:152 give measure and weight with (full) **justice**;-
007:029 Say: "My Lord hath commanded **justice**; and that
007:159 and do **justice** in the light of truth.
007:181 and dispense **justice** therewith.
010:004 that He may reward with **justice** those who
010:047 judged between them with **justice**, and they
010:054 will be with **justice**, and wrong
016:076 who commands **justice**, and is on the Straight Way?
016:090 Allah commands **justice**, the doing of good,
021:047 We shall set up scales of **justice** for the
023:041 Then the Blast overtook them with **justice**,
027:060 Nay, they are a people who swerve from **justice**.
031:015 in this life with **justice** (and consideration),
034:026 the matter between us (and you) in truth and **justice**:
038:026 so judge thou between men in truth (and **justice**):
039:075 in (perfect) **justice**, and the cry (on all sides)
040:020 And Allah will judge with (**Justice** and) Truth:
040:078 the matter was decided in truth and **justice**,
042:042 defying right and **justice**: for such
049:009 then make peace between them with **justice**, and be fair:
051:006 And verily Judgment and **Justice** will surely come to pass.
051:012 Day of Judgment and **Justice**?"
055:007 and He has set up the balance (of **Justice**),
055:009 So establish weight with **justice** and fall
057:025 that men may stand forth in **justice**;
060:010 He judges (with **justice**) between you.
065:002 endued with **justice**, and establish the evidence
072:014 that swerve from **justice**.

JUSTIFICATION

077:006 Whether of **Justification** or of Warning;-

JUSTLY

002:143 an Ummah **justly** balanced.
004:003 be able to deal **justly** (with them),
004:003 be able to deal **justly** with the orphans,
006:152 whenever ye speak, speak **justly**, even if
009:013 it is Allah Whom ye should **justly** fear, if ye believe!
022:018 the chastisement is **justly** due.
026:183 And withhold not things **justly** due to men,
038:014 came **justly** and inevitably (on them).
039:019 one against whom the decree of Punishment is **justly** due
042:015 to judge **justly** between you.
059:023 the **justly** Proud, Glory to Allah! (high is He)
060:008 and **justly** with them: for Allah

K

KA'BA
005:095 brought to the **Ka'ba**, of a domestic animal
005:097 Allah made the **Ka'ba**, the Sacred House, a means

KAF
019:001 **Kaf**. Ha. Ya. 'Ain. Sad.

KAFUR
076:005 of a Cup (of Wine) mixed with **Kafur**,-

KEEN
073:006 is a time when impression is more **keen** and speech

KEEP
002:019 in their ears to **keep** out the stunning
002:222 who **keep** themselves pure and clean.
002:222 so **keep** away from women in their courses,
002:229 be unable to **keep** the limits ordained by Allah,
002:229 unable to **keep** the limits ordained by Allah
002:230 they feel they can **keep** the limits ordained by Allah.
003:076 Nay,-Those that **keep** their plighted faith
004:063 so **keep** clear of them but admonish them,
004:081 so **keep** clear of them, and put thy trust in Allah,
004:167 and **keep** off (men) from the way of Allah,
005:089 But **keep** to your oaths.
006:026 and themselves they **keep** away; but they
007:111 They said: "**Keep** him and his brother in suspense
007:193 ye call them or ye **keep** silent.
008:001 so fear Allah, and **keep** straight the relations
008:030 plotted against thee, to **keep** thee in bonds,
008:034 when they **keep** out (men) from the Sacred Mosque-
010:107 there is none can **keep** back his favour: He causeth
011:086 But I am not set over you to **keep** watch!"
012:077 Joseph **keep** locked in his heart, revealing not
017:079 And as for the night **keep** awake a part of it
017:100 behold, ye would **keep** them back, for fear
018:028 And **keep** yourself content with those who call
018:055 And what is there to **keep** back men from believing,
018:076 about anything after this, **keep** me not in thy company:
020:058 not fail to **keep**-neither we nor thou-in a place
021:042 Say, "Who can **keep** you safe by night and by day
022:025 and would **keep** back (men) from the
022:035 perseverance over their afflictions, **keep** up regular prayer,
023:113 but ask those who **keep** account."
024:033 not the wherewith for marriage **keep** themselves chaste,
026:036 They said: "**Keep** him and his brother in suspense
033:018 who **keep** back (men) and those who say to their
039:038 some Mercy for me, can they **keep** back His Mercy?"
040:025 with him, and **keep** alive their females," but the
044:021 at least **keep** yourselves away from me."
073:008 But **keep** in remembrance the name of the Lord,
073:020 He knoweth that ye are unable to **keep** count thereof.
074:004 And thy garments **keep** free from stain!
074:055 Let any who will, **keep** it in remembrance!
074:056 But none will **keep** it in remembrance except as
080:012 Therefore let whose will, **keep** it in remembrance.
082:016 And they will not be able to **keep** away therefrom.

KEEPER
012:055 I am a good **keeper**, knowledgeable.

KEEPERS
039:071 And its **Keepers** will say, "Did not messengers
039:073 and its **Keepers** will say: "Peace be upon you!
040:049 Those in the Fire will say to the **Keepers** of Hell:
067:008 its **Keepers** will ask, "Did no Warner come to you?"
083:033 But they had not been sent as **Keepers** over them!

KEEPING
020:042 either of you, in **keeping** Me in remembrance.
028:023 who were **keeping** back (their flocks).

KEEPS
011:008 they are sure to say, "What **keeps** it back?"
039:042 He **keeps** back (from returning to life), but the

KEPT
002:103 If they had **kept** their Faith
013:033 but they are **kept** back (thereby) from the Path.
017:094 What **kept** men back from Belief when Guidance
020:015 I have almost **kept** it hidden-for every soul
020:062 over their affair, but they **kept** their talk secret.
020:092 (Moses) said: "O Aaron! what **kept** thee back,
027:017 and they were all **kept** in order and ranks.
027:024 and has **kept** them away from the Path,-so they
027:083 and they shall be **kept** in ranks,-
028:004 but he **kept** alive their females: for he
029:038 and **kept** them back from the path,
032:017 of the eye are **kept** hidden (in reserve) for them-
034:014 which **kept** (slowly) gnawing away at his staff:
034:032 "Was it we who **kept** you back from Guidance
080:014 Exalted (in dignity), **kept** pure and holy,
082:005 it hath sent forward and (what it hath) **kept** back.
098:002 rehearsing scriptures **kept** pure and holy:

KEYS
006:059 With Him are the **keys** of the Unseen,
024:061 or in houses of which the **keys** are in
028:076 that their very **keys** would have been a burden
039:063 To Him belong the **keys** of the heavens and the
042:012 To Him belong the **keys** of the heavens and the

KIDNAP
008:026 and afraid that men might despoil and **kidnap** you;

KILL
004:029 nor **kill** (or destroy) yourselves:
004:092 Never should a Believer **kill** a Believer; except
005:095 O ye who believe! **kill** not game, while in
006:151 **kill** not your children on a plea of want;-
017:031 **Kill** not your children for fear of want:
026:003 It may be thou will **kill** thy self with grief,
060:012 that they will not **kill** their children,

KILLED
004:157 but they **killed** him not, nor crucified him.
004:157 for of a surety they **killed** him not:
004:157 "We **killed** Christ Jesus the son of Mary,
005:003 that which hath been **killed** by strangling, or by
005:095 domestic animal equivalent to the one he **killed**.
028:015 and Moses struck him with his fist and **killed** him.
081:009 For what crime she was **killed**;

KILLING
017:031 Verily the **killing** of them is a great sin.

KILLS
004:092 and whoever **kills** a Believer by mistake it is
004:093 If a man **kills** a Believer intentionally

KILN
028:038 therefore, O Haman! light me a (**kiln** to bake bricks)

KIN

002:177 for your **kin**, for orphans,
002:180 to parents and next of **kin**,
003:068 nearest of **kin** to Abraham, are those
004:036 those in need, neighbors who are of **kin**, neighbors
004:135 even as against yourselves, or your parents, or your **kin**,
005:107 nearest in **kin** from among those who claim
009:113 for Pagans, even though they be of **kin**, after it
016:090 of good, and giving to kith and **kin**, and He
042:023 ask of you for this except the love of those near of **kin**."
047:022 and break your ties of kith and **kin**?

KIND

002:061 we cannot endure one **kind** of food (always);
002:263 **Kind** words and the covering of faults
005:013 for Allah loveth those who are **kind**.
006:099 each similar (in **kind**) yet different
006:141 similar (in **kind**) and different (in variety):
007:057 and produce every **kind** of harvest therewith:
007:058 springs up produce, (rich) after its **kind**:
009:117 for He is unto them Most **Kind**, Most Merciful.
009:128 to the Believers is he most **kind** and merciful.
011:040 "Embark therein, of each **kind** two, male and female,
013:003 and fruit of every **kind** He made in pairs,
016:007 for your Lord is indeed Most **Kind**, Most Merciful.
016:011 and every **kind** of fruit: Verily in this is a Sign
017:023 and that ye be **kind** to parents.
017:089 in this Qur'an, every **kind** of similitude:
018:054 every **kind** of similitude: but man is, in most
019:014 And **kind** to his parents, and he
019:032 "(He) hath made me **kind** to my mother, and not
022:005 forth every **kind** of beautiful growth (in pairs).
022:065 for Allah is Most **Kind** and Most Merciful to man.
026:058 Treasures, and every **kind** of honorable position;
030:058 for men in this Qur'an. Every **kind** of Parable:
031:010 every **kind** of noble creature, in pairs.
035:012 Yet from each (**kind** of water) do ye eat flesh fresh and
036:036 own (human) **kind** and (other) things of which
037:146 a spreading plant of the Gourd **kind**.
038:037 every **kind** of builder and diver,-
038:058 And other Penalties of a similar **kind**, to match
039:027 in this Qur'an every **kind** of Parable, in order
043:013 ye may remember the (**kind**) favour of your Lord,
044:010 a **kind** of smoke (or mist) plainly visible.
044:055 There can they call for every **kind** of fruit
050:007 every **kind** of beautiful growth (in pairs)-
055:052 In them will be Fruits of every **kind**, two and two.
057:009 And verily, Allah is to you Most **Kind** and Merciful.
064:011 No **kind** of calamity can occur, except by
082:011 **Kind** and honorable, writing down (your deeds):
104:001 Woe to every (**kind** of) scandal-monger and backbiter,

KINDLE

005:064 Every time they **kindle** the fire of war, Allah
036:080 when behold! ye **kindle** therewith (your own fires)!
056:071 See ye the Fire which ye **kindle**?

KINDLED

002:017 a man who **kindled** a fire;
081:012 When the Blazing Fire is **kindled** to fierce heat;
104:006 (It is) the Fire of Allah **kindled** (to a blaze),

KINDLY

060:008 of your homes, from dealing **kindly** and justly

KINDNESS

002:083 treat with **kindness** your parents
002:143 most surely full of **kindness**, Most Merciful.

KINDNESS (continued)

002:207 and Allah is full of **kindness** to (His) devotees.
002:229 or separate with **kindness**.
003:030 and Allah is full of **kindness** to those that serve Him."
004:005 and speak to them words of **kindness** and justice.
004:008 and speak to them words of **kindness** and justice.
004:019 with them on a footing of **kindness** and equity
016:047 for thy Lord is indeed full of **kindness** and mercy.
017:024 And, out of **kindness**, lower to them the wing
017:028 yet speak to them a word of easy **kindness**.
018:086 to punish them, or to treat them with **kindness**."
024:020 is full of **kindness** and mercy,
029:008 We have enjoined on man **kindness** to parents:
046:015 We have enjoined on man **kindness** to his parents:
059:010 Full of **Kindness**, Most Merciful."
090:017 of **kindness** and compassion.

KINDRED

002:083 your parents and **kindred**,
002:215 is for parents and **kindred** and orphans
008:075 But **kindred** by blood have prior rights against
009:024 yours sons, your brothers, your mates, or your **kindred**:
017:026 And render to the **kindred** their due rights,
030:038 So give what is due to **kindred**, the needy
058:022 or their brothers, or their **kindred**.
059:007 to His Messenger, and to **kindred** and orphans,
070:013 His **kindred** who sheltered him.

KINDS

002:164 in the beasts of all **kinds** that He scatters through the
002:266 and all **kinds** of fruit,
006:099 with it We produce vegetation of all **kinds**:
006:141 and tilth with produce of all **kinds**, and olives
007:096 to them (all **kinds** of) blessings from
011:024 These two **kinds** (of men) may be compared
015:019 and produced therein all **kinds** of things in due balance.
025:009 See what **kinds** of companions they make for thee!
026:007 how many noble things of all **kinds** we have
028:048 They say: "Two **kinds** of sorcery, each assisting
028:057 fruits of all **kinds**,-a provision
031:010 beasts of all **kinds**.
047:015 In it there are for them all **kinds** of fruits,

KINE

012:043 (in a vision) seven fat **kine**, whom seven
012:046 of seven fat **kine** whom seven lean ones devour,

KING

002:246 "Appoint for us a **King**, that we may fight in the cause
002:247 "Allah hath appointed Talut as **king** over you."
012:043 The **king** (of Egypt) said: "I do see (in a vision)
012:050 So the **king** said: "Bring ye him unto me." But when
012:051 (The **king**) said (to the ladies): "What was your
012:054 So the **king** said: "Bring him unto me; I will take
012:072 They said: "We miss the great beaker of the **king**;
012:076 by the law of the **king** except that Allah
018:079 there was after them a certain **king** who seized on every
019:085 like a band (presented before a **king** for honours).
020:114 High above all is Allah, the **King**, the Truth!
023:116 Therefore exalted be Allah the **King**, the Reality;
114:002 The **King** (or Ruler) of Mankind,

KINGDOM

002:102 Satans recited over Solomon's **Kingdom**.
004:054 and conferred upon them a great **kingdom**.
006:075 the **kingdom** of the heavens and the earth,
007:185 Do they see nothing in the **kingdom** of the

KINGDOM (continued)
020:120   and to a **kingdom** that never decays?"
038:020   We strengthened his **kingdom**, and gave
038:035   and grant me a **Kingdom**, which, will not

KINGS
005:020   made you **kings**, and gave you what He had not
027:034   She said: "**Kings**, when they enter a country,

KINSFOLK
004:036   and do good to parents, **kinsfolk**, orphans, those

KINSHIP
009:008   the ties either of **kinship** or of covenant?
009:010   the ties either of **kinship** or of covenant!
037:158   And they have invented a **kinship** between Him

KINSMEN
024:022   by oath against helping their **kinsmen**, those in
026:214   And admonish the nearest **kinsmen**,

KITH
016:090   and giving to **kith** and kin, and He
047:022   and break your ties of **kith** and kin?

KNEE
045:028   And thou wilt see every nation bowing the **knee**:

KNEE-SIGHTED
029:038   from the Path, though they were **keen-sighted**.

KNEES
019:068   on their **knees** round about Hell;
019:072   the wrong-doers therein, (humbled) to their **knees**.

KNEW
002:060   Each group **knew** its own place for water.
002:065   And well ye **knew** those amongst you
002:102   And they **knew** that the buyers of (magic)
002:102   if they but **knew**!
002:103   reward from Allah if they but **knew**!
002:184   if ye only **knew**.
002:239   which ye **knew** not (before).
002:280   that is best for you if ye only **knew**.
003:036   And Allah **knew** best what she brought forth-
006:091   which ye **knew** not-neither ye nor your fathers."
007:160   each group **knew** its own place for water.
009:041   That is best for you, if ye (but) **knew**.
010:029   we certainly **knew** nothing of your worship of us!"
011:049   nor thy People **knew** them.
012:003   among those who **knew** it not.
012:058   and he **knew** them, but they **knew** him not.
016:078   when ye **knew** nothing; and He gave you hearing
016:095   (a prize) far better for you, if ye only **knew**.
021:039   If only the Unbelievers **knew** (the time)
026:197   the Learned of the Children of Israel **knew** it (as true)?
029:041   is the Spider's house;-if they but **knew**.
029:064   that is life indeed, if they but **knew**.
036:026   my People **knew** (what I know)!-
039:026   of the Hereafter, if they only **knew**!
041:022   that Allah **knew** not many of the things that ye
048:018   He **knew** what was in their hearts, and He
048:027   For He **knew** what ye **knew** not, and He granted, besides
056:076   if ye but **knew**,-
061:011   for you, if ye but **knew**!
062:009   that is best for you if ye but **knew**!
068:033   in the Hereafter,-if only they **knew**!
071:004   put forward: if ye only **knew**."
096:005   Taught man that which he **knew** not.

KNEWEST
004:113   taught thee what thou **knewest** not (before):

KNEWEST (continued)
042:052   thou **knewest** not (before) what was Revelation,

KNIFE
012:031   she gave each of them a **knife**: and she

KNOCKS
021:018   and it **knocks** out its brain, and behold,

KNOTS
113:004   From the mischief of those who blow on **knots**;

KNOW
002:013   they are the fools but they do not **know**.
002:022   unto Allah when ye **know** (the truth).
002:026   Those who believe **know** that it is the truth
002:030   He said: "I **know** what ye **know** not."
002:033   and I **know** what ye reveal and what ye conceal?"
002:033   that I **know** the secrets of the heaven and earth,
002:042   when ye **know** (what it is).
002:077   **Know** they not that Allah knoweth what
002:078   who **know** not the Book,
002:080   ye say of Allah what ye do not **know**?"
002:101   as if (it had been something) they did not **know**!
002:113   what those say who **know** not,
002:140   Say: Do ye **know** better than Allah?
002:144   The people of the book **know** well that
002:146   conceal the truth which they themselves **know**.
002:146   of the Book **know** this as they **know** their own sons;
002:194   and **know** that Allah is with those
002:196   And **know** that Allah, is strict in punishment.
002:203   Then fear Allah, and **know** that ye will surely
002:209   then **know** that Allah is Exalted in Power, Wise.
002:216   But Allah knoweth, and ye **know** not.
002:223   and **know** that ye are to meet Him
002:230   which He makes plain to those who **know**.
002:231   and **know** that Allah is well acquainted
002:232   and Allah knows, and ye **know** not.
002:233   But fear Allah and **know** that Allah sees well
002:235   and **know** that Allah is Oft Forgiving, Most Forbearing.
002:235   And **know** that Allah knoweth
002:244   and **know** that Allah heareth and knoweth all things.
002:259   he said: "I **know** that Allah hath power
002:260   Then **know** that Allah is Exalted in Power, Wise."
002:267   And **know** that Allah is free of all wants,
002:273   Thou shalt **know** them by their (unfailing) mark:
003:066   It is Allah Who knows, and ye who **know** not!
003:075   and (well) they **know** it.
003:078   and (well) they **know** it!
003:140   that Allah may **know** those that believe,
004:011   Ye **know** not whether your parents or your children
005:034   **know** that Allah is Oft-Forgiving, Most Merciful.
005:092   **know** ye that it is Our Messenger's duty to proclaim
005:097   that ye may **know** that Allah hath knowledge of what
005:098   **Know** ye that Allah is strict in punishment and
005:113   and to **know** that thou hast indeed told us
005:116   though I **know** not what is in Thine.
006:020   given the Book **know** this as they **know** their own sons.
006:033   We **know** indeed the grief which their words
006:050   nor do I **know** what is hidden.
006:053   Doth not Allah **know** best those who are grateful?.
006:067   and soon shall ye **know** it."
006:081   (Tell me) if you **know**.
006:097   We detail Our Signs for people who **know**.
006:105   We may make the matter clear to those who **know**.
006:114   They **know** full well, to whom
006:135   soon will ye **know** who it is whose end

KNOW (continued)

007:028   do ye say of Allah what ye **know** not?"
007:032   in detail for those who **know**.
007:038   He will say: "Doubled for all": but this ye do not **know**.
007:046   who would **know** every one by his marks: they will
007:048   they will **know** from their marks, saying:
007:062   and I **know** from Allah something that ye **know** not.
007:075   "**Know** ye indeed that Salih is a messenger
007:123   but soon shall ye **know** (the consequences).
007:182   to ruin while they **know** not.
007:187   is with Allah (alone), but most men **know** not."
008:024   and **know** that Allah cometh in between
008:025   and **know** that Allah is strict in punishment.
008:028   And **know** ye that your possessions and your
008:041   And **know** that out of all the booty that ye
008:060   and others besides, whom ye may not **know**,
008:060   but whom Allah doth **know**.
009:002   but **know** ye that ye cannot frustrate Allah
009:003   if ye turn away, **know** ye that ye cannot frustrate Allah,
009:036   But **know** that Allah is with those
009:042   for Allah doth **know** that they are lying.
009:063   **Know** they not that for those who oppose
009:078   **Know** they not that Allah doth **know** their secret
009:093   so they **know** not.
009:101   thou knowest them not: We **know** them: twice shall
009:104   **Know** they not that Allah doth accept repentance
009:123   and **know** that Allah is with those who fear Him.
010:005   in detail, for those who **know**.
010:005   that ye might **know** the number of years and the
010:020   "The Unseen is only for Allah (to **Know**).
010:068   Say ye about Allah what ye **know** not?
010:089   and follow not the path of those who **know** not."
011:014   **know** ye that this Revelation is sent down
011:031   nor do I **know** what is hidden, nor claim
011:039   "But soon will ye **know** who it is on whom
011:079   They said: "Well dost thou **know** we have no need
011:093   soon will ye **know** who it is on whom descends the
012:021   but most among mankind **know** it not.
012:046   and that they may **know**."
012:051   no evil **know** we against him!"
012:052   may **know** that I have never been false to him
012:062   so they should **know** it only when they
012:068   but most men **know** not.
012:073   "By Allah! well **ye know** that we came not to make
012:080   "**Know** ye not that your father did take an oath
012:081   we bear witness only to what we **know**, and we
012:086   and I **know** from Allah that which ye **know** not.
012:089   He said: "**Know** ye how ye dealt with Joseph,
012:096   'I **know** from Allah that which ye **know** not?"
013:008   Allah doth **know** what every female (womb)
013:019   Is then one who doth **know** that that which
013:031   the Believers **know**, that, had Allah (so) willed,
013:042   and soon will the Unbelievers **know** who gets
014:038   "O our Lord! truly Thou dost **know** what we
014:052   and may **know** that He is One God: let men
015:003   soon for they will soon **know**.
015:096   another god: but soon will they come to **know**.
015:097   We do indeed **know** how thy heart is distressed
016:019   And Allah doth **know** what ye conceal, and what
016:021   nor do thy **know** when they will be raised up.
016:022   refuse to **know** and they are arrogant.
016:023   Undoubtedly Allah doth **know** what they conceal,
016:038   but most among mankind **know** it not.

KNOW (continued)

016:055   but soon will ye **know** (your folly)!
016:056   And they (even) assign to things they do not **know**,
016:070   so that they **know** nothing after having
016:074   for Allah knoweth, and ye **know** not.
016:075   But most of them do **know** not
016:103   We **know** indeed that they say, "It is a man that teaches
017:012   may **know** the number and count of the years:
017:030   for He doth **know** and regard all His servants.
017:047   We **know** best what it is they listen, when they
018:021   to the people, that they might **know** that the
018:022   it is but few that **know** their (real case)."
019:070   And certainly We **know** best those who are most
020:071   So shall ye **know** for certain, which of
020:104   We **know** best what they will say, when the
020:135   ye **know** who it is that is on the straight
021:007   if ye **know** this not, ask of those
021:024   But most of them **know** not the Truth, and so
021:081   for We do **know** all things.
021:109   but I **know** not whether that which ye are
021:111   "I **know** not but that it may be a trial for you,
022:005   so that they **know** nothing after having
023:084   and all beings therein? (Say) if ye **know**!"
023:088   but is not protected (of any)? (Say) if ye **know**."
024:019   Allah knows, and ye **know** not.
024:033   if ye **know** any good in them; yea, give
024:035   and Allah doth **know** all things.
024:063   Allah doth **know** those of you
024:064   Well doth He **know** what ye are
024:064   of what they did: for Allah doth **know** all things.
025:042   Soon will they **know**, when they
026:006   so they will **know** soon (enough) the truth
026:049   But soon shall ye **know**!
026:112   He said: "And what do I **know** as to what they do?
026:132   on you freely all that ye **know**.
026:227   And soon will the unjust **know** what vicissitudes their
027:061   Nay, most of them **know** not.
027:093   so that ye shall **know** them": and thy
028:013   but most of them do not **know**.
028:013   and that she might **know** that the promise
028:038   I **know** for you but myself: therefore O Haman!
028:050   **know** that they only follow their own lusts:
028:075   then shall they **know** that the Truth is with Allah
028:078   Did he not **know** that Allah had destroyed,
029:003   and Allah will certainly **know** those who are
029:010   Does not Allah **know** best all that
029:032   They said: "We **know** well who is there: we will
029:042   Verily Allah doth **know** of (everything)
029:066   But soon will they **know**.
030:007   They **know** but the outer (things) in the
030:022   are Signs for those who **know**.
030:030   but most among mankind **know** not.
030:034   but soon will ye **know** (your folly).
030:056   the Day of Resurrection: but ye-ye did not **know**!"
031:034   Nor does any one **know** what it is that he
031:034   nor does anyone **know** in what land he is to die.
033:005   But if ye **know** not their father's
033:050   We **know** what We have appointed for them
034:028   but most men **know** not.
034:036   to whom He pleases, but most men **know** not."
036:016   They said: "Our Lord doth **know** that we have been
036:026   my People knew (what I **know**)!-
036:076   Verily We **know** what they hide

KNOW (continued)

037:158   but the Jinns **know** (quite well) that they
037:170   they reject it: but soon will they **know**!
038:088   "And ye shall certainly **know** the truth
039:009   those who **know** and those who do not **know**?
039:039   I will do (my part): but soon will ye **know**-
039:052   **Know** they not that Allah enlarges the provision
040:057   than the creation of men: yet most men **know** not.
040:070   but soon shall they **know**,-
042:018   and **know** that it is the Truth.
042:035   But let those **know**, who dispute
043:089   and say "Peace!" but soon shall they **know**!
044:039   but most of them do not **know**.
045:018   of those who **know** not.
045:026   there is no doubt": but most men not **know**.
045:032   ye used to say, 'We **know** not what is the Hour:
046:009   nor do I **know** what will be done with me or with you.
047:019   **Know**, therefore, that there is no god but Allah,
047:030   but surely thou wilt **know** them by the tone of their speech!
048:025   ye did not **know** that ye were trampling down
049:007   And **know** that among you is Allah's Messenger:
049:013   ye may **know** each other (not that ye may despise each
050:004   We already **know** how much of them the earth
050:016   and We **know** what suggestions his soul makes to him:
050:045   We **know** best what they say; and thou
052:047   but most of them **know** not.
054:026   Ah! they will **know** on the morrow, which is
056:061   creating you (again) in (Forms) that ye **know** not.
056:062   And ye certainly **know** already the first form
057:017   **Know** ye (all) that Allah giveth life to the
057:020   **Know** ye (all), that the life of this world
057:029   That the People of the Book may **know** that they
058:007   Seest thou not that Allah doth **know** (all) that is
060:001   for I **know** full well all that ye conceal
061:005   and insult me, though ye **know** that I am
063:008   but the Hypocrites **know** not.
065:012   that ye may **know** that Allah has power
067:014   Should He not **know**,-He that created?
067:017   so that ye shall **know** how (terrible) was My warning?
067:029   so soon will ye **know** which (of us) it is
069:049   And We certainly **know** that there are amongst you
070:039   out of the (base matter) they **know**!
072:024   they are promised,-then will they **know** who it
072:025   Say: "I **know** not whether the (Punishment) which ye
072:028   "That he may **know** that they have (truly) brought
073:020   The Lord doth **know** that thou standest forth
074:031   and none can **know** the forces
078:004   Verily, they shall soon (come to) **know**!
078:005   Verily, verily they shall soon (come to) **know**!
081:014   (Then) shall each soul **know** what it has put forward.
082:005   (Then) shall each soul **know** what it hath sent
082:012   They **know** all that ye do.
100:009   Does he not **know**,-when that which is in the
102:003   But nay, ye soon shall **know** (the reality).
102:004   Again, ye soon shall **know**!
102:005   Nay, were ye to **know** with certainty of mind,

KNOWER

009:105   soon will ye be brought back to the **Knower** of what
032:006   Such as He, the **knower** of all things, hidden and
039:046   **Knower** of all that is hidden
062:008   be sent back to the **Knower** of things
064:018   **Knower** of what is hidden and what is open,

KNOWEST

002:106   **knowest** thou not that Allah hath power
002:107   **Knowest** thou not that to Allah belongeth
003:035   for Thou hearest and **knowest** all things."
005:040   **Knowest** thou not that to Allah (alone) belongeth
005:109   it is Thou who **knowest** in full all that is hidden.
005:116   Thou **knowest** what is in my heart, though I
005:116   For Thou **knowest** in full all that is hidden.
009:101   thou **knowest** them not: We know them: twice shall
011:079   indeed thou **knowest** quite well what we want!"
017:102   Moses said, "Thou **knowest** well that these things
019:065   **knowest** thou of any who is worthy of the same name
021:065   (they said), "Thou **knowest** full well that these
022:070   **Knowest** thou not that Allah knows all
026:019   which (thou **knowest**) thou didst, and thou
065:001   thou **knowest** not if perchance Allah

KNOWETH

002:077   Know they not that Allah **knoweth** what
002:158   He Who recognizeth and **knoweth**.
002:187   Allah **knoweth** what ye used to do secretly
002:197   (be sure) Allah **knoweth** it.
002:215   Allah **knoweth** it well.
002:216   But Allah **knoweth**, and ye know not.
002:224   heareth and **knoweth** all things.
002:227   Allah heareth and **knoweth** all things.
002:235   Allah **knoweth** what is in your hearts,
002:244   and know that Allah heareth and **knoweth** all things.
002:247   Allah is All-embracing, and He **knoweth** all things."
002:255   He **knoweth** what (appeareth to his creatures as)
002:256   And Allah heareth and **knoweth** all things.
002:261   and He **knoweth** all things.
002:268   and He **knoweth** all things.
002:273   be assured Allah **knoweth** it well.
002:283   And Allah **knoweth** all that ye do.
003:034   and Allah heareth and **knoweth** all things.
003:073   and He **knoweth** all things."
003:092   and whatever ye give, Allah **knoweth** it well.
003:115   for Allah **knoweth** well those that do right.
003:119   Allah **knoweth** well all the secrets of the heart."
003:121   and Allah heareth and **knoweth** all things.
003:154   for Allah **knoweth** well the secrets of your hearts.
004:070   and sufficient is it that Allah **knoweth** all.
004:147   and **knoweth** all things.
004:148   for Allah is He who heareth and **knoweth** all things.
005:007   for Allah **knoweth** well the secrets of your hearts.
005:054   and He **knoweth** all things.
005:061   But Allah **knoweth** fully all that they hide.
005:076   that heareth and **knoweth** all things."
005:099   but Allah **knoweth** all that ye reveal and ye conceal.
006:003   and He **knoweth** the (recompense) which
006:003   He **knoweth** what ye hide, and what ye reveal,
006:013   Who heareth and **knoweth** all things.
006:058   But Allah **knoweth** best those who do wrong."
006:059   He **knoweth** whatever there is on the earth
006:059   the treasures that none **knoweth** but He.
006:073   He **knoweth** the Unseen as well
006:115   for He is the one Who heareth and **knoweth** all.
006:117   Thy Lord **knoweth** best who strayeth
006:117   He **knoweth** best those who are rightly guided.
006:119   Thy Lord **knoweth** best who transgress.
006:124   Allah **knoweth** best where to place His mission.
007:200   for he heareth and **knoweth** (all things).
008:017   He who heareth and **knoweth** (all things).

KNOWETH (continued)

008:042   is He Who heareth and **knoweth** (all things).
008:043   but Allah saved (you): for He **knoweth** well the
008:053   heareth and **knoweth** (all things)."
008:061   the One that heareth and **knoweth** (all things).
008:066   for He **knoweth** that there is a weak spot in you:
009:044   And Allah **knoweth** well those who do their duty.
009:047   But Allah **knoweth** well those who do wrong.
009:078   and that Allah **knoweth** well all thing unseen?
009:094   to Him Who **knoweth** what is hidden and what
009:098   that heareth and **knoweth** (all things).
009:103   and Allah is one who heareth and **knoweth**.
010:040   and thy Lord **knoweth** best those who
010:065   it is He Who heareth and **knoweth** (all things).
011:005   for He **knoweth** well the (inmost secrets) of the hearts.
011:005   He **knoweth** what they conceal, and what they reveal:
011:006   He **knoweth** its resting place and its
011:031   Allah **knoweth** best what is in their souls: I should,
011:111   For He **knoweth** well all that they do.
012:019   But Allah **knoweth** well all that they do!
012:034   verily He heareth and **knoweth** (all things).
012:077   and Allah **knoweth** best the truth of what ye assert!"
013:009   He **knoweth** the Unseen and that which is open:
013:033   Who standeth every soul (and **knoweth**) all that it doth,
013:033   will inform Him of something He **knoweth** not on earth,
013:042   He **knoweth** the doings of every soul: and soon
016:028   verily Allah **knoweth** all that ye did;
016:074   for Allah **knoweth**, and ye know not.
016:091   for Allah **knoweth** all that ye do.
016:125   for thy Lord **knoweth** best, who have
017:025   Your Lord **knoweth** best what is in your hearts:
017:054   It is your Lord that **knoweth** you best: if He
017:055   And it is your Lord that **knoweth** best all beings
018:022   Say thou: "My Lord **knoweth** best their number;
020:007   He **knoweth** what is secret and what is yet more hidden.
021:004   Say: "My Lord **knoweth** (every) word (spoken)
021:004   heareth and **knoweth** (all things)."
024:032   and He **knoweth** all things.
026:220   For it is He Who heareth and **knoweth** all things.
027:074   And verily thy Lord **knoweth** all that
039:007   For He **knoweth** well all that is in (men's) hearts.
039:070   and (Allah) **knoweth** best all that they do.
053:030   and He **knoweth** best those who receive guidance.
053:030   Verily thy Lord **knoweth** best those who
063:001   Yea, Allah **knoweth** that thou art
068:007   Verily it is the Lord that **knoweth** best, which
068:007   and He **knoweth** best those who receive
073:020   He **knoweth** that there may be (some)
073:020   He **knoweth** that ye are unable to keep count thereof.
087:007   for He **knoweth** what is manifest and what is hidden.
096:014   **Knoweth** he not that Allah doth see?

KNOWING

012:089   not **knowing** (what ye were doing)?"
015:086   is the All-Creator, **knowing** all things.
027:018   (under foot) without **knowing** it."
045:023   Allah has, **knowing** (him as such), left him

KNOWINGLY

002:075   and perverted it **knowingly** after they understood it.
002:188   and **knowingly** a little of (other) people's property.
003:135   persisting **knowingly** in (the wrong) they have done.
008:027   nor misappropriate **knowingly** things entrusted
016:028   "We did no evil (**knowingly**)."
044:032   above the nations, **knowingly**,

KNOWINGLY (continued)

058:014   and they swear to falsehood **knowingly**.

KNOWLEDGE

002:029   and of all things He hath perfect **knowledge**.
002:032   of **knowledge** we have none,
002:032   perfect in **knowledge** and wisdom."
002:118   Say those without **knowledge**:
002:120   desires after the **knowledge** which that reached thee,
002:145   If thou after the **knowledge** hath reached thee,
002:151   and in new **Knowledge**.
002:169   of Allah that of which ye have no **knowledge**.
002:246   But Allah has **knowledge** of those of those who do wrong.
002:247   abundantly with **knowledge** and bodily prowess:
002:255   aught of his **knowledge** except as He willeth.
003:007   are firmly grounded in **knowledge** say: "We believe in it;
003:018   and those endued with **knowledge**,
003:019   after **knowledge** had come to them.
003:061   now after (full) **knowledge** hath come to thee,
003:063   Allah hath full **knowledge** of those who do mischief.
003:066   which ye had some **Knowledge**!
003:066   in matters of which ye have no **knowledge**?
003:071   while ye have **knowledge**?
003:167   But Allah hath full **knowledge** of all they conceal.
004:017   for Allah is full of **knowledge** and wisdom.
004:025   and Allah hath full **knowledge** about your faith.
004:032   for Allah hath full **knowledge** of all things.
004:035   for Allah hath full **knowledge**, and is
004:039   For Allah hath full **knowledge** of them.
004:045   But Allah hath full **knowledge** of your enemies:
004:092   for Allah hath all **knowledge** and all wisdom.
004:104   And Allah is full of **knowledge** and wisdom.
004:111   for Allah is full of **knowledge** and wisdom.
004:157   are full of doubts, with no (certain) **knowledge**.
004:162   well-grounded in **knowledge**, and the Believers,
004:166   He hath sent from His (Own) **knowledge**, and
004:176   And Allah hath **knowledge** of all things.
005:097   that ye may know that Allah hath **knowledge** of what
005:104   were void of **knowledge** and guidance?.
005:109   They will say: "We have no **knowledge**: it is
006:059   Not a leaf doth fall but with His **knowledge**:
006:060   and hath **knowledge** of all that
006:080   my Lord comprehendeth in His **knowledge** all things.
006:083   for thy Lord is full of wisdom and **knowledge**.
006:100   and they falsely, having no **knowledge**, attribute
006:101   and He hath full **knowledge** of all things.
006:119   by low desires without **knowledge**.
006:128   For thy Lord is full of wisdom and **knowledge**.
006:139   for He is full of Wisdom and **Knowledge**.
006:140   from folly, without **knowledge**, and forbid
006:143   Tell me with **knowledge** if ye are truthful:
006:144   to lead astray men without **knowledge**?
006:148   Say: "Have ye any (certain) **Knowledge**?
007:007   their whole story with **knowledge**, for We
007:033   of which ye have no **knowledge**.
007:052   based on **knowledge**, Which We explained in detail,-
007:089   in His **knowledge** in Allah is our trust.
007:138   He said: "Surely ye are a people without **knowledge**."
007:187   Say: "The **knowledge** thereof is with my Lord (alone):
007:187   Say: "The **knowledge** thereof is with my Allah (alone),
007:188   If I had **knowledge** of the unseen, I should
008:071   who hath (full) **knowledge** and wisdom.
009:006   are men without **knowledge**.
009:060   and Allah is full of **knowledge** and wisdom.

KNOWLEDGE (continued)

009:115	should avoid, for Allah hath **knowledge** of all things.
010:039	that whose **knowledge** they cannot compass,
010:093	it was after **knowledge** had been
011:014	sent down (replete) with the **knowledge** of Allah,
011:046	So ask not of Me that of which thou hast no **knowledge**!
011:047	of which I have no **knowledge** and unless Thou
012:006	For thy Lord is full of **knowledge** and wisdom."
012:022	We gave him power and **knowledge**: thus do
012:068	full of **knowledge** (and experience): but most
012:076	with **knowledge** is One, the All-Knowing.
012:083	For He is indeed full of **knowledge** and wisdom."
012:100	He is full of **knowledge** and wisdom.
012:108	unto Allah,-with a certain **knowledge** I and
013:037	the **knowledge** which hath reached thee, then wouldst
013:043	and such as have **knowledge** of the Book."
015:025	for He is Perfect in Wisdom and **Knowledge**.
015:053	glad tidings of a son endowed with **knowledge**."
016:008	(other) things of which ye have no **knowledge**.
016:025	burdens of those without **knowledge**, whom they
016:027	with **knowledge** will say: "This Day, indeed, are
017:036	thou hast no **knowledge**; for surely the hearing,
017:085	of my Lord of **Knowledge** it is only a little
017:107	given **knowledge** beforehand, when it
018:005	No **knowledge** have they of such a thing, nor had
018:026	(the **knowledge** of) the secrets of the heavens
018:065	taught **knowledge** from Our own presence.
018:068	about things which are beyond your **knowledge**?"
019:043	to me hath come **knowledge** which hath not reached thee:
020:052	He replied: "The **knowledge** of that is with
020:098	all things He comprehends in His **Knowledge**.
020:114	"O my Lord! increase me in **knowledge**."
021:074	We gave Judgment and **Knowledge**, and We
021:079	to each (of them) We gave Judgment and **Knowledge**;
022:003	are such as dispute about Allah, without **knowledge**,
022:008	such a one as disputes about Allah, without **knowledge**,
022:052	for Allah is full of **knowledge** and wisdom:
022:054	And that those on whom **knowledge** has been
022:071	and of which they have (really) no **knowledge**:
024:015	of which ye had no **knowledge**; and ye
024:018	for Allah is full of **knowledge** and wisdom.
024:029	and Allah has **knowledge** of what ye
024:031	who have no carnal **knowledge** of women; and that
024:058	for Allah is full of **knowledge** and wisdom.
024:059	for Allah is full of **knowledge** and wisdom.
027:015	We gave **knowledge** to David and Solomon: and they
027:040	Said one who had **knowledge** of the Book: "I will
027:042	And **knowledge** was bestowed on us
027:052	Verily in this is a Sign for people of **knowledge**.
027:066	Nay, but their **knowledge** fails as to the Hereafter,
027:084	not in **knowledge**, or what was it ye did?"
028:014	We bestowed on him wisdom and **knowledge**: for thus
028:078	because of a certain **knowledge** which I have."
028:080	But those who had been granted (true) **knowledge** said:
029:008	anything of which thou hast no **knowledge**, obey them
029:043	those understand them who have **Knowledge**.
029:049	in the heats of those endowed with **knowledge**:
029:062	for Allah has full **knowledge** of all things.
030:029	devoid of **knowledge**.
030:054	and it is He Who has all **knowledge** and power.
030:056	But those endued with **knowledge** and faith
031:006	without **knowledge** (or meaning), to mislead
031:015	of which thou hast no **knowledge**, obey them not;

KNOWLEDGE (continued)

031:020	without **knowledge** and without guidance,
031:034	Verily the **knowledge** of the Hour is with Allah
031:034	is full **knowledge** and He is acquainted
033:001	verily Allah is full of **knowledge** and wisdom.
033:040	and Allah has full **knowledge** of all things.
033:054	has full **knowledge** of all things.
033:063	say, "The **knowledge** thereof is with Allah (alone)":
034:006	And those to whom **knowledge** has come see that
034:048	He that has full **knowledge** of (all)
035:011	but with His **knowledge**.
035:028	among His Servants who have **knowledge**:
035:038	full **knowledge** of all that is in (men's) hearts.
036:036	of which they have no **knowledge**.
036:081	of skill and **knowledge** (infinite)!
038:069	"No **knowledge** have I of the Exalted Chiefs,
039:029	But most of them have no **knowledge**.
039:049	because of a certain **knowledge** (I have)!"
040:002	is from Allah, Exalted in Power, Full of **Knowledge**,-
040:007	in Mercy and **Knowledge**.
040:042	partners of whom I have no **knowledge**; and I
040:083	they exulted in such **knowledge** (and skill)
041:012	of (Him) the Exalted in Might, Full of **knowledge**.
041:047	To Him is referred the **Knowledge** of the Hour
041:047	but by His **Knowledge**.
042:014	after **knowledge** reached them,-being insolent
042:050	for He is full of **knowledge** and power.
043:009	the Exalted in Power, Full of **Knowledge**';
043:020	Of that they have no **knowledge**!
043:084	Full of Wisdom and **Knowledge**.
043:085	with Him is the **knowledge** of the Hour
043:086	to the Truth, and with full **knowledge**.
043:088	(Allah has **knowledge**) of the (Prophet's) cry,
045:017	it was only after **knowledge** had been granted to
045:024	But of that they have no **knowledge**: they merely
046:004	or any remnant of **knowledge** (ye may have), if ye
046:023	He said: "The **Knowledge** (of when it will come)
047:016	they say to those who have received **Knowledge**:
048:004	and Allah is full of **Knowledge** and Wisdom;-
048:025	wound have accrued to you without (your) **knowledge**,
048:026	And Allah has full **knowledge** of all things.
049:008	and Allah is full of **Knowledge** and Wisdom.
049:013	And Allah has full **knowledge** and is well
049:016	He has full **knowledge** of all things.
051:028	a son endowed with **knowledge**.
051:030	and He is full of Wisdom and **Knowledge**."
053:028	But they have no **knowledge** therein.
053:030	That is their attainment of **Knowledge**.
053:035	What! Has he **knowledge** of the Unseen so that
057:003	and He has full **knowledge** of all things.
057:006	and He has full **knowledge** of the secrets
058:007	full **knowledge** of all things.
058:011	who believe and who have been granted **Knowledge**:
060:010	and Allah is Full **Knowledge** and Wisdom.
065:012	all things in (His) **Knowledge**.
066:002	Full of **Knowledge** and Wisdom.
067:013	(full) **knowledge**, of the secrets of (all) hearts.
067:026	Say: "As to the **knowledge** of the time, it is
076:030	for Allah is full of **Knowledge** and Wisdom.
081:024	a **knowledge** of the Unseen.
084:023	But Allah has full **Knowledge** of what they

KNOWLEDGEABLE

012:055	I am a good keeper, **knowledgeable**.

KNOWN

002:197 For Hajj are the months well **known**.
003:167 They said: "Had we **known** there would be a fight,
003:187 to make it **known** and clear to mankind and not
004:083 would have **known** it from them (direct).
005:107 But if it gets **known** that these two were guilty
005:116 Thou wouldst indeed have **known** it. Thou knowest
009:016 Allah has not yet **known** those among you who strive
010:016 nor should He have made it **known** to you.
015:024 To Us are **known** those of you who hasten forward,
015:066 And We made **known** this decree to him, that the
016:070 after having **known** (much): for Allah
018:021 Thus did We make their case **known** to the people,
022:005 after having **known** (much).
023:114 a little,-if ye had only **known**!
033:059 be **known** (as such) and not molested.
034:014 had **known** the unseen, they would
047:030 and thou shouldst have **known** them by their marks:
055:041 (For) the sinners will be **known** by their Marks:
066:003 and Allah made it **known** to him, he confirmed
067:013 or make it **known**, He certainly has (full) knowledge,

KNOWS

002:181 For Allah hears and **knows** (all things).
002:220 but Allah **knows** the man who means mischief
002:232 and Allah **knows**, and ye know not.
002:235 Allah **knows** that ye cherish them in your hearts:
002:270 be sure Allah **knows** it all.
003:007 but no one **knows** its true meanings except Allah.
003:029 in your hearts or reveal it, Allah **knows** it all:
003:029 He **knows** what is in the heavens,
003:066 It is Allah Who **knows**, and ye who know not!
004:063 Those men, Allah **knows** what is in their hearts;
010:018 of something He **knows** not, in the
014:009 None **knows** them but Allah.
016:101 for another,-and Allah **knows** best what He reveals
017:084 But your Lord **knows** best who it is that is best who it is
018:019 "Allah (alone) **knows** best how long ye have
018:021 their Lord **knows** best about them:
018:026 Say: "Allah **knows** best how long they stayed:
020:110 He **knows** what is before or after or behind them:
021:028 He **knows** what is before them, and what
021:110 "It is He Who **knows** what is open in speech
022:068 say, "Allah **knows** best what it is ye are doing."
022:070 Knowest thou not that Allah **knows** all that
022:076 He **knows** what is before them and what
023:092 He **knows** what is hidden and what is open:
024:019 Allah **knows**, and ye know not.
024:021 hears and **knows** (all things).
024:028 and Allah **knows** well all that ye do.
024:041 Each one **knows** its own (mode of) prayer and praise.
024:041 And Allah **knows** well all that they do.
024:060 and Allah is One Who sees and **knows** all things.
025:006 by Him Who **knows** the secret (that is) in the
026:188 He said: "My Lord **knows** best what ye do."
027:025 and **knows** what ye hide and what ye reveal.
027:065 except Allah, **knows** what is hidden: nor can
028:037 Moses said: "My Lord **knows** best who it is
028:056 and He **knows** best those who receive guidance.
028:069 And thy Lord **knows** all that their hearts
028:085 Say: "My Lord **knows** best who it is that brings
029:005 and He hears and **knows** (all things).
029:011 And Allah most certainly **knows** those who believe,
029:045 And Allah **knows** the (deeds)

KNOWS (continued)

029:052 He **knows** what is in the heavens and on earth.
029:060 for He hears and **knows** (all things).
031:023 of their deeds: for Allah **knows** well all that
031:034 and He Who **knows** what is in the wombs.
032:017 Now no person **knows** what delights of the eye
033:018 Verily Allah **knows** those among you who keep
033:051 and Allah **knows** (all) that is in your hearts:
034:002 He **knows** all that goes into the earth, and all
034:003 it will come upon you;-by Him Who **knows** the unseen,
034:026 the One Who **knows** all."
035:008 for Allah **knows** well all that they do!
035:038 Verily Allah **knows** (all) the hidden things
036:079 For He fully **knows** all creation.
040:019 (Allah) **knows** the treachery of the eyes, and all
041:036 He is the One Who hears and **knows** all things.
041:047 of the Hour (of Judgment: He **knows** all): no fruit
042:012 He will: for He **knows** full well all things.
042:024 For He **knows** well the secrets of all hearts.
042:025 and He **knows** all that ye do.
044:006 for He hears and **knows** (all things);
046:008 He **knows** best of that whereof ye talk (so glibly)!
047:019 for Allah **knows** how ye move about and how ye
047:026 but Allah **knows** their (inner) secrets.
047:030 And Allah **knows** all that ye do.
049:001 for Allah is He who hears and **knows** all things.
049:016 But Allah **knows** all that is in heavens and on earth:
049:018 "Verily Allah **knows** the Unseen of the heavens
053:032 He **knows** best who it is that guards against evil.
053:032 He **knows** you well when He brings you out
057:004 He **knows** what enters within the earth and what comes
059:022 no other god;-Who **knows** (all things) both secret
060:010 examine (and test) them: Allah **knows** best as to
062:007 And Allah **knows** well those that do wrong!
064:004 and He **knows** what ye conceal
064:004 He **knows** what is in the heavens and on earth;
064:004 yes, Allah **knows** well the (secrets) of (all) hearts.
064:011 for Allah **knows** all things.
066:003 He said, "He told me Who is the Knower, The Aware."
072:026 "He (alone) **knows** the Unseen, nor does

L

LABOUR
018:095 help me therefore with strength (and **labour**):
068:027 "Indeed we are deprived (of the fruits of our **labour**)!"
094:007 (from thine immediate task), still **labour** hard,

LABOURING
088:003 **Labouring** (hard), weary,-

LACK
005:103 but most of them **lack** wisdom.
049:004 most of them **lack** understanding.

LADDER
006:035 or a **ladder** to the skies and bring them a Sign,-
017:093 or thou mount a **ladder** right into the skies.
052:038 Or have they a **ladder**, by which

LADEN
002:019 is that of a rain-**laden** cloud from the sky:
035:018 heavily **laden** should call another to (bear)
037:140 (like a slave from captivity) to the ship (fully) **laden**,

LADIES
012:030 **Ladies** said in the City: "The wife of the great
012:050 the matter with the **ladies** who cut
012:051 (The king) said (to the **ladies**): "What was your
012:051 The **ladies** said: "Allah preserve us! no evil
033:053 And when ye ask (his **ladies**) for anything
033:055 There is no blame (on those **ladies** if they appear)
033:055 And, (**ladies**), fear Allah;

LAG
009:046 so He made them **lag** behind and they were told,
015:024 who hasten forward, and those who **lag** behind.
015:060 those who will **lag** behind."
029:032 she is of those who **lag** behind!"
029:033 she is of those who **lag** behind.

LAGGED
007:083 she was of those who **lagged** behind.
027:057 to be of those who **lagged** behind.
037:135 those who **lagged** behind:
048:011 The desert Arabs who **lagged** behind will say
048:015 Those who **lagged** behind (will say), when ye
048:016 Say to the desert Arabs who **lagged** behind: "Ye shall

LAID
002:233 shall have a burden **laid** on it greater than it can bear.
009:108 was **laid** from the first day on piety;
012:048 have **laid** by in advance for them,-(all) except
037:103 he had **laid** him prostrate on his forehead (for sacrifice),
068:042 The Day that the Shin shall be **laid** bare,
081:010 When the Scrolls are **laid** open;

LAKE
027:044 she saw it, she thought it was a **lake** of water,

LAM
007:001 Alif **Lam** Mim Sad.

LAME
024:061 nor in one born **lame**, nor in one
048:017 nor is there blame on the **lame**, nor is

LAMENT
007:093 but how shall I **lament** over a people

LAMP
024:035 His Light is as if there were a Niche and within it a **Lamp**:
024:035 the **Lamp** enclosed in Glass:
025:061 and placed therein a **lamp** and a Moon giving light;
033:046 and as a **Lamp** spreading Light.
071:016 as a (Glorious) **Lamp**?
078:013 And placed (therein) a blazing **lamp**.

LAMPS
067:005 and We have made such (**Lamps**) (as) missiles
067:005 adorned the lowest heaven with **Lamps**, and We

LANCES
005:094 of your hands and your **lances**, that he

LAND
002:273 And cannot move about in the **land**,
003:014 and (wealth of) cattle and well-tilled **land**.
003:196 of the unbelievers through the **land** deceive thee:
004:115 and **land** him in Hell, what an evil refuge!
005:021 "O my people! enter the holy **land** which Allah
005:022 They said: "O Moses! in this **land** are a people
005:026 the **land** be out of their reach for forty years:
005:026 in distraction will they wander through the **land**:
005:032 or for spreading mischief in the **land**-it would be
005:032 continued to commit excesses in the **land**.
005:033 for mischief through the **land** is: execution
005:033 from opposite sides, or exile from the **land**:
006:063 the dark recesses of **land** and sea, when ye call
006:097 through the dark spaces of **land** and sea:
007:057 We drive them to a **land** that is dead, make rain
007:058 From the **land** that is clean and good, by the
007:058 but from the **land** that is bad, springs up
007:074 and gave you habitations in the **land**: ye build
007:110 "His plan is to get you out of your **land**:
007:127 to spread mischief in the **land**, and to
008:026 a small (band), deemed weak through the **land**,
008:067 until he hath thoroughly subdued the **land**.
009:002 (as ye will), throughout the **land**, but know
009:025 but they availed you naught: the **land**.
010:014 Then We made you heirs in the **land** after them,
010:022 traverse through **land** and sea; till when ye
010:078 may have greatness in the **land**?
011:085 commit not evil in the **land** with intent
012:009 to some (unknown) **land**, that so the favour of your
012:021 Thus did We establish Joseph in the **land**, that We
012:055 the store-houses of the **land**: I am
012:056 power to Joseph in the **land**, to take
012:073 in the **land**, and we are no thieves!"
012:080 Therefore will I not leave this **land** until my
013:025 and work mischief in the **land**;-on them is the Curse;
013:041 the **land** from its outlying borders?
014:013 drive you out of our **land**, or ye shall
014:014 to abide in the **land**, and succeed them.
017:067 But when He brings you back safe to **land**, ye turn
017:068 beneath the earth when ye are on **land**, or that
017:070 provided them with transport on **land** and sea;
017:076 Their purpose was to scare thee off the **land**, in order to
017:104 "Dwell securely in the **land** (of promise)":
020:057 us out of our **land** with thy magic, O Moses?
020:063 their object is to drive you out from your **land** with their
021:044 the **land** (in their control) from its outlying
021:071 to the **land** which We have blessed for the nations.
021:081 to the **land** which We had blessed: for We

LAND (continued)

022:041   (They are) those who, if We establish them the **land**,
022:046   Do they not travel through the **land**, so that
024:055   that He will, of a surety, grant them in the **land**,
025:049   That with it We may give life to a dead **land**,
026:035   "His plan is to get you out of your **land** by his sorcery;
026:152   "Who make mischief in the **land**, and mend
026:183   nor do evil in the **land**, working mischief.
027:048   who made mischief in the **land**, and would
027:063   the depths of darkness on **land** and sea, and Who
028:004   in the **land** and divided its people into sections,
028:005   gracious to those who were being depressed in the **land**,
028:006   to establish a firm place for them in the **land**,
028:019   to become a tyrant in the **land**, and not
028:022   (the **land** of) Madyan, he said: "I do
028:039   And he was arrogant and insolent in the **land**,
028:057   we should be snatched away from our **land**."
028:077   and seek not (occasions for) mischief in the **land**:
029:065   them safely to (dry) **land**, behold, they give
030:003   In a **land** close by: but they, (even) after
030:041   Mischief has appeared on **land** and sea
031:032   But when He has delivered them safely to **land**,
031:034   nor does anyone know in what **land** he is to die.
033:027   and their goods, and of a **land** which ye had
035:009   and We drive them to a **land** that is dead,
035:043   in the **land** and their plotting of Evil.
039:074   and has given us (this) **land** in heritage:
040:004   through the **land** deceive thee!
040:021   and in the traces (they have left) in the **land**:
040:026   should cause mischief to appear in the **land**!"
040:029   ye have the upper hand in the **land**:
040:082   and in the traces (they have left) in the **land**:
041:015   Now the 'Ad behaved arrogantly through the **land**,
042:042   beyond bounds through the **land**, defying right
043:011   and We raise to life therewith a **land** that is dead;
047:022   that ye will do mischief in the **land**, and break
050:011   and We give (new) life therewith to **land** that is dead:
050:036   Then did they wander through the **land**: was there
062:010   then may ye disperse through the **land**, and seek
073:020   others travelling through the **land**, seeking of Allah's
089:008   not produced in (all) the **land**?

LAND-GAME

005:096   but forbidden is the pursuit of **land-game**:

LANDED

020:117   the Garden, so that thou art **landed** in misery.

LANDMARK

026:128   "Do ye build a **landmark** on every high place

LANDS

007:137   **lands** whereon We sent down our blessings.
007:137   inheritors of **lands** in both East and West,-
016:007   And they carry your heavy loads to **lands** that ye
033:027   And How made you heirs of their **lands**, their houses,
089:011   (All) these transgressed beyond bounds in the **lands**.

LANGUAGE

014:004   in the **language** of his (own) people, in order
041:044   (in a **language**) other than Arabic, they would

LANGUAGES

030:022   and the variations in your **languages** and your

LAPSE

038:025   So We forgave him this (**lapse**): he enjoyed,

LARGE

003:146   and with them (fought) **large** bands of godly men?

LARGE (continued)

004:007   whether the property be small or **large**,
012:014   devour him while we are (so **large**) a party,
033:050   and not for the Believers (at **large**); We know
034:013   Basins as **large** as wells, and (cooking)

LARGELY

009:075   they would give (**largely**) in charity, and be
063:010   have given (**largely**) in charity, and I

LAST

002:008   "We believe in Allah and the **Last** Day,"
002:062   and who believe in Allah and the **last** day,
002:094   Say: "If the **last** Home, with Allah, be for you specially,
002:126   believe in Allah and the **Last** Day."
002:177   believe in Allah and the **Last** Day,
002:228   if they have faith in Allah and the **Last** Day.
002:232   who believe in Allah and the **Last** Day.
002:264   neither in Allah nor in the **last** day.
003:114   They believe in Allah and the **Last** Day;
004:034   (and **last**) beat them (lightly);
004:038   in Allah and the **Last** Day:
004:039   if they had faith in Allah and in the **Last** Day,
004:059   if ye do believe in Allah and the **Last** Day:
004:162   and believe in Allah and in the **Last** Day:
005:069   any who believe in Allah and the **Last** Day,
005:114   for the first and the **last** of us-a solemn
006:045   the **last** remnant was cut off.
007:025   but from it shall ye be taken out (at **last**)."
007:038   Saith the **last** about the first: "Our Lord!
007:039   Then the first will say to the **last**: "See then!
009:018   as believe in Allah and the **Last** Day, establish
009:019   believe in Allah and the **Last** Day, and strive
009:029   nor the **Last** Day, nor hold that forbidden which
009:044   and the **Last** Day ask thee for no exemption from
009:045   and the **Last** Day, and whose hearts are in doubt,
009:077   (to **last**) till the day whereon they shall meet Him:
009:099   believe in Allah and The **Last** Day, and look
010:051   "Would ye then believe in it at **last**, when it
012:085   though reach the **last** extremity of illness,
015:066   that the **last** remnants of those (sinners)
024:002   if ye believe in Allah and the **Last** Day: and let
028:070   To Him be praise, at the first and the **last**:
029:036   serve Allah, and fear the **last** day: nor commit
035:035   settled us in a Home that will **last**: no toil
038:007   "We never heard (the like) of this in the **last** religion,
040:039   it is the Hereafter that is the Home that will **last**.
057:003   He is the First and the **Last**, the Evident
058:022   who believe in Allah and the **Last** Day, loving those
060:006   for those whose hope is Allah and in the **Last** Day.
065:002   to him who believes in Allah and the **Last** Day
095:007   make you deny the **Last** Judgment?
104:003   would make him **last** for ever!

LASTING

011:039   on whom will be unloosed a Chastisement **lasting**."
020:071   and the more **lasting** Punishment!"
042:036   that which is with Allah is better and more **lasting**
042:045   in a **lasting** Chastisement!"

LAT

053:019   Have ye seen **Lat**, an 'Uzza,

LATE

030:018   and on earth; and in the **late** afternoon and when

LATE-NIGHT

024:058   and after the **late-night** prayer: these are

LATELY
059:015   Like those who **lately** preceded them, they have

LATER
002:184   (should be made up) from days **later**.
002:185   (should be made up) by days **later**.
010:019   mankind was bout on nation, but differed (**later**).
021:093   But (**later** generations) cut off their affair
029:020   so will Allah produce a **later** creation: for Allah
037:078   for him among generations to come in **later** times:
037:108   (to come) in **later** times:
037:119   (to come) in **later** times:
037:129   (to come) in **later** times:
043:056   and an Example to **later** ages.
056:014   And a few from those of **later** times.
056:040   And a (goodly) number from those of **later** times.
056:049   Say: "Yea, those of old and those of **later** times,
057:010   before the Victory, (with those who did so **later**).
077:017   So shall We make **later** (generations) follow them.

LATEST
026:084   among the **latest** (generations);

LATTER
004:020   the **latter** a whole treasure for dower, take not
005:027   Said the **latter**: "Be sure I will slay thee."
033:037   when the **latter** have dissolved (their marriage)
049:011   the (**latter**) are better than the (former):
049:011   it may be that the (**latter**) are better than the
059:009   to the (**latter**), but give them preference over

LAUGH
009:082   Let them **laugh** a little: much will they weep:
049:011   let not some men among you **laugh** at others:
049:011   nor let some women **laugh** at others: it may be that
053:060   And will ye **laugh** and not weep,-
083:029   Those in sin used to **laugh** at those who believed,
083:034   will **laugh** at the Unbelievers:

LAUGHED
011:071   and she **laughed**: but We gave her Glad tidings
043:047   behold, they **laughed** at them.

LAUGHING
002:067   a **laughing**-stock of us?"
023:110   while ye were **laughing** at them!
080:039   **Laughing**, rejoicing.

LAUGHTER
053:043   That it is He who Granteth **Laughter** and Tears;

LAUNCH
024:004   And those who **launch** a charge against
024:006   And for those who **launch** a charge

LAW
002:093   and hearken (to the **law**)"
002:178   the **law** of equality is prescribed to you
002:179   In the **Law** of Equality there is (saving of)
002:194   there is the **law** of equality.
004:176   thus doth Allah make clear to you (His **law**),
005:044   by the Rabbis and the Doctors of **Law**:
005:048   have We prescribed a **Law** and an Open Way.
005:063   the doctors of laws forbid them from their
006:146   For those who followed the Jewish **Law**, We
006:151   except by way of justice and **law**: thus doth
012:076   by the **law** of the king except that Allah
017:033   for he is helped (by the **Law**).
029:061   and the moon (to His **Law**), they will
031:029   and the moon (to His **Law**), each running
035:013   and the moon (to His **Law**): each one

LAW (continued)
036:040   (its own) orbit (according to **Law**).
039:005   (to His **law**) each one follow a course for a

LAWFUL
002:085   not **lawful** for you to banish them.
002:168   eat of what is on earth, **lawful** and good;
002:228   and it is not **lawful** for them to hide
002:229   It is not **lawful** for you, (men),
003:050   And to make **lawful** to you part of what
003:093   All food was **lawful** to the Children of Israel,
004:024   except for these, all others are **lawful**,
004:160   which had been **lawful** for them; in that
005:001   **Lawful** unto you (for food) are all
005:004   Say: **Lawful** unto you are (all) things good and pure:
005:004   They ask thee what is **lawful** to them (as food).
005:005   The food of the People of the Book is **lawful** unto you
005:005   day are all things good and pure made **lawful** unto you.
005:005   (**Lawful** unto you in marriage) are (not only) chaste
005:005   and yours is **lawful** unto them.
005:087   made **lawful** for you, but commit no excess:
005:088   things which Allah hath provided for you **lawful** and good:
005:096   **Lawful** to you is the pursuit of water-game and
005:107   who claim a **lawful** right: let them swear
007:157   he allows them as **lawful** what is
008:069   But (now) enjoy what ye took in war, **lawful** and good:
009:037   for they make it **lawful** one year, and forbidden
009:037   and make such forbidden ones **lawful**.
010:059   some things thereof and (some things) **lawful**."
016:114   which Allah has provided for you, **lawful** and good;
016:116   "This is **lawful**, and this is forbidden,"
022:030   **Lawful** to you (for food in pilgrimage) are cattle
033:050   O prophet! We have made **lawful** to thee
033:052   It is not **lawful** for thee (to marry more)
060:010   the (Unbelievers) **lawful** (husbands) for them.
060:010   They are not **lawful** (wives) for the Unbelievers,
066:001   has made **lawful** to thee, thou seekst

LAY
002:286   our Lord! **Lay** not on us a burden like that
002:286   which Thou didst **lay** on those before us;
002:286   Our Lord! **lay** not on us a burden
006:125   thus doth Allah **lay** abomination on those
007:078   and they **lay** prostrate in their homes
007:091   and they **lay** prostrate in their
007:195   Or hands to **lay** hold with?
011:067   and they **lay** prostrate in homes before the morning,-
011:094   and they **lay** prostrate in their homes
018:017   while they **lay** in the open space in the
020:087   to thee, as far as **lay** in our power: but we
024:060   no blame on them if they **lay** aside their (outer) garments,
028:019   Then, when he was about to **lay** his hands on their
029:037   and they **lay** prostrate in their homes
035:010   Those that **lay** Plots of Evil,-

LAYER
011:082   baked clay, spread, **layer** on **layer**,-

LAYERS
039:016   above them, and **Layers** (of Fire) below them:
039:016   They shall have **Layers** of Fire above them,

LAYETH
009:109   that **layeth** his foundation on an undermined sand-cliff
009:109   Which then is best?-he that **layeth** his foundation on piety
104:002   Who pileth up wealth and **layeth** it by,

LAYS

035:011   or **lays** down (her load), but with
047:004   until the war **lays** down its burdens.

LAZILY

009:054   that they come not to prayer save **lazily** and that

LEAD

002:257   they will **lead** them forth into the depths of darkness.
003:069   But they shall **lead** astray (not you),
003:069   the People of the Book to **lead** you astray.
004:060   But Satan's wish is **to lead** them astray far away
004:102   and standest to **lead** them in prayer, let one
004:113   have plotted to **lead** thee astray.
004:113   only **lead** their own souls astray,
005:002   you out of the Sacred Mosque **lead** you to transgression
006:116   they will **lead** thee away from the Way of Allah.
006:137   in order to **lead** them to their
006:144   to **lead** astray men without knowledge?
007:182   We will **lead** them step by step to ruin
011:098   and **lead** them into the Fire, but woeful
014:001   in order that thou mightest **lead** mankind out of
016:006   in the evening, and as ye **lead** them froth
018:017   to **lead** him to the Right Way.
018:051   as helpers such as **lead** (men) astray!
018:096   "Bring me, that I may pour over it, molten **lead**."
020:120   he said, "O Adam! shall I **lead** thee to the Tree
022:004   turns to him for friendship, him will he **lead** astray,
022:009   in order to **lead** (men) astray from the
024:011   and to him who took on himself the **lead** among them,
025:029   "He did **lead** me astray from the Message
025:074   to **lead** the righteous."
030:053   Nor canst thou **lead** back the blind from their
036:062   "But he did **lead** astray a great multitude of you.
037:023   "Besides Allah, and **lead** them to the Way
037:162   Can **lead** (any) into temptation concerning Allah,
038:082   I will **lead** them all astray.
039:037   there can be none to **lead** astray.
040:038   I will **lead** you to the Path of Right.
057:009   that He may **lead** you from the depths
061:010   O ye who believe! shall I **lead** you to a bargain
065:011   that he may **lead** forth those who believe and do

LEADER

012:080   The **leader** among them said: "Know ye not
020:071   Surely this must be your **leader**.
026:049   Surely he is your **leader**, who has

LEADERS

006:123   Thus have We placed **leaders** in every town,
007:060   The **leaders** of his people said: "Ah! we see
007:066   The **leaders** of the unbelievers among
007:075   The **leaders** of the arrogant party among his
007:088   The **leaders**, the arrogant party among his people,
007:090   The **leaders**, the Unbelievers among his people,
021:073   And We made them **leaders**, guiding (men)
028:005   in the land, to make them **leaders** (in faith)
028:041   And We made them (but) **leaders** inviting to the Fire;
032:024   **Leaders**, giving guidance under Our command, so long
038:006   And the **leaders** among them go away (impatiently),

LEADEST

007:155   and Thou **leadest** whom Thou wilt

LEADETH

005:016   and **leadeth** them out of darkness, by His Will,

LEADING

006:126   This is the Way of thy Lord, **leading** straight:

LEADING (continued)

006:153   Verily, this is My Way, **leading** straight: follow
020:079   instead of **leading** them aright.
023:077   We open on them a gate **leading** to a severe Punishment:
043:031   sent down to some **leading** man in either of

LEADS

002:026   and many He **leads** into the right path,
002:257   he **leads** them forth into light.
014:004   So Allah **leads** astray those whom He
039:021   and **leads** it through springs in the earth?

LEAF

006:059   Not a **leaf** doth fall but with His knowledge:

LEAN

012:043   whom seven **lean** ones devour,-and seven
012:046   of seven fat kine whom seven **lean** ones devour,
020:018   He said, "It is my rod: on it I **lean**; with it
022:027   **lean** (on account of journeys) through deep

LEARN

002:183   that ye may (**learn**) self-restraint.
002:187   that they may **learn** self-restraint.
006:069   that they may (**learn** to) fear Allah.
006:151   thus doth He command you, that ye may **learn** wisdom.
009:122   that thus they (may **learn**) to guard
012:002   in order that ye may **learn** wisdom.
022:046   thus **learn** wisdom and their ears may thus **learn** to hear?
022:054   has been bestowed may **learn** that the (Qur'an)
040:058   Little do ye **learn** by admonition!
050:017   to **learn** (his doings) **learn** (and note them),
068:037   Or have ye a Book through which ye **learn**-

LEARNED

002:102   They **learned** from them the means
002:102   And they **learned** what harmed them,
006:156   that they **learned** by assiduous study;"
026:197   the **learned** of the Children of Israel knew it

LEARNING

005:082   because amongst these are men devoted to **learning**.

LEARNS

045:009   And when he **learns** something of Our Signs,

LEARNT

002:037   Then **learnt** Adam from his Lord certain words
006:105   may say, "Thou hast **learnt** this (from somebody),

LEAST

003:064   say ye: "Bear witness that we (at **least**) are Muslims
003:120   not the **least** harm will their cunning do to you;
003:144   not the **least** harm will he do to Allah;
003:167   or (at **least**) drive (the foe from your city)."
003:171   the Faithful to be lost (in the **Least**).
003:176   not the **least** harm will they do to Allah:
003:177   not the **least** harm will they do to Allah,
004:020   take not the **least** bit of it back:
004:024   the enjoyment you have of them as a duty; but if,
004:040   Allah is never unjust in the **least** degree:
004:077   never will ye be dealt unjustly in the very **least**!
004:086   more courteous, (at **least**) of equal courtesy.
004:113   and to thee they can do no harm in the **least**.
004:124   and not the **least** injustice will be done to them.
005:017   Say: "Who then hath the **least** power against Allah,
005:041   thou hast no authority in the **least** for him
005:042   If thou decline, they cannot hurt thee in the **least**.
006:134   nor can ye frustrate it (in the **least** bit).
006:159   thou hast no part in them in the **least**:
008:019   Not the **least** good will your

LEAST (continued)

009:039   but Him ye would not harm in the **least**..
011:057   "If ye turn away,-I (at **least**) have conveyed
011:057   and you will not harm Him in the **least**.
011:109   their portion without (the **least**) abatement.
012:068   in the **least** against (the Plan of) Allah:
017:071   will not be dealt with unjustly in the **least**.
018:033   and failed not in the **least** therein:
019:060   and will not be wronged in the **least**,-
021:047   dealt with unjustly in the **least**.
028:081   and he had not (the **least** little) party to
029:012   Never in the **least** will they bear their faults:
033:023   changed (their determination) in the **least**:
034:003   the **least** little atom in the Heavens or on earth:
034:039   and nothing do ye spend in the **least** (in His Cause)
035:018   not the **least** portion of it can be carried
036:054   be wronged in the **least**, and ye shall but be
039:069   be wronged (in the **least**).
040:049   us the Chastisement for a Day (at **least**)!"
041:046   nor is thy Lord ever unjust (in the **least**) to His servants.
044:021   at **least** keep yourselves away from me."
047:032   will not harm Allah in the **least**,
058:010   but he cannot harm them in the **least**, except as Allah
058:013   forgives you, then (at **least**) establish regular
072:024   in (his) helper and **least** important in point

LEAVE

002:180   if he **leave** any goods,
002:203   but if anyone hastens to **leave** in two days,
002:234   If any of you die and **leave** widows behind;
002:240   but if they **leave** (the residence),
002:240   Those of you who die and **leave** widows
003:049   and I bring the dead into life by Allah's **leave**;
003:049   and it becomes a bird by Allah's **leave**:
003:121   thou didst **leave** the household (early)
003:145   Nor can a soul die except be Allah's **leave**,
003:166   was with the **leave** of Allah, in order
003:179   Allah will not **leave** the Believers
004:012   In what ye **leave**, their share is a fourth, if ye **leave** no
004:012   In what your wives **leave**, your share is half,
004:012   but if they **leave** a child, ye get a fourth;
004:012   but if ye **leave** a child, they get an eighth;
004:016   If they repent and amend, **leave** them alone;
004:025   wed them with the **leave** of their owners,
004:064   in accordance with the **leave** of Allah.
004:066   sacrifice their lives or to **leave** their homes,
004:081   but when they **leave** thee, a section
004:115   We shall **leave** him in the path he has chosen,
004:129   so as to **leave** her (as it were)
004:176   those who **leave** no descendants or ascendants
005:022   (once) they **leave**, then shall we enter."
005:022   never shall we enter it until they **leave** it:
005:110   the dead by My **leave**. And behold!
005:110   as it were, the figure of a bird, by My **leave**.
005:110   and it becometh a bird by My **leave**.
005:110   and the lepers by My **leave**. And behold!
006:024   will **leave** them in the lurch.
006:070   **Leave** alone those who take their religion
006:091   then **leave** them to plunge in vain
006:110   We shall **leave** them in their trespasses,
006:112   so **leave** them and they forge.
006:125   those whom He willeth to **leave** straying,
006:137   but **leave** alone them and what they forged.
007:053   will **leave** them in the lurch.

LEAVE (continued)

007:073   so **leave** her to graze in Allah's earth,
007:127   "Wilt thou **leave** Moses and his people,
007:176   or if you **leave** him alone, he (still)
007:186   He will **leave** them in their trespasses, wandering
008:066   two thousand, with the **leave** of Allah:
009:086   and say: "**Leave** us (behind): we would
009:095   that ye may **leave** them alone.
009:095   So **leave** them alone: for they are an abomination,
010:003   except after His **leave** (hath been obtained).
010:011   But We **leave** those who rest not their hope
010:030   invented falsehoods will **leave** them in the lurch.
011:034   willeth to **leave** you astray: He is
011:064   a sign to you: **leave** her to feed on Allah's (free) earth,
011:087   command thee that we **leave** off the worship which our
011:087   or that we **leave** off doing what we like with our property?
011:105   shall speak except by His **leave**:
012:047   ye shall **leave** them in the ear,-except a
012:080   Therefore will I not **leave** this land until my
014:001   into light-by the **leave** of their Lord-to the
014:023   with the **leave** of their Lord.
014:025   by the **leave** of its Lord.
014:027   the Hereafter; but Allah will **leave**, to stray,
015:003   **Leave** them alone, to eat and enjoy and let
015:048   be asked to **leave**.
016:041   To those who **leave** their homes in the cause
016:061   their wrong-doing, He would not **leave**, on the
016:087   and all their inventions shall **leave** them in the lurch.
016:110   those who **leave** their homes after trials and persecutions
017:067   that ye call upon-besides Himself-**leave** you in the lurch!
018:047   nor shall We **leave** out any one of them.
018:099   On that day We shall **leave** them to surge
019:072   against evil, and We shall **leave** the wrong-doers
020:106   "He will **leave** them as plains smooth and level;
021:089   "O my Lord! **leave** me not without offspring,
022:058   Those who **leave** their homes in the cause of
022:065   on the earth except by His **leave**: for Allah
023:054   But **leave** them in their confused ignorance
024:053   they would **leave** (their homes).
024:062   so when they ask for thy **leave**, for some business
024:062   give **leave** to those of them whom thou wilt,
024:062   they do not depart until they have asked for his **leave**;
024:062   those who ask for the **leave** are those who believe
026:166   "And **leave** those whom Allah has created
028:075   will **leave** them in the lurch.
029:026   "I will **leave** home for the sake of my Lord:
033:013   ask for **leave** of the Prophet, saying, "Truly our
033:046   to Allah's (Grace) by His **leave**, and as
033:053   the Prophet's houses,-until **leave** is given you,-
034:012   in front of him, by the **leave** of his Lord, and if
035:032   by Allah's **leave**, foremost in good deeds; that is
035:045   He would not **leave** on the back of the (earth)
036:012   which they send before and that which they **leave** behind,
040:026   Said Pharaoh: "**Leave** me to slay Moses; and let
040:034   Thus doth Allah **leave** to stray such as transgress and
040:074   Thus does Allah **leave** the Unbelievers to stray.
040:078   by the **leave** of Allah: but when
041:048   to invoke aforetime will **leave** them in the lurch,
043:083   So **leave** them to babble and play (with vanities)
044:024   "And **leave** the sea as a furrow (divided): for they
052:045   So **leave** them alone until they encounter
053:026   has given **leave** for whom He pleases and that
059:005   it was by **leave** of Allah, and in

LEAVE (continued)

059:010 and **leave** not, in our hearts, rancor (or sense of injury)
062:009 and **leave** off business (and traffic):
062:011 they disperse headlong to it, and **leave** thee standing.
064:011 except by the **leave** of Allah: and if
065:001 nor shall (themselves) **leave**, except in case they are guilty
068:044 Then **leave** Me alone with such as reject
070:042 So **leave** them to plunge in vain talk and play
071:026 **Leave** not of the Unbelievers, a single
071:027 "For, if Thou dost **leave** (any of) them, they will
073:010 and **leave** them with noble (dignity).
073:011 And **leave** Me (alone to deal with) those in
074:011 **Leave** Me alone, (to deal) with the (creature)
074:028 and naught doth it **leave** alone!-
074:031 Thus doth Allah **leave** to stray whom He pleaseth,
075:021 And **leave** alone the Hereafter.

LEAVES

002:264 which **leaves** it (just) a bare stone.
004:143 Whom Allah **leaves** straying, never wilt
007:022 the **leaves** of the Garden over their bodies.
013:033 Allah **leaves** to stray, no one can guide.
016:037 yet Allah guideth not such as He **leaves** to stray,
016:093 but He **leaves** straying whom He pleases,
017:097 but he whom He **leaves** astray-for such wilt thou
018:049 It **leaves** out nothing small or great,
020:121 for their covering, **leaves** from the Garden:
023:041 as rubbish of dead **leaves**.
030:029 whom Allah **leaves** astray?
035:008 For Allah **leaves** to stray whom He wills,
039:023 but such as Allah **leaves** to stray, can have
039:036 For such as Allah **leaves** to stray, there can
040:033 any whom Allah **leaves** to stray,
042:044 For any whom Allah **leaves** astray, there is
042:046 and for any whom Allah **leaves** to stray, there is
042:050 and He **leaves** barren whom He will: for He
055:012 Also corn with (its) **leaves** and stalk for fodder,

LEAVETH

006:039 whom Allah willeth, He **leaveth** to wander:
013:027 Say: "Truly Allah **leaveth**, to stray, whom He

LEAVING

004:117 (The pagans), **leaving** Him, call but
004:176 That dies, **leaving** a sister but no child, she

LED

002:206 he is **led** by arrogance to (more) crime.
005:030 soul of the other **led** him to the murder of his brother:
009:037 the Unbelievers are **led** to wrong thereby:
011:098 be the place to which they are **led**!
014:036 they have indeed **led** astray many among mankind:
020:079 Pharaoh **led** his people astray instead of
020:085 the Samiri has **led** them astray."
025:017 "Was it ye who **led** these my servants astray,
028:063 are the ones whom we **led** astray: we **led** them astray,
037:032 "We **led** you astray: for truly we were ourselves astray."
039:071 The Unbelievers will be **led** to Hell in groups;
039:073 will be **led** to the Garden in groups: until behold,
040:037 and the plot of Pharaoh **led** to nothing but
057:014 will reply, "True! but ye **led** yourselves into
074:042 "What **led** you into Hell-Fire?"

LEECH-LIKE

022:005 then out of a **leech-like** clot, then out
040:067 then from a **leech-like** clot; then does
075:038 Then did he become a **leech-like** clot; then did
096:002 Created man, out of a **leech-like** clot:

LEFT

002:017 and **left** them in utter darkness,
002:248 and the relics **left** by the family of Moses
003:028 shall have no relation **left** with Allah except by way of
003:170 and with regard to those **left** behind, who have
003:195 those who have **left** their homes, and were driven
004:007 From what is **left** by parents and those nearest
004:009 if they had **left** a helpless family behind:
004:011 if the deceased **left** brothers (or sisters),
004:011 if the deceased **left** children; if no children
004:012 has **left** neither ascendants nor descendants,
004:012 but has **left** a brother or a sister, each one
004:033 to property **left** by parents and relatives.
004:176 if (such a deceased was) a woman, who **left** no child,
006:023 There will then be (**left**) no excuse
006:094 Ye have **left** behind you all (the favours)
006:094 and your (pet) fancies have **left** you in the lurch!"
007:017 from their right and their **left**: nor wilt
007:037 They will reply, "They have **left** us in the lurch,"
007:079 So Salih **left** them, saying: "O my people!
007:093 So Shu'aib **left** them, saying: "O my people!
009:016 Do you think that you would be **left** alone while
009:081 Those who were **left** behind (in the Tabuk expedition)
009:118 who were **left** Behind; (they felt guilty)
011:021 they forged have **left** them in the lurch!
011:086 'That which is **left** you by Allah is best for you,
012:017 and **left** Joseph with our things: and the wolf
012:094 When the Caravan **left** (Egypt), their father
016:048 the right and the **left**, prostrating themselves to Allah,
018:017 turning away from them to the **left**, while they
018:018 We turned them on their right and on their **left** sides:
018:091 (He **left** them) as they were: We completely
024:022 and those who have **left** their homes in Allah's cause:
026:146 "Will ye be **left** secure, in (the enjoyment of) all that
029:002 Do men think that they will be **left** alone on saying, "We
029:035 And We have **left** thereof an evident Sign,
034:015 their home-land-two Gardens to the right and to the **left**.
037:078 And We **left** (this blessing) for him
037:108 And We **left** for him among **generations** (to come)
037:119 And We **left** for them among **generations** (to come)
037:129 And We **left** for him among **generations** (to come)
040:021 and in the traces (they have **left**) in the land:
040:074 "They have **left** us in the lurch: nay, we
040:082 and in the traces (they have **left**) in the land:
043:028 And he **left** it as a Word to endure among those
044:025 and springs they **left** behind.
045:023 Allah has knowing (him as such) **left** him astray,
046:028 Nay, they **left** them in the lurch:
050:017 on the right and one on the **left**.
051:037 And We **left** there a Signs for such as fear
051:042 It **left** nothing whatever that it came up against,
053:051 And the Thamud, He **left** no trace of them.
054:015 And We have **left** this as a Sign (for all time):
056:009 And the Companions of the **Left** Hand,-what will be
056:009 what will be the Companions of the **Left** Hand?
056:041 what will be the Companions of the **Left** Hand!
056:041 The Companions of the **Left** Hand,-what will be
056:065 And ye would be **left** in wonderment,
056:066 (Saying), "We are indeed **left** with debts
059:005 tender palm-trees, or **left** them standing on their roots,
069:008 Then seest thou any of them **left** surviving?
069:025 given his Record in his **left** hand, will say: "Ah! would
070:037 From the right and from the **left**, in crowds?

LEFT (continued)
074:031 and that no doubts may be **left** for the People
075:036 be **left** uncontrolled, (without purpose)?
081:004 she-camels, ten months with young, are **left** untended;
090:019 they are the (unhappy) Companions of the **Left** Hand.

LEG
075:029 And one **leg** will be joined with another:

LEGACIES
004:011 after the payment of **legacies** and debts.
004:012 after payment of **legacies** and debts.
004:012 after payment of **legacies** and debts;

LEGACY
051:053 Is this the **legacy** they have transmitted, one to

LEGAL
004:176 They ask thee for a **legal** decision, say:

LEGS
024:045 some that walk on two **legs**: and some
027:044 and she (tucked up her skirts), uncovering her **legs**.
038:033 over (their) **legs** and their necks.

LEND
028:086 therefore **lend** not thou support in any way

LENGTH
004:077 When (at **length**) the order for fighting
006:061 At **length**, when death approaches one of you.
008:036 at **length** they will be overcome: and the
010:052 "At **length** will be said to the wrong-doers:
010:090 At **length**, when overwhelmed with the flood, he said
011:040 At **length**, behold! there came Our Command,
012:070 At **length** when he had furnished them forth
012:076 at **length** He brought it out of
015:061 At **length** when the messengers arrived among
018:019 (At **length**) they (all) said, "Allah (alone)
018:096 At **length**, when he had filled up the space
019:027 At **length** she brought the (babe) to her people,
019:075 they will at **length** realize who is worst in position
023:015 After that, at **length**, ye will die.
026:206 Yet there comes to them at **length** the (Punishment)
027:018 At **length**, when they came to a valley of ants,
033:060 for any **length** of time:
034:019 At **length** We made them as a tale (that is told),
035:011 Nor is a man long-lived granted **length** of days,
040:034 at **length**, when he died, ye said:
041:020 At **length**, when they reach the (Fire),
043:038 At **length**, when (such a one) comes to Us, he says
043:055 When at **length** they provoked Us, We exacted
046:015 At **length**, when he reaches the age
047:004 at **length**, when ye have thoroughly subdued them,
067:027 At **length**, when they see it close at hand,
069:032 whereof the **length** is seventy cubits!
072:024 At **length**, when they see (with their own eyes)
075:007 At **length**, when the Sight is dazed,
080:033 At **length**, when there comes the Deafening Noise,-

LENTILS
002:061 its garlic, **lentils**, and onions."

LEPERS
003:049 and I heal those born blind, and the **lepers**,
005:110 and the **lepers** by My leave. And behold!

LESS
005:055 Your (real) friends are (no **less** than) Allah, His
012:104 it is no **less** than a Message for all creatures.
018:039 If thou dost see me **less** than thee in wealth and sons,
029:014 a thousand years **less** fifty: but the

LESS (continued)
034:003 nor is there anything **less** than that, or greater, but is
034:046 he is no **less** than a Warner to you, in face
036:069 this is no **less** than a Message and a Qur'an
038:087 "This is no **less** than a Reminder
053:004 It is no **less** than inspiration sent down to him:
068:052 But it is nothing **less** than a Message
073:003 Half of it,-or a little **less**,
081:027 Verily this is no **less** than a Message
083:003 or weight to men, give **less** than due.

LESSER
053:032 indecent deeds, save **lesser** offences,-verily thy

LESSON
002:066 and a **lesson** to those who fear Allah.
003:013 In this is a **lesson** for such as have eyes to see."
007:100 is it not a guiding (**lesson**) that, if We
032:026 Does it not teach them a **lesson**, how many
079:026 Verily in this is a **lesson** for whosoever

LESSONS
047:003 their **lessons** by similitudes.
069:012 should bear its (**lessons**) in remembrance.

LEST
003:073 (fear ye) **lest** a revelation be sent to someone
004:135 Follow not the lusts (of your hearts) **lest** ye swerve,
004:176 thus doth Allah make clear to you (His law), **lest** ye err.
005:019 **lest** ye should say: "There came unto us no bringer
005:049 but beware of them **lest** they beguile thee from
005:052 saying: "We do fear **lest** a change
006:070 with it (Al-Qur-an) **lest** a soul is caught in its
006:108 call upon besides Allah, **lest** they out of spite revile Allah
006:156 **Lest** ye should say: "The Book was sent down
006:157 Or **lest** ye should say: "If the Book
007:019 approach not this tree, **lest** you become of the unjust."
007:020 only forbade you this tree, **lest** ye should become angels
007:172 (This), **lest** ye should say on the Day of Judgment: "Of
007:173 Or **lest** ye should say: "Our fathers
008:046 into disputes, **lest** ye lose heart and your power depart;
009:064 The Hypocrites are afraid **lest** a Sura should be
010:083 and his chiefs, **lest** they should persecute them:
011:046 I give thee counsel, **lest** thou become one of the
011:089 cause you to sin, **lest** ye suffer a fate similar to that of the
012:005 thy vision to thy brothers, **lest** they concoct a plot against
012:013 I fear **lest** the wolf should devour him
016:015 mountains standing firm, **lest** it should shake
016:092 to deceive one another, **lest** one party should be more
017:039 object of worship, **lest** thou shouldst be thrown into Hell,
017:046 their hearts (and minds) **lest** they should
019:045 "O my father! I fear **lest** a Chastisement afflict
020:016 divert thee therefrom, **lest** thou perish!"...
020:045 or **lest** he transgress all bounds."
020:045 "Our Lord! we fear **lest** He hasten with insolence
020:061 ye a lie against Allah, **lest** He destroy you (at once)
020:081 commit no excess therein, **lest** My Wrath should descend
020:094 Truly I feared **lest** thou shouldst say, 'Thou hast
021:031 mountains standing firm, **lest** it should shake with them,
023:098 O my Lord! **lest** they should come near me."
024:063 the Messenger's order, **lest** some trial befall them,
026:156 "Touch her not with harm, **lest** the Chastisement of a
027:018 your habitations, **lest** Solomon and his host
028:033 among them, and I fear **lest** they slay me.
031:010 standing firm, **lest** it should shake with you;
033:032 be not too complaisant of speech, **lest** one in whose heart
035:041 and the earth, **lest** they cease (to function):

LEST (continued)

039:056   "**Lest** the soul should (then) say: `Ah! woe

039:057   "Or (**lest**) it should say: `If only had guided me,

039:058   "Or (**lest**) it should say when it (actually) sees

040:026   What I fear is **lest** he should change your religion,

040:026   or **lest** he should cause mischief to appear in the land!"

041:022   not seek to hide yourselves, **lest** your hearing, your sight,

049:002   speak aloud to one another, **lest** your deeds become vain

049:006   ascertain the truth, **lest** ye harm people

LET

002:049   slaughtered your sons and **let** your women-folk live;

002:186   supplicant when he calleth on Me: **let** them also, with a

002:193   But if they cease, **let** there be no hostility

002:197   that duty therein, **let** there be no obscenity,

002:256   **Let** there be no compulsion in religion.

002:282   himself to dictate, **let** his guardian dictate faithfully.

002:282   as between the parties: **let** not the scribe refuse to write:

002:282   but **let** him fear Allah his Lord and not diminish aught

002:282   as Allah has taught him, so **let** him write.

002:282   **Let** him who incurs the liability dictate,

002:282   reduce them to writing **let** a scribe write down faithfully

002:282   and **let** neither scribe nor witness suffer harm.

002:283   and **let** him fear Allah his Lord.

002:283   with another, **let** the trustee (faithfully) discharge his trust,

003:008   "**let** not our hearts deviate now after Thou

003:028   **Let** not the Believers take for friends

003:061   then **let** us earnestly pray.

003:061   say: "Come! **let** us gather together,

003:104   **Let** there arise out of you a band of people

003:160   In Allah, then, **let** Believers put their trust.

003:176   **Let** not those grieve thee who rush headlong

003:178   **Let** not the Unbelievers think that our respite

003:180   And **let** not those who covetously withhold of the

003:196   **Let** not the strutting about of the Unbelievers

004:006   but if he is poor, **let** him have for himself what is just

004:006   If the guardian is well-off, **let** him claim no remuneration,

004:009   **Let** those (disposing of an estate) have same fear

004:009   **let** them fear Allah, and speak appropriate words.

004:029   but **let** there be amongst you traffic

004:074   **Let** those fight in the cause of Allah who sell

004:102   And **let** the other party come up which hath not yet

004:102   their prostrations, **let** them take their positions in the rear.

004:102   **let** them pray with thee, taking all precautions,

004:102   **let** one party of them stand up (in prayer) with thee.

005:002   and **let** not the hatred of some people

005:008   and **let** not the hatred of others to you

005:011   And on Allah **let** Believers put (all) their trust.

005:029   "For me, I intend to **let** thee draw on thyself

005:041   O Messenger! **let** not those grieve thee, who race

005:047   **Let** the people of the Gospel Judge by what

005:103   or a she-camel **let** loose for free pasture, or idol

005:106   and **let** them both swear by Allah: "We will not

005:107   sin (of perjury) **let** two others stand forth in their places,-

005:107   **let** them swear by Allah: "We affirm that our witness is

006:113   To such (deceit) **let** the hearts of those incline,

006:113   and **let** them earn from it what they may.

006:113   who no faith in the Hereafter: and **let** them delight in it,

007:002   so **let** thy heart be oppressed no more

007:027   **Let** not Satan seduce you, in the same

007:073   and **let** her come to no harm, or ye shall

007:105   so **let** the children of Israel depart along with me."

007:194   and **let** them listen to your prayer, if ye

008:059   **Let** not the Unbelievers think that they

LET (continued)

009:028   so **let** them not, after this years of theirs, approach the

009:051   and on Allah **let** the believers put their trust.

009:055   **Let** not their wealth nor their children

009:082   **Let** them laugh a little: much will they weep:

009:085   Nor **let** their wealth nor their children

009:123   and **let** them find harshness in you: and know

010:058   And in His Mercy,-in that **let** them rejoice":

010:065   **Let** not their speech grieve thee: for all

011:081   and **let** not any of you look back: but thy wife

011:089   "And O my people! **let** not my dissent (from you)

012:019   and he **let** down his bucket (into the well).

012:067   and **let** all that trust put their trust on Him."

012:092   He said: "This day **let** no reproach be (cast)

014:006   slaughtered your sons, and **let** your women-folk

014:011   And on Allah **let** all men of faith put their trust.

014:052   that He is One Allah: **let** men of understanding take heed.

015:003   and **let** (false) Hope distract them:

015:012   Even so do We **let** it creep into the

015:065   **let** no one amongst you look back, but pass on

016:126   And if ye punish, **let** your punishment be proportionate

017:033   but **let** him not exceed bounds in the matter

017:080   Say: "O my Lord! **let** my entry be by the Gate

018:019   and **let** him not inform anyone about you.

018:019   and **let** him behave with care and courtesy,

018:019   **let** him find out which is the best food (to be had)

018:021   "**Let** us surely build a place of worship over them."

018:028   and **let** not thine eyes pass beyond them,

018:029   **let** him who will, believe, and **let** him who will, reject

018:110   expects to meet his Lord, **let** him work righteousness,

019:025   it will **let** fall fresh ripe dates upon thee.

020:016   "Therefore **let** not such as believe not therein

020:059   the Festival, and **let** the people be assembled

020:117   so **let** him not get you both out of the Garden,

021:005   **Let** him then bring us a Sign like the ones

021:096   are **let** through (their barrier), and they

022:015   then **let** him see whether his plan

022:015   and the Hereafter, **let** him stretch out a rope

022:029   "Then **let** them complete the rites prescribed

022:067   **let** them not then dispute with thee on the matter,

024:002   **let** not compassion move you in their case,

024:002   and **let** a party of the Believers witness their punishment.

024:006   **let** one of them testify four times by Allah that he is of

024:022   **Let** not those among you who are endued with grace

024:022   **let** them forgive and overlook: do you not wish that Allah

024:033   **Let** those who find not the wherewithal for

024:058   O ye who believe! **let** those whom your right

024:059   come of age, **let** them (also) ask for permission,

024:063   then **let** those beware who withstand the

025:053   It is He Who has **let** free the two bodies

026:087   "And **let** me not be in disgrace on the Day

026:205   Seest thou? If we do **let** them enjoy (this life)

027:041   **Let** us see whether she is guided (to the truth)

028:028   of the two terms I fulfil, **let** there be no injustice to me.

028:087   **Let** no one turn you away from Allah's revelations

030:060   nor **let** those excite thee, who have

031:023   But if any reject Faith, **let** not his rejection grieve thee:

031:033   nor **let** the Chief Deceiver deceive you about Allah.

031:033   **let** not then this present life deceive you,

035:005   **let** not then this present life deceive you,

035:005   nor **let** the Chief Deceiver deceive you about Allah.

035:008   So **let** not thy soul be vested in regret

036:076   **Let** not their speech, then, grieve thee.

LET (continued)

037:061 For the like of this **let** all strive, who wish
038:010 If so, **let** them mount up with the ropes and means
040:004 **Let** not, then, their strutting about through the
040:026 and **let** him Call on his Lord!
042:035 But **let** those know, who dispute
043:062 **Let** not the Satan hinder you: for he
047:004 He will never **let** their deeds be lost.
049:011 nor **let** some women laugh at others.
049:011 O ye who believe! **let** not some men among you laugh at
051:059 then **let** them not ask Me to hasten (that portion)!
052:034 **Let** them then produce a saying like unto it,-
052:038 Then **let** (such a) listener of theirs
055:019 He has **let** free the two Seas meeting together:
057:013 **Let** us borrow (a light) from your Light!"
058:010 and on Allah **let** the Believers put their trust.
059:018 and **let** every soul look to what (provision) he has
060:010 and **let** the (Unbelievers) ask for what they
061:005 Allah **let** their hearts go wrong.
063:009 O ye who believe! **let** not your riches or your children
064:013 and on Allah, therefore, **let** the Believers put their trust.
065:006 **let** another woman suckle (the child) on the (father's)
065:006 **Let** the women live (in 'Iddat) in the same style as ye
065:007 **Let** the man of means spend according to his means:
065:007 resources are restricted, **let** him spend according
068:024 "**Let** not a single indigent person break in upon
068:041 Then **let** them produce their "partners" if they are
073:019 Therefore, whoso will, **let** him take a (straight)
074:055 **Let** any who will, keep it in remembrance!
076:029 whosoever will, **let** him take a (straight) Path to his Lord.
078:039 whoso will, **let** him take a (straight) Return
080:012 Therefore **let** whose will, keep it in remembrance.
080:024 Then **let** man look at his Food, (and how We provide it):
083:026 and for this **let** those aspire, who have
085:016 Doer (without **let**) of all that He intends.
086:005 Now **let** man but think from what he is created!
096:015 **Let** him beware! If he desist not, We will
096:017 Then, **let** him call (for help) to his
106:003 **Let** them worship the Lord of this House,

LETS

040:067 then **lets** you (grow and) reach your age of full strength;
040:067 then **lets** you become old,-through of you there are some
040:067 and **lets** you reach a Term appointed;
047:004 but (He **lets** you fight) in order to test you,

LETTER

027:028 Go thou, with this **letter** of mine, and deliver
027:029 a **letter** worthy of respect.

LETTING

050:044 rent asunder, **letting** them hurrying out: that will

LEVEL

018:047 and thou wilt see the earth as a **level** stretch,
020:106 "He will **leave** them as plains smooth and level;

LEVELLED

007:137 and We **levelled** to the ground the great
091:014 crushed them for their sin and **levelled** them.

LEWDNESS

004:015 If any of your women are guilty of **lewdness**,
004:016 If two persons among you are guilty of **lewdness**,
004:019 except where they have been guilty of open **lewdness**;
005:005 and desire chastity, not **lewdness**.
007:080 "Do ye commit **lewdness** such as no people
029:028 commit **lewdness**, such as no people in Creation
065:001 they are guilty of some open **lewdness**, those are

LIABILITY

002:282 Let him who incurs the **liability** dictate,

LIABLE

002:282 If the party **liable** is mentally deficient,

LIAR

007:066 and "We think thou art a **liar**!"
011:093 the Chastisement of ignominy, and who is a **liar**!
012:026 then is her tale true, and he is a **liar**!
012:027 then is she the **liar**, and he is telling the truth!"
026:186 and indeed we think thou art a **liar**!
028:038 I think (Moses) is a **liar**!"
040:028 And if he be a **liar**, on him is
040:037 but surely, I think (Moses) is a **liar**!"
054:025 Nay, he is a **liar** an insolent one!
054:026 which is the **liar** the insolent one!

LIARS

006:028 for they are indeed **liars**.
009:043 and thou hadst proved the **liars**?
009:107 that they are certainly **liars**.
011:027 in fact we think ye are **liars**!"
012:110 and (come to) think that they were treated as **liars**,
016:086 at them (and say): "Indeed ye are **liars**!"
023:090 but they indeed are **liars**.
024:013 (stand forth) themselves as **liars**!
025:019 "Now have they proved you **liars** in what ye say:
026:223 They listen eagerly and most of them are **liars**.
029:012 in fact they are **liars**!
037:152 But they are **liars**!
058:018 No, indeed! they are but **liars**!
059:011 But Allah is witness that they are indeed **liars**.
063:001 the Hypocrites are indeed **liars**.

LIBERALITY

002:237 And do not forget **liberality** between yourselves.

LICE

007:133 Wholesale Death, Locusts, **lice**, Frogs,

LIE

002:010 because they **lie** (to themselves).
002:206 an evil bed indeed (to **lie** on)!
003:012 an evil bed indeed (to **lie** on)!
003:061 And invoke the curse of Allah on those who **lie**!
003:075 but they tell a **lie** against Allah,
003:078 it is they who tell a **lie** against Allah,
003:094 invent a **lie** and attribute it to Allah,
003:197 what an evil bed (to **lie** on)!
004:050 Behold! how they invent a **lie** against Allah!
005:041 men who will listen to any **lie**,-will listen even
005:103 who invent a **lie** against Allah, but most
006:021 who inventeth a **lie** against Allah or
006:024 Behold! how they **lie** against themselves but
006:024 but the (**lie**) which they invented will leave
006:093 one who inventeth a **lie** against Allah, or saith,
006:116 they do nothing but **lie**.
006:138 forging a **lie** against Allah's name: soon will
006:144 than one who invents a **lie** against Allah, to lead
006:148 Ye do nothing but **lie**."
007:016 lo! I will **lie** in wait for them on Thy
007:037 who forges a **lie** against Allah or rejects
007:089 "We should indeed forge a **lie** against Allah, if
007:145 homes of the wicked, (how they **lie** desolate)."
009:005 beleaguer them, and **lie** in wait for them
010:017 as forge a **lie** against Allah, or deny
010:066 and they do nothing but **lie**.
010:069 Say: "Those who forge a **lie** against Allah

LIE (continued)

011:005   that they may **lie** hid from Him!
011:018   those who forge a **lie** against Allah?
013:010   whether he **lie** hid by night
016:105   it is they who **lie**!
020:061   forge not ye a **lie** against Allah, lest He
023:038   "He is only a man who invents a **lie** against Allah,
024:007   of Allah on himself if he tells a **lie**.
024:008   that (her husband) is telling a **lie**;
024:011   Those who brought forward the **lie** are a body
024:012   and say, "This (charge) is an obvious **lie**?"
025:004   "Naught is this but a **lie** which he has forged,
029:068   who invents a **lie** against Allah or rejects
032:010   And they say: "What! when we **lie**, hidden and
036:015   Ye do nothing but **lie**."
038:056   an evil bed (indeed, to **lie** on)!-
039:032   one who utters a **lie** concerning Allah and rejects
040:028   on him is (the sin of) his **lie**; but, if he
043:020   They do nothing but **lie**!
092:009   And gives the **lie** to the Best,-
092:016   Who give the **lie** to Truth and turn their backs.

LIED

009:077   and because they **lied** (again and again).
011:018   "These are the ones who **lied** against their Lord!
012:074   if ye are (proved) to have **lied**?"
027:027   whether thou hast told the truth or **lied**!

LIARS

016:039   may realize that they were **liars**.

LIES

006:093   for that ye used to tell **lies** against Allah,
006:140   inventing (**lies**) against Allah.
008:028   and that it is Allah with whom **lies** your highest reward.
010:060   And what think those who forge **lies** against Allah,
028:075   and the (**lies**) which they invented will leave
038:004   "This is a sorcerer telling **lies**!
039:060   see those who told **lies** against Allah;-their faces
040:024   but they called (him) "a sorcerer telling **lies**!"...
040:028   not one who transgresses and **lies**!
072:004   who used to utter extravagant **lies** against Allah;

LIEU

071:025   and they found-in **lieu** of Allah-none to help them.

LIFE

002:028   and will again bring you to **life**;
002:028   Seeing that ye were without **life**,
002:028   and He gave you **life**;
002:073   Thus Allah bringeth the dead to **life**
002:085   but disgrace in this **life**?
002:086   buy the **life** of this world at the price
002:096   be given a **life** of a thousand years:
002:096   but the grant of such **life** will not
002:096   of all people, most greedy of **life**,
002:164   and the **life** which He gives therewith
002:179   there is (saving of) **Life** to you.
002:204   whose speech about this world's **life** may
002:207   gives his **life** to earn the pleasure of Allah;
002:212   The **life** of this world is alluring
002:217   no fruit in this **life** and in the Hereafter;
002:220   (Their bearings) on this **life** and the Hereafter.
002:243   Allah said to them: "Die." Then He restored them to **life**.
002:258   "My Lord is He Who Giveth **life** and death."
002:258   He said: "I give **life** and death."
002:259   shall Allah bring it (ever) to **life**,
002:260   "My Lord! show me how thou givest **life** to the dead.

LIFE (continued)

003:014   Such are the possessions of this world's **life**;
003:049   and I bring the dead into **life** by Allah's leave;
003:117   What they spend in the **life** of this (material) world may
003:145   If any do desire a reward in **life**, We shall give it to him;
003:156   It is Allah that gives **Life** and Death,
003:185   for the **life** of this world is but goods
004:074   who sell the **life** of this world for the Hereafter.
004:094   Coveting the perishable goods of this **life**:
004:134   (both) of this **life** and of the Hereafter:
004:134   If any one desires a reward in this **life**,
004:146   mend (their **life**), hold fast to Allah,
005:032   he saved the **life** of the whole people.
005:032   and if anyone saved a **life**, it would be as
005:045   "**Life** for life, eye for eye, nose for nose,
006:029   "There is nothing except our **life** on this earth,
006:032   Nothing is the **life** of this world but play
006:070   and are deceived by the **life** of this world.
006:122   to whom We gave **life**, and a light
006:130   It was the **life** of this world that deceived them.
006:151   whether open or secret; take not **life**,
006:162   my **life** and my death, are (all) for Allah,
007:010   for the fulfillment of your **life**: small are
007:032   Say: they are, in the **life** of this world,
007:051   and were deceived by the **life** of the world."
007:152   and with shame in this **life**: thus do
007:156   in this **life** and in the Hereafter: for we
007:158   it is He that giveth both **life** and death.
008:024   to that which will give you **life**; and know
009:038   But little is the comfort of this **life**, as compared with the
009:038   Do ye prefer the **life** of this world to the Hereafter?
009:055   Wish is to punish them with these things in this **life**,
009:074   a grievous chastisement in this **life** and in
009:116   He giveth **life** and He taketh it.
010:007   with the **life** of the Present, and those
010:023   an enjoyment of the **life** of the Present: in the end,
010:024   The likeness of the **life** of the present is as
010:031   "Who it is that sustains you (in **life**) from the sky
010:056   Is it He who giveth **life** and who taketh it,
010:064   in the **life** of the Present and in the Hereafter:
010:088   in the **life** of the Present, and so,
010:098   in the **life** of the Present, and permitted
010:098   enjoy (their **life**) for a while.
011:015   Those who desire the **life** of the Present
011:060   by a Curse in this **Life**,-and on the Day of Judgment.
011:099   this (**life**) and on the Day of Judgment: and woeful
011:116   of the good things of **life** which were given them,
013:026   (The worldly) rejoice in the **life** of this world:
013:026   but the **life** of this world is but little comfort compared
013:034   For them is a Penalty in the **life** of this world,
014:003   Those who prefer the **life** of this world
015:023   And verily, it is We Who give **life**, and Who
015:072   Verily, by thy **life** (O Prophet), in their
016:065   the skies, and gives therewith **life** to the earth
016:097   to him will We give a **life** that is
016:107   This because they love the **life** of this world
017:016   are given the good things of this **life** (to be obedient)
017:018   transitory things (of this **life**), We readily
017:023   old age in thy **life**, say not to them a word
017:033   Nor take **life**-which Allah has made sacred-
017:033   in the matter of taking **life**:
017:075   (of punishment) in this **life**, and an
018:028   and glitter of this **Life**; nor obey

LIFE (continued)

018:045	of the **life** of this world: it is like
018:046	of the **life** of this world: but the
018:104	in this **life**, while they thought that they were
019:015	he will be raised up to **life** (again)!
019:033	I shall be raised up to **life** (again)!"
020:072	decree (touching) the **life** of this world.
020:097	but thy (punishment) in this **life** will be that
020:124	a **life** narrowed down, and We shall raise him up
020:131	the splendor of the **life** of this world,
021:013	of this **life** which were given you, and to
021:034	before thee permanent **life** (here): if then
021:044	of this **life** to these men and their fathers
022:005	but when We pour down rain on it, it is stirred (to **life**),
022:006	it is He Who gives **life** to the dead,
022:009	for him there is disgrace in this **life**, and on
022:024	(in this **life**) to the purest of speeches;
022:066	and will again give you **life**: truly man
022:066	It is He Who gave you **life**, will cause
023:033	of this **life**, said: "He is no more than a man
023:037	"There is nothing but our **life** in this world!
023:080	It is He Who gives **life** and death, and to
023:099	he says: "O my Lord! send me back to (**life**),-
024:019	in this **life** and in the Hereafter: Allah knows,
024:023	are cursed in this **life** and in the Hereafter:
024:033	a gain in the goods of this **life**.
025:003	they control Death nor **Life** nor Resurrection.
025:018	good things (in **life**), until they
025:023	they did (in this **life**), and We shall make such
025:049	That with it We may give **life** to a dead land,
025:068	nor slay such **life** as Allah has made sacred,
026:018	many years of thy **life**?
026:205	(this **life**) for a few years,
028:014	and was firmly established (in **life**), We bestowed
028:058	which exulted in their **life** (of ease and plenty)!
028:060	are but the conveniences of this **life** and the
028:061	the good things of this **life**, but who, on the
028:067	But any that (in this **life**) had repented,
028:079	Said those whose aim is the **Life** of this World:
029:025	between yourselves in this **life**; but on
029:027	and We granted him his reward in this **life**;
029:045	is the greatest (thing in **life**) without doubt.
029:063	and gives **life** therewith to the earth after its
029:064	that is **life** indeed, if they but knew.
029:064	What is the **life** of this world but amusement
030:007	they know but the outer (things) in the **life** of this world:
030:019	and Who gives **life** to the earth after it is dead:
030:024	and with it gives **life** to the earth after it
030:040	and again He will give you **life**.
030:050	Allah's Mercy!-how He gives **life** to the earth
030:050	verily the Same will give **life** to the men
031:015	in this **life** with justice (and consideration),
031:033	let not then this present **life** deceive you,
033:028	"If it be that ye desire the **life** of this world,
035:005	let not them this present **life** deceive you,
035:011	nor is a part cut off from his **life**, but is in a Book
035:037	Did we not give you long enough **life** so that
036:012	Verily We shall give **life** to the dead,
036:033	We do give it **life**, and produce
036:068	If We grant long **life** to any, We cause
036:078	"Who can give **life** to (dry) bones and decomposed
036:079	Say, "He will give them **life** Who created
037:148	to enjoy (their **life**) for a while.

LIFE (continued)

039:007	of all that ye did (in this **life**). For He
039:026	of humiliation in the present **life**, but greater
039:042	He keeps back (from returning to **life**), but the
039:065	truly fruitless will be thy work (in **life**), and thou
040:011	and twice hast Thou given us **Life**!
040:039	"O my people! This **life** of the present is nothing
040:051	who believe, (both) in this world's **life** and on
040:068	It is He Who gives **Life** and Death; and when
040:077	and whether We show thee (in this **life**) some part
041:016	them a taste of a Chastisement of humiliation in this **life**;
041:031	"We are your protectors in this **life** and in
041:039	can surely give **life** to (men) who are dead.
041:039	gives **life** to the (dead) earth can surely
041:039	it is stirred to **life** and yields increase.
042:009	and it is He Who gives **life** to the dead:
042:036	is (but) the enjoyment of this **Life**:
043:011	and We raise to **life** therewith a land that is dead;
043:029	of this **life** to these (men) and their fathers,
043:032	them their livelihood in the **life** of this world:
043:035	all this was nothing but enjoyment of the present **life**:
043:072	ye are made heirs for your (good) deeds (in **life**).
044:008	it is He Who gives **life** and gives death,-the Lord
045:021	their **Life** and their death?
045:024	but our **life** in this world?
045:026	Say: "It is Allah Who gives you **life**, then gives
045:035	and the **life** of this world deceived you."
046:016	which was made to them (in this **life**).
046:020	in the **life** of the world, and ye
046:033	is able to give **life** to the dead?
047:036	The **life** of this world is but play and amusement:
050:011	and We give (new) **life** therewith to land
050:034	this is a Day of Eternal **Life**!"
050:043	Verily it is We Who give **Life** and Death;
053:025	and the Former **life**.
053:029	nothing but the **life** of this world.
053:044	That it is He who Granteth Death and **Life**;
056:024	A Reward for the Deeds of their past (**Life**).
057:002	it is He Who gives **life** and Death; and He
057:017	Know ye (all) that Allah giveth **life** to the earth after its
057:020	Know ye (all), that the **life** of this world
057:020	And what is the **life** of this world,
067:002	He Who created Death and **Life**, that He
068:033	Such is the Punishment (in this **life**); but greater
069:021	And he will be in a **life** of Bliss,
073:011	those in possession of the good thing of **life**,
074:014	To whom I made (**life**) smooth and comfortable!
075:020	Nay, (ye men!) but ye love the fleeting **life**,
075:040	the power to give **life** to the dead?
076:027	the fleeting **life**, and put away behind them
079:025	in the Hereafter, as in this **life**.
079:038	And had preferred the **life** of this world,
085:013	and He can restore (**life**).
086:008	Surely (Allah) able to bring him back (to **life**)!
087:016	Nay (behold), ye prefer the **life** of this world;
089:024	sent forth (Good Deeds) for (this) my (Future) **Life**."
101:007	Will be in a **life** of good pleasure and satisfaction.

LIFE-TIME

013:040	(within thy **life-time**) part of what We promised

LIFELESS

016:021	(They are things) dead, **lifeless**: nor do thy
022:005	barren and **lifeless**, but when We pour down rain

LIFETIME
010:016 A whole **lifetime** before this have I tarried
010:046 (realized in thy **lifetime**) some part of what We promise
023:093 (in my **lifetime**) that which they are warned

LIFT
051:002 And those that **lift** and bear away heavy weights;

LIGHT
002:017 Allah took away their **light**
002:020 every time the **light** (helps) them,
002:257 from **light** they will lead them forth
002:257 he leads them·forth into **light**.
002:265 and if it receives not heavy rain, **light** moisture suffice it.
003:107 they will be in (the **light** of) Allah's Mercy;
004:174 sent unto you a **light** (that is) manifest.
005:015 a (new) **Light** and a perspicuous Book,
005:016 by His Will, unto the **light**, guideth them
005:044 therein was guidance and **light**.
005:046 therein was guidance and **light**.
006:001 and made the Darkness and the **Light**.
006:091 A **light** and guidance to man: but ye
006:122 and a **Light** whereby he can walk
007:009 Those whose scale will be **light**, will find
007:157 the **Light** which is sent down with him,-it is
007:159 and do justice in the **light** of truth.
007:189 she bears a **light** burden and carries
009:032 Allah's **light** with their mouths, but Allah
009:032 His **light** should be perfected, even though
009:043 in a clear **light**, and thou hadst
009:064 But verily Allah will bring to **light** all that
009:127 Allah hath turned their hearts (from the **light**);
010:005 and the moon to be a **light** (of beauty),
013:016 Or the depths of darkness equal with **Light**?"
014:001 into **light**-by the leave of their Lord-to the
014:005 thy people from the depths of darkness into **light**,
016:080 which ye find so **light** (and handy) when ye
021:048 And a **Light** and a Message for those
023:103 But those whose balance is **light**, will be
024:015 and ye thought it to be a **light** matter, while it
024:035 Allah is the **Light** of the heavens and the earth.
024:035 **Light** upon **Light**!
024:035 Allah doth guide whom he will to His **Light**::
024:035 The parable of His **Light** is as it there were a Niche
024:036 (Lit is such a **Light**) in houses,
024:040 For any to whom Allah giveth not **light**, there in no **light**!
025:061 a lamp and a Moon giving **light**;
027:007 a burning brand (to **light** our fuel), that ye
027:086 and the Day to give them **light**?
028:038 therefore, O Haman! **light** me a (kiln to bake bricks)
028:071 who can give you **light**?
033:043 the depths of Darkness into **Light**:
033:046 and as a Lamp spreading **Light**.
035:020 Nor are the depths of Darkness and the **Light**;
039:022 received **light** from Allah,
039:069 with the **light** of its Lord: the Record
040:061 and the Day, as to give you **light**.
040:067 then does He get you out (into the **light**) as a
042:052 but We have made the (Qur'an) a **Light**, wherewith
047:029 will not bring to **light** all their rancor?
056:081 ye would hold in **light** esteem?
057:009 the depths of Darkness into the **Light**.
057:012 how their **Light** runs forward before their
057:013 Let us borrow (a **light**) from your **Light**!"
057:013 Then seek a **light** (where ye can)!"

LIGHT (continued)
057:019 their Reward and their **Light**, but those
057:028 He will provide for you a **light** by which
061:008 Allah's **Light** (by blowing) with their mouths:
061:008 His **Light**, even though the Unbelievers may detest
064:008 and His Messenger, and in the **Light** which We
065:011 of Darkness into **Light**.
066:008 perfect our **light** for us and grant us Forgiveness:
066:008 Their **Light** will run forward before them and by
071:016 "`And made the moon a **light** in their midst, and made
079:029 and its splendor doth He bring out (with **light**).
081:001 When the sun (with its spacious **light**) is folded up;
083:015 Verily, from (the **Light** of) their Lord, that Day,
092:001 By the Night as it conceals (the **light**);
093:001 By the Glorious Morning **Light**.
101:008 will be (found) **light**,-

LIGHTED
002:017 when it **lighted** all around him,

LIGHTEN
004:028 Allah doth wish to **lighten** your (burdens):
040:049 "Pray to your Lord to **lighten** us the

LIGHTENED
002:086 their chastisement shall not be **lightened**
002:162 Their penalty will not be **lightened**,
003:088 nor will their punishment be **lightened**,
008:066 For the present, Allah hath **lightened** your (burden),
035:036 nor shall its Chastisement be **lightened** for them.
043:075 Nowise will the (punishment) be **lightened** for them,

LIGHTER
032:021 of the **lighter** Chastisement before the greater

LIGHTLY
004:034 (and last) beat them (**lightly**);
009:041 Go ye forth, (whether equipped) **lightly** or heavily,

LIGHTNING
002:019 and thunder and **lightning**:
002:020 The **lightning** all but snatches away their sight:
004:153 by thunder and **lightning**.
013:012 It is He Who doth show you the **lightning**, by way
024:043 The vivid flash of His **lightning** well-nigh
030:024 He shows you the **lightning**, by way
069:005 by a terrible storm of thunder and **lightning**!

LIGHTS
007:203 This is (nothing but) **lights** from your Lord, and
041:012 And We adorned the lower heaven with **lights**,

LIKE
002:015 so they will wander.**like** blind ones (to and fro).
002:023 then produce a Sura **like** thereunto;
002:074 they became **like** a rock
002:085 behave **like** this but disgrace
002:113 **Like** unto their word is what those
002:164 trail **like** their slaves between the sky
002:171 is as if one were to shout **like** a goat-herd,
002:264 They are in Parable **like** a hard, barren rock,
002:264 **like** those who spend their wealth to be seen of men,
002:275 "Trade is **like** usury,"
002:286 Lay not on us a burden **like** that which Thou didst lay on
003:036 "And is not the male **like** the female.
003:073 someone (else) **like** unto that which was sent unto you?
003:105 Be not **like** those who are divided amongst themselves
003:112 pitched over them (**like** a tent) wherever they are found,
003:156 O ye who believe! Be not **like** the Unbelievers,
003:162 the good pleasure of Allah **like** the man who draws

LIKE (continued)

003:180   tied to their necks **like** a twisted collar,
004:001   scattered (**like** seeds) countless men and women;
004:140   if ye did, ye would be **like** them.
005:103   Who instituted (superstitions **like** those of) a slit-ear
006:038   but (forms part of) communities **like** you.
006:071   **like** one whom the Satans have made into a fool,
006:093   reveal the **like** of what Allah hath revealed?"
006:122   be **like** him who is in the depths of darkness,
006:124   one (exactly) **like** those receive by Allah's messengers."
007:057   the Winds **like** heralds of glad tidings,
007:138   a god **like** unto the gods they have."
007:179   They are **like** cattle,- nay more
007:189   and made his mate of **like** nature, in order
007:194   besides Allah are servants **like** unto you:
008:021   Nor be **like** those who say, "We hear,"
008:031   if we wish, we could say (words) **like** these:
008:047   And be not **like** those who started from their
010:024   and We make it **like** a harvest clean-mown,
010:027   will have a reward of **like** evil: ignominy will
010:038   Say: "Bring then a Sura **like** unto it, and call
010:077   Is it sorcery (**like**) this?
011:013   "Bring ye ten Suras forged, **like** unto it,
011:017   Can they be (**like**) those who accept a Clear
011:027   (in) thee nothing but a man **like** ourselves:
011:042   on the waves (towering) **like** mountains, and Noah
011:087   off doing what we **like** with our property?
013:017   For the scum disappears **like** froth cast out;
013:019   from thy Lord is the Truth, **like** one who is blind?
013:033   every soul (and knoweth) all that it doth, (**like** any others)?
014:010   than human, **like** ourselves!
014:011   "True, we are human **like** yourselves, but Allah
014:024   a goodly Word **like** a goodly tree,
015:019   And the earth We have spread out (**like** a carpet);
016:017   Is then He Who creates **like** one that creates not?
016:092   And be not **like** a woman who breaks
016:112   (closing in on it) **like** a garment (from every side),
017:029   Make not thy hand tied (**like** a niggard's) to thy neck,
017:088   were to gather together to produce the **like** of this Qur'an,
017:088   they could not produce the **like** thereof,
017:094   "Has Allah sent a man (**like** us) to be (His)
017:099   has power to create the **like** of them (anew)?
018:029   **like** the walls and roof of a tent, will hem them in:
018:029   they will be granted water **like** melted brass,
018:045   it is **like** the rain which We send down
018:099   to surge **like** waves on one another: the trumpet
018:109   even it we added another ocean **like** it, for its aid."
018:110   Say: "I am but a man **like** yourselves, but the
019:085   **like** a band (presented before a king for honours).
019:086   sinners to Hell, (**like** thirsty cattle driven down to water,-
020:053   the earth **like** a carpet spread out; has enabled
021:003   "Is this (one) more than a man **like** yourselves?
021:005   Let him then bring us a Sign **like** the ones
021:104   the heavens **like** a scroll rolled up for books (completed);-
022:005   then out of a leech-**like** clot,
022:031   or the wind had swooped (**like** a bird on its prey)
022:047   sight of thy Lord is **like** a thousand years
023:024   than a man **like** yourselves: his wish
023:033   a man **like** yourselves; he eats
023:034   "If ye obey a man **like** yourselves, behold, it is
023:047   "Shall we believe in two men **like** ourselves?
023:067   the (Qur'an), **like** one telling fables by night,"
024:039   their deeds are **like** a mirage in sandy

LIKE (continued)

024:040   Or (the Unbelievers' state) is **like** the depths
024:063   among yourselves **like** the summons of one of you to
025:044   They are only **like** cattle;-nay, they are
026:063   became **like** the huge, firm mass of a mountain.
026:130   "And when ye strike you strike **like** tyrants.
026:154   "Thou art no more than a mortal **like** us:
026:186   "Thou art no more than a mortal **like** us,
028:036   never did we hear the **like** among our
028:048   sent to him, **like** those which were sent to Moses?"
028:079   "Oh! that we had the **like** of what Qarun has got!"
031:032   When a wave covers them **like** the canopy
033:019   their eyes revolving, **like** one who faints from death:
033:032   ye are not **like** any of the (other) women:
033:033   make not a dazzling display, **like** that of the former Times
033:069   O ye who believe! be ye not **like** those who hurt Moses,
035:014   (O man!) can inform you **like** Him who is All-Aware.
036:015   the (people) said: "Ye are only men **like** ourselves;
036:029   and behold! they were (**like** ashes) quenched and silent.
036:039   she returns **like** the old (and withered)
036:081   the heavens and the earth able to create the **like** thereof?"-
037:054   He said: "Would ye **like** to look down?"
037:061   For the **like** of this let all strive, who wish
037:065   are **like** the heads of devils:
037:140   When he ran away (**like** slave from captivity)
038:007   "We never heard (the **like**) of this in the
039:006   then created of **like** nature, his mate;
039:009   hope in the Mercy of his Lord (**like** one who does Not)?
039:024   and receive it by his face, (**like** one guarded therefrom)?
040:030   for you something **like** the Day (of disaster)
040:031   "Something **like** the fate of the people of Noah,
040:040   but by the **like** thereof:
040:050   They will reply, "Then pray (as ye **like**)!
041:006   Say thou: "I am but a man **like** you:
041:013   you of a thunderbolt **like** the thunderbolt of the 'Ad
041:025   intimate companions (of **like** nature), who made
042:011   there is nothing whatever **like** unto Him, and He
044:045   **Like** molten brass; it will boil in their insides,
044:046   **Like** the boiling of scalding water.
047:038   then they would not be **like** you!
048:029   **like** a seed which sends forth its blade,
049:012   Would any of you **like** to eat the flesh of his dead brother?
051:052   But they said (of him) in **like** manner, "A sorcerer,
051:059   their is **like** unto the portion of their fellows
052:034   Let them then produce a saying **like** unto it,-
054:007   (torpid) **like** locusts scattered abroad,
054:031   Mighty Blast, and they became **like** the dry
054:050   is but a single Word,-**like** the twinkling of an eye.
054:051   have We destroyed gangs **like** unto you:
055:014   sounding clay **like** unto pottery.
055:037   and it becomes red **like** ointment:
055:058   **Like** unto rubies and coral.
056:023   **Like** unto Pearls well-guarded.
056:055   "Indeed ye shall drink **like** diseased camels
057:016   not become **like** those to whom was given The Book
059:015   **Like** those who lately preceded them, they have
059:016   (Their allies deceived them), **like** Satan, when he
059:019   And be ye not **like** those who forgot Allah; and He
068:020   became, by the morning, **like** a dark and desolate spot,
068:035   of Faith **like** the People of Sin?
068:048   and be not **like** the Companion of the Fish,-
070:008   The Day that the sky will be **like** molten brass,
070:009   And the mountains will be **like** wool,

LIKE (continued)

081:003 When the mountains vanish (**like** a mirage);
081:007 the souls are sorted out, (Being joined, **like** with **like**);
089:008 The **like** of which were not produced
101:004 will be **like** moths Scattered about,
101:005 And the mountains will be **like** carded wool.
105:005 Then did He make them **like** an empty field
112:004 And there is none **like** unto Him.

LIKENED

003:117 may be **likened** to a Wind which brings a nipping frost:

LIKENESS

002:265 And the **likeness** of those who spend
004:157 Only a **likeness** of that was shown to them.
010:024 The **likeness** of the life of the present is as
043:017 as a **likeness** to (Allah) Most Gracious, his face

LIKES

076:028 but, when We will, We shall exchange their **likes**.

LIKETH

039:007 but He **liketh** not ingratitude from His servants:

LIKEWISE

002:194 transgress ye **likewise** against him.
006:112 **Likewise** did We make for every Messenger
011:038 on you with ridicule **likewise**!
013:017 or utensils therewith, there is a scum **likewise**.
017:080 and **likewise** my exit by the Gate
050:040 and (so **likewise**) after the prostration.

LIKING

012:033 to my **liking** than that to which they invite me:

LIMIT

006:067 "For every Prophecy is a **limit** of time, and soon

LIMITED

019:084 a (**limited**) number (of days).
056:033 Whose season is not **limited**, nor (supply)

LIMITS

002:173 nor transgressing due **limits**,
002:178 the **limits** shall be in grave chastisement.
002:187 Those are **limits** (set by) Allah:
002:190 those who fight you but do not transgress **limits**;
002:229 unable to keep the **limits** ordained by Allah
002:229 if any do transgress the **limits** ordained by Allah,
002:229 these are the **limits** ordained by Allah;
002:229 be unable to keep the **limits** ordained by Allah,
002:230 keep the **limits** ordained by Allah.
002:230 Such are the **limits** ordained by Allah,
004:013 Those are **limits** set by Allah: those who
004:014 and transgress His **limits** will be admitted
006:145 nor transgressing due **limits**,-thy Lord
009:112 forbid evil; and observe the **limits** set by Allah;-
016:115 nor transgressing due **limits**,-then Allah
023:007 those **limits** are transgressors;-
026:166 Nay, ye are a people transgressing (all **limits**)!"
058:004 Those are **limits** (set by) Allah.
065:001 and any who transgresses the **limits** of Allah,
065:001 those are **limits** set by Allah:
069:011 the water (of Noah's Flood) overflowed beyond its **limits**,

LINE

022:036 over them as they **line** up (for sacrifice):
057:026 and established in their **line** Prophethood and

LINEAGE

025:054 has He established relationships of **lineage** and marriage:

LINGERED

012:042 and (Joseph) **lingered** in prison a few (more) years.
026:171 Except an old woman who **lingered** behind.

LININGS

055:054 whose inner **linings** will be of rich brocade:

LION

074:051 Fleeing from a **lion**!

LIPS

003:167 saying with their **lips** what was not in their hearts.
004:081 They have "Obedience" on their **lips**;
005:041 "We believe" with their **lips** but whose
023:104 with their **lips** displaced.
090:009 And a tongue, and a pair of **lips**?

LIQUID

014:050 Their garments of **liquid** pitch, and their

LISTEN

002:171 to things that **listen** to nothing but calls and cries:
002:186 with a will, **listen** to My call, and believe in Me:
003:100 if ye **listen** to a faction among the People of the Book,
005:041 men who will **listen** to any lie,-will **listen** even to others
005:083 And when they **listen** to the revelation
005:108 But fear Allah, and **listen** (to His counsel):
006:025 who (pretend to) **listen** to thee; but We
006:036 Those who **listen** (in truth), be sure,
007:194 and let them **listen** to your prayer, if ye
007:204 When the Qur'an is read, **listen** to it with attention,
008:021 "We hear," but **listen** not:
008:023 if He had made them **listen**, they would
008:023 He would indeed have made them **listen**: (as it is),
010:042 (pretend to) **listen** to thee:
010:067 for those who **listen** (to His Message).
014:022 I cannot **listen** to your cries, nor can ye **listen** to mine.
016:065 verily in this is a Sign for those who **listen**.
017:047 when they **listen** to thee; and when
017:047 We know best what it is they **listen**,
018:052 but they will not **listen** to them; and We
020:013 "I have chosen thee: **listen**, then to the
021:002 but they **listen** to it as in jest,-
022:073 **Listen** to it!
025:044 Or thinkest thou that most of them **listen** or understand?
025:052 Therefore **listen** not to the Unbelievers,
026:015 We are with you, and will **listen** (to your call).
026:025 "Do ye not **listen** (to what he says)?"
026:072 He said: "Do they **listen** to you when ye
026:223 They **listen** eagerly and most of them are liars.
027:080 Truly thou canst not cause the Dead to **listen**,
027:081 to **listen** who believe in Our Signs, so they
028:064 but they will not **listen** to them; and they
032:026 do they not then **listen**?
035:014 they will not **listen** to your call, and if
035:014 and if they were to **listen**, they cannot
036:025 of you (all): **listen**, then, to me!"
039:018 Those who **listen** to the Word, and follow
041:026 The Unbelievers say: "**Listen** not to this Qur'an,
046:029 they stood in the presence they said, "**Listen** in silence!"
047:016 And among them are men who **listen** to thee,
050:041 And **listen** the Day when the Caller will call
052:038 they can (climb up to heaven and) **listen** (to its secrets)?
064:016 So fear Allah as much as ye can; **listen** and obey;

LISTENED

003:168 "If only they had **listened** to us,
009:047 among you who would have **listened** to them.
014:022 call you, but ye **listened** to me; then reproach

LISTENED (continued)
021:076 (to Us) aforetime: We **listened** to his (prayer)
021:084 So We **listened** to him: We removed the distress that was
021:088 So We **listened** to him: and delivered him from distress:
021:090 So We **listened** to him: and We granted him Yahya:
040:018 wrong-doers have, who could be **listened** to.
067:010 "Had we but **listened** or used our intelligence,
072:001 a company of Jinns **listened** (to the Qur'an).
072:013 'And as for us, since we have **listened** to the

LISTENER
052:038 Then let (such a) **listener** of theirs

LISTENEST
063:004 thou **listenest** to their words.

LISTENING
005:042 (They are fond of) **listening** to falsehood,
046:029 of Jinns (quietly) **listening** to the Qur'an:

LISTENS
009:061 Say, "He **listens** to what is best for you;
027:062 Or, Who **listens** to the distressed when he calls
042:026 And He **listens** to those who believe and do
072:009 but any who **listens** now will find a flaming fire

LIT
003:106 some faces will be (**lit** up with) white,
003:107 But those whose faces will be (**lit** with) white,
024:035 glass as it were a brilliant star: **lit** from a blessed Tree,
024:036 (**Lit** is such a Light) in houses, which Allah

LITTLE
002:088 is on them for their blasphemy: **little** is it they believe.
002:188 and knowingly a **little** of (other) people's property.
002:264 on which is a **little** soil;
003:197 **Little** is it for enjoyment; their Ultimate
004:142 but **little** do they hold Allah in remembrance;
004:155 and **little** is it they believe;
005:094 make a trial of you in a **little** matter of game
007:003 **Little** it is ye remember of admonition.
007:086 but remember how ye were **little**, and He
009:038 But **little** is the comfort of this life,
009:082 Let them laugh a **little**: much will they weep:
010:070 A **little** enjoyment in this world!-and the,
010:091 but a **little** while before, wast thou
012:005 Said (the father): "My (dear) **little** son! relate
012:047 except a **little**, of which ye shall eat.
012:048 (all) except a **little** which ye shall have
013:026 is but **little** comfort compared to the Hereafter.
016:045 seize them from directions they **little** perceive?
017:052 ye tarried but a **little** while!"
017:074 thou wouldst nearly have inclined to them a **little**.
017:076 except for a **little** while.
017:085 a **little** that is communicated to you, (O men!)"
023:040 (Allah) said: "In but a **little** while, they are
023:078 feeling and understanding: **little** thanks it is ye give!
023:114 "Ye stayed not but a **little**,-if ye had only known!
027:062 **Little** it is that ye heed!
028:081 and he had not (the least **little**) party to
031:024 We grant them their pleasure for a **little** while:
032:009 sight and understanding **little** thanks do ye give!
033:018 for just a **little** while,
033:020 they would fight but **little**.
034:003 the least **little** atom in the Heavens or on earth:
034:014 his death except a **little** worm of the earth,
037:056 thou wast **little** short of bringing me to perdition!
037:174 So turn thou away from them for a **little** while,
037:178 So turn thou away from them for a **little** while,

LITTLE (continued)
038:044 "And take in thy hand a **little** grass, and strike
039:008 Say, "Enjoy the disbelief for a **little** while:
040:058 **Little** do ye learn by admonition!
048:015 Nay, but **little** do they understand (such things).
051:017 They were in the habit of sleeping but **little** by night,
051:043 "Enjoy (your brief day) for a **little** while!"
053:034 Gives a **little**, then hardens (his heart)?
059:002 **Little** did ye think that they would get out:
059:002 them from quarters from which they **little** expected (it),
063:010 Why didst Thou not give me respite for a **little** while?
067:023 and understanding: **little** thanks it is ye give.
068:044 We draw them on **little** by **little** from directions
069:041 It is not the word of a poet: **little** it is ye believe!
069:042 of a soothsayer: **little** admonition it is ye receive.
073:003 Half of it,-or a **little** less,
073:004 Or a **little** more; and recite the Qur'an in slow,
073:011 and bear with them for a **little** while.
077:046 enjoy yourselves (but) a **little** while, for that

LIVE
002:049 let your women-folk **live**;
003:169 Nay, they **live**, finding their sustenance
004:019 on the contrary **live** with them
007:020 or such beings as **live** for ever."
007:025 He said: "Therein shall ye **live**, and therein
008:042 might **live** after a Clear Sign (had been given).
014:006 slaughtered your sons, and let your women-folk **live**:
019:031 on me Prayer and Charity as long as I **live**;
020:074 therein shall he neither die or **live**.
021:034 would they **live** permanently?
022:036 (beg not but) **live** in contentment, and such
023:037 We shall die and we **live**!
023:057 Verily those who **live** in awe for fear
026:081 and then to **live** (again);
027:061 or, who has made the earth firm to **live** in;
040:034 and **live** in doubt,-
045:024 We shall die and we **live**, and nothing
050:003 When we die and become dust, (shall we **live** again?)
065:006 Let the women **live** (in 'iddat) in the same
065:006 in the same style as ye **live**, according to
087:013 In which he will then neither die nor **live**.

LIVED
008:042 and those who **lived** might live after a Clear Sign
024:055 after the fear in which they (**lived**), to one
033:062 who **lived** aforetime: no change wilt thou find
035:024 without a warner having **lived** among them (in the past).

LIVELIHOOD
002:036 and your means of **livelihood** for a time."
007:024 and your means of **livelihood**,-for a time."
021:111 and grant of (worldly) **livelihood** (to you) for a time.
030:023 (make for **livelihood**) out of His Bounty:
043:032 them their **livelihood** in the life of this world:
056:082 And have ye made it your **livelihood** that ye

LIVELY
020:066 of their magic-began to be in **lively** motion!

LIVES
002:155 some loss in goods, **lives** and the fruits (of your toil),
003:101 and among you **lives** the Messenger?
004:066 sacrifice their **lives** or to leave their homes,
006:038 (that **lives**) on the earth, nor a being
006:048 so those who believe and mend (their **lives**),-
007:035 those who are righteous and mend (their **lives**),
009:120 their own **lives** to his: because nothing

LIVES (continued)

016:028 "(Namely) those whose **lives** the angels take in
016:032 (Namely) those whose **lives** the angels take in
025:058 And put thy trust in Him Who **lives** and dies not;

LIVING

002:154 Nay, they are **living**,
002:255 Allah! There is no god but He, the **living**,
003:002 the **Living**, the Self-Subsisting,
003:027 and Thou bringest the dead out of the **living**;
003:027 Thou bringest the **Living** out of the dead,
006:095 He causeth the **living** to issue from the dead.
006:095 cause the dead to issue from the **living**.
010:031 and the dead from the **living**?
010:031 brings out the **living** from the dead and the
016:061 on the (earth), a single **living** creature:
020:111 The **Living**, The Self-Subsisting, The Sustainer,
021:030 We made from water every **living** thing.
024:029 fault on your part to enter houses not used for **living** in,
026:129 fine buildings in the hope of **living** therein (for ever)?
030:019 and brings out the dead from the **living**,
030:019 It is He Who brings out the **living** from the dead,
035:022 Nor are alike those that are **living** and those that are dead.
035:045 of the (earth) a single **living** creature:
040:065 He is the **living** (One): There is no god but He:
042:029 and the **living** creatures that He has scattered
077:026 The **living** and the dead,

LO

002:098 **Lo**! Allah is an enemy to those who
003:158 **Lo**! it is unto Allah that ye are brought together.
004:131 But if ye deny Him, **lo**! unto Allah belong all
006:044 when **lo**! they were plunged in despair!
006:054 **lo**! He is Oft-Forgiving, Most Merciful.
006:074 **Lo**! Abraham said to his father Azar: "Takest thou idols
007:016 **lo**! I will lie in wait for them on Thy Straight way:
007:201 bring Allah to remembrance when **lo**! they
008:048 **lo**! I fear Allah; for Allah is strict in punishment."
008:048 and said: "**Lo**! I am clear of you; **lo**! I see what ye see not;
008:049 **Lo**! the Hypocrites and those in whose heart
023:030 (for men to understand); **lo**! We put (men) to test.
023:077 then **Lo**! they will be plunged in despair therein!
036:053 a single Blast, when **lo**! they will

LOAD

012:065 camel's **load** (of grain to our provisions).
012:072 is (the reward of) a camel-**load**; I will
022:002 shall drop her **load** (unformed): thou shalt
035:011 or lays down (her **load**), but with
035:018 to (bear) his **load**, not the
052:040 are burdened with a **load** of debt?-
068:046 with a **load** of debt?-

LOADED

036:041 their race (through the flood) in the **loaded** Ark;

LOADS

016:007 And they carry your heavy **loads** to lands that ye

LOAN

002:245 Who is he that will **loan** to Allah a beautiful **loan**,
005:012 and **loan** to Allah a beautiful **loan**, verily I will
057:011 Who is he that will **loan** to Allah a beautiful **Loan**?
057:018 a Beautiful **Loan**, it shall be increased manifold
057:018 men and women, and **loan** to Allah a beautiful
064:017 If ye **loan** to Allah a beautiful **loan**, He will
073:020 and give zakat; and **loan** to Allah a Beautiful **Loan**.

LOATHED

028:042 be among the **loathed** (and despised).

LOCKED

012:077 Joseph keep **locked** in his heart, revealing not
100:010 And that which is (**locked** up) in (human)

LOCKS

047:024 or is that there are **locks** upon their hearts?

LOCUSTS

007:133 Wholesale Death, **Locusts**, lice, Frogs, and
054:007 (torpid) like **locusts** scattered abroad,

LODGED

053:046 From a seed when **lodged** (in its place);

LOFTIEST

030:027 To Him belongs the **loftiest** similitude (We can think of)

LOFTY

019:050 and We granted them **lofty** honour on the tongue
019:057 And We raised him to a **lofty** station.
022:045 and neglected, and castles **lofty** and well-built?
027:044 She was asked to enter the **lofty** Palace:
028:038 and build me a **lofty** palace, that I
029:058 a Home in Heaven,-**lofty** mansions beneath which
039:020 their Lord, that **lofty** mansions, one above
040:036 a **lofty** palace, that I may attain the ways
045:008 to him, yet is obstinate and **lofty**, as if
055:024 smoothly through the seas, **lofty** as mountains:
077:027 standing firm, **lofty** (in stature); and provided
080:030 And enclosed Gardens, dense with **lofty** trees,
089:007 Of the (city of) Iram, with **lofty** pillars,

LOINS

004:023 your son proceeding from your **loins**;
007:172 from their **loins**-their descendants, and made

LOLLS

007:176 he **lolls** out his tongue, or if
007:176 he (still) **lolls** out his tongue.

LONG

002:259 He said: "How **long** didst thou tarry (thus)?"
003:113 they rehearse the Signs of Allah all night **long**,
005:024 never enter it as **long** as they are in it.
005:084 we **long** for our Lord to admit us to
005:096 as **long** as ye are in the Sacred Precincts or in
007:155 been Thy Will Thou couldst have destroyed, **long** before,
009:007 As **long** as these stand true to you, stand ye true to them:
009:042 have followed thee, but the distance was **long**,
011:078 and they had been **long** in the habit
011:107 They will dwell therein so **long** as the heavens
011:108 so **long** as the heavens and the earth endure,
012:045 (so **long**) a space of time, said: "I will tell
013:030 a People before whom (**long** since) have (other)
014:003 they are astray by a **long** distance.
018:019 "How **long** have ye stayed (here)?"
018:019 "Allah (alone) knows best how **long** ye have
018:026 Say: "Allah knows best how **long** they stayed:
019:031 on me Prayer and Charity as **long** as I live;
019:046 now get away from me for a good **long** while!"
020:086 Did then the promise seem to you **long** (in coming)?
021:044 grew **long** for them; see they
028:045 and **long** were the ages that passed over them;
030:010 In the **long** run evil will be the End of those
032:024 so **long** as they persevered with patience
035:037 Did We not give you **long** enough life so that
036:068 If We grant **long** life to any, We cause
057:016 The Book aforetime, but **long** ages passed over

LONG (continued)

068:045   A (**long**) respite will I grant them: truly powerful
070:038   Does every man of them **long** to enter
076:001   Has there not been over Man a **long** period of Time,
076:026   and glorify Him a **long** night through.

LONG-EXTENDED

056:030   In shade **long-extended**,

LONG-LIVED

035:011   Nor is a man **long-lived** granted length of days,

LONGER

011:036   So grieve no **longer** over their (evil) deeds.
020:103   "Ye tarried not **longer** than ten (days);"
020:104   will say: "Ye tarried not **longer** than a day!"
034:019   place **longer** distances between our journey-stages":
038:003   no **longer** time for being save!

LONGING

007:056   and **longing** (in your hearts): for the
020:131   Nor strain thine eyes in **longing** for the

LOOK

002:259   but **look** at thy food and thy drink; they show no signs of
002:259   **look** further at the bones, how We bring them together
002:259   and **look** at thy donkey: and that We may make of thee a
002:266   not strong (enough to **look**, after themselves)
003:077   or **look** at them on the Day of Judgment,
004:046   and "Do hear"; and "Do **look** at us":
007:143   that I may **look** upon Thee." Allah said: "By no
007:143   but **look** upon the mount; if it abide
008:067   Ye **look** for the temporal goods of this world;
009:098   Some of the Bedouin Arabs **look** upon their payments
009:099   and **look** on their payments as pious gifts bringing
009:127   they **look** at each other, (saying), "Doth anyone
010:043   And among them are some who **look** at thee:
011:038   we (in our turn) can **look** down on you with
011:081   and let not any of you **look** back: but thy
015:065   let no one amongst you **look** back, but pass on
016:048   Do they not **look** at Allah's creation.
016:079   Do they not **look** at the birds, held poised
020:097   now **look** at thy god, of whom thou hast become a
026:007   Do they not **look** at the earth,-how many
037:054   He said: "Would ye like to **look** down?"
040:037   the heavens, and that I may **look** up to the God
047:020   is a disease looking at thee with a **look** of one
050:006   Do they not **look** at the sky above them?-
059:018   and let every soul **look** to what (provision) he has
078:027   For that they used not to **look** for any account
080:024   Then let man **look** at his Food,
088:017   Do they not **look** at the Camels, how they are made?-

LOOKED

018:018   if thou hadst **looked** at them, thou wouldst
037:055   He **looked** down and saw him in the midst

LOOKEST

063:004   When thou **lookest** at them, their bodies
076:020   And when thou **lookest**, it is there thou wilt see a

LOOKETH

008:067   but Allah **looketh** to the Hereafter:
096:007   In that he **looketh** upon himself as self-sufficient.

LOOKING

007:198   Thou wilt see them **looking** at thee, but they see not.
028:021   He therefore got away therefrom **looking** about, in a state
033:019   thou wilt see them **looking** to thee, their eyes
035:043   Now are they but **looking** for the way
039:068   they will be standing and **looking** on!

LOOKING (continued)

042:045   humbleness (and) **looking** with a stealthy glance.
047:020   is a disease **looking** at thee with a look of one
048:011   in (**looking** after) our flocks and heads, and our
051:044   seized them, even while they were **looking** on.
056:084   And ye the while (sit) **looking** on,-
075:023   **Looking** towards their Lord;

LOOKS

035:008   so that he **looks** upon it as good, (equal to one

LOOSE

005:103   or a she-camel let **loose** for free pasture, or idol

LORD

002:005   from their **Lord**,
002:026   that it is the truth from their **Lord**;
002:030   Behold, thy **Lord** said to the angels:
002:037   and his **Lord** turned towards him;
002:037   Then learnt Adam from his **Lord** certain words
002:046   that they are to meet their **Lord**,
002:049   therein was a tremendous trial from your **Lord**.
002:061   so beseech thy **Lord** for us to produce for us
002:062   shall have their reward with their **Lord**
002:068   They said: "Beseech on our behalf thy **Lord**
002:069   They said: "Beseech on our behalf thy **Lord**
002:070   They said, "Beseech on our behalf thy **Lord**
002:076   in argument about it before your **Lord**?"
002:105   for Allah is **Lord** of grace abounding.
002:105   come down to you from your **Lord**.
002:112   he will get his reward with his **Lord**;
002:124   Abraham was tried by his **Lord** with certain Commands,
002:126   remember Abraham said: "My **Lord**, make this a City
002:127   "Our **Lord**! accept (this service) from us:
002:128   "Our **Lord**! make of us Muslims,
002:129   "Our **Lord**! send amongst them a Messenger
002:131   Behold! his **Lord** said to him: "Submit
002:131   to the **Lord** and Cherisher of the Universe."
002:136   (all) Prophets from their **Lord**:
002:139   seeing that He is our **Lord** and your **Lord**;
002:144   that is the truth from their **Lord**,
002:147   The truth is from thy **Lord**,
002:149   that is indeed the truth from thy **Lord**.
002:157   (descend) blessings from their **Lord**, and Mercy.
002:178   This is a concession and a Mercy from your **Lord**.
002:198   the bounty of your **Lord** (during pilgrimage).
002:200   "Our **Lord**! Give us (thy bounties) in this world!"
002:201   "Our **Lord**! give us good in this world
002:248   of security from your **Lord**,
002:250   they prayed: "Our **Lord**! Pour out constancy on us
002:258   "My **Lord** is He Who Giveth life and death."
002:258   to one who disputed with Abraham about his **Lord**,
002:260   "My **Lord**! show me how thou givest life to the dead.
002:262   for them their reward is with their **Lord**;
002:274   have their reward with their **Lord**:
002:275   admonition from their **Lord**, desist,
002:277   will have their reward with their **Lord**:
002:282   but let him fear Allah his **Lord**
002:283   and let him fear Allah his **Lord**.
002:285   hath been revealed to him from his **Lord**,
002:285   (We seek) Thy forgiveness, our **Lord**,
002:286   our **Lord**! Lay not on us a burden like that
002:286   (Pray:) "Our **Lord**! Condemn us not if we
002:286   Our **Lord**! lay not on us a burden
003:004   and Allah is Exalted in Might, **Lord** of Retribution.
003:007   the whole of it is from our **Lord**:"

LORD (continued)

003:008 "Our **Lord**!" (they say), "let not our hearts
003:009 "Our **Lord**! Thou art He that will gather mankind
003:015 nearness to their **Lord** with rivers flowing beneath;
003:016 "Our **Lord**! we have indeed believed:
003:026 Say: "O Allah! **Lord** of Power (and Rule),
003:035 "O my **Lord**! I do dedicate unto thee what is in
003:036 "O my **Lord**! behold! I am delivered
003:037 Right graciously did her **Lord** accept her:
003:038 saying: "O my **Lord**! Grant unto me
003:038 There did Zakariya pray to his **Lord**, saying:
003:040 He said: "O my **Lord**! how shall I have a son,
003:041 of thy **Lord** again and again,
003:041 He said: "O my **Lord**! Give me a Sign!"
003:043 "O Mary! worship thy **Lord** devoutly;
003:047 She said: "O my **Lord**! how shall I have a son
003:049 I have come to you, with a Sign from your **Lord**,
003:050 I have come to you with a Sign from your **Lord**.
003:051 "It is Allah who is my **Lord** and your **Lord**;
003:053 "Our **Lord**! we believe in what thou hast revealed,
003:060 the truth (comes) from thy **Lord** alone;
003:073 should engage you in argument before your **Lord**?
003:074 for Allah is the **Lord** of bounties unbounded.
003:084 and the Prophets, from their **Lord**;
003:125 your **Lord** would help you with five thousand angels
003:133 for forgiveness from your **Lord** and for a Garden
003:136 is forgiveness from their **Lord**, and Gardens
003:147 "Our **Lord** forgive us our sins and anything
003:169 finding their sustenance from their **Lord**.
003:174 and Allah is the **Lord** of bounties unbounded.
003:191 (with the saying): "Our **Lord** not for naught
003:192 "Our **Lord**! any whom Thou dost admit to the Fire,
003:193 'Believe ye in the Lord', and we have believed.
003:193 Our **Lord**! Forgive us our sins, blot out
003:193 "Our **Lord**! We have heard the call
003:194 "Our **Lord**! grant us what Thou didst promise
003:195 And their **Lord** hath accepted of them,
003:198 On the other hand, for those who fear their **Lord**,
003:199 For them is a reward with their **Lord**,
004:001 O mankind! fear your Guardian **Lord**, Who created
004:065 But no, by thy **Lord**, they can have no (real) Faith.
004:075 "Our **Lord**! rescue us from this town.
004:077 they say: "Our **Lord**! why hast Thou ordered
004:174 from your **Lord** for We have sent unto you
005:002 and good pleasure of their **Lord**.
005:024 Go thou, and thy **Lord**, and fight
005:025 He said: "O my **Lord**! I have power
005:066 that was sent to them from their **Lord**, they
005:067 which hath been sent to thee from thy **Lord**.
005:068 that cometh to thee from thy **Lord**,
005:068 that has come to you from your **Lord**."
005:072 my **Lord** and your **Lord**."
005:083 they pray: "Our **Lord**! we believe; write us
005:084 we long for our **Lord** to admit us to
005:095 for Allah is Exalted, and **lord** of Retribution.
005:112 Can thy **Lord** send down to us a Table set
005:114 "O Allah our **Lord**! send us from heaven a table
005:117 'Worship Allah, my **Lord** and your Lord':
006:001 (others) as equal with their Guardian **Lord**.
006:004 of the Signs of their **Lord** reach them, but they
006:015 Say: "I would, if I disobeyed my **Lord**, indeed
006:023 "By Allah Our **Lord**, we were not those
006:027 Then would we not reject the Signs of our **Lord**,

LORD (continued)

006:030 They will say: "Yea, by our **Lord**!" He will say:
006:030 to stand before their **Lord**! He will say:
006:037 a Sign sent down to him from his **Lord**?"
006:038 gathered to their **Lord** in the end.
006:051 brought (to judgment) before their **Lord**:
006:052 on their **Lord** morning and evening, seeking
006:054 "Peace be on you: your **Lord** hath inscribed for
006:057 a clear Sign from my **Lord**, but ye
006:071 to submit ourselves to the **Lord** of the worlds;
006:076 he saw a star: he said: "This is my **Lord**."
006:077 He said: "This is my **Lord**." But when
006:077 "Unless my **Lord** guide me, I shall
006:078 he said: "This is my **Lord**; this is
006:080 my **Lord** comprehendeth in His knowledge all things.
006:080 unless my **Lord** willeth, (nothing can happen),
006:083 for thy **Lord** is full of wisdom and knowledge.
006:102 That is Allah, your **Lord**! There is no
006:104 from your **Lord** proofs (to open your eyes):
006:106 by inspiration from thy **Lord**: there is
006:108 In the end will they return to their **Lord** and He
006:112 If thy **Lord** had so willed, they would
006:114 from thy **Lord** in truth.
006:115 The Word of thy **Lord** doth find its fulfillment
006:117 Thy **Lord** knoweth best who strayeth
006:119 Thy **Lord** knoweth best those who transgress.
006:126 This is the way of thy **Lord**, leading
006:127 a Home of Peace with their **Lord**: He will
006:128 For thy **Lord** is full of wisdom and knowledge.
006:128 "Our **Lord**! we made profit from each other:
006:131 for thy **Lord** would not destroy the towns
006:132 for thy **Lord** is not unmindful of
006:133 Thy **Lord** is Self-sufficient, full of Mercy:
006:145 thy **Lord** is Oft-Forgiving, Most Merciful.
006:147 say: "Your **Lord** is full of Mercy All-embracing;
006:150 as equal with their Guardian **Lord**.
006:154 in the meeting with their **Lord**.
006:157 a Clear (Sign) from your **Lord**,-and a
006:158 if the angels come to them or thy **Lord** (Himself),
006:158 or certain of the Signs of thy **Lord**!
006:158 The day that certain of the signs of thy **Lord** do come,
006:161 Say: "Verily, my **Lord** hath guided me
006:164 for (my) **Lord** other than Allah.
006:165 for thy **Lord** is quick in punishment: yet He
007:003 given unto you from your **Lord**, and follow
007:020 he said: "Your **Lord** only forbade
007:022 And their **Lord** called unto them: "Did I not
007:023 They said: "Our **Lord**! we have wronged
007:029 Say: "My **Lord** hath commanded justice; and that
007:033 my **Lord** hath indeed forbidden are:
007:038 "Our **Lord**! it is these that misled us: so give
007:043 the Messengers of our **Lord** brought unto us."
007:044 the promises of our **Lord** to us true: have you
007:047 they will say: "Our **Lord**! send us
007:053 "The Messengers of our **Lord** did indeed
007:054 Your Guardian **Lord** is Allah, Who created
007:055 Call on your **Lord** with humility and in private:
007:061 from the **Lord** and Cherisher of the Worlds!"
007:062 the Message of my **Lord**.
007:063 come to you a reminder from your **Lord**, through
007:067 from the **Lord** and Cherisher of the Worlds!"
007:068 "I but convey to you the messages of my **Lord**:
007:069 from your **Lord** through a man of your

LORD (continued)

007:071   have already come upon you from your **Lord**:
007:073   a clear (Sign) from your **Lord**! This she-camel
007:075   is a messenger from his **Lord**?"
007:077   the order of their **Lord**, saying: "O Salih!
007:079   I was sent by my **Lord**: I gave you
007:085   a clear (Sign) from your **Lord**!
007:089   in the will of Allah, our **Lord**.
007:089   Our **Lord**! Decide thou between us and our
007:089   Our **Lord** comprehends all things in His
007:093   I was sent by my **Lord**: I gave you
007:104   I am a messenger from the **Lord** of the worlds,-
007:105   from your **Lord** with a clear (Sign): so let
007:121   Saying: "We believe in the **Lord** of the Worlds.
007:122   "The **Lord** of Moses and Aaron."
007:125   "For us, we are but sent back unto our **Lord**."
007:126   in the Signs of our **Lord** when they reached us!
007:126   Our **Lord**! pour out on us patience
007:129   He said: "It may be that your **Lord** will destroy
007:134   call on thy **Lord** in virtue
007:137   The fair promise of the **Lord** was fulfilled
007:141   in that was a momentous trial from your **Lord**.
007:142   thus was completed the term with his **Lord**, forty
007:143   When his **Lord** manifested Himself to the mount,
007:143   his **Lord** addressed him,
007:143   he said: "O my **Lord**! show (Thyself)
007:149   they said: "If our **Lord** have not mercy upon us
007:150   on the judgment of your **Lord**?"
007:151   Moses prayed: "O my **Lord**! forgive me
007:152   with wrath from their **Lord**, and with
007:153   verily Thy **Lord** is thereafter Oft-forgiving,
007:154   Guidance and Mercy for such as fear their **Lord**.
007:155   he prayed: "O my **Lord**! if it had been Thy will
007:164   our duty to your **Lord** and perchance
007:167   Thy **Lord** is quick in retribution, but He
007:167   Behold! thy **Lord** did declare that He
007:172   When thy **Lord** drew forth from the
007:172   "Am I not your **Lord** (who cherishes and sustains you)?"
007:187   "The knowledge thereof is with my **Lord** (alone):
007:189   they both pray to Allah their **Lord** (saying):
007:203   This is (nothing but) lights from your **Lord**,
007:203   is revealed to me from my **Lord**: this is
007:205   bring thy **Lord** to remembrance in thy
007:206   Those who are near to thy **Lord**, disdain not
008:002   and put (all) their trust in their **Lord**;
008:004   they have grades of dignity their **Lord**, and forgiveness,
008:005   Just as thy **Lord** ordered thee out of
008:009   the assistance of your **Lord**.
008:012   Remember the **Lord** inspired the angels
008:029   is the **Lord** of grace unbounded.
008:054   the Signs of their **Lord** so We destroyed them
009:021   Their **Lord** doth give them glad tidings of a
009:031   and (they take as their **Lord**) Christ the son of Mary;
009:129   He the **Lord** of the Throne Supreme!"
010:002   that they have before their **Lord** the good
010:003   This is Allah your **Lord**; Him therefore serve ye:
010:003   Verily your **Lord** is Allah, Who created
010:009   and work righteousness, their **Lord** will guide
010:015   if I were to disobey my **Lord**, I should myself
010:019   from thy **Lord**, their differences would have been
010:020   sent down to him from his **Lord**?"
010:030   their rightful **Lord**, and their invented falsehoods
010:032   Such is Allah, your true **Lord**: apart from

LORD (continued)

010:033   Thus is the Word of thy **Lord** proved true
010:037   from the **Lord** of the Worlds.
010:040   and thy **Lord** knoweth best those who
010:053   "Is that true?" Say: "Aye! by my **Lord**! It is
010:057   to you an admonition from your **Lord** and a
010:061   Nor is hidden from thy **Lord** (so much as)
010:085   Our **Lord**! make us not a trial for those
010:088   Moses prayed: "Our **Lord**! Thou hast indeed bestowed
010:088   our **Lord** they mislead (men) from Thy Path.
010:088   Deface our **Lord** the features of their wealth,
010:094   the Truth hath indeed come to thee from thy **Lord**:
010:096   of thy **Lord** hath been verified would not believe-
010:108   reached you from your **Lord**!
011:003   the forgiveness of your **Lord**, and turn
011:017   be (like) those who accept a Clear (Sign) from their **Lord**,
011:017   in doubt thereon: for it is the Truth from thy **Lord**:
011:018   "These are the one who lied against their **Lord**!
011:018   They will be brought before their **Lord**,
011:023   and humble themselves before their **Lord**-they will
011:028   from my **Lord** and that He hath sent Mercy unto me
011:029   for verily they are to meet their **Lord**, and ye
011:034   He is your **Lord**! and to Him will ye return!
011:041   For my **Lord** is, be sure, Oft-forgiving, Most Merciful!"
011:045   "O my **Lord**! surely my son is of my family and Thy
011:045   And Noah called upon his **Lord** and said: "O my
011:047   Noah said: "O my **Lord**! I do seek refuge with Thee,
011:052   "And O my people! Ask forgiveness of your **Lord**,
011:056   "I put my trust in Allah, my **Lord** and your **Lord**!
011:056   Verily, it is my **Lord** that is on a Straight Path.
011:057   For my **Lord** hath care and watch over all things."
011:057   My **Lord** will make another People to succeed you,
011:059   they rejected the Signs of their **Lord** and Cherisher;
011:060   For the 'Ad rejected their **Lord** and Cherisher!
011:061   for my **Lord** is (always) near, ready to answer."
011:063   If I have a Clear (Sign) from my **Lord** and He
011:066   For thy **Lord**-He is the Strong One, and the Mighty.
011:068   For the Thamud rejected their **Lord** and Cherisher!
011:076   The decree of thy **Lord** hath gone forth: for them
011:081   we are Messengers from thy **Lord**! By no means
011:083   Marked from thy **Lord**; nor are they ever far
011:088   I have a Clear (Sign) from my **Lord**, and He
011:090   "But ask forgiveness of you **Lord**, and turn
011:090   for my **Lord** is indeed Full of mercy
011:092   But verily my **Lord** encompasseth all that ye do!
011:101   when there issued the decree of thy **Lord**:
011:102   Such is the chastisement of thy **Lord** when He
011:107   heavens and the earth endure, except as thy **Lord** willeth:
011:107   for thy **Lord** is the (sure) Accomplisher
011:108   heavens and the earth endure, except as thy **Lord** willeth:
011:110   had gone forth before from thy **Lord** the matter
011:111   your **Lord** pay back (in full the recompense)
011:117   Nor would thy **Lord** be the One to destroy
011:118   If thy **Lord** had so willed, He could
011:119   and the Word of thy **Lord** shall be fulfilled:
011:119   Except those on whom thy **Lord** hath bestowed
011:123   and thy **Lord** is not unmindful of aught that ye do.
012:006   "Thus will thy **Lord** choose thee and teach thee
012:006   For thy **Lord** is full of knowledge and wisdom."
012:023   "Allah forbid! truly (thy husband) is my **lord**!
012:024   but that he saw the evidence of his **Lord**:
012:025   they both found her **lord** near the door.
012:033   He said: "O my **Lord**! the prison is dearer to my

LORD (continued)

012:034 So his **Lord** hearkened to him (in his prayer),
012:037 which my **Lord** hath taught me I have (I assure you)
012:041 he will pour out the wine for his **lord** to drink:
012:042 but Satan made him forget to mention him to his **lord**:
012:042 he said: "Mention me to thy **lord**."
012:050 "Go thou back to thy **lord**, and ask him, 'What was the
012:050 For my **Lord** is certainly well aware
012:053 certainly incites evil, unless my **Lord** do bestow
012:053 my **Lord** is Oft-Forgiving, Most Merciful.
012:098 He said: "Soon will I ask my **Lord** for forgiveness
012:100 Verily my **Lord** is gracious to whom He wills
012:101 "O my **Lord**! Thou hast indeed bestowed on me
013:001 unto thee from thy **Lord** is the Truth; but most
013:002 in the meeting with your **Lord**.
013:005 those who deny their **Lord**!
013:006 But verily thy **Lord** is full of forgiveness
013:006 and verily thy **Lord** is (also) strict in punishment.
013:007 a Sign sent down to him from his **Lord**?"
013:016 Say: "Who is the **Lord** and Sustainer of the
013:018 For those who respond to their **Lord**, are (all)
013:019 unto thee from thy **Lord** is the Truth, like one
013:021 to be joined, hold their **Lord** in awe, and fear
013:022 seeking the countenance their **Lord**;
013:027 a Sign sent down to him from his **Lord**?"
013:030 Say: "He is my **Lord**! There is no god but He!
014:001 into light-by the leave of their **Lord**-to the
014:006 a tremendous trial from your **Lord**."
014:007 And remember! your **Lord** caused to be declared
014:013 But their **Lord** inspired (this Message) to them:
014:018 their **Lord** is that their works are as ashes,
014:023 with the leave of their **Lord**.
014:025 by the leave of its **Lord**.
014:035 Remember Abraham said: "O my **Lord**! make this
014:036 "O my **Lord**! they have indeed led astray
014:037 "O our **Lord**! I have made some of my offspring
014:037 O our **Lord**! that they may establish regular
014:038 "O our **Lord**! truly Thou dost know what we
014:039 for truly my **Lord** is He, the Hearer of Prayer!
014:040 "O my **Lord**! make me one who establishes
014:040 O our **Lord**! and accept Thou my Prayer.
014:041 "O our **Lord**! cover (us) with Thy Forgiveness-me,
014:044 "Our **Lord**! respite us (if only) for a short Term:
014:047 the **Lord** of Retribution.
015:025 Assuredly it is thy **Lord** who will gather them
015:028 Behold! thy **Lord** said to the angels: "I am about to create
015:036 (Iblis) said: "O my **Lord**! give me then respite
015:039 (Iblis) said: "O my **Lord**! because Thou hast
015:056 the mercy of his **Lord**, but such as go astray?"
015:086 For verily it is thy **Lord** Who is the All-Creator,
015:092 Therefore, by the **Lord**, We will, of a surety
015:098 But celebrate the praises of thy **Lord** and be
015:099 And serve thy **Lord** until there come unto thee
016:007 for your **Lord** is indeed Most Kind, Most Merciful.
016:024 "What is it that your **Lord** has revealed?"
016:030 "What is it that your **Lord** has revealed?"
016:033 there comes the Command of thy **Lord** (for their doom)?
016:042 in patience, and put their trust on their **Lord**.
016:047 for thy **Lord** is indeed full of kindness and mercy.
016:049 for none are arrogant (before their **Lord**).
016:050 They all fear their **Lord**, high above
016:054 to other gods to join with their **Lord**-
016:068 And thy **Lord** taught the Bee to build

LORD (continued)

016:069 Thy **Lord** made smooth: there issues from within
016:086 they will say: "Our **Lord**! these are our `partners',
016:099 who believe and put their trust in their **Lord**.
016:102 the revelation from thy **Lord** in Truth, in order
016:110 But verily thy **Lord**,-to those who leave their
016:110 and patiently persevere,-thy **Lord**, after all
016:119 and make amends,-thy **Lord** after all this, is
016:119 But verily thy **Lord**, to those
016:125 Invite (all) to the Way of thy **Lord** with wisdom
016:125 for thy **Lord** knoweth best, who have
017:008 It may be that your **Lord** may (yet) show Mercy
017:012 Bounty from your **Lord** and that ye may know
017:017 And enough is thy **Lord** to note
017:020 the bounties of thy **Lord** are not
017:020 Of the bounties of thy **Lord** We bestow
017:023 Thy **Lord** hath decreed that ye worship none but Him,
017:024 "My **Lord**! bestow on them Thy Mercy even as they
017:025 Your **Lord** knoweth best what is in your hearts:
017:027 his **Lord** (Himself) ungrateful.
017:028 from thy **Lord** which thou dost expect, yet speak
017:030 Verily thy **Lord** doth provide sustenance in
017:038 is hateful in the sight of thy **Lord**.
017:039 (precepts of) wisdom, which thy **Lord** has revealed
017:040 Has then your **Lord**, (O Pagans!) preferred for
017:042 to the **Lord** of the Throne!
017:046 when thou dost mention thy **Lord**-and Him
017:054 It is your **Lord** that knoweth you best: if He
017:055 And it is your **Lord** that knoweth best all beings
017:057 means of access to their **Lord**,-as to who
017:057 for the Wrath of thy **Lord** is something
017:060 thy **Lord** doth encompass mankind round about:
017:065 Enough is thy **Lord** for a disposer
017:066 Your **Lord** is He that maketh the Ship go smoothly
017:079 soon will thy **Lord** raise thee
017:080 Say: "O my **Lord**! let my entry be by the Gate
017:084 to his own disposition: but your **Lord** knows best
017:085 of my **Lord** of Knowledge it is only a little
017:087 Except for Mercy from thy **Lord**; for His
017:093 Say: "Glory to my **Lord**! am I aught
017:100 the Treasures of the Mercy of my **Lord**, behold
017:102 by none but the **Lord** of the heavens and the earth
017:108 Truly has the promise of our **Lord** been fulfilled!"
017:108 And they say: "Glory to our **Lord**! Truly has
018:010 to the Cave: they said, "Our **Lord**! bestow on us
018:013 in their **Lord**, and We increased them in guidance:
018:014 "Our **Lord** is the **Lord** of the heavens and of
018:016 your **Lord** will shower His mercies
018:021 their **Lord** knows best about them:
018:022 Say thou: "My **Lord** knoweth best their number;
018:024 and remember thy **Lord** when thou forgettest,
018:024 "I hope that my **Lord** will guide me ever closer
018:027 what has been revealed to thee of the book of thy **Lord**:
018:028 who call on their **Lord** morning and evening,
018:029 Say, "The Truth is from your **Lord**" let him
018:036 even if I am brought back to my **Lord**.
018:038 and none shall I associate with my **Lord**.
018:038 "But as for my part Allah is my **Lord**, and none
018:040 "It may be that my **Lord** will give me something
018:042 to my **Lord** and Cherisher!"
018:046 are best in the sight of thy **Lord**, as rewards,
018:048 And they will be marshalled before thy **Lord** in ranks,
018:049 thy **Lord** treat with injustice.

LORD (continued)

018:050 and he broke the Command of his **Lord**.
018:055 for forgiveness from their **Lord** but that
018:057 who is reminded of the Signs of his **Lord** but turns
018:058 But your **Lord** is Most Forgiving, Full of Mercy.
018:081 "So we desired that their **Lord** would give them
018:082 so thy **Lord** desired that they should attain their
018:082 a mercy (and favour) from thy **Lord**.
018:087 then shall he be sent back to his **Lord**;
018:095 which my **Lord** has established me is better (than tribute):
018:098 and the promise of My **Lord** is true."
018:098 He said: "This is a mercy from my **Lord**: but when
018:098 but when the promise of my **Lord** comes to pass,
018:105 of their **Lord** and the fact of their having to
018:109 were ink (wherewith to write out) the words of my **Lord**,
018:109 the ocean be exhausted than would the words of my **Lord**,
018:110 whoever expects to meet his **Lord**, let him
018:110 and in the worship of his **Lord**, admit no one
019:002 of thy **Lord** to His Servant Zakariya.
019:003 Behold! he cried to his **Lord** in secret.
019:004 Praying: "O my **Lord**! infirm indeed are my bones,
019:004 am I unblest, O my **Lord**, in my prayer to Thee!
019:006 and make him, O my **Lord**! one with
019:008 He said: "O my **Lord**! how shall I have a son,
019:009 thy **Lord** saith, "That is easy for Me: I did
019:010 (Zakariya) said "O my **Lord**! give me a Sign,"
019:019 "Nay, I am only a messenger from thy **Lord**, (to announce)
019:021 thy **Lord** saith, 'That is easy for Me: and (We wish) to
019:024 "Grieve not! for thy **Lord** hath provided
019:036 Verily, Allah is my **Lord** and your **Lord**:
019:047 I will pray to my **Lord** for thy forgiveness: for He
019:048 I will call on my **Lord** perhaps, by my prayer to my **Lord**,
019:055 acceptable in the sight of his **Lord**.
019:064 and thy **Lord** never doth forget,-
019:064 but by command of thy **Lord**: to Him belongeth
019:065 **Lord** of the heavens and of the earth, and of
019:068 So, by thy **Lord**, without doubt, We shall
019:071 this is, with thy **Lord**, a Decree
019:076 Good Deeds are best in the sight of thy **Lord**, as rewards,
020:012 "Verily I am thy **Lord**! Therefore put off
020:025 (Moses) said: "O my **Lord**! expand me my breast;"
020:045 "Our **Lord**! we fear lest He hasten with insolence
020:047 indeed, have we come from thy **Lord**!
020:047 'Verily we are messengers sent by thy **Lord**:
020:049 "Who then, O Moses, is the **Lord** of you two?"
020:050 He said: "Our **Lord** is He Who gave to each (created)
020:052 my **Lord** never errs, nor forgets,-
020:052 "The knowledge of that is with my **Lord**, duly recorded:
020:070 "We believe in the **Lord** of Aaron and Moses."
020:073 For us, we have believed in our **Lord**: may He
020:074 Verily he who comes to his **Lord** as a sinner
020:084 O my **Lord**, to please Thee."
020:086 He said: "O my people! did not your **Lord** make a
020:086 that Wrath should descend from your **Lord** on you,
020:090 for verily your **Lord** is (Allah) Most Gracious:
020:105 say, "My **Lord** will uproot them and scatter
020:114 "O my **Lord**! increase me in knowledge."
020:121 thus did Adam disobey His **Lord**, and fell into error.
020:122 But his **Lord** chose him (for His Grace):
020:125 will say: "O my **Lord**! why hast Thou raised me up blind,
020:127 and believes not in the Signs of his **Lord**:
020:129 that went forth before from thy **Lord**,
020:130 the praises of thy **Lord**, before the

LORD (continued)

020:131 but the provision of thy **Lord** is better
020:133 a Sign from His **Lord**?"
020:134 "Our **Lord**! if only Thou hadst sent us a messenger,
021:002 a renewed Message from their **Lord**, but they
021:004 Say: "My **Lord** knoweth (every) word (spoken)
021:022 the **Lord** of the Throne: (high is He)
021:042 the remembrance of their **Lord**.
021:046 a breath of the Wrath of thy **Lord** do touch them,
021:049 Those who fear their **Lord** in their
021:056 He said, "Nay, your **Lord** is the **Lord** of the
021:083 And (remember) Job, when he cried to his **Lord** "Truly
021:089 "O my **Lord**! leave me not without offspring,
021:089 when he cried to his **Lord**: "O my **Lord**! leave me
021:092 Your **Lord** and Cherisher: therefore serve
021:112 "Our **Lord** Most Gracious is the One Whose
021:112 Say: "O my **Lord**! judge Thou in truth!"
022:001 O mankind! Fear your **Lord**! For the convulsion
022:019 but those who deny (their **Lord**),-for them
022:019 each other about their **Lord**: but those
022:030 in the sight of his **Lord**, Lawful to
022:040 that they say, "Our **Lord** is Allah."
022:047 sight of thy **Lord** is like a thousand years
022:054 the (Qur'an) is the Truth from the **Lord**, and that
022:067 but do thou invite (them) to thy **Lord**:
022:077 bow down, prostrate yourselves, and adore your **Lord**;
023:026 (Noah) said: "O my **Lord**! help me: for that
023:029 And say: "O my **Lord**! enable me
023:039 (The prophet) said: "O my **Lord**! help me: for that
023:052 is a single Ummah and I am your **Lord** and Cherisher:
023:057 for fear of their **Lord**;
023:058 Those who believe in the Signs of their **Lord**;
023:059 partners with their **Lord**;
023:060 because they will return to their **Lord**;-
023:072 But the recompense of thy **Lord** is best:
023:076 but they humbled not themselves to their **Lord**,
023:086 seven heavens, and the **Lord** of the Mighty Throne?"
023:086 Say: "Who is the **Lord** of the seven heavens,
023:093 Say: "O my **Lord**! if Thou wilt show me (in my lifetime)
023:094 "Then, O my **Lord**! put me not amongst the
023:097 And say: "O my **Lord**! I seek refuge with Thee from
023:098 O my **Lord**! lest they should come near me."
023:099 he says: "O my **Lord**! send me back to (life),-
023:106 They will say: "Our **Lord**! our misfortune
023:107 "Our **Lord**! bring us out of this: if ever
023:109 'Our **Lord**! we believe; then do Thou forgive us,
023:116 the **Lord** of the Throne of Honour!
023:117 and his reckoning will be only with his **Lord**!
023:118 So say: "O my **Lord**! grant Thou forgiveness
024:016 glory to Thee (our **Lord**) this is a most serious slander!"
025:016 a promise binding upon thy **Lord**."
025:021 or (why) do we not see our **Lord**?"
025:030 "O my **Lord**, Truly my people treated this Qur'an
025:031 but enough is the **Lord** to guide and to help.
025:045 Hast thou not seen how thy **Lord**?-doth prolong
025:054 for thy **Lord** has power (over all things).
025:055 is a helper (of Evil), against his own **Lord**!
025:057 may take a (straight) Path to his **Lord**."
025:064 in adoration of their **Lord** prostrate and standing;
025:065 Those who say, "Our **Lord**! avert from
025:073 with the Signs of their **Lord**, droop not down
025:074 "Our **Lord**! Grant unto us wives and offspring
025:077 "My **Lord** would not concern Himself with you

LORD (continued)

026:009	And verily, thy **Lord** is He, the Exalted
026:010	Behold, thy **Lord** called Moses: "Go to the
026:012	He said: "O my **Lord**! I do fear
026:016	by the **Lord** and Cherisher of all the Worlds;
026:021	I feared you; but my **Lord** has (since) invested me
026:023	Pharaoh said: "And what is the **Lord** and Cherisher
026:024	(Moses) said: "The **Lord** and Cherisher of the
026:026	(Moses) said: "Your **Lord** and the **Lord** of your
026:028	(Moses) said: "**Lord** of the East and the West,
026:047	Saying: "We believe in the **Lord** of the Worlds.
026:048	"The **Lord** of Moses and Aaron."
026:050	we shall but return to our **Lord**!
026:051	our **Lord** will forgive us our faults, since we
026:062	my **Lord** is with me! Soon will
026:068	And verily thy **Lord** is He, the Exalted
026:077	not so the **Lord** and Cherisher of the Worlds;
026:083	"O my **Lord**! bestow wisdom on me, and join
026:098	with the **Lord** of the Worlds;
026:104	And verily the **Lord** is He, the Exalted
026:109	my reward is only from the **Lord** of the Worlds:
026:113	"Their account is only with my **Lord**, if ye
026:117	He said: "O my **Lord**! truly my
026:122	And verily thy **Lord** is He, the Exalted
026:127	my reward is only from the **Lord** of the Worlds.
026:140	And verily thy **Lord** is He, the Exalted
026:145	my reward is only from the **Lord** of the Worlds.
026:159	And verily thy **Lord** is He, the Exalted
026:164	my reward is only from the **Lord** of the Worlds.
026:169	"O my **Lord**! deliver me and my family
026:175	And verily thy **Lord** is He, the Exalted
026:180	my reward is only from the **Lord** of the Worlds.
026:188	He said: "My **Lord** knows best what ye do."
026:191	And verily thy **Lord** is He, the Exalted
026:192	from the **Lord** of the Worlds:
027:008	the **Lord** of the Worlds!
027:019	and he said: "O my **Lord**! so order
027:026	**Lord** of the Throne Supreme!"
027:040	truly my **Lord** is Free of All Needs, Supreme in
027:040	"This is by the grace of my **Lord**!-to test
027:044	She said: "O my **Lord**! I have indeed
027:044	with Solomon, to the **Lord** of the Worlds."
027:073	But verily thy **Lord** is full of
027:074	And verily thy **Lord** knoweth all that
027:078	Verily thy **Lord** will decide between them
027:091	the **Lord** of this City, Him Who has
027:093	and thy **Lord** is not unmindful of all that ye do.
028:016	He prayed: "O my **Lord**! I have
028:017	He said: "O my **Lord**! for that Thou hast bestowed
028:021	He prayed: "O my **Lord**! save me
028:022	"I do hope that my **Lord** will show me
028:024	and said: "O my **Lord**! truly am I
028:030	Verily I am Allah, the **Lord** of the Worlds..:
028:032	from thy **Lord** to Pharaoh and his Chiefs: for truly
028:033	He said: "O my **Lord**! I have slain a man among them,
028:037	Moses said: "My **Lord** knows best who it is
028:046	as a Mercy from thy **Lord**, to give
028:047	they might say: "Our **Lord**! why didst
028:053	for it is the Truth from our **Lord**: indeed we
028:059	Nor was thy **Lord** the one to destroy a town
028:063	be proved, will say: "Our **Lord**! these are
028:068	Thy **Lord** does create and choose as He pleases:
028:069	And thy **Lord** knows all that their hearts

LORD (continued)

028:079	For he is truly a **lord** of mighty good fortune."
028:085	Say: "My **Lord** knows best who it is that brings
028:086	except as a Mercy from thy **Lord**: therefore lend
028:087	and invite (men) to thy **Lord** and be not
029:010	And if help comes (to thee) from thy **lord**, they are sure
029:026	"I will leave home for the sake of my **Lord**:
029:030	He said: "O my **Lord**! help Thou me against
029:050	sent down to him from his **Lord**?"
029:059	and put their trust in their **Lord** and Cherisher.
030:008	with their **Lord** (at the Resurrection)!
030:033	other gods besides their **Lord**,-
030:033	they cry to their **Lord**, turning back
031:005	These are on (true) guidance from their **Lord**;
031:033	O mankind! do your duty to your **Lord** and fear
032:002	from the **Lord** of the Worlds.
032:003	Nay, it is the Truth from thy **Lord**, that thou
032:010	Nay, they deny the meeting with their **Lord**!
032:011	then shall ye be brought back to your **Lord**."
032:012	the guilty one will bend low their heads before their **Lord**,
032:012	(saying): "Our **Lord**! We have seen and we have heard:
032:015	and celebrate the praises of their **Lord**, nor are
032:016	the while they call on their **Lord**, in Fear
032:022	than one to whom are recited the Signs of his **Lord**,?
032:025	Verily thy **Lord** will judge between them on the
033:002	to thee by inspiration from thy **Lord**: for Allah
033:067	And they would say: "Our **Lord**! We obeyed
033:068	"Our **Lord**! give them Double Chastisement
034:003	say, "Nay! but most surely, by my **Lord**, it will
034:006	to thee from thy **Lord**-that is the Truth, and that
034:012	in front of him, by the leave of his **Lord**, and if
034:015	by your **Lord**, and be grateful to Him:
034:015	and a **Lord** Oft-Forgiving!"
034:019	But they said: "Our **Lord**! place longer
034:021	and thy **Lord** doth watch over all things.
034:023	'What is it that your **Lord** commanded?'
034:026	Say: "Our **Lord** will gather us together and will
034:031	to stand before their **Lord**, throwing back
034:036	Say: "Verily my **Lord** enlarges and restricts
034:039	Say: "Verily my **Lord** enlarges and restricts
034:048	Say: "Verily my **Lord** doth cast the Truth,-
034:050	it is because of the inspiration of my **Lord** to me:
035:013	Such is Allah your **Lord**: to Him belongs the Dominion.
035:018	fear their **Lord** unseen and establish regular
035:034	for Our **Lord** is indeed Oft-Forgiving ready to
035:037	"Our **Lord**! Bring us out: we shall work righteousness.
035:039	for the Unbelievers in the sight of their **Lord**:
036:016	They said: "Our **Lord** doth know that we have been
036:025	"For me, I have faith in the **Lord** of you (all):
036:027	"For that my **Lord** has granted me Forgiveness
036:046	from among the Signs of their **Lord**, but they
036:051	(men) will rush forth to their **Lord**!
036:058	from a **Lord** Most Merciful!
037:005	**Lord** of the heavens and of the earth, and all
037:005	and **Lord** of every point at the rising of the sun!
037:031	against us, the Word of our **Lord** that we
037:057	"Had it not been for the Grace of my **Lord**, I should
037:084	Behold, He approached his **Lord** with a sound heart.
037:087	about the **Lord** of the Worlds?"
037:099	He said: "I will go to my **Lord**! He will
037:100	"O my **Lord**! grant me a righteous (son)!"
037:126	and the **Lord** and Cherisher of your fathers of old?"
037:126	"Allah, your **Lord** and Cherisher and the

LORD (continued)

037:149   is it that thy **Lord** has (only) daughters,
037:180   Glory to thy **Lord**, the **Lord** of Honour and Power!
037:182   the **Lord** and Cherisher of the Worlds.
038:009   of the Mercy of thy **Lord**,-the Exalted
038:012   and 'Ad, and Pharaoh the **Lord** of Stakes.
038:016   They say: "Our **Lord**! Hasten to us our sentence
038:024   he asked forgiveness of his **Lord**, fell down, bowing
038:032   to the remembrance of my **Lord**."
038:035   He said, "O my **Lord**! Forgive me, and grant me
038:041   behold he cried to his **Lord**: "Satan has
038:061   They will say: "Our **Lord**! Whoever brought
038:066   "The **Lord** of the heavens and the earth, and all
038:071   Behold, thy **Lord** said to the angels: "I am
038:079   (Iblis) said: "O my **Lord**! give me then respite
039:006   your **Lord** and Cherisher: to Him belongs
039:006   then how are ye turned away (from your true **Lord**)?
039:007   In the End, to your **Lord** is your return, when He
039:008   he crieth unto his **Lord**, turning to Him
039:009   and who places his hope in the Mercy of his **Lord**-
039:010   Fear your **Lord**: good is (the reward) for those
039:013   Say: "I would, if I disobeyed my **Lord**, indeed have fear
039:020   But it is for those who fear their **Lord**, that lofty mansions,
039:023   who fear their **Lord** tremble thereat; then their
039:031   in the presence of your **Lord**.
039:034   in the presence of their **Lord**: such is
039:037   Is not Allah Exalted in Power, **Lord** of Retribution?
039:054   "Turn ye to your **Lord** (in repentance) and submit
039:055   to you from your **Lord**, before the
039:069   with the light of its **Lord**: the Record
039:071   the Signs of your **Lord**, and warning
039:073   And those who feared their **Lord** will be led
039:075   "Praise be to Allah, the **Lord** of the Worlds!"
039:075   singing Glory and Praise to their **Lord**.
040:006   Thus was the Word of thy **Lord** proved true
040:007   "Our **Lord**! Thou embracest all things, in Mercy
040:007   and Praise to their **Lord**; believe in
040:008   "And grant, our **Lord**! That they enter the
040:011   They will say:" Our **Lord**! twice hast Thou made us
040:015   (He is) the **Lord** of the Throne: by His Command
040:026   and let him Call on his **Lord**!
040:027   called upon my **Lord** and your **Lord** (for protection)
040:028   with Clear (Signs) from your **Lord**?
040:028   "Will ye slay a man because he says, 'My **Lord** is Allah'?-
040:049   "Pray to your **Lord** to lighten us the Chastisement
040:055   and celebrate the Praises of thy **Lord** in the evening and
040:060   And your **Lord** says: "Call on Me; I will
040:062   Such is Allah, your **Lord**, the Creator
040:064   So Glory to Allah, the **Lord** of the Worlds!
040:064   such is Allah your **Lord**.
040:065   Praise be to Allah, **Lord** of the Worlds!
040:066   (in Islam) to the **Lord** of the Worlds."
040:066   that the Clear Signs have come to me from my **Lord**;
041:009   He is the **Lord** of (all) the Worlds.
041:014   They said, "If our **Lord** had so pleased, He would
041:023   did entertain concerning your **Lord**, hath brought
041:029   "Our **Lord**! Show us those, among Jinns
041:030   "Our **Lord** is Allah," and, further, stand straight
041:038   presence of thy **Lord** are those who celebrate
041:043   surely thy **Lord** has at His command (all) Forgiveness
041:045   Had it not been for a Word that went forth from thy **Lord**,
041:046   nor is thy **Lord** ever unjust (in the least)
041:050   but if I am brought back to my **Lord**, I have

LORD (continued)

041:053   enough that thy **Lord** doth witness all things?
041:054   in doubt concerning the Meeting with their **Lord**?
042:005   and the angels celebrate the Praises of their **Lord**,
042:010   Such is Allah my **Lord**: in Him
042:014   not been for a Word that went forth before from my **Lord**,
042:015   Allah is Our **Lord** and your **Lord**!
042:016   futile is their argument in the sight of their **Lord**:
042:022   before their **Lord**, all that they wish for.
042:036   their trust in their **Lord**:
042:038   Those who respond to their **Lord**, and establish
042:047   Respond ye to your **Lord**, before there
043:013   ye may remember the (kind) favour of your **Lord**,
043:014   "And to Our **Lord**, surely, must we turn back!"
043:032   But the Mercy of thy **Lord** in better than the (wealth)
043:032   Is it they who would portion out the Mercy of thy **Lord**?
043:035   the Hereafter, in the sight of thy **Lord**, is for the Righteous.
043:046   "I am a messenger of the **Lord** of the Worlds."
043:049   invoke thy **Lord** for us according to his
043:064   He is my **Lord** and your **Lord**: so worship ye Him:
043:077   "O Malik! would that thy **Lord** put and end to us!"
043:082   the **Lord** of the Throne!
043:082   Glory to the **Lord** of the heavens and the earth,
043:088   (Prophet's) cry, "O my **Lord**! Truly these
044:006   As a Mercy from thy **Lord**: for He
044:007   The **Lord** of the heavens and the earth and all
044:008   the **Lord** and Cherisher to you and your
044:012   "Our **Lord**! remove the Chastisement from us,
044:020   I have sought safety with my **Lord** and your **Lord**,
044:022   he cried to his **Lord**: "These are indeed a people given
044:057   As a Bounty from thy **Lord**!
045:011   and for those who reject the Signs of their **Lord**,
045:015   be brought back to your **Lord**.
045:017   Verily thy **Lord** will judge between them on the
045:030   their **Lord** will admit them to His Mercy:
045:036   **Lord** of the heavens and **Lord** of the earth,
045:036   **Lord** and Cherisher of all the worlds!
046:013   Verily those who say, "Our **Lord** is Allah,"
046:015   He says, "O my **Lord**! grant me that I may be grateful
046:025   "Everything will it destroy by the command of its **Lord**!"
046:034   "Is this not the Truth?" They will say, "Yea, by our **Lord**!"
047:002   down to Muhammad-for it is the Truth from their **Lord**,-
047:003   while those who believe follow the Truth from their **Lord**:
047:014   Is then one who is on a clear (Path) from his **Lord**,
047:015   and Forgiveness from their **Lord**, (can those in such Bliss)
050:027   "Our **Lord**! I did not make him transgress, but he
050:039   and celebrate the praises of thy **Lord**, before the rising
051:016   which their **Lord** gives them, because, before
051:023   Then, by the **Lord** of heaven and earth, this is
051:030   They said, "Even so has thy **Lord** spoken:
051:034   "Marked as from thy **Lord** for those who trespass
051:044   But they insolently defied the Command of their **Lord**:
051:058   Allah is He Who gives (all) Sustenance,-**Lord** of Power,
052:007   Verily, the Chastisement of thy **Lord** will indeed
052:018   and their **Lord** shall deliver them from the Chastisement
052:018   the (Bliss) which their **Lord** hath bestowed on them,
052:029   Therefore Remind for by the Grace of thy **Lord**, thou art
052:037   Or are the Treasures of thy **Lord** with them,
052:048   the praises of thy **Lord** the while thou standest forth,
052:048   Now wait in patience the command of thy **Lord**: for verily
053:018   of the Signs of his **Lord**, the Greatest!
053:023   to them Guidance from their **Lord**!
053:030   Verily thy **Lord** knoweth best those who

LORD (continued)

053:032 verily thy **Lord** is ample in forgiveness.
053:042 That to thy **Lord** is the final Goal;
053:049 That He is the **Lord** of Sirius (the Mighty Star);
053:055 Then which of the favours of thy **Lord**, (O man),
054:010 Then he called on his **Lord**: "I am one overcome:
055:013 Then which of the favours of your **Lord** will ye deny?
055:016 Then which of the favours of your **Lord** will ye deny?
055:017 and **Lord** of the two Wests:
055:017 (He is) **Lord** of the two Easts and **Lord**
055:018 Then which of the favours of your **Lord** will ye deny?
055:021 Then which of the favours of your **Lord** will ye deny?
055:023 Then which of the favours of your **Lord** will ye deny?
055:025 Then which of the favours of your **Lord** will ye deny?
055:027 thy **Lord**,-full of Majesty, Bounty and Honour.
055:028 Then which of the favours of your **Lord** will ye deny?
055:030 Then which of the favours of your **Lord** will ye deny?
055:032 Then which of the favours of your **Lord** will ye deny?
055:034 Then which of the favours of your **Lord** will ye deny?
055:036 Then which of the favours of your **Lord** will ye deny?
055:038 Then which of the favours of your **Lord** will ye deny?
055:040 Then which of the favours of your **Lord** will ye deny?
055:042 Then which of the favours of your **Lord** will ye deny?
055:045 Then which of the favours of your **Lord** will ye deny?
055:046 Seat of) their **Lord**, there will be two Gardens-
055:047 Then which of the favours of your **Lord** will ye deny?-
055:049 Then which of the favours of your **Lord** will ye deny?-
055:051 Then which of the favours of your **Lord** will ye deny?-
055:053 Then which of the favours of your **Lord** will ye deny?
055:055 Then which of the favours of your **Lord** will ye deny?
055:057 Then which of the favours of your **Lord** will ye deny?
055:059 Then which of the favours of your **Lord** will ye deny?
055:061 Then which of the favours of your **Lord** will ye deny?
055:063 Then which of the favours of your **Lord** will ye deny?
055:065 Then which of the favours of your **Lord** will ye deny?
055:067 Then which of the favours of your **Lord** will ye deny?
055:069 Then which of the favours of your **Lord** will ye deny?
055:071 Then which of the favours of your **Lord** will ye deny?
055:073 Then which of the favours of your **Lord** will ye deny?
055:075 Then which of the favours of your **Lord** will ye deny?
055:077 Then which of the favours of your **Lord** will ye deny?
055:078 Blessed be the name of thy **Lord**, full of
056:074 Then glorify the name of the **Lord**, the Supreme!
056:080 A Revelation from the **Lord** of the Worlds.
056:096 So glorify the name of thy **Lord**, the Supreme.
057:008 you to believe in your **Lord** and has indeed taken
057:019 in the eye of their **Lord**:
057:021 Be ye foremost (in seeking) forgiveness from your **Lord**,
057:021 and Allah is the **Lord** of Grace abounding.
057:029 For Allah is the **Lord** of Grace abounding.
059:010 Our **Lord**! Thou art indeed Full of Kindness,
059:010 "Our **Lord**! Forgive us, and our brethren who came
059:016 I do fear Allah, the **Lord** of the Worlds!"
060:001 ye believe in Allah your **Lord**!
060:004 "Our **Lord**! in Thee do we trust, and to
060:005 "Our **Lord**! Make us not a (test and) trial for the
060:005 but forgive us, our **Lord**! For Thou art the Exalted in
062:004 and Allah is the **Lord** of the highest bounty.
063:010 and he should say, "O my **Lord**! Why didst
064:007 Say: "Yea, by my **Lord**, ye shall
065:001 and fear Allah your **Lord**:
065:008 of their **Lord** and of His messengers, did We
066:008 that your **Lord** will remove from you your

LORD (continued)

066:008 while they say, "Our **Lord**! perfect our light
066:011 behold, she said: "O my **Lord**! build for me,
066:012 to the truth of the words of her **Lord** and of His
067:006 For those who reject their **Lord** (and Cherisher)
067:012 As for those who fear their **Lord** unseen, for them
068:002 Thou art not, by the grace of thy **Lord**, mad or
068:007 Verily it is thy **Lord** that knoweth best,
068:019 there came on the (garden) a visitation from thy **Lord**,
068:029 They said: "Glory to our **Lord**! Verily we
068:032 "It may be that our **Lord** will give us in exchange
068:034 of Delight, with their **Lord**.
068:048 So wait with patience for the Command thy **Lord**,
068:049 Had not Grace from His **Lord** reached him, he would
068:050 Thus did his **Lord** choose him and make him
069:010 And disobeyed (each) the messenger of their **Lord**
069:017 bear the Throne of thy **Lord** above them.
069:043 from the **Lord** of the Worlds.
069:052 So glorify the name of thy **Lord** Most High.
070:003 (A Penalty) from Allah, **Lord** of the Ways of Ascent.
070:027 And those who fear the punishment of their **Lord**,-
070:040 Now I do call to witness the **Lord** of all points
071:005 He said: "O my **Lord**! I have called to my People
071:010 "Saying, `Ask forgiveness from your **Lord**, for He
071:021 Noah said: "O my **Lord**! they have disobeyed me,
071:026 And Noah said: "O my **Lord**! Leave not
071:028 "O my **Lord**! Forgive me, my parents, all who
072:002 any (gods) with our **Lord**,
072:003 'And exalted is the Majesty of our **Lord**: He has
072:010 or whether their **Lord** (really) intends to guide
072:013 and any who believes in his **Lord** has no fear,
072:017 the remembrance of his **Lord**, He will
072:020 Say: "I do no more than invoke my **Lord**, and I
072:025 or whether my **Lord** will appoint for it
072:028 the Messages of their **Lord** and He encompasses
073:008 the **Lord** and devote thyself to Him wholeheartedly.
073:009 (He is) **Lord** of the East and the West: there is
073:019 a (straight) path to his **Lord**!
073:020 The **Lord** doth know that thou standest forth
074:003 And thy **Lord** do thou magnify!
074:031 the forces of the **Lord**, except He, and this
074:056 He is the **Lord** of Righteousness, and the
074:056 and the **Lord** of Forgiveness.
075:012 Before thy **Lord** (alone), that Day
075:023 Looking towards their **Lord**;
075:030 That Day the Drive will be (all) to thy **Lord**!
076:010 and distress from the side of our **Lord**."
076:021 and their **Lord** will give to them to drink a pure drink.
076:024 to the Command of thy **Lord**, and obey
076:025 of thy **Lord** morning and evening,
076:029 let him take a (straight) Path to his **Lord**.
078:036 Recompense from thy **Lord**, a Gift,
078:037 (From) the **Lord** of the heavens and the earth,
078:039 a (straight) Return to his **Lord**!
079:005 Then arrange to do (the commands of their **Lord**),-
079:016 Behold, thy **Lord** did call to him in the sacred
079:019 "`And that I guide thee to thy **Lord**, so thou
079:024 Saying, "I am your **Lord**, Most High."
079:044 With they **Lord** is the final end of it.
081:020 by the **Lord** of the Throne,
082:006 from thy **Lord** Most Beneficent?-
083:006 will stand before the **Lord** of the Worlds?
083:015 Verily, from (the Light of) their **Lord**, that Day,

LORD (continued)

084:002 And hearkens to (the Command of) its **Lord**,-and it
084:005 And hearkens to (the Command of) its **Lord**,-and it
084:006 ever toiling on towards the **Lord**-painfully toiling,
084:015 Nay, nay! for his **Lord** was (ever) watchful of him!
085:012 Truly strong is the Grip of thy **Lord**.
085:015 **Lord** of the Throne full of all Glory,
089:006 Seest thou not how thy **Lord** dealt with
089:010 And with Pharaoh, **lord** of Stakes?
089:013 Therefore did thy **Lord** pour on them a scourge
089:014 For thy **Lord** is watchful.
089:015 "My **Lord** hath honoured me."
089:015 Now, as for man, when his **Lord** trieth him,
089:016 "My **Lord** hath humiliated me!"
089:022 And thy **Lord** cometh, and His angels,
089:028 "Come back thou to thy **Lord**,-well pleased
091:014 So their **Lord**, crushed them
092:020 for the countenance of their **Lord** Most High;
093:011 But the Bounty of thy **Lord**-rehearse and proclaim!
094:008 And to thy **Lord** turn (all) thy attention.
096:001 of thy **Lord** and Cherisher, Who created-
096:003 Proclaim! And thy **Lord** is Most Bountiful,-
096:008 Verily, to thy **Lord** is the return (of all).
098:008 all this for such as fear their **Lord** and Cherisher.
099:005 For that thy **Lord** will have given her inspiration.
100:006 Truly Man is to his **Lord**, ungrateful;
100:011 That their **Lord** had been well-acquainted
105:001 Seest thou not how thy **Lord** dealt with the
106:003 Let them worship the **Lord** of this House,
108:002 Therefore to thy **Lord** turn in Prayer and Sacrifice.
110:003 Celebrate the Praises of thy **Lord**, and pray
113:001 Say: I seek refuge with the **Lord** of the Dawn,
114:001 the **Lord** and Cherisher of Mankind,

LORD'S

007:044 have you also found your **Lord's** promises true?"
010:099 If it had been the **Lord's** Will, they would
070:028 For their **Lord's** punishment is not a thing
074:007 But, for thy **Lord's** (Cause), be patient
079:040 their **Lord's** (tribunal) and had restrained (their)

LORDED

023:091 and some would have **lorded** it over others!

LORDS

003:064 among ourselves, **lords** and patrons other than Allah."
003:080 to take angels and prophets for **Lords** and Patrons.
009:031 their anchorites to be their **lords** beside Allah.
012:039 (I ask you): are many **lords** differing among

LOSE

003:139 So **lose** not heart, nor fall into despair:
004:044 and wish that ye should **lose** the right path.
007:178 such are the persons who **lose**.
008:046 lest ye **lose** heart and your power depart; and be
011:022 ones who will **lose** most in the Hereafter!
018:103 tell you of those who **lose** most in respect of their deeds?
020:123 will not **lose** his way, nor fall into misery.
022:011 they **lose** both this world and the Hereafter:
039:015 who **lose** their own souls and their people on the
040:085 the rejecters of Allah **lose** (utterly)!
042:045 who **lose** themselves and their families.
058:019 Truly, it is the Party of Satan that will **lose**.

LOSERS

007:149 we shall indeed be among the **Losers**.
009:069 and they are the **losers**.
011:047 I should indeed be among the **losers**!"

LOSERS (continued)

012:014 a party, then should we be the **losers**!
016:109 they will be the **losers**.
021:070 but We made them the Greater **losers**.
029:052 and reject Allah, that are **losers**.
039:065 and thou wilt surely be among the **losers**.
063:009 If any act thus, surely they are the **losers**.

LOSING

081:002 When the stars fall, **losing** their lustre;

LOSS

002:027 These cause **loss** (only) to themselves.
002:121 the **loss** is their own.
002:155 some **loss** in goods,
003:149 (from Faith) to your own **loss**.
004:012 so that no **loss** is caused (to anyone).
004:119 hath of a surety suffered a **loss** that is manifest.
007:030 others have deserved the **loss** of their way,
010:108 do so to their own **loss**:
017:015 who goeth astray doth so to his own **loss**:
017:082 to the unjust it causes nothing but **loss** after **loss**.
022:011 world and the Hereafter: that is indeed the manifest **loss**,
026:181 Give just measure, and cause not **loss** (to others
027:005 will be the greatest **loss**.
034:050 I only stray to the **loss** of my own soul: but if
035:039 to (their own) **loss**.
039:015 Ah! that is indeed the (real and) evident **Loss**!"
039:015 Say: "Truly, those in **loss** are those who lose
039:063 it is they who will be in **loss**.
042:045 will say: "Those are indeed in **loss** who lose
047:035 in **loss** for your (good) deeds.
048:011 you some **loss** or to give you some profit?
064:009 a day of mutual **loss** and gain (among you).
071:021 no Increase but only **Loss**.
079:012 be a return with **loss**!"
103:002 Verily Man is in **loss**,

LOST

002:016 and they have **lost** true direction.
002:064 ye had surely been among the **lost**.
003:085 in the ranks of those who have **lost**.
003:146 But they never **lost** heart if they met
003:171 the Faithful to be **lost** (in the Least).
003:195 I suffer to be **lost** the work of any of you,
005:005 those who have **lost** (all spiritual good).
005:030 and became (himself) one of the **lost** ones.
005:102 and on that account **lost** their faith.
006:012 It is they who have **lost** their own souls,
006:020 Those who have **lost** their own souls refuse
006:031 **Lost** indeed are they who treat it as a falsehood
006:140 **Lost** are those who slay their children,
007:023 we shall certainly be **lost**."
007:053 In fact they will have **lost** their souls, and the
008:037 They will be the ones to have **lost**.
009:120 the reward to be **lost** of those who do good;-
010:045 assuredly those will be **lost** who denied
011:021 They are the ones who have **lost** their own souls:
012:056 and We suffer not, to be **lost**, the reward
012:090 never will Allah suffer the reward to be **lost**, of those
023:034 behold, it is certain ye will be **lost**.
023:103 will be those who have **lost** their souls;
032:010 hidden and **lost**, in the earth, shall we
041:023 and (now) have ye become of those utterly **lost**!"
041:025 against them; for they are utterly **lost**.
041:049 he gives up all hope (and) is **lost** in despair.

LOST (continued)

046:018 for they will be (utterly) **lost**.
047:004 He will never let their deeds be **lost**.
067:030 some morning **lost** (in the underground earth),
068:026 they said: "We have surely **lost** our way:

LOT

002:162 nor will respite be their (**lot**).
003:088 nor respite be their (**lot**);
006:086 And Isma'il and Elisha, and Jonah, and **Lot**:
011:101 (to their **lot**) but perdition!
014:015 the **lot** of every powerful obstinate transgressor.
021:100 There, sobbing will be their **lot**, nor will
042:020 but he has no share or **lot** in the Hereafter.
056:060 We have decreed Death to be your common **lot**,
059:009 even though poverty was their (own **lot**).

LOTE-TREE

053:014 Near the **Lote-tree** of the utmost boundary.
053:016 Behold, the **Lote-tree** was shrouded with

LOTE-TREES

034:016 and some few (stunted) **Lote-trees**.
056:028 (They will be) among **lote-trees** without thorns,

LOTS

003:044 when they cast **lots** with pens,
037:141 He (agreed to) cast **lots**, and he

LOUD-VOICED

013:013 He flingeth the **loud-voiced** thunder-bolts,

LOUDNESS

007:205 and remember without **loudness** in words,

LOVE

002:093 filled (with the **love**) of the Calf
002:165 overflowing in their **love** for Allah.
002:165 they **love** them as they should **love** Allah.
002:177 out of **love** for Him,
002:216 and that ye **love** a thing which is bad for you.
003:014 the **love** of things they covet: women and sons;
003:031 Allah will **love** you and forgive you your sins:
003:031 Say: "If ye do **love** Allah, follow me:
003:092 unless ye give (freely) of that which ye **love**:
003:103 He joined your hearts in **love**,
003:119 but they **love** you not,
003:119 Ah! ye are those who **love** them,
003:188 and **love** to be praised for what they have not done,
005:054 whom He will **love** as they will **love** him,
005:082 and nearest among them in **love** to the Believers
006:076 "I **love** not those that set."
007:079 but ye **love** not good counsellors!"
007:189 in order that he might dwell with her (in **love**).
009:007 for Allah doth **love** the righteous.
009:023 your brothers if they **love** infidelity above Faith:
009:108 In it are men who **love** to be purified; and Allah
012:030 to seduce her slave truly he inspired her with violent **love**:
014:037 among men with **love** towards them, and feed
016:107 This because they **love** the life of this world
019:096 will The Most Gracious bestow **Love**.
020:039 but I endued thee with **love** from Me: and (this)
024:019 Those who **love** (to see) scandal circulate
029:025 out of mutual **love** and regard between yourselves
030:021 and He has put **love** and mercy between your (hearts):
042:023 for this except the **love** of those near of kin."
056:037 Full of **love** (for their mates), equal in age,-
060:001 offering them (your) **love**, even though
061:013 which ye do **love**,-help from Allah and a speedy
075:020 Nay, (ye men!) but ye **love** the fleeting life,

LOVE (continued)

076:008 And they feed, for the **love** of Allah, the indigent,
076:027 As to these, they **love** the fleeting life,
089:020 And ye **love** wealth with inordinate **love**!
100:008 And violent is he in his **love** of wealth.

LOVED

012:008 are **loved** more by our father than we: but we

LOVERS

004:069 the Sincere (**lovers** of Truth), the martyres,
005:005 Taking them as **lovers**.

LOVES

002:222 For Allah **loves** those who turn to Him constantly
002:222 and He **loves** those who keep themselves pure
003:076 verily Allah **loves** those who act aright.
003:134 for Allah **loves** those who do good:
003:146 And Allah **loves** those who are firm and steadfast.
003:159 For Allah **loves** those who put their trust (in Him).
028:077 for Allah **loves** not those who do mischief."
030:045 For He **loves** not those who reject Faith.
049:009 for Allah **loves** those who are fair (and just).
061:004 Truly Allah **loves** those who fight in His Cause

LOVEST

028:056 to guide everyone whom thou **lovest**:

LOVETH

002:190 for Allah **loveth** not transgressors.
002:195 for Allah **loveth** those who do good.
002:205 but Allah **loveth** not mischief.
002:276 for He **loveth** not any ungrateful Sinner.
003:032 Allah **loveth** not those who reject Faith.
003:057 but Allah **loveth** not those who do wrong.
003:140 And Allah **loveth** not those that do wrong.
003:148 For Allah **loveth** those who do good.
004:036 for Allah **loveth** not the arrogant,
004:107 for Allah **loveth** not one given to perfidy and sin:
004:148 Allah **loveth** not the shouting of evil
005:013 for Allah **loveth** those who are kind.
005:042 For Allah **loveth** those who judge in equity.
005:064 And Allah **loveth** not those who do mischief.
005:087 for Allah **loveth** not those given to excess.
005:093 For Allah **loveth** those who do good.
006:141 for Allah **loveth** not the wasters.
007:031 for Allah **loveth** not the wasters.
007:055 For Allah **loveth** not those who trespass
008:058 for Allah **loveth** not the treacherous.
009:004 for Allah **loveth** the righteous.
009:108 and Allah **loveth** those who make themselves pure.
016:023 verily He **loveth** not the arrogant.
022:038 verily, Allah **loveth** not any that is
028:076 "Exult not, for Allah **loveth** not those who
031:018 for Allah **loveth** not any arrogant boaster.
042:040 for (Allah) **loveth** not those who do wrong.
057:023 For Allah **loveth** not any vainglorious boaster,-
060:008 for Allah **loveth** those who are just.

LOVING

058:022 **loving** those who oppose Allah and His Messenger,

LOVING-KINDNESS

011:090 of mercy and **loving-kindness**."
085:014 Full of **loving-kindness**,

LOW

003:026 and thou bringest **low** whom Thou pleasest:
006:099 clusters of dates hanging **low** and near:
006:119 by **low** desires without knowledge.

LOW (continued)
012:020 in such **low** estimation did they hold him!
017:110 nor speak it in a **low** tone, but seek
020:088 the image of the calf: it seemed to **low**: so they said:
032:012 the guilty ones will bend **low** their heads before
056:003 (Many) will it bring **low**; (many) will it exalt;
068:023 So they departed, conversing in secret **low** tones,
069:023 The Fruits whereof (will hang in bunches) **low** and near.
076:014 And the shades of the (Garden) will come **low** over them,
076:014 the bunches (of fruit) there, will hang **low** easy to reach.
095:005 Then do We abase him (to be) the lowest of the **low**,

LOWER
008:042 and the caravan on **lower** ground than ye.
015:088 but **lower** thy wing (in gentleness)
017:024 And, out of kindness, **lower** to them the wing
024:030 should **lower** their gaze and guard their modesty:
024:031 they should **lower** their gaze and guard
026:215 And **lower** thy wing to the Believers who follow thee.
031:019 and **lower** thy voice; for the harshest
036:039 (and withered) **lower** part of date-stalk.
037:006 the **lower** heaven with beauty (in) the stars,-
041:012 And We adorned the **lower** heaven with lights,
049:003 Those that **lower** their voice in the presence
079:040 restrained (their) soul from **lower** Desires,

LOWERED
070:044 Their eyes **lowered** in dejection,-ignominy covering

LOWEST
004:145 the **lowest** depths of the Fire: no helper
067:005 adorned the **lowest** heaven with Lamps, and We
095:005 Then do We abase him (to be) the **lowest** of the low,

LOWING
007:148 having **lowing** sound did they not see that it could

LOWLY
005:054 as they will love Him,- **lowly** with the Believers,
075:037 Was he not a drop of sperm emitted (in **lowly** form)?

LUMINOUS
024:035 whose Oil is well-nigh **luminous**, though fire

LUMP
023:014 then of that clot We made a (foetus) **lump**;
023:014 We made out of that **lump** bones and clothed the bones

LUQMAN
031:012 We bestowed (in the past) wisdom on **Luqman**:
031:013 Behold, **Luqman** said to his son admonishing him
031:016 "O my son! (said **Luqman**), "If there be (but) the weight

LURCH
006:024 will leave them in the **lurch**.
006:094 and your (pet) fancies have left you in the **lurch**!"
007:037 They will reply, "They have left us in the **lurch**,"
007:053 will leave them in the **lurch**.
010:030 invented falsehoods will leave them in the **lurch**.
011:021 they forged have left them in the **lurch**!
016:087 leave them in the **lurch**.
017:067 leave you in the **lurch**!
028:075 will leave them in the **lurch**.
040:074 "They have left us in the **lurch**: nay, we
041:048 they used to invoke aforetime will leave them in the **lurch**,
046:028 Nay, they left them in the **lurch**: but that

LURKETH
006:013 (or **lurketh**) in the Night and the Day.

LURKING
015:047 any **lurking** sense of injury: (they will be)

LUSCIOUS
087:004 (green and **luscious**) pasture,

LUSTRE
081:002 When the stars fall, losing their **lustre**;

LUSTROUS
044:054 to maidens with beautiful, big, and **lustrous** eyes.
052:020 with beautiful, big and **lustrous** eyes.
056:022 with beautiful, big, and **lustrous** eyes,-

LUSTS
004:027 who follow their **lusts** is that ye should turn
004:135 Follow not the **lusts** (of your hearts), lest
007:081 "For ye practice your **lusts** on men in
019:059 and followed after **lusts** soon, then, will they
020:016 not therein but follow their own lust, divert thee
027:055 really approach men in your **lusts** rather than women?
028:050 who is more astray than one who follows his own **lusts**,
028:050 know that they only follow their own **lusts**:
047:014 and such as follow their own **lusts**?
047:016 Allah has sealed, and who follow their own **lusts**.
054:003 and follow their (own) **lusts** but every matter

LUT
007:080 We also (sent) **Lut**: he said to his people: "Do ye commit
011:070 been sent against the people of **Lut**."
011:077 When Our Messengers came to **Lut**, he was
011:081 (The Messengers) said "O **Lut**! we are Messengers
011:089 the people of **Lut** far off from you!
015:059 "Excepting the adherents of **Lut**: them we
015:061 arrived among the adherents of **Lut**.
015:068 **Lut** said: "These are my guests: disgrace me not:
021:071 and (his nephew) **Lut** (and directed them) to the
021:074 And to **Lut**, too, We gave
022:043 And those of Abraham and **Lut**;
026:160 The people of **Lut** rejected the messengers.
026:161 Behold, their brother **Lut** said to them: "Will ye
026:167 O **Lut**! thou wilt assuredly be cast out!"
027:054 (We also sent) **Lut** (as a Messenger): behold, he
027:056 "Drive out the followers of **Lut** from your city:
029:026 But **Lut** believed Him: he said: "I will leave home for
029:028 And (remember) **Lut**: behold, he said to his people:
029:032 He said: "But there is **Lut** there."
029:033 And when Our Messengers came to **Lut**, he was
037:133 So also was **Lut** among those sent (by us).
038:013 And Thamud, and the People of **Lut**, and the
050:013 The 'Ad, Pharaoh, the Brethren of **Lut**,
054:033 The People of **Lut** rejected (his) Warning.
054:036 And (**Lut**) did warn them of Our violent Seizure
066:010 the wife of Noah and the wife of **Lut**: they were

LUT'S
011:074 with Us for **Lut's** people.
054:034 (Which destroyed them), except, **Lut's** household:

LUXURIOUS
078:016 And gardens of **luxurious** growth?

LUXURY
056:045 to be indulged, before that, in sinful **luxury**,

LYING
003:191 and **lying** down on their sides, and contemplate
004:103 or **lying** down on your sides;
009:042 for Allah doth know that they are **lying**.
010:012 (in all postures)-**lying** down on his side, or sitting,
022:045 And how many wells are **lying** idle and neglected,
026:222 They descend on every **lying**, wicked person
069:007 the (whole) people **lying** overthrown in its (path),
096:016 A **lying**, sinful forelock!

M

MACES
022:021   In addition there will be **maces** of iron

MAD
015:006   Truly thou art **mad** (or possessed)!
015:067   came in (**mad**) joy (at news of the young men).
068:002   by the grace of thy Lord, **mad** or possessed.

MADE
002:022   who has **made** the earth your couch,
002:029   and **made** them into seven firmaments;
002:066   So We **made** it an example to their own time,
002:118   We have indeed **made** clear the Signs
002:125   Remember We **made** the house a place of assembly
002:143   Thus have We **made** of you an Ummah
002:159   after We have **made** it clear
002:177   to fulfil the contracts which ye have **made**;
002:178   But if any remission is **made** by the brother
002:184   (should be **made** up) from days later.
002:185   (should be **made** up) by days later.
003:037   He **made** her grow in purity and beauty:
003:093   except what Israel **made** unlawful for himself
003:118   We have **made** plain to you the Signs,
003:126   Allah **made** it but a message of hope for you,
003:187   And vile was the bargain they **made**!
004:042   wish that the earth were **made** one with them:
004:073   a fine thing should I then have **made** of it!"
004:160   We **made** unlawful for them certain (foods)
005:005   things good and pure **made** lawful unto you.
005:013   We cursed them, and **made** their hearts grow hard:
005:020   when He produced prophets among you, **made** you kings,
005:048   He would have **made** you a single People,
005:087   the good things which Allah hath **made** lawful for you,
005:097   Allah **made** the Ka'ba, the Sacred House, a means
005:101   about things which, if **made** plain to you, may
005:101   they will be **made** plain to you: Allah will
006:001   and **made** the Darkness and the Light.
006:009   If We had **made** it an angel, We should
006:027   when they shall be **made** to stand by the Fire!
006:030   when they shall be **made** to stand before
006:043   and Satan **made** their (sinful) acts
006:071   have **made** into a fool, wandering bewildered
006:107   but We **made** thee not one to
006:108   Thus have We **made** alluring to each
006:128   "Our Lord! we **made** profit from each other:
006:137   their "partners" **made** alluring the slaughter
006:151   which Allah hath **made** sacred, except by
006:165   It is He Who hath **made** you the inheritors
007:027   We **made** the Satans friends (only) to
007:043   Ye have been **made** its inheritors, for your
007:069   He **made** you inheritors after the people
007:074   "And remember how He **made** you inheritors
007:103   of those who **made** mischief.
007:118   And all that they did was **made** of no effect.
007:137   And We **made** a people, considered weak
007:143   He **made** it as dust and Moses fell down in a swoon.
007:148   The people of Moses **made**, in his absence, out of

MADE (continued)
007:172   and **made** them testify concerning
007:179   Many are the Jinns and men We have **made** for Hell:
007:189   and **made** his mate of like nature, in order
008:006   the truth after it was **made** manifest, as if
008:010   Allah **made** it but a message of hope, and an
008:023   (as it is), if He had **made** them listen, they would
008:023   He would indeed have **made** them listen:
008:042   Even if ye had **made** a mutual appointment to meet,
008:044   and He **made** you appear as contemptible in
008:048   Remember Satan **made** their (sinful) acts
009:007   whom ye **made** a treaty near the sacred mosque?
009:046   they would certainly have **made** some preparation
009:046   so He **made** them lag behind and they were told,
009:047   your (strength) but only (**made** for) disorder,
009:075   Amongst them are men who **made** a Covenant
009:090   desert Arabs (also), Men who **made** excuses and
009:114   a promise he had **made** to him.
010:005   It is He Who **made** the sun to be a shining glory
010:014   Then We **made** you heirs in the land after them,
010:016   nor should He have **made** it known to you.
010:067   He it is that hath **made** you the Night
010:073   and We **made** them inherit (the earth), while We
011:118   He could have **made** mankind one People: but they
012:018   "Nay, but your minds have **made** up a tale (that may pass)
012:023   He **made** my sojourn agreeable! Truly
012:042   But Satan **made** him forget to mention him
012:066   (and **made** powerless) and when they had sworn
012:100   Allah hath **made** it come true!
013:003   and fruit of every kind He **made** in pairs,
013:031   or the dead were **made** to speak,
014:032   it is He Who hath **made** the ships subject to you,
014:032   and the rivers (also) hath He **made** subject to you.
014:033   And He hath **made** subject to you the sun and the moon,
014:033   the Night and the Day hath He (also) **made** subject you.
014:037   "O our Lord! I have **made** some of my offspring
014:046   Mighty indeed were the plots which they **made**,
015:016   and **made** them fair-seeming to (all) beholders;
015:066   And We **made** known this decree to him, that the
015:091   (So also on such) who have **made** Qur'an into shreds
016:012   He has **made** subject to you the Night and the Day;
016:014   It is He Who has **made** the sea subject, that ye
016:063   Satan **made**, (to the wicked), their own acts seem alluring:
016:069   and follow the ways of Thy Lord **made** smooth:
016:072   And Allah has **made** for you mates of your own nature,
016:072   and **made** for you, out of them, sons and daughters
016:080   It is Allah who **made** your habitations homes of
016:080   and **made** for you out of the skins of animals,
016:081   of the hills He **made** some for your shelter;
016:081   It is Allah Who **made** out of the things He created,
016:081   He **made** you garments to protect you
016:091   indeed ye have **made** Allah your surety; for Allah
016:112   so Allah **made** it taste of hunger and terror
016:124   The Sabbath was only **made** (strict) for those
017:002   and **made** it a Guide to the Children of Israel,
017:006   in resources and sons, and **made** you the more
017:008   and We have **made** Hell a prison for those who reject
017:012   We have **made** the Night and the Day as two (of Our)
017:012   Sign of the Day We have **made** bright that ye may seek
017:012   the Sign of the Night have **We made** dark while the Sign
017:033   Nor take life-which Allah has **made** sacred-except for
017:055   and We **made** some of the Prophets to excel others
017:073   they would certainly have **made** thee (their) friend!

MADE (continued)

017:075	In that case We should have **made** thee taste
018:002	(He hath **made** it) Straight (and Clear) in order
018:007	That which is on earth We have **made** but as
018:048	not fulfil the appointment **made** to you to meet (Us)!":
018:063	none but Satan **made** me forget to tell (you)
018:096	when he had **made** it (red) as fire, he said:
018:097	Thus were they **made** powerless to scale it
019:030	He hath given me revelation and **made** me a prophet:
019:031	"And He hath **made** me Blessed wheresoever I be,
019:032	"(He) hath **made** me kind to my mother, and not
019:049	We **made** a prophet.
019:052	and **made** him draw near to Us,
019:097	So have We **made** the (Qur'an) easy in thine
020:053	"He Who has **made** for you the earth
020:080	and We **made** a Covenant with you on the
020:083	"What **made** thee hasten in advance of thy people,
020:087	but we were **made** to carry the weight of the
021:015	till We **made** them as a field that is mown,
021:030	We **made** from water every living thing.
021:031	and We have **made** therein broad highways
021:032	And We have **made** the heavens as a canopy
021:070	but We **made** them the Greater losers.
021:072	and We **made** righteous men of every one (of them).
021:073	And We **made** them leaders, guiding (men)
021:079	that **made** the hills and the birds
021:081	(It was Our power that **made**) the violent
021:091	and We **made** her and her son a Sign for all peoples.
022:025	which We have **made** (open) to (all) men-
022:036	The sacrificial camels We have **made** for you
022:036	thus have we **made** animals subject to you,
022:037	He has thus **made** them subject to you, that ye
022:039	To those against whom war is **made**, permission is
022:054	and their hearts may be **made** humbly (open)
022:065	Allah has **made** subject to you (men) all that is on the
023:014	then of that clot We **made** a (foetus) lump;
023:014	We **made** out of that lump bones and clothed the bones
023:014	Then We **made** the sperm into a clot of congealed blood;
023:017	And We have **made**, above you, seven tracts;
023:041	and We **made** them as rubbish of dead leaves
023:044	We **made** them as a tale (that is told):
023:044	so We **made** them follow each other (in punishment):
023:050	And We **made** the son of Mary and his mother
023:110	that (ridicule of) them **made** you forget My Message while
025:020	We have **made** some of you as a trial for others:
025:031	Thus have We **made** for every prophet an enemy
025:037	We drowned them, and We **made** them as a Sign
025:053	yet has He **made** a barrier between them,
025:061	Blessed is He Who **made** Constellations in the skies,
025:062	And it is He Who **made** the Night and the Day
025:068	nor slay such life as Allah has **made** sacred, except for
026:059	Thus it was, but We **made** the Children of Israel
026:064	And We **made** the other party approach thither.
027:004	We have **made** their deeds pleasing in their eyes;
027:024	Satan has **made** their deeds seem pleasing
027:048	in the City nine men, who **made** mischief in the land,
027:061	Or, who has **made** the earth firm to live in;
027:061	**made** rivers in its midst; set thereon mountains
027:061	and **made** a separating bar between the two seas
027:086	See they not that We have **made** the Night for them to
028:041	And We **made** them (but) leaders inviting
028:042	In this world We **made** a Curse to follow them:
028:061	one to whom We have **made** a goodly promise,

MADE (continued)

028:073	has **made** for you Night and Day,-that ye
029:015	and We **made** the (Ark) a Sign
029:038	Satan **made** their deeds alluring to them,
029:067	We have **made** a Sanctuary secure, and that
030:015	shall be **made** happy in a Mead (of Delight).
030:030	the nature in which Allah has **made** mankind:
030:048	then when He has **made** them reach such of his servants
031:020	and has **made** His bounties flow to you in exceeding
032:008	And **made** his progeny from a quintessence
032:023	and We **made** it a guide to the Children of Israel.
033:004	Allah has not **made** for any man two hearts
033:004	nor has He **made** your wives whom ye divorce
033:004	nor has He **made** your adopted sons your sons.
033:019	and so Allah has **made** their deeds of none effect:
033:026	and some ye **made** captives.
033:027	And He **made** you heirs of their lands,
033:050	O prophet! We have **made** lawful to thee
034:010	and We **made** the iron soft for Him;-
034:012	and We **made** a Font of molten brass to flow for him:
034:012	And to Solomon (We **made**) the Wind (obedient):
034:012	We **made** him taste of the Chastisement of the Blazing
034:019	At length We **made** them as a tale (that is told),
034:031	the wrong-doers will be **made** to stand before
035:001	Who **made** the angels messengers with wings,-
035:008	then to whom the evil of his conduct is **made** alluring,
035:011	then He **made** you in pairs.
035:039	He it is that has **made** you inheritors
036:035	their hands that **made** this:
037:063	For We have truly **made** it (as) a trial
037:067	be given a mixture **made** of boiling water.
037:077	And **made** his progeny to endure (on this earth);
037:098	but We **made** them the ones most humiliated!
038:005	"Has he **made** the gods (all) into one God?
038:018	It was We that **made** the hills declare, in unison
038:053	Such is the promise **made** to you
039:067	No just estimate have they **made** of Allah,
040:011	"Our Lord! twice has Thou **made** us to die, and twice
040:037	Thus was **made** alluring, in Pharaoh's eyes, the evil of
040:061	It is Allah Who has **made** the Night for you,
040:064	It is Allah Who has **made** for you the earth
040:064	and **made** your shapes beautiful,-and has
040:079	It is Allah Who **made** cattle for you, that ye
041:025	who **made** alluring to them what was before them
041:036	to discord is **made** to thee by the Satan,
042:008	He could have **made** them a single people; but He
042:011	He had **made** for you pairs from among yourselves,
042:052	but We have **made** the (Qur'an) a Light, wherewith
043:003	We have **made** it a Qur'an in Arabic, that ye
043:010	and has **made** for you roads (and channels)
043:010	(Yea, the same that) has **made** for you the earth
043:012	and has **made** for you ships and cattle
043:056	And We **made** them (a people) of the Past and an
043:059	and We **made** him an example to the
043:072	ye are **made** heirs for your (good) deeds (in life).
044:004	In that (night) is **made** distinct every affair
044:028	And We **made** other people inherit (those things)!
044:058	Verily, We have **made** this (Qur'an) easy, in thy tongue,
046:016	which was **made** to them (in this life).
047:006	He has **made** known for them.
047:009	so He has **made** their deeds fruitless.
047:023	has cursed for He has **made** them deaf and blinded
047:028	so He **made** their deeds of no effect.

MADE (continued)

048:026 and **made** them stick close to the command
049:007 and He has **made** hateful to you unbelief,
049:007 and has **made** it beautiful in your hearts, and He
049:013 and **made** you into nations and tribes, that ye
050:006 How We have **made** it and adorned it,
054:013 We bore him on an (Ark) **made** of broad planks
054:017 And We have indeed **made** the Qur'an easy to
054:022 But We have indeed **made** the Qur'an easy to
054:032 And We have indeed **made** the Qur'an easy to
054:040 And We have indeed **made** the Qur'an easy to
056:036 And **made** them virgin-pure (and undefiled),-
056:073 We have **made** it a reminder and an article
056:082 And have ye **made** it your livelihood that ye
057:007 of the (substance) whereof He has **made** you heirs.
058:016 They have **made** their oaths a screen
058:019 so he has **made** them forgot the remembrance
059:006 for this ye **made** no expedition with either
059:019 and He **made** them forget themselves!
063:002 They have **made** their oaths a screen
064:003 and **made** your shapes beautiful:
066:001 to be forbidden that which Allah has **made** lawful to thee,
066:003 and Allah **made** it known to him, he confirmed
067:005 and We have **made** such (Lamps) (as) missiles
067:015 It is He Who has **made** the earth manageable for you,
067:023 and **made** for you the faculties of hearing
068:018 But **made** no reservation, ("If it be Allah's Will").
069:007 He **made** it rage against them seven nights
069:027 "Ah! would that (Death) had **made** an end of me!
071:016 and **made** the sun as a (Glorious) Lamp?
071:016 "`And **made** the moon a light in their midst,
071:019 "`And Allah has **made** the earth for you as a carpet
071:025 and were **made** to enter the Fire and they found-
074:014 To whom I **made** (life) smooth and comfortable!
075:039 And of him He **made** two sexes, male and female.
076:016 Crystal-clear, **made** of silver:
076:028 and We have **made** their frame strong; but, when
077:025 Have We not **made** the earth (as a place)
077:027 And **made** therein mountains standing firm,
078:006 Have We not **made** the earth as a wide expanse,
078:009 And **made** your sleep for rest,
078:010 And **made** the night as a covering,
078:011 And **made** the day as a means of subsistence?
079:023 Then he collected (his men) and **made** a proclamation,
079:025 (and **made** an) example of him,-in the Hereafter,
080:017 Woe to man! what hath **made** him reject Allah?
088:017 Do they not look at the Camels, how they are **made**?-
090:008 Have We not **made** for him a pair of eyes?-
090:011 But he hath **made** not haste on the path that is steep.
093:008 and **made** thee independent.
100:010 in (human) breasts is **made** manifest-
104:008 It shall be **made** into a vault over them,

MADE-UP

038:007 this is nothing but a **made-up** tale!

MADINAH

009:101 as well as among the **Madinah** folk:
009:120 for the people of **Madinah** and the Bedouin Arabs of the
059:009 had homes (in **Madinah**) and had adopted the Faith,-
063:007 till they disperse (and quit **Madinah**).
063:008 They say, "If we return to **Madinah**, surely the

MADLY

070:036 the Unbelievers that they rush **madly** before thee-

MADMAN

026:027 who has been sent to you is a veritable **madman**!"

MADNESS

002:275 the Satan by his touch hath driven to **madness**.
007:184 Their Companion is not seized with **madness**:
034:008 or is he afflicted with **madness**."
054:024 Truly should we then be in error and **madness**.
054:047 the ones in error and **madness**.
068:006 Which of you is afflicted with **madness**.

MADYAN

007:085 To the **Madyan** people We sent Shu'aib, one of
009:070 the people of Abraham, the men of **Madyan**, and the
011:084 To the **Madyan** people (We sent) Shu'aib, one of
011:095 So away with **Madyan** as were Thamud gone away.
022:044 And the Companions **Madyan** people;
028:022 when he turned his face towards (the land of) **Madyan**,
028:023 the watering (place) in **Madyan**, he found
028:045 but thou wast not a dweller among the people of **Madyan**,
029:036 To the **Madyan** (people) (We sent) their brother Shu'aib.

MAGIANS

022:017 and the Sabians, Christians, **Magians**, and Polytheists,-

MAGIC

002:102 And they knew that the buyers of (**magic**)
002:102 but Satans disbelieved, teaching men **magic**,
005:110 'This is nothing but evident **magic**'.
006:007 "This is nothing but obvious **magic**!"
007:116 and they showed a great (feat of) **magic**.
020:057 us out of our land with thy **magic**, O Moses?
020:058 "But we can surely produce **magic** to match thine!
020:063 object is to drive you out from your land with their **magic**,
020:066 so it seemed to him on account of their **magic**-
020:071 Who has taught you **magic**!
020:073 and the **magic** to which thou didst compel us:
034:043 "This is nothing but evident **magic**!
052:015 "Is this then a **magic**, or is it ye that do not see?
054:002 and say, "This is (but) continuous **magic**."
074:024 but **magic** derived from of old;"

MAGICIAN

020:069 and the **magician** succeeds not.

MAGICIAN'S

020:069 what they have faked in but a **magician's** trick:

MAGICIANS

020:063 They said: "These two are certainly (expert) **magicians**:
020:070 So the **magicians** were thrown down to prostration:

MAGNIFICENT

017:009 that they shall have a **magnificent** reward;
027:023 every requisite; and she has a **magnificent** throne.
035:007 and a **magnificent** Reward.
042:022 That will indeed be the **magnificent** Bounty (of Allah).
076:020 see a Bliss and a Realm **Magnificent**.

MAGNIFY

017:111 Yea, **magnify** Him for His greatness and glory!"
074:003 And thy Lord do thou **magnify**!

MAGOG

018:094 the Gog and **Magog** (people) do great mischief
021:096 Gog and **Magog** (people) are let through (their barrier),

MAIDENS

044:054 to **maidens** with beautiful, big, and lustrous eyes.
052:020 and We shall wed them to **maidens**, with beautiful,
055:056 In them will be (**Maidens**), Chaste, restraining
055:070 In them will be fair (**Maidens**), good, beautiful;-
055:072 **Maidens** restrained (as to their glances),

MAIDENS (continued)

078:033 **Maidens** of Equal Age;

MAIDS

024:033 But force not your **maids** to prostitution when they desire

MAIL

016:081 and coats of **mail** to protect you from your
021:080 the making of coats of **mail** for your benefit,
034:011 (Commanding), "Make thou coats of **mail**, balancing well

MAIN

005:033 and strive with might and **main** for mischief
005:035 and strive (with might and **main**) in His cause:
009:016 those among you who strive with might and **main**,
009:019 and strive with might and **main** in the cause of Allah!
009:020 and strive with might and **main**, in Allah's
029:006 And if any strive (with might and **main**), they do

MAINTAIN

009:017 to **maintain** the mosques of Allah while they witness

MAINTAINED

009:018 visited and **maintained** by such as believe

MAINTAINERS

004:034 Men are the protectors and **maintainers** of women,

MAINTENANCE

002:240 a year's **maintenance** without expulsion;
009:019 or the **maintenance** of the Sacred Mosque,

MAJESTY

019:035 (the **majesty** of) Allah that He should beget
019:092 the **majesty** of The Most Gracious that He
045:037 And unto Him (alone) belongeth **Majesty** in the
055:027 thy Lord,-full of **Majesty**, Bounty and Honour.
055:078 full of **Majesty**, Bounty and Honour.
071:013 that ye are not conscious of Allah's **Majesty**,-
072:003 'And exalted is the **Majesty** of our Lord:

MAKE

002:011 "**Make** not mischief on the earth,"
002:012 the ones who **make** mischief,
002:030 Thou place therein one who will **make** mischief and
002:036 Then did Satan **make** them slip from the (garden),
002:068 to **make** plain to us what heifer it is!"
002:069 to **make** plain to us her colour."
002:070 to **make** plain to us what she is:
002:079 and for the gain they **make** thereby.
002:100 every time they **make** a Covenant,
002:124 He said: "I will **make** thee an Imam
002:126 "My Lord **make** this a City of Peace,
002:128 "Our Lord! **make** of us Muslims,
002:136 we **make** no difference between one another of them:
002:143 And never would Allah **make** your faith of no effect.
002:160 Except those who repent and **make** amends
002:180 that he **make** a bequest to parents and next of kin.
002:181 the guilt shall be on those who **make** the change.
002:187 Thus doth Allah **make** clear His Signs to men:
002:195 and **make** not your own hands contribute
002:196 he must **make** an offering such as he can afford,
002:219 Thus doth Allah **make** clear to you His Signs:
002:224 And **make** not Allah's (name) an excuse
002:235 There is no blame on you if ye **make** an indirect
002:235 but do not **make** a secret contract with them
002:242 Thus doth Allah **make** clear His Signs to you:
002:250 on us and **make** our steps firm:
002:259 and that We may **make** of thee a Sign unto the people.
002:266 Thus doth Allah **make** clear to you
002:270 or whatever you vow to **make**,

MAKE (continued)

002:271 and **make** them reach those (really) in need,
002:282 whenever ye **make** a commercial contract;
002:285 "We **make** no distinction (they say) between
003:049 in that I **make** for you out of clay, as it were,
003:050 And to **make** lawful to you part of what
003:055 I will **make** those who follow thee superior
003:084 we **make** no distinction between one and another
003:089 And **make** amends; for verily Allah
003:099 seeking to **make** it crooked,
003:103 Thus doth Allah **make** His Signs clear to you:
003:156 This that Allah may **make** it a cause of sighs
003:187 to **make** it known and clear to mankind and not
004:006 **Make** trial of orphans until they reach
004:026 Allah doth wish to **make** clear to you and
004:065 until they **make** thee judge in all disputes between them.
004:146 and **make** their religious devotion sincere to Allah:
004:152 and **make** no distinction between any of the messengers,
004:176 thus doth Allah **make** clear to you (His law),
005:006 but to **make** you clean, and to complete His favour
005:008 to you **make** you swerve to wrong and depart form
005:087 O ye who believe! **make** not unlawful the good
005:089 Thus doth Allah **make** clear to you His Signs,
005:094 Allah doth but **make** a trial of you in a little matter of
006:091 No just estimate of Allah do they **make** when they say:
006:091 but ye **make** it into (separate) sheets for show,
006:100 Yet they **make** the Jinns equals with Allah,
006:105 We may **make** the matter clear to those who know.
006:109 but what will **make** you (Muslims) realize
006:112 Likewise did We **make** for every Messenger
006:129 Thus do We **make** the wrong-doers turn to
007:045 desiring to **make** something crooked:
007:057 them to a land that is dead, **make** rain to descend thereon,
007:086 and seek to **make** it crooked;
007:129 and **make** you inheritors in the earth;
007:150 did ye **make** haste to bring on the judgment of your lord.
007:150 **Make** not the enemies rejoice over my misfortune,
007:163 thus did We **make** a trial of them, for they were given to
008:056 thou didst **make** a covenant, but they
008:060 Against them **make** ready your strength to the
009:037 for they **make** it lawful one year, and forbidden
009:037 and **make** such forbidden ones lawful.
009:066 **Make** ye no excuses: ye have rejected Faith
009:108 and Allah loveth those who **make** themselves pure.
010:021 Our messengers record all the plots that ye **make**!"
010:021 When We **make** mankind taste of some mercy after
010:024 and We **make** it like a harvest clean-mown,
010:039 thus did those before them **make** charges of falsehood:
010:042 but canst thou **make** the deaf to hear,-even though
010:067 and the Day to **make** things visible (to you).
010:070 Then shall We **make** them taste the severest
010:081 Allah will surely **make** it of no effect:
010:081 the work of those who **make** mischief.
010:085 Our Lord! **make** us not a trial for those
010:087 **make** your dwellings into places of worship,
011:057 My Lord will **make** another People to succeed you,
011:120 with it We **make** firm they heart:
012:021 said to his wife: "**Make** his stay (among us) honourable:
012:073 know that we came not to **make** mischief in the land,
013:004 yet some of them We **make** more excellent
013:017 to **make** ornaments or utensils therewith,
013:040 thy duty is to (**make** the Message) reach them:
014:003 (men) from the Path of Allah and seek to **make** it crooked:

MAKE (continued)

014:004   in order to **make** (things) clear to them.
014:035   "O my Lord! **make** this city one of peace and security:
014:040   "O my Lord! **make** me one who establishes
015:039   I will **make** (wrong) fair-seeming to them on
016:064   so that thou shouldst **make** clear to them
016:084   be allowed to **make** amends.
016:092   will certainly **make** clear to you (the truth of) that wherein
016:093   If Allah so willed, He could **make** you all one People:
016:119   but who thereafter repent and **make** amends,-
017:014   thy soul this day to **make** out an account
017:029   **Make** not thy hand tied (like a niggard's)
017:064   **make** assaults on them with thy cavalry and thy infantry:
017:064   them wealth and children: and **make** promises to them."
018:008   Verily what is on earth We shall **make** but as
018:021   Thus did We **make** their case known to the people,
018:052   and We shall **make** for them a place
018:098   He will **make** it into dust; and the promise of my Lord
019:006   and **make** him, O my Lord! one with whom Thou art
019:084   So **make** no haste against them, for We
020:032   "And **make** him share my task:
020:058   So **make** a tryst between us and thee,
020:086   did not your Lord **make** a handsome promise to you?
022:009   We shall **make** him taste the chastisement of burning
022:053   That He may **make** the suggestions thrown in
024:030   that will **make** for greater purity for them:
024:033   in order that ye may **make** a gain in the goods of this
024:046   have indeed sent down Signs that **make** things manifest:
024:058   thus does Allah **make** clear the Signs to you:
024:059   thus does Allah **make** clear His Signs to you:
024:060   provided they **make** not wanton display of their
024:061   thus does Allah **make** clear the Signs to you: that you
025:009   See what kinds of companions they **make** for thee!
025:023   **make** such deeds as floating dust scattered about.
025:045   Then do We **make** the sun its guide;
025:045   If He willed, He could **make** it stationary!
026:085   "**Make** me one of the inheritors of the Garden of Bliss;
026:152   "Who **make** mischief in the land, and mend
027:034   despoil it, and **make** the noblest of its people its meanest
027:049   that we shall **make** a secret night attack on him
028:005   to **make** them leaders (in faith) and **make** them heirs,
028:007   and We shall **make** him one of Our messengers."
028:071   Say: See ye? If Allah were to **make** the night
028:072   Say: see ye? If Allah were to **make** the Day
030:023   the quest that ye (**make** for livelihood) out of His Bounty:
030:044   will **make** provision for themselves (in heaven):
030:052   So verily thou canst not **make** the dead to hear,
030:052   nor canst thou **make** the deaf to hear the call,
030:053   only those wilt thou **make** to hear, who believe in Our
030:057   nor will they be allowed to **make** amends.
031:015   "But if they strive to **make** thee join in
032:021   And indeed We will **make** them taste of the
033:005   but there is no blame on you if ye **make** a mistake therein:
033:033   and to **make** you pure and spotless.
033:033   and **make** not a dazzling display, like that of the former
033:037   in thy heart that which Allah was about **make** manifest:
033:063   and what will **make** thee understand?-perchance the Hour
033:070   and **make** your utterance straight forward:
033:071   That He may **make** your conduct whole and sound
034:011   (Commanding), "**Make** thou coats of mail,
035:022   Allah can **make** any that He wills to hear;
035:022   but thou canst not **make** those to hear who are (buried)
037:117   which helps to **make** things clear;

MAKE (continued)

038:026   O David! We did indeed **make** thee a vicegerent
042:013   in Religion, and **make** no divisions therein:
042:017   will **make** thee realize that perhaps the Hour
043:019   And they **make** into females angels who themselves
043:040   Canst thou then **make** the deaf to hear, or give
043:054   Thus did he **make** fools of his people, and they
043:060   We could **make** angels from amongst you,
043:063   with Wisdom, and in order to **make** clear to you
045:021   Ill is the judgment that they **make**.
045:021   evil deeds think that We shall **make** them as equal with
045:035   shall not be taken out thence, nor can the **make** amends.
047:032   but He will **make** their deeds of no effect.
047:033   and **make** not vain your deeds!
048:028   the Religion of Truth, to **make** it prevail over all religion:
049:009   then **make** peace between them with justice,
049:009   fall into a fight, **make** ye peace between them:
049:010   so **make** peace and reconciliation between your two
050:027   "Our Lord! I did not **make** him transgress, but he
051:051   And **make** not another an object of worship
056:065   Were it Our Will, we could **make** it broken orts.
056:070   Our Will, We could **make** it saltish (and unpalatable):
058:011   (spread out and) **make** room: (ample) room will Allah
058:011   when ye are told to **make** room in the assemblies,
059:007   (merely) **make** a circuit between the wealth among you.
060:005   "Our Lord! **Make** us not a (test and) trial for
061:009   That He **make** it prevail over all religion,
065:004   He will **make** things easy for them.
066:007   "O ye Unbelievers! **make** no excuses this Day!
067:013   And whether ye hide your word or **make** it known,
068:050   and **make** him of the company of the Righteous.
069:003   And what will **make** thee realize what the
069:012   That We might **make** it a Reminder unto you,
072:019   they just **make** round him a dense crowd."
072:026   nor does He **make** any one acquainted with
073:017   a Day that will **make** children hoary-headed?-
075:016   the (Qur'an) to **make** haste therewith.
075:019   to explain it (and **make** it clear):
075:038   then did (Allah) **make** and fashion (him)
077:017   So shall We **make** later (generations) follow them.
080:020   Then doth He **make** His path smooth for him;
080:037   to **make** him indifferent to the others.
087:005   And then doth **make** it (but) swarthy stubble.
087:008   And We will **make** it easy for thee (to follow)
092:007   We will indeed **make** smooth for him
092:010   We will indeed **make** smooth for him
095:007   can after this, **make** you deny the Last Judgment?
098:004   Nor did the People of the Book **make** schisms, until after
104:003   would **make** him last for ever!
105:002   Did He not **make** their treacherous plan go astray?
105:005   Then did He **make** them like an empty field

MAKER

002:054   for you in the sight of your **Maker**.
002:054   so turn (in repentance) to your **Maker**,
006:014   the **Maker** of the heavens and the earth?

MAKERS

085:004   Woe to the **makers** of the pit (of Fire),

MAKES

002:221   and **makes** His Signs clear to mankind:
002:230   which He **makes** plain to those who know.
002:265   but **makes** it yield a double increase of harvest,
004:120   Satan **makes** them promises, and creates in them false
005:075   See how Allah doth **makes** His Signs clear to them;

MAKES (continued)

006:068 If Satan ever **makes** thee forget,
006:096 He **makes** the night for rest and tranquillity,
008:018 He Who **makes** feeble the Plans and stratagems
009:115 until He **makes** clear to them as to what they should avoid,
014:021 to us it **makes** no difference (now) whether
015:001 of a Qur'an that **makes** things clear.
024:018 Allah is the (very) Truth, that **makes** all things manifest.
024:028 go back: that **makes** for greater purity for yourselves;
024:043 Seest thou not that Allah **makes** the clouds
024:043 then **makes** them into a heap?
025:047 And He it is Who **makes** the Night as a Robe
025:047 and **makes** the Day (as it were) a Resurrection.
026:002 These are Verses of the Book that **makes** (things) clear.
027:001 a Book that **makes** (things) clear;
027:062 and **makes** you (mankind) inheritors of the earth?
028:002 These are Verses of the Book that **makes** (things) clear.
033:053 that **makes** for greater purity for your hearts and for theirs.
036:078 And he **makes** comparisons for Us, and forgets
039:005 He **makes** the Night overlap the Day, and the
039:021 then He **makes** it dry up and crumble
042:040 but if a person forgives and **makes** reconciliation,
043:002 By the Book that **makes** things clear,-
044:002 By the Book that **makes** things clear;-
048:029 a seed which sends forth its blade, then **makes** it strong;
050:016 and We know what suggestion his soul **makes** to him:
072:027 and then He **makes** a band of watchers march before

MAKEST

002:067 They said: "**Makest** thou a laughing-stock
005:110 And behold! thou **makest** out of clay, as it were,

MAKETH

006:097 It is He Who **maketh** the stars
006:125 He **maketh** their breast close and constricted,
017:066 Your Lord is He that **maketh** the Ship go smoothly

MAKING

002:196 And seven days on his return, **making** ten days in all.
002:224 or **making** peace between persons;
002:232 That is (the course **making** for) most virtue
005:019 Now hath come unto you, **making** (things) clear unto you,
005:106 when **making** bequests,-two just men of your own
007:029 and call upon Him, **making** your devotion sincere
014:030 But verily ye are **making** straightway for Hell!"
018:040 from heaven, **making** it (but) slippery sand!
021:080 the **making** of coats of mail for your benefit,
024:034 have already sent down to you verses **making** things clear,
029:065 **making** their devotion sincerely (and exclusively) to Him;
034:013 They worked for him as he desired, (**making**) Arches,
036:069 and a Qur'an **making** things clear:
043:029 and a Messenger **making** things clear.
076:006 do drink, **making** it flow in unstinted abundance.

MAKKAH

048:024 from them in the midst of **Makkah**, after that

MALE

003:036 "And is not the **male** like the female.
003:195 be he **male** or female: ye are members,
004:011 to the **male**, a portion equal to that of two females:
004:124 be they **male** or female, and have faith, they
004:176 the **male** having twice the share of the female,
005:038 As to the thief, **male** or female, cut off
007:127 He said: "Their **male** children will we slay;
007:141 of punishment who slew your **male** children and
011:040 kind two, **male** and female, and your family-
023:027 of every species, **male** and female, and thy

MALE (continued)

024:031 or **male** attendants free of sexual desires.
024:032 and the virtuous ones among your slaves, **male** or female:
042:049 He bestows (children) **male** or female according to
049:013 a single (pair) of a **male** and a female,
053:021 What! for you the **male** sex, and for him, the female?
053:045 That He did create in pairs-**male** and female,
075:039 And of him He made two sexes, **male** and female.
092:003 By the creation of **male** and female;-

MALES

006:143 say, hath He forbidden the two **males**, or the
006:144 say, hath He forbidden the two **males**, or the
026:165 will ye approach **males**,
042:050 Or He bestows both **males** and females,

MALICIOUS

012:031 When she heard of their **malicious** talk, she sent

MALIK

043:077 They will cry: "O **Malik**! would that thy Lord

MAN

002:017 a **man** who kindled a fire;
002:072 Remember ye slew a **man** and fell into a dispute
002:102 the means to sow discord between **man** and wife.
002:204 There is the type of **man** whose speech
002:207 And there is the type of **man** who gives his life
002:220 means mischief from the **man** who means good.
002:220 but Allah knows the **man** who means mischief
002:221 a **man** slave who believes is better
002:273 the ignorant **man** thinks, because of their modesty,
002:282 not two men, then a **man** and two women,
003:041 shalt speak to no **man** for three days but with signals.
003:047 how shall I have a son when **man** hath touched Me?"
003:079 It is not (possible) that a **man**, to whom is given the Book,
003:162 the **man** who draws on Himself the wrath of Allah,
003:162 Is the **man** who follows the good pleasure of Allah
004:012 If the **man** or woman whose inheritance
004:028 for **man** was created weak in (resolution).
004:079 Whatever good, (O **man**!) happens to thee,
004:093 If a **man** kills a Believer intentionally,
004:176 If it is a **man**. That dies,
006:009 We should have sent him as a **man**.
006:091 A light and guidance to **man**:
006:091 send down to **man** (by way of revelation)":
007:063 through a **man** of your own people, to warn
007:069 from your Lord through a **man** of your
007:175 Relate to them the story of the **man** to whom
008:024 in between a **man** and his heart,
009:049 Among them is (many) a **man** who says: "Grant me
010:002 sent Our inspiration to a **man** from among themselves?
010:012 When trouble toucheth a **man**, he crieth
010:044 Verily Allah will not deal unjustly with **man** in aught:
010:044 it is **man** that wrongs his own soul.
011:009 If We give **man** a taste of mercy from Ourselves,
011:027 (in) thee nothing but a **man** like ourselves:
011:072 and my husband here is an old **man**?
011:078 a single right-minded **man**?"
012:005 for Satan is to **man** an avowed enemy!
012:019 Good news! Here is a (fine) young **man**!
012:021 The **man** in Egypt who bought him, said to his wife:
012:032 the **man** about whom ye did blame me!
012:045 But the **man** who had been released, one of
012:046 "O Joseph!" (he said), "O **man** of truth! Expound
014:034 Verily, **man** is given up to injustice
015:026 We created **man** from sounding clay, from mud

MAN (continued)

015:028 "I am about to create **man**, from sounding
015:033 "I am not one to prostrate myself to **man**,
016:002 (saying): "Warn (**Man**) that there is no god but I:
016:004 and behold this same (**man**) becomes an open disputer!
016:004 He has created **man** from a sperm-drop and behold
016:075 and (the other) a **man** on whom We have bestowed goodly
016:076 is such a **man** equal with one who commands justice,
016:097 Whoever works righteousness, **man** or woman, and has
016:103 "It is a **man** that teaches him."
017:011 as he prays for good for **man** is given to haste.
017:011 **Man** prays for evil as fervently as he prays
017:022 or thou (O **man**!) wilt sit in disgrace
017:047 "Ye follow none other than a **man** bewitched!"
017:053 for Satan is to **man** an avowed enemy.
017:067 Most ungrateful is **man**!
017:083 Yet when We bestow Our favours on **man**, he turns
017:089 And We have explained to **man**, in this Qur'an,
017:093 am I aught but a **man**,-a messenger?"
017:094 "Has Allah sent a **man** (like us) to be (His)
017:100 for **man** is (ever) niggardly!"
018:034 (Abundant) was the produce this **man** had:
018:037 a sperm-drop, then fashioned thee into a **man**?
018:054 but **man** is, in most things, contentious.
018:082 their father had been a righteous **man**:
018:110 Say: "I am but a **man** like yourselves,
019:010 "Shall be that thou shalt speak to no **man** for three nights,
019:017 and he appeared before her as a **man** in all respects.
019:020 seeing that no **man** has touched me, and I am
019:026 And if thou dost see any **man**, say, 'I have vowed a fast
019:028 "O sister of Aaron! thy father was not a **man** of evil,
019:041 (the story of) Abraham: he was a **man** of Truth, a prophet.
019:056 he was a **man** of truth (and sincerity),
019:066 **Man** says: "What! when I am dead, shall I
019:067 But does not **man** call to mind that We
019:077 Has thou then seen the (sort of) **man** who rejects Our
020:040 Then thou didst slay a **man**, but We
020:111 the **man** that carries iniquity (on his back).
021:003 "Is this (one) more than a **man** like yourselves?
021:034 We granted not to any **man** before thee
021:037 **Man** is a creature of haste: soon (enough)
022:065 for Allah is Most Kind and Most Merciful to **man**.
022:066 truly **man** is a most ungrateful creature!
023:012 **Man** We did create from a quintessence (of clay);
023:024 "He is no more that a **man** like yourselves:
023:025 (and some said): "He is only a **man** possessed:
023:033 "He is no more than a **man** like yourselves; he eats
023:034 "If ye obey a **man** like yourselves, behold, it is
023:038 "He is only a **man** who invents a lie against Allah,
024:002 The woman and the **man** guilty of fornication,-
024:011 to every **man** among them (will come the punishment)
024:039 which the **man** parched with thirst mistakes for water;
024:040 if a **man** stretches out his hand, he can hardly see it!
025:008 "Ye follow none other than a **man** bewitched."
025:029 Ah! the Satan is but a traitor to **man**!
025:054 It is He Who has created **man** from water: then has
028:015 Now the **man** of his own people appealed to him against
028:018 the **man** who had, the day before, sought his
028:019 the **man** said: "O Moses! is it thy intention to slay me
028:019 to stay me as thou slewest a **man** yesterday?
028:020 And there came a **man**, running, from the
028:023 and our father is a very old **man**."
028:026 to employ is the (**man**) who is strong and trusty."

MAN (continued)

028:033 He said: "O my Lord! I have slain a **man** among them,
029:008 We have enjoined on **man** kindness to parents:
030:050 Then behold (O **man**!) the tokens of Allah's Mercy!-
031:014 And We have enjoined on **man** (to be good) to his parents:
032:007 the creation of **man** from clay,
032:018 Is then the **man** who believes no better than the
032:018 than the **man** who is rebellious and wicked?
033:004 Allah has not made for any **man** two hearts
033:036 It is not fitting for a Believer, **man** or woman, when a
033:072 being afraid thereof: but **man** undertook it:
034:007 "Shall we point out to you a **man** that will
034:021 except that We might test the **man** who believes
034:043 a man who wishes to hinder you from the
035:011 Nor is a **man** long-lived granted length of days,
035:014 And none, (O **man**!) can inform you like Him
036:020 a **man**, saying, "O my People! obey the messengers:
036:077 Doth not **man** see that it is We Who created
038:017 and remember Our Servant David, the **man** of strength:
038:023 "This **man** is my brother; he has
038:071 "I am about to create **man** from clay:
039:008 When some trouble toucheth **man** he crieth unto his Lord,
039:008 (**man**) doth forget what he cried and prayed for before,
039:029 and a **man** belonging entirely to one master:
039:029 a **man** belonging to many partners at variance
039:049 Now, when trouble touches **man**, he cries to Us;
040:028 said: "Will ye slay a **man** because he says,
040:028 A Believer, a **man** from among the people of Pharaoh,
040:030 Then said the **man** who believed: "O my People!
040:038 The **man** who believed said further: "O my People!
040:040 whether **man** or woman-and is a believer-such will
041:006 Say thou: "I am but a **man** like you:
041:049 **Man** does not weary of asking for good (things),
041:051 When We bestow favours on **man**, he turns
042:048 And truly, when We give **man** a taste of Mercy
042:048 truly then is **man** ungrateful!
042:051 It is not fitting for a **man** that Allah
043:015 Truly is **man** clearly unthankful.
043:031 sent down to some leading **man** in either of
044:014 "Tutored (by others), a **man** possessed!"
046:015 We have enjoined on **man** kindness to his parents:
050:016 It was We who created **man**, and We
053:024 Nay, shall **man** have (just) anything
053:039 That **man** can have nothing but what he strives for;
053:055 (O **man**), wilt thou dispute about?
054:024 For they said: "What! a **man**! a solitary
055:003 He has created **man**:
055:014 He created **man** from sounding clay
055:039 will be asked of **man** or Jinn as to his sin,
055:056 whom no **man** or Jinn before them has touched;-
055:074 Whom no **man** or Jinn before them has touched;-
056:083 when (the soul of the dying **man**) reaches the throat,
059:016 when he says to **man**, "Disbelieve": but when
059:016 but when (**man**) disbelieves, Satan says,
065:007 Let the **man** of means spend according to his means:
065:007 and the **man** whose resources are restricted, let him
070:019 Truly **man** was created very impatient;
070:038 Does every **man** of them long to enter
072:005 'But we do think that no **man** or Jinn should say aught
074:029 Darkening and changing the colour of **man**!
075:003 Does **man** think that We cannot assemble his bones?
075:005 But **man** wishes to do wrong (even) in the
075:010 That Day will **Man** say "Where is the refuge?"

MAN (continued)

075:013 That Day will **Man** be told (all) that
075:014 Nay, **man** will be evidence against himself,
075:034 Woe to thee, (O **man**!) yea, woe!
075:035 Again, woe to thee, (O **man**!), yea woe!
075:036 Does **Man** think that he will be left uncontrolled,
076:001 Has there not been over **Man** a long period of Time,
076:002 Verily We created **Man** from a drop of mingled sperm,
078:040 the Day when **man** will see (the Deeds) which his hands
079:035 The Day when **Man** shall remember (all) that
080:002 the blind **man** (interrupting).
080:017 Woe to **man**! what hath made him reject Allah?
080:024 Then let **man** look at his Food, (and how We provide it):
080:034 That Day shall a **man** flee from his own brother,
082:006 O **man**! what has seduced thee from thy Lord
084:006 O thou **man**! verily thou art ever toiling on
086:005 Now let **man** but think from what he is created!
086:010 (**Man**) will have no power, and no helper.
089:015 Now, as for **man**, when his Lord trieth him,
089:023 is brought (face to face),-on the Day will **man** remember,
090:004 Verily We have created **Man** into toil and struggle.
091:012 Behold, the most wicked **man** among them
095:004 We have indeed created **man** in the best of molds,
096:002 Created **man**, out of a leech-like clot:
096:005 Taught **man** that which he knew not.
096:006 Nay, but **man** doth transgress all bounds,
099:003 And **man** cries (distressed): 'What is the matter with her?'-
100:006 Truly **Man** is to his Lord, ungrateful;
103:002 Verily **Man** is in loss,

MAN'S

002:237 Or (the **man's** half) is remitted by him
002:237 and the remission (of the **man's** half)
017:013 Every **man's** fate We have fastened on his
077:001 one after another (to **man's** profit);

MAN-POWER

017:006 the more numerous in **man-power**.

MANAGE

004:005 which Allah has assigned to you to **manage**,
088:022 Thou art not one to **manage** (their) affairs.

MANAGEABLE

067:015 It is He Who has made the earth **manageable** for you,

MANAT

053:020 And another, the third (goddess), **Manat**?

MANHOOD

012:022 When Joseph attained his full **manhood**, We gave

MANIFEST

002:099 We have sent down to thee **manifest** Signs (ayat);
002:109 become **manifest** unto them:
003:097 In it are Signs **manifest**; the Station of Abraham;
003:164 while, before that, they had been in **manifest** error.
004:020 would ye take it by slander and a **manifest** sin?
004:050 but that by itself is a **manifest** sin!
004:119 hath of a surety suffered a loss that is **manifest**.
004:153 and gave Moses **manifest** proofs of authority.
004:174 sent unto you a light (that is) **manifest**.
006:028 will become **manifest** what before they concealed.
006:074 For I see thee and thy people in **manifest** error."
007:022 their shameful parts became **manifest** to them,
008:006 the truth after it was made **manifest**, as if
009:048 and the Decree of Allah became **manifest**, much to
011:096 and an authority **manifest**,
012:051 "Now is the truth the truth **manifest** (to all):

MANIFEST (continued)

015:085 the Hour is surely coming (when this will be **manifest**).
016:039 He may **manifest** to them the truth of that
019:038 but the unjust to-day are in error **manifest**!
021:054 in **manifest** error-ye and your fathers."
022:005 in order that We may **manifest** (Our Power) to you;
022:011 that is indeed the **manifest** loss,
023:045 and authority **manifest**,
024:025 that makes all things **manifest**.
024:046 that make things **manifest**: and Allah
026:097 "'By Allah, we were truly in an error **manifest**,
027:013 visibly they said: "This is sorcery **manifest**!"
027:016 this is indeed Grace **manifest** (from Allah)."
027:079 for thou art on (the Path of) **manifest** Truth.
028:085 and who is in **manifest** error."
031:011 nay, but the Transgressors are in **manifest** error.
033:037 in thy heart that which Allah was about to make **manifest**:
034:024 on right guidance or in **manifest** error!"
036:024 "I would indeed, then be in **manifest** Error.
036:047 Ye are in nothing but **manifest** error."
037:156 Or have ye an authority **manifest**?
040:023 with Our Signs and Authority **manifest**,
041:053 until it becomes **manifest** to them that this
043:040 or to such as (wander) in **manifest** error?
044:019 for I come to you with authority **manifest**.
044:033 in which there was a **manifest** trial.
045:030 that will be the **manifest** triumph.
046:032 besides Allah: such are in **manifest** error."
048:001 Verily We have granted thee a **manifest** Victory:
051:038 with authority **manifest**.
052:038 of theirs produce a **manifest** proof.
057:009 to His Servants **manifest** Signs, that He
062:002 before, in **manifest** error;-
067:029 (of us) it is that is in **manifest** error."
087:007 for He knoweth what is **manifest** and what is hidden.
100:010 in (human) breasts is made **manifest**-

MANIFESTED

007:143 When his Lord **manifested** Himself to the mount, He

MANIFESTLY

002:055 in thee until we see Allah **manifestly**,"
028:015 for he is an enemy that **manifestly** misleads!"
028:018 "Thou art truly, one erring **manifestly**."
039:022 of Allah! they are **manifestly** wandering (in error)!

MANIFOLD

002:261 Allah giveth **manifold** increase to whom He pleaseth:
057:011 increase it **manifold** to his credit,
057:018 increased **manifold** (to their credit), and they

MANKIND

002:161 and the curse of angels, and of all **mankind**;
002:164 for the profit of **mankind**;
002:185 as a guide to **mankind**,
002:213 **Mankind** was one single nation.
002:221 and makes His Signs clear to **mankind**:
002:243 For Allah is full of bounty to **mankind**,
003:003 Before this, as a guide to **mankind**,
003:009 gather **mankind** together against a Day about which
003:021 and slay those who teach just dealing with **mankind**,
003:087 curse of Allah, of His angels, and of all **mankind**;
003:110 Ye are the best of Peoples, evolved for **mankind**.
003:187 to make it known and clear to **mankind** and not
004:001 O **mankind**! fear your Guardian Lord, Who created
004:054 Or do they envy **mankind** for what
004:079 sent thee as a Messenger to (instruct) **mankind**.

MANKIND (continued)

004:133 If it were His Will, He could destroy you, O **mankind**,
004:165 that **mankind**, after (the coming) of the messengers,
004:170 O **mankind**! the Messengers hath come to you
004:174 O **mankind**! verily there hath come to you
010:002 That he should warn **mankind** (of their danger),
010:019 **Mankind** was but one nation, but differed (later).
010:021 When We make **mankind** taste of some mercy
010:023 O **mankind**! your insolence is against your own
010:057 O **mankind**! there hath come to you an admonition from
010:060 Verily; Allah is full of Bounty to **mankind**, but most of
010:061 and whatever deed ye (**mankind**) may be doing,-
010:092 But verily, many among **mankind** are heedless
010:099 Wilt thou then compel **mankind**, against their
011:103 that is a Day for which **mankind** will be
011:118 He could have made **mankind** one People:
012:021 but most among **mankind** know it not.
012:038 that (comes) of the grace of Allah to us and to **mankind**:
012:103 Yet no faith will the greater part of **mankind** have,
013:006 full of forgiveness for **mankind** for their
013:017 the good of **mankind** remains on the earth.
013:031 He could have guided all **mankind** (to the Right)?
014:001 in order that thou mightest lead **mankind** out of
014:036 led astray many among **mankind**:
014:044 So warn **mankind** of the Day when the Wrath
014:052 Here is a Message for **mankind**: that they
016:038 but most among **mankind** know it not.
017:060 thy Lord doth encompass **mankind** round about:
017:088 Say: "If the whole of **mankind** and Jinns were to
018:054 for the benefit of **mankind**, every kind
021:001 Closer and closer to **mankind** comes their Reckoning:
022:001 O **mankind**! Fear your Lord! For the convulsion
022:002 thou shalt see **mankind** as in a drunken riot,
022:005 O **mankind**! if ye have a doubt about the
022:018 and a great number among **mankind**?
022:078 and ye be witness for **mankind**!
025:037 as a Sign of **mankind**; and We
027:062 and makes you (**mankind**) inheritors of the earth?
027:073 full of grace to **mankind**: yet most
027:082 because **mankind** had no faith in Our Signs.
029:043 And such are the Parables We set forth for **mankind**,
030:030 the nature in which Allah has made **mankind**:
030:030 but most among **mankind** know not.
031:033 O **mankind**! do your duty to your Lord and fear
034:028 as a (Messenger) to all **mankind**, giving them
035:002 doth bestow on **mankind** none can withhold:
039:041 in Truth, for (instructing) **mankind**.
046:006 And when **mankind** are gathered together
049:013 O **mankind**! We created you from a single (pair)
057:025 as well as many benefits for **mankind**, that Allah
069:011 carried you (**mankind**), in the floating (Ark),
072:006 'True, there were persons among **mankind** who took
074:031 and this is no other than a Reminder to **mankind**.
074:036 A warning to **mankind**,-
083:006 A Day when (all) **mankind** will stand before
114:001 the Lord and Cherisher of **Mankind**,
114:002 The King (or Ruler) of **Mankind**,
114:003 The God (or Judge) of **Mankind**,-
114:005 Who whispers into the hearts of **Mankind**,-

MANNA

002:057 and sent down to you **manna** and quails,
007:160 and sent down to them **manna** and quails, (saying):
020:080 and We sent down to you **Manna** and quails:

MANNER

002:234 just and reasonable **manner**.
002:239 in the **manner** He has taught you,
005:004 in the **manner** directed to you by Allah:
005:095 (the Message) in the clearest **manner**.
007:027 in the same **manner** as he got your parents
007:089 nor could we by any **manner** of means return
008:052 "(Deeds) after the **manner** of the people
008:054 "(Deeds) after the **manner** of the people
012:068 in the **manner** their father had enjoined, it did
016:048 and all that in the humblest **manner**?
017:026 in the **manner** of a spendthrift.
033:004 Such is (only) your (**manner** of) speech by your mouths.
033:028 in a handsome **manner**."
033:049 and release them in a handsome **manner**.
051:052 But they said (of him) in like **manner**, "A sorcerer,

MANSION

066:011 a **mansion** in the Garden, and save

MANSIONS

009:072 and beautiful **mansions** in Gardens of everlasting
029:058 a Home in Heaven,-lofty **mansions** beneath which
039:020 their Lord, that lofty **mansions**, one above
061:012 and to beautiful **mansions** in Gardens of Eternity:

MANTLE

074:001 O thou wrapped up (in a **mantle**)!

MANY

002:026 and **many** He leads into the right path,
002:026 By it He causes **many** to stray,
002:211 how **many** Clear (Signs) We have sent them.
002:245 unto his credit and multiply **many** times?
003:144 **many** were the Messengers that passed away before Him.
003:146 How **many** of the Prophets fought (in Allah's way),
004:100 finds in the earth **many** a refuge.
004:160 and that they hindered **many** from Allah's Way;
005:032 yet, even after that, **many** of them continued
005:060 these are (**many** times) worse in rank, and far
005:062 **Many** of them dost thou see, racing each
005:066 but **many** of them follow a course that is evil.
005:071 yet again **many** of them became blind and deaf.
005:075 **many** were the Messengers that passed away
005:077 who misled **many**, and strayed themselves
005:080 Thou seest **many** of them turning in friendship
006:006 See they not how **many** of those before them
006:010 Mocked were (**many**) Messengers before thee;
006:042 (Messengers) to **many** nations, and We
006:119 But **many** do mislead (men) by low
007:004 How **many** towns have We destroyed
007:179 **Many** are the Jinns and men, We have
008:043 if He had shown them to thee as **many**, ye would
009:009 and (**many**) have they hindered from His Way:
009:025 in **many** battle-fields and on the day of Hunain:
009:034 There are indeed **many** among the priests and anchorites,
009:049 Among them is (**many**) a man who says: "Grant me
010:074 We sent (**many**) messengers to their Peoples:
010:092 But verily, **many** among mankind are heedless
011:017 yet **many** among men do not believe!
012:039 (I ask you): are **many** lords differing among themselves
012:105 And how **many** Signs in the heavens and the earth
013:006 before them, (**many**) exemplary punishments!
013:032 Mocked were (**many**) messengers before thee:
014:036 led astray **many** among mankind:
014:045 and We put forth (**many**) Parables in your behalf!"
017:017 How **many** generations have We destroyed after Noah?

MANY (continued)

019:074 But how **many** (countless) generations before them
019:098 But how **many** (countless) generation before
020:128 how **many** generations before them We destroyed,
021:011 How **many** were the towns. We utterly destroyed
021:041 Mocked were (**many**) Messengers before thee;
022:045 How **many** populations have We destroyed, which were
022:045 And how **many** wells are lying idle and neglected,
022:048 And to how **many** populations did I give respite,
023:091 (if there were **many** gods), behold, each god
025:038 and **many** a generation between them.
026:007 how **many** noble things of all kinds we have
026:018 didst thou not stay in our midst **many** years of thy life?
027:015 Who has favoured us above **many** of His servants
028:058 And how **many** towns We destroyed, which exulted
029:060 How **many** are the creatures that carry
030:008 yet are there truly **many** among men who deny
032:026 how **many** generations We destroyed before them,
036:031 See they not how **many** generations before them
037:071 And truly before them, **many** of the ancients went astray;-
038:003 How **many** generations before them did We destroy?
038:012 Before them (were **many** who) rejected messengers,-
038:024 truly **many** are the Partners (in business) who wrong
039:029 a man belonging to **many** partners at variance
041:022 that Allah knew not **many** of the things that ye
042:030 and for **many** (a sin) He grants forgiveness.
043:006 But how **many** were the prophets We sent
044:025 How **many** were the gardens and springs
047:013 And how **many** cities, with more
048:019 And **many** gains will they acquire (besides):
048:020 Allah has promised you **many** gains that ye
049:007 were he, in **many** matters, to follow your (wishes),
050:036 But how **many** generations before them did We
056:003 (**Many**) will it bring low; (**many**) will it exalt;
057:016 For **many** among them are rebellious
057:025 as well as **many** benefits for mankind, that Allah
057:026 but **many** of them became rebellious transgressors.
057:027 but **many** of them are rebellious transgressors.
065:008 How **many** populations that insolently opposed
071:024 "They have already misled **many**; and grant

MANY-SO-EVER

053:026 How **many-so-ever** be the angels in the heavens,

MARCH

044:023 "**March** forth with My servants by night: for ye
072:027 makes a band of watchers **march** before him and behind

MARCHED

041:019 they will be **marched** in ranks.

MARCHING

077:033 yellow camels (**marching** swiftly)."

MARK

002:189 Say: They are but signs to **mark** fixed periods
002:273 Thou shalt know them by their (unfailing) **mark**:
005:002 nor the garlands that **mark** out such animals,
005:097 and the garlands that **mark** them:
071:024 the wrong-doers but in straying (from their **mark**)."

MARKED

003:125 with five thousand angels clearly **marked**.
004:118 "I will take of Thy servants a portion **marked** off:
011:083 **Marked** from thy Lord; nor are they ever far
051:034 "**Marked** as from thy Lord for those who trespass

MARKETS

025:020 (men) who ate food and walked through the **markets**.

MARKS

007:046 who would know every one by his **marks**:
007:048 they will know from their **marks**, saying:
016:016 And **marks** and sign-posts; and by
047:030 and thou shouldst have known them by their **marks**:
048:029 On their faces are their **marks**, (being) the
055:041 (For) the sinners will be known by their **Marks**:

MARRIAGE

002:235 nor resolve on the tie of **marriage** till the term prescribed
002:237 by him in whose hands is the **marriage** tie;
004:005 (on **marriage**) their dower as an obligation;
004:006 until they reach the age of **marriage**;
004:023 Prohibited to you (for **marriage**) are: your mother,
004:024 provided ye seek (them in **marriage**) with
005:005 (Lawful unto you in **marriage**) are (not only)
023:006 in the **marriage** bond, or (the captives)
024:033 the wherewithal for **marriage** keep themselves
024:060 elderly women as are past the prospect of **marriage**,-
025:054 He established relationships of lineage and **marriage**:
033:037 in (the matter of) **marriage** with the wives
033:037 Then when Zaid had dissolved (his **marriage**) with her,
033:037 We joined her in **marriage** to thee: in order
033:037 the latter have dissolved (their **marriage**) with them.
060:010 the ties (**marriage** contract) of Unbelieving women:

MARRIED

002:230 until after she has **married** another husband
004:022 your fathers **married**, except what is past:
004:024 Also (prohibited are) women already **married**,
066:005 previously **married** or virgins.

MARRY

002:221 Do not **marry** unbelieving women (idolaters),
002:221 Nor **marry** (your girls) to unbelievers
004:003 **marry** women of your choice, two, or three, or four;
004:022 And **marry** not women whom your fathers married,
004:127 and yet whom ye desire to **marry**,
011:078 they are purer for you (if ye **marry**)!
015:071 "There are my daughters (to **marry**), if ye must act (so)."
024:032 **Marry** those among you who are single,
033:049 O ye who believe! when ye **marry** believing women,
033:052 It is not lawful for thee (to **marry** more) women after
033:053 or that ye should **marry** his widows after him
060:010 if ye **marry** them on payment of their dower to them.

MARRYING

002:232 from **marrying** their (former) husbands,

MARSHALLED

014:021 They will all be **marshalled** before Allah together:
014:048 and (men) will be **marshalled** forth, before Allah,
018:048 And they will be **marshalled** before thy Lord
027:017 And before Solomon were **marshalled** his hosts,-

MARTYR-WITNESSES

003:140 from your ranks **Martyr-witnesses** (to Truth).

MARTYRDOM

009:052 than one of two glorious things-(**martyrdom** or victory)?

MARTYRES

004:069 the Sincere (lovers of Truth), the **martyres**, and the

MARTYRS

003:170 the (**Martyrs**) glory in the fact that on them is no fear,
057:019 and the **martyrs**, in the eyes of their Lord:

MARUT

002:102 at Babylon to the angels Harut and **Marut**.

MARVEL

013:005 If thou dost **marvel** (at their want of faith),

MARVEL (continued)
037:012   Truly dost thou **marvel**, while they ridicule,

MARVELOUS
018:063   the sea in a **marvelous** way!"

MARWA
002:158   Behold! Safa and **Marwa** are among

MARY
002:087   We gave Jesus the son of **Mary** clear (Signs)
002:253   to Jesus the son of **Mary**, We gave Clear (Signs),
003:036   I have named her **Mary**,
003:037   He said: "O **Mary**! whence (comes) this to you?"
003:042   "O **Mary**! Allah hath chosen thee and purified thee
003:043   "O **Mary**! worship thy Lord devoutly;
003:044   should be charged with the care of **Mary**:
003:045   his name will be Christ Jesus, the son of **Mary**,
003:045   "O **Mary**! Allah giveth thee glad tidings
004:156   that they uttered against **Mary** a grave false charge;
004:157   "We killed Christ Jesus the son of **Mary**,
004:171   and His Word, which He bestowed on **Mary**,
004:171   Christ Jesus the son of **Mary** was (no more than)
005:017   to destroy Christ the son of **Mary**, his mother,
005:017   say that Allah is Christ the son of **Mary**.
005:046   We sent Jesus the son of **Mary**, confirming the Torah
005:072   "Allah is Christ the son of **Mary**."
005:075   Christ the son of **Mary** was no more
005:078   and of Jesus the son of **Mary**: because they
005:110   "O Jesus the son of **Mary**! recount my favour
005:112   "O Jesus the son of **Mary**! Can thy Lord
005:114   Said Jesus the son of **Mary**: "O Allah
005:116   "O Jesus the son of **Mary**! didst thou say unto men,
009:031   And (they take as their Lord) Christ the son of **Mary**;
019:016   Relate in the Book (the story of) **Mary**, when she
019:027   "O **Mary**! truly a strange thing hast thou brought!
019:034   Such (was) Jesus the son of **Mary**: (it is)
023:050   And We made the son of **Mary** and his mother
033:007   Moses, and Jesus the son of **Mary**: We took
043:057   When (Jesus) the son of **Mary** is held up as·an
057:027   son of **Mary**, and bestowed on him the Gospel;
061:006   And remember, Jesus, the son of **Mary**, said:
061:014   as said Jesus, the son of **Mary**, to the
066:012   And **Mary** the daughter of 'Imran, who guarded

MASS
026:063   became like the huge, firm **mass** of a mountain.

MASSES
024:043   mountain **masses** (of clouds) wherein is hail:

MASTER
001:004   **Master** of the Day of Judgment.
016:076   a wearisome burden is he to his **master**; whichever way
039:029   and a man belonging entirely to one **master**:

MASTERY
003:139   for ye must gain **mastery** if ye are true in Faith.
008:057   If ye gain the **mastery** over them in war,

MATCH
020:058   "But we can surely produce magic to **match** thine!
038:058   And other Penalties of a similar kind, to **match** them!

MATE
004:001   created, out of it, his **mate**, and from them
007:189   and made his **mate** of like nature, in order
039:006   of like nature, his **mate**;

MATERIAL
003:117   life of this (**material**) world may be likened
028:060   The (**material**) things which ye are given are but

MATERNAL
033:050   of thy **maternal** uncles and aunts, who migrated with

MATES
009:024   your sons, your brothers, your **mates**, or your
016:072   And Allah has made for you **mates** of your own
026:166   has created for you to be your **mates**?
030:021   that He created for you **mates** from among
056:037   Full of love (for their **mates**), equal in age,-

MATTER
002:065   in the **matter** of the Sabbath:
002:117   when He decreeth a **matter** He saith to it:
003:047   when He hath decreed a **matter**,
003:061   If any one disputes in this manner with thee,
003:186   then that indeed is a **matter** of great Resolution.
004:083   some **matter** touching (public) safety or fear,
004:154   "Transgress not in the **matter** of the Sabbath."
005:094   make a trial of you in a little **matter** of game
006:008   the **matter** would be settled at once, and no
006:009   caused them confusion in a **matter** which they have
006:058   the **matter** would be settled at once
006:105   We may make the **matter** clear to those who know.
007:163   Behold! they transgressed in the **matter** of the Sabbath,
008:038   is already (a **matter** of warning for them).
008:042   that Allah might accomplish a **matter** already decided;
008:044   that Allah might accomplish a **matter** already decided
009:038   O ye who believe! what is the **matter** with you,
009:040   If ye help not (the Prophet), (it is no **matter**):
009:058   slander thee in the **matter** of (the distribution of) the
010:002   Is it a **matter** of wonderment to men that We
010:035   What then is the **matter** with you? How judge ye?
010:047   the **matter** will be judged between them with justice,
011:044   And the water abated, and the **matter** was ended.
011:110   the **matter** would have been decided between them:
012:041   (So) hath been decreed that **matter** whereof ye
012:050   "What was the **matter** with the ladies who cut their
014:020   Nor is that for Allah any great **matter**.
014:022   And Satan will say when the **matter** is decided:
016:077   And the **matter** of the Hour (of Judgment) is as
017:033   in the **matter** of taking life:
017:051   "Or any created **matter** which, in your minds,
017:086   thy affair in that **matter** as against Us,-
018:022   except on a **matter** that is clear, nor consult
019:021   it is a **matter** (so) decreed."
019:035   When He determines a **matter**, He only says
019:039   when the **matter** will be determined: for (behold),
020:007   If thou pronounce the word aloud, (it is no **matter**):
021:078   when they gave judgment in the **matter** of the field into
021:079   the (right) understanding of the **matter**:
022:067   let them not dispute with thee on the **matter**, but do thou
024:002   in a **matter** prescribed by Allah, if ye believe in Allah
024:015   and ye thought it to be a light **matter**, while it was most
024:062   a **matter** requiring collective action,
026:050   They said: "No **matter**! for us, we shall
028:023   He said: "What is the **matter** with you?" They said:
028:068   no choice have they (in the **matter**): Glory to Allah!
033:036   man or woman, when a **matter** has been decided
033:037   in (the **matter** of) marriage with the wives
034:026   the **matter** between us (and you) in truth
037:025   "'What is the **matter** with you that ye
037:092   "What is the **matter** with you that ye
037:154   What is the **matter** with you? How judge ye?
040:057   and the earth is a greater (**matter**) than the
040:078   the **matter** was decided in truth and justice,

MATTER (continued)

041:038 but if the (Unbelievers) are arrogant, (no **matter**):
042:014 the **matter** would have been settled between them:
042:021 the **matter** would have been decided between them
047:021 and when a **matter** is resolved on, it were best for them
047:026 "We will obey you in part of (this) **matter**";
054:003 but every **matter** has its appointed time.
054:053 Every **matter**, small and great, is on record.
060:012 and that they will nor disobey thee in any just **matter**,-
066:003 When the Prophet disclosed a **matter** in confidence
068:036 What is the **matter** with you? How judge ye?
070:036 Now what is the **matter** with the Unbelievers
070:039 out of the (base **matter**) they know!
071:013 "'What is the **matter** with you, the ye are not conscious
074:049 Then what is the **matter** with them that they
084:020 What then is the **matter** with them, that they
099:003 'What is the **matter** with her?'-

MATTERS

002:213 in **matters** wherein they differed;
003:055 between you of the **matters** wherein ye dispute.
003:066 to disputing (even) in **matters** of which ye had
003:066 in **matters** of which ye have no knowledge?
003:109 to Allah do all **matters** return.
005:048 the truth of the **matters** in which ye dispute;
007:145 in the Tablets in all **matters**, Admonition
008:044 and unto Allah are all **matters** returned.
009:048 and upset **matters** for thee,-until
009:094 the true state of **matters** concerning you: it is
022:069 concerning the **matters** in which ye differ."
027:076 the **matters** in which they disagree.
032:025 in the **matters** wherein they differ (among themselves).
038:069 discuss (**matters**) among themselves.
039:046 in those **matters** about which they have differed."
045:017 as to those **matters** in which they set up differences.
049:007 in many **matters**, to follow your (wishes),
057:023 over **matters** that pass you by, nor exult

MATURITY

003:046 in childhood and in **maturity**.

MAY

002:021 that ye **may** become righteous,
002:063 perchance ye **may** fear Allah."
002:073 perchance ye **may** understand.
002:076 that they **may** engage you in argument
002:150 and that I **may** complete My favours on you,
002:150 and ye **may** (consent to) be guided.
002:179 that ye **may** restrain yourselves.
002:183 that ye **may** (learn) self-restraint.
002:186 that they **may** walk in the right way.
002:187 that they **may** learn self-restraint.
002:188 with intent that ye **may** eat up wrongfully
002:189 and fear Allah: that ye **may** prosper.
002:196 such as ye **may** find,
002:204 life **may** dazzle thee,
002:219 His Signs: in order that ye **may** consider-
002:221 that they **may** receive admonition.
002:222 ye **may** approach them as ordained for you
002:239 or riding, (as **may** be most convenient),
002:242 in order that ye **may** understand.
002:246 that we **may** fight in the cause of Allah."
002:259 and that We **may** make of thee a Sign
002:266 clear to you (His) Signs; that ye **may** consider.
002:267 out of it ye **may** give away something,
002:283 a pledge with possession (**may** serve the purpose).

MAY (continued)

003:028 that ye **may** guard yourselves from them.
003:072 perchance they **may** (themselves) turn back;
003:103 that ye **may** be guided.
003:117 life of this (material) world **may** be likened
003:123 then fear Allah; thus **may** ye show your gratitude.
003:130 that ye **may** (really) prosper.
003:132 that ye **may** obtain mercy.
003:140 that Allah **may** know those that believe,
003:140 and that He **may** take to Himself from your ranks
003:147 and anything we **may** have done that transgressed
003:156 This that Allah **may** make it a cause of sighs
003:178 that they **may** grow in their iniquity:
003:200 and fear Allah; that ye **may** prosper.
004:019 that ye **may** take away part of the dower
004:019 it **may** be that ye dislike a thing,
004:025 they **may** wed believing girls from among those
004:046 "We hear and we disobey"; and "Here, **may** you not hear";
004:056 that they **may** taste the Chastisement:
004:084 It **may** be that Allah will restrain
004:101 for fear the Unbelievers **may** attack you:
004:109 whose behalf ye **may** contend in this world;
005:002 the state of pilgrimage, ye **may** hunt, and let not
005:006 that ye **may** be grateful.
005:035 and main in His cause: that ye **may** prosper.
005:089 that ye **may** be grateful.
005:090 eschew such (abomination), that ye **may** prosper.
005:094 that He **may** test who feareth Him unseen:
005:095 that he **may** taste of the penalty of his deed.
005:097 that ye **may** know that Allah hath knowledge of what
005:100 O ye that understand that (so) ye **may** prosper."
005:100 of the bad **may** dazzle thee;
005:101 about things which, if made plan to **may** cause you trouble.
005:108 that they **may** give the evidence in its true
005:113 and that we ourselves **may** be witnesses
005:114 that there **may** be for us-for the first
006:019 that I **may** warn you and all whom it reaches.
006:051 that they **may** guard (against evil).
006:055 that the way of the sinners **may** be shown up.
006:065 that they **may** understand.
006:069 that they **may** (learn to) fear Allah.
006:097 that ye **may** guide yourselves, with their
006:105 they **may** say, "Thou hast learnt this (from somebody),
006:105 We **may** make the matter clear to those who know.
006:113 and let them earn from it what they **may**.
006:151 thus doth He command you, that ye **may** learn wisdom.
006:152 thus doth He command you, that ye **may** remember.
006:153 thus doth He command you, that ye **may** be righteous.
006:155 that ye **may** receive mercy:
006:165 that He **may** try you in the
007:026 that they **may** receive admonition!
007:057 perchance ye **may** remember.
007:063 to warn you,-so that ye **may** fear Allah
007:069 that so ye **may** prosper."
007:070 that we **may** worship Allah alone, and give up
007:129 that so He **may** see how ye act."
007:129 He said: "It **may** be that your Lord will destroy
007:143 that I **may** look upon Thee." Allah said: "By no
007:158 follow him that (so) ye **may** be guided."
007:164 and perchance they **may** fear Him."
007:171 what is therein; perchance ye **may** fear Allah".
007:174 and perchance they **may** turn (Unto Us).
007:176 so relate the story; perchance they **may** reflect.

MAY (continued)

007:185 (Do they not see) that it **may** well be that their term is
007:204 and hold your peace: that ye **may** receive Mercy.
008:037 In order that Allah **may** separate the impure
008:041 that ye **may** acquire (in war), a fifth share
008:045 much (and often); that ye **may** prosper.
008:057 those who follow them, that they **may** remember.
008:060 and others besides, whom ye **may** not know,
009:006 so that he **may** hear the Word of Allah; and then
009:012 that thus they **may** be restrained.
009:032 even though the Unbelievers **may** detest (it).
009:033 the Pagans **may** detest (it).
009:055 and that their souls **may** perish in their (very) denial
009:085 and that their souls **may** depart while they
009:095 that ye **may** leave them alone.
009:096 that ye **may** be pleased with them.
009:121 that Allah **may** requite them with the best
009:122 that thus they (**may** learn) to guard
010:004 that He **may** reward with justice those who
010:061 and whatever deed ye (mankind) **may** be doing,-
010:067 the Night that ye **may** rest therein, and the Day
010:078 that thou and thy brother **may** have greatness in the land?
010:082 however much the Sinners **may** hate it!"
011:003 that He **may** grant you enjoyment,
011:005 that they **may** lie hid from Him!
011:013 Or they **may** say, "He forged it." Say, "Bring ye
011:024 These two kinds (of men) **may** be compared to the blind
011:054 some of our gods **may** have seized thee with evil."
012:002 in order that ye **may** learn wisdom.
012:009 of your father **may** be given to you alone:
012:021 **may** be he will bring us much good,
012:018 made up a tale (that **may** pass) with you, (for me)
012:046 that I **may** return to the people, and that they **may** know."
012:052 in order that he **may** know that I have never been false
012:063 that we **may** get our measure;
012:083 **May** be Allah will bring them (back)
013:002 that ye **may** believe with certainty in the
014:010 in order that He **may** forgive you your sins
014:012 all the hurt you **may** cause us.
014:025 in order that they **may** receive admonition.
014:031 that they **may** establish regular prayers, and spend
014:032 subject to you, that they **may** sail through the
014:037 so that they **may** give thanks.
014:037 O our Lord! that they **may** establish regular prayer:
014:051 That Allah **may** requite each soul
014:052 and **may** know that He is One God: let men
014:052 that they **may** take warning therefrom,
016:014 and that ye **may** extract therefrom ornaments
016:014 that ye **may** eat thereof flesh that is
016:014 and that ye **may** be grateful.
016:014 that plough the waves, that ye **may** seek (thus)
016:015 that ye **may** guide yourselves;
016:025 That they **may** bear, on the Day of Judgment,
016:039 the rejecters of Truth **may** realize that they were liars.
016:039 He **may** manifest to them the truth of that
016:044 and that they **may** give thought.
016:046 Or that He **may** not call them to account in the
016:047 Or that He **may** not call them to account by a
016:078 that ye **may** give thanks (to Allah).
016:081 on you, that ye **may** surrender to His Will
016:090 that ye **may** receive admonition.
016:094 and ye **may** have to taste the evil (consequences)
016:094 the result that someone's foot **may** slip after it was firmly

MAY (continued)

016:116 for any false thing that your tongues **may** put forth,
017:008 It **may** be that your Lord **may** (yet) show Mercy
017:012 and that ye **may** know the number and count of the years:
017:012 Day We have made bright that ye **may** seek bounty from
017:041 in order that they **may** receive admonition,
017:066 in order that ye **may** seek of His Bounty.
018:002 and that He **may** give Glad Tidings to the
018:002 in order that He **may** warn (the godless) of a
018:004 Further, that He **may** warn those (also) who say,
018:007 in order that We **may** test them-as to which
018:019 to you, (that ye **may** satisfy your hunger therewith)
018:040 "It **may** be that my Lord will give me something
018:066 Moses said to him: "**May** I follow thee, on the
018:096 he said: "Bring me, that I **may** pour over it,
020:023 "In order that We **may** show thee of
020:028 "So they **may** understand what I say:
020:033 "That we **may** celebrate Thy praise without stint,
020:044 perchance he **may** take warning or fear (Allah)."
020:073 have believed in our Lord: **may** He forgive us our faults,
020:113 or that it **may** cause their remembrance (of Him).
020:113 in order that they **may** fear Allah, or that
020:130 and at the sides of the day: that thou **may** be pleased.
021:013 in order that ye **may** be called to account.
021:031 that they **may** find their way.
021:040 Nay, it **may** come to them all of a sudden
021:061 that they **may** bear witness:"
021:111 "I know not but that it **may** be a trial for you,
022:005 in order that We **may** manifest (Our Power) to you;
022:005 (foster you) that ye **may** reach your age of full strength;
022:028 "That they **may** witness the benefits (provided)
022:036 We made animals subject to you, that ye **may** be grateful.
022:037 that ye **may** glorify Allah for His guidance to you:
022:046 so that their hearts (and mind) **may** thus learn wisdom
022:046 and their ears **may** thus learn to hear?
022:053 That He **may** make the suggestions thrown in
022:054 and their hearts **may** be made humbly (open)
022:054 and that they **may** believe therein,
022:054 has been bestowed **may** learn that the (Qur'an)
022:077 and do good; that ye **may** prosper.
022:078 that the Messenger **may** be a witness for you,
023:100 "In order that I **may** work righteousness in the
024:001 in order that ye **may** receive admonition.
024:017 that ye **may** never repeat such (conduct), if ye
024:027 in order that ye **may** heed (what is seemly).
024:031 that ye **may** be successful.
024:033 desire chastity, in order that ye **may** make a gain
024:038 That Allah **may** reward them according to the
024:048 in order that He **may** judge between them, behold,
024:051 He **may** judge between them,
024:056 that ye **may** receive mercy.
024:061 that ye **may** understand.
025:001 that it **may** be an admonition to all creatures;-
025:032 that We **may** strengthen thy heart thereby,
025:049 That with it We **may** give life to a dead land,
025:050 amongst them, in order that they **may** be mindful
025:057 each one who will **may** take a (straight) Path to his Lord."
026:003 It **may** be thou will kill thy self with grief,
026:014 of crime against me; and I fear they **may** slay me."
026:040 "That we **may** follow the sorcerers if they win?"
027:007 that ye **may** warm yourselves."
027:019 and that I **may** work the righteousness that will
027:019 so order me that I **may** be grateful for Thy favours,

MAY (continued)

027:039   the purpose, and **may** be trusted."
027:046   ye **may** hope to receive mercy."
027:072   Say: "It **may** be that some of the events
027:072   hasten on **may** be (close) in your pursuit!
028:009   It **may** be that he will be of use to us, or we
028:009   or we **may** adopt him as a son."
028:025   he **may** reward thee for having watered (our
028:029   burning firebrand, that ye **may** warm yourselves."
028:034   for I fear that they **may** accuse me of falsehood."
028:038   that I **may** mount up to the god of Moses:
028:046   in order that they **may** receive admonition.
028:049   a better Guide than either of them, that I **may** follow it!
028:051   in order that they **may** receive admonition.
028:073   made for you Night and Day,-that ye **may** rest therein,
028:073   and that ye **may** seek of His Grace;-
028:073   and in order that ye **may** be grateful.
030:021   that ye **may** dwell in tranquillity with them,
030:041   in order that they **may** turn back (from Evil).
030:041   that (Allah) **may** give them a taste of some
030:045   That He **may** reward those who believe and work
030:046   that the ships **may** sail by His Command and that
030:046   in order that ye **may** be grateful.
030:046   and that ye **may** seek of His Bounty:
031:031   that He **may** show you of His Signs?
032:003   in order that they **may** be rightly guided.
032:021   they **may** (repent and) return.
033:008   That (Allah) **may** question the Truthful about their
033:024   That Allah **may** reward the men of Truth
033:037   in order that (in future) there **may** be no difficulty to the
033:043   that He **may** bring you out from the depths
033:071   That He **may** make your conduct whole and sound
034:004   That He **may** reward those who believe and work
034:046   (it **may** be) in pairs, or (it **may** be) singly,-
035:006   that they **may** become Companions of the Blazing Fire.
035:012   that ye **may** seek (thus) of the Bounty of Allah
035:012   of Allah that ye **may** be grateful.
036:035   That they **may** enjoy the fruits of this
036:045   in order that ye **may** receive Mercy," (they turn back).
036:070   and that the word **may** be proved true against those who
036:070   That it **may** give admonition to any (who are) alive,
038:029   and that men of understanding **may** receive admonition.
038:029   that they **may** meditate on its Signs, and that
039:003   they **may** bring us nearer to Allah."
039:027   in order that they **may** receive admonition.
039:028   in order that they **may** guard against Evil.
040:014   even though the Unbelievers **may** detest it.
040:015   that it **may** warn (men) of the Day
040:036   a lofty palace, that I **may** attain the ways
040:037   and that I **may** look up to the God of Moses:
040:061   Who has made the Night for you, that ye **may** rest therein,
040:067   a Term appointed: in order that ye **may** understand.
040:079   that ye **may** use some for riding and some for food;
040:080   that ye **may** through them attain to any need
040:080   to any need (there **may** be) in your hearts;
041:026   that ye **may** gain the upper hand!"
043:003   that ye **may** be able to understand.
043:010   in order that ye **may** find guidance (on the way);
043:013   In order that ye **may** sit firm and square
043:013   ye **may** remember the (kind) favour of your Lord,
043:028   that they **may** turn back (to Allah).
043:032   so that some **may** command work from others.
044:058   in thy tongue, in order that they **may** give heed.

MAY (continued)

045:010   nor any protectors they **may** have taken to themselves
045:010   and of no profit to them is anything they **may** have earned,
045:012   ye **may** seek of His Bounty, and that ye **may** be grateful.
045:012   that ship **may** sail through it by His command,
045:022   each soul **may** find the recompense of what it has earned,
046:004   or any remnant of knowledge (ye **may** have),
046:015   and that I **may** work righteousness such as Thou
046:015   grant me that I **may** be grateful for Thy favour
046:019   (Allah) **may** recompense their deeds;
046:027   the Signs in various ways, that they **may** turn (to Us).
048:002   That Allah **may** forgive thee thy faults of the
048:003   And that Allah **may** help thee with powerful help.
048:004   that they **may** add Faith to their Faith;-
048:005   That He **may** admit the men and women who believe,
048:006   And that He **may** punish the Hypocrites,
048:009   In order that ye (O men) **may** believe in Allah and His
048:009   that ye **may** assist and honor him, and celebrate
048:020   that is **may** be a Sign for the Believers,
048:020   and that He **may** guide you to a Straight Path;
048:025   that He **may** admit to His mercy whom He will.
049:002   as ye **may** speak aloud to one another,
049:010   And fear Allah, that ye **may** receive Mercy.
049:011   it **may** be that the (latter) are better than the (former):
049:011   it **may** be that the (latter) are better than the (former):
049:013   you into nations and tribes, that ye **may** know each other
049:013   know each other (not that ye **may** despise each other).
051:049   that ye **may** receive instruction.
051:056   that they **may** serve Me.
055:008   In order that ye **may** not transgress (due) balance.
056:020   And with fruits, any that they **may** select;
056:021   And the flesh of fowls, any that they **may** desire.
057:004   And He is with you wherever ye **may** be.
057:009   that He **may** lead you from the depths
057:017   plainly to you, that ye **may** understand.
057:023   In order that ye **may** not despair over matters
057:025   that Allah **may** test who it is that will help,
057:025   that men **may** stand forth in justice;
057:029   That the People of the Book **may** know that they
058:004   This, that ye **may** show your faith in Allah and His
058:010   by Satan, in order that he **may** cause grief to the
059:007   in order that it **may** not (Merely) make a circuit
059:021   which We propound to men, that they **may** reflect.
060:007   It **may** be that Allah will Establish friendship
061:008   even though the Unbelievers **may** detest (it).
061:009   even though the Pagans **may** detest (it).
062:010   and remember Allah frequently that ye **may** prosper.
062:010   then **may** ye disperse through the land, and seek
064:015   Your riches and your children **may** be but a trial:
065:011   clear explanations, that he **may** lead forth those
065:012   that ye **may** know that Allah has power
066:005   It **may** be, if he divorced you (all), that Allah
067:002   that He **may** try which of you is best in deed:
068:032   "It **may** be that our Lord will give us in exchange
071:004   "So He **may** forgive you your sins and give you
071:020   That ye **may** go about therein, in spacious roads."
072:028   "That he **may** know that they have (truly) brought
073:020   that there **may** be (some) among you in ill-health;
073:020   therefore, as much of the Qur'an as **may** be easy (for you);
073:020   therefore, of the Qur'an as much as **may** be easy for you.
074:031   that the People of the Book **may** arrive at certainty,
074:031   and that no doubts **may** be left for the People
074:031   and the Believers **may** increase in Faith,-

MAY (continued)

074:031 and the Unbelievers **may** say, "What doth Allah intend
078:015 That We **may** produce therewith grain and vegetables,
090:006 He **may** say (boastfully): "Wealth have I squandered in

MAYBE

017:051 Say, "**Maybe** it will be quite soon!

MAYEST

006:092 that thou **mayest** warn the Mother
010:061 In whatever business thou **mayest** be, and whatever
010:061 and whatever portion thou **mayest** be reciting
010:092 that thou **mayest** be a Sign to those
011:012 Perchance thou **mayest** (feel the inclination)
016:044 that thou **mayest** explain clearly to men
019:097 that with it thou **mayest** give glad tidings
020:039 in order that thou **mayest** be reared under Mine eye.
026:194 To thy heart and mind that thou **mayest** admonish
032:003 that thou **mayest** admonish a people to whom
033:051 Thou **mayest** defer (the turn of) any of them
033:051 and thou **mayest** receive any thou pleasest:
036:006 In order that thou **mayest** warn a people,
042:007 that thou **mayest** warn the Mother of Cities
046:015 such as Thou **mayest** approve; and be

MAZES

040:050 in (**mazes** of) error!"

ME

002:031 and said: "Tell **Me** the names of these
002:038 there comes to you guidance from **Me**,
002:040 and fulfil your Covenant with **Me**
002:040 and fear none but **Me**.
002:041 and fear **Me**, and **Me** alone.
002:067 He said: "Allah save **me** from being
002:131 "Submit (thy will to **Me**):"
002:132 in the state of submission (to **Me**).
002:133 "What will ye worship after **me**?"
002:150 so fear them not, but fear **Me**;
002:152 Then do ye remember **Me**; I will remember you.
002:152 Be grateful to **Me**, and reject not Faith.
002:186 of every suppliant when he calleth on **Me**:
002:186 When My servants ask thee concerning **Me**,
002:186 listen to My call, and believe in **Me**:
002:197 So fear **Me**, O ye that are wise.
002:249 only those who taste not of it go with **me**;
002:260 "My Lord! show **me** how thou givest life to the dead.
003:020 to Allah and so have those who follow **me**."
003:031 Say: "If ye do love Allah, follow **me**:
003:035 so accept this of **me**: for Thou hearest and knowest
003:038 Grant unto **me** from Thee a progeny that is pure:
003:041 He said: "O my Lord! Give **me** a Sign!"
003:047 how shall I have a son when man hath touched **Me**?"
003:050 So fear Allah, and obey **me**.
003:050 to attest the Torah which was before **me**.
003:055 then shall ye all return to **Me**,
003:175 but fear **Me**, if ye have Faith.
003:183 Say: "There came to you Messengers before **me**,
005:003 yet fear them not but fear **Me**.
005:028 "If thou dost stretch thy hand against **me**, to slay **me**,
005:028 it is not for **me** to stretch my hand against thee to slay
005:029 "For **me**, I intend to let thee draw on thyself
005:031 "Woe is **me**!" said he: "Was I not even able
005:044 therefore fear not men, but fear **Me**, and sell not
005:111 to have faith in **Me** and Mine Messenger: they said
005:116 say unto men, "Take **me** and my mother for two
005:117 when Thou didst take **me** up, thou wast

ME (continued)

005:117 except what Thou didst command **me** to say, to wit,
006:019 Say: "Allah is Witness between **me** and you:
006:019 revealed to **me** by inspiration that I may
006:050 nor do I but follow what is revealed to **me**."
006:050 with **me** are the treasures of Allah,
006:057 Say: "For **me**, I (work) on a clear Sign
006:058 the matter would be settled at once between you and **me**.
006:077 "Unless my Lord guide **me**, I shall surely be among those
006:079 "For **me**, I have set my face, firmly and truly, towards
006:080 He said: "(Come) ye to dispute with **me**, about Allah,
006:080 when He (Himself) hath guided **me**? I
006:081 (Tell **me**) if you know.
006:143 Tell **me** with knowledge if ye are truthful:
006:145 received by **me** by inspiration any (meat)
006:161 guided **me** to a way that is straight,-a religion
007:012 thou didst create **me** from fire and him from clay."
007:014 He said: "Give **me** respite till the day
007:016 thrown **me** out (of the Way),
007:061 He said: "O my people! there is no error in **me**:
007:067 there is no folly in **me**" but (I am)
007:071 dispute ye with **me** over names
007:105 so let the children of Israel depart along with **me**."
007:142 "Act for **me** amongst my people: do right,
007:143 He said: "O my Lord! show (Thyself) to **me**,
007:143 "By no means canst thou see **Me** (direct);
007:143 if it abide in its place, then shalt thou see **Me**."
007:150 nor count thou **me** amongst the people of sin."
007:150 The people did indeed reckon **me** as naught,
007:150 and went near to slaying **me**!
007:151 forgive **me** and my brother!
007:155 long before, both them and **me**:
007:188 and no evil should have touched **me**:
007:195 scheme (your worst) against **me**, and give **me** no respite!
007:203 is revealed to **me** from my Lord:
009:049 "Grant **me** exemption and draw **me** not into trial."
009:083 say: "Never shall ye come out with **me**, nor fight
009:083 nor fight an enemy with **me**:
009:129 Say: "Allah sufficeth **me**: there is no god
010:015 Say: "It is not for **me**, of my own
010:015 I follow naught but what is revealed unto **me**:
010:041 say: "My work to **me**, and yours to you!
010:071 Then pass your sentence on **me**, and give **me** no respite.
010:079 Said Pharaoh: "Bring **me** every sorcerer well versed."
011:010 "All evil has departed from **me**:" behold! he
011:028 and that He hath sent Mercy unto **me** from Him,
011:030 help **me** against Allah if I drove them away?
011:031 "I tell you not that with **me** are the Treasures
011:035 Say: "If I had forged it, on **me** were my sin!
011:037 and address **Me** no (further) on behalf
011:043 to some mountain: it will save **me** from the water."
011:046 So ask not of **Me** that of which thou hast
011:047 and unless Thou forgive **me** and have
011:047 and have Mercy on **me**, I should indeed
011:051 My reward is from none but Him who created **Me**:
011:055 So scheme (your worst) against **me**, all of you,
011:055 all of you, and give **me** no respite.
011:063 who then can help **me** against Allah if I were to disobey
011:063 and He hath sent Mercy unto **me** from Himself,-
011:072 She said: "Alas for **me**! Shall I bear a child,
011:078 and cover **me** not with shame about my guests!
011:088 and He hath given **me** sustenance (pure and)
012:004 I saw them prostrate themselves to **me**!"

ME (continued)

012:013 (Jacob) said: "Really it saddens **me** that ye
012:018 (For **me**) patience is most fitting: against that
012:026 seduce **me**-from my (true) self."
012:032 the man about whom ye did blame **me**!
012:033 unless Thou turn away their snare from **me**, I should feel
012:033 is dearer to my liking than that to which they invite **me**:
012:037 part of the (Duty) which my Lord hath taught **me** I have
012:042 he said: "Mention **me** to thy lord."
012:043 O ye chiefs! expound to **me** my vision if it be
012:045 of its interpretation: send ye **me** (therefore)."
012:050 So the king said: "Bring ye him unto **me**."
012:054 So the king said: "Bring him unto **me**; I will take
012:055 (Joseph) said: "Set **me** over the store-houses
012:059 he said: "Bring unto **me** a brother ye have,
012:060 ye shall have no measure (of corn) from **me**,
012:060 "Now if ye bring him not to **me**, ye shall
012:060 nor shall ye (even) come near **me**."
012:066 send him with you until ye swear a solemn oath to **me**,
012:066 you will be sure to bring him back to **me** unless ye are
012:080 until my father permits **me**, or Allah judges for **me**;
012:083 Allah will bring them (back) all to **me** (in the end).
012:083 So patience is most fitting (for **me**).
012:093 Then come ye (here) to **me** together with
012:094 nay, think **me** not a dotard."
012:100 sown enmity between **me** and my brothers.
012:100 He took **me** out of prison and brought
012:100 He was indeed good to **me** when He took
012:101 (as a Muslim), and unite **me** with the righteous."
012:101 and taught **me** something of the interpretation of
012:101 Thou hast indeed bestowed on **me** some power,
012:108 I and whoever follows **me**.
013:043 between **me** and you is Allah,
014:022 I reject your former act in associating **me** with Allah.
014:022 then reproach not **me**, but reproach your own souls,
014:022 over you except to call you, but ye listened to **me**;
014:035 and preserve **me** and my sons from worshipping idols.
014:036 and he that disobeys **me**,-but thou
014:036 he then who follows my (ways) is of **me**,
014:039 unto **me** in old age Isma'il and Isaac: for truly
014:040 "O my Lord! make **me** one who establishes
014:041 Thy Forgiveness-**me**, my parents and (all)
015:036 (Iblis) said: "O my Lord! give **me** then respite
015:039 because Thou hast put **me** in the wrong, I will
015:041 (Allah) said: "This is for **me** a straight path.
015:054 He said: "Do ye give **me** such glad tidings even though
015:054 even though old age has seized **me**?
015:068 Lut said: "These are my guests: disgrace **me** not:
015:069 "But fear Allah, and shame **me** not."
016:002 so do your duty unto **Me**."
016:051 then fear **Me** (and **Me** alone)."
017:002 "Take not other than **Me** as Disposer
017:024 even as they cherished **me** in childhood."
017:062 one whom thou hast honoured above **me**!
017:062 If Thou wilt but respite **me** to the Day
017:080 and grant **me** from Thee an authority to aid (**me**)."
017:096 "Enough is Allah for a witness between **me** and you:
018:024 "I hope that my Lord will guide **me** ever closer
018:039 If thou dost see **me** less than thee in wealth and sons,
018:040 my Lord will give **me** something better than thy garden,
018:042 and he could only say, "Woe is **me**! Would I had
018:050 take him and his progeny as protectors rather than **Me**?
018:051 nor is it for **Me** to take as helpers

ME (continued)

018:063 none but Satan made **me** forget to tell (you)
018:066 thou teach **me** something of the (Higher) Truth which
018:067 be able to have patience with **me**!
018:069 Moses said: "Thou wilt find **me**, if Allah
018:070 follow **me**, ask **me** no questions about anything
018:072 thou canst have no patience with **me**?"
018:073 Moses said: "Rebuke **me** not for forgetting,
018:073 nor grieve **me** by raising difficulties in my case."
018:075 thou canst have no patience with **me**?"
018:076 about anything after this, keep **me** not in thy company:
018:078 "This is the parting between **me** and thee:
018:095 help **me** therefore with strength (and labour):
018:095 "(The power) in which my Lord has established **me** is
018:096 he said: "Bring **me**, that I may pour over it,
018:096 "Bring **me** blocks of iron."
018:101 a veil from Remembrance of **Me**, and who
018:102 that they can take My servants as protectors besides **Me**?
018:110 (but) the inspiration has come to **me**, that your
019:005 (and colleagues) (will do) after **me**: but my
019:005 so give **me** an heir as from Thyself,-
019:006 "(One that) will (truly) inherit **me**, and inherit
019:009 thy Lord saith, "That is easy for **Me**: I did
019:010 (Zakariya) said "O my Lord! give **me** a Sign,"
019:020 seeing that no man has touched **me**, and I am
019:021 thy Lord saith, 'That is easy for **Me**:
019:030 He hath given **me** revelation and made **me** a prophet:
019:031 on **me** Prayer and Charity as long as I live;
019:031 "And He hath made **me** Blessed wheresoever I be,
019:032 "(He) hath made **me** kind to my mother, and not
019:033 "So Peace is on **me** the day I was born, the day
019:043 so follow **me**: I will guide thee to a Way that
019:043 "O my father! to **me** hath come knowledge which
019:046 now get away from **me** for a good long while!"
019:047 for He is to **me** Most Gracious.
020:014 so serve thou **Me** (only), and establish
020:025 (Moses) said: "O my Lord! expand **me** my breast;"
020:026 "Ease my task for **me**;
020:029 "And give **me** a Minister from my family,
020:039 up by one who is an enemy to **Me** and an enemy to him':
020:039 but I endued thee with love from **Me**:
020:042 either of you, in keeping **Me** in remembrance.
020:086 and so ye broke your promise to **me**?"
020:090 so follow **me** and obey my command."
020:093 "From following **me**? Didst thou then disobey me order?"
020:094 Seize (**me**) not by my beard nor by
020:096 thus did my soul suggest to **me**."
020:097 'Touch **me** not'; and moreover (for a future penalty) thou
020:114 "O my Lord! increase **me** in knowledge."
020:123 As is sure, there comes to you guidance from **Me**,
020:125 why hast thou raised **me** up blind, while I
021:024 and the Message of those before **me**."
021:024 this is the Message of those with **me** and the
021:025 therefore worship and serve **Me**.
021:037 so ask **Me** not to hasten them!
021:083 He cried to his Lord "Truly distress has seized **me**,
021:089 "O my Lord! leave **me** not without offspring,
021:092 therefore serve **Me** (and no other).
021:108 Say: "What has come to **me** by inspiration
022:026 (saying) "Associate not anything (in worship) with **Me**;
022:048 To **Me** is the destination (of all).
023:026 (Noah) said: "O my Lord! help **me**: for that
023:026 for that they accuse **me** of falsehood!

ME (continued)

023:027 and address **Me** not in favour of the wrong-doers:
023:029 enable **me** to disembark with Thy blessing:
023:039 for that they accuse **me** of falsehood."
023:039 (The prophet) said: "O my Lord! help **me**: for that
023:052 therefore fear **Me** (and no other).
023:093 Say: "O my Lord! if Thou wilt show **me** (in my lifetime)
023:094 "Then, O my Lord! put **me** not amongst the people who
023:098 O my Lord! lest they should come near **me**."
023:099 he says: "O my Lord! send **me** back to (life),-
023:108 and speak ye not to **Me**!
024:055 'They will worship **Me** (along) and not
024:055 and not associate aught with **Me**.'
025:028 "Ah! woe is **me**! would that I had never taken
025:029 Message (of Allah) after it had come to **me**!
025:029 "He did lead **me** astray from the Message (of Allah)
026:012 I do fear that they will charge **me** with falsehood:
026:014 of crime against **me**; and I fear they may slay **me**."
026:021 invested **me** with judgment (and wisdom) and
026:021 and appointed **me** as one of the messengers.
026:022 this is the favour with which thou dost reproach **me**,-)
026:029 (Pharaoh) said: "If thou takest any god other than **me**,
026:062 (Moses) said: "By no means! my Lord is with **me**!
026:062 Soon will He guide **me**!
026:077 "For they are enemies to **me**;
026:078 "Who created **me**, and it is He Who guides **me**;
026:079 "Who gives **me** food and drink,
026:080 "And when I am ill, it is He Who cures **me**;
026:081 "Who will cause **me** to die, and then
026:082 will forgive **me** my faults on the Day of Judgment.
026:083 and join **me** with the righteous;
026:083 "O my Lord! bestow wisdom on **me**, and join
026:084 "Grant **me** honorable mention on the tongue
026:085 "Make **me** one of the inheritors of the
026:087 "And let **me** not be in disgrace on the Day
026:108 "So fear Allah, and obey **me**.
026:110 "So fear Allah, and obey **me**."
026:117 truly my people have rejected **me**.
026:118 between **me** and them openly, and deliver
026:118 and deliver **me** and those of the Believers
026:118 the Believers who are with **me**."
026:126 "So fear Allah, and obey **me**.
026:131 "Now fear Allah, and obey **me**.
026:144 So fear Allah, and obey **me**.
026:150 "But fear Allah, and obey **me**;
026:163 "So fear Allah, and obey **me**.
026:169 "O my Lord! deliver **me** and my family
026:179 "So fear Allah, and obey **me**.
027:019 and admit **me**, by Thy Grace, to the ranks of thy
027:019 so order **me** that I may be grateful for Thy favours,
027:019 which thou has bestowed on **me** and on my parents,
027:021 unless he bring **me** a clear reason (for absence)."
027:029 here is-delivered to **me**-a letter worthy of respect.
027:031 but come to **me** in submission (to the true Religion).'"
027:031 "'Be ye not arrogant against **me**, but come
027:032 She said: "Ye chiefs! advise **me** in (this) my affair:
027:036 But that Which Allah has given **me** is better than that
027:036 he said: "Will ye give **me** abundance in wealth?
027:038 before they come to **me** in submission?"
027:038 which of you can bring **me** her throne before they
027:040 to test **me** whether I am grateful or ungrateful!
027:091 For **me**, I have been commanded to serve the Lord
028:009 "(Here is) a joy of the eye, for **me** and for thee:

ME (continued)

028:016 Do Thou then forgive **me**!"
028:017 Thou hast bestowed Thy Grace on **me**, never shall
028:019 to slay **me** as thou slewest a man yesterday?
028:021 save **me** from people given to wrong-doing."
028:022 will show **me** the smooth and straight Path."
028:024 any good that Thou dost send **me**!"
028:027 thou wilt find **me**, indeed, if Allah wills, one of the
028:027 on condition that thou serve **me** for eight years,
028:028 "Be that (the agreement) between **me** and thee:
028:028 let there be no injustice to **me**.
028:033 slain a man among them, and I fear lest they slay **me**.
028:034 to confirm (and strengthen) **me**:
028:034 for I fear that they may accuse **me** of falsehood."
028:034 so send him with **me** as a helper, to confirm
028:038 and build **me** a lofty palace, that I
028:038 therefore, O Haman! light **me** a (kiln to bake bricks)
028:078 He said: "This has been given to **me** because of
029:008 Ye have (all) to return to **Me**, and I will
029:008 to join with **Me** (in worship) anything of which
029:030 "O my Lord help Thou **me** against people who do
029:052 a Witness between **me** and you: He knows
029:056 therefore serve ye **Me**- (and **Me** alone)!
031:011 now show **Me** what is there that others
031:014 to **Me** is (thy final) Goal.
031:014 "Show gratitude to **Me** and to thy parents:
031:015 strive to thee join in worship with **Me** things of which
031:015 and follow the way of those who turn to **Me**:
031:015 in the End the return of you all is to **Me**,
032:013 but the Word from **Me** will come true, "I Will fill Hell
034:027 Say: "Show **me** those whom ye have joined with
034:050 it is because of the inspiration of my Lord to **me**:
035:040 Show **me** what it is they have created in the (wide) earth.
036:022 Who created **me**, and to Whom ye shall (all) be
036:023 of no use whatever will be their intercession for **me**,
036:023 Most Gracious should intend some adversity for **me**,
036:023 nor can they deliver **me**.
036:025 listen, then, to **me**!"
036:025 "For **me**, I have faith in the Lord of you (all):
036:026 He said: "Ah **me**! would that my People knew
036:027 and has enrolled **me** among those held in honour!"
036:027 "From That my Lord has granted **me** Forgiveness
036:061 "And that ye should worship **Me**, (for that)
037:056 little short of bringing **me** to perdition!
037:099 He will surely guide **me**!
037:100 "O my Lord! grant **me** a righteous (son)!"
037:102 thou will find **me**, if Allah so will one of the steadfast."
038:023 and he overcame **me** in the argument."
038:033 "Bring them back to **me**."
038:035 He said, "O my Lord! Forgive **me**, and grant
038:035 will not belong to another after **me**:
038:035 and grant **me** a Kingdom, which, will not
038:041 "Satan has afflicted **me** with distress and suffering"!
038:070 "Only this has been revealed to **me**: that I
038:076 Thou createdst **me** from fire, and him Thou createdst
038:079 (Iblis) said: "O my Lord! give **me** then respite
039:016 "O my servants! Then fear ye **Me**!"
039:038 remove His affliction or is He will some Mercy for **me**,
039:038 Say: "Sufficient is Allah for **me**!
039:038 can they, if Allah wills some affliction for **me**,
039:049 he says, "This has been given to **me** because of
039:056 say: 'Ah! woe is **me**!-in that I neglected (my Duty)
039:057 'If only Allah had guided **me**, I should

ME (continued)

039:064 some one other than Allah that ye order **me** to worship,
040:026 Said Pharaoh: "Leave **me** to slay Moses; and let
040:036 Pharaoh said: "O Haman! Build **me** a lofty palace,
040:038 "O my People! follow **me**: I will lead you to the Path of
040:041 how (strange) it is for **me** to call you to Salvation while
040:041 while ye call **me** to the Fire!
040:042 "Ye do call upon **me** to blaspheme against Allah,
040:043 "Without doubt ye do call **me** to one who
040:060 to serve **Me** will surely enter Hell abased."
040:060 And your Lord says: "Call on **Me**; I will answer your
040:066 that the Clear Signs have come to **me** from my Lord;
041:006 it is revealed to **me** by inspiration, that your
041:047 "Where are the Partners (ye attributed) to **Me**?"
043:027 and He will certainly guide **me**."
043:027 "(I worship) only Him Who made **me**, and He
043:038 "Would that between **me** and thee were the distance
043:051 the dominion of Egypt belong to **me**, (witness)
043:061 have no doubt about the (Hour), but follow ye **Me**:
043:063 therefore fear Allah and obey **me**.
044:018 Saying: "Restore to **me** the servants of Allah: I am
044:020 "For **me**, I have sought Safety with my Lord
044:020 my Lord and your Lord, against your injuring **me**.
044:021 at least keep yourselves away from **me**."
044:021 "If ye believe **me** not, at least keep
046:004 Show **me** what it is they have created on earth,
046:004 Bring **me** a Book (revealed) before this, or any remnant
046:008 Enough is He for a witness between **me** and you!
046:008 then can ye have no power to help **me** against Allah.
046:009 nor do I know what will be done with **me** or with you.
046:009 I follow but that which is revealed to **me** by inspiration;
046:015 and be gracious to **me** in my issue.
046:015 Thy favour which Thou hast bestowed upon **me**,
046:015 "O my Lord! grant **me** that I may be grateful for Thy
046:017 have passed before **me** (without rising again)?"
046:017 Do ye hold out the promise to **me** that I shall be raised
049:017 "Count not your Islam as favour upon **me**:
050:023 "Here is (his record) ready with **me**!"
050:029 "The Word changes not before **Me**, and I
051:056 that they may serve **Me**.
051:057 nor do I require that they should feed **Me**.
051:059 then let them not ask **Me** to hasten (that portion)!
054:010 "I am one overcome: do thou then help (**me**)!"
061:005 "O my people! why do ye vex and insult **me**,
061:006 giving Glad Tidings of a messenger to come after **me**,
061:006 confirming the Taurat (which came) before **me**,
063:010 Why didst thou not give **me** respite for a little while!
066:003 He said, "He told **me** Who is the Knower, The Aware."
066:011 and save **me** from Pharaoh and his doings, and save
066:011 build for **me**, in nearness to Thee, a mansion
066:011 and save **me** from those that do wrong";
067:028 to destroy **me**, and those with **me**, or if
068:044 Then leave **Me** alone with such as reject
069:020 that my Account would (one Day) reach **me**!"
069:025 "Ah! would that my record had not been given to **me**!
069:027 "Ah! would that (Death) had made an end of **me**!
069:028 "Of no profit to **me** has been my wealth!
069:029 "My power has perished from **me**!"...
071:003 "That ye should worship Allah, fear Him, and obey **me**:
071:021 Noah said: "O my Lord they have disobeyed **me**,
071:028 "O my Lord! Forgive **me**, my parents, all who
072:001 Say: It has been revealed to **me** that a company
072:022 "No one can deliver **me** from Allah (if i were to disobey

ME (continued)

073:011 And leave **Me** (alone to deal with) those in
074:011 Leave **Me** alone, (to deal) with the (creature)
077:039 Now, if ye have a trick (or plot), use it against **Me**!
078:040 will say, "Woe unto **me**! Would that
089:015 "My Lord hath honoured **me**."
089:016 "My Lord hath humiliated **me**!"
109:006 To you be your Way, and to **me** mine.

MEAD

030:015 shall be made happy in a **Mead** (of Delight).

MEADOWS

042:022 righteous deeds will be in the **Meadows** of the Gardens:

MEAL

011:070 not reaching towards the (**meal**), he felt
018:062 "Bring us our early **meal**; truly we have
033:053 until leave is given you,- for a **meal**, (and then)
033:053 and when ye have taken your **meal**, disperse,

MEAN

005:067 Allah will defend thee from men (who **mean** mischief).
068:010 Obey not every **mean**,-swearer,

MEANER

063:008 honourable (element) will expel therefrom the **meaner**."

MEANEST

007:013 the **meanest** (of creatures)."
011:027 but the **meanest** among us, apparently nor
026:111 when it is the **meanest** that follow thee?"
027:034 make the noblest of its people **meanest** thus do

MEANING

003:007 basic or fundamental clear (in **meaning**);
011:001 with verses fundamental (of established **meaning**),
012:036 "Tell us" (they said) "the truth and **meaning** thereof:
012:037 to you the truth and **meaning** of this ere it befall you.
031:006 without knowledge (or **meaning**), to mislead
047:020 of decisive **meaning** is revealed, and fighting

MEANINGS

003:007 but no one knows its true **meanings** except Allah.

MEANS

002:026 "What **means** Allah by this similitude?"
002:036 and your **means** of livelihood for a time."
002:102 the **means** to sow discord between man and wife.
002:220 man who **means** mischief from the man who **means** good.
002:236 and the poor according to his **means**;
002:236 the wealthy according to his **means**,
002:251 one set of people by **means** of another,
003:092 By no **means** shall ye attain righteousness unless
003:108 and Allah **means** no injustice to any
004:025 the **means** wherewith to wed free believing women,
004:034 and because they support them from their **means**.
004:034 seek not against them **means** (of annoyance):
004:092 For those who find this beyond their **means**,
004:098 and children who have no **means** in their power,
005:035 seek the **means** of approach unto Him, and strive
005:089 If that is beyond your **means**, fast for three days.
005:097 a **means** of support for men, as also
007:010 and provided you therein with **means** for the
007:024 and your **means** of livelihood,-for a time."
007:089 nor could we by any manner of **means** return
007:143 Allah said: "By no **means** canst thou
009:079 who give according to their **means**,-and throw
011:081 By no **means** shall they reach thee!
015:020 And We have provided therein **means** of subsistence,-
016:075 (By no **means**); praise be to Allah.

MEANS (continued)

017:057   do seek (for themselves) **means** of access to their Lord,-
018:053   no **means** will they find to turn away therefrom.
018:084   and We gave him the ways and the **means** to all ends.
021:069   and (a **means** of)) safety for Abraham!"
022:040   of people by **means** of another, there would
023:100   in the things I neglected."-"By no **means**! it is
024:022   with grace and amplitude of **means** resolve by oath
024:032   Allah will give them **means** out of His grace:
024:033   out of the **means** which Allah has given to you.
024:033   until Allah gives them **means** out of His grace.
026:015   Allah said: "By no **means**! proceed them, both of
026:062   (Moses said: "By no **means**! my Lord
034:027   have joined with Him as partners: by no **means** (can ye).
038:010   and **means** (to reach that end)!
040:005   to seize him, and disputed by **means** of vanities,
040:036   the ways and **means**-
040:037   "The ways and **means** of (reaching) the heavens,
042:011   by this **means** does He multiply you:
046:028   as a **means** of access (to Allah)?
058:004   And if any has not (the **means**), he should fast two
065:006   in the same style as ye live, according to your **means**:
065:007   Let the man of **means** spend according to his **means**:
070:015   By no **means**! for it would be the Blazing Fire-
070:039   By no **means**! for We have created them out of
072:012   by no **means** frustrate Allah throughout the earth,
072:017   "That We might try them by that (**means**).
074:016   By no **means**! For to Our Signs he has
074:053   By no **means**! But they fear not the Hereafter.
075:011   By no **means**! No place of safety!
078:011   And made the day as a **means** of subsistence?
080:011   By no **means** (should it be so)!
080:023   By no **means** hath he fulfilled what Allah
083:014   By no **means**! but on their hearts is the
104:004   By no **means**! He will be sure to be thrown

MEANT

004:062   "We **meant** no more than good-will and conciliation!"
025:018   not **meant** was it for us that we should take
026:211   It is not **meant** for them, nor is
036:069   in Poetry, nor is it **meant** for him:
053:010   to His Servant-(conveyed) what He (**meant**) to convey.

MEASURE

003:008   Grantor of bounties without **measure**.
003:027   to whom Thou pleasest, without **measure**."
003:037   to whom He pleases, without **measure**."
003:179   ye have a reward great without **measure**.
006:152   give **measure** and weight with (full) justice;-
007:085   Give just **measure** and weight, nor withhold
010:026   (reward)-yea, more (than in **measure**)!
011:084   And give not short **measure** or weight: I see you
011:085   "And O my people! give just **measure** and weight,
012:059   I pay out full **measure**, and that
012:060   ye shall have no **measure** (of corn) from me,
012:063   that we may get our **measure**; and we will indeed take
012:063   "O our father! No more **measure** of grain shall we get
012:088   so pay us full **measure**, (we pray thee), and treat
013:017   and the channels flow, each according to its **measure**:
013:026   Allah doth enlarge, or grant by (strict) **measure**,
017:035   Give full **measure** when ye **measure**, and weigh
017:043   they say! Exalted and Great (beyond **measure**)!
020:015   by the **measure** of its Endeavour.
022:040   is commemorated in abundant **measure**.
023:018   the sky according to (due) **measure**, and We

MEASURE (continued)

024:038   for those whom He will, without **measure**.
026:181   Give just **measure**, and cause not loss (to others by fraud).
029:062   by (strict) **measure**, (as He pleases):
031:020   flow to you in exceeding **measure**, (both) seen
032:005   on a Day, the **measure** of which is a thousand
038:009   the Grantor of Bounties without **measure**?
038:035   of Bounties (without **measure**)."
039:010   will truly receive a reward without **measure**!"
040:040   have abundance without **measure**.
042:027   in due **measure** as He pleases:
043:011   rain from the sky in due **measure**;-and We
054:049   We created in proportion and **measure**.
070:004   unto Him in a Day the **measure** whereof is (as)
073:020   But Allah doth appoint Night and Day in due **measure**.
076:016   they will determine the **measure** thereof
083:002   by **measure** from men, exact full **measure**,
083:003   when they have to give by **measure** or weight to men,

MEASURED

010:005   and **measured** out stages for it, that ye might
036:039   And the Moon,-We have **measured** for her stations
041:010   and **measured** therein its sustenance in four Days,
073:004   and recite the Qur'an in slow, **measured** rhythmic tones.
087:003   Who hath **measured**. And granted guidance;

MEASURES

002:212   His abundance without **measures** on whom He will.
015:021   thereof in due and ascertainable **measures**.

MEAT

002:173   He hath only forbidden you dead **meat**,
005:003   (forbidden) also is the division (of **meat**) by
005:003   dead **meat**, blood, the flesh of swine, and that
006:142   for burden and some for **meat**:
006:145   (**meat**) on which a name has been invoked, other than
006:145   unless it be dead **meat**, or blood poured forth,
006:145   any (**meat**) forbidden to be eaten by one who wishes
016:005   and numerous benefits, and of their (**meat**) ye eat.
016:115   He has only forbidden you dead **meat**, and blood,
022:037   It is not their **meat** nor their blood, that reaches
023:021   and of their (**meat**) ye eat;
052:022   of fruit and **meat**, anything they shall desire.

MEATS

006:118   So eat of (**meats**) on which Allah's name
006:119   Why should ye not eat of (**meats**) on which
006:121   Eat not of (**meats**) on which Allah's name

MEDITATE

004:081   a section of them **meditate** all night on things
038:029   that they may **meditate** on its Signs, and that

MEDITATED

003:122   Remember two of your parties **meditated** cowardice;
009:074   and they **meditated** a plot which they

MEDLEY

012:044   They said: "A confused **medley** of dreams: and we

MEDLEYS

021:005   "Nay," they say, "(these are) **medleys** of dreams!

MEED

006:164   Every soul draws the **meed** of its
030:041   and sea because of (the **meed**) that the hands
035:030   For He will pay them their **meed**, nay, He will

MEEDS

036:054   but be repaid the **meeds** of your past Deeds.

MEET

002:014   When they **meet** those who believe.

MEET (continued)

002:046   that they are to **meet** their Lord,
002:076   Behold! when they **meet** the men of Faith,
002:076   but when they **meet** each other in private,
002:223   to **meet** Him (in the Hereafter),
002:249   convinced that they must **meet** Allah,
002:250   When they advanced to **meet** Goliath and his forces,
003:119   when they **meet** you, they say, "We believe";
004:036   the Companion by your side, the way-farer (ye **meet**),
004:086   **meet** it with a greeting still more courteous, (or at least)
006:031   as a falsehood that they must **meet** Allah,-
008:015   O ye who believe! when ye **meet** the Unbelievers
008:042   Even if ye had made a mutual appointment to **meet**,
008:045   when ye **meet** a force, be firm, and call
009:077   (to last) till the Day whereon they shall **meet** Him:
011:029   for verily they are to **meet** their Lord, and ye
017:047   and when they **meet** in private behold, the wicked
018:048   made to you to **meet** (Us)!":
018:105   having to **meet** Him (in the Hereafter): vain will
018:110   whoever expects to **meet** his Lord, let him
021:103   but the angels will **meet** them (with mutual greetings):
025:021   Those who do not hope to **meet** Us (for Judgment)
027:037   as they will never be able to **meet**: we shall
033:044   salutation on the day they **meet** Him will be "peace!";
043:083   (with vanities) until they **meet** that Day of theirs,
047:004   Therefore, when ye **meet** the Unbelievers (in fight),
084:006   painfully toiling, but thou shalt **meet** Him.

MEETING

006:130   and warning you of the **meeting** of this
006:154   in the **meeting** with their Lord.
007:051   as they forgot the **meeting** of this
007:147   and the **Meeting** in the Hereafter,-vain are
007:155   of his people for Our place of **meeting**:
008:041   the Day of the **meeting** of the two forces.
010:007   on their **meeting** with Us, but are
010:011   their hope of their **meeting** with Us, in their
010:015   on their **meeting** with Us, say: "Bring
010:045   who denied the **meeting** with Allah and refused
013:002   in the **meeting** with your Lord.
023:033   who disbelieved and denied the **Meeting** in the
029:005   in the **meeting** with Allah, the term
029:023   and the **Meeting**, with Him (in the Hereafter),-
030:008   who deny the **meeting** with their Lord
030:016   and the **meeting** of the Hereafter,-such shall
032:010   Nay, they deny the **meeting** with their Lord!
032:014   "Taste ye then-for ye forgot the **Meeting** of this
039:071   and warning you of the **Meeting** of this Day
040:015   of the Day of Mutual **Meeting**,-
041:054   doubt concerning the **Meeting** with their Lord?
045:034   the **meeting** of this day of yours!
055:019   He has let free the two Seas **meeting** together:
056:050   for the **meeting** appointed for a Day Well-known.

MEETING-PLACE

011:017   the Fire will be their promised **meeting-place**.:

MEETS

025:068   and any that does this (not only) **meets** punishment

MELTED

018:029   like **melted** brass, that will scald their
022:020   With it will be **melted** what is within their

MEMBERS

002:217   and drive out its **members.**
003:195   ye are **members**, one of another;
028:059   a population except when its **members** practice iniquity.

MEMBERS (continued)

033:033   ye **Members** of the Family, and to make

MEMORY

069:012   (that should hear the tale and) retain its **memory** should

MEN

002:024   whose fuel is **Men** and Stones,
002:075   Can ye (O ye **men** of Faith) entertain
002:076   Behold! when they meet the **men** of Faith,
002:102   teaching **men** magic,
002:125   of assembly for **men** and a place of safety;
002:165   Yet there are **men** who take (for worship)
002:179   O ye **men** of understanding;
002:187   Thus doth Allah make clear His Signs to **men**:
002:189   fixed periods of time in (the affairs of) **men**.
002:200   There are **men** who say: "Our Lord! Give us
002:201   And there are **men** who say: "Our Lord! give us
002:219   and some profit, for **men**;
002:228   but **men** have a degree over them
002:229   It is not lawful for you, (**men**),
002:264   spend their wealth to be seen of **men**,
002:269   receive admonition but **men** of understanding.
002:282   it there are not two **men**, then a man and two women,
002:282   And get two witnesses, out or your own **men**.
002:285   as do the **men** of faith,
003:007   the Message except **men** of understanding.
003:014   Fair in the eyes of **men** is the love of things
003:068   Without doubt, among **men**, the nearest of kin
003:093   if ye be **men** of truth."
003:096   appointed for **men** was that at Bakka:
003:097   pilgrimage thereto is a duty **men** owe to Allah,
003:112   (of protection) from Allah and from **men**;
003:117   harvest of **men** who have wronged their own souls:
003:134   who restrain anger, and pardon (all) **men**;
003:138   Here is a plain statement to **men**,
003:140   We give to **men** and **men** by turns:
003:146   and with them (fought) large bands of godly **men**?
003:173   Those to whom **men** said: "A great army
003:190   there are indeed Signs for **men** of understanding,
003:191   **Men** who remember Allah, standing, sitting,
004:001   scattered (like seeds) countless **men** and women;
004:007   a share for **men** and a share for women,
004:032   to **men** is allotted what they earn,
004:034   **Men** are the protectors and maintainers of women,
004:038   to be seen of **men**, and have no faith in Allah
004:052   They are (**men**) whom Allah hath cursed:
004:063   Those **men**, Allah knows what is in their hearts;
004:072   There are certainly among you **men** who would tarry
004:075   **Men**, women, and children, whose cry is: "Our Lord!
004:077   behold! a section of them feared **men** as, or even
004:097   Such **men** will find their abode in Hell.
004:098   weak and oppressed, **men**, women, and children who
004:109   Ah! these are the sort of **men** on whose behalf
004:115   a path other than that becoming to **men** of Faith,
004:142   to be seen of **men**, but little
004:167   and keep off (**men**) from the way of Allah, have
005:011   unto you when certain **men** formed the design to
005:018   Nay, ye are but **men**, of the **men** He hath created:
005:023   (But) among (their) God-fearing **men** were two
005:041   or it be among the Jews-**men** who will listen to any lie,-
005:044   therefore fear not **men**, but fear Me, and sell not
005:049   And truly most **men** are rebellious.
005:053   "Are these the **men** who swore their strongest
005:067   Allah will defend thee from **men** (who mean mischief).

MEN (continued)

005:082 Strongest among **men** in enmity to the Believers
005:082 because amongst these are **men** devoted to learning.
005:082 And **men** who have renounced the world, and they
005:095 As adjudged by two just **men** among you; or by
005:097 a means of support for **men**, as also
005:106 when making bequests,-two just **men** of your own
005:109 ye received (from **men** to your teaching)?"
005:116 say unto **men**, "Take me and my mother for two
006:068 When thou seest **men** engaged in vain
006:089 These were the **men** to whom We gave the Book,
006:112 satans among **men** and Jinns, inspiring each other
006:119 But many do mislead (**men**) by low desires without
006:122 and a Light whereby he can walk amongst **men**,
006:123 its wicked **men**, to plot (and burrow) therein:
006:128 much (toll) did ye take of **men**."
006:128 Their friends amongst **men** will say: "Our Lord!
006:130 "O ye assembly of Jinns and **men**! came there
006:139 is specially reserved (for food) for our **men**,
006:144 to lead astray **men** without knowledge?
007:003 Follow (O **men**!) the revelation given unto
007:038 who passed away before you-**men** and Jinns,-into the Fire.
007:045 "Those who would hinder (**men**) from the path of Allah
007:046 and on the Heights will be **men** who would
007:048 The **men** on the Heights will call to certain **men** whom
007:049 not the **men** whom you swore that Allah with His Mercy
007:081 on **men** in preference to women:
007:082 these are indeed **men** who want
007:092 the **men** who rejected Shu'aib-
007:092 The **men** who rejected Shu'aib became as if
007:102 not **men** (true) to their covenant: but most
007:111 and send to the cities **men** to collect-
007:144 chosen thee above (other) **men**, by the
007:158 Say: "O **men**! I am sent unto you all, as the
007:173 the deeds of **men** who followed falsehood?"
007:179 Many are the Jinns and **men**, We have
007:180 but shun such **men** as distort His names:
007:187 is with Allah (alone), but most **men** know not."
008:026 and afraid that **men** might despoil and kidnap you;
008:034 No **men** can be its guardians
008:034 when they keep out (**men**) from the Sacred Mosque-
008:036 to hinder (**men**) from the path of Allah,
008:047 and to hinder (**men**) from the path of Allah:
008:047 started from their homes insolently and to be seen of **men**,
008:048 said: "No one among **men** can overcome you this day,
009:006 are **men** without knowledge.
009:034 devour the wealth of **men** and hinder (them) from the
009:058 And among them are **men** who slander thee
009:061 Among them are **men** who molest the Prophet and say,
009:067 The Hypocrites, **men** and women, are alike:
009:068 Hypocrites **men** and women, and the rejecters of Faith,
009:070 the people of Abraham, the **men** of Madyan, and the
009:071 The Believers, **men** and women, are protectors,
009:072 Allah hath promised to Believers, **men** and women,
009:075 Amongst them are **men** who made a Covenant
009:090 desert Arabs (also), **Men** who made excuses and
009:108 In it are **men** who love to be purified; and Allah
010:002 Is it a matter of wonderment to **men** that We
010:011 If Allah were to hasten for **men** the ill
010:024 which provides food for **men** and animals:
010:088 and so, our Lord they mislead (**men**) from Thy Path.
010:102 of the **men** who passed away before them?
010:104 Say: "O ye **men**! if ye are in doubt

MEN (continued)

010:108 Say: "O ye **men**! now Truth hath reached you
011:017 yet many among **men** do not believe!
011:019 "Those who would hinder (**men**) from the path of
011:024 These two kinds (of **men**) may be compared
011:109 Be not then in doubt as to what these **men** worship.
011:116 of the generations before you, **men** of righteousness who
011:116 who prohibited **men** from mischief in the earth
011:119 "I will fill Hell with Jinns and **men** all together."
012:036 Now with him there came into the prison two young **men**.
012:038 yet most **men** are not grateful.
012:040 but Most **men** understand not.
012:068 but most **men** know not.
012:109 (as Messengers) any but **men**, whom We did inspire,-
012:109 did inspire,-(**men**) from the people of the towns.
012:111 instruction for **men** endued with understanding.
013:001 but most **men** believe not.
013:013 Yet these (are the **men**) the while they are disputing
014:003 who hinder (**men**) from the Path of Allah and seek
014:011 And on Allah let all **men** of faith put their trust.
014:025 So Allah sets forth parables for **men**, in order
014:030 (idols) as equal to Allah, to mislead (**men**) from the Path!
014:037 among **men** with love towards them, and feed
014:045 of **men** who wronged themselves ye were
014:048 and (**men**) will be marshalled forth,
014:052 let **men** of understanding take heed.
015:067 came in (mad) joy (at news of the young **men**).
016:005 And cattle He has created for you (**men**): from them
016:012 for **men** who are wise.
016:013 is a Sign for **men** who mindful.
016:016 and by the stars (**men**) guide themselves.
016:043 And before thee We sent none but **men**, to whom
016:044 mayest explain clearly to **men** what is sent for them,
016:061 It Allah were to punish **men** for their wrong-doing,
016:069 a drink of varying colours, wherein is healing for **men**:
016:075 Allah sets forth the Parable (of two **men**): one a slave
016:076 Allah sets forth (another) Parable of two **men**:
016:088 Those who reject Allah and hinder (**men**) from the Path
016:094 evil (consequences) of having hindered (**men**) from the
017:059 only because the **men** of former generations treated them
017:060 which We showed thee, but as a trail for **men**,-
017:085 a little that is communicated to you, (O **men**!)"
017:089 yet the greater part of **men** refuse (to receive it)
017:094 What kept **men** back from Belief when Guidance
017:106 recite it to **men** at intervals:
018:032 set forth to them the parable of two **men**: for one of them
018:034 more honour and power in (my following of) **men**."
018:051 as helpers such as lead (**men**) astray!
018:055 And what is there to keep back **men** from believing,
018:079 certain **men** in dire want: they plied
019:021 unto **men** and a Mercy from Us': it is
020:054 Signs for **men** endued with understanding.
020:128 Is it not a guidance to such **men** (to call to mind) how
020:128 in this are Signs for **men** endued with understanding.
021:007 Before thee, also, the messengers We sent were but **men**,
021:010 We have revealed for you (O **men**!) a book
021:044 the good things of this life to these **men** and their fathers
021:072 and We made righteous **men** of every one (of them).
021:073 We made them leaders guiding (**men**) by Our Command,
021:085 and Zul-Kifl, all (**men**) of constancy and patience;
022:003 And yet among **men** there are such as dispute
022:008 Yet there is among **men** such a one as disputes
022:009 in order to lead (**men**) astray from the

MEN (continued)

022:011 There are among **men** some who serve Allah, as it
022:025 to (all) **men**-equal is the dweller there and the
022:025 and would keep back (**men**) from the
022:027 "And proclaim the Pilgrimage among **men**: they will
022:049 Say: "O **men**! I am (sent) to you only to give
022:065 made subject to you (**men**) all that is on the
022:073 O **men**! Here is a parable set forth!
022:075 Allah chooses Messengers from angles and from **men**:
023:030 Verily in this there are Signs (for **men** to understand);
023:030 lo! We put (**men**) to test.
023:047 They said: "Shall we believe in two **men** like ourselves?
024:004 for such **men** are wicked transgressors;-
024:012 Why did not the Believers-**men** and women-when ye
024:013 such **men**, in the sight of Allah, (stand forth) themselves
024:026 Women impure are for **men** impure,
024:026 women of purity are for **men** of purity, and **men** of purity:
024:026 and **men** impure are for women impure,
024:030 Say to the believing **men** that they should lower
024:035 Allah doth set forth Parables for **men**:
024:037 By **men** whom neither trade nor sale can divert
025:020 before thee were all (**men**) who ate food
025:049 cattle and **men** in great numbers.
025:050 be mindful but most **men** are averse (to aught)
026:087 on the Day when (**men**) will be raised up;-
026:183 "And withhold not things justly due to **men**, nor do evil
027:017 his hosts,-of Jinns and **men** and birds, and they
027:038 He said (to his own **men**): "Ye Chiefs! which of
027:048 There were in the City nine **men**, who made
027:055 "Would ye really approach **men** in your
027:056 these are indeed **men** who want to be clean and pure!"
028:008 their hosts were **men** of sin.
028:015 and he found there two **men** fighting,-one of
028:023 he found there a group of **men** watering (their flocks),
028:026 truly the best of **men** for thee to employ
028:043 Insight to **men** and Guidance and Mercy, that they
028:076 a burden to a body of strong **men**.
028:087 and invite (**men**) to thy Lord and be not
029:002 Do **men** think that they will be left alone
029:010 Then there are among **men** such as say, "We believe
029:029 "Do ye indeed approach **men**, and cut
029:031 for truly they are wicked **men**."
029:067 and that **men** are being snatched away from all
030:006 but most **men** understand not.
030:008 yet are there truly many among **men** who deny
030:014 that Day shall (all **men**) be sorted out.
030:020 behold, ye are **men** scattered (far and wide)!
030:033 When trouble touches **men**, they cry
030:036 When We give **men** a taste of Mercy, they exult
030:041 the hands of **men** have earned, that (Allah)
030:043 on that Day shall **men** be divided (in two).
030:050 verily the Same will give life to the **men** who are dead:
030:058 Verily We have propounded for **men**, in this
031:006 to mislead (**men**) from the Path of Allah and throw
031:006 But there are, among **men**, those who
031:018 "And swell not thy cheek (for pride) at **men**.
031:020 Yet there are among **men** those who dispute
032:013 "I will fill Hell with Jinns and **men** all together."
033:013 "Ye **men** of Yathrib! Ye cannot
033:018 who keep back (**men**) and those who say to their
033:019 Such **men** have no faith, and so
033:023 Among the Believers are **men** who have been true
033:024 That Allah may reward the **men** of Truth

MEN (continued)

033:035 for **men** and women who humble themselves,
033:035 and for **men** and women who engage much in Allah's
033:035 for **men** and women who give who give in charity,
033:035 Muslim **men** and women,-for believing **men** and women,
033:035 for **men** and women who are patient and constant,
033:035 for **men** and women who fast,
033:035 for **men** and women who guard their chastity,
033:035 for devout **men** and women, for true **men** and women,
033:039 to call (**men**) to account.
033:040 Muhammad is not the father of any of your **men**,
033:058 And those who annoy believing **men** and women
033:063 **Men** ask thee concerning the Hour: say, "The knowledge
033:073 Allah turns in Mercy to the Believers, **men** and women:
033:073 and the Unbelievers, **men** and women,
033:073 that Allah has to punish the Hypocrites, **men** and women,
034:028 but most **men** understand not.
034:036 to whom He pleases, but most **men** know not."
034:040 "Was it you that these **men** used to worship?"
035:003 O **men**! remember the grace of Allah unto you!
035:005 O **men**! certainly the promise of Allah is true,
035:015 O ye **men**! it is ye that have need of Allah:
035:028 And so amongst **men** and beasts and cattle,
035:045 If Allah were to punish **men** according to what
036:015 The (people) said: "Ye are only **men** like ourselves;
036:051 from the sepulchres (**men**) will rush forth to their Lord!
037:147 to a hundred thousand (**men**) or more.
038:026 so judge thou between **men** in truth (and justice):
038:029 and that **men** of understanding may receive admonition.
038:062 that we see not **men** who we used to number
039:021 of remembrance to **men** of understanding.
039:027 We have put forth for **men**, in the Qur'an every kind of
039:033 such are the **men** who do right.
039:042 It is Allah that takes the souls (of **men**) at death;
040:015 that it may warn (**men**) of the Day
040:019 and all that hearts (of **men**) conceal.
040:020 but those whom (**men**) invoke besides Him, will not
040:054 A Guide and a Message to **men** of understanding.
040:057 than the creation of **men**: yet most **men** know not.
040:059 therein is no doubt: yet most **men** believe not.
040:061 Verily Allah is Full of Grace and bounty to **men**:
040:061 yet most **men** give no thanks.
041:025 generations of Jinns and **men**, who have
041:029 among Jinns and **men**, who misled us: we shall
041:033 who calls (**men**) to Allah, work righteousness,
041:039 can surely give life to (**men**) who are dead.
042:028 (even) after (**men**) have given up all hope,
042:034 of the (evil) which (the **men**) have earned:
042:042 oppress **men** with wrong-doing and insolently
042:052 and verily Thou dost guide (**men**) to the Straight Way,-
043:008 So We destroyed **men**-stronger in power than these;-
043:029 of this life to these (**men**) and their fathers,
043:033 And were it not that (all) **men** might become
045:020 These are clear evidences to **men**, and a
045:026 there is no doubt": but most **men** not know.
046:006 hostile to them and deny that (**men**) had worshipped them.
046:011 good thing, (such **men**) would not have gone to it
046:018 previous generations of Jinns and **men**, that have
047:001 Those who reject Allah and hinder (**men**) from the
047:003 thus does Allah set forth for **men** their lessons
047:016 And among them are **men** who listen to thee,
047:016 Such are **men** whose hearts Allah has
047:019 for thy fault, and for the **men** and women who

MEN (continued)

047:023 Such are the **men** whom Allah has cursed
047:032 Those who disbelieve, hinder (**men**) from the
047:034 Those who disbelieve, and hinder (**men**) from the
048:005 That He may admit the **men** and women who believe,
048:006 the Hypocrites, **men** and women, and the
048:006 and the Polytheists, **men** and women, who think
048:009 In order that ye (O **men**) may believe
048:020 and He has restrained the hands of **men** from you;
048:025 believing **men** and believing women whom ye did
049:011 O ye who believe! let not some **men** among you
051:056 I have only created Jinns and **men**, that they
054:020 Plucking out **men** as if they were roots of
055:033 O ye assembly of Jinns and **men**! If it be
057:008 if ye are **men** of faith.
057:012 The Day shalt thou see the believing **men** and the
057:013 The day will the Hypocrites-**men** and women-say to
057:018 For those who give in Charity, **men** and women,
057:024 and commend covetousness to **men**.
057:025 that **men** may stand forth in justice;
058:002 If any **men** among you divorce their wives by Zihar
058:016 thus they obstruct (**men**) from the Path of Allah:
059:013 This is because they are **men** devoid of understanding.
059:021 Such are the similitudes which We propound to **men**,
062:006 to the exclusion of (other) **men**, then express
063:002 thus they obstruct (**men**) from the path of Allah:
065:010 O ye **men** of understanding-who have believed!-
066:006 whose fuel is **Men** and Stones, over which
067:018 But indeed **men** before them rejected (My warning):
068:001 Nun. By the Pen and by the (Record) which (**men**) write,-
068:007 knoweth best, which (among **men**) hath strayed
070:041 Substitute for them better (**men**) than they;
071:021 disobeyed me, but they follow (**men**) whose wealth
071:028 and (all) believing **men** and believing women:
073:015 We have sent to you, (O **men**!) a Messenger,
075:020 Nay, (ye **men**!) but ye love the fleeting life,
077:016 Did We not destroy the **men** of old (for their evil)?
077:018 Thus do We deal with **men** of sin.
079:023 Then he collected (his **men**) and made a proclamation,
083:002 by measure from **men**, exact full measure,
083:003 or weight to **men**, give less than due.
085:010 Those who persecute the Believers **men** and women,
099:006 On that Day will **men** proceed in groups sorted out,
101:004 (It is) a Day whereon **Men** will be like
114:006 Among Jinns and among **Men**.

MEN'S

004:128 even though **men's** souls are swayed by greed.
004:161 and that they devoured **men's** wealth wrongfully;
016:068 and in (**men's**) habitations;
029:010 they treat **men's** oppression as if it were the Wrath of
031:023 all that is in (**men's**) hearts.
035:038 full knowledge of all that is in (**men's**) hearts.
039:007 For He knoweth well all that is in (**men's**) hearts.

MEND

004:146 Except for those who repent, **mend** (their life), hold fast
006:048 so those who believe and **mend** (their lives),-
007:035 those who are righteous and **mend** (their lives),
024:005 and **mend** (their conduct): for Allah
026:152 and **mend** not (their ways)."

MENTALLY

002:282 If the party liable is **mentally** deficient,

MENTION

012:042 But Satan made him forget to **mention** him to his lord:
012:042 he said: "**Mention** me to thy lord."
017:046 when thou dost **mention** thy Lord-and Him
019:002 (This is) a **mention** of the Mercy of thy Lord
019:041 Also **mention** in the Book (the story of) Abraham:
019:051 Also **mention** in the Book (the story of) Moses:
019:054 Also **mention** in the Book (the story of) Isma'il:
019:056 Also **mention** in the Book Idris: he was
021:036 the **mention** of The Most Gracious!
026:084 "Grant me honorable **mention** on the tongue
046:021 **Mention** (Hud) one of 'Ad's (own) brethren:

MENTIONED

007:157 whom they find **mentioned** in their own (Scriptures),-
008:002 when Allah is **mentioned**, fell a tremor
016:118 such things as We have **mentioned** to thee before:
017:060 as also the Cursed Tree (**mentioned**) in the Qur'an:
022:030 are cattle except those **mentioned** to you
022:035 when Allah is **mentioned**, are filled
039:045 When Allah, Alone is **mentioned**, the hearts
039:045 but when (gods) other than He are **mentioned**, behold,
047:020 and fighting is **mentioned** therein, thou wilt
076:001 when he was nothing-(not even) **mentioned**?

MERCIES

007:017 gratitude (for Thy **mercies**)."
018:016 His **mercies** on you and dispose of your affair

MERCIFUL

001:001 In the name of Allah, Most Gracious, Most **Merciful**.
001:003 Most Gracious, Most **Merciful**.
002:000 In the name of Allah, Most Gracious, Most **Merciful**.
002:037 for He is Oft-Returning, Most **Merciful**.
002:054 for He is Oft-returning, Most **Merciful**.
002:143 most surely full of kindness, Most **Merciful**.
002:160 for I am Oft-Returning, Most **Merciful**.
002:163 Most Gracious, Most **Merciful**.
002:173 For Allah is Oft-Forgiving, Most **Merciful**.
002:182 for Allah is Oft-Forgiving, Most **Merciful**.
002:192 Allah is Oft-Forgiving, Most **Merciful**.
002:199 For Allah is Oft-forgiving, Most **Merciful**.
002:218 and Allah is Oft-Forgiving, Most **Merciful**.
002:226 Allah is Oft-Forgiving, Most **Merciful**.
003:000 In the name of Allah, Most Gracious, Most **Merciful**.
003:031 for Allah is Oft-Forgiving, Most **Merciful**.
003:089 for verily Allah is Oft-Forgiving, Most **Merciful**.
003:129 but Allah is Oft-Forgiving, Most **Merciful**.
004:000 In the name of Allah, Most Gracious, Most **Merciful**.
004:016 for Allah is Oft-returning, Most **Merciful**.
004:023 for Allah is Oft-Forgiving, Most **Merciful**.
004:025 And Allah is Oft-forgiving, Most **Merciful**.
004:029 for verily Allah hath been to you Most **Merciful**.
004:064 found Allah indeed Oft-Returning, Most **Merciful**.
004:096 For Allah is Oft-Forgiving. Most **Merciful**.
004:100 and Allah is Oft-Forgiving, Most **Merciful**.
004:106 for Allah is Oft-Forgiving, Most **Merciful**.
004:110 he will find Allah Oft-Forgiving, Most **Merciful**.
004:129 Allah is Oft-Forgiving, Most **Merciful**.
004:152 for Allah is Oft-Forgiving, Most **Merciful**.
005:000 In the name of Allah, Most Gracious, Most **Merciful**.
005:003 Allah is indeed Oft-Forgiving, Most **Merciful**.
005:034 know that Allah is Oft-Forgiving, Most **Merciful**.
005:039 for Allah is Oft-Forgiving, Most **Merciful**.
005:074 For Allah is Oft-Forgiving, Most **Merciful**.
005:098 and that Allah is Oft-Forgiving, Most **Merciful**.

MERCIFUL (continued)

006:000 In the name of Allah, Most Gracious, Most **Merciful**.
006:054 lo! He is Oft-Forgiving, Most **Merciful**.
006:145 thy Lord is Oft-Forgiving, Most **Merciful**.
006:165 yet He is indeed Oft-Forgiving, Most **Merciful**.
007:000 In the name of Allah, Most Gracious, Most **Merciful**.
007:151 For Thou art the Most **Merciful** of those
007:153 thereafter Oft-Forgiving, Most **Merciful**.
007:167 but He is also Oft-Forgiving, Most **Merciful**.
008:000 In the name of Allah, Most Gracious, Most **Merciful**.
008:069 for Allah is Oft-Forgiving, Most **Merciful**.
008:070 for Allah Is Oft-Forgiving, Most **Merciful**."
009:005 for Allah is Oft-Forgiving, Most **Merciful**.
009:027 for Allah is Oft-Forgiving, Most **Merciful**.
009:091 and Allah is Oft-Forgiving, Most **Merciful**.
009:099 for Allah is Oft-Forgiving, Most **Merciful**.
009:102 for Allah is Oft-Forgiving, Most **Merciful**.
009:104 the Oft-Returning, Most **Merciful**?
009:117 for He is unto them Most Kind, Most **Merciful**.
009:118 for Allah is Oft-Returning, Most **Merciful**.
009:128 to the Believers is he most kind and **merciful**.
010:000 In the name of Allah, Most Gracious, Most **Merciful**.
010:107 And He is the Oft-Forgiving, Most **Merciful**.
011:000 In the name of Allah, Most Gracious, Most **Merciful**.
011:041 be sure, Oft-Forgiving, Most **Merciful**!"
012:000 In the name of Allah, Most Gracious, Most **Merciful**.
012:053 my Lord is Oft-Forgiving, Most **Merciful**.
012:064 (of him), and He is the Most **Merciful** of those
012:092 and He is the Most **Merciful** of those
012:098 for He is indeed Oft-Forgiving, **Merciful**."
013:000 In the name of Allah, Most Gracious, Most **Merciful**.
014:000 In the name of Allah, Most Gracious, Most **Merciful**.
014:036 but thou art indeed Oft-Forgiving, Most **Merciful**.
015:000 In the name of Allah, Most Gracious, Most **Merciful**.
015:049 I am indeed the Oft-Forgiving, Most **Merciful**;
016:000 In the name of Allah, Most Gracious, Most **Merciful**.
016:007 for your Lord is indeed Most Kind, Most **Merciful**.
016:018 Oft-Forgiving, Most **Merciful**.
016:110 after all this is Oft-Forgiving, Most **Merciful**.
016:115 then Allah is Oft-Forgiving, Most **Merciful**.
016:119 all this, is Oft-Forgiving, Most **Merciful**.
017:000 In the name of Allah, Most Gracious, Most **Merciful**.
017:066 For He is unto you Most **Merciful**.
018:000 In the name of Allah, Most Gracious, Most **Merciful**.
019:000 In the name of Allah, Most Gracious, Most **Merciful**.
020:000 In the name of Allah, Most Gracious, Most **Merciful**.
021:000 In the name of Allah, Most Gracious, Most **Merciful**.
021:083 seized me, but Thou art the Most **Merciful** of those
021:083 of those that are **merciful**."
022:000 In the name of Allah, Most Gracious, Most **Merciful**.
022:065 for Allah is Most Kind and Most **Merciful** to man.
023:000 In the name of Allah, Most Gracious, Most **Merciful**.
024:000 In the name of Allah, Most Gracious, Most **Merciful**.
024:005 for Allah is Oft-Forgiving, Most **Merciful**.
024:022 For Allah is Oft-Forgiving, Most **Merciful**.
024:033 is Allah Oft-Forgiving, Most **Merciful** (to them).
024:062 for Allah is Oft-Forgiving, Most **Merciful**.
025:000 In the name of Allah, Most Gracious, Most **Merciful**.
025:006 verily He is Oft-Forgiving, Most **Merciful**."
025:070 and Allah is Oft-Forgiving, Most **Merciful**,
026:000 In the name of Allah, Most Gracious, Most **Merciful**.
026:009 the Exalted in Might, Most **Merciful**.
026:068 the Exalted in Might, Most **Merciful**.

MERCIFUL (continued)

026:104 the Exalted in Might, Most **Merciful**.
026:122 the Exalted in Might, Most **Merciful**.
026:140 the Exalted in Might, Most **Merciful**.
026:159 the Exalted in Might, Most **Merciful**.
026:175 the Exalted in Might, Most **Merciful**.
026:191 The Exalted in Might, Most **Merciful**
026:217 on the Exalted in Might, the **Merciful**,-
027:000 In the name of Allah, Most Gracious, Most **Merciful**.
027:011 truly, I am Oft-Forgiving, Most **Merciful**.
027:030 Most Gracious, Most **Merciful**:
028:000 In the name of Allah, Most Gracious, Most **Merciful**.
028:016 for He is the Oft-Forgiving, Most **Merciful**.
029:000 In the name of Allah, Most Gracious, Most **Merciful**.
030:000 In the name of Allah, Most Gracious, Most **Merciful**.
030:005 and He is Exalted in Might, Most **Merciful**.
031:000 In the name of Allah, Most Gracious, Most **Merciful**.
032:000 In the name of Allah, Most Gracious, Most **Merciful**.
032:006 the Exalted (in power), the **Merciful**;-
033:000 In the name of Allah, Most Gracious, Most **Merciful**.
033:005 is Oft-Returning, Most **Merciful**.
033:024 for Allah is Oft-Forgiving, Most **Merciful**.
033:050 And Allah is Oft-Forgiving, Most **Merciful**.
033:059 and Allah is Oft-Forgiving, Most **Merciful**.
033:073 for Allah is Oft-Forgiving, Most **Merciful**.
034:000 In the name of Allah, Most Gracious, Most **Merciful**.
034:002 and He is the Most **Merciful**, the Oft-Forgiving.
035:000 In the name of Allah, Most Gracious, Most **Merciful**.
036:000 In the name of Allah, Most Gracious, Most **Merciful**.
036:005 by (Him), the Exalted in Might, Most **Merciful**.
036:058 from a Lord Most **Merciful**!
037:000 In the name of Allah, Most Gracious, Most **Merciful**.
038:000 In the name of Allah, Most Gracious, Most **Merciful**.
039:000 In the name of Allah, Most Gracious, Most **Merciful**.
039:053 for He is Oft-Forgiving, Most **Merciful**.
040:000 In the name of Allah, Most Gracious, Most **Merciful**.
041:000 In the name of Allah, Most Gracious, Most **Merciful**.
041:002 A revelation from The Most Gracious, Most **Merciful**;-
041:032 Oft-Forgiving, Most **Merciful**!"
042:000 In the name of Allah, Most Gracious, Most **Merciful**.
042:005 the Oft-Forgiving, Most **Merciful**.
043:000 In the name of Allah, Most Gracious, Most **Merciful**.
044:000 In the name of Allah, Most Gracious, Most **Merciful**.
044:042 for He is exalted in Might, Most **Merciful**.
045:000 In the name of Allah, Most Gracious, Most **Merciful**.
046:000 In the name of Allah, Most Gracious, Most **Merciful**.
046:008 Oft-Forgiving, Most **Merciful**."
047:000 In the name of Allah, Most Gracious, Most **Merciful**.
048:000 In the name of Allah, Most Gracious, Most **Merciful**.
048:014 but Allah is Oft-Forgiving, Most **Merciful**.
049:000 In the name of Allah, Most Gracious, Most **Merciful**.
049:005 but Allah is Oft-Forgiving, Most **Merciful**.
049:012 Oft-returning, Most **Merciful**.
049:014 for Allah is Oft-Forgiving, Most **Merciful**."
050:000 In the name of Allah, Most Gracious, Most **Merciful**.
051:000 In the name of Allah, Most Gracious, Most **Merciful**.
052:000 In the name of Allah, Most Gracious, Most **Merciful**.
052:028 the Beneficent, the **Merciful**!"
053:000 In the name of Allah, Most Gracious, Most **Merciful**.
054:000 In the name of Allah, Most Gracious, Most **Merciful**.
055:000 In the name of Allah, Most Gracious, Most **Merciful**.
056:000 In the name of Allah, Most Gracious, Most **Merciful**.
057:000 In the name of Allah, Most Gracious, Most **Merciful**.

MERCIFUL (continued)

057:009 And verily, Allah is to you Most Kind and **Merciful**.
057:028 is Oft-Forgiving, Most **Merciful**:
058:000 In the name of Allah, Most Gracious, Most **Merciful**.
058:012 Allah is Oft-Forgiving, Most **Merciful**.
059:000 In the name of Allah, Most Gracious, Most **Merciful**.
059:010 Full of Kindness, Most **Merciful**."
059:022 He, Most Gracious, Most **Merciful**.
060:000 In the name of Allah, Most Gracious, Most **Merciful**.
060:007 and Allah is Oft-Forgiving, Most **Merciful**.
060:012 for Allah is Oft-Forgiving, Most **Merciful**.
061:000 In the name of Allah, Most Gracious, Most **Merciful**.
062:000 In the name of Allah, Most Gracious, Most **Merciful**.
063:000 In the name of Allah, Most Gracious, Most **Merciful**.
064:000 In the name of Allah, Most Gracious, Most **Merciful**.
064:014 verily Allah is Oft-Forgiving, Most **Merciful**.
065:000 In the name of Allah, Most Gracious, Most **Merciful**.
066:000 In the name of Allah, Most Gracious, Most **Merciful**.
066:001 But Allah is Oft-Forgiving, Most **Merciful**.
067:000 In the name of Allah, Most Gracious, Most **Merciful**.
067:020 (even as) an army, besides The Most **Merciful**?
068:000 In the name of Allah, Most Gracious, Most **Merciful**.
069:000 In the name of Allah, Most Gracious, Most **Merciful**.
070:000 In the name of Allah, Most Gracious, Most **Merciful**.
071:000 In the name of Allah, Most Gracious, Most **Merciful**.
072:000 In the name of Allah, Most Gracious, Most **Merciful**.
073:000 In the name of Allah, Most Gracious, Most **Merciful**.
073:020 for Allah is Oft-Forgiving, Most **Merciful**.
074:000 In the name of Allah, Most Gracious, Most **Merciful**.
075:000 In the name of Allah, Most Gracious, Most **Merciful**.
076:000 In the name of Allah, Most Gracious, Most **Merciful**.
077:000 In the name of Allah, Most Gracious, Most **Merciful**.
078:000 In the name of Allah, Most Gracious, Most **Merciful**.
079:000 In the name of Allah, Most Gracious, Most **Merciful**.
080:000 In the name of Allah, Most Gracious, Most **Merciful**.
081:000 In the name of Allah, Most Gracious, Most **Merciful**.
082:000 In the name of Allah, Most Gracious, Most **Merciful**.
083:000 In the name of Allah, Most Gracious, Most **Merciful**.
084:000 In the name of Allah, Most Gracious, Most **Merciful**.
085:000 In the name of Allah, Most Gracious, Most **Merciful**.
086:000 In the name of Allah, Most Gracious, Most **Merciful**.
087:000 In the name of Allah, Most Gracious, Most **Merciful**.
088:000 In the name of Allah, Most Gracious, Most **Merciful**.
089:000 In the name of Allah, Most Gracious, Most **Merciful**.
090:000 In the name of Allah, Most Gracious, Most **Merciful**.
091:000 In the name of Allah, Most Gracious, Most **Merciful**.
092:000 In the name of Allah, Most Gracious, Most **Merciful**.
093:000 In the name of Allah, Most Gracious, Most **Merciful**.
094:000 In the name of Allah, Most Gracious, Most **Merciful**.
095:000 In the name of Allah, Most Gracious, Most **Merciful**.
096:000 In the name of Allah, Most Gracious, Most **Merciful**.
097:000 In the name of Allah, Most Gracious, Most **Merciful**.
098:000 In the name of Allah, Most Gracious, Most **Merciful**.
099:000 In the name of Allah, Most Gracious, Most **Merciful**.
100:000 In the name of Allah, Most Gracious, Most **Merciful**.
101:000 In the name of Allah, Most Gracious, Most **Merciful**.
102:000 In the name of Allah, Most Gracious, Most **Merciful**.
103:000 In the name of Allah, Most Gracious, Most **Merciful**.
104:000 In the name of Allah, Most Gracious, Most **Merciful**.
105:000 In the name of Allah, Most Gracious, Most **Merciful**.
106:000 In the name of Allah, Most Gracious, Most **Merciful**.
107:000 In the name of Allah, Most Gracious, Most **Merciful**.
108:000 In the name of Allah, Most Gracious, Most **Merciful**.

MERCIFUL (continued)

109:000 In the name of Allah, Most Gracious, Most **Merciful**.
110:000 In the name of Allah, Most Gracious, Most **Merciful**.
111:000 In the name of Allah, Most Gracious, Most **Merciful**.
112:000 In the name of Allah, Most Gracious, Most **Merciful**.
113:000 In the name of Allah, Most Gracious, Most **Merciful**.
114:000 In the name of Allah, Most Gracious, Most **Merciful**.

MERCY

002:064 the Grace and **Mercy** of Allah to you
002:105 for His special **Mercy** whom He will
002:128 and turn unto us (in **Mercy**);
002:157 (descend) blessings from their Lord, and **Mercy**.
002:178 This is a concession and a **Mercy** from your Lord.
002:218 they have the hope of the **Mercy** of Allah;
002:286 Have **mercy** on us.
003:008 but grant us **mercy** from Thee:
003:074 For His **Mercy** He specially chooseth
003:107 they will be in (the light of) Allah's **Mercy**;
003:128 whether He turn in **mercy** to them, or punish them;
003:132 that ye may obtain **mercy**.
003:157 forgiveness and **mercy** from Allah are far better
003:159 It is part of the **Mercy** of Allah that thou
004:017 to them will Allah turn in **mercy**;
004:026 and (He doth wish to) turn to you (in **Mercy**):
004:083 the Grace and **Mercy** of Allah unto you,
004:096 and Forgiveness and **Mercy**.
004:113 But for the Grace of Allah to thee and His **Mercy**,
004:175 to **Mercy** and Grace from Himself, and guide
005:071 yet Allah (in **mercy**) turned to them: yet again
006:012 inscribed for Himself (the rule of) **Mercy**.
006:016 it is due to Allah's **Mercy**; and that
006:054 inscribed for Himself (the rule of) **Mercy**:
006:133 Thy Lord is Self-sufficient, full of **Mercy**:
006:147 say: "Your Lord is full of **Mercy** All-embracing;
006:154 and a guide and a **mercy**, that they
006:155 that ye may receive **mercy**:
006:157 and a guide and a **mercy**: then who
007:023 and bestow not upon us Thy **Mercy**, we shall
007:049 that Allah with His **Mercy** would never bless?
007:052 a guide and a **mercy** to all who believe.
007:056 for the **Mercy** of Allah is (always)
007:057 going before His **mercy**: when they
007:063 fear Allah and haply receive His **Mercy**?"
007:072 by Our **Mercy** and We cut off the roots
007:149 they said: "If our Lord have not **mercy** upon us
007:151 of those who sow **mercy**!"
007:151 Admit us to Thy **mercy**! For Thou art
007:154 Guidance and **Mercy** for such as fear their Lord.
007:155 so forgive us and give us Thy **mercy**; for Thou
007:156 but My **Mercy** extendeth to all things.
007:156 That (**Mercy**) I shall ordain for those
007:203 and Guidance, and **Mercy**, for any who have Faith."
007:204 and hold your peace: that ye may receive **Mercy**.
009:015 For Allah will turn (in **mercy**) to whom He will:
009:021 of a **Mercy** from Himself, of His good pleasure.
009:027 turn (in **mercy**) to whom He will: for Allah
009:061 and is a **Mercy** to those of you who believe."
009:071 on them will Allah pour His **mercy**:
009:099 soon will Allah admit them to His **Mercy**:
009:102 Perhaps Allah will turn unto them (in **mercy**):
009:106 or turn in **mercy** to them: and Allah
009:118 (He turned in **mercy** also) to the three who were
010:021 of some **mercy** after adversity hath touched them,

MERCY (continued)

010:057	who believe, a Guidance and a **Mercy**.
010:058	And in His **Mercy**,-in that let them rejoice":
010:086	"And deliver us by Thy **Mercy** from those
011:009	If We give man a taste of **mercy** from Ourselves,
011:017	before him is the Book of Moses-a guide and a **mercy**?
011:028	but that the **Mercy** hath been obscured from your sight?
011:028	from my Lord and that He hath sent **Mercy** unto me
011:043	any but those on whom He hath **mercy**!"-
011:047	and have **Mercy** on me, I should indeed
011:063	and He hath sent **Mercy** unto me from Himself,-
011:090	of **mercy** and loving-kindness."
011:094	believed with him, by (special) **Mercy** from Us:
011:119	those on whom thy Lord hath bestowed His **Mercy**:
012:053	unless my Lord do bestow His **Mercy**:
012:056	We bestow of Our **mercy** on whom We please, and We
012:064	of those who show **mercy**!"
012:087	and never give up hope of Allah's soothing **Mercy**:
012:087	truly no one despairs of Allah's soothing **Mercy**,
012:092	of those who show **mercy**?
012:111	and a Guide and a **Mercy** to any such as believe.
015:056	"And who despairs of the **mercy** of his Lord,
016:047	for thy Lord is indeed full of kindness and **mercy**.
016:064	a guide and a **mercy** to those who believe.
016:089	the book explaining all things, a **Mercy**, and Glad Tidings
017:008	It may be that your Lord may (yet) show **Mercy** unto you;
017:024	"My Lord! bestow on them Thy **Mercy** even as they
017:028	from them in pursuit of the **Mercy** from thy Lord
017:054	if He please, He granteth you **mercy**,
017:057	they hope for His **Mercy** and fear His Wrath:
017:082	and a **mercy** to those who believe:
017:087	Except for **Mercy** from thy Lord; for His
017:100	the Treasures of the **Mercy** of my Lord, behold
018:010	bestow on us **Mercy** from Thyself, and dispose
018:058	But your Lord is Most Forgiving, Full of **Mercy**.
018:065	On whom We had bestowed **Mercy** from Ourselves
018:082	a **mercy** (and favour) from thy Lord.
018:098	He said: "This is a **mercy** from my Lord: but when
019:002	(This is) a mention of the **Mercy** of thy Lord
019:021	unto men and a **Mercy** from Us':
019:050	And We bestowed of Our **Mercy** on them, and We
019:053	And, out of Our **Mercy**, We gave him his brother
021:075	And We admitted him to Our **Mercy**: for he
021:086	We admitted them to Our **Mercy**: for they
021:107	We sent thee not, but as a **mercy** for all creatures.
023:075	If We had **mercy** on them and removed
023:109	forgive us, and have **mercy** upon us:
023:109	for Thou art the best of those Who show **mercy**!'
023:118	for Thou art the Best of those who show **mercy**!"
023:118	grant thou forgiveness and **mercy**!
024:010	If it were not for Allah's grace and **mercy** on you,
024:014	and **mercy** of Allah on you, in this
024:020	is full of kindness and **mercy**,
024:020	Were it not for the grace and **mercy** of Allah
024:021	for the grace and **mercy** of Allah on you, not one
024:056	that ye may receive **mercy**.
025:048	going before His **Mercy**, and We
027:046	ye may hope to receive **mercy**."
027:063	as heralds of glad tidings, going before His **Mercy**?
027:077	and a **Mercy** to those who believe.
028:043	Insight to men and Guidance and **Mercy**, that they
028:046	as a **Mercy** from thy Lord, to give
028:073	It is out of His **Mercy** that He has made

MERCY (continued)

028:086	except as a **Mercy** from thy Lord: therefore lend
029:021	and He grants **mercy** to whom He pleases,
029:023	it is they who shall despair of My **mercy**:
029:051	Verily, in it is **Mercy** and Reminder to those
030:021	and He has put love and **mercy** between your (hearts):
030:033	but when He gives them a taste of **Mercy** from Himself,
030:036	When We give men a taste of **Mercy**, they exult
030:046	giving you a taste of His **Mercy**,-that the
030:050	Allah's **Mercy**!-how He gives life to the earth
031:003	A Guide and a **Mercy** to the Doers of Good,-
033:017	to give you Punishment or to give you **Mercy**?"
033:024	be His Will, or turn to them in **Mercy**:
033:043	and He is Full of **Mercy** to the Believers.
033:073	and Allah turns in **Mercy** to the Believers,
035:002	What Allah out of His **Mercy** doth bestow
036:044	Except by way of **Mercy** from Us, and by
036:045	ye may receive **Mercy**," (they turn back).
038:003	In the end they cried (for **mercy**)-
038:009	Or have they the Treasures of the **Mercy** of thy Lord,-
039:009	and who places his hope in the **Mercy** of his Lord-
039:038	remove His affliction or is He wills some **Mercy** for me,
039:038	can they keep back His **Mercy**?" Say: "Sufficient is Allah
039:053	Despair not of the **Mercy** of Allah: for Allah
040:007	Thou embracest all things, in **Mercy** and Knowledge.
040:009	Thou have bestowed **Mercy** indeed: and that
040:077	or We take thy soul (to Our **Mercy**) (before that),
041:050	When We give him a taste of some **mercy** from Us,
042:008	but He admits whom He will to His **Mercy**; and the
042:028	and scatters His **Mercy** (far and wide).
042:048	when We give man a taste of a **Mercy** from Us,
043:032	Is it they who would portion out the **Mercy** of thy Lord?
043:032	But the **Mercy** of thy Lord in better than the (wealth)
044:006	As a **Mercy** from thy Lord: for He
044:042	Except such as receive Allah's **Mercy**: for He
045:020	and a Guidance and **Mercy** to those of assured Faith.
045:030	to His **Mercy**: that will be the manifest triumph.
046:012	as a guide and a **mercy**; and this Book
048:025	that He may admit to His **mercy** whom He will.
049:010	And fear Allah, that ye may receive **Mercy**.
057:013	Within it will be **Mercy** throughout, and without
057:027	hearts of those who followed him compassion and **Mercy**.
057:028	a double portion of His **Mercy**: He will
067:011	but far from Allah's **mercy** are the Companions
067:028	or if He bestows His **Mercy** on us,-yet who
073:020	So He hath turned to you (in **mercy**):
076:031	He will admit to His **Mercy** Whom He will; but the
079:003	And by those who glide along (on errands of **mercy**),

MERE

002:249	a **mere** sip out of the hand is excused."
006:070	their religion to be **mere** play and amusement,
007:051	to be **mere** amusement and play, and were
030:032	and become (**mere**) Sects,-each party
064:006	"Shall (**mere**) human beings direct us?"
078:040	"Woe unto me! Would that I were (**mere**) dust!"

MERELY

009:090	and His Messenger (**Merely**) sat behind: soon will
030:029	Nay, the wrong-doers (**merely**) fellow their
044:038	the earth, and all between them, **merely** in (idle) sport:
045:024	of that they have no knowledge: they **merely** conjecture:
059:007	in order that it may not (**Merely**) make a circuit

MERGES

022:061 into Day, and He **merges** Day in Night, and verily
022:061 That is because Allah **merges** Night into Day,
031:029 Seest thou not that Allah **merges** Night into Day
031:029 into Day and He **merges** Day into Night; that He
035:013 He **merges** Night into Day, and He
035:013 and He **merges** Day into Night, and He
057:006 and He **merges** Day into Night; and He
057:006 He **merges** Night into Day, and He

MERIT

011:003 on all who abound in **merit**!
011:027 apparently nor do we see in you (all) any **merit** above us:
041:050 "This is due to my (**merit**): I think

MESSAGE

003:007 the **Message** except men of understanding.
003:020 thy duty is to convey the **Message**;
003:049 the Children of Israel, (with this **message**):
003:058 of the Signs and the **Message** of Wisdom."
003:126 Allah made it but a **message** of hope for you,
004:140 the **Message** of Allah held in defiance and ridicule,
005:013 of the **Message** that was sent them, nor wilt
005:014 forgot a good part of the **Message** that was
005:067 O Messenger! proclaim the (**Message**) which hath
005:092 to proclaim (the **Message**) in the clearest manner.
005:099 but to proclaim (the **message**).
006:007 a written (**Message**) on parchment, so that
006:145 Say: "I find not in the **Message** received by
007:006 to whom Our **Message** was sent and those
007:062 "I but convey to you" the **Message** of my Lord.
007:068 "I but convey to you the messages of my Lord:
007:069 hath come to you a **message** from your Lord
007:079 convey to you the **message** for which I was
007:087 who believes in the **message** with which
007:185 In what **message** after this will they then believe?
008:010 Allah made it but a **message** of hope, and an
008:012 the angels (with the **message**): "I am with you:
010:067 for those who listen (to His **Message**).
010:087 with this **message**: "Provide dwellings for your
011:051 no reward for this (**Message**).
011:057 have conveyed the **Message** with which I was
011:120 a **message** of remembrance to those who believe.
012:015 (this **Message**): 'Of a surety thou shall (one day)
012:104 than a **Message** for all creatures.
013:040 thy duty is to (make the **Message**) reach them:
014:013 But their Lord inspired (this **Message**) to them:
014:052 Here is a **Message** for mankind: that they
015:006 "O thou to whom the **Message** is being revealed!
015:009 We have, without doubt, sent down the **Message**;
015:013 they do not believe in the **Message**,
016:035 but to preach the Clear **Message**?
016:043 ask of those who possess the **Message**.
016:044 and We have sent down unto thee (also) the **Message**;
016:082 thy duty is only to preach the Clear **Message**.
018:006 if they believe not in this **Message**.
020:038 by inspiration, the **message**:
020:049 (When this **message** was delivered), (Pharaoh) said:
020:124 My **Message**, verily for him is a life narrowed
021:002 a renewed **Message** from their Lord, but they
021:007 ask of those who possess the **Message**.
021:024 this is the **Message** of those with me and the
021:024 and the **Message** of those before me."
021:048 And a Light and a **Message** for those
021:050 And this is a blessed **Message** which We

MESSAGE (continued)

021:105 after the **Message** (given to Moses): My servants
021:106 Verily in the (Qur'an) is a **Message** for people
021:109 say: "I have proclaimed the **Message** to you all
023:027 So We inspired him (with this **message**); "Construct the
023:110 made you forget My **Message** while ye
024:054 is only to preach the clear (**Message**)".
025:018 until they forgot the **Message**: for they
025:029 the **Message** (of Allah) after it had come to me!
026:005 a newly-revealed **message** from the Most Gracious,
026:006 They have indeed rejected (the **Message**): so they
027:059 He has chosen (for his **Message**).
028:086 in any way to those who reject (Allah's **Message**).
029:018 "And if ye reject (the **Message**), so did
034:034 "We believe not in the (**message**) with which
036:011 as follows the **Message** and fears the Most
036:017 to deliver the clear Messenger."
036:069 this is no less than a **Message** and a Qur'an
037:003 Those who thus proclaim the **message** (of Allah)!
037:037 (the **Message** of) the messengers (before him).
037:168 a **message** from those of old,
038:008 "What! Has the **Message** been sent to him-
038:008 But they are in doubt concerning My (own) **Message**!
038:049 This is a **message** (of admonition): and verily
039:021 Truly, in this, is a **Message** of remembrance
039:023 the most beautiful **message** in the form of a Book,
041:014 so we disbelieve in the **Message** you were sent with.
041:041 Those who reject the **Message** when it comes to them
042:048 Thy duty is but to convey (the **Message**).
046:011 who believe: "If (this **Message**) were a good thing,
046:035 (Thine but) to deliver the **Message**:
050:037 Verily in this is a **Message** for any that has
052:033 Or do they say, "He fabricated the (**Message**)?"
053:029 away from Our **Message** and desire nothing but
054:025 "Is It that the **Message** is sent to him, of all
056:081 Is it such a **Message** that ye would hold
064:006 So they rejected (the **Message**) and turned away.
064:012 to deliver (the **Message**) clearly and openly.
065:010 sent down to you a **Message**,-
067:009 'Allah never sent down any (**Message**): ye are in
068:044 Then leave Me alone with such as reject this **Message**:
068:051 trip thee up with their eyes when they hear the **Message**;
068:052 But it is nothing less that a **Message** to all the worlds.
069:043 (This is) a **Message** sent down from the
069:048 But verily this is a **Message** for the God-fearing.
072:016 (And Allah's **Message** is): "If they (the Pagans) had
077:050 Then what **Message**, after that, will they believe in?
080:011 For it is indeed a **Message** of remembrance.
081:027 a **Message** to (all) the Worlds:
087:006 By degrees shall We teach thee (the **Message**),
097:001 indeed revealed this (**Message**) in the night of Power:

MESSAGES

007:093 convey to you the **Messages** for which I was
007:144 by the **messages** I (have given thee) and the
033:039 who preach the **Messages** of Allah, and fear
072:023 from Allah and His **Messages**: for any
072:028 the **Messages** of their Lord and He encompasses

MESSENGER

002:087 comes to you an **Messenger** with what ye
002:101 a **Messenger** from Allah,
002:108 Would ye question your **Messenger**
002:129 a **Messenger** of their own,
002:143 who followed the **Messenger** from those who

MESSENGER (continued)

002:143 and the **Messenger** a witness over yourselves;
002:151 a **Messenger** of your own,
002:214 that even the **Messenger** and those of faith
002:279 notice of war from Allah and His **Messenger**:
002:285 The **Messenger** believeth in what hath been
003:032 Say: "Obey Allah and His **Messenger**": but if they
003:049 "And (appoint him) a **Messenger** to the Children
003:053 and we follow the **Messenger**;
003:081 then comes to you an **Messenger**, confirming
003:086 and bore witness that the **Messenger** was true
003:101 and among you lives the **Messenger**?
003:132 And obey Allah and the **Messenger**;
003:144 Muhammad is no more than a **Messenger**:
003:153 and the **Messenger** in your rear
003:164 among them a **Messenger** from among themselves,
003:172 the call of Allah and the **Messenger**, even after
003:179 but He chooses of his Messengers whom He pleases.
003:183 our promise not to believe in a **messenger** unless he
004:013 those who obey Allah and His **Messenger** will be
004:014 But those who disobey Allah and His **Messenger**
004:042 and disobey the **Messenger** will wish that
004:059 obey Allah, and obey the **Messenger**, and those
004:059 refer it to Allah and His **Messenger**, if ye
004:061 And to the **Messenger**":
004:064 and the **Messenger** had asked forgiveness for them,
004:064 We sent not a **Messenger**, but to be obeyed,
004:069 All who obey Allah and the **Messenger** are in the
004:079 sent thee as a **Messenger** to (instruct) mankind.
004:080 He who obeys the **Messenger**, obeys Allah:
004:083 If they had only referred it to the **Messenger**
004:100 for Allah and His **Messenger**,
004:102 When thou (O **Messenger**) art with them,
004:115 If anyone contends with the **Messenger** even after
004:136 believe in Allah and His **Messenger**,
004:136 He hath sent to His **Messenger** and the scripture
004:136 His Books, His **Messenger**, and the Day
004:157 the **Messenger** of Allah";
004:170 O mankind! the **Messenger** hath come to you in truth
004:171 was (no more than) an **Messenger** of Allah,
005:015 there hath come to you Our **Messenger**, revealing
005:019 making (things) clear unto you, Our **Messenger**,
005:033 who wage war against Allah and His **Messenger**,
005:041 O **Messenger**! let not those grieve thee, who race
005:055 His **Messenger**, and the Believers,-those who
005:056 (for friendship) to Allah, His **Messenger**,
005:067 O **Messenger**! proclaim the (Message) which hath
005:070 a **Messenger** with what they themselves desired not
005:075 Christ the son of Mary was no more than an **Messenger**;
005:083 the revelation received by the **Messenger**,
005:092 Obey Allah, and obey the **Messenger**.
005:104 to what Allah hath revealed; come to the **Messenger**":
005:111 to have faith in Me and Mine **Messenger**:
006:112 for every **Messenger** an enemy,-satans among
007:061 on the contrary I am a **messenger** from the
007:067 but (I am) a **Messenger** from the Lord
007:075 is a **messenger** from his Lord?" They said
007:077 if thou art a **Messenger** (of Allah)!"
007:104 I am a **messenger** from the Lord of the worlds,-
007:157 "Those who follow the **Messenger**, the unlettered
007:158 as the **Messenger** of Allah, to Whom
007:158 So believe in Allah and His **Messenger**.
008:001 spoils are at the disposal of Allah and the **Messenger**:

MESSENGER (continued)

008:001 obey Allah and His **Messenger**, it ye do believe."
008:013 if any contend against Allah and His **Messenger**.
008:013 they contended against Allah and His **Messenger**:
008:020 O ye who believe! obey Allah and His **Messenger**,
008:024 give your response to Allah and His **Messenger**,
008:027 the trust of Allah and the **Messenger**,
008:041 a fifth share is assigned to Allah,-and to the **Messenger**,
008:046 And obey Allah and His **Messenger**; and fall
008:071 against thee, (O **Messenger**!), they have
009:001 from Allah and His **Messenger**, to those
009:003 that Allah and His **Messenger** dissolve (treaty)
009:003 And an announcement from Allah His **Messenger**,
009:007 before Allah and His **Messenger**, with the
009:013 plotted to expel the **Messenger**, and attack
009:016 and protectors except Allah, His **Messenger**,
009:024 than Allah or His **Messenger**, or the striving
009:026 the **Messenger** and on the Believers, and sent
009:029 by Allah and His **Messenger**, nor acknowledge
009:033 His **Messenger** with Guidance and the
009:054 they reject Allah and His **Messenger**; that they
009:059 Allah and His **Messenger** will soon
009:059 what Allah and His **Messenger** gave them, and had
009:062 should please Allah and His **Messenger**, if they
009:063 who oppose Allah and His **Messenger**, is the
009:065 and His **Messenger**, that ye were mocking?"
009:070 To them came their **Messenger** with Clear Signs.
009:071 pay zakat and obey Allah and His **Messenger**.
009:074 Allah and His **Messenger** had enriched them!
009:080 rejected Allah and His **Messenger**:
009:081 in their sitting back behind the **Messenger** of Allah:
009:084 for they rejected Allah and His **Messenger**,
009:086 and fight along with His **Messenger**, those with
009:088 But the **Messenger**, and those who believe
009:090 and His **Messenger** (Merely) sat behind: soon will
009:091 (in duty) to Allah and His **Messenger**: no ground
009:094 and His **Messenger** will observe: in the end
009:097 sent down to His **Messenger**:
009:099 and obtaining the prayers of the **Messenger**.
009:105 and His **Messenger**, and the Believers: soon will
009:107 who warred against Allah and His **Messenger** aforetime.
009:120 behind Allah's **Messenger**, nor to prefer their own
009:128 a **Messenger** from amongst yourselves: it grieves
010:047 To every people (was sent) an **Messenger**: when their
010:047 when their **Messenger** comes (before them),
012:050 But when the **messenger** came to him, (Joseph) said:
013:038 a **messenger** to bring a Sign except as Allah
013:043 The Unbelievers say: "No **messenger** art thou."
014:004 We sent not a **messenger** except (to teach) in the
015:011 But never came a **messenger** to them
016:036 every People a **messenger**, (with the Command),
016:113 And there came to them a **Messenger** from among
017:015 We had sent a **messenger** (to give warning).
017:093 am I aught but a man,-a **messenger**?"
017:094 to be (His) **Messenger**?"
017:095 an angel for a **messenger**."
019:019 He said: "Nay, I am only a **messenger** from thy Lord,
019:051 And He was a **messenger** and a prophet.
019:054 and he was a **messenger** (and) a prophet.
020:096 from the footprint of the **Messenger**, and threw
020:134 "Our Lord! If only Thou hadst sent us a **messenger**,
021:025 Not a **messenger** did We send before thee
022:015 help him (His **Messenger**) in this world and the

MESSENGER (continued)

022:052 Never did We send a **messenger** or a prophet
022:078 that the **Messenger** may be a witness for you,
023:032 And We sent to them a **messenger** from among
023:044 a people their **messenger**, they accused
023:044 Then sent We Our messengers in succession:
023:051 O ye **messenger**! enjoy (all) things good and pure,
023:069 their **Messenger**, that they deny him?
024:047 and in the **Messenger**, and we obey": but even
024:048 When they are summoned to Allah and His **Messenger**,
024:050 that Allah and His **Messenger** will deal
024:051 His **Messenger**, in order that He may judge
024:052 His **Messenger**, and fear Allah and do right,
024:054 Say: "Obey Allah, and obey the **Messenger**: but if
024:056 and give zakat and obey the **Messenger**; that ye
024:062 for the leave are those who believe and His **Messenger**;
024:062 are believers, who believe in Allah and His **Messenger**:
024:063 of the **Messenger** among yourselves like the
025:007 And they say: "What sort of a **messenger** is this,
025:027 a (straight) path with the **Messenger**!
025:030 Then the **Messenger** will say: "O my Lord,
025:041 "Is this the one whom Allah has sent as a **messenger**?"
026:027 (Pharaoh) said: "Truly your **messenger** who has
026:107 "I am to you a trustworthy **messenger**.
026:125 "I am to you a **messenger** worthy of all trust.
026:143 I am to you a **messenger** worthy of all trust.
026:162 "I am to you a **messenger** worthy of all trust.
026:178 "I am to you a **messenger** worthy of all trust.
027:054 (We also sent) Lut (as a **Messenger**): behold, he
028:047 "Our Lord! why didst Thou not send us a **messenger**?
028:059 to its Centre a **messenger**, rehearsing to
029:018 and the duty of the **messenger** is only
033:012 say: "Allah and His **Messenger** promised us nothing
033:021 Ye have indeed in the **Messenger** of Allah
033:022 and His **Messenger** told us what was true."
033:022 "This is what Allah and His **Messenger** had promised
033:029 His **Messenger**, and the Home of the Hereafter,
033:031 and His **Messenger**, and work righteousness,-to her
033:033 and obey Allah and His **Messenger**.
033:036 been decided by Allah and His **Messenger**, to have
033:036 and His **Messenger**, he is indeed on a clearly
033:040 your men, but (he is) the **Messenger** of Allah,
033:053 ye should annoy Allah's **Messenger**, or that
033:057 and his **Messenger**-Allah has cursed them in this
033:066 we had obeyed Allah and obeyed the **Messenger**!"
033:071 he that obeys Allah and His **Messenger** has already
034:028 as a (**Messenger**) to all mankind, giving them
036:030 There comes not a **messenger** to them
040:034 ye said: 'No **messenger** will Allah send after him.'
040:078 for any **messenger** to bring a Sign except by the
041:044 What! a foreign (tongue) and (a **Messenger**) an Arab?"
042:051 or by the sending of a **Messenger** to reveal,
043:029 and a **Messenger** making things clear.
043:046 "I am a **messenger** of the Lord of the Worlds."
044:013 Seeing that a **Messenger** explaining things clearly
044:017 a **Messenger** most honorable,
044:018 I am to you a **messenger** worthy of all trust;
047:032 and resist the **Messenger**, after Guidance
047:033 and obey the **Messenger**, and make
048:009 may believe in Allah and His **Messenger**, that ye
048:012 "Nay, ye thought that the **Messenger** and the
048:013 And if any believe not in Allah and His **Messenger**,
048:017 but he that obeys Allah and His **Messenger**,- (Allah) will

MESSENGER (continued)

048:026 to His **Messenger** and to the Believers, and made
048:027 Truly did Allah fulfil the vision for His **Messenger**:
048:028 His **Messenger** with Guidance and the Religion
048:029 Muhammad is the **Messenger** of Allah; and those
049:001 not yourselves forward before Allah and His **Messenger**;
049:003 in the presence of Allah's **Messenger**,-their hearts
049:007 And know that among you is Allah's **Messenger**:
049:014 But if ye obey Allah and His **Messenger**, He will
049:015 and His **Messenger**, and have never since doubted,
050:001 (Thou art Allah's **Messenger**).
051:052 Similarly, no **messenger** came to the Peoples
054:009 the People of Noah rejected (their **messenger**):
057:007 Believe in Allah and His **Messenger**, and spend
057:008 And the **Messenger** invites you to believe in your Lord
057:028 Fear Allah, and believe in His **Messenger**,
058:004 may show your faith in Allah and His **Messenger**.
058:005 and His **Messenger** will be humbled to dust,
058:008 and disobedience to the **Messenger**.
058:009 and disobedience to the **Messenger**;
058:012 when ye consult the **Messenger** in private,
058:013 and obey Allah and His **Messenger**.
058:020 Allah and His **Messenger** will be among those
058:022 Loving those who oppose Allah and His **Messenger**,
059:004 That is because they resisted Allah and His **Messenger**:
059:006 What Allah has bestowed on His **Messenger**
059:007 What Allah has bestowed on His **Messenger**
059:007 belongs to Allah,-to His **Messenger**, and to kindred
059:007 So take what the **Messenger** gives you,
059:008 And aiding Allah and His **Messenger**:
060:001 driven out the **Messenger** and yourselves
061:005 I am the **messenger** of Allah (sent) to you?"
061:006 glad Tidings of a **messenger** to come after me,
061:006 I am the **messenger** of Allah (sent) to you,
061:009 It is He Who has sent His **Messenger** with Guidance
061:011 That ye believe in Allah and His **Messenger**, and that ye
062:002 the Unlettered a **messenger** from among themselves,
063:001 bear witness that thou art indeed the **Messenger** of Allah."
063:001 Allah knoweth thou art indeed His **Messenger**.
063:005 "Come, the **Messenger** of Allah will pray for your
063:007 nothing on those who are with Allah's **Messenger**,
063:008 But honour belongs to Allah and His **Messenger**,
064:008 Believe, therefore, in Allah and His **Messenger**,
064:012 So obey Allah, and obey His **Messenger**;
064:012 the duty of Our **Messenger** is but to deliver
065:011 A **Messenger**, who rehearses to you the Signs
069:010 And disobeyed (each) the **messenger** of their Lord;
069:040 of a honoured **messenger**;
069:044 And if the **messenger** were to invent any sayings
072:023 for any that disobey Allah and His **Messenger**,-
072:027 "Except a **messenger** whom He has chosen:
073:015 We have sent to you, (O men)! a **Messenger**, to be a
073:015 even as We sent a **messenger** to Pharaoh.
073:016 But Pharaoh disobeyed the **messenger**; so We
081:019 of a most honorable **Messenger**,
091:013 But the **messenger** of Allah said to them: "It is a She-
098:002 **Messenger** from Allah, rehearsing scriptures kept pure

MESSENGER'S

005:095 know ye that it is Our **Messenger's** duty to
005:099 The **Messenger's** duty is but to proclaim
024:054 The **Messenger's** duty is only to preach the clear
024:063 who withstand the **Messenger's** order, lest some

MESSENGERS

002:061 and slaying His **Messengers** without just cause.
002:087 a succession of **Messengers**;
002:177 and the Angels, and the Book, and the **Messengers**;
002:213 And Allah sent **Messengers** with glad tidings
002:252 verily thou art one of the **Messengers**.
002:253 Those **Messengers** We endowed with gifts,
002:285 between one and another of His **Messengers**."
002:285 His Angles, His books, and His **Messengers**.
003:144 many were the **Messengers** that passed away before Him.
003:179 So believe in Allah and His **Messengers**:
003:183 Say: "There came to you **Messengers** before me,
003:184 so were rejected **messengers** before thee,
003:194 Thou didst promise unto us through Thy **Messengers**,
004:150 and wish to separate between Allah and His **Messengers**,
004:150 Those who deny Allah and His **Messengers**,
004:152 and His **messengers** and make no distinction
004:152 make no distinction between any of the **messengers**,
004:155 that they slew the **Messengers** in defiance of right;
004:163 and the **Messengers** after him: We sent
004:164 Of some **messengers** We have already told thee
004:165 after (the coming) of the **messengers**,
004:165 **Messengers** who gave good news as well
004:171 so believe in Allah and His **Messengers**.
005:012 pay Zakat believe in My **Messengers**, honour and
005:019 after the break in (the series of) **Messengers**,
005:032 Our **Messengers** with Clear Signs, yet, even after
005:070 the Children of Israel and sent them **Messengers**.
005:075 many were the **Messengers** that passed
005:109 gather the **Messengers** together, and ask:
006:010 Mocked were (many) **Messengers** before thee;
006:034 Rejected were the **Messengers** before thee:
006:034 some account of those **Messengers**.
006:042 Before thee We sent (**Messengers**) to many nations,
006:048 We send the **Messengers** only to give
006:124 like those receive by Allah's **messengers**."
006:130 came there not unto you **messengers** from amongst you,
006:131 (The **messengers** were sent) thus, for thy Lord
007:035 come to you **messengers** from amongst you, rehearsing
007:037 until, when Our **messengers** (of death) arrive
007:043 the **Messengers** of our Lord brought unto us."
007:053 "The **Messengers** of our Lord did indeed
007:101 their **Messengers** with clear (Signs); but they
010:013 their **Messengers** came to them with Clear Signs,
010:021 Verily, Our **messengers** record all the plots that ye
010:074 after him We sent (many) **messengers** to their Peoples:
010:103 Our **messengers** and those who believe:
011:059 disobeyed His **Messengers**; and followed
011:069 There came Our **Messengers** to Abraham
011:077 When Our **Messengers** came to Lut, he was
011:081 (The **Messengers**) said "O Lut! we are **Messengers** from
011:120 the stories of the **messengers**,-with it
012:109 (as **Messengers**) any but men, whom We did inspire,-
012:110 until, when the **messengers** give up hope (of their people)
013:032 Mocked were (many) **messengers** before thee:
013:038 We did send **messengers** before thee, and appointed
014:009 To them came **Messengers** with Clear (Signs);
014:010 Their **messengers** said: "Is there a doubt
014:011 Their **messengers** said to them: "True, we are
014:013 And the Unbelievers said to their **messengers**: "Be sure
014:044 we will answer Thy Call, and follow the **messengers**!"
014:047 that Allah would fail His **messengers** in His promise:
015:010 We did send **messengers** before thee amongst

MESSENGERS (continued)

015:057 O ye **messengers** (of Allah)?"
015:061 At length when the **messengers** arrived among
015:080 Rocky Tract also rejected the **Messengers**:
016:035 but to preach the Clear Message?
017:077 (This was Our) way with the **messengers** We sent
018:056 We only send the **Messengers** to give glad tidings
018:106 and took My Signs and My **Messengers** by way of jest.
020:047 'Verily we are **Messengers** sent by thy Lord:
021:007 Before thee, also, the **messengers** We sent
021:041 Mocked were (many) **Messengers** before thee;
022:075 Allah chooses **Messengers** from angels and from
023:024 if Allah had wished (to send **messengers**), He could have
025:020 And the **messengers** whom We sent before thee
025:037 when they rejected the **messengers**, We drowned
026:021 (and wisdom) and appointed me as one of the **messengers**.
026:105 The people of Noah rejected the **messengers**.
026:123 The 'Ad (people) rejected the **messengers**.
026:141 The Thamud (people) rejected the **messengers**.
026:160 The people of Lut rejected the **messengers**.
026:176 The Companions of the Wood rejected the **messengers**.
027:010 those called as **messengers** have no fear,-
028:007 and We shall make him one of Our **messengers**."
028:045 Who send **messengers** (with inspiration).
028:065 ye gave to the **messengers**?"
029:031 When Our **Messengers** came to Abraham with the
029:033 And when Our **Messengers** came to Lut, he was
030:009 there came to them their **messengers** with Clear
030:047 before thee, **messengers** to their (respective) peoples,
034:044 nor sent **messengers** to them before thee as Warners.
034:045 My **messengers**, how (terrible) was My punishment!
035:001 the angels **messengers** with wings,-two, or three
035:004 so were **messengers** rejected before thee:
035:025 to whom came their **messengers** with Clear Signs,
036:003 Thou art indeed one of the **messengers**,
036:013 Behold, there came **messengers** to it.
036:014 When We (first) sent to them two **messengers**,
036:020 a man, saying, "O my People! obey the **messengers**:
036:052 the word of the **messengers**!"
037:037 and he confirms (the Message of) the **messengers**
037:181 And Peace on the **messengers**!
038:012 Before them (were many who) rejected **messengers**,-
038:014 Not one (of them) but the **messengers**, but My
039:071 "Did not **messengers** come to you from among
040:022 to them their **messengers** with Clear (Signs),
040:050 to you your **messengers** with Clear Signs?"
040:051 help Our **messengers** and those who believe,
040:070 We sent Our **messengers**: but soon
040:078 We did aforetime send **messengers** before thee:
040:083 For when their **messengers** came to them
041:014 Behold, the **messengers** came to them, from before
041:043 that was not said to the **messengers** before thee:
043:045 And question thou Our **messengers** whom We
043:080 Indeed (We do), and Our **Messengers** are by them,
046:009 Say: "I am not an innovation among the **messengers**,
046:035 as did (all) **messengers** of firm resolution;
050:014 each one (of them) rejected the **messengers**, and My
051:031 "And what, O ye **Messengers**, is your errand (now)?"
057:019 and His **messengers**-they are the Truthful and the
057:021 and His **messengers**: that is the Grace of Allah,
057:025 We sent aforetime our **messengers** with Clear Signs
057:025 who it is that will help, unseen, Him and His **messengers**:
057:027 We followed them up with (others of) Our **messengers**:

MESSENGERS (continued)

058:021 "It is I and My **messengers** who must prevail":
059:006 but Allah gives power to His **messengers** over any
064:006 to them **messengers** with Clear Signs, but they
065:008 of their Lord and of His **messengers**, did We
077:011 And when the **messengers** are (all) appointed

MET

003:013 a Sign in the two armies that **met** (in combat):
003:146 if they **met** with disaster in Allah's way,
003:155 on the day the two hosts **met**, it was Satan
003:166 What ye suffered on the day the two armies **met**,
008:042 but (thus ye **met**), that Allah might accomplish a matter
008:044 And remember when ye **met**, He showed
018:074 when they **met** a young man, he slew
022:073 if they all **met** together for the purpose!
025:075 be **met** with salutations and peace,
054:012 so the waters **met** (and rose) to the extent decreed.

METED

030:047 We **meted** out Retribution: and it

METTLE

047:031 and We shall try your reported (**mettle**).

MICHAEL

002:098 to Gabriel and **Michael**,

MIDDLE

002:238 Especially the **Middle** Prayer;
017:110 but seek a **middle** course between."
035:032 some who follow a **middle** course; and some who are

MIDDLING

002:068 but of **middling** age;

MIDIAN

020:040 thou tarry a number of years with the people of **Midian**.

MIDST

006:039 in the **midst** of darkness profound: whom Allah
006:044 in the **midst** of their enjoyment of Our gifts,
009:047 to and fro in your **midst** and sowing sedition among you,
011:102 the **midst** of their wrong: grievous, indeed,
016:046 in the **midst** of their goings to and fro,
016:079 held poised in the **midst** of (the air and) the sky?
016:113 seized them even in the **midst** of their iniquities.
017:091 in their **midst**, carrying abundant water;
018:017 in the **midst** of the Cave.
018:033 the least therein: in the **midst** of them We caused
024:043 issue forth from their **midst**.
026:018 and didst thou not stay in our **midst** many years
027:061 made rivers in its **midst**; set thereon
030:048 until thou seest rain-drops issue from the **midst** thereof:
033:020 and if they were in your **midst**, they would
037:055 in the **midst** of the Fire.
041:026 in the **midst** of its (reading), that ye
044:047 and drag him into the **midst** of the Blazing Fire!
051:015 they will be in the **midst** of Gardens and Springs,
054:054 they will be in the **midst** of Gardens and Rivers.
055:044 In its **midst** and in the **midst** of boiling hot water will
056:042 (They will be) in the **midst** of a fierce
065:012 through the **midst** of them (all) descends
071:016 "'And made the moon a light in their **midst**, and made
100:005 penetrate forthwith into the **midst** (of the foe) En masse;-

MIDWAY

004:150 and wish to take a course **midway**,

MIGHT

002:129 for Thou art the Exalted in **Might**, the Wise."
002:143 That ye **might** be witnesses over the nations,

MIGHT (continued)

003:004 and Allah is Exalted in **Might**, Lord of Retribution.
003:006 the Exalted and **Might**, the Wise.
003:127 That He **might** cut off a fringe of the Unbelievers
003:154 but (all this was) that Allah **might** test what
003:166 in order that He **might** test the Believers,
004:084 strongest in **might** and in punishment.
005:033 and strive with **might** and main for mischief
005:035 and strive with **might** and main in His cause:
006:075 that he **might** have certitude.
006:154 that they **might** believe in the meeting with their Lord.
007:094 in order that they **might** call in humility.
007:130 that they **might** receive admonition.
007:168 in order that they **might** turn (to Us).
007:189 in order that he **might** dwell with her
008:008 That He **might** establish Truth and prove
008:017 in order the He **might** confer on the Believers
008:026 and afraid that men **might** despoil and kidnap you;
008:026 that ye **might** be grateful.
008:042 and those who lived **might** live after a Clear Sign
008:042 who died **might** die after a Clear Sign (had been given),
008:042 that Allah **might** accomplish a matter already
008:044 That Allah **might** accomplish a matter
008:049 behold! Allah is Exalted in **might**, Wise.
008:063 for He is Exalted in **might**, Wise.
008:067 and Allah is Exalted in **might**, Wise.
009:016 strive with **might** and main, and take
009:019 and strive with **might** and main in the
009:020 and strive with **might** and main, in Allah's
009:040 Exalted in **might**, Wise.
009:118 that they **might** repent: for Allah
010:005 that ye **might** know the number of years and the
011:007 that He **might** try you, which of you is best in conduct.
012:021 that We **might** teach him the interpretation
012:024 that We **might** turn away from him (all) evil
012:062 in order that they **might** come back.
017:001 We did Bless,-in order that We **might** show him
018:019 that they **might** question each other.
018:021 to the people, that they **might** know that the
019:012 "O Yahya! take hold of the Book with **might**":
020:040 that her eye **might** be cooled and she
021:058 that they **might** turn (and address themselves) to it.
022:034 that they **might** celebrate the name of Allah
022:040 Exalted in **Might**, (able to enforce His Will).
023:049 in order that they **might** receive guidance.
026:009 the Exalted in **Might**, Most Merciful.
026:044 "By the **might** of Pharaoh, it is
026:068 the Exalted in **Might**, Most Merciful.
026:104 the Exalted in **Might**, Most Merciful.
026:122 the Exalted in **Might**, Most Merciful.
026:140 the Exalted in **Might**, Most Merciful.
026:159 the Exalted in **Might**, Most Merciful.
026:175 the Exalted in **Might**, Most Merciful.
026:191 The Exalted in **Might**, Most Merciful
026:217 on the Exalted in **Might**, the Merciful,-
027:009 the Exalted in **Might**, the Wise!...
027:078 and He is Exalted in **Might**, All-knowing.
028:010 so that she **might** remain a (firm) believer.
028:013 and that she **might** know that the promise
028:013 that her eye **might** be comforted, that she
028:013 that she **might** not grieve, and that
028:043 that they **might** receive admonition.
028:047 they **might** say: "Our Lord! why didst

MIGHT (continued)

029:006 And if any strive (with **might** and main), they do
029:026 for He is Exalted in **Might**, and Wise."
030:005 and He is Exalted in **Might**, Most Merciful.
030:027 for He is Exalted in **Might**, Full of Wisdom.
033:025 full of Strength, Exalted in **Might**.
034:006 to the Path of the Exalted (in **Might**), Worthy of all praise.
034:021 except that We **might** test the man who believes
035:028 Exalted in **Might**, Oft-Forgiving.
036:005 by (Him), the Exalted in **Might**, Most Merciful.
036:038 the Exalted in **Might**, the All-Knowing.
036:074 (hoping) that they **might** be helped!
038:066 and all between-Exalted in **Might**, Ever-Forgiving.
040:008 the Exalted in **Might**, Full of Wisdom.
040:084 But when they saw Our **Might**, they said
041:012 of (Him) the Exalted in **Might**, Full of knowledge.
041:016 that We **might** give them a taste of a Chastisement
043:033 were it not that (all) men **might** become of one community
043:048 in order that they **might** turn (to Us).
044:042 for He is exalted in **Might**, Most Merciful.
051:039 But (pharaoh) turned back on account of his **might**,
051:047 We have built the Firmament with **might**:
057:001 for He is the Exalted in **Might**, the Wise.
057:025 Full of Strength, Exalted in **Might**.
057:025 in which is great **might**, as well as
059:001 for He is the Exalted in **Might**, the Wise.
059:005 and in order that He **might** cover with shame
059:023 the Exalted in **Might**, the Irresistible, the justly
059:024 and He is the Exalted in **Might**, the Wise.
060:005 the Exalted in **Might**, the Wise."
061:001 the Exalted in **Might**, the Wise.
062:001 the Holy One, the Exalted in **Might**, the Wise.
062:003 is Exalted in **Might**, Wise.
064:018 is open, Exalted in **Might**, Full of Wisdom.
067:002 the Exalted in **Might**, Oft-Forgiving;
069:012 That We **might** make it a Reminder unto you,
072:017 "That We **might** try them by that (means).
080:003 but that perchance he **might** grow purity?
080:004 and the Reminder **might** profit him?
080:004 Or that he **might** receive admonition,

MIGHTEST

004:105 that thou **mightest** judge between people by that
007:002 warn (the erring) and a reminder the Believers.
009:103 that so thou **mightest** purify and sanctify them;
013:030 in order that thou **mightest** rehearse unto them what We
014:001 in order that thou **mightest** lead mankind out of
017:106 in order that thou **mightest** recite it
018:094 in order that thou **mightest** erect a barrier
071:007 that thou **mightest** forgive them, they have

MIGHTIER

009:069 they were **mightier** than you in power and more

MIGHTY

005:054 lowly with the Believers, **mighty** against the Rejecters,
005:119 **mighty** Triumph (the fulfillment of all desires).
006:015 the Chastisement of a **Mighty** Day.
006:016 and that would be a **Mighty** Triumph.
010:083 was **mighty** on the earth and one who
011:066 For thy Lord-He is the Strong One, and the **Mighty**.
011:067 The (**mighty**) Blast overtook the wrong-doers,
011:094 but the (**mighty**) Blast did seize the
012:028 Truly, **mighty** is your snare!
013:013 about Allah, He is **Mighty** in Power.
014:046 **Mighty** indeed were the plots which they made,

MIGHTY (continued)

015:073 But the (**mighty**) Blast overtook
015:083 But the (**mighty**) Blast seized them of a morning,
016:094 and a **mighty** Wrath descend on you.
017:004 with **mighty** arrogance (and twice would they be
022:074 for Allah is Powerful and **Mighty**.
023:086 seven heavens, and the Lord of the **Mighty** Throne?"
025:021 and **mighty** is the insolence of their impiety!
028:079 For he is truly a lord of **mighty** good fortune."
029:037 then the **mighty** Blast seized them, and they
029:040 some were caught by a (**mighty**) Blast; some We
036:029 It was no more than a single **mighty** Blast,
038:015 These (to-day) only wait for a single **mighty** Blast,
038:075 the high (and **mighty**) ones?"
039:013 the Chastisement of a **Mighty** Day."
042:019 and He is the Strong, the **Mighty**.
044:016 The day we shall seize you with a **mighty** onslaught:
044:049 Truly thou art **Mighty**, full of honour!
046:021 the Chastisement of a **Mighty** Day."
050:042 a (**mighty**) Blast in (very) truth): that will
053:005 He was taught by one **Mighty** in Power,
053:049 That He is the Lord of Sirius (the **Mighty** Star);
054:031 **For We sent against them a single Mighty** Blast,
054:042 the seizure of a **Mighty**, Powerful.
056:076 And that is indeed a **mighty** adjuration if ye
058:021 who must prevail": for Allah is Strong, **Mighty**.
074:035 This is but one of the **mighty** (Portents),
083:005 On a **Mighty** Day,
088:024 Allah will chastise him with a **mighty** Chastisement.

MIGRATED

033:050 who **migrated** with thee; and any

MILDLY

020:044 "But speak to him **mildly**; perchance he

MILK

016:066 We produce, for your drink, **milk**, pure and
023:021 We produce (**milk**) for you to drink; there are,
036:073 and they get (**milk**) to drink.
047:015 rivers of **milk** of which the taste never changes;

MIM

007:001 Alif Lam **Mim** Sad.
026:001 Ta Sin **Mim**.
028:001 Ta. Sin. **Mim**.
040:001 Ha-**Mim**.
041:001 Ha-**Mim**.
042:001 Ha-**Mim**;
043:001 Ha-**Mim**.
044:001 Ha **Mim**.
045:001 Ha-**Mim**.
046:001 Ha-**Mim**.

MIND

002:040 call to **mind** the (special) favour
002:046 Who bear in **mind** the certainty
002:047 call to **mind** the (special) favour
002:122 call to **mind** the special favour
002:238 Allah in a devout (frame of **mind**).
007:200 If a suggestion from Satan assail thy (**mind**), seek refuge
008:026 Call to **mind** when ye were a small (band),
010:071 "O my People, if it be hard on your (**mind**) that I
011:074 When fear had passed from (the **mind** of) Abraham
014:006 "Call to **mind** the favour of Allah to you
019:067 But does not man call to **mind** that We
020:067 So Moses conceived in his **mind** a (sort of) fear.
020:128 (to call to **mind**) how many generations before

MIND (continued)

022:046   so that their hearts (and **mind**) may thus learn
053:011   The (Prophet's) (**mind** and) heart in no way
102:005   with certainty of **mind**, (ye would beware)!

MINDFUL

007:172   "Of this we were never **mindful**":
011:114   that is a reminder to the **mindful**.
016:013   is a Sign for men who **mindful**.
025:050   be **mindful** but most men are averse (to aught)
025:062   for such as desire to be **mindful** or to show

MINDS

002:284   your **minds** or conceal it,
003:154   They hide in their **minds** what they
004:009   have the same fear in their **minds** as they would
012:018   He said: "Nay, but your **minds** have made up
017:046   their hearts (and **minds**) lest they should
017:051   in your **minds**, is hardest (to be raised up),-
030:008   Do they not reflect in their own **minds**?
048:027   if Allah wills, with **minds** secure, heads shaved,
092:019   And have in their **minds** no favour from anyone

MINE

005:111   to have faith in Me and **Mine** Messenger: they said
006:066   Say: "Not **mine** is the responsibility for
014:022   nor can ye listen to **mine**.
020:039   mayest be reared under **Mine** eye.
027:028   Go thou, with this letter of **mine**, and deliver
109:006   To you be your Way, and to me **mine**.

MINGLED

017:104   in a **mingled** crowd.
076:002   Verily We created man from a drop of **mingled** sperm,

MINGLING

010:024   by its **mingling** arises the produce of the earth-

MINISTER

020:029   "And give me a **Minister** from my family,
025:035   his brother Aaron with him as **Minister**;

MIRACLE

004:153   for an even greater (**miracle**), for they said:
005:113   be witnesses to the **miracle**.

MIRAGE

024:039   their deeds are like a **mirage** in sandy
078:020   as if they were a **mirage**.
081:003   When the mountains vanish (like a **mirage**);

MISAPPROPRIATE

008:027   nor **misappropriate** knowingly things entrusted

MISAPPROPRIATED

003:161   restore what he **misappropriated**;

MISBELIEVER

025:055   the **misbeliever** is a helper (of Evil), against his

MISBELIEVERS

025:004   But the **Misbelievers** say: "Naught is this but a lie which
025:026   it will be a Day of dire difficulty for the **Misbelievers**.

MISBELIEVING

059:011   say to their **misbelieving** brethren among the

MISCHIEF

002:011   "Make not **mischief** on the earth,"
002:012   the ones who make **mischief**,
002:027   and do **mischief** on earth:
002:030   make **mischief** therein and shed blood?
002:060   evil nor **mischief** on the (face of the) earth.
002:205   but Allah loveth not **mischief**.
002:205   to spread **mischief** through the earth

002:220   means **mischief** from the man who means good.
002:251   the earth would indeed be full of **mischief**,

MISCHIEF (continued)

003:063   Allah hath full knowledge of those who do **mischief**.
005:032   or for spreading **mischief** in the land-it would be
005:033   for **mischief** through the land is:
005:064   And Allah loveth not those who do **mischief**.
005:064   but they (ever) strive to do **mischief** on earth.
005:067   from men (who mean **mischief**).
007:056   Do no **mischief** on the earth, after it
007:074   and refrain from evil and **mischief** on the earth."
007:085   and do no **mischief** on the earth after it
007:086   And see what was the end of those who did **mischief**.
007:103   of those who made **mischief**.
007:127   to spread **mischief** in the land, and to
007:142   the way of those who do **mischief**."
008:073   and great **mischief**.
009:107   by way of **mischief** and infidelity-to disunite
010:040   those who are out for **mischief**.
010:081   the work of those who make **mischief**.
010:091   and thou didst **mischief** (and violence)!
011:085   with intent to do **mischief**.
011:116   who prohibited men from **mischief** in the earth
012:073   know that we came not to make **mischief** in the land,
013:025   to be joined, and work **mischief** in the land;
016:088   for that they used to spread **mischief**.
017:004   that twice would they do **mischief** on the earth
018:094   do great **mischief** on earth: shall we
026:152   "Who make **mischief** in the land, and mend
026:183   in the land, working **mischief**.
027:048   who made **mischief** in the land, and would
028:077   for Allah loves not those who do **mischief**."
028:077   and seek not (occasions for) **mischief** in the land:
028:083   high-handedness or **mischief** on earth:
029:030   help Thou me against people who do **mischief**!"
029:036   with intent to do **mischief**."
030:041   **Mischief** has appeared on land and sea
038:028   the same as those who do **mischief** on earth?
040:026   should cause **mischief** to appear in the land!"
047:022   that ye will do **mischief** in the land, and break
056:025   nor any **mischief**,-
089:012   And heaped therein **mischief** (on **mischief**).
113:002   From the **mischief** of created things;
113:003   From the **mischief** of Darkness as it overspreads;
113:004   From the **mischief** of those who blow on knots;
113:005   And from the **mischief** of the envious one
114:004   From the **mischief** of the Whisperer (of Evil),

MISDEEDS

005:013   but forgive them and overlook (their **misdeeds**):
007:096   and We brought them to book for their **misdeeds**.
029:007   blot out all **misdeeds** that they have committed,
058:016   a screen (for their **misdeeds**): thus they
063:002   a screen (for their **misdeeds**): thus they

MISER

092:008   But he who is a greedy **miser** and thinks

MISERABLE

002:079   to traffic with it for a **miserable** price!
002:090   **Miserable** is the price for which
002:174   and purchase for them a **miserable** profit,
003:187   and purchased with it some **miserable** gain!
003:199   the Signs of Allah for a **miserable** gain!
005:044   and sell not My Signs for a **miserable** price.
009:009   they sold for a **miserable** price, and (many)

MISERABLE (continued)

012:020 The (Brethren) sold him a **miserable** price,-for a few
016:095 Nor sell the Covenant of Allah a **miserable** price:
028:058 after them, are deserted,-all but a (**miserable**) few!

MISERS

009:076 they became **misers**, and turned back

MISERY

002:061 They were covered with humiliation and **misery**:
013:018 what a bed of **misery**!
016:027 covered with Shame and **Misery**,-
020:117 the Garden, so that thou art landed in **misery**.
020:123 will not lose his way, nor fall into **misery**.
040:052 and the Home of **Misery**.
092:010 for him the Path to **Misery**;

MISFORTUNE

003:120 but if some **misfortune** overtakes you,
004:062 How then, when they are seized by **misfortune**.
004:072 if a **misfortune** befalls you, they say: "Allah
007:150 Make not the enemies rejoice over my **misfortune**,
009:050 but if a **misfortune** befalls thee, they say
023:106 our **misfortune** overwhelmed us, and we
042:030 Whatever **misfortune** happens to you, is because
057:022 No **misfortune** can happen on earth or in your

MISGUIDED

007:179 nay more **misguided**: for they

MISLEAD

004:119 "I will **mislead** them, and I will create
006:119 But many do **mislead** (men) by low
009:115 And Allah will not **mislead** a people after He
010:088 our Lord they **mislead** (men) from Thy Path.
014:030 to **mislead** (men) from the Path!
031:006 to **mislead** (men) from the Path of Allah and throw
038:026 thou the lust (of thy heart), for it will **mislead** thee
071:027 they will but **mislead** Thy devotees, and they

MISLEADERS

038:060 (The followers shall cry to the **misleaders**:) "Nay, ye (too)!

MISLEADING

039:008 thus **misleading** others from Allah's Path.

MISLEADS

028:015 for he is an enemy that manifestly **misleads**!"

MISLED

005:077 who **misled** many, and strayed themselves
007:038 "Our Lord! it is these that **misled** us: so give
008:049 their religion has **misled** them."
016:025 burdens of those without knowledge, whom they **misled**.
025:042 who it is that is most **misled** in Path!
025:042 "He indeed would well-high have **misled** us from our
033:067 and they **misled** us as to the (right) path.
041:029 among Jinns and men, who **misled** us: we shall
053:002 Your Companion is neither astray nor being **misled**,
071:024 "They have already **misled** many; and grant

MISS

012:071 "What is it that ye **miss**?"
012:072 They said: "We **miss** the great beaker of the king;

MISSED

019:059 a posterity who **missed** prayers and followed

MISSILES

067:005 (as) **missiles** to drive away Satans, and have

MISSION

005:067 wouldst not have fulfilled and proclaimed His **Mission**.
006:124 Allah knoweth best where to place His **mission**.
011:025 We sent Noah to his People (with a **mission**):

MISSION (continued)

014:009 "We do deny (the **mission**) on which ye have
016:035 But what is the **mission** of messengers but to
036:014 on a **mission** to you."
036:016 we have been sent on a **mission** to you:
037:147 And We sent him (on a **mission**) to a
040:034 of the (**mission**) for which he had come:
046:023 I proclaim to you the **mission** on which I have

MIST

044:010 a kind of smoke (or **mist**) plainly visible.

MISTAKE

004:092 Never should a Believer kill a Believer except by **mistake**,
004:092 whoever kills a Believer by **mistake** it is ordained that
033:005 on you if ye make a **mistake** therein:

MISTAKES

024:039 parched with thirst **mistakes** for water;

MISTRUST

011:070 he felt some **mistrust** of them, and conceived

MITIGATED

016:085 no way be **mitigated**, nor will

MIX

002:220 if ye **mix** their affairs with yours,
006:082 and **mix** not their beliefs with wrong-that are

MIXED

006:146 or is **mixed** up with a bone: this in
009:102 they have **mixed** an act that was good with another
076:005 of a Cup (of Wine) **mixed** with Kafur,-
076:017 of a Cup **mixed** with Zanjabil,-

MIXING

004:002 (by **mixing** it up) with your own.

MIXTURE

037:067 be given a **mixture** made of boiling water.
083:027 With it will be (given) a **mixture** of Tasnim:

MOCK

006:005 the news of what they used to **mock** at.
009:064 Say: "**Mock** ye! But verily Allah will bring to light all
011:008 which they used to **mock** at!
036:030 to them but they **mock** Him!
039:048 which they used to **mock** at!
045:033 by that which they used to **mock** at!
046:026 they used to **mock** at!

MOCKED

006:010 **Mocked** were (many) Messengers before thee;
006:010 by the thing that they **mocked**.
013:032 **Mocked** were (many) messengers before thee: but I
015:011 to them but they **mocked** him.
021:041 hemmed in by the thing that they **mocked**.
021:041 **Mocked** were (many) Messengers before thee;
026:006 the truth of what they **mocked** at!
039:056 towards Allah, and was but among those who **mocked**!'
043:007 to them but they **mocked** him.

MOCKERY

002:015 Allah will throw back their **mockery** on them,
005:057 for a **mockery** or sport,-whether among those who
005:058 they take it (but) as **mockery** and sport; that is
025:041 in **mockery**: "Is this the one whom Allah has sent
037:014 And, when they see a Sign, turn it to **mockery**,
083:030 used to wink at each other (in **mockery**);

MOCKING

009:065 and His Messenger, that ye were **mocking**?"

MODE

024:041 Each knows its own (**mode** of) prayer and praise.

MODEL
016:120   Abraham was indeed a **model**, devoutly obedient

MODERATE
031:019   "And be **moderate** in thy pace, and lower

MODEST
024:060   but it is best for them to be **modest**:

MODESTY
002:273   because of their **modesty**,
023:005   Who guard their **modesty**,
024:030   they should lower their gaze and guard their **modesty**:
024:031   they should lower their gaze and guard their **modesty**;

MOISTURE
002:265   light **moisture** suffice it.

MOLDED
015:026   from mud **molded** into shape;
015:028   form sounding clay, from mud **molded** into shape;
015:033   sounding clay, from mud **moulded** into shape."

MOLDS
095:004   We have indeed created man in the best of **molds**,

MOLEST
009:061   Among them are men who **molest** the Prophet and say,
009:061   But those who **molest** the Prophet will have

MOLESTED
033:059   be known (as such) and not **molested**.

MOLTEN
018:096   over it, **molten** lead."
034:012   a Font of **molten** brass to flow for him; and there
044:045   Like **molten** brass; it will boil in their insides,
055:035   A flame of fire (to burn) and a (flash of) **molten** brass.
070:008   The Day that the sky will be like **molten** brass,

MOMENT
003:159   and consult them in affairs (of **moment**).

MOMENTOUS
002:143   Indeed it was (a change) **momentous**,
007:141   in that was a **momentous** trial from your Lord.
037:107   And We ransomed him with a **momentous** sacrifice:

MONASTERIES
022:040   pulled down **monasteries**, churches, synagogues,

MONASTICISM
057:027   But the **Monasticism** which they

MONEY
018:019   with this **money** of yours to the town: let him

MONSTROUS
019:089   Indeed ye have put forth a thing most **monstrous**!

MONTH
002:185   Ramadhan is the (**month**) in which
002:185   during that **month** should spent it in fasting,
002:194   The prohibited **month** for the prohibited **month**,
002:217   concerning fighting in the Prohibited **Month**.
005:002   nor of the Sacred **Month**, nor of the
009:037   Verily the transposing (of a prohibited **month**) is an

MONTH'S
034:012   its early morning (stride) was a **month's** (journey),
034:012   and its evening (stride) a **month's** (journey);

MONTHLY
002:228   concerning themselves for three **monthly** periods,
065:004   the age of **monthly** courses, for them

MONTHS
002:197   For Hajj are the **months** well known.
002:226   a waiting for four **months** is ordained;
002:234   concerning themselves four **months** and ten days
004:092   (is prescribed) a fast for two **months** running:

MONTHS (continued)
005:097   as also the Sacred **Months**, the animals
009:002   Go ye, then, for four **months**, (as you will),
009:005   But when the forbidden **months** are past, then fight
009:036   The number of **months** in the sight of Allah
009:037   in order to agree with the number of **months** forbidden
046:015   to his weaning is (a period of) thirty **months**.
058:004   two **months** consecutively before they touch each
065:004   if ye have any doubt, is three **months**, and those
081:004   When the she-camels, ten **months** with young,
097:003   is better than a thousand **Months**.

MONUMENT
002:198   praises of Allah at the Sacred **Monument**,

MOON
006:077   When he saw the **moon** rising in splendor, He said:
006:077   But when the **moon** set, he said: "Unless my
006:096   and the sun and **moon** for the
007:054   and the sun, the **moon**, and the stars, (all) are
010:005   shining glory and the **moon** to be a light
012:004   and the sun and the **moon**: I saw
013:002   He has subjected the sun and the **moon**! each one
014:033   the sun and the **moon**, both diligently
016:012   and the Day; the Sun and the **Moon**; and the
021:033   and the Day, and the sun and the **moon**: all (the
022:018   and on earth,-the sun, the **moon**, the stars;
025:061   a lamp and a **Moon** giving light;
029:061   and the **moon** (to His Law), they will
031:029   and the **moon** (to His Law), each running
035:013   and the **moon** (to His Law): each one
036:039   And the **Moon**,-We have measured for her stations
036:040   to catch up the **Moon**, nor can
039:005   He has subjected the sun and the **moon** (to His law):
041:037   the Night and the Day, and the Sun and the **Moon**.
041:037   Prostrate not to the sun and the **moon**, but prostrate to,
054:001   and the **moon** was cleft asunder.
055:005   The sun and the **moon** follow courses
071:016   "And made the **moon** a light in their midst, and made
074:032   Nay, verily: by the **Moon**,
075:008   And the **moon** is buried in darkness.
075:009   And the sun and **moon** are joined together,-
084:018   And the **Moon** in her Fullness:
091:002   By the **Moon** as she follow him;

MOONS
002:189   They ask thee concerning the New **Moons**.

MORALS
068:004   And surely thou hast sublime **morals**.

MORE
002:088   (which preserve Allah's word, we need no **more**)"
002:096   even **more** than the idolaters:
002:114   And who is **more** unjust than he who forbids
002:140   Ah! who is **more** unjust than those
002:167   "If only we had one **more** chance,
002:184   But he that will give **more**, of his own free will,
002:193   there is no **more** Persecution
002:200   yea, with far **more** heart and soul.
002:206   he is led by arrogance to (**more**) crime.
002:282   and **more** convenient to prevent doubts among yourselves,
002:282   it is juster in the sight of Allah, **more** suitable as evidence,
003:144   Muhammad is no **more** than a Messenger:
004:003   That will be **more** suitable, to prevent you
004:011   if only daughters, two or **more**, their share
004:012   but if **more** than two, they share in a third;
004:032   gifts **more** freely on some of you than on others:

MORE (continued)

004:034 the one **more** (strength) than the other,
004:046 it would have been better for them, and **more** proper;
004:062 "We meant no **more** than good-will and conciliation!"
004:077 or even **more** than, they should have feared Allah:
004:086 is offered meet it with a greeting still **more** courteous,
004:171 was (no **more** than) an Messenger of Allah,
004:173 He will give their (due) rewards,-and **more**, out of His
005:060 and far **more** astray from the even Path!"
005:075 was no **more** than an Messenger; many were
006:021 Who doth **more** wrong than he who inventeth
006:081 hath **more** right to security?
006:093 Who can be **more** wicked than one who
006:144 But who doth **more** wrong than one
006:157 then who could do **more** wrong than one
007:002 no **more** by any difficulty on that account,-
007:037 Who is **more** unjust than one who forges
007:114 He said: "Yea, (and **more**),-for ye shall
007:142 and completed (the period) with ten (**more**):
007:155 This is no **more** than Thy trial: by it Thou
007:179 nay **more** misguided: for they
008:039 there is no **more** persecution, and religion
009:013 Nay, it is Allah whom ye should **more** justly fear,
009:062 but it is **more** fitting that they should please
009:069 and **more** flourishing in wealth and children.
009:108 it is **more** worthy of thy standing forth
009:111 and who is **more** faithful to his to his Covenant than Allah?
010:017 Who doth **more** wrong than such as forge
010:026 do right is a goodly (reward)-yea, **more** (than in measure)!
010:035 gives guidance to Truth **more** worthy to be followed,
011:018 Who doth **more** wrong than those who
011:092 of **more** consideration with you than Allah?
012:008 are loved **more** by our father than we: but we
012:032 and (what is **more**) be in the company of the vilest!"
012:042 and (Joseph) lingered in prison a few (**more**) years.
012:063 No **more** measure of grain shall we get
012:065 they said: "O our father! What (**more**) can we desire?
012:065 so we shall get (**more**) food for our family;
013:004 yet some of them We make **more** excellent than others to
013:014 besides Him hear them no **more** than if they
013:018 all that is in the heavens and on earth, and as much **more**,
014:007 "If ye are grateful, I will add **more** (favours) unto you;
014:010 They said: "Ah! ye are no **more** then human,
016:071 of sustenance **more** freely on some of you than on others
016:071 those **more** favoured are not going to throw back their
016:092 lest one party should be **more** numerous then another:
017:006 the **more** numerous in man-power.
017:021 See how We have bestowed **more** on some than on others;
017:021 is **more** in rank and gradation and **more** in excellence.
018:015 Who doth **more** wrong than such as invent
018:025 three hundred years, and nine (**more**).
018:034 "**More** wealth have I than you, and **more** honour and
018:057 And who doth **more** wrong than one who is reminded
020:007 knoweth what is secret and what is yet **more** hidden.
020:071 which of us can give the **more** severe and the
020:071 and the **more** lasting Punishment!"
020:127 of the Hereafter is far **more** grievous and **more** enduring.
020:131 but the provision of thy Lord is better and **more** enduring.
021:003 "Is this (one) **more** than a man like yourselves?
021:047 And if there be (no **more** than) the weight
023:024 "He is no **more** than a man than a man like yourselves:
023:033 "He is no **more** than a man than a man like yourselves:
023:101 there will be no **more** relationships between

MORE (continued)

024:038 and add even **more** for them out of His Grace:
024:053 obedience is (**more**) reasonable; verily, Allah is
026:042 He said: "Yea, (and **more**),-for ye
026:154 "Thou art no **more** than a mortal like us:
026:186 "Thou art no **more** than a mortal like us,
028:034 he is **more** eloquent in speech than I: so send
028:050 and who is **more** astray than one who follows their
028:060 but that which is with Allah is better and **more** enduring:
029:068 And who does **more** wrong than he who invents
032:022 And who does **more** wrong than one to whom
033:016 no **more** than a brief (respite) will ye be allowed to enjoy!"
033:037 but it is **more** fitting that thou shouldst, fear Allah.
033:052 (to marry **more**) women after this,
034:035 They said: "We have **more** in wealth and in sons,
035:030 nay, He will give them (even) **more** out of
035:042 they would be **more** rightly guided
036:029 It was no **more** than a single mighty Blast,
036:053 It will be no **more** than a single Blast,
037:011 are they the **more** difficult to create, or the
037:147 to a hundred thousand (men) or **more**.
039:032 Who, then, doth **more** wrong than one who
039:047 had all that there is on earth, and as much **more**,
040:082 They were **more** numerous than these
041:016 but the Penalty of the Hereafter will be **more** humiliating
041:052 Who is **more** astray than one who is in a schism far
042:036 but that which is with Allah is better and **more** lasting:
043:059 He was no **more** than a servant: We granted
046:005 And who is **more** astray than one who invokes,
046:035 tarried **more** than an hour in a single day.
047:013 with **more** power than thy city which has driven
047:020 But **more** fitting for them-
050:030 It will say, "Are there any **more** (to come)?"
050:031 nigh to the righteous,-no **more** a thing distant.
050:035 all that they wish,-and there is **more** with Us.
058:007 five but he is the sixth,-nor between fewer not **more**,
063:008 surely the **more** honourable (element) will expel
068:028 Said one of them, **more** just (than the rest):
072:020 Say: "I do no **more** than invoke my Lord, and I
073:004 Or a little **more**; and recite the Qur'an in slow,
073:006 and speech **more** certain.
073:006 is a time when impression is **more** keen and speech
074:015 Yet is he greedy-that I should add (yet **more**);
075:019 Nay **more**, it is for Us to explain it
079:027 Are ye the **more** difficult to create or the
087:017 But the Hereafter is better and **more** enduring.
098:005 And they have been commanded no **more** than this:
102:001 diverts you (from the **more** serious things),

MOREOVER

006:154 **Moreover**, We gave Moses the Book, completing
008:063 And (**moreover**) He hath put affection
015:017 And (**moreover**) we have guarded them from every
016:053 and **moreover**, when ye are touched by distress,
017:075 and **moreover** thou wouldst have found none
020:097 'Touch me not'; and **moreover** (for a future penalty)
035:037 And (**moreover**) the warner came to you.
079:030 And the earth, **moreover**; hath He

MORN

079:046 or (at most till) the following **morn**!
097:005 Peace!...This until the rise of **Morn**!

MORNING

003:017 forgiveness in the early hours of the **morning**
003:041 and glorify Him in the evening and in the **morning**."

MORNING (continued)

003:072 "Believe in the **morning** what is revealed
003:121 (Remember that **morning**) thou didst leave
006:052 on their Lord **morning** and evening, seeking
007:078 in their homes in the **morning**!
007:091 in their homes before the **morning**!
011:067 prostrate in their homes before the **morning**,-
011:081 **Morning** is their time appointed:
011:081 time appointed: is not the **morning** nigh?"
011:094 in their homes by the **morning**,-
015:066 those (sinners) should be cut off by the **morning**.
015:083 But the (mighty) Blast seized them of a **morning**,
016:006 lead them forth to pasture in the **morning**.
017:078 in **morning** prayer for the recital of dawn
018:028 who call on their Lord **morning** and evening,
019:011 in the **morning** and in the evening.
019:062 their sustenance, **morning** and evening.
024:058 before **morning** prayer; the while
025:005 before him **morning** and evening."
028:018 In the **morning**, he was in the city, fearful and
029:037 in their homes in the **morning**.
030:017 ye rise in the **morning**;
033:042 And glorify Him **morning** and evening.
034:012 its early **morning** (stride) was a month's (journey),
037:177 Evil will be the **morning** for those who were
040:046 the Fire will they be brought, **morning** and evening:
040:055 in the evening and in the **morning**.
046:025 Then by the **morning** they-nothing was to be seen
048:009 and celebrate His praises **morning** and evening.
067:030 some **morning** lost (in the underground earth),
068:017 of the (garden) in the **morning**.
068:020 So the (garden) became, by the **morning**, like a
068:021 As the **morning** broke, they called out, one to
068:022 in the **morning**, if ye would gather the fruits."
068:025 And they opened the **morning**, strong in
076:025 of thy Lord **morning** and evening,
093:001 By the Glorious **Morning** Light.
100:003 And push home the charge in the **morning**,

MORNINGS

007:205 in the **mornings** and evenings; and be not
013:015 so do their shadows in the **mornings** and evenings.
024:036 is he glorified in the **mornings** and in the evenings,

MORROW

028:082 His position the day before began to say on the **morrow**:
031:034 that he will earn on the **morrow**: nor does
054:026 Ah! they will know on the **morrow**, which is
054:038 Early on the **morrow** an abiding Chastisement
059:018 he has sent forth for the **morrow**.

MORSEL

022:005 then out a **morsel** of flesh, partly formed

MORTAL

012:031 "Allah preserve us! no **mortal** is this!
026:154 "Thou art no more than a **mortal** like us:
026:186 "Thou art no more than a **mortal** like us,
074:025 "This is nothing but the word of a **mortal**!"

MOSES

002:051 appointed forty nights for **Moses**,
002:053 And remember We gave **Moses** the Scripture
002:054 And remember **Moses** said to his people: "O my people!
002:055 "O **Moses**! we shall never believe in thee
002:060 And remember **Moses** prayed for water
002:061 And remember ye said: "O **Moses**! we cannot endure one
002:067 remember **Moses** said to his people: "Allah commands

MOSES (continued)

002:087 We gave **Moses** the Book
002:092 There came to you **Moses** with clear (Signs);
002:108 as **Moses** was questioned of old?
002:136 and that given to **Moses** and Jesus,
002:246 Children of Israel after (the time of) **Moses**
002:248 the family of **Moses** and the family of Aaron,
003:003 Torah (of **Moses**) and the Gospel (of Jesus).
003:084 given to **Moses**, Jesus, and the Prophets
004:153 indeed they asked **Moses** for an even
004:153 and gave **Moses** manifest proofs of authority.
004:164 and to **Moses** Allah spoke direct;
005:020 Remember **Moses** said to his people: "O my people!
005:022 They said: "O **Moses**! in this land are a people
005:024 They said: O "**Moses**! we shall never enter it
005:044 It was We who revealed the Torah (to **Moses**):
006:084 Solomon, Job, Joseph, **Moses**, and Aaron: thus do
006:091 the Book which **Moses** brought?-A light
006:154 Moreover, We gave **Moses** the Book, completing
007:103 Then after them We sent **Moses** with Our Signs
007:104 **Moses** said: "O Pharaoh! I am
007:107 Then (**Moses**) threw his rod, and behold!
007:115 They said: "O **Moses**! wilt thou throw (first),
007:116 Said **Moses**: "Throw ye (first)."
007:117 We revealed to **Moses** "Throw thy rod": and behold!
007:122 "The Lord of **Moses** and Aaron."
007:127 "Wilt thou leave **Moses** and his people,
007:128 Said **Moses** to his people: "Pray for help
007:131 connected with **Moses** and those with Him!
007:132 They said (to **Moses**): "Whatever be
007:134 they said: "O **Moses**! on our behalf call on
007:138 They said: "O **Moses**! fashion for us a god
007:142 We appointed for **Moses** thirty nights,
007:142 And **Moses** had charged his brother Aaron
007:143 He made it as dust and **Moses** fell down in a swoon.
007:143 When **Moses** came to the place appointed by Us,
007:144 (Allah) said: "O **Moses**! I have chosen thee
007:148 The people of **Moses** made, in his absence, out of
007:150 When **Moses** came back to his people, angry and
007:151 **Moses** prayed: "O my Lord! forgive me
007:154 When the anger of **Moses** was appeased, he took
007:155 And **Moses** chose seventy of his people
007:159 Of the people of **Moses** there is
007:160 We directed **Moses** by inspiration, when his
010:075 **Moses** and Aaron to Pharaoh and his
010:077 Said **Moses**: "Say ye (this) about the Truth when it
010:080 **Moses** said to them: "Throw ye what ye (wish)
010:081 **Moses** said: "What ye have brought is sorcery:
010:083 But none believed in **Moses** except some
010:084 **Moses** said: "O my People! if ye do
010:087 We inspired **Moses** and his brother with this
010:088 **Moses** prayed: "Our Lord! Thou hast indeed bestowed
010:089 (O **Moses** and Aaron)! So stand ye straight,
011:017 and before him is the Book of **Moses**-a guide
011:096 And We sent **Moses**, with Our Clear (Signs) and an
011:110 We certainly gave the Book to **Moses**,
014:005 We sent **Moses** with Our Signs (and the command).
014:006 Remember! **Moses** said to his people: "Call to mind
014:008 And **Moses** said: "If ye show ingratitude, ye and
017:002 We gave **Moses** the Book, and made
017:101 To **Moses** We did give nine Clear Signs:
017:101 Pharaoh said to him: "O **Moses**! I consider thee,
017:102 **Moses** said, "Thou knowest well that these things

MOSES (continued)

018:060 Behold, **Moses** said to his attendant, "I will not give up
018:062 **Moses** said to his attendant: "Bring us our early meal;
018:064 **Moses** said: "That was what we were seeking after":
018:066 **Moses** said to him: "May I follow thee, on the
018:069 **Moses** said: "Thou wilt find me, if Allah
018:071 Said **Moses**: "Hast thou scuttled it in order to drown
018:073 **Moses** said: "Rebuke me not for forgetting,
018:074 **Moses** said: "Hast thou slain an innocent person
018:076 (**Moses**) said: "If ever I ask thee about anything
018:077 (**Moses**) said: "If thou hadst wished, surely thou
019:051 (the story of) **Moses**: for he was specially chosen.
020:009 Has the story of **Moses** reached thee?
020:011 he was called "O **Moses**!
020:017 And what is that in thy right hand, O **Moses**?"
020:019 (Allah) said, "Throw it, O **Moses**!"
020:025 (**Moses**) said: "O my Lord! expand me my breast;"
020:036 (Allah) said: "Granted is thy prayer, O **Moses**!"
020:040 Then didst thou come hither as ordained, O **Moses**!
020:045 They (**Moses** and Aaron) said: "Our Lord!
020:049 (Pharaoh) said: "Who, then, O **Moses**, is the
020:057 us out of our land with thy magic, O **Moses**?
020:059 **Moses** said: "Your tryst is the Day of the Festival,
020:061 **Moses** said to them: "Woe to you! Forge
020:065 They said: "O **Moses**! whether wilt thou that thou
020:067 So **Moses** conceived in his mind a (sort of) fear.
020:070 "We believe in the Lord of Aaron and **Moses**."
020:077 We sent an inspiration to **Moses**: "Travel by
020:083 (When **Moses** was up on the mount, Allah said):
020:083 in advance of thy people, O **Moses**?"
020:086 and the god of **Moses**, but (**Moses**) has forgotten!"
020:091 to it until **Moses** returns to us."
020:092 (**Moses**) said: "O Aaron! what kept thee back,
020:095 (**Moses**) said: "What then is thy case, O Samiri?"
020:097 (**Moses**) said: "Get thee gone! but thy (punishment)
021:048 In the past We granted to **Moses** and Aaron
021:105 after the Message (given to **Moses**): My servants
022:044 and **Moses** was rejected (in the same way).
023:045 Then We sent **Moses** and his brother Aaron,
023:049 And We gave **Moses** the Book, in order
025:035 (Before this), We sent **Moses** the Book,
026:010 Behold, thy Lord called **Moses**: "Go to the people of
026:020 **Moses**: "I did it then, when I was in error.
026:024 (**Moses**) said: "The Lord and Cherisher of the
026:026 (**Moses**) said: "Your Lord and the Lord of your
026:028 (**Moses**) said: "Lord of the East and the West,
026:030 (**Moses**) said: "Even if I showed you something
026:032 So (**Moses**) threw his rod, and behold,
026:043 **Moses** said to them: "Throw ye-
026:045 Then **Moses** threw his rod, when, behold,
026:048 "The Lord of **Moses** and Aaron."
026:052 By inspiration We told **Moses**: "Travel by night with
026:061 the people of **Moses** said: "We are sure to be overtaken."
026:062 (**Moses** said: "By no means! my Lord
026:063 Then We told **Moses** by inspiration: "Strike the sea with
026:065 We delivered **Moses** and all who were with him;
027:007 Behold! **Moses** said to his family: "I perceive a fire;
027:009 "O **Moses**! verily, I am Allah, the Exalted
027:010 "O **Moses**!" (it was said), fear not:
028:003 the story of **Moses** and Pharaoh in Truth,
028:007 mother of **Moses**: "Suckle (thy child), but when
028:008 (it was intended) that (**Moses**) should be
028:010 And the heart of the mother of **Moses** became void:

MOSES (continued)

028:011 And she said to the sister of (**Moses**), "Trace him."
028:015 and **Moses** struck him with his fist and killed
028:018 **Moses** said to him: "Thou art truly, one erring manifestly."
028:019 "O **Moses**! is it thy intention to slay me
028:020 He said: "O **Moses**! the Chiefs are taking counsel
028:029 Now when **Moses** had fulfilled the term, and was
028:030 "O **Moses**! Verily I am Allah, the Lord of the Worlds...
028:031 "O **Moses**!" (It was said), "Draw near, and fear not:
028:036 When **Moses** came to them with Our Clear Signs,
028:037 **Moses** said: "My Lord knows best who it is
028:038 that I may mount up to the god of **Moses**:
028:038 I think (**Moses**) is a liar!"
028:043 We did reveal to **Moses** the Book after We
028:044 when We decreed the commission to **Moses**, nor wast
028:046 side of (the Mountain of) Tur when We called (to **Moses**).
028:048 which were formerly sent to **Moses**?
028:048 like those which were sent to **Moses**?"
028:076 Qarun was doubtless, of the people of **Moses**;
029:039 there came to them **Moses** with Clear Sings,
032:023 We did indeed aforetime give the Book to **Moses**:
033:007 from Noah, Abraham, **Moses**, and Jesus the son of Mary:
033:069 those who hurt **Moses**, but Allah cleared him
037:114 Our favour on **Moses** and Aaron,
037:120 "Peace and salutation to **Moses** and Aaron!"
040:023 Of old We sent **Moses**, with Our Signs
040:026 Said Pharaoh: "Leave me to slay **Moses**;
040:027 **Moses** said: "I have indeed called upon my Lord
040:037 but surely, I think (**Moses**) is a liar!"
040:037 and that I may look up to the God of **Moses**;
040:053 We did aforetime give **Moses** the Guidance,
041:045 We certainly gave **Moses** the book aforetime:
042:013 on Abraham, **Moses**, and Jesus: namely, that
043:046 We did send **Moses** aforetime, with Our Signs,
043:052 "Am I not better than this (**Moses**), who is
046:012 And before this, was the Book of **Moses** as a guide and
046:030 we have heard a Book revealed after **Moses**,
051:038 And in **Moses** (was another Sign): behold, We sent
053:036 is he not acquainted with what is in the books of **Moses**-
061:005 And remember, **Moses** said to his people: "O my people!
079:015 Has the story of **Moses** reached thee?
079:020 Then did (**Moses**) show him the Great Sign.
087:019 The Books of Abraham and **Moses**.

MOSQUE

002:144 in the direction of the Sacred **Mosque**:
002:149 in the direction of the Sacred **Mosque**;
002:150 in the direction of the Sacred **Mosque**;
002:191 but fight them not at the Sacred **Mosque**,
002:196 is not in (the precincts of) the Sacred **Mosque**.
002:217 to prevent access to the Sacred **Mosque**,
004:043 except when you are passing by (through the **mosque**),
005:002 shutting you out of the Sacred **Mosque** lead you
008:034 the Sacred **Mosque**-and they are not its guardians?
009:007 with whom ye made a treaty near the sacred **mosque**?
009:019 or the maintenance of the Sacred **Mosque**,
009:028 after this year of theirs, approach the Sacred **Mosque**.
009:107 And there are those who put up a **mosque** by way
009:108 There is a **mosque** whose foundation was laid
017:001 from the Sacred **Mosque** to the Farthest **Mosque** whose
022:025 and from the Sacred **Mosque**, which We
048:025 and hindered you from the Sacred **Mosque** and the
048:027 ye shall enter the Sacred **Mosque**, if Allah

MOSQUES

002:187	while ye are in retreat in the **mosques**.
009:017	to maintain the **mosques** of Allah
009:018	The **mosques** of Allah shall be visited and
022:040	churches, synagogues, and **mosques**, in which

MOST

001:001	In the name of Allah, **Most** Gracious, **Most** Merciful.
001:003	**Most** Gracious, **Most** Merciful.
002:000	In the name of Allah, **Most** Gracious, **Most** Merciful.
002:037	for He is Oft-Returning, **Most** Merciful.
002:054	for He is Oft-returning, **Most** Merciful.
002:085	the **most** grievous chastisement
002:096	of all people, **most** greedy of life,
002:100	Nay, **most** of them are faithless.
002:143	all people **most** surely full of kindness, **Most** Merciful.
002:160	for I am Oft-Returning, **Most** Merciful.
002:163	**Most** Gracious, **Most** Merciful.
002:173	For Allah is Oft-Forgiving, **Most** Merciful.
002:182	for Allah is Oft-Forgiving, **Most** Merciful.
002:192	Allah is Oft-Forgiving, **Most** Merciful.
002:199	For Allah is Oft-forgiving, **Most** Merciful.
002:204	yet is he the **most** contentious of enemies.
002:218	and Allah is Oft-Forgiving, **Most** Merciful.
002:225	and He is Oft-Forgiving, **Most** Forbearing.
002:226	Allah is Oft-Forgiving, **Most** Merciful.
002:232	(the course making for) **most** virtue and purity amongst
002:235	and know that Allah is Oft Forgiving, **Most** Forbearing.
002:239	or riding, (as may be **most** convenient),
002:243	but **most** of them are ungrateful.
002:255	For He is the **Most** High, the Supreme (in glory).
002:256	hath grasped the **most** trustworthy hand-hold,
002:263	and he is **Most** Forbearing.
003:000	In the name of Allah, **Most** Gracious, **Most** Merciful.
003:031	for Allah is Oft-Forgiving, **Most** Merciful.
003:089	for verily Allah is Oft-Forgiving, **Most** Merciful.
003:110	but **most** of them are perverted transgressors.
003:129	but Allah is Oft-Forgiving, **Most** Merciful.
003:155	for Allah is Oft-Forgiving, **Most** Forbearing.
004:000	In the name of Allah, **Most** Gracious, **Most** Merciful.
004:012	and Allah is All-Knowing, **Most** Forbearing.
004:016	for Allah is Oft-returning, **Most** Merciful.
004:018	a chastisement **most** grievous.
004:023	for Allah is Oft-Forgiving, **Most** Merciful.
004:025	And Allah is Oft-forgiving, **Most** Merciful.
004:029	for verily Allah hath been to you **Most** Merciful.
004:031	If ye (but) eschew the **most** heinous of the things
004:034	for Allah is **Most** High, Great (above you all).
004:048	a sin **most** heinous indeed.
004:059	that is best, and **most** suitable for final determination.
004:064	found Allah indeed Oft-Returning, **Most** Merciful.
004:096	For Allah is Oft-Forgiving. **Most** Merciful.
004:100	and Allah is Oft-Forgiving, **Most** Merciful.
004:106	for Allah is Oft-Forgiving, **Most** Merciful.
004:110	he will find Allah Oft-Forgiving, **Most** Merciful.
004:114	In **most** of their secret talks there is no good:
004:129	Allah is Oft-forgiving, **Most** Merciful.
004:152	for Allah is Oft-Forgiving, **Most** Merciful.
005:000	In the name of Allah, **Most** Gracious, **Most** Merciful.
005:003	Allah is indeed Oft-Forgiving, **Most** Merciful.
005:034	know that Allah is Oft-Forgiving, **Most** Merciful.
005:039	for Allah is Oft-Forgiving, **Most** Merciful.
005:049	And truly **most** men are rebellious.
005:059	and (perhaps) that **most** of you are rebellious

MOST (continued)

005:064	from Allah increaseth in **most** of them their
005:068	that increaseth in **most** of them their
005:074	For Allah is Oft-forgiving, **Most** Merciful.
005:081	but **most** of them are rebellious wrong-doers.
005:098	and that Allah is Oft-Forgiving, **Most** Merciful.
005:101	for Allah is Oft-Forgiving, **Most** Forbearing
005:103	but **most** of them lack wisdom.
005:108	That is **most** suitable: that they
006:000	In the name of Allah, **Most** Gracious, **Most** Merciful.
006:019	Say: "What thing is **most** weighty in evidence?"
006:037	but **most** of them understand not."
006:054	lo! He is Oft-Forgiving, **Most** Merciful.
006:070	and for punishment, one **most** grievous: for they
006:111	But **most** of them ignore (the truth).
006:137	of **most** of the Pagans, their "partners"!
006:145	thy Lord is Oft-Forgiving, **Most** Merciful.
006:165	yet He is indeed Oft-Forgiving, **Most** Merciful.
007:000	In the name of Allah, **Most** Gracious, **Most** Merciful.
007:017	nor wilt Thou find, in **most** of them, gratitude
007:102	but **most** of them We found rebellious and disobedient.
007:102	**Most** of them We found not men (true) to their covenant:
007:131	but **most** of them do not understand!
007:151	For Thou art the **Most** Merciful of those
007:153	thereafter Oft-Forgiving, **Most** Merciful.
007:167	but He is also Oft-Forgiving, **Most** Merciful.
007:180	The **most** beautiful names belong to Allah: so call
007:187	is with Allah (alone), but **most** men know not."
008:000	In the name of Allah, **Most** Gracious, **Most** Merciful.
008:034	but **most** of them do not understand.
008:069	for Allah is Oft-Forgiving, **Most** Merciful.
008:070	for Allah Is Oft-Forgiving, **Most** Merciful."
008:074	and a provision **most** generous.
009:005	for Allah is Oft-Forgiving, **Most** Merciful.
009:008	and **most** of them are rebellious and wicked.
009:027	for Allah is Oft-Forgiving, **Most** Merciful.
009:034	announce unto them a **most** grievous chastisement-
009:091	and Allah is Oft-Forgiving, **Most** Merciful.
009:097	and **most** fitted to be in ignorance of the command
009:099	for Allah is Oft-Forgiving, **Most** Merciful.
009:102	for Allah is Oft-Forgiving, **Most** Merciful.
009:104	the Oft-Returning, **Most** Merciful?
009:114	for Abraham was **most** tender hearted, forbearing.
009:117	for He is unto them **Most** Kind, **Most** Merciful.
009:118	for Allah is Oft-Returning, **Most** Merciful.
009:128	to the Believers is he **most** kind and merciful.
010:000	In the name of Allah, **Most** Gracious, **Most** Merciful.
010:036	But **most** of them follow nothing but conjecture:
010:055	Yet **most** of them do not understand.
010:060	to mankind, but **most** of them are ungrateful.
010:107	And He is the Oft-Forgiving, **Most** Merciful.
011:000	In the name of Allah, **Most** Gracious, **Most** Merciful.
011:022	ones who will lose **most** in the Hereafter!
011:041	For my Lord is, be sure, Oft-Forgiving, **Most** Merciful!"
012:000	In the name of Allah, **Most** Gracious, **Most** Merciful.
012:003	the **most** beautiful of stories, in that
012:018	(For me) patience is **most** fitting: against that
012:021	but **most** among mankind know it not.
012:038	and to mankind: yet **most** men are not grateful.
012:040	but **Most** men understand not.
012:053	my Lord is Oft-Forgiving, **Most** Merciful.
012:064	and He is the **Most** Merciful of those
012:068	but **most** men know not.

MOST (continued)

012:083 So patience is **most** fitting (for me).
012:092 and He is the **Most** Merciful of those
012:098 for He is indeed Oft-Forgiving, Merciful."
012:106 And **most** of them believe not in Allah
013:000 In the name of Allah, **Most** Gracious, **Most** Merciful.
013:001 but **most** men believe not.
013:009 He is the Great, the **Most** High.
013:030 yet do they reject (Him), the **Most** Gracious!
014:000 In the name of Allah, **Most** Gracious, **Most** Merciful.
014:036 but thou art indeed Oft-Forgiving, **Most** Merciful.
015:000 In the name of Allah, **Most** Gracious, **Most** Merciful.
015:049 I am indeed the Oft-Forgiving, **Most** Merciful;
015:050 will be indeed the **most** grievous Chastisement.
016:000 In the name of Allah, **Most** Gracious, **Most** Merciful.
016:007 for your Lord is indeed **Most** Kind, **Most** Merciful.
016:018 Oft-Forgiving, **Most** Merciful.
016:038 but **most** among mankind know it not.
016:062 that the reward **most** fair is for themselves:
016:063 a **most** grievous chastisement.
016:075 But **most** of them understand not.
016:083 and **most** of them are (creatures) ungrateful.
016:101 but **most** of them understand not.
016:110 after all this is Oft-Forgiving, **Most** Merciful.
016:115 then Allah is Oft-Forgiving, **Most** Merciful.
016:117 a **most** grievous Chastisement.
016:119 thy Lord after all this, is Oft-Forgiving, **Most** Merciful.
016:125 are best and **most** gracious:
017:000 In the name of Allah, **Most** Gracious, **Most** Merciful.
017:003 Verily he was a devotee **most** grateful.
017:009 to that which is **most** right (or stable),
017:025 **Most** Forgiving to those who turn to Him
017:040 Truly ye utter a **most** dreadful saying!
017:044 Verily He is Oft-Forbearing, **Most** Forgiving!
017:066 For He is unto you **Most** Merciful.
017:067 **Most** ungrateful is man!
017:072 and **most** astray from the Path.
017:110 the **Most** Beautiful Names.
018:000 In the name of Allah, **Most** Gracious, **Most** Merciful.
018:054 but man is, in **most** things, contentious.
018:058 But your Lord is **Most** Forgiving, Full of Mercy.
018:103 lose **most** in respect of their deeds?
019:000 In the name of Allah, **Most** Gracious, **Most** Merciful.
019:018 "I seek refuge from thee to (Allah) **Most** Gracious:
019:026 say, I have vowed a fast to (Allah) **Most** Gracious,
019:044 for Satan is a rebel against (Allah) **Most** Gracious.
019:045 a Chastisement afflict thee from (Allah) **Most** Gracious,
019:047 for He is to me **Most** Gracious.
019:055 Prayer and Zakat and he was **most** acceptable in
019:058 (Allah) **Most** Gracious were rehearsed to them,
019:061 (Allah) **Most** Gracious has promised to His
019:069 against (Allah) **Most** Gracious.
019:070 are **most** worthy of being burned therein.
019:075 (Allah) **Most** Gracious extends (the rope)
019:078 or has he taken a promise with the **Most** Gracious?
019:085 We shall gather the righteous to (Allah) **Most** Gracious,
019:087 permission (or promise) from (Allah) **Most** Gracious.
019:088 They say: "The **Most** Gracious has begotten a son!"
019:089 Indeed ye have put forth a thing **most** monstrous!
019:091 That they attributed a son to The **Most** Gracious.
019:092 the majesty of The **Most** Gracious that He
019:093 to The **Most** Gracious as a servant.
019:096 will The **Most** Gracious bestow Love.

MOST (continued)

020:000 In the name of Allah, **Most** Gracious, **Most** Merciful.
020:005 The **Most** Gracious is firmly established
020:008 To Him belong the **Most** Beautiful Names.
020:063 and to do away with your **most** cherished way.
020:073 for Allah is Best and **Most** Abiding."
020:090 for verily your Lord is (Allah) **Most** Gracious:
020:108 and the voices will be hushed to The **Most** Gracious:
020:109 has been granted by The **Most** Gracious and whose
021:000 In the name of Allah, **Most** Gracious, **Most** Merciful.
021:024 But **most** of them know not the Truth, and so
021:026 And they say: "The **Most** Gracious has taken a son."
021:036 the mention of The **Most** Gracious!
021:042 and by day from (the Wrath of) The **Most** Gracious?"
021:049 in their **most** secret thoughts, and who
021:083 but Thou art the **Most** Merciful of those
021:112 "Our Lord **Most** Gracious is the One Whose
022:000 In the name of Allah, **Most** Gracious, **Most** Merciful.
022:025 We cause to taste of a **most** grievous chastisement.
022:039 Allah is **Most** powerful for their aid;
022:050 is forgiveness and a sustenance **most** generous.
022:059 All-Knowing, **Most** Forbearing.
022:062 **Most** High, **Most** Great.
022:065 for Allah is **Most** Kind and **Most** Merciful to man.
022:066 truly man is a **most** ungrateful creature!
023:000 In the name of Allah, **Most** Gracious, **Most** Merciful.
023:070 but **most** of them hate the Truth.
024:000 In the name of Allah, **Most** Gracious, **Most** Merciful.
024:005 for Allah is Oft-Forgiving, **Most** Merciful.
024:015 while it was **most** serious in the sight of Allah.
024:016 this is a **most** serious slander!"
024:022 For Allah is Oft-Forgiving, **Most** Merciful.
024:033 is Allah Oft-Forgiving, **Most** Merciful (to them).
024:062 for Allah is Oft-Forgiving, **Most** Merciful.
025:000 In the name of Allah, **Most** Gracious, **Most** Merciful.
025:006 verily He is Oft-Forgiving, **Most** Merciful."
025:026 shall be (wholly) for The **Most** Gracious:
025:034 and, as to path, **most** astray.
025:042 who it is that is **most** misled in Path!
025:044 Or thinkest thou that **most** of them listen
025:050 be mindful but **most** men are averse (to aught)
025:059 on the Throne: Allah **Most** Gracious: ask thou
025:060 they say, "And what is (Allah) **Most** Gracious?
025:060 "Adore ye The **Most** Gracious!",
025:063 (Allah) **Most** Gracious are those who walk on
025:070 and Allah is Oft-Forgiving, **Most** Merciful,
026:000 In the name of Allah, **Most** Gracious, **Most** Merciful.
026:005 the **Most** Gracious, but they turn away therefrom.
026:008 but **most** of them do not believe.
026:009 the Exalted in Might, **Most** Merciful.
026:067 but **most** of them do not believe.
026:068 the Exalted in Might, **Most** Merciful.
026:103 but **most** of them do not believe.
026:104 the Exalted in Might, **Most** Merciful.
026:121 but **most** of them do not believe.
026:122 the Exalted in Might, **Most** Merciful.
026:139 but **most** of them do not believe.
026:140 the Exalted in Might, **Most** Merciful.
026:158 but **most** of them do not believe.
026:159 the Exalted in Might, **Most** Merciful.
026:174 but **most** of them do not believe.
026:175 the Exalted in Might, **Most** Merciful.
026:190 but **most** of them do not believe.

MOST (continued)

026:191   The Exalted in Might, **Most** Merciful
026:223   They listen eagerly and **most** of them are liars.
027:000   In the name of Allah, **Most** Gracious, **Most** Merciful.
027:011   truly, I am Oft-Forgiving, **Most** Merciful.
027:030   'In the name of Allah, **Most** Gracious, **Most** Merciful:
027:061   Nay, **most** of them know not.
027:073   yet **most** of them are ungrateful.
027:076   to the Children of Israel **most** of the matters
028:000   In the name of Allah, **Most** Gracious, **Most** Merciful.
028:013   but **most** of them do not know.
028:016   for He is the Oft-Forgiving, **Most** Merciful.
028:057   But **most** of them understand not.
029:000   In the name of Allah, **Most** Gracious, **Most** Merciful.
029:011   And Allah **most** certainly knows those who believe,
029:023   they who will (suffer) a **most** grievous Chastisement.
029:063   But **most** of them understand not.
030:000   In the name of Allah, **Most** Gracious, **Most** Merciful.
030:005   and He is Exalted in Might, **Most** Merciful.
030:006   but **most** men understand not.
030:027   and for Him it is **most** easy.
030:030   but **most** among mankind know not.
030:042   End of those before (you): **most** of them were idolaters.
031:000   In the name of Allah, **Most** Gracious, **Most** Merciful.
031:025   But **most** of them know not.
031:030   and because Allah,-He is the **Most** High, **Most** Great.
032:000   In the name of Allah, **Most** Gracious, **Most** Merciful.
033:000   In the name of Allah, **Most** Gracious, **Most** Merciful.
033:005   is Oft-Returning, **Most** Merciful.
033:024   for Allah is Oft-Forgiving, **Most** Merciful.
033:050   And Allah is Oft-Forgiving, **Most** Merciful.
033:051   All-knowing, **Most** Forbearing.
033:059   their persons (when out of doors): that is **most** convenient,
033:059   and Allah is Oft-Forgiving, **Most** Merciful.
033:073   for Allah is Oft-Forgiving, **Most** Merciful.
034:000   In the name of Allah, **Most** Gracious, **Most** Merciful.
034:002   and He is the **Most** Merciful, the Oft-Forgiving.
034:003   say, "Nay! but **most** surely, by my Lord, it will
034:004   and a Sustenance **Most** Generous."
034:023   and He is the **Most** High, **Most** Great.'
034:028   but **most** men understand not.
034:036   to whom He pleases, but **most** men know not."
034:041   they worshipped the Jinns: **most** of them believe in them."
035:000   In the name of Allah, **Most** Gracious, **Most** Merciful.
035:030   Oft-Forgiving, **Most** Ready to appreciate (service).
035:041   verily He is **Most** Forbearing, Oft-Forgiving.
036:000   In the name of Allah, **Most** Gracious, **Most** Merciful.
036:005   by (Him), the Exalted in Might, **Most** Merciful.
036:011   of Forgiveness and a Reward **most** generous.
036:011   the **Most** Gracious, unseen: given such a one,
036:015   and the **Most** Gracious sends no sort of revelation:
036:023   If The **Most** Gracious should intend some
036:052   "This is what The **Most** Gracious had promised.
036:058   from a Lord **Most** Merciful!
037:000   In the name of Allah, **Most** Gracious, **Most** Merciful.
037:098   the ones **most** humiliated!
038:000   In the name of Allah, **Most** Gracious, **Most** Merciful.
039:000   In the name of Allah, **Most** Gracious, **Most** Merciful.
039:023   the **most** beautiful message in the form of a Book,
039:029   But **most** of them have no knowledge.
039:049   but **most** of them understand not!
039:053   for He is Oft-Forgiving, **Most** Merciful.
040:000   In the name of Allah, **Most** Gracious, **Most** Merciful.

MOST (continued)

040:012   with Allah, **Most** High, **Most** Great!"
040:057   than the creation of men: yet **most** men know not.
040:059   therein is no doubt: yet **most** men believe not.
040:061   yet **most** men give no thanks.
040:085   with His servants (from the **most** ancient times).
041:000   In the name of Allah, **Most** Gracious, **Most** Merciful.
041:002   A revelation from The **Most** Gracious, **Most** Merciful;-
041:004   yet **most** of them turn away, and so
041:032   Oft-Forgiving, **Most** Merciful!"
041:043   a **most** Grievous Chastisement.
042:000   In the name of Allah, **Most** Gracious, **Most** Merciful.
042:004   and He is **Most** High, **Most** Great.
042:005   the Oft-Forgiving, **Most** Merciful.
042:051   what Allah wills: for He is **Most** High, **Most** Wise.
043:000   In the name of Allah, **Most** Gracious, **Most** Merciful.
043:017   as a likeness to (Allah) **Most** Gracious, his face
043:020   the will of (Allah) **Most** Gracious, we should
043:033   himself from remembrance of the **Most** Gracious,
043:036   from remembrance of the **Most** Gracious, We appoint
043:045   other than The **Most** Gracious, to be worshipped?
043:078   but **most** of you have a hatred for Truth.
043:081   Say: "If The **Most** Gracious had a son, I would
044:000   In the name of Allah, **Most** Gracious, **Most** Merciful.
044:017   a Messenger **most** honorable,
044:039   just ends: but **most** of them do not know.
044:042   for He is exalted in Might, **Most** Merciful.
045:000   In the name of Allah, **Most** Gracious, **Most** Merciful.
045:026   there is no doubt": but **most** men not know.
046:000   In the name of Allah, **Most** Gracious, **Most** Merciful.
046:008   Oft-Forgiving, **Most** Merciful."
047:000   In the name of Allah, **Most** Gracious, **Most** Merciful.
048:000   In the name of Allah, **Most** Gracious, **Most** Merciful.
048:014   but Allah is Oft-Forgiving, **Most** Merciful.
049:000   In the name of Allah, **Most** Gracious, **Most** Merciful.
049:004   the Inner Apartments-**most** of them lack understanding.
049:005   but Allah is Oft-Forgiving, **Most** Merciful.
049:012   Oft-returning, **Most** Merciful.
049:013   is (he who is) the **most** righteous of you.
049:013   Verily the **most** honoured of you in the sight of Allah
049:014   for Allah is Oft-Forgiving, **Most** Merciful."
050:000   In the name of Allah, **Most** Gracious, **Most** Merciful.
050:033   "Who feared The **Most** Gracious unseen, and brought
051:000   In the name of Allah, **Most** Gracious, **Most** Merciful.
052:000   In the name of Allah, **Most** Gracious, **Most** Merciful.
052:047   but **most** of them know not.
053:000   In the name of Allah, **Most** Gracious, **Most** Merciful.
053:022   a division **most** unfair!
053:052   were (all) **most** unjust and **most** insolent transgressors,
054:000   In the name of Allah, **Most** Gracious, **Most** Merciful.
054:046   and that Hour will be **most** grievous and **most** bitter.
055:000   In the name of Allah, **Most** Gracious, **Most** Merciful.
055:001   The **Most** Gracious!
056:000   In the name of Allah, **Most** Gracious, **Most** Merciful.
056:077   That this is indeed a Qur'an **most** honourable,
057:000   In the name of Allah, **Most** Gracious, **Most** Merciful.
057:009   And verily, Allah is to you **Most** Kind and Merciful.
057:028   is Oft-Forgiving, **Most** Merciful:
058:000   In the name of Allah, **Most** Gracious, **Most** Merciful.
058:012   and **most** conducive to purity (of conduct).
058:012   Allah is Oft-Forgiving, **Most** Merciful.
058:020   among those **most** humiliated.
059:000   In the name of Allah, **Most** Gracious, **Most** Merciful.

MOST (continued)

059:010   Full of Kindness, **Most** Merciful."
059:022   both secret and open; He, **Most** Gracious, **Most** Merciful.
059:024   to Him belong the **Most** Beautiful Names:
060:000   In the name of Allah, **Most** Gracious, **Most** Merciful.
060:007   and Allah is Oft-Forgiving, **Most** Merciful.
060:012   for Allah is Oft-Forgiving, **Most** Merciful.
061:000   In the name of Allah, **Most** Gracious, **Most** Merciful.
062:000   In the name of Allah, **Most** Gracious, **Most** Merciful.
063:000   In the name of Allah, **Most** Gracious, **Most** Merciful.
064:000   In the name of Allah, **Most** Gracious, **Most** Merciful.
064:014   verily Allah is Oft-Forgiving, **Most** Merciful.
064:017   for Allah is All-Thankful, **Most** Forbearing,-
065:000   In the name of Allah, **Most** Gracious, **Most** Merciful.
065:011   a **most** excellent provision.
066:000   In the name of Allah, **Most** Gracious, **Most** Merciful.
066:001   But Allah is Oft-Forgiving, **Most** Merciful.
067:000   In the name of Allah, **Most** Gracious, **Most** Merciful.
067:003   wilt thou see in the Creation The **Most** Gracious.
067:019   uphold them except The **Most** Gracious: truly it
067:020   (even as) an army, besides The **Most** Merciful?
067:029   Say: "He is The **Most** Gracious: we have
068:000   In the name of Allah, **Most** Gracious, **Most** Merciful.
069:000   In the name of Allah, **Most** Gracious, **Most** Merciful.
069:033   "This was he that would not believe in Allah **Most** High,
069:052   So glorify the name of thy Lord **Most** High.
070:000   In the name of Allah, **Most** Gracious, **Most** Merciful.
071:000   In the name of Allah, **Most** Gracious, **Most** Merciful.
072:000   In the name of Allah, **Most** Gracious, **Most** Merciful.
073:000   In the name of Allah, **Most** Gracious, **Most** Merciful.
073:020   for Allah is Oft-Forgiving, **Most** Merciful.
074:000   In the name of Allah, **Most** Gracious, **Most** Merciful.
075:000   In the name of Allah, **Most** Gracious, **Most** Merciful.
076:000   In the name of Allah, **Most** Gracious, **Most** Merciful.
077:000   In the name of Allah, **Most** Gracious, **Most** Merciful.
078:000   In the name of Allah, **Most** Gracious, **Most** Merciful.
078:037   The **Most** Gracious: none shall have power to argue
078:038   permitted by The **Most** Gracious, and he
079:000   In the name of Allah, **Most** Gracious, **Most** Merciful.
079:024   Saying, "I am your Lord, **Most** High."
079:046   or (at **most** till) the following morn!
080:000   In the name of Allah, **Most** Gracious, **Most** Merciful.
081:000   In the name of Allah, **Most** Gracious, **Most** Merciful.
081:019   of a **most** honorable Messenger,
082:000   In the name of Allah, **Most** Gracious, **Most** Merciful.
082:006   from thy Lord **Most** Beneficent?-
083:000   In the name of Allah, **Most** Gracious, **Most** Merciful.
084:000   In the name of Allah, **Most** Gracious, **Most** Merciful.
085:000   In the name of Allah, **Most** Gracious, **Most** Merciful.
086:000   In the name of Allah, **Most** Gracious, **Most** Merciful.
087:000   In the name of Allah, **Most** Gracious, **Most** Merciful.
087:001   Glorify the name of thy Guardian-Lord, **Most** High,
087:011   the **most** unfortunate one,
088:000   In the name of Allah, **Most** Gracious, **Most** Merciful.
089:000   In the name of Allah, **Most** Gracious, **Most** Merciful.
090:000   In the name of Allah, **Most** Gracious, **Most** Merciful.
091:000   In the name of Allah, **Most** Gracious, **Most** Merciful.
091:012   Behold, the **most** wicked man among them
092:000   In the name of Allah, **Most** Gracious, **Most** Merciful.
092:015   None shall reach it but those **most** unfortunate ones
092:017   But those **most** devoted to Allah shall be
092:020   for the countenance of their Lord **Most** High;
093:000   In the name of Allah, **Most** Gracious, **Most** Merciful.

MOST (continued)

094:000   In the name of Allah, **Most** Gracious, **Most** Merciful.
095:000   In the name of Allah, **Most** Gracious, **Most** Merciful.
096:000   In the name of Allah, **Most** Gracious, **Most** Merciful.
096:003   Proclaim! And thy Lord is **Most** Bountiful,-
097:000   In the name of Allah, **Most** Gracious, **Most** Merciful.
098:000   In the name of Allah, **Most** Gracious, **Most** Merciful.
099:000   In the name of Allah, **Most** Gracious, **Most** Merciful.
100:000   In the name of Allah, **Most** Gracious, **Most** Merciful.
101:000   In the name of Allah, **Most** Gracious, **Most** Merciful.
102:000   In the name of Allah, **Most** Gracious, **Most** Merciful.
103:000   In the name of Allah, **Most** Gracious, **Most** Merciful.
104:000   In the name of Allah, **Most** Gracious, **Most** Merciful.
105:000   In the name of Allah, **Most** Gracious, **Most** Merciful.
106:000   In the name of Allah, **Most** Gracious, **Most** Merciful.
107:000   In the name of Allah, **Most** Gracious, **Most** Merciful.
108:000   In the name of Allah, **Most** Gracious, **Most** Merciful.
109:000   In the name of Allah, **Most** Gracious, **Most** Merciful.
110:000   In the name of Allah, **Most** Gracious, **Most** Merciful.
111:000   In the name of Allah, **Most** Gracious, **Most** Merciful.
112:000   In the name of Allah, **Most** Gracious, **Most** Merciful.
113:000   In the name of Allah, **Most** Gracious, **Most** Merciful.
114:000   In the name of Allah, **Most** Gracious, **Most** Merciful.

MOST-MERCIFUL

002:128   the Oft-Returning, **Most-Merciful**.

MOTHER

002:233   No **mother** shall be treated unfairly
002:233   (the foster **mother**) what ye offered,
004:011   the **mother** has a third:
004:011   brothers (or sisters), the **mother** has a sixth.
004:023   your **mother**, daughters, sisters, father's sisters,
005:017   to destroy Christ the son of Mary, his **mother**,
005:075   His **mother** was a woman of truth.
005:110   recount my favour to thee and to thy **mother**.
005:116   say unto men, "Take me and my **mother** for two
006:092   the **Mother** of Cities and all around her.
007:150   Aaron said: "Son of my **mother**! The people
012:059   of the same father as yourselves, (but a different **mother**):
013:039   with Him is the **Mother** of the Book.
019:028   a man of evil, nor thy **mother** a woman unchaste!"
019:032   "(He) hath made me kind to my **mother**, and not
020:038   "Behold! We sent to thy **mother**, by inspiration,
020:040   So We brought thee back to thy **mother**, that her
020:094   (Aaron) replied: "O son of my **mother**! Seize (me)
022:002   every **mother** giving suck shall forget
023:050   And We made the son of Mary and his **mother** as a Sign:
028:007   We sent this inspiration to the **mother** of Moses: "Suckle
028:010   And the heart of the **mother** of Moses became void:
028:013   Thus did We restore him to his **mother**, that her
031:014   in travail upon travail did his **mother** bear him.
042:007   that thou mayest warn the **Mother** of Cities
043:004   And verily, it is in the **Mother** of the Book,
046:015   in pain did his **mother** bear him,
080:035   And from his **mother**, and his father,

MOTHER'S

004:023   father's sisters, **mother's** sisters; brother's daughters,
024:061   or your **mother's** brothers, or your **mother's** sisters,

MOTHERS

002:233   The **mothers** shall give suck to their offspring
004:023   foster-sisters; your wives, **mothers**;
016:078   from the wombs of your **mothers** when ye
024:061   or your **mothers**, or your brothers,
033:004   ye divorce by Zihar your **mothers**:

MOTHERS (continued)

033:006   and his wives are their **mothers**.
039:006   of your **mothers**, in stages, one after
058:002   none can be their **mothers** except those
058:002   they cannot be their **mothers**:
058:002   you divorce their wives by Zihar (calling them **mothers**),

MOTHERS'

053:032   and when ye are hidden in your **mothers'** wombs.

MOTHS

101:004   will be like **moths** Scattered about,

MOTION

020:020   it was a snake, active in **motion**.
020:066   of their magic-began to be in lively **motion**!

MOTIONLESS

042:033   then would they become **motionless** on the back

MOULDETH

080:019   and then **mouldeth** him in due Proportions;

MOUNT

002:063   and We raised above you the **Mount** (Sinai)
002:093   and We raised above you the **Mount** (Sinai):
002:198   Then when ye pour down from (**Mount**) 'Arafat,
004:154   We raised over them the **Mount** (Sinai);
007:143   but look upon the **mount**; if it abide
007:143   He made it as dust and Moses fell down in a swoon.
007:171   When We raised the **mount** over them, as if
011:044   rested on **Mount** Judi and the word went forth:
017:093   or thou **mount** a ladder right into the skies.
019:052   right side of **Mount** (Sinai), and made
020:080   on the right side of **Mount** (Sinai), and We
020:083   (When Moses was up on the **mount**, Allah said):
023:020   a tree springing out of **Mount** Sinai, which produces oil,
028:029   he perceived a fire in the direction of **Mount** Tur.
028:038   that I may **mount** up to the god of Moses:
035:010   To Him **mount** up (all) Words of Purity:
038:010   If so, **mount** up with the ropes and means
052:001   By the **Mount** (of Revelation);
074:017   Soon will I visit him with a **mount** of calamities!
095:002   And the **Mount** of Sinai,
104:007   The which doth **mount** (Right) to the Hearts:

MOUNTAIN

011:043   The son replied: "I will betake myself to some **mountain**:
022:027   through deep and distant **mountain** highways;
024:043   He sends down from the sky **mountain** masses (of clouds)
026:063   became like the huge, firm mass of a **mountain**.
028:046   (the **Mountain** of) Tur when We called (to Moses).
059:021   Had We sent down this Qur'an on a **mountain**,

MOUNTAIN-SIDES

018:096   filled up the space between the two steep **mountain-sides**,

MOUNTAINS

007:074   and carve out homes in the **mountains**;
011:042   on the waves (towering) like **mountains**, and Noah
013:003   and set thereon **mountains** standing firm,
013:031   with which **mountains** were moved,
015:019   set thereon **mountains** firm and immovable;
015:082   Out of the **mountains** did they hew (their) edifices,
016:015   And He has set up on the earth **mountains** standing firm,
017:037   nor reach the **mountains** in height.
018:047   On the Day We shall remove the **mountains**, and thou
018:093   between two **mountains**, he found, beneath them,
019:090   and the **mountains** to fall down in utter ruin.
020:105   They ask thee concerning the **mountains**:
021:031   broad highways (between **mountains**) for them

MOUNTAINS (continued)

021:031   And We have set on the earth **mountains** standing firm,
026:149   "And ye carve house out of (rocky) **mountains** with great
027:061   set thereon **mountains** immovable; and made
027:088   Thou seest the **mountains** and thinkest them
031:010   He set on the earth **mountains** standing firm,
033:072   to the Heavens and the Earth and the **Mountains**:
034:010   "O ye **Mountains**! echo ye back the Praises of Allah
035:027   the **mountains** are tracts white and red,
041:010   He set on the (earth), **mountains** standing firm,
042:032   smooth-running through the ocean, (tall) as **mountains**.
050:007   and set thereon **mountains** standing firm,
052:010   And the **mountains** will move.
055:024   sailing smoothly through the seas, lofty as **mountains**:
056:005   And the **mountains** shall be crumbled to atoms,
069:014   and its **mountains**, and they are crushed at one
070:009   And the **mountains** will be like wool,
073:014   The Day the earth and the **mountains** will be
073:014   And the **mountains** will be as a heap of sand
077:010   When the **mountains** are scattered (to the winds)
077:027   And made therein **mountains** standing firm,
078:007   And the **mountains** as pegs?
078:020   And the **mountains** shall vanish, as if
079:032   And the **mountains** hath He firmly fixed;-
081:003   When the **mountains** vanish (like a mirage);
088:019   And at the **Mountains**, how they are fixed firm?-
101:005   And the **mountains** will be like carded wool.

MOUNTED

022:027   and (**mounted**) on every kind of camel,

MOUNTING

017:093   even believe in thy **mounting** until thou

MOUNTS

009:092   to thee to be provided with **mounts**.
009:092   "I can find no **mounts** for you," they turned
013:017   the foam that **mounts** up to the surface.
057:004   what comes down from heaven and what **mounts** up to

MOUTHS

003:118   rank hatred has already appeared from their **mouths**;
009:008   With (fair words from) their **mouths** they please
009:030   That is a saying from their **mouths**;
009:032   would they extinguish Allah's light with their **mouths**,
013:014   for water to reach their **mouths** but it reaches them not:
014:009   but they put their hands up to their **mouths**, and said:
018:005   a grievous thing that issues from their **mouths** as a saying.
024:015   and said out of your **mouths** things of which ye
033:004   (manner of) speech by your **mouths**.
036:065   that Day shall We set a seal on their **mouths**.
061:008   to extinguish Allah's Light (by bowing) with their **mouths**:

MOVE

002:273   And cannot **move** about in the land,
004:097   to **move** yourselves away (form evil)?"
011:041   Ark in the name of Allah, whether it **move** or be a rest!
020:128   in whose haunts they (now) **move**?
024:002   let not compassion **move** you in their case,
024:043   the clouds **move** gently, then joins
024:058   to **move** about attending to each other: thus does
036:067   have been unable to **move** about, nor could
047:019   for Allah knows how ye **move** about and how ye
052:010   And the mountains will **move**.
075:016   **Move** not thy tongue concerning the (Qur'an)

MOVED

003:154   their own feelings, **moved** by wrong suspicions of Allah-

MOVED (continued)
013:031 with which mountains were **moved**,
033:032 should be **moved** with desire:
069:014 And the earth is **moved**, and its mountains,

MOVEMENTS
026:219 And thy **movements** among those who

MOVING
011:006 There is no **moving** creature on earth but its
011:056 There is not a **moving** creature, but He hath grasp of its
016:049 whether **moving** creatures or the angels:
027:010 But when he saw it **moving** (of its own accord)
028:031 But when he saw it **moving** (of its own accord)

MOWN
011:100 and some have been **mown** down (by the sickle of time).
021:015 till We made them as a field that is **mown**, as ashes silent

MUCH
002:219 They ask thee how **much** they are to spend;
003:091 · as **much** gold as the earth contains,
003:186 certainly hear **much** that will grieve you,
004:082 found therein **much** discrepancy.
005:015 revealing to you **much** that ye used to
005:015 and passing over **much** (that is now unnecessary):
005:041 who have never so **much** as come to thee.
005:060 something **much** worse than this, (as judged)
006:025 in so **much** that when they come to thee, they (but)
006:091 while ye conceal **much** (of its contents):
006:128 "O ye assembly of Jinns **much** (toll) did ye take of men."
006:160 ten times as **much** to his credit: he that
008:045 and call Allah in remembrance **much** (and often);
009:048 Decree of Allah became manifest, **much** to their disgust.
009:082 Let them laugh a little: **much** will they weep:
010:061 (so **much** as) the weight of an atom on the
010:082 however **much** the Sinners may hate it!"
011:032 and (**much**) hast thou prolonged the dispute with us:
011:034 **much** as I desire to give you (good) counsel,
011:091 They said: "O Shu'aib! **much** of what thou sayest
012:021 may be he will bring us **much** good,
013:008 how **much** the wombs fall short (of their time or number)
013:018 and as **much** more, (in vain) would they offer it for
016:070 after having known (**much**):
018:062 truly we have suffered **much** fatigue at this
019:098 or hear (so **much** as) a whisper of them?
022:005 after having known (**much**).
022:036 in them is (**much**) good for you:
023:110 so **much** so that (ridicule of) them made you
026:227 engaged **much** in the remembrance of Allah,
033:021 and who remember Allah **much**.
033:035 who engage **much** in Allah's remembrance, for them
033:041 with **much** remembrance;
039:047 there is on earth, and as **much** more, (in vain)
041:050 I have (**much**) good (stored) in His sight!"
042:034 but **much** doth He forgive.
049:012 O ye who believe! avoid suspicion as **much** (as possible):
050:004 We already know how **much** of them the earth
051:023 as **much** as the fact that ye can speak
064:016 So fear Allah as **much** as ye can; listen and
073:020 Read ye, therefore, as **much** of the Qur'an as may
073:020 of the Qur'an as **much** as may be easy for you.

MUCH-FREQUENTED
052:004 By the **much-frequented** House;

MUD
015:026 from **mud** molded into shape;

MUD (continued)
015:028 from sounding clay, from **mud** molded into shape;
015:033 sounding clay, from **mud** moulded into shape."

MUHAJIRS
009:117 the Prophet, the **Muhajirs**, and the Ansar,-who
033:006 than (the Brotherhood of) Believers and **Muhajirs**:
059:008 indigent **Muhajirs**, those who were expelled from

MUHAMMAD
003:144 **Muhammad** is no more than a Messenger:
033:040 **Muhammad** is not the father of any of your men,
047:002 sent down to **Muhammad**-for it is the Truth from their
048:029 **Muhammad** is the Messenger of Allah;

MULES
016:008 And (He has created) horses, **mules**, and donkeys,

MULTIPLIED
003:130 doubled and **multiplied**; but fear Allah;
007:095 until they grew and **multiplied**, and began
007:188 I should have **multiplied** all good, and no
008:019 will your forces be to you even if they were **multiplied**:
016:013 He has **multiplied** in varying colours (and qualities),
023:079 And He has **multiplied** you through the earth,
030:039 who will get a recompense **multiplied**.
034:037 is a **multiplied** Reward for their deeds,
067:024 Say: "It is He Who has **multiplied** you through

MULTIPLY
002:245 unto his credit and **multiply** many times?
042:011 by this means does He **multiply** you:

MULTIPLYING
057:020 boasting and **multiplying**, (in rivalry)

MULTITUDE
002:199 it is usual for the **multitude** so to do,
026:056 "But we are a **multitude** amply fore-warned."
036:062 "But he did lead astray a great **multitude** of you.
054:045 Soon will their **multitude** be put to flight,

MURDER
002:178 prescribed to you in cases of **murder**:
005:030 soul of the other led him to the **murder** of his brother:
005:032 unless it be for **murder** or for spreading

MURDERED
005:030 he **murdered** him, and became (himself) one of the lost

MURKY
018:086 a spring of **murky** water: near it
038:057 a fluid dark, **murky**, intensely cold!-
078:025 dark, **murky**, intensely cold,-

MURMURING
020:108 so that thou hearest not but **murmuring**.

MUSK
083:026 The seal thereof will be **Musk**: and for this

MUSLIM
002:128 and of our progeny a people **Muslim**,
012:101 my soul as one submitting to Thy Will (as a **Muslim**),
033:035 For **Muslim** men and women,-for believing
051:036 except one (**Muslim**) household:

MUSLIMS
002:128 "Our Lord! make of us **Muslims**,
003:052 and do thou bear witness that we are **Muslims**.
003:064 are **Muslims** (bowing to Allah's Will)."
004:131 and you (O **Muslims**) to fear Allah, but if
005:111 we bow to Allah as Muslims'."
006:109 but what will make you (**Muslims**) realize
007:126 as **Muslims** (who bow to Thy Will)"!
015:002 wish that they had been **Muslims**.

MUSLIMS (continued)

016:089 a Mercy, and Glad Tidings to **Muslims**.
016:102 and as a Guide and Glad tidings to **Muslims**.
022:078 It is He Who has named you **Muslims**, both before
028:053 indeed we have been **Muslims** (bowing to Allah's Will)
059:005 Whether ye cut down (O ye **Muslims**!) of the tender

MUST

002:196 he **must** make an offering such as he can afford,
002:249 convinced that they **must** meet Allah,
003:139 for ye **must** gain mastery if ye are true in Faith.
004:047 for the decision of Allah **must** be carried out.
004:159 but **must** believe in Him before his death;
005:056 the party of Allah that **must** certainly triumph.
006:031 as a falsehood that they **must** meet Allah,-
007:037 appointed **must** reach them from the Book (of Decrees):
012:010 but if ye **must** do something, throw him
014:022 For wrong-doers there **must** be a grievous Chastisement.
015:071 "There are my daughters (to marry), if ye **must** act (so)."
016:039 (They **must** be raised up), in order that He may
016:096 What is with you **must** vanish: what is with Allah will
019:061 for His promise **must** (necessarily) come to pass.
019:071 a Decree which **must** be accomplished.
019:093 and the earth but **must** come to The Most Gracious
020:061 the forger **must** suffer failure!
020:071 Surely this **must** be your leader.
020:129 (their punishment) **must** necessarily have come;
021:035 to Us **must** ye return.
021:059 He **must** indeed be one of the unjust one.
022:067 appointed rites which they **must** follow: let them
025:040 And the (Unbelievers) **must** indeed have passed
033:015 a covenant with Allah **must** (surely) be answered for.
033:037 And Allah's command **must** be fulfilled.
037:024 "But stop them, for they **must** be asked:
037:173 And that Our forces,-they surely **must** conquer.
042:022 and (the burden of) that **must** (necessarily) fall
043:014 "And to Our Lord, surely, **Must** We turn back!"
058:021 "It is I and My messengers who **must** prevail":
073:018 His Promise needs **must** be accomplished.
077:007 Assuredly, what ye are promised **must** come to pass.
084:002 (the Command of) its Lord, and it **must** needs (do so);-
084:005 (the Command of) its Lord, and it **must** needs (do so);-

MUSTARD

021:047 the weight of a **mustard** seed, We will

MUSTARD-SEED

031:016 the weight of a **mustard-seed** and it were (hidden)

MUSTER

027:020 And he took a **muster** of the Birds; and he

MUTUAL

002:233 If they both decide on weaning, by **mutual** consent,
004:001 through Whom ye demand your **mutual** (rights),
004:029 you traffic and trade by **mutual** good-will:
004:092 with whom ye have a treaty of **mutual** alliance,
006:065 you a taste of **mutual** vengeance-each from the other."
008:042 Even if ye had made a **mutual** appointment to meet,
008:072 ye have a treaty of **mutual** alliance.
009:001 ye have contracted **mutual** alliances:-
014:031 neither **mutual** bargaining, nor befriending.
016:081 from your (**mutual**) violence.
018:034 in the course of a **mutual** argument: "More wealth
021:103 but the angels will meet them (with **mutual** greetings):
026:096 "They will say there in their **mutual** bickerings:
027:049 They said: "Swear a **mutual** oath by Allah that we
029:025 out of **mutual** love and regard between yourselves

MUTUAL (continued)

038:064 That is true-the **mutual** recriminations of the
040:015 of the Day of **Mutual** Meeting,-
040:032 a Day when there will be **mutual** calling (and wiling),-
042:038 who (conduct) their affairs by **mutual** Consultation;
052:025 engaging in **mutual** enquiry.
057:020 adornment and **mutual** boasting and multiplying,
064:009 a day of **mutual** loss and gain (among you).
065:006 and take **mutual** counsel together, according to
102:001 The **mutual** rivalry for piling up (the good things in this
103:003 in the **mutual** enjoining of Truth,

MUTUALLY

002:232 if they **mutually** agree on equitable terms.
004:024 ye agree **mutually** (to vary it),
017:064 and thy infantry; **mutually** share with them wealth

MY

002:038 whosoever follows **My** guidance,
002:040 and I shall fulfil **My** Covenant with you,
002:041 nor sell **My** Signs for a small price:
002:054 "O **my** people! Ye have indeed wronged yourselves
002:124 He pleaded: "And also (Imams) from **my** offspring!"
002:124 He answered: "But **My** Promise is not
002:125 should sanctify **My** House for those who compass it round,
002:126 And remember Abraham said: "**My** Lord,
002:131 He said: "I submit (**my** will) to the Lord
002:132 "O **my** sons! Allah hath chosen the Faith for you;
002:150 and that I may complete **My** favours on you,
002:186 When **My** servants ask thee concerning Me,
002:186 listen to **My** call, and believe in Me:
002:249 he goes not with **my** army;
002:258 "**My** Lord is He Who Giveth life and death."
002:260 He said: "Yea! but to satisfy **my** own heart."
002:260 "**My** Lord! show me how thou givest life to the dead.
003:020 say: "I have submitted **my** whole self to Allah
003:035 what is in **my** womb for Thy special service:
003:035 "O **my** Lord! I do dedicate unto thee what is in
003:036 "O **my** Lord! behold! I am delivered
003:038 saying: "O **my** Lord! Grant unto me
003:040 He said: "O **my** Lord! how shall I have a son,
003:040 seeing I am very old, and **my** wife is barren?"
003:041 He said: "O **my** Lord! Give me a Sign!"
003:047 She said: "O **my** Lord! how shall I have a son
003:051 "It is Allah who is **my** Lord and your Lord;
003:052 "Who will be **my** helpers to (the work of) Allah?"
003:079 "Be ye **my** worshippers rather than Allah's":
003:081 and take **My** covenant as binding on you?"
003:195 or suffered harm in **My** cause, and fought
005:003 completed **my** favour upon you, and have chosen
005:012 pay Zakat believe in **My** Messengers, honour and
005:020 "O **my** people! call in remembrance the favour
005:021 "O **my** people! enter the holy land which Allah
005:025 He said: "O **my** Lord! I have power
005:025 I have power only over myself and **my** bother:
005:028 to stretch **my** hand against thee to slay thee:
005:029 thee draw on thyself **my** sin as well as thine,
005:031 and to hide the naked body of **my** brother?"
005:044 and sell not **My** Signs for a miserable price.
005:072 worship Allah, **my** Lord and your Lord."
005:110 the figure of a bird, the dead by **My** leave.
005:110 recount **my** favour to thee and to thy mother.
005:110 and it becometh a bird by **My** leave.
005:110 and the lepers by **My** leave.
005:110 as it were, the figure of a bird, by **My** leave.

MY (continued)

005:116 say unto men, "Take me and **my** mother for two
005:116 Thou knowest what is in **my** heart, though I
005:117 'Worship Allah, **my** Lord and your Lord':
006:014 Say: "Shall I take for **my** protector any other
006:015 Say: "I would, if I disobeyed **my** Lord, indeed
006:057 a clear Sign from **my** Lord, but ye
006:057 What ye would see hastened is not in **my** power.
006:058 see hastened were in **my** power, the matter
006:076 he saw a star: he said: "This is **my** Lord."
006:077 "Unless **my** Lord guide me, I shall
006:077 He said: "This is **my** Lord." But when
006:078 "O **my** people! I am indeed free from your (guilt)
006:078 he said: "This is **my** Lord; this is
006:079 "For me, I have set **my** face, firmly
006:080 **my** Lord comprehendeth in His knowledge all things.
006:080 unless **my** Lord willeth, (nothing can happen),
006:130 setting forth unto you **My** Signs and warning
006:135 "O **my** people! do whatever ye can: I will do (**my** part):
006:153 Verily, this is **My** Way, leading straight:
006:161 Say: "Verily, **my** Lord hath guided me
006:162 Say: "Truly, **my** prayer and **my** service of sacrifice,
006:162 **my** life and **my** death, are (all) for Allah,
006:164 Say: "Shall I seek for (**my**) Lord other than Allah.
007:029 Say: "**My** Lord hath commanded justice; and that
007:033 Say: "The things that **my** Lord hath indeed forbidden are:
007:035 rehearsing **My** Signs unto you,-those who
007:059 He said: "O **my** people! worship Allah!
007:061 He said: "O **my** people! there is no error in me:
007:062 Sincere is **my** advice to you, and I
007:062 "I but convey to you" the Message of **my** Lord.
007:065 He said: "O **my** people! worship Allah! ye have
007:067 He said: "O **my** people! there is no folly in me"
007:068 "I but convey to you the messages of **my** Lord:
007:073 he said: "O **my** people! worship Allah; ye have
007:079 saying: "O **my** people! I indeed convey to you
007:079 I was sent by **my** Lord: I gave you
007:085 he said: "O **my** people! worship Allah; ye have
007:093 saying: "O **my** people! I did indeed convey to
007:093 I was sent by **my** Lord: I gave you
007:114 (raised to posts) nearest (to **my** person)."
007:142 "Act for me amongst **my** people: do right,
007:143 He said: "O **my** Lord! show (Thyself) to me, that
007:146 them will I turn away from **My** Signs: even if
007:150 that ye have done in **my** place in **my** absence:
007:150 Make not the enemies rejoice over **my** misfortune,
007:150 Aaron said: "Son of **my** mother! The people
007:151 forgive me and **my** brother!
007:151 Moses prayed: "O **my** Lord! forgive me
007:155 he prayed: "O **my** Lord! if it had been Thy will
007:156 but **My** Mercy extendeth to all things.
007:156 He said: "I afflict **My** punishment on whom
007:183 for **My** scheme is strong (and unfailing).
007:187 Say: "The knowledge thereof is with **my** Lord (alone):
007:196 "For **my** Protector is Allah, Who revealed
007:203 is revealed to me from **my** Lord: this is
009:129 there is no god but He: On him is **my** trust,-He the
010:015 if I were to disobey **my** Lord, I should myself
010:015 of **my** own accord, to change it: I follow
010:041 say: "**My** work to me, and yours to you!
010:053 "Is that true?" Say: "Aye! by **my** Lord!
010:071 "O **my** People, if it be hard on your (mind) that I
010:071 yet I put **my** trust in Allah get ye then

MY (continued)

010:072 have I asked of you: **my** reward is only due from Allah,
010:084 Moses said: "O **my** People! if ye do (really) believe in
010:104 Say: "O ye men! if ye are in doubt as to **my** religion,
011:028 from **my** Lord and that He hath sent Mercy unto me
011:028 He said: "O **my** people! see ye if (it be that)
011:029 "And O **my** People! I ask you for no wealth in return:
011:029 **my** reward is from none but Allah:
011:030 "And O **my** People! who would help me
011:034 "Of no profit will be **my** counsel to you, much as
011:035 Say: "If I had forged it, on me were **my** sin!
011:041 For **my** Lord is, be sure, Oft-Forgiving,
011:042 "O **my** son! embark with us, and be not with the
011:045 "O **my** Lord! surely **my** son is of **my** family and Thy
011:047 Noah said: "O **my** Lord! I do seek refuge with Thee,
011:050 He said: "O **my** people! worship Allah! ye have
011:051 **My** reward is from none but Him Who created Me:
011:051 "O **my** people! I ask of you no reward
011:052 "And O **my** people! ask forgiveness of your Lord,
011:056 Verily, it is **my** Lord that is on a Straight Path.
011:056 "I put **my** trust in Allah, **my** Lord and your Lord!
011:057 **My** Lord will make another People to succeed you,
011:057 For **my** Lord hath care and watch over all things."
011:061 for **my** Lord is (always) near, ready to answer."
011:061 He said: "O **my** people! worship Allah: ye have
011:063 He said: "O **my** people! Do ye see?-If I have
011:063 If I have a Clear (Sign) from **my** Lord and He
011:063 What then would ye add to **my** (portion) but perdition?
011:064 "And O **my** people! this she-camel of Allah
011:072 and **my** husband here is an old man?
011:078 He said: "O **my** people! here are **my** daughters:
011:078 and cover me not with disgrace about **my** guests!
011:084 he said: "O **my** people! worship Allah: ye have
011:085 "And O **my** people! give just measure and weight,
011:088 see ye whether I have a Clear (Sign) from **my** Lord,
011:088 I only desire (your) betterment to the best of **my** power;
011:088 and **my** success (in **my** task) can only come from Allah.
011:088 He said: "O **my** people! see ye whether I have
011:089 "And O **my** people! let not **my** dissent (from you)
011:090 for **my** Lord is indeed Full of mercy
011:092 He said: "O **my** people! is then **my** family of more
011:092 But verily **my** Lord encompasseth all that ye do!
011:093 I will do (**my** part): soon will ye know who it is on whom
011:093 "And O **my** people! do whatever ye can:
012:004 "O **my** father! I did see eleven stars and the
012:005 Said (the father): "**My** (dear) little son! relate not thy
012:023 "Allah forbid! truly (thy husband) is **my** lord!
012:023 he made **my** sojourn agreeable! Truly to no good come
012:026 seduce me-from **my** (true) self."
012:032 And now, if he doth not **my** bidding, he shall
012:033 "O **my** Lord! the prison is dearer to **my** liking than
012:036 (in a dream) carrying bread on **my** head, and birds
012:037 which **my** Lord hath taught me I have (I assure you)
012:038 "And I follow the ways of **my** fathers,-Abraham, Isaac,
012:039 "O **my** two companions of the prison! (I ask you):
012:041 "O **my** two companions of the prison!
012:043 O ye chiefs! expound to me **my** vision if it be
012:050 For **my** Lord is certainly well aware
012:053 incites evil, unless **my** Lord do bestow His Mercy:
012:053 but surely **my** Lord is Oft-Forgiving, Most Merciful.
012:054 I will take him specially to serve about **my** own person."
012:067 Further he said; "O **my** sons! enter not all by one gate:
012:067 on Him do I put **my** trust: and let all that trust put

012:067 against Allah (with **my** advice):
012:080 until **my** father permits me, or Allah
012:084 "How great is **my** grief for Joseph!"
012:086 "I only complain of **my** distraction and anguish to Allah,
012:087 "O **my** sons! go ye and enquire about Joseph
012:090 He said: "I am Joseph, and this is **my** brother:
012:093 and cast it over the face of **my** father: he will
012:093 "Go with this **my** shirt, and cast it
012:098 He said: "Soon will I ask **my** Lord for forgiveness
012:100 He said: "O **my** father! this is the fulfillment
012:100 the fulfillment of **my** vision of old!
012:100 sown enmity between me and **my** brothers.
012:100 Verily **my** Lord is gracious to whom He wills
012:101 Take Thou **my** soul (at death) as one submitting
012:101 Thou art **my** Protector in this world and in
012:101 "O **my** Lord! Thou hast indeed bestowed on me
012:108 Say thou: "This **my** Way; I do invite unto Allah,-
013:030 On Him is **my** trust, and to Him I turn!"
013:030 Say: "He is **my** Lord! There is no god but He!
013:032 then how (terrible) was **My** requital!
013:036 Unto Him do I call, and unto Him is **my** return."
014:007 truly **My** punishment is terrible indeed."
014:014 stand before **My** tribunal,-such as fear **My** Punishment."
014:022 but I failed in **my** promise to you.
014:031 Speak to **My** servants who have believed, that they
014:035 and preserve me and **my** sons from worshipping idols.
014:035 Abraham said: "O **my** Lord! make this make this city one
014:036 "O **my** Lord! they have indeed led astray many among
014:036 he then who follows **my** (ways) is of me, and he
014:037 I have made some of **my** offspring to dwell in a valley
014:039 for truly **my** Lord is He, the Hearer of Prayer!
014:040 "O **my** Lord! make me one who establishes
014:040 O our Lord! and accept Thou **my** Prayer.
014:040 and also (raise such) among **my** offspring,
014:041 Thy Forgiveness-me, **my** parents and (all)
015:029 and breathed into him of **My** spirit, fall ye down
015:036 (Iblis) said: "O **my** Lord! give me then respite
015:039 (Iblis) said: "O **my** Lord! because Thou hast
015:042 "For over **My** servants no authority shalt thou have,
015:049 Tell **My** servants that I am indeed the
015:050 And that **My** Chastisement will be indeed
015:068 Lut said: "These are **my** guests: disgrace me not:
015:071 He said: "There are **my** daughters (to marry),
016:027 and say: "Where are **My** `partners' concerning whom
017:024 "**My** Lord! bestow on them Thy Mercy even as they
017:053 Say to **My** servants that they should (only) say
017:062 under **my** sway-all but a few!"
017:065 "As for **My** servants, no authority
017:080 and likewise **my** exit by the Gate
017:080 Say: "O **my** Lord! let **my** entry be by the Gate
017:085 of **my** Lord of Knowledge it is only a little
017:093 Say: "Glory to **my** Lord! am I aught
017:100 the Treasures of the Mercy of **my** Lord, behold
018:022 Say thou: "**My** Lord knoweth best their number;
018:024 "I hope that **my** Lord will guide me ever closer
018:034 more honour and power in (**my** following of) men."
018:036 even if I am brought back to **my** Lord.
018:038 "But as for **my** part Allah is **my** Lord, and none
018:038 and none shall I associate with **my** Lord.
018:040 "It may be that **my** Lord will give me something
018:042 to **my** Lord and Cherisher!"
018:052 "Call on those whom ye thought to be **My** partners,"

018:056 and they treat **My** Signs and warnings as a jest.
018:073 by raising difficulties in **my** case."
018:076 received (full) excuse from **my** side."
018:082 I did it not of **my** own accord.
018:095 "(The power) in which **my** Lord has established me is
018:098 He said: "This is a mercy from **my** Lord: but when
018:098 but when the promise of **my** Lord comes to pass,
018:098 and the promise of **My** Lord is true."
018:102 can take **my** servants as protectors besides Me?
018:106 and took **My** Signs and **My** Messengers by way of jest.
018:109 the ocean be exhausted than would the words of **my** Lord,
018:109 were ink (wherewith to write out) the words of **my** Lord,
019:004 Praying: "O **my** Lord! infirm indeed are **my** bones,
019:004 and the hair of **my** head doth glisten with grey:
019:004 but never am I unblest, O **my** Lord, in **my** prayer to Thee!
019:005 "Now I fear (what) **my** relatives (and colleagues) will do
019:005 but **my** wife is barren: so give me an heir as from Thyself,-
019:006 and make him, O **my** Lord! one with whom thou art
019:008 when **my** wife is barren and I have grown quite decrepit
019:008 He said: "O **my** Lord! how shall I have a son,
019:010 (Zakariya) said "O **my** Lord! give me a Sign,"
019:032 "(He) hath made me kind to **my** mother,
019:036 Verily, Allah is **my** Lord and your Lord:
019:042 "O **my** father! why worship that which heareth not
019:043 "O **my** father! to me hath come knowledge which
019:044 "O **my** father! serve not Satan: for Satan
019:045 "O **my** father! I fear lest a Chastisement afflict
019:046 "Art thou shrinking from **my** gods, O Abraham?
019:047 I will pray to **my** Lord for thy forgiveness: for He
019:048 I will call on **my** Lord perhaps, by **my** prayer to **my** Lord,
020:014 and establish regular prayer for **My** remembrance.
020:018 He said, "It is **my** rod: on it I lean; with it
020:018 with it I beat down fodder for **my** flocks;
020:025 (Moses) said: "O **my** Lord! expand me **my** breast;"
020:026 "Ease **my** task for me;
020:027 "And remove the impediment from **my** speech.
020:029 "And give me a Minister from **my** family,
020:030 "Aaron, **my** brother;
020:031 "Add to **my** strength through him,
020:032 "And make him share **my** task:
020:042 Go, thou and thy brother, with **My** Signs, and slacken
020:052 **my** Lord never errs, nor forgets,-
020:052 "The knowledge of that is with **my** Lord, duly recorded:
020:077 "Travel by night with **my** servants, and strike
020:081 lest **My** Wrath should descend on you:
020:081 and those on whom descends **My** Wrath do perish indeed!
020:084 I hastened to Thee, O **my** Lord, to please Thee."
020:084 He replied: "Behold, they are close on **my** footsteps:
020:086 He said: "O **my** people! did not your Lord make a
020:090 so follow me and obey **my** command."
020:090 said to them: "O **my** people! ye are being tested
020:093 Didst thou then disobey **my** order?"
020:094 and thou didst not observe **my** word!'"
020:094 Seize (me) not by **my** beard nor by (the hair of) **my** head!
020:094 (Aaron) replied: "O son of **my** mother! Seize (me)
020:096 thus did **my** soul suggest to me."
020:105 say, "**My** Lord will uproot them and scatter
020:114 "O **my** Lord! increase me in knowledge."
020:123 whosoever follows **My** guidance, will not lose his way,
020:124 "But whosoever turns away from **My** Message, verily for
020:125 will say: "O **my** Lord! why hast thou raised me up blind,
021:004 Say: "**My** Lord knoweth (every) word (spoken)

MY (continued)

021:037	soon (enough) will I show you **My** Signs;
021:089	"O **my** Lord! leave me not without offspring,
021:105	**My** servants, the righteous, shall inherit the earth."
021:112	Say: "O **my** Lord! judge Thou in truth!"
022:026	and sanctify **My** House for those who
022:044	but how (terrible) was **My** punishment (of them)!
023:023	"O **my** people! worship Allah! Ye have
023:026	(Noah) said: "O **my** Lord! help me: for that
023:029	And say: "O **my** Lord! enable me to disembark with Thy
023:039	(The prophet) said: "O **my** Lord! help me: for that
023:066	"**My** Signs used to be rehearsed to you, but ye
023:093	"O **my** Lord! if Thou wilt show me (in **my** lifetime) that
023:094	"Then, O **my** Lord! put me not amongst the
023:097	And say: "O **my** Lord! I seek refuge with Thee from
023:098	O **my** Lord! lest they should come near me."
023:099	he says: "O **my** Lord! send me back to (life),-
023:105	"Were not **My** Signs rehearsed to you, and ye
023:109	"A part of **My** servants there was, who used
023:110	made you forget **My** Message while ye
023:118	So say: "O **my** Lord! grant Thou forgiveness
025:017	"Was it ye who led these **My** servants astray, or did they
025:030	"O **my** Lord, Truly **my** people treated this Qur'an
025:077	"**My** Lord would not concern Himself with you
026:012	"O **my** Lord! I do fear that they will charge me with
026:013	"**My** breast will be straitened.
026:013	And **my** tongue will not speak (plainly): so send
026:021	I feared you; but **my** Lord has (since) invested me
026:042	(raised to posts) nearest (to **my** person)."
026:052	"Travel by night with **My** servants; for surely
026:062	(Moses) said: "By no means! **My** Lord is with me!
026:082	will forgive me **my** faults on the Day of Judgment.
026:083	"O **my** Lord! bestow wisdom on me, and join
026:086	"Forgive **my** father, for that he is among those astray;
026:109	**my** reward is only from the Lord of the Worlds:
026:113	"Their account is only with **my** Lord, if ye
026:117	He said: "O **my** Lord! truly **my** people have rejected me.
026:127	**my** reward is only from the Lord of the Worlds.
026:145	**my** reward is only from the Lord of the Worlds.
026:164	**my** reward is only from the Lord of the Worlds.
026:169	"O **my** Lord! deliver me and **my** family from such things
026:180	**my** reward is only from the Lord of the Worlds.
026:188	He said: "**My** Lord knows best what ye do."
027:01	he said: "O **my** Lord! so order me that I may be grateful
027:019	which Thou has bestowed on me and on **my** parents,
027:032	advise me in (this) **my** affair:
027:035	(wait) to see what (answer) return (**my**) ambassadors."
027:040	truly **my** Lord is Free of All Needs, Supreme in
027:040	"This is by the grace of **my** Lord!-to test
027:044	She said: "O **my** Lord! I have indeed wronged **my** soul:
027:046	He said: "O **my** people! why ask ye to hasten
027:084	"Did ye reject **My** signs, though ye comprehended them
028:016	He prayed: "O **my** Lord! I have indeed wronged by soul!
028:017	He said: "O **my** Lord! for that Thou hast bestowed
028:021	He prayed: "O **my** Lord! save me
028:022	"I do hope that **my** Lord will show me
028:024	and said: "O **my** Lord! truly am I
028:025	She said: "**My** father invites thee that he may
028:026	Said one of the (damsels): "O **my** (dear) father!
028:027	one of these **my** daughters to thee, on condition
028:033	He said: "O **my** Lord! I have slain a man among them,
028:034	"And **my** brother Aaron-he is more
028:037	Moses said: "**My** Lord knows best who it is

MY (continued)

028:062	and say: "Where are **my** `partners'?-whom ye
028:074	He will say: "Where are **My** `partners' whom ye
028:085	Say: "**My** Lord knows best who it is that brings
029:023	shall despair of **My** mercy: it is they who
029:026	"I will leave home for the sake **of my** Lord:
029:030	He said: "O **my** Lord! help Thou me against
029:036	Then he said: "O **my** people! serve Allah,
029:056	O **My** servants who believe! truly, spacious is **My** Earth:
031:013	admonishing him "O **my** son! join not in worship (others)
031:016	"O **my** son! (said Luqman), "If there be (but) the weight
031:017	"O **my** son! establish regular prayer, enjoin what
034:003	say, "Nay! but most surely, by **my** Lord, it will
034:013	but few of **My** servants are grateful!"
034:036	Say: "Verily **my** Lord enlarges and restricts
034:039	Say: "Verily **my** Lord enlarges and restricts
034:045	yet when they rejected **My** messengers,
034:045	how (terrible) was **My** punishment!
034:047	**my** reward is only due from Allah:
034:048	Say: "Verily **my** Lord doth cast the Truth,-
034:050	I only stray to the loss of **my** own soul:
034:050	it is because of the inspiration of **my** Lord to me:
035:026	and how (terrible) was **My** punishment.
036:020	a man, saying, "O **my** People! obey the messengers:
036:026	"Ah me! Would that **my** People knew (what I know)!-
036:027	"For that **my** Lord has granted me Forgiveness
037:057	"Had it not been for the Grace of **my** Lord, I should
037:099	He said: "I will go to **my** Lord! He will surely guide me!
037:100	"O **my** Lord! grant me a righteous (son)!"
037:102	"O **my** father! do as thou art commanded:
037:102	he said: "O **my** son! I have seen in a dream
038:008	Nay, they have not yet tasted **My** Punishment!
038:008	But they are in doubt concerning **My** (own) Message!
038:014	but **My** Punishment came justly and inevitably
038:023	"This man is **my** brother; he has nine and ninety ewes,
038:023	'Commit her to **my** care,' and he overcame me
038:032	"Truly do I prefer wealth to the remembrance of **my** Lord."
038:035	He said, "O **my** Lord! Forgive me, and grant me
038:072	and breathed into him of **My** spirit,
038:075	whom I have created with **My** hands?
038:078	"And **My** Curse shall be on thee till the
038:079	(Iblis) said: "O **my** Lord! give me then respite
039:010	Say: "O ye **my** servants who believe! Fear your
039:013	Say: "I would, if I disobeyed **my** Lord, indeed have fear
039:014	with **my** sincere (and exclusive) devotion:
039:016	"O **my** servants! Then fear ye Me!"
039:017	So announce the Good News to **My** Servants,-
039:039	I will do (**my** part): but soon will ye know-
039:039	Say: "O **my** people! Do whatever ye can:
039:053	Say: "O **my** Servants who have transgressed against
039:056	in that I neglected (**my** duty) towards Allah,
039:059	'Nay, but there came to thee **My** Signs, and thou didst
040:005	And how (terrible), was **My** Requital!
040:027	"I have indeed called upon **my** Lord and your Lord
040:028	"Will ye slay a man because he says, '**My** Lord is Allah'?-
040:029	"O **my** people! yours is the dominion this day:
040:030	"O **my** People! truly I do fear for you something
040:032	"And, O **my** People! I fear for you a Day
040:038	"O **my** People! follow me: I will
040:039	"O **my** people! This life of the present is nothing
040:041	"And O **my** People! how (strange) it is for me
040:044	**My** (own) affair I commit to Allah:
040:066	that the Clear Signs have come to me from **my** Lord;

MY (continued)

041:050 but if I am brought back to **my** Lord, I have
041:050 "This is due to **my** (merit): I think
042:010 Such is Allah **my** Lord: in Him
043:051 (witness) these streams flowing underneath **my** (palace)?
043:051 saying: "O **my** people! Does not the dominion
043:064 "For Allah; He is **my** Lord and your Lord:
043:068 **My** devotees! no fear shall be on you today,
043:088 (Prophet's) cry, "O **my** Lord! Truly these are a people
044:020 I have sought safety with **my** Lord and your Lord,
044:023 "March forth with **My** servants by night: for ye
046:015 He says, "O **my** Lord! grant me that I may be grateful
046:015 and be gracious to me in **my** issue.
046:015 Thou hast bestowed upon me, and upon both **my** parents,
050:014 and **My** warning was duly fulfilled (in them).
050:028 "Dispute not with each other in **My** Presence:
050:029 and I do not the least injustice to **My** Servants."
050:045 such as fear **My** Warning!
054:016 how (terrible) was **My** Chastisement and **My** Warning?
054:018 then how terrible was **my** Chastisement and **My** Warning?
054:021 how (terrible) was **My** Chastisement and **My** Warning?
054:030 how (terrible) was **My** Chastisement and **My** Warning?
054:037 "Now taste ye **My** Wrath and **My** Warning."
054:039 "So taste ye **My** Chastisement and **My** Warning."·
058:021 "It is I and **My** messenger who must prevail":
060:001 and to seek **My** Good Pleasure, showing friendship
060:001 If ye have come out to strive in **My** Way and seek
060:001 O ye who believe! take not **My** enemies and yours
061:005 "O **my** people! why do ye vex and insult me,
061:014 "Who will be **my** helpers to (the work of) Allah?"
063:010 "O **my** Lord! Why didst Thou not give respite for a little
064:007 Say: "Yea, by **my** Lord, ye shall surely be raised up;
066:011 she said: "O **my** Lord! build for me, in nearness to Thee,
067:017 so that ye shall know how (terrible) was **My** warning?
067:018 But indeed men before them rejected (**My** warning):
067:018 then how (terrible) was **My** punishment (of them)?
068:045 truly powerful is **My** Plan.
069:019 "Ah here! read ye **my** Record!
069:020 that **my** Account would (one Day) reach me!"
069:025 "Ah! would that **my** record had not been given to me!
069:026 "And that I had never realized how **my** account (stood)!
069:028 "Of no profit to me has been **my** wealth!
069:029 "**My** power has perished from me!"...
071:002 He said: "O **my** People! I am to you a Warner,
071:005 "O **my** Lord! I have called to **my** People night and day:
071:006 "But **my** call only increases (their) flight
071:021 Noah said: "O **my** Lord! they have disobeyed me,
071:026 Noah said: "O **my** Lord! Leave not of the Unbelievers
071:028 "O **my** Lord! Forgive me, **my** parents, all who enter
071:028 all who enter **my** house in Faith, and (all) believing men
072:020 Say: "I do no more than invoke **my** Lord, and I
072:021 Say: "It is not in **my** power to cause you harm,
072:025 or whether **my** Lord will appoint for it a distant term.
089:015 "**My** Lord hath honoured me."
089:016 "**My** Lord hath humiliated me!"
089:024 sent forth (Good Deeds) for (this) **my** (Future) Life."
089:029 "Enter thou, then, among **my** Devotees!
089:030 "Yea, enter thou **my** Heaven!"

MYSELF

003:055 "O Jesus! I will take thee and raise thee to **Myself**
005:025 I have power only over **myself** and my bother:
007:188 or harm to **myself** except as Allah willeth.
010:015 I should **myself** fear the Chastisement

MYSELF (continued)

010:049 or profit to **myself** except as Allah willeth.
011:043 The son replied: "I will be take **myself** to some
011:080 or that I could betake **myself** to some powerful support."
012:036 Said one of them: "I see **myself** (in a dream)
012:036 Said the other: "I see **myself** (in a dream)
012:053 "Yet I do not absolve **myself** (of blame):
015:033 (Iblis) said: "I am not one to prostrate **myself** to man,
018:070 about anything until I **myself** speak to thee
020:041 "And I have prepared thee for **Myself** (for service)."
028:038 I know for you but **myself**: therefore O Haman!
040:029 "I but point out to you that which I see (**myself**);
043:026 "I do indeed clear **myself** of what ye worship:

N

NAKED
005:031   and to hide the **naked** body of my brother?"
005:031   the **naked** body of his brother.
020:118   for thee not to go hungry nor to go **naked**,
037:145   the **naked** shore in a state of sickness,
068:049   on the **naked** shore, in disgrace.

NAKEDNESS
020:121   and so their **nakedness** appeared to them:

NAME
001:001   In the **name** of Allah, Most Gracious, Most Merciful.
002:000   In the **name** of Allah, Most Gracious, Most Merciful.
002:030   Thy praises and glorify Thy Holy (**name**)?"
002:114   His **name** should be celebrated?
002:173   any other **name** hath been invoked besides that Allah,
002:224   And make not Allah's (**name**) an excuse
003:000   In the **name** of Allah, Most Gracious, Most Merciful.
003:045   his **name** will be Christ Jesus, the son of Mary,
004:000   In the **name** of Allah, Most Gracious, Most Merciful.
005:000   In the **name** of Allah, Most Gracious, Most Merciful.
005:003   hath been invoked the **name** of other than Allah;
005:004   but pronounce the **name** of Allah over it: and fear
006:000   In the **name** of Allah, Most Gracious, Most Merciful.
006:118   on which Allah's **name** hath been pronounced,
006:119   on which Allah's **name** hath been pronounced,
006:121   Allah's **name** hath not been pronounced:
006:138   forging a lie against Allah's **name**: soon will
006:138   the **name** of Allah is not pronounced:-forging
006:145   (meat) on which a **name** has been invoked, other
007:000   In the **name** of Allah, Most Gracious, Most Merciful.
008:000   In the **name** of Allah, Most Gracious, Most Merciful.
010:000   In the **name** of Allah, Most Gracious, Most Merciful.
011:000   In the **name** of Allah, Most Gracious, Most Merciful.
011:041   in the **name** of Allah, whether it move or be
012:000   In the **name** of Allah, Most Gracious, Most Merciful.
012:066   you until ye swear a solemn oath to me, in Allah's **name**,
012:080   an oath from you in Allah's **name**, and how
013:000   In the **name** of Allah, Most Gracious, Most Merciful.
013:033   Say: "But **name** them! is it that ye will inform
014:000   In the **name** of Allah, Most Gracious, Most Merciful.
015:000   In the **name** of Allah, Most Gracious, Most Merciful.
016:000   In the **name** of Allah, Most Gracious, Most Merciful.
016:115   and any (food) over which the **name** of other than
017:000   In the **name** of Allah, Most Gracious, Most Merciful.
017:073   Our **name** something quite different: (in that case)
017:110   by whatever **name** ye call upon Him, (it is well):
018:000   In the **name** of Allah, Most Gracious, Most Merciful.
019:000   In the **name** of Allah, Most Gracious, Most Merciful.
019:007   good news of a son: his **name** shall be Yahya:
019:007   none by that **name** have We conferred distinction before."
019:065   thou of any who is worthy of the same **Name** as He?
020:000   In the **name** of Allah, Most Gracious, Most Merciful.
021:000   In the **name** of Allah, Most Gracious, Most Merciful.
022:000   In the **name** of Allah, Most Gracious, Most Merciful.
022:028   and celebrate the **name** of Allah, through the
022:034   that they might celebrate the **name** of Allah
022:036   then pronounce the **name** of Allah over them

NAME (continued)
022:040   in which the **name** of Allah is commemorated
023:000   In the **name** of Allah, Most Gracious, Most Merciful.
024:000   In the **name** of Allah, Most Gracious, Most Merciful.
024:036   for the celebration in them, of His **name**:
025:000   In the **name** of Allah, Most Gracious, Most Merciful.
026:000   In the **name** of Allah, Most Gracious, Most Merciful.
027:000   In the **name** of Allah, Most Gracious, Most Merciful.
027:030   'In the **name** of Allah, Most Gracious,
028:000   In the **name** of Allah, Most Gracious, Most Merciful.
029:000   In the **name** of Allah, Most Gracious, Most Merciful.
030:000   In the **name** of Allah, Most Gracious, Most Merciful.
031:000   In the **name** of Allah, Most Gracious, Most Merciful.
032:000   In the **name** of Allah, Most Gracious, Most Merciful.
033:000   In the **name** of Allah, Most Gracious, Most Merciful.
034:000   In the **name** of Allah, Most Gracious, Most Merciful.
035:000   In the **name** of Allah, Most Gracious, Most Merciful.
036:000   In the **name** of Allah, Most Gracious, Most Merciful.
037:000   In the **name** of Allah, Most Gracious, Most Merciful.
038:000   In the **name** of Allah, Most Gracious, Most Merciful.
039:000   In the **name** of Allah, Most Gracious, Most Merciful.
040:000   In the **name** of Allah, Most Gracious, Most Merciful.
041:000   In the **name** of Allah, Most Gracious, Most Merciful.
042:000   In the **name** of Allah, Most Gracious, Most Merciful.
043:000   In the **name** of Allah, Most Gracious, Most Merciful.
044:000   In the **name** of Allah, Most Gracious, Most Merciful.
045:000   In the **name** of Allah, Most Gracious, Most Merciful.
046:000   In the **name** of Allah, Most Gracious, Most Merciful.
047:000   In the **name** of Allah, Most Gracious, Most Merciful.
048:000   In the **name** of Allah, Most Gracious, Most Merciful.
049:000   In the **name** of Allah, Most Gracious, Most Merciful.
049:011   ill-seeming is a **name** connoting wickedness,
050:000   In the **name** of Allah, Most Gracious, Most Merciful.
051:000   In the **name** of Allah, Most Gracious, Most Merciful.
052:000   In the **name** of Allah, Most Gracious, Most Merciful.
053:000   In the **name** of Allah, Most Gracious, Most Merciful.
053:027   **name** the angels with female names.
054:000   In the **name** of Allah, Most Gracious, Most Merciful.
055:000   In the **name** of Allah, Most Gracious, Most Merciful.
055:078   Blessed be the **name** of thy Lord, full of
056:000   In the **name** of Allah, Most Gracious, Most Merciful.
056:074   Then glorify the **name** of the Lord, the Supreme!
056:096   So glorify the **name** of thy Lord, the Supreme.
057:000   In the **name** of Allah, Most Gracious, Most Merciful.
058:000   In the **name** of Allah, Most Gracious, Most Merciful.
059:000   In the **name** of Allah, Most Gracious, Most Merciful.
060:000   In the **name** of Allah, Most Gracious, Most Merciful.
061:000   In the **name** of Allah, Most Gracious, Most Merciful.
061:006   after me, whose **name** shall be Ahmad.
062:000   In the **name** of Allah, Most Gracious, Most Merciful.
063:000   In the **name** of Allah, Most Gracious, Most Merciful.
064:000   In the **name** of Allah, Most Gracious, Most Merciful.
065:000   In the **name** of Allah, Most Gracious, Most Merciful.
066:000   In the **name** of Allah, Most Gracious, Most Merciful.
067:000   In the **name** of Allah, Most Gracious, Most Merciful.
068:000   In the **name** of Allah, Most Gracious, Most Merciful.
069:000   In the **name** of Allah, Most Gracious, Most Merciful.
069:044   any sayings in Our **name**,
069:052   So glorify the **name** of thy Lord Most High.
070:000   In the **name** of Allah, Most Gracious, Most Merciful.
071:000   In the **name** of Allah, Most Gracious, Most Merciful.
072:000   In the **name** of Allah, Most Gracious, Most Merciful.
073:000   In the **name** of Allah, Most Gracious, Most Merciful.

NAME (continued)

073:008   But keep in remembrance the **name** of the Lord,
074:000   In the **name** of Allah, Most Gracious, Most Merciful.
075:000   In the **name** of Allah, Most Gracious, Most Merciful.
076:000   In the **name** of Allah, Most Gracious, Most Merciful.
076:025   And celebrate the **name** of thy Lord
077:000   In the **name** of Allah, Most Gracious, Most Merciful.
078:000   In the **name** of Allah, Most Gracious, Most Merciful.
079:000   In the **name** of Allah, Most Gracious, Most Merciful.
080:000   In the **name** of Allah, Most Gracious, Most Merciful.
081:000   In the **name** of Allah, Most Gracious, Most Merciful.
082:000   In the **name** of Allah, Most Gracious, Most Merciful.
083:000   In the **name** of Allah, Most Gracious, Most Merciful.
084:000   In the **name** of Allah, Most Gracious, Most Merciful.
085:000   In the **name** of Allah, Most Gracious, Most Merciful.
086:000   In the **name** of Allah, Most Gracious, Most Merciful.
087:000   In the **name** of Allah, Most Gracious, Most Merciful.
087:001   Glorify the **name** of thy Guardian-Lord, Most High,
087:015   And remembers the **name** of their Guardian-Lord,
088:000   In the **name** of Allah, Most Gracious, Most Merciful.
089:000   In the **name** of Allah, Most Gracious, Most Merciful.
090:000   In the **name** of Allah, Most Gracious, Most Merciful.
091:000   In the **name** of Allah, Most Gracious, Most Merciful.
092:000   In the **name** of Allah, Most Gracious, Most Merciful.
093:000   In the **name** of Allah, Most Gracious, Most Merciful.
094:000   In the **name** of Allah, Most Gracious, Most Merciful.
095:000   In the **name** of Allah, Most Gracious, Most Merciful.
096:000   In the **name** of Allah, Most Gracious, Most Merciful.
096:001   Proclaim! (or Read!) in the **name** of thy Lord
097:000   In the **name** of Allah, Most Gracious, Most Merciful.
098:000   In the **name** of Allah, Most Gracious, Most Merciful.
099:000   In the **name** of Allah, Most Gracious, Most Merciful.
100:000   In the **name** of Allah, Most Gracious, Most Merciful.
101:000   In the **name** of Allah, Most Gracious, Most Merciful.
102:000   In the **name** of Allah, Most Gracious, Most Merciful.
103:000   In the **name** of Allah, Most Gracious, Most Merciful.
104:000   In the **name** of Allah, Most Gracious, Most Merciful.
105:000   In the **name** of Allah, Most Gracious, Most Merciful.
106:000   In the **name** of Allah, Most Gracious, Most Merciful.
107:000   In the **name** of Allah, Most Gracious, Most Merciful.
108:000   In the **name** of Allah, Most Gracious, Most Merciful.
109:000   In the **name** of Allah, Most Gracious, Most Merciful.
110:000   In the **name** of Allah, Most Gracious, Most Merciful.
111:000   In the **name** of Allah, Most Gracious, Most Merciful.
112:000   In the **name** of Allah, Most Gracious, Most Merciful.
113:000   In the **name** of Allah, Most Gracious, Most Merciful.
114:000   In the **name** of Allah, Most Gracious, Most Merciful.

NAMED

003:036   I have **named** her Mary,
005:001   with the exception **named**:
012:040   is nothing but names which ye have **named**, ye and
022:078   It is He Who has **named** you Muslims, both before

NAMELY

003:016   (**Namely**), those who say: "Our Lord!
016:028   "(**Namely**) those whose lives the angels take in
016:032   (**Namely**) those whose lives the angels take in
042:013   **namely**, that ye should remain steadfast in Religion,
053:038   **Namely**, that no bearer of burdens can bear

NAMES

002:031   And He taught Adam the **names** of all things;
002:031   "Tell Me the **names** of these if ye are right."
002:033   He said: "O Adam! tell them their **names**."
002:033   "When he had told them their **names**,

NAMES (continued)

007:071   dispute ye with me over **names** which ye have devised-
007:180   but shun such men as distort His **names**:
007:180   The most beautiful **names** belong to Allah: so call
012:040   is nothing but **names** which ye have named,
017:110   for to Him belong the Most Beautiful **Names**.
020:008   To Him belong the Most Beautiful **Names**.
033:005   But if ye know not their father's **names**, (then they are)
053:023   These are nothing but **names** which ye
053:027   name the angels with female **names**.
059:024   to Him belong the Most Beautiful **Names**:

NARRATED

028:025   So when he came to him and **narrated** the story, he said:

NARROWED

020:124   a life **narrowed** down, and We shall raise him up

NASR

071:023   Wadd nor Suwa, neither Yaguth nor Yauq, nor **Nasr'**;-

NATION

002:213   Mankind was one single **nation**.
010:019   Mankind was but one **nation**, but differed (later).
045:028   every **nation** will be called to its
045:028   And thou wilt see every **nation** bowing the knee:

NATIONS

002:143   That ye might be witnesses over the **nations**,
003:042   chosen thee above the women of all **nations**.
006:042   Before thee We sent (Messengers) to many **nations**,
006:042   We afflicted the **nations** with suffering and adversity,
006:086   and to all We gave favour above the **nations**:
006:090   this is but a Reminder to the **nations**."
007:069   and gave you a stature tall among the **nations**.
007:140   you with gifts above the **nations**?"
007:160   We divided them into twelve tribes or **nations**.
021:071   to the land which We have blessed for the **nations**.
035:042   would be more tightly guided than anyone of the **nations**:
037:079   "Peace and salutation to Noah among the **nations**!"
044:032   And We chose them aforetime above the **nations**,
045:016   and We favoured them above the **nations**.
049:013   and made you into **nations** and tribes, that ye

NATURAL

004:077   to our (**natural**) term, near (enough)?

NATURE

004:119   and deface the (fair) **nature** created by Allah."
005:108   in its true **nature** and shape, or else
007:189   and made his mate of like **nature**, in order
016:072   of your own **nature**, and made for you, out of
017:081   for Falsehood is (by its **nature**) bound to perish."
030:030   the **nature** in which Allah has made mankind:
036:068   We cause him to be reversed in **nature**: will they
039:006   of like **nature**, his mate; and He
041:025   intimate companions (of like **nature**), who made

NAUGHT

002:113   "The Jews have **naught** (to stand) upon";
002:113   "The Christians have **naught** (to stand) upon";
002:174   they swallow into themselves **naught** but Fire;
003:191   not for **naught** hast Thou created (all) this!
006:052   and in **naught** are they accountable for thee,
006:052   In **naught** art thou accountable for them,
007:150   The people did indeed reckon me as **naught**,
009:025   but they availed you **naught**; the land.
010:015   I follow **naught** but what is revealed unto me:
025:004   "**Naught** is this but a lie which he has forged,
029:024   So **naught** was the answer of (Abraham's) people
037:039   And you are requited **naught** save what ye did.

NAUGHT (continued)

047:001 their deeds will Allah bring to **naught**.
047:008 and (Allah) will bring their deeds to **naught**.
074:028 **Naught** doth it permit to endure, and **naught** doth it leave

NAY

002:013 **Nay** of a surety they are the fools
002:045 **Nay**, seek (Allah's) help with
002:081 **Nay**, those who seek gain in Evil,
002:088 **Nay**, Allah's curse is on them
002:100 **Nay**, most of them are faithless.
002:112 **Nay**, whoever submits his whole self
002:116 **Nay**, to Him belongs all that is in
002:135 Say thou: "**Nay**! (I would rather) the Religion
002:154 **Nay**, they are living,
002:170 they say: "**Nay**! we shall follow
002:259 He said "**Nay**, thou hast tarried
003:076 **Nay**,-Those that keep their plighted faith
003:150 **Nay**, Allah is your Protector, and He
003:169 **Nay**, they live, finding their sustenance
003:180 **Nay**, it will be the worse of them:
004:049 **Nay**-but Allah doth purify whom He pleaseth.
004:139 **Nay**, all honor is with Allah.
004:147 **Nay**, it is Allah that recognizeth (all good),
004:155 **nay**, Allah hath set the seal on their hearts
004:158 **Nay**, Allah raised him up unto Himself;
005:018 **Nay**, ye are but men, of the men
005:064 **Nay**, both His hands are widely outstretched:
006:014 Say: "**Nay**! but I am commanded to be the first
006:019 Say: "**Nay**! I cannot bear witness!"
006:041 "**Nay**,-On Him would ye call, and if
007:028 say: "**Nay** Allah never commands what is Indecent:
007:179 They are like cattle,-**nay** more misguided: for they are
009:013 **Nay**, it is Allah whom ye should more justly fear,
010:039 **Nay**, they charge with falsehood that whose
012:018 He said: "**Nay**, but your minds have made up
012:083 Jacob said: "**Nay**, but ye have yourselves contrived
012:094 **nay**, think me not a dotard."
013:013 **Nay**, thunder repeateth His praises, and so
013:033 **Nay**! to those who believe not, their devising
015:015 **nay**, we have been bewitched
016:028 (The angels will reply), "**Nay**, but verily Allah
016:033 **nay**, they wronged their own souls.
016:038 raise up those who die: **nay**, but it is a promise
017:050 Say: "(**Nay**!) be ye stones or iron,
019:019 He said: "**Nay**, I am only a messenger from thy Lord,
019:079 **Nay**! We shall record what he says, and We
020:066 He said, "**Nay**, throw ye first!" Then behold
021:005 "**Nay**," they say, "(these are) medleys of dreams!-
021:005 **Nay**, He forged it!-**Nay**, He is (but) a poet!"
021:018 **Nay**, We hurl the Truth against falsehood,
021:040 **Nay**, it may come to them all of a sudden
021:044 **Nay**, We gave the good things of this life
021:056 He said, "**Nay**, your Lord is the Lord of the
021:063 He said: "**Nay**, this was done by this
021:097 **nay**, we truly did wrong!"
023:056 **Nay**, they do not perceive.
023:070 **Nay**, he has brought them the Truth, but most
023:071 **Nay**, We have sent them their admonition, but they
024:050 **Nay**, it is they themselves who do wrong.
025:011 **Nay**, they deny the Hour (of the Judgment to come):
025:044 **nay**, they are farther astray from the way.
026:074 They said: "**Nay**, but we found our fathers
026:166 **Nay**, ye are a people transgressing (all limits)!"

NAY (continued)

027:036 **Nay** it is ye who rejoice in your gift!
027:055 **Nay**, ye are a people (grossly) ignorant!"
027:060 **Nay**, they are a people who swerve from justice.
027:061 **Nay**, most of them know not.
027:066 **nay**, they are blind thereunto!
027:066 **Nay**, but their knowledge fails as to the Hereafter,
029:049 **Nay**, here are Signs self-evident in the hearts
030:029 **Nay**, the wrong-doers (merely) fellow their
031:011 **nay**, but the Transgressors are in manifest error.
031:021 "**Nay**, we shall follow the ways that we found
032:003 **Nay**, it is the Truth from thy Lord, that thou
032:010 **Nay**, they deny the meeting with their Lord!
034:003 say, "**Nay**! but most surely, by my Lord, it will
034:008 **Nay**, it is those who believe not in the Hereafter,
034:027 **Nay**, He is Allah, the Exalted in Power, the Wise."
034:032 **Nay**, rather it was ye who transgressed."
034:033 "**Nay**! it was a plot (of yours) by day
034:041 **Nay**, but they worshipped the Jinns:
035:030 **nay**, He will give them (even) more out of
035:040 **Nay**, the wrong-doers promise each other nothing
036:019 **Nay**, but ye are a people transgressing all bounds!"
037:026 **Nay**, but that day they shall submit (to Judgment);
037:029 They will reply: "**Nay**, ye yourselves had no Faith!
037:030 **Nay**, it was ye who were a people in
037:037 **Nay**! he has come with the (very) Truth,
038:008 **Nay**, they have not yet tasted My Punishment!
038:060 (The followers shall cry to the misleaders:) "**Nay**, ye (too)!
039:049 **Nay**, but this is but a trial, but most
039:051 **Nay**, the evil results of their deeds overtook them.
039:059 "(The reply will be) `**Nay**, but there came to thee
039:066 **Nay**, but worship Allah, and be
040:074 **nay**, we invoked not, of old, anything (that had real
043:022 **Nay**! they say: "We found Our fathers following
043:077 "**Nay**, but ye shall abide!"
046:024 "**Nay**, it is the (calamity) ye were
046:028 **Nay**, they left them in the lurch:
048:012 "**Nay**, ye thought that the Messenger and the
048:015 **Nay**, but little do they understand (such things).
049:012 **Nay**, ye would abhor it...
049:017 **Nay**, Allah has conferred a favour upon you that He has
051:053 **Nay**, they are themselves a people transgressing beyond
052:033 **Nay**, they have no faith!
052:036 **Nay**, they have no firm belief.
053:024 **Nay**, shall man have (just) anything
053:036 **Nay**, is he not acquainted with what is in
054:025 **Nay**, he is a liar an insolent one!
054:046 **Nay**, the Hour (of Judgment) is the time promised
067:020 **Nay**, who is there that can help you, (even as)
067:021 **Nay**, they obstinately persist in insolent impiety
068:003 **Nay**, verily for thee is a Reward unfailing:
074:032 **Nay**, verily: by the Moon,
074:054 **Nay**, this surely is an admonition:
075:004 **Nay**, We are able to put together in perfect order
075:014 **Nay**, man will be evidence against himself,
075:019 **Nay** more, it is for Us to explain it
075:020 **Nay**, (ye men!) but ye love the fleeting life,
082:009 **Nay**! but ye do Reject The Judgment!
083:007 **Nay**! Surely the Record of the Wicked is (preserved)
083:018 **Nay**, verily the Record of the Righteous is
084:015 **Nay**, **nay**! for his Lord was (ever) watchful of him!
085:021 **Nay**, this is a Glorious Qur'an,
087:016 **Nay** (behold), ye prefer the life of this world;

NAY (continued)

089:017 **Nay, nay**! But ye honour not the orphans!
089:021 **Nay**! When the earth is pounded to powder,
090:000 **Nay** I do swear by this City;-
096:006 **Nay**, but man doth transgress all bounds,
096:019 **Nay**, heed him not: but prostrate
102:003 But **nay**, ye soon shall know (the reality).
102:005 **Nay**, were ye to know with certainty of mind,

NEAR

002:214 Ah! Verily, the help of Allah is (always) **near**!
004:077 to our (natural) term, **near** (enough)?
005:106 even though the (beneficiary) be our **near** relation:
006:099 clusters of dates hanging low and **near**:
006:152 even if a **near** relative is concerned;
007:056 is (always) **near** to those who do good.
007:150 and went **near** to slaying me!
007:206 Those who are **near** to thy Lord, disdain not
008:041 and to **near** relatives, orphans, the needy,
008:048 can overcome you this day, while I am **near** to you":
009:007 whom ye made a treaty **near** the sacred mosque?
009:123 Fight the Unbelievers who are **near** to you, and let
011:061 for my Lord is (always) **near**, ready to answer."
012:025 they both found her lord **near** the door.
012:060 nor shall ye (even) come **near** me."
014:017 but never well he be **near** swallowing it
018:086 set in a spring of murky water: **near** it he found a People:
019:018 (come not **near**) if thou dost fear Allah."
019:052 and made him draw **near** to Us, for converse
021:109 ye are promised is **near** or far.
022:033 place of sacrifice is **near** the Ancient House.
023:098 O my Lord! lest they should come **near** me."
026:090 the Garden will be brought **near**,
026:148 with spathes **near** breaking (with the weight of fruit)?
028:031 "O Moses!" (It was said), "Draw **near**, and fear
034:050 all things, and is (ever) **near**."
034:051 from a position (quite) **near**.
038:025 he enjoyed, indeed, a **Near** Approach to Us, and a
038:040 And he enjoyed, indeed, a **Near** Approach to Us,
040:018 drawing **near**, when the Hearts will (come)
042:023 for this except the love of those **near** of kin."
050:041 will call out from a place quite **near**,-
053:014 **Near** the Lote-tree of the utmost boundary.
053:015 **Near** it is the Garden of Abode.
055:054 will be **Near** (and easy of reach).
069:023 The Fruits whereof (will hang in bunches) low and **near**.
070:007 But We see it (quite) **near**.
072:025 which ye are promised is **near**, or whether
078:040 of a Chastisement **near**,-the Day when man will see
081:013 And when the Garden is brought **near**;-

NEARER

003:167 They were that day **nearer** to Unbelief than of Faith,
009:099 gifts bringing them **nearer** to Allah and obtaining
009:099 Aye, indeed they bring them **nearer** (to Him):
022:013 is **nearer** than his profit: evil, indeed, is the
034:037 that will bring you **nearer** to Us in degree:
039:003 they may bring us **nearer** to Allah."
050:016 for We are **nearer** to him than (his) jugular vein.
053:009 two bow-lengths or (even) **nearer**;
056:085 But We are **nearer** to him than ye, and yet see not,-

NEAREST

002:237 if the **nearest** to righteousness.
003:045 and (of the company of) those **nearest** to Allah;
003:068 among men, the **nearest** of kin to Abraham,

NEAREST (continued)

004:007 and those **nearest** related there is a share for
004:011 or your children are **nearest** to you in benefit.
004:172 nor do the angels, those **nearest** (to Allah):
005:082 and **nearest** among them in love to the Believers
005:107 **nearest** in kin from among those who claim a lawful right:
007:114 (raised to posts) **nearest** (to my person)."
017:057 means of access to their Lord,-as to who are **nearest**:
021:017 surely have taken it from the things **nearest** to Us,
026:042 (raised to posts) **nearest** (to my person)."
026:214 And admonish the **nearest** kinsmen,
056:011 These will be those **Nearest** to Allah:
056:088 Thus, then, if he be of those **Nearest** to Allah,
083:021 To which bear witness those **Nearest** (to Allah).
083:028 whereof drink those **Nearest** to Allah.

NEARLY

009:117 of them had **nearly** swerved (from duty), but He
017:074 thou wouldst **nearly** have inclined to them a little.
022:072 They **nearly** attack with violence those who
035:018 even though he be **nearly** related.

NEARNESS

003:015 are Gardens in **nearness** to their Lord with rivers flowing
066:011 build for me, in **nearness** to Thee, a mansion

NECESSARILY

019:061 for His promise must (**necessarily**) come to pass.
020:129 (their punishment) must **necessarily** have come;
042:022 and (the burden of) that must (**necessarily**) fall on them.

NECESSITATING

002:196 in his scalp, (**necessitating** shaving),

NECESSITY

002:173 but if one is forced by **necessity**,
006:119 except under compulsion of **necessity**?
006:145 if a person is forced by **necessity**, without wilful
016:115 But if one is forced by **necessity**, without wilful

NECK

017:013 Every man's fate We have fastened on his own **neck**:
017:029 (like a niggard's) to thy **neck**,
111:005 round her (own) **neck**!

NECKS

003:180 tied to their **necks** like a twisted collar,
008:012 smite ye above their **necks** and smite
013:005 They are those round whose **necks** will be
014:043 They running forward with **necks** outstretched,
026:004 bend their **necks** in humility.
034:033 We shall put yokes on the **necks** of the Unbelievers:
036:008 We have put yokes round their **necks** right up
038:033 over (their) legs and their **necks**.
040:071 When the yokes (shall be) round their **necks**,
047:004 ye meet the Unbelievers (in fight), Smite at their **necks**,

NEED

002:083 and orphans and those in **need**;
002:088 (which preserve Allah's word, we **need** no more)"
002:271 and make them reach those (really) in **need**,
002:273 (Charity is) for those in **need**, who,
003:097 Allah stands not in **need** of any of His creatures.
004:036 those in **need**, neighbors who are of kin, neighbors
011:079 "Well dost thou know we have no **need** of thy daughters:
028:024 truly am I in (desperate) **need** of any good that
035:015 O ye men! It is ye that have **need** of Allah:
039:007 truly Allah hath no **need** of you;
040:080 to any **need** (there may be) in your hearts;
093:008 And He found thee in **need**, and made

NEEDFUL
036:028   nor was it **needful** for Us so to do.

NEEDLE
007:040   pass through the eye of the **needle**:

NEEDS
002:219   say: "What is beyond your **needs**."
005:114   for thou art the best Sustainer (of our **needs**)."
017:111   nor (**needs**) He any to protect
027:040   truly my Lord is Free of All **Needs**, Supreme in
029:006   for Allah is free of all **needs** from all creation.
055:029   Of Him seeks (its need) every creature
057:024   free of all **needs**, worthy of all praise.
062:011   And Allah is the Best to provide (for all **needs**)."
064:006   and Allah.is free of all **needs**, worthy of all praise.
073:018   His Promise **needs** must be accomplished.
084:002   (the Command of) its Lord, and it must **needs** (do so);-
084:005   (the Command of) its Lord, and it must **needs** (do so);-
107:007   But refuse (to supply) (even) neighborly **needs**.

NEEDY
002:177   for the **needy**, for the wayfarer,
008:041   to near relatives, Orphans, the **needy**, and the wayfarer,-
009:060   Alms are for the poor and the **needy**, and those
030:038   So give what is due to kindred, the **needy**,
047:038   and it is ye that are **needy**.
059:007   and orphans, the **needy** and the wayfarer; in order
070:025   For the (**needy**) who asks and him who is deprived

NEGLECT
018:028   permitted to **neglect** the remembrance of Us,
025:030   this Qur'an with **neglect**."

NEGLECTED
006:031   and they say: "Ah! woe unto us that we **neglected**;
022:045   And how many wells are lying idle and **neglected**,
023:100   in the things I **neglected**."- "By no means! it is
039:056   in that I **neglected** (my duty) towards Allah,

NEGLECTFUL
107:005   Who are **neglectful** of their Prayers,

NEGLIGENT
004:102   if ye were **negligent** of your arms and your baggage,
019:039   for (behold), they are **negligent** and they do not believe!

NEIGHBORING
013:004   (diverse though) **neighboring**, and gardens

NEIGHBORLY
107:007   But refuse (to supply) (even) **neighborly** needs.

NEIGHBORS
004:036   those in need, **neighbors** who are of kin,
004:036   **neighbors** who are strangers, the Companion
033:060   be able to stay in it as thy **neighbors** for any

NEIGHBOURHOOD
009:120   the Bedouin Arabs of the **neighbourhood**, to stay behind

NEITHER
002:068   should be **neither** too old nor too young,
002:102   But **neither** of these taught anyone
002:107   have **neither** patron nor helper.
002:120   thou find **neither** Protector nor Helper against Allah.
002:264   but believe **neither** in Allah nor in the last day.
002:282   and let **neither** scribe nor witness suffer harm.
003:010   **neither** their possessions nor their (numerous) progeny
003:116   **neither** their possessions nor their (numerous) progeny
004:012   has left **neither** ascendants nor descendants,
004:143   belonging **neither** to these nor those whom Allah
006:071   things that can do us **neither** good nor harm,
006:091   which ye knew not-**neither** ye nor your fathers."

NEITHER (continued)
007:148   that it could **neither** speak to them, nor show
010:101   but **neither** Signs nor Warners profit those
010:106   such can **neither** profit thee nor hurt thee:
011:049   before this, **neither** thou nor thy People knew them.
013:037   then wouldst thou find **neither** protector nor
014:031   there will be **neither** mutual bargaining, nor befriending.
015:005   **Neither** can a people anticipate its Term,
016:035   **neither** we nor our fathers,-nor should We have prescribed
017:056   they have **neither** the power to remove your troubles
017:110   **Neither** speak thy Prayer aloud, nor speak
020:058   not fail to keep-**neither** we nor thou-in a place
020:074   for him is Hell: therein shall he **neither** die or live.
021:066   besides Allah, things that can **neither** be of
022:012   besides Allah, as can **neither** hurt nor profit
024:035   **neither** of the East nor of the West, whose Oil
024:037   By men whom **neither** trade nor sale can divert
025:055   things that can **neither** profit them nor harm them:
026:088   "The Day whereon **neither** wealth nor sons will avail,
034:031   "We shall **neither** believe in this scripture nor in (any)
037:161   For, verily, **neither** ye nor those ye worship
044:029   And **neither** heaven nor earth shed a tear over them:
048:022   find **neither** protector nor helper.
053:002   Your Companion is **neither** astray nor being misled,
056:044   **Neither** cool nor refreshing:
058:014   They are **neither** of you nor of them, and they
071:023   'Abandon not your gods: abandon **neither** Wadd nor
071:023   Wadd nor Suwa, **neither** Yaguth nor Yauq, nor Nasr';-
072:003   He has taken **neither** a wife nor a son.
076:013   they will see there **neither** the sun's (excessive heat)
081:024   **Neither** doth he withhold Grudgingly a knowledge
087:013   In which he will then **neither** die nor live.
088:007   Which will **neither** nourish nor satisfy hunger.

NEPHEW
021:071   and (his **nephew**) Lut (and directed them) to the

NEVER
002:055   "O Moses! we shall **never** believe in thee
002:080   for He **never** breaks His promise?
002:095   But they will **never** seek for death,
002:105   It is **never** the wish of those without
002:120   **Never** will the Jews or the Christians
002:143   And **never** would Allah make your faith
002:256   the most trustworthy hand-hold, that **never** breaks.
003:009   for Allah **never** fails in His promise."
003:085   (submission to Allah) **never** will it be accepted of him;
003:090   **never** will their repentance be accepted;
003:091   **never** would be accepted from any such as much
003:135   And are **never** obstinate in persisting knowingly
003:146   But they **never** lost heart if they met
003:182   for Allah **never** do injustice to those who serve Him."
003:192   and **never** will wrong-doers find any helpers!
003:194   for thou **never** breakest Thy promise."
003:195   "Never will I suffer to be lost the work of any of you,
004:040   Allah is **never** unjust in the least degree:
004:042   but **never** will they hide a single fact from Allah!
004:073   as if there had **never** been ties of affection
004:077   **never** will ye be dealt unjustly in the very least!
004:088   **never** shalt thou find the Way.
004:092   **Never** should a Believer kill a Believer; except
004:129   Ye are **never** able to do justice between wives
004:141   And **never** will Allah grant to the Unbelievers
004:143   **never** wilt thou find for him the Way.
005:022   **never** shall we enter it until they leave it:

NEVER (continued)

005:024 we shall **never** enter it as long as they are in it.
005:036 it would **never** be accepted of them.
005:037 but **never** will they get out therefrom:
005:041 who have **never** so much as come to thee.
005:054 and **never** afraid of the reproaches
005:081 **never** would they have taken them for friends
005:116 **never** could I say what I had no right (to say).
005:117 "**Never** said I to them aught except what Thou
006:004 But **never** did a single one of the Signs
006:021 But verily the wrong-doers **never** shall prosper.
006:029 and **never** shall we be raised up again."
006:061 and they **never** fail in their duty.
006:079 and the earth, and **never** shall I give
006:114 **Never** be then of those who doubt.
006:122 from which he can **never** come out?
006:147 from people in guilt **never** will His wrath be turned back.
007:007 for We were **never** absent (at any time or place).
007:028 say: "Nay Allah **never** commands what is Indecent:
007:043 **never** could we have found guidance, had it not been for
007:049 that Allah with His Mercy would **never** bless?
007:092 became as if they had **never** been in the homes
007:132 we shall **never** believe in thee."
007:170 **never** shall We suffer the reward of the righteous to
007:172 "Of this we were **never** mindful":
007:202 and **never** relax (their efforts).
008:015 **never** turn your backs to them.
008:051 For Allah is **never** unjust to His servants."
008:053 "Because Allah will **never** change the Grace
008:059 they will **never** frustrate (them).
009:083 say: "**Never** shall ye come out with me, nor fight
009:108 **Never** stand thou forth therein.
009:110 is **never** free from suspicion and shakiness
010:012 on his way as if he had **never** cried to Us for the
010:017 But **never** will prosper those who sin.
010:069 against Allah will **never** prosper."
010:105 and **never** in any wise be of the Unbelievers;
011:068 As if they had **never** dwelt and flourished there.
011:095 As if they had **never** dwelt and flourished there!
012:017 But thou wilt **never** believe us even though
012:038 and **never** could we attribute any partners
012:052 and that Allah will **never** guide the snare
012:052 may know that I have **never** been false to him
012:066 (Jacob) said: "**Never** will I send him with you
012:085 They said: "By Allah! (**never**) wilt thou cease
012:087 and **never** give up hope of Allah's soothing Mercy:
012:090 **never** will Allah suffer the reward to be lost, of those
012:108 Glory to Allah! and **never** will I join gods
012:110 But **never** will be warded off Our punishment
013:011 Verily **never** will Allah change the condition
013:031 But the Unbelievers,-**never** will disaster cease to
013:038 and it was **never** the part of a messenger
014:017 but **never** well he be near swallowing it
014:034 **never** will ye be able to number them.
014:047 **Never** think that Allah would fail His messengers
015:004 **Never** did We destroy a population that had not
015:011 But **never** came a messenger to them
016:018 **never** would ye be able to number them:
016:116 who ascribe false things to Allah, will **never** prosper.
017:048 and **never** can they find a way.
018:014 **never** shall we call upon any god other than Him:
018:020 and in that case ye would **never** attain prosperity."
018:041 underground so that thou wilt **never** be able to find it."

NEVER (continued)

018:042 Would I had **never** ascribed partners to my
018:057 even then will they **never** accept guidance.
019:004 doth glisten with grey: but **never** am I unblest,
019:064 and thy Lord **never** doth forget,-
020:052 my Lord **never** errs, nor forgets,-
020:072 They said: "**Never** shall we prefer thee to what
020:120 and to a kingdom that **never** decays?"
021:002 **Never** comes (aught) to them of a renewed Message
022:031 and **never** assigning partners to Him:
022:052 **Never** did We send a messenger or a prophet
023:017 and We are **never** unmindful of (Our) Creation.
023:024 sent down angels: **never** did we hear such a thing
023:037 But we shall **never** be raised up again!
023:062 They will **never** be wronged.
024:017 that ye may **never** repeat such (conduct), if ye
024:057 **Never** think thou that the Unbelievers can escape
025:009 and **never** a way will they be able to find!
025:028 "Ah! woe in me! **never** taken such a one for a friend!
026:208 **Never** did We destroy a town but had its warners-
026:209 and We **never** are unjust.
027:037 whit such hosts as they will **never** be able to meet:
028:017 **never** shall I be a help to those who sin!"
028:036 **never** did we hear the like among our fathers of old!"
028:082 will assuredly **never** prosper."
029:012 **Never** in the least will they bear their faults:
030:006 **Never** does Allah fail from His promise: but most
033:023 but they have **never** changed (their determination) in the
034:003 "**Never** to us will come the Hour":
034:017 and **never** do We give (such) requital except to such
034:034 **Never** did We send a Warner to a population,
035:024 and there **never** was a people, without a warner having
035:029 a Commerce that will **never** fail:
038:007 "We **never** heard (the like) of this in the
038:054 such will be Our Bounty (to you); it will **never** fail;-
039:020 **never** doth Allah fail in (His) promise.
039:047 which they could **never** have counted upon!
040:031 but Allah **never** wishes injustice to His Servants.
040:056 (the quest of) greatness, which they shall **never** attain to:
041:008 deeds of righteousness is a reward that will **never** fail.
041:038 And they **never** flag (nor feel themselves above it)
043:007 And **never** came there a prophet to them
043:013 for we could **never** be able to do it.
046:033 and **never** wearied with their creation,
047:004 He will **never** let their deeds be lost,
047:015 in it are rivers of milk of which the taste **never** changes;
047:035 and will **never** put you in loss
048:012 and the Believers would **never** return to their
049:015 and His Messenger, and have **never** since doubted,
053:017 (His) sight **never** swerved, nor did it go wrong!
059:011 and we will **never** hearken to any one
059:012 If they are expelled, **never** will they go out
059:012 are attacked (in fight), they will **never** help them;
062:007 But **never** will they express their desire
065:003 provides for him from (sources) he **never** could expect.
067:009 'Allah **never** sent down any (Message): ye are in
069:026 "And that I had **never** realized how my account (stood)!
084:025 for them is a Reward that will **never** fail.

NEVERTHELESS

033:006 **nevertheless** do ye what is just to your closest friends:

NEW

002:151 and in **new** Knowledge.
002:189 They ask thee concerning the **New** Moons.

NEW (continued)

005:013   barring a few-ever bent on (**new**) deceits:
005:015   a (**new**) Light and a perspicuous Book,
006:089   to a **new** People who reject them not.
007:038   Every time a **new** People enters, it curses
014:019   (in your place) a **new** Creation?
017:049   be raised up (to be) a **new** creation?"
017:098   really be raised up (to be) a **new** Creation?"
021:104   shall We produce a **new** one:
023:068   or has anything (**new**) come to them
028:045   But We raised up (**new**) generations, and long
034:007   that ye shall (then be raised) in a **New** Creation?
035:016   He could blot you out and bring in a **New** Creation:
050:011   and We give (**new**) life therewith to land that is dead:
050:015   be in confused doubt about a **new** Creation?
055:029   every day in (**new**) Splendor doth He (shine)!
065:001   about thereafter some **new** situation.

NEWLY-REVEALED

026:005   a **newly-revealed** message from the Most Gracious,

NEWS

004:165   Messengers who gave good **news** as well
006:005   the **news** of what they used to mock at.
006:048   only to give good **news** and to warn: so those
010:002   and give the good **news** to the Believers that they
012:019   Good **news**! Here is a (fine) young man!
012:096   Then when the bearer of the good **news** came, he cast
015:054   Of what, then, is your good **news**?"
015:067   came in (mad) joy (at **news** of the young men).
016:058   When **news** is brought to one of them, of (the birth of)
016:059   because of the bad **news** he has had!
019:007   We give thee good **news** of a son: his name
022:034   the Good **News** to those who humble themselves,
022:037   the Good **News** to all who do good.
029:031   Our messengers came to Abraham with the good **news**,
033:020   and seeking **news** about you (from a safe distance);
037:101   So We gave him the good **news** of a forbearing son.
037:112   And We gave him the good **news** of Isaac-
039:017   and turn to Allah (in repentance), Good **News**:
039:017   so announce the Good **News** to My Servants,-
041:004   Giving Good **News** and Admonition: yet most
043:017   When **news** is brought to one of them of
049:006   if a sinner comes to you with any **news**, ascertain the
057:012   (their greeting will be): "Good **News** for you this Day!
078:002   Concerning the Great **News**,

NEXT

002:180   that he make a bequest to parents and **next** of kin,
004:034   admonish them (first), (**next**), refuse to share their beds,
005:008   Be just: that is **next** to Piety: and fear

NICETY

007:008   be true (to a **nicety**):

NICHE

024:035   is as if there were a **Niche** and within it a Lamp:

NICKNAMES

049:011   nor call each other by (offensive) **nicknames**:

NIGGARD'S

017:029   Make not thy hand tied (like a **niggard's**) to thy neck,

NIGGARDLINESS

004:037   enjoin **niggardliness** on others,

NIGGARDLY

004:037   (Nor) those who are **niggardly**,
017:100   for man is (ever) **niggardly**!"
025:067   are not extravagant and not **niggardly**, but hold

NIGGARDLY (continued)

047:038   but among you are some that are **niggardly**.
047:038   But any who are **niggardly** are so at the expense of their
070:021   And **niggardly** when good reaches him;-

NIGH

006:151   come not **nigh** to indecent deeds, whether
006:152   And come not **nigh** to the orphan's property,
007:185   it may well be that their term **nigh** drawing to an end?
011:081   morning is their time appointed: is not the morning **nigh**?"
017:032   Nor come **nigh** to adultery: for it is an indecent (deed)
017:034   Come not **nigh** to the orphan's property
021:097   draw **nigh** (of fulfillment): then behold! the eyes
033:063   make thee understand?-perchance the Hour is **nigh**!
050:031   And the Garden will be brought **nigh** to the righteous,-
053:057   The (Hour) ever approaching draws **nigh**:
054:001   The Hour (of Judgment) is **nigh**, and the
073:020   standest forth (to prayer) **nigh** two-thirds of the night,

NIGHER

033:051   This were **nigher** to the cooling of their eyes,

NIGHT

002:164   in the alternation of the **Night** and the Day;
002:187   Permitted to you on the **night** of the fasts,
002:187   then complete your fast till the **night** appears;
002:187   approach not **night** thereto.
002:274   spend of their goods by **night** and by day,
003:027   "Thou causest the **Night** to gain on the Day.
003:027   And Thou causest the Day to gain on the **Night**;
003:113   they rehearse the Signs of Allah all **night** long,
003:190   and the alternation of **Night** and Day,
004:081   a section of them meditate all **night** on things
004:108   while He is with them when they plot by **night**.
006:013   (or lurketh) in the **Night** and the Day.
006:060   It is He Who doth take your souls by **night**,
006:076   When the **night** covered him over, he saw
006:096   He makes the **night** for rest and tranquillity,
007:004   Our punishment took them on a sudden by **night** or
007:054   He draweth the **night** as a veil O'er the day,
007:097   Our wrath by **night** while they were asleep?
010:006   Verily in the alternation of the **Night** and the Day,
010:024   there reaches it Our command by **night** or by day,
010:027   with pieces from the depth of the darkness of **Night**:
010:050   should come to you by **night** or by day,-
010:067   the **Night** that ye may rest therein, and the Day
011:081   with thy family while yet a part of the **night** remains,
011:114   two ends of the day and at the approaches of the **night**:
012:016   in the early part of the **night**, weeping.
013:003   He draweth the **Night** as a veil o'er the Day.
013:010   whether he lie hid by **night** or walk freely by day.
014:033   and the **Night** and the Day hath He (also)
015:065   "Then travel by **night** with thy household,
015:065   when a portion of the **night** (yet remains),
016:012   He has made subject to you the **Night** and the Day;
017:001   His Servant for a Journey by **night** from the
017:012   We have made the **Night** and the Day as two
017:012   the Sign of the **Night** have We made dark
017:078   at the sun's decline till the darkness the **night**,
017:079   And as for the **night** keep awake a part of it
020:077   "Travel by **night** with my servants, and strike
020:130   Yea, celebrate them for part of the hours of the **night**,
021:020   They celebrate His praises **night** and day,
021:033   It is He Who created the **Night** and the
021:042   Say, "Who can keep you safe by **night** and by day
021:078   of certain people had strayed by **night**:

NIGHT (continued)

022:061 and He merges Day in **Night**, and verily
022:061 That is because Allah merges **Night** into Day,
023:067 about the (Qur'an), like one telling fables by **night**,"
023:080 and to Him (is due) the alternation of **Night** and Day:
024:044 It is Allah Who alternates the **Night** and the Day:
025:047 And He it is Who makes the **Night** as a Robe
025:062 And it is He Who made the **Night** and the Day
025:064 Those who spend the **night** in adoration
026:052 "Travel by **night** with My servants; for surely
027:049 that we shall make a secret **night** attack on him
027:086 made the **Night** for them to rest in and the
028:071 the **Night** perpetual over you to the Day
028:072 who can give you a **Night** in which ye can rest?
028:073 has made for you **Night** and Day,-that ye
030:023 that ye take by **night** and by day, and the
031:029 Seest thou not that Allah merges **Night** into Day
031:029 into Day and He merges Day into **Night**;
034:018 secure, by **night** and by day."
034:033 "nay! it was a plot (of yours) by day and by **night**:
035:013 He merges **Night** into Day, and He
035:013 and He merges Day into **Night**, and He
036:037 And a Sign for them is the **Night**: We withdraw
036:040 nor can the **Night** outstrip the Day:
037:138 And by **night**: will ye not understand?
038:032 Until (the sun) was hidden in the veil (of **Night**):
039:005 He makes the **Night** overlap the Day, and the
039:005 and the Day overlap the **Night**:
039:009 the hours of the **night** prostrating himself
040:061 It is Allah Who has made the **Night** for you,
041:037 Among His Signs are the **Night** and the Day,
041:038 who celebrate His praises by **night** and by day.
044:003 We sent it down during a blessed **night**:
044:004 In that (**night**) is made distinct every affair
044:023 "March forth with My servants by **night**: for ye
045:005 And in the alternation of **Night** and Day,
050:040 And during part of the **night**, (also), celebrate
051:017 They were in the habit of sleeping but little by **night**,
052:049 And for part of the **night** also praise thou Him,-
057:006 He merges **Night** into Day, and He
057:006 and He merges Day into **Night**; and He
071:005 to my People **night** and day:
073:002 Stand (to pray) by **night**, but not all **night**,-
073:006 Truly the rising by **night** is a time
073:020 nigh two-thirds of the **night**, or half
073:020 or half the **night**, or a third of the **night**,
073:020 But Allah doth appoint **Night** and Day
074:033 And by the **Night** as it retreateth,
076:026 and glorify Him a long **night** through.
076:026 And part of the **night**, prostrate thyself to Him;
078:010 And made the **night** as a covering,
079:029 Its **night** doth He endow with darkness,
081:017 And the **Night** as it dissipates;
084:017 The **Night** and its Homing;
089:004 And by the **Night** when it passeth away;-
091:004 By the **Night** as it conceals it;
092:001 By the **Night** as it conceals (the light);
093:002 And by the **Night** when it is still,-
097:001 this (Message) in the **night** of Power:
097:002 what the **Night** of Power is?
097:003 The **Night** of Power is better

NIGHT-VISITANT

086:001 By the Sky and the **Night-Visitant** (therein);

NIGHT-VISITANT (continued)

086:002 to thee what the **Night-Visitant** is?-

NIGHTLY

004:081 But Allah records their **nightly** (plots):

NIGHTS

002:051 appointed forty **nights** for Moses,
007:142 thus was completed the term with his Lord, forty **nights**.
007:142 We appointed for Moses thirty **nights**, and completed
019:010 "Shall be that thou shalt speak to no man for three **nights**,
069:007 seven **nights** and eight days in succession:
089:002 By the ten **Nights**;

NINE

017:101 To Moses We did give **nine** Clear Signs:
018:025 three hundred years, and **nine** (more).
027:012 (these are) among the **nine** Signs (thou wilt take)
027:048 There were in the City **nine** men, who made
038:023 he has **nine** and ninety ewes, and I

NINETEEN

074:030 Over it are **Nineteen**.

NINETY

038:023 he has nine and **ninety** ewes, and I

NIPPING

003:117 likened to a Wind which brings a **nipping** frost:

NO

002:038 on them shall be **no** fear,
002:057 (but they rebelled); to Us they did **no** harm,
002:060 and do **no** evil nor mischief
002:062 on them shall be **no** fear,
002:084 shed **no** blood amongst you,
002:088 (which preserve Allah's word, we need **no** more)"
002:102 would have **no** share in the happiness
002:112 on such shall be **no** fear,
002:119 but of thee **no** question shall be asked
002:136 we make **no** difference between one of them:
002:143 make your faith of **no** effect.
002:150 that there be **no** ground of dispute
002:158 it is **no** sin in them.
002:163 there is **no** god but He,
002:169 of Allah that of which ye have **no** knowledge.
002:182 there is **no** wrong in Him;
002:189 It is **no** virtue if ye enter your houses
002:193 But if they cease, let there be **no** hostility
002:193 there is **no** more Persecution
002:197 let there be **no** obscenity, nor wickedness,
002:198 It is **no** crime in you if ye seek of the bounty
002:200 But they will have **no** portion in the Hereafter.
002:203 there is **no** blame on him,
002:217 works will bear **no** fruit in this life and in the Hereafter;
002:229 there is **no** blame on either of them
002:230 In that case there is **no** blame on either of them if they
002:233 **No** mother shall be treated unfairly
002:233 **No** soul shall have a burden laid on it
002:233 There is **no** blame on them,
002:233 for your offspring there is **no** blame on you,
002:234 there is **no** blame on you if they dispose
002:235 There is **no** blame on you if ye make an indirect
002:236 There is **no** blame on you if ye divorce women
002:240 there is **no** blame on you for what they do
002:254 when **no** bargaining (will avail),
002:255 Allah! There is **no** god but He, the living,
002:255 **No** slumber can seize Him nor sleep.
002:255 and He feeleth **no** fatigue in guarding

NO (continued)

002:256 Let there be **no** compulsion in religion.
002:259 they show **no** signs of age;
002:262 on them shall be **no** fear, nor shall they grieve.
002:270 But the wrong-doers have **no** helpers.
002:274 on them shall be **no** fear, nor shall they grieve.
002:277 on them shall be **no** fear,
002:282 there is **no** blame on you if ye reduce it
002:285 "We make **no** distinction (they say) between
002:286 On **no** soul doth Allah place a burden
003:002 Allah! there is **no** god but He,
003:006 There is **no** god but He,
003:007 but **no** one knows its true meanings except Allah.
003:009 a Day about which there in **no** doubt;
003:011 (their plight will be) **no** better than that of the people
003:018 There is **no** god but He:
003:018 There is **no** god but He the Exalted in Power,
003:022 works will bear **no** fruit in this world and in the Hereafter,
003:025 against a Day about which there is **no** doubt,
003:028 if any do that, shall have **no** relation left
003:041 "Shall be that thou shalt speak **no** man for three days
003:047 how shall I have a son when **no** man hath touched Me?"
003:062 there is **no** god except Allah;
003:064 that we associate **no** partners with Him;
003:065 Have ye **no** understanding?
003:066 in matters of which ye have **no** knowledge?
003:073 "And believe **no** one unless he follows your religion."
003:075 "there is **no** way over us as to the Unlettered people,"
003:077 they shall have **no** portion in the Hereafter:
003:078 but it is **no** part of the Book;
003:084 we make **no** distinction between one and another
003:091 and they will find on helpers.
003:092 By **no** means shall ye attain righteousness unless
003:108 and Allah means **no** injustice to any of His creatures.
003:111 They will do you **no** harm, barring a trifling
003:111 and **no** help shall they get.
003:126 (in any case) there is **no** victory except from Allah,
003:144 Muhammad is **no** more than a Messenger:
003:151 for which He had sent **no** authority:
003:161 **No** prophet could (ever) dishonestly
003:170 the fact that on them is **no** fear,
003:174 Grace and Bounty from Allah: **no** harm ever touched them:
003:176 Plan is that He will give them **no** portion in the Hereafter,
004:006 let him claim **no** remuneration,
004:011 if **no** children, and the parents are
004:012 your share is a half, if they leave **no** child;
004:012 their share is a fourth, if ye leave **no** child;
004:012 so that **no** loss is caused (to anyone).
004:018 Of **no** effect is the repentance of those
004:023 ye have gone in;-**no** prohibition if ye have not gone in;
004:024 there is **no** blame on you, and Allah
004:032 And in **no** wise covet those things in which
004:038 to be seen of men, and have **no** faith in Allah
004:043 and ye find **no** water, then take for yourselves clean sand
004:052 thou wilt find, have **no** one to help.
004:062 "We meant **no** more than good-will and conciliation!"
004:065 And find in their souls **no** resistance against thy decisions,
004:065 But **no**, by thy Lord, they can have **no** (real) Faith.
004:087 about which there is **no** doubt.
004:087 Allah! There is **no** god but He: of a surety
004:089 take **no** friends or helpers from their ranks:
004:090 Allah hath opened **no** way for you (to war against them).
004:098 and children who have **no** means in their power,

NO (continued)

004:101 there is **no** blame on you if ye shorten
004:102 But there is **no** blame on you if ye put away
004:113 and to thee they can do **no** harm in the least.
004:114 In most of their secret talks there is **no** good:
004:121 and from it they will find **no** way of escape.
004:128 there is **no** blame on them if they arrange
004:145 depths of the fire: **no** helper wilt thou find for them;
004:152 make **no** distinction between any of the messengers,
004:157 are full of doubts, with **no** (certain) knowledge.
004:165 should have **no** plea against Allah: for Allah
004:171 was (**no** more than) an Messenger of Allah,
004:171 commit **no** excesses in your religion: nor say
004:176 if (such a deceased was) a woman, who left **no** child,
004:176 those who leave **no** descendants or ascendants
004:176 That dies, leaving a sister but **no** child,
005:003 with **no** inclination to transgression,
005:006 and you find **no** water, then take for yourselves clean
005:019 unto us **no** bringer of glad tidings and **no** warner.
005:041 thou hast **no** authority in the least for him
005:041 but whose hearts have **no** faith;
005:055 Your (real) friends are (**no** less than) Allah,
005:059 disapprove of us for **no** other reason than that we believe
005:068 ye have **no** ground to stand upon unless ye stand
005:069 on them shall be **no** fear, nor shall they grieve.
005:071 They thought there would be **no** trial (or punishment);
005:072 There will for the wrong-doers be **no** one to help.
005:073 for there is **no** god except One God.
005:075 was **no** more than an Messenger; many were
005:076 something which hath **no** power either to harm or benefit
005:087 made lawful for you, but commit **no** excess:
005:093 there is **no** blame for what they ate
005:105 **No** hurt can come to you from those who stray.
005:109 They will say: "We have **no** knowledge:
005:116 never could I say what I had **no** right (to say).
006:008 and **no** respite would be granted them.
006:012 there is **no** doubt whatever, it is they
006:023 There will then be (left) **no** excuse for them but to say:
006:048 upon them shall be **no** fear, nor shall they grieve.
006:051 except for Him they will have **no** protector nor intercessor:
006:069 On their account **no** responsibility falls on
006:070 will find for itself **no** protector or intercessor except Allah:
006:090 Say: "**No** reward for this do I ask of you:
006:091 **No** just estimate of Allah do they
006:100 and they falsely, having **no** knowledge, attribute
006:101 when He hath **no** consort?
006:102 There is **no** god but He, the Creator
006:103 **No** vision can grasp Him, but His grasp
006:106 there is **no** god but He:
006:113 who have **no** faith in the Hereafter:
006:140 and heeded **no** guidance.
006:152 **no** burden do We place on any soul, but that which it
006:158 **no** good will it do to a soul to believe then,
006:159 thou hast **no** part in them in the least:
006:160 **No** wrong shall be done unto them.
006:163 **No** partner hath He: this am I commanded,
006:164 **no** bearer of burdens can bear the burden of another.
007:002 **no** more by any difficulty on that account,-that
007:005 **no** cry did they utter but this: "Indeed
007:033 of which ye have **no** knowledge.
007:033 for which He hath given **no** authority; and saying
007:035 on them shall be **no** fear, nor shall they grieve.
007:039 "See then! **no** advantage have ye over us; so taste

NO (continued)

007:040 **no** opening will there be of the gates
007:042 **no** burden do We place on any soul, but that
007:049 Enter ye the Garden: **no** fear shall be on you, nor
007:053 Have we **no** intercessors now to
007:059 worship Allah! ye have **no** other god but Him. I
007:061 He said: "O my people! there is **no** error in me: on
007:065 ye have **no** other god but Him. Will ye
007:067 there is **no** folly in me" but (I am)
007:073 ye have **no** other god but Him. Now hath
007:073 and let her come to **no** harm, or ye shall
007:080 **no** people in creation (ever) committed before you?
007:082 And his people gave **no** answer but this: they said,
007:085 ye have **no** other god but Him. Now hath come
007:085 and do **no** mischief on the earth after it
007:099 against Allah's devising but **no** one can fell
007:118 And all that they did was made of **no** effect.
007:137 considered weak (and of **no** account), inheritors
007:143 Allah said: "By **no** means canst thou
007:155 This is **no** more than Thy trial: by it Thou
007:158 there is **no** god but He: it is He
007:160 (but they rebelled): to Us they did **no** harm, but
007:163 but on the day they had **no** Sabbath, they came
007:186 there can be **no** guide; He will
007:188 Say: "I have **no** power over any good or harm
007:188 and **no** evil should have touched me: I am
007:192 **No** aid can they give them, nor can
007:195 and give me **no** respite!
008:010 (in any case) there is **no** help except from Allah:
008:034 its guardians? **No** men can be its guardians
008:039 there is **no** more persecution, and religion
008:046 and fall into **no** disputes, lest ye
008:048 and said: "**No** one among men can overcome
008:072 ye owe **no** duty of protection to them
009:017 The works of such bear **no** fruit: in Fire
009:031 one God: there is **no** god but He. Praise and
009:040 (it is **no** matter): for Allah did indeed help him,
009:040 "Have **no** fear, for Allah is with us": then Allah
009:044 **no** exemption from fighting with their goods
009:066 Make ye **no** excuses: ye have rejected Faith
009:091 **no** ground (of complaint) can there be against
009:091 or ill, or who find **no** resources to spend (on the
009:091 There is **no** blame on those who are infirm, or ill,
009:092 **no** resources wherewith to provide the expenses.
009:092 "I can find **no** mounts for you," they turned
009:094 Say thou: "Present **no** excuses: we shall
009:116 Except for Him ye have **no** protector nor helper.
009:118 **no** fleeing from Allah (and **no** refuge)
009:118 (and **no** refuge) but to Himself. Then He
009:126 and they take **no** heed.
009:129 there is **no** god but He: On him is my trust,-He the
010:003 **No** intercessor (can plead with Him) except after
010:026 **No** darkness nor abasement shall cover
010:027 **no** defender will they have from (the wrath of)
010:036 can be of **no** avail against Truth. Verily Allah
010:037 wherein there is **no** doubt-from the
010:049 Say: "I have **no** power over any harm or profit
010:054 and **no** wrong will be done unto them.
010:062 there is **no** fear, nor shall they grieve;
010:064 the Hereafter: **no** change can there be in the
010:068 and on earth! **No** warrant have ye for this!
010:071 on me, and give me **no** respite.
010:072 **no** reward have I asked of you: my reward

NO (continued)

010:081 of **no** effect: for Allah prospereth not the work
010:090 **no** god except Him Who the Children
010:094 so be in **no** wise of those in doubt.
010:100 **No** soul can believe, except by
011:006 There is **no** moving creature on earth but its
011:014 of Allah, and that there is **no** god but He! Will ye
011:016 and of **no** effect are the deeds that they do!
011:029 I ask you for **no** wealth in return: my reward
011:034 "Of **no** profit will be my counsel to you, much as
011:036 So grieve **no** longer over their (evil) deeds.
011:037 and address Me **no** (further) on behalf
011:046 thou hast **no** knowledge! I give thee counsel,
011:047 of which I have **no** knowledge and unless Thou
011:050 ye have **no** other god but Him. You are
011:051 **no** reward for this (Message). My reward
011:053 They said: "O Hud! **no** Clear (Sign) hast thou
011:055 all of you, and give me **no** respite.
011:061 ye have **no** other god but Him. It is He Who
011:064 (free) earth, and inflict **no** harm on her, or a
011:079 **no** need of thy daughters: indeed thou
011:081 By **no** means shall they reach thee! Now travel
011:084 ye have **no** other god but Him. And give
011:091 that thou hast **no** strength! Were it not
011:091 For thou hast among us **no** great position!"
011:101 whom they invoked, profited them **no** whit when there
011:105 The day it arrives, **no** soul shall speak
011:113 and ye have **no** protectors other than Allah,
012:023 Truly to **no** good come those who do wrong!"
012:031 "Allah preserve us! **no** mortal is this! This is
012:040 hath sent down **no** authority: the Command
012:051 **no** evil know we against him!" Said the 'Aziz's
012:060 ye shall have **no** measure (of corn) from me,
012:063 **No** more measure of grain shall we get (unless we
012:073 in the land, and we are **no** thieves!"
012:080 Now when they saw **no** hope of his (yielding),
012:087 soothing Mercy: truly **no** one despairs of Allah's
012:087 except those who have **no** faith."
012:092 He said: "This day let **no** reproach be (cast)
012:103 Yet **no** faith will the greater part of mankind have,
012:104 for this: it is **no** lest than a Message
012:104 And **no** reward dost thou ask of them for this:
013:011 **no** turning it back, nor will they find, besides
013:014 besides Him hear them **no** more than if they
013:016 such as have **no** power either for good or for
013:030 Say: "He is my Lord! There is **no** god but He!
013:033 Allah leaves to stray, **no** one can guide.
013:043 The Unbelievers say: "**No** messenger art thou."
014:010 They said: "Ah! ye are **no** more then human,
014:018 **no** power have they over aught that they
014:021 to us it makes **no** difference (now) whether
014:021 for ourselves there is **no** way of escape."
014:022 I had **no** authority over you except to call you,
014:026 it has **no** stability.
014:044 to swear aforetime that ye suffer **no** decline?
015:008 behold! **no** respite would they have!
015:042 "For over My servants **no** authority shalt thou have,
015:048 There **no** sense of fatigue shall touch them,
015:065 let **no** one amongst you look back, but pass on
015:084 And of **no** avail to them was all that they did
016:002 (saying): "Warn (Man) that there is **no** god but I:
016:008 (other) things of which ye have **no** knowledge.
016:028 "We did **no** evil (knowingly)." (The angels will

NO (continued)

016:053 And ye have **no** good thing but is from Allah:
016:073 such as have **no** power of providing them,
016:075 (By **no** means); praise be to Allah. But most
016:075 the dominion of another; he has **no** power of any
016:076 with **no** power of any sort; a wearisome burden
016:076 directs him, he brings **no** good: is such
016:084 then will **no** excuse be accepted from Unbelievers,
016:085 **no** way be mitigated, nor will
016:099 **No** authority has he over those who believe
016:108 and they take **no** heed.
016:118 We did them **no** wrong, but they
017:015 own loss: **no** bearer of burdens can bear
017:036 thou hast **no** knowledge; for surely the hearing,
017:065 **no** authority shalt thou have over them."
017:068 so that ye shall find **no** protector?
017:069 so that ye find **no** helper therein against Us?
017:077 thou wilt find **no** change in Our ways.
017:093 the skies. **No**, we shall not even believe
017:097 wilt thou find **no** protector besides Him. On the
017:099 **no** doubt. But the unjust refuse (to receive it)
017:111 **no** son, and has **no** partner in (His) dominion:
018:001 and hath allowed therein **no** Crookedness:
018:005 **No** knowledge have they of such a thing, nor had
018:017 for him wilt thou find **no** protector to lead
018:021 and that there can be **no** doubt about the
018:026 They have **no** protector other than Him; nor does
018:039 (be done)! There is **no** power but from Allah!'
018:053 fall therein; **no** means will they find to turn
018:058 beyond which they will find **no** refuge.
018:070 follow me, ask me **no** questions about anything
018:072 thou canst have **no** patience with me?"
018:075 thou canst have **no** patience with me?"
018:090 **no** covering protection against the sun.
018:108 **no** change will they wish for from them.
018:110 admit **no** one as partner."
019:010 to **no** man for three nights, although thou
019:020 seeing that **no** man has touched me, and I am
019:026 into **no** talk with any human being.'"
019:084 So make **no** haste against them, for We
020:007 (it is **no** matter): for verily He knoweth what
020:008 Allah! there is **no** god but He! To Him
020:014 "Verily, I am Allah: there is **no** god but I:
020:081 but commit **no** excess therein, lest My Wrath
020:089 and that it had **no** power either to harm
020:098 there is **no** god but He: all things
020:108 the Caller (straight): **no** crookedness in him:
020:109 On that Day shall **no** intercession avail except for
020:112 and has faith, will have **no** fear of harm nor of
020:115 and We found on his part **no** firm resolve.
021:008 ate **no** food, nor were they immortals.
021:025 that there is **no** god but I; therefore worship
021:028 and they offer **no** intercession except for
021:039 and (when) **no** help can reach them!
021:040 **no** power will they have then to avert it,
021:043 from Us? They have **no** power to aid themselves,
021:047 And if there be (**no** more than) the weight
021:067 that ye worship besides Allah! Have ye **no** sense?"
021:087 **no** power over him! But he
021:087 of darkness, "There is **no** god but Thou: Glory to
021:092 therefore serve Me (and **no** other).
021:103 them **no** grief: but the angels will meet them
022:007 there can be **no** doubt about it, or about

NO (continued)

022:040 of right,-(for **no** cause) except that they
022:060 to **no** greater extent than the injury he received,
022:071 and of which they have (really) **no** knowledge:
022:071 for those that do wrong there is **no** helper.
022:071 things for which **no** authority has been sent down to them,
022:073 they would have **no** power to release it from the fly:
022:078 and has imposed **no** difficulties on you
023:023 Ye have **no** other god but Him.
023:024 his people said: "He is **no** more than a man
023:032 (saying), "Worship Allah! ye have **no** other god
023:033 of this life, said: "He is **no** more than a man
023:043 **No** people can hasten their term, nor can
023:052 and Cherisher: therefore fear Me (and **no** other).
023:062 On **no** soul do We place a burden greater than
023:091 **No** son did Allah beget, nor is
023:100 in the things I neglected."-"By **no** means! it is
023:101 there will be **no** more relationships between
023:116 there is **no** god but He, the Lord
023:117 he has **no** authority thereof; and his
024:006 and have (in support) **no** evidence but their own,-
024:015 of which ye had **no** knowledge; and ye
024:028 If ye find **no** one in the house, enter not
024:029 It is **no** fault on your part to enter houses
024:031 who have **no** carnal knowledge of women; and that
024:040 not light, there in **no** light!
024:051 is **no** other than this: they said, "We hear
024:060 there is **no** blame on them if they lay aside
024:061 It is **no** fault in the blind nor in
024:061 friend of yours: there is **no** blame on you,
025:002 **no** son has He begotten, nor has He
025:003 that have **no** control of hurt or good
025:022 **no** joy will there be to the sinners that Day:
025:033 And **no** question do they bring to thee but We
025:041 they treat thee **no** otherwise than in mockery:
025:057 Say: "**No** reward do I ask of you for it but this:
025:072 Those who witness **no** falsehood, and, if
026:015 Allah said: "By **no** means! proceed them, both of
026:050 They said: "**No** matter! for us, we shall
026:062 (Moses said: "By **no** means! my Lord
026:109 "**No** reward do I ask of you for it: my reward
026:127 "**No** reward do I ask of you for it: my reward
026:137 "This is **no** other than a customary device
026:145 **No** reward do I ask of you for it: my reward
026:154 "Thou art **no** more than a mortal like us:
026:164 "**No** reward do I ask of you for it: my reward
026:180 "**No** reward do I ask of you for it: my reward
026:181 Give just measure, and cause **no** loss (to others
026:186 "Thou art **no** more than a mortal like us,
027:010 those called as messengers have **no** fear,-
027:024 so they receive **no** guidance,-
027:026 "Allah!-there is **no** god but He!-Lord of
027:032 **no** affair have I decided except in your presence."
027:043 for she was (sprung) of a people that had **no** faith.
027:056 But his people gave **no** other answer but this:
027:082 because mankind had **no** faith in Our Signs.
028:028 let there be **no** injustice to me.
028:038 Pharaoh said: "O Chiefs! **no** god do I know
028:041 **no** help shall they find.
028:046 **no** warner had come before thee: in order
028:068 as He pleases: **no** choice have they (in the
028:070 And He is Allah: there is **no** god but He. To Him
028:087 Let **no** one turn you away from Allah's revelations

NO (continued)

028:088 There is **no** god but He.
029:008 **no** knowledge, obey them not. Ye have
029:017 have **no** power to give you sustenance: then seek
029:028 commit lewdness, such as **no** people in Creation
029:029 gave **no** answer but this: they said: "Bring us
030:013 **No** intercessor will they have among their
030:029 To them there will be **no** helpers.
030:030 made mankind: **no** change (there is) in the work
030:039 **no** increase with Allah: but that
030:043 **no** chance of averting: on that Day
030:057 So on that Day **no** excuse of theirs will avail
030:060 who have (themselves) **no** certainty of faith.
031:015 of which thou hast **no** knowledge, obey them not;
031:028 is in **no** wise but as an individual soul: for Allah
031:033 when **no** father can avail aught for his son, nor a
032:002 in which there is **no** doubt,-from the
032:003 to whom **no** warner has come before thee: in order
032:017 Now **no** person knows what delights of the eye
032:018 Is then the man who believes **no** better than the
032:029 **no** profit will it be to Unbelievers if they
033:005 or your friends. But there is **no** blame on you
033:016 (ye do escape), **no** more than a brief (respite)
033:019 Such men have **no** faith, and so
033:025 **no** advantage did they gain, and enough
033:037 be **no** difficulty to the Believers in (the
033:038 There can be **no** difficulty to the Prophet
033:049 **no** period of 'Iddat have ye to count in respect
033:050 be **no** difficulty for thee. And Allah is
033:051 thou pleasest: and there is **no** blame on thee
033:055 There is **no** blame (on those ladies if they appear)
033:062 who lived aforetime: **no** change wilt thou find
033:065 **no** protector will they find, nor helper.
034:021 But he had **no** authority over them,-except that
034:022 **no** (sort of) share have they therein, nor is
034:022 they have **no** power,-not the weight of an atom,-
034:023 "**No** intercession can avail with Him, except for
034:027 by **no** means (can ye). Nay, He is
034:042 So on that Day **no** power shall they have
034:046 he is **no** less than a Warner to you, in face
034:051 but then there will be **no** escape (for them),
035:003 There is **no** god but He: how then
035:011 And **no** female conceives, or lays down
035:023 Thou art **no** other than a warner.
035:035 **no** toil nor sense of weariness shall touch
035:036 **no** term shall be determined for them, so they
035:037 for the Wrong-doers there is **no** helper."
035:043 **no** turning off wilt thou find in Allah's way
035:043 But **no** change wilt thou find in Allah's way
036:015 sends **no** sort of revelation: ye do
036:021 "Obey those who ask **no** reward of you
036:023 of **no** use whatever will be their intercession
036:029 It was **no** more than a single mighty Blast,
036:036 of which they have **no** knowledge.
036:043 **no** helper (to hear their cry), nor could
036:050 **No** (chance) will they then have, by will,
036:053 It will be **no** more than a single Blast,
036:069 this is **no** less than a Message and a Qur'an
037:013 And, when they are admonished, pay **no** heed,-
037:029 They will reply: "Nay, ye yourselves had **no** Faith!
037:035 there is **no** god except Allah, would puff
038:003 **no** longer time for being save!
038:015 will brook **no** delay.

NO (continued)

038:039 **no** account will be asked."
038:059 with you! **No** welcome for them! Truly, they
038:060 **No** welcome for you! It is ye
038:065 **no** god is there but Allah, the One
038:069 "**No** knowledge have I of the Exalted Chiefs,
038:086 Say: "**No** reward do I ask of you
038:087 "This is **no** less than a Reminder
039:006 There is **no** god but He: then how
039:007 **No** bearer of burdens can bear the burden
039:007 truly Allah hath **no** need of you; but He
039:022 (**no** better than one hard-hearted)?
039:029 But most of them have **no** knowledge.
039:036 there can be **no** guide.
039:043 **no** power whatever and **no** intelligence?"
039:050 was of **no** profit to them.
039:061 **no** evil shall touch them, nor shall they grieve.
039:067 **No** just estimate have they made of Allah,
040:003 There is **no** god but He: to Him is the Final Goal.
040:017 **no** injustice will there be that Day, for Allah
040:018 to choke (them); **no** intimate friend nor intercessors
040:033 and flee: **no** defender shall ye have from Allah:
040:034 ye said: '**No** messenger will Allah send after him.'
040:042 partners of whom I have **no** knowledge; and I
040:043 one who has **no** claim to be called to, whether in
040:052 The Day when **no** profit will it be to Wrong-doers
040:059 therein is **no** doubt: yet most men believe not.
040:061 to men: yet most men give **no** thanks.
040:062 there is **no** god but He: then how
040:065 There is **no** god but He: call upon
040:082 they accomplished was of **no** profit to them.
041:016 more humiliating still: and they will find **no** help.
041:035 And **no** one will be granted such goodness except
041:038 are arrogant, (**no** matter): for in the presence of
041:042 **No** falsehood can approach it from before
041:047 **no** fruit comes out of its sheath, nor does
041:048 that they have **no** way of escape.
042:007 of which there is **no** doubt: (when) some
042:008 **no** protector nor helper.
042:013 in Religion, and make **no** divisions therein:
042:015 There is **no** contention between us and you.
042:020 but he has **no** share or lot in the Hereafter.
042:023 Say: "**No** reward do I ask of you for this
042:035 that there is for them **no** way of escape.
042:041 to him, against such there is **no** cause of blame.
042:044 there is **no** protector thereafter. And thou
042:046 there is **no** way (to the Goal).
042:046 And **no** protectors have they to help them,
042:047 That Day there will be for you **no** place of refuge
042:047 will be **no** putting back, because of
043:020 **no** knowledge! They do nothing but lie!
043:059 He was **no** more than a servant: We granted
043:061 therefore have **no** doubt about the (Hour),
043:068 My devotees! **no** fear shall be on you today,
043:086 **no** power of intercession;-only he
044:008 There is **no** god but He: it is He
044:041 The Day when **no** protector can avail his client
044:041 his client in aught, and **no** help can they receive,
045:010 and of **no** profit to them is anything they may
045:019 They will be of **no** use to thee in the sight
045:024 But of that they have **no** knowledge: they merely
045:026 there is **no** doubt": but most men not know.
045:032 and we have **no** firm assurance.'"

NO (continued)

045:032 there was **no** doubt about its (coming),
045:034 and **no** helpers have ye!
046:008 then can ye have **no** power to help me against Allah.
046:013 on them shall be **no** fear, nor shall they grieve.
046:019 and **no** injustice will be done to them.
046:026 heart and intellect: but of **no** profit to them
046:028 Why then was **no** help forthcoming to them
046:032 and **no** protectors can he have besides Allah:
046:035 and be in **no** haste about the (Unbelievers).
047:011 but those who reject Allah have **no** protector.
047:014 from his Lord, **no** better than one to whom the evil
047:019 Know, therefore, that there is **no** god but Allah,
047:028 so He made their deeds of **no** effect.
047:032 their deeds of **no** effect.
048:017 **No** blame is there on the blind, nor is
048:023 already in the past: **no** change wilt thou find
049:014 Say, "Ye have **no** faith; but ye
050:006 and adorned it, and there is **no** flaws in it?
050:031 nigh to the righteous,-**no** more a thing distant.
051:052 Similarly, **no** messenger came to the Peoples
051:057 **No** sustenance do I require of them, nor do
052:029 of thy Lord, thou art **no** soothsayer nor possessed.
052:033 Nay, they have **no** faith!
052:036 Nay, they have **no** firm belief.
052:046 avail them nothing and **no** help shall be given them.
053:004 It is **no** less than inspiration sent down to him:
053:011 in **no** way falsified that which he saw.
053:023 for which Allah has sent down **no** authority (whatever).
053:028 But they have **no** knowledge therein.
053:038 Namely, that **no** bearer of burdens can bear
053:051 And the Thamud, He left **no** trace of them.
053:058 **No** one but Allah can disclose it.
055:035 **No** defense will ye have:
055:039 On that Day **no** question will be asked
055:056 whom **no** man or Jinn before them has touched;-
055:074 Whom **no** man or Jinn before them has touched;-
056:002 Then will **no** (soul) deny its coming.
056:019 **No** after-ache will they receive therefrom, nor will
056:025 **No** frivolity will they hear therein, nor any
057:015 "This Day shall **no** ransom be accepted of you,
057:022 **No** misfortune can happen on earth or in your
057:029 that they have **no** power whatever over the Grace
058:017 Of **no** profit whatever to them, against Allah,
058:018 **No**, indeed! they are but liars!
059:006 for this ye made **no** expedition with either
059:009 and entertain **no** desire, in their hearts
059:012 so they will receive **no** help.
059:022 Allah is He, than Whom there is **no** other god;-Who knows
059:023 Allah is He, than Whom there is **no** other god;-
060:003 Of **no** profit to you will be your relatives
060:004 **no** power (to get) aught on thy behalf from Allah."
060:010 And there will be **no** blame on you if ye marry
063:011 But to **no** soul will Allah grant respite when the
064:011 **No** kind of calamity can occur, except by
064:013 Allah! there is **no** god but He: and on
065:004 and for those who have **no** courses (it is the same)
065:007 has given him. Allah puts **no** burden on any
066:007 make **no** excuses this Day! Ye are being but
067:003 one above another: **no** want of proportion wilt thou
067:008 its Keepers will ask, "Did **no** Warner come to you?"
068:018 But made **no** reservation, ("If it be Allah's Will").
069:028 "Of **no** profit to me has been my wealth!

NO (continued)

069:035 "So **no** friend hath he here this Day.
070:010 And **no** friend will ask after a friend,
070:015 By **no** means! for it would be the Blazing Fire-
070:039 By **no** means! for We have created them out of
071:021 **no** Increase but only Loss.
071:024 and grant Thou **no** increase to the wrong-doers
071:028 wrong-doers grant Thou **no** increase but in
072:005 'But we do think that **no** man or Jinn
072:012 by **no** means frustrate Allah throughout the earth,
072:013 has **no** fear, either of a short (account) or of
072:020 Say: "I do **no** more than invoke my Lord, and I
072:022 Say: "**No** one can deliver me from Allah
073:009 there is **no** god but He: take Him
074:016 By **no** means! For to Our Signs he has
074:031 and that **no** doubts may be left for the People
074:031 and this is **no** other than a Reminder to mankind.
074:048 Then will **no** intercession of (any)
074:053 By **no** means! But they fear not the Hereafter.
075:011 By **no** means! **No** place of safety!
076:009 of Allah alone: **no** reward do we desire from you,
077:031 and is of **no** use against the fierce Blaze.
077:031 "(Which yields) **no** shade of coolness, and is
078:030 for **no** increase shall We grant you, except in
078:035 **No** Vanity shall they hear therein, nor Untruth;-
080:007 Though it is **no** blame to thee if he grow
080:011 By **no** means (should it be so)! For it
080:023 By **no** means hath he fulfilled what Allah
081:027 Verily this is **no** less than a Message
082:019 (It will be) the Day when **no** soul shall have
083:014 By **no** means! but on their hearts is the
085:008 **no** other reason than that they believed in Allah,
086:004 There is **no** soul but has a protector over it.
086:010 (Man) will have **no** power, and **no** helper.
088:006 **No** food will there be for them but a bitter Dhari
088:011 Where they shall hear **no** (word) of vanity:
091:015 And for Him is **no** fear of its consequences.
092:019 And have in their minds **no** favour from anyone
098:005 And they have been commanded **no** more than this:
104:004 By **no** means! He will be sure to be thrown
111:002 **No** profit to him from all his wealth, and all

NOAH

003:033 Allah did choose Adam and **Noah**,
004:163 as We sent it to **Noah** and the Messengers after
006:084 and before him, We guided **Noah**, and among
007:059 We sent **Noah** to his people. He said: "O my people!
007:069 the people of **Noah**, and gave you
009:070 The people of **Noah**, and Ad,
010:071 Relate to them the story of **Noah**.
011:025 We sent **Noah** to his People (with a mission)
011:032 They said: "O **Noah**! thou hast disputed with us,
011:036 It was revealed to **Noah**: "None of thy People
011:042 and **Noah** called out to his son, who had
011:043 the water." **Noah** said: "This day nothing can
011:045 And **Noah** called upon his Lord and said: "O my
011:046 He said: "O **Noah**! he is not of thy family: for his
011:047 **Noah** said: "O my Lord! I do seek refuge with Thee,
011:048 The word came: "O **Noah**! come down (from the Ark)
011:089 of the people of **Noah** or of Hud or of Salih,
014:009 before you? Of the People of **Noah**, and 'Ad,
017:003 whom We carried (in the Ark) with **Noah**!
017:017 Hoe many generations have We destroyed after **Noah**?
019:058 (in the Ark) with **Noah**, and of

NOAH (continued)

021:076 (Remember) **Noah**, when he cried (to Us) aforetime:
022:042 their prophets),-the People of **Noah**, and 'Ad
023:023 and certainly We sent **Noah** to his people:
023:026 (**Noah**) said: "O my Lord! help me: for that
025:037 And the people of **Noah**,-when they
026:105 The people of **Noah** rejected the messengers.
026:106 Behold, their brother **Noah** said to them: "Will ye
026:116 O **Noah**! thou shalt be stone (to death)."
029:014 We did sent **Noah** to his people, and he
033:007 and from thee: from **Noah**, Abraham, Moses, and
037:075 (In the days of old), **Noah** cried to Us, and We
037:079 "Peace and salutation to **Noah** among the nations!"
038:012 rejected messengers,-the People of **Noah**, and 'Ad,
040:005 who denied (the Signs),- the People of **Noah**, and the
040:031 "Something like the fate of the People of **Noah**, the 'Ad,
042:013 for you as that which He enjoined on **Noah**-the which
050:012 by the people of **Noah**, the Companions
051:046 So were the people of **Noah** before them: for they
053:052 And before them, the people of **Noah**, for that
054:009 of **Noah** rejected (their messenger): they rejected
057:026 And We sent **Noah** and Abraham, and established
066:010 to the Unbelievers, the wife of **Noah** and the wife
071:001 We sent **Noah** to his People (with the Command):
071:021 **Noah** said: "O my Lord! they have disobeyed me,
071:026 And **Noah** said: "O my Lord! Leave not

NOAH'S

069:011 **Noah's** flood) overflowed beyond its limits,

NOBLE

003:039 and (be besides) **noble**, chaste, and a Prophet,
012:031 This is none other than a **noble** angel!"
026:007 how many **noble** things of all kinds we have
031:010 every kind of **noble** creature, in pairs.
044:026 And corn-fields and **noble** buildings,
073:010 and leave them with **noble** (dignity).

NOBLEST

027:034 make the **noblest** of its people meanest thus do

NOISE

069:004 disbelieved in the day of **Noise** and Clamour!
080:033 At length, when there comes the Deafening **Noise**,-

NON-ARABS

026:198 Had We revealed it to any of the **non-Arabs**,

NONE

002:032 of knowledge we have **none**,
002:040 and fear **none** but Me.
002:083 worship **none** but Allah;
002:099 and **none** reject them but those who
002:106 **None** of Our revelations do We abrogate
002:111 And they say: "**None** shall enter Paradise
002:269 but **none** will receive admonition
002:281 and **none** shall be dealt with unjustly.
003:007 and **none** will grasp the Message
003:064 that we worship **none** but Allah;
003:160 If Allah helps you, **none** can overcome you:
003:161 and **none** shall be dealt with unjustly.
004:094 you a salutation: "Thou art **none** of a Believer!"
004:159 And there is **none** of the People of the Book
006:017 **none** can remove it but He; if He
006:034 there is **none** that can alter the Words
006:057 The Command rests with **none** but Allah: He
006:059 the treasures that **none** knoweth but He. He
006:070 **none** will be accepted: such is (the end of)

NONE (continued)

006:093 when he hath received **none**, or (again)
006:115 **none** can change His Words: for He
006:138 and **none** should eat of them except those
006:164 of its acts on **none** but itself: no bearer
007:187 **none** but He can reveal as to
009:016 and take **none** for friends and protectors
009:018 and fear **none** (at all) except Allah.
009:074 **none** on earth to protect or help them.
010:083 But **none** believed in Moses except some
010:107 there is **none** can keep back his favour: He causeth
010:107 there is **none** can remove it but He: if He
011:002 worship **none** but Allah. (Say:) "Verily I am
011:026 "That ye serve **none** but Allah: verily I do
011:029 my reward is from **none** but Allah: but I
011:036 "**None** of thy People will believe except those
011:051 My reward is from **none** but Him Who created Me:
011:116 (but there were **none**) except a few among them whom
012:031 This is **none** other than a noble angel!"
012:040 the Command is for **none** but Allah: He hath
012:040 He hath commanded that ye worship **none** but Him:
012:067 **none** can command except Allah: on Him
013:034 and defender have they **none** against Allah.
013:041 (Where) Allah commands, there is **none** to put
014:009 **None** knows them but Allah. To them came
016:037 to stray, and there is **none** to help them.
016:043 And before thee We sent **none** but men, to whom
016:049 for **none** are arrogant (before their Lord).
016:111 and **none** will be unjustly dealt with.
017:023 Thy Lord hath decreed that ye worship **none** but Him,
017:047 "Ye follow **none** other than a man bewitched!"
017:075 found **none** to help thee against Us!
017:086 then wouldst thou find **none** to plead thy affair
017:102 by **none** but the Lord of the heavens and the earth
018:027 thy Lord: **none** can change His Words, and **none**
018:027 and **none** wilt thou find as a refuge
018:038 and **none** shall I associate with my Lord.
018:063 **none** but Satan made me forget to tell (you)
018:074 who had slain **none**? Truly a foul
019:007 his name shall be Yahya: on **none** by that name
019:087 **None** shall have the power of intercession,
022:018 **none** can rise to honor: for Allah
024:003 **none** can have sexual relations with her but an
025:008 "Ye follow **none** other than a man bewitched."
026:100 "`Now, then, we have **none** to intercede (for us),
027:065 Say: **None** in the heavens or on earth, except
028:080 but this **none** shall attain, save those
029:025 the Fire, and ye shall have **none** to help."
029:047 and **none** but Unbelievers reject Our Signs.
029:049 with knowledge: and **none** but the unjust
031:032 and wrong). But **none** reject Our Signs except only
032:004 on the Throne: ye have **none**, besides Him,
033:014 with **none** but a brief delay!
033:019 of **none** effect: and that is easy of Allah.
033:039 and fear Him, and fear **none** but Allah.
035:002 doth bestow on mankind **none** can withhold:
035:002 **none** can grant, apart from Him: and He
035:014 And **none**, (O man!) can inform you like Him
035:041 should fail. There is **none**-not one-
039:023 can have **none** to guide.
039:037 there can be **none** to lead astray. Is not Allah
040:004 **None** can dispute about the Signs of Allah
040:021 and **none** had they to defend them against Allah.

NONE (continued)

040:033   to stray, there is **none** to guide...
041:014   (preaching): "Serve **none** but Allah." They said,
041:035   **none** but persons of the greatest good fortune.
045:022   it has earned, and **none** of them shall be wronged.
046:021   "Worship ye **none** other than Allah: truly I
047:013   And there was **none** to aid them.
052:008   There is **none** can avert it;-
056:079   Which **none** shall touch but those who are clean:
058:002   **none** can be their mothers except those
067:019   and folding them in? **None** can uphold them
069:037   "Which **none** do eat but those in sin."
070:002   is **none** to ward off,-
071:025   and they found-in lieu of Allah-**none** to help them.
071:027   and they will breed **none** but wicked
074:031   He pleaseth; and **none** can know the forces
074:031   And We have set **none** but angels as guardians
074:056   But **none** will keep it in remembrance except as
078:037   The Most Gracious: **none** shall have power to argue
078:038   **none** shall speak except any who permitted by
083:012   And **none** can deny it but the Transgressor
089:025   such as **none** (else) can inflict,
089:026   And His bonds will be such as **none** (other) can bind.
090:005   Thinketh he, that **none** hath power over him?
090:007   Thinketh he that **none** beholdeth him?
092:015   **None** shall reach it but those most unfortunate ones
112:004   And there is **none** like unto Him.

NONSENSE

023:067   "In arrogance: talking **nonsense** about the (Qur'an),

NOONDAY

024:058   for the **noonday** heat; and after

NOR

002:038   **nor** shall they grieve.
002:041   **nor** sell My Signs for a small price:
002:042   **nor** conceal the Truth when ye know
002:048   **nor** shall intercession be accepted for her,
002:048   **nor** shall compensation be taken from her.
002:048   **nor** shall anyone be helped (from outside).
002:060   evil **nor** mischief on the (face of the) earth.
002:062   **nor** shall they grieve.
002:068   should be neither too old **nor** too young,
002:084   **nor** turn out your own people
002:086   **nor** shall they be helped.
002:105   **nor** of the polytheists.
002:107   have neither patron **nor** helper.
002:112   **nor** shall they grieve.
002:120   neither Protector **nor** Helper against Allah.
002:123   **nor** shall compensation be accepted from her
002:123   **nor** shall intercession profit her
002:123   **nor** shall anyone be helped (from outside)
002:144   **nor** is Allah unmindful of what they do.
002:145   **nor** indeed will they follow
002:145   **nor** art thou going to follow their Qiblah;
002:162   **nor** will respite be their (lot).
002:167   **Nor** will there be a way for them
002:173   **nor** transgressing due limits,
002:174   **nor** purify them;
002:188   **nor** use it as bait for the judges,
002:197   **nor** wrangling in the Hajj.
002:197   let there be no obscenity, **nor** wickedness,
002:217   **Nor** will they cease fighting you until
002:221   **Nor** marry (your girls) to unbelievers
002:233   **Nor** father on account of his child,

NOR (continued)

002:235   **nor** resolve on the tie of marriage
002:254   **nor** friendship **nor** intercession.
002:255   No slumber can seize Him **nor** sleep.
002:255   **Nor** shall they compass aught of his knowledge
002:258   **Nor** doth Allah give guidance to a people unjust.
002:262   on them shall be no fear, **nor** shall they grieve.
002:264   neither in Allah **nor** in the last day.
002:274   on them shall be no fear, **nor** shall they grieve.
002:277   **nor** shall they grieve.
002:282   and let neither scribe **nor** witness suffer harm.
003:010   neither their possessions **nor** their (numerous)
003:019   **nor** did the People of the Book
003:022   **nor** will they have anyone to help.
003:044   **nor** wast thou with them when they dispute
003:056   **nor** will they have anyone to help.
003:067   Abraham was a Jew **nor** yet a Christian;
003:077   **nor** will He cleanse them (of sin):
003:077   **nor** will Allah (deign to) speak to them
003:080   **Nor** would he instruct you to take angels
003:088   **nor** will their punishment be lightened,
003:088   **nor** respite be their (lot);
003:116   neither their possessions **nor** their (numerous)
003:139   So lose heart, **nor** fall into despair:
003:145   **Nor** can a soul die except by Allah's leave,
003:146   **nor** did they weaken (in will) **nor** give in.
003:170   **nor** have they (cause to) grieve.
003:179   **Nor** will He disclose to you the secrets
004:002   **nor** substitute (your) worthless things
004:006   **nor** in haste against their growing up.
004:012   has left neither ascendants **nor** descendants,
004:018   **nor** of those who die rejecting faith:
004:019   **Nor** should ye treat them with harshness,
004:025   **nor** taking adulterous: when they
004:029   **nor** kill (or destroy) yourselves:
004:037   (**Nor**) those who are niggardly, enjoin
004:038   (**Nor**) those who spend of their substance, to be
004:043   **nor** in a state of ceremonial impurity except
004:091   **nor** give you guarantees of peace besides
004:098   **nor** can they find a way (to escape).
004:123   **Nor** will he find, besides Allah,
004:123   **nor** those of the people of the Book (can prevail):
004:137   **nor** guide them on the Way.
004:143   belonging neither to these **nor** those whom Allah
004:157   but they killed him , **nor** crucified him.
004:168   **nor** guide them to any way-
004:171   **nor** say of Allah aught but truth.
004:172   **nor** do the angels, those nearest (to Allah):
004:173   **nor** will they find, besides Allah, any to
005:002   **nor** the garlands that mark out such animals,
005:002   **nor** of the animals brought for sacrifice,
005:002   **nor** the people resorting to the Sacred House,
005:002   **nor** of the Sacred Month,
005:013   **nor** wilt thou cease to find them-barring a few,
005:069   on them shall be no fear, **nor** shall they grieve.
005:077   **nor** follow the vain desire of people who went
005:079   **Nor** did they forbid one another the iniquities
006:038   **nor** a being that flies on its wings, but
006:048   upon them shall be no fear, **nor** shall they grieve.
006:050   **Nor** do I tell you I am an angel.
006:050   **nor** do I know what is hidden.
006:051   no protector **nor** intercessor: that they

NOR (continued)

006:059	nor anything fresh or dry (green or withered),
006:071	things that can do us neither good nor harm, and
006:091	which ye knew -neither ye nor your fathers."
006:107	nor art thou set over them to dispose
006:134	nor can ye frustrate it (in the least bit).
006:145	nor transgressing due limits,-thy Lord
006:148	nor would our fathers; nor should
006:148	nor should we have had any forbidden thing."
006:150	nor follow thou the vain desires of such
006:158	nor earned righteousness through its Faith.
007:017	nor wilt Thou find, in most of them, gratitude
007:034	nor (an hour) can they advance (it in anticipation).
007:035	on them shall be no fear, nor shall they grieve.
007:040	nor will they enter the Garden, until the
007:049	nor shall ye grieve."
007:085	nor withhold from the people the things
007:089	nor could we by any manner of means return
007:148	nor show them the Way?
007:150	nor count thou me amongst the people of sin."
007:192	nor can they aid themselves!
008:021	Nor be like those who say, "We hear,"
008:027	nor misappropriate knowingly things entrusted
008:033	nor was He going to send it whilst they
009:004	nor aided any one against you. So fulfil
009:029	nor acknowledge the religion of Truth, from among
009:029	nor the Last Day, nor hold that forbidden which
009:055	nor their children dazzle thee: in reality
009:083	nor fight an enemy with me: for ye
009:084	nor stand at his grave; for they
009:084	Nor do thou ever pray for any of them that dies,
009:085	Nor let their wealth nor their children dazzle thee:
009:092	Nor (is there blame) on those who came to thee
009:116	Except for Him ye have no protector nor helper.
009:120	behind Allah's Messenger, nor to prefer their own
009:121	Nor could they spend anything (for the Cause),
009:121	nor cut across a valley, but the deed
010:016	nor should He have made it known to you. A whole
010:018	what can hurt them nor profit them, and they
010:026	No darkness nor abasement shall cover
010:061	Nor is hidden from thy Lord (so much as)
010:062	there is no fear, nor shall they grieve;
010:095	Nor be of those who reject the Signs of Allah,
010:101	but neither Signs nor Warners profit those
010:106	nor hurt thee: if thou dost, behold! thou shalt
010:106	"Nor call on any, other than Allah,-such can
011:020	They could hear, nor could they see!
011:020	nor have they protectors besides Allah!
011:027	nor do we see that any follow thee but the
011:027	apparently nor do we see in you (all) any
011:031	Nor yet do I say, of those whom your eyes
011:031	nor claim I to be an angel.
011:031	nor do I know what is hidden,
011:049	nor thy People knew them
011:053	Nor shall we believe in thee!
011:083	Marked from thy Lord; nor are they ever far
011:085	and weight, nor withhold from the people
011:089	or of Salih, nor are the people of Lut
011:101	nor did they add aught (to their
011:104	Nor shall We delay it but for a term appointed.
011:113	than Allah, nor shall ye be helped.
011:117	Nor would thy Lord be the One to destroy
012:053	"Nor do I absolve my own self (of blame):

NOR (continued)

012:060	from me, nor shall ye (even) come near me."
012:102	nor wast thou (present) with them when they
012:109	Nor did We send before thee (as Messengers)
013:011	no turning it back, nor will they find, besides
013:037	protector nor defender against Allah.
014:020	Nor is that for Allah any great matter.
014:022	nor can ye listen to mine.
014:031	neither mutual bargaining, nor befriending.
015:005	anticipate its Term, nor delay it.
015:048	touch them, nor shall they (ever) be asked
015:088	on certain classes of them, nor grieve over them:
016:021	nor do thy know when they will be raised up.
016:035	nor should we have prescribed prohibitions other
016:035	neither we nor our fathers,-
016:084	nor will they be allowed to make amends.
016:085	nor will they them receive respite.
016:095	Nor sell the Covenant of Allah for a miserable
016:115	nor transgressing due limits,-then Allah
016:127	the help from Allah; nor grieve over them:
017:015	nor would We punish until, We had sent
017:023	a word of contempt, nor repel them but address
017:029	nor stretch it forth to its utmost reach,
017:032	Nor come nigh to adultery: for it is
017:033	Nor take life-which Allah has made sacred-
017:037	nor reach the mountains in height.
017:037	Nor walk on the earth with insolence: for thou
017:056	from you nor to change them."
017:110	nor speak it in a low tone, but seek
017:111	(His) dominion: nor (needs) He any to protect
018:005	nor had their fathers.
018:022	nor consult any of them about (the affair of) the Sleepers.
018:023	Nor say of anything, "I shall be
018:026	nor does He share His Command with any
018:028	nor obey any whose heart We have permitted to
018:036	"Nor do I deem that the Hour (of Judgment)
018:043	against Allah, nor was he able to deliver himself.
018:043	Nor had he numbers to help him against Allah,
018:047	nor shall We leave out any one of them.
018:051	own creation: nor is it for Me to take as helpers
018:055	come to them, nor from praying for forgiveness
018:069	nor shall I disobey thee in aught."
018:073	for forgetting, nor grieve me by raising
018:105	vain will be their works, nor shall We, on the
019:028	a man of evil, nor thy mother a woman unchaste!"
020:052	my Lord never errs, nor forgets,-
020:058	fail to keep-neither we nor thou-in a place
020:074	is Hell: therein shall he neither die nor live.
020:094	nor by (the hair of) my head!
020:112	nor of any curtailment (of what is his due).
020:118	for thee to go hungry nor to go naked,
020:119	"Nor to suffer from thirst, nor from the sun's heat."
020:123	will lose his way, nor fall into misery.
020:131	Nor strain thine eyes in longing for the
021:008	ate no food, nor were they immortals.
021:008	Nor did We give them bodies that ate no food,
021:019	nor are they (ever) weary of His service):
021:020	nor do they ever flag or intermit.
021:039	the Fire from their faces, nor yet from their backs,
021:040	to avert it, nor will they (then) get respite.
021:043	to aid themselves, nor can they be defended
021:066	be of any good to you nor do you harm?
021:100	nor will they there hear (aught else).

NOR (continued)

022:012   **nor** profit them: that is straying far indeed
022:037   It is their meat **nor** their blood, that reaches
023:043   **nor** can they delay (it).
023:076   their Lord, **nor** do they submissively entreat
023:091   **nor** is there any god along with Him:
023:101   **nor** will one ask after another!
024:035   neither of the East **nor** of the West, whose Oil
024:037   **nor** from regular Prayer,
024:037   **nor** from paying zakat their (only) fear is for
024:037   By men whom neither trade **nor** sale can divert
024:061   **nor** in one afflicted with illness, **nor** in yourselves,
024:061   **nor** in one born lame,
025:002   **nor** has He a partner in His dominion:
025:003   **nor** can they control Death **nor** Life **nor** Resurrection.
025:019   (your penalty) **nor** (get) help."
025:055   things that can neither profit them **nor** harm them:
025:068   any other god, **nor** slay such life as Allah
026:088   "The Day whereon neither wealth **nor** sons will avail,
026:101   "'**Nor** a single intimate friend.
026:183   due to men, **nor** do evil in the land,
027:065   **nor** can they perceive when they shall be
027:070   **nor** distress thyself because of their plots.
027:080   **nor** canst thou cause the Deaf
027:081   **Nor** canst thou be a guide to the Blind,
028:007   but fear **nor** grieve: for We
028:044   **nor** wast thou a witness (of those events).
028:046   **Nor** wast thou at the side of (the Mountain
028:059   **nor** are We going to destroy a population except
028:059   **Nor** was thy Lord the one to destroy a town
028:077   **nor** forget thy portion in this world: but do
028:081   **nor** could he defend himself.
029:022   "on earth **nor** in heaven will ye be able
029:022   (His Plan), **nor** have ye, beside Allah,
029:033   "Fear thou , **nor** grieve: we are
029:036   **nor** commit evil on the earth, with intent
029:048   **nor** art thou (able) to transcribe it with
030:052   the dead to hear, **nor** canst thou make the deaf
030:053   **Nor** canst thou lead back the blind from their
030:057   **nor** will they be allowed to make amends.
030:060   **nor** let those excite thee, who have
031:018   **Nor** walk in insolence through the earth:
031:033   **nor** a son avail aught for his father.
031:033   **nor** let the Chief Deceiver
031:034   **nor** does anyone know in what land he is to die.
031:034   **Nor** does any one know what it is that he
032:015   **nor** are they (ever) puffed up with pride.
032:029   **Nor** will they be granted a respite."
033:004   **nor** has He made your wives whom ye divorce
033:004   **nor** has He made your adopted sons your sons.
033:017   **Nor** will they find for themselves,
033:052   **nor** to change them for (other) wives, even though
033:053   **Nor** is it right for you that ye should
033:065   no protector will they find, **nor** helper.
034:003   or on earth: **nor** is there anything less than
034:022   **nor** is any of them a helper to Allah.
034:025   **nor** shall we be questioned as to
034:030   for an hour **nor** put forward."
034:031   **nor** in (any) that (came) before it."
034:037   It is your wealth **nor** your sons, that will
034:044   **nor** sent messengers to them before thee as Warners.
035:005   life deceive you, **nor** let the Chief Deceiver
035:011   **Nor** is a man long-lived granted length of days,

NOR (continued)

035:011   **nor** is a part cut off from his life,
035:012   **Nor** are the two seas alike,-the one
035:017   **Nor** is that (at all) difficult for Allah.
035:018   **Nor** can a bearer of burdens bear another's
035:020   **Nor** are the depths of Darkness and the Light;
035:021   **Nor** are the (chilly) shade and the (genial)
035:022   **Nor** are alike those that are living
035:035   no toil **nor** sense of weariness shall touch
035:036   **nor** shall its Chastisement be lightened for them.
035:044   **Nor** is Allah to be frustrated by anything whatever
036:023   **nor** can they deliver me.
036:028   from heaven, **nor** was it needful for Us so to do.
036:040   **nor** can the Night outstrip the Day: each (just)
036:043   **nor** could they be delivered,
036:050   **nor** to return to their own people!
036:067   **nor** could they have returned (after error).
036:069   in Poetry, **nor** is it meant for him: this is
037:030   "**Nor** had we any authority over you.
037:047   **nor** will they suffer intoxication therefrom.
037:161   For, verily, neither ye **nor** those ye worship
038:026   (and justice): **nor** follow thou the lust (of thy
038:086   of you for this (Qur'an), **nor** am I a pretender.
039:041   **Nor** art thou set a Custodian
039:061   no evil shall touch them, **nor** shall they grieve.
040:018   **nor** intercessors will the wrong-doers have,
040:029   I see (myself); **nor** do I guide you but to
040:058   **nor** are (equal) those who believe and work
041:030   (they suggest), "**Nor** grieve!
041:034   **Nor** can Goodness and Evil be equal.
041:038   (**nor** feel themselves above it).
041:046   **nor** is thy Lord ever unjust (in the least)
041:047   **nor** does a female conceive (within her womb)
041:047   (within her womb) **nor** bring forth (young), but by
042:008   no protector **nor** helper.
042:015   art commanded, **nor** follow thou their vain desires;
042:031   **Nor** can ye escape through the earth; **nor** have
042:031   **nor** have ye, besides Allah, anyone to
042:047   of refuge **nor** will there be for you any room
043:068   you today, **nor** shall ye grieve,-
044:029   And neither heaven **nor** earth shed a tear over them:
044:029   over them: **nor** were they given a respite (again).
044:056   **Nor** will they there taste Death, except the
045:010   **nor** any protectors they may have taken to
045:035   out thence, **nor** can the make amends.
046:009   **nor** do I know what will be done
046:013   no fear, **nor** shall they grieve.
048:017   **nor** on one ill (if he joins the war):
048:017   **nor** is there blame on the lame,
048:022   find neither protector **nor** helper.
049:002   **nor** speak aloud to him in talk,
049:011   **nor** call each other by (offensive) nicknames:
049:011   **nor** defame **nor** be sarcastic to each
049:011   **nor** let some women laugh at
049:012   **nor** speak ill of each other behind their backs.
050:038   **nor** did any sense of weariness touch Us.
051:045   (on their feet), **nor** could they help themselves.
051:057   **nor** do I require that they should feed Me.
052:021   **nor** shall We deprive them (of the fruit)
052:029   thou art no soothsayer **nor** possessed.
053:002   Your Companion is neither astray **nor** being misled,
053:003   **Nor** does he say (aught) of (his own) Desire.
053:017   (His) sight never swerved, **nor** did it go wrong!

NOR (continued)

056:019 **nor** will they suffer intoxication:
056:025 **nor** any mischief,-
056:033 **nor** (supply) forbidden,
056:044 Neither cool **nor** refreshing:
057:015 **nor** of those who rejected Allah.
057:023 **nor** exult over favours bestowed upon you.
058:007 **nor** between fewer more, but He
058:007 **nor** between five but He makes the sixth,-
058:014 They are neither of you **nor** of them, and they
058:017 **nor** their sons: they will be Companions of the
060:008 (your) Faith **nor** drive you out of your homes,
060:010 for the Unbelievers, **nor** are the (Unbelievers)
065:001 their houses, **nor** shall they (themselves)
069:036 "**Nor** hath he any food except the foul pus
069:042 **Nor** is it the word of a soothsayer:
069:047 **Nor** could any of you withhold him (from Our wrath).
071:023 Wadd **nor** Suwa, neither Yaguth **nor** Yauq, **nor** Nasr';-
072:003 He has taken neither a wife **nor** a son.
072:012 **nor** can we escape Him by flight.
072:022 **nor** should I find refuge except in Him.
072:026 **nor** does He make any one acquainted with
074:006 **Nor** expect, in giving, any increase (for thyself)!
074:044 "**Nor** were we of those who fed the indigent;
075:031 So he gave nothing in charity, **nor** did he pray!-
076:009 no reward do we desire from you, **nor** thanks.
076:013 (excessive heat) **nor** excessive cold.
077:036 **Nor** will it be open to them to put forth pleas.
078:024 Nothing cool shall they taste therein, **nor** any drink,
078:035 No Vanity shall they hear therein, **nor** Untruth;-
081:025 **Nor** is it the word of a Satan accursed.
087:013 In which he will then neither die **nor** live.
088:007 Which will neither nourish **nor** satisfy hunger.
089:018 **Nor** do ye encourage one another to feed the poor!-
092:011 **Nor** will his wealth profit him when he falls
093:003 **nor** is He displeased.
093:010 **Nor** repulse him who asks;
098:004 **Nor** did the people of the Book make schisms,
109:003 **Nor** will ye worship that which I worship.
109:005 **Nor** will ye worship that which I worship.
112:003 He begetteth not, **nor** is He begotten;

NOSE

005:045 **nose** for **nose**, ear for ear, tooth for tooth,

NOT

001:007 Those whose (portion) is **not** wrath,
001:007 and who go **not** astray.
002:006 whether thou warn them or do **not** warn them;
002:006 or do **not** warn them; they will **not** believe.
002:008 but they do **not** (really) believe.
002:009 themselves and realize (it) **not**!
002:011 "Make **not** mischief on the earth,"
002:012 but they realize (it) **not**.
002:013 they are the fools but they do **not** know.
002:017 so they could **not** see.
002:018 they will **not** return (to the path).
002:022 then set **not** up rivals unto Allah
002:026 Allah disdains **not** to use
002:026 but He causes **not** to stray,
002:030 He said: "I know what ye know **not**."
002:033 Allah said: "Did I **not** tell you that
002:034 **not** so Iblis, he refused and was haughty:
002:035 but approach **not** this tree,
002:041 and be **not** the first to reject faith therein,

NOT (continued)

002:042 And cover **not** Truth with falsehood,
002:044 Will ye **not** understand?
002:048 a day when one soul shall **not** avail another
002:064 had it **not** been for the Grace
002:071 He said: "He says, a heifer **not** trained
002:074 And Allah is **not** unmindful of what ye do.
002:076 Do ye **not** understand (their aim)?
002:077 Know they **not** that Allah knoweth what
002:078 who know **not** the Book,
002:080 ye say of Allah what ye do **not** know?"
002:080 **not** touch us but for few numbered days:"
002:085 though it was **not** lawful for you
002:085 For Allah is **not** unmindful of what ye do.
002:086 their chastisement shall **not** be lightened
002:087 with what ye yourselves desire **not**,
002:094 and **not** for anyone else,
002:096 will **not** save him from (due) chastisement
002:100 Is it **not** (the case) that every time
002:101 something) they did **not** know!
002:102 so do **not** blaspheme."
002:102 **Not** what profited them.
002:102 Solomon did **not** disbelieve but Satans
002:102 But they could **not** thus harm anyone except
002:104 O ye of Faith! say **not** (to the Prophet)
002:106 knowest thou **not** that Allah hath power
002:107 Knowest thou **not** that to Allah belongeth
002:113 what those say who know **not**,
002:114 It was **not** fitting that such should
002:118 "Why speaketh **not** Allah unto Us?
002:118 Or why cometh **not** Us a Sign?"
002:123 a day when one soul shall **not** avail another,
002:124 is **not** within the reach of evil-doers."
002:132 then die **not** except in the state
002:134 ye shall **not** be asked about what they did.
002:135 and he joined **not** gods with Allah."
002:140 But Allah is **not** unmindful of what ye do!
002:141 Ye shall **not** be asked!
002:145 they would **not** follow thy Qiblah;
002:147 so be **not** at all in doubt.
002:149 And Allah is **not** unmindful of what ye do.
002:150 so fear them **not**, but fear Me;
002:152 Be grateful to Me, and reject **not** Faith.
002:154 And say **not** of those who are slain
002:154 though ye perceive (it) **not**.
002:162 Their penalty will **not** be lightened,
002:168 and do **not** the footsteps of Satan for he
002:174 Allah will **not** address them on the Day
002:177 It is **not** righteousness that ye turn your faces
002:185 He does **not** want to put you to difficulties.
002:187 but do **not** associate with your wives while
002:187 approach **not** night thereto.
002:188 And do **not** eat up your property
002:190 those who fight you but do **not** transgress limits;
002:190 for Allah loveth **not** transgressors.
002:191 but fight them **not** at the Sacred Mosque,
002:195 and make **not** your own hands contribute
002:196 and do **not** shave your heads until
002:196 is **not** in (the precincts of) the Sacred Mosque.
002:205 but Allah loveth **not** mischief.
002:208 and follow **not** the footsteps of the Satan
002:213 did **not** differ among themselves,
002:216 But Allah knoweth, and ye know **not**.

NOT (continued)

002:221 Do **not** marry unbelieving women (idolaters),
002:222 and do **not** approach them until they are clean.
002:224 And make **not** Allah's (name) an excuse
002:225 Allah will **not** call you to account
002:228 and it is **not** lawful for them to hide
002:229 It is **not** lawful for you, (men),
002:229 so do **not** transgress them
002:231 but do **not** take them back to injure them,
002:231 Do **not** treat Allah's Signs as a jest,
002:232 do **not** prevent them from marrying
002:232 and Allah knows, and ye knows **not**.
002:235 but do **not** make a secret contract with them
002:237 And do **not** forget liberality between yourselves.
002:239 which ye knew **not** (before).
002:243 Didst thou **not** turn thy vision
002:246 Hast thou **not** turned thy vision to the chiefs
002:246 that ye will **not** fight?"
002:246 He said: "Is it **not** possible if ye were
002:247 and he is **not** even gifted with wealth
002:249 only those who taste **not** of it go with me;
002:249 he goes **not** with my army;
002:251 And did **not** Allah check one set of people
002:253 they would **not** have fought each other;
002:253 succeeding generations would **not** have fought
002:258 Hast thou **not** turned thy thought to one
002:260 He said: "Dost thou **not** then believe?"
002:262 and follow **not** up their gifts with reminders
002:264 O ye who believe! cancel **not** your charity
002:264 And Allah guideth **not** those who reject faith.
002:265 and if it receives **not** heavy rain,
002:266 **not** strong (enough to look, after themselves)
002:267 and do **not** even aim at anything which is bad,
002:267 when ye yourselves would **not** receive it
002:272 and ye shall **not** be dealt with unjustly.
002:272 It is **not** for you to guide them
002:273 they beg **not** importunately from all and sundry.
002:275 **not** stand except as stands one whom the Satan
002:276 for He loveth **not** any ungrateful Sinner.
002:279 and ye shall **not** be dealt with unjustly.
002:279 ye shall have your capital sums: deal **not** unjustly,
002:279 If ye do it **not**, take notice of war
002:282 let **not** the scribe refuse to write:
002:282 Disdain **not** to reduce to writing
002:282 if ye reduce it **not** to writing.
002:282 The witnesses should **not** refuse when
002:282 **not** two men, then a man and two women,
002:282 and **not** diminish aught of what he owes.
002:283 Conceal **not** evidence; for whoever conceals it,
002:286 (Pray:) "Our Lord! Condemn us **not** if we
002:286 Our Lord! lay **not** on us a burden
002:286 our Lord! Lay **not** on us a burden like that
003:007 that is **not** entirely clear.
003:007 others are **not** entirely clear.
003:008 "let **not** our hearts deviate now after Thou
003:023 Hast thou **not** turned thy thought to those who
003:024 **not** touch us but for a few numbered days":
003:028 Let **not** the Believers take for friends
003:032 Allah loveth **not** those who reject Faith.
003:044 thou wast **not** with them when they cast
003:057 but Allah loveth **not** those who do wrong.
003:060 so be **not** of those who doubt
003:064 that we erect **not**, from among ourselves,

NOT (continued)

003:065 were **not** revealed till after him?
003:066 It is Allah Who knows, and ye who know **not**!
003:067 Abraham was **not** a Jew nor yet a Christian;
003:067 And he joined **not** gods with Allah.
003:069 but themselves, and they do **not** perceive!
003:069 But they shall lead astray (**not** you),
003:075 will **not** repay it unless thou constantly
003:078 but it is **not** from Allah:
003:079 It is **not** (possible) that a man,
003:086 But Allah guides **not** a people unjust.
003:095 he was **not** of the Pagans."
003:097 Allah stands **not** in need of any of His creatures.
003:099 But Allah is **not** unmindful of all that ye do."
003:102 and die **not** except in a state of Islam.
003:103 and be **not** divided among yourselves;
003:105 Be **not** like those who are divided amongst themselves
003:113 **Not** all of them are alike: of the People
003:117 it is **not** Allah that hath wronged them,
003:118 O ye who believe! take **not** into your intimacy
003:118 they will **not** fail to corrupt you.
003:119 but they love you **not**,
003:120 **not** the least harm will their cunning do to you;
003:124 Is it **not** enough for you that Allah should help
003:128 **Not** for thee, (but for Allah), is the decision:
003:130 O ye who believe! devour **not** usury,
003:139 So lose **not** heart, nor fall into despair:
003:140 And Allah loveth **not** those that do wrong.
003:144 **not** the least harm will he do to Allah;
003:153 to teach you **not** to grieve for (the booty)
003:154 we should **not** have been in the slaughter here."
003:154 what they dare **not** reveal to thee.
003:156 O ye who believe! Be **not** like the Unbelievers,
003:156 they would **not** have died, or been slain."
003:167 saying with their lips what was **not** in their hearts.
003:168 they would **not** have been slain."
003:169 Think **not** of those who are slain
003:170 who have **not** yet joined them (in their bliss),
003:171 suffereth **not** the reward of the Faithful
003:175 be ye **not** afraid of them, but fear
003:176 **not** the least harm will they do to Allah:
003:176 Let **not** those grieve thee who rush headlong
003:177 **not** the least harm will they do to Allah,
003:178 Let **not** the Unbelievers think that our respite
003:179 Allah will **not** leave the Believers
003:180 And let **not** those who covetously withhold of the
003:183 our promise **not** to believe in a messenger unless he
003:187 and **not** to hide it; but they threw
003:188 Think **not** that those who exult in what
003:188 think **not** that they can escape the Chastisement.
003:188 and love to be praised for what they have **not** done,
003:191 **not** for naught hast Thou created (all) this!
003:196 Let **not** the strutting about of the Unbelievers
003:199 they will **not** sell the Signs of Allah
004:002 and devour **not** their substance (by mixing it up)
004:003 If ye fear that ye shall **not** be able
004:003 but if ye fear that ye shall **not** be able
004:005 give **not** your property which Allah has assigned
004:006 but consume it **not** wastefully, nor in haste
004:011 Ye know **not** whether your parents or your children
004:020 take **not** the least bit of it back:
004:022 And marry **not** women whom your fathers married,
004:023 no prohibition if ye have **not** gone in;

NOT (continued)

004:024 desiring chastity, **not** fornication.
004:025 If any of you have **not** the means wherewith
004:025 they should be chaste, **not** fornicators,
004:029 O ye who believe! eat **not** up your property
004:034 seek **not** against them means (of annoyance):
004:036 for Allah loveth **not** the arrogant,
004:036 Serve Allah, and join **not** any partners with Him;
004:043 O ye who believe! approach **not** prayers in a state
004:044 Hast thou **not** turned thy thought to those who
004:046 and "Hear what is **not** heard"; and "Ra'ina"
004:048 Allah forgiveth **not** that partners
004:049 and they will **not** be wronged a whit.
004:049 Hast thou **not** turned thy thought to those
004:051 Hast thou **not** turned thy thought to those who
004:053 Behold, they give **not** a farthing to
004:060 Hast thou **not** turned thy thought to those who
004:064 We sent **not** a Messenger, but to be obeyed,
004:072 in that we were **not** present among them."
004:075 And why should ye **not** fight in the cause
004:077 Wouldst Thou **not** grant us respite to our
004:077 Hast thou **not** turned thy thought to those who
004:080 We have **not** sent thee to watch over them.
004:082 Do they **not** ponder on the Qur'an?
004:083 Were it **not** for the Grace
004:089 so take **not** friends from their ranks until
004:090 withdraw from you but fight you **not**, and
004:091 if they withdraw **not** from you nor give you
004:094 and say **not** to anyone who offers you a
004:095 **Not** equal are those Believers who sit (at home),
004:097 They say: "Was **not** the earth of Allah spacious
004:102 which hath **not** yet prayed and let them
004:104 And slacken **not** in following up the enemy: if
004:104 but you hope from Allah, what they have **not**.
004:105 so be **not** an advocate for those who
004:107 for Allah loveth **not** one given to perfidy and sin:
004:107 Contend **not** on behalf of such as
004:113 taught thee what thou knewest **not** (before):
004:116 Allah forgiveth **not** (the sin of) joining
004:123 **Not** your desires, nor those
004:124 and **not** the least injustice will be done to them.
004:127 to whom ye give **not** the portions prescribed, and
004:127 There is **not** a good deed which ye do, but
004:129 but turn **not** away (from a woman) altogether, so as
004:135 Follow **not** the lusts (of your hearts), lest
004:137 Allah will **not** forgive them nor
004:140 ye are **not** to sit with them unless they
004:141 they say: "Were we **not** with you?"
004:141 "Did we **not** gain an advantage over you.
004:141 And did we **not** guard you from the Believers?"
004:144 O ye who believe! take **not** for friends
004:148 Allah loveth **not** the shouting of evil
004:154 "Transgress **not** in the matter of the Sabbath."
004:157 for of a surety they killed him **not**:
004:157 but they killed him **not**, nor crucified him.
004:164 told thee the story; of others We have **not**;
004:168 Allah will **not** forgive them nor guide
004:171 Say **not** "Three": desist: it will be
004:172 Christ disdaineth **not** to serve and worship Allah,
005:002 but help ye **not** one another in sin and rancor:
005:002 O ye who believe! violate **not** the sanctity
005:002 and let **not** the hatred of some people
005:003 yet fear them **not** but fear Me.

NOT (continued)

005:005 are (**not** only) chaste women who are believers, but
005:005 and desire chastity, **not** lewdness.
005:006 Allah doth **not** wish to place you in a difficulty,
005:008 and let **not** the hatred of others to you
005:020 He had **not** given to any other among the peoples.
005:021 and turn **not** back ignominiously, for then
005:026 but sorrow thou **not** over these rebellious people."
005:027 it was accepted from one, but **not** from the other.
005:028 to slay me, it is **not** for me to stretch my hand
005:031 "Was I **not** even able to be as this raven, and to
005:040 Knowest thou **not** that to Allah (alone) belongeth
005:041 For such it is **not** Allah's will
005:041 but if **not**, beware!"
005:041 O Messenger! let **not** those grieve thee, who race
005:043 For they are **not** (really) people of Faith.
005:044 and sell **not** My Signs for a miserable price.
005:044 therefore fear **not** men, but fear Me, and sell **not**
005:048 and follow **not** their vain desires, diverging
005:049 and follow **not** their vain desires, but beware
005:051 Verily Allah guideth **not** a people unjust.
005:051 O ye who believe! take **not** the Jews and the
005:057 take **not** for friends and protectors those who
005:063 Why do **not** the Rabbis and the doctors of laws
005:064 And Allah loveth **not** those who do mischief.
005:067 For Allah guideth **not** those who reject Faith.
005:067 If thou didst **not**, thou wouldst **not**
005:067 thou wouldst **not** have fulfilled and proclaimed
005:068 But sorrow thou **not** over (these)
005:070 desired **not**-some (of theses) they called impostors,
005:073 If they desist **not** from their word (of blasphemy),
005:074 Why turn they **not** to Allah, and seek
005:077 exceed **not** in your religion the bounds
005:082 and they are **not** arrogant.
005:084 "What cause can we have **not** to believe in Allah
005:087 for Allah loveth **not** those given to excess.
005:087 O ye who believe! make **not** unlawful the good
005:089 Allah will **not** call you to account
005:091 and from prayer: will ye **not** then abstain?
005:095 O ye who believe! kill **not** game, while in
005:100 Say: "**Not** equal are things that are bad and
005:101 O ye who believe! ask **not** questions about things
005:103 It was **not** Allah Who instituted
005:106 "We will **not** take for it a price even though
005:106 we shall hide **not** the evidence we owe to Allah if
005:107 and that we have **not** trespassed (beyond the truth):
005:108 for Allah guideth **not** a rebellious people.
005:115 such as I have **not** inflicted on anyone
005:116 though I know **not** what is in Thine.
006:006 See they **not** how many of those before them
006:006 in strength such as We have **not** given to you-for
006:008 They say: "Why is **not** an angel sent down to him?"
006:012 that will **not** believer.
006:014 And He is that feedeth but is **not** fed."
006:014 and be **not** thou of the company of those
006:023 **not** those who joined gods with Allah."
006:025 so they understand it **not**, and deafness
006:025 they will **not** believe in them; in so much
006:026 and they perceive it **not**.
006:027 Then would we **not** reject the Signs of our Lord,
006:030 He will say: "Is **not** this the truth?"
006:032 Will ye **not** then understand?
006:033 it is **not** thee they reject: it is the

NOT (continued)

006:035	so be **not** thou amongst those who are swayed
006:037	but most of them understand **not**."
006:037	They say: "Why is **not** a Sign sent down
006:038	There is **not** an animal (that lives)
006:043	why then did they **not** call (Allah) in humility?
006:049	for that they ceased **not** from transgressing.
006:050	Say: "I tell you **not** that with me
006:050	Will ye then consider **not**?
006:052	Send **not** away those who call on their Lord
006:053	Doth **not** Allah know best those who are grateful?.
006:056	and be **not** of the company
006:056	Say: "I will **not** follow your vain desires:
006:057	What ye would see hastened is **not** in my power.
006:059	there is **not** a grain in the darkness
006:059	**Not** a leaf doth fall but with His knowledge:
006:066	Say: "**Not** mine is the responsibility for
006:068	sit **not** thou in the company of those who do wrong.
006:076	"I love **not** those that set."
006:080	Will ye **not** (yourselves) be admonished?
006:080	I fear **not** (the beings) ye associate with Allah:
006:081	when ye fear **not** to give partners
006:082	and mix **not** their beliefs with wrong-that are
006:089	to a new People who reject them **not**.
006:091	which ye knew **not**-neither ye nor your fathers."
006:094	We see **not** with you your intercessors whom ye
006:104	I am **not** (here) to watch over your doings."
006:107	**not** one to watch over their doings, nor art
006:107	they would **not** have taken false gods: but We
006:108	Revile **not** ye those whom they call
006:109	they will **not** believe."?
006:111	they are **not** the ones to believe, unless it
006:112	they would **not** have done it: so leave
006:119	Why should ye **not** eat of (meats) on which
006:121	Allah's name hath **not** been pronounced: that
006:121	Eat **not** of (meats) on which Allah's name
006:123	and they perceive it **not**.
006:124	"We shall **not** believe until we receive
006:130	came there **not** unto you messengers
006:131	for thy Lord would **not** destroy the towns
006:132	**not** unmindful of anything that they do.
006:135	the wrong-doers will **not** prosper."
006:136	reacheth **not** Allah, whilst the share
006:137	they would **not** have done so: but leave
006:138	the name of Allah is **not** pronounced:-forging
006:141	But waste **not** by excess: for Allah
006:141	for Allah loveth **not** the wasters.
006:142	and follow **not** the footsteps of Satan: for he
006:145	For Allah guideth **not** people who do wrong.
006:145	Say: "I find **not** in the Message received by
006:148	we should **not** have given partners to Him, nor
006:150	be **not** thou amongst them: nor follow
006:150	and such as believe **not** in the Hereafter: for
006:151	join **not** anything with Him: be good
006:151	kill **not** your children on a plea of want;-We
006:151	come **not** nigh to indecent deeds, whether
006:151	whether open or secret; take **not** life, which
006:152	And come **not** nigh to the orphan's property,
006:153	follow it: follow **not** (other) paths: they will
006:158	if it believed **not** before nor earned
006:161	and he (certainly) joined **not** gods with Allah."
007:003	and follow **not**, as friends
007:011	and they prostrated, **not** so Iblis; he refused

NOT (continued)

007:013	it is **not** for thee to be arrogant here: get out,
007:019	but approach **not** this tree, lest you
007:022	"Did I **not** forbid you that tree, and tell
007:023	if Thou forgive us **not** and bestow **not**
007:023	and bestow **not** upon us Thy Mercy, we shall
007:027	Let **not** Satan seduce you, in the same
007:028	do ye say of Allah what ye know **not**?"
007:031	for Allah loveth **not** the wasters.
007:031	eat and drink: but waste **not** by excess, for
007:034	**not** an hour can they cause delay, nor (an hour)
007:038	but this ye do **not** understand.
007:043	had it **not** been for the guidance of Allah:
007:046	"Peace be upon you": they have **not** entered it,
007:047	send us **not** to the company of the wrong-doers."
007:049	"Behold! are these **not** the men whom
007:055	For Allah loveth **not** those who trespass
007:056	Do **not** mischief on the earth, after it
007:062	and I know from Allah something that ye know **not**.
007:065	Will ye **not** fear (Allah)?"
007:072	and did **not** believe.
007:079	but ye love **not** good counsellors!"
007:086	"And squat **not** on every road, breathing
007:087	and a party which does **not** believe,
007:095	while they realized **not** (their peril).
007:100	so that they could **not** hear?
007:100	is it **not** a guiding (lesson) that, if We
007:101	but they would **not** believe what they
007:102	**not** men (true) to their covenant:
007:131	but most of them do **not** understand!
007:142	do right, and follow **not** the way
007:146	they will **not** believe in them; and if
007:146	they will **not** adopt it as the Way; but if
007:148	having lowing sound did they **not** see that it could
007:149	they said: "If our Lord have **not** mercy upon us
007:150	Make **not** the enemies rejoice over my misfortune,
007:163	they came **not**: thus did We make a trial
007:169	Will ye **not** understand?
007:169	that they would **not** ascribe to Allah
007:169	Was **not** the Covenant of the Book
007:172	"Am I **not** your Lord (who cherishes
007:179	and ears wherewith they hear **not**.
007:179	eyes wherewith they see **not**, and ears
007:179	They have hearts wherewith they understand **not**,
007:184	Their Companion is **not** seized with madness: he is
007:184	Do they **not** reflect?
007:185	(Do they **not** see) that it may well be
007:187	is with Allah (alone), but most men know **not**."
007:193	If ye call them to guidance, they will **not** obey:
007:198	If thou call them to guidance, they hear **not**.
007:198	looking at thee, but they see **not**.
007:203	If thou bring them **not** a revelation, they say:
007:203	they say: "Why hast thou **not** got it together?"
007:205	and be **not** thou of those who are unheedful.
007:206	disdain **not** to worship Him: they glorify
008:017	It is **not** ye who slew them; it was Allah:
008:017	it was **not** thy act, but Allah's: in order
008:019	**Not** the least good will your
008:020	and His Messenger, and turn **not** away from him
008:021	"We hear," but listen **not**:
008:022	and the dumb,-those who understand **not**.
008:025	**not** in particular (only) those of you who do wrong:
008:027	O ye that believe! betray **not** the trust

NOT (continued)

008:033 But Allah was **not** going to send them
008:034 but most of them do **not** understand.
008:034 the Sacred Mosque-and they are **not** its guardians?
008:034 that Allah should **not** punish them, when they
008:047 And be **not** like those who started from their
008:048 lo! I see what ye see **not**; lo! I
008:055 they will **not** believe.
008:056 every time, and they have **not** the fear (of Allah).
008:058 for Allah loveth **not** the treacherous.
008:059 Let **not** the Unbelievers think that they
008:060 and others besides, whom ye may **not** know, but
008:060 unto you, and ye shall **not** be treated unjustly.
008:063 **not** if thou hadst spent all that is in the earth,
008:067 It is **not** fitting for a Prophet that he
008:068 Had it **not** been for a previous ordainment
008:072 who believed but did **not** emigrate ye owe
009:004 have **not** subsequently failed you in aught, nor
009:004 (But the treaties are) **not** dissolved with those
009:008 over you, they respect **not** in you the ties
009:010 In a Believer they respect **not** the ties
009:013 Will ye **not** fight people who violated
009:016 alone while Allah has **not** yet known those
009:017 It is **not** for such as join gods with Allah,
009:019 and Allah guides **not** those who do wrong.
009:019 They are **not** equal in the sight of Allah: and
009:023 O ye who believe! Take **not** for protectors
009:024 His decision: and Allah guides **not** the rebellious.
009:026 and sent down forces which ye saw **not**: He punished
009:028 are unclean; so let them **not**, after this
009:029 Fight those who believe **not** in Allah nor the
009:032 but Allah will **not** allow but that His light
009:034 and spend it **not** in the Way of Allah: announce
009:036 that is the right religion so wrong **not** yourselves therein,
009:037 But Allah guideth **not** those who reject Faith.
009:039 but Him ye would **not** harm in the
009:040 with forces which ye saw **not**, and humbled
009:040 If ye help **not** (the Prophet), (it is no matter):
009:045 who believe **not** in Allah and the Last Day,
009:047 they would **not** have added to your (strength)
009:049 "Grant me exemption and draw me **not** into trial."
009:049 Have they **not** fallen into trial
009:053 willingly or unwillingly: **not** from you will it
009:054 are **not** accepted are: that they reject Allah
009:054 that they come **not** to prayer save lazily and that
009:055 Let **not** their wealth nor their children
009:056 but they are **not** of you: yet they
009:058 they are pleased, but if **not**, behold!
009:063 Know they **not** that for those who oppose
009:070 It is **not** Allah Who wrongs
009:070 Hath **not** the story reached them of those
009:078 Know they **not** that Allah doth know their secret
009:080 Whether thou ask for their forgiveness, or **not**,
009:080 and Allah guideth **not** those who are
009:080 for their forgiveness, Allah will **not** forgive them:
009:081 they said, "Go **not** forth in the heat."
009:087 their hearts are sealed and so they understand **not**.
009:093 so they know **not**.
009:094 we shall **not** believe you: Allah hath
009:096 Allah is **not** pleased with those who disobey.
009:101 thou knowest them **not**: We know them: twice shall
009:104 Know they **not** that Allah doth accept repentance
009:109 And Allah guideth **not** people that do wrong.

NOT (continued)

009:113 It is **not** fitting, for the Prophet and those
009:115 And Allah will **not** mislead a people after He
009:120 from an enemy: for Allah suffereth **not** the reward
009:120 It was **not** fitting for the people of Madinah
009:122 It is **not** for the Believers to go forth together:
009:126 Yet they turn **not** in repentance, and they
009:126 See they **not** that they are tried
009:127 for they are a people that understand **not**.
010:003 will you **not** receive admonition?
010:007 and those who heed **not** Our Signs,-
010:007 Those who rest **not** their hope on their
010:011 But We leave those who rest **not** their hope
010:013 but they would **not** believe!
010:015 those who rest **not** their hope on their
010:015 Say: "It is **not** for me, of my own
010:016 I should **not** have rehearsed it to you, nor should
010:016 I tarried amongst you: will ye **not** then understand?"
010:018 what can hurt them **not** nor profit them, and they
010:018 of something He knows **not**, in the
010:019 Had it **not** been for a Word
010:020 They say: "Why is **not** a Sign sent down
010:024 as if it had **not** flourished only the day before!
010:028 "It was **not** us that ye worshipped!"
010:031 Say, "Will ye **not** then show piety (to Him)?"
010:033 verily they will **not** believe.
010:035 he who finds **not** guidance (himself) unless he is guided?
010:037 This Qur'an is **not** such as can be produced by
010:040 believe therein, and some who do **not**:
010:043 the blind,-even though they will **not** see?
010:044 Verily Allah will **not** deal unjustly with
010:047 and they will **not** be wronged.
010:049 **not** an hour can they cause delay,
010:049 **not** (an hour) can they advance (it in anticipation).
010:055 Is it **not** (the case) that to Allah belongeth
010:055 Is it **not** (the case) that Allah's promise
010:055 Yet most of them do **not** understand.
010:061 And **not** the smallest and **not** the greatest
010:065 Let **not** their speech grieve thee: for all
010:068 for this! Say ye about Allah what ye know **not**?
010:071 so your plan be **not** to you dark and dubious.
010:073 those who were warned (but heeded **not**)!
010:074 but they would **not** believe what they had
010:077 But sorcerers will **not** prosper."
010:078 But **not** we shall believe in you!"
010:081 of no effect: for Allah prospereth **not** the work
010:085 Our Lord! make us **not** a trial for those
010:088 so they will **not** believe until they see
010:089 and follow **not** the path of those who know **not**."
010:096 of thy Lord hath been verified would **not** believe-
010:100 on those who will **not** understand.
010:101 profit those who believe **not**.
010:104 (behold!) I worship **not** what ye worship
010:108 and I am **not** (set) over you
011:011 **Not** so do those who show patience and constancy,
011:012 lest they say, "Why is **not** a treasure sent down
011:012 sent down unto him, or why does **not** an angel
011:014 answer **not** your (call), know ye
011:017 meeting-place. Be **not** then in doubt thereon:
011:017 thy Lord: yet many among men do **not** believe!
011:020 They could **not** hear, nor could they see!
011:020 They will **not** escape in earth, nor have
011:024 Will ye **not** them take heed?

NOT (continued)

011:029	but I will **not** drive away (in contempt)
011:030	them away? Will ye **not** then take heed?
011:031	"I tell you **not** that with me are the
011:031	will **not** grant them (all) that is good:
011:033	ye will **not** be able to frustrate it!
011:042	and be **not** with the Unbelievers!"
011:046	So ask **not** of Me that of which thou hast
011:046	He said: "O Noah! he is **not** of thy family: for his
011:051	created Me: will ye **not** then understand?
011:052	so turn ye **not** back in sin!"
011:053	hast thou brought us, and we are **not** the ones
011:056	and your Lord! There is **not** a moving creature,
011:057	and you will **not** harm Him in the least. For my
011:065	(behold) there is a promise **not** to be belied!"
011:070	They said: "Fear **not**: we have been sent
011:070	he saw their hands **not** reaching towards the (meal),
011:076	O Abraham! seek **not** this. The decree
011:078	and cover me **not** with shame about my guests!
011:078	my guests! Is there **not** among you a single
011:081	time appointed: is **not** the morning nigh?"
011:081	and let **not** any of you look back: but thy
011:084	And give **not** short measure or weight: I see you
011:085	their due: commit **not** evil in the land with intent
011:086	But I am **not** set over you to keep watch!"
011:088	I wish **not**, in opposition to you, to do
011:089	"And O my people! let **not** my dissent (from you)
011:091	Were it **not** for thy family, we should
011:091	thou sayest we do **not** understand! In fact
011:097	and the command of Pharaoh was no rightly (guide).
011:101	It was **not** We that wronged them: they wronged
011:109	Be **not** then in doubt as to what these men worship.
011:110	had it **not** been that a Word had gone forth
011:112	(unto Allah); and transgress **not** (from the Path):
011:113	And incline **not** to those who do wrong, or the
011:115	For verily Allah will **not** suffer the reward
011:118	but they will **not** cease to differ,
011:121	Say to those who do **not** believe: "Do whatever
011:123	and thy Lord is **not** unmindful of aught that ye do.
012:003	among those who knew it **not**.
012:005	relate **not** thy vision to thy brother, last they
012:010	Said one of them: "Slay **not** Joseph, but if
012:011	why dost thou **not** trust us with Joseph,-seeing we
012:013	devour him while ye attend no to him."
012:015	this affair while they perceive **not**."
012:021	but most among mankind know it **not**.
012:032	And now, if he doth **not** my bidding, he shall
012:037	of a people that believe **not** in Allah and that
012:038	and to mankind: yet most men are **not** grateful.
012:040	but Most men understand **not**.
012:044	and we are **not** skilled in the interpretation
012:053	"Nor do I absolve my own self (of blame):
012:056	and We suffer **not**, to be lost, the reward
012:058	knew them, but they knew him **not**.
012:059	see you **not** that I pay out full measure,
012:060	"Now if ye bring him **not** to me, ye shall
012:067	**Not** that I can profit you aught against Allah
012:067	enter **not** all by one gate: enter ye
012:068	it did **not** profit them in the least
012:068	but most men know **not**.
012:069	so grieve **not** at aught of their doings."
012:073	know that we came **not** to make mischief in the land,
012:076	He could **not** take his brother by the law

NOT (continued)

012:077	revealing **not** the secrets to them he (simply)
012:080	Therefore will I **not** leave this land until my
012:080	"Know ye **not** that your father did take an oath
012:081	and we could **not** well guard against the unseen!
012:086	and I know from Allah that which ye know **not**.
012:089	**not** knowing (what ye were doing)?"
012:094	nay, think me **not** a dotard."
012:096	to you, 'I know from Allah that which ye know **not**?"
012:096	clear sight. He said: "Did I **not** say to you,
012:106	And most of them believe **not** in Allah without associating
012:107	while they perceive **not**?
012:109	Do they **not** travel through the earth,
012:109	Will ye **not** then understand?
012:111	It is **not** a tale invented
013:001	but most men believe **not**.
013:007	And the Unbelievers say: "Why is **not** a Sign
013:014	their mouths but it reaches them **not**: for the
013:018	But those who respond **not** to Him,-even if
013:020	and fail **not** in their plighted word;
013:027	The Unbelievers say: "Why is **not** a Sign
013:031	Do **not** the Believers know,
013:031	Allah will **not** fail in His promise.
013:033	He knoweth **not** on earth, or is it
013:033	Nay! to those who believe **not**, their devising
013:036	and **not** to join partners with Him. Unto Him
013:041	See they **not** that We gradually reduce the land
014:004	We sent **not** a messenger except (to teach) in the
014:009	Has **not** the story reached you, (O people!),
014:011	It is **not** for us to bring you an authority
014:012	Why we should **not** put our trust on Allah.
014:017	yet will he **not** die:
014:019	Seest thou **not** that Allah created the
014:022	then reproach **not** me, but reproach
014:024	Seest thou **not** how Allah sets forth a parable?
014:028	Hast thou **not** turned thy thought to those
014:042	Think **not** that Allah doth **not** heed the deeds
014:043	their gaze returning **not** towards them, and their
014:044	"What! were ye **not** wont to swear aforetime
015:004	had **not** a term decreed and assigned beforehand.
015:007	"Why bringest thou **not** angels to us if it be
015:008	We send **not** the angels down except for just cause:
015:013	That they **not** believe in the Message,
015:020	for whose sustenance ye are **not** responsible.
015:021	And there is **not** a thing but its (sources and)
015:022	though ye are **not** the guardians of its stores.
015:031	**Not** so Iblis: he refused to be among those
015:032	reason for **not** being among those who
015:033	(Iblis) said: "I am **not** one to prostrate
015:053	They said: "Fear **not**! we give thee glad tidings
015:055	in truth; be **not** then in despair!"
015:068	Lut said: "These are my guests: disgrace me **not**:
015:069	"But fear Allah, and shame me **not**."
015:070	They said: "Did we **not** forbid thee (to speak)
015:085	We created **not** the heavens, the earth, and all
015:088	Strain **not** thine eyes.
016:001	the Command of Allah: seek ye **not** them to hasten
016:007	that ye could **not** (otherwise) reach except with
016:017	Is then He Who creates like one that creates **not**?
016:017	Will ye **not** receive admonition?
016:022	as to those who believe **not** in the Hereafter,
016:023	verily He loveth **not** the arrogant.
016:026	from directions they did **not** perceive.

NOT (continued)

016:033 But Allah wronged them **not**: nay, they wronged
016:035 we should **not** have worshipped aught but Him-
016:037 yet Allah guideth **not** such as He leaves to stray,
016:038 by Allah, that Allah will **not** raise up
016:038 but most among mankind know it **not**.
016:043 if ye realize this **not**, ask of those
016:045 or that the Wrath will **not** seize them
016:045 will **not** cause the earth to swallow them up,
016:046 Or that He may **not** call them to account in the
016:047 Or that He may **not** call them to account by a
016:048 Do they **not** look at Allah's creation. Among
016:051 Allah has said: "Take **not** (for worship) two gods:
016:056 And they (even) assign, to thing they do **not** know,
016:060 To those who believe **not** in the Hereafter,
016:061 just as they would **not** be able to anticipate
016:061 they would **not** be able to delay (the punishment)
016:061 their wrong-doing, He would **not** leave, on the
016:071 are **not** going to throw back their gifts to those
016:074 for Allah knoweth, and ye know **not**.
016:074 Invent **not** similitudes for Allah: for Allah
016:075 But most of them understand **not**.
016:079 Do they **not** look at the birds, held poised
016:091 and break **not** your oaths after ye have
016:092 And be **not** like a woman who breaks
016:094 And take **not** your oaths, to practice
016:101 but most of them understand **not**.
016:104 of Allah,-Allah will **not** guide them, and theirs
016:104 Those who believe **not** in the Signs of Allah,-
016:105 It is those who believe **not** in the Signs of
016:107 and Allah will **not** guide those who reject Faith.
016:116 But say **not**-for any false thing that your
016:120 in faith, and he joined **not** gods with Allah.
016:123 in Faith, and he joined **not** gods with Allah."
016:127 over them: and distress **not** thyself because
017:002 "Take **not** other than Me as Disposer
017:010 And to those who believe **not** in the Hereafter,
017:020 are **not** closed (to anyone).
017:022 Take **not** with Allah another god; or thou
017:023 old age in thy life, say **not** to them a word
017:026 but squander **not** (your wealth) in the manner
017:029 Make **not** thy hand tied (like a niggard's)
017:031 Kill **not** your children for fear of want:
017:033 but let him **not** exceed bounds in the matter
017:034 Come **not** nigh to the orphan's property
017:036 And pursue **not** that of which thou hast
017:037 for thou canst **not** rend the earth
017:039 Take **not**, with Allah, another object of worship,
017:044 there is **not** a thing but celebrates His praise;
017:044 and yet ye understand **not** how they declare
017:045 believe **not** in the Hereafter, a veil invisible:
017:054 We have **not** sent thee to be a disposer
017:058 There is **not** a population but We shall destroy
017:068 or that He will **not** send against you a violent
017:068 **not** cause you to be swallowed up beneath the
017:069 **not** send you back a second time to sea and send
017:071 will **not** be dealt with unjustly in the least.
017:074 And had We **not** given thee strength, thou wouldst
017:076 but in that case they would **not** have stayed
017:088 they could **not** produce the like thereof,
017:090 They say: "We shall **not** believe in thee,
017:093 No, we shall **not** even believe
017:099 See they **not** that Allah, Who created

NOT (continued)

017:107 Say: "Whether ye believe in it or **not**, it is
018:006 if they believe **not** in this Message.
018:011 (so that they heard **not**):
018:015 why do they **not** bring forward an authority
018:019 and let him **not** inform anyone about you.
018:022 Enter **not**, therefore, into controversies
018:028 and let **not** thine eyes pass beyond them,
018:030 shall **not** suffer to perish the reward of any
018:033 its produce, and failed **not** in the least therein:
018:035 "I deem **not** that this will ever perish,"
018:039 "Why didst thou **not**, as thou wentest into thy
018:048 We shall **not** fulfil the appointment made to you
018:049 placed before them: and **not** one will thy Lord
018:051 and the earth, **not** (even) their own creation:
018:051 I called them **not** to witness the creation
018:052 but they will **not** listen to them; and We
018:057 they should understand this **not**, and over
018:060 "I will **not** give up until I reach the junction
018:067 (The other) said: "Verily thou wilt **not** be able
018:072 He answered: "Did I **not** tell thee that thou canst
018:073 Moses said: "Rebuke me **not** for forgetting,
018:075 He answered: "Did I **not** tell thee that thou canst
018:076 keep me **not** in thy company: then wouldst
018:082 I did it **not** of my own accord.
019:010 although thou art **not** dumb."
019:014 and he was **not** overbearing or rebellious.
019:018 (come **not** near) if thou dost fear Allah."
019:020 and I am **not** unchaste?"
019:024 "Grieve **not**! for thy Lord hath provided
019:028 "O sister of Aaron! thy father was **not** a man
019:032 and **not** overbearing or unblest;
019:035 It is **not** befitting to (the majesty of) Allah
019:039 and they do **not** believe!
019:042 which heareth **not** and seeth **not**, and can
019:043 knowledge which hath **not** reached thee: so follow
019:044 "O my father! serve **not** Satan: for Satan
019:046 O Abraham? If thou forbear **not**, I will
019:048 I shall be **not** unblest."!
019:060 and will **not** be wronged in the least,-
019:062 They will **not** there hear any vain discourse,
019:064 (The angels say:) "We descend **not** but by
019:067 But does **not** man call to mind that We
019:071 **Not** one of you but will pass over it: this is,
019:083 Seest thou **not** that We have set Satans
019:092 For it is **not** consonant with the majesty
019:093 **Not** one of the beings in the heavens and the
020:002 We have **not** sent down the Qur'an to thee to be
020:016 "Therefore let **not** such as believe **not** therein
020:016 **not** therein but follow their own lust, divert thee
020:021 (Allah) said, "Seize it, and fear **not**: We shall
020:040 and she should **not** grieve.
020:042 with My Signs, and slacken **not**, either of
020:046 He said: "Fear **not**: for I am with you: I hear
020:047 the Children of Israel with us, and afflict them **not**:
020:058 tryst between us and thee which we shall **not** fail to keep-
020:061 forge **not** ye a lie against Allah, lest He
020:068 We said: "Fear **not**! for thou hast indeed
020:069 a magician's trick: and the magician succeeds **not**.
020:086 He said: "O my people! did **not** your Lord make a
020:087 They said: "We broke **not** the promise to thee,
020:089 Could they **not** see that it could **not** return them a word
020:091 They had said: "We will **not** cease to worship it,

NOT (continued)

020:094	Seize (me) **not** by my beard nor by
020:094	and thou didst **not** observe my word!'"
020:096	He replied: "I saw what they saw **not**: so I
020:097	a promise that will **not** fail: now look
020:097	'Touch me **not**'; and moreover (for a future penalty)
020:103	each other: "Ye tarried **not** longer than ten (days);"
020:104	will say: "Ye tarried **not** longer than a day!"
020:108	so that thou hearest **not** but murmuring.
020:110	or behind them: but they shall comprehend Him **not**.
020:114	Be **not** in haste with the Qur'an
020:116	but **not** Iblis: he refused.
020:117	so let him **not** get you both out of the Garden,
020:118	for thee **not** to go hungry nor to go naked,
020:123	will **not** lose his way, nor fall into misery.
020:127	and believes **not** in the Signs of his Lord:
020:128	Is it **not** a guidance to such men (to call
020:129	Had it **not** been for a Word that went forth
020:132	We ask thee **not** to provide sustenance: We provide
020:133	Has **not** a Clear Sign come to them of all
020:133	They say: "Why does he **not** bring us a Sign
021:001	their Reckoning: yet they heel **not** and they
021:006	(As to those) before them, **not** one of the towns
021:007	if ye know this **not**, ask of those
021:010	Will ye **not** then understand?
021:013	Flee **not**, but return to the good things of this
021:015	And that cry of theirs ceased **not**, till We
021:016	**Not** for (idle) sport did We create the heavens
021:019	are **not** too proud to serve Him, nor are
021:024	But most of them know **not** the Truth, and so
021:025	**Not** a messenger did We send before thee
021:027	They speak **not** before He speaks, and they
021:030	Will they **not** then believe?
021:030	Do **not** the Unbelievers see that the heavens
021:034	We granted **not** to any man before thee
021:036	they treat thee **not** except with ridicule.
021:037	so ask Me **not** to hasten them!
021:039	(the time) when they will **not** be able to ward
021:044	see they **not** that We gradually reduce the land
021:045	**not** hear the call, (even) when they are warned!
021:047	so that **not** a soul will be dealt with
021:065	that these (idols) do **not** speak!"
021:089	"O my Lord! leave me **not** without offspring,
021:094	and has Faith,-his endeavour will **not** be rejected:
021:095	that they shall **not** return,
021:099	they would **not** have got there! But each
021:102	**Not** the slightest sound will they hear of Hell:
021:107	We sent thee **not**, but as a mercy for all creatures.
021:109	but I know **not** whether that which ye are
021:111	"I know **not** but that it may be a trial for you,
022:002	a drunken riot, yet **not** drunk:
022:010	for verily Allah is **not** unjust to His servants.
022:015	If any think that Allah will **not** help him
022:018	Seest thou **not** that to Allah prostrate all things
022:026	"Associate **not** anything (in worship) with Me;
022:036	(beg **not** but) live in contentment, and such
022:037	It is **not** their meat nor their blood, that reaches
022:038	verily, Allah loveth **not** any that is unfaithful,
022:040	Did **not** Allah check one set of people
022:046	Truly it is **not** the eyes that are blind, but the
022:046	Do they **not** travel through the land, so that
022:047	But Allah will **not** fail in His promise.
022:055	Those who reject Faith will **not** cease to be

NOT (continued)

022:063	Seest thou **not** that Allah sends down
022:065	Seest thou **not** that Allah has made subject
022:067	let them **not** then dispute with thee on the matter,
022:070	Knowest thou **not** that Allah knows all that is in
022:074	No just estimate have they made of Allah:
023:023	will ye **not** fear (Him)?"
023:027	and address Me **not** in favour of the wrong-doers:
023:032	Will ye **not** fear (Him)?"
023:038	against Allah, but we are **not** the ones to believe
023:044	a people that will **not** believe!
023:056	Nay, they do **not** perceive.
023:059	Those who join **not** (in worship) partners with
023:065	"Groan **not** in supplication this day; for ye
023:065	for ye shall certainly **not** be helped by Us.
023:068	come to them that did **not** come to their
023:068	Do they **not** ponder over the Word (of Allah),
023:069	Or do they **not** recognize their Messenger,
023:074	And verily those who believe **not** in the Hereafter
023:076	but they humbled **not** themselves to their Lord,
023:080	of Night and Day: will ye **not** then understand?
023:085	Say: "Yet will ye **not** receive admonition?"
023:087	Say: "Will ye **not** then fear?"
023:088	but is **not** protected (of any)? (Say) if ye know."
023:094	"Then, O my Lord! put me **not** amongst the
023:105	"Were **not** My Signs rehearsed to you, and ye
023:108	and speak ye **not** to Me!
023:114	He will say: "Ye stayed **not** but a little,-
023:115	and that ye would **not** be brought back
023:117	shall **not** prosper.
024:002	a hundred stripes: let **not** compassion move you
024:004	and produce **not** four witnesses,
024:010	If it were **not** for God's grace and mercy on you,
024:011	think it **not** to be an evil to you;
024:012	Why did **not** the Believers-men and women-
024:013	Why did they **not** bring four witnesses to prove it?
024:013	to prove it? When they have **not** brought the
024:014	Were it **not** for the grace and mercy
024:016	"It is **not** right of us to speak of this:
024:016	And why did ye **not**, when ye heard
024:019	Allah knows, and ye know **not**.
024:020	Were it **not** for the grace and mercy of Allah
024:021	**not** one of you would ever have been pure:
024:021	and wrong: and were it **not** for the grace
024:021	O ye who believe! follow **not** Satan's footsteps:
024:022	Let **not** those among you who are endued with grace
024:022	do you **not** wish that Allah should forgive you?
024:027	enter **not** houses other than your own, until ye
024:028	enter **not** until permission is given to you:
024:029	to enter houses **not** used for living in,
024:031	and that they should **not** strike their feet
024:031	over their bosoms and **not** display their beauty
024:031	that they should **not** display their beauty
024:033	Let those who find **not** the wherewithal for
024:033	But force **not** your maids to prostitution when they
024:040	For any to whom Allah giveth **not** light, there in no light!
024:041	Seest thou **not** that it is Allah Whose praises
024:043	Seest thou **not** that Allah makes the clouds
024:047	turn away: they are **not** (really) Believers.
024:053	Say: "Swear ye **not**; obedience is
024:055	and **not** associate aught with Me.'
024:058	have **not** come of age ask your permission
024:058	it is **not** wrong for you or for them to move

NOT (continued)

024:060 provided they make **not** wanton display of their
024:062 they do **not** depart until they have asked
024:063 Deem **not** the summons of the Messenger
025:007 Why has **not** an angel been sent down to him
025:008 or why has he (**not**) a garden for enjoyment?"
025:008 "Or (why) has **not** a treasure been bestowed
025:014 "This day plead **not** for a single destruction:
025:018 "Glory to Thee! **not** meant was it for us that we should
025:021 to us, or (why) do we **not** see Our Lord?"
025:021 Those who do **not** hope to meet Us (for Judgment)
025:021 "Why are **not** the angels sent down to us,
025:032 "Why is **not** the Qur'an revealed to him
025:040 did they **not** then see it (with their own eyes)?
025:040 But they expect **not** to be raised again.
025:042 had it **not** been that we were constant to them!"-
025:045 Hast thou **not** seen how thy Lord?-doth prolong
025:052 Therefore listen **not** to the Unbelievers,
025:053 a partition that is **not** to be passed.
025:058 And put thy trust in Him Who lives and dies **not**;
025:067 are **not** extravagant and **not** niggardly,
025:068 Those who invoke **not**, with Allah, any other
025:068 except for just cause, **not** commit fornication;-
025:068 and any that does this (**not** only) meets punishment
025:073 droop **not** down at them as if they were deaf
025:077 "My Lord would **not** concern Himself with you
026:003 with grief, that they do **not** become Believers.
026:005 But there comes **not** to them a newly-revealed
026:007 Do they **not** look at the earth,-how many
026:008 but most of them do **not** believe.
026:011 "The people of Pharaoh: will they **not** fear Allah?"
026:013 And my tongue will **not** speak (plainly): so send
026:018 and didst thou **not** stay in our midst many years
026:018 (Pharaoh) said: "Did we **not** cherish thee as a
026:025 "Do ye **not** listen (to what he says)?"
026:067 but most of them do **not** believe.
026:077 **not** so the Lord and Cherisher of the Worlds;
026:087 "And let me **not** be in disgrace on the Day
026:103 but most of them do **not** believe.
026:106 "Will ye **not** fear (Allah)?
026:114 "I am **not** one to drive away those who believe.
026:116 They said: "If thou desist **not**, O Noah!
026:121 but most of them do **not** believe.
026:124 "Will ye **not** fear (Allah)?
026:136 be **not** among (our) Admonishers!
026:138 "And we are **not** the ones to receive Pains and
026:139 but most of them do **not** believe.
026:142 said to them: "Will you **not** fear (Allah)?
026:151 "And follow **not** the bidding of those
026:152 and mend **not** (their ways)."
026:156 "Touch her **not** with harm, lest the
026:158 but most of them do **not** believe.
026:161 "Will ye **not** fear (Allah)?
026:167 They said: "If thou desist **not**, O Lut!
026:173 on those who were admonished (but heeded **not**)!
026:174 but most of them do **not** believe.
026:177 "Will ye **not** fear (Allah)?
026:183 And withhold **not** things justly due to men,
026:190 but most of them do **not** believe.
026:197 Is it **not** a Sign to them that the learned
026:199 they would **not** have believed in it.
026:201 They will **not** believe in it until they see
026:202 of a sudden, while they perceive it **not**;

NOT (continued)

026:207 It will profit them **not** the enjoyment
026:210 The Satans did **not** bring it down:
026:211 It is **not** meant for them, nor is
026:213 So call **not** on any other god with Allah,
026:225 Seest thou **not** that they wander distracted
026:226 And that they say what they practice **not**?-
027:004 As to those who believe **not** in the Hereafter,
027:010 and retraced **not** his steps: "O Moses! "(it was said),
027:010 fear **not**: truly, in My presence, those called as
027:020 and he said: "Why is it I see **not** the Hoopoe?
027:022 But the Hoopoe tarried **not** far:
027:022 "I have compassed which thou has **not** compassed,
027:025 So that they worship **not** Allah Who brings forth
027:031 "'Be ye **not** arrogant against me, but come
027:041 those who are **not** rightly guided."
027:048 and would **not** reform.
027:049 'We were **not** present at the slaughter of his
027:050 even while they perceived it **not**.
027:058 on those who were admonished (but heeded **not**)!
027:060 and delight: it is **not** in your power to cause
027:061 Nay, most of them know **not**.
027:070 But grieve **not** over them, nor distress
027:080 Truly thou canst **not** cause the Dead to listen,
027:084 though ye comprehended **not** in knowledge, or what was
027:086 See they **not** that We have made the Night
027:093 and thy Lord is **not** unmindful of all that ye do.
028:007 but fear **not** nor grieve: for We
028:009 for me and for thee: slay him **not**. It may
028:009 And they perceived **not** (what they were doing)!
028:010 had We **not** strengthened her heart (with faith),
028:011 from a distance and they perceived **not**.
028:013 but most of them do **not** know.
028:013 that she might **not** grieve, and that
028:015 when its people were **not** watching: and he
028:019 and **not** to be one who sets things right!"
028:025 he said: "Fear thou **not**: (well) hast
028:027 But I intend **not** to place thee under a difficulty:
028:031 and fear **not**: for thou art of those who are secure.
028:031 and retraced **not** his steps: "O Moses
028:035 so they shall **not** be able to touch you: with Our
028:037 that the wrong-doers will **not** prosper."
028:039 they would **not** have to return to Us!"
028:044 Thou wast **not** on the Western Side when We
028:045 over them; but thou wast **not** a dweller
028:047 why didst Thou **not** send us a messenger?
028:047 If (We had) **not** (sent thee to the Quraish),
028:048 "Why are **not** (Signs) sent to him, like those
028:048 Do they **not** then reject (the Signs) which were
028:050 For Allah guides **not** people given to wrong-doing.
028:050 But if they hearken **not** to thee, know that
028:055 peace be to you: we seek **not** the ignorant."
028:056 It is true thou wilt **not** be able to guide
028:057 Have We **not** established for them
028:057 But most of them understand **not**.
028:060 will ye **not** then be wise?
028:063 It was **not** us they worshipped."
028:064 but they will **not** listen to them; and they
028:066 will **not** be able (even) to question each other.
028:071 Will ye **not** then hearken?
028:072 Night in which ye can rest? Will ye **not** then see?
028:076 "Exult **not**, for Allah loveth **not** those who
028:077 for Allah loves **not** those who do mischief."

NOT (continued)

028:077	to thee, and seek **not** (occasions for) mischief
028:078	Did he **not** know that Allah had destroyed,
028:078	But the wicked are **not** called (immediately)
028:081	and he had **not** (the least little) party to
028:082	Had it **not** been that Allah was gracious to us,
028:083	give to those who intend **not** high-handedness
028:086	And thou hadst **not** expected that the Book
028:086	therefore lend **not** thou support in any way
028:087	and be **not** of the company of these who
028:088	And call **not**, besides Allah, on another
029:002	and that they will **not** be tested?
029:008	no knowledge, obey them **not**.
029:010	Does **not** Allah know best all that
029:019	See they **not** how Allah originates creation,
029:022	"**Not** on earth nor in heaven will ye be able
029:033	"Fear thou **not**, nor grieve: we are
029:039	on the earth; yet they cold **not** overreach (Us).
029:040	it was **not** Allah Who wronged them: they wronged
029:046	And dispute ye **not** with the People of the Book,
029:048	And thou wast **not** (able) to recite a Book
029:050	Yet they say: "Why are **not** Signs sent down
029:051	And is it **not** enough for them that We have
029:053	had it **not** been for a term (of respite)
029:053	reach them,-of a sudden, while they perceive **not**!
029:060	that carry **not** their own sustenance?
029:063	But most of them understand **not**.
029:067	Do they **not** then see that We have made
029:068	Is there **not** a home in Hell
030:006	but most men understand **not**.
030:008	Do they **not** reflect in their own minds?
030:008	**Not** but in truth and for a term appointed,
030:009	Do they **not** travel through the earth, and see
030:009	it was **not** Allah Who wronged them, but they
030:030	but most among mankind know **not**.
030:031	and be **not** ye among those who join gods with Allah,-
030:037	See they **not** that Allah enlarges the provision
030:045	For He loves **not** those who reject Faith.
030:052	So verily thou canst **not** make the dead to hear,
030:055	swear that they tarried **not** but an hour:
030:056	the Day of Resurrection: but ye-ye did **not** know!"
030:059	of those who understand **not**.
031:007	as if he heard them **not**,
031:013	admonishing him "O my son! join **not** in worship
031:015	obey them **not**; yet bear them company in this
031:018	"And swell **not** thy cheek (for pride) at men.
031:018	for Allah loveth **not** any arrogant boaster.
031:020	Do ye **not** see that Allah has subjected to your
031:023	let **not** his rejection grieve thee: to Us
031:025	But most of them know **not**.
031:027	to its (supply), yet would **not** the Words of Allah
031:029	Seest thou **not** that Allah merges Night into Day
031:031	Seest thou **not** that the ships sail through the
031:033	let **not** then this present life deceive you,
032:004	will lye **not** then receive admonition?
032:023	be **not** then in doubt of its reaching
032:026	do they **not** then listen?
032:026	Does it **not** teach them a lesson, how many
032:027	And do they **not** see that We do drive Rain
032:027	Have they **not** the vision?
033:001	and hearken **not** to the Unbelievers and the
033:004	Allah has **not** made for any man two hearts
033:005	But if ye know **not** their father's names,

NOT (continued)

033:009	and forces that ye saw **not**: but Allah
033:013	though they were **not** exposed:
033:015	with Allah **not** to turn their backs, and a
033:016	Say: "Running away will **not** profit you if ye
033:018	but come **not** to the fight except for just
033:020	have **not** withdrawn; and if the Confederates
033:027	ye had **not** frequented (before).
033:032	be **not** too complaisant of speech, lest one
033:032	O Consorts of the Prophet! ye are **not** like any
033:033	and make **not** a dazzling display, like that
033:036	It is **not** fitting for a Believer, man or woman,
033:040	Muhammad is **not** the father of any of your men,
033:048	And obey **not** (the behests) of the Unbelievers
033:050	and **not** for the Believers (at large); We know
033:052	It is **not** lawful for thee (to marry more)
033:053	but Allah is **not** shy (to tell you) the truth.
033:053	(and then) **not** (so early as) to wait
033:053	O ye who Believe! enter **not** the Prophet's houses,-
033:059	be known (as such) and **not** molested. And Allah
033:060	in the City, desist **not**, We shall
033:060	against them: then will they **not** be able to
033:069	O ye who believe! be ye **not** like those who
034:003	the unseen,-from Whom is **not** hidden the least
034:008	Nay, it is those who believe **not** in the Hereafter,
034:009	See they **not** what is before them and behind
034:014	they would **not** have tarried in the humiliating
034:022	they have no power,-**not** the weight of an atom,-
034:025	Say: "Ye shall **not** be questioned as to our sins,
034:028	We have **not** sent thee but as a (Messenger)
034:028	but most men understand **not**.
034:031	the arrogant ones: "Had it **not** been for you,
034:034	"We believe **not** in the (message) with which
034:036	to whom He pleases, but most men know **not**."
034:037	It is **not** your wealth nor your sons, that will
034:041	Thou art our protector-**not** them. Nay, but
034:044	But We had **not** given them Books which they
034:045	(the Truth); these have **not** received a tenth
034:046	your Companion is **not** possessed: he is
034:049	and Falsehood showeth **not** its face and will
035:005	is true, let **not** then this present life deceive
035:008	So let **not** thy soul be vested in regret
035:013	besides Him own **not** a straw.
035:014	they will **not** listen to your call, and if
035:018	**not** the least portion of it can be carried
035:019	The blind and the seeing are **not** alike;
035:022	to hear; but thou canst **not** make those to hear
035:027	Seest thou **not** that Allah sends down
035:037	Did we **not** give you long enough life so that
035:037	**not** the (deeds) we used to do!"-"Did we **not**
035:041	There is none-**not** one-can sustain them thereafter:
035:044	Do they **not** travel through the earth, and see
035:045	He would **not** leave on the back of the (earth)
036:006	were **not** warned, and who therefore remain
036:007	for they do **not** believe.
036:010	admonish them: they will **not** believe.
036:010	admonish them or thou do **not** admonish them:
036:018	desist **not**, we will certainly stone you,
036:022	"Why should **not** I serve Him Who created me,
036:028	And We sent **not** down against his People,
036:030	There comes **not** a messenger to them
036:031	**Not** to them will they return:
036:031	See they **not** how many generations before them

NOT (continued)

036:035   of this (artistry): it was **not** their hands
036:035   will they **not** then give thanks?
036:040   It is **not** permitted to the Sun to catch
036:046   **Not** a Sign comes to them from among
036:049   They will **not** (have to) wait for aught but a
036:054   Then, on that Day, **not** a soul will be wronged
036:060   "Did I **not** enjoin on you, O ye children of Adam,
036:060   that ye should **not** worship Satan; for that he was to you
036:062   Did ye **not**, then understand?
036:068   will they **not** then understand?
036:069   We have **not** instructed the (Prophet) in Poetry,
036:071   See they **not** that it is We Who have created
036:073   Will they **not** then be grateful?
036:075   They have **not** the power to help them: and they
036:076   Let **not** their speech, then, grieve thee.
036:077   Doth **not** man see that it is We Who created
036:081   "Is **not** He Who created the heavens and the
037:008   (So) they should **not** strain their ears in the
037:025   that ye help **not** each other?'"
037:057   "Had it **not** been for the Grace of my Lord,
037:058   "Is it (the case) that we shall **not** die,
037:059   and that we shall **not** be punished?"
037:091   and said, "Will ye **not** eat (of the offerings before you)?
037:092   "What is the matter with you that ye speak **not**?"
037:124   "Will ye **not** fear (Allah)?
037:138   And by night: will ye **not** understand?
037:143   Had it **not** been that he (repented and)
037:155   Will ye **not** then receive admonition?
037:160   **Not** (so do) the servants of Allah, the chosen ones.
037:164   (The angels) "**Not** one of us but has a place appointed:
037:177   who were warned (and heeded **not**)!
038:008   Nay, they have **not** yet tasted My Punishment!
038:014   **Not** one (of them) but rejected the messengers,
038:022   with truth, and treat us **not** with injustice,
038:022   they said: "Fear **not**: We are two disputants,
038:024   each other: **not** so do those who believe
038:027   **Not** without purpose did We create
038:035   will **not** belong to another after me: for Thou
038:044   and strike therewith: and break **not** (thy oath)."
038:062   that we see **not** men who we used to number
038:074   **Not** so Iblis: he was haughty, and became
039:003   But Allah guides **not** such as are
039:003   Is it **not** to Allah that sincere devotion is due?
039:005   Is **not** He the Exalted in Power-He Who
039:007   but He liketh **not** ingratitude from His servants:
039:009   hope in the Mercy of his Lord-(like one who does **Not**)?
039:009   those who know and those who do **not** know?
039:017   Those who eschew Taghut and fall **not** into its worship,
039:021   Seest thou **not** that Allah sends down rain
039:025   from directions they did **not** perceive.
039:032   Is there **not** in Hell an abode
039:036   Is **not** Allah enough for His servant?
039:037   Is **not** Allah Exalted in Power, Lord of Retribution?
039:042   and those that die **not** (He takes) during their
039:045   the hearts of those who believe **not** in the
039:049   but most of them understand **not**!
039:051   them (too), and they shall **not** escape!
039:052   Know they **not** that Allah enlarges the provision
039:053   Despair **not** of the Mercy of Allah: for Allah
039:054   comes on you: after that ye shall **not** be helped.
039:055   of a sudden, while ye perceive **not**!-
039:060   is there **not** in Hell an abode for the Haughty?

NOT (continued)

039:069   and they will **not** be wronged (in the least).
039:071   "Did **not** messengers come to you from among
040:004   Let **not**, then, their strutting about through the
040:016   **not** a single thing concerning them
040:020   will **not** (be in a position) to judge at all.
040:021   Do they **not** travel through the earth and see
040:027   one who believes **not** in the Day of Account!"
040:028   truly Allah **guides not** one who transgresses and lies!
040:034   but ye ceased **not** to doubt of the (mission)
040:040   "He that works evil will **not** be requited but by
040:050   They will say: "Did there **not** come to you
040:057   than the creation of men: yet most men know **not**.
040:058   **Not** equal are the blind and those who
040:059   therein is no doubt: yet most men believe **not**.
040:069   Seest thou **not** those that dispute concerning
040:074   we invoked **not**, of old, anything (that had real existence)."
040:078   It was **not** (possible) for any messenger to bring a Sign
040:078   and some whose story We have **not** related to thee.
040:082   Do they **not** travel through the earth and see
040:085   was **not** going to profit them.
041:004   and so they hear **not**.
041:007   Those who pay **not** zakat, and who
041:015   What! did they **not** see that Allah,
041:022   that Allah knew **not** many of the things that ye
041:022   "Ye did **not** seek to hide yourselves, lest your
041:024   their suit shall **not** be granted.
041:026   The Unbelievers say: "Listen **not** to this Qur'an,
041:030   to time): "Fear ye **not**!" (they suggest),
041:037   Prostrate **not** to the sun and the moon,
041:040   are **not** hidden from Us.
041:041   to them (are **not** hidden from Us).
041:043   Nothing is said to thee that was **not** said to the
041:044   "Why are **not** its verses explained in detail?
041:044   and for those who believe **not**, there is
041:045   Had it **not** been for a Word
041:047   "We do assure Thee **not** one of us can bear witness!"
041:049   Man does **not** weary of asking for good (things),
041:050   I think **not** that the Hour (of Judgment)
041:053   Is it **not** enough that thy Lord doth witness all things?
042:006   and thou art **not** the disposer
042:014   Had it **not** been for a Word that went forth before
042:018   who believe **not** in it: those who
042:021   Had it **not** been for the Decree
042:039   (are **not** cowed but) help and defend themselves.
042:040   from Allah: for (Allah) loveth **not** those who
042:048   We have **not** sent thee as a guard over them.
042:051   It is **not** fitting for a man that Allah
042:052   to thee: thou knewest **not** (before) what was
043:020   we should **not** have worshipped such (deities)!"
043:031   Also, they say: "Why is **not** this Qur'an sent down
043:033   And were it **not** that (all) men might become
043:051   saying: "O my people! Does **not** the dominion
043:051   What! see ye **not** then?
043:052   "Am I **not** better than this (Moses), who is
043:053   on him, or (why) come (**not**) with him
043:053   "Then why are **not** gold bracelets bestowed on him,
043:062   Let **not** the Satan hinder you: for he
043:066   of a sudden, while they perceive **not**?
043:080   Or do they think that We hear **not** their secrets
043:088   Truly these are a people who believe **not**!"
044:019   "And be **not** arrogant as against Allah: for I
044:021   "If ye believe me **not**, at least keep

NOT (continued)

044:035 and we shall **not** be raised again.
044:038 We created **not** the heavens, the earth,
044:039 We created them **not** except for just ends:
044:039 just ends: but most of them do **not** know.
045:008 as if he had **not** heard them: then announce
045:014 to forgive those who do **not** hope for
045:018 of those who know **not**.
045:018 and follow **not** the desires of those
045:023 Will ye **not** then receive admonition?
045:026 there is no doubt": but most men **not** know.
045:031 "Were **not** Our Signs rehearsed to you?
045:032 ye used to say, 'We know **not** what is the Hour:
045:035 therefore, they shall **not** be taken out thence,
046:003 We created **not** the heavens and the earth and all
046:005 such as will **not** answer him to the Day of Judgment,
046:009 Say: "I am **not** an innovation among the messengers,
046:010 Allah guides **not** a people unjust."
046:011 good thing, (such men) would **not** have gone to it
046:011 and seeing that they guide **not** themselves thereby,
046:026 We have **not** given to you (ye Quraish)!
046:032 "If any does **not** hearken to the one who invites
046:033 See they **not** that Allah, Who created
046:034 (they will be asked), "Is this **not** the Truth?"
046:035 (it will be) as if they had **not** tarried more
047:010 Do they **not** travel through the earth, and see
047:020 "Why is **not** a Sura sent down (for us)?"
047:024 Do they **not** then earnestly seek to understand
047:029 will **not** bring to light all their rancor?
047:032 to them, will **not** harm Allah in the least,
047:033 and make **not** vain your deeds!
047:034 then die disbelieving,-Allah will **not** forgive them.
047:035 Be **not** weary and faint-hearted crying for peace,
047:036 and will **not** ask you (to give up) your possession.
047:038 then they would **not** be like you!
048:011 what is **not** in their hearts. Say: "Who then
048:013 And if any believe **not** in Allah and His Messenger,
048:015 Say: "**Not** thus will ye follow us: Allah has
048:017 nor on one ill (if he joins **not** the war): but he
048:021 which are **not** within your power, but which
048:025 whom ye did **not** know that ye were trampling down
048:025 Had there **not** been believing men and believing women
048:027 ye knew **not**, and He granted, besides this,
049:001 O ye who believe! put **not** yourselves forward
049:002 become vain and ye perceive **not**.
049:002 O ye who believe! raise **not** your voices
049:011 has believed: and those who do **not** desist are
049:011 O ye who believe! let **not** some men among you
049:012 and spy **not** on each other, nor speak
049:013 know each other (**not** that ye may despise each other).
049:014 He will **not** belittle aught of your deeds:
049:014 our wills to Allah,' for **not** yet has Faith
049:017 Say, "Count **not** your Islam as a favour upon me:
050:006 Do they **not** look at the sky above them?-
050:018 **Not** a word does he utter but there is a
050:027 "Our Lord! I did **not** make him transgress, but he
050:028 He will say: "Dispute **not** with each other
050:029 "The Word changes **not** before Me, and I
050:029 and I do **not** the least injustice to My Servants."
050:045 and thou art **not** one to compel them by force.
051:021 As also in your own selves: will ye **not** then see?
051:027 He said, "Will ye **not** eat?"
051:028 They said, "Fear **not**," and they gave him

NOT (continued)

051:028 (When they did **not** eat), He conceived
051:036 But We found **not** there any except one
051:045 Then they could **not** even stand (on their feet),
051:051 And make **not** another an object of worship
051:054 So turn away from them: **not** thine is the blame.
051:059 then let them **not** ask Me to hasten (that portion)!
052:015 "Is this then a magic, or is it ye that do **not** see?
052:016 whether ye bear it with patience, or **not**:
052:026 we were **not** without fear for the sake of our people.
052:047 but most of them know **not**.
053:027 Those who believe **not** in the Hereafter,
053:032 Therefore hold **not** yourselves purified: He knows
053:036 Nay, is he **not** acquainted with what is in
053:060 And will ye laugh and **not** weep,-
054:005 but (the preaching of) Warners profits them **not**.
055:008 In order that ye may **not** transgress (due) balance.
055:009 and fall **not** short in the balance.
055:020 which they do **not** transgress:
055:033 pass ye! **not** without authority shall
056:033 Whose season is **not** limited, nor (supply)
056:057 why will ye **not** admit the Truth?
056:060 your common lot, and We are **not** to be frustrated
056:061 creating you (again) in (Forms) that ye know **not**.
056:062 why then do ye **not** take heed?
056:070 then why do ye **not** give thanks?
056:083 Then why do ye **not** (intervene) when (the soul
056:085 But We are nearer to him than ye, and yet see **not**,-
056:086 Then why do you **not**,-if you are
057:008 How is it with you that you **not** believe in Allah?-
057:010 **Not** equal among you are those who spent (freely)
057:010 spend **not** in the cause of Allah?-For to Allah
057:014 (Those without) will call out, "Were we **not** with you?"
057:016 **not** become like those to whom was given The Book
057:016 Has **not** the time arrived for the Believers
057:023 In order that ye may **not** despair over matters
057:023 **not** any vainglorious boaster,-
057:027 We did **not** prescribe for them: (We commanded)
057:027 but that they did **not** foster as they
058:004 And if any has **not** (the means), he should
058:007 Seest thou **not** that Allah doth know (all) that is
058:007 There is **not** a secret consultation
058:008 they salute thee, **not** as Allah salutes thee,
058:008 "Why does **not** Allah Punish us for our words?"
058:008 Seest thou **not** those who were forbidden secret
058:009   do it **not** for iniquity and hostility,
058:012 But if ye find **not** (the wherewithal),
058:013 If, then, ye do **not** so, and Allah forgives you,
058:014 Seest thou **not** those who turn (in friendship)
058:022 Thou wilt **not** find any people who believe
059:003 And had it **not** been that Allah has decreed
059:007 in order that it may **not** (Merely) make a circuit
059:010 and leave **not**, in our hearts, rancor (or sense of injury)
059:011 Hast thou **not** observed the Hypocrites say to
059:014 They will **not** fight you (even) together, except in
059:019 And be ye **not** like those who forgot Allah; and He
059:020 **Not** equal are the Companions of the Fire and the
060:001 O ye who believe! take **not** My enemies and yours
060:004 and Him alone": but **not** when Abraham said to
060:005 "Our Lord! Make us **not** a (test and) trial for
060:008 Allah forbids you **not**, with regard to those who
060:008 to those who fight you **not** for (your) Faith
060:010 then send them **not** back to the Unbelievers.

NOT (continued)

060:010 They are **not** lawful (wives) for the Unbelievers,
060:010 But hold **not** to the ties (marriage contract) of
060:012 that they will **not** steal, that they will **not** commit adultery
060:012 that they **will not** utter slander, intentionally forging
060:012 that they will **not** kill their kill their children,
060:012 that they will **not** associate in worship any other thing
060:012 and that they will **not** disobey thee in any just matter,-
060:013 O ye who believe! turn **not** (for friendship)
061:002 O ye who believe! why say ye that which ye do **not**?
061:003 of Allah that ye say that which ye do **not**.
061:005 For Allah guides **not** those who are rebellious
061:007 And Allah guides **not** those who do wrong.
062:003 who have **not** already joined them:
062:005 and Allah guides **not** people who do wrong.
062:005 which carries huge tomes (but understands them **not**).
063:003 therefore they understand **not**.
063:006 Truly Allah guides **not** rebellious transgressors.
063:006 Allah will **not** forgive them.
063:006 for their forgiveness or **not**.
063:007 but the Hypocrites understand **not**.
063:008 but the Hypocrites know **not**.
063:009 O ye who believe! let **not** your riches or your
063:010 Why didst thou **not** give me respite for a
064:005 Has **not** the story reached you, of those
064:007 will **not** be raised up (for Judgment).
065:001 your Lord: and turn them **not** out of their houses,
065:001 (own) soul: thou knowest **not** if perchance Allah
065:006 according to your means: annoy them **not**, so as
065:008 did We **not** then call to account,-to severe
066:006 who flinch **not** (from executing) the Commands they
066:008 the Day that Allah will **not** permit to be
067:010 our intelligence, we should **not** (now) be among
067:014 Should He **not** know,-He that created?
067:016 is in heaven will **not** cause you to be swallowed
067:017 is in Heaven will **not** send against you a violent
067:019 Do they **not** observe the birds above them,
068:002 Thou art **not**, by the grace of thy Lord, mad or
068:008 So obey **not** to those who deny (the Truth).
068:010 Obey **not** every mean,-swearer,
068:024 "Let **not** a single indigent person break in upon
068:028 "Did I **not** say to you, 'Why **not** glorify (Allah)?'"
068:042 to prostrate, but they shall **not** be able,-
068:044 from directions they perceive **not**.
068:048 thy Lord, and be **not** like the Companion
068:049 Had **not** Grace from His Lord reached him, he would
069:018 **not** an act of yours that ye hide will be hidden.
069:025 "Ah! would that my record had **not** been given to me!
069:033 "This was he that would **not** believe in Allah Most High,
069:034 "And would **not** encourage the feeding
069:039 And what ye see **not**,
069:041 It is **not** the word of a poet: little it
070:022 **Not** so those devoted to Prayer:-
070:028 For their Lord's punishment is **not** a thing
070:030 hands possess,-for (then) they are **not** to be blamed,
070:041 and We are **not** to be defeated
071:013 that ye are **not** conscious of Allah's majesty,-
071:015 "`See ye **not** how Allah has created the seven
071:023 'Abandon **not** your gods: abandon neither Wadd nor
071:026 Leave **not** of the Unbelievers, a single
072:002 We shall **not** join (in worship) any (gods)
072:007 ye thought, that Allah would **not** raise up any one
072:010 'And we understand **not** whether ill is intended

NOT (continued)

072:018 for Allah (alone): so invoke **not** any one along
072:020 and I join **not** with Him any (false god)."
072:021 Say: "It is **not** in my power to cause you harm,
072:025 Say: "I know **not** whether the (Punishment) which ye
073:002 Stand (to pray) by night, but **not** all night,-
074:043 They will say: "We were **not** of those who prayed;
074:053 By no means! But they fear **not** the Hereafter.
075:016 Move **not** thy tongue concerning the (Qur'an)
075:037 Was he **not** a drop of sperm emitted (in lowly form)?
075:040 Has **not** He, (the same), the power
076:001 Has there **not** been over Man a long period of Time,
076:001 of Time, when he was nothing-(**not** even) mentioned?
076:024 and obey **not** to the sinner or the ingrate
076:030 But ye will **not**, except as Allah wills; for Allah
077:016 Did We **not** destroy the men of old (for their evil)?
077:020 Have We **not** created you from a fluid
077:025 Have We **not** made the earth (as a place)
077:035 shall **not** be able to speak,
077:048 "Prostrate yourselves!" They do **not** so.
078:006 Have We **not** made the earth as a wide expanse,
078:008 And (have We **not**) created you in pairs,
078:012 And (have We **not**) built over you
078:014 And do We **not** send down from the clouds
078:027 For that they used **not** to look for any account
080:007 if he grow **not** in purity.
081:022 And (O people!) your Companion is **not** one possessed;
081:029 But ye shall **not** will Except as Allah wills,-
082:016 And they will **not** be able to keep away therefrom.
083:004 Do they **not** think that they will be raised up?-
083:033 But they had **not** been sent as Keepers over them!
083:036 Will **not** the Unbelievers have been paid back
084:014 would **not** have to return (to Us)!
084:020 that they believe **not**?-
084:021 they fall **not** prostrate.
085:010 men and women, and do **not** turn in repentance,
086:014 It is **not** a thing for amusement.
087:006 (the Message), so thou shalt **not** forget,
088:017 Do they **not** look at the Camels, how they are made?-
088:022 Thou art **not** one to manage (their) affairs.
089:005 Is there (**not**) in these an adjuration (or evidence)
089:006 Seest thou **not** how thy Lord dealt with the 'Ad (people),-
089:008 The like of which were **not** produced in (all) the land?
089:017 Nay, nay! But ye honour **not** the orphans!
090:008 Have We **not** made for him a pair of eyes?-
090:011 But he hath made **not** haste on the
091:013 And (bar her **not** from) having her drink!"
093:003 Thy Guardian-Lord Hath **not** forsaken thee, nor is
093:006 Did He **not** find thee an orphan and give
093:009 Therefore, treat **not** the orphan with harshness,
094:001 Have We **not** expanded thee thy breast?-
095:008 Is **not** Allah the wisest of Judges?
096:005 Taught man that which he knew **not**.
096:014 Knoweth he **not** that Allah doth see?
096:015 Let him beware! If he desist **not**, We will
096:019 Nay, heed him **not**: but prostrate
098:001 were **not** going to depart (from their ways)
100:009 Does he **not** know,-when that which is in the
105:001 Seest thou **not** how thy Lord dealt with the
105:002 Did He **not** make their treacherous plan go astray?
107:003 And encourages **not** the feeding of the indigent.
109:002 I worship **not** that which ye worship,
109:004 And I will **not** worship that which

NOT (continued)

112:003 He begetteth **not**, nor is He begotten;

NOTABLE

016:103 point to is **notable** foreign, while this

NOTE

017:017 to **note** and see the sins of His servants.

050:017 appointed to learn (his doings) learn (and **note** them),

NOTED

054:052 All that they do is **noted** in (their)

NOTHING

002:078 and they do **nothing** but conjecture.

002:114 For them there is **nothing** but disgrace

002:167 as (**nothing** but) regrets.

002:171 listen to **nothing** but calls and cries:

002:264 do **nothing** with aught they have earned.

003:005 From Allah, verily **nothing** is hidden

003:115 **nothing** will be rejected of them;

004:120 but Satan's promises are **nothing** but deception.

005:053 and they will fall into (**nothing** but) ruin.

005:110 'This is **nothing** but evident magic'.

006:007 "This is **nothing** but obvious magic!"

006:025 "These are **nothing** but tales of the ancients."

006:029 "There is **nothing** except our life on this earth,

006:032 **Nothing** is the life of this world but play

006:038 **Nothing** have We omitted from the Book, and they

006:080 unless my Lord willeth, (**nothing** can happen), my

006:091 "**Nothing** doth Allah send down to man

006:116 they do **nothing** but lie.

006:116 They follow **nothing** but conjecture: they do

006:148 Ye follow **nothing** but conjecture: Ye do **nothing** but lie."

007:058 springs up **nothing** but that which is scanty, thus

007:105 to say **nothing** but truth about Allah. Now have

007:129 They said: "We have had (**nothing** but) trouble,

007:185 Do they see **nothing** in the kingdom of the

007:191 as partners things that can create **nothing**, but

007:203 This is (**nothing** but) lights from your Lord, and

008:031 like these: these are **nothing** but tales

008:035 is **nothing** but whistling and clapping of hands:

009:012 for their oaths are **nothing** to them; that thus

009:051 Say: "**Nothing** will happen to us except what

009:074 **nothing** (evil), but indeed they uttered blasphemy,

009:107 their intention is **nothing** but good; but Allah

009:120 because **nothing** could they suffer or do, but was

010:029 knew **nothing** of your worship of us!"

010:036 But most of them follow **nothing** but conjecture:

010:066 They follow **nothing** but conjecture, and they

010:066 and they do **nothing** but lie.

011:007 to say, "This is **nothing** but obvious sorcery!"

011:008 reaches them, **nothing** will turn it away from them,

011:016 is **nothing** in the Hereafter but the Fire: vain are

011:027 (in) thee **nothing** but a man like ourselves: nor do

011:043 **nothing** can save, from the Command of Allah,

011:054 "We say **nothing** but that (perhaps) some of

011:106 therein (**nothing** but) the heaving of sighs and sobs:

011:109 these men worship. They worship **nothing** but what

012:040 is **nothing** but names which ye have named, ye and

013:014 is **nothing** but vain prayer.

014:038 for **nothing** whatever is hidden from Allah,

016:020 create **nothing** and are themselves created.

016:070 so that they know **nothing** after having

016:078 when ye knew **nothing**; and He gave you hearing

016:079 **Nothing** holds them up but (the power of) Allah.

017:064 But Satan promises them **nothing** but deceit.

NOTHING (continued)

017:082 **nothing** but loss after loss.

017:094 was **nothing** but this: they said, "Has Allah

018:005 What they say in **nothing** but falsehood!

018:049 It leaves out **nothing** small or great, but

019:009 when thou hadst been **nothing**!'"

019:042 and can profit thee **nothing**?

019:067 that We created him before out of **nothing**?

020:107 **Nothing** crooked or curved wilt thou see

021:056 He Who created them (from **nothing**): and I

022:005 old age, so that they know **nothing** after having

023:037 "There is **nothing** but our life in this world!

023:083 They are **nothing** but tales of the ancients!"

024:039 he finds it to be **nothing**: but he

025:003 gods that can create **nothing** but are

027:068 these are **nothing** but tales of the ancients."

027:075 And there is **nothing** hidden in heaven or earth,

028:036 "This is **nothing** but sorcery faked up: never did

030:058 "Ye do **nothing** but talk vanities."

033:012 us **nothing** but delusion!"

033:013 not exposed: they intended **nothing** but to run away.

034:014 (Solomon's) death, **nothing** showed them his death

034:039 and **nothing** do ye spend in the least (in His

034:043 "This is **nothing** but evident magic!

035:040 **nothing** but delusions.

036:015 Ye do **nothing** but lie."

036:047 Ye are in **nothing** but manifest error."

037:015 And say, "This is **nothing** but evident sorcery!

038:007 this is **nothing** but a made-up tale!

040:025 in **nothing** but errors (and delusions)!...

040:037 to **nothing** but perdition (for him).

040:039 is **nothing** but (temporary) enjoyment:

040:050 is **nothing** but (futile wandering) in (mazes of) error!"

040:056 there is **nothing** in their breasts but (the quest of)

041:043 **Nothing** is said to thee that was not said to the

042:011 there is **nothing** whatever like unto Him, and He

043:020 They do **nothing** but lie!

043:035 But all this were **nothing** but enjoyment of the

043:039 it will avail you **nothing**, that day,

044:035 "There is **nothing** beyond our first death, and we

045:024 and **nothing** but Time can destroy us."

045:025 their argument is **nothing** but this:

046:017 "This is **nothing** but tales of the ancients!"

046:025 **nothing** was to be seen but (the ruins of)

051:042 It left **nothing** whatever that it came up against,

052:035 Were they created of **nothing**, or were

052:046 avail them **nothing** and no help shall be given them.

053:023 These are **nothing** but names which ye

053:023 They follow **nothing** but conjecture and what

053:026 will avail **nothing** except after Allah has given

053:028 and conjecture avails **nothing** against Truth.

053:028 They follow **nothing** but conjecture; and conjecture

053:029 and desire **nothing** but the life of this world.

053:039 That man can have **nothing** but what he strives for;

056:066 with debts (for **nothing**):

063:007 "Spend **nothing** on those who are with

066:010 and they profited **nothing** before Allah on their

067:009 ye are in **nothing** but a grave error!'"

067:020 The Most Merciful? In **nothing** but delusion are

068:052 But it is **nothing** less than a Message

074:024 Then said he: "This is **nothing** but magic

074:025 "This is **nothing** but the word of a mortal!"

075:031 So he gave **nothing** in charity, nor did he pray!-

NOTHING (continued)

076:001 of Time, when he was **nothing**-(not even) mentioned?
078:024 **Nothing** cool shall they taste therein,

NOTICE

002:279 **notice** of war from Allah and His Messenger:
022:072 thou wilt **notice** a denial on the faces of the Unbelievers!

NOURISH

028:012 the people of a house that will **nourish** and bring
088:007 Which will neither **nourish** nor satisfy hunger.

NOW

002:068 **now** do what ye are commanded!"
002:071 They said: "**Now** hast thou brought the truth."
002:083 and ye backslide (even **now**).
002:144 **now** shall We turn thee to a Qiblah
002:187 so **now** associate with them,
003:008 deviate **now** after Thou hast guided us,
003:061 **now** after (full) knowledge hath come to thee,
003:143 **now** ye have seen it with your own eyes
003:179 the Believers in the state in which ye are **now**,
004:018 and he says, "**Now** have I repented indeed";
004:047 believe in what We have (**now**) revealed, confirming
005:015 and passing over much (that is **now** unnecessary):
005:019 but **now** hath come unto you a bringer
005:019 **now** hath come unto you, making (things) clear
006:005 And **now** they reject the truth
006:094 so **now** all relations between you
006:104 "**Now** have come to you, from your Lord
006:157 **Now** then hath come unto you a Clear (Sign)
007:053 Have we no intercessors **now** to intercede on our behalf?
007:073 **Now** hath come unto you a clear
007:085 **Now** hath come unto you a clear
007:105 **Now** have I come unto you (people), from your
008:019 **now** hath the judgment come to you: if you
008:038 if (**now**) they desist (from Unbelief), their
008:069 But (**now**) enjoy what ye took in war, lawful
009:083 then sit ye (**now**) with those who stay behind."
009:128 **Now** hath come unto you a Messenger
010:051 (It will then be said): 'Ah! **now**? and ye wanted
010:091 (It was said to him): "Ah **now**!-but a little
010:108 Say: "O ye men! **now** Truth hath reached you
011:032 **now** bring upon us what thou threatenest us with,
011:038 He said: "If ye ridicule us **now**, we (in our turn)
011:062 Dost thou (**now**) forbid us the worship of what
011:078 for you (if ye marry)! **Now** fear Allah, and cover
011:081 **Now** travel with thy family while yet a part
012:023 and she fastened the doors, and said: "**Now** come,"
012:032 And **now**, if he doth not my bidding, he shall
012:036 **Now** with him there came into the prison
012:045 and who **now** remembered him after (so long)
012:051 Said the 'Aziz's wife: "**Now** is the truth manifest
012:060 "**Now** if ye bring him not to me, ye shall
012:063 **Now** when they returned to their father, they said:
012:069 **Now** when they came into Joseph's presence,
012:080 **Now** when they saw no hope of his (yielding),
012:088 we have (**now**) brought but scanty capital: so pay
013:024 **Now** how excellent is the final Home!"
014:021 to us it makes no difference (**now**) whether we rage,
017:081 And say: "Truth has (**now**) arrived, and Falsehood
018:019 **Now** send ye then one of you with this money
018:042 his property, which had (**now**) tumbled to pieces
018:048 (with the announcement), "**Now** have ye come to Us
018:055 **now** that guidance has come to them,
018:078 between me and thee: **now** I will tell thee the

NOW (continued)

019:005 "**Now** I fear (what) my relatives (and colleagues)
019:046 **now** get away from me for a good long while!"
019:098 a single one of them (**now**) or hear
020:022 **Now** draw thy hand close to thy side: it shall
020:097 **now** look at thy god, of whom thou hast become a
020:128 in whose haunts they (**now**) move? Verily, in
025:019 "**Now** have they proved you liars in what ye say:
026:039 "Are ye (**now**) assembled?"-
026:100 "**Now**, then, we have none to intercede (for us),
026:102 "**Now** if we only had a chance of return, we shall
026:131 "**Now** fear Allah, and obey me.
026:187 "**Now** cause a piece of the sky to fall on us,
027:010 "**Now** do thou throw thy rod!" But when
027:012 "**Now** put thy hand into thy bosom, and it
027:036 **Now** when (the embassy) came to Solomon, he said:
027:044 I do (**now**) submit (in Islam), with Solomon,
027:052 **Now** such were their houses,-in utter
028:015 of his foes. **Now** the man of his own people
028:029 **Now** when Moses had fulfilled the term, and was
028:031 "**Now** do thou throw thy rod!" But when
028:040 **now** behold what was the End of those
028:048 But (**now**), when the Truth has come to them
028:051 **Now** have We brought them the word in order
028:058 **Now** those habitations of theirs, after them,
029:065 **Now**, if they embark on a boat, they call
031:011 **now** show Me what is there that others
032:012 **now** then send us back (to the world):
032:012 work righteousness: for we do indeed (**now**) believe."
032:017 **Now** no person knows what delights of the eye
032:026 (**now**) go to and fro?
034:052 "We do believe (**now**) in the (truth)"; but how
035:043 **Now** are they but looking for the way
037:031 "So **now** has been proved true, against us,
037:102 **now** see what is thy view!"
037:149 **Now** ask them their opinion: is it
037:170 But (**now** that the Qur'an has come), they reject
038:022 the other: decide **now** between us with truth,
038:060 **Now** evil is (this) place to stay in!"
039:049 **Now**, when trouble touches man, he cries to Us;
040:011 **Now** have we recognized our sins:
040:025 **Now**, when he brought them in Truth, from Us,
040:044 "Soon will ye remember what I say to you (**now**).
041:015 **Now** the 'Ad behaved arrogantly through the land,
041:023 and (**now**) have ye become of those utterly lost!"
042:015 **Now** then, for that (reason), call (them to the Faith),
043:025 **now** see what was the end of those who rejected (Truth)!
043:063 he said: "**Now** have I come to you with Wisdom,
050:022 **now** have We removed thy veil, and sharp
051:031 O ye Messengers, is your errand (**now**)?"
052:048 **Now** await in patience the command of thy Lord:
054:037 (They heard): "**Now** taste ye My Wrath
060:007 those whom ye (**now**) hold as enemies.
067:010 we should not (**now**) be among the Companions
070:036 **Now** what is the matter with the Unbelievers
070:040 **Now** I do call to witness the Lord of all points
072:009 but any who listens **now** will find a
072:014 **Now** those who submit their wills-they have
077:039 **Now**, if ye have a trick (or plot),
079:010 They say (**now**): "What! shall we indeed be returned
086:005 **Now** let man but think from what he is created!
089:015 **Now**, as for man, when his Lord trieth him,

NOWISE

010:005   **Nowise** did Allah create this but in truth
043:075   **Nowise** will the (punishment) be lightened for them,
043:076   **Nowise** shall We be unjust to them: But it

NUMBER

002:109   Quite a **number** of the people of the Book
002:184   (Fasting) for a fixed **number** of days;
002:184   the prescribed **number** (should be made up)
002:243   though they were thousands (in **number**),
003:013   these saw with their own eyes twice their **number**.
009:036   The **number** of months in the sight of Allah
009:037   in order to agree with the **number** of months
010:005   that ye might know the **number** of years and the
013:008   (of their time or **number**) or do exceed.
014:034   never will ye be able to **number** them.
016:018   never would ye be able to **number** them:
017:012   may know the **number** and count of the years:
018:011   for a **number** of years, in the cave
018:022   "My Lord knoweth best their **number**; it is but few that
019:084   a (limited) **number** (of days).
020:040   Then didst thou tarry a **number** of years with the
021:084   and doubled their **number**,-as a Grace
022:018   But a great **number** are (also)
022:018   the animals; and a great **number** among mankind?
023:112   He will say: "What **number** of years did ye
038:043   and doubled their **number**,-as a Grace from Us,
038:062   to **number** among the bad ones?
056:013   A **number** of people from those of old,
056:039   A (goodly) **number** from those of old,
056:040   And a (goodly) **number** from those of later times.
065:012   and of the earth a similar **number**, through the
074:031   and We have fixed their **number** only as trial

NUMBERED

002:080   not touch us but for few **numbered** days:"
003:024   not touch us but for a few **numbered** days":
004:146   if so they will be (**numbered**) with the Believers.
019:094   and hath **numbered** them (all) exactly.

NUMBERS

009:025   your great **numbers** elated you, but they
018:043   Nor had he **numbers** to help him against Allah,
025:049   cattle and men in great **numbers**.
030:009   and populated it in greater **numbers** than these
072:024   in point of **numbers**.

NUMEROUS

003:010   their (**numerous**) progeny will avail them aught
003:116   their (**numerous**) progeny will avail them aught
016:005   and **numerous** benefits, and of their (meat) ye eat.
016:092   more **numerous** then another: for Allah
017:006   the more **numerous** in man-power.
023:021   in them, (besides), **numerous** (other) benefits for you;
040:082   They were more **numerous** than these
051:007   By the Sky with (its) **numerous** Paths,
068:014   Because he possesses wealth and (**numerous**) sons.

NUN

068:001   **Nun**. By the Pen and by the (Record) which (men)

NURSE

020:040   who will **nurse** and rear the (child)?'

O

O

002:021 O ye people! worship your Guardian-Lord,
002:033 He said: "O Adam! tell them their names."
002:035 And We said: "O Adam! dwell thou and thy wife
002:040 O children of Israel! call to mind
002:047 O children of Israel! call to mind
002:054 "O my people! Ye have indeed wronged yourselves
002:055 "O Moses! we shall never believe in thee
002:061 And remember ye said: "O Moses!
002:075 Can ye (O ye men of Faith) entertain
002:104 O ye of Faith! say not (to the Prophet)
002:122 O Children of Israel! call to mind
002:132 "O my sons! Allah hath chosen the Faith for you;
002:153 O ye who believe! seek help with
002:168 O ye people! eat of what is on earth,
002:172 O ye who believe! eat of the good things
002:178 O ye who believe! the law of equality
002:179 O ye men of understanding;
002:183 O ye who believe! fasting is prescribed to you
002:197 So fear Me, O ye that are wise.
002:208 O ye who believe! enter into Islam
002:254 O ye who believe! spend out of (the bounties)
002:264 O ye who believe! cancel not your charity
002:267 O ye who believe! give of the good things
002:278 O ye who believe! fear Allah,
002:282 O ye who believe! when ye deal with each other,
003:026 Say: "O Allah! Lord of Power (and Rule),
003:035 "O my Lord! I do dedicate unto thee what is in
003:036 "O my Lord! behold! I am delivered
003:037 He said: "O Mary! whence (comes) this to you?"
003:038 saying: "O my Lord! Grant unto me
003:040 He said: "O my Lord! how shall I have a son,
003:041 He said: "O my Lord! Give me a Sign!"
003:042 "O Mary! Allah hath chosen thee and purified thee
003:043 "O Mary! worship thy Lord devoutly;
003:044 (O Prophet!) by inspiration:
003:045 "O Mary! Allah giveth thee glad tidings
003:047 She said: "O my Lord! how shall I have a son
003:055 "O Jesus! I will take thee and raise thee to Myself
003:064 Say: "O people of the Book!
003:098 Say: "O people of the Book!
003:099 Say: "O ye People of the Book!
003:100 O ye who believe! if ye listen to a faction
003:102 O ye who believe! fear Allah as He should be feared,
003:118 O ye who believe! take not into your intimacy
003:130 O ye who believe! devour not usury,
003:149 O ye who believe! If ye obey the Unbelievers,
003:156 O ye who believe! Be not like the Unbelievers,
003:200 O ye who believe! Persevere in patience
004:001 O mankind! fear your Guardian Lord, Who created
004:019 O ye who believe! ye are forbidden to inherit
004:029 O ye who believe! eat not up your property
004:043 O ye who believe! approach not prayers in a state
004:047 O ye people of the Book! believe in what
004:059 O ye who believe! obey Allah, and obey
004:071 O ye who believe! take your precautions.

O (continued)

004:078 "This is from thee" (O Prophet).
004:079 Whatever good, (O man!) happens to thee,
004:094 O ye who believe! when ye go out in the cause
004:102 When thou (O Messenger) art with them, and
004:131 and you (O Muslims) to fear Allah, but if
004:133 O mankind, and create another race: for He
004:135 O ye who believe! stand out firmly for justice, as
004:136 O ye who believe! believe in Allah
004:144 O ye who believe! take not for friends
004:170 O mankind! the Messengers hath come to you
004:171 O people of the Book! commit no excesses
004:174 O mankind! verily there hath come to you
005:001 O ye who believe! fulfil (all) obligations.
005:002 O ye who believe! violate not the sanctity
005:006 O ye who believe! when ye prepare for prayer, wash
005:008 O ye who believe! stand out firmly for Allah, as
005:011 O ye who believe! call in remembrance
005:015 O People of the Book! there hath come
005:019 O People of the Book! now hath come
005:020 "O my people! call in remembrance the favour
005:021 "O my people! enter the holy land which Allah
005:022 They said: "O Moses! in this land are a people
005:024 They said: "O Moses! we shall never enter it
005:025 He said: "O my Lord! I have power
005:035 O ye who believe! do your duty to Allah, seek
005:041 O Messenger! let not those grieve thee, who race
005:051 O ye who believe! take not the Jews and the
005:054 O ye who believe! if any from among you turn
005:057 O ye who believe! take not for friends
005:059 Say: "O People of the Book! do ye disapprove
005:067 O Messenger! proclaim the (Message) which hath
005:068 Say: "O People of the Book! ye have
005:072 "O children of Israel! worship Allah, my Lord
005:077 Say: "O people of the Book! exceed not
005:087 O ye who believe! make not unlawful the good
005:090 O ye who believe! intoxicants and
005:094 O ye who believe! Allah doth but make a trial
005:095 O ye who believe! kill not game, while in
005:100 O ye that understand that (so) ye may prosper."
005:101 O ye who believe! ask not questions about things
005:105 O ye who believe! guard your own souls: if ye
005:106 O ye who believe! when death
005:110 "O Jesus the son of Mary! recount my favour
005:112 "O Jesus the son of Mary! Can thy Lord
005:114 "O Allah our Lord! send us from heaven a table
005:116 "O Jesus the son of Mary! didst thou say unto men,
006:078 "O my people! I am indeed free from your (guilt)
006:128 (and say): "O ye assembly of Jinns much (toll)
006:130 "O ye assembly of Jinns and men! came there
006:135 Say: "O my people! do whatever ye can: I will
007:003 Follow (O men!) the revelation given unto
007:019 O Adam! dwell thou and thy wife
007:026 O ye children of Adam! We have bestowed
007:027 O ye children of Adam! Let not
007:031 O children of Adam! wear your
007:035 O ye children of Adam! whenever there come to you
007:059 He said: "O my people! worship Allah!
007:061 He said: "O my people! there is no error in me: on
007:065 He said: "O my people! worship Allah! ye have
007:067 He said: "O my people! there is
007:073 he said: "O my people! worship Allah; ye have
007:077 saying: "O Salih! bring about thy threats, if

O (continued)

007:079   saying: "**O** my people! I indeed convey to you
007:085   he said: "**O** my people! worship Allah; ye have
007:088   said: "**O** Shu'aib! we shall certainly drive thee
007:093   saying: "**O** my people! I did indeed convey to
007:104   Moses said: "**O** Pharaoh! I am
007:115   They said: "**O** Moses! wilt thou throw (first), or
007:134   they said: "**O** Moses! on our behalf call on
007:138   They said: "**O** Moses! fashion for us a god
007:143   He said: "**O** my Lord! show (Thyself) to me, that
007:144   (Allah) said: "**O** Moses! I have chosen thee
007:151   Moses prayed: "**O** my Lord! forgive me
007:155   he prayed: "**O** my Lord! if it had been Thy will
007:158   Say: "**O** men! I am sent unto you all, as the
007:205   And do thou (**O** reader!) bring thy
008:015   **O** ye who believe! when ye meet the Unbelievers
008:019   (**O** Unbelievers!) if ye prayed for victory
008:020   **O** ye who believe! obey Allah and His Messenger,
008:024   **O** ye who believe! give your response
008:027   **O** ye that believe! betray not the trust
008:029   **O** ye who believe! if ye fear Allah, He will
008:032   Remember how they said: "**O** Allah! if this
008:045   **O** ye who believe! when ye
008:064   **O** Prophet! Sufficient unto thee is Allah,-
008:065   **O** Prophet! rouse the Believers to the fight.
008:070   **O** Prophet! say to those who are captives
008:071   against thee, (**O** Messenger!), they have
009:023   **O** ye who believe! Take not for protectors
009:028   **O** ye who believe! Truly the Pagans are unclean;
009:034   **O** ye who believe! There are indeed many among
009:038   **O** ye who believe! what is the matter with you,
009:073   **O** Prophet! strive hard against the Unbelievers
009:119   **O** ye who Believe! Fear Allah and be
009:123   **O** ye who believe! Fight the Unbelievers who are
010:010   "Glory to Thee, **O** Allah!" and "Peace" will be
010:023   **O** mankind! your insolence is against your own
010:057   **O** mankind! there hath come to you
010:071   "**O** my People, if it be hard on your (mind) that I
010:084   Moses said: "**O** my People! if ye do
010:089   (**O** Moses and Aaron)! So stand ye straight, and
010:104   Say: "**O** ye men! if ye are in doubt
010:108   Say: "**O** ye men! now Truth hath reached you
011:028   He said: "**O** my people! see ye if (it be that)
011:029   "And **O** my People! I ask you
011:030   "And **O** my People! who would help me
011:032   They said: "**O** Noah! thou hast disputed with us,
011:042   (from the rest): "**O** my son! embark with us, and be
011:044   swallow up thy water, and **O** sky! withhold (thy
011:044   Then the word went forth: "**O** earth! swallow up
011:045   "**O** my Lord! surely my son is of my family and Thy
011:046   He said: "**O** Noah! he is not of thy family: for his
011:047   Noah said: "**O** my Lord! I do seek refuge with Thee,
011:048   The word came: "**O** Noah! come down (from the
011:050   He said: "**O** my people! worship Allah! ye have
011:051   "**O** my people! I ask of you no reward
011:052   "And **O** my people! ask forgiveness of your Lord,
011:053   They said: "**O** Hud! no Clear (Sign) hast thou
011:061   He said: "**O** my people! worship Allah: ye have
011:062   They said: "**O** Salih! thou hast been of us!-
011:063   He said: "**O** my people! Do ye see?-If I have
011:064   "And **O** my people! this she-camel of Allah
011:073   **O** ye people of the house! For He is indeed
011:076   **O** Abraham! seek not this. The decree

O (continued)

011:078   He said: "**O** my people! here are my daughters:
011:081   (The Messengers) said "**O** Lut! we are Messengers
011:084   he said: "**O** my people! worship Allah: ye have
011:085   "And **O** my people! give just measure and weight,
011:088   He said: "**O** my people! see ye whether I have
011:089   "And **O** my people! let not my dissent (from you)
011:091   They said: "**O** Shu'aib! much of what thou sayest
011:092   He said: "**O** my people! is then my family of more
011:093   "And **O** my people! do whatever ye can: I will
012:004   "**O** my father! I did see eleven stars and the
012:011   They said: "**O** our father! why dost
012:029   "**O** Joseph, pass this over! (**O** wife),
012:029   (**O** wife), ask forgiveness for thy sin, for truly
012:033   He said: "**O** my Lord! the prison is dearer to my
012:039   "**O** my two companions of the prison! (I ask you):
012:041   "**O** my two companions of the prison! As to
012:043   **O** ye chiefs! expound to me my vision if it be
012:046   "Joseph!" (he said), "**O** man of truth! Expound
012:063   they said: "**O** our father! No more measure
012:065   They said: "**O** our father! What (more)
012:067   Further he said; "**O** my sons! enter not
012:070   Then shouted out a Crier: "**O** ye (in the
012:078   They said: " **O** exalted one! Behold! he has
012:081   and say, '**O** our father! behold! thy son
012:087   "**O** my sons! go ye and enquire about Joseph
012:088   "**O** exalted one! distress has seized us
012:097   They said: "**O** our father! ask for
012:100   He said: "**O** my father! this is the fulfillment
012:101   **O** Thou Creator of the heavens and the earth! Thou
012:101   "**O** my Lord! Thou hast indeed bestowed on me
014:009   (**O** people!), of those who (went) before you?
014:035   Remember Abraham said: "**O** my Lord! make this
014:036   "**O** my Lord! they have indeed led astray
014:037   "**O** our Lord! I have made some of my offspring
014:037   **O** our Lord! that they may establish regular
014:038   "**O** our Lord! truly Thou dost know what we
014:040   "**O** my Lord! make me one who establishes
014:040   **O** our Lord! and accept Thou my Prayer.
014:041   "**O** our Lord! cover (us) with Thy Forgiveness-me,
015:006   They say: "**O** thou to whom the Message
015:032   (Allah) said: "**O** Iblis! what is your reason for
015:036   (Iblis) said: "**O** my Lord! give me then respite
015:039   (Iblis) said: "**O** my Lord! because Thou hast
015:057   **O** ye messengers (of Allah)?"
015:072   Verily, by thy life (**O** Prophet), in their
017:003   **O** ye that are sprung from those whom We
017:022   or thou (**O** man!) wilt sit in disgrace
017:040   Has then your Lord, (**O** Pagans!) preferred for
017:080   Say: "**O** my Lord! let my entry be by the Gate
017:085   a little that is communicated to you, (**O** men!)"
017:101   Pharaoh said to him: "**O** Moses! I consider thee,
017:102   **O** Pharaoh, to be one doomed to destruction!"
018:086   We said: "**O** Zul-Qarnain! (thou hast authority),
018:094   They said: "**O** Zul-Qarnain! the Gog and Magog
019:004   Praying: "**O** my Lord! infirm indeed are my bones,
019:004   am I unblest, **O** my Lord, in my prayer to Thee!
019:006   and make him, **O** my Lord! one with
019:007   (His prayer was answered): "**O** Zakariya! We give
019:008   He said: "**O** my Lord! how shall I have a son,
019:010   (Zakariya) said "**O** my Lord! give me a Sign,"
019:012   "**O** Yahya! take hold of the Book with might":
019:027   "**O** Mary! truly a strange thing hast thou brought!

O (continued)

019:028	"O sister of Aaron! thy father was not a man
019:042	"O my father! why worship that which heareth not
019:043	"O my father! to me hath come knowledge which
019:044	"O my father! serve not Satan: for Satan
019:045	"O my father! I fear lest a Chastisement afflict
019:046	O Abraham? If thou forbear not, I will
020:011	he was called "O Moses!
020:017	And what is that in thy right hand, O Moses?"
020:019	(Allah) said, "Throw it, O Moses!"
020:025	(Moses) said: "O my Lord! expand me my breast;"
020:036	(Allah) said: "Granted is thy prayer, O Moses!"
020:040	Then didst thou come hither as ordained, O Moses!
020:049	(Pharaoh) said: "Who, then, O Moses, is the
020:057	us out of our land with thy magic, O Moses?
020:065	They said: "O Moses! whether wilt thou that thou
020:080	O ye Children of Israel! We delivered
020:083	in advance of thy people, O Moses?"
020:084	O my Lord, to please Thee."
020:086	He said: "O my people! did not your Lord make a
020:090	said to them: "O my people! ye are being tested
020:092	(Moses) said: "O Aaron! what kept thee back,
020:094	(Aaron) replied: "O son of my mother! Seize (me)
020:095	(Moses) said: "What then is thy case, O Samiri?"
020:114	"O my Lord! increase me in knowledge."
020:117	Then We said: "O Adam! verily, this is
020:120	he said, "O Adam! shall I lead thee to the Tree
020:125	He will say: "O my Lord! why hast
021:010	We have revealed for you (O men!) a book
021:062	did this with our gods, O Abraham?"
021:069	We said, "O Fire! be thou cool, and (a means
021:089	"O my Lord! leave me not without offspring,
021:112	Say: "O my Lord! judge Thou in truth!" "Our Lord
022:001	O mankind! Fear your Lord! For the convulsion
022:005	O mankind! if ye have a doubt about the
022:049	Say: "O men! I am (sent) to you only to give
022:073	O men! Here is a parable set forth!
022:077	O ye who believe! bow down, prostrate yourselves,
023:023	"O my people! worship Allah! Ye have
023:026	(Noah) said: "O my Lord! help me: for that
023:029	And say: "O my Lord! enable me
023:039	(The prophet) said: "O my Lord! help me: for that
023:051	O ye messenger! enjoy (all) things good and pure,
023:093	Say: "O my Lord! if Thou wilt show me (in my
023:094	"Then, O my Lord! put me not amongst the
023:097	And say: "O my Lord! I seek refuge with Thee from
023:098	O my Lord! lest they should come near me."
023:099	he says: "O my Lord! send me back to (life),-
023:118	So say: "O my Lord! grant Thou forgiveness
024:021	O ye who believe! follow not Satan's footsteps:
024:027	O ye who believe! enter not houses
024:031	And O ye Believers! turn ye all together towards
024:058	O ye who believe! let those whom your right
025:030	"O my Lord, Truly my people treated this Qur'an
026:012	He said: "O my Lord! I do fear
026:083	"O my Lord! bestow wisdom on me, and join
026:116	O Noah! thou shalt be stone (to death)."
026:117	He said: "O my Lord! truly my
026:167	O Lut! thou wilt assuredly be cast out!"
026:169	"O my Lord! deliver me and my family
026:221	Shall I inform you, (O people!), on whom
027:009	"O Moses! verily, I am Allah, the Exalted
027:010	"O Moses!" (it was said), fear not:
027:016	He said: "O ye people! we have been taught
027:018	"O ye ants, get into your habitations,
027:019	and he said: "O my Lord! so order
027:044	She said: "O my Lord! I have indeed
027:046	He said: "O my people! why ask ye to hasten
028:016	He prayed: "O my Lord! I have
028:017	He said: "O my Lord! for that Thou hast bestowed
028:019	"O Moses! is it thy intention to slay me
028:020	He said: "O Moses! the Chiefs are taking counsel
028:021	He prayed: "O my Lord! save me
028:024	and said: "O my Lord! truly am I
028:026	Said one of the (damsels): "O my (dear) father!
028:030	hallowed ground: "O Moses! Verily I am
028:031	"O Moses!" (It was said), "Draw near, and fear
028:033	He said: "O my Lord! I have slain a man among them,
028:038	therefore, O Haman! light me a (kiln to bake
028:038	Pharaoh said: "O Chiefs! no god do I know
029:030	He said: "O my Lord! help Thou me against
029:036	Then he said: "O my people! serve Allah,
029:056	O My servants who believe! truly, spacious
030:050	Then behold (O man!) the tokens of Allah's Mercy!-
031:013	admonishing him "O my son! join not in worship
031:016	"O my son! (said Luqman), "If there
031:017	"O my son! establish regular prayer, enjoin what
031:033	O mankind! do your duty to your Lord and fear
033:001	O Prophet! Fear Allah, and hearken
033:009	O ye who believe! Remember the
033:028	O Prophet! say to thy Consorts: "If it
033:030	O Consorts of the Prophet! if any of you were
033:032	O Consorts of the Prophet! ye are not like any
033:041	O ye who believe! remember Allah, with much
033:045	O Prophet! Truly We have sent thee as a Witness,
033:049	O ye who believe! when ye marry believing women,
033:050	O prophet! We have made lawful to thee
033:053	O ye who Believe! enter not the Prophet's houses,-
033:056	on the Prophet: O ye that believe! send ye
033:059	O Prophet! Tell thy wives and daughters, and the
033:069	O ye who believe! be ye not like those who
033:070	O ye who believe! fear Allah, and make
034:010	on David from Us: "O ye Mountains! echo ye
035:003	O men! remember the grace of Allah unto you!
035:005	O men! certainly the promise of Allah is true,
035:014	And none, (O man!) can inform you like Him
035:015	O ye men! it is ye that have need of Allah:
036:020	a man, saying, "O my People! obey the messengers:
036:059	And O ye in sin! get ye apart this Day!
036:060	"Did I not enjoin on you, O ye children of Adam,
037:100	"O my Lord! grant me a righteous (son)!"
037:102	he said: "O my son! I have seen in a dream
037:102	"O my father! do as thou art commanded: thou will
037:104	We called out to him, "O Abraham!
038:026	O David! We did indeed make thee a vicegerent
038:035	He said, "O my Lord! Forgive me, and grant me
038:075	(Allah) said: "O Iblis! what prevents thee from
038:079	(Iblis) said: "O my Lord! give me then respite
039:010	Say: "O ye my servants who believe! Fear your
039:016	"O my servants! Then fear ye Me!"
039:039	Say: "O my people! Do whatever ye can: I will
039:046	Say: "O Allah! Creator of the heavens and the
039:053	Say: "O my Servants who have transgressed against
039:064	O ye ignorant ones?"
040:029	"O my people! yours is the dominion this day:

O (continued)

040:030 "O my People! truly I do fear for you something
040:032 "And, O my People! I fear for you a Day
040:036 Pharaoh said: "O Haman! Build me a lofty palace,
040:038 "O my People! follow me: I will
040:039 "O my people! This life of the present is nothing
040:041 "And O my People! how (strange) it is for me
043:049 And they said, "O thou Sorcerer! invoke thy
043:051 saying: "O my people! Does not the dominion
043:077 They will cry: "O Malik! would that thy Lord
043:088 (Prophet's) cry, "O my Lord! Truly these
046:015 forty years, He says, "O my Lord! grant me
046:030 They said, "O our people! We have
046:031 "O our people, hearken to the one who invites
047:007 O ye who believe! if ye will
047:033 O ye who believe! obey Allah, and obey
048:009 In order that ye (O men) may believe
049:001 O ye who believe! put not yourselves forward
049:002 O ye who believe! raise not your voices
049:006 O ye who believe! if a sinner comes to you
049:011 O ye who believe! let not some men among you
049:012 O ye who believe! avoid suspicion as much
049:013 O mankind! We created you from a single (pair
051:031 O ye Messengers, is your errand (now)?"
053:055 (O man), wilt thou dispute about?
054:006 Therefore, (O Prophet,) turn away from them.
054:027 So watch them, (O Salih), and possess
054:043 (O Quraish), better than they? Or have
055:031 O both ye worlds!
055:033 O ye assembly of Jinns and men! If it be
055:035 On you will be sent (O ye evil ones twain)!
056:051 "Then will ye truly,- O ye that go wrong,
057:028 O ye that believe! fear Allah, and believe
058:009 O ye who believe! when ye hold secret counsel,
058:011 O ye who believe! When ye are told to make room
058:012 O ye who believe! When ye consult the Messenger
059:002 O ye with eyes (to see)!
059:005 Whether ye cut down (O ye Muslims!) of the tender
059:018 O ye who believe! Fear Allah, and let
060:001 O ye who believe! take not My enemies and yours
060:010 O ye who believe! when there come to you
060:012 O Prophet! when believing women come to thee
060:013 O ye who believe! turn not (for friendship)
061:002 O ye who believe! why say ye that which
061:005 "O my people! why do ye vex and insult me,
061:006 said: "O Children of Israel! I am the messenger
061:010 O ye who believe! shall I lead you to a bargain
061:014 O ye who believe! be ye helpers of Allah: as said
062:006 Say: "O ye of Jewry! if ye think that ye are
062:009 O ye who believe! when the call is proclaimed
063:009 O ye who believe! let not your riches or your
063:010 and he should say, "O my Lord! Why didst
064:014 O ye who believe! truly, among your wives
065:001 O Prophet! when ye do divorce women, divorce them
065:010 O ye men of understanding-who have believed!-
066:001 O Prophet! why holdest thou to be forbidden
066:006 O ye who believe! save yourselves and your
066:007 (It will be said), "O ye Unbelievers! make no
066:008 O ye who believe! turn to Allah with sincere
066:009 O Prophet! Strive hard against the Unbelievers
066:011 behold, she said: "O my Lord! build for me,
071:002 He said: "O my People! I am to you a Warner,
071:005 He said: "O my Lord! I have called to my People

O (continued)

071:021 Noah said: "O my Lord! they have disobeyed me,
071:026 And Noah said: "O my Lord! Leave not
071:028 "O my Lord! Forgive me, my parents, all who
073:001 O thou folded in garments!
073:015 We have sent to you, (O men!) a Messenger,
074:001 O thou wrapped up (in a mantle)!
075:034 Woe to thee, (O man!) yea, woe!
075:035 Again, woe to thee, (O man!), yea woe!
077:046 (O ye Unjust!) Eat ye and enjoy yourselves (but)
081:022 And (O people!) your Companion is not one possessed;
082:006 O man! what has seduced thee from thy Lord
084:006 O thou man! verily thou art ever toiling on
089:027 "O (thou) soul, in (complete) rest and satisfaction!
109:001 Say: O ye that reject Faith!

O'ER

007:054 He draweth the night as a veil O'er the day, each
013:003 O'er the Day. Behold, verily in these things

OATH

002:226 an oath for abstention from their wives,
012:066 they had sworn their solemn oath, he said:
012:066 with you until ye swear a solemn oath to me,
012:080 an oath from you in Allah's name, and how
024:007 And the fifth (oath) (should be) that he
024:008 four times (with an oath) by Allah, that (her
024:009 And the fifth (oath) should be that she solemnly
024:022 by oath against helping their kinsmen, those in
027:049 They said: "Swear a mutual oath by Allah that we
038:044 (thy oath)." Truly We found him full of patience
048:010 His oath, does so to the harm of his own soul,
060:012 to thee to take the oath of fealty to thee,
068:039 on oath, reaching to the Day of Judgment,

OATHS

002:224 an excuse in your oaths against doing good,
002:225 to account for thoughtlessness in your oaths,
005:053 who swore their strongest oaths by Allah, that
005:089 But keep to your oaths. Thus doth
005:089 That is the expiation for the oaths ye have sworn.
005:089 to account for what is void in your oaths, but
005:089 to account for your deliberate oaths: for
005:108 that other oaths would be taken after their oaths.
005:108 that other oaths would be taken after their oaths.
006:109 They swear their strongest oaths by Allah, that
009:012 for their oaths are nothing to them; that thus
009:012 their oaths after their covenant, and taunt
009:013 who violated their oaths, plotted to
016:038 They swear their strongest oaths by Allah,
016:091 and break not your oaths after ye have
016:092 Using your oaths to deceive one another, lest one
016:094 And take not your oaths, to practice
024:053 They swear their strongest oaths by Allah that,
035:042 They swore their strongest oaths by Allah
058:016 They have made their oaths a screen
063:002 They have made their oaths a screen
066:002 the expiration of your oaths (in some cases):

OBEDIENCE

004:034 but if they return to obedience, seek not
004:081 They have "Obedience" on their lips; but
024:053 obedience is (more) reasonable; verily, Allah is
033:022 and their zeal in obedience.
041:011 "We do come (together), in willing obedience."
048:016 show obedience, Allah will grant you a goodly

OBEDIENT

004:034   are devoutly **obedient**, and guard
016:120   devoutly **obedient** to Allah, (and) true in faith,
017:016   (to be **obedient**) but they continued to
030:026   all are devoutly **obedient** to Him.
034:012   the Wind (**obedient**): its early morning (stride)

OBEISANCE

015:029   fall ye down in **obeisance** unto him."

OBEY

002:285   And they say: "We hear, and we **obey**:
003:032   Say: "**Obey** Allah and His Messenger": but if they
003:050   So fear Allah, and **obey** me.
003:132   And **obey** Allah and the Messenger;
003:149   O ye who believe! If ye **obey** the Unbelievers,
004:013   those who **obey** Allah and His Messenger will be
004:046   If only they had said: "We hear and we **obey**"; and
004:059   **obey** Allah, and **obey** the Messenger, and those
004:069   All who **obey** Allah and the Messenger are in the
005:007   when ye said: "We hear and we **obey**":
005:092   **Obey** Allah, and **obey** the Messenger. And beware
006:121   if ye were to **obey** them, ye would
007:193   they will not **obey**: for you
008:001   **obey** Allah and His Allah, it ye do believe."
008:020   O ye who believe! **obey** Allah and His Messenger,
008:046   And **obey** Allah and His Messenger; and fall
009:071   regular prayers, pay Zakat and **obey** Allah and His
018:028   nor **obey** any whose heart We have permitted to
020:090   Most Gracious: so follow me and **obey** my command."
023:034   "If ye **obey** a man like yourselves, behold, it is
024:047   and in the Messenger, and we **obey**": but even
024:051   "We hear and we **obey**": it is
024:052   It is such as **obey** Allah and His Messenger,
024:054   If ye **obey** him, ye shall be on right guidance.
024:054   Say: "**Obey** Allah, and **obey** the Messenger: but if
024:056   and give zakat and **obey** the Messenger; that ye
026:108   "So fear Allah, and **obey** me.
026:110   "So fear Allah, and **obey** me."
026:126   "So fear Allah, and **obey** me.
026:131   "Now fear Allah, and **obey** me.
026:144   So fear Allah, and **obey** me.
026:150   "But fear Allah, and **obey** me;
026:163   "So fear Allah, and **obey** me.
026:179   "So fear Allah, and **obey** me.
029:008   no knowledge, **obey** them not. Ye have
031:015   **obey** them not; yet bear them company in this
033:033   and **obey** Allah and His Messenger. And Allah
033:048   And **obey** not (the behests) of the Unbelievers
036:020   a man, saying, "O my People! **obey** the messengers:
036:021   "**Obey** those who ask no reward of you
043:063   ye dispute: therefore fear Allah and **obey** me.
047:021   Were it to **obey** and say what is just, and when
047:026   "We will **obey** you in part of (this) matter";
047:033   O ye who believe! **obey** Allah, and **obey**
047:033   and **obey** the Messenger, and make
049:014   But if ye **obey** Allah and His Messenger, He will
058:013   and **obey** Allah and His Messenger. And Allah
064:012   So **obey** Allah, and **obey** His Messenger; but if
064:016   listen and **obey**; and spend in charity for the
068:008   So **obey** not to those who deny (the Truth).
068:010   **Obey** not every mean,-swearer,
071:003   fear Him, and **obey** me:
076:024   and **obey** not to the sinner or the ingrate

OBEYED

004:064   We sent not a Messenger, but to be **obeyed**,
033:066   we had **obeyed** Allah and **obeyed** the Messenger!"
033:066   we had **obeyed** Allah and **obeyed** the Messenger!"
033:067   We **obeyed** our chiefs and our great ones, and they
043:054   and they **obeyed** him: truly were

OBEYETH

002:158   And if anyone **obeyeth** his own

OBEYS

004:080   He who obeys the Messenger, **obeys** Allah: but
033:071   he that **obeys** Allah and His Messenger has already
048:017   but he that **obeys** Allah and His Messenger,-

OBJECT

003:141   Allah's **object** also is to purge those
017:039   with Allah, another **object** of worship, lest thou
020:063   their **object** is to drive you out from your land
040:012   as the Only (**object** of worship) ye did
051:051   And make not another an **object** of worship

OBLIGATION

004:005   (on marriage) their dower as an **obligation**;

OBLIGATIONS

002:282   future **obligations** in a fixed period of time,
005:001   O ye who believe! fulfil (all) **obligations**.
009:003   dissolve (treaty) **obligations** with the Pagans.
062:005   in those (**obligations**), is that of a donkey
062:005   entrusted with the (**obligations** of) Taurat,

OBLITERATE

040:005   of vanities, therewith to **obliterate** the Truth:

OBSCENITY

002:197   let there be no **obscenity**, nor wickedness,

OBSCURE

028:066   will be **obscure** to them and they will not

OBSCURED

011:028   hath been **obscured** from your sight? Shall we

OBSERVANCE

016:124   its **observance**); but Allah will judge between

OBSERVANT

035:031   well acquainted and fully **Observant**.

OBSERVE

009:071   what is evil: they **observe** regular prayers,
009:094   and His Messenger will **observe**: in the end
009:105   soon will Allah **observe** your work, and His
009:112   forbid evil; and **observe** the limits set by Allah;-
020:094   and thou didst not **observe** my word!'"
023:008   Those who faithfully **observe** their trust
067:019   Do they not **observe** the birds above them,

OBSERVED

059:011   Hast thou not **observed** the Hypocrites say to

OBSTINATE

003:135   And are never **obstinate** in persisting knowingly
005:064   them their **obstinate** rebellion and blasphemy.
005:068   them their **obstinate** rebellion and blasphemy.
009:057   thereto with an **obstinate** rush.
009:101   they are **obstinate** in hypocrisy: thou knowest
011:059   every powerful, **obstinate** transgressor.
014:015   the lot of every powerful **obstinate** transgressor.
018:080   them by **obstinate** rebellion and ingratitude
019:069   worst in **obstinate** rebellion against (Allah)
022:003   and follow every Satan **obstinate** in rebellion!
037:007   against all **obstinate** rebellious Satans.
037:030   a people in **obstinate** rebellion!

OBSTINATE (continued)
045:008   to him, yet is **obstinate** and lofty, as if
071:007   with their garments, grown **obstinate**, and given

OBSTINATELY
023:075   on them, they would **obstinately** persist in their
056:046   And persisted **obstinately** in wickedness supreme!
067:021   Nay, they **obstinately** persist in insolent impiety

OBSTRUCT
003:099   why **obstruct** ye those who believe,
058:016   thus they **obstruct** (men) from the Path of Allah:
063:002   thus they **obstruct** (men) from the path of Allah:

OBTAIN
003:132   that ye may **obtain** mercy.

OBTAINED
010:003   except after His leave (hath been **obtained**). This

OBTAINING
009:099   and **obtaining** the prayers of the Messenger. Aye,

OBVIOUS
006:007   "This is nothing but **obvious** magic!"
011:007   to say, "This is nothing but **obvious** sorcery!"
024:012   and say, "This (charge) is an **obvious** lie?"

OBVIOUSLY
012:008   Really our father is **obviously** in error!
037:113   do right, and (some) that **obviously** do wrong,

OCCASION
004:154   and (on another **occasion**) We said: "Enter
009:083   on the first **occasion**: then sit
020:002   to be (an **occasion**) for thy distress,

OCCASIONED
006:041   which **occasioned** your call upon Him, and ye

OCCASIONS
024:058   your presence), on three **occasions**: before morning
028:077   to thee, and seek not (**occasions** for) mischief

OCCUPANTS
006:131   their **occupants** were unwarned.

OCCUPATION
073:007   prolonged **occupation** with ordinary duties:

OCCUR
007:187   as to when it will **occur**. Heavy were
064:011   No kind of calamity can **occur**, except by

OCCURRED
012:035   Then it **occurred** to them after they had seen

OCEAN
002:164   the ships through the **Ocean** for the profit
018:109   my Lord, sooner would the **ocean** be exhausted than
018:109   my Lord, even if we added another **ocean** like it,
018:109   Say: "If the **ocean** were ink (wherewith to write
024:040   deep **ocean**, overwhelmed with billow topped by
031:027   and the **Ocean** (were ink), with seven
031:031   the **Ocean** by the grace of Allah?-that He
042:032   smooth-running through the **ocean**, (tall) as
042:033   on the back of the (**ocean**). Verily in
052:006   And by the **Ocean** filled with Swell;-

OCEANS
031:027   with seven **Oceans** behind it to add to its (supply),
081:006   When the **oceans** boil over with a swell;
082:003   When the **Oceans** are suffered to burst forth;

ODD
089:003   By the Even and **Odd** (contrasted);

ODIOUS
004:022   it was shameful and **odious**, an abominable

ODIUM
035:039   but adds to the **odium** for the Unbelievers

OF (See Appendix)

OFF
002:166   relations between them would be cut **off**.
003:026   and Thou strippest **off** power from whom
003:119   they bite **off** the very tips of their fingers
003:127   That He might cut **off** a fringe of the Unbelievers
004:088   Allah hath cast them **off** for their (evil) deeds.
004:118   "I will take of Thy servants a portion marked **off**:
004:167   and keep **off** (men) from the way of Allah, have
005:033   or the cutting **off** of hands and feet from opposite
005:038   cut **off** his or her hands: a retribution
006:045   the last remnant was cut **off**. Praise be to
006:094   between you have been cut **off**, and your
007:072   by Our Mercy and We cut **off** the roots
007:124   "Be sure I will cut **off** your hands and your
008:007   and to cut **off** the roots of the Unbelievers;-
008:012   and smite all their finger-tips **off** them."
011:087   leave **off** the worship which our fathers practiced,
011:087   **off** doing what we like with our property? Truly,
011:089   the people of Lut far **off** from you!
012:041   from **off** his head. (So) hath
012:110   But never will be warded **off** Our punishment
013:022   secretly and openly; and turn **off** Evil with good:
015:066   those (sinners) should be cut **off** by the morning.
017:076   Their purpose was to scare thee **off** the land,
018:041   run **off** underground so that thou wilt never
020:012   Therefore put **off** thy shoes: thou art
020:071   Be sure I will cut **off** your hands and feet
021:039   to ward **off** the Fire from their faces, not yet
021:093   But (later generations) cut **off** their affair
022:015   (himself) **off**: then let him see whether his plan
023:018   to drain it **off** (with ease).
023:053   But people have cut **off** their affair (of unity),
025:012   When it sees them from a place far **off**, they will
026:049   Be sure I will cut **off** your hands and your
029:029   and cut **off** the highway?-And practise
034:052   from a position (so) far **off**,-
034:053   with regard to the Unseen from a position far **off**?
035:011   of days, nor is a part cut **off** from his life,
035:043   no turning **off** wilt thou find in Allah's way
039:016   warn **off** His servants: "O My Servants!
039:024   Is, then, one who has to ward **off** the brunt
062:009   and leave **off** business (and traffic): that is
068:049   he would indeed have been cast **off** on the
069:046   And We should certainly then cut **off** the artery
070:002   is none to ward **off**,-
108:003   he will be cut **off** (from Future Hope).

OFFENCE
002:217   Say: "Fighting therein is a grave (**offense**);
002:275   (the **offense**) are Companion of the Fire:

OFFENCES
053:032   indecent deeds, save lesser **offences**,-verily thy

OFFENSIVE
049:011   by (**offensive**) nicknames: ill-seeming is a name

OFFER
002:196   or freed the poor, or **offer** sacrifice;
002:235   an indirect **offer** of betrothal or hold it
003:091   though they should **offer** it for ransom.
004:144   do ye wish to **offer** Allah an open
009:054   and that they **offer** contributions unwillingly.

OFFER (continued)

013:018 would they **offer** it for ransom.
016:028 they **offer** submission (with the pretense), "We did
021:028 and they **offer** no intercession except for
033:072 We did indeed **offer** the Trust to the Heavens
037:102 in a dream that I **offer** thee in sacrifice:
039:047 (in vain) would they **offer** it for ransom from the

OFFERED

002:071 Then they **offered** her in sacrifice,
002:233 (the foster mother) what ye **offered**,
004:086 When a (courteous) greeting is **offered** you,
006:070 if it **offered** every ransom (or reparation), none

OFFERING

002:196 he must make an **offering** such as he can afford,
002:196 until the **offering** reaches the place
002:196 send an **offering** for sacrifice,
005:095 the compensation is an **offering**, brought to
010:022 sincerely **offering** (their) duty unto Him, saying:
031:032 **offering** Him sincere devotion. But when
039:002 so serve Allah, **offering** Him sincere devotion.
060:001 **offering** them (your) love, even though
098:005 **offering** Him sincere devotion, being True

OFFERINGS

005:097 the animals for **offerings**, and the garlands
037:091 (of the **offerings** before you)?

OFFERS

004:094 and say not to anyone who **offers** you a

OFFICE

003:079 And the Prophetic **Office**,

OFFSPRING

002:124 He pleaded: "And also (Imams) from my **offspring**!"
002:233 suck to their **offspring** for two whole years,
002:233 for your **offspring** there is no blame on you,
003:034 **Offspring**, one of the other:
003:036 and I commend her and her **offspring** to Thy
013:023 their spouses, and their **offspring** and angels
014:037 of my **offspring** to dwell in a valley without
014:040 and also (raise such) among my **offspring**, O our
021:089 without **offspring**, though Thou art the best
025:074 and **offspring** who will be the comfort of our
065:006 and if they suckle your (**offspring**), give them

OFT

002:249 said: "How **oft**, by Allah's will,
054:051 And (**oft**) in the past, have We destroyed

OFT-FORBEARING

017:044 Verily He is **Oft-Forbearing**, Most Forgiving!

OFT-FORGIVING

002:173 For god is **Oft-Forgiving**, Most Merciful.
002:182 for Allah is **Oft-Forgiving**, Most Merciful.
002:192 Allah is **Oft-Forgiving**, Most Merciful.
002:199 For Allah is **Oft-Forgiving**, Most Merciful.
002:218 and Allah is **Oft-Forgiving**, Most Merciful.
002:225 and He is **Oft-Forgiving**, Most Forbearing.
002:226 Allah is **Oft-Forgiving**, Most Merciful.
002:235 know that Allah is **Oft-Forgiving**, Most Forbearing.
003:031 for Allah is **Oft-Forgiving**, Most Merciful.
003:089 for verily Allah is **Oft-Forgiving**, Most Merciful.
003:129 but Allah is **Oft-Forgiving**, Most Merciful.
003:155 for Allah is **Oft-Forgiving**, Most Forbearing.
004:023 for Allah is **Oft-Forgiving**, Most Merciful.
004:025 And Allah is Oft-forgiving, Most Merciful.
004:096 For Allah is **Oft-Forgiving**. Most Merciful.

OFT-FORGIVING (continued)

004:100 and Allah is **Oft-Forgiving**, Most Merciful.
004:106 for Allah is **Oft-Forgiving**, Most Merciful.
004:110 he will find Allah **Oft-Forgiving**, Most Merciful.
004:129 Allah is **Oft-Forgiving**, Most Merciful.
004:152 for Allah is **Oft-Forgiving**, Most Merciful.
005:003 Allah is indeed **Oft-Forgiving**, Most Merciful.
005:034 know that Allah is **Oft-Forgiving**, Most Merciful.
005:039 for Allah is **Oft-Forgiving**, Most Merciful.
005:074 For Allah is Oft-forgiving, Most Merciful.
005:098 and that Allah is **Oft-Forgiving**, Most Merciful.
005:101 for Allah is **Oft-Forgiving**, Most Forbearing
006:054 lo! He is **Oft-Forgiving**, Most Merciful.
006:145 thy Lord is **Oft-Forgiving**, Most Merciful.
006:165 yet He is indeed **Oft-Forgiving**, Most Merciful.
007:153 thereafter **Oft-Forgiving**, Most Merciful.
007:167 but He is also **Oft-Forgiving**, Most Merciful.
008:070 for Allah Is **Oft-Forgiving**, Most Merciful."
008:069 for Allah is **Oft-Forgiving**, Most Merciful.
009:005 for Allah is **Oft-Forgiving**, Most Merciful.
009:027 for Allah is **Oft-Forgiving**, Most Merciful.
009:091 and Allah is **Oft-Forgiving**, Most Merciful.
009:099 for Allah is **Oft-Forgiving**, Most Merciful.
009:102 for Allah is **Oft-Forgiving**, Most Merciful.
010:107 And He is the **Oft-Forgiving**, Most Merciful.
011:041 be sure, **Oft-Forgiving**, Most Merciful!"
012:053 my Lord is **Oft-Forgiving**, Most Merciful.
012:098 for He is indeed **Oft-Forgiving**, Merciful."
014:036 but thou art indeed **Oft-Forgiving**, Most Merciful.
015:049 I am indeed the **Oft-Forgiving**, Most Merciful;
016:018 **Oft-Forgiving**, Most Merciful.
016:110 after all this is **Oft-Forgiving**, Most Merciful.
016:115 then Allah is **Oft-Forgiving**, Most Merciful.
016:119 all this, is **Oft-Forgiving**, Most Merciful.
024:005 for Allah is **Oft-Forgiving**, Most Merciful.
024:022 For Allah is **Oft-Forgiving**, Most Merciful.
024:033 is Allah **Oft-Forgiving**, Most Merciful (to them).
024:062 for Allah is **Oft-Forgiving**, Most Merciful.
025:006 verily He is **Oft-Forgiving**, Most Merciful."
025:070 and Allah is **Oft-Forgiving**, Most Merciful,
027:011 truly, I am **Oft-Forgiving**, Most Merciful.
028:016 for He is the **Oft-Forgiving**, Most Merciful.
033:024 for Allah is **Oft-Forgiving**, Most Merciful.
033:050 And Allah is **Oft-Forgiving**, Most Merciful.
033:059 and Allah is **Oft-Forgiving**, Most Merciful.
033:073 for Allah is **Oft-Forgiving**, Most Merciful.
034:002 and He is the Most Merciful, the **Oft-Forgiving**.
034:015 and a Lord **Oft-Forgiving**!"
035:028 Exalted in Might, **Oft-Forgiving**.
035:030 **Oft-Forgiving**, Most Ready to appreciate (service).
035:034 for Our Lord is indeed **Oft-Forgiving** ready to
035:041 verily He is Most Forbearing, **Oft-Forgiving**.
039:053 for He is **Oft-Forgiving**, Most Merciful.
041:032 **Oft-Forgiving**, Most Merciful!"
042:005 the **Oft-Forgiving**, Most Merciful.
042:023 for Allah is **Oft-Forgiving**, Grateful.
046:008 **Oft-Forgiving**, Most Merciful."
048:014 but Allah is **Oft-Forgiving**, Most Merciful.
049:005 but Allah is **Oft-Forgiving**, Most Merciful.
049:014 for Allah is **Oft-Forgiving**, Most Merciful."
057:028 is **Oft-Forgiving**, Most Merciful:
058:012 Allah is **Oft-Forgiving**, Most Merciful.
060:007 and Allah is **Oft-Forgiving**, Most Merciful.

OFT-FORGIVING (continued)

060:012 for Allah is **Oft-Forgiving**, Most Merciful.
064:014 verily Allah is **Oft-Forgiving**, Most Merciful.
066:001 But Allah is **Oft-Forgiving**, Most Merciful.
067:002 the Exalted in Might, **Oft-Forgiving**;
071:010 for He is **Oft-Forgiving**;
073:020 for Allah is **Oft-Forgiving**, Most Merciful.
085:014 And He is the **Oft-Forgiving**, Full of

OFT-RELENTING

002:128 the **Oft-Returning**, Most-Merciful.

OFT-REPEATED

015:087 Seven **Oft-Repeated** (verses) and the Grand Qur'an.
025:014 plead for destruction **oft-repeated**!"
079:007 Followed by **oft-repeated** (commotions):

OFT-RETURNING

002:037 for He is **Oft-Returning**, Most Merciful.
002:054 for He is **Oft-returning**, Most Merciful.
002:160 for I am **Oft-Returning**, Most Merciful.
004:016 for Allah is **Oft-returning**, Most Merciful.
004:064 found Allah indeed **Oft-Returning**, Most Merciful.
009:104 the **Oft-Returning**, Most Merciful?
009:118 for Allah is **Oft-Returning**, Most Merciful.
024:010 on you, and that Allah is **Oft-Returning**, Full of
033:005 is **Oft-Returning**, Most Merciful.
049:012 **Oft-returning**, Most Merciful.
110:003 for He is **Oft-Returning** (in forgiveness).

OFTEN

004:056 as **often** as their skins are roasted through.
008:045 much (and **often**); that ye may prosper.
015:002 **Often** will those who disbelieve, wish that

OH

002:259 He said: "**Oh**! how shall Allah bring it
004:073 "**Oh**! I wish I had been with them: a fine
011:087 They said: "**Oh** Shu'aib! Does thy prayer
012:017 They said: "**Oh** our father! we went
025:027 "**Oh**! would that I had taken a (straight) path
028:079 this World: "**Oh**! that we had the like of what

OIL

012:049 will press (wine and **oil**)."
023:020 Mount Sinai, which produces **oil**, and relish
024:035 whose **Oil is** well-nigh luminous, though fire

OINTMENT

055:037 and it becomes red like **ointment**:

OLD

002:068 should be neither too **old** nor too young,
002:089 although from of **old** they had prayed
002:108 as Moses was questioned of **old**?
002:266 while he is stricken with **old** age,
003:040 seeing I am very **old**, and my wife is barren?"
005:110 to the people in childhood and in **old** age. Behold!
009:030 Unbelievers of **old** used to say. Allah's cures
011:072 and my husband here is an **old** man? That would
011:072 a child, seeing I am an **old** woman, and my husband
012:095 in thine **old** wandering illusion."
012:100 the fulfillment of my vision of **old**! Allah hath
014:039 unto me in **old** age Isma'il and Isaac: for truly
015:010 thee amongst the sects of **old**:
015:054 glad tidings even though **old** age has seized me?
017:023 **old** age in thy life, say not to them a word
019:008 and I have grown quite decrepit from **old** age?"
021:005 the ones that were sent to (prophets) of **old**!"
022:005 **old** age, so that they know nothing after having

OLD (continued)

023:024 among our ancestors of **old**."
023:068 to their fathers of **old**?
026:171 Except an **old** woman who lingered behind.
028:023 (their flocks): and our father is a very **old** man."
028:036 among our fathers of **old**!"
033:038 of Allah amongst those of **old** that have
036:039 she returns like the **old** (and withered)
037:017 "And also our fathers of **old**?"
037:075 (In the days of **old**), Noah cried to Us, and We
037:114 Again, (of **old**). We bestowed Our favour
037:126 and the Lord and Cherisher of your fathers of **old**?"
037:135 Except an **old** woman who was among those who
037:168 a message from those of **old**,
040:023 Of **old** We sent Moses, with Our Signs
040:067 then lets you become **old**,-through of
040:074 nay, we invoked not, of **old**, anything (that
043:006 We sent amongst the peoples of **old**?
043:008 the example of the peoples of **old**.
046:011 "This is an (**old**), **old** falsehood!"
046:011 "This is an (**old**), **old** falsehood!"
051:029 "A barren **old** woman!"
052:028 of **old**: truly it is He, the Beneficent
053:056 of the (series of) Warners of **old**!
056:013 A number of people from those of **old**,
056:039 A (goodly) number from those of **old**,
056:048 "(We) and our fathers of **old**?"
056:049 Say: "Yea, those of **old** and those of later times,
067:005 And We have, (from of **old**), adorned the
074:024 but magic derived from of **old**;"
077:016 Did We not destroy the men of **old** (for their evil)?

OLIVE

024:035 lit from a blessed Tree, an **Olive**, neither of
095:001 By the Fig and the **Olive**,

OLIVES

006:099 and **olives**, and pomegranates, each similar
006:141 and **olives** and pomegranates, similar
016:011 **olives**, date-palms, grapes, and every kind of
080:029 And **Olives** and Dates,

OMEN

027:047 They said: "Ill **omen** do we augur from thee
027:047 He said: "Your ill **omen** is with Allah; yea, ye
036:018 an evil **omen** from you: if ye desist not,
036:019 an evil **omen**), if ye are admonished? Nay, but

OMENS

007:131 they ascribed it to evil **omens** connected with
007:131 Behold! in truth the **omens** of evil are theirs
036:019 They said: "Your evil **omens** are with yourselves:

OMITTED

006:038 Nothing have We **omitted** from the Book, and they

OMNIPOTENT

054:055 In a sure abode with a Sovereign **Omnipotent**.

OMNISCIENT

006:096 the Exalted in Power, the **Omniscient**.

ON

001:007 The way of those **on** whom thou hast bestowed
002:005 They are **on** (true) guidance,
002:007 seal **on** their hearts and **on** their hearing,
002:007 and **on** their eyes is a veil;
002:007 Allah hath set a seal **on** their hearts
002:011 "Make not mischief **on** the earth,"
002:015 Allah will throw back their mockery **on** them,

ON (continued)

002:020 and when the darkness grows **on** them,
002:027 and do mischief **on** earth:
002:029 for you all things that are **on** earth;
002:030 "I will create a vicegerent **on** earth."
002:036 **On** earth will be your dwelling place
002:038 **on** them shall be no fear,
002:044 Do ye enjoin right conduct **on** the people,
002:059 so We sent **on** the transgressors
002:060 evil nor mischief **on** the (face of the) earth.
002:061 This because they went **on** rejecting
002:061 they drew **on** themselves the wrath of Allah.
002:061 rebelled and went **on** transgressing.
002:062 **on** them shall be no fear,
002:068 They said: "Beseech **on** our behalf thy Lord
002:069 They said: "Beseech **on** our behalf thy Lord
002:070 They said, "Beseech **on** our behalf thy Lord
002:085 and **on** the Day of Judgment
002:088 is **on** them for their blasphemy;
002:089 is **on** those without Faith.
002:090 **on** themselves Wrath upon Wrath.
002:095 their hands have sent **on** before them.
002:095 **on** account of the (sins) which their hands
002:112 **on** such shall be no fear,
002:113 in their quarrel **on** the Day of Judgment.
002:116 that is in the heavens and the earth:
002:137 they are indeed **on** the right path;
002:143 who would turn **on** their heels (from the Faith).
002:150 that are bent **on** wickedness;
002:150 and that I may complete My favours **on** you,
002:157 They are those **on** whom (descend)
002:159 **on** them shall be Allah's curse,
002:161 **on** them is Allah's curse,
002:168 O ye people! eat of what is **on** earth,
002:173 and that **on** which any other name
002:174 **on** the Day of Resurrection,
002:181 the guilt shall be **on** those who make the change.
002:182 wrong-doing **on** the part of the testator.
002:184 but if any of you is ill, or **on** a journey,
002:185 but if any one is ill, or **on** a journey,
002:186 of every suppliant when he calleth **on** Me:
002:187 Permitted to you **on** the night of the fasts,
002:193 And fight them **on** until there is no more
002:196 to continue the 'Umra **on** to the Hajj.
002:196 And seven days **on** his return,
002:201 and save us from the torment **on** the Fire!"
002:203 there is no blame **on** him,
002:203 and if anyone stays **on**,
002:206 an evil bed indeed (to lie **on**)!
002:212 His abundance without measures **on** whom He will.
002:212 above them **on** the Day of Resurrection;
002:220 (Their bearings) **on** this life and the Hereafter.
002:229 hold together **on** equitable terms,
002:229 there is no blame **on** either of them
002:230 no blame **on** either of them if they re-unite,
002:231 but solemnly rehearse Allah's favours **on** you,
002:231 or set them free **on** equitable terms;
002:231 either take them back **on** equitable terms
002:232 if they mutually agree **on** equitable terms.
002:233 If they both decide **on** weaning,
002:233 Nor father **on** account of his child,
002:233 laid **on** it greater than it can bear.
002:233 There is no blame **on** them,

ON (continued)

002:233 of their food and clothing **on** equitable terms.
002:233 if ye decide **on** a foster-mother for your offspring
002:233 for your offspring there is no blame **on** you,
002:233 **on** equitable terms.
002:233 treated unfairly **on** account of her child.
002:234 there is no blame **on** you if they dispose
002:235 nor resolve **on** the tie of marriage
002:235 There is no blame **on** you if ye make an indirect
002:236 but bestow **on** them (a suitable gift),
002:236 There is no blame **on** you if ye divorce women
002:239 If ye fear (an enemy), pray **on** foot,
002:240 there is no blame **on** you for what they do
002:241 suitable Gift this is duty **on** the righteous.
002:250 **on** us and make our steps firm:
002:255 His are all things in the heavens and **on** earth.
002:260 **on** every hill, and call to them:
002:262 **on** them shall be no fear, nor shall they grieve.
002:264 **on** which is a little soil;
002:264 **on** it falls a heavy rain,
002:265 heavy rain falls **on** it but makes it yield
002:274 **on** them shall be no fear, nor shall they grieve.
002:277 **on** them shall be no fear,
002:282 ye carry out **on** the spot among yourselves,
002:282 there is no blame **on** you if ye reduce it
002:282 refuse when they are called **on** (for evidence).
002:283 deposits a thing **on** trust with another,
002:283 If ye are **on** a journey, and cannot find a scribe,
002:284 that is in the heavens and **on** earth.
002:286 lay **on** those before us;
002:286 Have mercy **on** us.
002:286 our Lord! Lay not **on** us a burden like that
002:286 Our Lord! lay not **on** us a burden
002:286 **On** no soul doth Allah place a burden
003:005 is hidden **on** earth or in the heavens.
003:012 an evil bed indeed (to lie **on**)!
003:018 standing firm **on** justice.
003:027 "Thou causest the Night to gain **on** the Day.
003:027 And Thou causest the Day to gain **on** the Night;
003:029 in the heavens, and what is **on** earth.
003:030 "**On** the day when every soul will be confronted
003:052 unbelief **on** their part he said: "Who will be
003:061 And invoke the curse of Allah **on** those who lie!
003:077 or look at them **on** the Day of Judgment,
003:079 **on** the contrary (he would say): "Be ye worshippers
003:081 and take My covenant as binding **on** you?"
003:083 While all creatures in the heavens and **on** earth have,
003:087 **on** them (rests) the curse of Allah,
003:090 And then go **on** adding to their defiance of Faith,
003:103 and remember with gratitude Allah's favour **on** you;
003:103 and ye were **on** the brink of the Pit of Fire,
003:106 **On** the day when some faces will be
003:112 they draw **on** themselves wrath from Allah.
003:125 rush here **on** you in hot haste,
003:129 that is in the heavens and **on** earth.
003:144 but Allah (**on** the other hand) will swiftly
003:144 If any did turn back **on** his heels,
003:144 will ye then turn back **on** your heels?
003:149 they will drive you back **on** your heels,
003:154 He sent down calm **on** a band of you
003:155 **on** the day the two hosts met, it was Satan
003:161 he shall, **on** the Day of Judgment, restore
003:162 the man who draws **on** Himself the wrath of Allah,

ON (continued)

003:164 **on** the Believers when He sent among them
003:166 What ye suffered **on** the day the two armies met,
003:170 the fact that **on** them is no fear,
003:180 **on** the Day of Judgment.
003:182 which your hands sent **on** before ye:
003:185 and only **on** the Day of Judgment shall you
003:191 and lying down **on** their sides, and contemplate
003:194 and save us from shame **on** the Day of Judgment:
003:197 what an evil bed (to lie **on**)!
003:198 **On** the other hand, for those who fear their Lord,
004:005 (**on** marriage) their dower as an obligation;
004:019 with them **on** a footing of kindness and equity
004:019 **on** the contrary live with them
004:024 there is no blame **on** you, and Allah
004:032 gifts more freely **on** some of you than **on** others:
004:034 As to those women **on** whose part ye fear
004:037 hide the bounties which Allah hath bestowed **on** them;
004:037 enjoin niggardliness **on** others, hide
004:039 And what burden were it **on** them if they had faith
004:042 **On** that day those who reject Faith and
004:043 or **on** a journey, or one of you cometh from
004:069 those **on** whom is the Grace of Allah, of the
004:081 **on** things very different from what
004:081 They have "Obedience" **on** their lips; but
004:082 Do they not ponder **on** the Qur'an?
004:087 gather you together **on** the Day of Judgement,
004:089 and thus be **on** the same footing (as they):
004:094 till Allah conferred **on** you His favours:
004:101 there is no blame **on** you if ye shorten
004:102 But there is no blame **on** you if ye put away
004:103 or lying down **on** your sides; but
004:103 **on** Believers at stated times.
004:107 Contend not **on** behalf of such as
004:109 **on** their behalf **on** the Day of Judgment, or
004:109 Ah! these are the sort of men **on** whose behalf
004:112 and throws it **on** to one that is innocent,
004:112 He carries (**on** himself) (both)
004:126 in the heavens and **on** earth: and He
004:128 there is no blame **on** them if they arrange
004:128 or desertion **on** her husband's part, there
004:131 belong all things in the heavens and **on** earth.
004:131 in the heavens and **on** earth.
004:132 all things in the heavens and **on** earth, and
004:137 and go **on** increasing in Unbelief, Allah will
004:137 nor guide them **on** the Way.
004:141 betwixt you **on** the Day of Judgment.
004:154 and (**on** another occasion) We said: "Enter
004:155 **on** their hearts for their blasphemy, and
004:159 and **on** the Day of Judgment He will be
004:170 in the heavens and **on** earth: and Allah
004:171 in the heavens and **on** earth.
004:171 and His Word, which He bestowed **on** Mary, and
005:002 transgression (and hostility **on** your part).
005:003 and that **on** which hath been invoked
005:003 that which is sacrificed **on** stone (altars);
005:006 But if ye are ill, or **on** a journey, or one
005:011 And **on** Allah let Believers put (all) their trust.
005:013 barring a few-ever bent **on** (new) deceits: but
005:017 and all-every one that is **on** the earth?
005:023 were two **on** whom Allah had bestowed His Grace:
005:023 But **on** Allah put your trust if ye have faith."
005:029 thee draw **on** thyself my sin as well as thine, for

ON (continued)

005:032 **On** that account: We ordained
005:036 if they had everything **on** earth, and twice
005:054 which He will bestow **on** whom He pleaseth.
005:064 but they (ever) strive to do mischief **on** earth.
005:066 a party **on** the right course: but many
005:069 **on** them shall be no fear, nor shall they grieve.
005:078 Curses were pronounced **on** those among
005:080 that Allah's wrath is **on** them, and in torment
005:089 **on** a scale of the average for the food
005:093 **On** those who believe and do deeds
005:097 of what is in the heavens and **on** earth and that
005:102 and **on** that account lost their faith.
005:109 **On** the day when Allah will gather the
005:115 **on** anyone among all the peoples.
005:119 "This is a day **on** which the truthful will profit
006:006 Generations We had established **on** the earth, in
006:007 a written (Message) **on** parchment, so that
006:012 is in the heavens and **on** earth?" Say:
006:016 "**On** that day, if the penalty
006:022 **On** the day shall We gather them all together: We
006:025 but We have thrown veils **on** their hearts, so
006:029 "There is nothing except our life **on** this earth,
006:031 until **on** a sudden the hour is **on** them, and they
006:031 for they bear their burdens **on** their backs; and
006:035 If their spurning is hard **on** thee, yet if
006:038 nor a being that flies **on** its wings, but
006:038 (that lives) **on** the earth, nor a being
006:039 He placeth **on** the Way that is Straight.
006:041 "Nay,-**On** Him would ye call, and if
006:043 **On** the contrary their hearts became hardened, and
006:044 **on** a sudden, We called them to account, when lo!
006:052 **on** their Lord morning and evening, seeking
006:054 "Peace be **on** you: your Lord hath inscribed for
006:057 Say: "For me, I (work) **on** a clear Sign
006:059 **on** the earth and in the sea. Not a
006:065 send calamities **on** you, from above and below, or
006:069 **On** their account no responsibility falls **on**
006:069 falls **on** the righteous, but (their duty)
006:071 Say: "Shall we call **on** others besides Allah,-
006:071 and turn **on** our heels after receiving
006:082 for they are **on** (right) guidance."
006:094 all (the favours) which We bestowed **on** you: We
006:116 the common run of those **on** earth, they will
006:118 **on** which Allah's name hath been pronounced, if
006:119 **on** which Allah's name hath been pronounced, when
006:121 Eat not of (meats) **on** which Allah's name
006:125 **on** those who refuse to believe.
006:128 **On** the day when He will gather them
006:138 and cattle **on** which (at slaughter) the name
006:141 **on** the day that the harvest is gathered. But
006:145 (meat) **on** which a name has been invoked, other
006:151 kill not your children **on** a plea of want;-We
006:152 no burden do We place **on** any soul, but that
006:164 of its acts **on** none but itself: no bearer
007:002 no more by any difficulty **on** that account,-that
007:004 Our punishment took them **on** a sudden by night or
007:010 placed you with authority **on** earth, and provided
007:016 for them **on** Thy Straight Way:
007:024 **On** earth will be your dwelling-place and your
007:032 (and) purely for them **on** the Day of Judgment.
007:035 **on** them shall be no fear, nor shall they grieve.
007:042 no burden do We place **on** any soul, but that

ON (continued)

007:044	"The curse of Allah is **on** the wrong-doers;
007:046	and **on** the Heights will be men who would
007:048	The men **on** the Heights will call
007:049	Enter ye the Garden: no fear shall be **on** you, nor
007:052	based **on** knowledge, Which We explained in detail,-
007:053	now to intercede **on** our behalf? Or could
007:053	**On** the day when it is fulfilled those who
007:054	then He settled Himself **on** the Throne: He draweth
007:055	Call **on** your Lord with humility and in private:
007:056	Do no mischief **on** the earth, after it
007:056	but call **on** Him with fear and longing
007:061	**on** the contrary I am a messenger from the
007:074	and refrain from evil and mischief **on** the earth."
007:081	**on** men in preference to women: ye are
007:084	**on** them a shower (of brimstone): then see
007:085	and do no mischief **on** the earth after it
007:086	"And squat not **on** every road, breathing
007:124	and your feet **on** opposite sides, and I
007:126	**on** us simply because we believed in the Signs
007:126	Our Lord! pour out **on** us patience
007:132	to work therewith the sorcery **on** us, we shall
007:133	So We sent **on** them: Wholesale Death,
007:134	And when the Plague fell **on** them, they said:
007:134	call **on** thy Lord in virtue
007:134	they said: "O Moses! **on** our behalf call **on**
007:146	**on** the earth in defiance of right-them will I
007:150	**on** the judgment of your Lord?" He put down
007:156	**on** whom I will; but My Mercy
007:162	so We sent **on** them a plague from heaven. For
007:163	but **on** the day they had no Sabbath, they came
007:163	for **on** the day of their Sabbath their fish
007:168	into sections **on** this earth. There are
007:171	to fall **on** them (We said): "Hold firmly
007:172	lest ye should say **on** the Day of Judgment: "Of
007:178	he is **on** the right path: whom He
007:180	so call **on** Him by them; but shun
008:009	of the angels, ranks **on** ranks."
008:011	and He caused rain to descend **on** you from heaven,
008:016	he draws **on** himself the wrath of Allah, and his
008:016	to them **on** such a day-unless it
008:017	in order the He might confer **on** the Believers
008:032	rain down **on** us a shower of stones from the sky,
008:037	Put the impure, one **on** another, heap them
008:039	And fight them **on** until there is no
008:041	to our Servant **on** the Day of Discrimination-
008:042	and the caravan **on** lower ground than ye. Even if
008:042	the valley, and they **on** the farther side, and the
008:042	Remember ye were **on** the hither side of the valley,
008:048	he turned **on** his heels, and said:
008:053	**on** a people until they change what is in their
008:058	(so as to be) **on** equal terms: for Allah
008:073	tumult and oppression **on** earth, and great
009:003	**on** the day of the Great Pilgrimage,-that Allah
009:018	It is they who are expected to be **on** true guidance.
009:025	in many battle-fields and **on** the day of Hunain:
009:026	the Messenger and **on** the Believers, and sent
009:026	But Allah did pour His calm **on** the Messenger
009:030	Allah's curse be **on** them: how they
009:035	**On** the Day when it will be heated
009:042	(and weighed) **on** them. They would
009:049	Hell surrounds the Unbelievers (**on** all sides).
009:051	He is our Protector": and **on** Allah let the

ON (continued)

009:071	and His Messenger. **On** them will Allah pour His
009:074	none **on** earth to protect or help them.
009:075	**on** them of His bounty; they would
009:079	and throw ridicule **on** them,-Allah will
009:079	Allah will throw back their ridicule **on** them: and
009:083	**on** the first occasion: then sit
009:091	(**on** the Cause), if they are sincere (in duty)
009:091	There is no blame **on** those who are infirm, or ill,
009:092	Nor (is there blame) **on** those who came to thee
009:098	**on** them be the disaster of Evil: for Allah
009:099	and look **on** their payments as pious gifts bringing
009:103	sanctify them; and pray **on** their behalf. Verily
009:108	was laid from the first day **on** piety; it is
009:109	his foundation **on** piety to Allah and His
009:109	layeth his foundation **on** an undermined sand-cliff
009:111	a promise binding **on** Him in Truth, through the
009:129	there is no god but He: **On** him is my trust,-He the
010:003	**on** the Throne. Regulating and governing
010:007	**on** their meeting with Us, but are
010:011	as they would fain hasten **on** the good,-then would
010:011	their hope **on** their meeting with Us, in their
010:012	**on** his way as if he had never cried to Us for the
010:012	lying down **on** his side, or sitting, or standing.
010:015	**on** their meeting with Us, say: "Bring
010:018	in the heaven or **on** earth?-Glory to Him! and far
010:037	**on** the contrary it is a confirmation of
010:045	And **on** the day when He will gather them together:
010:051	and ye wanted (aforetime) to hasten it **on**!"
010:054	if it possessed all that is **on** earth, would fain
010:055	the heavens and **on** earth? Is it not
010:060	against Allah, **on** the Day of Judgment?
010:061	**on** the earth or in heaven. And not
010:062	Behold! verily **on** the friends of Allah there is
010:066	all creatures, in the heavens and **on** earth. What
010:068	and **on** earth! No warrant have ye for this!
010:071	"O my People, if it be hard **on** your (mind) that I
010:071	**on** me, and give me no respite.
010:083	was mighty **on** the earth and one who
010:088	indeed bestowed **on** Pharaoh and his Chiefs
010:093	**on** the Day of Judgment.
010:099	all who are **on** earth! Wilt thou
010:100	**on** those who will not understand.
010:101	in the heavens and **on** earth"; but neither
010:103	thus is it fitting **on** Our part that We
010:106	"Nor call **on** any, other than Allah,-such can
011:003	**on** all who abound in merit! But if
011:006	but its sustenance dependeth **on** Allah: He knoweth
011:006	There is no moving creature **on** earth but its
011:008	Ah! **On** the day it (actually) reaches them,
011:018	is **on** those who do wrong!-
011:033	**on** you if He wills-and then, ye will
011:035	Say: "If I had forged it, **on** me were my sin!
011:037	**on** behalf of those who are in sin: for they
011:038	they threw ridicule **on** him. He said: "If ye
011:038	**on** you with ridicule likewise!
011:039	**on** whom will descend a Chastisement that will
011:039	**on** whom will be unloosed a Chastisement lasting."
011:041	So he said: "Embark ye **on** the Ark, in the
011:042	**on** the waves (towering) like mountains, and Noah
011:043	of Allah, any but those **on** whom He hath mercy!"-
011:044	rested **on** Mount Judi and the word went forth:
011:047	and have Mercy **on** me, I should indeed

ON (continued)

011:048 and Blessing **on** thee and **on** some of the Peoples
011:053 **on** thy word! Nor shall we believe in thee!
011:056 Verily, it is my Lord that is **on** a Straight Path.
011:060 in this Life,-and **on** the Day of Judgment. Ah!
011:064 leave her to feed **on** Allah's (free) earth,
011:064 (free) earth, and inflict no harm **on** her, or a
011:073 and His blessings **on** you, O ye people
011:077 he was grieved **on** their account and felt himself
011:082 baked clay, spread, layer **on** layer,-
011:082 down **on** them brimstones hard as baked clay,
011:093 soon will ye know who it is **on** whom descends the
011:098 **on** the Day of Judgment, and lead
011:099 this (life) and **on** the Day of Judgment: and woeful
011:119 Except those **on** whom thy Lord hath bestowed
012:036 (in a dream) carrying bread **on** my head, and birds
012:056 We bestow of Our mercy **on** whom We please, and We
012:067 and let all that trust put their trust **on** Him."
012:067 **on** Him do I put my trust: and let
012:092 be (cast) **on** you: Allah will forgive you, and He
012:100 And he raised his parents high **on** the throne
012:101 bestowed **on** me some power, and taught me
013:002 then He established Himself **on** the Throne. He has
013:006 They ask thee to hasten **on** the evil
013:017 the good of mankind remains **on** the earth. Thus
013:018 in the heavens and **on** earth, and as much
013:025 in the land;-**on** them is the Curse; for them
013:030 but He! **On** Him is my trust, and to Him I turn!"
013:033 He knoweth not **on** earth, or is it
014:002 in the heavens and **on** earth! But alas
014:008 ye and all **on** earth together,-yet is Allah
014:009 "We do deny (the mission) **on** which ye have
014:011 And **on** Allah let all men of faith put their trust.
014:012 **on** Allah. Indeed He has guided us to the Ways
014:012 should put their trust **on** Allah."
014:018 blows furiously **on** a tempestuous day: no power
014:018 as ashes, **on** which the wind blows furiously
014:038 from Allah, whether **on** earth or in heaven.
014:041 **on** the Day that the Reckoning will be established!"
015:035 **on** thee till the Day of Judgment."
015:039 to them **on** the earth, and I will
015:047 (joyfully) facing each other **on** raised couches.
015:057 the business **on** which ye (Have come), O ye
015:065 but pass **on** whither ye are ordered."
015:074 **on** them brimstones hard as baked clay.
015:076 And the (cities were) right **on** the high-road.
015:079 They were both **on** an open highway, plain to see.
015:088 **on** certain classes of them, nor grieve over them:
015:090 sent down **on** those who divided (Scripture
015:091 (So also **on** such) as have made Qur'an into
016:010 the vegetation **on** which ye feed your cattle.
016:013 And the things **on** this earth which He has
016:015 And He has set up **on** the earth mountains standing
016:025 That they may bear, **on** the Day of Judgment,
016:026 fell down **on** them from above; and the Wrath
016:027 Then, **on** the Day of Judgment, He will
016:032 saying (to them), "Peace be **on** you; enter ye
016:036 and some **on** whom Error became inevitably
016:038 a promise (binding) **on** Him in truth: but most
016:042 in patience, and put their trust **on** their Lord.
016:049 is in the heavens and **on** earth, whether moving
016:052 the heavens and **on** earth, and to Him
016:055 the favours We have bestowed **on** them! Then enjoy

ON (continued)

016:059 **on** (sufferance and) Contempt, or bury it
016:059 Ah! what an evil (choice) they decide **on**!
016:061 **on** the (earth), a single living creature: but He
016:062 to be hastened **on** into it!
016:068 to build its cells in hills, **on** trees, and in
016:071 of sustenance more freely **on** some of you than
016:071 you than **on** others; those more favoured are not
016:075 **on** whom We have bestowed goodly favours from
016:076 who commands justice, and is **on** the Straight Way?
016:081 **on** you, that ye may surrender to His Will
016:084 **On** the Day We shall raise from all Peoples
016:089 **On** the day We shall raise from all peoples
016:092 and **on** the Day of Judgment He will certainly
016:094 and a mighty Wrath descend **on** you.
016:096 **on** those who patiently persevere, their reward
016:097 and We will bestow **on** such their reward
016:106 to Unbelief,-**on** them is Wrath from Allah,
016:111 **On** the Day every soul will come up pleading
016:112 **on** it) like a garment (from every side), because
016:124 judge between them **on** the Day of Judgment as to
017:004 **on** the earth and be elated with mighty arrogance
017:013 **on** his own neck: **On** the Day of Judgment We shall
017:020 We bestow freely **on** all-these as well as those:
017:021 than **on** others; but verily the Hereafter is more
017:021 See how We have bestowed more **on** some than **on**
017:024 "My Lord! bestow **on** them Thy Mercy even as they
017:034 will be enquired into (**on** the Day of Reckoning).
017:037 Nor walk **on** the earth with insolence: for thou
017:046 they turn **on** their backs, fleeing (from the Truth).
017:052 "It will be **on** a Day when He will call you,
017:055 and **on** earth: and We made some of the Prophets
017:056 Say: "Call **on** those-besides Him-whom ye fancy:
017:064 (seductive) voice; make assaults **on** them with
017:068 beneath the earth when ye are **on** land, or that
017:070 provided them with transport **on** land and sea;
017:070 and conferred **on** them special favours, above a
017:071 **On** the day We shall call together all human
017:083 Yet when We bestow Our favours **on** man, he turns
017:083 he turns away and becomes remote **on** his side
017:084 is best guided **on** the Way."
017:095 **on** earth, angels walking about in peace and quite,
017:097 that is **on** true guidance; but he
017:097 **On** the Day of Judgment We shall gather them
017:097 gather them together, prone **on** their faces,
017:107 fall down **on** their faces in humble prostration,
017:109 They fall down **on** their faces in tears, and it
018:007 That which is **on** earth We have made but as
018:008 Verily what is **on** earth We shall make but as
018:010 bestow **on** us Mercy from Thyself, and dispose
018:016 His mercies **on** you and dispose of your affair
018:018 two forelegs **on** the threshold: if thou
018:018 and We turned them **on** their right and their
018:022 except **on** a matter that is clear, nor consult
018:028 who call **on** their Lord morning and evening,
018:029 the drink! How uncomfortable a couch to recline **on**!
018:031 recline therein **on** raised thrones. How good
018:031 How beautiful a couch to recline **on**!
018:040 and that He will send **on** thy garden thunderbolts
018:042 over what he had spent **on** his property,
018:047 **On** the Day We shall remove the mountains, and thou
018:052 **On** the Day He will say, "Call **on**
018:052 My partners," and they will call **on** them, but they

ON (continued)

018:052 "Call **on** those whom ye thought to be My partners,"
018:062 When they had passed **on** (some distance), Moses said
018:064 **on** their footsteps, following (the path they
018:065 **On** whom We had bestowed Mercy from Ourselves
018:066 **on** the footing that thou teach me something
018:077 **on** the point of falling down, but he
018:079 they plied **on** the water: I but
018:079 king who seized **on** every boat by force.
018:084 Verily We established his power **on** earth, and We
018:090 the sun, he found it rising **on** a people for whom
018:094 do great mischief **on** earth: shall we
018:099 to surge like waves **on** one another: the trumpet
018:099 **On** that day We shall leave them to surge
018:105 **on** the Day of Judgment, give them any Weight.
019:007 his name shall be Yahya: **on** none by that name
019:015 So Peace **on** him the day he was born, the day
019:031 **on** me Prayer and Charity as long as I live;
019:033 "So Peace is **on** me the day I was born, the day
019:047 Abraham said: "Peace be **on** thee: I will
019:048 besides Allah: I will call **on** my Lord perhaps,
019:049 besides Allah, We bestowed **on** him Isaac and Jacob,
019:050 **on** the tongue of truth.
019:050 And We bestowed of Our Mercy **on** them, and We
019:055 He used to enjoin **on** his people Prayer and Zakat
019:058 **on** whom Allah did bestow His Grace,-of the
019:068 **on** their knees round about Hell;
019:083 set Satans **on** against the Unbelievers, to incite
019:095 to him singly **on** the Day of Judgment.
019:096 **On** those who believe and work deeds
020:004 the earth and the heavens **on** high.
020:005 is firmly established **on** the throne.
020:006 in the heavens and **on** earth, and all
020:018 He said, "It is my rod: **on** it I lean; with it
020:037 **on** thee another time (before).
020:039 the river will cast him up **on** the bank, and he
020:066 so it seemed to him **on** account of their magic-
020:071 **on** trunks of palm-trees: so shall
020:071 and feet **on** opposite sides, and I
020:080 **on** the right side of Mount (Sinai), and We
020:081 lest My Wrath should descend **on** you: and those
020:081 and those **on** whom descends My Wrath
020:082 and do right,-who, in fine, are **on** true guidance."
020:083 (When Moses was up **on** the mount, Allah said):
020:084 **on** my footsteps: I hastened to Thee, O my Lord
020:086 **on** you, and so ye broke your promise to me?"
020:100 **on** the Day of Judgement;
020:101 be to them **on** that Day,-
020:108 **On** that Day will they follow the caller
020:109 **On** that Day shall no intercession avail except for
020:111 the man that carries iniquity (**on** his back).
020:115 and We found **on** his part no firm resolve.
020:124 him up blind **on** the Day of Judgment."
020:132 Enjoin prayer **on** thy people, and be
020:135 ye know who it is that is **on** the straight
021:004 and **on** earth: He is the One that heareth and
021:019 in the heavens and **on** earth: even those
021:031 And We have set **on** the earth mountains standing
021:051 We bestowed aforetime **on** Abraham his rectitude
021:072 And We bestowed **on** him Isaac and, as an
021:084 We removed the distress that was **on** him, and We
021:090 they used to call **on** Us in yearning and awe.
021:095 But there is a ban **on** any population which We

ON (continued)

022:005 down rain **on** it, it is stirred (to life),
022:009 and **on** the Day of Judgment We shall make him
022:011 they turn **on** their faces: they lose
022:011 as it were, **on** the verge: if good
022:012 They call **on** such deities, besides Allah,
022:013 (Perhaps) they call **on** one whose hurt is nearer
022:017 Allah will judge between them **on** the Day of
022:018 and **on** earth,-the sun, the moon, the stars;
022:027 and (mounted) **on** every kind of camel, lean (**on**
022:027 they will come to thee **on** foot and (mounted)
022:027 lean (**on** account of journeys) through deep
022:031 or the wind had swooped (like a bird **on** its prey)
022:036 **on** their sides (after slaughter), eat ye
022:045 They tumbled down **on** their roofs. And how
022:047 Yet they ask thee to hasten **on** the Punishment!
022:054 And that those **on** whom knowledge has been
022:056 **On** that Day the Dominion will be that of Allah:
022:058 **on** them will Allah bestow verily a goodly
022:064 the heavens and **on** earth: for verily
022:065 **on** the earth, and the ships that sail through
022:065 **on** the earth except by His leave: for Allah
022:067 assuredly **on** the Right Way.
022:067 let them not then dispute with thee **on** the matter,
022:069 "Allah will judge between you **on** the Day of Judgment
022:070 Allah knows all that is in heaven and **on** earth?
022:072 thou wilt notice a denial **on** the faces of the Unbelievers!
022:073 Those **on** whom, besides Allah ye call,
022:078 **on** you in religion; it is the religion of your
023:016 Again, **on** the Day of Judgment, will ye
023:022 And **on** them, as well as in ships, ye ride.
023:027 take thou **on** board pairs of every species,
023:028 **on** the Ark-thou and those with thee,-say: "Praise
023:033 in the Hereafter, and **on** whom We had bestowed
023:050 **on** high ground, affording rest and security
023:056 We would hasten them **on** in every good? Nay, they
023:062 **On** no soul do We place a burden greater than
023:066 but ye used to turn back **on** your heels-
023:075 If We had mercy **on** them and removed
023:075 **on** them, they would obstinately persist in their
023:076 We inflicted Punishment **on** them, but they
023:077 Until We open **on** them a gate leading to
023:081 **On** the contrary they say things similar to
023:112 did ye stay **on** earth?"
024:007 of Allah **on** himself if he tells a lie.
024:009 **on** herself if (her accuser) is telling the truth.
024:010 **on** you, and that Allah is Oft-Returning, Full of
024:011 and to him who took **on** himself the lead among them,
024:011 **on** the contrary it is good for you: to every
024:014 and mercy of Allah **on** you, in this
024:015 Behold, ye received it **on** your tongues, and said
024:020 of Allah **on** you, and that Allah is full of
024:021 for the grace and mercy of Allah **on** you, not one
024:024 **On** the Day when their tongues, their hands,
024:025 **On** that Day Allah will pay them back (all) their
024:029 It is no fault **on** your part to enter houses
024:041 and **on** earth do celebrate, and the
024:045 and some that walk **on** four. Allah creates
024:045 that creep **on** their bellies; some that
024:045 some that walk **on** two legs: and some
024:049 But if the right is **on** their side, they come
024:054 the duty placed **on** him and ye
024:054 If ye obey him, ye shall be **on** right guidance.

ON (continued)

024:054 and ye for that placed **on** you. If ye
024:058 your presence), **on** three occasions: before morning
024:060 there is no blame **on** them if they lay aside
024:061 **on** you, whether ye eat in company or separately.
024:062 when they are with him **on** a matter requiring
024:063 or a grievous Chastisement be inflicted **on** them.
024:064 and **on** earth. Well doth He know what ye are
025:008 been bestowed **on** him, or why
025:018 **on** them and their fathers, good things
025:034 to Hell (prone) **on** their faces,-they will
025:040 have passed by the town **on** which was rained
025:059 **on** the Throne: Allah Most Gracious: ask thou
025:063 who walk **on** the earth in humility, and when
025:069 (But) the Chastisement **on** the Day of Judgment
025:077 with you but for your call **on** Him: but ye
026:049 and your feet **on** opposite sides, and I
026:071 and we remain constantly in attendance **on** them."
026:072 when ye call (**on** them),
026:082 will forgive me my faults **on** the Day of Judgment.
026:083 "O my Lord! bestow wisdom **on** me, and join
026:084 **on** the tongue of truth among the
026:087 **on** the Day when (men) will be raised up;-
026:128 "Do ye build a landmark **on** every high place
026:132 **on** you freely all that ye know.
026:133 "Freely has He bestowed **on** you cattle and sons,-
026:155 (severally) **on** a day appointed.
026:173 **on** those who were admonished (but heeded not)!
026:173 We rained down **on** them a shower (of brimstone):
026:187 to fall **on** us, if thou art truthful!"
026:204 to be hastened **on**?
026:213 So call not **on** any other god with Allah,
026:217 **on** the Exalted in Might, the Merciful,-
026:221 **on** whom it is that the Satans descend?
026:222 They descend **on** every lying, wicked person
027:019 **on** me and **on** my parents, and that
027:042 **on** us in advance of this, and we
027:046 to hasten **on** the evil before the good? If only
027:049 **on** him and his people, and that
027:058 And We rained down **on** them a shower (of brimstone):
027:058 **on** those who were admonished (but heeded not)!
027:059 and Peace **on** His servants whom He has chosen
027:062 when it calls **on** Him, and Who
027:063 the depths of darkness **on** land and sea, and Who
027:065 Say: None in the heavens or **on** earth, except
027:072 the events which ye wish to hasten **on**
027:079 for thou art **on** (the Path of) manifest Truth.
027:087 **on** earth, except such as Allah will please
028:014 We bestowed **on** him wisdom and knowledge: for thus
028:017 Thou hast bestowed Thy Grace **on** me, never shall
028:019 **on** their enemy, the man said: "O Moses!
028:026 (dear) father! engage him **on** wages: truly the
028:027 **on** condition that thou serve me for eight years,
028:041 and **on** the Day of Judgment no help
028:042 to follow them: and **on** the Day of Judgment
028:044 Thou wast not **on** the Western Side when We
028:061 **on** the Day of Judgment, is to be
028:074 The Day that He will call **on** them, He will
028:076 We had bestowed **on** him, that their
028:077 which Allah has bestowed **on** thee, the Home
028:082 the day before began to say **on** the morrow:
028:083 high-handedness or mischief **on** earth: and the
028:088 **on** another god. There is no god but He.

029:002 left alone **on** saying, "We believe", and that
029:008 We have enjoined **on** man kindness to parents:
029:013 and **on** the Day of Judgement they will
029:022 "Not **on** earth nor in heaven will ye be able
029:025 but **on** the Day of Judgement ye shall
029:033 he was grieved **on** their account, and felt
029:034 **on** the people of this township a Punishment
029:036 nor commit evil **on** the earth, with intent
029:039 **on** the earth; yet they cold not overreach (Us).
029:052 and **on** earth." And it is those who believe
029:053 They ask thee to hasten **on** the Punishment
029:054 They ask thee to hasten **on** the Punishment:
029:055 **On** the Day that the Punishment shall cover
029:065 they call **on** Allah, making their
029:065 Now, if they embark **on** a boat, they call
030:004 **on** that Day shall the Believers rejoice-
030:012 **On** the Day that the Hour will come, the guilty
030:014 **On** the Day that the Hour will come, that Day
030:018 and **on** earth; and in the late afternoon and when
030:026 is in the heavens and **on** earth: all are
030:028 We have bestowed **on** you? Do ye
030:034 **on** them! Then enjoy (your brief day); but soon
030:041 Mischief has appeared **on** land and sea
030:043 **on** that Day shall men be divided (in two).
030:055 **On** the Day that the Hour (of reckoning)
030:057 So **on** that Day no excuse of theirs will avail
031:005 These are **on** (true) guidance from their Lord;
031:006 and throw ridicule (**on** the Path): for such
031:010 and produce **on** the earth every kind
031:010 He set **on** the earth mountains standing firm,
031:012 wisdom **on** Luqman: "Show (thy) gratitude to Allah."
031:014 And We have enjoined **on** man (to be
031:016 or **on** earth, Allah will bring it forth: for Allah
031:020 and **on** earth, and has made His bounties flow to
031:027 And if all the trees **on** earth were pens and the
031:034 that he will earn **on** the morrow: nor does
032:004 **on** the Throne: ye have none, besides Him,
032:005 **on** a Day, the measure of which is a thousand
032:016 We have bestowed **on** them.
032:016 the while they call **on** their Lord, in Fear
032:025 **on** the Day of Judgement, in the matters wherein
032:029 Say: "**On** the Day of Decision, no profit
033:005 **on** you if ye make a mistake therein: (what counts
033:009 **on** you hosts (to overwhelm you): but We
033:009 (bestowed) **on** you, when there came down **on** you
033:010 Behold! they came **on** you from above you
033:036 **on** a clearly wrong Path.
033:043 He it is Who sends blessings **on** you, as do
033:044 Their salutation **on** the Day they meet
033:051 **on** thee if thou invite one whose (turn)
033:055 There is no blame (**on** those ladies if they appear)
033:056 **on** the Prophet: O ye that believe! send ye
033:056 send ye blessings **on** him, and salute
033:058 (**on** themselves) a calumny and a glaring sin.
033:061 They shall have a curse **on** them: wherever they
034:001 all things in the heavens and **on** earth: to Him
034:003 or **on** earth: nor is there anything less than
034:010 **on** David from Us: "O ye Mountains! echo ye
034:018 Between them and the Cities **on** which We had
034:020 And **on** them did Satan prove true his idea,
034:022 of an atom,-in the heavens or **on** earth: no (sort
034:024 **on** right guidance or in manifest error!"

ON (continued)

034:031   **on** one another! Those who were deemed weak
034:033   We shall put yokes **on** the necks of the Unbelievers:
034:037   in the dwellings **on** high!
034:040   **On** the Day He will gather them all together,
034:042   So **on** that Day no power shall they have
034:046   Say: "I do admonish you **on** one point: that ye
035:002   doth bestow **on** mankind none can withhold:
035:014   **On** the Day of Judgement they will
035:039   be **on** his own self their disbelief: but adds
035:043   **On** account of their arrogance in the land
035:044   in the heavens or **on** earth: for He
035:045   He would not leave **on** the back of the (earth)
036:004   **On** a Straight Way.
036:014   **on** a mission to you."
036:016   we have been sent **on** a mission to you:
036:018   indeed will be inflicted **on** you by us."
036:042   similar (vessels) **on** which they ride.
036:054   Then, **on** that Day, not a soul will be wronged
036:056   be in pleasant shade, reclining **on** raised couches;
036:060   "Did I not enjoin **on** you, O ye children of Adam,
036:065   **on** their mouths. But their hands will speak
037:018   be humiliated (**on** account of your evil)."
037:044   Facing each other **on** raised couches.
037:051   "I had an intimate companion (**on** the earth),
037:067   Then **on** top of that they will be given
037:069   Truly they found their fathers **on** the wrong Path;
037:070   So they (too) were rushed down **on** their footsteps!
037:077   And made his progeny to endure (**on** this earth);
037:103   prostrate **on** his forehead (for sacrifice),
037:114   Our favour **on** Moses and Aaron,
037:145   But We cast him forth **on** the naked shore
037:147   And We sent him (**on** a mission) to a
037:176   Do they wish (indeed) to hurry **on** Our Punishment?
037:181   And Peace **on** the messengers!
038:014   came justly and inevitably (**on** them).
038:026   a vicegerent **on** earth: so judge
038:028   **on** earth? Shall We treat those who guard
038:029   that they may meditate **on** its Signs, and that
038:034   We placed **on** his throne a body but he
038:039   (**on** others) or withhold them, no account
038:056   an evil bed (indeed, to lie **on**)!-
038:078   "And My Curse shall be **on** thee till the
039:015   **on** the Day of Judgement: Ah! that is
039:024   **on** the Day of Judgment (and receive
039:031   dispute **on** the Day of Judgment, in the
039:040   and **on** whom descends a Chastisement that abides."
039:042   during their sleep: those **on** whom He has passed
039:047   **on** the Day of Judgment: but something
039:047   there is **on** earth, and as much more, (in vain)
039:054   comes **on** you: after that ye shall not be helped.
039:055   before the Chastisement comes **on** you-of a
039:060   **On** the Day of Judgement wilt thou see those
039:067   **on** the Day of Judgement the whole of the earth
039:068   and **on** earth will swoon, except such
039:068   they will be standing and looking **on**!
039:075   (**on** all sides) will be, "Praise be to Allah,
039:075   **on** all sides, singing Glory and Praise to their
040:009   from ills that Day,-**on** them wilt Thou have
040:026   and let him Call **on** his Lord! What I
040:028   **on** him is (the sin of) his lie; but, if he
040:028   then will fall **on** you something of the
040:045   encompassed **on** all sides the People of Pharaoh.

ON (continued)

040:046   and (the Sentence will be) **on** the Day when the
040:047   can ye then take (**on** yourselves) from us
040:051   and **on** the Day when the Witnesses will stand forth,-
040:056   **on** them,-there is nothing in their breasts but (the
040:060   And your Lord says: "Call **on** Me; I will
040:075   **on** the earth in things other than the Truth,
040:078   there and then, those who stood **on** Falsehoods.
040:080   and **on** them and **on** ships ye are carried.
041:010   above it, and bestowed blessings **on** the earth,
041:010   He set **on** the (earth), mountains standing
041:030   the angels descend **on** them (from time to time):
041:040   **on** the Day of Judgement? Do what
041:051   **on** his side (instead of coming to Us); and when
041:051   When We bestow favours **on** man, he turns
042:004   in the heavens and **on** earth: and He is
042:005   for (all) beings **on** earth: Behold! Verily
042:013   for you as that which He enjoined **on** Noah-the which
042:013   **on** Abraham, Moses, and Jesus: namely, that
042:016   of their Lord: **on** them is Wrath, and for
042:022   (necessarily) fall **on** them. But those
042:022   **on** account of what they have earned, and (the
042:033   **on** the back of the (ocean). Verily in
042:038   of what We bestow **on** them for Sustenance;
042:039   oppressive wrong is inflicted **on** them, (are not
042:045   **On** the Day of Judgement. Behold! Truly
042:048   to him, **on** account of the deeds which his hands
042:053   **on** earth. Behold (how) all affairs tend
043:008   than these;-and (thus) has passed **on** the example
043:010   in order that ye may find guidance (**on** the way);
043:012   and cattle **on** which ye ride,
043:013   and square **on** their backs, and when
043:033   **on** which to go up,
043:034   and couches (of silver) **on** which they could recline,
043:043   verily thou art **on** a Straight Way.
043:053   **on** him, or (why) come (not) with him
043:060   amongst you, succeeding each other **on** the earth.
043:063   to you some of the (points) **on** which ye dispute:
043:066   that it should come **on** them all of a sudden,
043:067   Friends **on** that Day will be foes, one to
043:068   My devotees! no fear shall be **on** you today,
043:084   and God **on** earth; and He is Full of Wisdom
045:013   and **on** earth: behold, in that are Signs
045:017   **on** the Day of Judgement as to those matters in
045:018   Then We put thee **on** the (right) Way of Religion:
045:023   and put a cover **on** his sight. Who, then,
045:029   **on** record all that ye did."
046:004   they have created **on** earth, or have
046:013   (**on** that Path),-**on** them shall be no fear,
046:015   We have enjoined **on** man kindness to his parents:
046:017   his parents, "Fie **on** you! Do ye
046:020   **on** earth without just cause, and that
046:020   And **on** the Day that the Unbelievers will be
046:023   I proclaim to you the mission **on** which I have
046:026   when they went **on** rejecting the Signs of Allah:
046:034   And **on** the Day that the Unbelievers will be
046:035   the (Unbelievers). **On** the Day that they see
047:004   (the captives) firmly: therefore (is the time for)
047:010   **on** them, and similar (fates await) those who
047:014   Is then one who is **on** a clear (Path) from his Lord,
047:017   **on** them their Piety and Restraint (from evil).
047:018   that it should come **on** them of a sudden?
047:021   and when a matter is resolved **on**, it were

ON (continued)

048:002 and guide thee **on** the Straight Way;
048:006 **On** them is a round of Evil: the Wrath of
048:006 the Wrath of Allah is **on** them: He has cursed
048:011 (to intervene) **on** your behalf with Allah,
048:017 No blame is there **on** the blind, nor is
048:017 nor is there blame **on** the lame, nor is
048:017 nor **on** one ill (if he joins not the war): but he
048:018 Allah's Good Pleasure was **on** the Believers
048:025 trampling down and **on** whose account a guilt
048:029 **On** their faces are their marks, (being) the
048:029 and it stands **on** its own stem, (filling) the
049:012 and spy not **on** each other, nor speak
049:016 is in the heavens and **on** earth: He has
049:017 They impress **on** thee as favour that they
050:017 **on** the right and one **on** the left.
051:020 **On** the earth are Signs for those of assured Faith,
051:033 "To bring **on**, **on** them (a shower of) stones of
051:039 But (Pharaoh) turned back **on** account of his might,
051:044 seized them, even while they were looking **on**.
051:045 (on their feet), nor could they help themselves.
052:009 **On** the Day when the firmament will be
052:018 their Lord hath bestowed **on** them, and their
052:022 And We shall bestow **on** them, of fruit
052:044 of the sky falling (**on** them), they would
053:031 in the heavens and **on** earth: so that
054:010 Then he called **on** his Lord: "I am one
054:013 But We bore him **on** an (Ark) made of
054:019 **on** a Day of bitter ill-luck,
054:026 Ah! they will know **on** the morrow, which is
054:038 Early **on** the morrow an abiding Chastisement
054:048 through the Fire **on** their faces, (they will hear):
054:053 Every matter, small and great, is **on** record.
055:026 All that is **on** earth will perish:
055:029 and **on** earth: every day in (new) Splendour
055:035 **On** you will be sent (O ye evil ones twain)!
055:039 **On** that Day no question will be asked
055:054 They will recline **on** Carpets, whose inner
055:076 Reclining **on** green Cushions and rich
056:015 (They will be) **on** couches encrusted (with gold
056:016 Reclining **on** them, facing each other.
056:034 And **on** couches raised high.
056:054 "And drink Boiling Water **on** top of it:
056:056 **on** the Day of Requital!
056:084 And ye the while (sit) looking **on**,-
057:001 and **on** earth,-declares the Praises and Glory
057:004 **on** the Throne. He knows what enters within the
057:021 of Allah, which He bestows **on** whom He pleases:
057:022 No misfortune can happen **on** earth or in your
057:026 and some of them were **on** right guidance, but many
057:027 son of Mary, and bestowed **on** him the Gospel;
057:027 Yet We bestowed, **on** those among them who believed,
057:028 and He will bestow **on** you a double portion
057:029 His Hand, to bestow it **on** whomsoever He wills.
058:003 to their wives then wish to go back **on** the words
058:006 **On** the Day that Allah will raise
058:007 and **on** earth? There is not a secret consultation
058:007 them what they did **on** the Day of Judgment.
058:010 and **on** Allah let the Believers put their trust.
059:001 and **on** earth, declares the Praises and Glory
059:005 left them standing **on** their roots, it was
059:006 What Allah has bestowed **on** His Messenger (and taken
059:007 What Allah has bestowed **on** His Messenger (and taken

059:021 **on** a mountain, verily, thou wouldst have seen
059:024 and **on** earth, doth declare His Praises and Glory:
060:001 and have (**on** the contrary) driven out
060:003 **on** the Day of Judgment: He will judge between you:
060:004 no power (to get) aught **on** thy behalf from Allah."
060:010 And there will be no blame **on** you if ye marry
060:010 if ye marry them **on** payment of their dower to them.
060:010 have spent **on** their dowers, and let
060:010 what they have spent (**on** their dower). And there
060:010 (on their dowers of women who came over to you).
060:011 they had spent (**on** their dower). And fear
060:013 (for friendship) to people **on** whom is the Wrath
061:001 and **on** earth, declares the Praises and Glory
062:001 and **on** earth, doth declare the Praises and Glory
062:004 which He bestows **on** whom He will: and Allah
062:007 have sent **on** before them! And Allah
062:009 is proclaimed to prayer **on** Friday (the Day
063:003 so a seal was set **on** their hearts: therefore
063:004 The curse of Allah be **on** them! How are
063:004 (unable to stand **on** their own). They think
063:007 "Spend nothing **on** those who are with
063:010 We have bestowed **on** you, before Death
064:001 and **on** earth, doth declare the Praises and Glory
064:004 and **on** earth: and He knows what ye conceal
064:013 and **on** Allah, therefore, let the Believers
065:002 **on** equitable terms or part with them **on** equitable
065:002 **on** equitable terms; and take for witness
065:006 then spend (your substance) **on** them until they
065:006 (the child) **on** the (father's) behalf.
065:007 **on** any person beyond what He has given him.
066:010 **on** their account, but were told: "Enter ye
067:022 or one who walks evenly **on** a Straight Way?
067:028 or if He bestows His Mercy **on** us,-yet who
068:016 Soon shall We brand (the beast) **on** the snout!
068:019 Then there came, **on** the (garden) a visitation
068:039 **on** oath, reaching to the Day of Judgment,
068:044 We draw them **on** little by little from directions
068:049 **on** the naked shore, in disgrace.
069:013 Then, when one Blast is sounded **on** the Trumpet,
069:015 **On** that Day shall the (Great) Event come to pass,
069:017 And the angels will be **on** its sides, and eight
069:022 In a Garden **on** high,
070:014 And all, all that is **on** earth,-so it
071:012 and bestow **on** you Rivers (of flowing water).
071:012 and sons; and bestow **on** you Gardens and bestow
071:026 a single one **on** earth!
072:010 is intended to those **on** earth, or whether
072:016 **on** the (right) Way, We should
072:016 **on** them Rain in abundance.
075:025 to be inflicted **on** them;
075:032 But **on** the contrary, He rejected
076:013 **on** raised couches, they will see there neither
078:029 And all things have We preserved **on** record.
079:003 And by those who glide along (**on** errands of mercy),
079:028 **On** high hath He raised its canopy, and He
082:015 Which they will enter **on** the Day of Judgment,
083:005 **On** a Mighty Day,
083:014 By no means! but **on** their hearts is the
083:023 **On** raised couches will they command a sight
083:034 But **on** this Day the Believers will laugh
083:035 **On** raised couches they will command (a sight)
084:006 ever toiling **on** towards the Lord-painfully toiling,

ON (continued)

084:022 But **on** the contrary the Unbelievers reject (it).
088:010 In a Garden **on** high,
088:013 (of dignity), raised **on** high,
089:012 And heaped therein mischief (**on** mischief).
089:013 Therefore did thy Lord pour **on** them a scourge
089:023 (face to face),-**on** that Day will man remember,
090:011 **on** the path that is steep.
090:020 **On** them will be Fire Vaulted over (all round).
096:011 Seest thou if He is **on** (the road of) Guidance?-
096:018 We will call **on** the angels of punishment
097:004 **on** every errand:
099:004 **On** that Day will she declare her tidings:
099:006 **On** that Day will men proceed in groups sorted out,
113:004 From the mischief of those who blow **on** knots;

ONCE

004:154 and (**once** again) We commanded them: "Transgress
005:002 of some people in (**once**) shutting you out
005:022 (**once**) they leave, then shall we enter."
005:023 when **once** ye are in, victory will be yours; but
006:008 the matter would be settled at **once**, and no
006:058 at **once** between you and me. But Allah
009:126 are tried every year **once** or twice? Yet they
010:011 then would their respite be settled at **once**. But
013:011 but when (**once**) Allah willeth a people's
018:058 (at **once**) to account for what they have earned,
020:021 We shall return it at **once** to its
020:055 and from it shall We bring you out **once** again.
020:061 lest He destroy you (at **once**) utterly by
025:032 to him all at **once**?" Thus (is
037:021 whose truth ye (**once**) denied!"
042:021 between them (at **once**): but verily the wrong-doers

ONE

002:030 therein **one** who will make mischief
002:048 a day when **one** soul shall not avail another
002:061 we cannot endure **one** kind of food (always);
002:096 each **one** of them wishes he could be
002:123 a day when **one** soul shall not avail another,
002:133 the **one** (True) God;
002:136 between **one** and another of them:
002:163 And your God is **One** God:
002:167 "If only we had **one** more chance,
002:171 is as if **one** were to shout like a goat-herd,
002:173 but if **one** is forced by necessity,
002:184 the feeding of **one** that is indigent.
002:185 but if any **one** is ill, or on a journey,
002:185 So every **one** of you who is present (at his home)
002:194 If then any **one** transgresses the prohibition
002:196 if any **one** wishes to continue
002:197 If any **one** undertakes that duty therein,
002:213 Mankind was **one** single nation.
002:224 for Allah is **one** who heareth and knoweth
002:249 hath a small force vanquished a big **one**?
002:251 **one** set of people by means of another,
002:252 verily thou art **one** of the Messengers.
002:258 to **one** who disputed with Abraham about his Lord,
002:259 of **one** who passed by a hamlet,
002:275 not stand except as stands **one** whom the Satan
002:282 so that if **one** of them errs.
002:283 And if **one** of you deposits a thing
002:285 between **one** and another of His Messengers."
002:285 each **one** (of them) believeth in Allah,
003:007 but no **one** knows its true meanings except Allah.

ONE (continued)

003:013 **one** was fighting in the cause of Allah,
003:034 Offspring, **one** of the other:
003:061 If any **one** disputes in this manner with thee,
003:073 "And believe no **one** unless he follows your religion."
003:084 between **one** and another among them,
003:153 **one** distress after another by way of requital,
003:165 smote (your enemies) with **one** twice as great,
003:193 the call of **one** calling (us) to Faith,
003:195 ye are members, **one** of another;
004:003 then only **one**, or that which
004:011 if only **one**, her share is a half.
004:012 each **one** of the two gets a sixth;
004:018 until death faces **one** of them, and he says,
004:020 **one** wife in place of another, even if
004:023 and two sisters in wedlock at **one** and the same time,
004:025 Ye are **one** from another: wed them
004:034 the **one** more (strength) than the other, and
004:035 appoint (two) arbiters, **one** from his family,
004:042 wish that the earth were made **one** with them:
004:043 or on a journey, or **one** of you cometh from
004:052 thou wilt find, have no **one** to help.
004:075 and raise for us from Thee **one** who will help!"
004:075 and raise for us from Thee **one** who will protect;
004:102 let **one** party of them stand up
004:107 for Allah loveth not **one** given to perfidy and sin:
004:112 and throws it on to **one** that is innocent,
004:114 but if **one** exhorts to a deed of charity or
004:116 **one** who joins other gods with Allah, hath
004:125 than **one** who submits his whole self to Allah,
004:134 If any **one** desires a reward in this life, in
004:148 except by **one** who has been wronged, for Allah
004:171 for Allah is **One** God: glory be to him:
005:002 but help ye not **one** another in sin and rancor:
005:002 Help ye **one** another in righteousness and piety,
005:006 or **one** of you cometh from the privy or ye have
005:014 the **one** and the other, to the Day of Judgement.
005:027 it was accepted from **one**, but not from the other.
005:030 and became (himself) **one** of the lost ones.
005:037 their Chastisement will be **one** that endures.
005:072 There will for the wrong-doers be no **one** to help.
005:073 for there is no god except **One** God.
005:073 Allah is **one** of three in a Trinity: for there
005:079 Nor did they forbid **one** another the iniquities
005:095 domestic animal equivalent to the **one** he killed.
006:004 But never did a single **one** of the Signs
006:013 For He is the **One** Who heareth
006:019 Say: "But in truth He is the **One** God. And
006:025 if they saw every **one** of the Signs, they will
006:052 and thus be (**one**) of the unjust.
006:061 At length, when death approaches **one** of you. Our
006:070 and for punishment, **one** most grievous: for they
006:071 like **one** whom the Satans have made
006:093 **one** who inventeth a lie against Allah, or saith,
006:095 And He is the **one** to cause the dead
006:107 not **one** to watch over their doings, nor art
006:115 for He is the **one** Who heareth and knoweth all.
006:124 we receive **one** (exactly) like those
006:144 than **one** who invents a lie against Allah, to lead
006:145 by **one** who wishes to eat it, unless it
006:157 than **one** who rejecteth Allah's Signs, and turneth
007:037 Who is more unjust than **one** who forges
007:065 **one** of their (own) brethren: he said: "O my

ONE (continued)

007:073	**one** of their own brethren: he said: "O my
007:085	**one** of their own brethren: he said:
007:099	against Allah's devising but no **one** can fell
007:105	**One** for whom it is right to say nothing
008:007	Behold! Allah promised you **one** of the two
008:007	ye wished that the **one** unarmed should be yours,
008:037	Put the impure, **one** on another, heap them
008:048	and said: "No **one** among men can overcome
008:061	the **One** that heareth and knoweth (all things).
008:072	**one** of another. As to those who believed
008:073	**one** of another: unless ye do this, (protect each
009:004	nor aided any **one** against you. So fulfil
009:006	If **one** amongst the Pagans ask thee for asylum,
009:031	**one** God: there is no god but He. Praise and
009:037	for they make it lawful **one** year, and forbidden
009:052	other than **one** of two glorious things-(martyrdom
009:071	are protectors, **one** of another: they enjoin
009:103	and Allah is **one** who heareth and knoweth.
009:107	and in preparation for **one** who warred against
010:019	Mankind was but **one** nation, but differed (later).
010:028	**One** Day shall We gather them all together. Then
010:083	and **one** who transgressed all bounds.
011:001	in detail, from **One** Who is Wise and Well-
011:046	**one** of the ignorants!"
011:050	**one** of their own brethren. He said: "O my
011:061	**one** of their own brethren. He said: "O my
011:066	For thy Lord-He is the Strong **One**, and the Mighty.
011:084	**one** of their own brethren: he said: "O my people!
011:087	Truly, thou art the **one** that forbeareth with
011:117	Nor would thy Lord be the **One** to destroy
011:118	He could have made mankind **one** People: but they
012:010	Said **one** of them: "Slay not Joseph, but if
012:015	(**one** day) tell them the truth of this affair
012:017	we went racing with **one** another, and left
012:024	for he was **one** of Our servants chosen.
012:025	punishment for **one** who formed an evil
012:026	And **one** of her household saw (this)
012:036	Said **one** of them: "I see myself (in a dream)
012:036	for we see thou art **one** that doth good (to all)."
012:039	or Allah the **One**, Supreme and Irresistible?
012:041	As to **one** of you, he will pour out the wine
012:042	And of the two, to that **one** whom he considered
012:045	**one** of the two (who had been in prison) and who
012:067	enter not all by **one** gate: enter ye
012:076	with knowledge is **One**, the All-Knowing.
012:078	They said: "O exalted **one**! Behold! he has
012:078	so take **one** of us in his place: for we
012:087	soothing Mercy: truly no **one** despairs of Allah's
012:088	"O exalted **one**! distress has seized us
012:101	as **one** submitting to Thy Will (as a Muslim),
012:102	Such is **one** of the stories of what happened unseen,
013:002	each **one** runs (its course) for a term appointed.
013:016	of all things: He is the **One**, the Supreme
013:019	like **one** who is blind? It is
013:019	Is then **one** who doth know that that which
013:031	(this would be the **one**!) But, truly,
013:033	Allah leaves to stray, no **one** can guide.
014:016	In front of such a **one** is Hell, and he
014:035	make this city **one** of peace and security:
014:040	"O my Lord! make me **one** who establishes
014:048	the **One**, the Irresistible;
014:048	**One** day the Earth will be changed to a

ONE (continued)

014:052	and may know that He is **One** God: let men
015:033	(Iblis) said: "I am not **one** to prostrate
015:065	let no **one** amongst you look back, but pass on
016:017	Is then He Who creates like **one** that creates not?
016:022	Your God is **One** God: as to those
016:051	two gods: for He is just **one** God: then fear Me
016:058	When news is brought to **one** of them, of (the
016:075	(of two men): **one** a slave under the dominion
016:076	of two men: **one** of them dumb, with no
016:076	is such a man equal with **one** who commands justice,
016:092	lest **one** party should be more numerous
016:092	Using your oaths to deceive **one** another, lest **one**
016:093	you all **one** People: but He leaves straying whom
016:098	seek Allah's protection from Satan the Rejected **one**.
016:101	When We substitute **one** revelation for another,-
016:106	Any **one** who, after accepting Faith in Allah,
016:115	But if **one** is forced by necessity, without wilful
017:001	for He is the **One** Who heareth
017:023	Whether **one** or both of them attain old age
017:061	he said, "Shall I prostrate to **one** whom Thou
017:062	**one** whom thou hast honoured above me! If Thou
017:102	O Pharaoh, to be **one** doomed to destruction!"
018:019	Said **one** of them, "How long
018:019	Now send ye then **one** of you with this money
018:028	of Us, **one** who follows his own desires, and his
018:032	of two men: for **one** of them We provided two
018:044	from Allah, the True **One**. He is
018:047	nor shall We leave out any **one** of them.
018:049	placed before them: and not **one** will thy Lord
018:050	except Iblis. He was **one** of the Jinns, and he
018:057	And who doth more wrong than **one** who is reminded
018:065	So they found **one** of Our servants. On whom
018:085	**One** (such) way he followed,
018:099	to surge like waves on **one** another: the trumpet
018:110	admit no **one** as partner."
018:110	that your God is **one** God: whoever expects
019:006	**one** with whom Thou art well-pleased!"
019:006	"(**One** that) will (truly) inherit me, and inherit
019:029	They said: "How can we talk to **one** who is
019:049	Isaac and Jacob, and each **one** of them We made
019:071	Not **one** of you but will pass over it: this is,
019:087	of intercession, but such a **one** as has received
019:093	Not **one** of the beings in the heavens and the
019:095	And every **one** of them will come to him singly
019:098	a single **one** of them (now) or hear
020:039	and he will be taken up by **one** who is an enemy
020:040	and saith, 'Shall I show you **one** who will nurse
020:062	So they disputed, **one** with another, over their
020:123	with enmity **one** to another; but if, as is sure,
020:135	Say: "Each **one** (of us), is waiting: wait ye,
021:003	"Is this (**one**) more than a man like yourselves?
021:004	and on earth: He is the **One** that heareth and
021:006	(As to those) before them, not **one** of the towns
021:029	such a **one** We should reward with Hell: thus do
021:030	joined together (as **one** unit of Creation), before
021:036	"The **one** who talks of your gods?" And they
021:055	or are you **one** of those who jest?"
021:059	be **one** of the unjust **one**.
021:062	They said, "Art thou the **one** that did this
021:063	by this the biggest **one**! Ask them,
021:072	of every **one** (of them).
021:075	for he was **one** of the Righteous.

ONE (continued)

021:093	their affair (of unity), **one** from another:
021:099	But each **one** will abide therein.
021:104	shall We produce a new **one**: a promise
021:108	is **One** God: will ye therefore bow to His
021:112	the **One** Whose assistance should be sought against
022:008	Yet there is among men such a **one** as disputes
022:013	(Perhaps) they call on **one** whose hurt is nearer
022:034	for food). But your God is **One** God: submit then
022:040	Did not Allah check **one** set of people
022:060	That (is so). And if **one** has retaliated to no
022:060	for Allah is **One** that blots out (sins)
023:067	the (Qur'an), like **one** telling fables by night,"
023:099	Until, when death comes to **one** of them, he says:
023:101	nor will **one** ask after another!
024:006	but their own,-let **one** of them testify four
024:021	not **one** of you would ever have been pure:
024:021	whom He pleases: and Allah is **One** Who hears and
024:028	If ye find no **one** in the house, enter not
024:040	**one** above another: if a man
024:041	wings outspread? Each **one** knows its own (mode
024:055	to **one** of security and peace: 'They will
024:055	their religion-the **one** which He has chosen
024:060	and Allah is **One** Who sees and knows all things.
024:061	nor in **one** afflicted with illness, nor in
024:061	nor in **one** born lame, nor in **one**
024:063	like the summons of **one** of you to another:
025:020	For Allah is **One** Who sees (all things).
025:028	never taken such a **one** for a friend!
025:039	To teach **one** We set forth parables and examples;
025:039	and examples; and each **one** We broke to utter
025:041	in mockery: "Is this the **one** whom Allah has sent
025:043	Seest thou such a **one** as taketh for his god
025:053	**one** palatable and sweet, and the
025:057	but this: that each **one** who will may take
026:021	wisdom) and appointed me as **one** of the messengers.
026:085	"Make me **one** of the inheritors of the
026:114	"I am not **one** to drive away those who believe.
026:185	They said: "Thou art only **one** of those bewitched!
027:006	from **One** Who All-Wise, All-Knowing.
027:018	of ants, **one** of the ants said: "O ye ants,
027:040	Said **one** who had knowledge of the Book: "I will
027:041	(to the truth) or is **one** of those who
028:007	and We shall make him **one** of Our messengers."
028:015	**one** of his own people, and the other, of his
028:018	"Thou art truly, **one** erring manifestly."
028:019	and not to be **one** who sets things right!"
028:025	Afterwards **one** of the (damsels) came (back)
028:026	Said **one** of the (damsels): "O my (dear) father!
028:027	indeed, if Allah wills, **one** of the righteous."
028:027	**one** of these my daughters to thee, on condition
028:050	**one** who follows his own lusts, devoid of
028:059	Nor was thy Lord the **one** to destroy a town
028:061	and **one** to whom We have given the good
028:061	**one** to whom We have made a goodly promise,
028:067	be **one** of the successful.
028:087	Let no **one** turn you away from Allah's revelations
029:040	Each **one** of them We seized for his crime:
029:046	Our God and your God is **one**; and it
030:040	any single **one** of these things? Glory to Him!
031:007	a **one**, he turns away in arrogance, as if
031:034	Nor does any **one** know what it is that he
032:022	And who does more wrong than **one** to whom

ONE (continued)

033:019	like **one** who faints from death: but when
033:032	lest **one** in whose heart is a disease should be
033:036	if any **one** disobeys Allah and His Messenger,
033:037	Behold! thou didst say to **one** who had received
033:046	And as **one** who invites to Allah's (Grace)
033:051	on thee if thou invite **one** whose (turn)
034:026	and He is the **One** to decide, the **One**
034:026	the **One** Who knows all."
034:031	on **one** another! Those who were deemed weak
034:046	Say: "I do admonish you on **one** point: that ye
035:008	(equal to **one** who is rightly guided)? For Allah
035:012	the **one** palatable, sweet, and pleasant to drink,
035:013	each **one** runs its course for a term appointed.
035:015	the **One** Free of all wants, worthy of all praise.
035:018	bear another's burden. If **one** heavily laden
035:036	for them. Thus do We reward every ungrateful **one**!
035:041	**one**-can sustain them thereafter: verily He
036:003	Thou art indeed **one** of the messengers,
036:011	a **one**, therefore, good tidings, of Forgiveness
036:011	Thou canst but admonish such a **one** as follows
036:032	But each **one** of them all-will be
037:004	Verily, verily, your God is **One**!-
037:027	And they will turn to **one** another, and question
037:027	and question **one** another.
037:050	Then they will turn to **one** another and question
037:050	and question **one** another.
037:051	**One** of them will say: "I had an
037:081	For he was **one** of Our believing Servants.
037:102	if Allah so wills **one** of the steadfast."
037:111	For he was **one** of Our believing Servants.
037:112	of Isaac-a prophet,-**one** of the Righteous.
037:132	For He was **one** of Our believing Servants.
037:164	(The angels) "Not **one** of us but has a
038:005	into **one** God? Truly this is a strange thing!"
038:014	Not **one** (of them) but rejected the messengers,
038:022	two disputants, **one** of whom has wronged the other:
038:023	and I have (but) **one**: ye he says, 'Commit her
038:065	the **One**, Supreme and Irresistible,-
038:074	and became **one** of those who reject Faith.
038:075	Art thou haughty? Or art thou **one** of the high
038:075	thee from prostrating thyself to **one** whom I
038:085	with thee and those that follow thee,-every **one**."
039:004	He is Allah, the **One**, the Overpowering.
039:005	(to His law) each **one** follow a course for a
039:006	**one** after another, in three veils of darkness.
039:008	little while: verily thou art (**one**) of the
039:009	Is **one** who worships devoutly during the hours
039:009	(like **one** who does Not)? Say: "Are those
039:019	Is, then, **one** against whom the decree of Punishment
039:019	Wouldst thou, then, deliver **one** (who is)
039:019	(equal to **one** who eschews evil)? Wouldst thou,
039:020	**one** above another have been built: beneath them
039:022	Is **one** whose heart Allah has opened to Islam,
039:022	(no better than **one** hard-hearted)? Woe to those
039:024	(like **one** guarded therefrom)? It will
039:024	Is, then, **one** who has to ward off the brunt
039:029	to **one** master: are these two equal in comparison?
039:030	Truly thou wilt die (**one** day) and truly
039:030	and truly they (too) will die (**one** day).
039:032	**one** who utters a lie concerning Allah and rejects
039:059	and became **one** of those who reject Faith!'"
039:068	(to exempt). Then will a second **one** be sounded,

ONE (continued)

040:016 That of Allah, the **One**, the Overpowering!
040:027 **one** who believes not in the Day of Account!"
040:028 not **one** who transgresses and lies!
040:043 **one** who has no claim to be called to, whether in
040:065 He is the living (**One**): There is
040:084 the **One** God-and we reject the partners we used
041:006 that your God is **One** God: so take
041:032 "A hospitable gift from **One** Oft-Forgiving,
041:033 Who is better in speech than **one** who calls
041:035 And no **one** will be granted such goodness except
041:036 He is the **One** Who hears and knows all things.
041:042 it is sent down by **One** Full of Wisdom, Worthy of
041:047 "We do assure Thee not **one** of us can bear witness!"
041:052 reject it? Who is more astray than **one** who is in
042:011 and He is the **One** that hears and sees.
042:014 being insolent to **one** another. Had it
042:025 He is the **One** that accepts repentance from His
042:028 He is the **One** that sends down rain (even) after
043:017 When news is brought to **one** of them of
043:018 Is then **one** brought up among trinkets, and unable
043:033 might become of **one** community We would provide,
043:038 At length, when (such a **one**) comes to Us, he says
043:067 **one** to another,-except the Righteous
045:019 as) Protectors, **one** to another: but Allah
045:023 Then seest thou such a **one** as takes as his god
046:005 And who is more astray than **one** who invokes,
046:017 But (there is **one**) who says to his parents,
046:021 Mention (Hud) **one** of 'Ad's (own) brethren:
046:031 "O our people, hearken to the **one** who invites
046:032 "If any does not hearken to the **one** who invites
047:014 Is then **one** who is on a clear (Path) from his Lord,
047:014 from his Lord, no better than **one** to whom the evil
047:020 of **one** in swoon at the approach of death.
048:010 their hands: then any **one** who violates His oath,
048:010 his own soul, and any **one** who fulfils what he
048:017 nor on **one** ill (if he joins not the war): but he
049:002 **one** another, lest your deeds become vain
049:009 the **one** that transgresses until it complies
049:009 between them: but if **one** them transgresses beyond
049:011 (to be used of **one**) after he has believed:
050:010 piled **one** over another;-
050:014 each **one** (of them) rejected the messengers,
050:017 on the right and **one** on the left.
050:017 (and note them), **one** sitting on the right
050:032 for everyone penitent heedful **one**,
050:045 and thou art not **one** to compel them by force.
051:036 except **one** (Muslim) household:
051:039 "A sorcerer, or **one** possessed!"
051:052 "A sorcerer, or **one** possessed"!
051:053 **one** to another? Nay, they are themselves a
052:023 **one** with another, a cup free of frivolity,
053:005 He was taught by **one** Mighty in Power,
053:033 Seest thou **one** who turns back,
053:058 No **one** but Allah can disclose it.
054:009 "Here is **one** possessed!", and he was driven out.
054:010 "I am **one** overcome: do thou then help (me)!"
054:014 (and care): a recompense to **one** who had been
054:024 Shall we follow such a **one**? Truly should
054:024 a solitary **one** from among ourselves! Shall we
054:025 Nay, he is a liar an insolent **one**!
054:026 which is the liar the insolent **one**!
054:031 the dry stubble used by **one** who pens cattle.

ONE (continued)

056:029 (or fruits) piled **one** above another,-
057:009 He is the **One** Who Sends to His Servants
058:003 (it is ordained that such a **one**) should free
059:004 and His Messenger: and if any **one** resists Allah,
059:011 to any **one** in your affair; AND IF
059:023 the Holy **One**, the Source of Peace (and Perfection).
061:007 Who doth greater wrong than **one** who forges
062:001 the Holy **One**, the Exalted in Might, the Wise.
063:010 and I should have been **one** of the doers of good."
066:003 in confidence to **one** of his consorts, and she
066:004 **one** among those who believe,-and furthermore,
066:012 and was **one** of the devout (Servants).
067:003 **one** above another: no want of proportion wilt thou
067:022 Is then **one** who walks headlong, with his
067:022 or **one** who walks evenly on a Straight Way?
068:021 **one** to another,-
068:028 Said **one** of them, more just (than the rest):
068:030 Then they turned, **one** against another, in reproach.
069:013 Then, when **one** Blast is sounded on the Trumpet,
069:014 at **one** stroke,-
069:020 that my Account would (**one** Day) reach me!"
071:015 the seven heavens **one** above another,
071:026 a single **one** on earth!
072:007 any **one** (to Judgment).
072:018 for Allah (alone): so invoke not any **one** along
072:022 Say: "No **one** can deliver me from Allah (if I
072:026 nor does He make any **one** acquainted with
073:014 The Day the earth and the mountains will be
074:035 This is but **one** of the mighty (Portents),
074:052 Forsooth, each **one** of them wants to be given
075:029 And **one** leg will be joined with another:
077:001 **one** after another (to man's profit);
077:004 Then separate them, **one** from another,
080:005 As to **one** who regards himself as self-sufficient,
080:037 Each **one** of them, that Day, will have
081:022 And (O people!) your Companion is not **one** possessed;
085:003 By **one** that witnesses, and the
087:011 the most unfortunate **one**,
088:021 for thou art **one** to remind.
088:022 Thou art not **one** to manage (their) affairs.
089:018 Nor do ye encourage **one** another to feed the poor!-
096:009 Seest thou **one** who forbids-
107:001 Seest thou **one** who denies the Judgment (to come)?
107:002 Then such is the **one** who repulses the orphan,
112:001 Say: He is Allah, the **One**;
113:005 the envious **one** as he practices envy.

ONE'S

005:041 If any **one's** trial is intended by Allah, thou
054:028 each **one's** right to drink being brought forward

ONES

002:011 only **ones** that put things right!"
002:012 the **ones** who make mischief,
002:014 but when they are alone with their evil **ones**,
002:015 like blind **ones** (to and fro).
002:121 they are the **ones** that believe therein:
002:157 and they are the **ones** that receive guidance.
002:175 They are the **ones** who buy Error
002:249 he and the faithful **ones** with him,
003:104 they are the **ones** to attain felicity.
003:168 (They are) the **ones** that say, (of their brethren
004:002 worthless things for (their) good **ones**;
004:141 (These are) the **ones** who wait and watch about you:

ONES (continued)

005:030 and became (himself) one of the lost **ones**.
006:111 they are not the **ones** to believe, unless it
007:155 the deeds of the foolish **ones** among us?
007:202 But their brethren (the evil **ones**) plunge them
008:037 into Hell. They will be the **ones** to have lost.
009:037 and make such forbidden **ones** lawful. The evil
011:018 "These are the **ones** who lied against their Lord!
011:021 They are the **ones** who have lost their own souls:
011:022 **ones** who will lose most in the Hereafter!
011:029 and ye I see are the ignorant **ones**!
011:053 the **ones** to desert our gods on thy word!
012:043 whom seven lean **ones** devour,-and seven
012:046 **ones** devour, and of seven green ears of corn and
012:052 the snare of the false **ones**.
017:019 the **ones** whose striving will be thanked (by Allah).
021:005 the **ones** that were sent to (prophets) of old!"
021:064 and said, "Surely ye are the **ones** in the wrong."
021:086 for they were of the Righteous **ones**.
022:028 the distressed **ones** in want.
023:038 against Allah, but we are not the **ones** to believe
023:111 they are indeed the **ones** that have achieved Bliss."
024:032 and the virtuous **ones** among your slaves,
025:075 Those are the **ones** who will be rewarded
026:138 "And we are not the **ones** to receive Pains and
028:063 these are the **ones** whom we led astray: we led
031:005 are the **ones** who will prosper.
032:012 the guilty **ones** will bend low their heads before
033:067 We obeyed our chiefs and our great **ones**, and they
034:031 the arrogant **ones**: "Had it not been for you,
034:032 The arrogant **ones** will say to those who had
034:033 will say to the arrogant **ones**: Nay! it was
034:034 **ones** among them said: "We believe
034:037 these are the **ones** for whom there is a
036:078 and decomposed **ones** (at that)?"
037:098 the **ones** most humiliated!
037:160 Not (so do) the servants of Allah, the chosen **ones**.
038:062 to number among the bad **ones**?
038:075 the high (and mighty) **ones**?"
039:018 **ones** endued with understanding.
039:018 those are the **ones** whom Allah has guided,
039:064 O ye ignorant **ones**?"
040:047 The weak **ones** (who followed) will say to those
043:023 the wealthy **ones** among them said: "We found
048:025 They are the **ones** who disbelieved and hindered
049:015 Such are the sincere **ones**.
054:047 the **ones** in error and madness.
055:035 evil **ones** twain)! a flame of fire (to burn)
058:004 indigent **ones**. This, that ye may show your
059:009 they are the **ones** that achieve prosperity.
061:014 the **ones** that prevailed.
063:007 They are the **ones** who say, "Spend nothing
064:016 they are the **ones** that achieve prosperity.
070:035 Such will be the honoured **ones** in the
071:027 but wicked ungrateful **ones**.
072:004 'There were some foolish **ones** among us, who used
092:015 None shall reach it but those most unfortunate **ones**

ONIONS

002:061 its garlic, lentils, and **onions**."

ONLY

002:009 but they **only** deceive themselves
002:011 **only** ones that put things right!"
002:014 we (were) **only** jesting."

ONLY (continued)

002:027 These cause loss (**only**) to themselves.
002:085 Then is it **only** a part of the Book
002:102 "We are **only** for trial,
002:120 that is the (**only**) guidance."
002:143 **only** to test those who followed
002:165 If **only** the unrighteous could see,
002:167 "If **only** we had one more chance,
002:173 He hath **only** forbidden you dead meat,
002:184 if ye **only** knew.
002:229 A divorce is **only** permissible twice: after that,
002:249 **only** those who taste not of it go with me;
002:272 and ye shall **only** do so seeking
002:280 that is best for you if ye **only** knew.
003:110 If **only** the People of the Book had faith,
003:118 They **only** desire for you to suffer:
003:168 "If **only** they had listened to us,
003:173 so fear them": but it **only** increased their Faith:
003:175 It is **only** the Satan that suggests to you
003:185 **Only** he who is saved far from the fire and
003:185 and **only** on the Day of Judgment shall you
004:003 then **only** one, or that which
004:011 and the parents are the (**only**) heirs,
004:011 if **only** one, her share is a half.
004:011 if **only** daughters, two or more, their share
004:046 If **only** they had said: "We hear and we obey"; and
004:064 If they had **only**, when they were unjust
004:083 If they had **only** referred it to the Messenger
004:084 thou art held responsible **only** for thyself, and
004:113 **only** lead their own souls astray,
004:157 But **only** conjecture to follow, for of a surety
004:157 **Only** a likeness of that was shown to them.
005:005 are (not **only**) chaste women who are believers, but
005:025 I have power **only** over myself and my bother: so
005:065 If **only** the people of the Book had believed
005:066 If **only** they had stood fast by the Torah, the
005:081 If **only** they had believed in Allah, in the
005:113 They said: "We **only** wish to eat thereof
006:026 but they **only** destroy themselves and they
006:048 **only** to give good news and to warn: so those
006:063 'If He **only** delivers us from these (dangers), (We
006:070 they will have for drink (**only**) boiling water, and
006:071 is the (**only**) guidance, and we have
006:123 but they **only** plot against their own souls, and
006:157 "If the Book had **only** been sent down to us, we
006:160 he that doeth evil shall **only** be recompensed
007:020 "Your Lord **only** forbade you this tree, lest
007:027 (**only**) to those without Faith.
007:127 (**only**) their females will we save alive; and
007:187 **Only**, all of a sudden, will it come to you." They
008:025 not in particular (**only**) those of you who do wrong:
008:035 (its **only** answer can be), "Taste ye
008:036 have (**only**) regrets and sighs; at length
009:042 "If we **only** could, we should certainly have come
009:045 **Only** those ask thee for exemption who believe
009:047 your (strength) but **only** (made for) disorder,
009:054 The **only** reasons why their contributions are not
009:059 If **only** they had been content with what Allah
009:065 "We were **only** talking idly and in play." Say:
009:074 **only** return for the bounty with which Allah and
009:081 If **only** they could understand!
009:093 The ground (of complaint) is **only** against such as
009:114 father's forgiveness **only** because of a promise

ONLY (continued)

010:020 Say: "The Unseen is **only** for Allah (to Know).
010:024 as if it had not flourished **only** the day before!
010:072 my reward is **only** due from Allah, and I
010:098 If **only** there had been a single township
011:012 But thou art there **only** to warn! It is Allah
011:040 But **only** a few believed with him.
011:050 You are **only** forgers.
011:088 I **only** desire (your) betterment to the
011:088 (in my task) can **only** come from Allah. In Him I
011:116 If **only** there had been of the generations
012:062 so they should know it **only** when they
012:068 it served **only** to satisfy Jacob's heartfelt desire.
012:081 we bear witness **only** to what we know, and we
012:086 He said: "I **only** complain of my distraction
014:044 "Our Lord! respite us (if **only**) for a short Term:
015:015 They would **only** say: "Our eyes have been
015:021 are with Us; but We **only** send down thereof in
016:041 if they **only** realize (this)!
016:082 thy duty is **only** to preach the Clear Message.
016:095 (a prize) far better for you, if ye **only** knew.
016:100 His authority is over those **only**, who take
016:115 He has **only** forbidden you dead meat, and blood,
016:124 The Sabbath was **only** made (strict) for those
017:041 receive admonition, but it **only** increases their
017:053 (**only**) say those things that are best: for Satan
017:059 the Signs, **only** because the men of former
017:059 We **only** sent the Signs by way of frightening
017:060 but it **only** increases their inordinate
017:085 of my Lord of Knowledge it is **only** a little
017:099 them (anew)? **Only** He has decreed a term
018:006 Thou wouldst **only**, perchance, fret thyself
018:042 and he could **only** say, "Woe is me! Would I had
018:044 There, the (**only**) protection comes from Allah,
018:045 it is (**only**) Allah Who prevails over all things.
018:056 We **only** send the Messengers to give glad tidings
019:019 He said: "Nay, I am **only** a messenger from thy Lord,
019:035 He **only** says to it, "Be," and it is.
019:062 vain discourse, but **only** salutations of Peace:
020:003 But **only** as an admonition to those
020:014 but I: so serve thou Me (**only**), and establish
020:072 to degree: for thou canst **only** decree (touching)
020:134 "Our Lord! if **only** Thou hadst sent us a messenger,
021:039 If **only** the Unbelievers knew (the time)
021:073 they constantly served Us (and Us **only**).
022:044 and (**only**) after that did I punish them:
022:049 Say: "O men! I am (sent) to you **only** to give
023:025 (And some said:) "He is **only** a man possessed,
023:038 "He is **only** a man who invents a lie against Allah,
023:114 a little,-if ye had **only** known!
023:117 and his reckoning will be **only** with his Lord!
024:037 nor from paying zakat their (**only**) fear is for
024:053 by Allah that, if **only** thou wouldst command
024:054 he is **only** responsible for the duty placed
024:054 is **only** to preach the clear (Message)".
024:062 **Only** those are Believers who believe in Allah
025:044 They are **only** like cattle;-nay, they are
025:056 But thee We **only** sent to give
025:068 and any that does this (not **only**) meets punishment
026:028 If ye **only** had sense!"
026:051 "**Only**, our desire is that our Lord will
026:089 "But **only** he (will prosper) that brings
026:099 "And our seducers were **only** those who were

ONLY (continued)

026:102 "Now if we **only** had a chance of return, we shall
026:109 my reward is **only** from the Lord of the Worlds:
026:113 "Their account is **only** with my Lord, if ye
026:115 "I am sent **only** as a plain warner."
026:127 my reward is **only** from the Lord of the Worlds.
026:145 my reward is **only** from the Lord of the Worlds.
026:153 They said: "Thou art **only** the of those bewitched!
026:164 my reward is **only** from the Lord of the Worlds.
026:180 my reward is **only** from the Lord of the Worlds.
026:185 They said: "Thou art **only** one of those bewitched!
027:046 If **only** ye ask Allah for forgiveness, ye may
027:081 from straying: **only** those wilt thou get to listen
027:092 say: "I am **only** a Warner."
028:019 a man yesterday? Thou **only** desire to become a
028:050 know that they **only** follow their own lusts:
028:064 If **only** they had been open to guidance!'
028:084 the doers of evil are **only** punished (to the
029:018 is **only** to preach publicly (and clearly)."
029:043 forth for mankind, but **only** those understand
030:053 from their straying: **only** those wilt thou make
031:032 except **only** a perfidious ungrateful (wretch)!
032:012 If **only** thou couldst see when the guilty ones
032:015 **Only** those believe in Our Signs who, when they
033:004 your sons. Such is (**only**) your (manner of)
033:022 And it **only** added to their faith and their
033:033 And Allah **only** wishes to remove all abomination
033:050 this **only** for thee, and not
034:033 of the Unbelievers: it would **only** be a requital
034:037 in degree: but **only** those who believe and work
034:043 "This is **only** a falsehood invented!" And the
034:043 to them, they say, "This is **only** a man who
034:047 it is yours: my reward is **only** due from Allah:
034:050 I **only** stray to the loss of my own soul: but if
035:006 He **only** invites his adherents, that they
035:042 to them, it has **only** increased their aversion.
035:043 will hem in **only** the authors thereof. Now are
036:015 The (people) said: "Ye are **only** men like ourselves;
036:017 "And Our duty is **only** to deliver
037:149 (**only**) daughters, and they have sons?-
037:168 "If **only** we had had before us a message
038:015 These (to-day) **only** wait for a single mighty Blast,
038:070 "**Only** this has been revealed to me: that I
039:003 "We **only** serve them in order that they may
039:026 of the Hereafter, if they **only** knew!
039:057 'If **only** Allah had guided me, I should
039:058 'If **only** I had another chance I should
040:012 as the **Only** (object of worship) ye did
040:013 from the sky: but **only** those receive admonition
040:052 but they will (**only**) have the Curse and the Home
042:014 And they became divided **only** after knowledge
042:018 **Only** those wish to hasten it who believe
042:042 The blame is **only** against those who oppress men
043:027 "(I worship) **only** Him Who made me, and He
043:058 **only** by way of disputation: yea, they
043:066 Do they **only** wait for the Hour-that it
043:086 **only** he who bears witness to the Truth,
045:017 it was **only** after knowledge had been granted to
045:019 it is **only** wrong-doers (that stand as) Protectors,
045:032 the Hour: we **only** think it a conjecture, and we
046:023 will come) is **only** with Allah: I proclaim
047:018 Do they then **only** wait for the Hour,-that it
049:005 If **only** they had patience until thou

ONLY (continued)
049:014 but ye (**only**) say, 'We have submitted our wills
049:015 **Only** those are Believers who have
051:056 I have **only** created Jinns and men, that they
052:039 Or has He **only** daughters and ye have sons?
052:044 they would (**only**) say: "Clouds gathered in heaps!"
056:026 **Only** the saying, "Peace! Peace."
057:027 (We commanded) **only** the seeking for the Good
058:010 Secret counsels are **only** (inspired) by Satan,
060:009 Allah **only** forbids you, with regard to those who
068:033 in the Hereafter,-if **only** they knew!
071:004 put forward: if ye **only** knew."
071:006 "But my call **only** increases (their) flight
071:007 they have (**only**) thrust their fingers into their
071:021 no Increase but **only** Loss.
072:016 "If they (the pagans) had (**only**) remained on the
074:031 and We have fixed their number **only** as trial
076:010 "We **only** fear a Day of frowning and distress
092:020 But **only** the desire to seek for the countenance

ONSLAUGHT
044:016 a mighty **onslaught**: We will indeed (then) exact

OPEN
004:019 except where they have been guilty of **open** lewdness;
004:101 for the Unbelievers are unto you **open** enemies.
004:144 an **open** proof against yourselves?
005:048 have We prescribed a Law and an **Open** Way.
006:073 as well as that which is **open**. For He is
006:104 from your Lord proofs (to **open** your eyes): if
006:120 Eschew all sin, **open** or secret: those who
006:151 whether **open** or secret; take not life, which
007:033 indecent deeds, whether **open** or secret; sins
007:074 palaces and castles in (**open**) plains, and
009:005 then **open** the way for them: for Allah
009:094 and what is **open**: then will He show you
009:105 of what is hidden and what is **open**: then will He
013:009 which is **open**: He is the Great, the Most High.
015:079 They were both on an **open** highway, plain to see.
016:004 becomes an **open** disputer!
016:106 but such as **open** their breast to Unbelief,-
017:013 which he will see spread **open**.
018:017 while they lay in the **open** space in the
021:003 to witchcraft with your eyes **open**?"
021:110 "It is He Who knows what is **open** in speech
022:025 which We have made (**open**) to (all) men-
022:054 humbly (**open**) to it: for verily Allah is the
023:077 Until We **open** on them a gate leading to
023:092 is **open**: too high is He for the partners
028:064 If only they had been **open** to guidance!'
032:006 hidden and **open**, the Exalted
036:077 Yet behold! he (stands forth) as an **open** adversary!
038:050 will (ever) be **open** to them;
039:046 is hidden and **open**! It is Thou that wilt judge
039:069 placed (**open**); the prophets and the witnesses
046:009 I am but a Warner **open** and clear."
051:050 I am from Him a Warner to you, clear and **open**!
051:051 I am from Him a Warner to you, clear and **open**!
059:022 both secret and **open**; He Most Gracious
062:008 of things secret and **open**: and He
064:018 is **open**, Exalted in Might, Full of Wisdom.
065:001 they are guilty of some **open** lewdness, those are
071:002 a Warner, clear and **open**:
077:036 Nor will it be **open** to them to put forth pleas.
079:014 When, behold, they will be brought out to the **open**.

OPEN (continued)
081:010 When the Scrolls are laid **open**;

OPENED
004:090 then Allah hath **opened** no way
006:044 We **opened** to them the gates of all (good)
007:096 We should indeed have **opened** out to them
012:065 Then when they **opened** their baggage, they found
015:014 Even if We **opened** out to them a gate
039:022 Is one whose heart Allah has **opened** to Islam,
039:071 arrive there, its gates will be **opened**. And its
039:073 its gates will be **opened**; and its Keepers
054:011 So We **opened** the gates of heaven, with water
068:025 And they **opened** the morning, strong in
078:019 And the heavens shall be **opened** as if

OPENETH
006:125 He **openeth** their breast to Islam; those whom

OPENING
007:040 no **opening** will there be of the gates

OPENLY
002:160 make amends and **openly** declare (the Truth):
004:149 Whether you do **openly** a good deed or conceal
006:047 whether suddenly or **openly**, will any
007:133 and Blood: Signs **openly** self-explained: but they
007:163 **openly** (holding up their heads,) but on
013:010 it **openly**; whether he lie hid by night
013:022 secretly and **openly**; and turn off Evil with good:
014:031 secretly and **openly**, before the coming of a Day
015:089 warneth **openly** and without ambiguity,"-
015:094 Therefore expound **openly** what thou art commanded,
016:087 That day shall they (**openly**) show (their)
026:118 between me and them **openly**, and deliver
035:029 secretly and **openly**, hope for a Commerce
064:012 to deliver (the Message) clearly and **openly**.

OPENS
086:012 And by the Earth which **opens** out (for the gushing

OPINION
037:011 Just ask their **opinion:** are they
037:149 Now ask them their **opinion**: is it
051:008 Truly ye are of varying **opinion**.

OPPOSE
009:063 who **oppose** Allah and His Messenger, is the
058:005 Those who **oppose** (the commands of) Allah and His
058:020 Those who **oppose** (the commands of) Allah and
058:022 loving those who **oppose** Allah and His Messenger,

OPPOSED
065:008 insolently **opposed** the command of their Lord

OPPOSITE
005:033 from **opposite** sides, or exile from the land:
007:124 and your feet on **opposite** sides, and I
007:168 and some that are the **opposite**. We have
020:071 and feet on **opposite** sides, and I
026:049 and your feet on **opposite** sides, and I

OPPOSITION
011:088 I wish not, in **opposition** to you, to do
038:002 in Self-glory and **opposition**.

OPPRESS
042:042 **oppress** men with wrong-doing and insolently

OPPRESSED
004:075 being weak, are ill-treated (and **oppressed**)?
004:097 "Weak and **oppressed** were we in the earth."
004:098 weak and **oppressed**, men, women, and children who
004:127 the children who are weak and **oppressed**: that

OPPRESSED (continued)

007:002 so let thy heart be **oppressed** no more

OPPRESSION

002:193 except to those who practice **oppression**.
002:217 Tumult and **oppression** are worse than slaughter.
008:073 tumult and **oppression** on earth, and great
010:085 for those who practice **oppression**;
016:041 after suffering **oppression**,-We will assuredly
029:010 men's **oppression** as if it were the Wrath of Allah!

OPPRESSIVE

042:039 **oppressive** wrong is inflicted on them, (are not

OPPRESSORS

004:075 Whose people are **oppressors**; and raise for us
008:054 for they were all **oppressors** and wrong-doers.

OPTION

033:036 to have any **option** about their decision: if any

OR

002:006 whether thou warn them **or** do not warn them;
002:019 **Or** (another similitude) is that of
002:023 and call your witnesses **or** helpers
002:035 **or** ye run into harm and transgression."
002:071 to till the soil **or** water the fields;
002:080 **Or** is it that ye say of Allah
002:106 something better **or** similar:
002:106 We abrogate **or** cause to be forgotten,
002:111 Paradise unless he be a Jew **or** a Christian."
002:118 **Or** why cometh not Us a Sign?"
002:120 Never will the Jews **or** the Christians
002:125 **or** prostrate themselves (there
002:125 **or** use it as a retreat, **or** bow,
002:135 They say: "Become Jews **or** Christians
002:140 **Or** do ye say that Abraham,
002:140 and the Tribes were Jews **or** Christians?
002:158 the House in the Season **or** at other times,
002:177 in pain (**or** suffering) and adversity,
002:177 ye turn your faces toward East **or** West;
002:182 But if anyone fears partiality **or** wrong-doing
002:184 but if any of you is ill, **or** on a journey,
002:185 but if any one is ill, **or** on a journey,
002:196 **or** freed the poor, **or** offer sacrifice;
002:196 Hajj **or** 'umra in the service of Allah,
002:196 **or** had an ailment in his scalp,
002:214 **Or** do ye think that ye shall enter
002:223 so approach your tilth when **or** how ye will;
002:224 **or** making peace between persons;
002:224 **or** acting rightly, **or** making peace
002:229 **or** separate with kindness.
002:231 **or** to take undue advantage;
002:231 **or** set them free on equitable terms;
002:235 betrothal **or** hold it in your hearts.
002:236 **or** the fixation of their dower;
002:237 **Or** (the man's half) is remitted by him
002:239 **or** riding, (as may be most convenient),
002:245 It is Allah that giveth (you) want **or** Plenty,
002:255 before **or** after **or** behind them.
002:259 He said: "(Perhaps) a day **or** part of a day."
002:259 **Or** (take) the similitude of one
002:262 with reminders of their generosity **or** with injury,
002:264 your generosity **or** by injury-like those
002:270 **or** whatever you vow to make,
002:273 seeking (for trade **or** work):
002:282 whether it be small **or** big:
002:282 **or** weak, **or** unable himself to dictate,

OR (continued)

002:284 your minds **or** conceal it,
002:286 if we forget **or** fall into error;
003:005 is hidden on earth **or** in the heavens.
003:007 basic **or** fundamental clear (in meaning);
003:025 without (favour **or**) injustice?
003:028 take for friends **or** helpers Unbelievers rather
003:029 in your hearts **or** reveal it, Allah knows it all:
003:073 **Or** that those (receiving such revelation)
003:077 **or** look at them on the Day of Judgment,
003:083 willing **or** unwilling, bowed to His Will
003:127 of the Unbelievers **or** expose them to infamy,
003:128 whether He turn in mercy to them, **or** punish them;
003:134 whether in prosperity, **or** in adversity;
003:135 an act of indecency **or** wronged their own souls.
003:144 If he died **or** were slain,
003:156 through the earth **or** engaged in fighting:
003:156 they would not have died, **or** been slain."
003:157 And if ye are slain, **or** die, in the way of Allah,
003:158 And if ye die, **or** are slain,
003:159 Wert thou severe **or** harsh-hearted, they would
003:167 **or** (at least) drive (the foe from your city)."
003:195 be he male **or** female: ye are members,
004:003 **or** that which your right hands possess.
004:003 marry women of your choice, two, **or** three, **or** four;
004:007 whether the property be small **or** large,
004:008 other relatives, of orphans, **or** poor, are present,
004:011 if only daughters, two **or** more, their share
004:011 brothers (**or** sisters), the mother has a sixth.
004:011 **or** your children are nearest to you in benefit.
004:012 If the man **or** woman whose inheritance
004:012 but has left a brother **or** a sister, each one
004:015 **or** Allah ordain for them some (other) way.
004:029 nor kill (**or** destroy) yourselves:
004:043 **or** on a journey, **or** one of you cometh from
004:043 **or** ye have been in contact with women, and
004:043 **or** on a journey, **or** one of you cometh from
004:043 then take for yourselves clean sand (**or** earth),
004:047 and turn them hindwards, **or** curse them as We
004:053 Have they a share in dominion **or** power?
004:054 **Or** do they envy mankind for what
004:066 sacrifice their lives **or** to leave their homes,
004:071 **or** go forth all together.
004:074 whether he is slain **or** gets victory, soon shall
004:077 **or** even more than, they should have feared Allah:
004:083 safety **or** fear, they divulge it.
004:083 **or** to those charged with authority among them,
004:089 take no friends **or** helpers from their ranks:
004:090 you **or** fighting their own people.
004:090 **or** those who approach you with hearts restraining
004:102 the inconvenience of rain **or** because ye are ill;
004:103 **or** lying down on your sides; but
004:109 **or** who will carry their affairs through?
004:110 If anyone does evil **or** wrongs his own soul but
004:112 But if anyone earns a fault **or** a sin and throws
004:114 **or** goodness **or** conciliation between people
004:123 besides Allah, any protector **or** helper.
004:124 be they male **or** female, and have faith, they
004:128 **or** desertion on her husband's part, there
004:135 **or** decline to do justice, verily Allah
004:135 **or** your kin, and whether it be
004:135 and whether it be (against) rich **or** poor: for
004:135 even as against yourselves, **or** your parents, **or**

OR (continued)

004:149 or conceal it **or** cover evil with pardon, surely
004:173 any to protect **or** help them.
004:176 **or** ascendants as heirs.
005:001 the Sacred Precincts **or** in the state of Pilgrimage.
005:003 **or** by being gored to death; that which
005:003 **or** by a violent blow, **or** a headlong fall, **or** by
005:006 But if ye are ill, **or** on a journey, **or** one
005:006 **or** ye have been in contact with women, and you
005:006 **or** one of you cometh from the privy **or** ye have
005:006 then take for yourselves clean sand **or** earth, and
005:032 **or** for spreading mischief in the land-it would be
005:033 execution **or** crucifixion, **or** the cutting
005:033 from opposite sides, **or** exile from the land:
005:033 **or** the cutting off of hands and feet from opposite
005:038 As to the thief, male **or** female, cut off
005:038 cut off his **or** her hands: a retribution
005:041 **or** it be among the Jews, men who listen
005:042 either judge between them, **or** decline to interfere.
005:052 **or** a decision from Him then will they regret of
005:057 **or** among those who reject Faith: but fear
005:057 for a mockery **or** sport,-whether among those who
005:071 no trial (**or** punishment); so they became
005:076 no power either to harm **or** benefit you? But
005:089 **or** clothe them; **or** give a slave his freedom.
005:095 **or** by way of atonement, the feeding
005:095 while in the Sacred Precincts **or** in the state
005:095 **or** its equivalent in fasts: that he
005:096 **or** in the state of pilgrimage and fear Allah,
005:103 **or** a she-camel let loose for free pasture, **or** idol
005:103 **or** idol sacrifices for twin-births in animals, **or**
005:103 **or** stallion-camels freed from work: it is
005:106 of your own (brotherhood) **or** others from outside
005:108 **or** else they would fear that other oaths
006:013 (**or** lurketh) in the Night and the Day. For He
006:021 **or** rejecteth his Signs? But verily
006:035 **or** a ladder to the skies and bring them a Sign,-
006:040 **or** the Hour (that ye dread), would ye then
006:047 whether suddenly **or** openly, will any
006:059 the darkness (**or** depths) of the earth, nor
006:059 nor anything fresh **or** dry (green **or** withered),
006:065 **or** to cover you with confusion
006:070 no protector **or** intercessor except Allah: if it
006:070 if it offered every ransom (**or** reparation), none
006:093 **or** saith, "I have received inspiration," when
006:093 **or** (again) who saith, "I can reveal the like of
006:099 (**or** spathes) (come) clusters of dates
006:120 Eschew all sin, open **or** secret: those who
006:132 (**or** ranks) according to their deeds: for thy
006:138 forbidden to yoke **or** burden, and cattle
006:143 **or** the two females, **or** (the young) which the
006:144 **or** the two females, **or** (the young) which the
006:145 **or** the flesh of swine,-for it is
006:145 **or** blood poured forth, **or** the
006:145 for it is an abomination,-**or** what is impious,
006:146 **or** is mixed up with a bone: this in
006:146 their backs **or** their entrails, **or** is
006:151 whether open **or** secret; take not life, which
006:157 **Or** lest ye should say: "If the Book
006:158 **or** certain of the Signs of thy Lord! The day
006:158 **or** thy Lord (Himself), **or** certain
007:003 as friends **or** protectors, other than Him.
007:004 **or** while they slept for their afternoon rest.

OR (continued)

007:007 for We were never absent (at any time **or** place).
007:020 **or** such beings as live for ever."
007:033 sins and trespasses against truth **or** reason;
007:033 indecent deeds, whether open **or** secret; sins
007:037 **or** rejects His Signs? For such
007:050 "Pour down to us water **or** anything that Allah
007:053 **Or** could we be sent back? Then should
007:073 **or** ye shall be seized with a grievous punishment."
007:088 **or** else ye (thou and they) shall have
007:098 **Or** else did they feel secure against its
007:115 **or** shall we have the (first) throw?"
007:160 We divided them into twelve tribes **or** nations. We
007:164 destroy **or** visit with a terrible punishment?"-
007:173 **Or** lest ye should say: "Our fathers
007:176 **or** if you leave him alone, he (still)
007:188 **or** harm to myself except as Allah willeth. If
007:193 ye call them **or** ye keep silent.
007:195 **Or** hands to lay hold with? **Or** eyes
007:195 **Or** eyes to see with? **Or** ears
007:195 **Or** ears to hear with? Say: "Call your
008:016 **or** to retreat to a troop (of his own)-he draws
008:030 in bonds, **or** slay thee, **or** get
008:030 **or** get the out (of they home). They plot
008:032 from the sky, **or** send us a grievous chastisement."
009:008 the ties either of kinship **or** of covenant? With
009:010 the ties either of kinship **or** of covenant! It is
009:019 to pilgrims, **or** the maintenance of the Sacred
009:024 **or** your kindred: the wealth that ye have gained;
009:024 than Allah **or** His Messenger, **or** the striving
009:024 ye fear a decline: **or** the dwellings in which
009:024 **or** the striving in His cause;-then wait
009:041 lightly **or** heavily, and strive and struggle,
009:052 from Him, **or** by our hands. So wait (expectant);
009:052 (martyrdom **or** victory)? But we
009:053 willingly **or** unwillingly: not from you will it
009:057 **or** caves, **or** a place of concealment, they would
009:074 none on earth to protect **or** help them.
009:080 **or** not, (their sin is unforgivable): if thou
009:091 **or** ill, **or** who find no resources to spend (on the
009:106 **or** turn in mercy to them: and Allah
009:109 and His good pleasure?-**or** he that layeth his
009:120 **or** fatigue, **or** hunger, in the Cause of Allah,
009:120 because nothing could they suffer **or** do, but was
009:120 **or** fatigue, **or** hunger, in the Cause of Allah,
009:120 **or** trod paths to raise the ire of the Unbelievers,
009:120 the Unbelievers, **or** gain any gain from an
009:121 (for the Cause)-small **or** great-nor cut
009:126 are tried every year once **or** twice? Yet they
010:012 lying down on his side, **or** sitting, **or** standing.
010:012 **or** standing. But when We have removed his
010:015 than this, **or** change this." Say: "It is not
010:017 **or** deny His Signs? But never
010:018 in the heaven **or** on earth?-Glory to Him! and far
010:024 **or** by day, and We make it like a harvest clean-mown,
010:031 **Or** who is it that has power over hearing and sight?
010:035 to be followed, **or** he who finds not guidance
010:038 **Or** do they say, "He forged it"? Say: "Bring
010:046 We promise them,-**or** We take thy soul (before that),-
010:049 **or** profit to myself except as Allah willeth.
010:050 **or** by day,-what portion of it would the Sinners
010:059 **or** do ye forge (things) to attribute to Allah?"
010:061 on the earth **or** in heaven. And not

OR (continued)

010:095	Signs of Allah, **or** thou shalt be of those
011:012	sent down unto him, **or** why does not an angel
011:013	**Or** they may say, "He forged it." Say, "Bring ye
011:035	**Or** do they say, "He has forged it?" Say:
011:041	**or** be at rest! For my Lord is, be sure,
011:064	**or** a swift Punishment will seize you!
011:080	to suppress you **or** that I could betake myself to
011:084	And give not short measure **or** weight: I see you
011:087	fathers practiced, **or** that we leave off doing
011:089	of the people of Noah **or** of Hud **or** of Salih,
011:089	**or** of Salih, nor are the people of Lut
011:113	**or** the Fire will touch you; and ye have
012:009	"Slay ye Joseph **or** cast him out to some
012:021	much good, **or** we shall adopt him as a son." Thus
012:025	but prison **or** a grievous chastisement?"
012:039	**or** Allah the One, Supreme and Irresistible?
012:056	when, **or** where he pleased. We bestow
012:080	**or** Allah judges for me; and He
012:085	of illness, **or** until thou die!"
012:107	**Or** of the coming against them of the (final)
013:004	out of single roots **or** otherwise: watered with
013:008	(of their time **or** number) **or** do exceed. Every
013:010	of you conceal his speech **or** declare it openly;
013:010	by night **or** walk freely by day.
013:015	with good-will **or** in spite of themselves: so do
013:016	**or** for harm to themselves?" Say: "Are the
013:016	who see? **Or** the depths of darkness equal with
013:016	equal with Light?" **Or** do the assign to Allah
013:017	to make ornaments **or** utensils therewith, there is
013:026	Allah doth enlarge, **or** grant by (strict) measure,
013:031	**or** the earth were cloven asunder, **or** the dead
013:031	**or** the dead were made to speak, (this would
013:031	**or** to settle close to their homes, until the
013:033	**or** is it (just) a show of words?" Nay! to those
013:038	(**or** commanded). For each period is an appointment.
013:039	Allah doth blot out **or** confirm what He pleaseth:
013:040	We promised them **or** take to Us thy soul (before
014:013	**or** ye shall return to our religion." But their
014:021	(now) whether we rage, **or** bear (these torments)
014:038	from Allah, whether on earth **or** in heaven.
015:006	Truly thou art mad (**or** possessed)!
016:033	**or** there comes the Command of thy Lord
016:045	them up, **or** that the Wrath will not seize them
016:046	**Or** that He may not call them to account in the
016:047	**Or** that He may not call them to account by a
016:049	whether moving creatures **or** the angels: for more
016:059	**or** bury it in the dust? Ah! what an
016:073	with anything in heavens **or** earth, and cannot
016:077	is as the twinkling of an eye, **or** even quicker:
016:097	man **or** woman, and has Faith, verily, to him
017:009	(**or** stable), and giveth the glad tidings to the
017:022	**or** thou (O man!) wilt sit in disgrace
017:023	Whether one **or** both of them attain old age
017:033	(to demand Qisas **or** to forgive): but let
017:050	Say: "(Nay!) be ye stones **or** iron,
017:051	"**Or** any created matter which, in your minds,
017:054	**or** if He please, punishment: We have not
017:058	the Day of Judgment **or** punish it with a dreadful
017:068	**or** that He will not send against you a violent
017:069	**Or** do ye feel secure that He will not send
017:091	"**Or** (until) thou have a garden of date trees
017:092	"**Or** thou cause the sky to fall in pieces, as thou

OR (continued)

017:092	against us; **or** thou bring Allah and the angels
017:093	**or** thou mount a ladder right into the skies.
017:093	"**Or** thou have a house adorned with gold, **or** thou
017:107	Say: "Whether ye believe in it **or** not, it is
017:110	**or** call upon Rahman: by whatever
018:008	(without growth **or** herbage).
018:009	**Or** dost thou reflect that the Companions
018:019	a day, **or** part of a day." At length)
018:020	they would stone you **or** force you to return
018:041	"**Or** the water of the garden will run off
018:049	**or** great, but takes account thereof! They will
018:055	**or** the Wrath be brought to them face to face?
018:060	**or** (until) I spend years and years in travel."
018:086	to punish them, **or** to treat them with kindness."
018:097	to scale it **or** to dig through it.
019:014	and he was not overbearing **or** rebellious.
019:032	and not overbearing **or** unblest;
019:075	**or** in (the approach of) the Hour,-they will
019:078	**or** has he taken a promise with the Most Gracious?
019:087	has received permission (**or** promise) from (Allah)
019:098	**or** hear (so much as) a whisper of them?
020:010	**or** find some guidance at the fire."
020:022	(**or** stain)-as another Sign,-
020:044	perchance he may take warning **or** fear (Allah)."
020:045	**or** lest he transgress all bounds."
020:065	thou throw (first) **or** that we be the first
020:086	(in coming)? **Or** did ye desire that Wrath should
020:089	to harm them **or** to do them good?
020:107	Nothing crooked **or** curved wilt thou see
020:110	**or** behind them: but they shall comprehend Him not.
020:110	He knows what is before **or** after **or** behind them:
020:113	**or** that it may cause their remembrance (of Him).
021:020	nor do they ever flag **or** intermit.
021:021	**Or** have they taken (for worship) gods from
021:024	**Or** have they taken for worship (other) gods
021:043	**Or** have they gods that can guard them from Us?
021:055	**or** are you one of those who jest?"
021:109	ye are promised is near **or** far.
022:007	**or** about (the fact) that Allah will raise up
022:026	**or** stand up, **or** bow, **or** prostrate
022:026	**or** prostrate themselves (therein in prayer).
022:031	**or** the wind had swooped (like a bird on its prey)
022:052	**or** a prophet before thee, but, when he
022:055	**or** there comes to them the Chastisement
022:058	cause of Allah, and are slain **or** die,-on them
023:006	**or** (the captives) whom their right hands
023:068	(of Allah), **or** has anything (new) come to them
023:069	**Or** do they not recognize their Messenger,
023:070	**Or** do they say, "He is possessed"? Nay, he
023:072	**Or** is it that thou asked them for some recompense?
023:113	**or** part of a day: but ask those
024:003	an adulteress **or** idolatress, and the
024:003	but an adulterer **or** an idolater; to the
024:031	**or** their brothers' sons, **or** their sisters'
024:031	**or** male attendants free of sexual desires.
024:031	**or** their sisters' sons, **or** their women, **or** the
024:031	sexual desires. **Or** small children who have no
024:031	**or** the slaves whom their right hands possess,
024:031	**or** their sisters' sons, **or** their women, **or** the
024:032	your slaves, male **or** female: if they
024:040	**Or** (the Unbelievers' state) is like the depths
024:050	**or** are they in fear, that Allah

OR (continued)

024:050 **Or** do they doubt, **or** are
024:058 it is not wrong for you **or** for them to move
024:061 **or** your father's brothers, **or** your
024:061 a greeting **or** blessing and purity as from Allah.
024:061 **or** separately. But if ye enter houses,
024:061 **or** your mothers, **or** your brothers, **or** your
024:061 **or** your sisters, **or** your
024:061 **or** your mother's sisters, **or** in
024:061 **or** your mother's brothers, **or** in
024:061 **or** in the house of a sincere friend of yours:
024:061 **or** your fathers's sisters, **or** your
024:061 **or** in houses of which the keys are in
024:061 **or** those of your fathers, **or** your
024:063 **or** a grievous Chastisement be inflicted on them.
025:003 **or** good to themselves; nor can they control
025:008 "**Or** (why) has not a treasure been bestowed
025:008 **or** why has he (not) a garden for enjoyment?"
025:015 Say: "Is that best, **or** the eternal Garden,
025:017 **or** did they stray from the Path themselves?"
025:021 to us, **or** (why) do we not see Our Lord?"
025:043 (**or** impulse)? Could thou be a disposer of affairs
025:044 **Or** thinkest thou that most of them listen
025:044 of them listen **or** understand? They are
025:062 **or** to show their gratitude.
025:073 they were deaf **or** blind;
026:073 "**Or** do you good **or** harm?"
026:093 **or** help themselves?'"
026:136 whether thou admonish us **or** be not
026:213 with Allah, **or** thou wilt be among those who
027:007 some information, **or** I will bring you a burning
027:012 without stain (**or** harm): (these are)
027:020 the Hoopoe? **Or** is he among the absentees?
027:021 **or** execute him, unless he bring me a clear
027:027 whether thou hast told the truth **or** lied!
027:040 **or** ungrateful! And if any is grateful, truly his
027:041 (to the truth) **or** is one of those who
027:059 **or** the false gods they associate (with Him)?
027:060 **Or**, who has created the heaven and the earth,
027:061 **Or**, who has made the earth firm to live in;
027:062 **Or**, Who listens to the distressed when he calls
027:063 **Or**, Who guides you through the depths of
027:064 **Or**, Who originates Creation, then repeats
027:065 Say: None in the heavens **or** on earth, except
027:075 **or** earth, but is (recorded) in a clear record.
027:084 not in knowledge, **or** what was it ye did?"
028:009 **or** we may adopt him as a son." And they
028:029 some information, **or** a burning firebrand,
028:032 without stain (**or** harm), and draw
028:082 **or** restricts it, to any of His servants He pleases!
028:083 high-handedness **or** mischief on earth: and the
029:022 beside Allah, any protector **or** helper."
029:024 "Slay him **or** burn him." But Allah
029:068 **or** rejects the Truth when it reaches him?
030:035 **Or** have We sent down authority to them,
031:006 without knowledge (**or** meaning), to mislead
031:016 in a rock, **or** (anywhere) in the heavens **or** on
031:016 **or** on earth, Allah will bring it forth: for Allah
031:028 And your creation **or** your resurrection is in no
032:003 **Or** do they say, "He has forged it"? Nay, it
032:004 besides Him, to protect **or** intercede (for you):
033:005 **or** your friends. But there is no blame on you
033:016 **or** slaughter; and even if (ye do escape),

OR (continued)

033:017 any protector **or** helper.
033:017 to give you punishment **or** to give you Mercy?"
033:024 be His Will, **or** turn to them in Mercy: for Allah
033:036 man **or** woman, when a matter has been decided
033:053 **or** that ye should marry his widows after him
033:054 **or** conceal it, verily Allah has knowledge
033:055 **or** the (slaves) whom their right hands possess.
033:055 sisters' sons, **or** their women, **or** the
033:055 **or** their brothers' sons, **or** their sisters' sons,
033:055 **or** their sons, their brothers, **or** their
034:003 **or** on earth: nor is there anything less than
034:003 less than that, **or** greater, but is
034:008 **or** is he afflicted with madness." Nay, it is
034:009 them up, **or** cause a piece of the sky to fall
034:022 of an atom,-in the heavens **or** on earth: no (sort
034:024 on right guidance **or** in manifest error!"
034:024 it is that either we **or** ye are on right
034:042 for profit **or** harm: and We
034:046 **or** (it may be) singly,-and reflect
035:001 two, **or** three, **or** four (Pairs): He adds
035:003 you Sustenance from heaven **or** earth? There is
035:011 **or** lays down (her load), but with
035:040 **Or** have they a share in the heavens? **Or** have
035:040 **Or** have We given them a Book from which
035:044 in the heavens **or** on earth: for He
036:010 admonish them **or** thou do not admonish them:
037:011 **or** the (other) beings We have created?
037:062 **or** the Tree of Zaqqum?
037:147 to a hundred thousand (men) **or** more.
037:150 **Or** that We created the angels female, and they
037:156 **Or** have ye an authority manifest?
038:009 **Or** have they the Treasures of the Mercy
038:010 **Or** have they the dominion of the heavens
038:039 (on others) **or** withhold them, no account
038:063 **or** have (our) eyes failed to perceive them?"
038:075 Art thou haughty? **Or** art thou one of the high
039:009 prostrating himself **or** standing (in adoration),
039:038 remove His affliction **or** if He wills some Mercy
039:052 the provision **or** restricts it, for any
039:057 "**Or** (lest) it should say: `If only
039:058 "**Or** (lest) it should say when it (actually) sees
040:026 change your religion, **or** lest he should cause
040:040 whether man **or** woman-and is a believer-such will
040:043 whether in this world, **or** the Hereafter;
040:077 **or** We take thy soul (to Our Mercy) (before that),
041:011 **or** unwillingly." They said: "We do come
041:040 **or** he that comes safe through, on the
041:042 from before **or** behind it: it is
042:020 but he has no share **or** lot in the Hereafter.
042:031 anyone to protect **or** to help.
042:034 **Or** He can cause them to perish because of the
042:049 He bestows (children) male **or** female according to
042:050 **Or** He bestows both males and females, and He
042:051 **or** by the sending of a Messenger to reveal,
042:051 by inspiration, **or** from behind a veil, **or** by
043:040 **or** give direction to the blind **or** to such
043:040 **or** to such as (wander) in manifest error?
043:042 **Or** We shall show thee that (accomplished) which We
043:053 on him, **or** (why) come (not) with him
043:058 **or** He?" This they set forth to thee, only by
043:080 **Or** do they think that We hear not their secrets
044:010 a kind of smoke (**or** mist) plainly visible.

OR (continued)

045:014 recompense (for good **or** ill) each People according to
046:004 **or** any remnant of knowledge (ye may have), if ye
046:004 **or** have they a share in the heavens? Bring me
046:008 **Or** do they say, "He has forged it"? Say:
046:009 be done with me **or** with you. I follow
047:004 time for) either generosity **or** ransom: until the
047:024 **or** is that there are locks upon their hearts?
047:029 **Or** do those in whose hearts is a disease,
048:011 you some loss **or** to give you some profit?
048:016 **or** they shall submit. Then if ye show obedience,
050:037 **or** who gives ear and earnestly witnesses.
051:039 "A sorcerer, **or** one possessed!"
051:052 "A sorcerer, **or** one possessed"!
052:015 "Is this then a magic, **or** is it ye that do not see?
052:016 **or** not: ye but receive the recompense of your
052:030 **Or** do they say:-"A Poet! we await for him
052:032 to this, **or** are they but a people transgressing
052:033 **Or** do they say, "He fabricated the (Message)?"
052:035 **or** were they themselves the creators?
052:036 **Or** did they create the heavens and the earth?
052:037 **Or** are the Treasures of thy Lord with them,
052:037 with them, **or** have they control over them.
052:038 **Or** have they a ladder, by which
052:039 **Or** has He only daughters and ye have sons?
052:040 **Or** is it that thou dost ask for a reward,
052:041 **Or** that the Unseen is in their hands, and they
052:042 **Or** do they intend a plot (against thee)?
052:043 **Or** have they a god other then Allah? Exalted is
053:009 two bow-lengths **or** (even) nearer;
054:043 **Or** have ye an immunity in the Sacred Books?
054:044 **Or** do they say: "We acting together
055:039 will be asked of man **or** Jinn as to his sin,
055:056 whom no man **or** Jinn before them has touched;-
055:074 Whom no man **or** Jinn before them has touched;-
056:029 (**or** fruits) piled one above another,-
056:059 Is it ye who create it, **or** are We the Creators?
056:064 Is it ye that cause it to grow, **or** are We the Cause?
056:069 from the Cloud, **or** do We?
056:072 which feeds the fire, **or** do We grow it?
057:022 **or** in your souls but is recorded in a Book before
058:022 were their fathers **or** their sons, **or** their
058:022 **or** their brothers, **or** their kindred. For such
059:005 of the tender palm-trees, **Or** ye left them
059:006 with either cavalry **or** camelry: but Allah
059:010 rancor (**or** sense of injury) against those
059:014 **or** from behind walls. Strong is
060:001 and yours as friends (**or** protectors),-offering
060:012 (**or** fornication), that they will not kill their
062:011 than any pastime **or** bargain! And Allah
062:011 **or** some pastime, they disperse headlong to it,
063:006 for their forgiveness **or** not. Allah will
063:009 **or** your children divert you from the
065:002 on equitable terms **or** part with them on equitable
066:005 previously married **or** virgins.
067:010 "Had we but listened **or** used our intelligence,
067:013 **or** make it known, He certainly has (full) knowledge,
067:017 **Or** do ye feel secure that He Who is in
067:021 **Or** who is there that can provide you
067:022 **or** one who walks evenly on a Straight Way?
067:028 **or** if He bestows His Mercy on us,-yet who
068:002 mad **or** possessed.
068:037 **Or** have ye a Book through which ye learn-

OR (continued)

068:039 **Or** have ye Covenants with Us on oath,
068:041 **Or** have they some "Partners" (in Godhead)?
068:046 **Or** is it that thou dost ask them for a reward,
068:047 **Or** that the Unseen is in their hands, so that
072:005 **or** Jinn should say aught that is untrue
072:010 **or** whether their Lord (really) intends to guide
072:013 **or** of any injustice.
072:021 you harm, **or** to bring you to right conduct."
072:025 **or** whether my Lord will appoint for it
073:003 Half of it,-**or** a little less,
073:004 **Or** a little more; and recite the Qur'an in slow,
073:020 **or** half the night, **or** a third of the night, so do
074:037 **or** to follow behind;-
076:003 whether he be grateful **or** ungrateful.
076:024 **or** the ingrate among them.
077:006 Whether of Justification **or** of Warning;-
077:039 (**or** plot), use it against Me!
079:046 **or** (at most till) the following morn!
080:004 **Or** that he might receive admonition, and the
081:016 Go straight, **or** hide;
083:003 **or** weight to men, give less than due.
086:012 **or** the sprouting of vegetation),-
089:005 (**or** evidence) for those who understand?
090:014 **Or** the giving of food in a day of privation
090:016 **Or** to the indigent (down) in the dust.
096:001 Proclaim! (**or** Read!) in the name of thy Lord
096:012 **Or** enjoins Righteousness?
114:002 The King (**or** Ruler) of Mankind,
114:003 The God (**or** Judge) of Mankind,-

ORBIT

036:040 (its own) **orbit** (according to Law).

ORCHARDS

027:060 well-planted **orchards** full of beauty and delight:
036:034 And We produce therein **orchards** with date-palms

ORDAIN

004:015 or Allah **ordain** for them some (other) way.
007:156 That (Mercy) I shall **ordain** for those
007:156 "And **ordain** for us that which is good, in this

ORDAINED

002:187 and seek what Allah hath **ordained** for you,
002:222 **ordained** for you by Allah for Allah
002:226 a waiting for four months is **ordained**;
002:229 be unable to keep the limits **ordained** by Allah,
002:229 if any do transgress the limits **ordained** by Allah,
002:229 these are the limits **ordained** by Allah;
002:229 unable to keep the limits **ordained** by Allah
002:230 Such are the limits **ordained** by Allah,
002:230 keep the limits **ordained** by Allah.
004:011 These are settled portions **ordained** by Allah:
004:012 Thus is it **ordained** by Allah;
004:024 Thus hath Allah **ordained** (prohibitions) against you:
004:092 it is **ordained** that he should free
005:032 We **ordained** for the Children of Israel that if
005:045 We **ordained** therein for them: "Life for life,
007:145 And We **ordained** for him in the
009:036 so **ordained** by Him the day He created
009:060 (thus is it) **ordained** by Allah, and Allah
020:040 Then didst thou come hither as **ordained**, O Moses!
024:001 and which We have **ordained**: in it
028:012 And We **ordained** that he refused suck at first,
028:085 Verily He Who **ordained** the Qur'an for thee,

ORDAINED (continued)

029:027 and Jacob, and **ordained** among his progeny
035:011 a Book (**ordained**). All this is easy to Allah.
057:027 the Gospel; and We **ordained** in the hearts of those
058:003 (it is **ordained** that such a one) should free
066:002 Allah has already **ordained** for you, the expiation

ORDAINMENT

008:068 a previous **ordainment** from Allah, a severe
042:047 because of (the **ordainment** of) Allah! That Day

ORDER

002:219 His Signs: in **order** that ye may consider-
002:242 in **order** that ye may understand.
003:152 from your foes in **order** to test you.
003:152 and fell to disputing about the **order**,
003:166 in **order** that He might test the Believers,
004:077 the **order** for fighting was issued to them, behold!
004:119 I will **order** them to slit the ears of cattle,
006:137 in **order** to lead them to their
007:020 in **order** to reveal to them their shame that
007:056 after it hath been set in **order**, but call
007:077 the **order** of their Lord, saying: "O Salih!
007:085 after it has been set in **order**: that will
007:094 in **order** that they might call in humility.
007:168 in **order** that they might turn (to Us).
007:189 in **order** that he might dwell with her
008:017 in **order** the He might confer on the Believers
008:037 In **order** that Allah may separate the impure
009:037 in **order** to agree with the number of months
009:062 In **order** to please you: but it
010:078 in **order** that thou and thy brother may have
012:002 in **order** that ye may learn wisdom.
012:024 his Lord: thus (did We **order**) that We might
012:052 "This (say I), in **order** that he may know
012:062 in **order** that they might come back.
013:030 passed away; in **order** that thou mightest rehearse
014:001 in **order** that thou mightest lead mankind out of
014:004 in **order** to make (things) clear to them.
014:010 in **order** that He may forgive you your sins
014:025 in **order** that they may receive admonition.
014:037 by Thy Sacred House; in **order**, O our Lord,
016:039 (They must be raised up), in **order** that He may
016:102 in **order** to strengthen those who believe, and as
017:001 We did Bless,-in **order** that We might show him
017:041 in **order** that they may receive admonition,
017:066 in **order** that ye may seek of His Bounty.
017:076 the land, in **order** to expel thee; but in
017:106 in **order** that thou mightest recite it
018:002 in **order** that He may warn (the godless) of a
018:007 in **order** that We may test them-as to which
018:012 Then We roused them, in **order** to test which of
018:056 with vain argument, in **order** therewith to weaken
018:071 "Hast thou scuttled it in **order** to drown
018:088 as We **order** it by our command."
018:094 in **order** that thou mightest erect a barrier
020:023 "In **order** that We may show thee of
020:039 and (this) in **order** that thou mayest be
020:093 Didst thou then disobey my **order**?"
020:113 in **order** that they may fear Allah, or that
021:013 in **order** that ye may be called to account.
021:081 (tamely) for Solomon, to his **order**, to the
022:005 in **order** that We may manifest (Our Power) to you;
022:009 in **order** to lead (men) astray from the
023:049 in **order** that they might receive guidance.

ORDER (continued)

023:100 "In **order** that I may work righteousness in the
024:001 in **order** that ye may receive admonition.
024:027 in **order** that ye may heed (what is seemly).
024:031 their feet in **order** to draw attention to their
024:033 desire chastity, in **order** that ye may make a gain
024:048 in **order** that He may judge between them, behold,
024:051 His Messenger, in **order** that He may judge
024:063 who withstand the Messenger's **order**, lest some
025:050 amongst them, in **order** that they may be mindful
027:017 and they were all kept in **order** and ranks.
027:019 so **order** me that I may be grateful for Thy favours,
027:088 in perfect **order**: for He
028:046 in **order** that they may receive admonition.
028:051 in **order** that they may receive admonition.
028:073 and in **order** that ye may be grateful.
030:041 in **order** that they may turn back (from Evil).
030:046 in **order** that ye may be grateful.
032:003 in **order** that they may be rightly guided.
032:021 the greater Chastisement in **order** that they may
033:037 in **order** that (in future) there may be no
033:050 in **order** that there should be no difficulty
036:006 In **order** that thou mayest warn a people,
036:045 will be after you, in **order** that ye may
038:036 to flow gently to his **order**, whithersoever he
039:003 "We only serve them in **order** that they may
039:027 in **order** that they may receive admonition.
039:028 in **order** that they may guard against Evil.
039:064 that ye **order** me to worship, O ye
040:067 a Term appointed: in **order** that ye may understand.
043:010 in **order** that ye may find guidance (on the way);
043:013 In **order** that ye may sit firm and square
043:048 in **order** that they might turn (to Us).
043:063 with Wisdom, and in **order** to make clear to you
044:058 in thy tongue, in **order** that they may give heed.
045:022 for just ends, and in **order** that each soul my
046:019 (have done), and in **order** that (Allah) may
046:022 They said: "Hast thou come in **order** to turn
047:004 but (He lets you fight) in **order** to test you,
048:009 In **order** that ye (O men) may believe
055:008 In **order** that ye may not transgress (due) balance.
057:023 In **order** that ye may not despair over matters
058:010 by Satan, in **order** that he may cause grief to the
059:005 and in **order** that He might cover with shame
059:007 in **order** that it may not (Merely) make a circuit
074:031 in **order** that the People of the Book may arrive
075:004 in perfect **order** the very tips of his fingers.
076:002 of mingled sperm, in **order** to try him: so We
079:028 and He hath given it **order** and perfection.
087:002 given **order** and proportion;
091:007 and **order** given to it;

ORDERED

002:027 has **ordered** to be joined,
004:060 though they were **ordered** to reject him.
004:066 If We had **ordered** them to sacrifice their lives
004:077 why hast Thou **ordered** us to fight?
006:144 Allah **ordered** you such a thing? But who
008:005 Just as thy Lord **ordered** thee out of
015:065 but pass on whither ye are **ordered**."
025:002 and **ordered** them in due proportions.
034:033 Behold! ye (constantly) **ordered** us to be

ORDERING

006:096 such is the judgment and **ordering** of (Him),

ORDINANCES
006:146 for We are True (in Our **ordinances**).

ORDINARILY
024:031 what (**ordinarily**) appear thereof; that they
073:007 prolonged occupation with **ordinary** duties:

ORE
013:017 (**ore**) which they heat in the fire, to make

ORIGIN
036:078 and forgets his own (**Origin** and) Creation:

ORIGINATE
010:034 can any **originate** creation and repeat it?" Say:
029:020 see how Allah did **originate** creation; so will

ORIGINATED
043:027 "(I worship) only Him Who **originated** me, and He

ORIGINATES
010:034 **originates** Creation and repeats it: then how
027:064 Or, Who **originates** Creation, then repeats
029:019 **originates** creation, then repeats it: truly that

ORIGINATOR
002:117 The **Originator** of the heavens
006:101 Wonderful **Originator** of the heavens
035:001 the **Originator** of the heavens and the earth,
059:024 the **Originator**, the Fashioner, to Him belong

ORNAMENTS
007:148 out of their **ornaments**, the body
010:024 its golden **ornaments** and is decked out (in beauty):
013:017 to make **ornaments** or utensils therewith, there is
016:014 therefrom **ornaments** to wear; and thou
020:087 of the **ornaments** of the (whole) people, and we
024:031 their beauty and **ornaments** except what (ordinarily)
024:031 to their hidden **ornaments**. And O ye
035:012 and tender, and ye extract **ornaments** to wear;

ORPHAN
076:008 the indigent, the **orphan**, and the captive,-
090:015 To the **orphan** with claims of relationship,
093:006 Did He not find thee an **orphan** and give
093:009 Therefore, treat not the **orphan** with harshness,
107:002 Then such is the one who repulses the **orphan**,

ORPHAN'S
006:152 And come not nigh to the **orphan's** property,
017:034 **orphan's** property except to improve it, until he

ORPHANED
004:127 concerning the **orphaned** women to whom

ORPHANS
002:083 and **orphans** and those in need;
002:177 for your kin, for **orphans**,
002:215 is for parents and kindred and **orphans**
002:220 They ask thee concerning **orphans**.
004:002 To **orphans** restore their property
004:003 be able to deal justly with the **orphans**,
004:006 Make trial of **orphans** until they reach
004:008 other relatives, of **orphans**, or poor, are present,
004:010 property of **orphans**, eat up a fire into
004:036 and do good to parents, kinsfolk, **orphans**, those
004:127 that ye stand firm for justice to **orphans**.
008:041 and to near relatives, **orphans**, the needy,
018:082 two youths, **orphans**, in the Town; there was
059:007 and **orphans**, the needy and the wayfarer; in order
089:017 Nay, nay! But ye honour not the **orphans**!

ORTS
056:065 We could make it broken **orts**.

OTHER
002:076 but when they meet each **other** in private,
002:158 the House in the Season or at **other** times,
002:173 and that on which any **other** name
002:188 and knowingly a little of (**other**) people's property.
002:253 have fought among each **other**,
002:253 they would not have fought each **other**;
002:282 O ye who believe! when ye deal with each **other**,
002:282 The **other** can remind her.
003:013 the **other** resisting Allah;
003:019 except through envy of each **other**,
003:034 Offspring, one of the **other**:
003:064 lords and patrons **other** than Allah."
003:083 Do they seek for **other** than the Religion of Allah?
003:085 a religion **other** than Islam (submission to Allah)
003:144 but Allah (on the **other** hand) will swiftly
003:198 On the **other** hand, for those who fear their Lord,
003:200 vie in such perseverance: strengthen each **other**;
004:008 **other** relatives, of orphans, or poor, are present,
004:015 or Allah ordain for them some (**other**) way.
004:021 when ye have gone in unto each **other**,
004:034 the one more (strength) than the **other**, and
004:035 and the **other** from hers; if they seek
004:082 Had it been from **other** than Allah, they
004:102 And let the **other** party come up which hath
004:115 a path **other** than that becoming to men of Faith,
004:116 one who joins **other** gods with Allah, hath
004:116 He pleaseth **other** sins than this: one
004:116 (the sin of) joining **other** gods with Him:
005:003 hath been invoked the name of **other** than Allah;
005:014 the one and the **other**, to the Day of Judgement.
005:020 He had not given to any **other** among the peoples.
005:027 it was accepted from one, but not from the **other**.
005:030 The (selfish) soul of the **other** led him
005:041 who race each **other** into Unbelief: (whether it be)
005:051 they are but friends and protectors to each **other**.
005:059 no **other** reason than that we believer in Allah,
005:062 racing each **other** in sin and transgression and
005:072 Whoever joins **other** gods with Allah,-Allah will
005:108 that **other** oaths would be taken after their oaths.
006:014 any **other** than Allah, the Maker of
006:040 would ye then call upon **other** than Allah?-
006:046 who-a god **other** than Allah-could restore
006:056 **other** than Allah, whom ye call upon." Say:
006:064 from these and all (**other**) distresses: and yet
006:065 mutual vengeance-each from the **other**." See how
006:088 If they were to join **other** gods with Him, all
006:112 inspiring each **other** with flowery discourses
006:114 Say: "Shall I seek for judge **other** than Allah?-
006:128 "Our Lord! we made profit from each **other**: but
006:129 turn to each **other**, because of what they earn.
006:133 you up from the posterity of **other** people.
006:145 **other** than Allah's." But (even so)
006:153 follow it: follow not (**other**) paths: they will
006:164 for (my) Lord **other** than Allah. When
007:003 as friends or protectors, **other** than Him.
007:038 until they follow each **other**, all into the Fire.
007:054 each seeking the **other** in rapid succession: and
007:059 worship Allah! ye have not **other** god but Him. I
007:065 ye have no **other** god but Him. Will ye
007:073 ye have no **other** god but Him. Now hath
007:085 ye have no **other** god but Him. Now hath come
007:140 a god **other** than Allah, when it is

OTHER (continued)

007:144   chosen thee above (**other**) men, by the
008:048   came in sight of each **other**, he turned
008:073   (protect each **other**), there would be tumult and
008:075   rights against each **other** in the Book
009:052   **other** than one of two glorious things-(martyrdom
009:127   they look at each **other**, (saying), "Doth anyone
010:015   say: "Bring us a Qur'an **other** than this,
010:037   be produced by **other** than Allah; on the contrary
010:045   they will recognize each **other**: assuredly those
010:066   as His "partners" **other** than Allah? They follow
010:104   ye worship **other** than Allah! But I worship Allah-
010:106   "Nor call on any, **other** than Allah,-such can
011:013   whomsoever ye can, **other** than Allah!-if ye
011:048   be **other**) Peoples to whom We shall grant their
011:050   ye have no **other** god but Him. You are
011:055   "**Other** gods as partners! So scheme
011:061   ye have not **other** god but Him. It is He Who
011:084   ye have no **other** god but Him. And give
011:101   the deities, **other** than Allah, whom they
011:113   and ye have no protectors **other** than Allah,
012:025   So they both raced each **other** to the door, and she
012:031   This is none **other** than a noble angel!"
012:036   Said the **other**: "I see myself (in a dream)
012:041   as for the **other**, he will hang from the cross,
012:064   with any result **other** than when I trusted you with
012:079   **other** than him with whom we found our property:
013:016   (for worship) protectors **other** than Him, such as
013:030   have (**other**) Peoples (gone and) passed away;
015:047   (joyfully) facing each **other** on raised couches.
016:008   (**other**) things of which ye have no knowledge.
016:035   prohibitions **other** than His." So did
016:052   then will ye fear **other** than Allah?
016:054   to **other** gods to join with their Lord-
016:075   of any sort; and (the **other**) a man on whom
016:115   **other** than Allah has been invoked. But if
017:002   "Take not **other** than Me as Disposer
017:042   Say: if there had been (**other**) gods with Him,-
017:047   "Ye follow none **other** than a man bewitched!"
017:088   each **other** with help and support.
018:014   upon any god **other** then Him: if we did;
018:015   for worship gods **other** than Him: why do
018:016   and the things they worship **other** than Allah,
018:019   that they might question each **other**. Said one
018:026   They have no protector **other** than Him; nor does
018:027   as a refuge **other** than Him.
018:067   (The **other**) said: "Verily thou wilt not be able
018:070   The **other** said: "If then thou wouldst follow me,
019:081   gods **other** than Allah, to give
020:018   and in it I find **other** uses."
020:077   and without (any **other**) fear."
020:103   each **other**: "Ye tarried not longer than ten (days);"
021:011   in their places **other** peoples?
021:022   and the earth, **other** gods besides Allah,
021:024   (**other**) gods besides Him? Say, "Bring
021:082   for him, and did **other** work besides; and it
021:092   therefore serve Me (and no **other**).
022:019   each **other** about their Lord: but those
023:021   numerous (**other**) benefits for you; and of
023:023   Ye have no **other** god but Him. Will ye
023:032   no **other** god but Him. Will ye not fear (Him)?"
023:042   Then We raised after them **other** generations.
023:044   so We made them follow each **other** (in punishment):

OTHER (continued)

023:052   and Cherisher: therefore fear Me (and no **other**).
023:117   any **other** god, he has
024:027   enter not houses **other** than your own, until ye
024:029   living in, which serve some (**other**) use for you:
024:051   is no **other** than this: they said, "We hear
024:058   to move about attending to each **other**: thus does
024:061   enter houses, salute each **other**-a greeting of
025:008   "Ye follow none **other** than a man bewitched."
025:053   and the **other** salt and bitter; yet has
025:062   and the Day to follow each **other**: for such
025:068   any **other** god, nor slay such life as Allah
026:029   any god **other** than me, I will
026:061   saw each **other**, the people of Moses said: "We are
026:064   And We made the **other** party approach thither.
026:137   "This is no **other** than a customary device
026:213   So call not on any **other** god with Allah,
027:045   they became two factions quarreling with each **other**.
027:056   But his people gave no **other** answer but this:
027:090   "Do ye receive a reward **other** than that which
028:015   one of his own people, and the **other**, of his
028:048   each assisting the **other**!" And they say:
028:066   will not be able (even) to question each **other**.
028:071   what god is there **other** than Allah, who can
028:072   what god is there **other** than Allah, who can
029:013   and (**other**) burdens along with their own, and on
029:025   ye shall disown each **other** and curse each **other**:
029:025   curse each **other**: and your abode will be the Fire,
029:041   take protectors **other** than Allah is that
030:028   Do ye fear them as ye fear each **other**? Thus do
030:033   **other** gods besides their Lord,-
030:039   of (**other**) people, will have no increase with
033:006   Blood-relations among each **other** have closer
033:032   like any of the (**other**) women: if ye
033:052   nor to change them for (**other**) wives, even though
034:022   Say: "Call upon **other** (gods) whom ye fancy,
034:042   they have over each **other**, for profit
035:003   **other** than Allah, to give you sustenance
035:012   to drink, and the **other**, salt and bitter.
035:018   be carried (by the **other**), even though
035:023   Thou art no **other** than a warner.
035:040   the wrong-doers promise each **other** nothing but
036:023   "Shall I take (**other**) gods besides Him?
036:036   own (human) kind and (**other**) things of which
036:073   And they have (**other**) profits from them
036:074   Yet they take (for worship) gods **other** than Allah,
037:011   or the (**other**) beings We have created?
037:025   that ye help not each **other**?'"
037:044   Facing each **other** on raised couches.
037:086   "Is it a Falsehood-gods **other** than Allah
038:022   the **other**: decide now between us with truth,
038:024   each **other**: not so do those who believe
038:058   And **other** Penalties of a similar kind, to match
039:003   protectors **other** than Allah (say): "We only
039:029   at variance with each **other**, and a man
039:036   with **other** (gods) besides Him! For such
039:045   with disgust, but when (gods) **other** than He
039:064   Say: "Is it someone **other** than Allah that ye
040:047   each **other** in the Fire! The weak ones
040:075   on the earth in things **other** than the Truth,
040:080   for food; and there are (**other**) advantages in
041:044   (in a language) **other** than Arabic, they would
042:013   worship **other** things than Allah, hard is

OTHER (continued)

042:046 to help them, **other** than Allah: and for
043:045 **other** than The Most Gracious, to be worshipped?
043:060 amongst you, succeeding each **other** on the earth.
044:028 And We made **other** people inherit (those things)!
044:053 rich brocade, they will face each **other**;
046:021 "Worship ye none **other** than Allah: truly I
048:021 And **other** gains (there are), which are
048:029 (but) compassionate amongst each **other**. Thou wilt
049:009 the **other**, then fight ye (all) against the one
049:011 to each **other**, nor call each **other** by (offensive)
049:012 and spy not on each **other**, nor speak
049:012 nor speak ill of each **other** behind their backs.
049:013 that ye may know each **other** (not that
049:013 (not that ye may despise each **other**). Verily the
050:028 with each **other** in My Presence: I had
051:023 ye can speak intelligently to each **other**.
052:025 They will advance to each **other**, engaging in
052:043 Or have they a god **other** then Allah? Exalted is
055:060 Is there any Reward for Good-**other** than Good?
055:062 there are two **other** Gardens,-
056:016 Reclining on them, facing each **other**.
058:003 each **other**: this are ye admonished to perform:
058:004 touch each **other**, but if any is unable to do so,
059:022 no **other** god;-Who knows (all things) both secret
059:023 no **other** god;-the Sovereign, the Holy One,
060:011 of a woman from the **other** side). Then pay
060:012 any **other** thing whatever with Allah, that they
062:006 to the exclusion of (**other**) men, then express
066:004 each **other** against him, truly Allah
070:011 each **other**,-the sinner's desire will be: would that
071:023 "And they have said (to each **other**), `Abandon not
074:031 and this is no **other** than a Reminder to mankind.
074:040 they will question each **other**,
080:040 And **other** faces that Day will be dust-stained;
083:030 used to wink at each **other** (in mockery);
085:008 no **other** reason than that they believed in Allah,
088:008 (**Other**) faces that Day will be joyful,
089:026 And His bonds will be such as none (**other**) can bind.

OTHER'S

002:145 they follow each **other's** Qiblah.
021:080 from each **other's** violence: will ye

OTHERS

002:013 "Believe as the **others** believe"
002:047 and that I preferred you to all **others**.
002:074 **others** there are which when split
002:074 and **others** which sink for fear of Allah.
002:087 and **others** ye slay!
002:122 and that I preferred you to all **others**.
002:165 (for worship) **others** besides Allah,
002:229 such persons wrong (themselves as well as **others**).
002:253 with gifts, some above **others**:
002:253 **others** He raised to degrees (of honor);
002:253 some believing and **others** rejecting.
003:007 **others** are not entirely clear.
003:075 **others**, who, if entrusted with a single silver coin,
003:140 be sure a similar wound hath touched the **others**.
004:024 except for these, all **others** are lawful,
004:032 gifts more freely on some of you than on **others**:
004:037 enjoin niggardliness on **others**, hide
004:091 **Others** you will find that wish to be secure from
004:150 saying: "We believe in some but reject **others**":
004:164 told thee the story; of **others** We have not;

OTHERS (continued)

005:008 and let not the hatred of **others** to you
005:041 will listen ever to **others** who have never so much
005:106 of your own (brotherhood) or **others** from outside
005:107 Let two **others** stand forth in their places,-
006:001 (**others**) as equal with their Guardian Lord.
006:019 (your blasphemy of) joining **others** with Him."
006:026 **Others** they forbid it and themselves
006:053 Thus did We test some of them by **others**, that
006:071 Say: "Shall we call on **others** besides Allah,-
006:150 for they hold **others** as equal
006:165 some above **others**: that He may
007:030 **others** have deserved the loss of their way, in
007:181 who direct (**others**) with truth, and dispense
007:190 they ascribe to **others** a share in the gift
008:060 and **others** besides, whom ye may not know, but
009:039 grievous penalty, and put **others** in your place;
009:066 We will punish **others** amongst you, for that
009:102 **Others** (there are who) have acknowledged
009:106 There are (yet) **others**, held in suspense for the
012:043 and seven (**others**) withered. O ye chiefs!
012:046 of corn and (seven) **others** withered: that I
012:106 (**others** as partners) with Him!
013:004 more excellent than **others** to eat. Behold!
013:014 any **others** that they call upon besides Him
013:033 it doth, (like any **others**)? And yet they ascribe
016:071 you than on **others**; those more favoured are not
016:073 And worship **others** than Allah,-such as
017:021 than on **others**; but verily the Hereafter is more
017:055 of the Prophets to excel **others** and We gave
018:022 (**others**) say they were five, the dog
018:022 (yet **others**) say they were seven, the dog
020:053 of plants each separate from the **others**.
023:091 lorded it over **others**! Glory to
025:004 has forged, and **others** have helped him at it."
025:018 should take for protectors **others** besides Thee:
025:020 as a trial for **others**: will ye
026:066 But We drowned the **others**.
026:181 (to **others** by fraud).
027:043 the worship of **others** besides Allah: for she
029:065 they give a share (of their worship to **others**)!-
031:011 that **others** besides Him have created: nay, but
031:013 in worship (**others**) with Allah: for false
038:038 As also **others** bound together in fetters.
038:039 (on **others**) or withhold them, no account
039:008 unto Allah, thus misleading **others** from Allah's
039:043 intercessors **others** besides Allah? Say: "Even
042:006 **others** besides Him,-Allah doth watch over them;
043:032 of them above **others** in ranks, so that
043:032 from **others**. But the Mercy of thy Lord in better
044:014 "Tutored (by **others**), a man possessed!"
047:004 to test you, some with **others**. But those
049:011 among you laugh at **others**: it may
049:011 laugh at **others**: it may be that the (latter)
057:014 "Were we not with you?" (The **others**) will reply,
057:027 them up with (**others** of) Our messengers: We sent
060:009 and support (**others**) in driving you out,
062:003 Along with **others** of them, who have not already
066:010 with (**others**) that enter!"
073:020 yet **others** fighting in Allah's Cause. Read ye,
073:020 in ill-health; **others** traveling through the land,
080:037 to make him indifferent to the **others**.

OTHERWISE

013:004   out of single roots or **otherwise**: watered with
016:007   that ye could not (**otherwise**) reach except with
025:041   they treat thee no **otherwise** than in mockery:

OUGHT

022:078   And strive in His cause as ye **ought** to strive,

OUR

002:023   revealed from time to **our** servants
002:039   reject Faith and belie **Our** Signs,
002:059   infringed (**Our** command) repeatedly.
002:068   They said: "Beseech on **our** behalf thy Lord
002:069   They said: "Beseech on **our** behalf thy Lord
002:070   They said, "Beseech on **our** behalf thy Lord
002:088   They say, "**Our** hearts are the wrappings
002:106   None of **Our** revelations do We abrogate
002:127   "**Our** Lord! accept (this service) from us:
002:128   "**Our** Lord! make of us Muslims,
002:128   and of **our** progeny a people Muslim,
002:128   and show us **our** places for the celebration
002:129   "**Our** Lord! send amongst them a Messenger
002:138   (**Our** religion) takes its hue from Allah
002:139   for **our** doings and ye for yours;
002:139   sincere (in **our** faith) in Him?
002:139   seeing that He is **our** Lord and your Lord;
002:151   rehearsing to you **Our** Signs,
002:156   and to Him is **our** return":
002:170   shall follow the ways of **our** fathers."
002:200   "**Our** Lord! Give us (thy bounties) in this world!"
002:201   "**Our** Lord! give us good in this world
002:246   turned out of **our** homes and **our** families?"
002:250   they prayed: "**Our** Lord! Pour out constancy on us
002:250   on us and make **our** steps firm:
002:285   (We seek) Thy forgiveness, **our** Lord,
002:286   Blot out **our** signs.
002:286   (Pray:) "**Our** Lord! Condemn us not if we
002:286   **Our** Lord! lay not on us a burden
002:286   Thou art **our** protector;
002:286   **our** Lord! Lay not on us a burden like that
003:007   the whole of it is from **our** Lord:"
003:008   "let not **our** hearts deviate now after Thou
003:008   "**Our** Lord!" (they say), "let not **our** hearts
003:009   "**Our** Lord! Thou art He that will gather mankind
003:011   they denied **Our** Signs, and Allah called them
003:016   "**Our** Lord! we have indeed believed:
003:016   forgive us, then, **our** sins, and save us
003:053   "**Our** Lord! we believe in what thou hast revealed,
003:061   **our** sons and your sons, **our** women and your women,
003:084   and to Allah do we bow **our** will (in Islam)."
003:147   "**Our** Lord forgive us **our** sins and anything
003:147   that transgressed **our** duty:
003:147   establish **our** feet firmly, and help us
003:178   **our** respite to them is good for themselves:
003:183   **our** promise not to believe in a messenger unless he
003:191   (with the saying): "**Our** Lord not for naught
003:192   "**Our** Lord! any whom Thou dost admit to the Fire,
003:193   "**Our** Lord! We have heard the call
003:193   **Our** Lord! Forgive us **our** sins, blot out
003:193   blot out from us **our** iniquities, and take
003:193   **Our** Lord! Forgive us **our** sins, blot out
003:193   and take to Thyself **our** souls in the company
003:194   "**Our** Lord! grant us what Thou didst promise
004:056   Those who reject **Our** Signs, We shall soon
004:075   "**Our** Lord! rescue us from this town.

OUR (continued)

004:077   to **our** (natural) term, near (enough)?
004:077   they say: "**Our** Lord! why hast Thou ordered
004:155   that they said, "**Our** hearts are the Wrappings; nay,
005:010   Those who reject faith and deny **Our** Signs will be
005:015   there hath come to you **Our** Messenger, revealing
005:019   after the break in (the series of) **our** Messengers,
005:019   making (things) clear unto you, **Our** Messenger,
005:032   **Our** Messengers with Clear Signs, yet, even after
005:083   they pray: "**Our** Lord! we believe; write us
005:084   we long for **our** Lord to admit us to
005:086   and belie **Our** Signs, they shall be
005:095   know ye that it is **Our** Messenger's duty to
005:104   the ways we found **our** fathers following." What
005:106   even though the (beneficiary) be **our** near relation:
005:107   "We affirm that **our** witness is truer than that
005:113   to eat thereof and satisfy **our** hearts, and to know
005:114   "O Allah **our** Lord! send us from heaven a table
005:114   for thou art the best Sustainer (of **our** needs)."
005:114   and provide for **our** sustenance, for thou
006:023   "By Allah **Our** Lord, we were not those
006:027   Then would we not reject the Signs of **our** Lord,
006:029   "There is nothing except **our** life on this earth,
006:030   They will say: "Yea, by **our** Lord!" He will say:
006:034   until **Our** aid did reach them: there is none
006:039   Those who reject **Our** Signs are deaf and dumb,-
006:044   in the midst of their enjoyment of **Our** gifts, on
006:049   But those who reject **Our** Signs,-them shall
006:049   them shall **our** punishment touch, for that
006:054   who believe in **Our** Signs, say: "Peace be on you:
006:061   **Our** angels take his soul, and they never
006:063   (we vow) we shall truly show **our** gratitude.'?"
006:068   in vain discourse about **Our** Signs, turn away
006:071   and turn on **our** heels after receiving
006:083   That was **Our** argument which We gave
006:097   We detail **Our** Signs for people who know.
006:098   We detail **Our** signs for people who understand.
006:128   "**Our** Lord! we made profit from each other: but
006:128   but (alas!) we reached **our** term-which Thou
006:136   and this for **Our** "partners"! But the
006:139   is specially reserved (for food) for **our** men, and
006:139   and forbidden to **our** women; but if
006:146   for We are True (in **Our** ordinances).
006:148   nor would **our** fathers; nor should
006:148   until they tasted of **Our** wrath. Say:
006:150   of such as treat **Our** Signs as falsehoods, and
006:154   completing (**Our** favour) to those who
006:156   and for **our** part, we remained
006:157   those who turn away from **Our** Signs, with
007:004   **Our** punishment took them on a sudden by night or
007:005   When (thus) **Our** punishment took them, no cry
007:006   to whom **Our** Message was sent and those
007:009   for that they wrongfully treated **Our** Signs.
007:023   we have wronged **our** own souls: if Thou
007:023   They said: "**Our** Lord! we have wronged
007:028   they say: "We found **our** fathers doing so"; and
007:036   But those who reject **Our** Signs and treat
007:037   until, when **Our** messengers (of death) arrive
007:038   "**Our** Lord! it is these that misled us: so give
007:040   To those who reject **Our** Signs and treat
007:040   such is **Our** reward for those in sin.
007:041   such is **Our** requital of those who do wrong.
007:043   the Messengers of **our** Lord brought unto us."

OUR (continued)

007:044 the promises of **our** Lord to us true: have you
007:047 they will say: "**Our** Lord! send us
007:051 and as they were wont to reject **Our** Signs.
007:053 from **our** behavior in the past." In fact
007:053 "The Messengers of **our** Lord did indeed
007:053 now to intercede on **our** behalf? Or could
007:064 those who rejected **Our** Signs, they were
007:070 which **our** fathers used to worship. Bring us
007:072 the roots of those who rejected **Our** Signs and
007:072 by **Our** Mercy and We cut off the roots
007:076 The arrogant party said: "For **our** part, we
007:088 drive thee out of **our** city-(thee) and those
007:088 shall have to return to **our** religion." He said:
007:089 and **our** people in truth, for thou
007:089 in His knowledge in Allah is **our** trust. **Our**
007:089 **Our** Lord! Decide thou between us and **our**
007:089 **Our** Lord comprehends all things in His
007:089 in the will of Allah, **our** Lord. **Our** Lord
007:095 "**Our** fathers (too) were touched by suffering
007:097 **Our** wrath by night while they were asleep?
007:103 with **Our** Signs to Pharaoh and his chiefs. But
007:112 And bring up to thee all (**our**) sorcerers well-versed."
007:125 "For us, we are but sent back unto **our** Lord."
007:126 and take **our** souls unto Thee as Muslims
007:126 **Our** Lord! pour out on us patience
007:126 in the Signs of **our** Lord when they reached us!
007:134 they said: "O Moses! on **our** behalf call on
007:136 because they rejected **Our** Signs, and failed
007:137 lands whereon We sent down **our** blessings. The
007:146 For they have rejected **Our** Signs, and failed
007:147 Those who reject **Our** Signs and the Meeting
007:149 they said: "If **our** Lord have not mercy upon us
007:155 Thou art **our** Protector: so forgive us
007:155 of his people for **Our** place of meeting: when
007:156 and pay Zakat and those who believe in **Our** Signs;
007:164 **our** duty to your Lord and perchance
007:173 "**Our** fathers before us took false gods, but we
007:175 to whom We sent **Our** Signs, but he
007:176 If it had been **Our** Will, We should
007:176 We should have elevated him with **Our** Signs; but he
007:176 of those who reject **Our** Signs; so relate
007:177 who reject **Our** signs and wrong their own souls.
007:182 Those who reject **Our** signs, We shall
008:031 When **Our** Signs are rehearsed to them, they say:
008:041 to **our** Servant on the Day of Discrimination-
009:050 **our** precautions beforehand," and they
009:051 He is **our** Protector": and on Allah let the
009:052 from Him, or by **our** hands. So wait (expectant);
009:059 to Allah do we turn **our** hopes!" (That would
010:002 that We have set **Our** inspiration to a man
010:007 and those who heed not **Our** Signs,-
010:015 But when **Our** Clear Signs are rehearsed unto them,
010:018 and they say: "These are **our** intercessors with
010:021 to plotting against **Our** Signs! Say: "Swifter
010:021 Verily, **Our** messengers record all the plots
010:022 from this, we shall truly show **our** gratitude!
010:024 there reaches it **Our** command by night or by day,
010:073 those who rejected **Our** Signs. Then see
010:075 and his chiefs with **Our** Signs. But they
010:078 We found **our** fathers following,-in order
010:085 **Our** Lord! make us not a trial for those
010:085 They said: "In Allah do we put **our** trust. **Our** Lord

OUR (continued)

010:088 from Thy Path. Deface **our** Lord the features
010:088 and so, **our** Lord they mislead (men) from Thy Path.
010:088 Moses prayed: "**Our** Lord! Thou hast indeed bestowed
010:092 are heedless of **Our** Signs!
010:103 thus is it fitting on **Our** part that We
010:103 **Our** messengers and those who believe: thus is
011:010 (**Our**) favours after adversity hath touched him,
011:037 **Our** eyes and **Our** inspiration, and address Me
011:038 we (in **our** turn) can look down on you with
011:040 **Our** Command, and the fountains of the earth
011:053 the ones to desert **our** gods on thy word!
011:054 some of **our** gods may have seized thee with evil."
011:058 So when **Our** decree issued, We saved Hud
011:062 of what **our** fathers worshipped? But we
011:062 of us!-a center of **our** hopes hitherto! Dost thou
011:066 When **Our** Decree issued, We saved Salih
011:069 There came **Our** Messengers to Abraham
011:077 When **Our** Messengers came to Lut, he was
011:082 When **Our** decree issued, We turned (the cities)
011:087 off doing what we like with **our** property? Truly,
011:087 leave off the worship which **our** fathers practiced,
011:094 When **Our** decree issued, We saved Shu'aib
011:096 And We sent Moses, with **Our** Clear (Signs) and an
011:121 "Do whatever ye can: we shall do **our** part;
012:008 are loved more by **our** father than we: but we
012:008 Really **our** father is obviously in error!
012:011 They said: "O **our** father! why dost
012:017 and left Joseph with **our** things: and the wolf
012:017 They said: "Oh **our** father! we went
012:024 for he was one of **Our** servants chosen.
012:056 We bestow of **Our** mercy on whom We please, and We
012:063 (unless we take **our** brother): so send **our**
012:063 they said: "O **our** father! No more measure
012:063 that we may get **our** measure; and we
012:063 so send **our** brother with us, that we
012:065 camel's load (of grain to **our** provisions). This
012:065 get (more) for **our** family; we shall take care
012:065 take care of **our** brother; and add
012:065 They said: "O **our** father! What (more)
012:065 This **our** stock-in-trade has been
012:068 For he was, by **Our** instruction, full of
012:079 **our** property: indeed (if we did so), we should
012:081 and say, 'O **our** father! behold! thy son
012:088 seized us and **our** family: we have
012:097 They said: "O **our** father! ask for
012:097 ask for us forgiveness for **our** sins, for we
012:110 as liars, there reaches them **Our** help, and those
012:110 **Our** punishment from those who are in sin.
013:040 reach them: it is **Our** part to call them to account.
014:005 We sent Moses with **Our** Signs (and the
014:010 **our** fathers used to worship; then bring
014:012 Why we should not put **our** trust on Allah.
014:013 or ye shall return to **our** religion." But their
014:013 drive you out of **our** land, or ye shall
014:037 O **our** Lord! that they may establish regular
014:037 "O **our** Lord! I have made some of my offspring
014:038 "O **our** Lord! truly Thou dost know what we
014:040 O **our** Lord! and accept Thou my Prayer.
014:041 "O **our** Lord! cover (us) with Thy Forgiveness-me,
014:044 "**Our** Lord! respite us (if only) for a short Term:
015:015 They would only say: "**Our** eyes have been
015:081 We sent them **Our** Signs, but they

OUR (continued)

016:035 neither we nor **our** fathers,-nor should
016:063 (**our** prophets) to Peoples before thee; but Satan
016:086 **our** 'partners', those whom we used to invoke
016:086 they will say: "**Our** Lord! these are **our** `partners',
017:001 show him some of **Our** Signs: for he
017:005 **Our** servants given to terrible warfare:
017:008 (to **Our** punishments): and We have made Hell
017:012 as two (of **Our**) Signs: the Sign of
017:070 above a great part of **Our** Creation.
017:073 **Our** name something quite different: (in that case)
017:077 (This was **Our**) way with the messengers We sent
017:077 thou wilt find no change in **Our** ways.
017:083 Yet when We bestow **Our** favours on man, he turns
017:086 If it were **Our** Will, We could
017:098 because they rejected **Our** Signs, and said,
017:108 Truly has the promise of **our** Lord been fulfilled!"
017:108 And they say: "Glory to **our** Lord! Truly has
018:009 wonders among **Our** Signs?
018:010 and dispose of **our** affair for us in the right way!
018:010 to the Cave: they said, "**Our** Lord! bestow on us
018:014 "**Our** Lord is the Lord of the heavens and of
018:015 "These **our** people have taken for worship
018:062 at this (stage of) **our** journey."
018:062 "Bring us **our** early meal; truly we have
018:065 So they found one of **Our** servants. On whom
018:065 taught knowledge form **Our** own presence.
018:088 as We order it by **our** command."
019:017 from them: then We sent to her **Our** angel, and he
019:050 And We bestowed of **Our** Mercy on them, and We
019:053 And, out of **Our** Mercy, We gave him his brother
019:063 **Our** Servants who guard against evil.
019:073 When **Our** Clear Signs are rehearsed to them,
019:077 man who rejects **Our** Signs, yet says: "I shall
020:023 show thee of **Our** Greater Signs.
020:045 "**Our** Lord! we fear lest He hasten with insolence
020:050 He said: "**Our** Lord is He Who gave to each (created)
020:056 And We showed Pharaoh all **Our** Signs, but he
020:057 us out of **our** land with thy magic, O Moses?
020:073 may He forgive us **our** faults, and the
020:073 For us, we have believed in **our** Lord: may He
020:087 to thee, as far as lay in **our** power: but we
020:126 when **Our** Signs came unto thee, forgot them:
020:134 "**Our** Lord! if only Thou hadst sent us a messenger,
021:009 Then We fulfilled to them **Our** promise, and We
021:012 **Our** Punishment (coming), behold, they (tried to)
021:017 If it had been **Our** wish to take (just) a pastime,
021:053 They said, "We found **our** father worshipping them."
021:059 to **our** gods? He must indeed be one of
021:062 did this with **our** gods, O Abraham?"
021:073 guiding (men) by **Our** Command, and We
021:075 And We admitted him to **Our** Mercy: for he
021:077 who rejected **Our** Signs: truly they
021:079 and the birds celebrate **Our** praises, with David:
021:079 and Knowledge; it was **Our** power that made the
021:081 (It was **Our** power that made) the violent
021:086 We admitted them to **Our** Mercy: for they
021:091 from **Our** spirit, and We made her and her son
021:112 "**Our** Lord Most Gracious is the One Whose
022:005 in order that We may manifest (**Our** Power) to you;
022:040 that they say, "**Our** Lord is Allah." Did not
022:051 **Our** Signs, to frustrate them,-they will
022:057 and deny **Our** Signs, there will

OUR (continued)

022:072 When **Our** Clear Signs are rehearsed to them,
022:072 those who rehearse **Our** Signs to them.
023:017 unmindful of (**Our**) Creation.
023:024 among **our** ancestors of old."
023:027 within **Our** sight and under **Our** guidance: then when
023:027 then when comes **Our** command, and the
023:037 "There is nothing but **our** life in this world!
023:044 Then sent We **Our** messengers in succession:
023:045 his brother Aaron, with **Our** Signs and authority
023:083 and to **our** fathers before! They are nothing
023:106 They will say: "**Our** Lord! **our** misfortune
023:106 **our** misfortune overwhelmed us, and we
023:107 "**Our** Lord! bring us out of this: if ever
023:109 '**Our** Lord! we believe; then do Thou forgive us,
024:016 of this: glory to Thee (**our** Lord) this is
025:021 **our** Lord?" Indeed they have an arrogant
025:036 **Our** Signs": and those (people) We destroyed
025:042 misled us from **our** gods, had it
025:051 Had it been **Our** Will, We could
025:065 Those who say, "**Our** Lord! avert from
025:074 of **our** eyes, and give us (the grace) to lead
025:074 "**Our** Lord! Grant unto us wives and offspring
026:004 If (such) were **Our** Will, We could
026:015 both of you, with **Our** Signs; We are
026:018 and didst thou not stay in **our** midst many years
026:037 (**our**) sorcerers well-versed."
026:050 we shall but return to **our** Lord!
026:051 "Only, **our** desire is that **our** Lord will
026:051 **our** Lord will forgive us **our** faults, since we
026:074 **our** fathers doing thus (what we do)."
026:099 "`And **our** seducers were only those who were
026:136 be not among (**our**) Admonishers!
026:204 Do they then ask for **Our** Chastisement to be
027:007 a burning brand (to light **our** fuel), that ye
027:013 But when **Our** Signs came to them, visibly they
027:067 become dust,-we and **our** fathers,-shall we
027:068 we and **our** fathers before (us): these are
027:081 to listen who believe in **Our** Signs, so they
027:082 because mankind had no faith in **Our** Signs.
027:083 those who reject **Our** Signs, and they
028:007 and We shall make him one of **Our** messengers."
028:023 They said: "We cannot water (**our** flocks) until the
028:023 (their flocks): and **our** father is a very old man."
028:025 watered (**our** flocks) for us." So when
028:035 with **Our** Signs shall ye triumph,-you two
028:036 among **our** fathers of old!"
028:036 **Our** Clear Signs, they said: "This is
028:045 of Madyan, rehearsing **Our** Signs to them;
028:047 they might say: "**Our** Lord! why didst
028:053 for it is the Truth from **our** Lord: indeed we
028:055 "To us **our** deeds, and to you yours; peace be
028:057 from **our** land." Have We not established for them
028:059 rehearsing to them **Our** Signs; nor are
028:063 be proved, will say: "**Our** Lord! these are
029:012 who believe: "Follow **our** path, and we
029:031 When **Our** Messengers came to Abraham with the
029:033 And when **Our** Messengers came to Lut, he was
029:046 **Our** God and your God is one; and it
029:047 and none but Unbelievers reject **Our** Signs.
029:049 the unjust reject **Our** Signs.
029:066 Disdaining ungratefully **Our** gifts and giving
029:069 to **Our** Paths: for verily Allah is with those

OUR (continued)

029:069 And those who strive in **Our** (Cause),-We will
030:016 and falsely denied **Our** Signs and the meeting
030:053 in **Our** Signs and submit (their wills in Islam).
031:007 When **Our** Signs are rehearsed to such a one,
031:021 we found **our** fathers (following)." What! even
031:032 and wrong). But none reject **Our** Signs except only
032:012 "**Our** Lord! We have seen and we have heard:
032:015 Only those believe in **Our** Signs who, when they
032:024 Leaders, giving guidance under **Our** command, so long
032:024 have faith in **Our** Signs.
033:013 "Truly **our** houses are bare and exposed,"
033:067 And they would say: "**Our** Lord! We obeyed
033:067 We obeyed **our** chiefs and **our** great ones, and they
033:068 "**Our** Lord! give them Double Chastisement
034:005 **Our** Signs, to frustrate them,-for such
034:012 from **Our** command, We made him taste of the
034:018 We had poured **Our** blessings, We had
034:019 **our** journey-stages": but they wronged
034:019 But they said: "**Our** Lord! place longer
034:025 **our** sins, nor shall we be questioned as to
034:026 Say: "**Our** Lord will gather us together and will
034:038 Those who strive against **Our** Signs, to frustrate
034:041 Thou art **our** protector-not them. Nay, but
034:043 When **Our** Clear Signs are rehearsed to them,
035:032 for inheritance to such of **Our** servants as We
035:034 for **Our** Lord is indeed Oft-Forgiving ready to
035:037 (for assistance): "**Our** Lord! Bring us
036:016 They said: "**Our** Lord doth know that we have been
036:017 "And **Our** duty is only to deliver
036:043 If it were **Our** Will, We could drown them;
036:052 Who hath raised us up from **our** beds of repose?...
036:066 If it had been **Our** Will, We could
036:067 And if it had been **Our** Will, We could
036:071 among the things which **Our** hands have
037:017 "And also **our** fathers of old?"
037:031 taste (the punishment of **our** sins):
037:031 against us, the Word of **our** Lord that we
037:036 **our** gods for the sake of a Poet possessed?"
037:059 "Except **our** first death, and that
037:081 For he was one of **Our** believing Servants.
037:111 For he was one of **Our** believing Servants.
037:114 **Our** favour on Moses and Aaron,
037:122 For they were two of **Our** believing Servants.
037:132 For He was one of **Our** believing Servants.
037:171 before (this) to **Our** Servants sent (by Us),
037:171 Already has **Our** Word been passed before (this)
037:173 And that **Our** forces,-they surely must conquer.
037:176 Do they wish (indeed) to hurry on **Our** Punishment?
038:016 They say: "**Our** Lord! Hasten to us **our** sentence
038:016 **our** sentence (even) before the Day of Account!"
038:017 and remember **Our** Servant David, the man
038:018 in unison with him, **Our** Praises, at eventide
038:039 "Such are **Our** Bounties: whether thou
038:041 Commemorate **Our** servant Job, behold he
038:045 And commemorate **Our** Servants Abraham, Isaac,
038:047 They were, in **Our** sight, truly, of the
038:054 Truly such will be **Our** Bounty (to you); it will
038:061 They will say: "**Our** Lord! Whoever brought
038:063 or have (**our**) eyes failed to perceive them?"
040:007 "**Our** Lord! Thou embracest all things, in Mercy
040:008 "And grant, **our** Lord! That they enter the
040:011 They will say:" **Our** Lord! twice hast Thou made us

OUR (continued)

040:011 **our** sins: is there any way out (of this)?"
040:023 with **Our** Signs and Authority manifest,
040:043 or the Hereafter; **our** Return will be to Allah;
040:051 help **Our** messengers and those who believe,
040:070 We sent **Our** messengers: but soon
040:077 or We take thy soul (to **Our** Mercy) (before that),
040:084 But when they saw **Our** Might, they said
040:085 when they (actually) saw **Our** Punishment was not
041:005 They say: "**Our** hearts are under veils, (concealed)
041:005 invite us, and in **our** ears is a deadness,
041:014 They said, "If **our** Lord had so pleased, He would
041:015 But they continued to reject **Our** Signs!
041:028 wont to reject **Our** Signs.
041:029 "**Our** Lord! Show us those, among Jinns
041:029 we shall crush them beneath **our** feet, so that
041:030 "**Our** Lord is Allah," and, further, stand straight
041:040 Those who pervert the Truth in **Our** Signs are not
041:053 Soon will We show them **Our** Signs in the (furthest)
042:015 Allah is **Our** Lord and your Lord! For us
042:015 **Our** deeds, and for you for your deeds. There is
042:015 and to Him is (**Our**) final goal.
042:035 who dispute about **Our** Signs, that there
042:052 by **Our** command, sent inspiration to thee:
042:052 wherewith We guide such of **Our** servants as We will;
043:013 Who has subjected these to **Our** (use), for we
043:014 "And to **Our** Lord, surely, Must We turn back!"
043:022 Nay! they say: "We found **Our** fathers following
043:023 "We found **Our** fathers following a certain
043:045 And question thou **Our** messengers whom We
043:046 with **Our** Signs, to Pharaoh and his Chiefs:
043:047 But when he came to them with **Our** Signs, behold,
043:058 And they say, " Are **Our** gods best, or He?"
043:059 We granted **Our** favour to him, and We
043:060 And if it were **Our** Will, We could
043:069 Those who have believed in **Our** Signs and submitted
043:080 Indeed (We do), and **Our** Messengers are by them,
044:012 (They will say:) "**Our** Lord! remove the
044:035 "There is nothing beyond **our** first death, and we
044:036 "Then bring (back) **our** forefathers if what
045:009 of **Our** Signs, he takes them in jest: for such
045:024 but **our** life in this world? We shall
045:025 **our** forefathers, if what ye say is true!"
045:025 And when **Our** Clear Signs are rehearsed to them,
045:029 "This **Our** Record speaks about you with truth:
045:031 "Were not **Our** Signs rehearsed to you? But ye
046:007 When **Our** Clear Signs are rehearsed to them,
046:013 Verily those who say, "**Our** Lord is Allah,"
046:022 to turn us aside from **our** gods? Then bring
046:030 They said, "O **our** people! We have
046:031 "O **our** people, hearken to the one who invites
046:034 "Yea, by **our** Lord!" (He will say): "Then taste
048:011 and **our** families: do thou then ask forgiveness
048:011 in (looking after) **our** flocks and heads, and **our**
049:014 **our** wills to Allah,' for not yet has Faith
050:003 Return far (from **our** understanding)."
050:027 "**Our** Lord! I did not make him transgress, but he
052:026 not without fear for the sake of **our** people.
052:048 in **Our** eyes: and celebrate the praises of thy Lord
053:029 away from **Our** Message and desire nothing but
054:009 they rejected **Our** servant and said, "Here is
054:014 She floats under **Our** eyes (and care):
054:036 And (Lut) did warn them of **Our** violent Seizure

OUR (continued)

054:042	The (people) rejected all **Our** Signs; but We
054:050	And **Our** Command is but a single Word,-like the
056:048	"(We) and **our** fathers of old?"
056:065	Were it **Our** Will, we could make it broken orts.
056:070	Were it **Our** Will, We could make it saltish
057:014	ye waited (to **our** ruin); ye doubted
057:019	**Our** Signs,-they are the Companions of Hell-Fire.
057:025	We sent aforetime **our** messengers with Clear
057:027	them up with (others of) **Our** messengers: We sent
058:008	for **our** words. Enough for them is Hell: in it
059:010	"**Our** Lord! Forgive us, and **our** brethren who came
059:010	**Our** Lord! Thou art indeed Full of
059:010	"**Our** Lord! Forgive us, and **our** brethren who came
059:010	and leave not, in **our** hearts, rancor (or sense
060:004	to Thee is (**our**) final Return.
060:004	"**Our** Lord! in Thee do we trust, and to
060:005	"**Our** Lord! Make us not a (test and) trial for
060:005	**our** Lord! For Thou art the Exalted in Might
064:010	and treat **Our** Signs as falsehoods, they will
064:012	the duty of **Our** Messenger is but to deliver
066:008	perfect **our** light for us and grant us Forgiveness:
066:008	while they say, "**Our** Lord! perfect **our** light
066:010	of **Our** righteous servants but they betrayed their
066:012	of **Our** spirit; and she testified to the truth
067:010	**our** intelligence, we should not (now) be among
067:029	and on Him have we put **our** trust: so, soon
068:015	When to him are rehearsed **Our** Signs, "Tales of
068:026	they said: "We have surely lost **our** way:
068:027	(of the fruits of **our** labor)!"
068:029	They said: "Glory to **our** Lord! Verily we
068:032	"It may be that **our** Lord will give us in exchange
069:044	any sayings in **Our** name,
069:047	Nor could any of you withhold him (from **Our** wrath).
070:041	to be defeated (in **Our** Plan).
072:002	any (gods) with **our** Lord,
072:003	'And exalted is the Majesty of **our** Lord: He has
074:016	By no means! For to **Our** Signs he has
076:010	and distress from the side of **our** Lord."
078:028	But they (impudently) treated **Our** Signs as false
079:010	be returned to (**our**) former state?-
083:013	When **Our** Signs are rehearsed to him, he says,
090:019	But those who reject **Our** Signs, they are

OURSELVES

002:167	we would clear **ourselves** of them,
003:061	**ourselves** and yourselves:
003:064	that we erect not, from among **ourselves**,
004:067	given them from **Ourselves** a great reward;
005:113	and that we **ourselves** may be witnesses
006:071	to submit **ourselves** to the Lord of the worlds;
006:130	"We bear witness against **ourselves**." It was
011:009	from **Ourselves**, and then withdraw it from him,
011:027	(in) thee nothing but a man like **ourselves**: nor do
011:094	from Us: but the (mighty) Blast did seize the
014:010	than human, like **ourselves**! Ye wish
014:021	for **ourselves** there is no way of escape."
016:075	favours from **Ourselves**, and he spends thereof
018:063	when we betook **ourselves** to the rock? I did
018:065	from **Ourselves** and whom We had taught knowledge
020:091	to worship it, will devote **ourselves** to it
021:084	as a Grace from **Ourselves**, and a thing
023:047	two men like **ourselves**? And their
025:046	towards **Ourselves**,- a contraction by easy stages.

OURSELVES (continued)

028:048	to them from **Ourselves**, they say, "Why are
028:057	a provision from **Ourselves**? But most
028:063	as we were astray **ourselves**:
028:063	we free **ourselves** (from them) to you.
036:015	like **ourselves**; and the Most Gracious sends no
037:032	for truly we were **ourselves** astray."
043:022	and we do guide **ourselves** by their footsteps."
054:024	a solitary one from among **ourselves**! Shall we
054:044	"We acting together can defend **ourselves**"?

OUT

002:003	and spend **out** of what We have provided
002:019	in their ears to keep **out** the stunning
002:036	and get them **out** of the state (of felicity)
002:084	nor turn **out** your own people
002:167	a way for them **out** of the Fire.
002:177	**out** of love for Him,
002:191	and turn them **out** from where
002:191	from where they have turned you **out**;
002:217	and drive **out** its members.
002:246	turned **out** of our homes and our families?"
002:249	a mere sip **out** of the hand is excused."
002:250	they prayed: "Our Lord! Pour **out** constancy on us
002:254	O ye who believe! spend **out** of (the bounties)
002:256	Truth stands **out** clear from Error;
002:267	**out** of it ye may give away something,
002:282	And get two witnesses, **out** or your own men.
002:282	ye carry **out** on the spot among yourselves,
002:286	Blot **out** our signs.
003:025	and each soul will be paid **out** just what
003:027	Thou bringest the Living **out** of the dead,
003:027	and Thou bringest the dead **out** of the living;
003:049	in that I make for you **out** of clay, as it were,
003:103	by the Rope which Allah (stretches **out** for you),
003:104	Let there arise **out** of you a band of people
003:111	if they come **out** to fight you, they will show
003:155	But Allah has blotted **out** (their fault):
003:193	blot **out** from us our iniquities, and take
003:195	verily, I will blot **out** from them their iniquities,
003:195	and were drive **out** therefrom, or suffered harm
004:001	created, **out** of it, his mate, and from them
004:008	are present, give them **out** of the (property), and
004:039	and they spent **out** of what Allah
004:043	For Allah doth blot **out** sins and forgive
004:047	for the decision of Allah must be carries **out**.
004:078	"Wherever ye are, death will find you **out**, even
004:088	For those whom Allah hath thrown **out** of the Way,
004:088	whom Allah hath thrown **out** of the Way?
004:094	O ye who believe! when ye go **out** in the cause
004:099	for Allah doth blot **out** (sins) and
004:135	O ye who believe! stand **out** firmly for justice, as
004:173	and more, **out** of His bounty: but those
005:002	nor the garlands that mark **out** such animals, nor
005:002	shutting you **out** of the Sacred Mosque lead you
005:008	O ye who believe! stand **out** firmly for Allah, as
005:011	the design to stretch **out** their hands against you,
005:012	verily I will wipe **out** from you your evils, and
005:016	and leadeth them **out** of darkness, by His Will,
005:026	the land be **out** of their reach for forty years:
005:037	Their wish will be to get **out** of the Fire, but
005:037	but never will they get **out** therefrom: their
005:060	Say: "Shall I point **out** to you something
005:061	and they go **out** with the same.

OUT (continued)

005:065   blotted **out** their iniquities and admitted
005:110   And behold! thou makest **out** of clay, as it
006:006   for whom We poured **out** rain from the
006:099   close-compounded grain **out** of the date-palm
006:099   **out** of which We produce, close-compounded
006:108   lest they **out** of spite revile Allah
006:122   from which he can never come **out**? Thus
006:136   **Out** of what Allah hath produced in abundance
007:013   get **out**, for thou art of the meanest
007:016   thrown me **out** (of the Way),
007:018   (Allah) said: "Get **out** from this, disgraced
007:025   but from it shall ye be taken **out** (at last)."
007:027   he got your parents **out** of the Garden, stripping
007:044   will call **out** to the Companions of the Fire: "We
007:046   they will call **out** to the
007:074   and carve **out** homes in the mountains; so bring
007:082   they said, "Drive them **out** of your city: these are
007:088   drive thee **out** of our city-(thee) and those
007:096   We should indeed have opened **out** to them
007:108   And he drew **out** his hand, and behold!
007:110   "His plan is to get you **out** of your land: then
007:123   to drive **out** its people: but soon
007:126   Our Lord! pour **out** on us patience
007:148   **out** of their ornaments, the body
007:160   **out** of it there gushed forth twelve springs: each
007:176   he (still) lolls **out** his tongue. That is the
007:176   he lolls **out** his tongue, or if
008:003   and spend (freely) **out** of the gifts We have
008:005   **out** of the house in truth, even though
008:030   or get the **out** (of they home). They plot
008:034   when they keep **out** (men) from the Sacred Mosque-
008:041   And know that **out** of all the booty that ye
009:028   enrich you, if He wills, **out** of His bounty,
009:040   him **out**: being the second of the two they
009:042   have come **out** with you," they would destroy their
009:046   If they had intended to come **out**, they would
009:047   If they had come **out** with you, they would
009:074   which they were enable to carry **out**: this revenge
009:083   to come **out** (with thee), say: "Never
009:083   say: "Never shall ye come **out** with me, nor fight
010:005   and measured **out** stages for it, that ye might
010:024   its golden ornaments and is decked **out** (in beauty):
010:031   brings **out** the living from the dead and the
010:040   those who are **out** for mischief.
011:042   and Noah called **out** to his son, who had
012:009   "Slay ye Joseph or cast him **out** to some
012:020   counted **out**: in such low estimation did they
012:031   and she said (to Joseph), "Come **out** before them."
012:041   **out** the wine for his lord to drink: as to
012:059   I pay **out** full measure, and that
012:070   Then shouted **out** a Crier: "O ye (in) the
012:076   **out** of his brother's baggage. Thus did We
012:100   He took me **out** of prison and brought
012:100   and brought you (all here) **out** of the desert,
013:003   And it is He Who spread **out** the earth, and set
013:004   **out** of single roots or otherwise: watered with
013:017   cast **out**; while that which is for the good
013:022   spend, **out** of (the gifts) We have bestowed
013:039   Allah doth blot **out** or confirm what He pleaseth:
014:001   **out** of the depths of darkness into light-by
014:005   (and the command). "Bring **out** thy people from
014:013   drive you **out** of our land, or ye shall

OUT (continued)

014:031   and spend (in charity) **out** of the Sustenance
014:032   and with it bringeth **out** fruits wherewith
015:014   Even if We opened **out** to them a gate
015:016   It is We who have set **out** constellations in
015:019   And the earth We have spread **out** (like a carpet);
015:034   (Allah) said: "Then get thee **out** from here;
015:082   **Out** of the mountains did they hew (their) edifices,
016:010   from it ye drink, and **out** (grows) the vegetation
016:056   do not know, a portion **out** of that which We have
016:067   and the vine, ye get **out** strong drink,
016:072   **out** of them, sons and daughters and grandchildren,
016:080   (in your travels); and **out** of their wool,
016:080   and made for you **out** of the skins of animals,
016:081   **out** of the things He created, some things
017:013   We shall bring **out** for him a scroll, which he
017:014   thy soul this day to make **out** an account
017:024   And, **out** of kindness, lower to them the wing
017:042   sought **out** a way in submitting to the
018:019   let him find **out** which is the best food
018:037   **out** of dust, then **out** of a sperm-drop,
018:047   nor shall We leave **out** any one of them.
018:049   It leaves **out** nothing small or great, but
018:082   and get **out** their treasure-a mercy
018:100   for Unbelievers to see, all spread **out**,-
018:109   Say: "If the ocean were ink (wherewith to write **out**)
019:011   So Zakariya came **out** to his people from his
019:053   And, **out** of Our Mercy, We gave him his brother
019:067   that We created him before **out** of nothing?
019:069   Then shall We certainly drag **out** from every
019:084   for We but count **out** to them a (limited)
020:053   the earth like a carpet spread **out**; has enabled
020:055   and from it shall We bring you **out** once again.
020:057   us **out** of our land with thy magic, O Moses?
020:063   their object is to drive you **out** from your land
020:088   "Then he brought **out** (of the fire) before the
020:117   so let him not get you both **out** of the Garden,
021:018   and it knocks **out** its brain, and behold,
022:005   then **out** of a leech-like clot, then **out**
022:005   appointed term, then do We bring you **out** as babes,
022:005   then **out** a morsel of flesh, partly formed
022:005   **out** of dust, then **out** of sperm, then **out**
022:014   for Allah carries **out** all that He desires.
022:015   and the Hereafter, let him stretch **out** a rope
022:018   for Allah carries **out** all that He wills.
022:019   of Fire: over their heads will be poured **out**
022:019   for them will be cut **out** a garment of Fire:
022:035   and spend (in charity) **out** of what We have
022:060   **out** (sins) and forgives (again and again).
023:014   then We developed **out** of it another creature:
023:014   a (foetus) lump; then We made **out** of that lump
023:020   Also a tree springing **out** of Mount Sinai,
023:107   "Our Lord! bring us **out** of this: if ever
024:015   and said **out** of your mouths things of which ye
024:032   Allah will give them means **out** of His grace:
024:033   **out** of the means which Allah has given to you.
024:033   until Allah gives them means **out** of His grace.
024:038   and add even more for them **out** of His Grace:
024:040   if a man stretches **out** his hand, he can
026:033   And he drew **out** his hand, and behold
026:035   "His plan is to get you **out** of your land
026:149   "And ye carve house **out** of (rocky) mountains
026:167   O Lut! thou wilt assuredly be cast **out**!"

OUT (continued)

027:014 them wrongfully and **out** of pride: so see
027:056 "Drive **out** the followers of Lut from your city:
028:012 and) said: "Shall I point **out** to you the people
028:038 to bake bricks) **out** of clay, and build
028:054 **out** of what We have given them.
028:073 It is **out** of His Mercy that He has made
029:007 blot **out** all misdeeds that they have committed,
029:025 **out** of mutual love and regard between yourselves
030:014 that Day shall (all men) be sorted **out**.
030:019 the dead, and brings **out** the dead for the living,
030:019 It is He Who brings **out** the living from the dead,
030:019 and thus shall ye be brought **out** (from the dead).
030:023 (make for livelihood) **out** of His Bounty: verily
030:045 and work righteous deeds, **out** of His Bounty.
030:047 We meted **out** Retribution: and it
032:016 (in charity) **out** of the sustenance which We have
033:043 that He may bring you **out** from the depths
033:050 thy right hand possesses **out** of the captives
033:059 (when **out** of doors): that is most convenient,
034:002 and all that comes **out** thereof; all that
034:007 "Shall we point **out** to you a man that will
035:002 What Allah **out** of His Mercy doth bestow
035:016 you **out** and bring in a New Creation:
035:027 With it We then bring **out** produce of various
035:029 and spend (in Charity) **out** of what We have
035:030 **out** of His Bounty; for He is Oft-Forgiving,
035:035 "Who has, **out** of His bounty, settled us
035:037 Bring us **out**: we shall work righteousness, not the
036:066 We could surely have blotted **out** their eyes;
036:080 **out** of the green tree, when behold!
037:011 **out** of a sticky clay!
037:021 "This is the Day of Sorting **Out**, whose truth
037:064 **out** of the bottom of Hell-fire:
037:104 We called **out** to him, "O Abraham!
037:151 Behold they say, **out** of their own invention,
038:077 (Allah) said: "Then get thee **out** from here:
039:004 He pleased **out** of those whom He doth create:
040:011 our sins: is there any way **out** (of this)?"
040:029 "I but point **out** to you that which I see (myself);
040:067 then does He get you **out** (into the light) as a
041:047 no fruit comes **out** of its sheath, nor does
042:024 And Allah blots **out** falsehood, and proves
042:038 by mutual Consultation; who spend **out** of what
043:010 the earth spread **out**, and has
043:016 What! Has He taken Daughters **out** of what He
043:032 Is it they who would portion **out** the Mercy
043:032 It is We Who portion **out** between them their
044:040 Verily the Day of Sorting **Out** is the
045:035 **out** thence, nor can the make amends.
046:017 Do ye hold **out** the promise to me that I shall
046:020 and ye took your pleasure **out** of them: but to-day
047:013 which has driven thee **out**, have We
047:016 to thee, till when they go **out** from thee,
047:037 and He would bring **out** all your ill-feeling.
049:004 Those who shout **out** to thee from without
049:005 until thou couldst come **out** to them, it would
050:007 And the earth-We have spread it **out**, and set
050:041 will call **out** from a place quite near,-
050:044 rent asunder, from (men) hurrying **out**: that will
051:026 to his household, brought **out** a fatted calf.
051:048 And We have spread **out** the (spacious) earth:
051:048 (spacious) earth: how excellently We do spread **out**!

OUT (continued)

053:032 you **out** of the earth, and when
054:009 "Here is one possessed!", and he was driven **out**.
054:020 Plucking **out** men as if they were roots of
055:010 It is He Who has spread **out** the earth
055:022 **Out** of them come Pearls and Coral:
056:007 And ye shall be sorted **out** into three classes.
056:018 and cups (filled) **out** of clear-flowing fountains:
057:004 **out** of it, what comes down from heaven and what
057:007 and spend (in charity) **out** of the (substance)
057:014 (Those without) will call **out**, "Were we
058:011 (spread **out** and) make room: (ample) room
059:002 It is He who got **out** the Unbelievers among the
059:002 that they would get **out**: and they
059:011 "If ye are expelled, We too will go **out** with you,
059:012 go **out** with them; and if they are attacked
060:001 If ye have come **out** to strive in My Way and seek
060:001 driven **out** the Messenger and yourselves (from your
060:008 (your) Faith nor drive you **out** of your homes,
060:009 and drive you **out** of your homes, and support
060:009 you **out**, from turning to them (for friendship
063:010 **out** of the substance which We have bestowed
065:001 your Lord: and turn them not **out** of their houses,
065:002 fear Allah, He (ever) prepares a way **out**,
067:004 to thee dull and discomfited, in a state worn **out**.
068:021 As the morning broke, they called **out**, one to
068:048 when he cried **out** in agony.
070:016 Plucking **out** (his being) right to the skull!-
070:039 **out** of the (base matter) they know!
071:019 as a carpet (spread **out**),
072:014 they have sought **out** (the path) of right conduct:
073:014 a heap of sand poured **out** and flowing down.
074:052 to be given scrolls (of revelation) spread **out**!
077:013 For the Day of Sorting **out**.
077:014 what is the Day of Sorting **out**?
077:038 That will be a Day of Sorting **out**! We shall
078:017 Verily the Day of Sorting **Out** is a thing appointed,-
079:001 By the (angels) who tear **out** (the souls of
079:002 By those who gently draw **out** (the souls
079:014 When, behold, they will be brought **out** to the open.
079:029 and its splendor doth He bring **out** (with light).
079:031 He draweth **out** therefrom its water and its pasture,
081:007 When the souls are sorted **out**, (Being joined,
084:003 And when the Earth is flattened **out**,
086:012 And by the Earth which opens **out** (for the gushing
087:004 And Who bringeth **out** the (green and
088:016 And rich carpets (All) spread **out**.
088:020 And at the Earth, how it is spread **out**?
089:009 who cut **out** (huge) rocks in the valley?-
096:002 Created man, **out** of a leech-like clot:
099:006 sorted **out**, to be shown the Deeds that they

OUTER

024:060 lay aside their (**outer**) garments, provided they
030:007 They know but the **outer** (things) in the
033:059 **outer** garments over their persons (when out

OUTLYING

013:041 the land from its **outlying** borders? (Where) Allah
021:044 its **outlying** borders? Is it then they who will

OUTSIDE

002:048 nor shall anyone be helped (from **outside**).
002:123 nor shall anyone be helped (from **outside**)
003:118 into your intimacy those **outside** your ranks:

OUTSIDE (continued)

005:106   from **outside** if ye are journeying through
024:058   times of undress: **outside** those times it is

OUTSPREAD

024:041   wings **outspread**? Each one knows its own (mode

OUTSTRETCHED

005:064   Nay, both His hands are widely **outstretched**: He
014:043   necks **outstretched**, their heads uplifted, their
104:009   In columns **outstretched**.

OUTSTRIP

029:004   who practise Evil think that they will **outstrip** Us?
036:040   nor can the Night **outstrip** the Day: each (just)

OVEN

023:027   and the **oven** gushes forth, take thou

OVER

002:020   for Allah hath power **over** all things.
002:102   Satans recited **over** Solomon's Kingdom.
002:106   Allah hath power **over** all things?
002:109   for Allah hath power **over** all things.
002:143   That ye might be witnesses **over** the nations,
002:143   and the Messenger a witness **over** yourselves;
002:148   For Allah hath power **over** all things.
002:228   but men have a degree **over** them
002:247   "Allah hath appointed Talut as king **over** you."
002:247   authority **over** us when we are better fitted
002:255   **over** the heavens and the earth,
002:259   Allah hath power **over** all things."
002:284   For Allah hath power **over** all things.
002:286   grant us victory **over** the unbelievers.
003:026   Verily, **over** all things Thou hast power.
003:029   And Allah has power **over** all things.
003:075   no way **over** us as to the Unlettered people,"
003:112   Shame is pitched **over** them (like a tent)
003:112   And pitched **over** them is (the tent of) destitution.
003:159   so pass **over** (their faults), and ask for (Allah's)
003:165   for Allah hath power **over** all things."
003:189   and Allah hath power **over** all things.
004:001   for Allah ever watches **over** you.
004:080   We have not sent thee to watch **over** them.
004:085   and Allah hath power **over** all things.
004:090   He could have given them power **over** you, and
004:141   "Did we not gain an advantage **over** you.
004:141   Unbelievers a way (to triumph) **over** the Believers.
004:154   We raised **over** them the Mount (Sinai);
005:004   but pronounce the name of Allah **over** it: and fear
005:015   and passing **over** much (that is now unnecessary):
005:017   For Allah hath power **over** all things."
005:019   and Allah hath power **over** all things.
005:025   I have power only **over** myself and my bother: so
005:026   but sorrow thou not **over** these rebellious people."
005:040   and Allah hath power **over** all things.
005:068   **over** (these) people without Faith.
005:117   thou wast the Watcher **over** them, and Thou
005:117   and I was a witness **over** them whilst I
005:120   and it is He who hath power **over** all things.
006:017   He hath power **over** all things.
006:018   Irresistibly Supreme **over** His servants. And
006:061   Supreme **over** His servants and He sets guardians
006:061   and He sets guardians **over** you. At length
006:076   When the night covered him **over**, he saw
006:103   but His grasp is **over** all vision; He is
006:104   I am not (here) to watch **over** your doings."

OVER (continued)

006:107   not one to watch **over** their doings, nor art
006:107   nor art thou set **over** them to dispose
007:022   the leaves of the Garden **over** their bodies. And
007:039   "See then! no advantage have ye **over** us; so taste
007:071   **over** names which ye have devised-ye and
007:093   but how shall I lament **over** a people
007:127   and we have **over** them (power) irresistible.
007:150   Make not the enemies rejoice **over** my misfortune,
007:171   When We raised the mount **over** them, as if
007:188   Say: "I have no power **over** any good or harm
008:041   For Allah hath power **over** all things.
008:057   If ye gain the mastery **over** them in war,
008:071   given (thee) power **over** them. And Allah
009:008   **over** you, they respect not in you the ties
009:014   (to victory) **over** them, heal the
009:033   to cause it to prevail **over** all religion,
009:039   hath power **over** all things.
009:128   should suffer, ardently anxious is he **over** you: to
010:024   powers of disposal **over** it: there reaches
010:031   Or who is it that has power **over** hearing and sight?
010:049   Say: "I have no power **over** any harm or profit
010:108   **over** you to arrange your affairs."
011:004   and He hath power **over** all things."
011:007   and His Throne was **over** the Waters-that He
011:036   So grieve no longer **over** their (evil) deeds.
011:057   For my Lord hath care and watch **over** all things."
011:086   But I am not set **over** you to keep watch!"
012:021   power and control **over** His affairs; but most
012:029   "O Joseph, pass this **over**! (O wife),
012:055   (Joseph) said: "Set me **over** the store-houses
012:066   he said: "**Over** all that we say, be Allah
012:076   whom We please: but **over** all endued with knowledge
012:093   and cast it **over** the face of my father: he will
012:096   news came, he cast (the shirt) **over** his face,
013:033   Is then He Who standeth **over** every soul
014:018   no power have they **over** aught that they
014:022   I had no authority **over** you except to call you,
015:042   "For **over** My servants no authority shalt thou have,
015:088   **over** them: but lower thy wing (in gentleness)
016:077   even quicker: for Allah hath power **over** all things.
016:099   No authority has he **over** those who believe
016:100   His authority is **over** those only, who take
016:115   and any (food) **over** which the name of other than
016:127   **over** them: and distress not thyself because
017:006   **over** them: We gave you increase in resources
017:046   And We put coverings **over** their hearts
017:065   **over** them." Enough is thy Lord for a disposer
018:011   Then We drew (a veil) **over** their ears, for a
018:021   "Let us surely build a place of worship **over** them."
018:021   **over** them": their Lord knows best about them:
018:021   **over** their affair said, "Let us
018:042   **over** what he had spent on his property,
018:045   it is (only) Allah Who prevails **over** all things.
018:057   and **over** their ears, deafness. If thou
018:057   veils **over** their hearts so that they should
018:078   (those things) **over** which thou was unable
018:082   of (those things) **over** which thou wast unable
018:096   **over** it, molten lead."
019:071   Not one of you but will pass **over** it: this is,
020:062   **over** their affair, but they kept their talk secret.
021:087   no power **over** him! But he
022:006   and it is He Who has power **over** all things.

OVER (continued)

022:019 of Fire: **over** their heads will be poured out
022:028 **over** the cattle which He has provided for
022:034 of Allah **over** the sustenance He gave them
022:035 **over** their afflictions, keep up
022:036 **over** them as they line up (for sacrifice):
023:024 **over** you: if Allah had wished (to send
023:068 Do they not ponder **over** the Word (of Allah),
023:091 lorded it **over** others! Glory to
024:031 **over** their bosoms and not display their beauty
024:045 for verily Allah has power **over** all things.
025:054 for thy Lord has power (**over** all things).
027:023 **over** them and provided with every requisite;
027:070 But grieve not **over** them, nor distress
028:045 **over** them; but thou wast not a dweller
028:071 the Night perpetual **over** you to the Day
028:072 the Day perpetual **over** you to the
029:020 for Allah has power **over** all things.
030:050 for He has power **over** all things.
033:019 Covetous **over** you. Then when
033:027 And Allah has power **over** all things.
033:052 watch **over** all things.
033:059 outer garments **over** their persons (when out
033:066 turned **over** in the Fire, they will say:
034:021 But he had no authority **over** them,-except that
034:021 and thy Lord doth watch **over** all things.
034:038 **over** into Chastisement.
034:042 they have **over** each other, for profit
035:001 for Allah has power **over** all things.
037:030 "Nor had we any authority **over** you. Nay, it
037:146 And We caused to grow **over** him, a spreading
038:021 **over** the wall of the private chamber;
038:033 **over** (their) legs and their necks.
039:041 a Custodian **over** them.
040:044 watches **over** His Servants."
041:039 who are dead. For He has power **over** all things.
042:006 **over** them; and thou art not the disposer
042:009 it is He Who has power **over** all things.
042:048 **over** them. Thy duty is but to convey
043:042 for verily We shall prevail **over** them.
044:029 **over** them: nor were they given a respite (again).
044:048 "Then pour **over** his head the Chastisement
046:033 Yea, verily He has power **over** all things.
048:010 to Allah: the Hand of Allah is **over** their hands:
048:021 and Allah has power **over** all things.
048:024 **over** them. And Allah sees well all that ye do.
048:028 to make it **over** all religion: and enough
050:010 piled one **over** another;-
051:013 be tried (and tested) **over** the Fire!
052:037 with them, or have they control **over** them.
057:002 and He has Power **over** all things.
057:016 passed **over** them and their hearts grew hard?
057:023 nor exult **over** favours bestowed upon you.
057:023 **over** matters that pass you by, nor exult
057:029 **over** the Grace of Allah, that (His)
059:006 and Allah has power **over** all things.
059:006 **over** any He pleases: and Allah
059:009 preference **over** themselves, even though
060:007 For Allah has power (**over** all things); and Allah
060:010 (on their dowers of women who came **over** to you).
060:011 your turn (by the coming **over** of a woman
061:009 That He make it prevail **over** all religion,
064:001 and He has power **over** all things.

OVER (continued)

065:012 Allah has power **over** all things, and that
066:003 he confirmed part thereof and passed **over** a part.
066:006 **over** which are (appointed) angels stern (and)
066:008 us Forgiveness: for Thou hast power **over** all things."
067:001 and He **over** all things Hath Power;-
067:019 truly it is He that watches **over** all things.
070:044 ignominy covering them (all **over**)! Such is
074:030 **Over** it are Nineteen.
076:001 Has there not been **over** Man a long period of Time,
076:011 and will shed **over** them brightness and a
076:014 will come low **over** them, and the bunches
078:012 **over** you the seven firmaments,
081:006 When the oceans boil **over** with a swell;
082:010 But verily **over** you (are appointed angels)
083:033 But they had not been sent as Keepers **over** them!
085:006 Behold! they sat **over** against the (fire),
086:004 There is no soul but has a protector **over** it.
090:005 Thinketh he, that none hath power **over** him?
090:020 On them will be Fire Vaulted **over** (all round).
104:008 It shall be made into a vault **over** them,

OVERBEARING

019:014 and he was not **overbearing** or rebellious.
019:032 and not **overbearing** or unblest;

OVERCAME

038:023 and he **overcame** me in the argument."

OVERCOME

003:154 a band of you **overcome** with slumber,
003:160 If Allah helps you, none can **overcome** you:
008:036 at length they will be **overcome**: and the
008:048 can **overcome** you this day, while I
054:010 "I am one **overcome**: do thou then help (me)!"
060:002 If they **overcome** you they would behave to you

OVERFLOWED

069:011 Noah's flood) **overflowed** beyond its limits,

OVERFLOWING

002:165 **overflowing** in their love for Allah.
002:269 granted receiveth indeed a benefit **overflowing**;
005:083 thou wilt see their eyes **overflowing** with tears,

OVERLAP

039:005 and the Day **overlap** the Night: He has
039:005 He makes the Night **overlap** the Day, and the

OVERLOOK

002:109 but forgive and **overlook**,
005:013 but forgive them and **overlook** (their misdeeds):
015:085 So **overlook** (any human faults) with gracious
024:022 let them forgive and **overlook**: do you
064:014 But if ye forgive and **overlook**, and cover

OVERPOWERING

039:004 He is Allah, the One, the **Overpowering**.
040:016 That of Allah, the One, the **Overpowering**!

OVERREACH

029:039 on the earth; yet they cold not **overreach** (Us).

OVERSHADOWING

026:189 of **overshadowing** gloom seized them, and that

OVERSPREADS

113:003 From the mischief of Darkness as it **overspreads**;

OVERTAKE

018:055 the ancients to **overtake** them, or the
039:051 of their deeds will soon **overtake** them (too),
062:008 will truly **overtake** you: then will ye be sent

OVERTAKEN
006:124   be **overtaken** by humiliation before Allah, and
020:077   of being **overtaken** (by Pharaoh) and without
026:061   "We are sure to be **overtaken**."

OVERTAKES
003:120   but if some misfortune **overtakes** you,

OVERTHROWN
005:021   for then will ye be **overthrown**, to your own ruin."
009:070   and the cities **overthrown**. To them
053:053   the **Overthrown** Cities (of Sodom and Gomorrah),
069:007   the (whole) people lying **overthrown** in its (path),
069:009   and the Cities **Overthrown**, committed habitual Sin,

OVERTOOK
011:067   The (mighty) Blast **overtook** the wrong-doers,
015:073   **overtook** them at sunrise,
016:034   **overtook** them, and that every (Wrath) at which
023:041   Then the Blast **overtook** them with justice,
039:051   **overtook** them. And the wrong-doers of this

OVERWHELM
033:009   on you hosts (to **overwhelm** you): but We

OVERWHELMED
007:064   But We **overwhelmed** in the flood those who
007:152   will indeed be **overwhelmed** with wrath
010:022   being **overwhelmed**: they pray unto Allah, sincerely
010:090   At length, when **overwhelmed** with the flood, he said
011:037   **overwhelmed** (in the flood)."
020:078   completely **overwhelmed** them and covered them up.
023:106   our misfortune **overwhelmed** us, and we
024:040   deep ocean, **overwhelmed** with billow topped by
029:014   but the Deluge **overwhelmed** them while they
037:082   Then the rest We **overwhelmed** in the Flood.
043:075   will they be there **overwhelmed**.

OVERWHELMING
079:034   the great, **overwhelming** (Event),-
088:001   of the **Overwhelming** (Event)?

OWE
003:077   they **owe** to Allah and their own solemn plighted
003:097   pilgrimage thereto is a duty men **owe** to Allah,
005:106   we shall hide not the evidence we **owe** to Allah if
008:072   ye **owe** no duty of protection to them

OWES
002:282   and not diminish aught of what he **owes**.

OWN
002:057   but they harmed their **own** selves.
002:060   Each group knew its **own** place for water.
002:066   So We made it an example to their **own** time,
002:078   but (see therein their **own**) desires,
002:079   the Book with their **own** hands,
002:084   your **own** people from your homes:
002:121   the loss is their **own**.
002:129   a Messenger of their **own**,
002:146   know this as they know their **own** sons;
002:151   a Messenger of your **own**,
002:158   his **own** impulse to Good,
002:184   But he that will give more, of his **own** free will,
002:195   and make not your **own** hands contribute
002:231   if anyone does that, He wrongs his **own** soul.
002:260   He said: "Yea! but to satisfy my **own** heart."
002:272   ye give benefits your **own** souls,
002:282   And get two witnesses, out or your **own** men.
003:013   these saw with their **own** eyes twice their number.
003:024   deceive them as to their **own** religion.

OWN (continued)
003:077   they owe to Allah and their **own** solemn plighted
003:117   harvest of men who have wronged their **own** souls:
003:135   an act of indecency or wronged their **own** souls.
003:143   with your **own** eyes (and flinch!).
003:149   (from Faith) to your **own** loss.
003:154   stirred to anxiety by their **own** feelings,
003:168   Say: "Avert death from your **own** selves,
004:002   (by mixing it up) with your **own**.
004:005   but if they, of their **own** good pleasure, remit
004:009   as they would have for their **own** if they had left
004:010   eat up a fire into their **own** bodies:
004:040   and giveth from His **Own** self a great reward.
004:090   you or fighting their **own** people.
004:107   such as betray their **own** souls; for Allah
004:110   If anyone does evil or wrongs his **own** soul but
004:111   he earns it against his **own** soul: for Allah
004:113   only lead their **own** souls astray,
004:166   He hath sent from His (**Own**) knowledge, and
005:021   for then will ye be overthrown, to your **own** ruin."
005:043   when they have (their **own**) Torah before them?
005:105   O ye who believe! guard your **own** souls: if ye
005:106   of your **own** (brotherhood) or others from outside
006:012   It is they who have lost their **own** souls, that
006:020   Those who have lost their **own** souls refuse
006:020   know this as they know their **own** sons. Their
006:028   Yea, in their **own** (eyes) will become
006:070   is caught in its **own** ruin by its **own** action: it
006:070   deliver themselves to ruin by their **own** acts: they
006:070   is caught in its **own** ruin by its **own** action: it
006:104   it will be to his **own** (harm): I am not
006:104   it will be for (the good of) his **own** soul: if
006:108   alluring to each people its **own** doings. In the
006:122   their **own** deeds seem pleasing.
006:123   but they only plot against their **own** souls, and
006:137   to their **own** destruction, and cause
007:023   we have wronged our **own** souls: if Thou
007:063   through a man of your **own** people, to warn
007:065   one of their (**own**) brethren: he said: "O my
007:069   of your **own** people, to warn you? Call
007:073   one of their **own** brethren: he said: "O my
007:085   one of their **own** brethren: he said:
007:157   whom they find mentioned in their **own** (Scriptures),-
007:160   each group knew its **own** place for water. We gave
007:160   but they harmed their **own** souls.
007:176   and followed his **own** vain desires.
007:177   who reject Our signs and wrong their **own** souls.
008:016   or to retreat to a troop (of his **own**)-he draws
008:051   which your (**own**) hands sent forth. For Allah
008:053   is in their (**own**) souls: and verily
009:017   their **own** souls to infidelity. The works
009:042   destroy their **own** souls; for Allah
009:070   Who wrongs them, but they wrong their **own** souls.
009:120   their **own** lives to his: because nothing
010:015   of my **own** accord, to change it: I follow
010:023   your **own** souls,-an enjoyment of the life of the
010:044   it is man that wrongs his **own** soul.
010:108   do so to their **own** loss: and I am
010:108   **own** souls; those who stray, do so
011:021   **own** souls: and the (fancies) they forged
011:050   one of their **own** brethren. He said: "O my
011:061   one of their **own** brethren. He said: "O my
011:084   one of their **own** brethren: he said: "O my people!

OWN (continued)

011:101　they wronged their **own** souls: the deities,
012:054　to serve about my **own** person." Therefore when
012:069　(**own**) brother; so grieve not at aught
014:004　in the language of his (**own**) people, in order
014:022　but reproach your **own** souls. I cannot
016:025　Day of Judgment, their **own** burdens in full,
016:028　their **own** souls." Then would they offer
016:033　nay, they wronged their **own** souls.
016:063　their **own** acts seem alluring: he is their
016:072　of your **own** nature, and made for you, out of
017:013　on his **own** neck: On the Day of Judgment We shall
017:014　"Read thine (**own**) record: sufficient is thy soul
017:015　receiveth it for his **own** benefit: who goeth
017:015　**own** loss: no bearer of burdens can bear
017:084　to his **own** disposition: but your Lord knows best
018:028　of Us, one who follows his **own** desires, and his
018:051　**own** creation: nor is it for Me to take as helpers
018:065　taught knowledge form Our **own** presence.
018:082　I did it not of my **own** accord. Such is
019:097　in thine **own** tongue, that with
020:016　not therein but follow their **own** lust, divert thee
024:006　but their **own**,-let one of them testify four
024:027　enter not houses other than your **own**, until ye
024:041　**own** (mode of) prayer and praise. And Allah
024:061　that ye should eat in your **own** houses, or those
025:040　**own** eyes)? But they expect not to be raised again.
025:043　for his god his **own** passion (or impulse)?
025:055　is a helper (of Evil), against his **own** Lord!
027:010　(of its **own** accord) as if it had been a snake,
027:038　He said (to his **own** men): "Ye Chiefs! which of
027:040　his **own** soul; but if any is ungrateful, truly my
027:092　their **own** souls, and if any stray, say: "I
028:015　one of his **own** people, and the other, of his
028:015　his **own** people appealed to him against his foe,
028:031　**own** accord) as if it had been a snake, he turned
028:050　**own** lusts: and who is more astray than one who
028:050　one who follows his **own** lusts, devoid of
029:006　they do so for their **own** soul: for Allah
029:013　They will bear their **own** burdens, and other
029:013　and (other) burdens along with their **own**, and on
029:060　that carry not their **own** sustenance? It is
030:008　Do they not reflect in their **own** minds? Not but
030:009　but they wronged their **own** souls.
030:009　to their **own** destruction): it was
030:029　fellow their **own** desires being devoid of
030:036　their (**own**) hands have sent forth, behold,
031:012　does so to the profit of his **own** soul: but if
033:006　the Believers than their **own** selves, and his
034:050　I only stray to the loss of my **own** soul: but if
035:013　besides Him **own** not a straw.
035:018　for the benefit of his **own** soul; and the
035:032　**own** souls; some who follow a middle course
035:039　to (their **own**) loss.
035:039　be on his **own** self their disbelief: but adds
036:036　**own** (human) kind and (other) things of which
036:040　(its **own**) orbit (according to Law).
036:050　nor to return to their **own** people!
036:078　and forgets his **own** (Origin and) Creation:
036:080　when behold! ye kindle therewith (your **own** fires)!
037:151　Behold they say, out of their **own** invention,
038:008　My (**own**) Message! Nay, they
039:015　who lose their **own** souls and their people on the

OWN (continued)

039:041　benefits his **own** soul: but he
039:041　his **own** soul. Nor art thou set a Custodian
040:044　to you (now). My (**own**) affair I commit to Allah:
041:046　his **own** soul; whoever works evil, it is
041:046　it is against his **own** soul: nor is
041:053　and in their **own** souls, until it
045:015　**own** soul). In the end will ye (all) be brought
045:015　it is to his **own** benefit; if he
045:023　as his god his **own** vain desire? Allah has
046:021　(**own**) brethren: behold, he wanted his people
047:014　and such as follow their **own** lusts?
047:016　Allah has sealed, and who follow their **own** lusts.
047:038　of their **own** souls. But Allah is free of all
048:010　his **own** soul, and any one who fulfils what he
048:029　and it stands on its **own** stem, (filling) the
051:021　As also in your **own** selves: will ye not then see?
052:016　of your (**own**) deeds."
053:003　Nor does he say (aught) of (his **own**) Desire.
053:023　and what their **own** souls desire!-Even though
054:003　and follow their (**own**) lusts but every matter
059:002　by their **own** hands and the hands of the Believers.
059:009　of their **own** souls,-they are
059:009　even though poverty was their (**own** lot). And those
063:004　(unable to stand on their **own**). They think
064:016　for the benefit of your **own** souls: and those
064:016　of their **own** souls,-they are the
065:001　(**own**) soul: thou knowest not if perchance Allah
072:024　(with their **own** eyes) that which they are promised,-
080:034　That Day shall a man flee from his **own** brother,
080:037　will have enough concern (of his **own**) to make
083:031　to their **own** people, they would return jesting;
111:005　round her (**own**) neck!

OWNERS

004:025　wed them with the leave of their **owners**,
079:009　Cast down will be (their **owners'**) eyes.

OX

006:146　the **ox** and the sheep, except what

OXEN

006:144　Of camels a pair, and of **oxen** a pair; say,

P

PACE
031:019   "And be moderate in thy **pace**, and lower
PADDLE
052:012   That play (and **paddle**) in shallow trifles.
PAGAN
029:047   of these (**pagan** Arabs): and none
PAGANS
003:095   he was not of the **Pagans**."
004:117   (The **pagans**), leaving Him, call but
005:082   the Jews and **Pagans**; and nearest among them
006:121   ye would indeed be **Pagans**.
006:137   of most of the **Pagans**, their "partners"!
009:001   to those of the **Pagans** with whom ye have
009:003   dissolve (treaty) obligations with the **Pagans**.
009:004   with those **Pagans** with whom ye have entered
009:005   then fight and slay the **Pagans** wherever ye
009:006   If one amongst the **Pagans** ask thee for asylum,
009:007   with the **Pagans**, except those with whom ye
009:028   O ye who believe! Truly the **Pagans** are unclean;
009:033   the **Pagans** may detest (it).
009:036   the **Pagans** all together as they fight
009:113   for **Pagans**, even though they be of kin, after it
017:040   Has then your Lord, (O **Pagans**!) preferred for
061:009   all religion, even though the **Pagans** may detest
072:016   "If they (the **pagans**) had (only) remained on the
PAID
002:281   Then shall every soul be **paid** what it earned,
003:025   and each soul will be **paid** out just what
003:185   shall you be **paid** your full recompense.
004:092   blood-money should be **paid** to his family, and
033:050   **paid** their dowers; and those whom thy right
039:070   And to every soul will be **paid** in full
083:036   **paid** back for what they did?
PAIN
002:177   in **pain** (or suffering) and adversity,
039:047   from the **pain** of the Chastisement on the
046:015   bear him, and in **pain** did she give him birth.
046:015   to his parents: in **pain** did his mother bear him,
PAINFUL
034:005   for such will be a Chastisement of **Painful** wrath.
PAINFULLY
084:006   **painfully** toiling, but thou shalt meet Him.
PAINS
019:023   And the **pains** of childbirth drove her to the
026:138   to receive **Pains** and Chastisement!"
PAIR
006:143   of sheep a **pair**, and of goats a **pair**, say,
006:144   Of camels a **pair**, and of oxen a **pair**; say,
049:013   a single (**pair**) of a male and a female, and made
090:008   Have We not made for him a **pair** of eyes?-
090:009   And a tongue, and a **pair** of lips?
PAIRS
006:143   (Take) eight (head of cattle) in (four) **pairs**: of
013:003   in **pairs**, two and two: He draweth the Night
020:053   With it have We produced divers **pairs** of plants

PAIRS (continued)
022:005   forth every kind of beautiful growth (in **pairs**).
023:027   take thou on board **pairs** of every species,
031:010   every kind of noble creature, in **pairs**.
034:046   (it may be) in **pairs**, or (it may
035:001   two, or three, or four (**Pairs**): He adds
035:011   then He made you in **pairs**. And no
036:036   in **pairs** all things that the earth produces,
039:006   eight head of cattle in **pairs**: He creates
042:011   and **pairs** among cattle: by this
042:011   **pairs** from among yourselves, and **pairs**
043:012   That has created **pairs** in all things, and has
050:007   every kind of beautiful growth (in **pairs**)-
051:049   And of every thing We have created **pairs**: that ye
053:045   That He did create in **pairs**-male and female,
078:008   And (have We not) created you in **pairs**,
PALACE
027:044   the lofty **Palace**: but when she saw it,
027:044   He said: "This is but a **palace** paved smooth
028:038   and build me a lofty **palace**, that I
040:036   a lofty **palace**, that I may attain the ways
043:051   underneath my (**palace**)? What! see ye not then?
PALACES
007:074   **palaces** and castles in (open) plains, and
025:010   and He could give thee **Palaces** (secure to
PALATABLE
025:053   one **palatable** and sweet, and the
035:012   the one **palatable**, sweet, and pleasant to drink,
PALM
013:004   with corn, and **palm** trees-growing out of single
PALM-FIBRE
054:013   made of broad planks and caulked with **palm-fibre**:
PALM-LEAF
111:005   A twisted rope of **palm-leaf** fibre round her
PALM-TREE
019:023   to the trunk of a **palm-tree**: she cried
019:024   from beneath the (**palm-tree**): "Grieve not!
019:025   the trunk of the **palm-tree**: it will
PALM-TREES
020:071   on trunks of **palm-trees**: so shall
050:010   And tall (and stately) **palm-trees**, with shoots
054:020   roots of **palm-trees** torn up (from the ground).
059:005   of the tender **palm-trees**, Or ye left them
069:007   roots of hollow **palm-trees** tumbled down!
PALTRY
016:117   a **paltry** profit; but they will have a most
PANIC
002:177   and throughout all periods of **panic**.
PANTING
100:001   By the (Steeds) that run, with **panting** (breath),
PARABLE
002:171   The **parable** of those who reject Faith
002:261   The **parable** of those who spend their wealth
002:264   They are in **Parable** like a hard, barren rock,
013:035   The **parable** of the Garden which the righteous
014:018   The **parable** of those who reject their Lord
014:024   a **parable**?-a goodly Word like a goodly tree,
014:026   And the **parable** of an evil Word is that
016:075   Allah sets forth the **Parable** (of two men):
016:076   Allah sets forth (another) **Parable** of two men:
016:112   Allah sets forth a **parable**: a city
018:032   Set forth to them the **parable** of two men:

PARABLE (continued)

022:073 O men! Here is a **parable** set forth!
024:035 and the earth. The **parable** of His Light is as
029:041 The **parable** of those who take protectors
030:058 in this Qur'an. Every kind of **Parable**: but if
036:013 a **parable**, the (story of) the Companions of the
039:027 in this Qur'an every kind of **Parable**, in order
039:029 Allah puts forth a **Parable**-a man belonging

PARABLES

013:017 Thus doth Allah (by **parables**) show forth
013:017 Thus doth Allah set forth **parables**.
014:025 So Allah sets forth **parables** for men, in order
014:045 (many) **Parables** in your behalf!"
024:035 His Light: Allah doth set forth **Parables** for men:
025:039 To teach one We set forth **parables** and examples;
029:043 And such are the **Parables** We set forth for

PARADISE

002:111 **Paradise** unless he be a Jew or a Christian."
009:111 (of **Paradise**): they fight in His Cause, and slay
018:107 for their entertainment, the Gardens of **Paradise**,
023:011 Who will inherit **Paradise**: they will

PARCHED

024:039 **parched** with thirst mistakes for water;
032:027 drive Rain to **parched** soil (bare of herbage),

PARCHMENT

006:007 a written (Message) on **parchment**, so that
052:003 In a **parchment** unfolded;

PARDON

003:134 who restrain anger, and **pardon** (all) men;
004:149 or conceal it or cover evil with **pardon**, surely
008:033 whilst they could ask for **pardon**.
009:066 If We **pardon** some of you, We will
041:024 And if they beg for **pardon**, their suit

PARDONED

002:275 shall be **pardoned** for the past;

PARDONING

004:149 surely Allah is ever **pardoning** Powerful.

PARENTS

002:083 your **parents** and kindred,
002:180 to **parents** and next of kin,
002:215 is for **parents** and kindred and orphans
004:007 From what is left by **parents** and those nearest
004:011 For **parents**, a sixth share
004:011 and the **parents** are the (only) heirs,
004:011 Ye know not whether your **parents** or your children
004:033 to property left by **parents** and relatives.
004:036 and do good to **parents**, kinsfolk, orphans, those
004:135 even as against yourselves, or your **parents**, or
006:151 be good to your **parents**; kill not
007:027 he got your **parents** out of the Garden, stripping
012:099 a home for his **parents** with himself, and said:
012:100 And he raised his **parents** high on the throne
014:041 Thy Forgiveness-me, my **parents** and (all)
017:023 but Him, and that ye be kind to **parents**. Whether
018:080 his **parents** were people of Faith, and we
019:014 And kind to his **parents**, and he
027:019 on me and on my **parents**, and that
029:008 kindness to **parents**: but if they (either of
031:014 "Show gratitude to Me and to thy **parents**: to Me
031:014 (to be good) to his **parents**: in travail
046:015 upon me, and upon both my **parents**, and that
046:015 to his **parents**: in pain did his mother bear him,

PARENTS (continued)

046:017 his **parents**, "Fie on you! Do ye
071:028 "O my Lord! Forgive me, my **parents**, all who

PART

002:085 a **part** of the Book that ye believe in,
002:182 wrong-doing on the **part** of the testator.
002:259 He said: "(Perhaps) a day or **part** of a day."
003:007 perversity follow the **part** thereof that is not
003:044 This is **part** of the tidings of the things unseen,
003:050 **part** of what was (before) forbidden to you;
003:052 unbelief on their **part** he said: "Who will be
003:078 but it is no **part** of the Book;
003:078 you would think it is a **part** of the Book,
003:159 It is **part** of the Mercy of Allah that thou
004:005 remit any **part** of it to you, take it
004:019 that ye may take away **part** of the dower
004:034 whose **part** ye fear disloyalty and ill-conduct,
004:128 or desertion on her husband's **part**, there
005:002 transgression (and hostility on your **part**).
005:013 (right) places and forget a good **part** of the
005:014 forgot a good **part** of the Message that was
006:038 but (forms **part** of) communities like you. Nothing
006:135 I will do (my **part**): soon will ye know
006:156 and for our **part**, we remained
006:159 thou hast no **part** in them in the least: their
007:076 The arrogant party said: "For our **part**, we
009:058 If they are given **part** thereof, they are pleased,
009:117 after that the hearts of a **part** of them had
010:046 thy lifetime) some **part** of what We promise them,-
010:103 thus is it fitting on Our **part** that We
011:012 the inclination) to give up a **part** of what
011:081 a **part** of the night remains, and let not
011:093 I will do (my **part**): soon will ye
011:121 "Do whatever ye can: we shall do our **part**;
012:016 in the early **part** of the night, weeping.
012:037 That is **part** of the (Duty) which my
012:103 Yet no faith will the greater **part** of mankind have,
013:036 those who reject a **part** thereof. Say "I am
013:038 and it was never the **part** of a messenger
013:040 (within thy lifetime) **part** of what We promised
013:040 reach them: it is Our **part** to call them to account.
017:070 above a great **part** of Our Creation.
017:079 a **part** of it as an additional prayer for thee:
017:089 of similitude: yet the greater **part** of men refuse
018:019 a day, or **part** of a day." At length)
018:038 "But as for my **part** Allah is my Lord, and none
020:115 and We found on his **part** no firm resolve.
020:130 celebrate them for **part** of the hours of the night,
023:109 "A **part** of My servants there was, who used
023:113 or **part** of a day: but ask those
024:029 It is no fault on your **part** to enter houses
026:063 So it divided, and each separate **part** became like
035:011 of days, nor is a **part** cut off from his life,
036:007 the greater **part** of them; for they
036:020 from the farthest **part** of the City, a man,
036:039 (and withered) lower **part** of date-stalk.
039:039 I will do (my **part**): but soon will ye know-
040:077 some **part** of what We promise them,- or We
047:026 "We will obey you in **part** of (this) matter";
050:040 And during **part** of the night, (also), celebrate
052:049 And for **part** of the night also praise thou Him,-
053:007 While he was in the highest **part** of the horizon:
059:008 (Some **part** is due) to the indigent Muhajirs,

PART (continued)

065:002   on equitable terms or **part** with them on equitable
066:003   a **part**. Then when he told her thereof, she said,
066:003   he confirmed **part** thereof and passed over a **part**.
076:026   And **part** of the night, prostrate thyself to Him;

PART-WORSHIP

030:033   some of them pay **part-worship** to other gods
030:035   to which they pay **part-worship**?
040:073   ye gave **part-worship**-

PARTIALITY

002:182   But if anyone fears **partiality** or wrong-doing

PARTICULAR

008:025   not in **particular** (only) those of you who do wrong:

PARTIES

002:182   settlement among (the **parties** concerned),
002:229   the **parties** should either hold together
002:229   except when both **parties** fear that
002:282   write down faithfully as between the **parties**:
003:122   Remember two of your **parties** meditated cowardice;
004:071   And either go forth in **parties** or go
004:088   into two **parties** about the Hypocrites?
006:081   Which of (us) two **parties** hath more
008:007   the two **parties**, that it should be yours: ye wished
018:012   which of the two **parties** was best at calculating
020:131   for enjoyment to **parties** of them, the splendour
049:009   If two **parties** among the Believers fall into

PARTING

018:078   He answered: "This is the **parting** between me
075:028   (the Time) of **Parting**;

PARTISANS

034:054   as was in the past with their **partisans**: for they

PARTITION

023:100   Before them is a **Partition** till the Day
025:053   between them, a **partition** that is not

PARTLY

005:003   (**partly**) eaten by a wild animal; unless
022:005   **partly** formed and **partly** unformed, in order

PARTNER

004:085   becomes a **partner** therein: and
006:163   No **partner** hath He: this am I commanded, and
017:111   no son, and has no **partner** in (His) dominion:
018:110   admit no one as **partner**."
025:002   nor has He a **partner** in His dominion: it is

PARTNERS

003:064   that we associate no **partners** with Him;
003:151   for that they joined **partners** with Allah,
003:186   and from those who worship **partners** besides Allah.
004:036   Serve Allah, and join not any **partners** with Him;
004:048   that **partners** should be set up with him; but
004:048   to set up **partners** with Allah is to devise a sin
006:022   who ascribed **partners** (to Us): "Where are
006:022   "Where are the **partners** whom ye
006:078   from your (guilt) of giving **partners** to Allah.
006:079   I give **partners** to Allah."
006:081   to give **partners** to Allah without any warrant
006:094   whom ye thought to be **partners** in your affairs: so
006:136   But the share of their "**partners**" reacheth
006:136   and this for Our "**partners**"! But the
006:136   Allah reacheth their "**partners**"! Evil
006:137   their "**partners**" made alluring the slaughter
006:148   Those who give **partners** (to Allah) will say:
006:148   we should not have given **partners** to Him, nor

PARTNERS (continued)

007:033   assigning of **partners** to Allah, for which
007:190   the **partners** the ascribe to Him.
007:191   as **partners** things that can create nothing, but
009:031   from having the **partners** they associate (with Him).
010:018   the **partners** they ascribe (to Him)!"
010:028   ye and those ye joined as '**partners**'." We shall
010:028   and their "**partners**" shall say: "It was not
010:034   Say: "Of your `**partners**,' can any originate
010:035   Say: "Of your '**partners**' is there any that
010:066   as His "**partners**" other than Allah? They follow
010:071   about your plan and among your **Partners**, so your
011:055   "Other gods as **partners**! So scheme
012:038   any **partners** whatever to Allah: that comes
012:106   (others as **partners**) with Him!
013:016   to Allah **partners** who have created (anything)
013:033   they ascribe **partners** to Allah. Say: "But
013:036   and not to join **partners** with Him. Unto Him
016:001   the **partners** they ascribe unto Him!
016:003   above having the **partners** they ascribe to Him!
016:027   and say: "Where are My `**partners**' concerning whom
016:086   our '**partners**', those whom we used to invoke
016:086   When those who gave **partners** to Allah will see
016:086   will see their "**partners**," they will
016:100   who join **partners** with Allah.
018:042   Would I had never ascribed **partners** to my
018:052   My **partners**," and they will call on them, but they
022:031   if anyone assigns **partners** to Allah, he is
022:031   and never assigning **partners** to Him: if anyone
023:059   **partners** with their Lord;
023:092   for the **partners** they attribute to Him!
028:062   and say: "Where are my `**partners**'?-whom ye
028:064   "Call upon your `**partners**' (for help)": they will
028:068   and far is He above the **partners** they ascribe
028:074   He will say: "Where are My `**partners**' whom ye
030:013   among their "**Partners**," and they
030:013   and they will (themselves) reject their "**Partners**."
030:028   do ye have **partners** among those whom your
030:040   your (false) "**Partners**" who can do any single
030:040   the **partners** they attribute (to Him)!
034:027   joined with Him as **partners**: by no means
035:040   Say: "Have ye seen (these) `**partners**' of yours
038:024   the **Partners** (in business) who wrong each other:
039:029   a man belonging to many **partners** at variance
039:067   High is He above the **Partners** they attribute to Him!
040:012   **partners** were joined to Him, ye believed!
040:042   **partners** of whom I have no knowledge; and I
040:084   the One God-and we reject the **partners** we used
041:047   "Where are the **partners** (ye attributed) to Me?"
042:021   What! have they **partners** (in godhead), who have
043:039   that day, that ye shall be **partners** in punishment!
059:023   the **partners** they attribute to Him.
068:041   Or have they some "**Partners**" (in Godhead)?
068:041   produce their "**partners**," if they are truthful!

PARTNERSHIP

035:014   they will reject your "**Partnership**." And none,

PARTS

007:022   their shameful **parts** became manifest to them, and
015:090   divided (Scripture into arbitrary **parts**),-
017:005   very inmost **parts** of your homes; and it
017:106   (into **parts** from time to time), in order

PARTY

002:075 Seeing that a **party** of them heard
002:085 and banish a **party** of you from their homes;
002:100 some **party** among them throw it aside?
002:101 a **party** of the people of the Book
002:282 If the **party** liable is mentally deficient,
003:023 but a **party** of them turn back
004:102 let one **party** of them stand up
004:102 And let the other **party** come up which hath
004:113 a **party** of them would certainly have plotted
005:056 the **party** of Allah that must certainly triumph.
005:066 a **party** on the right course: but many
006:065 with confusion in **party** strife, giving you
007:075 The leaders of the arrogant **party** among his
007:076 The arrogant **party** said: "For our part, we
007:087 and a **party** which does not believe, hold
007:087 "And if there is a **party** among you who believes
007:088 The leaders, the arrogant **party** among his people,
008:005 even though a **party** among the Believers
012:014 a **party**, then should we be the losers!
016:092 lest one **party** should be more numerous
023:053 each **party** rejoices in that which is with itself.
024:002 and let a **party** of the Believers
026:064 And We made the other **party** approach thither.
028:081 **party** to help him against Allah, nor could
030:032 each **party** rejoicing in that which is with itself!
033:013 Behold! A **party** among them said: "Ye men
034:020 all but a **party** that believed.
037:083 Verily from his **party** was Abraham.
058:019 They are the **Party** of Satan. Truly, it
058:019 Truly, it is the **Party** of Satan that will lose.
058:022 They are the **Party** of Allah. Truly it
058:022 Truly it is the **Party** of Allah that will
073:020 and so doth a **party** of those with thee. But Allah

PASS

003:159 so **pass** over (their faults), and ask for (Allah's)
006:134 unto you will come to **pass**: nor can
007:040 **pass** through the eye of the needle: such is
010:048 to **pass**-if ye speak the truth?"
010:051 when it actually cometh to **pass**? (It will
010:071 and dubious. Then **pass** your sentence on me,
012:018 made up a tale (that may **pass**) with you, (for me)
012:029 "O Joseph, **pass** this over! (O wife),
012:105 and the earth do they **pass** by? Yet they
013:006 yet have come to **pass**, before them,
013:031 come to **pass**, for, verily, Allah will not fail
015:065 but **pass** on whither ye are ordered."
016:001 (Inevitable) cometh (to **pass**) the Command
017:005 came to **pass**, We sent against you Our servants
017:007 came to **pass**, (We permitted your enemies)
017:104 came to **pass**, We gathered you together in a
018:028 and let not thine eyes **pass** beyond them,
018:098 comes to **pass**, He will make it into dust; and the
019:061 for His promise must (necessarily) come to **pass**.
019:071 Not one of you but will **pass** over it: this is,
021:031 for them to **pass** through: that they
021:038 come to **pass**, if ye are telling the truth?"
025:072 and, if they **pass** by futility, they **pass**
025:072 they **pass** by it with honourable (avoidance);
027:071 (come to **pass**)? If ye are truthful."
027:088 but they shall **pass** away as the clouds **pass** away:
027:088 **pass** away: (such is) the artistry of Allah,
033:014 have brought it to **pass**, with none

PASS (continued)

034:029 (come to **pass**) if ye are telling the truth?"
036:048 this promise (come to **pass**), if what
037:137 Verily, ye **pass** by their (sites), by day-
038:033 Then began he to **pass** his hand over (their)
040:046 when the Hour comes to **pass**: "Cast ye
046:016 and **pass** by their ill deeds: (they shall
051:006 will surely come to **pass**.
052:007 will indeed come to **pass**;-
055:033 If it be ye can **pass** beyond the zones
055:033 **pass** ye! not without authority shall
055:033 authority shall ye be able to **pass**!
056:001 When the Event Inevitable cometh to **pass**,
057:023 over matters that **pass** you by, nor exult
069:015 On that Day shall the (Great) Event come to **pass**,
077:007 Assuredly, what ye are promised must come to **pass**.

PASSED

002:134 That was a People that hath **passed** away.
002:141 That was a people that hath **passed** away.
002:214 came to those who **passed** away before you?
002:259 of one who **passed** by a hamlet,
003:137 that have **passed** away before you:
003:144 many were the Messengers that **passed** away before Him.
005:075 that **passed** away before him. His mother
007:038 of the Peoples who **passed** away before you-men
007:175 but he **passed** them by: so Satan
010:102 of the men who **passed** away before them? Say:
011:038 his People **passed** by him, they threw
011:074 When fear had **passed** from (the mind of) Abraham
013:030 **passed** away; in order that thou mightest rehearse
018:062 When they had **passed** on (some distance), Moses said
024:034 people who **passed** away before you, and an
025:040 have **passed** by the town on which was rained
025:053 is not to be **passed**.
028:045 and long were the ages that **passed** over them;
033:038 that have **passed** away. And the
037:045 Round will be **passed** to them a Cup from a
037:171 Already has Our Word been **passed** before (this)
039:042 has **passed** the decree of death, He keeps
041:025 who have **passed** away, is proved against them;
043:008 than these;-and (thus) has **passed** on the example
043:071 To them will be **passed** round, dishes and
046:017 even though generations have **passed** before me
046:018 that have **passed** away; for they
057:016 **passed** over them and their hearts grew hard?
065:004 Such of your women as have **passed** the age
066:003 he confirmed part thereof and **passed** over a part.
076:015 And amongst them will be **passed** round vessels of
083:030 And whenever they **passed** by them, used to

PASSES

015:023 remain Inheritors (after all else **passes** away).

PASSETH

010:012 removed his affliction, he **passeth** on his way
089:004 And by the Night when it **passeth** away;-

PASSING

004:043 except when you are **passing** by (through the mosque),
005:015 and **passing** over much (that is now unnecessary):
009:064 showing them what is (really **passing**) in their

PASSION

012:024 And (with **passion**) did she desire him, and he
025:043 for his god his own **passion** (or impulse)?

PAST

002:275 shall be pardoned for the **past**;
004:022 your fathers married, except what is **past**:
004:023 except for what is **past**;
005:093 they ate (in the **past**), when they guard themselves
005:095 Allah forgives what is **past**: for repetition
007:053 from our behavior in the **past**." In fact
008:038 their **past** would be forgiven them; but if
009:005 But when the forbidden months are **past**, then fight
021:048 In the **past** We granted to Moses and Aaron
024:060 Such elderly women as are **past** the prospect
030:004 with Allah is the Command in the **Past** and in
031:012 We bestowed (in the **past**) wisdom on Luqman:
033:019 but when the fear is **past**, they will
034:054 as was in the **past** with their partisans: for they
035:024 lived among them (in the **past**).
036:054 but be repaid the meeds of your **past** Deeds.
043:056 And We made them (a people) of the **Past** and an
048:002 of the **past** and those to follow; fulfil His
048:023 already in the **past**: no change wilt thou find
054:051 And (oft) in the **past**, have We destroyed
056:024 A Reward for the Deeds of their **past** (Life).
057:028 (your **past**): for Allah is Oft-Forgiving,

PASTIME

021:017 a **pastime**, We should surely have taken it from
057:020 and a **pastime**, adornment and mutual boasting and
062:011 than any **pastime** or bargain! And Allah
062:011 or some **pastime**, they disperse headlong to it,

PASTURE

005:103 or a she-camel let loose for free **pasture**, or idol
016:006 lead them forth to **pasture** in the morning.
020:054 Eat (for yourselves) and **pasture** your cattle:
079:031 He draweth out therefrom its water and its **pasture**,
087:004 (green and luscious) **pasture**,

PATERNAL

033:050 and daughters of thy **paternal** uncles and aunts,

PATH

002:018 they will not return (to the **path**).
002:026 except those who forsake (the **path**),
002:026 and many He leads into the right **path**,
002:137 they are indeed on the right **path**;
002:213 to a **path** that is straight.
002:217 to the **path** of Allah to deny Him,
002:218 in the **path** of Allah,
002:272 the right **path** whom He pleaseth.
002:272 guide them to the right **path**.
003:099 who believe, from the **path** of Allah,
004:044 and wish that ye should lose the right **path**.
004:115 We shall leave him in the **path** he has chosen,
004:115 a **path** other than that becoming to men of Faith,
004:167 have verily strayed far, far away from the **Path**.
005:012 truly wandered from the **path** of rectitude."
005:016 guideth them to a **Path** that is Straight.
005:060 and far more astray from the even **Path**!"
006:056 if I did, I would stray from the **path**, and be
006:071 (vainly) guiding him to the **Path**."
006:153 they will scatter you about from His (great) **path**:
006:161 the **Path** (trod) by Abraham the true in faith, and
007:045 from the **path** of Allah desiring to make
007:086 the **path** of Allah those who believe in Him, and
007:155 Thou wilt into the right **path**. Thou art
007:178 he is on the right **path**: whom He

PATH (continued)

008:036 to hinder (men) from the **path** of Allah, and so
008:047 hinder (men) from the **path** of Allah: for Allah
010:088 from Thy **Path**. Deface our Lord the features
010:089 and follow not the **path** of those who know not."
011:019 **path** of Allah and wish it to be crooked: "These
011:056 Verily, it is my Lord that is on a Straight **Path**.
011:112 the straight **path**) as thou art commanded,-thou and
011:112 (from the **Path**): for He seeth well all that ye do.
013:033 from the **Path**. And those whom Allah leads
014:003 who hinder (men) from the **Path** of Allah and seek
014:030 to Allah, to mislead (men) from the **Path**! Say:
015:041 (Allah) said: "This is for me a straight **path**.
016:009 Allah alone can show the right **path** but there
016:088 (men) from the **Path** of Allah-for them will We
016:094 (men) from the **Path** of Allah, and a
016:125 who have strayed from His **Path**, and who
017:072 and most astray from the **Path**.
018:064 (the **path** they had come).
020:077 and strike a dry **path** for them through the sea,
022:009 from the **Path** of Allah: for him
022:024 to the **path** of Him Who is Worthy of (all) Praise.
025:017 or did they stray from the **Path** themselves?"
025:027 a (straight) **path** with the Messenger!
025:034 and, as to **path**, most astray.
025:042 who it is that is most misled in **Path**!
025:057 may take a (straight) **Path** to his Lord."
027:024 and has kept them away from the **Path**,-so they
027:079 for thou art on (the **Path** of) manifest Truth.
028:022 will show me the smooth and straight **Path**."
029:012 who believe: "Follow our **path**, and we
029:038 from the **Path**, though they were keen-sighted.
031:006 and throw ridicule (on the **Path**): for such
031:006 to mislead (men) from the **Path** of Allah and throw
033:036 on a clearly wrong **Path**.
033:067 and they misled us as to the (right) **path**.
034:006 and that it guides to the **path** of the
036:066 raced to the **Path**, but how
037:069 Truly they found their fathers on the wrong **Path**;
038:022 with injustice, but guide us to the even **Path**.
038:026 the **Path** of Allah, is a Chastisement
038:026 thee from the **Path** of Allah: for those
039:008 from Allah's **Path**. Say, "Enjoy
040:007 in repentance, and follow Thy **Path**; and preserve
040:029 but to the **Path** of Right!"
040:037 and he was hindered from the **Path**; and the
040:038 I will lead you to the **Path** of Right.
041:006 so take the straight **path** unto Him and ask for
043:037 the **Path**, but they think that they are being
046:013 (on that **Path**),-on them shall be no fear,
046:030 and to a Straight **Path**.
047:001 from the **Path** of Allah,-their deeds
047:014 Is then one who is on a clear (**Path**) from his Lord,
047:032 from the **Path** of Allah, and resist
047:034 from the **Path** of Allah, then die
047:038 the **Path**), He will substitute in your stead
048:020 you to a Straight **Path**;
053:030 those who stray from His **path**, and He
057:028 your **path**), and He will forgive you (your past):
058:016 **Path** of Allah: therefore shall they have
060:001 has strayed from the Straight **Path**.
063:002 thus they obstruct (men) from the **path** of Allah:
068:007 hath strayed from His **Path**: and He

PATH (continued)
069:007 in its (**path**), as if they had been roots of
072:014 they have sought out (the **path**) of right conduct:
073:019 a (straight) **path** to his Lord!
076:029 let him take a (straight) **Path** to his Lord.
080:020 Then doth He make His **path** smooth for him;
087:008 (to follow) the simple (**Path**).
090:011 on the **path** that is steep.
090:012 to thee the **path** that is steep?-
092:007 for him the **path** to Ease.
092:010 for him the **Path** to Misery;

PATHS
006:153 follow it: follow not (other) **paths**: they will
009:120 or trod **paths** to raise the ire of the Unbelievers,
029:069 to Our **Paths**: for verily Allah is with those
051:007 By the Sky with (its) numerous **Paths**,
072:011 we follow divergent **paths**.

PATIENCE
003:017 Those who show **patience**, (firmness and self-control);
003:200 Persevere in **patience** and constancy:
006:034 with **patience** and constancy they bore their
007:087 hold yourselves in **patience** until Allah
007:126 **patience** and constancy, and take
007:128 and (wait) in **patience** and constancy: for the
007:137 because they had **patience** and constancy, and We
011:011 Not so do those who show **patience** and constancy,
011:115 And be steadfast in **patience**; for verily
012:018 (For me) **patience** is most fitting: against that
012:083 for you. So **patience** is most fitting (for me).
013:024 in **patience**! Now how excellent is the final Home!"
014:012 We shall certainly bear with **patience** all the
014:021 (these torments) with **patience**: for ourselves
016:042 in **patience**, and put their trust on their Lord.
016:126 but if ye show **patience**, that is indeed
016:127 for thy **patience** is but with the help
018:067 be able to have **patience** with me!
018:068 "For how canst thou have **patience** about things
018:072 thou canst have no **patience** with me?"
018:075 thou canst have no **patience** with me?"
018:078 wast unable to hold **patience**.
018:082 thou wast unable to hold **patience**."
021:085 and Zul-kifl, all (men) of constancy and **patience**;
023:025 **patience**) with him for a time."
023:111 for their **patience** and constancy: they are
025:020 will ye have **patience**? For Allah
029:059 Those who persevere in **patience**, and put
032:024 with **patience** and continued to have faith
038:017 Have **patience** at what they say, and remember
038:044 of **patience** and constancy. How excellent
040:077 So persevere in **patience**! For the
041:024 If, then, they have **patience**, the Fire
041:035 exercise **patience** and self-restraint,-none but
042:043 But indeed if any show **patience** and forgive,
047:031 and persevere in **patience**; and We
049:005 If only they had **patience** until thou
050:039 Bear, then with **patience**, all that they say,
052:016 to you whether ye bear it with **patience**, or not:
052:048 Now await in **patience** the command of thy Lord:
054:027 and possess thyself in **patience**!
068:048 So wait with **patience** for the command of thy Lord,
070:005 a **Patience** of beautiful (contentment).
070:005 Therefore do thou hold **Patience**,-a **Patience**
073:010 And have **patience** with what they say, and leave

PATIENCE (continued)
090:017 and enjoin **patience**, (constancy, and self-restraint),
103:003 and of **Patience** and Constancy.

PATIENT
002:045 with **patient** perseverance and prayer:
002:153 with **patient** Perseverance and Prayer:
002:177 and to be firm and **patient**,
003:120 But if ye are **patient** and do right,
008:046 and be **patient** and persevering: for Allah
008:065 amongst you, **patient** and persevering, they will
008:066 **patient** and persevering, they will vanquish
010:109 and be **patient** and constant, till Allah
012:090 behold, he that is righteous and **patient**,-never
014:005 firmly **patient** and constant,-grateful and
016:126 for those who are **patient**.
016:127 And do thou be **patient**, for thy
018:069 if Allah so will, (truly) **patient**: nor shall
019:065 and **patient** in His worship: knowest thou
020:130 Therefore be **patient** with what they say,
022:035 who show **patient** perseverance over their
025:075 **patient** constancy; therein shall they be met
031:017 and bear with **patient** constancy whatever betide
033:035 for men and women who are **patient** and constant,
074:007 be **patient** and constant!
076:012 And because they were **patient** and constant, He will
076:024 Therefore be **patient** with constancy to the

PATIENTLY
002:153 for God is with those who **patiently** persevere.
002:155 to those who **patiently** persevere,
003:186 persevere **patiently**, and guard against evil,
008:046 for Allah is with those who **patiently** persevere.
008:066 for Allah is with those who **patiently** persevere.
011:049 So persevere **patiently**: for the End
013:022 Those who **patiently** persevere, seeking the
016:096 on those who **patiently** persevere, their reward
016:110 and **patiently** persevere,-thy Lord, after all
030:060 So **patiently** persevere: for verily
034:019 (soul that is) **patiently** constant and grateful.
039:010 Those who **patiently** persevere will truly
040:055 **Patiently**, then, persevere: for the Promise
042:033 everyone who **patiently** perseveres and is grateful.
046:035 Therefore **patiently** persevere, as did

PATRON
002:107 have neither **patron** nor helper.
016:063 he is also their **patron** to-day, so but
016:100 who take him as **patron** and who join
022:013 is the **patron**, and evil the companion (for help)!

PATRONS
002:257 the **patrons** are the Tagut from light
003:064 lords and **patrons** other than Allah."
003:080 to take angels and prophets for Lords and **Patrons**.

PAVED
027:044 **paved** smooth with slabs of glass." She said:

PAVILIONS
055:072 their glances), in (goodly) **pavilions**:-

PAY
002:233 provided ye **pay** (the foster mother)
003:057 Allah will **pay** them (in full) their reward;
003:075 will (readily) **pay** it back;
004:092 And **pay** blood-money to the deceased's family,
004:162 regular prayer and **pay** Zakat and believe in
005:012 **pay** Zakat believe in My Messengers, honour and

PAY (continued)

005:055 and **pay** Zakat and they bow down
007:156 and **pay** Zakat and those who believe in Our Signs;
009:005 regular prayers. And **pay** Zakat, then open
009:011 establish regular prayers, and **pay** Zakat they are
009:018 establish regular prayers, and **pay** Zakat, and fear
009:029 until they **pay** Jizya with willing submission,
009:071 regular prayers, **pay** Zakat and obey Allah and His
011:015 to them We shall **pay** (the price of) their deeds
011:109 **pay** them back (in full) their portion
011:111 your Lord **pay** back (in full the recompense)
012:059 I **pay** out full measure, and that
012:088 so **pay** us full measure, (we pray thee), and treat
024:025 On that Day Allah will **pay** them back (all) their
024:039 and Allah will **pay** him his account: and Allah
030:033 some of them **pay** part-worship to other gods
030:035 to which they **pay** part-worship?
035:030 For He will **pay** them their meed, nay, He will
037:013 And, when they are admonished, **pay** no heed,-
041:007 Those who **pay** not zakat, and who
060:010 for them. But **pay** the Unbelievers what they
060:011 Then **pay** to those whose wives have deserted

PAYING

024:037 nor from **paying** zakat their (only) fear is for

PAYMENT

004:011 after the **payment** of legacies and debts.
004:012 after **payment** of legacies and debts;
060:010 if ye marry them on **payment** of their dower to them.

PAYMENTS

009:098 their **payments** as a fine, and watch
009:099 and look on their **payments** as pious gifts bringing

PEACE

002:126 make this a City of **Peace**,
002:224 or making **peace** between persons;
004:090 between whom and you there is a treaty (of **peace**),
004:090 and (instead) send you (guarantees of) **peace**, then
004:091 nor give you guarantees of **peace** besides
005:016 His good pleasure to ways of **peace** and safety,
006:054 "**Peace** be on you: your Lord hath inscribed for
006:127 a Home of **Peace** with their Lord: He will
007:046 "**Peace** be upon you": they have not entered it, but
007:204 and hold your **peace**: that ye may receive Mercy.
008:061 do thou (also) incline towards **peace**, and trust
008:061 But if the enemy incline towards **peace**, do thou
009:040 then Allah sent down His **peace** upon him,
010:010 "Glory to Thee, O Allah!" and "**Peace**" will be
010:025 But Allah doth call to the Home of **Peace**: He doth
011:048 (from the Ark) with **Peace** from Us, and Blessing
011:069 "**Peace**!" and hastened to entertain them with
011:069 They said, "**Peace**!" He answered, "**Peace**!" and
013:024 "**Peace** unto you for that ye persevered in patience!
014:023 their greeting therein will be: "**Peace**!"
014:035 make this city one of **peace** and security:
015:046 "Enter ye here in **Peace** and Security."
015:052 and said, "**Peace**!" He said, "We feel
016:032 saying (to them), "**Peace** be on you; enter ye
017:095 on earth, angels walking about in **peace** and quite,
019:015 So **Peace** on him the day he was born, the day
019:033 "So **Peace** is on me the day I was born, the day
019:047 Abraham said: "**Peace** be on thee: I will
019:062 of **Peace**: and they will have therein their
020:047 And **peace** to all who follow guidance!

PEACE (continued)

024:055 to one of security and **peace**: 'They will
025:063 they say, "**Peace**!"
025:075 be met with salutations and **peace**,
027:059 and **Peace** on His servants whom He has chosen
028:055 **peace** be to you: we seek not the ignorant."
033:044 they meet Him will be "**peace**!"; and He
036:058 "**Peace**!"-a Word (of salutation) from a
037:079 "**Peace** and salutation to Noah among the nations!"
037:109 "**Peace** and salutation to Abraham!"
037:120 "**Peace** and salutation to Moses and Aaron!"
037:130 "**Peace** and salutation to such as Elias!"
037:181 And **Peace** on the messengers!
039:073 and its Keepers will say: "**Peace** be upon you!
043:089 and say "**Peace**!" but soon shall they know!
044:055 of fruit in **peace** and security;
047:035 for **peace**, when ye are the Uppermost: for Allah
049:009 fall into a fight, make ye **peace** between them:
049:009 then make **peace** between them with justice,
049:010 **peace** and reconciliation between your two
050:034 "Enter ye therein in **Peace** and Security; this Day
051:025 and said: "**Peace**!" He said, "**Peace**!" (And thought
056:026 Only the saying, "**Peace**! **Peace**."
056:091 "**Peace** be unto thee," from the Companions
059:023 the Holy One, the Source of **Peace** (and Perfection).
097:005 **Peace**!...This until the rise of Morn!

PEACEFUL

002:196 and when ye are in **peaceful** conditions (again),

PEARLS

022:023 with bracelets of gold and **pearls**; and their
035:033 with bracelets of gold and **pearls**; and their
052:024 as **Pearls** well-guarded.
055:022 Out of them come **Pearls** and Coral:
056:023 Like unto **Pearls** well-guarded.
076:019 thou wouldst think them scattered **Pearls**.

PEGS

078:007 And the mountains as **pegs**?

PEN

068:001 Nun. By the **Pen** and by the (Record) which (men)
096:004 He Who taught (the use of) the **Pen**,-

PENALTIES

038:058 And other **Penalties** of a similar kind, to match

PENALTY

002:162 Their **penalty** will not be lightened,
005:095 that he may taste of the **penalty** of his deed.
006:016 if the **penalty** is averted from any, it is
009:039 grievous **penalty**, and put others in your place;
012:074 shall be the **penalty** of this, if ye are
012:075 They said: "The **penalty** should be that he in whose
013:034 For them is a **Penalty** in the life of this world,
020:097 (for a future **penalty**) thou hast a promise that
025:019 (your **penalty**) nor (get) help." And whoever
040:046 into the severest **Penalty**"
041:016 in this life; but the **Penalty** of the Hereafter
042:045 to the (**Penalty**), abject in humbleness (and)
069:010 with an abundant **Penalty**.
070:003 (A **Penalty**) from Allah, Lord of the Ways of Ascent.

PENETRATE

100:005 And **penetrate** forthwith into the midst

PENETRATED

019:078 Has he **penetrated** to the Unseen, or he has

PENITENCE

011:075   and given to **penitence**.
013:027   to himself those who turn to Him in **penitence**,-
017:025   turn to Him again and again (in true **penitence**).

PENITENT

050:032   for everyone **penitent** heedful one,

PENS

003:044   when they cast lots with **pens**,
031:027   And if all the trees on earth were **pens** and the
054:031   the dry stubble used by one who **pens** cattle.

PEOPLE

002:008   Of the **people** there are some who say
002:021   O ye **people**! worship your Guardian-Lord,
002:036   And We said: "Get ye down, (all you **people**),
002:044   Do ye enjoin right conduct on the **people**,
002:049   delivered you from the **people** of Pharaoh:
002:050   drowned Pharaoh's **people** within your very sight.
002:054   "O my **people**! Ye have indeed wronged yourselves
002:054   And remember Moses said to his **people**:
002:060   for water for his **people**;
002:067   And remember Moses said to his **people**:
002:083   speak fair to the **people**;
002:084   your own **people** from your homes:
002:085   After this it is ye, the same **people**,
002:086   These are the **people** who buy the life
002:096   of all **people**, most greedy of life,
002:101   a party of the **people** of the Book
002:105   without Faith among the **people** of the Book
002:109   Quite a number of the **people** of the Book
002:109   wish they could turn you (**people**)
002:118   the Signs unto any **people** who hold
002:118   So said the **people** before them
002:124   an Imam to the **people**."
002:126   and feed its **People** with fruits,
002:128   and of our progeny a **people** Muslim,
002:134   That was a **People** that hath passed away.
002:141   That was a **people** that hath passed away.
002:142   The Fools among the **people** will say:
002:143   For Allah is to all **people** most surely
002:144   The **people** of the book know well that
002:145   the **people** of the Book all the Signs
002:146   The **people** of the Book know this
002:150   of dispute against you among the **people**,
002:159   clear for the **People** in the Book,
002:164   Signs for a **people** that are wise.
002:168   O ye **people**! eat of what is on earth,
002:177   Such are the **people** of truth, the God-fearing.
002:213   to judge between **people** in matters
002:213   but the **People** of the Book,
002:251   one set of **people** by means of another,
002:258   Nor doth Allah give guidance to a **people** unjust.
002:259   make of thee a Sign unto the **people**.
003:011   the **people** of Pharaoh, and their predecessors:
003:019   nor did the **People** of the Book
003:020   And say to the **People** of the Book
003:033   and the family of 'Imran above all **people**,
003:046   "He shall speak to the **people** in childhood
003:064   Say: "O **people** of the Book!
003:065   Ye **people** of the Book! why dispute ye about Abraham,
003:069   the **People** of the Book to lead you astray.
003:070   Ye **People** of the Book!
003:071   Ye **People** of the Book!

PEOPLE (continued)

003:072   A section of the **People** of the Book say: "Believe
003:075   no way over us as to the Unlettered **people**,"
003:075   Among the **People** of the Book are some who,
003:079   should say to **people**: "Be ye my worshippers
003:086   But Allah guides not a **people** unjust.
003:098   Say: "O **people** of the Book!
003:099   Say: "O ye **People** of the Book!
003:100   listen to a faction among the **People** of the Book,
003:104   a band of **people** inviting to all that is good,
003:110   If only the **People** of the Book had faith,
003:113   of the **People** of the book are a portion that stand
003:187   a Covenant from the **People** of the Book,
003:199   among the **people** of the Book, those who
004:041   How then if We brought from each **People** a witness,
004:041   a witness against these **People**!
004:047   O ye **people** of the Book! believe in what
004:054   the **people** of Abraham the Book and Wisdom, and
004:058   and when ye judge between **people** that ye
004:075   Whose **people** are oppressors; and raise for us
004:078   But what hath come to these **people**.
004:090   you or fighting their own **people**.
004:091   secure from you as well as that of their **people**:
004:092   to a **people** at war with you, and he was Believer,
004:092   If he belonged to a **people** with whom
004:105   that thou mightest judge between **people** by that
004:108   They seek to hide themselves from the **people** but
004:114   between **people** (secrecy is permissible): to him
004:123   nor those of the **people** of the Book (can prevail):
004:131   the **people** of the Book before you, and you
004:153   The **people** of the Book ask thee to cause
004:159   And there is none of the **People** of the Book
004:171   O **people** of the Book! commit no excesses
005:002   nor the **people** resorting to the Sacred House,
005:002   of some **people** in (once) shutting you out
005:005   but chaste women among the **People** of the Book,
005:005   The food of the **People** of the Book is lawful
005:015   O **People** of the Book! there hath come
005:019   O **people** of the Book! now hath come
005:020   "O my **people**! call in remembrance the favour
005:020   Remember Moses said to his **people**: "O my **people**!
005:021   "O my **people**! enter the holy land which Allah
005:022   are a **people** of exceeding strength: never shall
005:025   so separate us from this rebellious **people**!"
005:026   but sorrow thou not over these rebellious **people**."
005:032   it would be as if he slew the whole **people**: and if
005:032   he saved the life of the whole **people**.
005:043   For they are not (really) **people** of Faith.
005:047   Let the **people** of the Gospel Judge by what
005:048   He would have made you a single **People**, but
005:050   But who, for a **people** whose faith is assured, can
005:051   Verily Allah guideth not a **people** unjust.
005:054   soon will Allah produce a **people** whom He will
005:058   a **people** without understanding.
005:059   Say: "O **People** of the Book! do ye disapprove
005:065   If only the **people** of the Book had believed
005:068   over (these) **people** without Faith.
005:068   Say: "O **People** of the Book! ye have
005:077   of **people** who went wrong in times gone by,-who
005:077   Say: "O **people** of the Book! exceed not
005:102   Some **people** before you did ask such questions, and
005:108   for Allah guideth not a rebellious **people**.
005:110   to the **people** in childhood and in old age. Behold!

PEOPLE (continued)

006:066 But thy **people** reject this, though it is
006:074 For I see thee and thy **people** in manifest error."
006:078 "O my **people**! I am indeed free from your (guilt)
006:080 His **people** disputed with him. He said:
006:083 (to use) against his **people**: We raise
006:089 to a new **People** who reject them not.
006:097 We detail Our Signs for **people** who know.
006:098 We detail Our signs for **people** who understand.
006:099 are signs for **people** who believe.
006:108 alluring to each **people** its own doings. In the
006:133 you up from the posterity of other **people**.
006:135 Say: "O my **people**! do whatever ye can: I will
006:145 For Allah guideth not **people** who do wrong.
006:147 but from **people** in guilt never will
007:034 To every **People** is a term. Appointed: when their
007:038 Every time a new **People** enters, it curses
007:059 We sent Noah to his **people**. He said: "O
007:059 He said: "O my **people**! worship Allah!
007:060 The leaders of his **people** said: "Ah! we see
007:061 He said: "O my **people**! there is no error in me: on
007:063 through a man of your own **people**, to warn
007:064 they were indeed a blind **people**!
007:065 He said: "O my **people**! worship Allah! ye have
007:065 To the 'Ad **people**, (We sent) Hud, one of
007:066 among his **people** said: "Ah! we see
007:067 He said: "O my **people**! there is
007:069 the **people** of Noah, and gave you
007:069 of your own **people**, to warn you? Call
007:073 he said: "O my **people**! worship Allah; ye have
007:073 To the Thamud **people** (We sent) Salih, one of
007:074 inheritors after the 'Ad **people** and gave
007:075 among his **people** said to those who were
007:079 saying: "O my **people**! I indeed convey to you
007:080 We also (sent) Lut: he said to his **people**: "Do
007:080 no **people** in creation (ever) committed before you?
007:081 ye are indeed a **people** transgressing beyond bounds."
007:082 And his **people** gave no answer but this: they said,
007:085 To the Madyan **people** We sent Shu'aib, one of
007:085 he said: "O my **people**! worship Allah; ye have
007:085 nor withhold from the **people** the things
007:088 The leaders, the arrogant party among his **people**,
007:089 and our **people** in truth, for thou
007:090 The leaders, the Unbelievers among his **people**,
007:093 saying: "O my **people**! I did indeed convey to
007:093 a **people** who refuse to believe!"
007:094 We took up its **people** in suffering
007:096 If the **people** of the towns had but
007:097 Did the **people** of the towns feel secure
007:105 Now have I come unto you (**people**), from your
007:109 Said the Chiefs of the **people** of Pharaoh: "This
007:116 they bewitched the eyes of the **people**, and
007:123 to drive out its **people**: but soon
007:127 "Wilt thou leave Moses and his **people**, to
007:127 Said the chiefs of Pharaoh's **people**: "Wilt
007:128 Said Moses to his **people**: "Pray for help
007:130 We punished the **people** of Pharaoh with years
007:133 a **people** given to sin.
007:137 And We made a **people**, considered weak
007:137 which Pharaoh and his **people** erected
007:138 They came upon a **people** devoted entirely
007:138 He said: "Surely ye are a **people** without knowledge."
007:141 you from Pharaoh's **people**, who afflicted

PEOPLE (continued)

007:142 "Act for me amongst my **people**: do right,
007:145 and enjoin the **people** to hold fast by the
007:148 The **people** of Moses made, in his absence, out of
007:150 The **people** did indeed reckon me as naught, and
007:150 When Moses came back to his **people**, angry and
007:150 nor count thou me amongst the **people** of sin."
007:155 of his **people** for Our place of meeting: when
007:159 Of the **people** of Moses there is
007:160 when his (thirsty) **people** asked him for Water:
007:164 preach to a **people** whom Allah will destroy or
007:177 Evil as an example are **people** who reject
007:181 Of those We have created are **people** who direct
008:049 say: "These **people**,-their religion has
008:052 the **people** of Pharaoh and of those before them:
008:053 on a **people** until they change what is in their
008:054 the **people** of Pharaoh and those before them":
008:054 and We drowned the **people** of Pharaoh: for they
008:065 for these are a **people** without understanding.
008:072 except against a **people** with whom ye have
009:003 His Messenger, to the **people** (assembled) on the
009:013 Will ye not fight **people** who violated
009:020 They are the **people** who will achieve (salvation).
009:029 from among the **People** of the Book, until they
009:053 a **people** rebellious and wicked."
009:070 the **people** of Abraham, the men of Madyan, and the
009:070 of those before them? The **people** of Noah, and Ad,
009:109 And Allah guideth not **people** that do wrong.
009:115 And Allah will not mislead a **people** after He
009:120 It was not fitting for the **people** of Madinah
009:122 and admonish the **people** when they return to them,-
009:127 for they are a **people** that understand not.
010:024 (in beauty): the **people** to whom it belongs think
010:047 To every **people** (was sent) an Messenger: when their
010:049 Allah willeth. To every **People** is a term appointed:
010:071 "O my **People**, if it be hard on your (mind) that I
010:071 Behold! he said to his **People**: "O my **People**,
010:075 But they were arrogant: they were a wicked **people**.
010:083 except some children of his **People**, because of
010:084 Moses said: "O my **People**! if ye do
010:087 for your **People** in Egypt, make your dewllings
010:098 except the **people** of Jonah? When they
011:025 We sent Noah to his **People** (with a
011:027 among his **people** said: "We see (in) thee
011:028 He said: "O my **people**! see ye if (it be that)
011:029 "And O my **People**! I ask you
011:030 "And O my **People**! who would help me
011:036 "None of thy **People** will believe except those
011:038 his **People** passed by him, they threw
011:049 nor thy **People** knew them. So persevere
011:050 To the 'Ad **People** (We sent) Hud, one of
011:050 He said: "O my **people**! worship Allah! ye have
011:051 "O my **people**! I ask of you no reward
011:052 "And O my **people**! ask forgiveness of your Lord,
011:057 make another **People** to succeed you, and you
011:059 Such were the 'Ad **People**: they rejected
011:060 Away with the 'Ad the **People** of Hud!
011:061 To the Thamud **People** (We sent) Salih, one of
011:061 He said: "O my **people**! worship Allah: ye have
011:063 He said: "O my **people**! Do ye see?-If I have
011:064 "And O my **people**! this she-camel of Allah
011:070 been sent against the **people** of Lut."
011:073 O ye **people** of the house! For He is indeed

PEOPLE (continued)

011:074	with Us for Lut's **people**.
011:078	He said: "O my **people**! here are my daughters:
011:078	And his **people** came rushing towards him, and they
011:081	to the **people**. Morning is their time appointed:
011:084	he said: "O my **people**! worship Allah: ye have
011:084	To the Madyan **people** (We sent) Shu'aib, one of
011:085	"And O my **people**! give just measure and weight,
011:085	the **people** the things that are their due:
011:088	He said: "O my **people**! see ye whether I have
011:089	"And O my **people**! let not my dissent (from you)
011:089	of the **people** of Noah or of Hud or of Salih,
011:089	the **people** of Lut far off from you!
011:092	He said: "O my **people**! is then my family of more
011:093	"And O my **people**! do whatever ye can: I will
011:098	He will go before his **people** on the
011:117	their **people** are righteous.
011:118	He could have made mankind one **People**: but they
012:037	of a **people** that believe not in Allah and that
012:046	that I may return to the **people**, and that
012:049	a year in which the **people** will have abundant
012:062	when they return to their **people**, in order
012:109	did inspire,-(men) from the **people** of the towns.
012:110	(of their **people**) and (come to) think that they
013:007	and to every **people** a guide.
013:011	the condition of a **people** until they
013:030	a **People** before whom (long since) have (other)
014:004	in the language of his (own) **people**, in order
014:005	thy **people** from the depths of darkness into light,
014:006	Remember! Moses said to his **people**: "Call to mind
014:006	the **people** of Pharaoh: they set you hard task
014:009	(O **people**!), of those who (went) before you?
014:009	before you? Of the **People** of Noah, and 'Ad,
014:028	and caused their **people** to descend to the
015:005	Neither can a **people** anticipate its Term,
015:058	to a **people** (deep) in sin,
016:036	and eschew Evil": of the **people** were some whom
016:036	every **People** a messenger, (with the Command),
016:059	his **people**, because of the bad news he has had!
016:089	against these (thy **people**): and We
016:093	you all one **People**: but He leaves straying whom
016:112	because of the (evil) which (its **people**) wrought.
018:015	"These our **people** have taken for worship
018:021	to the **people**, that they might know that the
018:080	his parents were **people** of Faith, and we
018:086	near it he found a **People**: We said:
018:090	the sun, he found it rising on a **people** for whom
018:093	beneath them, a **people** who scarcely
018:094	the Gog and Magog (**people**) do great mischief
019:011	So Zakariya came out to his **people** from his
019:027	to her **people**, carrying him (in her arms),
019:055	He used to enjoin on his **people** Prayer and Zakat
019:097	and warnings to **people** given to contention.
020:040	with the **people** of Midian. Then didst
020:059	the Festival, and let the **people** be assembled
020:079	Pharaoh led his **people** astray instead of
020:083	in advance of thy **people**, O Moses?"
020:085	(Allah) said: "We have tested thy **people** in thy
020:086	He said: "O my **people**! did not your Lord make a
020:086	So Moses returned to his **people** in state
020:087	of the ornaments of the (whole) **people**, and we
020:088	before the (**people**) the image of a calf: it seemed
020:090	said to them: "O my **people**! ye are being tested

PEOPLE (continued)

020:132	Enjoin prayer on thy **people**, and be
021:052	and his **people**, "What are these images, to which
021:061	the eyes of the **people**, that they
021:074	truly they were a **people** given to Evil,
021:074	given to Evil, a rebellious **people**.
021:077	truly they were a **people** given to Evil: so We
021:077	We helped him against **people** who rejected
021:078	of certain **people** had strayed by night: We did
021:084	and We restored his **people** to him, and doubled
021:096	Until the Gog and Magog (**people**) are let
021:106	for **people** who would (truly) worship Allah.
022:034	To every **people** did We appoint rites (of
022:040	of **people** by means of another, there would
022:042	their prophets),-the **People** of Noah, and 'Ad
022:044	Madyan **people**; and Moses was rejected (in the
022:067	To every **People** have We appointed rites
023:023	to his **people**: he said, "O my **people**!
023:023	"O my **people**! worship Allah! Ye have
023:024	his **people** said: "He is no more than a man
023:028	Who has saved us from the **people** who do wrong."
023:033	And the chiefs of his **people**, who disbelieved
023:041	So away with the **people** who do wrong!
023:043	No **people** can hasten their term, nor can
023:044	a **people** their messenger, they accused
023:044	a **people** that will not believe!
023:046	they were an arrogant **people**.
023:047	And their **people** are subject to us!"
023:053	But **people** have cut off their affair (of unity),
023:094	amongst the **people** who do wrong!"
023:106	and we became a **people** astray!
024:012	the affair,-though well of their **people** and say,
024:026	**people** say: for them there is forgiveness, and a
024:034	**people** who passed away before you, and an
025:018	for they were a **people** destroyed."
025:030	"O my Lord, Truly my **people** treated this Qur'an
025:036	Our Signs": and those (**people**) We destroyed
025:036	to the **people** who have rejected Our Signs":
025:037	And the **people** of Noah,-when they
026:010	"Go to the **people** of iniquity,-
026:011	"The **people** of Pharaoh: will they not fear Allah?"
026:039	And the **people** were told: "Are ye
026:061	saw each other, the **people** of Moses said: "We are
026:070	and his **people**: "What worship ye?"
026:105	The **people** of Noah rejected the messengers.
026:117	truly my **people** have rejected me.
026:123	The 'Ad (**people**) rejected the messengers.
026:141	The Thamud (**people**) rejected the messengers.
026:160	The **people** of Lut rejected the messengers.
026:166	Nay, ye are a **people** transgressing (all limits)!"
026:221	Shall I inform you, (O **people**!), on whom
027:012	and his **people**: for they are a **people**
027:012	a **people** rebellious in transgression."
027:016	He said: "O ye **people**! we have been taught
027:024	"I found her and her **people** worshipping the
027:034	make the noblest of its **people** meanest thus do
027:043	for she was (sprung) of a **people** that had no faith.
027:046	He said: "O my **people**! why ask ye to hasten
027:047	yea, ye are a **people** under trial."
027:049	on him and his **people**, and that
027:049	of his **people**, and we are
027:051	destroyed them and their **people**, (all of them).
027:052	Verily in this is a Sign for **people** of knowledge.

PEOPLE (continued)

027:054   behold, he said to his **people**, "Do ye
027:055   Nay, ye are a **people** (grossly) ignorant!"
027:056   But his **people** gave no other answer but this:
027:060   Nay, they are a **people** who swerve from justice.
027:083   from every **people** a troop of those who reject
027:086   for any **people** that believe!
028:003   in Truth, for **people** who believe.
028:004   in the land and divided its **people** into sections,
028:008   Then the **people** of Pharaoh picked him up
028:012   the **people** of a house that will nourish and bring
028:015   one of his own **people**, and the other, of his
028:015   his own **people** appealed to him against his foe,
028:015   when its **people** were not watching: and he
028:021   save me from **people** given to wrong-doing."
028:025   (well) hast thou escaped from unjust **people**."
028:032   for truly they are a **people** rebellious and wicked."
028:045   a dweller among the **people** of Madyan,
028:046   to give warning to a **people** to whom no warner
028:050   For Allah guides not **people** given to wrong-doing.
028:075   And from each **people** shall We draw a witness,
028:076   Behold, his **people** said to him: "Exult not,
028:076   Qarun was doubtless, of the **people** of Moses;
028:079   So he went forth among his **people** in the
029:014   We did sent Noah to his **people**, and he
029:016   he said to his **people**, "Serve Allah
029:024   Verily in this are Signs for **people** who believe.
029:024   (Abraham's) **people** except that they said: "Slay him
029:028   he said to his **people**: "Ye do commit lewdness,
029:028   commit lewdness, such as no **people** in Creation
029:029   your councils?" But his **people** gave no answer
029:030   me against **people** who do mischief!"
029:031   the **people** of this township: for truly
029:034   on the **people** of this township a Punishment
029:035   for any **people** who (care to) understand.
029:036   Then he said: "O my **people**! serve Allah,
029:036   To the Madyan (**people**) (We sent)
029:038   the Thamud (**people**): clearly will appear to you
029:046   And dispute ye not with the **People** of the Book,
029:047   So the **People** of the Book believe therein,
030:028   to a **people** that understand.
030:039   of (other) **people**, will have no increase with
032:003   that thou mayest admonish a **people** to whom
033:026   And those of the **people** of the Book who aided
033:037   the **people**, but it is more fitting that thou
035:024   a **people**, without a warner having lived among
036:006   warn a **people**, whose fathers were not warned,
036:015   The (**people**) said: "Ye are only men like ourselves;
036:018   The (**people**) said: "For us, We augur an evil
036:019   Nay, but ye are a **people** transgressing all bounds!"
036:020   a man, saying, "O my **People**! obey the messengers:
036:026   my **People** knew (what I know)!-
036:028   his **People**, after Him, any hosts from heaven,
036:050   nor to return to their own **people**!
037:030   a **people** in obstinate rebellion!
037:076   And We delivered him and his **people** from the
037:085   his **people**, "What is that which ye worship?
037:115   and their **people** from (their) Great distress.
037:124   Behold, he said to his **people**, "Will ye
038:012   rejected messengers,-the **People** of Noah, and 'Ad,
038:013   And Thamud, and the **People** of Lut, and the
038:043   And We gave him (back) his **people** and double
038:064   of the **People** of the Fire!

PEOPLE (continued)

039:015   who lose their own souls and their **people** on the
039:039   Say: "O my **people**! Do whatever ye can: I will
040:005   after them; and every **People** plotted against
040:005   But (there were **people**) before them, who denied
040:005   who denied (the Signs),-the **People** of Noah,
040:028   A Believer, a man from among the **people** of Pharaoh,
040:029   "O my **people**! yours is the dominion this day:
040:030   "O my **People**! truly I do fear for you something
040:031   "Something like the fate of the **people** of Noah,
040:032   "And, O my **People**! I fear for you a Day
040:038   "O my **People**! follow me: I will
040:039   "O my **people**! This life of the present is nothing
040:041   "And O my **People**! how (strange) it is for me
040:045   encompassed on all sides the **People** of Pharaoh.
040:046   "Cast ye the **People** of Pharaoh into the
041:003   for **people** who understand;-
042:008   He could have made them a single **people**; but He
043:005   a **people** transgressing beyond bounds?
043:023   a Warner before thee to any **people**, the wealthy
043:026   and his **people**: "I do indeed clear myself of what
043:044   for thee and for thy **people**; and soon
043:051   And Pharaoh proclaimed among his **people**, saying:
043:051   saying: "O my **people**! Does not the dominion
043:054   Thus did he make fools of his **people**, and they
043:054   truly were they a **people** rebellious (against Allah).
043:056   And We made them (a **people**) of the Past and an
043:057   as an example, behold thy **people** raise a clamour
043:058   they are a contentious **people**.
043:088   Truly these are a **people** who believe not!"
044:011   Enveloping the **people**: this will
044:017   We did, before them, try the **people** of Pharaoh:
044:022   "These are indeed a **people** given to sin."
044:028   And We made other **people** inherit (those things)!
044:037   What! are they better than the **people** of Tubba
045:014   or ill) each **People** according to what
045:031   and were a **people** given to sin!
046:010   Allah guides not a **people** unjust."
046:021   his **people** beside the winding Sand-tracts:
046:023   but I see that ye are a **people** in ignorance!"...
046:029   to their **people**, to warn them.
046:030   They said, "O our **people**! We have
046:031   "O our **people**, hearken to the one who invites
047:038   in your stead another **people**; then they
048:012   evil thought, for ye are a **people** doomed to perish."
048:016   (to fight) against a **people** given to vehement war
049:006   harm **people** unwittingly, and afterwards
050:012   by the **people** of Noah, the Companions
050:014   and the **people** of Tubba'; each one
051:025   (And thought, "These seem) unusual **people**."
051:032   a **people** (deep) in sin;-
051:041   And in the 'Ad (**people**) (was another
051:046   So were the **people** of Noah before them: for they
051:053   themselves a **people** transgressing beyond bounds!
052:026   not without fear for the sake of our **people**.
052:032   a **people** transgressing beyond bounds?
053:050   the (powerful) ancient 'Ad (**people**),
053:052   And before them, the **people** of Noah, for that
054:009   Before them the **People** of Noah rejected
054:018   The 'Ad (**people**) (too) rejected (Truth): then how
054:025   of all **people** amongst us? Nay, he is
054:033   The **People** of Lut rejected (his) Warning.
054:041   To the **people** of Pharaoh, too, aforetime,

PEOPLE (continued)

054:042 The (**people**) rejected all Our Signs; but We
056:013 A number of **people** from those of old,
057:029 That the **People** of the Book may know that they
058:022 Thou wilt not find any **people** who believe
059:002 among the **People** of the Book from their homes
059:007 (and taken away) from the **people** of the townships,-
059:011 among the **People** the **People** of the Book?-"If ye
059:014 that is because they are a **people** devoid of wisdom.
060:004 with him, when they said to their **people**: "We are
060:013 (for friendship) to **people** on whom is the Wrath
061:005 And remember, Moses said to his **people**: "O my
061:005 "O my **people**! why do ye vex and insult me,
062:005 Evil is the similitude of **people** who falsify
062:005 and Allah guides not **people** who do wrong.
068:017 the **People** of the Garden, when they
068:035 Shall We then treat the **People** of Faith
068:035 of Faith like the **People** of Sin?
069:004 The Thamud and the 'Ad **people** disbelieved in
069:007 the (whole) **people** lying overthrown in its (path),
071:001 We sent Noah to his **People** (with the Command):
071:001 thy **People** before there comes to them
071:002 He said: "O my **People**! I am to you a Warner,
071:005 to my **People** night and day:
074:031 in order that the **People** of the Book may arrive
074:031 for the **People** of the book and the Believers,
081:022 And (O **people**!) your Companion is not one possessed;
083:031 to their own **people**, they would return jesting;
083:032 "Behold! these are the **people** truly astray!"
084:009 And he will turn to his **people**, rejoicing!
084:013 Truly, did he go about among his **people**, rejoicing!
089:006 dealt with the 'Ad (**people**),-
089:009 And with the Thamud (**people**), who cut
091:011 The Thamud (**people**) rejected (their prophet)
098:001 Those who disbelieve, among the **People** of the
098:004 Nor did the **people** of the Book make schisms,
098:006 Those who disbelieve, among the **People** of the
110:002 And thou dost see the **People** enter Allah's

PEOPLE'S

002:188 and knowingly a little of (other) **people's** property.
013:011 a **people's** punishment, there can be no turning

PEOPLES

003:110 Ye are the best of **Peoples**, evolved for mankind.
005:020 He had not given to any other among the **peoples**.
005:115 on anyone among all the **peoples**.
006:156 sent down to two **Peoples** before us, and for
007:038 of the **Peoples** who passed away before you-men
010:074 (many) messengers to their **Peoples**: they brought
011:048 be other) **Peoples** to whom We shall grant their
011:048 the **Peoples** (who will spring) from those
013:030 have (other) **Peoples** (gone and) passed away;
016:063 (our prophets) to **Peoples** before thee; but Satan
016:084 from all **Peoples** a Witness: then will
016:089 all **peoples** a witness against them, from amongst
021:011 in their places other **peoples**?
021:091 and her son a Sign for all **peoples**.
022:042 the **Peoples** before them (with their prophets),-
026:196 in the revealed Books of former **peoples**.
029:015 a Sign for all **Peoples**!
030:047 messengers to their (respective) **peoples**, and they
043:006 We sent amongst the **peoples** of old?
043:008 the example of the **peoples** of old.
051:052 the **Peoples** before them, but they said (of him)

PERCEIVE

002:154 though ye **perceive** (it) not.
003:069 but themselves, and they do not **perceive**!
006:026 and they **perceive** it not.
006:123 and they **perceive** it not.
012:015 this affair while they **perceive** not."
012:107 while they **perceive** not?
016:026 from directions they did not **perceive**.
016:045 seize them from directions they little **perceive**?
020:010 "Tarry ye; I **perceive** a fire; perhaps I can
023:056 Nay, they do not **perceive**.
026:202 of a sudden, while they **perceive** it not;
027:007 "I **perceive** a fire; soon will
027:065 nor can they **perceive** when they shall be
028:029 "Tarry ye; I **perceive** a fire; I hope
029:053 reach them,-of a sudden, while they **perceive** not!
038:063 or have (our) eyes failed to **perceive** them?"
039:025 from directions they did not **perceive**.
039:055 of a sudden, while ye **perceive** not!-
041:048 in the lurch, and they will **perceive** that they
043:066 of a sudden, while they **perceive** not?
049:002 become vain and ye **perceive** not.
068:044 from directions they **perceive** not.

PERCEIVED

009:118 and they **perceived** that there is no fleeing
027:050 even while they **perceived** it not.
028:009 And they **perceived** not (what they were doing)!
028:011 from a distance and they **perceived** not.
028:029 he **perceived** a fire in the direction of Mount Tur.

PERCHANCE

002:063 **perchance** ye may fear Allah."
002:073 **perchance** ye may understand.
002:185 and **perchance** ye shall be grateful.
003:072 **perchance** they may (themselves) turn back;
007:057 **perchance** ye may remember.
007:164 and **perchance** they may fear Him."
007:171 what is therein; **perchance** ye may fear Allah".
007:174 and **perchance** they may turn (Unto Us).
007:176 so relate the story; **perchance** they may reflect.
011:012 **Perchance** thou mayest (feel the inclination)
018:006 Thou wouldst only, **perchance**, fret thyself
020:044 **perchance** he may take warning or fear (Allah)."
033:063 make thee understand?-**perchance** the Hour is nigh!
065:001 **perchance** Allah will bring about thereafter
080:003 but that **perchance** he might Grow purity?

PERDITION

007:009 will find their souls in **perdition**, for that
011:063 to my (portion) but **perdition**?
011:101 (to their lot) but **perdition**!
014:028 to the House of **perdition**?-
018:052 a place of common **perdition**.
037:056 little short of bringing me to **perdition**!
040:037 to nothing but **perdition** (for him).
065:009 of their conduct was **Perdition**.
071:028 but in **Perdition**!"
084:011 Soon will he cry for **Perdition**,

PERFECT

002:029 and of all things He hath **perfect** knowledge.
002:032 **perfect** in knowledge and wisdom."
012:006 of stories (and events) and **perfect** His favour
015:025 for He is **Perfect** in Wisdom and Knowledge.
027:088 in **perfect** order: for He

PERFECT (continued)
039:075 in (**perfect**) justice, and the cry (on all sides)
066:008 **perfect** our light for us and grant us Forgiveness:
075:004 in **perfect** order the very tips of his fingers.

PERFECTED
005:003 This day have I **perfected** your religion for you,
009:032 His light should be **perfected**, even though
012:006 of Jacob-even as He **perfected** it to thy fathers

PERFECTION
059:023 (and **Perfection**). The Guardian of Faith,
079:028 and He hath given it order and **perfection**.

PERFIDIOUS
031:032 except only a **perfidious** ungrateful (wretch)!

PERFIDY
004:107 for Allah loveth not one given to **perfidy** and sin:

PERFORM
058:003 to **perform**: and Allah is well-acquainted with
076:007 They **perform** (their) vows, and they fear

PERFORMED
004:103 When ye have **performed** the prayers, remember

PERHAPS
002:259 He said: "(**Perhaps**) a day or part of a day."
005:052 Ah! **perhaps** Allah will give (thee) victory, or a
005:059 and (**perhaps**) that most of you are rebellious
009:102 **Perhaps** Allah will turn unto them (in mercy): for
011:054 "We say nothing but that (**perhaps**) some of
018:019 They said, "We have stayed (**perhaps**) a day,
019:048 my Lord **perhaps**, by my prayer to my Lord, I shall
020:010 **perhaps** I can bring you some burning brand
022:013 (**Perhaps**) they call on one whose hurt is nearer
042:017 will make thee realize that **perhaps** the Hour

PERIL
007:095 while they realized not (their **peril**).

PERIOD
002:185 (He wants you) to complete the prescribed **period**,
002:185 the prescribed **period** (should be made up)
002:228 better right to take them back in that **period**,
002:282 future obligations in a fixed **period** of time,
002:282 to writing (your contract) for a future **period**,
007:142 and completed (the **period**) with ten (more): thus
012:048 (**period**) seven dreadful (years), which will
012:049 "Then will come after that (**period**) a year
013:038 (or commanded). For each **period** is an appointment.
021:044 and their fathers until the **period** grew long for
033:049 no **period** of 'Iddat have ye to count in respect
046:015 to his weaning is (a **period** of) thirty months.
065:004 for them the prescribed **period**, if ye
065:004 are pregnant, their **period** is until they deliver
076:001 Has there not been over Man a long **period** of Time,
077:022 For a **period** (of gestation), determined?

PERIODS
002:177 and throughout all **periods** of panic.
002:189 fixed **periods** of time in (the affairs of) men.
002:228 concerning themselves for three monthly **periods**,
065:001 divorce them at their prescribed **periods**, and count
065:001 prescribed **periods**: for fear Allah your Lord:

PERISH
003:119 Say: "**Perish** in your rage; Allah knoweth
007:170 of the righteous to **perish**.
009:055 may **perish** in their (very) denial of Allah.
010:095 be of those who **perish**.
011:115 the reward of the righteous to **perish**.

PERISH (continued)
014:013 the wrong-doers to **perish**!
017:081 for Falsehood is (by its nature) bound to **perish**."
018:030 shall not suffer to **perish** the reward of any
018:035 "I deem not that this will ever **perish**,"
020:016 divert thee therefrom, lest thou **perish**!"...
020:081 My Wrath do **perish** indeed!
021:018 and behold, falsehood doth **perish**! Ah! woe
028:088 will **perish** except His Face. To Him
042:034 Or He can cause them to **perish** because of the
045:027 that Day will the followers of Falsehood **perish**!
048:012 evil thought, for ye are a people doomed to **perish**."
055:026 All that is on earth will **perish**:
111:001 **Perish** the hands of the Father of Flame! **Perish** he!

PERISHABLE
004:094 Coveting the **perishable** goods of this life: with

PERISHED
017:081 and Falsehood **perished**: for Falsehood
040:078 and justice, and there **perished**, there and
069:029 "My power has **perished** from me!"...

PERJURY
005:107 were guilty of the sin (of **perjury**), let two

PERMANENT
021:034 before thee **permanent** life (here): if then

PERMANENTLY
021:034 would they live **permanently**?

PERMISSIBLE
002:229 A divorce is only **permissible** twice: after that,
004:114 between people (secrecy is **permissible**): to him

PERMISSION
002:102 anyone except by Allah's **permission**.
003:152 His **permission** were about to annihilate your enemy,
004:025 This (**permission**) is for those
007:123 before I give you **permission**? Surely this
009:083 of them, and they ask thy **permission** to come
019:087 has received **permission** (or promise) from (Allah)
020:071 before I give you **permission**? Surely this
020:109 except for those for whom **permission** has been
022:039 **permission** is given (to fight), because they
024:027 until ye have asked **permission** and saluted
024:028 enter not until **permission** is given to you:
024:058 **permission** (before they come to your presence),
024:059 ask for **permission**, as do those before them:
026:049 I give you **permission**? Surely he
034:023 has granted **permission**. So far
042:021 some religion without the **permission** of Allah?
042:051 to reveal, with Allah's **permission**, what Allah
097:004 and the Spirit by Allah's **permission**, on every

PERMIT
048:015 (in war): "**Permit** us to follow you." They wish
066:008 the Day that Allah will not **permit** to be
074:028 Naught doth it **permit** to endure, and naught

PERMITS
012:080 until my father **permits** me, or Allah
014:011 an authority except as Allah **permits**. And on
058:010 in the least, except as Allah **permits**; and on

PERMITTED
002:187 **Permitted** to you on the night of the fasts,
002:275 **permitted** trade and forbidden usury.
010:059 Say: "Hath Allah indeed **permitted** you, or do
010:098 and **permitted** them to enjoy (their
013:038 except as Allah **permitted** (or commanded).

PERMITTED (continued)
017:007 came to pass, (We **permitted** your enemies)
018:028 **permitted** to neglect the remembrance of Us,
024:036 which Allah hath **permitted** to be raised to honour;
036:040 It is not **permitted** to the Sun to catch
037:148 And they believed; so We **permitted** them to enjoy
078:038 **permitted** by The Most Gracious, and he

PERMITTETH
002:255 in His presence except as He **permitteth**?

PERPETUAL
013:023 Gardens of **perpetual** bliss: they shall
013:035 **perpetual** is the fruits thereof and the
028:071 the Night **perpetual** over you to the Day
028:072 the Day **perpetual** over you to the
037:009 is a **perpetual** chastisement,
056:017 youths of **perpetual** (freshness),
076:019 (serve) youths of **perpetual** (freshness): if thou

PERSECUTE
010:083 **persecute** them; and certainly Pharaoh was mighty
085:010 Those who **persecute** the Believers, men and women,

PERSECUTION
002:191 for **Persecution** is worse than slaughter;
002:193 there is no more **Persecution**
008:039 there is no more **persecution**, and religion

PERSECUTIONS
006:034 bore their rejection and their **persecution** until
016:110 and **persecutions**,-and who thereafter strive and

PERSEVERANCE
002:045 with patient **perseverance** and prayer:
002:153 with patient **Perseverance** and Prayer:
003:200 vie in such **perseverance**: strengthen each other;
022:035 who show patient **perseverance** over their

PERSEVERE
002:153 for God is with those who patiently **persevere**.
002:155 to those who patiently **persevere**,
002:249 Allah is with those who steadfastly **persevere**."
003:186 **persevere** patiently, and guard against evil,
003:200 **Persevere** in patience and constancy:
008:046 for Allah is with those who patiently **persevere**.
008:066 for Allah is with those who patiently **persevere**.
011:049 So **persevere** patiently: for the End
013:022 Those who patiently **persevere**, seeking the
016:042 (They are) those who **persevere** in patience,
016:096 on those who patiently **persevere**, their reward
016:110 and patiently **persevere**,-thy Lord, after all
028:080 save those who steadfastly **persevere** (in good)."
029:059 Those who **persevere** in patience, and put
030:060 So patiently **persevere**: for verily
031:031 who constantly **persevere** and give thanks.
039:010 Those who patiently **persevere** will truly
040:055 Patiently, then, **persevere**: for the Promise
040:077 So **persevere** in patience! For the
046:035 Therefore patiently **persevere**, as did
047:031 and **persevere** in patience; and We

PERSEVERED
013:024 "Peace unto you for that ye **persevered** in patience!
028:054 for that they have **persevered**, that they
032:024 so long as they **persevered** with patience

PERSEVERES
042:033 everyone who patiently **perseveres** and is grateful.

PERSEVERING
008:046 and be patient and **persevering**: for Allah

PERSEVERING (continued)
008:065 amongst you, patient and **persevering**, they will
008:066 patient and **persevering**, they will vanquish

PERSIST
008:038 but if they **persist**, the punishment
023:075 on them, they would obstinately **persist** in their
067:021 Nay, they obstinately **persist** in insolent impiety
085:019 And yet the Unbelievers (**persist**) in rejecting

PERSISTED
005:078 because they disobeyed and **persisted** in Excesses.
006:070 for they **persisted** in rejecting Allah.
011:116 given them, and **persisted** in sin.
015:081 but they **persisted** in turning away from them.
029:014 them while they (**persisted** in) sin.
056:046 And **persisted** obstinately in wickedness supreme!

PERSISTENT
004:117 they call but upon Satan the **persistent** rebel!

PERSISTENTLY
036:064 for that ye (**persistently**) rejected (Truth)."

PERSISTING
003:135 **persisting** knowingly in (the wrong) they have done.

PERSON
003:161 If any **person** acts dishonestly he shall,
004:001 Who created you from a single **person**,
005:032 that if anyone slew a **person**-unless it be for
006:145 if a **person** is forced by necessity, without
007:114 (raised to posts) nearest (to my **person**)."
007:189 created you from a single **person**, and made
012:054 to serve about my own **person**." Therefore when
013:011 For each (such **person**) there are
018:026 with any **person** whatsoever.
018:074 "Hast thou slain an innocent **person** who had
026:042 (raised to posts) nearest (to my **person**)."
026:222 They descend on every lying, wicked **person**
032:017 Now no **person** knows what delights of the eye
039:006 a single **person**: then created, of like
042:040 but if a **person** forgives and makes reconciliation,
065:007 on any **person** beyond what He has given him.
068:024 "Let not a single indigent **person** break in upon

PERSONAL
033:006 have closer **personal** ties, in the

PERSONS
002:224 or making peace between **persons**;
002:229 such **persons** wrong (themselves as well as others).
004:016 If two **persons** among you are guilty of lewdness,
004:095 with their goods and **persons** than to those who
004:095 with their goods and their **persons**.
005:089 for expiation, feed then indigent **persons**, on
007:178 such are the **persons** who lose.
008:072 with their property and their **persons**, in the
009:020 and their **persons**, have the highest rank in
009:041 and your **persons**, in the cause of Allah. That is
009:044 with their goods and **persons**. And Allah
009:081 with their goods and their **persons**, in the
009:088 fight with their wealth and their **persons**: for
009:111 their **persons** and their good; for theirs
017:018 We will, to such **persons** as We will: in the
025:070 of such **persons** into good, and Allah
033:059 outer garments over their **persons** (when out
038:008 to him-(of all **persons**) among us?." But they
041:035 none but **persons** of the greatest good fortune.
049:015 with their belongings and their **persons** in the

PERSONS (continued)

057:024   Such **persons** as are covetous and commend
061:011   and your **persons**: that will be best for you,
065:002   for witness two **persons** from among you, endued with
072:006   who took shelter with **persons** among the Jinns,
072:006   'True, there were **persons** among mankind who took

PERSPICUOUS

005:015   a (new) Light and a **perspicuous** Book,
007:184   he is but a **perspicuous** warner.
012:001   of the **Perspicuous** Book.
026:195   In the **perspicuous** Arabic tongue.
034:003   but is in the Record **Perspicuous**:

PERVERSE

002:099   but those who are **perverse**.
009:067   Verily the Hypocrites are rebellious and **perverse**.
009:084   and died in a state of **perverse** rebellion.

PERVERSELY

009:080   who are **perversely** rebellious.

PERVERSITY

003:007   **perversity** follow the part thereof that is not

PERVERT

041:040   Those who **pervert** the Truth in Our Signs are not

PERVERTED

002:075   and **perverted** it knowingly
003:082   they are **perverted** transgressors.
003:110   but most of them are **perverted** transgressors.
035:003   how then are ye **perverted**?

PET

006:094   and your (**pet**) fancies have left you in the lurch!"

PETITION

022:073   feeble are those who **petition** and those
022:073   those who **petition** and those whom they petition!

PHARAOH

002:049   delivered you from the people of **Pharaoh**:
003:011   the people of **Pharaoh**, and their predecessors:
007:103   with Our Signs to **Pharaoh** and his chiefs. But
007:104   Moses said: "O **Pharaoh**! I am
007:106   (**Pharaoh**) said: "If indeed thou hast
007:109   Said the Chiefs of the people of **Pharaoh**: "This
007:113   So there came the sorcerers to **Pharaoh**: they said:
007:123   Said **Pharaoh**: "Believe ye in him before I
007:130   We punished the people of **Pharaoh** with years
007:137   which **Pharaoh** and his people erected
008:052   the people of **Pharaoh** and of those before them:
008:054   the people of **Pharaoh** and those before them":
008:054   and We drowned the people of **Pharaoh**: for they
010:075   Moses and Aaron to **Pharaoh** and his
010:079   Said **Pharaoh**: "Bring me every sorcerer well versed."
010:083   because of the fear of **Pharaoh** and his chiefs,
010:083   persecute them; and certainly **Pharaoh** was mighty
010:088   indeed bestowed on **Pharaoh** and his Chiefs
010:090   across the sea: **Pharaoh** and his hosts followed
011:097   but they followed the command of **Pharaoh**, and the
011:097   Unto **Pharaoh** and his Chiefs: but they
011:097   and the command of **Pharaoh** was no rightly (guide).
014:006   the people of **Pharaoh**: they set you hard task
017:101   **Pharaoh** said to him: "O Moses! I consider thee,
017:102   O **Pharaoh**, to be one doomed to destruction!"
020:024   "Go thou to **Pharaoh**, for he
020:043   "Go, both of you, to **Pharaoh**, for he
020:049   (**Pharaoh**) said: "Who, then, O Moses, is the
020:051   (**Pharaoh**) said: "What then is the condition of

PHARAOH (continued)

020:056   And We showed **Pharaoh** all Our Signs, but he
020:060   So **Pharaoh** withdrew: he concerted his plan,
020:071   (**Pharaoh**) said: "Believe ye in Him before I
020:077   of being overtaken (by **Pharaoh**) and without
020:078   Then **Pharaoh** pursued them with his forces,
020:079   **Pharaoh** led his people astray instead of
023:046   To **Pharaoh** and his Chiefs: but these
026:011   "The people of **Pharaoh**: will they not fear Allah?"
026:016   to **Pharaoh**, and say: 'We have been sent by the
026:018   (**Pharaoh**) said: "Did we not cherish thee as a
026:023   **Pharaoh** said: "And what is the Lord and Cherisher
026:025   (**Pharaoh**) said to those around:
026:027   (**Pharaoh**) said: "Truly your messenger who has
026:029   (**Pharaoh**) said: "If thou takest any god other
026:031   (**Pharaoh**) said: "Show it then, if thou
026:034   (**Pharaoh**) said to the Chiefs around him:
026:041   they said to **Pharaoh**: "Of course-shall we
026:044   "By the might of **Pharaoh**, it is
026:049   Said (**Pharaoh**): "Believe ye in Him before I give
026:053   Then **Pharaoh** sent heralds to (all) the Cities,
027:012   (thou wilt take) to **Pharaoh** and his people:
028:003   the story of Moses and **Pharaoh** in Truth,
028:004   Truly **Pharaoh** elated himself in the land
028:006   in the land, and to show **Pharaoh**, Haman, and
028:008   for **Pharaoh** and Haman and (all) their hosts
028:008   Then the people of **Pharaoh** picked him up
028:009   The wife of **Pharaoh** said: "(Here is)
028:032   from thy Lord to **Pharaoh** and his Chiefs: for truly
028:038   **Pharaoh** said: "O Chiefs! no god do I know
029:039   (Remember also) Qarun, **Pharaoh**, and Haman:
038:012   and 'Ad, and **Pharaoh** the Lord of Stakes.
040:024   To **Pharaoh**, Haman, and Qarun; but they
040:026   Said **Pharaoh**: "Leave me to slay Moses; and let
040:028   of **Pharaoh**, who had concealed his faith, said:
040:029   should it befall us?" **Pharaoh** said: "I but
040:036   **Pharaoh** said: "O Haman! Build me a lofty palace,
040:037   and the plot of **Pharaoh** led to nothing but
040:045   encompassed on all sides the People of **Pharaoh**.
040:046   "Cast ye the People of **Pharaoh** into the
043:046   with Our Signs, to **Pharaoh** and his Chiefs:
043:051   And **Pharaoh** proclaimed among his people, saying:
044:017   of **Pharaoh**: there came to them a messenger
044:031   Inflicted by **Pharaoh**, for he was arrogant (even)
050:013   The 'Ad, **Pharaoh**, the Brethren of Lut,
051:038   Behold, We sent him to **Pharaoh**, with authority
051:039   But (**Pharaoh**) turned back on account of his might,
054:041   To the people of **Pharaoh**, too, aforetime,
066:011   and save me from **Pharaoh** and his doings, and save
066:011   to those who believe, the wife of **Pharaoh**: behold
069:009   And **Pharaoh**, and those before him, and the
073:015   a messenger to **Pharaoh**.
073:016   But **Pharaoh** disobeyed the messenger; so We
079:017   "Go thou to **Pharaoh**, for he has
079:021   But (**Pharaoh**) rejected it and disobeyed (guidance);
085:018   Of **Pharaoh** and the Thamud?
089:010   And with **Pharaoh**, lord of Stakes?

PHARAOH'S

002:050   drowned **Pharaoh's** people within your very sight.
007:127   Said the chiefs of **Pharaoh's** people: "Wilt
007:141   you from **Pharaoh's** people, who afflicted
040:037   in **Pharaoh's** eyes, the evil of his deeds, and he

PICKED
012:010 he will be **picked** up by some caravan of travellers."
028:008 **picked** him up (from the river): (it was
PIECE
002:073 "Strike the (body) with a **piece** of the (heifer)."
026:187 "Now cause a **piece** of the sky to fall on us,
034:009 them up, or cause a **piece** of the sky to fall
052:044 Were they to see a **piece** of the sky falling
PIECES
002:260 tie them (cut them into **pieces**),
009:109 And it doth crumble to **pieces** with him, into the
009:109 sand-cliff ready to crumble to **pieces**? And it
009:110 until their hearts are cut to **pieces**. And Allah
010:027 as it were, with **pieces** from the depth of the
017:092 "Or thou cause the sky to fall in **pieces**, as thou
018:042 to **pieces** to its very foundations, and he
021:058 So he broke them to **pieces**, (all) but
034:007 all scattered to **pieces** in disintegration, that ye
047:015 so that it cuts up their bowels (to **pieces**)?
063:004 **pieces** of timber propped up, (unable to
104:004 to be thrown into that which Breaks to **Pieces**.
104:005 That which Breaks to **Pieces**?
PIERCING
037:010 by a flaming fire, of **piercing** brightness.
086:003 (It is) the Star of **piercing** brightness;-
PIETY
005:002 Help ye one another in righteousness and **piety**,
005:008 Be just: that is next to **Piety**: and fear
009:108 was laid from the first day on **piety**; it is
009:109 his foundation on **piety** to Allah and His
010:031 Say, "Will ye not then show **piety** (to Him)?"
010:105 face towards Religion with true **piety**, and never
022:032 come truly from **piety** of heart.
022:037 it is your **piety** that reaches Him: He has
047:017 on them their **Piety** and Restraint (from evil).
049:003 their hearts has Allah tested of **piety**: for them
PILED
050:010 **piled** one over another;-
056:029 (or fruits) **piled** one above another,-
PILETH
104:002 Who **pileth** up wealth and layeth it by,
PILGRIMAGE
002:189 And for **Pilgrimage**.
002:198 the bounty of your Lord (during **pilgrimage**).
003:097 **pilgrimage** thereto is a duty men owe to Allah,
005:001 the Sacred Precincts or in the state of **Pilgrimage**.
005:002 the state of **pilgrimage**, ye may hunt, and let not
005:095 in the state of **pilgrimage** if any of you
005:096 or in the state of **pilgrimage** and fear Allah,
009:003 on the day of the Great **Pilgrimage**,-that Allah
022:027 "And proclaim the **Pilgrimage** among men: they will
022:030 Such (is the **Pilgrimage**): whoever honours
022:030 Lawful to you (for food in **pilgrimage**) are cattle
PILGRIMS
009:019 to **pilgrims**, or the maintenance of the Sacred
PILING
102:001 The mutual rivalry for **piling** up (the good
PILLARS
013:002 without any **pillars** that ye can see; then He
031:010 any **pillars** that ye can see; He set
089:007 Of the (city of) Iram, with lofty **pillars**,

PIOUS
009:019 (the **pious** service of) those who believe in Allah
009:099 and look on their payments as **pious** gifts bringing
080:016 Honorable and **Pious** and Just.
PIT
003:103 and ye were on the brink of the **Pit** of Fire,
085:004 Woe to the makers of the **pit** (of Fire),
092:011 when he falls headlong (into the **Pit**).
101:009 Will have his home in a (bottomless) **pit**.
PITCH
014:050 Their garments of liquid **pitch**, and their
PITCHED
003:112 And **pitched** over them is (the tent of) destitution.
003:112 Shame is **pitched** over them (like a tent)
PITY
019:013 And **pity** (for all creatures) as from Us,
PLACE
002:030 They said, "Wilt thou **place** therein
002:036 On earth will be your dwelling **place**
002:060 Each group knew its own **place** for water.
002:125 the Station of Abraham as a **place** of prayer;
002:125 of assembly for men and a **place** of safety;
002:125 Remember We made the house a **place** of assembly
002:175 buy error in **place** of Guidance and Torment
002:175 and Torment in **place** of Forgiveness.
002:196 the **place** of sacrifice.
002:199 Then return from the **place** whence it is usual
002:286 **place** a burden greater than it can bear.
003:154 to the **place** of their death":
004:020 one wife in **place** of another, even if
005:006 Allah doth not wish to **place** you in a difficulty,
006:098 then there is a resting **place** and a repository: We
006:124 Allah knoweth best where to **place** His mission.
006:133 and in your **place** appoint whom He will
006:152 no burden do We **place** on any soul, but that
007:007 for We were never absent (at any time or **place**).
007:029 (to Him) at every time and **place** of prayer, and
007:031 at every time and **place** of prayer: eat and
007:042 no burden do We **place** on any soul, but that
007:143 When Moses came to the **place** appointed by Us, and
007:143 if it abide in its **place**, then shalt
007:150 that ye have done in my **place** in my absence: did
007:155 of his people for Our **place** of meeting: when
007:160 each group knew its own **place** for water. We gave
009:039 your **place**; but Him ye would not harm in the
009:057 or caves, or a **place** of concealment, they would
009:057 If they could find a **place** to flee to, or caves,
010:028 joined gods (with Us): "To your **place**! ye and
010:100 and He will **place** abomination on those
011:006 He knoweth its resting **place** and its
011:098 be the **place** to which they are led!
012:078 so take one of us in his **place**: for we
013:029 and a beautiful **place** of (final) return."
014:019 (in your **place**) a new Creation?
014:029 an evil **place** to stay in!
016:112 from every **place**: yet was it ungrateful for the
018:021 "Let us surely build a **place** of worship over them."
018:052 a **place** of common perdition.
019:016 to a **place** in the East.
019:022 with him to a remote **place**.
020:058 in a **place** where both shall have even chances."
020:107 thou see in their **place**."

PLACE (continued)

022:031   its prey) and thrown him into a far-distant **place**.
022:033   **place** of sacrifice is near the Ancient House.
022:059   to a **place** with which they shall be well pleased:
023:013   in a **place** of rest, firmly fixed;
023:062   On no soul do We **place** a burden greater than
025:012   When it sees them from a **place** far off, they will
025:013   into a constricted **place** therein, they will
025:066   and as a **place** to rest in";
025:075   **place** in heaven, because of their patient
025:076   an abode and **place** of rest!
026:128   high **place** to amuse yourselves?
027:011   to take the **place** of evil, truly, I am
028:006   To establish a firm **place** for them in the land,
028:023   the watering (**place**) in Madyan, he found
028:027   But I intend not to **place** thee under a difficulty:
028:085   to the **Place** of Return. Say: "My Lord
034:019   **place** longer distances between our journey-stages":
036:038   And the Sun runs unto a resting **place**, for Him:
037:164   but has a **place** appointed;
038:025   and a beautiful **place** of (final) Return.
038:040   to Us, and a beautiful **Place** of (final) Return.
038:049   is a beautiful **place** of (final) Return,-
038:055   will be an evil **place** of (final) Return!-
038:060   upon us! Now evil is (this) **place** to stay in!"
040:064   the earth as a resting **place**, and the
041:044   called from a **place** far distant!"
042:047   That Day there will be for you no **place** of refuge
048:025   detained from reaching their **place** of sacrifice.
050:036   was there any **place** of escape (for them)?
050:041   will call out from a **place** quite near,-
053:046   From a seed when lodged (in its **place**);
057:015   the Fire: that is the proper **place** to claim you:
075:011   By no means! No **place** of safety!
075:012   that Day will be the **place** of rest.
077:021   The which We placed in a **place** of rest,
077:025   (as a **place**) to draw together
078:021   Truly Hell is as a **place** of ambush
078:022   For the transgressors a **place** of destination:

PLACED

002:031   then He **placed** them before the angles,
005:064   Amongst them We have **placed** enmity and hatred
006:123   Thus have We **placed** leaders in every town, its
007:010   **placed** you with authority on earth, and provided
018:032   the two We **placed** tillage.
018:049   will be **placed** (before you); and thou
018:049   **placed** before them: and not one will thy Lord
019:017   She **placed** a screen (to screen herself) from them:
023:013   Then We **placed** him as (a drop of) sperm in a
024:054   and ye for that **placed** on you. If ye
024:054   the duty **placed** on him and ye
025:061   in the skies, and **placed** therein a Lamp
026:091   the Fire will be **placed** in full view;
027:040   **placed** firmly before him, he said: "This is
034:018   We had **placed** Cities in prominent positions,
034:054   is **placed** a barrier, as was
038:034   We **placed** on his throne a body but he
039:069   **placed** (open); the prophets and the witnesses
046:020   will be **placed** before the Fire, (it will
046:034   will be **placed** before the Fire, (they will
051:027   And **placed** it before them... He said,
077:021   The which We **placed** in a place of rest,
078:013   And **placed** (therein) a blazing lamp.

PLACED (continued)

079:036   And Hell-Fire shall be **placed** in full view
088:014   Goblets **placed** (ready),

PLACES

002:114   that in **places** for the worship of Allah,
002:128   and show us our **places** for the celebration
004:046   those who displace words from their (right) **places**,
005:013   (right) **places** and forget a good part of the
005:041   They change the words from their (right) **places**;
005:107   Let two others stand forth in their **places**,-
010:087   make your dwellings into **places** of worship,
021:011   in their **places** other peoples?
025:024   and have the fairest of **places** for repose.
034:013   (in their **places**): "Exercise thanks sons of
036:067   in their **places**; then should they have been
039:009   the Hereafter, and who **places** his hope in the
072:018   "And the **places** of worship are for Allah (alone):

PLACETH

006:039   He **placeth** on the Way that is Straight.

PLAGUE

002:059   the transgressors a **plague** from heaven,
007:134   And when the **Plague** fell on them, they said:
007:134   if thou wilt remove the **Plague** from us, we
007:135   But when We removed the **Plague** from them
007:162   so We sent on them a **plague** from heaven. For

PLAIN

002:068   to make **plain** to us what heifer it is!"
002:069   to make **plain** to us her colour."
002:070   to make **plain** to us what she is:
002:230   which He makes **plain** to those who know.
003:118   We have made **plain** to you the Signs,
003:138   Here is a **plain** statement to men,
005:043   Therein is the (**plain**) command of Allah; yet even
005:101   about things which, if made **plain** to you, may
005:101   they will be made **plain** to you: Allah will
007:107   **plain** (for all to see)!
015:079   They were both on an open highway, **plain** to see.
024:018   And Allah makes the Signs **plain** to you: for Allah
026:032   **plain** (for all to see)!
026:115   "I am sent only as a **plain** warner."
067:026   it is with Allah alone: I am a **plain** warner."

PLAINLY

004:115   **plainly** conveyed to him, and follows a path
019:038   How **plainly** will they see and hear, the Day
026:013   And my tongue will not speak (**plainly**): so send
034:014   the Jinns saw **plainly** that if they had known
038:070   that I am to give warning **plainly** and publicly."
044:010   a kind of smoke (or mist) **plainly** visible.
057:017   **plainly** to you, that ye may understand.

PLAINS

007:074   palaces and castles in (open) **plains**, and
020:106   "He will leave them as **plains** smooth and level;

PLAN

003:176   Allah's **Plan** is that He will give them no portion
005:001   according to His Will and **Plan**.
005:048   but (His **Plan** is) to test you in what He
005:091   Satan's **plan** is (but) to excite enmity
006:111   unless it is in Allah's **Plan**. But most
007:099   can feel secure from the **Plan** of Allah, except
007:110   "His **plan** is to get you out of your land: then
008:030   They plot and **plan**, and Allah too plans, but the
010:021   Say: "Swifter to **plan** is Allah! Verily, Our

PLAN (continued)

010:071 so your **plan** be not to you dark and dubious.
010:071 about your **plan** and among your Partners, so your
012:068 in the least against (the **Plan** of) Allah: it served
012:076 Thus did We **plan** for Joseph. He could not
020:060 his **plan**, and then came (back).
020:064 "Therefore concert your **plan**, and then
021:057 **plan** against your idols-after ye
022:015 his **plan** will remove that which enrages (him)!
026:035 "His **plan** is to get you out of your land
029:022 (His **Plan**), nor have ye, beside Allah,
043:079 some **Plan** (among themselves)? But it
068:045 truly powerful is My **Plan**.
070:041 to be defeated (in Our **Plan**).
105:002 Did He not make their treacherous **plan** go astray?

PLANETS

081:015 So verily I call to witness the **Planets**-that recede,

PLANKS

054:013 made of broad **planks** and caulked with palm-fibre:

PLANNED

003:054 And (the unbelievers) plotted and **planned**,
003:054 and Allah too **planned**,
007:123 have **planned** in the city to drive
021:070 Then they **planned** against him: but We
027:050 They plotted and **planned**, but We
027:050 but We too **planned**, even while

PLANNERS

003:054 and the best of **planners** is Allah.
008:030 but the best of **planners** is Allah.

PLANNETH

011:107 Accomplisher of what He **planneth**.

PLANNING

086:016 And I am **planning** a scheme,

PLANS

008:018 He Who makes feeble the **Plans** and stratagems
008:030 They plot and **plan**, and Allah too plans, but the
012:102 when they concerted their **plans** together in the

PLANT

008:011 and to **plant** your feet firmly therewith.
037:146 a spreading **plant** of the Gourd kind.
047:007 He will help you, and **plant** your feet firmly.

PLANTED

016:094 may slip after it was firmly **planted**; and ye

PLANTS

020:053 of **plants** each separate from the others.
055:012 for fodder, and sweet-smelling **plants**.

PLAY

006:032 but **play** and amusement. But best
006:070 their religion to be mere **play** and amusement, and
007:051 to be mere amusement and **play**, and were
009:065 "We were only talking idly and in **play**." Say:
012:012 enjoy himself and **play**, and we
029:064 but amusement and **play**? But verily
043:083 So leave them to babble and **play** (with vanities)
044:009 Yet they **play** about in doubt.
047:036 The life of this world is but **play** and amusement:
052:012 That **play** (and paddle) in shallow trifles.
057:020 of this world is but **play** and a pastime,
070:042 and **play** about, until they encounter that Day

PLAYED

007:098 while they **played** about (care-free)?

PLEA

004:165 should have no **plea** against Allah: for Allah
006:151 kill not your children on a **plea** of want;-We
008:034 But what **plea** have they that Allah
027:085 be unable to speak (in **plea**).

PLEAD

010:003 No intercessor (can **plead** with Him) except after
011:074 reached him, he began to **plead** with Us for
017:086 then wouldst thou find none to **plead** thy affair
025:013 they will **plead** for destruction there and then!
025:014 "This day **plead** not for a single destruction:
025:014 **plead** for destruction oft-repeated!"

PLEADED

002:124 He **pleaded**: "And also (Imams) from my offspring!"

PLEADING

016:111 up **pleading** for itself, and every

PLEADS

058:001 of the woman who **pleads** with thee concerning her

PLEAS

077:036 Nor will it be open to them to put forth **pleas**.

PLEASANT

016:031 (**pleasant**) rivers: they will have therein all
035:012 the one palatable, sweet, and **pleasant** to drink,
036:056 be in **pleasant** shade, reclining on raised couches;
044:027 And **pleasant** things wherein they had

PLEASE

002:144 a Qiblah that shall **please** thee.
002:265 to **please** Allah and to strengthen their souls,
009:008 they **please** you, but their hearts are averse
009:062 In order to **please** you: but it
009:062 should **please** Allah and His Messenger, if they
012:056 We bestow of Our mercy on whom We **please**, and We
012:076 whom We **please**: but over all endued with knowledge
012:099 in safety if it **please** Allah."
015:091 Qur'an into shreds (as they **please**).
017:054 if He **please**, He granteth you mercy, or if
017:054 or if He **please**, punishment: We have not
020:084 O my Lord, to **please** Thee."
027:019 that will **please** Thee: and admit me,
027:087 will **please** (to exempt): and all
039:068 except such as it will **please** Allah (to exempt).
063:004 their bodies **please** thee; and when
066:001 thou seekest to **please** thy consorts? But Allah

PLEASED

004:090 If Allah had **pleased**, He could have
009:058 they are **pleased**, but if not, behold!
009:096 that ye may be **pleased** with them. But if
009:096 Allah is not **pleased** with those who disobey.
009:096 But if ye are **pleased** with them. Allah is not
010:007 but are **pleased** and satisfied with the life
012:056 when, or where he **pleased**. We bestow
020:130 of the day: that thou may be **pleased**.
022:059 well **pleased**: for Allah is All-Knowing,
035:016 If He so **pleased**, He could blot you out
039:004 He **pleased** out of those whom He doth create:
039:007 He is **pleased** with you. No bearer
041:014 They said, "If our Lord had so **pleased**, He would
058:022 Allah will be well **pleased** with them, and they
088:009 **Pleased** with their Striving,-
089:028 well **pleased** (thyself), and well-pleasing unto Him!
098:008 Allah well **pleased** with them, and they

PLEASES

002:090   send it to any of His servants He **pleases**:
003:006   shapes you in the wombs as He **pleases**.
003:037   to whom He **pleases**, without measure."
003:179   but He chooses of his Messengers whom He **pleases**.
014:004   whom He **pleases** and He is Exalted in power,
014:004   those whom He **pleases** and guides whom He **pleases**
014:011   to such of His servants as He **pleases**. It is
016:093   straying whom He **pleases**, and He guides
016:093   and He guides whom He **pleases**: but ye
024:021   whom He **pleases**: and Allah is One Who hears and
024:043   from whom He **pleases**. The vivid
024:043   He **pleases** and He turns it away from whom
028:068   as He **pleases**: no choice have they (in the
028:082   He **pleases**! Had it not been that Allah was
029:021   He **pleases**, and towards Him are ye turned.
029:021   "He punishes whom He **pleases**, and He
029:062   by (strict) measure, (as He **pleases**): for Allah
029:062   of His servants He **pleases**; and He
030:037   to whomsoever He **pleases**? Verily in that are Signs
034:036   to whom He **pleases**, but most men know not."
034:039   of His servants as He **pleases**: and nothing
035:001   He adds to Creation as He **pleases**: for Allah
039:023   He guides therewith whom He **pleases**, but such
039:052   for any He **pleases**? Verily, in this
040:015   His servants He **pleases**, that is
042:013   those whom He **pleases**, and guides
042:019   He gives Sustenance to whom He **pleases**: and He
042:027   in due measure as He **pleases**: for He
053:026   has given leave for whom He **pleases** and that
057:021   He **pleases**: and Allah is the Lord
059:006   over any He **pleases**: and Allah

PLEASEST

003:026   Thou enduest with honour whom Thou **pleasest**,
003:026   and thou bringest low whom Thou **pleasest**:
003:026   thou givest power to whom Thou **pleasest**,
003:026   Thou strippest off Power from whom Thou **pleasest**:
003:027   to whom Thou **pleasest**, without measure."
033:051   any of them that thou **pleasest**, and thou
033:051   thou **pleasest**: and there is no blame on thee

PLEASETH

002:247   Allah granteth His authority to whom He **pleaseth**;
002:261   manifold increase to whom He **pleaseth**:
002:269   He granteth wisdom to whom He **pleaseth**;
002:272   the right path whom He **pleaseth**.
002:284   and punisheth whom He **pleaseth**.
002:284   He forgiveth whom He **pleaseth**,
003:013   with His aid whom He **pleaseth**.
003:073   He granteth them to whom He **pleaseth**:
003:074   specially chooseth whom He **pleaseth**:
003:129   He forgiveth whom He **pleaseth** and punisheth
003:129   and punisheth whom He **pleaseth**;
004:048   to whom He **pleaseth**;
004:049   Nay-but Allah doth purify whom He **pleaseth**.
004:116   He **pleaseth** other sins than this: one
005:017   He createth what He **pleaseth**.
005:018   He forgiveth whom He **pleaseth**, and He
005:018   and He punisheth whom He **Pleaseth**: and to Allah
005:040   He punisheth whom He **pleaseth**, and He forgiveth
005:040   and He forgiveth whom he **pleaseth**: and Allah
005:054   which He will bestow on whom He **pleaseth**.
005:064   (of His Bounty) as He **pleaseth**.
006:088   He giveth that guidance to whom He **pleaseth**, of

PLEASETH (continued)

007:128   such of His servants as He **pleaseth**; and the
010:025   He doth guide whom He **pleaseth** to a way
010:107   whomsoever of His servants He **pleaseth**. And He
013:026   He **pleaseth**. (The worldly) rejoice in the life
013:039   He **pleaseth**: with Him is the Mother of the Book.
016:002   to such of His servants as He **pleaseth**, (saying):
017:030   He **pleaseth**, and He straiten it for He doth
074:031   whom He **pleaseth**, and guide whom He **pleaseth**;
074:031   He **pleaseth**; and none can know the forces

PLEASING

006:122   their own deeds seem **pleasing**.
009:037   The evil of their course seems **pleasing** to them.
013:033   their devising seems **pleasing**, but they
027:004   We have made their deeds **pleasing** in their eyes;
027:024   seem **pleasing** in their eyes, and has
047:014   the evil of his conduct seems **pleasing**, and such
048:012   to their families; this seemed **pleasing** in your

PLEASURE

002:126   for a while will I grant them their **pleasure**,
002:207   gives his life to earn the **pleasure** of Allah;
003:015   the good **pleasure** of Allah.
003:162   the good **pleasure** of Allah like the man who draws
003:174   for they followed the good **pleasure** of Allah:
004:005   but if they, of their own good **pleasure**, remit
004:114   seeking the good **pleasure** of Allah, We
005:002   and good **pleasure** of their Lord.
005:016   His good **pleasure** to ways of peace and safety,
009:021   His good **pleasure**. And of Gardens for them,
009:072   **Pleasure** of Allah: that is the supreme triumph.
009:109   and His good **pleasure**?-or he that layeth his
017:071   will read it (with **pleasure**), and they will not
031:024   We grant them their **pleasure** for a little while:
038:051   therein can they call (at **pleasure**) for fruit
046:020   and ye took your **pleasure** out of them: but to-day
047:028   hated Allah's good **pleasure**; so He
048:018   Allah's Good **Pleasure** was on the Believers
048:029   and (His) Good **Pleasure**. On their faces
057:020   and (His) Good **Pleasure** (for the devotees of Allah).
057:027   the Good **pleasure** of Allah; but that
059:008   from Allah and (His) Good **Pleasure**, and aiding
060:001   and to seek My Good **Pleasure**, showing friendship
101:007   Will be in a life of good **pleasure** and satisfaction.

PLEASURES

011:048   grant their **pleasures** (for a time), but in

PLEDGE

002:283   a **pledge** with possession (may serve the purpose).
052:021   (Yet) is each individual in **pledge** for his deeds.
074:038   Every soul will be (held) in **pledge** for its deeds.

PLENTIFUL

055:064   Dark green in colour (from **plentiful** watering).

PLENTY

002:058   and eat of the **plenty** therein as ye wish;
002:245   It is Allah that giveth (you) want or **Plenty**,
028:058   (of ease and **plenty**)! Now those

PLIANT

068:009   be **pliant**: so would thy be **pliant**.

PLIED

018:079   they **plied** on the water: I but

PLIGHT

003:011   (Their **plight** will be) no better than that
004:097   They say: "In what (**plight**) were ye?"

PLIGHT (continued)
025:034 they will be in an evil **plight**, and, as
048:010 to thee **plight** their fealty in truth to Allah:
048:010 Verily those who **plight** their fealty to thee

PLIGHTED
003:076 their **plighted** faith and act aright,
003:077 solemn **plighted** word for a small price,
013:020 and fail not in their **plighted** word;
013:025 of Allah, after having **plighted** their word

PLOT
004:108 while He is with them when they **plot** by night.
006:123 to **plot** (and burrow) therein: but they
006:123 but they only **plot** against their own souls, and
008:030 They **plot** and plan, and Allah too plans, but the
009:074 and they meditated a **plot** which they
012:005 lest they concoct a **plot** against thee: for Satan
016:026 **plot** (against Allah' Way): but Allah
027:051 of their **plot**!-this, that We destroyed them
034:033 "Nay! it was a **plot** (of yours) by day
040:037 and the **plot** of Pharaoh led to nothing but
052:042 who disbelieve are themselves ensnared in a **Plot**.
052:042 Or do they intend a **plot** (against thee)?
071:022 "And they have devised a tremendous **Plot**.
077:039 (or **plot**), use it against Me!

PLOTS
004:081 But Allah records their nightly (**plots**): so keep
006:124 and a severe chastisement, for all their **plots**.
010:021 all the **plots** that ye make!"
012:102 in the process of weaving their **plots**.
013:042 devise **plots**; but in all things Allah is the
014:046 they made, but their **plots** were (well) within
014:046 Mighty indeed were the **plots** which they made,
016:045 (**plots**) feel secure that Allah will not cause
016:127 not thyself because of their **plots**.
027:070 nor distress thyself because of their **plots**.
035:010 of Righteousness. Those that lay **Plots** of Evil,-
040:025 but the **plots** of Unbelievers (end) in nothing

PLOTTED
003:054 And (the unbelievers) **plotted** and planned,
004:113 have **plotted** to lead thee astray.
008:030 **plotted** against thee, to keep thee in bonds,
009:013 **plotted** to expel the Messenger, and attack
009:048 Indeed they had **plotted** sedition before, and upset
027:050 They **plotted** and planned, but We
037:098 (This failing), they then **plotted** against him,
040:005 **plotted** against their prophet, to seize
040:045 that they **plotted** (against him), but the

PLOTTING
010:021 to **plotting** against Our Signs! Say: "Swifter
035:010 and the **plotting** of such will be void (of result).
035:043 of Evil. But the **plotting** of Evil will hem
035:043 in the land and their **plotting** of Evil.
052:046 The Day when their **plotting** will avail them
086:015 As for them, they are but **plotting** a scheme,

PLOUGH
016:014 that **plough** the waves, that ye may seek (thus)
035:012 therein that **plough** the waves, that ye

PLUCKING
054:020 **Plucking** out men as if they were roots of
070:016 **Plucking** out (his being) right to the skull!-

PLUNGE
006:091 then leave them to **plunge** in vain

PLUNGE (continued)
007:202 **plunge** them deeper into error, and never
070:042 So leave them to **plunge** in vain talk and play

PLUNGED
006:044 when lo! they were **plunged** in despair!
023:077 then Lo! they will be **plunged** in despair therein!
036:037 and behold they are **plunged** in darkness;

POET
021:005 Nay, He is (but) a **poet**!" Let him
037:036 our gods for the sake of a **Poet** possessed?"
052:030 Or do they say:-"A **Poet**! we await for him
069:041 It is not the word of a **poet**: little it

POETRY
036:069 in **Poetry**, nor is it meant for him: this is

POETS
026:224 And the **Poets**,- it is those straying in Evil,

POINT
003:044 when they dispute (the **point**).
005:060 Say: "Shall I **point** out to you something
016:103 **point** to is notable foreign, while this
018:077 on the **point** of falling down, but he
019:073 is best in **point** of position and fairer
021:032 the Signs which these things (**point** to)!
028:012 and) said: "Shall I **point** out to you the people
034:007 "Shall we **point** out to you a man that will
034:046 Say: "I do admonish you on one **point**: that ye
037:005 and Lord of every **point** at the rising of the sun!
040:029 "I but **point** out to you that which I see (myself);
072:024 in **point** of numbers.

POINTED
019:029 But she **pointed** to the babe. They said
022:026 Behold! We **pointed** the site, to Abraham, of the

POINTS
043:063 to you some of the (**points**) on which ye dispute:
070:040 of all **points** in the East and the West that We

POISED
016:079 held **poised** in the midst of (the air

POLLUTION
002:222 Say: They are a hurt and a **pollution**:

POLYTHEISTS
002:105 nor of the **polytheists**.
022:017 Magians, and **Polytheists**,-Allah will
048:006 and the **Polytheists**, men and women, who think
098:001 of the Book and among the **Polytheists**, were not
098:006 of the Book and among the **Polytheists**, will be

POMEGRANATES
006:099 and olives, and **pomegranates**, each similar
006:141 and olives and **pomegranates**, similar
055:068 In them will be Fruits, and dates and **pomegranates**:

POMP
018:028 beyond them, seeking the **pomp** and glitter of

PONDER
004:082 Do they not **ponder** on the Qur'an?
023:068 Do they not **ponder** over the Word (of Allah),

POOR
002:196 or freed the **poor**, or offer sacrifice;
002:236 and the **poor** according to his means;
004:006 But if he is **poor** let him have for himself
004:008 other relatives, of orphans, or **poor**, are present,
004:135 and whether it be (against) rich or **poor**: for
009:060 Alms are for the **poor** and the needy, and those

POOR (continued)

089:018 Nor do ye encourage one another to feed the **poor**!-

POPULATED

030:009 and **populated** it in greater numbers than these

POPULATION

015:004 Never did We destroy a **population** that had not
017:058 There is not a **population** but We shall destroy
021:095 But there is a ban on any **population** which We
028:059 a **population** except when its members practice
034:034 to a **population**, but the wealthy ones among

POPULATIONS

022:045 How many **populations** have We destroyed, which were
022:048 And to how many **populations** did I give respite,
065:008 How many **populations** that insolently opposed

PORTENTS

074:035 This is but one of the mighty (**Portents**),
077:012 For what Day are these (**Portents**) deferred?

PORTION

001:007 Those whose (**portion**) is not wrath,
002:025 that their **portion** is Gardens,
002:058 (the **portion** of) those who do good."
002:200 But they will have no **portion** in the Hereafter.
002:260 then put a **portion** of them: on every hill,
003:023 those who have been given a **portion** of the Book?
003:077 they shall have no **portion** in the Hereafter:
003:113 are a **portion** that stand (for the right);
003:176 no **portion** in the Hereafter, but a severe punishment.
004:011 to the male, a **portion** equal to that of two females:
004:033 give their due **portion**.
004:044 to those who were given a **portion** of the Book?
004:051 to those who were given a **portion** of the Book?
004:118 "I will take of Thy servants a **portion** marked off:
007:037 For such, their **portion** appointed must reach
007:161 (the **portion** of) those who do good."
009:069 They had their enjoyment of their **portion**: and ye
010:050 or by day,-what **portion** of it would the Sinners
010:061 and whatever **portion** thou mayest be reciting
011:063 to my (**portion**) but perdition?
011:109 their **portion** without (the least) abatement.
012:003 this (**portion** of the) Qur'an: before this,
015:065 when a **portion** of the night (yet remains), and do
016:056 do not know, a **portion** out of that which We have
017:075 and an equal **portion** in death: and moreover
017:075 thee taste double **portion** (of punishment)
028:077 nor forget thy **portion** in this world: but do
035:018 not the least **portion** of it can be carried
043:032 It is We Who **portion** out between them their
043:032 Is it they who would **portion** out the Mercy
051:059 is like unto the **portion** of their fellows
051:059 then let them not ask Me to hasten (that **portion**)!
051:059 For the wrong-doers, their **portion** is like
057:028 a double **portion** of His Mercy: He will
061:014 and a **portion** disbelieved: but We gave power to
061:014 Allah's helpers!" Then a **portion** of the Children

PORTIONS

004:011 These are settled **portions** ordained by Allah:
004:127 to whom ye give not the **portions** prescribed, and

POSITION

007:027 from a **position** where ye cannot see them: We
011:091 For thou hast among us no great **position**!"
019:073 is best in point of **position** and fairer
019:075 who is worst in **position**, and who

POSITION (continued)

026:058 Treasures, and every kind of honorable **position**;
028:082 And those who had envied his **position** the day
034:051 from a **position** (quite) near.
034:052 from a **position** (so) far off,-
034:053 with regard to the Unseen from a **position** far off?
040:020 will not (be in a **position**) to judge at all.
044:051 in a **position** of Security,

POSITIONS

004:102 let them take their **positions** in the rear.
034:018 in prominent **positions**, and between them We had

POSITIVELY

027:049 and we are **positively** telling the truth.'"

POSSESS

004:003 or that which your right hands **possess**.
004:024 except those whom your right hands **possess**:
004:025 from among those whom your right hand **possess**:
004:036 and what your right hands **possess**: for
016:043 ask of those who **possess** the Message.
016:071 to those whom their right hands **possess**, so as
021:007 ask of those who **possess** the Message.
023:006 right hands **possess**,-for (in their case) they are
024:031 right hands **possess**, or male attendants free
024:058 whom your right hands **possess**, and the
030:028 whom your right hands **possess**, to share
033:050 the captives whom their right hands **possess**;-
033:052 right hand should **possess** (as handmaidens):
033:055 right hands **possess**. And, (ladies), fear Allah;
054:027 and **possess** thyself in patience!
070:030 hands **possess**,-for (then) they are not to be blamed,

POSSESSED

010:054 if it **possessed** all that is on earth, would fain
015:006 Truly thou art mad (or **possessed**)!
023:025 a man **possessed**: wait (and have patience) with
023:070 Or do they say, "He is **possessed**"? Nay, he
034:046 your Companion is not **possessed**: he is
037:036 our gods for the sake of a Poet **possessed**?"
044:014 "Tutored (by others), a man **possessed**!"
051:039 "A sorcerer, or one **possessed**!"
051:052 "A sorcerer, or one **possessed**"!
052:029 of thy Lord, thou art no soothsayer nor **possessed**.
054:009 "Here is one **possessed**!", and he was driven out.
068:002 mad or **possessed**.
068:051 Surely he is **possessed**!"
081:022 And (O people!) your Companion is not one **possessed**;

POSSESSES

033:050 thy right hand **possesses** out of the captives
068:014 Because he **possesses** wealth and (numerous) sons.

POSSESSION

002:283 a pledge with **possession** (may serve the purpose).
012:056 to take **possession** therein as, when, or
024:061 are in your **possession**, or in
073:011 those in **possession** of the good things of life,

POSSESSIONS

003:010 neither their **possessions** nor their (numerous)
003:014 Such are the **possessions** of this world's life;
003:116 neither their **possessions** nor their (numerous)
003:186 and tested in your **possessions** and in yourselves;
008:028 And know ye that your **possessions** and your
047:036 and will not ask you (to give up) your **possessions**.

POSSESSORS

007:100 in succession to its (previous) **possessors**, is it

POSSESSORS (continued)
038:045 **possessors** of Power and Vision.

POSSIBLE
002:216 But it is **possible** that ye dislike a thing
002:246 He said: "Is it not **possible** if ye were
003:079 It is not (**possible**) that a man,
009:121 requite them with the best (**possible** reward).
040:078 to thee. It was not (**possible**) for any
049:012 as much (as **possible**): for suspicion in

POSSIBLY
006:019 Can ye **possibly** bear witness that besides
016:073 and cannot **possibly** have such power?

POST
003:121 to **post** the Faithful at their stations for battler:

POSTERITY
002:066 and to their **posterity**,
006:133 you up from the **posterity** of other people.
012:006 His favour to thee and to the **posterity** of Jacob-
019:006 and inherit the **posterity** of Jacob; and make
019:058 and of the **posterity** of Abraham and Israel-
019:058 of the **posterity** of Adam, and of those
019:059 a **posterity** who missed prayers and followed
040:008 their **posterity**! For Thou art (He), the Exalted

POSTS
007:114 (raised to **posts**) nearest (to my person)."
026:042 (raised to **posts**) nearest (to my person)."

POSTURE
007:161 and enter the gate in a **posture** of humility: We

POSTURES
010:012 he crieth unto Us (in all **postures**)-lying down

POT-HERBS
002:061 its **pot-herbs**, and cucumbers,

POTTERY
055:014 sounding clay like unto **pottery**.

POUNDED
089:021 Nay! When the earth is **pounded** to powder,

POUR
002:198 Then when ye **pour** down from (Mount) 'Arafat,
002:250 they prayed: "Our Lord! **Pour** out constancy on us
007:050 "**Pour** down to us water or anything that Allah
007:126 Our Lord! **pour** out on us patience
009:026 But Allah did **pour** His calm on the Messenger
009:071 On them will Allah **pour** His mercy:
012:041 As to one of you, he will **pour** out the wine
018:096 he said: "Bring me, that I may **pour** over it,
022:005 barren and lifeless, but when We **pour** down rain
044:048 "Then **pour** over his head the Chastisement
080:025 For that We **pour** forth water in abundance,
089:013 Therefore did thy Lord **pour** on them a scourge

POURED
006:006 for whom We **poured** out rain from the
006:145 or blood **poured** forth, or the
022:019 of Fire: over their heads will be **poured** out
034:018 We had **poured** Our blessings, We had
073:014 a heap of sand **poured** out and flowing down.

POURING
011:052 the skies **pouring** abundant rain, and strength
054:011 with water **pouring** forth.
055:066 **pouring** forth water in continuous abundance:

POVERTY
002:268 Satan threatens you with **poverty** and bids

POVERTY (continued)
009:028 And if ye fear **poverty**, soon will Allah enrich you,
024:032 if they are in **poverty**, Allah will
059:009 even though **poverty** was their (own lot). And those

POWDER
089:021 Nay! When the earth is pounded to **powder**,

POWER
002:020 for Allah hath **power** over all things.
002:106 Allah hath **power** over all things?
002:109 for Allah hath **power** over all things.
002:148 For Allah hath **power** over all things.
002:165 that to Allah belongs all **power**,
002:209 then know that Allah is Exalted in **Power**, Wise.
002:220 He is indeed Exalted in **Power**, Wise."
002:228 and Allah is Exalted in **Power**, Wise.
002:240 And Allah is Exalted in **Power**, Wise.
002:251 and Allah gave him **power** and wisdom
002:258 because Allah had granted Him **Power**?
002:259 Allah hath **power** over all things."
002:260 Then know that Allah is Exalted in **Power**, Wise."
002:284 For Allah hath **power** over all things.
003:018 the Exalted in **Power**, the Wise.
003:026 Verily, over all things Thou hast **power**.
003:026 thou givest **power** to whom Thou pleasest,
003:026 and Thou strippest off **power** from whom
003:026 Say: "O Allah! Lord of **Power** (and Rule),
003:029 And Allah has **power** over all things.
003:062 the Exalted in **Power**, the Wise.
003:165 for Allah hath **power** over all things."
003:189 and Allah hath **power** over all things.
004:053 Have they a share in dominion or **power**?
004:056 for Allah is Exalted in **Power**, Wise.
004:085 and Allah hath **power** over all things.
004:090 He could have given them **power** over you, and
004:098 and children who have no means in their **power**,
004:133 for He hath **power** this to do.
004:158 and Allah is Exalted in **Power**, Wise;
004:165 for Allah is Exalted in **Power**, Wise.
005:017 Say: "Who then hath the least **power** against Allah,
005:017 For Allah hath **power** over all things."
005:019 and Allah hath **power** over all things.
005:025 I have **power** only over myself and my bother: so
005:034 before they fall into your **power**: in that
005:038 and Allah is Exalted in **Power** full of Wisdom.
005:040 and Allah hath **power** over all things.
005:076 no **power** either to harm or benefit you? But
005:118 Thou art the Exalted in **power**, the Wise.
005:120 and it is He who hath **power** over all things.
006:017 He hath **power** over all things.
006:037 **power** to send down a Sign: but most
006:057 What ye would see hastened is not in my **power**.
006:058 see hastened were in my **power**, the matter
006:065 Say: "He hath **power** to send calamities
006:096 the Exalted in **Power**, the Omniscient.
006:102 and He hath **power** to dispose
006:109 are in the **power** of Allah: but what
007:127 and we have over them (**power**) irresistible.
007:188 Say: "I have no **power** over any good or harm
008:010 Exalted in **Power**, Wide.
008:041 For Allah hath **power** over all things.
008:046 lest ye lose heart and your **power** depart; and be
008:060 to the utmost of your **power**, including
008:071 given (thee) **power** over them. And Allah

POWER (continued)

009:039	hath **power** over all things.
009:069	they were mightier than you in **power** and more
009:071	His mercy: for Allah is Exalted in **power**, Wise.
010:031	Or who is it that has **power** over hearing and sight?
010:049	Say: "I have no **power** over any harm or profit
010:065	for all **power** and honour belong to Allah: it is
011:004	and He hath **power** over all things."
011:080	He said: "Would that I had **power** to suppress you
011:088	to the best of my **power**; and my success (in my
012:021	**power** and control over His affairs; but most
012:022	We gave him **power** and knowledge: thus do
012:056	**power** to Joseph in the land, to take
012:101	bestowed on me some **power**, and taught me
013:013	about Allah, He is Mighty in **Power**.
013:016	such as have no **power** either for good or for
014:001	in **Power**, Worthy of all Praise!-
014:004	is Exalted in **power**, Full of Wisdom.
014:018	no **power** have they over aught that they
014:030	Say: "Enjoy (your brief **power**)! But verily
014:047	for Allah is Exalted in **power**,-the Lord
016:060	for He is the Exalted in **Power**, Full of Wisdom.
016:073	such as have no **power** of providing them,
016:073	and cannot possibly have such **power**?
016:075	the dominion of another; he has no **power** of any
016:076	with no **power** of any sort; a wearisome burden
016:077	even quicker: for Allah hath **power** over all things.
016:079	Nothing holds them up but (the **power** of) Allah.
017:007	all that fell into their **power**.
017:056	the **power** to remove your troubles from you
017:099	has **power** to create the like of them (anew)?
018:034	more honour and **power** in (my following of) men."
018:039	(be done)! There is no **power** but from Allah!'
018:084	Verily We established his **power** on earth, and We
018:095	He said: "(The **power**) in which my Lord has
019:081	to give them **power** and glory!
019:087	None shall have the **power** of intercession,
020:087	to thee, as far as lay in our **power**: but we
020:089	and that it had no **power** either to harm
021:040	no **power** will they have then to avert it,
021:043	from Us? They have no **power** to aid themselves,
021:079	and Knowledge; it was Our **power** that made the
021:081	(It was Our **power** that made) the violent
021:087	no **power** over him! But he
022:005	in order that We may manifest (Our **Power**) to you;
022:006	and it is He Who has **power** over all things.
022:073	they would have no **power** to release it from the fly:
024:045	for verily Allah has **power** over all things.
024:055	inheritance (of **power**), as He granted
025:054	for thy Lord has **power** (over all things).
026:211	not meant for them, nor is it in their **power**
027:060	and delight: it is not in your **power** to cause
029:017	have no **power** to give you sustenance: then seek
029:020	for Allah has **power** over all things.
029:042	and He is Exalted (in **power**), Wise.
030:050	for He has **power** over all things.
030:054	and it is He Who has all knowledge and **power**.
031:009	is true: and He is Exalted in **power**, Wise.
031:027	for Allah is Exalted in **power**, Full of Wisdom.
032:006	the Exalted (in **power**), the Merciful;-
033:027	And Allah has **power** over all things.
034:022	they have no **power**,-not the weight of an atom,-
034:027	Nay, He is Allah, the Exalted in **Power**, the Wise."

POWER (continued)

034:042	So on that Day no **power** shall they have
035:001	for Allah has **power** over all things.
035:002	and He is the Exalted in **Power**, Full of Wisdom.
035:010	If any do seek for glory and **power**,-to Allah
035:010	to Allah belong all glory and **power**. To Him
036:075	They have not the **power** to help them: and they
037:180	Honour and **Power**! (He is free) from what
038:009	the Exalted in **Power**, the Grantor
038:036	Then We subjected the Wind to his **power**, to flow
038:045	possessors of **Power** and Vision.
038:082	(Iblis) said: "Then, by Thy **Power**, I will
039:001	from Allah, the Exalted in **Power**, Full of Wisdom.
039:005	Is not He the Exalted in **Power**-He Who
039:037	Is not Allah Exalted in **Power**, Lord of Retribution?
039:043	no **power** whatever and no intelligence?"
040:002	is from Allah, Exalted in **Power**, Full of Knowledge,-
040:042	in **Power**, Who forgives again and again!
041:039	who are dead. For He has **power** over all things.
041:041	and indeed it is a Book of exalted **power**.
042:003	Allah, Exalted in **Power**, Full of Wisdom.
042:009	it is He Who has **power** over all things.
042:029	and He has **power** to gather them together
042:050	for He is full of knowledge and **power**.
043:008	So We destroyed men-stronger in **power** than these;-
043:009	by (Him), the Exalted in **Power**, Full of Knowledge';
043:086	no **power** of intercession;-only he
045:002	is from Allah the Exalted in **Power**, Full of Wisdom.
045:016	the **Power** of Command, and Prophethood;
045:037	and He is Exalted in **Power**, Full of Wisdom!
046:002	is from Allah the Exalted in **Power**, Full of Wisdom.
046:008	then can ye have no **power** to help me against Allah.
046:026	in a (prosperity and) **power** which We have
046:033	Yea, verily He has **power** over all things.
047:013	with more **power** than thy city which has driven
048:007	and Allah is Exalted in **Power**, Full of Wisdom.
048:011	Say: "Who then has any **power** at all (to intervene)
048:019	Exalted in **Power**, Full of Wisdom.
048:021	and Allah has **power** over all things.
048:021	which are not within your **power**, but which
050:036	stronger in **power** than they? Then did
051:047	and We indeed have vast **power**.
051:058	Lord of **Power**,-Steadfast (for ever).
053:005	He was taught by one Mighty in **Power**,
057:002	and He has **Power** over all things.
057:029	that they have no **power** whatever over the Grace
059:006	and Allah has **power** over all things.
059:006	but Allah gives **power** to His Messenger over any
060:004	no **power** (to get) aught on thy behalf from Allah."
060:007	For Allah has **power** (over all things); and Allah
061:014	**power** to those who believed against their enemies,
064:001	and He has **power** over all things.
065:012	Allah has **power** over all things, and that
066:008	us Forgiveness: for Thou hast **power** over all things."
067:001	and He over all things Hath **Power**;-
069:029	"My **power** has perished from me!"...
072:021	Say: "It is not in my **power** to cause you harm,
075:040	the **power** to give life to the dead?
078:037	The Most Gracious: none shall have **power** to argue
081:020	Endued with **Power**, held in honour by the Lord
082:019	shall have **power** (to do) aught for another: for the
085:008	Exalted in **Power**, worthy of all Praise!
086:010	(Man) will have no **power**, and no helper.

POWER (continued)

090:005   Thinketh he, that none hath **power** over him?
097:001   this (Message) in the night of **Power**:
097:002   what the Night of **Power** is?
097:003   The Night of **Power** is better

POWERFUL

004:149   surely Allah is ever pardoning **Powerful**.
011:059   every **powerful**, obstinate transgressor.
011:080   myself to some **powerful** support."
014:015   the lot of every **powerful** obstinate transgressor.
022:039   Allah is Most **powerful** for their aid;
022:074   for Allah is **Powerful** and Mighty.
048:003   And that Allah may help thee with **powerful** help.
053:050   the (**powerful**) ancient 'Ad (people),
054:042   of a Mighty, **Powerful**.
068:045   truly **powerful** is My Plan.

POWERLESS

007:075   who were reckoned **powerless**-those among
011:077   and felt himself **powerless** (to protect) them.
012:066   (and made **powerless**) and when they had sworn
018:097   Thus were they made **powerless** to scale it
029:033   and felt himself **powerless** (to protect) them:

POWERS

010:024   **powers** of disposal over it: there reaches

PRACTICE

002:044   and forget to **practice** it yourselves,
004:025   that ye **practice** self-restraint.
004:128   But if ye do good and **practice** self-restraint,
004:129   and **practice** self-restraint, Allah
007:081   "For ye **practice** your lusts on men in
007:139   and vain is the (worship) which they **practice**."
010:085   for those who **practice** oppression;
016:094   to **practice** deception between yourselves. With
026:226   And that they say what they **practice** not?-
028:059   members **practice** iniquity.
029:004   Do those who **practice** evil think that they
029:029   And **practice** wickedness (even) in your councils?"
033:038   It was the **practice** (approved) of Allah
033:039   (It is the **practice** of those) who preach
033:062   wilt thou find in the **practice** (approved) of
033:062   (Such was) the **practice** (approved) of Allah
048:023   (Such has been) the **practice** of Allah already in
048:023   thou find in the **practice** of Allah.

PRACTICED

006:127   because they **practiced** (righteousness).
011:087   fathers **practiced**, or that we leave off doing
021:074   the town which **practiced** abominations: truly they
027:052   **practiced** wrong-doing. Verily in this
027:053   and **practiced** righteousness.
034:043   fathers **practiced**." And they say, "This is
041:018   who believed and **practiced** righteousness.

PRACTICES

113:005   the envious one as he **practices** envy.

PRACTICING

011:078   the habit of **practicing** abominations. He said:

PRACTISE

002:193   except to those who **practise** oppression.

PRAISE

001:002   **Praise** be to Allah,
002:267   and Worthy of all **praise**.
004:131   worthy of all **praise**.
006:001   **Praise** be to Allah, Who created the heavens

PRAISE (continued)

006:045   **Praise** be to Allah, the Cherisher of the Worlds.
006:100   **praise** and glory be to Him! (for He is)
007:043   and they shall say: "**Praise** be to Allah, Who
009:031   **Praise** and glory to Him: (far is He) from having
009:112   and **praise** Him; that wander in devotion to the
010:010   "**Praise** be to Allah, the Cherisher
011:073   all **praise**, full of all glory!"
014:001   in Power, Worthy of all **Praise**!-
014:008   Worthy of all **praise**.
014:039   "**Praise** be to Allah, who hath granted unto me
016:075   (By no means); **praise** be to Allah. But most
017:044   a thing but celebrates His **praise**; and yet
017:052   (His call) with (words of) His **praise**, and ye
017:079   raise thee to a Station of **Praise** and Glory!
017:111   Say: "**Praise** be to Allah Who begets no son,
018:001   **Praise** be to Allah, Who hath sent to His
020:033   "That we may celebrate Thy **praise** without stint,
022:024   to the path of Him Who is Worthy of (all) **Praise**.
022:064   all wants, worthy of all **praise**.
023:028   say: "**Praise** be to Allah, Who has
024:041   own (mode of) prayer and **praise**. And Allah
025:058   His **praise**; and enough is He to be acquainted
027:015   and they both said: "**Praise** be to Allah, Who has
027:059   Say: **Praise** be to Allah, and Peace
027:093   And say: "**Praise** be to Allah, Who will
028:070   To him be **praise**, at the first and the last:
029:063   Say, "**Praise** be to Allah!" But most
030:018   Yea, To Him be **praise**, in the heavens and on
031:012   worthy of all **praise**.
031:025   certainly say, "Allah." Say: "**Praise** be to Allah!"
031:026   worthy of all **praise**.
034:001   **Praise** be to Allah, to Whom belong all things
034:001   to Him be **Praise** in the Hereafter: and He
034:006   of the Exalted (in Might), Worthy of all **praise**.
035:001   **Praise** be to Allah, the Originator
035:015   the One Free of all wants, worthy of all **praise**.
035:034   And they will say: "**Praise** be to Allah, Who has
037:182   And **praise** to Allah, the Lord and
039:029   in comparison? **Praise** be to Allah! But most
039:074   They will say: "**Praise** be to Allah, Who has
039:075   on all sides, singing Glory and **Praise** to their
039:075   (on all sides) will be, "**Praise** be to Allah,
040:007   and **Praise** to their Lord; believe in
040:065   sincere devotion. **Praise** be to Allah, Lord of
041:042   Worthy of all **Praise**.
042:028   Worthy of all **Praise**.
045:036   Then **Praise** be to Allah, Lord of the
052:049   And for part of the night also **praise** thou Him,-
057:024   free of all needs, worthy of all **praise**.
060:006   of all Wants, Worthy, of all **Praise**.
064:001   Dominion, and to Him belongs **Praise**: and He
064:006   of all needs, worthy of all **praise**.
085:008   Exalted in Power, worthy of all **Praise**!

PRAISED

003:188   and love to be **praised** for what they have not done,

PRAISES

002:030   Thy **praises** and glorify Thy Holy (name)?"
002:198   and celebrate His **praises** as He
002:198   **praises** of Allah at the Sacred Monument,
002:200   the **praises** of your fathers,
002:200   celebrate the **praises** of Allah,
002:239   celebrate Allah's **praises** in the manner

PRAISES (continued)

003:041   Then celebrate the **praises** of thy Lord
013:013   Nay, thunder repeateth His **praises**, and so
015:098   But celebrate the **praises** of thy Lord and be
019:011   by signs to celebrate Allah's **praises** in the
020:130   the **praises** of thy Lord, before the
021:020   They celebrate His **praises** night and day, nor do
021:079   and the birds celebrate Our **praises**, with David:
024:041   Whose **praises** all beings in the heavens and on
032:015   and celebrate the **praises** of their Lord, nor are
034:010   echo ye back the **Praises** of Allah with him!
038:018   in unison with him, Our **Praises**, at eventide
040:055   and celebrate the **Praises** of thy Lord in the
041:038   who celebrate His **praises** by night and by day.
042:005   and the angels celebrate the **Praises** of their Lord,
048:009   and celebrate His **praises** morning and evening.
050:039   they say, and celebrate the **praises** of they Lord,
050:040   (also), celebrate His **praises**, and (so likewise)
052:048   in Our eyes: and celebrate the **praises** of thy Lord
057:001   and on earth,-declares the **Praises** and Glory
059:001   and on earth, declares the **Praises** and Glory
059:024   and on earth, doth declare His **Praises** and Glory:
061:001   and on earth, declares the **Praises** and Glory
062:001   and on earth, doth declare the **Praises** and Glory
064:001   and on earth, doth declare the **Praises** and Glory
110:003   Celebrate the **Praises** of thy Lord, and pray

PRAY

002:239   If ye fear (an enemy), **pray** on foot,
002:286   (**Pray**:) "Our Lord! Condemn us not if we
003:017   and who **pray** for forgiveness in the early hours
003:038   There did Zakariya **pray** to his Lord, saying:
003:061   then let us earnestly **pray**.
004:102   let them **pray** with thee, taking all precautions,
005:083   they **pray**: "Our Lord! we believe; write us
007:128   "**Pray** for help from Allah," and (wait)
007:189   they both **pray** to Allah their Lord (saying):
009:084   Nor do thou ever **pray** for any of them that dies,
009:103   sanctify them; and **pray** on their behalf. Verily
009:113   that they should **pray** for forgiveness for Pagans,
010:022   being overwhelmed: they **pray** unto Allah, sincerely
012:088   so pay us full measure, (we **pray** thee), and treat
019:047   I will **pray** to my Lord for thy forgiveness: for He
023:109   who used to **pray**, 'Our Lord!
025:074   And those who **pray**, "Our Lord!
040:049   of Hell: "**Pray** to your Lord to lighten us the
040:050   They will reply, "Then **pray** (as ye like)! But the
042:005   their Lord, and **pray** for forgiveness for all
060:004   said to his father: "I will **pray** for forgiveness
060:012   receive their fealty, and **pray** to Allah for the
063:005   "Come, the Messenger of Allah will **pray** for your
063:006   It is equal to them whether thou **pray** for their
073:002   Stand (to **pray**) by night, but not all night,-
075:031   So he gave nothing in charity, nor did he **pray**!-
096:010   A votary when he (turns) to **pray**?
110:003   and **pray** for His Forgiveness: for he

PRAYED

002:060   And remember Moses **prayed** for water
002:089   **prayed** for victory against those
002:250   they **prayed**: "Our Lord! Pour out constancy on us
004:102   which hath not yet **prayed** and let them
007:151   Moses **prayed**: "O my Lord! forgive me
007:155   he **prayed**: "O my Lord! if it had been Thy will
008:019   (O Unbelievers!) if ye **prayed** for victory

PRAYED (continued)

009:114   And Abraham **prayed** for his father's forgiveness
010:088   Moses **prayed**: "Our Lord! Thou hast indeed bestowed
028:016   He **prayed**: "O my Lord! I have
028:021   He **prayed**: "O my Lord! save me
039:008   and **prayed** for before, and he
060:004   from Allah." (They **prayed**): "Our Lord!
074:043   They will say: "We were not of those who **prayed**;

PRAYER

002:003   are steadfast in **prayer**,
002:043   And be steadfast in **prayer**: give Zakat,
002:045   with patient perseverance and **prayer**:
002:083   be steadfast in **prayer**; and Give Zakat.
002:110   **prayer** and give Zakat:
002:125   or prostrate themselves (therein in **prayer**).
002:125   the Station of Abraham as a place of **prayer**;
002:127   the House (with this **prayer**):
002:153   with patient Perseverance and **Prayer**:
002:177   to be steadfast in **prayer**,
002:186   I respond to every **prayer** of every suppliant
002:238   Especially the Middle **Prayer**;
003:038   for Thou art He that heareth **prayer**!
003:039   While he was standing in **prayer** in the chamber,
003:043   (in **prayer**) with those who bow down."
004:102   stand up (in **prayer**) with thee.
004:102   and standest to lead them in **prayer**, let one
004:142   When they stand up to **prayer**, they stand
004:162   regular **prayer** and pay Zakat and believe in
005:006   O ye who believe! when ye prepare for **prayer**, wash
005:058   When ye proclaim your call to **prayer**, they take
005:085   And for this their **prayer** hath Allah
005:091   and from **prayer**: will ye not then abstain?
005:106   detain them both after **prayer**, and let
006:162   Say: "Truly, my **prayer** and my
007:029   (to Him) at every time and place of **prayer**, and
007:031   at every time and place of **prayer**: eat and
007:170   by the Book and establish regular **prayer**,-never
007:194   and let them listen to your **prayer**, if ye
008:035   Their **prayer** at the house (of Allah) is nothing
009:054   that they come not to **prayer** save lazily and that
009:108   standing forth (for **prayer**) therein. In it
009:112   in **prayer**; that enjoin good and forbid evil;
010:010   (This will be) their **prayer** therein: "Glory to
010:010   and the end of their **prayer** will be: "Praise be to
010:089   Allah said: "Accepted is your **prayer** (O Moses
011:087   Does thy **prayer** command thee that we leave off
012:034   (in his **prayer**), and turned away from him
013:014   To Him is due the true **prayer** any others
013:014   for the **prayer** of those without Faith is nothing
013:014   is nothing but vain **prayer**.
014:037   may establish regular **prayer**: so fill
014:039   for truly my Lord is He, the Hearer of **Prayer**!
014:040   O our Lord! and accept Thou my **Prayer**.
014:040   who establishes regular **Prayer**, and also
017:078   in morning **prayer** for the recital of dawn
017:079   a part of it as an additional **prayer** for thee:
017:110   Neither speak thy **Prayer** aloud, nor speak
019:004   am I unblest, O my Lord, in my **prayer** to Thee!
019:007   (His **prayer** was answered): "O Zakariya! We give
019:031   on me **Prayer** and Charity as long as I live;
019:048   my Lord perhaps, by my **prayer** to my Lord, I shall
019:055   **Prayer** and Zakat and he was most acceptable in
020:014   and establish regular **prayer** for My remembrance.

PRAYER (continued)

020:036   (Allah) said: "Granted is thy **prayer**, O Moses!"
020:132   Enjoin **prayer** on thy people, and be
021:076   to his (**prayer**) and delivered him and his
022:026   or prostrate themselves (therein in **prayer**).
022:035   keep up regular **prayer**, and spend
022:041   the land, establish regular **prayer** and give
022:078   regular **Prayer**, give zakat and hold fast
024:037   nor from regular **Prayer**, nor from
024:041   own (mode of) **prayer** and praise. And Allah
024:056   So establish regular **Prayer** and give zakat
024:058   and after the late-night **prayer**: these are
024:058   before morning **prayer**; the while
026:218   Who seeth thee standing forth (in **prayer**),
029:045   and establish Regular **Prayer**:
029:045   for **Prayer** restrains from shameful and evil
031:004   Those who establish regular **Prayer**, and give
031:017   "O my son! establish regular **prayer**, enjoin what
033:033   regular **Prayer** and give zakat and obey
035:014   they cannot answer your (**prayer**). On the Day
035:018   establish regular **Prayer**. And whoever
035:029   of Allah, establish regular **Prayer**, and spend
037:075   and We are the Best to hear **prayer**.
040:050   But the **Prayer** of those without Faith is nothing
040:060   I will answer your (**Prayer**): but those
041:051   (he comes) full of prolonged **prayer**!
042:038   and establish regular **prayer**; who (conduct)
048:029   (in **prayer**), seeking Grace from Allah and (His)
058:001   her complaint (in **prayer**) to Allah: and Allah
058:013   establish regular **prayer**; give zakat and obey
062:009   is proclaimed to **prayer** on Friday (the Day
062:010   And when the **Prayer** is finished, then may
070:022   Not so those devoted to **Prayer**:-
070:023   Those who remain steadfast to their **prayer**;
073:020   standest forth (to **prayer**) nigh two-thirds
073:020   and establish regular **Prayer** and give zakat;
098:005   to establish regular **Prayer**; and to
108:002   Therefore to thy Lord turn in **Prayer** and Sacrifice.

PRAYERS

002:238   Guard strictly your (habit of) **prayers**.
002:277   and establish regular **prayers** and give Zakat,
004:043   O ye who believe! approach not **prayers** in a state
004:077   but establish regular **prayers** and spend
004:101   if ye shorten your **prayers**, for fear
004:103   set up regular **Prayers**: for such
004:103   for such **prayers** are enjoined on Believers
004:103   When ye have performed the **prayers**, remember
005:012   if ye (but) establish regular **Prayers**, pay Zakat
005:055   those who establish regular **prayers** and pay
006:072   "To establish regular **prayers** and
006:092   and they are constant in guarding their **Prayers**.
008:003   Who establish regular **prayers** and spend
009:005   regular **prayers**. And pay Zakat, then open
009:011   establish regular **prayers**, and pay Zakat they are
009:018   establish regular **prayers**, and pay Zakat, and fear
009:071   regular **prayers**, pay Zakat and obey Allah and His
009:099   and obtaining the **prayers** of the Messenger. Aye,
009:103   Verily thy **prayers** are a source of security
010:087   of worship, and establish regular **prayers**: and give
011:114   And establish regular **prayers** at the two ends
013:022   establish regular **prayers**; spend, out of
014:031   that they may establish regular **prayers**, and spend
017:078   Establish regular **prayers**-at the sun's decline

PRAYERS (continued)

019:059   a posterity who missed **prayers** and followed
021:073   good deeds, to establish regular **prayers**, and to
023:002   Those who humble themselves in their **prayers**;
023:009   And who (strictly) guard their **prayers**;-
027:003   Those who establish regular **prayers** and give
030:031   and fear Him: establish regular **prayers**, and be
107:005   Who are neglectful of their **Prayers**,

PRAYING

018:055   come to them, nor from **praying** for forgiveness
019:004   **Praying**: "O my Lord! infirm indeed are my bones,
051:018   they (were found) **praying** for Forgiveness;

PRAYS

017:011   Man prays for evil as fervently as he **prays**
017:011   as he **prays** for good for man is given to haste.
087:015   their Guardian-Lord, and **prays**.

PREACH

007:164   **preach** to a people whom Allah will destroy or
011:003   "(And to **preach** thus), `Seek ye the forgiveness
016:035   but to **preach** the Clear Message?
016:082   thy duty is only to **preach** the Clear Message.
024:054   is only to **preach** the clear (Message)".
029:018   is only to **preach** publicly (and clearly)."
033:039   who **preach** the Messages of Allah, and fear

PREACHERS

007:164   Said the **preachers**: "To discharge our duty

PREACHING

016:125   with wisdom and beautiful **preaching**; and argue
041:014   (**preaching**): "Serve none but Allah." They said,
054:005   but (the **preaching** of) Warners profits them not.

PRECAUTION

003:028   left with Allah except by way of **precaution**,
004:102   but take (every) **precaution** for yourselves.

PRECAUTIONS

004:071   O ye who believe! take your **precautions**.
004:102   taking all **precautions**, and bearing arms: the
009:050   our **precautions** beforehand," and they

PRECEDED

059:015   Like those who lately **preceded** them, they have

PRECEPTS

007:145   by the best in the **precepts**: soon shall I
017:039   (**precepts** of) wisdom, which thy Lord has revealed

PRECINCTS

002:196   is not in (the **precincts** of) the Sacred Mosque.
005:001   the Sacred **Precincts** or in the state of Pilgrimage.
005:002   of the Sacred **Precincts** and of the state
005:095   while in the Sacred **Precincts** or in the state
005:096   as long as ye are in the Sacred **Precincts** or in
017:001   Farthest Mosque whose **precincts** We did Bless,-

PRECIOUS

056:015   (with gold and **precious** stones),

PRECISELY

066:006   but do (**precisely**) what they are commanded.

PREDECESSORS

003:011   the people of Pharaoh, and their **predecessors**:
034:045   And their **predecessors** rejected (the Truth);
035:025   so did their **predecessors**, to whom

PREFER

009:038   Do ye **prefer** the life of this world to the
009:087   They **prefer** to be with (the women), who remain
009:093   are rich. They **prefer** to stay with the (women)

PREFER (continued)

009:120   behind Allah's Messenger, nor to **prefer** their own
014:003   Those who **prefer** the life of this world
020:072   They said: "Never shall we **prefer** thee to what
038:032   And he said, "Truly do I **prefer** wealth to the
087:016   Nay (behold), ye **prefer** the life of this world;

PREFERENCE

007:030   the Satans in **preference** to Allah, for their
007:081   on men in **preference** to women: ye are
013:006   the evil in **preference** to the good yet have
059:009   **preference** over themselves, even though

PREFERRED

002:047   and that I **preferred** you to all others.
002:122   and that I **preferred** you to all others.
009:083   for ye **preferred** to sit inactive on the
012:091   Allah **preferred** thee above us, and we
017:040   **preferred** for you sons, and taken for Himself
041:017   but they **preferred** blindness (of heart) to Guidance:
079:038   And had **preferred** the life of this world,

PREGNANT

022:002   and every **pregnant** female shall drop her
065:004   are **pregnant**, their period is until they deliver
065:006   And if they are **pregnant**, then spend

PREPARATION

009:046   some **preparation** therefor: but Allah was averse
009:107   and in **preparation** for one who warred against
033:053   to wait for its **preparation**: but when

PREPARE

005:006   O ye who believe! when ye **prepare** for prayer, wash

PREPARED

002:024   which is **prepared** for those who reject faith.
003:131   **prepared** for those who reject Faith.
003:133   **prepared** for the righteous.
004:018   for them have We **prepared** a chastisement
004:037   for We have **prepared**, for those who resist Faith,
004:093   and a dreadful chastisement is **prepared** for him.
004:102   Allah hath **prepared** a humiliating punishment.
004:151   and We have **prepared** for Unbelievers
004:161   We have **prepared** for those among them who reject
009:089   Allah hath **prepared** for them Gardens under which
009:100   hath He **prepared** Gardens under which rivers flow,
012:031   she sent for them and **prepared** a banquet for them:
017:010   that We have **prepared** for them a Chastisement
018:029   for the wrong-doers We have **prepared** a Fire
018:102   besides Me? Verily We have **prepared** Hell for the
020:041   "And I have **prepared** thee for Myself (for service)."
025:011   to come): but We have **prepared** a Blazing
025:037   and We have **prepared** for (all) wrong-doers
033:008   has **prepared** for the Unbelievers a grievous
033:029   **prepared** for the well-doers amongst you
033:031   and We have **prepared** for her
033:035   for them has Allah **prepared** forgiveness and
033:044   and He has **prepared** for them a generous Reward.
033:057   and has **prepared** for them a humiliating Punishment.
033:064   the Unbelievers and **prepared** for them
048:013   His Messenger, We have **prepared**, for those
057:021   **prepared** for those who believe in Allah and His
058:015   Allah has **prepared** for them a severe Chastisement:
065:010   Allah has **prepared** for them a severe Punishment
067:005   and have **prepared** for them the Chastisement
076:004   **prepared** Chains, Yokes, and a Blazing Fire.
076:031   He **prepared** a grievous Chastisement.

PREPARES

065:002   fear Allah, He (ever) **prepares** a way out,

PRESCRIBE

057:027   We did not **prescribe** for them: (We commanded)

PRESCRIBED

002:178   **prescribed** to you in cases of murder:
002:180   It is **prescribed**, when death approaches
002:183   O ye who believe! fasting is **prescribed** to you
002:183   as it was **prescribed** to those before you,
002:184   the **prescribed** number (should be made up)
002:185   (He wants you) to complete the **prescribed** period,
002:185   the **prescribed** period (should be made up)
002:216   Fighting is **prescribed** for you,
002:235   marriage till the term **prescribed** is fulfilled.
004:024   but if, after a dower is **prescribed**, ye agree
004:092   (is **prescribed**) a fast for two months running:
004:127   to whom ye give not the portions **prescribed**, and
005:048   have We **prescribed** a Law and an Open Way.
016:035   nor should we have **prescribed** prohibitions other
022:029   the rites **prescribed** for them, fulfil their
024:002   in a matter **prescribed** by Allah, if ye
065:001   divorce them at their **prescribed** periods, and count
065:001   **prescribed** periods: for fear Allah your Lord:
065:004   for them the **prescribed** period, if ye

PRESENCE

002:255   in His **presence** except as He permitteth?
004:006   take witnesses in their **presence**:
012:058   they entered his **presence**, and he knew them,
012:069   Joseph's **presence**, he received his (full) brother
012:088   into (Joseph's) **presence** they said: "O exalted
012:094   scent the **presence** of Joseph: nay, think
012:099   the **presence** of Joseph, he provided a home for
015:052   When they entered his **presence** and said,
018:065   taught knowledge form Our own **presence**.
024:058   your **presence**), on three occasions: before morning
027:010   fear not: truly, in My **presence**, those called
027:032   no affair have I decided except in your **presence**."
039:031   in the **presence** of your Lord.
039:034   in the **presence** of their Lord: such is
041:038   **presence** of thy Lord are those who celebrate
046:029   in the **presence** thereof, they said, "Listen in
049:003   in the **presence** of Allah's Messenger,-their hearts
050:028   with each other in My **Presence**: I had
051:025   Behold, they entered His **presence**, and said:

PRESENT

002:185   So every one of you who is **present** (at his home)
004:008   are **present**, give them out of the (property), and
004:072   in that we were not **present** among them."
006:144   Were ye **present** when Allah ordered
008:066   For the **present**, Allah hath lightened your
009:094   Say thou: "**Present** no excuses: we shall
009:094   They will **present** their excuses to you when ye
010:007   with the life of the **Present**, and those
010:023   of the **Present**: in the end, to Us
010:024   The likeness of the life of the **present** is as
010:064   in the life of the **Present** and in the Hereafter:
010:088   in the life of the **Present**, and so,
010:098   in the life of the **Present**, and permitted
011:015   the **Present** and its glitter,-to them
012:102   nor wast thou (**present**) with them when they
018:100   And We shall **present** Hell that day for Unbelievers
027:035   But I am going to send him a **present**, and wait

PRESENT (continued)

027:049 'We were not **present** at the slaughter of his
031:033 let not then this **present** life deceive you,
033:049 so give them a **present**, and release
035:005 is true, let not then this **present** life deceive
039:026 of humiliation in the **present** life, but greater
040:039 "O my people! This life of the **present** is nothing
040:052 to Wrong-doers to **present** their excuses, but they
043:035 of the **present** life: the Hereafter, in the sight
093:004 for thee than the **present**.

PRESENTED

005:027 Behold! they each **presented** a sacrifice (to Allah):
019:085 like a band (**presented** before a king for honours).

PRESERVE

002:088 (which **preserve** Allah's word, we need no more)"
012:031 "Allah **preserve** us! no mortal is this! This is
012:051 The ladies said: "Allah **preserve** us! no evil
014:035 and security: and **preserve** me and my sons
040:007 and **preserve** them from the Chastisement of the
040:009 "And **preserve** them from (all) ills; and any
040:009 and any whom Thou dost **preserve** from ills
044:056 and He will **preserve** them from the Chastisement

PRESERVED

078:029 And all things have We **preserved** on record.
083:007 is (**preserved**) in Sijjin.
083:018 the Righteous is (**preserved**) in 'Illiyin.
085:022 (Inscribed) in a Tablet **Preserved**!

PRESERVER

059:023 of Faith, the **Preserver** of Safety, the Exalted

PRESERVING

002:255 fatigue in guarding and **preserving** them

PRESS

002:019 they **press** their fingers in their ears
012:049 will **press** (wine and oil)."
047:037 of them, and **press** you, ye would covetously
074:037 To any of you that chooses to **press** forward, or to
079:004 Then **press** forward as in a race,

PRESSING

012:036 (in a dream) **pressing** wine." Said the other:

PRESUMPTION

004:153 but they were seized for their **presumption**, with

PRETENCE

016:028 they offer submission (with the **pretence**), "We did

PRETEND

006:025 who (**pretend** to) listen to thee; but We
010:042 (**pretend** to) listen to thee: but canst

PRETENDER

038:086 of you for this (Qur'an), nor am I a **pretender**.

PREVAIL

004:123 nor those of the people of the Book (can **prevail**):
009:033 to cause it to **prevail** over all religion,
048:028 to make it **prevail** over all religion:
058:021 who must **prevail**": for Allah is Strong, Mighty.

PREVAIL

061:009 That He make it **prevail** over all religion,

PREVAILED

018:021 about them: those who **prevailed** over their
061:014 the ones that **prevailed**.

PREVAILS

018:045 it is (only) Allah Who **prevails** over all things.

PREVENT

002:217 of Allah to **prevent** access to the path
002:217 to **prevent** access to the Sacred Mosque,
002:232 do not **prevent** them from marrying
002:282 to **prevent** doubts among yourselves
004:003 to **prevent** you from doing injustice.
027:081 to the Blind, (to **prevent** them) from straying:

PREVENTED

002:196 but if ye are **prevented** (from completing it),
007:012 (Allah) said: "What **prevented** thee from

PREVENTION

033:051 of their eyes, the **prevention** of their grief,

PREVENTS

038:075 (Allah) said: "O Iblis! what **prevents** thee from

PREVIOUS

007:100 in succession to its (**previous**) possessors, is it
008:068 a **previous** ordainment from Allah, a severe
020:051 condition of **previous** generations?"
041:025 and the word among the **previous** generations of
046:018 **previous** generations of Jinns and men, that have

PREVIOUSLY

066:005 **previously** married or virgins.

PREY

005:004 the beasts and birds of **prey**, training them
022:031 its **prey**) and thrown him into a far-distant place.

PRICE

002:041 nor sell My Signs for a small **price**:
002:079 to traffic with it for a miserable **price**!
002:086 at the **price** of Hereafter:
002:090 Miserable is the **price** for which
002:102 And vile was the **price** for which they
003:077 solemn plighted word for a small **price**,
003:177 Those who purchase Unbelief at the **price** of Faith,
005:044 and sell not My Signs for a miserable **price**.
005:106 "We will not take for it a **price** even though
009:009 they sold for a miserable **price**, and (many)
011:015 to them We shall pay (the **price** of) their deeds
012:020 a miserable **price**,-for a few dirhams counted out:
016:095 a miserable **price**: for with Allah is (a prize)

PRIDE

002:087 ye are puffed up with **pride**?
007:137 erected (with such **pride**).
011:010 behold! he falls into exultation and **pride**.
016:006 And ye have a sense of **pride** and beauty in them
027:014 them wrongfully and out of **pride**: so see
028:079 in the (**pride** of his worldly) glitter. Said those
031:018 "And swell not thy cheek (for **pride**) at men.
032:015 nor are they (ever) puffed up with **pride**.
037:035 would puff themselves up with **Pride**,

PRIED

072:008 'And we **pried** into the (secrets of) heaven;

PRIESTS

009:031 They take their **priests** and their anchorites
009:034 many among the **priests** and anchorites, who in

PRIOR

008:075 But kindred by blood have **prior** rights against

PRISON

012:025 but **prison** or a grievous chastisement?"
012:032 he shall certainly be cast into **prison**, and (what
012:033 He said: "O my Lord! the **prison** is dearer to my
012:036 into the **prison** two young men. Said one

PRISON (continued)

012:039   "O my two companions of the **prison**! (I ask you):

012:041   "O my two companions of the **prison**! As to

012:042   and (Joseph) lingered in **prison** a few (more) years.

012:045   one of the two (who had been in **prison**) and who

012:100   He took me out of **prison** and brought

017:008   made Hell a **prison** for those who reject

026:029   I will certainly put thee in **prison**!"

PRISONERS

008:067   that he should have **prisoners** of war until he

PRIVATE

002:076   but when they meet each other in **private**,

007:055   Call on your Lord with humility and in **private**:

012:080   they held a conference in **private**. The leader

017:047   and when they meet in **private** behold, the wicked

021:003   **private** counsels, (saying), "Is this (one)

038:021   over the wall of the **private** chamber;

043:080   their secrets and their **private** counsels? Indeed

058:012   the Messenger in **private**, spend something

058:012   your **private** consultation. That will

058:013   your **private** consultation (with him)? If, then,

071:009   in public and secretly in **private**,

PRIVATELY

016:075   spends thereof (freely), **privately** and publicly:

PRIVATION

090:014   Or the giving of food in a day of **privation**

PRIVY

004:043   you cometh from the **privy**, or ye have been

005:006   or one of you cometh from the **privy** or ye have

PRIZE

016:095   (a **prize**) far better for you, if ye only knew.

PROCEED

026:015   Allah said: "By no means! **proceed** them, both of

099:006   On that Day will men **proceed** in groups sorted out,

PROCEEDED

018:071   So they both **proceeded**: until, when they

018:074   Then they **proceeded**: until, when they

018:077   Then they **proceeded**: until, when they

PROCEEDING

004:023   your son **proceeding** from your loins;

004:171   and a Spirit **proceeding** from Him: so believe

086:007   **Proceeding** from between the backbone and the ribs:

PROCESS

010:004   It is He Who beginneth the **process** of Creation,

012:102   in the **process** of weaving their plots.

016:047   by a **process** of slow wastage-for thy

PROCESSION

043:053   with him angels accompanying him in **procession**?"

PROCLAIM

005:058   When ye **proclaim** your call to prayer, they take

005:067   O Messenger! **proclaim** the (Message) which hath

005:095   duty to **proclaim** (the Message)

005:099   but to **proclaim** (the message). But Allah

007:044   but a Crier shall **proclaim** between them: "The curse

009:003   frustrate Allah, and **proclaim** a grievous

009:112   So **proclaim** the glad tidings to the Believers.

022:027   "And **proclaim** the Pilgrimage among men: they will

022:037   guidance to you: and **proclaim** the Good News

037:003   Those who thus **proclaim** the message (of Allah)!

046:023   I **proclaim** to you the mission on which I have

PROCLAIM (continued)

093:011   But the Bounty of thy Lord-rehearse and **proclaim**!

096:001   **Proclaim**! (or Read!) in the name of thy Lord

096:003   **Proclaim**! And thy Lord is Most Bountiful,-

PROCLAIMED

005:067   and **proclaimed** His Mission. And Allah

021:109   say: "I have **proclaimed** the Message to you all

043:051   And Pharaoh **proclaimed** among his people, saying:

062:009   is **proclaimed** to prayer on Friday (the Day

PROCLAMATION

079:023   Then he collected (his men) and made a **proclamation**,

PRODUCE

002:023   then **produce** a Sura like thereunto;

002:061   to **produce** for us of what the earth groweth,

002:111   Say: "**Produce** your proof if ye are truthful."

005:054   soon will Allah **produce** a people whom He will

006:099   from some We **produce** green (crops), out of

006:099   out of which We **produce**, close-compounded

006:099   with it We **produce** vegetation of all kinds: from

006:141   and tilth with **produce** of all kinds, and olives

006:148   If so, **produce** it before us. Ye follow

007:057   and **produce** every kind of harvest therewith: thus

007:058   springs up **produce**, (rich) after its kind: but

010:024   arises the **produce** of the earth-which provides

016:066   We **produce**, for your drink, milk, pure and

016:069   Then to eat of all the **produce** (of the

017:088   were to gather together to **produce** the like

017:088   they could not **produce** the like thereof, even if

018:033   its **produce**, and failed not in the least therein:

018:034   (Abundant) was the **produce** this man had: he said

020:058   "But we can surely **produce** magic to match thine!

021:104   shall We **produce** a new one: a promise

023:021   We **produce** (milk) for you to drink; there are,

024:004   and **produce** not four witnesses, (to support

028:075   "**Produce** your Proof": then shall

029:020   so will Allah **produce** a later creation: for Allah

031:010   and **produce** on the earth every kind

032:027   (bare of herbage), and **produce** therewith crops,

035:027   With it We then bring out **produce** of various

036:033   and **produce** grain therefrom, of which ye do eat.

036:034   And We **produce** therein orchards with date-palms

039:021   therewith, **produce** of various colours: then it

050:009   and We **produce** therewith Gardens and Grain

052:034   Let them then **produce** a saying like unto it,-

052:038   of theirs **produce** a manifest proof.

068:041   **produce** their "partners," if they are truthful!

078:015   That We may **produce** therewith grain and vegetables,

080:027   And **produce** therein grain,

PRODUCED

002:267   the fruits of the earth which We have **produced** for you,

005:020   when He **produced** prophets among you, made you

006:098   **produced** you from a single soul: then there

006:136   Out of what Allah hath **produced** in abundance

007:032   which He hath **produced** for His servants, and

008:063   have **produced** that affection, but Allah

010:037   be **produced** by other than Allah; on the contrary

011:061   It is He Who hath **produced** you from the earth

015:019   and **produced** therein all kinds of things in due balance.

020:053   With it have We **produced** divers pairs of plants

021:104   We **produced** the first Creation, shall We

026:007   we have **produced** therein?

050:007   standing firm, and **produced** therein every kind

PRODUCED (continued)

071:017 "'And Allah has **produced** you from the earth,
089:008 not **produced** in (all) the land?

PRODUCES

012:072 the king; for him who **produces** it. Is (the
016:011 With it He **produces** for you corn, olives, date-
023:020 Mount Sinai, which **produces** oil, and relish
036:036 the earth **produces**, as well as their own (human)
036:080 "The same Who **produces** for you fire out of

PRODUCETH

006:141 It is He who **produceth** gardens, with

PRODUCING

034:016 (rows) into "gardens" **producing** bitter fruit,
055:011 **producing** spathes (enclosing dates);

PROFANITY

022:025 is **profanity** wrongfully them will We created

PROFESS

002:113 Yet they (**profess**) to study the (same) Book.

PROFESSING

040:085 But their **professing** the Faith when they

PROFIT

002:123 nor shall intercession **profit** her
002:164 for the **profit** of mankind;
002:174 and purchase for them a miserable **profit**,
002:219 and some **profit**, for men;
002:219 but the sin is greater than the **profit**."
005:119 will **profit** from their truth: theirs are
006:128 "Our Lord! we made **profit** from each other: but
007:048 saying: "Of what **profit** to you were your hoards
010:018 what can hurt them not nor **profit** them, and they
010:049 or **profit** to myself except as Allah willeth.
010:101 **profit** those who believe not.
010:106 such can neither **profit** thee nor hurt thee:
011:034 "Of no **profit** will be my counsel to you, much as
012:067 Not that I can **profit** you aught against Allah
012:068 it did not **profit** them in the least
016:117 a paltry **profit**; but they will have a most
019:042 and can **profit** thee nothing?
022:012 nor **profit** them: that is straying far indeed
022:013 is nearer than his **profit**: evil, indeed, is the
025:055 things that can neither **profit** them nor harm them:
026:207 It will **profit** them not the enjoyment
031:012 does so to the **profit** of his own soul: but if
032:029 no **profit** will it be to Unbelievers if they
033:016 Say: "Running away will not **profit** you if ye
034:042 for **profit** or harm: and We
039:050 was of no **profit** to them.
040:052 The Day when no **profit** will it be to Wrong-doers
040:082 they accomplished was of no **profit** to them.
040:085 was not going to **profit** them. (Such has
045:010 and of no **profit** to them is anything they may
046:026 heart and intellect: but of no **profit** to them
048:011 some **profit**? But Allah is well acquainted with
052:019 "Eat and drink ye, with **profit** and health,
058:017 Of no **profit** whatever to them, against Allah,
060:003 Of no **profit** to you will be your relatives
069:028 "Of no **profit** to me has been my wealth!
074:048 of (any) intercessors **profit** them.
077:001 one after another (to man's **profit**);
080:004 and the Reminder might **profit** him?
081:028 (With **profit**) to whoever among you wills to
089:023 that remembrance **profit** him?

PROFIT (continued)

092:011 Nor will his wealth **profit** him when he falls
111:002 No **profit** to him from all his wealth, and all

PROFITED

002:102 Not what **profited** them.
010:098 should have **profited** it,-except the people
011:101 whom they invoked, **profited** them no whit when there
066:010 and they **profited** nothing before Allah on their

PROFITLESS

002:016 but their traffic is **profitless**,

PROFITS

004:094 with Allah are **profits** and spoils abundant.
036:073 And they have (other) **profits** from them
054:005 but (the preaching of) Warners **profits** them not.
087:009 the admonition **profits** (the hearer).

PROFOUND

006:039 in the midst of darkness **profound**: whom Allah

PROGENY

002:128 and of our **progeny** a people Muslim,
002:205 and destroy crops and **progeny**
003:010 their (numerous) **progeny** will avail them aught
003:038 Grant unto me from Thee a **progeny** that is pure:
003:116 their (numerous) **progeny** will avail them aught
006:084 and among his **progeny**, David, Solomon,
006:087 and **progeny** and brethren: We chose them, and
008:028 and your **progeny** are but a trial: and that
018:050 and his **progeny** as protectors rather than Me?
029:027 his **progeny** Prophethood and Revelation, and We
032:008 And made his **progeny** from a quintessence
037:077 And made his **progeny** to endure (on this earth);
037:113 but of their **progeny** are (some) that do right,

PROHIBITED

002:194 The **prohibited** month for the **prohibited** month,
002:194 and so for all things **prohibited**,
002:194 The **prohibited** month for the **prohibited** month,
002:217 concerning fighting in the **Prohibited** Month.
004:023 **Prohibited** to you (for marriage) are: your mother,
004:024 Also (**prohibited** are) women already married,
006:151 Allah hath (really) **prohibited** you from": join
009:037 **prohibited** month) is an addition to Unbelief:
011:116 men of righteousness who **prohibited** men from
016:118 To the Jews We **prohibited** such things as We

PROHIBITION

002:194 transgresses the **prohibition** against you,
004:023 no **prohibition** if ye have not gone in;

PROHIBITIONS

004:024 Thus hath Allah ordained (**prohibitions**) against you:
007:166 they transgressed (all) **prohibitions**, We said
016:035 **prohibitions** other than His." So did

PROHIBITS

007:157 what is good (and pure) and **prohibits** them from
059:007 **prohibits** you. And fear Allah; for Allah

PROLONG

025:045 doth **prolong** the Shadow! If He willed,

PROLONGED

011:032 **prolonged** the dispute with us: now bring
041:051 (he comes) full of **prolonged** prayer!
073:007 **prolonged** occupation with ordinary duties:

PROMINENT

034:018 in **prominent** positions, and between them We had

PROMISE

002:080	Say: "Have ye taken a **promise** from Allah,
002:080	for He never breaks His **promise**?
002:124	He answered: "But My **Promise** is not
003:009	for Allah never fails in His **promise**."
003:152	His **promise** to you when we with His permission
003:183	our **promise** not to believe in a messenger unless he
003:194	for thou never breakest Thy **promise**."
003:194	Thou didst **promise** unto us through Thy Messengers,
004:122	Allah's **promise** is the truth, and whose
007:134	in virtue of his **promise** to thee: if thou
007:137	The fair **promise** of the Lord was fulfilled
009:111	a **promise** binding on Him in Truth, through the
009:114	a **promise** he had made to him. But when
010:004	The **promise** of Allah is true and sure. It is He
010:046	We **promise** them,-or We take thy soul (before that),-
010:048	They say: "When will this **promise** come to pass-
010:055	that Allah's **promise** is assuredly true? Yet most
011:045	and Thy **promise** is true, and Thou art
011:065	(behold) there is a **promise** not to be belied!"
013:031	not fail in His **promise**.
013:031	until the **Promise** of Allah come to pass,
014:022	a **promise** of truth: I too promised, but I
014:022	but I failed in my **promise** to you. I had no
014:047	His messengers in His **promise**: for Allah
016:038	a **promise** (binding) on Him in truth: but most
017:104	in the land (of **promise**)": but when
017:108	Truly has the **promise** of our Lord been fulfilled!"
018:021	that the **promise** of Allah it true, and that
018:098	and the **promise** of My Lord is true."
018:098	but when the **promise** of my Lord comes to pass,
019:061	for His **promise** must (necessarily) come to pass.
019:078	or has he taken a **promise** with the Most Gracious?
019:087	has received permission (or **promise**) from (Allah)
020:086	make a handsome **promise** to you? Did then
020:086	on you, and so ye broke your **promise** to me?"
020:086	Did then the **promise** seem to you long (in coming)?
020:087	They said: "We broke not the **promise** to thee,
020:097	a **promise** that will not fail: now look
021:009	Then We fulfilled to them Our **promise**, and We
021:038	They say: "When will this **promise** come to pass,
021:097	Then will the True **Promise** draw nigh
021:104	a **promise** We have undertaken: truly shall
022:047	in His **promise**. Verily a Day in the sight of
023:035	"Does he **promise** that when ye die and become
025:016	a **promise** binding upon thy Lord."
027:071	They also say: "When will this **promise** (come to
028:013	the **promise** of Allah is true: but most
028:061	a goodly **promise**, and who is going to reach
030:006	Never does Allah fall from His **promise**: but most
030:006	(It is) the **promise** of Allah. Never does
030:060	for verily the **promise** of Allah is true: nor let
031:009	To dwell therein. The **promise** of Allah is true:
031:033	Verily, the **promise** of Allah is true: let not
034:029	They say: "When will this **promise** (come to pass)
035:005	O men! certainly the **promise** of Allah is true,
035:040	the wrong-doers **promise** each other nothing but
036:048	this **promise** (come to pass), if what
038:053	Such is the **promise** made to you
039:020	(such is) the **promise** of Allah: never doth
039:020	never doth Allah fail in (His) **promise**.
039:074	Who has truly fulfilled His **promise** to us,
040:055	for the **Promise** of Allah is true: and ask

PROMISE (continued)

040:077	some part of what We **promise** them,- or We
040:077	For the **Promise** of Allah is true: and whether
045:032	"And when it was said that the **promise** of Allah
046:016	of the Garden: a **promise** of truth, which was
046:017	have Faith! For the **promise** of Allah is true."
046:017	Do ye hold out the **promise** to me that I shall
057:014	ye doubted (Allah's **promise**); and (your
067:025	They ask: When will this **promise** be (fulfilled)?
067:027	**promise** fulfilled), which ye were calling for!"
073:018	His **Promise** needs must be accomplished.

PROMISED

004:095	Unto all (in Faith) hath Allah **promised** good: but
005:009	hath Allah **promised** forgiveness and a great reward.
006:134	All that hath been **promised** unto you
008:007	Behold! Allah **promised** you one of the two
009:068	Allah hath **promised** the Hypocrites, men and women,
009:072	Allah hath **promised** to Believers, men and women,
011:017	the Fire will be their **promised** meeting place.
013:035	the righteous are **promised**! beneath it
013:040	We **promised** them or take to Us thy soul (before
014:022	a promise of truth: I too **promised**, but I
015:043	the **promised** abode for them all!
019:054	(strictly) true to what he **promised**, and he
019:061	(Allah) Most Gracious has **promised** to His
021:103	(the Day) that ye were **promised**."
021:109	ye are **promised** is near or far.
022:072	Allah has **promised** it to the Unbelievers!
023:036	"Far, very far is that which ye are **promised**!
023:083	"Such things have been **promised** to us and to
024:055	Allah has **promised**, to those among you who believe
025:015	eternal Garden, **promised** to the righteous?
026:206	the (Punishment) which they were **promised**!
027:068	"It is true we were **promised** this,-we and
033:012	His Messenger **promised** us nothing but delusion!"
033:022	had **promised** us, and Allah and His Messenger
036:052	had **promised**. And true was the word
036:063	"This is the Hell of which ye were **promised**!
040:008	which Thou hast **promised** to them, and to
041:030	the which ye were **promised**!
043:042	which We have **promised** them: for verily
043:083	of theirs, which they have been **promised**.
046:035	they see the (Punishment) **promised** them, (it will
047:015	which the righteous are **promised**: in it are
048:020	Allah has **promised** you many gains that ye
048:029	at him. Allah has **promised** those among them
050:032	"This is what was **promised** for you,-for every
051:005	Verily that which ye are **promised** is true;
051:022	as (also) that which ye are **promised**.
051:060	they have been **promised**!
053:047	That He hath **promised** a Second Creation
054:046	the time **promised** them (for their full recompense):
057:010	has Allah **promised** a goodly (reward). And Allah
070:042	that Day of theirs which they have been **promised**!
070:044	Such is the Day the which they are **promised**!
072:024	they are **promised**,-then will they know who it
072:025	which ye are **promised** is near, or whether
077:007	Assuredly, what ye are **promised** must come to pass.
085:002	By the **promised** Day (of Judgment);

PROMISES

004:120	but Satan's **promises** are nothing but deception.
004:120	Satan makes them **promises**, and creates
007:044	have you also found your Lord's **promises** true?"

PROMISES (continued)

007:044   the **promises** of our Lord to us true: have you
017:064   But Satan **promises** them nothing but deceit.
017:064   and make **promises** to them." But Satan

PROMISETH

002:268   Allah **promiseth** you His forgiveness and bounties.

PROMULGATED

075:018   follow thou its recital (as **promulgated**):

PRONE

017:097   gather them together, **prone** on their faces,
025:034   to Hell (**prone**) on their faces,-they will

PRONOUNCE

005:004   but **pronounce** the name of Allah over it: and fear
020:007   If thou **pronounce** the word aloud, (it is
022:036   then **pronounce** the name of Allah over them
058:003   But those who **pronounce** the word "Zihar" to their

PRONOUNCED

005:078   Curses were **pronounced** on those among
006:118   on which Allah's name hath been **pronounced**, if
006:119   on which Allah's name hath been **pronounced**, when
006:121   Allah's name hath not been **pronounced**: that
006:138   the name of Allah is not **pronounced**:-forging
039:069   and a just decision **pronounced** between them;

PROOF

002:111   Say: "Produce your **proof** if ye are truthful."
004:144   an open **proof** against yourselves?
004:174   come to you a convincing **proof** from your Lord
021:024   "Bring your convincing **proof**: this is
028:075   "Produce your **Proof**": then shall
052:038   of theirs produce a manifest **proof**.

PROOFS

004:153   and gave Moses manifest **proofs** of authority.
006:104   from your Lord **proofs** (to open your eyes): if

PROPER

002:189   Enter houses through the **proper** doors:
004:046   it would have been better for them, and more **proper**;
004:083   the **proper** investigators would have known
005:023   they said: "Assault them at the (**proper**) Gate:
005:077   the bounds (of what is **proper**), trespassing
006:141   but render the dues that are **proper** on the
057:015   the Fire: that is the **proper** place to claim you:

PROPERTY

002:188   your **property** among yourselves for vanities,
002:188   and knowingly a little of (other) people's **property**.
004:002   their **property** (when they reach their age),
004:005   give not your **property** which Allah has assigned
004:006   When ye release their **property** to them, take
004:006   release their **property** to them;
004:007   whether the **property** be small or large,
004:008   are present, give them out of the (**property**), and
004:010   **property** of orphans, eat up a fire into
004:024   with gifts from your **property**, desiring
004:029   your **property** among yourselves in vanities:
004:033   to **property** left by parents and relatives.
006:152   And come not nigh to the orphan's **property**,
008:072   with their **property** and their persons, in the
011:087   off doing what we like with our **property**? Truly,
012:079   our **property**: indeed (if we did so), we should
017:034   orphan's **property** except to improve it, until he
018:042   his **property**, which had (now) tumbled to pieces
030:039   for increase through the **property** of (other)
059:008   their **property**, while seeking Grace from Allah

PROPHECY

006:067   "For every **Prophecy** is a limit of time, and soon

PROPHET

002:104   (to the **Prophet**) Ra'ina,
002:246   They said to a **Prophet** (that was) among them:
002:247   Their **Prophet** said to them: "Allah hath appointed
002:248   And (further) their **Prophet** said to them: "A Sign
003:039   and (be besides) noble, chaste, and a **Prophet**,
003:044   (O **Prophet**!) by inspiration:
003:068   as are also this **Prophet** and those who believe:
003:161   No **prophet** could (ever) dishonestly
004:078   "This is from thee" (O **Prophet**).
005:081   in the **Prophet**, and in what hath been
007:094   Whenever We sent a **prophet** to a town, We took
007:157   the unlettered **Prophet**, whom they find
007:158   The unlettered **Prophet**, who believeth in
008:064   O **Prophet**! Sufficient unto thee is Allah,-
008:065   O **Prophet**! rouse the Believers to the fight.
008:067   It is not fitting for a **Prophet** that he
008:070   O **Prophet**! say to those who are captives
009:040   If ye help not (the **Prophet**), (it is no matter):
009:061   Among them are men who molest the **Prophet** and say,
009:061   But those who molest the **Prophet** will have
009:073   O **Prophet**! strive hard against the Unbelievers
009:113   It is not fitting, for the **Prophet** and those
009:117   the **Prophet**, the Muhajirs, and the Ansar,-who
015:072   Verily, by thy life (O **Prophet**), in their
019:030   He hath given me revelation and made me a **prophet**:
019:041   a man of Truth, a **prophet**.
019:049   We made a **prophet**.
019:051   and he was a messenger and a **prophet**.
019:053   his brother Aaron, (also) a **prophet**.
019:054   and he was a messenger (and) a **prophet**.
019:056   a man of truth (and sincerity) (and) a **prophet**:
022:052   or a **prophet** before thee, but, when he
023:039   (The **prophet**) said: "O my Lord! help me: for that
025:031   Thus have We made for every **prophet** an enemy
033:001   O **Prophet**! Fear Allah, and hearken
033:006   The **Prophet** is closer to the Believers
033:013   ask for leave of the **Prophet**, saying, "Truly our
033:028   O **Prophet**! say to thy Consorts: "If it
033:030   O Consorts of the **Prophet**! if any of you were
033:032   O Consorts of the **Prophet**! ye are not like any
033:038   to the **Prophet** in what Allah has indicated
033:045   O **Prophet**! Truly We have sent thee as a Witness,
033:050   the **Prophet** wishes to wed her;-this only
033:050   gives herself to the **Prophet** if the **Prophet**
033:050   O **prophet**! We have made lawful to thee
033:053   the **Prophet**: he is shy to dismiss you, but Allah
033:056   on the **Prophet**: O ye that believe! send ye
033:059   O **prophet**! Tell thy wives and daughters, and the
036:069   We have not instructed the (**Prophet**) in Poetry,
037:112   of Isaac-a **prophet**,-one of the Righteous.
040:005   plotted against their **prophet**, to seize
043:007   And never came there a **prophet** to them
049:002   of the **Prophet**, nor speak aloud to him in talk,
054:006   Therefore, (O **Prophet**,) turn away from them.
060:012   O **Prophet**! when believing women come to thee
065:001   O **Prophet**! when ye do divorce women, divorce them
066:001   O **Prophet**! why holdest thou to be forbidden
066:003   When the **Prophet** disclosed a matter in confidence
066:008   to be humiliated the **Prophet** and those who
066:009   O **Prophet**! strive hard against the Unbelievers

PROPHET (continued)
080:001   The (**Prophet**) frowned and turned away,
091:011   (their **prophet**) through their inordinate wrong-doing.
091:014   (as a false **prophet**), and they hamstrung her.

PROPHET'S
033:053   the **Prophet's** houses,-until leave is given you,-
043:088   (**Prophet's**) cry, "O my Lord! Truly these
053:011   The (**Prophet's**) (mind and) heart in no way

PROPHETHOOD
006:089   and Judgement, and **Prophethood**: if these
029:027   his progeny **Prophethood** and Revelation, and We
045:016   and **Prophethood**; We gave them, for Sustenance
057:026   **Prophethood** and Revelation: and some

PROPHETIC
003:079   And the **Prophetic** Office,

PROPHETS
002:091   the **prophets** of Allah in times gone by,
002:098   and His angels and **prophets**,
002:136   (all) **Prophets** from their Lord:
003:021   and in defiance of right, slay the **prophets**,
003:080   to take angels and **prophets** for Lords and Patrons.
003:081   Behold! Allah took the covenant of the **Prophets**,
003:084   and the **Prophets**, from their Lord;
003:112   and slew the **Prophets** in defiance of right:
003:146   How many of the **Prophets** fought (in Allah's way),
003:181   of slaying the **Prophets** in defiance of right,
004:069   of the **Prophets** (who teach), the Sincere
005:020   when He produced **prophets** among you, made you
005:044   by the **Prophets** who bowed (as in Islam)
006:090   Those were the (**prophets**) who
016:063   (our **prophets**) to Peoples before thee; but Satan
017:055   of the **Prophets** to excel others and We gave
019:058   Those were some of the **prophets** on whom
021:005   the ones that were sent to (**prophets**) of old!"
022:042   their **prophets**),-the People of Noah, and 'Ad
033:007   the **Prophets** their Covenant: and from
033:040   of Allah, and the Seal of the **Prophets**: and Allah
039:069   placed (open); the **prophets** and the witnesses
043:006   But how many were the **prophets** We sent
043:024   ye (**prophets**) are sent with."

PROPORTION
013:008   in (due) **proportion**.
015:029   (in due **proportion**) and breathed into him
032:009   in due **proportion**, and breathed into him of His
034:018   in due **proportion**: "Travel therein, secure, by
054:049   We created in **proportion** and measure.
065:003   for all things has Allah appointed a due **proportion**.
067:003   one above another: no want of **proportion** wilt thou
075:038   and fashion (him) in due **proportion**.
082:007   fashioned thee in due **proportion**, and gave
087:002   given order and **proportion**;
091:007   By the Soul, and the **proportion** and order

PROPORTIONATE
016:126   let your punishment be **proportionate** to the

PROPORTIONS
025:002   and ordered them in due **proportions**.
039:005   in true (**proportions**): He makes
080:019   and then mouldeth him in due **Proportions**;

PROPOUND
030:028   He does **propound** to you a similitude from
041:047   The Day that (Allah) will **propound** to them
059:021   such are the similitudes which We **propound** to men,

PROPOUNDED
030:058   Verily We have **propounded** for men, in this

PROPPED
063:004   pieces of timber **propped** up, (unable to

PROSPECT
024:060   the **prospect** of marriage,-there is

PROSPER
002:005   and it is these who will **prosper**.
002:189   and fear Allah: that ye may **prosper**.
003:130   that ye may (really) **prosper**.
003:200   and fear Allah; that ye may **prosper**.
005:035   and main in His cause: that ye may **prosper**.
005:090   eschew such (abomination), that ye may **prosper**.
005:100   O ye that understand that (so) ye may **prosper**."
006:021   But verily the wrong-doers never shall **prosper**.
006:135   the wrong-doers will not **prosper**."
007:008   will be heavy, will **prosper**:
007:069   that so ye may **prosper**."
007:157   it is they who will **prosper**."
008:045   much (and often); that ye may **prosper**.
009:088   and it is they who will **prosper**.
010:017   But never will **prosper** those who sin.
010:069   against Allah will never **prosper**."
010:077   But sorcerers will not **prosper**."
016:116   to Allah, will never **prosper**.
022:077   your Lord; and do good; that ye may **prosper**.
023:117   shall not **prosper**.
024:051   it is such as these that will **prosper**.
026:089   "But only he (will **prosper**) that brings
028:037   that the wrong-doers will not **prosper**."
028:082   will assuredly never **prosper**."
030:038   and it is they who will **prosper**.
031:005   are the ones who will **prosper**.
062:010   and remember Allah frequently that ye may **prosper**.
087:014   But he will **prosper** who purify himself.

PROSPERETH
010:081   of no effect: for Allah **prospereth** not the work

PROSPERITY
003:134   whether in **prosperity**, or in adversity;
007:095   their suffering into **prosperity**, until they
007:168   with both **prosperity** and adversity: in order
011:084   I see you in **prosperity**, but I fear for you
018:020   and in that case ye would never attain **prosperity**."
046:026   in a (**prosperity** and) power which We have
059:009   they are the ones that achieve **prosperity**.
064:016   they are the ones that achieve **prosperity**.

PROSTITUTION
024:033   maids to **prostitution** when they desire chastity,

PROSTRATE
002:125   or **prostrate** themselves (therein in prayer).
003:043   **prostrate** thyself, and bow down (in prayer)
003:113   and they **prostrate** themselves in adoration.
007:011   then We bade the angels **prostrate** to Adam, and
007:011   he refused to be of those who **prostrate**.
007:078   and they lay **prostrate** in their homes
007:091   and they lay **prostrate** in their
007:120   But the sorcerers fell down **prostrate** in adoration.
007:206   they glorify Him and **prostrate** before Him.
009:112   that bow down and **prostrate** themselves in prayer;
011:067   **prostrate** in their homes before the morning,-
011:094   and they lay **prostrate** in their homes
012:004   I saw them **prostrate** themselves to me!"

PROSTRATE (continued)

013:015 do **prostrate** themselves to Allah-with good-will
015:033 to **prostrate** myself to man, Whom Thou
015:098 and be of those who **prostrate** themselves in
016:049 And to Allah doth **prostrate** all that is in
017:061 "**Prostrate** unto Adam": they prostrated
017:061 he said, "Shall I **prostrate** to one whom Thou
018:050 "**Prostrate** to Adam": they prostrated except Iblis.
019:058 in **prostrate** adoration and in tears.
020:116 "**Prostrate** yourselves to Adam," they prostrated
022:018 Seest thou not that to Allah **prostrate** all things
022:026 or **prostrate** themselves (therein in prayer).
022:077 **prostrate** yourselves, and adore your Lord,
025:064 in adoration of their Lord **prostrate** and standing;
026:046 **prostrate** in adoration,
026:219 those who **prostrate** themselves.
029:037 and they lay **prostrate** in their homes
037:103 **prostrate** on his forehead (for sacrifice),
041:037 and the moon, but **prostrate** to Allah,
041:037 **Prostrate** not to the sun and the moon,
048:029 and **prostrate** themselves (in prayer),
068:042 to **prostrate**, but they shall not be able,-
076:026 And part of the night, **prostrate** thyself to Him;
077:048 "**Prostrate** yourselves!" They do not so.
084:021 they fall not **prostrate**.
096:019 but **prostrate** down in adoration, and bring

PROSTRATED

007:011 and they **prostrated** , not so Iblis; he refused
015:030 So the angels **prostrated** themselves, all of
015:031 among those who **prostrated** themselves.
015:032 those who **prostrated** themselves?"
017:061 they **prostrated** except Iblis: he said,
018:050 "Prostrate to Adam": they **prostrated** except Iblis.
020:116 they **prostrated** themselves, but not
038:073 So the angels **prostrated** themselves, all of

PROSTRATING

002:058 and enter the gate **prostrating**,
007:012 thee from **prostrating** when I commanded thee?"
016:048 and the left, **prostrating** themselves to Allah,
038:075 thee from **prostrating** thyself to one whom I
039:009 **prostrating** himself or standing (in adoration),

PROSTRATION

012:100 in **prostration** (all) before him. He said:
017:107 fall down on their faces in humble **prostration**,
020:070 to **prostration**: they said, "We believe
038:024 (in **prostration**), and turned (to Allah in repentance).
038:072 fall ye down in **prostration** unto him."
048:029 (being) the traces of their **prostration**. This is
050:040 and (so likewise) after the **prostration**.
053:062 But fall ye down in **prostration** to Allah,

PROSTRATIONS

004:102 when they finish their **prostrations**, let them

PROTECT

004:075 and raise for us from Thee one who will **protect**;
004:135 for Allah can best **protect** both.
004:173 any to **protect** or help them.
008:040 the Best to **protect** and the Best to help.
008:073 (**protect** each other), there would be tumult and
009:074 none on earth to **protect** or help them.
011:077 (to **protect**) them. He said: "This is
013:011 besides Him, any to **protect**.
016:081 to **protect** you from heat, and coats

PROTECT (continued)

016:081 and coats of mail to **protect** you from your
017:111 to **protect** Him from humiliation: yea, magnify
021:068 They said, "Burn him and **protect** your gods,
022:078 the Best to **protect** and the Best to help!
029:033 (to **protect**) them: but they said: "Fear not
032:004 besides Him, to **protect** or intercede (for you):
042:031 anyone to **protect** or to help.
082:010 (are appointed angels) to **protect** you,-

PROTECTED

023:088 but is not **protected** (of any)? (Say) if ye know."

PROTECTION

003:036 to Thy **protection** from Satan the Rejected."
003:112 (of **protection**) from Allah and from men;
005:044 the **protection** of Allah's Book, and the were
008:072 ye owe no duty of **protection** to them
016:098 seek Allah's **protection** from Satan the Rejected one.
018:044 There, the (only) **protection** comes from Allah,
018:090 no covering **protection** against the sun.
040:027 (for **protection**) from every arrogant one who
060:009 (for friendship and **protection**). It is

PROTECTOR

002:120 neither **Protector** nor Helper against Allah.
002:257 Allah is the **Protector** of those who have faith:
002:286 Thou art our **protector**;
003:068 and Allah is the **Protector** of those who have faith.
003:122 but Allah was their **Protector**,
003:150 Nay, Allah is your **Protector**, and He
004:045 Allah is enough for a **Protector**, and Allah
004:123 besides Allah, any **protector** or helper.
006:014 Say: "Shall I take for my **protector** any other
006:051 no **protector** nor intercessor: that they
006:062 their True **Protector**, surely His is
006:070 no **protector** or intercessor except Allah: if it
007:155 Thou art our **Protector**: so forgive us
007:196 "For my **Protector** is Allah, Who revealed
008:040 be sure that Allah is your **Protector**-
009:051 He is our **Protector**": and on Allah let the
009:116 Except for Him ye have no **protector** nor helper.
012:101 Thou art my **Protector** in this world and in
013:037 **protector** nor defender against Allah.
017:068 so that ye shall find no **protector**?
017:097 wilt thou find no **protector** besides Him. On the
018:017 for him wilt thou find no **protector** to lead
018:026 They have no **protector** other than Him; nor does
022:078 He is your **Protector**-the best
029:022 beside Allah, any **protector** or helper."
033:017 any **protector** or helper.
033:065 no **protector** will they find, nor helper.
034:041 Thou art our **protector**-not them. Nay, but
042:008 no **protector** nor helper.
042:009 But it is Allah,-He is the **Protector**, and it
042:028 and wide). And He is the **Protector**, Worthy of
042:044 there is no **protector** thereafter. And thou
044:041 The Day when no **protector** can avail his client
045:019 but Allah is the **Protector** of the Righteous.
047:011 but those who reject Allah have no **protector**.
047:011 That is because Allah is the **Protector** of those
048:022 find neither **protector** nor helper.
066:002 is your **Protector**, and He is Full of Knowledge
066:004 truly Allah is his **Protector**, and Gabriel,
086:004 There is no soul but has a **protector** over it.

PROTECTORS

004:034 Men are the **protectors** and maintainers of women,
005:051 they are but friends and **protectors** to each other.
005:051 and the Christians for your friends and **protectors**:
005:057 take not for friends and **protectors** those who
005:081 for friends and **protectors**, but most of them
007:003 as friends or **protectors**, other than Him.
007:030 for their friends and **protectors**, and think
008:072 these are (all) friends and **protectors**, one of
008:073 The Unbelievers are **protectors**, one of another:
009:016 and **protectors** except Allah, His Messenger, and
009:023 for **protectors** your fathers and your brothers
009:071 are **protectors**, one of another: they enjoin
011:020 nor have they **protectors** besides Allah! Their
011:113 and ye have no **protectors** other than Allah,
013:016 (for worship) **protectors** other than Him, such as
018:050 and his progeny as **protectors** rather than Me?
018:102 can take my servants as **protectors** besides Me?
025:018 should take for **protectors** others besides Thee:
029:041 take **protectors** other than Allah is that
039:003 **protectors** other than Allah (say): "We only
041:031 "We are your **protectors** in this life and in
042:006 And those who take as **protectors** others besides
042:009 (for worship) **protectors** besides Him? But is
042:046 And no **protectors** have they to help them,
045:010 nor any **protectors** they may have taken to
045:019 as) **Protectors**, one to another: but Allah
046:032 and no **protectors** can he have besides Allah:
060:001 and yours as friends (or **protectors**),-offering

PROTECTS

023:088 Who **protects** (all), but is

PROUD

021:019 are not too **proud** to serve Him, nor are
059:023 the justly **Proud**, Glory to Allah! (high is He)

PROVE

006:150 to **prove** that Allah did forbid so and so." If
008:008 and **prove** Falsehood false, distasteful though
010:082 doth **prove** and establish the Truth, however much
024:013 to **prove** it? When they have not brought the
034:020 And on them did Satan **prove** true his idea,

PROVED

009:043 and thou hadst **proved** the liars?
010:033 **proved** true against those who rebel: verily they
012:074 if ye are (**proved**) to have lied?"
017:016 the word is **proved** true against them; then We
025:019 "Now have they **proved** you liars in what ye say:
028:063 be **proved**, will say: "Our Lord! these are
036:007 The Word is **proved** true against the greater
036:070 may be **proved** true against those who
037:031 "So now has been **proved** true, against us,
039:071 has been **proved** true against the Unbelievers!"
040:006 **proved** true against the Unbelievers; that truly
041:025 who have passed away, is **proved** against them;
046:018 the word **proved** true among the previous generations

PROVES

042:024 and **proves** the Truth by His Words. For He

PROVIDE

004:130 Allah will **provide** abundance for each of them
005:114 and **provide** for our sustenance, for thou
006:151 We **provide** sustenance for and for them;-come
007:050 that Allah doth **provide** for your sustenance." They
009:092 no resources wherewith to **provide** the expenses.

PROVIDE (continued)

010:087 with this message: "**Provide** dwellings for your
012:059 and that I do **provide** the best hospitality?
017:030 Verily thy Lord doth **provide** sustenance in
017:031 of want: We shall **provide**, sustenance for them
020:132 We **provide** it for thee. But the
020:132 We ask thee not to **provide** sustenance: We **provide**
024:038 His Grace: for Allah doth **provide** for those
033:028 then come! I will **provide** for your enjoyment
043:033 would **provide**, for everyone that blasphemes
057:028 He will **provide** for you a light by which
058:011 (Ample) room will Allah **provide** for you.
062:011 And Allah is the Best to **provide** (for all needs)."
067:021 **provide** you with Sustenance if He were to
080:024 (and how We **provide** it):

PROVIDED

002:003 We have **provided** for them.
002:057 the good things We have **provided** for you:"
002:060 the sustenance **provided** by Allah,
002:172 the good things that We have **provided** for you.
002:230 **provided** they feel that they can keep the limits
002:233 **provided** ye pay (the foster mother)
002:240 **provided** it is reasonable.
002:254 (the bounties) We have **provided** for you,
003:170 They rejoice in the bounty **provided** by Allah:
004:024 **provided** ye seek (them in marriage) with
004:091 in their case We have **provided** you with a clear
005:088 which Allah hath **provided** for you, lawful
006:140 hath **provided** for them, inventing
006:142 eat what Allah hath **provided** for you, and
007:010 and **provided** you therein with means for the
007:032 (which He hath **provided**) for sustenance? Say:
007:160 We have **provided** for you": (but they rebelled);
008:026 and kidnap you; but He **provided** a safe asylum
009:092 to thee to be **provided** with mount. And when
010:093 and **provided** for them sustenance of the best:
012:099 the presence of Joseph, he **provided** a home for
015:020 And We have **provided** therein means of subsistence,-
016:072 and grandchildren, and **provided** for you sustenance
016:114 which Allah has **provided** for you, lawful and good;
017:018 in the end have We **provided** Hell for them:
017:070 **provided** them with transport on land and sea;
018:032 We **provided** two gardens of grape-vines and
018:090 for whom We had **provided** no covering protection
019:024 hath **provided** a rivulet beneath thee;
020:081 We have **provided** for your sustenance, but commit
022:028 the benefits (**provided**) for them, and celebrate
022:028 **provided** for them for sacrifice): then eat
024:060 **provided** they make not wanton display of their
027:023 ruling over them and **provided** with every requisite;
030:040 further, He has **provided** for your sustenance;
034:015 "Eat of the Sustenance (**provided**) by your Lord,
035:029 We have **provided** for them, secretly and
036:047 which Allah has **provided** you," the Unbelievers
040:064 and has **provided** for you Sustenance, of things
041:012 with lights, and (**provided** it) with guard.
077:027 and **provided** for you water sweet (and wholesome)?

PROVIDES

003:037 for Allah **provides** sustenance to whom He pleases,
010:024 which **provides** food for men and animals: (it grows)
065:003 And He **provides** for him from (sources) he never
106:004 Who **provides** them with food against hunger,

PROVIDING
015:022 from the shy, therewith **providing** you with water
016:073 **providing** them, for sustenance, with anything
032:027 therewith crops, **providing** food for their cattle
068:039 of Judgment, (**providing**) that ye shall have

PROVISION
002:197 And take a **provision** (with you) for the journey,
008:074 and a **provision** most generous.
020:118 "There is therein (enough **provision**) for thee
020:131 but the **provision** of thy Lord is better
022:058 He Who bestows the best **Provision**.
022:058 a goodly **Provision**: truly Allah is He Who
024:026 and a **provision** honorable.
028:057 a **provision** from Ourselves? But most
028:082 Who enlarges the **provision** or restricts it,
030:037 the **provision** and restricts it, to whomsoever
030:044 will make **provision** for themselves (in heaven):
034:036 and restricts the **provision** to whom He pleases,
039:052 the **provision** or restricts it, for any
042:027 the **provision** for His Servants, they would
059:018 and let every soul look to what (**provision**) he has
065:011 a most excellent **provision**.
067:021 were to withhold His **provision**? Nay, they
079:033 A **provision** for you and your cattle.
080:032 A **provision** for you and your cattle.

PROVISIONS
002:197 but the best of **provisions** is right conduct.
012:059 them forth with **provisions** (suitable) for them,
012:065 camel's load (of grain to our **provisions**). This
012:070 them forth with **provisions** (suitable) for them,

PROVOKED
043:055 When at length they **provoked** Us, We exacted

PROWESS
002:247 abundantly with knowledge and bodily **prowess**:

PSALMS
004:163 and to David We gave the **Psalms**.
017:055 and We gave to David the **Psalms**.
021:105 Before this We wrote in the **Psalms**, after the

PUBLIC
002:274 in secret and in **public**,
004:083 some matter touching (**public**) safety or fear,
004:148 shouting of evil words in **public** speech, except
004:153 for they said: "Show us Allah in **public**," but
071:009 in **public** and secretly in private,

PUBLICLY
014:007 to be declared (**publicly**): "If ye are grateful,

PUBLICLY
016:075 and **publicly**: are the two equal? (By no means);
029:018 is only to preach **publicly** (and clearly)."
038:070 that I am to give warning plainly and **publicly**."

PUFF
037:035 would **puff** themselves up with Pride,

PUFFED
002:087 ye are **puffed** up with pride?
032:015 nor are they (ever) **puffed** up with pride.
089:015 and gifts, then saith he, (**puffed** up), "My Lord

PULLED
022:040 **pulled** down monasteries, churches, synagogues,

PUNISH
003:056 I will **punish** them with severe chastisement
003:128 whether He turn in mercy to them, or **punish** them;

PUNISH (continued)
004:016 **punish** them both.
004:173 He will **punish** with a grievous chastisement: nor
005:018 Say: "Why then doth He **punish** you for your sins?
005:049 it is Allah's purpose to **punish** them.
005:095 for repetition Allah will **punish** him for Allah
005:115 I will **punish** him with a chastisement such as I
005:118 "If Thou dost **punish** them, they are
006:139 He will soon **punish** them: for He is
007:100 We could **punish** them (too) for their sins, and
008:034 that Allah should not **punish** them, when they
009:014 **punish** them by your hands, and disgrace
009:039 He will **punish** you with a grievous penalty,
009:055 **punish** them with these things in this life,
009:066 We will **punish** other amongst you, for that
009:074 Allah will **punish** them with a grievous chastisement
009:085 Allah's Wish is to **punish** them with these things
009:101 twice shall We **punish** them: and in
009:106 whether He will **punish** them, or turn in mercy
012:075 Thus it is We **punish** the wrong-doers!
016:061 It Allah were to **punish** men for their wrong-doing,
016:126 And if ye **punish**, let your
017:015 nor would We **punish** until, We had sent
017:058 the Day of Judgment or **punish** it with a dreadful
018:086 to **punish** them, or to treat them with kindness."
018:087 we **punish**; then shall he be sent back to his Lord;
018:087 to his Lord; and He will **punish** him with
022:021 of iron (to **punish**) them.
022:044 **punish** them: but how (terrible) was My punishment
027:021 "I will certainly **punish** him with a
033:024 and **punish** the Hypocrites if that be His Will,
033:073 has to **punish** the Hypocrites, men and women,
035:026 In the end did I **punish** those who rejected Faith:
035:045 If Allah were to **punish** men according to what
048:006 And that He may **punish** the Hypocrites,
048:016 He will **punish** you with a grievous Chastisement."
048:017 (Allah) will **punish** him with a grievous Chastisement.
058:008 "Why does not Allah **Punish** us for our words?
079:025 But Allah did **punish** him, (and made an)

PUNISHED
007:130 We **punished** the people of Pharaoh with years
008:052 and Allah **punished** them for their crimes: for Allah
009:026 He **punished** the Unbelievers: thus doth
013:032 I **punished** them: then how (terrible) was My
017:004 (and twice would they be **punished**)!
022:048 **punished** them. To Me is the destination (of all).
026:214 those who will be **punished**.
028:084 **punished** (to the extent) of their deeds.
037:059 and that we shall not be **punished**?"
048:025 We should certainly have **punished** the Unbelievers
059:003 He would certainly have **punished** them in this
069:010 of their Lord; so He **punished** them with an

PUNISHES
029:021 "He **punishes** whom He pleases, and He
048:014 and He **punishes** whom He wills: but Allah

PUNISHETH
002:284 and **punisheth** whom He pleaseth.
003:129 and **punisheth** whom He pleaseth;
005:018 and He **punisheth** whom He Pleaseth: and to Allah
005:040 He **punisheth** whom He pleaseth, and He forgiveth

PUNISHMENT
002:104 Faith is a grievous **punishment**.

PUNISHMENT (continued)

002:165   and Allah will strongly enforce the **Punishment**:
002:165   Behold, they would see the **Punishment**:
002:196   And know that Allah, is strict in **punishment**.
002:211   Allah is strict in **punishment**.
003:011   For Allah is strict in **punishment**.
003:088   nor will their **punishment** be lightened,
003:176   no portion in the Hereafter, but a severe **punishment**.
003:177   but they will have a grievous **punishment**.
003:178   but they will have a shameful **punishment**.
004:014   and they shall have a humiliating **punishment**.
004:025   their **punishment** is half that for free women.
004:037   a **Punishment** that steeps them in contempt;
004:084   strongest in might and in **punishment**.
004:102   Allah hath prepared a humiliating **punishment**.
004:147   What can Allah gain by your **punishment**.
004:151   for Unbelievers a humiliating **punishment**.
005:002   fear Allah: for Allah is strict in **punishment**.
005:033   The **punishment** of those who wage war against
005:033   and a heavy **punishment** is theirs in the Hereafter;
005:038   and exemplary **punishment** from Allah, and Allah
005:041   and in the Hereafter a heavy **punishment**.
005:071   no trial (or **punishment**); so they became
005:098   Know ye that Allah is strict in **punishment** and
006:040   if there come upon you the **Punishment** of Allah,
006:047   if the **Punishment** of Allah comes to you, whether
006:049   them shall our **punishment** touch, for that
006:070   and for **punishment**, one most grievous: for they
006:165   for thy Lord is quick in **punishment**: yet He
007:004   Our **punishment** took them on a sudden by night or
007:005   When (thus) Our **punishment** took them, no cry
007:038   so give them a double **punishment** in the Fire."
007:141   of **punishment** who slew your male children and
007:059   I fear for you the **Punishment** of a dreadful Day!"
007:071   He said: "**Punishment** and wrath have already
007:073   or ye shall be seized with a grievous **punishment**."
007:156   He said: "I afflict My **punishment** on whom
007:164   destroy or visit with a terrible **punishment**?"-
007:165   with a grievous **punishment**, because they
008:013   Allah is strict in **punishment**.
008:014   "Taste ye then of the (**punishment**): for those
008:025   Allah is strict in **punishment**.
008:038   the **punishment** of those before them is already
008:048   for Allah is strict in **punishment**."
008:052   for Allah is Strong, and Strict in **punishment**:
008:068   a severe **punishment** would have reached you
009:052   that Allah will send His **punishment** from Him
009:068   And an enduring **punishment**,-
010:050   Say: "Do ye see-if His **punishment** should come
010:052   'Taste ye the enduring **punishment**!
011:026   the **punishment** of a Grievous Day."
011:064   or a swift **Punishment** will seize you!
012:025   **punishment** for one who formed an evil
012:110   Our **punishment** from those who are in sin.
013:006   and verily thy Lord is (also) strict in **punishment**.
013:011   a people's **punishment**, there can be no turning
014:007   truly My **punishment** is terrible indeed."
014:014   My tribunal,-such as fear My **Punishment**."
016:061   (the **punishment**) for a single hour, just as
016:126   let your **punishment** be proportionate to the
017:054   or if He please, **punishment**: We have not
017:075   (of **punishment**) in this life, and an
018:002   of a terrible **Punishment** from Him, and that

PUNISHMENT (continued)

018:058   have hastened their **Punishment**: but they
018:087   him with a **punishment** unheard-of (before).
019:075   (being fulfilled)-either in **punishment** or in
019:079   and We Shall add and add to his **punishment**.
020:071   and the more lasting **Punishment**!"
020:097   but thy (**punishment**) in this life will be that
020:129   (their **punishment**) must necessarily have come;
020:134   Had We destroyed them a **punishment** before this,
021:012   Our **Punishment** (coming), behold, they (tried to)
022:044   My **punishment** (of them)!
022:047   the **Punishment**! But Allah will not fail in His
022:057   there will be a humiliating **Punishment**.
023:044   (in **punishment**): We made them as a tale
023:064   Until, when We seize in **Punishment** those of
023:076   We inflicted **Punishment** on them, but they
023:077   leading to a severe **Punishment**: then Lo!
024:002   the Believers witness their **punishment**.
024:008   But it would avert the **punishment** from the wife,
024:011   the **punishment**) of the sin that he earned, and to
025:068   and any that does this (not only) meets **punishment**
025:077   and soon will come the inevitable (**punishment**)!"
026:189   Then the **punishment** of a day of overshadowing
026:206   the (**Punishment**) which they were promised!
027:021   with a severe **punishment**, or execute
028:061   is to be among those brought up (for **punishment**)?
029:034   a **Punishment** from heaven, because they
029:053   the **Punishment** (for them): had it
029:053   the **Punishment** would certainly have come to them:
029:054   the **Punishment**: but, of a surety, Hell will
029:055   On the Day that the **Punishment** shall cover
030:016   such shall be brought forth to **Punishment**.
033:017   to give you **punishment** or to give you Mercy?"
033:030   unseemly conduct, the **Punishment** would be
033:057   and has prepared for them a humiliating **Punishment**.
034:045   My messengers, how (terrible) was My **punishment**!
035:026   was My **punishment**.
036:018   stone you, and a grievous **punishment** indeed will
037:031   taste (the **punishment** of our sins):
037:127   be called up (for **punishment**),
037:176   Do they wish (indeed) to hurry on Our **Punishment**?
038:008   Nay, they have not yet tasted My **Punishment**!
038:014   the messengers, but My **Punishment** came justly
039:019   against whom the degree of **Punishment** is justly due
039:025   the **Punishment** came to them from directions
039:026   but greater is the **Punishment** of the Hereafter,
040:003   is strict in **Punishment**, and is
040:022   full of Strength, Severe **Punishment**.
040:029   us from the **Punishment** of Allah, should it
040:085   when they (actually) saw Our **Punishment** was not
043:039   that day, that ye shall be partners in **punishment**!
043:048   and We seized them with **Punishment**, in order
043:074   The Sinners will be in the **Punishment** of Hell,
043:075   Nowise will the (**punishment**) be lightened for them,
044:030   of Israel from humiliating **Punishment**,
046:035   they see the (**Punishment**) promised them,
048:025   with a grievous **punishment**.
052:047   there is another **punishment** besides this: but most
057:013   will be (wrath and) **Punishment**!
059:003   the **Punishment** of the Fire,
059:004   resists Allah, verily Allah is severe in **Punishment**.
059:007   for Allah is strict in **Punishment**.
065:010   a severe **Punishment** (in the Hereafter).

PUNISHMENT (continued)
067:018   was My **punishment** (of them)?
068:033   Such is the **Punishment** (in this life); but greater
068:033   but greater is the **Punishment** in the Hereafter,-
070:027   And those who fear the **punishment** of their Lord,-
070:028   For their Lord's **punishment** is not a thing
072:025   Say: "I know not whether the (**Punishment**) which ye
073:016   so We seized him with a heavy **Punishment**.
096:018   of **punishment** (to deal with him)!

PUNISHMENTS
013:006   before them, (many) exemplary **punishments**!
014:006   hard tasks and **punishments**, slaughtered your
017:008   (to Our **punishments**): and We have made Hell
037:053   receive rewards and **punishments**?'"

PURCHASE
002:174   and **purchase** for them a miserable profit,
003:177   Those who **purchase** Unbelief at the price of Faith,
031:006   those who **purchase** idle tales, without knowledge

PURCHASED
003:187   and **purchased** with it some miserable gain!
009:111   Allah hath **purchased** of the Believers their persons

PURE
002:069   **pure** and rich in tone,
002:130   Him We chose and rendered **pure** in this world:
002:222   who keep themselves **pure** and clean.
003:038   Grant unto me from Thee a progeny that is **pure**:
005:004   Say: Lawful unto you are (all) things good and **pure**:
005:005   things good and **pure** made lawful unto you.
007:032   and the things, clean and **pure**, (which He
007:082   who want to be clean and **pure**!"
007:157   what is good (and **pure**) and prohibits them from
008:037   the impure from the **pure**. Put the impure,
009:108   and Allah loveth those who make themselves **pure**.
011:088   (**pure** and) good as from Himself? I wish not,
016:066   **pure** and agreeable to those who drink it.
016:097   that is good and **pure**, and We
016:103   while this is Arabic, **pure** and clear.
017:070   things good and **pure**; and conferred
019:019   the gift of a **pure** son."
023:051   good and **pure**, and work righteousness: for I
024:021   been **pure**: but Allah doth purify whom He pleases:
025:048   and We send down **pure** water from the sky,-
027:056   men who want to be clean and **pure**!"
033:033   and to make you **pure** and spotless.
040:064   of things **pure** and good;-such is Allah
045:016   for Sustenance things good and **pure**; and We
047:015   and rivers of honey **pure** and clear. In it
056:036   And made them virgin-**pure** (and undefiled),-
076:021   to them to drink a **pure** drink.
080:014   Exalted (in dignity), kept **pure** and holy,
083:025   Their thirst will be slaked with **Pure** Wine sealed;
098:002   rehearsing scriptures kept **pure** and holy:

PURELY
007:032   (and) **purely** for them on the Day of Judgment.

PURER
011:078   my daughters: they are **purer** for you

PUREST
022:024   (in this life) to the **purest** of speeches;

PURGE
003:141   to **purge** those that are true in Faith
003:154   and **purge** what is in your hearts.

PURIFIED
002:025   and they have therein spouses (**purified**);
002:222   But when they have **purified** themselves,
003:015   with spouses **purified** and the good pleasure
003:042   and **purified** thee-chosen thee above the women
004:057   therein shall they have spouses **purified**
009:108   In it are men who love to be **purified**; and Allah
038:083   sincere and **purified** (by Thy grace)."
053:032   not yourselves **purified**: He knows
079:018   thou shouldst be **purified** (from sin)?-

PURIFIES
035:018   And whoever **purifies** himself does so for the
091:009   Truly he succeeds that **purifies** it,

PURIFY
002:129   and **purify** them:
002:174   nor **purify** them;
004:049   Nay-but Allah doth **purify** whom He pleaseth.
005:041   Allah's will to **purify** their hearts.
009:103   that so thou mightest **purify** and sanctify them;
020:076   who **purify** themselves (from evil).
024:021   been pure: but Allah doth **purify** whom He pleases:
062:002   His Signs, to **purify** them, and to instruct
087:014   But he will prosper who **purify** himself.

PURIFYING
002:151   and **purifying** you,
003:164   **purifying** them, and instructing them in Scripture

PURITY
002:232   most virtue and **purity** amongst you,
003:037   He made her grow in **purity** and beauty:
004:049   to those who claim **purity** for themselves?
016:032   take in a state of **purity**, saying (to them),
018:081   in **purity** (of conduct) and closer in affection.
019:013   as from Us, and **purity**: he was devout,
024:026   and women of **purity** are for men of **purity**, and men
024:026   women of **purity**: these are
024:026   and men of **purity** are for women of **purity**:
024:028   **purity** for yourselves: and Allah
024:030   greater **purity** for them: and Allah
024:061   a greeting or blessing and **purity** as from Allah.
033:053   that makes for greater **purity** for your
035:010   To Him mount up (all) Words of **Purity**: it is
058:012   and most conducive to **purity** (of conduct).
080:003   but that perchance he might Grow **purity**?
080:007   if he grow not in **purity**.

PURPOSE
002:176   the Book are in a schism far (from the **purpose**).
002:283   a pledge with possession (may serve the **purpose**).
003:127   frustrated of their **purpose**.
005:049   it is Allah's **purpose** to punish them.
017:073   And their **purpose** was to tempt thee away from
017:076   Their **purpose** was to scare thee off the land,
022:025   and any whose **purpose** therein is profanity
022:073   if they all met together for the **purpose**!
027:039   the **purpose**, and may be trusted."
031:017   firmness (of **purpose**) in (the conduct of) affairs.
038:027   Not without **purpose** did We create
038:046   a special (**purpose**)-the remembrance of the
041:052   who is in schism far (from any **purpose**)?"
065:003   accomplish His **purpose**: verily, for all things
075:036   be left uncontrolled, (without **purpose**)?

PURSE'S
009:067   and tighten their **purse's** strings. They have

PURSUE
017:036   And **pursue** not that of which thou hast
PURSUED
011:060   And they were **pursued** by a Curse in this Life,-
011:116   But the wrong-doers **pursued** the enjoyment of the
015:018   by stealth, is **pursued** by a fiery comet,
020:078   Then Pharaoh **pursued** them with his forces,
026:052   for surely ye shall be **pursued**.”
026:060   So they **pursued** them at sunrise.
037:010   by stealth, and they are **pursued** be a flaming
044:023   for ye are sure to be **pursued**.
PURSUING
014:033   both diligently **pursuing** their courses: and the
PURSUIT
005:096   Lawful to you is the **pursuit** of water-game and
005:096   but forbidden is the **pursuit** of land-game: as long
017:028   from them in **pursuit** of the Mercy from thy Lord
027:072   hasten on may be (close) in your **pursuit**!
PUS
069:036   the foul **pus** from the washing of wounds,
PUSH
100:003   And **push** home the charge in the morning,
PUT
002:011   only ones that **put** things right!”
002:185   He does not want to **put** you to difficulties.
002:220   He could have **put** you into difficulties:
002:260   then **put** a portion of them: on every hill,
003:122   the Faithful (ever) **put** their trust.
003:159   For Allah loves those who **put** their trust (in Him).
003:159   **put** thy trust in Allah.
003:160   In Allah, then, let Believers **put** their trust.
004:081   so keep clear of them, and **put** thy trust in Allah,
004:102   **put** away your arms because of the inconvenience
005:011   And on Allah let Believers **put** (all) their trust.
005:023   But on Allah **put** your trust if ye have faith.”
007:150   He **put** down the Tablets, seized his brother
008:002   and **put** (all) their trust in their Lord;
008:037   **Put** the impure, one on another, heap them
008:063   **put** affection between their hearts: not if
009:039   grievous penalty, and **put** others in your place;
009:051   let the believers **put** their trust.
009:077   So He hath **put** as a consequence hypocrisy into
009:107   And there are those who **put** up a mosque by way
010:071   yet I **put** my trust in Allah get ye then
010:084   then in Him **put** your trust if ye
010:085   They said: “In Allah do we **put** our trust. Our Lord
011:056   “I **put** my trust in Allah, my Lord and your Lord!
011:123   so worship Him, and **put** thy trust in Him: and thy
012:015   and We **put** into his heart (this Message):
012:062   And (Joseph) told his servants to **put** their stock-
012:067   and let all that trust **put** their trust on Him.”
012:067   on Him do I **put** my trust: and let
012:070   (suitable) for them, he **put** the drinking cup into
013:041   to **put** back His command: and He
014:009   Clear (Signs); but they **put** their hands up to
014:011   And on Allah let all men of faith **put** their trust.
014:012   For those who **put** their trust should **put**
014:012   Why we should not **put** our trust on Allah.
014:012   should **put** their trust on Allah.”
014:019   remove you and **put** (in your place)
014:045   with them; and We **put** forth (many) Parables
015:039   and I will **put** them all in the wrong,-

PUT (continued)
015:039   because Thou hast **put** me in the wrong, I will
015:042   **put** themselves in the wrong and follow thee.”
016:042   in patience, and **put** their trust on their Lord.
016:099   who believe and **put** their trust in their Lord.
016:116   that your tongues may **put** forth, “This is
017:045   We **put**, between thee and those who believe not
017:046   And We **put** coverings over their hearts
017:060   We **put** fear (and warning) into them, but it
019:089   Indeed ye have **put** forth a thing most monstrous!
020:012   Therefore **put** off thy shoes: thou art
020:134   we were humbled and **put** to shame.”
023:030   (for men to understand); lo! We **put** (men) to test.
023:094   “Then, O my Lord! **put** me not amongst the
025:004   **put** forward an iniquity and a falsehood.
025:058   And **put** thy trust in Him Who lives and dies not;
026:029   I will certainly **put** thee in prison!”
026:217   And **put** thy trust on the Exalted
027:012   “Now **put** thy hand into thy bosom, and it
027:079   So **put** thy trust in Allah: for thou
029:059   and **put** their trust in their Lord and Cherisher.
030:021   with them, and He has **put** love and mercy
032:011   Say: “The Angel of Death, **put** in charge of you,
033:003   And **put** thy trust in Allah, and enough
033:048   their insolence but **put** thy trust in Allah.
034:030   for a Day, which ye cannot **put** back for an hour
034:030   for an hour nor **put** forward.”
034:033   We shall **put** yokes on the necks of the Unbelievers:
036:008   We have **put** yokes round their necks right up
036:009   And We have **put** a bar in front of them and a
038:011   and they will be **put** to flight.
039:027   We have **put** forth for men, in the
039:038   for me! In Him trust those who **put** their trust.”
042:036   who believe and **put** their trust in their Lord:
043:077   thy Lord **put** and end to us!” He will say, “Nay,
045:018   Then We **put** thee on the (right) Way of Religion:
045:023   and **put** a cover on his sight. Who, then,
045:029   with truth: for We were wont to **put** on record
047:022   if ye were **put** in authority, that ye
047:035   and will never **put** you in loss
049:001   O ye who believe! **put** not yourselves forward
054:045   Soon will their multitude be **put** to flight,
057:013   So a wall will be **put** up betwixt them, with a
058:010   and on Allah let the Believers **put** their trust.
064:013   let the Believers **put** their trust.
067:029   and on Him have we **put** our trust: so, soon
070:011   Though they will be **put** in sight of each other,-
071:004   **put** forward: if ye only knew.”
075:004   Nay, We are able to **put** together in perfect order
075:013   and all that he **put** back.
075:013   (all) that he **put** forward, and all
075:015   Even though he were to **put** up his excuses.
076:027   the fleeting life, and **put** away behind them
077:036   Nor will it be open to them to **put** forth pleas.
081:014   (Then) shall each soul know what it has **put** forward.
082:008   does He **put** thee together.
PUTS
022:005   (to life), it swells, and it **puts** forth every
039:029   Allah **puts** forth a Parable-a man belonging
065:003   And if anyone **puts** his trust in Allah,
065:007   has given him. Allah **puts** no burden on any
PUTTETH
080:021   and **putteth** him in his Grave;

PUTTING

042:047   will be no **putting** back, because of

Q

QAF
042:002   'Ain. Sin. **Qaf**.
050:001   **Qaf**. By the Glorious Qur'an (Thou art

QARUN
028:076   **Qarun** was doubtless, of the people of Moses;
028:079   of what **Qarun** has got! For he is
029:039   (Remember also) **Qarun**, Pharaoh, and Haman:
040:024   To Pharaoh, Haman, and **Qarun**; but they

QIBLAH
002:142   the **Qiblah** to which they were used?"
002:143   the **Qiblah** to which thou wast used,
002:144   a **Qiblah** that shall please thee.
002:145   they would not follow thy **Qiblah**;
002:145   nor art thou going to follow their **Qiblah**;
002:145   they follow each other's **Qiblah**.

QISAS
017:033   (to demand **Qisas** or to forgive): but let

QUAILS
002:057   and sent down to you manna and **quails**,
007:160   and sent down to them manna and **quails**, (saying):
020:080   and We sent down to you Manna and **quails**:

QUAKE
034:051   will **quake** with terror: but then

QUAKING
007:155   when they were seized with violent **quaking**, he

QUALITIES
016:013   colours (and **qualities**); Verily in this is a Sign

QUANTITY
012:065   This is but a small **quantity**.

QUARREL
002:113   in their **quarrel** on the Day of Judgment.

QUARRELLING
027:045   they became two factions **quarreling** with each other.

QUARTER
014:017   from every **quarter**, yet will he not die;

QUARTERS
059:002   came to them from **quarters** from which they little

QUEEN
027:029   (The **Queen**) said: "Ye chiefs! here is-

QUENCHED
021:015   is mown, as ashes silent and **quenched**.
036:029   (like ashes) **quenched** and silent.

QUEST
030:023   and the **quest** that ye (make for
040:056   but (the **quest** of) greatness, which they

QUESTION
002:108   Would ye **question** your Messenger
002:119   but of thee no **question** shall be asked
002:210   and the **question** is (thus) settled?
004:012   whose inheritance is in **question**, has left
007:006   Then shall We **question** those to whom
009:065   If thou dost **question** them, they declare
018:019   that they might **question** each other. Said one
025:033   And no **question** do they bring to thee but We

QUESTION (continued)
028:066   will not be able (even) to **question** each other.
033:008   That (Allah) may **question** the Truthful about their
037:027   and **question** one another.
037:050   and **question** one another.
041:047   to them the (**question**), "Where are
043:009   If thou wert to **question** them, 'Who created
043:045   And **question** thou Our messengers whom We
055:039   On that Day no **question** will be asked
074:040   they will **question** each other,

QUESTIONED
002:108   as Moses was **questioned** of old?
017:036   all of those shall be **questioned** of.
021:023   but they will be **questioned** (for theirs).
021:023   He cannot be **questioned** for His acts, by they
034:025   Say: "Ye shall not be **questioned** as to our sins,
034:025   our sins, nor shall we be **questioned** as to
081:008   Buried alive, is **questioned**-
102:008   Then, shall ye be **Questioned** that Day about the

QUESTIONER
070:001   A **questioner** asked about a Chastisement to befall-

QUESTIONS
002:210   all **questions** go back (for decision).
005:101   O ye who believe! ask not **questions** about things
005:102   Some people before you did ask such **questions**, and
018:070   follow me, ask me no **questions** about anything
075:006   He **questions**: "When is the Day of Resurrection?"

QUICK
002:202   and Allah is **quick** in account.
003:133   Be **quick** in the race for forgiveness
006:165   for thy Lord is **quick** in punishment: yet He
007:167   Thy Lord is **quick** in retribution, but He
021:090   **quick** in doing in good works: they used

QUICKER
016:077   even **quicker**: for Allah hath power over all things.

QUICKLY
020:069   right hand: **quickly** will it swallow up that which
051:026   Then he turned **quickly** to his household,

QUIET
016:080   homes of rest and **quiet** for you; and made
016:112   a city enjoying security and **quiet**, abundantly
017:095   and **quiet**, We should certainly have sent them

QUIETLY
033:033   And stay **quietly** in your houses, and make
046:029   of Jinns (**quietly**) listening to the Qur'an:

QUINTESSENCE
023:012   Man We did create from a **quintessence** (of clay);
032:008   a **quintessence** of despised fluid.

QUIT
063:007   till they disperse (and **quit** Madinah). But to

QUITE
002:109   **Quite** a number of the people of the Book
011:079   indeed thou knowest **quite** well what we want!"
017:051   Say, "Maybe it will be **quite** soon!
017:073   Our name something **quite** different: (in that case)
019:008   and I have grown **quite** decrepit from old age?"
024:064   Be **quite** sure that to Allah doth belong
034:051   from a position (**quite**) near.
037:158   but the Jinns know (**quite** well) that they
050:041   will call out from a place **quite** near,-
050:044   **quite** easy for Us.
070:007   But We see it (**quite**) near.

QUR'AN

002:062	Those who believe (in the **Qur'an**)
002:185	in which was sent down the **Qur'an**,
004:082	Do they not ponder on the **Qur'an**?
005:069	Those who believe (in the **Qur'an**). Those who
005:101	when the **Qur'an** is being revealed, they will
006:019	this **Qur'an** hath been revealed to me
007:204	When the **Qur'an** is read, listen to
009:111	and the **Qur'an**: and who is more faithful to his
010:015	say: "Bring us a **Qur'an** other than this,
010:037	This **Qur'an** is not such as can be produced by
010:061	be reciting from the **Qur'an**,-and whatever
012:002	We have sent it down as an Arabic **Qur'an**, in order
012:003	this (portion of the) **Qur'an**: before this,
013:031	If there were a **Qur'an** with which mountains
015:001	of a **Qur'an** that makes things clear.
015:087	Seven Oft-Repeated (verses) and the Grand **Qur'an**.
015:091	**Qur'an** into shreds (as they please).
016:098	When thou dost read the **Qur'an,** seek Allah's
017:009	Verily this **Qur'an** doth guide to that which
017:041	in various (ways) in this **Qur'an**, in order
017:045	When thou dost recite the **Qur'an**, We put,
017:046	they should understand the **Qur'an**, and deafness
017:046	and Him alone-in the **Qur'an**, they turn
017:060	(mentioned) in the **Qur'an**: We put
017:078	the night, and the recital of the **Qur'an** in the
017:082	of the **Qur'an** that which is a healing and a mercy
017:088	the like of this **Qur'an**, they could not
017:089	in this **Qur'an**, every kind of similitude:
017:105	We sent down the (**Qur'an**) in Truth, and in
017:106	(It is) a **Qur'an** which We have divided (into parts
018:054	We have explained in detail in this **Qur'an**, for the
019:097	So have We made the (**Qur'an**) easy in thine
020:002	We have not sent down the **Qur'an** to thee to be
020:113	an Arabic **Qur'an**-and explained therein in detail
020:114	the **Qur'an** before its revelation to thee
021:106	Verily in the (**Qur'an**) is a Message for people
022:017	Those who believe (in the **Qur'an**), those who
022:054	the (**Qur'an**) is the Truth from the Lord, and that
023:067	the (**Qur'an**), like one telling fables by night,"
025:006	Say: "The (**Qur'an**) was sent down by Him
025:030	this **Qur'an** with neglect."
025:032	"Why is not the **Qur'an** revealed to him
025:052	with the (**Qur'an**).
027:001	These are verses of the **Qur'an**,-A Book
027:006	As to thee, thou receivest the **Qur'an** from One
027:076	Verily this **Qur'an** doth explain to the
027:092	And to rehearse the **Qur'an**: and if
028:085	Verily He Who ordained the **Qur'an** for thee,
030:058	in this **Qur'an**. Every kind of Parable: but if
036:002	By the **Qur'an**, full of Wisdom,-
036:069	and a **Qur'an** making things clear:
037:170	But (now that the **Qur'an** has come), they reject
038:001	Sad: By the **Qur'an**, full of Admonition:
038:086	of you for this (**Qur'an**), nor am I a pretender.
039:027	in this **Qur'an** every kind of Parable, in order
039:028	(It is) a **Qur'an** in Arabic, without any
041:003	in detail;-a **Qur'an** in Arabic, for people
041:026	this **Qur'an**, but talk at random in the midst
041:044	Had We sent this as a **Qur'an** (in a language)
042:007	to thee an Arabic **Qur'an**: that thou
042:052	but We have made the (**Qur'an**) a Light, wherewith
043:003	We have made it a **Qur'an** in Arabic, that ye

QUR'AN (continued)

043:031	Also, they say: "Why is not this **Qur'an** sent down
043:044	The (**Qur'an**) is indeed a Reminder for thee
044:058	Verily, We have made this (**Qur'an**) easy, in thy
046:029	the **Qur'an**: when they stood in the presence
047:024	not then earnestly seek to understand the **Qur'an**
050:001	Qaf. By the Glorious **Qur'an** (Thou art
050:045	by force. So admonish with the **Qur'an** such as
054:017	And We have indeed made the **Qur'an** easy to
054:022	But We have indeed made the **Qur'an** easy to
054:032	And We have indeed made the **Qur'an** easy to
054:040	And We have indeed made the **Qur'an** easy to
055:002	It is He Who has taught the **Qur'an**.
056:077	That this is indeed a **Qur'an** most honourable,
059:021	Had We sent down this **Qur'an** on a mountain,
072:001	(to the **Qur'an**). They said, 'We have really
073:004	Or a little more; and recite the **Qur'an** in slow,
073:020	of the **Qur'an** as much as may be easy for you.
073:020	Read ye, therefore, as much of the **Qur'an** as may
075:016	the (**Qur'an**) to make haste therewith.
076:023	the **Qur'an** to thee by stages.
084:021	And when the **Qur'an** is read to them, they fall
085:021	Nay, this is a Glorious **Qur'an**,

QURAISH

028:047	to the **Quraish**),-in case a calamity should seize
044:034	As to these (**Quraish**), they say forsooth:
046:026	We have not given to you (ye **Quraish**)! and We
054:043	(O **Quraish**), better than they? Or have
106:001	For the familiarity of the **Quraish**,

R

RA'INA

002:104 (to the Prophet) **Ra'ina**,
004:046 and "**Ra'ina**" with a twist of their tongues

RABBIS

005:044 by the **Rabbis** and the Doctors of Law: for to
005:063 Why do not the **Rabbis** and the doctors of laws

RACE

002:148 (as in a **race**) towards all that is good.
003:133 Be quick in the **race** for forgiveness
004:133 O mankind, and create another **race**: for He
005:041 who **race** each other into Unbelief: (whether it be)
005:048 so strive as in a **race** in all virtues.
015:027 And the Jinn **race**, We had created before, from the
036:041 their **race** (through the flood) in the loaded Ark;
079:004 Then press forward as in a **race**,

RACED

012:025 So they both **raced** each other to the door, and she
036:066 **raced** to the Path, but how

RACING

005:062 **racing** each other in sin and transgression and
012:017 we went **racing** with one another, and left

RAFFLING

005:003 by **raffling** with arrows: that is impiety.

RAGE

003:119 Say: "Perish in your **rage**; Allah knoweth
003:119 of their fingers at you in their **rage**.
014:021 (now) whether we **rage**, or bear (these torments)
048:029 it fills the Unbelievers with **rage** at him.
069:007 He made it **rage** against them seven nights

RAGING

025:012 they will hear its fury and its **raging** sigh.
056:055 diseased camels **raging** with thirst!

RAHMAN

017:110 or call upon **Rahman**: by whatever

RAIMENT

007:026 We have bestowed **raiment** upon you to
007:026 but the **raiment** of righteousness-that is the best.
007:027 stripping them of their **raiment**, to expose

RAIN

002:019 is that of a **rain**-laden cloud from the sky:
002:022 and sent down **rain** from the heavens;
002:164 in the **rain** which Allah sends down
002:264 on it falls a heavy **rain**,
002:265 and if it receives not heavy **rain**,
002:265 heavy **rain** falls on it but makes it yield
004:102 the inconvenience of **rain** or because ye are ill;
006:006 **rain** from the skies in abundance, and gave
006:099 sendeth down **rain** from the skies: with it
007:057 make **rain** to descend thereon, and produce
008:011 and He caused **rain** to descend on you from heaven,
008:032 **rain** down on us a shower of stones from the sky,
010:024 is as the **rain** which We send down from the skies:
011:044 withhold (thy **rain**)!" And the water abated, and

RAIN (continued)

011:052 the skies pouring abundant **rain**, and strength
013:012 the clouds, heavy with (fertilizing) **rain**!
014:032 and sendeth down **rain** from the skies, and with it
015:022 then cause the **rain** to descend from the shy,
016:010 It is He Who sends down **rain** from the sky: from it
016:065 And Allah sends down **rain** from the skies,
018:045 it is like the **rain** which We send down
022:005 down **rain** on it, it is stirred (to life),
022:063 sends down **rain** from the sky, and forthwith
024:043 Then wilt thou see **rain** issue forth
027:060 **rain** from the sky? Yea, with
029:063 that sends down **rain** from the sky, and gives
030:024 and He sends down **rain** from the sky and with
030:049 (the **rain**)-just before this-they were
031:010 We send down **rain** from the sky, and produce
031:034 It is He Who sends down **rain**, and He
032:027 drive **Rain** to parched soil (bare of herbage),
035:027 sends down **rain** from the sky? With it
039:021 down **rain** from the sky, and leads
041:039 but when We send down **rain** to it, it is
042:028 He is the One that sends down **rain** (even) after
043:011 **rain** from the sky in due measure;-and We
046:024 us **rain**!" "Nay, it is the (calamity) ye were
050:009 **Rain** charged with blessing, and We
056:069 Do ye bring it Down (in **rain**) from the Cloud,
057:020 Here is a similitude: how **rain** and the growth
071:011 "`He will send **rain** to you in abundance;
072:016 on them **Rain** in abundance.
086:011 By the Firmament which giveth returns **rain**,

RAIN-DROPS

030:048 seest **rain-drops** issue from the midst thereof:

RAINED

007:084 And We **rained** down on them
011:082 (the cities) upside down, and **rained** down on them
015:074 upside down, and **rained** down on them brimstones
025:040 was **rained** a shower of evil: did they
026:173 We **rained** down on them a shower (of brimstone):
027:058 And We **rained** down on them a shower (of brimstone):

RAISE

003:055 "O Jesus! I will take thee and **raise** thee to Myself
004:075 and **raise** for us from Thee one who will protect;
004:075 and **raise** for us from Thee one who will help!"
006:036 Allah will **raise** them up: then will they
006:060 by day doth He **raise** you up again; that a term
006:083 We **raise** whom We will, degree after degree: for
007:057 thus shall We **raise** up the dead: perchance
009:120 or trod paths to **raise** the ire of the Unbelievers,
012:076 We **raise** to degrees (of wisdom) whom We please:
013:012 it is He Who doth **raise** up the clouds,
014:040 and also (**raise** such) among my offspring, O our
016:038 **raise** up those who die: nay, but it is a promise
016:084 On the Day We shall **raise** from all Peoples
016:089 On the day We shall **raise** from all peoples
017:079 **raise** thee to a Station of Praise and Glory!
020:124 a life narrowed down, and We shall **raise** him up
021:021 gods from the earth who can **raise** (the dead)?
022:007 **raise** up all who are in the graves.
030:048 and they **raise** the Clouds: then does
035:009 so that they **raise** up the Clouds, and We
043:011 and We **raise** to life therewith a land that is dead;
043:032 this world: and We **raise** some of them above

RAISE (continued)

043:057 as an example, behold thy people **raise** a clamour
049:002 O ye who believe! **raise** not your voices
058:006 will **raise** them all up (again) and tell them
058:011 **raise** up, to (suitable) ranks (and degrees),
058:018 The Day will Allah **raise** them all up
071:018 into the (earth), and **raise** you forth (again at
072:007 ye thought, that Allah would not **raise** up any one
080:022 He will **raise** him up (again).
100:004 And **raise** the dust in clouds the while,

RAISED

002:056 Then We **raised** you up after your death;
002:063 and We **raised** above you the Mount (Sinai)
002:093 and We **raised** above you the mount (Sinai):
002:127 **raised** the foundations of the House
002:253 others He **raised** to degrees (of honor);
002:259 then **raised** him up (again).
004:154 We **raised** over them the Mount (Sinai);
004:158 Nay, Allah **raised** him up unto Himself; and
006:006 and **raised** in their wake fresh generations
006:029 and never shall we be **raised** up again."
006:133 even as He **raised** you up
006:165 He hath **raised** you in ranks, some above
007:014 respite till the day they are **raised** up."
007:114 (**raised** to posts) nearest (to my person)."
007:171 When We **raised** the mount over them, as if
011:007 "Ye shall indeed be **raised** up after death,
012:100 And he **raised** his parents high on the throne
013:002 Allah is He Who **raised** the heavens without any
015:036 then respite till the Day the (dead) are **raised**."
015:047 (joyfully) facing each other on **raised** couches.
016:021 nor do thy know when they will be **raised** up.
016:039 (They must be **raised** up), in order that He may
017:049 be **raised** up (to be) a new creation?"
017:051 **raised** up)-(yet shall ye be **raised** up)!" Then will
017:098 really be **raised** up (to be) a new Creation?"
018:019 We **raised** them up (from sleep), that they
018:031 recline therein on **raised** thrones. How good
019:015 he will be **raised** up to life (again)!
019:033 I shall be **raised** up to life (again)!"
019:057 And We **raised** him to a lofty station.
019:066 shall I then be **raised** up alive?"
020:125 why hast thou **raised** me up blind, while I
021:026 They are (but) servants **raised** to honour.
023:016 will ye be **raised** up.
023:031 Then We **raised** after them another generation.
023:037 But we shall never be **raised** up again!
023:042 Then We **raised** after them other generations.
023:082 could we really be **raised** up again?
023:100 the Day they are **raised** up.
024:036 which Allah hath permitted to be **raised** to honour;
025:040 own eyes)? But they expect not to be **raised** again.
026:042 (**raised** to posts) nearest (to my person)."
026:087 on the Day when (men) will be **raised** up;-
027:065 shall be **raised** up (for Judgment).
027:067 shall we really be **raised** (from the dead)?
028:045 But We **raised** up (new) generations, and long
034:007 that ye shall (then be **raised**) in a New Creation?
036:052 Who hath **raised** us up from our beds of repose?...
036:056 be in pleasant shade, reclining on **raised** couches;
037:016 and bones, shall we (then) be **raised** up (again)?
037:044 Facing each other on **raised** couches.
038:079 then respite till the Day the (dead) are **raised**."

RAISED (continued)

043:011 be **raised** (from the dead);-
044:035 and we shall not be **raised** again.
046:017 I shall be **raised** up, even though
052:005 By the Canopy **Raised** High;
055:007 And the Firmament has He **raised** high, and He
056:034 And on couches **raised** high.
056:047 and bones, shall we then indeed be **raised** up again?-
064:007 will not be **raised** up (for Judgment). Say: "Yea,
064:007 ye shall surely be **raised** up: then shall
076:013 on **raised** couches, they will see there neither
079:028 On high hath He **raised** its canopy, and He
083:004 Do they not think that they will be **raised** up?-
083:023 On **raised** couches will they command a sight
083:035 On **raised** couches they will command (a sight)
088:013 (of dignity), **raised** on high,
088:018 And at the Sky, how it is **raised** high?-
094:004 And **raised** high the esteem (in which)

RAISING

018:073 by **raising** difficulties in my case."
053:047 a Second Creation (**raising** of the Dead);

RAMADHAN

002:185 **Ramadhan** is the (month) in which

RAN

037:140 When he **ran** away (like a slave from captivity)

RANCOR

004:030 If any do that in **rancor** and injustice, soon
005:002 but help ye not one another in sin and **rancor**:
047:029 will not bring to light all their **rancor**?
059:010 **rancor** (or sense of injury) against those
007:043 from their hearts any **rancour**; beneath

RANDOM

041:026 this Qur'an, but talk at **random** in the midst

RANGE

037:001 By those who **range** themselves in ranks,

RANGED

037:165 "And we are verily **ranged** in ranks (for service);

RANK

003:118 **rank** hatred has already appeared from their mouths;
005:060 these are (many times) worse in **rank**, and far
009:020 highest **rank** in the sight of Allah: they are
017:021 is more in **rank** and gradation and more
025:050 (to aught) but (**rank**) ingratitude.
057:010 so later). Those are higher in **rank** than those
089:022 and His angels, **rank** upon **rank**,

RANKS

002:130 the Hereafter in the **ranks** of the Righteous.
003:085 in the **ranks** of those who have lost.
003:114 they are in the **ranks** of the righteous.
003:118 into your intimacy those outside your **ranks**:
003:140 from your **ranks** Martyr-witnesses (to Truth).
004:089 so take not friends from their **ranks** until
004:089 take no friends or helpers from their **ranks**:
004:096 **Ranks** specially bestowed by Him, and
005:005 in the **ranks** of those who have lost
006:085 all in the **ranks** of the Righteous:
006:132 (or **ranks**) according to their deeds: for thy
006:165 He hath raised you in **ranks**, some above
008:009 of the angels, **ranks** on **ranks**."
010:104 to be (in the **ranks**) of the Believers,
012:033 and join the **ranks** of the ignorant."
016:122 in the **ranks** of the Righteous.

RANKS (continued)

018:048 before thy Lord in **ranks**, (with the
020:064 And then assemble in (serried) **ranks**: he wins
020:075 for them are **ranks** exalted,-
025:025 descending (in **ranks**),-
027:017 and they were all kept in order and **ranks**.
027:019 to the **ranks** of Thy righteous Servants."
027:083 and they shall be kept in **ranks**,-
037:001 By those who range themselves in **ranks**,
037:165 "And we are verily ranged in **ranks** (for service);
041:019 they will be marched in **ranks**.
043:032 of them above others in **ranks**, so that
052:020 on couches arranged in **ranks**, and We
058:011 raise up, to (suitable) **ranks** (and degrees),
078:038 will stand forth in **ranks**, none shall

RANSOM

002:085 ye **ransom** them,
002:177 and for the **ransom** of slaves;
002:184 is a **ransom**,
003:091 though they should offer it for **ransom**.
005:036 and twice repeated, to give as **ransom** for the
006:070 if it offered every **ransom** (or reparation), none
008:068 reached you for the (**ransom**) that ye took.
010:054 would fain give it in **ransom**: they would
013:018 would they offer it for **ransom**. For them
039:047 (in vain) would they offer it for **ransom** from the
047:004 time for) either generosity or **ransom**: until the
057:015 "This Day shall no **ransom** be accepted of you,

RANSOMED

037:107 And We **ransomed** him with a momentous sacrifice:

RAPID

007:054 each seeking the other in **rapid** succession: and

RASS

025:038 and the Companions of the **Rass**, and many
050:012 the Companions of the **Rass**, the Thamud,

RATHER

002:135 Say thou: "Nay! (I would **rather**) the Religion
003:028 Unbelievers **rather** than Believers:
003:079 "Be ye my worshippers **rather** than Allah's":
004:139 Unbelievers **rather** than believers: it is
004:144 for friends Unbelievers **rather** than Believers: do
018:050 **rather** than Me? And they are enemies to you!
027:055 in your lusts **rather** than women? Nay, ye
034:032 Nay, **rather** it was ye who transgressed."
037:153 Did He (then) choose daughters **rather** than sons?

RATIFIED

002:027 Allah's Covenant after it is **ratified**,
002:084 and this ye solemnly **ratified**.
005:007 and His Covenant, which He **ratified** with you,

RAVEN

005:031 Then Allah sent a **raven**, who scratched
005:031 "Was I not even able to be as this **raven**, and to

REACH

002:124 is not within the **reach** of evil-doers."
002:271 and make them **reach** those (really) in need,
004:002 their property (when they **reach** their age),
004:006 until they **reach** the age of marriage;
004:063 and speak to them a word to **reach** their very souls.
005:026 the land be out of their **reach** for forty years:
005:094 of game well within **reach** of your hands and
006:004 of the Signs of their Lord **reach** them, but they
006:034 until Our aid did **reach** them: there is none

REACH (continued)

007:037 must **reach** them from the Book (of Decrees): until
010:107 He causeth it to **reach** whomsoever of His
011:048 a grievous Chastisement **reach** them from Us."
011:081 By no means shall they **reach** thee! Now travel
012:085 though **reach** the last extremity of illness,
013:014 their hands for water to **reach** their mouths
013:040 **reach** them: it is Our part to call them to account.
014:024 and its branches (**reach**) to the heavens,-
014:044 when the Wrath will **reach** them: then will
016:007 that ye could not (otherwise) **reach** except with
017:029 utmost **reach**, so that thou become blameworthy
017:037 rend the earth asunder, nor **reach** the mountains
018:060 "I will not give up until I **reach** the junction
021:039 and (when) no help can **reach** them!
022:005 may **reach** your age of full strength; and some
028:061 to **reach** its (fulfillment), and one
029:053 **reach** them,-of a sudden, while they perceive not!
030:017 when ye **reach** eventide and when ye rise
030:048 made them **reach** such of his servants as He wills,
038:010 and means (to **reach** that end)!
040:067 die before;-and lets you **reach** a Term appointed;
040:067 **reach** your age of full strength; then lets
041:020 At length, when they **reach** the (Fire),
055:054 will be Near (and easy of **reach**).
069:020 that my Account would (one Day) **reach** me!"
076:014 will hang low easy to **reach**.

REACHED

002:120 the knowledge which hat **reached** thee,
002:145 If thou after the knowledge hath **reached** thee,
006:043 When the suffering **reached** them from Us, why
006:128 but (alas!) we **reached** our term-which Thou
007:034 Appointed: when their term is **reached**, not an
007:126 in the Signs of our Lord when they **reached** us!
008:068 **reached** you for the (ransom) that ye took.
009:070 Hath not the story **reached** them of those
010:039 **reached** them: thus did those before them make
010:049 a term appointed: when their term is **reached**, not
010:077 when it hath (actually) **reached** you? Is it
010:108 **reached** you from your Lord! Those, who
011:074 **reached** him, he began to plead with Us for
013:037 the knowledge which hath **reached** thee, then wouldst
014:009 Has not the story **reached** you, (O people!),
018:061 But when they **reached** the Junction, they forgot
018:086 Until, when he **reached** the setting of the sun,
018:093 Until, when he **reached** (a tract) between two
019:043 knowledge which hath not **reached** thee: so follow
020:009 Has the story of Moses **reached** thee?
028:014 When he **reached** full age, and was
034:032 from Guidance after it **reached** you? Nay, rather,
037:102 Then, when (the son) **reached** (the age of)
038:021 **reached** thee? Behold, they climbed over the
040:035 that hath **reached** them, very hateful (is such
042:014 after knowledge **reached** them,-being insolent
051:024 Has the story **reached** thee, of the honoured
064:005 Has not the story **reached** you, of those
068:049 Had not Grace from His Lord **reached** him, he would
079:015 Has the story of Moses **reached** thee?
085:017 Has the story **reached** thee, of the Forces-
088:001 Has the story **reached** thee, of the

REACHES

002:196 until the offering **reaches** the place
006:005 the truth when it **reaches** them: but soon

REACHES (continued)

006:019 that I may warn you and all whom it **reaches**. Can
006:149 the argument that **reaches** home: if it had
010:024 there **reaches** it Our command by night or by day,
011:008 **reaches** them, nothing will turn it away from them,
012:110 as liars, there **reaches** them Our help, and those
013:014 their mouths but it **reaches** them not: for the
022:037 that **reaches** Allah: it is your
022:037 it is your piety that **reaches** Him: He has
029:068 it **reaches** him? Is there not a home in Hell
046:015 thirty months. At length, when he **reaches** the age
056:083 when (the soul of the dying man) **reaches** the throat,
070:021 And niggardly when good **reaches** him;-
075:026 Yea, when (the soul) **reaches** to the collar-bone

REACHETH

006:136 **reacheth** not Allah, whilst the share
006:136 Allah **reacheth** their "partners"! Evil

REACHING

011:070 not **reaching** towards the (meal), he felt
032:023 of its **reaching** (thee): and We made
040:037 "The ways and means of (**reaching**) the heavens,
048:025 detained from **reaching** their place of sacrifice.
068:039 on oath, **reaching** to the Day of Judgment,

READ

003:078 (as they **read**) so that you would think
006:059 a Record Clear (to those who can **read**).
007:204 When the Qur'an is **read**, listen to
016:098 When thou dost **read** the Qur'an, seek Allah's
017:014 "**Read** thine (own) record: sufficient is thy soul
017:071 will **read** it (with pleasure), and they will not
017:093 a book that we could **read**." Say: "Glory
069:019 "Ah here! **read** ye my Record!
073:020 (in mercy): **read** ye, therefore, of the Qur'an
073:020 **Read** ye, therefore, as much of the Qur'an as may
084:021 And when the Qur'an is **read** to them, they fall
096:001 Proclaim! (or **Read**!) in the name of thy Lord

READER

007:205 And do thou (O **reader**!) bring thy

READILY

003:075 will (**readily**) pay it back;
017:018 We **readily** grant them-such things as We will,
010:094 then ask those who have been **reading** the Book
041:026 in the midst of its (**reading**), that ye
046:029 (**reading**) was finished, they returned to their

READY

008:060 Against them make **ready** your strength to the
009:109 sand-cliff **ready** to crumble to pieces? And it
011:061 for my Lord is (always) near, **ready** to answer."
035:030 Oft-Forgiving, Most **Ready** to appreciate (service).
035:034 **Ready** to appreciate (service):
048:006 He has cursed them and got Hell **ready** for them:
050:023 "Here is (his record) **ready** with me!"·
088:014 Goblets placed (**ready**),

REAL

004:060 Their (**real**) wish is to resort together for
004:065 But no, by thy Lord, they can have no (**real**) Faith.
005:055 Your (**real**) friends are (no less than) Allah, His
018:022 know their (**real** case)." Enter not,
034:008 (**real**) Chastisement, and in farthest Error.
039:015 Ah! that is indeed the (**real** and) evident Loss!"
040:074 anything (that had **real** existence)." Thus does

REALITY

009:055 in **reality** Allah's plan is to punish them
022:006 This is so, because Allah is the **Reality**: it is
022:062 That is because Allah-He is the **Reality**; and those
023:116 the King, the **Reality**; there is no
040:069 How are they turned away (from **Reality**)?-
069:001 The Sure **Reality**!
069:002 What is the Sure **Reality**?
069:003 what the Sure **Reality** is?
083:017 "This is the (**reality**) which ye rejected as false!"
084:005 (then will come Home the full **Reality**).
102:003 But nay, ye soon shall know (the **reality**).

REALIZE

002:009 themselves and **realize** (it) not!
002:012 but they **realize** (it) not.
006:109 **realize** that even if a (special) Sign came, they
016:039 may **realize** that they were liars.
016:041 if they only **realize** (this)!
016:043 if ye **realize** this not, ask of those
019:075 they will at length **realize** who is worst
024:025 and they will **realize** that Allah is the
042:017 will make thee **realize** that perhaps the Hour
069:003 And what will make thee **realize** what the

REALIZED

007:095 while they **realized** not (their peril).
010:046 Whether We show thee (**realized** in thy lifetime)
069:026 "And that I had never **realized** how my

REALLY

002:008 but they do not (**really**) believe.
002:014 they say: "We are **really** with you,
002:271 and make them reach those (**really**) in need,
003:130 that ye may (**really**) prosper.
004:098 Except those who are (**really**) weak and oppressed,
005:043 For they are not (**really**) people of Faith.
006:151 Allah hath (**really**) prohibited you from": join
009:064 showing them what is (**really** passing) in their
010:084 if ye do (**really**) believe in Allah, then in Him
011:062 But we are **really** in suspicious (disquieting)
012:008 **Really** our father is obviously in error!
012:013 (Jacob) said: "**Really** it saddens me that ye
014:009 ye have been sent, and we are **really** in suspicious
017:049 to bones and dust, should we **really** be raised up
017:098 **really** be raised up (to be) a new Creation?"
022:071 and of which they have (**really**) no knowledge:
023:082 could we **really** be raised up again?
024:047 turn away: they are not (**really**) Believers.
027:055 "Would ye **really** approach men in your
027:067 shall we **really** be raised (from the dead)?
037:052 "Who used to say, Do you **really** believe?
041:052 is (**really**) from Allah, and yet do ye reject it?
043:037 Such (Satans) **really** hinder them from the Path,
044:012 for We do **really** believe!"
069:020 "I did **really** understand that my Account
072:001 'We have **really** heard a wonderful Recital!
072:010 or whether their Lord (**really**) intends to guide

REALM

076:020 see a Bliss and a **Realm** Magnificent.

REAP

002:134 They shall **reap** the fruit of what they did,
002:141 They shall **reap** the fruit of what they did,
012:047 and the harvests that ye **reap**, ye shall

REAR

003:153 in your **rear** was calling you back.
004:102 let them take their positions in the **rear**.
020:040 who will nurse and **rear** the (child)?' So We
057:013 "Turn ye back to your **rear**! Then seek

REARED

020:039 mayest be **reared** under Mine eye.

REASON

005:059 no other **reason** than that we believer in Allah,
007:033 sins and trespasses against truth or **reason**;
015:032 **reason** for not being among those who
027:021 me a clear **reason** (for absence)."
028:039 in the land, beyond **reason**,-he and
041:015 the land, against (all) truth and **reason**, and said
042:015 Now then, for that (**reason**), call (them to
070:025 is deprived (for some **reason** from asking);
085:008 no other **reason** than that they believed in Allah,

REASONABLE

002:178 then grant any **reasonable** demand,
002:180 according to **reasonable** usage;
002:234 just and **reasonable** manner.
002:236 a gift of a **reasonable** amount is due
002:240 provided it is **reasonable**.
004:006 let him have for himself what is just and **reasonable**.
004:025 according to what is **reasonable**:
024:053 obedience is (more) **reasonable**; verily, Allah is
065:006 and **reasonable**. And if ye find yourselves

REASONS

009:054 The only **reasons** why their contributions are not

REBEL

004:117 they call but upon Satan the persistent **rebel**!
005:047 by what Allah hath revealed, they are indeed **rebel**.
010:033 proved true against those who **rebel**: verily they
019:044 for Satan is a **rebel** against (Allah) Most Gracious.

REBELLED

002:057 (but they **rebelled**); to Us they did no harm,
002:061 **rebelled** and went on transgressing.
003:112 this because they **rebelled** and transgressed
007:160 (but they **rebelled**): to Us they did no harm, but

REBELLION

005:064 them their obstinate **rebellion** and blasphemy.
005:068 them their obstinate **rebellion** and blasphemy.
009:084 and died in a state of perverse **rebellion**.
010:091 wast thou in **rebellion**!-and thou
016:090 and evil and **rebellion**: He instructs you, that ye
018:080 them by obstinate **rebellion** and ingratitude
019:069 worst in obstinate **rebellion** against (Allah)
022:003 and follow every Satan obstinate in **rebellion**!
037:030 a people in obstinate **rebellion**!
049:007 and **rebellion**: such indeed are those who

REBELLIOUS

005:025 so separate us from this **rebellious** people!"
005:026 but sorrow thou not over these **rebellious** people."
005:049 And truly most men are **rebellious**.
005:059 are **rebellious** and disobedient?"
005:081 but most of them are **rebellious** wrong-doers.
005:108 for Allah guideth not a **rebellious** people.
007:102 We found **rebellious** and disobedient.
009:008 and most of them are **rebellious** and wicked.
009:024 His decision: and Allah guides not the **rebellious**.
009:053 a people **rebellious** and wicked."
009:067 Verily the Hypocrites are **rebellious** and perverse.

REBELLIOUS (continued)

009:080 who are perversely **rebellious**.
019:014 and he was not overbearing or **rebellious**.
021:074 given to Evil, a **rebellious** people.
024:055 they are **rebellious** and wicked.
027:012 a people **rebellious** in transgression."
028:032 for truly they are a people **rebellious** and wicked."
029:034 because they have been wickedly **rebellious**."
032:018 than the man who is **rebellious** and wicked?
032:020 As to those who are **rebellious** and wicked,
037:007 against all obstinate **rebellious** Satans.
043:054 truly were they a people **rebellious** (against Allah).
057:016 are **rebellious** transgressors.
057:026 but many of them became **rebellious** transgressors.
057:027 but many of them are **rebellious** transgressors.
059:005 cover with shame the **rebellious** transgressors.
059:019 Such are the **rebellious** transgressors!
061:005 are **rebellious** transgressors.
063:006 Truly Allah guides not **rebellious** transgressors.

REBUKE

018:073 Moses said: "**Rebuke** me not for forgetting,
046:017 (and **rebuke** the son): "Woe to thee! have Faith!

REBUTTED

037:141 and he was of the **rebutted**:

RECEDE

081:015 So verily I call to witness the Planets-that **recede**,

RECEIVE

002:157 and they are the ones that **receive** guidance.
002:221 that they may **receive** admonition.
002:267 **receive** it except with closed eyes.
002:269 **receive** admonition but men of understanding.
003:161 **receive** its due whatever it earned,
006:056 the company of those who **receive** guidance."
006:093 This day shall ye **receive** your reward,-
006:124 we **receive** one (exactly) like those
006:126 the Signs for those who **receive** admonition.
006:155 that ye may **receive** mercy:
007:026 that they may **receive** admonition!
007:030 and think that they **receive** guidance.
007:063 fear Allah and haply **receive** His Mercy?"
007:130 that they might **receive** admonition.
007:204 and hold your peace: that ye may **receive** Mercy.
010:003 will you not **receive** admonition?
010:045 and refused to **receive** true guidance.
010:108 Those, who **receive** guidance, do so for
013:019 with understanding that **receive** admonition;-
014:025 in order that they may **receive** admonition.
016:017 creates not? Will ye not **receive** admonition?
016:085 nor will they then **receive** respite.
016:090 that ye may **receive** admonition.
016:125 and who **receive** guidance.
017:041 **receive** admonition, but it only increases their
017:089 men refuse (to **receive** it) except with ingratitude!
017:099 (to **receive** it) except with ingratitude.
020:015 for every soul to **receive** its reward by the
023:049 in order that they might **receive** guidance.
023:085 Say: "Yet will ye not **receive** admonition?"
024:001 in order that ye may **receive** admonition.
024:056 that ye may **receive** mercy.
026:138 to **receive** Pains and Chastisement!"
027:024 so they **receive** no guidance,-
027:046 ye may hope to **receive** mercy."
027:090 "Do ye **receive** a reward other than that which

RECEIVE (continued)

028:043   that they might **receive** admonition.
028:046   in order that they may **receive** admonition.
028:051   in order that they may **receive** admonition.
028:056   and He knows best those who **receive** guidance.
032:004   (for you): will lye not then **receive** admonition?
033:051   and thou mayest **receive** any thou pleasest:
034:050   but if I **receive** guidance, it is
034:052   but how could they **receive** (Faith) from a
035:037   **receive** admonition? And (moreover) the warner
036:045   ye may **receive** Mercy," (they turn back).
037:053   **receive** rewards and punishments?'"
037:155   Will ye not then **receive** admonition?
038:029   and that men of understanding may **receive** admonition.
039:009   endued with understanding that **receive** admonition.
039:010   will truly **receive** a reward without measure!"
039:024   (and **receive** it) on his face, (like one
039:027   in order that they may **receive** admonition.
040:013   **receive** admonition who turn (to Allah).
041:030   But **receive** the Glad Tidings of the
044:041   his client in aught, and no help can they **receive**,
044:042   Except such as **receive** Allah's Mercy: for He
045:023   Will ye not then **receive** admonition?
047:017   But to those who **receive** Guidance, He increases
049:010   And fear Allah, that ye may **receive** Mercy.
052:016   or not: ye but **receive** the recompense of your
053:030   and He knoweth best those who **receive** guidance.
054:015   that will **receive** admonition?
054:017   then is there any that will **receive** admonition?
054:022   then is there any that will **receive** admonition?
054:032   then is there any that will **receive** admonition?
054:040   then is there any that will **receive** admonition?
054:051   then is there any that will **receive** admonition?
056:019   No after-ache will they **receive** therefrom, nor will
059:012   so they will **receive** no help.
060:012   **receive** their fealty, and pray to Allah for the
066:006   they **receive** from Allah, but do
068:007   who **receive** (True) Guidance.
069:042   of a soothsayer: little admonition it is ye **receive**.
072:023   "Unless I deliver what I **receive** from Allah
080:004   Or that he might **receive** admonition, and the
083:002   Those who, when they have to **receive** by measure

RECEIVED

002:151   A similar (favour have ye already **received**)
003:186   from those who **received** the Book before you
005:057   those who **received** the Scripture before you, or
005:060   by the treatment it **received** from Allah?
005:083   the revelation **received** by the Messenger, thou
005:109   ye **received** (from men to your teaching)?"
006:034   Already hast thou **received** some account
006:044   the warning they had **received**, We opened
006:090   who **received** Allah's guidance. Follow the
006:090   Follow the guidance they **received**; say: "No
006:093   or saith, "I have **received** inspiration," when
006:093   when he hath **received** none, or (again)
006:124   like those **received** by Allah's messengers." Allah
006:145   **received** by me by inspiration any (meat)
007:069   the benefits (ye have **received**) from Allah: that
007:074   the benefits (ye have **received**) from Allah, and
007:190   in the gift they have **received**: but Allah
012:069   Joseph's presence, he **received** his (full) brother
014:021   **received** the guidance of Allah, we should
018:076   **received** (full) excuse from my side."

RECEIVED (continued)

019:087   has **received** permission (or promise) from (Allah)
020:135   and who it is that has **received** guidance."
022:060   he **received**, and is again set upon inordinately.
023:064   those of them who **received** the good things
024:015   Behold, ye **received** it on your tongues, and said
030:049   Even though, before they **received** (the rain)-
033:037   had **received** the grace of Allah and thy favour:
034:045   (the Truth); these have not **received** a tenth
039:022   **received** light from Allah, (no better than
047:016   **received** Knowledge: "What is it he said just then?"

RECEIVES

002:265   and if it **receives** not heavy rain,
009:104   and **receives** their gifts of charity, and that
039:041   He, then, that **receives** guidance benefits his

RECEIVEST

027:006   As to thee, thou **receivest** the Qur'an from One

RECEIVETH

002:269   granted **receiveth** indeed a benefit overflowing;
017:015   Who **receiveth** guidance, receiveth it
017:015   **receiveth** it for his own benefit: who goeth

RECEIVING

002:275   Those who after **receiving** admonition
003:073   Or that those (**receiving** such revelation)
003:105   and fall into disputation after **receiving** Clear Signs:
006:071   heels after **receiving** guidance from Allah?-

RECENTLY

009:060   have been (**recently**) reconciled (to Truth);

RECESSES

006:063   the dark **recesses** of land and sea, when ye call

RECITAL

017:078   in morning prayer for the **recital** of dawn
017:078   the night, and the **recital** of the Qur'an in the
053:059   Do ye then wonder at this **recital**?
072:001   'We have really heard a wonderful **Recital**!
075:018   follow thou its **recital** (as promulgated):

RECITE

005:027   **Recite** to them the truth of the story
017:045   When thou dost **recite** the Qur'an, We put,
017:106   **recite** it to men at intervals: We have
018:027   And **recite** (and teach) what has been revealed
029:045   **Recite** what is sent of the Book by inspiration
029:048   And thou wast not (able) to **recite** a Book
033:034   And **recite** what is rehearsed to you
073:004   Or a little more; and **recite** the Qur'an in slow,
075:017   It is for Us to collect it and to **recite** it:

RECITED

002:102   Satans **recited** over Solomon's Kingdom.
017:107   when it is **recited** to them, fall down
026:199   And had he **recited** it to them, they would
028:053   And when it is **recited** to them, they say:
032:015   when they are **recited** to them fall down
032:022   to whom are **recited** the Signs of his Lord,
075:018   But when We have **recited** it, follow thou

RECITING

010:061   be **reciting** from the Qur'an,-and whatever

RECKON

007:150   The people did indeed **reckon** me as naught, and

RECKONED

007:075   who were **reckoned** powerless-those among
009:120   but was **reckoned** to their credit as a deed
058:006   Allah has **reckoned** and which they forgot, For Allah

RECKONING

006:096 for the **reckoning** (of time): such is
013:018 For them will the **reckoning** be terrible:
013:021 and fear the terrible **reckoning**;
014:041 on the Day that the **Reckoning** will be established!"
017:034 will be enquired into (on the Day of **Reckoning**).
018:040 **reckoning**) from heaven, making it (but)
021:001 their **Reckoning**: yet they heel not and they
022:047 a thousand years of your **reckoning**.
023:117 and his **reckoning** will be only with his Lord!
030:055 (of **reckoning**) will be established,
032:005 a thousand years of your **reckoning**.
084:008 Soon will his account be taken by an easy **reckoning**,

RECLINE

018:029 the drink! How uncomfortable a couch to **recline** on!
018:031 **recline** therein on raised thrones. How good
018:031 How beautiful a couch to **recline** on!
038:051 Therein will they **recline** (at ease); therein can
043:034 and couches (of silver) on which they could **recline**,
052:020 They will **recline** (with ease) on couches
055:054 They will **recline** on Carpets, whose inner

RECLINING

036:056 be in pleasant shade, **reclining** on raised couches;
055:076 **Reclining** on green Cushions and rich
056:016 **Reclining** on them, facing each other.
076:013 **Reclining** in the (Garden) on raised couches,

RECOGNIZETH

002:158 He Who **recognizes** and knoweth.
004:147 Nay, it is Allah that **recognizeth** (all good), and

RECOGNITION

004:047 fame of some (of you) beyond all **recognition**,

RECOGNIZE

005:083 with tears, for they **recognize** the truth: they
010:045 they will **recognize** each other: assuredly those
016:083 They **recognize** the favours of Allah; then they
023:069 Or do they not **recognize** their Messenger,
083:024 Thou wilt **recognize** in their Faces the beaming

RECOGNIZED

002:089 that which they (should) have **recognized**,
040:011 us Life! Now have we **recognized** our sins:
070:024 And those in whose wealth is a **recognized** right
076:022 and your Endeavour is accepted and **recognized**."

RECOLLECTION

006:068 then after **recollection**, sit not thou

RECOMMENDS

004:085 and whoever **recommends** and helps an evil cause,

RECOMPENSE

003:136 how excellent a **recompense** for those who work
003:185 shall you be paid your full **recompense**.
004:093 his **recompense** is Hell, to abide
005:085 Such is the **recompense** of those who do good.
006:003 the (**recompense**) which ye earn (by your deeds).
006:120 due **recompense** for their "earnings."
006:146 this in **recompense** for their wilful disobedience:
007:152 thus do We **recompense** those who invent
009:082 they weep: a **recompense** for the (evil)
009:095 **recompense** for the (evil) that they did.
010:052 the **recompense** of what ye earned!'"
011:111 the **recompense**) of their deeds: for He
017:063 you (all)-an ample **recompense**.
017:063 be the **recompense** of you (all)-
017:098 That is their **recompense**, because they

RECOMPENSE (continued)

018:031 How good the **recompense**! How beautiful
018:077 exacted some **recompense** for it!"
020:127 And thus do We **recompense** him who transgresses
023:072 some **recompense**? But the **recompense** of thy Lord
030:039 who will get a **recompense** multiplied.
042:040 The **recompense** for an injury is an injury
045:014 it is for Him to **recompense** (for good or ill)
045:022 soul may find the **recompense** of what it has earned,
046:014 (for aye): **recompense** for their (good) deeds.
046:019 (Allah) may **recompense** their deeds; and no
046:025 Thus do We **recompense** those given to sin!
047:036 He will grant you your **recompense**, and will
052:016 or not: ye but receive the **recompense** of your
054:014 (and care): a **recompense** to one who had been
054:046 full **recompense**): and that Hour will be most
065:006 give them their **recompense**: and take
078:026 A fitting **recompense** (for them).
078:036 **Recompense** from thy Lord, a Gift,

RECOMPENSED

006:160 be **recompensed** according to his evil: no wrong
016:111 and every soul will be **recompensed** (fully) for
045:028 ye be **recompensed** for all that ye did!
046:020 but to-day shall ye be **recompensed** with a

RECONCILED

009:060 have been (recently) **reconciled** (to Truth);

RECONCILIATION

002:228 if they wish for **reconciliation**.
004:035 Allah will cause their **reconciliation**:
042:040 makes **reconciliation**, his reward is due from Allah:
049:010 peace and **reconciliation** between your two

RECORD

003:181 We shall certainly **record** their word
006:059 a **Record** Clear (to those who can read).
010:021 Verily, Our messengers **record** all the plots
010:061 are recorded in a clear **Record**.
011:006 all is in a clear **Record**.
017:014 "Read thine (own) **record**: sufficient is thy soul
017:058 That is written in the (eternal) **Record**.
017:071 given their **record** in their right hand will read
019:079 Nay! We shall **record** what he says, and We
021:094 be rejected: We shall **record** it in his favour.
022:070 Indeed it is all in a **record**,
023:062 before Us is a **record** which clearly speaks
027:075 or earth, but is (recorded) in a clear **record**.
034:003 but is in the **Record** Perspicuous:
036:012 and We **record** that which they sent before
039:069 the **Record** (of Deeds) will be placed (open);
043:080 are by them, to **record**.
045:028 called to its **Record**: "This Day shall ye be
045:029 on **record** all that ye did."
045:029 "This Our **Record** speaks about you with truth:
050:004 with Us is a **Record** guarding (the full account).
050:023 "Here is (his **record**) ready with me!"
054:053 Every matter, small and great, is on **record**.
068:001 Nun. By the Pen and by the (**Record**) which (men)
069:019 Then He that will be given his **Record** in his
069:019 "Ah here! read ye my **Record**!
069:025 And he that will be given his **Record** in his
069:025 "Ah! would that my **record** had not been given to me!
078:029 And all things have We preserved on **record**.
083:007 Nay! Surely the **Record** of the Wicked is (preserved)
083:018 Nay, verily the **Record** of the Righteous is

RECORD (continued)
084:007 Then he who is given his **Record** in his Right hand,
084:010 But he who is given his **Record** behind his back,-

RECORDED
010:061 are **recorded** in a clear Record.
018:049 is (**recorded**) therein; they will say, "Ah! woe
020:052 is with my Lord, duly **recorded**: my Lord
027:075 or earth, but is (**recorded**) in a clear record.
043:019 Their evidence will be **recorded**, and they
057:022 or in your souls but is **recorded** in a Book before

RECORDS
004:081 But Allah **records** their nightly (plots): so keep

RECOUNT
005:110 **recount** my favour to thee and to thy mother.
007:007 And verily We shall **recount** their whole

RECOVERED
007:143 When he **recovered** his senses he said: "Glory be

RECRIMINATIONS
038:064 That is true,-the mutual **recriminations** of the

RECTITUDE
005:012 truly wandered from the path of **rectitude**."
021:051 **rectitude** of conduct, and well

RED
018:096 when he had made it (**red**) as fire, he said:
035:027 and **red**, of various shades of colour, and black
055:037 and it becomes **red** like ointment:

REDEEM
070:011 would that he could **redeem** himself from the

REDUCE
002:282 if ye **reduce** it no to writing.
002:282 Disdain not to **reduce** to writing
002:282 **reduce** them to writing.
013:041 See they not that We gradually **reduce** the land
021:044 see they not that We gradually **reduce** the land

REDUCED
017:049 They say: "What! when we are **reduced** to bones
017:098 and said, "When we are **reduced** to bones
051:042 up against, but **reduced** it to ruin and rottenness.

REFER
004:059 **refer** it to Allah and His Messenger, if ye

REFERRED
004:083 If they had only **referred** it to the Messenger
041:047 To Him is **referred** the Knowledge of the Hour

REFLECT
007:176 so relate the story; perchance they may **reflect**.
007:184 Do they not **reflect**? Their Companion
010:024 the Signs in detail for those who **reflect**.
018:009 Or dost thou **reflect** that the Companions
030:008 Do they not **reflect** in their own minds? Not but
030:021 verily in that are Signs for those who **reflect**.
034:046 and **reflect** (within yourselves): your Companion
039:042 are Signs for those who **reflect**.
045:013 are Signs indeed for those who **reflect**.
051:049 We have created pairs: that ye may **reflect**.
059:021 to men, that they may **reflect**.

REFLECTED
074:021 Then he **reflected**;

REFORM
027:048 and would not **reform**.

REFRACTORY
074:016 he has been **refractory**!

REFRAIN
003:172 and **refrain** from wrong have a great reward;
007:074 and **refrain** from evil and mischief on the earth."
017:059 And We **refrain** from sending the Signs,
059:007 gives you, and **refrain** from what He prohibits you.

REFRESHING
038:042 cool and **refreshing**, and (water) to drink."
056:044 Neither cool nor **refreshing**:

REFUGE
003:162 and whose abode is in Hell? A woeful **refuge**!
004:097 What an evil **refuge**!
004:100 finds in the earth many a **refuge**.
004:115 and land him in Hell, what an evil **refuge**!
007:200 thy (mind), seek **refuge** with Allah; for He
008:016 and his abode is Hell, an evil **refuge** (indeed)!
009:073 Their abode is hell, an evil **refuge** indeed.
009:118 (and no **refuge**) but to Himself. Then He
011:047 Noah said: "O my Lord! I do seek **refuge** with Thee,
018:027 as a **refuge** other than Him.
018:058 beyond which they will find no **refuge**.
019:018 She said: "I seek **refuge** from thee to (Allah)
023:097 And say: "O my Lord! I seek **refuge** with Thee from
023:098 "And I seek **refuge** with Thee, O my Lord!
024:057 is the Fire,-and it is indeed an evil **refuge**!
040:056 seek **refuge**, then, in Allah: it is He
041:036 by the Satan, seek **refuge** in Allah. He is
042:047 of **refuge** nor will there be for you any room
057:015 to claim you: and an evil **refuge** it is!"
059:009 as came to them for **refuge**, and entertain
066:009 Their abode is Hell,-an evil **refuge** (indeed).
072:022 nor should I find **refuge** except in Him.
075:010 That Day will Man say "Where is the **refuge**?"
113:001 Say: I seek **refuge** with the Lord of the Dawn,
114:001 Say: I seek **refuge** with the Lord

REFUGEE
004:100 as a **refugee** from home for Allah and

REFUGEES
060:010 to you believing women **refugees**, examine (and

REFUSE
002:246 we **refuse** to fight in the cause of Allah,
002:282 let not the scribe **refuse** to write:
002:282 **refuse** when they are called on (for evidence).
004:034 (next), **refuse** to share their beds,
006:020 **refuse** therefore to believer.
006:125 on those who **refuse** to believe.
007:093 a people who **refuse** to believe!"
008:040 If they **refuse**, be sure
016:022 **refuse** to know and they are arrogant.
017:089 men **refuse** (to receive it) except with ingratitude!
017:099 no doubt. But the unjust **refuse** (to receive it)
020:056 but he did reject and **refuse**.
040:010 to the Faith and ye used to **refuse**."
107:007 But **refuse** (to supply) (even) neighborly needs.

REFUSED
002:034 not so Iblis, he **refused** and was haughty:
002:089 they **refused** to believe in it
006:110 even as they **refused** to believe in this
007:011 he **refused** to be of those who prostrate.
010:045 and **refused** to receive true guidance.
015:031 Not so Iblis: he **refused** to be among those
018:077 but they **refused** them hospitality. They found
020:116 but not Iblis: he **refused**.

REFUSED (continued)
028:012 And We ordained that he **refused** suck at first,
033:072 and the Mountains: but they **refused** to undertake
068:043 while they were whole, (and had **refused**).

REGAINED
012:096 his face, and he forthwith **regained** clear sight.

REGARD
003:170 and with **regard** to those left behind, who have
017:030 for He doth know and **regard** all His servants.
029:025 out of mutual love and **regard** between yourselves
034:053 with **regard** to the Unseen from a position far off?
060:008 Allah forbids you not, with **regard** to those who
060:009 Allah only forbids you, with **regard** to those who

REGARDS
004:011 as **regards** your children's (inheritance):
080:005 As to one who **regards** himself as self-sufficient,

REGIONS
041:053 in the (furthest) **regions** (of the earth), and in

REGISTER
083:009 (There is) a **Register** (fully) inscribed.
083:020 (There is) a **Register** (fully) inscribed.

REGRET
005:052 they **regret** of the thoughts which they secretly
035:008 in **regret** for them: for Allah

REGRETS
002:167 as (nothing but) **regrets**.
003:156 a cause of sighs and **regrets** in their hearts.
005:031 Then he became full of **regrets**.
008:036 have (only) **regrets** and sighs; at length
026:157 then did they become full of **regrets**.

REGULAR
002:277 and establish **regular** prayers and give Zakat,
004:077 and spend in **regular** Zakat?
004:077 but establish **regular** prayers and spend
004:103 set up **regular** Prayers: for such
004:162 **regular** prayer and pay Zakat and believe in
005:012 if ye (but) establish **regular** Prayers, pay Zakat
005:055 those who establish **regular** prayers and pay
006:072 "To establish **regular** prayers and
007:170 by the Book and establish **regular** prayer,-never
008:003 Who establish **regular** prayers and spend
009:005 **regular** prayers. And pay Zakat, then open
009:011 establish **regular** prayers, and pay Zakat they are
009:018 establish **regular** prayers, and pay Zakat, and fear
009:071 **regular** prayers, pay Zakat and obey Allah and His
010:087 of worship, and establish **regular** prayers: and give
011:114 And establish **regular** prayers at the two ends
013:022 establish **regular** prayers; spend, out of
014:031 that they may establish **regular** prayers, and spend
014:037 may establish **regular** prayer: so fill
014:040 who establishes **regular** Prayer, and also
017:078 Establish **regular** prayers-at the sun's decline
020:014 and establish **regular** prayer for My remembrance.
021:073 good deeds, to establish **regular** prayers, and to
022:035 keep up **regular** prayer, and spend
022:041 the land, establish **regular** prayer and give
022:078 **regular** Prayer, give zakat and hold fast
024:037 nor from **regular** Prayer, nor from
024:056 So establish **regular** Prayer and give zakat
027:003 Those who establish **regular** prayers and give
029:045 and establish **Regular** Prayer: for Prayer
030:031 and fear Him: establish **regular** prayers, and be

REGULAR (continued)
031:004 Those who establish **regular** Prayer, and give
031:017 "O my son! establish **regular** prayer, enjoin what
033:033 **regular** Prayer and give zakat and obey
035:018 establish **regular** Prayer. And whoever
035:029 of Allah, establish **regular** Prayer, and spend
042:038 and establish **regular** prayer; who (conduct)
058:013 establish **regular** prayer; give zakat and obey
073:020 and establish **regular** Prayer and give zakat;
098:005 to establish **regular** Prayer; and to

REGULATE
013:002 He doth **regulate** all affairs, explaining the

REGULATES
010:031 And who is it that rules and **regulates** all affairs?"

REGULATING
010:003 **regulating** and governing all things. No

REHEARSE
002:129 Who shall **rehearse** Thy Signs to them
002:231 but solemnly **rehearse** Allah's favours on you,
002:252 We **rehearse** them to thee in truth:
003:058 "This is what we **rehearse** unto thee of the Signs
003:108 We **rehearse** them to thee in Truth:
003:113 they **rehearse** the Signs of Allah all night long,
006:151 Say: "Come, I will **rehearse** what Allah hath
013:030 mightest **rehearse** unto them what We send down
018:083 Say, "I will **rehearse** to you something
022:072 those who **rehearse** Our Signs to them.
026:069 And **rehearse** to them (something of)
027:092 And to **rehearse** the Qur'an: and if
028:003 We **rehearse** to thee some of the story
035:029 Those who **rehearse** the Book of Allah,
045:006 which We **rehearse** to thee in truth: then in
062:002 among themselves, to **rehearse** to them His Signs,
093:011 But the Bounty of thy Lord-**rehearse** and proclaim!

REHEARSED
003:101 while unto you are **rehearsed** the Signs of Allah,
004:127 been **rehearsed** unto you in the Book, concerning
008:002 His revelations **rehearsed**, find their faith
008:031 When Our Signs are **rehearsed** to them, they say:
010:015 But when Our Clear Signs are **rehearsed** unto them,
010:016 I should not have **rehearsed** it to you, nor should
019:058 (Allah) Most Gracious were **rehearsed** to them,
019:073 When Our Clear Signs are **rehearsed** to them,
022:072 When Our Clear Signs are **rehearsed** to them,
023:066 "My Signs used to be **rehearsed** to you, but ye
023:105 "Were not My Signs **rehearsed** to you, and ye
025:032 **rehearsed** it to thee in slow, well-arranged
029:051 the Book which is **rehearsed** to them? Verily,
031:007 When Our Signs are **rehearsed** to such a one,
033:034 And recite what is **rehearsed** to you
034:043 When Our Clear Signs are **rehearsed** to them,
045:008 He hears the Signs of Allah **rehearsed** to him,
045:025 And when Our Clear Signs are **rehearsed** to them,
045:031 "Were not Our Signs **rehearsed** to you? But ye
046:007 When Our Clear Signs are **rehearsed** to them,
068:015 When to him are **rehearsed** Our Signs, "Tales of
083:013 When Our Signs are **rehearsed** to him, he says,

REHEARSES
065:011 A Messenger, who **rehearses** to you the Signs

REHEARSING
002:151 **rehearsing** to you Our Signs,
003:164 **rehearsing** unto them the Signs of Allah,

REHEARSING (continued)

007:035   **rehearsing** My Signs unto you,-those who
028:045   of Madyan, **rehearsing** Our Signs to them;
028:059   **rehearsing** to them Our Signs; nor are
039:071   from among yourselves, **rehearsing** to you the Signs
098:002   **rehearsing** scriptures kept pure and holy:

REJECT

002:006   As to those who **reject** Faith,
002:024   which is prepared for those who **reject** faith.
002:026   but those who **reject** Faith say:
002:028   How can ye **reject** the faith in Allah?
002:034   he was of those who **reject** Faith.
002:039   **reject** Faith and belie Our Signs,
002:041   and be not the first to **reject** faith therein,
002:085   and do ye **reject** the rest?
002:090   Chastisement of those who **reject** Faith.
002:091   yet they **reject** all besides,
002:098   those who **reject** Faith.
002:099   and none **reject** them but those who
002:121   those who **reject** faith therein,
002:126   He said: "(Yea), and such as **reject** Faith,
002:152   Be grateful to Me, and **reject** not Faith.
002:161   Those who **reject** Faith, and die rejecting,
002:171   The parable of those who **reject** Faith
002:191   Such is the reward of those who **reject** faith.
002:212   is alluring to those who **reject** faith,
002:250   help us against those that **reject** faith."
002:254   Those who **reject** Faith-they are the wrong-doers
002:257   Of those who **reject** faith the patrons
002:264   And Allah guideth not those who **reject** faith.
003:004   Then those who **reject** Faith in the Signs
003:010   Those who **reject** faith,
003:012   Say to those who **reject** Faith: "Soon
003:032   Allah loveth not those who **reject** Faith.
003:055   who follow thee superior to those who **reject** faith,
003:056   "As to those who **reject** faith,
003:070   Why **reject** ye the Signs of Allah,
003:072   but **reject** it at the end of the day:
003:086   who **reject** faith after they accepted it and bore
003:090   But those who **reject** faith after they accepted it.
003:091   As to those who **reject** faith, and die rejecting,
003:098   why **reject** ye the Signs of Allah,
003:106   "Did ye **reject** Faith after accepting it?
003:116   Those who **reject** faith, neither their
003:131   prepared for those who **reject** Faith.
003:184   Then if they **reject** thee, so were rejected
004:042   On that day those who **reject** Faith and
004:056   Those who **reject** Our Signs, We shall soon
004:060   though they were ordered to **reject** him.
004:076   and those who **reject** Faith fight in the cause
004:089   They but wish that ye should **reject** Faith.
004:137   Those who believe, then **reject** Faith, then
004:137   then believe (again) and (again) **reject** Faith, and
004:150   saying: "We believe in some but **reject** others":
004:161   who **reject** faith a grievous chastisement.
004:167   Those who **reject** Faith and keep off
004:168   Those who **reject** Faith and do wrong,-Allah will
004:170   But if ye **reject** Faith, to Allah belong
005:003   This day have those who **reject** Faith given up
005:010   Those who **reject** faith and deny Our Signs will be
005:036   As to those who **reject** Faith,-if they had
005:057   or among those who **reject** Faith: but fear
005:067   For Allah guideth not those who **reject** Faith.

REJECT (continued)

005:086   But those who **reject** Faith and belie
006:001   Yet those who **reject** Faith hold (others)
006:005   And now they **reject** the truth
006:027   Then would we not **reject** the Signs of our Lord,
006:033   it is not thee they **reject**: it is the
006:039   Those who **reject** Our Signs are deaf and dumb,-
006:049   But those who **reject** Our Signs,-them shall
006:057   but ye **reject** Him. What Ye
006:066   But thy people **reject** this, though it is
006:089   if these (their descendants) **reject** them, behold!
006:089   to a new People who **reject** them not.
006:093   and scornfully to **reject** of His Signs!"
007:036   But those who **reject** Our Signs and treat
007:040   To those who **reject** Our Signs and treat
007:051   and as they were wont to **reject** Our Signs.
007:076   we **reject** what ye believe in."
007:101   the heart of those who **reject** Faith.
007:147   Those who **reject** Our Signs and the Meeting
007:176   of those who **reject** Our Signs; so relate
007:177   who **reject** Our signs and wrong their own souls.
007:182   Those who **reject** Our signs, We shall
008:014   for those who **reject** is the chastisement
008:055   sight of Allah are those who **reject** Him: they will
009:002   with shame those who **reject** Him.
009:003   a grievous chastisement to those who **reject** Faith.
009:037   not those who **reject** Faith.
009:054   they **reject** Allah and His Messenger; that they
010:004   because they did **reject** Him.
010:004   but those who **reject** Him will have draughts of
010:086   from those who **reject** (Thee)."
010:095   Nor be of those who **reject** the Signs of Allah,
011:017   the Sects that **reject** it,-the Fire
013:030   yet do they **reject** (Him), the Most Gracious! Say:
013:036   those who **reject** a part thereof. Say "I am
014:018   The parable of those who **reject** their Lord
014:022   I **reject** your former act in associating
016:088   Those who **reject** Allah and hinder (men) from
016:107   and Allah will not guide those who **reject** Faith.
017:008   who **reject** (all Faith).
018:029   and let him who will, **reject** (it): for the
019:082   Instead, they shall **reject** their worship,
020:048   those who **reject** and turn away.'"
020:056   but he did **reject** and refuse.
021:050   will ye then **reject** it?
022:055   Those who **reject** Faith will not cease to be
022:057   And for those who **reject** Faith and deny
024:004   and **reject** their evidence ever after: for such
024:055   If any do **reject** Faith after this, they are
025:032   Those who **reject** Faith say: "Why is not
027:083   those who **reject** Our Signs, and they
027:084   "Did ye **reject** My signs, though ye
028:048   And they say: "For us, we **reject** all (such things)!"
028:048   Do they not then **reject** (the Signs) which were
028:082   us up! Ah! those who **reject** Allah will assuredly
028:086   in any way to those who **reject** (Allah's Message).
029:018   "And if ye **reject** (the Message), so did
029:023   Those who **reject** the Signs of Allah and the
029:047   and none but Unbelievers **reject** Our Signs.
029:049   the unjust **reject** Our Signs.
029:052   and **reject** Allah, that are losers.
029:067   is vain, and **reject** the Grace of Allah?
029:068   a home in Hell for those who **reject** Faith?

REJECT (continued)

030:013 and they will (themselves) **reject** their "Partners."
030:044 Those who **reject** Faith will suffer from that
030:045 those who **reject** Faith.
031:023 But if any **reject** Faith, let not
031:032 and wrong). But none **reject** Our Signs except only
032:020 to **reject** as false."
034:053 Seeing that they did **reject** faith (entirely)
035:004 And if they **reject** thee, so were
035:007 For those who **reject** Allah, is a
035:014 they will **reject** your "Partnership." And none,
035:025 And if they **reject** thee, so did
035:036 But those who **reject** (Allah)-for them
036:070 those who **reject** (Truth).
037:170 they **reject** it: but soon will they know!
038:074 and became one of those who **reject** Faith.
039:007 It ye **reject** (Allah), truly Allah
039:059 and became one of those who **reject** Faith!'"
039:059 **reject** them: thou wast haughty, and became
039:063 and the earth: and those who **reject** the Signs
040:012 ye did **reject** Faith, but when partners were
040:063 to **reject** the Signs of Allah.
040:070 Those who **reject** the Book and the
040:084 the One God-and we **reject** the partners we used
041:015 But they continued to **reject** Our Signs!
041:028 wont to **reject** Our Signs.
041:041 Those who **reject** the Message when it comes to them
041:052 **reject** it? Who is more astray than one who is in
043:030 they said: "This is sorcery, and we do **reject** it."
045:011 who **reject** the Signs of their Lord, is a
045:031 But as to those who **reject** Allah, (to them
046:003 but those who **reject** Faith turn away
046:010 from Allah, and ye **reject** it, and a
047:001 Those who **reject** Allah and hinder (men) from the
047:003 **reject** Allah follow falsehood. While those
047:008 But those who **reject** (Allah),- for them
047:010 those who **reject** Allah.
047:011 but those who **reject** Allah have no protector.
047:012 while those who **reject** Allah will enjoy (this
048:013 for those who **reject** Allah, a Blazing fire!
054:003 They **reject** (the warning) and follow
057:019 but those who **reject** Allah and deny Our Signs,-
058:004 **Reject** (Him), there is a grievous Chastisement.
060:002 ye should **reject** the Truth.
064:010 But those who **reject** Faith and treat
067:006 For those who **reject** their Lord (and Cherisher)
068:044 as **reject** this Message: by degrees shall We draw
069:049 amongst you those that **reject** (it).
077:029 which ye used to **reject** as false!
080:017 Woe to man! what hath made him **reject** Allah?
082:009 Nay! but ye do **Reject** The Judgment!
084:022 But on the contrary the Unbelievers **reject** (it).
090:019 But those who **reject** Our Signs, they are
109:001 Say: O ye that **reject** Faith!

REJECTED

002:065 "Be ye apes, despised and **rejected**."
002:258 who (in arrogance) **rejected** Faith.
003:036 to Thy protection from Satan the **Rejected**."
003:112 This because they **rejected** the Signs of Allah,
003:115 nothing will be **rejected** of them;
003:137 what was the end of those who **rejected** Truth.
003:184 so were **rejected** messengers before thee,
004:155 that they **rejected** the Signs of Allah; that they

REJECTED (continued)

004:156 That they **rejected** Faith: that they uttered
005:078 who **rejected** Faith, by the tongue
006:011 what was the end of those who **rejected** Truth."
006:030 the Chastisement, because ye **rejected** Faith."
006:034 **Rejected** were the Messengers before thee: with
006:130 they bear witness that they **rejected** Faith.
007:037 that they had **rejected** Allah.
007:050 hath Allah forbidden to those who **rejected** Him;
007:064 But they **rejected** him, and We
007:064 those who **rejected** Our Signs, they were
007:072 the roots of those who **rejected** Our Signs and
007:092 the men who **rejected** Shu'aib-
007:092 The men who **rejected** Shu'aib became as if
007:096 but they **rejected** (the truth), and We
007:101 what they had **rejected** before. Thus doth
007:103 But they wrongfully **rejected** them: so see
007:136 because they **rejected** Our Signs, and failed
007:146 For they have **rejected** Our Signs, and failed
007:166 "Be ye apes, despised and **rejected**."
008:052 before them: they **rejected** the Signs of Allah, and
009:066 **rejected** Faith after ye had accepted it. If We
009:080 **rejected** Allah and His Messenger: and Allah
009:084 for they **rejected** Allah and His Messenger, and
010:073 those who **rejected** Our Signs. Then see
010:073 They **rejected** him, but We delivered him, and those
010:074 they had already **rejected** beforehand. Thus do
011:059 they **rejected** the Signs of their Lord and
011:060 **rejected** their Lord and Cherisher! Away with
011:068 For the Thamud **rejected** their Lord and Cherisher!
015:034 from here; for thou art **rejected**, accursed.
015:080 Rocky Tract also **rejected** the Messengers:
016:098 seek Allah's protection from Satan the **Rejected** one.
016:113 falsely **rejected** him; so the Wrath seized them
017:018 burn therein, disgraced and **rejected**.
017:039 into Hell, blameworthy and **rejected**.
017:098 because they **rejected** Our Signs, and said,
018:106 because they **rejected** Faith, and took
021:077 who **rejected** Our Signs: truly they
021:094 be **rejected**: We shall record it in his favour.
022:025 As to those who have **rejected** (Allah), and would
022:044 Madyan people; and Moses was **rejected** (in the
023:048 So they **rejected** them and they became of those
025:036 to the people who have **rejected** Our Signs":
025:037 when they **rejected** the messengers, We drowned
025:077 but ye have indeed **rejected** (Him), and soon
026:006 They have indeed **rejected** (the Message): so they
026:105 The people of Noah **rejected** the messengers.
026:117 truly my people have **rejected** me.
026:123 The 'Ad (people) **rejected** the messengers.
026:139 So they **rejected** him, and We
026:141 The Thamud (people) **rejected** the messengers.
026:160 The people of Lut **rejected** the messengers.
026:176 **rejected** the messengers.
026:189 But they **rejected** him. Then the
029:037 But they **rejected** him: then the
030:009 with Clear (Signs), (which they **rejected**, to their
030:010 for that they **rejected** the Signs of Allah,
030:016 And those who have **rejected** Faith and falsely
034:017 **rejected** Faith: and never do We give (such)
034:045 yet when they **rejected** My messengers,
034:045 And their predecessors **rejected** (the Truth);
035:004 so were messengers **rejected** before thee:

REJECTED (continued)

035:026 who **rejected** Faith: and how (terrible) was My
036:014 two messengers, they **rejected** them: but We
036:064 for that ye (persistently) **rejected** (Truth)."
037:127 But they **rejected** him, and they
038:012 **rejected** messengers,-the People of Noah, and 'Ad,
038:014 Not one (of them) but **rejected** the messengers,
038:077 from here: for thou art **rejected**, accursed.
039:025 **rejected** (revelation), and so the Punishment
040:022 **rejected** them: so Allah called them to account:
043:025 those who **rejected** (Truth)!
050:014 each one (of them) **rejected** the messengers,
054:009 they **rejected** Our servant and said, "Here is
054:009 of Noah **rejected** (their messenger): they **rejected**
054:014 had been **rejected** (with scorn)!
054:018 The 'Ad (people) (too) **rejected** (Truth): then how
054:023 The Thamud (also) **rejected** (their) Warners.
054:033 The People of Lut **rejected** (his) Warning.
054:042 The (people) **rejected** all Our Signs; but We
057:015 who **rejected** Allah. Your abode is the Fire:
060:001 even though they have **rejected** the truth
060:004 we have **rejected** you, and there
063:003 then they **rejected** Faith: so a seal
064:005 of those who **rejected** Faith aforetime? So they
064:006 So they **rejected** (the Message) and turned away.
067:009 but we **rejected** him and said, 'Allah never sent
067:018 But indeed men before them **rejected** (My warning):
075:032 He **rejected** Truth and turned away!
079:021 But (Pharaoh) **rejected** it and disobeyed (guidance);
083:017 "This is the (reality) which ye **rejected** as false!"
091:011 The Thamud (people) **rejected** (their prophet)
091:014 Then they **rejected** him (as a false prophet),

REJECTERS

002:019 But Allah is ever round the **rejecters** of Faith!
005:054 mighty against the **Rejecters**, fighting in
009:068 men and women, and the **rejecters** of Faith, the fire
016:039 and that the **rejecters** of Truth may realize
025:077 Say (to the **rejecters**): "My Lord
029:054 Hell will encompass the **rejecters** of Faith!-
034:017 as are ungrateful **rejecters**.
040:085 the **rejecters** of Allah lose (utterly)!
052:011 Then woe that Day to the **rejecters** (of Truth);-
076:004 For the **Rejecters** We have prepared Chains, Yokes,
077:015 Ah woe, that Day, to the **Rejecters** of Truth!
077:019 Ah woe, that Day, to the **Rejecters** of Truth!
077:024 Ah woe, that Day, to the **Rejecters** of Truth!
077:028 Ah woe, that Day, to the **Rejecters** of Truth!
077:034 Ah woe, that Day, to the **Rejecters** of Truth!
077:037 Ah woe, that Day, to the **Rejecters** of Truth!
077:040 Ah woe, that Day, to the **Rejecters** of Truth!
077:045 Ah woe, that Day, to the **Rejecters** of Truth!
077:047 Ah woe, that Day, to the **Rejecters** of Truth!
077:049 Ah woe, that Day, to the **Rejecters** of Truth!
080:042 Such will be the **Rejecters** of Allah, the Doers

REJECTETH

006:021 or **rejecteth** his Signs? But verily
006:157 than one who **rejecteth** Allah's Signs, and turneth

REJECTING

002:061 **rejecting** the Signs of Allah and slaying
002:161 Those who reject Faith, and die **rejecting**,
002:253 some believing and others **rejecting**.
003:091 As to those who reject faith, and die **rejecting**,
003:106 Taste then the Chastisement for **rejecting** Faith.

REJECTING (continued)

004:018 nor of those who die **rejecting** faith:
006:070 for they persisted in **rejecting** Allah.
046:026 when they went on **rejecting** the Signs of Allah:
085:019 in **rejecting** (the Truth)!

REJECTION

006:034 bore their **rejection** and their persecution until
030:044 from that **rejection**: and those
031:023 let not his **rejection** grieve thee: to Us

REJECTOR

050:024 every contumacious **Rejector** (of Allah)!

REJECTS

002:256 whoever **rejects** Tagut and believes in Allah
005:005 If anyone **rejects** faith, fruitless is his work,
007:037 or **rejects** His Signs? For such
007:178 whom He **rejects** from His guidance. Such are
007:186 To such as Allah **rejects** from His guidance, there
019:077 man who **rejects** Our Signs, yet says: "I shall
029:068 or **rejects** the Truth when it reaches him?
039:032 and **rejects** the Truth when it comes to him!

REJOICE

003:120 they **rejoice** at it.
003:170 They **rejoice** in the bounty provided by Allah:
003:171 They **rejoice** in the Grace and the Bounty
007:150 Make not the enemies **rejoice** over my misfortune,
009:111 Then **rejoice** in the bargain which ye have
009:112 set by Allah;-(there do **rejoice**). So proclaim
009:124 is increased, and they do **rejoice**.
010:022 and they **rejoice** thereat; then comes
010:058 them **rejoice**": that is better than the (wealth)
013:026 He pleaseth. (The worldly) **rejoice** in the life
013:036 **rejoice** at what hath been revealed unto thee:
027:036 Nay it is ye who **rejoice** in your gift!
030:004 on that Day shall the Believers **rejoice**-
030:048 as He wills, behold, they do **rejoice**!-
040:075 "That was because ye were wont to **rejoice** on the

REJOICED

009:081 (in the Tabuk expedition) **rejoiced** in their

REJOICES

023:053 each party **rejoices** in that which is with itself.

REJOICING

009:050 and they turn away **rejoicing**.
030:032 each party **rejoicing** in that which is with itself!
043:070 ye and your wives, in (beauty and) **rejoicing**.
080:039 Laughing, **rejoicing**.
084:009 And he will turn to his people, **rejoicing**!
084:013 Truly, did he go about among his people, **rejoicing**!

RELAPSE

006:028 they would certainly **relapse** to the things

RELATE

007:101 We (thus) **relate** unto thee: there came
007:175 **Relate** to them the story of the man to whom
007:176 so **relate** the story; perchance they may reflect.
010:071 **Relate** to them the story of Noah. Behold! he
011:100 of communities which We **relate** unto thee: of them
011:120 All that We **relate** to thee of the stories
012:003 We do **relate** unto thee the most beautiful
012:005 **relate** not thy vision to thy brother, last they
018:013 We **relate** to thee their story in truth: they were
019:016 **Relate** in the Book (the story of) Mary, when she
020:099 Thus do We **relate** to thee some stories

RELATED

004:007 and those nearest **related** there is a share for
035:018 even though he be nearly **related**. Thou canst
040:078 and some whose story We have not **related** to thee.
040:078 whose story We have **related** to thee, and some

RELATION

003:028 if any do that, shall have no **relation** left
005:106 even though the (beneficiary) be our near **relation**:

RELATIONS

002:166 **relations** between them would be cut off.
006:094 so now all **relations** between you
008:001 the **relations** between yourselves: obey Allah
024:003 sexual **relations** with any but an adulteress
024:003 none can have sexual **relations** with her but an

RELATIONSHIP

090:015 To the orphan with claims of **relationship**,

RELATIONSHIPS

023:101 **relationships** between them that day, nor will
025:054 then has He established **relationships** of lineage

RELATIVE

006:152 even if a near **relative** is concerned; and fulfil

RELATIVES

004:008 other **relatives**, of orphans, or poor, are present,
004:033 to property left by parents and **relatives**.
008:041 and to near **relatives**, orphans, the needy,
019:005 "Now I fear (what) my **relatives** (and colleagues)
060:003 your **relatives** and your children on the Day

RELAX

007:202 and never **relax** (their efforts).

RELEASE

004:006 **release** their property to them;
004:006 When ye **release** their property to them, take
022:073 they would have no power to **release** it from the fly:
033:049 and **release** them in a handsome manner.

RELEASED

012:045 But the man who had been **released**, one of
034:016 the flood (**released**) from the Dams, and We

RELEASES

007:157 He **releases** them from their heavy burdens and from

RELIABLE

004:015 take the evidence of four (**reliable**) witnesses

RELICS

002:248 and the **relics** left by the family of Moses

RELIEF

018:029 **relief** they will be granted water like melted
065:007 Allah will soon grant **relief**.
094:005 So, verily, with every difficulty, there is **relief**:
094:006 Verily, with every difficulty there is **relief**.

RELIEVES

027:062 and Who **relieves** his suffering, and makes

RELIGION

038:007 in the last **religion**, this is
002:120 unless thou follow their form of **religion**.
002:130 the **religion** of Abraham but such as debase
002:135 the **Religion** of Abraham the True,
002:138 (Our **religion**) takes its hue from Allah
002:193 and the **religion** becomes Allah's.
002:256 Let there be no compulsion in **religion**.
003:019 The **Religion** before Allah is Islam
003:024 deceive them as to their own **religion**.
003:073 "And believe no one unless he follows your **religion**."
003:083 Do they seek for other than the **Religion** of Allah?

RELIGION (continued)

003:085 a **religion** other than Islam (submission to Allah)
003:095 follow the **religion** of Abraham, the sane in faith:
004:125 Who can be better in **religion** than one
004:171 commit no excesses in your **religion**: nor say
005:003 This day have I perfected your **religion** for you,
005:003 given up all hope of your **religion**: yet fear
005:003 and have chosen for you Islam as your **religion**.
005:057 those who take your **religion** for a mockery
005:077 exceed not in your **religion** the bounds
006:070 their **religion** to be mere play and amusement, and
006:137 and cause confusion in their **religion**. If
006:159 As for those who divide their **religion** and
006:161 a **religion** of right,-the Path (trod)
007:051 "Such as took their **religion** to be
007:088 shall have to return to our **religion**." He said:
007:089 if we returned to your **religion** after Allah
008:039 and **religion** becomes Allah's in its entirety
008:049 their **religion** has misled them." But if
008:072 but if they seek your aid in **religion**, it is
009:029 nor acknowledge the **religion** of Truth, from among
009:033 all **religion**, even though the Pagans
009:033 and the **Religion** of Truth, to cause
009:036 that is the right **religion** so wrong not yourselves
009:122 to devote themselves to studies in **religion**, and
010:104 in doubt as to my **religion**, (behold!) I
010:105 face towards **Religion** with true piety, and never
012:040 but Him: that is the right **religion**, but most
014:013 or ye shall return to our **religion**." But their
016:052 and to Him is the **religion** always: then will
018:020 to return to their **religion**, and in
022:078 on you in **religion**; it is the **religion** of your
024:055 their **religion**-the one which He has chosen
027:031 (to the true **Religion**).'"
030:030 to the **religion** being upright, the nature
030:030 that is the true **Religion**: but most
030:032 Those who split up their **Religion**, and become
030:043 the right **Religion**, before there come from Allah
040:026 change your **religion**, or lest he should cause
042:013 in **Religion**, and make no divisions therein:
042:013 The same **religion** has He established for you
042:021 some **religion** without the permission of Allah?
043:022 fathers following a certain **religion**, and we
043:023 a certain **religion**, and we will certainly
045:017 in affairs (of **Religion**): it was
045:018 of **Religion**: so follow thou that (Way),
048:028 and the **Religion** of Truth, to make
048:028 to make it over all **religion**: and enough
049:016 your **Religion**?" But Allah knows all that is in
061:009 all **religion**, even though the Pagans may detest
061:009 with Guidance and the **Religion** of Truth. That He
098:005 and that is the **Religion** Right and Straight.
110:002 enter Allah's **Religion** in crowds,

RELIGIOUS

004:146 **religious** devotions sincere to Allah: if so

RELISH

023:020 and **relish** for those who use it for food.

REMAIN

003:125 "Yea,-if ye **remain** firm, and act aright,
009:087 who **remain** behind (at home): their hearts
009:093 the (women} who **remain** behind: Allah hath
011:081 but thy wife (will **remain** behind): to her
015:023 **remain** Inheritors (after all else passes away).

REMAIN (continued)

018:003 Wherein they shall **remain** forever:
026:071 and we **remain** constantly in attendance on them."
028:010 (with faith), so that she might **remain** a (firm)
036:006 therefore **remain** heedless (of the Signs of Allah).
038:006 "Walk ye away, and **remain** constant to your gods!
042:013 Namely, that ye should **remain** steadfast in Religion,
046:013 is Allah," and **remain** firm (on that Path),-
070:023 Those who **remain** steadfast to their prayer;

REMAINED

003:142 (in His cause) and **remained** steadfast?
003:154 Say: "Even if you had **remained** in your homes,
006:156 we **remained** unacquainted with all that they
018:042 (with ruin), and he **remained** twisting and
026:120 Thereafter We drowned those who **remained** behind.
037:144 He would certainly have **remained** inside the
041:045 but they **remained** in suspicious disquieting doubt
072:016 "If they (the pagans) had (only) **remained** on the

REMAINING

016:106 **remaining** firm in Faith,-but such

REMAINS

002:278 **remains** of your demand for usury,
010:032 apart from the Truth, what (**remains**) but error?
011:081 a part of the night **remains**, and let not
013:017 the good of mankind **remains** on the earth. Thus
015:065 when a portion of the night (yet **remains**), and do

REMARRY

002:230 he cannot, after that, **re-marry** her until

REMEMBER

002:049 And **remember**, We delivered you
002:050 And **remember** We divided the sea for you
002:051 And **remember** We appointed forty nights
002:053 And **remember** We gave Moses the Scripture
002:054 And **remember** Moses said to his people:
002:055 And **remember** ye said: "O Moses!
002:058 And **remember** We said: "Enter this town,
002:060 And **remember** Moses prayed for water
002:061 And **remember** ye said: "O Moses!
002:063 And **remember** We took your Covenant
002:067 And **remember** Moses said to his people:
002:072 **Remember** ye slew a man and fell into a dispute
002:083 And **remember** We took a Covenant
002:084 And **remember** We took your Covenant
002:093 And **remember** We took your Covenant
002:124 And **remember** that Abraham was tried
002:125 **Remember** We made the house a place of assembly
002:126 And **remember** Abraham said: "My Lord,
002:127 And **remember** Abraham and Isma'il raised
002:152 Then do ye **remember** Me; I will **remember** you.
002:203 **Remember** Allah during the Appointed Days
003:103 and **remember** with gratitude Allah's favour on you;
003:121 (**Remember** that morning) thou didst leave
003:122 **Remember** two of your parties meditated cowardice;
003:124 **Remember** thou saidst to the faithful: "Is it not
003:135 **Remember** Allah and ask for forgiveness
003:187 And **remember** Allah took a Covenant from
003:191 Men who **remember** Allah, standing, sitting,
004:103 **remember** Allah, standing, sitting down, or
004:127 and (**remember**) what hath been rehearsed unto you
005:020 **Remember** Moses said to his people: "O my people!
006:152 thus doth He command you, that ye may **remember**.
007:003 Little it is ye **remember** of admonition.
007:057 perchance ye may **remember**.

REMEMBER (continued)

007:074 "And **remember** how He made you inheritors
007:086 but **remember** how ye were little, and He
007:141 And **remember**, We rescued you from
007:161 And **remember** it was said to them: "Dwell in
007:205 and **remember** without loudness in words, in the
008:009 **Remember** ye implored the assistance
008:011 **Remember** He covered you with drowsiness, to give
008:012 **Remember** the Lord inspired the angels
008:030 **Remember** how the Unbelievers plotted against
008:032 **Remember** how they said: "O Allah! if this
008:042 **Remember** ye were on the hither side of the valley,
008:043 **Remember** in thy dream Allah showed them
008:044 And **remember** when ye met, He showed
008:048 **Remember** Satan made their (sinful) acts
008:057 those who follow them, that they may **remember**.
008:072 and (**remember**) Allah seeth all that ye do.
012:085 thou cease to **remember** Joseph until though reach
014:006 **Remember**! Moses said to his people: "Call to mind
014:007 And **remember**! your Lord caused to be declared
014:035 **Remember** Abraham said: "O my Lord! make this
018:024 and **remember** thy Lord when thou forgettest,
020:034 "And **remember** Thee without stint:
021:076 (**Remember**) Noah, when he cried (to Us) aforetime:
021:078 And **remember** David and Solomon, when they
021:083 And (**remember**) Job, when he cried to his Lord
021:085 And (**remember**) Isma'il, Idris, and Zul-kifl,
021:087 And **remember** Zun-nun, when he departed in wrath:
021:089 And (**remember**) Zakariya, when he cried
021:091 And (**remember**) her who guarded her chastity:
029:028 And (**remember**) Lut: behold, he said to his people:
029:038 **Remember** also the 'Ad and the Thamud
029:039 (**Remember** also) Qarun, Pharaoh, and Haman:
033:007 And **remember** We took from the Prophets
033:009 **Remember** the Grace of Allah, (bestowed) on
033:021 and who **remember** Allah much.
033:041 O ye who believe! **remember** Allah, with much
035:003 O men! **remember** the grace of Allah unto you!
038:017 and **remember** Our Servant David, the man
040:044 "Soon will ye **remember** what I say to you (now).
043:013 ye may **remember** the (kind) favour of your Lord,
054:017 easy to understand and **remember**: then is
054:022 easy to understand and **remember**: then is
054:032 easy to understand and **remember**: then is
054:040 easy to understand and **remember**: then is
061:005 And **remember**, Moses said to his people: "O my
061:006 And **remember**, Jesus, the son of Mary, said:
062:010 and **remember** Allah frequently that ye may prosper.
079:035 The Day when Man shall **remember** (all) that
089:023 man **remember**, but how will that remembrance

REMEMBERED

012:045 and who now **remembered** him after (so long)

REMEMBERS

087:015 And **remembers** the name of their Guardian-Lord,

REMEMBRANCE

002:063 (ever) to **remembrance** what is therein,
004:142 but little do they hold Allah in **remembrance**;
005:007 And call in **remembrance** the favour of Allah
005:011 call in **remembrance** the favour of Allah unto you
005:020 "O my people! call in **remembrance** the favour
005:091 and hinder you from the **remembrance** of Allah, and
007:069 Call in **remembrance** that He made you
007:069 Call in **remembrance** the benefits

REMEMBRANCE (continued)

007:074	so bring to **remembrance** the benefits
007:171	and bring (even) to **remembrance** what is
007:201	bring Allah to **remembrance** when lo! they
007:205	bring thy Lord to **remembrance** in thy
008:045	and call Allah in **remembrance** much (and often);
011:120	a message of **remembrance** to those who believe.
013:028	the **remembrance** of Allah: for without
013:028	for without doubt in the **remembrance** of Allah
018:028	permitted to neglect the **remembrance** of Us,
018:101	a veil from **Remembrance** of Me, and who
020:014	and establish regular prayer for My **remembrance**.
020:042	either of you, in keeping Me in **remembrance**.
020:113	or that it may cause their **remembrance** (of Him).
021:042	the **remembrance** of their Lord.
024:037	can divert from the **Remembrance** of Allah, nor from
026:227	in the **remembrance** of Allah, and defend
029:045	and evil deeds; and **remembrance** of Allah is the
033:035	who engage much in Allah's **remembrance**, for them
033:041	with much **remembrance**;
038:032	to the **remembrance** of my Lord." Until (the
038:046	a special (purpose)-the **remembrance** of the
039:021	of **remembrance** to men of understanding.
039:022	hardened against the **remembrance** of Allah!
039:023	do soften to the **remembrance** of Allah. Such is
043:036	from **remembrance** of the Most Gracious, We appoint
057:016	the **remembrance** of Allah and of the Truth which
058:019	the **remembrance** of Allah. They are
062:009	to the **Remembrance** of Allah, and leave
063:009	from the **remembrance** of Allah. If any
069:012	should bear its (lessons) in **remembrance**.
072:017	the **remembrance** of his Lord, He will
073:008	But keep in **remembrance** the name of the Lord,
074:055	Let any who will, keep it in **remembrance**!
074:056	But none will keep it in **remembrance** except as
080:011	For it is indeed a Message of **remembrance**.
080:012	Therefore let whose will, keep it in **remembrance**.
089:023	that **remembrance** profit him?

REMIND

002:282	The other can **remind** her.
006:069	but (their duty) is to **remind** them, that they
010:071	and **remind** (you) the Signs of Allah,- yet I put
014:005	into light, and **remind** them of the Days
051:055	But **remind**: for reminding benefits the Believers.
052:029	Therefore **Remind** for by the Grace of thy Lord,
088:021	Therefore do thou **remind**, for thou
088:021	for thou art one to **remind**.

REMINDED

018:057	who is **reminded** of the Signs of his Lord but turns

REMINDER

006:090	this is but a **Reminder** to the nations."
007:002	warn (the erring) and a **reminder** the Believers.
007:063	come to you a **reminder** from your Lord, through
011:114	that is a **reminder** to the mindful.
020:099	for We have sent thee a **reminder** from Us.
026:209	By way of **reminder**; and We
029:051	Verily, in it is Mercy and **Reminder** to those
038:087	a **Reminder** to (all) the Worlds.
040:054	A Guide and a **Reminder** to men of understanding.
043:005	Shall We then take away the **Reminder** from you
043:044	The (Qur'an) is indeed a **Reminder** for thee
044:013	How shall they have the **Reminder**. Seeing that
047:018	to them, how shall they have their **Reminder**?

REMINDER (continued)

050:008	For an insight and **Reminder** to every
056:073	We have made it a **reminder** and an article
069:012	That We might make it a **Reminder** unto you,
074:031	and this is no other than a **Reminder** to mankind.
077:005	Then spread abroad a **Reminder**,
080:004	and the **Reminder** might profit him?

REMINDERS

002:262	with **reminders** of their generosity or with injury,
002:264	your charity by **reminders** of your generosity

REMINDING

051:055	But remind: for **reminding** benefits the Believers.

REMISSION

002:178	But if any **remission** is made by the brother
002:237	and the **remission** (of the man's half)

REMIT

002:237	unless they **remit** it.
002:280	But if ye **remit** it by way of charity,
004:005	**remit** any part of it to you, take it
004:031	We shall **remit** your evil deeds, and admit
004:092	unless they **remit** it freely.
039:035	So that Allah will **remit** from them (even) the

REMITS

005:045	But if anyone **remits** the retaliation by way of charity,

REMITTED

002:237	Or (the man's half) is **remitted** by him

REMNANT

006:045	the last **remnant** was cut off. Praise be to
046:004	or any **remnant** of knowledge (ye may have), if ye

REMNANTS

015:066	that the last **remnants** of those (sinners)

REMORSE

034:033	They are filled with **remorse**. When they

REMOTE

017:083	he turns away and becomes **remote** on his side
019:022	with him to a **remote** place.
041:051	he turns away, and gets himself **remote** on his side

REMOVE

002:271	it will **remove** from you some of
006:017	none can **remove** it but He; if He
006:041	He would **remove** (the distress) which occasioned
007:043	And We shall **remove** from their hearts
007:134	if thou wilt **remove** the Plague from us, we
008:011	to **remove** from you the stain of Satan, to
008:029	**remove** from you (all) evil deeds and forgive you:
010:107	there is none can **remove** it but He: if He
011:114	**remove** those that are evil: that is a
014:019	**remove** you and put (in your place)
015:047	And We shall **remove** from their hearts any lurking
017:056	the power to **remove** your troubles from you
017:103	So he resolved to **remove** them from the
018:047	On the Day We shall **remove** the mountains, and thou
020:027	"And **remove** the impediment from my speech.
022:015	his plan will **remove** that which enrages (him)!
033:033	And Allah only wishes to **remove** all abomination
039:038	**remove** His affliction or if He wills some Mercy
044:012	**remove** the Chastisement from us for We
044:015	We shall indeed **remove** the Chastisement for a
047:002	He **remove** from them their ills and improve
048:005	and **remove** their sins from them; and that
064:009	He will **remove** from them their ills, and He
065:005	He will **remove** his evil deeds from him
066:008	that your Lord will **remove** from you your

REMOVED
007:135 But when We **removed** the Plague from them
010:012 **removed** his affliction, he passeth on his way
010:098 When they believed, We **removed** from them
021:084 We **removed** the distress that was on him, and We
021:101 will be **removed** far therefrom.
023:075 and **removed** the distress which is on them,
034:023 when terror is **removed** from their hearts (at the
035:034 Who has **removed** from us (all) sorrow: for our
043:050 But when We **removed** the Chastisement from them,
050:022 of this; now have We **removed** thy veil, and sharp
092:017 shall be **removed** far from it,-
094:002 And **removed** from thee thy burden

REMOVES
016:054 Yet, when He **removes** the distress from you,

REMUNERATION
004:006 let him claim no **remuneration**,

REND
017:037 **rend** the earth asunder, nor reach the mountains

RENDER
003:081 do ye believe him and **render** him help."
003:100 **render** you apostates after ye have believed!
004:058 Allah doth command you to **render** back your trusts
006:141 but **render** the dues that are proper on the
017:026 And **render** to the kindred their due rights,
018:079 I but wished to **render** it unserviceable, for there
018:094 shall we then **render** thee tribute in order that

RENDERED
002:130 Him We chose and **rendered** pure in this world:
002:272 shall be **rendered** back to you,

RENDERS
002:116 everything **renders** worship to Him.

RENEGADES
004:089 But if they turn **renegades**, seize them

RENEWED
013:005 creation **renewed**?" They are those who deny
021:002 a **renewed** Message from their Lord, but they
032:010 a Creation **renewed**?" Nay, they

RENOUNCED
005:082 And men who have **renounced** the world, and they

RENT
012:026 is **rent** from the front, then is her tale true,
025:025 **rent** asunder with clouds, and angels
042:005 The heavens are almost **rent** asunder from above
050:044 **rent** asunder, from (men) hurrying out: that will
055:037 When the sky is **rent** asunder, and it becomes
069:016 And the sky will be **rent** asunder, for it
084:001 When the Sky is **rent** asunder,

REPAID
008:060 the cause of Allah, shall be **repaid** unto you,
036:054 but be **repaid** the meeds of your past Deeds.

REPARATION
006:070 if it offered every ransom (or **reparation**), none

REPAY
002:280 easy for him to **repay**.
003:075 will not **repay** it unless thou constantly

REPEAT
002:275 but those who **repeat** (the offense)
010:034 can any originate creation and **repeat** it?" Say:
024:017 that ye may never **repeat** such (conduct), if ye

REPEATED
005:036 and twice **repeated**, to give as ransom for the

REPEATEDLY
002:059 infringed (Our command) **repeatedly**.
007:162 For that they **repeatedly** transgressed.

REPEATETH
010:004 of Creation, and **repeateth** it, that He
013:013 Nay, thunder **repeateth** His praises, and so

REPEATING
039:023 (yet) **repeating** (its teaching in various aspects):

REPEATS
010:034 originates Creation and **repeats** it: then how
027:064 then **repeats** it, and Who gives you sustenance
029:019 originates creation, then **repeats** it: truly that
030:011 then **repeats** it; then shall ye be brought
030:027 of) creation; then **repeats** it; and for

REPEL
017:023 a word of contempt, nor **repel** them but address
023:096 **Repel** evil with that which is best: We are
041:034 **Repel** (Evil) with what is better: then will

REPELLING
037:002 Those who are strong in **repelling** (evil),

REPENT
002:160 Except those who **repent** and make amends
002:279 but if ye **repent** ye shall have
003:089 Except for those that **repent** (even) after that.
004:016 If they **repent** and amend, leave them alone;
004:017 who do evil in ignorance and **repent** soon afterwards;
004:146 Except for those who **repent**, mend (their life),
005:034 Except for those who **repent** before they
005:039 But if the thief **repent** after his crime, and amend
007:153 but **repent** thereafter and (truly) believe,-
009:003 If, then, ye **repent**, it were best for you; but if
009:005 but if they **repent**, and establish regular prayers.
009:011 But (even so), if they **repent**, establish regular
009:074 If they **repent**, it will be best for them: but if
009:118 that they might **repent**: for Allah
016:119 but who thereafter **repent** and make amends,-
019:060 Except those who **repent** and believe, and work
020:082 to those who **repent**, believe, and do right,-
024:005 Except those who **repent** thereafter and mend
032:021 they may (**repent** and) return.

REPENTANCE
002:054 so turn (in **repentance**) to your Maker,
003:090 never will their **repentance** be accepted;
004:017 Allah accepts the **repentance** of those who do evil
004:018 Of no effect is the **repentance** of those
004:092 by way of **repentance** to Allah: for Allah
007:143 To Thee I turn in **repentance**, and I
009:104 accept **repentance** from His votaries and receives
009:112 in **repentance**: that serve Him, and praise Him;
009:126 Yet they turn not in **repentance**, and they
010:054 they would declare (their) **repentance** when they
011:003 and turn to Him in **repentance**; that He
011:052 (in **repentance**): He will send you the skies
011:061 and turn to Him (in **repentance**): for my
011:090 and turn unto Him (in **repentance**): for my Lord
024:031 all together towards Allah in **repentance** that ye
025:071 has truly turned to Allah in **repentance**:
030:031 Turn ye in **repentance** to Him, and fear
030:033 turning back to Him in **repentance**: but when
034:009 that turns to Allah (in **repentance**).

REPENTANCE (continued)

038:017 turned (in **repentance** to Allah).
038:024 (in prostration), and turned (to Allah in **repentance**).
038:030 the Servant! Ever did he turn (to Us in **repentance**)!
039:008 turning to Him in **repentance**: but when
039:017 to Allah (in **repentance**),-for them is Good News:
039:054 "Turn ye to your Lord (in **repentance**) and submit
040:003 Who forgiveth Sin, accepteth **Repentance**, is Severe
040:007 in **repentance**, and follow Thy Path; and preserve
042:025 He is the One that accepts **repentance** from His
049:006 of **repentance** for what ye have done.
060:004 and to Thee do we turn in **repentance**: to Thee
066:004 If ye two turn in **repentance** to Allah,
066:005 in **repentance**, who worship (in humility),
066:008 with sincere **repentance**: in the hope that your
068:032 for we do turn to Him (in **repentance**)!"
085:010 turn in **repentance**, will have the Chastisement

REPENTED

004:018 and he says, "Now have I **repented** indeed";
006:054 and thereafter **repented**, and amended
007:149 When they **repented**, and saw that
028:067 had **repented**, believed, and worked righteousness,
037:143 (**repented** and) glorified Allah,

REPENTS

025:070 Unless he **repents**, believers, and works
025:071 And whoever **repents** and does good has truly

REPETITION

005:095 for **repetition** Allah will punish him for Allah

REPLACES

034:039 (in His Cause) but He **replaces** it: for He

REPLETE

011:014 sent down (**replete**) with the knowledge of Allah,

REPLIED

011:043 The son **replied**: "I will be take myself to some
018:063 He **replied**: "Sawest thou (what happened) when we
019:046 (The father) **replied**: "Art thou shrinking
020:052 He **replied**: "The knowledge of that is with
020:084 He **replied**: "Behold, they are close on my footsteps:
020:094 (Aaron) **replied**: "O son of my mother! Seize (me)
020:096 He **replied**: "I saw what they saw not: so I

REPLY

004:097 They **reply**: "Weak and oppressed
006:040 (**Reply**) if ye are truthful!
007:037 They will **reply**, "They have left us in the lurch,"
014:021 They will **reply**, "If we had received the
016:028 (The angels will **reply**), "Nay, but verily Allah
029:061 they will certainly **reply**, "Allah." How are
029:063 they will certainly **reply**, "Allah!" Say, "Praise
037:029 They will **reply**: "Nay, ye yourselves had no Faith!
039:059 "(The **reply** will be) `Nay, but there came to thee
040:050 They will **reply**, "Then pray (as ye like)! But the
040:074 "Besides Allah?" They will **reply**: "They have
043:009 to **reply**, 'They were created by (Him),
044:023 (The **reply** came): "March forth
057:014 will **reply**, "True! but ye led yourselves into

REPORTED

047:031 and We shall try your **reported** (mettle).

REPOSE

025:024 and have the fairest of places for **repose**.
025:047 and Sleep as **Repose**, and makes
036:052 Who hath raised us up from our beds of **repose**?...

REPOSITORY

006:098 then there is a resting place and a **repository**: We

REPROACH

012:092 He said: "This day let no **reproach** be (cast)
014:022 but **reproach** your own souls. I cannot
014:022 then **reproach** not me, but **reproach**
026:022 thou dost **reproach** me,-that you
068:030 Then they turned, one against another, in **reproach**.

REPROACHES

005:054 the **reproaches** of such as find fault.

REPULSE

093:010 Nor **repulse** him who asks;

REPULSED

037:009 **Repulsed**. And for them is a

REPULSES

107:002 Then such is the one who **repulses** the orphan,

REQUIRE

051:057 nor do I **require** that they should feed Me.
051:057 No sustenance do I **require** of them, nor do

REQUIRING

024:062 a matter **requiring** collective action, they do

REQUISITE

027:023 every **requisite**; and she has a magnificent throne.

REQUITAL

003:153 one distress after another by way of **requital**,
007:041 such is Our **requital** of those who do wrong.
013:032 was My **requital**!
034:017 give (such) **requital** except to such as are
034:017 That was the **Requital** We gave them because
034:033 be a **requital** for their (ill) Deeds.
040:005 seized them! And how (terrible), was My **Requital**!
041:028 Such is the **requital** of the enemies of Allah,-
041:028 a (fit) **requital**, for that they were wont to
056:056 on the Day of **Requital**!

REQUITE

006:138 soon will He **requite** them for what they forged.
006:157 In good time shall We **requite** those who
009:121 **requite** them with the best (possible reward).
010:013 not believe! Thus do We **requite** those who sin!
014:051 That Allah may **requite** each soul
041:027 and We will **requite** them for the worst

REQUITED

004:123 whoever works evil, will be **requited** accordingly.
007:180 for what they do, they will soon be **requited**.
037:039 And you are **requited** naught save what ye did.
040:017 That Day will every soul be **requited** for what
040:040 "He that works evil will not be **requited** but by
066:007 Ye are being but **requited** for all that ye did!"

RESCUE

004:075 "Our Lord! **rescue** us from this town.

RESCUED

007:089 after Allah hath **rescued** us therefrom; nor
007:141 And remember, We **rescued** you from
007:165 We **rescued** those who forbade evil; but We

RESERVATION

068:018 But made no **reservation**, ("If it be Allah's Will").

RESERVE

032:017 of the eye are kept hidden (in **reserve**) for them-

RESERVED

006:139 is specially **reserved** (for food) for our men, and

RESIDE
034:037 their deeds, while secure they (**reside**) in the
RESIDENCE
002:240 but if they leave (the **residence**),
RESIST
003:141 of blessings those that **resist** Faith.
003:147 and help us against those that **resist** Faith."
004:037 for We have prepared, for those who **resist** Faith,
047:032 and **resist** the Messenger, after Guidance
RESISTANCE
004:065 no **resistance** against thy decisions, but
RESISTED
059:004 That is because they **resisted** Allah and His
RESISTETH
005:012 **resisteth** faith, he hath truly wandered from
005:115 but if any of you after that **resisteth** faith, I
RESISTING
003:013 the other **resisting** Allah;
RESISTS
059:004 **resists** Allah, verily Allah is severe in Punishment.
RESOLUTION
003:186 then that indeed is a matter of great **Resolution**.
004:028 for man was created weak in (**resolution**).
042:043 an affair of great **resolution**.
046:035 as did (all) messengers of firm **resolution**; and be
RESOLVE
002:235 nor **resolve** on the tie of marriage
020:115 and We found on his part no firm **resolve**.
024:022 with grace and amplitude of means **resolve** by oath
068:025 strong in an (unjust) **resolve**.
RESOLVED
017:103 So he **resolved** to remove them from the
047:021 and when a matter is **resolved** on, it were
068:017 when they **resolved** to gather the fruits of the
RESORT
004:060 Their (real) wish is to **resort** together for
RESORTING
005:002 nor the people **resorting** to the Sacred House,
RESOURCES
009:091 or ill, or who find no **resources** to spend (on the
RESOURCES
009:092 no **resources** wherewith to provide the expenses.
017:006 in **resources** and sons, and made you the more
065:007 **resources** are restricted, let him spend according
074:012 To whom I granted **resources** in abundance,
RESPECT
009:008 over you, they **respect** not in you the ties
009:010 In a Believer they **respect** not the ties
016:071 so as to be equal in that **respect**. Will they
018:103 lose most in **respect** of their deeds?
019:076 **respect** of (their) eventual returns."
027:029 a letter worthy of **respect**.
033:049 in **respect** of them: so give
033:056 and salute him with all **respect**.
035:031 with **respect** to his servants-well acquainted
042:023 of good in **respect** thereof: for Allah
057:014 And the Deceiver deceived you in **respect** of Allah.
070:032 And those who **respect** their trusts and covenants;
RESPECTIVE
017:071 (**respective**) Imams: those who are given their

RESPECTIVE (continued)
030:047 messengers to their (**respective**) peoples, and they
RESPECTIVELY
066:010 they were (**respectively**) under two of Our
RESPECTS
019:017 and he appeared before her as a man in all **respects**.
RESPITE
002:162 nor will **respite** be their (lot).
003:088 nor **respite** be their (lot);
003:178 our **respite** to them is good for themselves:
003:178 We grant them **respite** that they may grow
004:077 Wouldst Thou not grant us **respite** to our
006:008 and no **respite** would be granted them.
007:014 He said: "Give me **respite** till the day
007:015 "Be thou among those who have **respite**."
007:183 **Respite** will I grant unto them: for My
007:195 and give me no **respite**!
010:011 then would their **respite** be settled at once. But
010:071 on me, and give me no **respite**.
011:055 all of you, and give me no **respite**.
012:110 (**Respite** will be granted) until, when the
013:032 but I granted **respite** to the Unbelievers,
014:010 your sins and give you **respite** for a term
014:042 He but giveth them **respite** against a Day when
014:044 "Our Lord! **respite** us (if only) for a short Term:
015:008 behold! no **respite** would they have!
015:036 then **respite** till the Day the (dead) are raised."
015:037 (Allah) said: "**Respite** is granted thee-
016:061 but He gives them **respite** for a stated Term:
016:085 nor will they then receive **respite**.
017:062 If Thou wilt but **respite** me to the Day
020:129 a term appointed (for **respite**).
021:040 to avert it, nor will they (then) get **respite**.
022:044 **respite** to the Unbelievers, and (only) after
022:048 give **respite**, which were given to wrong-doing?
029:053 (of **respite**) appointed, the Punishment
032:029 Nor will they be granted a **respite**."
033:016 a brief (**respite**) will ye be allowed to enjoy!"
035:045 but he gives them **respite** for a stated Term:
038:079 then **respite** till the Day the (dead) are raised."
038:080 (Allah) said: "**Respite** then is granted thee-
044:029 over them: nor were they given a **respite** (again).
063:010 Why didst thou not give me **respite** for a
063:011 But to no soul will Allah grant **respite** when the
068:045 A (long) **respite** will I grant them: truly powerful
071:004 and give you **respite** for a stated Term: for when
086:017 give **respite** to them gently (for a while).
RESPITED
026:203 Then they will say: "Shall we be **respited**?"
RESPOND
002:186 I **respond** to every prayer of every suppliant
013:018 For those who **respond** to their Lord, are (all)
013:018 But those who **respond** no to Him,-even if
042:038 Those who **respond** to their Lord, and establish
042:047 **Respond** ye to your Lord, before there
RESPONSE
005:109 and ask: "What was the **response** ye received
008:024 give your **response** to Allah and His Messenger,
RESPONSIBILITY
006:066 the **responsibility** for arranging your affairs;
006:069 On their account no **responsibility** falls on
010:041 Ye are free from **responsibility** for what I do,

RESPONSIBILITY (continued)

026:216 "I am free (of **responsibility**) for what ye do!"
042:015 For us (is the **responsibility** for) Our deeds,

RESPONSIBLE

002:139 that we are **responsible** for our doings
004:084 thou art held **responsible** only for thyself, and
015:020 for whose sustenance ye are not **responsible**.
024:054 he is only **responsible** for the duty placed

REST

002:085 and do ye reject the **rest**?
006:096 He makes the night for **rest** and tranquillity, and
007:004 or while they slept for their afternoon **rest**.
010:007 Those who **rest** not their hope on their
010:011 But We leave those who **rest** not their hope
010:015 unto them, those who **rest** not their hope on their
010:067 the Night that ye may **rest** therein, and the Day
011:041 or be at **rest**! For my Lord is, be sure,
011:042 (from the **rest**): "O my son! embark with us, and be
016:080 homes of **rest** and quiet for you; and made
022:005 to **rest** in the wombs for an appointed term,
023:013 in a place of **rest**, firmly fixed;
023:050 on high ground, affording **rest** and security
025:066 and as a place to **rest** in";
025:076 an abode and place of **rest**!
026:172 Then the **rest** We destroyed utterly.
027:086 made the Night for them to **rest** in and the
028:072 ye can **rest**? Will ye not then see?
028:073 that ye may **rest** therein, and that
037:082 Then the **rest** We overwhelmed in the Flood.
037:136 Then We destroyed the **rest**.
039:042 but the **rest** He sends (to their
040:061 for you, that ye may **rest** therein, and the Day,
056:089 (There is for him) **Rest** and Satisfaction, and a
068:028 (than the **rest**): "Did I not say to you,
075:012 that Day will be the place of **rest**.
077:021 of **rest**, firmly fixed,
078:009 And made your sleep for **rest**,
089:027 "O (thou) soul, in (complete) **rest** and satisfaction!

RESTED

011:044 **rested** on Mount Judi and the word went forth:

RESTING

006:098 then there is a **resting** place and a repository: We
011:006 He knoweth its **resting** place and its
036:038 And the Sun runs unto a **resting** place, for Him:
040:064 the earth as a **resting** place, and the

RESTORE

003:161 **restore** what he misappropriated;
004:002 To orphans **restore** their property
006:046 could **restore** them to you?" See how We
028:007 for We shall **restore** him to thee, and We
028:013 Thus did We **restore** him to his mother, that her
044:018 Saying: "**Restore** to me the servants of Allah: I am
075:027 "Who is a magician (to **restore** him)?"
085:013 and He can **restore** (life).

RESTORED

002:243 "Die." Then He **restored** them to life.
021:084 and We **restored** his people to him, and doubled

RESTRAIN

002:179 that ye may **restrain** yourselves.
002:194 Allah is with those who **restrain** themselves
003:134 who **restrain** anger, and pardon (all) men;
004:084 will **restrain** the fury of the Unbelievers; for

RESTRAIN (continued)

005:110 And behold! I did **restrain** the Children of Israel
009:036 with those who **restrain** themselves.
016:128 **restrain** themselves, and those who do good.

RESTRAINED

009:012 that thus they may be **restrained**.
048:020 and He has **restrained** the hands of men from you;
048:024 And it is He who has **restrained** their hands
055:072 Maidens **restrained** (as to their glances),
079:040 **restrained** (their) soul from lower Desires,

RESTRAINING

004:090 hearts **restraining** them from fighting you or
004:091 besides **restraining** their hands, seize them
037:048 chaste women; **restraining** their glances, with big
038:052 chaste women **restraining** their glances,
055:056 Chaste, **restraining** their glances, whom no

RESTRAINS

029:045 for Prayer **restrains** from shameful and evil

RESTRAINT

047:017 on them their Piety and **Restraint** (from evil).

RESTRICT

065:006 so as to **restrict** them. And if

RESTRICTED

002:273 in Allah's cause are **restricted** (from travel).
065:007 resources are **restricted**, let him spend according

RESTRICTING

089:016 **restricting** his subsistence for him, then saith

RESTRICTS

028:082 or **restricts** it, to any of His servants He pleases!
030:037 the provision and **restricts** it, to whomsoever
034:036 and **restricts** the provision to whom He pleases,
034:039 and **restricts** the Sustenance to such of His
039:052 the provision or **restricts** it, for any
042:012 and **restricts** the Sustenance to whom He will:

RESTS

003:087 on them (**rests**) the curse of Allah,
006:057 The Command **rests** with none but Allah: He
022:041 and forbid wrong: with Allah **rests** the end

RESULT

005:080 forward before them (with the **result**), that Allah's
012:064 with any **result** other than when I trusted you with
016:094 With the **result** that someone's foot may slip
020:121 In the **result**, they both ate of the tree, and so
033:073 (With the **result**) that Allah has to punish
035:010 and the plotting of such will be void (of **result**).
048:029 and delight. As a **result**, it fills
059:015 they have tasted the evil **result** of their conduct;
064:005 So they tasted the evil **result** of their conduct;
065:009 Then did they taste the evil **result** of their

RESULTS

016:034 But the evil **results** of their deeds overtook them,
039:051 Nay, the evil **results** of their deeds overtook them.
039:051 of this (generation)-the evil **results** of their

RESURRECTION

002:174 on the Day of **Resurrection**,
002:212 above them on the Day of **Resurrection**;
003:055 to the Day of **Resurrection**:
022:005 about the **Resurrection**, (consider) that
025:003 they control Death nor Life nor **Resurrection**.
025:047 and makes the Day (as it were) a **Resurrection**.
030:008 with their Lord (at the **Resurrection**)!

RESURRECTION (continued)

030:056 the Day of **Resurrection**: but ye-ye did not know!"
030:056 of **Resurrection**, and this is the Day of
031:028 And your creation or your **resurrection** is in no
035:009 even so (will be) the **Resurrection**!
037:144 inside the Fish till the Day of **Resurrection**.
046:006 (at the **Resurrection**), they will be hostile
050:011 thus will be the **Resurrection**.
050:042 that will be the day of **Resurrection**.
067:015 which He furnishes: but unto Him is the **Resurrection**.
071:018 (again at the **Resurrection**)?
075:001 I do swear by the **Resurrection** Day;
075:006 He questions: "When is the Day of **Resurrection**?"

RETAIN

016:059 he has had! Shall he **retain** it on (sufferance
033:037 and thy favour: "**Retain** thou (in wedlock) thy wife
069:012 hear the tale and) **retain** its memory should bear

RETALIATED

022:060 That (is so). And if one has **retaliated** to no

RETALIATION

005:045 But if anyone remits the **retaliation** by way of charity, i

RETIRED

019:022 So she conceived him, and she **retired** with him

RETRACED

027:010 and **retraced** not his steps: "O Moses!"
028:031 and **retraced** not his steps: "O Moses

RETREAT

002:125 or use it as a **retreat**, or bow,
002:187 while ye are in **retreat** in the mosques.
008:016 or to **retreat** to a troop (of his own)-he draws
009:025 did constrain you, and ye turned back in **retreat**.
027:010 a snake, he turn back in **retreat**, and retraced
027:080 (especially) when they turn back in **retreat**.
028:031 he turned back in **retreat**, and retraced

RETREATETH

074:033 And by the Night as it **retreateth**,

RETRIBUTION

003:004 and Allah is Exalted in Might, Lord of **Retribution**.
005:038 a **retribution** for their deeds and exemplary
005:095 for Allah is Exalted, and lord of **Retribution**.
007:136 So We exacted **retribution** from them: We drowned
007:167 Thy Lord is quick in **retribution**, but He
014:047 the Lord of **Retribution**.
015:079 So We exacted **retribution** from them. They were
030:047 We meted out **Retribution**: and it
032:022 who transgress We shall exact (Due) **Retribution**.
039:037 Is not Allah Exalted in Power, Lord of **Retribution**?
043:025 So We exacted **retribution** from them: now see
043:041 We shall be sure to exact **retribution** from them,
043:055 We exacted **retribution** from them, and We
044:016 (then) exact **retribution**!
047:004 exacted **retribution** from them (Himself); but He

RETURN

002:018 they will not **return** (to the path).
002:028 and again to Him will ye **return**.
002:046 and that they are to **return** to Him.
002:156 and to Him is our **return**":
002:196 And seven days on his **return**,
002:199 Then **return** from the place whence it is usual
002:226 if then they **return**,
002:245 and to Him shall be your **return**.
003:014 the best of the goals (to **return** to).

RETURN (continued)

003:055 then shall ye all **return** to Me,
003:109 to Allah do all matters **return**.
004:034 but if they **return** to obedience, seek not
005:105 The **return** of you all is to Allah: it is
006:060 in the end unto Him will be your **return**, then
006:108 In the end will they **return** to their Lord and He
006:164 Your **return** in the end is toward Allah: He will
007:029 so shall ye **return**."
007:088 shall have to **return** to our religion." He said:
007:089 **return** thereto unless it be as in the will
008:019 if ye **return** (to the attack), so shall We.
009:074 only **return** for the bounty with which Allah and
009:094 when ye **return** to them. Say thou:
009:095 when ye **return** to them, that ye
009:111 for theirs (in **return**) is the Garden (of Paradise):
009:122 and admonish the people when they **return** to them,-
010:004 To Him will be your **return**-of all of you. The
010:023 to Us is your **return**, and We
010:046 their **return**: ultimately Allah is witness to all
010:070 and, then, to Us will be their **return**. Then shall
011:004 "To Allah is your **return**, and He
011:029 I ask you for no wealth in **return**: my reward
011:034 He is your Lord! and to Him will ye **return**!
012:046 that I may **return** to the people, and that
013:029 and a beautiful place of (final) **return**."
013:036 Unto Him do I call, and unto Him is my **return**."
014:013 or ye shall **return** to our religion." But their
017:051 to **return**?" Say: "He Who created you first!"
018:020 to **return** to their religion, and in
019:080 To Us shall **return** all that he talks of, and he
020:021 We shall **return** it at once to its
020:055 and into it shall We **return** you, and from
020:089 not **return** them a word (for answer), and that
021:013 Flee not, but **return** to the good things of this
021:035 to Us must ye **return**.
021:093 from another: (yet) will they all **return** to Us.
021:095 that they shall not **return**,
023:060 because they will **return** to their Lord;-
023:107 if ever we **return** (to evil), then shall
024:042 and to Allah is the **return**.
026:050 we shall but **return** to our Lord!
026:102 "`Now if we only had a chance of **return**, we shall
027:028 and (wait to) see what answer they **return**"...
027:035 what (answer) **return** (my) ambassadors."
028:039 they would not have to **return** to Us!"
028:085 to the Place of **Return**. Say: "My Lord
029:008 Ye have (all) to **return** to Me, and I will
029:017 to Him will be your **return**.
031:015 in the End the **return** of you all is to Me,
031:022 and to Allah shall all things **return**.
031:023 to Us is their **return**, and We
032:021 they may (repent and) **return**.
034:049 and will not **return**."
036:031 Not to them will they **return**:
036:050 nor to **return** to their own people!
037:068 Then shall their **return** be to the (Blazing) Fire.
038:025 and a beautiful place of (final) **Return**.
038:040 to Us, and a beautiful Place of (final) **Return**.
038:049 is a beautiful place of (final) **Return**,-
038:055 will be an evil place of (final) **Return**!-
039:007 In the End, to your Lord is your **return**, when He
040:043 or the Hereafter; our **Return** will be to Allah;

RETURN (continued)
040:077 that they shall (all) **return**.
041:021 the first time, and unto Him were ye to **return**.
042:044 say: "Is there any way (to effect) a **return**?"
048:012 and the Believers would never **return** to their
050:003 **Return** far (from our understanding)."
050:043 and to Us is the Final **Return**-
060:004 to Thee is (our) final **Return**.
063:008 They say, "If we **return** to Madinah, surely the
064:003 and to Him is the final **Return**.
071:018 "And in the End He will **return** you into the
078:039 a (straight) **Return** to his Lord!
079:012 be a **return** with loss!"
083:031 to their own people, they would **return** jesting;
084:014 would not have to **return** (to Us)!
088:025 For to Us will be their **Return**;
092:019 is expected in **return**,
096:008 Verily, to thy Lord is the **return** (of all).

RETURNED
003:174 And they **returned** with Grace and Bounty from Allah:
006:028 But if they were **returned**, they would
006:036 then will they be **returned** unto Him.
006:062 Then are men **returned** unto Allah, their True
007:089 if we **returned** to your religion after Allah
008:044 and unto Allah are all matters **returned**.
012:062 when they **returned** to their people, in order
012:063 Now when they **returned** to their father, they said:
012:065 had been **returned** to them. They said:
012:065 has been **returned** to us: so we shall get (more)
012:082 and the caravan in which we **returned**, and (you
019:040 to Us will they all be **returned**.
020:086 So Moses **returned** to his people in state
035:004 before thee: to Allah all affairs are **returned**.
036:067 nor could they have **returned** (after error).
046:029 (reading) was finished, they **returned** to their
079:010 be **returned** to (our) former state?-
083:031 And when they **returned** to their own people,

RETURNING
014:043 their gaze **returning** not towards them, and their
039:042 He keeps back (from **returning** to life), but the
086:011 By the Firmament which giveth **returning** rain,

RETURNS
019:076 respect o (their) eventual **returns**."
020:091 to it until Moses **returns** to us."
027:040 thy glance **returns** to thee. Then when
036:039 she **returns** like the old (and withered)

RE-UNITE
002:230 no blame on either of them if they **re-unite**,

REVEAL
002:033 and I know what ye **reveal** and what ye conceal?"
002:041 And believe in what I **reveal**,
002:077 what they conceal and what they **reveal**?
003:029 in your hearts or **reveal** it, Allah knows it all:
003:044 which We **reveal** unto thee (O Prophet!)
003:154 what they dare not **reveal** to thee.
005:099 but Allah knoweth all that ye **reveal** and ye conceal.
006:003 He knoweth what ye hide, and what ye **reveal**, and
006:093 **reveal** the like of what Allah hath revealed?"
007:020 in order to **reveal** to them their shame that
007:187 none but He can **reveal** as to
011:005 and what they **reveal**: for He knoweth well the
012:003 in that We **reveal** to thee this (portion
012:037 I will surely **reveal** to you the truth and meaning

REVEAL (continued)
012:102 happened unseen, which We **reveal** by inspiration
014:038 what we conceal and what we **reveal**: for nothing
016:019 and what ye **reveal**.
016:023 they conceal, and what they **reveal**: Verily He
024:029 of what ye **reveal** and what ye conceal.
025:033 but We **reveal** to thee the truth and the best
027:025 and knows what ye hide and what ye **reveal**.
027:074 as well as all that they **reveal**.
028:043 We did **reveal** to Moses the Book after We
028:069 their hearts conceal and all that they **reveal**.
033:054 Whether ye **reveal** anything or conceal it,
042:051 to **reveal**, with Allah's permission, what Allah
060:001 ye conceal and all that ye **reveal**. And any
064:004 what ye conceal and what ye **reveal**: yea, Allah

REVEALED
002:023 **revealed** from time to our servants
002:076 what Allah hath **revealed** to you,
002:170 "Follow what Allah hath **revealed**,"
002:285 hath been **revealed** to him form his Lord,
003:053 "Our Lord! we believe in what thou hast **revealed**,
003:065 were not **revealed** till after him?
003:072 what is **revealed** to the Believers,
003:084 and in what has been **revealed** to us and what
003:084 and what was **revealed** to Abraham, Isma'il;
003:093 for himself before the Torah was **revealed**.
004:047 believe in what We have (now) **revealed**, confirming
004:061 "Come to what Allah hath **revealed**. And
004:162 believe in what hath been **revealed** to thee and
004:162 and what was **revealed** before thee: and
005:005 **revealed** before your time, when you
005:044 by what Allah hath **revealed**, they are Unbelievers.
005:044 It was We who **revealed** the Torah (to Moses):
005:045 by what Allah hath **revealed**, they are wrong-doers.
005:047 by what Allah hath **revealed**, they are indeed rebel.
005:047 by what Allah hath **revealed** therein.
005:048 so judge between them by what Allah hath **revealed**,
005:049 between them by what Allah hath **revealed**, and
005:081 hath been **revealed** to him, never would they
005:101 when the Qur'an is being **revealed**, they will
005:104 "Come to what Allah hath **revealed**; come to
006:019 **revealed** to me by inspiration that I may
006:050 I but follow what is **revealed** to me." Say:
006:093 reveal the like of what Allah hath **revealed**?"
006:155 which We have **revealed** as a blessing: so follow
007:002 A Book **revealed** unto thee,- so let
007:117 We **revealed** to Moses "Throw thy rod": and behold!
007:196 Who **revealed** the Book, (from time to time), and He
007:203 is **revealed** to me from my Lord: this is
009:064 all that ye fear (should be **revealed**)."
010:015 I follow naught but what is **revealed** unto me: if I
010:094 We have **revealed** unto thee, then ask
011:012 of what is **revealed** unto thee, and thy
011:036 It was **revealed** to Noah: "None of thy People
011:049 of the Unseen, which We have **revealed** unto thee:
013:001 that which hath been **revealed** unto thee
013:019 that which hath been **revealed** unto thee from
013:036 rejoice at what hath been **revealed** unto thee:
013:037 Thus have We **revealed** it to be a judgment
014:001 A Book which We have **revealed** unto thee, in order
015:006 the Message is being **revealed**! Truly thou
016:024 has **revealed**?" they say, "Tales of the ancients!"
016:030 "What is it that your Lord has **revealed**?" they say

REVEALED (continued)

016:123   Then We **revealed** to thee "Follow the ways
017:039   has **revealed** to thee. Take not, with Allah,
017:073   away from that which We had **revealed** unto thee,
017:106   We have **revealed** it by stages.
018:027   been **revealed** to thee of the Book of thy Lord:
020:048   'Verily it has been **revealed** to us that the
021:010   We have **revealed** for you (O men!) a book
025:032   Thus (is it **revealed**), that We may
025:032   "Why is not the Qur'an **revealed** to him
026:196   in the **revealed** Books of former peoples.
026:198   Had We **revealed** it to any of the non-Arabs,
028:087   have been **revealed** to thee: and invite
035:031   confirming what was (**revealed**) before it:
035:031   That which We have **revealed** to thee of the Book
038:070   "Only this has been **revealed** to me: that I
039:002   Verily it is We Who have **revealed** the Book
039:023   Allah has **revealed** (from time to time) the most
039:041   Verily We have **revealed** the Book to thee in Truth,
039:055   "And follow the Best that which **revealed** to you
039:065   But it has already been **revealed** to thee,-as it
041:006   it is **revealed** to me by inspiration, that your
046:004   Bring me a Book (**revealed**) before this, or any
046:009   I follow but that which is **revealed** to me
046:030   We have heard a Book **revealed** after Moses,
047:020   of decisive meaning is **revealed**, and fighting
047:026   who hate what Allah has **revealed**, "We will
057:016   the Truth which has been **revealed** (to them),
072:001   Say: It has been **revealed** to me that a company
097:001   We have indeed **revealed** this (Message)

REVEALING

005:015   **revealing** to you much that ye used to
012:077   **revealing** not the secrets to them he (simply)

REVEALS

016:101   He **reveals** (in stages),-they say, "Thou art

REVELATION

002:004   the **Revelation** sent to thee,
002:041   confirming the **revelation** which is with you,
002:090   (the **revelation**) which Allah has sent down,
002:097   (**revelation**) to they heart by Allah's will,
002:136   and the **revelation** given to us,
003:073   **revelation** be sent to someone (else) like unto that
003:073   Or that those (receiving such **revelation**)
003:199   those who believe in Allah, in the **revelation** to you,
003:199   and in the **revelation** to them, bowing
005:059   and the **revelation** that hath come to us
005:064   But the **revelation** that cometh to thee from Allah
005:066   the Gospel, and all the **revelation** that was
005:068   It is the **revelation** that cometh to thee
005:068   The Gospel, and all the **revelation** that has
005:083   the **revelation** received by the Messenger, thou
006:091   send down to man (by way of **revelation**)": say:
007:003   Follow (O men!) the **revelation** given unto
007:075   in the **revelation** which hath been sent
007:144   take then the (**revelation**) which I give thee, and
007:203   If thou bring them not a **revelation**, they say:
008:041   the **revelation** We sent down to our Servant
011:014   know ye that this **Revelation** is sent down
015:001   These are the Ayats of **Revelation**,-of a Qur'an
016:101   When We substitute one **revelation** for another,-
016:102   the **revelation** from thy Lord in Truth, in order
019:030   He hath given me **revelation** and made me a prophet:
020:004   A **revelation** from Him Who created the earth

REVELATION (continued)

020:114   the Qur'an before its **revelation** to thee
020:133   of all that was in the former Books of **revelation**?
021:045   to **revelation**": but the deaf will not hear the
022:055   to be in doubt concerning (**Revelation**) until the
022:078   both before and in this (**Revelation**); that the
026:192   Verily this is a **Revelation** from the
028:052   before this,-they do believe in this (**Revelation**);
029:027   his progeny Prophethood and **Revelation**, and We
029:046   "We believe in the **Revelation** which has
031:021   the (**revelation**) that Allah has sent down,
032:002   (This is) the **revelation** of the Book in which
034:006   see that the (**Revelation**) sent down to thee
036:005   (It is a **Revelation**) sent down by (Him),
036:015   sends no sort of **revelation**: ye do
039:001   The **revelation** of this Book is from Allah,
039:025   rejected (**revelation**), and so the Punishment
040:002   The **revelation** of this Book is from Allah,
041:002   A **revelation** from The Most Gracious, Most Merciful;-
041:052   Say: "See ye if the (**Revelation**) is (really)
042:052   what was **revelation**, and what was Faith; but We
043:043   So hold thou fast to the **Revelation** sent down
045:002   The **revelation** of the book is from Allah
046:002   The **revelation** of the Book is from Allah
047:002   and believe in the (**Revelation**) sent down
047:009   That is because they hate the **Revelation** of Allah;
052:001   By the Mount (of **Revelation**);
056:080   A **Revelation** from the Lord of the Worlds.
057:026   Prophethood and **Revelation**: and some
069:050   But truly (**Revelation**) is a cause of sorrow
074:052   to be given scrolls (of **revelation**) spread out!

REVELATIONS

002:106   None of Our **revelations** do We abrogate
002:174   Those who conceal Allah's **revelations** in the Book,
004:060   they believe in the **revelations** that have come
006:092   (the **revelations**) which came before it: that
008:002   His **revelations** rehearsed, find their faith
010:037   a confirmation of (**revelations**) that went before
028:087   from Allah's **revelations** after they have been
040:070   and the (**revelations**) with which We sent
044:005   For We (ever) send (**revelations**),
066:012   and of His **Revelations**, and was
087:018   of the earliest (**Revelations**),-

REVENGE

009:074   this **revenge** of theirs was (their) only return

REVERENCE

021:028   and **reverence** of His (glory).

REVERSED

036:068   We cause him to be **reversed** in nature: will they

REVERT

017:008   (to your sins), We shall **revert** (to Our
017:008   show Mercy unto you; but it ye **revert** (to your
044:015   will **revert** (to your ways).
058:008   forbidden secret counsels yet **revert** to that

REVILE

006:108   **revile** Allah in their ignorance. Thus
006:108   **Revile** not ye those whom they call

REVIVE

035:009   that is dead, and **revive** the earth therewith

REVIVES

045:005   and **revives** therewith the earth after its death,

REVOLVING

033:019 their eyes **revolving**, like one who faints from death:

REWARD

002:062 shall have their **reward** with their Lord
002:085 But what is the **reward** for those
002:103 **reward** from Allah if they but knew!
002:112 he will get his **reward** with his Lord;
002:191 Such is the **reward** of those who reject faith.
002:262 for them their **reward** is with their Lord;
002:274 have their **reward** with their Lord:
002:277 will have their **reward** with their Lord:
003:057 Allah will pay them (in full) their **reward**;
003:087 Of such the **reward** is that on them (rests)
003:136 For such the **reward** is forgiveness
003:144 will swiftly **reward** those who (serve him)
003:145 If any do desire a **reward** in this life,
003:145 and if any do desire a **reward** in the Hereafter,
003:145 And swiftly shall We **reward** those that
003:148 And Allah gave them a **reward** in this world,
003:148 and the excellent **reward** of the Hereafter.
003:171 suffereth not the **reward** of the Faithful
003:172 and refrain from wrong have a great **reward**;
003:179 ye have a **reward** great without measure.
003:195 a **reward** from Allah, and from Allah
003:199 For them is a **reward** with their Lord,
004:040 and giveth from His Own self a great **reward**.
004:067 given them from Ourselves a great **reward**;
004:074 soon shall We give him a **reward** of great (value).
004:095 those who sit at home by a great **reward**.
004:100 his **reward** becomes due and sure with Allah:
004:114 We shall soon give a **reward** of the highest (value).
004:134 in Allah's (gift) is the **reward** (both) of
004:134 If any one desires a **reward** in this life, in
004:146 to the Believers a **reward** of immense value.
004:162 to them shall We soon give a great **reward**.
005:009 hath Allah promised forgiveness and a great **reward**.
005:029 and that is the **reward** of those who do wrong."
006:084 thus do We **reward** those who do good:
006:090 Say: "No **reward** for this do I ask of you: this
006:093 This day shall ye receive your **reward**,-
007:040 such is Our **reward** for those in sin.
007:113 a (suitable) **reward** if we win!"
007:170 never shall We suffer the **reward** of the
008:028 whom lies your highest **reward**.
009:022 Verily with Allah is a **reward**, the greatest
009:026 thus doth He **reward** those without Faith.
009:120 the **reward** to be lost of those who do good;-
009:121 requite them with the best (possible **reward**).
010:004 that He may **reward** with justice those who
010:026 (**reward**)-yea, more (than in measure)! No
010:027 will have a **reward** of like evil: ignominy will
010:072 my **reward** is only due from Allah, and I
010:072 no **reward** have I asked of you: my **reward**
011:011 (of sins) and a great **reward**.
011:029 my **reward** is from none but Allah: but I
011:051 no **reward** for this (Message). My **reward**
011:051 My **reward** is from none but Him Who created Me:
011:115 the **reward** of the righteous to perish.
012:022 thus do We **reward** those who do right.
012:056 the **reward** of those who do good.
012:057 But verily the **reward** of the Hereafter
012:072 is (the **reward** of) a camel-load; I will
012:088 for Allah doth **reward** the charitable."

REWARD (continued)

012:090 never will Allah suffer the **reward** to be lost,
012:104 And no **reward** dost thou ask of them for this:
016:031 thus doth Allah **reward** the righteous,-
016:041 in this world; but truly the **reward** of the
016:062 that the **reward** most fair is for themselves:
016:096 their **reward** according to the best
016:097 their **reward** according to the best
017:009 have a magnificent **reward**;
018:002 shall have a goodly **Reward**.
018:030 shall not suffer to perish the **reward** of any
018:044 He is the Best to **reward**, and the Best
018:088 a goodly **reward**, and easy will be his task as We
018:106 That is their **reward**, Hell; because they
020:015 for every soul to receiver its **reward** by the
020:076 for aye: such is the **reward** of those who purify
021:029 such a one We should **reward** with Hell: thus do
021:029 thus do We **reward** those who do wrong.
024:038 That Allah may **reward** them according to the
025:015 a **reward** as well as a final abode.
025:057 Say: "No **reward** do I ask of you for it but this:
026:041 shall we have a (suitable) **reward** if we win?"
026:109 my **reward** is only from the Lord of the Worlds:
026:109 "No **reward** do I ask of you for it: my **reward**
026:127 my **reward** is only from the Lord of the Worlds.
026:127 "No **reward** do I ask of you for it: my **reward**
026:145 my **reward** is only from the Lord of the Worlds.
026:145 No **reward** do I ask of you for it: my **reward**
026:164 "No **reward** do I ask of you for it: my **reward**
026:164 my **reward** is only from the Lord of the Worlds.
026:180 my **reward** is only from the Lord of the Worlds.
026:180 "No **reward** do I ask of you for it: my **reward**
027:090 "Do ye receive a **reward** other than that which
028:014 for thus do We **reward** those who do good.
028:025 he may **reward** thee for having watered (our
028:054 Twice will they be given their **reward**, for that
028:080 The **reward** of Allah (in the Hereafter) is best
028:084 If any does good, the **reward** to him is better
029:007 have committed, and We shall **reward** them according
029:027 and We granted him his **reward** in this life;
029:058 an excellent **reward** for those who do (good)!-
030:045 That He may **reward** those who believe and work
032:017 for them-as a **reward** for their (good) Deeds.
033:024 That Allah may **reward** the men of Truth
033:029 amongst you a great **reward**.
033:031 to her shall We grant her **reward** twice: and We
033:035 forgiveness and great **reward**.
033:044 and He has prepared for them a generous **Reward**.
034:004 That He may **reward** those who believe and work
034:037 is a multiplied **Reward** for their deeds,
034:047 Say: "Whatever **reward** do I ask of you: it is
034:047 it is yours: my **reward** is only due from Allah:
035:007 and a magnificent **Reward**.
035:036 for them. Thus do We **reward** every ungrateful one!
036:011 of Forgiveness and a **Reward** most generous.
036:021 "Obey those who ask no **reward** of you
037:080 Thus indeed do We **reward** those who do right.
037:105 the dream!"-thus indeed do We **reward** those who
037:110 Thus indeed do We **reward** those who do right.
037:121 Thus indeed do We **reward** those who do right.
037:131 Thus indeed do We **reward** those who do right.
038:086 Say: "No **reward** do I ask of you
039:010 will truly receive a **reward** without measure!"

REWARD (continued)

039:010 Fear your Lord: good is (the **reward**) for those
039:034 such is the **reward** of those who do good:
039:035 and give them their **reward** according to the
039:074 as we will: how excellent a **reward** for those who
041:008 deeds of righteousness is a **reward** that will
042:023 Say: "No **reward** do I ask of you for this
042:040 makes reconciliation, his **reward** is due from Allah:
048:010 Allah will soon grant him a great **Reward**.
048:016 a goodly **reward**, but if ye turn back as ye
048:029 and a great **Reward**.
049:003 for them is Forgiveness and a great **Reward**.
052:040 a **reward**, so that they are burdened
053:041 Then will he be rewarded with a **reward** complete;
054:035 Thus do We **reward** those who give thanks.
055:060 Is there any **Reward** for Good-other than Good?
056:024 A **Reward** for the Deeds of their past (Life).
057:007 for them is a great **Reward**.
057:010 has Allah promised a goodly (**reward**). And Allah
057:011 and he will have (besides) a generous **reward**.
057:018 and they shall have (besides) a generous **reward**.
057:019 their **Reward** and their Light, but those
057:027 who believed, their (due) **reward**, but many
059:017 Such is the **reward** of wrong-doers.
064:015 with Him is the highest **Reward**.
065:005 from him and will enlarge his **reward**.
067:012 for them is Forgiveness and a great **Reward**.
068:003 Nay, verily for thee is a **Reward** unfailing:
068:046 a **reward**, so that they are burdened with a load
073:020 Yea, better and greater, in **Reward**, and seek ye
076:009 of Allah alone: no **reward** do we desire from you,
076:012 He will **reward** them with a Garden and (garments
076:022 "Verily this is a **Reward** for you, and your
077:044 Thus do We certainly **reward** the Doers of Good.
084:025 for them is a **Reward** that will never fail.
092:019 from anyone for which a **reward** is expected
095:006 for they shall have a **reward** unfailing.
098:008 Their **reward** is with Allah:

REWARDED

005:085 hath Allah **rewarded** them with Gardens, with
007:147 **rewarded** except as they have wrought?
023:111 "I have **rewarded** them this day for their
025:075 be **rewarded** with the highest place in heaven,
048:018 and He **rewarded** them with a speedy Victory;
053:041 Then will he be **rewarded** with a reward complete;

REWARDS

003:195 and from Allah is the best of **rewards**.
004:152 We shall soon give their (due) **rewards**: for Allah
004:173 He will give their (due) **rewards**,-and more,
018:046 of thy Lord, as **rewards**, and best
019:076 thy Lord, as **rewards**, and best in respect of
037:053 receive **rewards** and punishments?'"
053:031 so that He **rewards** those who do evil,
053:031 and He **rewards** those who do good, with what

RHYTHMIC

073:004 in slow, measured **rhythmic** tones.

RIBS

086:007 Proceeding from between the backbone and the **ribs**:

RICH

002:069 pure and **rich** in tone,
003:181 "Truly, Allah is indigent and we are **rich**!"
004:135 and whether it be (against) **rich** or poor: for

RICH (continued)

007:058 springs up produce, (**rich**) after its kind: but
009:093 are **rich**. They prefer to stay with the (women)
016:080 their hair, **rich** stuff and articles of convenience
044:053 **rich** brocade, they will face each other;
055:054 **rich** brocade: the Fruit of the Gardens will be
055:076 and **rich** Carpets of beauty.
088:016 And **rich** carpets (All) spread out.

RICHES

028:076 those who exult (in **riches**).
028:078 in amount (of **riches**) they had collected? But the
057:020 **riches** and children. Here is a
058:017 against Allah, will be their **riches** nor their
063:009 O ye who believe! let not your **riches** or your
064:015 Your **riches** and your children may be but a trial:

RIDE

016:008 and donkeys, for you to **ride** and as an adornment;
023:022 And on them, as well as in ships, ye **ride**.
036:042 similar (vessels) on which they **ride**.
043:012 and cattle on which ye **ride**,

RIDICULE

004:140 the Message of Allah held in defiance and **ridicule**,
009:079 and throw **ridicule** on them,-Allah will
009:079 Allah will throw back their **ridicule** on them: and
011:038 they threw **ridicule** on him. He said: "If ye
011:038 He said: "If ye **ridicule** us now, we (in our turn)
011:038 on you with **ridicule** likewise!
021:036 with **ridicule**. "Is this," (they say), "The one
023:110 "But ye treated them with **ridicule**, so much
023:110 so much so that (**ridicule** of) them made you
030:010 and held them up to **ridicule**.
031:006 and throw **ridicule** (on the Path): for such
034:007 The Unbelievers say (in **ridicule**): "Shall we
037:012 Truly dost thou marvel, while they **ridicule**,
038:063 "Did we treat them (as such) in **ridicule**, or have
043:057 a clamor thereat (in **ridicule**)!

RIDING

002:239 or **riding**, (as may be most convenient),
040:079 that ye may use some for **riding** and some for food;

RIGHT

002:011 only ones that put things **right**!"
002:026 and many He leads into the **right** path,
002:031 names of these if ye are **right**."
002:044 Do ye enjoin **right** conduct on the people,
002:053 and the criterion (between **right** and wrong),
002:137 they are indeed on the **right** path;
002:185 guidance and judgment (between **right** and wrong).
002:186 that they may walk in the **right** way.
002:197 but the best of provisions is **right** conduct.
002:203 if his aims is to do **right**.
002:228 better **right** to take them back in that period,
002:236 is due from those who wish to do the **right** thing.
002:272 guide them to the **right** path.
002:272 the **right** path whom He pleaseth.
003:003 Criterion (of judgement between **right** and wrong).
003:020 If they do, they are in **right** guidance,
003:021 and in defiance of **right**, slay the prophets,
003:037 **Right** graciously did her Lord accept her:
003:104 enjoining what is **right**, and forbidding
003:110 Enjoining what is **right**, forbidding what is wrong,
003:112 and slew the Prophets in defiance of **right**:
003:113 are a portion that stand (for the **right**);
003:114 they enjoin what is **right**, and forbid

RIGHT (continued)

003:115 for Allah knoweth well those that do **right**.
003:120 But if ye are patient and do **right**,
003:172 those who do **right** and refrain from wrong
003:179 and if ye believe and do **right**, ye have
003:181 of slaying the Prophets in defiance of **right**,
004:003 or that which your **right** hands possess.
004:005 take it and enjoy it with **right** good cheer.
004:024 except those whom your **right** hands possess:
004:025 from among those whom your **right** hand possess:
004:033 To those also, to whom your **right** hand was pledged,
004:036 and what your **right** hands possess: for
004:044 and wish that ye should lose the **right** path.
004:046 those who displace words from their (**right**) places,
004:051 in the (**right**) way than the Believers!
004:060 lead them astray far away (from the **Right**).
004:077 the Hereafter is the best for those who do **right**:
004:116 hath strayed far, far away (from the **Right**).
004:155 that they slew the Messengers in defiance of **right**;
005:013 (**right**) places and forget a good part of the
005:041 They change the words from their (**right**) places;
005:066 a party on the **right** course: but many
005:105 if ye follow (**right**) guidance. No hurt
005:107 who claim a lawful **right**: let them swear
005:116 never could I say what I had no **right** (to say).
006:081 hath more **right** to security? (Tell me)
006:082 for they are on (**right**) guidance."
006:154 those who would do **right**, and explaining
006:161 a religion of **right**,-the Path (trod)
007:017 from their **right** and their left: nor wilt
007:105 One for whom it is **right** to say nothing
007:142 do **right**, and follow not the way
007:146 on the earth in defiance of **right**-them will I
007:146 and if they see the way of **right** conduct, they
007:155 Thou wilt into the **right** path. Thou art
007:156 for those who do **right**, and pay
007:178 he is on the **right** path: whom He
007:199 Hold to forgiveness; command what is **right**; but
008:029 (to judge between **right** and wrong), remove from
009:036 that is the **right** religion so wrong not yourselves
009:059 (That would been the **right** course).
009:091 be against such as do **right**: and Allah
010:023 through the earth in defiance of **right**! O Mankind!
010:026 To those who do **right** is a goodly (reward)-yea,
012:022 thus do We reward those who do **right**.
012:040 but Him: that is the **right** religion, but most
012:090 to be lost, of those who do **right**."
012:109 for those who do **right**. Will ye
013:031 all mankind (to the **Right**)?
015:076 And the (cities were) **right** on the high-road.
016:009 Allah alone can show the **right** path but there
016:048 turn round, from the **right** and the left,
016:071 to those whom their **right** hands possess, so as
017:009 to that which is most **right** (or stable),
017:071 given their record in their **right** hand will read
017:093 or thou mount a ladder **right** into the skies.
018:010 and dispose of our affair for us in the **right** way!
018:017 when it rose, declining to the **right** from their
018:017 to lead him to the **Right** Way.
018:018 and We turned them on their **right** and their
018:024 ever closer (even) than this to the **right** course."
019:052 **right** side of Mount (Sinai), and made
020:017 And what is that in thy **right** hand, O Moses?"

020:069 **right** hand: quickly will it swallow up that which
020:082 and do **right**,-who, in fine, are no true guidance."
021:048 for those who would do **right**,-
021:079 the (**right**) understanding of the matter: to each
022:040 of **right**,-(for no cause) except that they
022:041 and give zakat, enjoin the **right** and forbid
022:067 assuredly on the **Right** Way.
022:074 They do not have the **right** estimate of Allah:
023:006 **right** hands possess,-for (in their case) they are
024:016 "It is not **right** of us to speak of this:
024:031 **right** hands possess, or male attendants free
024:049 But if the **right** is on their side, they come
024:052 and do **right**, that will triumph.
024:054 **right** guidance. The Messenger's duty is only
024:058 whom your **right** hands possess, and the
025:026 That Day, the dominion **right** by shall be
026:155 she has a **right** of watering, and ye
026:155 and ye have a **right** of watering, (severally) on
028:019 and not to be one who sets things **right**!"
028:030 he was called from the **right** bank of the valley,
029:048 it with thy **right** hand: in that case, indeed,
029:069 is with those who do **right**.
030:028 whom your **right** hands possess, to share
030:043 the **right** Religion, before there come from Allah
031:032 those that falter between (**right** and wrong).
033:004 and He shows the (**right**) Way.
033:050 the captives whom their **right** hands possess;-
033:050 thy **right** hand possesses out of the captives
033:052 **right** hand should possess (as handmaidens):
033:053 Nor is it **right** for you that ye should
033:055 **right** hands possess. And, (ladies), fear Allah;
033:067 and they misled us as to the (**right**) path.
034:015 to the **right** and to the left. "Eat of the
034:024 on **right** guidance or in manifest error!"
036:008 **right** up to their chins, so that
037:028 to come to us from the **right** hand."
037:080 Thus indeed do We reward those who do **right**.
037:093 striking (them) with the **right** hand.
037:105 those who do **right**.
037:110 Thus indeed do We reward those who do **right**.
037:113 do **right**, and (some) that obviously do wrong,
037:121 Thus indeed do We reward those who do **right**.
037:131 Thus indeed do We reward those who do **right**.
038:028 the same as those who turn aside from the **right**?
039:033 such are the men who do **right**.
039:044 (the **right** to grant) Intercession: to Him
039:067 up in his **right** hand: Glory to Him! High is
040:018 will (come) **right** up to the Throats to choke
040:029 but to the Path of **Right**!"
040:038 I will lead you to the Path of **Right**.
042:042 defying **right** and justice: for such
045:018 Then We put thee on the (**right**) Way of Religion:
046:012 and as Glad Tidings to those who do **right**.
050:017 on the **right** and one on the left.
054:028 each one's **right** to drink being brought forward
056:008 what will be the Companions of the **Right** Hand?
056:008 the Companions of the **Right** Hand;-what will be
056:027 what will be the Companions of the **Right** Hand!
056:027 The Companions of the **Right** Hand,-what will be
056:038 For the Companions of the **Right** Hand.
056:090 And if he be of the Companions of the **Right** Hand,
056:091 from the Companions of the **Right** Hand.

RIGHT (continued)

057:012 before their **right** hands: (their greeting will be)
057:025 the book and the Balance (of **Right** and Wrong),
057:026 and some of them were on **right** guidance, but many
066:008 and by their **right** hands, while they say,
069:019 in his **right** hand will say: "Ah here!
069:045 We should certainly seize him by his **right** hand
070:016 Plucking out (his being) **right** to the skull!-
070:017 and turn away their faces (from the **Right**),
070:024 And those in whose wealth is a recognized **right**
070:030 and the (captives) whom their **right** hands possess,-
070:037 From the **right** and from the left, in crowds?
071:006 (their) flight (from the **Right**)."
072:002 'It gives guidance to the **Right**, and we
072:010 to guide them to **right** conduct.
072:014 they have sought out (the path) of **right** conduct:
072:016 on the (**right**) Way, We should
072:021 you harm, or to bring you to **right** conduct."
074:039 Except the Companions of the **Right** Hand.
078:038 and he will say what is **right**.
084:007 Then he who is given his Record in his **Right** hand,
090:018 Such are the Companions of the **Right** Hand.
091:008 And its inspiration as to its wrong and its **right**;
098:003 Wherein are books **right** and straight.
098:005 and that is the Religion **Right** and Straight.
104:007 The which doth mount (**Right**) to the Hearts:

RIGHT-MINDED

011:078 a single **right-minded** man?"
011:087 forbeareth with faults and is **right-minded**!

RIGHTEOUS

002:021 that ye may become **righteous**,
002:130 the Hereafter in the ranks of the **Righteous**.
002:212 But the **righteous** will be above them
002:241 suitable Gift this is duty on the **righteous**.
003:015 For the **righteous** are Gardens in nearness to
003:039 of the (goodly) company of the **righteous**."
003:046 (of the company) of the **righteous**."
003:114 they are in the ranks of the **righteous**.
003:133 prepared for the **righteous**.
003:193 in the company of the **righteous**.
003:198 is the best (bliss) for the **righteous**.
004:034 Therefore the **righteous** women are devoutly
004:069 the martyres, and the **Righteous** (who do good):
005:027 the sacrifice of those who are **righteous**.
005:065 had believed and been **righteous**. We
005:084 to admit us to the company of the **righteous**?"
006:032 for those who are **righteous**. Will ye not
006:069 falls on the **righteous**, but (their duty)
006:085 all in the ranks of the **Righteous**:
006:153 thus doth He command you, that ye may be **righteous**.
006:155 so follow it and be **righteous**, that ye
007:035 those who are **righteous** and mend (their lives),
007:128 and the end is (best) for the **righteous**.
007:168 that are the **righteous**, and some
007:169 But best for the **righteous** is the Home
007:170 of the **righteous** to perish.
007:196 and He will befriend the **righteous**.
008:034 its guardians except the **righteous**; but most
009:004 for Allah loveth the **righteous**.
009:007 for Allah doth love the **righteous**.
009:075 and be truly amongst those who are **righteous**.
011:049 for the End is for those who are **righteous**.
011:115 the reward of the **righteous** to perish.

RIGHTEOUS (continued)

011:117 their people are **righteous**.
012:009 for you to be **righteous** after that!"
012:090 behold, he that is **righteous** and patient,-
012:101 (as a Muslim), and unite me with the **righteous**.""
013:023 the **righteous** among their fathers, their spouses,
013:035 the **righteous** are promised! beneath it
013:035 such is the End of the **Righteous**; and the End
015:045 The **righteous** (will be) amid Gardens and fountains
016:030 excellent indeed is the Home of the **righteous**,-
016:030 To the **righteous** (when) it is said, "What is
016:031 thus doth Allah reward the **righteous**,-
016:122 in the ranks of the **Righteous**.
018:002 **righteous** deeds, that they shall have
018:030 of any who do a (single) **righteous** deed.
018:082 their father had been a **righteous** man: so thy
018:107 work **righteous** deeds, they have, for their
019:085 The day We shall gather the **righteous** to (Allah)
019:097 glad tidings to the **righteous**, and warnings
020:075 who have worked **righteous** deeds,-for them
021:072 Jacob, and We made **righteous** men of every
021:075 for he was one of the **Righteous**.
021:086 for they were of the **Righteous** ones.
021:105 My servants, the **righteous**, shall inherit
022:014 who believe and work **righteous** deeds, to Gardens,
022:023 and work **righteous** deeds, to Gardens
022:056 **righteous** deeds will be in Gardens of Delight.
024:055 who believe and work **righteous** deeds, that He
025:015 the **righteous**? For them, that is a reward
025:070 and works **righteous** deeds, for Allah
025:074 to lead the **righteous**."
026:083 and join me with the **righteous**;
026:090 "To the **righteous**, the Garden
027:019 to the ranks of Thy **righteous** Servants."
028:027 indeed, if Allah wills, one of the **righteous**."
028:083 and the End is (best) for the **righteous**.
029:007 **righteous** deeds,-from them shall We blot out
029:009 **righteous** deeds,-them shall We admit to the
029:009 to the company of the **Righteous**.
029:027 in the Hereafter of the **Righteous**.
030:015 and worked **righteous** deeds, shall be
030:045 and work **righteous** deeds, out of His Bounty.
031:008 For those who believe and work **righteous** deeds,
032:019 do **righteous** deeds, are Gardens as hospitable
035:007 **righteous** deeds, is Forgiveness, and a
037:100 "O my Lord! grant me a **righteous** (son)!"
037:112 of Isaac-a prophet,-one of the **Righteous**.
038:049 and verily, for the **Righteous**, is a beautiful
039:057 I should certainly have been among the **righteous**!'
039:061 But Allah will deliver the **righteous** for they
040:008 and to the **righteous** among their fathers,
040:040 and he that works a **righteous** deed-whether man
042:022 **righteous** deeds will be in the Meadows of the
042:023 who believe and do **righteous** deeds. Say: "No
043:035 in the sight of thy Lord, is for the **Righteous**.
043:067 one to another,-except the **Righteous**
044:051 As to the **Righteous** (they will be) in a
045:015 If anyone does a **righteous** deed, it is
045:019 but Allah is the Protector of the **Righteous**.
045:021 **righteous** deeds,-that equal will be their Life
045:030 and did **righteous** deeds, their Lord
047:012 and do **righteous** deeds, to Gardens
047:015 which the **righteous** are promised: in it are

RIGHTEOUS (continued)

048:029 and do **righteous** deeds Forgiveness, and a
049:013 the most **righteous** of you. And Allah
050:031 nigh to the **righteous**,-no more a thing distant.
051:015 As to the **Righteous**, they will be in the midst
052:017 As to the **Righteous**, they will be in Gardens,
054:054 As to the **Righteous**, they will be in the midst
065:011 and do **righteous** deeds from the depths of Darkness
066:004 and Gabriel, and (every) **righteous** one among
066:010 of Our **righteous** servants but they betrayed their
068:034 Verily, for the **righteous** are Gardens of Delight,
068:050 and make him of the company of the **Righteous**.
072:011 are **righteous**, and some the contrary: we follow
076:005 As to the **Righteous**, they shall drink of a Cup
077:041 As to the **Righteous**, they shall
078:031 Verily for the **righteous** there will
082:013 As for the **Righteous**, they will be in Bliss;
083:018 the **Righteous** is (preserved) in 'Illiyin.
083:022 Truly the **Righteous** will be in Bliss:
084:025 and work **righteous** deeds: for them
085:011 **righteous** deeds, will be Gardens. Beneath which
089:027 (To the **righteous** soul will be said:) "O (thou)
095:006 do **righteous** deeds: for they
098:007 do **righteous** deeds,-they are the best of creatures.
103:003 do **righteous** deeds, and (join together) in the

RIGHTEOUSNESS

002:025 who believe and work **righteousness**,
002:062 and work **righteousness**,
002:082 have faith and work **righteousness**,
002:177 It is not **righteousness** that ye turn your faces
002:177 but it is **righteousness**-to believe in Allah
002:237 if the nearest to **righteousness**.
002:277 and do deeds of **righteousness**,
003:057 "As to those who believe and work **righteousness**,
003:092 By no means shall ye attain **righteousness** unless
004:057 and do deeds of **righteousness**, We shall
004:122 and do deeds of **righteousness**, We shall soon
004:124 If any do deeds of **righteousness**, be they
004:173 and do deeds of **righteousness**, He will
005:002 Help ye one another in **righteousness** and piety,
005:009 deeds of **righteousness** hath Allah promised
005:069 and work **righteousness**,-on them shall
005:093 and do deeds of **righteousness** there is no
005:093 and do deeds of **righteousness**,-then again
006:127 because they practiced (**righteousness**).
006:158 nor earned **righteousness** through its Faith. Say:
007:026 but the raiment of **righteousness**-that is the best.
007:042 But those who believe and work **righteousness**,-
007:043 for your deeds (of **righteousness**)."
009:105 And say: "Work (**righteousness**): soon will
009:120 as a deed of **righteousness**,-whether they suffered
010:004 those who believe and work **righteousness**, but those
010:005 but in truth and **righteousness**. (Thus) doth
010:009 and work **righteousness**, their Lord will guide
011:011 and constancy, and work **righteousness**; for them
011:023 and work **righteousness**, and humble
011:116 men of **righteousness** who prohibited men from
012:057 who believe, and are constant in **righteousness**.
013:029 work **righteousness**, is (ever) blessedness, and a
014:023 and work **righteousness** will be admitted to
016:097 Whoever works **righteousness**, man or
017:009 of **righteousness**, that they shall have a
017:025 of **righteousness**, verily He is Most Forgiving

RIGHTEOUSNESS (continued)

018:030 and work **righteousness**, verily We shall not
018:088 works **righteousness**-he shall have a goodly reward,
018:110 let him work **righteousness**, and in the
019:060 and work **righteousness**: for these
019:096 and work deeds of **righteousness**, will The
020:112 But he who works deeds of **righteousness**, and has
020:132 the Hereafter is for **righteousness**.
021:094 Whoever works any act of **righteousness** and has
022:050 work **righteousness**, for them is forgiveness
023:051 good and pure, and work **righteousness**: for I
023:100 "In order that I may work **righteousness** in the
026:227 work **righteousness**, engaged much in the
027:019 and that I may work the **righteousness** that will
027:053 and practiced **righteousness**.
028:067 and worked **righteousness**, haply he shall be one
028:080 and work **righteousness**: but this
029:058 and work deeds of **righteousness**-to them
030:044 and those who work **righteousness** will make
032:012 work **righteousness**: for we do indeed (now) believe."
033:031 and His Messenger, and work **righteousness**,-to her
034:004 and work deeds of **righteousness**: for such
034:011 of chain armour, and work ye **righteousness**; for be
034:037 and work **Righteousness**-these are
035:010 of **Righteousness**. Those that lay Plots of Evil,-
035:037 Bring us out: we shall work **righteousness**, not the
038:024 of **righteousness**, and how few are they?"
038:028 and work deeds of **righteousness**, the same
039:074 for those who work (**righteousness**)!"
040:058 and work deeds of **righteousness**, and those
041:008 deeds of **righteousness** is a reward that will
041:018 who believed and practiced **righteousness**.
041:033 works **righteousness**, and says, "I am of
041:046 Whoever works **righteousness** benefits his own soul;
042:026 and do deeds of **righteousness**, and gives
046:015 and that I may work **righteousness** such as Thou
047:002 work deeds of **righteousness**, and believe
049:007 those who walk in **righteousness**;-
058:009 **righteousness** and self-restraint; and fear Allah,
064:009 in Allah and work **righteousness**,-He will
065:011 and work **righteousness**, He will admit to Gardens
074:056 He is the Lord of **Righteousness**, and the
077:043 heart's content: for that ye worked (**Righteousness**).
096:012 Or enjoins **Righteousness**?

RIGHTFUL

010:030 their **rightful** Lord, and their invented falsehoods

RIGHTLY

002:224 or acting **rightly**, or making peace
006:117 He knoweth best those who are **rightly** guided.
011:097 and the command of Pharaoh was no **rightly** (guide).
018:017 he whom Allah guides is **rightly** guided; but he
027:041 those who are not **rightly** guided."
032:003 in order that they may be **rightly** guided.
035:008 (equal to one who is **rightly** guided)? For Allah
035:042 **rightly** guided than anyone of the nations:

RIGHTS

002:228 **rights** similar to the **rights** against them,
004:001 through Whom ye demand your mutual (**rights**),
008:075 **rights** against each other in the Book
017:026 due **rights**, as (also) to those in want, and to

RINGS

034:011   of mail, balancing well the **rings** of chain

RIOT

022:002   a drunken **riot**, yet not drunk: but dreadful

RIPE

019:025   it will let fall fresh **ripe** dates upon thee.

RIPENESS

006:099   and the **ripeness** thereof. Behold!

RISE

002:258   do thou then cause it to **rise** from the West."
002:258   Allah that causeth the sun to **rise** from the East,
022:018   none can **rise** to honor: for Allah
027:039   thou **rise** from thy Council: indeed I
030:017   ye **rise** in the morning;
058:011   **rise** up, **rise** up: Allah will raise up,
097:005   Peace!...This until the **rise** of Morn!

RISING

006:077   When he saw the moon **rising** in splendor, He said:
006:078   When he saw the sun **rising** (in splendor), he
018:090   the sun, he found it **rising** on a people for whom
018:090   Until, when he came to the **rising** of the sun,
020:130   before the **rising** of the sun, and before
037:005   and Lord of every point at the **rising** of the sun!
046:017   before me (without **rising** again)?" And they
050:039   of thy Lord, before the **rising** of the sun
073:006   Truly the **rising** by night is a time

RITES

002:128   for the celebration of (due) **rites**;
002:200   So when ye have accomplished your **rites**,
005:002   the sanctity of the **rites** of Allah, nor of
022:029   the **rites** prescribed for them, fulfil their
022:030   whoever honours the sacred **rites** of Allah,
022:032   and whoever holds in honour the **Rites** of Allah,
022:034   **rites** (of sacrifice), that they
022:067   appointed **rites** which they must follow: let them

RIVALRY

057:020   (in **rivalry**) among yourselves, riches and
102:001   The mutual **rivalry** for piling up (the good

RIVALS

002:022   then set not up **rivals** unto Allah
039:008   and he doth set up **rivals** unto Allah,

RIVER

002:249   When they crossed the **river**,
018:033   We caused a **river** to flow.
020:039   the **river** will cast him up on the bank, and he
020:039   and throw (the chest) into the **river**: the **river**
028:007   cast him into the **river**, but fear
028:008   picked him up (from the **river**): (it was

RIVERS

002:025   beneath which **rivers** flow.
002:074   some from which **rivers** gush forth;
003:015   nearness to their Lord with **rivers** flowing beneath;
003:136   and Gardens with **rivers** flowing underneath,
003:195   into Gardens with **rivers** flowing beneath;
003:198   are Gardens, with **rivers** flowing beneath;
004:013   **rivers** flowing beneath, to abide therein
004:057   with **rivers** flowing beneath, their eternal home:
004:122   with **rivers** flowing beneath, to dwell
005:012   with **rivers** flowing beneath; but if any
005:085   with **rivers** flowing underneath, their eternal home.
005:119   with **rivers** flowing beneath, their eternal home:
007:043   beneath them will be **rivers** flowing;-and they

RIVERS (continued)

009:072   **rivers** flow, to dwell therein, and beautiful
009:089   under which **rivers** flow, to dwell therein: that is
009:100   **rivers** flow, to dwell therein for ever: that is
010:009   beneath them will flow **rivers** in Gardens of Bliss.
013:003   standing firm, and (flowing) **rivers**: and fruit
013:035   beneath if flow **rivers**: perpetual is
014:023   **rivers** flow,-to dwell therein for aye with the
014:032   and the **rivers** (also) hath He made subject to you.
016:015   should shake with you; and **rivers** and ways; that ye
016:031   (pleasant) **rivers**: they will have therein all
017:091   and cause **rivers** to gush forth in their midst,
018:031   **rivers** will flow; they will be adorned therein
020:076   flow **rivers**: they will dwell therein for aye:
022:014   to Gardens, beneath which **rivers** flow: for Allah
022:023   to Gardens beneath which **rivers** flow: they shall
025:010   Gardens beneath which **rivers** flow; and He
027:061   to live in; made **rivers** in its midst; set thereon
029:058   beneath which flow **rivers**,-to dwell therein
039:020   beneath them flow **rivers**: (such is
047:012   to Gardens beneath which **rivers** flow; while those
047:015   never changes; **rivers** of wine, a joy to
047:015   **rivers** of milk of which the taste never changes;
047:015   in it are **rivers** of water unstalling; **rivers** of
047:015   and **rivers** of honey pure and clear. In it
048:005   **rivers** flow, to dwell therein for aye, and remove
048:017   him to Gardens beneath which **rivers** flow; and he
054:054   they will be in the midst of Gardens and **Rivers**.
057:012   flow **rivers**! To dwell therein for aye! This is
058:022   beneath which **Rivers** flow, to dwell
061:012   which **rivers** flow, and to beautiful mansions in
064:009   beneath which **rivers** flow, to dwell therein
065:011   to Gardens beneath which **rivers** flow, to dwell
066:008   to Gardens beneath which **rivers** flow,-the Day
071:012   and bestow on you **Rivers** (of flowing water).
085:011   Beneath which **Rivers** flow: that is
098:008   **rivers** flow; they will dwell therein for ever

RIVULET

019:024   hath provided a **rivulet** beneath thee;

ROAD

007:086   "And squat not on every **road**, breathing
096:011   Seest thou if He is on (the **road** of) Guidance?-

ROADS

020:053   by **roads** (and channels); and has sent
043:010   and has made for you **roads** (and channels)
071:020   That ye may go about therein, in spacious **roads**."

ROASTED

004:056   as often as their skins are **roasted** through.
011:069   them with **roasted** calf.

ROBE

025:047   as a **robe** for you, and Sleep

ROCK

002:060   We said "strike the **rock** with thy staff."
002:074   they became like a **rock**
002:264   They are in Parable like a hard, barren **rock**,
007:160   for Water: "Strike the **rock** with thy staff": out
018:063   when we betook ourselves to the **rock**? I did
031:016   in a **rock**, or (anywhere) in the heavens or on

ROCKS

002:074   For among **rocks** there are some
089:009   who cut out (huge) **rocks** in the valley?-

ROCKY
015:080   **Rocky** Tract also rejected the Messengers:
026:149   (**rocky**) mountains with great skill.

ROD
007:107   Then (Moses) threw his **rod**, and behold!
007:117   We revealed to Moses "Throw thy **rod**": and behold!
020:018   He said, "It is my **rod**: on it I lean; with it
026:032   So (Moses) threw his **rod**, and behold,
026:045   Then Moses threw his **rod**, when, behold,
026:063   "Strike the sea with thy **rod**." So it
027:010   "Now do thou throw thy **rod**!" But when
028:031   "Now do thou throw thy **rod**!" But when

RODS
020:066   Then behold their ropes and their **rods**-so it
026:044   and their **rods**, and said: "By the

ROLL
021:104   The Day that we **roll** up the heavens like a

ROLLED
021:104   like a scroll **rolled** up for books (completed);-
039:067   and the heavens will be **rolled** up in his

ROMANS
030:002   The **Romans** Empire has been defeated-

ROOF
016:026   from their foundations, and the **roof** fell down
018:029   like the walls and **roof** of a tent, will hem

ROOFS
002:259   all in ruins to its **roofs**.
022:045   They tumbled down on their **roofs**. And how
043:033   Most Gracious, silver **roofs** for their houses,

ROOM
042:047   any **room** for denial (of your sins)!
058:011   (Ample) **room** will Allah provide for you.
058:011   (spread out and) make **room**: (ample) room

ROOM
058:011   to make **room** in the assemblies, (spread out

ROOT
014:024   a goodly tree, whose **root** is firmly fixed, and its
014:026   It is torn up by the **root** from the surface

ROOTS
007:072   the **roots** of those who rejected Our Signs and
008:007   and to cut off the **roots** of the Unbelievers;-
013:004   out of single **roots** or otherwise: watered with
054:020   **roots** of palm-trees torn up (from the ground).
059:005   left them standing on their **roots**, it was
069:007   **roots** of hollow palm-trees tumbled down!

ROPE
002:015   and give them **rope** in their trespasses;
003:103   by the **Rope** which Allah (stretches out for you),
019:075   (the **rope**) to them, until, when they see the
022:015   a **rope** to the ceiling and cut (himself) off:
111:005   A twisted **rope** of palm-leaf fibre round her

ROPES
020:066   Then behold their **ropes** and their rods-so it
026:044   So they threw their **ropes** and their rods,
038:010   mount up with the **ropes** and means

ROSE
018:017   when it **rose**, declining to the right from their
054:012   (and **rose**) to the extent decreed.

ROTTEN
079:011   "What!-when we shall have become **rotten** bones?"

ROTTENNESS
051:042   up against, but reduced it to ruin and **rottenness**.

ROUND
002:019   But Allah is ever **round** the rejecters of Faith!
002:081   and are girt **round** by their sins,
002:125   My House for those who compass it **round**,
002:158   should compass them **round**,
003:120   for Allah compasseth **round** about all that they do.
004:108   and Allah doth compass **round** all that they do.
009:101   **round** about you are Hypocrites, as well as
011:084   that will compass (you) all **round**.
013:005   They are those **round** whose necks will be
016:048   turn **round**, from the right and the left,
017:060   **round** about: We granted the Vision which We
019:068   on their knees **round** about Hell;
022:026   for those who compass it **round**, or stand up,
036:008   We have put yokes **round** their necks right up
037:045   **Round** will be passed to them a Cup from a
040:071   When the yokes (shall be) **round** their necks,
043:071   To them will be passed **round**, dishes and
046:027   We destroyed aforetime towns **round** about you;
048:006   On them is a **round** of Evil: the Wrath of
052:024   **Round** about them will serve, (devoted) to
055:044   of boiling hot water will they wander **round**!
056:017   **Round** about them will (serve) youths of
072:019   they just make **round** him a dense crowd."
076:015   And amongst them will be passed **round** vessels of
076:019   And **round** about them will (serve) youths
090:020   On them will be Fire Vaulted over (all **round**).
111:005   **round** her (own) neck!

ROUNDED
021:033   each in its **rounded** course.

ROUSE
004:084   and **rouse** the Believers.
008:065   O Prophet! **rouse** the Believers to the fight.

ROUSED
018:012   Then We **roused** them, in order to test which of

ROUTED
002:251   By Allah's will they **routed** them:

ROWS
034:016   (**rows**) into "gardens" producing bitter fruit,
088:015   And Cushions set in **rows**,

RUB
004:043   and **rub** therewith your faces and hands.
005:006   **rub** your heads (with water); and wash your
005:006   and **rub** therewith your faces and hands.

RUBBISH
023:041   as **rubbish** of dead leaves. So away

RUBIES
055:058   Like unto **rubies** and coral.

RUDDY
084:016   So I do call to witness the **ruddy** glow of Sunset;

RUIN
002:114   whose zeal is (in fact) to **ruin** them?
005:021   for then will ye be overthrown, to your own **ruin**."
005:053   and they will fall into (nothing but) **ruin**.
006:070   deliver themselves to **ruin** by their own acts: they
006:070   is caught in its own **ruin** by its own action: it
007:099   except those (doomed) to **ruin**!
007:182   to **ruin** while they know not.
011:065   (then will be your **ruin**) (behold) there is a promise
018:042   (with **ruin**), and he remained twisting and

RUIN (continued)

023:071 therein would have been in **ruin**. Nay, we
027:052 in utter **ruin**,-because they practised wrong-doing.
051:042 up against, but reduced it to **ruin** and rottenness.
057:014 ye waited (to our **ruin**); ye doubted

RUINED

007:090 "If ye follow Shu'aib, be sure then ye are **ruined**!
007:092 it was they who were **ruined**!
024:010 Full of Wisdom,-(ye would be **ruined** indeed).
024:020 (ye would be **ruined** indeed).

RUINS

002:259 all in **ruins** to its roofs.
046:025 (the **ruins** of) their houses! Thus do

RULE

003:026 Say: "O Allah! Lord of Power (and **Rule**),
006:012 inscribed for Himself (the **rule** of) Mercy. That
006:054 inscribed for Himself (the **rule** of) Mercy: verily,

RULER

114:002 The King (or **Ruler**) of Mankind,

RULES

010:031 And who is it that **rules** and regulates all affairs?"

RULING

027:023 "I found (there) a woman **ruling** over them

RUN

002:035 or ye **run** into harm and transgression."
005:052 they **run** about amongst them, saying:
006:116 the common **run** of those on earth, they will
018:041 **run** off underground so that thou wilt never
030:010 In the long **run** evil will be the End of those
033:013 not exposed: they intended nothing but to **run** away.
066:008 Their Light will **run** forward before them and by
100:001 By the (Steeds) that **run**, with panting (breath),

RUNNING

004:092 (is prescribed) a fast for two months **running**:
014:043 They **running** forward with necks outstretched,
028:020 And there came a man, **running**, from the
031:029 each **running** its course for a term appointed;
033:016 Say: "**Running** away will not profit you if ye
033:016 if ye are **running** away from death or slaughter;
036:020 Then there came **running**, from the

RUNS

013:002 each one **runs** (its course) for a term appointed.
035:013 each one **runs** its course for a term appointed.
036:038 And the Sun **runs** unto a resting place, for Him:
057:012 how their Light **runs** forward before their

RUSH

003:125 **rush** here on you in hot haste,
003:176 who **rush** headlong into Unbelief:
004:102 to assault you in a single **rush**.
009:057 thereto with an obstinate **rush**.
036:051 (men) will **rush** forth to their Lord!
070:036 the Unbelievers that they **rush** madly before thee-

RUSHED

024:014 seized you in that ye **rushed** glibly into
037:070 So they (too) were **rushed** down on their footsteps!

RUSHING

011:078 And his people came **rushing** towards him, and they
038:059 Here is a troop **rushing** headlong with you!
070:043 as if they were **rushing** to a goal-post

S

SABA
027:022 from **Saba** with tidings true.
034:015 There was, for **Saba**', aforetime, a Sign

SABBATH
002:065 in the matter of the **Sabbath**:
004:154 "Transgress not in the matter of the **Sabbath**."
007:163 the matter of the **Sabbath**, for on the
007:163 for on the day of their **Sabbath** their fish
007:163 but on the day they had no **Sabbath**, they came
016:124 The **Sabbath** was only made (strict) for those

SABBATH-BREAKERS
004:047 as We cursed the **Sabbath-breakers**:

SABIANS
002:062 and the Christians and the **Sabians**,
005:069 and the **Sabians** and the Christians,-any who
022:017 and the **Sabians**, Christians, Magians, and

SACRED
002:144 in the direction of the **Sacred** Mosque:
002:149 in the direction of the **Sacred** Mosque;
002:150 in the direction of the **Sacred** Mosque;
002:191 but fight them not at the **Sacred** Mosque,
002:196 is not in (the precincts of) the **Sacred** Mosque.
002:198 praises of Allah at the **Sacred** Monument,
002:217 to prevent access to the **Sacred** Mosque,
005:001 the **Sacred** Precincts or in the state of Pilgrimage.
005:002 nor the people resorting to the **Sacred** House,
005:002 of the **Sacred** Precincts and of the state
005:002 shutting you out of the **Sacred** Mosque lead you
005:002 nor of the **Sacred** Month, nor of the
005:095 while in the **Sacred** Precincts or in the state
005:096 as long as ye are in the **Sacred** Precincts or in
005:097 as also the **Sacred** Months, the animals
005:097 Allah made the Ka'ba, the **Sacred** House, a means
006:151 which Allah hath made **sacred**, except by
008:034 the **Sacred** Mosque-and they are not its guardians?
009:007 the **sacred** mosque? As long as these stand true
009:019 the **Sacred** Mosque, equal to (the pious service
009:028 approach the **Sacred** Mosque. And if ye fear
009:036 of them four are **sacred**; that is
014:037 by Thy **Sacred** House; in order, O our Lord,
017:001 from the **Sacred** Mosque to the Farthest Mosque
017:033 made **sacred**-except for just cause. And if
020:012 thou art in the **sacred** valley Tuwa.
022:025 and from the **Sacred** Mosque, which We
022:026 of the (**Sacred**) House, (saying): "Associate not
022:030 whoever honours the **sacred** rites of Allah,
025:068 has made **sacred**, except for
048:025 and hindered you from the **Sacred** Mosque and the
048:027 ye shall enter the **Sacred** Mosque, if Allah
054:043 Or have ye an immunity in the **Sacred** Books?
079:016 in the **sacred** valley to Tuwa:-

SACRIFICE
002:067 "Allah commands that ye **sacrifice** a heifer.
002:071 Then they offered her in **sacrifice**,
002:196 the place of **sacrifice**.

SACRIFICE (continued)
002:196 or freed the poor, or offer **sacrifice**;
002:196 send an offering for **sacrifice**,
003:183 unless he showed us a **sacrifice** consumed by fire
004:066 **sacrifice** their lives or to leave their homes,
005:002 nor of the animals brought for **sacrifice**, nor the
005:027 the **sacrifice** of those who are righteous.
005:027 a **sacrifice** (to Allah): it was accepted
006:162 and my service of **sacrifice**, my life
022:028 provided for them for **sacrifice**): then eat
022:032 of Allah, (in the **sacrifice** of animals),
022:033 place of **sacrifice** is near the Ancient House.
022:034 rites (of **sacrifice**), that they
022:036 (for **sacrifice**): when they are down on their
037:102 in **sacrifice**: now see what is thy view!"
037:103 prostrate on his forehead (for **sacrifice**),
037:107 And We ransomed him with a momentous **sacrifice**:
048:025 of **sacrifice**. Had there not been believing men
108:002 Therefore to thy Lord turn in Prayer and **Sacrifice**.

SACRIFICED
005:003 that which is **sacrificed** on stone (altars);

SACRIFICES
005:103 or idol **sacrifices** for twin-births in animals, or

SACRIFICIAL
022:036 The **sacrificial** camels We have made for you
048:025 and the **sacrificial** animals, detained from

SACRIFICING
005:090 intoxicants and gambling, **sacrificing** to stones,

SAD
007:001 Alif Lam Mim **Sad**.
019:001 Kaf. Ha. Ya. 'Ain. **Sad**.
038:001 **Sad**: By the Qur'an, full of Admonition:
075:024 And some faces, that Day, will be **sad** and dismal,

SADDENS
012:013 (Jacob) said: "Really it **saddens** me that ye

SADDLE-BAG
012:070 cup into his brother's **saddle-bag**. Then shouted
012:075 in whose **saddle-bag** it is found, should be

SADDLE-BAGS
012:062 had bartered) into their **saddle-bags**, so they

SAFA
002:158 Behold! **Safa** and Marwa are among

SAFE
008:026 a **safe** asylum for you, strengthened you
017:067 But when He brings you back **safe** to land, ye turn
021:042 Say, "Who can keep you **safe** by night and by day
033:020 about you (from a **safe** distance); and if
041:040 or he that comes **safe** through, on the

SAFELY
029:065 them **safely** to (dry) land, behold, they give
031:032 But when He has delivered them **safely** to land,
002:125 of assembly for men and a place of **safety**;
004:083 **safety** or fear, they divulge it.
005:016 His good pleasure to ways of peace and **safety**,
005:048 and guarding it in **safety**: so judge
007:138 (with **safety**) across the sea. They came
012:099 in **safety** if it please Allah."
012:110 into **safety**. But never will be warded off Our
021:069 and (a means of)) **safety** for Abraham!"
044:020 "For me, I have sought **Safety** with my Lord
059:023 of Faith, the Preserver of **Safety**, the Exalted
075:011 By no means! No place of **safety**!

SAID

002:011	When it is **said** to them: "Make not mischief
002:013	When it is **said** to them: "Believe
002:030	Behold, thy Lord **said** to the angels:
002:030	He **said**: "I know what ye know not."
002:030	They **said**, "Wilt thou place therein
002:031	and **said**: "Tell Me the names of these
002:032	They **said**: "Glory to Thee,
002:033	Allah **said**: "Did I not tell you that
002:033	He **said**: "O Adam! tell them their names."
002:034	And behold, We **said** to the angels:
002:035	And We **said**: "O Adam! dwell thou and thy wife
002:036	And We **said**: "Get ye down, (all you people),
002:038	We **said**: "Get ye down all from here;
002:054	And remember Moses **said** to his people:
002:055	And remember ye **said**: "O Moses!
002:058	And remember We **said**: "Enter this town,
002:060	We **said** "strike the rock with thy staff."
002:061	And remember ye **said**: "O Moses!
002:061	He **said**: "Will ye exchange the better
002:065	We **said** to them: "Be ye apes,
002:067	And remember Moses **said** to his people:
002:067	He **said**: "Allah save me from being
002:067	They **said**: "Makest thou a laughing-stock
002:068	They **said**: "Beseech on our behalf thy Lord
002:068	He **said**: "He says: The heifer should be
002:069	He **said**: "He says, a fawn-coloured heifer,
002:069	They **said**: "Beseech on our behalf thy Lord
002:070	They **said**, "Beseech on our behalf thy Lord
002:071	He **said**: "He says, a heifer not trained
002:071	They **said**: "Now hast thou brought the truth."
002:073	So We **said**: "Strike the (body)
002:091	When it is **said** to them,
002:093	they **said**: "We hear, and we disobey":
002:118	So **said** the people before them
002:124	He **said**: "I will make thee an Imam
002:126	He **said**: "(Yea), and such as reject Faith,
002:126	And remember Abraham **said**: "My Lord,
002:131	Behold! his Lord **said** to him: "Submit
002:131	He **said**: "I submit (my will) to the Lord
002:133	They **said**: "We shall worship thy God
002:133	Behold, he **said** to his sons: "What
002:170	When it is **said** to them: "Follow what Allah
002:206	When it is **said** to him, "Fear God,"
002:243	Allah **said** to them: "Die:" Then He restored them
002:246	They **said** to a Prophet (that was) among them:
002:246	They **said**: "How could we refuse to fight
002:246	He **said**: "Is it not possible if ye were
002:247	Their Prophet **said** to them: "Allah hath appointed
002:247	He **said**: "Allah hath chosen him above you.
002:248	And (further) their Prophet **said** to them: "A Sign
002:249	they **said**: "This day we cannot cope
002:249	he **said**: "Allah will test you at the stream;
002:249	**said**: "How oft, by Allah's will,
002:258	He **said**: "I give life and death."
002:258	Abraham **said**: "My Lord is He Who Giveth
002:258	**Said** Abraham: "But it is Allah that causeth
002:259	He **said** "Nay, thou hast tarried
002:259	He **said**: "How long didst thou tarry (thus)?"
002:259	he **said**: "I know that Allah hath power
002:259	He **said**: "(Perhaps) a day or part of a day."
002:259	He **said**: "Oh! how shall Allah bring it
002:260	Behold! Abraham **said**: "My Lord! show me how

SAID (continued)

002:260	He **said**: "Take four birds;
002:260	He **said**: "Dost thou not then believe?"
002:260	He **said**: "Yea! but to satisfy my own heart."
003:035	Behold! wife of 'Imran **said**: "O my Lord!
003:036	When she was delivered, she **said**: "O my Lord!
003:037	He **said**: "O Mary! whence (comes) this to you?"
003:037	She **said**: "From Allah: for Allah provides
003:040	He **said**: "O my Lord! how shall I have a son,
003:041	He **said**: "O my Lord! Give me a Sign!"
003:042	Behold! the angels **said**: "O Mary!
003:045	Behold! the angels **said** "O Mary!
003:047	She **said**: "O my Lord! how shall I have a son
003:047	He **said**: "Even so; Allah createth what He willeth:
003:052	**Said** the Disciples: "We are Allah's helpers
003:052	unbelief on their part he **said**: "Who will be
003:055	Behold! Allah **said**: "O Jesus! I will take thee
003:059	then **said** to him: "Be": and he was.
003:081	He **said**: "Then bear witness, and I am with you
003:081	They **said**: "We agree."
003:081	Allah **said**: "Do ye agree, and take My covenant
003:106	(will be **said**): "Did ye reject Faith
003:147	All that they **said** was: "Our Lord forgive us
003:154	They **said**: "Have we any hand in the affair?
003:167	They **said**: "Had we known there would be a fight,
003:173	Those to whom men **said**: "A great army
003:173	They **said**: "For us Allah sufficeth,
003:183	They (also) **said**: "Allah took our promise
004:046	If only they had **said**: "We hear and we obey"; and
004:061	When it is **said** to them: "Come to what
004:118	Allah did curse him, but he **said**: "I will
004:153	for they **said**: "Show us Allah in public," but
004:154	We **said**: "Enter the gate with humility"; and
004:155	that they **said**, "Our hearts are the Wrappings; nay,
004:157	That they **said** (in boast), "We killed
005:007	when ye **said**: "We hear and we obey":
005:012	and Allah **said**: "I am with you: if ye (but)
005:020	Remember Moses **said** to his people: "O my people!
005:022	They **said**: "O Moses! in this land are a people
005:023	they **said**: "Assault them at the (proper) Gate:
005:024	They **said**: O "Moses! we shall never enter it
005:025	He **said**: "O my Lord! I have power
005:026	Allah **said**: "Therefore will the land
005:027	"Surely," **said** the former, "Allah doth accept
005:027	**Said** the latter: "Be sure I will slay thee."
005:031	"Woe is me!" **said** he: "Was I not even able
005:072	But **said** Christ: "O children of Israel!
005:104	When it is **said** to them: "Come to what Allah
005:110	and the unbelievers among them **said**: 'This is
005:111	they **said**, 'We have faith, and do thou
005:112	**Said** Jesus: "Fear Allah, if ye have faith."
005:112	Behold! the Disciples **said**: "O Jesus
005:113	They **said**: "We only wish to eat thereof
005:114	**Said** Jesus the son of Mary: "O Allah
005:115	Allah **said**: "I will send it down unto you: but
005:116	Had I **said** such a thing. Thou wouldst
005:117	"Never **said** I to them aught except what Thou
006:074	Lo! Abraham **said** to his father Azar: "Takest
006:076	he saw a star: he **said**: "This is my Lord." But
006:076	But when it set, he **said**: "I love not
006:077	He **said**: "This is my Lord." But when
006:077	But when the moon set, he **said**: "Unless my
006:078	he **said**: "This is my Lord; this is

SAID (continued)

006:078	But when the sun set, he **said**: "O my people!
006:080	He **said**: "(Come) ye to dispute with me, about
007:012	He **said**: "I am better than he: thou didst
007:012	(Allah) **said**: "What prevented thee from
007:013	(Allah) **said**: "Get thee down from it: it is not
007:014	He **said**: "Give me respite till the day
007:015	(Allah) **said**: "Be thou among those
007:016	He **said**: "Because Thou hast thrown me
007:018	(Allah) **said**: "Get out from this, disgraced
007:020	he **said**: "Your Lord only forbade
007:023	They **said**: "Our Lord! we have wronged
007:024	(Allah) **said**: "Get ye down, with enmity
007:025	He **said**: "Therein shall ye live, and therein
007:059	He **said**: "O my people! worship Allah!
007:060	The leaders of his people **said**: "Ah! we see
007:061	He **said**: "O my people! there is no error in me: on
007:065	He **said**: "O my people! worship Allah! ye have
007:066	among his people **said**: "Ah! we see
007:067	He **said**: "O my people! there is
007:070	They **said**: "Comest thou to us, that we
007:071	He **said**: "Punishment and wrath have already
007:073	he **said**: "O my people! worship Allah; ye have
007:075	among his people **said** to those who were
007:075	They **said**: "We do indeed believe in the
007:076	The arrogant party **said**: "For our part, we
007:080	We also (sent) Lut: he **said** to his people: "Do
007:082	they **said**, "Drive them out of your city: these are
007:085	he **said**: "O my people! worship Allah; ye have
007:088	He **said**: "What! even though we do detest (them)?
007:088	**said**: "O Shu'aib! we shall certainly drive thee
007:090	Unbelievers among his people, **said**: "If ye follow
007:104	Moses **said**: "O Pharaoh! I am
007:106	(Pharaoh) **said**: "If indeed thou hast
007:109	**Said** the Chiefs of the people of Pharaoh: "This
007:111	They **said**: "Keep him and his brother in suspense
007:113	they **said**, "Of course we shall have a (suitable)
007:114	He **said**: "Yea, (and more),-for ye shall
007:115	They **said**: "O Moses! wilt thou throw (first), or
007:116	**Said** Moses: "Throw ye (first)." So when
007:123	**Said** Pharaoh: "Believe ye in him before I
007:125	They **said**: "For us, we are
007:127	**Said** the chiefs of Pharaoh's people: "Wilt
007:127	He **said**: "Their male children will we slay; (only)
007:128	**Said** Moses to his people: "Pray for help
007:129	He **said**: "It may be that your Lord will destroy
007:129	They **said**: "We have had (nothing but) trouble,
007:131	they **said**, "This is due to us"; when gripped
007:132	They **said** (to Moses): "Whatever be
007:134	they **said**: "O Moses! on our behalf call on
007:138	He **said**: "Surely ye are a people without knowledge."
007:138	They **said**: "O Moses! fashion for us a god
007:140	He **said**: "Shall I seek for you a god
007:143	He **said**: "O my Lord! show (Thyself) to me, that
007:143	Allah **said**: "By no means canst thou
007:143	When he recovered his senses he **said**: "Glory be
007:144	(Allah) **said**: "O Moses! I have chosen thee
007:145	(and **said**): "Take and hold these with firmness,
007:149	they **said**: "If our Lord have not mercy upon us
007:150	angry and grieved, he **said**: "Evil it is that ye
007:150	Aaron **said**: "Son of my mother! The people
007:156	He **said**: "I afflict My punishment on whom
007:161	And remember it was **said** to them: "Dwell in

SAID (continued)

007:164	**Said** the preachers: "To discharge our duty
007:164	When some of them **said**: "Why do ye preach to a
007:166	We **said** to them: "Be ye apes,
007:171	to fall on them (We **said**): "Hold firmly
007:172	They **said**: "Yea! we do testify! (This), lest ye
008:014	Thus (will it be **said**): "Taste ye then
008:032	Remember how they **said**: "O Allah! if this
008:048	and **said**: "No one among men can overcome
008:048	and **said**: "Lo! I am clear of you; lo!
009:040	and he **said** to his companion, "Have no fear,
009:059	and had **said**, "Sufficient unto us is Allah!
009:074	They swear by Allah that they **said** nothing (evil),
009:081	they **said**, "Go not forth in the heat." Say,
010:051	(It will then be **said**): 'Ah! now? and ye wanted
010:052	"At length will be **said** to the wrong-doers:
010:071	Behold! he **said** to his People: "O my People,
010:076	they **said**: "This is indeed evident sorcery!"
010:077	**Said** Moses: "Say ye (this) about the Truth when it
010:078	They **said**: "Hast thou come to us to turn us
010:079	**Said** Pharaoh: "Bring me every sorcerer well versed."
010:080	Moses **said** to them: "Throw ye what ye (wish)
010:081	Moses **said**: "What ye have brought is sorcery:
010:084	Moses **said**: "O my People! if ye do
010:085	They **said**: "In Allah do we put our trust. Our Lord
010:089	Allah **said**: "Accepted is your prayer (O Moses
010:090	he **said**: "I believe that there is no god except
010:091	(It was **said** to him): "Ah now!-but a little
011:027	among his people **said**: "We see (in) thee
011:028	He **said**: "O my people! see ye if (it be that)
011:032	They **said**: "O Noah! thou hast disputed with us,
011:033	He **said**: "Truly, Allah will bring it on you
011:038	He **said**: "If ye ridicule us now, we (in our turn)
011:040	We **said**: "Embark therein, of each kind two,
011:041	So he **said**: "Embark ye on the Ark, in the
011:043	the water." Noah **said**: "This day nothing can
011:045	And Noah called upon his Lord and **said**: "O my
011:046	He **said**: "O Noah! he is not of thy family: for his
011:047	Noah **said**: "O my Lord! I do seek refuge with Thee,
011:050	He **said**: "O my people! worship Allah! ye have
011:053	They **said**: "O Hud! no Clear (Sign) hast thou
011:054	with evil." He **said**: "I call Allah to witness,
011:061	He **said**: "O my people! worship Allah: ye have
011:062	They **said**: "O Salih! thou hast been of us!-
011:063	He **said**: "O my people! Do ye see?-If I have
011:065	So he **said**: "Enjoy yourselves in your homes
011:069	They **said**, "Peace!" He answered, "Peace!" and
011:070	They **said**: "Fear not: we have been sent
011:072	She **said**: "Alas for me! Shall I bear a child,
011:073	They **said**: "Dost thou wonder at Allah's decree?
011:077	He **said**: "This is a distressful day."
011:078	He **said**: "O my people! here are my daughters:
011:079	They **said**: "Well dost thou know we have no need
011:080	He **said**: "Would that I had power to suppress you
011:081	(The Messengers) **said** "O Lut! we are Messengers
011:084	he **said**: "O my people! worship Allah: ye have
011:087	They **said**: "Oh Shu'aib! Does thy prayer
011:088	He **said**: "O my people! see ye whether I have
011:091	They **said**: "O Shu'aib! much of what thou sayest
011:092	He **said**: "O my people! is then my family of more
012:004	Behold, Joseph **said** to his father: "O my father!
012:005	**Said** (the father): "My (dear) little son! relate
012:008	They **said**: "Truly Joseph and his brother are loved

SAID (continued)

012:010 **Said** one of them: "Slay not Joseph, but if
012:011 They **said**: "O our father! why dost
012:013 (Jacob) **said**: "Really it saddens me that ye
012:014 They **said**: "If the wolf were to devour him
012:017 They **said**: "Oh our father! we went
012:018 He **said**: "Nay, but your minds have made up
012:019 (into the well). He **said**: "Ah there! Good news
012:021 The man in Egypt who bought him, **said** to his wife:
012:023 the doors, and **said**: "Now come," he **said**: "Allah
012:023 He **said**: "Allah forbid! truly (thy husband) is my
012:025 She **said**: "What is the (fitting) punishment for
012:026 He **said**: "It was she that sought to seduce me-
012:028 (her husband) **said**: "Behold! it is a snare
012:030 Ladies **said** in the City: "The wife of the great
012:031 their hands: they **said**, "Allah preserve us!
012:031 and she **said** (to Joseph), "Come out before them."
012:032 She **said**: "There before you is the man
012:033 He **said**: "O my Lord! the prison is dearer to my
012:036 **Said** the other: "I see myself (in a dream)
012:036 "Tell us" (they **said**) "the truth
012:036 **Said** one of them: "I see myself (in a dream)
012:037 He **said**: "Before any food comes (in due course)
012:042 he **said**: "Mention me to thy lord." But Satan
012:043 The king (of Egypt) **said**: "I do see (in a vision)
012:044 They **said**: "A confused medley of dreams: and we
012:045 **said**: "I will tell you the truth of its
012:046 "O Joseph!" (he **said**), "O man of truth! Expound
012:047 (Joseph) **said**: "For seven years shall ye
012:050 (Joseph) **said**: "Go thou back to thy lord,
012:050 So the king **said**: "Bring ye him unto me." But when
012:051 The ladies **said**: "Allah preserve us! no evil
012:051 **Said** the 'Aziz's wife: "Now is the truth manifest
012:051 (The king) **said** (to the ladies): "What was your
012:054 So the king **said**: "Bring him unto me; I will take
012:054 he **said**: "Be assured this day, thou art
012:055 (Joseph) **said**: "Set me over the store-houses
012:059 for them, he **said**: "Bring unto me a brother
012:061 They **said**: "We shall try to win him from
012:063 they **said**: "O our father! No more measure
012:064 He **said**: "Shall I trust you with him with any
012:065 They **said**: "O our father! What (more)
012:066 (Jacob) **said**: "Never will I send him with you
012:066 he **said**: "Over all that we say, be Allah
012:067 Further he **said**; "O my sons! enter not
012:069 He **said** (to him): "Behold! I am thy (own) brother;
012:071 They **said**, turning towards them: "What is it
012:072 They **said**: "We miss the great beaker of the king;
012:073 (The brothers) **said**: "By Allah! well ye know that
012:074 (The Egyptians) **said**: "What then shall be
012:075 They **said**: "The penalty should be that he in whose
012:077 He (simply) **said** (to himself): "Ye are
012:077 They **said**: "If he steals, there was a brother
012:078 They **said**: "O exalted one! Behold! he has
012:079 He **said**: "Allah forbid that we take other than
012:080 The leader among them **said**: "Know ye not
012:083 Jacob **said**: "Nay, but ye have yourselves contrived
012:084 And he turned away from them, and **said**: "How great
012:085 They **said**: "By Allah! (never) wilt thou cease
012:086 He **said**: "I only complain of my distraction
012:088 into (Joseph's) presence they **said**: "O exalted
012:089 He **said**: "Know ye how ye dealt with Joseph,
012:090 He **said**: "I am Joseph, and this is my brother:

SAID (continued)

012:090 They **said**: "Art thou indeed, Joseph?" He **said**
012:091 They **said**: "By Allah! indeed has Allah preferred
012:092 He **said**: "This day let no reproach be (cast)
012:094 their father **said**: "I do indeed scent the presence
012:095 They **said**: "By Allah! truly thou art in thine
012:096 clear sight. He **said**: "Did I not say to you,
012:097 They **said**: "O our father! ask for
012:098 He **said**: "Soon will I ask my Lord for forgiveness
012:099 and **said**: "Enter ye Egypt (all) in safety
012:100 He **said**: "O my father! this is the fulfillment
014:006 Remember! Moses **said** to his people: "Call to mind
014:008 And Moses **said**: "If ye show ingratitude, ye and
014:009 up to their mouths, and **said**: "We do deny
014:010 They **said**: "Ah! ye are no more then human,
014:010 Their messengers **said**: "Is there a doubt
014:011 Their messengers **said** to them: "True, we are
014:013 And the Unbelievers **said** to their messengers:
014:035 Remember Abraham **said**: "O my Lord! make this
015:028 Behold! thy Lord **said** to the angels: "I am
015:032 (Allah) **said**: "O Iblis! what is your reason for
015:033 (Iblis) **said**: "I am not one to prostrate
015:034 (Allah) **said**: "Then get thee out from here;
015:036 (Iblis) **said**: "O my Lord! give me then respite
015:037 (Allah) **said**: "Respite is granted thee-
015:039 (Iblis) **said**: "O my Lord! because Thou hast
015:041 (Allah) **said**: "This is for me a straight path.
015:052 When they entered his presence and **said**, "Peace!"
015:052 He **said**, "We feel afraid of you!"
015:053 They **said**: "Fear not! we give thee glad tidings
015:054 He **said**: "Do ye give me such glad tidings
015:055 They **said**: "We give thee glad tidings in truth;
015:056 He **said**: "And who despairs of the mercy
015:057 Abraham **said**: "What then is the business
015:058 They **said**: "We have been sent to a people
015:062 He **said**: "Ye appear to be uncommon folk."
015:063 They **said**: "Yea, we have come to thee
015:068 Lut **said**: "These are my guests: disgrace me not:
015:070 They **said**: "Did we not forbid thee (to speak)
015:071 He **said**: "There are my daughters (to marry),
016:024 When it is **said** to them, "What is it
016:030 To the righteous (when) it is **said**, "What is
016:051 Allah has **said**: "Take not (for worship) two gods:
017:014 (It will be **said** to him:) "Read thine
017:061 he **said**, "Shall I prostrate to one whom Thou
017:061 Behold! We **said** to the angels: "Prostrate unto
017:062 He **said**, "Seest Thou? This is the one whom
017:063 Allah **said**: "Go thy way; if any of them follow
017:094 was nothing but this: they **said**, "Has Allah
017:098 and **said**, "When we are reduced to bones
017:101 Pharaoh **said** to him: "O Moses! I consider thee,
017:102 Moses **said**, "Thou knowest well that these things
017:104 And We **said** thereafter to the Children of Israel,
018:010 to the Cave: they **said**, "Our Lord! bestow on us
018:014 Behold, they stood up and **said**: "Our Lord
018:019 They **said**, "We have stayed (perhaps) a day,
018:019 **Said** one of them, "How long
018:019 (At length) they (all) **said**, "Allah (alone)
018:021 (Some) **said**, "Construct a building over them":
018:021 over their affair **said**, "Let us
018:034 he **said** to his companion, in the course
018:035 wronged himself: he **said**, "I deem not
018:037 His companion **said** to him, in the course

SAID (continued)

018:050 Behold! We **said** to the angels, "Prostrate to Adam":
018:060 Behold, Moses **said** to his attendant, "I will
018:062 Moses **said** to his attendant: "Bring us
018:064 Moses **said**: "That was what we were seeking after":
018:066 Moses **said** to him: "May I follow thee, on the
018:067 (The other) **said**: "Verily thou wilt not be able
018:069 Moses **said**: "Thou wilt find me, if Allah
018:070 The other **said**: "If then thou wouldst follow me,
018:071 he scuttled it. **Said** Moses: "Hast thou scuttled
018:073 Moses **said**: "Rebuke me not for forgetting,
018:074 he slew him. Moses **said**: "Hast thou slain
018:076 (Moses) **said**: "If ever I ask thee about anything
018:077 (Moses) **said**: "If thou hadst wished, surely thou
018:086 We **said**: "O Zul-Qarnain! (thou hast authority),
018:087 He **said**: "Whoever doth wrong, him shall we punish;
018:094 They **said**: "O Zul-Qarnain! the Gog and Magog
018:095 He **said**: "(The power) in which my Lord has
018:096 steep mountain sides, he **said**, "Blow (with
018:096 he **said**: "Bring me, that I may pour over it,
018:098 He **said**: "This is a mercy from my Lord: but when
019:008 He **said**: "O my Lord! how shall I have a son,
019:009 He **said**: "So (it will be): thy Lord saith,
019:010 (Zakariya) **said** "O my Lord! give me a Sign,"
019:018 She **said**: "I seek refuge from thee to (Allah)
019:019 He **said**: "Nay, I am only a messenger from thy Lord,
019:020 She **said**: "How shall I have a son, seeing that
019:021 He **said**: "So (it will be): thy Lord saith,
019:027 (in her arms), they **said**: "O Mary!
019:029 They **said**: "How can we talk to one who is
019:030 He **said**: "I am indeed a servant of Allah: He hath
019:042 Behold, he **said** to his father: "O my father!
019:047 Abraham **said**: "Peace be on thee: I will
020:010 so he **said** to his family, "Tarry ye;
020:018 He **said**, "It is my rod: on it I lean; with it
020:019 (Allah) **said**, "Throw it, O Moses!"
020:021 (Allah) **said**, "Seize it, and fear not: We shall
020:025 (Moses) **said**: "O my Lord! expand me my breast;"
020:036 (Allah) **said**: "Granted is thy prayer, O Moses!"
020:045 They (Moses and Aaron) **said**: "Our Lord!
020:046 He **said**: "Fear not: for I am with you: I hear
020:049 (Pharaoh) **said**: "Who, then, O Moses, is the
020:050 He **said**: "Our Lord is He Who gave to each (created)
020:051 (Pharaoh) **said**: "What then is the condition of
020:057 He **said**: "Hast thou come to drive us out
020:059 Moses **said**: "Your tryst is the Day of the Festival,
020:061 Moses **said** to them: "Woe to you! Forge
020:063 They **said**: "These two are certainly (expert)
020:065 They **said**: "O Moses! whether wilt thou that thou
020:066 He **said**, "Nay, throw ye first!" Then behold
020:068 We **said**: "Fear not! for thou hast indeed
020:070 to prostration: they **said**, "We believe
020:071 (Pharaoh) **said**: "Believe ye in Him before I
020:072 They **said**: "Never shall we prefer thee to what
020:083 Allah **said**): "What made thee hasten in advance
020:085 (Allah) **said**: "We have tested thy people in thy
020:086 He **said**: "O my people! did not your Lord make a
020:087 They **said**: "We broke not the promise to thee,
020:088 it seemed to low: so they **said**: "This is
020:090 **said** to them: "O my people! ye are being tested
020:091 They had **said**: "We will not cease to worship it,
020:092 (Moses) **said**: "O Aaron! what kept thee back,
020:095 (Moses) **said**: "What then is thy case, O Samiri?"

SAID (continued)

020:097 (Moses) **said**: "Get thee gone! but thy (punishment)
020:116 When We **said** to the angels, "Prostrate yourselves
020:117 Then We **said**: "O Adam! verily, this is
020:120 he **said**, "O Adam! shall I lead thee to the Tree
020:123 He **said**: "Get ye down, both of you,-all together,
020:134 before this, they would have **said**: "Our Lord
021:014 They **said**: "Ah! woe to us! we were
021:052 Behold! he **said** to his father and his people,
021:053 They **said**, "We found our father worshipping them."
021:054 He **said**, "Indeed ye have been in manifest error-
021:055 They **said**, "Have you brought us the Truth, or are
021:056 He **said**, "Nay, your Lord is the Lord of the
021:059 They **said**, "Who has done this to our gods?
021:060 They **said**, "We heard a youth talk of them:
021:061 They **said**, "Then bring him before the eyes
021:062 They **said**, "Art thou the one that did this
021:063 He **said**: "Nay, this was done by this
021:064 and **said**, "Surely ye are the ones in the wrong."
021:065 (they **said**), "Thou knowest full well that these
021:066 (Abraham) **said**, "Do ye then worship, besides Allah,
021:068 They **said**, "Burn him and protect your gods,
021:069 We **said**, "O Fire! be thou cool, and (a means
022:010 (It will be **said**): "This is because of the deeds
022:022 and (it will be **said**), "Taste ye
023:023 to his people: he **said**, "O my people!
023:024 his people **said**: "He is no more than a man
023:025 (And some **said**:) "He is only a man possessed:
023:026 (Noah) **said**: "O my Lord! help me: for that
023:033 of this life, **said**: "He is no more than a man
023:039 (The prophet) **said**: "O my Lord! help me: for that
023:040 (Allah) **said**: "In but a little while, they are
023:047 They **said**: "Shall we believe in two men
023:065 (It will be **said**): "Groan not
023:081 similar to what the ancients **said**.
024:015 and **said** out of your mouths things of which ye
025:060 When it is **said** to them, "Adore ye
026:012 He **said**: "O my Lord! I do fear
026:015 Allah **said**: "By no means! proceed them, both of
026:018 (Pharaoh) **said**: "Did we not cherish thee as a
026:023 Pharaoh **said**: "And what is the Lord and Cherisher
026:024 (Moses) **said**: "The Lord and Cherisher of the
026:025 (Pharaoh) **said** to those around: "Do ye not
026:026 (Moses) **said**: "Your Lord and the Lord of your
026:027 (Pharaoh) **said**: "Truly your messenger who has
026:028 (Moses) **said**: "Lord of the East and the West,
026:029 (Pharaoh) **said**: "If thou takest any god other
026:030 (Moses) **said**: "Even if I showed you something
026:031 (Pharaoh) **said**: "Show it then, if thou
026:034 (Pharaoh) **said** to the Chiefs around him:
026:036 They **said**: "Keep him and his brother in suspense
026:041 they **said** to Pharaoh: "Of course-shall we
026:042 He **said**: "Yea, (and more),-for ye
026:043 Moses **said** to them: "Throw ye-
026:044 and their rods, and **said**: "By the
026:049 **Said** (Pharaoh): "Believe ye in Him before I give
026:050 They **said**: "No matter! for us, we shall
026:061 saw each other, the people of Moses **said**: "We are
026:062 (Moses **said**: "By no means! my Lord
026:070 Behold, he **said** to his father and his people:
026:071 They **said**: "We worship idols, and we
026:072 He **said**: "Do they listen to you when ye
026:074 They **said**: "Nay, but we found our fathers

SAID (continued)

026:075 He **said**: "Do ye then see whom ye
026:092 "And it shall be **said** to them: `Where are
026:106 Behold, their brother Noah **said** to them: "Will ye
026:111 They **said**: "Shall we believe in thee when it
026:112 He **said**: "And what do I know as to what they do?
026:116 They **said**: "If thou desist not, O Noah!
026:117 He **said**: "O my Lord! truly my
026:124 Behold, their brother Hud **said** to them: "Will ye
026:136 They **said**: "It is the same to us whether thou
026:142 **said** to them: "Will you not fear (Allah)?
026:153 They **said**: "Thou art only the of those bewitched!
026:155 He **said**: "Here is a she-camel: she has
026:161 Behold, their brother Lut **said** to them: "Will ye
026:167 They **said**: "If thou desist not, O Lut!
026:168 He **said**: "I do detest your doings."
026:177 Behold, Shu'aib **said** to them: "Will ye
026:185 They **said**: "Thou art only one of those bewitched!
026:188 He **said**: "My Lord knows best what ye do."
027:007 Behold! Moses **said** to his family: "I perceive
027:010 "O Moses!" (it was **said**), fear not:
027:013 visibly they **said**: "This is sorcery manifest!"
027:015 and they both **said**: "Praise be to Allah, Who has
027:016 He **said**: "O ye people! we have been taught
027:018 of ants, one of the ants **said**: "O ye ants,
027:019 and he **said**: "O my Lord! so order
027:020 and he **said**: "Why is it I see not the Hoopoe?
027:022 he (came up and) **said**: "I have compassed
027:027 (Solomon) **said**: "Soon shall we see whether thou
027:029 (The Queen) **said**: "Ye chiefs! here is-
027:032 She **said**: "Ye chiefs! advise me
027:033 They **said**: "We are endued with strength,
027:034 She **said**: "Kings, when they enter a country,
027:036 he **said**: "Will ye give me abundance in wealth?
027:038 He **said** (to his own men): "Ye Chiefs! which of
027:039 A stalwart of the Jinn **said**: "I will
027:040 **Said** one who had knowledge of the Book: "I will
027:040 placed firmly before him, he **said**: "This is
027:041 He **said**: "Disguise her throne, let us
027:042 "Is this thy throne?" She **said**, "It seems
027:044 He **said**: "This is but a palace paved smooth
027:044 She **said**: "O my Lord! I have indeed
027:046 He **said**: "O my people! why ask ye to hasten
027:047 They **said**: "Ill omen do we augur from thee
027:047 He **said**: "Your ill omen is with Allah; yea, ye
027:049 They **said**: "Swear a mutual oath by Allah that we
027:054 behold, he **said** to his people, "Do ye
027:056 but this: they **said**, "Drive out
028:009 The wife of Pharaoh **said**: "(Here is)
028:011 And she **said** to the sister of (Moses),
028:012 and) **said**: "Shall I point out to you the people
028:015 He **said**: "This is a work of Satan: for he
028:017 He **said**: "O my Lord! for that Thou hast bestowed
028:018 his help (again). Moses **said** to him: "Thou art
028:019 on their enemy, the man **said**: "O Moses!
028:020 He **said**: "O Moses! the Chiefs are taking counsel
028:022 (the land of) Madyan, he **said**: "I do
028:023 He **said**: "What is the matter with you?" They **said**:
028:023 They **said**: "We cannot water (our flocks) until the
028:024 and **said**: "O my Lord! truly am I
028:025 he **said**: "Fear thou not: (well) hast
028:025 She **said**: "My father invites thee that he may
028:026 **Said** one of the (damsels): "O my (dear) father!

SAID (continued)

028:027 He **said**: "I intended to wed one of these
028:028 He **said**: "Be that (the agreement) between me
028:029 of Mount Tur. He **said** to his family: "Tarry ye;
028:031 "O Moses!" (It was **said**), "Draw near, and fear
028:033 He **said**: "O my Lord! I have slain a man among them,
028:035 He **said**: "We will certainly strengthen thy arm
028:036 Our Clear Signs, they **said**: "This is
028:037 Moses **said**: "My Lord knows best who it is
028:038 Pharaoh **said**: "O Chiefs! no god do I know
028:064 It will be **said** (to them): "Call upon
028:076 Behold, his people **said** to him: "Exult not,
028:078 He **said**: "This has been given to me because of
028:079 **Said** those whose aim is the Life of this World:
028:080 (true) knowledge **said**: "Alas for you! The reward
029:016 he **said** to his people, "Serve Allah
029:024 (Abraham's) people except that they **said**: "Slay him
029:025 And He **said**: "For you, ye have taken (for worship)
029:026 But Lut believed Him: he **said**: "I will
029:028 he **said** to his people: "Ye do commit lewdness,
029:029 gave no answer but this: they **said**: "Bring us
029:030 He **said**: "O my Lord! help Thou me against
029:031 with the good news, they **said**: "We are
029:032 He **said**: "But there is Lut there." They **said**:
029:032 They **said**: "We know well who is there: we will
029:033 (to protect) them: but they **said**: "Fear not
029:036 Then he **said**: "O my people! serve Allah,
031:013 Behold, Luqman **said** to his son admonishing him
031:016 "O my son! (**said** Luqman), "If there
032:020 be forced thereinto, and it will be **said** to them:
033:013 Behold! A party among them **said**: "Ye men
033:022 the Confederate forces, they **said**: "This is
034:019 But they **said**: "Our Lord! place longer
034:034 ones among them **said**: "We believe
034:035 They **said**: "We have more in wealth and in sons,
036:014 they **said**, "Truly, we have been sent on a
036:015 The (people) **said**: "Ye are only men like ourselves;
036:016 They **said**: "Our Lord doth know that we have been
036:018 The (people) **said**: "For us, We augur an evil
036:019 They **said**: "Your evil omens are with yourselves:
036:026 It was **said**: "Enter thou the Garden." He **said**:
036:026 He **said**: "Ah me! would that my People knew
037:022 "Bring ye up," it shall be **said**, "The wrong-doers
037:054 He **said**: "Would ye like to look down?"
037:056 He **said**: "By Allah! thou wast little short
037:085 Behold, he **said** to his father and to his people,
037:089 And he **said**, "I am indeed sick (at heart)!"
037:091 and **said**, "Will ye not eat (of the offerings
037:095 He **said**: "Worship ye that which ye have
037:097 They **said**: "Build him a furnace, and throw
037:099 He **said**: "I will go to my Lord! He will
037:102 thy view!" (The son) **said**: "O my father!
037:102 he **said**: "O my son! I have seen in a dream
037:124 Behold, he **said** to his people, "Will ye
037:167 And there were those who **said**,
038:022 they **said**: "Fear not: We are two disputants,
038:024 (David) **said**: "He has undoubtedly wronged thee
038:032 And he **said**, "Truly do I prefer wealth to the
038:035 He **said**, "O my Lord! Forgive me, and grant me
038:071 Behold, thy Lord **said** to the angels: "I am
038:075 (Allah) **said**: "O Iblis! what prevents thee from
038:076 (Iblis) **said**: "I am better than he:
038:077 (Allah) **said**: "Then get thee out from here:

SAID (continued)

038:079   (Iblis) **said**: "O my Lord! give me then respite
038:080   (Allah) **said**: "Respite then is granted thee-
038:082   (Iblis) **said**: "Then, by Thy Power, I will
038:084   (Allah) **said**: "This is the Truth, and the
039:024   It will be **said** to the wrong-doers: "Taste ye
039:072   (To them) will be **said**: "Enter ye
040:025   from Us, they **said**, "Slay the
040:026   **Said** Pharaoh: "Leave me to slay Moses; and let
040:027   Moses **said**: "I have indeed called upon my Lord
040:028   **said**: "Will ye slay a man because he says,
040:029   should it befall us?" Pharaoh **said**: "I but
040:030   Then **said** the man who believed: "O my People!
040:034   ye **said**: 'No messenger will Allah send after him.'
040:036   Pharaoh **said**: "O Haman! Build me a lofty palace,
040:038   The man who believed **said** further: "O my People!
040:073   Then shall it be **said** to them: "Where are
040:084   they **said**: "We believe in Allah,-the One
041:011   or unwillingly." They **said**: "We do come
041:011   He **said** to it and to the earth: "Come ye
041:014   They **said**, "If our Lord had so pleased, He would
041:015   and **said**: "Who is superior to us in strength?"
041:043   Nothing is **said** to thee that was not
041:043   was not **said** to the messengers before thee:
041:044   they would have **said**: "Why are not
043:023   the wealthy ones among them **said**: "We found
043:024   He **said**: "What! even if I brought you better
043:024   They **said**: "For us, We deny that ye (prophets)
043:026   Behold! Abraham **said** to his father and his people:
043:030   they **said**: "This is sorcery, and we do reject it."
043:046   his Chiefs: he **said**, "I am a messenger
043:049   And they **said**, "O thou Sorcerer! invoke thy
043:063   he **said**: "Now have I come to you with Wisdom,
045:031   (to them will be **said**): "Were not Our
045:032   "And when it was **said** that the promise of Allah
045:034   It will also be **said**: "This Day We will forget
046:020   (it will be **said** to them): "Ye squandered
046:022   They **said**: "Hast thou come in order to turn
046:023   He **said**: "The Knowledge (of when it will come)
046:024   they **said**, "This cloud will give us rain!"
046:029   in the presence thereof, they **said**, "Listen in
046:030   They **said**, "O our people! We have
047:016   received Knowledge: "What is it he **said** just then?"
047:026   This, because they **said** to those who hate
050:022   (It will be **said**:) "Thou wast heedless of this;
051:025   Behold, they entered his presence, and **said**: "Peace!"
051:025   He **said**, "Peace!" (And thought, "These seem)
051:027   He **said**, "Will ye not eat?"
051:028   They **said**, "Fear not," and they gave him
051:029   she smote her forehead and **said**: "A barren
051:030   They **said**, "Even so has thy Lord spoken: and He
051:031   (Abraham) **said**: "And what, O ye Messengers,
051:032   They **said**, "We have been sent to a people
051:039   of his might, and **said**, "A sorcerer,
051:052   the Peoples before them, but they **said** (of him)
052:014   "This," it will be **said**, "Is the Fire,-
052:019   (To them will be **said**:) "Eat and
054:009   they rejected Our servant and **said**, "Here is
054:024   For they **said**: "What! a man! a solitary
057:013   your Light!" It will be **said**: "Turn Ye
060:004   with him, when they **said** to their people: "We are
060:004   **said** to his father: "I will pray for forgiveness
061:005   And remember, Moses **said** to his people: "O my

SAID (continued)

061:006   Clear Signs, they **said**, "This is evident sorcery!"
061:006   **said**: "O Children of Israel! I am the messenger
061:014   as **said** Jesus, the son of Mary, to the
061:014   **Said** the Disciples, "We are Allah's helpers!"
063:005   And when it is **said** to them, "Come, the
064:006   but they **said**: "Shall (mere)
066:003   He **said**, "He told me Who is the Knower, The Aware."
066:003   she **said**, "Who told thee this?" He **said**,
066:007   (It will be **said**), "O ye Unbelievers! make no
066:011   behold, she **said**: "O my Lord! build for me,
067:009   but we rejected him and **said**, 'Allah never sent
067:027   of the Unbelievers, and it will be **said** (to them):
068:026   they **said**: "We have surely lost our way:
068:028   **Said** one of them, more just (than the rest):
068:029   They **said**: "Glory to our Lord! Verily we
068:031   They **said**: "Alas for us! We have
071:002   He **said**: "O my People! I am to you a Warner,
071:005   He **said**: "O my Lord! I have called to my People
071:021   Noah **said**: "O my Lord! they have disobeyed me,
071:023   "And they have **said** (to each other), `Abandon not
071:026   And Noah **said**: "O my Lord! Leave not
072:001   (to the Qur'an). They **said**, 'We have really
074:024   Then **said** he: "This is nothing but magic
077:029   (It will be **said**:) "Depart ye to that which ye
077:048   And when it is **said** to them, "Prostrate yourselves!"
083:017   Further, it will be **said** to them: "This is the
089:027   (To the righteous soul will be **said**:) "O (thou)
091:013   But the messenger of Allah **said** to them: "It is

SAIDST

003:124   Remember thou **saidst** to the faithful: "Is it not
009:092   and when thou **saidst**, "I can find

SAIL

010:022   they **sail** with them with a favourable wind, and
014:032   subject to you, that they may **sail** through the
022:065   **sail** through the sea by His command? He withholds
030:046   that the ships may **sail** by His Command and that
031:031   Seest thou not that the ships **sail** through the
045:012   to you, that ship may **sail** through it by

SAILED

011:042   So the Ark **sailed** with them on the waves

SAILING

002:164   in the **sailing** of the ships
055:024   And His are the Ships **sailing** smoothly through

SAITH

002:117   He **saith** to it: "Be," and it is.
003:047   He but **saith** to it 'Be,' and it is!
006:073   the day He **saith**, "Be," Behold! it is. His
006:093   or **saith**, "I have received inspiration," when
006:093   or (again) who **saith**, "I can reveal the like of
007:038   **Saith** the last about the first: "Our Lord!
019:009   thy Lord **saith**, "That is easy for Me: I did
019:021   thy Lord **saith**, 'That is easy for Me: and (We
020:040   and **saith**, 'Shall I show you one who will nurse
089:015   and gifts, then **saith** he, (puffed up), "My Lord
089:016   then **saith** he (in despair), "My Lord

SAKE

029:026   "I will leave home for the **sake** of my Lord:
037:036   our gods for the **sake** of a Poet possessed?"
052:026   not without fear for the **sake** of our people.
076:009   (Saying), "We feed you for the **sake** of Allah alone:

SALE
024:037 By men whom neither trade nor **sale** can divert

SALIH
007:073 To the Thamud people (We sent) **Salih**, one of
007:075 "Know ye indeed that **Salih** is a messenger
007:077 saying: "O **Salih**! bring about thy threats, if
007:079 So **Salih** left them, saying: "O my people!
011:061 To the Thamud People (We sent) **Salih**, one of
011:062 They said: "O **Salih**! thou hast been of us!-
011:066 We saved **Salih** and those who believed with him,
011:089 or of **Salih**, nor are the people of Lut
026:142 Behold, their brother **Salih** said to them:
027:045 their brother **Salih**, saying, "Serve Allah":
054:027 So watch them, (O **Salih**), and possess

SALSABIL
076:018 A fountain there, called **Salsabil**.

SALT
025:053 and the other **salt** and bitter; yet has
035:012 **salt** and bitter. Yet from each (kind of

SALTISH
056:070 make it **saltish** (and unpalatable): then why

SALUTATION
004:094 you a **salutation**: "Thou art none of a Believer!"
013:023 from every gate (with the **salutation**)
033:044 Their **salutation** on the Day they meet
036:058 "Peace!"-a Word (of **salutation**) from a
037:079 "Peace and **salutation** to Noah among the nations!"
037:109 "Peace and **salutation** to Abraham!"
037:120 "Peace and **salutation** to Moses and Aaron!"
037:130 "Peace and **salutation** to such as Elias!"
056:091 (For him is the **salutation**), "Peace be

SALUTATIONS
019:062 vain discourse, but only **salutations** of Peace:
025:075 be met with **salutations** and peace,

SALUTE
024:061 enter houses, **salute** each other-a greeting of
033:056 and **salute** him with all respect.
058:008 they **salute** thee, not as Allah salutes thee,

SALUTED
024:027 and **saluted** those in them: that is

SALUTES
058:008 **salutes** thee, (but in crooked ways): and they

SALVATION
002:135 if ye would be guided (to **salvation**)."
003:191 **salvation** from the Chastisement of the Fire.
009:020 They are the people who will achieve (**salvation**).
039:061 for they have earned **salvation**: no evil
040:041 for me to call you to **Salvation** while ye call

SAME
002:006 it is the **same** to them whether thou
002:085 After this it is ye, the **same** people,
002:113 Yet they (profess) to **study** the (**same**) Book.
002:233 An heir shall be chargeable in the **same** way.
004:009 have the **same** fear in their minds as they would
004:023 and two sisters in wedlock at one and the **same** time,
004:089 and thus be on the **same** footing (as they):
005:061 and they go out with the **same**.
007:027 in the **same** manner as he got your parents
007:193 for you it is the **same** whether ye call
012:059 the **same** father as yourselves, (but a
012:065 and add (at the **same** time) a full camel's load
013:004 watered with the **same** water, yet some

SAME (continued)
013:010 It is the **same** (to Him) whether any of you
016:004 and behold this **same** (man) becomes an
019:065 of the **same** Name as He?
022:044 (in the **same** way). But I granted respite to
026:136 They said: "It is the **same** to us whether thou
027:042 "It seems the **same**. And knowledge
030:050 verily the **Same** will give life to the men
036:010 The **same** is to them whether thou admonish them
036:080 "The **same** Who produces for you fire out of
038:028 the **same** as those who turn aside from the right?
038:028 the **same** as those who do mischief on earth?
042:013 The **same** religion has He established for you
043:010 (Yea, the **same** that) has made for you the earth
043:023 Just in the **same** way, whenever We sent a Warner
052:016 "Burn ye therein: the **same** is it to you
065:004 (it is the **same**): for those who are pregnant,
065:006 in the **same** style as ye live, according to
075:040 Has not He, (the **same**), the power

SAMIRI
020:085 in thy absence: the **Samiri** has led them astray."
020:087 and that was what the **Samiri** suggested.
020:095 (Moses) said: "What then is thy case, O **Samiri**?"

SANCTIFIED
027:091 Him Who has **sanctified** it and to Whom

SANCTIFY
002:125 that they should **sanctify** My House
009:103 **sanctify** them; and pray on their behalf. Verily
022:026 with Me; and **sanctify** My House for those who

SANCTITY
005:002 the **sanctity** of the rites of Allah, nor of

SANCTUARY
028:057 for them a secure **Sanctuary**, to which
029:067 We have made a **Sanctuary** secure, and that

SAND
004:043 then take for yourselves clean **sand** (or earth),
005:006 then take for yourselves clean **sand** or earth, and
018:040 making it (but) slippery **sand**!
073:014 a heap of **sand** poured out and flowing down.

SAND-CLIFF
009:109 **sand-cliff** ready to crumble to pieces? And it

SAND-TRACTS
046:021 **Sand-tracts**: but there have been Warners before

SANDY
024:039 in **sandy** deserts, which the man parched with

SANE
003:095 follow the religion of Abraham, the **sane** in faith:

SARCASTIC
049:011 the (former): nor defame nor be **sarcastic** to each

SAT
009:090 and His Messenger (Merely) **sat** behind: soon will
085:006 Behold! they **sat** over against the (fire),

SATAN
002:036 Then did **Satan** make them slip from the (garden),
002:168 and do not the footsteps of **Satan** for he
002:208 the **Satan** for he is to you an avowed enemy.
002:268 **Satan** threatens you with poverty and bids
002:275 the **Satan** by his touch hath driven to madness.
003:036 to Thy protection from **Satan** the Rejected."
003:155 it was **Satan** who caused them to fail,
003:175 It is only the **Satan** that suggests to you
004:038 if any take the **Satan** for their intimate, what

SATAN (continued)

004:076	so fight ye against the friends, of **Satan**:
004:076	feeble indeed is the cunning of **Satan**.
004:083	all but a few of you would have followed **Satan**.
004:117	they call but upon **Satan** the persistent rebel!
004:119	Whoever, forsaking Allah, takes **Satan** for a friend,
004:120	**Satan** makes them promises, and creates
006:043	and **Satan** made their (sinful) acts
006:068	If **Satan** ever makes thee forget, then after
006:142	and follow not the footsteps of **Satan**: for he
007:020	Then began **Satan** to whisper
007:022	**Satan** was an avowed enemy unto you?"
007:027	Let not **Satan** seduce you, in the same
007:175	so **Satan** followed him up, and he went astray.
007:200	If a suggestion from **Satan** assail thy (mind),
007:201	from **Satan** assaults them, bring Allah
008:011	to remove from you the stain of **Satan**, to
008:048	Remember **Satan** made their (sinful) acts
012:005	for **Satan** is to man an avowed enemy!
012:042	But **Satan** made him forget to mention him
012:100	the desert, (even) after **Satan** had sown enmity
014:022	And **Satan** will say when the matter is decided:
015:017	from every accursed **Satan**.
016:063	but **Satan** made, (to the wicked), their own
016:098	seek Allah's protection from **Satan** the Rejected one.
017:027	the Satans. And the **Satan** is to his Lord
017:053	among them: for **Satan** is to man an avowed enemy.
017:053	for **Satan** doth sow dissensions among them:
017:064	But **Satan** promises them nothing but deceit.
018:063	none but **Satan** made me forget to tell (you)
019:044	for **Satan** is a rebel against (Allah) Most Gracious.
019:044	"O my father! serve not **Satan**: for **Satan**
019:045	so that thou become to **Satan** a friend."
020:120	But **Satan** whispered evil to him: he said,
022:003	and follow every **Satan** obstinate in rebellion!
022:004	About the (**Satan**) it is decreed that whoever
022:052	cancel anything (vain) that **Satan** throws in,
022:052	**Satan** threw some (vanity) into his desire:
022:053	thrown in by **Satan**, but a
024:021	follow the footsteps of **Satan**, he will
025:029	come to me! Ah! the **Satan** is but a traitor
027:024	**Satan** has made their deeds seem pleasing
028:015	He said: "This is a work of **Satan**: for he
029:038	**Satan** made their deeds alluring to them,
031:021	What! even if it is **Satan** beckoning them to the
034:020	And on them did **Satan** prove true his idea,
035:006	Verily **Satan** is an enemy to you: so treat him
036:060	not worship **Satan**; for that he was to you
038:041	"**Satan** has afflicted me with distress and suffering"!
041:036	by the **Satan**, seek refuge in Allah. He is
043:036	We appoint for him a **Satan**, to be
043:062	Let not the **Satan** hinder you: for he
047:025	to them,-**Satan** has instigated them and buoyed
058:010	by **Satan**, in order that he may cause grief to the
058:019	They are the Party of **Satan**. Truly, it
058:019	Truly, it is the Party of **Satan** that will lose.
058:019	**Satan** has got the better of them: so he
059:016	(Their allies deceived them), like **Satan**, when he
059:016	**Satan** says, "I am free of thee: I do
081:025	Nor is it the word of a **Satan** accursed.

SATAN'S

004:060	But **Satan's** wish is to lead them
004:120	but **Satan's** promises are nothing but deception.

SATAN'S (continued)

005:090	are an abomination,-of **Satan's** handiwork: eschew
005:091	**Satan's** plan is (but) to excite enmity
024:021	**Satan's** footsteps: if any will follow the

SATANS

002:102	**Satans** recited over Solomon's Kingdom.
002:102	but **Satans** disbelieved,
006:071	like one whom the **Satans** have made
006:112	**satans** among men and Jinns, inspiring each other
006:121	But the **satans** ever inspire their friends
007:027	We made the **Satans** friends (only) to
007:030	the **Satans** in preference to Allah, for their
017:027	the **Satans**. And the Satan is to his Lord
019:068	and (also) **Satans** (with them); then shall
019:083	set **Satans** on against the Unbelievers, to incite
023:097	with Thee from the suggestions of the **Satans**.
026:210	The **Satans** did not bring it down:
026:221	on whom it is that the **Satans** descend?
037:007	against all obstinate rebellious **Satans**.
038:037	As also the **Satans**, (including) every kind
043:037	Such (**Satans**) really hinder them from the Path,
067:005	(as) missiles to drive away **Satans**, and have

SATISFACTION

013:028	hearts find **satisfaction** in the remembrance
013:028	of Allah do hearts find **satisfaction**.
033:051	of their grief, and their **satisfaction**-that of
053:048	That it is He Who giveth wealth and **satisfaction**,
056:089	(There is for him) Rest and **Satisfaction**, and a
069:024	full **satisfaction**; because of the (good) that ye
089:027	"O (thou) soul, in (complete) rest and **satisfaction**!
092:021	And soon will they attain (complete) **satisfaction**.
101:007	Will be in a life of good pleasure and **satisfaction**.

SATISFIED

002:120	be **satisfied** with thee unless
010:007	but are pleased and **satisfied** with the life

SATISFY

002:260	He said: "Yea! but to **satisfy** my own heart."
005:113	to eat thereof and **satisfy** our hearts, and to know
012:068	it served only to **satisfy** Jacob's heartfelt desire.
018:019	to you, (that ye may **satisfy** your hunger therewith)
088:007	Which will neither nourish nor **satisfy** hunger.

SAVE

002:032	**save** what Thou hast taught Us:
002:067	He said: "Allah **save** me from being
002:096	will not **save** him from (due) chastisement
002:201	and **save** us from the torment on the Fire!"
003:016	and **save** us from the agony of the Fire;"
003:194	and **save** us from shame on the Day of Judgment:
007:127	(only) their females will we **save** alive; and
009:054	that they come not to prayer **save** lazily and that
010:092	"This day shall We **save** thee in thy body,
011:043	nothing can **save**, from the Command of Allah,
011:043	to some mountain: it will **save** me from the water."
012:032	firmly **save** himself guiltless! And now,
015:059	to **save** (from Harm),-all-
019:072	But We shall **save** those who guarded against evil,
028:021	**save** me from people given to wrong-doing."
028:080	**save** those who steadfastly persevere (in good)."
029:024	But Allah did **save** him from the Fire. Verily in
029:032	we will certainly **save** him and his following,-
029:033	we are (here) to **save** thee and thy following,
037:039	And you are requited naught **save** what ye did.
053:032	indecent deeds, **save** lesser offences,-verily thy

SAVE (continued)

061:010 **save** you from a grievous Chastisement?-
066:006 O ye who believe! **save** yourselves and your
066:011 and **save** me from those that do wrong";
066:011 and **save** me from Pharaoh and his doings, and **save**
078:025 **Save** a boiling fluid and a fluid, dark, murky,

SAVED

002:050 and **saved** you and drowned Pharaoh's people
003:103 and He **saved** you from it.
003:185 Only he who is **saved** far from the fire and
005:032 and if anyone **saved** a life, it would be as
005:032 he **saved** the life of the whole people.
007:072 We **saved** him and those who adhered to him, by Our
007:083 But We **saved** him and his family, except
007:141 and **saved** alive your females: in that
008:043 but Allah **saved** (you): for He knoweth well the
011:058 We **saved** them from a severe chastisement.
011:058 We **saved** Hud and those who believed with him,
011:066 We **saved** Salih and those who believed with him,
011:094 We **saved** Shu'aib and those who believed with him,
011:116 them whom We **saved** (from harm)? But the wrong-
012:042 he considered about to be **saved**, he said:
020:040 but We **saved** thee from trouble, and We
021:009 and We **saved** them and those whom We willed,
021:074 and We **saved** him from the town which
023:028 Who has **saved** us from the people who do wrong."
027:053 And We **saved** those who believed and practiced
027:057 But We **saved** him and his family, except his
029:015 But We **saved** him and the Companions of the Ark,
029:016 And (We also **saved**) Abraham: behold, he said
038:003 no longer time for being **saved**!
040:045 Then Allah **saved** him from (every) evil that they
059:009 And those **saved** from the covetousness of their
064:016 and those **saved** from the covetousness of their

SAVING

002:179 there is (**saving** of) Life to you.

SAW

003:013 these **saw** with their own eyes twice their number.
006:025 if they **saw** every one of the Signs, they will
006:076 he **saw** a star: he said: "This is my Lord." But
006:077 When he **saw** the moon rising in splendor, He said:
006:078 When he **saw** the sun rising (in splendor), he
007:149 and **saw** that they had erred, they said:
009:026 and sent down forces which ye **saw** not: He punished
009:040 with forces which ye **saw** not, and humbled
011:070 But when he **saw** their hands not reaching
012:004 I **saw** them prostrate themselves to me!"
012:024 but that he **saw** the evidence of his Lord:
012:026 **saw** (this) and bore witness, (thus):-
012:028 So when he **saw** his shirt,-that it
012:031 before them. When they **saw** him, they did
012:080 Now when they **saw** no hope of his (yielding),
020:010 Behold, he **saw** a fire: so he said
020:096 He replied: "I **saw** what they **saw** not: so I
026:061 **saw** each other, the people of Moses said: "We are
027:010 But when he **saw** it moving (of its own accord)
027:040 Then when (Solomon) **saw** it placed firmly
027:044 she **saw** it, she thought it was a lake of water,
028:031 But when he **saw** it moving (of its own accord)
033:009 and forces that ye **saw** not: but Allah
033:022 When the Believers **saw** the Confederate forces,
034:014 the Jinns **saw** plainly that if they had known
037:055 He looked down and **saw** him in the midst

SAW (continued)

040:084 But when they **saw** Our Might, they said
040:085 when they (actually) **saw** Our Punishment was not
046:024 Then, when they **saw** a could advancing towards
053:011 in no way falsified that which he **saw**.
053:012 with him concerning what he **saw**?
053:013 For indeed he **saw** him at a second descent,
068:026 But when they **saw** the (garden), they said:
081:023 And without doubt he **saw** him in the clear horizon.
083:032 And whenever they **saw** them, they would

SAWEST

018:063 He replied: "**Sawest** thou (what happened) when we
020:092 thee back, when thou **sawest** them going wrong.

SAY

002:008 Of the people there are some who **say**
002:011 they **say**: "Why, we are only ones
002:013 they **say**: "Shall we believe
002:014 they **say**: "We believe,"
002:014 they **say**: "We are really with you,
002:025 they **say**: "Why this is what we were fed
002:026 but those who reject Faith **say**:
002:058 and **say**: Forgive (us) We shall forgive you
002:076 they **say**: "Shall you tell them what Allah
002:076 they **say**: "We believe":
002:079 and then **say**: "This is from Allah,"
002:080 And they **say**: "The fire shall not touch us
002:080 ye **say** of Allah what ye do not know?"
002:080 **Say**: "Have ye taken a promise from Allah,
002:088 They **say**, "Our hearts are the wrappings
002:091 they **say**, "We believe in what was sent
002:091 **Say**: "Why then have ye slain the prophets
002:093 **Say**: "Vile indeed are the behests
002:094 **Say**: "If the last Home, with Allah,
002:097 **Say**: Whoever is an enemy to Gabriel
002:104 O ye of Faith! **say** not (to the Prophet)
002:104 but **say**, 'Unzurna and hearken (to him):
002:111 **Say**: "Produce your proof if ye are truthful."
002:111 And they **say**: "None shall enter Paradise
002:113 and the Christians **say**: "The Jews
002:113 what those **say** who know not,
002:113 The Jews **say**: "The Christians have
002:116 They **say**: "Allah hath begotten a son";
002:118 **Say** those without knowledge:
002:120 **Say**: "The guidance of Allah,
002:135 **Say** thou: "Nay! (I would rather) the Religion
002:135 They **say**: "Become Jews or Christians
002:136 **Say** ye: "We believer in Allah,
002:139 **Say**: Will ye dispute with us about Allah,
002:140 **Say**: Do ye know better than Allah?
002:140 Or do ye **say** that Abraham,
002:142 **Say**: To Allah belong both East and West:
002:142 The Fools among the people will **say**:
002:154 And **say** not of those who are slain
002:156 Who **say**, when afflicted with calamity:
002:167 And those who followed would **say**: "If only
002:169 and that ye should **say** of Allah
002:170 they **say**: "Nay! we shall follow
002:189 **Say**: They are but signs to mark fixed periods
002:200 There are men who **say**: "Our Lord! Give us
002:201 And there are men who **say**: "Our Lord! give us
002:215 **Say**: Whatever wealth ye spend that is good,
002:217 **Say**: "Fighting therein is a grave (offense);
002:219 **say**: "What is beyond your needs."

SAY (continued)

002:219   **Say**: "In them is great sin,
002:220   **Say**: "The best thing to do
002:222   **Say**: They are a hurt and a pollution:
002:247   They **say**: "How can he exercise authority
002:275   That is because they **say**: "Trade
002:285   "We make no distinction (they **say**) between
002:285   And they **say**: "We hear, and we obey:
003:007   in knowledge **say**: "We believe in it;
003:008   "Our Lord!" (they **say**), "let not our hearts
003:012   **Say** to those who reject Faith: "Soon
003:015   **Say**: shall I give you glad tidings of things
003:016   (Namely), those who **say**: "Our Lord!
003:020   And **say** to the People of the Book
003:020   **say**: "I have submitted my whole self to Allah
003:024   This because they **say**: "The Fire shall not touch us
003:026   **Say**: "O Allah! Lord of Power (and Rule),
003:029   **Say**: "Whether ye hide what is in your hearts
003:031   **Say**: "If ye do love Allah, follow me:
003:032   **Say**: "Obey Allah and His Messenger": but if they
003:061   **say**: "Come! let us gather together,
003:064   **Say**: "O people of the Book!
003:064   **say** ye: "Bear witness that we (at least) are Muslims
003:072   A section of the People of the Book **say**: "Believe
003:073   **Say**: "True guidance is the guidance of Allah:
003:073   **Say**: "All bounties are in the hand of Allah:
003:075   because, they **say**, "There is no way over us
003:078   and they **say** "That is from Allah"
003:079   on the contrary (he would **say**): "Be ye worshippers
003:079   should **say** to people: "Be ye my worshippers
003:084   **Say**: "We believe in Allah, and in what
003:093   **Say**: "Bring ye the Torah and **study** it,
003:095   **Say**: "Allah speaketh the truth: follow the religion
003:098   **Say**: "O people of the Book!
003:099   **Say**: "O ye People of the Book!
003:119   **Say**: "Perish in your rage; Allah knoweth
003:119   when they meet you, they **say**, "We believe";
003:154   They **say** (to themselves): "If we had anything
003:154   **Say**: "Even if you had remained in your homes,
003:154   **Say** thou: "Indeed, this affair is wholly Allah's."
003:156   who **say** of their brethren, when they
003:165   do ye **say**? "Whence is this?"
003:165   **Say** (to them): "It is from yourselves:
003:168   (They are) the ones that **say**, (of their brethren
003:168   **Say**: "Avert death from your own selves,
003:181   Allah hath heard the taunt of those who **say**:
003:181   and We shall **say**: "Taste ye the Chastisement
003:183   **Say**: "There came to you Messengers before me,
004:043   until ye can understand all that ye **say**,
004:046   and **say**: "We hear and we disobey"; and
004:051   and **say** to the Unbelievers that they are better
004:072   They **say**: "Allah did favour us in that we
004:073   they would be sure to **say**-as it there had never
004:077   **Say**: "Short is the enjoyment of this world: the
004:077   they **say**: "Our Lord! why hast Thou ordered
004:078   they **say**, "This is from Allah"; but
004:078   **Say**: "All things are from Allah."
004:078   but if evil, they **say**, "This is from
004:094   and **say** not to anyone who offers you a
004:097   They **say**: "In what (plight) were ye?"
004:097   They **say**: "Was not the earth of Allah spacious
004:127   **Say**: Allah doth instruct you about them: and
004:141   they **say**: "Were we not with you?"

SAY (continued)

004:141   they **say** (to them): "Did we not gain
004:171   **Say** not "Three": desist: it will be
004:171   nor **say** of Allah aught but truth.
004:176   **say**: Allah directs (thus) about those who leave
005:004   **Say**: Lawful unto you are (all) things good and pure:
005:017   **say** that Allah is Christ the son of Mary.
005:017   **Say**: "Who then hath the least power against Allah,
005:018   (Both) the Jews and the Christians **say**: "We are
005:018   **Say**: "Why then doth He punish you for your sins?
005:019   lest ye should **say**: "There came unto us no bringer
005:041   (whether it be) among those who **say**: "We believe"
005:041   they **say**, "If ye are given this, take it, but if
005:053   And those who believe will **say**: "Are these
005:059   **Say**: "O People of the Book! do ye disapprove
005:060   **Say**: "Shall I point out to you something
005:061   When they come to thee, they **say**: "We believe":
005:064   The Jews **say**: "Allah's hand is tied up," Be
005:068   **Say**: "O People of the Book! ye have
005:072   Certainly they disbelieve who **say**: "Allah is
005:073   They disbelieve who **say**: Allah is one
005:076   **Say**: Will ye worship, besides Allah, something
005:077   **Say**: "O people of the Book! exceed not
005:082   who **say**, "We are Christians:" because amongst
005:100   **Say**: "Not equal are things that are bad and
005:104   they **say**: "Enough for us are the ways
005:109   They will **say**: "We have no knowledge: it is
005:110   Then will Allah **say**: "O Jesus
005:116   And behold! Allah will **say** "O Jesus
005:116   **say** unto men, "Take me and my mother for two
005:116   He will **say**: "Glory to Thee! never could
005:116   never could I **say** what I had no right (to **say**).
005:117   except what Thou didst command me to **say**, to wit,
005:119   Allah will **say**: "This is a day
006:007   the Unbelievers would have been sure to **say**: "This
006:008   They **say**: "Why is not an angel sent down to him?"
006:011   **Say**: "Travel through the earth and see what was
006:012   **Say**: "To Allah. He hath inscribed for Himself
006:012   **Say**: "To whom belongeth all that is in the
006:014   **Say**: "Shall I take for my protector any other
006:014   **Say**: "Nay! but I am commanded to be the first
006:015   **Say**: "I would, if I disobeyed my Lord, indeed
006:019   **Say**: "Nay! I cannot bear witness!" **Say**:
006:019   **Say**: "Allah is Witness between me and you: this
006:019   **Say**: "What thing is most weighty in evidence?"
006:019   **Say**: "But in truth He is the One God. And
006:022   We shall **say** to those who ascribed partners
006:023   no excuse for them but to **say**: "By Allah
006:025   the Unbelievers **say**: "These are nothing
006:027   They will **say**: "Would that we
006:029   And they (sometimes) **say**: "There is nothing
006:030   They will **say**: "Yea, by our Lord!" He will **say**:
006:030   He will **say**: "Is not this the truth?" They will
006:030   He will **say**: "Taste ye then the Chastisement,
006:031   and they **say**: "Ah! woe unto us that we neglected;
006:037   **Say**: "Allah hath certainly power to send
006:037   They **say**: "Why is not a Sign sent down
006:040   **Say**: "Think ye to yourselves, if there come
006:046   **Say**: "Think ye, if Allah took away your hearing
006:047   **Say**: "Think ye, if the Punishment of Allah
006:050   **Say**: "Can the blind be held equal to the seeing?"
006:050   **Say**: "I tell you not that with me
006:053   that they should **say**: "Is it these
006:054   **Say** "Peace be on you: your Lord hath inscribed for

SAY (continued)

006:056   **Say**: "I will not follow your vain desires: if I
006:056   **Say**: "I am forbidden to worship those-other
006:057   **Say**: "For me, I (work) on a clear Sign
006:058   **Say**: "If what ye would see hastened
006:063   **Say**: "Who is it that delivereth you from the dark
006:064   **Say**: "It is Allah that delivereth you from these
006:065   **Say**: "He hath power to send calamities
006:066   **Say**: "Not mine is the responsibility for
006:071   **Say**: "Allah's guidance is the (only)
006:071   **Say**: "Shall we call on others besides Allah,-
006:090   **Say**: "No reward for this do I ask of you: this
006:091   do they make when they **say**: "Nothing
006:091   **Say**: "Who then sent down the Book
006:091   **Say**: "Allah (sent it down)": then leave
006:105   may **say**, "Thou hast learnt this (from somebody),
006:109   **Say**: "Certainly (all) Signs are in
006:114   **Say**: "Shall I seek for judge other than Allah?-
006:124   a Sign (from Allah), they **say**:" We shall
006:128   (and **say**): "O ye assembly of Jinns much (toll)
006:128   Their friends amongst men will **say**: "Our Lord!
006:128   He will **say**: "The Fire be your dwelling-place:
006:130   They will **say**: "We bear witness
006:135   **Say**: "O my people! do whatever ye can: I will
006:136   they **say**, according to their fancies: "This
006:138   except those whom-so they **say**-We wish; further,
006:138   And they **say** that such and such
006:139   They **say**: "What is in the wombs
006:143   **say**, hath He forbidden the two males, or the
006:144   **say**, hath He forbidden the two males, or the
006:145   **Say**: "I find not in the Message received by
006:147   **say**: "Your Lord is full of Mercy All-embracing;
006:148   will **say**: "If Allah had wished, we should
006:148   **Say**: "Have ye any (certain) Knowledge? If so,
006:149   **Say**: "With Allah is the argument
006:150   **Say**: "Bring forward your witnesses to prove
006:151   **Say**: "Come, I will rehearse what Allah hath
006:156   Lest ye should **say**: "The Book was sent down
006:157   Or lest ye should **say**: "If the Book
006:158   **Say**: "Wait ye: we too are waiting."
006:161   **Say**: "Verily, my Lord hath guided me
006:162   **Say**: "Truly, my prayer and my
006:164   **Say**: "Shall I seek for (my) Lord
007:028   **say**: "Nay Allah never commands what is Indecent:
007:028   do ye **say** of Allah what ye know not?"
007:028   they **say**: "We found our fathers doing so"; and
007:029   **Say**: "My Lord hath commanded justice; and that
007:032   **Say**: they are, in the life of this world, for
007:032   **Say**: Who hath forbidden the beautiful
007:033   **Say**: The things that my Lord
007:037   they **say**: "Where are the things that ye
007:038   He will **say**: "Doubled for all": but this
007:038   He will **say**: "Enter ye in the company of the
007:039   Then the first will **say** to the last: "See then!
007:043   and they shall **say**: "Praise be to Allah, Who
007:044   They shall **say**, "Yes"; but a Crier
007:047   they will **say**: "Our Lord! send us
007:050   They will **say**: "Both these things hath Allah
007:053   those who have forgotten it before will **say**: "The
007:095   and began to **say**: "Our fathers
007:105   to **say** nothing but truth about Allah. Now have
007:158   **Say**: "O men! I am sent unto you all, as the
007:161   as ye wish, but **say** forgive (us) and enter

SAY (continued)

007:172   lest ye should **say** on the Day of Judgment: "Of
007:173   Or lest ye should **say**: "Our fathers
007:187   **Say**: "The knowledge thereof is with
007:188   **Say**: "I have no power over any good or harm
007:195   **Say**: "Call your `god-partners', scheme
007:203   they **say**: "Why hast thou not got it together?"
007:203   **Say**: "I but follow what is revealed
008:001   **Say**: "(Such) spoils are at the disposal of
008:021   Nor be like those who **say**, "We hear,"
008:031   if we wished, we could **say** (words) like these:
008:031   they **say**: "We have heard this (before): if we
008:038   **Say** to the Unbelievers, if (now)
008:049   **say**: "These people,-their religion has
008:070   O Prophet! **say** to those who are captives
009:024   **Say**: If it be that your fathers, your sons,
009:030   Unbelievers of old used to **say**. Allah's cures
009:050   they **say**, "We took indeed our precautions
009:051   **Say**: "Nothing will happen to us except what
009:052   **Say**: "Can you expect for us (any fate) other than
009:053   **Say**: "Spend (for the cause) willingly
009:061   **Say**, "He listens to what is best for you;
009:061   and **say**, "He is (all) ear." **Say**, "He listens
009:064   in their hearts. **Say**: "Mock ye! But verily
009:065   **Say**: "Was it at Allah, and His Signs, and His
009:081   **Say**, "The fire of Hell is fiercer in heat." If
009:083   **say**: "Never shall ye come out with me, nor fight
009:086   and **say**: "Leave us (behind): we would
009:094   **Say** thou: "Present no excuses: we shall
009:105   And **say**: "Work (righteousness): soon will
009:124   some of them **say**: "Which of you has had his faith
009:129   **Say**: "Allah sufficeth me: there is no god
010:002   (but) **say** the Unbelievers: "This is
010:015   **Say**: "It is not for me, of my own
010:015   **say**: "Bring us a Qur'an other than this,
010:016   **Say**: "If Allah had so willed, I should
010:018   and they **say**: "These are our intercessors with
010:018   **Say**: "Do ye indeed inform Allah of something
010:020   **Say**: "The Unseen is only for Allah (to Know).
010:020   They **say**: "Why is not a Sign sent down
010:021   **Say**: "Swifter to plan is Allah! Verily, Our
010:028   Then shall We **say** to those who joined gods
010:028   and their "partners" shall **say**: "It was not
010:031   **Say**: "Who is it that sustains you (in life)
010:031   all affairs?" They will soon **say**: "Allah". **Say**,
010:031   **Say**, "Will ye not then show piety (to Him)?"
010:034   **Say**: "It is Allah Who originates Creation
010:034   **Say**: "Of your `partners,' can any originate
010:035   **Say**: "It is Allah Who gives guidance towards Truth.
010:035   **Say**: "Of your 'partners' is there any that
010:038   **Say**: "Bring then a Sura like unto it, and call
010:038   Or do they **say**, "He forged it"? **Say**: "Bring
010:041   **say**: "My work to me, and yours to you! Ye are
010:048   They **say**: "When will this promise come to pass-
010:049   **Say**: "I have no power over any harm or profit
010:050   **Say**: "Do ye see-if His punishment should come
010:053   "Is that true?" **Say**: "Aye! by my Lord! It is
010:058   **Say**: "In the Bounty of Allah. And in His
010:059   **Say**: "See ye what things Allah hath sent down
010:059   **Say**: "Hath Allah indeed permitted you, or do
010:068   for this! **Say** ye about Allah what ye know not?
010:068   They **say**, "Allah hath begotten a son!"-Glory be
010:069   **Say**: "Those who forge a lie against Allah

SAY (continued)

010:077	Said Moses: "**Say** ye (this) about the Truth when it
010:101	**Say**: "Behold all that is in the heavens
010:102	**Say**: "Wait ye then: for I too,
010:104	**Say**: "O ye men! if ye are in doubt
010:108	**Say**: "O ye men! now Truth hath reached you
011:002	(**Say**:) "Verily I am (sent) unto you from Him
011:007	to **say**, "This is nothing but obvious sorcery!"
011:007	But if thou wert to **say** to them, "Ye shall
011:008	they are sure to **say**, "What keeps it back?" Ah!
011:010	touched him, he is sure to **say**, "All evil has
011:012	lest they **say**, "Why is not a treasure sent down
011:013	Or they may **say**, "He forged it." **Say**, "Bring ye
011:013	**Say**, "Bring ye then ten Suras forged, like unto
011:018	and the witnesses will **say**. "These are the
011:031	Nor yet do I **say**, of those whom your eyes
011:035	Or do they **say**, "He has forged it?" **Say**:
011:035	**Say**: "If I had forged it, on me were my sin!
011:054	"We **say** nothing but that (perhaps) some of
011:121	**Say** to those who do not believe: "Do whatever
012:052	"This (**say** I), in order that he may know
012:066	he said: "Over all that we **say**, be Allah
012:081	and **say**, 'O our father! behold! thy son
012:096	clear sight. He said: "Did I not **say** to you,
012:108	**Say** thou: "This my Way; I do invite unto Allah,-
013:007	And the Unbelievers **say**: "Why is not a Sign
013:016	**Say**: "Who is the Lord and Sustainer of the
013:016	them similar? **Say**: "Allah is the Creator of all
013:016	**Say**: "(It is) Allah." **Say**: "Do ye then
013:016	**Say**: "Do ye then take (for worship) protectors
013:016	**Say**: "Are the blind equal with those who see?
013:027	**Say**: "Truly Allah leaveth, to stray, whom He
013:027	The Unbelievers **say**: "Why is not a Sign
013:030	**Say**: "He is my Lord! There is no god but He!
013:033	**Say**: "But name them! is it that ye will inform
013:036	**Say**: "I am commanded to worship Allah, and not
013:043	The Unbelievers **say**: "No messenger art thou."
013:043	art thou." **Say** "Enough for a witness between me
014:021	the weak **say** to those who were arrogant, "For us
014:022	And Satan will **say** when the matter is decided:
014:030	**Say**: "Enjoy (your brief power)! But verily
014:044	then will the wrong-doers **say**: "Our Lord!
015:006	They **say**: "O thou to whom the Message
015:015	They would only **say**: "Our eyes have been
015:089	And **say**: "I am indeed he that warneth openly
015:097	is distressed at what they **say**.
016:024	has revealed?" they **say**, "Tales of the ancients!"
016:027	and **say**: "Where are My `partners' concerning whom
016:027	with knowledge will **say**: "This Day, indeed, are
016:030	they **say**, "All that is good." To those
016:035	The worshippers of false gods **say**: "If Allah
016:040	We but **say** the Word, "Be," and it is.
016:086	they will **say**: "Our Lord! these are our `partners',
016:086	at them (and **say**): "Indeed ye are liars!"
016:101	He reveals (in stages),-they **say**, "Thou art
016:102	**Say**, the Holy Spirit has brought the revelation
016:103	We know indeed that they **say**, "It is
016:116	But **say** not-for any false thing that your
017:023	old age in thy life, **say** not to them a word
017:024	the wing of humility, and **say**: "My Lord!
017:042	**Say**: if there had been (other) gods with Him,-
017:042	with Him,-as they **say**,-behold, they would
017:043	they **say**! Exalted and Great (beyond measure)!

SAY (continued)

017:047	behold, the wicked **say**, "Ye follow none
017:049	They **say**: "What! when we are reduced to bones
017:050	**Say**: "(Nay!) be ye stones or iron,
017:051	**Say**, "Maybe it will be quite soon!
017:051	to return?" **Say**: "He Who created you first!"
017:051	their heads towards thee, and **say**, "When will
017:051	Then will they **say**: "Who will cause us to return?"
017:053	**Say** to My servants that they should (only) **say**
017:053	(only) **say** those things that are best: for Satan
017:056	**Say**: "Call on those-besides Him-whom ye fancy:
017:080	**Say**: "O my Lord! let my entry be by the Gate
017:081	And **say**: "Truth has (now) arrived, and Falsehood
017:084	**Say**: "Everyone acts according to his own
017:085	**Say**: "The Spirit is of the command of my Lord
017:088	**Say**: "If the whole of mankind and Jinns were to
017:090	They **say**: "We shall not believe in thee,
017:093	**Say**: "Glory to my Lord! am I aught
017:095	**Say**, "If there were settled, on earth,
017:096	**Say**: "Enough is Allah for a witness between me
017:100	**Say**: "If ye had control of the Treasures
017:107	**Say**: "Whether ye believe in it or not, it is
017:108	And they **say**: "Glory to our Lord! Truly has
017:110	**Say**: "Call upon Allah, or call
017:111	**Say**: "Praise be to Allah Who begets no son,
018:004	who **say**, "Allah hath begotten a son":
018:005	What they **say** in nothing but falsehood!
018:022	(yet others) **say** they were seven, the dog
018:022	(Some) **say** they were three, the dog
018:022	**Say** thou: "My Lord knoweth best their number;
018:022	(others) **say** they were five, the dog
018:023	Nor **say** of anything, "I shall be
018:024	thou forgettest, and **say**, "I hope
018:026	**Say**: "Allah knows best how long they stayed:
018:029	**Say**, "The Truth is from your Lord" let him
018:039	into thy garden, **say**: Allah's Will (be done)!
018:042	and he could only **say**, "Woe is me! Would I had
018:049	is (recorded) therein; they will **say**, "Ah! woe
018:052	On the Day He will **say**, "Call on
018:083	**Say**, "I will rehearse to you something
018:103	**Say**: "Shall we tell you of those who lose most
018:109	**Say**: "If the ocean were ink (wherewith to write
018:110	**Say**: "I am but a man like yourselves, but the
019:026	And if thou dost see any man, **say**, 'I have
019:064	(The angels **say**:) "We descend not but by
019:073	to them, the Unbelievers **say** to those who
019:075	**Say**: "whoever goes astray, (Allah) Most Gracious
019:088	They **say**: "The Most Gracious has begotten a son!"
020:028	"So they may understand what I **say**:
020:047	"So go ye both to him, and **say**, `Verily we
020:094	Truly I feared lest thou shouldst **say**, 'Thou hast
020:097	be that thou wilt **say**, 'Touch me not';
020:104	We know best what they will **say**, when the
020:104	will **say**: "Ye tarried not longer than a day!"
020:105	**say**, "My Lord will uproot them and scatter
020:114	to thee is completed, but **say**, "O my lord!
020:125	He will **say**: "O my Lord! why hast
020:126	(Allah) will **say**: "Thus didst thou, when Our
020:130	they **say**, and celebrate (constantly) the praises
020:133	They **say**: "Why does he not bring us a Sign
020:135	**Say**: "Each one (of us), is waiting: wait ye,
021:004	**Say**: "My Lord knoweth (every) word (spoken)
021:005	"Nay," they **say**, "(these are) medleys of dreams!

SAY (continued)

021:024	**Say**, "Bring your convincing proof: this is
021:026	And they **say**: "The Most Gracious has taken a son."
021:029	If any of them should **say**, "I am
021:036	with ridicule. "Is this," (they **say**), "The one
021:038	They **say**: "When will this promise come to pass,
021:042	**Say**, "Who can keep you safe by night and by day
021:045	**Say**, "I do but warn you according to revelation":
021:046	they will then **say**, "Woe to us! we did
021:108	**Say**: "What has come to me by inspiration
021:109	**say**: "I have proclaimed the Message to you all
021:112	**Say**: "O my Lord! judge Thou in truth!" "Our Lord
022:040	that they **say**, "Our Lord is Allah." Did not
022:049	**Say**: "O men! I am (sent) to you only to give
022:068	**say**, "Allah knows best what it is ye are doing."
022:072	**Say**, "Shall I tell you of something (far) worse than
023:028	**say**: "Praise be to Allah, Who has
023:029	And **say**: "O my Lord! enable me
023:070	Or do they **say**, "He is possessed"? Nay, he
023:081	On the contrary they **say** things similar to
023:082	They **say**: "What! when we die and become
023:084	and all beings therein? (**Say**) if ye know!"
023:084	**Say**: "To whom belong the earth and all
023:085	They will **say**, "To Allah!" **Say**: "Yet will
023:085	**Say**: "Yet will ye not receive admonition?"
023:086	**Say**: "Who is the Lord of the seven heavens,
023:087	They will **say**, "(They belong) to Allah." **Say**:
023:087	**Say**: "Will ye not then fear?"
023:088	but is not protected (of any)? (**Say**) if ye know."
023:088	**Say**: "Who is it in whose hands is the
023:089	**Say**: "Then how are ye deluded?"
023:089	They will **say**, "(It belongs) to Allah." **Say**:
023:093	**Say**: "O my Lord! if Thou wilt show me (in my
023:096	We are well acquainted with the things they **say**.
023:097	And **say**: "O my Lord! I seek refuge with Thee from
023:106	They will **say**: "Our Lord! our misfortune
023:108	He will **say**: "Be ye driven into it
023:112	He will **say**: "What number of years did ye
023:113	They will **say**: "We stayed a day or part
023:114	He will **say**: "Ye stayed not but a little,-
023:118	So **say**: "O my Lord! grant Thou forgiveness
024:012	and **say**, "This (charge) is an obvious lie?"
024:016	when ye heard it, **say**? "It is not
024:026	people **say**: for them there is forgiveness, and a
024:030	**Say** to the believing men that they should lower
024:031	And **say** to the believing women that they should
024:047	They **say**, "We believe in Allah and in the
024:051	is no other than this: they **say**, "We hear
024:053	**Say**: "Swear ye not; obedience is
024:054	**Say**: "Obey Allah, and obey the Messenger: but if
025:004	But the Misbelievers **say**: "Naught is
025:005	And they **say**: "Tales of the ancients, which he
025:006	**Say**: "The (Qur'an) was sent down by Him
025:007	And they **say**: "What sort of a messenger is this,
025:008	for enjoyment?" The wicked **say**: "Ye follow
025:015	**Say**: "Is that best, or the eternal Garden,
025:018	They will **say**: "Glory to Thee! not meant
025:019	ye **say**: so ye cannot avert (your penalty)
025:019	(Allah will **say**): "Now have
025:021	(for Judgment) **say**: "Why are not
025:022	that Day: the (angels) will **say**: "There is
025:027	will bite at his hands, he will **say**, "Oh! would
025:030	Then the Messenger will **say**: "O my Lord,

SAY (continued)

025:032	Those who reject Faith **say**: "Why is not
025:057	**Say**: "No reward do I ask of you for it but this:
025:060	They **say**, "And what is (Allah) Most Gracious?
025:063	they **say**, "Peace!"
025:065	Those who **say**, "Our Lord! avert from
025:077	**Say** (to the rejecters): "My Lord
026:016	to Pharaoh, and **say**: 'We have been sent by the
026:096	"They will **say** there in their mutual bickerings:
026:203	Then they will **say**: "Shall we be respited?"
026:216	Then if they disobey thee, **say**: "I am free
026:226	And that they **say** what they practice not?-
027:049	and that we shall then **say** to his heir (when he
027:059	**Say**: Praise be to Allah, and Peace
027:064	**Say**, "Bring forth your argument, if ye
027:065	**Say**: None in the heavens or on earth, except
027:067	The Unbelievers **say**:" What! when we become dust,-
027:069	**Say**: "Go ye through the earth and see what has
027:071	They also **say**: "When will this promise (come to
027:072	**Say**: "It may be that some of the events
027:084	the Judgment-Seat), (Allah) will **say**; "Did ye
027:092	**say**: "I am only a Warner."
027:093	And **say**: "Praise be to Allah, Who will
028:028	Be Allah a witness to what we **say**."
028:047	they might **say**: "Our Lord! why didst
028:048	And they **say**: "For us, we reject all (such things)!"
028:048	to them from Ourselves, they **say**, "Why are
028:048	They **say**: "Two kinds of sorcery, each assisting
028:049	**Say**: "Then bring ye a Book from Allah, which is
028:053	they **say**: "We believe therein, for it is
028:055	they turn away therefrom and **say**: "To us our
028:057	They **say**: "If we were to follow the guidance
028:062	and **say**: "Where are my `partners'?-whom ye
028:063	be proved, will **say**: "Our Lord! these are
028:065	and **say**: "What was the answer ye gave
028:071	**Say**: See ye? If Allah were to make the night
028:072	**Say**: see ye? If Allah were to make the Day
028:074	He will **say**: "Where are My `partners' whom ye
028:075	a witness, and We shall **say**: "Produce your
028:082	the day before began to **say** on the morrow:
028:085	**Say**: "My Lord knows best who it is that brings
029:010	to **say**, "We have (always) been with you!"
029:010	Then there are among men such as **say**, "We believe
029:012	And the Unbelievers **say** to those who believe:
029:020	**Say**: "Travel through the earth and see how
029:046	who do wrong but **say**, "We believe
029:050	Yet they **say**: "Why are not Signs sent down
029:050	**Say**: "The Signs are indeed with Allah: and I
029:052	**Say**: "Enough is Allah for a Witness
029:055	and (a Voice) shall **say**: "Taste ye
029:063	**Say**, "Praise be to Allah!" But most
030:042	**Say**: "Travel through the earth and see
030:056	and faith will **say**: "Indeed ye
030:058	the Unbelievers are sure to **say**, "Ye do
031:021	sent down, they **say**: "Nay, we shall
031:025	certainly **say**, "Allah." **Say**: "Praise be to Allah!"
032:003	Or do they **say**, "He has forged it"? Nay, it
032:010	And they **say**: "What! when we lie, hidden and
032:011	**Say**: "The Angel of Death, put in charge of you,
032:028	They **say**: "When will this decision be, if ye
032:029	**Say**: "On the Day of Decision, no profit
033:012	**say**: "Allah and His Messenger promised us nothing
033:016	**Say**: "Running away will not profit you if ye

SAY (continued)

033:017 **Say**: "Who is it that can screen you from Allah
033:018 who keep back (men) and those who **say** to their
033:028 O Prophet! **say** to thy Consorts: "If it
033:037 Behold! thou didst **say** to one who had received
033:063 **say**, "The knowledge thereof is with Allah (alone)":
033:066 they will **say**: "Woe to us! would that we had
033:067 And they would **say**: "Our Lord! We obeyed
034:003 **say**, "Nay! but most surely, by my Lord, it will
034:003 The Unbelievers **say**, "Never to us
034:007 The Unbelievers **say** (in ridicule): "Shall we
034:022 **Say**: "Call upon other (gods) whom ye fancy,
034:023 will they **say**, 'What is it that your Lord
034:023 your Lord commanded?' They will **say**, 'That which
034:024 **Say**: "Who gives you sustenance, from the
034:024 **Say**: "It is Allah; and certain it is that
034:025 **Say**: "Ye shall not be questioned as to our sins,
034:026 **Say**: "Our Lord will gather us together and will
034:027 **Say**: "Show me those whom ye have joined with
034:029 They **say**: "When will this promise (come to pass)
034:030 **Say**: "The appointment to you is for a Day,
034:031 The Unbelievers **say**: "We shall neither believe
034:031 deemed weak will **say** to the arrogant ones:
034:032 The arrogant ones will **say** to those who had
034:033 will **say** to the arrogant ones: Nay! it was
034:036 **Say**: "Verily my Lord enlarges and restricts
034:039 **Say**: "Verily my Lord enlarges and restricts
034:040 all together, and **say** to the angels, "Was it
034:041 They will **say**, "Glory to thee! Thou art
034:042 and We shall **say** to the wrong-doers, "Taste ye
034:043 And the Unbelievers **say** of the Truth when it
034:043 to them, they **say**, "This is only a man who
034:043 fathers practiced." And they **say**, "This is
034:046 **Say**: "I do admonish you on one point: that ye
034:047 **Say**: "Whatever reward do I ask of you: it is
034:048 **Say**: "Verily my Lord doth cast the Truth,-
034:049 **Say**: "The Truth has arrived, and Falsehood
034:050 **Say**: "If I am astray, I only stray to the loss
034:052 And they will **say**, "We do believe
035:034 And they will **say**: "Praise be to Allah, Who has
035:040 **Say**: "Have ye seen (these) `partners' of yours
036:047 the Unbelievers **say** to those who believe:
036:048 if what ye **say** is true?"
036:048 Further, they **say**, "When will this promise
036:052 of repose?... (A voice will **say**): "This is
036:052 They will **say**: "Ah! woe unto us! Who hath
036:079 **Say**, "He will give them life Who created
037:015 And **say**, "This is nothing but evident sorcery!
037:018 **Say** thou: "Yea, and ye shall then be humiliated
037:020 They will **say**, "Ah! woe to us! this is
037:021 (A voice will **say**,) "This is the Day
037:028 They will **say**: "It was ye who used to come
037:036 And **say**: "What! Shall we give up our gods
037:051 One of them will **say**: "I had an
037:052 "Who used to **say**, Do you really believe?
037:151 Behold they **say**, out of their own invention,
038:004 And the Unbelievers **say**, "This is a
038:016 They **say**: "Our Lord! Hasten to us our sentence
038:017 Have patience at what they **say**, and remember
038:061 They will **say**: "Our Lord! Whoever brought
038:062 And they will **say**: "How is it with us that we
038:065 **Say**: "Truly am I a Warner: no god
038:067 **Say**: "That is a Tremendous tidings.

SAY (continued)

038:084 and the Truth I **say**.
038:086 **Say**: "No reward do I ask of you
039:003 protectors other than Allah (**say**): "We only
039:008 **Say** "Enjoy thy disbelief for a little while:
039:009 **Say**: "Are those equal, those who
039:010 **Say**: "O ye my servants who believe! Fear your
039:011 **Say**: "Verily, I am commanded to serve Allah
039:013 **Say**: "I would, if I disobeyed my Lord,
039:014 **Say**: "It is Allah I serve, with my
039:015 **Say**: "Truly, those in loss are those who lose
039:038 His Mercy?" **Say**: "Sufficient is Allah for me!
039:038 they would be sure to **say**, "Allah." **Say**: "See
039:038 **Say**: "See ye then? The things
039:039 **Say**: "O my people! Do whatever ye can: I will
039:043 **Say**: "Even if they have no power whatever
039:044 **Say**: "To Allah belongs exclusively (the right
039:046 **Say**: "O Allah! Creator of the heavens and the
039:050 them **say**! But all that they did was of
039:053 **Say**: "O my Servants who have transgressed against
039:056 **say**: 'Ah! woe is me!-in that
039:057 "Or (lest) it should **say**: `If only
039:058 "Or (lest) it should **say** when it (actually) sees
039:064 **Say**: "Is it someone other than Allah that ye
039:071 And its Keepers will **say**, "Did not messengers
039:073 and its Keepers will **say**: "Peace be upon you!
039:074 They will **say**: "Praise be to Allah, Who has
040:011 They will **say**:" Our Lord! twice hast Thou made us
040:044 "Soon will ye remember what I **say** to you (now).
040:047 will **say** to those who had been arrogant, "We but
040:048 Those who had been arrogant will **say**: "We are
040:049 Those in the Fire will **say** to the Keepers of Hell:
040:050 They will **say**: "Did there not come to you
040:050 Clear Signs?" They will **say**: "Yes." They will
040:066 **Say**: "I have been forbidden to invoke those whom
041:005 They **say**: "Our hearts are under veils, (concealed)
041:006 **Say** thou: "I am but a man like you: it is
041:009 **Say**: Is it that ye Deny Him Who created the earth
041:013 But if they turn away, **say** thou: "I have warned
041:021 They will **say**: "Allah hath given us speech,-
041:021 They will **say** to their skins: "Why bear ye
041:026 The Unbelievers **say**: "Listen not to this Qur'an,
041:029 And the Unbelievers will **say**: "Our Lord!
041:030 In the case of those who **say**, "Our Lord
041:044 **Say**: "It is a guide and a healing to those
041:047 to Me?" They will **say**, "We do assure
041:050 has touched him, he is sure to **say**, "This is
041:052 **Say**: "See ye if the (Revelation) is (really)
042:015 vain desires; but **say**: "I believe in
042:023 **Say**: "No reward do I ask of you for this
042:024 What! Do they **say**, "He has forged
042:044 **say**: "Is there any way (to effect) a return?"
042:045 will **say**: "Those are indeed in loss who lose
043:013 of your Lord, and **say**, "Glory to Him Who has
043:020 ("Ah!") they **say**, "If it had been the will
043:022 Nay! they **say**: "We found Our fathers following
043:031 Also, they **say**: "Why is not this Qur'an sent down
043:058 And they **say**, " Are Our gods best, or He?"
043:077 thy Lord put and end to us!" He will **say**, "Nay,
043:081 **Say**: "If The Most Gracious had a son, I would
043:087 they will certainly **say**, Allah: how then
043:089 and **say** "Peace!" but soon shall they know!
044:012 (They will **say**:) "Our Lord! remove the

SAY (continued)

044:014	Yet they turn away from him and **say**: "Tutored (by
044:034	As to these (Quraish), they **say** forsooth:
044:036	if what ye **say** is true!"
045:024	And they **say**: "What is there but our life
045:025	but this: they **say**, "Bring (back) our forefathers,
045:025	our forefathers, if what ye **say** is true!"
045:026	**Say**: "It is Allah Who gives you life, then gives
045:032	ye used to **say**, 'We know not what is the Hour:
046:004	**Say**: "Do ye see what it is ye invoke beside Allah?
046:007	to them, the Unbelievers **say**, of the Truth
046:008	Or do they **say**, "He has forged it"? **Say**:
046:008	**Say**: "Had I forged it, then ye
046:009	**Say**: "I am not an innovation among the messengers,
046:010	**Say**: "See ye? If (this teaching) be from Allah,
046:011	themselves thereby, they will **say**, "This is
046:011	The Unbelievers **say** of those who believe:
046:013	Verily those who **say**, "Our Lord is Allah,"
046:034	the Truth?" They will **say**, "Yea, by
046:034	"Yea, by our Lord!" (He will **say**): "Then taste
047:016	from thee, they **say** to those who have received
047:020	Those who believe **say**, "Why is not
047:021	Were it to obey and **say** what is just, and when
048:011	They **say** with their tongues what is not
048:011	**Say**: "Who then has any power at all (to intervene)
048:011	will **say** to thee: "We were engaged in (looking
048:015	(this) beforehand": then they will **say**, "But ye
048:015	**Say**: "Not thus will ye follow us: Allah has
048:015	Those who lagged behind (will **say**), when ye
048:016	**Say** to the desert Arabs who lagged behind:
049:014	**Say**, "Ye have no faith; but ye
049:014	but ye (only) **say**, 'We have submitted our wills
049:014	The desert Arabs **say**, "We believe." **Say**, "Ye
049:016	**Say**: "What! Will ye tell Allah about your Religion?"
049:017	**Say**, "Count not your Islam as a favour upon me:
050:002	among themselves. So the Unbelievers **say**: "This is
050:023	And his companion will **say**: "Here is
050:027	His companion will **say**: "Our Lord!
050:028	He will **say**: "Dispute not with each other
050:030	It will **say**, "Are there any more (to come)?"
050:032	(A voice will **say**:) "This is what
050:039	they **say**, and celebrate the praises of they Lord,
050:045	We know best what they **say**; and thou
052:026	They will **say**: "Aforetime, We were not without
052:030	Or do they **say**:-" A Poet! we await for him
052:031	**Say** thou: "Await ye!-I too
052:033	Or do they **say**, "He fabricated the (Message)?"
052:044	they would (only) **say**: "Clouds gathered in heaps!"
053:003	Nor does he **say** (aught) of (his own) Desire.
054:002	and **say**, "This is (but) continuous magic."
054:008	this Day!" The Unbelievers will **say**.
054:044	Or do they **say**: "We acting together
056:047	And they used to **say**, "What! when we
056:049	**Say**: "Yea, those of old and those of later times,
057:013	**say** to the Believers: "Wait for us! Let us
058:008	and they **say** to themselves, "Why does not
059:010	And those who came after them **say**: "Our Lord!
059:011	**say** to their misbelieving brethren among the
061:002	O ye who believe! why **say** ye that which
061:003	of Allah that ye **say** that which ye do not.
062:006	**Say**: "O ye of Jewry! if ye think that ye are
062:008	**Say** "The Death from which ye flee will truly
062:011	**Say**: "That which Allah has is better than any

SAY (continued)

063:001	they **say**, "We bear witness that thou art
063:007	They are the ones who **say**, "Spend nothing
063:008	They **say**, "If we return to Madinah, surely the
063:010	and he should **say**, "O my Lord! Why didst
064:007	**Say**: "Yea, by my Lord, ye shall
066:008	while they **say**, "Our Lord! perfect our light
067:009	They will **say**: "Yes indeed: a Warner
067:010	They will further **say**: "Had we but
067:023	**Say**: "It is He Who has created you, and made
067:024	**Say**: "It is He Who has multiplied you through
067:026	**Say**: "As to the knowledge of the time, it is
067:028	**Say**: "See ye?-if Allah were to destroy me,
067:029	**Say**: "He is The Most Gracious: we have
067:030	**Say**: "See ye?-if your stream be some morning lost
068:028	(than the rest): "Did I not **say** to you,
068:051	the Message; and they **say**: "Surely he
069:019	in his right hand will **say**: "Ah here!
069:025	in his left hand, will **say**: "Ah! would
069:030	(The stern command will **say**): "Seize ye him,
072:001	**Say**: It has been revealed to me that a company
072:005	or Jinn should **say** aught that is untrue
072:020	**Say**: "I do no more than invoke my Lord, and I
072:021	**Say**: "It is not in my power to cause you harm,
072:022	**Say**: "No one can deliver me from Allah (if I
072:025	**Say**: "I know not whether the (Punishment) which ye
073:010	And have patience with what they **say**, and leave
074:031	and the Unbelievers may **say**, "What doth
074:043	They will **say**: "We were not of those who prayed;
075:010	That Day will Man **say** "Where is the refuge?"
078:038	and he will **say** what is right.
078:040	will **say**, "Woe unto me! Would that
079:010	They **say** (now): "What! shall we indeed be returned
079:012	They **say**: "It would, in that case, be a
079:018	"And **say** to him, `Wouldst thou that thou shouldst
083:032	they would **say**, "Behold!
089:024	He will **say**: "Ah! would that I had sent forth
090:006	He may **say** (boastfully): "Wealth have I
109:001	**Say**: O ye that reject Faith!
112:001	**Say**: He is Allah, the One;
113:001	**Say**: I seek refuge with the Lord of the Dawn,
114:001	**Say**: I seek refuge with the Lord

SAYEST

011:091	thou **sayest** we do not understand! In fact
017:092	as thou **sayest** (will happen), against us;

SAYING

002:057	**saying**: "Eat of the good things
002:063	(**saying**): "Hold firmly to what We have
002:093	(**saying**): "Hold firmly to what We given you,
002:102	taught anyone (such things without **saying**:
003:038	**saying**: "O my Lord! Grant unto me
003:081	**saying**: "I give you a Book and Wisdom:
003:167	**saying** with their lips what was not in their hearts.
003:191	(with the **saying**): "Our Lord not for naught
004:150	**saying**: "We believe in some but reject others":
005:052	**saying**: "We do fear lest a change
006:093	(**saying**), "Yield up your souls. This day
007:033	and **saying** things about Allah of which
007:048	**saying**: "Of what profit to you were your hoards
007:077	**saying**: "O Salih! bring about thy threats, if
007:079	**saying**: "O my people! I indeed convey to you
007:093	**saying**: "O my people! I did indeed convey to
007:121	**Saying**: "We believe in the Lord of the Worlds.

SAYING (continued)

007:160 (**saying**): "Eat of the good things We have
007:169 **saying** (for excuse): "(Everything) will
007:172 concerning themselves, (**saying**): "Am I
007:189 (**saying**): "If Thou givest us a goodly child, we
008:050 and their backs (**saying**): "Taste the
009:030 Son of Allah. That is a **saying** from their mouth;
009:127 (**saying**), "Doth anyone see you?" then they turn away:
010:022 **saying**, "If Thou dost deliver us from this,
013:005 want of faith), strange is their **saying**: "When
016:002 (**saying**): "Warn (Man) that there is no god but I:
016:032 **saying** (to them), "Peace be on you; enter ye
017:040 Truly ye utter a most dreadful **saying**!
018:005 from their mouths as a **saying**. What they
020:081 (**Saying**): "Eat of the good things We have
021:003 private counsels, (**saying**), "Is this (one)
022:026 of the (Sacred) House, (**saying**): "Associate not
023:032 from among themselves, (**saying**), "Worship Allah!
026:047 **Saying**: "We believe in the Lord of the Worlds.
026:054 (**Saying**): "These (Israelites) are but a small band,
027:045 their brother Salih, **saying**, "Serve Allah":
029:002 left alone on **saying**, "We believe", and that
032:012 (**saying**) "Our Lord! We have seen
033:013 ask for leave of the Prophet, **saying**, "Truly our
036:020 a man, **saying**, "O my People! obey the messengers:
038:006 away (impatiently), (**saying**), "Walk ye away,
043:051 **saying**: "O my people! Does not the dominion
044:018 **Saying**: "Restore to me the servants of Allah: I am
052:034 Let them then produce a **saying** like unto it,-
056:026 Only the **saying**, "Peace! Peace."
056:066 (**Saying**), "We are indeed left with debts
068:023 low tones, (**saying**)-
071:010 "**Saying**, `Ask forgiveness from your Lord, for He
076:009 (**Saying**), "We feed you for the sake of Allah alone:
079:024 **Saying**, "I am your Lord, Most High."

SAYINGS

069:044 any **sayings** in Our name,

SAYS

002:068 He said: "He **says**: The heifer should be
002:069 He said: "He **says**, a fawn-coloured heifer,
002:071 He said: "He **says**, a heifer not trained
004:018 and he **says**, "Now have I repented indeed";
009:049 Among them is (many) a man who **says**: "Grant me
019:035 He only **says** to it, "Be," and it is.
019:066 Man **says**: "What! when I am dead, shall I
019:077 man who rejects Our Signs, yet **says**: "I shall
019:079 Nay! We shall record what he **says**, and We
023:024 such a thing (as he **says**), among our
023:099 he **says**: "O my Lord! send me back to (life),-
023:100 it is but a word he **says**."-Before them
026:025 "Do ye not listen (to what he **says**)?"
036:078 and) Creation: he **says**, "Who can
038:023 and I have (but) one: ye he **says**, 'Commit her
039:049 he **says**, "This has been given to me because of
040:028 he **says**, 'My Lord is Allah'?-when he
040:060 And your Lord **says**: "Call on Me; I will
040:068 He **says** to it, "Be," and it is.
041:033 works righteousness, and **says**, "I am of
043:038 he **says** (to his evil-companion): 'Would that
046:015 forty years, He **says**, "O my Lord! grant me
046:017 is true." But he **says**, "This is
046:017 But (there is one) who **says** to his parents,
059:016 Satan **says**, "I am free of thee: I do

SAYS (continued)

059:016 when he **says** to man, "Disbelieve": but when
083:013 he **says**, "Tales of the Ancients!"

SCALD

018:029 **scald** their faces, how dreadful the drink!

SCALDING

044:046 Like the boiling of **scalding** water.

SCALE

005:089 on a **scale** of the average for the food
007:008 those whose **scale** (of good) will be
007:009 Those whose **scale** will be light, will find
018:097 to **scale** it or to dig through it.

SCALES

021:047 We shall set up **scales** of justice for the
026:182 And weigh with **scales** true and upright.

SCALP

002:196 in his **scalp**, (necessitating shaving),

SCANDAL

024:019 **scandal** circulate among the Believers, will have

SCANDAL-MONGER

104:001 Woe to every (kind of) **scandal-monger** and backbiter,

SCANTY

007:058 springs up nothing but that which is **scanty**, thus
012:088 we have (now) brought but **scanty** capital: so pay

SCARCE

024:035 though fire **scarce** touched it: Light upon

SCARCELY

002:071 and they **scarcely** did it.
018:093 who **scarcely** understood a word.
043:052 and can **scarcely** express himself clearly?

SCARE

017:076 Their purpose was to **scare** thee off the land,

SCATTER

006:153 they will **scatter** you about from His (great) path:
018:045 which the winds do **scatter**: it is (only)
020:097 a blazing fire and **scatter** it broadcast in the sea!
020:105 and **scatter** them as dust;
051:001 By the (Winds) that **scatter** broadcast;
077:003 And **scatter** (things) far and wide;

SCATTERED

004:001 **scattered** (like seeds) countless men and women;
025:023 make such deeds as floating dust **scattered** about.
030:020 behold, ye are men **scattered** (far and wide)!
031:010 with you; and He **scattered** through it beast of
034:007 all **scattered** to pieces in disintegration, that ye
034:019 all in **scattered** fragments. Verily in this
042:029 has **scattered** through them: and He
045:004 are **scattered** (through the earth), are Signs
054:007 (torpid) like locusts **scattered** abroad,
056:006 Becoming dust **scattered** abroad,
076:019 thou wouldst think them **scattered** Pearls.
077:010 When the mountains are **scattered** (to the winds)
082:002 When the Stars are **scattered**;
100:009 is in the graves is **Scattered** abroad
101:004 will be like moths **Scattered** about,

SCATTERS

002:164 kinds that He **scatters** through the earth;
042:028 all hope, and **scatters** His Mercy (far and wide).

SCENT

012:094 **scent** the presence of Joseph: nay, think

scheme 695 seal

SCHEME
007:183 for My **scheme** is strong (and unfailing).
007:195 **scheme** (your worst) against me, and give
011:055 So **scheme** (your worst) against me, all of you,
086:015 As for them, they are but plotting a **scheme**,
086:016 And I am planning a **scheme**,

SCHISM
002:137 it is they who are in **schism**;
002:176 the Book are in a **schism** far (from the purpose).
022:053 in a **schism** far (from the Truth):
041:052 who is in **schism** far (from any purpose)?"

SCHISMS
010:093 as to the **schisms** amongst them, on the Day
010:093 that they fell into **schisms**. Verily Allah
045:017 into **schisms**, though insolent envy among
098:004 make **schisms**, until after there came to them

SCOFF
002:212 and they **scoff** at those who believe.
015:095 unto thee against those who **scoff**.-
040:083 they were wont to **scoff** hemmed them in.

SCOFFED
016:034 at which they had **scoffed** hemmed them in.

SCOFFERS
006:010 but the **scoffers** were hemmed in by the thing
021:041 before thee; but their **scoffers** were hemmed in

SCORCHING
003:181 "Taste ye the Chastisement of the **scorching** Fire!
015:027 from the fire of a **scorching** wind.
052:027 the Chastisement of the **Scorching** Wind.

SCORN
054:014 had been rejected (with **scorn**)!

SCORNFULLY
006:093 and **scornfully** to reject of His Signs!"

SCOURGE
089:013 a **scourge** of diverse chastisement:

SCOWLED
074:022 Then he frowned and he **scowled**;

SCRATCHED
005:031 who **scratched** the ground, to show him how

SCREEN
019:017 She placed a **screen** (to **screen** herself) from them:
033:017 Say: "Who is it that can **screen** you from Allah
033:053 ask them from before a **screen**: that makes
041:005 is a **screen**: so do thou (what thou wilt); for us,
058:016 a **screen** (for their misdeeds): thus they
063:002 a **screen** (for their misdeeds): thus they

SCRIBE
002:282 Let a **scribe** write down faithfully
002:282 let not the **scribe** refuse to write:
002:282 and let neither **scribe** nor witness suffer harm.
002:283 and cannot find a **scribe**,

SCRIBES
080:015 (Written) by the hands of **scribes**-

SCRIPTURE
002:044 and yet ye study the **Scripture**?
002:053 And remember We gave Moses the **Scripture**
002:129 and instruct them in **Scripture** and Wisdom,
002:151 and instructing you in **Scripture** and Wisdom,
003:164 and instructing them in **Scripture** and Wisdom,
004:136 and the **scripture** which He sent
004:136 and the **scripture** which He hath sent

SCRIPTURE (continued)
005:048 To thee We sent the **Scripture** in truth, confirming
005:048 confirming the **scripture** that came before it, and
005:057 those who received the **Scripture** before you, or
015:090 divided (**Scripture** into arbitrary parts),-
034:031 neither believe in this **scripture** nor in (any)

SCRIPTURES
002:062 and those who follow the Jewish (**Scriptures**),
003:184 who came with Clear Signs, and the **Scriptures**.
005:069 Those who follow the Jewish (**Scriptures**), and
007:157 whom they find mentioned in their own (**Scriptures**),-
016:044 and **Scriptures** and We have sent down unto thee
022:017 those who follow the Jewish (**scriptures**), and the
035:025 Clear Signs, **Scriptures** and the illuminating
046:010 (with earlier **scriptures**), and has believed while
098:002 rehearsing **scriptures** kept pure and holy:

SCROLL
017:013 We shall bring out for him a **scroll**, which he
021:104 like a **scroll** rolled up for books (completed);-

SCROLLS
074:052 to be given **scrolls** (of revelation) spread out!
081:010 When the **Scrolls** are laid open;

SCUM
013:017 there is a **scum** likewise. Thus doth
013:017 For the **scum** disappears like froth cast out;

SCUTTLED
018:071 he **scuttled** it. Said Moses: "Hast thou scuttled
018:071 "Hast thou **scuttled** it in order to drown

SEA
002:050 And remember We divided the **sea** for you
006:059 on the earth and in the **sea**. Not a
006:063 the dark recesses of land and **sea**, when ye call
006:097 through the dark spaces of land and **sea**: We
007:136 We drowned them in the **sea**, because they
007:138 (with safety) across the **sea**. They came
007:163 the town standing close by the **sea**. Behold!
010:022 traverse through land and **sea**; till when ye
010:090 across the **sea**: Pharaoh and his hosts followed
014:032 through the **sea** by His Command; and the
016:014 It is He Who has made the **sea** subject, that ye
017:066 go smoothly for you through the **sea**, in order
017:067 When distress seizes you at **sea**, those that
017:069 to **sea** and send against you a heavy gale
017:070 with transport on land and **sea**; given them
018:061 the **sea** (straight) as in a tunnel.
018:063 the **sea** in a marvelous way!"
020:077 through the **sea**, without fear of being overtaken
020:097 a blazing fire and scatter it broadcast in the **sea**!
022:065 sail through the **sea** by His command? He withholds
026:063 "Strike the **sea** with thy rod." So it
027:063 the depths of darkness on land and **sea**, and Who
028:040 and We flung them into the **sea**: now behold
030:041 and **sea** because of (the meed) that the hands
044:024 "And leave the **sea** as a furrow (divided): for they
045:012 It is Allah Who has subjected the **sea** to you,
051:040 and threw them into the **sea**: and his

SEAL
002:007 Allah hath set a **seal** on their hearts
004:155 nay, Allah hath set the **seal** on their hearts
007:100 and **seal** up their hearts so that they
007:101 Thus doth Allah **seal** up the heart
010:074 Thus do We **seal** the hearts of the transgressors.

SEAL (continued)

030:059   Thus does Allah **seal** up the hearts of those
033:040   of Allah, and the **Seal** of the Prophets: and Allah
036:065   That Day shall We set a **seal** on their mouths.
040:035   **seal** up every heart-of arrogant tyrinical."
042:024   He could **seal** up thy heart. And Allah
063:003   so a **seal** was set on their hearts: therefore
083:026   The **seal** thereof will be Musk: and for this

SEALED

006:046   and **sealed** up your hearts, who-a god
009:087   their hearts are **sealed** and so they understand not.
009:093   Allah hath **sealed** their hearts: so they
016:108   and eyes Allah has **sealed** up and they
045:023   left him astray, and **sealed** his hearing and his
047:016   Allah has **sealed**, and who follow their own lusts.
083:025   Their thirst will be slaked with Pure Wine **sealed**;

SEARCH

007:187   wert eager in **search** thereof: Say: "The
012:076   So he began (the **search**) with their baggage,

SEARCHING

003:007   seeking discord, and **searching** for interpretation,

SEAS

018:060   the junction of the two **seas** or (until)
027:061   the two **seas** (can there be another) god besides
035:012   Nor are the two **seas** alike,-the one
055:019   He has let free the two **Seas** meeting together:
055:024   smoothly through the **seas**, lofty as mountains:

SEASON

002:158   the House in the **Season** or at other times,
006:141   eat of their fruit in their **season**, but render
056:033   Whose **season** is not limited, nor (supply)

SEAT

055:046   **Seat** of) their Lord, there will be two Gardens-

SEATED

043:013   and when so **seated**, ye may

SECOND

009:040   him out: being the **second** of the two they
017:007   so when the **second** of the warnings came to pass,
017:069   not send you back a **second** time to sea and send
017:104   but when the **second** of the warnings came to pass,
039:068   (to exempt). Then will a **second** one be sounded,
053:013   For indeed he saw him at a **second** descent,
053:047   a **Second** Creation (raising of the Dead);
067:004   Again turn thy vision a **second** time: (thy) vision

SECRECY

004:114   between people (**secrecy** is permissible): to him

SECRET

002:235   but do not make a **secret** contract with them
002:274   in **secret** and in public,
004:114   In most of their **secret** talks there is no good:
006:063   in humility and in **secret**: 'If He only
006:120   Eschew all sin, open or **secret**: those who
006:151   whether open or **secret**; take not life, which
007:033   indecent deeds, whether open or **secret**; sins
009:078   their **secret** (thoughts) and their **secret** counsels,
009:078   **secret** counsels, And that Allah knoweth well all
019:003   Behold! he cried to his Lord in **secret**.
019:052   for converse in **secret**.
020:007   knoweth what is **secret** and what is yet more hidden.
020:062   over their affair, but they kept their talk **secret**.
021:049   in their most **secret** thoughts, and who
025:006   by Him Who knows the **secret** (that is) in the

SECRET (continued)

027:049   that we shall make a **secret** night attack on him
058:007   a **secret** consultation between three, but He is
058:008   (to do)? And they hold **secret** counsels among
058:008   forbidden **secret** counsels yet revert to that
058:009   **secret** counsel, do it not for iniquity and
058:010   **Secret** counsels are only (inspired) by Satan,
059:022   both **secret** and open; He Most Gracious
060:001   showing friendship unto them in **secret**: for I
062:008   of things **secret** and open: and He
068:023   So they departed, conversing in **secret** low tones,
086:009   The Day that (all) things **secret** will be tested,

SECRETE

084:023   of what they **secrete** (in their breasts).

SECRETLY

002:187   used to do **secretly** among yourselves:
005:052   which they **secretly** harboured in their hearts.
013:022   **secretly** and openly; and turn off Evil with good:
014:031   **secretly** and openly, before the coming of a Day
035:029   **secretly** and openly, hope for a Commerce
071:009   in public and **secretly** in private,

SECRETS

002:033   that I know the **secrets** of the heaven and earth,
003:119   Allah knoweth well all the **secrets** of the heart."
003:154   for Allah knoweth well the **secrets** of your hearts.
003:179   to you the **secrets** of the Unseen,
005:007   for Allah knoweth well the **secrets** of your hearts.
008:043   well the (**secrets**) of (all) hearts.
011:005   knoweth well the (inmost **secrets**) of the hearts.
011:123   unseen (**secrets**) of the heavens and the earth,
012:077   revealing not the **secrets** to them he (simply)
018:026   (the knowledge of) the **secrets** of the heavens
042:024   For He knows well the **secrets** of all hearts.
043:080   their **secrets** and their private counsels? Indeed
047:026   their (inner) **secrets**.
052:038   and) listen (to its **secrets**)? Then let
057:006   of the **secrets** of (all) hearts.
064:004   yes, Allah knows well the (**secrets**) of (all) hearts.
067:013   (full) knowledge, of the **secrets** of (all) hearts.
072:008   (**secrets** of) heaven; but we found it filled with
072:026   acquainted with His **Secrets**.-

SECT

019:069   from every **sect** all those who were worst in

SECTION

003:069   It is the wish of a **section** of the People
003:072   A **section** of the People of the Book say: "Believe
003:078   a **section** who distort the Book with their tongues;
004:077   behold! a **section** of them feared men as, or even
004:081   a **section** of them meditate all night on things
007:159   there is a **section** who guide and do justice

SECTIONS

007:168   into **sections** on this earth. There are
028:004   into **sections**, depressing a group among them:

SECTS

006:159   and break up into **sects**, thou hast
011:017   the **Sects** that reject it,-the Fire
015:010   thee amongst the **sects** of old:
019:037   But the **sects** differ among themselves: and woe
023:053   (of unity), between them, into **sects**: each party
030:032   and become (mere) **Sects**,-each party
043:065   But **sects** from among themselves fell into

SECURE

004:091 secure from you as well as that of their people:
007:097 feel secure against the coming of Our wrath
007:098 Or else did they feel secure against its
007:099 can feel secure from the Plan of Allah, except
007:099 Did they then fell secure against Allah's
009:006 be secure, that is because they are men
012:107 Do they then feel secure from the coming against
015:082 (their) edifices, (feeling themselves) secure.
016:045 (plots) feel secure that Allah will not cause
017:068 Do ye then feel secure that He will not cause
017:069 Or do ye feel secure that He will not send
025:010 (secure to dwell in).
026:146 "Will ye be left secure, in (the
027:089 be secure from terror that Day.
028:031 and fear not: for thou art of those who are secure.
028:057 for them a secure Sanctuary, to which
029:067 We have made a Sanctuary secure, and that
034:018 secure, by night and by day."
034:037 their deeds, while secure they (reside) in the
048:027 if Allah wills, with minds secure, heads shaved,
067:016 Do ye feel secure that He Who is in heaven
067:017 Or do ye feel secure that He Who is in
070:028 a thing to feel secure from:-

SECURELY

017:104 Children of Israel, "Dwell securely in the land

SECURITY

002:239 but when ye are in security,
002:248 of security from your Lord,
003:097 whoever enters it attains security;
006:081 hath more right to security? (Tell me)
006:082 that are (truly) in security, for they
009:103 of security for them: and Allah is One
014:035 and security: and preserve me and my sons
015:046 "Enter ye here in Peace and Security."
016:112 a city enjoying security and quiet, abundantly
023:050 and security and furnished with springs.
024:055 to one of security and peace: 'They will
044:051 in a position of Security,
044:055 of fruit in peace and security;
050:034 "Enter ye therein in Peace and Security; this Day
095:003 And this City of Security,-
106:004 security against fear (of danger).

SEDITION

009:047 midst and sowing sedition among you, and there
009:048 Indeed they had plotted sedition before, and upset
033:014 to sedition. They would certainly have brought
033:060 and those who stir up sedition in the City,

SEDUCE

007:027 Let not Satan seduce you, in the same
012:023 sought to seduce him and she fastened the doors,
012:026 seduce me-from my (true) self." And one
012:030 the (great) 'Aziz is seeking to seduce her slave
012:032 I did seek to seduce him from his
012:051 it was I who sought to seduce him he is indeed
012:051 when ye did seek to seduce Joseph"? The ladies

SEDUCED

082:006 O man! what has seduced thee from thy Lord

SEDUCERS

026:099 "'And our seducers were only those who were

SEDUCTIVE

017:064 (seductive) voice; make assaults on them with

SEE

002:017 so they could not see.
002:055 in thee until we see Allah manifestly,"
002:078 but (see therein their own) desires,
002:144 We see the turning of thy face
002:165 Behold, they would see the Punishment:
002:165 If only the unrighteous could see,
002:166 they would see the Chastisement
003:013 In this is a lesson for such as have eyes to see."
003:037 Every time that he entered her chamber to see her,
003:137 travel through the earth, and see what was the end
005:062 Many of them dost thou see, racing each
005:075 See how Allah doth makes His Signs
005:075 yet see in what ways they are deluded
005:083 thou wilt see their eyes overflowing with tears,
006:006 See they not how many of those before them
006:011 Say: "Travel through the earth and see what was
006:027 If thou couldst but see when they
006:030 If thou couldst but see when they
006:046 See how We explain the Signs by various
006:057 What ye would see hastened is not in my power.
006:058 see hastened were in my power, the matter
006:065 See how We explain the Signs in diverse ways; that
006:074 For I see thee and thy people in manifest error."
006:093 If thou couldst but see how the wicked
006:094 We see not with you your intercessors whom ye
006:104 if any will see, it will be
006:158 Are they waiting to see if the
007:027 from a position where ye cannot see them: We
007:027 for he and his tribe see you from a position
007:039 "See then! no advantage have ye over us; so taste
007:060 "Ah! we see thee evident error."
007:066 "Ah! we see thou art in folly!" and "We think
007:084 then see what was the end of those who
007:086 And see what was the end of those who did mischief.
007:103 so see what was the end of those
007:107 plain (for all to see)!
007:129 that so He may see how ye act."
007:143 then shalt thou see Me." When his Lord
007:143 canst thou see Me (direct); but look
007:146 even if they see all the Signs, they will not
007:146 and if they see the way of right conduct, they
007:146 but if they see the way of error, that is
007:148 having lowing sound did they not see that it could
007:179 eyes wherewith they see not, and ears
007:185 (Do they not see) that it may well be
007:185 Do they see nothing in the kingdom of the
007:195 Or eyes to see with? Or ears
007:198 looking at thee, but they see not.
007:198 they hear not. Thou wilt see them looking at
007:201 they see (aright)!
008:006 being driven to death while they see it.
008:039 verily Allah doth see all that they do.
008:048 lo! I see what ye see not; lo! I
008:050 If thou couldst see, when the
009:126 See they not that they are tried
009:127 (saying), "Doth anyone see you?" then they turn away:
010:014 after them, to see how ye would behave!
010:030 There will every soul see (the fruits of)
010:039 but see what was the end of those who did wrong!
010:043 the blind,-even though they will not see?
010:050 Say: "Do ye see-if His punishment should come
010:054 when they see the Chastisement: but the

SEE (continued)

010:059   Say: "**See** ye what things Allah hath sent down

010:073   Then **see** what was the end of those who

010:088   until they **see** the grievous Chastisement."

010:097   until they **see** (for themselves)

011:020   They could not hear, nor could they **see**!

011:024   and those who can **see** and hear well. Are they

011:027   apparently nor do we **see** in you (all) any

011:027   among his people said: "We **see** (in) thee

011:027   nor do we **see** that any follow thee but the

011:028   He said: "O my people! **see** ye if (it be that)

011:029   and ye I **see** are the ignorant ones!

011:063   He said: "O my people! Do ye **see**?-If I have

011:084   I **see** you in prosperity, but I fear for you

011:088   He said: "O my people! **see** ye whether I have

011:091   In fact among us we **see** that thou hast no strength!

012:004   "O my father! I did **see** eleven stars and the

012:030   we **see** she is evidently going astray."

012:036   Said one of them: "I **see** myself (in a dream)

012:036   Said the other: "I **see** myself (in a dream)

012:036   for we **see** thou art one that doth good (to all)."

012:043   The king (of Egypt) said: "I do **see** (in a vision)

012:059   (but a different mother): **see** you not that I pay

012:078   for we **see** that thou art (gracious) in doing good."

012:093   he will come to **see** (clearly). Then come

012:109   through the earth, and **see** what was the end of

013:002   without any pillars that ye can **see**; then He

013:016   who **see**? Or the depths of darkness equal with

013:041   **See** they not that We gradually reduce the land

014:049   And thou wilt **see** the Sinners that day

015:018   a fiery comet, bright (to **see**).

015:079   They were both on an open highway, plain to **see**.

016:036   So travel through the earth, and **see** what was

016:085   **see** the Chastisement then will it in no way

016:086   will **see** their "partners," they will

017:013   which he will **see** spread open.

017:017   to note and **see** the sins of His servants.

017:021   **See** how We have bestowed more on some than on

017:048   **See** what similes thy strike for thee: but they

017:099   **See** they not that Allah, Who created

018:039   but from Allah!' If thou dost **see** me less than

018:047   and thou wilt **see** the earth as a level stretch,

018:049   and thou wilt **see** the sinful in great terror

018:053   And the Sinful shall **see** the Fire and apprehend

018:100   for Unbelievers to **see**, all spread out,-

019:026   And if thou dost **see** any man, say, 'I have

019:038   How plainly will they **see** and hear, the Day

019:075   **see** the warning of Allah (being fulfilled)-

020:046   I hear and **see** (everything).

020:089   Could they not **see** that it could not return

020:107   thou **see** in their place."

021:030   Do not the Unbelievers **see** that the heavens

021:036   When the Unbelievers **see** thee, they treat

021:044   **see** they not that We gradually reduce the land

022:002   The Day ye shall **see** it, every mother

022:002   thou shalt **see** mankind as in a drunken riot,

022:015   (himself) off: then let him **see** whether his plan

024:019   Those who love (to **see**) scandal circulate

024:040   he can hardly **see** it! For any

024:043   Then wilt thou **see** rain issue forth

025:009   **See** what kinds of companions they make for thee!

025:021   to us, or (why) do we not **see** Our Lord?"

025:022   The Day they **see** the angels,-no joy

025:040   did they not then **see** it (with their own eyes)?

025:041   When they **see** thee, they treat

025:042   when they **see** the Chastisement, who it

026:032   plain (for all to **see**)!

026:075   He said: "Do ye then **see** whom ye

026:201   they **see** the grievous Chastisement

027:014   so **see** what was the end of those who

027:020   and he said: "Why is it I **see** not the Hoopoe?

027:027   (Solomon) said: "Soon shall we **see** whether thou

027:028   and (wait to) **see** what answer they return"...

027:035   and (wait) to **see** with what (answer)

027:041   let us **see** whether she is guided (to the truth)

027:051   Then **see** what was the end of their plot!-

027:054   though ye **see** (its iniquity)?

027:069   Say: "Go ye through the earth and **see** what has

027:086   **See** they not that We have made the Night

028:064   and they will **see** the Chastisement (before them);

028:071   Say: **See** ye? If Allah were to make the night

028:072   Say: **see** ye? If Allah were to make the Day

028:072   ye can rest? Will ye not then **see**?

029:019   **See** they not how Allah originates creation,

029:020   **see** how Allah did originate creation; so will

029:067   Do they not then **see** that We have made

030:009   and **see** what was the End of those before them?

030:037   **See** they not that Allah enlarges the provision

030:042   and **see** what was the End of those before (you):

030:051   they **see** (their tilth) turn yellow,-behold, they

031:010   any pillars that ye can **see**; He set

031:020   Do ye not **see** that Allah has subjected to your

032:012   If only thou couldst **see** when the guilty ones

032:027   And do they not **see** that We do drive Rain

033:019   thou wilt **see** them looking to thee, their eyes

034:006   **see** that the (Revelation) sent down to thee

034:009   **See** they not what is before them and behind

034:011   for be sure I **see** (clearly) all that ye do."

034:031   Couldst thou but **see** when the wrong-doers

034:033   When they **see** the Chastisement: We shall

034:051   If thou couldst but **see** when they will quake

035:044   and **see** what was the End of those before them,-

036:009   so that they cannot **see**.

036:031   **See** they not how many generations before them

036:071   **See** they not that it is We Who have created

036:077   Doth not man **see** that it is We Who created

037:014   And, when they **see** a Sign, turn it to mockery,

037:019   they will begin to **see**!

037:073   Then **see** what was the end of those

037:102   in sacrifice: now **see** what is thy view!"

037:175   and they soon shall **see** (how thou farest)!

037:179   and they soon shall **see** (how thou farest)!

038:062   that we **see** not men who we used to number

039:021   then it withers; thou wilt **see** it grow yellow;

039:038   Say: "**See** ye then? The things

039:060   **see** those who told lies against Allah;-their faces

039:075   And thou wilt **see** the angels surrounding the

040:021   and **see** what was the End of those before them?

040:029   I **see** (myself); nor do I guide you but to

040:058   and those who (clearly) **see**: nor are

040:082   and **see** what was the end of those before them?

041:015   in strength?" What! did they not **see** that Allah,

041:052   Say: "**See** ye if the (Revelation) is (really)

042:022   Thou wilt **see** the wrong-doers in fear on account

042:044   And thou wilt **see** the wrong-doers, when in

SEE (continued)

042:045 And thou wilt **see** them brought forward to the
043:025 now **see** what was the end of those who
043:051 underneath my (palace)? What! **see** ye not then?
045:028 And thou wilt **see** every nation bowing the knee:
046:004 Say: "Do ye **see** what it is ye invoke beside Allah?
046:010 Say: "**See** ye? If (this teaching) be from Allah,
046:023 but I **see** that ye are a people in ignorance!"...
046:033 **See** they not that Allah, Who created
046:035 they **see** the (Punishment) promised them, (it will
047:010 and **see** what was the End of those before them
047:020 thou wilt **see** those in whose hearts is a disease
048:029 Thou wilt **see** them bow and prostrate themselves
051:021 As also in your own selves: will ye not then **see**?
052:015 "Is this then a magic, or is it ye that do not **see**?
052:044 Were they to **see** a piece of the sky falling
053:018 For truly did he **see**, of the Signs
053:035 so that he can **see**?
054:002 But if they **see** a Sign, they turn away, and say,
056:058 Do ye then **see**? The (human Seed) that ye emit,-
056:063 **See** ye the seed that ye sow in the ground?
056:068 **See** ye the water which ye drink?
056:071 **See** ye the Fire which ye kindle?
056:085 But We are nearer to him than ye, and yet **see** not,-
057:012 The Day shalt thou **see** the believing men and the
057:020 thou wilt **see** it grow yellow; then it becomes
059:002 O ye with eyes (to **see**)!
062:011 But when they **see** some bargain or some pastime,
063:005 **see** them turning away their faces in arrogance.
067:003 wilt thou **see** in the Creation of The Most Gracious.
067:027 At length, when they **see** it close at hand,
067:028 Say: "**See** ye?-if Allah were to destroy me,
067:030 Say: "**See** ye?-if your stream be some morning lost
068:005 Soon wilt thou **see** and they will **see**,
069:007 so that thou couldst **see** the (whole) people
069:038 So I do call to witness what ye **see**
069:039 And what ye **see** not,
070:006 They **see** the (Day) indeed as a far-off (event):
070:007 But We **see** it (quite) near.
071:015 "**See** ye not how Allah has created the seven
072:024 At length, when they **see** (with their own eyes)
076:013 on raised couches, they will **see** there neither
076:020 **see** a Bliss and a Realm Magnificent.
078:040 man will **see** (the Deeds) which his hands have sent
079:046 The Day they **see** it, (it will be)
096:014 Knoweth he not that Allah doth **see**?
099:007 an atom's weight of good, **see** it!
099:008 an atom's weight of evil, shall **see** it.
102:006 Ye shall certainly **see** Hell-fire!
102:007 Again, ye shall **see** it with certainty of sight!
110:002 And thou dost **see** the People enter Allah's

SEED

021:047 the weight of a mustard **seed**, We will
048:029 like a **seed** which sends forth its blade,
056:058 Do ye then see? The (human **Seed**) that ye emit,-
056:063 See ye the **seed** that ye sow in the ground?

SEED-GRAIN

006:095 It is Allah Who causeth the **seed-grain** and the

SEEDS

004:001 scattered (like **seeds**) countless men and women;
052:021 and whose **seeds** follow them in Faith,-to them

SEEING

002:020 their faculty of hearing and **seeing**;
002:028 **Seeing** that ye were without life,
002:075 **Seeing** that a party of them heard
002:139 **seeing** that He is our Lord and your Lord;
002:246 **seeing** that we were turned out of our homes
003:040 **seeing** I am very old, and my wife is barren?"
005:084 which has come to us, **seeing** that we long for
006:050 Say: "Can the blind be held equal to the **seeing**?"
009:008 **seeing** that if they get an advantage over you,
011:072 a child, **seeing** I am an old woman, and my husband
012:011 **seeing** we are indeed his sincere well-wishers?
019:020 **seeing** that no man has touched me, and I am
020:035 For Thou art ever **seeing**."
034:053 **Seeing** that they did reject faith (entirely)
035:019 The blind and the **seeing** are not alike;
040:010 to yourselves, **seeing** that ye were called to the
040:066 **seeing** that the Clear Signs have come to me
044:013 **Seeing** that a Messenger explaining things clearly
046:011 and **seeing** that they guide not themselves thereby,
046:026 (faculties of) hearing, **seeing**, heart and
067:023 of hearing, **seeing**, and understanding:
068:043 **seeing** that they had been summoned aforetime
071:014 "**Seeing** that it is He that has created you

SEEK

001:005 Thee do we worship, and Thine aid we **seek**.
002:045 Nay, **seek** (Allah's) help with
002:081 Nay, those who **seek** gain in Evil,
002:094 then **seek** ye for death,
002:095 But they will never **seek** for death,
002:153 O ye who believe! **seek** help with
002:176 **seek** causes of dispute in the Book
002:187 and **seek** what Allah hath ordained for you,
002:198 It is no crime in you if ye **seek** of the bounty
002:285 (We **seek**) Thy forgiveness, our Lord,
003:083 Do they **seek** for other than the Religion of Allah?
004:024 provided ye **seek** (them in marriage) with
004:034 **seek** not against them means (of annoyance):
004:035 if they **seek** to set things aright, Allah
004:106 But **seek** the forgiveness of Allah; for Allah
004:108 They **seek** to hide themselves from the people but
004:139 is it honor they **seek** among them?
004:142 The Hypocrites-they **seek** to deceive Allah but it
005:016 Wherewith Allah guideth all who **seek** His good
005:035 **seek** the means of approach unto Him, and strive
005:050 Do they then **seek** after a judgment of
005:074 and **seek** His forgiveness?
006:035 yet if thou wert able to **seek** a tunnel
006:114 Say: "Shall I **seek** for judge other than Allah?-
006:164 Say: "Shall I **seek** for (my) Lord
007:086 and **seek** to make it crooked; but
007:140 He said: "Shall I **seek** for you a god
007:200 thy (mind), **seek** refuge with Allah; for He
008:072 but if they **seek** your aid in religion, it is
010:053 They **seek** to be informed by thee: "Is that true?"
011:003 "(And to preach thus), `**Seek** ye the forgiveness
011:047 Noah said: "O my Lord! I do **seek** refuge with Thee,
011:076 O Abraham! **seek** not this. The decree
012:032 I did **seek** to seduce him from his
012:051 when ye did **seek** to seduce Joseph"? The ladies
014:003 Allah and **seek** to make it crooked: they are
016:001 the Command of Allah: **seek** ye not them to hasten
016:014 **seek** (thus) of the bounty of Allah and that

SEEK (continued)

016:098   seek Allah's protection from Satan the Rejected one.
017:012   We have made bright that ye may seek bounty from
017:057   do seek (for themselves) means of access
017:066   in order that ye may seek of His Bounty.
017:110   but seek a middle course between."
019:018   She said: "I seek refuge from thee to (Allah)
019:076   those who seek guidance: and the
023:097   And say: "O my Lord! I seek refuge with Thee from
023:098   "And I seek refuge with Thee, O my Lord!
028:055   peace be to you: we seek not the ignorant."
028:073   and that ye may seek of His Grace;-and in
028:077   to thee, and seek not (occasions for) mischief
028:077   "But seek, with the (wealth) which Allah
029:017   then seek ye sustenance from Allah, serve Him,
030:038   that is best for those who seek the Countenance,
030:046   and that ye may seek of His Bounty: in order
033:029   But if ye seek Allah and His Messenger,
035:010   If any do seek for glory and power,-to Allah
035:012   that ye may seek (thus) of the Bounty of Allah
040:056   seek refuge, then, in Allah: it is He
041:022   "Ye did not seek to hide yourselves, lest your
041:036   by the Satan, seek refuge in Allah. He is
045:012   it by His command, that ye may seek of His Bounty,
046:017   And they two seek Allah's aid, (and rebuke
047:024   earnestly seek to understand the Qur'an, or is that
057:013   Then seek a light (where ye can)!" So a wall
060:001   and to seek My Good Pleasure, showing friendship
062:010   and seek of the Bounty of Allah: and remember
073:020   and seek ye the Grace of Allah: for Allah
092:020   But only the desire to seek for the countenance
113:001   Say: I seek refuge with the Lord of the Dawn,
114:001   Say: I seek refuge with the Lord

SEEKERS

012:007   are Signs for Seekers (after Truth).

SEEKEST

066:001   thou seekest to please thy consorts? But Allah

SEEKING

002:265   those who spend their wealth seeking to please
002:272   do so seeking the "Face" of Allah.
002:273   seeking (for trade or work):
003:007   seeking discord, and searching for interpretation,
003:099   seeking to make it crooked,
004:114   seeking the good pleasure of Allah, We
005:002   seeking of the bounty and good pleasure
006:052   seeking His Face. In naught
007:054   each seeking the other in rapid succession: and
012:030   the (great) 'Aziz is seeking to seduce her slave
013:022   seeking the countenance their Lord; establish
018:028   and evening, seeking his Face; and let
018:028   beyond them, seeking the pomp and glitter of
018:064   seeking after": so they went back on their
030:039   seeking the Countenance of Allah, (will increase):
033:020   the Bedouins, and seeking news about you
033:053   disperse, without seeking familiar talk.
048:029   (in prayer), seeking Grace from Allah and (His)
057:021   Be ye foremost (in seeking) forgiveness from your
057:027   (We commanded) only the seeking for the Good
059:008   their property, while seeking Grace from Allah
073:020   the land, seeking of Allah's bounty; yet others

SEEKS

004:110   but afterwards seeks Allah's forgiveness, he

SEEKS (continued)

027:049   (when he seeks vengeance): 'We were
055:029   Of Him seeks (its need) every creature

SEEM

006:043   (sinful) acts seem alluring to them.
006:122   their own deeds seem pleasing.
008:048   (sinful) acts seem alluring to them, and said:
010:012   seem fair in their eyes!
016:063   their own acts seem alluring: he is their
020:086   Did then the promise seem to you long (in coming)?
027:024   seem pleasing in their eyes, and has
028:066   will be obscure to them and they will not
051:025   (And thought, "These seem) unusual people."

SEEMED

009:118   that the earth seemed constrained to them, for all
009:118   and their (very) Souls seemed straitened to them,-
013:016   so that the creation seemed to them similar?
020:066   so it seemed to him on account of their magic-
020:088   it seemed to low: so they said: "This is
048:012   to their families; this seemed pleasing in your

SEEMLY

024:027   in order that ye may heed (what is seemly).

SEEMS

009:037   The evil of their course seems pleasing to them.
013:033   their devising seems pleasing, but they
027:042   "It seems the same. And knowledge
047:014   the evil of his conduct seems pleasing, and such

SEEN

002:264   spend their wealth to be seen of men,
003:143   now ye have seen it with your own eyes
004:038   to be seen of men, and have no faith in Allah
004:142   to be seen of men, but little
008:047   and to be seen of men, and to hinder (men) from
009:043   who told the truth were seen by thee in a clear
012:035   they had seen the Signs, (that it was best)
018:017   Thou wouldst have seen the sun, when it rose,
019:077   Hast thou then seen the (sort of) man who
025:045   Hast thou not seen how thy Lord?-doth prolong
031:020   (both) seen and unseen? Yet there are
032:012   "Our Lord! We have seen and we have heard:
035:040   Say: "Have ye seen (these) `partners' of yours
036:066   but how could they have seen?
037:102   he said: "O my son! I have seen in a dream
046:025   nothing was to be seen but (the ruins of)
053:019   Have ye seen Lat, an 'Uzza,
059:021   have seen it humble itself and cleave
107:006   Those who (want but) to be seen,

SEES

002:096   for Allah sees well all that they do.
002:110   for Allah sees well all that ye do.
002:233   that Allah sees well what ye do.
002:237   For Allah sees well all that ye do.
003:156   and Allah sees well all that ye do.
003:163   and Allah sees well all that they do.
005:071   But Allah sees well all that they do.
017:096   and He sees (all things)."
018:026   how clearly He sees, how finely He hears
022:061   Who hears and sees (all things).
022:075   He Who hears and sees (all things).
024:060   and Allah is One Who sees and knows all things.
025:012   When it sees them from a place far off, they will
025:020   For Allah is One Who sees (all things).

SEES (continued)

031:028 for Allah is He Who hears and **sees** (all things).
033:009 but Allah **sees** (clearly) all that ye do.
039:058 (actually) **sees** the Chastisement: 'If only
040:020 Who hears and **sees** (all things).
040:056 it is He Who hears and **sees** (all things).
042:011 and He is the One that hears and **sees**.
048:024 over them. And Allah **sees** well all that ye do.
049:018 and Allah **sees** well all that ye do."
057:004 may be. And Allah **sees** well all that ye do.
058:001 for Allah hears and **sees** (all things).
060:003 between you: for Allah **sees** well all that ye do.
064:002 are Believers: and Allah see well all that ye do.
079:036 in full view for him who **sees**.-

SEEST

004:061 thou **seest** the Hypocrites avert their faces
005:052 thou **seest** how eagerly they run about
005:080 Thou **seest** many of them turning in friendship
006:068 When thou **seest** men engaged in vain
014:019 **Seest** thou not that Allah created the
014:024 **Seest** thou not how Allah sets forth a parable?
016:014 and thou **seest** the ships therein that plough
017:062 He said, "**Seest** Thou? This is the one whom
019:083 **Seest** thou not that We have set Satans
022:005 And (further), thou **seest** the earth barren and
022:018 **Seest** thou not that to Allah prostrate all things
022:063 **Seest** thou not that Allah sends down
022:065 **Seest** thou not that Allah has made **subject**
024:041 **Seest** thou not that it is Allah Whose praises
024:043 **Seest** thou not that Allah makes the clouds
025:043 **Seest** thou such a one as taketh for his god
026:205 **Seest** thou? If we do let them enjoy (this life)
026:225 **Seest** thou not that they wander distracted
027:088 Thou **seest** the mountains and thinkest them
030:048 **seest** rain-drops issue from the midst thereof:
031:029 **Seest** thou not that Allah merges Night into Day
031:031 **Seest** thou not that the ships sail through the
035:012 to wear; and thou **seest** the ships therein that
035:027 **Seest** thou not that Allah sends down
039:021 **Seest** thou not that Allah sends down rain
040:069 **Seest** thou not those that dispute concerning
041:039 thou **seest** the earth humble; but when
045:023 Then **seest** thou such a one as takes as his god
053:033 **Seest** thou one who turns back,
058:007 **Seest** thou not that Allah doth know (all) that is
058:008 **Seest** thou not those who were forbidden secret
058:014 **Seest** thou not those who turn (in friendship)
067:003 vision again: **Seest** thou any flaw?
069:008 Then **seest** thou any of them left surviving?
076:019 if thou **seest** them, thou wouldst think
089:006 **Seest** thou not how thy Lord dealt with
096:009 **Seest** thou one who forbids-
096:011 **Seest** thou if He is on (the road of) Guidance?-
096:013 **Seest** thou if he denies (Truth) and turns away?
105:001 **Seest** thou not how thy Lord dealt with the
107:001 **Seest** thou one who denies the Judgment (to come)?

SEETH

002:265 Allah **seeth** well whatever ye do.
004:058 For Allah is He Who heareth and **seeth** all things.
004:134 for Allah is He that heareth and **seeth** (all things).
008:072 and (remember) Allah **seeth** all that ye do.
011:112 (from the Path): for He **seeth** well all that ye do.
017:001 Who heareth and **seeth** (all things).

SEETH (continued)

019:042 which heareth not and **seeth** not, and can
026:218 Who **seeth** thee standing forth (in prayer),
041:040 **seeth** (clearly) all that ye do.

SEIZE

002:255 No slumber can **seize** Him nor sleep.
004:089 **seize** them and slay them wherever ye find them;
004:091 **seize** them and slay them wherever ye get them:
007:169 came their way, they would (again) **seize** them. Was
009:005 wherever ye find them, and **seize** them, beleaguer
009:090 **seize** the Unbelievers among them.
011:064 or a swift Punishment will **seize** you!
011:094 did **seize** the wrong-doers, and they
013:031 cease to **seize** them for their (ill) deeds, or to
016:045 **seize** them from directions they little perceive?
020:021 (Allah) said, "**Seize** it, and fear not: We shall
020:094 **Seize** (me) not by my beard nor by
023:064 Until, when We **seize** in Punishment those of
026:156 lest the Chastisement of a Great Day **seize** you."
028:047 should **seize** them for (the deeds) that their
036:049 it will **seize** them while they are yet disputing
040:005 to **seize** him, and disputed by means of vanities,
044:016 The day We shall **seize** you with a mighty onslaught:
044:047 (A voice will cry:) "**Seize** ye him and drag him
069:030 "**Seize** ye him, and bind ye him,
069:045 We should certainly **seize** him by his right hand

SEIZED

002:055 thereupon, thunderbolt **seized** you.
004:062 How then, when they are **seized** by misfortune.
004:153 but they were **seized** for their presumption, with
007:073 or ye shall be **seized** with a grievous punishment."
007:150 **seized** his brother by (the hair of) his head, and
007:155 when they were **seized** with violent quaking, he
007:184 Their Companion is not **seized** with madness: he is
011:054 some of our gods may have **seized** thee with evil."
012:088 **seized** us and our family: we have
015:054 **seized** me? Of what, then, is your good news?"
015:083 But the (mighty) Blast **seized** them of a morning,
016:026 and the Wrath **seized** them from directions
016:113 **seized** them even in the midst of their iniquities.
018:079 king who **seized** on every boat by force.
021:083 **seized** me, but Thou art the Most Merciful of those
024:014 **seized** you in that ye rushed glibly into
026:158 But the Chastisement **seized** them. Verily in
026:189 of overshadowing gloom **seized** them, and that
028:040 So We **seized** him and his hosts, and We
029:037 then the mighty Blast **seized** them, and they
029:040 Each one of them We **seized** for his crime:
033:061 they shall be **seized** and slain.
034:051 (for them), and they will be **seized** from a
040:005 **seized** them! And how (terrible), was My Requital!
041:017 **seized** them, because of what they had earned.
043:048 and We **seized** them with Punishment, in order
051:044 **seized** them, even while they were looking on.
054:038 an abiding Chastisement **seized** them:
054:042 but We **seized** them with the Seizure of a Mighty,
055:041 be **seized** by their forelocks and their feet.
073:016 so We **seized** him with a heavy Punishment.

SEIZES

017:067 When distress **seizes** you at sea, those that
017:083 and when Evil **seizes** him he gives himself
041:051 and when Evil **seizes** him, (he comes) full

SEIZURE

054:036 violent **Seizure** but they disputed about the Warning.
054:042 but We seized them with the **Seizure** of a Mighty,

SELECT

056:020 And with fruits, any that they may **select**;

SELF

002:112 whole **self** to Allah and is a doer of good,
003:020 say: "I have submitted my whole **self** to Allah
004:040 and giveth from His Own **self** a great reward.
004:125 than one who submits his whole **self** to Allah,
012:026 seduce me-from my (true) **self**." And one
012:032 from his (true) **self** but he did firmly save
031:022 Whoever submits his whole **self** to Allah, and is
035:039 be on his own **self** their disbelief: but adds

SELF-CONTROL

003:017 Those who show patience, (firmness and **self-control**);

SELF-EVIDENT

029:049 Nay, here are Signs **self-evident** in the hearts

SELF-EXPLAINED

007:133 and Blood: Signs openly **self-explained**: but they

SELF-GLORY

038:002 in **Self-glory** and opposition.

SELF-PURIFICATION

092:018 for increase in **self-purification**,

SELF-REPROACHING

075:002 And I do swear by the **self-reproaching** soul.

SELF-RESTRAINT

002:183 that ye may (learn) **self-restraint**.
002:187 that they may learn **self-restraint**.
004:025 that ye practice **self-restraint**.
004:128 But if ye do good and practice **self-restraint**,
004:129 and practice **self-restraint**, Allah
041:035 exercise patience and **self-restraint**,-none but
048:026 to the command of **self-restraint**; and well
058:009 righteousness and **self-restraint**; and fear Allah,
090:017 and **self-restraint**), and enjoin deeds of kindness

SELF-SUBSISTING

002:255 the **Self-subsisting**, Supported of all
003:002 the Living, the **Self-Subsisting**,
020:111 the Living, the **Self-Subsisting**, The Sustainer,

SELF-SUFFICIENT

006:133 Thy Lord is **Self-sufficient**, full of Mercy: if
010:068 Glory be to Him! He is **Self-Sufficient**! His are
080:005 As to one who regards himself as **self-sufficient**,
092:008 and thinks himself **self-sufficient**.
096:007 In that he looketh upon himself as **self-sufficient**.

SELFISH

002:109 have believed from **selfish** envy,
002:213 except through **selfish** contumacy.
005:030 The (**selfish**) soul of the other led him

SELL

002:041 nor **sell** My Signs for a small price:
002:102 which they did **sell** their souls,
003:077 As for those who **sell** the faith they owe to Allah
003:199 they will not **sell** the Signs of Allah
004:074 who **sell** the life of this world for the Hereafter.
005:044 and **sell** not My Signs for a miserable price.
016:095 Nor **sell** the Covenant of Allah for a miserable

SELVES

002:057 but they harmed their own **selves**.
003:168 Say: "Avert death from your own **selves**,

SELVES (continued)

007:029 and that ye set your whole **selves** (to Him)
033:006 the Believers than their own **selves**, and his
051:021 As also in your own **selves**: will ye not then see?

SEND

002:074 when split asunder **send** fort water;
002:090 **send** it to any of His servants He pleases:
002:110 **send** forth for your souls before you,
002:129 "Our Lord! **send** amongst them a Messenger
002:196 **send** an offering for sacrifice,
004:090 and (instead) **send** you (guarantees of) peace, then
005:112 Can thy Lord **send** down to us a Table set
005:114 "O Allah our Lord! **send** us from heaven a table
005:115 Allah said: "I will **send** it down unto you: but
006:008 If We did **send** down an angel, the matter
006:037 power to **send** down a Sign: but most
006:048 We **send** the Messengers only to give
006:052 **Send** not away those who call on their Lord
006:065 **send** calamities on you, from above and below, or
006:091 **send** down to man (by way of revelation)": say:
006:111 Even if We did **send** unto them angels, and the
007:047 **send** us not to the company of the wrong-doers."
007:111 and **send** to the cities men to collect-
007:134 and we shall **send** away the Children
007:167 that He would **send** against them, to the
008:032 from the sky, or **send** us a grievous chastisement."
008:033 nor was He going to **send** it whilst they
008:033 **send** them a Chastisement: whilst thou
009:052 that Allah will **send** His punishment from Him
010:024 is as the rain which We **send** down from the skies:
010:088 and **send** hardness to their hearts, so they
011:052 (in repentance): He will **send** you the skies
012:012 "**Send** him with us to-morrow to enjoy himself
012:045 of its interpretation: **send** ye me (therefore)."
012:063 so **send** our brother with us, that we
012:066 (Jacob) said: "Never will I **send** him with you
012:109 Nor did We **send** before thee (as Messengers)
013:030 We **send** down unto thee by inspiration; yet do
013:038 We did **send** messengers before thee, and appointed
015:008 We **send** not the angels down except for just cause:
015:010 We did **send** messengers before thee amongst
015:021 are with Us; but We only **send** down thereof in
015:022 And We **send** the fecundating winds, then cause
016:002 He doth **send** down His angels with inspiration
017:068 or that He will not **send** against you a violent
017:069 and **send** against you a heavy gale to drown you
017:069 not **send** you back a second time to sea and **send**
017:082 We **send** down (stage by stage) of the Qur'an
017:093 until thou **send** down to us a book that we
018:019 Now **send** ye then one of you with this money
018:040 and that He will **send** on thy garden thunderbolts
018:045 We **send** down from the skies: the earth's
018:056 We only **send** the Messengers to give glad tidings
020:047 thy Lord: **send** forth, therefore, the Children
021:025 Not a messenger did We **send** before thee
022:052 Never did We **send** a messenger or a prophet
023:018 And We **send** down water from the sky according
023:024 (to **send** messengers), He could have sent down
023:099 he says: "O my Lord! **send** me back to (life),-
025:048 and We **send** down pure water from the sky,-
026:004 We could **send** down to them from the sky a Sign,
026:013 so **send** unto Aaron.
026:017 "**Send** thou with us the Children of Israel.'"

SEND (continued)

027:035   But I am going to **send** him a present, and wait
028:024   any good that Thou dost **send** me!"
028:034   so **send** him with me as a helper, to confirm
028:045   Who **send** messengers (with inspiration).
028:047   why didst Thou not **send** us a messenger?
029:014   We did **send** Noah to his people, and he
030:047   We did indeed **send**, before thee, messengers to
030:051   And if We (but) **send** a Wind from which they see
031:010   We **send** down rain from the sky, and produce
032:012   we have heard: now then **send** us back (to the
033:056   **send** ye blessings on him, and salute
033:056   Allah and His Angels **send** blessings on the
034:034   Never did We **send** a Warner to a population,
040:015   by His Command doth He **send** the spirit
040:034   **send** after him.' Thus doth Allah leave to stray
040:078   We did aforetime **send** messengers before thee:
041:039   but when We **send** down rain to it, it is
042:003   Thus doth (He) **send** Inspiration to thee
043:046   We did **send** Moses aforetime, with Our Signs,
044:005   For We (ever) **send** (revelations),
050:009   And We **send** down from the sky Rain charged
054:027   For We will **send** the she-camel by way
060:010   then **send** them not back to the Unbelievers.
067:017   is in Heaven will not **send** against you a violent
071:011   "'He will **send** rain to you in abundance;
073:005   Soon shall We **send** down to thee a weighty Word.
073:020   **send** forth for yourselves, ye shall
078:014   And do We not **send** down from the clouds

SENDETH

006:099   **sendeth** down rain from the skies: with it
007:057   It is He Who **sendeth** the Winds
014:032   and **sendeth** down rain from the skies, and with it
040:013   and **sendeth** down sustenance for you from the sky:

SENDING

017:059   And We refrain from **sending** the Signs,
042:051   or by the **sending** of a Messenger to reveal,

SENDS

002:164   **sends** down from the skies,
013:017   He **sends** down water from the skies, and the
016:010   It is He Who **sends** down rain from the sky: from it
016:065   And Allah **sends** down rain from the skies,
022:063   **sends** down rain from the sky, and forthwith
024:043   And He **sends** down from the sky mountain masses
025:048   And He it is Who **sends** the Winds as heralds
027:060   and the earth, and who **sends** you down rain from
027:063   and who **sends** the winds as heralds of glad tidings,
029:063   that **sends** down rain from the sky, and gives
030:024   and He **sends** down rain from the sky and with
030:046   that He **sends** the Winds, as heralds
030:048   It is Allah Who **sends** the Winds, and they
031:034   It is He Who **sends** down rain, and He
033:043   He it is Who **sends** blessings on you, as do
035:009   It is Allah Who **sends** forth the Winds, so that
035:027   **sends** down rain from the sky? With it
036:015   **sends** no sort of revelation: ye do
039:021   Seest thou not that Allah **sends** down rain
039:042   but the rest He **sends** (to their
042:027   but He **sends** (it) down in due measure
042:028   He is the One that **sends** down rain (even) after
043:011   That **sends** down (from time to time) rain from
045:005   and the fact that Allah **sends** down Sustenance
048:029   like a seed which **sends** forth its blade,

SENDS (continued)

057:009   He is the One Who **Sends** to His Servants

SENSE

015:047   any lurking **sense** of injury: (they will be)
015:048   There no **sense** of fatigue shall touch them,
016:006   And ye have a **sense** of pride and beauty in them
021:067   that ye worship besides Allah! Have ye no **sense**?"
026:028   If ye only had **sense**!"
035:035   no toil nor **sense** of weariness shall touch
050:038   nor did any **sense** of weariness touch Us.
059:010   rancor (or **sense** of injury) against those

SENSES

007:143   When he recovered his **senses** he said: "Glory be

SENT

002:004   and **sent** before thy time,
002:004   the Revelation **sent** to thee,
002:022   and **sent** down rain from the heavens;
002:057   and **sent** down to you manna and quails,
002:059   so We **sent** on the transgressors
002:090   (the revelation) which Allah has **sent** down,
002:091   "Believe in what Allah hath **sent** down,"
002:091   what was **sent** down to us":
002:095   their hands have **sent** on before them.
002:099   We have **sent** down to thee manifest Signs
002:119   Verily We have **sent** thee in truth
002:151   in that We have **sent** among you a Messenger
002:159   (Signs) We have **sent** down, and the Guidance,
002:176   (Their doom is) because Allah **sent** down the Book
002:185   in which was **sent** down the Qur'an,
002:211   how many Clear (Signs) We have **sent** them.
002:213   And Allah **sent** Messengers with glad tidings
002:213   and with them He **sent** the Book in truth,
002:231   He **sent** down to you the Book and Wisdom,
003:003   It is He Who **sent** down to thee (step by step),
003:003   and He **sent** down the Torah (of Moses)
003:003   and He **sent** down the Criterion
003:007   He it is Who has **sent** down to thee the Book:
003:073   revelation be **sent** to someone (else) like unto that
003:073   like unto that which was **sent** unto you?
003:124   three thousand angels (specially) **sent** down?
003:151   for which He had **sent** no authority:
003:154   He **sent** down calm on a band of you
003:164   on the Believers when He **sent** among them
003:182   which your hands **sent** on before ye:
004:062   their hands have **sent** forth?
004:064   We **sent** not a Messenger, but to be obeyed,
004:079   **sent** thee as a Messenger to (instruct) mankind.
004:080   We have not **sent** thee to watch over them.
004:091   every time they are **sent** back to temptation, they
004:105   We have **sent** down to thee the Book in truth, that
004:113   For Allah hath **sent** down to thee the Book
004:136   He hath **sent** to His Messenger and the scripture
004:136   and the scripture which He **sent** to those before (him).
004:140   Already has He **sent** you word in the Book, that
004:163   We have **sent** thee inspiration, as We **sent**
004:163   We **sent** inspiration to Abraham.
004:163   as We **sent** it to Noah and the Messengers after
004:166   He hath **sent** unto thee He hath **sent**
004:166   He hath **sent** from His (Own) knowledge, and
004:174   **sent** unto you a light (that is) manifest.
005:013   of the Message that was **sent** them, nor wilt
005:014   that was **sent** them: so We stirred up enmity and
005:031   Then Allah **sent** a raven, who scratched

SENT (continued)

005:046   We **sent** Jesus the son of Mary, confirming the Torah
005:046   We **sent** him the Gospel: therein was
005:048   To thee We **sent** the Scripture in truth, confirming
005:049   (teaching) which Allah hath **sent** down to thee.
005:066   that was **sent** to them from their Lord, they
005:067   which hath been **sent** to thee from thy Lord.
005:070   the Children of Israel and **sent** them Messengers.
005:080   which their souls have **sent** forward before
006:007   If We had **sent** unto thee a written (Message)
006:008   They say: "Why is not an angel **sent** down to him?"
006:009   We should have **sent** him as a man. And We
006:027   "Would that we were but **sent** back! Then would
006:037   a Sign **sent** down to him from his Lord?" Say:
006:042   Before thee We **sent** (Messengers)
006:091   Say: "Who then **sent** down the Book
006:091   Say: "Allah (**sent** it down)": then leave
006:092   which We have **sent** down, bringing
006:114   that it hath been **sent** down from thy
006:114   Who hath **sent** unto you the Book, explained
006:131   (The messengers were **sent**) thus, for thy Lord
006:156   **sent** down to two Peoples before us, and for
006:157   "If the Book had only been **sent** down to us, we
007:006   and those by whom We **sent** it.
007:006   to whom Our Message was **sent** and those
007:052   For We had certainly **sent** unto them a Book, based
007:053   Or could we be **sent** back? Then should
007:059   We **sent** Noah to his people. He said: "O
007:065   To the 'Ad people, (We **sent**) Hud, one of
007:073   To the Thamud people (We **sent**) Salih, one of
007:075   been **sent** through him."
007:079   I was **sent** by my Lord: I gave you
007:080   We also (**sent**) Lut: he said to his people: "Do
007:085   To the Madyan people We **sent** Shu'aib, one of
007:087   with which I have been **sent**, and a party
007:093   I was **sent** by my Lord: I gave you
007:094   Whenever We **sent** a prophet to a town, We took
007:103   Then after them We **sent** Moses with Our Signs
007:125   "For us, we are but **sent** back unto our Lord."
007:133   So We **sent** on them: Wholesale Death,
007:137   lands whereon We **sent** down our blessings. The
007:157   the Light which is **sent** down with him,-it is
007:158   Say: "O men! I am **sent** unto you all, as the
007:160   and **sent** down to them manna and quails, (saying):
007:162   so We **sent** on them a plague from heaven. For
007:175   to whom We **sent** Our Signs, but he
008:041   the revelation We **sent** down to our Servant
008:051   which your (own) hands **sent** forth. For Allah
009:026   and **sent** down forces which ye saw not: He punished
009:033   It is He who hath **sent** His Messenger
009:040   then Allah **sent** down His peace upon him,
009:046   was averse to their being **sent** forth; so He
009:064   should be **sent** down about them, showing them
009:097   **sent** down to His Messenger: but Allah
009:101   be **sent** to a grievous Chastisement.
010:002   that We have **sent** Our inspiration to a man
010:020   **sent** down to him from his Lord?" Say:
010:030   (the fruits of) the deeds it **sent** before: they will
010:047   To every people (was **sent**) an Messenger: when their
010:059   **sent** down to you for sustenance? Yet ye
010:074   Then after him We **sent** (many) messengers
010:075   Then after them **sent** We Moses and Aaron
010:109   Follow thou the inspiration **sent** unto thee, and be

SENT (continued)

011:002   (Say:) "Verily I am (**sent**) unto you from Him
011:012   **sent** down unto him, or why does not an angel
011:014   **sent** down (replete) with the knowledge of Allah,
011:025   We **sent** Noah to his People (with a
011:028   from my Lord and that He hath **sent** Mercy unto me
011:050   To the 'Ad People (We **sent**) Hud, one of
011:057   I was **sent** to you. My Lord will make anther
011:061   To the Thamud People (We **sent**) Salih, one of
011:063   and He hath **sent** Mercy unto me from Himself,-
011:070   been **sent** against the people of Lut."
011:084   To the Madyan people (We **sent**) Shu'aib, one of
011:096   And We **sent** Moses, with Our Clear (Signs) and an
012:002   We have **sent** it down as an Arabic Qur'an, in order
012:019   they **sent** their water-carrier (for water), and he
012:031   she **sent** for them and prepared a banquet for them:
012:040   hath **sent** down no authority: the Command
013:007   a Sign **sent** down to him from his Lord?" But thou
013:027   a Sign **sent** down to him from his Lord?" Say:
013:030   Thus have We **sent** thee amongst a People
014:004   We **sent** not a messenger except (to teach) in the
014:005   We **sent** Moses with Our Signs (and the
014:009   ye have been **sent**, and we are really in suspicious
015:009   We have, without doubt, **sent** down the Message;
015:058   They said: "We have been **sent** to a people
015:081   We **sent** them Our Signs, but they
015:090   **sent** down on those who divided (Scripture
016:036   For We assuredly **sent** amongst every People
016:043   And before thee We **sent** were but men, to whom
016:044   and Scriptures and We have **sent** down unto thee
016:044   to men what is **sent** for them, and that
016:044   (We **sent** them) with Clear Signs and Scriptures
016:063   By Allah, We (also) **sent** (our prophets) to
016:064   And We **sent** down the Book to thee so that
016:070   **sent** back to a feeble age, so that
016:089   and We have **sent** down to thee the Book explaining
017:005   came to pass, We **sent** against you Our servants
017:015   We had **sent** a messenger (to give warning).
017:054   We have not **sent** thee to be a disposer
017:059   We only **sent** the Signs by way of frightening
017:059   as false: We **sent** the She-camel to the Thamud-
017:077   We **sent** before thee: thou wilt
017:086   We have **sent** thee by inspiration: then wouldst
017:094   "Has Allah **sent** a man (like us) to be (His)
017:095   **sent** them down from the heavens an angel
017:102   these things have been **sent** down by none
017:105   We **sent** down the (Qur'an) in Truth, and in
017:105   and We **sent** thee but to give Glad Tidings
018:001   Praise be to Allah, Who hath **sent** to His
018:057   have **sent** forth? Verily We have set veils over
018:087   we punish; then shall he be **sent** back to his Lord;
019:017   from them: then We **sent** to her Our angel, and he
020:002   We have not **sent** down the Qur'an to thee to be
020:038   "Behold! We **sent** to thy mother, by inspiration,
020:047   'Verily we are Messengers **sent** by thy Lord:
020:053   and has **sent** down water from the sky." With it
020:077   We **sent** an inspiration to Moses: "Travel by
020:080   and We **sent** down to you Manna and quails:
020:099   for We have **sent** thee a reminder from Us.
020:113   Thus have we **sent** this down-an Arabic Qur'an-
020:134   "Our Lord! if only Thou hadst **sent** us a messenger,
021:005   the ones that were **sent** to (prophets) of old!"
021:007   We **sent** were but men, to whom

SENT (continued)

021:025   **sent** by Us to him: that there
021:050   which We have **sent** down: will ye
021:107   We **sent** thee not, but as a mercy for all creatures.
022:005   and some are **sent** back to the feeblest old age,
022:010   of the deeds which thy hands **sent** forth, for verily
022:016   Thus have We **sent** down Clear Signs; and verily
022:049   Say: "O men! I am (**sent**) to you only to give
022:071   things for which no authority has been **sent** down to them,
023:023   and certainly We **sent** Noah to his people:
023:024   **sent** down angels: never did we hear such a thing
023:032   And We **sent** to them a messenger from among
023:044   Then **sent** We Our messengers in succession:
023:045   Then We **sent** Moses and his brother Aaron,
023:071   Nay, We have **sent** them their admonition, but they
023:090   We have **sent** them the Truth: but they
024:001   in it have We **sent** down Clear Signs, in order
024:001   A Sura which We have **sent** down and which
024:034   We have already **sent** down to you verses making
024:046   We have indeed **sent** down Signs that make
025:001   Blessed is He Who **sent** down the Criterion
025:006   Say: "The (Qur'an) was **sent** down by Him
025:007   Why has not an angel been **sent** down to him
025:020   And the messengers whom We **sent** before thee
025:021   "Why are not the angels **sent** down to us,
025:025   and angels shall be **sent** down, descending (in
025:035   (Before this), We **sent** Moses the Book,
025:041   has **sent** as a messenger?"
025:051   We could have **sent** a warner to every town.
025:056   But thee We only **sent** to give
026:016   to Pharaoh, and say: 'We have been **sent** by the
026:027   who has been **sent** to you is a veritable madman!"
026:053   Then Pharaoh **sent** heralds to (all) the Cities,
026:115   "I am **sent** only as a plain warner."
027:045   We **sent** (aforetime), to the Thamud, their brother
027:054   (We also **sent**) Lut (as a Messenger): behold, he
028:007   So We **sent** this inspiration to the mother of Moses:
028:046   (to Moses). Yet (art thou **sent**) as a Mercy
028:047   If (We had) not (**sent** thee to the Quraish),
028:047   that their hands have **sent** forth, they might
028:048   "Why are not (Signs) **sent** to him, like those
028:048   like those which were **sent** to Moses?"
028:048   which were formerly **sent** to Moses? They say:
028:052   Those to whom We **sent** the Book before this,-
028:059   a town until He had **sent** to its Centre
028:086   that the Book would be **sent** to thee except as
029:036   (We **sent**) their brother Shu'aib. Then he
029:040   We **sent** a violent tornado (with showers
029:045   Recite what is **sent** of the Book by inspiration
029:047   **sent** down the Book to thee. So the
029:050   **sent** down to him from his Lord?" Say: "The
029:051   We have **sent** down to thee the Book
030:035   Or have We **sent** down authority to them,
030:036   their (own) hands have **sent** forth, behold,
031:021   **sent** down, they say: "Nay, we shall
033:009   but We **sent** against them a hurricane and forces
033:045   O Prophet! Truly We have **sent** thee as a Witness,
034:006   see that the (Revelation) **sent** down to thee
034:016   and We **sent** against them the flood (released)
034:028   We have not **sent** thee but as a (Messenger)
034:034   with which ye have been **sent**."
034:044   nor **sent** messengers to them before thee as Warners.
035:024   Verily We have **sent** thee with truth, as a

SENT (continued)

036:005   (It is a Revelation) **sent** down by (Him), the
036:012   **sent** before and that which they leave behind,
036:014   they said, "Truly, we have been **sent** on a
036:014   When We (first) **sent** to them two messengers,
036:016   we have been **sent** on a mission to you:
036:028   And We **sent** not down against his People,
037:072   But We **sent** aforetime, among them, warners.
037:123   So also was Elias among those **sent** (by us).
037:133   So also was Lut among those **sent** (by us).
037:139   So also was Jonah among those **sent** (by Us).
037:147   And We **sent** him (on a mission) to a
037:171   before (this) to Our Servants **sent** (by Us),
038:008   "What! Has the Message been **sent** to him-
038:029   **sent** down unto thee, full of blessings, that they
039:006   and He **sent** down for you eight head
040:023   Of old We **sent** Moses, with Our Signs
040:070   We **sent** Our messengers: but soon
041:014   He would certainly have **sent** down angels: so we
041:014   so we disbelieve in the Message you were **sent** with.
041:016   So We **sent** against them a furious Wind
041:042   it is **sent** down by One Full of Wisdom, Worthy of
041:044   Had We **sent** this as a Qur'an (in a language)
042:007   Thus have We **sent** by inspiration to thee
042:013   the which We have **sent** by inspiration to thee-
042:015   **sent** down; and I am commanded to judge justly
042:017   It is Allah Who has **sent** down the Book in truth,
042:048   his hands have **sent** forth, truly then
042:048   We have not **sent** thee as a guard over them.
042:052   by Our command, **sent** inspiration to thee:
043:006   We **sent** amongst the peoples of old?
043:023   Just in the same way, whenever We **sent** a Warner
043:024   ye (prophets) are **sent** with."
043:031   **sent** down to some leading man in either of
043:043   **sent** down to thee: verily thou
043:045   whom We **sent** before thee; did We
044:003   We **sent** it down during a blessed night: for We
046:023   I have been **sent**: but I
047:002   **sent** down to Muhammad-for is the Truth from their
047:020   "Why is not a Sura **sent** down (for us)?"
048:004   It is He who **sent** down Tranquillity into the
048:008   We have truly **sent** thee as a witness, as a
048:018   and He **sent** down tranquillity to them, and He
048:026   Allah **sent** down His tranquillity to His
048:028   It is He who has **sent** His Messenger
050:028   I had already in advance **sent** you Warning.
051:032   They said, "We have been **sent** to a people
051:038   Behold, We **sent** him to Pharaoh, with authority
051:041   (was another Sign): behold, We **sent** against them
053:004   It is no less than inspiration **sent** down to him:
053:023   for which Allah has **sent** down no authority
054:019   For We **sent** against them a furious wind, on a
054:025   "Is It that the Message is **sent** to him, of all
054:031   For We **sent** against them a single Mighty Blast,
054:034   We **sent** against them a violent tornado with
055:035   On you will be **sent** (O ye evil ones twain)!
057:025   We **sent** aforetime our messengers with Clear
057:025   with Clear Signs and **sent** down with them the Book
057:025   in justice; and We **sent** down Iron, in which
057:026   And We **sent** Noah and Abraham, and established
057:027   We **sent** after them Jesus the son of Mary,
058:005   for We have already **sent** down Clear Signs.
059:018   he has **sent** forth for the morrow. Yea, fear

SENT (continued)

059:021 Had We **sent** down this Qur'an on a mountain,
061:005 I am the messenger of Allah (**sent**) to you?"
061:006 I am the messenger of Allah (**sent**) to you,
061:009 It is He Who has **sent** His Messenger with Guidance
062:002 It is He Who has **sent** amongst the Unlettered
062:007 have **sent** on before them! And Allah
062:008 be **sent** back to the Knower of things
064:008 which We have **sent** down. And Allah
065:005 which He has **sent** down to you: and if
065:010 **sent** down to you a Message,-
067:009 'Allah never **sent** down any (Message): ye are in
069:024 that ye **sent** before you, in the days
069:043 (This is) a Message **sent** down from the
071:001 We **sent** Noah to his People (with the Command):
073:015 concerning you, even as We **sent** a messenger
073:015 We have **sent** to you, (O men!) a Messenger,
076:023 It is We Who have **sent** down the Qur'an
077:001 By the (Winds) **Sent** Forth one after another
078:040 have **sent** forth, and the Unbeliever will say,
082:005 it hath **sent** forward and (what it hath) kept back.
083:033 But they had not been **sent** as Keepers over them!
089:024 **sent** forth (Good Deeds) for (this) my (Future) Life."
105:003 And He **sent** against them flights of Birds,

SENTENCE

010:071 and dubious. Then pass your **sentence** on me,
038:016 our **sentence** (even) before the Day of Account!"
040:046 and (the **Sentence** will be) on the Day when the
050:024 (The **sentence** will be:) "Throw, both of

SEPARATE

002:229 or **separate** with kindness.
004:130 But if they **separate** Allah will provide
004:150 and wish to **separate** between Allah
005:025 so **separate** us from this rebellious people!"
006:091 into (**separate**) sheets for show, while ye
008:037 In order that Allah may **separate** the impure
010:028 We shall **separate** them, and their
020:053 of plants each **separate** from the others.
026:063 So it divided, and each **separate** part became like
077:004 Then **separate** them, one from another,

SEPARATED

011:042 who had **separated** himself (from the rest):

SEPARATELY

024:061 or **separately**. But if ye enter houses,

SEPARATES

003:179 until He **separates** what is evil from what is good.

SEPARATING

027:061 and made a **separating** bar between the two seas

SEPULCHERS

036:051 when behold! from the **sepulchers** (men) will
070:043 from their **sepulchers** in sudden hast as if they

SERIES

005:019 after the break in the (the **series** of) Messengers,
053:056 of the (**series** of) Warners of old!

SERIOUS

024:015 while it was most **serious** in the sight of Allah.
024:016 this is a most **serious** slander!"
037:102 (the age of) (**serious**) work with him, he said:
102:001 diverts you (from the more **serious** things),

SERPENT

007:107 and behold! it was a **serpent**, plain
026:032 and behold, it was a **serpent**, plain (for

SERRIED

020:064 And then assemble in (**serried**) ranks: he wins

SERVANT

002:023 revealed from time to our **servant**
008:041 to our **Servant** on the Day of Discrimination-
017:001 His **Servant** for a Journey by night from the
018:001 to His **Servant** the Book, and hath
019:002 of thy Lord to His **Servant** Zakariya.
019:030 He said: "I am indeed a **servant** of Allah: He hath
019:093 to The Most Gracious as a **servant**.
025:001 the Criterion to His **servant**, that it
038:017 and remember Our **Servant** David, the man
038:030 the **Servant**! Ever did he turn (to Us in repentance)!
038:041 Commemorate Our **servant** Job, behold he
038:044 how excellent is the **servant**! Ever did
039:036 Is not Allah enough for His **servant**? But they
043:059 He was no more than a **servant**: We granted
050:008 to every **servant** turning (to Allah).
053:010 to His **Servant**-(conveyed) what He (meant) to convey.
054:009 they rejected Our **servant** and said, "Here is

SERVANTS

057:009 to His **Servants** manifest Signs, that He
002:090 send it to any of His **servants** He pleases:
002:186 When My **servants** ask thee concerning Me,
003:015 For in Allah's sight are (all) His **servants**,
003:020 and in Allah's sight are (all) His **servants**.
004:118 "I will take of Thy **servants** a portion marked off:
005:118 they are Thy **servants**: if Thou
006:088 of His **servants**, if they were
007:032 which He hath produced for His **servants**, and
007:128 such of His **servants** as He pleaseth; and the
007:194 besides Allah are **servants** like unto you: call
008:051 For Allah is never unjust to His **servants**."
010:107 whomsoever of His **servants** He pleaseth. And He
012:024 for he was one of Our **servants** chosen.
012:062 And (Joseph) told his **servants** to put their stock-
014:011 to such of His **servants** as He pleases. It is
014:031 Speak to My **servants** who have believed, that they
015:040 "Except Thy chosen **servants** among them,
015:042 "For over My **servants** no authority shalt thou have,
015:049 Tell My **servants** that I am indeed the
016:002 to such of His **servants** as He pleaseth, (saying):
017:005 Our **servants** given to terrible warfare:
017:017 to note and see the sins of His **servants**.
017:030 for He doth know and regard all His **servants**.
017:053 Say to My **servants** that they should (only) say
017:065 "As for My **servants**, no authority
017:096 well acquainted with His **servants**, and He
018:065 So they found one of Our **servants**. On whom
018:102 can take my **servants** as protectors besides Me?
019:061 to His **servants** in the Unseen: for His
019:063 Our **Servants** who guard against evil.
020:077 "Travel by night with my **servants**, and strike
021:026 They are (but) **servants** raised to honour.
021:105 My **servants**, the righteous, shall inherit
022:010 for verily Allah is not unjust to His **servants**.
023:109 "A part of My **servants** there was, who used
025:017 my **servants** astray, or did they
025:058 to be acquainted with the faults of His **servants**;-
025:063 And the **servants** of (Allah) Most Gracious
026:052 "Travel by night with My **servants**; for surely
027:015 of His **servants** who believe!"
027:019 to the ranks of Thy righteous **Servants**."

SERVANTS (continued)

027:059 and Peace on His **servants** whom He has chosen
028:082 or restricts it, to any of His **servants** He pleases!
029:056 O My **servants** who believe! truly, spacious
029:062 of His **servants** He pleases; and He
030:048 made them reach such of his **servants** as He wills,
034:013 of My **servants** are grateful!"
034:039 of His **servants** as He pleases: and nothing
035:028 fear Allah, among His **Servants**, who have
035:031 with respect to his **servants**-well acquainted
035:032 for inheritance to such of Our **servants** as We
035:045 in His sight all His **servants**.
036:030 Ah! alas for (My) **servants**! There comes
037:040 But the chosen **servants** of Allah,-
037:074 Except the chosen **servants** of Allah.
037:081 For he was one of Our believing **Servants**.
037:111 For he was one of Our believing **Servants**.
037:122 For they were two of Our believing **Servants**.
037:128 Except the chosen **Servants** of Allah (among them).
037:132 For He was one of Our believing **Servants**.
037:160 Not (so do) the **servants** of Allah, the chosen ones.
037:169 **Servants** of Allah, sincere (and devoted)!"
037:171 before (this) to Our **Servants** sent (by Us),
038:045 And commemorate Our **Servants** Abraham, Isaac,
038:083 "Except Thy **Servants** amongst them, sincere and
039:007 His **servants**: if ye are grateful, He is
039:010 Say: "O ye my **servants** who believe! Fear your
039:016 warn off His **servants**: "O My **Servants**!
039:016 "O my **servants**! Then fear ye Me!"
039:017 to My **Servants**,-
039:046 wilt judge between Thy **Servants** in those matters
039:053 Say: "O my **Servants** who have transgressed against
040:015 His **servants** He pleases, that is
040:031 but Allah never wishes injustice to His **Servants**.
040:044 watches over His **Servants**."
040:048 Truly, Allah has judged between (His) **Servants**!"
040:085 with His **servants** (from the most ancient times).
041:046 (in the least) to His **servants**.
042:019 Gracious is Allah to His **servants**: He gives
042:023 gives Glad Tidings to His **Servants** who believe
042:025 from His **Servants** and forgives sins: and He
042:027 for He is with His **Servants** well-acquainted,
042:027 the provision for His **Servants**, they would
042:052 wherewith We guide such of Our **servants** as We will;
043:015 of His **servants** a share with Him. Truly is
044:018 Saying: "Restore to me the **servants** of Allah: I am
044:023 "March forth with My **servants** by night: for ye
050:011 As sustenance for (Allah's) **Servants**; and We
050:029 and I do not the least injustice to My **Servants**."
066:010 of Our righteous **servants** but they betrayed their
066:012 and was one of the devout (**Servants**).

SERVE

002:283 a pledge with possession (may **serve** the purpose).
003:030 kindness to those that **serve** Him."
003:144 those who (**serve** him) with gratitude.
003:145 those that (**serve** us with) gratitude.
003:182 for Allah never do injustice those who **serve** Him."
004:036 **Serve** Allah, and join not any partners with Him;
004:172 Christ disdaineth not to **serve** and worship Allah,
009:112 in repentance: that **serve** Him, and praise Him;
010:003 Him therefore **serve** ye: will you not
010:018 They **serve**, besides Allah, what can
011:026 "That ye **serve** none but Allah: verily I do

SERVE (continued)

012:054 to **serve** about my own person." Therefore when
015:099 And **serve** thy Lord until there come unto thee
016:036 (with the Command), "**Serve** Allah and eschew Evil":
016:080 of convenience (to **serve** you) for a time.
016:114 if it is He whom ye **serve**.
019:036 and your Lord: Him therefore **serve** ye: this is
019:044 "O my father! **serve** not Satan: for Satan
020:014 but I: so **serve** thou Me (only), and establish
021:019 are not too proud to **serve** Him, nor are
021:025 therefore worship and **serve** Me.
021:084 for all who **serve** Us.
021:092 therefore **serve** Me (and no other).
022:011 There are among men some who **serve** Allah, as it
024:029 living in, which **serve** some (other) use for you:
027:045 "**Serve** Allah": but behold, they became
027:091 For me, I have been commanded to **serve** the Lord
028:027 on condition that thou **serve** me for eight years,
029:016 "**Serve** Allah and fear Him: that will
029:017 **serve** Him, and be grateful to Him: to Him
029:036 **serve** Allah, and fear the last day: nor commit
029:056 therefore **serve** ye Me-(and Me alone)!
036:022 "Why should not I **serve** Him Who created me,
036:044 (to **serve** them) for a time.
039:002 so **serve** Allah, offering Him sincere devotion.
039:003 "We only **serve** them in order that they may
039:011 to **serve** Allah with sincere devotion;
039:014 Say: "It is Allah I **serve**, with my
039:015 "**Serve** ye what ye will besides Him." Say:
040:060 to **serve** Me will surely enter Hell abased."
041:014 (preaching): "**Serve** none but Allah." They said,
041:037 if it is Him ye wish to **serve**.
043:019 who themselves **serve** Allah. Did they
051:056 that they may **serve** Me.
052:024 Round about them will **serve**, (devoted) to
056:017 Round about them will (**serve**) youths of
076:019 (**serve**) youths of perpetual (freshness): if thou

SERVED

012:068 it **served** only to satisfy Jacob's heartfelt desire.
021:073 they constantly **served** Us (and Us only).

SERVANTS

006:018 Irresistibly Supreme over His **servants**. And
006:061 Supreme over His **servants** and He sets guardians

SERVICE

002:127 "Our Lord! accept (this **service**) from us:
002:196 Hajj or 'Umra in the **service** of Allah,
003:035 what is in my womb for Thy special **service**:
006:162 and my **service** of sacrifice, my life
009:019 (the pious **service** of) those who believe in Allah
020:041 "And I have prepared thee for Myself (for **service**)."
021:019 nor are they (ever) weary of His **service**):
033:031 in the **service** of Allah and His Messenger,
035:030 Oft-Forgiving, Most Ready to appreciate (**service**).
035:034 Ready to appreciate (**service**):
037:165 "And we are verily ranged in ranks (for **service**);

SERVITUDE

013:005 will be yokes (of **servitude**): they will

SET

002:007 Allah hath **set** a seal on their hearts
002:022 then **set** not up rivals unto Allah
002:049 they **set** you hard tasks and chastisement,
002:187 Those are limits (**set** by) Allah:

SET (continued)

002:231   or **set** them free on equitable terms;
002:249   When Talut **set** forth with the armies,
002:251   one **set** of people by means of another,
004:013   Those are limits **set** by Allah: those who
004:035   if they seek to **set** things aright, Allah
004:048   that partners should be **set** up with him; but
004:048   to **set** up partners with Allah is to devise a sin
004:103   **set** up regular Prayers: for such
004:155   nay, Allah hath **set** the seal on their hearts
005:112   a Table **set** (with viands) from heaven?" Said
005:114   a table **set** (with viands), that there may
006:076   But when it **set**, he said: "I love not
006:076   "I love not those that **set**."
006:077   But when the moon **set**, he said: "Unless my
006:078   But when the sun **set**, he said: "O my people!
006:079   "For me, I have **set** my face, firmly
006:107   nor art thou **set** over them to dispose
007:029   and that ye **set** your whole selves (to Him)
007:056   after it hath been **set** in order, but call
007:085   after it has been **set** in order: that will
009:112   **set** by Allah;-(there do rejoice). So proclaim
010:105   "And further (thus): **set** thy face towards
010:108   and I am not (**set**) over you
011:086   But I am not **set** over you to keep watch!"
012:055   (Joseph) said: "**Set** me over the store-houses
013:003   and **set** thereon mountains standing firm,
013:017   Thus doth Allah **set** forth parables.
014:006   the people of Pharaoh: they **set** you hard task
014:030   And they **set** up (idols) as equal to Allah,
015:016   It is We who have **set** out constellations in
015:019   (like a carpet); **set** thereon mountains firm
016:015   And He has **set** up on the earth mountains standing
018:017   from their Cave, and when it **set**, turning away
018:032   **Set** forth to them the parable of two men:
018:045   **Set** forth to them the similitude of the
018:057   have sent forth? Verily We have **set** veils over
018:077   but he **set** it up straight. (Moses) said:
018:086   the sun, he found it **set** in a spring of murky
019:083   **set** Satans on against the Unbelievers, to incite
021:031   And We have **set** on the earth mountains standing
021:047   We shall **set** up scales of justice for the
022:040   Did not Allah check one **set** of people
022:060   he received, and is again **set** upon inordinately.
022:073   O men! Here is a parable **set** forth!
024:035   His Light: Allah doth **set** forth Parables for men:
025:039   To teach one We **set** forth parables and examples;
027:061   **set** thereon mountains immovable; and made
029:043   And such are the Parables We **set** forth for
030:030   So **set** thou thy face truly to the religion
030:043   But **set** thou thy face to the right Religion,
031:010   He **set** on the earth mountains standing firm,
033:028   your enjoyment and **set** you free in a
033:051   whose (turn) thou hadst **set** aside. This were
036:013   **Set** forth to them, by way of a parable,
036:065   That Day shall We **set** a seal on their mouths.
039:008   and he doth **set** up rivals unto Allah,
039:041   his own soul. Nor art thou **set** a Custodian
041:010   He **set** on the (earth), mountains standing
043:058   or He?" This they **set** forth to thee, only by
045:017   matters in which they **set** up differences.
047:003   thus does Allah **set** forth for men their lessons
048:015   when ye **set** forth to acquire booty (in war):

SET (continued)

050:007   and **set** thereon mountains standing firm,
050:026   "Who **set** up another god besides Allah: throw him
055:007   and He has **set** up the balance (of Justice),
058:004   (**set** by) Allah. For those who Reject (Him)
063:003   so a seal was **set** on their hearts: therefore
065:001   those are limits **set** by Allah: and any
074:031   And We have **set** none but angels as guardians
088:015   And Cushions **set** in rows,

SETS

006:061   and He **sets** guardians over you. At length
014:024   Seest thou not how Allah **sets** forth a parable?
014:025   So Allah **sets** forth parables for men, in order
016:075   Allah **sets** forth the Parable (of two men):
016:076   Allah **sets** forth (another) Parable of two men:
016:112   Allah **sets** forth a parable: a city
028:019   and not to be one who **sets** things right!"
043:017   them of (the birth of) what he **sets** up as a
066:010   Allah **sets** forth, for an example to the
066:011   And Allah **sets** forth, as an example to those

SETTING

006:130   **setting** forth unto you My Signs and warning
018:086   Until, when he reached the **setting** of the sun,
020:130   and before its **setting**; yea, celebrate them
021:011   their iniquities, **setting** up in their places
050:039   of the sun and before (its) **setting**,
052:049   and at the **setting** of the stars!
056:075   Furthermore I swear by the **setting** of the Stars,-

SETTLE

003:023   to **settle** their dispute,
013:031   or to **settle** close to their homes, until the
043:079   But it is We Who **settle** things.
055:031   Soon shall We **settle** your affairs, O both

SETTLED

002:210   and the question is (thus) **settled**?
004:011   These are **settled** portions ordained by Allah:
006:008   the matter would be **settled** at once, and no
006:058   the matter would be **settled** at once
007:054   then He **settled** Himself on the Throne: He draweth
010:011   then would their respite be **settled** at once. But
010:019   have been **settled** between them.
010:093   We **settled** the Children of Israel in a
011:061   the earth and **settled** you therein: then ask
017:095   Say, "If there were **settled**, on earth,
035:035   **settled** us in a Home that will last: no toil
041:045   would have been **settled** between them: but they
042:014   the matter would have been **settled** between them:
043:079   What! have they **settled** some Plan

SETTLEMENT

002:182   **settlement** among (the parties concerned),
004:128   **settlement** between themselves; and such
004:128   and such **settlement** is best; even though

SEVEN

002:029   and made them into **seven** firmaments;
002:196   And **seven** days on his return,
002:261   it groweth **seven** ears,
012:043   whom **seven** lean ones devour,-
012:043   (in a vision) **seven** fat kine,
012:043   and **seven** green ears of corn,
012:043   and **seven** (others) withered. O ye chiefs!
012:046   Expound to Us (the dream) of **seven** fat kine whom
012:046   whom **seven** lean ones devour,

SEVEN (continued)

012:046 and of seven green ears of corn and
012:046 of corn and (**seven**) others withered: that I
012:047 (Joseph) said: "For **seven** years shall ye
012:048 (period) **seven** dreadful (years), which will
015:044 To it are **seven** Gates: for each
015:087 **Seven** Oft-Repeated (verses) and the Grand Qur'an.
017:044 The **seven** heavens and the earth, and all
018:022 (yet others) say they were **seven**, the dog
023:017 **seven** tracts; and We are never unmindful of (Our)
023:086 **seven** heavens, and the Lord of the Mighty Throne?"
031:027 with **seven** Oceans behind it to add to its (supply),
041:012 So He completed them as **seven** firmaments in two
065:012 Allah is He Who created **seven** Firmaments and of
067:003 He Who created the **seven** heavens one above another:
069:007 **seven** nights and eight days in succession: so that
071:015 the **seven** heavens one above another,
078:012 over you the **seven** firmaments,

SEVENTY

007:155 And Moses chose **seventy** of his people
009:080 if thou ask **seventy** times for their forgiveness,
069:032 whereof the length is **seventy** cubits!

SEVERALLY

026:155 (**severally**) on a day appointed.

SEVERE

003:056 **severe** chastisement in this world and the Hereafter
003:159 Wert thou **severe** or harsh-hearted, they would
003:176 no portion in the Hereafter, but a **severe** punishment.
006:124 and a **severe** chastisement, for all their plots.
008:068 a **severe** punishment would have reached you
011:058 We saved them from a **severe** chastisement.
011:102 indeed, and **severe** is His chastisement.
020:071 which of us can give the more **severe** and the
023:077 leading to a **severe** Punishment: then Lo!
027:021 with a **severe** punishment, or execute
040:003 is **Severe** in Punishment, and is
040:022 full of Strength, **Severe** Punishment.
041:027 a taste of a **severe** Chastisement, and We
041:050 the taste of a **severe** Chastisement.
050:026 throw him into a **severe** Chastisement."
057:020 a Chastisement **severe** (for the devotees of wrong).
058:015 **severe** Chastisement: evil indeed are their deeds.
059:004 resists Allah, verily Allah is **severe** in Punishment.
065:008 to **severe** account?-and We chastised them with
065:010 a **severe** Punishment (in the Hereafter).
066:006 stern (and) **severe**, who flinch not (from

SEVEREST

003:004 will suffer the **severest** chastisement
010:070 the **severest** Chastisement for their disbelief.
040:046 into the **severest** Penalty"

SEW

007:022 and they began to **sew** together the leaves
020:121 to them: they began to **sew** together, for their

SEX

053:021 What! for you the male **sex**, and for

SEXES

075:039 And of him He made two **sexes**, male and female.

SEXUAL

024:003 none can have **sexual** relations with her but an
024:003 **sexual** relations with any but an adulteress
024:031 or male attendants free of **sexual** desires.

SHADE

002:057 And We gave You the **shade** of clouds
007:160 We gave them the **shade** of clouds, and sent
013:035 and the **shade** therein: such is
016:081 some things to give you **shade**; of the
028:024 then he turned back to the **shade**, and said:
035:021 Nor are the (chilly) **shade** and the (genial)
036:056 be in pleasant **shade**, reclining on raised couches;
056:030 In **shade** long-extended,
077:031 "(Which yields) no **shade** of coolness, and is

SHADES

004:057 We shall admit them to **shades**, cool
035:027 and red, of various **shades** of colour, and black
056:043 And in the **shades** of Black Smoke:
076:014 And the **shades** of the (Garden) will come
077:041 they shall be amidst (cool) **shades** and springs

SHADOW

025:045 doth prolong the **Shadow**! If He willed,
077:030 "Depart ye to a **Shadow** (of smoke ascending)

SHADOWS

013:015 so do their **shadows** in the mornings and evenings.
016:048 Among things,-how their **shadows** turn round,

SHAKE

014:046 even though they were such as to **shake** the hills!
016:015 should **shake** with you; and rivers and ways; that ye
019:025 "And **shake** towards thyself the trunk
021:031 lest it should **shake** with them, and We
031:010 standing firm, lest it should **shake** with you;

SHAKEN

002:214 and were so **shaken** in spirit that even the Messenger
033:011 Believers tried: they were **shaken** as by
056:004 When the earth shall be **shaken** to its depths,
099:001 When the Earth is **shaken** to her

SHAKES

067:016 when it **shakes** (as in an earthquake)?

SHAKINESS

009:110 and **shakiness** in their hearts, until their

SHAKING

033:011 as by a tremendous **shaking**.

SHALL

002:013 "**Shall** we believe as the fools believe?"-
002:038 on them **shall** be no fear,
002:038 nor **shall** they grieve.
002:039 they **shall** abide therein."
002:039 they **shall** be Companions of the Fire;
002:040 and I **shall** fulfil My Covenant with you,
002:048 nor **shall** compensation be taken from her.
002:048 Nor **shall** anyone be helped (from outside).
002:048 a day when one soul **shall** not avail another
002:048 nor **shall** intercession be accepted for her,
002:055 "O Moses! we **shall** never believe in thee
002:058 and say: Forgive (us) We **shall** forgive you
002:061 and ye **shall** find what ye want!"
002:062 nor **shall** they grieve.
002:062 **shall** have their reward with their Lord
002:062 on them **shall** be no fear,
002:076 they say: "**Shall** you tell them what Allah
002:080 And they say: "The fire **shall** not touch us
002:081 therein **shall** they abide (for ever).
002:082 therein **shall** they abide (for ever).
002:085 they **shall** be consigned to the most
002:086 nor **shall** they be helped.

SHALL (continued)

002:086 their chastisement **shall** not be lightened
002:095 But they **shall** will never seek for death,
002:110 ye **shall** find it with Allah:
002:111 And they say: "None **shall** enter Paradise
002:112 nor **shall** they grieve.
002:112 on such **shall** be no fear,
002:119 but of thee no question **shall** be asked
002:123 nor **shall** compensation be accepted from her
002:123 nor **shall** intercession profit her
002:123 nor **shall** anyone be helped (from outside)
002:123 a day when one soul **shall** not avail another,
002:129 Who **shall** rehearse Thy Signs to them
002:133 They said: "We **shall** worship thy God
002:134 ye **shall** not be asked about what they did.
002:134 They **shall** reap the fruit of what they did,
002:141 Ye **shall** not be asked!
002:141 They **shall** reap the fruit of what they did,
002:144 a Qiblah that **shall** please thee.
002:144 now **shall** We turn thee to a Qiblah
002:155 Be sure We **shall** test you with something
002:159 on them **shall** be Allah's curse,
002:170 **shall** follow the ways of our fathers."
002:178 the limits **shall** be in grave chastisement.
002:181 the guilt **shall** be on those who make the change.
002:185 and perchance ye **shall** be grateful.
002:214 ye **shall** enter the Garden (of Bliss)
002:228 Divorced women **shall** wait concerning themselves
002:228 And women **shall** have rights similar
002:233 The mothers **shall** give suck to their offspring
002:233 But he **shall** bear the cost of their food
002:233 No mother **shall** be treated unfairly
002:233 No soul **shall** have a burden laid on it
002:233 An heir **shall** be chargeable in the same way.
002:234 they **shall** wait concerning themselves
002:245 and to Him **shall** be your return.
002:248 **shall** come to you the Ark of the Covenant,
002:255 Nor **shall** they compass aught of his knowledge
002:259 **shall** Allah bring it (ever) to life,
002:262 on them **shall** be no fear, nor **shall** they grieve.
002:272 and ye **shall** not be dealt with unjustly.
002:272 and ye **shall** only do so seeking
002:272 **shall** be rendered back to you,
002:274 on them **shall** be no fear, nor **shall** they grieve.
002:275 **shall** be pardoned for the past;
002:277 on them **shall** be no fear,
002:277 nor **shall** they grieve.
002:279 ye **shall** have your capital sums:
002:279 and ye **shall** no be dealt with unjustly.
002:281 Then **shall** every soul be paid what it earned,
002:281 and none **shall** be dealt with unjustly.
002:281 when ye **shall** be brought back to Allah.
003:015 Say: **shall** I give you glad tidings of things
003:024 This because they say: "The Fire **shall** not touch us
003:028 if any do that, **shall** have no relation left
003:040 He said: "O my Lord! how **shall** I have a son,
003:041 "**Shall** be that thou shalt speak to no man
003:046 And he **shall** be (of the company)
003:046 "He **shall** speak to the people in childhood
003:047 how **shall** I have a son when man hath touched Me?"
003:055 then **shall** ye all return to Me,
003:069 But they **shall** lead astray (not you),
003:077 they **shall** have a grievous Chastisement.

SHALL (continued)

003:077 they **shall** have no portion in the Hereafter:
003:083 and to Him **shall** they all be brought back.
003:086 How **shall** Allah guide those who reject faith
003:092 By no means **shall** ye attain righteousness unless
003:111 and no help **shall** they get.
003:145 And swiftly **shall** We reward those that
003:145 We **shall** give it to him.
003:151 Soon **shall** We cast terror into the hearts
003:161 he **shall**, on the Day of Judgment, restore
003:161 then **shall** every soul receive its due
003:161 and none **shall** be dealt with unjustly.
003:181 We **shall** certainly record their word
003:181 and We **shall** say: "Taste ye the Chastisement
003:185 **shall** you be paid your full recompense.
003:185 Every soul **shall** have a taste of death:
003:186 Ye **shall** certainly be tried and tested
003:186 and ye **shall** certainly hear much
004:003 If ye fear that ye **shall** not be able
004:003 but if ye fear that ye **shall** not be able
004:014 and they **shall** have a humiliating punishment.
004:030 soon **shall** We cast them into the Fire:
004:031 We **shall** remit your evil deeds, and admit
004:056 We **shall** soon cast into the Fire:
004:056 We **shall** change them for fresh skins, that they
004:057 therein **shall** they have spouses purified
004:057 We **shall** admit them to shades, cool
004:057 We **shall** soon admit to Gardens, with rivers
004:074 soon **shall** We give him a reward of great (value).
004:114 We **shall** soon give a reward of the highest (value).
004:115 We **shall** leave him in the path he has chosen,
004:122 We **shall** soon admit them to Gardens, with rivers
004:152 We **shall** soon give their (due) rewards: for Allah
004:162 to them **shall** We soon give a great reward.
004:176 they **shall** have two-thirds of the inheritance
004:176 she **shall** have half the inheritance: if
005:022 never **shall** we enter it until they leave it: if
005:022 (once) they leave, then **shall** we enter."
005:024 They said: O "Moses! we **shall** never enter it
005:060 Say: "**Shall** I point out to you something
005:069 on them **shall** be no fear, nor **shall** they grieve.
005:069 on them **shall** be no fear, nor **shall** they grieve.
005:086 they **shall** be Companions of Hell-fire.
005:096 and fear Allah, to Whom ye **shall** be gathered back.
005:106 if we do, then behold! we **shall** be sinners.
005:106 we **shall** hide not the evidence we owe to Allah if
006:005 but soon **shall** come to them the news
006:014 Say: "**Shall** I take for my protector any other
006:021 But verily the wrong-doers never **shall** prosper.
006:022 We **shall** say to those who ascribed partners
006:022 On the day **shall** We gather them all together: We
006:027 when they **shall** be made to stand by the Fire!
006:029 and never **shall** we be raised up again."
006:030 when they **shall** be made to stand before
006:038 and they (all) **shall** be gathered to
006:048 upon them **shall** be no fear, nor **shall** they grieve.
006:049 them **shall** our punishment touch, for that
006:063 (we vow) we **shall** truly show our gratitude.'?"
006:067 and soon **shall** ye know it."
006:071 Say: "**Shall** we call on others besides Allah,-
006:072 that we **shall** be gathered together."
006:077 I **shall** surely be among those who go astray."
006:079 and the earth, and never **shall** I give

SHALL (continued)

006:089 behold! We **shall** entrust their charge to a new
006:093 This day **shall** ye receive your reward,-
006:108 and He **shall** then tell them the truth
006:110 We (too) **shall** turn to (confusion) their hearts
006:110 We **shall** leave them in their trespasses, to
006:114 Say: "**Shall** I seek for judge other than Allah?-
006:124 "We **shall** not believe until we receive
006:157 In good time **shall** We requite those who
006:160 he that doeth evil **shall** only be recompensed
006:160 No wrong **shall** be done unto them.
006:160 He that doeth good **shall** have ten times
006:164 Say: "**Shall** I seek for (my) Lord
007:006 Then **shall** We question those to whom
007:007 And verily We **shall** recount their whole
007:023 we **shall** certainly be lost."
007:025 and therein **shall** ye die: but from it
007:025 but from it **shall** ye be taken out (at last)."
007:025 He said: "Therein **shall** ye live, and therein
007:029 so **shall** ye return."
007:035 on them **shall** be no fear, nor **shall** they grieve.
007:043 and they **shall** say: "Praise be to Allah, Who
007:043 And We **shall** remove from their hearts
007:043 And they **shall** hear the cry: "Behold!
007:044 but a Crier **shall** proclaim between them: "The curse
007:044 They **shall** say, "Yes"; but a Crier
007:046 Between them **shall** be a veil, and on
007:047 When their eyes **shall** be turned towards
007:049 Enter ye the Garden: no fear **shall** be on you, nor
007:049 nor **shall** ye grieve."
007:051 That day **shall** We forget them as they
007:057 thus **shall** We raise up the dead: perchance
007:073 or ye **shall** be seized with a grievous punishment."
007:088 said: "O Shu'aib! we **shall** certainly drive thee
007:088 **shall** have to return to our religion." He said:
007:093 but how **shall** I lament over a people
007:113 they said, "Of course we **shall** have a (suitable)
007:114 for ye **shall** in that case be (raised to posts)
007:115 or **shall** we have the (first) throw?"
007:123 but soon **shall** ye know (the consequences).
007:132 we **shall** never believe in thee."
007:134 and we **shall** send away the Children
007:134 we **shall** truly believe in thee, and we
007:140 He said: "**Shall** I seek for you a god
007:145 soon **shall** I show you the homes of the
007:149 we **shall** indeed be among the Losers.
007:156 That (Mercy) I **shall** ordain for those
007:161 We **shall** forgive you your faults; We **shall**
007:161 We **shall** increase (the portion of)
007:170 never **shall** We suffer the reward of the
007:189 we vow we **shall** (ever) be grateful."
008:019 so **shall** We. Not the least good will your
008:024 ye **shall** (all) be gathered.
008:060 Whatever ye **shall** spend in the cause of Allah,
008:060 the cause of Allah, **shall** be repaid unto you,
008:060 unto you, and ye **shall** not be treated unjustly.
009:017 in Fire **shall** they dwell.
009:018 The mosques of Allah **shall** be visited and
009:063 Wherein they **shall** dwell. That is
009:068 the fire of Hell: therein **shall** they dwell:
009:074 and in the Hereafter: they **shall** have none on
009:077 (to last) till the day whereon they **shall** meet Him:
009:079 and they **shall** have a grievous chastisement.

SHALL (continued)

009:083 say: "Never **shall** ye come out with me, nor fight
009:094 we **shall** not believe you: Allah hath
009:101 and in addition **shall** they be sent
009:101 twice **shall** We punish them: and in
010:022 from this, we **shall** truly show our gratitude!
010:023 and We **shall** show you the truth of all that ye did.
010:026 **shall** cover their faces! They are Companions
010:028 Then **shall** We say to those who joined gods
010:028 and their "partners" **shall** say: "It was not
010:028 We **shall** separate them, and their
010:028 One Day **shall** We gather them all together. Then
010:056 and to Him **shall** ye all be brought back.
010:062 there is no fear, nor **shall** they grieve;
010:070 Then **shall** We make them taste the severest
010:078 But not we **shall** believe in you!"
010:092 "This day **shall** We save thee in thy body,
011:007 "Ye **shall** indeed be raised up after death,
011:015 to them We **shall** pay (the price of) their deeds
011:028 **Shall** we compel you to accept it when ye
011:048 be other) Peoples to whom We **shall** grant their
011:072 She said: "Alas for me! **Shall** I bear a child,
011:081 By no means **shall** they reach thee! Now travel
011:099 which **shall** be given (unto them)!
011:104 Nor **shall** We delay it but for a term appointed.
011:105 **shall** speak except by His leave: of those
011:106 Those who are wretched **shall** be in the Fire:
011:108 And those who are blessed **shall** be in the Garden:
011:109 before (them): but verily We **shall** pay them back
011:113 than Allah, nor **shall** ye be helped.
011:119 and the Word of thy Lord **shall** be fulfilled:
011:121 "Do whatever ye can: we **shall** do our part;
011:122 "And wait ye! we too **shall** wait."
012:012 and we **shall** take every care of him."
012:015 'Of a surety thou **shall** (one day) tell them
012:021 much good, or we **shall** adopt him as a son." Thus
012:032 he **shall** certainly be cast into prison, and (what
012:047 except a little, of which ye **shall** eat.
012:047 ye **shall** leave them in the ear,-except a
012:047 **shall** ye diligently sow as is your wont: and the
012:048 **shall** have (specially) guarded.
012:048 which will devour what ye **shall** have laid
012:060 ye **shall** have no measure (of corn) from me,
012:060 from me, nor **shall** ye (even) come near me."
012:061 They said: "We **shall** try to win him from
012:061 win him from his father: indeed we **shall** do it."
012:063 No more measure of grain **shall** we get (unless we
012:064 He said: "**Shall** I trust you with him with any
012:065 has been returned to us: so we **shall** get (more)
012:065 get (more) for our family; we **shall** take care
012:074 **shall** be the penalty of this, if ye are
013:005 **shall** we indeed then be in a creation renewed?"
013:023 they **shall** enter there, as well as the righteous
013:023 and angels **shall** enter unto them from every
013:040 Whether We **shall** show thee (within thy lifetime)
014:012 We **shall** certainly bear with patience all the
014:013 their messengers: "Be sure we **shall** drive you
014:013 to them: "Verily We **shall** cause the wrong-doers
014:013 or ye **shall** return to our religion." But their
014:014 "And verily We **shall** cause you to abide
014:014 when they **shall** stand before My tribunal,-such
015:035 "And the Curse **shall** be on thee
015:047 And We **shall** remove from their hearts any lurking

SHALL (continued)

015:048 There no sense of fatigue **shall** touch them,
015:048 touch them, nor **shall** they (ever) be asked
016:056 By Allah, ye **shall** certainly be called to account
016:059 he has had! **Shall** he retain it on (sufferance
016:063 so but they **shall** have a most grievous
016:084 On the Day We **shall** raise from all Peoples
016:087 and all their inventions **shall** leave them
016:087 That day **shall** they (openly) show (their)
016:089 On the day We **shall** raise from all peoples
016:089 from amongst themselves: and We **shall** bring thee
016:093 but ye **shall** certainly be called to account
017:008 (to your sins), We **shall** revert (to Our
017:009 of righteousness, that they **shall** have a
017:013 We **shall** bring out for him a scroll, which he
017:031 of want: We **shall** provide, sustenance for them
017:036 all of those **shall** be questioned of.
017:051 raised up)-(yet **shall** ye be raised up)!" Then will
017:058 We **shall** destroy it before the Day
017:061 he said, "**Shall** I prostrate to one whom Thou
017:068 so that ye **shall** find no protector?
017:071 On the day We **shall** call together all human
017:090 They say: "We **shall** not believe in thee,
017:093 the skies. No, we **shall** not even believe
017:097 We **shall** increase for them the fierceness
017:097 On the Day of Judgment We **shall** gather them
018:002 **shall** have a goodly Reward.
018:003 Wherein they **shall** remain forever:
018:008 Verily what is on earth We **shall** make but as
018:014 and of the earth: never **shall** we call upon any
018:023 "I **shall** be sure to do so and so to-morrow"
018:030 **shall** not suffer to perish the reward of any
018:036 I **shall** surely find (there) something better
018:038 and none **shall** I associate with my Lord.
018:047 On the Day We **shall** remove the mountains, and thou
018:047 a level stretch, and We **shall** gather them,
018:047 nor **shall** We leave out any one of them.
018:048 We **shall** not fulfil the appointment made to you
018:052 and We **shall** make for them a place
018:053 And the Sinful **shall** see the Fire and apprehend
018:069 nor **shall** I disobey thee in aught."
018:087 He said: "Whoever doth wrong, him **shall** we punish;
018:087 we punish; then **shall** he be sent back to his Lord;
018:088 works righteousness-he **shall** have a goodly reward,
018:094 **shall** we then render thee tribute in order that
018:099 and We **shall** collect them all together.
018:099 On that day We **shall** leave them to surge
018:100 And We **shall** present Hell that day for Unbelievers
018:103 Say: "**Shall** we tell you of those who lose most
018:105 vain will be their works, nor **shall** We, on the
018:108 Wherein they **shall** dwell (for aye): no change
019:007 his name **shall** be Yahya: on none by that name
019:008 He said: "O my Lord! how **shall** I have a son,
019:010 "**shall** be that thou shalt speak to no man
019:020 She said: "How **shall** I have a son, seeing that
019:033 I **shall** be raised up to life (again)!"
019:048 I **shall** be not unblest."!
019:066 **shall** I then be raised up alive?"
019:068 We **shall** gather them together, and (also)
019:068 then **shall** We bring them forth on their
019:069 Then **shall** We certainly drag out from every
019:072 But We **shall** save those who guarded against evil
019:072 against evil, and We **shall** leave the wrong-doers

SHALL (continued)

019:077 "I **shall** certainly be given wealth and children"?
019:079 Nay! We **shall** record what he says, and We
019:079 and We **Shall** add and add to his punishment.
019:080 To Us **shall** return all that he talks of, and he
019:080 and he **shall** appear before Us bare and alone.
019:082 Instead, they **shall** reject their worship,
019:085 The day We **shall** gather the righteous to (Allah)
019:086 And We **shall** drive the sinners to Hell,
019:087 None **shall** have the power of intercession,
020:021 We **shall** return it at once to its
020:022 it **shall** come forth white (and shining),
020:040 and saith, '**Shall** I show you one who will nurse
020:055 and into it **shall** We return you, and from
020:055 and from it **shall** We bring you out once again."
020:058 in a place where both **shall** have even chances."
020:058 between us and thee, which we **shall** not fail
020:071 So **shall** ye know for certain, which of
020:072 They said: "Never **shall** we prefer thee to what
020:074 is Hell: therein **shall** he neither die or live.
020:102 that Day, We **shall** gather the sinful, blear-eyed
020:109 On that Day **shall** no intercession avail except for
020:110 or behind them: but they **shall** comprehend Him not.
020:111 (All) faces **shall** be humbled before-the Living,
020:120 he said, "O Adam! **shall** I lead thee to the Tree
020:124 a life narrowed down, and We **shall** raise him up
020:135 wait ye, therefore, and soon **shall** ye know who
021:035 Every soul **shall** have a taste of death: and We
021:047 We **shall** set up scales of justice for the
021:094 be rejected: We **shall** record it in his favour.
021:095 that they **shall** not return,
021:104 truly **shall** We fulfil it.
021:104 **shall** We produce a new one: a promise
021:105 **shall** inherit the earth."
022:002 **shall** forget her suckling-babe, and every
022:002 **shall** drop her load (unformed): thou shalt
022:002 The Day ye **shall** see it, every mother
022:009 and on the Day of Judgment We **shall** make him
022:018 And such as Allah **shall** disgrace,-none can
022:023 they **shall** be adorned therein with bracelets
022:059 to a place with which they **shall** be well pleased:
022:072 Say, "**Shall** I tell you of something (far) worse than
023:027 the wrong-doers: for they **shall** be drowned
023:035 ye **shall** be brought forth (again)?
023:037 in this world! We **shall** die and we live! But we
023:037 But we **shall** never be raised up again!
023:047 They said: "**Shall** we believe in two men
023:065 for ye **shall** certainly not be helped by Us.
023:079 the earth, and to Him **shall** ye be gathered back.
023:107 then **shall** we be wrong-doers indeed!"
023:117 **shall** not prosper.
024:054 If ye obey him, ye **shall** be on right guidance.
025:019 him **shall** We cause to taste of a
025:023 And We **shall** turn to whatever deeds they did
025:023 they did (in this life), and We **shall** make such
025:025 and angels **shall** be sent down, descending (in
025:025 The Day the heaven **shall** be rent asunder
025:026 **shall** be (wholly) for The Most Gracious: it will
025:060 **Shall** we adore that which thou commandest us?"
025:075 patient constancy; therein **shall** they be met
026:041 **shall** we have a (suitable) reward if we win?"
026:042 for ye **shall** in that case be (raised to
026:049 But soon **shall** ye know! Be sure

SHALL (continued)

026:050 we **shall** but return to our Lord!
026:052 for surely ye **shall** be pursued."
026:092 "And it **shall** be said to them: `Where are
026:102 we **shall** truly be of those who believe!'"
026:111 They said: "**Shall** we believe in thee when it
026:203 Then they will say: "**Shall** we be respited?"
026:221 **Shall** I inform you, (O people!), on whom
027:027 (Solomon) said: "Soon **shall** we see whether thou
027:037 we **shall** expel them from there in disgrace,
027:037 we **shall** come to them with such hosts as they
027:049 and that we **shall** then say to his heir (when he
027:049 that we **shall** make a secret night attack on him
027:065 **shall** be raised up (for Judgment).
027:067 **shall** we really be raised (from the dead)?
027:082 We **shall** bring forth from the earth a beast
027:083 The Day We **shall** gather together from every
027:083 and they **shall** be kept in ranks,-
027:087 and all **shall** come to Him in utter humility.
027:088 but they **shall** pass away as the clouds pass away:
027:093 so that ye **shall** know them": and thy
028:007 and We **shall** make him one of Our messengers."
028:007 for We **shall** restore him to thee, and We
028:012 and) said: "**Shall** I point out to you the people
028:017 never **shall** I be a help to those who sin!"
028:035 so they **shall** not be able to touch you: with Our
028:035 with Our Signs **shall** ye triumph,-you two
028:041 no help **shall** they find.
028:067 and worked righteousness, haply he **shall** be one
028:070 and to Him **shall** ye (all) be brought back.
028:075 a witness, and We **shall** say: "Produce your
028:075 And from each people **shall** We draw a witness,
028:075 then **shall** they know that the Truth is
028:080 but this none **shall** attain, save those
028:083 That Home of the Hereafter We **shall** give to
029:007 righteous deeds,-from them **shall** We blot out
029:007 have committed, and We **shall** reward them according
029:009 righteous deeds,-them **shall** We admit to the
029:023 **shall** despair of My mercy: it is they who
029:025 the Fire, and ye **shall** have none to help."
029:025 ye **shall** disown each other and curse each other:
029:055 and (a Voice) **shall** say: "Taste ye
029:055 **shall** cover them from above them and from
029:057 in the end to Us **shall** ye be brought back.
029:057 Every soul **shall** have a taste of death: in the
029:058 to them **shall** We give a Home in Heaven,-
030:004 on that Day **shall** the Believers rejoice-
030:011 then repeats it; then **shall** ye be brought
030:014 that Day **shall** (all men) be sorted out.
030:015 **shall** be made happy in a Mead (of Delight).
030:016 such **shall** be brought forth to Punishment.
030:019 and thus **shall** ye be brought out (from the dead).
030:043 on that Day **shall** men be divided (in two).
031:021 "Nay, we **shall** follow the ways that we found
031:022 and to Allah **shall** all things return.
031:023 and We **shall** tell them the truth of their deeds:
031:024 a little while: in the end **shall** We drive them
032:010 **shall** we indeed be in a Creation renewed?"
032:011 then **shall** ye be brought back to your Lord."
032:022 who transgress We **shall** exact (Due) Retribution.
033:031 to her **shall** We grant her reward twice: and We
033:047 **shall** have from Allah a very great Bounty.
033:060 We **shall** certainly stir thee up against them:

SHALL (continued)

033:061 They **shall** have a curse on them: wherever they
033:061 they **shall** be seized and slain.
034:007 "**Shall** we point out to you a man that will
034:007 that ye **shall** (then be raised) in a New Creation?
034:025 our sins, nor **shall** we be questioned as to
034:025 Say: "Ye **shall** not be questioned as to our sins,
034:031 The Unbelievers say: "We **shall** neither believe
034:033 We **shall** put yokes on the necks of the Unbelievers:
034:042 and We **shall** say to the wrong-doers, "Taste ye
034:042 So on that Day no power **shall** they have
035:035 **shall** touch us therein."
035:036 no term **shall** be determined for them, so they
035:036 nor **shall** its Chastisement be lightened for them.
035:037 Bring us out: we **shall** work righteousness, not the
036:012 Verily We **shall** give life to the dead, And We
036:022 Who created me, and to Whom ye **shall** (all) be
036:023 "**Shall** I take (other) gods besides Him?
036:047 who believe: "**Shall** we then feed those whom,
036:051 The trumpet **shall** be sounded, when behold!
036:054 be wronged in the least, and ye **shall** but be
036:055 **shall** that Day have joy in all that they do;
036:057 they **shall** have whatever they call for;
036:065 That Day **shall** We set a seal on their mouths.
037:016 and bones, **shall** we (then) be raised up (again)?
037:018 Say thou: "Yea, and ye **shall** then be humiliated
037:022 "Bring ye up," it **shall** be said, "The wrong-doers
037:026 Nay, but that day they **shall** submit (to Judgment);
037:031 that we **shall** indeed (have to) taste (the
037:034 Verily that is how We **shall** deal with Sinners.
037:036 And say: "What! **Shall** we give up our gods
037:038 Ye **shall** indeed taste of the Grievous Chastisement;-
037:042 Fruits, and they (**shall** enjoy) honour and dignity,
037:053 and bones, **shall** we indeed receive rewards
037:058 "Is it (the case) that we **shall** not die,
037:059 and that we **shall** not be punished?"
037:068 Then **shall** their return be to the (Blazing) Fire.
037:175 and they soon **shall** see (how thou farest)!
037:179 and they soon **shall** see (how thou farest)!
038:028 on earth? **Shall** We treat those who guard
038:028 **Shall** We treat those who believe and work
038:057 Yea, such!-Then **shall** they taste it,-a boiling
038:059 Truly, they **shall** burn in the Fire!
038:060 (The followers **shall** cry to the misleaders:)
038:078 "And My Curse **shall** be on thee till the
038:088 "And ye **shall** certainly know the truth
039:016 They **shall** have Layers of Fire above them,
039:034 They **shall** have all that they wish for, in the
039:044 ye **shall** be brought back."
039:051 them (too), and they **shall** not escape!
039:054 comes on you: after that ye **shall** not be helped.
039:061 no evil **shall** touch them, nor **shall** they grieve.
040:033 A day when ye **shall** turn your backs and flee:
040:033 and flee: no defender **shall** ye have from Allah:
040:056 which they **shall** never attain to: seek refuge,
040:070 but soon **shall** they know,-
040:071 When the yokes (**shall** be) round their necks,
040:071 they **shall** be dragged along-
040:072 then in the Fire **shall** they be burned;
040:073 Then **shall** it be said to them: "Where are
040:077 that they **shall** (all) return.
041:005 for us, we **shall** do (what we will!)"
041:024 their suit **shall** not be granted.

SHALL (continued)

041:029   we **shall** crush them beneath our feet, so that
041:031   therein **shall** ye have all that ye ask for!-
041:031   your souls **shall** desire; therein **shall**
041:031   therein **shall** ye have all that your souls
041:050   they did, and We **shall** give them the taste
042:022   of the Gardens: they **shall** have, before their
042:023   We **shall** give Him an increase of good
043:005   **Shall** We then take away the Reminder from you
043:039   that day, that ye **shall** be partners in punishment!
043:041   We **shall** be sure to exact retribution from them,
043:042   Or We **shall** show thee that (accomplished) which We
043:044   and soon **shall** ye (all) be brought to account.
043:049   for We **shall** truly accept guidance."
043:061   And (Jesus) **shall** be a Sign (for the coming of)
043:068   My devotees! no fear **shall** be on you today,
043:068   you today, nor **shall** ye grieve,-
043:071   and ye **shall** abide therein (for aye).
043:073   Ye **shall** have therein abundance of fruit,
043:073   of fruit, from which ye **shall** eat.
043:076   Nowise **shall** We be unjust to them: But it
043:077   "Nay, but ye **shall** abide!"
043:085   And to Him **shall** ye be brought back.
043:089   and say "Peace!" but soon **shall** they know!
044:013   How **shall** they have the Reminder. Seeing that
044:015   We **shall** indeed remove the Chastisement for a
044:016   The day We **shall** seize you with a mighty onslaught:
044:035   and we **shall** not be raised again.
044:054   So; and We **shall** wed them to maidens
045:021   think that We **shall** hold them as equal with those
045:022   it has earned, and none of them **shall** be wronged.
045:024   We **shall** die and we live, and nothing
045:028   called to its Record: "This Day **shall** ye be
045:035   therefore, they **shall** not be taken out thence,
046:013   no fear, nor **shall** they grieve.
046:013   (on that Path),-on them **shall** be no fear,
046:014   Such **shall** be Companions of the Garden,
046:016   Such are they from whom We **shall** accept the best
046:016   (they **shall** be) among the Companions of the Garden:
046:017   I **shall** be raised up, even though
046:020   but to-day **shall** ye be recompensed with a
046:035   the Message: but **shall** any be destroyed except
047:015   be compared to such as **shall** dwell for ever
047:018   to them, how **shall** they have their Reminder?
047:031   and We **shall** try your reported (mettle).
047:031   And We **shall** try you until We test those among you
048:016   vehement war: then **shall** ye fight, or they
048:016   or they **shall** submit. Then if ye show obedience,
048:016   lagged behind: "Ye **shall** be summoned (to fight)
048:020   that ye **shall** acquire, and He
048:027   ye **shall** enter the Sacred Mosque, if Allah
050:003   (**shall** we live again?) That is
050:020   And the Trumpet **shall** be blown: that will
052:013   That Day **shall** they be thrust down to the
052:018   and their Lord **shall** deliver them from
052:020   and We **shall** wed them to maidens, with beautiful,
052:021   nor **shall** We deprive them (of the fruit)
052:021   to them **shall** We join their families: nor **shall**
052:022   of fruit and meat, anything they **shall** desire.
052:022   And We **shall** bestow on them, of fruit
052:023   They **shall** there exchange, one with
052:045   wherein they **shall** be thunderstruck.
052:046   avail them nothing and no help **shall** be given them.

SHALL (continued)

053:024   Nay, **shall** man have (just) anything
054:024   **Shall** we follow such a one? Truly should
055:031   Soon **shall** We settle your affairs, O both
055:033   authority **shall** ye be able to pass!
056:004   When the earth **shall** be shaken to its depths,
056:005   And the mountains **shall** be crumbled to atoms,
056:007   And ye **shall** be sorted out into three classes.
056:047   and bones, **shall** we then indeed be raised up again?-
056:055   "Indeed ye **shall** drink like diseased camels
056:079   Which none **shall** touch but those who are clean:
057:015   "This Day **shall** no ransom be accepted of you,
057:018   and they **shall** have (besides) a generous reward.
057:018   a Beautiful Loan, it **shall** be increased manifold
057:019   of their Lord: they **shall** have their Reward
057:028   by which ye **shall** walk (straight in your path),
058:009   and fear Allah, to whom ye **shall** be brought back.
058:016   Path of Allah: therefore **shall** they have
059:003   they **shall** (certainly) have the Punishment
061:006   after me, whose name **shall** be Ahmad. But when
061:010   O ye who believe! **shall** I lead you to a bargain
064:006   "**Shall** (mere) human beings direct us?" So they
064:007   then **shall** ye be told (the truth)
064:007   ye **shall** surely be raised up: then **shall**
065:001   their houses, nor **shall** they (themselves)
067:017   so that ye **shall** know how (terrible) was My warning?
067:024   and to Him **shall** ye be gathered together."
068:016   Soon **shall** We brand (the beast) on the snout!
068:035   **Shall** We then treat the People of Faith
068:038   That ye **shall** have, through it whatever ye choose?
068:039   that ye **shall** have whatever ye **shall** demand?
068:042   The Day that the Shin **shall** be laid bare,
068:042   to prostrate, but they **shall** not be able,-
068:042   laid bare, and they **shall** be summoned to prostrate,
068:044   as reject this Message: by degrees **shall** We draw
069:015   On that Day **shall** the (Great) Event come to pass,
069:018   That Day **shall** ye be brought to Judgment: not an
072:002   We **shall** not join (in worship) any (gods)
072:023   they **shall** dwell therein for ever."
073:005   Soon **shall** We send down to thee a weighty Word.
073:017   Then how **shall** ye, if ye deny (Allah),
073:020   ye **shall** find it with Allah. Yea, better
076:005   As to the Righteous, they **shall** drink of a Cup
076:028   but, when We will, We **shall** exchange their likes.
077:017   So **shall** We make later (generations) follow them.
077:035   **shall** not be able to speak,
077:038   We **shall** Gather you together and those before (you)!
077:041   they **shall** be amidst (cool) shades and springs
077:042   And (they **shall** have) fruits,-all they desire.
078:004   Verily, they **shall** soon (come to) know!
078:005   Verily, verily they **shall** soon (come to) know!
078:018   The Day that the Trumpet **shall** be sounded, and ye
078:018   and ye **shall** come forth in crowds;
078:019   And the heavens **shall** be opened as if
078:020   And the mountains **shall** vanish, as if
078:024   Nothing cool **shall** they taste therein,
078:030   for no increase **shall** We grant you, except in
078:035   No Vanity **shall** they hear therein, nor Untruth;-
078:037   The Most Gracious: none **shall** have power to argue
078:038   none **shall** speak except any who permitted by
079:010   They say (now): "What! **shall** we indeed be returned
079:011   "What!-when we **shall** have become rotten bones?"
079:035   The Day when Man **shall** remember (all) that

SHALL (continued)

079:036 And Hell-Fire **shall** be placed in full view
080:034 That Day **shall** a man flee from his own brother,
081:014 (Then) **shall** each soul know what it has put forward.
081:029 But ye **shall** not will Except as Allah wills,-
082:005 (Then) **shall** each soul know what it hath sent
082:019 **shall** have power (to do) aught for another: for the
084:019 Ye **shall** surely travel from stage to stage.
087:006 By degrees **shall** We teach thee (the Message),
088:011 Where they **shall** hear no (word) of vanity:
092:015 None **shall** reach it but those most unfortunate ones
092:017 **shall** be removed far from it,-
095:006 for they **shall** have a reward unfailing.
099:007 Then **shall** anyone who has done an atom's weight
099:008 an atom's weight of evil, **shall** see it.
102:003 But nay, ye soon **shall** know (the reality).
102:004 Again, ye soon **shall** know!
102:006 Ye **shall** certainly see Hell-fire!
102:007 Again, ye **shall** see it with certainty of sight!
102:008 Then, **shall** ye be Questioned that Day about the
104:008 It **shall** be made into a vault over them,
111:004 His wife **shall** carry the (crackling) wood-as fuel!

SHALLOW

052:012 That play (and paddle) in **shallow** trifles.

SHALT

002:273 Thou **shalt** know them by their (unfailing) mark:
003:041 that thou **shalt** speak to no man for three days
004:088 never **shalt** thou find the Way.
007:143 then **shalt** thou see Me."
010:095 Signs of Allah, or thou **shalt** be of those
010:106 thou **shalt** certainly be of those who do wrong."
015:042 **shalt** thou have, except such as put themselves
017:065 no authority **shalt** thou have over them."
019:010 "shall be that thou **shalt** speak to no man
022:002 thou **shalt** see mankind as in a drunken riot,
026:116 O Noah! thou **shalt** be stone (to death)."
057:012 The Day **shalt** thou see the believing men and the
084:006 painfully toiling, but thou **shalt** meet Him.
087:006 (the Message), so thou **shalt** not forget,
093:005 thou **shalt** be well-pleased.

SHAME

003:112 **Shame** is pitched over them (like a tent)
003:192 truly Thou coverest with **shame**,
003:194 and save us from **shame** on the Day of Judgment:
007:020 their **shame** that was hidden from them (before):
007:026 upon you to cover your **shame**, as well as
007:027 to expose their **shame**: for he
007:152 and with **shame** in this life: thus do
009:002 with **shame** those who reject Him.
011:039 that will cover them with **shame**,-on whom
011:078 and cover me not with **shame** about my guests!
015:069 "But fear Allah, and **shame** me not."
016:027 He will cover them with **shame**, and say:
016:027 covered with **Shame** and Misery,-
016:059 With **shame** does he hide himself from his people,
020:134 we were humbled and put to **shame**."
021:065 Then were they confounded with **shame**: (they said),
059:005 cover with **shame** the rebellious transgressors.

SHAMEFUL

002:169 For he commands you what is evil and **shameful**,
003:178 but they will have a **shameful** punishment.
004:022 it was **shameful** and odious, an abominable

SHAMEFUL (continued)

007:022 their **shameful** parts became manifest to them, and
029:045 for Prayer restrains from **shameful** and evil

SHAPE

005:108 in its true nature and **shape**, or else
007:011 and gave you **shape**; then We bade
015:026 from mud molded into **shape**;
015:028 form sounding clay, from mud molded into **shape**;
015:033 sounding clay, from mud moulded into **shape**."
040:064 and has given you **shape**-and made
064:003 and has given you **shape**, and made

SHAPES

003:006 **shapes** you in the wombs as He pleases.
040:064 and made your **shapes** beautiful,-and has
064:003 and made your **shapes** beautiful: and to Him

SHARE

002:102 would have no **share** in the happiness
004:007 a determinate **share**.
004:007 a **share** for men and a **share** for women,
004:011 their **share** is two-thirds of the inheritance;
004:011 a sixth **share** of the inheritance to each, if
004:011 if only one, her **share** is a half.
004:012 their **share** is a fourth, if ye leave no child;
004:012 your **share** is a half, if they leave no child;
004:012 but if more than two, they **share** in a third;
004:034 (next), refuse to **share** their beds,
004:053 Have they a **share** in dominion or power?
004:176 if there are brothers and sisters, (they **share**),
004:176 the male having twice the **share** of the female,
006:136 But the **share** of their "partners" reacheth
006:136 they assigned Him a **share**: They say,
006:136 whilst the **share** of Allah reacheth
007:190 they ascribe to others a **share** in the gift
008:041 a fifth **share** is assigned to Allah,-and to
017:064 and thy infantry; mutually **share** with them wealth
018:026 nor does He **share** His Command with any
020:032 "And make him **share** my task:
029:065 they give a **share** (of their worship to others)!-
030:028 to **share** as equals in the wealth We have
034:022 no (sort of) **share** have they therein, nor is
035:040 Or have they a **share** in the heavens? Or have
037:033 (all) **share** in the Chastisement.
040:047 from us some **share** of the Fire?"
042:020 but he has no **share** or lot in the Hereafter.
043:015 of His servants a **share** with Him. Truly is
046:004 or have they a **share** in the heavens? Bring me
051:019 a due **share** for the beggar and the deprived.

SHARERS

004:033 We have appointed **sharers** and heirs to property

SHARES

004:085 helps an evil cause, **shares** in its burden:
006:139 then all have **shares** therein. For their

SHARP

033:019 **sharp** tongues, covetous of goods. Such men
050:022 and **sharp** is thy sight this Day!"

SHAVE

002:196 and do not **shave** your heads until
048:027 heads **shaved**, hair cut short, and without fear.

SHAVING

002:196 in his scalp, (necessitating **shaving**),

SHE

002:070 to make plain to us what **she** is:

SHE (continued)

002:221 even though **she** allure you.
002:229 if **she** give something for her freedom
002:230 until after **she** has married another husband
003:036 When **she** was delivered, **she** said: "O my Lord!
003:036 And Allah knew best what **she** brought forth-
003:037 to the care of Zakariya was **she** assigned.
003:037 **She** said: "From Allah: for Allah provides
003:047 **She** said: "O my Lord! how shall I have a son
004:176 **she** shall have half the inheritance: if
007:083 **she** was of those who lagged behind.
007:189 **she** bears a light burden and carries
007:189 When **she** grows heavy, they both
011:071 and **she** laughed: but We gave her Glad tidings
011:072 **She** said: "Alas for me! Shall I bear a child,
012:023 sought to seduce him and **she** fastened the doors,
012:023 But **she**, in whose house he was, sought to
012:024 And (with passion) did **she** desire him, and he
012:025 **She** said: "What is the (fitting) punishment for
012:025 and **she** tore his shirt from the back: they both
012:026 He said: "It was **she** that sought to seduce me-
012:027 **she** the liar, and he is telling the truth!"
012:030 we see **she** is evidently going astray."
012:031 and **she** said (to Joseph), "Come out before them."
012:031 When **she** heard of their malicious talk, **she** sent
012:031 **she** sent for them and prepared a banquet for them:
012:031 for them: **she** gave each of them a knife: and **she**
012:032 **She** said: "There before you is the man
016:092 the yarn which **she** has spun, after it
019:016 when **she** withdrew from her family to a place
019:017 **She** placed a screen (to screen herself) from them:
019:018 **She** said: "I seek refuge from thee to (Allah)
019:020 **She** said: "How shall I have a son, seeing that
019:022 So **she** conceived him, and **she** retired with him
019:023 **she** cried (in her anguish): "Ah! would
019:027 At length **she** brought the (babe) to her people,
019:029 But **she** pointed to the babe. They said
020:040 and **she** should not grieve. Then thou
024:008 the wife, if **she** bears witness four times
024:009 **she** solemnly invokes the wrath of Allah on herself
026:155 **she** has a right of watering, and ye
027:023 every requisite; and **she** has a magnificent throne.
027:032 **She** said: "Ye chiefs! advise me
027:034 **She** said: "Kings, when they enter a country,
027:041 let us see whether **she** is guided (to the truth)
027:042 So when **she** arrived, **she** was asked, "Is this
027:042 "Is this thy throne?" **She** said, "It seems
027:043 for **she** was (sprung) of a people that had no faith.
027:044 **She** was asked to enter the lofty Palace:
027:044 **She** said: "O my Lord! I have indeed
027:044 **she** saw it, **she** thought it was a lake of water,
027:044 of water, and **she** (tucked up her skirts),
028:010 (with faith), so that **she** might remain a (firm)
028:010 became void: **she** was going almost to disclose
028:011 And **she** said to the sister of (Moses),
028:011 So **she** (the sister) watched him from a distance
028:013 and that **she** might know that the promise
028:013 that **she** might not grieve, and that
028:025 **She** said: "My father invites thee that he may
029:033 **she** is of those who lag behind.
036:039 **she** returns like the old (and withered)
046:015 bear him, and in pain did **she** give him birth.
051:029 **she** smote her forehead and said: "A barren

SHE (continued)

054:014 **She** floats under Our eyes (and care):
066:003 and **she** then divulged it (to another), and Allah
066:003 **she** said, "Who told thee this?" He said,
066:011 behold, **she** said: "O my Lord! build for me,
066:012 of Our spirit; and **she** testified to the truth
081:009 For what crime **she** was killed;
091:002 By the Moon as **she** follow him;
099:004 On that Day will **she** declare her tidings:

SHE-CAMEL

005:103 a slit-ear **she-camel**, or a **she-camel**
005:103 or a **she-camel** let loose for free pasture, or idol
007:073 This **she-camel** of Allah is a Sign unto you: so
007:077 Then they ham-strung the **she-camel**, and
011:064 "And O my people! this **she-camel** of Allah
017:059 as false: We sent the **She-camel** to the Thamud-
026:155 He said: "Here is a **she-camel**: she has
054:027 For We will send the **she-camel** by way
091:013 "It is a **She-camel** of Allah! And (bar

SHE-CAMELS

081:004 When the **she-camels**, ten months with young,

SHEATH

041:047 no fruit comes out of its **sheath**, nor does

SHEATHS

006:099 the date-palm and its **sheaths** (or spathes)

SHED

002:030 make mischief therein and **shed** blood?
002:084 **shed** no blood amongst you,
044:029 And neither heaven nor earth **shed** a tear over them:
076:011 and will **shed** over them brightness and a

SHEEP

006:143 of **sheep** a pair, and of goats a pair, say,
006:146 the ox and the **sheep**, except what
021:078 of the field into which the **sheep** of certain

SHEETS

006:091 into (separate) **sheets** for show, while ye

SHELTER

016:081 your **shelter**; He made you garments to protect you
023:050 We gave them both **shelter** on high ground,
024:063 under **shelter** of some excuse: then let
072:006 who took **shelter** with persons among the Jinns,
093:006 and give thee **shelter** (and care)?

SHELTERED

070:013 His kindred who **sheltered** him.

SHEPHERDS

028:023 until the **shepherds** take back (their flocks):

SHIN

068:042 The Day that the **Shin** shall be laid bare,

SHINE

039:069 And the Earth will **shine** with the light
055:029 (new) Splendor doth He (**shine**)!

SHINETH

074:034 And by the Dawn as it **shineth** forth,-

SHINING

010:005 **shining** glory and the moon to be a light
020:022 (and **shining**), without harm (or stain),-
056:018 With goblets, (**shining**) beakers, and cups

SHIP

017:066 Your Lord is He that maketh the **Ship** go smoothly
037:140 from captivity) to the **ship** (fully) laden,

SHIPS

002:164	the **ships** through the Ocean for the profit
010:022	till when ye even board **ships**;-they sail
014:032	it is He Who hath made the **ships** subject to you,
016:014	and thou seest the **ships** therein that plough
022:065	on the earth, and the **ships** that sail through
023:022	And on them, as well as in **ships**, ye ride.
030:046	that the **ships** may sail by His Command and that
031:031	Seest thou not that the **ships** sail through the
035:012	to wear; and thou seest the **ships** therein that
040:080	and on them and on **ships** ye are carried.
042:032	And among His Signs are the **ships**, smooth-running
043:012	and has made for you **ships** and cattle
045:012	that **ships** may sail through it by His command,
055:024	And His are the **Ships** sailing smoothly through

SHIRT

012:018	They stained his **shirt** with false blood. He said
012:025	and she tore his **shirt** from the back: they both
012:026	(thus)-"If it be that his **shirt** is rent
012:027	"But if it be that his **shirt** is torn
012:028	So when he saw his **shirt**,-that it
012:093	"Go with this my **shirt**, and cast it
012:096	news came, he cast (the **shirt**) over his face,

SHOES

020:012	Therefore put off thy **shoes**: thou art

SHOOTS

037:065	The **shoots** of its fruit-stalks are like
050:010	with **shoots** of fruit-stalks, piled one

SHORE

037:145	the naked **shore** in a state of sickness,
068:049	on the naked **shore**, in disgrace.

SHORT

004:077	Say: "**Short** is the enjoyment of this world: the
011:084	And give not **short** measure or weight: I see you
013:008	by how much the wombs fall **short** (of their
014:044	**short** Term: we will answer Thy Call, and follow
037:056	little **short** of bringing me to perdition!
048:027	heads shaved, hair cut **short**, and without fear.
055:009	and fall not **short** in the balance.
072:013	has no fear, either of a **short** (account) or of

SHORTEN

004:101	if ye **shorten** your prayers, for fear

SHORTNESS

007:130	and **shortness** of crops; that they might

SHOULD

002:068	**should** be neither too old nor too young,
002:089	that which they (**should**) have recognized,
002:090	Allah of His Grace **should** send it
002:105	That anything good **should** come down
002:114	**should** themselves enter them except in fear.
002:114	His name **should** be celebrated?
002:121	the Book study it as it **should** be studied:
002:125	that they **should** sanctify My House
002:158	**should** compass them round,
002:165	they love them as they **should** love Allah.
002:169	and that ye **should** say of Allah
002:184	(**should** be made up) from days later.
002:185	during that month **should** spent it in fasting,
002:185	(**should** be made up) by days later.
002:196	he **should** fast three days during the Hajj.
002:196	(he **should**) in compensation either fast,
002:215	They ask thee what they **should** spend (in charity).

SHOULD (continued)

002:229	the parties **should** either hold together
002:240	**should** bequeath for their widows a year's
002:266	**should** have a garden with date-palms
002:266	that it **should** be caught in a whirlwind,
002:282	The witnesses **should** not refuse when
003:044	**should** be charged with the care of Mary:
003:073	**should** engage you in argument before your Lord?
003:079	**should** say to people: "Be ye my worshippers
003:091	though they **should** offer it for ransom.
003:102	O ye who believe! fear Allah as He **should** be feared,
003:122	and in Allah **should** the Faithful
003:124	**should** help you with three thousand angels
003:125	even if the enemy **should** rush here
003:127	and they **should** then be turned back,
003:154	we **should** not have been in the slaughter here."
003:167	we **should** certainly have followed you."
004:019	Nor **should** ye treat them with harshness,
004:025	they **should** be chaste, not fornicators,
004:027	ye **should** turn away (from Him), far, far away.
004:044	and wish that ye **should** lose the right path.
004:048	that partners **should** be set up with him; but
004:067	And We **should** then have given them from
004:068	And We **should** have shown them the Straight Way.
004:073	a fine thing **should** I then have made of it!"
004:075	And why **should** ye not fight in the cause
004:077	or even more than, they **should** have feared Allah:
004:088	Why **should** ye be divided into two parties
004:089	They but wish that ye **should** reject Faith.
004:092	Never **should** a Believer kill a Believer; except
004:092	blood-money **should** be paid to his family, and
004:092	he **should** free a believing slave.
004:100	And abundance **should** he die as a refugee
004:165	**should** have no plea against Allah: for Allah
005:019	lest ye **should** say: "There came unto us no bringer
005:065	We **should** indeed have blotted out their
006:009	We **should** have sent him as a man. And We
006:009	and We **should** certainly have caused them confusion
006:053	that they **should** say: "Is it these
006:081	"How **should** I fear (the beings) ye
006:119	Why **should** ye not eat of (meats) on which
006:138	and none **should** eat of them except those
006:148	we **should** not have given partners to Him, nor
006:148	nor **should** we have had any forbidden thing." So
006:156	Lest ye **should** say: "The Book was sent down
006:157	Or lest ye **should** say: "If the Book
006:157	we **should** have followed its guidance
007:020	lest ye **should** become angels or such
007:053	Then **should** we behave differently from our
007:089	"We **should** indeed forge a lie against Allah, if
007:096	We **should** indeed have opened out to them
007:172	lest ye **should** say on the Day of Judgment: "Of
007:173	Or lest ye **should** say: "Our fathers
007:176	We **should** have elevated him with Our Signs; but he
007:188	and no evil **should** have touched me: I am
007:188	I **should** have multiplied all good, and no
008:007	the two parties, that it **should** be yours: ye wished
008:007	**should** be yours, but Allah willed to establish
008:034	that Allah **should** not punish them, when they
008:062	**Should** they intend to deceive thee,- verily
008:067	that he **should** have prisoners of war until he
009:013	Nay, it is Allah whom ye **should** more justly fear,
009:032	His light **should** be perfected, even though

SHOULD (continued)

009:042	"If we only could, we **should** certainly have come
009:062	**should** please Allah and His Messenger, if they
009:064	all that ye fear (**should** be revealed)."
009:064	**should** be sent down about them, showing them
009:113	that they **should** pray for forgiveness for Pagans,
009:115	**should** avoid, for Allah hath knowledge of all things.
009:128	**should** suffer, ardently anxious is he over you: to
010:002	That he **should** warn mankind (of their danger), and
010:015	I **should** myself fear the Chastisement
010:016	I **should** not have rehearsed it to you, nor **should**
010:016	nor **should** He have made it known to you. A whole
010:050	**should** come to you by night or by day,-what
010:071	that I **should** stay (with you) and remind
010:083	and his chiefs, lest they **should** persecute them:
010:098	**should** have profited it,-except the people
010:103	that We **should** deliver those who believe!
011:002	(It teacheth) that ye **should** worship none
011:031	I **should**, if I did, indeed be a wrong-doer."
011:047	I **should** indeed be among the losers!"
011:091	we **should** certainly have stoned thee! For thou
012:013	I fear lest the wolf **should** devour him
012:013	that ye **should** take him away: I fear
012:014	a party, then **should** we be the losers!
012:033	their snare from me, I **should** feel inclined towards
012:062	so they **should** know it only when they
012:075	**should** be held (as bondman) to atone
012:075	They said: "The penalty **should** be that he in whose
012:079	we **should** be acting wrongfully."
014:012	**should** put their trust on Allah."
014:012	Why we **should** not put our trust on Allah.
014:021	we **should** have given it to you: to us
014:044	to swear aforetime that ye **should** suffer no decline?
015:066	those (sinners) **should** be cut off by the morning.
016:015	**should** shake with you; and rivers and ways; that ye
016:035	nor **should** we have prescribed prohibitions other
016:035	"If Allah had so willed, we **should** not have
016:064	they differ, and that it **should** be a guide
016:092	lest one party **should** be more numerous
017:046	they **should** understand the Qur'an, and deafness
017:049	to bones and dust, **should** we really be raised up
017:053	Say to My servants that they **should** (only) say
017:075	In that case We **should** have made thee taste
017:095	and quiet, We **should** certainly have sent them
017:098	to bones and broken dust, **should** we really be
018:014	if we did; we **should** indeed have uttered
018:020	"For if thy **should** come upon you, they would
018:057	they **should** understand this not, and over
018:082	so thy Lord desired that they **should** attain their
019:035	**should** beget a son. Glory to Him! When He
019:092	that He **should** beget a son.
020:040	and she **should** not grieve. Then thou
020:081	lest My Wrath **should** descend on you: and those
020:086	that Wrath **should** descend from your Lord on you,
020:134	a messenger, we **should** certainly have followed
021:017	a pastime, We **should** surely have taken it from
021:029	such a one We **should** reward with Hell: thus do
021:029	If any of them **should** say, "I am
021:031	lest it **should** shake with them, and We
021:112	the One Whose assistance **should** be sought against
022:032	of animals), such (honour) **should** come truly
022:073	And if the fly **should** snatch away anything form them,
023:098	O my Lord! lest they **should** come near me."

SHOULD (continued)

024:007	And the fifth (oath) (**should** be) that he
024:009	And the fifth (oath) **should** be that she solemnly
024:022	do you not wish that Allah **should** forgive you?
024:030	**should** lower their gaze and guard their modesty:
024:031	that they **should** draw their veils over their
024:031	they **should** lower their gaze and guard
024:031	that they **should** not display their beauty
024:031	and that they **should** not strike their feet
024:061	that ye **should** eat in your own houses, or those
025:018	**should** take for protectors others besides Thee:
028:008	**should** be to them an adversary and a cause
028:047	**should** seize them for (the deeds) that their
028:047	a messenger? We **should** then have followed the
028:057	we **should** be snatched away from our land."
031:010	standing firm, lest it **should** shake with you;
033:020	the Confederates **should** come (again), they would
033:032	**should** be moved with desire: but speak
033:050	in order that there **should** be no difficulty
033:052	right hand **should** possess (as handmaidens):
033:053	ye **should** annoy Allah's Messenger, or that
033:053	or that ye **should** marry his widows after him
033:059	that they **should** cast their outer garments
033:059	most convenient, that they **should** be known
034:031	for you, we **should** certainly have been believers!"
035:018	heavily laden **should** call another to (bear)
035:036	so they **should** die, nor shall
035:037	so that he that would **should** receive admonition?
035:041	**should** fail. There is none-not one-
036:022	"Why **should** not I serve Him Who created me,
036:023	If The Most Gracious **should** intend some
036:060	of Adam, that ye **should** not worship Satan;
036:061	"And that ye **should** worship Me, (for that)
036:066	their eyes; then they **should** have raced to
036:067	in their places; then **should** they have been
037:008	(So) they **should** not strain their ears in the
037:057	my Lord, I **should** certainly have been among
037:169	"We **should** certainly have been Servants of Allah,
039:056	"Lest the soul **should** (then) say: `Ah! woe
039:057	"Or (lest) it **should** say: `If only
039:057	I **should** certainly have been among the righteous!'
039:058	"Or (lest) it **should** say when it (actually) sees
039:058	I **should** certainly be among those who do good!'
040:026	What I fear is lest he **should** change your
040:026	**should** cause mischief to appear in the land!"
040:029	**should** it befall us?" Pharaoh said: "I but
041:022	and your skins **should** bear witness against you!
042:013	Namely, that ye **should** remain steadfast in Religion,
042:051	that Allah **should** speak to him except by inspiration,
043:020	we **should** not have worshipped such (deities)!"
043:066	that it **should** come on them all of a sudden,
047:018	that it **should** come on them of a sudden?
048:022	If the Unbelievers **should** fight you, they would
048:025	We **should** certainly have punished the Unbelievers
050:015	the first Creation, that they **should** be in
051:057	nor do I require that they **should** feed Me.
054:024	Truly **should** we then be in error and madness.
056:082	that ye **should** declare it false?
057:016	(to them), and that they **should** not become
057:016	in all humility **should** engage in the remembrance
057:027	as they **should** have done. Yet We
058:003	**should** free a slave before they touch each other:
058:004	to do so, he **should** feed sixty indigent ones.

SHOULD (continued)

058:004   he **should** fast for two months consecutively
060:002   ye **should** reject the Truth.
063:010   for a little while? I **should** then have gave
063:010   and I **should** have been one of the doers of good."
063:010   and he **should** say, "O my Lord! Why didst
063:010   before Death **should** come to any of you and he
067:010   our intelligence, we **should** not (now) be among
067:014   **Should** He not know,-He that created? And He
069:012   **should** bear its (lessons) in remembrance.
069:012   unto you, and that ears (that **should** hear the
069:045   We **should** certainly seize him by his right hand
069:046   And We **should** certainly then cut off the artery
071:003   "That ye **should** worship Allah, fear Him,
072:005   or Jinn **should** say aught that is untrue
072:016   We **should** certainly have bestowed on them
072:022   nor **should** I find refuge except in Him.
074:015   Yet is he greedy-that I **should** add (yet more);
080:011   By no means (**should** it be so)! For it
098:001   (from their ways) until there **should** come to

SHOULDST

006:052   that thou **shouldst** turn them away, and thus
016:064   so that thou **shouldst** make clear to them
017:039   lest thou **shouldst** be thrown into Hell,
020:094   Truly I feared lest thou **shouldst** say, 'Thou hast
021:034   if then thou **shouldst** die, would they
033:037   that thou **shouldst** fear Allah. Then when
047:030   and thou **shouldst** have known them by their marks:
068:009   Their desire is that thou **shouldst** be pliant:
079:018   thou **shouldst** be purified (from sin)?-
079:019   so thou **shouldst** fear Him?'"

SHOUT

002:171   is as if one were to **shout** like a goat-herd,
049:004   Those who **shout** out to thee from without

SHOUTED

012:070   Then **shouted** out a Crier: "O ye (in) the

SHOUTING

004:148   **shouting** of evil words in public speech, except

SHOW

001:006   **Show** us the straight way.
002:128   and **show** us our places for the celebration
002:167   Thus will Allah **show** them (the fruits of)
002:175   Ah! what boldness (they **show**) for the Fire!
002:259   they **show** no signs of age;
002:260   "My Lord! **show** me how thou givest life to the dead.
002:284   Whether ye **show** what is in your minds
003:017   Those who **show** patience, (firmness and self-control);
003:111   they will **show** you their backs, and no help
003:123   then fear Allah; thus may ye **show** your gratitude.
004:153   for they said: "**Show** us Allah in public," but
005:014   **show** them what it is they have done.
005:031   to **show** him how to hide the naked body
005:048   it is He that will **show** you the truth
005:110   **show** them the Clear Signs, and the unbelievers
006:060   then will He **show** you the truth of all that ye did.
006:063   (we vow) we shall truly **show** our gratitude.'?
006:075   So also did We **show** Abraham the kingdom
006:091   into (separate) sheets for **show**, while ye
007:106   **show** it forth,-if thou tellest the truth."
007:143   He said: "O my Lord! **show** (Thyself) to me, that
007:145   soon shall I **show** you the homes of the
007:148   nor **show** them the Way? They took

SHOW (continued)

007:151   the Most Merciful of those who **show** mercy!"
009:094   He **show** you the truth of all that ye did."
009:105   then will He **show** you the truth of all that ye did."
010:022   from this, we shall truly **show** our gratitude!
010:023   and We shall **show** you the truth of all that ye did.
010:031   Say, "Will ye not then **show** piety (to Him)?"
010:046   Whether We **show** thee (realized in thy lifetime)
011:011   Not so do those who **show** patience and constancy,
012:064   of those who **show** mercy!"
012:092   of those who **show** mercy?
013:012   It is He Who doth **show** you the lightning, by way
013:017   **show** forth Truth and falsehood. For the
013:033   or is it (just) a **show** of words?" Nay! to those
013:040   Whether We shall **show** thee (within thy lifetime)
014:007   but if ye **show** ingratitude, truly My punishment
014:008   And Moses said: "If ye **show** ingratitude, ye and
016:009   Allah alone can **show** the right path but there
016:055   To **show** their ingratitude for the favours
016:087   **show** (their) submission to Allah; and all
016:126   but if ye **show** patience, that is indeed
017:001   **show** him some of Our Signs: for he
017:008   **show** Mercy unto you; but it ye revert (to your
018:007   but as a glittering **show** for it, in order
020:023   **show** thee of Our Greater Signs.
020:040   and saith, 'Shall I **show** you one who will nurse
021:037   soon (enough) will I **show** you My Signs; so ask
022:035   who **show** patient perseverance over their
023:093   Say: "O my Lord! if Thou wilt **show** me (in my
023:095   **show** thee (in fulfillment) that against which
023:109   for Thou art the best of those Who **show** mercy!'
023:118   for Thou art the Best of those who **show** mercy!"
025:062   or to **show** their gratitude.
026:031   (Pharaoh) said: "**Show** it then, if thou
027:093   Who will soon **show** you His Signs, so that
028:006   in the land, and to **show** Pharaoh, Haman, and
028:022   will **show** me the smooth and straight Path."
030:034   (As if) to **show** their ingratitude for the
030:052   when they **show** their backs and turn away.
031:011   now **show** Me what is there that others
031:012   wisdom on Luqman: "**Show** (thy) gratitude to Allah."
031:014   "**Show** gratitude to Me and to thy parents: to Me
031:031   that He may **show** you of His Signs? Verily is
034:027   Say: "**Show** me those whom ye have joined with
035:040   besides Allah? **Show** me what it is they have
040:077   and whether We **show** thee (in this life) some part
041:029   "Our Lord! **Show** us those, among Jinns
041:050   in His sight!" But We will **show** the Unbelievers
041:053   Soon will We **show** them Our Signs in the (furthest)
042:043   But indeed if any **show** patience and forgive,
043:042   Or We shall **show** thee that (accomplished) which We
046:004   beside Allah? **Show** me what it is they have
048:016   **show** obedience, Allah will grant you a goodly
054:045   to flight, and they will **show** their backs.
058:004   **show** your faith in Allah and His Messenger.
059:009   the Faith,-**show** their affection to such as came
079:020   Then did (Moses) **show** him the Great Sign.

SHOWED

003:183   unless he **showed** us a sacrifice consumed by fire
007:116   and they **showed** a great (feat of) magic.
008:043   **showed** them to thee as few: if He
008:044   He **showed** them to you as few in your eyes, and
016:121   He **showed** his gratitude for the favours of Allah,

SHOWED (continued)

017:060 which We **showed** thee, but as a trail for men,-
020:056 And We **showed** Pharaoh all Our Signs, but he
026:030 (Moses) said: "Even if I **showed** you something
034:014 (Solomon's) death, nothing **showed** them his death
043:048 We **showed** them Sign after Sign, each greater
076:003 We **showed** him the Way: whether he

SHOWER

007:084 on them a **shower** (of brimstone): then see
008:032 rain down on us a **shower** of stones from the sky,
018:016 the Cave: your Lord will **shower** His mercies
025:040 was rained a **shower** of evil: did they
026:173 We rained down on them a **shower** (of brimstone):
026:173 (of brimstone): and evil was the **shower** on those
027:058 And We rained down on them a **shower** (of brimstone):
027:058 (of brimstone): and evil was the **shower** on those
051:033 "To bring on, on them (a **shower** of) stones of

SHOWERS

017:068 a violent tornado (with **showers** of stones) so that
029:040 (with **showers** of stones); some were
054:034 tornado with **showers** of stones, (which destroyed
067:017 violent tornado (with **showers** of stones), so that

SHOWETH

002:073 and **showeth** you His Signs,
034:049 and Falsehood **showeth** not its face and will
040:013 He it is Who **showeth** you His Signs, and sendeth

SHOWING

009:064 **showing** them what is (really passing) in their
060:001 **showing** friendship unto them in secret: for I

SHOWN

002:259 When this was **shown** clearly to him,
003:101 will be **shown** a way that is straight.
004:068 And We should have **shown** them the Straight Way.
004:105 by that which Allah has **shown** thee; so be not
004:157 Only a likeness of that was **shown** to them.
006:055 that the way of the sinners may be **shown** up.
008:043 if He had **shown** them to thee as many, ye would
014:045 ye were clearly **shown** how We dealt with them;
046:027 about you; and We have **shown** the Signs in various
047:025 after Guidance was clearly **shown** to them,-
047:030 We could have **shown** them up to thee, and thou
047:032 after Guidance has been clearly **shown** to them,
057:017 Already have We **shown** the Signs plainly to you,
090:010 And **shown** him the two highways?
099:006 sorted out, to be **shown** the Deeds that they

SHOWS

017:097 every time it **shows** abatement, We shall
030:024 He **shows** you the lightning, by way
033:004 and He **shows** the (right) Way.
040:081 And He **shows** you (always) His Signs; then which
091:003 By the Day as it **shows** up (the Sun's) glory;

SHREDS

015:091 Qur'an into **shreds** (as they please).

SHRINKING

019:046 "Art thou **shrinking** from my gods, O Abraham?

SHROUDED

053:016 **shrouded** with what shrouds.

SHROUDS

053:016 shrouded with what **shrouds**.

SHU'AIB

007:085 To the Madyan people We sent **Shu'aib**, one of
007:088 said: "O **Shu'aib**! we shall certainly drive thee

SHU'AIB (continued)

007:090 said: "If ye follow **Shu'aib**, be sure
007:092 The men who rejected **Shu'aib** became as if
007:092 the men who rejected **Shu'aib**-
007:093 So **Shu'aib** left them, saying: "O my people!
011:084 To the Madyan people (We sent) **Shu'aib**, one of
011:087 They said: "Oh **Shu'aib**! Does thy prayer
011:091 They said: "O **Shu'aib**! much of what thou sayest
011:094 We saved **Shu'aib** and those who believed with him,
026:177 Behold, **Shu'aib** said to them: "Will ye
029:036 (We sent) their brother **Shu'aib**. Then he

SHUN

007:180 but **shun** such men as distort His names: for what
022:030 but **shun** the abomination of idols, and shun
022:030 and **shun** the word that is false,-
053:029 Therefore **shun** those who turn away from
074:005 And all abomination **shun**!

SHUTTING

005:002 **shutting** you out of the Sacred Mosque lead you

SHY

033:053 but Allah is not **shy** (to tell you) the truth.
033:053 the Prophet: he is **shy** to dismiss you, but Allah

SICK

037:089 And he said, "I am indeed **sick** (at heart)!"

SICKLE

011:100 (by the **sickle** of time).

SICKNESS

037:145 the naked shore in a state of **sickness**,

SIDE

003:153 without even casting a **side** glance at anyone,
004:036 the Companion by your **side**, the way-farer (ye meet),
008:042 the valley, and they on the farther **side**, and the
008:042 Remember ye were on the hither **side** of the valley,
010:012 lying down on his **side**, or sitting, or standing.
016:112 on it) like a garment (from every **side**), because
017:083 his **side** (instead of coming to Us), and when
018:076 received (full) excuse from my **side**."
019:052 right **side** of Mount (Sinai), and made
020:022 Now draw thy hand close to thy **side**: it shall
020:080 on the right **side** of Mount (Sinai), and We
022:009 (Disdainfully) bending his **side**, in order
024:049 But if the right is on their **side**, they come
028:032 to thy **side** (to guard) against fear. Those are
028:044 Thou wast not on the Western **Side** when We
028:046 Nor wast thou at the **side** of (the Mountain
037:008 and they are cast away from every **side**,
041:051 on his **side** (instead of coming to Us); and when
060:011 of a woman from the other **side**). Then pay
074:013 And sons to be by his **side**!-
076:010 and distress from the **side** of our Lord."

SIDES

003:191 and lying down on their **sides**, and contemplate
004:103 or lying down on your **sides**; but
005:033 from opposite **sides**, or exile from the land:
007:124 and your feet on opposite **sides**, and I
009:049 Hell surrounds the Unbelievers (on all **sides**).
010:022 and the waves come to them from all **sides**, and they
018:018 and their left **sides**: their dog
019:073 those who believe, "Which of the two **sides** is best
020:071 and feet on opposite **sides**, and I
020:130 of the night, and at the **sides** of the day;
022:036 on their **sides** (after slaughter), eat ye

SIDES (continued)

026:049   and your feet on opposite **sides**, and I
033:014   to them from the **sides** of the (City), and they
039:075   (on all **sides**) will be, "Praise be to Allah,
039:075   on all **sides**, singing Glory and Praise to their
040:045   encompassed on all **sides** the People of Pharaoh.
069:017   And the angels will be on its **sides**, and eight

SIGH

025:012   they will hear its fury and its raging **sigh**.

SIGHS

003:156   a cause of **sighs** and regrets in their hearts.
008:036   have (only) regrets and **sighs**; at length
011:106   therein (nothing but) the heaving of **sighs** and sobs:

SIGHT

002:020   The lightning all but snatches away their **sight**:
002:050   drowned Pharaoh's people within your very **sight**.
002:054   for you in the **sight** of your Maker.
002:217   but graver is it in the **sight** of Allah
002:282   it is juster in the **sight** of Allah,
003:015   For in Allah's **sight** are (all) His servants,
003:020   and in Allah's **sight** are (all) His servants.
003:152   in **sight** (of the Victory) which ye covet.
003:163   They are in varying grades in the **sight** of Allah,
006:046   took away your hearing and your **sight**, and sealed
007:131   are theirs in Allah's **sight**, but most
008:022   the **sight** of Allah are the deaf and the dumb,-
008:048   came in **sight** of each other, he turned
008:055   **sight** of Allah are those who reject Him: they will
009:019   They are not equal in the **sight** of Allah: and
009:020   highest rank in the **sight** of Allah: they are
009:036   **sight** of Allah is twelve (in a year)-so ordained
009:042   (in **sight**), and the journey easy, they would
010:031   hearing and **sight**? And who is it that brings out
011:028   hath been obscured from your **sight**? Shall we
012:096   clear **sight**. He said: "Did I not say to you,
014:046   (well) within the **sight** of Allah, even though
016:078   you hearing and **sight** and intelligence
017:036   for surely the hearing, the **sight**,
017:038   is hateful in the **sight** of thy Lord.
018:046   Good Deeds, are best in the **sight** of thy Lord,
019:055   acceptable in the **sight** of his Lord.
019:076   Good Deeds, are best in the **sight** of thy Lord,
020:125   while I had **sight** (before)?"
022:030   in the **sight** of his Lord, Lawful to
022:047   **sight** of thy Lord is like a thousand years
023:027   within Our **sight** and under Our guidance: then when
023:078   (the faculties of) hearing, **sight**, feeling and
024:013   in the **sight** of Allah, (stand forth)
024:015   while it was most serious in the **sight** of Allah.
024:043   well-nigh blinds the **sight**.
032:009   and **sight** (and understanding): little thanks
033:005   that is juster in the **sight** of Allah.
033:053   Truly such a thing is in Allah's **sight** an enormity.
033:069   was honorable in Allah's **sight**.
035:039   for the Unbelievers in the **sight** of their Lord:
035:045   in His **sight** all His servants.
038:047   They were, in Our **sight**, truly, of the
040:035   (is such conduct) in the **sight** of Allah and of
041:020   the (Fire), their hearing, their **sight**, and their
041:022   lest your hearing, your **sight**, and your skins
041:050   in His **sight**!" But We will show the Unbelievers
042:016   futile is their dispute in the **sight** of their
042:044   when in **sight** of the Chastisement, say: "Is there

SIGHT (continued)

043:035   in the **sight** of thy Lord, is for the Righteous.
045:019   the **sight** of Allah: it is
045:023   and put a cover on his **sight**. Who, then,
046:026   hearing, **sight**, and heart and intellect, when they
047:023   and blinded their **sight**.
048:005   and that is, in the **sight** of Allah, the grand
049:013   in the **sight** of Allah is (he who is) the most
050:022   and sharp is thy **sight** this Day!"
053:017   (His) **sight** never swerved, nor did it go wrong!
053:040   will soon come in **sight**;
061:003   Grievously hateful is it in the **sight** of Allah
070:011   Though they will be put in **sight** of each other,-
075:007   At length, when the **Sight** is dazed,
076:002   so We gave him (the gifts), of Hearing and **Sight**.
083:023   a **sight** (of all things):
083:035   (a **sight**) (of all things).
102:007   Again, ye shall see it with certainty of **sight**!

SIGN

002:118   Or why cometh not Us a **Sign**?"
002:248   "A **sign** of his authority is that there shall come
002:259   make of thee a **Sign** unto the people.
003:013   a **Sign** in the two armies that met (in combat):
003:041   "Thy **Sign**," was the answer, "Shall be that thou
003:041   He said: "O my Lord! Give me a **Sign**!"
003:049   Surely therein is a **Sign** for you if ye did believe.
003:049   I have come to you, with a **Sign** from your Lord,
003:050   I have come to you with a **Sign** from your Lord.
005:114   a solemn festival and a **Sign** from Thee; and
006:035   and bring them a **Sign**,-(what good?). If it
006:037   a **Sign** sent down to him from his Lord?" Say:
006:037   power to send down a **Sign**: but most
006:057   a clear **Sign** from my Lord, but ye
006:109   that if a (special) **Sign** came to them,
006:124   a **Sign** (from Allah), they say:" We shall
006:157   a Clear **Sign** from your Lord,-and a
007:073   a clear (**Sign**) from your Lord! This she-camel
007:073   This she-camel of Allah is a **Sign** unto you: so
007:085   a clear (**Sign**) from your Lord! Give just
007:105   from your Lord with a clear (**Sign**): so let
007:106   thou hast come with a **Sign**, show it
008:042   who died might die after a clear **Sign** (had been
008:042   might live after a Clear **Sign** (had been given).
010:020   They say: "Why is not a **Sign** sent down
010:092   a **Sign** to those who come after thee! But verily
010:097   Even if every **Sign** was brought unto them,-until
011:017   a Clear (**Sign**) from their Lord, and followed
011:028   (it be that) I have a Clear **Sign** from my Lord
011:053   They said: "O Hud! no Clear (**Sign**) hast thou
011:063   If I have a Clear (**Sign**) from my Lord and He
011:064   of Allah is a **sign** to you: leave her
011:088   I have a Clear (**Sign**) from my Lord, and He
011:103   In that is a **Sign** for those who fear
013:007   a **Sign** sent down to him from his Lord?" But thou
013:027   a **Sign** sent down to him from his Lord?" Say:
013:038   a messenger to bring a **Sign** except as Allah
015:077   Behold! in this is a **Sign** for those who believe!
016:011   is a **Sign** for those who give thought.
016:013   is a **Sign** for men who mindful.
016:065   verily in this is a **Sign** for those who listen.
016:066   find an instructive **Sign**. From what
016:067   in this also is a **Sign** for those who are wise.
016:069   for men: verily in this is a **Sign** for those

SIGN (continued)

017:012   made dark while the **Sign** of the Day We have
017:012   the **Sign** of the Night have We made dark
017:059   to the Thamud-a visible **Sign**-but they
019:010   "O my Lord! give me a **Sign**,"
019:010   "Thy **Sign**," was the answer, "Shall be
019:021   and (We wish) to appoint him as a **Sign** unto men
020:022   (or stain)-as another **Sign**,-
020:047   and afflict them not: with a **Sign**, indeed, have
020:133   Has not a Clear **Sign** come to them of all
020:133   a **Sign** from His Lord?" Has not
021:005   Let him then bring us a **Sign** like the ones
021:091   and her son a **Sign** for all peoples.
023:050   and his mother as a **Sign**: We gave
025:037   as a **Sign** of mankind; and We
026:004   a **Sign**, to which they would bend their necks
026:008   Verily, in this is a **Sign**: but most
026:067   Verily in this is a **Sign**: but most
026:103   Verily in this is a **Sign**, but most
026:121   Verily in this is a **Sign**: but most
026:139   Verily in this is a **Sign**: but most
026:154   like us: then bring us a **Sign**, if thou
026:158   Verily in this is a **Sign**: but most
026:174   Verily in this is a **Sign**: but most
026:190   Verily in that is a **Sign**: but most
026:197   Is it not a **Sign** to them that the learned
027:052   Verily in this is a **Sign** for people of knowledge.
029:015   a **Sign** for all Peoples!
029:035   an evident **Sign**, for any
029:044   verily in that is a **Sign** for those who believe.
030:058   but if thou bring to them any **Sign**, the Unbelievers
034:009   is a **Sign** for every devotee that turns
034:015   a **Sign** in their homeland-two Gardens to the
036:033   A **Sign** for them is the earth that is dead;
036:037   And a **Sign** for them is the Night: We withdraw
036:041   And a **Sign** for them is that We bore their race
036:046   Not a **Sign** comes to them from among
037:014   And, when they see a **Sign**, turn it to mockery,
040:078   for any messenger to bring a **Sign** except by the
043:048   We showed them **Sign** after **Sign**, each greater
043:061   And (Jesus) shall be a **Sign** (for the coming of)
048:020   from you; that is may be a **Sign** for the Believers,
051:038   And in Moses (was another **Sign**): behold, We sent
051:041   (was another **Sign**): behold, We sent against them
051:043   And in the Thamud (was another **Sign**): behold,
054:002   But if they see a **Sign**, they turn away, and say,
054:015   And We have left this as a **Sign** (for all time):
079:020   Then did (Moses) show him the Great **Sign**.

SIGN-POSTS

016:016   And marks and **sign-posts**; and by

SIGNALS

003:041   no man for three days but with **signals**.

SIGNS

002:039   reject Faith and belie Our **Signs**,
002:041   nor sell My **Signs** for a small price:
002:061   rejecting the **Signs** of Allah and slaying
002:073   and showeth you His **Signs**,
002:087   We gave Jesus the son of Mary clear (**Signs**)
002:092   There came to you Moses with clear (**Signs**);
002:099   manifest **Signs** (ayat);
002:118   the **Signs** unto any people who hold
002:129   Who shall rehearse Thy **Signs** to them
002:145   all the **Signs** (together),

SIGNS (continued)

002:151   rehearsing to you Our **Signs**,
002:159   (**Signs**) We have sent down, and the Guidance,
002:164   **Signs** for a people that are wise.
002:185   also clear (**Signs**) for guidance and judgment
002:187   Thus doth Allah make clear His **Signs** to men:
002:189   Say: They are but **signs** to mark fixed periods
002:209   the clear (**signs**) have come to you,
002:211   how many Clear (**Signs**) We have sent them.
002:213   after the clear **Signs** came to them,
002:219   Thus doth Allah make clear to you His **Signs**:
002:221   and makes His **Signs** clear to mankind:
002:231   Do not treat Allah's **Signs** as a jest,
002:242   Thus doth Allah make clear His **Signs** to you:
002:252   These are the **signs** of Allah:
002:253   to Jesus the son of Mary, We gave Clear (**Signs**),
002:253   after Clear (**Signs**) had come to them,
002:259   they show no **signs** of age;
002:266   clear to you (His) **Signs**; that ye may consider.
003:004   in the **Signs** of Allah will suffer
003:011   they denied Our **Signs**, and Allah called them
003:019   But if any deny the **Signs** of Allah,
003:021   As to those who deny the **Signs** of Allah,
003:058   of the **Signs** and the Message of Wisdom."
003:070   Why reject ye the **Signs** of Allah,
003:086   and that Clear **Signs** had come unto them?
003:097   In it are **Signs** manifest; the Station of Abraham;
003:098   why reject ye the **Signs** of Allah,
003:101   while unto you are rehearsed the **Signs** of Allah,
003:103   Thus doth Allah make His **Signs** clear to you:
003:105   and fall into disputation after receiving Clear **Signs**:
003:108   These are the **Signs** of Allah:
003:112   This because they rejected the **Signs** of Allah,
003:113   they rehearse the **Signs** of Allah all night long,
003:118   the **Signs**, if ye have wisdom.
003:164   rehearsing unto them the **Signs** of Allah,
003:183   with Clear **Signs** and even with what ye ask for:
003:184   who came with Clear **Signs**, and the Scriptures.
003:190   there are indeed **Signs** for men of understanding,
003:199   the **Signs** of Allah for a miserable gain!
004:056   Those who reject Our **Signs**, We shall soon
004:153   even after Clear **Signs** had come to them; even
004:155   that they rejected the **Signs** of Allah; that they
005:010   Those who reject faith and deny Our **Signs** will be
005:032   Our Messengers with Clear **Signs**, yet, even after
005:044   and sell not My **Signs** for a miserable price.
005:075   makes His **Signs** clear to them; yet see
005:086   and belie Our **Signs**, they shall be
005:089   Thus doth Allah make clear to you His **Signs**, that
005:110   show them the Clear **Signs**, and the unbelievers
006:004   of the **Signs** of their Lord reach them, but they
006:021   or rejecteth his **Signs**? But verily
006:025   if they saw every one of the **Signs**, they will
006:027   Then would we not reject the **Signs** of our Lord,
006:033   it is the **Signs** of Allah, which the wicked deny.
006:039   Those who reject Our **Signs** are deaf and dumb,-
006:046   We explain the **Signs** by various (symbols):
006:049   But those who reject Our **Signs**,-them shall
006:054   who believe in Our **Signs**, say: "Peace be on you:
006:055   Thus do We explain the **Signs** in detail: that
006:065   See how We explain the **Signs** in diverse ways; that
006:068   in vain discourse about Our **Signs**, turn away
006:093   and scornfully to reject of His **Signs**!"

SIGNS (continued)

006:097   We detail Our **Signs** for people who know.
006:098   We detail Our **signs** for people who understand.
006:099   are **signs** for people who believe.
006:105   the **Signs** by various (ways) that they may say,
006:109   Say: "Certainly (all) **Signs** are in the power
006:109   realize that even if a (special) **Signs** came,
006:118   if ye have faith in His **Signs.**
006:126   the **Signs** for those who receive admonition.
006:130   setting forth unto you My **Signs** and warning
006:150   of such as treat Our **Signs** as falsehoods, and
006:157   those who turn away from Our **Signs,** with
006:157   than one who rejecteth Allah's **Signs,** and turneth
006:158   The day that certain of the **Signs** of thy
006:158   or certain of the **Signs** of thy Lord! The day
007:009   for that they wrongfully treated Our **Signs.**
007:026   Such are among the **Signs** of Allah, that they
007:032   Thus do We explain the **Signs** in detail
007:035   rehearsing My **Signs** unto you,-those who
007:036   But those who reject Our **Signs** and treat
007:037   or rejects His **Signs**? For such
007:040   To those who reject Our **Signs** and treat
007:051   and as they were wont to reject Our **Signs.**
007:058   thus do We explain the **Signs** by various
007:064   those who rejected Our **Signs,** they were
007:072   the roots of those who rejected Our **Signs** and
007:101   their Messengers with clear (**Signs**); but they
007:103   with Our **Signs** to Pharaoh and his chiefs. But
007:126   in the **Signs** of our Lord when they reached us!
007:132   "Whatever be the **Signs** thou bringest, to work
007:133   and Blood: **Signs** openly self-explained: but they
007:136   because they rejected Our **Signs,** and failed
007:146   even if they see all the **Signs,** they will not
007:146   them will I turn away from My **Signs**: even if
007:146   For they have rejected Our **Signs,** and failed
007:147   Those who reject Our **Signs** and the Meeting
007:156   and pay Zakat and those who believe in Our **Signs**;
007:174   Thus do We explain the **Signs** in detail; and
007:175   to whom We sent Our **Signs,** but he
007:176   We should have elevated him with Our **Signs**; but he
007:176   of those who reject Our **Signs**; so relate
007:177   who reject Our **signs** and wrong their own souls.
007:182   Those who reject Our **signs,** We shall
008:031   When Our **Signs** are rehearsed to them, they say:
008:052   before them: they rejected the **Signs** of Allah, and
008:054   the **Signs** of their Lord so We destroyed them
009:011   (thus) do We explain **Signs** in detail, for those
009:065   Say: "Was it at Allah, and His **Signs,** and His
009:070   with Clear **Signs.** It is not Allah Who wrongs
010:005   (Thus) doth He explain His **Signs** in detail,
010:006   are **Signs** for those who fear Him.
010:007   and those who heed not Our **Signs,**-
010:013   with Clear **Signs,** but they would not believe!
010:015   But when Our Clear **Signs** are rehearsed unto them,
010:017   or deny His **Signs**? But never
010:021   to plotting against Our **Signs**! Say: "Swifter
010:024   the **Signs** in detail for those who reflect.
010:067   Verily in this are **Signs** for those
010:071   and remind (you) the **Signs** of Allah,- yet I put
010:073   those who rejected Our **Signs.** Then see
010:074   they brought them Clear **Signs,** but they
010:075   and his chiefs with Our **Signs.** But they
010:092   are heedless of Our **Signs**!

SIGNS (continued)

010:095   **Signs** of Allah, or thou shalt be of those
010:101   but neither **Signs** nor Warners profit those
011:059   they rejected the **Signs** of their Lord and
011:096   And We sent Moses, with Our Clear (**Signs**) and an
012:007   are **Signs** for Seekers (after Truth).
012:035   they had seen the **Signs,** (that it was best)
012:105   And how many **Signs** in the heavens and the earth
013:002   explaining the **Signs** in detail, that ye
013:003   in these things are **Signs** for those who consider!
013:004   there are **Signs** for those who understand!
014:005   there are **Signs** for such as are firmly patient
014:005   We sent Moses with Our **Signs** (and the
014:009   Clear (**Signs**); but they put their hands up to
015:075   Behold! in this are **Signs** for those
015:081   We sent them Our **Signs,** but they
016:012   His Command: verily in this are **Signs** for men
016:044   (We sent them) with Clear **Signs** and Scriptures
016:079   are **Signs** for those who believe.
016:104   Those who believe not in the **Signs** of Allah,-
016:105   the **Signs** of Allah, that forge falsehood: it is
017:001   show him some of Our **Signs**: for he
017:012   as two (of Our) **Signs**: the Sign of
017:059   the **Signs,** only because the men of former
017:059   We only sent the **Signs** by way of frightening
017:098   because they rejected Our **Signs,** and said,
017:101   To Moses We did give nine Clear **Signs**: ask the
018:009   wonders among Our **Signs**?
018:017   Such are among the **Signs** of Allah: he whom
018:056   My **Signs** and warnings as a jest.
018:057   who is reminded of the **Signs** of his Lord but turns
018:105   They are those who deny the **Signs** of their Lord
018:106   and took My **Signs** and My Messengers by way of jest.
019:011   by **signs** to celebrate Allah's praises in the
019:058   and chose. Whenever the **Signs** of (Allah) Most
019:073   When Our Clear **Signs** are rehearsed to them,
019:077   man who rejects Our **Signs,** yet says: "I shall
020:023   show thee of Our Greater **Signs.**
020:042   with My **Signs,** and slacken not, either of
020:054   **Signs** for men endued with understanding.
020:056   And We showed Pharaoh all Our **Signs,** but he
020:072   Clear **Signs** Him Who created us! So decree
020:126   when Our **Signs** came unto thee, forgot them:
020:127   and believes not in the **Signs** of his Lord:
020:128   Verily, in this are **Signs** for men
020:134   have followed Thy **Signs** before we were
021:032   the **Signs** which these things (point to)!
021:037   soon (enough) will I show you My **Signs**; so ask
021:077   who rejected Our **Signs**: truly they
022:016   Thus have We sent down Clear **Signs**; and verily
022:036   for you as among the **Signs** from Allah: in them
022:051   Our **Signs,** to frustrate them,-they will
022:052   (and establish) His **Signs**: for Allah
022:057   and deny Our **Signs,** there will
022:072   those who rehearse Our **Signs** to them.
022:072   When Our Clear **Signs** are rehearsed to them,
023:030   Verily in this there are **Signs** (for men
023:045   his brother Aaron, with Our **Signs** and authority
023:058   Those who believe in the **Signs** of their Lord;
023:066   "My **Signs** used to be rehearsed to you, but ye
023:105   "Were not My **Signs** rehearsed to you, and ye
024:001   in it have We sent down Clear **Signs,** in order
024:018   And Allah makes the **Signs** plain to you: for Allah

SIGNS (continued)

024:046   We have indeed sent down **Signs** that make
024:058   **Signs** to you: for Allah
024:059   make clear His **Signs** to you: for Allah
024:061   make clear the **Signs** to you: that you
025:036   Our **Signs**": and those (people) We destroyed
025:073   with the **Signs** of their Lord, droop not down
026:015   both of you, with Our **Signs**; We are
027:012   (these are) among the nine **Signs** (thou wilt take)
027:013   But when Our **Signs** came to them, visibly they
027:081   to listen who believe in Our **Signs**, so they
027:082   because mankind had no faith in Our **Signs**.
027:083   those who reject Our **Signs**, and they
027:084   "Did ye reject My **signs**, though ye
027:086   Verily in this are **Signs** for any people
027:093   Who will soon show you His **Signs**, so that
028:035   with Our **Signs** shall ye triumph,-you two
028:036   Our Clear **Signs**, they said: "This is
028:045   of Madyan, rehearsing Our **Signs** to them;
028:047   followed the **Signs** and been amongst those
028:048   "Why are not (**Signs**) sent to him, like those
028:048   Do they not then reject (the **Signs**) which were
028:059   rehearsing to them Our **Signs**; nor are
029:023   Those who reject the **Signs** of Allah and the
029:024   Verily in this are **Signs** for people who believe.
029:039   with Clear **Signs**, but they
029:047   and none but Unbelievers reject Our **Signs**.
029:049   Nay, here are **Signs** self-evident in the hearts
029:049   the unjust reject Our **Signs**.
029:050   Yet they say: "Why are not **Signs** sent down
029:050   Say: "The **Signs** are indeed with Allah: and I
030:009   with Clear (**Signs**), (which they rejected, to their
030:010   the **Signs** of Allah, and held
030:016   and falsely denied Our **Signs** and the meeting
030:020   Among His **Signs** is this, that He
030:021   verily in that are **Signs** for those who reflect.
030:021   And among His **Signs** is this, that He
030:022   And among His **Signs** is the creation of the
030:022   are **Signs** for those who know.
030:023   And among His **Signs** is the sleep that ye take
030:023   verily in that are **Signs** for those who hearken.
030:024   And among His **Signs**, He shows
030:024   are **Signs** for those who are wise.
030:025   And among His **Signs** is this, that heaven
030:028   Thus do We explain the **Signs** in detail to a
030:037   are **Signs** for those who believe.
030:046   Among His **Signs** is this, that He
030:047   and they came to them with Clear **Signs**:
030:053   in Our **Signs** and submit (their wills in Islam).
031:007   When Our **Signs** are rehearsed to such a one,
031:031   that He may show you of His **Signs**? Verily is
031:031   Verily in this are **Signs** for all who constantly
031:032   and wrong). But none reject Our **Signs** except only
032:015   Only those believe in Our **Signs** who, when they
032:022   to whom are recited the **Signs** of his Lord,
032:024   have faith in Our **Signs**.
032:026   Verily in that are **Signs**: do they
033:034   of the **Signs** of Allah and His Wisdom: for Allah
034:005   Our **Signs**, to frustrate them,-for such
034:019   Verily in this are **Signs** for every (soul that
034:038   Those who strive against Our **Signs**, to frustrate
034:043   When Our Clear **Signs** are rehearsed to them,
035:025   Clear **Signs**, Scriptures and the illuminating

SIGNS (continued)

036:006   therefore remain heedless (of the **Signs** of Allah).
036:046   from among the **Signs** of their Lord, but they
038:029   that they may meditate on its **Signs**, and that
039:042   are **Signs** for those who reflect.
039:052   Verily, in this are **signs** for those who believe!
039:059   to thee My **Signs**, and thou didst reject them:
039:063   the **Signs** of Allah,-it is they
039:071   the **Signs** of your Lord, and warning
040:004   None can dispute about the **Signs** of Allah
040:005   who denied (the **Signs**),-the People of Noah,
040:013   He it is Who showeth you His **Signs**, and sendeth
040:022   with Clear (**Signs**), but they rejected them:
040:023   with Our **Signs** and Authority manifest,
040:028   with Clear (**Signs**) from your Lord? And if
040:034   gone by, with Clear **Signs**, but ye
040:035   "(Such) as dispute about the **Signs** of Allah,
040:050   Clear **Signs**?" They will say: "Yes." They will
040:056   Those who dispute about the **Signs** of Allah
040:063   to reject the **Signs** of Allah.
040:066   seeing that the Clear **Signs** have come to me
040:069   dispute concerning the **signs** of Allah? How are
040:081   And He shows you (always) His **Signs**; then which
040:081   then which of the **Signs** of Allah will ye deny?
040:083   to them with Clear **Signs**, they exulted
041:015   But they continued to reject Our **Signs**!
041:028   wont to reject Our **Signs**.
041:037   Among His **Signs** are the Night and the Day, and the
041:039   And among His **Signs** is this: thou seest
041:040   Those who pervert the Truth in Our **Signs** are not
041:053   Soon will We show them Our **Signs** in the (furthest)
042:029   And among His **Signs** is the creation of the
042:032   And among His **Signs** are the ships, smooth-running
042:033   Verily in this are **Signs** for everyone who
042:035   who dispute about Our **Signs**, that there
043:046   with Our **Signs**, to Pharaoh and his Chiefs:
043:047   But when he came to them with Our **Signs**, behold,
043:063   When Jesus came with Clear **Signs**, he said:
043:069   Those who have believed in Our **Signs** and submitted
044:033   And granted them **Signs** in which
045:003   are **Signs** for those who believe.
045:004   are **Signs** for those of assured Faith.
045:005   the winds,- are **Signs** for those that are wise.
045:006   believe after Allah and His **Signs**?
045:006   Such are the **Signs** of Allah, which We
045:008   He hears the **Signs** of Allah rehearsed to him,
045:009   of Our **Signs**, he takes them in jest: for such
045:011   who reject the **Signs** of their Lord, is a
045:013   are **Signs** indeed for those who reflect.
045:017   And We granted them clear **Signs** in affairs
045:025   And when Our Clear **Signs** are rehearsed to them,
045:031   "Were not Our **Signs** rehearsed to you? But ye
045:035   the **Signs** of Allah in jest, and the
046:007   When Our Clear **Signs** are rehearsed to them,
046:026   when they went on rejecting the **Signs** of Allah:
046:027   about you; and We have shown the **Signs** in various
051:020   On the earth are **Signs** for those of assured Faith,
051:037   And We left there a **Signs** for such as fear
053:018   of the **Signs** of his Lord, the Greatest!
054:042   The (people) rejected all Our **Signs**; but We
057:009   to His Servants manifest **Signs**, that He
057:017   Already have We shown the **Signs** plainly to you,
057:019   Our **Signs**,-they are the Companions of Hell-Fire.

SIGNS (continued)
057:025 with Clear **Signs** and sent down with them the Book
058:005 Clear **Signs**. And the Unbelievers (will have)
061:006 Clear **Signs**, they said, "This is evident sorcery!"
062:002 His **Signs**, to purify them, and to instruct
062:005 who falsify the **Signs** of Allah: and Allah
064:006 to them messengers with Clear **Signs**, but they
064:010 and treat Our **Signs** as falsehoods, they will
065:011 the **Signs** of Allah containing clear explanations,
068:015 When to him are rehearsed Our **Signs**, "Tales of
074:016 By no means! For to Our **Signs** he has
078:028 But they (impudently) treated Our **Signs** as false
083:013 When Our **Signs** are rehearsed to him, he says,
090:019 But those who reject Our **Signs**, they are

SIJJIN
083:007 is (preserved) in **Sijjin**.
083:008 And what will explain to thee what **Sijjin** is?

SILENCE
046:029 "Listen in **silence**!" When the (reading) was

SILENT
007:193 ye call them or ye keep **silent**.
012:084 and he was suppressed with **silent** sorrow.
021:015 is mown, as ashes **silent** and quenched.
036:029 (like ashes) quenched and **silent**.

SILK
018:031 green garments of fine **silk** and heavy brocade;
022:023 and their garments there will be of **silk**.
035:033 and their garments there will be of **silk**.
044:053 Dressed in fine **silk** and in rich brocade,
076:012 and (garments of) **silk**.
076:021 of fine **silk** and heavy brocade, and they

SILVER
003:014 heaped-up hoards of gold and **silver**;
003:075 others, who, if entrusted with a single **silver** coin,
009:034 those who hoard gold and **silver** and spend
043:033 Most Gracious, **silver** roofs for their houses,
043:033 their houses, and (**silver**) stair-ways on which
043:034 and couches (of **silver**) on which they could recline,
043:034 And (**silver**) doors to their houses, and couches
076:015 vessels of **silver** and goblets of crystal,-
076:016 Crystal-clear, made of **silver**: they will
076:021 of **silver**; and their Lord will give to them

SIMILAR
002:106 something better or **similar**:
002:118 before them words of **similar** import.
002:151 A **similar** (favour have ye already received)
002:228 rights **similar** to the rights against them,
003:140 be sure a **similar** wound hath touched the others.
004:104 they are suffering **similar** hardships; but you
006:099 each **similar** (in kind) yet different
006:141 **similar** (in kind) and different (in variety):
007:169 (Even so), if **similar** vanities came their way,
011:089 lest ye suffer a fate **similar** to that of the
013:016 them **similar**? Say: "Allah is the Creator of all
023:081 **similar** to what the ancients said.
036:042 **similar** (vessels) on which they ride.
038:058 And other Penalties of a **similar** kind, to match
047:010 on them, and **similar** (fates await) those who
065:012 and of the earth a **similar** number, through the

SIMILARITY
046:010 of Israel testifies to its **similarity** (with earlier

SIMILARLY
029:062 and He (**similarly**) grants by (strict) measure,
051:052 **Similarly**, no messenger came to the Peoples

SIMILES
017:048 See what **similes** thy strike for thee: but they

SIMILITUDE
002:017 Their **similitude** is that of a man
002:019 Or (another **similitude**) is that of
002:025 for they are given things in **similitude**;
002:026 use the **similitude** of things,
002:026 "What means Allah by this **similitude**?"
002:259 Or (take) the **similitude** of one
003:059 The **similitude** of Jesus before Allah
007:176 His **similitude** is that of a dog: if you
007:176 That is the **similitude** of those who
016:060 of evil: to Allah applies the highest **similitude**:
016:060 in the Hereafter, applies the **similitude** of evil:
017:089 of **similitude**: yet the greater part of men refuse
018:045 Set forth to them the **similitude** of the
018:054 every kind of **similitude**: but man is, in most
030:027 To Him belongs the loftiest **similitude** (We can
030:028 a **similitude** from yourselves: do ye
048:029 and their **similitude** in the Gospel is: like a
048:029 This is their **similitude** in the Taurat; and their
057:020 Here is a **similitude**: how rain and the growth
062:005 Evil is the **similitude** of people who falsify
062:005 The **similitude** of those who were entrusted with

SIMILITUDES
016:074 Invent not **similitudes** for Allah: for Allah
047:003 their lessons by **similitudes**.
059:021 such are the **similitudes** which We propound to men,

SIMPLE
087:008 (to follow) the **simple** (Path).

SIMPLY
007:126 on us **simply** because we believed in the Signs
012:077 He (**simply**) said (to himself): "Ye are
060:001 (from your homes), (**simply**) because ye believe

SIN
002:158 it is no **sin** in them.
002:219 Say: "In them is great **sin**,
002:219 but the **sin** is greater than the profit."
002:283 his heart is tainted with **sin**.
003:077 nor will He cleanse them (of **sin**):
004:002 For this is indeed a great **sin**.
004:020 would ye take it by slander and a manifest **sin**?
004:025 for those among you who fear **sin**;
004:048 a **sin** most heinous indeed.
004:050 but that by itself is a manifest **sin**!
004:097 those who die in **sin** against their soul.
004:107 for Allah loveth not one given to perfidy and **sin**:
004:111 And if anyone earns **sin**, he earns it
004:112 (both) a false charge and a flagrant **sin**.
004:112 But if anyone earns a fault or a **sin** and throws
004:116 (the **sin** of) joining other gods with Him:
005:002 but help ye not one another in **sin** and rancor:
005:029 thee draw on thyself my **sin** as well as thine, for
005:062 racing each other in **sin** and transgression and
005:107 were guilty of the **sin** (of perjury), let two
006:120 those who earn **sin** will get due recompense
006:120 Eschew all **sin**, open or secret: those who
007:040 such is Our reward for those in **sin**.
007:084 those who indulged in **sin** and crime!

SIN (continued)

007:133 a people given to **sin**.
007:150 nor count thou me amongst the people of **sin**."
009:080 or not, (their **sin** is unforgivable): if thou
010:013 not believe! Thus do We requite those who **sin**!
010:017 But never will prosper those who **sin**.
011:035 my **sin**! And I am free of the sins of which
011:037 on behalf of those who are in **sin**: for they
011:052 so turn ye not back in **sin**!"
011:054 that I am free from the **sin** of ascribing, to Him,
011:089 (from you) cause you to **sin**, lest ye suffer
011:116 given them, and persisted in **sin**.
012:029 (O wife), ask forgiveness for thy **sin**, for truly
012:091 and we certainly have been guilty of **sin**!"
012:110 Our punishment from those who are in **sin**.
015:058 to a people (deep) in **sin**,
017:031 Verily the killing of them is a great **sin**.
024:011 the punishment) of the **sin** that he earned, and to
027:069 what has been the end of those guilty (of **sin**)."
028:008 their hosts were men of **sin**.
028:017 never shall I be a help to those who **sin**!"
029:014 them while they (persisted in) **sin**.
033:058 (on themselves) a calumny and a glaring **sin**.
034:028 and warning them (against **sin**), but most
036:059 And O ye in **sin**! get ye apart this Day!
040:003 Who forgiveth **Sin**, accepteth Repentance, is Severe
040:028 on him is (the **sin** of) his lie; but, if he
040:030 (of disaster) of the Confederates (in **sin**)!-
042:030 (a **sin**) He grants forgiveness.
044:022 "These are indeed a people given to **sin**."
044:037 they were guilty of **sin**.
045:031 and were a people given to **sin**!
046:025 Thus do We recompense those given to **sin**!
049:012 for suspicion in some cases is a **sin**: and spy
051:032 a people (deep) in **sin**;-
052:023 of frivolity, free from **sin**.
054:047 Truly those in **sin** are the ones in error
055:039 will be asked of man or Jinn as to his **sin**,
068:012 deep in **sin**.
068:035 of Faith like the People of **Sin**?
069:009 and the Cities Overthrown, committed habitual **Sin**,
069:037 "Which none do eat but those in **sin**."
077:018 Thus do We deal with men of **sin**.
079:018 thou shouldst be purified (from **sin**)?-
083:029 Those in **sin** used to laugh at those who believed,
091:014 crushed them for their **sin** and levelled them.

SIN.

026:001 Ta **Sin** Mim.
027:001 Ta. **Sin**.
028:001 Ta. **Sin**. Mim.
036:001 Ya - **Sin**.
042:002 'Ain. **Sin**. Qaf.

SINAI

002:063 and We raised above you the Mount (**Sinai**)
002:093 and We raised above you the mount (**Sinai**):
004:154 We raised over them the Mount (**Sinai**);
019:052 right side of Mount (**Sinai**), and made
020:080 on the right side of Mount (**Sinai**), and We
023:020 Mount **Sinai**, which produces oil, and relish
095:002 And the Mount of **Sinai**,

SINCE

013:030 a People before whom (long **since**) have (other)
026:021 I feared you; but my Lord has (**since**) invested me

SINCE (continued)

026:051 **since** we are the first to believe."
049:015 **since** doubted, but have striven with their
072:013 'And as for us, **since** we have listened to the

SINCERE

002:094 if ye are **sincere**."
002:139 **sincere** (in our faith) in Him?
004:069 the **Sincere** (lovers of Truth), the martyres,
004:146 religion devotions **sincere** to Allah: if so
007:021 that he was their **sincere** adviser.
007:029 making your devotion **sincere** such as He created
007:062 **Sincere** is my advice to you, and I
007:068 I am to you a **sincere** and trustworthy adviser".
009:091 (on the Cause), if they are **sincere** (in duty)
012:011 seeing we are indeed his **sincere** well-wishers?
024:061 or in the house of a **sincere** friend of yours:
028:020 for I do give thee **sincere** advice."
031:032 offering Him **sincere** devotion. But when
037:169 Servants of Allah, **sincere** (and devoted)!"
038:083 **sincere** and purified (by Thy grace)."
039:002 so serve Allah, offering Him **sincere** devotion.
039:003 Is it not to Allah that **sincere** devotion is due?
039:011 to serve Allah with **sincere** devotion;
039:014 with my **sincere** (and exclusive) devotion:
040:014 **sincere** devotion to Him, even though
040:065 **sincere** devotion. Praise be to Allah, Lord of
049:015 Such are the **sincere** ones.
049:017 if ye be true and **sincere**.
066:008 with **sincere** repentance: in the hope that your
098:005 offering Him **sincere** devotion, being True

SINCERELY

010:022 **sincerely** offering (their) duty unto Him, saying:
029:065 making their devotion **sincerely** (and exclusively)

SINCERITY

019:056 he was a man of truth (and **sincerity**),
022:078 to strive, (with **sincerity** and under discipline):
092:006 And (in all **sincerity**) testifies to the Best,-

SINFUL

005:063 **sinful** words and eating things forbidden?
006:043 (**sinful**) acts seem alluring to them.
008:048 (**sinful**) acts seem alluring to them, and said:
018:049 and thou wilt see the **sinful** in great terror
018:053 And the **Sinful** shall see the Fire and apprehend
020:102 that Day, We shall gather the **sinful**, blear-eyed
044:044 Will be the food of the **Sinful**,-
045:007 Woe to each **sinful** imposter.
056:045 to be indulged, before that, in **sinful** luxury,
096:016 A lying, **sinful** forelock!

SING

040:007 and those around it **sing** Glory and Praise

SINGING

039:075 on all sides, **singing** Glory and Praise to their

SINGLE

002:213 Mankind was one **single** nation.
003:075 others, who, if entrusted with a **single** silver coin,
003:165 What! when a **single** disaster smites you,
004:001 Who created you from a **single** person,
004:042 but never will they hide a **single** fact from Allah!
004:078 that they fail to understand a **single** fact?.
004:102 to assault you in a **single** rush.
005:048 He would have made you a **single** People, but
006:004 But never did a **single** one of the Signs

SINGLE (continued)

006:098 produced you from a **single** soul: then there
007:189 created you from a **single** person, and made
010:098 a **single** township (among those We warned), which
011:078 a **single** right-minded man?"
013:004 out of **single** roots or otherwise: watered with
013:008 Every **single** thing is with Him in (due)
016:061 (the punishment) for a **single** hour, just as
016:061 on the (earth), a **single** living creature: but He
016:061 to anticipate it (for a **single** hour).
018:030 of any who do a (**single**) righteous deed.
019:098 a **single** one of them (now) or hear
021:092 is a **single** Ummah, and I am your Lord
023:052 is a **single** Ummah and I am your Lord and Cherisher:
024:032 Marry those among you who are **single**,
025:014 a **single** destruction: plead for
026:101 "Nor a **single** intimate friend.
030:025 by a **single** call, from the earth, behold, ye
030:040 any **single** one of these things? Glory to Him!
035:045 of the (earth) a **single** living creature: but He
036:029 It was no more than a **single** mighty Blast,
036:049 but a **single** Blast: it will
036:053 a **single** Blast, when lo! they will
037:019 Then it will be a **single** (compelling) cry;
038:015 These (to-day) only wait for a **single** mighty Blast,
038:024 wronged thee in demanding thy (**single**) ewe to be
039:006 a **single** person: then created, of like
040:016 come forth: not a **single** thing concerning them
042:008 He could have made them a **single** people; but He
046:035 a **single** day. (Thine but) to deliver the Message:
049:010 a **single** Brotherhood: so make peace and
049:013 a **single** (pair) of a male and a female, and made
054:031 For We sent against them a **single** Mighty Blast,
054:050 And Our Command is but a **single** Word,-like the
068:024 "Let not a **single** indigent person break in upon
071:026 a **single** one on earth!
072:028 and takes account of every **single** thing."
079:013 a **single** (compelling) Cry.
079:046 but a **single** evening, or (at most till)

SINGLY

019:095 to him **singly** on the Day of Judgment.
034:046 or (it may be) **singly**,-and reflect

SINK

002:074 and others which **sink** for fear of Allah.

SINNED

010:054 Every soul that hath **sinned**, if it

SINNER

002:276 for He loveth not any ungrateful **Sinner**.
020:074 as a **sinner** (at judgment),-for him is Hell:
049:006 O ye who believe! if a **sinner** comes to you
076:024 and obey not to the **sinner** or the ingrate
083:012 the Transgressor beyond bounds, the **Sinner**!

SINNER'S

070:011 each other,-the **sinner's** desire will be: would that

SINNERS

005:106 if we do, then behold! we shall be **sinners**.
006:055 that the way of the **sinners** may be shown up.
009:066 for that they are **sinners**.
010:050 would the **Sinners** wish to hasten?
010:082 however much the **Sinners** may hate it!"
014:049 And thou wilt see the **Sinners** that day
015:012 into the hearts of the **sinners**-

SINNERS (continued)

015:044 is a (special) class (of **sinners**) assigned.
015:066 those (**sinners**) should be cut off by the morning.
017:105 Glad Tidings and to warn (**sinners**).
019:086 And We shall drive the **sinners** to Hell,
025:022 no joy will there be to the **sinners** that Day:
025:031 an enemy among the **sinners**: but enough
026:200 the hearts of the **Sinners**.
037:034 Verily that is how We shall deal with **Sinners**.
043:074 The **Sinners** will be in the Punishment of Hell,
055:041 (For) the **sinners** will be known by their Marks:
055:043 This is the Hell which the **Sinners** deny:
074:041 And (ask) of the **Sinners**:
077:046 for that ye are **Sinners**.

SINS

002:081 and are girt round by their **sins**,
002:095 on account of the (**sins**) which their hands
002:286 Blot out our **sins**.
003:011 and Allah called them to account for their **sins**.
003:016 forgive us, then, our **sins**, and save us
003:031 Allah will love you and forgive you your **sins**:
003:135 and who can forgive **sins** except Allah?
003:135 and ask for forgiveness for their **sins**,
003:147 "Our Lord forgive us our **sins** and anything
003:193 Our Lord! Forgive us our **sins**, blot out
004:043 **sins** and forgive again and again.
004:099 for Allah doth blot out (**sins**) and
004:116 He pleaseth other **sins** than this: one
005:018 Say: "Why then doth He punish you for your **sins**?
006:006 yet for their **sins** We destroyed them, and raised
007:004 We destroyed (for their **sins**)?
007:033 **sins** and trespasses against truth or reason;
007:100 We could punish them (too) for their **sins**, and
008:074 for them is the forgiveness of **sins** and a
011:011 (of **sins**) and a great reward.
011:035 my sin! And I am free of the **sins** of which
012:097 ask for us forgiveness for our **sins**, for we
014:010 your **sins** and give you respite for a term
017:008 (to your **sins**), We shall revert (to Our
017:017 to note and see the **sins** of His servants.
022:060 out (**sins**) and forgives (again and again).
025:039 to utter annihilation (for their **sins**).
028:078 called (immediately) to account for their **sins**.
033:071 and sound and forgive you your **sins**: he that
034:025 our **sins**, nor shall we be questioned as to
037:031 taste (the punishment of our **sins**):
039:053 for Allah forgives all **sins**: for He
040:011 our **sins**: is there any way out (of this)?"
040:021 to account for their **sins**, and none
042:025 from His Servants and forgives **sins**: and He
042:037 Those who avoid the greater **sins** and indecencies
042:047 any room for denial (of your **sins**)!
047:013 have We destroyed (for their **sins**)? And there
048:005 and remove their **sins** from them; and that
050:036 did We destroy (for their **Sins**),-stronger in
053:032 Those who avoid great **sins** and indecent deeds,
060:012 for the forgiveness (of their **sins**): for Allah
061:012 He will forgive you your **sins**, and admit
067:011 They will then confess their **sins**: but far
071:004 "So He may forgive you your **sins** and give you
071:025 Because of their **sins** they were drowned

SIP

002:249 a mere **sip** out of the hand is excused."

SIP (continued)
014:017 In gulps will he **sip** it, but never

SIRIUS
053:049 That He is the Lord of **Sirius** (the Mighty Star);

SISTER
004:012 but has left a brother or a **sister**, each one
004:176 That dies, leaving a **sister** but no child, she
019:028 "O **sister** of Aaron! thy father was not a man
020:040 "Behold! thy **sister** goeth forth and saith,
028:011 And she said to the **sister** of (Moses),
028:011 So she (the **sister**) watched him from a distance
028:012 at first, until (his **sister** came up and) said:

SISTER'S
004:023 **sister's** daughters; foster-mothers

SISTER-PEOPLE
007:038 it curses its **sister-People** (that went before),

SISTERS
004:011 brothers (or **sisters**), the mother has a sixth.
004:023 your mother, daughters, **sisters**, father's **sisters**,
004:023 and two **sisters** in wedlock at one and the same time,
004:023 mother's **sisters**; brother's daughters,
004:176 if there are two **sisters**, they shall
004:176 if there are brothers and **sisters**, (they share),
024:061 or your **sisters**, or your
024:061 or your fathers's **sisters**, or your
024:061 or your mother's **sisters**, or in

SISTERS'
024:031 or their **sisters'** sons, or their women,
033:055 **sisters'** sons, or their women, or the

SIT
003:168 while they themselves **sit** (at ease): "If only
004:095 those who **sit** at home by a great reward.
004:095 those who **sit** (at home).
004:095 Not equal are those Believers who **sit** (at home),
004:140 ye are not to **sit** with them unless they
005:024 and fight ye two, while we **sit** here.
006:068 **sit** not thou in the company of those who do wrong.
009:046 were told, "**Sit** ye among those who **sit** (inactive)."
009:083 then **sit** ye (now) with those who stay behind."
009:083 for ye preferred to **sit** inactive on the
009:086 we would be with those who **sit** (at home)."
017:022 or thou (O man!) wilt **sit** in disgrace
043:013 In order that ye may **sit** firm and square
056:084 And ye the while (**sit**) looking on,-
072:009 'We used, indeed, to **sit** there in (hidden)

SITE
022:026 Behold! We pointed the **site**, to Abraham, of the

SITES
037:137 Verily, ye pass by their (**sites**), by day-

SITTING
003:191 Men who remember Allah, standing, **sitting**,
004:103 remember Allah, standing, **sitting** down, or
009:081 in their **sitting** back behind the Messenger
010:012 lying down on his side, or **sitting**, or standing.
050:017 (and note them), one **sitting** on the right

SITUATED
012:077 "Ye are the worse **situated**: and Allah

SITUATION
033:011 In that **situation** were the Believers tried:
065:001 about thereafter some new **situation**.

SIX
007:054 and the earth in **six** days, then He
010:003 in **six** Days, then He established Himself on the
011:007 and the earth in **six** Days-and His Throne
025:059 in **six** days, then He established Himself on the
032:004 in **six** Days, then He established Himself on the
050:038 and all between them in **Six** Days, nor did
057:004 and the earth in **six** Days, then He

SIXTH
004:011 brothers (or sisters), the mother has a **sixth**.
004:011 a **sixth** share of the inheritance to each, if
004:012 each one of the two gets a **sixth**;
018:022 the dog being the **sixth**,-doubtfully guessing
058:007 the **sixth**,-nor between fewer not more, but He

SIXTY
058:004 to do so, he should feed **sixty** indigent ones.

SKIES
002:164 sends down from the **skies**,
006:006 rain from the **skies** in abundance, and gave
006:035 or a ladder to the **skies** and bring them a Sign,-
006:099 sendeth down rain from the **skies**: with it
006:125 as if they had to climb up to the **skies**: thus
010:024 from the **skies**: by its mingling arises the
011:052 the **skies** pouring abundant rain, and strength
013:017 He sends down water from the **skies**, and the
014:032 and sendeth down rain from the **skies**, and with it
016:065 the **skies**, and gives therewith life to the earth
017:093 the **skies**. No, we shall not even believe
018:045 We send down from the **skies**: the earth's
019:090 At it the **skies** are about to burst, the earth
025:061 in the **skies**, and placed therein a Lamp

SKILL
026:149 carve house out of (rocky) mountains with great **skill**.
036:081 of **skill** and knowledge (infinite)!
040:083 (and **skill**) as they had; but that

SKILLED
012:044 and we are not **skilled** in the interpretation

SKINS
004:056 as often as their **skins** are roasted through.
004:056 We shall change them for fresh **skins**, that they
016:080 and made for you out of the **skins** of animals,
022:020 within their bodies, as well as (their) **skins**.
039:023 various aspects): the **skins** of those who fear
039:023 then their **skins** and their hearts do soften
041:020 and their **skins** will bear witness against them,
041:021 They will say to their **skins**: "Why bear ye
041:022 and your **skins** should bear witness against you!

SKIRTS
027:044 and she (tucked up her **skirts**), uncovering her legs.

SKULL
070:016 Plucking out (his being) right to the **skull**!-

SKY
002:019 is that of a rain-laden cloud from the **sky**:
002:164 between the **sky** and the earth;
008:032 from the **sky**, or send us a grievous chastisement."
010:031 (in life) from the **sky** and from the earth?
011:044 swallow up thy water, and O **sky**!
015:022 cause the rain to descend from the **sky**,
016:010 It is He Who sends down rain from the **sky**:
016:079 in the mist of (the air and) the **sky**?
017:092 "Or thou cause the **sky** to fall in pieces,
020:053 and has sent down water from the **sky**."

SKY (continued)

022:063 sends down rain from the **sky**, and forthwith
022:065 He withholds the **sky** from falling on the earth
023:018 the **sky** according to (due) measure, and We
024:043 And He sends down from the **sky** mountain masses
025:048 and We send down pure water from the **sky**,-
026:004 We could send down to them from the **sky** a Sign,
026:187 "Now cause a piece of the **sky** to fall on us,
027:060 rain from the **sky**? Yea, with
029:063 that sends down rain from the **sky**, and gives
030:024 and He sends down rain from the **sky** and with
030:048 then does He spread them in the **sky** as He wills,
031:010 We send down rain from the **sky**, and produce
034:002 all that comes down from the **sky** and all
034:009 and behind them, of the **sky** and the earth?
034:009 a piece of the **sky** to fall upon them.
035:027 sends down rain from the **sky**?
039:021 down rain from the **sky**, and leads
040:013 from the **sky**: but only those receive admonition
040:064 and the **sky** as a canopy, and has given
041:011 Then He turned to the **sky**, and it
043:011 rain from the **sky** in due measure;-and We
044:010 that the **sky** will bring forth a kind of smoke
045:005 down Sustenance from the **sky**, and revives
050:006 Do they not look at the **sky** above them?-
050:009 And We send down from the **sky** Rain charged
051:007 By the **Sky** with (its) numerous Paths,
052:044 of the **sky** falling (on them), they would
055:037 When the **sky** is rent asunder, and it becomes
069:016 And the **sky** will be rent asunder, for it
070:008 The Day that the **sky** will be like molten brass,
073:018 Whereon the **sky** will be cleft asunder? His Promise
081:011 When the **sky** is unveiled:
082:001 When the **Sky** is cleft asunder;
084:001 When the **Sky** is rent asunder,
085:001 By the **Sky**, with its constellations;
086:001 By the **Sky** and the Night-Visitant (therein);
088:018 And at the **Sky**, how it is raised high?-

SLABS

027:044 paved smooth with **slabs** of glass." She said:

SLACKEN

004:104 And **slacken** not in following up the enemy: if
020:042 with My Signs, and **slacken** not, either of

SLAIN

002:091 Say: Why then have ye **slain** the prophets
002:154 are **slain** in the way of Allah:
002:178 by the brother of the **slain**,
003:144 If he died or were **slain**,
003:156 they would not have died, or been **slain**."
003:157 And if ye are **slain**, or die, in the way of Allah,
003:158 And if ye die, or are **slain**,
003:168 they would not have been **slain**."
003:168 (of their brethren **slain**), while they themselves
003:169 who are **slain** in Allah's way as dead.
003:195 and fought and were **slain**, verily,
004:074 whether he is **slain** or gets victory, soon shall
009:111 and slay and are **slain**: a promise
017:033 And if anyone is **slain** wrongfully, We have
018:074 "Hast thou **slain** an innocent person who had
018:074 who had **slain** none? Truly a foul
022:058 cause of Allah, and are **slain** or die,-on them
028:033 He said: "O my Lord! I have **slain** a man among them,
033:061 they shall be seized and **slain**.

SLAIN (continued)

047:004 But those who are **slain** in the way of Allah,

SLAKE

025:049 a dead land, and **slake** the thirst of things

SLAKED

083:025 Their thirst will be **slaked** with Pure Wine sealed;

SLANDER

004:020 would ye take it by **slander** and a manifest sin?
004:046 their tongues and a **slander** to Faith.
009:058 who **slander** thee in the matter of (the
009:079 Those who **slander** such of the Believers as give
024:016 this is a most serious **slander**!"
024:023 Those who **slander** chaste women, indiscreet
060:012 not utter **slander**, intentionally forging

SLANDERER

068:011 A **slanderer**, going about with calumnies,

SLAUGHTER

002:191 for Persecution is worse than **slaughter**;
002:217 Tumult and oppression are worse than **slaughter**.
003:154 we should not have been in the **slaughter** here."
005:003 unless ye are able to **slaughter** it (in due form);
006:137 the **slaughter** of their children, in order
006:138 and cattle on which (at **slaughter**) the name
022:036 on their sides (after **slaughter**), eat ye
027:049 'We were not present at the **slaughter** of his
033:016 or **slaughter**; and even if (ye do escape),

SLAUGHTERED

002:049 **slaughtered** your sons and let your women-folk
014:006 **slaughtered** your sons, and let your women-folk

SLAVE

002:178 the **slave** for the **slave**,
002:221 a man **slave** who believes is better
002:221 a **slave** woman who believes is better
004:092 and a believing **slave** be freed.
004:092 he should free a believing **slave**.
004:092 the freeing of a believing **slave** (is enough).
005:089 or clothe them; or give a **slave** his freedom.
012:030 her **slave** truly hath he inspired her with violent
016:075 (of two men): one a **slave** under the dominion
037:140 When he ran away (like **slave** from captivity)
058:003 should free a **slave** before they touch each other:

SLAVES

002:164 trail like their **slaves** between the sky
002:177 and for the ransom of **slaves**;
024:031 or the **slaves** whom their right hands possess,
024:032 your **slaves**, male or female: if they
024:033 His grace. And if any of yours **slaves** ask for
033:055 or the (**slaves**) whom their right hands possess.

SLAY

002:054 and **slay** yourselves (the wrong-doers);
002:085 who **slay** among yourselves,
002:087 and others ye **slay**!
002:191 but if they fight you, **slay** them.
002:191 And **slay** them wherever ye catch them,
003:021 and in defiance of right, **slay** the prophets,
003:021 and **slay** those who teach just dealing with mankind,
003:183 why then did ye **slay** them, if ye speak the truth?.
004:089 seize them and **slay** them wherever ye find them;
004:091 seize them and **slay** them wherever ye get them:
005:027 Said the latter: "Be sure I will **slay** thee."
005:028 to stretch my hand against thee to **slay** thee: for
005:028 to **slay** me, it is not for me to stretch my hand

SLAY (continued)

005:070 they called impostors, and some they **slay**.
006:140 Lost are those who **slay** their children, from
007:127 He said: "Their male children will we **slay**; (only)
008:030 in bonds, or **slay** thee, or get
009:005 then fight and **slay** the Pagans wherever ye
009:111 and **slay** and are slain: a promise
012:009 "**Slay** ye Joseph or cast him out to some
012:010 Said one of them: "**Slay** not Joseph, but if
020:040 Then thou didst **slay** a man, but We
025:068 any other god, nor **slay** such life as Allah
026:014 of crime against me; and I fear they may **slay** me."
028:009 for me and for thee: **slay** him not. It may
028:019 to **slay** me as thou slewest a man yesterday?
028:020 to **slay** thee: so get thee away, for I
028:033 among them, and I fear lest they **slay** me.
029:024 "**Slay** him or burn him." But Allah
040:025 "**Slay** the sons of those who believe with him,
040:026 Said Pharaoh: "Leave me to **slay** Moses; and let
040:028 said: "Will ye **slay** a man because he says,

SLAYING

002:061 and **slaying** His Messengers without just cause.
003:181 of **slaying** the Prophets in defiance of right,
007:150 and went near to **slaying** me! Make not the

SLEEP

002:255 No slumber can seize Him nor **sleep**.
018:019 We raised them up (from **sleep**), that they
025:047 and **Sleep** as Repose, and makes
030:023 And among His Signs is the **sleep** that ye take
032:016 They forsake their beds of **sleep**, the while
039:042 during their **sleep**: those on whom He has passed
078:009 And made your **sleep** for rest,

SLEEPERS

018:022 (the affair of) the **Sleepers**.

SLEEPING

051:017 They were in the habit of **sleeping** but little

SLEPT

007:004 or while they **slept** for their afternoon rest.

SLEW

002:072 Remember ye **slew** a man and fell into a dispute
002:251 and David **slew** Goliath;
003:112 and **slew** the Prophets in defiance of right:
004:155 that they **slew** the Messengers in defiance of right;
005:032 it would be as if he **slew** the whole people: and if
005:032 that if anyone **slew** a person-unless it be for
007:141 of punishment who **slew** your male children and
008:017 It is not ye who **slew** them; it was Allah:
018:074 he **slew** him. Moses said: "Hast thou slain
028:004 among them: their sons he **slew**, but he
033:026 (so that) some ye **slew**, and some

SLEWEST

028:019 to slay me as thou **slewest** a man yesterday?

SLIGHTEST

021:102 Not the **slightest** sound will they hear of Hell:

SLIP

002:036 Then did Satan make them **slip** from the (garden),
016:094 may **slip** after it was firmly planted; and ye
024:063 Allah doth know those of you who **slip** away under

SLIPPERY

018:040 making it (but) **slippery** sand!

SLIT

004:119 I will order them to **slit** the ears of cattle,

SLIT-EAR

005:103 a **slit-ear** she-camel, or a she-camel

SLOW

016:047 by a process of **slow** wastage-for thy
025:032 rehearsed it to thee in **slow**, well-arranged
073:004 in **slow**, measured rhythmic tones.

SLOWLY

034:014 of the earth, which kept (**slowly**) gnawing away

SLUMBER

002:255 No **slumber** can seize Him nor sleep.
003:154 a band of you overcome with **slumber**,

SMALL

002:041 nor sell My Signs for a **small** price:
002:246 they turned back except a **small** band among them.
002:249 hath a **small** force vanquished a big one?
002:282 whether it be **small** or big:
003:077 solemn plighted word for a **small** price,
004:007 whether the property be **small** or large,
007:010 **small** are the thanks that ye give!
008:026 a **small** (band), deemed weak through the land, and
009:121 (for the Cause)-**small** or great-nor cut
012:065 This is but a **small** quantity.
018:049 It leaves out nothing **small** or great, but
024:031 sexual desires. Or **small** children who have no
026:054 (Saying): "These (Israelites) are but a **small** band,
054:053 Every matter, **small** and great, is on record.

SMALLEST

010:061 And not the **smallest** and not the greatest

SMILED

027:019 So he **smiled**, amused at her speech; and she

SMITE

008:012 **smite** ye above their necks and smite
008:012 and **smite** all their finger-tips off them."
008:050 (how) they **smite** their faces and their backs
033:019 they will **smite** you with sharp tongues,
047:004 (in fight), **Smite** at their necks, at length
047:027 and **smite** their faces and their backs?

SMITES

003:165 What! when a single disaster **smites** you,

SMITTEN

027:087 will be sounded-then will be **smitten** with terror

SMOKE

018:029 a Fire whose (**smoke** and flames), like the
041:011 and it had been (as) **smoke**: He said
044:010 a kind of **smoke** (or mist) plainly visible.
055:015 And He created Jinns from fire free of **smoke**:
056:043 And in the shades of Black **Smoke**:
077:030 (of **smoke** ascending) in three columns,

SMOOTH

016:069 Thy Lord made **smooth**: there issues from within
020:106 "He will leave them as plains **smooth** and level;
027:044 paved **smooth** with slabs of glass." She said:
028:022 will show me the **smooth** and straight Path."
074:014 To whom I made (life) **smooth** and comfortable!
080:020 Then doth He make His path **smooth** for him;
092:007 We will indeed make **smooth** for him
092:010 We will indeed make **smooth** for him

SMOOTH-RUNNING

042:032 **smooth-running** through the ocean, (tall) as

SMOOTHLY

017:066 go **smoothly** for you through the sea, in order
055:024 **smoothly** through the seas, lofty as mountains:

SMOTE

003:165   **smote** (your enemies) with one twice as great,
051:029   she **smote** her forehead and said: "A barren

SNAKE

020:020   it was a **snake**, active in motion.
027:010   a **snake**, he turn back in retreat, and retraced
028:031   own accord) as if it had been a **snake**, he turned

SNARE

012:028   a **snare** of you women! Truly, mighty is your snare!
012:033   their **snare** from me, I should feel inclined towards
012:034   from him their **snare**: verily He heareth
012:050   well aware of their **snare**."
012:052   the **snare** of the false ones.

SNATCH

022:073   And if the fly should **snatch** away anything form them,
037:010   Except such as **snatch** away something by stealth,
054:037   **snatch** away his guests from him, but We

SNATCHED

022:031   and been **snatched** up by birds, or the
028:057   we should be **snatched** away from our land."
029:067   and that men are being **snatched** away from all

SNATCHES

002:020   The lightning all but **snatches** away their sight:

SNOUT

068:016   Soon shall We brand (the beast) on the **snout**!

SO

002:015   **so** they will wander like blind ones
002:017   **so** they could not see.
002:034   not **so** Iblis, he refused and was haughty:
002:054   **so** turn (in repentance) to your Maker,
002:059   **so** We sent on the transgressors
002:060   **So** eat and drink of the sustenance
002:061   **so** beseech thy Lord for us to produce for us
002:066   **So** We made it an example to their own time,
002:073   **So** We said: "Strike the (body)
002:102   **so** do not blaspheme."
002:118   **So** said the people before them
002:132   upon his sons and **so** did Jacob;
002:137   **So** if they believe as ye believe,
002:147   **so** be not at all in doubt.
002:150   **So** from whencesoever thou startest forth,
002:150   **so** fear them not, but fear Me;
002:158   **So** if those who visit the House
002:185   **So** every one of you who is present (at his home)
002:187   **so** now associate with them,
002:194   and **so** for all things prohibited,
002:197   **So** fear Me, O ye that are wise.
002:199   it is usual for the multitude **so** to do,
002:200   **So** when ye have accomplished your rites,
002:214   and were **so** shaken in spirit that even the Messenger
002:222   **so** keep away from women in their courses,
002:223   **so** approach your tilth when or how ye will;
002:229   **so** do not transgress them
002:230   **So** if a husband divorces his wife (irrevocably),
002:253   If Allah had **so** willed, they would not have
002:253   If Allah had **so** willed, succeeding generations
002:271   even **so** it is well,
002:272   do **so** seeking the "Face" of Allah.
002:282   as Allah has taught him, **so** let him write.
002:282   **So** fear Allah; for it is Allah
002:282   **so** that if one of them errs.
003:020   **So** if they dispute with thee,

SO (continued)

003:020   to Allah and **so** have those who follow me."
003:035   **so** accept this or me: for Thou hearest
003:047   He said: "Even **so**; Allah createth what He willeth:
003:050   **So** fear Allah, and obey me.
003:060   **so** be not of those who doubt
003:078   (as they read) **so** that you would think
003:103   **so** that by His Grace, Ye became brethren;
003:139   **So** lose not heart, nor fall into despair:
003:159   **so** pass over (their faults), and ask for (Allah's)
003:173   **so** fear them": but it only increased their Faith:
003:179   **So** believe in Allah and His Messengers:
003:184   **so** were rejected messengers before thee,
004:012   **so** that no loss is caused (to anyone).
004:063   **so** keep clear of them but admonish them,
004:076   **so** fight ye against the friends, of Satan:
004:081   **so** keep clear of them, and put thy trust in Allah,
004:089   **so** take not friends from their ranks until
004:105   **so** be not an advocate for those who
004:129   **so** as to leave her (as it were)
004:146   if **so** they will be (numbered) with the Believers.
004:153   even **so** We forgave them; and gave Moses
004:171   **so** believe in Allah and His Messengers.
005:011   **so** fear Allah.
005:014   that was sent them: **so** We stirred up enmity and
005:025   **so** separate us from this rebellious people!"
005:041   who have never **so** much as come to thee.
005:048   **so** judge between them by what Allah hath revealed,
005:048   If Allah had **so** willed, He would have
005:048   **so** strive as in a race in all virtues.
005:071   **so** they became blind and deaf; yet Allah
005:095   If any of you doth **so** intentionally, the
005:100   **so** fear Allah, O ye that understand that;
005:100   O ye that understand that (**so**) ye may prosper."
005:110   **So** that thou didst speak to the people
006:007   **so** that they could touch it with their hands, the
006:025   in **so** much that when they come to thee, they
006:025   **so** they understand it not, and deafness
006:035   **so** be not thou amongst those who are swayed
006:048   **so** those who believe and mend (their lives),-
006:075   **So** also did We show Abraham the kingdom
006:094   **so** now all relations between you
006:112   **so** leave them and they forge.
006:112   If thy Lord had **so** willed, they would
006:118   **So** eat of (meats) on which Allah's name
006:130   **So** against themselves will they bear
006:137   Even **so**, in the eyes of most
006:137   they would not have done **so**: but leave
006:138   except those whom-**so** they say-We wish; further,
006:145   But (even **so**), if a person
006:148   If **so**, produce it before us. Ye follow
006:148   **So** did their ancestors argue falsely, until
006:150   to prove that Allah did forbid **so** and **so**." If
006:155   **so** follow it and be righteous, that ye
007:002   **so** let thy heart be oppressed no more
007:011   and they prostrated, not **so** Iblis; he refused
007:022   **So** by deceit he brought about their fall: when
007:028   they say: "We found our fathers doing **so**"; and
007:029   **so** shall ye return."
007:038   **so** give them a double punishment in the Fire." He
007:039   **so** taste ye of the Chastisement
007:063   to warn you,-**so** that ye may fear Allah
007:069   that **so** ye may prosper."

007:070   if **so** be that thou tellest the truth!"
007:073   **so** leave her to graze in Allah's earth, and
007:074   **so** bring to remembrance the benefits
007:078   **So** the earthquake took them unawares, and they
007:079   **So** Salih left them, saying: "O my people!
007:093   **So** Shu'aib left them, saying: "O my people!
007:100   if We **so** willed, We could
007:100   **so** that they could not hear?
007:103   **so** see what was the end of those
007:105   **so** let the Children of Israel depart along with me."
007:113   **So** there came the sorcerers to Pharaoh: they said:
007:116   **So** when they threw, they bewitched
007:119   **So** they were vanquished there and then, and
007:129   that **so** He may see how ye act."
007:133   **So** We sent on them: Wholesale Death,
007:136   **So** We exacted retribution from them: We drowned
007:155   **so** forgive us and give us Thy mercy; for Thou
007:157   **So** it is those who believe in him, honor him,
007:158   **So** believe in Allah and His Messenger. The
007:158   follow him that (**so**) ye may be guided."
007:162   **so** We sent on them a plague from heaven. For
007:169   (Even **so**), if similar vanities came their way,
007:175   **so** Satan followed him up, and he went astray.
007:176   **so** relate the story; perchance they may reflect.
007:180   **so** call on Him by them; but shun
008:001   **so** fear Allah, and keep straight the relations
008:019   **so** shall We. Not the least good will your
008:036   and **so** will they continue to spend; but in
008:054   the Signs of their Lord **so** We destroyed them
008:058   (**so** as to be) on equal terms: for Allah
008:066   spot in you: but (even **so**), if there
008:071   against Allah, and **so** hath He given thee
009:004   **So** fulfil your engagements with them to the
009:006   **so** that he may hear the Word of Allah; and then
009:011   But (even **so**), if they repent, establish regular
009:023   above faith: if any of you do **so**, they do wrong.
009:028   are unclean; **so** let them not, after this
009:036   that is the right religion **so** wrong not yourselves
009:036   **so** ordained by Him the day He created
009:045   in doubt, **so** that they are tossed in their
009:046   **so** He made them lag behind and they were told,
009:052   **So** wait (expectant); we too will wait with you."
009:067   **so** He hath forgotten them. Verily the
009:077   **So** He hath put as a consequence hypocrisy into
009:087   their hearts are sealed and **so** they understand not.
009:093   **so** they know not.
009:095   **So** leave them alone: for they are an abomination,
009:103   that **so** thou mightest purify and sanctify them;
009:110   The foundation of those who **so** build is never
009:112   **So** proclaim the glad tidings to the Believers.
010:016   Say: "If Allah had **so** willed, I should
010:061   (**so** much as) the weight of an atom on the
010:071   **so** your plan be not to you dark and dubious.
010:088   **so** they will not believe until they see
010:088   and **so**, our Lord they mislead (men) from Thy Path.
010:089   (O Moses and Aaron)! **So** stand ye straight, and
010:094   thy Lord: **so** be in no wise of those in doubt.
010:098   which believed,-**so** its Faith should have
010:108   do **so** to their own loss: and I am
010:108   do **so** for the good of their own souls;
011:011   Not **so** do those who show patience and constancy,
011:036   **So** grieve no longer over their (evil) deeds.

011:041   **So** he said: "Embark ye on the Ark, in the
011:042   **So** the Ark floated with them on the waves
011:046   **So** ask not of Me that of which thou hast
011:049   **So** persevere patiently: for the End
011:052   **so** turn ye not back in sin!"
011:055   **So** scheme (your worst) against me, all of you,
011:058   **So** when Our decree issued, We saved Hud
011:065   **So** he said: "Enjoy yourselves in your homes
011:068   and Cherisher! **So** away with the Thamud!
011:095   flourished there! **So** away with Madyan as were
011:107   They will dwell therein **so** long as the heavens
011:108   **so** long as the heavens and the earth endure,
011:118   If thy Lord had **so** willed, He could
011:123   **so** worship Him, and put thy trust in Him: and thy
012:009   to some (unknown) land, that **so** the favour of your
012:014   devour him while we are (**so** large) a party,
012:015   **So** they did take him away, and they
012:019   **So** they concealed him as a treasure! But Allah
012:025   **So** they both raced each other to the door, and she
012:028   **So** when he saw his shirt,-that it
012:034   **So** his Lord hearkened to him (in his prayer),
012:041   (**So**) hath been decreed that matter whereof ye
012:045   (**so** long) a space of time, said: "I will tell
012:050   **So** the king said: "Bring ye him unto me." But when
012:054   **So** the king said: "Bring him unto me; I will take
012:062   **so** they should know it only when they
012:063   **so** send our brother with us, that we
012:065   has been returned to us: **so** we shall get (more)
012:069   (own) brother; **so** grieve not at aught
012:076   **So** he began (the search) with their baggage,
012:076   except that Allah willed it (**so**). We raise
012:078   **so** take one of us in his place: for we
012:079   our property: indeed (if we did **so**), we should
012:083   for you. **So** patience is most fitting (for me).
012:088   **so** pay us full measure, (we pray thee), and treat
013:013   and **so** do the angels, with awe: He flingeth
013:015   **so** do their shadows in the mornings and evenings.
013:016   **so** that the creation seemed to them similar?
013:017   the surface. Even **so**, from that (ore) which
013:026   (which He giveth) to whom **so** He pleaseth.
013:031   (**so**) willed, He could have guided all mankind
014:004   to them. **So** Allah leads astray those whom He
014:019   in Truth? If He **so** will, He can remove you
014:025   **So** Allah sets forth parables for men, in order
014:037   **so** that they may give thanks.
014:037   **so** fill the hearts of some among men
014:044   **So** warn mankind of the Day when the Wrath
014:048   to a different Earth, and **so** will be the Heavens,
015:012   Even **so** do We let it creep into the
015:030   **So** the angels prostrated themselves, all of
015:031   Not **so** Iblis: he refused to be among those
015:071   (to marry), if ye must act (**so**)."
015:079   **So** We exacted retribution from them. They were
015:085   **So** overlook (any human faults) with gracious
015:091   (**So** also on such) as have made Qur'an into
016:002   but I: **so** do your duty unto Me."
016:029   "**So** enter the gates of Hell, to dwell therein.
016:033   **So** did those who went before them. But Allah
016:035   "If Allah had **so** willed, we should not have
016:035   **So** did those who went before them. But what
016:036   **So** travel through the earth, and see what was
016:063   **so** but they shall have a most grievous

SO (continued)

016:064 so that thou shouldst make clear to them
016:070 so that they know nothing after having
016:071 so as to be equal in that respect. Will they
016:080 which ye find so light (and handy) when ye
016:093 If Allah so willed, He could make you all
016:112 so Allah made it taste of hunger and terror
016:113 falsely rejected him; so the Wrath seized them
016:114 So eat of the sustenance which Allah
016:116 so as to ascribe false things to Allah. For those
017:007 So when the second of the warnings came to pass,
017:015 who goeth astray doth so to his own loss:
017:016 continued to transgress; so that the word is
017:029 utmost reach, so that thou become blameworthy
017:068 so that ye shall find no protector?
017:069 so that ye find no helper therein against Us?
017:103 So he resolved to remove them from the
018:011 (so that they heard not):
018:023 "I shall be sure to do so and so to-morrow"
018:024 Except "If Allah so wills" and remember
018:025 So they stayed in their Cave three hundred years,
018:041 run off underground so that thou wilt never
018:042 So his fruits were encompassed (with ruin),
018:057 veils over their hearts so that they should
018:064 seeking after": so they went back on their
018:065 So they found one of Our servants. On whom
018:069 if Allah so will, (truly) patient: nor shall
018:071 So they both proceeded: until, when they
018:081 "So we desired that their Lord would give them
018:082 so thy Lord desired that they should attain their
019:005 so give me an heir as from Thyself,-
019:009 He said: "So (it will be): thy Lord saith,
019:011 So Zakariya came out to his people from his
019:015 So Peace on him the day he was born, the day
019:021 it is a matter (so) decreed."
019:021 He said: "So (it will be): thy Lord saith,
019:022 So she conceived him, and she retired with him
019:026 "So eat and drink and cool (thine) eye. And if
019:033 "So Peace is on me the day I was born, the day
019:043 so follow me: I will guide thee to a Way that
019:045 so that thou become to Satan a friend."
019:065 so worship Him, and be constant and patient
019:068 So, by thy Lord, without doubt, We shall
019:084 So make no haste against them, for We
019:097 So have We made the (Qur'an) easy in thine
019:098 or hear (so much as) a whisper of them?
020:010 so he said to his family, "Tarry ye;
020:014 but I: so serve thou Me (only), and establish
020:028 "So they may understand what I say:
020:040 So We brought thee back to thy mother, that her
020:047 "So go ye both to him, and say, `Verily we
020:058 to match thine! So make a tryst between us
020:060 So Pharaoh withdrew: he concerted his plan,
020:062 So they disputed, one with another, over their
020:066 so it seemed to him on account of their magic-
020:067 So Moses conceived in his mind a (sort of) fear.
020:070 So the magicians were thrown down to prostration:
020:071 So shall ye know for certain, which of
020:072 So decree whatever thou desirest to degree:
020:086 So Moses returned to his people in state
020:086 on you, and so ye broke your promise to me?"
020:088 it seemed to low: so they said: "This is
020:090 Most Gracious: so follow me and obey my command."

SO (continued)

020:096 so I took a handful (of dust) from the
020:108 so that thou hearest not but murmuring.
020:117 the Garden, so that thou art landed in misery.
020:117 so let him not get you both out of the Garden,
020:121 and so their nakedness appeared to them:
020:126 forgot them: so wilt thou, this day, be forgotten.
021:024 and so turn away.
021:037 so ask Me not to hasten them!
021:047 so that not a soul will be dealt with
021:052 to which ye are (so assiduously) devoted?"
021:058 So he broke them to pieces, (all) but
021:064 So they turned to themselves and said,
021:077 so We drowned them (in the Flood) all together.
021:084 So We listened to him: We removed
021:088 So We listened to him: and delivered
021:090 So We listened to him: and We him Yahya: We cured
021:104 so shall We produce a new one:
022:005 so that they know nothing after having
022:006 This is so, because Allah is the Reality:
022:030 so shun the abomination of idols,
022:042 If they disbelieve you so did the Peoples
022:046 so that their hearts (and mind) may thus learn
022:056 so those who believe and work righteous deeds
022:060 That (is so). And if one has retaliated to no
022:078 for mankind! So establish regular Prayer,
023:014 another creature: so blessed be Allah, the Best
023:027 So We inspired him (with this message);
023:041 So away with the people who do wrong!
023:044 (that is told): so away with a people
023:044 so We made them follow each other (in punishment):
023:048 So they rejected them and they became of those
023:110 so much so that (ridicule of) them made you
023:118 So say: "O my Lord! grant Thou forgiveness
024:056 So establish regular Prayer and give zakat
024:062 so when they ask for thy leave, for some
025:019 so ye cannot avert (your penalty)
026:006 so they will know soon (enough) the truth
026:013 so send unto Aaron.
026:016 "So go forth, both of you, to Pharaoh,
026:021 "So I fled from you (all) when I feared you;
026:032 So (Moses) threw his rod, and behold,
026:038 So the sorcerers were got together for the
026:041 So when the sorcerers arrived, they said
026:044 So they threw their ropes and their rods,
026:057 So We expelled them from gardens, springs,
026:060 So they pursued them at sunrise.
026:063 So it divided, and each separate part became like
026:077 not so the Lord and Cherisher of the Worlds;
026:108 "So fear Allah, and obey me.
026:110 "So fear Allah, and obey me."
026:119 So we delivered him and those with him. In the
026:126 "So fear Allah, and obey me.
026:139 So they rejected him, and We
026:144 So fear Allah, and obey me.
026:163 "So fear Allah, and obey me.
026:170 So We delivered him and his family,-all
026:179 "So fear Allah, and obey me.
026:213 So call not on any other god with Allah,
027:004 and so they wander blindly.
027:014 so see what was the end of those who
027:019 So he smiled, amused at her speech; and she
027:019 so order me that I may be grateful for Thy favours,

SO (continued)

027:024 so they receive no guidance,-
027:025 So that they worship not Allah Who brings forth
027:033 so consider what thou wilt command."
027:042 So when she arrived, she was asked, "Is this
027:079 So put thy trust in Allah: for thou
027:081 so they submit.
027:093 so that ye shall know them": and thy
028:007 So We sent this inspiration to the mother of Moses:
028:010 (with faith), so that she might remain a (firm)
028:011 So she (the sister) watched him from a distance
028:016 So (Allah) forgave him: for He
028:020 to slay thee: so get thee away, for I
028:024 So he watered (their flocks) for them; then he
028:025 So when he came to him and narrated the story,
028:034 so send him with me as a helper, to confirm
028:035 so they shall not be able to touch you: with Our
028:040 So We seized him and his hosts, and We
028:079 So he went forth among his people in the
029:006 they do so for their own soul: for Allah
029:018 so did generations before you: and the
029:020 so will Allah produce a later creation: for Allah
029:024 So naught was the answer of (Abraham's) people
029:047 So the People of the Book believe therein,
030:017 So (give) glory to Allah, when ye
030:030 So set thou thy face truly to the religion
030:038 So give what is due to kindred, the needy
030:052 So verily thou canst not make the dead to hear,
030:057 So on that Day no excuse of theirs will avail
030:060 So patiently persevere: for verily
031:012 to Allah." Any who is (so) grateful does so
031:012 does so to the profit of his own soul: but if
032:013 If We had so willed, We could
032:024 so long as they persevered with patience
032:030 So turn away from them, and wait: they too
033:019 and so Allah has made their deeds of none effect:
033:026 (so that) some ye slew, and some
033:049 so give them a present, and release
033:053 (and then) not (so early as) to wait
034:014 so when he fell down, the Jinns
034:023 So far (is this the case) that, when terror
034:042 So on that Day no power shall they have
034:052 from a position (so) far off,-
035:004 so were messengers rejected before thee:
035:006 so treat him as an enemy. He only
035:008 so that he looks upon it as good, (equal to one
035:008 So let not thy soul be vested in regret
035:009 so that they raise up the Clouds, and We
035:009 even so (will be) the Resurrection!
035:016 If He so pleased, He could blot you out
035:018 And whoever purifies himself does so for the
035:025 so did their predecessors, to whom
035:028 And so amongst men and beasts and cattle,
035:036 so they should die, nor shall
035:037 So taste ye (the fruit of your deeds): for the
035:037 so that he that would should receive admonition?
035:039 so, he who disbelieves his disbelief be on
036:008 so that they cannot bow their heads.
036:009 so that they cannot see.
036:028 from heaven, nor was it needful for Us so to do.
036:047 those whom, if Allah had so willed, He could
036:083 So glory to Him in Whose hands is the
037:002 Those who so are strong in repelling (evil),

SO (continued)

037:008 (So) they should not strain their ears in the
037:031 "So now has been proved true, against us,
037:070 So they (too) were rushed down on their footsteps!
037:090 So they turned away from him, and departed.
037:101 So We gave him the good news of a forbearing son.
037:102 if Allah so wills one of the steadfast."
037:103 So when they had both submitted (to Allah),
037:116 And We helped them, so they were victorious;
037:123 So also was Elias among those sent (by us).
037:133 So also was Lut among those sent (by us).
037:139 So also was Jonah among those sent (by Us).
037:148 And they believed; so We permitted them to enjoy
037:160 Not (so do) the servants of Allah, the chosen ones.
037:174 So turn thou away from them for a little while,
037:178 So turn thou away from them for a little while,
038:004 So they wonder that a Warner has come to them
038:010 and all between? If so, let them mount up
038:024 each other: not so do those who believe
038:025 So We forgave him this (lapse): he enjoyed,
038:026 so judge thou between men in truth (and justice):
038:073 So the angels prostrated themselves, all of
038:074 Not so Iblis: he was haughty, and became
039:002 so serve Allah, offering Him sincere devotion.
039:017 Good News: so announce the Good News to My
039:022 to Islam, so that he has received light
039:025 rejected (revelation), and so the Punishment
039:026 So Allah gave them a taste of humiliation
039:035 So that Allah will remit from them (even) the
040:022 rejected them: so Allah called them to account:
040:064 So Glory to Allah, the Lord of the Worlds!
040:077 So persevere in patience! For the
041:004 and so they hear not.
041:005 is a screen: so do thou (what thou wilt); for us,
041:006 so take the straight path unto Him and ask for
041:012 So He completed them as seven firmaments in two
041:014 so we disbelieve in the Message you were sent with.
041:014 They said, "If our Lord had so pleased, He would
041:016 So We sent against them a furious Wind
041:017 to Guidance: so the thunderbolt of the Chastisement
041:029 so that they become the vilest."
042:008 If Allah had so willed, He could
043:008 So We destroyed men-stronger in power than these;-
043:011 is dead; even so will ye be raised
043:013 and when so seated, ye may
043:025 So We exacted retribution from them: now see
043:032 so that some may command work from others.
043:043 So hold thou fast to the Revelation sent down
043:064 and your Lord: so worship ye Him: this is
043:083 So leave them to babble and play (with vanities)
044:054 So; and We shall wed them to maidens
044:059 So wait thou and watch; for they
045:018 of Religion: so follow thou that (Way),
046:008 whereof ye talk (so glibly)! Enough is He
047:009 of Allah; so He has made their deeds fruitless.
047:015 so that it cuts up their bowels (to pieces)?
047:028 so He made their deeds of no effect.
047:030 Had We so willed, We could have
047:038 are niggardly are so at the expense of their
048:010 His oath, does so to the harm of his own soul,
049:010 a single Brotherhood: so make peace and
050:002 among themselves. So the Unbelievers say: "This is
050:005 to them: so they are in a confused state.

SO (continued)

050:040 and (so likewise) after the prostration.
050:045 by force. **So** admonish with the Qur'an such as
051:030 They said, "Even **so** has thy Lord spoken: and He
051:040 **So** We took him and his forces, and threw
051:044 of their Lord: **so** the thunderbolt seized them,
051:046 **So** were the people of Noah before them: for they
051:054 **So** turn away from them: not thine is the blame.
052:040 a reward, **so** that they are burdened
052:045 **So** leave them alone until they encounter
053:010 **So** did (Allah) convey the inspiration to His
053:031 **so** that He rewards those who do evil,
053:035 **so** that he can see?
053:054 **So** that there covered it that which covered.
054:011 **So** We opened the gates of heaven, with water
054:012 with springs, **so** the waters met (and rose)
054:027 **So** watch them, (O Salih), and possess
054:039 "**So** taste ye My Chastisement and My Warning."
055:009 **So** establish weight with justice and fall
056:096 **So** glorify the name of thy Lord, the Supreme.
057:010 **so** later). Those are higher in rank than those
057:013 **So** a wall will be put up betwixt them, with a
058:004 to do **so**, he should feed sixty indigent ones.
058:013 If, then, ye do not **so**, and Allah forgives you,
058:019 **so** he has made them forgot the remembrance
059:002 **so** that they destroyed their dwellings by their
059:007 among you. **So** take what the Messenger gives you,
059:012 **so** they will receive no help.
061:013 and speedy victory. **So** give the Glad Tidings
063:003 **so** a seal was set on their hearts: therefore
063:004 **so** beware of them. The curse
064:005 **So** they tasted the evil result of their conduct;
064:006 **So** they rejected (the Message) and turned away.
064:012 **So** obey Allah, and obey His Messenger; but if
064:014 to yourselves: **so** beware of them! But if
064:016 **So** fear Allah as much as ye can; listen and
065:006 **so** as to restrict them. And if
066:004 **so** inclined; but is ye back up each other
067:003 The Most Gracious. **So** turn thy vision again:
067:015 for you, **so** traverse ye through its tracts
067:017 **so** that ye shall know how (terrible) was My warning?
067:029 **so** soon will ye know which (of us) it is
068:008 **So** obey not to those who deny (the Truth).
068:009 be pliant: **so** would thy be pliant.
068:020 **So** the (garden) became, by the morning, like a
068:023 **So** they departed, conversing in secret low tones,
068:046 a reward, **so** that they are burdened with a load
068:047 **so** that they can write it down?
068:048 **So** wait with patience for the command of thy Lord,
069:007 **so** that thou couldst see the (whole) people
069:010 of their Lord; **so** He punished them with an
069:035 "**So** no friend hath he here this Day.
069:038 **So** I do call to witness what ye see
069:052 **So** glorify the name of thy Lord Most High.
070:014 **so** it could deliver him:
070:022 Not **so** those devoted to Prayer:-
070:042 **So** leave them to plunge in vain talk and play
071:004 "**So** He may forgive you your sins and give you
071:008 "**So** I have called to them aloud;
072:018 for Allah (alone): **so** invoke not any one along
073:016 **so** We seized him with a heavy Punishment.
073:020 and **so** doth a party of those with thee. But Allah
073:020 count thereof. **So** He hath turned to you (in mercy):

SO (continued)

075:031 **So** he gave nothing in charity, nor did he pray!-
076:002 **so** We gave him (the gifts), of Hearing and Sight.
077:017 **So** shall We make later (generations) follow them.
077:048 "Prostrate yourselves!" They do not **so**.
078:030 "**So** taste ye (the fruits of your deeds); for no
079:019 **so** thou shouldst fear Him?'"
080:011 By no means (should it be **so**)! For it
081:015 **So** verily I call to witness the Planets-that recede,
084:002 and it must needs (do **so**);-
084:005 and it must needs (do **so**);-(then will
084:016 **So** I do call to witness the ruddy glow of Sunset;
084:024 **So** announce to them a Chastisement Grievous,
087:006 (the Message), **so** thou shalt not forget,
091:014 hamstrung her. **So** their Lord, crushed them
092:005 **So** he who gives (in charity) and fears (Allah),
094:005 **So**, verily, with every difficulty, there is relief:
107:004 **So** woe to the worshippers

SOAK

023:018 and We caused it to **soak** in the soil; and We

SOBBING

021:100 There, **sobbing** will be their lot, nor will

SOBS

011:106 therein (nothing but) the heaving of sighs and **sobs**:

SODOM

053:053 the Overthrown Cities (of **Sodom** and Gomorrah),

SOFT

016:080 their wool, and their **soft** fibers (between wool
034:010 and We made the iron **soft** for Him;-

SOFTEN

039:023 do **soften** to the remembrance of Allah. Such is

SOIL

002:071 to till the **soil** or water the fields;
002:264 on which is a little **soil**;
018:008 but as dust and dry **soil** (without growth
020:006 and all between them, and all beneath the **soil**.
023:018 and We caused it to soak in the **soil**; and We
030:009 in strength: they tilled the **soil** and populated
032:027 drive Rain to parched **soil** (bare of herbage),

SOJOURN

012:023 is my lord! He made my **sojourn** agreeable! Truly

SOLD

002:090 for which they have **sold** their souls,
009:009 they **sold** for a miserable price, and (many)
012:020 The (Brethren) **sold** him for a miserable price,-

SOLEMN

003:077 **solemn** plighted word for a small price,
004:021 and they have taken from you a **solemn** covenant?
004:154 And We took from them a **solemn** Covenant.
005:114 a **solemn** festival and a Sign from Thee; and
012:066 with you until ye swear a **solemn** oath to me,
012:066 they had sworn their **solemn** oath, he said:
033:007 We took from them a **solemn** Covenant:

SOLEMNLY

002:084 and this ye **solemnly** ratified.
002:231 but **solemnly** rehearse Allah's favours on you,
024:007 that he **solemnly** invokes the curse of Allah
024:009 she **solemnly** invokes the wrath of Allah on herself

SOLID

061:004 as if they were a **solid** cemented structure.

SOLITARY
054:024 a **solitary** one from among ourselves! Shall we

SOLOMON
002:102 **Solomon** did not disbelieve but Satans
004:163 to Jesus, Job, Jonah, Aaron, and **Solomon**, and to
006:084 **Solomon**, Job, Joseph, Moses, and Aaron: thus do
021:078 And remember David and **Solomon**, when they
021:079 To **Solomon** We inspired the (right)
021:081 (tamely) for **Solomon**, to his order, to the
027:015 We gave knowledge to David and **Solomon**: and they
027:016 And **Solomon** was David's heir. He said:
027:017 And before **Solomon** were marshalled his hosts,-
027:018 your habitations, lest **Solomon** and his host
027:027 (**Solomon**) said: "Soon shall we see whether thou
027:030 It is from **Solomon**, and is (as follows):
027:036 Now when (the embassy) came to **Solomon**, he said:
027:040 Then when (**Solomon**) saw it placed firmly
027:044 with **Solomon**, to the Lord of the Worlds."
034:012 And to **Solomon** (We made) the Wind (obedient):
038:030 To David We gave **Solomon** (for a son),-
038:034 And We did try **Solomon**: We placed

SOLOMON'S
002:102 Satans recited over **Solomon's** Kingdom.
034:014 (**Solomon's**) death, nothing showed them his death

SOME
002:008 Of the people there are **some** who say
002:074 **some** from which rivers gush forth;
002:087 **Some** ye called impostors,
002:100 **some** party among them throw it aside?
002:146 but **some** of them conceal the truth
002:155 **some** loss in goods,
002:219 and **some** profit, for men;
002:223 But do **some** good act for your souls beforehand;
002:253 **some** believing and others rejecting.
002:253 to **some** of them Allah spoke;
002:253 with gifts, **some** above others:
002:271 **some** of your (stains of) evil.
003:066 which ye had **some** Knowledge!
003:075 Among the People of the Book are **some** who,
003:106 and **some** faces will be (in the gloom of) black:
003:106 **some** faces will be (lit up with) white,
003:110 among them are **some** who have faith,
003:120 but if **some** misfortune overtakes you,
003:152 Among you are **some** that hanker after this world
003:152 and **some** that desire the Hereafter.
003:155 because of **some** (evil) they had done.
003:187 and purchased with it **some** miserable gain!
004:015 or Allah ordain for them **some** (other) way.
004:032 gifts more freely on **some** of you than on others:
004:047 fame of **some** (of you) beyond all recognition,
004:055 And **some** of them averted their faces from him:
004:055 **Some** of them believed.
004:078 If **some** good befalls them, they say, "This
004:083 **some** matter touching (public) safety or fear,
004:150 saying: "We believe in **some** but reject others":
004:164 Of **some** messengers We have already told thee
005:002 of **some** people in (once) shutting you out
005:049 that for **some** of their crimes it is Allah's
005:060 those of whom **some** He transformed into apes
005:070 they called impostors, and **some** they slay.
005:070 desired not-**some** (of theses) they called impostors,
005:102 **Some** people before you did ask such questions, and
006:025 Of them there are **some** who (pretend to)

SOME (continued)
006:034 **some** account of those Messengers.
006:053 Thus did We test **some** of them by other, that
006:099 from **some** We produce green (crops), out of
006:142 for burden and **some** for meat: eat what
006:142 Of the cattle are **some** for burden
006:165 **some** above others: that He may
007:030 **Some** He hath guided: others have
007:138 devoted entirely to **some** idols they had. They
007:164 When **some** of them said: "Why do ye preach to a
007:168 There are among them **some** that are
007:168 and **some** that are the opposite. We have
009:046 **some** preparation therefor: but Allah was averse
009:047 and there would have been **some** among you
009:066 If We pardon **some** of you, We will
009:098 **Some** of the Bedouin Arabs look upon their payments
009:099 But **some** of the Bedouin Arabs believe in Allah
009:124 **some** of them say: "Which of you has had his faith
010:021 of **some** mercy after adversity hath touched them,
010:040 believe therein, and **some** who do not: and thy
010:040 Of them there are **some** who believe therein,
010:042 Among them are **some** who (pretend to)
010:043 And among them are **some** who look at thee:
010:046 thy lifetime) **some** part of what We promise them,-
010:059 Yet ye hold forbidden **some** things thereof and (**some**
010:059 and (**some** things) lawful." Say: "Hath Allah
010:083 except **some** children of his People, because of
010:107 if He do design **some** benefit for thee, there is
011:043 to **some** mountain: it will save me from the water."
011:048 and Blessing on thee and on **some** of the Peoples
011:049 Such are **some** of the stories of the Unseen,
011:054 **some** of our gods may have seized thee with evil."
011:070 he felt **some** mistrust of them, and conceived
011:080 myself to **some** powerful support."
011:100 of them **some** are standing, and **some**
011:100 These are **some** of the stories of communities
011:100 and **some** have been mown down (by the
011:105 be wretched and **some** will be blessed.
011:105 of those (gathered) **some** will be wretched
012:009 to **some** (unknown) land, that so the favour of your
012:010 he will be picked up by **some** caravan of travellers."
012:101 bestowed on me **some** power, and taught me
013:004 yet **some** of them We make more excellent
014:010 then bring us **some** clear authority."
014:037 "O our Lord! I have made **some** of my offspring
014:037 so fill the hearts of **some** among men
016:036 **some** whom Allah guided, and **some**
016:036 and **some** on whom Error became inevitably
016:054 from you, behold! **some** of you turn to other gods
016:070 and of you there are **some** who are sent back
016:071 of sustenance more freely on **some** of you than
016:081 **some** things to give you shade; of the
016:081 of the hills He made **some** for your shelter;
017:001 show him **some** of Our Signs: for he
017:021 See how We have bestowed more on **some** than on
017:055 and on earth: and We made **some** of the Prophets
018:019 best food (to be had) and bring **some** to you,
018:021 (**Some**) said, "Construct a building over them":
018:022 (**Some**) say they were three, the dog
018:062 When they had passed on (**some** distance), Moses said
018:077 exacted **some** recompense for it!"
019:058 Those were **some** of the prophets on whom
020:010 perhaps I can bring you **some** burning brand

SOME (continued)

020:010 or find **some** guidance at the fire."
020:099 **some** stories of what happened before: for We
020:113 in detail **some** of the warnings, in order that
021:082 And of Satans were **some** who dived for him,
022:005 and **some** of you are called to die, and **some**
022:005 and **some** are sent back to the feeblest old age,
022:011 There are among men **some** who serve Allah, as it
022:052 Satan threw **some** (vanity) into his desire:
023:025 (And **some** said:) "He is only a man possessed:
023:072 **some** recompense? But the recompense of thy Lord
023:091 had created, and **some** would have lorded it over
024:029 living in, which serve **some** (other) use for you:
024:045 **some** that walk on two legs: and **some**
024:045 from water: of them there are **some** that creep
024:045 and **some** that walk on four. Allah creates
024:047 but even after that, **some** of them turn away:
024:048 behold, **some** of them decline (to come).
024:062 for **some** business of theirs, give leave
024:063 under shelter of **some** excuse: then let
024:063 lest **some** trial befall them, or a
025:020 the markets. We have made **some** of you as a
027:007 **some** information, or I will bring you a burning
027:072 Say: "It may be that **some** of the events
028:003 We rehearse to thee **some** of the story
028:029 **some** information, or a burning firebrand,
029:040 **some** We caused the earth to swallow up; and **some**
029:040 and **some** We drowned (in the waters): it was
029:040 his crime: of them, against **some** We sent
029:040 **some** were caught by a (mighty) Blast; **some** We
029:047 believe therein, as also do **some** of these
030:033 **some** of them pay part-worship to other gods
030:036 they exult thereat: and when **some** evil afflicts
030:041 of **some** of their deeds: in order
033:023 of them **some** have died and **some** (still) wait:
033:026 (so that) **some** ye slew, and **some**
033:026 and **some** ye made captives.
034:016 and **some** few (stunted) Lote-trees.
035:032 a middle course; and **some** who are, by Allah's
035:032 own souls; **some** who follow a middle course
035:032 among them **some** who wrong their own souls;
036:023 intend **some** adversity for me, of no
036:072 their (use)? Of them **some** do carry them
036:072 carry them and **some** they eat:
037:113 but of their progeny are (**some**) that do right,
037:113 do right, and (**some**) that obviously do wrong,
039:008 When **some** trouble toucheth man he crieth
039:038 **some** affliction for me, remove His
039:038 **some** Mercy for me, can they keep back His Mercy?"
040:047 from us **some** share of the Fire?"
040:067 though of you there are **some** who die before;-
040:077 **some** part of what We promise them,- or We
040:078 before thee: of them there are **some** whose story
040:078 and **some** whose story We have not related to thee.
040:079 that ye may use **some** for riding and **some** for food;
041:050 When We give him a taste of **some** mercy from Us,
041:050 from Us, after **some** adversity has touched him,
042:007 and **some** in the Blazing Fire.
042:007 (when) **some** will be in the Garden, and **some**
042:021 **some** religion without the permission of Allah?
042:048 exult thereat, but when **some** ill happens to him,
043:015 Yet they attribute to **some** of His servants
043:031 sent down to **some** leading man in either of

SOME (continued)

043:032 so that **some** may command work from others.
043:032 this world: and We raise **some** of them above
043:063 to you **some** of the (points) on which ye dispute:
043:079 **some** Plan (among themselves)? But it
047:004 to test you, **some** with others. But those
047:018 **some** tokens thereof, and when it comes to them
047:038 of Allah: but among you are **some** that are
048:011 **some** profit? But Allah is well acquainted with
048:011 you **some** loss or to give you **some** profit?
049:011 than the (former): nor let **some** women laugh at
049:011 O ye who believe! let not **some** men among you
049:012 for suspicion in **some** cases is a sin: and spy
052:030 for him **some** calamity (hatched) by Time!"
057:026 and **some** of them were on right guidance, but many
059:008 (**Some** part is due) to the indigent Muhajirs,
062:011 or **some** pastime, they disperse headlong to it,
062:011 But when they see **some** bargain or **some** pastime,
064:002 and of you are **some** that are Unbelievers,
064:002 are Unbelievers, and **some** that are Believers:
064:014 are (**some** that are) enemies to yourselves:
065:001 they are guilty of **some** open lewdness, those are
065:001 about thereafter **some** new situation.
066:002 (in **some** cases): and Allah is your Protector,
067:030 **some** morning lost (in the underground earth),
068:041 Or have they **some** "Partners" (in Godhead)?
070:025 is deprived (for **some** reason from asking);
072:004 'There were **some** foolish ones among us, who used
072:011 are righteous, and **some** the contrary: we follow
072:011 'There are among us **some** that are righteous,
072:014 'Amongst us are **some** that **submit** their wills
072:014 their wills (to Allah), and **some** that swerve
073:020 may be (**some**) among you in ill-health;
075:022 **Some** faces that Day, will beam
075:024 And **some** faces, that Day, will be sad and dismal,
075:025 In the thought that **some** back-breaking calamity
080:038 **Some** Faces that Day will be beaming.
088:002 **Some** faces, that Day, will be humiliated,

SOMEONE

003:073 revelation be sent to **someone** (else) like unto that
039:064 Say: "Is it **someone** other than Allah that ye

SOMEONE'S

016:094 With the result that **someone's** foot may slip

SOMETHING

002:101 **something**) they did not know!
002:106 **something** better or similar:
002:155 **something** of fear and hunger,
002:211 substitutes (**something** else),
002:229 if she give **something** for her freedom
002:267 out of it ye may give away **something**,
005:060 **something** much worse than this, (as judged)
005:076 **something** which hath no power either
007:045 desiring to make **something** crooked: they were
007:062 and I know from Allah **something** that ye know not.
008:070 He will give you **something** better than what
010:018 of **something** He knows not, in the
012:010 but if ye must do **something**, throw him
012:101 and taught me **something** of the interpretation
013:033 will inform Him of **something** He knoweth not
016:025 in full, and also (**something**) of the burdens of
017:057 is **something** to take heed of.
017:073 Our name **something** quite different: (in that case)
018:036 **something** better in exchange."

SOMETHING (continued)

018:040 me **something** better than thy garden, and that
018:066 me **something** of the (Higher) Truth which thou
018:083 you **something** of his story."
022:072 Say, "Shall I tell you of **something** (far) worse than
024:033 yea, give them **something** yourselves out of
026:030 you **something** clear (and) convincing?"
026:069 (**something** of) Abraham's story.
037:010 Except such as snatch away **something** by stealth,
039:047 but **something** will confront them from Allah,
040:028 then will fall on you **something** of the
040:030 for you **something** like the Day (of disaster)
040:031 "**Something** like the fate of the people of Noah,
045:009 And when he learns **something** of Our Signs,
058:012 spend **something** in charity before your private
058:018 they have **something** (to stand upon). No, indeed!
063:010 And spend **something** (in charity) out of

SOMETIMES

006:029 And they (**sometimes**) say: "There is nothing

SOMEWHAT

042:020 We grant **somewhat** thereof, but he

SON

002:087 We gave Jesus the **son** of Mary clear (Signs)
002:116 They say: "Allah hath begotten a **son**";
002:253 to Jesus the **son** of Mary, We gave Clear (Signs),
003:040 He said: "O my Lord! how shall I have a **son**,
003:045 his name will be Christ Jesus, the **son** of Mary,
003:047 how shall I have a **son** when man hath touched Me?"
004:157 "We killed Christ Jesus the **son** of Mary, the
004:171 Christ Jesus the **son** of Mary was (no more than)
004:171 (for Exalted is He) above having a **son**.
005:017 say that Allah is Christ the **son** of Mary.
005:017 to destroy Christ the **son** of Mary, his mother, and
005:046 We sent Jesus the **son** of Mary, confirming the Torah
005:072 "Allah is Christ the **son** of Mary." But said
005:075 Christ the **son** of Mary was no more
005:078 and of Jesus the **son** of Mary: because they
005:110 "O Jesus the **son** of Mary! recount my favour
005:112 "O Jesus the **son** of Mary! Can thy Lord
005:114 Said Jesus the **son** of Mary: "O Allah
005:116 "O Jesus the **son** of Mary! didst thou say unto men,
006:101 how can He have a **son** when He
007:150 Aaron said: "**Son** of my mother! The people
009:030 **Son** of Allah. That is a saying from their mouth,
009:030 The Jews call 'Uzair a **son** of Allah, and the
009:031 their Lord) Christ the **son** of Mary; yet they
010:068 They say, "Allah hath begotten a **son**!"-Glory be
011:042 (from the rest): "O my **son**! embark with us, and be
011:042 and Noah called out to his **son**, who had
011:043 The **son** replied: "I will be take myself to some
011:043 between them, and the **son** was among those who
011:045 "O my Lord! surely my **son** is of my family and Thy
012:005 Said (the father): "My (dear) little **son**! relate
012:021 much good, or we shall adopt him as a **son**." Thus
012:081 thy **son** committed theft! we bear witness
015:053 glad tidings of a **son** endowed with knowledge."
017:111 no **son**, and has no partner in (His) dominion:
018:004 who say, "Allah hath begotten a **son**":
018:081 give them in exchange (a **son**) better in purity
019:007 We give thee good news of a **son**: his name
019:008 have a **son**, when my wife is barren and I have
019:012 (To his **son** came the command): "O Yahya!
019:019 the gift of a pure **son**."

SON (continued)

019:020 She said: "How shall I have a **son**, seeing that
019:034 Such (was) Jesus the **son** of Mary: (it is)
019:035 should beget a **son**. Glory to Him! When He
019:088 They say: "The Most Gracious has begotten a **son**!"
019:091 That they attributed a **son** to The Most Gracious.
019:092 that He should beget a **son**.
020:094 (Aaron) replied: "O **son** of my mother! Seize (me)
021:091 and her **son** a Sign for all peoples.
023:050 And We made the **son** of Mary and his mother
023:091 No **son** did Allah beget, nor is
025:002 no **son** has He begotten, nor has He
028:009 or we may adopt him as a **son**." And they
031:013 admonishing him "O my **son**! join not in worship
031:013 Behold, Luqman said to his **son** admonishing him
031:016 "O my **son**! (said Luqman), "If there
031:017 "O my **son**! establish regular prayer, enjoin what
031:033 nor a **son** avail aught for his father. Verily, the
031:033 when no father can avail aught for his **son**, nor a
033:007 Moses, and Jesus the **son** of Mary: We took
037:100 "O my Lord! grant me a righteous (**son**)!"
037:101 So We gave him the good news of a forbearing **son**.
037:102 Then, when (the **son**) reached (the age of)
037:102 he said: "O my **son**! I have seen in a dream
037:102 thy view!" (The **son**) said: "O my father!
038:030 (for a **son**),-how excellent is the Servant!
039:004 a **son**, He could have chosen whom He pleased
043:057 When (Jesus) the **son** of Mary is held up as an
043:081 Say: "If The Most Gracious had a **son**, I would
046:017 (and rebuke the **son**): "Woe to thee! have Faith!
051:028 a **son** endowed with knowledge.
057:027 **son** of Mary, and bestowed on him the Gospel;
061:006 And remember, Jesus, the **son** of Mary, said:
061:014 as said Jesus, the **son** of Mary, to the
072:003 He has taken neither a wife nor a **son**.

SONS

002:049 slaughtered your **sons** and let your women-folk
002:132 "O my **sons**! Allah hath chosen the Faith for you;
002:132 upon his **sons** and so did Jacob;
002:133 Behold, he said to his **sons**: "What
002:146 know this as they know their own **sons**;
003:014 the love of things they covet: Women and **sons**;
003:061 our **sons** and your **sons**, our women and your women,
004:023 your **sons** proceeding from your loins;
005:018 "We are **sons** of Allah, and His beloved."
005:027 of the story of the two **sons** of Adam.
006:020 know this as they know their own **sons**.
006:100 attribute to Him **sons** and daughters, praise and
009:024 your **sons**, your brothers, your mates, or your
012:067 Further he said; "O my **sons**! enter not
012:087 "O my **sons**! go ye and enquire about Joseph
014:006 slaughtered your **sons**, and let your women-folk
014:035 **sons** from worshipping idols.
016:072 out of them, **sons** and daughters and grandchildren,
017:006 in resources and **sons**, and made you the more
017:040 preferred for you **sons**, and taken for Himself
017:070 We have honoured the **sons** of Adam; provided them
018:039 less than thee in wealth and **sons**,
018:046 Wealth and **sons** are allurements of the
023:055 granted them abundance of wealth and **sons**,
024:031 their husbands' fathers, their **sons**, their husbands'
024:031 or their brothers' **sons**, or their sisters'
024:031 or their sisters' **sons**, or their women, or the

SONS (continued)

024:031   their husbands' **sons**, their brothers or their
026:088   "The Day whereon neither wealth nor **sons** will avail,
026:133   "Freely has He bestowed on you cattle and **sons**,-
028:004   among them: their **sons** he slew, but he
033:004   your **sons**. Such is (only) your (manner of)
033:004   nor has He made your adopted **sons** your **sons**.
033:037   with the wives of their adopted **sons**, when the
033:055   sisters' **sons**, or their women, or the
033:055   or their **sons**, their brothers, or their
033:055   or their brothers' **sons**, or their sisters' **sons**,
034:013   **sons** of David, but few of My servants
034:035   and in **sons**, and we cannot be chastised."
034:037   It is not your wealth nor your **sons**, that will
037:149   (only) daughters, and they have **sons**?-
037:153   Did He (then) choose daughters rather than **sons**?
040:025   "Slay the **sons** of those who believe with him,
043:016   and granted to you **sons** for choice?
052:039   Or has He only daughters and ye have **sons**?
058:017   nor their **sons**: they will be Companions of the
058:022   were their fathers or their **sons**, or their
068:014   Because he possesses wealth and (numerous) **sons**.
071:012   and **sons**; and bestow on you Gardens and bestow
074:013   And **sons** to be by his side!-

SOON

002:126   but will **soon** drive them to the torment
003:012   "**Soon** will ye be vanquished
003:151   **Soon** shall We cast terror into the hearts
003:180   **soon** it will be tied to their necks
004:010   they will **soon** be enduring a blazing Fire!
004:017   who do evil in ignorance and repent **soon** afterwards;
004:030   **soon** shall We cast them into the Fire:
004:056   We shall **soon** cast into the Fire:
004:057   We shall **soon** admit to Gardens, with rivers
004:074   **soon** shall We give him a reward of great (value).
004:114   We shall **soon** give a reward of the highest (value).
004:122   We shall **soon** admit them to Gardens, with rivers
004:146   And **soon** will Allah grant to the Believers
004:152   We shall **soon** give their (due) rewards: for Allah
004:162   to them shall We **soon** give a great reward.
004:175   **soon** will He admit them to Mercy and Grace
005:014   And **soon** will Allah show them what
005:054   **soon** will Allah produce a people whom He will
006:005   but **soon** shall come to them the news
006:067   and **soon** shall ye know it."
006:124   **Soon** will the wicked be overtaken
006:135   **soon** will ye know who it is whose end
006:138   **soon** will He requite them for what they forged.
006:139   He will **soon** punish them: for He is
007:123   but **soon** shall ye know (the consequences).
007:145   **soon** shall I show you the homes of the
007:180   for what they do, they will **soon** be requited.
009:028   And if ye fear poverty, **soon** will Allah enrich you,
009:059   will **soon** give us of His bounty: to Allah
009:090   **Soon** will a grievous chastisement seize the
009:099   **soon** will Allah admit them to His Mercy: for Allah
009:105   **soon** will ye be brought back to the Knower of what
009:105   **soon** will Allah observe your work, and His
010:031   all affairs?" They will **soon** say: "Allah". Say,
011:039   "But **soon** will ye know who it is on whom
011:093   **soon** will ye know who it is on whom descends the
012:098   He said: "**Soon** will I ask my Lord for forgiveness
013:042   and **soon** will the Unbelievers know who gets

SOON (continued)

015:003   **soon** for they will **soon** know.
015:096   another god: but **soon** will they come to know.
016:055   but **soon** will ye know (your folly)!
017:051   Say, "Maybe it will be quite **soon**!
017:079   for thee: **soon** will thy Lord raise thee
018:045   but **soon** it becomes dry stubble, which the
019:059   and followed after lusts **soon**, then, will they
020:135   wait ye, therefore, and **soon** shall ye know who
021:037   **soon** (enough) will I show you My Signs; so ask
025:042   to them!"-**Soon** will they know, when they
025:077   and **soon** will come the inevitable (punishment)!"
026:006   so they will know **soon** (enough) the truth
026:049   But **soon** shall ye know! Be sure
026:062   **Soon** will He guide me!
026:227   And **soon** will the unjust know what
027:007   **soon** will I bring you from there some information,
027:027   (Solomon) said: "**Soon** shall we see whether thou
027:093   Who will **soon** show you His Signs, so that
029:066   (worldly) enjoyment! But **soon** will they know.
030:003   will **soon** be victorious-
030:034   but **soon** will ye know (your folly).
037:170   they reject it: but **soon** will they know!
037:175   and they **soon** shall see (how thou farest)!
037:179   and they **soon** shall see (how thou farest)!
039:039   I will do (my part): but **soon** will ye know-
039:051   of their deeds will **soon** overtake them (too),
040:044   "**Soon** will ye remember what I say to you (now).
040:070   but **soon** shall they know,-
041:053   **Soon** will We show them Our Signs in the (furthest)
043:044   and **soon** shall ye (all) be brought to account.
043:089   and say "Peace!" but **soon** shall they know!
047:005   **Soon** will He guide them and improve their condition,
048:010   Allah will **soon** grant him a great Reward.
053:040   will **soon** come in sight;
054:045   **Soon** will their multitude be put to flight,
055:031   **Soon** shall We settle your affairs, O both
057:020   the tillers; **soon** it withers; thou wilt
065:007   Allah will **soon** grant relief.
067:029   so **soon** will ye know which (of us) it is
068:005   **Soon** wilt thou see and they will see,
068:016   **Soon** shall We brand (the beast) on the snout!
073:005   **Soon** shall We send down to thee a weighty Word.
074:017   **Soon** will I visit him with a mount of calamities!
074:026   **Soon** will cast him into Hell-Fire!
078:004   Verily, they shall **soon** (come to) know!
078:005   Verily, verily they shall **soon** (come to) know!
084:008   **Soon** will his account be taken by an easy reckoning,
084:011   **Soon** will he cry for Perdition,
092:021   And **soon** will they attain (complete) satisfaction.
093:005   And **soon** will thy Guardian-Lord give thee
102:003   But nay, ye **soon** shall know (the reality).
102:004   Again, ye **soon** shall know!
111:003   Burnt **soon** will he be in a Fire of blazing Flame!

SOONER

018:109   my Lord, **sooner** would the ocean be exhausted than

SOOTHING

012:087   **soothing** Mercy: truly no one despairs of Allah's
012:087   of Allah's **soothing** Mercy, except those

SOOTHSAYER

052:029   of thy Lord, thou art no **soothsayer** nor possessed.
069:042   of a **soothsayer**: little admonition it is ye receive.

SORCERER

007:109   "This is indeed a **sorcerer** well-versed.
010:002   "This is indeed a evident **sorcerer**!"
010:079   Said Pharaoh: "Bring me every **sorcerer** well versed."
026:034   a **sorcerer** well-versed:
038:004   "This is a **sorcerer** telling lies!
040:024   but they called (him) "a **sorcerer** telling lies!"...
043:049   And they said, "O thou **Sorcerer**! invoke thy
051:039   "A **sorcerer**, or one possessed!"
051:052   "A **sorcerer**, or one possessed"!

SORCERERS

007:112   And bring up to thee all (our) **sorcerers** well-versed."
007:113   So there came the **sorcerers** to Pharaoh: they said:
007:120   But the **sorcerers** fell down prostrate in adoration.
010:077   But **sorcerers** will not prosper."
010:080   When the **sorcerers** came, Moses said
026:037   (our) **sorcerers** well-versed."
026:038   So the **sorcerers** were got together for the
026:040   "That we may follow the **sorcerers** if they win?"
026:041   So when the **sorcerers** arrived, they said
026:046   Then did the **sorcerers** fall down, prostrate in

SORCERY

004:051   They believe in **sorcery** and Tagut and say to the
007:132   to work therewith the **sorcery** on us, we shall
010:076   they said: "This is indeed evident **sorcery**!"
010:077   Is it **sorcery** (like) this? But sorcerers
010:081   is **sorcery**: Allah will surely make it of no effect:
011:007   to say, "This is nothing but obvious **sorcery**!"
015:015   been bewitched by **sorcery**."
017:101   to have been worked upon by **sorcery**!"
026:035   of your land by his **sorcery**; then what
026:049   who has taught you **sorcery**! But soon
027:013   visibly they said: "This is **sorcery** manifest!"
028:036   "This is nothing but **sorcery** faked up: never did
028:048   They say: "Two kinds of **sorcery**, each assisting
037:015   And say, "This is nothing but evident **sorcery**!
043:030   they said: "This is **sorcery**, and we do reject it."
046:007   "This is evident **sorcery**!"
061:006   Clear Signs, they said, "This is evident **sorcery**!"

SORROW

005:026   but **sorrow** thou not over these rebellious people."
005:068   But **sorrow** thou not over (these)
012:084   And his eyes became white with **sorrow**, and he
012:084   and he was suppressed with silent **sorrow**.
020:086   in state of anger and **sorrow**. He said:
028:008   and a cause of **sorrow**: for Pharaoh
035:034   Who has removed from us (all) **sorrow**: for our
069:050   of **sorrow** for the Unbelievers.

SORRY

023:040   they are sure to be **sorry**!"

SORT

004:109   Ah! these are the **sort** of men on whose behalf
016:075   of any **sort**; and (the other) a man on whom
016:076   with no power of any **sort**; a wearisome burden
019:077   Hast thou then seen the (**sort** of) man who
020:067   So Moses conceived in his mind a (**sort** of) fear.
023:091   (**sort** of) things they attribute to Him!
025:007   And they say: "What **sort** of a messenger is this,
034:022   no (**sort** of) share have they therein, nor is
036:015   sends no **sort** of revelation: ye do
050:003   That is a (**sort** of) Return far

SORTED

030:014   that Day shall (all men) be **sorted** out.
056:007   And ye shall be **sorted** out into three classes.
081:007   When the souls are **sorted** out, (Being joined,
099:006   **sorted** out, to be shown the Deeds that they

SORTING

037:021   "This is the Day of **Sorting** Out, whose truth
044:040   Verily the Day of **Sorting** Out is the
077:013   For the Day of **Sorting** out.
077:014   what is the Day of **Sorting** out?
077:038   That will be a Day of **Sorting** out! We shall
078:017   Verily the Day of **Sorting** Out is a thing appointed,-

SOUGHT

012:018   it is Allah (alone) whose help can be **sought**."
012:023   **sought** to seduce him and she fastened the doors,
012:026   He said: "It was she that **sought** to seduce me-
012:051   it was I who **sought** to seduce him he is indeed
014:015   But they **sought** victory and decision (there and
017:042   behold, they would certainly have **sought** out
021:112   **sought** against the blasphemies ye utter!
028:018   **sought** his help called aloud for his help (again).
044:020   "For me, I have **sought** Safety with my Lord
054:037   And they even **sought** to snatch away
072:014   they have **sought** out (the path) of right conduct:

SOUL

002:048   a day when one **soul** shall not avail another
002:123   a day when one **soul** shall not avail another,
002:200   yea, with far more heart and **soul**.
002:231   if anyone does that, He wrongs his own **soul**.
002:233   No **soul** shall have a burden laid on it
002:281   Then shall every **soul** be paid what it earned,
002:286   On no **soul** doth Allah place a burden
003:025   and each **soul** will be paid out just what
003:030   "On the day when every **soul** will be confronted
003:145   Nor can a **soul** die except by Allah's leave,
003:161   then shall every **soul** receive its due
003:185   Every **soul** shall have a taste of death:
004:110   If anyone does evil or wrongs his own **soul** but
004:111   he earns it against his own **soul**: for Allah
005:030   The (selfish) **soul** of the other led him
006:061   Our angels take his **soul**, and they never
006:070   with it (Al-Qur-an) lest a **soul** is caught in its
006:098   produced you from a single **soul**: then there
006:104   it will be for (the good of) his own **soul**: if
006:152   no burden do We place on any **soul**, but that
006:158   to a **soul** to believe then, if it
006:164   Every **soul** draws the meed of its
007:042   no burden do We place on any **soul**, but that
007:205   in thy (very) **soul**, with humility and remember
010:030   There will every **soul** see (the fruits of)
010:044   it is man that wrongs his own **soul**.
010:046   We promise them,-or We take thy **soul** (before that),-
010:054   Every **soul** that hath sinned, if it
010:100   No **soul** can believe, except by
011:105   The day it arrives, no **soul** shall speak
012:053   (of blame): the (human) **soul** certainly incites
012:101   Take Thou my **soul** (at death) as one submitting
013:033   every **soul** (and knoweth) all that it doth,
013:040   thy **soul** (before it is all accomplished), thy duty
013:042   He knoweth the doings of every **soul**: and soon
014:051   each **soul** according to its deserts; and verily
016:111   On the Day every **soul** will come up pleading
016:111   and every **soul** will be recompensed (fully) for

SOUL (continued)

017:014   thy **soul** this day to make out an account
020:015   for every **soul** to receiver its reward by the
020:096   thus did my **soul** suggest to me."
021:035   Every **soul** shall have a taste of death: and We
021:047   so that not a **soul** will be dealt with
023:062   On no **soul** do We place a burden greater than
027:040   his own **soul**; but if any is ungrateful, truly my
027:044   I have indeed wronged my **soul**: I do
028:016   I have indeed wronged by **soul**! Do Thou
029:057   Every **soul** shall have a taste of death: in the
031:012   does so to the profit of his own **soul**: but if
031:028   is in no wise but as an individual **soul**: for Allah
032:013   every **soul** its true guidance: but the
034:019   (**soul** that is) patiently constant and grateful.
034:050   I only stray to the loss of my own **soul**: but if
035:008   So let not thy **soul** be vested in regret
035:018   for the benefit of his own **soul**; and the
036:054   Then, on that Day, not a **soul** will be wronged
039:041   his own **soul**. Nor art thou set a Custodian
039:041   benefits his own **soul**: but he
039:056   "Lest the **soul** should (then) say: `Ah! woe
039:070   And to every **soul** will be paid in full
040:017   That Day will every **soul** be requited for what
040:077   or We take thy **soul** (to Our Mercy) (before that),
041:046   his own **soul**; whoever works evil, it is
041:046   it is against his own **soul**: nor is
045:015   own **soul**). In the end will ye (all) be brought
045:022   **soul** may find the recompense of what it has earned,
048:010   his own **soul**, and any one who fulfils what he
050:016   and We know what suggestions his **soul** makes to him:
050:021   And there will come forth every **soul**: with each
056:002   Then will no (**soul**) deny its coming.
056:083   when (the **soul** of the dying man) reaches the throat,
056:087   Call back the **soul**, if ye are
059:018   and let every **soul** look to what (provision) he has
063:011   But to no **soul** will Allah grant respite when the
065:001   (own) **soul**: thou knowest not if perchance Allah
074:038   Every **soul** will be (held) in pledge for its deeds.
075:002   And I do swear by the self-reproaching **soul**.
075:026   Yea, when (the **soul**) reaches to the collar-bone
079:040   restrained (their) **soul** from lower Desires,
081:014   (Then) shall each **soul** know what it has put forward.
082:005   (Then) shall each **soul** know what it hath sent
082:019   (It will be) the Day when no **soul** shall have
086:004   There is no **soul** but has a protector over it.
089:027   (To the righteous **soul** will be said:) "O (thou)
089:027   "O (thou) **soul**, in (complete) rest and satisfaction!
091:007   By the **Soul**, and the proportion and order

SOULS

002:090   for which they have sold their **souls**,
002:102   which they did sell their **souls**,
002:110   send forth for your **souls** before you,
002:130   as debase their **souls** with folly?
002:223   But do some good act for your **souls** beforehand;
002:265   to please Allah and to strengthen their **souls**,
002:272   ye give benefits your own **souls**,
003:117   harvest of men who have wronged their own **souls**:
003:135   an act of indecency or wronged their own **souls**.
003:193   and take to Thyself our **souls** in the company
004:063   and speak to them a word to reach their very **souls**.
004:065   And find in their **souls** no resistance
004:097   those who die in sin against their **souls**.

SOULS (continued)

004:097   When angels take the **souls** of those who die
004:107   such as betray their own **souls**; for Allah
004:113   only lead their own **souls** astray,
004:128   even though men's **souls** are swayed by greed.
005:080   which their **souls** have sent forward before
005:105   O ye who believe! guard your own **souls**: if ye
006:012   It is they who have lost their own **souls**, that
006:020   Those who have lost their own **souls** refuse
006:060   It is He Who doth take your **souls** by night, and
006:093   (saying), "Yield up your **souls**. This day
006:123   but they only plot against their own **souls**, and
007:009   will find their **souls** in perdition, for that
007:023   we have wronged our own **souls**: if Thou
007:037   arrive and take their **souls**, they say:
007:053   In fact they will have lost their **souls**, and the
007:126   and take our **souls** unto Thee as Muslims
007:160   but they harmed their own **souls**.
007:177   who reject Our signs and wrong their own **souls**.
008:050   when the angels take the **souls** of the
008:053   is in their (own) **souls**: and verily
009:017   their own **souls** to infidelity. The works
009:042   destroy their own **souls**; for Allah
009:055   in this life, and that their **souls** may perish
009:070   Who wrongs them, but they wrong their own **souls**.
009:085   and that their **souls** may depart while they
009:118   and their (very) **Souls** seemed straitened to them,-
010:023   your own **souls**,-an enjoyment of the life of the
010:104   your **souls** (at death): I am commanded to be
010:108   own **souls**; those who stray, do so
011:021   own **souls**: and the (fancies) they forged
011:031   Allah knoweth best what is in their **souls**: I should,
011:101   they wronged their own **souls**: the deities,
014:022   but reproach your own **souls**.
016:007   except with **souls** distressed: for your Lord
016:028   take in a state of wrong-doing to their own **souls**."
016:033   nay, they wronged their own **souls**.
016:070   and takes your **souls** at death; and of you
021:102   of Hell: what their **souls** desired, in that
023:103   their **souls**; in Hell will they abide.
027:014   though their **souls** acknowledged them wrongfully
027:092   their own **souls**, and if any stray, say: "I
029:006   they do so for their own **souls**: for Allah
030:009   but they wronged their own **souls**.
032:011   of you, will (duly) take your **souls**: then shall
035:032   own **souls**; some who follow a middle course
039:015   who lose their own **souls** and their people on the
039:042   It is Allah that takes the **souls** (of men)
039:053   transgressed against their **souls**! Despair not
041:053   and in their own **souls**, until it
043:071   the **souls** could desire, all that
047:027   take their **souls** at death, and smite
047:038   of their own **souls**. But Allah is free of all
053:023   and what their own **souls** desire!-Even though
057:022   or in your **souls** but is recorded in a Book before
059:009   of their own **souls**,-they are
064:016   for the benefit of your own **souls**: and those
064:016   of their own **souls**,-they are the
079:001   (the **souls** of the wicked) with violence;
079:002   (the **souls** of the blessed);
081:007   When the **souls** are sorted out, (Being joined,

SOUND

002:071   **sound** and without blemish."

SOUND (continued)

004:006   if then ye find **sound** judgment in them, release
007:148   having lowing **sound** did they not see that it could
021:102   Not the slightest **sound** will they hear of Hell:
026:089   that brings to Allah a **sound** heart;
033:071   and **sound** and forgive you your sins: he that
037:084   Behold, He approached his Lord with a **sound** heart.
038:020   and **sound** judgment in speech and decision.

SOUNDED

020:102   The Day when the Trumpet will be **sounded**: that Day,
027:087   will be **sounded**-then will be smitten with terror
036:051   The trumpet shall be **sounded**, when behold!
039:068   be **sounded**, when, behold, they will
039:068   The Trumpet will (just) be **sounded**, when all
069:013   Then, when one Blast is **sounded** on the Trumpet,
074:008   Finally when the Trumpet is **sounded**,
078:018   The Day that the Trumpet shall be **sounded**, and ye

SOUNDING

015:026   We created man from **sounding** clay, from mud
015:028   form **sounding** clay, from mud molded into shape;
015:033   **sounding** clay, from mud moulded into shape.”
055:014   **sounding** clay like unto pottery.

SOUNDS

031:019   for the harshest of **sounds** without doubt is the

SOURCE

009:103   Verily thy prayers are a **source** of security
059:023   the Holy One, the **Source** of Peace (and Perfection).

SOURCES

015:021   (**sources** and) treasures (inexhaustible) are with
065:003   And He provides for him from (**sources**) he never

SOVEREIGN

054:055   In a sure abode with a **Sovereign** Omnipotent.
059:023   no other god;-the **Sovereign**, the Holy One,
062:001   and Glory of Allah,-the **Sovereign**, the Holy One,

SOVEREIGNTY

023:088   is the **sovereignty** of all things,-Who protects

SOW

002:102   the means to **sow** discord between man and wife.
012:047   shall ye diligently **sow** as is your wont: and the
017:053   for Satan doth **sow** dissensions among them:
056:063   See ye the seed that ye **sow** in the ground?

SOWERS

048:029   (filling) the **sowers** with wonder and delight.

SOWING

009:047   midst and **sowing** sedition among you, and there

SOWN

012:100   **sown** enmity between me and my brothers. Verily
013:004   and gardens of vines and fields **sown** with corn,

SPACE

012:045   (so long) a **space** of time, said: “I will tell
018:017   lay in the open **space** in the midst of the Cave.
018:096   the **space** between the two steep mountain-sides,

SPACES

006:097   through the dark **spaces** of land and sea:

SPACIOUS

004:097   **spacious** enough for you to move yourselves
029:056   truly, **spacious** is My Earth: therefore serve
039:010   **Spacious** is Allah's earth! Those who
051:048   (**spacious**) earth: how excellently We do spread out!
071:020   That ye may go about therein, in **spacious** roads.”

SPACIOUS (continued)

081:001   When the sun (with its **spacious** light) is folded up;

SPARKS

077:032   “Indeed it throws about **sparks** (huge) as Forts,
100:002   And strike **sparks** of fire,

SPATHES

006:099   (or **spathes**) (come) clusters of dates
026:148   with **spathes** near breaking (with the
055:011   producing **spathes** (enclosing dates);

SPEAK

002:083   **speak** fair to the people;
002:235   **speak** to them in terms honourable,
003:041   that thou shalt **speak** to no man for three days
003:046   “He shall **speak** to the people in childhood
003:077   nor will Allah (deign to) **speak** to them
003:168   if ye **speak** the truth.”
003:183   why then did ye slay them, if ye **speak** the truth?.
004:005   and **speak** to them words of kindness and justice.
004:008   and **speak** to them words of kindness and justice.
004:009   let them fear Allah, and **speak** appropriate words.
004:063   and **speak** to them a word to reach their very souls.
005:110   So that thou didst **speak** to the people
006:111   and the dead did **speak** unto them, and We
006:152   whenever ye **speak**, **speak** justly, even if
007:148   that it could neither **speak** to them, nor show
008:020   from him when ye hear (him **speak**).
010:038   besides Allah, if it be ye **speak** the truth!”
010:048   to pass-if ye **speak** the truth?”
011:013   if ye **speak** the truth!
011:105   shall **speak** except by His leave: of those
013:031   or the dead were made to **speak**, (this would
014:031   **Speak** to My servants who have believed, that they
015:070   (to **speak**) for all and sundry?”
017:028   yet **speak** to them a word of easy kindness.
017:110   Neither **speak** thy Prayer aloud, nor **speak**
017:110   nor **speak** it in a low tone, but seek
018:070   **speak** to thee concerning it.”
019:010   “shall be that thou shalt **speak** to no man
020:044   “But **speak** to him mildly; perchance he
021:027   They **speak** not before He speaks, and they
021:065   that these (idols) do not **speak**!”
023:108   and **speak** ye not to Me!
024:006   of those who **speak** the Truth.
024:016   “It is not right of us to **speak** of this:
026:013   And my tongue will not **speak** (plainly): so send
027:082   a beast to **speak** unto them because mankind had
027:085   be unable to **speak** (in plea).
033:032   but **speak** ye a speech (that is) just.
036:065   will **speak** to Us, and their feet bear witness,
037:092   that ye **speak** not?”
042:051   that Allah should **speak** to him except by inspiration,
049:002   in talk, as ye may **speak** aloud to one another,
049:002   of the Prophet, nor **speak** aloud to him in talk,
049:012   nor **speak** ill of each other behind their backs.
051:023   ye can **speak** intelligently to each other.
052:034   like unto it,-if (it be) they **speak** the Truth!
063:004   and when they **speak**, thou listenest
077:035   shall not be able to **speak**,
078:038   none shall **speak** except any who permitted by

SPEAKEST

011:032   us with, if thou **speakest** the truth!”

SPEAKETH
002:118 "Why **speaketh** not Allah unto Us?
003:095 Say: "Allah **speaketh** the truth: follow the religion

SPEAKS
021:027 They speak not before He **speaks**, and they
023:062 clearly **speaks** the truth. They will
030:035 to them, **speaks** to them the things to which
045:029 "This Our Record **speaks** about you with truth:

SPECIAL
002:040 call to mind the (**special**) favour
002:047 call to mind the (**special**) favour
002:105 for His **special** Mercy whom He will
002:122 the **special** favour which I bestowed upon you,
003:035 what is in my womb for Thy **special** service:
006:109 realize that even if a (**special**) Sign came, they
006:109 that if a (**special**) Sign came to them, by it
011:058 with him, by (**special**) Grace from Us: We saved
011:066 with him, by (**special**) Grace from Us-and from
011:094 believed with him, by (**special**) Mercy from Us:
015:044 is a (**special**) class (of sinners) assigned.
017:070 and conferred on them **special** favours, above a
038:046 a **special** (purpose)-the remembrance of the
056:035 We have created them of **special** creation.

SPECIALLY
002:094 be for you **specially**,
003:074 **specially** chooseth whom He pleaseth:
003:124 three thousand angels (**specially**) sent down?
004:096 Ranks **specially** bestowed by Him, and
006:139 is **specially** reserved (for food) for our men, and
012:048 shall have (**specially**) guarded.
012:054 I will take him **specially** to serve about
019:051 **specially** chosen. And He was a messenger and a

SPECIES
023:027 of every **species**, male and female, and thy

SPECIOUSNESS
009:118 for all its **speciousness**, and their

SPEECH
002:204 whose **speech** about this world's life may
004:148 shouting of evil words in public **speech**, except
010:065 Let not their **speech** grieve thee: for all
013:010 of you conceal his **speech** or declare it openly;
020:027 "And remove the impediment from my **speech**.
021:110 in **speech** and what ye hide (in your hearts).
027:016 been taught the **speech** of Birds, and we
027:019 So he smiled, amused at her **speech**; and she
028:034 he is more eloquent in **speech** than I: so send
033:004 (manner of) **speech** by your mouths. But Allah
033:032 but speak ye a **speech** (that is) just.
033:032 be not too complaisant of **speech**, lest one
036:076 Let not their **speech**, then, grieve thee.
038:020 and sound judgment in **speech** and decision.
041:021 us speech,-(He) Who giveth **speech** to everything:
041:033 Who is better in **speech** than one who calls
047:030 know them by the tone of their **speech**! And Allah
055:004 He has taught him an intelligent **speech**.
073:006 and **speech** more certain.

SPEECHES
022:024 of **speeches**; they have been guided to the Path

SPEED
002:260 they will come to thee (flying) with **speed**.

SPEEDY
048:018 and He rewarded them with a **speedy** Victory;

SPEEDY (continued)
048:027 besides this, a **speedy** victory.
061:013 and **speedy** victory. So give the Glad Tidings

SPEND
002:003 and **spend** out of what We have provided
002:177 to **spend** of your substance,
002:195 And **spend** of your substance in the cause
002:215 They ask thee what they should **spend** (in charity).
002:215 Say: Whatever wealth ye **spend** that is good,
002:219 They ask thee how much they are to **spend**;
002:254 O ye who believe! **spend** out of (the bounties)
002:261 **spend** their wealth in the way of Allah
002:262 Those who **spend** their wealth in the cause
002:264 **spend** their wealth to be seen of men,
002:265 those who **spend** their wealth seeking to please
002:270 And whatever ye **spend** in charity or whatever
002:274 **spend** of their goods by night and by day,
003:017 who **spend** (in the way of God);
003:117 What they **spend** in the life of this
003:134 Those who **spend** (freely), whether in prosperity,
004:038 (Nor) those who **spend** of their substance, to be
004:077 and **spend** in regular Zakat?
008:003 and **spend** (freely) out of the gifts We have
008:036 and so will they continue to **spend**; but in
008:036 The Unbelievers **spend** their wealth to hinder
008:060 Whatever ye shall **spend** in the cause of Allah,
009:034 and **spend** it not in the Way of Allah: announce
009:053 Say: "**Spend** (for the cause) willingly
009:091 or ill, or who find no resources to **spend** (on the
009:121 Nor could they **spend** anything (for the Cause),
013:022 **spend**, out of (the gifts) We have bestowed
014:031 and **spend** (in charity) out of the Sustenance
018:060 or (until) I **spend** years and years in travel."
022:035 and **spend** (in charity) out of what We have
025:064 Those who **spend** the night in adoration
025:067 Those who, when they **spend**, are not
028:054 and that they **spend** (in charity) out of
032:016 in Fear and Hope: and they **spend** (in charity)
034:039 and nothing do ye **spend** in the least (in His
035:029 and **spend** (in Charity) out of what We have
036:047 "**Spend** ye of (the bounties) with which Allah
042:038 by mutual Consultation; who **spend** out of what
047:038 Behold, ye are those invited to **spend** (of your
057:007 who believe and **spend** (in charity),-for them
057:007 and **spend** (in charity) out of the (substance)
057:010 **spend** not in the cause of Allah?-For to Allah
058:012 **spend** something in charity before your private
063:007 "**Spend** nothing on those who are with
063:010 And **spend** something (in charity) out of
064:016 listen and obey; and **spend** in charity for the
065:006 then **spend** (your substance) on them until they
065:007 Let the man of means **spend** according to his means:
065:007 **spend** according to what Allah has given him.
092:018 Those who **spend** their wealth for increase

SPENDETH
005:064 He giveth and **spendeth** (of His Bounty)

SPENDING
017:100 for fear or **spending** them: for man
058:013 **spending** sums in charity before your private

SPENDS
016:075 **spends** thereof (freely), privately and publicly:

SPENDTHRIFT
017:026 in the manner of a **spendthrift**.

SPENDTHRIFTS
017:027 Verily **spendthrifts** are brothers of the Satans.

SPENT
002:185 during that month should **spent** it in fasting,
004:039 and they **spent** out of what Allah
008:063 not if thou hadst **spent** all that is in the earth,
018:042 over what he had **spent** on his property,
057:010 who **spent** (freely) and fought, before the
057:010 than those who **spent** (freely) and fought
060:010 what they have **spent** on their dowers, and let
060:010 what they have **spent** (on their dower). And there
060:010 have **spent** on their dowers, and let
060:011 they had **spent** (on their dower). And fear

SPERM
022:005 out of dust, then out of **sperm**, then out
023:013 Then We placed him as (a drop of) **sperm** in a
023:014 Then We made the **sperm** into a clot of
036:077 We Who created Him from **sperm**? Yet behold!
075:037 Was he not a drop of **sperm** emitted (in lowly form)?
076:002 of mingled **sperm**, in order to try him: so We

SPERM-DROP
016:004 He has created man from a **sperm-drop** and behold
018:037 a **sperm-drop**, then fashioned thee into a man?
035:011 then from a **sperm-drop**; then He made
040:067 then from a **sperm-drop**, then from
053:046 From a **sperm-drop** when lodged (in its place);
080:019 From a **sperm-drop**: He hath created him, and then

SPIDER
029:041 is that of the **Spider**, who builds

SPIDER'S
029:041 is the **Spider's** house;-if they but knew.

SPIRIT
002:087 and strengthened him with the holy **spirit**.
002:214 and were so shaken in **spirit** that even the Messenger
002:253 and strengthened him with the Holy **Spirit**.
004:171 and a **Spirit** proceeding from Him: so believe
005:110 Behold! I strengthened thee with the Holy **Spirit**.
015:029 into him of My **spirit**, fall ye down
016:102 Say, the Holy **Spirit** has brought the revelation
017:085 Say: "The **Spirit** is of the command of my Lord
017:085 They ask thee concerning the **Spirit**. Say: "The
021:091 from Our **spirit**, and We made her and her son
026:193 With it came down the Truthful **spirit**
032:009 of His **spirit**. And He gave you (the faculties
038:072 and breathed into him of My **spirit**, fall ye
040:015 the **spirit** (of inspiration) to any of His servants
058:022 them with a **spirit** from Himself. And He will
059:014 (**spirit**) amongst themselves: thou wouldst
066:012 of Our **spirit**; and she testified to the truth
070:004 The angels and the **Spirit** ascend unto Him
078:038 The Day that the **Spirit** and the angels will stand
097:004 and the **Spirit** by Allah's permission, on every

SPIRITUAL
005:005 those who have lost (all **spiritual** good).

SPITE
006:108 lest they out of **spite** revile Allah
010:090 hosts followed them in insolence and **spite**. At
013:015 with good-will or in **spite** of themselves: so do

SPLENDOR
006:077 When he saw the moon rising in **splendor**, He said:

SPLENDOR (continued)
006:078 When he saw the sun rising (in **splendor**), he
010:088 and his Chiefs **splendor** and wealth in the life
020:131 the **splendor** of the life of this world,
055:029 (new) **Splendor** doth He (shine)!
079:029 and its **splendor** doth He bring out (with light).
091:001 By the Sun and his (glorious) **splendor**;

SPLIT
002:074 when **split** asunder send fort water;
006:095 and the date-stone to **split** and sprout. He
019:090 the earth to **split** asunder, and the
030:032 Those who **split** up their Religion, and become
080:026 And We **split** the earth in fragments,

SPOILS
004:094 with Allah are profits and **spoils** abundant.
008:001 (things taken as) **spoils** of war. Say: "(Such)
008:001 Say: "(Such) **spoils** are at the disposal of

SPOKE
002:253 to some of them Allah **spoke**;
004:164 and to Moses Allah **spoke** direct;

SPOKEN
007:144 and the words I (have **spoken** to thee); take then
012:054 Therefore when he had **spoken** to him, he said:
021:004 word (**spoken**) in the heavens and the earth:
051:030 They said, "Even so has thy Lord **spoken**: and He
071:009 "Further I have **spoken** to them in public

SPORT
005:057 for a mockery or **sport**,-whether among those who
005:058 they take it (but) as mockery and **sport**;
021:016 Not for (idle) **sport** did We create the heavens
044:038 merely in (idle) **sport**:

SPOT
002:282 ye carry out on the **spot** among yourselves,
008:066 **spot** in you: but (even so), if there
068:020 like a dark and desolate **spot**, (Whose fruit

SPOTLESS
033:033 and to make you pure and **spotless**.

SPOUSES
002:025 and they have therein **spouses** (purified);
003:015 with **spouses** purified and the good pleasure
004:057 therein shall they have **spouses** purified
013:023 their **spouses**, and their offspring and angels

SPREAD
002:205 to **spread** mischief through the earth
007:127 to **spread** mischief in the land, and to
011:082 baked clay, **spread**, layer on layer,-
013:003 And it is He Who **spread** out the earth, and set
015:019 And the earth We have **spread** out (like a carpet);
016:088 for that they used to **spread** mischief.
017:013 which he will see **spread** open.
018:100 for Unbelievers to see, all **spread** out,-
020:053 the earth like a carpet **spread** out; has enabled
030:048 then does He **spread** them in the sky as He wills,
043:010 the earth **spread** out, and has
050:007 And the earth-We have **spread** it out, and set
051:048 And We have **spread** out the (spacious) earth:
051:048 (spacious) earth: how excellently We do **spread** out!
055:010 It is He Who has **spread** out the earth
058:011 (**spread** out and) make room: (ample) room
071:019 as a carpet (**spread** out),
074:052 to be given scrolls (of revelation) **spread** out!
077:005 Then **spread** abroad a Reminder,

SPREAD (continued)

088:016 And rich carpets (All) **spread** out.
088:020 And at the Earth, how it is **spread** out?

SPREADING

005:032 or for **spreading** mischief in the land-it would be
033:046 and as a Lamp **spreading** Light.
037:146 a **spreading** plant of the Gourd kind.
067:019 above them, **spreading** their wings and folding

SPRING

011:048 the Peoples (who will **spring**) from those
017:090 in thee, until thou cause a **spring** to gush
018:086 a **spring** of murky water: near it
083:028 A **spring**, from (the waters) whereof drink
088:005 to drink, of a boiling hot **spring**,
088:012 Therein will be a bubbling **spring**:

SPRINGING

023:020 Also a tree **springing** out of Mount Sinai,

SPRINGS

002:060 Then gushed forth therefrom twelve **springs**.
007:058 **springs** up nothing but that which is scanty, thus
007:058 **springs** up produce, (rich) after its kind: but
007:160 out of it there gushed forth twelve **springs**: each
023:050 and security and furnished with **springs**.
026:057 So We expelled them from gardens, **springs**,
026:134 "And Gardens and **Springs**.
026:147 "Gardens and **Springs**,
036:034 and We cause **springs** to gush forth therein.
037:064 For it is a tree that **springs** out of
039:021 and leads it through **springs** in the earth?
044:025 and **springs** they left behind.
044:052 Among Gardens and **Springs**;
051:015 they will be in the midst of Gardens and **Springs**,
054:012 with **springs**, so the waters met (and rose)
055:050 In them (each) will be two **Springs** flowing (free);
055:066 In them (each) will be two **springs** pouring forth
077:041 and **springs** (of water).
086:012 (for the gushing of **springs** or the sprouting

SPROUT

006:095 and the date-stone to split and **sprout**. He

SPROUTING

086:012 or the **sprouting** of vegetation),-

SPRUNG

017:003 O ye that are **sprung** from those whom We
027:043 for she was (**sprung**) of a people that had no faith.

SPUN

016:092 the yarn which she has **spun**, after it

SPURNING

006:035 If their **spurning** is hard on thee, yet if

SPY

049:012 and **spy** not on each other, nor speak

SQUANDER

017:026 but **squander** not (your wealth) in the manner

SQUANDERED

046:020 "Ye **squandered** your good things in the life
090:006 "Wealth have I **squandered** in abundance!"

SQUARE

043:013 and **square** on their backs, and when

SQUAT

007:086 "And **squat** not on every road, breathing

STABILITY

014:026 it has no **stability**.

STABLE

017:009 (or **stable**), and giveth the glad tidings to the

STAFF

002:060 We said "strike the rock with thy **staff**."
007:160 for Water: "Strike the rock with thy **staff**": out
034:014 gnawing away at his **staff**: so when

STAGE

017:082 We send down (**stage** by **stage**) of the Qur'an
018:062 at this (**stage** of) our journey."
084:019 Ye shall surely travel from **stage** to **stage**.

STAGES

010:005 and measured out **stages** for it, that ye might
016:101 He reveals (in **stages**),-they say, "Thou art
017:106 We have revealed it by **stages**.
025:032 well-arranged **stages**, gradually.
025:046 towards Ourselves,- a contraction by easy **stages**.
034:018 We had appointed **stages** of journey in due
039:006 of your mothers, in **stages**, one after
071:014 created you in diverse **stages**?
076:023 the Qur'an to thee by **stages**.

STAIN

008:011 to remove from you the **stain** of Satan, to
020:022 (or **stain**)-as another Sign,-
027:012 without **stain** (or harm): (these are)
028:032 without **stain** (or harm), and draw
074:004 And thy garments keep free from **stain**!
083:014 is the **stain** of the (ill) which they do!

STAINED

012:018 They **stained** his shirt with false blood. He said

STAINS

002:271 some of your (**stains** of) evil.

STAIR-WAYS

043:033 their houses, and (silver) **stair-ways** on which

STAKES

038:012 and 'Ad, and Pharaoh the Lord of **Stakes**.
089:010 And with Pharaoh, lord of **Stakes**?

STALK

055:012 Also corn with (its) leaves and **stalk** for fodder,
075:033 Then did he **stalk** to his family in full conceit!

STALKS

105:005 an empty field of **stalks** and straw,

STALLION-CAMELS

005:103 or **stallion-camels** freed from work: it is

STALWART

027:039 A **stalwart** of the Jinn said: "I will

STAND

002:020 they **stand** still.
002:113 "The Jews have naught (to **stand**) upon";
002:113 "The Christians have naught (to **stand**) upon";
002:238 and **stand** before Allah in a devout
002:275 not **stand** except as stands one whom the Satan
003:113 are a portion that **stand** (for the right);
004:102 **stand** up (in prayer) with thee.
004:127 that ye **stand** firm for justice to orphans.
004:135 O ye who believe! **stand** out firmly for justice, as
004:142 When they **stand** up to prayer, they **stand**
004:142 they **stand** without earnestness, to be seen
005:008 O ye who believe! **stand** out firmly for Allah, as
005:068 ye have no ground to **stand** upon unless ye **stand**
005:068 unless ye **stand** fast by the Torah.
005:107 Let two others **stand** forth in their places,-
006:030 to **stand** before their Lord! He will say:

STAND (continued)

009:007 As long as these **stand** true to you,
009:007 **stand** ye true to them: for Allah
009:084 that dies, nor **stand** at his grave; for they
009:108 Never **stand** thou forth therein. There is
010:089 (O Moses and Aaron)! So **stand** ye straight,
011:112 Therefore **stand** firm (in the straight path)
014:014 when they shall **stand** before My tribunal,-such
021:028 well-pleased and they **stand** in awe and reverence
022:026 or **stand** up, or bow, or prostrate
024:013 (**stand** forth) themselves as liars!
030:025 that heaven and earth **stand** by His command:
033:013 Ye cannot **stand** (the attack)! Therefore go
034:031 to **stand** before their Lord, throwing back
034:046 that ye do **stand** up before Allah,-(it may be)
040:051 and on the Day when the Witnesses will **stand** forth,-
041:030 **stand** straight and steadfast, the angels
042:015 and **stand** steadfast as thou art commanded,
045:019 it is only wrong-doers (that **stand** as) Protectors,
051:045 Then they could not even **stand** (on their feet),
055:046 they will **stand** before (the Judgment Seat of)
057:025 and Wrong), that men may **stand** forth in justice;
058:018 they have something (to **stand** upon). No, indeed!
063:004 (unable to **stand** on their own). They think
068:040 will **stand** surety of that!
070:033 And those who **stand** firm in their testimonies;
073:002 **Stand** (to pray) by night, but not all night,-
078:038 will **stand** forth in ranks, none shall
083:006 will **stand** before the Lord of the Worlds?

STANDARD

005:044 By its **standard** have been judged the Jews, by the

STANDEST

004:102 and **standest** to lead them in prayer, let one
052:048 of thy Lord the while thou **standest** forth,
073:020 **standest** forth (to prayer) nigh two-thirds

STANDETH

013:033 Is then He Who **standeth** over every soul

STANDING

003:018 **standing** firm on justice.
003:039 While he was **standing** in prayer in the chamber,
003:191 Men who remember Allah, **standing**, sitting,
004:103 remember Allah, **standing**, sitting down, or
007:163 the town **standing** close by the sea. Behold!
009:108 **standing** forth (for prayer) therein. In it
010:012 or **standing**. But when We have removed his
011:071 And his wife was **standing** (there), and she
011:100 of them some are **standing**, and some
012:054 thou art of high **standing** with us, invested with
013:003 **standing** firm, and (flowing) rivers: and fruit
016:015 mountains **standing** firm, lest it should shake
021:031 mountains **standing** firm, lest it should
025:064 in adoration of their Lord prostrate and **standing**;
026:218 Who seeth thee **standing** forth (in prayer),
031:010 **standing** firm, lest it should shake with you;
039:009 prostrating himself or **standing** (in adoration),
039:068 they will be **standing** and looking on!
041:010 mountains **standing** firm, high above it,
050:007 **standing** firm, and produced therein every kind
059:005 left them **standing** on their roots, it was
062:011 to it, and leave thee **standing**. Say: "That which
077:027 **standing** firm, lofty (in stature); and provided
079:040 the fear of **standing** before their Lord's (tribunal)

STANDS

002:256 Truth **stands** out clear from Error;
002:275 not stand except as **stands** one whom the Satan
003:097 Allah **stands** not in need of any of His creatures.
014:027 **stands** firm, in this world and in the Hereafter:
036:077 Yet behold! he (**stands** forth) as an open adversary!
048:029 and it **stands** on its own stem, (filling) the

STAR

006:076 he saw a **star**: he said: "This is my Lord." But
024:035 the glass as it were a brilliant **star**: lit from
053:001 By the **Star** when it goes down,-
053:049 That He is the Lord of Sirius (the Mighty **Star**);
086:003 (It is) the **Star** of piercing brightness;-

STARE

014:042 a Day when the eyes will fixedly **stare** in horror,-
021:097 will fixedly **stare** in horror: "Ah! woe to us!

STARS

006:097 the **stars** (as beacons) for you, that ye
007:054 and the sun, the moon, and the **stars**, (all) are
012:004 "O my father! I did see eleven **stars** and the
016:012 and the **Stars** are in subjection by His Command:
016:016 and by the **stars** (men) guide themselves.
022:018 the **stars**; the hills, the trees, the animals;
037:006 the lower heaven with beauty (in) the **stars**,-
037:088 Then did he cast a glance at the **Stars**,
052:049 and at the setting of the **stars**!
056:075 Furthermore I swear by the setting of the **Stars**,-
077:008 Then when the **stars** become dim;
081:002 When the **stars** fall, losing their lustre;
082:002 When the **Stars** are scattered;

STARTED

008:047 And be not like those who **started** from their

STARTEST

002:149 From whencesoever thou **startest** forth,
002:150 So from whencesoever thou **startest** forth,

STARTS

011:038 Forthwith he **starts** constructing the Ark:

STATE

002:036 the **state** (of felicity) in which they had been.
002:132 in the **state** of submission (to Me).
003:102 and die not except in a **state** of Islam.
003:179 the Believers in the **state** in which ye are now,
004:043 in a **state** of intoxication, until
004:043 nor in a **state** of ceremonial impurity except
005:001 the Sacred Precincts or in the **state** of Pilgrimage.
005:002 the **state** of pilgrimage, ye may hunt, and let not
005:006 If ye are in a **state** of ceremonial impurity, bathe
005:096 or in the **state** of pilgrimage and fear Allah,
009:084 and died in a **state** of perverse rebellion.
009:094 the true **state** of matters concerning you: it is
009:125 and they will die in a **state** of Unbelief.
016:028 take in a **state** of wrong-doing to their own
016:032 take in a **state** of purity, saying (to them),
018:019 Such (being their **state**), We raised
020:086 in **state** of anger and sorrow. He said:
020:101 They will abide in this (**state**): and grievous
022:032 Such (is his **state**): and whoever
024:040 Or (the Unbelievers' **state**) is like the depths
024:055 and that He will change (their **state**), after the
028:021 looking about, in a **state** of fear. He prayed:
030:054 in a **state** of (helpless) weakness, then gave
037:145 the naked shore in a **state** of sickness,

STATE (continued)
050:005   to them: so they are in a confused **state**.
067:004   to thee dull and discomfited, in a **state** worn out.
079:010   be returned to (our) former **state**?-

STATED
004:103   on Believers at **stated** times.
006:002   and then decreed a **stated** term (for you). And
016:061   a **stated** Term: when their Term expires, they would
035:045   a **stated** Term: when their Term expires,
071:004   and give you respite for a **stated** Term: for when

STATELY
050:010   And tall (and **stately**) palm-trees, with shoots
053:006   For he appeared (in **stately** form)

STATEMENT
003:138   Here is a plain **statement** to men,
019:034   (it is) a **statement** of truth, about which
058:001   (and accepted) the **statement** of the woman

STATION
002:125   the **Station** of Abraham as a place of prayer;
003:097   In it are Signs manifest; the **Station** of Abraham;
017:079   raise thee to a **Station** of Praise and Glory!
019:057   And We raised him to a lofty **station**.

STATIONARY
025:045   it **stationary**! Then do We make the sun its guide;

STATIONS
003:121   to post the Faithful at their **stations** for battler:
036:039   for her **stations** (to traverse) till she returns
072:009   in (hidden) **stations**, to (steal) a hearing;

STATURE
007:069   and gave you a **stature** tall among
077:027   standing firm, lofty (in **stature**); and provided

STAY
009:072   of everlasting **stay** but the greatest bliss
009:083   then sit ye (now) with those who **stay** behind."
009:093   are rich. They prefer to **stay** with the (women)
009:120   of the neighbourhood, to **stay** behind Allah's
010:071   that I should **stay** (with you) and remind
012:021   his wife: "Make his **stay** (among us) honourable:
012:069   (full) brother to **stay** with him. He said
014:029   an evil place to **stay** in!
023:112   did ye **stay** on earth?"
026:018   and didst thou not **stay** in our midst many years
033:033   And **stay** quietly in your houses, and make
033:060   be able to **stay** in it as thy neighbors for any
038:060   upon us! Now evil is (this) place to **stay** in!"

STAYED
003:156   "If they had **stayed** with us, they would
017:076   have **stayed** (therein) after thee, except for
018:019   ye have **stayed** here... Now send
018:019   They said, "We have **stayed** (perhaps) a day,
018:019   "How long have ye **stayed** (here)?" They said,
018:025   So they **stayed** in their Cave three hundred years,
018:026   they **stayed**: with Him is (the knowledge of)
023:113   They will say: "We **stayed** a day or part
023:114   He will say: "Ye **stayed** not but a little,-

STAYS
002:203   and if anyone **stays** on,

STEAD
047:038   in your **stead** another people; then they

STEADFAST
002:003   are **steadfast** in prayer,
002:043   And be **steadfast** in prayer: give Zakat,

STEADFAST (continued)
002:083   be **steadfast** in prayer; and Give Zakat.
002:110   And be **steadfast** in prayer
002:177   to be **steadfast** in prayer,
003:142   (in His cause) and remained **steadfast**?
003:146   And Allah loves those who are firm and **steadfast**.
011:115   And be **steadfast** in patience; for verily
037:102   if Allah so wills one of the **steadfast**."
041:030   stand straight and **steadfast**, the angels
042:013   Namely, that ye should remain **steadfast** in Religion,
042:015   and stand **steadfast** as thou art commanded,
051:058   Lord of Power,-**Steadfast** (for ever).
070:023   Those who remain **steadfast** to their prayer;

STEADFASTLY
002:249   Allah is with those who **steadfastly** persevere."
028:080   save those who **steadfastly** persevere (in good)."

STEAL
012:077   a brother of his who did **steal** before (him)."
060:012   that they will not **steal**, that they
072:009   in (hidden) stations, to (**steal**) a hearing;

STEALS
012:077   They said: "If he **steals**, there was a brother

STEALTH
015:018   by **stealth**, is pursued by a fiery comet,
037:010   by **stealth**, and they are pursued be a flaming

STEALTHY
042:045   a **stealthy** glance. And the Believers will say:

STEEDS
008:060   including **steeds** of war, to strike terror
100:001   By the (**Steeds**) that run, with panting (breath),

STEEP
018:096   **steep** mountain sides, he said, "Blow (with
090:011   on the path that is **steep**.
090:012   to thee the path that is **steep**?-

STEEPED
007:133   but they were **steeped** in arrogance, a people
026:099   who were **steeped** in guilt.
038:002   But the Unbelievers (are **steeped**) in Self-glory

STEEPS
004:037   a Punishment that **steeps** them in contempt;

STEM
048:029   and it stands on its own **stem**, (filling) the

STEP
003:003   (**step** by **step**), in truth, the Book,
007:182   We will lead them **step** by **step** to ruin

STEP-DAUGHTERS
004:023   your **step-daughters** under your guardianship,

STEPS
002:250   on us and make our **steps** firm:
027:010   and retraced not his **steps**: "O Moses!"
028:031   and retraced not his **steps**: "O Moses
037:094   with hurried **steps**, to him.

STERN
066:006   **stern** (and) severe, who flinch not (from
069:030   (The **stern** command will say): "Seize ye him,
072:008   filled with **stern** guards and flaming fires.

STICK
048:026   and made them **stick** close to the command

STICKY
037:011   out of a **sticky** clay!

STILL
002:020 they stand **still**.
004:086 meet it with a greeting **still** more courteous,
007:046 but they **still** hoped. To (enter it).
007:176 he (**still**) lolls out his tongue. That is the
009:015 And **still** the indignation of their heart. For
033:023 (**still**) wait: but they have never changed (their
041:016 more humiliating **still**: and they will find no help.
042:033 He can **still** the Wind: then would
093:002 And by the Night when it is **still**,-
094:007 (from thine immediate task), **still** labor hard,

STILL-BORN
006:139 but if it is **still-born** then all

STINT
020:033 "That we may celebrate Thy praise without **stint**,
020:034 "And remember Thee without **stint**:

STIR
033:060 and those who **stir** up sedition in the City,
033:060 We shall certainly **stir** thee up against them:

STIRRED
003:154 **stirred** to anxiety by their own feelings,
005:014 that was sent them: so We **stirred** up enmity and
022:005 down rain on it, it is **stirred** (to life),
041:039 it is **stirred** to life and yields increase.

STOCK
002:067 a laughing-**stock** of us?"

STOCK-IN-TRADE
012:062 their **stock-in-trade** (with which they had bartered)
012:065 This our **stock-in-trade** has been
012:065 they found their **stock-in-trade** had been

STONE
002:264 which leaves it (just) a bare **stone**.
005:003 that which is sacrificed on **stone** (altars);
018:020 they would **stone** you or force you to return
019:046 I will indeed **stone** thee: now get
036:018 **stone** you, and a grievous punishment indeed will

STONED
011:091 we should certainly have **stoned** thee! For thou
026:116 O Noah! thou shalt be **stoned** (to death)."

STONES
002:024 whose fuel is Men and **Stones**,
005:090 intoxicants and gambling, sacrificing to **stones**,
008:032 rain down on us a shower of **stones** from the sky,
017:050 Say: "(Nay!) be ye **stones** or iron,
017:068 a violent tornado (with showers of **stones**) so that
029:040 (with showers of **stones**); some were
051:033 **stones** of clay (brimstone),
054:034 tornado with showers of **stones**, (which destroyed
056:015 (with gold and precious **stones**),
066:006 whose fuel is Men and **Stones**, over which
067:017 violent tornado (with showers of **stones**), so that
105:004 Striking them with **stones** of baked clay.

STOOD
005:066 If only they had **stood** fast by the Torah, the
018:014 Behold, they **stood** up and said: "Our Lord
040:078 there and then, those who **stood** on Falsehoods.
046:029 the Qur'an: when they **stood** in the presence
069:026 how my account (**stood**)!
072:019 Devotee of Allah **stood** up to invoke Him,

STOODEST
003:075 unless thou constantly **stoodest** demanding,

STOP
016:080 when ye travel and when ye **stop** (in your
037:024 "But **stop** them, for they must be asked:

STORE
003:049 and what ye **store** in your houses.
003:091 For such is (in **store**) a chastisement grievous,

STORE-HOUSES
012:055 the **store-houses** of the land: I am

STORED
041:050 I have (much) good (**stored**) in His sight!"

STORES
015:022 though ye are not the guardians of its **stores**.

STORIES
011:049 Such are some of the **stories** of the Unseen,
011:100 These are some of the **stories** of communities
011:120 the **stories** of the messengers,-with it
012:003 the most beautiful of **stories**, in that
012:006 of **stories** (and events) and perfect His favour
012:021 the interpretation of **stories** (and events).
012:102 Such is one of the **stories** of what happened unseen,
012:111 There is, in their **stories**, instruction for
020:099 some **stories** of what happened before: for We

STORM
069:005 by a terrible **storm** of thunder and lightning!

STORMY
010:022 then comes a **stormy** wind and the waves

STORY
004:164 told thee the **story**; of others We have not;
005:027 of the **story** of the two sons of Adam.
007:007 their whole **story** with knowledge, for We
007:101 Such were the towns whose **story** We (thus)
007:175 Relate to them the **story** of the man to whom
007:176 so relate the **story**; perchance they may reflect.
009:070 Hath not the **story** reached them of those
010:071 Relate to them the **story** of Noah. Behold! he
012:083 yourselves contrived a **story** (good enough) for you.
014:009 Has not the **story** reached you, (O people!),
018:013 We relate to thee their **story** in truth: they were
018:083 you something of his **story**."
019:016 Relate in the Book (the **story** of) Mary, when she
019:041 (the **story** of) Abraham: he was a man of Truth,
019:051 (the **story** of) Moses: for he was specially chosen.
019:054 (the **story** of) Isma'il: he was (strictly) true
020:009 Has the **story** of Moses reached thee?
024:034 an illustration from (the **story** of) people who
026:069 (something of) Abraham's **story**.
028:003 the **story** of Moses and Pharaoh in Truth,
028:025 narrated the **story**, he said:
036:013 a parable, the (**story** of) the Companions of the
038:021 Has the **Story** of the Disputants reached thee?
040:078 and some whose **story** We have not related to thee.
040:078 whose **story** We have related to thee, and some
051:024 Has the **story** reached thee, of the honoured
064:005 Has not the **story** reached you, of those
079:015 Has the **story** of Moses reached thee?
085:017 Has the **story** reached thee, of the Forces-
088:001 Has the **story** reached thee, of the

STRAIGHT
001:006 Show us the **straight** way.
002:142 a Way that is **straight**.
002:213 to a path that is **straight**.
003:051 This is a Way that is **straight**."

STRAIGHT (continued)

003:101   will be shown a way that is **straight**.
004:068   And We should have shown them the **Straight** Way.
004:175   and guide them to Himself by a **straight** Way.
005:016   guideth them to a Path that is **Straight**.
006:039   He placeth on the Way that is **Straight**.
006:087   and We guided them to a **straight** Way.
006:126   leading **straight**: We have detailed the Signs
006:153   Verily, this is My Way, leading **straight**: follow
006:161   guided me to a way that is **straight**,-a religion
007:016   for them on Thy **Straight** Way:
008:001   so fear Allah, and keep **straight** the relations
010:025   to a Way that is **straight**.
010:089   (O Moses and Aaron)! So stand ye **straight**, and
011:056   Verily, it is my Lord that is on a **Straight** Path.
011:112   the **straight** path) as thou art commanded,-thou and
015:041   (Allah) said: "This is for me a **straight** path.
016:076   who commands justice, and is on the **Straight** Way?
016:121   and guided him to a **Straight** Way.
017:035   is **straight**: that is better and fairer in the
018:002   (He hath made it) **Straight** (and Clear) in order
018:061   the sea (**straight**) as in a tunnel.
018:077   but he set it up **straight**. (Moses) said:
019:036   this is a Way that is **straight**.
019:043   a Way that is even and **straight**.
020:108   the Caller (**straight**): no crookedness in him:
020:135   the **straight** and even way, and who
022:054   to the **Straight** Way.
023:073   But verily thou callest them to the **Straight** Way;
024:046   to a Way that is **straight**.
025:027   a (**straight**) path with the Messenger!
025:057   may take a (**straight**) Path to his Lord."
028:022   will show me the smooth and **straight** Path."
033:070   and make your utterance **straight** forward:
036:004   On a **Straight** Way.
036:061   (for that) this was the **Straight** Way?
037:118   And We guided them to the **Straight** Way.
041:006   so take the **straight** path unto Him and ask for
041:030   stand **straight** and steadfast, the angels
042:052   (men) to the **Straight** Way,-
043:043   verily thou art on a **Straight** Way.
043:061   this is a **Straight** Way.
043:064   this is a **Straight** Way."
046:030   and to a **Straight** Path.
048:002   and guide thee on the **Straight** Way;
048:020   you to a **Straight** Path;
057:028   by which ye shall walk (**straight** in your path),
060:001   has strayed from the **Straight** Path.
067:022   or one who walks evenly on a **Straight** Way?
073:019   a (**straight**) path to his Lord!
076:029   let him take a (**straight**) Path to his Lord.
078:039   a (**straight**) Return to his Lord!
081:016   Go **straight**, or hide;
081:028   wills to go **straight**:
098:003   Wherein are books right and **straight**.
098:005   and that is the Religion Right and **Straight**.

STRAIGHTWAY

009:057   they would turn **straightway** thereto with
014:030   But verily ye are making **straightway** for Hell!"
026:045   when behold, it **straightway** swallows up all the
030:025   behold, ye (**straightway**) come forth.

STRAIN

015:088   **Strain** not thine eyes. (Wistfully) at what We

STRAIN (continued)

020:131   Nor **strain** thine eyes in longing for the
037:008   (So) they should not **strain** their ears in the

STRAITEN

017:030   He pleaseth, and He **straiten** it for He doth

STRAITENED

009:118   and their (very) Souls seemed **straitened** to them,-
011:012   and thy heart feeleth **straitened** lest they say,
026:013   "My breast will be **straitened**. And my

STRANDS

016:092   who breaks into untwisted **strands** the yarn

STRANGE

013:005   want of faith), **strange** is their saying: "When
018:071   Truly a **strange** thing hast thou done!"
038:005   into one God? Truly this is a **strange** thing!"
040:041   "And O my People! how (**strange**) it is for me

STRANGERS

004:036   neighbors who are **strangers**, the Companion

STRANGLING

005:003   that which hath been killed by **strangling**, or by

STRATAGEM

008:016   unless it be in a **stratagem** of war, or to
009:005   for them in every **stratagem** (of war); but if

STRATAGEMS

008:018   and **stratagems** of the Unbelievers.

STRAW

035:013   besides Him own not a **straw**.
105:005   and **straw** (of which the corn) has been eaten up.

STRAY

002:026   By it He causes many to **stray**,
002:026   but He causes not to **stray**,
005:105   no hurt can come to you from those who **stray**.
006:056   if I did, I would **stray** from the path, and be
007:155   by it Thou causest whom Thou wilt to **stray**, and
010:108   own souls; those who **stray**, do so
013:027   Say: "Truly Allah leaveth, to **stray**, whom He
013:033   Allah leaves to **stray**, no one can guide.
014:027   to **stray**, those who do wrong: Allah doeth
016:037   to **stray**, and there is none to help them.
018:017   but he whom Allah leaves to **stray**,-for him
025:017   or did they **stray** from the Path themselves?"
027:092   their own souls, and if any **stray**, say: "I
034:050   I only **stray** to the loss of my own soul: but if
035:008   For Allah leaves to **stray** whom He wills,
039:023   but such as Allah leaves to **stray**, can have
039:036   For such as Allah leaves to **stray**, there can
040:033   to **stray**, there is none to guide...
040:034   leave to **stray** such as transgress and live
040:074   Thus does Allah leave the Unbelievers to **stray**.
042:046   And for any whom Allah leaves to **stray**,
053:030   those who **stray** from His path, and He
074:031   Thus doth Allah leave to **stray** whom He pleaseth,

STRAYED

002:108   hath **strayed** without doubt from the even way.
004:116   hath **strayed** far, far away (from the Right).
004:167   have verily **strayed** far, far away from the Path.
005:077   and **strayed** themselves from the even Way.
016:125   who have **strayed** from His Path, and who
021:078   of certain people had **strayed** by night: We did
060:001   has **strayed** from the Straight Path.
068:007   hath **strayed** from His Path: and He

STRAYETH
006:117   who **strayeth** from His Way: He knoweth

STRAYING
004:143   Whom Allah leaves **straying**, never wilt
006:125   those whom He willeth to leave **straying**, He
014:018   that is the **straying** far, far (from the goal).
016:093   **straying** whom He pleases, and He guides
022:012   nor profit them: that is **straying** far indeed
026:091   "And to those **straying** in evil, the Fire
026:094   they and those **straying** in evil,
026:224   **straying** in Evil, who follow them:
027:081   from **straying**: only those wilt thou get to listen
030:053   from their **straying**: only those wilt thou make
071:024   the wrong-doers but in **straying** (from their mark)."

STRAYS
039:041   but he that **strays** injures his own soul.

STREAM
002:249   he said: "Allah will test you at the **stream**;
067:030   Say: "See ye?-if your **stream** be some morning lost

STREAMING
009:092   they turned back, their eyes **streaming** with tears

STREAMS
002:266   and vines and **streams** flowing underneath,
006:006   and gave **streams** flowing beneath their (feet): yet
043:051   (witness) these **streams** flowing underneath my

STREETS
025:007   and walks through the **streets**? Why has

STRENGTH
002:286   than we have the **strength** to bear.
004:034   the one more (**strength**) than the other, and
005:022   are a people of exceeding **strength**: never shall
006:006   in **strength** such as We have not given to you-for
006:152   until he attain the age of full **strength**; give
008:060   Against them make ready your **strength** to the
009:047   your (**strength**) but only (made for) disorder,
011:052   and add **strength** to your **strength**: so turn ye
011:091   that thou hast no **strength**! Were it not
014:027   Allah will establish in **strength** those who
017:034   full **strength**; and fulfil (every) engagement,
017:074   And had We not given thee **strength**, thou wouldst
018:014   We gave **strength** to their hearts: behold, they
018:082   attain their age of full **strength** and get out
018:095   help me therefore with **strength** (and labour):
020:031   "Add to my **strength** through him,
022:005   may reach your age of full **strength**; and some
022:040   is Full of **Strength**, Exalted in Might, (able to
027:033   with **strength**, and given to vehement war: but the
027:039   indeed I have full **strength** for the purpose,
028:078   to him in **strength** and greater in amount
030:009   in **strength**: they tilled the soil and populated
030:054   after weakness, then, after **strength**, gave you
030:054   then gave (you) **strength** after weakness,
033:025   full of **Strength**, Exalted in might.
035:044   to them in **strength**? Nor is Allah to be
038:017   the man of **strength**: for he ever turned (in
040:021   to them in **strength**, and in
040:022   full of **Strength**, Severe Punishment.
040:067   reach your age of full **strength**; then lets
040:082   than these and superior in **strength** and in
041:015   in **strength**?" What! did they not see that Allah,
041:015   was superior to them in **strength**? But they
046:015   the age of full **strength** and attains forty years,

STRENGTH (continued)
057:025   Full of **Strength**, Exalted in Might.

STRENGTHEN
002:265   to please Allah and to **strengthen** their souls,
003:200   vie in such perseverance: **strengthen** each other;
004:066   to **strengthen** their (faith).
008:011   to **strengthen** your hearts, and to plant
016:102   in order to **strengthen** those who believe, and as
025:032   that We may **strengthen** thy heart thereby,
028:034   to confirm (and **strengthen**) me: for I fear
028:035   He said: "We will certainly **strengthen** thy arm

STRENGTHENED
002:087   and **strengthened** him with the holy spirit.
002:253   and **strengthened** him with the Holy Spirit.
005:110   Behold! I **strengthened** thee with the Holy Spirit.
008:002   find their faith **strengthened**, and put (all)
008:026   **strengthened** you with His aid, and gave you
008:062   He it is that hath **strengthened** thee with His
009:040   upon him, and **strengthened** him with forces
028:010   had We not **strengthened** her heart (with faith),
036:014   but We **strengthened** them with a third: they said
038:020   We **strengthened** his kingdom, and gave
058:022   in their hearts, and **strengthened** them with

STRENUOUSNESS
025:052   them with the utmost **strenuousness**, with the

STRETCH
005:011   the design to **stretch** out their hands against you,
005:028   to **stretch** my hand against thee to slay thee: for
005:028   "If thou dost **stretch** thy hand against me, to slay
006:093   the angels **stretch** forth their hands, (saying),
013:014   if they were to **stretch** forth their hands
017:029   nor **stretch** it forth to its utmost reach,
018:047   a level **stretch**, and We shall gather them,
022:015   and the Hereafter, let him **stretch** out a rope
060:002   to you as enemies, and **stretch** forth their hands

STRETCHES
003:103   by the Rope which Allah (**stretches** out for you),
024:040   if a man **stretches** out his hand, he can

STRETCHING
018:018   their dog **stretching** forth his two fore-legs

STRICKEN
002:266   while he is **stricken** with old age,

STRICT
002:196   And know that Allah, is **strict** in punishment.
002:211   Allah is **strict** in punishment.
003:011   For Allah is **strict** in punishment.
005:002   fear Allah: for Allah is **strict** in punishment.
005:098   Know ye that Allah is **strict** in punishment and
008:013   Allah is **strict** in punishment.
008:025   Allah is **strict** in punishment.
008:048   for Allah is **strict** in punishment."
008:052   for Allah is Strong, and **Strict** in punishment:
013:006   and verily thy Lord is (also) **strict** in punishment.
013:026   by (**strict**) measure, the Sustenance (which He
016:124   The Sabbath was only made (**strict**) for those
029:062   by (**strict**) measure, (as He pleases): for Allah
059:007   for Allah is **strict** in Punishment.

STRICTLY
002:238   Guard **strictly** your (habit of) prayers.
019:054   (**strictly**) true to what he promised, and he
023:009   And who (**strictly**) guard their prayer;-
070:034   And those who (**strictly**) guard their worship;-

STRIDE
034:012 morning (**stride**) was a month's (journey), and its
034:012 and its evening (**stride**) was a month's (journey);

STRIFE
006:065 with confusion in party **strife**, giving you

STRIKE
002:060 We said "**strike** the rock with thy staff."
002:073 "**Strike** the (body) with a piece of the (heifer)."
007:160 for Water: "**Strike** the rock with thy staff": out
008:060 to **strike** terror into (the hearts of) the enemies,
017:048 See what similes thy **strike** for thee: but they
020:077 and **strike** a dry path for them through the sea,
024:031 and that they should not **strike** their feet
026:063 "**Strike** the sea with thy rod." So it
026:130 "And when ye **strike** you **strike** like tyrants.
038:042 "**Strike** with thy foot: here is (water)
038:044 and **strike** therewith: and break not (thy oath)."
100:002 And **strike** sparks of fire,

STRIKES
003:117 it **strikes** and destroys the harvest of men
024:043 is hail: He **strikes** therewith whom He pleases

STRIKETH
013:013 and therewith He **striketh** whomsoever He will.

STRIKING
037:093 **striking** (them) with the right hand.
105:004 **Striking** them with stones of baked clay.

STRING
077:033 "As if there were (a **string** of) yellow camels

STRINGS
009:067 and tighten their purse's **strings**. They have

STRIPES
024:002 a hundred **stripes**: let not compassion move you
024:004 flog them with eighty **stripes**; and reject

STRIPPEST
003:026 and Thou **strippest** off power from whom

STRIPPING
007:027 **stripping** them of their raiment,

STRIVE
002:148 then **strive** together (as in a race)
003:136 for those who work (and **strive**)!
004:095 to those who **strive** and fight with their goods
004:095 And those who **strive** and fight in the cause
004:095 but those who **strive** and fight hath He
005:033 and **strive** with might and main for mischief
005:035 and **strive** with might and main in His cause: that
005:048 so **strive** as in a race in all virtues.
005:064 but they (ever) **strive** to do mischief on earth.
009:016 **strive** with might and main, and take
009:019 and **strive** with might and main in the
009:020 and **strive** with might and main, in Allah's
009:041 lightly or heavily, and **strive** and struggle,
009:073 O Prophet! **strive** hard against the Unbelievers
009:081 they hated to **strive** and fight, with their
009:086 to believe in Allah and to **strive** and fight
009:088 who believe with him, **strive** and fight with
016:110 **strive** and fight for the Faith and patiently
017:019 and **strive** therefor with all due striving,
022:051 "But those who **strive** against Our Signs,
022:078 And **strive** in His cause as ye ought to **strive**,
022:078 to **strive**, (with sincerity and under discipline):
025:052 the Unbelievers, but **strive** against them with
029:006 And if any **strive** (with might and main), they do

STRIVE (continued)
029:008 (either of them) **strive** (to force) to join
029:069 And those who **strive** in Our (Cause),-We will
031:015 "But if they **strive** to make thee join in
034:005 But those who **strive** against Our Signs,
034:038 Those who **strive** against Our Signs, to frustrate
037:061 For the like of this let all **strive**, who wish
037:061 who wish to **strive**.
047:031 among you who **strive** their utmost and persevere
060:001 If ye have come out to **strive** in My Way and seek
061:011 ye **strive** (your utmost) in the Cause of Allah,
066:009 O Prophet! **strive** hard against the Unbelievers
092:004 Verily, (the ends) ye **strive** for are diverse.

STRIVEN
049:015 since doubted, but have **striven** with their

STRIVES
053:039 That man can have nothing but what he **strives** for;

STRIVING
009:024 or the **striving** in His cause;-then wait
017:019 due **striving**, and Faith,-they are the ones
017:019 the ones whose **striving** will be thanked (by Allah).
053:040 That (the fruit of) his **striving** will soon
079:022 **striving** hard (against Allah).
080:008 But as to him who came to thee **striving** earnestly,
088:009 Pleased with their **Striving**,-

STROKE
069:014 and they are crushed at one **stroke**,-

STRONG
002:266 not **strong** (enough to look, after themselves)
004:078 even if ye are in towers built up **strong** and high!"
007:183 for My scheme is **strong** (and unfailing).
008:052 for Allah is **Strong**, and Strict in punishment:
011:066 For thy Lord-He is the **Strong** One, and the Mighty.
016:067 **strong** drink, and wholesome food: behold, in this
016:092 after it has become **strong**. Using your oaths
018:095 a **strong** barrier between you and them:
028:026 to employ is the (man) who is **strong** and trusty."
028:076 a burden to a body of **strong** men. Behold, his
037:002 Those who are **strong** in repelling (evil),
042:019 and He is the **Strong**, the Mighty.
048:029 are **strong** against Unbelievers, (but) compassionate
048:029 its blade, then makes it **strong**; it then
058:021 who must prevail": for Allah is **Strong**, Mighty.
059:014 **Strong** is their fighting (spirit) amongst
068:025 **strong** in an (unjust) resolve.
076:028 and We have made their frame **strong**; but, when
085:012 Truly **strong** is the Grip of thy Lord.

STRONGER
043:008 So We destroyed men-**stronger** in power than these;-
050:036 **stronger** in power than they? Then did

STRONGEST
004:084 **strongest** in might and in punishment.
005:053 who swore their **strongest** oaths by Allah, that
005:082 **Strongest** among men in enmity to the Believers
006:109 They swear their **strongest** oaths by Allah, that
016:038 They swear their **strongest** oaths by Allah,
024:053 They swear their **strongest** oaths by Allah that,
035:042 They swore their **strongest** oaths by Allah

STRONGHOLDS
033:026 down from their **strongholds** and cast terror

STRONGLY
002:165 and Allah will **strongly** enforce the Punishment:

STROVE
002:218   and fought (and **strove** and struggled)
079:035   (all) that he **strove** for,

STRUCK
007:116   and **struck** terror into them: and they showed
028:015   and Moses **struck** him with his fist and killed
030:012   the guilty will be **struck** dumb with despair.

STRUCTURE
061:004   as if they were a solid cemented **structure**.
091:005   By the Firmament and its (wonderful) **structure**;

STRUCTURES
016:026   but Allah took their **structures** from their

STRUGGLE
009:041   and **struggle**, with your goods and your person,
090:004   Verily We have created Man into toil and **struggle**.

STRUGGLED
002:218   and fought (and strove and **struggled**)

STRUTTING
003:196   Let not the **strutting** about of the Unbelievers
040:004   Let not, then, their **strutting** about through the

STUBBLE
018:045   but soon it becomes dry **stubble**, which the
054:031   the dry **stubble** used by one who pens cattle.
087:005   And then doth make it (but) swarthy **stubble**.

STUDIED
002:121   the Book study it as it should be **studied**:
003:079   and ye have **studied** it earnestly."

STUDIES
009:122   to devote themselves to **studies** in religion, and

STUDY
002:044   and yet ye **study** the Scripture?
002:113   Yet they (profess) to **study** the (same) Book.
002:121   the Book **study** it as it should be studied:
003:093   Say: "Bring ye the Torah and **study** it,
006:156   that they learned by assiduous **study**;"
007:169   And they **study** what is in the Book. But best
034:044   which they could **study**, nor sent

STUFF
016:080   their hair, rich **stuff** and articles of convenience
080:018   From what **stuff** Hath He created him?

STUMBLE
006:110   to (**stumble** blindly).

STUNNING
002:019   the **stunning** thunder-clap,

STUNTED
034:016   and some few (**stunted**) Lote-trees.

STUPOR
050:019   And the **stupor** of death comes in truth.

STYLE
065:006   in the same **style** as ye live, according to

SUBDUED
008:067   until he hath thoroughly **subdued** the land.
009:029   willing submission, and feel themselves **subdued**.
047:004   **subdued** them, blind (the captives) firmly:

SUBJECT
014:032   and the rivers (also) hath He made **subject** to you.
014:032   **subject** to you, that they may sail through the
014:033   And He hath made **subject** to you the sun
014:033   hath He (also) made **subject** you.
016:012   He has made **subject** to you the Night and the Day;
016:014   It is He Who hath made the sea **subject**, that ye

SUBJECT (continued)
022:036   thus have we made animals **subject** to you,
022:037   He has thus made them **subject** to you, that ye
022:065   made **subject** to you (men) all that is on the
023:047   And their people are **subject** to us!"
085:003   and the **subject** of the witness;-

SUBJECTED
013:002   He has **subjected** the sun and the moon! each one
029:061   and the earth and **subjected** the sun and the moon
031:020   Do ye not see that Allah has **subjected** to your
031:029   that He has **subjected** the sun and the moon
035:013   and He has **subjected** the sun and the moon
036:072   And that We have **subjected** them to their (use)?
038:036   Then We **subjected** the Wind to his power, to flow
039:005   He has **subjected** the sun and the moon (to His
043:013   Who has **subjected** these to Our (use), for we
045:012   It is Allah Who has **subjected** the sea to you,
045:013   And He has **subjected** to you, as from

SUBJECTION
016:012   and the Stars are in **subjection** by His Command:

SUBLIME
068:004   And surely thou hast **sublime** morals.

SUBMISSION
002:132   in the state of **submission** (to Me).
003:019   Allah is Islam (**submission** to His Will):
003:085   a religion other than Islam (**submission** to Allah)
009:029   willing **submission**, and feel themselves subdued.
016:028   they offer **submission** (with the pretense), "We did
016:087   show (their) **submission** to Allah; and all
024:049   they come to him with all **submission**.
027:031   but come to me in **submission** (to the
027:038   before they come to me in **submission**?"

SUBMISSIVELY
023:076   **submissively** entreat (Him)!

SUBMIT
002:131   "**Submit** (thy will to Me):"
002:131   He said: "I **submit** (my will) to the Lord
002:133   to Him do we **submit**."
002:136   and we **submit** to Allah.
003:020   "Do ye (also) **submit** yourselves?"
006:071   to **submit** ourselves to the Lord of the worlds;
006:163   those who **submit** to His Will.
010:072   of those who **submit** to Allah's Will (in Islam)."
010:084   if ye **submit** (your will to His)."
010:090   I am of those who **submit** (to Allah in Islam)."
011:014   Will ye even then **submit** (to Islam)?"
022:034   **submit** then your wills to Him (in Islam):
027:044   I do (now) **submit** (in Islam), with Solomon,
027:081   so they **submit**.
029:046   and it is to Him we **submit** (in Islam)."
030:053   in Our Signs and **submit** (their wills in Islam).
037:026   Nay, but that day they shall **submit** (to Judgment);
039:012   of those who **submit** to Allah in Islam."
039:054   and **submit** to Him, before the Chastisement come on
040:066   and I have been commanded to **submit** (in Islam)
046:015   do I **submit** (to Thee) in Islam."
048:016   or they shall **submit**. Then if ye show obedience,
066:005   who **submit** (their wills), who believe, who are
072:014   'Amongst us are some that **submit** their wills
072:014   Now those who **submit** their wills-they have

SUBMITS
002:112   Nay, whoever **submits** his whole self

SUBMITS (continued)
004:125   than one who **submits** his whole self to Allah,
031:022   Whoever **submits** his whole self to Allah, and is
SUBMITTED
003:020   say: "I have **submitted** my whole self to Allah
027:042   and we have **submitted** to Allah (in Islam)."
037:103   So when they had both **submitted** (to Allah),
043:069   and **submitted** (to Us).
049:014   but ye (only) say, 'We have **submitted** our wills
SUBMITTING
012:101   as one **submitting** to Thy Will (as a Muslim),
017:042   sought out a way in **submitting** to the
SUBSEQUENTLY
008:075   And those who accept Faith **subsequently**, and
009:004   have not **subsequently** failed you in aught, nor
062:005   of) Taurat, but who **subsequently** failed in those
SUBSERVIANT
007:054   (all) are **subserviant** by His Command. Verily,
SUBSISTENCE
015:020   of **subsistence**,-for you and for those for whose
078:011   And made the day as a means of **subsistence**?
089:016   restricting his **subsistence** for him, then saith
SUBSTANCE
002:177   to spend of your **substance**,
002:195   your **substance** in the cause of Allah,
004:002   and devour not their **substance** (by mixing it up)
004:038   (Nor) those who spend of their **substance**, to be
047:038   (of your **substance**) in the Way of Allah:
057:007   of the (**substance**) whereof He has made you heirs.
063:010   out of the **substance** which We have bestowed
065:006   then spend (your **substance**) on them until they
SUBSTITUTE
002:106   but We **substitute** something better
004:002   nor **substitute** (your) worthless things
016:101   When We **substitute** one revelation for another,-
017:073   unto thee, to **substitute** in Our name something
047:038   the Path), He will **substitute** in your stead
070:041   **Substitute** for them better (men) than they;
SUBSTITUTED
027:011   and have thereafter **substituted** good to take
SUBSTITUTES
002:211   **substitutes** (something else),
SUBTLE
006:103   He is **subtle** well-aware.
031:016   for Allah is **subtle** and aware.
067:014   And He is The **Subtle** The Aware.
SUCCEED
006:006   fresh generations (to **succeed** them).
011:057   make another People to **succeed** you, and you
014:014   to abide in the land, and **succeed** them. This for
SUCCEEDED
003:185   and admitted to the Garden will have **succeeded**:
007:169   After them **succeeded** an (evil) generation: they
SUCCEEDING
002:253   **succeeding** generations would not have fought
043:060   amongst you, **succeeding** each other on the earth.
SUCCEEDS
020:069   a magician's trick: and the magician **succeeds** not.
091:009   Truly he **succeeds** that purifies it,
SUCCESS
004:141   But if the Unbelievers gain a **success**, they say

SUCCESS (continued)
011:088   to the best of my power; and my **success** (in my
018:044   and the Best to give **success**.
058:022   that will achieve **Success**.
SUCCESSFUL
023:001   **Successful** indeed are the Believers,-
023:102   (of good deeds) is heavy,-they will be **successful**.
024:031   that ye may be **successful**.
028:067   be one of the **successful**.
SUCCESSION
002:087   a **succession** of Messengers;
007:054   each seeking the other in rapid **succession**: and
007:100   in **succession** to its (previous) possessors, is it
013:011   there are (angels) in **succession**, before and
023:044   in **succession**: every time there came to a people
069:007   seven nights and eight days in **succession**: so that
SUCCESSORS
006:133   whom He will as your **successors**, even as
SUCCUMB
004:091   they **succumb** thereto: if they withdraw
SUCH
002:096   but the grant of **such** life will not
002:102   and **such** things as came down at Babylon
002:102   taught anyone (**such** things without saying:
002:112   on **such** shall be no fear,
002:114   It was not fitting that **such** should
002:126   He said: "(Yea), and **such** as reject Faith,
002:126   **such** of them as believe
002:130   the religion of Abraham but **such** as debase
002:177   **Such** are the people of truth, the God-fearing.
002:191   **Such** is the reward of those who reject faith.
002:196   **such** as ye may find,
002:196   he must make an offering **such** as he can afford,
002:214   without **such** (trials) as came to those
002:229   **such** persons wrong (themselves as well as others).
002:230   **Such** are the limits ordained by Allah,
002:282   If ye do (**such** harm), it would be
002:282   **such** as ye choose, for witnesses,
003:013   In this is a lesson for **such** as have eyes to see."
003:014   **Such** are the possessions of this world's life;
003:073   Or that those (receiving **such** revelation)
003:087   Of **such** the reward is that on them (rests)
003:091   never would be accepted from any **such** as much
003:091   For **such** is (in store) a chastisement grievous,
003:136   For **such** the reward is forgiveness
003:140   **Such** days (of varying fortunes) We give to men
003:200   vie in **such** perseverance: strengthen each other;
004:070   **Such** is the Bounty from Allah: and sufficient
004:097   **Such** men will find their abode in Hell.
004:103   for **such** prayers are enjoined on Believers
004:107   **such** as betray their own souls; for Allah
004:128   and **such** settlement is best; even though
004:176   if (**such** a deceased was) a woman, who left no child,
005:002   nor the garlands that mark out **such** animals, nor
005:041   For **such** it is not Allah's will
005:054   the reproaches of **such** as find fault.
005:085   **Such** is the recompense of those who do good.
005:090   eschew **such** (abomination), that ye may prosper.
005:102   Some people before you did ask **such** questions, and
005:115   **such** as I have not inflicted on anyone
005:116   Had I said **such** a thing. Thou wouldst
006:006   in strength **such** as We have not given to you-for

SUCH (continued)

006:070   **such** is (the end of) those who deliver themselves
006:096   **such** is the judgment and ordering of (Him), the
006:113   To **such** (deceit) let the hearts
006:138   **such** and **such** cattle and crops are forbidden, and
006:139   the wombs of **such** and **such** cattle is specially
006:144   Allah ordered you **such** a thing? But who
006:150   of **such** as treat Our Signs as falsehoods, and
006:150   If they bring **such** witnesses, be not
006:150   and **such** as believe not in the Hereafter: for
007:020   or **such** beings as live for ever."
007:026   **Such** are among the Signs of Allah, that they
007:029   **such** as He created you in the beginning, so
007:037   For **such**, their portion appointed must reach
007:040   **such** is Our reward for those in sin.
007:041   **such** is Our requital of those who do wrong.
007:051   "**Such** as took their religion to be
007:080   "Do ye commit lewdness **such** as no people
007:101   **Such** were the towns whose story We (thus)
007:128   **such** of His servants as He pleaseth; and the
007:137   erected (with **such** pride).
007:154   Guidance and Mercy for **such** as fear their Lord.
007:178   **such** are the persons who lose.
007:180   but shun **such** men as distort His names: for what
007:186   To **such** as Allah rejects from His guidance, there
008:001   Say: "(**Such**) spoils are at the disposal of
008:004   **Such** in truth are the Believers: they have
008:016   to them on **such** a day-unless it
009:008   How (can there be **such** a league), seeing that
009:017   The works of **such** bear no fruit: in Fire
009:017   It is not for **such** as join gods with Allah,
009:018   visited and maintained by **such** as believe,
009:037   and make **such** forbidden ones lawful. The evil
009:079   Those who slander **such** of the Believers as give
009:091   be against **such** as do right: and Allah
009:093   **such** as claim exemption while they are rich.
009:118   (they felt guilty) to **such** a degree that the earth
010:017   Who doth more wrong than **such** as forge
010:032   **Such** is Allah, your true Lord: apart from
010:037   This Qur'an is not **such** as can be produced by
010:106   **such** can neither profit thee nor hurt thee:
011:049   **Such** are some of the stories of the Unseen,
011:059   **Such** were the 'Ad People: they rejected
011:102   **Such** is the chastisement of thy Lord when He
012:020   counted out: in **such** low estimation did they
012:102   **Such** is one of the stories of what happened unseen,
012:111   and a Guide and a Mercy to any **such** as believe.
013:011   For each (**such** person) there are
013:016   **such** as have no power either for good or for
013:022   Evil with good: for **such** there is the final
013:035   **such** is the End of the Righteous; and the End
013:043   and **such** as have knowledge of the Book."
014:005   there are Signs for **such** as are firmly patient
014:011   to **such** of His servants as He pleases. It is
014:014   This for **such** as fear the Time when they
014:014   My tribunal,-**such** as fear My Punishment."
014:016   In front of **such** a one is Hell, and he
014:040   and also (raise **such**) among my offspring, O our
014:046   even though they were **such** as to shake the hills!
015:013   in the Message, **such** has been the way of those
015:042   shalt thou have, except **such** as put themselves
015:054   He said: "Do ye give me **such** glad tidings
015:056   the mercy of his Lord, but **such** as go astray?"

SUCH (continued)

015:084   they did (with **such** art and care)!
015:090   (Of just **such** wrath) as We sent down
015:091   (So also on **such**) as have made Qur'an into
016:002   to **such** of His servants as He pleaseth, (saying):
016:037   yet Allah guideth not **such** as He leaves to stray,
016:073   and cannot possibly have **such** power?
016:073   **such** as have no power of providing them,
016:076   is **such** a man equal with one who commands justice,
016:097   and We will bestow on **such** their reward
016:106   but **such** as open their breast to Unbelief,-
016:117   In **such** falsehood is but a paltry profit;
016:118   To the Jews We prohibited **such** things as We
017:018   We readily grant them-**such** things as We will,
017:018   We will, to **such** persons as We will: in the
017:038   Of all **such** things the evil is hateful
017:097   but he whom He leaves astray-for **such** wilt thou
018:005   No knowledge have they of **such** a thing, nor had
018:015   Who doth more wrong than **such** as invent
018:017   **Such** are among the Signs of Allah: he whom
018:019   **Such** (being their state), We raised
018:051   as helpers **such** as lead (men) astray!
018:059   **Such** were the towns We destroyed when they
018:082   **Such** is the interpretation of (those things)
018:085   One (**such**) way he followed,
019:034   **Such** (was) Jesus the son of Mary: (it is)
019:063   **Such** is the Garden which We give as an
019:087   of intercession, but **such** a one as has received
020:016   "Therefore let not **such** as believe not therein
020:075   But **such** as comes to Him as Believers who have
020:076   for aye: **such** is the reward of those who purify
020:128   Is it not a guidance to **such** men (to call
021:017   if We would do (**such** a thing)!
021:029   **such** a one We should reward with Hell: thus do
022:003   And yet among men there are **such** as dispute
022:008   Yet there is among men **such** a one as disputes
022:012   They call on **such** deities, besides Allah,
022:018   And **such** as Allah shall disgrace,-none can
022:018   are (also) **such** as unto whom the chastisement
022:030   **Such** (is the Pilgrimage): whoever honours
022:032   **Such** (is his state): and whoever
022:032   of animals), **such** (honour) should come truly
022:036   and **such** as beg with due humility: thus have
022:036   eat ye thereof, and feed **such** as (beg not but)
023:024   **such** a thing (as he says), among our
023:083   "**Such** things have been promised to us and to
024:003   to the Believers **such** a thing is forbidden.
024:004   for **such** men are wicked transgressors;-
024:013   brought the witnesses, **such** men, in the
024:017   that ye may never repeat **such** (conduct), if ye
024:033   yet, after **such** compulsion, is Allah
024:033   (for emancipation) give them **such** a deed if you
024:036   (Lit is **such** a Light) in houses, which Allah
024:051   it is **such** as these that will prosper.
024:052   It is **such** as obey Allah and His Messenger,
024:060   **Such** elderly women as are past the prospect
025:011   a Blazing Fire for **such** as deny the Hour:
025:023   make **such** deeds as floating dust scattered about.
025:028   never taken **such** a one for a friend!
025:043   Seest thou **such** a one as taketh for his god
025:059   of any acquainted (with **such** things).
025:062   for **such** as desire to be mindful or to show
025:068   any other god, nor slay **such** life as Allah

SUCH (continued)

025:070 of **such** persons into good, and Allah
026:004 If (**such**) were Our Will, We could
026:059 the Children of Israel inheritors of **such** things.
026:169 and my family from **such** things as they do!"
027:005 **Such** are they for whom a grievous Chastisement
027:037 we shall come to them with **such** hosts as they
027:052 Now **such** were their houses,-in utter
027:087 on earth, except **such** as Allah will please
027:088 pass away: (**such** is) the artistry of Allah,
028:048 And they say: "For us, we reject all (**such** things)!"
028:062 whom ye imagined (to be **such**)?"
028:074 whom ye imagined (to be **such**)?"
028:076 towards them: **such** were the treasures We had
029:010 Then there are among men **such** as say, "We believe
029:028 commit lewdness, **such** as no people in Creation
029:043 And **such** are the Parables We set forth for
030:016 **such** shall be brought forth to Punishment.
030:048 made them reach **such** of his servants as He wills,
031:006 for **such** there will be a humiliating Chastisement.
031:007 When Our Signs are rehearsed to **such** a one,
031:011 **Such** is the Creation of Allah: now show Me
032:006 **Such** as He, the knower of all things, hidden and
033:004 your sons. **Such** is (only) your (manner of)
033:006 **such** is the writing in the Book (of Allah).
033:019 **Such** men have no faith, and so
033:053 Truly **such** a thing is in Allah's sight an enormity.
033:053 familiar talk. **Such** (behavior) annoys the Prophet
033:059 be known (as **such**) and not molested. And Allah
033:062 (**Such** was) the practice (approved) of Allah
034:004 for **such** is Forgiveness and a
034:005 for **such** will be a Chastisement of Painful wrath.
034:017 give (**such**) requital except to **such** as are
034:039 and restricts the Sustenance to **such** of His
035:010 and the plotting of **such** will be void (of result).
035:013 a term appointed. **Such** is Allah your Lord:
035:018 Thou canst but warn **such** as fear their Lord
035:032 for inheritance to **such** of Our servants as We
036:011 the Most Gracious, unseen: given **such** a one,
036:011 Thou canst but admonish **such** a one as follows
037:010 Except **such** as snatch away something by stealth,
037:130 "Peace and salutation to **such** as Elias!"
037:163 Except **such** as are (themselves) going to
038:013 **such** were the Confederates.
038:039 "**Such** are Our Bounties: whether thou
038:053 **Such** is the promise made to you
038:054 Truly **such** will be Our Bounty (to you); it will
038:055 Yea, **such**! But-for the wrong-doers will be
038:057 Yea, **such**!-Then shall they taste it,-a boiling
038:063 "Did we treat them (as **such**) in ridicule, or have
039:003 But Allah guides not **such** as are
039:004 (He is above **such** things). He is Allah,
039:006 of darkness. **Such** is Allah, your Lord
039:020 (**such** is) the promise of Allah: never doth
039:023 **Such** is the guidance of Allah; He guides
039:023 but **such** as Allah leaves to stray, can have
039:033 **such** are the men who do right.
039:034 **such** is the reward of those who do good:
039:036 For **such** as Allah leaves to stray, there can
039:037 And **such** as Allah doth guide there can be
039:067 of Allah, **such** as is due to Him: on the
039:068 except **such** as it will please Allah (to exempt).
040:034 leave to stray **such** as transgress and live

SUCH (continued)

040:035 (is **such** conduct) in the sight of Allah and of
040:035 "(**Such**) as dispute about the Signs of Allah,
040:040 **such** will enter the Garden (of Bliss):
040:062 **Such** is Allah, your Lord, the Creator
040:064 **such** is Allah your Lord. So Glory
040:083 they exulted in **such** knowledge (and skill)
040:085 (**Such** has been) Allah's way of dealing with His
041:012 with guard. **Such** is the Decree of (Him)
041:028 **Such** is the requital of the enemies of Allah,-
041:035 And no one will be granted **such** goodness except
042:010 **Such** is Allah my Lord: in Him
042:041 to him, against **such** there is no cause of blame.
042:042 for **such** there will be a Chastisement grievous.
042:052 wherewith We guide **such** of Our servants as We will;
043:020 **such** (deities)!" Of that they have no knowledge!
043:037 **Such** (Satans) really hinder them from the Path,
043:038 At length, when (**such** a one) comes to Us, he says
043:040 or to **such** as (wander) in manifest error?
043:072 **Such** will be the Garden of which ye are made
044:027 they had taken **such** delight!
044:042 Except **such** as receive Allah's Mercy: for He
045:006 **Such** are the Signs of Allah, which We
045:009 for **such** there will be a humiliating Chastisement.
045:023 Allah has, knowing (him as **such**), left him
045:023 Then seest thou **such** a one as takes as his god
046:005 **such** as will not answer him to the Day of Judgment,
046:011 good thing, (**such** men) would not have gone to it
046:014 **Such** shall be Companions of the Garden,
046:015 **such** as Thou mayest approve; and be
046:016 **Such** are they from whom We shall accept the best
046:018 **Such** are they against whom is the word
046:032 besides Allah: **such** are in manifest error."
047:014 and **such** as follow their own lusts?
047:015 their Lord, (can those in **such** Bliss) be compared
047:015 be compared to **such** as shall dwell for ever
047:016 just then?" **Such** are men whose hearts Allah has
047:023 **Such** are the men whom Allah has cursed
048:015 Nay, but little do they understand (**such** things).
048:023 (**Such** has been) the practice of Allah already in
049:007 and rebellion: **such** indeed are those who
049:015 **Such** are the sincere ones.
050:045 **such** as fear My Warning!
051:009 the Truth) **such** as would be deluded.
051:037 And We left there a Signs for **such** as fear
052:038 Then let (**such** a) listener of theirs
053:022 Behold, **such** would be indeed a division
054:004 **such** tidings as contain a deterrent,
054:024 Shall we follow **such** a one? Truly should
055:046 But for **such** as fear the time when they will
056:056 **Such** will be their entertainment on the Day
056:081 Is it **such** a Message that ye would hold
057:024 **Such** persons as are covetous and commend
058:003 (it is ordained that **such** a one) should free
058:014 (in friendship) to **such** as have the Wrath of
058:022 For **such** He has written Faith in their hearts,
059:008 **such** are indeed the truthful;-
059:009 the Faith,-show their affection to **such** as came
059:017 **Such** is the reward of wrong-doers.
059:019 **Such** are the rebellious transgressors!
059:021 **such** are the similitudes which We propound to men,
060:009 It is **such** as turn to them (in these
060:010 to you). **Such** is the command of Allah: He judges

SUCH (continued)

062:004 **Such** is the Bounty of Allah, which He
065:002 **Such** is the admonition given to him who believes
065:004 **Such** of your women as have passed the age
067:005 and We have made **such** (Lamps) (as) missiles
067:006 of Hell: and evil is (**such**) destination.
068:033 **Such** is the Punishment (in this life); but greater
068:044 Then leave Me alone with **such** as reject
070:017 Inviting (all) **such** as turn their backs and turn
070:035 **Such** will be the honoured ones in the
070:044 **Such** is the Day the which they are promised!
079:037 Then, for **such** as had transgressed all bounds,
079:040 And for **such** as had entertained the fear
079:045 Thou art but a Warner for **such** as fear it.
080:042 **Such** will be the Rejecters of Allah, the Doers
089:025 such as none (else) can inflict,
089:026 And His bonds will be **such** as none (other) can bind.
090:018 **Such** are the Companions of the Right Hand.
095:006 Except **such** as believe and do righteous deeds:
098:008 all this for **such** as fear their Lord and Cherisher.
103:003 Except **such** as have Faith, and do righteous deeds,
107:002 Then **such** is the one who repulses the orphan,

SUCK

002:233 **suck** to their offspring for two whole years,
004:023 foster-mothers (who gave you **suck**),
022:002 every mother giving **suck** shall forget
028:012 And We ordained that he refused **suck** at first,

SUCKLE

028:007 mother of Moses: "**Suckle** (thy child), but when
065:006 and if they **suckle** your (offspring), give them
065:006 let another woman **suckle** (the child)

SUCKLING-BABE

022:002 shall forget her **suckling-babe**, and every

SUDDEN

006:031 until on a **sudden** the hour is on them, and they
006:044 on a **sudden**, We called them to account, when lo!
007:004 Our punishment took them on a **sudden** by night or
007:095 Behold! We called them to account of a **sudden**,
007:187 Only, all of a **sudden**, will it come to you." They
012:107 the (final) Hour all of a **sudden** while they
021:040 of a **sudden** and confound them: no power
026:202 of a **sudden**, while they perceive it not;
029:053 reach them,-of a **sudden**, while they perceive not!
039:055 of a **sudden**, while ye perceive not!-
043:066 of a **sudden**, while they perceive not?
047:018 a **sudden**? But already have come some tokens
070:043 from their sepulchers in **sudden** hast as if they

SUDDENLY

006:047 whether **suddenly** or openly, will any
022:055 comes **suddenly** upon them, or there

SUFFER

002:282 and let neither scribe nor witness **suffer** harm.
003:004 will **suffer** the severest chastisement
003:118 They only desire for you to **suffer**:
003:195 I **suffer** to be lost the work of any of you,
007:170 never shall We **suffer** the reward of the
009:120 because nothing could they **suffer** or do, but was
009:128 should **suffer**, ardently anxious is he over you: to
011:089 lest ye **suffer** a fate similar to that of the
011:115 For verily Allah will not **suffer** the reward
012:056 and We **suffer** not, to be lost, the reward
012:090 never will Allah **suffer** the reward to be lost,

SUFFER (continued)

014:044 to swear aforetime that ye **suffer** no decline?
018:030 shall not **suffer** to perish the reward of any
020:061 the forger must **suffer** failure!
020:119 "Nor to **suffer** from thirst, nor from
029:010 they **suffer** affliction in (the cause of) Allah,
029:023 they who will (**suffer**) a most grievous Chastisement.
030:044 Those who reject Faith will **suffer** from that
037:047 nor will they **suffer** intoxication therefrom.
049:007 certainly **suffer**: but Allah has endeared the
056:019 nor will they **suffer** intoxication:

SUFFERANCE

016:059 on (**sufferance** and) Contempt, or bury it

SUFFERED

002:218 who **suffered** exile and fought
003:166 What ye **suffered** on the day the two armies met,
003:195 or **suffered** harm in My cause, and fought
004:119 hath of a surety **suffered** a loss that is manifest.
009:120 whether they **suffered** thirst, or fatigue,
018:062 truly we have **suffered** much fatigue at this
082:003 When the Oceans are **suffered** to burst forth;

SUFFERETH

003:171 **suffereth** not the reward of the Faithful
009:120 for Allah **suffereth** not the reward to be lost

SUFFERING

002:177 in pain (or **suffering**) and adversity,
002:214 They encountered **suffering** and adversity,
004:104 if ye are **suffering** hardships, they are
004:104 they are **suffering** similar hardships; but you
006:042 and We afflicted the nations with **suffering** and
006:043 When the **suffering** reached them from Us, why
007:094 in **suffering** and adversity, in order
007:095 their **suffering** into prosperity, until they
007:095 touched by **suffering** and affluence".. Behold!
016:041 after **suffering** oppression,-We will assuredly
027:062 and Who relieves his **suffering**, and makes
038:041 "Satan has afflicted me with distress and **suffering**"!

SUFFERS

002:286 and it **suffers** every ill that it earns.

SUFFICE

002:137 but Allah will **suffice** thee as against them,

SUFFICETH

002:265 light moisture **sufficeth** it.
003:173 They said: "For us Allah **sufficeth**,
008:062 verily Allah **sufficeth** thee: He it is
009:129 Say: "Allah **sufficeth** me: there is no god

SUFFICIENT

004:070 and **sufficient** is it that Allah knoweth all.
008:064 O Prophet! **Sufficient** unto thee is Allah,-
009:059 and had said, "**Sufficient** unto us is Allah!
009:068 they dwell: **sufficient** is it for them: for them
015:095 For **sufficient** are We unto thee
017:014 "Read thine (own) record: **sufficient** is thy soul
039:038 His Mercy?" Say: "**Sufficient** is Allah for me!
065:003 in Allah, **sufficient** is (Allah) for him.
078:036 a Gift, (amply) **sufficient**,-

SUGGEST

020:096 thus did my soul **suggest** to me."
041:030 (they **suggest**), "Nor grieve! But receive

SUGGESTED

020:087 and that was what the Samiri **suggested**.

SUGGESTION
007:200 If a **suggestion** from Satan assail thy (mind),
SUGGESTIONS
007:020 to whisper **suggestions** to them, in order
022:053 That He may make the **suggestions** thrown in
023:097 with Thee from the **suggestions** of the Satans.
050:016 and We know what **suggestions** his soul makes to him:
SUGGESTS
003:175 **suggests** to you the fear of his votaries:
SUIT
041:024 their **suit** shall not be granted.
SUITABLE
002:236 but bestow on them (a **suitable** gift),
002:241 **suitable** Gift this is duty on the righteous.
002:282 more **suitable** as evidence,
004:003 That will be more **suitable**, to prevent you
004:059 most **suitable** for final determination.
005:108 That is most **suitable**: that they
007:113 a (**suitable**) reward if we win!"
012:059 them forth with provisions (**suitable**) for them,
012:070 (**suitable**) for them, he put the drinking cup into
026:041 shall we have a (**suitable**) reward if we win?"
054:028 brought forward (by **suitable** turns).
058:011 raise up, to (**suitable**) ranks (and degrees),
SUMMER
106:002 journeys by winter and **summer**,-
SUMMONED
024:048 When they are **summoned** to Allah and His
024:051 when **summoned** to Allah and His Messenger,
048:016 lagged behind: "Ye shall be **summoned** (to fight)
068:042 laid bare, and they shall be **summoned** to prostrate,
068:043 **summoned** aforetime to bow in adoration, while they
SUMMONS
024:063 Deem not the **summons** of the Messenger
024:063 like the **summons** of one of you to another:
SUMS
002:279 ye shall have your capital **sums**:
058:013 spending **sums** in charity before your private
SUN
002:258 Allah that causeth the **sun** to rise from the East,
006:078 But when the **sun** set, he said: "O my people!
006:078 When he saw the **sun** rising (in splendor), he
006:096 and the **sun** and moon for the
007:054 and the **sun**, the moon, and the stars, (all) are
010:005 It is He Who made the **sun** to be a shining glory
012:004 and the **sun** and the moon: I saw
013:002 He has subjected the **sun** and the moon! each one
014:033 the **sun** and the moon, both diligently
016:012 and the Day; the **Sun** and the Moon; and the
018:017 Thou wouldst have seen the **sun**, when it rose,
018:086 the **sun**, he found it set in a spring of murky
018:090 no covering protection against the **sun**.
018:090 the **sun**, he found it rising on a people for whom
020:059 be assembled when the **sun** is well up."
020:130 before the rising of the **sun**, and before
021:033 and the Day, and the **sun** and the moon: all (the
022:018 and on earth,-the **sun**, the moon, the stars;
025:045 it stationary! Then do We make the **sun** its guide;
027:024 worshipping the **sun** besides Allah: Satan has
029:061 and the earth and subjected the **sun** and the moon
031:029 that He has subjected the **sun** and the moon
035:013 and He has subjected the **sun** and the moon

SUN (continued)
035:021 and the (genial) heat of the **sun**:
036:038 And the **Sun** runs unto a resting place, for Him:
036:040 It is not permitted to the **Sun** to catch
037:005 and Lord of every point at the rising of the **sun**!
038:032 Until (the **sun**) was hidden in the veil (of Night):
039:005 He has subjected the **sun** and the moon (to His
041:037 Prostrate not to the **sun** and the moon,
041:037 and the **Sun** and the Moon. Prostrate not
050:039 of the **sun** and before (its) setting,
055:005 The **sun** and the moon follow courses
071:016 in their midst, and made the **sun** as a
075:009 And the **sun** and moon are joined together,-
081:001 When the **sun** (with its spacious light) is folded up;
091:001 By the **Sun** and his (glorious) splendor;
SUN'S
017:078 **sun's** decline till the darkness of the night,
020:119 nor from the **sun's** heat."
076:013 there neither the **sun's** (excessive heat)
091:003 By the Day as it shows up (the **Sun's**) glory;
SUNDER
002:027 and who **sunder** what Allah has ordered
SUNDRY
002:273 they beg not importunately from all and **sundry**.
015:070 (to speak) for all and **sundry**?"
SUNRISE
015:073 overtook them at **sunrise**,
026:060 So they pursued them at **sunrise**.
SUNSET
084:016 So I do call to witness the ruddy glow of **Sunset**;
SUPERIOR
003:055 who follow thee **superior** to those who reject faith,
028:078 (whole) generations,-which were **superior** to him
030:009 They were **superior** to them in strength:
035:044 before them,-though they were **superior** to them
040:021 before them? They were even **superior** to them
040:082 than these and **superior** in strength and in
041:015 was **superior** to them in strength? But they
041:015 and said: "Who is **superior** to us in strength?"
SUPERIORITY
023:024 his wish is to assert his **superiority** over you:
SUPERSTITIONS
005:103 Who instituted (**superstitions** like those of) a
006:139 attribution (of **superstitions** to Allah), He will
SUPPLIANT
002:186 of every **suppliant** when he calleth on Me:
SUPPLICATION
023:064 behold, they will groan in **supplication**!
023:065 "Groan not in **supplication** this day; for ye
SUPPLIED
003:037 he found her **supplied** with sustenance.
016:112 abundantly **supplied** with sustenance from every
085:005 Fire **supplied** (abundantly) with Fuel:
SUPPLY
031:027 to its (**supply**), yet would not the Words of Allah
056:033 nor (**supply**) forbidden,
067:030 underground earth), who then can **supply** you with
107:007 But refuse (to **supply**) (even) neighborly needs.
SUPPORT
003:013 but Allah doth **support** with His aid
004:034 and because they **support** them from their means.

SUPPORT (continued)

005:097 a means of **support** for men, as also
011:080 myself to some powerful **support**."
017:088 each other with help and **support**.
024:004 (to **support** their allegation),-flog them
024:006 and have (in **support**) no evidence but their own,-
028:086 therefore lend not thou **support** in any way
060:009 and **support** (others) in driving you out,

SUPPORTER

002:255 the Self-subsisting, **Supported** of all
003:002 the **Supporter** of all.

SUPPORTS

039:033 and he who confirms (and **supports**) it-such are

SUPPRESS

011:080 to **suppress** you or that I could betake myself to

SUPREME

002:255 For He is the Most High, the **Supreme** (in glory).
004:013 and that will be the **Supreme** achievement.
006:018 Irresistibly **Supreme** over His servants. And
006:061 **Supreme** over His servants and He sets guardians
009:063 That is the **supreme** disgrace.
009:072 Pleasure of Allah: that is the **supreme** triumph.
009:089 that is the **supreme** felicity.
009:100 that is the **supreme** Triumph.
009:111 that is the achievement **supreme**.
009:129 He the Lord of the Throne **Supreme**!"
010:064 This is indeed the **supreme** Triumph.
012:039 or Allah the One, **Supreme** and Irresistible?
013:016 the **Supreme** and Irresistible."
027:026 Lord of the Throne **Supreme**!"
027:040 **Supreme** in Honour!"
036:081 He is the Creator **Supreme**, of skill
037:060 Verily this is the **supreme** Triumph!
038:065 the One, **Supreme** and Irresistible,-
044:057 That will be the **supreme** achievement!
056:046 And persisted obstinately in wickedness **supreme**!
056:074 Then glorify the name of the Lord, the **Supreme**!
056:096 So glorify the name of thy Lord, the **Supreme**.
061:012 that is indeed the **supreme** Triumph.
064:009 that will be the **Supreme** Triumph.

SUPPRESSED

012:084 and he was **suppressed** with silent sorrow.

SURA

002:023 then produce a **Sura** like thereunto;
009:064 The Hypocrites are afraid lest a **Sura** should be
009:086 When a **Sura** comes down, enjoining them to believe
009:124 Whenever there cometh down a **Sura**, some of
009:127 Whenever there cometh down a **Sura**, they look
010:038 Say: "Bring then a **Sura** like unto it, and call
024:001 A **Sura** which We have sent down and which
047:020 "Why is not a **Sura** sent down (for us)?"
047:020 (for us)?" But when a **Sura** of decisive meaning

SURAS

011:013 Say, "Bring ye then ten **Suras** forged, like unto

SURE

002:002 in it is guidance **sure**; without doubt,
002:038 and if, as is **sure**,
002:155 Be **sure** We shall test you with something
002:158 be **sure** that Allah is He
002:197 (be **sure**) Allah knoweth it.
002:270 be **sure** Allah knows it all.
003:140 be **sure** a similar wound hath touched the others.

SURE (continued)

004:073 they would be **sure** to say-as it there had never
004:100 his reward becomes due and **sure** with Allah:
005:027 Said the latter: "Be **sure** I will slay thee."
006:007 the Unbelievers would have been **sure** to say: "This
006:036 be **sure**, will accept: as to the dead, Allah
007:090 be **sure** then ye are ruined!"
007:124 "Be **sure** I will cut off your hands and your
008:040 be **sure** that Allah is your Protector-
010:004 The promise of Allah is true and **sure**. It is He
011:007 after death, the Unbelievers would be **sure** to say,
011:008 they are **sure** to say, "What keeps it back?" Ah!
011:010 touched him, he is **sure** to say, "All evil has
011:041 be **sure**, Oft-Forgiving, Most Merciful!"
011:107 for thy Lord is the (**sure**) Accomplisher
012:066 be **sure** to bring him back to me unless ye are
014:013 their messengers: "Be **sure** we shall drive you
018:023 "I shall be **sure** to do so and so to-morrow"
020:071 Be **sure** I will cut off your hands and feet
020:123 as is **sure**, there comes to you guidance from Me,
023:040 they are **sure** to be sorry!"
024:064 Be quite **sure** that to Allah doth belong
026:049 Be **sure** I will cut off your hands and your
026:061 "We are **sure** to be overtaken."
027:003 and also have **sure** faith in the Hereafter.
027:037 "Go back to them, and be **sure** we shall come
029:010 (to thee) from thy lord, they are **sure** to say,
030:058 the Unbelievers are **sure** to say, "Ye do
031:004 **sure** faith in the Hereafter.
034:011 for be **sure** I see (clearly) all that ye do."
039:038 they would be **sure** to say, "Allah." Say: "See
041:050 has touched him, he is **sure** to say, "This is
043:009 and the earth?' They would be **sure** to reply,
043:041 We shall be **sure** to exact retribution from them,
044:023 for ye are **sure** to be pursued.
054:055 In a **sure** abode with a Sovereign Omnipotent.
069:001 The **Sure** Reality!
069:002 What is the **Sure** Reality?
069:003 what the **Sure** Reality is?
104:004 By no means! He will be **sure** to be thrown

SURELY

002:064 ye had **surely** been among the lost.
002:143 most **surely** full of kindness, Most Merciful.
002:203 ye will **surely** be gathered unto Him.
003:049 **Surely** therein is a Sign for you if ye did believe.
004:082 they would **surely** have found therein
004:149 **surely** Allah is ever pardoning Powerful.
005:027 "**Surely**," said the former, "Allah doth accept
006:062 **surely** His is the Command, and He
006:077 I shall **surely** be among those who go astray."
007:123 **Surely** this is a trick which ye have planned
007:138 He said: "**Surely** ye are a people without knowledge."
008:043 ye would **surely** have been discouraged, and ye
008:043 and ye would **surely** have disputed
010:081 is sorcery: Allah will **surely** make it of no effect:
011:045 "O my Lord! **surely** my son is of my family and Thy
012:037 I will **surely** reveal to you the truth and meaning
012:053 do bestow His Mercy: but **surely** certainly my Lord is
015:085 And the Hour is **surely** coming (when this
017:036 thou hast no knowledge; for **surely** the hearing,
017:062 I will **surely** bring his descendants under my sway-
018:021 "Let us **surely** build a place of worship over them."
018:036 I shall **surely** find (there) something better

SURELY (continued)

018:058 have earned, then **surely** He would have hastened
018:077 **surely** thou couldst have exacted some
020:058 "But we can **surely** produce magic to match thine!
020:071 **Surely** this must be your leader. Who has
021:017 a pastime, We should **surely** have taken it from
021:064 and said, "**Surely** ye are the ones in the wrong."
021:098 To it will ye (**surely**) come!
022:040 there would **surely** have been pulled down
026:049 **Surely** he is your leader, who has
026:052 for **surely** ye shall be pursued."
026:055 "And they have **surely** enraged us;
029:005 is **surely** coming: and He
033:015 must (**surely**) be answered for.
034:003 say, "Nay! but most **surely**, by my Lord, it will
036:066 We could **surely** have blotted out their eyes;
037:099 He will **surely** guide me!
037:173 And that Our forces,-they **surely** must conquer.
039:065 and thou wilt **surely** be among the losers.
040:037 but **surely**, I think (Moses) is a liar!"
040:060 to serve Me will **surely** enter Hell abased."
041:039 can **surely** give life to (men) who are dead.
041:043 **surely** thy Lord has at His command (all) Forgiveness
043:014 "And to Our Lord, **surely**, Must We turn back!"
047:030 by their marks: but **surely** thou wilt know them
051:006 will **surely** come to pass.
056:052 "Ye will **surely** taste of the Tree of Zaqqum.
063:008 **surely** the more honourable (element) will expel
063:009 If any act thus, **surely** they are the losers.
064:007 ye shall **surely** be raised up: then shall
065:003 for him. For Allah will **surely** accomplish His
068:004 And **surely** thou hast sublime morals.
068:026 they said: "We have **surely** lost our way:
068:051 **Surely** he is possessed!"
074:054 Nay, this **surely** is an admonition:
083:007 Nay! **Surely** the Record of the Wicked is (preserved)
084:019 Ye shall **surely** travel from stage to stage.
086:008 **Surely** (Allah) able to bring him back (to life)!

SURETY

002:012 Of a **surety**, they are the ones
002:013 Nay of a **surety** they are the fools
002:024 But if ye cannot-and of a **surety** ye cannot
004:087 of a **surety** He will gather you together
004:119 hath of a **surety** suffered a loss that is manifest.
004:157 for of a **surety** they killed him not:
011:111 And, of a **surety**, to all will your Lord
012:015 (this Message): 'Of a **surety** thou shall (one day)
015:092 of a **surety**, call them to account,
016:091 indeed ye have made Allah your **surety**; for Allah
024:055 that He will, of a **surety**, grant them
029:054 the Punishment: but, of a **surety**, Hell will
068:040 will stand **surety** of that!

SURFACE

013:017 the **surface**. Even so, from that (ore) which
014:026 from the **surface** of the earth: it has

SURGE

018:099 to **surge** like waves on one another: the trumpet

SURRENDER

016:081 on you, that ye may **surrender** to His Will

SURROUNDED

018:032 grape-vines and **surrounded** the with date-palms;

SURROUNDING

039:075 **surrounding** the Throne (Divine) on all sides,

SURROUNDS

009:049 Hell **surrounds** the Unbelievers (on all sides).

SURVIVING

069:008 Then seest thou any of them left **surviving**?

SUSPENSE

007:111 in **suspense** (for a while); and send
009:106 There are (yet) others, held in **suspense** for the
026:036 in **suspense** (for a while), and dispatch

SUSPICION

009:110 is never free from **suspicion** and shakiness
049:012 for **suspicion** in some cases is a sin: and spy
049:012 O ye who believe! avoid **suspicion** as much

SUSPICIONS

003:154 **suspicions** due to Ignorance.
003:154 moved by wrong **suspicions** of Allah-**suspicions**
050:025 cast doubts and **suspicions**;

SUSPICIOUS

011:062 **suspicious** (disquieting) doubt as to that
011:110 is **suspicious** doubt concerning it.
014:009 in **suspicious** (disquieting) doubt as to that
034:054 in **suspicious** (disquieting) doubt.
041:045 but they remained in **suspicious** disquieting doubt
042:014 are in **suspicious** (disquieting) doubt concerning it.

SUSTAIN

035:041 one-can **sustain** them thereafter: verily He

SUSTAINER

001:002 the Cherisher and **Sustainer** of the Worlds:
005:114 for thou art the best **Sustainer** (of our needs)."
007:054 the Cherisher and **Sustainer** of the Worlds!
010:010 the Cherisher and **Sustainer** of the Worlds!"
013:016 Say: "Who is the Lord and **Sustainer** of the
020:111 The **Sustainer**, helpless indeed will be the man

SUSTAINS

007:172 (who cherishes and **sustains** you)?"-They said:
010:031 Say: "Who is it that **sustains** you (in life)
035:041 It is Allah Who **sustains** the heavens and the

SUSTENANCE

002:022 fruits for your **sustenance**;
002:060 the **sustenance** provided by Allah,
003:027 and Thou givest **sustenance** to whom Thou pleasest,
003:037 he found her supplied with **sustenance**.
003:037 for Allah provides **sustenance** to whom He pleases,
003:169 finding their **sustenance** from their Lord.
004:039 what Allah hath given them for **sustenance**?
005:114 and provide for our **sustenance**, for thou
006:151 We provide **sustenance** for and for them;-come
007:032 (which He hath provided) for **sustenance**? Say:
007:050 that Allah doth provide for your **sustenance**." They
008:003 We have given them for **sustenance**:
008:004 and generous **sustenance**:
008:026 and gave you good things for **sustenance**: that ye
010:059 sent down to you for **sustenance**? Yet ye
010:093 and provided for them **sustenance** of the best:
011:006 but its **sustenance** dependeth on Allah: He knoweth
011:088 and He hath given me **sustenance** (pure and)
013:022 We have bestowed for their **sustenance**, secretly
013:026 by (strict) measure, the **Sustenance** (which He
014:031 the **Sustenance** We have given them, secretly and
015:020 for whose **sustenance** ye are not responsible.
016:056 We have bestowed for their **sustenance**! By Allah,

SUSTENANCE (continued)

016:071 of **sustenance** more freely on some of you than
016:072 you **sustenance** of the best: will they
016:073 providing them, for **sustenance**, with anything
016:112 abundantly supplied with **sustenance** from every
016:114 So eat of the **sustenance** which Allah
017:030 **sustenance** in abundance for whom He pleaseth,
017:031 of want: We shall provide, **sustenance** for them
017:070 and sea; given them for **sustenance** things good
019:062 their **sustenance**, morning and evening.
020:081 We have provided for your **sustenance**, but commit
020:132 We ask thee not to provide **sustenance**: We provide
022:034 of Allah over the **sustenance** He gave them
022:050 is forgiveness and a **sustenance** most generous.
023:072 He is the Best of those who give **sustenance**.
027:064 you **sustenance** from heaven and earth? (Can there
029:017 have no power to give you **sustenance**: then seek
029:017 then seek ye **sustenance** from Allah, serve Him,
029:060 that carry not their own **sustenance**? It is
029:062 Allah enlarges the **sustenance** (which He
030:040 your **sustenance**; then He will cause you to die;
032:016 (in charity) out of the **sustenance** which We have
033:031 for her a generous **Sustenance**.
034:004 and a **Sustenance** Most Generous."
034:015 "Eat of the **Sustenance** (provided) by your Lord,
034:024 Say: "Who gives you **sustenance**, from the
034:039 for He is the Best of those Who grant **Sustenance**.
034:039 and restricts the **Sustenance** to such of His
035:003 you **Sustenance** from heaven or earth? There is
037:041 For them is a **Sustenance** determined,
040:013 and sendeth down **sustenance** for you from the sky:
040:064 and has provided for you **Sustenance**, of things
041:010 its **sustenance** in four Days, alike for
042:012 and restricts the **Sustenance** to whom He will:
042:019 He gives **Sustenance** to whom He pleases: and He
042:038 of what We bestow on them for **Sustenance**;
045:005 down **Sustenance** from the shy, and revives
045:016 for **Sustenance** things good and pure; and We
050:011 As **sustenance** for (Allah's) Servants; and We
051:022 And in heaven is your **Sustenance**, as (also)
051:057 No **sustenance** do I require of them, nor do
051:058 For Allah is He Who gives (all) **Sustenance**,-
067:015 its tracts and enjoy of the **Sustenance** which He
067:021 provide you with **Sustenance** if He were to

SUWA

071:023 Wadd nor **Suwa**, neither Yaguth nor Yauq, nor Nasr';-

SWALLOW

002:174 they **swallow** into themselves naught but Fire;
011:044 **swallow** up thy water, and O sky! withhold (thy
016:045 will not cause the earth to **swallow** them up,
020:069 right hand: quickly will it **swallow** up that which
028:081 Then We caused the earth to **swallow** up him
028:082 He could have caused the earth to **swallow** us up!
029:040 some We caused the earth to **swallow** up; and some
034:009 We could cause the earth to **swallow** them up,
037:142 Then the big Fish did **swallow** him, and he

SWALLOWED

017:068 not cause you to be **swallowed** up beneath the
067:016 to be **swallowed** up by the earth when it shales

SWALLOWING

014:017 **swallowing** it down his throat; death will come

SWALLOWS

007:117 and behold! it **swallows** up all the
026:045 when behold, it straightway **swallows** up all the

SWARM

021:096 and they swiftly **swarm** from every hill.

SWARTHY

087:005 And then doth make it (but) **swarthy** stubble.

SWAY

017:062 under my **sway**-all but a few!"

SWAYED

004:128 even though men's souls are **swayed** by greed.
006:035 who are **swayed** by ignorance (and impatience)!

SWEAR

005:106 and let them both **swear** by Allah: "We will not
005:107 let them **swear** by Allah: "We affirm that
006:109 They **swear** their strongest oaths by Allah, that
009:042 They would indeed **swear** by Allah, "If we only
009:056 They **swear** by Allah that they are indeed of you;
009:062 To you they **swear** by Allah. In order
009:074 They **swear** by Allah that they said nothing (evil),
009:095 They will **swear** to you by Allah, when ye
009:096 They will **swear** unto you, that ye
009:107 They will indeed **swear** that their intention
012:066 with you until ye **swear** a solemn oath to me,
014:044 to **swear** aforetime that ye suffer no decline?
016:038 They **swear** their strongest oaths by Allah,
024:053 They **swear** their strongest oaths by Allah that,
024:053 Say: "**Swear** ye not; obedience is
027:049 They said: "**Swear** a mutual oath by Allah that we
030:055 **swear** that they tarried not but an hour:
056:075 Furthermore I **swear** by the setting of the Stars,-
058:014 and they **swear** to falsehood knowingly.
058:018 then will they **swear** to Him as they **swear** to you:
058:018 **swear** to you: and they think that they have
075:001 I do **swear** by the Resurrection Day;
075:002 And I do **swear** by the self-reproaching soul.
090:001 Nay I do **swear** by this City;-

SWEARER

068:010 Obey not every mean,-**swearer**,

SWEARING

004:062 Then they come to thee, **swearing** by Allah: "We

SWEET

025:053 one palatable and **sweet**, and the
035:012 the one palatable, **sweet**, and pleasant to drink,
077:027 and provided for you water **sweet** (and wholesome)?

SWEET-SMELLING

055:012 for fodder, and **sweet-smelling** plants.

SWELL

031:018 "And **swell** not thy cheek (for pride) at men.
052:006 And by the Ocean filled with **Swell**;-
081:006 When the oceans boil over with a **swell**;

SWELLS

022:005 (to life), it **swells**, and it puts forth every

SWEPT

068:019 (which **swept** away) all around, while they

SWERVE

004:135 lest ye **swerve**, and if ye distort (Justice) or
005:008 to you make you **swerve** to wrong and depart form
027:060 Nay, they are a people who **swerve** from justice.
072:014 that **swerve** from justice. Now those
072:015 'But those who **swerve**,-they are

SWERVED
009:117 of them had nearly **swerved** (from duty), but He
033:010 and behold, the eyes **swerved** and the hearts
053:017 (His) sight never **swerved**, nor did it go wrong!

SWIFT
003:019 Allah is **swift** in calling to account.
003:199 and Allah is **swift** in account.
005:004 and fear Allah; for Allah is **swift** in taking account.
011:064 or a **swift** Punishment will seize you!
013:041 and He is **swift** in calling to account.
014:051 and verily Allah is **Swift** in calling account.
024:039 and Allah is **swift** in taking account.
038:031 highest breeding; and **swift** of foot;
040:017 for Allah is **Swift** in taking account.

SWIFTER
010:021 Say: "**Swifter** to plan is Allah! Verily, Our

SWIFTEST
006:062 and He is the **Swiftest** in taking account.

SWIFTLY
003:144 will **swiftly** reward those who (serve him)
003:145 And **swiftly** shall We reward those that
021:096 and they **swiftly** swarm from every hill.
077:033 yellow camels (marching **swiftly**)."

SWIM
021:033 All (the celestial bodies) **swim** along, each in

SWIMS
036:040 each (just) **swims** along in (its own) orbit

SWINE
002:173 and blood, and the flesh of **swine**,
005:003 dead meat, blood, the flesh of **swine**, and that
005:060 He transformed into apes and **swine**, those who
006:145 or the flesh of **swine**,-for it is
016:115 and blood, and the flesh of **swine**, and any

SWOON
007:143 He made it as dust and Moses fell down in a **swoon**.
039:068 and on earth will **swoon**, except such
047:020 of one in **swoon** at the approach of death.

SWOOPED
022:031 or the wind had **swooped** (like a bird on its prey)

SWORD
054:029 and he took a **sword** in hand, and hamstrung (her).

SWORE
005:053 who **swore** their strongest oaths by Allah, that
007:021 And he **swore** to them both, that he
007:049 the men whom you **swore** that Allah with
035:042 They **swore** their strongest oaths by Allah
048:018 The Believers when they **swore** Fealty to thee

SWORN
005:089 That is the expiation for the oaths ye have **sworn**.
012:066 they had **sworn** their solemn oath, he said:

SYMBOL
002:248 **Symbol** for you if ye indeed have faith."

SYMBOLS
002:158 are among the **Symbols** of Allah.
006:046 by various (**symbols**): Yet they turn aside.
007:058 by various (**symbols**) to those who are grateful.

SYNAGOGUES
022:040 churches, **synagogues**, and mosques, in which

T

TA
020:001 **Ta-Ha**.
026:001 **Ta** Sin Mim.
027:001 **Ta**. Sin.
028:001 **Ta**. Sin. Mim.

TABLE
005:112 a **Table** set (with viands) from heaven?" Said
005:114 a **table** set (with viands), that there may

TABLET
085:022 (Inscribed) in a **Tablet** Preserved!

TABLETS
007:145 in the **Tablets** in all matters, Admonition
007:150 He put down the **Tablets**, seized his brother
007:154 he took up the **tablets**: in the writing

TABUK
009:081 (in the **Tabuk** expedition) rejoiced in their

TAGHUT
039:017 Those who eschew **Taghut** and fall not into

TAGUT
002:256 whoever rejects **Tagut** and believes in Allah
002:257 the patrons are the **Tagut** from light
004:051 They believe in sorcery and **Tagut** and say to the
004:060 To the Evil (**Tagut**), though they were ordered
004:076 fight in the cause of Evil (**Tagut**): so fight
005:060 those who worshipped Evil (**Tagut**)-these are

TAINTED
002:283 his heart is **tainted** with sin.

TAKE
002:020 He could **take** away their faculty
002:125 and **take** ye the Station of Abraham
002:165 Yet there are men who **take** (for worship)
002:197 And **take** a provision (with you) for the journey,
002:226 For those who **take** an oath for abstention
002:228 better right to **take** them back in that period,
002:229 to **take** back any of your gifts from (your wives),
002:231 either **take** them back on equitable terms
002:231 or to **take** undue advantage;
002:231 but do not **take** them back to injure them,
002:235 and **take** heed of Him;
002:259 Or (**take**) the similitude of one
002:260 He said: "**Take** four birds;
002:279 If ye do it not, **take** notice of war
002:282 But **take** witnesses whenever ye make
003:028 **take** for friends or helpers Unbelievers rather
003:055 "O Jesus! I will **take** thee and raise thee to Myself
003:080 to **take** angels and prophets for Lords and Patrons.
003:081 and **take** My covenant as binding on you?"
003:118 O ye who believe! **take** not into your intimacy
003:140 and that He may **take** to Himself from your ranks
003:193 and **take** to Thyself our souls in the company
004:005 **take** it and enjoy it with right good cheer.
004:006 **take** witnesses in their presence:
004:015 **take** the evidence of four (reliable) witnesses
004:019 that ye may **take** away part of the dower

TAKE (continued)
004:019 and equity if ye **take** a dislike to them it may
004:020 **take** not the least bit of it back:
004:020 But if ye decide to **take** one wife
004:020 would ye **take** it by slander and a manifest sin?
004:021 And how could ye **take** it when ye
004:038 if any **take** the Satan for their intimate, what
004:043 then **take** for yourselves clean sand (or earth),
004:071 O ye who believe! **take** your precautions.
004:089 **take** no friends or helpers from their ranks:
004:089 so **take** not friends from their ranks until
004:097 When angels **take** the souls of those who die
004:102 let them **take** their positions in the rear.
004:102 but **take** (every) precaution for yourselves.
004:118 "I will **take** of Thy servants a portion marked off:
004:125 For Allah did **take** Abraham for a friend.
004:139 Those who **take** for friends Unbelievers rather
004:144 O ye who believe! **take** not for friends
004:150 and wish to **take** a course midway,
005:006 then **take** for yourselves clean sand or earth, and
005:012 Allah did aforetime **take** a Covenant from
005:014 We did **take** a Covenant, but they forgot a good
005:041 they say, "If ye are given this, **take** it, but if
005:051 O ye who believe! **take** not the Jews and the
005:057 **take** not for friends and protectors those who
005:057 those who **take** your religion for a mockery
005:058 they **take** it (but) as mockery and sport; that is
005:106 (**take**) witnesses among yourselves when making
005:106 "We will not **take** for it a price even though
005:116 say unto men, "**Take** me and my mother for two
005:117 when Thou didst **take** me up, thou wast
006:014 Say: "Shall I **take** for my protector any other
006:060 It is He Who doth **take** your souls by night, and
006:061 Our angels **take** his soul, and they never
006:070 Leave alone those who **take** their religion
006:128 much (toll) did ye **take** of men." Their friends
006:143 (**Take**) eight (head of cattle) in (four) pairs: of
006:151 whether open or secret; **take** not life, which
007:037 arrive and **take** their souls, they say:
007:126 and **take** our souls unto Thee as Muslims
007:136 and failed to **take** warning from them.
007:144 **take** then the (revelation) which I give thee, and
007:145 (and said): "**Take** and hold these with firmness,
007:146 and failed to **take** warning from them.
008:050 when the angels **take** the souls of the
009:016 and **take** none for friends and protectors
009:023 O ye who believe! **Take** not for protectors
009:031 beside Allah. And (they **take** as their Lord)
009:031 They **take** their priests and their anchorites
009:103 Of their goods **take** alms, that so
009:126 and they **take** no heed.
010:021 touched them, behold! they **take** to plotting
010:046 We promise them,-or We **take** thy soul (before that),-
010:104 But I worship Allah-who will **take** your souls
011:024 Will ye not them **take** heed?
011:030 them away? Will ye not then **take** heed?
011:043 The son replied: "I will be **take** myself to some
012:012 and we shall **take** every care of him."
012:013 that ye should **take** him away: I fear
012:015 So they did **take** him away, and they
012:054 I will **take** him specially to serve about
012:056 to **take** possession therein as, when, or
012:063 (unless we **take** our brother): so send our

TAKE (continued)

012:063	and we will indeed **take** every care of him."
012:064	But Allah is the best to **take** care (of him),
012:065	**take** care of our brother; and add
012:076	He could not **take** his brother by the law
012:078	so **take** one of us in his place: for we
012:079	He said: "Allah forbid that we **take** other than
012:080	"Know ye not that your father did **take** an oath
012:101	**Take** Thou my soul (at death) as one submitting
013:016	Say: "Do ye then **take** (for worship) protectors
013:040	We promised them or **take** to Us thy soul (before
014:052	let men of understanding **take** heed.
014:052	that they may **take** warning therefrom, and may
016:028	**take** in a state of wrong-doing to their own
016:032	**take** in a state of purity, saying (to them),
016:051	Allah has said: "**Take** not (for worship) two gods:
016:094	And **take** not your oaths, to practice
016:100	who **take** him as patron and who join
016:108	and they **take** no heed.
017:001	Glory to (Allah) Who did **take** His Servant
017:002	"**Take** not other than Me as Disposer
017:022	**Take** not with Allah another god; or thou
017:033	Nor **take** life-which Allah has made sacred-
017:039	has revealed to thee. **Take** not, with Allah,
017:057	is something to **take** heed of.
017:086	We could **take** away that which We have sent thee
018:050	Will ye then **take** him and his progeny
018:051	own creation: nor is it for Me to **take** as helpers
018:102	can **take** my servants as protectors besides Me?
019:012	"O Yahya! **take** hold of the Book with might":
019:094	He does **take** and account of them (all), and hath
020:044	perchance he may **take** warning or fear (Allah)."
021:017	If it had been Our wish to **take** (just) a pastime,
021:047	and enough are We to **take** account.
023:027	**take** thou on board pairs of every species,
025:018	should **take** for protectors others besides Thee:
025:057	may **take** a (straight) Path to his Lord."
026:227	know what vicissitudes their affairs will **take**!
027:011	to **take** the place of evil, truly, I am
027:012	(thou wilt **take**) to Pharaoh and his people:
028:012	and **take** care of him."
028:023	until the shepherds **take** back (their flocks):
029:041	**take** protectors other than Allah is that
030:023	that ye **take** by night and by day, and the
032:011	of you, will (duly) **take** your souls: then shall
033:026	who aided them-Allah did **take** them down from
036:023	"Shall I **take** (other) gods besides Him?
036:074	Yet they **take** (for worship) gods other than Allah,
038:044	"And **take** in thy hand a little grass, and strike
039:003	is due? But those who **take** for protectors
039:004	Had Allah wished to **take** to Himself a son,
039:043	What! Do they **take** for intercessors others
040:047	can ye then **take** (on yourselves) from us
040:077	or We **take** thy soul (to Our Mercy) (before that),
041:006	so **take** the straight path unto Him and ask for
042:006	And those who **take** as protectors others besides
043:005	Shall We then **take** away the Reminder from you
043:041	Even if We **take** thee away, We shall
045:035	"This, because ye used to **take** the Signs
047:027	**take** their souls at death, and smite
056:062	why then do ye not **take** heed?
059:002	of the Believers. **Take** warning, then, O ye
059:007	among you. So **take** what the Messenger gives you,

TAKE (continued)

060:001	O ye who believe! **take** not My enemies and yours
060:012	to thee to **take** the oath of fealty to thee,
065:002	term appointed, either **take** them back on equitable
065:002	on equitable terms; and **take** for witness
065:006	and **take** mutual counsel together, according to
073:009	**take** Him therefore for (thy) Disposer of Affairs.
073:019	Therefore, whoso will, let him **take** a (straight)
076:029	let him **take** a (straight) Path to his Lord.
078:039	whoso will, let him **take** a (straight) Return
092:012	Verily We **take** upon Us to guide,

TAKEN

002:048	nor shall compensation be **taken** from her.
002:080	Say: "Have ye **taken** a promise from Allah,
003:159	Then, when thou hast **taken** a decision,
004:021	and they have **taken** from you a solemn covenant?
004:025	when they are **taken** in wedlock,
005:081	never would they have **taken** them for friends
005:108	that other oaths would be **taken** after their oaths.
006:107	they would not have **taken** false gods: but We
007:025	but from it shall ye be **taken** out (at last)."
007:169	of the Book **taken** from them, that they
008:001	(things **taken** as) spoils of war. Say: "(Such)
008:070	than what has been **taken** from you, and He
017:040	preferred for you sons, and **taken** for Himself
018:015	"These our people have **taken** for worship
019:078	or has he **taken** a promise with the Most Gracious?
019:081	And they have **taken** (for worship) gods other
020:039	and he will be **taken** up by one who is an enemy
020:115	**taken** the covenant of Adam, but he forgot: and We
021:017	a pastime, We should surely have **taken** it from
021:021	Or have they **taken** (for worship) gods from
021:024	Or have they **taken** for worship (other) gods
021:026	**taken** a son." Glory to Him! They are
023:091	each god would have **taken** away what he had created,
025:003	Yet have they **taken**, besides Him, gods that
025:027	"Oh! would that I had **taken** a (straight) path
025:028	never **taken** such a one for a friend!
029:025	And He said: "For you, ye have **taken** (for worship)
033:053	and when ye have **taken** your meal, disperse,
036:012	We **taken** account. In a clear Book (of evidence).
042:009	What! Have they **taken** (for worship)
043:016	What! Has He **taken** Daughters out of what He
044:027	they had **taken** such delight!
045:010	have **taken** to themselves besides Allah: for them
045:035	therefore, they shall not be **taken** out thence,
057:008	indeed **taken** your Convenant, if ye
059:006	(and **taken** away) from them-for this
059:007	(and **taken** away) from the people of the townships,-
072:003	He has **taken** neither a wife nor a son.
084:008	Soon will his account be **taken** by an easy reckoning,

TAKES

002:138	(Our religion) **takes** its hue from Allah
004:086	Allah **takes** careful account of all things.
004:119	Whoever, forsaking Allah, **takes** Satan for a friend,
004:176	her brother **takes** her inheritance: if there
016:070	and **takes** your souls at death; and of you
018:049	or great, but **takes** account thereof! They will
039:009	(in adoration), who **takes** heed of the Hereafter,
039:042	and those that die not (He **takes**) during their
039:042	It is Allah that **takes** the souls (of men)
045:009	of Our Signs, he **takes** them in jest: for such
045:023	Then seest thou such a one as **takes** as his god

TAKES (continued)
050:004 the earth **takes** away: with Us
072:028 and **takes** account of every single thing."

TAKEST
006:074 "**Takest** thou idols for gods? For I see
026:029 (Pharaoh) said: "If thou **takest** any god other

TAKETH
009:116 He giveth life and He **taketh** it. Except for
010:056 Is it He who giveth life and who **taketh** it, and to
025:043 Seest thou such a one as **taketh** for his god

TAKING
004:006 but all-sufficient is Allah in **taking** account.
004:025 nor **taking** adulterous: when they
004:102 **taking** all precautions, and bearing arms: the
004:102 **Taking** their arms with them:
005:004 and fear Allah; for Allah is swift in **taking** account.
005:005 **Taking** them as lovers.
006:062 and He is the Swiftest in **taking** account.
017:033 in the matter of **taking** life: for he
024:039 and Allah is swift in **taking** account.
028:020 are **taking** counsel together about thee, to slay
040:017 for Allah is Swift in **taking** account.
051:016 **Taking** joy in the things which their

TALE
012:018 made up a **tale** (that may pass) with you, (for me)
012:026 her **tale** true, and he is a liar!
012:111 a **tale** invented, but a confirmation of what
023:044 (in punishment): We made them as a **tale** (that is
034:019 At length We made then as a **tale** (that is told),
038:007 this is nothing but a made-up **tale**!
069:012 hear the **tale** and) retain its memory should bear

TALES
006:025 "These are nothing but **tales** of the ancients."
008:031 but **tales** of the ancients."
016:024 has revealed?" they say, "**Tales** of the ancients!"
023:083 They are nothing but **tales** of the ancients!"
025:005 And they say: "**Tales** of the ancients, which he
027:068 these are nothing but **tales** of the ancients."
031:006 those who purchase idle **tales**, without knowledge
046:017 "This is nothing but **tales** of the ancients!"
068:015 "**Tales** of the Ancients," he cries!
083:013 he says, "**Tales** of the Ancients!"

TALH
056:029 Among **Talh** trees with flowers (or fruits)

TALK
009:069 in idle **talk** as they did. They!-their works
012:031 When she heard of their malicious **talk**, she sent
019:026 into no **talk** with any human being.'"
019:029 They said: "How can we **talk** to one who is
020:062 over their affair, but they kept their **talk** secret.
021:060 **talk** of them: he is called Abraham."
021:063 Ask them, if they can **talk**."
023:003 Who avoid vain **talk**;
028:055 And when they hear vain **talk**, they turn
030:058 "Ye do nothing but **talk** vanities."
033:053 familiar **talk**. Such (behavior) annoys the Prophet
041:026 this Qur'an, but **talk** at random in the midst
046:008 whereof ye **talk** (so glibly)! Enough is He
049:002 in **talk**, as ye may speak aloud to one another,
070:042 So leave them to plunge in vain **talk** and play
074:045 "But we used to **talk** vanities with vain talkers;

TALKED
006:022 whom ye (invented and) **talked** about?"

TALKERS
029:048 indeed, would the **talkers** of vanities have doubt.
074:045 "But we used to talk vanities with vain **talkers**;

TALKING
009:065 "We were only **talking** idly and in play." Say:
023:067 "In arrogance: **talking** nonsense about the (Qur'an),

TALKS
004:114 In most of their secret **talks** there is no good:
019:080 To Us shall return all that he **talks** of, and he
021:036 "The one who **talks** of your gods?" And they

TALL
007:069 **tall** among the nations. Call in remembrance
042:032 (**tall**) as mountains.
050:010 And **tall** (and stately) palm-trees, with shoots

TALUT
002:247 "Allah hath appointed **Talut** as king over you."
002:249 When **Talut** set forth with the armies,

TAMARISKS
034:016 bitter fruit, and **tamarisks**, and some few

TAMELY
021:081 (**tamely**) for Solomon, to his order, to the

TARRIED
002:259 hast **tarried** thus a hundred years:
010:016 I **tarried** amongst you: will ye not then understand?"
010:045 had **tarried** but an hour of a day: they will
017:052 ye **tarried** but a little while!"
018:012 at calculating the term of years they had **tarried**!
020:103 each other: "Ye **tarried** not longer than ten (days);"
020:104 will say: "Ye **tarried** not longer than a day!"
027:022 But the Hoopoe **tarried** not far: he (came
029:014 and he **tarried** among them a thousand years
030:055 swear that they **tarried** not but an hour:
034:014 they would not have **tarried** in the humiliating
046:035 **tarried** more than an hour in a single day.
079:046 (it will be) as if they had **tarried** but a single

TARRY
002:259 He said: "How long didst thou **tarry** (thus)?"
004:072 men who would **tarry** behind: if a
020:010 "**Tarry** ye; I perceive a fire; perhaps I can
020:040 Then didst thou **tarry** a number of years with the
028:029 "**Tarry** ye; I perceive a fire; I hope
030:056 "Indeed ye did **tarry**, within Allah's Decree,

TASK
011:088 (in my **task**) can only come from Allah. In Him I
018:088 a goodly reward, and easy will be his **task** as We
020:026 "Ease my **task** for me;
020:032 "And make him share my **task**:
034:014 in the humiliating Chastisement (of their **Task**).
094:007 (from thine immediate **task**), still labor hard,

TASKS
002:049 they set you hard **tasks** and chastisement,
014:006 hard **tasks** and punishments, slaughtered your

TASNIM
083:027 With it will be (given) a mixture of **Tasnim**:

TASTE
002:249 only those who **taste** not of it go with me;
003:106 **Taste** then the Chastisement for rejecting Faith.
003:181 "**Taste** ye the Chastisement of the scorching Fire!
003:185 Every soul shall have a **taste** of death:
004:056 that they may **taste** the Chastisement:

TASTE (continued)

005:095 that he may **taste** of the penalty of his deed.
006:030 He will say: "**Taste** ye then the Chastisement,
006:065 giving you a **taste** of mutual vengeance-
007:039 so **taste** ye of the Chastisement
008:014 "**Taste** ye then of the (punishment): for those
008:035 "**Taste** ye the Chastisement because ye blasphemed."
008:050 "**Taste** the chastisement of the blazing Fire-
009:035 **taste** ye, then, the (treasures) ye hoarded!"
010:021 When We make mankind **taste** of some mercy
010:052 the wrong-doers: '**Taste** ye the enduring punishment!
010:070 Then shall We make them **taste** the severest
011:009 If We give man a **taste** of mercy from Ourselves,
011:010 But if We give him a **taste** of (Our) favours
016:094 and ye may have to **taste** the evil (consequences)
016:112 so Allah made it **taste** of hunger and terror
017:075 thee **taste** double portion (of punishment)
021:035 Every soul shall have a **taste** of death: and We
022:009 make him **taste** the chastisement of burning (Fire).
022:022 "**Taste** ye the Chastisement of Burning!"
022:025 We cause to **taste** of a most grievous chastisement.
025:019 him shall We cause to **taste** of a
029:055 "**Taste** ye (the fruits) of your deeds!"
029:057 Every soul shall have a **taste** of death: in the
030:033 but when He gives them a **taste** of Mercy
030:036 When We give men a **taste** of Mercy, they exult
030:041 that (Allah) may give them a **taste** of some
030:046 giving you a **taste** of His Mercy,-that the
032:014 "**Taste** ye then-for ye forgot the Meeting of this
032:014 **taste** ye the Chastisement of Eternity for your
032:020 to them: "**Taste** ye the Chastisement of the Fire,
032:021 And indeed We will make them **taste** of the
034:012 from Our command, We made him **taste** of the
034:042 "**Taste** ye the Chastisement of the Fire,-the which
035:037 So **taste** ye (the fruit of your deeds): for the
037:031 **taste** (the punishment of our sins):
037:038 Ye shall indeed **taste** of the Grievous Chastisement;-
037:046 Crystal-white, of a **taste** delicious to those
038:057 Yea, such!-Then shall they **taste** it,-a boiling
039:024 "**Taste** ye (the fruits of) what ye earned!"
039:026 So Allah gave them a **taste** of humiliation
041:016 that We might give them a **taste** of a Chastisement
041:027 a **taste** of a severe Chastisement,
041:050 the **taste** of a severe Chastisement.
041:050 When We give him a **taste** of some mercy from Us,
042:048 And truly, when We give man a **taste** of Mercy
044:049 "**Taste** thou (this)! Truly thou
044:056 Nor will they there **taste** Death, except the
046:034 "Then **taste** ye the Chastisement, for that
047:015 rivers of milk of which the **taste** never changes;
051:014 "**Taste** ye your trial! this is what
054:037 (They heard): "Now **taste** ye My Wrath
054:039 "So **taste** ye My Chastisement and My Warning."
054:048 (they will hear): "**Taste** ye the touch of Hell!"
056:052 "Ye will surely **taste** of the Tree of Zaqqum.
065:009 Then did they **taste** the evil result of their
078:024 **taste** therein, nor any drink,
078:030 "So **taste** ye (the fruits of your deeds); for no

TASTED

006:148 until they **tasted** of Our wrath. Say:
007:022 when they **tasted** of the tree, their shameful
038:008 Nay, they have not yet **tasted** My Punishment!
059:015 they have **tasted** the evil result of their conduct;

TASTED (continued)

064:005 So they **tasted** the evil result of their conduct;

TAUGHT

002:031 And He **taught** Adam the names of all things;
002:032 save what Thou hast **taught** Us:
002:102 **taught** anyone (such things without saying:
002:239 in the manner He has **taught** you,
002:251 and **taught** him whatever (else) He willed.
002:282 as Allah has **taught** him, so let him write.
003:079 for ye have **taught** the Book and ye have
004:113 **taught** thee what thou knewest not (before):
005:004 and what ye have **taught** the beasts
005:110 Behold! I **taught** thee the Book and Wisdom, the
006:091 therein were ye **taught** that which ye knew
006:106 Follow what thou art **taught** by inspiration
012:037 which my Lord hath **taught** me I have (I assure
012:101 and **taught** me something of the interpretation
016:068 And thy Lord **taught** the Bee to build
018:065 **taught** knowledge form Our own presence.
018:066 which thou hast been **taught**?"
020:071 who has **taught** you magic! Be sure
021:080 It was We Who **taught** him the making of
026:049 who has **taught** you sorcery! But soon
027:016 been **taught** the speech of Birds, and we
053:005 He was **taught** by one Mighty in Power,
055:002 It is He Who has **taught** the Qur'an.
055:004 He has **taught** him an intelligent speech.
096:004 He Who **taught** (the use of) the Pen,-
096:005 **Taught** man that which he knew not.

TAUNT

003:181 Allah hath heard the **taunt** of those who say:

TAURAT

007:157 in the **Taurat** and the Gospel; for he
048:029 This is their similitude in the **Taurat**; and their
061:006 to you confirming the **Taurat** (which came)
062:005 of) **Taurat**, but who subsequently failed in those

TEACH

003:021 and slay those who **teach** just dealing with mankind,
003:048 "And Allah will **teach** him the Book and Wisdom,
003:153 to **teach** you not to grieve for (the booty)
004:069 of the Prophets (who **teach**), the Sincere
012:006 and **teach** thee the interpretation of stories
012:021 that We might **teach** him the interpretation
014:004 We sent not a messenger except (to **teach**) in the
018:027 And recite (and **teach**) what has been revealed
018:066 on the footing that thou **teach** me something
025:039 To **teach** one We set forth parables and examples;
032:026 Does it not **teach** them a lesson, how many
087:006 By degrees shall We **teach** thee (the Message),

TEACHES

002:282 for it is Allah that **teaches** you.
016:103 "It is a man that **teaches** him." The tongue

TEACHETH

011:002 (It **teacheth**) that ye should worship none

TEACHING

002:102 **teaching** men magic,
004:058 the **teaching** which He giveth you!
005:049 (**teaching**) which Allah hath sent down to thee.
005:109 ye received (from men to your **teaching**)?"
039:023 (yet) repeating (its **teaching** in various aspects):
046:010 Say: "See ye? If (this **teaching**) be from Allah,

TEAR

044:029   And neither heaven nor earth shed a **tear** over them:
079:001   By the (angels) who **tear** out (the souls of

TEARS

005:083   with **tears**, for they recognize the truth: they
009:092   with **tears** of grief that they had no resources
017:109   They fall down on their faces in **tears**, and it
019:058   in prostrate adoration and in **tears**.
053:043   That it is He who Granteth Laughter and **Tears**;

TELL

002:031   and said: "**Tell** Me the names of these
002:033   He said: "O Adam! **tell** them their names."
002:033   Allah said: "Did I not **tell** you that
002:076   they say: "Shall you **tell** them what Allah
003:075   but they **tell** a lie against Allah,
003:078   it is they who **tell** a lie against Allah,
006:050   Say: "I **tell** you not that with me
006:050   Nor do I **tell** you I am an angel. I but follow
006:081   (**Tell** me) if you know.
006:093   for that ye used to **tell** lies against Allah, and
006:108   and He shall then **tell** them the truth
006:143   **Tell** me with knowledge if ye are truthful:
006:159   He will in the end **tell** them the truth
006:164   He will **tell** you the truth of things
007:022   and **tell** you that Satan was an
011:031   "I **tell** you not that with me are the
012:015   (one day) **tell** them the truth of this affair
012:017   even though we **tell** the truth."
012:036   "**Tell** us" (they said) "the truth
012:045   said: "I will **tell** you the truth of its
015:049   **Tell** My servants that I am indeed the
015:051   **Tell** them about the guests of Abraham.
015:064   and assuredly we **tell** the truth.
018:063   to **tell** (you) about it: it took
018:072   He answered: "Did I not **tell** thee that thou canst
018:075   He answered: "Did I not **tell** thee that thou canst
018:078   between me and thee: now I will **tell** thee the
018:103   Say: "Shall we **tell** you of those who lose most
022:072   Say, "Shall I **tell** you of something (far) worse
024:064   to Him, He will **tell** them the truth of what
029:008   and I will **tell** you (the truth) of all that ye did.
031:015   is to Me, and I will **tell** you all that ye did."
031:023   and We shall **tell** them the truth of their deeds:
033:053   but Allah is not shy (to **tell** you) the truth.
033:059   O prophet! **Tell** thy wives and daughters, and the
034:007   that will **tell** you, when ye are all scattered
039:007   when He will **tell** you the truth of all
045:014   **Tell** those who believe, to forgive
049:016   Say: "What! Will ye **tell** Allah about your Religion?"
054:028   And **tell** them that the water is to be divided
058:006   and **tell** them of their deeds (which) Allah has
058:007   they be: in the end will He **tell** them what
062:008   and He will **tell** you the things that ye did!"
080:003   But what could **tell** thee but that perchance

TELLEST

004:081   from what thou **tellest** them.
007:070   if so be that thou **tellest** the truth!"
007:106   show it forth,-if thou **tellest** the truth."
026:031   if thou **tellest** the truth!"
026:154   if thou **tellest** the truth!"
029:029   if thou **tellest** the truth."

TELLING

012:027   she the liar, and he is **telling** the truth!"

TELLING (continued)

012:082   and (you will find) we are indeed **telling** the truth."
021:038   come to pass, if ye are **telling** the truth?"
023:067   the (Qur'an), like one **telling** fables by night,"
024:008   that (her husband) is **telling** a lie;
024:009   on herself if (her accuser) is **telling** the truth.
027:049   and we are positively **telling** the truth.'"
027:064   if ye are **telling** the truth!"
032:028   if ye are **telling** the truth?"
034:029   (come to pass) if ye are **telling** the truth?"
038:004   "This is a sorcerer **telling** lies!
040:024   but they called (him) "a sorcerer **telling** lies!"...
040:028   but, if he is **telling** the Truth, then will
046:004   if ye are **telling** the truth!"
046:022   if thou art **telling** the truth!"
067:025   be (fulfilled)? If ye are **telling** the truth.

TELLS

024:007   of Allah on himself if he **tells** a lie.
033:004   But Allah **tells** (you) the Truth, and He

TEMPESTUOUS

014:018   blows furiously on a **tempestuous** day: no power
077:002   Which then blow violently in **tempestuous** Gusts,

TEMPLE

017:007   and to enter your **Temple** as they had

TEMPORAL

008:067   Ye look for the **temporal** goods of this world;

TEMPORARY

011:006   and its **temporary** deposit: all is
040:039   is nothing but (**temporary**) enjoyment: it is

TEMPT

017:073   And their purpose was to **tempt** thee away from

TEMPTATION

004:091   every time they are sent back to **temptation**, they
037:162   Can lead (any) into **temptation** concerning Allah,
057:014   yourselves into **temptation**; ye waited

TEN

002:196   making **ten** days in all.
002:234   concerning themselves four months and **ten** days
005:089   for expiation, feed **ten** indigent persons,
006:160   **ten** times as much to his credit: he that
007:142   and completed (the period) with **ten** (more): thus
011:013   Say, "Bring ye then **ten** Suras forged, like unto
020:103   each other: "Ye tarried not longer than **ten** (days);"
028:027   **ten** years, it will be (grace) from thee. But I
081:004   When the she-camels, **ten** months with young,
089:002   By the **ten** Nights;

TEND

042:053   all affairs **tend** towards Allah!

TENDER

009:114   for Abraham was most **tender** hearted, forbearing.
016:014   that is fresh and **tender**, and that
035:012   and **tender**, and ye extract ornaments to wear;
059:005   of the **tender** palm-trees, Or ye left them

TENDING

042:014   (**tending**) to a Term appointed, the matter

TENT

003:112   And pitched over them is (the **tent** of) destitution.
003:112   (like a **tent**) wherever they are found,
018:029   like the walls and roof of a **tent**,

TENTH

034:045   a **tenth** of what We had granted to those:

TENTS
016:080 of animals, (**tents** for) dwellings, which ye
TERM
002:231 (are about to) fulfil the **term** of their ('Iddat),
002:232 and they fulfil the **term** of their ('Iddat),
002:233 for him who desires to complete the **term**.
002:234 when they have fulfilled their **term**,
002:235 marriage till the **term** prescribed is fulfilled.
003:145 the **term** being fixed as by writing.
004:077 to our (natural) **term**, near (enough)?
006:002 And there is with Him another determined **term**;
006:002 and then decreed a stated **term** (for you).
006:060 that a **term** appointed be fulfilled;
006:128 but (alas!) we reached our **term**-which Thou
007:034 To every People is a **term**. Appointed: when their
007:034 Appointed: when their **term** is reached, not an
007:135 from them according to a fixed **term** which they
007:142 thus was completed the **term** with his Lord, forty
007:185 may well be that their **term** is nigh drawing
009:004 to the end of their **term**: for Allah
010:049 To every people a **term** appointed:
010:049 when their **term** is reached,
011:003 good (and true), for a **term** appointed,
011:008 for them for a definite **term**, they are
011:104 Nor shall We delay it but for a **term** appointed.
013:002 for a **term** appointed. He doth
014:010 for a **term** appointed!" They said: "Ah!
014:044 short **Term**: we will answer Thy Call, and follow
015:004 had not a **term** decreed and assigned beforehand.
015:005 anticipate its **Term**, nor delay it.
016:061 But He gives them respite for a stated **Term**:
016:061 when their **Term** expires,
017:099 a **term** appointed, of which there is no doubt.
018:012 at calculating the **term** of years they had tarried!
020:129 a **term** appointed (for respite).
022:005 appointed **term**, then do We bring you out as babes,
022:033 a **term** appointed: in the end their place of
023:043 No people can hasten their **term**, nor can
028:029 Now when Moses had fulfilled the **term**, and was
029:005 the **Term** (appointed) by Allah is surely coming:
029:053 had it not been for a **term** (of respite)
030:008 a **term** appointed, did Allah create the heavens
031:029 a **term** appointed; and that Allah is well
035:013 a **term** appointed. Such is Allah your Lord:
035:036 no **term** shall be determined for them, so they
035:045 a stated **Term**: when their **Term** expires,
035:045 **Term** expires, verily Allah has in His sight
039:042 a **term** appointed. Verily in this are Signs
040:067 a **Term** appointed: in order that ye may understand.
042:014 (tending) to a **Term** appointed, the matter
046:003 and for a **term** appointed: but those
065:002 **term** appointed, either take them back on equitable
071:004 and give you respite for a stated **Term**: for when
071:004 For when the **Term** given by Allah is accomplished,
072:025 for it a distant **term**.

TERMS
002:229 hold together on equitable **terms**,
002:231 either take them back on equitable **terms**
002:231 or set them free on equitable **terms**;
002:232 if they mutually agree on equitable **terms**.
002:233 on equitable **terms**.
002:233 of their food and clothing on equitable **terms**.
002:235 speak to them in **terms** honourable,

TERMS (continued)
003:064 come to common **terms** as between us and you:
008:058 (so as to be) on equal **terms**: for Allah
017:023 but address them in **terms** of honour.
028:028 whichever of the two **terms** I fulfil, let there
065:002 on equitable **terms**; and take for witness
065:002 on equitable **terms** or part with them on equitable

TERRIBLE
007:164 destroy or visit with a **terrible** punishment?"-
013:018 be **terrible**: their abode will be Hell,-what a
013:021 and fear the **terrible** reckoning;
013:025 for them is the **terrible** Home!
013:032 I punished them: then how (**terrible**) was My
014:002 for a **terrible** Chastisement (their Unfaith
014:007 truly My punishment is **terrible** indeed."
017:005 **terrible** warfare: they entered the very inmost
018:002 of a **terrible** Punishment from Him, and that
022:001 (of judgment) will be a thing **terrible**!
022:044 punish them: but how (**terrible**) was My punishment
034:045 My messengers, how (**terrible**) was My punishment!
034:046 in face of a **terrible** Chastisement."
035:007 is a **terrible** Chastisement: but for
035:010 a Chastisement **terrible**; and the plotting
035:026 who rejected Faith: and how (**terrible**) was My
040:005 seized them! And how (**terrible**), was My Requital!
042:016 and for them will be a Chastisement **Terrible**.
042:026 is a **terrible** Chastisement.
054:006 to a **terrible** affair,
054:016 But how (**terrible**) was My Chastisement and My
054:018 then how **terrible** was my Chastisement and My
054:021 Yea, how (**terrible**) was my Chastisement and my
054:030 Ah! how (**terrible**) was My Chastisement and My
067:007 they will hear the (**terrible**) drawing in of its
067:017 so that ye shall know how (**terrible**) was My warning?
067:018 (My warning): then how (**terrible**) was My
069:005 by a **terrible** storm of thunder and lightning!

TERRIFIED
038:022 and he was **terrified** of them, they said:
TERRITORY
034:015 a **territory** fair and happy, and a Lord
TERROR
002:019 the while they are in **terror** of death.
003:151 **terror** into the hearts of the Unbelievers,
007:116 and struck **terror** into them: and they showed
008:012 the Believers: I will instill **terror** into the
008:060 to strike **terror** into (the hearts of) the enemies,
016:112 and **terror** (in extremes) (closing in on it) like
018:018 filled with **terror** of them.
018:049 in great **terror** because of what is (recorded)
020:102 blear-eyed (with **terror**).
021:103 The Great **Terror** will bring them no grief:
027:087 with **terror** those who are in the heavens,
027:089 be secure from **terror** that Day.
033:026 cast **terror** into their hearts, (so that)
034:023 when **terror** is removed from their hearts (at the
034:051 will quake with **terror**: but then
059:002 and cast **terror** into their hearts, so that

TEST
002:143 only to **test** those who followed
002:155 Be sure We shall **test** you with something
002:249 he said: "Allah will **test** you at the stream;
003:152 from your foes in order to **test** you.
003:154 **test** what is in your breasts and purge

TEST (continued)

003:166 in order that He might **test** the Believers,
005:048 but (His Plan is) to **test** you in what He
005:094 that He may **test** who feareth Him unseen: any
006:053 Thus did We **test** some of them by other, that
016:092 for Allah will **test** you by this; and on
018:007 in order that We may **test** them-as to which
018:012 Then We roused them, in order to **test** which of
020:131 of this world, through which We **test** them: but the
021:035 and We **test** you by evil and by good
023:030 (for men to understand); lo! We put (men) to **test.**
027:040 to **test** me whether I am grateful or ungrateful!
029:003 We did **test** those before them, and Allah
034:021 except that We might **test** the man who believes
047:004 to **test** you, some with others. But those
047:031 And We shall try you until We **test** those among you
057:025 that Allah may **test** who it is that will help,
060:005 "Our Lord! Make us not a **(test** and) trial for
060:010 examine (and **test)** them: Allah knows best as to

TESTATOR

002:182 wrong-doing on the part of the **testator.**

TESTED

003:186 and **tested** in your possessions and in yourselves;
020:085 (Allah) said: "We have **tested** thy people in thy
020:090 being **tested** in this: for verily
029:002 and that they will not be **tested**?
049:003 their hearts has Allah **tested** of piety: for them
051:013 be tried (and **tested)** over the Fire!
086:009 The Day that (all) things secret will be **tested,**

TESTIFIED

066:012 of Our spirit; and she **testified** to the truth

TESTIFIES

046:010 of Israel **testifies** to its similarity (with earlier
092:006 And (in all sincerity) **testifies** to the Best,-

TESTIFY

004:015 and if they **testify,** confine them to houses
007:172 and made them **testify** concerning
007:172 They said: "Yea! we do **testify!** (This), lest ye
024:006 **testify** four times by Allah that he is of those

TESTIMONIES

070:033 And those who stand firm in their **testimonies;**

TESTIMONY

002:140 the **testimony** they have from Allah?
011:103 that will be a Day of **Testimony.**

TESTING

003:142 **testing** those of you who fought hard

THAMUD

007:073 To the **Thamud** people (We sent) Salih, one of
009:070 and 'Ad, and **Thamud;** the people
011:061 To the **Thamud** People (We sent) Salih, one of
011:068 and Cherisher! So away with the **Thamud!**
011:068 For the **Thamud** rejected their Lord and Cherisher!
011:095 as were **Thamud** gone away.
014:009 and 'Ad, and **Thamud?** And of those who (came)
017:059 to the **Thamud**-a visible Sign-but they
022:042 and 'Ad, and **Thamud;**
025:038 As also 'Ad and **Thamud,** and the
026:141 The **Thamud** (people) rejected the messengers.
027:045 We sent (aforetime), to the **Thamud,** their brother
029:038 the **Thamud** (people): clearly will appear to you
038:013 And **Thamud,** and the People of Lut, and the
040:031 of Noah, the 'Ad, and the **Thamud,** and those

THAMUD (continued)

041:013 like the thunderbolt of the 'Ad and the **Thamud!**"
041:017 As to the **Thamud,** We gave them guidance, but they
050:012 the Companions of the Rass, the **Thamud,**
051:043 And in the **Thamud** (was another Sign): behold,
053:051 And the **Thamud,** He left no trace of them.
054:023 The **Thamud** (also) rejected (their) Warners.
069:004 The **Thamud** and the 'Ad people disbelieved in
069:005 But the **Thamud,**-they were destroyed by a terrible
085:018 Of Pharaoh and the **Thamud?**
089:009 And with the **Thamud** (people), who cut
091:011 The **Thamud** (people) rejected (their prophet)

THAN

002:096 even more **than** the idolaters:
002:114 And who is more unjust **than** he who forbids
002:138 and who is give a better hue **than** Allah.
002:140 Ah! who is more unjust **than** those
002:140 Say: Do ye know better **than** Allah?
002:191 for Persecution is worse **than** slaughter;
002:217 Tumult and oppression are worse **than** slaughter.
002:219 but the sin is greater **than** the profit."
002:221 is better **than** an unbeliever,
002:221 is better **than** an unbelieving woman,
002:233 laid on it greater **than** it can bear.
002:247 better fitted **than** he to exercise authority,
002:263 **than** charity followed by injury.
002:286 place a burden greater **than** it can bear.
002:286 **than** we have the strength to bear.
003:011 no better **than** that of the people of Pharaoh,
003:015 glad tidings of things far better **than** those?
003:028 Unbelievers rather **than** Believers:
003:064 lords and patrons other **than** Allah."
003:079 "Be ye my worshippers rather **than** Allah's":
003:083 Do they seek for other **than** the Religion of Allah?
003:085 a religion other **than** Islam (submission to Allah)
003:144 Muhammad is no more **than** a Messenger:
003:157 are far better **than** all they could amass.
003:167 They were that day nearer to Unbelief **than** of Faith,
004:012 but if more **than** two, they share in a third;
004:032 gifts more freely on some of you **than** on others:
004:034 the one more (strength) **than** the other, and
004:051 in the (right) way **than** the Believers!
004:062 "We meant no more **than** good-will and conciliation!"
004:077 or even more **than,** they should have feared Allah:
004:082 Had it been from other **than** Allah, they
004:087 And whose word can be truer **than** Allah's?
004:095 with their goods and persons **than** to those who
004:115 a path other **than** that becoming to men of Faith,
004:116 He pleaseth other sins **than** this: one
004:122 and whose word can be truer **than** Allah's?
004:125 **than** one who submits his whole self to Allah,
004:139 Unbelievers rather **than** believers: it is
004:144 for friends Unbelievers rather **than** Believers: do
004:171 was (no more **than)** an Messenger of Allah, and
005:003 hath been invoked the name of other **than** Allah;
005:050 can give better judgment **than** Allah?
005:055 Your (real) friends are (no less **than)** Allah, His
005:059 no other reason **than** that we believer in Allah,
005:060 something much worse **than** this, (as judged)
005:075 was no more **than** an Messenger; many were
005:107 **than** that of those two, and that
006:014 any other **than** Allah, the Maker of
006:021 Who doth more wrong **than** he who inventeth

THAN (continued)

006:040   would ye then call upon other **than** Allah?-
006:046   who-a god other **than** Allah-could restore
006:056   other **than** Allah, whom ye call upon." Say:
006:093   Who can be more wicked **than** one who
006:114   Say: "Shall I seek for judge other **than** Allah?-
006:144   **than** one who invents a lie against Allah, to lead
006:145   other **than** Allah's." But (even so)
006:157   its guidance better **than** they." Now then
006:157   **than** one who rejecteth Allah's Signs, and turneth
006:164   for (my) Lord other **than** Allah. When
007:003   as friends or protectors, other **than** Him.
007:012   He said: "I am better **than** he: thou didst
007:037   Who is more unjust **than** one who forges
007:140   a god other **than** Allah, when it is
007:155   This is no more **than** Thy trial: by it Thou
008:042   and the caravan on lower ground **than** ye. Even if
008:070   **than** what has been taken from you, and He
009:024   **than** Allah or His Messenger, or the striving
009:052   other **than** one of two glorious things-(martyrdom
009:069   they were mightier **than** you in power and more
009:111   faithful to his Covenant **than** Allah? Then rejoice
010:015   **than** this, or change this." Say: "It is not
010:017   Who doth more wrong **than** such as forge
010:026   (reward)-yea, more (**than** in measure)! No
010:037   be produced by other **than** Allah; on the contrary
010:058   them rejoice": that is better **than** the (wealth)
010:066   as His "partners" other **than** Allah? They follow
010:104   ye worship other **than** Allah! But I worship Allah-
010:106   "Nor call on any, other **than** Allah,-such can
011:013   whomsoever ye can, other **than** Allah!-if ye
011:018   Who doth more wrong **than** those who
011:092   of more consideration with you **than** Allah? For ye
011:101   the deities, other **than** Allah, whom they
011:113   **than** Allah, nor shall ye be helped.
012:008   are loved more by our father **than** we: but we
012:031   This is none other **than** a noble angel!"
012:033   to my liking **than** that to which they invite me:
012:064   with any result other **than** when I trusted you with
012:079   other **than** him with whom we found our property:
012:104   **than** a Message for all creatures.
013:004   more excellent **than** others to eat. Behold!
013:014   besides Him hear them no more **than** if they
013:016   (for worship) protectors other **than** Him, such as
014:010   **than** human, like ourselves! Ye wish
016:035   prohibitions other **than** His." So did
016:052   then will ye fear other **than** Allah?
016:071   you **than** on others; those more favoured are not
016:073   And worship others **than** Allah,-such as
016:092   one party should be more numerous **than** another:
016:107   this world better **than** the Hereafter:
016:115   other **than** Allah has been invoked.
017:002   "Take not other **than** Me as Disposer
017:021   We have bestowed more on some **than** on others;
017:047   "Ye follow none other **than** a man bewitched!"
018:014   upon any god other **than** Him: if we did;
018:015   for worship gods other **than** Him: why do
018:015   Who doth more wrong **than** such as invent
018:016   **than** Allah, betake yourself to the Cave:
018:024   ever closer (even) **than** this to the right course."
018:026   They have no protector other **than** Him; nor does
018:027   as a refuge other **than** Him.
018:034   "More wealth have I **than** you, and more honour

THAN (continued)

018:039   less **than** thee in wealth and sons,
018:040   me something better **than** thy garden, and that
018:050   rather **than** Me? And they are enemies to you!
018:057   And who doth more wrong **than** one who is reminded
018:095   is better (**than** tribute): help me
018:109   be exhausted **than** would the words of my Lord,
019:081   gods other **than** Allah, to give
020:103   each other: "Ye tarried not longer **than** ten (days);"
020:104   will say: "Ye tarried not longer **than** a day!"
021:003   "Is this (one) more **than** a man like yourselves?
021:047   And if there be (no more **than**) the weight
022:013   is nearer **than** his profit: evil, indeed, is the
022:060   to no greater extent **than** the injury he received,
022:072   Say, "Shall I tell you of something (far) worse **than**
023:024   **than** a man like yourselves: his wish
023:033   of this life, said: "He is no more **than** a man
023:062   greater **than** it can bear: before Us
024:027   enter not houses other **than** your own, until ye
024:051   is no other **than** this: they said, "We hear
025:008   "Ye follow none other **than** a man bewitched."
025:010   (things) **than** those,-Gardens beneath
025:041   they treat thee no otherwise **than** in mockery:
026:029   any god other **than** me, I will
026:137   "This is no other **than** a customary device
026:154   "Thou art no more **than** a mortal like us:
026:186   "Thou art no more **than** a mortal like us,
027:036   has given me is better **than** that which He has
027:055   in your lusts rather **than** women? Nay, ye
027:089   **than** it. And they will be secure
027:090   "Do ye receive a reward other **than** that which
028:034   he is more eloquent in speech **than** I: so send
028:049   which is a better Guide **than** either of them,
028:050   own lusts: and who is more astray **than** one who
028:071   what god is there other **than** Allah, who can
028:072   what god is there other **than** Allah, who can
028:084   is better **than** his deed; but if
029:041   take protectors other **than** Allah is that
029:068   And who does more wrong **than** he who invents
030:009   **than** these have done: there came
032:018   **than** the man who is rebellious and wicked?
032:022   And who does more wrong **than** one to whom
033:006   **than** (the Brotherhood of) Believers and Muhajirs:
033:006   the Believers **than** their own selves, and his
033:016   (ye do escape), no more **than** a brief (respite)
034:003   less **than** that, or greater, but is
034:046   he is no less **than** a Warner to you, in face
035:003   other **than** Allah, to give you sustenance
035:023   Thou art no other **than** a warner.
035:042   rightly guided **than** anyone of the nations:
036:029   It was no more **than** a single mighty Blast,
036:053   It will be no more **than** a single Blast,
036:069   this is no less **than** a Message and a Qur'an
036:074   **than** Allah, (hoping) that they might be helped!
037:086   **than** Allah that ye desire?
037:153   Did He (then) choose daughters rather **than** sons?
038:076   **than** he: Thou createdst me from fire, and him
038:087   "This is no less **than** a Reminder
039:003   protectors other **than** Allah (say): "We only
039:022   (no better **than** one hard-hearted)? Woe to those
039:032   Who, then, doth more wrong **than** one who
039:045   **than** He are mentioned, behold, they are

THAN (continued)

039:064 Say: "Is it someone other **than** Allah that ye
040:057 **than** the creation of men: yet most men know not.
040:075 on the earth in things other **than** the Truth,
040:082 **than** these and superior in strength and in
041:033 Who is better in speech **than** one who calls
041:044 (in a language) other **than** Arabic, they would
041:052 reject it? Who is more astray **than** one who is in
042:013 worship other things **than** Allah, hard is
042:046 to help them, other **than** Allah: and for
043:008 **than** these;-and (thus) has passed on the example
043:024 you better guidance **than** that which ye found
043:032 is better **than** the (wealth) which they amass.
043:045 other **than** The Most Gracious, to be worshipped?
043:052 "Am I not better **than** this (Moses), who is
043:059 He was no more **than** a servant: We granted
044:037 What! are they better **than** the people of Tubba
046:005 And who is more astray **than** one who invokes,
046:021 "Worship ye none other **than** Allah: truly I
046:035 tarried more **than** an hour in a single day.
047:013 with more power **than** thy city which has driven
047:014 from his Lord, no better **than** one to whom the evil
049:011 the (latter) are better **than** the (former):
049:011 **than** the (former): nor let some women laugh at
050:016 to him **than** (his) jugular vein.
050:036 stronger in power **than** they? Then did
053:004 It is no less **than** inspiration sent down to him:
054:043 (O Quraish), better **than** they? Or have
055:060 Is there any Reward for Good-other **than** Good?
056:085 But We are nearer to him **than** ye, and yet see not,-
057:010 **than** those who spent (freely) and fought
059:013 in their hearts, **than** Allah. This is
059:022 Allah is He, **than** Whom there is no other god;-
059:023 Allah is He, **than** Whom there is no other god;-
061:007 Who doth greater wrong **than** one who forges
062:011 **than** any pastime or bargain! And Allah
066:005 in exchange Consorts better **than** you,-who submit
068:028 (**than** the rest): "Did I not say to you,
068:032 in exchange a better (garden) **than** this: for we
068:052 But it is nothing less **than** a Message
070:041 **than** they; and We are not to be defeated
072:020 Say: "I do no more **than** invoke my Lord, and I
074:031 and this is no other **than** a Reminder to mankind.
081:027 Verily this is no less **than** a Message
083:003 or weight to men, give less **than** due.
085:008 no other reason **than** that they believed in Allah,
093:004 for thee **than** the present.
097:003 is better **than** a thousand Months.
098:005 **than** this: to worship Allah, offering Him

THANKED

017:019 the ones whose striving will be **thanked** (by Allah).

THANKS

007:010 small are the **thanks** that ye give!
007:144 and be of those who give **thanks**."
014:037 so that they may give **thanks**.
016:078 that ye may give **thanks** (to Allah).
023:078 little **thanks** it is ye give!
031:031 who constantly persevere and give **thanks**.
032:009 little **thanks** do ye give!
034:013 (in their places): "Exercise **thanks** sons of
036:035 will they not then give **thanks**?
039:066 and be of those who give **thanks**.
040:061 to men: yet most men give no **thanks**.

THANKS (continued)

054:035 Thus do We reward those who give **thanks**.
056:070 then why do ye not give **thanks**?
067:023 and understanding: little **thanks** it is ye give.
076:009 from you, nor **thanks**.

THAT

002:011 only ones **that** put things right!"
002:017 Their similitude is **that** of a man
002:019 is **that** of a rain-laden cloud from the sky:
002:021 **that** ye may become righteous,
002:025 **that** their portion is Gardens,
002:026 **that** it is the truth from their Lord;
002:028 Seeing **that** ye were without life,
002:029 for you all things **that** are on earth;
002:033 **that** I know the secrets of the heaven and earth,
002:046 **that** they are to meet their Lord,
002:046 and **that** they are to return to Him.
002:047 and **that** I preferred you to all others.
002:054 **that** will be better for you
002:059 for **that** they infringed (Our command)
002:059 the word from **that** which had been given them;
002:067 "Allah commands **that** ye sacrifice a heifer.
002:075 Seeing **that** a party of them heard
002:075 entertain the hope **that** they will believe
002:076 **that** they may engage you in argument
002:077 Know they not **that** Allah knoweth what
002:080 Or is it **that** ye say of Allah
002:085 a part of the Book **that** ye believe in,
002:087 Is it **that** whenever there comes to you
002:089 **that** which they (should) have recognized,
002:090 in insolent envy **that** Allah of His grace
002:090 in **that** they deny (the revelation)
002:092 yet ye worshipped the Calf (even) after **that**,
002:096 for Allah sees well all **that** they do.
002:100 Is it not (the case) **that** every time
002:102 And they knew **that** the buyers of (magic)
002:105 **That** anything good should come down
002:106 knowest thou not **that** Allah hath power
002:107 Knowest thou not **that** to Allah belongeth
002:110 for Allah sees well all **that** ye do.
002:114 **that** in places for the worship of Allah,
002:114 It was not fitting **that** such should
002:116 **that** is in the heavens and the earth:
002:120 **that** is the (only) guidance."
002:121 they are the ones **that** believe therein:
002:122 and **that** I preferred you to all others.
002:124 And remember **that** Abraham was tried
002:125 **that** they should sanctify My House
002:134 **That** was a People **that** hath passed away.
002:136 and **that** given to (all) Prophets
002:136 and **that** given to Moses and Jesus,
002:139 seeing **that** He is our Lord and your Lord;
002:139 and **that** we are sincere
002:139 **that** we are responsible for our doings
002:140 Or do ye say **that** Abraham,
002:141 **That** was a people **that** hath passed away.
002:142 a Way **that** is straight.
002:143 **That** ye might be witnesses over the nations,
002:144 turn your faces in **that** direction.
002:144 a Qiblah **that** shall please thee.
002:144 The people of the book know well **that**
002:144 **that** is the truth from their Lord,
002:148 (as in a race) towards all **that** is good.

THAT (continued)

002:149 **that** is indeed the truth from thy Lord.
002:150 **that** there be no ground of dispute
002:150 and **that** I may complete My favours on you,
002:150 **that** are bent on wickedness;
002:151 in **that** We have sent among you a Messenger
002:157 and they are the ones **that** receive guidance.
002:158 be sure **that** Allah is He
002:164 gives therewith to an earth **that** is dead;
002:164 kinds **that** He scatters through the earth;
002:164 Signs for a people **that** are wise.
002:165 **that** to Allah belongs all power,
002:169 and **that** ye should say of Allah
002:169 of Allah **that** of which ye have no knowledge.
002:171 to things **that** listen to nothing
002:172 the good things **that** We have provided for you.
002:173 and **that** on which any other name
002:173 name hath been invoked besides **that** Allah,
002:177 It is not righteousness **that** ye turn your faces
002:179 **that** ye may restrain yourselves.
002:180 **that** he make a bequest to parents
002:183 **that** ye may (learn) self-restraint.
002:184 the feeding of one **that** is indigent.
002:184 But he **that** will give more, of his own free will,
002:184 And it is better for you **that** ye fast,
002:185 and to glorify Him in **that** He has guide you;
002:185 during **that** month should spent it in fasting,
002:186 **that** they may walk in the right way.
002:187 **that** they may learn self-restraint.
002:188 with intent **that** ye may eat up wrongfully
002:189 and fear Allah: **that** ye may prosper.
002:194 and know **that** Allah is with those
002:196 And know **that** Allah, is strict in punishment.
002:197 So fear Me, O ye **that** are wise.
002:197 If any one undertakes **that** duty therein,
002:203 Then fear Allah, and know **that** ye will surely
002:209 then know **that** Allah is Exalted in Power, Wise.
002:213 to a path **that** is straight.
002:213 concerning **that** wherein they differed.
002:214 Or do ye think **that** ye shall enter
002:214 **that** even the Messenger and those of faith
002:215 And whatever ye do **that** is good,
002:215 Say: Whatever wealth ye spend **that** is good,
002:216 and **that** ye love a thing which is bad for you.
002:216 But it is possible **that** ye dislike a thing
002:219 His Signs: in order **that** ye may consider-
002:221 **that** they may receive admonition.
002:223 and know **that** ye are to meet Him
002:228 better right to take them back in **that** period,
002:229 fear **that** they would be unable to keep
002:229 If ye (judges) do indeed fear **that** they would be
002:229 A divorce is only permissible twice: after **that**,
002:230 In **that** case there is no blame
002:230 provided they feel **that** they can keep the limits
002:230 he cannot, after **that**, re-marry her until
002:231 and the fact **that** He sent down to you
002:231 if anyone does **that**, He wrongs his own soul.
002:231 and know **that** Allah is well acquainted
002:232 **That** is (the course making for) most virtue
002:233 **that** Allah sees well what ye do.
002:235 Allah knows **that** ye cherish them in your hearts:
002:235 and know **that** Allah is Oft Forgiving, Most Forbearing.
002:235 And know **that** Allah knoweth

THAT (continued)

002:235 with them except **that** you speak to them
002:237 For Allah sees well all **that** ye do.
002:242 in order **that** ye may understand.
002:244 and know **that** Allah heareth and knoweth all things.
002:245 It is Allah **that** giveth (you) want or Plenty,
002:245 Who is he **that** will loan to Allah a beautiful loan,
002:246 **that** we may fight in the cause of Allah."
002:246 **that** ye will not fight?"
002:246 They said to a Prophet (**that** was) among them:
002:246 seeing **that** we were turned out of our homes
002:248 "A sign of his authority is **that** there shall come
002:249 convinced **that** they must meet Allah,
002:250 help us against those **that** reject faith."
002:256 **that** never breaks.
002:258 Allah **that** causeth the sun to rise from the East,
002:259 he said: "I know **that** Allah hath power
002:259 and **that** We may make of thee a Sign
002:260 Then know **that** Allah is Exalted in Power, Wise."
002:261 the way of Allah is **that** of a grain of corn:
002:266 **that** it should be caught in a whirlwind,
002:266 Does any of you wish **that** he should have
002:266 clear to you (His) Signs; **that** ye may consider.
002:267 And know **that** Allah is free of all wants,
002:271 **that** is best for you:
002:273 **that** they are free from want.
002:275 **That** is because they say: "Trade
002:280 **that** is best for you if ye only knew.
002:282 so **that** if one of them errs.
002:282 for it is Allah **that** teaches you.
002:283 And Allah knoweth all **that** ye do.
002:284 **that** is in the heavens and on earth.
002:286 It gets every good **that** it earns,
002:286 and it suffers every ill **that** it earns.
002:286 like **that** which Thou didst lay on those
003:007 **that** is not entirely clear.
003:009 "Our Lord! Thou art He **that** will gather mankind
003:011 no better than **that** of the people of Pharaoh,
003:013 a Sign in the two armies **that** met (in combat):
003:018 **that** is the witness of Allah, His angels,
003:028 **that** ye may guard yourselves from them.
003:028 if any do **that**, shall have no relation left
003:030 kindness to those **that** serve Him."
003:037 Every time **that** he entered her chamber to see her,
003:038 Grant unto me from Thee a progeny **that** is pure:
003:038 for Thou art He **that** heareth prayer!
003:041 **that** thou shalt speak to no man for three days
003:049 in **that** I make for you out of clay, as it were,
003:051 This is a Way **that** is straight."
003:052 and do thou bear witness **that** we are Muslims.
003:059 Jesus before Allah is as **that** of Adam;
003:064 **that** we erect not, from among ourselves,
003:064 **that** we worship none but Allah;
003:064 **that** we associate no partners with Him;
003:064 say ye: "Bear witness **that** we (at least) are Muslims
003:073 Or **that** those (receiving such revelation)
003:073 like unto **that** which was sent unto you?
003:076 Nay,-Those **that** keep their plighted faith
003:078 and they say "**That** is from Allah"
003:078 (as they read) so **that** you would think
003:079 **that** a man, to whom is given the Book, and Wisdom.
003:086 and bore witness **that** the Messenger was true
003:086 and **that** Clear Signs had come unto them?

THAT (continued)

003:087   Of such the reward is **that** on them (rests)
003:088   In **that** will they dwell; nor will their punishment
003:089   Except for those **that** repent (even) after **that**.
003:092   unless ye give (freely) of **that** which ye love:
003:096   appointed for men was **that** at Bakka:
003:099   But Allah is not unmindful of all **that** ye do."
003:101   will be shown a way **that** is straight.
003:103   **that** ye may be guided.
003:103   so **that** by His Grace, Ye became brethren;
003:104   a band of people inviting to all **that** is good,
003:109   **that** is in the heavens and earth:
003:113   are a portion **that** stand (for the right);
003:115   for Allah knoweth well those **that** do right.
003:115   Of the good **that** they do, nothing
003:117   it is not Allah **that** hath wronged them,
003:120   If aught **that** is good befalls you, it grieves them;
003:120   for Allah compasseth round about all **that** they do.
003:121   (Remember **that** morning) thou didst leave
003:124   Is it not enough for you **that** Allah should help
003:127   **That** He might cut off a fringe of the Unbelievers
003:129   **that** is in the heavens and on earth.
003:130   **that** ye may (really) prosper.
003:132   **that** ye may obtain mercy.
003:133   and for a Garden whose width is **that** (of the whole)
003:137   **that** have passed away before you:
003:140   **that** Allah may know those **that** believe,
003:140   And Allah loveth not those **that** do wrong.
003:140   and **that** He may take to Himself from your ranks
003:141   to purge those **that** are true in Faith
003:141   of blessings those **that** resist Faith.
003:142   Did ye think **that** ye would enter Heaven
003:144   many were the Messengers **that** passed away before Him.
003:145   those **that** (serve us with) gratitude.
003:147   **that** transgressed our duty:
003:147   All **that** they said was: "Our Lord forgive us
003:147   and help us against those **that** resist Faith."
003:151   for **that** they joined partners with Allah,
003:152   and some **that** desire the Hereafter.
003:152   Among you are some **that** hanker after this world
003:153   and for (the ill) **that** had befallen you.
003:153   (the booty) **that** had escaped you and for (the ill)
003:153   For Allah is well aware of all **that** ye do.
003:154   but (all this was) **that** Allah might test what
003:156   It is Allah **that** gives Life and Death,
003:156   This **that** Allah may make it a cause of sighs
003:156   and Allah sees well all **that** ye do.
003:158   Lo! it is unto Allah **that** ye are brought together.
003:159   **that** thou dost deal gently with them.
003:160   **that** can help you?
003:160   if He forsakes you, who is there, after **that**,
003:163   and Allah sees well all **that** they do.
003:164   while, before **that**, they had been in manifest error.
003:166   in order **that** He might test the Believers,
003:167   They were **that** day nearer to Unbelief than of Faith,
003:168   (They are) the ones **that** say, (of their brethren
003:170   the fact **that** on them is no fear,
003:171   and in the fact **that** Allah suffereth not
003:175   It is only the Satan **that** suggests to you
003:176   Allah's Plan is **that** He will give them no portion
003:178   **that** they may grow in their iniquity:
003:178   Let not the Unbelievers think **that** our respite
003:180   and Allah is well acquainted with all **that** ye do.

THAT (continued)

003:180   think **that** it is good for them:
003:186   certainly hear much **that** will grieve you,
003:186   then **that** indeed is a matter of great Resolution.
003:188   think not **that** they can escape the Chastisement.
003:188   Think not **that** those who exult in what
003:198   and **that** which is from Allah is the best (bliss)
003:200   and fear Allah; **that** ye may prosper.
004:001   and be heedful the wombs (**that** bore you):
004:003   but if ye fear **that** ye shall not be able
004:003   or **that** which your right hands possess.
004:003   **That** will be more suitable, to prevent you
004:003   If ye fear **that** ye shall not be able
004:011   to the male, a portion equal to **that** of two females:
004:012   so **that** no loss is caused (to anyone).
004:013   and **that** will be the Supreme achievement.
004:019   it may be **that** ye dislike a thing,
004:019   **that** ye may take away part of the dower
004:025   **that** ye practice self-restraint.
004:025   their punishment is half **that** for free women.
004:027   who follow their lusts is **that** ye should turn
004:030   If any do **that** in rancor and injustice, soon
004:037   a Punishment **that** steeps them in contempt;
004:042   wish **that** the earth were made one with them:
004:042   On **that** day those who reject Faith and
004:043   until ye can understand all **that** ye say,
004:044   and wish **that** ye should lose the right path.
004:048   **that** partners should be set up with him; but
004:050   but **that** by itself is a manifest sin!
004:051   and say to the Unbelievers **that** they are better
004:056   **that** they may taste the Chastisement:
004:058   **that** ye judge with justice: verily
004:059   **that** is best, and most suitable
004:060   to those who declare **that** they believe in
004:060   **that** have come to thee and to those before thee?
004:070   and sufficient is it **that** Allah knoweth all.
004:072   in **that** we were not present among them."
004:078   **That** they fail to understand a single fact?.
004:084   It may be **that** Allah will restrain
004:089   They but wish **that** ye should reject Faith.
004:091   Others you will find **that** wish to be secure from
004:091   secure from you as well as **that** of their people:
004:092   it is ordained **that** he should free
004:094   for Allah is well aware of all **that** ye do.
004:099   For these, there is hope **that** Allah will forgive:
004:105   by **that** which Allah has shown thee; so be not
004:105   **that** thou mightest judge between people by **that**
004:108   In words **that** He cannot approve: and Allah
004:108   and Allah doth compass round all **that** they do.
004:112   and throws it on to one **that** is innocent,
004:115   a path other than **that** becoming to men of Faith,
004:119   hath of a surety suffered a loss **that** is manifest.
004:126   and He it is **that** encompasseth all things.
004:127   **that** ye stand firm for justice to orphans.
004:128   Allah is well-acquainted with all **that** ye do.
004:130   for Allah is He **that** careth for all and is Wise.
004:134   for Allah is He **that** heareth and seeth (all things).
004:135   verily Allah is well-acquainted with all **that** ye do.
004:138   **that** there is for them a grievous Chastisement.
004:140   **that** when ye hear the Message of Allah
004:143   (They are) wavering between this and **that** belonging
004:147   Nay, it is Allah **that** recognizeth (all good), and
004:155   **that** they said, "Our hearts are the Wrappings;

THAT (continued)

004:155   in **that** they broke their Covenant;
004:155   **that** they slew the Messengers in defiance of right;
004:155   **that** they rejected the Signs of Allah;
004:156   **that** they uttered against Mary a grave false charge;
004:156   **That** they rejected Faith:
004:157   **That** they said (in boast), "We killed
004:157   Only a likeness of **that** was shown to them.
004:160   and **that** they hindered many from Allah's Way;
004:161   and **that** they devoured men's wealth wrongfully;
004:161   **That** they took usury, though they were forbidden;
004:165   as well as warning, **that** mankind, after
004:166   But Allah beareth witness **that** what He hath
004:174   sent unto you a light (**that** is) manifest.
004:176   **That** dies, leaving a sister but no child, she
005:002   nor the garlands **that** mark out such animals, nor
005:003   **that** which hath been killed by strangling, or by
005:003   **that** which is sacrificed on stone (altars);
005:003   by raffling with arrows: **that** is impiety.
005:003   and **that** on which hath been invoked
005:003   **that** which hath been (partly) eaten
005:006   **that** ye may be grateful.
005:008   For Allah is well-acquainted with all **that** ye do.
005:008   Be just: **that** is next to Piety: and fear
005:013   of the Message **that** was sent them, nor wilt
005:014   **that** was sent them: so We stirred up enmity and
005:015   and passing over much (**that** is now unnecessary):
005:015   **that** ye used to hide in the Book, and
005:016   guideth them to a Path **that** is Straight.
005:017   and all-every one **that** is on the earth?
005:017   and all **that** is between.
005:017   say **that** Allah is Christ the son of Mary.
005:017   They disbelieved indeed those **that** say **that** Allah
005:018   and all **that** is between: and unto Him
005:029   and **that** is the reward of those who do wrong."
005:032   On **that** account: We ordained
005:032   **that** if anyone slew a person-unless it be for
005:032   yet, even after **that**, many of them continued
005:033   **that** is their disgrace in this world, and a heavy
005:034   know **that** Allah is Oft-Forgiving, Most Merciful.
005:034   in **that** case, know **that** Allah
005:035   and main in His cause: **that** ye may prosper.
005:037   their Chastisement will be one **that** endures.
005:040   Knowest thou not **that** to Allah (alone) belongeth
005:043   yet even after **that**, they would turn away.
005:046   confirming the Torah **that** had come before him: We
005:046   **that** had come before him: a guidance and
005:048   it is He **that** will show you the truth
005:048   confirming the scripture **that** came before it, and
005:048   diverging form the truth **that** hath come to thee.
005:049   beguile thee from any of **that** (teaching) which
005:049   **that** for some of their crimes it is Allah's
005:051   And he amongst you **that** turns to them
005:053   All **that** they do will be in vain, and they
005:053   **That** they were with you?"
005:054   **That** is the Grace of Allah, which He will
005:056   the party of Allah **that** must certainly triumph.
005:058   **that** is because they are a people
005:059   no other reason than **that** we believer in Allah,
005:059   come to us and **that** which came before (us), and
005:059   and (perhaps) **that** most of you are rebellious
005:059   and the revelation **that** hath come to us
005:061   But Allah knoweth fully all **that** they hide.

THAT (continued)

005:062   Evil indeed are the things **that** they do.
005:064   But the revelation **that** cometh to thee from Allah
005:066   **that** was sent to them from their Lord, they
005:066   but many of them follow a course **that** is evil.
005:068   **that** cometh to thee from thy Lord,
005:068   **that** has come to you from your Lord."
005:068   **that** increaseth in most of them their
005:071   But Allah sees well all **that** they do.
005:075   **that** passed away before him. His mother
005:076   **that** heareth and knoweth all things."
005:080   **that** Allah's wrath is on them, and in torment
005:084   which has come to us, seeing **that** we long for
005:089   **that** ye may be grateful.
005:089   **That** is the expiation for the oaths ye have sworn.
005:089   If **that** is beyond your means, fast for three days.
005:090   eschew such (abomination), **that** ye may prosper.
005:094   **that** He may test who feareth Him unseen: any
005:095   know ye **that** it is Our Messenger's duty to
005:095   **that** he may taste of the penalty of his deed.
005:097   **that** ye may know **that** Allah hath knowledge of what
005:097   and **that** Allah is well acquainted with all things.
005:097   and the garlands **that** mark them:
005:098   and **that** Allah is Oft-Forgiving, Most Merciful.
005:098   Know ye **that** Allah is strict in punishment and
005:099   but Allah knoweth all **that** ye reveal and ye conceal.
005:100   O ye **that** understand **that** (so) ye may prosper."
005:100   and things **that** are good, even though
005:100   Say: "Not equal are things **that** are bad and
005:100   O ye **that** understand **that** (so) ye may prosper."
005:102   and on **that** account lost their faith.
005:105   it is He **that** will inform you of all **that** ye do.
005:107   But if it gets known **that** these two were guilty
005:107   than **that** of those two,
005:107   "We affirm **that** our witness is truer than **that**
005:107   and **that** we have not trespassed (beyond the truth):
005:108   **that** other oaths would be taken after their oaths.
005:108   **that** they may give the evidence in its true
005:108   **That** is most suitable:
005:109   it is Thou who knowest in full all **that** is hidden.
005:110   So **that** thou didst speak to the people
005:111   and do thou bear witness **that** we bow to Allah
005:113   and to know **that** thou hast indeed told us
005:113   and **that** we ourselves may be witnesses
005:114   **that** there may be for us-for the first
005:115   but if any of you after **that** resisteth faith, I
005:116   For Thou knowest in full all **that** is hidden.
005:119   and they with Allah: **that** is the mighty Triumph
005:120   and all **that** is therein, and it is He
006:007   so **that** they could touch it with their hands, the
006:010   by the thing **that** they mocked.
006:012   Say: "To whom belongeth all **that** is in the
006:012   **that** will not believer.
006:012   **That** He will gather you together for
006:013   "To Him belongeth all **that** dwelleth (or lurketh)
006:014   And He is **that** feedeth but is not fed." Say:
006:016   and **that** would be a Mighty Triumph.
006:016   "On **that** day, if the penalty
006:019   **that** I may warn you and all whom it reaches.
006:019   **that** besides Allah there is another gods?"
006:025   in so much **that** when they come to thee, they
006:027   "Would **that** we were but sent back! Then would
006:031   and they say: "Ah! woe unto us **that** we neglected;

THAT (continued)

006:031	as a falsehood **that** they must meet Allah,-
006:031	and evil indeed are the burdens **that** they bear!
006:034	there is none **that** can alter the Words
006:038	(**that** lives) on the earth, nor a being
006:038	nor a being **that** flies on its wings, but
006:039	He placeth on the Way **that** is Straight.
006:040	or the Hour (**that** ye dread), would ye then
006:042	**that** they call (Allah) in humility.
006:049	for **that** they ceased not from transgressing.
006:050	Say: "I tell you not **that** with me
006:051	**that** they may guard (against evil).
006:051	**that** they will be brought (to judgment)
006:052	**that** thou shouldst turn them away, and thus
006:053	Is it these then **that** Allah hath favoured
006:053	**that** they should say: "Is it these
006:055	**that** the way of the sinners may be shown up.
006:059	the treasures **that** none knoweth but He. He
006:060	then will He show you the truth of all **that** ye did.
006:060	**that** a term appointed be fulfilled; in the end
006:060	all **that** ye have done by day: by day doth
006:063	Say: "Who is it **that** delivereth you from the dark
006:064	Say: "It is Allah **that** delivereth you from these
006:065	**that** they may understand.
006:069	**that** they may (learn to) fear Allah.
006:071	things **that** can do us neither good nor harm, and
006:072	**that** we shall be gathered together."
006:073	as well as **that** which is open. For He is
006:075	**that** he might have certitude.
006:076	"I love not those **that** set."
006:082	**that** are (truly) in security, for they
006:083	**That** was Our argument which We gave
006:088	all **that** they did would be vain for them.
006:088	He giveth **that** guidance to whom He pleaseth, of
006:091	therein were ye taught **that** which ye knew
006:092	**that** thou mayest warn the Mother
006:093	for **that** ye used to tell lies against Allah, and
006:095	**That** is Allah: then how are ye
006:096	He it is **that** cleaveth the daybreak
006:097	**that** ye may guide yourselves, with their
006:102	**That** is Allah, your Lord! There is no
006:105	this (from somebody), and **that** We may make the
006:105	the Signs by various (ways) **that** they may say,
006:108	the truth of all **that** they did.
006:109	**that** if a (special) Sign came to them, by it
006:109	realize **that** even if a (special) Sign came, they
006:114	**that** it hath been sent down from thy
006:121	**that** would be impiety. But the
006:130	they bear witness **that** they rejected Faith.
006:130	It was the life of this world **that** deceived them.
006:132	not unmindful of anything **that** they do.
006:134	All **that** hath been promised unto you
006:135	certain it is **that** the wrong-doers
006:138	And they say **that** such and such
006:141	on the day **that** the harvest is gathered.
006:141	but render the dues **that** are proper on the
006:149	the argument **that** reaches home: if it had
006:150	to prove **that** Allah did forbid so and so."
006:151	thus doth He command you, **that** ye may learn wisdom.
006:152	but **that** which it can bear;-whenever ye speak
006:152	thus doth He command you, **that** ye may remember.
006:153	thus doth He command you, **that** ye may be righteous.
006:154	**that** they might believe in the

THAT (continued)

006:155	**that** ye may receive mercy:
006:156	**that** they learned by assiduous study;"
006:158	The day **that** certain of the Signs of thy
006:159	the truth of all **that** they did.
006:160	He **that** doeth good shall have ten times
006:160	he **that** doeth evil shall only be recompensed
006:161	guided me to a way **that** is straight,-a religion
006:164	Cherisher of all things (**that** exist)?" Every
006:165	**that** He may try you in the
007:002	**that** with it thou mightest warn
007:002	no more by any difficulty on **that** account,-
007:008	The balance **that** day will be true
007:009	for **that** they wrongfully treated Our Signs.
007:010	small are the thanks **that** ye give!
007:020	their shame **that** was hidden from them (before):
007:021	**that** he was their sincere adviser.
007:022	"Did I not forbid you **that** tree, and tell
007:022	and tell you **that** Satan was an
007:026	but the raiment of righteousness-**that** is the best.
007:026	**that** they may receive admonition!
007:029	and **that** ye set your whole selves (to Him)
007:030	and think **that** they receive guidance.
007:030	In **that** they took the Satans in
007:033	Say: The things **that** my Lord
007:037	**that** they had rejected Allah.
007:037	**that** ye used to invoke besides Allah?"
007:038	"Our Lord! it is these **that** misled us: so give
007:038	it curses its sister-People (**that** went before),
007:039	the Chastisement for all **that** ye did!"
007:042	but **that** which it can bear,-they will be
007:043	indeed it was the truth **that** the Messengers
007:049	**that** Allah with His Mercy would never bless?
007:050	**that** Allah doth provide for your sustenance." They
007:051	**That** day shall We forget them as they
007:057	We drive them to a land **that** is dead, make rain
007:058	but from the land **that** is bad, springs up
007:058	From the land **that** is clean and good, by the
007:058	springs up nothing but **that** which is scanty, thus
007:062	and I know from Allah something **that** ye know not.
007:063	"Do ye wonder **that** there hath come to you
007:063	to warn you,-so **that** ye may fear Allah
007:069	Call in remembrance **that** He made you
007:069	"Do ye wonder **that** there hath come
007:069	**that** so ye may prosper."
007:070	if so be **that** thou tellest the truth!"
007:070	**that** we may worship Allah alone, and give up
007:070	and give up **that** which our fathers
007:075	"Know ye indeed **that** Salih is a messenger
007:085	**that** will be best for you, if ye have Faith.
007:085	the things **that** are their due; and do
007:094	in order **that** they might call in humility.
007:100	is it not a guiding (lesson) **that**, if We
007:100	so **that** they could not hear?
007:114	for ye shall in **that** case be (raised to posts)
007:118	And all **that** they did was made of no effect.
007:129	**that** so He may see how ye act."
007:129	He said: "It may be **that** your Lord will destroy
007:130	**that** they might receive admonition.
007:141	in **that** was a momentous trial from your Lord.
007:143	**that** I may look upon Thee." Allah said: "By no
007:146	**that** is the Way they will adopt. For they
007:148	**that** it could neither speak to them, nor show

THAT (continued)

007:149   and saw **that** they had erred, they said:
007:150   **that** ye have done in my place in my absence:
007:156   **That** (Mercy) I shall ordain for those
007:156   "And ordain for us **that** which is good, in this
007:157   and from the yokes **that** are upon them.
007:158   follow him **that** (so) ye may be guided."
007:158   it is He **that** giveth both life and death.
007:162   For **that** they repeatedly transgressed.
007:162   changed the word from **that** which had
007:165   **that** had been given them, We rescued
007:167   **that** He would send against them, to the
007:168   and some **that** are the opposite. We have
007:168   **that** are the righteous, and some
007:168   in order **that** they might turn (to Us).
007:169   **that** they would not ascribe to Allah
007:176   His similitude is **that** of a dog: if you
007:176   **That** is the similitude of those who
007:185   (Do they not see) **that** it may well be
007:185   and all **that** Allah hath created? (Do they
007:185   may well be **that** their term is nigh drawing
007:189   in order **that** he might dwell with her
007:191   as partners things **that** can create nothing, but
007:204   and hold your peace: **that** ye may receive Mercy.
008:007   the two parties, **that** it should be yours: ye wished
008:007   ye wished **that** the one unarmed should be yours,
008:008   **That** He might establish Truth and prove
008:017   in order **that** He might confer on the Believers
008:018   **That**, and also because Allah is He Who
008:024   and **that** it is He to Whom ye shall
008:024   to **that** which will give you life; and know
008:024   and know **that** Allah cometh in between
008:025   who do wrong: and know **that** Allah is strict
008:026   **that** ye might be grateful.
008:026   and afraid **that** men might despoil and kidnap you;
008:027   O ye **that** believe! betray not the trust
008:028   and **that** it is Allah with whom lies
008:028   And know ye **that** your possessions and your
008:034   **that** Allah should not punish them, when they
008:037   In order **that** Allah may separate the impure
008:039   verily Allah doth see all **that** they do.
008:040   be sure **that** Allah is your Protector-
008:041   **that** ye may acquire (in war), a fifth share
008:041   And know **that** out of all the booty **that** ye
008:042   **that** Allah might accomplish a matter already
008:042   a matter already decided; **that** those who died
008:044   **That** Allah might accomplish a matter
008:045   much (and often); **that** ye may prosper.
008:047   for Allah compasseth all **that** they do.
008:057   those who follow them, **that** they may remember.
008:059   **that** they have escaped, they will
008:061   the One **that** heareth and knoweth (all things).
008:062   He it is **that** hath strengthened thee with His
008:063   not if thou hadst spent all **that** is in the earth,
008:063   have produced **that** affection, but Allah
008:066   for He knoweth **that** there is a weak spot in you:
008:067   **that** he should have prisoners of war until he
008:068   reached you for the (ransom) **that** ye took.
008:072   and (remember) Allah seeth all **that** ye do.
009:002   but **that** Allah will cover with shame
009:002   but know ye **that** ye cannot frustrate Allah
009:003   know ye **that** ye cannot frustrate Allah,
009:003   **that** Allah and His Messenger dissolve (treaty)

THAT (continued)

009:006   be secure, **that** is because they are men
009:006   so **that** he may hear the Word of Allah; and then
009:008   seeing **that** if they get an advantage over you,
009:012   **that** thus they may be restrained.
009:016   Do you think **that** you would be left alone while
009:016   with (all) **that** ye do.
009:021   for them, wherein are delights **that** endure:
009:024   or your kindred: the wealth **that** ye have gained;
009:024   Say: If it be **that** your fathers, your sons,
009:025   For all **that** it is wide, did constrain
009:029   nor the Last Day, nor hold **that** forbidden which
009:030   Son of Allah. **That** is a saying from their mouth;
009:032   but Allah will not allow but **that** His light
009:036   **that** is the right religion so wrong not yourselves
009:036   But know **that** Allah is with those
009:038   with you, **that** when ye are asked to go forth in
009:041   **That** is best for you, if ye (but) knew.
009:042   for Allah doth know **that** they are lying.
009:045   in doubt, so **that** they are tossed in their
009:052   **that** Allah will send His punishment from Him
009:054   are not accepted are: **that** they reject Allah
009:054   **that** they come not to prayer save lazily and
009:054   and **that** they offer contributions unwillingly.
009:055   in this life, and **that** their souls may perish
009:056   They swear by Allah **that** they are indeed of you;
009:059   (**That** would been the right course).
009:062   but it is more fitting **that** they should please
009:063   **That** is the supreme disgrace.
009:063   Know they not **that** for those who oppose
009:064   all **that** ye fear (should be revealed)."
009:065   and His Messenger, **that** ye were mocking?"
009:066   for **that** they are sinners.
009:072   Pleasure of Allah: **that** is the supreme triumph.
009:074   They swear by Allah **that** they said nothing (evil),
009:075   a Covenant with Allah, **that** if He bestowed on them
009:078   secret counsels, And **that** Allah knoweth well all
009:078   Know they not **that** Allah doth know their secret
009:082   the (evil) **that** they do.
009:084   **that** dies, nor stand at his grave; for they
009:085   and **that** their souls may depart while they
009:089   **that** is the supreme felicity.
009:092   with tears of grief **that** they had no resources
009:094   He show you the truth of all **that** ye did."
009:094   it is your action **that** Allah and His Messenger
009:095   **that** ye may leave them alone. So leave
009:095   recompense for the (evil) **that** they did.
009:096   **that** ye may be pleased with them. But if
009:098   **that** heareth and knoweth (all things).
009:100   **that** is the supreme Triumph.
009:102   with another **that** was evil. Perhaps Allah
009:102   they have mixed an act **that** was good with another
009:103   **that** so thou mightest purify and sanctify them;
009:104   and **that** Allah is verily He, the Oft-Returning,
009:104   Know they not **that** Allah doth accept repentance
009:105   then will He show you the truth of all **that** ye did."
009:107   **that** they are certainly liars.
009:107   They will indeed swear **that** their intention
009:109   And Allah guideth not people **that** do wrong.
009:109   and His good pleasure?-or he **that** layeth his
009:109   Which then is best?-he **that** layeth his foundation
009:111   **that** is the achievement supreme.
009:112   **that** bow down and prostrate themselves in prayer;

THAT (continued)

009:112	and praise Him; **that** wander in devotion to the
009:112	in repentance: **that** serve Him, and praise Him;
009:112	in prayer; **that** enjoin good and forbid evil;
009:112	Those **that** turn (to Allah) in repentance:
009:113	**that** they should pray for forgiveness for Pagans,
009:113	after it is clear to them **that** they are
009:114	**that** he was an enemy to Allah, he dissociated
009:117	after **that** the hearts of a part of them had
009:118	**that** the earth seemed constrained to them, for all
009:118	and they perceived **that** there is no fleeing
009:118	**that** they might repent: for Allah
009:121	their credit; **that** Allah may requite them
009:122	to them,-**that** thus they (may learn) to guard
009:123	and know **that** Allah is with those who fear Him.
009:126	See they not **that** they are tried
009:127	for they are a people **that** understand not.
009:128	it grieves him **that** ye should suffer, ardently
010:002	**that** We have set Our inspiration to a man
010:002	**That** he should warn mankind (of their danger), and
010:002	**that** they have before their Lord the good
010:004	**that** He may reward with justice those who
010:005	**that** ye might know the number of years and the
010:006	and in all **that** Allah hath created, in the
010:012	for the affliction **that** touched him! Thus do
010:019	for a word **that** went forth before from thy Lord,
010:021	all the plots **that** ye make!"
010:023	and We shall show you the truth of all **that** ye did.
010:025	to a Way **that** is straight.
010:028	"It was not us **that** ye worshipped!"
010:031	And who is it **that** rules and regulates all affairs?"
010:031	Say: "Who is it **that** sustains you (in life)
010:031	Or who is it **that** has power over hearing and sight?
010:031	hearing and sight? And who is it **that** brings out
010:035	any **that** can give guidance towards Truth?" Say:
010:036	Verily Allah is well aware of all **that** they do.
010:037	**that** went before it, and a fuller
010:039	**that** whose knowledge they cannot compass,
010:044	it is man **that** wrongs his own soul.
010:046	(before **that**)-in any case, to Us is their return:
010:046	to all **that** they do.
010:053	"Is **that** true?" Say: "Aye! by my Lord! It is
010:054	if it possessed all **that** is on earth, would fain
010:054	Every soul **that** hath sinned, if it
010:055	Is it not (the case) **that** to Allah belongeth
010:055	**that** Allah's promise is assuredly true? Yet most
010:058	them rejoice": **that** is better than the (wealth)
010:058	And in His Mercy,-in **that** let them rejoice":
010:067	He it is **that** hath made you the Night
010:067	the Night **that** ye may rest therein, and the Day
010:071	**that** I should stay (with you) and remind
010:078	in order **that** thou and thy brother may have
010:090	he said: "I believe **that** there is no god except
010:092	thy body, **that** thou mayest be a Sign to those
010:093	**that** they fell into schisms. Verily Allah
010:101	Say: "Behold all **that** is in the heavens
010:103	**that** We should deliver those who believe!
011:002	(It teacheth) **that** ye should worship none
011:003	**that** He may grant you enjoyment, good (and
011:005	**that** they may lie hid from Him! Ah! even
011:007	**that** He might try you, which of you
011:008	completely encircled by **that** which they
011:012	It is Allah **that** arrangeth all affairs!

THAT (continued)

011:014	of Allah, and **that** there is no god but He!
011:014	know ye **that** this Revelation is sent down
011:016	and of no effect are the deeds **that** they do!
011:017	the Sects **that** reject it,-the Fire
011:026	"**That** ye serve none but Allah: verily I do
011:027	nor do we see **that** any follow thee but the
011:028	unto me from Him, but **that** the Mercy hath been
011:028	(it be **that**) I have a Clear Sign from my Lord
011:028	from my Lord and **that** He hath sent Mercy unto me
011:031	will not grant them (all) **that** is good: Allah
011:031	"I tell you not **that** with me are the
011:031	your eyes do despise **that** Allah will not
011:034	(good) counsel, if it be **that** Allah willeth to
011:038	the Ark: every time **that** the Chiefs of his People
011:039	**that** will cover them with shame,-on whom
011:046	So ask not of Me **that** of which thou hast
011:047	with Thee, from asking Thee for **that** of which
011:054	**that** I am free from the sin of ascribing, to Him,
011:054	"We say nothing but **that** (perhaps) some of
011:056	Verily, it is my Lord **that** is on a Straight Path.
011:062	to **that** to which thou invitest us."
011:066	and from the Ignominy of **that** Day. For thy Lord
011:072	**That** would indeed be a wonderful thing!"
011:076	**that** cannot be turned back!
011:080	to suppress you or **that** I could betake myself to
011:080	He said: "Would **that** I had power to suppress you
011:084	**that** will compass (you) all round.
011:085	the people the things **that** are their due:
011:086	'**That** which is left you by Allah is best for you,
011:087	Does thy prayer command thee **that** we leave off
011:087	Truly, thou art the one **that** forbeareth with
011:087	fathers practiced, or **that** we leave off doing
011:088	to do **that** which I forbid you to do. I only
011:089	lest ye suffer a fate similar to **that** of the
011:091	**that** thou hast no strength! Were it not
011:092	But verily my Lord encompasseth all **that** ye do!
011:101	It was not We **that** wronged them: they wronged
011:103	**that** is a Day for which mankind will be
011:103	**that** will be a Day of Testimony.
011:103	In **that** is a Sign for those who fear
011:110	had it not been **that** a Word had gone forth
011:111	For He knoweth well all **that** they do.
011:112	(from the Path): for He seeth well all **that** ye do.
011:114	**that** is a reminder to the mindful.
011:114	remove those **that** are evil: **that** is a
011:114	for those things **that** are good remove those
011:120	All **that** We relate to thee of the stories
011:123	and thy Lord is not unmindful of aught **that** ye do.
012:002	in order **that** ye may learn wisdom.
012:003	in **that** We reveal to thee this (portion
012:009	for you to be righteous after **that**!"
012:009	to some (unknown) land, **that** so the favour of your
012:013	**that** ye should take him away: I fear
012:018	made up a tale (**that** may pass) with you, (for me)
012:018	against **that** which ye assert, it is
012:019	But Allah knoweth well all **that** they do!
012:021	**that** We might teach him the interpretation
012:024	**that** We might turn away from him (all) evil
012:024	but **that** he saw the evidence of his Lord:
012:026	(thus)-"If it be **that** his shirt is rent
012:026	He said: "It was she **that** sought to seduce me-
012:027	"But if it be **that** his shirt is torn

THAT (continued)

012:028   **that** it was torn at the back, (her husband)
012:033   to my liking than **that** to which they invite me:
012:035   (**that** it was best) to imprison him for a time.
012:036   for we see thou art one **that** doth good (to all)."
012:037   and **that** (even) deny the Hereafter.
012:037   **That** is part of the (Duty) which my
012:037   of a people **that** believe not in Allah and **that**
012:038   **that** (comes) of the grace of Allah to us and to
012:040   He hath commanded **that** ye worship none but Him:
012:040   but Him: **that** is the right religion, but most
012:041   (So) hath been decreed **that** matter whereof ye
012:042   And of the two, to **that** one whom he considered
012:043   if it be **that** ye can interpret visions."
012:046   and **that** they may know."
012:046   **that** I may return to the people,
012:047   and the harvests **that** ye reap, ye shall
012:048   "Then will come after **that** (period) seven
012:049   "Then will come after **that** (period) a year
012:052   may know **that** I have never been false to him
012:052   "This (say I), in order **that** he may know
012:052   and **that** Allah will never guide the snare
012:059   and **that** I do provide the best hospitality?
012:059   (but a different mother): see you not **that** I pay
012:062   in order **that** they might come back.
012:063   **that** we may get our measure; and we
012:066   to me, in Allah's name, **that** ye will be sure to
012:066   he said: "Over all **that** we say, be Allah
012:067   and let all **that** trust put their trust on Him."
012:067   Not **that** I can profit you aught against Allah
012:071   "What is it **that** ye miss?"
012:073   know **that** we came not to make mischief in the land,
012:075   They said: "The penalty should be **that** he in whose
012:076   except **that** Allah willed it (so). We raise
012:078   for we see **that** thou art (gracious) in doing good."
012:079   He said: "Allah forbid **that** we take other than
012:080   "Know ye not **that** your father did take an oath
012:086   and I know from Allah **that** which ye know not.
012:090   behold, he **that** is righteous and patient,-
012:096   to you, 'I know from Allah **that** which ye know not?'
012:110   think **that** they were treated as liars,
013:001   **that** which hath been revealed unto thee
013:002   without any pillars **that** ye can see; then He
013:002   **that** ye may believe with certainty in the
013:009   He knoweth the Unseen and **that** which is open:
013:014   any others **that** they call upon besides Him
013:016   so **that** the creation seemed to them similar?
013:017   the surface. Even so, from **that** (ore) which
013:017   cast out; while **that** which is for the good
013:017   the foam **that** mounts up to the surface.
013:018   even if they had all **that** is in the heavens
013:019   with understanding **that** receive admonition;-
013:019   Is then one who doth know **that that** which hath be
013:024   "Peace unto you for **that** ye persevered in patience!
013:030   passed away; in order **that** thou mightest rehearse
013:031   the Believers know, **that**, had Allah (so) willed,
013:033   every soul (and knoweth) all **that** it doth,
013:033   Say: "But name them! is it **that** ye will inform
013:041   See they not **that** We gradually reduce the land
014:001   in order **that** thou mightest lead mankind out of
014:009   as to **that** to which ye invite us."
014:010   in order **that** He may forgive you your sins
014:018   their Lord is **that** their works are as ashes,

THAT (continued)

014:018   **that** is the straying far, far (from the goal).
014:018   **that** they have earned:
014:019   Seest thou not **that** Allah created the
014:020   Nor is **that** for Allah any great matter.
014:025   in order **that** they may receive admonition.
014:026   is **that** of an evil tree: it is torn
014:027   those who believe, with the Word **that** stands firm,
014:031   **that** they may establish regular prayers, and spend
014:032   subject to you, **that** they may sail through the
014:034   And He giveth you of all **that** ye ask for. But if
014:036   and he **that** disobeys me,-but thou
014:037   so **that** they may give thanks.
014:037   O our Lord! **that** they may establish regular
014:041   on the Day **that** the Reckoning will be established!"
014:042   Think not **that** Allah doth not heed the deeds
014:044   to swear aforetime **that** ye suffer no decline?
014:047   Never think **that** Allah would fail His messengers
014:049   **that** day bound together in fetters:-
014:051   **That** Allah may requite each soul
014:052   and may know **that** He is One God: let men
014:052   **that** they may take warning therefrom, and may
015:001   of a Qur'an **that** makes things clear.
015:002   wish **that** they had been Muslims.
015:004   Never did We destroy a population **that** had not
015:007   if it be **that** thou hast the Truth?"
015:018   But any **that** gains a hearing by stealth,
015:049   Tell My servants **that** I am indeed the
015:050   And **that** My Chastisement will be indeed
015:063   to thee to accomplish **that** of which they doubt.
015:066   **that** the last remnants of those (sinners)
015:084   And of no avail to them was all **that** they did
015:089   And say: "I am indeed he **that** warneth openly
015:099   come unto thee the Hour **that** is Certain.
016:002   (saying): "Warn (Man) **that** there is no god but I:
016:007   **that** ye could not (otherwise) reach except with
016:009   but there are ways **that** turn aside: if Allah
016:014   and **that** ye may extract therefrom ornaments
016:014   **that** is fresh and tender, and **that**
016:014   and **that** ye may be grateful.
016:014   **that** plough the waves, **that** ye may seek (thus)
016:014   **that** ye may eat thereof flesh **that** is
016:014   **that** plough the waves, **that** ye may seek (thus)
016:015   **that** ye may guide yourselves;
016:017   Is then He Who creates like one **that** creates not?
016:024   "What is it **that** your Lord has revealed?"
016:025   **That** they may bear, on the Day of Judgment,
016:028   verily Allah knoweth all **that** ye did;
016:030   "What is it **that** your Lord has revealed?" they say
016:030   they say, "All **that** is good." To those
016:031   therein all **that** they wish: thus doth
016:034   overtook them, and **that** every (Wrath) at which
016:038   by Allah, **that** Allah will not raise up
016:039   of **that** wherein they differ, and **that**
016:039   may realize **that** they were liars.
016:039   and **that** the rejectors of Truth may realize
016:039   (They must be raised up), in order **that** He may
016:044   and **that** they may give thought.
016:044   **that** thou mayest explain clearly to men
016:045   them up, or **that** the Wrath will not seize them
016:045   (plots) feel secure **that** Allah will not cause
016:046   Or **that** He may not call them to account in the
016:047   Or **that** He may not call them to account by a

THAT (continued)

016:048   to Allah, and all **that** in the humblest manner?
016:049   And to Allah doth prostrate all **that** is in
016:050   all **that** they are commanded.
016:056   do not know, a portion out of **that** which We have
016:062   **that** the reward most fair is for themselves:
016:064   so **that** thou shouldst make clear to them
016:064   they differ, and **that** it should be a guide
016:070   so **that** they know nothing after having
016:071   so as to be equal in **that** respect. Will they
016:078   **that** ye may give thanks (to Allah).
016:081   on you, **that** ye may surrender to His Will
016:087   **That** day shall they (openly) show (their)
016:088   for **that** they used to spread mischief.
016:090   **that** ye may receive admonition.
016:091   for Allah knoweth all **that** ye do.
016:092   (the truth of) **that** wherein ye disagree.
016:094   With the result **that** someone's foot may slip
016:097   **that** is good and pure, and We
016:103   "It is a man **that** teaches him." The tongue
016:103   We know indeed **that** they say, "It is
016:105   the Signs of Allah, **that** forge falsehood: it is
016:116   **that** your tongues may put forth, "This is
016:125   and argue with them in ways **that** are best
016:126   to the wrong **that** has been done to you: but if
016:126   **that** is indeed the best (course) for those
017:001   We did Bless,-in order **that** We might show him
017:003   O ye **that** are sprung from those whom We
017:004   **that** twice would they do mischief on the earth
017:007   all **that** fell into their power.
017:008   It may be **that** your Lord may (yet) show Mercy
017:009   to **that** which is most right (or stable),
017:009   of righteousness, **that** they shall have a
017:010   **that** We have prepared for them a Chastisement
017:012   We have made bright **that** ye may seek bounty from
017:012   Bounty from your Lord and **that** ye may know
017:016   continued to transgress; so **that** the word is
017:023   but Him, and **that** ye be kind to parents. Whether
017:023   Thy Lord hath decreed **that** ye worship none but Him,
017:029   utmost reach, so **that** thou become blameworthy
017:035   is straight: **that** is better and fairer in the
017:035   and weigh with a balance **that** is straight:
017:036   And pursue not **that** of which thou hast
017:041   in order **that** they may receive admonition,
017:043   Glory to Him! He is high above all **that** they say!
017:051   "When will **that** be?" Say, "May be
017:052   and ye will think **that** ye tarried
017:053   Say to My servants **that** they should (only) say
017:053   (only) say those things **that** are best: for Satan
017:054   It is your Lord **that** knoweth you best: if He
017:055   And it is your Lord **that** knoweth best all beings
017:055   all beings **that** are in the heavens and on earth:
017:058   **That** is written in the (eternal) Record.
017:060   Behold! We told thee **that** thy Lord doth
017:066   Your Lord is He **that** maketh the Ship go smoothly
017:066   in order **that** ye may seek of His Bounty.
017:067   those **that** ye call upon-besides Himself-leave you
017:068   Do ye then feel secure **that** He will not cause
017:068   or **that** He will not send against you a violent
017:068   so **that** ye shall find no protector?
017:069   so **that** ye find no helper therein against Us?
017:069   Or do ye feel secure **that** He will not send
017:073   (in **that** case), behold! they would

THAT (continued)

017:073   away from **that** which We had revealed unto thee,
017:075   In **that** case We should have made thee taste
017:076   but in **that** case they would not have stayed
017:082   of the Qur'an **that** which is a healing and a mercy
017:084   knows best who it is **that** is best
017:085   a little **that** is communicated to you, (O men!)"
017:086   thy affair in **that** matter as against Us,-
017:086   We could take away **that** which We have sent thee
017:093   a book **that** we could read." Say: "Glory
017:097   **that** is on true guidance; but he
017:097   **That** is their recompense, because they
017:099   See they not **that** Allah, Who created
017:102   Moses said, "Thou knowest well **that** these things
017:106   in order **that** thou mightest recite it
017:107   it is true **that** those who were given knowledge
018:002   in order **that** He may warn (the godless) of a
018:002   and **that** He may give Glad Tidings to the
018:002   righteous deeds, **that** they shall have
018:004   Further, **that** He may warn those (also) who say,
018:005   It is a grievous thing **that** issues from their
018:007   **That** which is on earth We have made but as
018:007   in order **that** We may test them-as to which
018:009   Or dost thou reflect **that** the Companions
018:011   (so **that** they heard not):
018:019   to you, (**that** ye may satisfy your hunger therewith)
018:019   **that** they might question each other. Said one
018:020   and in **that** case ye would never attain prosperity."
018:021   to the people, **that** they might know **that** the
018:021   and **that** there can be no doubt about the
018:021   **that** the promise of Allah it true, and **that**
018:022   their number; it is but few **that** know their
018:022   except on a matter **that** is clear, nor consult
018:024   "I hope **that** my Lord will guide me ever closer
018:029   like melted brass, **that** will scald their
018:035   "I deem not **that** this will ever perish,"
018:036   "Nor do I deem **that** the Hour (of Judgment)
018:040   "It may be **that** my Lord will give me something
018:040   and **that** He will send on thy garden thunderbolts
018:041   run off underground so **that** thou wilt never
018:046   but the things **that** endure, Good Deeds,
018:049   They will find all **that** they did, placed before
018:053   and apprehend **that** they have to fall therein;
018:055   from believing, now **that** guidance has come to them,
018:055   but **that** (they wait for) the ways of the ancients
018:057   veils over their hearts so **that** they should
018:064   Moses said: "**That** was what we were seeking after":
018:066   on the footing **that** thou teach me something
018:072   He answered: "Did I not tell thee **that** thou canst
018:075   He answered: "Did I not tell thee **that** thou canst
018:080   and we feared **that** he would grieve them by
018:081   "So we desired **that** their Lord would give them
018:082   so thy Lord desired **that** they should attain their
018:094   in order **that** thou mightest erect a barrier
018:096   he said: "Bring me, **that** I may pour over it,
018:099   On **that** day We shall leave them to surge
018:100   And We shall present Hell **that** day for Unbelievers
018:102   Do the Unbelievers think **that** they can take
018:104   in this life, while they thought **that** they were
018:106   **That** is their reward, Hell; because they
018:110   **that** your God is one God: whoever expects
019:006   "(One **that**) will (truly) inherit me, and inherit
019:007   **that** name have We conferred distinction before."

THAT (continued)

019:009	thy Lord saith, "**That** is easy for Me: I did
019:010	"shall be **that** thou shalt speak to no man
019:015	the day **that** he dies, and the day **that** he will
019:020	seeing **that** no man has touched me, and I am
019:021	thy Lord saith, '**That** is easy for Me: and (We
019:023	would **that** I had been a thing forgotten."
019:023	"Ah! would **that** I had died before this! would **that**
019:033	the day **that** I die, and the day **that** I shall
019:035	(the majesty of) Allah **that** He should beget
019:036	this is a Way **that** is straight.
019:038	the Day **that** they will appear before Us!
019:042	"O my father! why worship **that** which heareth not
019:043	a Way **that** is even and straight.
019:045	so **that** thou become to Satan a friend."
019:065	and of all **that** is between them: so worship
019:067	**that** We created him before out of nothing?
019:076	and the things **that** endure, Good Deeds,
019:080	To Us shall return all **that** he talks of, and he
019:083	Seest thou not **that** We have set Satans
019:091	**That** they attributed a son to The Most Gracious.
019:092	**that** He should beget a son.
019:097	**that** with it thou mayest give glad tidings
020:017	And what is **that** in thy right hand, O Moses?"
020:023	"In order **that** We may show thee of
020:033	"**That** we may celebrate Thy praise without stint,
020:039	and (this) in order **that** thou mayest be
020:040	**that** her eye might be cooled and she
020:048	**that** the Chastisement (awaits) those who
020:052	He replied: "The knowledge of **that** is with
020:065	thou throw (first) or **that** we be the first
020:065	They said: "O Moses! whether wilt thou **that** thou
020:069	**that** which they have faked: what they
020:069	"Throw **that** which is in thy right hand:
020:082	He **that** forgives again and again, to those
020:086	**that** Wrath should descend from your Lord on you,
020:087	and **that** was what the Samiri suggested.
020:089	and **that** it had no power either to harm
020:089	Could they not see **that** it could not return
020:097	be **that** thou wilt say, 'Touch me not';
020:097	a promise **that** will not fail: now look
020:101	be to them on **that** Day,-
020:102	**that** Day, We shall gather the sinful, blear-eyed
020:108	On **that** Day will they follow the caller
020:108	so **that** thou hearest not but murmuring.
020:109	On **that** Day shall no intercession avail except for
020:111	the man **that** carries iniquity (on his back).
020:113	in order **that** they may fear Allah, or **that**
020:113	or **that** it may cause their remembrance (of Him).
020:117	the Garden, so **that** thou art landed in misery.
020:120	and to a kingdom **that** never decays?"
020:129	**that** went forth before from thy Lord, (their
020:130	of the day: **that** thou may be pleased.
020:133	of all **that** was in the former Books of revelation?
020:135	and who it is **that** has received guidance."
020:135	ye know who it is **that** is on the straight
021:004	and on earth: He is the One **that** heareth and
021:005	the ones **that** were sent to (prophets) of old!"
021:008	Nor did We give them bodies **that** ate no food,
021:013	in order **that** ye may be called to account.
021:015	till We made them as a field **that** is mown,
021:015	And **that** cry of theirs ceased not, till We
021:016	the heavens and the earth and all **that** is between!

THAT (continued)

021:025	**that** there is no god but I; therefore worship
021:030	Do not the Unbelievers see **that** the heavens
021:031	**that** they may find their way.
021:041	hemmed in by the thing **that** they mocked.
021:043	Or have they gods **that** can guard them from Us?
021:044	see they not **that** We gradually reduce the land
021:047	so **that** not a soul will be dealt with
021:058	**that** they might turn (and address themselves) to it.
021:061	**that** they may bear witness:"
021:062	They said, "Art thou the one **that** did this
021:065	**that** these (idols) do not speak!"
021:066	besides Allah, things **that** can neither be of
021:067	**that** ye worship besides Allah! Have ye no sense?"
021:079	**that** made the hills and the birds
021:081	(It was Our power **that** made) the violent
021:083	of those **that** are merciful."
021:084	We removed the distress **that** was on him, and We
021:087	in wrath: he imagined **that** We had no power
021:095	**that** they shall not return,
021:098	and the (false) gods **that** ye worship besides Allah,
021:102	in **that** will they dwell.
021:103	(the Day) **that** ye were promised."
021:104	The Day **that** we roll up the heavens like a
021:108	by inspiration is **that** your God is one God:
021:109	but I know not whether **that** which ye are
021:111	"I know not but **that** it may be a trial for you,
022:004	**that** whoever turns to him for friendship,
022:005	as babes, then (foster you) **that** ye may reach
022:005	in order **that** We may manifest (Our Power) to you;
022:005	(consider) **that** We created you out of dust,
022:005	old age, so **that** they know nothing after having
022:007	or about (the fact) **that** Allah will raise up
022:011	the Hereafter: **that** is indeed the manifest loss,
022:012	nor profit them: **that** is straying far indeed
022:014	for Allah carries out all **that** He desires.
022:015	his plan will remove **that** which enrages (him)!
022:015	If any think **that** Allah will not help him
022:018	Seest thou not **that** to Allah prostrate all things
022:018	all things **that** are in the heavens and on earth,-
022:018	for Allah carries out all **that** He wills.
022:028	"**That** they may witness the benefits (provided)
022:030	and shun the word **that** is false,-
022:034	**that** they might celebrate the name of Allah
022:036	to you, **that** ye may be grateful.
022:037	**that** reaches Allah: it is your
022:037	**that** ye may glorify Allah for His guidance to you:
022:037	it is your piety **that** reaches Him: He has
022:038	**that** is unfaithful, ungrateful.
022:040	**that** they say, "Our Lord is Allah." Did not
022:044	and (only) after **that** did I punish them:
022:046	Truly it is not the eyes **that** are blind, but the
022:046	so **that** their hearts (and mind) may thus learn
022:053	**That** He may make the suggestions thrown in
022:054	has been bestowed may learn **that** the (Qur'an)
022:054	And **that** those on whom knowledge has been
022:054	and **that** they may believe therein, and their
022:056	On **that** Day the Dominion will be **that** of Allah:
022:060	**That** (is so). And if one has retaliated to no
022:060	for Allah is One **that** blots out (sins)
022:061	**That** is because Allah merges Night into Day,
022:062	**That** is because Allah-He is the Reality; and those

THAT (continued)

022:063   Seest thou not **that** Allah sends down
022:064   To Him belongs all **that** is in the heavens
022:065   made subject to you (men) all **that** is on the
022:065   Seest thou not **that** Allah has made subject
022:065   on the earth, and the ships **that** sail through
022:070   Knowest thou not **that** Allah knows all **that**
022:070   Allah knows all **that** is in heaven and on earth?
022:070   and **that** is easy for Allah.
022:071   for those **that** do wrong there is no helper.
022:072   And evil is **that** destination!"
022:077   your Lord; and do good; **that** ye may prosper.
022:078   **that** the Messenger may be a witness for you,
023:014   then of **that** clot We made a (foetus) lump;
023:014   of **that** lump bones and clothed the bones
023:015   After **that**, at length, ye will die.
023:026   for **that** they accuse me of falsehood!
023:035   "Does he promise **that** when ye die and become
023:036   "Far, very far is **that** which ye are promised!
023:039   for **that** they accuse me of falsehood."
023:044   (**that** is told): so away with a people
023:044   a people **that** will not believe!
023:049   in order **that** they might receive guidance.
023:051   for I am well-acquainted with (all) **that** you do.
023:053   each party rejoices in **that** which is with itself.
023:055   Do they think **that** because We have granted them
023:063   and there are, besides **that**, deeds of theirs,
023:068   come to them **that** did not come to their
023:069   their Messenger, **that** they deny him?
023:072   Or is it **that** thou asked them for some recompense?
023:074   in the Hereafter are deviating from **that** Way.
023:093   (in my lifetime) **that** which they are warned
023:095   show thee (in fulfillment) **that** against which
023:096   Repel evil with **that** which is best: We are
023:100   "In order **that** I may work righteousness in the
023:101   relationships between them **that** day, nor will
023:110   so much so **that** (ridicule of) them made you
023:111   they are indeed the ones **that** have achieved Bliss."
023:115   "Did ye then think **that** We had created you
023:115   and **that** ye would not be brought back
024:001   in order **that** ye may receive admonition.
024:006   testify four times by Allah **that** he is of those
024:007   **that** he solemnly invokes the curse of Allah
024:008   **that** (her husband) is telling a lie;
024:009   And the fifth (oath) should be **that** she solemnly
024:010   on you, and **that** Allah is Oft-Returning, Full of
024:011   the punishment) of the sin **that** he earned, and to
024:014   seized you in **that** ye rushed glibly into
024:017   **that** ye may never repeat such (conduct), if ye
024:020   of Allah on you, and **that** Allah is full of
024:022   do you not wish **that** Allah should forgive you?
024:025   **that** makes all things manifest.
024:025   On **that** Day Allah will pay them back (all) their
024:025   and they will realize **that** Allah is the
024:027   **that** is best for you, in order
024:027   in order **that** ye may heed (what is seemly).
024:028   and Allah knows well all **that** ye do.
024:028   go back: **that** makes for greater purity for
024:030   Say to the believing men **that** they should lower
024:030   their modesty: **that** will make for greater purity
024:030   and Allah is well acquainted with all **that** they do.
024:031   **that** they should draw their veils over their
024:031   **that** ye may be successful.

THAT (continued)

024:031   **that** they should not display their beauty
024:031   and **that** they should not strike their feet
024:031   And say to the believing women **that** they should
024:033   desire chastity, in order **that** ye may make a gain
024:038   **That** Allah may reward them according to the
024:041   And Allah knows well all **that** they do.
024:041   Seest thou not **that** it is Allah Whose praises
024:043   Seest thou not **that** Allah makes the clouds
024:045   some **that** walk on two legs: and some
024:045   **that** creep on their bellies;
024:045   and some **that** walk on four.
024:046   to a Way **that** is straight.
024:046   **that** make things manifest: and Allah
024:047   but even after **that**, some of them turn away:
024:048   in order **that** He may judge between them, behold,
024:050   Is it **that** there is a disease in their hearts?
024:050   **that** Allah and His Messenger will deal
024:051   it is such as these **that** will prosper.
024:051   His Messenger, in order **that** He may judge
024:052   and do right, **that** will triumph.
024:053   by Allah **that**, if only thou wouldst command
024:053   Allah is well acquainted with all **that** ye do."
024:054   and ye for **that** placed on you. If ye
024:055   **that** He will, of a surety, grant them
024:055   **that** He will establish in authority their religion
024:055   and **that** He will change (their state), after the
024:056   **that** ye may receive mercy.
024:057   Never think thou **that** the Unbelievers can escape
024:061   **that** ye should eat in your own houses, or those
024:061   **that** ye may understand.
024:064   Be quite sure **that** to Allah doth belong
025:001   **that** it may be an admonition to all creatures;-
025:003   **that** have no control of hurt or good
025:003   gods **that** can create nothing but are
025:006   by Him Who knows the secret (**that** is) in the
025:010   Blessed is He Who, if **that** were His Will,
025:015   the righteous? For them, **that** is a reward
025:015   Say: "Is **that** best, or the eternal Garden,
025:016   all **that** they wish for: they will
025:018   not meant was it for us **that** we should take
025:022   **that** Day: the (angels) will say: "There is
025:024   be well, **that** Day, in their abode, and have
025:026   **That** Day, the dominion right by shall be
025:027   "Oh! would **that** I had taken a (straight) path
025:027   The Day **that** the wrong-doer will bite
025:028   "Ah! woe is me! would **that** I had never taken
025:032   **that** We may strengthen thy heart thereby,
025:042   had it not been **that** we were constant to them!"-
025:042   who it is **that** is most misled in Path!
025:044   Or thinkest thou **that** most of them listen
025:049   **That** with it We may give life to a dead land,
025:050   amongst them, in order **that** they may be mindful
025:053   between them, a partition **that** is not
025:055   things **that** can neither profit them nor harm them:
025:057   but this: **that** each one who will may take
025:059   and the earth and all **that** is between, in six
025:060   Shall we adore **that** which thou commandest us?"
025:068   and any **that** does this (not only) meets punishment
026:002   **that** makes (things) clear.
026:003   with grief, **that** they do not become Believers.
026:012   I do fear **that** they will charge me with falsehood:
026:022   **that** you hast enslaved the Children of Israel!"

THAT (continued)

026:040 "**That** we may follow the sorcerers if they win?"
026:042 for ye shall in **that** case be (raised to
026:043 "Throw ye-**that** which ye are about to throw!"
026:051 "Only, our desire is **that** our Lord will
026:086 for **that** he is among those astray;
026:089 **that** brings to Allah a sound heart;
026:111 when it is the meanest **that** follow thee?"
026:132 on you freely all **that** ye know.
026:146 in (the enjoyment of) all **that** ye have here?-
026:189 and **that** was the Chastisement of a Great Day.
026:190 Verily in **that** is a Sign: but most
026:194 To thy heart and mind **that** thou mayest admonish
026:197 Is it not a Sign to them **that** the learned
026:221 on whom it is **that** the Satans descend?
026:225 Seest thou not **that** they wander distracted
026:226 And **that** they say what they practice not?-
027:001 a Book **that** makes (things) clear;
027:007 **that** ye may warm yourselves."
027:019 so order me **that** I may be grateful for Thy favours,
027:019 and **that** I may work the righteousness **that** will
027:019 **that** will please Thee: and admit me,
027:025 So **that** they worship not Allah Who brings forth
027:036 has given me is better than **that** which He has
027:036 in wealth? But **that** which Allah has given me
027:043 for she was (sprung) of a people **that** had no faith.
027:047 from thee and those **that** are with thee." He said:
027:049 **that** we shall make a secret night attack on him
027:049 and **that** we shall then say to his heir (when he
027:051 of their plot!-this, **that** We destroyed them
027:062 god besides Allah? Little it is **that** ye heed!
027:072 Say: "It may be **that** some of the events
027:074 as well as all **that** they reveal.
027:074 all **that** their hearts do hide, as well
027:086 for any people **that** believe!
027:086 See they not **that** We have made the Night
027:087 And the Day **that** the Trumpet will be sounded
027:088 for He is well acquainted with all **that** ye do.
027:089 be secure from terror **that** Day.
027:090 **that** which ye have earned by your deeds?"
027:093 and thy Lord is not unmindful of all **that** ye do.
027:093 so **that** ye shall know them": and thy
028:002 **that** makes (things) clear.
028:008 (it was intended) **that** (Moses) should be
028:009 It may be **that** he will be of use to us, or we
028:010 (with faith), so **that** she might remain a (firm)
028:012 the people of a house **that** will nourish and bring
028:012 And We ordained **that** he refused suck at first,
028:013 **that** she might not grieve, and **that**
028:013 and **that** she might know **that** the promise
028:013 **that** her eye might be comforted, **that** she
028:013 and **that** she might know **that** the promise
028:015 for he is an enemy **that** manifestly misleads!"
028:017 He said: "O my Lord! for **that** Thou hast bestowed
028:022 "I do hope **that** my Lord will show me
028:024 any good **that** Thou dost send me!"
028:025 She said: "My father invites thee **that** he may
028:027 on condition **that** thou serve me for eight years,
028:028 He said: "Be **that** (the agreement) between me
028:029 burning firebrand, **that** ye may warm yourselves."
028:034 for I fear **that** they may accuse me of falsehood."
028:037 **that** the wrong-doers will not prosper."
028:037 who it is **that** comes with guidance from Him

THAT (continued)

028:038 **that** I may mount up to the god of Moses: but as
028:039 he and his hosts: they thought **that** they would
028:043 **that** they might receive admonition.
028:045 and long were the ages **that** passed over them;
028:046 in order **that** they may receive admonition.
028:047 **that** their hands have sent forth, they might
028:049 of them, **that** I may follow it! (Do), if
028:050 know **that** they only follow their own lusts:
028:051 in order **that** they may receive admonition.
028:054 for **that** they have persevered, **that** they
028:054 **that** they avert Evil with Good, and **that**
028:054 and **that** they spend (in charity) out of
028:060 but **that** which is with Allah is better
028:062 **That** Day (Allah) will call to them, and say:
028:065 **That** Day (Allah) will call to them, and say:
028:066 Then the arguments **that** day will be obscure
028:067 But any **that** (in this life) had repented,
028:069 And thy Lord knows all **that** their hearts
028:069 their hearts conceal and all **that** they reveal.
028:073 and in order **that** ye may be grateful.
028:073 **that** ye may rest therein, and **that**
028:073 and **that** ye may seek of His Grace;-and in
028:073 It is out of His Mercy **that** He has made
028:074 The Day **that** He will call on them, He will
028:075 then shall they know **that** the Truth is
028:076 **that** their very keys would have been a burden
028:078 I have." Did he not know **that** Allah had destroyed,
028:079 this World: "Oh! **that** we had the like of what
028:082 He pleases! Had it not been **that** Allah was
028:083 **That** Home of the Hereafter We shall give to
028:085 **that** brings true guidance, and who
028:086 **that** the Book would be sent to thee except as
028:088 but He. Everything (**that** exists) will perish
029:002 and **that** they will not be tested?
029:002 Do men think **that** they will be left alone
029:004 **that** they will get the better of us? Evil is
029:007 blot out all misdeeds **that** they have committed,
029:008 and I will tell you (the truth) of all **that** ye did.
029:010 all **that** is in the hearts of all Creation?
029:016 **that** will be best for you-if ye understand!
029:017 The things **that** ye worship besides Allah have no
029:019 truly **that** is easy for Allah.
029:024 (Abraham's) people except **that** they said: "Slay him
029:041 is **that** of the Spider, who builds
029:042 of (everything) whatever **that** they call upon
029:044 verily in **that** is a Sign for those who believe.
029:045 the (deeds) **that** ye do.
029:046 and in **that** which came do to you; Our God
029:047 And thus (it is) **that** We have sent down
029:048 In **that** case, indeed, would the talkers of vanities
029:051 And is it not enough for them **that** We have
029:052 and reject Allah, **that** are losers.
029:055 On the Day **that** the Punishment shall cover
029:060 **that** carry not their own sustenance? It is
029:063 **that** sends down rain from the sky, and gives
029:064 **that** is life indeed, if they but knew.
029:067 and **that** men are being snatched away from all
029:067 Then, do they believe in **that** which is vain,
029:067 Do they not then see **that** We have made
030:004 on **that** Day shall the Believers rejoice-
030:010 for **that** they rejected the Signs of Allah,
030:014 **that** Day shall (all men) be sorted out.

THAT (continued)

030:020 **that** He created you from dust; and then,-behold,
030:021 verily in **that** are Signs for those who reflect.
030:021 **that** ye may dwell in tranquillity with them,
030:021 **that** He created for you mates from among
030:022 and your colours: verily in **that** are Signs
030:023 verily in **that** are Signs for those who hearken.
030:023 **that** ye take by night and by day, and the
030:023 and the quest **that** ye (make for
030:024 after it is dead: verily in **that** are Signs
030:025 **that** heaven and earth stand by His command:
030:026 To Him belongs every being **that** is in the
030:028 to a people **that** understand.
030:030 **that** is the true Religion: but most
030:032 each party rejoicing in **that** which is with itself!
030:037 to whomsoever He pleases? Verily in **that** are Signs
030:037 See they not **that** Allah enlarges the provision
030:038 **that** is best for those who seek the Countenance,
030:039 **That** which you give in usury for increase
030:039 but **that** which you give for charity, seeking the
030:041 in order **that** they may turn back (from Evil).
030:041 **that** (Allah) may give them a taste of some
030:041 and sea because of (the meed) **that** the hands
030:043 on **that** Day shall men be divided (in two).
030:044 from **that** rejection: and those
030:045 **That** He may reward those who believe and work
030:046 and **that** ye may seek of His Bounty: in order
030:046 in order **that** ye may be grateful.
030:046 **that** the ships may sail by His Command and **that**
030:046 **that** He sends the Winds, as heralds
030:055 On the Day **that** the Hour (of reckoning)
030:055 swear **that** they tarried not but an hour:
030:057 So on **that** Day no excuse of theirs will avail
031:010 any pillars **that** ye can see; He set
031:011 **that** others besides Him have created: nay, but
031:015 is to Me, and I will tell you all **that** ye did."
031:020 Do ye not see **that** Allah has subjected to your
031:021 the (revelation) **that** Allah has sent down,
031:021 "Nay, we shall follow the ways **that** we found
031:023 all **that** is in (men's) hearts.
031:025 who it is **that** created the heavens and the earth.
031:026 (**that** is) free of all wants, worthy of
031:029 **that** He has subjected the sun and the moon
031:029 is well acquainted with all **that** ye do?
031:029 a term appointed; and **that** Allah is well
031:029 Seest thou not **that** Allah merges Night into Day
031:030 **That** is because Allah is the Truth and because
031:031 **that** He may show you of His Signs? Verily is
031:031 Seest thou not **that** the ships sail through the
031:032 those **that** falter between (right and wrong).
031:034 **that** he will earn on the morrow: nor does
032:003 **that** thou mayest admonish a people to whom
032:003 in order **that** they may be rightly guided.
032:021 the greater Chastisement in order **that** they may
032:026 Verily in **that** are Signs: do they
032:027 And do they not see **that** We do drive Rain
033:002 with (all) **that** ye do.
033:002 But follow **that** which comes to thee by
033:005 **that** is juster in the sight of Allah.
033:008 **That** (Allah) may question the Truthful about their
033:009 but Allah sees (clearly) all **that** ye do.
033:009 and forces **that** ye saw not: but Allah
033:011 In **that** situation were the Believers tried:

THAT (continued)

033:017 Say: "Who is it **that** can screen you from Allah
033:019 of none effect: and **that** is easy of Allah.
033:020 They think **that** the Confederates have not
033:024 **That** Allah may reward the men of Truth
033:024 and punish the Hypocrites if **that** be His Will,
033:026 (so **that**) some ye slew, and some
033:028 "If it be **that** ye desire the life of this world,
033:030 and **that** is easy for Allah.
033:031 But any of you **that** is devout in the service
033:032 but speak ye a speech (**that** is) just.
033:033 like **that** of the former Times of Ignorance;
033:037 in order **that** (in future) there may be no
033:037 **that** thou shouldst fear Allah. Then when
033:037 **that** which Allah was about to make manifest:
033:038 **that** have passed away. And the
033:043 **that** He may bring you out from the depths
033:047 to the Believers, **that** they shall have
033:050 in order **that** there should be no difficulty
033:051 **that** of all of them-with **that** which thou hast
033:051 and Allah knows (all) **that** is in your hearts:
033:051 any of them **that** thou pleasest, and thou
033:053 or **that** ye should marry his widows after him
033:053 **that** makes for greater purity for your
033:053 Nor is it right for you **that** ye should
033:056 on the Prophet: O ye **that** believe! send ye
033:059 (when out of doors): **that** is most convenient,
033:059 **that** they should cast their outer garments
033:059 most convenient, **that** they should be known
033:066 would **that** we had obeyed Allah and obeyed
033:066 The Day **that** their faces will be turned over
033:071 he **that** obeys Allah and His Messenger has already
033:071 **That** He may make your conduct whole and sound
033:073 (With the result) **that** Allah has to punish
034:002 and all **that** ascends thereto and He
034:002 and all **that** comes out thereof; all **that**
034:002 all **that** comes down from the sky and all
034:002 He knows all **that** goes into the earth, and all
034:003 less than **that**, or greater, but is
034:004 **That** He may reward those who believe and work
034:006 to thee from thy Lord-**that** is the Truth, and **that**
034:006 see **that** the (Revelation) sent down to thee
034:006 and **that** it guides to the path of the
034:007 **that** ye shall (then be raised) in a New Creation?
034:007 **that** will tell you, when ye are all scattered
034:008 in the Hereafter, **that** are in (real) Chastisement,
034:009 **that** turns to Allah (in repentance).
034:011 for be sure I see (clearly) all **that** ye do."
034:012 and there were Jinns **that** worked in front of him,
034:014 the Jinns saw plainly **that** if they had known
034:017 **That** was the Requital We gave them because
034:019 (soul **that** is) patiently constant and grateful.
034:019 (**that** is told), and We dispersed them all in
034:020 all but a party **that** believed.
034:021 except **that** We might test the man who believes
034:023 'That' which is true and just; and He
034:023 will they say, 'What is it **that** your Lord
034:023 So far (is this the case) **that**, when terror
034:024 it is **that** either we or ye are on right
034:031 nor in (any) **that** (came) before it." Couldst thou
034:037 **that** will bring you nearer to Us in degree:
034:040 "Was it you **that** these men used to worship?"
034:042 So on **that** Day no power shall they have

THAT (continued)

034:046   **that** ye do stand up before Allah,-(it may be)
034:048   of (all) **that** is hidden."
034:048   the Truth,-He **that** has full knowledge of (all)
034:053   and **that** they cast (conjectures) with regard
034:053   Seeing **that** they did reject faith (entirely)
035:006   **that** they may become Companions of the Blazing Fire.
035:008   so **that** he looks upon it as good, (equal to one
035:008   for Allah knows well all **that** they do!
035:009   so **that** they raise up the Clouds, and We
035:009   **that** is dead, and revive the earth therewith
035:010   of Righteousness. Those **that** lay Plots of Evil,-
035:012   therein **that** plough the waves, **that** ye
035:012   **that** ye may seek (thus) of the Bounty of Allah
035:012   of Allah **that** ye may be grateful.
035:015   O ye men! it is ye **that** have need of Allah:
035:017   Nor is **that** (at all) difficult for Allah.
035:022   Allah can make any **that** He wills to hear;
035:022   are living and those **that** are dead. Allah can
035:022   Nor are alike those **that** are living
035:027   Seest thou not **that** Allah sends down
035:029   a Commerce **that** will never fail:
035:031   **That** which We have revealed to thee of the Book
035:032   **that** is the highest Grace.
035:035   settled us in a Home **that** will last: no toil
035:037   so **that** he **that** would should receive admonition?
035:038   full knowledge of all **that** is in (men's) hearts.
035:039   He it is **that** has made you inheritors
035:042   by Allah **that** if a warner came to them,
036:006   In order **that** thou mayest warn a people,
036:008   so **that** they cannot bow their heads.
036:009   so **that** they cannot see.
036:012   and We record **that** which they sent before
036:012   sent before and **that** which they leave behind,
036:016   They said: "Our Lord doth know **that** we have been
036:026   He said: "Ah me! would **that** my People knew
036:027   "For **that** my Lord has granted me Forgiveness
036:033   A Sign for them is the earth **that** is dead;
036:035   their hands **that** made this: will they
036:035   **That** they may enjoy the fruits of this
036:036   in pairs all things **that** the earth produces,
036:038   for Him: **that** is the decree of (Him), the Exalted
036:041   And a Sign for them is **that** We bore their race
036:045   When they are told, "Fear ye **that** which is
036:045   which is before you and **that** which will be
036:045   will be after you, in order **that** ye may
036:054   Then, on **that** Day, not a soul will be wronged
036:055   shall **that** Day have joy in all **that** they do;
036:060   of Adam, **that** ye should not worship Satan;
036:060   not worship Satan; for **that** he was to you
036:061   (for **that**) this was the Straight Way?
036:061   "And **that** ye should worship Me, (for **that**)
036:064   for **that** ye (persistently) rejected (Truth)."
036:065   **That** Day shall We set a seal on their mouths.
036:065   bear witness, to all **that** they did.
036:070   (who are) alive, and **that** the word may be
036:070   **That** it may give admonition to any (who are)
036:071   See they not **that** it is We Who have created
036:072   And **that** We have subjected them to their (use)?
036:074   than Allah, (hoping) **that** they might be helped!
036:077   Doth not man see **that** it is We Who created
036:078   and decomposed ones (at **that**)?"
037:025   **that** ye help not each other?'"

THAT (continued)

037:026   Nay, but **that** day they shall submit (to Judgment);
037:031   **that** we shall indeed (have to) taste (the
037:033   Truly, **that** day, they will (all) share
037:034   Verily **that** is how We shall deal with Sinners.
037:035   For they, when they were told **that** there is
037:058   "Is it (the case) **that** we shall not die,
037:059   and **that** we shall not be punished?"
037:062   Is **that** the better entertainment or the
037:064   For it is a tree **that** springs out of
037:067   Then on top of **that** they will be given
037:085   his people, "What is **that** which ye worship?
037:086   than Allah **that** ye desire?
037:092   **that** ye speak not?"
037:095   He said: "Worship ye **that** which ye have
037:102   in a dream **that** I offer thee in sacrifice:
037:113   but of their progeny are (some) **that** do right,
037:113   do right, and (some) **that** obviously do wrong,
037:143   Had it not been **that** he (repented and)
037:149   is it **that** thy Lord has (only) daughters,
037:150   Or **that** We created the angels female, and they
037:158   **that** they will be brought before Him.
037:170   But (now **that** the Qur'an has come), they reject
037:172   **That** they would certainly be assisted,
037:173   And **that** Our forces,-they surely must conquer.
038:004   So they wonder **that** a Warner has come to them
038:010   and means (to reach **that** end)!
038:018   It was We **that** made the hills declare, in unison
038:024   are they?." And David gathered **that** We had
038:026   for **that** they forget the Day of Account.
038:027   all between! **That** were the thought of Unbelievers!
038:029   **that** they may meditate on its Signs, and **that**
038:029   and **that** men of understanding may receive admonition.
038:062   **that** we see not men who we used to number
038:064   **That** is true-the mutual recriminations of the
038:067   Say: "**That** is a Tremendous tidings.
038:070   **that** I am to give warning plainly and publicly."
038:085   with thee and those **that** follow thee,-every one."
038:085   "**That** I will certainly fill Hell with thee
039:003   "We only serve them in order **that** they may
039:003   Is it not to Allah **that** sincere devotion is due?
039:003   in **that** wherein they differ. But Allah
039:007   of all **that** ye did (in this life). For He
039:007   For He knoweth well all **that** is in (men's) hearts.
039:009   endued with understanding **that** receive admonition.
039:015   Ah! **that** is indeed the (real and) evident Loss!"
039:020   their Lord, **that** lofty mansions, one above
039:021   Seest thou not **that** Allah sends down rain
039:022   to Islam, so **that** he has received light
039:027   in order **that** they may receive admonition.
039:028   in order **that** they may guard against Evil.
039:034   They shall have all **that** they wish for, in the
039:035   So **that** Allah will remit from them (even) the
039:038   **that** created the heavens and the earth, they would
039:038   The things **that** ye invoke besides Allah,-
039:040   and on whom descends a Chastisement **that** abides."
039:041   but he **that** strays injures his own soul.
039:041   He, then, **that** receives guidance benefits his
039:042   It is Allah **that** takes the souls (of men)
039:042   and those **that** die not (He takes) during their
039:044   in the End, it is to Him **that** ye shall
039:046   is hidden and open! It is Thou **that** wilt judge
039:046   and the earth! Knower of all **that** is hidden

THAT (continued)

039:047	Even if the wrong-doers had all **that** there is
039:048	be (completely) encircled by **that** which they
039:050	them say! But all **that** they did was of
039:052	Know they not **that** Allah enlarges the provision
039:054	comes on you: after **that** ye shall not be helped.
039:055	"And follow the Best **that** which revealed to you
039:056	in **that** I neglected (my duty) towards Allah,
039:064	**that** ye order me to worship, O ye
039:068	when all **that** are in the heavens and on
039:070	and (Allah) knoweth best all **that** they do.
040:005	the Truth; but it was I **that** seized them!
040:006	**that** truly they are Companions of Fire!
040:008	"And grant, our Lord! **That** they enter the
040:009	from ills **that** Day,-on them wilt Thou have
040:009	and **that** will be truly the highest Achievement.
040:010	to yourselves, seeing **that** ye were called to the
040:015	**that** it may warn (men) of the Day
040:016	**That** of Allah, the One, the Overpowering!
040:016	Whose will be the Dominion **that** Day?
040:017	**That** Day will every soul be requited for what
040:017	no injustice will there be **that** Day, for Allah
040:018	Warn them of the Day **that** is (ever) drawing near,
040:019	and all **that** hearts (of men) conceal.
040:022	**That** was because there came to them
040:029	"I but point out to you **that** which I see (myself);
040:035	**that** hath reached them, very hateful (is such
040:036	a lofty palace, **that** I may attain the ways
040:037	the heavens, and **that** I may look up to the God
040:039	it is the Hereafter **that** is the Home **that** will last.
040:040	"He **that** works evil will not be requited but by
040:040	and he **that** works a righteous deed-whether man
040:045	**that** they plotted (against him), but the
040:061	for you, **that** ye may rest therein, and the Day,
040:066	seeing **that** the Clear Signs have come to me
040:067	a Term appointed: in order **that** ye may understand.
040:069	Seest thou not those **that** dispute concerning
040:074	anything (**that** had real existence)." Thus does
040:075	the Truth, and **that** ye were wont to be insolent.
040:075	"**That** was because ye were wont to rejoice on the
040:077	**that** they shall (all) return.
040:077	(before **that**),-(in any case) it is to Us **that** they
040:079	**that** ye may use some for riding and some for food;
040:080	**that** ye may through them attain to any need
040:082	in the land: yet all **that** they accomplished was
040:083	but **that** very (Wrath) at which they were
041:005	(concealed) from **that** to which thou dost invite us,
041:006	**that** your God is One God: so take
041:008	**that** will never fail.
041:009	Say: Is it **that** ye Deny Him Who created the earth
041:015	**that** Allah, Who created them, was superior
041:016	**that** We might give them a taste of a Chastisement
041:019	The Day **that** the enemies of Allah will be
041:022	**that** Allah knew not many of the things **that** ye
041:022	**that** ye used to do!
041:026	**that** ye may gain the upper hand!"
041:028	a (fit) requital, for **that** they were wont to
041:029	so **that** they become the vilest."
041:031	therein shall ye have all **that** ye ask for!-
041:031	therein shall ye have all **that** your souls
041:040	seeth (clearly) all **that** ye do.
041:040	or he **that** comes safe through, on the
041:040	he **that** is cast into the Fire, or he

THAT (continued)

041:043	Nothing is said to thee **that** was not said to the
041:045	for a Word **that** went forth before from thy Lord,
041:047	The Day **that** (Allah) will propound to them
041:048	**that** they have no way of escape.
041:050	the Unbelievers the truth of all **that** they did,
041:050	I think not **that** the Hour (of Judgment)
041:053	enough **that** thy Lord doth witness all things?
041:053	**that** this is the Truth. Is it not enough **that**
041:054	**that** doth encompass all things!
042:004	To Him belongs all **that** is in the heavens
042:007	**that** thou mayest warn the Mother of Cities
042:011	and He is the One **that** hears and sees.
042:013	for you as **that** which He enjoined on Noah-the which
042:013	to thee-and **that** which We enjoined on Abraham,
042:013	Namely, **that** ye should remain steadfast in Religion,
042:014	Had it not been for a Word **that** went forth before
042:015	Now then, for **that** (reason), call (them to
042:017	will make thee realize **that** perhaps the Hour
042:018	Behold, verily those **that** dispute concerning
042:018	and know **that** it is the Truth. Behold, verily
042:020	his tilth; and to any **that** desires the tilth
042:020	To any **that** desires the tilth of the Hereafter,
042:022	wish for. **That** will indeed be the magnificent
042:022	before their Lord, all **that** they wish for.
042:022	and (the burden of) **that** must (necessarily) fall
042:023	**That** is (the Bounty) whereof Allah gives Glad
042:025	He is the One **that** accepts repentance from His
042:025	and He knows all **that** ye do.
042:028	He is the One **that** sends down rain (even) after
042:029	and the living creatures **that** He has scattered
042:035	**that** there is for them no way of escape.
042:036	but **that** which is with Allah is better
042:043	and forgive, **that** would truly be an affair
042:047	**That** Day there will be for you no place of refuge
042:051	**that** Allah should speak to him except by inspiration,
043:002	By the Book **that** makes things clear,-
043:003	**that** ye may be able to understand.
043:005	from you altogether, for **that** ye are a people
043:010	(Yea, the same **that**) has made for you the earth
043:010	in order **that** ye may find guidance (on the way);
043:011	and We raise to life therewith a land **that** is dead;
043:011	**That** sends down (from time to time) rain from
043:012	**That** has created pairs in all things, and has
043:013	In order **that** ye may sit firm and square
043:020	such (deities)!" Of **that** they have no knowledge!
043:024	you better guidance than **that** which ye found
043:024	They said: "For us, We deny **that** ye (prophets)
043:028	**that** they may turn back (to Allah).
043:032	so **that** some may command work from others.
043:033	**that** blasphemes against The Most Gracious,
043:033	And were it not **that** (all) men might become
043:037	the Path, but they think **that** they are being
043:038	"Would **that** between me and thee were the distance
043:039	**that** day, **that** ye shall be partners in punishment!
043:042	Or We shall show thee **that** (accomplished) which We
043:048	in order **that** they might turn (to Us).
043:066	**that** it should come on them all of a sudden,
043:067	Friends on **that** Day will be foes, one to
043:071	there will be there all **that** the souls
043:071	all **that** the eyes could delight in: and ye
043:077	They will cry: "O Malik! would **that** thy Lord
043:080	Or do they think **that** We hear not their secrets

THAT (continued)

043:083	(with vanities) until they meet **that** Day of theirs,
044:002	By the Book **that** makes things clear;-
044:004	In **that** (night) is made distinct every affair
044:010	**that** the sky will bring forth a kind of smoke
044:013	Seeing **that** a Messenger explaining things clearly
044:057	**That** will be the supreme achievement!
044:058	in thy tongue, in order **that** they may give heed.
045:004	and the fact **that** animals are scattered
045:005	and the fact **that** Allah sends down Sustenance
045:005	the winds,- are Signs for those **that** are wise.
045:012	of His Bounty, and **that** ye may be grateful.
045:012	it by His command, **that** ye may seek of His Bounty,
045:012	to you, **that** ship may sail through it by
045:013	as from Him, all **that** is in the heavens and on
045:013	and on earth: behold, in **that** are Signs
045:017	granted to them **that** they fell into schisms,
045:018	**that** (Way), and follow not the desires of those
045:019	it is only wrong-doers (**that** stand as) Protectors,
045:021	righteous deeds,-**that** equal will be their Life
045:021	think **that** We shall hold them as equal with those
045:021	Ill is the judgment **that** they make.
045:022	for just ends, and in order **that** each soul my
045:024	But of **that** they have no knowledge: they merely
045:027	and the Day **that** the Hour of Judgement
045:027	**that** Day will the followers of Falsehood perish!
045:028	ye be recompensed for all **that** ye did!
045:029	on record all **that** ye did."
045:030	to His Mercy: **that** will be the manifest triumph.
045:032	of Allah was true, and **that** the Hour-there was
045:032	"And when it was said **that** the promise of Allah
045:033	by **that** which they used to mock at!
045:035	deceived you." (From) **that** Day, therefore, they
046:003	turn away from **that** whereof they are warned.
046:006	be hostile to them and deny **that** (men) had
046:008	against Allah. He knows best of **that** whereof ye
046:009	I follow but **that** which is revealed to me
046:011	and seeing **that** they guide not themselves thereby,
046:013	(on **that** Path),-on them shall be no fear,
046:015	grant me **that** I may be grateful for Thy favour
046:015	and **that** I may work righteousness such as Thou
046:017	Do ye hold out the promise to me **that** I shall
046:018	**that** have passed away; for they
046:019	(have done), and in order **that** (Allah) may
046:020	and **that** ye (ever) transgressed."
046:020	for **that** ye were arrogant on earth
046:020	And on the Day **that** the Unbelievers will be
046:023	but I see **that** ye are a people in ignorance!"...
046:026	(completely) encircled by **that** which they used
046:027	in various ways, **that** they may turn (to Us).
046:028	but **that** was their Falsehood and their invention.
046:033	See they not **that** Allah, Who created
046:034	for **that** ye were wont to deny (Truth)!"
046:034	And on the Day **that** the Unbelievers will be
046:035	the (Unbelievers). On the Day **that** they see
047:009	**That** is because they hate the Revelation of Allah;
047:011	**That** is because Allah is the Protector of those
047:015	so **that** it cuts up their bowels (to pieces)?
047:018	**that** it should come on them of a sudden?
047:019	Know, therefore, **that** there is no god but Allah,
047:022	**that** ye will do mischief in the land, and break
047:024	or is **that** there are locks upon their hearts?
047:028	This because they followed **that** which displeased

THAT (continued)

047:029	is a disease, think **that** Allah will not
047:030	And Allah knows all **that** ye do.
047:038	of all wants, and it is ye **that** are needy.
047:038	**that** are niggardly. But any who are niggardly
048:002	**That** Allah may forgive thee thy faults of the
048:003	And **that** Allah may help thee with powerful help.
048:004	**that** they may add Faith to their Faith;-for to
048:005	**That** He may admit the men and women who believe,
048:005	and **that** is, in the sight of Allah, the grand
048:006	And **that** He may punish the Hypocrites,
048:009	**that** ye may assist and honor him, and celebrate
048:009	In order **that** ye (O men) may believe
048:011	acquainted with all **that** ye do.
048:012	"Nay, ye thought **that** the Messenger and the
048:017	but he **that** obeys Allah and His Messenger,-
048:020	from you; **that** is may be a Sign for the Believers,
048:020	**that** ye shall acquire, and He
048:020	the Believers, and **that** He may guide you to a
048:024	over them. And Allah sees well all **that** ye do.
048:024	after **that** He gave you the victory over them.
048:025	ye did not know **that** ye were trampling down
048:025	**that** He may admit to His mercy whom He will.
049:003	Those **that** lower their voice in the presence
049:007	And know **that** among you is Allah's Messenger:
049:009	the one **that** transgresses until it complies
049:010	And fear Allah, **that** ye may receive Mercy.
049:011	laugh at others: it may be **that** the (latter)
049:011	it may be **that** the (latter) are better than the
049:013	**that** ye may know each other (not **that**
049:013	(not **that** ye may despise each other). Verily the
049:016	your Religion?" But Allah knows all **that** is in
049:017	**that** they have embraced Islam. Say, "Count
049:017	a favour upon you **that** He has guided you
049:018	and Allah sees well all **that** ye do."
050:002	But they wonder **that** there has come to them
050:003	**That** is a (sort of) Return far
050:011	to land **that** is dead: thus will
050:015	the first Creation, **that** they should be in
050:020	**that** will be the Day whereof warning
050:035	all **that** they wish,-and there is more with Us.
050:037	**that** has a heart and understanding or who
050:039	Bear, then with patience, all **that** they say,
050:042	**that** will be the day of Resurrection.
050:044	**that** will be a gathering together,-quite easy
051:001	By the (Winds) **that** scatter broadcast;
051:002	And those **that** lift and bear away heavy weights;
051:003	And those **that** flow with ease and gentleness;
051:004	And those **that** distribute the affair;-
051:005	Verily **that** which ye are promised is true;
051:022	as (also) **that** which ye are promised.
051:023	as much as the fact **that** ye can speak
051:042	It left nothing whatever **that** it came up against,
051:049	**that** ye may receive instruction.
051:056	**that** they may serve Me.
051:057	nor do I require **that** they should feed Me.
051:059	then let them not ask Me to hasten (**that** portion)!
051:060	from **that** Day of theirs which they have been promised!
052:011	Then woe **that** Day to the rejecters (of Truth);-
052:012	**That** play (and paddle) in shallow trifles.
052:013	**That** Day shall they be thrust down to the
052:015	"Is this then a magic, or is it ye **that** do not see?
052:032	Is it **that** their intellects urges them to this,

THAT (continued)

052:040 a reward, so **that** they are burdened
052:040 Or is it **that** thou dost ask for a reward,
052:041 Or **that** the Unseen is in their hands, and they
052:045 they encounter **that** Day of theirs, wherein they
053:011 in no way falsified **that** which he saw.
053:026 and **that** he is acceptable to Him.
053:030 **That** is their attainment of Knowledge. Verily thy
053:031 so **that** He rewards those who do evil,
053:031 Yea, to Allah belongs all **that** is in the heavens
053:032 He knows best who it is **that** guards against evil.
053:035 so **that** he can see?
053:038 Namely, **that** no bearer of burdens can bear
053:039 **That** man can have nothing but what he strives for;
053:040 **That** (the fruit of) his striving will soon
053:042 **That** to thy Lord is the final Goal;
053:043 **That** it is He who Granteth Laughter and Tears;
053:044 **That** it is He who Granteth Death and Life;
053:045 **That** He did create in pairs-male and female,
053:047 **That** He hath promised a Second Creation
053:048 **That** it is He Who giveth wealth and satisfaction,
053:049 **That** He is the Lord of Sirius (the Mighty Star);
053:050 And **that** it is He Who destroyed the (powerful)
053:052 for **that** they were (all) most unjust and most
053:054 So **that** there covered it **that** which covered.
054:006 **that** the Caller will call (them) to a
054:015 **that** will receive admonition?
054:017 then is there any **that** will receive admonition?
054:022 then is there any **that** will receive admonition?
054:025 "Is It **that** the Message is sent to him, of all
054:028 And tell them **that** the water is to be divided
054:032 then is there any **that** will receive admonition?
054:040 then is there any **that** will receive admonition?
054:046 full recompense): and **that** Hour will be most
054:051 then is there any **that** will receive admonition?
054:052 All **that** they do is noted in (their)
055:008 In order **that** ye may not transgress (due) balance.
055:026 All **that** is on earth will perish:
055:039 On **that** Day no question will be asked
056:020 And with fruits, any **that** they may select;
056:021 And the flesh of fowls, any **that** they may desire.
056:045 For **that** they were wont to be indulged,
056:045 to be indulged, before **that**, in sinful luxury,
056:051 "Then will ye truly,-O ye **that** go wrong,
056:058 Do ye then see? The (human Seed) **that** ye emit,-
056:061 creating you (again) in (Forms) **that** ye know not.
056:063 See ye the seed **that** ye sow in the ground?
056:064 Is it ye **that** cause it to grow, or are We the Cause?
056:076 And **that** is indeed a mighty adjuration if ye
056:077 **That** this is indeed a Qur'an most honourable,
056:081 Is it such a Message **that** ye would hold
056:082 **that** ye should declare it false?
057:004 may be. And Allah sees well all **that** ye do.
057:008 How is it with you **that** you not believe in Allah?-
057:009 **that** He may lead you from the depths
057:010 How is it **that** you spend not in the cause of Allah?-
057:010 And Allah is well acquainted with all **that** ye do.
057:011 Who is he **that** will loan to Allah a beautiful Loan?
057:015 the Fire: **that** is the proper place to claim you:
057:016 the Believers **that** their hearts in all humility
057:016 (to them), and **that** they should not become
057:017 Know ye (all) **that** Allah giveth life to the
057:017 plainly to you, **that** ye may understand.

THAT (continued)

057:020 Know ye (all), **that** the life of this world
057:021 and His messengers: **that** is the Grace of Allah,
057:022 **that** is truly easy for Allah:
057:023 over matters **that** pass you by, nor exult
057:023 In order **that** ye may not despair over matters
057:025 **that** Allah may test who it is **that** will help,
057:025 and Wrong), **that** men may stand forth in justice;
057:027 but **that** they did not foster as they
057:028 O ye **that** believe! fear Allah, and believe
057:029 **that** (His) Grace is (entirely) in His Hand,
057:029 **that** they have no power whatever over the Grace
057:029 **That** the People of the Book may know **that** they
058:003 well-acquainted with (all) **that** ye do.
058:003 (it is ordained **that** such a one) should free
058:004 indigent ones. This, **that** ye may show your
058:006 On the Day **that** Allah will raise
058:007 Seest thou not **that** Allah doth know (all) **that** is
058:007 (all) **that** is in the heavens and on earth?
058:008 and evil is **that** destination!
058:008 to **that** which they were forbidden (to do)?
058:010 by Satan, in order **that** he may cause grief to the
058:012 **That** will be best for you, and most
058:013 and Allah is well-acquainted with all **that** ye do.
058:013 Is it **that** ye are afraid of spending sums
058:018 swear to you: and they think **that** they have
058:019 Truly, it is the Party of Satan **that** will lose.
058:022 **that** will achieve Success.
059:002 so **that** they destroyed their dwellings by their
059:002 and they thought **that** their fortresses would
059:002 **that** they would get out: and they
059:003 And had it not been **that** Allah has decreed
059:004 **That** is because they resisted Allah and His
059:005 and in order **that** He might cover with shame
059:007 in order **that** it may not (Merely) make a circuit
059:009 they are the ones **that** achieve prosperity.
059:011 But Allah is witness **that** they are indeed liars.
059:014 **that** is because they are a people devoid of wisdom.
059:017 **that** they will go into the Fire, dwelling therein
059:018 for Allah is well-acquainted with (all) **that** ye do.
059:020 **that** will achieve Felicity.
059:021 to men, **that** they may reflect.
060:001 the truth **that** has come to you, and have
060:001 ye conceal and all **that** ye reveal. And any
060:001 for I know full well all **that** ye conceal
060:001 And any of you **that** does this has strayed
060:002 for evil; and they desire **that** ye should
060:003 between you: for Allah sees well all **that** ye do.
060:007 It may be **that** Allah will Establish friendship
060:009 (in these circumstances), **that** do wrong.
060:010 **that** they are Believers, then send
060:012 **that** they will not steal, **that** they
060:012 fealty to thee, **that** they will not associate
060:012 and **that** they will not disobey thee in any
060:012 kill their children, **that** they will not utter
060:012 **that** they will not commit adultery (or fornication),
060:012 (or fornication), **that** they will not kill their
061:002 **that** which ye do not?
061:003 of Allah **that** ye say **that** which ye do not.
061:005 and insult me, though ye know **that** I am
061:009 **That** He make it prevail over all religion,
061:010 to a bargain **that** will save you
061:011 and His Messenger, and **that** ye strive

THAT (continued)

061:011   **That** ye believe in Allah and His Messenger,
061:011   and your persons: **that** will be best for you,
061:012   **that** is indeed the supreme Triumph.
061:014   the ones **that** prevailed.
062:005   in those (obligations), is **that** of a donkey
062:006   **that** ye are friends to Allah, to the
062:007   And Allah knows well those **that** do wrong!
062:008   and He will tell you the things **that** ye did!"
062:009   **that** is best for you if ye but knew!
062:010   and remember Allah frequently **that** ye may prosper.
062:011   Say: "**That** which Allah has is better than any
063:001   And Allah beareth witness **that** the Hypocrites
063:001   they say, "We bear witness **that** thou art
063:001   **that** thou art indeed His Messenger. And Allah
063:003   **That** is because they believed, then they
063:004   They think **that** every cry is against them.
063:011   acquainted with (all) **that** ye do.
064:002   are Believers: and Allah see well all **that** ye do.
064:002   and of you are some **that** are Unbelievers,
064:002   are Unbelievers, and some **that** are Believers:
064:006   **That** was because there came to them messengers
064:007   The Unbelievers think **that** they will not be
064:007   And **that** is easy for Allah."
064:007   (the truth) of all **that** ye did. And **that**
064:008   And Allah is well-acquainted with all **that** ye do.
064:009   The Day **that** He assembles you (all) for a day
064:009   for a day of Assembly,-**that** will be a day
064:009   **that** will be the Supreme Triumph.
064:010   and evil is **that** Goal.
064:014   are (some **that** are) enemies to yourselves:
064:016   they are the ones **that** achieve prosperity.
065:005   **That** is the Command of Allah, which He
065:008   How many populations **that** insolently opposed
065:011   clear explanations, **that** he may lead forth those
065:012   **that** ye may know **that** Allah has power
065:012   and **that** Allah comprehends all things
065:012   **that** ye may know **that** Allah has power
066:001   to be forbidden **that** which Allah has made
066:005   **that** Allah will give him in exchange Consorts
066:007   Ye are being but requited for all **that** ye did!"
066:008   the Day **that** Allah will not permit to be
066:008   **that** your Lord will remove from you your
066:010   with (others) **that** enter!"
066:011   and save me from those **that** do wrong";
067:002   **that** He may try which of you is best in deed:
067:014   Should He not know,-He **that** created? And He
067:016   Do ye feel secure **that** He Who is in heaven
067:017   so **that** ye shall know how (terrible) was My warning?
067:017   Or do ye feel secure **that** He Who is in
067:019   truly it is He **that** watches over all things.
067:020   Nay, who is there **that** can help you, (even as)
067:021   Or who is there **that** can provide you
067:029   (of us) it is **that** is in manifest error."
068:007   Verily it is thy Lord **that** knoweth best,
068:009   Their desire is **that** thou shouldst be pliant:
068:013   Violent (and cruel),-with all **that**, of a
068:032   "It may be **that** our Lord will give us in exchange
068:038   **That** ye shall have, through it whatever ye choose?
068:039   of Judgment, (providing) **that** ye shall have
068:040   will stand surety of **that**!
068:042   The Day **that** the Shin shall be laid bare,
068:043   seeing **that** they had been summoned aforetime

THAT (continued)

068:046   a reward, so **that** they are burdened with a load
068:046   Or is it **that** thou dost ask them for a reward,
068:047   so **that** they can write it down?
068:047   Or **that** the Unseen is in their hands, so **that**
069:007   so **that** thou couldst see the (whole) people
069:012   unto you, and **that** ears (**that** should hear the
069:012   **That** We might make it a Reminder unto you,
069:015   On **that** Day shall the (Great) Event come to pass,
069:016   for it will **that** Day be flimsy,
069:017   and eight will, **that** Day, bear the Throne
069:018   **That** Day shall ye be brought to Judgment: not an
069:018   not an act of yours **that** ye hide will be hidden.
069:019   Then He **that** will be given his Record in his
069:020   **that** my Account would (one Day) reach me!"
069:024   in the days **that** are gone!"
069:024   **that** ye sent before you, in the days
069:025   "Ah! would **that** my record had not been given to me!
069:025   And he **that** will be given his Record in his
069:026   "And **that** I had never realized how my
069:027   "Ah! would **that** (Death) had made an end of me!
069:033   "This was he **that** would not believe
069:040   **That** this is verily the word of a honoured
069:049   amongst you those **that** reject (it).
069:049   And We certainly know **that** there are amongst you
070:008   The Day **that** the sky will be like molten brass,
070:011   from the Chastisement of **that** Day by his children,
070:011   would **that** he could redeem himself from the
070:014   And all, all **that** is on earth,-so it
070:036   the Unbelievers **that** they rush madly before thee-
070:040   **that** We can certainly-
070:042   **that** Day of theirs which they have been promised!
071:003   "**That** ye should worship Allah, fear Him,
071:007   **that** thou mightest forgive them, they have
071:013   **that** ye are not conscious of Allah's majesty,-
071:014   "Seeing **that** it is He **that** has created you
071:020   **That** ye may go about therein, in spacious roads."
072:001   Say: It has been revealed to me **that** a company
072:005   or Jinn should say aught **that** is untrue
072:005   'But we do think **that** no man or Jinn
072:007   ye thought, **that** Allah would not raise up any one
072:011   'There are among us some **that** are righteous,
072:012   'But we think **that** we can by no means
072:014   'Amongst us are some **that** submit their wills
072:014   **that** swerve from justice. Now those
072:017   "**That** We might try them by **that** (means). But if
072:023   for any **that** disobey Allah and His Messenger,-
072:024   who it is **that** is weakest in (his) helper
072:024   (with their own eyes) **that** which they are promised,-
072:028   and He encompasses all **that** is with them, and takes
072:028   "**That** he may know **that** they have (truly) brought
073:013   And Food **that** chokes, and a Chastisement Grievous.
073:017   a Day **that** will make children hoary-headed?-
073:020   for you. He knoweth **that** there may be (some)
073:020   The Lord doth know **that** thou standest forth
073:020   He knoweth **that** ye are unable to keep count thereof.
074:009   **That** will be-**that** Day-a Day of Distress,-
074:015   Yet is he greedy-**that** I should add (yet more);
074:031   in order **that** the People of the Book may arrive
074:031   and **that** no doubts may be left for the People
074:031   and the Believers, and **that** those in whose heart
074:037   To any of you **that** chooses to press forward, or to
074:047   "Until there came to us (the Hour) **that** is certain."

THAT (continued)

074:049	**that** they turn away from admonition?-
075:003	Does man think **that** We cannot assemble his bones?
075:010	**That** Day will Man say "Where is the refuge?"
075:012	**that** Day will be the place of rest.
075:013	**That** Day will Man be told (all) **that**
075:013	(all) **that** he put forward, and all
075:013	and all **that** he put back.
075:022	Some faces **that** Day, will beam
075:024	And some faces, **that** Day, will be sad and dismal,
075:025	In the thought **that** some back-breaking calamity
075:028	And he will think **that** it was (the Time)
075:030	**That** Day the Drive will be (all) to thy Lord!
075:036	Does Man think **that** he will be left uncontrolled,
076:011	from the evil of **that** Day, and will
076:027	behind them a Day (**that** will be) hard.
077:015	Ah woe, **that** Day, to the Rejecters of Truth!
077:019	Ah woe, **that** Day, to the Rejecters of Truth!
077:024	Ah woe, **that** Day, to the Rejecters of Truth!
077:028	Ah woe, **that** Day, to the Rejecters of Truth!
077:029	(It will be said:) "Depart ye to **that** which ye
077:034	Ah woe, **that** Day, to the Rejecters of Truth!
077:035	**That** will be a Day when they shall not
077:037	Ah woe, **that** Day, to the Rejecters of Truth!
077:038	**That** will be a Day of Sorting out! We shall
077:040	Ah woe, **that** Day, to the Rejecters of Truth!
077:043	heart's content: for **that** ye worked (Righteousness).
077:045	Ah woe, **that** Day, to the Rejecters of Truth!
077:046	for **that** ye are Sinners.
077:047	Ah woe, **that** Day, to the Rejecters of Truth!
077:049	Ah woe, **that** Day, to the Rejecters of Truth!
077:050	Then what Message, after **that**, will they believe in?
078:015	**That** We may produce therewith grain and vegetables,
078:018	The Day **that** the Trumpet shall be sounded, and ye
078:027	For **that** they used not to look for any account
078:038	The Day **that** the Spirit and the angels will stand
078:039	**That** is the True Day: therefore, whoso will,
078:040	"Woe unto me! Would **that** I were (mere) dust!"
079:006	One Day everything **that** can be in commotion
079:008	Hearts **that** Day will be in agitation;
079:012	They say: "It would, in **that** case, be a
079:018	"And say to him, `Wouldst thou **that** thou shouldst
079:019	"`And **that** I guide thee to thy Lord, so thou
079:035	(all) **that** he strove for,
080:003	but **that** perchance he might Grow purity?
080:004	Or **that** he might receive admonition, and the
080:025	For **that** We pour forth water in abundance,
080:034	**That** Day shall a man flee from his own brother,
080:037	Each one of them, **that** Day, will have
080:038	Some Faces **that** Day will be beaming.
080:040	And other faces **that** Day will be dust-stained;
081:015	So verily I call to witness the Planets-**that** recede,
082:012	They know all **that** ye do.
082:019	for the Command, **that** Day, will be
083:001	Woe to those **that** deal in fraud,-
083:004	Do they not think **that** they will be raised up?-
083:010	Woe, **that** Day, to those **that** deny-
083:011	Those **that** deny the Day of Judgment.
083:015	**that** Day, will they be veiled.
084:014	Truly, did he think **that** he would not
084:020	**that** they believe not?-
084:025	for them is a Reward **that** will never fail.
085:003	By one **that** witnesses, and the

THAT (continued)

085:007	And they witnessed (all) **that** they were doing
085:008	no other reason than **that** they believed in Allah,
085:011	**that** is the great Triumph.
085:016	Doer (without let) of all **that** He intends.
086:009	The Day **that** (all) things secret will be tested,
086:013	**that** distinguishes (Good from Evil):
088:002	Some faces, **that** Day, will be humiliated,
088:008	(Other) faces **that** Day will be joyful,
089:023	And Hell, **that** Day, is brought (face to face),-
089:023	**that** remembrance profit him?
089:023	(face to face),-on **that** Day will man remember,
089:024	He will say: "Ah! would **that** I had sent forth
089:025	For, **that** Day, His Chastisement will be such as
090:003	And the begetter and **that** he begot;-
090:005	Thinketh he, **that** none hath power over him?
090:007	Thinketh he **that** none beholdeth him?
090:011	on the path **that** is steep.
090:012	to thee the path **that** is steep?-
091:009	Truly he succeeds **that** purifies it,
091:010	And he fails **that** corrupts it!
093:005	give thee (**that** wherewith) thou shalt
096:005	Taught man **that** which he knew not.
096:007	In **that** he looketh upon himself as self-sufficient.
096:014	Knoweth he not **that** Allah doth see?
098:005	and **that** is the Religion Right and Straight.
099:004	On **that** Day will she declare her tidings:
099:005	For **that** thy Lord will have given her inspiration.
099:006	On **that** Day will men proceed in groups sorted out,
099:006	**that** they (had done).
100:001	By the (Steeds) **that** run, with panting (breath),
100:007	And to **that** (fact) he bears witness (by his deeds);
100:009	Does he not know,-when **that** which is in the
100:010	And **that** which is (locked up) in (human)
100:011	well-acquainted with them, (Even to) **that** Day?
100:011	**That** their Lord had been well-acquainted
102:008	Then, shall ye be Questioned **that** Day about the
104:003	Thinking **that** his wealth would make him
104:004	to be thrown into **that** which Breaks to Pieces.
104:005	**That** which Breaks to Pieces?
109:001	Say: O ye **that** reject Faith!
109:002	I worship not **that** which ye worship,
109:003	Nor will ye worship **that** which I worship.
109:004	**that** which ye have been wont to worship,
109:005	Nor will ye worship **that** which I worship.

THE (See Appendix)

THEE

001:005	**Thee** do we worship, and Thine aid we seek.
002:004	And who believed in the Revelation sent to **thee**,
002:032	They said: "Glory to **Thee**,
002:055	in **thee** until we see Allah manifestly,"
002:099	We have sent down to **thee** manifest Signs
002:119	Verily We have sent **thee** in truth as a bearer of
002:119	but of **thee** no question shall be asked
002:120	the knowledge which hat reached **thee**,
002:120	be satisfied with **thee** unless thou follow their
002:124	He said: "I will make **thee** an Imam
002:137	but Allah will suffice **thee** as against them,
002:144	now shall We turn **thee** to a Qiblah
002:144	a Qiblah that shall please **thee**.
002:145	If thou after the knowledge hath reached **thee**,
002:186	When My servants ask **thee** concerning Me,
002:189	They ask **thee** concerning the New Moons.

THEE (continued)

002:204 whose speech about life may dazzle **thee**,
002:215 They ask **thee** what they should spend (in charity).
002:217 They ask **thee** concerning fighting
002:219 They ask **thee** how much they are to spend;
002:219 They ask **thee** concerning wine and gambling.
002:220 They ask **thee** concerning orphans.
002:222 They ask **thee** concerning women's courses.
002:252 We rehearse them to **thee** in truth:
002:255 Who is **thee** can intercede in His presence
002:259 make of **thee** a Sign unto the people.
002:260 they will come to **thee** (flying) with speed.
002:285 and to **Thee** is the end of all journeys."
003:003 It is He Who sent down to **thee** (step by step),
003:007 He it is Who has sent down to **thee** the Book:
003:020 So if they dispute with **thee**,
003:035 "O my Lord! I do dedicate unto **thee** what is in
003:038 Grant unto me from **Thee** a progeny that is pure:
003:039 "Allah doth give **thee** glad tidings of Yahya,
003:042 "O Mary! Allah hath chosen **thee** and purified **thee**
003:042 chosen **thee** above the women of all nations.
003:044 which We reveal unto **thee** (O Prophet!)
003:045 "O Mary! Allah giveth **thee** glad tidings
003:055 "O Jesus! I will take **thee** and raise **thee** to Myself
003:055 and clear **thee** (of the falsehoods)
003:055 who follow **thee** superior to those who reject faith,
003:058 "This is what we rehearse unto **thee** of the Signs
003:061 now after (full) knowledge hath come to **thee**,
003:061 If any one disputes in this manner with **thee**,
003:108 We rehearse them to **thee** in Truth:
003:128 Not for **thee**, (but for Allah), is the decision:
003:154 what they dare not reveal to **thee**.
003:159 they would have broken away from about **thee**:
003:176 Let not those grieve **thee** who rush headlong
003:184 Then if they reject **thee**, so were rejected
003:184 so were rejected messengers before **thee**,
003:191 Glory to **thee**! Give us salvation from
003:196 of the unbelievers through the land deceive **thee**:
004:041 and We brought **thee** as a witness
004:060 that have come to **thee** and to those before **thee**?
004:061 avert their faces from **thee** in disgust.
004:062 Then they come to **thee**, swearing by Allah: "We
004:064 come unto **thee** and asked Allah's forgiveness,
004:065 until they make **thee** judge in all disputes between
004:075 and raise for us from **Thee** one who will protect;
004:075 and raise for us from **Thee** one who will help!"
004:078 "This is from **thee**" (O Prophet).
004:079 sent **thee** as a Messenger to (instruct) mankind.
004:079 but whatever evil happens to **thee**, is from
004:079 Whatever good, (O man!) happens to **thee**, is from
004:080 We have not sent **thee** to watch over them.
004:081 but when they leave **thee**, a section of them
004:102 let them pray with **thee**, taking all precautions,
004:102 stand up (in prayer) with **thee**.
004:105 We have sent down to **thee** the Book in truth,
004:105 by that which Allah has shown **thee**; so be not
004:113 But for the Grace of Allah to **thee** and His Mercy,
004:113 would certainly have plotted to lead **thee** astray.
004:113 and to **thee** they can do no harm in the least.
004:113 and great is the Grace of Allah unto **thee**.
004:113 For Allah hath sent down to **thee** the Book
004:113 taught **thee** what thou knewest not (before):
004:153 The people of the Book ask **thee** to cause

THEE (continued)

004:162 believe in what hath been revealed to **thee** and
004:162 and what was revealed before **thee**:
004:163 We have sent **thee** inspiration, as We sent
004:164 told **thee** the story; of others We have not;
004:166 He hath sent unto **thee** He hath sent
004:176 They ask **thee** for a legal decision,
005:004 They ask **thee** what is lawful to them (as food).
005:027 Said the latter: "Be sure I will slay **thee**."
005:028 to stretch my hand against **thee** to slay **thee**:
005:029 **thee** draw on thyself my sin as well as thine,
005:041 who have never so much as come to **thee**.
005:041 O Messenger! let not those grieve **thee**, who race
005:042 If they do come to **thee**, either judge
005:042 If thou decline, they cannot hurt **thee** in the least.
005:043 But why do they come to **thee** for decision,
005:048 diverging form the truth that hath come to **thee**.
005:048 To **thee** We sent the Scripture in truth, confirming
005:049 beguile **thee** from any of that (teaching) which
005:049 (teaching) which Allah hath sent down to **thee**.
005:052 Ah! perhaps Allah will give (**thee**) victory, or a
005:061 When they come to **thee**, they say: "We believe":
005:064 But the revelation that cometh to **thee** from Allah
005:067 And Allah will defend **thee** from men
005:067 which hath been sent to **thee** from thy Lord.
005:068 that cometh to **thee** from thy Lord,
005:100 the abundance of the bad may dazzle **thee**;
005:110 recount my favour to **thee** and to thy mother.
005:110 Behold! I taught **thee** the Book and Wisdom,
005:110 (violence to) **thee** when thou didst show them
005:110 Behold! I strengthened **thee** with the Holy Spirit.
005:114 a solemn festival and a Sign from **Thee**;
005:116 He will say: "Glory to **Thee**! never could
006:007 If We had sent unto **thee** a written (Message)
006:010 Mocked were (many) Messengers before **thee**;
006:017 if He touch **thee** with happiness, He hath
006:017 "If Allah touch **thee** with affliction, none can
006:025 in so much that when they come to **thee**, they
006:025 they (but) dispute with **thee**;
006:025 there are some who (pretend to) listen to **thee**;
006:033 the grief which their words do cause **thee**:
006:033 it is not **thee** they reject: it is the
006:034 Rejected were the Messengers before **thee**:
006:035 If their spurning is hard on **thee**,
006:042 Before **thee** We sent (Messengers)
006:052 and in naught are they accountable for **thee**,
006:054 When those come to **thee** who believe
006:068 If Satan ever makes **thee** forget,
006:074 For I see **thee** and thy people in manifest error."
006:107 but We made **thee** not one to watch over their doings,
006:116 they will lead **thee** away from the Way of Allah.
006:147 If they accuse **thee** of falsehood,
007:002 A Book revealed unto **thee**,- so let
007:012 **thee** from prostrating when I commanded **thee**?"
007:013 (Allah) said: "Get **thee** down from it: it is not
007:013 it is not for **thee** to be arrogant here: get out,
007:018 If any of them follow **thee**,-Hell will I fill with you all.
007:060 "Ah! we see **thee** evident error."
007:088 we shall certainly drive **thee** out of our city-
007:088 (**thee**) and those who believe with **thee**;
007:101 We (thus) relate unto **thee**:
007:112 And bring up to **thee** all (our) sorcerers well-versed."

THEE (continued)

007:126 and take our souls unto **Thee** as Muslims
007:127 and to abandon **thee** and thy gods?"
007:132 we shall never believe in **thee**."
007:134 the Children of Israel with **thee**."
007:134 we shall truly believe in **thee**, and we
007:134 in virtue of his promise to **thee**: if thou
007:143 To **Thee** I turn in repentance, and I
007:143 "Glory be to **Thee**!
007:143 that I may look upon **Thee**."
007:144 and the words I (have spoken to **thee**);
007:144 chosen **thee** above (other) men,
007:144 take then the (revelation) which I give **thee**,
007:144 by the messages I (have given **thee**) and the
007:156 for we have turned unto **Thee**."
007:187 They ask **thee** as if thou wert eager in search
007:187 They ask **thee** about the (final) Hour-when will
007:198 thou will see them looking at **thee**,
008:001 They ask **thee** concerning (things taken as)
008:005 Just as thy Lord ordered **thee** out of
008:006 Disputing with **thee** concerning the truth
008:030 Remember how the Unbelievers plotted against **thee**,
008:030 to keep **thee** in bonds, or slay **thee**,
008:030 or get **thee** out (of they home).
008:032 if this is indeed the truth from **Thee**,
008:043 if He had shown them to **thee** as many,
008:043 in thy dream Allah showed them to **thee** as few:
008:062 Should they intend to deceive **thee**,-
008:062 verily Allah sufficeth **thee**:
008:062 He it is that hath strengthened **thee** with His aid
008:064 and unto those who follow **thee** among the Believers.
008:064 O Prophet! Sufficient unto **thee** is Allah,-
008:071 But if they have treacherous designs against **thee**,
008:071 and so hath He given (**thee**) power over them.
009:006 If one amongst the Pagans ask **thee** for asylum,
009:042 they would (ali) without doubt followed **thee**,
009:043 who told the truth were seen by **thee** in a clear
009:043 God give **thee** grace!
009:044 and the Last Day ask **thee** for no exemption from
009:045 Only those ask **thee** for exemption who believe
009:048 and upset matters for **thee**,-
009:050 If good befalls **thee**, it grieves them;
009:050 but if a misfortune befalls **thee**,
009:055 Let not their wealth nor their children dazzle **thee**:
009:058 who slander **thee** in the matter of
009:083 and they ask thy permission to come out (with **thee**),
009:083 If, then, Allah bring **thee** back to any of them,
009:085 Nor let their wealth nor their children dazzle **thee**:
009:086 and influence among them ask **thee** for exemption,
009:092 on those who came to **thee** to be provided with mount.
010:010 "Glory to **Thee**, O Allah!" and "Peace" will be
010:041 If they charge **thee** with falsehood, say: "My work
010:042 Among them are some who (pretend to) listen to **thee**:
010:043 And among them are some who look at **thee**:
010:046 Whether We show **thee** (realized in thy lifetime)
010:053 They seek to be informed by **thee**: "Is that true?"
010:065 Let not their speech grieve **thee**:
010:086 from those who reject (**Thee**)."
010:092 a Sign to those who come after **thee**!
010:092 "This day shall We save **thee** in thy body,
010:094 who have been reading the Book from before **thee**:
010:094 We have revealed unto **thee**, then ask
010:094 the Truth hath indeed come to **thee** from thy Lord:

THEE (continued)

010:106 such can neither profit **thee** nor hurt **thee**:
010:107 if He do design some benefit for **thee**, there is
010:107 If Allah do touch **thee** with hurt, there is
010:109 Follow thou the inspiration sent unto **thee**,
011:012 to give up a part of what is revealed unto **thee**,
011:027 nor do we see that any follow **thee** but the
011:027 (in) **thee** nothing but a man like ourselves: nor do
011:046 I give **thee** counsel, lest thou become on of the
011:047 Noah said: "'O my Lord! I do seek refuge with **Thee**,
011:047 from asking **Thee** for that of which I have no knowledge
011:048 the Peoples (who will spring) from those with **thee**:
011:048 and Blessing on **thee** and on some of the Peoples
011:049 which We have revealed unto **thee**:
011:053 Nor shall we believe in **thee**!
011:054 some of our gods may have seized **thee** with evil."
011:081 By no means shall they reach **thee**!
011:087 Does thy prayer command **thee** that we leave off
011:091 we should certainly have stoned **thee**! For thou
011:100 the stories of communities which We relate unto **thee**:
011:112 thou and those who with **thee** turn (unto Allah);
011:120 in them there cometh to **thee** the Truth, as well
011:120 All that We relate to **thee** of the stories
012:003 in that We reveal to **thee** this (portion of the) Qur-an:
012:003 We do relate unto **thee** the most beautiful
012:005 lest they concoct a plot against **thee**:
012:006 His favour to **thee** and to the posterity of Jacob-
012:006 and teach **thee** the interpretation of stories
012:006 "Thus will thy Lord choose **thee** and teach
012:088 so pay us full measure, (we pray **thee**),
012:091 Allah preferred **thee** above us, and we
012:102 which We reveal by inspiration unto **thee**:
012:109 Nor did We send before **thee** (as Messengers)
013:001 been revealed unto **thee** from thy Lord is the Truth;
013:006 They ask **thee** to hasten on the evil
013:030 Thus have We sent **thee** amongst a People
013:030 We send down unto **thee** by inspiration; yet do
013:032 Mocked were (many) messengers before **thee**: but I
013:036 rejoice at what hath been revealed unto **thee**:
013:037 after the knowledge which hath reached **thee**,
013:038 We did send messengers before **thee**, and appointed
013:040 Whether We shall show **thee** (within thy lifetime)
014:001 A Book which We have revealed unto **thee**, in order
015:010 send messengers before **thee** amongst the sects of old:
015:034 (Allah) said: "Then get **thee** out from here;
015:035 the Curse shall be on **thee** till the Day of Judgment."
015:037 (Allah) said: "Respite is granted **thee**-
015:042 put themselves in the wrong and follow **thee**."
015:053 They said: "Fear not! we give **thee** glad tidings
015:055 They said: "We give **thee** glad tidings in truth;
015:063 to **thee** to accomplish that of which they doubt.
015:064 "We have come to **thee** with the Truth and assuredly
015:070 They said: "Did we not forbid **thee** (to speak)
015:087 And We have bestowed upon **thee** the Seven
015:095 sufficient are We unto **thee** against those who scoff.-
015:099 come unto **thee** the Hour that is Certain.
016:043 And before **thee** We sent were but men, to whom
016:044 We have sent down unto **thee** (also) the Message;
016:063 We (also) sent (our prophets) to Peoples before **thee**:
016:064 And We sent down the Book to **thee** so that
016:086 those whom we used to invoke besides **Thee**."
016:089 bring **thee** as a witness against these (thy people);
016:089 and We have sent down to **thee** the Book explaining

THEE (continued)

016:118   as We have mentioned to **thee** before:
016:123   Then We revealed to **thee** "Follow the ways
017:014   this day to make out an account against **thee**."
017:039   which thy Lord has revealed to **thee**.
017:045   We put, between **thee** and those who believe not
017:047   when they listen to **thee**;
017:048   See what similes thy strike for **thee**:
017:051   their heads towards **thee**, and say, "When will
017:054   We have not sent **thee** to be a disposer
017:060   Behold! We told **thee** that thy Lord doth
017:060   We granted the Vision which We showed **thee**,
017:063   if any of them follow **thee**, verily Hell will be the
017:073   And their purpose was to tempt **thee** away from
017:073   from that which We had revealed unto **thee**,
017:073   they would certainly have made **thee** (their) friend!
017:074   And had We not given **thee** strength, thou wouldst
017:075   found none to help **thee** against Us!
017:075   made **thee** taste double portion (of punishment)
017:076   they would not have stayed (therein) after **thee**,
017:076   Their purpose was to scare **thee** off the land,
017:076   in order to expel **thee**;
017:077   with the messengers We sent before **thee**:
017:079   raise **thee** to a Station of Praise and Glory!
017:079   keep awake a part of it as an additional prayer for **thee**:
017:080   and grant me from **Thee** an authority to aid (me)."
017:085   They ask **thee** concerning the Spirit.
017:086   We have sent **thee** by inspiration:
017:087   for His Bounty is to **thee** (indeed) great.
017:090   They say: "We shall not believe in **thee**,
017:101   "O Moses! I consider **thee**, indeed, to have
017:102   and I consider **thee**, indeed, O Pharaoh,
017:105   and We sent **thee** but to give Glad Tidings
018:013   We relate to **thee** their story in truth: they were
018:027   been revealed to **thee** of the Book of thy Lord:
018:037   a sperm-drop, then fashioned **thee** into a man?
018:037   "Dost thou deny Him Who created **thee** out of dust,
018:039   If thou dost see me less than **thee** in wealth and sons,
018:066   Moses said to him: "May I follow **thee**, on the
018:069   nor shall I disobey **thee** in aught."
018:070   until I Myself speak to **thee** concerning it."
018:072   He answered: "Did I not tell **thee** that thou canst
018:075   He answered: "Did I not tell **thee** that thou canst
018:076   (Moses) said: "If ever I ask **thee** about anything
018:078   now will I tell **thee** the interpretation of (those things)
018:078   "This is the parting between me and **thee**:
018:083   They ask **thee** concerning Zul-Qarnain.
018:094   shall we then render **thee** tribute in order that
019:004   am I unblest, O my Lord, in my prayer to **Thee**!
019:007   We give **thee** good news of a son: his name
019:009   I did indeed create **thee** before, when thou
019:018   She said: "I seek refuge from **thee** to (Allah)
019:019   from thy Lord, (to announce) to **thee** the gift
019:024   for thy Lord hath provided a rivulet beneath **thee**;
019:025   it will let fall fresh ripe dates upon **thee**.
019:042   and can profit **thee** nothing?
019:043   I will guide **thee** to a Way that is even and straight.
019:043   knowledge which hath not reached **thee**:
019:045   a Chastisement afflict **thee** from (Allah)
019:046   I will indeed stone **thee**: now get
019:047   Abraham said: "Peace be on **thee**: I will
020:002   We have not sent down the Qur'an to **thee** to be
020:009   Has the story of Moses reached **thee**?

THEE (continued)

020:013   "I have chosen **thee**: listen, then to the
020:013   then to the inspiration (given to **thee**).
020:016   divert **thee** therefrom, lest thou perish!"...
020:023   show **thee** of Our Greater Signs.
020:034   "And remember **Thee** without stint:
020:037   We conferred a favour on **thee** another time (before).
020:039   but I endued **thee** with love from Me:
020:040   So We brought **thee** back to thy mother, that her
020:040   and We tired **thee** in various ways.
020:040   but We saved **thee** from trouble, and We
020:041   "And I have prepared **thee** for Myself (for service)."
020:058   So make a tryst between us and **thee**,
020:072   They said: "Never shall we prefer **thee** to what
020:083   "What made **thee** hasten in advance of thy people
020:084   I hastened to **Thee**, O my Lord to please **Thee**."
020:087   They said: "We broke not the promise to **thee**,
020:092   "O Aaron! what kept **thee** back, (Moses) said:
020:097   (Moses) said: "Get **thee** gone! but thy (punishment)
020:099   for We have sent **thee** a reminder from Us.
020:099   Thus do We relate to **thee** some stories
020:105   They ask **thee** concerning the mountains: say, "My
020:114   the Qur-an before its revelation to **thee** is completed,
020:117   this is an enemy to **thee** and thy wife: so let
020:118   for **thee** not to go hungry nor to go naked,
020:120   he said, "O Adam! shall I lead **thee** to the Tree
020:126   when Our Signs came unto **thee**, forgot them:
020:132   We ask **thee** not to provide sustenance:
020:132   We provide it for **thee**.
021:007   Before **thee**, also, the messengers We sent
021:025   before **thee** without this inspiration sent by
021:034   not to any man before **thee** permanent life (here):
021:036   When the Unbelievers see **thee**, they treat
021:036   they treat **thee** not except with ridicule.
021:041   Mocked were (many) messengers before **thee**;
021:087   Glory to **Thee**: I was indeed wrong!"
021:107   We sent **thee** not, but as a mercy for all creatures.
022:027   they will come to **thee** on foot and (mounted)
022:047   Yet they ask **thee** to hasten on the Punishment!
022:052   Never did We send a messenger or a prophet before **thee**,
022:067   let them not then dispute with **thee** on the matter,
022:068   If they do wrangle with **thee**,
023:028   on the Ark-thou and those with **thee**,-say: "Praise
023:095   show **thee** (in fulfillment) that against which
023:097   with **Thee** from the suggestions of the Satans.
023:098   "And I seek refuge with **Thee**, O my Lord!
024:016   glory to **Thee** (our Lord) this is a most serious slander!"
025:009   for **thee**! But they have gone astray, and never
025:010   and He could give **thee** Palaces (secure to dwell in).
025:010   His Will, could give **thee** better (things) than
025:018   that we should not take for protectors besides **Thee**:
025:018   They will say: "Glory to **Thee**! not meant
025:020   before **thee** were all (men) who ate food
025:032   and We have rehearsed it to **thee** in slow,
025:033   And no question do they bring to **thee** but
025:033   but We reveal to **thee** the truth and the best
025:041   they treat **thee** no otherwise than in mockery:
025:041   When they see **thee**, they treat
025:056   But **thee** We only sent to give glad tidings
026:018   (Pharaoh) said: "Did we not cherish **thee** as a
026:029   I will certainly put **thee** in prison!"
026:037   "And bring up to **thee** all (our) sorcerers
026:111   They said: "Shall we believe in **thee** when it

THEE (continued)

026:111   when it is the meanest that follow **thee**?"

026:215   And lower thy wing to the Believers who follow **thee**.

026:216   Then if they disobey **thee**, say: "I am free

026:218   Who seeth **thee** standing forth (in prayer),

027:006   As to **thee**, thou receivest the Qur'an from One

027:019   I may work the righteousness that will please **Thee**:

027:022   and I have come to **thee** from Saba with tidings true.

027:033   but the command is with **thee**; so consider

027:039   "I will bring it to **thee** before thou rise

027:040   "I will bring it to **thee** before even thy glance

027:040   thy glance returns to **thee**.

027:047   from **thee** and those that are with **thee**."

028:003   We rehearse to **thee** some of the story

028:007   for We shall restore him to **thee**, and We

028:009   "(Here is) a joy of the eye, for me and for **thee**:

028:020   are taking counsel together about **thee**, to slay

028:020   to slay **thee**: so get **thee** away, for I

028:025   She said: "My father invites **thee** that he may

028:025   he may reward **thee** for having watered (our

028:026   truly the best of men for **thee** to employ

028:027   But I intend not to place **thee** under a difficulty:

028:027   it will be (grace) from **thee**.

028:027   one of these my daughters to **thee**, on condition

028:028   "Be that (the agreement) between me and **thee**:

028:046   no warner had come before **thee**: in order

028:047   If (We had) not (sent **thee** to the Quraish),

028:050   But if they hearken not to **thee**, know that

028:057   "If we were to follow the guidance with **thee**,

028:077   with the (wealth) which Allah has bestowed on **thee**,

028:077   as Allah has been good to **thee**,

028:085   Verily He Who ordained the Qur-an for **thee**,

028:085   will bring **thee** back to the Place of Return.

028:086   that the Book would be sent to **thee** except as

028:087   revelations after they have been revealed to **thee**:

029:008   (either of them) strive (to force) **thee** to join with Me

029:010   And if help comes (to **thee**) from thy Lord,

029:033   we are (here) to save **thee** and thy following,

029:045   Recite what is sent of the Book by inspiration to **thee**,

029:047   thus (it is) that We have sent down the Book to **thee**.

029:051   We have sent down to **thee** the Book

029:053   They ask **thee** to hasten on the Punishment

029:054   They ask **thee** to hasten on the Punishment:

030:047   We did indeed send, before **thee**, messengers to

030:060   nor let those excite **thee**, who have

031:017   and bear with patient constancy whatever betide **thee**;

031:023   let not his rejection grieve **thee**: to Us

032:003   to whom no warner has come before **thee**:

032:023   be not then in doubt of its reaching (**thee**):

033:002   to **thee** by inspiration from thy Lord: for Allah

033:007   from the Prophets their Covenant: and from **thee**:

033:019   thou wilt see them looking to **thee**, their eyes

033:037   We joined her in marriage to **thee**: in order

033:045   O Prophet! Truly We have sent **thee** as a Witness,

033:050   made lawful to **thee** thy wives to whom thou hast

033:050   who migrated with **thee**; and any

033:050   in order that there should be no difficulty for **thee**.

033:050   the captives of war whom Allah has assigned to **thee**;

033:050   this only for **thee**, and not

033:051   and there is no blame on **thee** if thou invite one whose

033:052   It is not lawful for **thee** (to marry more)

033:052   even though their beauty attract **thee**,

033:060   We shall certainly stir **thee** up against them:

THEE (continued)

033:063   Men ask **thee** concerning the Hour: say, "The

033:063   what will make **thee** understand?-

034:006   to **thee** from thy Lord-that is the Truth, and that

034:028   We have not sent **thee** but as a (Messenger)

034:041   They will say, "Glory to **thee**! Thou art

034:044   nor sent messengers to them before **thee** as Warners.

035:004   so were the messengers rejected before **thee**:

035:004   And if they reject **thee**, so were

035:024   Verily We have sent **thee** with truth, as a

035:025   And if they reject **thee**, so did

035:031   That which We have revealed to **thee** of the Book

036:076   Let not their speech, then, grieve **thee**.

037:102   in a dream that I offer **thee** in sacrifice:

038:021   Has the Story of the Disputants reached **thee**?

038:024   wronged **thee** in demanding thy (single) ewe to be

038:026   O David! We did indeed make **thee** a vicegerent

038:026   for it will mislead **thee** from the Path of Allah:

038:029   (Here is) a Book which We have sent down unto **thee**,

038:075   "O Iblis! what prevents **thee** from prostrating thyself

038:077   (Allah) said: "Then get **thee** out from here:

038:078   "And My Curse shall be on **thee** till the

038:080   (Allah) said: "Respite then is granted **thee**-

038:085   with **thee** and those that follow **thee**,-every one."

039:002   We Who have revealed the Book to **thee** in Truth:

039:036   But they try to frighten **thee** with other

039:041   Verily We have revealed the Book to **thee** in Truth,

039:059   `Nay but there came to **thee** My Signs,

039:065   as it was to those before **thee**,-"

039:065   But it has already been revealed to **thee**,-as it

040:004   their strutting about through the land deceive **thee**!

040:077   and whether We show **thee** (in this life) some part

040:078   whose story We have related to **thee**,

040:078   we did aforetime send messengers before **thee**:

040:078   and some whose story We have not related to **thee**.

041:005   and between us and **thee** is a screen:

041:034   and **thee** was hatred become as it were thy

041:036   to discord is made to **thee** by the Satan,

041:043   to the messengers before **thee**: surely thy

041:043   Nothing is said to **thee** that was not said to the

041:047   "We do assure **Thee** not one of us can bear witness!"

042:003   inspiration to **thee** as (He did) to those before **thee**,-

042:007   We sent by inspiration to **thee** an Arabic Qur'an:

042:013   The which We have sent by inspiration to **thee**-

042:017   will make **thee** realize that perhaps the Hour

042:048   We have not sent **thee** as a guard over them.

042:052   by Our command, sent to **thee**:

043:023   whenever We sent a Warner before **thee** to any people,

043:038   "Would that between me and **thee** were the distance

043:041   Even if We take **thee** away, We shall

043:042   Or We shall show **thee** that (accomplished) which We

043:043   So hold thou fast to the Revelation sent down to **thee**:

043:044   a Reminder for **thee** and for thy people;

043:045   our messengers whom We sent before **thee**;

043:049   for us according to his covenant with **thee**;

043:058   This they set forth to **thee**, only by

045:006   which We rehearse to **thee** in truth: then in

045:018   Then We put **thee** on the (right) Way of Religion:

045:019   They will be of no use to **thee** in the sight

046:015   do I submit (to **Thee**) in Islam."

046:015   Truly have I turned to **Thee** and truly do I

046:017   (and rebuke the son): "Woe to **thee**! have Faith!

046:029   Behold, We turned towards **thee** a company of Jinns

THEE (continued)

047:016   And among them are men who listen to **thee**,
047:016   till when they go out from **thee**,
047:020   is a disease looking at **thee** with a look of one
047:030   We could have shown them up to **thee**, and thou
048:001   Verily We have granted **thee** a manifest Victory:
048:002   and guide **thee** on the Straight Way;
048:002   fulfil His favour to **thee**; and guide
048:002   That Allah may forgive **thee** thy faults of the
048:003   And that Allah may help **thee** with powerful help.
048:008   We have truly sent **thee** as a witness, as a
048:010   to **thee** plight their fealty in truth to Allah:
048:011   The desert Arabs who lagged behind will say to **thee**:
048:018   when they swore Fealty to **thee** under the Tree:
049:004   Those who shout out to **thee** from without
049:017   They impress on **thee** as favour that they
051:024   Has the story reached **thee**, of the honoured
052:042   Or do they intend a plot (against **thee**)?
056:091   "Peace be unto **thee**," from the Companions
058:001   of the woman who pleads with **thee** concerning her
058:008   not as Allah salute **thee**, (but in crooked ways):
058:008   And when they come to **thee**, they salute **thee**,
059:016   Satan says, "I am free of **thee**: I do
060:004   "I will pray for forgiveness for **thee**,
060:004   to **Thee** is (our) final Return.
060:004   "Our Lord! in **Thee** do we trust, and to
060:004   and to **Thee** do we turn in repentance:
060:012   and that they will not disobey **thee** in any
060:012   to **thee** to take the oath of fealty to **thee**,
062:011   and leave **thee** standing.
063:001   When the Hypocrites come to **thee**, they say,
063:004   their bodies please **thee**;
066:001   that which Allah has made lawful to **thee**,
066:003   she said, "Who told **thee** this?"
066:011   build for me, in nearness to **Thee**, a mansion
067:004   thy vision will come back to **thee** dull and discomfited,
068:003   Nay, verily for **thee** is a Reward unfailing:
068:051   the Unbelievers would almost trip **thee** with their eyes
069:003   And what will make **thee** realize what the
070:036   the Unbelievers that they rush madly before **thee**-
073:005   Soon shall We send down to **thee** a weighty Word.
073:007   True, there is for **thee** by day prolonged occupation
073:020   and so doth a party of those with **thee**.
074:027   And what will explain to **thee** what Hell-Fire is?
075:034   Woe to **thee**, (O man!) yea, woe!
075:035   Again, woe to **thee**, (O man!), yea woe!
076:023   Who have sent down the Qur'an to **thee** by stages.
077:014   And what will explain to **thee** what is the Day of
079:015   Has the story of Moses reached **thee**?
079:019   "`And that I guide **thee** to thy Lord,
079:042   They ask **thee** about the Hour,-'When will
080:003   But what could tell **thee** but that perchance
080:007   Though it is no blame to **thee** if he grow
080:008   But as to him who came to **thee** striving earnestly,
082:006   O man! what has seduced **thee** from thy Lord
082:007   and gave **thee** a just bias;
082:007   fashioned **thee** in due proportion,
082:007   Him Who created **thee**,
082:008   does He put **thee** together.
082:017   And what will explain to **thee** what the
082:018   Again, what will explain to **thee** what the
083:008   And what will explain to **thee** what Sijjin is?
083:019   And what will explain to **thee** what 'Illiyin is?

THEE (continued)

085:017   Has the story reached **thee**, of the Forces-
086:002   what will explain to **thee** what the Night-Visitant is?-
087:006   By degrees shall We teach **thee** (the Message),
087:008   And We will make it easy for **thee** (to follow)
088:001   Has the story reached **thee**, of the
090:012   what will explain to **thee** the path that is steep?-
093:003   Thy Guardian-Lord Hath not forsaken **thee**, nor is
093:004   the Hereafter will be better for **thee** than the present.
093:005   soon will thy Guardian-Lord give **thee** (that wherewith)
093:006   Did He not find **thee** an orphan and give
093:006   and give **thee** shelter (and care)?
093:007   and He gave **thee** guidance.
093:007   And He found **thee** wandering, and He
093:008   And He found **thee** in need, and made
093:008   and made **thee** independent.
094:001   Have We not expanded **thee** thy breast?-
094:002   And removed from **thee** thy burden
101:003   will explain to **thee** what the (Day) of Clamour is?
101:010   And what will explain to **Thee** what this is?
104:005   And what will explain to **thee** That which
108:001   To **thee** have We granted the Abundance.
108:003   For he who hateth **thee**,-he will

THEFT

012:081   Behold! thy son committed **theft**! we bear witness

THEIR

002:004   and (in **their** hearts) have the assurance
020:005   They are on (true guidance), from **their** Lord,
002:007   seal on **their** hearts and on **their** hearing,
002:007   and on **their** eyes is a veil;
002:007   Allah hath set a seal on **their** hearts
002:010   and Allah has increased **their** disease,
002:010   In **their** hearts is a disease;
002:014   but when they are alone with **their** evil ones,
002:015   Allah will throw back **their** mockery on them,
002:015   and give them rope in **their** trespasses;
002:016   but **their** traffic is profitless,
002:017   Allah took away **their** light and left them
002:017   **Their** similitude is that of a man who kindled a fire;
002:019   in **their** ears to keep out the stunning
002:019   they press **their** fingers in **their** ears
002:020   The lightning all but snatches away **their** sight:
002:020   **their** faculty of hearing and seeing;
002:025   that **their** portion is Gardens,
002:026   that it is the truth from **their** Lord;
002:033   He said: "O Adam! tell them **their** names."
002:033   "When he had told them **their** names,
002:046   that they are to meet **their** Lord,
002:057   but they harmed **their** own selves.
002:062   shall have **their** reward with **their** Lord
002:066   So We made it an example to **their** own time
002:066   and to **their** posterity,
002:076   Do ye not understand (**their** aim)?
002:078   but (see therein **their** own) desires,
002:079   the Book with **their** own hands,
002:079   Woe to them for what **their** hands do write,
002:081   and are girt round by **their** sins,
002:085   and banish a party of you from **their** homes;
002:085   assist (**their** enemies) against them,
002:086   **their** chastisement shall not be lightened
002:088   Allah's curse is on them for **their** blasphemy;
002:090   for which they have sold **their** souls,
002:093   and **their** hearts were filled (with the love)

THEIR (continued)

002:093 because of **their** Faithlessness.
002:095 **their** hands have sent on before them.
002:101 Book of Allah behind **their** backs,
002:102 which they did sell **their** souls,
002:103 If they had kept **their** Faith
002:111 Those are **their** (vain) desires.
002:113 Like unto **their** word is what those say
002:113 in **their** quarrel on the Day of Judgment.
002:118 who hold firmly to Faith (in **their** hearts).
002:118 **Their** hearts are alike.
002:120 unless thou follow **their** form of religion.
002:120 follow **their** desires after the knowledge
002:121 the loss is **their** own.
002:126 for a while will I grant them **their** pleasure,
002:129 a Messenger of **their** own,
002:130 as debase **their** souls with folly?
002:136 and that given to (all) Prophets from **their** Lord:
002:143 who would turn on **their** heels (from the Faith).
002:144 that is the truth from **their** Lord,
002:145 wert to follow **their** (vain) desires,
002:145 nor art thou going to follow **their** Qiblah;
002:146 know this as they know **their** own sons;
002:157 (descend) blessings from **their** Lord, and Mercy.
002:162 **Their** penalty will not be lightened,
002:162 nor will respite be **their** (lot).
002:164 trail like **their** slaves between the sky
002:165 overflowing in **their** love for Allah.
002:167 (the fruits of) **their** deeds as (nothing but)
002:170 What! even though **their** fathers were void of
002:174 grievous will be **their** Chastisement.
002:176 (**Their** doom is) because Allah sent down the Book
002:187 They are your garments and ye are **their** garments.
002:217 turn back from **their** faith and die in unbelief,
002:217 **their** works will bear no fruit in this life
002:220 "The best thing to do is what is for **their** good;
002:220 (**Their** bearings) on this life and the Hereafter.
002:220 if ye mix **their** affairs with yours,
002:222 so keep away from women in **their** courses,
002:226 an oath for abstention from **their** wives,
002:227 But if **their** intention is firm for divorce,
002:228 to hide what Allah hath created in **their** wombs,
002:228 And **their** husbands have the better right
002:231 (are about to) fulfil the term of **their** ('Iddat),
002:232 from marrying **their** (former) husbands,
002:232 and they fulfil the term of **their** ('Iddat),
002:233 of **their** food and clothing on equitable terms.
002:233 suck to **their** offspring for two whole years,
002:234 when they have fulfilled **their** term,
002:236 or the fixation of **their** dower;
002:240 should bequeath for **their** widows a year's maintenance
002:243 thy vision to those who abandoned **their** homes,
002:247 **Their** Prophet said to them: "Allah hath appointed
002:248 And (further) **their** Prophet said to them: "A Sign
002:261 spend **their** wealth in the way of Allah
002:262 for them **their** reward is with **their** Lord;
002:262 with reminders of **their** generosity or with injury,
002:262 spend **their** wealth in the cause of Allah,
002:262 and follow not up **their** gifts with reminders
002:264 spend **their** wealth to be seen of men,
002:265 to please Allah and to strengthen **their** souls,
002:265 those who spend **their** wealth seeking to please
002:273 because of **their** modesty,

THEIR (continued)

002:273 Thou shalt know them by **their** (unfailing) mark:
002:274 have **their** reward with **their** Lord:
002:275 **their** case is for Allah (to judge);
002:275 admonition from **their** Lord, desist,
002:277 will have **their** reward with **their** Lord:
003:010 neither **their** possessions nor **their** (numerous)
003:010 **their** (numerous) progeny will avail them aught
003:011 and Allah called them to account for **their** sins.
003:011 the people of Pharaoh, and **their** predecessors:
003:013 these saw with **their** own eyes twice **their** number.
003:015 therein is **their** eternal home;
003:015 nearness to **their** Lord with rivers flowing beneath;
003:023 to settle **their** dispute,
003:024 deceive them as to **their** own religion.
003:024 for **their** forgeries deceive them
003:052 unbelief on **their** part he said: "Who will be
003:057 Allah will pay them (in full) **their** reward;
003:076 Those that keep **their** plighted faith and act aright,
003:077 they owe to Allah and **their** own solemn plighted
003:078 a section who distort the Book with **their** tongues;
003:084 and the Prophets, from **their** Lord;
003:088 nor will **their** punishment be lightened,
003:088 nor respite be **their** (lot);
003:090 And then go on adding to **their** defiance of Faith,
003:090 never will **their** repentance be accepted;
003:111 they will show you **their** backs, and no help
003:116 neither **their** possessions nor **their** (numerous)
003:117 harvest of men who have wronged **their** own souls:
003:118 what **their** hearts conceal is far worse.
003:118 rank hatred has already appeared from **their** mouths;
003:119 bite off the very tips of **their** fingers at you in **their** rage.
003:120 not the least harm will **their** cunning do to you;
003:121 to post the Faithful at **their** stations for battler:
003:122 but Allah was **their** Protector,
003:122 the Faithful (ever) put **their** trust.
003:127 frustrated of **their** purpose.
003:135 and ask for forgiveness for **their** sins,
003:135 an act of indecency or wronged **their** own souls.
003:136 is forgiveness from **their** Lord,
003:151 **their** abode will be the Fire:
003:154 They hide in **their** minds what they
003:154 stirred to anxiety by **their** own feelings,
003:154 to the place of **their** death":
003:155 But Allah has blotted out (**their** fault):
003:156 a cause of sighs and regrets in **their** hearts.
003:156 who say of **their** brethren, when they
003:159 For Allah loves those who put **their** trust (in Him).
003:159 so pass over (**their** faults),
003:160 In Allah, then, let Believers put **their** trust.
003:167 saying with **their** lips what was not in **their** hearts.
003:168 the ones that say (of **their** brethren slain),
003:169 finding **their** sustenance from **their** Lord.
003:170 who have not yet joined them (in **their** bliss),
003:173 but it only increased **their** Faith:
003:178 that they may grow in **their** iniquity:
003:180 tied to **their** necks like a twisted collar,
003:181 **their** word and (**their** act) of slaying the Prophets
003:187 but they threw it away behind **their** backs,
003:191 sitting, and lying down on **their** sides,
003:195 verily, I will blot out from them **their** iniquities,
003:195 those who have left **their** homes, and were driven
003:195 And **their** Lord hath accepted of them,

THEIR (continued)

003:197   **their** Ultimate abode is Hell: what an evil
003:198   On the other hand, for those who fear **their** Lord,
003:199   For them is a reward with **their** Lord,
004:002   **their** property (when they reach **their** age),
004:002   and devour not **their** substance (by mixing it up)
004:002   worthless things for (**their**) good ones;
004:005   but if they, of **their** own good pleasure, remit
004:005   (on marriage) **their** dower as an obligation;
004:006   nor in haste against **their** growing up.
004:006   take witnesses in **their** presence:
004:006   release **their** property to them;
004:006   When ye release **their** property to them, take
004:009   as they would have for **their** own if they had left
004:009   have the same fear in **their** minds as they would
004:010   eat up a fire into **their** own bodies:
004:011   **their** share is two-thirds of the inheritance;
004:012   **their** share is a fourth, if ye leave no child;
004:019   forbidden to inherit women against **their** will.
004:024   Give them **their** dowery for the enjoyment
004:025   **their** punishment is half that for free women.
004:025   and give them **their** dowers, according
004:025   wed them with the leave of **their** owners,
004:027   who follow **their** lusts is that ye should turn
004:033   give **their** due portion.
004:034   and because they support them from **their** means.
004:034   (next), refuse to share **their** beds,
004:035   Allah will cause **their** reconciliation:
004:038   if any take the Satan for **their** intimate,
004:038   (Nor) those who spend of **their** substance, to be
004:046   but Allah hath cursed them, for **their** Unbelief;
004:046   those who displace words from **their** (right) places,
004:046   **their** tongues and a slander to Faith.
004:053   they give nothing but farthing to **their** fellow-men!
004:055   And some of them averted **their** faces from him:
004:056   as often as **their** skins are roasted through.
004:057   with rivers flowing beneath, **their** eternal home:
004:060   **Their** (real) wish is to resort together for
004:060   together for judgment (in **their** disputes)
004:061   avert **their** faces from thee in disgust.
004:062   deeds which **their** hands have sent forth?
004:063   and speak to them a word to reach **their** very souls.
004:063   Those men, Allah knows what is in **their** hearts;
004:065   And find in **their** souls no resistance against
004:066   sacrifice **their** lives or to leave **their** homes,
004:066   would have gone farthest to strengthen **their** (faith).
004:069   Ah! How beautiful is **their** Company.
004:077   **their** hands (from fight) but establish regular
004:081   But Allah records **their** nightly (plots): so keep
004:081   They have "Obedience" on **their** lips; but
004:088   Allah hath cast them for **their** (evil) deeds.
004:089   take no friends or helpers from **their** ranks:
004:089   so take not friends from **their** ranks until
004:090   them from fighting you or fighting **their** own people.
004:091   secure from you as well as that of **their** people:
004:091   in **their** case We have provided you with a clear
004:091   besides restraining **their** hands, seize them
004:092   For those who find this beyond **their** means,
004:095   with **their** goods and **their** persons.
004:095   with **their** goods and persons than to those who
004:097   those who die in sin against **their** soul.
004:097   Such men will find **their** abode in Hell.
004:098   and children who have no means in **their** power,

THEIR (continued)

004:102   let them take **their** positions in the rear.
004:102   Taking **their** arms with them:
004:102   when they finish **their** prostrations, let them
004:105   those who betray **their** trust;
004:107   such as betray **their** own souls; for Allah
004:109   on **their** behalf on the Day of Judgment, or
004:109   or who will carry **their** affairs through?
004:113   only lead **their** own souls astray,
004:114   In most of **their** secret talks there is no good:
004:121   They (his dupes) will have **their** dwelling in hell,
004:146   and make **their** religion devotion sincere to Allah:
004:146   mend (**their** life), hold fast to Allah, and
004:152   We shall soon give **their** (due) rewards:
004:153   but they were seized for **their** presumption, with
004:154   And for **their** Covenant We raised over them
004:155   in that they broke **their** Covenant; that they
004:155   on **their** hearts for **their** blasphemy, and
004:173   He will give **their** (due) rewards,-and more,
005:002   and good pleasure of **their** Lord.
005:005   when ye give them **their** due dowers, and desire
005:011   but (Allah) held back **their** hands from you:
005:011   the design to stretch out **their** hands against you,
005:011   And on Allah let Believers put (all) **their** trust.
005:013   But because of **their** breach of **their** Covenant, We
005:013   they change the words from **their** (right) places
005:013   but forgive them and overlook (**their** misdeeds):
005:013   We cursed them, and made **their** hearts grow hard:
005:023   (But) among (**their**) God-fearing men were two
005:026   the land be out of **their** reach for forty years:
005:033   that is **their** disgrace in this world, and a heavy
005:037   **Their** wish will be to get out of the Fire,
005:037   **their** Chastisement will be one that endures.
005:038   a retribution for **their** deeds and exemplary
005:041   Allah's will to purify **their** hearts.
005:041   They change the words from **their** (right) places;
005:041   "We believe" with **their** lips but whose
005:043   when they have (**their** own) Torah before them?
005:046   And in **their** footsteps We sent Jesus
005:048   and follow not **their** vain desires, diverging
005:049   and follow not **their** vain desires, but beware
005:049   that for some of **their** crimes it is Allah's
005:052   which they secretly harboured in **their** hearts.
005:053   who swore **their** strongest oaths by Allah, that
005:062   transgression and **their** eating of things forbidden.
005:063   from **their** (habit of) uttering sinful words
005:063   Evil indeed are **their** works.
005:064   them **their** obstinate rebellion and blasphemy.
005:064   Be **their** hands tied up and be they
005:065   blotted out **their** iniquities and admitted
005:066   that was sent to them from **their** Lord,
005:066   from above them and form below **their** feet.
005:068   them **their** obstinate rebellion and blasphemy.
005:073   If they desist not from **their** word (of blasphemy),
005:075   They had both to eat **their** (daily) food.
005:080   which **their** souls have sent forward before
005:083   thou wilt see **their** eyes overflowing with tears,
005:085   And for this **their** prayer hath Allah
005:085   with rivers flowing underneath, **their** eternal home.
005:102   and on that account lost **their** faith.
005:104   What! even though **their** fathers were void
005:106   If ye doubt (**their** truth), detain them
005:107   Let two others stand forth in **their** places,-

THEIR (continued)

005:108 that other oaths would be taken after **their** oaths.
005:119 with rivers flowing beneath, **their** eternal home:
005:119 the truthful will profit from **their** truth:
006:001 (others) as equal with **their** Guardian Lord.
006:004 of the Signs of **their** Lord reach them, but they
006:006 and gave streams flowing beneath **their** (feet):
006:006 yet for **their** sins We destroyed them,
006:006 and raised in **their** wake fresh generations
006:007 so that they could touch it with **their** hands,
006:012 It is they who have lost **their** own souls,
006:020 know this as they know **their** own sons.
006:020 Those who have lost **their** own souls refuse
006:025 but We have thrown veils on **their** hearts,
006:025 and deafness in **their** ears;
006:028 Yea, in **their** own (eyes) will become manifest
006:030 they shall be made to stand before **their** Lord!
006:033 which **their** words do cause thee: it is not
006:034 bore **their** rejection and **their** persecution until
006:035 If **their** spurning is hard on thee,
006:038 gathered to **their** Lord in the end.
006:043 On the contrary **their** hearts became hardened, and
006:043 and Satan made **their** (sinful) acts seem alluring
006:044 in the midst of **their** enjoyment of Our gifts,
006:048 so those who believe and mend (**their** lives),-
006:051 brought (to judgment) before **their** Lord:
006:052 on **their** Lord morning and evening, seeking
006:061 and they never fail in **their** duty.
006:062 they are returned unto Allah, **their** True Protector,
006:069 but (**their** duty) is to remind them, that they
006:069 On **their** account no responsibility falls on
006:070 deliver themselves to ruin by **their** own acts:
006:070 **their** religion to be mere play and amusement,
006:082 and mix not **their** beliefs with wrong-
006:087 (To them) and to **their** fathers, and progeny
006:089 behold! We shall entrust **their** charge to a new
006:089 if these (**their** descendants) reject them, behold!
006:092 and they are constant in guarding **their** Prayers.
006:093 the angels stretch forth **their** hands, (saying),
006:097 that ye may guide yourselves, with **their** help,
006:107 to dispose of **their** affairs.
006:107 not one to watch over **their** doings,
006:108 In the end will they return to **their** Lord and He
006:108 they out of spite revile Allah in **their** ignorance.
006:109 They swear **their** strongest oaths by Allah,
006:110 We shall leave them in **their** trespasses,
006:110 turn to (confusion) **their** hearts and **their** eyes,
006:111 all things before **their** very eyes, they are
006:120 due recompense for **their** "earnings."
006:121 **their** friends to contend with you if ye
006:122 **their** own deeds seem pleasing.
006:123 but they only plot against **their** own souls,
006:124 and a severe chastisement, for all **their** plots.
006:125 He openeth **their** breast to Islam; those whom
006:125 He maketh **their** breast close and constricted,
006:127 a Home of Peace with **their** Lord:
006:127 He will be **their** Friend, because they
006:128 **Their** friends amongst men will say: "Our Lord!
006:131 **their** occupants were unwarned.
006:132 (or ranks) according to **their** deeds:
006:136 they say, according to **their** fancies: "This
006:136 But the share of **their** "partners" reacheth
006:136 Evil (and unjust) is **their** judgment.

THEIR (continued)

006:136 Allah reacheth **their** "partners"!
006:137 the slaughter of **their** children, in order
006:137 and cause confusion in **their** religion.
006:137 **their** "partners" made alluring the slaughter
006:137 in order to lead them to **their** own destruction,
006:139 For **their** (false) attribution
006:140 Lost are those who slay **their** children, from
006:141 eat of **their** fruit in **their** season,
006:146 except what adheres to **their** backs or **their** entrails,
006:146 this in recompense for **their** wilful disobedience:
006:148 So did **their** ancestors argue falsely, until
006:150 as equal with **their** Guardian Lord.
006:154 in the meeting with **their** Lord.
006:157 for **their** turning away.
006:159 **their** affair is with Allah:
006:159 As for those who divide **their** religion and
007:004 We destroyed (for **their** sins)?
007:004 or while they slept for **their** afternoon rest.
007:007 **their** whole story with knowledge,
007:009 will find **their** souls in perdition,
007:017 from **their** right and **their** left:
007:020 **their** shame that was hidden from them (before):
007:021 that he was **their** sincere adviser.
007:022 **their** shameful parts became manifest to them, and
007:022 the leaves of the Garden over **their** bodies. And
007:022 And **their** Lord called unto them: "Did I not
007:022 So by deceit he brought about **their** fall: when
007:027 stripping them of **their** raiment,
007:027 to expose **their** shame:
007:030 for **their** friends and protectors,
007:030 others have deserved the loss of **their** way, in
007:034 Appointed: when **their** term is reached, not an
007:035 those who are righteous and mend (**their** lives),
007:037 For such, **their** portion appointed must reach
007:037 messengers (of death) arrive and take **their** souls,
007:043 We shall remove from **their** hearts any rancour;
007:047 When **their** eyes shall be turned towards
007:048 they will know from **their** marks,
007:051 "Such as took **their** religion to be mere amusement
007:053 In fact they will have lost **their** souls, and the
007:065 one of **their** (own) brethren: he said: "O my
007:073 one of **their** own brethren: he said: "O my
007:077 the order of **their** Lord, saying: "O Salih!
007:078 they lay prostrate in **their** homes in the morning!
007:085 one of **their** own brethren: he said:
007:085 the things that are **their** due;
007:091 lay prostrate in **their** homes before the morning!
007:095 while they realized not (**their** peril).
007:095 **their** suffering into prosperity, until they
007:096 and We brought them to book for **their** misdeeds.
007:100 and seal up **their** hearts so that they
007:100 We could punish them (too) for **their** sins,
007:101 came to them **their** Messengers with clear (Signs);
007:102 not men (true) to **their** covenant:
007:127 He said: "**Their** male children will we slay; (only)
007:127 (only) **their** females will we save alive;
007:135 Behold! they broke **their** word!
007:147 vain are **their** deeds:
007:148 out of **their** ornaments, the body of the calf,
007:152 be overwhelmed with wrath from **their** Lord,
007:154 Guidance and Mercy for such as fear **their** Lord.
007:157 whom they find mentioned in **their** own (Scriptures),-

THEIR (continued)

007:157 He releases them from **their** heavy burdens and from
007:160 but they harmed **their** own souls.
007:163 **their** fish did come to them, openly
007:163 for on the day of **their** Sabbath
007:163 openly (holding up **their** heads,) but on
007:166 When in **their** insolence they transgressed
007:169 if similar vanities came **their** way, they would
007:172 from **their** loins-their descendants, and made
007:173 but we are (**their**) descendants after them:
007:177 who reject Our signs and wrong **their** own souls.
007:184 **Their** Companion is not seized with madness:
007:185 may well be that **their** term is nigh drawing
007:186 He will leave them in **their** trespasses, wandering
007:189 they both pray to Allah **their** Lord (saying):
007:202 and never relax (**their** efforts).
007:202 But **their** brethren (the evil ones) plunge them
008:002 and put (all) **their** trust in **their** Lord;
008:002 find **their** faith strengthened,
008:002 fell a tremor in **their** hearts,
008:004 they have grades of dignity with **their** Lord,
008:012 and smite all **their** finger-tips off them."
008:012 smite ye above **their** necks and smite
008:035 **Their** prayer at the house (of Allah) is nothing
008:036 The Unbelievers spend **their** wealth to hinder
008:038 **their** past would be forgiven them;
008:044 made you appear as contemptible in **their** eyes:
008:047 from **their** homes insolently and to be seen by men,
008:048 Remember Satan made **their** (sinful) acts seem alluring
008:049 **their** religion has misled them."
008:050 (how) they smite **their** faces and **their** backs
008:052 and Allah punished them for **their** crimes:
008:053 until they change what is in **their** (own) souls:
008:054 destroyed them for **their** crimes,
008:054 the Signs of **their** Lord so We destroyed them
008:056 but they break **their** covenant every time,
008:058 throw back (**their** covenant) to them,
008:063 put affection between **their** hearts:
008:072 with **their** property and **their** persons,
009:004 with them to the end of **their** term:
009:008 but **their** hearts are averse from you;
009:008 With (fair words from) **their** mouths they please
009:012 But if they violate **their** oaths after **their** covenant,
009:012 for **their** oaths are nothing to them;
009:013 Will ye not fight people who violated **their** oaths,
009:015 And still the indignation of **their** heart.
009:017 while they witness **their** own souls to infidelity.
009:020 with **their** goods and **their** persons,
009:021 **Their** Lord doth give them glad tidings of a
009:030 That is a saying from **their** mouths; (in this)
009:031 They take **their** priests and **their** anchorites
009:031 anchorites to be **their** lords beside Allah.
009:031 (they take as **their** Lord) Christ the son of Mary;
009:032 Allah's light with **their** mouths,
009:035 and with it will be branded **their** foreheads,
009:035 **their** flanks, and **their** backs,-"
009:037 The evil of **their** course seems pleasing to them.
009:042 they would destroy **their** own souls;
009:044 from fighting with **their** goods and persons.
009:044 And Allah knoweth well those who do **their** duty.
009:045 they are tossed in **their** doubts to and fro.
009:046 was averse to **their** being sent forth;
009:048 much to **their** disgust.

THEIR (continued)

009:051 let the believers put **their** trust.
009:054 The only reasons why **their** contributions are not
009:055 Let not **their** wealth nor **their** children
009:055 may perish in **their** (very) denial of Allah.
009:055 and that **their** souls may perish
009:064 what is (really passing) in **their** hearts.
009:067 and tighten **their** purse's strings.
009:069 They had **their** enjoyment of **their** portion:
009:069 They!-**their** works are fruitless in this world
009:070 Who wrongs them, but they wrong **their** own souls.
009:070 To them came **their** Messenger with Clear Signs.
009:073 **Their** abode is hell, an evil refuge indeed.
009:074 this revenge of theirs was (**their**) only return
009:074 but if they turn back (to **their** evil ways),
009:076 and turned back (from **their** Covenant),
009:077 **their** Covenant with Allah,
009:077 hath put as a consequence hypocrisy into **their** hearts,
009:079 who give according to **their** means,-
009:079 Allah will throw back **their** ridicule on them:
009:080 (**their** sin is unforgivable): if thou
009:080 if thou ask seventy times for **their** forgiveness,
009:080 Whether thou ask for **their** forgiveness, or not,
009:081 with **their** goods and **their** persons, in the
009:081 in **their** sitting back behind the Messenger
009:085 and that **their** souls may depart while they
009:085 Nor let **their** wealth nor **their** children
009:087 **their** hearts are sealed and so they understand not.
009:088 fight with **their** wealth and **their** persons:
009:092 **their** eyes streaming with tears of grief
009:093 Allah hath sealed **their** hearts: so they
009:094 They will present **their** excuses to you when ye
009:095 and Hell is **their** dwelling-place,
009:098 Bedouin Arabs look upon **their** payments as a fine,
009:099 and look on **their** payments as pious gifts bringing
009:100 those who forsook (**their**) homes) and of those who
009:102 have acknowledged **their** wrong-doings:
009:103 Of **their** goods take alms, that so
009:103 and pray on **their** behalf.
009:104 and receives **their** gifts of charity,
009:107 **their** intention is nothing but good;
009:110 and shakiness in **their** hearts,
009:110 until **their** hearts are cut to pieces.
009:111 **their** persons and **their** good;
009:118 and **their** (very) Souls seemed straitened to them,-
009:120 but was reckoned to **their** credit as a deed
009:120 nor to prefer **their** own lives to his:
009:121 but the deed is inscribed to **their** credit;
009:124 Yea, those who believe, **their** faith is increased,
009:125 it will add doubt to **their** doubt, and they
009:127 Allah has turned **their** hearts (from the light);
010:002 That he should warn mankind (of **their** danger),
010:002 that they have before **their** Lord the good
010:007 on **their** meeting with Us,
010:007 Those who rest not **their** hope on
010:008 **Their** abode is the Fire, because of
010:009 will guide them because of **their** Faith:
010:009 **their** Lord will guide
010:010 will be **their** greeting therein and the
010:010 and the end of **their** prayer will be: "Praise be to
010:010 (This will be) **their** prayer therein: "Glory to
010:011 in **their** trespasses, wandering in
010:011 **their** hope of **their** meeting with Us,

their
         798
         their

THEIR (continued)

010:011 then would **their** respite be settled at once.
010:012 seem fair in **their** eyes!
010:013 **their** Messengers came to them with Clear Signs,
010:015 on **their** meeting with Us, say: "Bring
010:015 unto them, those who rest not **their** hope on
010:019 **their** differences would have been settled
010:022 sincerely offering (**their**) duty unto Him,
010:026 darkness nor abasement shall cover **their** faces!
010:027 ignominy will cover **their** (faces):
010:027 **their** faces will be covered, as it were,
010:028 and **their** "partners" shall say: "It was not
010:030 will be brought back to Allah **their** rightful Lord,
010:030 and **their** invented falsehoods will leave them
010:046 in any case, to Us is **their** return:
010:047 when **their** Messenger comes (before them),
010:049 when **their** term is reached,
010:054 they would declare (**their**) repentance when they
010:065 Let not **their** speech grieve thee:
010:070 the severest Chastisement for **their** disbelief.
010:070 and, then, to Us will be **their** return.
010:074 after him We sent (many) messengers to **their** Peoples:
010:081 When they had had **their** throw, Moses said: "What ye
010:088 Deface Our Lord the features of **their** wealth,
010:088 and send hardness to **their** hearts,
010:098 and permitted them to enjoy (**their**) life for a while.
010:099 against **their** will, to believe!
010:108 do so to **their** own loss:
010:108 do so for the good of **their** own souls;
011:005 Behold! they fold up **their** hearts,
011:005 cover themselves with **their** garments,
011:015 **their** deeds therein,-without diminution.
011:017 a Clear (Sign) from **their** Lord, and followed
011:017 the Fire will be **their** promised meeting place.
011:018 They will be brought before **their** Lord,
011:018 "These are the ones who lied against **their** Lord!
011:020 **Their** chastisement will be doubled!
011:021 They are the ones who have lost **their** own souls:
011:023 and humble themselves before **their** Lord-
011:029 for verily they are to meet **their** Lord,
011:031 Allah knoweth best what is in **their** souls:
011:036 So grieve no longer over **their** (evil) deeds.
011:048 grant **their** pleasures (for a time),
011:050 (We sent) Hud, one of **their** own brethren.
011:059 they rejected the Signs of **their** Lord and Cherisher;
011:060 For the `Ad rejected **their** Lord and Cherisher!
011:061 (We sent) Salih, one of **their** own brethren.
011:067 prostrate in **their** homes before the morning,-
011:068 For the Thamud rejected **their** Lord and Cherisher!
011:070 But when he saw **their** hands not reaching
011:077 he was grieved on **their** account and felt himself
011:081 Morning is **their** time appointed:
011:084 (we sent) Shu'aib, one of **their** own brethren:
011:085 from the people the things that are their due:
011:094 and they lay prostrate in **their** homes by the morning,-
011:101 nor did they add aught (to **their** lot) but perdition!
011:101 they wronged **their** own souls:
011:102 He has chastises communities the midst of **their** wrong:
011:109 **their** portion without (the least) abatement.
011:109 but what **their** fathers worshipped before (them):
011:111 (in full the recompense) of **their** deeds:
011:117 **their** people are righteous.
012:015 of this **their** affair while they perceive not."

THEIR (continued)

012:016 Then they came to **their** father in the early part
012:019 they sent **their** water-carrier (for water), and he
012:031 and (in **their** amazement) cut **their** hands:
012:031 When she heard of **their** malicious talk, she sent
012:033 unless Thou turn away **their** snare from me,
012:034 and turned away from him **their** snare:
012:050 the matter with the ladies who cut **their** hands?'
012:050 for my Lord is certainly well aware of **their** snare."
012:062 when they return to **their** people,
012:062 (with which they had bartered) into **their** saddle-bags,
012:062 (Joseph) told his servants to put **their** stock-in-trade
012:063 Now when they returned to **their** father, they said:
012:065 Then when they opened **their** baggage, they found
012:065 they found **their** stock-in-trade had been returned
012:066 they had sworn **their** solemn oath, he said:
012:067 and let all that trust put **their** trust on Him."
012:068 in the manner **their** father had enjoined,
012:069 so grieve not at aught of **their** doings."
012:076 So he began (the search) with **their** baggage,
012:094 **their** father said: "I do indeed scent the presence
012:102 in the process of weaving **their** plots.
012:102 when they concerted **their** plans together in the
012:105 Yet they turn (**their** faces) away from them!
012:110 when the messengers give up hope (of **their** people)
012:111 There is, in **their** stories, instruction for
013:005 "When we are (actually) dust, strange is **their** saying:
013:005 They are those who deny **their** Lord!
013:005 If thou dost marvel (at **their** want of faith),
013:006 is full of forgiveness for mankind for **their** wrong-doing.
013:008 wombs fall short (of **their** time or number) or do exceed.
013:014 were to stretch forth **their** hands for water to reach
013:014 to reach **their** mouths but it reaches them not:
013:015 so do **their** shadows in the mornings and evenings.
013:018 **their** abode will be Hell,-what a
013:018 For those who respond to **their** Lord, are (all)
013:020 and fail not in **their** plighted word;
013:021 hold **their** Lord in awe, and fear the terrible reckoning;
013:022 seeking the countenance **their** Lord;
013:022 We have bestowed for **their** sustenance, secretly
013:023 and **their** offspring and angels shall enter unto them
013:023 the righteous among **their** fathers, **their** spouses,
013:025 after having plighted **their** word thereto,
013:031 cease to seize them for **their** (ill) deeds,
013:031 or to settle close to **their** homes, until the
013:033 **their** devising seems pleasing, but they
013:037 **their** (vain) desires after the knowledge which
014:001 into light-by the leave of **their** Lord-
014:002 a terrible Chastisement (**their** Unfaith will bring them)!-
014:009 but they put **their** hands up to **their** mouths,
014:010 **Their** messengers said: "Is there a doubt
014:011 And on Allah let all men of faith put **their** trust.
014:011 **Their** messengers said to them: "True, we are
014:012 For those who put **their** trust should put
014:012 should put **their** trust on Allah."
014:013 And the Unbelievers said to **their** messengers:
014:013 But **their** Lord inspired (this Message) to them:
014:018 reject **their** Lord is that **their** works are as ashes,
014:023 to dwell therein for aye with the leave of **their** Lord.
014:023 **Their** greeting therein will be: "Peace!"
014:028 and caused **their** people to descend to the House
014:033 both diligently pursuing **their** courses:
014:043 **their** gaze returning not towards them,

THEIR (continued)

014:043	and **their** hearts a (gaping) void!
014:043	with necks outstretched, **their** heads uplifted,
014:046	but **their** plots were (well) within the sight of Allah
014:050	and **their** faces covered with Fire;
014:050	**Their** garments of liquid pitch,
015:046	(**Their** greeting will be): "Enter ye here
015:047	And We shall remove from **their** hearts any lurking
015:072	in **their** wild intoxication, they wander in distraction,
015:082	Out of the mountains did they hew (**their**) edifices,
015:093	For all **their** deeds.
016:005	and of **their** (meat) ye eat.
016:022	**their** hearts refuse to know,
016:025	on the Day of Judgment, **their** own burdens in full,
016:026	Allah took **their** structures from **their** foundations,
016:028	Take in a state of wrong-doing to **their** own souls."
016:033	nay, they wronged **their** own souls.
016:033	there comes the Command of thy Lord (for **their** doom)?
016:034	But the evil results of **their** deeds overtook them,
016:037	If thou art anxious for **their** guidance,
016:038	They swear **their** strongest oaths by Allah,
016:041	To those who leave **their** homes in the cause
016:042	and put **their** trust on **their** Lord.
016:046	without a chance of **their** frustrating Him?-
016:046	in the midst of **their** goings to and fro,
016:048	Among things,-how **their** shadows turn round,
016:049	for none are arrogant (before **their** Lord).
016:050	They all fear **their** Lord,
016:054	you turn to other gods to join with **their** Lord-
016:055	To show **their** ingratitude for the favours
016:056	We have bestowed for **their** sustenance!
016:061	If Allah were to punish men for **their** wrong-doing,
016:061	when **their** Term expires, they would not be able
016:062	and **their** tongues assert the falsehood that the
016:063	**their** own acts seem alluring: he is **their** patron to-day,
016:066	From what is within **their** bodies,
016:069	from within **their** bodies a drink of varying
016:071	are not going to throw back **their** gifts to those
016:071	to those whom **their** right hands possess,
016:080	and out of **their** wool,
016:080	and **their** soft fibers (between wool and hair),
016:080	and **their** hair, rich stuff and articles of convenience
016:086	who gave partners of Allah will see **their** "partners,"
016:086	But they will throw back **their** word at them
016:087	and all **their** inventions shall leave them
016:087	show (**their**) submission to Allah;
016:096	Their reward according to the best of **their** actions.
016:097	**their** reward according to the best of **their** actions.
016:099	who believe and put **their** trust in **their** Lord.
016:106	but such as open **their** breast to Unbelief,-
016:110	leave **their** homes after trials and persecutions
016:113	seized them even in the midst of **their** iniquities.
016:124	as to **their** differences.
016:127	and distress not thyself because of **their** plots.
017:007	visit with destruction all that fell into **their** power.
017:026	And render to the kindred **their** due rights,
017:041	increases **their** flight (from the Truth)!
017:046	and deafness into **their** ears:
017:046	And We put coverings over **their** hearts (and minds)
017:046	they turn on **their** backs, fleeing (from the Truth).
017:051	then will they wag **their** heads towards thee,
017:054	a disposer of **their** affairs for them.
017:057	seek (for themselves) means of access to **their** Lord,-

THEIR (continued)

017:060	but it only increases **their** inordinate transgression!
017:071	all human beings with **their** (respective) Imams:
017:071	given **their** record in **their** right hand will read
017:073	they would certainly have made thee (**their**) friend!
017:073	And **their** purpose was to tempt thee away from
017:076	**Their** purpose was to scare thee off the land,
017:091	and cause rivers to gush forth in **their** midst,
017:097	gather them together, prone on **their** faces,
017:097	**their** abode will be Hell:
017:098	That is **their** recompense, because they
017:107	fall down on **their** faces in humble prostration,
017:109	They fall down on **their** faces in tears,
017:109	and it increases **their** (earnest) humility.
018:005	that issues from **their** mouths as a saying.
018:005	nor had **their** fathers.
018:011	Then We drew (a veil) over **their** ears,
018:013	We relate to thee **their** story in truth:
018:013	they were youths who believed in **their** Lord,
018:014	We gave strength to **their** hearts: behold, they
018:017	declining to the right from **their** Cave,
018:018	**their** dog stretching forth his two fore-legs
018:018	and We turned them on **their** right and **their** left sides:
018:018	**their** dog stretching forth his two fore-legs
018:019	Such (being **their** state), We raised
018:020	or force you to return to **their** religion,
018:021	those who prevailed over **their** affair said,
018:021	Thus did We make **their** case known to the people,
018:021	they dispute among themselves as to **their** affair.
018:021	**their** Lord knows best about them:
018:022	Say thou: "My Lord knoweth best **their** number;
018:022	it is but few that know **their** (real case)."
018:025	So they stayed in **their** Cave three hundred years,
018:028	who call on **their** Lord morning and evening,
018:029	that will scald **their** faces,
018:051	nor (even) **their** own creation:
018:055	nor from praying for forgiveness from **their** Lord
018:057	veils over **their** hearts so that they should
018:057	and over **their** ears, deafness.
018:058	have hastened **their** Punishment:
018:058	but they have **their** appointed time, beyond which
018:059	We fixed an appointed time for **their** destruction.
018:061	they forgot (about) **their** Fish, which took
018:064	so they went back on **their** footsteps,
018:081	"So we desired that **their** Lord would give them
018:082	**their** father had been a righteous man:
018:082	attain **their** age of full strength and get out
018:082	and get out **their** treasure-
018:102	for the Unbelievers for (**their**) entertainment.
018:103	lose most in respect of **their** deeds?
018:104	they were acquiring good by **their** works?"
018:105	vain will be **their** works, nor shall We, on the
018:106	That is **their** reward, Hell; because they
018:107	for **their** entertainment, the Gardens of Paradise,
019:062	and they will have therein **their** sustenance,
019:068	bring them forth on **their** knees round about Hell;
019:072	the wrong-doers therein, (humbled) to **their** knees.
019:076	respect of (**their**) eventual returns."
019:082	Instead, they shall reject **their** worship,
020:016	not therein but follow **their** own lust,
020:063	out from your land with **their** magic,
020:063	**their** object is to drive you out from
020:066	Then behold **their** ropes and **their** rods-

THEIR (continued)

020:066   so it seemed to him on account of **their** magic-
020:107   crooked or curved wilt thou see in **their** place."
020:113   or that it may cause **their** remembrance (of Him).
020:121   and so **their** nakedness appeared to them:
020:121   for **their** covering, leaves from the Garden:
020:129   (**their** punishment) must necessarily have come;
021:001   Closer and closer to mankind comes **their** Reckoning:
021:002   a renewed Message from **their** Lord, but they
021:003   The wrong-doers conceal **their** private counsels,
021:003   **Their** hearts toying as with trifles.
021:011   We utterly destroyed because of **their** iniquities,
021:011   setting up in **their** places other peoples?
021:031   that they may find **their** way.
021:039   to ward off the Fire from **their** faces,
021:039   not yet from **their** backs,
021:041   but **their** scoffers were hemmed in
021:042   turn away from the remembrance of **their** Lord.
021:044   the land (in **their** control) from its outlying
021:044   and **their** fathers until the period grew long for
021:049   Those who fear **their** Lord
021:049   in **their** most secret thoughts,
021:078   We did witness **their** judgment.
021:084   and doubled **their** number,-as a Grace
021:093   But (later generations) cut off **their** affair (of unity),
021:096   Gog and Magog (people) are let through (**their** barrier),
021:100   There, sobbing will be **their** lot,
021:102   what **their** souls desired, in that will they dwell.
022:011   they turn on **their** faces:
022:019   but those who deny (**their** Lord),-
022:019   antagonists dispute with each other about **their** Lord:
022:019   over **their** heads will be poured out boiling water.
022:020   within **their** bodies, as well as (**their**) skins.
022:023   and **their** garments there will be of silk.
022:029   fulfil **their** vows,
022:033   in the end **their** place of sacrifice is near the Ancient
022:035   who show patient perseverance over **their** afflictions,
022:036   when they are down on **their** sides (after slaughter),
022:037   It is not **their** meat nor **their** blood, that reaches
022:039   Allah is Most powerful for **their** aid;
022:040   expelled from **their** homes in defiance of right,-
022:042   so did the Peoples before them (with **their** prophets),-
022:045   They tumbled down on **their** roofs.
022:046   thus learn wisdom and **their** ears may thus
022:046   but the hearts which are in **their** breasts.
022:046   so that **their** hearts (and mind) may thus learn
022:054   and **their** hearts may be made humbly (open)
022:058   Those who leave **their** homes in the cause of Allah,
023:002   Those who humble themselves in **their** prayers;
023:005   Who guard **their** modesty,
023:006   for (in **their** case) they are free from blame,
023:006   or (the captives) whom **their** right hands possess,-
023:008   faithfully observe **their** trust and **their** covenants;
023:009   And who (strictly) guard **their** prayer;-
023:021   and of **their** (meat) ye eat;
023:021   from within **their** bodies We produce (milk)
023:043   No people can hasten **their** term,
023:044   every time there came to a people **their** messenger,
023:047   And **their** people are subject to us!"
023:053   But people have cut off **their** affair (of unity),
023:054   But leave them in **their** confused ignorance
023:057   Verily those who live in awe for fear of **their** Lord;
023:058   Those who believe in the Signs of **their** Lord;

THEIR (continued)

023:060   with **their** hearts full of fear,
023:060   because they will return to **their** Lord;-
023:060   And those who dispense **their** charity with
023:063   But **their** hearts are in confused ignorance
023:068   come to them that did no come to **their** fathers of old?
023:069   Or do they not recognize **their** Messenger,
023:071   but they turn away from **their** admonition.
023:071   If the Truth had been in accord with **their** desires,
023:071   Nay, We have sent them **their** admonition,
023:075   they would obstinately persist in **their** transgression,
023:076   but they humbled not themselves to **their** Lord,
023:103   will be those who have lost **their** souls;
023:104   The Fire will burn **their** faces, and they
023:104   with **their** lips displaced.
023:111   this day for **their** patience and constancy:
024:002   let not compassion move you in **their** case,
024:002   the Believers witness **their** punishment.
024:004   and reject **their** evidence ever after:
024:004   and produce not four (to support **their** allegation),-
024:005   those who repent thereafter and mend (**their** conduct):
024:006   and have (in support) no evidence but **their** own,-
024:006   And for those who lunch a charge against **their** wives,
024:012   the affair,-though well of **their** people and say,
024:022   by oath against helping **their** kinsmen,
024:022   left **their** homes in Allah's cause:
024:024   **their** hands, and **their** feet will bear witness
024:024   bear witness against them as to **their** actions.
024:024   On the Day when **their** tongues,
024:025   Allah will pay them back (all) **their** just dues,
024:030   should lower **their** gaze and guard **their** modesty:
024:031   to draw attention to **their** hidden ornaments.
024:031   that they should not strike **their** feet in order to draw
024:031   or **their** brothers' sons, or **their** sisters' sons,
024:031   or **their** women, or the
024:031   or the slaves whom **their** right hands possess,
024:031   **their** husbands' sons, **their** brothers or
024:031   **their** fathers, **their** husbands' fathers, **their** sons,
024:031   they should lower **their** gaze and guard **their** modesty;
024:031   and not display **their** beauty except to **their** husbands,
024:031   should not display **their** beauty and ornaments except
024:031   that they should draw **their** veils over **their** bosoms
024:031   to **their** husbands, **their** fathers, **their** husbands'
024:037   nor from paying zakat **their** (only) fear is for
024:038   reward them according to the best of **their** deeds,
024:039   **their** deeds are like a mirage in sandy deserts,
024:043   then wilt thou see rain issue forth from **their** midst.
024:045   of them thee are some that creep on **their** bellies;
024:049   But if the right is on **their** side, they come
024:050   Is it that there is a disease in **their** hearts?
024:053   they would leave (**their** homes).
024:053   They swear **their** strongest oaths by Allah that,
024:055   that he will establish in authority **their** religion-
024:055   and that He will change (**their** state),
024:057   can escape in the earth **their** abode is the Fire,-
024:060   they make not a wanton display of **their** beauty:
024:060   on them if they lay aside **their** (outer) garments,
024:062   and ask Allah for **their** forgiveness:
024:062   for some business of **their**,
025:018   on them and **their** fathers, good things (in life),
025:021   and mighty is the insolence of **their** impiety!
025:024   that Day, in **their** abode,
025:034   who will be gathered to Hell (prone) on **their** faces,-
025:039   We broke to utter annihilation (for **their** sins).

THEIR (continued)

025:040   did they not then see it (with **their** own eyes)?
025:062   to be mindful or to show **their** gratitude.
025:064   in adoration of **their** Lord prostrate and standing;
025:073   they are admonished with the Signs of **their** Lord,
025:075   because of **their** patient and constancy:
026:004   to which they would bend **their** necks in humility.
026:044   So they threw **their** ropes and **their** rods,
026:096   "They will say there in **their** mutual bickerings:
026:106   Behold, **their** brother Noah said to them: "Will ye
026:113   "**Their** account is only with my Lord, if ye
026:124   Behold, **their** brother Hud said to them: "Will ye
026:142   Behold, **their** brother Salih said to them: "Will you
026:152   and mend not (**their** ways)."
026:161   Behold, **their** brother Lut said to them: "Will ye
026:211   It is not meet for them, nor is it in **their** power
026:227   know what vicissitudes **their** affairs will take!
027:004   We have made **their** deeds pleasing in **their** eyes;
027:014   though **their** souls acknowledged them wrongfully
027:024   seem pleasing in **their** eyes,
027:024   Satan has made **their** deeds seem pleasing
027:045   **their** brother Salih, saying, "Serve Allah":
027:051   then see what was the end of **their** plot!-this,
027:051   destroyed them and **their** people, (all of them).
027:052   Now such were **their** houses,-in utter
027:066   Nay, but **their** knowledge fails as to the Hereafter,
027:070   nor distress thyself because of **their** plots.
027:074   all that **their** hearts do hide, as well
027:085   because of **their** wrong-doing,
027:090   **their** faces will be thrown headlong into the Fire:
027:092   they do it for the good of **their** own souls,
028:004   **their** sons he slew, but he kept alive **their** females:
028:006   show Pharaoh and Haman, and **their** hosts, what they
028:008   and Haman and (all) **their** hosts were men of sin.
028:019   when, he was about to lay his hands on **their** enemy,
028:023   watering (**their** flocks):
028:023   found there a group of men watering (**their** flocks),
028:023   two women who were keeping back (**their** flocks).
028:024   So he watered (**their** flocks) for them; then he
028:047   that **their** hands have sent forth, they might
028:050   know that they only follow **their** own lusts:
028:054   Twice will they be given **their** reward, for that
028:058   and We are **their** heirs!
028:058   which exulted in **their** life (of ease and plenty)!
028:069   **their** hearts conceal and all that they reveal.
028:076   that **their** very keys would have been a burden
028:078   called (immediately) to account for **their** sins.
028:084   punished (to the extent) of **their** deeds.
029:004   Evil is **their** judgment!
029:006   they do so for **their** own soul:
029:007   them according to the best of **their** deeds.
029:013   they will be called to account for **their** falsehoods.
029:013   They will bear **their** own burdens,
029:013   and (other) burdens along with **their** own, and on
029:033   he was grieved on **their** account, and felt
029:036   (We sent) **their** brother Shu'aib.
029:037   and they lay prostrate in **their** homes in the morning.
029:038   from (the traces of) **their** buildings (**their** fate):
029:038   Satan made **their** deeds alluring to them,
029:059   and put **their** trust in **their** Lord and Cherisher.
029:060   that carry not **their** own sustenance?
029:065   they give a share (of **their** worship to others)!-
029:065   making **their** devotion sincerely (and exclusively)

THEIR (continued)

030:008   deny the meeting with **their** Lord (at the Resurrection)!
030:008   Do they not reflect in **their** own minds?
030:009   (Which they rejected, to **their** own destruction):
030:009   there came to them **their** messengers with Clear
030:009   but they wronged **their** own souls.
030:013   No intercessor will they have among **their** "Partners,"
030:013   and they will (themselves) reject **their** "Partners."
030:029   fellow **their** own desires being devoid of knowledge.
030:032   Those who split up **their** Religion, and become
030:033   pay part-worship to other gods besides **their** Lord,-
030:033   they cry to **their** Lord,
030:034   (As if) to show **their** ingratitude for the
030:036   **their** (own) hands have sent forth, behold,
030:041   (Allah) may give them a taste of some of **their** deeds:
030:047   messengers to **their** (respective) peoples,
030:051   they see (**their** tilth) turn yellow,-behold, they
030:052   when they show **their** backs and turn away.
030:053   Nor canst thou lead back the blind from **their** straying:
030:053   in Our Signs and submit (**their** wills in Islam).
031:005   These are on (true) guidance from **their** Lord;
031:023   and We shall tell them the truth of **their** deeds:
031:023   to Us is **their** return,
031:024   We grant them **their** pleasure for a little while:
032:010   Nay, they deny the meeting with **their** Lord!
032:012   will bend low **their** heads before **their** Lord,!
032:015   and celebrate the praises of **their** Lord,
032:016   They forsake **their** beds of sleep,
032:016   the while they call on **their** Lord, in Fear
032:017   for them-as a reward for **their** (good) Deeds.
032:019   as hospitable homes, for **their** (good) deeds.
032:020   **their** abode will be the Fire:
032:027   providing food for **their** cattle and themselves?
033:005   Call them by after **their** fathers:
033:005   But if you know not **their** father's names,
033:006   and his wives are **their** mothers.
033:006   closer to the Believers than **their** own selves,
033:007   We took from the Prophets **their** Covenant:
033:008   about **their** truthfulness and He has prepared
033:015   with Allah not to turn **their** backs,
033:018   and those who say to **their** brethren, "Come along
033:019   **their** eyes revolving, like one who faints from death:
033:019   and so Allah has made **their** deeds of none effect:
033:022   And it only added to **their** faith and
033:022   and **their** zeal in obedience.
033:023   been true to **their** Covenant with Allah:
033:023   changed (**their** determination) in the least:
033:024   Allah may reward the men of Truth for **their** Truth,
033:025   Allah turned back the unbelievers for (all) **their** fury:
033:025   enough is Allah for the Believers in **their** fight.
033:026   down from **their** strongholds and cast terror
033:026   cast terror into **their** hearts, (so that)
033:027   of **their** lands, **their** houses, and **their** goods,
033:035   for men and women who guard **their** chastity,
033:036   to have any option about **their** decision:
033:037   with the wives of **their** adopted sons,
033:037   the latter have dissolved (**their** marriage) with them.
033:044   **Their** salutation on the Day they meet
033:048   **their** insolence but put thy trust in Allah.
033:050   for them as to **their** wives and the captives
033:050   the captives whom **their** right hands possess;-
033:050   thy wives to whom thou hast paid **their** dowers;
033:051   the prevention of **their** grief, and **their** satisfaction-

THEIR (continued)

033:051 this were nigher to the cooling of **their** eyes, ,
033:052 even though **their** beauty attract thee,
033:055 or **their** women,
033:055 or **their** brothers' sons, or **their** sisters' sons,
033:055 or the (slaves) whom **their** right hands possess.
033:055 (on those ladies if they appear) before **their** fathers or
033:059 that they should cast **their** outer garments
033:059 outer garments over **their** persons (when out of doors):
033:066 The Day that **their** faces will be turned over
034:013 and (cooking) Cauldrons fixed (in **their** places):
034:014 in the humiliating Chastisement (of **their** Task).
034:015 a Sign in **their** homeland-two Gardens to the
034:016 and We converted **their** two Garden (rows) into
034:023 when terror is removed from **their** hearts
034:031 wrong-doers will be made to stand before **their** Lord,
034:033 be a requital for **their** (ill) Deeds.
034:037 whom there is a multiplied Reward got **their** deeds,
034:045 And **their** predecessors rejected (the Truth);
034:054 as was in the past with **their** partisans:
034:054 And between them and **their** desires, is placed
035:018 fear **their** Lord unseen and establish regular
035:025 to whom came **their** messengers with Clear Signs,
035:025 so did **their** predecessors,
035:030 For He will pay them **their** meed,
035:032 among them some who wrong **their** own souls;
035:033 and **their** garments there will be of silk.
035:039 the odium for the Unbelievers in the sight of **their** Lord:
035:039 his disbelief be on his own self **their** disbelief:
035:039 **their** disbelief but adds to (**their** own) loss.
035:042   it has only increased **their** aversion.
035:042 They swore **their** strongest oaths by Allah
035:043 in the land and **their** plotting of Evil.
035:043 On account of **their** arrogance in the land
035:045 when **their** Term expires,
036:008 right up to **their** chins, so that
036:008 We have put yokes round **their** necks right up
036:008 so that they cannot bow **their** heads.
036:023 of no use whatever will be **their** intercession for me,
036:035 it was not **their** hands that made this:
036:036 as well as **their** own (human) kind and (other) things
036:041 We bore **their** race (through the flood) in the loaded Ark;
036:043 then would there be no helper (to hear **their** cry),
036:046 comes to them from among the Signs of **their** Lord,
036:050 to dispose (of **their** affairs),
036:050 nor to return to **their** own people!
036:051 (men) will rush forth to **their** Lord!
036:056 They and **their** associates will be in pleasant
036:065 That Day shall We set a seal on **their** mouths.
036:065 But **their** hands will speak to Us,
036:065 and **their** feet bear witness,
036:066 We could surely have blotted out **their** eyes;
036:067 We could have transformed them in **their** places;
036:071 which are under **their** dominion?-
036:072 And that We have subjected them to **their** (use)?
036:076 Let not **their** speech, then, grieve thee.
037:008 (So) they should not strain **their** ears in the
037:011 Just ask **their** opinion: are they
037:022 "The wrong-doers and **their** wives, and the
037:048 chaste women; restraining **their** glances,
037:066 they will eat thereof and fill **their** bellies therewith.
037:068 Then shall **their** return be to the (Blazing) Fire.
037:069 Truly they found **their** fathers on the wrong Path;

THEIR (continued)

037:070 So they (too) were rushed down on **their** footsteps!
037:091 Then did he turn to **their** gods and said,
037:113 but of **their** progeny are (some) that do right,
037:115 and **their** people from (**their**) Great distress.
037:137 Verily, ye pass by **their** (sites), by day-
037:148 to enjoy (**their** life) for a while.
037:149 Now ask them **their** opinion: is it
037:151 Behold they say, out of **their** own invention,
038:033 to pass his hand over (**their**) legs and **their** necks.
038:043 and doubled **their** number,-as a Grace from Us,
038:052 will be chaste women restraining **their** glances,
039:015 who lose **their** own souls and **their** people on the
039:020 But it is for those who fear **their** Lord,
039:023 who fear **their** Lord tremble thereat;
039:023 then **their** skins and **their** hearts do soften
039:034 in the presence of **their** Lord:
039:035 and give them **their** reward according to the
039:035 (even) the worst in **their** deeds and give
039:038 In Him trust those who put **their** trust."
039:042 rest He sends (to **their** bodies) for a term appointed.
039:042 and those that die not (He take) during **their** sleep:
039:048 For the evils of **their** Deeds will confront them,
039:051 Nay, the evil results of **their** deeds overtook them.
039:051 of **their** deeds will soon overtake them (too),
039:053 my Servants who have transgressed against **their** souls!
039:060 **their** faces will be turned black; is there
039:073 And those who feared **their** Lord will be led
039:075 singing Glory and Praise to **their** Lord.
040:004 Let not, then, **their** strutting about through the
040:005 plotted against **their** prophet, to seize
040:007 and those around it sing Glory and Praise to **their** Lord;
040:008 among **their** fathers, **their** wives, and **their** posterity!
040:021 but Allah did call them to account for **their** sins,
040:022 to them **their** messengers with Clear (Signs),
040:025 and keep alive **their** females,"
040:052 to Wrong-doers to present **their** excuses,
040:056 there is nothing in **their** breasts but (the quest of)
040:071 When the yokes (shall be) round **their** necks,
040:083 For when **their** messengers came to them
040:085 But **their** professing the Faith when they
041:020 witness against them, as to (all) **their** deeds.
041:020   **their** hearing, **their** sight, and **their** skins will bear
041:021 They will say to **their** skins: "Why bear ye
041:024 **their** suit shall not be granted.
041:027 for the worst of **their** deeds.
041:044 and it is blindness in **their** (eyes):
041:044 there is a deafness in **their** ears, and it
041:045 (**their** differences) would have been settled between
041:053 and in **their** own souls,
041:054 in doubt concerning the Meeting with **their** Lord?
042:005 and the angels celebrate the Praises of **their** Lord,
042:006 the disposer of **their** affairs.
042:015 art commanded, nor follow thou **their** vain desires;
042:016 futile is **their** dispute in the sight of **their** Lord:
042:036 for those who believe and put **their** trust in **their** Lord:
042:038 who (conduct) **their** affairs by mutual Consultation;
042:038 Those who respond to **their** Lord, and establish
042:045 who lose themselves and **their** families.
043:013 In order that ye may sit firm and square on **their** backs,
043:019 **Their** evidence will be recorded, and they
043:019 Did they witness **their** creation?
043:022 and we do guide ourselves by **their** footsteps."

THEIR (continued)

043:023 and we will certainly follow in **their** footsteps."
043:029 good tidings of this life to these (men) and **their** fathers,
043:032 them **their** livelihood in the life of this world:
043:033 silver roofs on **their** houses,
043:034 And (silver) doors to **their** houses, and couches
043:050 behold, they broke **their** word.
043:080 **their** secrets and **their** private counsels?
044:028 Thus (was **their** end)!
044:045 Like molten brass; it will boil in **their** insides,
045:011 and for those who reject the Signs of **their** Lord,
045:021 that equal will be **their** Life and **their** death?
045:025 **their** argument is nothing but this: they say , "Bring
045:030 **their** Lord will admit them to His Mercy:
046:005 are unconscious of **their** call (to them)?
046:014 recompense for **their** (good) deeds.
046:016 and pass by **their** ill deeds:
046:016 We shall accept the best of **their** deeds and
046:019 (Allah) may recompense **their** deeds;
046:024 they saw a cloud advancing towards **their** valleys,
046:025 nothing will be seen but (the ruins of) **their** houses!
046:026 to them were there (faculties of) hearing, sight,
046:028 but that was **their** Falsehood and **their** invention.
046:029 they returned to **their** people, to warn them.
046:033 and never wearied with **their** creation,
047:001 **their** deeds will Allah bring to naught.
047:002 from them **their** ills and improve **their** condition.
047:002 for it is the Truth from **their** Lord,-
047:003 Allah set forth foe men **their** lessons by similitudes.
047:003 those who believe follow the Truth from **their** Lord:
047:004 ye meet the Unbelievers (in fight), Smite at **their** necks,
047:004 He will never let **their** deeds be lost.
047:005 Soon will He guide them and improve **their** condition,
047:008 and (Allah) will bring **their** deeds to naught.
047:009 so He has made **their** deeds fruitless.
047:012 and the Fire will be **their** abode.
047:013 have We destroyed (for **their** sins)?
047:014 and such as follow **their** own lusts?
047:015 and forgiveness from **their** Lord,
047:015 so that it cuts up **their** bowels (to pieces)?
047:016 and who follow **their** own lusts.
047:017 He increases **their** Guidance, and bestows on them
047:017 on them **their** Piety and Restraint (from evil).
047:018 how shall they have **their** Reminder?
047:023 for He has made them deaf and blinded **their** sight.
047:024 or is that there are locks upon **their** hearts?
047:026 but Allah knows **their** (inner) secrets.
047:027 when the angels take **their** souls at death,
047:028 so He made **their** deeds of no effect.
047:029 will not bring to light all **their** rancor?
047:030 know them by the tone of **their** speech!
047:030 shouldst have known them by **their** marks:
047:031 among you who strive **their** utmost and persevere
047:032 but He will make **their** deeds of no effect.
047:038 are niggardly are so at the expense of **their** own souls.
048:004 that they may add Faith to **their** Faith;-
048:005 and remove **their** sins from them; at
048:010 to thee plight **their** fealty in truth to Allah:
048:010 the Hand of Allah is over **their** hands:
048:010 Verily those who plight **their** fealty to thee
048:011 what is not in **their** hearts.
048:011 They say with **their** tongues what is
048:012 and the Believers will never return to **their** families;

THEIR (continued)

048:018 He knew what was in **their** hearts,
048:022 they would certainly turn **their** backs;
048:024 **their** hands from you and your hand from them
048:025 detained from reaching **their** place of sacrifice.
048:026 While the Unbelievers got up in **their** hearts heat
048:029 and **their** similitude in the Gospel is:
048:029 This is **their** similitude in the Taurat;
048:029 (being) the traces of **their** prostration.
048:029 On **their** faces are **their** marks,
049:003 **their** hearts has Allah tested of piety:
049:003 Those that lower **their** voice in the presence
049:012 nor speak ill of each other behind **their** backs.
049:015 with **their** belongings and **their** persons in the
050:036 generations before did We destroy (for **their** Sins),-
051:016 Taking joy in the things which **their** Lord gives them,
051:019 And in **their** wealth there is a due share
051:044 But they insolently defied the Command of **their** Lord:
051:045 Then they could not even stand (on **their** feet),
051:059 For the wrong-doers, **their** portion is like unto
051:059 the portion of **their** fellows (of earlier generations):
052:018 and **their** Lord shall deliver them from the Chastisement
052:018 the (Bliss) which **their** Lord hath bestowed on them,
052:021 We deprive them (of the fruit) of aught of **their** works:
052:021 to them shall We join **their** families:
052:032 Is it that **their** intellects urges them to this,
052:041 Or that the Unseen is in **their** hands, and they
052:046 The Day when **their** plotting will avail them
053:023 has already come to them Guidance from **their** Lord!
053:026 **their** intercession will avail nothing except after Allah
053:030 That is **their** attainment of Knowledge.
053:031 He reward those who do evil, according to **their** deeds,
054:003 and follow **their** (own) lusts but every matter
054:007 humbled-from (**their**) graves,
054:007 They will come forth,-**their** eyes humbled-
054:009 the People of Noah rejected (**their** messenger):
054:023 The Thamud (also) rejected (**their**) Warners.
054:029 But they called to **their** companion, and he
054:037 but We blinded **their** eyes.
054:045 Soon will **their** multitude be put to flight,
054:045 and they will show **their** backs.
054:046 the time promised them (for **their** full recompense):
054:048 they will be dragged through the Fire on **their** faces,
054:052 All that they do note in (**their**) Books (of Deeds):
055:041 (For) the sinners will be known by **their** Marks:
055:041 be seized by **their** forelocks and **their** feet.
055:046 stand before (the Judgment Seat of) **their** Lord,
055:056 Chaste, restraining **their** glances, whom no
055:072 Maidens restrained (as to **their** glances), in (goodly)
056:024 A Reward for the Deeds of **their** past (Life).
056:037 Full of love (for **their** mates), equal in age,-
056:056 Such will be **their** entertainment on the Day
057:012 and by **their** right hands:
057:012 how **their** Light runs forward before them and
057:012 (**their** greeting will be): "Good News for you this Day!
057:016 the Believers that **their** hearts in all humility
057:016 passed over them and **their** hearts grew hard?
057:018 increased manifold (to **their** credit), and they
057:019 they shall have **their** Reward and **their** Light,
057:019 in the eye of **their** Lord:
057:026 and established in **their** line Prophethood and
057:027 Then, in **their** wake, We followed them up with
057:027 among them who believed, **their** (due) reward,

THEIR (continued)

058:002	none can be **their** mothers except those
058:002	they cannot be **their** mothers:
058:002	If any men among you divorce **their** wives by Zihar
058:003	to **their** wives then wish to go back on the words
058:006	and tell them of **their** deeds (which) Allah has
058:010	and on Allah let the Believers put **their** trust.
058:015	evil indeed are **their** deeds.
058:016	They have made **their** oaths a screen
058:016	a screen (for **their** misdeeds):
058:017	against Allah, will be **their** riches nor **their** sons:
058:022	even though they were **their** fathers or **their** sons,
058:022	or **their** brothers, or **their** kindred.
059:002	so that they destroyed **their** dwellings by
059:002	and they thought that **their** fortresses would
059:002	by **their** own hands and the hands of the Believers.
059:002	and cast terror into **their** hearts, so that
059:002	**their** homes at the first gathering (of the forces).
059:005	left them standing on **their** roots,
059:008	expelled from **their** homes and **their** property,
059:009	the covetousness of **their** own souls,-
059:009	even though poverty was **their** (own lot).
059:009	show **their** affection to such as came to them
059:009	in **their** hearts for things given to the (latter),
059:011	say to **their** misbelieving brethren among the People
059:012	they will turn **their** backs;
059:013	Of a truth ye arouse greater fear in **their** hearts, .
059:014	but **their** hearts are divided:
059:014	Strong is **their** fighting (spirit) amongst
059:015	they have tasted the evil result of **their** conduct;
059:016	(**Their** allies deceived them), like Satan, when he
060:004	when they said to **their** people: "We are clear of you
060:010	the Unbelievers what they have spent on **their** dowers,
060:010	ask for what they have spent (on **their** dower).
060:010	if ye marry them on payment of **their** dower to them.
060:010	Allah knows best as to **their** Faith:
060:011	the equivalent of what they had spent (on **their** dower).
060:012	that they will not kill **their** children,
060:012	then do thou receive **their** fealty,
060:012	and pray to Allah for the forgiveness (of **their** sins):
061:005	Allah let **their** hearts go wrong.
061:008	**Their** intention is to extinguish Allah's Light
061:008	(by blowing) with **their** mouths:
061:014	gave power to those who believed against **their** enemies,
062:007	because of the (deeds) **their** hands have sent
062:007	But never will they express **their** desire (for Death),
063:002	truly evil are **their** deeds.
063:002	They have made **their** oaths a screen
063:002	a screen (for **their** misdeeds): thus they
063:003	so a seal was set on **their** hearts:
063:004	timber propped up, (unable to stand on **their** own).
063:004	thou listenest to **their** words.
063:004	**their** bodies please thee;
063:005	see them turning away **their** faces in arrogance.
063:005	they turn aside **their** heads,
063:006	whether thou pray for **their** forgiveness or not.
064:005	So they tasted the evil result of **their** conduct;
064:009	He will remove from them **their** ills,
064:013	let the Believers put **their** trust.
064:014	and cover up (**their** faults),
064:016	saved from the covetousness of **their** own souls,-
065:001	divorce them at **their** prescribed periods,
065:001	and turn them not out of **their** houses,

THEIR (continued)

065:001	and count (accurately) **their** prescribed periods:
065:002	Thus when they fulfil **their** term appointed,
065:004	**their** period is until they deliver their burdens:
065:006	give them **their** recompense:
065:006	on them until they deliver **their** burden:
065:008	opposed the command of **their** Lord and of His
065:009	then did they taste the evil result of **their** conduct,
065:009	and the End of **their** conduct was Perdition.
066:005	who submit (**their** wills), who believe, who are devout;
066:008	**Their** Light will run forward before them and by
066:008	and by **their** right hands, while they say, "Our Lord!
066:009	**Their** abode is Hell,-an evil refuge (indeed).
066:010	and they profited nothing before Allah on **their** account,
066:010	righteous servants but they betrayed **their** (husbands),
067:006	For those who reject **their** Lord (and Cherisher)
067:011	They will then confess **their** sins:
067:012	As for those who fear **their** Lord unseen, for them
067:019	spreading **their** wings and folding then in?
068:009	**Their** desire is that thou shouldst be pliant:
068:034	are Gardens of Delight, with **their** Lord.
068:041	produce **their** "partners," if they are truthful!
068:043	**Their** eyes will be cast down,-ignominy will
068:047	Or that the Unseen is in **their** hands,
068:051	thee up with **their** eyes when they hear the Message;
069:010	of **their** Lord; so He punished them with an
070:017	and turn away **their** faces (from the Right),
070:017	Inviting (all) such as turn **their** backs and turn
070:023	Those who remain steadfast to **their** prayer;
070:027	And those who fear the punishment of **their** Lord,-
070:028	For **their** Lord's punishment is not a thing
070:029	And those who guard **their** chastity,
070:030	Except with **their** wives and the (captives)
070:030	and the (captives) whom **their** right hands possess,-
070:032	And those who respect **their** trusts and covenants;
070:033	And those who stand firm in **their** testimonies;
070:034	And those who (strictly) guard **their** worship;-
070:043	from **their** sepulchers in sudden hast as if they
070:044	**Their** eyes lowered in dejection,-ignominy covering
071:006	"But me call only increases (**their**) flight
071:007	they have (only) thrust **their** fingers into **their** ears,
071:007	covered themselves up with **their** garments,
071:016	"' And made the moon a light in **their** midst,
071:024	the wrong-doers but in straying (from **their** mark)."
071:025	Because of **their** sins they were drowned
072:010	or whether **their** Lord (really) intends to guide
072:014	Now those who submit **their** wills-they have
072:014	'Amongst us are some that submit **their** wills (to Allah),
072:024	(with **their** own eyes) that which they are promised,-
072:028	the Messages of **their** Lord and He encompasses
074:031	and We have fixed **their** number only as trial
075:023	Looking towards **their** Lord;
076:007	They perform (**their**) vows, and they fear
076:016	the measure thereof (according to **their** wishes).
076:021	and **their** Lord will give to them to drink a pure
076:028	and We have made **their** frame strong;
076:028	We shall exchange **their** likes.
077:016	Did We not destroy the men of old (for **their** evil)?
078:027	used not to look for any account (for **their** deeds),
079:005	Then arrange to do (the commands of **their** Lord),-
079:009	Cast down will be (**their** owners') eyes.
079:040	and had restrained (**their**) soul from lower Desires,

THEIR (continued)

079:040   the fear of standing before **their** Lord's (tribunal)
079:041   **Their** abode will be the Garden.
081:002   When the stars fall, losing **their** lustre;
083:014   By no means! but on **their** hearts is the stain
083:015   Verily, from (the Light of) **their** Lord, that Day,
083:024   Thou wilt recognize in **their** Faces the beaming
083:025   **Their** thirst will be slaked with Pure Wine sealed;
083:031   and when they returned to **their** own people,
084:023   knowledge of what they secrete (in **their** breasts).
087:015   And remember the name of his **their** Guardian-Lord,
088:009   Pleased with **their** Striving,-
088:022   Thou art not one to manage (**their**) affairs.
088:025   For to Us will be **their** Return;
091:011   The Thamud (people) rejected (**their** prophet)
091:011   through **their** inordinate wrong-doing.
091:014   crushed them for **their** sin and levelled them.
091:014   and they hamstrung her so **their** Lord,
092:016   Who give the lie to Truth and turn **their** backs.
092:018   Those who spend **their** wealth for increase
092:019   And have in **their** minds no favour from anyone
092:020   for the countenance of **their** Lord Most High;
098:001   were not going to depart (from **their** ways) until
098:008   **Their** reward is with Allah:
098:008   all this for such as fear **their** Lord and Cherisher.
100:011   That **their** Lord had been well-acquainted
105:002   Did He not make **their** treacherous plan go astray?
106:002   **Their** familiarity with the journeys by winter and
107:005   Who are neglectful of **their** Prayers,

THEIRS

005:033   and a heavy punishment is **theirs** in the Hereafter;
005:036   **Theirs** would be a grievous Chastisement.
005:119   **theirs** are Gardens, with rivers flowing beneath,-
007:051   as they forgot the meeting of this day of **theirs**,
007:131   in truth the omens of evil are **theirs** in Allah's sight,
009:028   so let them not, after this year of **theirs**, approach the
009:074   this revenge of **theirs** was (their) only return
009:111   for **theirs** (in return) is the Garden (of Paradise):
016:104   and **theirs** will be a grievous Chastisement.
016:106   and **theirs** will be a dreadful Chastisement.
021:015   And that cry of **theirs** ceased not, till We
021:023   but they will be questioned (for **theirs**).
023:063   and there are, beside that, deeds of **theirs**,
024:062   for some business of **theirs**,
027:005   and in the Hereafter **theirs** will be the greatest loss.
028:058   Now those habitations of **theirs**, after them,
030:003   (even) after (this) defeat of **theirs**,
030:057   So on that Day no excuse of **theirs** will avail
033:053   makes for greater purity for your hearts and for **theirs**.
043:083   play (with vanities) until they meet that Day of **theirs**,
051:060   the Day of **theirs** which they have been promised!
052:038   (such) listener of **theirs** produce a manifest proof.
052:045   leave them along until they encounter that Day of **theirs**,
070:042   that Day of **theirs** which they have been promised!

THEM

002:003   We have provided for **them**.
002:006   whether thou warn **them** or do not warn **them**;
002:006   it is the same to **them** whether thou
002:011   When it is said to **them**: "Make not mischief
002:013   When it is said to **them**: "Believe as the others believe:"
002:015   Allah will throw back their mockery on **them**,
002:015   and give **them** rope in their trespasses;
002:017   and left **them** in utter darkness,

THEM (continued)

002:020   and when the darkness grows on **them**,
002:020   every time the light (helps) **them**,
002:029   and made **them** into seven firmaments;
002:031   then He placed **them** before the angles,
002:033   "When he had told **them** their names,
002:033   He said: "O Adam! tell **them** their names."
002:036   and get **them** out of the state (of felicity)
002:036   Then did Satan make **them** slip from the (garden),
002:038   on **them** shall be no fear,
002:059   the word from that which had been given **them**;
002:062   on **them** shall be no fear,
002:065   We said to **them**: "Be ye apes,
002:075   Seeing that a party of **them** heard the word of Allah,
002:076   they say: "Shall you tell **them** what Allah hath revealed
002:078   And there are among **them** illiterates,
002:079   Woe to **them** for what their hands do write,
002:085   assist (their enemies) against **them**,
002:085   not lawful for you to banish **them**.
002:085   ye ransom **them**,
002:088   Allah's curse is on **them** for their blasphemy;
002:089   And when there comes; to **them** a Book from Allah,
002:089   confirming what is with **them**,
002:089   comes to **them** that which (should) have recognized
002:091   confirming what is with **them**.
002:091   When it is said to **them**, "Believe in what Allah
002:095   their hands have sent on before **them**.
002:096   Thou wilt indeed find **them**,
002:096   each one of **them** wishes he could be given life
002:099   and none reject **them** but those who are perverse.
002:100   Nay, most of **them** are faithless.
002:100   some party among **them** throw it aside?
002:101   And when came to **them** a Messenger
002:101   confirming what was with **them**,
002:102   They learned from **them** the means
002:102   And they learned what harmed **them**,
002:102   Not what profited **them**.
002:109   after the Truth hath become manifest unto **them**:
002:113   but Allah will judge between **them**
002:114   should themselves enter **them** except in fear.
002:114   For **them** there is nothing but disgrace
002:114   whose zeal is (in fact) to ruin **them**?
002:118   to the people before **them** words of similar import.
002:126   but will soon drive **them** to the torment of the Fire,-
002:126   such of **them** as believe in Allah and the Last Day'."
002:126   for a while will I grant **them** their pleasure,
002:129   "Our Lord! send amongst **them** a Messenger
002:129   and instruct **them** in Scripture and Wisdom,
002:129   Who shall rehearse Thy Signs to **them**
002:129   and purify **them**:
002:136   We make to difference between one and another of **them**:
002:137   but Allah will suffice thee as against **them**,
002:142   "What hath turned **them** from the Qiblah
002:146   but some of **them** conceal the truth
002:150   so fear **them** not, but fear Me;
002:150   except those of **them** that are bent on wickedness;
002:158   should compass **them** round,
002:158   it is no sin in **them**.
002:159   on **them** shall be Allah's curse,
002:160   to **them** I turn; for I am Oft-Returning, Most Merciful.
002:161   on **them** is Allah's curse,
002:165   they love **them** as they should love Allah.
002:166   clear themselves of those who follow (**them**):

THEM (continued)

002:166 relations between **them** would be cut off.
002:167 a way for **them** out of the Fire.
002:167 Thus will Allah show **them** (the fruits of)
002:167 we would clear ourselves of **them**,
002:170 When it is said to **them**: "Follow what Allah
002:174 and purchase for **them** a miserable profit,
002:174 Allah will not address **them** on the Day
002:174 nor purify **them**;
002:186 I am indeed close (to **them**):
002:186 let **them** also, with a will, listen to My call,
002:187 so now associate with **them**,
002:191 And slay **them** wherever ye catch **them**,
002:191 and turn **them** out from where they turned you out;
002:191 but fight **them** not at the Sacred Mosque,
002:191 but if they fight you, slay **them**.
002:193 And fight **them** on until there is no more
002:210 Allah comes to **them** in canopies of clouds,
002:211 how many Clear (Signs) We have sent **them**.
002:212 above **them** on the Day of Resurrection;
002:213 after the clear Signs came to **them**,
002:213 and with **them** He sent the Book in truth,
002:219 Say: "In **them** is great sin,
002:222 and do not approach **them** until they are clean.
002:222 ye may approach **them** as ordained for you
002:228 rights similar to the rights against **them**,
002:228 better right to take **them** back in that period,
002:228 and it is not lawful for **them** to hide what Allah
002:228 but men have a degree over **them**
002:229 so do not transgress **them** if any do transgress
002:229 there is no blame on either of **them** if she give
002:230 no blame on either of **them** if they re-unite,
002:231 but do not take **them** back to injure **them**,
002:231 either take **them** back on equitable terms
002:231 or set **them** free on equitable terms;
002:232 do not prevent **them** from marrying their (former)
002:233 There is no blame on **them**,
002:235 Allah knows that ye cherish **them** in your hearts:
002:235 a secret contract with **them** except that you speak
002:235 speak to **them** in terms honourable,
002:236 but bestow on **them** (a suitable gift),
002:237 And if ye divorce **them** before consummation,
002:237 then the half of the dower (is due to **them**),
002:237 but after the fixation of a dower for **them**,
002:243 Allah said to **them**: "Die:" Then He restored **them**
002:243 but most of **them** are ungrateful.
002:246 They said to a Prophet (that was) among **them**:
002:246 they turned back except a small band among **them**.
002:247 Their Prophet said to **them**: "Allah hath appointed
002:248 And (further) their Prophet said to **them**: "A Sign
002:251 By Allah's will they routed **them**:
002:252 We rehearse **them** to thee in truth:
002:253 to some of **them** Allah spoke;
002:253 after Clear (Signs) had come to **them**,
002:255 before or after or behind **them**.
002:255 feeleth no fatigue in guarding and preserving **them**
002:257 he leads **them** forth into light.
002:257 lead **them** forth into the depths of darkness.
002:259 how We bring **them** together and clothe **them**
002:259 and clothe **them** with flesh."
002:260 then put a portion of **them**:
002:260 on every hill, and call to **them**:
002:260 "Take four birds; tie **them** (cut **them** into pieces),

THEM (continued)

002:262 on **them** shall be no fear, nor shall they grieve.
002:262 for **them** their reward is with their Lord;
002:271 but if ye conceal **them**,
002:271 and make **them** reach those (really) in need,
002:272 guide **them** to the right path.
002:273 Thou shalt know **them** by their (unfailing) mark:
002:274 on **them** shall be no fear, nor shall they grieve.
002:277 on **them** shall be no fear,
002:282 so that if one of **them** errs.
002:282 reduce **them** to writing let a scribe write down
002:285 each one (of **them**) believeth in Allah,
003:010 will avail **them** aught against Allah:
003:011 and Allah called **them** to account for their sins.
003:019 after knowledge had come to **them**.
003:021 announce to **them** a grievous chastisement.
003:023 but a party of **them** turn back and decline
003:024 deceive **them** as to their own religion.
003:025 We gather **them** together against a Day
003:028 that ye may guard yourselves from **them**.
003:044 as to which of **them** should be charged with the care
003:044 nor wast thou with **them** when they dispute
003:044 thou wast not with **them** when they cast
003:056 I will punish **them** with severe chastisement
003:057 Allah will pay **them** (in full) their reward;
003:073 He granteth **them** to whom He pleaseth:
003:077 nor will He cleanse **them** (of sin):
003:077 nor will Allah (deign to) speak to **them**
003:077 or look at **them** on the Day of Judgment,
003:078 There is among **them** a section who distort
003:084 between one and another among **them**,
003:086 and that Clear Signs had come unto **them**?
003:087 on **them** (rests) the curse of Allah,
003:105 for **them** is a dreadful Chastisement,
003:108 We rehearse **them** to thee in Truth:
003:110 among **them** are some who have faith,
003:110 it were best for **them**:
003:110 but most of **them** are perverted transgressors.
003:112 Shame is pitched over **them** (like a tent)
003:112 And pitched over **them** is (the tent of) destitution.
003:113 Not all of **them** are alike:
003:115 nothing will be rejected of **them**;
003:116 will avail **them** aught against Allah:
003:117 it is not Allah that hath wronged **them**,
003:119 Ah! ye are those who love **them**,
003:120 If aught that is good befalls you, it grieves **them**;
003:127 of the Unbelievers or expose **them** to infamy,
003:128 whether He turn in mercy to **them**, or punish **them**;
003:146 and with **them** (fought) large bands of godly men?
003:148 And Allah gave **them** a reward in this world,
003:155 it was Satan who caused **them** to fail,
003:159 and ask for (Allah's) forgiveness for **them**;
003:159 that thou dost deal gently with **them**.
003:159 and consult **them** in affairs (of moment).
003:164 the Signs of Allah, purifying **them**,
003:164 and instructing **them** in Scripture and Wisdom,
003:164 among **them** a Messenger from among themselves,
003:164 rehearsing unto **them** the Signs of Allah,
003:165 Say (to **them**): "It is from yourselves:
003:170 who have not yet joined **them** (in their bliss),
003:170 the fact that on **them** is no fear,
003:173 "A great army is gathering against you, so fear **them**":
003:174 no harm ever touched **them**:

THEM (continued)

003:175 be ye not afraid of **them**, but fear Me,
003:176 Allah's Plan is that He will give **them** no portion
003:178 We grant **them** respite that they may grow
003:178 our respite to **them** is good for themselves:
003:180 Nay, it will be the worse of **them**:
003:180 think that it is good for **them**:
003:180 Allah hath given **them** of His Grace,
003:183 why then did ye slay **them**, if ye speak the truth?.
003:188 For **them** is a Chastisement grievous indeed.
003:195 and answered **them**: "Never will I suffer
003:195 and admit **them** into Gardens with rivers
003:195 verily, I will blot out from **them** their iniquities,
003:195 And their Lord hath accepted of **them**, and
003:199 and in the revelation to **them**,
003:199 For **them** is a reward with their Lord,
004:001 and from **them** twain scattered (like seeds)
004:003 be able to deal justly (with **them**),
004:005 but feed and clothe **them** therewith,
004:005 and speak to **them** words of kindness and justice.
004:006 if then ye find sound judgment in **them**, release
004:006 When ye release their property to **them**,
004:006 release their property to **them**;
004:008 give **them** out of the (property),
004:008 and speak to **them** words of kindness and justice.
004:009 let **them** fear Allah, and speak appropriate words.
004:015 to houses until death do claim **them**,
004:015 witnesses from amongst you against **them**;
004:015 or Allah ordain for **them** some (other) way.
004:015 and if they testify, confine **them** to houses
004:016 If they repent and amend, leave **them** alone;
004:016 punish **them** both.
004:017 to **them** will Allah turn in mercy;
004:018 for **them** have We prepared a chastisement
004:018 until death faces one of **them**, and he says,
004:019 take away a part of the dower ye have given **them**,
004:019 Nor should ye treat **them** with harshness,
004:019 live with **them** on a footing of kindness and equity
004:019 and equity if ye take a dislike to **them** it may be that
004:024 Give **them** their dowery for the enjoyment
004:024 provided ye seek (**them** in marriage) with
004:024 the enjoyment you have of **them** as a duty; but if,
004:025 and give **them** their dowers, according
004:025 wed **them** with the leave of their owners,
004:030 soon shall We cast **them** into the Fire:
004:034 (and last) beat **them** (lightly);
004:034 seek not against **them** means (of annoyance):
004:034 and because they support **them** from their means.
004:034 admonish **them** (first), (next), refuse to share their
004:034 what Allah would have **them** guard.
004:035 If ye fear a breach between **them** twain, appoint
004:037 a Punishment that steeps **them** in contempt;
004:037 hide the bounties which Allah hath bestowed on **them**;
004:039 For Allah hath full knowledge of **them**.
004:039 what Allah hath given **them** for sustenance?
004:039 And what burden were it on **them** if they had faith
004:042 wish that the earth were made one with **them**:
004:046 and but few of **them** will believe.
004:046 it would have been better for **them**, and more proper;
004:046 but Allah hath cursed **them**, for their Unbelief;
004:047 and turn **them** hindwards,
004:047 or curse **them** as We cursed the Sabbath-breakers,
004:054 for what Allah hath given **them** of His bounty?

THEM (continued)

004:054 and conferred upon **them** a great kingdom.
004:055 And some of **them** averted their faces from him:
004:055 Some of **them** believed.
004:056 We shall change **them** for fresh skins, that they
004:057 We shall admit **them** to shades, cool
004:060 lead **them** astray far away (from the Right).
004:061 When it is said to **them**: "Come to what Allah hath
004:063 so keep clear of **them** but admonish **them**,
004:063 and speak to **them** a word to reach their very souls.
004:064 and the Messenger had asked forgiveness for **them**,
004:065 but accept **them** with the fullest conviction.
004:065 judge in all disputes between **them**.
004:066 If We had ordered **them** to sacrifice their lives
004:066 it would have been best for **them**, and would
004:066 very few of **them** would have done it: but if
004:067 given **them** from Ourselves a great reward;
004:068 And We should have shown **them** the Straight Way.
004:072 in that we were not present among **them**."
004:073 "Oh! I wish I had been with **them**:
004:073 ties of affection between you and **them**,
004:077 behold! a section of **them** feared men as,
004:077 the order for fighting was issued to **them**,
004:078 If some good befalls **them**, they say, "This
004:080 We have not sent thee to watch over **them**.
004:081 a section of **them** meditate all night on things
004:081 things very different from what thou tellest **them**.
004:081 so keep clear of **them**, and put thy trust in Allah,
004:083 When there comes to **them** some matter
004:083 or to those charged with authority among **them**,
004:083 would have known it from **them** (direct).
004:088 Allah hath cast off **them** for their (evil) deeds.
004:089 seize **them** and slay **them** wherever ye find **them**;
004:090 no way for you (to war against **them**).
004:090 hearts restraining **them** from fighting you or
004:090 He could have given **them** power over you, and
004:091 seize **them** and slay **them** wherever ye get **them**:
004:091 We provided you with a clear argument against **them**.
004:102 let one party of **them** stand up (in prayer) with thee.
004:102 and standest to lead **them** in prayer, let one
004:102 let **them** pray with thee, taking all precautions,
004:102 When thou (O Messenger) art with **them**, and
004:102 Taking their arms with **them**:
004:102 let **them** take their positions in the rear.
004:108 while He is with **them** when they plot by night.
004:113 a party of **them** would certainly have plotted
004:119 and I will create in **them** false desires;
004:119 I will order **them** to slit the ears of cattle,
004:119 "I will mislead **them**, and I will
004:120 Satan makes **them** promises, and creates
004:120 and creates in **them** false hopes, but
004:122 We shall soon admit **them** to Gardens, with rivers
004:124 and not the least injustice will be done to **them**.
004:127 Say: Allah doth instruct you about **them**: and
004:128 there is no blame on **them** if they arrange
004:130 for each of **them** from His all-reaching bounty:
004:137 Allah will not forgive **them** nor
004:137 nor guide **them** on the Way.
004:138 that there is for **them** a grievous Chastisement.
004:139 is it honor they seek among **them**?
004:140 ye are not to sit with **them** unless they turn to
004:140 if ye did, ye would be like **them**.
004:141 they say (to **them**): "Did we not gain an advantage

808

THEM (continued)

004:142 to deceive Allah but it is Allah who deceive **them**.

004:145 no helper wilt thou find for **them**;

004:153 even after Clear Signs had come to **them**;

004:153 even so We forgave **them**; and gave Moses

004:153 to cause a book to descend to **them** from heaven:

004:154 And We took from **them** a solemn Covenant.

004:154 We raised over **them** the Mount (Sinai);

004:154 and (once again) We commanded **them**: "Transgress

004:157 Only a likeness of that was shown to **them**.

004:159 He will be a witness against **them**;

004:160 which had been lawful for **them**; in that

004:160 We made unlawful for **them** certain (foods)

004:161 We have prepared for those among **them** who reject

004:162 to **them** shall We soon give a great reward.

004:162 But those among **them** who are well-grounded

004:168 Allah will not forgive **them** nor guide

004:168 nor guide **them** to any way-

004:172 gather **them** all together unto Himself to (answer).

004:173 any to protect or help **them**.

004:175 and guide **them** to Himself by a straight Way.

004:175 soon will He admit **them** to Mercy and Grace

004:176 shall have two-thirds of the inheritance (between **them**):

005:003 yet fear **them** not but fear Me.

005:004 They ask thee what is lawful to **them** (as food).

005:004 training **them** to hunt in the manner directed

005:005 Taking **them** as lovers.

005:005 when ye give **them** their due dowers, and desire

005:005 is lawful unto you and yours is lawful unto **them**.

005:012 believe in My Messengers honour and assist **them**,

005:012 and We appointed twelve chieftains among **them**,

005:013 nor wilt thou cease to find **them**-barring a few,

005:013 but forgive **them** and overlook (their misdeeds):

005:013 We cursed **them**, and made their hearts grow hard:

005:013 and forgot a good part of the Message that was sent **them**,

005:014 and forgot a good part of the Message that was sent **them**:

005:014 show **them** what it is they have done.

005:016 guideth **them** to a Path that is Straight.

005:016 and leadeth **them** out of darkness, by His Will,

005:023 they said: "Assault **them** at the (proper) Gate:

005:027 Recite to **them** the truth of the story of the two sons

005:032 Then although there came to **them** Our Messengers

005:032 many of **them** continued to commit excesses in the land.

005:036 it would never be accepted of **them**.

005:041 For **them** there is disgrace in this world, and in

005:042 If thou judge, judge in equity between **them**.

005:042 either judge between **them**, or decline to interfere.

005:043 when they have (their own) Torah before **them**?-

005:044 for to **them** was entrusted the protection of Allah's

005:045 We ordained therein for **them**: "Life for life,

005:048 so judge between **them** by what Allah hath revealed,

005:049 it is Allah's purpose to punish **them**.

005:049 but beware of **them** lest they beguile thee from

005:049 between **them** by what Allah hath revealed, and

005:052 they run about amongst **them**, saying: "We do fear

005:062 Many of **them** dost thou see, racing each

005:063 the doctors of laws forbid **them** from their (habit of)

005:064 **them** their obstinate rebellion and blasphemy.

005:064 Amongst **them** We have placed enmity and hatred

005:065 and admitted **them** to Gardens of Bliss.

005:066 but many of **them** follow a course that is evil.

005:066 from above **them** and from below their feet.

005:066 There is from among **them** a party of the right course:

THEM (continued)

005:066 that was sent to **them** from their Lord,

005:068 **them** their obstinate rebellion and blasphemy.

005:069 on **them** shall be no fear, nor shall they grieve.

005:070 the Children of Israel and sent **them** Messengers.

005:070 Every time there came to **them** a Messenger

005:071 yet Allah (in mercy) turned to **them**: yet again

005:071 yet again many of **them** became blind and deaf.

005:073 chastisement will befall the disbelievers among **them**.

005:075 Allah doth makes His Signs clear to **them**;

005:080 souls have sent forward before **them** (with the result),

005:080 that Allah's wrath is on **them**, and in torment

005:080 Thou seest many of **them** turning in friendship

005:081 never would they have taken **them** for friends

005:081 but most of **them** are rebellious wrong-doers.

005:082 and nearest among **them** in love to the Believers

005:085 hath Allah rewarded **them** with Gardens, with

005:089 or clothe **them**; or give a slave his freedom.

005:097 and the garlands that mark **them**:

005:103 but most of **them** lack wisdom.

005:104 When it is said to **them**: "Come to what Allah

005:106 and let **them** both swear by Allah: "We will not

005:106 detain **them** both after prayer, and let

005:107 let **them** swear by Allah: "We affirm that

005:110 and the unbelievers among **them** said: 'This is

005:110 when thou didst show **them** the Clear Signs,

005:117 and I was a witness over **them** whilst I

005:117 whilst I dwelt amongst **them**;

005:117 "Never said I to **them** aught except what Thou

005:117 thou wast the Watcher over **them**,

005:118 "If Thou dost punish **them**, they are

005:118 if Thou dost forgive **them**, Thou art

005:119 Allah well-pleased with **them**, and they

006:004 of the Signs of their Lord reach **them**, but they

006:005 but soon shall come to **them** the news of what

006:005 they reject the truth when it reaches **them**:

006:006 how many of those before **them** We did destroy?-

006:006 in their wake fresh generations (to succeed **them**).

006:006 yet for their sins We destroyed **them**, and raised

006:008 and no respite would be granted **them**.

006:009 caused **them** confusion in a matter which they have

006:022 On the day shall We gather **them** all together:

006:023 no excuse for **them** but to say: "By Allah

006:024 will leave **them** in the lurch.

006:025 Of **them** there are some who (pretend to)

006:025 they will not believe in **them**;

006:031 until on a sudden the hour is on **them**, and they

006:034 and their persecution until Our aid did reach **them**:

006:035 He could gather **them** together unto true guidance:

006:035 or a ladder to the skies and bring **them** a Sign,-

006:036 Allah will raise **them** up: then will they

006:037 but most of **them** understand not."

006:043 When the suffering reached **them** from Us,

006:043 Satan made their (sinful) acts seem alluring to **them**.

006:044 We opened to **them** the gates of all (good)

006:048 upon **them** shall be no fear, nor shall they grieve.

006:049 **them** shall our punishment touch,

006:052 that thou shouldst turn **them** away, and thus

006:052 In naught art thou accountable for **them**, and in

006:053 Thus did We test some of **them** by others,

006:068 turn away from **them** unless they turn to a different

006:069 but (their duty) is to remind **them**,

006:070 But continue to admonish **them** with it (Al-Qur-an)

THEM (continued)

006:087	We chose **them**, and We guided **them** to a straight Way.
006:087	and We guided **them** to a straight Way.
006:087	(To **them**) and to their fathers, and progeny
006:088	all that they did would be vain for **them**.
006:089	to a new People who reject **them** not.
006:089	if these (their descendants) reject **them**, behold!
006:091	then leave **them** to plunge in vain discourse and trifling.
006:107	nor art thou set over **them** to dispose of their affairs.
006:108	and He shall then tell **them** the truth of all that they did.
006:109	that if a (special) Sign came to **them**,
006:110	We shall leave **them** in their trespasses, to
006:111	Even if We did send unto **them** angels,
006:111	But most of **them** ignore (the truth).
006:111	and the dead did speak unto **them**,
006:112	so leave **them** and they forge.
006:113	and let **them** delight in it, and let
006:113	and let **them** earn from it what they may.
006:121	if ye were to obey **them**, ye would
006:124	When there comes to **them** a Sign
006:127	For **them** will be a Home of Peace
006:128	On the day when He will gather **them** all together,
006:130	It was the life of this world that deceived **them**.
006:137	in order to lead **them** to their own destruction,
006:137	but leave alone **them** and what they forged.
006:138	soon will He requite **them** for what they forged.
006:138	and none should eat of **them** except those
006:139	He will soon punish **them**: for He is
006:140	and forbid food which Allah hath provided for **them**,
006:146	and We forbade **them** the fat of the ox
006:150	be not thou amongst **them**:
006:151	We provide sustenance for you and for **them**;-
006:158	Are they waiting to see if the angels come to **them**,
006:159	He will in the end tell **them** the truth
006:159	thou hast no part in **them** in the least:
006:160	No wrong shall be done unto **them**.
007:004	Our punishment took **them** on a sudden by night
007:005	When (thus) Our punishment took **them**, no cry
007:016	lo! I will lie in wait for **them** on Thy Straight Way:
007:017	nor wilt Thou find, in most of **them**, gratitude
007:017	and behind **them** from their right and from their left:
007:017	"Then will I assault **them** from before **them**
007:018	If any of **them** follow thee,-Hell will I fill with you all.
007:020	to whisper suggestions to **them**, in order
007:020	in order to reveal to **them** their shame that
007:020	their shame that was hidden from **them** (before):
007:021	And he swore to **them** both, that he
007:022	their shameful parts became manifest to **them**, and
007:022	And their Lord called unto **them**: "Did I not
007:027	stripping **them** of their raiment, to expose
007:027	from a position where ye cannot see **them**:
007:032	(and) purely for **them** on the Day of Judgment.
007:035	on **them** shall be no fear, nor shall they grieve.
007:036	who reject Our Signs and treat **them** with arrogance,-
007:037	must reach **them** from the Book (of Decrees): until
007:038	so give **them** a double punishment in the Fire."
007:040	and treat **them** with arrogance, no opening
007:041	For **them** there is hell, as a couch (below) and folds
007:043	beneath **them** will be rivers flowing;-and they
007:044	but a Crier shall proclaim between **them**: "The curse
007:046	Between **them** shall be a veil, and on
007:051	That day shall We forget **them** as they forgot the
007:052	For We had certainly sent unto **them** a Book, based

THEM (continued)

007:053	will leave **them** in the lurch.
007:057	We drive **them** to a land that is dead,
007:075	those among **them** who believe: "Know ye
007:078	So the earthquake took **them** unawares, and they
007:079	So Salih left **them**, saying: "O my people!
007:082	they said, "Drive **them** out of your city: these are
007:084	We rained down on **them** a shower (of brimstone):
007:088	He said: "What! even though we do detest (**them**)?
007:091	But the earthquake took **them** unawares, and they
007:093	So Shu'aib left **them**, saying: "O my people!
007:095	Behold! We called **them** to account of a sudden,
007:096	to **them** (all kinds of) blessings from heaven and earth;
007:096	and We brought **them** to book for their misdeeds.
007:100	We could punish **them** (too) for their sins, and
007:101	there came indeed to **them** their Messengers
007:102	Most of **them** We found not men (true) to their covenant:
007:102	but most of **them** We found rebellious and disobedient.
007:103	But they wrongfully rejected **them**:
007:103	Then after **them** We sent Moses with Our Signs
007:116	and struck terror into **them**:
007:127	and we have over **them** (power) irresistible.
007:131	but most of **them** do not understand!
007:133	So We sent on **them**: Wholesale Death,
007:134	And when the Plague fell on **them**, they said:
007:135	from **them** according to a fixed term which they
007:136	and failed to take warning from **them**.
007:136	We drowned **them** in the sea, because they
007:136	So We exacted retribution from **them**:
007:146	**them** will I turn away from My Signs:
007:146	they will not believe in **them**; and if
007:146	and failed to take warning from **them**.
007:148	that it could neither speak to **them**, nor show
007:148	nor show **them** the Way?
007:155	both **them** and me: wouldst thou destroy us for the
007:157	and forbids **them** what is evil:
007:157	and from the yokes that are upon **them**.
007:157	he allows **them** as lawful what is good and (pure)
007:157	He releases **them** from their heavy burdens and from
007:157	and prohibits **them** from what is bad (and impure):
007:157	for he commands **them** what is just and forbids
007:160	and sent down to **them** manna and quails, (saying):
007:160	We divided **them** into twelve tribes or nations.
007:160	We gave **them** the shade of clouds, and sent
007:161	And remember it was said to **them**: "Dwell in
007:162	changed the word which had been given **them**,
007:162	But the transgressors among **them** changed the
007:162	so We sent on **them** a plague from heaven.
007:163	thus did We make a trial of **them**,
007:163	their fish did come to **them**, openly
007:163	Ask **them** concerning the town standing close by the sea.
007:164	When some of **them** said: "Why do ye preach to a
007:165	disregarded the warnings that had been given **them**,
007:166	We said to **them**: "Be ye apes,
007:167	they Lord did declare that He would send against **them**,
007:167	who would be afflict **them** with grievous Chastisement.
007:168	We have tried **them** with both prosperity the righteous,
007:168	We broke **them** up into sections
007:168	There are among **them** some that are
007:169	was not the Covenant of the Book taken from **them**,
007:169	came their way, they would (again) seize **them**.
007:169	After **them** succeeded an (evil) generation:
007:171	to fall on **them** (We said): "Hold firmly

THEM (continued)

007:171 When We raised the mount over **them**, as if
007:172 and made **them** testify concerning themselves,
007:173 but we are (their) descendants after **them**:
007:175 but he passed **them** by: so Satan followed him up,
007:175 Relate to **them** the story of the man to whom We
007:180 so call on Him by **them**;
007:182 We will lead **them** step by step to ruin
007:183 Respite will I grant unto **them**: for My
007:186 He will leave **them** in their trespasses, wandering
007:190 But when He giveth **them** a goodly child, they
007:192 No aid can they give **them**, nor can
007:193 If ye call **them** to guidance, they will
007:193 it is the dame whether ye call **them** or ye keep silent.
007:194 call upon **them**, and let **them** listen to your prayer,
007:198 Thou wilt see **them** looking at thee,
007:198 If thou callest **them** to guidance, they hear
007:201 when a thought of evil from Satan assaults **them**,
007:202 (the evil ones) plunge **them** deeper into error,
007:203 If thou bring **them** not a revelation, they say:
008:003 We have given **them** for sustenance:
008:012 and smite all their finger-tips off **them**."
008:015 never turn your backs to **them**.
008:016 If any do turn his back to **them** on such a day-
008:017 It is not ye who slew **them**; it was Allah:
008:023 if He had made **them** listen, they would
008:023 He would indeed have made **them** listen:
008:023 If Allah had found in **them** any good,
008:031 When Our Signs are rehearsed to **them**,
008:033 whilst thou wast amongst **them**;
008:033 But Allah was not going send **them** a Chastisement:
008:034 but most of **them** do not understand.
008:034 what plea have they that Allah should not punish **them**,
008:037 heap **them** together, and cast **them** into Hell.
008:038 is already (a matter of warning for **them**).
008:038 the punishment of those before **them** is already
008:038 their past would be forgiven **them**; but if
008:039 And fight **them** on until there is no more persecution
008:043 in thy dream Allah showed **them** to thee as few:
008:043 if He had shown **them** to thee as many,
008:044 He showed **them** to you as few in your eyes, and
008:048 Satan made their (sinful) acts seem alluring to **them**,
008:049 their religion has misled **them**."
008:052 before **them**: they rejected the Signs of Allah, and
008:052 and Allah punished **them** for their crimes:
008:054 of the People of Pharaoh and those before **them**":
008:054 so We destroyed **them** for their crimes,
008:057 If ye gain the mastery over **them** in war,
008:057 disperse, with **them**, those who follow **them**,
008:058 throw back (their covenant) to **them**,
008:059 they will never frustrate (**them**).
008:060 Against **them** make ready your strength to the
008:071 and hath He given (thee) power over **them**.
008:072 it is your duty to help **them**, except against
008:072 no duty of protection to **them** until they emigrate;
008:072 who gave (**them**) asylum and aid,-
008:074 as well as those who give (**them**) asylum and aid,-
008:074 for **them** is the forgiveness of sins and a provision
009:004 So fulfil your engagements with **them** to the
009:005 and pay Zakat then open the way for **them**:
009:005 wherever ye find **them**, and seize **them**, beleaguer **them**,
009:005 and lie in wait for **them** in every stratagem (of war);
009:007 stand true to you, stand ye true to **them**:

THEM (continued)

009:008 and most of **them** are rebellious and wicked.
009:012 for their oaths are nothing to **them**;
009:013 Do ye fear **them**? Nay, it is Allah Whom ye should
009:014 and disgrace **them**, help you (to victory) over **them**,
009:014 Fight **them**, and Allah will punish **them** by your hands,
009:021 of His good pleasure. And of Gardens for **them**,
009:021 Their Lord doth give **them** glad tidings of a Mercy
009:028 so let **them** not, after this year of theirs, approach the
009:030 Allah's curse be on **them**:
009:034 announce unto **them** a most grievous chastisement-
009:034 of men and hinder (**them**) from the Way of Allah.
009:036 of **them** four are sacred;
009:037 The evil of their course seems pleasing to **them**.
009:042 but the distance was long, (and weighed) on **them**.
009:043 Why didst thou grant **them** exemption
009:046 so He made **them** lag behind and they were told,
009:047 among you who would have listened to **them**.
009:049 Among **them** is (many) a man who says: "Grant me
009:050 If good befalls thee, it grieves **them**;
009:055 punish **them** with these things in this life,
009:058 And among **them** are men who slander thee
009:059 what Allah and His Messenger gave **them**,
009:061 Among **them** are men who molest the Prophet and say,
009:064 showing **them** what is (really passing) in their
009:064 lest a Sura should be sent down about **them**,
009:065 If thou dost question **them**, they declare
009:067 so He hath forgotten **them**.
009:068 for **them** is the curse of Allah.
009:068 they dwell: sufficient is it for **them**:
009:070 To **them** came their Messenger with Clear Signs.
009:070 Who wrongs **them**, but they wrong their own souls.
009:070 Hath not the story reached **them** of those before **them**?
009:071 On **them** will Allah pour His mercy:
009:073 and be firm against **them**.
009:074 Allah will punish **them** with a grievous chastisement
009:074 Allah and His Messenger had enriched **them**!
009:074 none on earth to protect or help **them**.
009:074 If they repent, it will be best for **them**:
009:075 Amongst **them** are men who made a Covenant
009:075 that id He bestowed on **them** of His bounty;
009:079 Allah will throw back their ridicule on **them**:
009:079 and throw ridicule on **them**,-Allah will
009:080 Allah will not forgive **them**:
009:082 Let **them** laugh a little: much will they weep:
009:083 if, then, Allah bring thee back to any of **them**,
009:084 Nor do thou ever pray for any of **them** that dies,
009:085 Allah's Wish is to punish **them** with these things
009:086 and influence among **them** ask thee for exemption,
009:086 When a Sura comes down, enjoining **them** to believe
009:088 for **them** are (all) good things:
009:089 Allah hath prepared for **them** Gardens under which
009:090 seize the Unbelievers among **them**.
009:094 their excuses to you when ye return to **them**.
009:095 that ye may leave **them** alone.
009:095 So leave **them** alone: for they are an abomination,
009:095 when ye return to **them**,
009:096 that ye may be pleased with **them**.
009:096 But if ye are pleased with **them**.
009:098 on **them** be the disaster of Evil:
009:099 gifts bringing **them** nearer to Allah and obtaining
009:099 Aye, indeed they bring **them** nearer (to Him):
009:099 soon will Allah admit **them** to His Mercy: for Allah

THEM (continued)

009:100	as are they with him: for **them** hath He prepared
009:100	well-pleased is Allah with **them**,
009:100	those who follow **them** in (all) good deeds,
009:100	and of those who gave **them** aid,
009:101	thou knowest **them** not: We know **them**:
009:101	twice shall We punish **them**:
009:102	Perhaps Allah will turn unto **them** (in mercy):
009:103	that so thou mightest purify sanctify **them**;
009:103	verily thy prayers are a source of security for **them**:
009:106	whether He will punish **them**,
009:106	or turn in mercy to **them**:
009:113	after it is clear to **them** that they are companions of
009:115	makes clear to **them** as to what they should avoid,
009:115	after He hath Guided **them** until He makes clear
009:117	for He is unto **them** Most Kind, Most Merciful.
009:117	a part of **them** had nearly swerved (from duty),
009:117	but He turned to **them** (also):
009:118	and their (very) Souls seemed straitened to **them**,-
009:118	Then He turned to **them**, that they
009:118	that the earth seemed constrained to **them**,
009:121	requite **them** with the best (possible reward).
009:122	and admonish the people when they return to **them**,-
009:123	and let **them** find harshness in you:
009:124	some of **them** say: "Which of you has had his faith
010:009	will guide **them** because of their Faith:
010:009	beneath **them** will flow rivers in Gardens of Bliss.
010:013	their Messengers came to **them** with Clear Signs,
010:014	Then We made you heirs in the land after **them**,
010:015	But when Our Clear Signs are rehearsed unto **them**,
010:019	their differences would have been settled between **them**.
010:021	some mercy after adversity hath touched **them**,
010:022	they sail with **them** with a favourable wind,
010:022	and the waves come to **them** from all sides, and they
010:023	But when He delivereth **them**, behold! they
010:028	We shall separate **them**, and their "partners"
010:028	One Day shall We gather **them** all together.
010:030	invented falsehoods will leave **them** in the lurch.
010:036	But most of **them** follow nothing but conjecture:
010:039	did those before **them** make charges of falsehood:
010:039	before the interpretation thereof hath reached **them**
010:040	Of **them** there are some who believe therein,
010:042	Among **them** are some who (pretend to)
010:043	And among **them** are some who look at thee:
010:045	**them** together: (it will be) as if they had tarried
010:046	some part of what We promise **them**,-
010:047	the matter will be judged between **them** with justice,
010:047	when their Messenger comes (before **them**),
010:054	and no wrong will be done unto **them**.
010:054	but the judgment between **them** will be with justice,
010:055	Yet most of **them** do not understand.
010:058	in that let **them** rejoice":
010:060	but most of **them** are ungrateful.
010:064	For **them** are Glad Tidings, in the life
010:070	Then shall We make **them** taste the severest
010:071	Relate to **them** the story of Noah.
010:073	and We made **them** inherit (the earth),
010:074	they brought **them** Clear Signs,
010:075	Then after **them** sent We Moses and Aaron
010:076	When the Truth did come to **them** from Us,
010:080	Moses said to **them**: "Throw ye what ye (wish)
010:083	lest they should persecute **them**;
010:090	hosts followed **them** in insolence and spite.

THEM (continued)

010:093	Verily Allah will judge between **them** as to
010:093	it was after knowledge had been granted to **them**,
010:093	judge between them as to the schisms amongst **them**,
010:093	and provided for **them** sustenance of the best:
010:097	Even if every Sign was brought unto **them**,-until
010:098	from **them** the Chastisement of Ignominy in the
010:098	and permitted **them** to enjoy (their life) for a while.
010:102	of the men who passed away before **them**?
011:007	But if thou wert to say to **them**, "Ye shall
011:008	Ah! On the day it (actually) reaches **them**,
011:008	nothing will turn it away from **them**,
011:008	If We delay the chastisement for **them** for a definite term,
011:011	for **them** is forgiveness (of sins) and a great reward.
011:015	to **them** We shall pay (the price of) their deeds
011:021	the (fancies) they forged have left **them** in the lurch!
011:030	who would help me against Allah if I drove **them** away?
011:031	will not grant **them** (all) that is good:
011:039	a chastisement that will cover **them** with shame,-
011:042	So the Ark floated with **them** on the waves
011:043	and the waves came between **them**,
011:048	a grievous Chastisement reach **them** from Us."
011:049	neither thou nor thy People knew **them**.
011:058	We saved **them** from a severe chastisement.
011:069	and hastened to entertain **them** with roasted calf.
011:070	he felt some mistrust of **them**,
011:070	and conceived a fear of **them**.
011:076	for **them** there cometh a Chastisement that cannot
011:077	and felt himself powerless (to protect) **them**.
011:082	down on **them** brimstones hard as baked clay,
011:098	and lead **them** into the Fire but woeful indeed
011:099	and woeful is the gift which shall be given (unto **them**)!
011:100	of **them** some are standing,
011:101	profited **them** no whit when there issued the decree
011:101	It was not We that wronged **them**:
011:106	there will be for **them** therein (nothing but) the heaving
011:109	but verily We shall pay **them** back (in full) their portion
011:109	but what their fathers worshipped before (**them**):
011:110	the matter would have been decided between **them**:
011:116	of the good things of life which were given **them**,
011:116	a few among **them** whom We saved (from harm)?
011:119	and for this did He create **them**:
011:120	in **them** there cometh to thee the Truth, as well
012:004	I saw **them** prostrate themselves to me!"
012:010	Said one of **them**: "Slay not Joseph, but if
012:015	(one day) tell **them** the truth of this affair
012:031	and she said (to Joseph) "come out before **them**."
012:031	she gave each of **them** a knife:
012:031	she sent for **them** and prepared a banquet for **them**:
012:033	I should feel inclined towards **them** and join the
012:035	Then it occurred to **them** after they had seen
012:036	Said one of **them**: "I see myself (in a dream)
012:047	ye shall leave **them** in the ear,-
012:048	what ye shall have laid by in advance for **them**,-
012:058	and he knew **them**, but they knew him not.
012:059	And when he had furnished **them** forth with
012:059	provisions (suitable) for **them**,
012:065	their stock-in-trade had been returned to **them**.
012:068	it did not profit **them** in the least against Allah
012:070	At length when he furnished **them** forth with
012:070	with provisions (suitable) for **them**,
012:071	They said, turning towards **them**: "What is it
012:077	revealing not the secrets to **them** he (simply)
012:080	The leader among **them** said: "Know ye not

THEM (continued)

012:083 May be Allah will bring **them** (back) all to me
012:084 And he turned away from **them**, and said: "How great
012:102 nor wast thou (present) with **them** when they
012:104 And no reward dost thou ask of **them** for this:
012:105 Yet they turn (their faces) away from **them**!
012:106 And most of **them** believe not in Allah
012:107 the coming against **them** of the covering veil
012:107 Or of the coming against **them** of the (final) Hour
012:109 and see what was the end of those before **them**?
012:110 there reaches **them** Our help,
013:004 yet some of **them** We make more excellent
013:006 to the good yet have come to pass, before **them**,
013:014 besides Him hear **them** no more than if they
013:014 water to reach their mouths but it reaches **them** not:
013:016 so that the creation seemed to **them** similar?
013:018 For **them** will the reckoning be terrible:
013:023 and angels shall enter unto **them** from every
013:025 for **them** is the terrible Home!
013:025 and work mischief in the land;-on **them** is the Curse;
013:030 mightest rehearse unto **them** what We send down
013:031 cease to seize **them** for their (ill) deeds,
013:032 I punished **them**: then how (terrible) was My
013:033 Say: "But name **them**! is it that ye will inform
013:034 For **them** is a Penalty in the life of this world,
013:038 and appointed for **them** wives and children:
013:040 what We promised **them** or take to Us thy soul
013:040 Thy duty is to make (the Message) reach **them**:
013:040 it is Our part to call **them** to account.
013:042 Those before **them** did (also) devise plots;
014:002 a terrible Chastisement (their Unfaith will bring **them**)!-
014:004 in order to make thing clear to **them**.
014:005 and remind **them** of the Days of Allah."
014:009 None knows **them** but Allah.
014:009 and of those who (came) after **them**?
014:009 To **them** came Messengers with Clear (Signs);
014:011 Their messengers said to **them**: "True, we are
014:013 But their Lord inspired (this Message) to **them**:
014:014 to abide in the land, and succeed **them**.
014:031 the Sustenance We have given **them**,
014:034 never will ye be able to number **them**.
014:037 and feed **them** with Fruits:
014:037 some among men with love towards **them**,
014:042 He but giveth **them** respite against a Day when
014:043 their gaze returning not towards **them**,
014:044 the Day when the Wrath will reach **them**:
014:045 ye were clearly shown how We dealt with **them**;
015:003 and let (false) Hope distract **them**:
015:003 Leave **them** alone, to eat and enjoy and let
015:011 came a messenger to **them** but they mocked him.
015:013 such has been the way of those went before **them**.
015:014 Even if We opened out to **them** a gate from heaven,
015:016 and made **them** fair-seeming to (all) beholders;
015:017 And (moreover) we have guarded **them** from every
015:025 it is thy Lord who will gather **them** together:
015:030 all of **them** together:
015:039 and I will put **them** all in the wrong,-
015:039 I will make (wrong) to **them** on the earth,
015:040 "Except Thy chosen servants among **them**,
015:043 the promised abode for **them** all!
015:048 There no sense of fatigue shall touch **them**,
015:051 Tell **them** about the guests of Abraham.
015:059 **them** we are certainly (charged) to save

THEM (continued)

015:065 and do thou go behind **them**:
015:073 But the (mighty) Blast overtook **them** at sunrise,
015:074 on **them** brimstones hard as baked clay.
015:079 So We exacted retribution from **them**.
015:081 but they persisted in turning away from **them**.
015:081 We sent **them** Our Signs, but they
015:083 But the (mighty) Blast seized **them** of a morning,
015:084 And of no avail to **them** was all that they did
015:085 and all between **them**, but for just ends.
015:088 nor grieve over **them**:
015:088 We have bestowed on certain classes of **them**,
015:092 We will, of a surety, call **them** to account,
016:005 from **them** ye derive warmth, and numerous
016:006 ye have a sense of pride and beauty **them** as ye
016:006 ye drive **them** home in the evening,
016:006 lead **them** forth to pasture in the morning.
016:018 never would ye be able to number **them**:
016:024 When it is said to **them**, "What is it
016:026 and form the roof fell down on **them** from above;
016:026 Those before **them** did also plot (against Allah's Way)
016:026 and the Wrath seized **them** from directions
016:027 He will cover **them** with shame, and say:
016:031 beneath **them** flow (pleasant) rivers:
016:032 saying (to **them**), "Peace be on you; enter ye
016:033 the (ungodly) wait but for the angels to come to **them**,
016:033 So did those who went before **them**.
016:033 But Allah wronged **them** not: nay, they wronged
016:034 at which they had scoffed hemmed **them** in.
016:034 But the evil results of their deeds overtook **them**,
016:035 So did those who went before **them**.
016:037 and there is none to help **them**.
016:039 in order that He may manifest to **them** the truth
016:044 mayest explain clearly to men what is sent for **them**,
016:044 (We sent **them**) with Clear Signs and Scriptures
016:045 Allah will not cause the earth to swallow **them** up,
016:045 or that the Wrath will not seize **them** from directions
016:047 Or that He may not call **them** to account
016:050 They all fear their Lord, high above **them**,
016:055 the favours We have bestowed on **them**!
016:058 When news is brought to one of **them**,
016:061 but He gives **them** respite for a stated Term:
016:062 is for themselves: without doubt for **them** is the
016:064 to **them** those things in which they differ,
016:072 and made for you, out of **them**, sons and
016:073 such has no power of providing **them**,
016:075 But most of **them** understand not.
016:076 one of **them** dumb, with no power of any sort;
016:079 Nothing holds **them** up but (the power of) Allah.
016:083 and most of **them** are (creatures) ungrateful.
016:083 recognize the favours of Allah; then they deny **them**;
016:086 but they will throw back their words at **them** (and say):
016:087 leave **them** in the lurch.
016:088 for **them** will We add Chastisement to Chastisement;
016:089 shall raise from all peoples a witness against **them**,
016:091 break not your oaths after ye have confirmed **them**;
016:101 but most of **them** understand not.
016:104 Allah will not guide **them**,
016:106 on **them** is Wrath from Allah,
016:113 seized **them** even in the midst of their iniquities.
016:113 And there came to **them** a Messenger from among
016:118 We did **them** no wrong, but they
016:124 judge between **them** on the Day of Judgment as to

THEM (continued)

016:125   and argue with **them** in ways that are best
016:127   nor grieve over **them**:
017:006   Then did We grant you victory over **them**:
017:010   that We have prepared for **them** a Chastisement
017:016   then We destroy **them** utterly.
017:016   the word is proved true against **them**;
017:016   We command those among **them** who are given
017:018   Hell for **them**: they will burn therein,
017:018   We readily grant **them**-such things as We will,
017:023   nor repel **them** but address **them** in terms of honour.
017:023   Whether one or both of **them** attain old age
017:023   say not to **them** a word of contempt,
017:024   And, out of kindness, lower to **them** the wing
017:024   "My Lord! bestow on **them** Thy Mercy even as they
017:028   yet speak to **them** a word of easy kindness.
017:028   from **them** in pursuit of the Mercy from thy Lord
017:031   sustenance for **them** as well as for you.
017:031   Verily the killing of **them** is a great sin.
017:053   for Satan doth sow dissensions among **them**:
017:054   a disposer of their affairs for **them**.
017:056   your troubles from you nor to change **them**."
017:059   of former generations treated **them** as false:
017:060   We put fear (and warning) into **them**,
017:063   (Allah) said: "Go thy way, if any of **them** follow thee,
017:064   And Arouse those whom thou canst among **them**,
017:064   mutually share with **them** wealth and children;
017:064   assaults on **them** with thy cavalry and thy infantry;
017:064   But Satan promises **them** nothing but deceit.
017:064   and make promises to **them**."
017:065   no authority shalt thou have over **them**."
017:070   given **them** for sustenance things good and pure;
017:070   and conferred on **them** special favours,
017:070   provided **them** with transport on land and sea;
017:074   thou wouldst nearly have inclined to **them** a little.
017:094   man back from Belief when Guidance came to **them**,
017:095   We should certainly have sent **them** down from the
017:097   On the Day of judgment We shall gather **them** together,
017:097   We shall increase for **them** the fierceness of the Fire.
017:099   has power to create the like of **them** (anew)?
017:100   for fear or spending **them**:
017:100   behold, ye would keep **them** back,
017:101   when he came to **them**, Pharaoh said to him: "O Moses!
017:103   So he resolved to remove **them** from the face of the
017:107   when it is recited to **them**,
018:006   fret thyself to death, following after **them**, in grief,
018:007   as to which of **them** are best in conduct.
018:007   in order that We may test **them**-as to which
018:012   Then We roused **them**, in order to test which of
018:013   and We increased **them** in guidance:
018:016   "When ye turn away from **them** and the things
018:017   turning away from **them** to the left,
018:018   wouldst have certainly turned back from **them** in flight,
018:018   Thou wouldst have thought **them** awake, whilst they
018:018   and We turned **them** on their right and their
018:018   if thou hadst looked at **them**,
018:018   wouldst certainly have been filled with terror of **them**.
018:019   We raised **them** up (from sleep), that they
018:019   Said one of **them**, "How long have ye stayed (here)"
018:021   their Lord knows best about **them**:
018:021   "Let us surely build a place of worship over **them**."
018:021   (Some) said, "Construct a building over **them**":
018:022   consult any of **them** about (the affair of) the Sleepers.

THEM (continued)

018:022   the dog being the fourth among **them**;
018:022   therefore, into controversies concerning **them**,
018:028   and let not thine eyes pass beyond **them**,
018:029   like the walls and roof of a tent, will hem **them** in:
018:031   beneath **them** rivers will flow:
018:031   For **them** will be Gardens of Eternity;
018:032   Set forth to **them** the parable of two men:
018:032   grape-vines and surrounded **them** with date-palms;
018:032   for one of **them** We provided two gardens of grape-
018:033   in the midst of **them** We caused a river to flow.
018:045   Set forth to **them** the similitude of the life of this world
018:047   nor shall We leave out any one of **them**.
018:047   and We shall gather **them**, all together,
018:049   They will find all that they did, placed before **them**:
018:051   I called **them** not to witness the creation
018:052   My partners," and they will call on **them**,
018:052   but they will not listen to **them**;
018:052   and We shall make for **them** a place of common
018:055   now that guidance has come to **them**,
018:055   the ways of the ancients to overtake **them**,
018:055   or the Wrath be brought to **them** face to face?
018:057   If thou callest **them** to guidance, even then
018:057   the Signs of his Lord but turns away from **them**,
018:058   If He were to call **them** (at once) to account
018:077   they asked **them** for food,
018:077   but they refused **them** hospitality.
018:079   for there was after **them** a certain king who
018:080   that he would grieve **them** by obstinate rebellion
018:081   give **them** in exchange (a son) better in purity
018:091   (He left **them**) as they were:
018:093   beneath **them**, a people who scarcely understood
018:094   a barrier between us and **them**?
018:095   a strong barrier between you and **them**:
018:099   and We shall collect **them** all together.
018:099   On that day We shall leave **them** to surge
018:105   on the Day of Judgment, give **them** any Weight.
018:108   no change will they wish for from **them**.
019:011   he told **them** by signs to celebrate Allah's praises
019:017   She placed a screen (to screen herself) from **them**:
019:039   But warn **them** of the Day of Distress,
019:049   When he had turned away from **them** and from
019:049   Isaac and Jacob, and each one of **them** We made
019:050   And We bestowed of Our Mercy on **them**, and We
019:050   and We granted **them** lofty honour on the tongue
019:058   (Allah) Most Gracious were rehearsed to **them**,
019:059   But after **them** there followed a posterity
019:065   and of all that is between **them**:
019:068   and (also) Satans (with **them**);
019:068   We shall gather **them** together, and (also)
019:068   then shall We bring **them** forth on their knees
019:073   When Our Clear Signs are rehearsed to **them**,
019:074   (countless) generations before **them** have We destroyed,
019:075   (Allah) Most Gracious extends (the rope) to **them**,
019:081   to give **them** power and glory!
019:082   and become adversaries against **them**.
019:083   to incite **them** with fury?
019:084   for We but count out to **them** a (limited)
019:084   So make no haste against **them**, for We
019:094   He does take and account of **them** (all),
019:094   and hath numbered **them** (all) exactly.
019:095   And every one of **them** will come to him singly

THEM (continued)

019:098 Canst thou find a single one of **them** (now) or hear
019:098 (countless) generation before **them** have We destroyed?
019:098 or hear (so much as) a whisper of **them**?
020:006 and all between **them**,
020:047 and afflict **them** not:
020:075 for **them** are ranks exalted,-
020:077 and strike a dry path for **them** through the sea,
020:078 completely overwhelmed **them** and covered **them** up.
020:078 Then Pharaoh pursued **them** with his forces,
020:079 instead of leading **them** aright.
020:085 the Samiri has led **them** astray."
020:087 and we threw. **them** (into the fire),
020:089 no power either to harm **them** or to do **them** good?
020:089 that it could not return **them** a word (for answer),
020:090 said to **them**: "O my people! ye are being tested
020:092 when thou sawest **them** going wrong.
020:101 grievous will the burden be to **them** on that Day,-
020:104 when the best of **them** in judgment will say:
020:105 and scatter **them** as dust;
020:105 say, "My Lord will uproot **them** and scatter
020:106 "He will leave **them** as plains smooth and level;
020:110 He knows what is before or after or behind **them**:
020:121 and so their nakedness appeared to **them**:
020:126 when Our Signs came unto thee, forgot **them**:
020:128 how many generations before **them** We destroyed,
020:130 celebrate **them** for part of the hours of the night,
020:131 things We have given for enjoyment to parties of **them**,
020:131 the life of this world, through which We test **them**:
020:133 Has not a Clear Sign come to **them** of all
020:134 Had We destroyed **them** a punishment before this,
021:002 Never comes (aught) to **them** of a renewed Message
021:006 (As to those) before **them**, not one of the towns
021:008 Nor did We give **them** bodies that ate no food,
021:009 Then We fulfilled to **them** Our promise,
021:009 and We saved **them** and those whom We willed,
021:015 till We made **them** as a field that is mown,
021:024 But most of **them** know not the Truth,
021:028 and what is behind **them**, and they
021:028 He knows what is before **them**,
021:029 If any of **them** should say, "I am a god besides Him",
021:030 before We clove **them** asunder?
021:031 lest it should shake with **them**,
021:031 (between mountains) for **them** to pass through:
021:037 so ask Me not to hasten **them**!
021:039 and (when) no help can reach **them**!
021:040 Nay, it may come to **them** all of a sudden
021:040 of a sudden and confound **them**:
021:043 Or have they gods that can guard **them** from Us?
021:044 and their fathers until the period grew long for **them**;
021:046 a breath of the Wrath of thy Lord do touch **them**
021:053 They said, "We found our father worshipping **them**."
021:056 He Who created **them** (from nothing):
021:058 (all) but the biggest of **them**,
021:058 So he broke **them** to pieces, (all) but
021:060 They said, "We heard a youth talk of **them**:
021:063 Ask **them**, if they can talk."
021:070 but We made **them** the Greater losers.
021:071 and (his nephew) Lut (and directed **them**) to the
021:072 and We made righteous men of every one (of **them**).
021:073 And We made **them** leaders, guiding (men)
021:073 and We sent **them** inspiration to do good deeds,
021:077 so We drowned **them** (in the Flood) all together.

THEM (continued)

021:079 to each (of **them**) We gave Judgment and Knowledge;
021:082 and it was We Who guarded **them**.
021:086 We admitted **them** to Our Mercy:
021:103 The Great Terror will bring **them** no grief:
021:103 but the angels meet **them** (with mutual greetings):
022:011 but if a trial comes to **them**, they turn
022:011 if good befalls **them**, they are, therewith,
022:012 as can neither hurt nor profit **them**:
022:017 Allah will judge between **them** on the Day of
022:019 for **them** will be cut out a garment of Fire:
022:021 there will be maces of iron (to punish) **them**.
022:025 is profanity wrongfully **them** will We created
022:028 may witness the benefits (provided) for **them**,
022:028 which He has provided for **them** (for sacrifice):
022:029 "Then let **them** complete the rites prescribed for **them**
022:033 In **them** ye have benefits for a term appointed:
022:034 He gave **them** from animals (fit for food).
022:035 We have bestowed upon **them**.
022:036 in **them** is (much) good for you:
022:036 over **them** as they line up (for sacrifice):
022:037 He has thus made **them** subject to you, that ye
022:041 if We establish **them** in the land,
022:042 the Peoples before **them** (with their prophets),-
022:044 and only after that did I punish **them**:
022:044 My punishment (of **them**)!
022:048 In the end I punished **them**.
022:050 for **them** is forgiveness and a sustenance most
022:051 who strive against Our Signs, to frustrate **them**,-
022:055 the Hour (of Judgment) comes suddenly upon **them**,
022:055 or there comes to **them** the Chastisement
022:056 He will judge between **them**:
022:058 on **them** will Allah bestow verily a goodly Provision:
022:059 Verily He will admit **them** to a place with which they
022:067 but do thou invite (**them**) to thy Lord:
022:067 let **them** not then dispute with thee on the matter,
022:071 things for which no authority has been sent down to **them**,
022:072 those who rehearse Our Signs to **them**.
022:072 When Our Clear Signs are rehearsed to **them**,
022:073 And if the fly should snatch away anything from **them**,
022:076 He knows what is before **them** and what is behind **them**:
023:006 Except with those joined to **them** in the marriage bond,
023:019 and of **them** ye eat (and have enjoyment),-
023:019 in **them** have ye abundant fruits:
023:021 there are, in **them**, (besides), numerous other
023:022 And on **them**, as well as in ships, ye ride.
023:027 of **them** against whom the Word has already
023:031 Then We raised after **them** another generation.
023:032 And We sent to **them** a messenger from among
023:041 and We made **them** as rubbish of dead leaves
023:041 Then the Blast overtook **them** with justice,
023:042 Then We raised after **them** other generations.
023:044 so We made **them** follow each other (in punishment):
023:044 We made **them** as a tale (that is told):
023:048 So they rejected **them** and they became of those
023:050 We gave **them** both shelter on high ground,
023:053 people have cut off their affair (of unity), between **them**,
023:054 But leave **them** in their confused ignorance
023:055 granted **them** abundance of wealth and sons,
023:056 We would hasten **them** on in every good?
023:061 and these who are foremost in **them**.
023:064 those of **them** who received the good things
023:068 come to **them** that did not come to their

THEM (continued)

023:070	Nay, he has brought **them** the Truth,
023:070	but most of **them** hate the Truth.
023:071	Nay, We have sent **them** their admonition, but they
023:072	Or is it that thou asked **them** for some recompense?
023:073	But verily thou callest **them** to the Straight Way;
023:075	If We had mercy on **them** and removed the distress
023:075	the distress which is on **them**,
023:076	We inflicted Punishment on **them**, but they
023:077	Until We open on **them** a gate leading to a serve
023:090	We have sent **them** the Truth: but they
023:099	Until, when death comes to one of **them**, he says:
023:100	Before **them** is a Partition till the Day
023:101	be no more relationships between **them** that day,
023:105	and ye did but treat **them** as falsehoods?"
023:110	"But ye treated **them** with ridicule,
023:110	so much so that (ridicule of) **them** made you forget
023:110	while ye were laughing at **them**!
023:111	"I have rewarded **them** this day for their patience
024:002	flog each of **them** with a hundred stripes:
024:004	flog **them** with eighty stripes;
024:006	let one of **them** testify four times by Allah
024:011	and to him who took on himself the lead among **them**,
024:011	to every man among **them** (will come the punishment)
024:022	let **them** forgive and overlook:
024:023	for **them** is a grievous Chastisement-
024:024	bear witness against **them** as to their actions.
024:025	On that Day Allah will pay **them** back (all) their
024:026	people say: for **them** there is forgiveness, and a
024:027	ye have asked permission and saluted those in **them**:
024:032	Allah will give **them** means out of His grace:
024:033	(for emancipation) give **them** such a deed if you
024:033	is Allah Oft-Forgiving, Most Merciful (to **them**).
024:033	yea, give **them** something yourselves out of
024:033	if ye know any good in **them**;
024:033	until Allah gives **them** means out of His grace.
024:036	in **them** is He glorified in the mornings and in the
024:036	for the celebration, in **them**, of His name:
024:038	and add even more for **them** out of His Grace:
024:038	That Allah may reward **them** according to the
024:043	then joins **them** together, then makes **them** into a heap?
024:045	of **them** there are some that creep on their bellies;
024:047	but even after that, some of **them** turn away:
024:048	behold, some of **them** decline (to come).
024:048	in order that He may judge between **them**,
024:050	will deal unjustly with **them**?
024:051	He may judge between **them**,
024:053	if only thou wouldst command **them**,
024:055	as He granted it to those before **them**;
024:055	He has chosen for **them**;
024:055	grant **them** in the land, inheritance (of power),
024:058	it is not wrong for you or for **them** to move
024:059	as do those before **them**:
024:059	let **them** (also) ask for permission,
024:060	there is no blame on **them** if they lay aside
024:060	but it is best for **them** to be modest:
024:062	give leave to those of **them** whom thou wilt,
024:063	or a grievous Chastisement be inflicted on **them**.
024:063	lest some trial befall **them**, or a
024:064	He will tell **them** the truth of what they did:
025:002	and ordered **them** in due proportions.
025:012	When it sees **them** from a place far off, they will
025:015	For **them**, that is a reward as well as a final abode.

THEM (continued)

025:016	"For **them** there will be therein all that they wish for:
025:017	The Day He will gather **them** together as well as those
025:018	on **them** and their fathers,
025:037	We drowned **them**, and We made **them** as a Sign
025:038	and many a generation between **them**.
025:042	had it not been that we were constant to **them**!"
025:044	Or thinkest thou that most of **them** listen or understand?
025:050	And We have distributed the (water) amongst **them**,
025:052	but strive against **them** with the utmost strenuousness,
025:053	yet has He made a barrier between **them**,
025:055	things that can neither profit **them** nor harm **them**:
025:060	and it increases **them** in aversion.
025:060	When it is said to **them**, "Adore ye The Most
025:063	and when the ignorant address **them**, they say,
025:073	droop not down at **them** as if they were deaf
026:004	We could send down to **them** from the sky a Sign,
026:005	But there comes not to **them** a newly-revealed
026:008	but most of **them** do not believe.
026:043	Moses said to **them**: "Throw ye-
026:057	So We expelled **them** from gardens, springs,
026:060	So they pursued **them** at sunrise.
026:067	but most of **them** do not believe.
026:069	And rehearse to **them** (something of) Abraham's
026:071	and we remain constantly in attendance on **them**."
026:072	"Do they listen to you when ye call (on **them**),
026:092	"And it shall be said to **them**: `Where are the (gods)
026:103	but most of **them** do not believe.
026:106	Behold, their brother Noah said to **them**: "Will ye
026:118	"Judge thou, then, between me and **them** openly,
026:121	but most of **them** do not believe.
026:124	Behold, their brother Hud said to **them**: "Will ye
026:139	but most of **them** do not believe.
026:139	So they rejected him, and We destroyed **them**.
026:142	Behold, their brother Salih said to **them**: "Will you
026:158	but most of **them** do not believe.
026:158	But the Chastisement seized **them**.
026:161	Behold, their brother Lut said to **them**: "Will ye
026:173	We rained down on **them** a shower (of brimstone):
026:174	but most of **them** do not believe.
026:177	Behold, Shu'aib said to **them**: "Will ye
026:189	of a day of overshadowing gloom seized **them**,
026:190	but most of **them** do not believe.
026:197	Is it not a Sign to **them** that the learned
026:199	And had he recited it to **them**, they would
026:202	But the (Penalty) will come to **them** of a sudden,
026:205	If we do let **them** enjoy (this life) for a few years,
026:206	Yet there comes to **them** at length the (Punishment)
026:207	It will profit **them** not the enjoyment
026:211	It is not meant for **them**, nor is
026:223	They listen eagerly and most of **them** are liars.
026:224	straying in Evil, who follow **them**:
027:013	But when Our Signs came to **them**,
027:014	though their souls acknowledged **them** wrongfully
027:014	And they denied **them**,
027:023	a woman ruling over **them** and provided with every
027:024	and has kept **them** away from the Path,-so they
027:028	and deliver it to **them**:
027:028	then draw back from **them**, and (wait to)
027:037	we shall expel **them** from there in disgrace,
027:037	"Go back to **them**, and be sure we shall come
027:037	we shall come to **them** with such hosts as they
027:051	destroyed **them** and their people, all (of **them**).

THEM (continued)

027:058	And We rained down on **them** a shower (of brimstone):
027:060	power to cause the growth of the tress in **them**.
027:061	Nay, most of **them** know not.
027:070	But grieve not over **them**, nor distress
027:073	yet most of **them** are ungrateful.
027:078	the Lord will decide between **them** by His Decree:
027:081	be a guide to the Blind, (to prevent **them**) from straying:
027:082	a beast to speak unto **them** because mankind had
027:082	when the Word is fulfilled against **them** (the unjust),
027:084	though ye comprehended **them** not in knowledge,
027:085	And the Word is fulfilled against **them**,
027:086	made the Night for **them** to rest in and the
027:086	and the Day to give **them** light?
027:088	Thou seest the mountains and thinkest **them** firmly fixed:
027:093	so that ye shall know **them**":
028:004	depressing a group among **them**:
028:005	to make **them** leaders (in faith) and make **them** heirs,
028:006	To establish a firm place for **them** in the land,
028:006	what they were dreading from **them**.
028:008	should be to **them** an adversary and a cause
028:013	but most of **them** do not know.
028:023	and besides **them** he found two women who were
028:024	So he watered (their flocks) for **them**;
028:033	He said "O my Lord! i have slain a man among **them**,
028:036	When Moses came to **them** with Our Clear Signs,
028:040	and We flung **them** into the sea:
028:041	And We made **them** (but) leaders inviting
028:042	In this world We made a Curse to follow **them**:
028:045	rehearsing Our Signs to **them**;
028:045	and long were the ages that passed over **them**;
028:047	should seize **them** for (the deeds) that their
028:048	when the Truth has come to **them** from Ourselves,
028:049	which is a better guide than either of **them**,
028:051	Now have We brought **them** the word in order
028:053	And when it is recited to **them**, they say:
028:054	out of what We have given **them**.
028:057	But most of **them** understand not.
028:057	for **them** a secure Sanctuary, to which
028:058	Now those habitations of theirs, after **them**,
028:059	rehearsing to **them** Our Signs;
028:062	That Day (Allah) will call to **them**, and say:
028:063	we free ourselves (from **them**) to you.
028:063	we led **them** astray, as we were astray ourselves:
028:064	they will call upon **them**,
028:064	and they will see the Chastisement (before **them**);
028:064	but they will not listen to **them**;
028:064	It will be said (to **them**): "Call upon your 'partners'
028:065	That Day (Allah) will call to **them**, and say:
028:066	will be obscure to **them** and they will not
028:074	The Day that He will call on **them**, He will
028:075	will leave **them** in the lurch.
028:076	but he acted insolently towards **them**:
029:003	We did test those before **them**,
029:007	reward **them** according to the best of their deeds.
029:007	from **them** shall We blot out misdeeds that they
029:008	which thou hast no knowledge, obey **them** not.
029:008	but if (either of **them**) strive (to force) to join
029:009	**them** shall We admit to the to the company of
029:014	overwhelmed **them** while they (persisted in) sin.
029:014	and he tarried among **them** a thousand years
029:033	and felt himself powerless (to protect) **them**:
029:037	then the mighty Blast seized **them**, and they

THEM (continued)

029:038	Satan made their deeds alluring to **them**,
029:038	and kept **them** back from the path,
029:039	there came to **them** Moses with Clear Signs,
029:040	of **them**, against some We sent a violent tornado
029:040	it was not Allah Who wronged **them**: they wronged
029:040	Each one of **them** We seized for his crime:
029:043	those understand **them** who have Knowledge.
029:046	unless it be with those of **them** who do wrong
029:051	And is it not enough for **them** that We have
029:051	the Book which is rehearsed to **them**?
029:053	They ask thee to hasten the Punishment (for **them**):
029:053	the Punishment would have certainly come to **them**:
029:053	and it will certainly reach **them**,-of a sudden,
029:055	On the Day that the Punishment shall cover **them** from
029:055	above **them** and from below **them**,
029:058	to **them** shall We give a Home in Heaven,-
029:060	It is Allah Who feeds (both) **them** and you:
029:061	If indeed thou ask **them** who has created
029:063	And if indeed thou ask **them** who it is that sends
029:063	But most of **them** understand not.
029:065	but when He has delivered **them** safely to (dry) land,
029:067	men are being snatched away from all around **them**?
029:069	We will certainly guide **them** to Our Paths:
030:008	created the heavens and the earth and all between **them**:
030:009	and see the end of those before **them**?
030:009	They were superior to **them** in strength:
030:009	there came to **them** their messengers with Clear
030:009	it was not Allah Who wronged **them**, but they
030:010	and held **them** up to ridicule.
030:021	that ye may dwell in tranquillity with **them**,
030:028	Do ye fear **them** as ye fear each other?
030:029	To **them** there will be no helpers.
030:033	some of **them** pay part-worship to other gods
030:033	but when He gives **them** a taste of Mercy
030:034	for the (favours) We Have bestowed on **them**!
030:035	Or have We sent down authority to **them**,
030:035	which speaks to **them** the things to which
030:036	evil afflicts **them** because of what their (own)
030:041	that (Allah) may give **them** a taste of some
030:042	most of **them** were idolaters.
030:047	and they came to **them** with Clear Signs:
030:048	made **them** reach such of his servants as He wills,
030:048	then does He spread **them** in the sky as He wills,
030:048	and break **them** into fragments,
030:058	but if thou bring to **them** any Sign, the Unbelievers
031:007	as if he heard **them** not,
031:015	obey **them** not; yet bear **them** company in this life
031:020	a Book to enlighten **them**!
031:021	What! even if it is Satan beckoning **them** to the
031:023	and We shall tell **them** the truth of their deeds:
031:024	We grant **them** their pleasure for a little while:
031:024	drive **them** to a chastisement unrelenting.
031:025	to Allah!" But most of **them** know not.
031:025	If thou ask **them**, who it is that created the heavens
031:032	But when He has delivered **them** safely to land,
031:032	there are among **them** those that falter between
031:032	When a wave covers **them** like the canopy
032:004	and all between **them**, in six Days,
032:015	when they are recited to **them** fall down
032:016	the sustenance which We have bestowed on **them**.
032:017	of the eye are kept hidden (in reserve) for **them**-
032:020	and it will be said to **them**: "Taste ye the Chastisement

THEM (continued)

032:021 And indeed We will make **them** taste of the
032:024 And We appointed, from among **them**, Leaders,
032:025 Verily thy Lord will judge between **them** on the
032:026 Does it not teach **them** a lesson,
032:026 how many generations We destroyed before **them**,
032:030 So turn away from **them**, and wait:
033:005 Call **them** by after their fathers:
033:007 We took from **them** a solemn Covenant:
033:009 but We sent against **them** a hurricane and forces
033:013 Therefore go back!" and a band of **them** ask for
033:013 Behold! A party among **them** said: "Ye men
033:014 been effected to **them** from the sides of the (City),
033:019 thou wilt see **them** looking to thee, their eyes
033:023 of **them** some have died and some (still) wait:
033:024 or turn to **them** in Mercy:
033:026 And those of the people of the Book who aided **them**-
033:026 Allah did take **them** down from their strongholds
033:035 for **them** has Allah prepared forgiveness and
033:037 when the latter have dissolved (their marriage) with **them**.
033:044 and He has prepared for **them** a generous Reward.
033:049 and then divorce **them** before ye have touched **them**,
033:049 no period of `Iddat have ye to count in respect of **them**:
033:049 so give **them** a present, and release
033:049 and release **them** in a handsome manner.
033:050 for **them** as to their wives and the captives
033:051 defer (the turn) any of **them** that thou pleasest,
033:051 with that which thou hast to give **them**:
033:051 that of all of **them**-
033:052 nor to change **them** for (other) wives, even though
033:053 ask **them** from before a screen:
033:057 and has prepared for **them** a humiliating Punishment.
033:057 Allah has cursed **them** in this world and in the
033:060 We shall certainly stir thee up against **them**
033:061 They shall have a curse on **them**:
033:064 for **them** a Blazing Fire,-
033:068 and curse **them** with a very great Curse!"
033:068 "Our Lord! give **them** Double Chastisement
034:005 who strive against Our Signs, to frustrate **them**,-
034:009 or cause a piece of the sky to fall upon **them**.
034:009 See they not what is before **them** and behind **them**,
034:009 We could cause the earth to swallow **them** up,
034:012 and if any of **them** turned aside from Our command,
034:014 (Solomon's) death, nothing showed **them** his death
034:016 and We sent against **them** the flood (released)
034:017 **them** because they ungratefully rejected Faith:
034:018 in prominent positions, and between **them** We had
034:018 Between **them** and the Cities on which We had
034:019 At length We made **them** as a tale (that is told),
034:019 (that is told), and We dispersed **them** all in
034:020 And on **them** did Satan prove true his idea,
034:021 But he had no authority over **them**,-except that
034:022 nor is any of **them** a helper to Allah.
034:028 giving **them** glad tidings, and warning **them**
034:034 ones among **them** said: "We believe
034:038 to frustrate **them**, will be given over into
034:040 On the day He will gather **them** all together,
034:041 most of **them** believe in **them**."
034:043 to **them**, they say, "This is only a man who
034:043 when it comes to **them**, "This is nothing
034:044 nor sent messengers to **them** before thee as Warners.
034:044 But We had not given **them** Books which they
034:051 but then there will be no escape (for **them**),

THEM (continued)

034:054 And between **them** and their desires, is placed
035:008 in regret for **them**: for Allah
035:009 and We drive **them** to a land that is dead,
035:010 of Evil,-for **them** is a Chastisement terrible;
035:014 If ye invoke **them**, they will
035:024 lived among **them** (in the past).
035:029 We have provided for **them**, secretly and
035:030 For He will pay **them** their meed,
035:030 nay, He will give **them** (even) more out of
035:032 among **them** some who wrong their own souls;
035:036 no term shall be determined for **them**,
035:036 for **them** will be the Fire of Hell:
035:040 Or have We given **them** a Book from which
035:041 one-can sustain **them** thereafter: verily He
035:042 to **them**, it has only increased their aversion.
035:042 to **them**, they would be more rightly guided
035:044 though they were superior to **them** in strength?
035:044 and see what was the end of those before **them**,-
035:045 but he gives **them** respite for a stated Term:
036:007 the greater part of **them**; for they
036:009 and a bar behind **them**, and further, We have
036:009 And We have put a bar in front of **them** and a
036:009 We have covered **them** up: so that
036:010 The same is to **them** whether thou admonish **them**
036:010 or thou do not admonish **them**:
036:010 admonish **them**: they will not believe.
036:013 Set forth to **them**, by way of a parable,
036:014 but We strengthened **them** with a third:
036:014 two messengers, they rejected **them**:
036:014 When We (first) sent to **them** two messengers,
036:030 to **them** but they mock Him!
036:031 Not to **them** will they return:
036:031 before **them** We destroyed?
036:032 But each one of **them** all-will be
036:033 A Sign for **them** is the earth that is dead;
036:037 And a Sign for **them** is the Night:
036:041 And a Sign for **them** is that We bore their race
036:042 And We have created for **them** similar
036:043 drown **them**; then would there be no helper
036:044 (to serve **them**) for a time.
036:046 Not a Sign comes to **them** from among
036:049 it will seize **them** while they are yet disputing
036:057 (Every) fruit will be there for **them**;
036:067 We could have transformed **them** in their places;
036:071 have created for **them**-among the things
036:072 And that We have subjected **them** to their (use)?
036:072 Of **them** some do carry **them** and some they eat:
036:073 from **them** (besides), and they get (milk)
036:075 They have not the power to help **them**:
036:075 and they are a host brought up before **them**.
036:079 Say, "He will give **them** life Who created
036:079 Who created **them** for the first time!
037:005 and all between **them**, and Lord
037:009 And for **them** is a perpetual chastisement,
037:011 **Them** have We created out of a sticky clay!
037:023 "Besides Allah, and lead **them** to the Way
037:024 "But stop **them**, for they must be asked:
037:041 For **them** is a Sustenance determined,
037:045 Round will be passed to **them** a Cup from a
037:048 And beside **them** will be chaste women;
037:051 One of **them** will say: "I had an
037:071 And truly before **them**, many of

THEM (continued)

037:072 But We sent aforetime, among **them**, warners.
037:093 Then did he turn upon **them**, striking (**them**)
037:098 against him, but We made **them** the ones
037:115 And We delivered **them** and their people
037:116 And We helped **them**, so they were victorious;
037:117 And We gave **them** the Book which helps
037:118 And We guided **them** to the Straight Way.
037:119 And We left for **them** among generations (to come)
037:128 Except the chosen Servants of Allah (among **them**).
037:148 And they believed; so We permitted **them** to enjoy
037:149 Now ask **them** their opinion: is it
037:174 So turn thou away from **them** for a little while,
037:175 And watch **them** (how they fare), and they
037:177 their courtyards before **them**, Evil will
037:178 So turn thou away from **them** for a little while,
038:003 How many generations before **them** did We destroy?
038:004 to **them** from among themselves!
038:006 And the leaders among **them** go away (impatiently),
038:010 If so, let **them** mount up
038:012 Before **them** (were many who) rejected messengers,-
038:014 came justly and inevitably (on **them**).
038:014 Not one (of **them**) but rejected the messengers,
038:022 and he was terrified of **them**,
038:033 "Bring **them** back to me." Then began
038:039 whether thou bestow **them** (on others)
038:039 (on others) or withhold **them**, no account
038:046 Verily We did chose **them** for a special (purpose)-
038:048 each of **them** was of the company
038:050 will (ever) be open to **them**;
038:052 And beside **them** will be chaste women
038:058 of a similar kid, to match **them**!
038:059 No welcome for **them**! Truly, they
038:063 or have (our) eyes failed to perceive **them**?"
038:063 "Did we treat **them** (as such) in ridicule,
038:073 all of **them** together;
038:082 I will lead **them** all astray.
038:083 "Except Thy Servants amongst **them**, sincere and
039:003 Truly Allah will judge between **them** in that
039:003 "We only serve **them** in order that they may
039:016 and Layers (of Fire) below **them**: with this doth Allah
039:016 They shall have Layers of Fire above **them**,
039:017 to Allah (in repentance),-for **them** is Good News:
039:020 beneath **them** flow rivers:
039:025 Those before **them** (also) rejected (revelation),
039:025 the Punishment came to **them** from directions
039:026 So Allah gave **them** a taste of humiliation
039:029 But most of **them** have no knowledge.
039:035 and give **them** their reward according to the
039:035 So that Allah will remit from **them** (even) the
039:038 If indeed thou ask **them** who it is that created
039:041 a Custodian over **them**.
039:047 but something will confront **them** from Allah,
039:048 confront **them**, and they will be (completely)
039:049 but most of **them** understand not!
039:050 But all that they did was of no profit to **them**.
039:050 Thus did the (generations) before them say!
039:051 overtook **them**. And the wrong-doers of this
039:051 will soon overtake **them** (too),
039:059 reject **them**: thou wast haughty, and became
039:061 no evil shall touch **them**, nor shall they grieve.
039:069 between **them**; and they will not be wronged
039:072 (To **them**) will be said: "Enter ye

THEM (continued)

039:075 between **them** (at Judgment) will be in (perfect)
040:005 But (there were people) before **them**, who denied
040:005 and the Confederates after **them**;
040:005 but it was I who seized **them**!
040:007 and preserve **them** from the Chastisement of the
040:008 which Thou hast promised to **them**, and to
040:009 from ills that Day,-on **them** wilt Thou have
040:009 "And preserve **them** from (all) ills; and any
040:016 concerning **them** is hidden from Allah.
040:018 Warn **them** of the Day that is (ever) drawing near,
040:018 to choke (**them**); no intimate friend nor intercessors
040:021 what was the end of those before **them**?
040:021 but Allah did call **them** to account
040:021 and none had they to defend **them** against Allah.
040:021 They were even superior to **them** in strength, and in
040:022 to **them** their messengers with Clear (Signs),
040:022 rejected **them**: so Allah called **them** to account:
040:025 Now, when he brought **them** in Truth, from Us,
040:031 and those who came after **them**:
040:035 that hath reached **them**, very hateful
040:056 without any authority on **them**,-
040:073 Then shall it be said to **them**: "Where are
040:077 some part of what We promise **them**,-
040:078 before thee: of **them** there are some whose story
040:080 advantages in **them** for you (besides);
040:080 that ye may through **them** attain to any need
040:080 and on **them** and on ships ye are carried.
040:082 they accomplished was of no profit to **them**.
040:082 what was the end of those before **them**?
040:083 they were wont to scoff hemmed **them** in.
040:083 to **them** with Clear Signs, they exulted
040:085 was not going to profit **them**.
041:004 yet most of **them** turn away,
041:012 So He completed **them** as seven firmaments in two
041:014 Behold, the messengers came to **them**,
041:014 from before **them** and behind **them**, (preaching):
041:015 that Allah, Who created **them**,
041:015 was superior to **them** in strength?
041:016 that We might give **them** a taste of a Chastisement
041:016 So We sent against **them** a furious Wind
041:017 As to the Thamud, We gave **them** guidance, but they
041:017 seized **them**, because of what they had earned.
041:020 against **them**, as to (all) their deeds.
041:024 the Fire will be a Home for **them**!
041:025 alluring to **them** what was before **them** and behind **them**;
041:025 And We have destined for **them** intimate companions
041:025 against **them**; for they are utterly lost.
041:027 and We will requite **them** for the worst
041:028 for **them** the Eternal Home: a (fit)
041:029 we shall crush **them** beneath our feet, so that
041:030 the angels descend on **them** (from time to time):
041:037 to Allah, Who created **them**, if it
041:041 to **them** (are not hidden from Us).
041:045 would have been settled between **them**: but they
041:047 to **them** the (question), "Where are
041:048 to invoke aforetime will leave **them** in the lurch,
041:050 they did, and We shall give **them** the taste
041:053 Soon will We show **them** Our Signs in the (furthest)
041:053 until it becomes manifest to **them** that this
042:005 from above **them** (by His Glory):
042:006 Allah doth watch over **them**;
042:007 and warn (**them**) of the Day of Assembly, of which

THEM (continued)

042:008 He could have made **them** a single people; but He
042:013 to which thou callest **them**.
042:014 the matter would been settled between **them**:
042:014 who have inherited the Book after **them** are in
042:014 after knowledge reached **them**,-being insolent
042:015 call (**them** to the Faith),
042:016 and for **them** will be a Chastisement Terrible.
042:016 of their Lord: on **them** is Wrath, and for
042:021 would have been decided between **them** (at once):
042:022 (necessarily) fall on **them**.
042:026 gives **them** increase of His bounty:
042:029 **them** together when He wills.
042:029 has scattered through **them**:
042:034 Or He can cause **them** to perish because of the
042:035 that there is for **them** no way of escape.
042:038 of what We bestow on **them** for Sustenance;
042:039 oppressive wrong is inflicted on **them**,
042:045 And thou wilt see **them** brought forward to the
042:046 to help **them**, other than Allah:
042:048 We have not sent thee as a guard over **them**.
043:007 to **them** but they mocked him.
043:009 If thou wert to question **them**, 'Who created
043:017 **them** of (the birth of) what he sets up as a
043:021 What! have We given **them** a Book before this,
043:023 the wealthy ones among **them** said: "We found
043:025 So We exacted retribution from **them**: now see
043:029 has come to **them**, and a Messenger
043:030 But when the Truth came to **them**, they said:
043:032 of **them** above others in ranks,
043:032 between **them** their livelihood in the life of this world:
043:041 We shall be sure to exact retribution from **them**,
043:042 for verily We shall prevail over **them**.
043:042 which We have promised **them**: for verily
043:047 behold, they laughed at **them**.
043:047 But when he came to **them** with Our Signs, behold,
043:048 We showed **them** Sign after Sign, each greater
043:048 and We seized **them** with Punishment, in order
043:050 from **them**, behold, they broke their word.
043:055 We exacted retribution from **them**,
043:055 and We drowned **them** all.
043:056 And We made **them** (a people) of the Past
043:066 that it should come on **them** all of a sudden,
043:071 To **them** will be passed round, dishes and
043:075 will the (punishment) be lightened for **them**,
043:076 Nowise shall We be unjust to **them**:
043:080 are by **them**, to record.
043:083 So leave **them** to babble and play (with vanities)
043:085 and the earth, and all between **them**:
043:087 If thou ask **them**, Who Created **them**, they will
043:089 But turn away from **them**, and say "Peace!"
044:007 and all between **them**, if ye
044:013 things clearly has (already) come to **them**,-
044:017 there came to **them** a messenger
044:017 We did, before **them**, try the people of Pharaoh:
044:029 nor shed a tear over **them**:
044:032 And We chose **them** aforetime above the
044:033 And granted **them** Signs in which
044:037 and those who were before **them**?
044:037 We destroyed **them** because they were
044:038 the earth, and all between **them**, merely in
044:039 We created **them** not except for just ends:
044:039 but most of **them** do not know.

THEM (continued)

044:040 is the time appointed for all of **them**,-
044:054 and We shall wed **them** to maidens
044:056 and He will preserve **them** from the Chastisement
045:008 as if he had not heard **them**:
045:009 of Our Signs, he takes **them** in jest: for such
045:010 and of no profit to **them** is anything they may
045:010 In front of **them** is Hell:
045:010 for **them** is a tremendous Chastisement.
045:016 and We favoured **them** above the nations.
045:016 We gave **them**, for Sustenance
045:017 Verily thy Lord will judge between **them** on the
045:017 granted to **them** that they fell into schisms,
045:017 And We granted **them** clear Signs in affairs
045:021 think that We shall hold **them** as equal with those
045:022 and none of **them** shall be wronged.
045:025 Our Clear Signs are rehearsed to **them**,
045:030 their Lord will admit **them** to His Mercy:
045:031 (to **them** will be said): "Were not Our
045:033 Then will appear to **them** the evil (fruits)
046:003 and all between **them** but for just ends,
046:005 are unconscious of their call (to **them**)?
046:006 be hostile to **them** and deny that (men) had
046:006 (men) had worshipped **them**.
046:007 of the Truth when it comes to **them**: "This is
046:007 to **them**, the Unbelievers say, of the Truth
046:013 (on that Path),-on **them** shall be no fear,
046:016 which was made to **them** (in this life).
046:019 and no injustice will be done to **them**.
046:020 (it will be said to **them**): "Ye squandered
046:020 and ye took your pleasure out of **them**: but to-day
046:026 And We had firmly established **them** in a
046:026 and We had endowed **them** with (faculties of)
046:026 to **them** were there (faculties of) hearing, sight,
046:028 Nay, they left **them** in the lurch:
046:028 to **them** from those whom they worshipped as gods,
046:029 to their people, to warn **them**.
046:035 they see the (Punishment) promised **them**,
047:002 from **them** their ills and improve their condition.
047:004 when ye have thoroughly subdued **them**,
047:004 exacted retribution from **them** (Himself);
047:005 Soon will He guide **them** and improve their condition,
047:006 And admit **them** to the Garden which He has
047:006 He has made known for **them**.
047:008 for **them** is destruction, and (Allah) will
047:010 before **them** (who did evil)?
047:010 Allah brought utter destruction on **them**,
047:013 And there was none to aid **them**.
047:015 In it there are for **them** all kinds of fruits,
047:016 And among **them** are men who listen to thee,
047:017 on **them** their Piety and Restraint (from evil).
047:018 and when it comes to **them**,
047:018 that it should come on **them** of a sudden?
047:020 But more fitting for **them**-
047:021 it were best for **them** if they were true to Allah.
047:023 has cursed for He has made **them** deaf and blinded
047:025 Satan has instigated **them** and buoyed **them** up with
047:025 after Guidance was clearly shown to **them**,-
047:030 know **them** by the tone of their speech!
047:030 and thou shouldst have known **them** by their marks:
047:030 We could have shown **them** up to thee,
047:032 after Guidance has been clearly shown to **them**,
047:034 then die disbelieving,-Allah will not forgive **them**.

THEM (continued)

047:037   If He were to ask you for all of **them**,
048:005   and remove their sins from **them**; a
048:006   He has cursed **them** and got Hell ready for **them**:
048:006   the Wrath of Allah is on **them**: He has cursed
048:006   On **them** is a round of Evil:
048:018   and He sent down tranquillity to **them**,
048:018   and He rewarded **them** with a speedy Victory;
048:024   after that He gave you the victory over **them**.
048:024   from **them** in the midst of Makkah,
048:025   the Unbelievers among **them** with a
048:026   and made **them** stick close to the command
048:029   Allah has promised those among **them**
048:029   Thou wilt see **them** bow and prostrate themselves
048:029   among **them** who believe and do righteous
049:003   for **them** is Forgiveness and a great Reward.
049:004   most of **them** lack understanding.
049:005   it would be best for **them**: but Allah
049:005   until thou couldst come out to **them**, it would
049:009   but if one **them** transgresses beyond against
049:009   make ye peace between **them**:
049:009   then make peace between **them** with justice,
050:002   to **them** a Warner from among themselves.
050:004   We already know how much of **them** the earth
050:005   But they deny the truth when it comes to **them**:
050:006   Do they not look at the sky above **them**?-
050:012   Before **them** was denied (the Hereafter) by the
050:014   each one (of **them**) rejected the messengers,
050:014   duly fulfilled (in **them**).
050:017   (and note **them**), one sitting on the right
050:035   There will be for **them** therein all that
050:036   But how many generations before **them** did We
050:036   was there any place of escape (for **them**)?
050:038   and all between **them** in Six Days,
050:044   letting **them** hurrying out:
050:045   and thou art not one to compel **them** by force.
051:016   which their Lord gives **them**, because, before
051:027   And placed it before **them**...
051:028   He conceived a fear of **them**.
051:033   "To bring on, on **them** (a shower of) stones of
051:040   and threw **them** into the sea:
051:041   against **them** the devastating Wind:
051:044   seized **them**, even while they were looking on.
051:046   So were the people of Noah before **them**:
051:052   the Peoples before **them**, but they
051:054   So turn away from **them**: not thine is the blame.
051:057   No sustenance do I require of **them**, nor do
051:059   then let **them** not ask Me to hasten (that portion)!
052:018   their Lord hath bestowed on **them**,
052:018   **them** from the Chastisement of the Fire.
052:019   (To **them** will be said:) "Eat and
052:020   and We shall wed **them** to maidens, with beautiful,
052:021   nor shall We deprive **them** (of the fruit)
052:021   and whose seeds follow **them** in Faith,-
052:021   to **them** shall We join their families:
052:022   And We shall bestow on **them**, of fruit
052:024   Round about **them** will serve,
052:024   (devoted) to **them**, youths (handsome) as Pearls
052:032   Is it that their intellects urges **them** to this,
052:034   Let **them** then produce a saying like unto it,-
052:037   Or are the Treasures of thy Lord with **them**,
052:037   or have they control over **them**.
052:044   of the sky falling (on **them**), they would

THEM (continued)

052:045   So leave **them** alone until they encounter
052:046   avail **them** nothing and no help shall be given **them**.
052:047   but most of **them** know not.
053:023   to **them** Guidance from their Lord!
053:051   And the Thamud, He left no trace of **them**.
053:052   And before **them**, the people of Noah,
054:004   There have already come to **them** such tidings
054:005   but (the preaching of) Warners profits **them** not.
054:006   that the Caller will call (**them**) to a
054:006   Therefore , (O Prophet) turn away from **them**.
054:009   Before **them** the People of Noah rejected
054:019   For We sent against **them** a furious wind,
054:027   So watch **them**, (O Salih), and possess
054:027   by way of trial for **them**.
054:028   And tell **them** that the water is to be divided
054:028   to be divided between **them**: each one's
054:031   For We sent against **them** a single Mighty Blast,
054:034   We sent against **them** a violent tornado with
054:034   (which destroyed **them**), except Lut's household:
054:034   **them** We delivered by early Dawn,-
054:036   And (Lut) did warn **them** of Our violent Seizure
054:038   an abiding Chastisement seized **them**:
054:042   but We seized **them** with the Seizure of a Mighty,
054:046   the time promised **them** (for their full recompense):
055:020   Between **them** is a Barrier which they
055:022   Out of **them** come Pearls and Coral:
055:050   In **them** (each) will be two Springs flowing (free);
055:052   In **them** will be Fruits of every kind, two and two.
055:056   In **them** will be (Maidens), Chaste, restraining
055:056   whom no man or Jinn before **them** has touched;-
055:066   In **them** (each) will be two springs pouring forth
055:068   In **them** will be Fruits, and dates and pomegranates:
055:070   In **them** will be fair (Maidens), good, beautiful;-
055:074   Whom no man or Jinn before **them** has touched;-
056:016   Reclining on **them**, facing each other.
056:017   Round about **them** will (serve) youths of
056:035   We have created **them** of special creation.
056:036   And made **them** virgin-pure (and undefiled),-
057:007   for **them** is a great Reward.
057:012   how their Light runs forward before
057:013   So a wall will be put up betwixt **them**, with a
057:016   passed over **them** and their hearts grew hard?
057:016   For many among **them** are rebellious
057:016   of the Truth which has been revealed (to **them**),
057:025   with Clear Signs and sent down with **them** the Book
057:026   but many of **them** became rebellious transgressors.
057:026   and some of **them** were on right guidance, but many
057:027   We sent after **them** Jesus the son of Mary,
057:027   Yet We bestowed, on those among **them** who believed,
057:027   Then, in their wake, We followed **them** up with
057:027   but many of **them** are rebellious transgressors.
057:027   We did not prescribe for **them**:
058:002   except those who gave **them** birth.
058:002   by Zihar (calling **them** mothers), they cannot
058:005   as were those before **them**:
058:006   and tell **them** of their deeds (which) Allah has
058:006   will raise **them** all up (again)
058:007   **them** what they did on the Day of Judgment.
058:007   but He is the fourth among **them**,-
058:007   but He is with **them**, wheresoever they be:
058:008   Enough for **them** is Hell: in it
058:010   but he cannot harm **them** in the

THEM (continued)

058:014	They are neither of you nor of **them**, and they
058:014	the Wrath of Allah upon **them**?
058:015	Allah has prepared for **them** a severe Chastisement:
058:017	Of no profit whatever to **them**, against Allah,
058:018	The Day will Allah raise **them** all up
058:019	Satan has got the better of **them**:
058:019	so he has made **them** forgot the remembrance
058:022	and strengthened **them** with a spirit from Himself.
058:022	Allah will be well pleased with **them**, and they
058:022	And He will admit **them** to Gardens beneath which
059:002	came to **them** from quarters from which they little
059:002	fortresses would defend **them** from Allah!
059:003	He would certainly have punished **them** in this
059:003	has decreed banishment for **them**,
059:005	left **them** standing on their roots, it was
059:006	(and taken away) from **them**-for this
059:009	but give **them** preference over
059:009	And those who before **them**, had homes
059:009	as came to **them** for refuge, and entertain
059:010	And those who came after **them** say: "Our Lord!
059:012	never will they go out with **them**;
059:012	they will never help **them**;
059:012	and if they do help **them**, they will
059:015	(in the Hereafter there is) for **them** a grievous
059:015	Like those who lately preceded **them**,
059:016	(Their allies deceived **them**), like Satan, when he
059:019	and He made **them** forget themselves!
060:001	showing friendship unto **them** in secret: for I
060:001	offering **them** (your) love, even though
060:006	There was indeed in **them** an excellent example
060:008	and justly with **them**: for Allah
060:009	It is such as turn to **them** (in these circumstances),
060:009	from turning to **them** (for friendship and protection).
060:010	examine (and test) **them**: Allah knows best as to
060:010	then send **them** not back to the Unbelievers.
060:010	if ye marry **them** on payment of their dower to **them**.
060:010	the (Unbelievers) lawful (husbands) for **them**.
061:006	But when he came to **them** with Clear Signs,
062:002	His Signs, to purify **them**,
062:002	among themselves, to rehearse to **them** His Signs,
062:002	and to instruct **them** in the Book and Wisdom,-
062:003	who have not already joined **them**:
062:003	Along with others of **them**,
062:005	tomes (but understands **them** not).
062:007	have sent on before **them**!
063:004	When thou lookest at **them**, their bodies
063:004	They think that every cry is against **them**.
063:004	so beware of **them**.
063:004	The curse of Allah be on **them**! How are
063:005	And when it is said to **them**, "Come, the
063:005	see **them** turning away their faces in arrogance.
063:006	It is equal to **them** whether thou pray for their
063:006	Allah will not forgive **them**.
064:006	to **them** messengers with Clear Signs, but they
064:006	But Allah can do without (**them**):
064:009	and He will admit **them** to gardens beneath which
064:009	He will remove from **them** their ills, and He
064:014	so beware of **them**!
065:001	divorce **them** at their prescribed periods, and count
065:001	and turn **them** not out of their houses,
065:002	or part with **them** on equitable
065:002	either take **them** back on equitable

THEM (continued)

065:006	according to your means: annoy **them** not, so as
065:006	give **them** their recompense: and take
065:006	so as to restrict **them**.
065:006	then spend (your substance) on **them** until they
065:008	**them** with a horrible Chastisement.
065:010	Allah has prepared for **them** a severe Punishment
065:011	Allah has indeed granted for **them** a most
065:012	through the midst of **them** (all) descends
066:008	Their Light will run forward before **them** and by
066:009	and be harsh with **them**.
067:005	and have prepared for **them** the Chastisement
067:012	for **them** is Forgiveness and a great Reward.
067:018	But indeed men before **them** rejected (My warning):
067:018	was My punishment (of **them**)?
067:019	Do they not observe the birds above **them**,
067:019	spreading their wings and folding **them** in?
067:019	None can uphold **them** except The Most Gracious:
067:027	(to **them**): "This is (the promise fulfilled),
068:017	Verily We have tried **them** as We tried the People
068:028	Said one of **them**, more just (than the rest):
068:040	Ask thou of **them**, which of **them** will stand
068:041	Then let **them** produce their "partners"
068:043	ignominy will cover **them**; seeing that
068:044	We draw **them** on little by little from directions
068:045	A (long) respite will I grant **them**: truly powerful
068:046	Or is it that thou dost ask **them** for a reward,
069:007	He made it rage against **them** seven nights
069:008	Then seest thou any of **them** left surviving?
069:010	of their Lord; so He punished **them** with an
069:017	bear the Throne of thy Lord above **them**.
070:038	Does every man of **them** long to enter
070:039	By no means! for We have created **them** out of
070:041	Substitute for **them** better (men) than they;
070:042	So leave **them** to plunge in vain talk and play
070:043	a goal-post (fixed for **them**),-
070:044	ignominy covering **them** (all over)!
071:001	to **them** a grievous Chastisement."
071:007	"And every time I have called to **them**,
071:007	that thou mightest forgive **them**, they have
071:008	"So I have called to **them** aloud;
071:009	"Further I have spoken to **them** in public
071:021	whose wealth and children give **them** no Increase
071:025	and they found-in lieu of Allah-none to help **them**.
071:027	"For, if Thou dost leave (any of) **them**, they will
072:006	but they increased **them** into further
072:010	to guide **them** to right conduct.
072:016	on **them** Rain in abundance.
072:017	"That We might try **them** by that (means).
072:023	and His Messenger,-for **them** is Hell: they shall
072:028	and He encompasses all that is with **them**, and takes
073:010	and leave **them** with noble (dignity).
073:011	and bear with **them** for a little while.
073:012	With Us are Fetters (to bind **them**),
073:012	and a Fire (to burn **them**),
074:048	of (any) intercessors profit **them**.
074:049	Then what is the matter with **them** that they
074:052	Forsooth, each one of **them** wants to be given
075:025	to be inflicted on **them**;
076:011	and will shed over **them** brightness and a
076:011	But Allah will deliver **them** from the evil
076:012	He will reward **them** with a Garden and
076:014	will come low over **them**, and the bunches

THEM (continued)

076:015   And amongst **them** will be passed round vessels of
076:019   thou wouldst think **them** scattered Pearls.
076:019   And round about **them** will (serve) youths
076:019   if thou seest **them**, thou wouldst think
076:021   give to **them** to drink a pure drink.
076:021   Upon **them** will be green Garments of fine silk
076:024   or the ingrate among **them**.
076:027   behind **them** a Day (that will be) hard.
076:028   It is We Who created **them**, and We have
076:031   but the wrong-doers,-for **them** has He prepared
077:004   Then separate **them**, one from another,
077:017   So shall We make later (generations) follow **them**.
077:036   Nor will it be open to **them** to put forth pleas.
077:048   And when it is said to **them**, "Prostrate yourselves!"
078:026   A fitting recompense (for **them**).
080:037   Each one of **them**, that Day, will have
080:041   Blackness will cover **them**:
083:017   Further, it will be said to **them**: "This is the
083:030   And whenever they passed by **them**, used to
083:032   And whenever they saw **them**, they would
083:033   But they had not been sent as Keepers over **them**!
084:020   What then is the matter with **them**, that they
084:021   And when the Qur'an is read to **them**, they fall
084:024   So announce to **them** a Chastisement Grievous,
084:025   for **them** is a Reward that will never fail.
085:008   And they ill-treated **them** for no other reason
085:020   But Allah doth encompass **them** from behind!
086:015   As for **them**, they are but plotting a scheme,
086:017   give respite to **them** gently (for a while).
088:006   No food will there be for **them** but a bitter Dhari
088:026   Then it will be for Us to call **them** to account.
089:013   Therefore did thy Lord pour on **them** a scourge
090:020   On **them** will be Fire Vaulted over (all round).
091:012   among **them** was deputed (for impiety).
091:013   But the messenger of Allah said to **them**: "It is
091:014   crushed **them** for their sin and levelled **them**.
098:001   come to **them** Clear Evidence,-
098:004   came to **them** Clear Evidence.
098:008   Allah well pleased with **them**, and they
100:011   well-acquainted with **them**, (Even to) that Day?
104:008   It shall be made into a vault over **them**,
105:003   And He sent against **them** flights of Birds,
105:004   Striking **them** with stones of baked clay.
105:005   Then did He make **them** like an empty field
106:003   Let **them** worship the Lord of this House,
106:004   Who provides **them** with food against hunger,

THEME

004:140   unless they turn to a different **Theme**:
006:068   they turn to a different **theme**.

THEMSELVES

002:009   only deceive **themselves** and realize (it) not!
002:010   because they lie (to **themselves**).
002:027   These cause loss (only) to **themselves**.
002:061   they drew on **themselves** the wrath of Allah.
002:090   on **themselves** Wrath upon Wrath.
002:103   and guarded **themselves** from evil,
002:114   should **themselves** enter them except in fear.
002:125   or prostrate **themselves** (therein in prayer).
002:146   the truth which they **themselves** know.
002:166   clear **themselves** of those who follow (them):
002:167   as they have cleared **themselves** of us."
002:174   they swallow into **themselves** naught but Fire;

THEMSELVES (continued)

002:194   Allah is with those who restrain **themselves**
002:213   did not differ among **themselves**,
002:222   who keep **themselves** pure and clean.
002:222   But when they have purified **themselves**,
002:228   concerning **themselves** for three monthly periods,
002:229   such persons wrong (**themselves** as well as others).
002:234   dispose of **themselves** in a just and reasonable
002:234   concerning **themselves** four months and ten days
002:240   for what they do with **themselves**,
002:266   not strong (enough to look, after **themselves**)
003:010   they are **themselves** but fuel for the Fire.
003:069   but **themselves**, and they do not perceive!
003:072   perchance they may (**themselves**) turn back;
003:105   Be not like those who are divided amongst **themselves**
003:112   they draw on **themselves** wrath from Allah.
003:113   and they prostrate **themselves** in adoration.
003:117   but they wrong **themselves**.
003:154   They say (to **themselves**): "If we had anything
003:164   among them a Messenger from among **themselves**,
003:168   while they **themselves** sit (at ease):
003:178   our respite to them is good for **themselves**:
004:049   to those who claim purity for **themselves**?
004:064   were unjust to **themselves**, come unto thee
004:108   They seek to hide **themselves** from the people but
004:128   settlement between **themselves**; and such
005:014   From those, too, who call **themselves** Christians,
005:070   a Messenger with what they **themselves** desired not
005:077   and strayed **themselves** from the even Way.
005:093   guard **themselves** from evil and believe, and
005:093   then again, guard **themselves** from evil and do good.
006:024   Behold! how they lie against **themselves** but
006:026   but they only destroy **themselves** and they
006:026   and **themselves** they keep away;
006:070   deliver **themselves** to ruin by their own acts:
006:130   So against **themselves** will they bear
007:037   and they will bear witness against **themselves**,
007:169   but they chose (for **themselves**) the vanities
007:172   concerning **themselves**, (saying): "Am I
007:191   but are **themselves** created?
007:192   nor can they aid **themselves**!
007:197   and indeed to help **themselves**."
009:029   willing submission, and feel **themselves** subdued.
009:036   with those who restrain **themselves**.
009:079   as give **themselves** freely to (deeds of) charity,
009:108   and Allah loveth those who make **themselves** pure.
009:112   that bow down and prostrate **themselves** in prayer;
009:122   to guard **themselves** (against evil).
009:122   to devote **themselves** to studies in religion, and
010:002   to a man from among **themselves**?
010:097   (for **themselves**) the Chastisement Grievous.
011:005   cover **themselves** with their garments, He knoweth
011:023   and humble **themselves** before their Lord-they will
012:004   I saw them prostrate **themselves** to me!"
012:039   differing among **themselves** better,
013:011   until they change what is in **themselves** but when
013:015   do prostrate **themselves** to Allah-with good-will
013:015   with good-will or in spite of **themselves**:
013:016   or for harm to **themselves**?"
014:045   of men who wronged **themselves** ye were
015:030   So the angels prostrated **themselves**, all of
015:031   among those who prostrated **themselves**.
015:032   those who prostrated **themselves**?"

THEMSELVES (continued)

015:042 put **themselves** in the wrong and follow thee."
015:082 (their) edifices, (feeling **themselves**) secure.
015:098 **themselves** in adoration.
016:016 and by the stars (men) guide **themselves**.
016:020 create nothing and are **themselves** created.
016:048 and the left, prostrating **themselves** to Allah,
016:057 Glory be to Him!-and for **themselves** what they desire!
016:062 they hate (for **themselves**), and their
016:062 that the reward most fair is for **themselves**:
016:089 from amongst **themselves**: and We shall bring thee
016:113 from among **themselves**, but they falsely rejected
016:118 but they were used to doing wrong to **themselves**.
016:128 restrain **themselves**, and those who do good.
017:057 do seek (for **themselves**) means of access
018:010 Behold, the youths betook **themselves** to the cave:
018:021 Behold they dispute among **themselves** as to
019:037 But the sects differ among **themselves**:
020:076 who purify **themselves** (from evil).
020:116 they prostrated **themselves**, but not
021:043 to aid **themselves**, nor can they be defended
021:058 that they might turn (and address **themselves**) to it.
021:064 So they turned to **themselves** and said, "Surely
021:090 And humble **themselves** before Us.
022:026 or prostrate **themselves** (therein in prayer).
022:034 the Good News to those who humble **themselves**,
023:002 Those who humble **themselves** in their prayers;
023:032 from among **themselves**, (saying), "Worship Allah!
023:076 but they humbled not **themselves** to their Lord,
024:013 (stand forth) **themselves** as liars!
024:033 keep **themselves** chaste, until Allah
024:050 Nay, it is they **themselves** who do wrong.
025:003 or good to **themselves**; nor can they control
025:003 but are **themselves** created;
025:017 or did they stray from the Path **themselves**?"
025:021 have an arrogant conceit of **themselves**,
026:093 or help **themselves**?'"
026:219 those who prostrate **themselves**.
026:227 and defend **themselves** after they are
029:040 they wronged **themselves**.
029:066 and giving **themselves** up to (worldly) enjoyment!
030:013 and they will (**themselves**) reject their "Partners."
030:044 will make provision for **themselves** (in heaven):
030:060 who have (**themselves**) no certainty of faith.
032:025 matters wherein they differ (among **themselves**).
032:027 their cattle and **themselves**?
033:017 for **themselves**, besides Allah, any protector
033:035 who humble **themselves**, for men and women who give
033:058 (on **themselves**) a calumny and a glaring sin.
034:019 but they wronged **themselves** (therein).
036:021 and who are **themselves** guided.
036:021 of you (for **themselves**), and who
036:049 yet disputing among **themselves**!
037:001 By those who range **themselves** in ranks,
037:035 would puff **themselves** up with Pride,
037:163 Except such as are (**themselves**) going to
038:004 to them from among **themselves**!
038:069 discuss (matters) among **themselves**.
038:073 So the angels prostrated **themselves**, all of
041:038 (nor feel **themselves** above it).
042:039 (are not cowed but) help and defend **themselves**.
042:045 who lose **themselves** and their families.
043:019 who **themselves** serve Allah.

THEMSELVES (continued)

043:065 But sects from among **themselves** fell into
043:076 but it is they who have been unjust **themselves**.
043:079 some Plan (among **themselves**)?
045:010 have taken to **themselves** besides Allah: for them
045:017 envy among **themselves**.
046:011 **themselves** thereby, they will say, "This is
048:029 and prostrate **themselves** (in prayer),
050:002 there has come to them a Warner among **themselves**.
051:045 (on their feet), nor could they help **themselves**.
051:053 **themselves** a people transgressing beyond bounds!
052:035 or were they **themselves** the creators?
052:042 who disbelieve are **themselves** ensnared in a Plot.
057:027 which they invented for **themselves**,
058:008 and they say to **themselves**, "Why does not
058:008 counsels among **themselves** for iniquity
059:009 preference over **themselves**, even though
059:014 (spirit) amongst **themselves**: thou wouldst
059:019 and He made them forget **themselves**!
062:002 a messenger form among **themselves**, to rehearse
065:001 nor shall they (**themselves**) leave, except in case
071:007 and given **themselves** up to arrogance.
071:007 into their ears, covered **themselves** up with their

THEN

002:022 **then** set not up rivals unto Allah
002:023 **then** produce a Sura like thereunto;
002:024 **then** fear the fire whose fuel
002:028 **then** will He cause you to die,
002:029 **then** He turned to the heaven and made them
002:031 **then** He placed them before the angles,
002:036 **Then** did Satan make them slip from the (garden),
002:037 **Then** learnt Adam from his Lord certain words
002:048 **Then** guard yourselves against a day
002:052 Even **then** We did forgive you,
002:054 **Then** He turned towards you (in forgiveness):
002:056 **Then** We raised you up after your death;
002:060 **Then** gushed forth therefrom twelve springs.
002:071 **Then** they offered her in sacrifice,
002:079 **Then** woe to those who write the Book
002:079 and **then** say: "This is from Allah,"
002:083 **Then** did ye turn back,
002:085 **Then** is it only a part of the Book
002:091 Say: Why **then** have ye slain the prophets
002:094 **then** seek ye for death,
002:120 **then** wouldst thou find neither Protector
002:123 **Then** guard yourselves against a day
002:132 **then** die not except in the state of submission
002:144 Turn **then** thy face in the direction
002:145 **then** wert thou indeed (clearly) in the wrong.
002:148 **then** strive together (as in a race)
002:152 **Then** do ye remember Me; I will remember you.
002:166 **Then** would those who are followed clear
002:173 **then** is he guiltless.
002:178 **then** grant any reasonable demand,
002:187 **then** complete your fast till the night appears;
002:194 If **then** any one transgresses the prohibition
002:198 **Then** when ye pour down from (Mount) 'Arafat,
002:199 **Then** return from the place whence it is usual
002:203 **Then** fear Allah, and know that ye will surely
002:209 **then** know that Allah is Exalted in Power, Wise.
002:226 if **then** they return,
002:237 **then** the half of the dower (is due to them),
002:243 "Die." **Then** He restored them to life.

THEN (continued)

002:244 **Then** fight in the cause of Allah,
002:258 do thou **then** cause it to rise from the West."
002:259 **then** raised him up (again).
002:260 **then** put a portion of them: on every hill,
002:260 He said: "Dost thou not **then** believe?"
002:260 **Then** know that Allah is Exalted in Power, Wise."
002:281 **Then** shall every soul be paid what it earned,
002:282 not two men, **then** a man and two women,
003:004 **Then** those who reject Faith in the Signs
003:016 forgive us, **then**, our sins, and save us
003:041 **Then** celebrate the praises of thy Lord
003:051 **then** worship Him.
003:053 **then** write us down among those who bear witness."
003:055 **then** shall ye all return to Me,
003:059 **then** said to him: "Be": and he was.
003:061 **then** let us earnestly pray.
003:064 If **then** they turn back,
003:081 He said: "**Then** bear witness, and I am with you
003:081 **then** comes to you an Messenger, confirming
003:090 And **then** go on adding to their defiance of Faith,
003:106 Taste **then** the Chastisement for rejecting Faith.
003:123 **then** fear Allah; thus may ye show your gratitude.
003:127 and they should **then** be turned back,
003:144 will ye **then** turn back on your heels?
003:152 **Then** did He divert you from your foes
003:159 **Then**, when thou hast taken a decision,
003:160 In Allah, **then**, let Believers put their trust.
003:161 **then** shall every soul receive its due
003:183 why **then** did ye slay them, if ye speak the truth?.
003:184 **Then** if they reject thee, so were rejected
003:186 **then** that indeed is a matter of great Resolution.
004:003 **then** only one, or that which your right hand
004:006 if **then** ye find sound judgment in them, release
004:041 How **then** if We brought from each People a witness,
004:043 **then** take for yourselves clean sand (or earth),
004:062 How **then**, when they are seized by misfortune.
004:062 **Then** they come to thee, swearing by Allah: "We
004:067 And We should **then** have given them from
004:073 a fine thing should I **then** have made of it!"
004:084 **Then** fight in Allah's cause, thou art held
004:090 **then** Allah hath opened no way
004:137 **then** believe (again) and (again) reject Faith, and
004:137 Those who believe, **then** reject Faith,
004:175 **Then** those who believe in Allah, and hold
005:006 **then** take for yourselves clean sand or earth, and
005:017 Say: "Who **then** hath the least power against Allah,
005:018 Say: "Why **then** doth He punish you for your sins?
005:021 for **then** will ye be overthrown, to your own ruin."
005:022 (once) they leave, **then** shall we enter."
005:031 **Then** Allah sent a raven, who scratched
005:031 **Then** he became full of regrets.
005:032 **Then** although there came to them Our Messengers
005:050 Do they **then** seek after a judgment of (the Days of)
005:052 or a decision from Him **then** will they regret of
005:091 will ye not **then** abstain?
005:093 **then** again, guard themselves from evil and do good.
005:106 if we do, **then** behold! we shall be sinners.
005:110 **Then** will Allah say: "O Jesus the son of Mary!
006:002 and **then** decreed a stated term (for you).
006:023 There will **then** be (left) no excuse
006:027 **Then** would we not reject the Signs of our Lord,
006:030 He will say: "Taste ye **then** the Chastisement,

THEN (continued)

006:032 Will ye not **then** understand?
006:036 **then** will they be turned unto Him.
006:040 would ye **then** call upon other than Allah?-
006:043 why **then** did they not call (Allah) in humility?
006:050 Will ye **then** consider not?
006:053 Is it these **then** that Allah hath favoured
006:060 **then** will He show you the truth of all that ye did.
006:062 **Then** are men returned unto Allah,
006:068 **then** after recollection, sit not thou
006:091 **then** leave them to plunge in vain discourse
006:091 Say: "Who **then** sent down the Book
006:095 **then** how are ye deluded away from the truth?
006:098 **then** there is a resting place and a repository:
006:099 and (**then** there are) gardens of grapes, and
006:102 **then** worship ye Him: and He hath
006:108 and He shall **then** tell them the truth
006:114 Never be **then** of those who doubt.
006:139 **then** all have shares therein.
006:157 Now **then** hath come unto you a Clear (Sign)
006:157 **then** who could do more wrong than one
006:158 to a soul to believe **then**,
007:006 **Then** shall We question those to whom
007:011 **then** We bade the angels prostrate to Adam,
007:017 "**Then** will I assault them from before them
007:020 **Then** began Satan to whisper
007:039 **Then** the first will say to the last: "See **then**!
007:053 **Then** should we behave differently from our
007:054 **then** He settled Himself on the Throne:
007:071 **Then** wait: I am amongst you, also waiting."
007:077 **Then** they ham-strung the she-camel, and
007:084 **then** see what was the end of those who
007:090 "If ye follow Shu'aib, be sure **then** ye are ruined!
007:095 **Then** We changed their suffering
007:099 Did they **then** fell secure against Allah's
007:103 **Then** after them We sent Moses with Our Signs
007:107 **Then** (Moses) threw his rod, and behold!
007:110 **then** what is it ye counsel?"
007:119 So they were vanquished there and **then**,
007:143 **then** shalt thou see Me."
007:144 take **then** the (revelation) which I give thee,
007:173 wilt Thou **then** destroy us because of the deeds
007:185 In what message after this will they **then** believe?
008:014 "Taste ye **then** of the (punishment):
009:002 Go ye, **then**, for four months, (as you will),
009:003 If, **then**, ye repent, it were best for you; but if
009:005 **then** open the way for them: for Allah
009:005 **then** fight and slay the Pagans wherever ye
009:006 and **then** escort him to where he can be secure,
009:024 **then** wait until Allah brings about His Decision:
009:035 taste ye, **then**, the (treasures) ye hoarded!"
009:040 **then** Allah sent down His peace upon him,
009:083 If, **then**, Allah bring thee back to any of them,
009:083 **then** sit ye (now) with those who stay behind."
009:094 and what is open: **then** will He show you
009:105 **then** will He show you the truth of all that ye did."
009:109 Which **then** is best?-he that layeth his foundation
009:111 **Then** rejoice in the bargain which ye have
009:118 **Then** He turned to them, that they
009:127 (saying), "Doth anyone see you?" **then** they turn away:
010:003 in six Days, **then** He established Himself on the
010:011 **then** would their respite be settled at once.
010:014 **Then** We made you heirs in the land after them,

THEN (continued)

010:016 I tarried amongst you: will ye not **then** understand?"
010:020 **Then** wait ye: I too will wait with you."
010:022 **then** comes a stormy wind and the waves
010:028 **Then** shall We say to those who joined gods
010:031 Say, "Will ye not **then** show piety (to Him)?"
010:032 How **then** are ye turned away?
010:034 **then** how are ye deluded away (from the truth)?"
010:035 Is then He Who gives guidance to Truth
010:035 What **then** is the matter with you? How judge ye?
010:038 Say: "Bring **then** a Sura like unto it, and call
010:051 (It will **then** be said): 'Ah! now? and ye wanted
010:051 "Would ye **then** believe in it at last, when it
010:070 and, **then**, to Us will be their return.
010:070 **Then** shall We make them taste the severest
010:071 get ye **then** an agreement about your plan
010:071 **Then** pass your sentence on me,
010:073 **Then** see what was the end of those who
010:074 **Then** after him We sent (many) messengers
010:075 **Then** after them sent We Moses and Aaron
010:084 **then** in Him put your trust if ye
010:094 **then** ask those who have been reading the Book
010:099 Wilt thou **then** compel mankind, against their
010:102 Say: "Wait ye **then**: for I too, will wait with you."
010:102 Do they **then** expect (anything) but
011:003 But if ye turn away, **then** I fear for you
011:009 from Ourselves, and **then** withdraw it from him,
011:013 Say, "Bring ye **then** ten Suras forged, like unto
011:014 "If **then** they (your false gods) answer not
011:014 Will ye even **then** submit (to Islam)?"
011:017 Be not **then** in doubt thereon:
011:024 Will ye not them take heed?
011:030 them away? Will ye not **then** take heed?
011:033 and **then**, ye will not be able to frustrate it!
011:044 **Then** the word went forth: "O earth! swallow up
011:051 created Me: will ye not **then** understand?
011:061 **then** ask forgiveness of Him, and turn
011:063 What **then** would ye add to my (portion)
011:063 from Himself,-who **then** can help me against
011:065 (**then** will be your ruin): (behold) there is
011:092 He said: "O my people! is **then** my family of more
011:109 Be not **then** in doubt as to what these men worship.
012:014 **then** should we be the losers!
012:016 **Then** they came to their father in the
012:019 **Then** there came a caravan of travellers: they sent
012:026 is rent from the front, **then** is her tale true,
012:027 is torn from the back, **then** is she the liar,
012:035 **Then** it occurred to them after they had seen
012:048 "**Then** will come after that (period) seven
012:049 "**Then** will come after that (period) a year
012:058 **Then** came Joseph's brethren: they entered
012:065 **Then** when they opened their baggage, they found
012:070 **Then** shouted out a Crier: "O ye (in) the
012:074 (The Egyptians) said: "What **then** shall be
012:088 **Then**, when they came (back) into (Joseph's)
012:093 **Then** come ye (here) to me together with
012:096 **Then** when the bearer of the good news came,
012:107 Do they **then** feel secure from the coming against
012:109 Will ye not **then** understand?
013:002 **then** He established Himself on the Throne.
013:005 shall we indeed **then** be in a creation renewed?"
013:016 Say: "Do ye **then** take (for worship) protectors
013:019 Is **then** one who doth know that that which

THEN (continued)

013:032 I punished them: **then** how (terrible) was My
013:033 Is **then** He Who standeth over every soul
013:037 **then** wouldst thou find neither protector nor
014:010 **then** bring us some clear authority."
014:015 (there and **then**), and frustration was the lot
014:021 before Allah together: **then** will the weak say to
014:021 can ye **then** avail us at all against the
014:022 **then** reproach not me, but reproach
014:036 he **then** who follows my (ways) is of me, and he
014:044 **then** will the wrong-doers say: "Our Lord!
015:022 **then** cause the rain to descend from the shy,
015:034 (Allah) said: "**Then** get thee out from here;
015:036 **then** respite till the Day the (dead) are raised."
015:054 Of what, **then**, is your good news?"
015:055 in truth; be not **then** in despair!"
015:057 Abraham said: "What **then** is the business
015:065 "**Then** travel by night with thy household, when a
016:001 seek ye not **then** to hasten it:
016:017 Is **then** He Who creates like one that creates not?
016:027 **Then**, on the Day of Judgment, He will
016:028 **Then** would they offer submission
016:045 Do **then** those who devise evil (plots) feel
016:052 **then** will ye fear other than Allah?
016:055 **Then** enjoy (your brief day); but soon
016:069 **Then** to eat of all the produce (of the earth),
016:071 Will they **then** deny the favour of Allah?
016:072 will they **then** believe in vain things, and be
016:083 **then** they deny them; and most
016:084 **then** will no excuse be accepted from Unbelievers,
016:085 see the Chastisement **then** will it in no way
016:085 nor will they **then** receive respite.
016:115 **then** Allah is Oft-Forgiving, Most Merciful.
016:123 **Then** We revealed to thee "Follow the ways
017:006 **Then** did We grant you victory over them:
017:016 **then** We destroy them utterly.
017:040 Has **then** your Lord, (O Pagans!) preferred for
017:051 **Then** will they say: "Who will cause us to return?"
017:051 **Then** will they wag their heads
017:068 Do ye **then** feel secure that He will not cause
017:086 **then** wouldst thou find none to plead thy affair
018:011 **Then** We drew (a veil) over their ears, for a
018:012 **Then** We roused them, in order to test which of
018:019 Now send ye **then** one of you with this money
018:037 out of dust, **then** out of a sperm-drop,
018:037 **then** fashioned thee into a man?
018:050 Will ye **then** take him and his progeny
018:057 even **then** will they never accept guidance.
018:058 **then** surely He would have hastened their Punishment:
018:070 The other said: "If **then** thou wouldst follow me,
018:074 **Then** they proceeded: until, when they
018:076 **then** wouldst thou have received (full)
018:077 **Then** they proceeded: until, when they
018:087 **then** shall he be sent back to his Lord;
018:089 **Then** followed he (another) way,
018:092 **Then** followed he (another) way,
018:094 shall we **then** render thee tribute in order that
018:096 "Blow (with your bellows)" **then**, when he
019:017   **then** We sent to her Our angel, and he
019:059 and followed after lusts soon, **then**, will they
019:066 shall I **then** be raised up alive?"
019:068 **then** shall We bring them forth on their
019:069 **Then** shall We certainly drag out from every

THEN (continued)

019:077 Hast thou **then** seen the (sort of) man who
020:013 **then** to the inspiration (given to thee).
020:040 **Then** thou didst slay a man, but We
020:040 **Then** didst thou tarry a number of years with the
020:040 **Then** didst thou come hither as ordained, O Moses!
020:049 (Pharaoh) said: "Who, **then**, O Moses, is the
020:050 to each (created) thing its form **then**, gave (it) guidance."
020:051 (Pharaoh) said: "What **then** is the condition of
020:060 he concerted his plan, and **then** came (back).
020:064 And **then** assemble in (serried) ranks:
020:066 **Then** behold their ropes and their rods-so it
020:078 **Then** Pharaoh pursued them with his forces,
020:086 Did **then** the promise seem to you long (in coming)?
020:088 "**Then** he brought out (of the fire) before the
020:093 Didst thou **then** disobey my order?"
020:095 (Moses) said: "What **then** is thy case, O Samiri?"
020:117 **Then** We said: "O Adam! verily, this is
021:005 Let him **then** bring us a Sign like the ones
021:009 **Then** We fulfilled to them Our promise, and We
021:010 Will ye not **then** understand?
021:030 Will they not **then** believe?
021:034 if **then** thou shouldst die, would they
021:040 to avert it, nor will they (**then**) get respite.
021:040 no power will they have **then** to avert it,
021:044 Is it **then** they who will win?
021:046 they will **then** say, "Woe to us! we did
021:050 will ye **then** reject it?
021:061 They said, "**Then** bring him before the eyes
021:065 **Then** were they confounded with shame:
021:066 (Abraham) said, "Do ye **then** worship, besides Allah,
021:070 **Then** they planned against him: but We
021:080 will ye **then** be grateful?
021:097 **then** behold! the eyes of the Unbelievers will fixedly
021:097 **Then** will the True Promise draw nigh
022:005 **then** out a morsel of flesh, partly formed
022:005 **then** (foster you) that ye may reach your age of full
022:005 We created you out of dust, **then** out of sperm,
022:005 **then** out of a leech-like clot,
022:005 **then** do We bring you out as babes,
022:015 **then** let him see whether his plan will remove that
022:028 **then** eat ye thereof and feed the distressed
022:029 "**Then** let them complete the rites prescribed
022:034 submit **then** your wills to Him (in Islam):
022:036 **then** pronounce the name of Allah over them
022:058 in the cause of Allah, and are **then** slain or die,-
022:067 let them not **then** dispute with thee on the matter,
023:013 **Then** We placed him as (a drop of) sperm in a
023:014 **then** We developed out of it another creature:
023:014 **then** of that clot We made a (foetus) lump;
023:014 **then** We made out of that lump bones and clothed
023:014 **Then** We made the sperm into a clot of
023:027 **then** when comes Our command, and the
023:031 **Then** We raised after them another generation.
023:041 **Then** the Blast overtook them with justice,
023:042 **Then** We raised after them other generations.
023:044 **Then** sent We Our messengers in succession:
023:045 **Then** We sent Moses and his brother Aaron,
023:077 **then** Lo! they will be plunged in despair therein!
023:080 of Night and Day: will ye not **then** understand?
023:087 Say: "Will ye not **then** fear?"
023:089 Say: "**Then** how are ye deluded?"
023:094 "**Then**, O my Lord! put me not amongst the

THEN (continued)

023:101 **Then** when the Trumpet is blown, there will
023:102 **Then** those whose balance (of good deeds)
023:107 **then** shall we be wrong-doers indeed!"
023:109 'Our Lord! we believe; **then** do Thou forgive us,
023:115 "Did ye **then** think that We had created you
024:043 **then** joins them together, **then** makes them into a heap?
024:043 **Then** wilt thou see rain issue forth
024:063 **then** let those beware who withstand the
025:013 they will plead for destruction there and **then**!
025:030 **Then** the Messenger will say: "O my Lord,
025:040 did they not **then** see it (with their own eyes)?
025:045 **Then** do We make the sun its guide;
025:046 **Then** We draw it in towards Ourselves,-
025:054 **then** has He established relationships of lineage
025:059 **then** He established Himself on the Throne:
025:059 ask thou, **then**, about Him of any acquainted
026:015 Allah said: "By no means! proceed them, both of
026:020 Moses: "I did it **then**, when I was in error.
026:031 (Pharaoh) said: "Show it **then**, if thou
026:035 **then** what is it ye counsel?"
026:045 **Then** Moses threw his rod, when, behold,
026:046 **Then** did the sorcerers fall down, prostrate in
026:053 **Then** Pharaoh sent heralds to (all) the Cities,
026:063 **Then** We told Moses by inspiration: "Strike the
026:075 He said: "Do ye **then** see whom ye have been
026:081 and **then** to live (again);
026:094 "**Then** they will be thrown headlong into the (Fire),-
026:100 "'Now, **then**, we have none to intercede (for us),
026:118 "Judge thou, **then**, between me
026:154 like us: **then** bring us a Sign, if thou
026:157 **then** did they become full of regrets.
026:172 **Then** the rest We destroyed utterly.
026:189 **Then** the punishment of a day of overshadowing
026:203 **Then** they will say: "Shall we be respited?"
026:204 Do they **then** ask for Our Chastisement to be
026:216 **Then** if they disobey thee, say: "I am free
027:028 **then** draw back from them, and (wait to)
027:040 **Then** when (Solomon) saw it placed firmly
027:049 and that we shall **then** say to his heir
027:051 **Then** see what was the end of their plot!-
027:064 Or, who originates Creation, **then** repeats it,
027:087 **then** will be smitten with terror those who
028:008 **Then** the people of Pharaoh picked him up
028:016 Do Thou **then** forgive me!" So (Allah)
028:019 **Then**, when he was about to lay his hands on their
028:022 **Then** when he turned his face towards
028:024 **then** he turned back to the shade, and said:
028:047 We should **then** have followed the Signs
028:048 Do they not **then** reject (the Signs) which were
028:049 Say: "**Then** bring ye a Book from Allah, which is
028:060 will ye not **then** be wise?
028:066 **Then** the arguments that day will be obscure
028:071 Will ye not **then** hearken?
028:072 Will ye not **then** see?
028:075 **then** shall they know that the Truth is
028:081 **Then** We caused the earth to swallow up him
029:010 **Then** there are among men such as say, "We believe
029:017 **then** seek ye sustenance from Allah, serve Him,
029:019 originates creation, **then** repeats it: truly that
029:036 **Then** he said: "O my people! serve Allah,
029:037 **then** the mighty Blast seized them, and they
029:061 How are they **then** deluded away (from the truth)?

THEN (continued)

029:067   Do they not **then** see that We have made
029:067   **Then**, do they believe in that which is vain,
030:011   **then** repeats it; **then** shall ye be brought back to Him.
030:015   **Then** those who have believed and worked
030:020   that He created you from dust; and **then**,-behold,
030:025   by His command: **then** when He calls you,
030:027   It is He Who begins the creation; **then** repeats it;
030:034   **Then** enjoy (your brief day); but soon
030:040   **then** He will cause you to die;
030:047   **then**, to those who transgressed, We meted
030:048   **then** does He spread them in the sky as He wills,
030:048   **then** when He has made them reach such of His
030:050   **Then** behold (O man!) the tokens of Allah's Mercy!-
030:054   after weakness, **then**, after strength, gave you
030:054   **then** gave (you) strength after weakness,
031:033   let not **then** this present life deceive you,
032:004   **then** He established Himself on the Throne:
032:004   (for you): will ye not **then** receive admonition?
032:005   **then** it ascends unto Him, on a
032:011   **then** shall ye be brought back to your Lord."
032:012   we have heard: now **then** send us back (to the world):
032:014   "Taste ye **then**-for ye forgot the Meeting of this
032:018   Is **then** the man who believes no better than the
032:022   of his Lord, and who **then** turns away therefrom?
032:023   be not **then** in doubt of its reaching (thee):
032:026   do they not **then** listen?
032:029   if they (**then**) Believe!
033:005   (**then** they are) your brothers in faith,
033:019   **Then** when fear comes, thou wilt
033:028   **then** come! I will provide for your enjoyment
033:037   **Then** when Zaid had dissolved (his marriage)
033:047   **Then** give the glad tidings to the Believers,
033:049   believing women, and **then** divorce them before
033:053   (and **then**) not (so early as) to wait
033:060   **then** will they not be able to stay in it as thy neighbours
034:007   that ye shall (**then** be raised) in a New Creation?
034:014   **Then**, when We decreed (Solomon's) death,
034:023   (at the Day of Judgment, **then**) will they
034:051   but **then** there will be no escape (for them),
035:003   how **then** are ye perverted?
035:005   let not **then** this present life deceive
035:008   Is he, **then**, to whom the evil of his conduct
035:011   **then** from a sperm-drop; **then** He made you in pairs.
035:027   With it We **then** bring out produce of various
035:032   **Then** We have given the Book for inheritance
036:020   **Then** there came running, from the
036:024   "I would indeed, **then** be in manifest Error.
036:025   of you (all): listen, **then**, to me!"
036:035   will they not **then** give thanks?
036:043   **then** would there be no helper (to hear their cry),
036:047   who believe: "Shall we **then** feed those whom,
036:050   No (chance) will they **then** have, by will,
036:054   **Then**, on that Day, not a soul will be wronged
036:062   Did ye not, **then** understand?
036:066   **then** they should have raced to the Path,
036:067   **then** should they have been unable to move about,
036:068   will they not **then** understand?
036:073   Will they not **then** be grateful?
036:076   Let not their speech, **then**, grieve thee.
037:016   shall we (**then**) be raised up (again)?
037:018   Say thou: "Yea, and ye shall **then** be humiliated
037:019   **Then** it will be a single (compelling) cry;

THEN (continued)

037:050   **Then** they will turn to one another and question
037:067   **Then** on top of that they will be given
037:068   **Then** shall their return be to the (Blazing) Fire.
037:073   **Then** see what was the end of those who were warned
037:082   **Then** the rest We overwhelmed in the Flood.
037:087   "**Then** what is your idea about the Lord
037:088   **Then** did he cast a glance at the Stars,
037:091   **Then** did he turn to their gods and said,
037:093   **Then** did he turn upon them, striking (them)
037:094   **Then** came (the worshippers) with hurried
037:098   (This failing), they **then** plotted against him,
037:102   **Then**, when (the son) reached (the age of)
037:136   **Then** We destroyed the rest.
037:142   **Then** the big Fish did swallow him, and he
037:153   Did He (**then**) choose daughters rather than sons?
037:155   Will ye not **then** receive admonition?
037:157   **Then** bring ye your Book (of authority)
038:033   **Then** began he to pass his hand over (their)
038:036   **Then** We subjected the Wind to his power, to flow
038:057   Yea, such!-**Then** shall they taste it,-a boiling
038:077   (Allah) said: "**Then** get thee out from here:
038:079   **then** respite till the Day the (dead) are raised."
038:080   (Allah) said: "Respite **then** is granted thee-
038:082   (Iblis) said: "**Then**, by Thy Power, I will
039:006   a single person: **then** created, of like
039:006   **then** how are ye turned away (from your true Lord)?
039:016   "O my servants! **Then** fear ye Me!"
039:019   Is, **then**, one against whom the decree of Punishment
039:019   Wouldst thou, **then**, deliver one (who is)
039:021   **then** it withers; thou wilt see it grow yellow;
039:021   **then** He makes it dry up and crumble away.
039:021   **Then** He causes to grow, therewith,
039:023   **then** their skins and their hearts do soften
039:024   Is, **then**, one who has to ward off the brunt
039:032   Who, **then**, doth more wrong than one who
039:038   Say: "See ye **then**? The things
039:041   He, **then**, that receives guidance benefits his
039:056   "Lest the soul should (**then**) say: `Ah! woe
039:068   **Then** will a second one be sounded,
040:004   Let not, **then**, their strutting about through the
040:007   Forgive, **then**, those who turn in repentance,
040:014   Call ye, **then**, upon Allah with sincere devotion
040:028   **then** will fall on you something of the (calamity)
040:030   **Then** said the man who believed: "O my People!
040:045   **Then** Allah saved him from (every) evil that they
040:047   can ye **then** take (on yourselves) from us
040:050   They will reply, "**Then** pray (as ye like)!
040:055   Patiently, **then**, persevere: for the Promise
040:056   seek refuge, **then**, in Allah: it is He
040:062   **then** how ye are deluded away from the Truth!
040:067   **then** does He get you out (into the light) as a
040:067   as a child: **then** lets you (grow and) reach your
040:067   **then** from a sperm-drop, **then** from a leech-like clot;
040:067   **then** lets you become old,-through of
040:072   **then** in the Fire shall they be burned;
040:073   **Then** shall it be said to them: "Where are
040:078   there and **then**, those who stood on Falsehoods.
040:081   **then** which of the Signs of Allah will ye deny?
041:011   **Then** He turned to the sky, and it
041:024   If, **then**, they have patience, the Fire
041:034   **then** will he between whom and thee was
042:015   Now **then**, for that (reason), call (them to

THEN (continued)

042:033 **then** would they become motionless on the back
042:037 are angry even **then** forgive;
042:048 If **then** they turn away, We have not
042:048 truly **then** is man ungrateful!
043:005 Shall We **then** take away the Reminder from you
043:018 Is **then** one brought up among trinkets, and unable
043:040 Canst thou **then** make the deaf to hear, or give
043:048 each greater **then** its fellow, and We
043:051 What! see ye not **then**?
043:053 "**Then** why are not gold bracelets bestowed on him,
043:065 **then** woe to the wrong-doers, from the Chastisement
043:087 how **then** are they deluded away (from the Truth)?
044:010 **Then** watch thou for the Day that the sky will bring
044:016 (**then**) exact retribution!
044:022 **then** he cried to his Lord: "These are
044:036 "**Then** bring (back) our forefathers if what
044:048 "**Then** pour over his head the Chastisement
045:006 **then** in what exposition will they believe after
045:008 **then** announce to him a Chastisement Grievous!
045:018 **Then** We put thee on the (right) Way of Religion:
045:023 Will ye not **then** receive admonition?
045:023 Who, **then**, will guide him after Allah
045:023 **Then** seest thou such a one as takes as his god
045:026 **then** He will gather you together for the Day
045:026 **then** gives you death;
045:030 **Then**, as to those who believed and did
045:033 **Then** will appear to them the evil (fruits)
045:036 **Then** Praise be to Allah, Lord of the heavens
046:008 **then** can ye have no power to help me against Allah.
046:022 **Then** bring upon us the (calamity) with which
046:024 **Then**, when they saw a could advancing towards
046:025 **Then** by the morning they-nothing was
046:028 Why **then** was no help forthcoming to them
046:034 "**Then** taste ye the Chastisement,
047:014 Is **then** one who is on a clear (Path) from his Lord,
047:016 "What is it he said just **then**?"
047:018 Do they **then** only wait for the Hour,-that it
047:022 **Then**, is it to be expected of you, if ye
047:024 Do they not **then** earnestly seek to understand
047:034 **then** die disbelieving,- Allah will not forgive them.
047:038 **then** they would not be like you!
048:010 **then** any one who violates His oath,
048:011 Say: "Who **then** has any power at all (to intervene)
048:011 do thou **then** ask forgiveness for us."
048:015 **then** they will say, "But ye are jealous of us."
048:016 **Then** if ye show obedience,
048:016 **then** shall ye fight, or they
048:022 **then** would they find neither protector nor helper.
048:029 **then** makes it strong; it **then** becomes thick,
049:009 the other, **then** fight ye (all) against the one
049:009 **then** make peace between them with justice,
050:015 Were We **then** weary with the first Creation,
050:036 **Then** did they wander through the land:
050:039 Bear, **then** with patience, all that they say,
051:016 because, before **then**, they had done good deeds
051:021 As also in your own selves: will ye not **then** see?
051:023 **Then**, by the Lord of heaven and earth, this is
051:026 **Then** he turned quickly to his household,
051:035 **Then** We evacuated those of the Believers
051:045 **Then** they could not even stand (on their feet),
051:059 **then** let them not ask Me to hasten (that portion)!
051:060 Woe, **then**, to the Unbelievers, from the Day

THEN (continued)

052:011 **Then** woe that Day to the rejecters (of Truth);-
052:015 "Is this **then** a magic, or is it ye that do not see?
052:034 Let them **then** produce a saying like unto it,-
052:038 **Then** let (such a) listener of theirs produce a manifest
052:043 Or have they a god other **then** Allah?
053:008 **Then** he approached and came closer,
053:012 Will ye **then** dispute with him
053:034 Gives a little, **then** hardens (his heart)?
053:041 **Then** will he be rewarded with a reward complete;
053:055 **Then** which of the favours of thy Lord, (O man),
053:059 Do ye **then** wonder at this recital?
054:010 "I am one overcome: do thou **then** help (me)!"
054:010 **Then** he called on his Lord: "I am one
054:015 **then** is there any that will receive admonition?
054:017 **then** is there any that will receive admonition?
054:018 **then** how terrible was my Chastisement and My
054:022 **then** is there any that will receive admonition?
054:024 Truly should we **then** be in error and madness.
054:032 **then** is there any that will receive admonition?
054:040 **then** is there any that will receive admonition?
054:051 **then** is there any that will receive admonition?
055:013 **Then** which of the favours of your Lord
055:016 **Then** which of the favours of your Lord
055:018 **Then** which of the favours of your Lord
055:021 **Then** which of the favours of your Lord
055:023 **Then** which of the favours of your Lord
055:025 **Then** which of the favours of your Lord
055:028 **Then** which of the favours of your Lord
055:030 **Then** which of the favours of your Lord
055:032 **Then** which of the favours of your Lord
055:034 **Then** which of the favours of your Lord
055:036 **Then** which of the favours of your Lord
055:038 **Then** which of the favours of your Lord
055:040 **Then** which of the favours of your Lord
055:042 **Then** which of the favours of your Lord
055:045 **Then** which of the favours of your Lord
055:047 **Then** which of the favours of your Lord
055:049 **Then** which of the favours of your Lord
055:051 **Then** which of the favours of your Lord
055:053 **Then** which of the favours of your Lord
055:055 **Then** which of the favours of your Lord
055:057 **Then** which of the favours of your Lord
055:059 **Then** which of the favours of your Lord
055:061 **Then** which of the favours of your Lord
055:063 **Then** which of the favours of your Lord
055:065 **Then** which of the favours of your Lord
055:067 **Then** which of the favours of your Lord
055:069 **Then** which of the favours of your Lord
055:071 **Then** which of the favours of your Lord
055:073 **Then** which of the favour of your Lord
055:075 **Then** which of the favours of your Lord
055:077 **Then** which of the favours of your Lord
056:002 **Then** will no (soul) deny its coming.
056:008 **Then** (there will be) the Companions
056:047 shall we **then** indeed be raised up again?-
056:051 "**Then** will ye truly,-O ye that go wrong,
056:053 "**Then** will ye fill your insides therewith,
056:058 Do ye **then** see? The (human Seed) that ye emit,-
056:062 why **then** do ye not take heed?
056:070 **then** why do ye not give thanks?
056:074 **Then** glorify the name of the Lord, the Supreme!
056:083 **Then** why do ye not (intervene) when (the soul

THEN (continued)

056:086 **Then** why do you not,-if you are
056:088 Thus, **then**, if he be of those Nearest to Allah,
057:004 **then** He established Himself on the Throne.
057:013 **Then** seek a light (where ye can)!" So a wall
057:020 **then** it becomes dry and crumbles away.
057:027 **Then**, in their wake, We followed them up with
058:003 to their wives **then** wish to go back on the words
058:013 **then** (at least) establish regular prayer;
058:013 If, **then**, ye do not so, and Allah forgives you,
058:018 **then** will they swear to Him as they swear to you:
059:002 Take warning, **then**, O ye with eyes (to see)!
060:010 **then** send them not back to the Unbelievers.
060:011 **Then** pay to those whose wives have deserted
060:012 **then** do thou receive their fealty,
061:005 **Then** when they went wrong, Allah let
061:014 **Then** a portion of the Children of Israel believed,
062:006 **then** express your desire for Death, if ye
062:008 **then** will ye be sent back to the Knower of things
062:010 **then** may ye disperse through the land, and seek
063:003 **then** they rejected Faith: so a seal
063:010 I should **then** have given (largely) in charity,
064:007 **then** shall ye be told (the truth)
065:006 **then** spend (your substance) on them until they
065:008 did We not **then** call to account,-to severe
065:009 **Then** did they taste the evil result of their
066:003 and she **then** divulged it (to another), and Allah
066:003 **Then** when he told her thereof, she said,
067:011 They will **then** confess their sins: but far
067:018 (My warning): **then** how (terrible) was My punishment
067:022 Is **then** one who walks headlong, with his
067:030 who **then** can supply you with clear-flowing water?"
068:019 **Then** there came, on the (garden) a visitation
068:030 **Then** they turned, one against another, in reproach.
068:035 Shall We **then** treat the People of Faith
068:041 **Then** let them produce their "partners"
068:044 **Then** leave Me alone with such as reject
069:008 **Then** seest thou any of them left surviving?
069:013 **Then**, when one Blast is sounded on the Trumpet,
069:019 **Then** He that will be given his Record in his
069:046 And We should certainly **then** cut off the artery
070:030 hands possess,-for (**then**) they are not to be blamed,
072:024 they are promised,-**then** will they know who it
072:027 and **then** He makes a band of watchers march before
073:017 **Then** how shall ye, if ye deny (Allah),
074:021 **Then** he reflected;
074:022 **Then** he frowned and he scowled;
074:023 **Then** he turned back and was haughty;
074:024 **Then** said he: "This is nothing but magic
074:049 **Then** what is the matter with them that they
075:033 **Then** did he stalk to his family in full conceit!
075:038 **then** did (Allah) make and fashion (him)
075:038 **Then** did he become a leech-like clot;
077:002 Which **then** blow violently in tempestuous Gusts,
077:004 **Then** separate them, one from another,
077:005 **Then** spread abroad a Reminder,
077:008 **Then** when the stars become dim;
077:050 **Then** what Message, after that, will they believe in?
079:004 **Then** press forward as in a race,
079:005 **Then** arrange to do (the commands of their Lord),-
079:020 **Then** did (Moses) show him the Great Sign.
079:023 **Then** he collected (his men) and made a proclamation,
079:037 **Then**, for such as had transgressed all bounds,

THEN (continued)

080:019 and **then** mouldeth him in due Proportions;
080:020 **Then** doth He make His path smooth for him;
080:021 **Then** He causeth him to die, and putteth
080:022 **Then**, when it is His will, He will
080:024 **Then** let man look at his Food,
081:014 (**Then**) shall each soul know what it has put forward.
081:026 **Then** whither go ye?
082:005 (**Then**) shall each soul know what it hath sent
084:005 (**then** will come Home the full Reality).
084:007 **Then** he who is given his Record in his Right hand,
084:020 What **then** is the matter with them, that they
087:005 And **then** doth make it (but) swarthy stubble.
087:013 In which he will **then** neither die nor live.
088:026 **Then** it will be for Us to call them to account.
089:015 **then** saith he, (puffed up), "My Lord
089:016 **then** saith he (in despair), "My Lord
089:029 "Enter thou, **then**, among my Devotees!
090:017 **Then** will he be of those who believe, and enjoin
091:014 **Then** they rejected him (as a false prophet),
095:005 **Then** do We abase him (to be) the lowest of the low,
095:007 What **then**, can after this make you deny the Last
096:017 **Then**, let him call (for help) to his council (of comrades):
099:007 **Then** shall anyone who has done an atom's weight
101:006 **Then**, he whose balance (of good deeds) will be
102:008 **Then**, shall ye be Questioned that Day about the
105:005 **Then** did He make them like an empty field
107:002 **Then** such is the one who repulses the orphan,

THENCE

045:035 they shall not be taken out **thence**,

THENCEFORTH

002:074 **Thenceforth** were your hearts hardened:

THERE

002:008 Of the people **there** are some who say: "We believe
002:023 (if **there** are any) besides Allah,
002:038 **there** comes to you guidance from Me,
002:052 **there** was a chance for you to be grateful.
002:053 **there** was a chance for you to be guided aright.
002:074 For among rocks **there** are some
002:074 others **there** are which when split
002:078 And **there** are among them illiterates,
002:087 Is it that whenever **there** comes to you
002:089 And when **there** comes to them a Book
002:089 when **there** comes to them that which
002:092 **There** came to you Moses with clear (Signs);
002:101 And **there** when came to them a Messenger
002:114 For them **there** is nothing but disgrace
002:115 whithersoever ye turn, **there** is Allah's Face.
002:150 that **there** be no ground of dispute
002:163 **there** is no god but He,
002:165 Yet **there** are men who take (for worship)
002:167 Nor will **there** be a way for them
002:179 **there** is (saving of) Life to you.
002:182 **there** is no wrong in Him;
002:191 unless they (first) fight you **there**;
002:193 But if they cease, let **there** be no hostility
002:193 **there** is no more Persecution
002:194 **there** is the law of equality.
002:197 let **there** be no obscenity, nor wickedness,
002:200 **There** are men who say: "Our Lord! Give us
002:201 And **there** are men who say: "Our Lord! give us
002:203 **there** is no blame on him,
002:203 **there** is no blame on him,

THERE (continued)

002:204 **There** is the type of man whose speech
002:207 And **there** is the type of man who gives his life
002:229 **there** is no blame on either of them
002:230 In that case **there** is no blame
002:233 **There** is no blame on them,
002:233 for your offspring **there** is no blame on you,
002:234 **there** is no blame on you if they dispose
002:235 **There** is no blame on you if ye make an indirect
002:236 **There** is no blame on you if ye divorce women
002:240 **there** is no blame on you for what they do
002:248 "A sign of his authority is that **there** shall come
002:255 Allah! **There** is no god but He, the living,
002:256 Let **there** be no compulsion in religion.
002:282 And if **there** are not two men,
002:282 **there** is no blame on you if ye reduce it
003:002 Allah! **there** is no god but He,
003:006 **There** is no god but He,
003:009 a Day about which **there** in no doubt;
003:013 "**There** has already been for you a Sign
003:018 **There** is no god but He the Exalted in Power,
003:018 **There** is no god but He:
003:025 against a Day about which **there** is no doubt,
003:030 it will wish **there** were a great distance between
003:038 **There** did Zakariya pray to his Lord, saying:
003:062 **there** is no god except Allah;
003:075 because, they say, "**There** is no way over us
003:078 **There** is among them a section who distort
003:104 Let **there** arise out of you a band of people
003:126 (in any case) **there** is no victory except
003:137 **There** have been examples that have passed
003:153 **There** did Allah give you one distress
003:160 if He forsakes you, who is **there**, after that,
003:167 They said: "Had we known **there** would be a fight,
003:183 Say: "**There** came to you Messengers before me,
003:190 **there** are indeed Signs for men of understanding,
003:199 And **there** are, certainly, among the people
004:007 and those nearest related **there** is a share for
004:024 **there** is no blame on you, and Allah
004:029 but let **there** be amongst you traffic
004:040 if **there** is any good (done), He doubleth it, and
004:046 Of the Jews **there** are those who displace words
004:072 **There** are certainly among you men who
004:073 as if **there** had never been ties of affection
004:083 When **there** comes to them some matter
004:087 Allah! **There** is no god but He: of a surety
004:087 about which **there** is no doubt.
004:090 between whom and you **there** is a treaty (of peace),
004:099 For these, **there** is hope that Allah will forgive:
004:101 **there** is no blame on you if ye shorten
004:102 But **there** is no blame on you if ye put away
004:114 In most of their secret talks **there** is no good:
004:127 **There** is not a good deed which ye do, but
004:128 **there** is no blame on them if they arrange
004:138 that **there** is for them a grievous Chastisement.
004:159 And **there** is none of the People of the Book
004:174 O mankind! verily **there** hath come to you
004:176 if **there** are brothers and sisters, (they share),
004:176 if **there** are two sisters, they shall
005:015 **there** hath come to you Our Messenger, revealing
005:015 **There** hath come to you from Allah a (new)
005:019 lest ye should say: "**There** came unto us no bringer
005:032 Then although **there** came to them Our Messengers

THERE (continued)

005:041 For them **there** is disgrace in this world, and in
005:066 **There** is from among them a party of the right course:
005:070 Every time **there** came to them a Messenger
005:071 They thought **there** would be no trial
005:072 **There** will for the wrong-doers be no one to help.
005:073 for **there** is no god except One God.
005:093 **there** is no blame for what they ate (in the past),
005:114 that **there** may be for us-for the first and the last of us-
006:002 And **there** is with Him another determined term; yet
006:012 **there** is no doubt whatever, it is they
006:019 that besides Allah **there** is another gods?"
006:023 **There** will then be (left) no excuse
006:025 Of them **there** are some who (pretend to)
006:029 "**There** is nothing except our life on this earth,
006:034 **there** is none that can alter the Words
006:038 **There** is not an animal (that lives)
006:040 if **there** come upon you the Punishment of Allah,
006:059 **there** is not a grain in the darkness
006:059 He knoweth whatever **there** is on the earth
006:098 then **there** is a resting place and a repository:
006:099 and (then **there** are) gardens of grapes,
006:099 Behold! in these things **there** are signs
006:102 **There** is no god but He, the Creator
006:106 **there** is no god but He:
006:124 When **there** comes to them a Sign
006:130 came **there** not unto you messengers from amongst you
006:138 further, **there** are cattle forbidden to yoke or burden,
007:035 O ye children of Adam! whenever **there** come to you
007:040 no opening will **there** be of the gates
007:041 For them **there** is hell, as a couch
007:061 He said: "O my people! **there** is no error in me:
007:063 "Do ye wonder that **there** hath come to you
007:067 **there** is no folly in me" but (I am)
007:069 "Do ye wonder that **there** hath come to you a message
007:087 "And if **there** is a party among you who believes
007:101 **there** came indeed to them their Messengers
007:113 So **there** came the sorcerers to Pharaoh: they said:
007:119 So they were vanquished **there** and then,
007:158 **there** is no god but He: it is He
007:159 **there** is a section who guide and do justice
007:160 out of it **there** gushed forth twelve springs:
007:168 **There** are among them some that are
007:186 **there** can be no guide; He will
008:010 (in any case) **there** is no help except from Allah:
008:039 **there** is no more persecution, and religion
008:065 If **there** are twenty amongst you,
008:066 if **there** are a hundred of you, patient
008:066 for He knoweth that **there** is a weak spot in you:
008:073 (protect each other), **there** would be tumult and
009:007 How can **there** be a covenant before Allah
009:008 How (can **there** be such a league), seeing that
009:031 one God: **there** is no god but He.
009:034 And **there** are those who hoard gold and silver
009:034 O ye who believe! **There** are indeed many among
009:042 If **there** had been immediate gain (in sight),
009:047 and **there** would have been some among you
009:090 And **there** were, among the desert Arabs (also),
009:091 **There** is no blame on those who are infirm, or ill,
009:091 no ground (of complaint) can **there** be against
009:092 Nor (is **there** blame) on those who came to thee
009:102 Others (**there** are who) have acknowledged
009:106 **There** are (yet) others, held in suspense for the

THERE (continued)

009:107	And **there** are those who put up a mosque by way
009:108	**There** is a mosque whose foundation was laid
009:118	and they perceived that **there** is no fleeing
009:124	Whenever **there** cometh down a Sura, some of
009:127	Whenever **there** cometh down a Sura, they look
009:129	**there** is no god but He: On him is my trust,-
010:024	**there** reaches it Our command by night or by day,
010:030	**There** will every soul see (the fruits of)
010:035	Say: "Of your 'partners' is **there** any that
010:037	wherein **there** is no doubt-from the
010:040	Of them **there** are some who believe therein,
010:057	O mankind! **there** hath come to you an admonition
010:062	**there** is no fear, nor shall they grieve;
010:064	no change can **there** be in the words of Allah.
010:090	he said: "I believe that **there** is no god except
010:098	If only **there** had been a single township
010:107	**there** is none can remove it but He:
010:107	**there** is none can keep back his favour:
011:006	**There** is no moving creature on earth but its
011:012	But thou art **there** only to warn! It is Allah
011:014	and that **there** is no god but He!
011:016	They are those for whom **there** is nothing
011:040	At length, behold! **there** came Our Command,
011:048	from those with thee: but (**there** will be other)
011:056	**There** is not a moving creature,
011:065	(behold) **there** is a promise not to be belied!"
011:068	As if they had never dwelt and flourished **there**.
011:069	**There** came Our Messengers to Abraham
011:071	And his wife was standing (**there**), and she
011:076	for them **there** cometh a Chastisement that cannot
011:078	Is **there** not among you a single right-minded man?"
011:095	As if they had never dwelt and flourished **there**!
011:101	when **there** issued the decree of thy Lord: nor did
011:106	**there** will be for them therein (nothing but) the heaving
011:116	If only **there** had been of the generations
011:116	(but **there** were none) except a few among them whom
011:120	in them **there** cometh to thee the Truth, as well
012:009	(**there** will be time enough) for you
012:019	Then **there** came a caravan of travellers: they sent
012:019	He said: "Ah **there**! Good news! Here is a (fine)
012:032	She said: "**There** before you is the man
012:036	Now with him **there** came into the prison
012:077	They said: "If he steals, **there** was a brother
012:110	**there** reaches them Our help, and those
012:111	**There** is, in their stories, instruction for
013:003	in these things are Signs for those who consider!
013:004	**there** are Signs for those who understand!
013:011	**there** are (angels) in succession, before and
013:011	a people's punishment, **there** can be no turning
013:015	Whatever beings **there** are in the heavens
013:017	**there** is a scum likewise.
013:022	Evil with good: for such **there** is the final
013:023	they shall enter **there**, as well as the righteous
013:030	Say: "He is my Lord! **There** is no god but He!
013:031	If **there** were a Qur'an with which mountains
013:036	but **there** are among the clans those who
013:041	(Where) Allah commands, **there** is none to put
014:005	**there** are Signs for such as are firmly patient
014:010	Their messengers said: "Is **there** a doubt
014:015	But they sought victory and decision (**there** and then),
014:021	for ourselves **there** is no way of escape."
014:022	For wrong-doers **there** must be a grievous Chastisement."

014:031	of a Day in which **there** will be neither mutual
015:021	And **there** is not a thing but its (sources and)
015:048	**There** no sense of fatigue shall touch them,
015:071	He said: "**There** are my daughters (to marry),
015:099	And serve thy Lord until **there** come unto thee
016:002	(saying): "Warn (Man) that **there** is no god but I:
016:009	but **there** are ways that turn aside: if Allah
016:030	To those who do good, **there** is good in this world,
016:033	or **there** comes the Command of thy Lord
016:037	He leaves to stray, and **there** is none to help them.
016:069	**there** issues from within from within their bodies
016:070	and of you **there** are some who are sent back
016:113	And **there** came to them a Messenger from among
017:042	Say: if **there** had been (other) gods with Him,-
017:044	**there** is not a thing but celebrates His praise;
017:058	**There** is not a population but We shall destroy
017:095	Say, "If **there** were settled, on earth,
017:099	a term appointed, of which **there** is no doubt.
018:021	and that **there** can be no doubt about the
018:036	I shall surely find (**there**) something better
018:039	**There** is no power but from Allah!'
018:044	**There**, the (only) protection comes from Allah,
018:055	And what is **there** to keep back men from believing,
018:077	They found **there** a wall on the point
018:079	for **there** was after them a certain king who
018:082	**there** was, beneath it, a buried treasure, to which
019:059	But after them **there** followed a posterity
019:062	They will not **there** hear any vain discourse,
020:008	Allah! **there** is no god but He!
020:014	"Verily, I am Allah: **there** is no god but I:
020:098	**there** is no god but He: all things
020:118	"**There** is therein (enough provision) for thee
020:123	as is sure, **there** comes to you guidance from Me,
020:129	but **there** is a term appointed (for respite),
021:022	If **there** were, in the heavens and the earth,
021:022	**there** would have been ruin in both!
021:025	that **there** is no god but I; therefore worship
021:047	And if **there** be (no more than) the weight
021:087	"**There** is no god but Thou: Glory to
021:095	But **there** is a ban on any population which We
021:099	they would not have got **there**!
021:100	nor will they **there** hear (aught else).
021:100	**There**, sobbing will be their lot, nor will
022:003	And yet among men **there** are such as dispute
022:007	**there** can be no doubt about it, or about
022:008	Yet **there** is among men such a one as disputes
022:011	**There** are among men some who serve Allah, as it
022:021	In addition **there** will be maces of iron
022:023	and their garments **there** will be of silk.
022:025	to (all) men-equal is the dweller **there** and the
022:040	**there** would surely have been pulled down
022:055	or **there** comes to them the Chastisement
022:057	**there** will be a humiliating Punishment.
022:071	for those that do wrong **there** is no helper.
023:021	**there** are, in them, (besides), numerous other
023:030	Verily in this **there** are Signs (for men to understand)
023:037	"**There** is nothing but our life in this world!
023:044	every time **there** came to a people their messenger,
023:063	and **there** are, besides that, deeds of theirs,
023:091	nor is **there** any god along with Him
023:091	(if **there** were many gods), behold, each god
023:101	**there** will be no more relationships between

THERE (continued)

023:109 "A part of My servants **there** was, who used
023:116 **there** is no god but He, the Lord
024:026 people say: for them **there** is forgiveness, and a
024:035 is as if **there** were a Niche and within it a Lamp:
024:039 but he finds Allah **there**, and Allah
024:040 not light, **there** in no light!
024:045 of them **there** are some that creep on their bellies;
024:050 Is it that **there** is a disease in their hearts?
024:060 **there** is no blame on them if they lay aside
024:061 **there** is no blame on you,
025:013 they will plead for destruction **there** and then!
025:016 they will dwell (**there**) for aye:
025:016 "For them **there** will be therein all that
025:022 no joy will **there** be to the sinners that Day:
025:022 "**There** is a barrier forbidden (to you)
026:005 But **there** comes not to them a newly-revealed
026:096 "They will say **there** in their mutual bickerings:
026:206 Yet **there** comes to them at length the (Punishment)
027:007 soon will I bring you from **there** some information,
027:023 "I found (**there**) a woman ruling over them
027:026 "Allah!-**there** is no god but He!-Lord of
027:037 we shall expel them from **there** in disgrace,
027:048 **There** were in the City nine men, who made
027:060 (Can **there** be another) god besides Allah?
027:061 the two seas (can **there** be another) god besides Allah?
027:062 (Can **there** be another) god besides Allah?
027:063 (Can **there** be another) god besides Allah?-
027:064 (Can **there** be another) god besides Allah?
027:075 And **there** is nothing hidden in heaven or earth,
028:015 and he found **there** two men fighting,-one of
028:020 And **there** came a man, running, from the
028:023 he found **there** a group of men watering
028:028 let **there** be no injustice to me.
028:029 I hope to bring you from **there** some information,
028:070 And He is Allah: **there** is no god but He.
028:071 what god is **there** other than Allah, who can
028:072 what god is **there** other than Allah, who can
028:088 **There** is no god but He.
029:010 Then **there** are among men such as say, "We believe
029:032 He said: "But **there** is Lut **there**."
029:032 They said: "Well do we know who is **there**:
029:039 **there** came to them Moses with Clear Signs,
029:068 Is **there** not a home in Hell for those who rejected Faith?
030:008 yet are **there** truly many among men who deny
030:009 **there** came to them their messengers with Clear (Signs),
030:029 To them **there** will be no helpers.
030:030 made mankind: no change (**there** is) in the work
030:040 Are **there** any of your (false) "Partners"
030:043 from Allah the Day which **there** is no chance
030:043 before **there** come from Allah the Day which there is
031:006 for such **there** will be a humiliating Chastisement.
031:006 But **there** are, among men, those who
031:007 as if **there** were deafness in both his ears:
031:008 **there** will be Gardens of Bliss,-
031:011 now show Me what is **there** that others
031:016 "If **there** be (but) the weight of a mustard-seed
031:020 Yet **there** are among men those who dispute
031:032 **there** are among them those that falter
032:002 in which **there** is no doubt,-from the
033:005 But **there** is no blame on you if ye make a mistake
033:009 (bestowed) on you, when **there** came down on you
033:037 in order that (in future) **there** may be no

THERE (continued)

033:038 **There** can be no difficulty to the Prophet
033:050 in order that **there** should be no difficulty
033:051 thou pleasest: and **there** is no blame on thee
033:055 **There** is no blame (on those ladies if they appear)
034:003 nor is **there** anything less than that,
034:012 and **there** were Jinns that worked in front of him,
034:015 **There** was, for Saba', aforetime, a Sign
034:037 are the ones for whom **there** is a multiplied Reward
034:051 but then **there** will be no escape (for them),
035:003 unto you! Is **there** a Creator, other than
035:003 **There** is no god but He: how then
035:024 a warner: and **there** never was a people,
035:032 but **there** are among them some who wrong their
035:033 and their garments **there** will be of silk.
035:037 for the Wrong-doers **there** is no helper."
035:041 **There** is none-not one-can sustain them
036:013 Behold, **there** came messengers to it.
036:020 Then **there** came running, from the
036:030 **There** comes not a messenger to them
036:043 then would **there** be no helper (to hear their cry),
036:057 (Every) fruit will be **there** for them; they shall
037:035 **there** is no god except Allah,
037:057 been among those brought (**there**)!
037:167 And **there** were those who said,
038:003 (for mercy)-when **there** was no longer time
038:031 Behold, **there** were brought before him, at eventide,
038:065 no god is **there** but Allah, the One
039:006 **There** is no god but He: then how
039:032 Is **there** not in Hell an abode for the unbelievers?
039:036 **there** can be no guide.
039:037 And such as Allah doth guide **there** can be
039:047 Even if the wrong-doers had all that **there** is on earth,
039:059 "(The reply will be) `Nay, but **there** came to thee
039:060 is **there** not in Hell an abode for the Haughty?
039:071 arrive **there**, its gates will be opened.
039:073 until behold, they arrive **there**; its gates
040:003 **There** is no god but He: to Him is the Final Goal.
040:005 But (**there** were people) before them, who denied
040:011 our sins: is **there** any way out (of this)?"
040:017 no injustice will **there** be that Day, for Allah
040:022 That was because **there** came to them
040:032 a Day when **there** will be mutual calling
040:033 **there** is none to guide...
040:034 "And to you **there** came Joseph in times gone by,
040:050 They will say: "Did **there** not come to you
040:056 **there** is nothing in their breasts but (the quest of)
040:062 **there** is no god but He: then how
040:065 **There** is no god but He: call upon
040:067 though of you **there** are some who die before;-
040:078 before thee: of them **there** are some whose story
040:078 in truth and justice, and **there** perished,
040:078 **there** and then, those who stood on Falsehoods.
040:080 to any need (**there** may be) in your hearts; and on
040:080 for food; and **there** are (other) advantages in
041:044 **there** is a deafness in their ears, and it
042:007 of which **there** is no doubt: (when) some
042:011 **there** is nothing whatever like unto Him,
042:015 **There** is no contention between us and you.
042:026 for the Unbelievers **there** is a terrible Chastisement.
042:035 that **there** is for them no way of escape.
042:041 against such **there** is no cause of blame.
042:042 for such **there** will be a Chastisement grievous.

THERE (continued)

042:044 say: "Is **there** any way (to effect) a return?"
042:044 **there** is no protector thereafter.
042:046 **there** is no way (to the Goal).
042:047 before **there** come a Day which **there** will be no putting
042:047 That Day **there** will be for you no place of refuge
042:047 of refuge nor will **there** be for you any room
043:007 And never came **there** a prophet to them
043:071 **there** will be **there** all that the souls could desire,
043:075 will they be **there** overwhelmed.
044:008 **There** is no god but He: it is He
044:017 **there** came to them a messenger most honourable,
044:033 in which **there** was a manifest trial.
044:035 "**There** is nothing beyond our first death,
044:055 **There** can they call for every kind of fruit
044:056 Nor will they **there** taste Death, except the
045:009 for such **there** will be a humiliating Chastisement.
045:024 And they say: "What is **there** but our life
045:026 **there** is no doubt": but most men not know.
045:032 **there** was no doubt about its (coming), ye used
046:017 But (**there** is one) who says to his parents,
046:021 but **there** have been Warners before
047:013 And **there** was none to aid them.
047:015 In it **there** are for them all kinds of fruits,
047:019 Know, therefore, that **there** is no god but Allah,
048:017 nor is **there** blame on the lame, nor is
048:017 No blame is **there** on the blind,
048:021 And other gains (**there** are), which are
048:025 Had **there** not been believing men and believing women
050:002 But they wonder that **there** has come to them
050:006 and adorned it, and **there** is not flaws in it?
050:018 Not a word does he utter but **there** is a vigilant Guardian.
050:021 And **there** will come forth every soul: with each
050:030 It will say, "Are **there** any more (to come)?"
050:035 all that they wish,-and **there** is more with Us.
050:035 **There** will be for them therein all that
050:036 was **there** any place of escape (for them)?
051:019 And in their wealth **there** is a due share
051:035 the Believers who were **there**,
051:036 But We found not **there** any except one
051:037 And We left **there** a Signs for such as fear
052:008 **There** is none can avert it;-
052:023 They shall **there** exchange, one with
052:047 **there** is another punishment besides this: but most
053:023 Even though **there** has already come to them
054:004 **There** have already come to them such tidings
054:015 then is **there** any that will receive admonition?
054:017 then is **there** any that will receive admonition?
054:022 then is **there** any that will receive admonition?
054:032 then is **there** any that will receive admonition?
054:040 then is **there** any that will receive admonition?
054:051 then is **there** any that will receive admonition?
055:046 **there** will be two Gardens-
055:060 Is **there** any Reward for Good-other than Good?
055:062 **there** are two other Gardens,-
056:008 Then (**there** will be) the Companions
056:022 And (**there** will be) Companions with beautiful,
056:089 (**There** is for him) Rest and Satisfaction, and a
057:014 until **there** issued the Command of Allah.
058:004 Reject (Him), **there** is a grievous Chastisement.
058:007 **There** is not a secret consultation between three,
059:015 (in the Hereafter **there** is) for them a grievous
059:022 Allah is He, than Whom **there** is no other god;-

THERE (continued)

059:023 Allah is He, than Whom **there** is no other god;-
060:004 and **there** has arisen between us and you,
060:004 **There** is for you an excellent example (to follow)
060:006 **There** was indeed in them an excellent example
060:010 And **there** will be no blame on you if ye marry
060:010 O ye who believe! when **there** come to you
064:006 That was because **there** came to them messengers
064:013 Allah! **there** is no god but He:
067:020 Nay, who is **there** that can help you, (even as)
067:021 Or who is **there** that can provide you
068:019 Then **there** came, on the (garden) a visitation
069:049 And We certainly know that **there** are amongst you
070:002 The Unbelievers the which **there** is none
071:001 thy People before **there** comes to them
072:004 'There were some foolish ones among us, who used
072:006 'True, **there** were persons among mankind who took
072:009 'We used, indeed, to sit **there** in (hidden)
072:011 'There are among us some that are righteous,
073:007 True, **there** is for thee by day prolonged occupation
073:009 **there** is no god but He: take Him
073:020 He knoweth that **there** may be (some)
074:047 "Until **there** came to us (the Hour) that is certain."
075:027 And **there** will be a cry, "Who is a magician
076:001 Has **there** not been over Man a long period of Time,
076:013 **there** neither the sun's (excessive heat)
076:014 and the bunches (of fruit), **there**, will hang
076:017 And they will be given to drink **there** of a Cup
076:018 A fountain **there**, called Salsabil.
076:020 And when thou lookest, it is **there** thou wilt see a
077:033 "As if **there** were (a string of) yellow camels
078:019 as if **there** were doors,
078:031 **there** will be an Achievement,
079:034 Therefore, when **there** comes the great,
080:002 Because **there** came to him the blind
080:033 At length, when **there** comes the Deafening Noise,-
081:021 With authority **there**, (and) faithful of his trust.
083:009 (**There** is) a Register (fully) inscribed.
083:020 (**There** is) a Register (fully) inscribed.
086:004 **There** is no soul but has a protector over it.
088:006 No food will **there** be for them but a bitter Dhari
089:005 Is **there** (not) in these an adjuration (or evidence)
094:005 So, verily, with every difficulty, **there** is relief:
094:006 Verily, with every difficulty **there** is relief.
098:001 (from their ways) until **there** should come to
098:004 make schisms, until after **there** came to them
112:004 And **there** is none like unto Him.

THEREAFTER

002:064 But ye turned back **thereafter**:
005:094 any who transgress **thereafter** will have
006:054 and **thereafter** repented, and amended
007:153 **thereafter** Oft-Forgiving, Most Merciful.
007:153 but repent **thereafter** and (truly) believe,-
016:110 and who **thereafter** strive and fight for the Faith
016:119 but who **thereafter** repent and make amends,-
017:104 And We said **thereafter** to the Children of Israel,
024:005 Except those who repent **thereafter** and mend
026:120 **Thereafter** We drowned those who remained behind.
027:011 and have **thereafter** substituted good to take
030:051 they become, **thereafter**, ungrateful (Unbelievers)!
035:041 one-can sustain them **thereafter**:
042:044 there is no protector **thereafter**.
065:001 about **thereafter** some new situation.

THEREANENT
027:066   and uncertainty **thereanent**; nay,

THEREAT
010:022   and they rejoice **thereat**; then comes
030:036   they exult **thereat**: and when some evil afflicts
039:023   who fear their Lord tremble **thereat**; then their
042:048   exult **thereat**, but when some ill happens to him,
043:057   a clamor **thereat** (in ridicule)!

THEREBY
002:079   and for the gain they make **thereby**.
009:037   are led to wrong **thereby**: for they
013:033   but they are kept back (**thereby**) from the Path.
025:032   that We may strengthen thy heart **thereby**,
046:011   themselves **thereby**, they will say, "This is

THEREFOR
009:046   some preparation **therefor**: but Allah was averse
017:019   and strive **therefor** with all due striving,

THEREFORE
004:034   **Therefore** the righteous women are devoutly
004:090   **therefore** if they withdraw from you
004:094   **therefore** carefully investigate, for Allah
005:026   Allah said: "**Therefore** will the land
005:044   **therefore** fear not men, but fear Me, and sell not
006:020   refuse **therefore** to believer.
010:003   Him **therefore** serve ye: will you not
011:112   **Therefore** stand firm (in the straight path)
012:045   of its interpretation: send ye me (**therefore**)."
012:054   **Therefore** when he had spoken to him, he said:
012:080   **Therefore** will I not leave this land until my
015:092   **Therefore**, by the Lord, We will, of a surety
015:094   **Therefore** expound openly what thou art commanded,
018:022   Enter not, **therefore**, into controversies
018:095   help me **therefore** with strength (and labour):
019:036   and your Lord: Him **therefore** serve ye:
020:012   **Therefore** put off thy shoes: thou art
020:016   "**Therefore** let not such as believe not therein
020:047   send forth, **therefore**, the Children of Israel with us,
020:064   "**Therefore** concert your plan, and then
020:130   **Therefore** be patient with what they say,
021:025   **therefore** worship and serve Me.
021:092   **therefore** serve Me (and no other).
021:108   will ye **therefore** bow to His Will (in Islam)?"
023:052   **therefore** fear Me (and no other).
023:116   **Therefore** exalted be Allah, the King,
025:052   **Therefore** listen not to the Unbelievers,
028:021   He **therefore** got away therefrom, looking about,
028:038   **therefore**, O Haman! light me a (kiln to bake bricks)
028:086   **therefore** lend not thou support in any way
029:056   **therefore** serve ye Me-(and Me alone)!
033:013   **Therefore** go back!" and a band of them ask for
036:006   **therefore** remain heedless (of the Signs of Allah).
036:011   **therefore**, good tidings, of Forgiveness
043:061   **therefore** have no doubt about the (Hour),
043:063   **therefore** fear Allah and obey me.
045:035   **therefore**, they shall not be taken out thence,
046:035   **Therefore** patiently persevere, as did
047:004   **Therefore**, when ye meet the Unbelievers (in fight),
047:004   **therefore** (is the time for) either generosity or ransom:
047:019   Know, **therefore**, that there is no god but Allah,
051:050   **Therefore** flee unto Allah: I am
052:029   **Therefore** Remind for by the Grace of thy Lord,
053:029   **Therefore** shun those who turn away from
053:032   **Therefore** hold not yourselves purified:

THEREFORE (continued)
054:006   **Therefore**, (O Prophet,) turn away from them.
058:016   **therefore** shall they have a humiliating Chastisement,
063:003   **therefore** they understand not.
064:008   Believe, **therefore**, in Allah and His Messenger,
064:013   **therefore**, let the Believers put their trust.
065:010   **Therefore** fear Allah, O ye men of understanding-
070:005   **Therefore** do thou hold Patience,-a Patience
073:009   take Him **therefore** for (thy) Disposer of Affairs.
073:019   **Therefore**, whoso will, let him take a (straight)
073:020   read ye, **therefore**, of the Qur'an as much as may
073:020   Read ye, **therefore**, as much of the Qur'an as may
076:024   **Therefore** be patient with constancy to the
078:039   That is the True Day: **therefore**, whoso will,
079:034   **Therefore**, when there comes the great,
080:011   **Therefore** let whose will, keep it in remembrance.
086:017   **Therefore** grant a delay to the unbelievers:
087:009   **Therefore** give admonition in case the admonition
088:021   **Therefore** do thou remind, for thou
089:013   **Therefore** did thy Lord pour on them a scourge
092:014   **Therefore** do I warn you of a Fire blazing fiercely;
093:009   **Therefore**, treat not the orphan with harshness,
094:007   **Therefore**, when thou art free (from thine
108:002   **Therefore** to thy Lord turn in Prayer and Sacrifice.

THEREFROM
002:025   they are fed with fruits **therefrom**,
002:060   Then gushed forth **therefrom** twelve springs.
003:019   the Book dissent **therefrom** except through
003:195   and were drive out **therefrom**,
005:037   but never will they get out **therefrom**:
006:004   but they turned away **therefrom**.
006:157   and turneth away **therefrom**?
007:089   after Allah hath rescued us **therefrom**;
014:052   that they may take warning **therefrom**,
016:014   **therefrom** ornaments to wear;
018:053   to turn away **therefrom**.
020:010   burning brand **therefrom** or find some
020:016   divert thee **therefrom**, lest thou perish!"...
020:100   If any do turn away **therefrom**, verily they
021:101   will be removed far **therefrom**.
022:022   away **therefrom**, from anguish, they will
026:005   the Most Gracious, but they turn away **therefrom**.
028:021   He therefore got away **therefrom**, looking about,
028:055   they turn away **therefrom** and say: "To us our
032:020   get away **therefrom**, they will be forced
032:022   and who then turns away **therefrom**?
036:033   and produce grain **therefrom**, of which ye do eat.
036:037   We withdraw **therefrom** the Day, and behold
036:046   but they turn away **therefrom**.
037:047   nor will they suffer intoxication **therefrom**.
039:024   (like one guarded **therefrom**)?
056:019   No after-ache will they receive **therefrom**, nor will
063:008   will expel **therefrom** the meaner."
079:031   He draweth out **therefrom** its water and its pasture,
082:016   And they will not be able to keep away **therefrom**.

THEREIN
002:020   they walk **therein**,
002:025   and they abide **therein** (for ever).
002:025   and they have **therein** spouses (purified);
002:030   **therein** one who will make mischief
002:030   make mischief **therein** and shed blood?
002:035   things **therein** as (where and when) ye will;
002:039   they shall abide **therein**."

THEREIN (continued)

002:041	and be not the first to reject faith **therein**,
002:049	**therein** was a tremendous trial from your Lord.
002:058	and eat of the plenty **therein** as ye wish;
002:063	(ever) to remembrance what is **therein**,
002:078	but (see **therein** their own) desires,
002:081	**therein** shall they abide (for ever).
002:082	**therein** shall they abide (for ever).
002:121	those who reject faith **therein**,
002:121	they are the ones that believe **therein**:
002:125	or prostrate themselves (**therein** in prayer).
002:162	They will abide **therein**:
002:197	If any one undertakes that duty **therein**,
002:217	of the Fire and will abide **therein**.
002:217	Say: "Fighting **therein** is a grave (offense);
002:248	with (an assurance) **therein** of security
002:257	to dwell **therein** (for ever).
002:266	with fire **therein**, and be burnt up?
002:275	they will abide **therein** (for ever).
003:015	**therein** is their eternal home;
003:049	Surely **therein** is a Sign for you if ye did believe.
003:107	**therein** to dwell (for ever).
003:116	dwelling **therein** (for ever).
003:198	**therein** are they to dwell (for ever),
004:013	to abide **therein** (for ever) and that
004:014	will be admitted to a Fire, to abide **therein**:
004:057	**therein** shall they have spouses purified
004:082	found **therein** much discrepancy.
004:085	becomes a partner **therein**:
004:093	to abide **therein** (for ever):
004:122	to dwell **therein** for ever.
004:157	And those who differ **therein** are full of doubts,
004:169	to dwell **therein** for ever:
005:043	**Therein** is the (plain) command of Allah;
005:044	**therein** was guidance and light.
005:045	We ordained **therein** for them: "Life for life,
005:046	**therein** was guidance and light.
005:047	by what Allah hath revealed **therein**.
005:120	and all that is **therein**, and it is He
006:091	**therein** were ye taught that which ye knew
006:123	to plot (and burrow) **therein**:
006:128	you will dwell **therein** for ever, except as
006:139	then all have shares **therein**.
007:010	and provided you **therein** with means for the
007:025	and **therein** shall ye die:
007:025	He said: "**Therein** shall ye live,
007:036	to dwell **therein** (for ever).
007:042	**therein** to dwell (for ever).
007:161	"Dwell in this town and eat **therein** as ye wish,
007:171	what is **therein**; perchance ye may fear Allah".
009:022	They will dwell **therein** for ever.
009:036	not yourselves **therein**, and fight the Pagans all
009:068	the fire of Hell: **therein** shall they dwell:
009:072	rivers flow, to dwell **therein**, and beautiful
009:089	under which rivers flow, to dwell **therein**:
009:100	rivers flow, to dwell **therein** for ever:
009:108	Never stand thou forth **therein**.
009:108	standing forth (for prayer) **therein**:
010:010	will be their greeting **therein** and the end
010:010	(This will be) their prayer **therein**: "Glory to
010:026	they will abide **therein** (for aye)!
010:027	they will abide **therein** (for aye)!
010:040	believe **therein**, and some who do not:

THEREIN (continued)

010:061	when ye are deeply engrossed **therein**.
010:067	the Night that ye may rest **therein**, and the Day
011:015	their deeds **therein**,-without diminution.
011:016	vain are the designs they frame **therein**,
011:017	They believe **therein**; but those of the Sects
011:023	to dwell **therein** for aye!
011:040	We said: "Embark **therein**, of each kind two,
011:061	the earth and settled you **therein**:
011:106	**therein** (nothing but) the heaving of sighs and sobs:
011:107	They will dwell **therein** so long as the heavens
011:108	in the Garden: they will dwell **therein** so long as
011:110	to Moses, but differences arose **therein**:
012:056	to take possession **therein** as, when, or
013:005	to dwell **therein** (for aye)!
013:035	and the shade **therein**: such is
014:006	**therein** was a tremendous trial from your Lord."
014:023	their greeting **therein** will be: "Peace!"
014:023	to dwell **therein** for aye with the
014:029	They will burn **therein**,-an evil
015:014	to continue (all day) ascending **therein**,
015:019	and produced **therein** all kinds of things in due balance.
015:020	And We have provided **therein** means of subsistence,-
016:014	and thou seest the ships **therein** that plough
016:029	to dwell **therein**.
016:031	**therein** all that they wish: thus doth
017:018	burn **therein**, disgraced and rejected.
017:044	and all beings **therein**, declare His
017:069	so that ye find no helper **therein** against Us?
017:076	have stayed (**therein**) after thee, except for
018:001	and hath allowed **therein** no Crookedness:
018:031	be adorned **therein** with bracelets of gold,
018:031	recline **therein** on raised thrones.
018:033	the least **therein**: in the midst of them We caused
018:049	is (recorded) **therein**; they will say, "Ah! woe
018:053	apprehendthat they have to fall **therein**;
019:062	they will have **therein** their sustenance,
019:070	are most worthy of being burned **therein**.
019:072	the wrong-doers **therein**, (humbled) to their knees.
020:016	not **therein** but follow their own lust,
020:053	has enabled you to go about **therein** by roads
020:074	is Hell: **therein** shall he neither die or live.
020:076	they will dwell **therein** for aye:
020:081	but commit no excess **therein**, lest My Wrath
020:113	an Arabic Qur'an-and explained **therein** in detail
020:118	"There is **therein** (enough provision) for thee
020:132	and be constant **therein**.
021:031	and We have made **therein** broad highways
021:099	But each one will abide **therein**.
022:022	they will be forced back **therein**,
022:023	they shall be adorned **therein** with bracelets
022:025	and any whose purpose **therein** is profanity
022:026	or prostrate themselves (**therein** in prayer).
022:054	and that they may believe **therein**, and their
023:011	they will dwell **therein** (for ever).
023:071	**therein** would have been in ruin.
023:077	then Lo! they will be plunged in despair **therein**!
023:084	the earth and all beings **therein**?
023:104	and they will **therein** grin, with their
025:013	into a constricted place **therein**, they will
025:016	"For them there will be **therein** all that
025:061	in the skies, and placed **therein** a Lamp
025:069	and he will dwell **therein** in ignominy,-

THEREIN (continued)

025:075 **therein** shall they be met with salutations and peace,
025:076 Dwelling **therein**;-how beautiful an abode
026:007 we have produced **therein**?
026:129 of living **therein** (for ever)?
028:053 they say: "We believe **therein**, for it is
028:073 that ye may rest **therein**, and that
029:047 So the People of the Book believe **therein**,
029:058 to dwell **therein** for aye;-an excellent
031:009 To dwell **therein**. The promise of Allah is true:
033:005 on you if ye make a mistake **therein**:
033:065 To dwell **therein** for ever: no protector
034:018 "Travel **therein**, secure, by night and day."
034:019 but they wronged themselves (**therein**).
034:022 no (sort of) share have they **therein**, nor is
035:012 **therein** that plough the waves, that ye
035:033 **therein** will they be adorned with bracelets
035:035 shall touch us **therein**."
035:037 **Therein** will they cry aloud (for assistance):
036:034 and We cause springs to gush forth **therein**.
036:034 And We produce **therein** orchards with date-palms
038:051 **therein** can they call (at pleasure) for fruit
038:051 **Therein** will they recline (at ease);
038:056 Hell!-they will burn **therein**-an evil
039:028 without any crookedness (**therein**): in order
039:072 to dwell **therein**: and evil is (this) abode
039:073 Enter ye here, to dwell **therein**."
040:040 **therein** will they have abundance
040:059 **therein** is no doubt: yet most men believe not.
040:061 for you, that ye may rest **therein**, and the Day,
040:076 to dwell **therein**: and evil is (this) abode
041:010 the earth, and measured **therein** its sustenance
041:028 **therein** will be for them the Eternal Home:
041:031 **therein** shall ye have all that ye ask for!-
041:031 **therein** shall ye have all that your souls shall desire;
041:045 but disputes arose **therein**.
042:013 and make no divisions **therein**:
043:010 and has made for you roads (and channels) **therein**,
043:071 and ye shall abide **therein** (for aye).
043:073 Ye shall have **therein** abundance of fruit,
043:074 of Hell, to dwell **therein** (for aye):
046:014 of the Garden, dwelling **Therein** (for aye):
047:020 and fighting is mentioned **therein**, thou wilt
048:005 to dwell **therein** for aye, and remove
050:007 and produced **therein** every kind beautiful growth
050:034 "Enter ye **therein** in Peace and Security; this Day
050:035 There will be for them **therein** all that
052:016 "Burn ye **therein**: the same is it to you
053:028 But they have no knowledge **therein**.
055:011 **Therein** is fruit and date-palms, producing spathes
056:025 No frivolity will they hear **therein**, nor any
057:012 To dwell **therein** for aye! This is
057:013 with a gate **therein**.
058:017 of the Fire, to swell **therein** (for aye)!
058:022 to dwell **therein** (for ever).
059:017 dwelling **therein** for ever.
064:009 to dwell **therein** for ever: that will
064:010 to dwell **therein** for aye: and evil
065:011 to dwell **therein** for ever: Allah has
067:007 When they are cast **therein**, they will
067:008 every time a Group is cast **therein**, its Keepers
071:020 That ye may go about **therein**, in spacious roads."
072:002 and we have believed **therein**:

THEREIN (continued)

072:023 they shall dwell **therein** for ever."
077:027 And made **therein** mountains standing firm,
078:013 And placed (**therein**) a blazing lamp.
078:023 They will dwell **therein** for ages.
078:024 Nothing cool shall they taste **therein**, nor any drink,
078:035 No Vanity shall they hear **therein**, nor Untruth;-
080:027 And produce **therein** grain,
086:001 By the Sky and the Night-Visitant (**therein**);
088:012 **Therein** will be a bubbling spring:
088:013 **Therein** will be couches (of dignity),
089:012 And heaped **therein** mischief (on mischief).
092:015 None shall burn **therein** but those most unfortunate ones
097:004 **Therein** come down the angels and the Spirit
098:006 to dwell **therein** (for aye). They are
098:008 They will dwell **therein** for ever; Allah well

THEREINTO

032:020 be forced **thereinto**, and it will be said to them:

THEREOF

003:007 perversity follow the part **thereof** that is not
005:113 to eat **thereof** and satisfy our hearts, and to know
006:099 feast your eyes with the fruit and the ripeness **thereof**.
007:187 Say: "The knowledge **thereof** is with
007:187 wert eager in search **thereof**:
007:187 Say: "The knowledge **thereof** is with
009:058 If they are given part **thereof**, they are pleased,
010:039 the interpretation **thereof** hath reached them:
010:059 Yet ye hold forbidden some things **thereof** and
010:061 We are Witnesses **thereof** when ye
012:036 and birds are eating **thereof**."
012:036 "the truth and meaning **thereof**: for we
013:035 perpetual is the fruits **thereof** and the
013:036 those who reject a part **thereof**.
015:021 **thereof** in due and ascertainable measures.
016:014 that ye may eat **thereof** flesh that is
016:075 spends **thereof** (freely), privately and publicly:
017:088 they could not produce the like **thereof**, even if
018:049 but takes account **thereof**!
022:028 then eat ye **thereof** and feed the distressed
022:036 eat ye **thereof**, and feed such as (beg not but)
023:117 he has no authority **thereof**; and his
024:031 what (ordinarily) appear **thereof**; that they
025:033 and best explanation (**thereof**).
028:060 and the glitter **thereof**;
029:035 And We have left **thereof** an evident Sign,
030:048 until thou seest rain-drops issue from the midst **thereof**:
033:063 say, "The knowledge **thereof** is with Allah (alone)":
033:072 to undertake it, being afraid **thereof**:
034:002 and all that comes out **thereof**; all that
035:043 will hem in only the authors **thereof**.
036:081 able to create the like **thereof**?"
037:046 to those who drink (**thereof**),
037:066 Truly they will eat **thereof** and fill
040:040 but by the like **thereof**:
042:010 the decision **thereof** is with Allah:
042:020 We grant somewhat **thereof**, but he
042:023 of good in respect **thereof**: for Allah
046:029 in the presence **thereof**, they said, "Listen in
047:018 some tokens **thereof**, and when it comes to them
066:003 he confirmed part **thereof** and passed over a part.
066:003 Then when he told her **thereof**, she said,
073:020 ye are unable to keep count **thereof**.
076:016 **thereof** (according to their wishes).

THEREOF (continued)
079:043   with the declaration **thereof**?
083:026   The seal **thereof** will be Musk: and for this

THEREON
007:057   make rain to descend **thereon**, and produce
007:154   in the writing **thereon** was Guidance and Mercy
011:017   Be not then in doubt **thereon**: for it is the
013:003   and set **thereon** mountains standing firm,
015:019   (like a carpet); set **thereon** mountains firm
019:040   and all beings **thereon**: to Us will
027:061   set **thereon** mountains immovable; and made
041:045   disquieting doubt **thereon**.
050:007   and set **thereon** mountains standing firm,

THERETO
002:187   approach not night **thereto**.
003:097   pilgrimage **thereto** is a duty men owe to Allah,
004:091   they succumb **thereto**: if they withdraw
005:044   and they were witnesses **thereto**: therefore
007:089   return **thereto** unless it be as in the will
009:057   **thereto** with an obstinate rush.
013:025   their word **thereto** and cut asunder those things
034:002   and all that ascends **thereto** and He
037:150   and they are witnesses (**thereto**)?
042:040   is an injury equal **thereto** (in degree): but if

THEREUNTO
002:023   then produce a Sura like **thereunto**;
027:066   nay, they are blind **thereunto**!

THEREUPON
002:055   **thereupon** thunderbolt seized you.

THEREWITH
002:022   and brought forth **therewith** fruits
002:164   gives **therewith** to an earth that is dead;
004:005   but feed and clothe them **therewith**, and speak
004:043   and rub **therewith** your faces and hands.
004:127   but Allah is well-acquainted **therewith**.
005:006   and rub **therewith** your faces and hands.
007:057   and produce every kind of harvest **therewith**:
007:132   to work **therewith** the sorcery on us, we shall
007:181   and dispense justice **therewith**.
008:011   from heaven, to clean you **therewith**, to remove
008:011   and to plant your feet firmly **therewith**.
013:013   and **therewith** He striketh whomsoever He will.
013:017   to make ornaments or utensils **therewith**, there is
015:022   from the shy, **therewith** providing you with water
016:065   the skies, and gives **therewith** life to the earth
018:056   with vain argument, in order **therewith** to weaken
022:011   **therewith**, well content; but if
024:043   He strikes **therewith** whom He pleases
029:063   and gives life **therewith** to the earth after its
032:027   **therewith** crops, providing food for their cattle
035:009   the earth **therewith** after its death:
036:080   when behold! ye kindle **therewith** (your own fires)!
037:066   and fill their bellies **therewith**.
038:044   and strike **therewith**: and break not (thy oath)."
039:021   **therewith**, produce of various colours:
039:023   He guides **therewith** whom He pleases, but such
040:005   of vanities, **therewith** to obliterate the Truth:
043:011   and We raise to life **therewith** a land that is dead;
045:005   and revives **therewith** the earth after its death,
050:009   and We produce **therewith** Gardens and Grain
050:011   and We give (new) life **therewith** to land
056:053   "Then will ye fill your insides **therewith**,
075:016   the (Qur'an) to make haste **therewith**.

THEREWITH (continued)
078:015   That We may produce **therewith** grain and vegetables,

THESE
02:005   and it is **these** who will prosper.
002:016   **These** are they who have bartered
002:027   **These** cause loss (only) to themselves.
002:031   names of **these** if ye are right."
002:086   **These** are the people who buy the life
002:102   But neither of **these** taught anyone
002:202   To **these** will be allotted what they have earned.
002:223   and give (**these**) good tidings
002:229   **these** are the limits ordained by Allah;
002:252   **These** are the signs of Allah:
003:013   **these** saw with their own eyes twice their number.
003:108   **These** are the Signs of Allah:
003:167   **these** were told: "Come, fight in the way of Allah
004:011   **These** are settled portions ordained by Allah:
004:024   except for **these**, all others are lawful,
004:041   a witness against **these** People!
004:078   But what hath come to **these** people.
004:099   For **these**, there is hope that Allah will forgive:
004:109   Ah! **these** are the sort of men on whose behalf
004:141   (**These** are) the ones who wait and watch about you:
004:143   belonging neither to **these** nor those whom Allah
005:026   but sorrow thou not over **these** rebellious people."
005:053   "Are **these** the men who swore their strongest
005:060   **these** are (many times) worse in rank, and far
005:068   over (**these**) people without Faith
005:070   desired not-some (of theses) they called impostors,
005:082   because amongst **these** are men devoted to learning.
005:107   But if it gets known that **these** two were guilty
006:025   "**These** are nothing but tales of the ancients."
006:053   Is it **these** then that Allah hath favoured
006:063   'If He only delivers us from **these** (dangers),
006:064   from **these** and all (other) distresses: and yet
006:089   if **these** (their descendants) reject them, behold!
006:089   **These** were the men to whom We gave the Book, and
006:099   Behold! in **these** things there are signs
007:038   "Our Lord! it is **these** that misled us: so give
007:049   "Behold! are **these** not the men whom
007:050   They will say: "Both **these** things hath Allah
007:082   **these** are indeed men who want
007:139   "As to **these** folk,-the cult
007:145   (and said): "Take and hold **these** with firmness,
008:031   we could say (words like **these**:
008:031   **these** are nothing but tales of the ancients."
008:049   say: "**These** people,-their religion has
008:065   for **these** are a people without understanding.
008:072   **these** are (all) friends and protectors, one of
008:074   **these** are (all) in very truth the believers: for
009:007   As long as **these** stand true
009:055   punish them with **these** things in this life,
009:085   **these** things in this world, and that
009:112   set by Allah;-(these do rejoice). So proclaim
010:001   **These** are the Ayats of the Book of Wisdom.
010:018   and they say: "**These** are our intercessors with
010:061   the greatest of **these** things but are recorded
011:018   "**These** are the ones who lied against their Lord!
011:019   "**These** were they who denied the Hereafter!"
011:022   Without a doubt, **these** are the very ones who
011:024   **These** two kinds (of men) may be compared
011:100   **These** are some of the stories of communities
011:109   Be not then in doubt as to what **these** men worship.

THESE (continued)

012:001 Alif Lam Ra. **These** are the Verses of the
012:077 But **these** things did Joseph keep
013:001 **These** are the Verses of the Book: that which
013:003 in **these** things are Signs for those who consider!
013:004 Behold, verily in **these** things there are Signs
013:013 Yet **these** (are the men) the while
014:021 (**these** torments) with patience: for ourselves
015:001 **These** are the Ayats of Revelation,-of a Qur'an
015:068 Lut said: "**These** are my guests: disgrace me not:
016:086 they will say: "Our Lord! **these** are our `partners',
016:089 against **these** (thy people): and We
017:020 We bestow freely on all-**these** as well as those:
017:039 **These** are among the (precepts of) wisdom,
017:102 **these** things have been sent down by none
018:015 "**These** our people have taken for worship
019:060 for **these** will enter the Garden and will
020:063 They said: "**These** two are certainly (expert)
021:005 "Nay," they say, "(**these** are) medleys of dreams!
021:006 will **these** believe?
021:032 the Signs which **these** things (point to)!
021:044 of this life to **these** men and their fathers
021:052 and his people, "What are **these** images, to which
021:065 that **these** (idols) do not speak!"
021:079 it was We Who did (all **these** things).
021:090 **These** (three) were quick in doing
021:099 If **these** had been gods, they would
022:019 **These** two antagonists dispute with each other
023:010 **These** will be the heirs,
023:046 but **these** behaved insolently: they were
023:061 It is **these** who hasten in every good work,
023:061 good work, and **these** who are foremost in them.
024:026 **these** are not affected by what people say:
024:044 verily in **these** things is an instructive example
024:051 it is such as **these** that will prosper.
024:058 **these** are your three times of undress:
026:002 **These** are Verses of the Book that makes
026:054 (Saying): "**These** (Israelites) are but a small band,
027:001 **These** are verses of the Qur'an,-A Book
027:012 (**these** are) among the nine Signs (thou wilt take)
027:056 from your city: **these** are indeed men who
027:068 **these** are nothing but tales of the ancients."
028:002 **These** are Verses of the Book that makes
028:027 one of **these** my daughters to thee, on condition
028:061 Are (**these** two) alike?-one to whom
028:063 **these** are the ones whom we led astray:
029:047 as also do some of **these** (pagan Arabs)
030:009 in greater numbers than **these** have done:
030:039 it is **these** who will get a recompense multiplied.
030:040 any single one of **these** things? Glory to Him!
031:002 **These** are Verses of the Wise Book,-
031:005 and **these** are the ones who will prosper.
031:005 **These** are on (true) guidance from their Lord;
033:055 There is no blame (on those ladies if they appear)
034:037 **these** are the ones for whom there is a
034:040 "Was it you that **these** men used to worship?"
034:045 (the Truth); **these** have not received a tenth
035:040 Say: "Have ye seen (**these**) `partners' of yours
038:015 **These** (to-day) only wait for a single mighty Blast,
040:082 than **these** and superior in strength and in
043:008 stronger in power than **these**;-
043:013 Who has subjected **these** to Our (use), for we
043:029 of this life to **these** (men) and their fathers,

THESE (continued)

043:051 (witness) **these** streams flowing underneath my
043:088 Truly **these** are a people who believe not!"
044:022 "**These** are indeed a people given to sin."
044:034 As to **these** (Quraish), they say forsooth:
045:020 **These** are clear evidences to men, and a
048:020 and He has given you **these** beforehand; and He
051:025 (And thought, "**These** seem) unusual people."
053:023 **These** are nothing but names which ye
055:062 And besides **these** two, there are
056:011 **These** will be those Nearest to Allah:
060:009 (in **these** circumstances), that do wrong.
076:027 As to **these**, they love the fleeting life,
077:012 For what Day are **these** (Portents) deferred?
083:032 "Behold! **these** are the people truly astray!"
089:005 Is there (not) in **these** an adjuration (or evidence)
089:011 (All) **these** transgressed beyond bounds in the lands.

THEY

002:005 **They** are on (true) guidance,
002:006 or do not warn them; **they** will not believe.
002:007 great is the chastisement **they** (incur).
002:008 but **they** do not (really) believe.
002:009 Fain would **they** deceive Allah
002:009 but **they** only deceive themselves
002:010 because **they** lie (to themselves).
002:010 and grievous is the chastisement **they** (incur),
002:011 **they** say: "Why, we are only ones
002:012 Of a surety, **they** are the ones
002:012 but **they** realize (it) not.
002:013 **they** say: "Shall we believe as the fools believe?"
002:013 Nay of a surety **they** are the fools but **they** do not know.
002:014 When **they** meet those who believe.
002:014 but when **they** are alone with their evil ones,
002:014 **they** say: "We are really with you,
002:014 **they** say: "We believe,"
002:015 so **they** will wander like blind ones
002:016 and **they** have lost true direction.
002:016 These are **they** who have bartered
002:017 so **they** could not see.
002:018 **they** will not return (to the path).
002:019 the while **they** are in terror of death.
002:019 **they** press their fingers in their ears
002:020 **they** stand still.
002:020 **they** walk therein,
002:025 for **they** are given things in similitude;
002:025 and **they** have therein spouses (purified);
002:025 **they** say: "Why this is what we were fed
002:025 Every time **they** are fed with fruits
002:025 and **they** abide therein (for ever).
002:030 **They** said, "Wilt thou place therein
002:032 **They** said: "Glory to Thee,
002:034 "Bow down to Adam"; and **they** bowed down:
002:036 the state (of felicity) in which **they** had been.
002:038 nor shall **they** grieve.
002:039 **they** shall abide therein."
002:039 **they** shall be Companions of the Fire;
002:046 that **they** are to meet their Lord,
002:046 and that **they** are to return to Him.
002:049 **they** set you hard tasks and chastisement,
002:057 (but **they** rebelled); to Us **they** did no harm,
002:057 but **they** harmed their own selves.
002:059 for that **they** infringed (Our command)
002:061 This because **they** went on rejecting

THEY (continued)

002:061 **they** drew on themselves the wrath of Allah.
002:061 This because **they** rebelled
002:061 **They** were covered with humiliation and misery:
002:062 nor shall **they** grieve.
002:067 **They** said: "Makest thou a laughing-stock
002:068 **They** said: "Beseech on our behalf thy Lord
002:069 **They** said: "Beseech on our behalf thy Lord
002:070 **They** said, "Beseech on our behalf thy Lord
002:071 Then **they** offered her in sacrifice,
002:071 and **they** scarcely did it.
002:071 **They** said: "Now hast thou brought the truth."
002:074 **they** became like a rock
002:075 **they** will believe in you?
002:075 knowingly after **they** understood it.
002:076 **they** say: "Shall you tell them what Allah
002:076 but when **they** meet each other in private,
002:076 that **they** may engage you in argument
002:076 **they** say: "We believe":
002:076 Behold! when **they** meet the men of Faith,
002:077 what **they** conceal and what **they** reveal?
002:077 Know **they** not that Allah knoweth what
002:078 and **they** do nothing but conjecture.
002:079 and for the gain **they** make thereby.
002:080 And **they** say: "The fire shall not touch us
002:081 therein shall **they** abide (for ever).
002:081 **they** are Companions of the Fire,
002:082 therein shall **they** abide (for ever).
002:082 **they** are companions of the Garden,
002:085 and if **they** come to you as captives,
002:085 **they** shall be consigned to the most
002:086 nor shall **they** be helped.
002:088 **They** say, "Our hearts are the wrappings
002:088 little is it **they** believe.
002:089 **they** refused to believe in it
002:089 that which **they** (should) have recognized,
002:089 although from of old **they** had prayed
002:090 thus have **they** drawn on themselves
002:090 in that **they** deny (the revelation)
002:090 for which **they** have sold their souls.
002:091 yet **they** reject all besides,
002:091 **they** say, "We believe in what was sent
002:093 **they** said: "We hear, and we disobey":
002:095 But **they** will never seek for death,
002:096 for Allah sees well all that **they** do.
002:100 every time **they** make a Covenant,
002:101 (it had been something) **they** did not know!
002:102 And **they** knew that the buyers of (magic)
002:102 **They** learned from them the means
002:102 **They** followed what the Satans recited
002:102 And **they** learned what harmed them,
002:102 But **they** could not thus harm anyone except
002:102 which **they** did sell their souls,
002:102 if **they** but knew!
002:103 If **they** had kept their Faith
002:103 reward from Allah if **they** but knew!
002:109 wish **they** could turn you (people)
002:111 And **they** say: "None shall enter Paradise
002:112 nor shall **they** grieve.
002:113 Yet **they** (profess) to study the (same) Book.
002:116 **They** say: "Allah hath begotten a son";
002:121 **they** are the ones that believe therein:
002:125 that **they** should sanctify My House

THEY (continued)

002:133 **They** said: "We shall worship thy God
002:134 ye shall not be asked about what **they** did.
002:134 **They** shall reap the fruit of what **they** did,
002:135 **They** say: "Become Jews or Christians
002:137 but if **they** turn back,
002:137 it is **they** who are in schism;
002:137 **they** are indeed on the right path;
002:137 So if **they** believe as ye believe,
002:140 the testimony **they** have from Allah?
002:141 **They** shall reap the fruit of what **they** did,
002:141 About what **they** did!
002:142 the Qiblah to which **they** were used?"
002:144 nor is Allah unmindful of what **they** do.
002:145 **they** follow each other's Qiblah.
002:145 **they** would not follow thy Qiblah;
002:146 the truth which **they** themselves know.
002:146 know this as **they** know their own sons;
002:154 "**They** are dead."
002:154 Nay, **they** are living,
002:157 and **they** are the ones that receive guidance.
002:157 **They** are those on whom (descend)
002:162 **They** will abide therein:
002:164 and the clouds which **they** trail
002:165 **they** love them as **they** should love Allah.
002:165 Behold, **they** would see the Punishment:
002:166 **they** would see the Chastisement
002:167 as **they** have cleared themselves of us."
002:170 **they** say: "Nay! we shall follow
002:171 **they** are void of wisdom.
002:174 **they** swallow into themselves naught but Fire;
002:175 Ah! what boldness (**they** show) for the Fire!
002:175 **They** are the ones who buy Error
002:186 that **they** may walk in the right way.
002:187 **They** are your garments and ye are their garments.
002:187 that **they** may learn self-restraint.
002:189 **They** ask thee concerning the New Moons.
002:189 Say: **They** are but signs to mark fixed periods
002:191 from where **they** have turned you out;
002:191 unless **they** (first) fight you there;
002:191 but if **they** fight you, slay them.
002:192 But if **they** cease,
002:193 But if **they** cease, let there be no hostility
002:200 But **they** will have no portion in the Hereafter.
002:202 To these will be allotted what **they** have earned.
002:210 Will **they** wait until Allah comes to them
002:212 and **they** scoff at those who believe.
002:213 concerning that wherein **they** differed.
002:213 in matters wherein **they** differed;
002:215 **They** ask thee what **they** should spend (in charity).
002:217 until **they** turn you back from your faith
002:217 **They** ask thee concerning fighting
002:217 back from your faith if **they** can.
002:217 **they** will be Companions of the Fire
002:217 Nor will **they** cease fighting you until
002:218 **they** have the hope of the Mercy of Allah;
002:219 **They** ask thee concerning wine and gambling.
002:219 **They** ask thee how much **they** are to spend;
002:220 **they** are your brethren;
002:220 **They** ask thee concerning orphans.
002:221 marry (your girls) to unbelievers until **they** believe;
002:221 Do not marry unbelieving woman until **they** believe;
002:221 that **they** may receive admonition.

THEY (continued)

002:222 **They** ask thee concerning women's courses.
002:222 Say: **They** are a hurt and a pollution:
002:222 But when **they** have purified themselves,
002:222 and do not approach them until **they** are clean.
002:226 if then **they** return,
002:228 if **they** wish for reconciliation.
002:228 if **they** have faith in Allah and the Last Day.
002:229 If ye (judges) do indeed fear that **they** would be
002:229 fear that **they** would be unable to keep the limits
002:230 no blame on either of them if **they** re-unite,
002:230 provided **they** feel that **they** can keep the limits
002:231 When ye divorce women, and **they** (are about to)
002:232 and **they** fulfil the term of their ('Iddat),
002:232 if **they** mutually agree on equitable terms.
002:233 If **they** both decide on weaning,
002:234 there is no blame on you if **they** dispose of themselves
002:234 when **they** have fulfilled their term,
002:234 **they** shall wait concerning themselves four mouths
002:237 unless **they** remit it.
002:240 for what **they** do with themselves,
002:240 but if **they** leave (the residence),
002:243 though **they** were thousands (in number),
002:246 **They** said: "How could we refuse to fight
002:246 **they** turned back except a small band among them.
002:246 **they** said to a Prophet (that was) among them:
002:246 But when **they** were commanded to fight,
002:247 **They** say: "How can he exercise authority
002:249 "But **they** drank of it, except a few.
002:249 convinced that **they** must meet Allah,
002:249 **they** said: "This day we cannot cope
002:249 When **they** crossed the river,
002:250 **they** prayed: "Our Lord! Pour out constancy on us
002:250 When **they** advanced to meet Goliath
002:251 By Allah's will **they** routed them:
002:253 **they** would not have fought each other;
002:253 but **they** (chose) to wrangle,
002:254 Those who reject Faith-**they** are the wrong-doers
002:255 Nor shall **they** compass aught of his knowledge
002:257 from light **they** will lead them forth
002:257 **They** will be Companions of the fire,
002:259 **they** show no signs of age;
002:260 **they** will come to thee (flying) with speed.
002:262 on them shall be no fear, nor shall **they** grieve.
002:264 **They** are in Parable like a hard, barren rock,
002:264 do nothing with aught **they** have earned.
002:264 **They** will be able to do nothing
002:273 that **they** are free from want.
002:273 **they** beg not importunately from all and sundry.
002:274 on them shall be no fear, nor shall **they** grieve.
002:275 **they** will abide therein (for ever).
002:275 That is because **they** say: "Trade is like usury,"
002:277 nor shall **they** grieve.
002:282 refuse when **they** are called on (for evidence).
002:285 And **they** say: "We hear, and we obey:
002:285 "We make no distinction (**they** say) between
003:007 **they** are the foundation of the Book:
003:008 "Our Lord!" (**they** say), "let not our hearts
003:010 **they** are themselves but fuel for the Fire.
003:011 **they** denied Our Signs, and Allah called them
003:014 the love of things **they** covet: women and sons;
003:020 but if **they** turn back, thy duty
003:020 If **they** do, **they** are in right guidance,

THEY (continued)

003:020 So if **they** dispute with thee,
003:022 **They** are those whose works will bear no fruit
003:022 nor will **they** have anyone to help.
003:023 **They** are invited to the Book of Allah,
003:024 This because **they** say: "The Fire shall not touch us
003:025 But how (will **they** fare) when We gather them
003:032 but if **they** turn back, Allah loveth not
003:044 when **they** dispute (the point).
003:044 when **they** cast lots with pens,
003:056 nor will **they** have anyone to help.
003:063 But if **they** turn back,
003:064 If then **they** turn back,
003:069 But **they** shall lead astray (not you),
003:069 but themselves, and **they** do not perceive!
003:072 perchance **they** may (themselves) turn back;
003:075 and (well) **they** know it.
003:075 because, **they** say, "There is no way over us
003:075 but **they** tell a lie against Allah,
003:077 **they** shall have a grievous Chastisement.
003:077 **they** owe to Allah and their own solemn plighted
003:077 **they** shall have no portion in the Hereafter:
003:078 (as **they** read) so that you would think
003:078 and **they** say "That is from Allah"
003:078 it is **they** who tell a lie against Allah,
003:081 **They** said: "We agree."
003:082 **they** are perverted transgressors.
003:083 and to Him shall **they** all be brought back.
003:083 Do **they** seek for other than the Religion of Allah?
003:086 who reject faith after **they** accepted it and bore
003:088 In that will **they** dwell; nor will their punishment
003:090 But those who reject faith after **they** accepted it.
003:090 for **they** are those who have gone astray.
003:091 and **they** will find on helpers.
003:091 though **they** should offer it for ransom.
003:094 **they** are indeed unjust wrong-doers.
003:100 **they** would (indeed) render you apostates
003:104 **they** are the ones to attain felicity.
003:107 **they** will be in (the light of) Allah's Mercy;
003:111 and no help shall **they** get.
003:111 **They** will do you no harm, barring a trifling
003:111 if **they** come out to fight you,
003:111 **they** will show you their backs, and no help
003:112 this because **they** rebelled and transgressed
003:112 This because **they** rejected the Signs of Allah,
003:112 (like a tent) wherever **they** are found,
003:112 **they** draw on themselves wrath from Allah.
003:113 and **they** prostrate themselves in adoration.
003:113 **they** rehearse the Signs of Allah all night long,
003:114 and **they** (hasten in emulation) in (all)
003:114 **they** enjoin what is right, and forbid
003:114 **they** are in the ranks of the righteous.
003:114 **They** believe in Allah and the Last Day;
003:115 Of the good that **they** do, nothing
003:116 **they** will be companions of the Fire,
003:117 What **they** spend in the life of this (material) world
003:117 but **they** wrong themselves.
003:118 **They** only desire for you to suffer:
003:118 **they** will not fail to corrupt you.
003:119 when **they** meet you, **they** say, "We believe";
003:119 but when **they** are alone,
003:119 but **they** love you not,
003:119 **they** bite off the very tips of their fingers

THEY (continued)

003:120 **they** rejoice at it.
003:120 for Allah compasseth round about all that **they** do.
003:127 and **they** should then be turned back,
003:128 for **they** are indeed wrong-doers.
003:135 persisting knowingly in (the wrong) **they** have done.
003:146 if **they** met with disaster in Allah's way,
003:146 But **they** never lost heart if **they** met
003:146 nor did **they** weaken (in will) nor give in.
003:147 All that **they** said was: "Our Lord forgive us
003:149 **they** will drive you back on your heels,
003:151 for that **they** joined partners with Allah,
003:154 **They** say (to themselves): "If we had anything
003:154 **They** said: "Have we any hand in the affair?
003:154 what **they** dare not reveal to thee.
003:154 **They** hide in their minds what
003:155 because of some (evil) **they** had done.
003:156 "If **they** had stayed with us,
003:156 when **they** are travelling through the earth
003:156 **they** would not have died, or been slain."
003:157 are far better than all **they** could amass.
003:159 **they** would have broken away from about thee:
003:163 **They** are in varying grades in the sight of Allah,
003:163 and Allah sees well all that **they** do.
003:164 while, before that, **they** had been in manifest error.
003:167 But Allah hath full knowledge of all **they** conceal.
003:167 **They** said: "Had we known there would be a fight,
003:167 **They** were that day nearer to Unbelief than of Faith,
003:168 **they** would not have been slain."
003:168 (**They** are) the ones that say, (of their brethren slain),
003:168 "If only **they** had listened to us,
003:168 while **they** themselves sit (at ease):
003:169 Nay, **they** live, finding their sustenance
003:170 **They** rejoice in the bounty provided by Allah:
003:170 nor have **they** (cause to) grieve.
003:171 **They** rejoice in the Grace and the Bounty
003:173 **They** said: "For us Allah sufficeth,
003:174 for **they** followed the good pleasure of Allah:
003:174 And **they** returned with Grace and Bounty from Allah:
003:176 not the least harm will **they** do to Allah:
003:177 not the least harm will **they** do to Allah,
003:177 but **they** will have a grievous punishment.
003:178 that **they** may grow in their iniquity:
003:178 but **they** will have a shameful punishment.
003:183 **They** (also) said: "Allah took our promise
003:184 Then if **they** reject thee, so were rejected
003:187 And vile was the bargain **they** made!
003:187 but **they** threw it away behind their backs,
003:188 think not that **they** can escape the Chastisement.
003:188 who exult in what **they** have brought about,
003:188 and love to be praised for what **they** have not done,
003:198 therein are **they** to dwell (for ever),
003:199 **they** will not sell the Signs of Allah
004:002 their property (when **they** reach their age),
004:005 but if **they**, of their own good pleasure, remit
004:006 until **they** reach the age of marriage;
004:009 as **they** would have for their own if
004:009 if **they** had left a helpless family behind:
004:010 **they** will soon be enduring a blazing Fire!
004:012 but if ye leave a child, **they** get an eighth;
004:012 but if more than two, **they** share in a third;
004:012 your share is a half, if **they** leave no child;
004:012 but if **they** leave a child, ye get a fourth;

THEY (continued)

004:014 and **they** shall have a humiliating punishment.
004:015 and if **they** testify, confine them to houses
004:016 If **they** repent and amend, leave them alone;
004:019 except where **they** have been guilty of open lewdness;
004:021 and **they** have taken from you a solemn covenant?
004:025 if **they** commit indecency their punishment is
004:025 **they** should be chaste, not fornicators,
004:025 when **they** are taken in wedlock,
004:025 **they** may wed believing girls from among those
004:032 to men is allotted what **they** earn,
004:032 and to women what **they** earn:
004:034 but if **they** return to obedience, seek not
004:034 and because **they** support them from their means.
004:035 if **they** seek to set things aright, Allah
004:039 and **they** spent out of what Allah
004:039 if **they** had faith in Allah and in the Last Day,
004:042 but never will **they** hide a single fact from Allah!
004:044 **They** traffic in error, and wish
004:046 If only **they** had said: "We hear and we obey";
004:049 and **they** will not be wronged a whit.
004:050 Behold! how **they** invent a lie against Allah!
004:051 **They** believe in sorcery and Tagut and say to the
004:051 **they** are better guided in the (right) way
004:052 **They** are (men) whom Allah hath cursed:
004:053 Behold, **they** give not a farthing to
004:053 Have **they** a share in dominion or power?
004:054 Or do **they** envy mankind for what
004:056 that **they** may taste the Chastisement:
004:057 therein shall **they** have spouses purified
004:058 your trusts to those to whom **they** are due;
004:060 though **they** were ordered to reject him.
004:060 **they** believe in the revelations that have come
004:062 Then **they** come to thee, swearing by Allah: "We
004:062 How then, when **they** are seized by misfortune.
004:064 **they** would have found Allah indeed
004:064 If **they** had only, when **they** were unjust
004:065 until **they** make thee judge in all
004:065 But no, by thy Lord, **they** can have no (real) Faith.
004:066 but if **they** had done what **they** were (actually) told,
004:072 **They** say: "Allah did favour us in that we
004:073 **they** would be sure to say-as if there had never
004:077 or even more than, **they** should have feared Allah:
004:077 **they** say: "Our Lord! why hast Thou ordered
004:078 that **they** fail to understand a single fact?.
004:078 **they** say, "This is from Allah";
004:078 but if evil, **they** say, "This is from
004:081 **They** have "Obedience" on their lips; but
004:081 but when **they** leave thee, a section of them
004:082 Do **they** not ponder on the Qur'an?
004:082 **they** would surely have found therein
004:083 If **they** had only referred it to the Messenger
004:083 safety or fear, **they** divulge it.
004:089 **They** but wish that ye should reject Faith.
004:089 As **they** do, and thus be
004:089 and thus be on the same footing (as **they**):
004:089 until **they** flee in the way of Allah
004:089 But if **they** turn renegades, seize them
004:090 and **they** would have fought you: therefore
004:090 therefore if **they** withdraw from you
004:091 if **they** withdraw not from you nor give you
004:091 every time **they** are sent back to temptation,
004:091 **they** succumb thereto:

THEY (continued)

004:092 unless **they** remit it freely.
004:097 **They** reply: "Weak and oppressed
004:097 **They** say: "In what (plight) were ye?"
004:097 **They** say: "Was not the earth of Allah spacious
004:098 nor can **they** find a way (to escape).
004:102 when **they** finish their prostrations, let them
004:104 **they** are suffering similar hardships; but you
004:104 but you hope from Allah, what **they** have not.
004:108 and Allah doth compass round all that **they** do.
004:108 but **they** cannot hide from Allah, while
004:108 **They** seek to hide themselves from the people but
004:108 while He is with them when **they** plot by night.
004:113 and to thee **they** can do no harm in the least.
004:113 But (in fact) **they** will only lead
004:117 **they** call but upon Satan the persistent rebel!
004:121 **They** (his dupes) will have their dwelling in hell,
004:121 and from it **they** will find no way of escape.
004:124 be **they** male or female, and have faith,
004:124 **they** will enter Heaven,
004:127 **They** ask thy instruction concerning the Women.
004:128 if **they** arrange an amicable settlement between
004:130 But if **they** separate Allah will provide
004:139 is it honor **they** seek among them?
004:140 unless **they** turn to a different Theme:
004:141 **they** say (to them): "Did we not gain
004:141 **they** say: "Were we not with you?"
004:142 **they** stand without earnestness, to be seen
004:142 but little do **they** hold Allah in remembrance;
004:142 When **they** stand up to prayer,
004:142 The Hypocrites-**they** seek to deceive Allah but it
004:143 (**They** are) wavering between this and that belonging
004:146 if so **they** will be (numbered) with the Believers.
004:151 **They** are in truth Unbelievers; and We have
004:153 indeed **they** asked Moses for an even
004:153 but **they** were seized for their presumption,
004:153 for **they** said: "Show us Allah in public,"
004:153 Yet **they** worshipped the calf even after
004:155 that **they** slew the Messengers in defiance of right;
004:155 that **they** rejected the Signs of Allah;
004:155 that **they** said, "Our hearts are the Wrappings; n
004:155 in that **they** broke their Covenant;
004:155 (**They** have incurred divine displeasure):
004:155 and little is it **they** believe;
004:156 That **they** rejected Faith:
004:156 that **they** uttered against Mary a grave false charge;
004:157 but **they** killed him not, nor crucified him.
004:157 That **they** said (in boast), "We killed Christ Jesus
004:157 for of a surety **they** killed him not:
004:160 and that **they** hindered many from Allah's Way;
004:161 and that **they** devoured men's wealth wrongfully;
004:173 nor will **they** find, besides Allah, any to
004:176 if there are brothers and sisters, (**they** share),
004:176 **they** shall have two-thirds of the inheritance
004:176 **They** ask thee for a legal decision,
005:004 eat what **they** catch for you, but pronounce
005:004 **They** ask thee what is lawful to them (as food).
005:013 **they** change the words from their (right) places
005:014 show them what it is **they** have done.
005:014 We did take a Covenant, but **they** forgot a good
005:017 **They** disbelieved indeed those that say that Allah
005:022 (once) **they** leave, then shall we enter."
005:022 never shall we enter it until **they** leave it:

THEY (continued)

005:022 **They** said: "O Moses! in this land are a people
005:023 **they** said: "Assault them at the (proper) Gate:
005:024 never enter it as long as **they** are in it.
005:024 **They** said: O "Moses! we shall never enter it
005:026 in distraction will **they** wander through the land:
005:027 Behold! **they** each presented a sacrifice (to Allah):
005:034 before **they** fall into your power:
005:036 if **they** had everything on earth, and twice
005:037 but never will **they** get out therefrom:
005:041 **they** say, "If ye are given this, take it, but if
005:041 **They** change the words from their (right) places;
005:042 (**They** are fond of) listening to falsehood,
005:042 If **they** do come to thee, either judge
005:042 If thou decline, **they** cannot hurt thee in the least.
005:043 For **they** are not (really) people of Faith.
005:043 yet even after that, **they** would turn away.
005:043 But why do **they** come to thee for decision,
005:043 when **they** have (their own) Torah before them?
005:044 by what Allah hath revealed, **they** are Unbelievers.
005:044 and **they** were witnesses thereto:
005:045 by what Allah hath revealed, **they** are wrong-doers.
005:047 by what Allah hath revealed, **they** are indeed rebel.
005:049 but beware of them lest **they** beguile thee from
005:049 And if **they** turn away, be assured that for some
005:050 Do **they** then seek after a judgment of
005:051 **they** are but friends and protectors to each other.
005:052 which **they** secretly harboured in their hearts.
005:052 **they** regret of the thoughts which
005:052 **they** run about amongst them,
005:053 and **they** will fall into (nothing but) ruin.
005:053 That **they** were with you?"
005:053 All that **they** do will be in vain,
005:054 whom He will love as **they** will love him,
005:055 **they** bow down humbly (in worship).
005:058 **they** take it (but) as mockery and sport;
005:058 that is because **they** are a people without understanding.
005:061 When **they** come to thee, **they** say: "We believe":
005:061 **they** enter with a disbelief,
005:061 and **they** go out with the same.
005:061 But Allah knoweth fully all that **they** hide.
005:062 Evil indeed are the things that **they** do.
005:064 be **they** accursed for the (blasphemy) **they** utter.
005:064 but **they** (ever) strive to do mischief on earth.
005:064 Every time **they** kindle the fire of war, Allah
005:066 **they** would have eaten both from above them
005:066 If only **they** had stood fast by the Torah,
005:069 on them shall be no fear, nor shall **they** grieve.
005:070 some (of these) **they** called impostors,
005:070 and some **they** slay.
005:070 a Messenger with what **they** themselves desired not
005:071 But Allah sees well all that **they** do.
005:071 **They** thought there would be no trial
005:071 so **they** became blind and deaf; yet Allah
005:072 Certainly **they** disbelieve who say: "Allah is
005:073 If **they** desist not from their word (of blasphemy),
005:073 **They** disbelieve who say: Allah is one of three
005:074 Why turn **they** not to Allah, and seek
005:075 **They** had both to eat their (daily) food.
005:075 **they** are deluded away from the truth!
005:078 because **they** disobeyed and persisted in Excesses.
005:079 evil indeed were the deeds which **they** did.
005:079 the iniquities which **they** committed: evil indeed

THEY (continued)

005:079   Nor did **they** forbid one another the iniquities
005:080   and in torment will **they** abide.
005:081   never would **they** have taken them for friends
005:081   If only **they** had believed in Allah, in the
005:082   and **they** are not arrogant.
005:083   with tears, for **they** recognize the truth:
005:083   **they** pray: "Our Lord! we believe; write us
005:083   And when **they** listen to the revelation
005:086   **they** shall be Companions of Hell-fire.
005:093   **they** ate (in the past), when **they** guard themselves
005:101   **they** will be made plain to you: Allah will
005:104   **they** say: "Enough for us are the ways
005:108   that **they** may give the evidence in its true
005:108   or else **they** would fear that other oaths
005:109   **They** will say: "We have no knowledge: it is
005:111   **they** said, 'We have faith, and do thou
005:113   **They** said: "We only wish to eat thereof
005:118   **they** are Thy servants: if Thou
005:119   and **they** with Allah: that is the mighty Triumph
006:004   but **they** turned away therefrom.
006:005   the news of what **they** used to mock at.
006:005   And now **they** reject the truth
006:006   See **they** not how many of those before them
006:007   so that **they** could touch it with their hands,
006:008   **They** say: "Why is not an angel sent down to him?"
006:009   **they** have already covered with confusion.
006:010   by the thing that **they** mocked.
006:012   It is **they** who have lost their own souls,
006:020   know this as **they** know their own sons.
006:024   Behold! how **they** lie against themselves but
006:024   but the (lie) which **they** invented will leave
006:025   **they** (but) dispute with thee; the Unbelievers
006:025   in so much that when **they** come to thee,
006:025   so **they** understand it not, and deafness
006:025   if **they** saw every one of the Signs,
006:025   **they** will not believe in them; in so much
006:026   and **they** perceive it not.
006:026   Others **they** forbid it and themselves
006:026   but **they** only destroy themselves
006:026   and themselves **they** keep away;
006:027   when **they** shall be made to stand by the Fire!
006:027   **They** will say: "Would that we were sent back!
006:028   will become manifest what before **they** concealed.
006:028   for **they** are indeed liars.
006:028   But if **they** were returned,
006:028   to the things **they** were forbidden,
006:028   **they** would certainly relapse to the things
006:029   And **they** (sometimes) say: "There is nothing
006:030   when **they** shall be made to stand before
006:030   **They** will say: "Yea, by our Lord!" He will say:
006:031   Lost indeed are **they** who treat it as a falsehood
006:031   as a falsehood that **they** must meet Allah,-
006:031   for **they** bear their burdens on their backs;
006:031   and **they** say: "Ah! woe unto us that we neglected;
006:031   and evil indeed are the burdens that **they** bear!
006:033   it is not thee **they** reject: it is the
006:034   with patience and constancy **they** bore their
006:036   then will **they** be turned unto Him.
006:037   **They** say: "Why is not a Sign sent down
006:038   and **they** (all) shall be gathered to
006:042   that **they** call (Allah) in humility.
006:043   why then did **they** not call (Allah) in humility?

THEY (continued)

006:044   But when **they** forget the warning
006:044   when lo! **they** were plunged in despair!
006:044   the warning **they** had received, We opened
006:046   by various (symbols): Yet **they** turn aside.
006:048   upon them shall be no fear, nor shall **they** grieve.
006:049   for that **they** ceased not from transgressing.
006:051   that **they** will be brought (to judgment)
006:051   except from Him **they** will have no protector
006:051   that **they** may guard (against evil).
006:052   and in naught are **they** accountable for thee, that
006:053   that **they** should say: "Is it these
006:061   and **they** never fail in their duty.
006:062   Then are they returned unto Allah, their True
006:065   that **they** may understand.
006:068   **they** turn to a different theme.
006:069   that **they** may (learn to) fear Allah.
006:070   for **they** persisted in rejecting Allah.
006:070   **they** will have for drink (only) boiling water,
006:082   for **they** are on (right) guidance."
006:088   If **they** were to join other gods with Him,
006:088   all that **they** did would be vain for them.
006:090   Follow the guidance **they** received; say: "No
006:091   do **they** make when **they** say: "Nothing
006:092   and **they** are constant in guarding their Prayers.
006:099   when **they** begin to bear fruit, feast your
006:100   and **they** falsely, having no knowledge, attribute
006:100   (for He is) above what **they** attribute to Him!
006:100   Yet **they** make the Jinns
006:105   the Signs by various (ways) that **they** may say,
006:107   **they** would not have taken false gods:
006:108   In the end will **they** return to their Lord and He
006:108   **they** call upon besides Allah,
006:108   the truth of all that **they** did.
006:108   lest **they** out of spite revile Allah
006:109   **they** will not believe."?
006:109   by it **they** would believe.
006:109   **They** swear their strongest oaths by Allah, that
006:110   even as **they** refused to believe in this
006:111   **they** are not the ones to believe, unless it
006:112   **they** would not have done it: so leave
006:112   so leave them and **they** forge.
006:113   and let them earn from it what **they** may.
006:114   **They** know full well, to whom
006:116   **they** do nothing but lie.
006:116   **they** will lead thee away from the Way of Allah.
006:116   **They** follow nothing but conjecture:
006:123   but **they** only plot against their own souls,
006:123   and **they** perceive it not.
006:124   a Sign (from Allah), **they** say:" We shall
006:125   as if **they** had to climb up to the skies: thus
006:127   because **they** practiced (righteousness).
006:129   turn to each other, because of what **they** earn.
006:130   **they** bear witness that **they** rejected Faith.
006:130   **They** will say: "We bear witness
006:132   not unmindful of anything that **they** do.
006:136   **they** say, according to their fancies: "This
006:136   **they** assigned Him a share:
006:137   **they** would not have done so: but leave
006:137   but leave alone them and what **they** forged.
006:138   soon will He requite them for what **they** forged.
006:138   except those whom-so **they** say-We wish; further,
006:138   And **they** say that such and such

THEY (continued)

006:139 **They** say: "What is in the wombs
006:140 **They** have indeed gone astray and heeded
006:147 If **they** accuse thee of falsehood,
006:148 until **they** tasted of Our wrath.
006:150 for **they** hold others as equal
006:150 If **they** bring such witnesses, be not
006:153 **they** will scatter you about from His (great) path:
006:154 that **they** might believe in the
006:156 that **they** learned by assiduous study;"
006:157 its guidance better than **they**."
006:158 Are **they** waiting to see if the
006:159 the truth of all that **they** did.
007:004 or while **they** slept for their afternoon rest.
007:005 no cry did **they** utter but this: "Indeed
007:009 for that **they** wrongfully treated Our Signs.
007:011 and **they** prostrated, not so Iblis; he refused
007:014 respite till the day **they** are raised up."
007:022 and **they** began to sew together the leaves
007:022 when **they** tasted of the tree, their shameful
007:023 **They** said: "Our Lord! we have wronged
007:026 that **they** may receive admonition!
007:028 When **they** commit an indecency,
007:028 **they** say: "We found our fathers doing so";
007:030 In that **they** took the Satans in
007:030 and think that **they** receive guidance.
007:032 Say: **they** are, in the life of this world, for
007:034 not an hour can **they** cause delay, nor (an hour)
007:034 nor (an hour) can **they** advance (it in anticipation).
007:035 on them shall be no fear, nor shall **they** grieve.
007:036 **they** are Companions of the Fire, to dwell
007:037 **They** will reply, "**They** have left us in the lurch,"
007:037 that **they** had rejected Allah.
007:037 and **they** will bear witness against themselves, that
007:037 **they** say: "Where are the things that ye
007:038 until **they** follow each other, all into the Fire.
007:040 nor will **they** enter the Garden, until the
007:042 **they** will be Companions of the Garden, therein
007:043 and **they** shall say: "Praise be to Allah, Who
007:043 And **they** shall hear the cry: "Behold!
007:044 **They** shall say, "Yes"; but a Crier
007:045 **they** were those who denied the Hereafter."
007:046 **they** will call out to the Companions of the Garden,
007:046 "Peace be upon you": **they** have not entered it,
007:046 but **they** still hoped. To (enter it).
007:047 **they** will say: "Our Lord! send us
007:048 **they** will know from their marks,
007:050 **They** will say: "Both these things hath Allah
007:051 and as **they** were wont to reject Our Signs.
007:051 as **they** forgot the meeting of this
007:053 Are **they** waiting for its fulfillment?
007:053 and the things **they** forged will leave
007:053 In fact **they** will have lost their souls, and the
007:057 when **they** have carried the heavy-laden clouds.
007:064 **they** were indeed a blind people!
007:064 But **they** rejected him, and We
007:070 **They** said: "Comest thou to us, that we
007:075 **They** said: "We do indeed believe in the
007:077 Then **they** ham-strung the she-camel, and
007:078 and **they** lay prostrate in their homes
007:082 **they** said, "Drive them out of your city: these are
007:088 or else ye (thou and **they**) shall have
007:091 and **they** lay prostrate in their

THEY (continued)

007:092 became as if **they** had never been in the homes
007:092 it was **they** who were ruined!
007:092 in the homes where **they** had flourished:
007:094 in order that **they** might call in humility.
007:095 until **they** grew and multiplied, and began
007:095 while **they** realized not (their peril).
007:096 but **they** rejected (the truth), and We
007:097 Our wrath by night while **they** were asleep?
007:098 Or else did **they** feel secure against its
007:099 Did **they** then fell secure against Allah's
007:100 so that **they** could not hear?
007:101 but **they** would not believe what
007:101 what **they** had rejected before.
007:103 But **they** wrongfully rejected them: so see
007:111 **They** said: "Keep him and his brother in suspense
007:113 **they** said, "Of course we shall have a (suitable)
007:115 **They** said: "O Moses! wilt thou throw (first), or
007:116 and **they** showed a great (feat of) magic.
007:116 So when **they** threw, **they** bewitched the eyes
007:117 all the falsehoods which **they** fake!
007:118 And all that **they** did was made of no effect.
007:119 So **they** were vanquished there and then, and
007:125 **They** said: "For us, we are but sent back
007:126 in the Signs of our Lord when **they** reached us!
007:129 **They** said: "We have had (nothing but) trouble,
007:130 that **they** might receive admonition.
007:131 **they** ascribed it to evil omens connected with
007:131 **they** said, "This is due to us"; when gripped
007:132 **They** said (to Moses): "Whatever be
007:133 but **they** were steeped in arrogance, a people
007:134 **they** said: "O Moses! on our behalf call on
007:135 which **they** had to fulfill,-Behold!
007:135 Behold! **they** broke their word!
007:136 because **they** rejected Our Signs, and failed
007:137 because **they** had patience and constancy, and We
007:138 **They** came upon a people devoted entirely
007:138 **They** said: "O Moses! fashion for us a god
007:138 a god like unto the gods **they** have."
007:138 devoted entirely to some idols **they** had.
007:139 and vain is the (worship) which **they** practice."
007:139 the cult **they** are in is bound to destruction, and
007:145 homes of the wicked, (how **they** lie desolate)."
007:146 even if **they** see all the Signs,
007:146 but if **they** see the way of error, that is
007:146 **they** will not believe in them; and if
007:146 **they** will not adopt it as the Way; but if
007:146 and if **they** see the way of right conduct,
007:146 For **they** have rejected Our Signs, and failed
007:146 that is the Way **they** will adopt.
007:147 rewarded except as **they** have wrought?
007:147 can **they** expect to be rewarded except
007:148 having lowing sound did **they** not see that it could
007:149 When **they** repented, and saw that
007:149 and saw that **they** had erred,
007:149 **they** said: "If our Lord have not mercy upon us
007:155 when **they** were seized with violent quaking, he
007:157 whom **they** find mentioned in their own (Scriptures),-
007:157 it is **they** who will prosper."
007:160 (but **they** rebelled): to Us **they** did no harm, but
007:160 but **they** harmed their own souls.
007:162 For that **they** repeatedly transgressed.
007:163 for **they** were given to transgression.

THEY (continued)

007:163 **they** came not: thus did We make a trial
007:163 Behold! **they** transgressed in the matter
007:163 but on the day **they** had no Sabbath,
007:164 and perchance **they** may fear Him."
007:165 When **they** disregarded the warnings that had
007:165 because **they** were given to transgression.
007:166 **they** transgressed (all) prohibition, We said
007:168 in order that **they** might turn (to Us).
007:169 **they** inherited the Book,
007:169 but **they** chose (for themselves) the vanities
007:169 And **they** study what is in the Book.
007:169 came their way, **they** would (again) seize them.
007:169 that **they** would not ascribe to Allah
007:171 and **they** thought it was going to fall
007:172 **They** said: "Yea! we do testify! (This), lest ye
007:174 and perchance **they** may turn (Unto Us).
007:176 so relate the story; perchance **they** may reflect.
007:179 **They** have hearts wherewith **they** understand not,
007:179 **They** are like cattle,-
007:179 eyes wherewith **they** see not,
007:179 and ears wherewith **they** hear not.
007:179 for **they** are heedless (of warning).
007:180 for what **they** do, **they** will soon be requited.
007:182 to ruin while **they** know not.
007:184 Do **they** not reflect?
007:185 Do **they** see nothing in the kingdom of the
007:185 (Do **they** not see) that it may well be
007:185 In what message after this will **they** then believe?
007:187 **They** ask thee about the (final) Hour-when will
007:187 **They** ask thee as if thou wert eager
007:189 When **they** are united, she bears
007:189 **they** both pray to Allah their Lord (saying):
007:190 **they** ascribe to others a share in the gift
007:190 the partners **they** ascribe to Him.
007:190 in the gift **they** have received:
007:191 Do **they** indeed ascribe to Him as partners
007:192 No aid can **they** give them, nor can
007:192 nor can **they** aid themselves!
007:193 **they** will not obey: for you
007:195 Have **they** feet to walk with?
007:198 If thou call them to guidance, **they** hear not.
007:198 wilt see them looking at thee, but **they** see not.
007:201 when lo! **they** see (aright)!
007:203 **they** say: "Why hast thou not got it together?"
007:206 **they** glorify Him and prostrate before Him.
008:001 **They** ask thee concerning (things taken as)
008:002 and when **they** hear His revelations rehearsed,
008:004 **they** have grades of dignity with their Lord,
008:006 to death and **they** saw it.
008:006 as if **they** were being driven to death
008:013 This because **they** contended against Allah
008:019 even if **they** were multiplied: for verily
008:023 **they** would but have turned back
008:030 **They** plot and plan, and Allah too plans, but the
008:031 **they** say: "We have heard this (before): if we
008:032 Remember how **they** said: "O Allah! if this
008:033 whilst **they** could ask for pardon.
008:034 the Sacred Mosque-and **they** are not its guardians?
008:034 But what plea have **they** that Allah
008:034 when **they** keep out (men) from the Sacred Mosque-
008:036 at length **they** will be overcome:
008:036 and so will **they** continue to spend; but in

THEY (continued)

008:036 but in the end **they** will have (only)
008:037 **They** will be the ones to have lost.
008:038 but if **they** persist, the punishment
008:038 if (now) **they** desist (from Unbelief), their
008:039 verily Allah doth see all that **they** do.
008:039 in its entirety but if **they** cease, verily Allah
008:040 If **they** refuse, be sure
008:042 the valley, and **they** on the farther side, and the
008:047 for Allah compasseth all that **they** do.
008:050 (how) **they** smite their faces and their backs
008:052 **they** rejected the Signs of Allah, and
008:053 on a people until **they** change what is in their
008:054 **they** treated as false the Signs of their Lord
008:054 for **they** were all oppressors and wrong-doers.
008:055 **they** will not believe.
008:056 **They** are those with whom thou didst
008:056 and **they** have not the fear (of Allah).
008:056 but **they** break their covenant every time,
008:057 those who follow them, that **they** may remember.
008:059 **they** will never frustrate (them).
008:059 that **they** have escaped,
008:062 Should **they** intend to deceive thee,- verily
008:065 **they** will vanquish two hundred: if a hundred.
008:065 if a hundred. **They** will vanquish a thousand
008:066 and if a thousand, **they** will vanquish two thousand,
008:066 **they** will vanquish two hundred,
008:071 But if **they** have treacherous designs against thee,
008:071 **they** have already been in treason against Allah,
008:072 to them until **they** emigrate; but if
008:072 but if **they** seek your aid in religion, it is
008:075 in your company,-**they** are of you.
009:005 but if **they** repent, and establish regular prayers.
009:006 be secure, that is because **they** are men
009:008 **they** respect not in you the ties either of kinship
009:008 seeing that if **they** get an advantage over you,
009:008 **they** please you, but their hearts are averse
009:009 **they** sold for a miserable price, and (many)
009:009 and (many) have **they** hindered from His Way:
009:010 It is **they** who have transgressed all bounds.
009:010 In a Believer **they** respect not the ties
009:011 **they** are your brethren in Faith: (thus) do
009:011 But (even so), if **they** repent, establish regular
009:012 But if **they** violate their oaths
009:012 that thus **they** may be restrained.
009:017 in Fire shall **they** dwell.
009:017 of Allah while **they** witness against their own
009:018 It is **they** who are expected to be on true guidance.
009:019 **They** are not equal in the sight of Allah: and
009:020 **They** are the people who will achieve (salvation).
009:022 **They** will dwell therein for ever.
009:023 your brothers if **they** love infidelity above Faith:
009:023 if any of you do so, **they** do wrong.
009:025 but **they** availed you naught:
009:029 until **they** pay Jizya with willing submission,
009:030 how **they** are deluded away from the Truth!
009:030 **they** but imitate what the Unbelievers of old
009:031 from having the partners **they** associate (with Him).
009:031 **They** take their priests and their anchorites
009:031 yet **they** were commanded to worship but One God:
009:031 And (**they** take as their Lord) Christ the son of Mary;
009:032 Fain would **they** extinguish Allah's light

THEY (continued)

009:036 as **they** fight you all together.
009:037 for **they** make it lawful one year, and forbidden
009:040 the two **they** were in the Cave, and he
009:042 **they** would destroy their own souls;
009:042 for Allah doth know that **they** are lying.
009:042 **They** would indeed swear by Allah, "If we only
009:045 so that **they** are tossed in their doubt to and fro.
009:046 If **they** had intended to come out,
009:046 **they** would certainly have made some preparation
009:046 so He made them lag behind and **they** were told,
009:047 If **they** had come out with you,
009:047 **they** would not have added to your (strength)
009:048 Indeed **they** had plotted sedition before, and upset
009:049 Have **they** not fallen into trial already?
009:050 and **they** turn away rejoicing.
009:050 **they** say, "We took indeed our precautions
009:054 that **they** come not to prayer save lazily and that
009:054 **they** reject Allah and His Messenger;
009:054 and that **they** offer contributions unwillingly.
009:056 **They** swear by Allah that **they** are indeed of you;
009:056 but **they** are not of you: yet **they** are afraid (of you).
009:057 **they** would turn straightway thereto with
009:057 If **they** could find a place to flee to, or caves,
009:058 behold! **they** are indignant!
009:058 If **they** are given part thereof, **they** are pleased,
009:059 If only **they** had been content with what Allah
009:062 To you **they** swear by Allah.
009:062 if **they** are Believers.
009:062 but it is more fitting that **they** should please
009:063 Know **they** not that for those who oppose
009:063 Wherein **they** shall dwell.
009:065 **they** declare (with emphasis): "We were only
009:066 for that **they** are sinners.
009:067 **they** enjoin evil, and forbid what is just,
009:067 **They** have forgotten Allah; so He
009:068 therein shall **they** dwell:
009:069 **they** were mightier than you in power and more
009:069 **They** had their enjoyment of their portion: and ye
009:069 in idle talk as **they** did.
009:069 **They**!-their works are fruitless in this world
009:069 and **they** are the losers.
009:070 Who wrongs them, but **they** wrong their own souls.
009:071 **they** observe regular prayers,
009:071 **they** enjoin what is just, and forbid what is evil:
009:074 If **they** repent, it will be best for them: but if
009:074 **They** swear by Allah that **they** said nothing (evil),
009:074 nothing (evil), but indeed **they** uttered blasphemy,
009:074 uttered blasphemy, and **they** uttered it after
009:074 but if **they** turn back (to their evil ways), Allah
009:074 and **they** meditated a plot which
009:074 and in the Hereafter: **they** shall have none on
009:074 which **they** were enable to carry out: this revenge
009:075 **they** would give (largely) in charity, and be
009:076 **they** became covetous, and turned
009:077 because **they** broke their Covenant
009:077 (to last) till the day whereon **they** shall meet Him:
009:077 and because **they** lied (again and again).
009:078 Know **they** not that Allah doth know their secret
009:079 and **they** shall have a grievous chastisement.
009:080 because **they** have rejected Allah
009:081 **they** hated to strive and fight, with their
009:081 **they** said, "Go not forth in the heat."

THEY (continued)

009:081 If only **they** could understand!
009:082 the (evil) that **they** do.
009:082 much will **they** weep: a recompense for the (evil)
009:083 and **they** ask thy permission to come out (with thee),
009:084 for **they** rejected Allah and His Messenger, and
009:085 while **they** are unbelievers.
009:087 **They** prefer to be with (the women), who remain
009:087 their hearts are sealed and so **they** understand not.
009:088 and it is **they** who will prosper.
009:091 (on the Cause), if **they** are sincere (in duty)
009:092 with tears of grief that **they** had no resources
009:092 **they** turned back, their eyes streaming with tears
009:093 so **they** know not.
009:093 **They** prefer to stay with the (women)
009:093 such as claim exemption while **they** are rich.
009:094 **They** will present their excuses to you when ye
009:095 So leave them alone: for **they** are an abomination,
009:095 recompense for the (evil) that **they** did.
009:095 **They** will swear to you by Allah, when ye
009:096 **They** will swear unto you, that ye
009:099 Aye, indeed **they** bring them nearer (to Him): soon
009:100 as are **they** with him: for them hath He prepared
009:101 **they** are obstinate in hypocrisy: thou knowest
009:101 and in addition shall **they** be sent
009:102 **they** have mixed an act that was good with another
009:104 Know **they** not that Allah doth accept repentance
009:107 **They** will indeed swear that their intention
009:107 that **they** are certainly liars.
009:111 **they** fight in His Cause, and slay
009:113 for Pagans, even though **they** be of kin, after it
009:113 that **they** are companions of the Fire.
009:113 that **they** should pray for forgiveness for Pagans,
009:115 makes clear to them as to what **they** should avoid,
009:118 (**they** felt guilty) to such a degree that the earth
009:118 and **they** perceived that there is no fleeing
009:118 that **they** might repent: for Allah
009:120 because nothing could **they** suffer or do, but was
009:120 whether **they** suffered thirst, or fatigue,
009:121 Nor could **they** spend anything (for the Cause),
009:122 that thus **they** (may learn) to guard
009:122 and admonish the people when **they** return to them,-
009:124 is increased, and **they** do rejoice.
009:125 and **they** will die in a state of Unbelief.
009:126 See **they** not that **they** are tried
009:126 Yet **they** turn not in repentance,
009:126 and **they** take no heed.
009:127 (saying), "Doth anyone see you?" then **they** turn away:
009:127 for **they** are a people that understand not.
009:127 **they** look at each other, (saying), "Doth anyone
009:129 But if **they** turn away, Say: "Allah sufficeth me:
010:002 the good actions **they** have advanced (but) say
010:002 that **they** have before their Lord the good
010:004 because **they** did reject Him.
010:008 because of the (evil) **they** earned.
010:011 as **they** would fain hasten on the good,-
010:011 the ill (**they** have earned)
010:013 with Clear Signs, but **they** would not believe!
010:013 when **they** did wrong: their Messengers
010:018 the partners **they** ascribe (to Him)!"
010:018 **They** serve, besides Allah, what can
010:018 and **they** say: "These are our intercessors with
010:020 **They** say: "Why is not a Sign sent down

THEY (continued)

010:021 behold! **they** take to plotting against Our Signs!
010:022 **they** pray unto Allah, sincerely
010:022 and **they** think **they** are being overwhelmed:
010:022 and **they** rejoice thereat; then comes
010:022 **they** sail with them with a favourable wind, and
010:023 behold! **they** transgress insolently through the
010:024 it belongs think **they** have all powers of
010:026 **They** are Companions of the Garden;
010:026 **they** will abide therein (for aye)!
010:027 **they** are Inhabitants of the Fire:
010:027 **they** will abide therein (for aye)!
010:027 no defender will **they** have from (the wrath of)
010:030 **they** will be brought back to Allah their rightful
010:031 **They** will soon say: "Allah".
010:033 verily **they** will not believe.
010:036 Verily Allah is well aware of all that **they** do.
010:038 Or do **they** say, "He forged it"?
010:039 that whose knowledge **they** cannot compass,
010:039 Nay, **they** charge with falsehood that whose
010:041 If **they** charge thee with falsehood, say: "My work
010:042 even though **they** are without understanding.
010:043 the blind,-even though **they** will not see?
010:045 **they** will recognize each other: assuredly those
010:045 (it will be) as if **they** had tarried but and hour of a day:
010:046 to all that **they** do.
010:047 and **they** will not be wronged.
010:048 **They** say: "When will this promise come to pass-
010:049 not an hour can **they** cause delay, nor (an hour)
010:049 can **they** advance (it in anticipation).
010:053 **They** seek to be informed by thee: "Is that true?"
010:054 **they** would declare (their) repentance when
010:054 when **they** see the Chastisement: but the
010:058 the (wealth) **they** hoard.
010:062 there is no fear, nor shall **they** grieve;
010:066 and **they** do nothing but lie.
010:066 What do **they** follow who worship as His "partners"
010:066 **They** follow nothing but conjecture,
010:068 **They** say, "Allah hath begotten a son!"-Glory be
010:073 **They** rejected him, but We delivered him, and those
010:074 **they** would not believe what **they** had already rejected
010:074 **they** brought them Clear Signs,
010:075 But **they** were arrogant: **they** were a wicked people.
010:076 **they** said: "This is indeed evident sorcery!"
010:078 **They** said: "Hast thou come to us to turn us
010:081 When **they** had had their throw,
010:083 and his chiefs, lest **they** should persecute them:
010:085 **They** said: "In Allah do we put our trust.
010:088 until **they** see the grievous Chastisement."
010:088 so **they** will not believe until
010:088 and so, our Lord **they** mislead (men) from Thy Path.
010:093 that **they** fell into schisms.
010:097 until **they** see (for themselves)
010:098 When **they** believed, We removed from them
010:099 **they** would all have believed,-all who
010:102 Do **they** then expect (anything) but
011:005 and what **they** reveal: for He knoweth well the
011:005 that **they** may lie hid from Him!
011:005 Ah! even when **they** cover themselves
011:005 He knoweth what **they** conceal, and what
011:005 Behold! **they** fold up their hearts,
011:008 which **they** used to mock at!
011:008 **they** are sure to say, "What keeps it back?"

THEY (continued)

011:008 from them, and **they** will be completely encircled
011:012 lest **they** say, "Why is not a treasure sent down
011:013 Or **they** may say, "He forged it." Say, "Bring ye
011:014 "If then **they** (your false gods) answer not
011:016 **They** are those for whom there is nothing
011:016 vain are the designs **they** frame therein,
011:016 and of no effect are the deeds that **they** do!
011:017 **They** believe therein; but those of the Sects
011:017 Can **they** be (like) those who accept a Clear
011:018 **They** will be brought before their Lord, and the
011:019 "These were **they** who denied the Hereafter!"
011:020 **They** will not escape in earth, nor have
011:020 **They** could not hear, nor could **they** see!
011:020 nor have **they** protectors besides Allah!
011:021 **They** are the ones who have lost their own souls:
011:021 **they** forged have left them in the lurch!
011:023 **they** will be Companions of the Garden, to dwell
011:024 Are **they** equal when compared?
011:029 for verily **they** are to meet their Lord, and ye
011:032 **They** said: "O Noah! thou hast disputed with us,
011:035 Or do **they** say, "He has forged it?"
011:037 for **they** are about to be overwhelmed
011:038 **they** threw ridicule on him. He said: "If ye
011:053 **They** said: "O Hud! no Clear (Sign) hast thou
011:059 **they** rejected the Signs of their Lord and
011:060 And **they** were pursued by a Curse in this Life,-
011:062 **They** said: "O Salih! thou hast been of us!-
011:065 But **they** did ham-string her.
011:067 the wrong-doers, and **they** lay prostrate in
011:068 As if **they** had never dwelt and flourished there.
011:069 **They** said, "Peace!" He answered, "Peace!"
011:070 **They** said: "Fear not: we have been sent
011:073 **They** said: "Dost thou wonder at Allah's decree?
011:078 and **they** had been long in the habit
011:078 my daughters: **they** are purer for you
011:079 **They** said: "Well dost thou know we have no need
011:081 By no means shall **they** reach thee!
011:083 Marked from thy Lord; nor are **they** ever far
011:087 **They** said: "Oh Shu'aib! Does thy prayer
011:091 **They** said: "O Shu'aib! much of what thou sayest
011:094 and **they** lay prostrate in their homes
011:095 As if **they** had never dwelt and flourished there!
011:097 but **they** followed the command of Pharaoh, and the
011:098 be the place to which **they** are led!
011:099 And **they** are followed by a curse in this (life)
011:101 whom **they** invoked, profited them no whit when there
011:101 **they** wronged their own souls:
011:101 nor did **they** add aught (to their lot) but perdition!
011:107 **They** will dwell therein so long as the heavens
011:108 in the Garden: **they** will dwell therein so long as
011:109 **They** worship nothing but what their fathers worshipped
011:110 but **they** are in suspicious doubt concerning it.
011:111 For He knoweth well all that **they** do.
011:118 but **they** will not cease to differ,
012:005 lest **they** concoct a plot against thee: for Satan
012:008 **They** said: "Truly Joseph and his brother are loved
012:011 **They** said: "O our father! why dost
012:014 **They** said: "If the wolf were to devour him
012:015 and **they** all agreed to throw him down to the
012:015 So **they** did take him away,
012:015 this affair while **they** perceive not."
012:016 Then **they** came to their father in the

THEY (continued)

012:017 **They** said: "Oh our father! we went
012:018 **They** stained his shirt with false blood.
012:019 **they** sent their water-carrier (for water), and he
012:019 But Allah knoweth well all that **they** do!
012:019 So **they** concealed him as a treasure!
012:020 in such low estimation did **they** hold him!
012:025 So **they** both raced each other to the door, and she
012:025 **they** both found her lord near the door.
012:031 When **they** saw him, **they** did extol him,
012:031 **they** said, "Allah preserve us!
012:033 to my liking than that to which **they** invite me:
012:035 **they** had seen the Signs, (that it was best)
012:036 "Tell us" (**they** said) "the truth and meaning thereof:
012:044 **They** said: "A confused medley of dreams: and we
012:046 and that **they** may know."
012:049 and in which **they** will press (wine and oil).
012:058 knew them, but **they** knew him not.
012:058 **they** entered his presence, and he knew them,
012:061 **They** said: "We shall try to win him from
012:062 their stock-in-trade (with which **they** had bartered)
012:062 so **they** should know it only when
012:062 in order that **they** might come back.
012:062 when **they** return to their people, in order
012:063 **they** said: "O our father! No more measure
012:063 Now when **they** returned to their father,
012:065 **they** found their stock-in-trade had been
012:065 **They** said: "O our father! What (more)
012:065 Then when **they** opened their baggage,
012:066 **they** had sworn their solemn oath,
012:068 And when **they** entered in the manner
012:069 Now when **they** came into Joseph's presence,
012:071 **They** said, turning towards them: "What is it
012:072 **They** said: "We miss the great beaker of the king;
012:075 **They** said: "The penalty should be that he in whose
012:077 **They** said: "If he steals, there was a brother
012:078 **They** said: "O exalted one! Behold! he has
012:080 **they** held a conference in private.
012:080 Now when **they** saw no hope of his (yielding),
012:085 **They** said: "By Allah! (never) wilt thou cease
012:088 Then, when **they** came (back) into (Joseph's)
012:088 into (Joseph's) presence **they** said: "O exalted
012:090 **They** said: "Art thou indeed, Joseph?"
012:091 **They** said: "By Allah! indeed has Allah preferred
012:095 **They** said: "By Allah! truly thou art in thine
012:097 **They** said: "O our father! ask for
012:099 Then when **they** entered the presence of Joseph,
012:100 the throne and **they** fell down in prostration,
012:102 when **they** concerted their plans together in the
012:105 Yet **they** turn (their faces) away from them!
012:105 and the earth do **they** pass by?
012:107 while **they** perceive not?
012:107 Do **they** then feel secure from the coming against
012:109 Do **they** not travel through the earth, and see
012:110 think that **they** were treated as liars,
013:005 **they** will be Companions of the Fire, to dwell
013:005 **They** are those who deny their Lord!
013:005 **They** are those round whose necks will be
013:006 **They** ask thee to hasten on the evil
013:011 no turning it back, nor will **they** find, besides
013:011 until **they** change what is in themselves but when
013:011 **they** guard him by command of Allah.
013:013 the while **they** are disputing about Allah,

THEY (continued)

013:014 if **they** were to stretch forth their hands
013:014 any others that **they** call upon besides Him
013:016 Or do the assign to Allah partners who have created
013:017 (ore) which **they** heat in the fire, to make
013:018 even if **they** had all that is in the heavens
013:018 would **they** offer it for ransom.
013:023 **they** shall enter there, as well as the righteous
013:030 yet do **they** reject (Him), the Most Gracious!
013:033 **they** ascribe partners to Allah. Say: "But
013:033 but **they** are kept back (thereby) from the Path.
013:034 and defender have **they** none against Allah.
013:041 See **they** not that We gradually reduce the land
014:003 **they** are astray by a long distance.
014:006 the people of Pharaoh: **they** set you hard task
014:009 Clear (Signs); but **they** put their hands up to
014:010 **They** said: "Ah! ye are no more then human,
014:014 when **they** shall stand before My tribunal,-such
014:015 But **they** sought victory and decision
014:018 no power have **they** over aught that **they** have earned:
014:021 **They** will reply, "If we had received the
014:021 **They** will all be marshalled before Allah together:
014:025 in order that **they** may receive admonition.
014:029 **They** will burn therein,-an evil
014:030 And **they** set up (idols) as equal to Allah,
014:031 that **they** may establish regular prayers, and spend
014:032 subject to you, that **they** may sail through the
014:036 "O my Lord! **they** have indeed led astray
014:037 O our Lord! that **they** may establish regular
014:037 so that **they** may give thanks.
014:043 **They** running forward with necks outstretched,
014:046 Mighty indeed were the plots which **they** made,
014:046 even though **they** were such as to shake the hills!
014:052 that **they** may take warning therefrom, and may
015:002 wish that **they** had been Muslims.
015:003 soon for **they** will soon know.
015:006 **They** say: "O thou to whom the Message
015:008 if **they** came (to the ungodly),
015:008 behold! no respite would **they** have!
015:011 to them but **they** mocked him.
015:013 That **they** not believe in the Message,
015:014 and **they** were to continue (all day) ascending therein,
015:015 **They** would only say: "Our eyes have been
015:047 (**they** will be) brothers (joyfully) facing
015:048 touch them, nor shall **they** (ever) be asked
015:052 When **they** entered his presence and said,
015:053 **They** said: "Fear not! we give thee glad tidings
015:055 **They** said: "We give thee glad tidings in truth;
015:058 **They** said: "We have been sent to a people
015:063 to thee to accomplish that of which **they** doubt.
015:063 **They** said: "Yea, we have come to thee
015:070 **They** said: "Did we not forbid thee (to speak)
015:072 **they** wander in distraction, to and fro.
015:079 **They** were both on an open highway, plain to see.
015:081 but **they** persisted in turning away from them.
015:082 Out of the mountains did **they** hew (their) edifices,
015:084 **they** did (with such art and care)!
015:091 Qur'an into shreds (as **they** please).
015:096 another god: but soon will **they** come to know.
015:097 is distressed at what **they** say.
016:001 the partners **they** ascribe unto Him!
016:003 above having the partners **they** ascribe to Him!
016:007 And **they** carry your heavy loads to lands that ye

THEY (continued)

016:020 Those whom **they** invoke besides Allah create nothing
016:021 nor do thy know when **they** will be raised up.
016:021 (**They** are things) dead, lifeless:
016:022 refuse to know and **they** are arrogant.
016:023 **they** conceal, and what **they** reveal: Verily He
016:024 **they** say, "Tales of the ancients!"
016:025 the burdens **they** will bear!
016:025 whom **they** misled.
016:025 That **they** may bear, on the Day of Judgment,
016:026 from directions **they** did not perceive.
016:028 **they** offer submission (with the pretense), "We did
016:030 **they** say, "All that is good."
016:031 **they** will have therein all that they wish:
016:031 Gardens of Eternity which **they** will enter:
016:031 therein all that **they** wish: thus doth
016:033 nay, **they** wronged their own souls.
016:034 at which **they** had scoffed hemmed them in.
016:038 **They** swear their strongest oaths by Allah,
016:039 of that wherein **they** differ, and that
016:039 may realize that **they** were liars.
016:039 (**They** must be raised up), in order that He may
016:041 if **they** only realize (this)!
016:042 (**They** are) those who persevere in patience,
016:044 and that **they** may give thought.
016:045 seize them from directions **they** little perceive?
016:048 Do **they** not look at Allah's creation.
016:050 and **they** do all that **they** are commanded.
016:050 **They** all fear their Lord, high above
016:057 And **they** assign daughters for Allah!
016:057 Glory be to Him!-and for themselves what **they** desire!
016:059 Ah! what an evil (choice) **they** decide on!
016:061 **they** would not be able to delay (the punishment)
016:061 just as **they** would not be able to anticipate
016:062 is the Fire, and **they** will be the first to be
016:062 **They** attribute to Allah what **they** hate (for themselves),
016:063 so but **they** shall have a most grievous
016:064 **they** differ, and that it should be a guide
016:070 so that **they** know nothing after having
016:071 Will **they** then deny the favour of Allah?
016:072 will **they** then believe in vain things, and be
016:079 Do **they** not look at the birds, held poised
016:082 But if **they** turn away, thy duty
016:083 then **they** deny them; and most
016:083 **They** recognize the favours of Allah;
016:084 nor will **they** be allowed to make amends.
016:085 nor will **they** then receive respite.
016:086 But **they** will throw back their word at them
016:086 **they** will say: "Our Lord! these are our `partners',
016:087 That day shall **they** (openly) show (their)
016:088 for that **they** used to spread mischief.
016:101 He reveals (in stages),-**they** say, "Thou art
016:103 The tongue of him **they** wickedly point to
016:103 We know indeed that **they** say, "It is a man that
016:105 it is **they** who lie!
016:107 This because **they** love the life of this world
016:108 and **they** take no heed.
016:108 Those are **they** whose hearts, ears, and eyes
016:109 **they** will be the losers.
016:113 from among themselves, but **they** falsely rejected
016:117 but **they** will have a most
016:118 but **they** were used to doing wrong to themselves.
017:004 that twice would **they** do mischief on the earth

THEY (continued)

017:004 (and twice would **they** be punished)!
017:005 **they** entered the very inmost parts of your homes;
017:007 as **they** had entered it before, and to
017:009 of righteousness, that **they** shall have a
017:016 (to be obedient) but **they** continued to
017:018 Hell for them: **they** will burn therein,
017:019 due striving, and Faith,-**they** are the ones
017:024 even as **they** cherished me in childhood."
017:041 in order that **they** may receive admonition,
017:042 as **they** say,-behold, **they** would certainly have sought
017:043 **they** say! Exalted and Great (beyond measure)!
017:044 **they** declare His glory! Verily He is
017:046 **they** turn on their backs, fleeing (from the Truth).
017:046 **they** should understand the Qur'an, and deafness
017:047 and when **they** meet in private behold, the wicked
017:047 We know best what it is **they** listen,
017:047 when **they** listen to thee; and when
017:048 but **they** have gone astray, and never
017:048 and never can **they** find a way.
017:049 **They** say: "What! when we are reduced to bones
017:051 Then will **they** wag their heads towards thee,
017:051 Then will **they** say: "Who will cause us to return?"
017:053 Say to My servants that **they** should (only) say
017:056 whom ye fancy: **they** have neither the power
017:057 Those whom **they** call upon do seek
017:057 **they** hope for His Mercy and fear His Wrath:
017:059 but **they** treated her wrongfully:
017:061 **they** prostrated except Iblis: he said,
017:071 and **they** will not dealt with unjustly in the least.
017:073 **they** would certainly have made thee (their) friend!
017:076 but in that case **they** would not have stayed
017:085 **They** ask thee concerning the Spirit. Say: "The
017:088 even if **they** backed up each other
017:088 **they** could not produce the like thereof, even if
017:090 **They** say: "We shall not believe in thee,
017:094 was nothing but this: **they** said, "Has Allah
017:098 because **they** rejected Our Signs, and said,
017:099 See **they** not that Allah, Who created
017:108 And **they** say: "Glory to our Lord! Truly has
017:109 **They** fall down on their faces in tears, and it
018:002 righteous deeds, that **they** shall have
018:003 Wherein **they** shall remain forever:
018:005 No knowledge have **they** of such a thing, nor had
018:005 What **they** say in nothing but falsehood!
018:006 if **they** believe not in this Message.
018:010 to the Cave: **they** said, "Our Lord! bestow on us
018:011 (so that **they** heard not):
018:012 at calculating the term of years **they** had tarried!
018:013 **they** were youths who believed in their Lord,
018:014 Behold, **they** stood up and said: "Our Lord
018:015 why do **they** not bring forward an authority
018:015 for what **they** do?
018:016 and the things **they** worship other than Allah,
018:017 while **they** lay in the open space in the
018:018 whilst **they** were asleep, and We
018:019 **They** said, "We have stayed (perhaps) a day,
018:019 that **they** might question each other.
018:019 (At length) **they** (all) said, "Allah (alone)
018:020 **they** would stone you or force you to return
018:020 "For if thy should come upon you, **they** would
018:021 to the people, that **they** might know that the
018:021 Behold **they** dispute among themselves as to

THEY (continued)

018:022　(yet others) say **they** were seven, the dog
018:022　(Some) say **they** were three, the dog
018:022　(others) say **they** were five, the dog
018:025　So **they** stayed in their Cave three hundred years,
018:026　Say: "Allah knows best how long **they** stayed:
018:026　**They** have no protector other than Him; nor does
018:029　 if **they** implore relief **they** will be granted water
018:031　of gold, and **they** will wear green garments
018:031　rivers will flow; **they** will be adorned therein
018:031　and heavy brocade; **they** will recline therein
018:048　And **they** will be marshalled before thy Lord
018:049　is (recorded) therein; **they** will say, "Ah! woe
018:050　And **they** are enemies to you!
018:050　"Prostrate to Adam": **they** prostrated except Iblis.
018:052　but **they** will not listen to them;
018:052　to be My partners," and **they** will call on them,
018:053　and apprehend that **they** have to fall therein;
018:053　no means will **they** find to turn away therefrom.
018:055　but that (**they** wait for) the ways of the ancients
018:056　to weaken the truth, and **they** treat My Signs
018:057　even then will **they** never accept guidance.
018:057　**they** should understand this not, and over
018:058　beyond which **they** will find no refuge.
018:058　(at once) to account for what **they** have earned,
018:058　but **they** have their appointed time, beyond which
018:059　when **they** committed iniquities; but We
018:061　**they** forgot (about) their Fish, which took
018:061　But when **they** reached the Junction,
018:062　When **they** had passed on (some distance),
018:064　following (the path **they** had come).
018:064　so **they** went back on their footsteps,
018:065　So **they** found one of Our servants.
018:071　So **they** both proceeded: until,
018:071　when **they** were in the boat, he scuttled it.
018:074　when **they** met a young man, he slew
018:074　Then **they** proceeded: until,
018:077　**they** asked them for food,
018:077　**They** found there a wall on the point
018:077　when **they** came to the inhabitants of a town,
018:077　but **they** refused them hospitality.
018:077　Then **they** proceeded: until,
018:079　**they** plied on the water: I but
018:082　to which **they** were entitled; their father
018:082　so thy Lord desired that **they** should attain their
018:083　**They** ask thee concerning Zul-Qarnain. Say, "I
018:091　(He left them) as **they** were: We completely
018:094　**They** said: "O Zul-Qarnain! the Gog and Magog
018:097　Thus were **they** made powerless to scale it
018:102　Do the Unbelievers think that **they** can take
018:104　 while **they** thought that **they** were acquiring good
018:105　**They** are those who deny the Signs of their Lord
018:106　because **they** rejected Faith, and took
018:107　work righteous deeds, **they** have, for their
018:108　no change will **they** wish for from them.
018:108　Wherein **they** shall dwell (for aye):
019:027　(in her arms), **they** said: "O Mary!
019:029　**They** said: "How can we talk to one who is
019:034　about which **they** (vainly) dispute.
019:038　the Day that **they** will appear before Us!
019:038　How plainly will **they** see and hear,
019:039　**they** are negligent and **they** do not believe!
019:040　to Us will **they** all be returned.

THEY (continued)

019:049　and from those whom **they** worshipped besides Allah,
019:058　to them, **they** would fall down in prostrate
019:059　will **they** face Destruction,-
019:062　**They** will not there hear any vain discourse,
019:062　and **they** will have therein their sustenance,
019:075　**they** will at length realize who is worst
019:075　(the rope) to them, until, when **they** see the
019:081　And **they** have taken (for worship) gods other
019:082　Instead, **they** shall reject their worship,
019:088　**They** say: "The Most Gracious has begotten a son!"
019:091　That **they** attributed a son to The Most Gracious.
020:028　"So **they** may understand what I say:
020:045　**They** (Moses and Aaron) said: "Our Lord!
020:062　So **they** disputed, one with another, over their
020:062　over their affair, but **they** kept their talk secret.
020:063　**They** said: "These two are certainly (expert)
020:065　**They** said: "O Moses! whether wilt thou that thou
020:069　that which **they** have faked:
020:069　what **they** have faked is but a magician's trick:
020:070　**they** said, "We believe in the Lord of Aaron and Moses."
020:072　**They** said: "Never shall we prefer thee to what
020:076　flow rivers: **they** will dwell therein for aye:
020:084　He replied: "Behold, **they** are close on my footsteps:
020:087　**They** said: "We broke not the promise to thee,
020:088　it seemed to low: so **they** said: "This is your god,
020:089　Could **they** not see that it could not return
020:091　**They** had said: "We will not cease to worship it,
020:096　He replied: "I saw what **they** saw not: so I
020:100　verily **they** will bear a burden on the
020:101　**They** will abide in this (state): and grievous
020:103　In whispers will **they** consult each other:
020:104　We know best what **they** will say, when the
020:105　**They** ask thee concerning the mountains: say, "My
020:108　On that Day will **they** follow the caller
020:110　or behind them: but **they** shall comprehend Him not.
020:113　in order that **they** may fear Allah, or that
020:116　**they** prostrated themselves, but not
020:121　**they** began to sew together, for their
020:121　In the result, **they** both ate of the tree, and so
020:128　in whose haunts **they** (now) move?
020:130　**they** say, and celebrate (constantly) the praises
020:133　**They** say: "Why does he not bring us a Sign
020:134　**they** would have said: "Our Lord! If only thou
021:001　yet **they** heel not and **they** turn away.
021:002　but **they** listen to it as in jest,-
021:005　"Nay," **they** say, "(these are) medleys of dreams!
021:008　ate no food, nor were **they** immortals.
021:012　**they** (tried to) flee from it.
021:012　Yet, when **they** felt Our Punishment (coming),
021:014　**They** said: "Ah! woe to us! we were
021:019　nor are **they** (ever) weary (of His service):
021:020　nor do **they** ever flag or intermit.
021:020　**They** celebrate His praises night and day, nor do
021:021　Or have **they** taken (for worship) gods from
021:022　(high is He) above what **they** attribute to Him!
021:023　but **they** will be questioned (for theirs).
021:024　Or have **they** taken for worship (other) gods
021:026　And **they** say: "The Most Gracious has taken a son."
021:026　**They** are (but) servants raised to honour.
021:027　**They** speak not before He speaks,
021:027　and **they** act (in all things) by His command.
021:028　and **they** offer no intercession except for

THEY (continued)

021:030   Will **they** not then believe?
021:031   that **they** may find their way.
021:032   Yet do **they** turn away from the Signs
021:034   would **they** live permanently?
021:036   **they** treat thee not except with ridicule.
021:036   And **they** blaspheme at the mention of
021:036   "Is this," (**they** say), "The one who talks of your gods?"
021:038   **They** say: "When will this promise come to pass,
021:039   (the time) when **they** will not be able to ward
021:040   to avert it, nor will **they** (then) get respite.
021:040   no power will **they** have then to avert it,
021:041   hemmed in by the thing that **they** mocked.
021:042   Yet **they** turn away from the remembrance
021:043   Or have **they** gods that can guard them from Us?
021:043   nor can **they** be defended from Us.
021:043   **They** have no power to aid themselves,
021:044   Is it then **they** who will win?
021:044   see **they** not that We gradually reduce the land
021:045   not hear the call, (even) when **they** are warned!
021:046   **they** will then say, "Woe to us! we did
021:053   **They** said, "We found our father worshipping them."
021:055   **They** said, "Have you brought us the Truth, or are
021:058   that **they** might turn (and address themselves) to it.
021:059   **They** said, "Who has done this to our gods?
021:060   **They** said, "We heard a youth talk of them:
021:061   that **they** may bear witness:"
021:061   **They** said, "Then bring him before the eyes
021:062   **They** said, "Art thou the one that did this
021:063   Ask them, if **they** can talk."
021:064   So **they** turned to themselves and said,
021:065   (**they** said), "Thou knowest full well that these
021:065   Then were **they** confounded with shame:
021:068   **They** said, "Burn him and protect your gods,
021:070   Then **they** planned against him: but We
021:073   **they** constantly served Us (and Us only).
021:074   truly **they** were a people given to Evil,
021:077   truly **they** were a people given to Evil: so We
021:078   when **they** gave judgment in the matter of the
021:086   for **they** were of the Righteous ones.
021:090   **they** used to call on Us in yearning and awe.
021:093   from another: (yet) will **they** all return to Us.
021:095   that **they** shall not return,
021:096   and **they** swiftly swarm from every hill.
021:099   **they** would not have got there
021:100   nor will **they** there hear (aught else).
021:102   Not the slightest sound will **they** hear of Hell:
021:102   in that will **they** dwell.
021:109   But if **they** turn back, say: "I have
022:005   so that **they** know nothing after having known
022:011   **they** lose both this world and the Hereafter:
022:011   **they** turn on their faces:
022:011   if good befalls them, **they** are, therewith,
022:012   **They** call on such deities, besides Allah,
022:013   (Perhaps) **they** call on one whose hurt is nearer
022:022   Every time **they** wish to get away therefrom,
022:022   **they** will be forced back therein,
022:023   **they** shall be adorned therein with bracelets
022:024   **they** have been guided to the Path
022:024   For **they** have been guided (in this life)
022:027   **they** will come to thee on foot and (mounted)
022:028   "That **they** may witness the benefits (provided)
022:034   that **they** might celebrate the name of Allah

THEY (continued)

022:036   when **they** are down on their sides (after slaughter),
022:036   over them as **they** line up (for sacrifice):
022:039   because **they** are wronged;-and verily, Allah is
022:040   (**They** are) those who have been expelled from
022:040   that **they** say, "Our Lord is Allah." Did not
022:041   (**They** are) those who, if We establish them in the land,
022:042   If **they** disbelieve you so did the Peoples
022:045   **They** tumbled down on their roofs.
022:046   Do **they** not travel through the land, so that
022:047   Yet **they** ask thee to hasten on the Punishment!
022:051   **they** will be Companions of the Fire."
022:054   and that **they** may believe therein, and their
022:059   to a place with which **they** shall be well pleased:
022:062   **they** invoke,-**they** are but vain Falsehood:
022:067   appointed rites which **they** must follow: let them
022:068   If **they** do wrangle with thee,
022:071   and of which **they** have (really) no knowledge:
022:071   Yet **they** worship, besides Allah,
022:072   **They** nearly attack with violence those who rehearse
022:073   **they** would have no power to release it from the fly:
022:073   those who petition and those whom **they** petition!
022:073   if **they** all met together for the purpose!
022:074   No just estimate have **they** made of Allah:
023:006   **they** are free from blame,
023:011   **they** will dwell therein (for ever).
023:026   for that **they** accuse me of falsehood!
023:027   the wrong-doers: for **they** shall be drowned
023:039   for that **they** accuse me of falsehood."
023:040   **they** are sure to be sorry!"
023:043   nor can **they** delay (it).
023:044   **they** accused him of falsehood: so We
023:046   **they** were an arrogant people.
023:047   **They** said: "Shall we believe in two men
023:048   So **they** rejected them and **they** became of those
023:049   in order that **they** might receive guidance.
023:055   Do **they** think that because We have granted them
023:056   Nay, **they** do not perceive.
023:060   because **they** will return to their Lord;-
023:062   **They** will never be wronged.
023:063   deeds of theirs, which **they** will (continue)
023:064   behold, **they** will groan in supplication!
023:068   Do **they** not ponder over the Word (of Allah),
023:069   Or do **they** not recognize their Messenger,
023:069   their Messenger, that **they** deny him?
023:070   Or do **they** say, "He is possessed"? Nay, he
023:071   but **they** turn away from their admonition.
023:075   **they** would obstinately persist in their transgression,
023:076   but **they** humbled not themselves to their Lord,
023:076   nor do **they** submissively entreat (Him)!-
023:077   then Lo! **they** will be plunged in despair therein!
023:081   On the contrary **they** say things similar to
023:082   **They** say: "What! when we die and become
023:083   **They** are nothing but tales of the ancients!"
023:085   **They** will say, "To Allah!" Say: "Yet will
023:087   **They** will say, "(**They** belong) to Allah."
023:089   **They** will say, "(It belongs) to Allah."
023:090   but **they** indeed are liars.
023:091   (sort of) things **they** attribute to Him!
023:092   for the partners **they** attribute to Him!
023:093   **they** are warned against,-
023:095   against which **they** are warned.
023:096   We are well acquainted with the things **they** say.

THEY (continued)

023:098 O my Lord! lest **they** should come near me."
023:100 the Day **they** are raised up.
023:102 (of good deeds) is heavy,-**they** will be successful.
023:103 their souls; in Hell will **they** abide.
023:104 and **they** will therein grin, with their
023:106 **They** will say: "Our Lord! our misfortune
023:111 **they** are indeed the ones that have achieved Bliss."
023:113 **They** will say: "We stayed a day or part
024:013 When **they** have not brought the witnesses,
024:013 Why did **they** not bring four witnesses to prove it?
024:025 and **they** will realize that Allah is the
024:030 and Allah is well acquainted with all that **they** do.
024:030 Say to the believing men that **they** should lower
024:031 that **they** should not display their beauty
024:031 and that **they** should not strike their feet
024:031 **they** should lower their gaze and guard
024:031 that **they** should draw their veils over their
024:032 if **they** are in poverty, Allah will
024:033 maids to prostitution when **they** desire chastity,
024:041 And Allah knows well all that **they** do.
024:047 **They** say, "We believe in Allah and in the
024:047 turn away: **they** are not (really) Believers.
024:048 When **they** are summoned to Allah and His
024:049 **they** come to him with all submission.
024:050 Nay, it is **they** themselves who do wrong.
024:050 Or do **they** doubt, or are **they** in fear, that Allah
024:051 is no other than this: **they** said, "We hear
024:053 **they** would leave (their homes).
024:053 **They** swear their strongest oaths by Allah that,
024:055 `**They** will worship Me (along) and not
024:055 **they** are rebellious and wicked.
024:055 after the fear in which **they** (lived), to one
024:058 permission (before **they** come to your presence),
024:060 provided **they** make not wanton display of their
024:060 there is no blame on them if **they** lay aside
024:062 so when **they** ask for thy leave, for some
024:062 **they** do not depart until **they** have asked
024:062 when **they** are with him on a matter requiring
024:064 and one day **they** will be brought back to Him,
024:064 of what **they** did: for Allah doth know all things.
025:003 Yet have **they** taken, besides Him, gods that
025:003 **they** control Death nor Life nor Resurrection.
025:004 In truth it is **they** who have put forward
025:005 and **they** are dictated before him
025:005 And **they** say: "Tales of the ancients, which he
025:007 And **they** say: "What sort of a messenger is this,
025:009 See what kinds of companions **they** make for thee!
025:009 But **they** have gone astray, and never
025:009 and never a way will **they** be able to find!
025:011 Nay, **they** deny the Hour (of the Judgment to come):
025:012 **they** will hear its fury and its raging sigh.
025:013 And when **they** are cast, bound together, into a
025:013 **they** will plead for destruction there and then!
025:016 **they** will dwell (there) for aye: a promise
025:016 all that **they** wish for:
025:017 as well as those whom **they** worship besides Allah,
025:017 or did **they** stray from the Path themselves?"
025:018 **They** will say: "Glory to Thee! not meant
025:018 until **they** forgot the Message:
025:018 for **they** were a people destroyed."
025:019 "Now have **they** proved you liars in what ye say:
025:021 our Lord?" Indeed **they** have an arrogant

THEY (continued)

025:022 The Day **they** see the angels,-no joy
025:023 to whatever deeds they did **they** did (in this life),
025:033 And no question do **they** bring to thee but We
025:034 **they** will be in an evil plight, and, as
025:037 when **they** rejected the messengers, We drowned
025:040 own eyes)? But **they** expect not to be raised again.
025:040 did **they** not then see it (with their own eyes)?
025:041 **they** treat thee no otherwise than in mockery:
025:041 When **they** see thee, **they** treat
025:042 Soon will **they** know, when **they** see the Chastisement,
025:044 **they** are farther astray from the way.
025:044 **They** are only like cattle;-nay,
025:050 amongst them, in order that **they** may be mindful
025:055 Yet do **they** worship, besides Allah, things that
025:060 **They** say, "And what is (Allah) Most Gracious?
025:063 when the ignorant address them, **they** say, "Peace!"
025:067 Those who, when **they** spend, are not
025:072 and, if **they** pass by futility, **they** pass
025:072 **they** pass by it with honourable (avoidance);
025:073 Those who, when **they** are admonished with the
025:073 **they** were deaf or blind;
025:075 therein shall **they** be met with salutations and peace,
026:003 with grief, that **they** do not become Believers.
026:004 a Sign, to which **they** would bend their necks
026:005 the Most Gracious, but **they** turn away therefrom.
026:006 so **they** will know soon (enough) the truth
026:006 the truth of what **they** mocked at!
026:006 **They** have indeed rejected (the Message):
026:007 Do **they** not look at the earth,-how many
026:011 "The people of Pharaoh: will **they** not fear Allah?"
026:012 I do fear that **they** will charge me with falsehood:
026:014 "And (further), **they** have a charge of crime
026:014 of crime against me; and I fear **they** may slay me."
026:036 **They** said: "Keep him and his brother in suspense
026:040 "That we may follow the sorcerers if **they** win?"
026:041 **they** said to Pharaoh: "Of course-shall we
026:044 So **they** threw their ropes and their rods,
026:045 all the falsehoods which **they** fake!
026:050 **They** said: "No matter! for us, we shall
026:055 "And **they** are raging furiously against us;
026:060 So **they** pursued them at sunrise.
026:071 **They** said: "We worship idols, and we
026:072 He said: "Do **they** listen to you when ye
026:074 **They** said: "Nay, but we found our fathers
026:077 "For **they** are enemies to me; not so
026:093 "`Besides Allah? Can **they** help you or help
026:094 "Then **they** will be thrown headlong into
026:094 **they** and those straying in evil,
026:096 "**They** will say there in their mutual bickerings:
026:111 **They** said: "Shall we believe in thee when it
026:112 He said: "And what do I know as to what **they** do?
026:116 **They** said: "If thou desist not, O Noah!
026:136 **They** said: "It is the same to us whether thou
026:139 So **they** rejected him, and We
026:153 **They** said: "Thou art only the of those bewitched!
026:157 then did **they** become full of regrets.
026:157 But **they** ham-strung her: then did
026:167 **They** said: "If thou desist not, O Lut!
026:169 and my family from such things as **they** do!"
026:185 **They** said: "Thou art only one of those bewitched!
026:189 But **they** rejected him.
026:199 **they** would not have believed in it.

THEY (continued)

026:201 **they** see the grievous Chastisement
026:201 **They** will not believe in it until
026:202 of a sudden, while **they** perceive it not;
026:203 Then **they** will say: "Shall we be respited?"
026:204 Do **they** then ask for Our Chastisement to be
026:206 the (Punishment) which **they** were promised!
026:207 the enjoyment **they** were given
026:212 Indeed **they** are banished from hearing it.
026:216 Then if **they** disobey thee, say: "I am free
026:222 **They** descend on every lying, wicked person
026:223 **They** listen eagerly and most of them are liars.
026:225 Seest thou not that **they** wander distracted
026:227 **they** are unjustly attacked.
027:004 and so **they** wander blindly.
027:005 Such are **they** for whom a grievous Chastisement
027:012 for **they** are a people rebellious in transgression."
027:013 visibly **they** said: "This is sorcery manifest!"
027:014 And **they** denied them, though their
027:015 and **they** both said: "Praise be to Allah, Who has
027:017 and **they** were all kept in order and ranks.
027:018 At length, when **they** came to a valley of ants,
027:024 so **they** receive no guidance,-
027:025 So that **they** worship not Allah Who brings forth
027:028 and (wait to) see what answer **they** return"...
027:033 **They** said: "We are endued with strength,
027:034 thus do **they** behave.
027:034 She said: "Kings, when **they** enter a country,
027:037 in disgrace, and **they** will feel humbled (indeed)."
027:037 as **they** will never be able to meet: we shall
027:038 before **they** come to me in submission?"
027:045 **they** became two factions quarreling with each other.
027:047 **They** said: "Ill omen do we augur from thee
027:049 **They** said: "Swear a mutual oath by Allah that we
027:050 **They** plotted and planned, but We
027:050 even while **they** perceived it not.
027:052 in utter ruin,-because **they** practised wrong-doing.
027:056 but this: **they** said, "Drive out the followers of Lut
027:059 or the false gods **they** associate (with Him)?
027:060 Nay, **they** are a people who swerve from justice.
027:063 High is Allah above what **they** associate with Him!
027:065 nor can **they** perceive when **they** shall be
027:066 nay, **they** are blind thereunto!
027:066 the Hereafter, **they** are in doubt and uncertainty
027:071 **They** also say: "When will this promise (come to pass)?
027:074 as well as all that **they** reveal.
027:076 the matters in which **they** disagree.
027:080 (especially) when **they** turn back in retreat.
027:081 so **they** submit.
027:083 and **they** shall be kept in ranks,-
027:084 Until, when **they** come (before the Judgment-Seat),
027:085 their wrong-doing, and **they** will be unable
027:086 See **they** not that We have made the Night
027:088 but **they** shall pass away as the clouds pass away:
027:089 And **they** will be secure from terror that Day.
027:092 **they** do it for the good of their own souls,
028:006 what **they** were dreading from them.
028:009 And **they** perceived not (what **they** were doing)!
028:011 from a distance and **they** perceived not.
028:023 **They** said: "We cannot water (our flocks) until the
028:032 for truly **they** are a people rebellious and wicked."
028:033 among them, and I fear lest **they** slay me.
028:034 for I fear that **they** may accuse me of falsehood."

THEY (continued)

028:035 so **they** shall not be able to touch you: with Our
028:036 Our Clear Signs, **they** said: "This is
028:039 **they** thought that **they** would not have to return to Us!"
028:041 no help shall **they** find.
028:042 Day of Judgment **they** will be among the
028:043 that **they** might receive admonition.
028:046 in order that **they** may receive admonition.
028:047 **they** might say: "Our Lord! why didst
028:048 to them from Ourselves, **they** say, "Why are
028:048 And **they** say: "For us, we reject all (such things)!"
028:048 **They** say: "Two kinds of sorcery, each assisting
028:048 Do **they** not then reject (the Signs) which were
028:050 But if **they** hearken not to thee, know that
028:050 know that **they** only follow their own lusts:
028:051 in order that **they** may receive admonition.
028:052 before this,-**they** do believe in this (Revelation);
028:053 **they** say: "We believe therein, for it is
028:054 and that **they** spend (in charity) out of
028:054 for that **they** have persevered,
028:054 Twice will **they** be given their reward,
028:054 that **they** avert Evil with Good, and that
028:055 And when **they** hear vain talk,
028:055 **they** turn away therefrom and say: "To us our
028:057 **They** say: "If we were to follow the guidance
028:063 It was not us **they** worshipped."
028:064 **they** will call upon them,
028:064 (before them); (how **they** wish) 'If only
028:064 If only **they** had been open to guidance!'
028:064 and **they** will see the Chastisement (before them);
028:064 but **they** will not listen to them;
028:066 will be obscure to them and **they** will not
028:068 **they** ascribe (to Him)!
028:068 no choice have **they** (in the matter):
028:069 their hearts conceal and all that **they** reveal.
028:075 and the (lies) which **they** invented will leave
028:075 then shall **they** know that the Truth is
028:078 in amount (of riches) **they** had collected?
028:087 from Allah's revelations after **they** have been
029:002 Do men think that **they** will be left alone
029:002 and that **they** will not be tested?
029:004 that **they** will get the better of us?
029:006 **they** do so for their own soul: for Allah
029:007 blot out all misdeeds that **they** have committed,
029:008 but if **they** (either of them) strive (to force) thee
029:010 **they** suffer affliction in (the cause of) Allah,
029:010 **they** treat men's oppression as if it were Wrath of Allah!
029:010 **they** are sure to say, "We have (always) been with you!"
029:012 will **they** bear their faults: in fact **they** are liars!
029:013 **they** will be called to account for their falsehoods.
029:013 **They** will bear their own burdens, and other
029:014 them while **they** (persisted in) sin.
029:019 See **they** not how Allah originates creation,
029:023 (in the Hereafter),-it is **they** who shall despair
029:023 **they** who will (suffer) a most grievous Chastisement.
029:024 (Abraham's) people except that **they** said: "Slay him
029:029 gave no answer but this: **they** said: "Bring us
029:031 for truly **they** are wicked men."
029:031 with the good news, **they** said: "We are indeed going
029:032 **They** said: "We know well who is there: we will
029:033 but **they** said: "Fear thou not, nor grieve:
029:034 because **they** have been wickedly rebellious."
029:037 and **they** lay prostrate in their homes

THEY (continued)

029:037 But **they** rejected him: then the
029:038 from the Path, though **they** were keen-sighted.
029:039 but **they** behaved with insolence on the earth;
029:039 on the earth; yet **they** cold not overreach (Us).
029:040 **they** wronged themselves.
029:041 is the Spider's house;-if **they** but knew.
029:042 of (everything) whatever that **they** call upon
029:050 Yet **they** say: "Why are not Signs sent down
029:053 **They** ask thee to hasten on the Punishment
029:053· reach them,-of a sudden, while **they** perceive not!
029:054 **They** ask thee to hasten on the Punishment:
029:061 **they** will certainly reply, "Allah."
029:061 How are **they** then deluded away (from the truth)?
029:063 **they** will certainly reply, "Allah!" Say, "Praise
029:064 that is life indeed, if **they** but knew.
029:065 **they** give a share (of their worship to others)!-
029:065 Now, if **they** embark on a boat, **they** call on Allah,
029:066 (worldly) enjoyment! But soon will **they** know.
029:067 Do **they** not then see that We have made
029:067 Then, do **they** believe in that which is vain,
030:003 In a land close by: but **they**, (even) after
030:007 **They** know but the outer (things) in the
030:007 but of the Hereafter **they** are heedless.
030:008 Do **they** not reflect in their own minds?
030:009 Do **they** not travel through the earth, and see
030:009 (Signs), (which **they** rejected, to their own destruction):
030:009 **They** were superior to them in strength:
030:009 **they** tilled the soil and populated it in greater numbers
030:009 but **they** wronged their own souls.
030:010 for that **they** rejected the Signs of Allah,
030:013 and **they** will (themselves) reject their "Partners."
030:013 No intercessor will **they** have among their
030:033 **they** cry to their Lord, turning back
030:035 to which **they** pay part-worship?
030:036 **they** exult thereat: and when some evil afflicts
030:036 behold, **they** are in despair!
030:037 See **they** not that Allah enlarges the provision
030:038 and it is **they** who will prosper.
030:040 the partners **they** attribute (to Him)!
030:041 in order that **they** may turn back (from Evil).
030:047 and **they** came to them with Clear Signs: then, to
030:048 and **they** raise the Clouds: then does
030:048 as He wills, behold, **they** do rejoice!-
030:049 Even though, before **they** received (the rain)-
030:049 **they** were dumb with despair!
030:051 **they** see (their tilth) turn yellow,-behold,
030:051 **they** become, thereafter, ungrateful (Unbelievers)!
030:052 when **they** show their backs and turn away.
030:055 thus were **they** used to being deluded!
030:055 swear that **they** tarried not but an hour:
030:057 nor will **they** be allowed to make amends.
031:015 "But if **they** strive to make thee join in
031:021 When **they** are told to follow the (revelation)
031:021 sent down, **they** say: "Nay, we shall
031:025 and the earth. **They** will certainly say, "Allah."
031:030 and because whatever else **they** invoke besides
031:032 **they** call upon Allah, offering Him
032:003 in order that **they** may be rightly guided.
032:003 Or do **they** say, "He has forged it"? Nay, it
032:010 Nay, **they** deny the meeting with their Lord!
032:010 And **they** say: "What! when we lie, hidden and
032:015 when **they** are recited to them fall down

THEY (continued)

032:015 nor are **they** (ever) puffed up with pride.
032:016 the while **they** call on their Lord, in Fear
032:016 in Fear and Hope: and **they** spend (in charity)
032:016 **They** forsake their beds of sleep, the while
032:018 Not equal are **they**.
032:020 to get away therefrom **they** will be forced thereinto,
032:020 the Fire: every time **they** wish to get away
032:021 **they** may (repent and) return.
032:024 so long as **they** persevered with patience
032:025 matters wherein **they** differ (among themselves).
032:026 do **they** not then listen?
032:026 before them, in whose dwellings **they** (now) go
032:027 And do **they** not see that We do drive Rain
032:027 Have **they** not the vision?
032:028 **They** say: "When will this decision be, if ye
032:029 Nor will **they** be granted a respite."
032:029 if **they** (then) Believe!
032:030 **they** too are waiting.
033:005 (then they are) your Brothers in faith,
033:010 Behold! **they** came on you from above you
033:011 Believers tried: **they** were shaken as by
033:013 and exposed," though **they** were not exposed:
033:013 **they** intended nothing but to run away.
033:014 **They** would certainly have brought it to pass,
033:014 and **they** had been incited to sedition.
033:015 And yet **they** had already covenanted with Allah
033:017 Nor will **they** find for themselves,
033:019 **they** will smite you with sharp tongues,
033:020 **they** would wish **they** were in the deserts
033:020 **they** would fight but little.
033:020 and if **they** were in your midst,
033:020 **They** think that the Confederates have not
033:022 the Confederate forces, **they** said: "This is
033:023 but **they** have never changed (their determination)
033:025 no advantage did **they** gain, and enough
033:044 on the Day **they** meet Him will be "peace!";
033:047 to the Believers, that **they** shall have
033:055 (on those ladies, if **they** appear) before their fathers
033:059 most convenient, that **they** should be known
033:059 that **they** should cast their outer garments
033:060 against them: then will **they** not be able to
033:061 wherever **they** are found,
033:061 **They** shall have a curse on them:
033:061 **they** shall be seized and slain.
033:065 no protector will **they** find, nor helper.
033:066 **they** will say: "Woe to us! would that we had
033:067 And **they** would say: "Our Lord! We obeyed
033:067 and **they** misled us as to the (right) path.
033:069 Allah cleared him of the (calumnies) **they** had uttered:
033:072 and the Mountains: but **they** refused to undertake
034:009 See **they** not what is before them and behind
034:013 **They** worked for him as he desired,
034:014 **they** would not have tarried in the humiliating
034:014 the Jinns saw plainly that if **they** had known
034:016 But **they** turned away (from Allah), and We
034:017 them because **they** ungratefully rejected Faith:
034:019 but **they** wronged themselves (therein).
034:019 But **they** said: "Our Lord! place longer
034:020 his idea, and **they** followed him, all but
034:022 **they** have no power,-not the weight of an atom,-
034:022 no (sort of) share have **they** therein, nor is
034:023 **They** will say, 'That which true and just;

THEY (continued)

034:023   will **they** say, 'What is it that your Lord commanded?'
034:029   **They** say: "When will this promise (come to pass)
034:033   When **they** see the Chastisement: We shall
034:033   **They** are filled with remorse.
034:035   **They** said: "We have more in wealth and in sons,
034:037   their deeds, while secure **they** (reside) in the
034:041   **They** will say, "Glory to thee! Thou art
034:041   Nay, but **they** worshipped the Jinns:
034:042   **they** have over each other, for profit
034:043   to them, **they** say, "This is only a man who
034:043   And **they** say, "This is only a falsehood invented!"
034:044   which **they** could study, nor sent
034:045   yet when **they** rejected My messengers,
034:051   If thou couldst but see when **they** will quake
034:051   (for them), and **they** will be seized from a
034:052   but how could **they** receive (Faith) from a
034:052   And **they** will say, "We do believe
034:053   Seeing that **they** did reject faith (entirely)
034:053   and that **they** cast (conjectures) with regard
034:054   for **they** were indeed in suspicious
035:004   And if **they** reject thee, so were
035:006   that **they** may become Companions of the Blazing Fire.
035:008   for Allah knows well all that **they** do!
035:009   so that **they** raise up the Clouds, and We
035:014   **they** will not listen to your call, and if
035:014   and if **they** were to listen,
035:014   **they** cannot answer your (prayer).
035:014   **they** will reject your "Partnership."
035:025   And if **they** reject thee, so did
035:028   and cattle, are **they** of various colours.
035:033   Gardens of Eternity will **they** enter:
035:033   therein will **they** be adorned with bracelets
035:034   And **they** will say: "Praise be to Allah, Who has
035:036   so **they** should die, nor shall
035:037   Therein will **they** cry aloud (for assistance):
035:040   Or have **they** a share in the heavens?
035:040   from which **they** (can derive) clear (evidence)?-
035:040   **they** have created in the (wide) earth.
035:041   and if **they** should fail.
035:041   and the earth, lest **they** cease (to function):
035:042   to them, **they** would be more rightly guided
035:042   **They** swore their strongest oaths by Allah
035:043   Now are **they** but looking for the way
035:044   before them,-though **they** were superior to them
035:044   Do **they** not travel through the earth, and see
035:045   according to what **they** deserve, He would
036:007   for **they** do not believe.
036:008   so that **they** cannot bow their heads.
036:009   so that **they** cannot see.
036:010   admonish them: **they** will not believe.
036:012   and We record that which **they** sent before
036:012   sent before and that which **they** leave behind,
036:014   two messengers, **they** rejected them: but We
036:014   **they** said, "Truly, we have been sent on a
036:016   **They** said: "Our Lord doth know that we have been
036:019   **They** said: "Your evil omens are with yourselves:
036:023   nor can **they** deliver me.
036:029   mighty Blast, and behold! **they** were (like ashes)
036:030   to them but **they** mock Him!
036:031   See **they** not how many generations before them
036:031   Not to them will **they** return:
036:035   will **they** not then give thanks?

THEY (continued)

036:035   That **they** may enjoy the fruits of this
036:036   of which **they** have no knowledge.
036:037   and behold **they** are plunged in darkness;
036:042   similar (vessels) on which **they** ride.
036:043   nor could **they** be delivered,
036:045   When **they** are told, "Fear ye that which is
036:045   ye may receive Mercy," (**they** turn back).
036:046   but **they** turn away therefrom.
036:047   And when **they** are told, "Spend ye
036:048   Further, **they** say, "When will this promise
036:049   **They** will not (have to) wait for aught but a
036:049   it will seize them while **they** are yet disputing
036:050   No (chance) will **they** then have, by will,
036:052   **They** will say: "Ah! woe unto us! Who hath
036:053   **they** will all be brought up before Us!
036:055   shall that Day have joy in all that **they** do;
036:056   **They** and their associates will be in pleasant
036:057   **they** shall have whatever **they** call for;
036:065   bear witness, to all that **they** did.
036:066   their eyes; then **they** should have raced to
036:066   but how could **they** have seen?
036:067   nor could **they** have returned (after error).
036:067   then should **they** have been unable to move about,
036:068   will **they** not then understand?
036:071   See **they** not that it is We Who have created
036:072   carry them and some **they** eat:
036:073   Will **they** not then be grateful?
036:073   from them (besides), and **they** get (milk)
036:073   And **they** have (other) profits from them
036:074   Yet **they** take (for worship) gods other than Allah,
036:074   than Allah, (hoping) that **they** might be helped!
036:075   **They** have not the power to help them:
036:075   and **they** are a host brought up before them.
036:076   what **they** hide as well as what **they** disclose.
037:008   (So) **they** should not strain their ears in the
037:008   and **they** are cast away from every side,
037:010   and **they** are pursued be a flaming fire,
037:011   are **they** the more difficult to create, or the
037:012   Truly dost thou marvel, while **they** ridicule,
037:013   And, when **they** are admonished, pay no heed,-
037:014   And, when **they** see a Sign, turn it to mockery,
037:019   **they** will begin to see!
037:020   **They** will say, "Ah! woe to us! this is
037:022   and the things **they** worshipped-
037:024   "But stop them, for **they** must be asked:
037:026   Nay, but that day **they** shall submit (to Judgment);
037:027   And **they** will turn to one another, and question
037:028   **They** will say: "It was ye who used to come
037:029   **They** will reply: "Nay, ye yourselves had no Faith!
037:033   Truly, that day, **they** will (all) share
037:035   For **they**, when **they** were told that there is
037:042   Fruits, and **they** (shall enjoy) honour and dignity,
037:047   nor will **they** suffer intoxication therefrom.
037:049   As if **they** were (delicate) eggs closely guarded.
037:050   Then **they** will turn to one another and question
037:066   Truly **they** will eat thereof and fill
037:067   Then on top of that **they** will be given
037:069   Truly **they** found their fathers on the wrong Path;
037:070   So **they** (too) were rushed down on their footsteps!
037:090   So **they** turned away from him, and departed.
037:097   **They** said: "Build him a furnace, and throw
037:098   (This failing), **they** then plotted against him,

THEY (continued)

037:103	So when **they** had both submitted (to Allah),
037:116	And We helped them, so **they** were victorious;
037:122	For **they** were two of Our believing Servants.
037:127	and **they** will certainly be called up (for punishment),
037:127	But **they** rejected him,
037:148	And **they** believed; so We permitted them to enjoy
037:149	(only) daughters, and **they** have sons?-
037:150	and **they** are witnesses (thereto)?
037:151	Behold **they** say, out of their own invention,
037:152	But **they** are liars!
037:158	that **they** will be brought before Him.
037:158	And **they** have invented a kinship between Him
037:159	from the things **they** ascribe (to Him)!
037:170	**they** reject it: but soon will **they** know!
037:172	That **they** would certainly be assisted,
037:173	And that Our forces,-**they** surely must conquer.
037:175	and **they** soon shall see (how thou farest)!
037:175	And watch them (how **they** fare), and **they**
037:176	Do **they** wish (indeed) to hurry on Our Punishment?
037:179	and **they** soon shall see (how thou farest)!
037:179	And watch (how **they** fare) and **they**
037:180	from what **they** ascribe (to Him)!
038:003	In the end **they** cried (for mercy)
038:004	So **they** wonder that a Warner has come to them
038:008	Nay, **they** have not yet tasted My Punishment!
038:008	But **they** are in doubt concerning My (own)
038:009	Or have **they** the Treasures of the Mercy
038:010	Or have **they** the dominion of the heavens
038:011	**They** are but a host of confederates and
038:011	and **they** will be put to flight.
038:016	**They** say: "Our Lord! Hasten to us our sentence
038:017	Have patience at what **they** say, and remember
038:021	Behold, **they** climbed over the wall of the private
038:022	**they** said: "Fear not: We are two disputants,
038:022	When **they** entered the presence of David, and he
038:024	and how few are **they**?..."
038:026	for that **they** forget the Day of Account.
038:029	that **they** may meditate on its Signs, and that
038:047	**They** were, in Our sight, truly, of the
038:051	Therein will **they** recline (at ease);
038:051	therein can **they** call (at pleasure) for fruit
038:056	Hell!-**they** will burn therein-an evil
038:057	Yea, such!-Then shall **they** taste it,-a boiling
038:059	Truly, **they** shall burn in the Fire!
038:061	**They** will say: "Our Lord! Whoever brought
038:062	And **they** will say: "How is it with us that we
038:069	Exalted Chiefs, when **they** discuss (matters)
039:003	**they** may bring us nearer to Allah." Truly Allah
039:003	in that wherein **they** differ.
039:016	**They** shall have Layers of Fire above them,
039:022	**They** are manifestly wandering (in error)!
039:025	from directions **they** did not perceive.
039:026	of the Hereafter, if **they** only knew!
039:027	in order that **they** may receive admonition.
039:028	in order that **they** may guard against Evil.
039:030	and truly **they** (too) will die (one day).
039:034	**They** shall have all that **they** wish for, in the
039:035	to the best of what **they** have done.
039:036	But **they** try to frighten thee with other
039:038	**they** would be sure to say, "Allah." Say: "See
039:038	some Mercy for me, can **they** keep back His Mercy?"
039:038	can **they**, if Allah wills some affliction

THEY (continued)

039:043	What! Do **they** take for intercessors others
039:043	Say: "Even if **they** have no power whatever
039:045	**they** are filled with joy!
039:046	in those matters about which **they** have differed."
039:047	from Allah, which **they** could never have
039:047	(in vain) would **they** offer it for ransom from the
039:048	which **they** used to mock at!
039:048	confront them, and **they** will be (completely)
039:050	But all that **they** did was of profit to them.
039:051	them (too), and **they** shall not escape!
039:052	Know **they** not that Allah enlarges the provision
039:061	no evil shall touch them, nor shall **they** grieve.
039:061	for **they** have earned salvation:
039:063	it is **they** who will be in loss.
039:067	High is He above the Partners **they** attribute to Him!
039:067	No just estimate have **they** made of Allah,
039:068	**they** will be standing and looking on!
039:069	between them; and **they** will no be wronged
039:070	and (Allah) knoweth best all that **they** do.
039:071	in groups; until, when **they** arrive there,
039:073	until behold, **they** arrive there; its gates
039:074	**They** will say: "Praise be to Allah, Who has
040:006	that truly **they** are Companions of Fire!
040:008	"And grant, our Lord! That **they** enter the
040:011	**They** will say:" Our Lord! twice hast Thou made us
040:016	The Day whereon **they** will (all) come forth:
040:021	Do **they** not travel through the earth and see
040:021	**They** were even superior to them
040:021	and none had **they** to defend them against Allah.
040:021	and in the traces (**they** have left) in the land:
040:022	with Clear (Signs), but **they** rejected them:
040:024	but **they** called (him) "a sorcerer telling lies!"...
040:025	from Us, **they** said, "Slay the sons of those who
040:040	(of Bliss): therein will **they** have abundance
040:045	that **they** plotted (against him), but the
040:046	In front of the Fire will **they** be brought,
040:047	Behold, **they** will dispute with each other
040:050	Clear Signs?" **They** will say: "Yes."
040:050	**They** will say: "Did there not come to you
040:050	**They** will reply, "Then pray (as ye like)!
040:052	but **they** will (only) have the Curse and the Home
040:056	which **they** shall never attain to: seek refuge,
040:069	How are **they** turned away (from Reality)?-
040:070	but soon shall **they** know,-
040:071	**they** shall be dragged along-
040:072	then in the Fire shall **they** be burned;
040:074	**They** will reply: "**They** have left us in the lurch:
040:077	that **they** shall (all) return.
040:082	and in the traces (**they** have left) in the land:
040:082	Do **they** not travel through the earth and see
040:082	yet all that **they** accomplished was of no profit
040:082	**They** were more numerous than these
040:083	**they** exulted in such knowledge (and skill)
040:083	(and skill) as **they** had; but that
040:083	**they** were wont to scoff hemmed them in.
040:084	**they** said: "We believe in Allah,-the One
040:084	But when **they** saw Our Might,
040:085	when **they** (actually) saw Our Punishment was not
041:004	and so **they** hear not.
041:005	**They** say: "Our hearts are under veils, (concealed)
041:011	**They** said: "We do come (together),
041:013	But if **they** turn away, say thou: "I have warned

THEY (continued)

041:014 **They** said, "If our Lord had so pleased, He would
041:015 What! did **they** not see that Allah,
041:015 But **they** continued to reject Our Signs!
041:016 more humiliating still: and **they** will find no help.
041:017 seized them, because of what **they** had earned.
041:017 but **they** preferred blindness (of heart) to Guidance:
041:019 **they** will be marched in ranks.
041:020 At length, when **they** reach the (Fire),
041:021 **They** will say: "Allah hath given us speech,-
041:021 **They** will say to their skins: "Why bear ye
041:024 And if **they** beg for pardon, their suit
041:024 If, then, **they** have patience, the Fire
041:025 against them; for **they** are utterly lost.
041:028 a (fit) requital, for that **they** were wont to
041:029 so that **they** become the vilest."
041:030 "Fear ye not! (**they** suggest), "Nor grieve!
041:038 And **they** never flag (nor feel themselves above it).
041:044 **they** would have said: "Why are not its verses
041:044 **they** are (as it were) being called from
041:045 but **they** remained in suspicious disquieting doubt
041:047 **They** will say, "We do assure Thee not on of us can
041:048 The (deities) **they** used to invoke aforetime
041:048 and **they** will perceive that **they** have no way of escape.
041:050 the Unbelievers the truth of all that they did,
041:054 Ah indeed! are **they** in doubt concerning
042:009 What! Have **they** taken (for worship)
042:014 And **they** became divided only after knowledge
042:021 What! have **they** partners (in godhead), who have
042:022 on account of what **they** have earned,
042:022 of the Gardens: **they** shall have,
042:022 before their Lord, all that **they** wish for.
042:024 What! Do **they** say, "He has forged
042:027 **they** would indeed transgress beyond all bounds
042:033 then would **they** become motionless on the back
042:037 when **they** are angry even then forgive;
042:046 And no protectors have **they** to help them,
042:048 If then **they** turn away, We have not
043:007 to them but **they** mocked him.
043:009 and the earth?' **They** would be sure to reply,
043:009 to reply, '**They** were created by (Him),
043:015 Yet **they** attribute to some of His servants
043:019 Did **they** witness their creation?
043:019 and **they** will be called to account!
043:019 And **they** make into females angels who themselves
043:020 ("Ah!") **they** say, "If it had been the will
043:020 **They** do nothing but lie!
043:020 such (deities)!" Of that **they** have no knowledge!
043:021 before this, to which **they** are holding fast?
043:022 Nay! **they** say: "We found Our fathers following
043:024 **They** said: "For us, We deny that ye (prophets)
043:028 that **they** may turn back (to Allah).
043:030 **they** said: "This is sorcery, and we do reject it."
043:031 Also, **they** say: "Why is not this Qur'an sent down
043:032 Is it **they** who would portion out the Mercy
043:032 is better than the (wealth) which **they** amass.
043:034 and couches (of silver) on which **they** could recline,
043:037 but **they** think that **they** are being guided aright!
043:047 behold, **they** laughed at them.
043:048 in order that **they** might turn (to Us).
043:049 And **they** said, "O thou Sorcerer! invoke thy
043:050 from them, behold, **they** broke their word.
043:054 truly were **they** a people rebellious (against Allah).

THEY (continued)

043:054 he make fools of his people, and **they** obeyed him:
043:055 When at length **they** provoked Us, We exacted
043:058 And **they** say, " Are Our gods best, or He?"
043:058 This **they** set forth to thee, only by
043:058 **they** are a contentious people.
043:066 of a sudden, while **they** perceive not?
043:066 Do **they** only wait for the Hour-that it
043:075 will **they** be there overwhelmed.
043:076 but it is **they** who have been unjust themselves.
043:077 **They** will cry: "O Malik! would that thy Lord
043:079 What! have **they** settled some Plan
043:080 Or do **they** think that We hear not their secrets
043:082 He is free from the things **they** attribute (to Him)!
043:083 of theirs, which **they** have been promised.
043:083 (with vanities) until **they** meet that Day of theirs,
043:086 And those whom **they** invoke besides Allah have no
043:087 **they** will certainly say, Allah: how then
043:087 how then are **they** deluded away (from the Truth)?
043:089 and say "Peace!" but soon shall **they** know!
044:009 Yet **they** play about in doubt.
044:012 (**They** will say:) "Our Lord! remove the
044:013 How shall **they** have the Reminder. Seeing that
044:014 Yet **they** turn away from him and say: "Tutored
044:022 (But **they** were aggressive): then he
044:024 For **they** are a host (destined) to be drowned."
044:025 and springs **they** left behind.
044:027 **they** had taken such delight!
044:029 over them: nor were **they** given a respite (again).
044:034 As to these (Quraish), **they** say forsooth:
044:037 What! are **they** better than the people of Tubba
044:037 **they** were guilty of sin.
044:041 his client in aught, and no help can **they** receive,
044:051 As to the Righteous (**they** will be) in a
044:053 rich brocade, **they** will face each other;
044:055 There can **they** call for every kind of fruit
044:056 Nor will **they** there taste Death, except the
044:058 in thy tongue, in order that **they** may give heed.
044:059 for **they** (too) are waiting.
045:006 then in what exposition will **they** believe after
045:010 nor any protectors **they** may have taken to
045:010 **they** may have earned, nor any
045:014 to what **they** have earned.
045:017 matters in which **they** set up differences.
045:017 granted to them that **they** fell into schisms,
045:019 **They** will be of no use to thee in the sight
045:021 Ill is the judgment that **they** make.
045:024 But of that **they** have no knowledge:
045:024 And **they** say: "What is there but our life
045:024 **they** merely conjecture:
045:025 but this: **they** say, "Bring (back) our forefathers,
045:033 the evil (fruits) of what **they** did,
045:033 and **they** will be completely encircled by that
045:033 by that which **they** used to mock at!
045:035 out thence, nor can the make amends.
045:035 therefore, **they** shall not be taken out thence,
046:003 turn away from that whereof **they** are warned.
046:004 or have **they** a share in the heavens?
046:004 **they** have created on earth, or have
046:006 (at the Resurrection), **they** will be hostile
046:008 Or do **they** say, "He has forged it"?
046:011 **they** will say, "This is an (old), old falsehood!"
046:011 and seeing that **they** guide not themselves thereby,

THEY (continued)

046:013 no fear, nor shall **they** grieve.
046:016 (**they** shall be) among the Companions of the Garden:
046:016 Such are **they** from whom We shall accept the best
046:017 And **they** too seek Allah's aid,
046:018 Such are **they** against whom is the word
046:018 for **they** will be (utterly) lost.
046:019 according to the deeds which **they** (have done),
046:022 **They** said: "Hast thou come in order to turn
046:024 **they** said, "This cloud will give us rain!"
046:024 Then, when **they** saw a could advancing towards
046:025 Then by the morning **they**-nothing was
046:026 when **they** went on rejecting the Signs of Allah:
046:026 and **they** were (completely) encircled
046:026 **they** used to mock at!
046:027 in various ways, that **they** may turn (to Us).
046:028 Nay, **they** left them in the lurch: but that
046:028 to them from those whom **they** worshipped as gods,
046:029 **they** said, "Listen in silence!"
046:029 when **they** stood in the presence thereof,
046:029 (reading) was finished, **they** returned to their
046:030 **They** said, "O our people! We have
046:033 See **they** not that Allah, Who created
046:034 (**they** will be asked), "Is this not the Truth?"
046:034 **They** will say, "Yea, by our Lord"
046:035 (it will be) as if **they** had not tarried more
046:035 **they** see the (Punishment) promised them,
047:009 That is because **they** hate the Revelation of Allah;
047:010 Do **they** not travel through the earth, and see
047:016 to thee, till when **they** go out from thee,
047:016 from thee, **they** say to those who have received
047:018 Do **they** then only wait for the Hour,-that it
047:018 to them, how shall **they** have their Reminder?
047:021 it were best for them if **they** were true to Allah.
047:024 Do **they** not then earnestly seek to understand
047:026 This, because **they** said to those who hate
047:028 This because **they** followed that which displeased
047:028 and **they** hated Allah's good pleasure;
047:038 then **they** would not be like you!
048:004 that **they** may add Faith to their Faith;-for to
048:011 **They** say with their tongues what is not
048:015 (this) beforehand": then **they** will say, "But ye
048:015 **They** wish to change Allah's word: Say: "Not thus
048:015 Nay, but little do **they** understand (such things).
048:016 then shall ye fight, or **they** shall submit.
048:018 The Believers when **they** swore Fealty to thee
048:019 And many gains will **they** acquire (besides):
048:022 **they** would certainly turn their backs;
048:022 then would **they** find neither protector nor helper.
048:025 If **they** had been apart, We should
048:025 **They** are the ones who disbelieved and hindered
048:026 and well were **they** entitled to it
049:005 If only **they** had patience until thou
049:017 **They** impress on thee as favour that
049:017 that **they** have embraced Islam.
050:002 But **they** wonder that there has come to them
050:005 so **they** are in a confused state.
050:005 But **they** deny the truth when it comes to them:
050:006 Do **they** not look at the sky above them?-
050:015 the first Creation, that **they** should be in
050:035 all that **they** wish,-and there is more with Us.
050:036 stronger in power than **they**?
050:036 Then did **they** wander through the land: was there

THEY (continued)

050:039 **they** say, and celebrate the praises of **they** Lord,
050:042 The Day when **they** will hear a (mighty) Blast
050:045 We know best what **they** say; and thou
051:012 **They** ask, "When will be the Day of Judgement
051:013 (It will be) a Day when **they** will be tried
051:015 **they** will be in the midst of Gardens and Springs,
051:016 because, before then, **they** had done good deeds
051:017 **They** were in the habit of sleeping but little
051:018 **they** (were found) praying for Forgiveness;
051:025 Behold, **they** entered His presence,
051:028 **They** said, "Fear not," and **they** gave him
051:028 (When **they** did not eat), He conceived
051:030 **They** said, "Even so has thy Lord spoken: and He
051:032 **They** said, "We have been sent to a people
051:043 Behold, **they** were told "Enjoy (your brief day)
051:044 But **they** insolently defied the command of their
051:044 seized them, even while **they** were looking on.
051:045 Then **they** could not even stand (on their feet),
051:045 (on their feet), nor could **they** help themselves.
051:046 for **they** wickedly transgressed.
051:052 but **they** said (of him) in like manner,
051:053 Is this the legacy **they** have transmitted, one to
051:053 Nay, **they** are themselves a people transgressing
051:056 that **they** may serve Me.
051:057 nor do I require that **they** should feed Me.
051:060 **they** have been promised!
052:013 That Day shall **they** be thrust down to the
052:017 **they** will be in Gardens, and in Happiness,-
052:020 **They** will recline (with ease) on couches
052:022 of fruit and meat, anything **they** shall desire.
052:023 **They** shall there exchange, one with
052:025 **They** will advance to each other, engaging in
052:026 **They** will say: "Aforetime, We were not without
052:030 Or do **they** say:-"A Poet! we await for him
052:032 to this, or are **they** but a people transgressing
052:033 Nay, **they** have no faith!
052:033 Or do **they** say, "He fabricated the (Message)?"
052:034 like unto it,-if (it be) **they** speak the Truth!
052:035 or were **they** themselves the creators?
052:035 Were **they** created of nothing, or were
052:036 Or did **they** create the heavens and the earth?
052:036 Nay, **they** have no firm belief.
052:037 with them, or have **they** control over them.
052:038 by which **they** can (climb up to heaven and) listen
052:038 Or have **they** a ladder, by which
052:040 so that **they** are burdened with a load of debt?-
052:041 and **they** write it down?
052:042 Or do **they** intend a plot (against thee)?
052:043 the things **they** associate with Him!
052:043 Or have **they** a god other then Allah? Exalted is
052:044 Were **they** to see a piece of the sky falling
052:044 **they** would (only) say: "Clouds gathered in heaps!"
052:045 **they** encounter that Day of theirs,
052:045 wherein **they** shall be thunderstruck.
053:023 **They** follow nothings but conjecture and what
053:028 **They** follow nothing but conjecture; and conjecture
053:028 But **they** have no knowledge therein.
053:052 for that **they** were (all) most unjust and most
054:002 But if **they** see a Sign, **they** turn away,
054:003 **They** reject (the warning) and follow
054:007 **They** will come forth,-their eyes humbled-from
054:009 **they** rejected Our servant and said, "Here is

THEY (continued)

054:020 Plucking out men as if **they** were roots of
054:024 For **they** said: "What! a man! a solitary
054:026 Ah! **they** will know on the morrow, which is
054:029 But **they** called to their companion, and he
054:031 Mighty Blast, and **they** became like the dry
054:036 violent Seizure but **they** disputed about the Warning.
054:037 (**They** heard): "Now taste ye My Wrath
054:037 And **they** even sought to snatch away
054:043 (O Quraish), better than **they**?
054:044 Or do **they** say: "We acting together
054:045 to flight, and **they** will show their backs.
054:048 (**they** will hear): "Tastes ye the touch of Hell!"
054:048 The Day **they** will be dragged through the Fire
054:052 All that **they** do is noted in (their)
054:054 **they** will be in the midst of Gardens and Rivers.
055:020 which **they** do not transgress:
055:041 and **they** will be seized by their forelocks and their feet.
055:044 of boiling hot water will **they** wander round!
055:046 **they** will stand before (the Judgment Seat of)
055:054 **They** will recline on Carpets, whose inner
056:015 (**They** will be) on couches encrusted
056:019 nor will **they** suffer intoxication:
056:019 No after-ache will **they** receive therefrom, nor will
056:020 And with fruits, any that **they** may select;
056:021 And the flesh of fowls, any that **they** may desire.
056:025 No frivolity will **they** hear therein, nor any
056:028 (**They** will be) among lote-trees without thorns,
056:042 (**They** will be) in the midst of a fierce
056:045 For that **they** were wont to be indulged,
056:047 And **they** used to say, "What! when we
057:016 and that **they** should not become like those to whom
057:018 and **they** shall have (besides) a generous reward.
057:019 of their Lord: **they** shall have their Reward
057:019 Our Signs,-**they** are the Companions of Hell-Fire.
057:019 and His messengers-**they** are the Truthful and the
057:027 but that **they** did not foster as **they** should have done.
057:027 which **they** invented for themselves, We did not
057:029 that **they** have no power whatever over the Grace
058:002 And in fact **they** use words (both) iniquitous
058:002 **they** cannot be their mothers: none can
058:003 should free a slave before **they** touch each other:
058:003 then wish to go back on the words **they** uttered,-
058:004 two months consecutively before **they** touch each
058:006 Allah has reckoned and which **they** forgot, For Allah
058:007 them what **they** did on the Day of Judgment.
058:007 but he is with them, wheresoever **they** be:
058:008 to that which **they** were forbidden (to do)?
058:008 and **they** say to themselves, "Why does not
058:008 in it will **they** burn, and evil
058:008 And **they** hold secret counsels among
058:008 And when **they** come to thee, **they** salute thee,
058:014 **They** are neither of you nor of them,
058:014 and **they** swear to falsehood knowingly.
058:016 **they** have a humiliating Chastisement.
058:016 thus **they** obstruct (men) from the Path of Allah:
058:016 **They** have made their oaths a screen
058:017 nor their sons: **they** will be Companions of the
058:018 then will **they** swear to Him as **they** swear to you:
058:018 No, indeed! **they** are but liars!
058:018 and **they** think that **they** have something (to stand upon).
058:019 **They** are the Party of Satan.
058:022 Allah will be well pleased with them, and **they** with Him.

THEY (continued)

058:022 **They** are the Party of Allah.
058:022 even though **they** were their fathers or their sons,
059:002 **they** little expected (it), and cast
059:002 so that **they** destroyed their dwellings by their
059:002 that **they** would get out:
059:002 and **they** thought that their fortresses would
059:003 **they** shall (certainly) have the Punishment
059:004 That is because **they** resisted Allah and His
059:009 **they** are the ones that achieve prosperity.
059:011 But Allah is witness that **they** are indeed liars.
059:012 are attacked (in fight), **they** will never help them;
059:012 go out with them; and if **they** are attacked
059:012 help them; and if **they** do help them,
059:012 **they** will turn their backs;
059:012 so **they** will receive no help.
059:012 If **they** are expelled, never will **they** go out
059:013 This is because **they** are men devoid
059:014 **They** will not fight you (even) together, except in
059:014 thou wouldst think **they** were united, but their
059:014 that is because **they** are a people devoid of wisdom.
059:015 **they** have tasted the evil result of their conduct;
059:017 that **they** will go into the Fire, dwelling therein
059:021 to men, that **they** may reflect.
059:023 the partners **they** attribute to Him.
060:001 even though **they** have rejected the truth
060:002 and **they** desire that ye should reject the Truth.
060:002 If **they** overcome you **they** would behave to you
060:004 when **they** said to their people: "We are clear of you
060:004 (**They** prayed): "Our Lord! in Thee do we trust,
060:010 what **they** have spent on their dowers, and let
060:010 what **they** have spent (on their dower).
060:010 **They** are not lawful (wives) for the Unbelievers,
060:010 that **they** are Believers, then send
060:011 **they** had spent (on their dower).
060:012 that **they** will not steal,
060:012 fealty to thee, that **they** will not associate
060:012 that **they** will not utter slander,
060:012 that **they** will not kill their children,
060:012 that **they** will not commit adultery (or fornication),
060:012 and that **they** will not disobey thee in any
060:013 Of the Hereafter **they** are already in despair,
061:004 as if **they** were a solid cemented structure.
061:005 Then when **they** went wrong, Allah let
061:006 Clear Signs, **they** said, "This is evident sorcery!"
061:014 and **they** became the ones that prevailed.
062:002 and Wisdom,-although **they** had been, before, in
062:007 But never will **they** express their desire
062:011 or some pastime, **they** disperse headlong to it,
062:011 But when **they** see some bargain or some pastime,
063:001 **they** say, "We bear witness that thou art
063:002 thus **they** obstruct (men) from the path of Allah:
063:002 **They** have made their oaths a screen
063:003 therefore **they** understand not.
063:003 That is because **they** believed, then **they** rejected Faith:
063:004 **They** are as (worthless as hollow) pieces of
063:004 **They** are the enemies; so beware
063:004 How are **they** deluded (away from the Truth)!
063:004 **They** think that every cry is against them.
063:004 and when **they** speak, thou listenest
063:005 for your forgiveness," **they** turn aside their
063:007 till **they** disperse (and quit Madinah).
063:007 **They** are the ones who say, "Spend nothing

THEY (continued)

063:008 **They** say, "If we return to Madinah, surely the
063:009 If any act thus, surely **they** are the losers.
064:005 So **they** tasted the evil result of their conduct;
064:005 their conduct; and **they** had a grievous Chastisement.
064:006 So **they** rejected (the Message) and turned away.
064:006 but **they** said: "Shall (mere) human beings direct us?"
064:007 The Unbelievers think that **they** will not be
064:010 **they** will be Companions of the Fire, to dwell
064:016 **they** are the ones that achieve prosperity.
065:001 **they** are guilty of some open lewdness, those are
065:001 their houses, nor shall **they** (themselves) leave,
065:002 Thus when **they** fulfil their term appointed,
065:004 **they** deliver their burdens: and for
065:006 and if **they** suckle your (offspring), give them
065:006 until **they** deliver their burden: and if
065:006 And if **they** are pregnant, then spend
065:009 Then did **they** taste the evil result of their
066:006 **they** receive from Allah, but do
066:006 but do (precisely) what **they** are commanded.
066:008 while **they** say, "Our Lord! perfect our light
066:010 **they** betrayed their (husbands),
066:010 **they** were (respectively) under two of Our
066:010 and **they** profited nothing before Allah on their
067:007 **they** will hear the (terrible) drawing in of its
067:007 When **they** are cast therein,
067:009 **They** will say: "Yes indeed: a Warner
067:010 **They** will further say: "Had we but listened
067:011 **They** will then confess their sins: but far
067:019 Do **they** not observe the birds above them,
067:021 Nay, **they** obstinately persist in insolent impiety
067:025 **They** ask: When will this promise be (fulfilled)?
067:027 At length, when **they** see it close at hand,
068:005 Soon wilt thou see and **they** will see,
068:017 when **they** resolved to gather the fruits of the
068:019 while **they** were asleep.
068:021 As the morning broke, **they** called out, one to
068:023 So **they** departed, conversing in secret low tones,
068:025 And **they** opened the morning, strong in
068:026 **they** said: "We have surely lost our way:
068:026 But when **they** saw the (garden),
068:029 **They** said: "Glory to our Lord! Verily we
068:030 Then **they** turned, one against another, in reproach.
068:031 **They** said: "Alas for us! We have indeed transgressed!
068:033 in the Hereafter,-if only **they** knew!
068:041 produce their "partners," if **they** are truthful!
068:041 Or have **they** some "Partners" (in Godhead)?
068:042 to prostrate, but **they** shall not be able,-
068:042 laid bare, and **they** shall be summoned to prostrate,
068:043 while **they** were whole, (and had refused).
068:043 seeing that **they** had been summoned aforetime
068:044 from directions **they** perceive not.
068:046 so that **they** are burdened with a load
068:047 so that **they** can write it down?
068:051 thee up with their eyes when **they** hear the Message;
068:051 and **they** say: "Surely he is possessed!"
069:005 But the Thamud,-**they** were destroyed by a terrible
069:006 And the 'Ad,-**they** were destroyed by a furious
069:007 in its (path), as if **they** had been roots of
069:014 and its mountains, and **they** are crushed at one
070:006 **They** see the (Day) indeed as a far-off (event):
070:011 Though **they** will be put in sight of each other,-
070:030 hands possess,-for (then) **they** are not to be blamed,

THEY (continued)

070:036 the Unbelievers that **they** rush madly before thee-
070:039 out of the (base matter) **they** know!
070:041 Substitute for them better (men) than **they**;
070:042 that Day of theirs which **they** have been promised!
070:042 and play about, until **they** encounter that Day
070:043 The Day whereon **they** will issue from their
070:043 as if **they** were rushing to a goal-post
070:044 Such is the Day the which **they** are promised!
071:007 **they** have (only) thrust their fingers into their
071:021 Noah said: "O my Lord! **they** have disobeyed me,
071:021 but **they** follow (men) whose wealth and children
071:022 "And **they** have devised a tremendous Plot.
071:023 "And **they** have said (to each other), `Abandon not
071:024 "**They** have already misled many; and grant
071:025 and **they** found-in lieu of Allah-none to help them.
071:025 Because of their sins **they** were drowned
071:027 and **they** will breed none but wicked
071:027 **they** will but mislead Thy devotees,
072:001 **They** said, 'We have really heard a wonderful Recital!
072:006 but **they** increased them into further error.
072:007 'And **they** (came to) think as ye thought,
072:014 **they** have sought out (the path) of right conduct:
072:015 **they** are (but) fuel for Hell Fire'-
072:016 "If **they** (the pagans) had (only) remained on the
072:019 **they** just make round him a dense crowd."
072:023 **they** shall dwell therein for ever."
072:024 At length, when **they** see (with their own eyes)
072:024 **they** are promised,-then will **they** know who it
072:028 "That he may know that **they** have (truly) brought
073:010 And have patience with what **they** say, and leave
074:040 (**They** will be) in Gardens (of Delight);
074:040 **they** will question each other,
074:043 **They** will say: "We were not of those who prayed;
074:049 that **they** turn away from admonition?-
074:050 As if **they** were affrighted asses,
074:053 By no means! But **they** fear not the Hereafter.
076:005 As to the Righteous, **they** shall drink of a Cup
076:007 **They** perform (their) vows, and **they** fear
076:007 and **they** fear a Day whose evil flies far and wide.
076:008 And **they** feed, for the love of Allah, the indigent,
076:012 And because **they** were patient and constant, He will
076:013 on raised couches, **they** will see there neither
076:016 **they** will determine the measure thereof
076:017 And **they** will be given to drink there of a Cup
076:021 and **they** will be adorned with Bracelets of silver;
076:027 As to these, **they** love the fleeting life,
077:035 shall not be able to speak,
077:041 **they** shall be amidst (cool) shades and springs
077:042 And (**they** shall have) fruits,-all **they** desire.
077:048 "Prostrate yourselves!" **They** do not so.
077:050 Then what Message, after that, will **they** believe in?
078:001 Concerning what are **they** disputing?
078:003 About which **they** cannot agree.
078:004 Verily, **they** shall soon (come to) know!
078:005 Verily, verily **they** shall soon (come to) know!
078:020 as if **they** were a mirage.
078:023 **They** will dwell therein for ages.
078:024 Nothing cool shall **they** taste therein,
078:027 For that **they** used not to look for any account
078:028 But **they** (impudently) treated Our Signs as false
078:035 No Vanity shall **they** hear therein, nor Untruth;-
079:010 **They** say (now): "What! shall we indeed be returned

THEY (continued)

079:012 **They** say: "It would, in that case, be a
079:014 When, behold, **they** will be brought out to the open.
079:042 **They** ask thee about the Hour,-'When will
079:044 With **they** Lord is the final end of it.
079:046 (it will be) as if **they** had tarried but a single
079:046 The Day **they** see it, (it will be)
082:012 **They** know all that ye do.
082:013 As for the Righteous, **they** will be in Bliss;
082:014 And the Wicked-**they** will be in the Fire,
082:015 Which **they** will enter on the Day of Judgment,
082:016 And **they** will not be able to keep away therefrom.
083:002 Those who, when **they** have to receive by measure
083:003 But when **they** have to give by measure or weight
083:004 Do **they** not think that **they** will be raised up?-
083:014 is the stain of the (ill) which **they** do!
083:015 that Day, will **they** be veiled.
083:016 Further, **they** will enter the Fire of Hell.
083:023 On raised couches will **they** command a sight
083:030 And whenever **they** passed by them, used to
083:031 **they** would return jesting;
083:031 And when **they** returned to their own people,
083:032 **they** would say, "Behold! these are the people truly astray!"
083:032 And whenever **they** saw them,
083:033 But **they** had not been sent as Keepers over them!
083:035 On raised couches **they** will command (a sight)
083:036 paid back for what **they** did?
084:020 that **they** believe not?-
084:021 **they** fall not prostrate.
084:023 of what **they** secrete (in their breasts).
085:006 Behold! **they** sat over against the (fire),
085:007 And **they** witnessed (all) that **they** were doing
085:008 no other reason than that **they** believed in Allah,
085:008 And **they** ill-treated them for no other reason
085:010 **they** will have the Chastisement of the
086:015 As for them, **they** are but plotting a scheme,
088:004 The while **they** enter the Blazing Fire,-
088:005 The while **they** are given, to drink,
088:011 Where **they** shall hear no (word) of vanity:
088:017 Do **they** not look at the Camels, how **they** are made?-
088:019 And at the Mountains, how **they** are fixed firm?-
090:019 **they** are the (unhappy) Companions of the Left Hand.
091:014 Then **they** rejected him (as a false prophet),
091:014 (as a false prophet), and **they** hamstrung her.
092:021 And soon will **they** attain (complete) satisfaction.
095:006 for **they** shall have a reward unfailing.
098:005 And **they** have been commanded no more than this:
098:006 **They** are the worst of creatures.
098:007 do righteous deeds,-**they** are the best of creatures.
098:008 Allah well pleased with them, and **they** with Him:
098:008 **They** will dwell therein for ever;
099:006 to be shown the Deeds that **they** (had done).

THICK

048:029 it then becomes **thick**, and it stands

THIEF

005:038 As to the **thief**, male or female, cut off
005:039 But if the **thief** repent after his crime, and amend

THIEVES

012:070 ye are **thieves**, without doubt!"
012:073 in the land, and we are no **thieves**!"

THINE

001:005 Thee do we worship, and **Thine** aid we seek.

THINE (continued)

005:029 thee draw on thyself my sin as well as **thine**, for
005:116 though I know not what is in **Thine**.
012:095 in **thine** old wandering illusion."
015:088 Strain not **thine** eyes. (Wistfully) at
017:014 "Read **thine** (own) record: sufficient is thy soul
018:028 and let not **thine** eyes pass beyond them,
019:026 "So eat and drink and cool (**thine**) eye.
019:097 in **thine** own tongue, that with
020:058 "But we can surely produce magic to match **thine**!
020:131 Nor strain **thine** eyes in longing for the
026:019 "And thou didst a deed of **thine** which (thou knowest)
046:035 (**Thine** but) to deliver the Message:
051:054 So turn away from them: not **thine** is the blame.
094:007 (from **thine** immediate task), still labor hard,

THING

002:216 ye dislike a **thing** which is good for you,
002:216 and that ye love a **thing** which is bad for you.
002:220 Say: "The best **thing** to do is what is for their good;
002:236 is due from those who wish to do the right **thing**.
002:283 deposits a **thing** on trust with another,
004:019 it may be that ye dislike a **thing**,
004:073 a fine **thing** should I then have made of it!"
005:116 Had I said such a **thing**. Thou wouldst
006:010 by the **thing** that they mocked.
006:019 Say: "What **thing** is most weighty in evidence?"
006:144 Allah ordered you such a **thing**? But who
006:148 nor should we have had any forbidden **thing**."
011:072 That would indeed be a wonderful **thing**!"
013:008 Every single **thing** is with Him in (due)
015:021 And there is not a **thing** but its (sources and)
016:053 And ye have no good **thing** but is from Allah:
016:116 But say not-for any false **thing** that your
017:044 a **thing** but celebrates His praise; and yet
018:005 No knowledge have they of such a **thing**, nor had
018:005 It is a grievous **thing** that issues from their
018:071 Truly a strange **thing** hast thou done!"
018:074 Truly a foul (unheard-of) **thing** hast thou done!"
019:023 would that I had been a **thing** forgotten."
019:027 "O Mary! truly a strange **thing** hast thou brought!
019:089 Indeed ye have put forth a **thing** most monstrous!
020:050 to each (created) **thing** its form, then, gave (it)
021:017 if We would do (such a **thing**)!
021:030 We made from water every living **thing**.
021:041 hemmed in by the **thing** that they mocked.
021:084 and a **thing** for commemoration, for all
022:001 (of judgment) will be a **thing** terrible!
023:024 such a **thing** (as he says), among our
024:003 to the Believers such a **thing** is forbidden.
029:045 is the greatest (**thing** in life) without doubt.
033:053 Truly such a **thing** is in Allah's sight an enormity.
036:082 Verily, when He intends a **thing**, His Command
038:005 Truly this is a strange **thing**!"
038:006 a **thing** designed (against you)!
038:043 from Us, and a **thing** for commemoration, for all
040:016 come forth: not a single **thing** concerning them
046:011 "If (this Message) were a good **thing**,
050:002 "This is a wonderful **thing**!
050:019 "This **thing** which thou wast trying to escape!"
050:031 nigh to the righteous,-no more a **thing** distant.
051:049 And of every **thing** We have created pairs: that ye
060:012 any other **thing** whatever with Allah, that they
070:028 a **thing** to feel secure from:-

THING (continued)

072:028   and takes account of every single **thing**."
086:014   It is not a **thing** for amusement.

THINGS

002:011   only ones that put **things** right!"
002:020   for Allah hath power over all **things**.
002:025   for they are given **things** in similitude;
002:026   use the similitude of **things**,
002:029   and of all **things** He hath perfect knowledge.
002:029   for you all **things** that are on earth;
002:031   And He taught Adam the names of all **things**;
002:035   **things** therein as (where and when) ye will;
002:057   the good **things** We have provided for you:"
002:102   and such **things** as came down at Babylon
002:102   taught anyone (such **things**) without saying:
002:106   Allah hath power over all **things**?
002:109   for Allah hath power over all **things**.
002:148   For Allah hath power over all **things**.
002:171   to **things** that listen to nothing
002:172   the good **things** that We have provided for you.
002:181   For Allah hears and knows (all **things**).
002:194   and so for all **things** prohibited,
002:224   heareth and knoweth all **things**.
002:227   Allah heareth and knoweth all **things**.
002:231   well acquainted with all **things**.
002:244   and know that Allah heareth and knoweth all **things**.
002:247   Allah is All-embracing, and He knoweth all **things**."
002:255   His are all **things** in the heavens and on earth.
002:256   And Allah heareth and knoweth all **things**.
002:259   Allah hath power over all **things**."
002:261   and He knoweth all **things**.
002:267   good **things** which ye have (honorably) earned,
002:268   and He knoweth all **things**.
002:282   And Allah is well acquainted with all **things**.
002:284   For Allah hath power over all **things**.
003:014   the love of **things** they covet: women and sons;
003:015   glad tidings of **things** far better than those?
003:026   Verily, over all **things** Thou hast power.
003:029   And Allah has power over all **things**.
003:034   and Allah heareth and knoweth all **things**.
003:035   for Thou hearest and knoweth all **things**."
003:044   This is part of the tidings of the **things** unseen,
003:073   and He knoweth all **things**."
003:121   and Allah heareth and knoweth all **things**.
003:165   for Allah hath power over all **things**."
003:189   and Allah hath power over all **things**.
004:002   worthless **things** for (their) good ones;
004:031   of the **things** which ye are forbidden to do,
004:032   for Allah hath full knowledge of all **things**.
004:032   And in no wise covet those **things** in which
004:033   For truly Allah is witness to all **things**.
004:035   and is acquainted with all **things**.
004:035   if they seek to set **things** aright, Allah
004:058   For Allah is He Who heareth and seeth all **things**.
004:078   Say: "All **things** are from Allah."
004:081   on **things** very different from what thou tellest them.
004:085   and Allah hath power over all **things**.
004:086   Allah takes careful account of all **things**.
004:126   But to Allah belong all **things** in the
004:126   and He it is that encompasseth all **things**.
004:131   To Allah belong all **things** in the heavens and on earth.
004:132   all **things** in the heavens and on earth, and
004:147   and knoweth all **things**.

THINGS (continued)

004:148   for Allah is He who heareth and knoweth all **things**.
004:170   to Allah belong all **things** in the heavens
004:171   To Him belong all **things** in the
004:176   And Allah hath knowledge of all **things**.
005:004   Say: Lawful unto you are (all) **things** good and pure:
005:005   **things** good and pure made lawful unto you.
005:017   For Allah hath power over all **things**."
005:019   and Allah hath power over all **things**.
005:019   making (**things**) clear unto you, Our Messenger,
005:040   and Allah hath power over all **things**.
005:054   and He knoweth all **things**.
005:062   transgression and their eating of **things** forbidden.
005:062   Evil indeed are the **things** that they do.
005:063   sinful words and eating **things** forbidden?
005:076   that heareth and knoweth all **things**."
005:087   the good **things** which Allah hath made lawful
005:088   Eat of the **things** which Allah hath
005:097   and that Allah is well acquainted with all **things**.
005:100   Say: "Not equal are **things** that are bad and
005:100   and **things** that are good, even though
005:101   But if ye ask about **things** when the Qur'an
005:101   about **things** which, if made plain to you, may
005:117   and Thou art a Witness to all **things**.
005:120   and it is He who hath power over all **things**.
006:013   Who heareth and knoweth all **things**.
006:017   He hath power over all **things**.
006:018   and He is the Wise, acquainted with all **things**."
006:028   to the **things** they were forbidden, for they
006:044   the gates of all (good) **things**, until, in the
006:071   **things** that can do us neither good nor harm, and
006:073   well acquainted (with all **things**).
006:080   my Lord comprehendeth in His knowledge all **things**.
006:099   Behold! in these **things** there are signs
006:101   He created all **things**, and He hath
006:101   and He hath full knowledge of all **things**.
006:102   the Creator of all **things**: then worship
006:111   all **things** before their very eyes, they are
006:154   and explaining all **things** in detail,-and a
006:164   Cherisher of all **things** (that exist)?"
006:164   of **things** wherein ye disputed."
007:019   and enjoy (its good **things**) as ye wish: but
007:032   and the **things**, clean and pure,
007:033   and saying **things** about Allah of which
007:033   Say: The **things** that my Lord hath indeed forbidden
007:037   they say: "Where are the **things** that ye
007:050   They will say: "Both these **things** hath Allah
007:053   and the **things** they forged will leave
007:085   the **things** that are their due; and do
007:089   Our Lord comprehends all **things** in His
007:145   Admonition and explanation of all **things**,
007:156   but My Mercy extendeth to all **things**.
007:160   (saying): "Eat of the good **things** We have
007:191   as partners **things** that can create nothing, but
007:200   for he heareth and knoweth (all **things**).
008:001   (**things** taken as) spoils of war. Say: "(Such)
008:017   He who heareth and knoweth (all **things**).
008:026   and gave you good **things** for sustenance: that ye
008:027   **things** entrusted to you.
008:041   For Allah hath power over all **things**.
008:042   is He Who heareth and knoweth (all **things**).
008:053   heareth and knoweth (all **things**)."
008:061   the One that heareth and knoweth (all **things**).

THINGS (continued)

008:075	Verily Allah is well-acquainted with all **things**.
009:039	hath power over all **things**.
009:052	other than one of two glorious **things**-
009:055	punish them with these **things** in this life,
009:078	well all **things** unseen?
009:085	these **things** in this world, and that
009:088	for them are (all) good **things**: and it
009:098	that heareth and knoweth (all **things**).
009:115	should avoid, for Allah hath knowledge of all **things**.
010:003	regulating and governing all **things**.
010:059	and (some **things**) lawful." Say: "Hath Allah
010:059	Yet ye hold forbidden some **things** thereof and
010:059	Say: "See ye what **things** Allah hath sent down
010:059	or do ye forge (**things**) to attribute to Allah?"
010:061	the greatest of these **things** but are recorded
010:065	it is He Who heareth and knoweth (all **things**).
010:067	and the Day to make **things** visible (to you).
010:068	His are all **things** in the heavens and on earth!
011:001	and Well-Acquainted (with all **things**):
011:004	and He hath power over all **things**."
011:057	For my Lord hath care and watch over all **things**."
011:085	the people the **things** that are their due:
011:114	for those **things** that are good remove those
011:116	of the good **things** of life which were given them,
012:017	and left Joseph with our **things**: and the wolf
012:034	verily He heareth and knoweth (all **things**).
012:077	But these **things** did Joseph keep locked in his heart,
012:111	a detailed exposition of all **things**,
013:003	in these **things** are Signs for those who consider!
013:004	Behold, verily in these **things** there are Signs
013:016	Say: "Allah is the Creator of all **things**:
013:018	are (all) good **things**.
013:021	**things** which Allah hath commanded to be joined,
013:025	those **things** which Allah has commanded to be
013:031	the Command is with Allah in **things**!
013:042	devise plots; but in all **things** Allah is the
014:002	Of Allah, to Whom do belong all **things** in the
014:004	in order to make (**things**) clear to them.
015:001	of a Qur'an that makes **things** clear.
015:019	of **things** in due balance.
015:086	is the All-Creator, knowing all **things**.
016:008	(other) **things** of which ye have no knowledge.
016:013	And the **things** on this earth which He has
016:021	(They are **things**) dead, lifeless: nor do thy
016:048	Among **things**,-how their shadows turn round,
016:056	And they (even) assign, to **things** they do not know,
016:064	to them those **things** in which they differ,
016:072	will they then believe in vain **things**,
016:077	even quicker: for Allah hath power over all **things**.
016:081	out of the **things** He created,
016:081	some **things** to give you shade; of the
016:089	Book explaining all **things**, a guide a Mercy,
016:116	so as to ascribe false **things** to Allah.
016:116	For those who ascribe false **things** to Allah,
016:118	To the Jews We prohibited such **things** as We
017:001	Who heareth and seeth (all **things**).
017:012	all **things** have We explained in detail.
017:016	are given the good **things** of this life (to be
017:018	transitory **things** (of this life), We readily
017:018	We readily grant them-such **things** as We will,
017:038	Of all such **things** the evil is hateful
017:041	We have explained (**things**) in various (ways)

THINGS (continued)

017:053	(only) say those **things** that are best: for Satan
017:070	**things** good and pure; and conferred
017:096	and He sees (all **things**)."
017:102	these **things** have been sent down by none
018:016	and the **things** they worship other than Allah,
018:045	it is (only) Allah Who prevails over all **things**.
018:046	but the **things** that endure, Good Deeds,
018:054	in most **things**, contentious.
018:068	about **things** which are beyond your knowledge?"
018:078	(those **things**) over which thou was unable
018:082	of (those **things**) over which thou wast unable
019:076	and the **things** that endure, Good Deeds,
020:081	(Saying): "Eat of the good **things** We have
020:098	all **things** He comprehends in His Knowledge.
020:131	for the **things** We have given for enjoyment
021:004	heareth and knoweth (all **things**)."
021:013	Flee not, but return to the good **things** of this
021:017	it from the **things** nearest to Us, if We
021:018	(false) **things** ye ascribe (to Us).
021:027	and they act (in all **things**) by His command.
021:032	the Signs which these **things** (point to)!
021:044	Nay, We gave the good **things** of this life
021:066	besides Allah, **things** that can neither be of
021:067	"Fie upon you, and upon the **things** that ye
021:079	with David: it was We Who did (all these **things**).
021:081	for We do know all **things**.
022:006	and it is He Who has power over all **things**.
022:017	for Allah is witness of all **things**.
022:018	all **things** that are in the heavens and on earth,-
022:061	Who hears and sees (all **things**).
022:071	**things** for which no authority has been sent down to them,
022:075	He Who hears and sees (all **things**).
023:033	had bestowed the good **things** of this life,
023:051	O ye messenger! enjoy (all) **things** good and pure,
023:064	the good **things** of this world, behold, they
023:081	On the contrary they say **things** similar to
023:083	"Such **things** have been promised to us and to
023:088	is the sovereignty of all **things**,-Who protects
023:091	(sort of) **things** they attribute to Him!
023:096	We are well acquainted with the **things** they say.
023:100	in the **things** I neglected."-"By no means! it is
024:015	and said out of your mouths **things** of which ye
024:021	hears and knows (all **things**).
024:025	that makes all **things** manifest.
024:032	and He knoweth all **things**.
024:034	verses making **things** clear, an illustration
024:035	for men: and Allah doth know all **things**.
024:044	verily in these **things** is an instructive example
024:045	for verily Allah has power over all **things**.
024:046	that make **things** manifest: and Allah
024:060	and Allah is One Who sees and knows all **things**.
024:064	of what they did: for Allah doth know all **things**.
025:002	it is He Who created all **things**, and ordered
025:010	could give thee better (**things**) than those,-
025:018	good **things** (in life), until they
025:020	For Allah is One Who sees (all **things**).
025:049	of **things** We have created,-cattle and
025:054	for thy Lord has power (over all **things**).
025:055	**things** that can neither profit them nor harm them:
025:059	of any acquainted (with such **things**).
026:002	that makes (**things**) clear.
026:007	how many noble **things** of all kinds we have

THINGS (continued)

026:059 the Children of Israel inheritors of such **things**.
026:169 and my family from such **things** as they do!"
026:183 And withhold not **things** justly due to men,
026:220 For it is He Who heareth and knoweth all **things**.
027:001 a Book that makes (**things**) clear;
027:088 of Allah, Who disposes of all **things** in perfect
027:091 to Whom (belong) all **things**: and I
028:002 that makes (**things**) clear.
028:019 and not to be one who sets **things** right!"
028:048 And they say: "For us, we reject all (such **things**)!"
028:060 The (material) **things** which ye are given are but
028:061 the good **things** of this life, but who, on the
029:005 and He hears and knows (all **things**).
029:017 The **things** that ye worship besides Allah have no
029:020 for Allah has power over all **things**.
029:060 and you: for He hears and knows (all **things**).
029:062 for Allah has full knowledge of all **things**.
030:007 They know but the outer (**things**) in the
030:035 which speaks to them the **things** to which they pay
030:040 any single one of these **things**? Glory to Him!
030:050 for He has power over all **things**.
031:015 join in worship with Me **things** of which thou
031:020 to your (use) all **things** in the heavens and on
031:022 and to Allah shall all **things** return.
031:026 To Allah belong all **things** in heaven and earth:
031:028 for Allah is He Who hears and sees (all **things**).
031:034 is acquainted (with all **things**).
032:006 Such as He, the knower of all **things**, hidden and
032:007 He Who has created all **things** in the best way
033:027 And Allah has power over all **things**.
033:040 and Allah has full knowledge of all **things**.
033:052 watch over all **things**.
033:054 has full knowledge of all **things**.
033:055 fear Allah; for Allah is Witness to all **things**.
034:001 all **things** in the heavens and on earth: to Him
034:021 and thy Lord doth watch over all **things**.
034:047 from Allah: and He is Witness to all **things**."
034:050 it is He Who hears all **things**, and is (ever) near."
035:001 for Allah has power over all **things**.
035:038 the hidden **things** of the heavens and the earth:
036:012 leave behind, and of all **things** have We taken
036:036 in pairs all **things** that the earth produces,
036:036 own (human) kind and (other) **things** of which
036:069 and a Qur'an making **things** clear:
036:071 among the **things** which Our hands have
036:083 is the dominion of all **things**: and to Him
037:022 and the **things** they worshipped-
037:117 which helps to make **things** clear;
037:159 from the **things** they ascribe (to Him)!
039:004 (He is above such **things**). He is Allah,
039:038 The **things** ye invoke besides Allah,-can they,
039:062 Allah is the Creator of all **things**, and He
040:007 "Our Lord! Thou embracest all **things**, in Mercy
040:020 Who hears and sees (all **things**).
040:056 it is He Who hears and sees (all **things**).
040:062 the Creator of all **things**, there is
040:064 of **things** pure and good;-such is Allah
040:075 on the earth in **things** other than the Truth,
041:036 He is the One Who hears and knows all **things**.
041:039 For He has Power over all **things**.
041:049 Man does not weary of asking for good (**things**),
041:053 enough that thy Lord doth witness all **things**?

THINGS (continued)

041:054 that doth encompass all **things**!
042:009 it is He Who has power over all **things**.
042:012 He will: for He knows full well all **things**.
042:013 worship other **things** than Allah, hard is
042:030 is because of the **things** your hands have wrought,
043:002 By the Book that makes **things** clear,-
043:012 That has created pairs in all **things**, and has
043:029 and a Messenger making **things** clear.
043:029 Yea, I have given the good **things** of this life
043:079 But it is We Who settle **things**.
043:082 He is free from the **things** they attribute (to Him)!
044:002 By the Book that makes **things** clear;-
044:006 for He hears and knows (all **things**);
044:013 **things** clearly has (already) come to them,-
044:027 And pleasant **things** wherein they had
044:028 And We made other people inherit (those **things**)!
045:016 for Sustenance **things** good and pure; and We
046:020 "Ye squandered your good **things** in the life
046:033 Yea, verily He has power over all **things**.
048:015 Nay, but little do they understand (such **things**).
048:021 and Allah has power over all **things**.
048:026 And Allah has full knowledge of all **things**.
049:001 for Allah is He who hears and knows all **things**.
049:013 and is well acquainted (with all **things**).
049:016 He has full knowledge of all **things**.
051:016 Taking joy in the **things** which their
052:043 the **things** they associate with Him!
054:049 Verily, all **things** have We created
057:002 and He has Power over all **things**.
057:003 and He has full knowledge of all **things**.
058:001 for Allah hears and sees (all **things**).
058:006 for Allah is Witness to all **things**.
058:007 full knowledge of all **things**.
059:006 and Allah has power over all **things**.
059:009 in their hearts for **things** given to the (latter),
059:022 no other god;-Who knows (all **things**) both secret
060:007 For Allah has power (over all **things**); and Allah
062:008 of **things** secret and open:
062:008 and He will tell you the **things** that ye did!"
064:001 and He has power over all **things**.
064:011 for Allah knows all **things**.
065:003 for all **things** has Allah appointed a due proportion.
065:012 Allah has power over all **things**, and that
065:012 all **things** in (His) Knowledge.
066:008 us Forgiveness: for Thou hast power over all **things**."
067:001 and He over all **things** Hath Power;-
067:019 truly it is He that watches over all **things**.
073:011 those in possession of the good **things** of life,
077:003 And scatter (**things**) far and wide;
077:023 the Best to determine (**things**).
078:029 And all **things** have We preserved on record.
083:023 a sight (of all **things**):
083:035 (a sight) (of all **things**).
085:009 And Allah is Witness to all **things**.
086:009 The Day that (all) **things** secret will be tested,
102:001 diverts you (from the more serious **things**),
113:002 From the mischief of created **things**;

THINK

002:214 Or do ye **think** that ye shall enter
003:078 you would **think** it is a part of the Book,
003:142 Did ye **think** that ye would enter Heaven
003:169 **Think** not of those who are slain

THINK (continued)

003:178 Let not the Unbelievers **think** that our respite
003:180 **think** that it is good for them:
003:188 **think** not that they can escape the Chastisement.
003:188 **Think** not that those who exult in what
006:040 Say: "**Think** ye to yourselves, if there come
006:046 Say: "**Think** ye, if Allah took away your hearing
006:047 Say: "**Think** ye, if the Punishment of Allah
007:030 and **think** that they receive guidance.
007:066 and "We **think** thou art a liar!"
008:059 Let not the Unbelievers **think** that they
009:016 Do you **think** that you would be left alone while
010:022 and they **think** they are being overwhelmed:
010:024 it belongs **think** they have all powers of
010:060 And what **think** those who forge lies against Allah,
011:027 in fact we **think** ye are liars!"
012:094 nay, **think** me not a dotard."
012:110 **think** that they were treated as liars,
014:042 **Think** not that Allah doth not heed the deeds
014:047 Never **think** that Allah would fail His messengers
017:052 and ye will **think** that ye tarried
018:102 Do the Unbelievers **think** that they can take
022:015 If any **think** that Allah will not help him
023:055 Do they **think** that because We have granted them
023:115 "Did ye then **think** that We had created you
024:011 **think** it not to be an evil to you; on the
024:057 Never **think** thou that the Unbelievers can escape
026:186 like us, and indeed we **think** thou art a liar!
028:038 I **think** (Moses) is a liar!"
029:002 Do men **think** that they will be left alone
029:004 Do those who practice evil **think** that they
030:027 (We can **think** of) in the heavens and the earth:
033:020 They **think** that the Confederates have not
040:037 but surely, I **think** (Moses) is a liar!"
041:022 But ye did **think** that Allah knew not many of the
041:050 I **think** not that the Hour (of Judgment)
043:037 but they **think** that they are being guided aright!
043:080 Or do they **think** that We hear not their secrets
045:021 **think** that We shall hold them as equal with those
045:032 the Hour: we only **think** it a conjecture, and we
047:029 is a disease, **think** that Allah will not
048:006 who **think** an evil thought of Allah. On them
058:018 swear to you: and they **think** that they have
059:002 Little did ye **think** that they would get out:
059:014 thou wouldst **think** they were united, but their
062:006 Say: "O ye of Jewry! if ye **think** that ye are
063:004 They **think** that every cry is against them.
064:007 The Unbelievers **think** that they will not be
069:020 "I did really **think** that my Account
072:005 'But we do **think** that no man or Jinn
072:007 'And they (came to) **think** as ye thought,
072:012 'But we **think** that we can by no means
075:003 Does man **think** that We cannot assemble his bones?
075:028 And he will **think** that it was (the Time)
075:036 Does Man **think** that he will be left uncontrolled,
076:019 thou wouldst **think** them scattered Pearls.
083:004 Do they not **think** that they will be raised up?-
084:014 Truly, did he **think** that he would not
086:005 Now let man but **think** from what he is created!

THINKEST

025:044 Or **thinkest** thou that most of them listen
027:088 **thinkest** them firmly fixed: but they

THINKETH

090:005 **Thinketh** he, that none hath power over him?
090:007 **Thinketh** he that none beholdeth him?

THINKING

104:003 **Thinking** that his wealth would make him

THINKS

002:273 the ignorant man **thinks**, because of
092:008 and **thinks** himself self-sufficient.

THIRD

004:011 the mother has a **third**:
004:012 but if more than two, they share in a **third**;
036:014 but We strengthened them with a **third**:
053:020 And another, the **third** (goddess), Manat?
073:020 or half the night, or a **third** of the night, so do

THIRST

009:120 whether they suffered **thirst**, or fatigue,
020:119 "Nor to suffer from **thirst**, nor from
024:039 parched with **thirst** mistakes for water;
025:049 a dead land, and slake the **thirst** of things
056:055 diseased camels raging with **thirst**!
083:025 Their **thirst** will be slaked with Pure Wine sealed;

THIRSTY

007:160 when his (**thirsty**) people asked him for Water:
019:086 to Hell, (like **thirsty** cattle driven down to water,-)

THIRTY

007:142 We appointed for Moses **thirty** nights,
046:015 to his weaning is (a period of) **thirty** months.

THIS

002:002 **This** is the Book;
002:025 they say: "Why **this** is what we were fed
002:026 "What means Allah by **this** similitude?"
002:035 but approach not **this** tree,
002:058 And remember We said: "Enter **this** town,
002:061 **This** because They rebelled
002:061 **This** because they went on rejecting
002:079 and then say: "**This** is from Allah,"
002:083 the children of Israel (to **this** effect):
002:084 your Covenant (to **this** effect):
002:084 and **this** ye solemnly ratified.
002:084 and to **this** ye were witness.
002:085 behave like **this** but disgrace in **this** life?
002:085 After **this** it is ye, the same people,
002:086 buy the life of **this** world at the price
002:114 but disgrace in **this** world,
002:126 make **this** a City of Peace,
002:127 the House (with **this** prayer):
002:127 "Our Lord! accept (**this** service) from us:
002:130 Him We chose and rendered pure in **this** world:
002:146 know **this** as they know their own sons;
002:178 **This** is a concession and a Mercy from your Lord.
002:178 After **this** whoever exceeds the limits
002:180 **this** is due from the God-fearing.
002:196 **This** is for those whose household is not
002:200 "Our Lord! Give us (thy bounties) in **this** world!"
002:201 in **this** world and good in the Hereafter.
002:204 whose speech about **this** world's life may
002:212 The life of **this** world is alluring
002:217 no fruit in **this** life and in the Hereafter;
002:220 (Their bearings) on **this** life and the Hereafter.
002:232 **This** instruction is for all amongst you,
002:241 suitable Gift **this** is duty on the righteous.
002:248 In **this** is a Symbol for you

THIS (continued)

002:249	they said: "This day we cannot cope
002:259	When this was shown clearly to him,
002:259	after (this) its death?"
003:003	Before this, as a guide to mankind,
003:013	In this is a lesson for such as have eyes to see."
003:014	Such are the possessions of this world's life;
003:022	no fruit in this world and in the Hereafter,
003:024	This because they say: "The Fire shall not touch us
003:035	so accept this or me: for Thou hearest
003:037	He said: "O Mary! whence (comes) this to you?"
003:044	This is part of the tidings of the things unseen,
003:045	held in honour in this world and the Hereafter
003:049	the Children of Israel, (with this message):
003:051	This is a Way that is straight."
003:056	severe chastisement in this world and the Hereafter
003:058	"This is what we rehearse unto thee of the Signs
003:061	If any one disputes in this manner with thee,
003:062	This is the true account: there is no
003:068	as are also this Prophet and those who believe:
003:081	and take this My covenant as binding on you?"
003:082	If any turn back after this, they are
003:094	If any, after this, invent a lie
003:112	this because they rebelled and transgressed
003:112	This because they rejected the Signs of Allah,
003:117	life of this (material) world may be likened
003:145	If any do desire a reward in this life,
003:148	And Allah gave them a reward in this world,
003:152	Among you are some that hanker after this world
003:154	but (all this was) that Allah might test what
003:154	"If we had had anything to do with this affair,
003:154	Say thou: "Indeed, this affair is wholly Allah's."
003:156	This that Allah may make it a cause of sighs
003:165	do ye say?-"Whence is this?"
003:182	"This is because of the (unrighteous deeds) which
003:185	for the life of this world is but goods
003:191	not for naught hast Thou created (all) this!
004:002	For this is indeed a great sin.
004:025	This (permission) is for those
004:074	who sell the life of this world for the Hereafter.
004:075	"Our Lord! rescue us from this town.
004:077	Say: "Short is the enjoyment of this world:
004:078	they say, "This is from Allah"; but
004:078	"This is from thee" (O Prophet).
004:092	For those who find this beyond their means,
004:094	Coveting the perishable goods of this life: with
004:109	whose behalf ye may contend in this world;
004:114	to him who does this, seeking
004:116	He pleaseth other sins than this:
004:133	for He hath power this to do.
004:134	If any one desires a reward in this life, in
004:134	(both) of this life and of the Hereafter:
004:143	(They are) wavering between this and that belonging
004:169	and this to Allah is easy.
005:003	This day have I perfected your religion for you,
005:003	This day have those who reject Faith given up
005:005	This day are (all) things good and pure
005:012	but if any of you, after this, resisteth faith,
005:022	They said: "O Moses! in this land are a people
005:025	so separate us from this rebellious people!"
005:031	"Was I not even able to be as this raven, and to
005:033	that is their disgrace in this world, and a heavy
005:041	they say, "If ye are given this, take it, but if

005:041	For them there is disgrace in this world, and in
005:049	And this (He commands): Judge thou between them
005:060	something much worse than this, (as judged)
005:085	And for this their prayer hath Allah
005:110	'This is nothing but evident magic'.
005:119	"This is a day on which the truthful will profit
006:007	"This is nothing but obvious magic!"
006:019	this Qur'an hath been revealed to me
006:020	know this as they know their own sons.
006:029	"There is nothing except our life on this earth,
006:030	He will say: "Is not this the truth?" They will
006:032	Nothing is the life of this world but play
006:051	Give this warning to those in whose (hearts)
006:066	But thy people reject this, though it is
006:070	and are deceived by the life of this world.
006:076	he saw a star: he said: "This is my Lord."
006:077	He said: "This is my Lord." But when
006:078	he said: "This is my Lord;
006:078	this is the greatest (of all)." But when
006:088	This is the Guidance of Allah: He giveth
006:090	this is but a Reminder to the nations."
006:090	Say: "No reward for this do I ask of you:
006:092	And this is a Book which We
006:092	believe in this (Book), and they
006:093	This day shall ye receive your reward,-
006:105	"Thou hast learnt this (from somebody),
006:126	This is the way of thy Lord, leading
006:130	It was the life of this world that deceived them.
006:130	and warning you of the meeting of this day of yours?"
006:136	"This is for Allah, and this for Our "partners"!
006:146	this in recompense for their wilful disobedience:
006:153	Verily, this is My Way, leading straight: follow
006:155	And this is a Book which We have
006:163	No partner hath He: this am I commanded, and
007:005	no cry did they utter but this: "Indeed we did wrong."
007:018	(Allah) said: "Get out from this, disgraced
007:019	but approach not this tree, lest you
007:020	"Your Lord only forbade you this tree, lest
007:032	Say: they are, in the life of this world, for
007:038	but this ye do not understand.
007:043	Who hath guided us to this (felicity): never
007:051	of this day of theirs, and as they
007:073	This she-camel of Allah is a Sign unto you: so
007:082	And his people gave no answer but this: they said,
007:109	"This is indeed a sorcerer well-versed.
007:123	Surely this is a trick which ye have planned
007:131	they said, "This is due to us"; when gripped
007:152	and with shame in this life: thus do
007:155	This is no more than Thy trial: by it Thou
007:156	in this life and in the Hereafter: for we
007:161	"Dwell in this town and eat therein as ye wish,
007:168	into sections on this earth.
007:169	the vanities of this world, saying
007:172	"Of this we were never mindful":
007:172	They said: "Yea! we do testify! (This), lest ye
007:185	In what message after this will they then believe?
007:203	This is (nothing but) lights from your Lord, and
008:013	This because they contended against Allah
008:031	they say: "We have heard this (before): if we
008:032	if this is indeed the truth from Thee, rain down
008:048	can overcome you this day, while I
008:051	This is "Because of (the deeds) which your

THIS (continued)

008:067 Ye look for the temporal good of **this** world;
008:073 one of another: unless ye do **this**, (protect each
009:027 Again will Allah, after **this**, turn (in mercy)
009:028 after **this** year of theirs, approach the
009:030 from their mouths; (in **this**) they but imitate
009:035 "**This** is the (treasure) which ye hoarded for yourselves:
009:038 Do ye prefer the life of **this** world to the
009:038 comfort of **this** life, as compared
009:055 to punish them with these things in **this** life,
009:069 in **this** world and in the Hereafter, and they
009:074 a grievous chastisement in **this** life and in
009:074 **this** revenge of theirs was (their) only return
009:085 these things in **this** world, and that
010:002 "**This** is indeed a evident sorcerer!"
010:003 **This** is Allah your Lord; Him therefore serve ye:
010:005 Nowise did Allah create **this** but in truth
010:010 (**This** will be) their prayer therein: "Glory to
010:015 "Bring us a Qur-an other than **this**, or change **this**."
010:016 A whole lifetime before **this** have I tarried
010:022 saying, "If thou dost deliver us from **this**, we shall
010:037 **This** Qur'an is not such as can be produced by
010:048 They say: "When will **this** promise come to pass-
010:064 **This** is indeed the supreme Triumph.
010:067 Verily in **this** are Signs for those
010:068 No warrant have ye for **this**!
010:070 A little enjoyment in **this** world!-and the,
010:076 they said: "**This** is indeed evident sorcery!"
010:077 Is it sorcery (like) **this**? But sorcerers
010:077 Said Moses: "Say ye (**this**) about the Truth when it
010:087 We inspired Moses and his brother with **this** message:
010:092 "**This** day shall We save thee in thy body,
011:001 Alif Lam Ra. (**This** is) a Book, with verse
011:007 to say, "**This** is nothing but obvious sorcery!"
011:014 know ye that **this** Revelation is sent down
011:043 Noah said: "**This** day nothing can save,
011:049 unto thee: before **this**, neither thou nor thy
011:051 no reward for **this** (Message). My reward
011:060 in **this** Life,-and on the Day of Judgment.
011:064 "And O my people! **this** she-camel of Allah
011:076 O Abraham! seek not **this**.
011:077 He said: "**This** is a distressful day."
011:099 **this** (life) and on the Day of Judgment:
011:119 and for **this** did He create them:
012:003 **this** (portion of the) Qur'an:
012:003 before **this**, thou too was among those
012:015 **this** affair while they perceive not."
012:015 (**this** Message): "Of a surety thou shall (one day)
012:026 saw (**this**) and bore witness, (thus):-
012:029 "O Joseph, pass **this** over! (O wife),
012:031 **This** is none other than a noble angel!"
012:031 "Allah preserve us! no mortal is **this**!
012:037 and meaning of **this** ere it befall you.
012:052 "**This** (say I), in order that he may know
012:054 he said: "Be assured **this** day, thou art
012:065 **This** our stock-in-trade has been
012:065 **This** is but a small quantity.
012:074 shall be the penalty of **this**, if ye are
012:080 and how, before **this**, ye did fail in your duty
012:080 Therefore will I not leave **this** land until my
012:090 He said: "I am Joseph, and **this** is my brother:
012:092 He said: "**This** day let no reproach be (cast)
012:093 "Go with **this** my shirt, and cast it

THIS (continued)

012:100 He said: "O my father! **this** is the fulfillment
012:101 Thou art my Protector in **this** world and in
012:104 And no reward dost thou ask of them for **this**:
012:108 Say thou: "**This** my Way; I do invite unto Allah,-
013:026 but the life of **this** world is but
013:026 in the life of **this** world:
013:031 (**this** would be the one!) But, truly,
013:034 For them is a Penalty in the life of **this** world,
014:003 of **this** world to the Hereafter, who hinder
014:005 Verily in **this** there are Signs for such
014:013 But their Lord inspired (**this** Message) to them:
014:014 **This** for such as fear the Time when they
014:027 stands firm, in **this** world and in the Hereafter:
014:035 make **this** city one of peace and security:
015:041 (Allah) said: "**This** is for me a straight path.
015:066 And We made known **this** decree to him, that the
015:075 Behold! in **this** are Signs for those
015:077 Behold! in **this** is a Sign for those who believe!
015:085 the Hour is surely coming (when **this** will be manifest).
016:004 and behold **this** same (man) becomes an
016:011 and every kind of fruit: Verily in **this** is a Sign
016:012 His Command: verily in **this** are Signs for men
016:013 And the things on **this** earth which He has
016:013 colours (and qualities); Verily in **this** is a Sign
016:027 with knowledge will say: "**This** Day, indeed, are
016:030 in **this** world, and the Home of the Hereafter is
016:041 if they only realize (**this**)!
016:041 in **this** world; but truly the reward of the
016:043 if ye realize **this** not, ask of those
016:065 verily in **this** is a Sign for those who listen.
016:067 in **this** also is a Sign for those who are wise.
016:069 for men: verily in **this** is a Sign for those
016:079 Verily in **this** are Signs for those who believe.
016:092 for Allah will test you by **this**; and on
016:103 while **this** is Arabic, pure and clear.
016:107 **This** because they love the life of **this** world better
016:110 Thy Lord, after all **this** is Oft-Forgiving, Most Merciful.
016:116 "**This** is lawful, and **this** is forbidden,"
016:119 Thy Lord after all **this**, is Oft-Forgiving, Most Merciful.
016:122 And We gave him Good in **this** world, and he
017:009 Verily **this** Qur'an doth guide to that which
017:014 thy soul **this** day to make out an account
017:016 are given the good things of **this** life (to be obedient)
017:018 transitory things (of **this** life), We readily
017:041 in various (ways) in **this** Qur'an, in order
017:062 He said, "Seest Thou? **This** is the one whom
017:072 But those who were blind in **this** world, will be
017:075 (of punishment) in **this** life, and an
017:077 (**This** was Our) way with the messengers We sent
017:088 the like of **this** Qur'an, they could not
017:089 in **this** Qur'an, every kind of similitude:
017:094 was nothing but **this**: they said, "Has Allah
018:006 if they believe not in **this** Message.
018:019 with **this** money of yours to the town: let him
018:024 ever closer (even) than **this** to the right course."
018:028 and glitter of **this** Life; nor obey
018:034 (Abundant) was the produce **this** man had: he said
018:035 "I deem not that **this** will ever perish,"
018:045 of the life of **this** world: it is like
018:046 of the life of **this** world: but the
018:049 "Ah! woe to us! what a book is **this**! It leaves
018:054 We have explained in detail in **this** Qur'an, for the

THIS (continued)

018:057   they should understand **this** not, and over
018:062   at **this** (stage of) our journey."
018:076   about anything after **this**, keep me not
018:078   He answered: "**This** is the parting between me
018:098   He said: "**This** is a mercy from my Lord: but when
018:104   in **this** life, while they thought that they were
019:002   (**This** is) a mention of the Mercy of thy Lord
019:023   "Ah! would that I had died before **this**! would that
019:026   Most Gracious, and **this** day will I enter into no
019:036   **this** is a Way that is straight.
019:071   **this** is, with thy Lord, a Decree
020:039   and (**this**) in order that thou mayest be
020:049   (When **this** message was delivered), (Pharaoh) said:
020:054   your cattle: verily, in **this** are Signs for men
020:071   Surely **this** must be your leader. Who has
020:072   decree (touching) the life of **this** world.
020:088   "**This** is your god, and the god of Moses,
020:090   being tested in **this**: for verily
020:090   Aaron had already, before **this** said to them:
020:097   but thy (punishment) in **this** life will be that
020:101   They will abide in **this** (state): and grievous
020:113   Thus have we sent **this** down-an Arabic Qur'an-
020:117   **this** is an enemy to thee and thy wife: so let
020:126   forgot them: so wilt thou, **this** day, be forgotten.
020:128   Verily, in **this** are Signs for men
020:131   of **this** world, through which We test them: but the
020:134   before **this**, they would have said: "Our Lord
021:003   "Is **this** (one) more than a man like yourselves?
021:007   if ye know **this** not, ask of those
021:013   of **this** life which were given you, and to
021:024   **this** is the Message of those with me and the
021:025   before thee without **this** inspiration sent by
021:036   "Is **this**," (they say), "The one who talks of your gods?"
021:038   They say: "When will **this** promise come to pass,
021:044   of **this** life to these men and their fathers
021:050   And **this** is a blessed Message which We
021:056   and I am a witness to **this** (truth).
021:059   They said, "Who has done **this** to our gods?
021:062   did **this** with our gods, O Abraham?"
021:063   He said: "Nay, **this** was done by **this** the biggest one!
021:092   Verily, **this** Ummah of yours is a single Ummah,
021:097   we were indeed heedless of **this**;
021:103   "**This** is your Day,-(the day)
021:105   Before **this** We wrote in the Psalms, after the
022:006   **This** is so, because Allah is the Reality: it is
022:009   for him there is disgrace in **this** life, and on
022:010   (It will be said): "**This** is because of the deeds
022:011   they lose both **this** world and the Hereafter:
022:015   help him (His Messenger) in **this** world and the
022:024   (in **this** life) to the purest of speeches;
022:078   both before and in **this** (Revelation); that the
023:027   so We inspired him (with **this** message); "Construct
023:030   Verily in **this** there are Signs (for men
023:033   We had bestowed the good things of **this** life,
023:037   "There is nothing but our life in **this** world!
023:052   And verily **this** Ummah of yours is a single
023:063   in confused ignorance of **this**; and there
023:064   the good things of **this** world, behold, they
023:065   "Groan not in supplication **this** day; for ye
023:107   "Our Lord! bring us out of **this**: if ever
023:111   "I have rewarded them **this** day for their
024:012   and say, "**This** (charge) is an obvious lie?"

THIS (continued)

024:014   in **this** world and the Hereafter, a grievous
024:014   glibly into **this** affair.
024:016   "It is not right of us to speak of **this**:
024:016   glory to Thee (our Lord) **this** is a most serious slander!"
024:019   in **this** life and in the Hereafter: Allah knows,
024:023   are cursed in **this** life and in the Hereafter:
024:033   a gain in the goods of **this** life. But if
024:051   is no other than **this**: they said, "We hear
024:055   If any do reject Faith after **this**, they are
025:004   "Naught is **this** but a lie which he has forged,
025:007   And they say: "What sort of a messenger is **this**,
025:014   "**This** day plead not for a single destruction:
025:023   they did (in **this** life), and We shall make such
025:030   **this** Qur'an with neglect."
025:035   (Before **this**), We sent Moses the Book,
025:041   in mockery: "Is **this** the one whom Allah has sent
025:057   Say: "No reward do I ask of you for it but **this**:
025:068   and any that does **this** (not only) meets punishment
026:008   Verily, in **this** is a Sign: but most
026:022   "And **this** is the favour with which thou dost
026:034   "**This** is indeed a sorcerer well-versed:
026:067   Verily in **this** is a Sign: but most
026:103   Verily in **this** is a Sign, but most
026:121   Verily in **this** is a Sign: but most
026:137   "**This** is no other than a customary device
026:139   Verily in **this** is a Sign: but most
026:158   Verily in **this** is a Sign: but most
026:174   Verily in **this** is a Sign: but most
026:192   Verily **this** is a Revelation from the
026:205   (**this** life) for a few years,
027:013   visibly they said: "**This** is sorcery manifest!"
027:016   **this** is indeed Grace manifest (from Allah)."
027:028   Go thou, with **this** letter of mine, and deliver
027:032   advise me in (**this**) my affair: no affair
027:040   "**This** is by the grace of my Lord!-to test
027:042   "Is **this** thy throne?" She said, "It seems
027:042   on us in advance of **this**, and we
027:044   He said: "**This** is but a palace paved smooth
027:051   of their plot!-**this**, that We destroyed them
027:052   Verily in **this** is a Sign for people of knowledge.
027:056   But his people gave no other answer but **this**:
027:068   "It is true we were promised **this**,-we and
027:071   They also say: "When will **this** promise
027:076   Verily **this** Qur'an doth explain to the
027:086   Verily in **this** are Signs for any people
027:091   the Lord of **this** City, Him Who has
028:007   So We sent **this** inspiration to the mother of Moses:
028:015   He said: "**This** is a work of Satan: for he
028:036   "**This** is nothing but sorcery faked up: never did
028:042   In **this** world We made a Curse to follow them:
028:052   before **this**,-they do believe in **this** (Revelation);
028:053   (bowing to Allah's Will) from before **this**."
028:060   are but the conveniences of **this** life and the
028:061   the good things of **this** life, but who, on the
028:067   But any that (in **this** life) had repented,
028:077   nor forget thy portion in **this** world: but do
028:078   He said: "**This** has been given to me because of
028:079   Said those whose aim is the Life of **this** World:
028:080   but **this** none shall attain, save those
029:024   Verily in **this** are Signs for people who believe.
029:025   between yourselves in **this** life; but on
029:027   and We granted him his reward in **this** life;

THIS (continued)

029:029 gave no answer but **this**: they said: "Bring us the Wrath
029:031 the people of **this** township: for truly
029:034 on the people of **this** township a Punishment
029:048 a Book, before **this** (Book came), nor art
029:064 What is the life of **this** world but amusement
030:003 (even) after (**this**) defeat of theirs, will soon
030:007 in the life of **this** world: but of
030:020 Among His Signs is **this**, that He
030:021 And among His Signs is **this**, that He
030:025 And among His Signs is **this**, that heaven
030:046 Among His Signs is **this**, that He
030:049 (the rain)-just before **this**-they were
030:056 of Resurrection, and **this** is the Day of
030:058 in **this** Qur'an. Every kind of Parable: but if
031:015 in **this** life with justice (and consideration),
031:017 for **this** is firmness (of purpose) in (the conduct of)
031:031 Verily in **this** are Signs for all who constantly
031:033 let not then **this** present life deceive you,
032:002 (**This** is) the revelation of the Book in which
032:014 of **this** day of yours, and We
032:028 They say: "When will **this** decision be, if ye
033:022 "**This** is what Allah and His Messenger had promised
033:028 of **this** world, and its glitter,-then come!
033:050 **this** only for thee, and not
033:051 **This** were nigher to the cooling of their eyes,
033:052 (to marry more) women after **this**, not to
033:057 in **this** world and in the Hereafter, and has
034:009 Verily is **this** is a Sign fro every devotee that turns
034:019 Verily in **this** are Signs for every (soul that is)
034:023 So far (is **this** the case) that, when terror
034:029 They say: "When will **this** promise (come to pass)
034:031 neither believe in **this** scripture nor in (any)
034:043 "**This** is nothing but evident magic!
034:043 to them, they say, "**This** is only a man who
034:043 "**This** is only a falsehood invented!"
035:005 let not then **this** present life deceive you,
035:011 All **this** is easy to Allah.
036:019 with yourselves: (deem ye **this** an evil omen),
036:035 their hands that made **this**: will they
036:035 That they may enjoy the fruits of **this** (artistry):
036:048 **this** promise (come to pass), if what
036:052 "**This** is what The Most Gracious had promised.
036:059 And O ye in sin! get ye apart **this** Day!
036:061 (for that) **this** was the Straight Way?
036:063 "**This** is the Hell of which ye were promised!
036:064 "Embrace ye the (Fire) **this** Day, for that
036:069 **this** is no less than a Message and a Qur'an
037:015 And say, "**This** is nothing but evident sorcery!
037:020 **this** is the Day of Judgement!"
037:021 "**This** is the Day of Sorting Out, whose truth
037:060 Verily **this** is the supreme Triumph!
037:061 For the like of **this** let all strive, who wish
037:077 And made his progeny to endure (on **this** earth);
037:078 And We left (**this** blessing) for him
037:098 (**This** failing), they then plotted against him,
037:106 For **this** was a clear trial-
037:171 before (**this**) to Our Servants sent (by Us),
038:001 of Admonition: (**this** is the Truth).
038:004 "**This** is a sorcerer telling lies!
038:005 Truly **this** is a strange thing!"
038:006 For **this** is truly a thing designed (against you)!
038:007 **this** is nothing but a made-up tale!

THIS (continued)

038:007 "We never heard (the like) of **this** in the
038:023 "**This** man is my brother; he has
038:025 So We forgave him **this** (lapse): he enjoyed,
038:049 **This** is a message (of admonition): and verily
038:060 It is ye who have brought **this** upon us!
038:060 Now evil is (**this**) place to stay in!"
038:061 Whoever brought **this** upon us,-add to
038:070 "Only **this** has been revealed to me: that I
038:084 (Allah) said: "**This** is the Truth, and the
038:086 of you for **this** (Qur'an), nor am I a pretender.
038:087 "**This** is no less than a Reminder
039:001 The revelation of **this** Book is from Allah,
039:007 of all that ye did (in **this** life).
039:010 for those who do good in **this** world. Spacious is
039:016 with **this** doth Allah warn off His servants:
039:021 Truly, in **this**, is a Message of remembrance
039:042 Verily in **this** are Signs for those who reflect.
039:049 he says, "**This** has been given to me because of
039:049 Nay, but **this** is but a trial, but most
039:051 of **this** (generation)-the evil results of their
039:052 Verily, in **this** are signs for those who believe!
039:071 and warning you of the Meeting of **this** Day of yours?"
039:072 (**this**) abode of the arrogant!"
039:074 to us, and has given us (**this**) land in heritage:
040:002 The revelation of **this** Book is from Allah,
040:011 our sins: is there any way out (of **this**)?"
040:012 "**This** is because, when Allah was invoked as the
040:029 "O my People! yours is the dominion**this** day:
040:039 "O my people! **This** life of the present is nothing
040:043 whether in **this** world, or the Hereafter;
040:048 "We are all in **this** (Fire)! Truly, Allah has
040:051 who believe, (both) in **this** world's life and on
040:076 is (**this**) abode of the arrogant!"
040:077 and whether We show thee (in **this** life) some part
041:016 a taste of a Chastisement of humiliation in **this** life;
041:023 "But **this** thought of yours which ye did entertain
041:026 The Unbelievers say: "Listen not to **this** Qur'an,
041:031 "We are your protectors in **this** life and in
041:039 And among His Signs is **this**: thou seest
041:044 Had We sent **this** as a Qur'an (in a language)
041:050 "**This** is due to my (merit): I think
041:053 that **this** is the Truth. Is it not enough that
042:020 the tilth of **this** world, We grant
042:023 for **this** except the love of those near of kin."
042:033 Verily in **this** are Signs for everyone who
042:036 is (but) the enjoyment of **this** Life: but that
043:021 before **this**, to which they are holding fast?
043:029 of **this** life to these (men) and their fathers,
043:030 they said: "**This** is sorcery, and we do reject it."
043:031 Also, they say: "Why is not **this** Qur'an sent down
043:032 them and their livelihood in the life of **this** world:
043:035 But all **this** were nothing but enjoyment of the
043:052 "Am I not better than **this** (Moses), who is
043:058 **This** they set forth to thee, only by
043:061 **this** is a Straight Way.
043:064 **this** is a Straight Way."
044:011 **this** will be a Chastisement Grievous.
044:049 "Taste thou (**this**)! Truly thou
044:050 "Truly **this** is what ye used to doubt!"
044:058 Verily, We have made **this** (Qur'an) easy, in thy
045:011 **This** is (true) Guidance: and for those who reject
045:024 And they say: "What is it but our life in **this** world?

THIS (continued)

045:025   but **this**: they say, "Bring (back) our forefathers,
045:028   called to its Record: "**This** Day shall ye be
045:029   "**This** Our Record speaks about you with truth:
045:034   It will also be said: "**This** Day We will forget
045:034   the meeting of **this** day of yours! And Your
045:035   "**This**, because ye used to take the Signs
046:004   Bring me a Book (revealed) before **this**, or any
046:007   "**This** is evident sorcery!"
046:010   Say: "See ye? If (**this** teaching) be from Allah,
046:011   "**This** is an (old), old falsehood!"
046:011   who believe: "If (**this** Message) were a good thing,
046:012   And before **this**, was the Book of Moses as a
046:012   and **this** Book confirms it in the Arabic tongue;
046:016   which was made to them (in **this** life).
046:017   "**This** is nothing but tales of the ancients!"
046:024   they said, "**This** cloud will give us rain!"
046:034   (they will be asked), "Is **this** not the Truth?"
047:003   **This** because those who reject Allah
047:012   enjoy (**this** world) and eat as cattle eat; and the
047:026   **This**, because they said to those who hate
047:026   of (**this**) matter"; but Allah knows their (inner)
047:028   **This** because they followed that which displeased
047:036   The life of **this** world is but play and amusement:
048:012   to their families; **this** seemed pleasing in your
048:015   (**this**) beforehand": then they will say, "But ye
048:027   besides **this**, a speedy victory.
048:029   **This** is their similitude in the Taurat; and their
050:002   "**This** is a wonderful thing!
050:019   "**This** thing which thou wast trying to escape!"
050:022   and sharp is thy sight **this** Day!"
050:022   (It will be said:) "'Thou wast heedless of **this**;
050:032   "**This** is what was promised for you,-for every
050:034   **this** is a Day of Eternal Life!"
050:037   Verily in **this** is a Message for any that has
051:014   **this** is what ye used to ask to be hastened!"
051:023   **this** is the very Truth, as much as
051:053   Is **this** the legacy they have transmitted, one to
052:014   "**This**," it will be said, "Is the Fire,-
052:015   "Is **this** then a magic, or is it ye that do not see?
052:032   to **this**, or are they but a people transgressing
052:047   there is another punishment besides **this**: but most
053:029   nothing but the life of **this** world.
053:056   **This** is a Warner, of the
053:059   Do ye then wonder at **this** recital?
054:002   and say, "**This** is (but) continuous magic."
054:008   "Hard is **this** Day!" The Unbelievers will say.
054:015   And We have left **this** as a Sign (for all time):
055:043   **This** is the Hell which the Sinners deny:
056:077   That **this** is indeed a Qur'an most honourable,
056:095   Verily, **this** is the very Truth of assured Certainty.
057:012   **This** is indeed the highest Triumph.
057:012   (Their greeting will be): "Good News for **this** Day!
057:015   "**This** Day shall no ransom be accepted of you,
057:020   of **this** world, but goods and chattels of deception?
057:020   of **this** world is but play and a pastime,
058:003   each other: **this** are ye admonished to perform:
058:004   **This**, that ye may show your faith in Allah
059:003   He would certainly have punished them in **this** world:
059:006   for **this** ye made no expedition with either
059:013   **This** is because they are men devoid
059:021   Had We sent down **this** Qur'an on a mountain,
060:001   And any of you that does **this** has strayed

THIS (continued)

061:006   Clear Signs, they said, "**This** is evident sorcery!"
066:003   she said, "Who told thee **this**?" He said,
066:007   "O you who Unbelievers! make no excuses **this** Day!
067:025   They ask: When will **this** promise be (fulfilled)?
067:027   (to them): "**This** is (the promise fulfilled),
068:024   in upon you into the (garden) **this** day."
068:032   in exchange a better (garden) than **this**: for we
068:033   Such is the Punishment (in **this** life); but greater
068:044   as reject **this** Message: by degrees shall We draw
069:033   "**This** was he that would not believe
069:035   "So no friend hath he here **this** Day.
069:040   That **this** is verily the word of a honoured
069:043   (**This** is) a Message sent down from the
069:048   But verily **this** is a Message for the God-fearing.
070:031   beyond **this** are transgressors;-
073:019   Verily **this** is an Admonition: therefore, whoso
074:024   Then said he: "**This** is nothing but magic
074:025   "**This** is nothing but the word of a mortal!"
074:031   "What doth Allah intend by **this**?"
074:031   and **this** is no other than a Reminder to mankind.
074:035   **This** is but one of the mighty (Portents),
074:054   Nay, **this** surely is an admonition:
076:022   "Verily **this** is a Reward for you, and your
076:029   **This** is an admonition: whosoever will, let him
079:025   in the Hereafter, as in **this** life.
079:026   Verily in **this** is a lesson for whosoever
079:038   And had preferred the life of **this** world,
081:019   Verily **this** is the word of a most
081:027   Verily **this** is no less than a Message
083:017   "**This** is the (reality) which ye rejected as false!"
083:026   and for **this** let those aspire, who have
083:034   But on **this** Day the Believers will laugh
085:021   Nay, **this** is a Glorious Qur'an,
086:013   Behold **this** is the Word that distinguishes
087:016   Nay (behold), ye prefer the life of **this** world;
087:018   And **this** is in the Books of the
089:024   sent forth (Good Deeds) for (**this**) my (Future) Life."
090:001   Nay I do swear by **this** City;-
090:002   And thou art an inhabitant of **this** City;-
095:003   And **this** City of Security,-
095:007   What then, can after **this** make you
097:001   **this** (Message) in the night of Power:
097:005   Peace!...**This** until the rise of Morn!
098:005   And they have been commanded no more than **this**:
098:008   all **this** for such as fear their Lord and Cherisher.
101:010   And what will explain to Thee what **this** is?
102:001   (the good things of **this** world) diverts you
106:003   Let them worship the Lord of **this** House,

THITHER

002:150   turn your face **thither**:
026:064   And We made the other party approach **thither**.

THORNS

056:028   (They will be) among lote-trees without **thorns**,

THOROUGHLY

008:067   until he hath **thoroughly** subdued the land.
047:004   at length, when ye have **thoroughly** subdued them,

THOSE

001:007   **Those** whose (portion) is not wrath,
001:007   The way of **those** on whom thou hast bestowed
002:002   to **those** who fear Allah;
002:006   As to **those** who reject Faith,
002:009   deceive Allah and **those** who believe,

THOSE (continued)

002:014 When they meet **those** who believe.
002:021 who created you and **those** who came before you
002:024 which is prepared for **those** who reject faith.
002:025 But give glad tidings to **those** who believe
002:026 **Those** who believe know that it is the truth
002:026 except **those** who forsake (the path),
002:026 but **those** who reject Faith say: "What Means
002:027 **Those** who break Allah's Covenant
002:034 he was of **those** who reject Faith.
002:039 "But **those** who reject Faith
002:043 with **those** who bow down (in worship).
002:045 except to **those** who are humble.
002:058 (the portion of) **those** who do good."
002:062 **Those** who believe (in the Qur'an)
002:062 and **those** who follow the Jewish (Scriptures),
002:065 And well ye knew **those** amongst you
002:066 and a lesson to **those** who fear Allah.
002:079 Then woe to **those** who write the Book
002:081 Nay, **those** who seek gain in Evil,
002:082 But **those** who have faith
002:083 and orphans and **those** in need;
002:085 for **those** among you who behave like this
002:089 is on **those** without Faith.
002:089 **those** without Faith,
002:090 Chastisement of **those** who reject Faith.
002:097 glad tidings for **those** who believe,
002:098 **those** who reject Faith.
002:099 but **those** who are perverse.
002:104 to **those** without Faith
002:105 It is never the wish of **those** without
002:111 **Those** are their (vain) desires.
002:113 what **those** say who know not,
002:118 Say **those** without knowledge:
002:121 **Those** to whom We have given the Book
002:121 **those** who reject faith therein,
002:125 My House for **those** who compass it round,
002:140 **those** who conceal the testimony
002:143 from **those** who turn on their heels (from the Faith).
002:143 only to test **those** who followed the Messenger
002:143 except to **those** guided by Allah.
002:150 except **those** of them that are bent
002:153 for God is with **those** who patiently persevere.
002:154 And say not of **those** who are slain
002:155 to **those** who patiently persevere,
002:157 They are **those** on whom (descend)
002:158 So if **those** who visit the House
002:159 **Those** who conceal the clear (Signs)
002:159 and the curse of **those** entitled to curse.
002:160 Except **those** who repent and make amends
002:161 **Those** who reject Faith, and die rejecting,
002:165 But **those** of Faith are overflowing
002:166 clear themselves of **those** who follow (them):
002:166 Then would **those** who are followed clear
002:167 And **those** who followed would say: "If only
002:171 The parable of **those** who reject Faith
002:174 **Those** who conceal Allah's revelations in the Book,
002:176 the Book in truth but **those** who seek causes
002:177 for **those** who ask, and for the ransom of slaves;
002:181 the guilt shall be on **those** who make the change.
002:183 as it was prescribed to **those** before you,
002:184 For **those** who can do it (with hardship),
002:187 **Those** are limits (set by) Allah:

002:190 Fight in the cause of Allah **those** who fight you
002:191 Such is the reward of **those** who reject faith.
002:193 except to **those** who practice oppression.
002:194 Allah is with **those** who restrain themselves
002:195 for Allah loveth **those** who do good.
002:196 This is for **those** whose household is not
002:212 is alluring to **those** who reject faith,
002:212 and they scoff at **those** who believe.
002:214 came to **those** who passed away before you?
002:214 **those** of faith who were with him cried:
002:215 and **those** in want and for wayfarers.
002:218 **Those** who believed and **those** who suffered
002:222 For Allah loves **those** who turn to Him constantly
002:222 and He loves **those** who keep themselves pure
002:223 good tidings to **those** who believe.
002:226 For **those** who take an oath for abstention
002:230 which He makes plain to **those** who know.
002:236 is due from **those** who wish to do the right thing.
002:240 **Those** of you who die and leave widows
002:243 thy vision to **those** who abandoned their homes,
002:246 knowledge of **those** who do wrong.
002:249 Allah is with **those** who steadfastly persevere."
002:249 only **those** who taste not of it go with me;
002:249 But **those** who were convinced
002:250 help us against **those** that reject faith."
002:253 **Those** Messengers We endowed with gifts,
002:254 **Those** who reject Faith-they are the wrong-doers
002:257 Allah is the Protector of **those** who have faith:
002:257 Of **those** who reject faith the patrons
002:261 The parable of **those** who spend their wealth
002:262 **Those** who spend their wealth in the cause
002:264 And Allah guideth not **those** who reject faith.
002:264 like **those** who spend their wealth
002:265 **those** who spend their wealth seeking to please
002:271 and make them reach **those** (really) in need,
002:273 (Charity is) for **those** in need, who,
002:274 **Those** who (in charity) spend of their goods
002:275 **Those** who devour usury will not stand
002:275 but **those** who repeat (the offense)
002:275 **Those** who after receiving admonition
002:277 **Those** who believe, and do deeds
002:286 like that which Thou didst lay on **those** before us;
003:004 Then **those** who reject Faith in the Signs
003:007 And **those** who are firmly grounded in knowledge
003:007 But **those** in whose hearts is perversity follow
003:010 **Those** who reject faith,
003:012 Say to **those** who reject Faith: "Soon will ye be
003:015 glad tidings of things far better than **those**?
003:016 (Namely), **those** who say: "Our Lord!
003:017 **Those** who show patience, (firmness and self-control);
003:018 and **those** endued with knowledge,
003:020 the Book and to **those** who are unlearned:
003:020 to Allah and so have **those** who follow me."
003:021 and slay **those** who teach just dealing with mankind,
003:021 As to **those** who deny the Signs of Allah,
003:022 They are **those** whose works will bear no fruit
003:023 **those** who have been given a portion of the Book?
003:030 kindness to **those** that serve Him."
003:032 Allah loveth not **those** who reject Faith.
003:043 (in prayer) with **those** who bow down."
003:045 and (of the company) of **those** nearest to Allah;
003:049 and I heal **those** born blind, and the lepers,

THOSE (continued)

003:053 then write us down among **those** who bear witness."
003:055 who follow thee superior to **those** who reject faith,
003:055 I will make **those** who follow thee superior
003:055 (of the falsehoods) of **those** who blaspheme;
003:056 "As to **those** who reject faith,
003:057 but Allah loveth not **those** who do wrong.
003:057 "As to **those** who believe and work righteousness,
003:060 so be not of **those** who doubt
003:061 And invoke the curse of Allah on **those** who lie!
003:063 Allah hath full knowledge of **those** who do mischief.
003:066 Ah! Ye are **those** who fell to disputing (even)
003:068 as are also this Prophet and **those** who believe:
003:068 are **those** who follow him,
003:068 and Allah is the Protector of **those** who have faith.
003:073 Or that **those** (receiving such revelation)
003:076 verily Allah loves **those** who act aright.
003:076 Nay,-**Those** that keep their plighted faith
003:077 As for **those** who sell the faith they owe to Allah
003:085 in the ranks of **those** who have lost.
003:086 How shall Allah guide **those** who reject faith
003:089 Except for **those** that repent (even) after that.
003:090 But **those** who reject faith after they accepted it,
003:090 for they are **those** who have gone astray.
003:091 As to **those** who reject faith, and die rejecting,
003:097 **those** who can afford the journey;
003:099 why obstruct ye **those** who believe,
003:105 Be not like **those** who are divided amongst themselves
003:106 to **those** whose faces will be black,
003:107 But **those** whose faces will be (lit with) white,
003:115 for Allah knoweth well **those** that do right.
003:116 **Those** who reject faith, neither their
003:118 into your intimacy **those** outside your ranks:
003:119 Ah! ye are **those** who love them,
003:131 prepared for **those** who reject Faith.
003:134 **Those** who spend (freely), whether in prosperity,
003:134 for Allah loves **those** who do good:
003:135 And **those** who, having done an act of indecency
003:136 for **those** who work (and strive)!
003:137 what was the end of **those** who rejected Truth.
003:138 a guidance and instruction to **those** who fear Allah!
003:140 And Allah loveth not **those** that do wrong.
003:140 that Allah may know **those** that believe,
003:141 of blessings **those** that resist Faith.
003:141 to purge **those** that are true in Faith
003:142 testing **those** of you who fought hard
003:145 **those** that (serve us with) gratitude.
003:146 And Allah loves **those** who are firm and steadfast.
003:147 and help us against **those** that resist Faith."
003:148 For Allah loveth **those** who do good.
003:152 for Allah is full of grace to **those** who believe.
003:154 **those** for whom death was decreed would certainly
003:155 **Those** of you who turned back on the day
003:159 For Allah loves **those** who put their trust (in Him).
003:169 Think not of **those** who are slain
003:170 and with regard to **those** left behind, who have
003:172 **those** who do right and refrain from wrong
003:172 Of **those** who answered the call of Allah
003:172 **Those** to whom men said: "A great army
003:176 Let not **those** grieve thee who rush headlong
003:177 **Those** who purchase Unbelief at the price of Faith,
003:180 And let not **those** who covetously withhold of the
003:181 Allah hath heard the taunt of **those** who say:

THOSE (continued)

003:182 for Allah never do injustice to **those** who serve Him."
003:186 from **those** who received the Book before you
003:186 and from **those** who worship parties besides Allah.
003:188 Think not that **those** who exult in what
003:195 **those** who have left their homes, and were driven
003:198 On the other hand, for **those** who fear their Lord,
003:199 **those** who believe in Allah, in the revelation to you,
004:005 To **those** weak of understanding give not
004:007 and **those** nearest related there is a share for
004:009 Let **those** (disposing of an estate) have
004:010 **Those** who unjustly eat up the property of orphans,
004:013 **those** who obey Allah and His Messenger will be
004:013 **Those** are limits set by Allah:
004:014 But **those** who disobey Allah and His Messenger
004:017 Allah accepts the repentance of **those** who do evil
004:018 of **those** who continue to do evil, until death
004:018 nor of **those** who die rejecting faith:
004:023 (**those** who have been) wives of your son
004:024 except **those** whom your right hands possess:
004:025 from among **those** whom your right hand possess:
004:025 for **those** among you who fear sin;
004:026 and to guide you into the ways of **those** before you;
004:027 but the wish of **those** who follow
004:032 And in no wise covet **those** things in which
004:033 To **those** also, to whom your right hand was pledged,
004:034 As to **those** women on whose part ye fear
004:036 **those** in need, neighbors who are of kin, neighbors
004:037 for We have prepared, for **those** who resist Faith,
004:037 (Nor) **those** who are niggardly, enjoin
004:038 (Nor) **those** who spend of their substance, to be
004:042 On that day **those** who reject Faith and
004:044 to **those** who were given a portion of the Book?
004:046 **those** who displace words from their (right) places,
004:049 to **those** who claim purity for themselves?
004:051 to **those** who were given a portion of the Book?
004:052 and **those** whom Allah hath cursed, thou wilt find,
004:056 **Those** who reject Our Signs, We shall soon
004:057 But **those** who believe and do
004:058 your trusts to **those** to whom they are due;
004:059 and **those** charged with authority among you.
004:060 to **those** who declare that they believe in
004:060 that have come to thee and to **those** before thee?
004:063 **Those** men, Allah knows what is in their hearts;
004:069 **those** on whom is the Grace of Allah, of the
004:074 Let **those** fight in the cause of Allah who sell
004:075 the cause of Allah and of **those** who, being
004:076 **Those** who believe fight in the cause of Allah,
004:076 and **those** who reject Faith fight in the cause
004:077 the Hereafter is the best for **those** who do right:
004:077 to **those** who were told to hold back their hands
004:083 or to **those** charged with authority among them,
004:088 For **those** whom Allah hath thrown out of the Way,
004:088 Would ye guide **those** whom Allah
004:090 Except **those** who join a group between whom
004:090 or **those** who approach you with hearts restraining
004:092 For **those** who find this beyond their means,
004:095 to **those** who strive and fight with their goods
004:095 **those** who sit (at home) by a great reward.
004:095 except **those** who are disabled.
004:095 And **those** who strive and fight in the cause
004:095 but **those** who strive and fight hath He
004:095 Not equal are **those** Believers who sit (at home),

THOSE (continued)

004:095 **those** who sit (at home).

004:097 **those** who die in sin against their soul.

004:098 Except **those** who are (really) weak and oppressed,

004:105 **those** who betray their trust;

004:122 But **those** who believe and do deeds

004:123 nor **those** of the people of the Book (can prevail):

004:136 and the scripture which He sent to **those** before (him).

004:137 **Those** who believe, then reject Faith, then

004:139 **Those** who take for friends Unbelievers rather

004:140 and **those** who defy Faith-all in Hell;

004:143 belonging neither to these nor **those** whom Allah

004:146 Except for **those** who repent, mend (their life),

004:150 **Those** who deny Allah and his Messenger, and

004:152 To **those** who believe in Allah and His messengers

004:157 And **those** who differ therein are full of doubts,

004:161 We have prepared for **those** among them who reject

004:162 and (especially) **those** who establish regular prayer

004:162 But **those** among them who are well-grounded

004:167 **Those** who reject Faith and keep off

004:168 **Those** who reject Faith and do wrong,-Allah will

004:172 **those** who disdain His worship and are arrogant,

004:172 nor do the angels, **those** nearest (to Allah):

004:173 but **those** who are disdainful and arrogant, He will

004:173 But **those** who believe and do deeds

004:175 Then **those** who believe in Allah, and hold

004:176 **those** who leave no descendants or ascendants

005:003 This day have **those** who reject Faith given up

005:005 **those** who have lost (all spiritual good).

005:009 To **those** who believe and do deeds of righteousness

005:010 **Those** who reject faith and deny Our Signs will be

005:013 for Allah loveth **those** who are kind.

005:014 From **those**, too, who call themselves Christians,

005:017 They disbelieved indeed **those** that say that Allah

005:027 the sacrifice of **those** who are righteous.

005:029 and that is the reward of **those** who do wrong."

005:033 The punishment of **those** who wage war against

005:034 Except for **those** who repent before they

005:036 As to **those** who reject Faith,-if they had

005:041 (whether it be) among **those** who say: "We believe"

005:041 O Messenger! let not **those** grieve thee, who race

005:042 For Allah loveth **those** who judge in equity.

005:046 an admonition to **those** who fear Allah.

005:047 by what Allah hath revealed, they are indeed rebel.

005:052 **Those** in whose heart is a disease-thou seest how

005:055 **those** who establish regular prayers and pay

005:056 As to **those** who turn (for friendship)

005:057 **those** who received the Scripture before you, or

005:057 **those** who take your religion for a mockery

005:057 or among **those** who reject Faith: but fear

005:060 **those** who worshipped Evil (Tagut)-these are

005:060 **Those** who incurred the curse of Allah

005:060 **those** of whom some He transformed into apes

005:064 And Allah loveth not **those** who do mischief.

005:067 For Allah guideth not **those** who reject Faith.

005:069 **Those** who believe (in the Qur'an). **Those** who

005:069 **Those** who follow the Jewish (Scriptures), and

005:078 **those** among the Children of Israel who rejected

005:082 to the Believers wilt thou find **those** who say,

005:085 Such is the recompense of **those** who do good.

005:086 But **those** who reject Faith and belie

005:087 for Allah loveth not **those** given to excess.

005:093 On **those** who believe and do deeds

THOSE (continued)

005:093 For Allah loveth **those** who do good.

005:096 and **those** who travel; but forbidden

005:101 Allah will forgive **those**: for Allah

005:103 Who instituted (superstitions like **those** of) a

005:105 no hurt can come to you from **those** who stray.

005:107 nearest in kin from among **those** who claim

005:107 than that of **those** two, and that

005:110 and thou healest **those** born blind, and the

006:001 Yet **those** who reject Faith hold (others)

006:006 See they not how many of **those** before them

006:011 what was the end of **those** who rejected Truth."

006:014 of **those** who join gods with Allah."

006:014 the first of **those** who bow to Allah (in Islam),

006:020 **Those** to whom We have given the Book know this

006:020 **Those** who have lost their own souls refuse

006:022 We shall say to **those** who ascribed partners

006:023 not **those** who joined gods with Allah."

006:027 but would be amongst **those** who believe!"

006:032 for **those** who are righteous.

006:034 some account of **those** Messengers.

006:035 so be not thou amongst **those** who are swayed

006:036 **Those** who listen (in truth), be sure,

006:039 **Those** who reject Our Signs are deaf and dumb,-

006:047 will any be destroyed except **those** who do wrong?"

006:048 so **those** who believe and mend (their lives),-

006:049 But **those** who reject Our Signs,-them shall

006:051 Give this warning to **those** in whose (hearts)

006:052 Send not away **those** who call on their Lord

006:053 Doth not Allah know best **those** who are grateful?.

006:054 When **those** come to thee who believe

006:056 Say: "I am forbidden to worship **those**-other

006:056 the company of **those** who receive guidance."

006:058 But Allah knoweth best **those** who do wrong."

006:059 a Record Clear (to **those** who can read).

006:068 sit not thou in the company of **those** who do wrong.

006:070 such is (the end of) **those** who deliver themselves

006:070 Leave alone **those** who take their religion

006:076 "I love not **those** that set."

006:077 I shall surely be among **those** who go astray."

006:082 "It is **those** who believe and mix not

006:084 thus do We reward **those** who do good:

006:090 **Those** were the (prophets) who

006:092 **Those** who believe in the Hereafter believe in

006:105 We may make the matter clear to **those** who know.

006:106 **those** who join gods with Allah.

006:108 Revile not ye **those** whom they call

006:113 the hearts of **those** incline, who have

006:114 Never be then of **those** who doubt.

006:116 the common run of **those** on earth, they will

006:117 He knoweth best **those** who are rightly guided.

006:119 Thy Lord knoweth best **those** who transgress.

006:120 **those** who earn sin will get due recompense

006:122 Thus to **those** without Faith their own

006:124 like **those** receive by Allah's messengers."

006:125 on **those** who refuse to believe.

006:125 **those** whom He willeth to leave straying, He

006:125 **Those** whom Allah willeth to guide,- He openeth

006:126 the Signs for **those** who receive admonition.

006:138 except **those** whom-so they say-We wish; further,

006:140 Lost are **those** who slay their children, from

006:146 For **those** who followed the Jewish Law, We

006:148 **Those** who give partners (to Allah) will say:

THOSE (continued)

006:154 **those** who would do right, and explaining
006:157 **those** who turn away from Our Signs, with
006:159 As for **those** who divide their religion and
006:163 **those** who submit to His Will.
007:006 and **those** by whom We sent it.
007:006 Then shall We question **those** to whom
007:008 **those** whose scale (of good) will be
007:009 **Those** whose scale will be light, will find
007:011 he refused to be of **those** who prostrate.
007:015 "Be thou among **those** who have respite."
007:027 (only) to **those** without Faith.
007:032 for **those** who believe, (and) purely for
007:032 in detail for **those** who know.
007:035 **those** who are righteous and mend (their lives),
007:036 But **those** who reject Our Signs and treat
007:040 To **those** who reject Our Signs and treat
007:040 such is Our reward for **those** in sin.
007:041 such is Our requital of **those** who do wrong.
007:042 But **those** who believe and work righteousness,-
007:045 they were **those** who denied the Hereafter."
007:045 "**Those** who would hinder (men) from the
007:050 hath Allah forbidden to **those** who rejected Him;
007:053 **those** who have forgotten it before will say: "The
007:055 **those** who trespass beyond bounds.
007:056 is (always) near to **those** who do good.
007:058 by various (symbols) to **those** who are grateful.
007:064 **those** who rejected Our Signs, they were
007:064 and **those** with him, in the Ark: but We
007:072 We saved him and **those** who adhered to him, by Our
007:072 the roots of **those** who rejected Our Signs and
007:075 **those** among them who believe: "Know ye
007:075 among his people said to **those** who were
007:083 she was of **those** who lagged behind.
007:084 **those** who indulged in sin and crime!
007:086 And see what was the end of **those** who did mischief.
007:086 the path of Allah **those** who believe in Him, and
007:088 (thee) and **those** who believe with thee; or else
007:099 except **those** (doomed) to ruin!
007:100 To **those** who inherit the earth in succession
007:101 the heart of **those** who reject Faith.
007:103 of **those** who made mischief.
007:131 connected with Moses and **those** with Him!
007:142 the way of **those** who do mischief."
007:144 and be of **those** who give thanks."
007:146 **Those** who behave arrogantly on the earth
007:147 **Those** who reject Our Signs and the Meeting
007:151 of **those** who sow mercy!"
007:152 **Those** who took the calf (for worship) will
007:152 **those** who invent (falsehoods).
007:153 But **those** who do wrong but repent
007:155 for Thou art the best of **those** who forgive.
007:156 and pay Zakat and **those** who believe in Our Signs;
007:156 for **those** who do right, and pay
007:157 "**Those** who follow the Messenger, the unlettered
007:157 So it is **those** who believe in him, honor him,
007:161 (the portion of) **those** who do good."
007:165 We rescued **those** who forbade evil; but We
007:167 **those** who would afflict them with
007:170 As to **those** who hold fast by the Book
007:176 of **those** who reject Our Signs; so relate
007:181 Of **those** We have created are people who direct
007:182 **Those** who reject Our signs, We shall

THOSE (continued)

007:188 to **those** who have faith."
007:194 Verily **those** whom ye call upon besides Allah
007:197 "But **those** ye call upon besides Him, are unable
007:201 **Those** who fear Allah, when a thought
007:205 and be not thou of **those** who are unheedful.
007:206 **Those** who are near to thy Lord, disdain not
008:002 For, Believers are **those** who, when Allah
008:008 distasteful though it be to **those** in guilt.
008:014 for **those** who reject is the chastisement
008:019 for verily Allah is with **those** who believe!
008:021 Nor be like **those** who say, "We hear,"
008:022 and the dumb,-**those** who understand not.
008:025 not in particular (only) **those** of you who do wrong:
008:038 the punishment of **those** before them is already
008:042 (had been given), and **those** who lived might live
008:042 that **those** who died might die after a clear Sign
008:046 for Allah is with **those** who patiently persevere.
008:047 And be not like **those** who started from their
008:049 Lo! the Hypocrites and **those** in whose heart
008:052 the people of Pharaoh and of **those** before them:
008:054 the people of Pharaoh and **those** before them":
008:055 sight of Allah are **those** who reject Him: they will
008:056 They are **those** with whom thou didst
008:057 **those** who follow them, that they may remember.
008:064 is Allah,-and unto **those** who follow thee
008:066 for Allah is with **those** who patiently persevere.
008:070 O Prophet! say to **those** who are captives
008:072 As to **those** who believed but did not emigrate
008:072 as well as **those** who gave (them)
008:072 **Those** who believed, and emigrated and fought
008:074 **Those** who believe, and emigrate, and fight
008:074 as well as **those** who give (them) asylum and aid,-
008:075 And **those** who accept Faith subsequently, and
009:001 to **those** of the Pagans with whom ye have
009:002 with shame **those** who reject Him.
009:003 a grievous chastisement to **those** who reject Faith.
009:004 with **those** Pagans with whom ye have entered
009:007 with the Pagans, except **those** with whom ye
009:011 for **those** who understand.
009:016 known **those** among you who strive with
009:019 (the pious service of) **those** who believe in Allah
009:019 and Allah guides not **those** who do wrong.
009:020 **Those** who believe, and emigrate and strive
009:026 thus doth He reward **those** without Faith.
009:029 Fight **those** who believe not in Allah nor the
009:034 **those** who hoard gold and silver and spend
009:036 with **those** who restrain themselves.
009:037 not **those** who reject Faith.
009:043 grant them exemption until **those** who told
009:044 **Those** who believe in Allah and the Last Day
009:044 And Allah knoweth well **those** who do their duty.
009:045 Only **those** ask thee for exemption who believe
009:046 were told, "Sit ye among **those** who sit (inactive)."
009:047 But Allah knoweth well **those** who do wrong.
009:060 (to Truth); for **those** in bondage and in debt;
009:060 the (funds): for **those** whose hearts have been
009:060 and **those** employed to administer the (funds):
009:061 But **those** who molest the Prophet will have
009:061 and is a Mercy to **those** of you who believe."
009:063 Know they not that for **those** who oppose
009:069 and ye have of yours, as did **those** before you;
009:069 As in the case of **those** before you: they were

THOSE (continued)

009:070   Hath not the story reached them of **those** before them?-
009:075   and be truly amongst **those** who are righteous.
009:079   (deeds of) charity, as well as **those** who give
009:079   **Those** who slander such of the Believers as give
009:080   and Allah guideth not **those** who are
009:081   **Those** who were left behind (in the Tabuk expedition)
009:083   then sit ye (now) with **those** who stay behind."
009:086   **those** with wealth and influence among them
009:086   we would be with **those** who sit (at home)."
009:088   But the Messenger, and **those** who believe
009:090   and **those** who were false to Allah and His Messenger
009:091   There is no blame on **those** who are infirm, or ill,
009:092   Nor (is there blame) on **those** who came to thee
009:096   Allah is not pleased with **those** who disobey.
009:100   **those** who follow them in (all) good deeds,
009:100   **those** who gave them aid, and (also)
009:100   **those** who forsook (their homes) and of
009:107   And there are **those** who put up a mosque by way
009:108   and Allah loveth **those** who make themselves pure.
009:110   The foundation of **those** who so build is never
009:112   **Those** that turn (to Allah) in repentance:
009:113   and **those** who believe, that they
009:119   and be with **those** who are truthful.
009:120   the reward to be lost of **those** who do good;-
009:123   and know that Allah is with **those** who fear Him.
009:124   Yea, **those** who believe, their faith is increased,
009:125   But **those** in whose hearts is a disease,-it will
010:004   **those** who believe and work righteousness,
010:004   but **those** who reject Him will have draughts of
010:005   in detail, for **those** who know.
010:006   are Signs for **those** who fear Him.
010:007   **Those** who rest not their hope on their
010:007   and **those** who heed not Our Signs,-
010:009   **Those** who believe, and work righteousness,
010:011   But We leave **those** who rest not their hope
010:013   Thus do We requite **those** who sin!
010:015   **those** who rest not their hope on their meeting with Us,
010:017   But never will prosper **those** who sin.
010:024   the Signs in detail for **those** who reflect.
010:026   To **those** who do right is a goodly (reward)-yea,
010:027   But **those** who have earned evil will have
010:028   ye and **those** ye joined as 'partners'."
010:028   Then shall We say to **those** who joined gods
010:033   proved true against **those** who rebel: verily they
010:039   but see what was the end of **those** who did wrong!
010:039   thus did **those** before them make charges of falsehood:
010:040   **those** who are out for mischief.
010:045   assuredly **those** will be lost who denied
010:057   in your hearts,-and for **those** who believe,
010:060   And what think **those** who forge lies against Allah,
010:063   **Those** who believe and (constantly)
010:067   for **those** who listen (to His Message).
010:069   Say: "**Those** who forge a lie against Allah
010:072   of **those** who submit to Allah's Will (in Islam)."
010:073   and **those** with him, in the Ark, and We made
010:073   **those** who were warned (but heeded not)!
010:073   **those** who rejected Our Signs.
010:081   the work of **those** who make mischief.
010:085   for **those** who practice oppression;
010:086   from **those** who reject (Thee)."
010:087   and give Glad Tidings to **those** who believe!"
010:089   and follow not the path of **those** who know not."

THOSE (continued)

010:090   I am of **those** who submit (to Allah in Islam)."
010:092   a Sign to **those** who come after thee!
010:094   so be in no wise of **those** in doubt.
010:094   then ask **those** who have been reading the Book
010:095   Nor be of **those** who reject the Signs of Allah,
010:095   be of **those** who perish.
010:096   **Those** against whom the Word of thy Lord
010:098   a single township (among **those** We warmed), which
010:100   on **those** who will not understand.
010:101   profit **those** who believe not.
010:103   Our messengers and **those** who believe: thus is
010:103   that We should deliver **those** who believe!
010:106   thou shalt certainly be of **those** who do wrong."
010:108   **Those**, who receive guidance, do so for
010:108   **those** who stray, do so to their own loss:
011:011   Not so do **those** who show patience and constancy,
011:015   **Those** who desire the life of the Present
011:016   They are **those** for whom there is nothing
011:017   They believe therein; but **those** of the Sects
011:017   Can they be (like) **those** who accept a Clear
011:018   **those** who forge a lie against Allah? They will
011:018   Behold! the Curse of Allah is on **those** who do wrong!-
011:019   "**Those** who would hinder (men) from the path of
011:023   But **those** who believe and work righteousness,
011:024   and **those** who can see and hear well.
011:029   I will not drive away (in contempt) **those** who believe:
011:031   Nor yet do I say, of **those** whom your eyes
011:036   except **those** who have believed already!
011:037   on behalf of **those** who are in sin: for they
011:040   and your family-except **those** against whom
011:043   **those** who were drowned.
011:043   of Allah, any but **those** on whom He hath mercy!"-
011:044   "Away with **those** who do wrong!"
011:048   some of the people (who sill spring) from **those** with thee:
011:049   for the End is for **those** who are righteous.
011:058   We saved Hud and **those** who believed with him,
011:066   We saved Salih and **those** who believed with him,
011:083   ever far from **those** who do wrong!
011:094   We saved Shu'aib and **those** who believed with him,
011:103   In that is a Sign for **those** who fear
011:105   of **those** (gathered) some will be wretched
011:106   **Those** who are wretched shall be in the Fire:
011:108   And **those** who are blessed shall be in the Garden:
011:112   thou and **those** who with thee turn (unto Allah);
011:113   And incline not to **those** who do wrong, or the
011:114   for **those** things that are good remove
011:114   remove **those** that are evil: that is a
011:119   Except **those** on whom thy Lord hath bestowed
011:120   a message of remembrance to **those** who believe.
011:121   Say to **those** who do not believe: "Do whatever
012:003   among **those** who knew it not.
012:022   thus do We reward **those** who do right.
012:023   Truly to no good come **those** who do wrong!"
012:051   he is indeed of **those** who are (ever) true
012:056   the reward of **those** who do good.
012:057   the Hereafter is the best, for **those** who believe,
012:064   of **those** who show mercy!"
012:087   except **those** who have no faith."
012:090   to be lost, of **those** who do right."
012:092   of **those** who show mercy?
012:109   the end of **those** before them?
012:109   for **those** who do right. Will ye

THOSE (continued)

012:110	Our punishment from **those** who are in sin.
012:110	and **those** whom We will are delivered into safety.
013:003	in these things are Signs for **those** who consider!
013:004	there are Signs for **those** who understand!
013:005	**those** who deny their Lord! They are
013:005	They are **those** round whose necks will be
013:014	for the prayer of **those** without Faith is nothing
013:016	Say: "Are the blind equal with **those** who see?
013:018	For **those** who respond to their Lord, are (all)
013:018	But **those** who respond not to Him,-even if
013:019	It is **those** who are endued with understanding
013:020	**Those** who fulfil the Covenant of Allah and fail
013:021	**Those** who join together **those** things which
013:022	**Those** who patiently persevere, seeking the
013:025	**those** things which Allah has commanded to be
013:025	But **those** who break the Covenant of Allah,
013:027	to himself **those** who turn to Him in penitence,-
013:028	"**Those** who believe, and whose hearts find
013:029	"For **those** who believe and work righteousness,
013:033	Nay! to **those** who believe not, their devising
013:033	And **those** whom Allah leads astray,
013:036	**Those** to whom We have given the Book rejoice at
013:036	**those** who reject a part thereof.
013:042	**Those** before them did (also) devise plots;
014:003	**Those** who prefer the life of this world
014:004	**those** whom He pleases and guides whom He pleases
014:009	And of **those** who (came) after them?
014:009	(O people!), of **those** who (went) before you?
014:012	For **those** who put their trust should put
014:018	The parable of **those** who reject their Lord
014:021	the weak say to **those** who were arrogant, "For us
014:023	But **those** who believe and work righteousness
014:027	**those** who believe, with the Word that stands firm,
014:027	but Allah will leave, to stray, **those** who do wrong:
014:028	to **those** who have exchanged the favour of Allah.
014:042	the deeds of **those** who do wrong.
015:002	Often will **those** who disbelieve, wish that
015:013	of **those** went before them.
015:020	of subsistence,-for you and for **those** for whose
015:024	who hasten forward, and **those** who lag behind.
015:024	To Us are known **those** of you who hasten forward,
015:031	among **those** who prostrated themselves.
015:032	**those** who prostrated themselves?"
015:044	for each of **those** Gates is a (special) class
015:060	**those** who will lag behind."
015:066	**those** (sinners) should be cut off by the morning.
015:075	for **those** who by tokens do understand.
015:077	Behold! in this is a Sign for **those** who believe!
015:090	as We sent down on **those** who divided
015:094	**those** who join false gods with Allah.
015:095	unto thee against **those** who scoff.-
015:096	**Those** who adopt, with Allah, another god:
015:098	and be of **those** who prostrate themselves in
016:011	is a Sign for **those** who give thought.
016:020	**Those** whom they invoke besides Allah create nothing
016:022	as to **those** who believe not in the Hereafter,
016:025	burdens of **those** without knowledge, whom they
016:026	**Those** before them did also plot (against Allah's Way):
016:027	**Those** endued with knowledge will say: "This Day,
016:028	"(Namely) **those** whose lives the angels take in
016:030	To **those** who do good, there is good in this world,
016:032	(Namely) **those** whose lives the angels take in

THOSE (continued)

016:033	So did **those** who went before them. But Allah
016:035	So did **those** who went before them. But what
016:036	what was the end of **those** who denied (the Truth).
016:038	raise up **those** who die: nay, but it is a promise
016:041	To **those** who leave their homes in the cause
016:042	(They are) **those** who persevere in patience,
016:043	ask of **those** who possess the Message.
016:045	Do then **those** who devise evil (plots) feel
016:060	To **those** who believe not in the Hereafter,
016:064	to them **those** things in which they differ,
016:064	a guide and a mercy to **those** who believe.
016:065	verily in this is a Sign for **those** who listen.
016:066	pure and agreeable to **those** who drink it.
016:067	in this also is a Sign for **those** who are wise.
016:069	for **those** who give thought.
016:071	to **those** whom their right hands possess, so as
016:071	**those** more favoured are not going to throw back
016:079	are Signs for **those** who believe.
016:086	When **those** who gave partners to Allah will see
016:086	our 'partners', **those** whom we used to invoke
016:088	**Those** who reject Allah and hinder (men) from
016:096	on **those** who patiently persevere, their reward
016:099	No authority has he over **those** who believe
016:100	His authority is over **those** only, who take
016:102	in order to strengthen **those** who believe, and as
016:104	**Those** who believe not in the Signs of Allah,-
016:105	It is **those** who believe not in the Signs of
016:107	and Allah will not guide **those** who reject Faith.
016:108	**Those** are they whose hearts, ears, and eyes
016:110	But verily thy Lord,-to **those** who leave their
016:116	For **those** who ascribe false things to Allah,
016:119	to **those** who do wrong in ignorance, but who
016:124	for **those** who disagreed (as to its observance);
016:126	for **those** who are patient.
016:128	restrain themselves, and **those** who do good.
016:128	For Allah is with **those** who restrain themselves,
017:003	O ye that are sprung from **those** whom We
017:008	made Hell a prison for **those** who reject
017:010	And to **those** who believe not in the Hereafter,
017:016	We command **those** among them who are given
017:019	**Those** who do wish for the (things of)
017:020	We bestow freely on all-these as well as **those**:
017:025	Most Forgiving to **those** who turn to Him
017:026	due rights, as (also) to **those** in want, and to
017:036	all of **those** shall be questioned of.
017:045	We put, between thee and **those** who believe not
017:053	(only) say **those** things that are best: for Satan
017:056	Say: "Call on **those**-besides Him-whom ye fancy:
017:057	**Those** whom they call upon do seek
017:064	And Arouse **those** whom thou canst among them,
017:067	**those** that ye call upon-besides Himself-leave you
017:071	(respective) Imams: **those** who are given their
017:072	But **those** who were blind in this world, will be
017:082	and a mercy to **those** who believe:
017:107	it is true that **those** who were given knowledge
018:004	Further, that He may warn **those** (also) who say,
018:021	**those** who prevailed over their affair said, "Let us
018:028	And keep yourself content with **those** who call
018:030	As to **those** who believe and work righteousness,
018:033	Each of **those** gardens brought forth its produce,
018:052	"Call on **those** whom ye thought to be My partners,"
018:071	"Hast thou scuttled it in order to drown **those** in it?

THOSE (continued)

018:078   (**those** things) over which thou was unable
018:082   of (**those** things) over which thou wast unable
018:103   Say: "Shall we tell you of **those** who lose most
018:104   "**Those** whose efforts have been wasted in this life,
018:105   They are **those** who deny the Signs of their Lord
018:107   As to **those** who believe and work righteous deeds,
019:048   and from **those** whom ye invoke besides Allah:
019:049   and from **those** whom they worshipped besides Allah,
019:058   and of **those** whom We carried (in the Ark)
019:058   **Those** were some of the prophets on whom
019:058   and Israel-of **those** whom We guided and chose.
019:060   Except **those** who repent and believe, and work
019:061   Gardens of Eternity, **those** which (Allah) Most
019:063   as an inheritance to **those** of Our Servants
019:069   from every sect all **those** who were worst in
019:070   And certainly We know best **those** who are most
019:072   But We shall save **those** who guarded against evil,
019:073   **those** who believe, "Which of the two sides is best
019:076   **those** who seek guidance: and the
019:096   On **those** who believe and work deeds
020:003   to **those** who fear (Allah),
020:048   **those** who reject and turn away.'"
020:076   for aye: such is the reward of **those** who purify
020:081   and **those** on whom descends My Wrath
020:082   to **those** who repent, believe, and do right,-
020:109   except for **those** for whom permission has been
021:006   (As to **those**) before them, not one of the towns
021:007   ask of **those** who possess the Message.
021:009   **those** who transgressed beyond bounds.
021:009   and We saved them and **those** whom We willed,
021:019   even **those** who are with Him are not
021:024   and the Message of **those** before me." But most
021:024   this is the Message of **those** with me and the
021:028   except for **those** who with whom He is well-pleased
021:029   thus do We reward **those** who do wrong.
021:048   for **those** who would do right,-
021:049   **Those** who fear their Lord in their
021:055   or are you one of **those** who jest?"
021:083   of **those** that are merciful."
021:088   and thus do We deliver **those** who have faith.
021:101   **Those** for whom the Good (Record) from Us
022:014   Verily Allah will admit **those** who believe
022:017   **Those** who believe (in the Qur'an),
022:017   **those** who follow the Jewish (scriptures), and the
022:019   but **those** who deny (their Lord),-for them
022:023   Allah will admit **those** who believe and work
022:025   As to **those** who have rejected (Allah), and would
022:026   for **those** who compass it round, or stand up,
022:030   are cattle except **those** mentioned to you
022:034   the Good News to **those** who humble themselves,
022:035   To **those** whose hearts, when Allah
022:038   (from ill) **those** who believe: verily Allah
022:039   To **those** against whom war is made, permission is
022:040   (They are) **those** who have been expelled from
022:040   Allah will certainly aid **those** who aid His
022:041   (They are) **those** who, if We
022:043   And **those** of Abraham and Lut;
022:050   "**Those** who believe and work righteousness,
022:051   "But **those** who strive against Our Signs,
022:053   but a trial for **those** in whose hearts is a
022:054   And that **those** on whom knowledge has been
022:054   is the Guide of **those** who believe, to the

THOSE (continued)

022:055   **Those** who reject Faith will not cease to be
022:056   so **those** who believe and work righteous deeds
022:057   And for **those** who reject Faith and deny
022:058   **Those** who leave their homes in the cause of
022:062   and **those** besides Him whom they invoke,-
022:071   for **those** that do wrong there is no helper.
022:072   They nearly attack with violence **those** who rehearse
022:073   feeble are **those** who petition and
022:073   and **those** whom they petition!
022:073   **Those** on whom, besides Allah ye call,
023:002   **Those** who humble themselves in their prayers;
023:006   Except with **those** joined to them in the
023:007   But **those** whose desires exceed **those** limits are
023:008   **Those** who faithfully observe their trust
023:020   and relish for **those** who use it for food.
023:027   and thy family-except **those** of them
023:028   on the Ark-thou and **those** with thee,-say: "Praise
023:048   of **those** who were destroyed.
023:057   Verily **those** who live in awe for fear
023:058   **Those** who believe in the Signs of their Lord;
023:059   **Those** who join not (in worship) partners with
023:060   And **those** who dispense their charity with their
023:064   **those** of them who received the good things
023:072   He is the Best of **those** who give sustenance.
023:074   And verily **those** who believe not in the Hereafter
023:102   Then **those** whose balance (of good deeds)
023:103   But **those** whose balance is light, will be
023:103   will be **those** who have lost their souls;
023:109   for Thou art the best of **those** Who show mercy!'
023:113   but ask **those** who keep account."
023:118   for Thou art the Best of **those** who show mercy!"
024:004   And **those** who launch a charge against
024:005   Except **those** who repent thereafter and mend
024:006   And for **those** who launch a charge
024:006   of **those** who speak the Truth.
024:011   **Those** who brought forward the lie are a body
024:019   **Those** who love (to see) scandal circulate
024:022   Let not **those** among you who are endued with grace
024:022   **those** in want, and **those** who have left their
024:023   **Those** who slander chaste women, indiscreet
024:027   and saluted **those** in them: that is
024:032   Marry **those** among you who are single, and the
024:033   Let **those** who find not the wherewithal for
024:034   and an admonition for **those** who fear (Allah).
024:038   for **those** whom He will, without measure.
024:044   **those** who have vision!
024:055   Allah has promised, to **those** among you who believe
024:055   as He granted it to **those** before them; that He
024:058   times of undress: outside **those** times it is
024:058   O ye who believe! let **those** whom your right
024:059   ask for permission, as do **those** before them:
024:061   or **those** of your fathers, or your
024:062   give leave to **those** of them whom thou wilt,
024:062   **those** who ask for the leave are **those** who believe
024:062   Only **those** are Believers who believe in Allah
024:063   then let **those** beware who withstand the
025:010   could give thee better (things) than **those**,-
025:017   as well as **those** whom they worship besides Allah,
025:021   **Those** who do not hope to meet Us (for Judgment)
025:032   **Those** who reject Faith say: "Why is not
025:034   **Those** who will be gathered to Hell
025:036   Our Signs": and **those** (people) We destroyed

THOSE (continued)

025:063 (Allah) Most Gracious are **those** who walk on
025:064 **Those** who spend the night in adoration
025:065 **Those** who say, "Our Lord! avert from
025:067 but hold a just (balance) between **those** (extremes);
025:067 **Those** who, when they spend, are not
025:068 **Those** who invoke not, with Allah, any other
025:072 **Those** who witness no falsehood, and, if
025:073 **Those** who, when they are admonished with the
025:074 And **those** who pray, "Our Lord!
025:075 **Those** are the ones who will be rewarded
026:025 (Pharaoh) said to **those** around: "Do ye not
026:086 for that he is among **those** astray;
026:091 "And to **those** straying in evil, the Fire
026:094 they and **those** straying in evil,
026:099 "'And our seducers were only **those** who were
026:102 we shall truly be of **those** who believe!'"
026:114 "I am not one to drive away **those** who believe.
026:118 and deliver me and **those** of the Believers
026:119 So we delivered him and **those** with him.
026:120 Thereafter We drowned **those** who remained behind.
026:151 of **those** who are extravagant,-
026:153 They said: "Thou art only one of **those** bewitched!
026:166 "And leave **those** whom Allah has created
026:173 on **those** who were admonished (but heeded not)!
026:185 They said: "Thou art only one of **those** bewitched!
026:213 **those** who will be punished.
026:219 **those** who prostrate themselves.
026:224 And the Poets,- it is **those** straying in Evil,
026:227 Except **those** who believe, work righteousness,
027:003 **Those** who establish regular prayers and give
027:004 As to **those** who believe not in the Hereafter,
027:008 "Blessed are **those** in the Fire and **those** around:
027:010 **those** called as messengers have no fear,-
027:014 of **those** who acted corruptly!
027:041 **those** who are not rightly guided."
027:047 from thee and **those** that are with thee." He said:
027:053 And We saved **those** who believed and practiced
027:057 to be of **those** who lagged behind.
027:058 on **those** who were admonished (but heeded not)!
027:069 what has been the end of **those** guilty (of sin)."
027:077 and a Mercy to **those** who believe.
027:081 from straying: only **those** wilt thou get to listen
027:083 **those** who reject Our Signs, and they
027:087 with terror **those** who are in the heavens,
027:087 in the heavens, and **those** who are on earth,
027:091 and I am commanded to be of **those** who bow
028:005 **those** who were being depressed in the land,
028:014 for thus do We reward **those** who do good.
028:017 never shall I be a help to **those** who sin!"
028:031 and fear not: for thou art of **those** who are secure.
028:032 **Those** are the two credentials from thy Lord
028:035 you two as well as **those** who follow you."
028:040 of **those** who did wrong!
028:044 nor wast thou a witness (of **those** events).
028:047 amongst **those** who believe!"
028:048 like **those** which were sent to Moses?"
028:052 **Those** to whom We sent the Book before this,-
028:056 but Allah guides **those** whom He will
028:056 and He knows best **those** who receive guidance.
028:058 Now **those** habitations of theirs, after them,
028:061 is to be among **those** brought up (for punishment)?
028:063 **Those** against whom the charge will be proved,

THOSE (continued)

028:076 **those** who exult (in riches).
028:077 for Allah loves not **those** who do mischief."
028:079 Said **those** whose aim is the Life of this World:
028:080 is best for **those** who believe and work
028:080 save **those** who steadfastly persevere (in good)."
028:080 But **those** who had been granted (true) knowledge
028:082 Ah! **those** who reject Allah will assuredly
028:082 And **those** who had envied his position the day
028:083 give to **those** who intend not high-handedness
028:086 in any way to **those** who reject (Allah's Message).
028:087 these who join gods with Allah.
029:003 We did test **those** before them, and Allah
029:003 who are true from **those** who are false.
029:003 and Allah will certainly know **those** who are
029:004 Do **those** who practice evil think that they
029:005 For **those** whose hopes are in the meeting
029:007 **Those** who believe and work righteous deeds,-
029:009 And **those** who believe and work righteous deeds,-
029:011 And Allah most certainly knows **those** who believe,
029:011 **those** who are Hypocrites.
029:012 And the Unbelievers say to **those** who believe:
029:023 **Those** who reject the Signs of Allah and the
029:032 she is of **those** who lag behind!"
029:033 she is of **those** who lag behind.
029:041 The parable of **those** who take protectors
029:043 **those** understand them who have Knowledge.
029:044 verily in that is a Sign for **those** who believe.
029:046 unless it be with **those** of them who do wrong.
029:049 in the hearts of **those** endowed with knowledge:
029:051 to **those** who believe.
029:052 **those** who believe in vanities and reject Allah,
029:058 But **those** who believe and work deeds
029:058 an excellent reward for **those** who do (good)!-
029:059 **Those** who persevere in patience, and put
029:068 a home in Hell for **those** who reject Faith?
029:069 And **those** who strive in Our (Cause),-We will
029:069 is with **those** who do right.
030:009 and see what was the End of **those** before them?
030:010 In the long run evil will be the End of **those** who do evil;
030:015 Then **those** who have believed and worked
030:016 And **those** who have rejected Faith and falsely
030:021 verily in that are Signs for **those** who reflect.
030:022 are Signs for **those** who know.
030:023 verily in that are Signs for **those** who hearken.
030:024 are Signs for **those** who are wise.
030:028 do ye have partners among **those** whom your
030:029 But who will guide **those** whom Allah
030:031 and be not ye among **those** who join gods with Allah,-
030:032 **Those** who split up their Religion, and become
030:037 are Signs for **those** who believe.
030:038 that is best for **those** who seek the Countenance,
030:042 and see what was the End of **those** before (you):
030:044 and **those** who work righteousness will make
030:044 **Those** who reject Faith will suffer from that
030:045 **those** who reject Faith.
030:045 That He may reward **those** who believe and work
030:047 then, to **those** who transgressed, We meted
030:047 to aid **those** who believed.
030:053 only **those** wilt thou make to hear, will believe
030:056 But **those** endued with knowledge and faith
030:059 of **those** who understand not.
030:060 nor let **those** excite thee, who have

THOSE (continued)

031:004   **Those** who establish regular Prayer, and give
031:006   **those** who purchase idle tales, without knowledge
031:008   For **those** who believe and work righteous deeds,
031:015   of **those** who turn to Me: in the End
031:020   Yet there are among men **those** who dispute
031:032   **those** that falter between (right and wrong).
032:015   Only **those** believe in Our Signs who, when they
032:019   For **those** who believe and do righteous deeds,
032:020   As to **those** who are rebellious and wicked,
032:022   Verily from **those** who transgress We shall exact (due)
033:012   And behold! The Hypocrites and **those** in whose hearts
033:018   who keep back (men) and **those** who say to their
033:018   Verily Allah knows **those** among you who keep
033:026   And **those** of the people of the Book who aided
033:038   of Allah amongst **those** of old that have
033:039   (It is the practice of **those**) who preach
033:050   and **those** whom thy right hand possesses
033:057   **Those** who annoy Allah and his Messenger-
033:058   And **those** who annoy believing men and women
033:060   Truly, if the Hypocrites, and **those** in whose
033:060   and **those** who stir up sedition in the City,
033:062   of Allah among **those** who lived aforetime:
033:069   **those** who hurt Moses, but Allah cleared him
034:004   That He may reward **those** who believe and work
034:005   But **those** who strive against Our Signs,
034:006   And **those** to whom knowledge has come see that
034:008   Nay, it is **those** who believe not in the Hereafter,
034:023   except for **those** for whom He has granted
034:027   Say: "Show me **those** whom ye have joined with
034:031   **Those** who were deemed weak will say to the arrogant
034:032   The arrogant ones will say to **those** who had
034:033   **Those** who had been deemed weak will say to
034:037   but only **those** who believe and work righteousness
034:038   **Those** who strive against Our Signs, to frustrate
034:039   for He is the Best of **those** Who grant Sustenance.
034:045   a tenth of what We had granted to **those**: yet when
035:007   For **those** who reject Allah, is a
035:007   but for **those** who believe and work righteous deeds,
035:010   **Those** that lay Plots of Evil,-
035:013   And **those** whom ye invoke besides Him
035:022   but thou canst not make **those** to hear
035:022   Nor are alike **those** that are living
035:022   are living and **those** that are dead.
035:026   In the end did I punish **those** who rejected Faith:
035:028   **Those** truly fear Allah,
035:029   **Those** who rehearse the Book of Allah,
035:036   But **those** who reject (Allah)-for them
035:044   and see what was the End of **those** before them,-
036:021   "Obey **those** who ask no reward of you
036:027   me among **those** held in honour!"
036:047   **those** whom, if Allah had so willed, He could
036:047   the Unbelievers say to **those** who believe:
036:070   **those** who reject (Truth).
037:001   By **those** who range themselves in ranks,
037:003   **Those** who thus proclaim the message (of Allah)!
037:046   to **those** who drink (thereof),
037:057   been among **those** brought (there)!
037:073   of **those** who were warned,
037:080   Thus indeed do We reward **those** who do right.
037:105   **those** who do right.
037:110   Thus indeed do We reward **those** who do right.
037:121   Thus indeed do We reward **those** who do right.

THOSE (continued)

037:123   So also was Elias among **those** sent (by us).
037:131   Thus indeed do We reward **those** who do right.
037:133   So also was Lut among **those** sent (by us).
037:135   **those** who lagged behind:
037:139   So also was Jonah among **those** sent (by Us).
037:161   For, verily, neither ye nor **those** ye worship
037:166   "And we are verily **those** who declare
037:167   And there were **those** who said,
037:168   a message from **those** of old,
037:177   Evil will be the morning for **those** who were
038:024   not so do **those** who believe and work deeds
038:026   for **those** who wander astray from the Path
038:028   Shall We treat **those** who believe and work
038:028   the same as **those** who turn aside from the right?
038:028   the same as **those** who do mischief on earth?
038:028   Shall We treat **those** who guard against evil,
038:074   and became one of **those** who reject Faith.
038:085   with thee and **those** that follow thee,-every one."
039:003   But **those** who take for protectors
039:004   He pleased out of **those** whom He doth create:
039:009   Say: "Are **those** equal, **those** who know and
039:009   It is **those** who are endued with understanding
039:009   who know and **those** who do not know?
039:010   for **those** who do good in this world. Spacious is
039:010   **Those** who patiently persevere will truly
039:012   of **those** who submit to Allah in Islam."
039:015   Say: "Truly, **those** in loss are **those** who lose
039:017   **Those** who eschew Taghut and fall not into
039:018   **those** are the ones whom Allah has guided,
039:018   and **those** are the ones endued with understanding.
039:018   **Those** who listen to the Word, and follow
039:020   But it is for **those** who fear their Lord,
039:022   Woe to **those** whose hearts are hardened against
039:023   the skins of **those** who fear their Lord
039:025   **Those** before them (also) rejected (revelation),
039:034   such is the reward of **those** who do good:
039:038   In Him trust **those** who put their trust."
039:042   and **those** that die not (He takes) during their
039:042   are Signs for **those** who reflect.
039:042   **those** on whom He has passed the degree of death,
039:045   the hearts of **those** who believe not in the
039:046   in **those** matters about which they have differed."
039:052   Verily, in this are signs for **those** who believe!
039:056   towards Allah, and was but among **those** who mocked!'
039:058   I should certainly be among **those** who do good!'
039:059   and became one of **those** who reject Faith!'"
039:060   see **those** who told lies against Allah;-their faces
039:063   and **those** who reject the Signs
039:065   as it was to **those** before thee,-" If thou
039:066   and be of **those** who give thanks.
039:073   And **those** who feared their Lord will be led
039:074   for **those** who work (righteousness)!"
040:007   and **those** around it sing Glory and Praise
040:007   for **those** who believe: "Our Lord!
040:007   Forgive, then, **those** who turn in repentance,
040:007   **Those** who bear the Throne (of Allah)
040:013   but only **those** receive admonition who turn (to Allah).
040:020   but **those** whom (men) invoke besides
040:021   and see what was the End of **those** before them?
040:025   "Slay the sons of **those** who believe with him,
040:031   and **those** who came after them: but Allah
040:047   will say to **those** who had been arrogant, "We but

THOSE (continued)

040:048 **Those** who had been arrogant will say: "We are
040:049 **Those** in the Fire will say to the Keepers of Hell:
040:050 But the Prayer of **those** without Faith is nothing
040:051 help Our messengers and **those** who believe,
040:056 **Those** who dispute about the Signs of Allah
040:058 and **those** who (clearly) see: nor are
040:058 and **those** who do evil. Little do ye
040:058 nor are (equal) **those** who believe and work
040:060 but **those** who are too arrogant to serve Me
040:063 Thus are deluded **those** who are wont to reject
040:066 **those** whom ye invoke besides Allah,-seeing that
040:069 Seest thou not **those** that dispute concerning
040:070 **Those** who reject the Book and the
040:078 there and then, **those** who stood on Falsehoods.
040:082 and see what was the end of **those** before them?
041:006 And woe to **those** who join gods with Allah,-
041:007 **Those** who pay not zakat, and who
041:008 For **those** who believe and work deeds of
041:018 But We delivered **those** who believed
041:023 and (now) have ye become of **those** utterly lost!"
041:029 "Our Lord! Show us **those**, among Jinns
041:030 In the case of **those** who say, "Our Lord
041:033 "I am of **those** who bow in Islam"?
041:035 goodness except **those** who exercise patience
041:038 presence of thy Lord are **those** who celebrate
041:040 **Those** who pervert the Truth in Our Signs are not
041:041 **Those** who reject the Message when it comes to them
041:044 and a healing to **those** who believe;
041:044 and for **those** who believe not, there is
042:003 to thee as (He did) to **those** before thee,-Allah,
042:006 And **those** who take as protectors others besides
042:013 and guides to Himself **those** who turn (to Him).
042:013 **those** whom He pleases, and guides
042:013 to **those** who worship other things
042:014 but truly **those** who have inherited the Book
042:016 But **those** who dispute concerning Allah after He
042:018 Only **those** wish to hasten it who believe
042:018 Behold, verily **those** that dispute concerning
042:018 **those** who believe hold it in awe, and know
042:022 But **those** who believe and work righteous deeds
042:023 for this except the love of **those** near of kin."
042:026 And He listens to **those** who believe and do
042:035 But let **those** know, who dispute
042:036 (it is) for **those** who believe and put their trust
042:037 **Those** who avoid the greater sins and indecencies
042:038 **Those** who respond to their Lord, and establish
042:039 And **those** who, when an oppressive wrong
042:040 **those** who do wrong.
042:042 The blame is only against **those** who oppress men
042:045 will say: "**Those** are indeed in loss who lose
043:025 **those** who rejected (Truth)!
043:028 among **those** who came after him, that they
043:069 **Those** who have believed in Our Signs and submitted
043:086 And **those** whom they invoke besides Allah have no
044:028 And We made other people inherit (**those** things)!
044:037 of Tubba and **those** who were before them?
045:003 are Signs for **those** who believe.
045:004 are Signs for **those** of assured Faith.
045:005 the winds,- are Signs for **those** that are wise.
045:011 This is (true) Guidance: and for **those** who reject
045:013 are Signs indeed for **those** who reflect.
045:014 Tell **those** who believe, to forgive

THOSE (continued)

045:014 to forgive **those** who do not hope for
045:017 on the Day of Judgement as to **those** matters in
045:018 of **those** who know not.
045:020 and a Guidance and Mercy to **those** of assured Faith.
045:021 What! do **those** who do evil deeds think that
045:021 with **those** who believe and do righteous deeds,-
045:030 Then, as to **those** who believed and did
045:031 But as to **those** who reject Allah,
046:003 but **those** who reject Faith turn away
046:011 The Unbelievers say of **those** who believe:
046:012 and as Glad Tidings to **those** who do right.
046:013 Verily **those** who say, "Our Lord is Allah,"
046:025 Thus do We recompense **those** given to sin!
046:028 to them from **those** whom they worshipped as gods,
046:035 destroyed except **those** who transgress?
047:001 **Those** who reject Allah and hinder (men) from the
047:002 But **those** who believe and work deeds
047:003 While **those** who believe follow the Truth
047:003 This because **those** who reject Allah
047:004 But **those** who are slain in the way of Allah,
047:008 But **those** who reject (Allah),- for them
047:010 **those** who reject Allah.
047:010 and see what was the End of **those** before them
047:011 Allah is the protector of **those** who believe,
047:011 but **those** who reject Allah have no protector.
047:012 while **those** who reject Allah will enjoy (this world)
047:012 Verily Allah will admit **those** who believe and do
047:015 a joy to **those** who drink; and rivers
047:015 their Lord, (can **those** in such Bliss) be compared
047:016 from thee, they say to **those** who have received
047:017 But to **those** who receive Guidance, He increases
047:020 **Those** who believe say, "Why is not
047:020 thou wilt see **those** in whose hearts is a disease
047:025 **Those** who turn back as apostates after Guidance
047:026 This, because they said to **those** who hate
047:029 Or do **those** in whose hearts is a disease,
047:031 And We shall try you until We test **those** among you
047:032 **Those** who disbelieve, hinder (men) from the
047:034 **Those** who disbelieve, and hinder (men) from the
047:038 Behold, ye are **those** invited to spend (of your substance)
048:002 of the past and **those** to follow; fulfil His
048:010 Verily **those** who plight their fealty to thee
048:013 for **those** who reject Allah, a Blazing fire!
048:015 **Those** who lagged behind (will say), when ye
048:029 and **those** who are with him are strong
048:029 Allah has promised **those** among them who believe
049:003 **Those** that lower their voice in the presence
049:004 **Those** who shout out to thee from without
049:007 **those** who walk in righteousness;-
049:009 for Allah loves **those** who are fair (and just).
049:011 and **those** who do not desist are indeed doing wrong.
049:015 Only **those** are Believers who have
051:002 And **those** that lift and bear away heavy weights;
051:003 And **those** that flow with ease and gentleness;
051:004 And **those** that distribute the affair;-
051:011 **Those** who (flounder) heedless in a
051:020 On the earth are Signs for **those** of assured Faith,
051:034 "Marked as from thy Lord for **those** who trespass
051:035 Then We evacuated **those** of the Believers
052:021 And **those** who believe and whose seeds
052:042 But **those** who disbelieve are themselves ensnared
052:047 And verily, for **those** who do wrong, there is

THOSE (continued)

053:027 **Those** who believe not in the Hereafter,
053:029 Therefore shun **those** who turn away from
053:030 and He knoweth best **those** who receive guidance.
053:030 **those** who stray from His path, and He
053:031 so that He rewards **those** who do evil,
053:031 and He rewards **those** who do good, with what
053:032 **Those** who avoid great sins and indecent deeds,
054:035 Thus do We reward **those** who give thanks.
054:047 Truly **those** in sin are the ones in error
056:010 And **those** Foremost (in Faith) will be
056:011 These will be **those** Nearest to Allah:
056:013 A number of people from **those** of old,
056:014 And a few from **those** of later times.
056:039 A (goodly) number from **those** of old,
056:040 And a (goodly) number from **those** of later times.
056:049 Say: "Yea, **those** of old and **those** of later times,
056:079 Which none shall touch but **those** who are clean:
056:088 Thus, then, if he be of **those** Nearest to Allah,
056:092 And if he be of **those** who deny (the truth)
057:007 For, **those** of you who believe and spend (in charity),-
057:010 than **those** who spent (freely) and fought
057:010 before the Victory, (with **those** who did so later).
057:010 **Those** are higher in rank than **those** who spent
057:010 Not equal among you are **those** who spent (freely)
057:014 (**Those** without) will call out, "Were we
057:015 of you, nor of **those** who rejected Allah.
057:016 not become like **those** to whom was given The Book
057:018 For **those** who give in Charity, men and women,
057:019 And **those** who believe in Allah and His messengers-
057:019 but **those** who reject Allah and deny Our Signs,-
057:021 prepared for **those** who believe in Allah and His
057:027 Yet We bestowed, on **those** among them who believed,
057:027 of **those** who followed him Compassion and Mercy.
058:002 except **those** who gave them birth.
058:003 But **those** who pronounce the word "Zihar" to their
058:004 **Those** are limits (set by) Allah.
058:004 For **those** who Reject (Him), there is
058:005 as were **those** before them: for We
058:005 **Those** who oppose (the commands of) Allah and His
058:008 Seest thou not **those** who were forbidden secret
058:011 (and degrees), **those** of you who believe and who
058:014 Seest thou not **those** who turn (in friendship)
058:020 **Those** who oppose (the commands of) Allah and
058:020 among **those** most humiliated.
058:022 loving **those** who oppose Allah and His Messenger,
059:008 indigent Muhajirs, **those** who were expelled from
059:009 And **those** who before them, had homes
059:009 And **those** saved from the covetousness of their
059:010 against **those** who have believed.
059:010 And **those** who came after them say: "Our Lord!
059:015 Like **those** who lately preceded them, they have
059:019 And be ye not like **those** who forgot Allah; and He
060:004 (to follow) in Abraham and **those** with him,
060:006 for **those** whose hope is in Allah and in
060:007 **those** whom ye (now) hold as enemies.
060:008 for Allah loveth **those** who are just.
060:008 to **those** who fight you not for (your) Faith
060:009 to **those** who fight you for (your) Faith, and drive
060:011 Then pay to **those** whose wives have deserted
060:013 in despair about **those** (buried) in graves.
061:004 Truly Allah loves **those** who fight in His Cause
061:005 For Allah guides not **those** who are rebellious

THOSE (continued)

061:007 And Allah guides not **those** who do wrong.
061:014 power to **those** who believed against their enemies,
062:005 but who subsequently failed in **those** (obligations),
062:005 The similitude of **those** who were entrusted with
062:007 And Allah knows well **those** that do wrong!
063:007 "Spend nothing on **those** who are with
064:005 of **those** who rejected Faith aforetime?
064:009 And **those** who believe in Allah
064:010 But **those** who reject Faith and treat
064:016 and **those** saved from the covetousness of their
065:001 **those** are limits set by Allah: and any
065:002 And for **those** who fear Allah,
065:004 and for **those** who fear Allah, He will
065:004 and for **those** who have no courses (it is the same):
065:004 for **those** who are pregnant,
065:011 And **those** who believe in Allah and work
065:011 lead forth **those** who believe and do
066:004 one among **those** who believe,-and furthermore,
066:008 and **those** who believe with him,
066:011 to **those** who believe, the wife of Pharaoh: behold
066:011 and save me from **those** that do wrong";
067:006 For **those** who reject their Lord (and Cherisher)
067:012 As for **those** who fear their Lord unseen, for them
067:028 to destroy me, and **those** with me, or if
068:007 and He knoweth best **those** who receive
068:008 So obey not to **those** who deny (the Truth).
069:009 And Pharaoh, and **those** before him, and the
069:037 "Which none do eat but **those** in sin."
069:049 amongst you **those** that reject (it).
070:022 Not so **those** devoted to Prayer:-
070:023 **Those** who remain steadfast to their prayer;
070:024 And **those** in whose wealth is a recognized right
070:026 And **those** who hold to the truth of the
070:027 And **those** who fear the punishment of their Lord,-
070:029 And **those** who guard their chastity,
070:031 But **those** who trespass beyond this
070:032 And **those** who respect their trusts and covenants;
070:033 And **those** who stand firm in their testimonies;
070:034 And **those** who (strictly) guard their worship;-
072:010 is intended to **those** on earth, or whether
072:014 Now **those** who submit their wills-they have
072:015 'But **those** who swerve,-they are
073:011 **those** in possession of the good things of life,
073:020 and so doth a party of **those** with thee.
074:010 Far from easy for **those** without Faith.
074:031 and the Believers, and that **those** in whose heart
074:043 They will say: "We were not of **those** who prayed;
074:044 "Nor were we of **those** who fed the indigent;
077:038 We shall Gather you together and **those** before (you)!
079:002 By **those** who gently draw out (the souls of the blessed);
079:003 And by **those** who glide along (on errands of mercy),
083:001 Woe to **those** that deal in fraud,-
083:002 **Those** who, when they have to receive by measure
083:010 Woe, that Day, to **those** that deny-
083:011 **Those** that deny the Day of Judgment.
083:021 To which bear witness **those** Nearest (to Allah).
083:026 and for this let **those** aspire, who have
083:028 whereof drink **those** Nearest to Allah.
083:029 **Those** in sin used to laugh at **those** who believed,
084:025 Except to **those** who believe and work
085:010 **Those** who persecute the Believers, men and women,
085:011 For **those** who believe and do righteous deeds,

THOSE (continued)

089:005 (or evidence) for **those** who understand?

090:017 Then will he be of **those** who believe, and enjoin

090:019 But **those** who reject Our Signs, they are

092:015 None shall reach it but **those** most unfortunate ones

092:017 But **those** most devoted to Allah shall be

092:018 **Those** who spend their wealth for increase

098:001 **Those** who disbelieve, among the People of the

098:006 **Those** who disbelieve, among the People of the

098:007 **Those** who have faith and do righteous deeds,-

107:006 **Those** who (want but) to be seen,

113:004 From the mischief of **those** who blow on knots;

THOU

001:007 **Thou** hast bestowed Thy Grace,

002:006 whether **thou** warn them or do not warn them;

002:030 They said, "Wilt **thou** place therein

002:032 save what **Thou** hast taught Us:

002:032 in truth it is **Thou** who art perfect

002:035 dwell **thou** and thy wife in the Garden;

002:067 They said: "Makest **thou** a laughing-stock

002:071 They said: "Now hast **thou** brought the truth."

002:096 **Thou** wilt indeed find them,

002:106 knowest **thou** not that Allah hath power

002:107 Knowest **thou** not that to Allah belongeth

002:120 unless **thou** follow their form of religion.

002:120 then wouldst **thou** find neither Protector

002:120 Wert **thou** to follow their desires

002:127 for **thou** art the All-Hearing,

002:128 for **Thou** art the Oft-Returning,

002:129 for **Thou** art the Exalted in Might, the Wise."

002:135 Say **thou**: "Nay! (I would rather) the Religion

002:143 the Qiblah to which **thou** wast used,

002:145 If **thou** after the knowledge hath reached thee,

002:145 Even if **thou** wert to bring to the people

002:145 then wert **thou** indeed (clearly) in the wrong.

002:145 nor art **thou** going to follow their Qiblah;

002:149 From whencesoever **thou** startest forth,

002:150 So from whencesoever **thou** startest forth,

002:243 Didst **thou** not turn thy vision

002:246 Hast **thou** not turned thy vision to the chiefs

002:252 verily **thou** art one of the Messengers.

002:258 Hast **thou** not turned thy thought to one

002:258 do **thou** then cause it to rise from the West."

002:259 He said "Nay, **thou** hast tarried

002:259 He said: "How long didst **thou** tarry (thus)?"

002:260 He said: "Dost **thou** not then believe?"

002:260 "My Lord! show me how **thou** givest life to the dead.

002:273 **Thou** shalt know them by their (unfailing) mark:

002:286 like that which **Thou** didst lay on those

002:286 **Thou** art our protector;

003:008 for **Thou** art the Grantor of bounties

003:008 deviate now after **Thou** hast guided us,

003:009 "Our Lord! **Thou** art He that will gather mankind

003:023 Hast **thou** not turned thy thought to those who

003:026 and **thou** bringest low whom **Thou** pleasest:

003:026 Verily, over all things **Thou** hast power.

003:026 **Thou** enduest with honour whom **Thou** pleasest,

003:026 **Thou** strippest off power from whom **Thou** pleasest:

003:026 **thou** givest power to whom **Thou** pleasest,

003:027 to whom **Thou** pleasest, without measure."

003:027 and **Thou** givest sustenance to whom **Thou** pleasest,

003:027 and **Thou** bringest the dead out of the living;

003:027 **Thou** bringest the Living out of the dead,

THOU (continued)

003:027 And **Thou** causest the Day to gain on the Night;

003:027 "**Thou** causest the Night to gain on the Day.

003:035 for **Thou** hearest and knoweth all things."

003:038 for **Thou** art He that heareth prayer!

003:041 that **thou** shalt speak to no man for three days

003:044 nor wast **thou** with them when they dispute

003:044 **thou** wast not with them when they cast

003:052 and do **thou** bear witness that we are Muslims.

003:053 "Our Lord! we believe in what **thou** hast revealed,

003:075 unless **thou** constantly stoodest demanding,

003:121 **thou** didst leave the household (early)

003:124 Remember **thou** saidst to the faithful: "Is it not

003:154 Say **thou**: "Indeed, this affair is wholly Allah's."

003:159 Then, when **thou** hast taken a decision,

003:159 Wert **thou** severe or harsh-hearted, they would

003:159 that **thou** dost deal gently with them.

003:191 not for naught hast **Thou** created (all) this!

003:192 "Our Lord! any whom **Thou** dost admit to the Fire,

003:192 truly **Thou** coverest with shame,

003:194 for **thou** never breakest Thy promise."

003:194 **Thou** didst promise unto us through Thy Messengers,

004:044 Hast **thou** not turned thy thought to those who

004:049 Hast **thou** not turned thy thought to those

004:051 Hast **thou** not turned thy thought to those who

004:052 **thou** wilt find, have no one to help.

004:060 Hast **thou** not turned thy thought to those who

004:061 **thou** seest the Hypocrites avert their faces

004:077 Wouldst **Thou** not grant us respite to our

004:077 why hast **Thou** ordered us to fight?

004:077 Hast **thou** not turned thy thought to those who

004:081 from what **thou** tellest them.

004:084 **thou** art held responsible only for thyself, and

004:088 never shalt **thou** find the Way.

004:094 you a salutation: "**Thou** art none of a Believer!"

004:102 When **thou** (O Messenger) art with them, and

004:105 that **thou** mightest judge between people by that

004:113 taught thee what **thou** knewest not (before):

004:143 never wilt **thou** find for him the Way.

004:145 no helper wilt **thou** find for them;

005:013 nor wilt **thou** cease to find them-barring a few,

005:024 Go **thou**, and thy Lord, and fight

005:026 but sorrow **thou** not over these rebellious people."

005:028 "If **thou** dost stretch thy hand against me, to slay

005:029 for **thou** wilt be among the companions of the Fire,

005:040 Knowest **thou** not that to Allah (alone) belongeth

005:041 **thou** hast no authority in the least for him

005:042 If **thou** judge, judge in equity between them.

005:042 If **thou** decline, they cannot hurt thee in the least.

005:049 And this (He commands): Judge **thou** between them

005:052 **thou** seest how eagerly they run about

005:062 Many of them dost **thou** see, racing each

005:067 If **thou** didst not, **thou** wouldst not have fulfilled

005:068 But sorrow **thou** not over (these)

005:080 **Thou** seest many of them turning in friendship

005:082 to the Believers wilt **thou** find those who say,

005:082 to the Believers wilt **thou** find the Jews and

005:083 **thou** wilt see their eyes overflowing with tears,

005:109 it is **Thou** who knowest in full all that is hidden.

005:110 (violence to) thee when **thou** didst show them

005:110 And behold! **thou** bringest forth the dead

005:110 So that **thou** didst speak to the people

005:110 And behold! **thou** makest out of clay, as it

THOU (continued)

005:110   and **thou** healest those born blind, and the
005:110   And **thou** breathest into it, and it becometh
005:111   and do **thou** bear witness that we bow to Allah
005:113   and to know that **thou** hast indeed told us
005:114   for **thou** art the best Sustainer (of our needs)."
005:116   **Thou** wouldst indeed have known it.
005:116   **Thou** knowest what is in my heart, though I
005:116   For **Thou** knowest in full all that is hidden.
005:116   "O Jesus the son of Mary! didst **thou** say unto men,
005:117   except what **Thou** didst command me to say, to wit,
005:117   **thou** wast the Watcher over them,
005:117   when **Thou** didst take me up,
005:117   and **Thou** art a Witness to all things.
005:118   if **Thou** dost forgive them, **Thou** art the Exalted,
005:118   "If **Thou** dost punish them, they are
006:014   and be not **thou** of the company of those
006:027   If **thou** couldst but see when they
006:030   If **thou** couldst but see when they
006:034   Already hast **thou** received some account
006:035   yet if **thou** wert able to seek a tunnel
006:035   so be not **thou** amongst those who are swayed
006:052   that **thou** shouldst turn them away, and thus
006:068   When **thou** seest men engaged in vain
006:068   sit not **thou** in the company of those who do wrong.
006:074   "Takest **thou** idols for gods? For I see
006:092   that **thou** mayest warn the Mother
006:093   If **thou** couldst but see how the wicked
006:105   may say, "**Thou** hast learnt this (from somebody),
006:106   Follow what **thou** art taught by inspiration
006:107   nor art **thou** set over them to dispose
006:116   Wert **thou** to follow the common run
006:128   which **Thou** didst appoint for us."
006:150   nor follow **thou** the vain desires of such
006:150   be not **thou** amongst them:
006:159   **thou** hast no part in them in the least:
007:002   that with it **thou** mightest warn (the erring)
007:012   **thou** didst create me from fire and him from clay."
007:013   get out, for **thou** art of the meanest
007:015   (Allah) said: "Be **thou** among those who have respite."
007:016   He said: "Because **Thou** hast thrown me
007:017   nor wilt **Thou** find, in most of them, gratitude
007:019   O Adam! dwell **thou** and thy wife
007:023   if **Thou** forgive us not and bestow not
007:066   and "We think **thou** art a liar!"
007:066   "Ah! we see **thou** art in folly!" and "We think
007:070   if so be that **thou** tellest the truth!"
007:070   They said: "Comest **thou** to us, that we
007:070   Bring us what **thou** threatenest us with, if so
007:077   if **thou** art a Messenger (of Allah)!"
007:088   or else ye (**thou** and they) shall have
007:089   Our Lord! Decide **thou** between us and our
007:089   for **thou** art the best to decide."
007:106   show it forth,-if **thou** tellest the truth."
007:106   **thou** hast come with a Sign, show it
007:115   They said: "O Moses! wilt **thou** throw (first), or
007:126   "But **thou** dost wreak thy vengeance on us
007:127   "Wilt **thou** leave Moses and his people, to
007:129   both before and after **thou** comest to us."
007:132   "Whatever be the Signs **thou** bringest, to work
007:134   if **thou** wilt remove the Plague from us, we
007:143   then shalt **thou** see Me."
007:143   canst **thou** see Me (direct); but look

THOU (continued)

007:150   nor count **thou** me amongst the people of sin."
007:151   For **Thou** art the Most Merciful of those
007:155   by it **Thou** causest whom **Thou** wilt to stray, and
007:155   wouldst **Thou** destroy us for the deeds of the
007:155   and **Thou** leadest whom **Thou** wilt into the right
007:155   Thy will **thou** couldst have destroyed, long
007:155   **Thou** art our Protector: so forgive us
007:155   for **Thou** art the best of those who forgive.
007:173   wilt **Thou** then destroy us because of the deeds
007:187   They ask thee as if **thou** wert eager
007:189   (saying): "If **Thou** givest us a goodly child, we
007:198   **Thou** wilt see them looking at thee,
007:198   If **thou** callest them to guidance, they hear not.
007:203   they say: "Why hast **thou** not got it together?"
007:203   If **thou** bring them not a revelation, they say:
007:205   And do **thou** (O reader!) bring thy
007:205   and be not **thou** of those who are unheedful.
008:017   when **thou** threwest (a handful of dust),
008:033   whilst **thou** wast amongst them; nor was He
008:050   If **thou** couldst see, when the
008:056   **thou** didst make a covenant, but they
008:058   If **thou** fearest treachery from any group, throw
008:061   do **thou** (also) incline towards peace, and trust
008:063   not if **thou** hadst spent all that is in the earth,
008:063   couldst **thou** have produced that affection,
009:043   God give thee grace! Why didst **thou** grant them
009:043   and **thou** hadst proved the liars?
009:065   If **thou** dost question them, they declare
009:080   Whether **thou** ask for their forgiveness, or not,
009:080   if **thou** ask seventy times for their forgiveness,
009:084   Nor do **thou** ever pray for any of them that dies,
009:092   and when **thou** saidst, "I can find no mounts for you,"
009:094   Say **thou**: "Present no excuses: we shall
009:101   **thou** knowest them not: We know them: twice shall
009:103   that so **thou** mightest purify and sanctify them;
009:108   Never stand **thou** forth therein. There is
010:022   saying, "If **Thou** dost deliver us from this,
010:042   but canst **thou** make the deaf to hear,-even though
010:043   look at thee: but canst **thou** guide the blind,-
010:061   and whatever portion **thou** mayest be reciting
010:061   In whatever business **thou** mayest be, and whatever
010:078   They said: "Hast **thou** come to us to turn us
010:078   in order that **thou** and thy brother may have
010:088   Moses prayed: "Our Lord! **Thou** hast indeed bestowed
010:091   But a little while before, wast **thou** in rebellion!-
010:091   and **thou** didst mischief (and violence)!
010:092   thy body, that **thou** mayest be a Sign to those
010:094   If **thou** wert in doubt as to what We have
010:095   Signs of Allah, or **thou** shalt be of those
010:099   Wilt **thou** then compel mankind, against their
010:106   **thou** shalt certainly be of those who do wrong."
010:106   nor hurt thee: if **thou** dost, behold!
010:109   Follow **thou** the inspiration sent unto thee, and be
011:007   But if **thou** wert to say to them, "Ye shall
011:012   Perchance **thou** mayest (feel the inclination)
011:012   But **thou** art there only to warn! It is Allah
011:032   if **thou** speakest the truth!"
011:032   now bring upon us what **thou** threatenest us with,
011:032   and (much) hast **thou** prolonged the dispute with us:
011:032   They said: "O Noah! **thou** hast disputed with us,
011:045   and **Thou** art the Justest of Judges!"
011:046   I give thee counsel, lest **thou** become one of

THOU (continued)

011:046	ask not of Me that of which **thou** hast no knowledge!
011:047	and unless **Thou** forgive me and have
011:049	before this, neither **thou** nor thy People knew them.
011:053	"O Hud! No Clear (Sign) hast **thou** brought us,
011:062	They said: "O Salih! **thou** hast been of us!-
011:062	Dost **thou** (now) forbid us the worship of what
011:062	to that to which **thou** invitest us."
011:073	They said: "Dost **thou** wonder at Allah's decree?
011:079	indeed **thou** knowest quite well what we want!"
011:079	They said: "Well dost **thou** know we have no need
011:087	Truly, **thou** art the one that forbeareth with
011:091	**thou** sayest we do not understand!
011:091	that **thou** hast no strength!
011:091	For **thou** hast among us no great position!"
011:112	(in the straight path) as **thou** art commanded,-
011:112	**thou** and those who with thee turn (unto Allah);
012:003	before this, **thou** too was among those
012:011	why dost **thou** not trust us with Joseph,-seeing we
012:015	(this Message): 'Of a surety **thou** shall (one day)
012:017	But **thou** wilt never believe us even though
012:029	for truly **thou** hast been at fault!
012:033	unless **Thou** turn away their snare from me:
012:036	for we see **thou** art one that doth good (to all)."
012:050	(Joseph) said: "Go **thou** back to thy lord,
012:054	**thou** art of high standing with us, invested with
012:078	for we see that **thou** art (gracious) in doing good."
012:085	**thou** cease to remember Joseph until though reach
012:085	the last extremity of illness, or until **thou** die!"
012:090	They said: "Art **thou** indeed, Joseph?" He said
012:095	They said: "By Allah! truly **thou** art in thine
012:101	**Thou** art my Protector in this world and in
012:101	O **Thou** Creator of the heavens and the earth!
012:101	"O my Lord! **Thou** hast indeed bestowed on me
012:101	Take **Thou** my soul (at death) as one submitting
012:102	nor wast **thou** (present) with them when they
012:103	mankind have, however ardently **thou** dost desire it.
012:104	And no reward dost **thou** ask of them for this:
012:108	Say **thou**: "This my Way; I do invite unto Allah,-
013:005	If **thou** dost marvel (at their want of faith),
013:007	But **thou** art truly a warner, and to
013:030	passed away; in order that **thou** mightest rehearse
013:037	Wert **thou** to follow their (vain) desires
013:037	then wouldst **thou** find neither protector nor
013:043	The Unbelievers say: "No messenger art **thou**."
014:001	in order that **thou** mightest lead mankind out of
014:019	Seest **thou** not that Allah created the
014:024	Seest **thou** not how Allah sets forth a parable?
014:028	Hast **thou** not turned thy thought to those
014:036	but **thou** art indeed Oft-Forgiving, Most Merciful.
014:038	"O our Lord! truly **Thou** dost know what we
014:040	O our Lord! and accept **Thou** my Prayer.
014:049	And **thou** wilt see the Sinners that day
015:006	Truly **thou** art mad (or possessed)!
015:006	They say: "O **thou** to whom the Message
015:007	"Why bringest **thou** not angels to us if it be
015:007	if it be that **thou** hast the Truth?"
015:033	Whom **Thou** didst create from sounding clay,
015:034	from here; for **thou** art rejected, accursed.
015:039	because **Thou** hast put me in the wrong, I will
015:042	"For over My servants No authority shalt **thou** have,
015:065	and do **thou** go behind them: let no one
015:094	Therefore expound openly what **thou** art commanded,

THOU (continued)

016:014	and **thou** seest the ships therein that plough
016:037	If **thou** art anxious for their guidance, yet Allah
016:044	that **thou** mayest explain clearly to men
016:064	so that **thou** shouldst make clear to them
016:098	When **thou** dost read the Qur'an, seek Allah's
016:101	they say, "**Thou** art but a forger" but most
016:127	And do **thou** be patient, for thy
017:022	or **thou** (O man!) wilt sit in disgrace
017:028	from thy Lord which **thou** dost expect, yet speak
017:028	And even if **thou** hast to turn away from them
017:029	utmost reach, so that **thou** become blameworthy
017:036	**thou** hast no knowledge; for surely the hearing,
017:037	for **thou** canst not rend the earth
017:039	lest **thou** shouldst be thrown into Hell,
017:045	When **thou** dost recite the Qur'an, We put,
017:046	when **thou** dost mention thy Lord-and Him
017:061	whom **Thou** didst create from clay?"
017:062	If **Thou** wilt but respite me to the Day
017:062	He said, "Seest **Thou**? This is the one whom
017:062	one whom **thou** hast honoured above me!
017:064	And Arouse those whom **thou** canst among them,
017:065	no authority shalt **thou** have over them."
017:074	**thou** wouldst nearly have inclined to them a little.
017:075	and moreover **thou** wouldst have found none
017:077	**thou** wilt find no change in Our ways.
017:086	then wouldst **thou** find none to plead thy affair
017:090	until **thou** cause a spring to gush forth for us
017:091	"Or (until) **thou** have a garden of date trees
017:092	"Or **thou** cause the sky to fall in pieces,
017:092	as **thou** sayest (will happen), against us;
017:092	or **thou** bring Allah and the angels before (us)
017:093	until **thou** send down to us a book that we
017:093	"Or **thou** have a house adorned with gold,
017:093	or **thou** mount a ladder right into the skies.
017:097	wilt **thou** find no protector besides Him.
017:102	Moses said, "**Thou** knowest well that these things
017:106	in order that **thou** mightest recite it
018:006	**Thou** wouldst only, perchance, fret thyself
018:009	Or dost **thou** reflect that the Companions
018:017	**Thou** wouldst have seen the sun, when it rose,
018:017	for him wilt **thou** find no protector to lead
018:018	**thou** wouldst have certainly turned back
018:018	**Thou** wouldst have thought awake, whilst they
018:018	if **thou** hadst looked at them,
018:022	Say **thou**: "My Lord knoweth best their number;
018:024	When **thou** forgettest, and say, "I hope that me Lord
018:027	and none wilt **thou** find as a refuge
018:037	"Dost **thou** deny Him Who created thee out of dust,
018:039	If **thou** dost see me less than thee in wealth and sons,
018:039	"Why didst **thou** not, as **thou** wentest into thy garden,
018:041	run off underground so that **thou** wilt never
018:047	and **thou** wilt see the earth as a level stretch,
018:049	and **thou** wilt see the sinful in great terror
018:057	If **thou** callest them to guidance, even then
018:063	He replied: "Sawest **thou** (what happened) when we
018:066	on the footing that **thou** teach me something
018:066	which **thou** hast been taught?"
018:067	(The other) said: "Verily **thou** wilt not be able
018:068	"For how canst **thou** have patience about things
018:069	Moses said: "**Thou** wilt find me, if Allah
018:070	The other said: "If then **thou** wouldst follow me,
018:071	"Hast **thou** scuttled it in order to drown

THOU (continued)

018:071 Truly a strange thing hast **thou** done!"
018:072 **thou** canst have no patience with me?"
018:074 "Hast **thou** slain an innocent person who had
018:074 Truly a foul (unheard-of) thing hast **thou** done!"
018:075 **thou** canst have no patience with me?"
018:076 then wouldst **thou** have received (full)
018:077 (Moses) said: "If **thou** hadst wished,
018:077 surely **thou** couldst have exacted some
018:078 (those things) over which **thou** was unable
018:082 **thou** wast unable to hold patience."
018:086 (**thou** hast authority), either to punish them,
018:094 in order that **thou** mightest erect a barrier
019:006 one with whom **Thou** art well-pleased!"
019:009 when **thou** hadst been nothing!'"
019:010 although **thou** art not dumb."
019:010 "shall be that **thou** shalt speak to no man
019:018 (come not near) if **thou** dost fear Allah."
019:026 And if **thou** dost see any man, say, 'I have
019:027 "O Mary! truly a strange thing hast **thou** brought!
019:045 so that **thou** become to Satan a friend."
019:046 If **thou** forbear not, I will indeed stone thee:
019:046 "Art **thou** shrinking from my gods, O Abraham?
019:065 knowest **thou** of any who is worthy of the
019:077 Hast **thou** then seen the (sort of) man who
019:083 Seest **thou** not that We have set Satans
019:097 that with it **thou** mayest give glad tidings
019:098 Canst **thou** find a single one of them (now)
020:007 If **thou** pronounce the word aloud, (it is
020:012 **thou** art in the sacred valley Tuwa.
020:014 so serve **thou** Me (only), and establish
020:016 divert thee therefrom, lest **thou** perish!"...
020:024 "Go **thou** to Pharaoh, for he
020:035 For **Thou** art ever seeing."
020:039 and (this) in order that **thou** mayest be
020:040 Then **thou** didst slay a man, but We
020:040 Then didst **thou** come hither as ordained, O Moses!
020:040 Then didst **thou** tarry a number of years with the
020:042 "Go, **thou** and thy brother, with My
020:057 He said: "Hast **thou** come to drive us out
020:058 not fail to keep-neither we nor **thou**-in a place
020:065 They said: "O Moses! whether wilt **thou** that
020:065 **thou** throw (first) or that we be the first
020:068 We said: "Fear not! for **thou** hast indeed
020:072 for **thou** canst only decree (touching)
020:072 So decree whatever **thou** desirest to degree:
020:073 and the magic to which **thou** didst compel us:
020:092 thee back, when **thou** sawest them going wrong.
020:093 Didst **thou** then disobey my order?"
020:094 Truly I feared lest **thou** shouldst say, '**Thou** hast
020:094 and **thou** didst not observe my word!'"
020:097 now look at thy god, of whom **thou** hast become a
020:097 (for a future penalty) **thou** hast a promise that
020:097 be that **thou** wilt say, 'Touch me not';
020:107 **thou** see in their place."
020:108 so that **thou** hearest not but murmuring.
020:117 the Garden, so that **thou** art landed in misery.
020:125 why hast **thou** raised me up blind, while I
020:126 (Allah) will say: "Thus didst **thou**, when Our
020:126 forgot them: so wilt **thou**, this day, be forgotten.
020:130 of the day: that **thou** may be pleased.
020:134 "Our Lord! if only **Thou** hadst sent us a messenger,
021:034 if then **thou** shouldst die, would they

THOU (continued)

021:062 They said, "Art **thou** the one that did this
021:065 (they said), "**Thou** knowest full well that these
021:069 We said, "O Fire! be **thou** cool,
021:083 but **Thou** art the Most Merciful of those
021:087 "There is no god but **Thou**: Glory to
021:089 without offspring, though **Thou** art the best
021:112 Say: "O my Lord! judge **Thou** in truth!"
022:002 **thou** shalt see mankind as in a drunken riot,
022:005 And (further), **thou** seest the earth barren and
022:018 Seest **thou** not that to Allah prostrate all things
022:034 and give **thou** the good news to those who humble
022:063 Seest **thou** not that Allah sends down
022:065 Seest **thou** not that Allah has made subject
022:067 for **thou** art assuredly on the Right Way.
022:067 but do **thou** invite (them) to thy Lord:
022:070 Knowest **thou** not that Allah knows all that is
022:072 **thou** wilt notice a denial on the faces of the Unbelievers!
023:027 take **thou** on board pairs of every species,
023:028 on the Ark-**thou** and those with thee,-say: "Praise
023:028 And when **thou** hast embarked on the Ark-
023:029 Thy blessing: for **Thou** art the Best to enable
023:072 Or is it that **thou** asked them for some recompense?
023:073 But verily **thou** callest them to the Straight Way;
023:093 Say: "O my Lord! if **Thou** wilt show me (in my lifetime)
023:109 for **Thou** art the best of those Who show mercy!'
023:109 'Our Lord! we believe; then do **Thou** forgive us,
023:118 For **Thou** art the Best of those who show mercy!"
023:118 grant **thou** forgiveness and mercy!
024:041 Seest **thou** not that it is Allah Whose praises
024:043 Seest **thou** not that Allah makes the clouds
024:043 Then wilt **thou** see rain issue forth
024:053 by Allah that, if only **thou** wouldst command
024:057 Never think **thou** that the Unbelievers can escape
024:062 **thou** wilt, and ask Allah for their forgiveness;
025:018 besides Thee: but **Thou** didst bestow, on them
025:043 Could **thou** be a disposer of affairs for him?
025:043 Seest **thou** such a one as taketh for his god
025:044 Or thinkest **thou** that most of them listen
025:045 Hast **thou** not seen how thy Lord?-doth prolong
025:059 ask **thou**, then, about Him of any acquainted
025:060 Shall we adore that which **thou** commandest us?"
026:003 It may be **thou** will kill thy self with grief,
026:017 "'Send **thou** with us the Children of Israel.'"
026:018 and didst **thou** not stay in our midst many years
026:019 and **thou** art an ungrateful!"
026:019 "And **thou** didst a deed of thine which
026:019 which (**thou** knowest) **thou** didst,
026:022 **thou** dost reproach me,-that you
026:029 (Pharaoh) said: "If **thou** takest any god other
026:031 if **thou** tellest the truth!"
026:116 They said: "If **thou** desist not,
026:116 O Noah! **thou** shalt be stone (to death)."
026:118 "Judge **thou**, then, between me
026:136 whether **thou** admonish us or be not
026:153 They said: "**Thou** art only the of those bewitched!
026:154 if **thou** tellest the truth!"
026:154 "**Thou** art no more than a mortal like us:
026:167 O Lut! **thou** wilt assuredly be cast out!"
026:167 They said: "If **thou** desist not, O Lut!
026:185 They said: "**Thou** art only one of those bewitched!
026:186 "**Thou** art no more than a mortal like us,
026:186 like us, and indeed we think **thou** art a liar!

THOU (continued)

026:187	to fall on us, if **thou** art truthful!"
026:194	To thy heart and mind that **thou** mayest admonish
026:205	Seest **thou**? If we do let them enjoy (this life)
026:213	with Allah, or **thou** wilt be among those who
026:225	Seest **thou** not that they wander distracted
027:006	As to thee, **thou** receivest the Qur'an from One
027:010	"Now do **thou** throw thy rod!"
027:012	(**thou** wilt take) to Pharaoh and his people:
027:019	for Thy favours, which **Thou** has bestowed on me
027:022	"I have compassed which **thou** hast not compassed,
027:027	whether **thou** hast told the truth or lied!
027:028	Go **thou**, with this letter of mine, and deliver
027:033	so consider what **thou** wilt command."
027:039	**thou** rise from thy Council: indeed I
027:079	for **thou** art on (the Path of) manifest Truth.
027:080	Truly **thou** canst not cause the Dead to listen,
027:080	nor canst **thou** cause the Deaf to hear the call,
027:081	Nor canst **thou** be a guide to the Blind,
027:081	only those wilt **thou** get to listen who believe
027:088	**Thou** seest the mountains and thinkest them
028:007	but when **thou** hast fears about him, cast him
028:016	Do **Thou** then forgive me!" So (Allah)
028:017	**Thou** hast bestowed Thy Grace on me, never shall
028:018	"**Thou** art truly, one erring manifestly."
028:019	**Thou** only desire to become a tyrant in the land,
028:019	to slay me as **thou** slewest a man yesterday?
028:024	any good that **Thou** dost send me!"
028:025	(well) hast **thou** escaped from unjust people."
028:025	he said: "Fear **thou** not: (well) hast
028:027	on condition that **thou** serve me for eight years,
028:027	under a difficulty: **thou** wilt find me, indeed, if
028:027	for eight years, but if **thou** complete ten years,
028:031	"Now do **thou** throw thy rod!" But when
028:031	and fear not: for **thou** art of those who are secure.
028:044	**Thou** wast not on the Western Side when We
028:044	nor wast **thou** a witness (of those events).
028:045	but **thou** wast not a dweller among the people
028:046	Yet (art **thou** sent) as a Mercy from they Lord,
028:046	Nor wast **thou** at the side of (the Mountain of) Tur
028:047	why didst **Thou** not send us a messenger?
028:056	to guide everyone whom **thou** lovest: but Allah
028:056	It is true **thou** wilt not be able to guide
028:077	but do **thou** good, as Allah has been good to thee,
028:086	therefore lend not **thou** support in any way
028:086	And **thou** hadst not expected that the Book
029:008	anything of which **thou** hast no knowledge,
029:029	if **thou** tellest the truth."
029:030	He said: "O my Lord! help **Thou** me against
029:033	"Fear **thou** not, nor grieve: we are
029:048	nor art **thou** (able) to transcribe it with
029:048	And **thou** wast not (able) to recite a Book
029:061	If indeed **thou** ask them who has created
029:063	And if indeed **thou** ask them who it is that sends
030:030	So set **thou** thy face truly to the religion
030:043	But set **thou** thy face to the right Religion,
030:048	into fragments, until **thou** seest rain-drops
030:052	the dead to hear, nor canst **thou** make the deaf
030:052	So verily **thou** canst not make the dead to hear,
030:053	Nor canst **thou** lead back the blind from their
030:053	**thou** make to hear, who believe in Our Signs
030:058	but if **thou** bring to them any Sign, the Unbelievers
031:015	of which **thou** hast no knowledge, obey them not;

THOU (continued)

031:025	If **thou** ask them, who it
031:029	Seest **thou** not that Allah merges Night into Day
031:031	Seest **thou** not that the ships sail through the
032:003	that **thou** mayest admonish a people to whom
032:012	If only **thou** couldst see when the guilty ones
033:019	**thou** wilt see them looking to thee, their eyes
033:037	Behold! **thou** didst say to one who had received
033:037	But **thou** didst hide in thy heart that which
033:037	"Retain **thou** (in wedlock) thy wife,
033:037	make manifest: **thou** didst fear the people,
033:037	that **thou** shouldst fear Allah.
033:050	to thee thy wives to whom **thou** hast paid their
033:051	whose (turn) **thou** hadst set aside.
033:051	on thee if **thou** invite one whose (turn)
033:051	**Thou** mayest defer (the turn of) any of them
033:051	**thou** hast to give them: and Allah
033:051	any of them that **thou** pleasest,
033:051	and **thou** mayest receive any **thou** pleasest:
033:062	wilt **thou** find in the practice (approved) of
034:011	(Commanding), "Make **thou** coats of mail,
034:031	Couldst **thou** but see when the wrong-doers
034:041	**Thou** art our protector-not them.
034:051	If **thou** couldst but see when they will quake
035:012	and **thou** seest the ships therein that plough
035:018	**Thou** canst but warn such as fear their Lord
035:022	but **thou** canst not make those to hear who are
035:023	**Thou** art no other than a warner.
035:027	Seest **thou** not that Allah sends down
035:043	no turning off wilt **thou** find in Allah's way
035:043	But no change wilt **thou** find in Allah's way
036:003	**Thou** art indeed one of the messengers,
036:006	In order that **thou** mayest warn a people,
036:010	The same is to them whether **thou** admonish them
036:010	admonish them or **thou** do not admonish them:
036:011	**Thou** canst but admonish such a one as follows
036:026	It was said: "Enter **thou** the Garden."
037:012	Truly dost **thou** marvel, while they ridicule,
037:018	Say **thou**: "Yea, and ye shall then be humiliated
037:056	He said: "By Allah! **thou** wast little short
037:102	"O my father! do as **thou** art commanded:
037:102	**thou** will find me, if Allah
037:105	"**Thou** hast already fulfilled the dream!"-
037:174	So turn **thou** away from them for a little while,
037:175	and they soon shall see (how **thou** farest)!
037:178	So turn **thou** away from them for a little while,
037:179	and they soon shall see (how **thou** farest)!
038:026	nor follow **thou** the lust (of thy heart),
038:026	so judge **thou** between men in truth (and justice):
038:035	for **Thou** art the Grantor of Bounties
038:039	whether **thou** bestow them (on others)
038:075	Art **thou** haughty? Or art **thou** one of the high
038:076	**Thou** createdst me from fire, and him
038:076	and him **Thou** createdst from clay."
038:077	from here: for **thou** art rejected, accursed.
039:008	verily **thou** art (one) of the Companions of the Fire!"
039:019	Wouldst **thou**, then, deliver one (who is)
039:021	Seest **thou** not that Allah sends down rain
039:021	then it withers; **thou** wilt see it grow yellow;
039:030	Truly **thou** wilt die (one day) and truly
039:038	If indeed **thou** ask them who it is that created
039:041	Nor art **thou** set a Custodian over them.
039:046	It is **Thou** that wilt judge between Thy Servants

THOU (continued)

039:059   **thou** wast haughty, and became one of those who
039:059   to thee My Signs, and **thou** didst reject them:
039:060   On the Day of Judgement wilt **thou** see those
039:065   "If **thou** wert to join (gods with Allah),
039:065   and **thou** wilt surely be among the losers.
039:075   And **thou** wilt see the angels surrounding the
040:007   "Our Lord! **Thou** embracest all things, in Mercy
040:008   For **Thou** art (He), the Exalted in Might,
040:008   which **Thou** hast promised to them, and to
040:009   and any whom **Thou** dost preserve from ills
040:009   **Thou** have bestowed Mercy indeed: and that
040:011   They will say:" Our Lord! twice hast **Thou** made us
040:011   made us to die, and twice hast **Thou** given us Life!
040:069   Seest **thou** not those that dispute concerning
041:005   (concealed) from that to which **thou** dost invite us,
041:005   is a screen: so do **thou** (what **thou** wilt); for us,
041:006   Say **thou**: "I am but a man like you: it is
041:013   But if they turn away, say **thou**: "I have warned
041:039   **thou** seest the earth humble; but when
042:006   and **thou** art not the disposer of their affairs.
042:007   that **thou** mayest warn the Mother of Cities
042:013   hard is the (way) to which **thou** callest them.
042:015   nor follow **thou** their vain desires;
042:015   and stand steadfast as **thou** art commanded,
042:022   **Thou** wilt see the wrong-doers in fear on account
042:044   And **thou** wilt see the wrong-doers, when in
042:045   And **thou** wilt see them brought forward to the
042:052   **thou** knewest not (before) what was Revelation,
042:052   as We will; and verily **thou** dost guide (men)
043:009   If **thou** wert to question them, 'Who created
043:040   Canst **thou** then make the deaf to hear, or give
043:043   So hold **thou** fast to the Revelation sent down
043:043   verily **thou** art on a Straight Way.
043:045   And question **thou** Our messengers whom We
043:049   And they said, "O **thou** Sorcerer! invoke thy
043:087   If **thou** ask them, Who Created them, they will
044:010   Then watch **thou** for the Day that the
044:049   "Taste **thou** (this)! Truly **thou** art Mighty,
044:059   So wait **thou** and watch; for they
045:018   the (right) Way of Religion: so follow **thou** that (Way),
045:023   Then seest **thou** such a one as takes as his god
045:028   And **thou** wilt see every nation bowing the knee:
046:015   Thy favour which **Thou** hast bestowed upon me,
046:015   such as **Thou** mayest approve; and be
046:022   with which **thou** dost threaten us,
046:022   They said: "Hast **thou** come in order to turn
046:022   if **thou** art telling the truth!"
047:020   **thou** wilt see those in whose hearts is a disease
047:030   and **thou** shouldst have known them by their marks:
047:030   surely **thou** wilt know them by the tone of their speech!
048:011   and our families: do **thou** then ask forgiveness
048:023   **thou** find in the practice of Allah.
048:029   **Thou** wilt see them bow and prostrate themselves
049:005   until **thou** couldst come out to them, it would
050:001   (**Thou** art Allah's Messenger).
050:019   **thou** wast trying to escape!"
050:022   (It will be said:) "**Thou** wast heedless of this;
050:030   "Art **thou** filled to the full?" It will say,
050:045   and **thou** art not one to compel them by force.
052:029   of thy Lord, **thou** art no soothsayer nor possessed.
052:031   Say **thou**: "Await ye!-I too will wait along with you!"
052:040   Or is it that **thou** dost ask for a reward,

THOU (continued)

052:048   of thy Lord the while **thou** standest forth,
052:048   of thy Lord: for verily **thou** art in Our eyes:
052:049   also praise thou Him,-and at the setting of the stars!
053:033   Seest **thou** one who turns back,
053:055   (O man), wilt **thou** dispute about?
054:010   "I am one overcome: do **thou** then help (me)!"
057:012   The Day shalt **thou** see the believing men and the
057:020   **thou** wilt see it grow yellow; then it becomes
058:007   Seest **thou** not that Allah doth know (all) that is
058:008   Seest **thou** not those who were forbidden secret
058:014   Seest **thou** not those who turn (in friendship)
058:022   **Thou** wilt not find any people who believe
059:010   Our Lord! **Thou** art indeed Full of
059:011   Hast **thou** not observed the Hypocrites say to
059:014   **thou** wouldst think they were united, but their
059:021   on a mountain, verily, **thou** wouldst have seen
060:005   For **Thou** art the Exalted in Might
060:012   in any just matter,-then so **thou** receive their fealty,
063:001   that **thou** art indeed His Messenger. And Allah
063:001   **thou** art indeed the Messenger of Allah."
063:004   **thou** listenest to their words. They are
063:004   When **thou** lookest at them, their bodies
063:005   and **thou** wouldst see them turning away their faces
063:006   It is equal to them whether **thou** pray for their
063:010   Why didst **thou** not give me respite for a
065:001   (own) soul: **thou** knowest not if perchance Allah
066:001   O Prophet! why holdest **thou** to be forbidden
066:001   **thou** seekest to please thy consorts?
066:008   us Forgiveness: for **Thou** hast power over all things."
067:003   wilt **thou** see in the Creation of The Most Gracious.
067:003   vision again: Seest **thou** any flaw?
068:002   **Thou** art not, by the grace of thy Lord, mad or
068:004   And surely **thou** hast sublime morals.
068:005   Soon wilt **thou** see and they will see,
068:009   Their desire is that **thou** shouldst be pliant:
068:040   Ask **thou** of them, which of them will stand
068:046   Or is it that **thou** dost ask them for a reward,
069:007   so that **thou** couldst see the (whole) people
069:008   Then seest **thou** any of them left surviving?
070:005   Therefore do **thou** hold Patience,-a Patience
071:001   (with the Command): "Do **thou** warn thy People
071:007   that **thou** mightest forgive them, they have
071:024   and grant **Thou** no increase to the wrong-doers
071:027   "For, if **Thou** dost leave (any of) them, they will
071:028   wrong-doers grant **Thou** no increase but in
073:001   O **thou** folded in garments!
073:020   The Lord doth know that **thou** standest forth
074:001   O **thou** wrapped up (in a mantle)!
074:003   And thy Lord do **thou** magnify!
075:018   follow **thou** its recital (as promulgated):
076:019   if **thou** seest them,
076:019   **thou** wouldst think them scattered Pearls.
076:020   And when **thou** lookest, it is there **thou** wilt see a
079:017   "Go **thou** to Pharaoh, for he has
079:018   `Wouldst **thou** that **thou** shouldst be purified (from sin)?-
079:019   so **thou** shouldst fear Him?'"
079:043   Wherein art **thou** (concerned) with the
079:045   **Thou** art but a Warner for such as fear it.
080:006   To him dost **thou** attend;
080:010   Of him wast **thou** unmindful.
083:024   **Thou** wilt recognize in their Faces the beaming
084:006   painfully toiling, but **thou** shalt meet Him.

THOU (continued)

084:006 O **thou** man! verily **thou** art ever toiling on
087:006 (the Message), so **thou** shalt not forget,
088:021 Therefore do **thou** remind,
088:021 for **thou** art one to remind.
088:022 **Thou** art not one to manage (their) affairs.
089:006 Seest **thou** not how thy Lord dealt with
089:027 "O (**thou**) soul, in (complete) rest and satisfaction!
089:028 "Come back **thou** to thy Lord,-well pleased
089:029 "Enter **thou**, then, among my Devotees!
089:030 "Yea, enter **thou** my Heaven!"
090:002 And **thou** art an inhabitant of this City;-
093:005 **thou** shalt be well-pleased.
094:004 (in which) **thou** (art held)?
094:007 when **thou** art free (from thine immediate task),
096:009 Seest **thou** one who forbids-
096:011 Seest **thou** if He is on (the road of) Guidance?-
096:013 Seest **thou** if he denies (Truth) and turns away?
105:001 Seest **thou** not how thy Lord dealt with the
107:001 Seest **thou** one who denies the Judgment (to come)?
110:002 And **thou** dost see the People enter Allah's

THOUGH

002:085 **though** it was not lawful for you
002:154 **though** ye perceive (it) not.
002:170 What! even **though** their fathers were
002:198 even **though**, before this, ye went astray.
002:221 even **though** she allure you.
002:221 even **though** he allure you.
002:243 **though** they were thousands (in number),
003:091 **though** they should offer it for ransom.
003:119 **though** ye believe in the whole of the Book,
004:060 **though** they were ordered to reject him.
004:128 even **though** men's souls are swayed by greed.
004:161 That they took usury, **though** they were forbidden;
005:100 even **though** the abundance of the bad
005:104 What! even **though** their fathers were void
005:106 even **though** the (beneficiary) be our near relation:
005:116 **though** I know not what is in Thine.
006:066 **though** it is the Truth. Say: "Not mine
006:100 **though** Allah did create the Jinns; and they
007:088 He said: "What! even **though** we do detest (them)?
008:005 even **though** a party among the Believers
008:008 distasteful **though** it be to those in guilt.
009:032 even **though** the Unbelievers may detest (it).
009:033 all religion, even **though** the Pagans
009:113 for Pagans, even **though** they be of kin, after it
010:042 even **though** they are without understanding.
010:043 the blind,-even **though** they will not see?
012:017 even **though** we tell the truth."
012:085 **though** reach the last extremity of illness,
013:004 (diverse **though**) neighboring, and gardens
014:046 even **though** they were such as to shake the hills!
015:022 **though** ye are not the guardians of its stores.
015:054 glad tidings even **though** old age has seized me?
021:089 without offspring, **though** Thou art the best
024:035 **though** fire scarce touched it: Light upon
027:014 **though** their souls acknowledged them wrongfully
027:054 **though** ye see (its iniquity)?
027:084 **though** ye comprehended them not in knowledge,
029:038 from the Path, **though** they were keen-sighted.
030:049 Even **though**, before they received (the rain)-
033:013 and exposed," **though** they were not exposed:
033:052 even **though** their beauty attract thee,

THOUGH (continued)

035:018 even **though** he be nearly related.
035:044 **though** they were superior to them in strength?
040:014 even **though** the Unbelievers may detest it.
040:067 **though** of you there are some who die before;-
046:017 even **though** generations have passed before me
053:023 Even **though** there has already come to them
058:022 even **though** they were their fathers and sons,
059:009 even **though** poverty was their (own lot).
060:001 even **though** they have rejected the truth
060:004 for forgiveness for thee, **though** I have no power
061:005 and insult me, **though** ye know that I am
061:008 His Light, even **though** the Unbelievers may detest
061:009 all religion, even **though** the Pagans may detest
070:011 **Though** they will be put in sight of each other,-
075:015 Even **though** he were to put up his excuses.
080:007 **Though** it is no blame to thee if he grow

THOUGHT

002:258 Hast thou not turned thy **thought** to one
003:023 Hast thou not turned thy **thought** to those who
004:044 Hast thou not turned thy **thought** to those who
004:049 Hast thou not turned thy **thought** to those
004:051 Hast thou not turned thy **thought** to those who
004:060 Hast thou not turned thy **thought** to those who
004:077 Hast thou not turned thy **thought** to those who
005:071 They **thought** there would be no trial
006:094 whom ye **thought** to be partners in your affairs:
007:171 and they **thought** it was going to fall
007:201 when a **thought** of evil from Satan
016:011 is a Sign for those who give **thought**.
016:044 and that they may give **thought**.
016:069 for those who give **thought**.
018:018 Thou wouldst have **thought** awake, whilst they
018:048 created you first: aye, ye **thought** We shall not
018:052 "Call on those whom ye **thought** to be My partners,"
018:104 in this life, while they **thought** that they were
024:012 the affair,-**thought** well of their people and say,
024:015 and ye **thought** it to be a light matter, while it
027:044 she saw it, she **thought** it was a lake of water,
028:039 he and his hosts: they **thought** that they would
038:027 That were the **thought** of Unbelievers!
041:023 "But this **thought** of yours which ye did entertain
048:006 who think an evil **thought** of Allah.
048:012 "Nay, ye **thought** that the Messenger and the
048:012 evil **thought**, for ye are a people doomed to perish."
051:025 (And **thought**, "These seem) unusual people."
059:002 and they **thought** that their fortresses would
072:007 ye **thought**, that Allah would not raise up any one
074:018 For he **thought** and he determined;-
075:025 In the **thought** that some back-breaking calamity

THOUGHTLESSNESS

002:225 to account for **thoughtlessness** in your oaths,

THOUGHTS

005:052 they regret of the **thoughts** which they secretly
009:078 their secret (**thoughts**) and their secret counsels,
021:049 in their most secret **thoughts**, and who
033:010 (vain) **thoughts** about Allah!

THOUSAND

002:096 be given a life of a **thousand** years:
003:124 three **thousand** angels (specially) sent down?
003:125 with five **thousand** angels clearly marked.
008:009 "I will assist you with a **thousand** of the angels,
008:065 a **thousand** of the Unbelievers: for these

THOUSAND (continued)

008:066 and if a **thousand**, they will vanquish two **thousand**,
022:047 a **thousand** years of your reckoning.
029:014 a **thousand** years less fifty: but the
032:005 a **thousand** years of your reckoning.
037:147 to a hundred **thousand** (men) or more.
070:004 is (as) fifty **thousand** years:
097:003 is better than a **thousand** Months.

THOUSANDS

002:243 though they were **thousands** (in number),

THREAD

002:187 until the white **thread** of dawn appear to you
002:187 appear to you distinct from its black **thread**;

THREATEN

046:022 with which thou dost **threaten** us, if thou

THREATENEST

007:070 Bring us what thou **threatenest** us with, if so
011:032 now bring upon us what thou **threatenest** us with,

THREATENS

002:268 Satan **threatens** you with poverty and bids

THREATS

007:077 saying: "O Salih! bring about thy **threats**, if
007:086 "And squat not on every road, breathing **threats**,

THREE

002:196 he should fast **three** days during the Hajj.
002:228 concerning themselves for **three** monthly periods,
003:041 no man for **three** days but with signals.
003:124 **three** thousand angels (specially) sent down?
004:003 marry women of your choice, two, or **three**, or four;
004:171 Say not "**Three**": desist: it will be
005:073 Allah is one of **three** in a Trinity: for there
005:089 If that is beyond your means, fast for **three** days.
006:084 all (**three**) We guided: and before
009:118 (He turned in mercy also) to the **three** who were
011:065 in your homes for **three** days: (then will be your ruin):
018:022 (Some) say they were **three**, the dog
018:025 **three** hundred years, and nine (more).
019:010 to no man for **three** nights, although thou
021:090 for him. These (**three**) were quick in doing
024:058 these are your **three** times of undress:
024:058 (before they come to your presence), on **three** occasions:
035:001 two, or **three**, or four (Pairs): He adds
039:006 one after another, in **three** veils of darkness.
056:007 And ye shall be sorted out into **three** classes.
058:007 a secret consultation between **three**, but He is
065:004 if ye have any doubt, is **three** months, and those
077:030 (of smoke ascending) in **three** columns,

THRESHOLD

018:018 two forelegs on the **threshold**: if thou

THREW

002:101 **threw** away the Book of Allah
003:187 but they **threw** it away behind their backs,
007:107 Then (Moses) **threw** his rod, and behold!
007:116 So when they **threw**, they bewitched
011:038 they **threw** ridicule on him. He said: "If ye
020:020 He **threw** it, and behold! it was a sneak,
020:087 and we **threw** them (into the fire), and that
020:096 and **threw** it (into the calf): thus did
022:052 Satan **threw** some (vanity) into his desire:
026:032 So (Moses) **threw** his rod, and behold,
026:044 So they **threw** their ropes and their rods,
026:045 Then Moses **threw** his rod, when, behold,

THREW (continued)

051:040 and **threw** them into the sea: and his

THREWEST

008:017 it was Allah: when thou **threwest** (a handful)

THROAT

014:017 swallowing it down his **throat**; death will come
056:083 when (the soul of the dying man) reaches the **throat**,

THROATS

033:010 and the hearts gaped up to the **throats**, and ye
040:018 will (come) right up to the **Throats** to choke

THRONE

002:255 His **throne** doth extend over the heavens
007:054 then He settled Himself on the **Throne**: He draweth
009:129 He the Lord of the **Throne** Supreme!"
010:003 then He established Himself on the **Throne**.
011:007 and His **Throne** was over the Waters-that He
012:100 the **throne** and they fell down in prostration,
013:002 then He established Himself on the **Throne**. He has
017:042 to the Lord of the **Throne**!
020:005 is firmly established on the **throne**.
021:022 the Lord of the **Throne**: (high is He)
023:086 seven heavens, and the Lord of the Mighty **Throne**?"
023:116 the Lord of the **Throne** of Honour!
025:059 then He established Himself on the **Throne**:
027:023 every requisite; and she has a magnificent **throne**.
027:026 Lord of the **Throne** Supreme!"
027:038 which of you can bring me her **throne** before they
027:041 He said: "Disguise her **throne**, let us
027:042 "Is this thy **throne**?" She said, "It seems
032:004 on the **Throne**: ye have none, besides Him,
038:034 We placed on his **throne** a body but he
039:075 surrounding the **Throne** (Divine) on all sides,
040:007 Those who bear the **Throne** (of Allah) and those
040:015 (He is) the Lord of the **Throne**: by His Command
043:082 and the earth, the Lord of the **Throne**! He is
057:004 then He established Himself on the **Throne**.
069:017 bear the **Throne** of thy Lord above them.
081:020 by the Lord of the **Throne**,
085:015 Lord of the **Throne** full of all Glory,

THRONES

018:031 recline therein on raised **thrones**. How good

THROUGH

002:164 kinds that He scatters **through** the earth;
002:164 the ships **through** the Ocean for the profit
002:189 Enter houses **through** the proper doors:
002:205 to spread mischief **through** the earth
002:213 except **through** selfish contumacy.
003:019 except **through** envy of each other,
003:137 travel **through** the earth, and see what was the end
003:156 **through** the earth or engaged in fighting:
003:194 Thou didst promise unto us **through** Thy Messengers,
003:196 of the unbelievers **through** the land deceive thee:
004:001 **through** Whom ye demand your mutual (rights),
004:019 about **through** it a great deal of good.
004:043 except when you are passing by (**through** the mosque),
004:056 as often as their skins are roasted **through**.
004:101 When ye travel **through** the earth, there is
004:109 or who will carry their affairs **through**?
004:132 and enough is Allah to carry **through** all affairs.
005:026 in distraction will they wander **through** the land:
005:033 for mischief **through** the land is: execution or
005:106 journeying **through** the earth, and the chance

THROUGH (continued)

006:011	Say: "Travel **through** the earth and see what was
006:071	wandering bewildered **through** the earth, his
006:097	**through** the dark spaces of land and sea: We
006:158	nor earned righteousness **through** its Faith.
007:040	pass **through** the eye of the needle: such is
007:063	**through** a man of your own people, to warn
007:069	from your Lord **through** a man of your
007:075	been sent **through** him."
007:187	Heavy were its burden **through** the heavens
008:026	a small (band), deemed weak **through** the land, and
009:111	**through** the Torah, the Gospel, and the Qur'an:
010:022	traverse **through** land and sea; till when ye
010:023	**through** the earth in defiance of right!
012:109	**through** the earth, and see what was the end of
014:032	**through** the sea by His Command; and the
016:036	So travel **through** the earth, and see what was
017:066	go smoothly for you **through** the sea, in order
018:061	which took its course **through** the sea
018:063	it took its course **through** the sea
018:097	to scale it or to dig **through** it.
020:031	"Add to my strength **through** him,
020:077	**through** the sea, without fear of being overtaken
020:131	of this world, **through** which We test them: but the
021:031	for them to pass **through**: that they
021:087	But he cried **through** the depths of darkness,
021:096	are let **through** (their barrier), and they
022:027	**through** deep and distant mountain highways;
022:028	**through** the Days appointed, over the
022:046	Do they not travel **through** the land, so that
022:065	sail **through** the sea by His command?
023:079	And He has multiplied you **through** the earth,
025:007	who eats food, and walks **through** the streets?
025:020	who ate food and walked **through** the markets.
027:063	Or, Who guides you **through** the depths of
027:069	Say: "Go ye **through** the earth and see what has
028:035	thy arm **through** thy brother, and invest
029:020	Say: "Travel **through** the earth and see how
030:009	Do they not travel **through** the earth, and see
030:039	for increase **through** the property of (other)
030:042	Say: "Travel **through** the earth and see
031:010	and He scattered **through** it beast of
031:018	Nor walk in insolence **through** the earth:
031:031	ships sail **through** the Ocean by the grace of Allah?
035:044	Do they not travel **through** the earth, and see
036:041	their race (**through** the flood) in the loaded Ark;
039:021	and leads it **through** springs in the earth?
040:004	strutting about **through** the land deceive thee!
040:021	Do they not travel **through** the earth and see
040:080	that ye may **through** them attain to any need
040:082	Do they not travel **through** the earth and see
041:015	Now the 'Ad behaved arrogantly **through** the land,
041:016	a furious Wind **through** days of disaster, that We
041:040	or he that comes safe **through**, on the
042:027	all bounds **through** the earth; but He
042:029	has scattered **through** them: and He
042:031	Nor can ye escape **through** the earth; nor have
042:032	smooth-running **through** the ocean, (tall) as
042:042	beyond bounds **through** the land, defying right
045:004	are scattered (**through** the earth), are Signs
045:012	that ship may sail **through** it by
045:017	into schisms, **through** insolent envy among
047:010	Do they not travel **through** the earth, and see

THROUGH (continued)

050:036	Then did they wander **through** the land: was there
051:009	**Through** which are deluded (away from the Truth)
054:048	**through** the Fire on their faces, (they will hear):
055:024	smoothly **through** the seas, lofty as mountains:
062:010	then may ye disperse **through** the land, and seek
065:012	**through** the midst of them (all) descends
067:015	so traverse ye **through** its tracts
067:024	Say: "It is He Who has multiplied you **through** the earth,
068:037	Or have ye a Book **through** which ye learn-
068:038	That ye shall have, **through** it whatever ye choose?
073:020	in ill-health; others traveling **through** the land,
076:026	to Him; and glorify Him a long night **through**.
091:011	(their prophet) **through** their inordinate wrong-doing.

THROUGHOUT

002:177	and **throughout** all periods of panic.
009:002	(as ye will), **throughout** the land, but know
057:013	Within it will be Mercy **throughout**, and without
072:012	by no means frustrate Allah **throughout** the earth,

THROW

002:015	Allah will **throw** back their mockery on them,
002:100	some party among them **throw** it aside?
007:115	or shall we have the (first) **throw**?"
007:115	They said: "O Moses! wilt thou **throw** (first), or
007:116	Said Moses: "**Throw** ye (first)." So when
007:117	We revealed to Moses "**Throw** thy rod": and behold!
008:058	**throw** back (their covenant) to them,
009:079	and **throw** ridicule on them,-Allah will
009:079	Allah will **throw** back their ridicule on them:
010:080	ye (wish) to **throw**!"
010:080	Moses said to them: "**Throw** ye what ye (wish)
010:081	When they had had their **throw**, Moses said:
012:010	**throw** him down to the bottom of the well: he will
012:015	and they all agreed to **throw** him down to the
016:071	are not going to **throw** back their gifts to those
016:086	But they will **throw** back their word at them
020:019	(Allah) said, "**Throw** it, O Moses!"
020:039	"'**Throw** (the child) into the chest,
020:039	and **throw** (the chest) into the river:
020:065	thou **throw** (first) or that we be the first to throw?"
020:066	He said, "Nay, **throw** ye first!" Then behold
020:069	"**Throw** that which is in thy right hand:
026:043	"**Throw** ye-that which ye are about to **throw**!"
027:010	"Now do thou **throw** thy rod!" But when
028:031	"Now do thou **throw** thy rod!" But when
031:006	and **throw** ridicule (on the Path): for such
037:097	and **throw** him into the blazing fire!"
050:024	"**Throw**, both of you, into Hell every contumacious
050:026	**throw** him into a severe Chastisement."

THROWING

034:031	**throwing** back the word (of blame) on one another!

THROWN

004:088	whom Allah hath **thrown** out of the Way?
004:088	For those whom Allah hath **thrown** out of the Way,
006:025	but We have **thrown** veils on their hearts, so
007:016	**thrown** me out of (the Way),
017:039	lest thou shouldst be **thrown** into Hell,
020:070	So the magicians were **thrown** down to prostration:
022:031	and **thrown** him into a far-distant place.
022:053	**thrown** in by Satan, but a
026:094	"Then they will be **thrown** headlong into
027:090	will be **thrown** headlong into the Fire:
104:004	to be **thrown** into that which Breaks to Pieces.

THROWS

004:112 and **throws** it on to one that is innocent,
022:052 Allah will cancel anything (vain) that Satan **throws** in,
077:032 "Indeed it **throws** about sparks (huge) as Forts,
099:002 And the Earth **throws** up her burden (from within),

THRUST

028:032 "**Thrust** thy hand into thy bosom, and it
052:013 That Day shall they be **thrust** down to the
071:007 they have (only) **thrust** their fingers into their

THUNDER

002:019 and **thunder** and lightning:
004:153 by **thunder** and lightning.
013:013 Nay, **thunder** repeateth His praises, and so
069:005 by a terrible storm of **thunder** and lightning!

THUNDER-BOLTS

013:013 He flingeth the loud-voiced **thunder-bolts**, and

THUNDER-CLAP

002:019 the stunning **thunder-clap**,

THUNDERBOLT

002:055 thereupon, **thunderbolt** seized you.
041:013 "I have warned you of a **thunderbolt** like the
041:013 like the **thunderbolt** of the 'Ad and the Thamud!"
041:017 so the **thunderbolt** of the Chastisement
051:044 of their Lord: so the **thunderbolt** seized them,

THUNDERBOLTS

018:040 garden **thunderbolts** (by way of reckoning) from

THUNDERSTRUCK

052:045 wherein they shall be **thunderstruck**.

THUS

002:073 **Thus** Allah bringeth the dead to life
002:090 **thus** have they drawn on themselves
002:102 But they could not **thus** harm anyone except
002:143 **Thus** have We made of you an Ummah
002:167 **Thus** will Allah show them (the fruits of)
002:187 **Thus** doth Allah make clear His Signs to men:
002:210 and the question is (**thus**) settled?
002:219 **Thus** doth Allah make clear to you His Signs:
002:242 **Thus** doth Allah make clear His Signs to you:
002:258 **Thus** was he confounded who (in arrogance)
002:259 hast tarried **thus** a hundred years:
002:259 He said: "How long didst thou tarry (**thus**)?"
002:266 **Thus** doth Allah make clear to you
003:040 "**Thus**," was the answer, "Doth Allah accomplish
003:103 **Thus** doth Allah make His Signs clear to you:
003:123 then fear Allah; **thus** may ye show your gratitude.
004:011 Allah (**thus**) directs you as regards
004:012 **Thus** is it ordained by Allah;
004:024 **Thus** hath Allah ordained (prohibitions) against you:
004:089 and **thus** be on the same footing (as they):
004:094 Even **thus** were ye yourselves before, till Allah
004:176 say: Allah directs (**thus**) about those who leave
004:176 **thus** doth Allah make clear to you (His law),
005:089 **Thus** doth Allah make clear to you His Signs, that
005:106 and the chance of death befalls you (**thus**).
006:052 and **thus** be (one) of the unjust.
006:053 **Thus** did We test some of them by others,
006:055 **Thus** do We explain the Signs in detail:
006:084 **thus** do We reward those who do good:
006:105 **Thus** do We explain the Signs
006:108 **Thus** have We made alluring to each
006:122 **Thus** to those without Faith their own
006:123 **Thus** have We placed leaders in every town,

THUS (continued)

006:125 **thus** doth Allah lay abomination on those
006:129 **Thus** do We make the wrong-doers turn to
006:131 (The messengers were sent) **thus**, for thy Lord
006:151 **thus** doth He command you, that ye may learn wisdom.
006:152 **thus** doth He command you, that ye may remember.
006:153 **thus** doth He command you, that ye may be righteous.
007:005 When (**thus**) Our punishment took them, no cry
007:028 and "Allah commanded us **thus**": say: "Nay
007:032 **Thus** do We explain the Signs in detail
007:057 **thus** shall We raise up the dead: perchance
007:058 **thus** do We explain the Signs by various
007:101 We (**thus**) relate unto thee: there came
007:101 **Thus** doth Allah seal up the heart
007:118 **Thus** truth was confirmed. And all that
007:142 **thus** was completed the term with his Lord, forty
007:152 **thus** do We recompense those who invent
007:163 **thus** did We make a trial of them,
007:174 **Thus** do We explain the Signs in detail; and
008:014 **Thus** (will it be said): "Taste ye then
008:042 but (**thus** ye met), that Allah might accomplish
009:011 (**thus**) do We explain Signs in detail, for those
009:012 that **thus** they may be restrained.
009:026 **thus** doth He reward those without Faith.
009:060 (**thus** is it) ordained by Allah, and Allah
009:122 that **thus** they (may learn) to guard
010:005 (**Thus**) doth He explain His Signs in detail,
010:012 **Thus** do the deeds of transgressors seem fair
010:013 **Thus** do We requite those who sin!
010:024 **Thus** do We explain the Signs
010:033 **Thus** is the Word of thy Lord proved true
010:039 **thus** did those before them make charges of falsehood:
010:074 **Thus** do We seal the hearts of the transgressors.
010:103 **thus** is it fitting on Our part that We
010:105 "And further (**thus**): set thy face towards
011:003 "(And to preach **thus**), `Seek ye the forgiveness
012:006 "**Thus** will thy Lord choose thee and teach thee
012:021 **Thus** did We establish Joseph in the land, that We
012:022 **thus** do We reward those who do right.
012:024 **thus** (did We order) that We might turn away from him
012:026 (**thus**)-" If it be that his shirt is rent
012:056 **Thus** did We give established power to Joseph
012:075 **Thus** it is We punish the wrong-doers!
012:076 **Thus** did We plan for Joseph. He could not
013:017 **Thus** doth Allah set forth parables.
013:017 **Thus** doth Allah (by parables) show forth
013:030 **Thus** have We sent thee amongst a People
013:037 **Thus** have We revealed it to be a judgment
016:014 seek (**thus**) of the bounty of Allah and that
016:029 **Thus** evil indeed is the abode
016:031 **thus** doth Allah reward the righteous,-
016:081 **Thus** does He complete his favours on you,
018:021 **Thus** did We make their case known to the people,
018:097 **Thus** were they made powerless to scale it
020:096 **thus** did my soul suggest to me."
020:099 **Thus** do We relate to thee some stories
020:113 **Thus** have we sent this down-an Arabic Qur'an-
020:121 **thus** did Adam disobey His Lord,
020:126 (Allah) will say: "**Thus** didst thou, when Our
020:127 And **thus** do We recompense him who transgresses
021:029 **thus** do We reward those who do wrong.
021:088 and **thus** do We deliver those who have faith.
022:016 **Thus** have We sent down Clear Signs; and verily

THUS (continued)

022:036 **thus** have We made animals subject to you,
022:037 He has **thus** made them subject to you, that ye
022:046 so that their hearts (and minds) may **thus** learn wisdom
022:046 and their ears may **thus** learn to hear?
024:058 **thus** does Allah make clear the Signs to you:
024:059 **thus** does Allah make clear His Signs to you:
024:061 **Thus** does Allah make clear the Signs to you:
025:031 **Thus** have We made for every prophet an enemy
025:032 **Thus** (is it revealed), that We may
026:059 **Thus** it was, but We made the Children of Israel
026:074 our fathers doing **thus** (what we do)."
026:200 **Thus** have We caused it to enter the hearts
027:034 **thus** do they behave.
028:013 **Thus** did We restore him to his mother, that her
028:014 for **thus** do We reward those who do good.
029:047 And **thus** (it is) that We have sent down
030:019 and **thus** shall ye be brought out (from the dead).
030:028 **Thus** do We explain the Signs in detail to a
030:055 **thus** were they used to being deluded!
030:059 **Thus** does Allah seal up the hearts of those
035:012 that ye may seek (**thus**) of the Bounty of Allah
035:036 **Thus** do We reward every ungrateful one!
037:003 Those who **thus** proclaim the message (of Allah)!
037:080 **Thus** indeed do We reward those who do right.
037:105 **thus** indeed do We reward those who
037:110 **Thus** indeed do We reward those who do right.
037:121 **Thus** indeed do We reward those who do right.
037:131 **Thus** indeed do We reward those who do right.
039:008 **thus** misleading others from Allah's Path.
039:050 **Thus** did the (generations) before them say!
040:006 **Thus** was the Word of thy Lord proved true
040:034 **Thus** doth Allah leave to stray
040:035 **Thus** doth Allah seal up every heart-
040:037 **Thus** was made alluring, in Pharaoh's
040:063 **Thus** are deluded those who are wont to reject
040:074 **Thus** does Allah leave the Unbelievers to stray.
040:085 And even **thus** did the rejecters of Allah
042:003 **Thus** doth (He) send Inspiration to thee
042:007 **Thus** have We sent by inspiration to thee
042:052 And **thus** have We, by Our command, sent
043:008 and (**thus**) has passed on the example
043:054 **Thus** did he make fools of his people, and they
044:028 **Thus** (was their end)! And We
046:025 **Thus** do We recompense those given to sin!
047:003 **thus** does Allah set forth for men their lessons
047:004 **Thus** (are ye commanded): but if
048:015 Say: "Not **thus** will ye follow us: Allah has
050:011 **thus** will be the Resurrection.
054:035 **Thus** do We reward those who give thanks.
056:088 **Thus**, then, if he be of those Nearest to Allah,
058:016 **thus** they obstruct (men) from the Path of Allah:
063:002 **thus** they obstruct (men) from the path of Allah:
063:009 If any act **thus**, surely they are the losers.
065:002 **Thus** when they fulfil their term appointed,
068:050 **Thus** did his Lord choose him and make him
074:031 **Thus** doth Allah leave to stray whom He pleaseth,
077:018 **Thus** do We deal with men of sin.
077:044 **Thus** do We certainly reward the Doers of Good.

THY

001:007 hast bestowed **Thy** Grace,
002:004 and sent before **thy** time,
002:030 Behold, **thy** Lord said to the angels:

THY (continued)

002:030 **Thy** praises and glorify **Thy** Holy (name)?"
002:035 dwell thou and **thy** wife in the Garden;
002:060 We said "strike the rock with **thy** staff."
002:061 so beseech **thy** Lord for us to produce for us
002:068 They said: "Beseech on our behalf **thy** Lord
002:069 They said: "Beseech on our behalf **thy** Lord
002:070 They said, "Beseech on our behalf **thy** Lord
002:097 (revelation) to **thy** heart by Allah's will,
002:128 bowing to **Thy** (Will),
002:128 bowing to **Thy** (Will);
002:129 Who shall rehearse **Thy** Signs to them
002:131 "Submit (**thy** will to Me):"
002:133 worship **thy** God and the God of **thy** fathers,
002:144 Turn then **thy** face in the direction
002:144 **thy** face (for guidance) to the heavens:
002:145 they would not follow **thy** Qiblah;
002:147 The truth is from **thy** Lord,
002:149 turn **thy** face in the direction of the
002:149 that is indeed the truth from **thy** Lord.
002:150 turn **thy** face in the direction
002:200 "Our Lord! Give us (**thy** bounties) in this world!"
002:243 **thy** vision to those who abandoned their homes,
002:246 Hast thou not turned **thy** vision to the chiefs
002:258 Hast thou not turned **thy** thought to one
002:259 but look at **thy** food and **thy** drink;
002:259 and look at **thy** donkey:
002:285 (We seek) **Thy** forgiveness, our Lord,
003:020 **thy** duty is to convey the Message;
003:023 Hast thou not turned **thy** thought to those who
003:026 in **Thy** hand is all Good.
003:035 what is in my womb for **Thy** special service:
003:036 to **Thy** protection from Satan the Rejected."
003:041 "**Thy** Sign," was the answer, "Shall be that thou
003:041 of **thy** Lord again and again,
003:043 "O Mary! worship **thy** Lord devoutly;
003:060 the truth (comes) from **thy** Lord alone;
003:159 put **thy** trust in Allah.
003:194 for thou never breakest **Thy** promise."
003:194 Thou didst promise unto us through **Thy** Messengers,
004:044 Hast thou not turned **thy** thought to those who
004:049 Hast thou not turned **thy** thought to those
004:051 Hast thou not turned **thy** thought to those who
004:060 Hast thou not turned **thy** thought to those who
004:065 no resistance against **thy** decisions, but
004:065 But no, by **thy** Lord, they can have no (real) Faith.
004:077 Hast thou not turned **thy** thought to those who
004:081 so keep clear of them, and put **thy** trust in Allah,
004:118 "I will take of **Thy** servants a portion marked off:
004:127 They ask **thy** instruction concerning the Women.
005:024 Go thou, and **thy** Lord, and fight
005:028 "If thou dost stretch **thy** hand against me, to slay
005:067 which hath been sent to thee from **thy** Lord.
005:068 that cometh to thee from **thy** Lord, that
005:110 recount my favour to thee and to **thy** mother.
005:112 Can **thy** Lord send down to us a Table set
005:118 they are **Thy** servants: if Thou
006:066 But **thy** people reject this, though it is
006:074 For I see thee and **thy** people in manifest error."
006:083 for **thy** Lord is full of wisdom and knowledge.
006:106 by inspiration from **thy** Lord:
006:112 If **thy** Lord had so willed, they would
006:114 that it hath been sent down from **thy** Lord in truth.

THY (continued)

006:115	The Word of **thy** Lord doth find its fulfillment
006:117	**Thy** Lord knoweth best who strayeth
006:119	**Thy** Lord knoweth best those who transgress.
006:126	This is the way of **thy** Lord, leading
006:128	For **thy** Lord is full of wisdom and knowledge.
006:131	for **thy** Lord would not destroy the towns
006:132	for **thy** Lord is not unmindful of
006:133	**Thy** Lord is Self-sufficient, full of Mercy:
006:145	**thy** Lord is Oft-Forgiving, Most Merciful.
006:158	if the angels come to them, or **thy** Lord (Himself),
006:158	The day that certain Signs of **thy** Lord do come,
006:158	or certain of the Signs of **thy** Lord!
006:165	for **thy** Lord is quick in punishment:
007:002	so let **thy** heart be oppressed no more
007:016	for them on **Thy** Straight Way:
007:017	gratitude (for **Thy** mercies)."
007:019	and **thy** wife in the Garden, and enjoy
007:023	and bestow not upon us **Thy** Mercy, we shall
007:077	saying: "O Salih! bring about **thy** threats,
007:117	We revealed to Moses "Throw **thy** rod": and behold!
007:126	"But thou dost wreak **thy** vengeance on us
007:126	as Muslims (who bow to **Thy** Will)"!
007:127	and to abandon thee and **thy** gods?"
007:132	to work therewith **thy** sorcery on us, we shall
007:134	call on **thy** Lord in virtue
007:137	The fair promise of **thy** Lord was fulfilled
007:145	and enjoin **thy** people to hold fast by the
007:151	Admit us to **Thy** mercy! For Thou art
007:153	verily **Thy** Lord is thereafter Oft-forgiving,
007:155	This is no more than **Thy** trial: by it Thou
007:155	if it had been **Thy** Will thou couldst have destroyed,
007:155	so forgive us and give us **Thy** mercy; for Thou
007:160	"Strike the rock with **thy** staff":
007:167	Behold! **thy** Lord did declare that He
007:167	**Thy** Lord is quick in retribution, but He
007:172	When **thy** Lord drew forth from the Children
007:200	If a suggestion from Satan assail **thy** (mind),
007:205	bring **thy** Lord to remembrance in **thy** (very) soul,
007:206	Those who are near to **thy** Lord, disdain not
008:005	Just as **thy** Lord ordered thee out of **thy** house in truth,
008:012	Remember **thy** Lord inspired the angels
008:017	it was not **thy** act, but Allah's: in order
008:030	or get **thy** out (of they home).
008:043	Remember in **thy** dream Allah showed them
009:009	evil indeed are the deeds **thy** have done.
009:083	and they ask **thy** permission to come out (with thee),
009:103	Verily **thy** prayers are a source of security
009:108	it is more worthy of **thy** standing forth
010:019	from **thy** Lord, their differences would have been
010:033	Thus is the Word of **thy** Lord proved true
010:040	and **thy** Lord knoweth best those who
010:046	We promise them,-or We take **thy** soul (before that),-
010:046	Whether We show thee (Realized in **thy** lifetime)
010:078	in order that thou and **thy** brother may have
010:086	"And deliver us by **Thy** Mercy from those
010:088	Our Lord they mislead (men) from **Thy** Path.
010:092	"This day shall We save thee in **thy** body,
010:094	the Truth hath come indeed come to thee from **thy** Lord:
010:096	of **thy** Lord hath been verified would not believe-
010:099	If it had been **thy** Lord's Will, they would
010:105	"And further (thus): set **thy** face towards
011:012	and **thy** heart feeleth straitened lest they say,

011:017	for it is the Truth from **thy** Lord:
011:036	"None of **thy** People will believe except those
011:044	"O earth! swallow up **thy** water,
011:044	and O sky! withhold (**thy** rain)!"
011:045	and **Thy** promise is true, and Thou art
011:046	He said: "O Noah! he is not of **thy** family: for his
011:049	neither thou nor **thy** People knew them.
011:053	the ones to desert out gods on **thy** word!
011:066	For **thy** Lord-He is the Strong One, and the Mighty.
011:076	The decree of **thy** Lord hath gone forth: for them
011:079	"Well dost thou know we have no need of **thy** daughters:
011:081	we are Messengers from **thy** Lord! By no means
011:081	Now travel with **thy** family while yet a part
011:081	but **thy** wife (will remain behind): to her
011:083	Marked from **thy** Lord; nor are they ever far
011:087	Does **thy** prayer command thee that we leave off
011:091	Were it not for **thy** family, we should
011:101	when there issued the decree of **thy** Lord:
011:102	Such is the chastisement of **thy** Lord when He
011:107	except as **thy** Lord willeth: for **thy** Lord
011:107	for **thy** Lord is the (sure) Accomplisher
011:108	except as **thy** Lord willeth: a gift without break.
011:110	had gone forth before from **thy** Lord the matter
011:117	Nor would **thy** Lord be the One to destroy
011:118	If **thy** Lord had so willed, He could
011:119	Except those on whom **thy** Lord hath bestowed
011:119	and the Word of **thy** Lord shall be fulfilled:
011:120	with it We make firm **thy** heart: in them
011:123	so worship Him, and put **thy** trust in Him:
011:123	and **thy** Lord is not unmindful of aught that ye do.
012:005	relate not **thy** vision to **thy** brother, last they
012:006	"Thus will **thy** Lord choose thee and teach thee
012:006	For **thy** Lord is full of knowledge and wisdom."
012:006	**thy** fathers Abraham and Isaac aforetime!
012:023	He said: "Allah forbid! truly (**thy** husband) is my
012:025	an evil design against **thy** wife, but prison
012:029	(O wife), ask forgiveness for **thy** sin, for truly
012:042	he said: "Mention me to **thy** lord." But Satan
012:050	**thy** lord, and ask him, 'What was the matter
012:069	He said (to him): "Behold! I am **thy** (own) brother;
012:081	**thy** son committed theft! we bear witness
012:101	as one submitting to **Thy** Will (as a Muslim),
013:001	unto thee from **thy** Lord is the Truth; but most
013:006	and verily **thy** Lord is (also) strict in punishment.
013:006	But verily **thy** Lord is full of forgiveness
013:019	unto thee from **thy** Lord is the Truth, like one
013:040	(within **thy** lifetime) part of what We promised
013:040	**thy** duty is to (make the Message) reach them:
013:040	take to Us **thy** soul (before it is all accomplished),
014:005	**thy** people from the depths of darkness into light,
014:028	Hast thou not turned **thy** thought to those
014:037	by **Thy** Sacred House; in order, O our Lord,
014:041	**Thy** Forgiveness-me, my parents and (all)
014:044	we will answer **Thy** Call, and follow
015:025	Assuredly it is **thy** Lord who will gather them
015:028	Behold! **thy** Lord said to the angels: "I am
015:040	"Except **Thy** chosen servants among them,
015:065	"Then travel by night with **thy** household, when a
015:072	Verily, by **thy** life (O Prophet), in their
015:086	For verily it is **thy** Lord Who is the All-Creator,
015:088	but lower **thy** wing (in gentleness)
015:092	Therefore, by **thy** Lord, We will, of a surety

THY (continued)

015:097   We do indeed know how **thy** heart is distressed
015:098   But celebrate the praises of **thy** Lord and be
015:099   And serve **thy** Lord until there come unto thee
016:021   nor do **thy** know when they will be raised up.
016:033   there comes the Command of **thy** Lord (for their doom)?
016:047   for **thy** Lord is indeed full of kindness and mercy.
016:068   And **thy** Lord taught the Bee to build
016:069   **Thy** Lord made smooth: there issues from within
016:082   **thy** duty is only to preach the Clear Message.
016:089   as a witness against these (**thy** people):
016:102   the revelation from **thy** Lord in Truth, in order
016:110   **thy** Lord, after all this is Oft-Forgiving,
016:110   But verily **thy** Lord,-to those who leave their
016:119   **thy** Lord after all this, is Oft-Forgiving,
016:119   But verily **thy** Lord, to those
016:125   for **thy** Lord knoweth best, who have
016:125   Invite (all) to the Way of **thy** Lord with wisdom
016:127   for **thy** patience is but with the help
017:014   **thy** soul this day to make out an account
017:017   And enough is **thy** Lord to note and see the sins
017:020   the bounties of **thy** Lord are not closed (to anyone).
017:020   Of the bounties of **thy** Lord We bestow
017:023   old age in **thy** life, say not to them a word
017:023   **Thy** Lord hath decreed that ye worship none but Him,
017:024   "My Lord! bestow on them **Thy** Mercy even as they
017:028   from **thy** Lord which thou dost expect, yet speak
017:029   Make not **thy** hand tied (like a niggard's) to **thy** neck,
017:030   Verily **thy** Lord doth provide sustenance in
017:038   is hateful in the sight of **thy** Lord.
017:039   (precepts of) wisdom, which **thy** Lord has revealed
017:046   when thou dost mention **thy** Lord-and Him
017:048   See what similes **thy** strike for thee: but they
017:057   for the Wrath of **thy** Lord is something to take heed of.
017:060   **thy** Lord doth encompass mankind round about:
017:063   Allah said: "Go **thy** way; if any of them follow
017:064   among them, with **thy** (seductive) voice;
017:064   them with **thy** cavalry and **thy** infantry;
017:065   Enough is **thy** Lord for a disposer
017:079   soon will **thy** Lord raise thee to a Station
017:086   none to plead **thy** affair in that matter as against Us,-
017:087   Except for Mercy from **thy** Lord; for His
017:093   even believe in **thy** mounting until thou
017:110   Neither speak **thy** Prayer aloud, nor speak
018:024   and remember **thy** Lord when thou forgettest,
018:027   what has been revealed to thee of the Book of **thy** Lord:
018:039   as thou wentest into **thy** garden,
018:040   me something better than **thy** garden, and that
018:040   and that He will send on **thy** garden thunderbolts
018:046   are best in the sight of **thy** Lord, as rewards,
018:048   And they will be marshalled before **thy** Lord in ranks,
018:049   And not one will **thy** Lord treat with injustice.
018:076   keep me not in **thy** company:
018:082   a mercy (and favour) from **thy** Lord.
018:082   so **thy** Lord desired that they should attain their
019:002   of **thy** Lord to His Servant Zakariya.
019:009   **thy** Lord saith, "That is easy for Me: I did
019:010   "**Thy** Sign," was the answer, "shall be
019:019   from **thy** Lord, (to announce) to thee the gift
019:021   **thy** Lord saith, 'That is easy for Me:
019:024   "Grieve not! for **thy** Lord hath provided
019:028   "O sister of Aaron! **thy** father was not a man of evil,
019:028   nor **thy** mother a woman unchaste!"

THY (continued)

019:047   I will pray to my Lord for **thy** forgiveness: for He
019:064   but by command of **thy** Lord: to Him belongeth
019:064   and **thy** Lord never doth forget,-
019:068   So, by **thy** Lord, without doubt, We shall
019:071   this is, with **thy** Lord, a Decree
019:076   are best in the sight of **thy** Lord, as rewards,
020:002   to be (an occasion) for **thy** distress,
020:012   "Verily I am **thy** Lord! Therefore put off **thy** shoes:
020:017   And what is that in **thy** right hand, O Moses?"
020:022   Now draw **thy** hand close to **thy** side: it shall
020:033   "That we may celebrate **Thy** praise without stint,
020:036   (Allah) said: "Granted is **thy** prayer, O Moses!"
020:038   "Behold! We sent to **thy** mother, by inspiration,
020:040   So We brought thee back to **thy** mother, that her
020:040   "Behold! **thy** sister goeth forth and saith,
020:042   "Go, thou and **thy** brother, with My
020:047   'Verily we are Messengers sent by **thy** Lord:
020:047   indeed, have we come from **thy** Lord!
020:057   us out of our land with **thy** magic, O Moses?
020:069   "Throw that which is in **thy** right hand:
020:083   in advance of **thy** people, O Moses?"
020:085   (Allah) said: "We have tested **thy** people
020:085   in **thy** absence: the Samiri has led them astray."
020:095   (Moses) said: "What then is **thy** case, O Samiri?"
020:097   now look at **thy** god, of whom thou hast become a
020:097   but **thy** (punishment) in this life will be that
020:117   this is an enemy to thee and **thy** wife: so let
020:129   that went forth before from **thy** Lord,
020:130   the praises of **thy** Lord, before the
020:131   but the provision of **thy** Lord is better
020:132   Enjoin prayer on **thy** people, and be
020:134   have followed **Thy** Signs before we were
021:046   breath of the Wrath of **thy** Lord do touch them,
022:010   of the deeds which **thy** hands sent forth, for verily
022:047   a Day in the sight of **thy** Lord is like a thousand years
022:054   the (Qur'an) is the Truth from **thy** Lord, and that
022:067   but do not invite (them) to **thy** Lord:
023:027   male and female, and **thy** family-except those of them
023:029   **Thy** blessing: for Thou art the Best to enable
023:072   But the recompense of **thy** Lord is best: He is
024:062   those who ask for **thy** leave are those who
024:062   so when they ask for **thy** leave, for some
025:016   a promise binding upon **thy** Lord."
025:031   but enough is **thy** Lord to guide and to help.
025:032   that We may strengthen **thy** heart thereby,
025:045   Hast thou not seen how **thy** Lord?-doth prolong
025:054   for **thy** Lord has power (over all things).
025:058   And put **thy** trust in Him Who lives and dies not;
026:003   It may be thou will kill **thy** self with grief,
026:009   And verily, **thy** Lord is He, the Exalted
026:010   Behold, **thy** Lord called Moses: "Go to the
026:018   didst thou not stay in our midst many years of **thy** life?
026:063   "Strike the sea with **thy** rod." So it
026:068   And verily **thy** Lord is He, the Exalted
026:104   And verily the Lord is He, the Exalted
026:122   And verily **thy** Lord is He, the Exalted
026:140   And verily **thy** Lord is He, the Exalted
026:159   And verily **thy** Lord is He, the Exalted
026:175   And verily **thy** Lord is He, the Exalted
026:191   And verily **thy** Lord is He, the Exalted
026:194   To **thy** heart and mind that thou mayest admonish
026:214   And admonish **thy** nearest kinsmen,

THY (continued)

026:215 And lower **thy** wing to the Believers who follow thee.
026:217 And put **thy** trust on the Exalted
026:219 And **thy** movements among those who
027:010 "Now do thou throw **thy** rod!" But when
027:012 "Now put **thy** hand into **thy** bosom, and it
027:019 to the ranks of **Thy** righteous Servants."
027:019 for **Thy** favours, which Thou has bestowed on me
027:019 and admit me, by **Thy** Grace, to the
027:039 thou rise from **thy** Council: indeed I
027:040 "I will bring it to thee before **thy** glance returns to thee.
027:042 "Is this **thy** throne?" She said, "It seems
027:073 But verily **thy** Lord is full of grace to mankind:
027:074 And verily **thy** Lord knoweth all that
027:078 Verily **thy** Lord will decide between them
027:079 So put **thy** trust in Allah: for thou
027:093 and **thy** Lord is not unmindful of all that ye do.
028:007 to the mother of Moses: "Suckle (**thy** child),
028:017 Thou hast bestowed **Thy** Grace on me, never shall
028:019 "O Moses! is it **thy** intention to slay me
028:031 "Now do thou throw **thy** rod!" But when
028:032 from **thy** Lord to Pharaoh and his Chiefs: for truly
028:032 and draw **thy** hand close to **thy** side (to guard)
028:032 "Thrust **thy** hand into **thy** bosom, and it
028:035 "We will certainly strengthen **thy** arm through **thy** brother,
028:046 as a Mercy from **thy** Lord, to give
028:059 Nor was **thy** Lord the one to destroy a town
028:068 **Thy** Lord does create and choose as He pleases:
028:069 And **thy** Lord knows all that their hearts
028:077 nor forget **thy** portion in this world: but do
028:086 except as a Mercy from **thy** Lord: therefore lend
028:087 and invite (men) to **thy** Lord and be not
029:010 And if help comes (to thee) from **thy** lord,
029:033 and **thy** following, except **thy** wife: she is
029:048 nor art thou (able) to transcribe it with **thy** right hand:
030:030 So set thou **thy** face truly to the religion
030:043 But set thou **thy** face to the right Religion,
031:012 wisdom on Luqman: "Show (**thy**) gratitude to Allah."
031:014 to Me is (**thy** final) Goal.
031:014 "Show gratitude to Me and to **thy** parents: to Me
031:018 "And swell not **thy** cheek (for pride) at men.
031:019 "And be moderate in **thy** pace, and lower **thy** voice;
032:003 Nay, it is the Truth from **thy** Lord, that thou
032:025 Verily **thy** Lord will judge between them on the
033:002 to thee by inspiration from **thy** Lord: for Allah
033:003 And put **thy** trust in Allah, and enough
033:028 O Prophet! say to **thy** Consorts: "If it
033:037 But thou didst hide in **thy** heart that which
033:037 who had received the grace of Allah and **thy** favour:
033:037 "Retain thou (in wedlock) **thy** wife,
033:048 their insolence but put **thy** trust in Allah.
033:050 and aunts, and daughters of **thy** maternal uncles
033:050 to thee **thy** wives to whom thou hast paid their
033:050 **thy** right hand possesses out of the captives
033:050 and daughters of **thy** paternal uncles and aunts,
033:052 attract thee, except any **thy** right hand should
033:059 O prophet! Tell **thy** wives and daughters, and the
033:060 be able to stay in it as **thy** neighbors for any
034:006 to thee from **thy** Lord-that is the Truth, and that
034:021 and **thy** Lord doth watch over all things.
035:008 So let not **thy** soul be vested in regret
037:102 now see what is in **thy** view!"
037:149 is it that **thy** Lord has (only) daughters,

THY (continued)

037:180 Glory to **thy** Lord, the Lord of Honour and Power!
038:009 of the Mercy of **thy** Lord,-the Exalted
038:024 wronged thee in demanding **thy** (single) ewe to be
038:026 nor follow thou the lust (of **thy** heart), for it will
038:042 "Strike with **thy** foot: here is (water)
038:044 and break not (**thy** oath)."
038:044 "And take in **thy** hand a little grass, and strike
038:071 Behold, **thy** Lord said to the angels: "I am
038:082 (Iblis) said: "Then, by **Thy** Power, I will
038:083 "Except **Thy** Servants amongst them, sincere and
038:083 sincere and purified (by **Thy** grace)."
039:008 Say "Enjoy **thy** disbelief for a little while:
039:046 wilt judge between **Thy** Servants in those matters
039:065 truly fruitless will be **thy** work (in life), and thou
040:006 Thus was the Word of **thy** Lord proved true
040:007 in repentance, and follow **Thy** Path; and preserve
040:055 and ask forgiveness for **thy** fault,
040:055 and celebrate the Praises of **thy** Lord in the
040:077 or We take **thy** soul (to Our Mercy) (before that),
041:034 became as it were **thy** friend and intimate!
041:038 presence of **thy** Lord are those who celebrate
041:043 surely **thy** Lord has at His command (all) Forgiveness
041:045 been for a Word that went forth before from **thy** Lord,
041:046 nor is **thy** Lord ever unjust (in the least)
041:053 enough that **thy** Lord doth witness all things?
042:014 for a Word that went forth before from **thy** Lord,
042:024 He could seal up **thy** heart. And Allah
042:048 **Thy** duty is but to convey (the Message).
043:032 But the Mercy of **thy** Lord in better
043:032 the Mercy of **thy** Lord? It is
043:035 in the sight of **thy** Lord, is for the Righteous.
043:044 for thee and for **thy** people; and soon
043:049 invoke **thy** Lord for us according to his
043:057 as an example, behold **thy** people raise a clamour
043:077 **thy** Lord put and end to us!" He will say, "Nay,
044:006 As a Mercy from **thy** Lord: for He
044:057 As a Bounty from **thy** Lord! That will
044:058 Verily, We made this (Qur-an) in **thy** tongue, in order
045:017 Verily **thy** Lord will judge between them on the
046:015 **Thy** favour which Thou hast bestowed upon me,
047:013 with more power than **thy** city which has driven
047:019 and ask forgiveness for **thy** fault, and for the men
048:002 That Allah may forgive thee **thy** faults of the
050:022 now have We removed **thy** veil,
050:022 and sharp is **thy** sight this Day!"
050:039 and celebrate the praises of **thy** Lord, before the
051:030 They said, "Even so has **thy** Lord spoken:
051:034 "Marked as from **thy** Lord for those who trespass
052:007 Verily, the Chastisement of **thy** Lord will indeed
052:029 Therefore Remind for by the Grace of **thy** Lord,
052:037 Or are the Treasures of **thy** Lord with them,
052:048 Now await in patience the command of **thy** Lord:
052:048 the praises of **thy** Lord the while thou standest forth,
053:030 Verily **thy** Lord knoweth best those who
053:032 verily **thy** Lord is ample in forgiveness. He knows
053:042 That to **thy** Lord is the final Goal;
053:055 Then which of the favours of **thy** Lord, (O man),
055:027 But will abide (for ever) the Face of **thy** Lord,
055:078 Blessed be the name of **thy** Lord, full of
056:074 Then glorify the name of **thy** Lord, the Supreme!
056:096 So glorify the name of **thy** Lord, the Supreme.
060:004 no power (to get) aught on **thy** behalf from Allah."

THY (continued)

066:001   thou seekest to please **thy** consorts?
067:003   So turn **thy** vision again:
067:004   (**thy**) vision will come back to thee dull
067:004   Again turn **thy** vision a second time:
068:002   Thou art not, by the grace of **thy** Lord, mad or
068:007   Verily it is **thy** Lord that knoweth best,
068:009   be pliant: so would **thy** be pliant.
068:019   a visitation from **thy** Lord, (which swept
068:048   So wait with patience for the Command of **thy** Lord,
069:017   bear the Throne of **thy** Lord above them.
069:052   So glorify the name of **thy** Lord Most High.
071:001   **thy** People before there comes to them
071:027   they will but mislead **Thy** devotees, and they
073:009   take Him therefore for (**thy**) Disposer of Affairs.
074:002   Arise and deliver **thy** warning!
074:003   And **thy** Lord do thou magnify!
074:004   And **thy** garments keep free from stain!
074:007   But, for **thy** Lord's (Cause), be patient
074:031   the forces of **thy** Lord, except He, and this
075:012   Before **thy** Lord (alone), that Day
075:016   Move not **thy** tongue concerning the (Qur'an)
075:030   That Day the Drive will be (all) to **thy** Lord!
076:024   to the Command of **thy** Lord, and obey
076:025   of **thy** Lord morning and evening,
078:036   Recompense from **thy** Lord, a Gift,
079:016   Behold, **thy** Lord did call to him in the sacred
079:019   "And that I guide thee to **thy** Lord, so thou
082:006   from **thy** Lord Most Beneficent?-
085:012   Truly strong is the Grip of **thy** Lord.
087:001   Glorify the name of **thy** Guardian-Lord, Most High,
089:006   Seest thou not how **thy** Lord dealt with
089:013   Therefore did **thy** Lord pour on them a scourge
089:014   For **thy** Lord is watchful.
089:022   And **thy** Lord cometh, and His angels,
089:028   "Come back thou to **thy** Lord,-well pleased
093:005   And soon will **thy** Guardian-Lord give thee
093:011   But the Bounty of **thy** Lord-rehearse and proclaim!
094:001   Have We not expanded thee **thy** breast?-
094:002   And removed from thee **thy** burden
094:003   The which did gall **thy** back?-
094:008   And to **thy** Lord turn (all) **thy** attention.
096:001   of **thy** Lord and Cherisher, Who created-
096:003   Proclaim! And **thy** Lord is Most Bountiful,-
096:008   Verily, to **thy** Lord is the return (of all).
099:005   For that **thy** Lord will have given her inspiration.
105:001   Seest thou not how **thy** Lord dealt with the
108:002   Therefore to **thy** Lord turn in Prayer and Sacrifice.
110:003   Celebrate the Praises of **thy** Lord, and pray

THYSELF

003:043   prostrate **thyself**, and bow down (in prayer)
003:193   and take to **Thyself** our souls in the company
004:079   is from **thyself** and We have sent thee as
004:084   thou art held responsible only for **thyself**, and
005:029   thee draw on **thyself** my sin as well as thine, for
007:143   He said: "O my Lord! show (**Thyself**) to me, that
016:127   and distress not **thyself** because of their plots.
018:006   fret **thyself** to death, following after them,
018:010   bestow on us Mercy from **Thyself**, and dispose
019:005   so give me an heir as from **Thyself**,-
019:025   "And shake towards **thyself** the trunk
027:070   nor distress **thyself** because of their plots.
038:075   thee from prostrating **thyself** to one whom I

THYSELF (continued)

054:027   and possess **thyself** in patience!
073:008   the Lord and devote **thyself** to Him wholeheartedly.
074:006   Nor expect, in giving, any increase (for **thyself**)!
076:026   And part of the night, prostrate **thyself** to Him;
089:028   well pleased (**thyself**), and well-pleasing unto Him!
096:019   and bring **thyself** the closer (to Allah)!

TIDINGS

002:025   But give glad **tidings** to those who believe
002:097   glad **tidings** for those who believe,
002:119   glad **tidings** and a warner:
002:155   but give glad **tidings** to those
002:213   with glad **tidings** and warnings;
002:223   good **tidings** to those who believe.
003:015   glad **tidings** of things far better than those?
003:039   "Allah doth give thee glad **tidings** of Yahya,
003:044   This is part of the **tidings** of the things unseen,
003:045   glad **tidings** of a Word from Him:
004:138   To the Hypocrites give the glad **tidings** that
005:019   unto us no bringer of glad **tidings** and no warner.
005:019   a bringer of glad **tidings** and a warner.
007:053   did indeed bring true (**tidings**).
007:057   the Winds like heralds of glad **tidings**, going
007:188   and a bringer of glad **tidings** to those
009:021   Their Lord doth give them glad **tidings** of a
009:112   So proclaim the glad **tidings** to the Believers.
010:064   For them are Glad **Tidings**, in the life
010:087   and give Glad **Tidings** to those who believe!"
011:002   from Him to warn and to bring glad **tidings**:
011:069   to Abraham with glad **tidings**. They said,
011:071   glad **tidings** of Isaac, and after him, of Jacob.
011:074   Abraham and the glad **tidings** had reached him,
015:053   glad **tidings** of a son endowed with knowledge."
015:054   glad **tidings** even though old age has seized me?
015:055   They said: "We give thee glad **tidings** in truth;
016:089   a Mercy, and Glad **Tidings** to Muslims.
016:102   and as a Guide and Glad **tidings** to Muslims.
017:009   and giveth the glad **tidings** to the Believers
017:105   Glad **Tidings** and to warn (sinners).
018:002   and that He may give Glad **Tidings** to the
018:056   glad **tidings** and to give warnings: but the
019:097   glad **tidings** to the righteous, and warnings
025:048   as heralds of glad **tidings**, going before
025:056   to give glad **tidings** and warnings.
027:002   A Guide; and Glad **Tidings** for the Believers,
027:022   from Saba with **tidings** true.
027:063   of glad **tidings**, going before His Mercy?
030:046   as heralds go Glad **Tidings**, giving you
033:045   as a Witness, a Bearer of Glad **Tidings**, and a
033:047   Then give the glad **tidings** to the Believers,
034:028   giving them glad **tidings**, and warning
035:024   as a bearer of glad **tidings**, and as a warner:
036:011   a one, therefore, good **tidings**, of Forgiveness
038:067   Say: "That is a Tremendous **tidings**.
041:030   But receive the Glad **Tidings** of the
042:023   gives Glad **Tidings** to His Servants who believe
046:012   and as Glad **Tidings** to those who do right.
048:008   as a bringer of Glad **Tidings**, and as a Warner:
051:028   gave him glad **tidings** of a son endowed
054:004   such **tidings** as contain a deterrent,
061:006   glad **Tidings** of a messenger to come after me,
061:013   the Glad **Tidings** to the Believers.
099:004   On that Day will she declare her **tidings**:

TIE

002:235   nor resolve on the **tie** of marriage till the
002:237   by him in whose hands is the marriage **tie**;
002:260   **tie** them (cut them into pieces),

TIED

003:180   **tied** to their necks like a twisted collar,
005:064   Be their hands **tied** up and be they
005:064   The Jews say: "Allah's hand is **tied** up,"
017:029   Make not thy hand **tied** (like a niggard's)

TIES

004:073   **ties** of affection between you and them,
009:008   the **ties** either of kinship or of covenant?
009:010   the **ties** either of kinship or of covenant!
033:006   have closer personal **ties**, in the
047:022   and break your **ties** of kith and kin?
060:010   the **ties** (marriage contract) of Unbelieving women:

TIGHTEN

009:067   and **tighten** their purse's strings.

TILL

002:071   to **till** the soil or water the fields;
002:109   **till** Allah brings about His command;
002:187   then complete your fast **till** the night appears;
002:235   marriage **till** the term prescribed is fulfilled.
002:280   grant him time **till** it is easy for him
003:065   were not revealed **till** after him?
004:094   **till** Allah conferred on you His favours:
005:064   enmity and hatred **till** the Day of Judgment.
007:014   respite **till** the day they are raised up."
009:077   (to last) **till** the day whereon they shall meet Him:
010:022   **till** when ye even board ships;-they sail
010:024   (it grows) **till** the earth is clad with its golden
010:109   **till** Allah doth decide: for He
015:035   on thee **till** the Day of Judgment."
015:036   then respite **till** the Day the (dead) are raised."
015:038   "**Till** the Day of the Time Appointed."
017:078   sun's decline **till** the darkness of the night,
021:015   **till** We made them as a field that is mown,
023:100   Before them is a Partition **till** the Day
036:039   for her stations (to traverse) **till** she returns
037:144   inside the Fish **till** the Day of Resurrection.
038:078   **till** the Day of Judgement."
038:079   then respite **till** the Day the (dead) are raised."
038:081   "**Till** the day of the Time Appointed."
047:016   to thee, **till** when they go out from thee,
063:007   **till** they disperse (and quit Madinah).
079:046   or (at most **till**) the following morn!

TILLAGE

018:032   the two We placed **tillage**.

TILLED

030:009   they **tilled** the soil and populated it

TILLERS

057:020   delight (the hearts of) the **tillers**;

TILTH

002:223   Your wives are as a **tilth** unto you
002:223   so approach your **tilth** when or how ye will;
006:136   in abundance in **tilth** and in cattle, they
006:141   and **tilth** with produce of all kinds, and olives
030:051   they see (their **tilth**) turn yellow,-behold, they
042:020   We give increase in his **tilth**;
042:020   and to any that desires the **tilth** of this world,
042:020   To any that desires the **tilth** of the Hereafter,
068:022   "Go ye to your **tilth** (betimes) in the morning,

TIMBER

063:004   pieces of **timber** propped up,

TIME

002:004   and sent before thy **time**,
002:020   every **time** the light (helps) them,
002:023   revealed from **time** to our servants
002:025   Every **time** they are fed with fruits
002:036   and your means of livelihood for a **time**."
002:066   So We made it an example to their own **time**,
002:100   every **time** they make a Covenant,
002:189   fixed periods of **time** in (the affairs of) men.
002:246   Children of Israel after (the **time** of) Moses
002:280   grant him **time** till it is easy for him
002:282   future obligations in a fixed period of **time**,
003:037   Every **time** that he entered her chamber to see her,
004:008   But if at the **time** of division other relatives,
004:023   and two sisters in wedlock at one and the same **time**,
004:091   every **time** they are sent back to temptation, they
005:005   revealed before your **time**, when you
005:064   Every **time** they kindle the fire of war, Allah
005:070   Every **time** there came to them a Messenger
006:067   "For every Prophecy is a limit of **time**, and soon
006:094   and alone as We created you for the first **time**:
006:096   for the reckoning (of **time**): such is
006:157   In good **time** shall We requite those who
007:007   for We were never absent (at any **time** or place).
007:024   and your means of livelihood,-for a **time**."
007:029   (to Him) at every **time** and place of prayer, and
007:031   at every **time** and place of prayer:
007:038   Every **time** a new People enters, it curses
007:187   when will be its appointed **time**? Say: "The
007:196   Who revealed the Book, (from **time** to **time**), and He
008:056   every **time**, and they have not the fear (of Allah).
009:117   who followed Him in a **time** of distress,
010:005   know the number of years and the count (of **time**).
011:038   every **time** that the Chiefs of his People
011:048   grant their pleasures (for a **time**), but in
011:081   Morning is their **time** appointed:
011:100   some have been mown down (by the sickle of **time**).
012:009   you alone: (there will be **time** enough) for you
012:035   (that it was best) to imprison him for a **time**.
012:045   (so long) a space of **time**, said: "I will tell
012:065   and add (at the same **time**) a full camel's load
013:008   (of their **time** or number) or do exceed.
014:014   This for such as fear the **Time** when they
015:038   "Till the Day of the **Time** Appointed."
016:080   of convenience (to serve you) for a **time**.
017:069   not send you back a second **time** to sea and send
017:097   every **time** it shows abatement, We shall
017:106   which We have divided (into parts from **time** to **time**),
018:058   but they have their appointed **time**, beyond which
018:059   but We fixed an appointed **time** for their
020:037   on thee another **time** (before).
021:039   (the **time**) when they will not be able to ward
021:111   livelihood (to you) for a **time**.
022:022   Every **time** they wish to get away therefrom,
023:025   wait (and have patience) with him for a **time**."
023:044   in succession: every **time** there came to a people
023:054   confused ignorance for a **time**.
028:015   And he entered the City at a **time** when its
032:020   the Fire: every **time** they wish to get away
033:053   ye should marry his widows after him at any **time**.
033:060   for any length of **time**:

TIME (continued)

036:044 (to serve them) for a **time**.
036:079 Who created them for the first **time**!
038:003 no longer **time** for being save!
038:081 "Till the day of the **Time** Appointed."
039:005 each one follows a course for a **time** appointed.
039:023 Allah has revealed (from **time** to **time**) the most
041:021 He created you for the first **time**, and unto Him
041:030 the angels descend on them (from **time** to **time**):
041:036 And if (at any **time**) an incitement to discord
043:011 That sends down (from **time** to **time**) rain from
044:040 is the **time** appointed for all of them,-
045:024 and nothing but **Time** can destroy us."
047:004 therefore (is the **time** for) either generosity or ransom:
052:030 for him some calamity (hatched) by **Time**!"
053:061 Wasting your **time** in vanities?
054:003 but every matter has its appointed **time**.
054:015 And We have left this as a Sign (for all **time**):
054:046 the **time** promised them (for their full recompense):
055:046 But for such as fear the **time** when they will
057:016 Has not the **time** arrived for the Believers
063:011 when the **time** appointed (for it) has come;
067:004 Again turn vision a second **time**: (thy) vision
067:008 every **time** a Group is cast therein, its Keepers
067:026 Say: "As to the knowledge of the **time**, it is
071:007 "And every **time** I have called to them, that thou
073:006 is a **time** when impression is more keen and speech
075:005 (even) in the **time** in front of him.
075:028 And he will think it was (the **Time**) of Parting;
076:001 Has there not been over man a long period of **Time**,
077:011 are (all) appointed a **time** (to collect);-
079:042 'When will be its appointed **time**?'
103:001 By the **time**,

TIMES

002:091 the prophets of Allah in **times** gone by,
002:158 the House in the Season or at other **times**,
002:245 unto his credit and multiply many **times**?
004:103 on Believers at stated **times**.
005:060 these are (many **times**) worse in rank, and far
005:077 of people who went wrong in **times** gone by,-
006:160 ten **times** as much to his credit: he that
007:131 But when good (**times**) came, they said,
009:080 if thou ask seventy **times** for their forgiveness,
014:025 It brings forth its fruit at all **times**, by the
024:006 testify four **times** by Allah that he is of those
024:008 four **times** (with an oath) by Allah,
024:058 these are your three **times** of undress:
024:058 outside those **times** it is not wrong for you or them
033:033 like that of the former **Times** of Ignorance;
037:078 for him among generations to come in later **times**:
037:108 (to come) in later **times**:
037:119 (to come) in later **times**:
037:129 (to come) in later **times**:
040:034 "And to you there came Joseph in **times** gone by,
040:085 ancient **times**). And even thou did the rejecters
056:014 And a few from those of later **times**.
056:040 And a (goodly) number from those of later **times**.
056:049 Say: "Yea, those of old and those of later **times**,

TIPS

003:119 they bite off the very **tips** of their fingers
075:004 in perfect order the very **tips** of his fingers.

TIRED

020:040 and We **tired** thee in various ways.

TO (See Appendix)
TO-DAY

016:063 he is also their patron **to-day**, so but
019:038 But the unjust **to-day** are in error manifest!
020:064 he wins (all along) **to-day** who gains
038:015 These (**to-day**) only wait for a single mighty Blast,
046:020 but **to-day** shall ye be recompensed with a

TO-MORROW

012:012 "Send him with us **to-morrow** to enjoy himself
018:023 "I shall be sure to do so and so **to-morrow**"

TODAY

043:068 My devotees! No fear shall be on you **today**,

TOGETHER

002:148 then strive **together** (as in a race)
002:148 Allah will bring you **together**.
002:229 hold **together** on equitable terms,
002:259 how We bring them **together** and clothe them
003:009 gather mankind **together** against a Day about which
003:012 vanquished and gathered **together** to Hell,
003:025 We gather them **together** against a Day
003:061 say: "Come! let us gather **together**,
003:103 And hold fast, all **together**, by the Rope
003:158 Lo! it is unto Allah that ye are brought **together**.
004:060 **together** for judgment (in their disputes) To the
004:071 or go forth all **together**.
004:087 gather you **together** on the Day of Judgement,
004:172 gather them all **together** unto Himself to (answer).
005:109 gather the Messengers **together**, and ask:
006:012 That He will gather you **together** for
006:022 On the day shall We gather them all **together**: We
006:035 He could gather them **together** unto true guidance:
006:072 that we shall be gathered **together**."
006:111 and We gathered **together** all things
006:128 gather them all **together**, (and say):
007:022 and they began to sew **together** the leaves
007:203 they say: "Why hast thou not got it **together**?"
008:036 gathered **together** to Hell;-
008:037 heap them **together**, and cast them into Hell.
009:036 as they fight you all **together**. But know
009:036 the Pagans all **together** as they fight
009:122 it is not for the Believers to go forth **together**:
010:028 One Day shall We gather them all **together**.
010:045 And on the day when He will gather them **together**:
011:103 is a Day for which mankind will be gathered **together**:
011:119 with Jinns and men all **together**."
012:093 **together** with all your family."
012:102 when they concerted their plans **together** in the
013:021 Those who join **together** those things which
014:008 ye and all on earth **together**,-yet is Allah
014:021 before Allah **together**: then will the weak say to
014:049 that day bound **together** in fetters:-
015:025 gather them **together**: for He
015:030 all of them **together**:
017:071 On the day We shall call **together** all human
017:088 were to gather **together** to produce the like
017:097 gather them **together**, prone on their faces,
017:104 came to pass, We gathered you **together** in a
018:047 gather them, all **together**, nor shall
018:099 and We shall collect them all **together**.
019:068 We shall gather them **together**, and (also)
020:121 to them: they began to sew **together**, for their

TOGETHER (continued)

020:123   He said: "Get ye down both of you,-all **together**,
021:030   joined **together** (as one unit of Creation), before
021:077   so We drowned them (in the Flood) all **together**.
022:073   if they all met **together** for the purpose!
024:031   all **together** towards Allah in repentance that ye
024:043   then joins them **together**, then makes
025:013   And when they are cast, bound **together**, into a
025:017   The Day He will gather them **together** as well
026:038   So the sorcerers were got **together** for the
026:095   "And the whole hosts of Iblis **together**.
027:083   The Day We shall gather **together** from every
028:020   are taking counsel **together** about thee, to slay
032:013   "I will fill Hell with Jinns and men all **together**."
034:026   Say: "Our Lord will gather us **together** and will
034:040   On the Day He will gather them all **together**,
038:038   As also others bound **together** in fetters.
038:073   all of them **together**;
041:011   "Come ye **together**, willingly or unwillingly."
041:011   "We do come (**together**), in willing obedience."
041:019   will be gathered **together** to the Fire, they will
042:015   Allah will bring us **together**, and to
042:029   them **together** when He wills.
045:026   then He will gather you **together** for the Day
046:006   And when mankind are gathered **together**
050:044   that will be a gathering **together**,-quite easy
054:044   "We acting **together** can defend ourselves"?
055:019   He has let free the two Seas meeting **together**:
056:050   "All will certainly be gathered **together** for the
059:014   They will not fight you (even) **together**, except in
065:006   and take mutual counsel **together**, according to
067:024   and to Him shall ye be gathered **together**."
075:004   Nay, We are able to put **together** in perfect order
075:009   And the sun and moon are joined **together**,-
077:025   (as a place) to draw **together**
077:038   We shall Gather you **together** and those before (you)!
081:005   herded **together** (in human habitations);
082:008   does He put thee **together**.
103:003   do righteous deeds, and (join **together**) in the

TOIL

002:155   lives and the fruits (of your **toil**),
035:035   no **toil** nor sense of weariness shall touch
090:004   Verily We have created Man into **toil** and struggle.

TOILING

084:006   ever **toiling** on towards the Lord-painfully toiling,
084:006   painfully **toiling**, but thou shalt meet Him.

TOKENS

015:075   for those who by **tokens** do understand.
030:050   Then behold (O man!) the **tokens** of Allah's Mercy!-
047:018   some **tokens** thereof, and when it comes to them

TOLD

002:033   "When he had **told** them their names,
003:167   these were **told**: "Come, fight in the way of Allah
004:066   what they were (actually) **told**, it would
004:077   to those who were **told** to hold back their hands
004:164   Of some messengers We have already **told** thee the story;
005:113   and to know that thou has indeed **told** us the truth;
009:043   who **told** the truth were seen by thee in a clear
009:046   and they were **told**, "Sit ye among those who sit
012:062   And (Joseph) **told** his servants to put their stock-
017:060   Behold! We **told** thee that thy Lord doth
019:011   he **told** them by signs to celebrate Allah's praises
023:044   We made them as a tale (that is **told**):

TOLD (continued)

026:039   And the people were **told**: "Are ye
026:052   By inspiration We **told** Moses: "Travel by
026:063   Then We **told** Moses by inspiration: "Strike the
027:027   whether thou hast **told** the truth or lied!
031:021   When they are **told** to follow the (revelation)
033:022   and His Messenger **told** us what was true."
034:019   At length We made them as a tale (that is **told**),
036:045   When they are **told**, "Fear ye that which is
036:047   And when they are **told**, "Spend ye
037:035   For they, when they were **told** that there is
039:060   see those who **told** lies against Allah;-their faces
051:043   Behold, they were **told** "Enjoy (your brief day)
058:011   And when ye are **told** to rise up,
058:011   O ye who believe! When ye are **told** to make room
064:007   then shall ye be **told** (the truth)
066:003   He said, "He **told** me Who is the Knower, The Aware."
066:003   she said, "Who **told** thee this?"
066:003   Then when he **told** her thereof,
066:010   on their account, but were **told**: "Enter ye
075:013   That Day will Man be **told** (all) that

TOLL

006:128   much (**toll**) did ye take of men."

TOMES

062:005   which carries huge **tomes** (but understands them not).

TONE

002:069   pure and rich in **tone**,
017:110   nor speak it in a low **tone**, but seek
047:030   know them by the **tone** of their speech! And Allah

TONES

068:023   conversing in secret low **tones**, (saying)-
073:004   in slow, measured rhythmic **tones**.

TONGUE

005:078   by the **tongue** of David and of Jesus
007:176   he (still) lolls out his **tongue**.
007:176   he lolls out his **tongue**, or if
016:103   The **tongue** of him they wickedly point to
019:050   on the **tongue** of truth.
019:097   in thine own **tongue**, that with
026:013   And my **tongue** will not speak (plainly): so send
026:084   on the **tongue** of truth among the
026:195   In the perspicuous Arabic **tongue**.
041:044   What! a foreign (**tongue**) and (a Messenger) an Arab?"
044:058   in thy **tongue**, in order that they may give heed.
046:012   the Arabic **tongue**; to admonish the unjust, and as
075:016   Move not thy **tongue** concerning the (Qur'an)
090:009   And a **tongue**, and a pair of lips?

TONGUES

003:078   a section who distort the Book with their **tongues**;
004:046   their **tongues** and a slander to Faith.
016:062   and their **tongues** assert the falsehood that the
016:116   that your **tongues** may put forth, "This is
024:015   Behold, ye received it on your **tongues**, and said
024:024   On the Day when their **tongues**, their hands,
033:019   they will smite you sharp **tongues**,
048:011   They say with their **tongues** what is not
060:002   their hands and their **tongues** against you for evil;

TOO

002:068   should be neither **too** old nor **too** young,
003:054   and Allah **too** planned,
005:014   From those, **too**, who call themselves Christians,
006:110   We (**too**) shall turn to (confusion) their hearts

TOO (continued)

006:158   Say: "Wait ye: we **too** are waiting."
007:095   "Our fathers (**too**) were touched by suffering
007:100   We could punish them (**too**) for their sins, and
008:030   They plot and plan, and Allah **too** plans, but the
009:052   So wait (expectant); we **too** will wait with you."
010:020   I **too** will wait with you."
010:102   for I **too**, will wait with you."
011:093   for I **too** am watching with you!"
011:122   "And wait ye! we **too** shall wait."
012:003   before this, thou **too** was among those
014:022   a promise of truth: I **too** promised, but I
016:066   And verily in cattle (**too**) will ye find an
021:019   are not **too** proud to serve Him, nor are
021:074   And to Lut, **too**, We gave
023:021   And in cattle (**too**) ye have an instructive example:
023:092   is open: **too** high is He for the partners
027:050   but We **too** planned, even while
032:014   and We **too** will forget you-taste ye
032:030   they **too** are waiting.
033:032   be not **too** complaisant of speech, lest one
037:070   So they (**too**) were rushed down on their footsteps!
038:060   "Nay, ye (**too**)! No welcome for you!
039:030   and truly they (**too**) will die (one day).
039:051   results of their deeds will sone overtake them (**too**),
040:060   but those who are **too** arrogant to serve Me
044:059   for they (**too**) are waiting.
052:031   I **too** will wait along with you!"
054:018   The 'Ad (people) (**too**) rejected (Truth): then how
054:041   To the People of Pharaoh, **too**, aforetime, came Warners
059:011   "If ye are expelled, We **too** will go out with you,

TOOK

002:017   Allah **took** away their light
002:051   ye **took** the calf (for worship),
002:063   And remember We **took** your Covenant
002:083   And remember We **took** a Covenant
002:084   And remember We **took** your Covenant
002:093   And remember We **took** your Covenant
003:081   Behold! Allah **took** the covenant of the Prophets,
003:183   They (also) said: "Allah **took** our promise
003:187   And remember Allah **took** a Covenant from
004:154   And We **took** from them a solemn Covenant.
004:161   That they **took** usury, though they were forbidden;
005:070   We **took** the Covenant of the Children
006:046   **took** away your hearing and your sight, and sealed
007:004   Our punishment **took** them on a sudden by night or
007:005   When (thus) Our punishment **took** them, no cry
007:030   In that they **took** the Satans in
007:051   "Such as **took** their religion to be
007:078   So the earthquake **took** them unawares, and they
007:091   But the earthquake **took** them unawares, and they
007:094   We **took** up its people in suffering
007:095   Behold! We **took** them to account of a sudden,
007:138   We **took** the Children of Israel (with safety)
007:148   They **took** it for worship and they did wrong.
007:152   Those who **took** the calf (for worship) will
007:154   he **took** up the tablets: in the writing
007:173   "Our fathers before us **took** false gods, but we
008:068   reached you for the (ransom) that ye **took**.
008:069   But (now) enjoy what ye **took** in war, lawful
009:050   they say, "We **took** indeed our precautions
010:090   We **took** the Children of Israel across the sea:
012:100   He **took** me out of prison and brought

TOOK (continued)

016:026   but Allah **took** their structures from their
018:061   which **took** its course through the sea
018:063   it **took** its course through the sea
018:106   and **took** My Signs and My Messengers by way of jest.
020:096   so I **took** a handful (of dust) from the
024:011   and to him who **took** on himself the lead among them,
027:020   And he **took** a muster of the Birds; and he
033:007   And remember We **took** from the Prophets
033:007   We **took** from them a solemn Covenant:
046:020   and ye **took** your pleasure out of them: but to-day
051:040   So We **took** him and his forces, and threw
054:029   and he **took** a sword in hand, and hamstrung (her).
072:006   who **took** shelter with persons among the Jinns,

TOOTH

005:045   **tooth** for **tooth**, and wounds equal for equal."

TOP

037:067   Then on **top** of that they will be given
056:054   "And drink Boiling Water on **top** of it:

TOPPED

024:040   **topped** by billow, **topped** by (dark) clouds:

TORAH

003:003   **Torah** (of Moses) and the Gospel (of Jesus).
003:048   the Book and Wisdom, the **Torah** and the Gospel.
003:050   to attest the **Torah** which was before me.
003:065   when the **Torah** and the Gospel were not revealed
003:093   for himself before the **Torah** was revealed.
003:093   Say: "Bring ye the **Torah** and study it,
005:043   when they have (their own) **Torah** before them?
005:044   It was We who revealed the **Torah** (to Moses):
005:046   And confirmation of the **Torah** that had
005:046   confirming the **Torah** that had come before him: We
005:066   If only they had stood fast by the **Torah**, the
005:068   unless ye stand fast by the **Torah**.
005:110   the **Torah** and the Gospel. And behold!
009:111   through the **Torah**, the Gospel, and the Qur'an:

TORE

012:025   and she **tore** his shirt from the back: they both

TORMENT

002:114   an exceeding **torment**.
002:126   to the **torment** of Fire,
002:175   and **Torment** in place of Forgiveness.
002:201   and save us from the **torment** on the Fire!"
005:080   and in **torment** will they abide.

TORMENTS

014:021   (these **torments**) with patience: for ourselves

TORN

012:027   is **torn** from the back, then is she the liar,
012:028   that it was **torn** at the back, (her husband)
014:026   It is **torn** up by the root from the surface
054:020   roots of palm-trees **torn** up (from the ground).

TORNADO

017:068   a violent **tornado** (with showers of stones) so that
029:040   We sent a violent **tornado** (with showers of sones)
054:034   a violent **tornado** with showers of stones,
067:017   violent **tornado** (with showers of stones), so that

TORPID

054:007   (**torpid**) like locusts scattered abroad,

TORRENT

013:017   but the **torrent** bears away the foam that

TOSSED
009:045   so that they are **tossed** in their doubts to and fro.

TOUCH
002:080   not **touch** us but for few numbered days:"
002:275   the Satan by his **touch** hath driven to madness.
003:024   not **touch** us but for a few numbered days":
006:007   so that they could **touch** it with their hands, the
006:017   "If Allah **touch** thee with affliction, none can
006:017   if He **touch** thee with happiness, He hath
006:049   them shall our punishment **touch**, for that
010:107   If Allah do **touch** thee with hurt, there is
011:113   or the Fire will **touch** you; and ye have
015:048   **touch** them, nor shall they (ever) be asked
020:097   '**Touch** me not'; and moreover (for a future penalty)
021:046   of thy Lord do **touch** them, they will
026:156   "**Touch** her not with harm, lest the
028:035   so they shall not be able to **touch** you:
035:035   shall **touch** us therein."
039:061   no evil shall **touch** them, nor shall they grieve.
050:038   nor did any sense of weariness **touch** Us.
054:048   (they will hear): "Tastes ye the **touch** of Hell!"
056:079   Which none shall **touch** but those who are clean:
058:003   should free a slave before they **touch** each other:
058:004   two months consecutively before they **touch** each other,

TOUCHED
003:047   how shall I have a son when man hath **touched** Me?"
003:140   be sure a similar wound hath **touched** the others.
003:140   If a wound hath **touched** you, be sure a similar
003:174   no harm ever **touched** them: for they followed
007:095   **fathers (too) were touched** by suffering and affluence"
007:188   and no evil should have **touched** me:
010:012   for the affliction that **touched** him!
010:021   taste of some mercy after adversity hath **touched** them,
011:010   favours after adversity hath **touched** him,
016:053   are **touched** by distress, unto Him
019:020   seeing that no man has **touched** me, and I am
024:035   though fire scarce **touched** it:
033:049   them before ye have **touched** them, no period
041:050   after some adversity has **touched** him,
055:056   whom no man or Jinn before them has **touched**;-
055:074   Whom no man or Jinn before them has **touched**;-

TOUCHES
030:033   When trouble **touches** men, they cry
039:049   Now, when trouble **touches** man, he cries to Us;
041:049   good (things), but if ill **touches** him, he gives
070:020   Fretful when evil **touches** him;

TOUCHETH
010:012   When trouble **toucheth** a man, he crieth
039:008   When some trouble **toucheth** man he crieth

TOUCHING
004:083   some matter **touching** (public) safety or fear,
020:072   decree (**touching**) the life of this world.

TOWARD
002:177   ye turn your faces **toward** East or West;
006:079   firmly and truly, **toward** Him Who
006:164   Your return in the end is **toward** Allah: He will

TOWARDS
002:037   and his Lord turned **towards** him;
002:054   Then He turned **towards** you (in forgiveness):
002:148   (as in a race) **towards** all that is good.
007:047   turned **towards** the Companions of the Fire, they
008:061   But if the enemy incline **towards** peace, do thou

TOWARDS (continued)
008:061   do thou (also) incline **towards** peace, and trust
010:035   any that can give guidance **towards** Truth?"
010:035   is there any that can give any guidance **towards** Truth.
010:105   face **towards** Religion with true piety, and never
011:070   not reaching **towards** the (meal), he felt
011:078   And his people came rushing **towards** him, and they
012:033   inclined **towards** them and join the
012:071   They said, turning **towards** them: "What is it
014:037   among men with love **towards** them, and feed
014:043   their gaze returning not **towards** them, and their
017:051   their heads **towards** thee, and say, "When will
018:016   of your affair **towards** comfort and ease."
019:025   "And shake **towards** thyself the trunk
024:031   all together **towards** Allah in repentance that ye
025:046   Then We draw it in **towards** Ourselves,-
028:022   Then when he turned his face **towards** (the land of)
028:076   but he acted insolently **towards** them:
029:021   He pleases, and **towards** Him are ye turned.
039:056   in that I neglected (my Duty) **towards** Allah,
042:053   all affairs tend **towards** Allah!
046:024   advancing **towards** their valleys, they said,
046:029   Behold, We turned **towards** thee a company of Jinns
054:008   with eyes transfixed, **towards** the Caller!-
075:023   Looking **towards** their Lord;
084:006   ever toiling on **towards** the Lord-painfully toiling,

TOWERING
011:042   on the waves (**towering**) like mountains, and Noah

TOWERS
004:078   even if ye are in **towers** built up strong and high!"

TOWN
002:058   And remember We said: "Enter this **town**,
002:061   Go ye down to any **town**,
004:075   "Our Lord! rescue us from this **town**.
006:123   Thus have We placed leaders in every **town**, its
007:094   Whenever We sent a prophet to a **town**, We took
007:161   "Dwell in this **town** and eat therein as ye wish,
007:163   the **town** standing close by the sea. Behold!
012:082   Ask at the **town** where we have been and the
017:016   When We decide to destroy a **town**, We command
018:019   with this money of yours to the **town**:
018:077   when they came to the inhabitants of a **town**,
018:082   two youths, orphans, in the **Town**; there was
021:074   the **town** which practiced abominations: truly they
025:040   have passed by the **town** on which was rained
025:051   We could have sent a warner to every **town**.
026:208   Never did We destroy a **town** but had its warners-
028:059   a **town** until He had sent to its Centre

TOWNS
006:131   the **towns** unjustly whilst their occupants
007:004   How many **towns** have We destroyed
007:096   If the people of the **towns** had but
007:097   Did the people of the **towns** feel secure
007:101   Such were the **towns** whose story We (thus)
011:117   to destroy the **towns** unjustly while their people
012:109   (men) from the peoples of the **towns**.
018:059   Such were the **towns** We destroyed when they
021:006   the **towns** which We destroyed believed: will these
021:011   How many were the **towns**. We utterly
028:058   And how many **towns** We destroyed, which exulted
046:027   We destroyed aforetime **towns** round about you;

TOWNSHIP
010:098 a single **township** (among those We warmed),
029:031 the people of this **township**: for truly
029:034 on the people of this **township** a Punishment

TOWNSHIPS
059:007 the **townships**,-belongs to Allah,-to His Messenger,
059:014 except in fortified **townships**, or from

TOYING
021:003 Their hearts **toying** as with trifles.

TRACE
028:011 And she said to the sister of (Moses), "**Trace** him."
053:051 And the Thamud, He left no **trace** of them.

TRACES
029:038 to you from (the **traces**) of their buildings
040:021 and in the **traces** (they have left) in the land:
040:082 and in the **traces** (they have left) in the land:
048:029 (being) the **traces** of their prostration. This is

TRACT
015:080 Rocky **Tract** also rejected the Messengers:
018:093 Until, when he reached (a **tract**) between two

TRACTS
013:004 And in the earth are **tracts** (diverse though)
023:017 And We have made, above you, seven **tracts**;
035:027 the mountains are **tracts** white and red,
067:015 so traverse ye through its **tracts** and enjoy

TRADE
002:273 seeking (for **trade** or work):
002:275 permitted **trade** and forbidden usury.
002:275 "**Trade is** like usury,"
004:029 you traffic and **trade** by mutual good-will:
024:037 By men whom neither **trade** nor sale can divert

TRAFFIC
002:016 but their **traffic** is profitless,
002:079 to **traffic** with it for a miserable price!
004:029 you **traffic** and trade by mutual good-will:
004:044 They **traffic** in error, and wish
062:009 and leave off business (and **traffic**):

TRAIL
002:164 and the clouds which they **trail** like their slaves

TRAIN
002:210 with angels (in His **train**)

TRAINED
002:071 He said: "He says, a heifer not **trained**

TRAINING
005:004 **training** them to hunt in the manner directed

TRAITOR
025:029 a **traitor** to man!

TRAMPLING
048:025 **trampling** down and on whose account a guilt

TRANQUILLITY
006:096 He makes the night for rest and **tranquillity**,
030:021 that ye may dwell in **tranquillity** with them,
048:004 It is He who sent down **Tranquillity** into the
048:018 and He sent down **tranquillity** to them, and He
048:026 Allah sent down His **tranquillity** to His

TRANSACTION
002:282 but if it be a **transaction** which ye carry out

TRANSACTIONS
002:282 in **transactions** involving future obligations

TRANSCRIBE
029:048 nor art thou (able) to **transcribe** it with

TRANSFIXED
054:008 Hastening, with eyes **transfixed**, towards the

TRANSFORMED
005:060 He **transformed** into apes and swine, those who
036:067 We could have **transformed** them in their places;

TRANSGRESS
002:190 those who fight you but do not **transgress** limits;
002:194 **transgress** ye likewise against him.
002:229 so do not **transgress** them
002:229 if any do **transgress** the limits ordained by Allah,
004:014 and **transgress** His limits will be admitted
004:154 "**Transgress** not in the matter of the Sabbath."
005:094 any who **transgress** thereafter will have
006:119 Thy Lord knoweth best those who **transgress**.
010:023 behold! they **transgress** insolently through the
011:112 and **transgress** not (from the Path):
017:016 continued to **transgress**; so that the word is
020:045 or lest he **transgress** all bounds."
032:022 who **transgress** We shall exact (Due) Retribution.
040:034 leave to stray such as **transgress** and live
042:027 they would indeed **transgress** beyond all bounds
042:042 and insolently **transgress** beyond bounds
046:035 destroyed except those who **transgress**?
050:027 "Our Lord! I did not make him **transgress**, but he
055:008 In order that ye may not **transgress** (due) balance.
055:020 which they do not **transgress**:
096:006 Nay, but man doth **transgress** all bounds,

TRANSGRESSED
002:065 amongst you who **transgressed** in the matter
003:112 and **transgressed** beyond bounds.
003:147 that **transgressed** our duty:
007:162 For that they repeatedly **transgressed**.
007:163 Behold! they **transgressed** in the matter
007:166 they **transgressed** (all) prohibition, We said
009:010 It is they who have **transgressed** all bounds.
010:083 and one who **transgressed** all bounds.
020:024 for he had indeed **transgressed** all bounds."
020:043 for he has indeed **transgressed** all bounds;
021:009 those who **transgressed** beyond bounds.
030:047 then, to those who **transgressed**, We meted
034:032 Nay, rather it was ye who **transgressed**."
039:053 Servants who have **transgressed** against their souls!
046:020 and that ye (ever) **transgressed**."
050:025 "Who forbade what was good, **transgressed** all bounds,
051:046 for they wickedly **transgressed**.
068:031 We have indeed **transgressed**!
079:017 for he has indeed **transgressed** all bounds:
079:037 Then, for such as had **transgressed** all bounds,
089:011 (All) these **transgressed** beyond bounds in the lands.

TRANSGRESSES
002:194 If then any one **transgresses** the prohibition against you,
020:127 him who **transgresses** beyond bounds and believes
040:028 not one who **transgresses** and lies!
049:009 the one that **transgresses** until it complies
049:009 **transgresses** beyond bounds against the other,
065:001 and any who **transgresses** the limits of Allah,

TRANSGRESSING
002:061 rebelled and went on **transgressing**.
002:173 nor **transgressing** due limits,
006:049 for that they ceased not from **transgressing**.
006:145 nor **transgressing** due limits,-thy Lord
007:081 ye are indeed a people **transgressing** beyond bounds."
016:115 nor **transgressing** due limits,-then Allah

TRANSGRESSING (continued)

026:166 Nay, ye are a people **transgressing** (all limits)!"
036:019 Nay, but ye are a people **transgressing** all bounds!"
043:005 a people **transgressing** beyond bounds?
051:053 themselves a people **transgressing** beyond bounds!
052:032 a people **transgressing** beyond bounds?
068:012 (all) good, **transgressing** beyond bounds, deep in

TRANSGRESSION

002:035 or ye run into harm and **transgression**."
002:085 in guilt and **transgression**;
005:002 **transgression** (and hostility on your part).
005:003 with no inclination to **transgression**, Allah is
005:062 **transgression** and their eating of things forbidden.
007:163 for they were given to **transgression**.
007:165 because they were given to **transgression**.
017:060 their inordinate **transgression**!
023:075 they would obstinately persist in their **transgression**,
027:012 a people rebellious in **transgression**."

TRANSGRESSOR

011:059 every powerful, obstinate **transgressor**.
014:015 the lot of every powerful obstinate **transgressor**.
083:012 the **Transgressor** beyond bounds, the Sinner!

TRANSGRESSORS

002:059 But the **transgressors** changed the word
002:059 so We sent on the **transgressors**
002:190 for Allah loveth not **transgressors**.
003:082 they are perverted **transgressors**.
003:110 but most of them are perverted **transgressors**.
007:162 But the **transgressors** among them changed the
010:012 Thus do the deeds of **transgressors** seem fair
010:074 Thus do We seal the hearts of the **transgressors**.
023:007 those limits are **transgressors**;-
024:004 for such men are wicked **transgressors**;-
030:055 be established, the **transgressors** will swear that
030:057 will avail the **Transgressors**, nor will
031:011 nay, but the **Transgressors** are in manifest error.
040:043 to Allah; and the **Transgressors** will be
044:031 arrogant (even) among inordinate **transgressors**.
053:052 and most insolent **transgressors**,
057:016 are rebellious **transgressors**.
057:026 but many of them became rebellious **transgressors**.
057:027 but many of them are rebellious **transgressors**.
059:005 cover with shame the rebellious **transgressors**.
059:019 Such are the rebellious **transgressors**!
061:005 Allah guides not those who are rebellious **transgressors**.
063:006 Truly Allah guides not rebellious **transgressors**.
070:031 beyond this are **transgressors**;-
078:022 For the **transgressors** a place of destination:

TRANSITORY

017:018 **transitory** things (of this life), We readily

TRANSMITTED

051:053 Is this the legacy they have **transmitted**, one to

TRANSPORT

017:070 provided them with **transport** on land and sea;

TRANSPOSING

009:037 Verily the **transposing** (of a prohibited month)

TRAVAIL

031:014 in **travail** upon **travail** did his mother bear him.

TRAVEL

002:273 in Allah's cause are restricted (from **travel**).
003:137 **travel** through the earth, and see what was the end
004:101 When ye **travel** through the earth, there is

TRAVEL (continued)

005:096 for the benefit of yourselves and those who **travel**;
006:011 Say: "**Travel** through the earth and see what was
011:081 Now **travel** with thy family while yet a part
012:109 Do they not **travel** through the earth,
015:065 "Then **travel** by night with thy household, when a
016:036 So **travel** through the earth, and see what was
016:080 when ye **travel** and when ye stop (in your travels),
018:060 or (until) I spend years and years in **travel**."
020:077 "**Travel** by night with my servants, and strike
022:046 Do they not **travel** through the land, so that
026:052 "**Travel** by night with My servants; for surely
029:020 Say: "**Travel** through the earth and see how
030:009 Do they not **travel** through the earth, and see
030:042 Say: "**Travel** through the earth and see
034:018 "**Travel** therein, secure, by night and by day."
035:044 Do they not **travel** through the earth, and see
040:021 Do they not **travel** through the earth and see
040:082 Do they not **travel** through the earth and see
047:010 Do they not **travel** through the earth, and see
084:019 Ye shall surely **travel** from stage to stage.

TRAVELLERS

012:010 he will be picked up by some caravan of **travellers**."
012:019 Then there came a caravan of **travellers**: they sent

TRAVELLING

003:156 when they are **travelling** through the earth
028:029 and was **travelling** with his family, he perceived
073:020 in ill-health; others **traveling** through the land,

TRAVELS

016:080 and when you stop (in your **travels**);

TRAVERSE

010:022 **traverse** through land and sea; till when ye
036:039 for her stations (to **traverse**) till she returns
067:015 so **traverse** ye through its tracts and enjoy

TREACHEROUS

008:058 for Allah loveth not the **treacherous**.
008:071 But if they have **treacherous** designs against thee,
105:002 Did He not make their **treacherous** plan go astray?

TREACHERY

008:058 If thou fearest **treachery** from any group, throw
040:019 (Allah) knows the **treachery** of the eyes, and all

TREASON

008:071 they have already been in **treason** against Allah,

TREASURE

004:020 the latter a whole **treasure** for dower, take not
009:035 (**treasure**) which ye hoarded for yourselves:
011:012 lest they say, "Why is not a **treasure** sent down
012:019 So they concealed him as a **treasure**! But Allah
018:082 there was, beneath it, a buried **treasure**, to which
018:082 and get out their **treasure**-a mercy
025:008 "Or (why) has not a **treasure** been bestowed

TREASURES

006:050 with me are the **treasures** of Allah, nor do I
006:059 the **treasures** that none knoweth but He.
009:035 taste ye, then, the (**treasures**) ye hoarded!"
011:031 are the **Treasures** of Allah, nor do
015:021 (sources and) **treasures** (inexhaustible) are with
017:100 the **Treasures** of the Mercy of my Lord, behold
026:058 **Treasures**, and every kind of honorable position;
028:076 such were the **treasures** We had bestowed on him,
038:009 Or have they the **Treasures** of the Mercy
052:037 Or are the **Treasures** of thy Lord with them,

TREASURES (continued)
063:007 But to Allah belong the **treasures** of the

TREAT
002:083 **treat** with kindness your parents
002:231 Do not **treat** Allah's Signs as a jest,
004:019 Nor should ye **treat** them with harshness,
006:031 Lost indeed are they who **treat** it as a falsehood
006:150 of such as **treat** Our Signs as falsehoods, and
007:036 and **treat** them with arrogance,-they are
007:040 and **treat** them with arrogance, no opening
012:088 and **treat** it as charity to us; for Allah
018:049 thy Lord **treat** with injustice.
018:056 to weaken the truth, and they **treat** My Signs
018:086 to punish them, or to **treat** them with kindness."
021:036 they **treat** thee not except with ridicule.
023:105 and ye did but **treat** them as falsehoods?"
025:041 they **treat** thee no otherwise than in mockery:
029:010 they **treat** men's oppression as if it were the Wrath
035:006 so **treat** him as an enemy.
038:022 with truth, and **treat** us not with injustice,
038:028 Shall We **treat** those who believe and work
038:028 Shall We **treat** those who guard against evil,
038:063 "Did we **treat** them (as such) in ridicule, or have
064:010 and **treat** Our Signs as falsehoods, they will
068:035 Shall We then **treat** the People of Faith
093:009 Therefore, **treat** not the orphan with harshness,

TREATED
002:233 **treated** unfairly on account of her child.
007:009 for that they wrongfully **treated** Our Signs.
008:054 they **treated** as false the Signs of their Lord so We
008:060 unto you, and ye shall not be **treated** unjustly.
012:110 think that they were **treated** as liars,
017:059 but they **treated** her wrongfully: We only
017:059 of former generations **treated** them as false:
023:110 "But ye **treated** them with ridicule, so much
025:030 "O my Lord, Truly my people **treated** this Qur'an
078:028 But they (impudently) **treated** Our Signs as false

TREATIES
009:004 (But the **treaties** are) not dissolved with those

TREATMENT
005:060 by the **treatment** it received from Allah?

TREATY
004:090 between whom and you there is a **treaty** (of peace),
004:092 with whom ye have a **treaty** of mutual alliance,
008:072 ye have a **treaty** of mutual alliance.
009:003 dissolve (**treaty**) obligations with the Pagans.
009:007 whom ye made a **treaty** near the sacred mosque?

TREE
002:035 but approach not this **tree**,
007:019 but approach not this **tree**, lest you
007:020 "Your Lord only forbade you this **tree**, lest
007:022 "Did I not forbid you that **tree**, and tell
007:022 when they tasted of the **tree**, their shameful
014:024 a goodly **tree**, whose root is firmly fixed, and its
014:026 And the parable of an evil Word is that of an evil **tree**:
017:060 as also the Cursed **Tree** (mentioned) in the Qur-an:
020:120 to the **Tree** of Eternity and to a kingdom
020:121 In the result, they both ate of the **tree**, and so
023:020 Also a **tree** springing out of Mount Sinai,
024:035 lit from a blessed **Tree**, an Olive, neither of
028:030 of the valley, from a **tree** in hallowed ground:
036:080 out of the green **tree**, when behold!
037:062 or the **Tree** of Zaqqum?

TREE (continued)
037:064 For it is a **tree** that springs out of
044:043 Verily the **tree** of Zaqqum
048:018 to thee under the **Tree**: He knew
056:052 "Ye will surely taste of the **Tree** of Zaqqum.
056:072 Is it ye who grow the **tree** which feeds the fire,

TREES
016:068 to build its cells in hills, on **trees**, and in
017:091 of date **trees** and vines, and cause rivers
022:018 the stars; the hills, the **trees**, the animals;
027:060 to cause the growth of the **trees** in them.
031:027 And if all the **trees** on earth were pens and the
055:006 And the herbs and the **trees**-both (alike)
056:029 Among Talh **trees** with flowers (or fruits)
080:030 And enclosed Gardens, dense with lofty **trees**,

TREES-GROWING
013:004 with corn, and palm **trees-growing** out of single

TRELLISES
006:141 with **trellises** and without, and dates, and tilth

TREMBLE
039:023 who fear their Lord **tremble** thereat; then their

TREMENDOUS
002:049 therein was a **tremendous** trial from your Lord.
014:006 a **tremendous** trial from your Lord."
033:011 as by a **tremendous** shaking.
038:067 Say: "That is a **Tremendous** tidings.
045:010 for them is a **tremendous** Chastisement.
071:022 "And they have devised a **tremendous** Plot.

TREMOR
008:002 fell a **tremor** in their hearts, and when

TRESPASS
007:055 those who **trespass** beyond bounds.
051:034 who **trespass** beyond bounds."
070:031 But those who **trespass** beyond this

TRESPASSED
005:107 and that we have not **trespassed** (beyond the truth):

TRESPASSES
002:015 and give them rope in their **trespasses**;
006:110 We shall leave them in their **trespasses**, to
007:033 sins and **trespasses** against truth or reason;
007:186 He will leave them in their **trespasses**, wandering
010:011 in their **trespasses**, wandering in

TRESPASSING
005:077 **trespassing** beyond the truth, nor follow the vain

TRIAL
002:049 therein was a tremendous **trial** from your Lord.
002:102 "We are only for **trial**,
004:006 Make **trial** of orphans until they reach
005:041 If any one's **trial** is intended by Allah, thou
005:071 They thought there would be no **trial** (or punishment);
005:094 make a **trial** of you in a little matter of game
007:141 in that was a momentous **trial** from your Lord.
007:155 This is no more than Thy **trial**: by it Thou
007:163 thus We made a **trial** of them, for they were
008:025 And fear the **trial** which affecteth not in
008:028 and your progeny are but a **trial**:
009:049 "Grant me exemption and draw me not into **trial**."
009:049 Have they not fallen into **trial** already?
010:085 Our Lord! make us not a **trial** for those
014:006 a tremendous **trial** from your Lord."
017:060 which We showed thee, but as a **trail** for men,-

TRIAL (continued)

021:035 and by good by way of **trial**.
021:111 "I know not but that it may be a **trial** for you,
022:011 but if a **trial** comes to them, they turn
022:053 but a **trial** for those in whose hearts is a
024:063 lest some **trial** befall them, or a
025:020 We have made some of you as a **trial** for others:
027:047 yea, ye are a people under **trial**."
037:063 have truly made it (as) a **trial** for the wrong-doers.
037:106 For this was a clear **trial**-
039:049 Nay, but this is but a **trial**, but most
044:033 in which there was a manifest **trial**.
051:014 "Taste ye your **trial**! this is what
054:027 by way of **trial** for them.
060:005 Make us not a (test and) **trial** for the Unbelievers,
064:015 Your riches and your children may be but a **trial**:
074:031 have fixed their number only as **trial** for Unbelievers,-

TRIALS

002:214 without such (**trials**) as came to those
016:110 leave their homes after **trials** and persecutions

TRIBE

007:027 for he and his **tribe** see you from a position

TRIBES

002:136 and to Abraham, Isma'il, Isaac, Jacob, and the **Tribes**,
002:140 and the **Tribes** were Jews or Christians?
003:084 Abraham, Isma'il; Isaac, Jacob, and the **Tribes**,
004:163 Isma'il, Isaac, Jacob and the **Tribes**, to Jesus,
007:160 We divided them into twelve **tribes** or nations.
049:013 and made you into nations and **tribes**, that ye

TRIBUNAL

014:014 the time when they shall stand before My **tribunal**,-
079:040 their Lord's (**tribunal**) and had restrained (their)

TRIBUTE

018:094 shall we then render thee **tribute** in order that
018:095 my Lord has established me is better (than **tribute**):
028:057 to which are brought as **tribute** fruits of

TRICK

007:123 Surely this is a **trick** which ye have planned
020:069 a magician's **trick**: and the magician succeeds not.
077:039 Now, if ye have a **trick** (or plot),

TRIED

002:124 was **tried** by his lord with certain Commands,
003:186 Ye shall certainly be **tried** and tested
007:168 We have **tried** them with both prosperity
009:126 not that they are **tried** every year once or twice?
021:012 they (**tried** to) flee from it.
033:011 In that situation were the Believers **tried**:
038:024 We had **tried** him: he asked forgiveness of his Lord,
051:013 be **tried** (and tested) over the Fire!
068:017 Verily We have **tried** them as We **tried** the People

TRIETH

089:015 Now, as for man, when his Lord **trieth** him,
089:016 But when He **trieth** him, restricting his

TRIFLES

021:003 Their hearts toying as with **trifles**.
052:012 That play (and paddle) in shallow **trifles**.

TRIFLING

003:111 barring a **trifling** annoyance;
006:091 in vain discourse and **trifling**.

TRINITY

005:073 Allah is one of three in a **Trinity**: for there

TRINKETS

043:018 Is then one brought up among **trinkets**, and unable

TRIP

068:051 And the Unbelievers would almost **trip** thee up

TRIUMPH

004:141 Unbelievers a way (to **triumph**) over the Believers.
005:056 the party of Allah that must certainly **triumph**.
005:119 mighty **Triumph** (the fulfillment of all desires).
006:016 and that would be a Mighty **Triumph**.
009:072 Pleasure of Allah: that is the supreme **triumph**.
009:089 that is the supreme **triumph**.
009:100 that is the supreme **Triumph**.
010:064 This is indeed the supreme **Triumph**.
024:052 and do right, that will **triumph**.
028:035 with Our Signs shall ye **triumph**,-you two
037:060 Verily this is the supreme **Triumph**!
045:030 to His Mercy: that will be the manifest **triumph**.
048:005 the grand **triumph**,
057:012 This is indeed the highest **Triumph**.
061:012 that is indeed the supreme **Triumph**.
064:009 that will be the Supreme **Triumph**.
085:011 that is the great **Triumph**.

TROD

006:161 the Path (**trod**) by Abraham the true in faith,
009:120 or **trod** paths to raise the ire of the Unbelievers,

TROOP

008:016 or to retreat to a **troop** (of his own)-he draws
027:083 from every people a **troop** of those who reject
038:059 Here is a **troop** rushing headlong with you!

TROUBLE

005:101 if made plain to you, may cause you **trouble**.
007:129 They said: "We have had (nothing but) **trouble**,
010:012 When **trouble** toucheth a man, he crieth
020:040 but We saved thee from **trouble**, and We
030:033 When **trouble** touches men, they cry
039:008 When some **trouble** toucheth man he crieth
039:049 Now, when **trouble** touches man, he cries to Us;

TROUBLES

017:056 the power to remove your **troubles** from you

TRUE

002:005 They are on (**true**) guidance,
002:016 and they have lost **true** direction.
002:133 the one (**True**) God;
002:135 the Religion of Abraham the **True**,
003:007 but no one knows its **true** meanings except Allah.
003:017 who are **true** (in word and deed);
003:062 This is the **true** account: there is no
003:073 Say: "**True** guidance is the guidance of Allah:
003:086 and bore witness that the Messenger was **true**
003:139 for ye must gain mastery if ye are **true** in Faith.
003:141 **true** in faith and deprive of blessings
004:125 way of Abraham the **true** in faith?
005:108 in its **true** nature and shape, or else
006:035 He could gather them together unto **true** guidance:
006:062 their **True** Protector, surely His is
006:146 for We are **True** (in Our ordinances).
006:161 the Path (trod) by Abraham the **true** in faith,
007:008 The balance that day will be **true** (to a nicety):
007:044 the promises of our Lord to us **true**: have you
007:044 have you also found your Lord's promises **true**?"
007:053 did indeed bring **true** (tidings).
007:102 not men (**true**) to their covenant: but most

TRUE (continued)

009:007   stand **true** to you, stand ye **true** to them: for Allah
009:018   It is they who are expected to be on **true** guidance.
009:094   the **true** state of matters concerning you:
010:004   The promise of Allah is **true** and sure.
010:032   Such is Allah, your **true** Lord:
010:033   proved **true** against those who rebel:
010:045   and refused to receive **true** guidance.
010:053   "Is that **true**?" Say: "Aye! by my Lord! It is
010:055   that Allah's promise is assuredly **true**? Yet most
010:105   face towards Religion with **true** piety, and never
011:003   good (and **true**), for a term appointed, and bestow
011:045   and Thy promise is **true**, and Thou art
012:026   seduce me-from my (**true**) self."
012:026   then is her tale **true**, and he is a liar!
012:032   from his (**true**) self but he did firmly save
012:051   he is indeed of those who are (ever) **true** (and virtuous).
012:100   Allah hath made it come **true**! He was
013:014   To Him is due the **true** prayer any others
014:011   "**True**, we are human like yourselves, but Allah
016:120   devoutly obedient to Allah, (and) **true** in faith,
016:123   "Follow the ways of Abraham the **True** in Faith,
017:016   the word is proved **true** against them; then We
017:025   turn to Him again and again (in **true** penitence).
017:097   that is on **true** guidance; but he
017:107   it is **true** that those who were given knowledge
018:021   that the promise of Allah it **true**, and that
018:044   from Allah, the **True** One. He is
018:098   and the promise of My Lord is **true**."
019:054   (strictly) **true** to what he promised, and he
020:082   and do right,-who, in fine, are no **true** guidance."
021:097   Then will the **True** Promise draw nigh
022:031   Being **true** in faith to Allah, and never
024:017   if ye are (**true**) Believers.
026:182   And weigh with scales **true** and upright.
026:197   of the Children of Israel knew it (as **true**)?
027:022   from Saba with tidings **true**.
027:031   but come to me in submission (to the **true** Religion).'"
027:068   "It is **true** we were promised this,-we and
028:013   the promise of Allah is **true**: but most
028:056   It is **true** thou wilt not be able to guide
028:080   those who had been granted (**true**) knowledge said:
028:085   that brings **true** guidance, and who
029:003   who are **true** from those who are false.
030:030   that is the **true** Religion: but most
030:060   for verily the promise of Allah is **true**: nor let
031:005   These are on (**true**) guidance from their Lord;
031:009   The promise of Allah is **true**:
031:033   Verily, the promise of Allah is **true**:
032:013   certainly have brought every soul its **true** guidance:
032:013   but the Word from Me will come **true**, "I Will
033:022   and His Messenger told us what was **true**."
033:023   been **true** to their Covenant with Allah:
033:035   for **true** men and women, for men
034:020   And on them did Satan prove **true** his idea,
034:023   'That which is **true** and just; and He
035:005   O men! certainly the promise of Allah is **true**,
036:007   The Word is proved **true** against the greater
036:048   if what ye say is **true**?"
036:052   And **true** was the word of the messengers!"
036:070   may be proved **true** against those who
037:031   "So now has been proved **true**, against us,
038:034   but he did turn (to Us in **true** devotion):

TRUE (continued)

038:064   That is **true**,-the mutual recriminations of the
039:005   the heavens and the earth in **true** (proportions):
039:006   then how are ye turned away (from your **true** Lord)?
039:071   The answer will be: "**True**: but the Decree
039:071   has been proved **true** against the Unbelievers!"
040:006   proved **true** against the Unbelievers; that truly
040:055   for the Promise of Allah is **true**:
040:077   For the Promise of Allah is **true**:
044:036   if what ye say is **true**!"
045:011   This is (**true**) Guidance: and for those who reject
045:025   our forefathers, if what ye say is **true**!"
045:032   when it was said that the promise of Allah was **true**,
046:017   For the promise of Allah is **true**."
046:018   the word proved **true** among the previous generations
047:021   it were best for them if they were **true** to Allah.
049:017   if ye be **true** and sincere.
051:005   Verily that which ye are promised is **true**;
056:087   if ye are **true** (in your claim of Independence)?
057:014   will reply, "**True**! but ye led yourselves into
068:007   who receive (**True**) Guidance.
072:006   '**True**, there were persons among mankind who took
073:007   **True**, there is for thee by day prolonged occupation
078:039   That is the **True** Day: therefore, whoso will,
098:005   being **True** (in faith); to establish

TRUER

004:087   And whose word can be **truer** than Allah's?
004:122   and whose word can be **truer** than Allah's?
005:107   "We affirm that our witness is **truer** than that

TRULY

003:079   Him (Who is **truly** the Cherisher of all)
003:181   "**Truly**, Allah is indigent and we are rich!"
003:192   **truly** Thou coverest with shame,
004:033   For **truly** Allah is witness to all things.
005:012   he hath **truly** wandered from the path of rectitude."
005:049   And **truly** most men are rebellious.
006:019   And I **truly** am innocent of (your blasphemy of)
006:063   (we vow) we shall **truly** show our gratitude.'?"
006:079   firmly and **truly**, toward Him Who
006:082   that are (**truly**) in security, for they
006:162   Say: "**Truly**, my prayer and my
007:134   we shall **truly** believe in thee, and we
007:153   but repent thereafter and (**truly**) believe,-
009:028   O ye who believe! **Truly** the Pagans are unclean;
009:075   and be **truly** amongst those who are righteous.
010:022   from this, we shall **truly** show our gratitude!
010:036   **truly** conjecture can be of no avail against Truth.
011:033   He said: "**Truly**, Allah will bring it on you
011:087   **Truly**, thou art the one that forbeareth with
012:008   They said: "**Truly** Joseph and his brother are loved
012:023   **Truly** to no good come those who do wrong!"
012:023   He said: "Allah forbid! **truly** (thy husband) is my
012:028   **Truly**, mighty is your snare!
012:029   for **truly** thou hast been at fault!
012:030   her slave **truly** hath he inspired her with violent
012:087   **truly** no one despairs of Allah's soothing Mercy,
012:095   They said: "By Allah! **truly** thou art in thine
012:097   for we were **truly** at fault."
013:007   But thou art **truly** a warner, and to
013:027   Say: "**Truly** Allah leaveth, to stray, whom He
013:031   But, **truly**, the Command is with Allah
013:034   this world, but harder, **truly** is the Chastisement
014:007   **truly** My punishment is terrible indeed."

TRULY (continued)

014:038	"O our Lord! **truly** Thou dost know what we
014:039	for **truly** my Lord is He, the Hearer of Prayer!
015:006	**Truly** thou art mad (or possessed)!
016:041	but **truly** the reward of the Hereafter will be greater.
017:040	**Truly** ye utter a most dreadful saying!
017:108	**Truly** has the promise of our Lord been fulfilled!"
018:062	**truly** we have suffered much fatigue at this
018:069	if Allah so will, (**truly**) patient: nor shall
018:071	**Truly** a strange thing hast thou done!"
018:074	**Truly** a foul (unheard-of) thing hast thou done!"
019:006	"(One that) will (**truly**) inherit me, and inherit
019:027	"O Mary! **truly** a strange thing hast thou brought!
020:094	**Truly** I feared lest thou shouldst say, 'Thou hast
021:074	**truly** they were a people given to Evil,
021:077	**truly** they were a people given to Evil: so We
021:083	to his Lord "**Truly** distress has seized me,
021:097	nay, we **truly** did wrong!"
021:104	**truly** shall We fulfil it.
021:106	for people who would (**truly**) worship Allah.
022:032	come **truly** from piety of heart.
022:046	**Truly** it is not the eyes that are blind, but the
022:058	**truly** Allah is He Who bestows the best Provision.
022:066	**truly** man is a most ungrateful creature!
023:071	with their desires, **truly** the heavens and the
025:030	"O my Lord, **Truly** my people treated this Qur'an
025:071	has **truly** turned to Allah in repentance:
026:027	(Pharaoh) said: "**Truly** your messenger who has
026:097	"'By Allah, we were **truly** in an error manifest,
026:102	we shall **truly** be of those who believe!'"
026:117	**truly** my people have rejected me.
026:135	"**Truly** I fear for you the Chastisement
027:010	fear not: **truly**, in My presence, those called
027:011	**truly**, I am Oft-Forgiving, Most Merciful.
027:040	**truly** my Lord is Free of All Needs, Supreme in
027:040	**truly** his gratitude is (a gain) for his own soul;
027:080	**Truly** thou canst not cause the Dead to listen,
028:004	**Truly** Pharaoh elated himself in the land
028:018	"Thou art **truly**, one erring manifestly."
028:024	**truly** am I in (desperate) need of any good that
028:026	**truly** the best of men for thee to employ
028:032	for **truly** they are a people rebellious and wicked."
028:079	For he is **truly** a lord of mighty good fortune."
029:019	**truly** that is easy for Allah.
029:031	for **truly** they are wicked men."
029:041	but **truly** the flimsiest of houses is the
029:056	O My servants who believe! **truly**, spacious is My Earth:
030:008	yet are there **truly** many among men who deny
030:030	So set thou thy face **truly** to the religion
033:013	"**Truly** our houses are bare and exposed,"
033:045	O Prophet! **Truly** We have sent thee as a Witness,
033:053	**Truly** such a thing is in Allah's sight an enormity.
033:060	**Truly**, if the Hypocrites, and those in whose
035:028	Those **truly** fear Allah,
036:014	they said, "**Truly**, we have been sent on a
037:012	**Truly** dost thou marvel, while they ridicule,
037:032	for **truly** we were ourselves astray."
037:033	**Truly**, that day, they will (all) share
037:063	For We have **truly** made it (as) a trial
037:066	**Truly** they will eat thereof and fill
037:069	**Truly** they found their fathers on the wrong Path;
037:071	And **truly** before them, many of
038:005	**Truly** this is a strange thing!"

TRULY (continued)

038:006	For this is **truly** a thing designed (against you)!
038:024	**truly** many are the Partners (in business) who wrong
038:032	And he said, "**Truly** do I prefer wealth to the
038:044	**Truly** We found him full of patience and constancy.
038:047	They were, in Our sight, **truly**, of the
038:054	**Truly** such will be Our Bounty (to you); it will
038:059	**Truly**, they shall burn in the Fire!
038:065	Say: "**Truly** am I a Warner: no god
039:003	**Truly** Allah will judge between them in that
039:007	**truly** Allah hath no need of you; but He
039:010	will **truly** receive a reward without measure!"
039:015	Say: "**Truly**, those in loss are those who lose
039:021	**Truly**, in this, is a Message of remembrance
039:030	and **truly** they (too) will die (one day).
039:030	**Truly** thou wilt die (one day)
039:065	**truly** fruitless will be thy work (in life),
039:074	Who has **truly** fulfilled His promise to us,
040:006	that **truly** they are Companions of Fire!
040:009	and that will be **truly** the highest Achievement.
040:028	**truly** Allah guides not one who transgresses and lies!
040:030	"O my People! **truly** I do fear for you something
040:048	**Truly**, Allah has judged between (His) Servants!"
041:039	**Truly**, He Who gives life to the (dead) earth
042:014	but **truly** those who have inherited the Book
042:043	that would **truly** be an affair of great resolution.
042:045	Behold! **Truly** the wrong-doers are in a
042:048	**truly** then is man ungrateful!
042:048	And **truly**, when We give man a taste of Mercy
043:015	**Truly** is man clearly unthankful.
043:049	for We shall **truly** accept guidance."
043:054	**truly** were they a people rebellious (against Allah).
043:088	**Truly** these are a people who believe not!"
044:015	for a while, (but) **truly** ye will revert
044:049	**Truly** thou art Mighty, full of honour!
044:050	"**Truly** this is what ye used to doubt!"
046:010	(how unjust ye are!) **truly**, Allah guides
046:015	**Truly** have I turned to Thee and **truly** do I
046:021	**truly** I fear for you the Chastisement
048:008	We have **truly** sent thee as a witness, as a
048:026	**Truly** did Allah fulfil the vision
051:008	**Truly** ye are of varying opinion.
052:028	"**Truly** we did call unto Him from of old:
052:028	**truly** it is He, the Beneficent , the Merciful!"
053:018	For **truly** did he see, of the Signs
054:024	**Truly** should we then be in error and madness.
054:047	**Truly** those in sin are the ones in error
056:051	"Then will ye **truly**,-O ye that go wrong,
057:022	that is **truly** easy for Allah:
058:002	but **truly** Allah is All-Pardoning, All-Forgiving.
058:019	**Truly**, it is the Party of Satan that will lose.
058:022	**Truly** it is the Party of Allah that will
060:006	But if any turn away, **truly** Allah is Free of all
061:004	**Truly** Allah loves those who fight in His Cause
062:008	"The Death form which ye flee will **truly** overtake you:
063:002	**truly** evil are their deeds.
063:006	**Truly** Allah guides not rebellious transgressors.
064:014	O ye who believe! **truly**, among your wives
066:004	**truly** Allah is his Protector, and Gabriel,
067:019	**truly** it is He that watches over all things.
068:045	**truly** powerful is My Plan.
069:050	But **truly** (Revelation) is a cause of sorrow
070:019	**Truly** man was created very impatient;

TRULY (continued)
072:028 (truly) brought and delivered the Messages
073:006 Truly the rising by night is a time
078:021 Truly Hell is as a place of ambush
083:022 Truly the Righteous will be in Bliss:
083:032 "Behold! these are the people truly astray!"
084:013 Truly, did he go about among his people, rejoicing!
084:014 Truly, did he think that he would not
085:012 Truly strong is the Grip of thy Lord.
091:009 Truly he succeeds that purifies it,
100:006 Truly Man is to his Lord, ungrateful;

TRUMPET
006:073 the day the trumpet will be blown. He knoweth
018:099 the trumpet will be blown, and We
020:102 The Day when the Trumpet will be sounded: that Day,
023:101 Then when the Trumpet is blown, there will
027:087 And the Day that the Trumpet will be sounded
036:051 The trumpet shall be sounded, when behold!
039:068 The Trumpet will (just) be sounded, when all
050:020 And the Trumpet shall be blown: that will
069:013 Then, when one Blast is sounded on the Trumpet,
074:008 Finally when the Trumpet is sounded,
078:018 The Day that the Trumpet shall be sounded, and ye

TRUNK
019:023 to the trunk of a palm-tree: she cried
019:025 the trunk of the palm-tree: it will

TRUNKS
020:071 on trunks of palm-trees: so shall

TRUST
002:283 let the trustee (faithfully) discharge his trust,
002:283 deposits a thing on trust with another,
003:122 the Faithful (ever) put their trust.
003:159 put thy trust in Allah.
003:159 For Allah loves those who put their trust (in Him).
003:160 In Allah, then, let Believers put their trust.
004:081 so keep clear of them, and put thy trust in Allah,
004:105 those who betray their trust;
005:011 And on Allah let Believers put (all) their trust.
005:023 But on Allah put your trust if ye have faith."
007:089 in His knowledge in Allah is our trust.
008:002 and put (all) their trust in their Lord;
008:027 the trust of Allah and the Messenger, nor
008:049 But if any trust in Allah, behold! Allah
008:061 and trust in Allah: for He is the One
009:051 let the believers put their trust.
009:129 there is no god but He: On him is my trust,-
010:071 yet I put my trust in Allah get ye then
010:084 then in Him put your trust if ye
010:085 They said: "In Allah do we put our trust.
011:056 "I put my trust in Allah, my Lord and your Lord!
011:088 In Him I trust, and unto Him I turn.
011:123 so worship Him, and put thy trust in Him:
012:011 why dost thou not trust us with Joseph,-seeing we
012:054 invested with all trust."
012:064 He said: "Shall I trust you with him with any
012:067 on Him do I put my trust:
012:067 and let all that trust put their trust on Him."
013:030 On Him is my trust, and to Him I turn!"
014:011 And on Allah let all men of faith put their trust.
014:012 Why we should not put our trust on Allah.
014:012 For those who put their trust should put
014:012 should put their trust on Allah."
016:042 in patience, and put their trust on their Lord.

TRUST (continued)
016:099 who believe and put their trust in their Lord.
023:008 their trust and their covenants;
025:058 And put thy trust in Him Who lives and dies not;
026:125 "I am to you a messenger worthy of all trust.
026:143 I am to you a messenger worthy of all trust.
026:162 "I am to you a messenger worthy of all trust.
026:178 "I am to you a messenger worthy of all trust.
026:217 And put thy trust on the Exalted
027:079 So put thy trust in Allah: for thou
029:059 and put their trust in their Lord and Cherisher.
033:003 And put thy trust in Allah, and enough
033:048 their insolence but put thy trust in Allah.
033:072 We did indeed offer the Trust to the Heavens
039:038 In Him trust those who put their trust."
042:010 in Him I trust, and to Him I turn.
042:036 their trust in their Lord:
044:018 I am to you a messenger worthy of all trust;
058:010 and on Allah let the Believers put their trust.
060:004 "Our Lord! in Thee do we trust, and to
064:013 let the Believers put their trust.
065:003 And if anyone puts his trust in Allah,
067:029 and on Him have we put our trust: so, soon
081:021 With authority there, (and) faithful of his trust.

TRUSTED
012:064 with any result other than when I trusted you with
027:039 the purpose, and may be trusted."

TRUSTEE
002:283 let the trustee (faithfully) discharge his trust,

TRUSTS
004:058 your trusts to those to whom they are due;
070:032 And those who respect their trusts and covenants;

TRUSTWORTHY
002:256 hath grasped the most trustworthy hand-hold,
007:068 I am to you a sincere and trustworthy adviser".
026:107 "I am to you a trustworthy messenger.

TRUSTY
028:026 to employ is the (man) who is strong and trusty."

TRUTH
002:022 unto Allah when ye know (the truth).
002:026 that it is the truth from their Lord;
002:032 in truth it is Thou who art perfect
002:042 nor conceal the Truth when ye know
002:042 And cover not Truth with falsehood,
002:071 They said: "Now hast thou brought the truth."
002:091 even if it be Truth confirming
002:109 after the truth hath become manifest
002:119 in truth as a bearer of glad tidings
002:144 that is the truth from their Lord,
002:146 the truth which they themselves know.
002:147 The truth is from thy Lord,
002:149 that is indeed the truth from thy Lord.
002:160 make amends and openly declare (the Truth):
002:176 the Book in truth but those who seek causes
002:177 Such are the people of truth, the God-fearing.
002:213 and with them He sent the Book in truth,
002:213 guided the Believers to the Truth,
002:252 We rehearse them to thee in truth:
002:256 Truth stands out clear from Error;
003:003 (step by step), in truth, the Book,
003:039 confirming the truth of a Word from Allah,
003:060 the truth (comes) from thy Lord alone;

TRUTH (continued)

003:071 and conceal the **Truth**,
003:071 Why do ye clothe **truth** with falsehood,
003:093 if ye be men of **truth**."
003:095 Say: "Allah speaketh the **truth**: follow the religion
003:108 We rehearse them to thee in **Truth**:
003:137 what was the end of those who rejected **Truth**.
003:140 from your ranks Martyr-witnesses (to **Truth**).
003:168 if ye speak the **truth**."
003:183 why then did ye slay them, if ye speak the **truth**?.
004:069 the Sincere (lovers of **Truth**), the martyres,
004:105 We have sent down to thee the Book in **truth**,
004:122 Allah's promise is the **truth**, and whose
004:151 They are in **truth** Unbelievers; and We have
004:170 to you in **truth** from Allah: believe in him:
004:171 nor say of Allah aught but **truth**.
005:027 Recite to them the **truth** of the story
005:048 the **truth** of the matters in which ye dispute;
005:048 To thee We sent the Scripture in **truth**, confirming
005:048 diverging from the **truth** that hath come to thee.
005:075 His mother was a woman of **truth**.
005:075 they are deluded away from the **truth**!
005:077 trespassing beyond the **truth**, nor follow
005:083 with tears, for they recognize the **truth**: they
005:084 believe in Allah and the **truth** which has
005:106 If ye doubt (their **truth**), detain them
005:107 trespassed (beyond the **truth**): if we did,
005:113 that thou has indeed told us the **truth**;
005:119 will profit from their **truth**:
006:005 the **truth** when it reaches them: but soon
006:011 what was the end of those who rejected **Truth**."
006:019 Say: "But in **truth** He is the One God.
006:030 He will say: "Is not this the **truth**?"
006:036 Those who listen (in **truth**), be sure,
006:057 He declares the **Truth**, and He is
006:060 then will He show you the **truth** of all that ye did.
006:066 though it is the **Truth**.
006:073 He Who created the heavens and the earth with **truth**:
006:073 His Word is the **Truth**.
006:095 then how are ye deluded away from the **truth**?
006:108 the **truth** of all that they did.
006:111 But most of them ignore (the **truth**).
006:114 that it hath been sent down from thy Lord in **truth**.
006:115 its fulfillment in **truth** and in justice:
006:159 the **truth** of all that they did.
006:164 He will tell you the **truth** of things
007:033 sins and trespasses against **truth** or reason;
007:043 indeed it was the **truth** that the Messengers
007:070 if so be that thou tellest the **truth**!"
007:089 and our people in **truth**, for thou
007:096 but they rejected (the **truth**), and We
007:105 to say nothing but **truth** about Allah.
007:106 show it forth,-if thou tellest the **truth**."
007:118 Thus **truth** was confirmed. And all that
007:131 Behold! in **truth** the omens of evil are theirs
007:159 and do justice in the light of **truth**.
007:169 to Allah anything but the **truth**?
007:181 who direct (others) with **truth**, and dispense
008:004 Such in **truth** are the Believers: they have
008:005 out of the house in **truth**, even though
008:006 the **truth** after it was made manifest, as if
008:007 to establish the **Truth** according to His words,
008:032 if this is indeed the **truth** from Thee, rain down

TRUTH (continued)

008:074 these are (all) in very **truth** the believers:
009:029 nor acknowledge the religion of **Truth**, from among
009:030 how they are deluded away from the **Truth**!
009:033 and the Religion of **Truth**, to cause
009:043 who told the **truth** were seen by thee in a clear
009:048 until the **Truth** arrived, and the Decree
009:060 hearts have been (recently) reconciled (to **Truth**);
009:094 He show you the **truth** of all that ye did."
009:105 then will He show you the **truth** of all that ye did."
009:111 a promise binding on Him in **Truth**, through the
010:005 Allah created this but in **truth** and righteousness.
010:023 and We shall show you the **truth** of all that ye did.
010:032 apart from the **Truth**, what (remains) but error?
010:034 then how are ye deluded away (from the **truth**)?"
010:035 any that can give guidance towards **Truth**?"
010:035 gives guidance to **Truth** more worthy to be followed,
010:035 is there any that can give any guidance towards **Truth**.
010:036 can be of no avail against **Truth**.
010:038 besides Allah, if it be ye speak the **truth**!"
010:048 to pass-if ye speak the **truth**?"
010:053 It is the very **truth**!
010:076 When the **Truth** did come to them from Us, they said:
010:077 Said Moses: "Say ye (this) about the **Truth** when it
010:082 doth prove and establish the **Truth**, however much
010:094 the **Truth** hath indeed come to thee from thy Lord:
010:108 Say: "O ye men! now **Truth** hath reached you
011:013 if ye speak the **truth**!
011:017 doubt thereon: for it is the **Truth** from thy Lord:
011:032 us with, if thou speakest the **truth**!"
011:120 in them there cometh to thee the **Truth**, as well
012:007 are Signs for Seekers (after **Truth**).
012:015 (one day) tell them the **truth** of this affair
012:017 even though we tell the **truth**."
012:027 she the liar, and he is telling the **truth**!"
012:036 "the **truth** and meaning thereof:
012:037 I will surely reveal to you the **truth** and meaning
012:045 said: "I will tell you the **truth** of its
012:046 "O Joseph!" (he said), "O man of **truth**! Expound
012:051 the **truth** manifest (to all): it was I
012:077 and Allah knoweth best the **truth** of what ye assert!"
012:082 and (you will find) we are indeed telling the **truth**."
013:001 unto thee from thy Lord is the **Truth**; but most
013:017 show forth **Truth** and falsehood.
013:019 unto thee from thy Lord is the **Truth**, like one
014:019 created the heavens and the earth in **Truth**?
014:022 a promise of **truth**: I too promised, but I
015:007 if it be that thou hast the **Truth**?"
015:055 They said: "We give thee glad tidings in **truth**;
015:064 and assuredly we tell the **truth**.
015:064 "We have come to thee with the **Truth**
016:003 and the earth with **truth** far is He above having
016:036 what was the end of those who denied (the **Truth**).
016:038 a promise (binding) on Him in **truth**: but most
016:039 and that the rejectors of **Truth** may realize
016:039 He may manifest to them the **truth** of that
016:092 (the **truth** of) that wherein ye disagree.
016:102 the revelation from thy Lord in **Truth**, in order
017:041 increases their flight (from the **Truth**)!
017:046 they turn on their backs, fleeing (from the **Truth**).
017:080 the Gate of **Truth** and Honor; and grant
017:080 by the Gate of **Truth** and Honor, and likewise
017:081 And say: "**Truth** has (now) arrived, and Falsehood

TRUTH (continued)

017:105 and in **Truth** has it descended:
017:105 We sent down the (Qur'an) in **Truth**,
018:013 We relate to thee their story in **truth**: they were
018:029 Say, "The **Truth** is from your Lord" let him
018:056 to weaken the **truth**, and they treat My Signs
018:066 me something of the (Higher) **Truth** which thou
019:034 (it is) a statement of **truth**, about which
019:041 a man of **Truth**, a prophet.
019:050 on the tongue of **truth**.
019:056 he was a man of **truth** (and sincerity), (and) a
020:114 High above all is Allah, the King, the **Truth**!
021:018 Nay, We hurl the **Truth** against falsehood, and it
021:024 But most of them know not the **Truth**, and so
021:038 come to pass, if ye are telling the **truth**?"
021:055 They said, "Have you brought us the **Truth**, or are
021:056 and I am a witness to this (**truth**).
021:109 to you all alike and in **truth**; but I
021:112 Say: "O my Lord! judge Thou in **truth**!"
022:053 in a schism far (from the **Truth**):
022:054 the (Qur'an) is the **Truth** from the Lord, and that
023:062 clearly shows the **truth**.
023:070 Nay, he has brought them the **Truth**, but most
023:070 but most of them hate the **Truth**.
023:071 If the **Truth** had been in accord with their
023:090 We have sent them the **Truth**: but they
024:006 of those who speak the **Truth**.
024:009 on herself if (her accuser) is telling the **truth**.
024:025 is the (very) **Truth**, that makes
024:064 to Him, He will tell them the **truth** of what
025:004 at it." In **truth** it is they who have put forward
025:033 but We reveal to thee the **truth** and the best
026:006 the **truth** of what they mocked at!
026:031 if thou tellest the **truth**!"
026:084 on the tongue of **truth** among the
026:154 if thou tellest the **truth**!"
027:027 whether thou hast told the **truth** or lied!
027:041 (to the **truth**) or is one of those who
027:049 and we are positively telling the **truth**.'"
027:064 if ye are telling the **truth**!"
027:079 for thou art on (the Path of) manifest **Truth**.
028:003 some of the story of Moses and Pharaoh in **Truth**,
028:048 But (now), when the **Truth** has come to them
028:053 for it is the **Truth** from our Lord:
028:075 the **Truth** is with Allah (alone), and the
029:008 and I will tell you (the **truth**) of all that ye did.
029:029 if thou tellest the **truth**."
029:044 and the earth in **truth**:
029:061 How are they then deluded away (from the **truth**)?
029:068 or rejects the **Truth** when it reaches him?
030:008 Not but in **truth** and for a term appointed,
031:023 and We shall tell them the **truth** of their deeds:
031:030 That is because Allah is the **Truth** and because
032:003 Nay, it is the **Truth** from thy Lord, that thou
032:028 if ye are telling the **truth**?"
033:004 But Allah tells (you) the **Truth**, and He
033:024 of **Truth** for their **Truth**, and punish
033:053 but Allah is not shy (to tell you) the **truth**.
034:006 to thee from thy Lord-that is the **Truth**, and that
034:026 between us (and you) in **truth** and justice:
034:029 (come to pass) if ye are telling the **truth**?"
034:043 And the Unbelievers say of the **Truth** when it
034:045 And their predecessors rejected (the **Truth**);

TRUTH (continued)

034:048 Say: "Verily my Lord doth cast the **Truth**,-
034:049 Say: "The **Truth** has arrived, and Falsehood
034:052 "We do believe (now) in the (**truth**)"; but how
035:024 Verily We have sent thee with **truth**, as a
035:031 of the Book is the **Truth**,-confirming what
036:064 for that ye (persistently) rejected (**Truth**)."
036:070 those who reject (**Truth**).
037:021 whose **truth** ye (once) denied!"
037:037 Nay! he has come with the (very) **Truth**,
038:001 of Admonition: (this is the **Truth**).
038:022 decide now between us with **truth**,
038:026 so judge thou between men in **truth** (and justice):
038:084 (Allah) said: "This is the **Truth**, and the **Truth** I say.
038:088 the **truth** of it (all) after a while."
039:002 the Book to thee in **Truth**:
039:007 when He will tell you the **truth** of all
039:032 and rejects the **Truth** when it comes to him!
039:033 And he who brings the **Truth** and he
039:041 Verily We have revealed the Book to thee in **Truth**,
040:005 therewith to obliterate the **Truth**;
040:020 And Allah will judge with (Justice and) **Truth**:
040:025 Now, when he brought them in **Truth**, from Us,
040:028 but, if he is telling the **Truth**, then will
040:062 then how ye are deluded away from the **Truth**!
040:075 on the earth in things other than the **Truth**,
040:078 the matter was decided in **truth** and justice,
041:015 the land, against (all) **truth** and reason, and said
041:040 Those who pervert the **Truth** in Our Signs are not
041:050 the Unbelievers the **truth** of all that they did,
041:053 until it becomes manifest to them that this is the **Truth**.
042:017 It is Allah Who has sent down the Book in **truth**,
042:018 and know that it is the **Truth**.
042:024 and proves the **Truth** by His Words.
043:025 those who rejected (**Truth**)!
043:029 and their fathers, until the **Truth** has come
043:030 But when the **Truth** came to them, they said:
043:078 Verily We have brought the **truth** to you:
043:078 but most of you have a hatred for **Truth**.
043:086 only he who bears witness to the **Truth**,
043:087 how then are they deluded away (from the **Truth**)?
045:006 which We rehearse to thee in **truth**:
045:029 "This Our Record speaks about you with **truth**:
046:004 if ye are telling the **truth**!"
046:007 of the **Truth** when it comes to them:
046:016 a promise of **truth**, which was made to them
046:022 if thou art telling the **truth**!"
046:030 it guides to the **Truth** and to a Straight Path.
046:034 for that ye were wont to deny (**Truth**)!"
046:034 (they will be asked), "Is this not the **Truth**?"
047:002 for it is the **Truth** from their Lord,-
047:003 those who believe follow the **Truth** from their Lord:
048:010 to thee plight their fealty in **truth** to Allah:
048:028 and the Religion of **Truth**, to make
049:006 ascertain the **truth**, lest ye harm people
050:005 But they deny the **truth** when it comes to them:
050:019 And the stupor of death comes in **truth**.
050:042 a (mighty) Blast in (very) **truth**): that will
051:009 Through which are deluded (away form the **Truth**)
051:023 this is the very **Truth**, as much as
052:011 Then woe that Day to the rejecters (of **Truth**);-
052:034 like unto it,-if (it be) they speak the **Truth**!
053:028 and conjecture avails nothing against **Truth**.

TRUTH (continued)

054:018 The 'Ad (people) (too) rejected (**Truth**):
056:051 go wrong, and deny (the **truth**);
056:057 why will ye not admit the **Truth**?
056:092 And if he be of those who deny (the **truth**)
056:095 Verily, this is the very **Truth** of assured Certainty.
057:016 the **Truth** which has been revealed (to them),
059:013 Of a **truth** ye arouse greater fear in their hearts,
060:001 the **truth** that has come to you, and have
060:002 ye should reject the **Truth**.
061:009 with Guidance and the Religion of **Truth**.
063:004 How are they deluded (away from the **Truth**)!
064:003 and the earth with the **truth**, and has
064:007 (the **truth**) of all that ye did.
066:012 to the **truth** of the words of her Lord and of His
067:021 in insolent impiety and flight (from the **Truth**).
067:025 be (fulfilled)? If ye are telling the **truth**.
068:008 So obey not to those who deny (the **Truth**).
069:051 But verily it is **Truth** of assured certainty.
070:026 And those who hold to the **truth** of the
073:011 of life, (who (yet) deny the **Truth**);
075:032 He rejected **Truth** and turned away!
077:015 Ah woe, that Day, to the Rejecters of **Truth**!
077:019 Ah woe, that Day, to the Rejecters of **Truth**!
077:024 Ah woe, that Day, to the Rejecters of **Truth**!
077:028 Ah woe, that Day, to the Rejecters of **Truth**!
077:034 Ah woe, that Day, to the Rejecters of **Truth**!
077:037 Ah woe, that Day, to the Rejecters of **Truth**!
077:040 Ah woe, that Day, to the Rejecters of **Truth**!
077:045 Ah woe, that Day, to the Rejecters of **Truth**!
077:047 Ah woe, that Day, to the Rejecters of **Truth**!
077:049 Ah woe, that Day, to the Rejecters of **Truth**!
085:019 in rejecting (the **Truth**)!
092:016 Who give the lie to **Truth** and turn their backs.
096:013 Seest thou if he denies (**Truth**) and turns away?
103:003 in the mutual enjoining of **Truth**, and of

TRUTHFUL

002:023 if ye are **truthful**.
002:111 Say: "Produce your proof if ye are **truthful**."
005:119 "This is a day on which the **truthful** will profit
006:040 (Reply) if ye are **truthful**!
006:143 Tell me with knowledge if ye are **truthful**:
007:194 if ye are (indeed) **truthful**!
009:119 and be with those who are **truthful**.
026:187 to fall on us, if thou art **truthful**!"
026:193 With it came down the **Truthful** spirit
027:071 (come to pass)? If ye are **truthful**."
028:049 (Do), if ye are **truthful**!"
033:008 That (Allah) may question the **Truthful** about their
037:157 (of authority) if ye be **truthful**!
057:019 and His messengers-they are the **Truthful** and the
059:008 such are indeed the **truthful**;-
062:006 if ye are **truthful**!"
068:041 produce their "partners," if they are **truthful**!

TRUTHFULNESS

033:008 about their **truthfulness** and He has prepared

TRY

006:165 that He may **try** you in the
011:007 that He might **try** you, which of you
012:061 They said: "We shall **try** to win him from
038:034 And We did **try** Solomon: We placed
039:036 But they **try** to frighten thee with other
044:017 We did, before them, **try** the people of Pharaoh:

TRY (continued)

047:031 and We shall **try** your reported (mettle).
047:031 And We shall **try** you until We test those among you
067:002 that He may **try** which of you is best in deed:
072:017 "That We might **try** them by that (means).
076:002 of mingled sperm, in order to **try** him: so We

TRYING

050:019 thou wast **trying** to escape!"

TRYST

020:058 So make a **tryst** between us
020:059 Moses said: "Your **tryst** is the Day of the Festival,

TUBBA

044:037 of **Tubba** and those who were before them?
050:014 and the people of **Tubba'**; each one

TUCKED

027:044 of water, and she (**tucked** up her skirts),

TUMBLED

018:042 his property, which had (now) **tumbled** to pieces
022:045 They **tumbled** down on their roofs. And how
069:007 roots of hollow palm-trees **tumbled** down!

TUMULT

002:217 **Tumult** and oppression are worse than slaughter.
008:073 **tumult** and oppression on earth, and great

TUNNEL

006:035 a **tunnel** in the ground or a ladder
018:061 the sea (straight) as in a **tunnel**.

TUR

028:029 he perceived a fire in the direction of Mount **Tur**.
028:046 (the Mountain of) **Tur** when We called (to Moses).

TURN

002:054 so **turn** (in repentance) to your Maker,
002:083 Then did ye **turn** back,
002:084 nor **turn** out your own people
002:109 wish they could **turn** you (people)
002:115 whithersoever ye **turn**,
002:128 and **turn** unto us (in Mercy);
002:137 but if they **turn** back,
002:143 who would **turn** on their heels (from the Faith).
002:144 now shall We **turn** thee to a Qiblah
002:144 **turn** your faces in that direction.
002:144 **Turn** then thy face in the direction
002:149 **turn** thy face in the direction of the
002:150 **turn** your face thither:
002:150 **turn** thy face in the direction
002:160 to them I **turn**;
002:177 ye **turn** your faces toward East or West;
002:191 and **turn** them out from where
002:217 **turn** back from their faith and die in unbelief,
002:217 until they **turn** you back from your faith
002:222 For Allah loves those who **turn** to Him constantly
002:243 Didst thou not **turn** thy vision
003:020 but if they **turn** back, thy duty
003:023 **turn** back and decline (the arbitration).
003:032 but if they **turn** back, Allah loveth not
003:063 But if they **turn** back,
003:064 If then they **turn** back,
003:072 perchance they may (themselves) **turn** back;
003:082 If any **turn** back after this, they are
003:128 whether He **turn** in mercy to them, or punish them;
003:144 If any did **turn** back on his heels,
003:144 will ye then **turn** back on your heels?
003:149 and ye will **turn** back (from Faith)

TURN (continued)

004:017	to them will Allah **turn** in mercy;
004:026	and (He doth wish to) **turn** to you (in Mercy):
004:027	ye should **turn** away (from Him), far, far away.
004:027	Allah doth wish to **turn** to you, but
004:047	and **turn** them hindwards, or curse them as We
004:080	but if any **turn** away, We have not
004:089	But if they **turn** renegades, seize them
004:129	but **turn** not away (from a woman) altogether, so as
004:140	unless they **turn** to a different Theme: if ye did,
005:021	and **turn** not back ignominiously, for then
005:043	yet even after that, they would **turn** away.
005:049	And if they **turn** away, be assured that for some
005:054	you **turn** back from his Faith, soon will
005:056	As to those who **turn** (for friendship)
005:074	Why **turn** they not to Allah, and seek
005:095	and beware (of evil): if ye do **turn** back, know
006:046	by various (symbols): Yet they **turn** aside.
006:052	that thou shouldst **turn** them away, and thus
006:068	**turn** away from them unless they
006:068	they **turn** to a different theme.
006:071	and **turn** on our heels after receiving
006:106	and **turn** aside from those who
006:110	We (too) shall **turn** to (confusion) their hearts
006:129	the wrong-doers **turn** to each other, because of what
006:157	those who **turn** away from Our Signs,
007:143	To Thee I **turn** in repentance, and I
007:146	them will I **turn** away from My Signs:
007:168	in order that they might **turn** (to Us).
007:174	and perchance they may **turn** (Unto Us).
007:199	but **turn** away from the ignorant.
008:015	never **turn** your backs to them.
008:016	If any do **turn** his back to them
008:020	and **turn** not away from him when ye hear (him speak).
009:003	but if ye **turn** away, know ye
009:015	For Allah will **turn** (in mercy) to whom He will:
009:027	**turn** (in mercy) to whom He will: for Allah
009:050	and they **turn** away rejoicing.
009:057	they would **turn** straightway thereto with
009:059	to Allah do we **turn** our hopes!"
009:074	but if they **turn** back (to their evil ways), Allah
009:102	Perhaps Allah will **turn** unto them (in mercy):
009:106	or **turn** in mercy to them: and Allah
009:112	Those that **turn** (to Allah) in repentance:
009:126	Yet they **turn** not in repentance, and they
009:127	"Doth anyone see you?" Then they **turn** away:
009:129	But if they **turn** away, Say: "Allah sufficeth me:
010:072	"But if ye **turn** back, (consider):
010:078	to **turn** us away from the ways We found
011:003	and **turn** to Him in repentance; that He
011:003	But if ye **turn** away, then I fear for you
011:008	reaches them, nothing will **turn** it away from them,
011:038	we (in our **turn**) can look down on you with
011:052	so **turn** ye not back in sin!"
011:052	your Lord, and **turn** to Him (in repentance):
011:057	"If ye **turn** away,-I (at least) have conveyed
011:061	and **turn** to Him (in repentance):
011:088	In Him I trust, and unto Him I **turn**.
011:090	and **turn** unto Him (in repentance): for my Lord
011:112	thou and those who with thee **turn** (unto Allah);
012:024	that We might **turn** away from him (all) evil
012:033	unless Thou **turn** away their snare
012:081	"**Turn** ye back to your father, and say,

TURN (continued)

012:105	Yet they **turn** (their faces) away from them!
013:022	secretly and openly; and **turn** off Evil with good:
013:027	to himself those who **turn** to Him in penitence,-
013:030	On Him is my trust, and to Him I **turn**!"
014:010	Ye wish to **turn** us away from what our fathers
015:094	art commanded, and **turn** away from those who
016:009	but there are ways that **turn** aside:
016:048	how their shadows **turn** round, from the right
016:054	behold! some of you **turn** to other gods
016:082	But if they **turn** away, thy duty
017:025	**turn** to Him again and again (in true penitence).
017:028	And even if thou hast to **turn** away from them
017:046	they **turn** on their backs, fleeing (from the Truth).
017:067	ye **turn** away (from Him).
018:016	"When ye **turn** away from them and the things
018:053	no means will they find to **turn** away therefrom.
019:048	"And I will **turn** away from you (all) and from
020:048	those who reject and **turn** away.'"
020:100	If any do **turn** away therefrom, verily they
021:001	and they **turn** away.
021:024	and so **turn** away.
021:032	Yet do they **turn** away from the Signs
021:042	Yet they **turn** away from the remembrance
021:057	after ye go away and **turn** your backs"...
021:058	that they might **turn** (and address themselves) to it.
021:109	But if they **turn** back, say: "I have
022:011	they **turn** on their faces:
023:066	but ye used to **turn** back on your heels-
023:071	but they **turn** away from their admonition.
024:031	And O ye Believers! **turn** ye all together towards
024:047	some of them **turn** away: they are not (really) Believers.
024:054	but if ye **turn** away, he is
025:023	And We shall **turn** to whatever deeds they did
026:005	the Most Gracious, but they **turn** away therefrom.
027:080	(especially) when they **turn** back in retreat.
028:055	they **turn** away therefrom and say: "To us our
028:087	Let no one **turn** you away from Allah's revelations
030:031	**Turn** ye in repentance to Him, and fear
030:041	in order that they may **turn** back (from Evil).
030:051	they see (their tilth) **turn** yellow,-behold, they
030:052	when they show their backs and **turn** away.
031:015	of those who **turn** to Me: in the End
032:030	So **turn** away from them, and wait: they too
033:015	with Allah not to **turn** their backs, and a
033:024	be His Will, or **turn** to them in Mercy: for Allah
033:051	Thou mayest defer (the **turn** of) any of them
033:051	whose (**turn**) thou hadst set aside.
036:045	ye may receive Mercy," (they **turn** back).
036:046	but they **turn** away therefrom.
037:014	And, when they see a Sign, **turn** it to mockery,
037:027	And they will **turn** to one another, and question
037:050	Then they will **turn** to one another and question
037:091	Then did he **turn** to their gods and said,
037:093	Then did he **turn** upon them, striking (them)
037:174	So **turn** thou away from them for a little while,
037:178	So **turn** thou away from them for a little while,
038:019	all with him did **turn** (to Allah).
038:028	the same as those who **turn** aside from the right?
038:030	Ever did he **turn** (to Us in repentance)!
038:034	but he did **turn** (to Us in true devotion):
038:044	Ever did he **turn** (to Us)!
038:068	"From which ye do **turn** away!

TURN (continued)

039:017 not into its worship,-and **turn** to Allah
039:054 "**Turn** ye to your Lord (in repentance) and submit
040:007 Forgive, then, those who **turn** in repentance,
040:013 receive admonition who **turn** (to Allah).
040:033 A day when ye shall **turn** your backs and flee:
041:004 yet most of them **turn** away, and so
041:013 But if they **turn** away, say thou: "I have warned
042:010 in Him I trust, and to Him I **turn**.
042:013 and guides to Himself those who **turn** (to Him).
042:048 If then they **turn** away, We have not
043:014 "And to Our Lord, surely, must We **turn** back!"
043:028 that they may **turn** back (to Allah).
043:048 in order that they might **turn** (to Us).
043:089 But **turn** away from them, and say "Peace!"
044:014 Yet they **turn** away from him and say: "Tutored
046:003 **turn** away from that whereof they are warned.
046:022 to **turn** us aside from our gods?
046:027 in various ways, that they may **turn** (to Us).
047:025 Those who **turn** back as apostates after Guidance
047:038 If ye **turn** back (from the Path),
048:016 a goodly reward, but if ye **turn** back as ye
048:022 they would certainly **turn** their backs;
051:054 So **turn** away from them: not thine is the blame.
053:029 Therefore shun those who **turn** away from
054:002 But if they see a Sign, they **turn** away, and say,
054:006 Therefore, (O Prophet,) **turn** away from them.
057:013 "**Turn** ye back to your rear! Then seek
057:024 And if any **turn** back (from Allah's Way),
058:014 Seest thou not those who **turn** (in friendship)
059:012 they will **turn** their backs; so they
060:004 and to Thee do we **turn** in repentance:
060:006 But if any **turn** away, truly Allah is Free of all
060:009 It is such as **turn** to them (in these circumstances),
060:011 deserts you to the Unbelievers, and you have your **turn**
060:013 O ye who believe! **turn** not (for friendship)
063:005 for your forgiveness," they **turn** aside their
064:012 but if ye **turn** back, the duty
065:001 and **turn** them not out of their houses,
066:004 If ye two **turn** in repentance to Allah,
066:005 who are devout; who **turn** to Allah in repentance,
066:008 O ye who believe! **turn** to Allah with sincere
067:003 So **turn** thy vision again:
067:004 Again **turn** thy vision a second time:
068:032 for we do **turn** to Him (in repentance)!"
070:017 Inviting (all) such as **turn** their backs and
070:017 and **turn** away their faces (from the Right),
074:049 that they **turn** away from admonition?-
084:009 And he will **turn** to his people, rejoicing!
085:010 and do not **turn** in repentance, will have the
088:023 But if any **turn** away and disbelieve,-
092:016 Who give the lie to Truth and **turn** their backs.
094:008 And to thy Lord **turn** (all) thy attention.
108:002 Therefore to thy Lord **turn** in Prayer and Sacrifice.

TURNED

002:029 then He **turned** to the heaven and made them
002:037 and his Lord **turned** towards him;
002:054 Then He **turned** towards you (in forgiveness):
002:064 But ye **turned** back thereafter:
002:142 "What hath **turned** them from the Qiblah
002:187 but He **turned** to you and forgave you:
002:191 from where they have **turned** you out;
002:246 **turned** out of our homes and our families?"

TURNED (continued)

002:246 they **turned** back except a small band among them.
002:246 Hast thou not **turned** thy vision to the chiefs
002:258 Hast thou not **turned** thy thought to one
003:023 Hast thou not **turned** thy thought to those who
003:127 and they should then be **turned** back,
003:155 Those of you who **turned** back on the day
004:044 Hast thou not **turned** thy thought to those who
004:049 Hast thou not **turned** thy thought to those
004:051 Hast thou not **turned** thy thought to those who
004:060 Hast thou not **turned** thy thought to those who
004:077 Hast thou not **turned** thy thought to those who
005:071 yet Allah (in mercy) **turned** to them:
006:004 but they **turned** away therefrom.
006:147 never will His wrath be **turned** back.
007:047 **turned** towards the Companions of the Fire,
007:119 and **turned** about humble.
007:156 for we have **turned** unto Thee."
008:023 **turned** back and declined (faith).
008:048 he **turned** on his heels, and said:
009:025 did constrain you, and ye **turned** back in retreat.
009:076 and **turned** back (from their Covenant), averse
009:092 they **turned** back, their eyes streaming with tears
009:117 but He **turned** to them (also): for He
009:117 Allah **turned** with favour to the Prophet,
009:118 (He **turned** in mercy also) to the three who were
009:118 Then He **turned** to them, that they
009:127 Allah hath **turned** their hearts (from the light):
010:032 How then are ye **turned** away?
011:076 a Chastisement that cannot be **turned** back!
011:082 When Our decree issued, We **turned** (the cities)
012:034 (in his prayer), and **turned** away from him their snare:
012:084 And he **turned** away from them, and said: "How great
014:028 Hast thou not **turned** thy thought to those
015:074 And We **turned** (the Cities) upside down,
018:018 **turned** back from them in flight, and wouldst
018:018 and We **turned** them on their right and their
019:049 When he had **turned** away from them and from
020:122 He **turned** to him, and gave him guidance.
021:064 So they **turned** to themselves and said,
024:037 the Day when hearts and eyes will be **turned** about,-
025:071 has truly **turned** to Allah in repentance:
027:010 a snake, he **turned** back in retreat, and retraced
028:022 Then when he **turned** his face towards (the land of)
028:024 then he **turned** back to the shade, and said:
028:031 he **turned** back in retreat, and retraced
029:021 He pleases, and towards Him are ye **turned**.
033:025 And Allah **turned** back the Unbelievers for (all)
033:066 The Day that their faces will be **turned** over in the Fire,
034:012 and if any of them **turned** aside from Our command,
034:016 But they **turned** away (from Allah), and We
037:090 So they **turned** away from him, and departed.
038:017 for he ever **turned** (in repentance to Allah).
038:024 (in prostration), and **turned** (to Allah in repentance).
039:006 then how are ye **turned** away (from your true Lord)?
039:060 their faces will be **turned** black; is there
040:069 How are they **turned** away (from Reality)?-
041:011 Then He **turned** to the sky, and it
046:015 Truly have I **turned** to Thee and truly do I
046:029 Behold, We **turned** towards thee a company of Jinns
050:033 and brought a heart **turned** in devotion (to Him):
051:026 Then he **turned** quickly to his household,
051:039 But (Pharaoh) **turned** back on account of his might,

TURNED (continued)

064:006 So they rejected (the Message) and **turned** away.
068:030 Then they **turned**, one against another, in reproach.
073:020 So He hath **turned** to you (in mercy):
074:023 Then he **turned** back and was haughty;
075:032 He rejected Truth and **turned** away!
079:022 Further, he **turned** his back, striving hard
080:001 The (Prophet) frowned and **turned** away,
082:004 And when the Graves are **turned** upside down;-

TURNETH

005:039 Allah **turneth** to him in forgiveness; for Allah
006:157 and **turneth** away therefrom?

TURNING

002:144 We see the **turning** of thy face
005:080 Thou seest many of them **turning** in friendship
006:157 with a dreadful chastisement for their **turning** away.
012:071 They said, **turning** towards them: "What is it
013:011 no **turning** it back, nor will they find, besides
015:081 but they persisted in **turning** away from them.
018:017 **turning** away from them to the left, while they
018:042 twisting and **turning** his hands over what
030:033 **turning** back to Him in repentance: but when
035:043 no **turning** off wilt thou find in Allah's way
039:008 **turning** to Him in repentance:
050:008 to every servant **turning** (to Allah).
060:009 from **turning** to them (for friendship and protection).
063:005 see them **turning** away their faces in arrogance.

TURNS

002:130 And who **turns** away from the religion
002:148 To each is a goal to which Allah **turns** him;
002:205 When he **turns** his back,
003:140 We give to men and men by **turns**:
005:051 And he amongst you that **turns** to them
017:083 he **turns** away and becomes remote on his side
018:057 but **turns** away from them, forgetting the
020:124 "But whosoever **turns** away from My Message,
022:004 that whoever **turns** to him for friendship,
024:043 He pleases and He **turns** it away from whom
031:007 a one, he **turns** away in arrogance, as if
032:022 of his Lord, and who then **turns** away therefrom?
033:073 men and women, and Allah **turns** in Mercy to the
034:009 that **turns** to Allah (in repentance).
041:051 he **turns** away, and gets himself remote on his side
048:017 and he who **turns** back, (Allah) will
053:033 Seest thou one who **turns** back,
054:028 brought forward (by suitable **turns**).
072:017 But if any **turns** away from the remembrance
096:010 A votary when he (**turns**) to pray?
096:013 Seest thou if he denies (Truth) and **turns** away?

TUTORED

044:014 "**Tutored** (by others), a man possessed!"

TUWA

020:012 thou art in the sacred valley **Tuwa**.
079:016 in the sacred valley to **Tuwa**:-

TWAIN

004:001 and from them **twain** scattered (like seeds)
004:035 If ye fear a breach between them **twain**, appoint
012:041 whereof ye **twain** do enquire."
031:014 And in years **twain** was his weaning:
055:035 On you will be sent (O ye evil ones **twain**)! a flame

TWELVE

002:060 Then gushed forth therefrom **twelve** springs.

TWELVE (continued)

005:012 and We appointed **twelve** chieftains among them,
007:160 We divided them into **twelve** tribes or nations.
007:160 out of it there gushed forth **twelve** springs:
009:036 sight of Allah is **twelve** (in a year)-so ordained

TWENTY

008:065 If there are **twenty** amongst you,

TWICE

002:229 A divorce is only permissible **twice**: after that,
003:013 these saw with their own eyes **twice** their number.
003:165 smote (your enemies) with one **twice** as great,
004:176 the male having **twice** the share of the female,
005:036 and **twice** repeated, to give as ransom for the
009:101 **twice** shall We punish them:
009:126 are tried every year once or **twice**?
017:004 (and **twice** would they be punished)!
017:004 that **twice** would they do mischief on the earth
028:054 **Twice** will they be given their reward, for that
033:031 to her shall We grant her reward **twice**: and We
040:011 made us to die, and **twice** hast Thou given us Life!
040:011 They will say:" Our Lord! **twice** hast Thou made us

TWIN-BIRTHS

005:103 or idol sacrifices for **twin-births** in animals, or

TWINKLING

016:077 is as the **twinkling** of an eye, or even quicker:
054:050 like the **twinkling** of an eye.

TWIST

004:046 and "Ra'ina" with a **twist** of their tongues

TWISTED

003:180 tied to their necks like a **twisted** collar,
111:005 A **twisted** rope of palm-leaf fibre round her

TWISTING

018:042 **twisting** and turning his hands over what

TWO

002:203 but if anyone hastens to leave in **two** days,
002:233 suck to their offspring for **two** whole years,
002:282 not **two** men, then a man and **two** women,
002:282 And get **two** witnesses, out or your own men.
003:013 a Sign in the **two** armies that met (in combat):
003:122 Remember **two** of your parties meditated cowardice;
003:155 on the day the **two** hosts met, it was Satan
003:166 What ye suffered on the day the **two** armies met,
004:003 marry women of your choice, **two**, or three, or four;
004:011 to the male, a portion equal to that of **two** females:
004:011 if only daughters, **two** or more, their share
004:012 each one of the **two** gets a sixth;
004:012 but if more than **two**, they share in a third;
004:016 If **two** persons among you are guilty of lewdness,
004:023 and **two** sisters in wedlock at one and the same time,
004:035 appoint (**two**) arbiters, one from his family,
004:088 into **two** parties about the Hypocrites?
004:092 (is prescribed) a fast for **two** months running:
004:176 if there are **two** sisters, they shall
005:023 were **two** on whom Allah had bestowed His Grace:
005:024 and fight ye **two**, while we sit here.
005:027 of the story of the **two** sons of Adam.
005:095 As adjudged by **two** just men among you; or by
005:106 when making bequests,-**two** just men of your own
005:107 But if it gets known that these **two** were guilty
005:107 our witness is truer than that of those **two**, and that
005:107 Let **two** others stand forth in their places,-
005:116 'Take me and my mother for **two** gods beside Allah?"

TWO (continued)

006:081   Which of (us) **two** parties hath more
006:143   or the **two** females, or (the young) which the
006:143   which the wombs of the **two** females enclose?
006:144   say, hath He forbidden the **two** males, or the
006:144   or the **two** females, or (the young) which the
006:144   which the wombs of the **two** females enclose?-
006:156   sent down to **two** Peoples before us, and for
008:007   Behold! Allah promised you one of the **two** parties,
008:041   the Day of the meeting of the **two** forces.
008:048   but when the **two** forces came in sight
008:065   they will vanquish **two** hundred:
008:066   they will vanquish **two** hundred,
008:066   and if a thousand, **two** thousand, with the leave
009:040   the **two** they were in the Cave, and he
009:052   other than one of **two** glorious things-
011:024   These **two** kinds (of men) may be compared
011:040   of each kind **two**, male and female, and your family-
011:114   And establish regular prayers at the **two** ends of the day
012:036   into the prison **two** young men.
012:039   "O my **two** companions of the prison! (I ask you):
012:041   "O my **two** companions of the prison!
012:042   And of the **two**, to that one whom he considered
012:045   one of the **two** (who had been in prison) and who
013:003   and fruit of every kind He made in pairs, **two** and **two**:
016:051   Allah has said: "Take not (for worship) **two** gods:
016:075   Allah sets forth the Parable (of **two** men):
016:075   are the **two** equal? (By no means);
016:076   Allah sets forth (another) Parable of **two** men:
017:012   made the Night and the Day as **two** (of Our) Signs:
018:012   which of the **two** parties was best at calculating
018:018   **two** forelegs on the threshold:
018:032   We provided **two** gardens of grape-vines and
018:032   Set forth to them the parable of **two** men:
018:032   in between the **two** We placed tillage.
018:060   the junction of the **two** seas or (until)
018:082   "As for he wall, it belonged **two** youths,
018:093   between **two** mountains, he found, beneath them,
018:096   the space between the **two** steep mountain-sides,
019:073   those who believe, "Which of the **two** sides is best
020:049   is the Lord of you **two**?"
020:063   They said: "These **two** are certainly (expert)
022:019   These **two** antagonists dispute with each other
023:047   They said: "Shall we believe in **two** men like ourselves?"
024:045   some that walk on **two** legs: and some
025:053   the **two** bodies of flowing water: one palatable
026:061   And when the **two** bodies saw each other,
027:045   they became **two** factions quarreling with each other.
027:061   the **two** seas (can there be another) god besides
028:015   and he found there **two** men fighting,-one of
028:023   and besides them he found **two** women who were
028:028   whichever of the **two** terms I fulfil, let there
028:032   Those are the **two** credentials from thy Lord
028:035   you **two** as well as those who follow you."
028:048   They say: "**Two** kinds of sorcery, each assisting
028:061   Are (these **two**) alike?-one to whom
030:043   on that Day shall men be divided (in **two**).
033:004   Allah has not made for any man **two** hearts in his breast:
034:015   a Sign in their homeland-**two** Gardens to the
034:016   and We converted their **two** Garden (rows) into
035:001   **two**, or three, or four (Pairs):
035:012   Nor are the **two** seas alike,-the one
036:014   When We (first) sent to them **two** messengers,

TWO (continued)

037:122   For they were **two** of Our believing Servants.
038:022   they said: "Fear not, we are **two** disputants,
039:029   to one master: are these **two** equal in comparison?
041:009   deny Him Who created the earth in **two** Days?
041:012   So He completed them as seven firmaments in **two** Days,
043:031   in either of the **two** (Chief) cities?"
046:017   And they **two** seek Allah's aid, (and rebuke
049:009   If **two** parties among the Believers fall into
049:010   your **two** (contending) brothers;
050:017   Behold, **two** (guardian angels) appointed to learn
053:009   And was at a distance of **two** bow-lengths or (even) nearer;
055:017   (He is) Lord of the **two** Easts and Lord of the **two** Wests:
055:019   He has let free the **two** Seas meeting together:
055:046   there will be **two** Gardens-
055:050   In them (each) will be **two** Springs flowing (free);
055:052   In them will be Fruits of every kind, **two** and **two**.
055:062   And besides these **two**, there are **two** other Gardens,-
055:066   In them (each) will be **two** springs pouring forth
058:004   **two** months consecutively before they touch each
065:002   for witness **two** persons from among you, endued with
066:004   If ye **two** turn in repentance to Allah,
066:010   they were (respectively) under **two** of Our
075:039   And of him He made **two** sexes, male and female.
090:010   And shown him the **two** highways?

TWO-THIRDS

004:011   their share is **two-thirds** of the inheritance;
004:176   they shall have **two-thirds** of the inheritance
073:020   nigh **two-thirds** of the night, or half

TYPE

002:204   There is the **type** of man whose speech
002:207   And there is the **type** of man who gives his life

TYRANT

028:019   to become a **tyrant** in the land, and not

TYRANTS

026:130   "And when ye strike you strike like **tyrants**.

TYRINICAL

040:035   seal up every heart-of arrogant **tyrinical**."

U

ULTIMATE
003:197 their **Ultimate** abode is Hell: what an evil

ULTIMATELY
010:046 **ultimately** Allah is witness to all that they do.

UMMAH
002:143 an **Ummah** justly balanced.
021:092 Verily, this **Ummah** of yours is a single **Ummah**,
023:052 And verily this **Ummah** of yours is a single **Ummah**

'UMRA
002:196 Hajj or **'Umra** in the service of Allah,
002:196 to continue the **'Umra** on to the Hajj.

UNABLE
002:229 be **unable** to keep the limits ordained by Allah,
002:229 **unable** to keep the limits ordained by Allah
002:282 or weak, or **unable** himself to dictate,
007:197 are **unable** to help you, and indeed
009:074 which they were **unable** to carry out: this revenge
018:078 wast **unable** to hold patience.
018:082 thou wast **unable** to hold patience."
018:101 and who had been **unable** even to hear.
027:085 be **unable** to speak (in plea).
036:067 have been **unable** to move about, nor could
043:018 and **unable** to give a clear account in a dispute
058:004 touch each other, but if any is **unable** to do so,
063:004 (**unable** to stand on their own).
073:020 He knoweth that ye are **unable** to keep count thereof.

UNACQUAINTED
006:156 we remained **unacquainted** with all that they

UNARMED
008:007 ye wished that the one **unarmed** should be yours,

UNAWARES
007:078 So the earthquake took them **unawares**, and they
007:091 But the earthquake took them **unawares**, and they

UNBELIEF
002:108 But whoever changeth from Faith to **Unbelief**,
002:217 turn back from their faith and die in **unbelief**,
003:052 **unbelief** on their part he said: "Who will be
003:080 What! would he bid you to **unbelief** after ye have
003:167 They were that day nearer to **Unbelief** than of Faith,
003:176 who rush headlong into **Unbelief**:
003:177 Those who purchase **Unbelief** at the price of Faith,
004:046 but Allah hath cursed them, for their **Unbelief**;
004:137 and go on increasing in **Unbelief**, Allah will
005:041 who race each other into **Unbelief**: (whether it be)
008:038 if (now) they desist (from **Unbelief**), their
009:037 (of a prohibited month) is an addition to **Unbelief**:
009:097 in **unbelief** and hypocrisy, and most fitted
009:125 and they will die in a state of **Unbelief**.
016:106 after accepting faith in Allah, utters **Unbelief**,-
016:106 but such as open their breast to **Unbelief**,-
049:007 and He has made hateful to you **unbelief**, wrongdoing,

UNBELIEVER
002:221 is better than an **unbeliever**,
078:040 have sent forth, and the **Unbeliever** will say,

UNBELIEVERS
002:221 **Unbelievers** do (but) beckon you to the Fire.
002:221 to **unbelievers** until they believe;
002:286 grant us victory over the **unbelievers**.
003:028 **Unbelievers** rather than Believers:
003:054 And (the **unbelievers**) plotted and planned,
003:127 of the **Unbelievers** or expose them to infamy,
003:149 O ye who believe! If ye obey the **Unbelievers**,
003:151 terror into the hearts of the **Unbelievers**,
003:156 O ye who believe! Be not like the **Unbelievers**,
003:178 Let not the **Unbelievers** think that our respite
003:196 of the **unbelievers** through the land deceive thee:
004:051 and say to the **Unbelievers** that they are better
004:084 will restrain the fury of the **Unbelievers**;
004:101 for the **Unbelievers** are unto you open enemies.
004:101 for fear the **Unbelievers** may attack you:
004:102 the **Unbelievers** wish, if ye were negligent of
004:102 For the **Unbelievers** Allah hath prepared
004:139 Those who take for friends **Unbelievers** rather than
004:141 But if the **Unbelievers** gain a success, they say
004:141 **Unbelievers** a way (to triumph) over the Believers.
004:144 for friends **Unbelievers** rather than Believers:
004:151 They are in truth **Unbelievers**; and We have
004:151 for **Unbelievers** a humiliating punishment.
005:044 by what Allah hath revealed, they are **Unbelievers**.
005:080 in friendship to the **Unbelievers**.
005:110 and the **unbelievers** among them said: 'This is
006:007 the **Unbelievers** would have been sure to say:
006:025 the **Unbelievers** say: "These are nothing
007:066 The leaders of the **unbelievers** among
007:090 The leaders, the **Unbelievers** among his people,
008:007 and to cut off the roots of the **Unbelievers**;-
008:012 into the hearts of the **Unbelievers**:
008:015 the **Unbelievers** in hostile array, never turn
008:018 and stratagems of the **Unbelievers**.
008:019 (O **Unbelievers**!) if ye prayed for victory
008:030 Remember how the **Unbelievers** plotted against
008:036 and the **Unbelievers** will be gathered together
008:036 The **Unbelievers** spend their wealth to hinder
008:038 Say to the **Unbelievers**, if (now)
008:050 of the **Unbelievers** (at death), (how) they
008:059 Let not the **Unbelievers** think that they
008:065 a thousand of the **Unbelievers**:
008:073 The **Unbelievers** are protectors, one of another:
009:026 He punished the **Unbelievers**: thus doth
009:030 **Unbelievers** of old used to say.
009:032 even though the **Unbelievers** may detest (it).
009:037 to Unbelief: the **Unbelievers** are led
009:040 the word of the **Unbelievers**.
009:040 help him, when the **Unbelievers** drove him out:
009:049 Hell surrounds the **Unbelievers** (on all sides).
009:073 the **Unbelievers** and the Hypocrites, and be
009:085 while they are **unbelievers**.
009:090 seize the **Unbelievers** among them.
009:120 or trod paths to raise the ire of the **Unbelievers**,
009:123 O ye who believe! Fight the **Unbelievers** who are
010:002 (but) say the **Unbelievers**: "This is
010:105 and never in any wise be of the **Unbelievers**;
011:007 after death, the **Unbelievers** would be sure to say,
011:027 But the Chiefs of the **Unbelievers** among his
011:042 and be not with the **Unbelievers**!"
013:007 And the **Unbelievers** say: "Why is not a Sign
013:027 The **Unbelievers** say: "Why is not a Sign

UNBELIEVERS (continued)

013:031 But the **Unbelievers**,-never will disaster cease to
013:032 but I granted respite to the **Unbelievers**, and finally
013:035 and the End of **Unbelievers** is the Fire.
013:042 and soon will the **Unbelievers** know who gets
013:043 The **Unbelievers** say: "No messenger art thou."
014:002 But alas for the **Unbelievers** for a
014:013 And the **Unbelievers** said to their messengers:
016:027 indeed, are the **Unbelievers** covered with
016:084 then will no excuse be accepted from **Unbelievers**,
018:056 but the **Unbelievers** dispute with vain argument,
018:100 for **Unbelievers** to see, all spread out,-
018:101 (**Unbelievers**) whose eyes had been under a veil
018:102 Do the **Unbelievers** think that they can take
018:102 for the **Unbelievers** for (their) entertainment.
019:037 and woe to the **Unbelievers** because of the
019:073 the **Unbelievers** say to those who believe,
019:083 set Satans on against the **Unbelievers**, to incite
021:030 Do not the **Unbelievers** see that the heavens
021:036 When the **Unbelievers** see thee, they treat
021:039 If only the **Unbelievers** knew (the time)
021:097 the eyes of the **Unbelievers** will fixedly
021:098 Verily ye, (**Unbelievers**), and the false
022:044 respite to the **Unbelievers**, and (only) after
022:072 thou wilt notice a denial on the faces of the **Unbelievers**!
022:072 Allah has promised it to the **Unbelievers**!
023:024 The chiefs of the **Unbelievers** among his people
023:117 And verily the **Unbelievers** shall not prosper
024:039 But the **Unbelievers**,-their deeds
024:057 Never think thou that the **Unbelievers** can escape
025:040 And the (**Unbelievers**) must indeed have passed
025:052 Therefore listen not to the **Unbelievers**, but strive
027:067 The **Unbelievers** say:" What! when we become dust,-
029:012 And the **Unbelievers** say to those who believe:
029:047 and none but **Unbelievers** reject Our Signs.
030:051 they become, thereafter, ungrateful (**Unbelievers**)!
030:058 the **Unbelievers** are sure to say, "Ye do
032:029 no profit will it be to **Unbelievers** if they
033:001 and hearken not to the **Unbelievers** and the
033:008 has prepared for the **Unbelievers** a grievous
033:025 And Allah turned back the **Unbelievers** for (all)
033:048 of the **Unbelievers** and the Hypocrites,
033:064 the **Unbelievers** and prepared for them
033:073 men and women, and the **Unbelievers**, men and
034:003 The **Unbelievers** say, "Never to us
034:007 The **Unbelievers** say (in ridicule): "Shall we
034:031 The **Unbelievers** say: "We shall neither believe
034:033 We shall put yokes on the necks of the **Unbelievers**:
034:043 And the **Unbelievers** say of the Truth when it
035:039 for the **Unbelievers** in the sight of their Lord:
036:047 the **Unbelievers** say to those who believe:
038:002 But the **Unbelievers** (are steeped) in Self-glory
038:004 And the **Unbelievers** say, "This is a
038:027 That were the thought of **Unbelievers**!
038:027 But woe to the **Unbelievers** because of the Fire (of Hell)!
039:032 an abode for the **unbelievers**?
039:071 The **Unbelievers** will be led to Hell in groups;
039:071 has been proved true against the **Unbelievers**!"
040:004 about the Signs of Allah but the **Unbelievers**.
040:006 proved true against the **Unbelievers**;
040:010 The **Unbelievers** will be addressed: "Greater was
040:014 even though the **Unbelievers** may detest it.
040:025 but the plots of **Unbelievers** (end) in nothing

UNBELIEVERS (continued)

040:074 Thus does Allah leave the **Unbelievers** to stray.
041:026 The **Unbelievers** say: "Listen not to this Qur'an,
041:027 But We will certainly give the **Unbelievers** a taste
041:029 And the **Unbelievers** will say: "Our Lord!
041:038 But if they (**Unbelievers**) are arrogant,
041:050 the **Unbelievers** the truth of all that they did,
042:026 but for the **Unbelievers** there is a
046:007 to them, the **Unbelievers** say, of the Truth
046:011 The **Unbelievers** say of those who believe:
046:020 And on the Day that the **Unbelievers** will be
046:034 And on the Day that the **Unbelievers** will be
046:035 and be in no haste about the (**Unbelievers**).
047:004 Therefore, when ye meet the **Unbelievers** (in fight),
048:022 If the **Unbelievers** should fight you, they would
048:025 the **Unbelievers** among them with a
048:026 While the **Unbelievers** got up in their hearts
048:029 are strong against **Unbelievers**, (but) compassionate
048:029 it fills the **Unbelievers** with rage at him.
050:002 So the **Unbelievers** say: "This is a wonderful thing!
051:060 Woe, then, to the **Unbelievers**, from the Day
054:008 'Hard in this Day!" The **Unbelievers** will say.
054:043 Are your **Unbelievers**, (O Quraish),
058:005 And the **Unbelievers** (will have) a humiliating
059:002 It is He who got out the **Unbelievers** among the
060:005 trial for the **Unbelievers**, but forgive us, our Lord!
060:010 They are not lawful (wives) for the **Unbelievers**,
060:010 and let the (**Unbelievers**) ask for what they
060:010 then send them not back to the **Unbelievers**.
060:010 nor are the (**Unbelievers**) lawful (husbands) for them.
060:010 But pay the **Unbelievers** what they have spent
060:011 And if any of your wives deserts you to the **Unbelievers**,
060:013 in despair, just as the **Unbelievers** are in despair
061:008 His Light, even though the **Unbelievers** may detest
064:002 and of you some are **Unbelievers**, and some that
064:007 The **Unbelievers** think that they will not be
066:007 (It will be said), "O ye **Unbelievers**! make no
066:009 the **Unbelievers** and the Hypocrites, and be
066:010 to the **Unbelievers**, the wife of Noah and the wife
067:020 delusion are the **Unbelievers**.
067:027 of the **Unbelievers**, and it will be said (to them):
067:028 yet who can deliver the **Unbelievers** from a
068:051 And the **Unbelievers** would almost trip thee up
069:050 of sorrow for the **Unbelievers**.
070:002 The **Unbelievers** the which there is none
070:036 the **Unbelievers** that they rush madly before thee-
071:026 Leave not of the **Unbelievers**, a single
074:031 as trial for **Unbelievers**,-in order
074:031 and the **Unbelievers** may say, "What doth
083:034 will laugh at the **Unbelievers**:
083:036 Will not the **Unbelievers** have been paid back
084:022 But on the contrary the **Unbelievers** reject (it).
085:019 And yet the **Unbelievers** (persist) in rejecting
086:017 Therefore grant a delay to the **unbelievers**:

UNBELIEVERS'

024:040 Or (the **Unbelievers'** state) is like the depths

UNBELIEVING

002:221 Do not marry **unbelieving** women (idolaters),
002:221 is better than an **unbelieving** woman,
060:010 not to the ties (marriage contract) of **unbelieving** women:

UNBLEST

019:004 am I **unblest**, O my Lord, in my prayer to Thee!
019:032 and not overbearing or **unblest**;

UNBLEST (continued)
019:048   I shall be not **unblest**."!
UNBOUNDED
003:074   for Allah is the Lord of bounties **unbounded**.
003:174   and Allah is the Lord of bounties **unbounded**.
008:029   is the Lord of grace **unbounded**.
UNCERTAINTY
027:066   and **uncertainty** thereanent; nay, they
UNCHASTE
019:020   and I am not **unchaste**?"
019:028   a man of evil, nor thy mother a woman **unchaste**!"
UNCLEAN
009:028   O ye who believe! Truly the Pagans are **unclean**;
UNCLES
033:050   and daughters of thy paternal **uncles** and aunts,
033:050   maternal **uncles** and aunts, who migrated
UNCOMFORTABLE
018:029   the drink! How **uncomfortable** a couch to recline on!
UNCOMMON
015:062   He said: "Ye appear to be **uncommon** folk."
UNCONSCIOUS
046:005   are **unconscious** of their call (to them)?
UNCONTROLLED
075:036   be left **uncontrolled**, (without purpose)?
UNCOVERING
027:044   and she (tucked up her skirts), **uncovering** her legs.
UNDEFILED
056:036   And made them virgin-pure (and **undefiled**),-
UNDER
003:112   except when **under** a covenant (of protection)
004:023   your step-daughters **under** your guardianship, born
006:119   except **under** compulsion of necessity?
009:072   men and women, Gardens **under** which rivers flow,
009:089   **under** which rivers flow, to dwell therein: that is
009:100   hath He prepared Gardens **under** which rivers flow,
011:037   "But construct an Ark **under** Our eyes
016:075   (of two men): one a slave **under** the dominion
016:106   except **under** compulsion, his heart remaining firm
017:062   I will surely bring his descendants **under** my sway-
018:101   (Unbelievers) whose eyes had been **under** a veil
020:039   mayest be reared **under** Mine eye.
022:078   ought to strive, (with sincerity and **under** discipline):
023:027   within Our sight and **under** Our guidance: then when
024:063   you who slip away **under** shelter of some excuse:
027:018   (**under** foot) without knowing it."
027:047   yea, ye are a people **under** trial."
028:027   But I intend not to place thee **under** a difficulty:
032:024   Leaders, giving guidance **under** Our command, so long
036:071   which are **under** their dominion?-
041:005   They say: "Our hearts are **under** veils, (concealed)
048:018   to thee **under** the Tree: He knew
054:014   She floats **under** Our eyes (and care):
066:010   they were (respectively) **under** two of Our
UNDERGO
072:017   He will cause him to **undergo** ever-growing
UNDERGROUND
018:041   run off **underground** so that thou wilt never
067:030   stream be some morning lost (in the **underground** earth),
UNDERMINED
009:109   layeth his foundation on an **undermined** sand-cliff

UNDERNEATH
002:266   and vines and streams flowing **underneath**,
003:136   and Gardens with rivers flowing **underneath**,
005:085   with rivers flowing **underneath**, their eternal home.
043:051   (witness) these streams flowing **underneath** my (palace)?
UNDERSTAND
002:044   Will ye not **understand**?
002:073   perchance ye may **understand**.
002:076   Do ye not **understand** (their aim)?
002:242   in order that ye may **understand**.
004:043   until ye can **understand** all that ye say,
004:078   that they fail to **understand** a single fact?.
005:100   O ye that **understand** that (so) ye may prosper."
006:025   so they **understand** it not, and deafness
006:032   Will ye not then **understand**?
006:037   but most of them **understand** not."
006:065   that they may **understand**.
006:098   We detail Our signs for people who **understand**.
007:131   but most of them do not **understand**!
007:169   Will ye not **understand**?
007:179   They have hearts wherewith they **understand** not,
008:022   and the dumb,-those who **understand** not.
008:034   but most of them do not **understand**.
009:011   for those who **understand**.
009:081   If only they could **understand**!
009:087   their hearts are sealed and so they **understand** not.
009:127   for they are a people that **understand** not.
010:016   I tarried amongst you: will ye not then **understand**?"
010:100   on those who will not **understand**.
011:051   created Me: will ye not then **understand**?
011:091   thou sayest we do not **understand**!
012:040   but Most men **understand** not.
012:109   Will ye not then **understand**?
013:004   there are Signs for those who **understand**!
015:075   for those who by tokens do **understand**.
016:101   but most of them **understand** not.
017:044   and yet ye **understand** not how they declare
017:046   they should **understand** the Qur'an, and deafness
018:057   they should **understand** this not, and over
020:028   "So they may **understand** what I say:
021:010   Will ye not then **understand**?
023:030   (for men to **understand**); lo! We put (men) to test.
023:080   of Night and Day: will ye not then **understand**?
024:061   that ye may **understand**.
025:044   of them listen or **understand**?
026:113   if ye could (but) **understand**.
028:057   But most of them **understand** not.
029:016   that will be best for you-if ye **understand**!
029:035   for any people who (care to) **understand**.
029:043   those **understand** them who have Knowledge.
029:063   But most of them **understand** not.
030:006   but most men **understand** not.
030:028   to a people that **understand**.
030:059   of those who **understand** not.
031:025   to Allah!" But most of them know not.
033:063   make thee **understand**?-perchance the Hour is nigh!
036:062   Did ye not, then **understand**?
036:068   will they not then **understand**?
037:138   And by night: will ye not **understand**?
039:049   but most of them **understand** not!
040:067   a Term appointed: in order that ye may **understand**.
041:003   for people who **understand**;-
043:003   that ye may be able to **understand**.

UNDERSTAND (continued)

047:024 to **understand** the Qur'an, or is that
048:015 Nay, but little do they **understand** (such things).
054:017 easy to **understand** and remember: then is
054:022 easy to **understand** and remember: then is
054:032 easy to **understand** and remember: then is
054:040 easy to **understand** and remember: then is
057:017 plainly to you, that ye may **understand**.
063:003 therefore they **understand** not.
063:007 but the Hypocrites **understand** not.
072:010 'And we **understand** not whether ill is intended
089:005 (or evidence) for those who **understand**?

UNDERSTANDING

002:179 O ye men of **understanding**;
002:269 receive admonition but men of **understanding**.
003:007 the Message except men of **understanding**.
003:065 Have ye no **understanding**?
003:190 there are indeed Signs for men of **understanding**,
004:005 To those weak of **understanding** give not
004:129 If ye come to a friendly **understanding**, and
005:058 a people without **understanding**.
008:065 for these are a people without **understanding**.
010:042 even though they are without **understanding**.
012:111 instruction for men endued with **understanding**.
013:019 with **understanding** that receive admonition;-
014:052 let men of **understanding** take heed.
020:054 Signs for men endued with **understanding**.
020:128 for men endued with **understanding**.
021:079 the (right) **understanding** of the matter:
023:078 hearing, sight, feeling and **understanding**:
032:009 (the faculties of) hearing, and sight and **understanding**
038:029 and that men of **understanding** may receive admonition.
038:043 for all who have **Understanding**.
039:009 endued with **understanding** that receive admonition.
039:018 ones endued with **understanding**.
039:021 of remembrance to men of **understanding**.
040:054 A Guide and a Message to men of **understanding**.
045:023 and his heart (and **understanding**), and put
049:004 most of them lack **understanding**.
050:003 Return far (from our **understanding**)."
050:037 that has a heart and **understanding** or who
059:013 men devoid of **understanding**.
065:010 O ye men of **understanding**-who have believed!-
067:023 the faculties of hearing, sight, and **understanding**:

UNDERSTANDS

062:005 which carries huge tomes (but **understands** them not).

UNDERSTOOD

002:075 knowingly after they **understood** it.
018:091 We completely **understood** what was before him.
018:093 who scarcely **understood** a word.

UNDERTAKE

033:072 to **undertake** it, being afraid thereof: ·

UNDERTAKEN

021:104 a promise We have **undertaken**: truly shall

UNDERTAKES

002:197 If any one **undertakes** that duty therein,

UNDERTOOK

033:072 but man **undertook** it: he was

UNDESERVEDLY

033:058 and women **undeservedly**, bear (on themselves)

UNDIVIDED

006:146 We forbade every (animal) with **undivided** hoof,

UNDOUBTEDLY

016:023 **Undoubtedly** Allah doth know what they conceal,
038:024 (David) said: "He has **undoubtedly** wronged thee

UNDRESS

024:058 times of **undress**: outside those times it is

UNDUE

002:231 or to take **undue** advantage;

UNFAILING

002:273 Thou shalt know them by their (**unfailing**) mark:
007:183 for My scheme is strong (and **unfailing**).
068:003 Nay, verily for thee is a Reward **unfailing**:
095:006 for they shall have a reward **unfailing**.

UNFAIR

053:022 a division most **unfair**!

UNFAIRLY

002:233 treated **unfairly** on account of her child.

UNFAITH

009:012 fight ye the chiefs of **Unfaith**: for their
014:002 (their **Unfaith** will bring them)!-

UNFAITHFUL

022:038 that is **unfaithful**, ungrateful.

UNFOLDED

052:003 In a parchment **unfolded**;

UNFORGIVABLE

009:080 or not, (their sin is **unforgivable**): if thou

UNFORMED

022:002 shall drop her load (**unformed**): thou shalt
022:005 partly formed and partly **unformed**, in order

UNFORTUNATE

087:011 the most **unfortunate** one,
092:015 None shall reach it but those most **unfortunate** ones

UNGODLY

015:008 (to the **ungodly**), behold! no respite
016:033 Do the (**ungodly**) wait but for the angels

UNGRATEFUL

002:243 but most of them are **ungrateful**.
002:276 for He loveth not any **ungrateful** Sinner.
010:060 to mankind, but most of them are **ungrateful**.
016:072 and be **ungrateful** for Allah's favours?-
016:083 and most of them are (creatures) **ungrateful**.
016:112 yet was it **ungrateful** for the favours of Allah:
017:027 his Lord (Himself) **ungrateful**.
017:067 Most **ungrateful** is man!
022:038 that is unfaithful, **ungrateful**.
022:066 truly man is a most **ungrateful** creature!
026:019 and thou art an **ungrateful**!"
027:040 his own soul; but if any is **ungrateful**, truly my
027:040 to test me whether I am grateful or **ungrateful**!
027:073 yet most of them are **ungrateful**.
030:051 they become, thereafter, **ungrateful** (Unbelievers)!
031:012 but if any is **ungrateful**, verily Allah
031:032 except only a perfidious **ungrateful** (wretch)!
034:017 as are **ungrateful** rejecters.
034:033 to be **ungrateful** to Allah and to attribute
035:036 Thus do We reward every **ungrateful** one!
039:003 as are false and **ungrateful**.
042:048 truly then is man **ungrateful**!
071:027 but wicked **ungrateful** ones.
076:003 whether he be grateful or **ungrateful**.
100:006 Truly Man is to his Lord, **ungrateful**;

UNGRATEFULLY
029:066 Disdaining **ungratefully** Our gifts and giving
034:017 them because they **ungratefully** rejected Faith:

UNHAPPY
090:019 they are the (**unhappy**) Companions of the Left Hand.

UNHEARD-OF
018:074 Truly a foul (**unheard-of**) thing hast thou done!"
018:087 him with a punishment **unheard-of** (before).

UNHEEDFUL
007:205 and be not thou of those who are **unheedful**.

UNISON
038:018 in **unison** with him, Our Praises, at eventide

UNIT
021:030 joined together (as one **unit** of Creation), before

UNITE
012:101 (as a Muslim), and **unite** me with the righteous."""

UNITED
007:189 When they are **united**, she bears
059:014 thou wouldst think they were **united**, but their

UNITY
021:093 their affair (of **unity**), one from another:
023:053 But people have cut off their affair (of **unity**),

UNIVERSE
002:131 to the Lord and Cherisher of the **Universe**."

UNJUST
002:114 And who is more **unjust** than he who forbids
002:140 Ah! who is more **unjust** than those
002:258 Nor doth Allah give guidance to a people **unjust**.
003:086 But Allah guides not a people **unjust**.
003:094 they are indeed **unjust** wrong-doers.
004:040 Allah is never **unjust** in the least degree:
004:064 were **unjust** to themselves, come unto thee
005:051 Verily Allah guideth not a people **unjust**.
006:052 and thus be (one) of the **unjust**.
006:136 Evil (and **unjust**) is their judgment.
007:019 lest you become of the **unjust**."
007:037 Who is more **unjust** than one who forges
008:051 For Allah is never **unjust** to His servants."
017:082 to the **unjust** it causes nothing but
017:099 But the **unjust** refuse (to receive it)
019:038 But the **unjust** to-day are in
021:059 be one of the **unjust** one.
022:010 for verily Allah is not **unjust** to His servants.
026:209 and We never are **unjust**.
026:227 And soon will the **unjust** know what
027:082 against them (the **unjust**), We shall
028:025 (well) hast thou escaped from **unjust** people."
029:049 the **unjust** reject Our Signs.
033:072 he was indeed **unjust** and foolish;-
041:046 nor is thy Lord ever **unjust** (in the least)
043:076 but it is they who have been **unjust** themselves.
043:076 Nowise shall We be **unjust** to them: But it
046:010 (how **unjust** ye are!) truly, Allah guides
046:010 Allah guides not a people **unjust**."
046:012 the Arabic tongue; to admonish the **unjust**, and as
053:052 for that they were (all) most **unjust** and most
068:025 strong in an (**unjust**) resolve.
077:046 (O ye **Unjust**!) Eat ye and enjoy yourselves (but)

UNJUSTLY
002:272 and ye shall not be dealt with **unjustly**.
002:279 and ye shall no be dealt with **unjustly**.
002:279 deal not **unjustly**,

UNJUSTLY (continued)
002:281 and none shall be dealt with **unjustly**.
003:161 and none shall be dealt with **unjustly**.
004:010 Those who **unjustly** eat up the property of orphans,
004:077 never will ye be dealt **unjustly** in the very least!
006:131 the towns **unjustly** whilst their occupants
008:060 unto you, and ye shall not be treated **unjustly**.
010:044 Verily Allah will not deal **unjustly** with man in aught:
011:117 to destroy the towns **unjustly** while their people
016:111 and none will be **unjustly** dealt with.
017:071 will not be dealt with **unjustly** in the least.
021:047 dealt with **unjustly** in the least.
024:050 will deal **unjustly** with them?
026:227 they are **unjustly** attacked.

UNKNOWN
012:009 to some (**unknown**) land, that so the favour of your
018:022 doubtfully guessing at the **unknown**; (yet others)
051:025 (And thought, "These seem) **unknown** people."

UNLAWFUL
003:093 except what Israel made **unlawful** for himself
004:160 We made **unlawful** for them certain (foods)
005:087 O ye who believe! make not **unlawful** the good

UNLEARNED
003:020 the Book and to those who are **unlearned**:

UNLESS
002:111 Paradise **unless** he be a Jew or a Christian."
002:120 **unless** thou follow their form of religion.
002:191 **unless** they (first) fight you there;
002:237 **unless** they remit it.
003:073 "And believe no one **unless** he follows your religion."
003:075 **unless** thou constantly stoodest demanding,
003:092 **unless** ye give (freely) of that which ye love:
003:183 **unless** he showed us a sacrifice consumed by fire
004:092 **unless** they remit it freely.
004:140 **unless** they turn to a different Theme: if ye did,
005:003 **unless** ye are able to slaughter it (in due form);
005:032 **unless** it be for murder or for spreading
005:068 **unless** ye stand fast by the Torah.
006:068 turn away from them **unless** they turn
006:077 "**Unless** my Lord guide me, I shall
006:080 **unless** my Lord willeth, (nothing can happen), my
006:111 **unless** it is in Allah's Plan.
006:145 **unless** it be dead meat, or blood
007:089 return thereto **unless** it be as in the will
008:016 **unless** it be in a stratagem of war, or to
008:073 **unless** ye do this, (protect each other),
009:039 **Unless** ye go forth, He will
010:035 not guidance (himself) **unless** he is guided?
011:047 and **unless** Thou forgive me and have
012:033 **unless** Thou turn away their snare
012:053 certainly incites evil, **unless** my Lord do bestow
012:063 of grain shall we get (**unless** we take our brother):
012:066 **unless** ye are yourselves hemmed in
025:070 **Unless** he repents, believers, and works
027:021 or execute him, **unless** he bring me a clear
029:046 **unless** it be with those of them who do wrong
060:004 for ever,-**unless** ye believe in Allah and Him
072:023 "**Unless** I deliver what I receive from Allah

UNLETTERED
003:075 no way over us as to the **Unlettered** people,"
007:157 the **unlettered** Prophet, whom they find
007:158 The **unlettered** Prophet, who believeth in
062:002 the **Unlettered** a messenger from among themselves,

UNLOOSED
011:039 on whom will be **unloosed** a Chastisement lasting."

UNMINDFUL
002:074 And Allah is not **unmindful** of what ye do.
002:085 For Allah is not **unmindful** of what ye do.
002:140 But Allah is not **unmindful** of what ye do!
002:144 nor is Allah **unmindful** of what they do.
002:149 And Allah is not **unmindful** of what ye do.
003:099 But Allah is not **unmindful** of all that ye do."
006:132 not **unmindful** of anything that they do.
011:123 and thy Lord is not **unmindful** of aught that ye do.
023:017 and We are never **unmindful** of (Our) Creation.
027:093 and thy Lord is not **unmindful** of all that ye do.
080:010 Of him wast thou **unmindful**.

UNNECESSARY
005:015 and passing over much (that is now **unnecessary**):

UNNOTICED
007:189 and carries it about (**unnoticed**).

UNPALATABLE
056:070 make it saltish (and **unpalatable**):

UNRELENTING
014:017 will be a chastisement **unrelenting**.
031:024 drive them to a chastisement **unrelenting**.

UNRIGHTEOUS
002:165 If only the **unrighteous** could see,
003:182 "This is because of the (**unrighteous** deeds) which
011:046 for his conduct is **unrighteous**.

UNRULY
021:081 the violent (**unruly**) wind flow (tamely) for

UNSEEMLY
002:268 and bids you to conduct **unseemly**.
033:030 if any of you were guilty of evident **unseemly** conduct,

UNSEEN
002:003 Who believe in the **Unseen**,
003:044 This is part of the tidings of the things **unseen**,
003:179 to you the secrets of the **Unseen**,
005:094 that He may test who feareth Him **unseen**:
006:059 With Him are the keys of the **Unseen**,
006:073 He knoweth the **Unseen** as well
007:188 If I had knowledge of the **unseen**, I should
009:078 well all things **unseen**?
010:020 Say: "The **Unseen** is only for Allah (to Know).
011:049 of the **Unseen**, which We have revealed unto thee:
011:123 **unseen** (secrets) of the heavens and the earth,
012:081 and we could not well guard against the **unseen**!
012:102 happened **unseen**, which We reveal by inspiration
013:009 He knoweth the **Unseen** and that which is open:
016:077 To Allah belongeth the **Unseen** of the heavens
019:061 to His servants in the **Unseen**: for His
019:078 Has he penetrated to the **Unseen**, or he has
031:020 in exceeding measure, (both) seen and **unseen**?
034:003 by Him who knows the **unseen**,-
034:014 had known the **unseen**, they would
034:053 with regard to the **Unseen** from a position far off?
035:018 fear their Lord **unseen** and establish regular
036:011 the Most Gracious, **unseen**: given such a one,
049:018 "Verily Allah knows the **Unseen** of the heavens
050:033 "Who feared The Most Gracious **unseen**, and brought
052:041 Or that the **Unseen** is in their hands, and they
053:035 What! Has he knowledge of the **Unseen** so that
057:025 will help, **unseen** Him and His messengers:
067:012 As for those who fear their Lord **unseen**, for them

UNSEEN (continued)
068:047 Or that the **Unseen** is in their hands, so that
072:026 "He (alone) knows the **Unseen**, nor does
081:024 a knowledge of the **Unseen**.

UNSERVICEABLE
018:079 I but wished to render it **unserviceable**, for there

UNSTALLING
047:015 in it are rivers of water **unstalling**; rivers of

UNSTINTED
076:006 do drink, making it flow in **unstinted** abundance.

UNTENDED
081:004 with young, are left **untended**;

UNTHANKFUL
043:015 Truly is man clearly **unthankful**.

UNTIL
002:055 in thee **until** we see Allah manifestly,"
002:187 **until** the white thread of dawn appear to you
002:193 And fight them on **until** there is no more
002:196 **until** the offering reaches the place
002:210 Will they wait **until** Allah comes to them
002:217 **until** they turn you back from your faith
002:221 Do not marry unbelieving woman **until** they believe:
002:221 nor marry (your girls) to unbelievers **until** they believe;
002:222 and do not approach them **until** they are clean.
002:230 **until** after she has married another husband
003:152 **until** ye flinched and fell to disputing
003:179 **until** He separates what is evil from what is good.
004:006 **until** they reach the age of marriage;
004:015 to houses **until** death do claim them, or
004:018 **until** death faces one of them, and he says,
004:043 **until** after washing your whole body if ye are ill,
004:043 **until** ye can understand all that ye say,
004:065 **until** they make thee judge in all
004:089 **until** they flee in the way of Allah
005:022 never shall we enter it **until** they leave it:
006:031 **until** on a sudden the hour is on them, and they
006:034 **until** Our aid did reach them: there is none
006:044 the gates of all (good) things, **until**, in the
006:124 "We shall not believe **until** we receive
006:148 **until** they tasted of Our wrath.
006:152 **until** he attain the age of full strength;
007:037 **until**, when Our messengers (of death) arrive
007:038 **until** they follow each other, all into the Fire.
007:040 **until** the camel can pass through
007:087 **until** Allah doth decide between us: for He
007:095 **until** they grew and multiplied, and began
008:039 And fight them on **until** there is no
008:053 on a people **until** they change what is in their
008:067 **until** he hath thoroughly subdued the land.
008:072 to them **until** they emigrate; but if
009:024 then wait **until** Allah brings about His Decision:
009:029 **until** they pay Jizya with willing submission,
009:043 grant them exemption **until** those who told
009:048 **until** the Truth arrived, and the Decree
009:110 **until** their hearts are cut to pieces.
009:115 after He hath Guided them **until** He makes clear
010:088 **until** they see the grievous Chastisement."
010:097 **until** they see (for themselves)
012:066 with you **until** ye swear a solemn oath to me,
012:080 **until** my father permits me, or Allah
012:085 of illness, or **until** thou die!"
012:085 thou cease to remember Joseph **until** though reach

UNTIL (continued)

012:110 (Respite will be granted) **until**, when the
013:011 **until** they change what is in themselves but when
013:031 **until** the Promise of Allah come to pass,
015:099 And serve thy Lord **until** there come unto thee
017:015 nor would We punish **until**, We had sent
017:034 **until** he attains the age of full strength;
017:090 in thee, **until** thou cause a spring to gush
017:091 "Or (**until**) thou have a garden of date trees
017:093 **until** thou send down to us a book that we
018:060 or (**until**) I spend years and years in travel."
018:060 "I will not give up **until** I reach the junction
018:070 about anything **until** I myself speak to thee
018:071 So they both proceeded: **until**, when they
018:074 Then they proceeded: **until**, when they
018:077 Then they proceeded: **until**, when they
018:086 **Until**, when he reached the setting of the sun,
018:090 **Until**, when he came to the rising of the sun,
018:093 **Until**, when he reached (a tract) between two
019:075 (the rope) to them, **until**, when they see the
020:091 to it **until** Moses returns to us."
021:044 and their fathers **until** the period grew long for
021:096 **Until** the Gog and Magog (people) are let
022:055 **until** the Hour (of Judgment) comes suddenly
023:064 **Until**, when We seize in Punishment those of
023:077 **Until** We open on them a gate leading to
023:099 **Until**, when death comes to one of them, he says:
024:027 **until** ye have asked permission and saluted
024:028 enter not **until** permission is given to you:
024:033 **until** Allah gives them means out of His grace.
024:039 for water; **until** when he comes up to it,
024:062 they do not depart **until** they have asked
025:018 **until** they forgot the Message: for they
026:201 They will not believe in it **until** they see
027:084 **Until**, when they come (before the Judgment-Seat),
028:012 at first, **until** (his sister came up and) said:
028:023 **until** the shepherds take back (their flocks):
028:059 a town **until** He had sent to its Centre
030:048 into fragments, **until** thou seest rain-drops
033:053 the Prophet's houses,-**until** leave is given you,-
038:032 **Until** (the sun) was hidden in the veil (of Night):
039:071 in groups; **until**, when they arrive there,
039:073 **until** behold, they arrive there; its gates
041:053 **until** it becomes manifest to them that this
043:029 and their fathers, **until** the Truth has come
043:083 (with vanities) **until** they meet that Day of theirs,
047:004 **until** the war lays down its burdens.
047:031 And We shall try you **until** We test those among you
049:005 **until** thou couldst come out to them, it would
049:009 the one that transgresses **until** it complies
052:045 So leave them alone **until** they encounter
057:014 **until** there issued the Command of Allah.
065:004 are pregnant, their period is **until** they deliver
065:006 **until** they deliver their burden:
070:042 and play about, **until** they encounter that Day
074:047 "**Until** there came to us (the Hour) that is certain."
097:005 Peace!...This **until** the rise of Morn!
098:001 (from their ways) **until** there should come to
098:004 make schisms, **until** after there came to them
102:002 **Until** ye visit the graves.

UNTO

002:022 set not up rivals **unto** Allah when ye know (the truth).
002:109 become manifest **unto** them:

UNTO (continued)

002:113 Like **unto** their word is what those
002:118 Or why cometh not **unto** Us a Sign?"
002:118 "Why speaketh not Allah **unto** Us?
002:118 the Signs **unto** any people who hold
002:128 and turn **unto** us (in Mercy);
002:203 ye will surely be gathered **unto** Him.
002:223 Your wives are as a tilth **unto** you
002:245 will double **unto** his credit and multiply many times?
002:259 make of thee a Sign **unto** the people.
003:038 Grant **unto** me from Thee a progeny that is pure:
003:039 the angels called **unto** him: "Allah doth give thee
003:044 which We reveal **unto** thee (O Prophet!)
003:058 "This is what we rehearse **unto** thee of the Signs
003:073 like **unto** that which was sent **unto** you?
003:086 and that Clear Signs had come **unto** them?
003:101 while **unto** you are rehearsed the Signs of Allah,
003:158 Lo! it is **unto** Allah that ye are brought together.
003:164 rehearsing **unto** them the Signs of Allah,
003:194 Thou didst promise **unto** us through Thy Messengers,
004:021 when ye have gone in **unto** each other,
004:064 come **unto** thee and asked Allah's forgiveness,
004:083 the Grace and Mercy of Allah **unto** you,
004:095 **Unto** all (in Faith) hath Allah promised good:
004:101 for the Unbelievers are **unto** you open enemies.
004:113 and great is the Grace of Allah **unto** thee.
004:127 been rehearsed **unto** you in the Book, concerning
004:131 But if ye deny Him, lo! **unto** Allah belong all
004:132 Yea, **unto** Allah belong all things
004:158 Nay, Allah raised him up **unto** Himself;
004:166 He hath sent **unto** thee He hath sent
004:172 gather them all together **unto** Himself to (answer).
004:174 sent **unto** you a light (that is) manifest.
005:001 Lawful **unto** you (for food) are all
005:004 Say: Lawful **unto** you are (all) things good and pure:
005:005 (Lawful **unto** you in marriage) are (not only)
005:005 things good and pure made lawful **unto** you.
005:005 is lawful **unto** you and yours is lawful **unto** them.
005:007 the favour of Allah **unto** you, and His Covenant,
005:011 the favor of Allah **unto** you when certain men formed
005:016 by His Will, **unto** the light, guideth them
005:018 and **unto** Him is the final goal (of all)."
005:019 now hath come **unto** you, making (things) clear **unto** you,
005:019 "There came **unto** us no bringer of glad tidings and no
005:019 but now hath come **unto** you a bringer of glad tidings
005:020 the favour of Allah **unto** you, when He produced
005:021 which Allah hath assigned **unto** you, and turn
005:035 seek the means of approach **unto** Him, and strive
005:115 Allah said: "I will send it down **unto** you:
005:116 say **unto** men, "Take me and my mother for two
006:007 If We had sent **unto** thee a written (Message)
006:031 and they say: "Ah! woe **unto** us that we neglected;
006:035 He could gather them together **unto** true guidance:
006:036 then will they be turned **unto** Him.
006:060 in the end **unto** Him will be your return,
006:062 Then are men returned **unto** Allah, their True
006:111 Even if We did send **unto** them angels, and the
006:111 and the dead did speak **unto** them, and We
006:114 Who hath sent **unto** you the Book, explained
006:130 setting forth **unto** you My Signs and warning
006:130 came there not **unto** you messengers
006:134 All that hath been promised **unto** you will come to pass:
006:157 Now then hath come **unto** you a Clear (Sign)

UNTO (continued)

006:160 No wrong shall be done **unto** them.
007:002 A Book revealed **unto** thee,- so let
007:003 given **unto** you from your Lord, and follow
007:022 Satan was an avowed enemy **unto** you?"
007:022 And their Lord called **unto** them: "Did I not
007:035 rehearsing My Signs **unto** you,-those who
007:043 the Messengers of our Lord brought **unto** us."
007:052 For We had certainly sent **unto** them a Book,
007:073 Now hath come **unto** you a clear
007:073 This she-camel of Allah is a Sign **unto** you:
007:085 Now hath come **unto** you a clear
007:101 We (thus) relate **unto** thee: there came
007:105 Now have I come **unto** you (people), from your
007:125 "For us, we are but sent back **unto** our Lord."
007:126 and take our souls **unto** Thee as Muslims
007:138 a god like **unto** the gods they have."
007:156 for we have turned **unto** Thee."
007:158 Say: "O men! I am sent **unto** you all, as the
007:174 and perchance they may turn (**Unto** Us).
007:183 Respite will I grant **unto** them:
007:194 besides Allah are servants like **unto** you:
008:044 and **unto** Allah are all matters returned.
008:060 shall be repaid **unto** you, and ye shall not be treated
008:064 O Prophet! Sufficient **unto** thee is Allah,-
008:064 and **unto** those who follow thee among the Believers.
009:034 announce **unto** them a most grievous chastisement-
009:059 and had said, "Sufficient **unto** us is Allah!
009:096 They will swear **unto** you, that ye
009:102 Perhaps Allah will turn **unto** them (in mercy):
009:116 **Unto** Allah belongeth the dominion of the
009:117 for He is **unto** them Most Kind, Most Merciful.
009:128 Now hath come **unto** you a Messenger
010:012 he crieth **unto** Us (in all postures)-lying down
010:015 But when Our clear Signs are rehearsed **unto** them,
010:015 I follow naught but what is revealed **unto** me:
010:022 they pray **unto** Allah,
010:022 sincerely offering (their) duty **unto** Him, saying:
010:038 Say: "Bring then a Sura like **unto** it, and call
010:054 and no wrong will be done **unto** them.
010:094 We have revealed **unto** thee, then ask
010:097 Even if every Sign was brought **unto** them,-
010:109 Follow thou the inspiration sent **unto** thee, and be
011:002 (Say:) "Verily I am (sent) **unto** you from Him
011:012 sent down **unto** him, or why does not an angel
011:012 of what is revealed **unto** thee, and thy
011:013 "Bring ye then ten Suras forged, like **unto** it,
011:028 and that He hath sent Mercy **unto** me from Him,
011:049 stories of the unseen, which We have revealed **unto** thee:
011:063 and He hath sent Mercy **unto** me from Himself,-
011:088 In Him I trust, and **unto** Him I turn.
011:090 and turn **unto** Him (in repentance): for my Lord
011:097 **Unto** Pharaoh and his Chiefs: but they followed
011:099 which shall be given (**unto** them)!
011:100 of communities which We relate **unto** thee:
011:112 thou and those who with thee (**unto** Allah);
012:003 We do relate **unto** thee the most beautiful
012:050 So the king said: "Bring ye him **unto** me."
012:054 So the king said: "Bring him **unto** me; I will take
012:059 for them, he said: "Bring **unto** me a brother
012:102 which We revealed by inspiration **unto** thee:
012:108 Say thou: "This is My Way; I do invite **unto** Allah,-
013:001 **unto** thee from thy Lord is the Truth; but most

UNTO (continued)

013:019 **unto** thee from thy Lord is the Truth, like one
013:023 and angels shall enter **unto** them from every
013:024 "Peace **unto** you for that ye persevered in patience!
013:030 mightest rehearse **unto** them what We send down
013:030 We send down **unto** thee by inspiration;
013:036 rejoice at what hath been revealed **unto** thee:
013:036 **Unto** Him do I call, and **unto** Him is my return."
014:001 A Book which We have revealed **unto** thee, in order
014:007 I will add more (favours) **unto** you; but if ye
014:039 Who hath granted **unto** me in old age Isma'il and Isaac:
015:029 fall ye down in obeisance **unto** him."
015:095 For sufficient are We **unto** thee against those who
015:099 come **unto** thee the Hour that is Certain.
016:001 the partners they ascribe **unto** Him!
016:002 so do your duty **unto** Me."
016:044 and We have sent down **unto** thee (also) the Message;
016:053 **unto** Him ye cry with groans;
017:008 It may be that your Lord may (yet) show Mercy **unto** you;
017:061 "Prostrate **unto** Adam": they prostrated
017:066 For He is **unto** you Most Merciful.
017:073 thee away from the which We had revealed **unto** thee,
019:021 as a Sign **unto** men and a Mercy from Us':
020:126 when Our Signs came **unto** thee, forgot them:
022:018 are (also) such as **unto** whom the chastisement
025:074 "Our Lord! Grant **unto** us wives and offspring
026:013 so send **unto** Aaron.
027:082 a beast to speak **unto** them because mankind had
032:005 then it ascends **unto** Him, on a day the measure
035:003 O men! Remember the grace of Allah **unto** you!
036:038 And the Sun runs **unto** a resting place, for Him:
036:052 They will say: "Ah! woe **unto** us! Who hath
038:029 sent down **unto** thee, full of blessings, that they
038:072 fall ye down in prostrated **unto** him."
039:008 he crieth **unto** his Lord, turning to Him
039:008 and he doth set up Rivals **unto** Allah, thus misleading
041:006 so take the straight path **unto** Him and ask for
041:021 the first time, and **unto** Him were ye to return.
042:011 there is nothing whatever like **unto** Him, and He
045:037 And **unto** Him (alone) belongeth Majesty in the
051:050 Therefore flee **unto** Allah:
051:059 is like **unto** the portion of their fellows
052:028 "Truly we did call **unto** Him from of old:
052:034 like **unto** it,-if (it be) they speak the Truth!
054:051 have We destroyed gangs like **unto** you:
055:014 sounding clay like **unto** pottery.
055:058 Like **unto** rubies and coral.
056:023 Like **unto** Pearls well-guarded.
056:091 "Peace be **unto** thee," from the Companions
060:001 showing friendship **unto** them in secret:
067:015 which He furnishes: but **unto** Him is the Resurrection.
069:012 That We might make it a Reminder **unto** you,
070:004 **unto** Him in a Day the measure whereof is (as)
078:040 will say, "Woe **unto** me! Would that
089:028 well pleased (thyself), and well-pleasing **unto** Him!
092:013 And verily **unto** Us (belong) the End
112:004 And there is none like **unto** Him.

UNTRUE

072:005 man or jinn should say aught that is **untrue** against

UNTRUTH

078:035 No Vanity shall they hear therein, nor **Untruth**;-

UNTWISTED

016:092   who breaks into **untwisted** strands the yarn

UNVEILED

081:011   When the sky is **unveiled**:

UNWARNED

006:131   their occupants were **unwarned**.

UNWILLING

003:083   willing or **unwilling**, bowed to His Will

UNWILLINGLY

009:053   Say: "'Spend (for the Cause) willingly or **unwillingly**:

009:054   and that they offer contributions **unwillingly**.

041:011   "Come ye together, willingly or **unwillingly**."

UNWITTINGLY

049:006   harm people **unwittingly**, and afterwards

'UNZURNA

002:104   but say, **'Unzurna** and hearken (to him):

UP

002:022   then set not **up** rivals unto Allah

002:056   Then We raised you **up** after your death;

002:087   and followed him **up** with a succession

002:087   ye are puffed **up** with pride?

002:184   (should be made **up**) from days later.

002:185   (should be made **up**) by days later.

002:188   And do not eat **up** your property

002:188   with intent that ye may eat **up** wrongfully

002:259   then raised him **up** (again).

002:262   and follow not **up** their gifts with reminders

002:266   with fire therein, and be burnt **up**?

002:278   and give **up** what remains of your demand

003:106   some faces will be (lit **up** with) white,

003:153   Behold! ye were climbing **up** the high ground,

004:002   (by mixing it **up**) with your own.

004:006   nor in haste against their growing **up**.

004:010   eat **up** a fire into their own bodies:

004:010   Those who unjustly eat **up** the property of orphans,

004:029   O ye who believe! eat not **up** your property

004:048   that partners should be set **up** with him;

004:048   to set **up** partners with Allah is to devise a sin

004:078   even if ye are in towers built **up** strong and high!"

004:102   And let the other party come **up** which hath

004:102   stand **up** (in prayer) with thee.

004:103   set **up** regular Prayers: for such prayers

004:104   And slacken not in following **up** the enemy:

004:142   When they stand **up** to prayer, they stand

004:158   Nay, Allah raised him **up** unto Himself;

005:003   given **up** all hope of your religion: yet fear

005:014   so We stirred **up** enmity and hatred

005:064   Be their hands tied **up** and be they

005:064   The Jews say: "Allah's hand is tied **up**,"

005:117   when Thou didst take me **up**, thou wast

006:029   and never shall we be raised **up** again."

006:036   Allah will raise them **up**: then will they

006:046   and sealed **up** your hearts, who-a god

006:055   that the way of the sinners may be shown **up**.

006:060   by day doth He raise you **up** again;

006:093   (saying), "Yield **up** your souls. This day

006:125   as if they had to climb **up** to the skies:

006:133   He raised you **up** from the posterity of other people.

006:146   or is mixed **up** with a bone:

006:159   and break **up** into sects, thou hast

007:014   respite till the day they are raised **up**."

007:057   thus shall We raise **up** the dead:

UP (continued)

007:058   springs **up** produce, (rich) after its kind:

007:058   springs **up** nothing but that which is scanty,

007:070   and give **up** that which our fathers

007:094   We took **up** its people in suffering

007:100   and seal **up** their hearts so that they

007:101   Thus doth Allah seal **up** the heart

007:112   And bring **up** to thee all (our) sorcerers well-versed."

007:117   and behold! it swallows **up** all the

007:142   his brother Aaron (before he went **up**):

007:154   he took **up** the tablets:

007:163   openly (holding **up** their heads,) but on

007:168   We broke them **up** into sections

007:175   so Satan followed him **up**, and he went astray.

009:107   And there are those who put **up** a mosque by way

011:005   Behold! they fold **up** their hearts, that they

011:007   "Ye shall indeed be raised **up** after death,

011:012   (feel the inclination) to give **up** a part of what

011:044   swallow **up** thy water, and O sky! withhold

012:010   he will be picked **up** by some caravan of travellers."

012:018   made **up** a tale (that may pass) with you, (for me)

012:087   and never give **up** hope of Allah's soothing Mercy:

012:110   when the messengers give **up** hope (of their people)

013:012   it is He Who doth raise **up** the clouds,

013:017   the foam that mounts **up** to the surface.

014:009   but they put their hands **up** to their mouths,

014:026   It is torn **up** by the root from the surface

014:030   And they set **up** (idols) as equal to Allah,

014:034   Verily, man is given **up** to injustice and ingratitude.

016:015   And He has set **up** on the earth mountains standing

016:018   If ye would count **up** the favours of Allah,

016:021   nor do thy know when they will be raised **up**.

016:038   that Allah will not raise **up** those who die:

016:039   (They must be raised **up**), in order that He may

016:045   that Allah will not cause the earth to swallow them **up**,

016:079   Nothing holds them **up** but (the power of) Allah.

016:108   and eyes Allah has sealed **up** and they

016:111   On the Day every soul will come **up** pleading for itself,

017:049   be raised **up** (to be) a new creation?"

017:051   is hardest (to be raised **up**)-(yet shall ye be raised **up**)!"

017:068   not cause you to be swallowed **up** beneath the

017:083   he gives himself **up** to despair!

017:088   even if they backed **up** each other

017:098   really be raised **up** (to be) a new Creation?"

018:014   Behold, they stood **up** and said: "Our Lord

018:019   We raised them **up** (from sleep), that they

018:060   "I will not give **up** until I reach the junction

018:077   but he set it **up** straight.

018:096   At length, when he had filled **up** the space

019:015   he will be raised **up** to life (again)!

019:033   I shall be raised **up** to life (again)!"

019:066   shall I then be raised **up** alive?"

020:039   the river will cast him **up** on the bank, and he

020:039   and he will be taken **up** by one who is an enemy

020:059   be assembled when the sun is well **up**."

020:069   quickly will it swallow **up** that which

020:078   completely overwhelmed them and covered them **up**.

020:083   (When Moses was **up** on the mount, Allah said):

020:124   We shall raise him **up** blind on the Day of Judgment."

020:125   why hast thou raised me **up** blind, while I

021:011   setting **up** in their places other peoples

021:047   We shall set **up** scales of justice for the

021:104   like a scroll rolled **up** for books (completed);-

UP (continued)

021:104	The Day that we roll **up** the heavens like a
022:007	raise **up** all who are in the graves.
022:026	or stand **up**, or bow, or prostrate
022:031	and been snatched **up** by birds, or the
022:035	keep **up** regular prayer, and spend
022:036	over them as they line **up** (for sacrifice):
023:016	will ye be raised **up**.
023:037	But we shall never be raised **up** again!
023:082	could we really be raised **up** again?
023:100	the Day they are raised **up**.
024:039	for water; until when he comes **up** to it,
026:037	"And bring **up** to thee all (our) sorcerers
026:045	when behold, it straightway swallows **up** all the
026:087	on the Day when (men) will be raised **up**;-
027:022	he (came **up** and) said: "I have compassed
027:044	of water, and she (tucked **up** her skirts),
027:065	shall be raised **up** (for Judgment).
028:008	picked him **up** (from the river):
028:012	at first, until (his sister came **up** and) said:
028:012	and bring him **up** for you and take
028:036	"This is nothing but sorcery faked **up**:
028:038	that I may mount **up** to the god of Moses:
028:045	But We raised **up** (new) generations, and long
028:061	is to be among those brought **up** (for punishment)?
028:081	We caused the earth to swallow **up** him and his house;
028:082	He could have caused the earth to swallow us **up**!
029:040	some We caused the earth to swallow **up**; and some
029:066	and giving themselves **up** to (worldly) enjoyment!
030:010	and held them **up** to ridicule.
030:032	Those who split **up** their Religion, and become
030:059	Thus does Allah seal **up** the hearts of those
032:015	nor are they (ever) puffed **up** with pride.
033:010	and the hearts gaped **up** to the throats, and ye
033:060	and those who stir **up** sedition in the City,
033:060	We shall certainly stir thee **up** against them:
034:009	We could cause the earth to swallow them **up**,
034:046	that ye do stand **up** before Allah,-(it may be)
035:009	so that they raise **up** the Clouds, and We
035:010	To Him mount **up** (all) Words of Purity: it is
036:008	right **up** to their chins, so that
036:009	We have covered them **up**: so that
036:040	to catch **up** the Moon, nor can
036:052	Who hath raised us **up** from our beds of repose?...
036:053	they will all be brought **up** before Us!
036:075	and they are a host brought **up** before them.
037:016	and bones, shall we (then) be raised **up** (again)?
037:022	"Bring ye **up**," it shall be said, "The wrong-doers
037:035	would puff themselves **up** with Pride,
037:036	And say: "What! Shall we give **up** our gods
037:127	be called **up** (for punishment),
038:010	mount **up** with the ropes and means
039:008	and he doth set **up** rivals unto Allah,
039:021	then He makes it dry **up** and crumble away.
039:067	and the heavens will be rolled **up** in his right hand:
040:018	will (come) right **up** to the Throats to choke
040:035	seal **up** every heart-of arrogant tyrinical."
040:037	and that I may look **up** to the God of Moses:
041:049	he gives **up** all hope (and) is lost in despair.
042:024	He could seal **up** thy heart.
042:028	(even) after (men) have given **up** all hope,
043:017	(the birth of) what he sets **up** as a likeness to (Allah)
043:018	Is then one brought **up** among trinkets, and unable

UP (continued)

043:033	and (silver) stair-ways on which to go **up**,
043:057	When (Jesus) the son of Mary is held **up** as an
045:017	matters in which they set **up** differences.
046:017	I shall be raised **up**, even though
047:015	so that it cuts **up** their bowels (to pieces)?
047:025	and buoyed them **up** with false hopes.
047:030	We could have shown them **up** to thee, and thou
047:036	and will not ask you (to give **up**) your possession.
048:026	While the Unbelievers got **up** in their hearts
050:026	"Who set **up** another god besides Allah: throw him
051:042	It left nothing whatever that it came **up** against,
052:038	by which they can (climb **up** to heaven and) listen
054:020	roots of palm-trees torn **up** (from the ground).
055:007	and He has set **up** the balance (of Justice),
056:047	and bones, shall we then indeed be raised **up** again?-
057:004	and what mounts **up** to it.
057:013	So a wall will be put **up** betwixt them, with a
057:027	We followed them **up** with (others of) Our messengers:
058:006	will raise them all **up** (again) and tell them
058:011	raise **up**, to (suitable) ranks (and degrees),
058:011	rise **up**, rise **up**: Allah will raise **up**,
058:018	The Day will Allah raise them all **up** (for Judgment):
063:004	as (worthless as hollow) pieces of timber propped **up**,
064:007	will not be raised **up** (for Judgment).
064:007	ye shall surely be raised **up**: then shall
064:014	and cover **up** (their faults), verily Allah
066:004	but is ye back **up** each other against him,
066:004	and furthermore, the angels,-will back (him) **up**.
067:016	to be swallowed **up** by the earth when it shales
068:051	thee **up** with their eyes when they hear the Message;
071:007	and given themselves **up** to arrogance.
071:007	covered themselves **up** with their garments,
072:007	ye thought, that Allah would not raise **up** any one
072:019	"'Yet when the Devotee of Allah stood up to invoke him,
074:001	O thou wrapped **up** (in a mantle)!
075:015	Even though he were to put **up** his excuses.
080:022	He will raise him **up** (again).
081:001	When the sun (with its spacious light) is folded **up**;
083:004	Do they not think that they will be raised **up**?-
089:015	then saith he, (puffed **up**), "My Lord hath honoured me."
091:003	By the Day as it shows **up** (the Sun's) glory;
099:002	And the Earth throws **up** her burden (from within),
100:010	And that which is (locked **up**) in (human)
102:001	mutual rivalry for piling **up** (the good things of this world)
104:002	Who pileth **up** wealth and layeth it by,
105:005	and straw (of which the corn) has been eaten **up**.

UPHOLD

067:019	None can **uphold** them except The Most Gracious:

UPLIFTED

014:043	necks outstretched, their heads **uplifted**,

UPON

002:040	favour which I bestowed **upon** you,
002:047	favour which I bestowed **upon** you,
002:090	on themselves Wrath **upon** Wrath.
002:113	"The Jews have naught (to stand) **upon**";
002:113	"The Christians have naught (to stand) **upon**";
002:122	the special favour which I bestowed **upon** you,
002:132	And Abraham enjoined **upon** his sons and so did Jacob;
002:216	Fighting is prescribed **upon** you,
004:054	and conferred **upon** them a great kingdom.
004:093	and the wrath and the curse of Allah are **upon** him,
004:117	(The Pagans), leaving Him, call but **upon** female deities:

UPON (continued)

004:117	they call but **upon** Satan the persistent rebel!
005:003	completed my favour **upon** you, and have chosen
005:068	ye have no ground to stand **upon** unless ye stand
006:040	if there come **upon** you the Punishment of Allah,
006:040	would ye then call **upon** other than Allah?-
006:041	which occasioned your call **upon** Him, and ye
006:048	**upon** them shall be no fear, nor shall they grieve.
006:056	other than Allah, whom ye call **upon**."
006:063	when ye call **upon** Him in humility
006:108	they call **upon** besides Allah, lest they
007:023	and bestow not **upon** us Thy Mercy, we shall
007:026	We have bestowed raiment **upon** you to cover your shame,
007:029	and call **upon** Him, making your devotion
007:071	have already come **upon** you from your Lord:
007:138	They came **upon** a people devoted entirely
007:143	that I may look **upon** Thee." Allah said: "By no
007:143	but look **upon** the mount; if it abide
007:149	"If our Lord have not mercy **upon** us and forgive us,
007:157	and from the yokes that are **upon** them.
007:194	call **upon** them, and let them listen to your prayer.
007:194	Verily those whom ye call **upon** besides Allah
007:197	"But those ye call **upon** besides Him, are unable
009:040	then Allah sent down His peace **upon** him, a
009:098	Some of the Bedouin Arabs look **upon** their payments
011:032	now bring **upon** us what thou threatenest us with,
011:045	And Noah called **upon** his Lord and said: "O my
013:014	any others that they call **upon** besides Him
015:087	And We have bestowed **upon** thee the Seven Oft-
017:057	Those whom they call **upon** do seek
017:067	those that ye call **upon**-besides Himself-leave you
017:101	to have been worked **upon** by sorcery!"
017:110	by whatever name ye call **upon** Him, (it is well):
017:110	"Call **upon** Allah, or call **upon** Rahman: by whatever
018:014	never shall we call **upon** any god other then Him:
018:020	"For if thy should come **upon** you, they would
019:025	it will let fall fresh ripe dates **upon** thee.
021:067	"Fie **upon** you, and **upon** the things that ye
022:035	We have bestowed **upon** them.
022:055	comes suddenly **upon** them, or there
022:060	and is again set **upon** inordinately.
023:109	forgive us, and have mercy **upon** us: for Thou
024:035	Light **upon** Light! Allah doth
024:064	what ye are intent **upon**:
025:016	a promise binding **upon** thy Lord."
028:064	they will call **upon** them, but they
028:064	"Call **upon** your `partners' (for help)":
029:042	whatever that they call **upon** besides Him:
030:047	and it was a duty incumbent **upon** Us to aid
031:014	in travail **upon** travail did his mother bear him.
031:032	they call **upon** Allah, offering Him
034:003	it will come **upon** you;-by Him Who knows the unseen,
034:009	or cause a piece of the sky to fall **upon** them.
034:022	Say: "Call **upon** other (gods) whom ye fancy,
035:008	so that he looks **upon** it as good,
035:040	of yours whom ye call **upon** besides Allah?
037:093	Then did he turn **upon** them, striking (them)
037:125	"Will ye call **upon** Baal and forsake
037:177	But when it descends **upon** their courtyards
038:060	It is ye who have brought this **upon** us!
038:061	Whoever brought this **upon** us,-add to
039:008	when He bestoweth a favour **upon** him as from Himself,
039:047	never have counted **upon**!

UPON (continued)

039:049	but when We bestow a favour **upon** him as from Us,
039:073	And its Keepers will say: "Peace be **upon** you!
040:014	Call ye, then, **upon** Allah with sincere devotion
040:027	Moses said: "I have indeed called **upon** my Lord
040:042	"Ye do call **upon** me to blaspheme against Allah,
040:065	call **upon** Him, giving Him sincere devotion.
040:068	and when He decides **upon** an affair, He says
046:015	Thy favour which Thou hast bestowed **upon** me,
046:015	and **upon** both my parents, and that I may work
046:022	Then bring **upon** us the (calamity) with which
047:024	or is that there are locks **upon** their hearts?
049:017	say, "Count not your Islam as a favour **upon** me:
049:017	Nay, Allah has conferred a favour **upon** you
052:020	on couches arranged in ranks, and We
057:023	nor exult over favours bestowed **upon** you.
058:014	the Wrath of Allah **upon** them?
058:018	they have something (to stand **upon**).
068:024	break in **upon** you into the (garden) this day."
076:021	**Upon** them will be green Garments of fine silk
089:022	and His angels, rank **upon** rank,
092:012	Verily We take **upon** Us to guide,
096:007	In that he looketh **upon** himself as self-sufficient.

UPPER

020:064	who gains the **upper** hand."
020:068	hast indeed the **upper** hand:
040:029	this day: ye have the **upper** hand in the land:
041:026	that ye may gain the **upper** hand!"

UPPERMOST

047:035	for peace, when ye are the **Uppermost**:

UPRIGHT

003:067	but he was **Upright**.
026:182	And weigh with scales true and **upright**.
030:030	to the religion being **upright**, the nature

UPROOT

020:105	say, "My Lord will **uproot** them and scatter

UPSET

009:048	and **upset** matters for thee,-until the Truth arrived

UPSIDE

011:082	We turned (the cities) **upside** down,
015:074	And We turned (the cities) **upside** down,
082:004	And when the Graves are turned **upside** down;-

URGES

052:032	Is it that their intellects **urges** them to this,

US

001:006	Show **us** the straight way.
002:032	save what Thou hast taught **Us**:
002:057	(but they rebelled); to **Us** they did no harm,
002:058	and say: Forgive (**us**) We shall forgive you
002:061	to produce for **us** of what the earth groweth,
002:061	so beseech thy Lord for **us** to produce
002:067	a laughing-stock of **us**?"
002:068	to make plain to **us** what heifer it is!"
002:069	to make plain to **us** her colour."
002:070	to **us** are all heifers alike:
002:070	to make plain to **us** what she is:
002:080	not touch **us** but for few numbered days:"
002:091	what was sent down to **us**":
002:118	Or why cometh not **Us** a Sign?"
002:118	"Why speaketh not Allah unto **Us**?
002:127	"Our Lord! accept (this service) from **us**:
002:128	"Our Lord! make of **us** Muslims,

US (continued)

002:128 and show **us** our places for the celebration
002:128 and turn unto **us** (in Mercy);
002:136 and the revelation given to **us**,
002:139 Say: Will ye dispute with **us** about Allah,
002:167 as they have cleared themselves of **us**."
002:200 "Our Lord! Give **us** (thy bounties) in this world!"
002:201 "Our Lord! give **us** good in this world
002:201 and save **us** from the torment on the Fire!"
002:246 "Appoint for **us** a king,
002:247 authority over **us** when we are better fitted
002:250 help **us** against those that reject faith."
002:250 pour out constancy on **us** and make our steps firm:
002:286 Have mercy on **us**.
002:286 our Lord! Lay not on **us** a burden like that
002:286 And grant **us** forgiveness.
002:286 Our Lord! lay not on **us** a burden greater
002:286 grant **us** victory over the unbelievers.
002:286 which Thou didst lay on those before **us**;
002:286 (Pray:) "Our Lord! Condemn **us** not if we
003:008 but grant **us** mercy from Thee:
003:008 deviate now after Thou hast guided **us**,
003:016 and save **us** from the agony of the Fire;"
003:016 forgive **us**, then, our sins,
003:024 not touch **us** but for a few numbered days":
003:053 then write **us** down among those who bear witness."
003:061 then let **us** earnestly pray.
003:061 say: "Come! let **us** gather together,
003:064 come to common terms as between **us** and you:
003:075 no way over **us** as to the Unlettered people,"
003:084 and in what has been revealed to **us** and what
003:145 those that (serve **us** with) gratitude.
003:147 "Our Lord forgive **us** our sins and anything
003:147 and help **us** against those that resist Faith."
003:156 "If they had stayed with **us**, they would
003:168 "If only they had listened to **us**,
003:173 They said: "For **us** Allah sufficeth,
003:183 unless he showed **us** a sacrifice consumed by fire
003:191 Glory to thee! Give **us** salvation from
003:193 Our Lord! Forgive **us** our sins, blot out
003:193 the call of one calling (**us**) to Faith,
003:193 blot out from **us** our iniquities, and take
003:194 Thou didst promise unto **us** through Thy Messengers,
003:194 and save **us** from shame on the Day of Judgment:
003:194 "Our Lord! grant **us** what Thou didst promise
004:046 and "Do hear"; and "Do look at **us**":
004:072 They say: "Allah did favour **us** in that we
004:075 and raise for **us** from Thee one who will help!"
004:075 and raise for **us** from Thee one who will protect;
004:075 "Our Lord! rescue **us** from this town.
004:077 Wouldst Thou not grant **us** respite to our
004:077 why hast Thou ordered **us** to fight?
004:153 for they said: "Show **us** Allah in public,"
005:019 unto **us** no bringer of glad tidings and no warner.
005:025 so separate **us** from this rebellious people!"
005:052 a change of fortune bring **us** disaster."
005:059 come to **us** and that which came before (**us**),
005:059 do ye disapprove of **us** for no other reason
005:083 write **us** down among the witnesses.
005:084 which has come to **us**, seeing that we long for
005:084 to admit **us** to the company of the righteous?"
005:104 they say: "Enough for **us** are the ways
005:112 Can thy Lord send down to **us** a Table set

US (continued)

005:113 and to know that thou has indeed told **us** the truth;
005:114 "O Allah our Lord! send **us** from heaven a table
005:114 that there may be for **us**-for the first
005:114 for the first and the last of **us**-a solemn
006:022 who ascribed partners (to **Us**): "Where are
006:031 and they say: "Ah! woe unto **us** that we neglected;
006:043 When the suffering reached them from **Us**,
006:053 Allah hath favoured from amongst **us**?"
006:063 'If He only delivers **us** from these (dangers),
006:071 things that can do **us** neither good nor harm,
006:071 his friends calling 'Come to **us**',
006:081 Which of (**us**) two parties hath more
006:094 "And behold! ye come to **Us** bare and alone
006:128 which Thou didst appoint for **us**."
006:148 If so, produce it before **us**.
006:156 sent down to two Peoples before **us**, and for
006:157 "If the Book had only been sent down to **us**,
007:023 and bestow not upon **us** Thy Mercy, we shall
007:023 if Thou forgive **us** not and bestow not
007:028 and "Allah commanded **us** thus": say: "Nay
007:037 They will reply, "They have left **us** in the lurch,"
007:038 "Our Lord! it is these that misled **us**: so give
007:039 "See then! no advantage have ye over **us**;
007:043 Who hath guided **us** to this (felicity):
007:043 the Messengers of our Lord brought unto **us**."
007:044 the promises of our Lord to **us** true: have you
007:047 send **us** not to the company of the wrong-doers."
007:050 "Pour down to **us** water or anything that Allah
007:070 They said: "Comest thou to **us**, that we
007:070 Bring **us** what thou threatenest **us** with, if so
007:087 until Allah doth decide between **us**: for He
007:089 after Allah hath rescued **us** therefrom;
007:089 Our Lord! Decide thou between **us** and our
007:125 "For **us**, we are but sent back unto our Lord."
007:126 thy vengeance on **us** simply because we believed
007:126 in the Signs of our Lord when they reached **us**!
007:126 Our Lord! pour out on **us** patience
007:129 both before and after thou comest to **us**."
007:131 they said, "This is due to **us**"; when gripped
007:132 to work therewith the sorcery on **us**, we shall
007:134 if thou wilt remove the Plague from **us**,
007:138 They said: "O Moses! fashion for **us** a god
007:143 When Moses came to the place appointed by **Us**,
007:149 "If our Lord have not mercy upon **us** and forgive **us**,
007:151 Admit **us** to Thy mercy! For Thou art
007:155 so forgive **us** and give **us** Thy mercy; for Thou
007:155 of the foolish ones among **us**?
007:155 wouldst Thou destroy **us** for the deeds of the
007:156 "And ordain for **us** that which is good, in this
007:160 (but they rebelled): to **Us** they did no harm,
007:161 as ye wish, but say forgive (**us**) and enter
007:168 in order that they might turn (to **Us**).
007:169 "(Everything) will be forgiven **us**."
007:173 "Our fathers before **us** took false gods, but we
007:173 wilt Thou then destroy **us** because of the deeds
007:174 and perchance they may turn (Unto **Us**).
007:189 (saying): "If Thou givest **us** a goodly child,
008:032 rain down on **us** a shower of stones from the sky,
008:032 or send **us** a grievous chastisement."
009:040 "Have no fear, for Allah is with **us**":
009:051 except what Allah has decreed for **us**:
009:051 Say: "Nothing will happen to **us** except what

US (continued)

US (continued)

009:052	Say: "Can you expect for **us** (any fate) other than
009:059	and His Messenger will soon give **us** of His bounty:
009:059	and had said, "Sufficient unto **us** is Allah!
009:086	and say: "Leave **us** (behind): we would
009:094	Allah hath already informed **us** of the true state
010:007	on their meeting with **Us**, but are
010:011	their hope of their meeting with **Us**, in their
010:012	on his way as if he had never cried to **Us** for the
010:012	he crieth unto **Us** (in all postures)-lying down
010:015	say: "Bring **us** a Qur'an other than this,
010:015	those who rest not their hope on their meeting with **Us**,
010:022	saying, "If Thou dost deliver **us** from this,
010:023	to **Us** is your return, and We
010:028	Then shall We say to those who joined gods (with **Us**):
010:028	"It was not **us** that ye worshipped!"
010:029	"Enough is Allah for a witness between **us** and you:
010:029	knew nothing of your worship of **us**!"
010:046	(before that)-in any case, to **Us** is their return:
010:070	and, then, to **Us** will be their return.
010:076	When the Truth did come to them from **Us**,
010:078	They said: "Hast thou come to **us** to turn
010:078	to turn **us** away from the ways We found
010:085	Our Lord! make **us** not a trial for those
010:086	"And deliver **us** by Thy Mercy from those
011:027	nor so we see in you (all) any merit above **us**:
011:027	but the meanest among **us**, apparently nor
011:032	and (much) hast thou prolonged the dispute with **us**:
011:032	now bring upon **us** what thou threatenest **us** with,
011:032	They said: "O Noah! Thou hast disputed with **us**,
011:038	He said: "If ye ridicule **us** now, we (in our turn)
011:042	"O my son! embark with **us**, and be
011:048	(from the Ark) with Peace from **Us**, and Blessing
011:048	a grievous Chastisement reach them from **Us**."
011:053	"O Hud! No clear (Sign) hast thou brought **us**,
011:058	with him, by (special) Grace from **Us**:
011:062	to that to which thou invitest **us**."
011:062	Dost thou (now) forbid **us** the worship of what
011:062	They Said: "O Salih! thou hast been of **us**!-
011:066	with him, by (special) Grace from **Us**-and from
011:074	he began to plead with **Us** for Lut's people.
011:091	For thou hast among **us** no great position!"
011:091	In fact among **us** we see that thou hast no strength!
012:011	why dost thou not trust **us** with Joseph,-seeing we
012:012	"Send him with **us** to-morrow to enjoy himself
012:017	But thou wilt never believe **us** even though
012:021	may be he will bring **us** much good,
012:021	"Make his stay (among **us**) honourable:
012:031	"Allah preserve **us**! no mortal is this!
012:036	"Tell **us**" (they said) "the truth and meaning thereof:
012:038	that (comes) of the grace of Allah to **us** and to
012:046	Expound to **us** (the dream) of seven
012:051	The ladies said: "Allah preserve **us**! no evil
012:063	so send our brother with **us**, that we
012:065	This our stock-in-trade has been returned to **us**:
012:078	so take one of **us** in his place: for we
012:088	and treat it as charity to **us**; for Allah
012:088	so pay **us** full measure, (we pray thee), and treat
012:088	seized **us** and our family: we have
012:090	Allah has indeed been gracious to **us** (all):
012:091	Allah preferred thee above **us**, and we
012:097	ask for **us** forgiveness for our sins, for we
013:040	We promised them or take to **Us** thy soul (before
014:009	as to that to which ye invite **us**."
014:010	Ye wish to turn **us** away from what our fathers
014:010	then bring **us** some clear authority."
014:011	It is not for **us** to bring you an authority
014:012	all the hurt you may cause **us**.
014:012	Indeed He has guided **us** to the Ways
014:021	"For **us**, we but followed you;
014:021	can ye then avail **us** at all against the
014:021	to **us** it makes no difference (now) whether
014:041	"O our Lord! cover (**us**) with Thy Forgiveness-me,
014:044	"Our Lord! respite **us** (if only) for a short Term:
015:007	"Why bringest thou not angels to **us** if it be
015:021	(sources and) treasures (inexhaustible) are with **Us**;
015:024	To **Us** are known those of you who hasten forward,
017:051	Then will they say: "Who will cause **us** to return?"
017:069	so that ye find no helper therein against **Us**?
017:075	found none to help thee against **Us**!
017:083	his side (instead of coming to **Us**), and when
017:086	thy affair in that matter as against **Us**,-
017:090	to gush forth for **us** from the earth,
017:092	and the angels before (**us**) face to face;
017:092	as thou sayest (will happen), against **us**;
017:093	until thou send down to **us** a book that we
017:094	"Has Allah sent a man (like **us**) to be (His
018:010	bestow on **us** Mercy from Thyself, and dispose
018:010	and dispose of our affair for **us** in the right way!
018:021	"Let **us** surely build a place of worship over them."
018:028	have permitted to neglect the remembrance of **Us**,
018:048	come to **Us** (bare) as We created you first:
018:048	made to you to meet (**Us**)!":
018:049	"Ah! woe to **us**! what a book is this!
018:062	"Bring **us** our early meal; truly we have
018:094	a barrier between **us** and them?
019:013	And pity (for all creatures) as from **Us**, and purity:
019:021	unto men and a Mercy from **Us**':
019:038	the Day that they will appear before **Us**!
019:040	to **Us** will they all be returned.
019:052	and made him draw near to **Us**, for converse
019:064	and what is behind **us**, and what
019:064	to Him belongeth what is before **us** and what
019:080	and he shall appear before **Us** bare and alone.
019:080	To **Us** shall return all that he talks of, and he
020:045	with insolence against **us**, or lest
020:047	the Children of Israel with **us**, and afflict
020:048	'Verily it has been revealed to **us** that the
020:057	"Hast thou come to drive **us** out of our land
020:058	between **us** and thee, which we shall not fail
020:071	which of **us** can give the more severe and the
020:072	Clear Signs Him Who created **us**! So decree
020:072	to what has come to **us** of the Clear Signs
020:073	may He forgive **us** our faults,
020:073	and the magic to which thou didst compel **us**:
020:073	For **us**, we have believed in our Lord:
020:091	to it until Moses returns to **us**."
020:099	for We have sent thee a reminder from **Us**.
020:133	They say: "Why does he not bring **us** a Sign
020:134	"Our Lord! if only Thou hadst sent **us** a messenger,
020:135	Say: "Each one (of **us**), is waiting: wait ye,
021:005	Let him then bring **us** a Sign like the ones
021:014	They said: "Ah! woe to **us**! we were
021:017	it from the things nearest to **Us**, if We
021:018	(false) things ye ascribe (to **Us**).

US (continued)

021:025	sent by **Us** to him: that there
021:035	to **Us** must ye return.
021:043	Or have they gods that can guard them from **Us**?
021:043	be defended from **Us**.
021:046	they will then say, "Woe to **us**! we did
021:055	They said, "Have you brought **us** the Truth, or are
021:073	they constantly served **Us** (and **Us** only).
021:076	(Remember) Noah, when he cried (to **Us**) aforetime:
021:084	for all who serve **Us**.
021:090	they used to call on **Us** in yearning and awe.
021:090	And humble themselves before **Us**.
021:093	(yet) will they all return to **Us**.
021:097	"Ah! woe to **us**! we were indeed heedless of this;
021:101	Those for whom the Good from **Us** has gone before,
023:028	Who has saved **us** from the people who do wrong."
023:029	to enable **us** to disembark."
023:047	And their people are subject to **us**!"
023:062	before **Us** is a record which clearly speaks
023:065	for ye shall certainly not be helped by **Us**.
023:083	"Such things have been promised to **us** and to
023:106	our misfortune overwhelmed **us**, and we
023:107	"Our Lord! bring **us** out of this:
023:109	forgive **us**, and have mercy upon **us**: for Thou
023:115	brought back to **Us** (for account)"?
024:016	"It is not right of **us** to speak of this:
025:018	not meant was it for **us** that we should take
025:021	Those who do not hope to meet **Us** (for Judgment)
025:021	"Why are not the angels sent down to **us**,
025:042	misled **us** from our gods, had it
025:060	Shall we adore that which thou commandest **us**?"
025:065	avert from **us** the Wrath of Hell, for its
025:074	"Our Lord! Grant unto **us** wives and offspring
025:074	of our eyes, and give **us** (the grace) to lead
026:017	"'Send thou with **us** the Children of Israel.'"
026:018	as a child among **us**, and didst
026:050	They said: "No matter! for **us**, we shall
026:051	our Lord will forgive **us** our faults, since we
026:055	"And they are raging furiously against **us**;
026:100	"'Now, then, we have none to intercede (for **us**),
026:136	whether thou admonish **us** or be not
026:136	They said: "It is the same to **us** whether thou
026:154	"Thou art no more than a mortal like **us**:
026:154	then bring **us** a Sign, if thou tellest the truth!"
026:186	"Thou art no more than a mortal like **us**, and indeed
026:187	"Now cause a piece of the sky to fall on **us**,
027:015	Who has favoured **us** above many of His servants
027:041	let **us** see whether she is guided (to the truth)
027:042	knowledge was bestowed on **us** in advance of this,
027:068	we and our fathers before (**us**): these are
028:009	It may be that he will be of use to **us**, or we
028:025	watered (our flocks) for **us**."
028:039	they would not have to return to **Us**!"
028:047	why didst Thou not send **us** a messenger?
028:048	And they say: "For **us**, we reject all (such things)!"
028:055	"To **us** our deeds, and to you yours; peace be
028:063	It was not **us** they worshipped."
028:082	He could have caused the earth to swallow **us** up!
028:082	Allah was gracious to **us**, He could
029:004	that they will get the better of **us**?
029:029	"Bring **us** the Wrath of Allah if thou
029:039	yet they cold not overreach (**Us**).
029:046	which has come down to **us** and in that

US (continued)

029:057	in the end to **Us** shall ye be brought back.
030:047	and it was a duty incumbent upon **Us** to aid
031:023	to **Us** is their return, and We
032:012	we have heard: now then send **us** back (to the
033:012	and His Messenger promised **us** nothing but delusion!"
033:018	to their brethren, "Come along to **us**," but come
033:022	"This is what Allah and His Messenger had promised **us**,
033:022	and Allah and His Messenger told **us** what was true."
033:066	they will say: "Woe to **us**! would that we had
033:067	and they misled **us** as to the (right) path.
034:003	"Never to **us** will come the Hour": say, "Nay!
034:010	We bestowed Grace aforetime on David from **Us**: "
034:026	the matter between **us** (and you) in truth
034:026	Say: "Our Lord will gather **us** together and will
034:033	Behold! ye (constantly) ordered **us** to be
034:037	that will bring you nearer to **Us** in degree:
035:034	Who has removed from **us** (all) sorrow:
035:035	shall touch **us** therein."
035:035	settled **us** in a Home that will last:
035:037	Bring **us** out: we shall work righteousness, not the
036:018	indeed will be inflicted on you by **us**."
036:018	The (people) said: "For **us**, We augur an evil
036:028	from heaven, nor was it needful for **Us** so to do.
036:032	will be brought before **Us** (for judgment).
036:044	Except by way of Mercy from **Us**, and by
036:052	They will say: "Ah! woe unto **us**!
036:052	Who hath raised **us** up from our beds of repose?...
036:053	they will all be brought up before **Us**!
036:065	will speak to **Us**, and their feet bear witness,
036:078	And he makes comparisons for **Us**, and forgets
037:020	They will say, "Ah! woe to **us**! this is
037:028	to come to **us** from the right hand."
037:031	"So now has been prove true, against **us**,
037:075	(In the days of old), Noah cried to **Us**, and We
037:123	So also was Elias among those sent (by **us**).
037:133	So also was Lut among those sent (by **us**).
037:139	So also was Jonah among those sent (by **Us**).
037:164	(The angels) "Not one of **us** but has a
037:168	"If only we had before **us** a message
037:171	before (this) to Our Servants sent (by **Us**),
038:008	to him-(of all persons) among **us**?."
038:016	They say: "Our Lord! Hasten to **us** our sentence
038:022	but guide **us** to the even Path.
038:022	decide now between **us** with truth,
038:022	with truth, and treat **us** not with injustice,
038:025	he enjoyed, indeed, a Near Approach to **Us**,
038:030	the Servant! Ever did he turn (to **Us** in repentance)!
038:034	but he did turn (to **Us** in true devotion):
038:040	and he enjoyed, indeed, a Near Approach to **Us**,
038:044	Ever did he turn (to **Us**)!
038:060	It is ye who have brought this upon **us**!
038:061	Whoever brought this upon **us**,-add to
038:062	And they will say: "How is it with **us** that we
039:003	they may bring **us** nearer to Allah."
039:049	Now, when trouble touches man, he cries to **Us**;
039:049	upon him as from **Us**, he say,
039:074	Who has truly fulfilled His promise to **us**,
039:074	and has given **us** (this) land in heritage:
040:011	made **us** to die, and twice hast Thou given **us** Life!
040:025	Now we have brought them the Truth from **Us**,
040:029	should it befall **us**?"
040:029	but who will help **us** from the Punishment of Allah,

US (continued)

040:047	from us some share of the Fire?"
040:049	"Pray to your Lord to lighten us the Chastisement
040:074	"They have left us in the lurch: nay, we
040:077	(in any case) it is to Us that they shall (all) return.
041:005	for us, we shall do (what we will!)"
041:005	(concealed) from that to which thou dost invite us,
041:005	and between us and thee is a screen:
041:015	and said: "Who is superior to us in strength?"
041:021	"Why bear ye witness against us?"
041:021	They will say: Allah hath given us speech,-
041:029	"Our Lord! Show us those, among Jinns
041:029	among Jinns and men, who misled us: we shall
041:040	pervert the Truth in our Signs are not hidden from Us.
041:041	to them (are not hidden from Us).
041:047	"We do assure Thee not one of us can bear witness!"
041:050	When We give him a taste of some mercy from Us, ,
041:051	on his side (instead of coming to Us); and when
042:015	Allah will bring us together, and to
042:015	There is no contention between us and you.
042:015	For us (is the responsibility for) Our deeds,
042:048	of Mercy from Us, he doth exult thereat,
043:004	of the Book, with Us, high (in dignity),
043:024	They said: "For us, We deny that ye (prophets)
043:038	At length, when (such a one) comes to Us, he says
043:048	in order that they might turn (to Us).
043:049	invoke thy Lord for us according to his
043:055	When at length they provoked Us, We exacted
043:069	and submitted (to Us).
043:077	thy Lord put and end to us!" He will say, "Nay,
044:005	By command, from Us. For We
044:012	remove the Chastisement from us for We
045:024	and nothing but Time can destroy us."
046:011	(such men) would not have gone to it first, before us!"
046:022	Then bring upon us the (calamity) with which
046:022	with which thou dost threaten us, if thou
046:022	to turn us aside from our gods?
046:024	They said, "This cloud will give us rain!"
046:027	in various ways, that they may turn (to Us).
046:032	who invites (Us) to Allah, he cannot
047:020	"Why is not a Sura sent down (for us)?"
048:011	do thou then ask forgiveness for us."
048:015	Say: "Not thus will ye follow us: Allah has
048:015	"But ye are jealous of us." Nay, but little
048:015	(in war): "Permit us to follow you."
050:004	with Us is a Record guarding (the full account).
050:035	all that they wish,-and there is more with Us.
050:038	nor did any sense of weariness touch Us.
050:043	and to Us is the Final Return-
050:044	quite easy for Us.
052:027	"But Allah has been good to us, and has
052:027	and has delivered us from the Chastisement
054:025	of all people amongst us?
054:035	As a Grace from Us: Thus do We
057:013	Let us borrow (a light) from your Light!"
057:013	say to the Believers: "Wait for us!
058:008	"Why does not Allah Punish us for our words?"
059:010	"Our Lord! Forgive us, and our brethren who came
059:010	who came before us into the Faith and leave not,
060:004	between us and you, enmity and hatred for ever,-
060:005	"Our Lord! Make us not a (test and) trial for
060:005	trial for the Unbelievers, but forgive us, our Lord!
064:006	"Shall (mere) human beings direct us?"

US (continued)

066:008	perfect our light for us and grant us Forgiveness:
067:009	a Warner did come to us, but we
067:028	or if He bestows His Mercy on us,-yet who
067:029	will ye know which (of us) it is that is in manifest error."
068:031	They said: "Alas for us! We have
068:032	"It may be that our Lord will give us in exchange
068:039	Or have ye Covenants with Us on oath,
072:004	'There were some foolish ones among us, who used
072:011	'There are among us some that are righteous,
072:013	'And as for us, since we have listened to the
072:014	'Amongst us are some that submit their wills
073:012	With Us are Fetters (to bind them), and a Fire
074:047	"Until there came to us (the Hour) that is certain."
075:017	It is for Us to collect it and to recite it:
075:019	Nay more, it is for Us to explain it
084:014	would not have to return (to Us)!
088:025	For to Us will be their Return;
088:026	Then it will be for Us to call them to account.
092:012	Verily We take upon Us to guide,
092:013	And verily unto Us (belong) the End

USAGE

002:180	according to reasonable usage;

USE

002:026	Allah disdains not to use the similitude of things,
002:125	or use it as a retreat, or bow,
002:188	nor use it as bait for the judges,
005:096	and its use for food,-for the
006:083	(to use) against his people: We raise
023:020	and relish for those who use it for food.
024:029	living in, which serve some (other) use for you:
028:009	It may be that he will be of use to us, or we
031:020	to your (use) all things in the heavens and on
036:023	of no use whatever will be their intercession
036:072	And that We have subjected them to their (use)?
040:079	that ye may use some for riding and some for food;
043:013	Who has subjected these to Our (use), for we
045:019	They will be of no use to thee in the sight
058:002	And in fact they use words (both) iniquitous
070:018	And collect (wealth) and hide it (from use)!
077:031	and is of no use against the fierce Blaze.
077:039	(or plot), use it against Me!
096:004	He Who taught (the use of) the Pen,-

USED

002:142	the Qiblah to which they were used?"
002:143	the Qiblah to which thou wast used,
002:187	used to do secretly among yourselves:
002:200	as ye used to celebrate the praises
005:015	that ye used to hide in the Book, and
006:005	the news of what they used to mock at.
006:093	for that ye used to tell lies against Allah, and
007:037	that ye used to invoke besides Allah?"
007:070	which our fathers used to worship.
009:030	Unbelievers of old used to say.
011:008	which they used to mock at!
014:010	our fathers used to worship; then bring
016:027	concerning whom ye used to dispute (with the godly)?"
016:086	our 'partners', those whom we used to invoke
016:088	for that they used to spread mischief.
016:118	but they were used to doing wrong to themselves.
019:055	He used to enjoin on his people Prayer and Zakat
021:090	they used to call on Us in yearning and awe.
023:066	but ye used to turn back on your heels-

USED (continued)
023:066 "My Signs **used** to be rehearsed to you, but ye
023:109 who **used** to pray, 'Our Lord!
024:029 to enter houses not **used** for living in,
030:055 an hour: thus were they **used** to being deluded!
034:040 "Was it you that these men **used** to worship?"
035:037 not the (deeds) we **used** to do!"-
037:028 They will say: "It was ye who **used** to come
037:052 "Who **used** to say, Do you really believe?
038:062 that we see not men who we **used** to number
039:048 which they **used** to mock at!
040:010 to the Faith and ye **used** to refuse."
040:084 we **used** to join with Him."
041:022 that ye **used** to do!
041:048 The (deities) they **used** to invoke aforetime
044:050 "Truly this is what ye **used** to doubt!"
045:032 ye **used** to say, 'We know not what is the Hour:
045:033 by that which they **used** to mock at!
045:035 "This, because ye **used** to take the Signs
046:026 they **used** to mock at!
049:011 (to be **used** of one) after he has believed:
051:014 this is what ye **used** to ask to be hastened!"
054:031 the dry stubble **used** by one who pens cattle.
056:047 And they **used** to say, "What! when we
067:010 "Had we but listened or **used** our intelligence,
072:004 who **used** to utter extravagant lies against Allah;
072:009 'We **used**, indeed, to sit there in (hidden)
074:045 "But we **used** to talk vanities with vain talkers;
074:046 "And we **used** to deny the Day of Judgment,
077:029 which ye **used** to reject as false!
078:027 For that they **used** not to look for any account
083:029 Those in sin **used** to laugh at those who believed,
083:030 **used** to wink at each other (in mockery);

USES
020:018 and in it I find other **uses**."

USING
016:092 **Using** your oaths to deceive one another, lest one

USUAL
002:199 it is **usual** for the multitude so to do,

USURY
002:275 "Trade is like **usury**,"
002:275 Those who devour **usury** will not stand
002:275 permitted trade and forbidden **usury**.
002:276 Allah will deprive **usury** of all blessing,
002:278 remains of your demand for **usury**,
003:130 O ye who believe! devour not **usury**,
004:161 That they took **usury**, though they were forbidden;
030:039 That which you give in **usury** for increase

UTENSILS
013:017 to make ornaments or **utensils** therewith, there is

UTMOST
008:060 to the **utmost** of your power, including
017:029 nor stretch it forth to its **utmost** reach,
025:052 them with the **utmost** strenuousness, with the
047:031 among you who strive their **utmost** and persevere
053:014 Near the Lote-tree of the **utmost** boundary.
061:011 ye strive (your **utmost**) in the Cause of Allah,
099:001 to her (**utmost**) convulsion,

UTTER
002:017 and left them in **utter** darkness,
005:064 be they accursed for the (blasphemy) they **utter**.
007:005 no cry did they **utter** but this: "Indeed

UTTER (continued)
017:040 Truly ye **utter** a most dreadful saying!
019:090 and the mountains to fall down in **utter** ruin.
021:112 sought against the blasphemies ye **utter**!
025:036 We destroyed with **utter** destruction.
025:039 to **utter** annihilation (for their sins).
027:052 in **utter** ruin,-because they practised wrong-doing.
027:087 and all shall come to Him in **utter** humility.
047:010 Allah brought **utter** destruction on them,
050:018 Not a word does he **utter** but there is a
060:012 not **utter** slander, intentionally forging
072:004 who used to **utter** extravagant lies against Allah;

UTTERANCE
033:070 and make your **utterance** straight forward:

UTTERED
004:156 that they **uttered** against Mary a grave false charge;
009:074 but indeed they **uttered** blasphemy,
009:074 and they **uttered** it after accepting Islam:
018:014 have **uttered** an enormity!"
033:069 Allah cleared him of the (calumnies) they had **uttered**:
058:003 then wish to go back on the words they **uttered**,-

UTTERING
005:063 from their (habit of) **uttering** sinful words

UTTERLY
017:016 then We destroy them **utterly**.
020:061 lest He destroy you (at once) **utterly** by chastisement:
021:011 We **utterly** destroyed because of their iniquities,
026:172 Then the rest We destroyed **utterly**.
040:085 the rejecters of Allah lose (**utterly**)!
041:023 and (now) have ye become of those **utterly** lost!"
041:025 against them; for they are **utterly** lost.
046:018 for they will be (**utterly**) lost.

UTTERS
016:106 in Allah, **utters** Unbelief,-except under
039:032 one who **utters** a lie concerning Allah and rejects

'UZAIR
009:030 The Jews call **'Uzair** a son of Allah, and the

'UZZA
053:019 Have ye seen Lat, and **'Uzza**,

V

VAIN

002:111	Those are their (**vain**) desires.
002:145	wert to follow their (**vain**) desires,
005:048	and follow not their **vain** desires,
005:049	and follow not their **vain** desires, but beware
005:053	All that they do will be in **vain**, and they
005:077	nor follow the **vain** desire of people who went
006:056	Say: "I will not follow your **vain** desires:
006:068	in **vain** discourse about Our Signs,
006:088	all that they did would be **vain** for them.
006:091	leave them to plunge in **vain** discourse and trifling.
006:150	nor follow thou the **vain** desires of such
007:139	and **vain** is the (worship) which they practice."
007:147	**vain** are their deeds:
007:176	and followed his own **vain** desires.
011:016	**vain** are the designs they frame therein,
013:014	without faith is nothing but **vain** prayer.
013:018	(in **vain**) would they offer it for ransom.
013:037	their (**vain**) desires after the knowledge which
016:072	will they then believe in **vain** things, and be
018:056	but the Unbeliever dispute with **vain** argument,
018:105	**vain** will be their works,
019:062	They will not there hear any **vain** discourse,
022:052	cancel anything (**vain**) that Satan throws in,
022:062	they are but **vain** Falsehood:
023:003	Who avoid **vain** talk;
028:055	And when they hear **vain** talk, they turn
029:067	Then, do they believe in that which is **vain**,
033:010	and they imagined various (**vain**) thoughts about Allah!
039:047	(in **vain**) would they offer it for ransom from the
042:015	nor follow thou their **vain** desires;
045:023	a one as takes as his god his own **vain** desire?
047:033	and make not **vain** your deeds!
049:002	lest your deeds become **vain** and ye perceive not.
070:042	So leave them to plunge in **vain** talk and play
074:045	"But we used to talk vanities with **vain** talkers;

VAINGLORIOUS

004:036	the **vainglorious**;
057:023	not any **vainglorious** boaster,-

VAINLY

006:071	(**vainly**) guiding him to the Path."
019:034	about which they (**vainly**) dispute.

VALLEY

008:042	Remember ye were on the hither side of the **valley**,
009:121	nor cut across a **valley**,
014:037	in a **valley** without cultivation,
020:012	thou art in the sacred **valley** Tuwa.
026:225	wander distracted in every **valley**?-
027:018	At length, when they came to a **valley** of ants,
028:030	he was called from the right bank of the **valley**,
048:024	from them in the **valley** of Makkah, after that
079:016	to him in the sacred **valley** of Tuwa:-
089:009	who cut out (huge) rocks in the **valley**?-

VALLEYS

046:024	advancing towards their **valleys**, they said,

VALUE

004:074	soon shall We give him a reward of great (**value**).
004:114	We shall soon give a reward of the highest (**value**).
004:146	to the Believers a reward of immense **value**.

VANGUARD

009:100	The **vanguard** (of Islam)-the first of those who

VANISH

016:096	What is with you must **vanish**:
078:020	And the mountains shall **vanish**, as if
081:003	When the mountains **vanish** (like a mirage);

VANITIES

002:188	your property among yourselves for **vanities**,
004:029	your property among yourselves in **vanities**:
007:169	the **vanities** of this world,
007:169	(Even so), if similar **vanities** came their way,
029:048	indeed, would the talkers of **vanities** have doubt.
029:052	those who believe in **vanities** and reject Allah,
030:058	"Ye do nothing but talk **vanities**."
040:005	and dispute by means of **vanities**,
043:083	(with **vanities**) until they meet that Day of theirs,
053:061	Wasting your time in **vanities**?
074:045	"But we used to talk **vanities** with vain talkers;

VANITY

022:052	Satan threw some (**vanity**) into his desire:
078:035	No **Vanity** shall they hear therein, nor Untruth;-
088:011	Where they shall hear no (word) of **vanity**:

VANQUISH

008:065	They will **vanquish** a thousand of the Unbelievers:
008:065	they will **vanquish** two hundred: if a hundred.
008:066	and if a thousand, they will **vanquish** two thousand,
008:066	they will **vanquish** two hundred, and if a thousand,

VANQUISHED

002:249	hath a small force **vanquished** a big one?
003:012	**vanquished** and gathered together to Hell,
007:119	So they were **vanquished** there and then, and

VARIANCE

039:029	at **variance** with each other, and a man

VARIATIONS

030:022	and the **variations** in your languages and your

VARIETY

006:099	each similar (in kind) yet different (in **variety**):
006:141	similar (in kind) and different (in **variety**):

VARIOUS

006:046	See how We explain the Signs by **various** (symbols):
006:105	the Signs by **various** (ways) that they may say,
007:058	by **various** (symbols) to those who are grateful.
017:041	in **various** (ways) in this Qur'an, in order
020:040	and We tired thee in **various** ways.
033:010	and ye imagined **various** (vain) thoughts
035:027	of **various** shades of colour,
035:027	With it We then bring out produce of **various** colours,
035:028	are they of **various** colours.
039:021	produce of **various** colours: then it
039:023	(yet) repeating (its teaching **various** aspects):
046:027	and We have shown the Signs in **various** ways,

VARY

004:024	ye agree mutually (to **vary** it),

VARYING

003:140	Such days (of **varying** fortunes) We give to men
003:163	They are in **varying** grades in the sight of Allah,
016:013	He has multiplied in **varying** colours
016:069	from within their bodies a drink of **varying** colours,

VARYING (continued)
051:008 Truly ye are of **varying** opinion.

VAST
024:040 the depths of darkness in a **vast** deep ocean,
051:047 and We indeed have **vast** power.

VAULT
104:008 It shall be made into a **vault** over them,

VAULTED
090:020 On them will be Fire **Vaulted** over (all round).

VEGETABLES
078:015 That We may produce therewith grain and **vegetables**,

VEGETATION
006:099 with it We produce **vegetation** of all kinds: from
016:010 the **vegetation** on which ye feed your cattle.
018:045 the earth's **vegetation** absorbs it,
080:028 And Grapes and the fresh **vegetation**,
086:012 gushing of springs or the sprouting of **vegetation**),-

VEHEMENT
027:033 and given to **vehement** war: but the
048:016 (to fight) against a people given to **vehement** war:

VEIL
002:007 and on their eyes is a **veil**;
007:046 Between them shall be a **veil**, and on
007:054 He draweth the night as a **veil** O'er the day,
012:107 of the covering **veil** of the wrath of Allah.
013:003 He draweth the Night as a **veil** o'er the Day.
017:045 believe not in the Hereafter, a **veil** invisible:
018:011 Then We drew (a **veil**) over their ears,
018:101 eyes had been under a **veil** from Remembrance of Me,
038:032 Until (the sun) was hidden in the **veil** (of Night):
042:051 by inspiration, or from behind a **veil**, or by
050:022 of this; now have We removed thy **veil**, and sharp

VEILED
083:015 that Day, will they be **veiled**.

VEILS
006:025 but We have thrown **veils** on their hearts,
018:057 **veils** over their hearts so that they should
024:031 that they should draw their **veils** over their
039:006 in three **veils** of darkness.
041:005 They say: "Our hearts are under **veils**, (concealed)

VEIN
050:016 for We are nearer to him than (his) jugular **vein**.

VENERABLE
012:078 he has a father, aged and **venerable**,

VENGEANCE
006:065 giving you a taste of mutual **vengeance**-
007:126 "But thou dost wreak thy **vengeance** on us
027:049 we shall then say to his heir (when he seeks **vengeance**):

VERGE
022:011 as it were, on the **verge**:

VERIFIED
010:096 of thy Lord hath been **verified** would not believe-

VERILY
002:119 **Verily** We have sent thee in truth
002:214 Ah! **Verily**, the help of Allah is (always) near!
002:252 **verily** thou art one of the Messengers.
003:005 **verily** nothing is hidden on earth or in the heavens
003:026 **Verily**, over all things Thou hast power.
003:076 **verily** Allah loves those who act aright.
003:089 for **verily** Allah is Oft-Forgiving, Most Merciful.
003:195 **verily**, I will blot out from them their iniquities,

VERILY (continued)
004:029 for **verily** Allah hath been to you Most Merciful.
004:058 **verily** how excellent is the teaching
004:131 **Verily** We have directed the people
004:135 **verily** Allah is well-acquainted with all that ye do.
004:167 have **verily** strayed far, far away from the Path.
004:174 O mankind! **verily** there hath come to you
005:012 **verily** I will wipe out from you your evils, and
005:051 **Verily** Allah guideth not a people unjust.
005:073 **verily** a grievous chastisement will befall the
006:021 But **verily** the wrong-doers never shall prosper.
006:054 **verily**, if any of you did evil in ignorance,
006:153 **Verily**, this is My Way, leading straight:
006:161 Say: "**Verily**, my Lord hath guided me
007:007 And **verily** We shall recount their whole
007:054 **Verily**, His are the Creation and the Command,
007:153 **verily** Thy Lord is thereafter Oft-forgiving,
007:194 **Verily** those whom ye call upon besides Allah
008:019 for **verily** Allah is with those who believe!
008:039 **verily** Allah doth see all that they do.
008:042 And **verily** Allah is He who knoweth (all things).
008:053 and **verily** Allah is He Who heareth and
008:062 **verily** Allah sufficeth thee:
008:075 **Verily** Allah is well-acquainted with all things.
009:022 **Verily** with Allah is a reward, the greatest
009:037 **Verily** the transposing (of a prohibited month)
009:064 But **verily** Allah will bring to light all that
009:067 **Verily** the Hypocrites are rebellious and perverse.
009:103 **Verily** thy prayers are a source of security
009:104 and that Allah is **verily** He, the Oft-Returning,
010:003 **Verily** your Lord is Allah, Who created
010:006 **Verily**, in the alternation of the Night
010:021 **Verily**, Our messengers record all the plots
010:033 **verily** they will not believe.
010:036 **Verily** Allah is well aware of all that they do.
010:044 **Verily** Allah will not deal unjustly with
010:060 **Verily** Allah is full of Bounty to mankind,
010:062 Behold! **verily** on the friends of Allah there is
010:066 Behold! **verily** to Allah belong all creatures,
010:067 **Verily** in this are Signs for those
010:092 But **verily**, many among mankind are heedless
010:093 **Verily** Allah will judge between them as to
011:002 (Say:) "**Verily** I am (sent) unto you from Him
011:026 **Verily** I do fear for you the punishment
011:029 for **verily** they are to meet their Lord, and ye
011:056 **Verily**, it is my Lord that is on a Straight Path.
011:092 But **verily** my Lord encompasseth all that ye do!
011:109 but **verily** We shall pay them back
011:115 For **verily** Allah will not suffer the reward
012:007 **Verily** in Joseph and his brethren are Signs
012:034 **verily** He heareth and knoweth (all things).
012:057 But **verily** the reward of the Hereafter
012:100 **Verily** my Lord is gracious to whom He wills
012:100 for **verily** He is full of knowledge and wisdom.
013:003 Behold, **verily** in these things there are Signs
013:004 Behold, **verily** in these things there are Signs
013:006 But **verily** thy Lord is full of forgiveness
013:006 and **verily** thy Lord is (also) strict in punishment.
013:011 **Verily** never will Allah change the condition
013:031 come to pass, for, **verily**, Allah will not fail
014:005 **Verily** in this there are Signs
014:013 "**Verily** We shall cause the wrong-doers
014:014 "And **verily** We shall cause you to abide

VERILY (continued)

014:030   But **verily** ye are making straightway for Hell!"
014:034   **Verily**, man is given up to injustice
014:051   and **verily** Allah is Swift in calling account.
015:023   And **verily**, it is We Who give life,
015:043   And **verily**, Hell is the promised
015:072   **Verily**, by thy life (O Prophet),
015:086   For **verily** it is thy Lord Who is the All-Creator,
016:011   **Verily** in this is a Sign for those who give thought.
016:012   His Command: **verily** in this are Signs for men
016:013   **Verily** in this is a Sign for men who are mindful.
016:023   **verily** He loveth not the arrogant.
016:028   **verily** Allah knoweth all that ye did;
016:065   **verily** in this is a Sign for those who listen.
016:066   And **verily** in cattle (too) will ye find an
016:069   **verily** in this is a Sign for those who give thought.
016:079   **Verily** in this are Signs for those who believe.
016:097   and has Faith, **verily**, to him will We give a life
016:110   But **verily** thy Lord,-to those who leave their
016:119   But **verily** thy Lord, to those
017:003   **Verily** he was a devotee most grateful.
017:009   **Verily** this Qur'an doth guide to that which
017:021   but **verily** the Hereafter is more
017:025   **verily** He is Most Forgiving
017:027   **Verily** spendthrifts are brothers of the Satans.
017:030   **Verily** thy Lord doth provide sustenance in
017:031   **Verily** the killing of them is a great sin.
017:044   **Verily** He is Oft-Forbearing, Most Forgiving!
017:063   **verily** Hell will be the recompense of you (all)-
018:008   **Verily** what is on earth We shall make but as
018:030   **verily** We shall not suffer to perish the reward
018:057   **Verily** We have set veils over their hearts
018:067   "**Verily** thou wilt not be able to have patience
018:084   **Verily** We established his power on earth,
018:102   **Verily** We have prepared Hell for the
019:036   **Verily**, Allah is my Lord and your Lord:
020:007   for **verily** He knoweth what is secret
020:012   "**Verily** I am thy Lord! Therefore put off
020:014   "**Verily**, I am Allah: there is no god but I:
020:015   "**Verily** the Hour is coming-I have almost
020:047   '**Verily** we are Messengers sent by thy Lord:
020:048   '**Verily** it has been revealed to us that the
020:054   **verily**, in this are Signs for men
020:074   **Verily** he who comes to his Lord as a sinner
020:090   for **verily** your Lord is (Allah) Most Gracious:
020:100   **verily** they will bear a burden on the
020:117   Then We said: "O Adam! **verily**, this is
020:124   My Message, **verily** for him is a life narrowed
020:128   **Verily**, in this are Signs for men
021:092   **Verily**, this Ummah of yours is a single Ummah,
021:098   **Verily** ye, (Unbelievers), and the false
021:106   **Verily** in the (Qur'an) is a Message for people
022:007   And **verily** the Hour will come: there can
022:010   for **verily** Allah is not unjust to His servants.
022:014   **Verily** Allah will admit those who believe
022:016   and **verily** Allah doth guide whom He will!
022:038   **Verily** Allah will defend (from ill)
022:038   **verily**, Allah loveth not any that is
022:039   and **verily** Allah is Most powerful for their aid;
022:040   for **verily** Allah is full of Strength,
022:047   **Verily** a Day in the sight of is like a thousand years
022:053   **verily** the wrong-doers are in a schism
022:054   for **verily** Allah is the Guide for those who believe,

VERILY (continued)

022:058   on them will Allah bestow **verily** a goodly Provision:
022:059   **Verily** He will admit them to a place with which
022:061   and **verily** it is Allah Who hear and sees (all things)
022:062   **verily** Allah is He, Most High,
022:064   for **verily** Allah,-He is Free of all wants,
023:030   **Verily** in this there are Signs (for men to understand);
023:052   And **verily** this Ummah of yours is a single Ummah
023:057   **Verily** those who live in awe for fear
023:073   But **verily** thou callest them to the Straight Way;
023:074   And **verily** those who believe not in the Hereafter
023:117   And **verily** the Unbelievers shall not
024:044   **verily** in these things is an instructive example
024:045   for **verily** Allah has power over all things.
024:053   **verily**, Allah is well acquainted with all that you do."
025:006   **verily** He is Oft-Forgiving, Most Merciful."
026:008   **Verily**, in this is a Sign: but most
026:009   And **verily**, thy Lord is He, the Exalted
026:067   **Verily** in this is a Sign: but most
026:068   And **verily** thy Lord is He, the Exalted
026:103   **Verily** in this is a Sign, but most
026:104   And **verily** the Lord is He, the Exalted
026:121   **Verily** in this is a Sign: but most
026:122   And **verily** thy Lord is He, the Exalted
026:139   **Verily** in this is a Sign: but most
026:140   And **verily** thy Lord is He, the Exalted
026:158   **Verily** in this is a Sign: but most
026:159   And **verily** thy Lord is He, the Exalted
026:174   **Verily** in this is a Sign: but most
026:175   And **verily** thy Lord is He, the Exalted
026:190   **Verily** in that is a Sign: but most
026:191   And **verily** thy Lord is He, the Exalted
026:192   **Verily** this is a Revelation from the Lord
027:009   "O Moses! **verily**, I am Allah, the Exalted
027:052   **Verily** in this is a Sign for people of knowledge.
027:073   But **verily** thy Lord is full of grace to mankind
027:074   And **verily** thy Lord knoweth all that
027:076   **Verily** this Qur'an doth explain to the
027:078   **Verily** thy Lord will decide between them
027:086   **Verily** in this are Signs for any people
028:030   **Verily** I am Allah, the Lord of the Worlds...
028:085   **Verily** He Who ordained the Qur'an for thee,
029:024   **Verily** in this are Signs for people who believe.
029:042   **Verily** Allah doth know of (everything)
029:044   **verily** in that is a Sign for those who believe.
029:051   **Verily**, in it is Mercy and Reminder to those
029:064   But **verily** the Home in the Hereafter,-
029:069   for **verily** Allah is with those who do right.
030:021   **verily** in that are Signs for those who reflect.
030:022   **verily** in that are Signs for those who know.
030:023   **verily** in that are Signs for those who hearken.
030:024   **verily** in that are Signs for those who are wise.
030:037   to whomsoever He pleases? **Verily** in that are Signs
030:050   **verily** the Same will give life to the men
030:052   So **verily** thou canst not make the dead to hear,
030:058   **Verily** We have propounded for men, in this
030:060   for **verily** the promise of Allah is true: nor let
031:012   **verily** Allah is free of all wants, worthy of
031:026   **verily** Allah is He (that is) free of all wants,
031:031   **Verily** in this are Signs for all who constantly
031:033   **Verily**, the promise of Allah is true: let not
031:034   **Verily** with Allah is full knowledge
031:034   **Verily** the knowledge of the Hour is with Allah

VERILY (continued)

032:022 **Verily** from those who transgress We shall exact (due)
032:025 **Verily** thy Lord will judge between them on the
032:026 **Verily** in that are Signs:
033:001 **verily** Allah is full of knowledge and wisdom.
033:018 **Verily** Allah knows those among you who keep
033:029 **verily** Allah has prepared for the wrong-doers
033:054 **verily** Allah has knowledge of all things.
033:064 **Verily** Allah has cursed the Unbelievers
034:009 **Verily** is this is a Sign for every devotee
034:019 **Verily** in this are Signs for every (soul that
034:036 Say: "**Verily** my Lord enlarges and restricts
034:039 Say: "**Verily** my Lord enlarges and restricts
034:048 Say: "**Verily** my Lord doth cast the Truth,-
035:006 **Verily** Satan is an enemy to you: so treat him
035:024 **Verily** We have sent thee with truth,
035:038 **Verily** Allah knows (all) the hidden things
035:038 **verily** He has full knowledge of all that is in (men's)
035:041 **verily** He is Most Forbearing, Oft-Forgiving.
035:045 **verily** Allah has in His sight all His servants.
036:012 **Verily** We shall give life to the dead,
036:055 **Verily** the Companions of the Garden shall that
036:076 **Verily** We know what they hide as well as
036:082 **Verily**, when He intends a thing, His Command
037:004 **Verily, verily,** your God is One!-
037:004 **Verily, verily,** your God is One!-
037:034 **Verily** that is how We shall deal with Sinners.
037:060 **Verily** this is the supreme Triumph!
037:083 **Verily** from his party was Abraham.
037:137 **Verily**, ye pass by their (sites), by day-
037:161 For, **verily**, neither ye nor those ye worship
037:165 "And we are **verily** ranged in ranks (for service);
037:166 "And we are **verily** those who declare
038:046 **Verily** We did chose them for a special (purpose)-
038:049 and **verily**, for the Righteous, is a beautiful
039:002 **Verily** it is We Who have revealed the Book
039:008 **verily** thou art (one) of the Companions of the Fire!"
039:011 Say: "**Verily**, I am commanded to serve Allah
039:041 **Verily** We have revealed the Book to thee in Truth,
039:042 **Verily** in this are Signs for those who reflect.
039:052 **Verily**, in this are signs for those who believe!
040:020 **Verily** it is Allah (alone) Who hears
040:061 **Verily** Allah is Full of Grace and Bounty to men:
041:040 **Verily** He seeth (clearly) all that you do.
042:005 Behold! **Verily** Allah is He, the Oft-Forgiving,
042:018 Behold, **verily** those that dispute concerning
042:021 but **verily** the wrong-doers will have a grievous
042:033 **Verily** in this are Signs for everyone who patiently
042:052 and **verily** thou dost guide (men) to the Straight Way,-
043:004 And **verily**, it is in the Mother of the Book,
043:042 for **verily** We shall prevail over them.
043:043 **verily** thou art on a Straight Way.
043:078 **Verily** We have brought the truth to you:
044:040 **Verily** the Day of Sorting Out is the time appointed
044:043 **Verily** the tree of Zaqqum
044:058 **Verily**, We have made this (Qur'an) easy,
045:003 **Verily** in the heavens and the earth, are Signs
045:017 **Verily** thy Lord will judge between them on the
046:013 **Verily** those who say, "Our Lord is Allah,"
046:033 Yea, **verily** He has power over all things.
047:012 **Verily** Allah will admit those who believe and do
048:001 **Verily** We have granted thee a manifest Victory:
048:010 **Verily** those who plight their fealty to thee

VERILY (continued)

049:013 **Verily** the most honoured of you in the sight
049:018 "**Verily** Allah knows the Unseen of the heavens
050:037 **Verily** in this is a Message for any that has
050:043 **Verily** it is We Who give Life and Death;
051:005 **Verily** that which ye are promised is true;
051:006 And **verily** Judgment and Justice will surely come to pass.
052:007 **Verily**, the Chastisement of thy Lord will indeed
052:047 And **verily**, for those who do wrong, there is
052:048 for **verily** thou art in Our eyes:
053:030 **Verily** thy Lord knoweth best those who stray
053:032 **verily** thy Lord is ample in forgiveness
054:049 **Verily**, all things have We created in proportion
056:095 **Verily**, this is the very Truth of assured Certainty.
057:009 And **verily**, Allah is to you Most Kind and Merciful.
057:024 **verily** Allah is free of all needs,
059:004 **verily** Allah is severe in Punishment.
059:021 **verily**, thou wouldst have seen it humble itself
064:014 **verily** Allah is Oft-Forgiving, Most Merciful.
065:001 does **verily** wrong his (own) soul:
065:003 **verily**, for all things has Allah appointed a due
068:003 Nay, **verily** for thee is a Reward unfailing:
068:007 **Verily** it is thy Lord that knoweth best,
068:017 **Verily** We have tried them as We tried the People
068:029 **Verily** we have been doing wrong!"
068:034 **Verily**, for the righteous are Gardens of Delight,
069:040 That this is **verily** the word of a honoured
069:048 But **verily** this is a Message for the God-fearing.
069:051 But **verily** it is Truth of assured certainty.
073:019 **Verily** this is an Admonition: therefore, whoso
074:032 Nay, **verily**: by the Moon,
076:002 **Verily** We created Man from a drop of mingled sperm,
076:022 "**Verily** this is a Reward for you, and your
078:004 **Verily**, they shall soon (come to) know!
078:005 **Verily, verily** they shall soon (come to) know!
078:017 **Verily** the Day of Sorting Out is a thing appointed,-
078:031 **Verily** for the righteous there will an Achievement,
078:040 **Verily**, We have warned you of a Chastisement near,-
079:013 But **verily**, it will be but a single (compelling) Cry,
079:026 **Verily** in this is a lesson for whosoever feareth (Allah).
081:015 So **verily** I call to witness the Planets-that recede,
081:019 **Verily** this is the word of a most honourable
081:027 **Verily** this is no less than a Message
082:010 But **verily** over you (are appointed angels)
083:015 **Verily**, from (the Light of) their Lord, that Day,
083:018 Nay, **verily** the Record of the Righteous is
084:006 O thou man! **verily** thou art ever toiling on
090:004 **Verily** We have created Man into toil and struggle.
092:004 **Verily**, (the ends) ye strive for are diverse.
092:012 **Verily** We take upon Us to guide,
092:013 And **verily** unto Us (belong) the End and the
093:004 And **verily** the hereafter will be better for thee
094:005 So, **verily**, with every difficulty, there is relief:
094:006 **Verily**, with every difficulty there is relief.
096:008 **Verily**, to thy Lord is the return (of all).
103:002 **Verily** Man is in loss,

VERITABLE

026:027 who has been sent to you is a **veritable** madman!"

VERSED

010:079 Said Pharaoh: "Bring me every sorcerer well **versed**."

VERSES

003:007 in it are **verses** basic or fundamental
011:001 with **verses** fundamental (of established meaning),

VERSES (continued)

012:001 Alif Lam Ra. These are the **Verses** of the
013:001 These are the **Verses** of the Book: that which
015:087 Seven Oft-Repeated (**verses**) and the Grand Qur'an.
024:034 sent down to you **verses** making things clear,
026:002 These are **Verses** of the Book that makes
027:001 These are **verses** of the Qur'an,-A Book
028:002 These are **Verses** of the Book that makes
031:002 These are **Verses** of the Wise Book,-
041:003 A Book, whereof the **verses** are explained in detail;
041:044 "Why are not its **verses** explained in detail?

VERY

002:050 drowned Pharaoh's people within your **very** sight.
003:040 seeing I am **very** old, and my wife is barren?"
003:119 they bite off the **very** tips of their fingers
004:063 and speak to them a word to reach their **very** souls.
004:066 **very** few of them would have done it:
004:077 never will ye be dealt unjustly in the **very** least!
004:081 on things **very** different from what they tellest them.
006:111 all things before their **very** eyes,
007:205 Bring thy Lord to remembrance in thy (**very**) soul,
008:074 these are (all) in **very** truth the believers:
009:055 may perish in their (**very**) denial of Allah.
009:118 and their (**very**) Souls seemed straitened to them,-
010:053 It is the **very** truth!
011:022 Without a doubt, these are the **very** ones who
017:005 **very** inmost parts of your homes;
018:042 had (now) tumbled to pieces to its **very** foundations,
023:036 "Far, **very** far is that which ye are promised!
024:025 that Allah is the (**very**) Truth,
028:023 and our father is a **very** old man."
028:076 that their **very** keys would have been a burden
033:047 shall have from Allah a **very** great Bounty.
033:068 and curse with a **very** great Curse!"
037:037 Nay! he has come with the (**very**) Truth,
040:035 **very** hateful (is such conduct) in the sight of Allah
040:083 but that **very** (Wrath) at which they were
050:042 a (mighty) Blast in (**very**) truth):
051:023 this is the **very** Truth,
056:095 Verily, this is the **very** Truth of assured Certainty.
070:019 Truly man was created **very** impatient;
075:004 in perfect order the **very** tips of his fingers.
085:013 It is He Who Creates from the **very** beginning,

VESSELS

036:042 similar (**vessels**) on which they ride.
076:015 **vessels** of silver and goblets of crystal,-

VESTED

035:008 So let not thy soul be **vested** in regret

VEX

061:005 "O my people! why do ye **vex** and insult me,

VIANDS

005:112 a Table set (with **viands**) from heaven?"
005:114 send us form heaven a table set (with **viands**),

VICEGERENT

002:030 "I will create a **vicegerent** on earth."
038:026 a **vicegerent** on earth: so judge

VICISSITUDES

026:227 know what **vicissitudes** their affairs will take!

VICTORIOUS

030:003 will soon be **victorious**-
037:116 And We helped them, so they were **victorious**;

VICTORY

002:089 prayed for **victory** against those without Faith,-
002:286 grant us **victory** over the unbelievers.
003:126 no **victory** except from Allah, the Exalted,
003:152 in sight (of the **Victory**) which ye covet.
004:074 whether he is slain or gets **victory**, soon shall
004:141 if ye do gain a **victory** from Allah,
005:023 when once ye are in, **victory** will be yours;
005:052 Ah! perhaps Allah will give (thee) **victory**, or a
008:019 if ye prayed for **victory** and judgment,
009:014 and disgrace them help you (to **victory**) over them,
009:052 of two glorious things-(martyrdom or **victory**)?
014:015 But they sought **victory** and decision
017:006 Then did We grant you **victory** over them:
030:005 He gives **victory** to whom He will, and He
033:071 has already attained the great **victory**.
048:001 Verily We have granted thee a manifest **Victory**:
048:018 and He rewarded them with a speedy **Victory**;
048:024 after that He gave you the **victory** over them.
048:027 besides this, a speedy **victory**.
057:010 before the **Victory**, (with those who did so later).
061:013 and speedy **victory**. So give the Glad Tidings
110:001 When comes the Help of Allah, and **Victory**,

VIE

003:200 **vie** in such perseverance: strengthen each other;

VIEW

026:091 the Fire will be placed in full **view**;
037:102 now see what is thy **view**!"
079:036 in full **view** for him who sees.-

VIGILANT

028:018 fearful and **vigilant** when behold, the man
050:018 does he utter but there is a **vigilant** Guardian.

VILE

002:093 Say: "**Vile** indeed are the behests
002:102 And **vile** was the price for which they
003:187 And **vile** was the bargain they made!

VILEST

012:032 and (what is more) be in the company of the **vilest**!"
041:029 so that they become the **vilest**."

VINE

016:067 and the **vine**, ye get out strong drink,

VINES

002:266 and **vines** and streams flowing underneath,
013:004 and gardens of **vines** and fields sown with corn,
017:091 a garden of date trees and **vines**,
023:019 for you gardens of date-palms and **vines**: in them
036:034 produce therein orchards with date-palms and **Vines**,

VIOLATE

005:002 O ye who believe! **violate** not the sanctity
009:012 But if they **violate** their oaths

VIOLATED

009:013 who **violated** their oaths, plotted to

VIOLATES

048:010 their hands: then any one who **violates** His oath,

VIOLENCE

005:110 (**violence** to) thee when thou didst show them
010:091 and thou didst mischief (and **violence**)!
016:081 from your (mutual) **violence**.
021:080 from each other's **violence**: will ye
022:072 They nearly attack with **violence** those who rehearse
079:001 (the souls of the wicked) with **violence**;

VIOLENT
005:003 or by a **violent** blow, or a headlong fall,
007:155 when they were seized with **violent** quaking,
012:030 truly has he inspired her with **violent** love:
017:068 a **violent** tornado (with showers of stones) so that
021:081 the **violent** (unruly) wind flow (tamely) for
029:040 We sent a **violent** tornado (with showers of stones)
054:034 We sent against them a **violent** tornado with
054:036 **violent** Seizure but they disputed about the Warning.
067:017 **violent** tornado (with showers of stones), so that
068:013 **Violent** (and cruel),-with all that, of a
069:006 by a furious wind, exceedingly **violent**;
073:014 and the mountains will be in **violent** commotion.
079:006 in commotion will be in **violent** commotion,
100:008 And **violent** is he in his love of wealth.

VIOLENTLY
077:002 Which then blow **violently** in tempestuous Gusts,

VIRGIN
056:036 And made them **virgin**-pure (and undefiled),-

VIRGINS
066:005 previously married or **virgins**.

VIRTUE
002:189 it is **virtue** if ye fear Allah.
002:189 It is no **virtue** if ye enter your houses
002:232 most **virtue** and purity amongst you,
007:134 in **virtue** of his promise to thee: if thou

VIRTUES
005:048 so strive as in a race in all **virtues**.

VIRTUOUS
012:051 (ever) true (and **virtuous**).
024:032 and the **virtuous** ones among your slaves,

VISIBLE
010:067 and the Day to make things **visible** (to you).
017:059 to the Thamud-a **visible** Sign-but they
044:010 a kind of smoke (or mist) plainly **visible**.

VISIBLY
027:013 **visibly** they said: "This is sorcery manifest!"

VISION
002:243 thy **vision** to those who abandoned their homes,
002:246 Hast thou not turned thy **vision** to the chiefs ·
006:103 No **vision** can grasp Him, but
006:103 but His grasp is over all **vision**; He is
012:005 relate not thy **vision** to thy brother,
012:043 O ye chiefs! expound to me my **vision** if it be
012:043 (in a **vision**) seven fat kine, whom seven
012:100 the fulfillment of my **vision** of old!
017:060 We granted the **Vision** which We showed thee,
024:044 is an instructive example those who have **vision**!
032:027 Have they not the **vision**?
038:045 possessors of Power and **Vision**.
048:027 the **vision** for His Messenger:
067:003 So turn thy **vision** again: Seest thou any flaw?
067:004 Again turn thy **vision** a second time:
067:004 (thy) **vision** will come back to thee dull

VISIONS
012:043 if it be that ye can interpret **visions**."

VISIT
002:158 So if those who **visit** the House
007:164 destroy or **visit** with a terrible punishment?"-
017:007 and to **visit** with destruction all that
074:017 Soon will I **visit** him with a mount of calamities!
102:002 Until ye **visit** the graves.

VISITATION
068:019 on the (garden) a **visitation** from thy Lord,

VISITED
007:165 but We **visited** the wrong-doers with a
009:018 **visited** and maintained by such as believe

VISITOR
022:025 and the **visitor** from the country-and any

VIVID
024:043 The **vivid** flash of His lightning well-nigh

VOICE
017:064 with thy (seductive) **voice**;
019:024 But (a **voice**) cried to her from beneath
027:008 a **voice** was heard: "Blessed are
029:055 and (a **Voice**) shall say: "Taste ye
031:019 and lower thy **voice**; for the harshest
036:052 (A **voice** will say): "This is what The Most Gracious
037:021 (A **voice** will say,) "This is the Day of Sorting out,
044:047 (A **voice** will cry:) "Seize ye him and drag him
049:002 your voices above the **voice** of the Prophet,
049:003 Those that lower their **voice** in the presence
050:032 (A **voice** will say:) "This is what was promised for you,-

VOICES
020:108 and the **voices** will be hushed to The Most Gracious:
049:002 your **voices** above the voice of the Prophet,

VOID
002:170 fathers were **void** of wisdom and guidance?.
002:171 they are **void** of wisdom.
005:089 to account for what is **void** in your oaths,
005:104 were **void** of knowledge and guidance?
014:043 and their hearts a (gaping) **void**!
028:010 And the heart of the mother of Moses became **void**:
035:010 and the plotting of such will be **void** (of result).

VOTARIES
003:175 suggests to you the fear of his **votaries**:
009:104 accept repentance from His **votaries** and receives

VOTARY
096:010 A **votary** when he (turns) to pray?

VOW
002:270 or whatever you **vow** to make,
006:063 (we **vow**) we shall truly show our gratitude.'?"
007:189 we **vow** we shall (ever) be grateful."

VOWED
019:026 'I have **vowed** a fast to (Allah) Most Gracious,

VOWS
022:029 fulfil their **vows**, and (again) circumambulate
076:007 They perform (their) **vows**, and they fear

WADD
071:023   **Wadd** nor Suwa, neither Yaguth nor Yauq, nor Nasr';-

WAG
017:051   Then will they **wag** their heads towards thee.

WAGE
005:033   who **wage** war against Allah and His Messenger,

WAGES
028:026   (dear) father! engage him on **wages**:

WAILING
040:032   mutual calling (and **wiling**),-

WAIT
002:210   Will they **wait** until Allah comes to them
002:228   Divorced women shall **wait** concerning themselves
002:234   they shall **wait** concerning themselves four months
004:141   (These are) the ones who **wait** and watch about you:
006:158   Say: "**Wait** ye: we too are waiting."
007:016   I will lie in **wait** for them on Thy Straight Way:
007:071   Then **wait**: I am amongst you, also waiting."
007:128   and (**wait**) in patience and constancy: for the
009:005   and lie in **wait** for them in every stratagem (of war);
009:024   then **wait** until Allah brings about His Decision:
009:052   So **wait** (expectant); we too will **wait** with you."
010:020   Then **wait** ye: I too will **wait** with you."
010:102   Say: "**Wait** ye then: for I too, will **wait** with you."
011:122   "And **wait** ye! we too shall **wait**."
016:033   Do the (ungodly) **wait** but for the angels
018:055   but that (they **wait** for) the ways of the ancients
020:135   **wait** ye, therefore, and soon shall ye know who
023:025   **wait** (and have patience) with him for a time."
027:028   and (**wait** to) see what answer they return"...
027:035   and (**wait**) to see with what (answer)
032:030   So turn away from them, and **wait**: they too are waiting
033:023   of them some have died and some (still) **wait**:
033:053   to **wait** for its preparation: but when
036:049   They will not (have to) **wait** for aught but a
038:015   These (to-day) only **wait** for a single mighty Blast,
043:066   Do they only **wait** for the Hour-that it
044:059   So **wait** thou and watch; for they
047:018   Do they then only **wait** for the Hour,-that it
052:031   I too will **wait** along with you!"
054:006   (And **wait** for) the Day that the Caller will call (them)
057:013   say to the Believers: "**Wait** for us! Let us
068:048   So **wait** with patience for the command of thy Lord,

WAITED
057:014   ye **waited** (to our ruin); ye doubted

WAITING
002:226   a **waiting** for four months is ordained;
006:158   Are they **waiting** to see if the
006:158   Say: "Wait ye: we too are **waiting**."
007:053   Are they **waiting** for its fulfillment?
007:071   Then wait: I am amongst you, also **waiting**."
020:135   Say: "Each one (of us), is **waiting**: wait ye,
027:005   a grievous Chastisement is (**waiting**):
032:030   they too are **waiting**.
044:059   for they (too) are **waiting**.

WAKE
006:006   and raised in their **wake** fresh generations
057:027   Then, in their **wake**, We followed them up with

WALK
002:020   every time the light (helps) them, they **walk** therein,
002:186   that they may **walk** in the right way.
006:122   he can **walk** amongst men,
007:195   Have they feet to **walk** with?
013:010   by night or **walk** freely by day.
017:037   Nor **walk** on the earth with insolence: for thou
024:045   and some that **walk** on four.
024:045   some that **walk** on two legs: and some
025:063   who **walk** on the earth in humility, and when
031:018   at men. Nor **walk** in insolence through the earth:
038:006   "**Walk** ye away, and remain constant to your gods!
049:007   those who **walk** in righteousness;-
057:028   by which ye shall **walk** (straight in your path),

WALKED
025:020   who ate food and **walked** through the markets.

WALKING
017:095   on earth, angels **walking** about in peace and quite,
028:025   came (back) to him, **walking** bashfully.

WALKS
025:007   and **walks** through the streets?
067:022   Is then one who **walks** headlong, with his
067:022   or one who **walks** evenly on a Straight Way?

WALL
018:077   They found there a **wall** on the point of falling down
018:082   "As for the **wall**, it belonged to two youths,
038:021   over the **wall** of the private chamber;
057:013   So a **wall** will be put up betwixt them, with a

WALLS
018:029   like the **walls** and roof of a tent, will hem
059:014   except in fortified townships, or from behind **walls**.

WANDER
002:015   so they will **wander** like blind ones
005:026   in distraction will they **wander** through the land:
006:039   whom Allah willeth, He leaveth to **wander**
009:112   that **wander** in devotion to Cause of Allah;
015:072   they **wander** in distraction, to and fro.
026:225   **wander** distracted in every valley?-
027:004   and so they **wander** blindly.
038:026   for those who **wander** astray from the Path
043:040   or to such as (**wander**) in manifest error?
050:036   Then did they **wander** through the land:
055:044   of boiling hot water will they **wander** round!

WANDERED
005:012   truly **wandered** from the path of rectitude."

WANDERING
006:071   **wandering** bewildered through the earth,
007:186   **wandering** in distraction.
010:011   **wandering** in distraction blindly.
012:095   in thine old **wandering** illusion."
023:075   **wandering** in distraction to and fro.
033:020   in the deserts (**wandering**) among the Bedouins,
039:022   they are manifestly **wandering** (in error)!
040:050   without faith is nothing but (futile **wandering**)
093:007   And He found thee **wandering**,

WANT
002:061   and ye shall find what ye **want**!"
002:185   He does not **want** to put you to difficulties.
002:215   and those in **want** and for wayfarers.

WANT (continued)

002:245 It is Allah that giveth (you) **want** or Plenty,
006:151 kill not your children on a plea of **want**;-
007:082 who **want** to be clean and pure!"
011:079 indeed thou knowest quite well what we **want**!"
013:005 If thou dost marvel (at their **want** of faith),
017:026 as (also) to those in **want**,
017:031 Kill not your children for fear of **want**:
018:079 it belonged to certain men in dire **want**:
022:028 the distressed ones in **want**.
024:022 those in **want**, and those who have left
027:056 men who **want** to be clean and pure!"
033:053 And when you (his ladies) for anything ye **want**,
067:003 no **want** of proportion wilt thou see in the Creation
107:006 Those who (**want** but) to be seen,

WANTED

010:051 and ye **wanted** (aforetime) to hasten it on!"

WANTON

024:060 provided they make not **wanton** display of their

WANTS

002:185 (He **wants** you) to complete the prescribed period,
002:263 Allah is free of all **wants**,
002:267 And know that Allah is free of all **wants**,
004:131 and Allah is free of all **wants**, worthy
014:008 yet is Allah Free of all **wants**, Worthy of
022:064 He is free of all **wants**, worthy of all praise.
031:012 verily Allah is free of all **wants**, worthy of
031:026 verily Allah is He (that is) free of all **wants**, worthy of
035:015 the One Free of all **wants**, worthy of all praise.
047:038 But Allah is free of all **wants**, and it is ye that are needy.
060:006 truly Allah is free of all **Wants**, Worthy, of all Praise.
074:052 Forsooth, each one of them **wants** to be given

WAR

002:279 notice of **war** from Allah and His Messenger:
004:090 no way for you (to **war** against them).
004:092 to a people at **war** with you,,
005:033 who wage **war** against Allah and His Messenger,
005:064 Every time they kindle the fire of **war**,
008:001 (things taken as) spoils of **war**.
008:016 unless it be in a stratagem of **war**,
008:041 all the booty that ye may acquire (in **war**),
008:057 If ye gain the mastery over them in **war**,
008:060 including steeds of **war**,
008:067 that he should have prisoners of **war** until he
008:069 But (now) enjoy what ye took in **war**,
009:005 for them in every stratagem (of **war**);
022:039 To those against whom **war** is made,
027:033 and given to vehement **war**:
033:050 the captives of **war** whom Allah has assigned
047:004 until the **war** lays down its burdens.
048:015 when ye set forth to acquire booty (in **war**):
048:016 (to fight) against a people given to vehement **war**:
048:017 nor on one ill (if he joins not the **war**):

WARD

021:039 to **ward** off the Fire from their faces,
039:024 Is, then, one who has to **ward** off the brunt
070:002 the which there is none is none to **ward** off,-

WARDED

012:110 But never will be **warded** off Our punishment from those

WARFARE

017:005 sent against you Our servants given to terrible **warfare**:

WARM

027:007 that ye may **warm** yourselves."
028:029 burning firebrand, that ye may **warm** yourselves."

WARMTH

016:005 from them ye derive **warmth**,

WARN

002:006 whether thou **warn** them or do not **warn** them;
006:019 that I may **warn** you and all whom it reaches.
006:048 only to give good news and to **warn**:
006:092 that thou mayest **warn** the Mother
007:002 **warn** (the erring) and a reminder the Believers.
007:063 to **warn** you,-so that ye may fear Allah
007:069 of your own people, to **warn** you?
010:002 That he should **warn** mankind (of their danger),
011:002 from Him to **warn** and to bring glad tidings:
011:012 But thou art there only to **warn**!
014:044 So **warn** mankind of the Day when the Wrath
016:002 (saying): "**Warn** (Man) that there is no god but I:
017:105 Glad Tidings and to **warn** (sinners).
018:002 in order that He may **warn** (the godless) of a
018:004 Further, that He may **warn** those (also) who say,
019:039 But **warn** them of the Day of Distress, when the
021:045 Say, "I do but **warn** you according to revelation":
035:018 Thou canst but **warn** such as fear their Lord
036:006 **warn** a people, whose fathers were not warned,
039:016 with this doth Allah **warn** off His servants:
040:015 that it may **warn** (men) of the Day
040:018 **Warn** them of the Day that is (ever) drawing near,
042:007 and **warn** (them) of the Day of Assembly,
042:007 that thou mayest **warn** the Mother of Cities
044:003 for We (ever) wish to **warn** (against Evil).
046:029 to their people, to **warn** them.
054:036 And (Lut) did **warn** them of Our violent Seizure
071:001 (with the Command): "Do thou **warn** thy People
092:014 Therefore do I **warn** you of a Fire blazing fiercely;

WARNED

010:073 those who were **warned** (but heeded not)!
010:098 a single township (among those We **warned**), which
021:045 not hear the call, (even) when they are **warned**!
023:093 (in my lifetime) that which they are **warned** against,-
023:095 (in fulfillment) against which they are **warned**.
036:006 whose fathers were not **warned**,
037:073 then see what was he End of those who were **warned**,
037:177 morning for those who were **warned** (and heeded not)!
041:013 "I have **warned** you of a thunderbolt like the
046:003 turn away from that whereof they are **warned**.
046:021 behold, he **warned** his people
078:040 Verily, We have **warned** you of a Chastisement near,-

WARNER

002:119 in truth as a bearer of glad tidings and a **warner**:
005:019 unto us no bringer of glad tidings and no **warner**.
005:019 a bringer of glad tidings and a **warner**.
007:184 he is but a perspicuous **warner**.
007:188 I am but a **warner**, and a bringer
011:025 "I have come to you as a clear **warner**.
013:007 But thou art truly a **warner**,
025:051 We could have sent a **warner** to every town.
026:115 "I am sent only as a plain **warner**."
027:092 say: "I am only a **Warner**."
028:046 no **warner** had come before thee:
029:050 and I am indeed a clear **Warner**."
032:003 to whom no **warner** has come before thee:
033:045 a Bearer of Glad Tidings, and a **Warner**,-

WARNER (continued)

034:034   Never did We send a **Warner** to a population,
034:046   he is no less than a **Warner** to you,
035:023   Thou art no other than a **warner**.
035:024   and as a **warner**:
035:024   without a **warner** having lived among
035:037   And (moreover) the **warner** came to you.
035:042   but when a **warner** came to them,
035:042   by Allah that if a **warner** came to them,
038:004   So they wonder that a **Warner** has come to them
038:065   Say: "Truly am I a **Warner**:
043:023   a **Warner** before thee to any people,
046:009   I am but a **Warner** open and clear."
048:008   as a bringer of Glad Tidings, and as a **Warner**:
050:002   to them a **Warner** from among themselves.
051:050   I am from Him a **Warner** to you, clear and open!
051:051   I am from Him a **Warner** to you, clear and open!
053:056   This is a **Warner**, of the (series of) Warners of old!
067:008   its Keepers will ask, "Did no **Warner** come to you?"
067:009   a **Warner** did come to us, but we
067:026   I am a plain **warner**."
071:002   a **Warner**, clear and open:
079:045   Thou art but a **Warner** for such as fear it.

WARNERS

010:101   but neither Signs nor **Warners** profit those
026:208   Never did We destroy a town but had its **warners**-
034:044   nor sent messengers to them before thee as **Warners**.
037:072   But We sent aforetime, among them, **warners**.
046:021   **Warners** before him and after him:
053:056   of the (series of) **Warners** of old!
054:005   but (the preaching of) **Warners** profits them not.
054:023   The Thamud (also) rejected (their) **Warners**.
054:041   too, aforetime, came **Warners** (from Allah).

WARNETH

015:089   **warneth** openly and without ambiguity,"-

WARNING

004:165   Messengers who gave good news as well as **warning**,
006:044   the **warning** they had received,
006:051   Give this **warning** to those in whose (hearts)
006:130   and **warning** you of the meeting of this
007:136   and failed to take **warning** from them.
007:146   and failed to take **warning** from them.
007:179   for they are heedless (of **warning**).
008:038   is already (a matter of **warning** for them).
014:052   that they may take **warning** therefrom,
017:005   and it was a **warning** (completely) fulfilled.
017:015   We had sent a messenger (to give **warning**).
017:059   of frightening (and **warning** from evil).
017:060   We put fear (and **warning**) into them,
019:075   see the **warning** of Allah (being fulfilled)-
020:044   perchance he may take **warning** or fear (Allah)."
022:049   I am (sent) to you only to give a clear **warning**:
028:046   to give **warning** to a people to whom no warner
034:028   and **warning** them (against sin), but most
038:070   that I am to give **warning** plainly and publicly."
039:071   and **warning** you of the Meeting of this Day
050:014   and My **warning** was duly fulfilled
050:020   whereof **warning** (had been given).
050:028   I had already in advance sent you **Warning**.
050:045   such as fear My **Warning**!
054:003   They reject (the **warning**) and follow
054:016   how (terrible) was My Chastisement and My **Warning**?
054:018   how (terrible) was My Chastisement and my **Warning**!

WARNING (continued)

054:021   how (terrible) was My Chastisement and my **Warning**!
054:030   how (terrible) was My Chastisement and My **Warning**!
054:033   The People of Lut rejected (his) **Warning**.
054:036   violent Seizure but they disputed about the **Warning**.
054:037   My Wrath and My **Warning**."
054:039   "So taste ye My Chastisement and My **Warning**."
059:002   Take **warning**, then, O ye with eyes (to see)!
067:017   so that ye shall know how (terrible) was My **warning**?
067:018   But indeed men before them rejected (My **warning**):
074:002   Arise and deliver thy **warning**!
074:036   A **warning** to mankind,-
077:006   Whether of Justification or of **Warning**;-

WARNINGS

002:213   with glad tidings and **warnings**;
007:165   When they disregarded the **warnings** that had
017:005   When the first of the **warnings** came to pass,
017:007   so when the second of the **warnings** came to pass,
017:104   but when the second of the **warnings** came to pass,
018:056   glad tidings and to give **warnings**:
018:056   My Signs and **warnings** as a jest.
019:097   and **warnings** to people given to contention.
020:113   in detail some of the **warnings**, in order that
025:056   to give glad tidings and **warnings**.

WARNS

040:028   of the (calamity) of which he **warns** you:

WARRANT

006:081   without any **warrant** having been given to you?
010:068   No **warrant** have ye for this!

WARRED

009:107   **warred** against Allah and His Messenger aforetime.

WAS

002:034   he **was** of those who reject Faith.
002:034   not so Iblis, he refused and **was** haughty:
002:049   therein **was** a tremendous trial from your Lord.
002:052   there **was** a chance for you to be grateful.
002:053   there **was** a chance for you to be guided aright.
002:072   but Allah **was** to bring forth what ye did hide.
002:085   though it **was** not lawful for you
002:091   what **was** sent down to us":
002:101   confirming what **was** with them,
002:102   And vile **was** the price for which they
002:108   as Moses **was** questioned of old?
002:114   It **was** not fitting that such should
002:124   **was** tried by his lord with certain Commands,
002:134   That **was** a People that hath passed away.
002:141   That **was** a people that hath passed away.
002:143   Indeed it **was** (a change) momentous,
002:183   as it **was** prescribed to those before you,
002:185   in which **was** sent down the Qur'an,
002:213   Mankind **was** one single nation.
002:246   They said to a Prophet (that **was**) among them:
002:258   Thus **was** he confounded who (in arrogance)
002:259   When this **was** shown clearly to him,
003:013   one **was** fighting in the cause of Allah,
003:036   When she **was** delivered, she said: "O my Lord!
003:037   to the care of Zakariya **was** she assigned.
003:039   While he **was** standing in prayer in the chamber,
003:040   "Thus," **was** the answer, "Doth Allah accomplish
003:041   "Thy Sign," **was** the answer, "Shall be that thou
003:050   to attest the Torah which **was** before me.
003:050   part of what **was** (before) forbidden to you;
003:059   then said to him: "Be": and he **was**.

WAS (continued)

003:067	Abraham **was** not a Jew nor yet a Christian;
003:067	but he **was** Upright.
003:073	like unto that which **was** sent unto you?
003:084	and what **was** revealed to Abraham, Isma'il;
003:086	and bore witness that the Messenger **was** true
003:093	All food **was** lawful to the Children of Israel,
003:093	for himself before the Torah **was** revealed.
003:095	he **was** not of the Pagans."
003:096	appointed for men **was** that at Bakka:
003:122	but Allah **was** their Protector,
003:137	what **was** the end of those who rejected Truth.
003:147	All that they said **was**: "Our Lord forgive us
003:153	in your rear **was** calling you back.
003:154	those for whom death **was** decreed would certainly
003:154	but (all this **was**) that Allah might test what
003:154	while another band **was** stirred to anxiety
003:155	it **was** Satan who caused them to fail,
003:166	**was** with the leave of Allah,
003:167	saying with their lips what **was** not in their hearts.
003:187	And vile **was** the bargain they made!
004:022	it **was** shameful and odious, an abominable
004:028	for man **was** created weak in (resolution).
004:033	To those also, to whom your right hand **was** pledged,
004:047	confirming what **was** (already) with you,
004:077	the order for fighting **was** issued to them, behold!
004:092	to a people at war with you, and he **was** a Believer,
004:097	They say: "**Was** not the earth of Allah spacious
004:157	Only a likeness of that **was** shown to them.
004:162	and what **was** revealed before thee:
004:171	**was** (no more than) an Messenger of Allah,
004:176	if (such a deceased **was**) a woman, who left no child,
005:013	of the Message that **was** sent them,
005:014	forgot a good part of the message that **was** sent them:
005:027	it **was** accepted from one, but not from the other.
005:031	"**Was** I not even able to be as this raven,
005:044	It **was** We who revealed the Torah (to Moses):
005:044	for to them **was** entrusted the protection
005:044	therein **was** guidance and light.
005:046	therein **was** guidance and light.
005:066	that **was** sent to them from their Lord,
005:075	His mother **was** a woman of truth.
005:075	**was** no more than an Messenger;
005:103	It **was** not Allah Who instituted
005:109	and ask: "What **was** the response ye received
005:117	and I **was** a witness over them whilst I
006:011	what **was** the end of those who rejected Truth."
006:045	the last remnant **was** cut off.
006:083	That **was** Our argument which We gave
006:122	Can he who **was** dead, to whom
006:130	It **was** the life of this world that deceived them.
006:156	Lest ye should say: "The Book **was** sent down
007:006	to whom Our Message **was** sent and those
007:020	their shame that **was** hidden from them (before):
007:021	that he **was** their sincere adviser.
007:022	Satan **was** an avowed enemy unto you?"
007:043	indeed it **was** the truth that the Messengers
007:079	I **was** sent by my Lord: I gave you
007:083	she **was** of those who lagged behind.
007:084	then see what **was** the end of those who
007:086	And see what **was** the end of those who did mischief.
007:092	it **was** they who were ruined!
007:093	I **was** sent by my Lord: I gave you

WAS (continued)

007:103	so see what **was** the end of those
007:107	and behold! it **was** a serpent, plain
007:108	and behold! it **was** white to all beholders!
007:118	And all that they did **was** made of no effect.
007:118	Thus truth **was** confirmed.
007:137	of thy Lord **was** fulfilled for the Children of Israel,
007:141	in that **was** a momentous trial from your Lord.
007:142	thus **was** completed the term with his Lord,
007:154	in the writing thereon **was** Guidance and Mercy
007:154	When the anger of Moses **was** appeased, he took
007:161	And remember it **was** said to them: "Dwell in
007:169	**Was** not the Covenant of the Book
007:171	and they thought it **was** going to fall
008:006	the truth after it **was** made manifest,
008:017	It is not you who slew them; it **was** Allah:
008:017	it **was** not thy act, but Allah's:
008:033	But Allah **was** not going to send them
008:033	nor **was** He going to send it whilst they
009:042	followed thee, but the distance **was** long,
009:046	but Allah **was** averse to their being sent forth;
009:065	Say: "**Was** it at Allah, and His Signs,
009:074	this revenge of theirs **was** (their) only return
009:102	with another that **was** evil.
009:102	they have mixed an act that **was** good with another
009:108	whose foundation **was** laid from the first day on piety;
009:114	that he **was** an enemy to Allah,
009:114	for Abraham **was** most tender hearted, forbearing.
009:120	but **was** reckoned to their credit as a deed
009:120	It **was** not fitting for the people of Madinah
010:019	Mankind **was** but one nation, but differed (later).
010:028	"It **was** not us that ye worshipped!"
010:039	but see what **was** the end of those who did wrong!
010:047	To every people (**was** sent) an Messenger:
010:073	Then see what **was** the end of those who
010:083	Pharaoh **was** mighty on the earth and one who
010:091	(It **was** said to him): "Ah now!-but a little
010:093	it **was** after knowledge had been
010:097	Even if every Sign **was** brought unto them,-
011:007	and His Throne **was** over the Waters-that He
011:036	It **was** revealed to Noah: "None of thy People
011:043	and the son **was** among those who were drowned.
011:044	and the matter **was** ended.
011:057	I **was** sent to you.
011:071	And his wife **was** standing (there), and she
011:075	For Abraham **was**, without doubt, forbearing
011:077	he **was** grieved on their account and felt himself
011:097	and the command of Pharaoh **was** no rightly (guide).
011:101	It **was** not We that wronged them: they wronged
012:003	thou too **was** among those who knew it not.
012:023	But she, in whose house he **was**, sought to
012:024	for he **was** one of Our servants chosen.
012:026	He said: "It **was** she that sought to seduce me-
012:028	that it **was** torn at the back, (her husband)
012:035	(that it **was** best) to imprison him for a time.
012:050	thy lord, and ask him, 'What **was** the matter
012:051	"What **was** your affair when ye did seek to seduce
012:051	it **was** I who sought to seduce him he is indeed
012:068	For he **was**, by Our instruction, full of
012:077	They said: "If he steals, there **was** a brother
012:084	and he **was** suppressed with silent sorrow.
012:100	He **was** indeed good to me when He took
012:109	and see what **was** the end of those before them?

WAS (continued)

013:032 | then how (terrible) **was** My requital!
013:038 | and it **was** never the part of a messenger
014:006 | there **was** a tremendous trial
014:015 | and frustration **was** the lot of every powerful
014:022 | "It **was** Allah Who gave you a promise
015:084 | And of no avail to them **was** all that they did
016:036 | what **was** the end of those who denied (the Truth).
016:094 | may slip after it **was** firmly planted;
016:112 | yet **was** it ungrateful for the favors of Allah:
016:120 | Abraham **was** indeed a model, devoutly obedient
016:124 | The Sabbath **was** only made (strict) for those
017:003 | Verily he **was** a devotee most grateful.
017:005 | and it **was** a warning (completely) fulfilled.
017:073 | And their purpose **was** to tempt thee away from
017:076 | Their purpose **was** to scare thee off the land,
017:077 | (This **was** Our) way with the messengers We sent
017:094 | **was** nothing but this: they said, "Has Allah
018:012 | which of the two parties **was** best at calculating
018:034 | (Abundant) **was** the produce this man had:
018:043 | nor **was** he able to deliver himself.
018:050 | He **was** one of the Jinns, and he
018:064 | Moses said: "That **was** what we were seeking after":
018:079 | for there **was** after them a certain king who
018:082 | there **was**, beneath it, a buried treasure, to which
018:091 | We completely understood what **was** before him.
019:007 | (His prayer **was** answered): "O Zakariya! We give
019:010 | "Thy Sign," **was** the answer, "shall be
019:013 | as from Us, and purity: he **was** devout,
019:014 | and he **was** not overbearing or rebellious.
019:015 | So Peace on him the day he **was** born, the day
019:028 | "O sister of Aaron! thy father **was** not a man
019:033 | "So Peace is on me the day I **was** born, the day
019:034 | Such (**was**) Jesus the son of Mary:
019:041 | (the story of) Abraham: he **was** a man of Truth,
019:051 | (the story of) Moses: for he **was** specially chosen.
019:051 | And He **was** a messenger and a prophet.
019:054 | (the story of) Isma'il: he **was** (strictly) true
019:054 | and he **was** a messenger (and) a prophet.
019:055 | Prayer and Zakat and he **was** most acceptable in
019:056 | he **was** a man of truth (and sincerity),
020:011 | he **was** called "O Moses!
020:020 | it **was** a snake, active in motion.
020:049 | (When this message **was** delivered), (Pharaoh) said:
020:083 | (When Moses **was** up on the mount, Allah said):
020:087 | and that **was** what the Samiri suggested.
020:133 | of all that **was** in the former Books of revelation?
021:063 | He said: "Nay, this **was** done by this
021:075 | for he **was** one of the Righteous.
021:079 | it **was** Our power that made the
021:079 | it **was** We Who did (all these things).
021:080 | It **was** We Who taught him the making of
021:081 | (It **was** Our power that made) the violent
021:082 | and it **was** We Who guarded them.
021:084 | We removed the distress that **was** on him, and We
021:087 | Glory to Thee: I **was** indeed wrong!"
022:044 | but how (terrible) **was** My punishment
022:044 | and Moses **was** rejected (in the same way).
023:109 | "A part of My servants there **was**, who used
024:015 | while it **was** most serious in the sight of Allah.
025:006 | Say: "The (Qur'an) **was** sent down by Him
025:017 | "**Was** it ye who led these my servants astray,
025:018 | not meant **was** it for us that we should take

WAS (continued)

025:040 | by the town on which **was** rained a shower of evil:
026:020 | Moses: "I did it then, when I **was** in error.
026:032 | and behold, it **was** a serpent, plain
026:033 | and behold, it **was** white to all beholders!
026:059 | Thus it **was**, but We made the Children of Israel
026:173 | and evil **was** the shower on those who were
026:189 | and that **was** the Chastisement of a Great Day.
027:008 | a voice **was** heard: "Blessed are
027:010 | "O Moses!" (it **was** said), fear not:
027:014 | so see what **was** the end of those who
027:016 | And Solomon **was** David's heir.
027:042 | So when she arrived, she **was** asked, "Is this
027:042 | And knowledge **was** bestowed on us
027:043 | for she **was** (sprung) of a people that had no faith.
027:044 | She **was** asked to enter the lofty Palace:
027:044 | she saw it, she thought it **was** a lake of water,
027:051 | Then see what **was** the end of their plot!-
027:058 | and evil **was** the shower on those who were
027:084 | or what **was** it ye did?"
028:004 | for he **was** indeed an evil-doer.
028:008 | (it **was** intended) that (Moses) should be
028:010 | she **was** going almost to disclose his (case),
028:014 | and **was** firmly established (in life),
028:018 | In the morning, he **was** in the city, fearful and
028:019 | Then, when he **was** about to lay his hands on their
028:029 | and **was** travelling with his family,
028:030 | he **was** called from the right bank of the valley,
028:031 | "O Moses!" (It **was** said), "Draw near, and fear
028:039 | And he **was** arrogant and insolent in the land,
028:040 | now behold what **was** the End of those
028:059 | Nor **was** thy Lord the one to destroy a town
028:063 | It **was** not us they worshipped."
028:065 | and say: "What **was** the answer ye gave
028:076 | Qarun **was** doubtless, of the people of Moses;
028:082 | Allah **was** gracious to us, He could
029:024 | So naught **was** the answer of (Abraham's) people
029:033 | he **was** grieved on their account, and felt
029:040 | it **was** not Allah Who wronged them: they wronged
030:009 | it **was** not Allah Who wronged them, but they
030:009 | and see what **was** the End of those before them?
030:042 | and see what **was** the End of those before (you):
030:047 | and it **was** a duty incumbent upon Us to aid
031:014 | And in years twain **was** his weaning:
033:022 | and His Messenger told us what **was** true."
033:037 | that which Allah **was** about to make manifest:
033:038 | It **was** the practice (approved) of Allah
033:062 | (Such **was**) the practice (approved) of Allah
033:069 | and he **was** honorable in Allah's sight.
033:072 | he **was** indeed unjust and foolish;-
034:012 | and its evening (stride) **was** a month's (journey);
034:012 | morning (stride) **was** a month's (journey), and its
034:015 | There **was**, for Saba', aforetime, a Sign
034:017 | That **was** the Requital We gave them because
034:032 | Nay, rather it **was** ye who transgressed."
034:032 | "**Was** it we who kept you back from Guidance
034:033 | "Nay! it **was** a plot (of yours) by day
034:040 | "**Was** it you that these men used to worship?"
034:045 | My messengers, how (terrible) **was** My punishment!
034:054 | as **was** in the past with their partisans:
035:024 | and there never **was** a people,
035:026 | and who (terrible) **was** My punishment.
035:031 | confirming what **was** (revealed) before it:

WAS (continued)

035:044 and see what **was** the End of those before them,-
036:026 It **was** said: "Enter thou the Garden."
036:028 nor **was** it needful for Us so to do.
036:029 It **was** no more than a single mighty Blast,
036:035 it **was** not their hands that made this:
036:052 And true **was** the word of the messengers!"
036:060 for that he **was** to you an enemy avowed?-
036:061 (for that) this **was** the Straight Way?
037:028 They will say: "It **was** ye who used to come
037:030 Nay, it **was** ye who were a people in
037:073 Then see what **was** the end of those
037:081 For he **was** one of Our believing Servants.
037:083 Verily from his party **was** Abraham.
037:106 For this **was** a clear trial-
037:111 For he **was** one of Our believing Servants.
037:123 So also **was** Elias among those sent (by us).
037:132 For He **was** one of Our believing Servants.
037:133 So also **was** Lut among those sent (by us).
037:135 Except an old woman who **was** among those who
037:139 So also **was** Jonah among those sent (by Us).
037:141 and he **was** of the rebutted:
038:003 when there **was** no longer time for being saved!
038:018 It **was** We that made the hills declare, in unison
038:022 and he **was** terrified of them,
038:032 Until (the sun) **was** hidden in the veil (of Night):
038:048 each of them **was** of the company of the Good.
038:074 Not so Iblis: he **was** haughty, and became
039:050 all that they did **was** of no profit to them.
039:055 "And follow the Best that which **was** revealed to you
039:056 and **was** but among those who mocked!'
039:065 as it **was** to those before thee,-
040:005 but it **was** I that seized them!
040:005 And how (terrible), **was** My Requital!
040:006 Thus **was** the Word of thy Lord proved true
040:010 "Greater **was** the aversion of Allah to you
040:012 "This is because, when Allah **was** invoked as the
040:021 and see what **was** the End of those before them?
040:022 That **was** because there came to them
040:037 Thus **was** made alluring, in Pharaoh's
040:037 and he **was** hindered from the Path;
040:075 "That **was** because ye were wont to rejoice on the
040:078 It **was** not (possible) for any messenger to bring
040:078 the matter **was** decided in truth and justice,
040:082 all that they accomplished **was** of no profit to them.
040:082 and see what **was** the end of those before them?
040:085 saw Our Punishment **was** not going to profit them.
041:015 **was** superior to them in strength?
041:025 **was** before them and behind them;
041:034 and thee **was** hatred become as it were thy
041:043 Nothing is said to thee that **was** not said to the
042:052 what **was** revelation, and what **was** Faith;
043:005 He **was** no more than a servant:
043:025 now see what **was** the end of those who
043:035 But all this **was** nothing but enjoyment of the
044:028 Thus (**was** their end)!
044:031 Inflicted by Pharaoh, for he **was** arrogant (even)
044:033 in which there **was** a manifest trial.
045:017 it **was** only after knowledge had been granted to
045:032 promise of Allah **was** true, and that the Hour-
045:032 "And when it **was** said that the promise of
045:032 there **was** no doubt about its (coming),
046:012 And before this, **was** the Book of Moses as a

WAS (continued)

046:016 which **was** made to them (in this life).
046:025 nothing **was** to be seen but (the ruins of)
046:028 but that **was** their Falsehood and their invention.
046:028 Why then **was** no help forthcoming to them
046:029 When the (reading) **was** finished, they returned
047:010 and see what **was** the End of those before them
047:013 And there **was** none to aid them.
047:025 after Guidance **was** clearly shown to them,-
048:018 He knew what **was** in their hearts, and He
048:018 Allah's Good Pleasure **was** on the Believers
050:012 Before them **was** denied (the Hereafter) by the
050:014 and My warning **was** duly fulfilled (in them).
050:016 It **was** We who created man, and We
050:019 "This **was** the thing which thou wast trying to escape!"
050:025 "Who forbade what **was** good, transgressed all
050:027 but he **was** (himself) far astray."
050:032 "This is what **was** promised for you,-for every
050:036 **was** there any place of escape (for them)?
051:038 And in Moses (**was** another Sign): behold, We sent
051:040 and his **was** the blame.
051:041 And in the `Ad (people) (**was** another Sign):
051:043 And in the Thamud (**was** another Sign): behold,
053:005 He **was** taught by one Mighty in Power,
053:007 While he **was** in the highest part of the horizon:
053:009 And **was** at a distance of but two bow-lengths
053:016 Behold, the Lote-tree **was** shrouded with
054:001 and the moon **was** cleft asunder.
054:009 "Here is one possessed!", and he **was** driven out.
054:016 But how (terrible) **was** My Chastisement and My
054:018 then how terrible **was** my Chastisement and My
054:021 Yea, how (terrible) **was** my Chastisement and my
054:030 Ah! how (terrible) **was** My Chastisement and My
057:016 not become like those to whom **was** given The Book
059:005 it **was** by leave of Allah,
059:009 even though poverty **was** their (own lot).
060:006 There **was** indeed in them an excellent example
063:003 so a seal **was** set on their hearts: therefore
064:006 That **was** because there came to them messengers
065:009 of their conduct **was** Perdition.
066:012 and **was** one of the devout (Servants).
067:017 so that ye shall know how (terrible) **was** My warning?
067:018 **was** My punishment (of them)?
069:033 "This **was** he that would not believe
070:019 Truly man **was** created very impatient;
074:023 Then he turned back and **was** haughty;
075:025 back-breaking calamity **was** about to be
075:028 And he will think that it **was** (the Time)
075:037 **Was** he not a drop of sperm emitted (in lowly form)?
076:001 when he **was** nothing-(not even) mentioned?
081:009 For what crime she **was** killed;
084:015 Nay, nay! for his Lord **was** (ever) watchful of him!
091:012 among them **was** deputed (for impiety).

WASH

005:006 **wash** your faces, and your hands (and arms)
005:006 and (**wash**) your feet to the ankles.
038:042 here is (water) wherein to **wash**, cool and

WASHING

004:043 until after **washing** your whole body if ye are ill,
069:036 the foul pus from the **washing** of wounds,

WAST

002:143 the Qiblah to which thou **wast** used,
003:044 thou nor **wast** thou with them when they dispute

WAST (continued)

003:044 thou **wast** not with them when they cast lots
005:117 thou **wast** the Watcher over them, and Thou
008:033 whilst thou **wast** amongst them; nor was He
010:091 **wast** thou in rebellion!-and thou
012:102 nor **wast** thou (present) with them when they
018:078 **wast** unable to hold patience.
018:082 thou **wast** unable to hold patience."
028:044 Thou **wast** not on the Western Side when We
028:044 nor **wast** thou a witness (of those events).
028:045 but thou **wast** not a dweller among the people
028:046 Nor **wast** thou at the side of (the Mountain of) Tur
029:048 And thou **wast** not (able) to recite a Book
037:056 He said: "By Allah! thou **wast** little short of bring
039:059 thou **wast** haughty, and became one of them who reject
050:019 thou **wast** trying to escape!"
050:022 (It will be said:) "Thou **wast** heedless of this;
080:010 Of him **wast** thou unmindful.

WASTAGE

016:047 by a process of slow **wastage**-for thy

WASTE

006:141 But **waste** not by excess: for Allah
007:031 eat and drink: but **waste** not by excess, for

WASTED

018:104 "Those whose efforts have been **wasted** in this life,

WASTEFULLY

004:006 but consume it not **wastefully**, nor in haste

WASTERS

006:141 for Allah loveth not the **wasters**.
007:031 for Allah loveth not the **wasters**.

WASTING

053:061 **Wasting** your time in vanities?

WATCH

004:080 We have not sent thee to **watch** over them.
004:141 (These are) the ones who wait and **watch** about you:
006:104 I am not (here) to **watch** over your doings."
006:107 not one to **watch** over their doings, nor art
009:098 and **watch** for disasters for you:
011:057 For my Lord hath care and **watch** over all things."
011:086 But I am not set over you to keep **watch**!"
011:093 And **watch** ye! for I too am watch ye!
033:052 **watch** over all things.
034:021 and thy Lord doth **watch** over all things.
037:175 And **watch** them (how they fare), and they
037:179 And **watch** (how they fare) and they
042:006 Allah doth **watch** over them;
044:010 Then **watch** thou for the Day that the
044:059 So wait thou and **watch**; for they
054:027 So **watch** them, (O Salih), and possess

WATCHED

028:011 So she (the sister) **watched** him from a distance

WATCHER

005:117 thou wast the **Watcher** over them, and Thou

WATCHERS

072:027 and then He makes a band of **watchers** march before

WATCHES

004:001 for Allah ever **watches** over you.
040:044 **watches** over His Servants."
067:019 truly it is He that **watches** over all things.

WATCHFUL

042:027 well-acquainted, **Watchful**.
084:015 Nay, nay! for his Lord was (ever) **watchful** of him!

WATCHFUL (continued)

089:014 For thy Lord is **watchful**.

WATCHING

011:093 for I too am **watching** with you!"
028:015 when its people were not **watching**:
072:009 find a flaming fire **watching** him in ambush.

WATER

002:060 Each group knew its own place for **water**.
002:060 for **water** for his people;
002:071 to till the soil or **water** the fields;
002:074 when split asunder send fort **water**;
002:249 if any drinks of its **water**,
004:043 and ye find no **water**, then take
005:006 rub your heads (with **water**); and wash your
005:006 and you find no **water**, then take
006:070 they will have for drink (only) boiling **water**,
007:050 "Pour down to us **water** or anything that Allah
007:160 for **Water**: "Strike the rock with thy staff":
007:160 each group knew its own place for **water**.
011:043 it will save me from the **water**."
011:044 "O earth! swallow up thy **water**,
011:044 O sky! withhold (thy rain)!"
012:019 they sent their **water**-carrier (for **water**),
012:049 a year in which the people will have abundant **water**,
013:004 watered with the same **water**, yet some
013:014 their hands for **water** to reach their mouths
013:017 He sends down **water** from the skies, and the
014:016 and he is given, for drink, boiling fetid **water**.
015:022 therewith proving you with **water** (in abundance),
015:045 and fountains (of clear-flowing **water**).
017:091 in their midst, carrying abundant **water**;
018:029 relief they will be granted **water** like melted
018:041 "Or the **water** of the garden will run off
018:079 they plied on the **water**: I but
018:086 a spring of murky **water**: near it
019:086 driven down to **water**),-
020:053 and has sent down **water** from the sky."
021:030 We made from **water** every living thing.
022:019 over their heads will be poured out boiling **water**.
023:018 And We send down **water** from the sky according
024:039 which the man parched with thirst mistakes for **water**;
024:045 And Allah has created every animal from **water**:
025:048 and We send down pure **water** from the sky,-
025:050 And We have distributed the (**water**) amongst them,
025:053 the two bodies of flowing **water**: one palatable
025:054 It is He Who has created man from **water**:
027:044 she thought it was a lake of **water**,
028:023 They said: "We cannot **water** (our flocks) until the
035:012 (kind of **water**) do ye eat flesh fresh and tender,
037:067 be given a mixture made of boiling **water**.
038:042 here is (**water**) wherein to wash, cool and
038:042 cool and refreshing, and (**water**) to drink."
044:046 Like the boiling of scalding **water**.
044:048 the Chastisement of Boiling **Water**;
047:015 and be given, to drink, boiling **water**,
047:015 in it are rivers of **water** installing;
054:011 with **water** pouring forth.
054:028 And tell them that the **water** is to be divided
055:044 of boiling hot **water** will they wander round!
055:066 pouring forth **water** in continuous abundance:
056:031 By **water** flowing constantly,
056:042 of a fierce Blast of Fire and in Boiling **Water**,
056:054 "And drink Boiling **Water** on top of it:

WATER (continued)

056:068   See ye the **water** which ye drink?
056:093   For him is Entertainment with Boiling **Water**,
067:030   you with clear-flowing **water**?"
069:011   We, when the **water** (of Noah's flood) overflowed
071:012   and bestow on you Rivers (of flowing **water**).
077:027   and provided for you **water** sweet (and wholesome)?
077:041   and springs (of **water**).
078:014   send down from the clouds **water** in abundance,
079:031   He draweth out therefrom its **water** and its pasture,
080:025   For that We pour forth **water** in abundance,

WATER-CARRIER

012:019   they sent their **water-carrier** (for water), and he

WATER-GAME

005:096   Lawful to you is the pursuit of **water-game** and

WATERED

013:004   **watered** with the same water, yet some
028:024   So he **watered** (their flocks) for them; then he
028:025   may reward thee for having **watered** (our flocks) for us."

WATERING

026:155   she has a right of **watering**,
026:155   and ye have a right of **watering**, (severally) on
028:023   men **watering** (their flocks), and besides
028:023   the **watering** (place) in Madyan, he found
055:064   Dark green in colour (from plentiful **watering**).

WATERS

011:007   and His Throne was over the **Waters**-that He
020:078   but the **waters** completely overwhelmed them
029:040   and some We drowned (in the **waters**): it was
054:012   so the **waters** met (and rose) to the extent decreed.
083:028   A spring, from (the **waters**) whereof drink

WAVE

031:032   When a **wave** covers them like the canopy

WAVERING

004:143   (They are) **wavering** between this and that belonging

WAVES

010:022   and the **waves** come to them from all sides, and they
011:042   on the **waves** (towering) like mountains, and Noah
011:043   He hath mercy!"-And the **waves** came between them,
016:014   and thou seest the ships therein that plough the **waves**,
018:099   to surge like **waves** on one another: the trumpet
035:012   and thou seest the ships therein that plough the **waves**,

WAY

001:006   Show us the straight **way**.
001:007   The **way** of those on whom thou hast bestowed
002:108   hath strayed without doubt from the even **way**.
002:142   a **Way** that is straight.
002:154   are slain in the **way** of Allah:
002:167   a **way** for them out of the Fire.
002:186   that they may walk in the right **way**.
002:233   An heir shall be chargeable in the same **way**.
002:261   the **way** of Allah is that of a grain of corn:
002:280   But if ye remit it by **way** of charity,
003:017   who spend (in the **way** of God);
003:028   left with Allah except by **way** of precaution,
003:051   This is a **Way** that is straight."
003:075   no **way** over us as to the Unlettered people,"
003:101   will be shown a **way** that is straight.
003:146   if they met with disaster in Allah's **way**,
003:146   How many of the Prophets fought (in Allah's **way**),
003:153   one distress after another by **way** of requital,
003:157   And if ye are slain, or die, in the **way** of Allah,

WAY (continued)

003:167   these were told: "Come, fight in the **way** of Allah
003:169   who are slain in Allah's **way** as dead.
004:015   or Allah ordain for them some (other) **way**.
004:051   in the (right) **way** than the Believers!
004:068   And We should have shown them the Straight **Way**.
004:088   never shalt thou find the **Way**.
004:088   For those whom Allah hath thrown out of the **Way**,
004:088   whom Allah hath thrown out of the **Way**?
004:089   the **way** of Allah (from what is forbidden).
004:090   no **way** for you (to war against them).
004:092   by **way** of repentance to Allah: for Allah
004:098   nor can they find a **way** (to escape).
004:121   and from it they will find no **way** of escape.
004:125   **way** of Abraham the true in faith?
004:137   nor guide them on the **Way**.
004:141   Unbelievers a **way** (to triumph) over the Believers.
004:143   never wilt thou find for him the **Way**.
004:160   and that they hindered many from Allah's **Way**;
004:167   and keep off (men) from the **way** of Allah,
004:168   nor guide them to any **way**-
004:169   Except the **way** of Hell, to dwell
004:175   and guide them to Himself by a straight **Way**.
005:045   by **way** of charity, it is an act
005:048   have We prescribed a Law and an Open **Way**.
005:054   fighting in the **way** of Allah, and never afraid
005:077   and strayed themselves from the even **Way**.
005:095   or by **way** of atonement, the feeding
006:039   He placeth on the **Way** that is Straight.
006:055   that the **way** of the sinners may be shown up.
006:087   and We guided them to a straight **Way**.
006:091   send down to man (by **way** of revelation)":
006:112   flowery discourses by **way** of deception.
006:116   they will lead thee away from the **Way** of Allah.
006:117   who strayeth from His **Way**: He knoweth
006:126   This is the **way** of thy Lord, leading
006:151   except by **way** of justice and law: thus doth
006:153   Verily, this is My **Way**, leading straight: follow
006:161   guided me to a **way** that is straight,-a religion
007:016   for them on Thy Straight **Way**:
007:016   thrown me out (of the **Way**),
007:030   others have deserved the loss of their **way**,
007:142   the **way** of those who do mischief."
007:146   they will not adopt it as the **Way**;
007:146   and if they see the **way** of right conduct,
007:146   but if they see the **way** of error, that is
007:146   that is the **Way** they will adopt. For they
007:148   nor show them the **Way**?
007:169   came their **way**, they would (again) seize them.
009:005   then open the **way** for them: for Allah
009:009   and (many) have they hindered from His **Way**:
009:034   and hinder (them) from the **Way** of Allah.
009:034   and spend it not in the **Way** of Allah: announce
009:107   by **way** of mischief and infidelity-to disunite
010:012   on his **way** as if he had never cried to Us for the
010:025   to a **Way** that is straight.
012:108   Say thou: "This my **Way**; I do invite unto Allah,-
013:012   by **way** both of fear and of hope:
014:001   to the **Way** of (Him) the Exalted in Power,
014:021   for ourselves there is no **way** of escape."
015:013   such has been the **way** of those who went before
016:026   plot (against Allah' **Way**): but Allah
016:076   who commands justice, and is on the Straight **Way**?

WAY (continued)

016:076 his master; whichever **way** he directs him,
016:085 then will it in no **way** be mitigated, nor will
016:121 and guided him to a Straight **Way**.
016:125 Invite (all) to the **Way** of thy Lord with wisdom
017:032 for it is an indecent (deed) and an **way**.
017:042 sought out a **way** in submitting to the
017:048 and never can they find a **way**.
017:059 We only sent the Signs by **way** of frightening
017:063 Allah said: "Go thy **way**; if any of them follow
017:077 (This was Our) **way** with the messengers We sent
017:084 is best guided on the **Way**."
018:010 and dispose of our affair for us in the right **way**!
018:017 to lead him to the Right **Way**.
018:040 garden thunderbolts (by **way** of reckoning) from
018:063 the sea in a marvelous **way**!"
018:085 One (such) **way** he followed,
018:089 Then followed he (another) **way**,
018:092 Then followed he (another) **way**,
018:106 and took My Signs and My Messengers by **way** of jest.
019:036 this is a **Way** that is straight.
019:043 a **Way** that is even and straight.
020:063 and to do away with your most cherished **way**.
020:123 will not lose his **way**, nor fall into misery.
020:135 the straight and even **way**, and who
021:031 that they may find their **way**.
021:035 and We test you by evil and by good by **way** of trial.
022:012 far indeed (from the **Way**)!
022:025 from the **Way** of Allah, and from
022:044 and Moses was rejected (in the same **way**).
022:054 to the Straight **Way**.
022:067 assuredly on the Right **Way**.
023:073 But verily thou callest them to the Straight **Way**;
023:074 in the Hereafter are deviating from that **Way**.
024:046 to a **Way** that is straight.
025:009 and never a **way** will they be able to find!
026:209 By **way** of reminder; and We
028:086 in any **way** to those who reject (Allah's Message).
029:046 of the Book, except in the best **way**, unless it
030:024 by **way** both of fear and of hope, and He
031:015 and follow the **way** of those who turn to Me:
032:007 the best **way** and He began the creation of man
033:004 and He shows the (right) **Way**.
035:043 But no change wilt thou find in Allah's **way** (of dealing):
035:043 the **way** the ancients were dealt with?
036:004 On a Straight **Way**.
036:013 Set forth to them, by **way** of a parable,
036:044 Except by **way** of Mercy from Us, and by
036:044 and by **way** of (worldly) convenience (to serve them)
036:061 (for that) this was the Straight **Way**?
037:023 the **Way** to the (Fierce) Fire!
037:118 And We guided them to the Straight **Way**.
040:011 our sins: is there any **way** out (of this)?"
040:085 (Such has been) Allah's **way** of dealing with His
041:048 that they have no **way** of escape.
042:013 hard is the (**way**) to which thou callest them.
042:035 that there is for them no **way** of escape.
042:044 say: "Is there any **way** (to effect) a return?"
042:046 there is no **way** (to the Goal).
042:052 (men) to the Straight **Way**,-
042:053 The **Way** of Allah, to whom belongs whatever is
043:010 in order that ye may find guidance (on the **way**);
043:023 Just in the same **way**, whenever We sent a Warner

WAY (continued)

043:043 verily thou art on a Straight **Way**.
043:058 only by **way** of disputation:
043:061 this is a Straight **Way**.
043:064 this is a Straight **Way**."
045:018 that (**Way**), and follow not the desires of those
045:018 Then We put thee on the (right) **Way** of Religion:
047:004 But those who are slain in the **way** of Allah,-
047:038 (of your substance) in the **Way** of Allah:
048:002 and guide thee on the Straight **Way**;
048:025 (Allah would have allowed you to force your **way**,
053:011 in no **way** falsified that which he saw.
054:027 For We will send the she-camel by **way** of trial for them.
057:024 And if any turn back (from Allah's **Way**), verily Allah
060:001 If ye have come out to strive in My **Way** and seek
065:002 fear Allah, He (ever) prepares a **way** out,
067:022 or one who walks evenly on a Straight **Way**?
068:026 they said: "We have surely lost our **way**:
072:016 they (the Pagans) had (only) remained on the (right) **Way**,
076:003 We showed him the **Way**: whether he
109:006 To you be your **Way**, and to me mine.

WAY-FARER

004:036 the Companion by your side, the **way-farer** (ye meet),

WAYFARER

002:177 for the needy, for the **wayfarer**,
008:041 the needy, and the **wayfarer**,-
009:060 and for the **wayfarer**: (thus it is) ordained by Allah.
017:026 and to the **wayfarer**: but squander not
030:038 the needy, and the **wayfarer**, that is best
059:007 and orphans, the needy and the **wayfarer**; in order

WAYFARERS

002:215 and those in want and for **wayfarers**.

WAYS

002:170 shall follow the **ways** of our fathers."
004:026 and to guide you into the **ways** of those before you;
005:016 His good pleasure to **ways** of peace and safety,
005:075 yet see in what **ways** they are deluded
005:104 the **ways** we found our fathers following."
006:065 See how We explain the Signs in diverse **ways**;
006:105 the Signs by various (**ways**) that they may say,
007:048 were your hoards and your arrogant **ways**?
009:074 but if they turn back (to their evil **ways**),
010:078 to turn us away from the **ways** We found
012:037 (I assure you) abandoned the **ways** of a people
012:038 "And I follow the **ways** of my fathers,-Abraham,
014:012 to the **Ways** we (follow).
014:036 he then who follows my (**ways**) is of me, and he
016:009 but there are **ways** that turn aside: if Allah
016:015 should shake with you; and rivers and **ways**;
016:069 (of the earth), and follow the **ways** of Thy Lord
016:123 "Follow the **ways** of Abraham the True in Faith,
016:125 and argue with them in **ways** that are best
017:041 in various (**ways**) in this Qur'an, in order
017:077 thou wilt find no change in Our **ways**.
018:055 but that (they wait for) the **ways** of the ancients
018:084 and We gave him the **ways** and the means to all ends.
020:040 and We tired thee in various **ways**.
026:152 and mend not (their **ways**)."
031:021 "Nay, we shall follow the **ways** that we found
040:036 that I may attain the **ways** and means-
040:037 "The **ways** and means of (reaching) the heavens,
044:015 will revert (to your **ways**).
046:027 the Signs in various **ways**, that they may turn (to Us).

WAYS (continued)

058:008 salutes thee, (but in crooked **ways**): and they
070:003 (A Penalty) from Allah, Lord of the **Ways** of Ascent.
098:001 (from their **ways**) until there should come to

WE

001:005 Thee do **we** worship, and Thine aid **we** seek.
002:003 **We** have provided for them.
002:008 "**We** believe in Allah and the Last Day,"
002:011 they say: "Why, **we** are only ones that put things right."
002:013 they say: "Shall **we** believe as the fool believe?"-
002:014 they say: "**We** believe," but when they are alone
002:014 "**We** are really with you **we** (were) only jesting."
002:023 in doubt as to what **We** have revealed
002:025 **we** were fed with before,"
002:030 Whilst **we** do celebrate Thy praises
002:032 of knowledge **we** have none,
002:034 And behold, **We** said to the angels:
002:035 And **We** said: "O Adam! dwell thou and thy wife
002:036 And **We** said: "Get ye down, (all you people),
002:038 **We** said: "Get ye down all from here;
002:049 And remember, **We** delivered you
002:050 And remember **We** divided the sea for you
002:051 And remember **We** appointed forty nights
002:052 Even then **We** did forgive you,
002:053 And remember **We** gave Moses the Scripture
002:055 "O Moses! **we** shall never believe in thee
002:055 in thee until **we** see Allah manifestly,"
002:056 Then **We** raised you up after your death;
002:057 And **We** gave You the shade of clouds
002:057 the good things **We** have provided for you:"
002:058 And remember **We** said: "Enter this town,
002:058 and say: Forgive (us) **We** shall forgive you
002:059 so **We** sent on the transgressors
002:060 **We** said "strike the rock with thy staff."
002:061 **we** cannot endure one kind of food (always);
002:063 **We** have given you and bring (ever) to
002:063 and **We** raised above you the Mount (Sinai)
002:063 And remember **We** took your Covenant
002:065 **We** said to them: "Be ye apes,
002:066 So **We** made it an example to their own time,
002:070 **we** wish indeed for guidance if Allah wills."
002:073 So **We** said: "Strike the (body)
002:076 they say: "**We** believe":
002:083 And remember **We** took a Covenant
002:084 And remember **We** took your Covenant
002:087 **We** gave Jesus the son of Mary clear (Signs)
002:087 **We** gave Moses the Book
002:088 (which preserve Allah's word, **we** need no more)"
002:091 they say, "**We** believe in what was sent
002:093 (saying): "Hold firmly to what **We** given you,
002:093 and **We** raised above you the mount (Sinai):
002:093 they said: "**We** hear, and **we** disobey":
002:093 And remember **We** took your Covenant
002:093 they said: "**We** hear, and **we** disobey":
002:099 **We** have sent down to thee manifest Signs
002:102 "**We** are only for trial,
002:106 **We** abrogate or cause to be forgotten,
002:106 but **We** substitute something better
002:118 **We** have indeed made clear the Signs
002:119 Verily **We** have sent thee in truth
002:121 Those to whom **We** have given the Book
002:125 and **We** covenanted with Abraham and Isma'il,
002:125 Remember **We** made the house a place of assembly

WE (continued)

002:130 Him **We** chose and rendered pure in this world:
002:133 They said: "**We** shall worship thy God
002:133 to Him do **we** submit."
002:136 and **we** submit to Allah.
002:136 **we** make no difference between one
002:136 Say ye: "**We** believer in Allah,
002:138 and it is He. Whom **we** worship.
002:139 and that **we** are sincere
002:139 that **we** are responsible for our doings
002:143 Thus have **We** made of you an Ummah
002:143 and **We** appointed the Qiblah
002:144 now shall **We** turn thee to a Qiblah
002:144 **We** see the turning of thy face
002:151 in that **We** have sent among you a Messenger
002:155 Be sure **We** shall test you with something
002:156 To Allah **we** belong,
002:159 after **We** have made it clear
002:159 (Signs) **We** have sent down, and the Guidance,
002:167 "If only **we** had one more chance,
002:167 **we** would clear ourselves of them,
002:170 they say: "Nay! **we** shall follow
002:172 the good things that **We** have provided for you.
002:211 how many Clear (Signs) **We** have sent them.
002:246 seeing that **we** were turned out of our homes
002:246 **we** refuse to fight in the cause of Allah,
002:246 that **we** may fight in the cause of Allah."
002:247 authority over us when **we** are better fitted
002:249 they said: "This day **we** cannot cope
002:252 **We** rehearse them to thee in truth:
002:253 to Jesus the son of Mary, **We** gave Clear (Signs),
002:253 Those Messengers **We** endowed with gifts,
002:254 (the bounties) **We** have provided for you,
002:259 and that **We** may make of thee a Sign
002:259 how **We** bring them together and clothe them
002:267 the fruits of the earth which **We** have produced for you,
002:285 And they say: "**We** hear, and **we** obey:
002:285 (**We** seek) Thy forgiveness, our Lord,
002:285 "**We** make no distinction (they say) between
002:286 if **we** forget or fall into error;
002:286 than **we** have the strength to bear.
003:007 in knowledge say: "**We** believe in it;
003:016 "Our Lord! **we** have indeed believed:
003:025 **We** gather them together against a Day
003:044 which **We** reveal unto thee (O Prophet!)
003:052 and do thou bear witness that **we** are Muslims.
003:052 "**We** are Allah's helpers, **We** believe in Allah,
003:053 and **we** follow the Messenger;
003:053 "Our Lord! **we** believe in what thou hast revealed,
003:058 "This is what **we** rehearse unto thee of the Signs
003:064 that **we** associate no partners with Him;
003:064 say ye: "Bear witness that **we** (at least) are Muslims
003:064 that **we** erect not, from among ourselves,
003:064 that **we** worship none but Allah;
003:081 They said: "**We** agree."
003:084 and to Allah do **we** bow our will (in Islam)."
003:084 **we** make no distinction between one and another
003:084 Say: "**We** believe in Allah, and in what
003:108 **We** rehearse them to thee in Truth:
003:118 **We** have made plain to you the Signs,
003:119 when they meet you, they say, "**We** believe";
003:140 **We** give to men and men by turns:
003:145 And swiftly shall **We** reward those that

WE (continued)

003:145 **We** shall give it to him;
003:145 **We** shall give it to him.
003:147 and anything **we** may have done that transgressed
003:151 Soon shall **We** cast terror into the hearts
003:152 His promise to you when **we** with His permission
003:154 "If **we** had had anything to do with this affair,
003:154 They said: "Have **we** any hand in the affair?
003:154 **we** should not have been in the slaughter here."
003:167 **we** should certainly have followed you."
003:167 They said: "Had **we** known there would be a fight,
003:178 **We** grant them respite that they may grow
003:181 and **We** shall say: "Taste ye the Chastisement
003:181 **We** shall certainly record their word
003:181 "Truly, Allah is indigent and **we** are rich!"
003:193 "Our Lord! **We** have heard the call
003:193 'Believe ye in the Lord', and **we** have believed.
004:018 for them have **We** prepared a chastisement
004:030 soon shall **We** cast them into the Fire:
004:031 **We** shall remit your evil deeds, and admit
004:033 **We** have appointed sharers and heirs to property
004:037 for **We** have prepared, for those who resist Faith,
004:041 How then if **We** brought from each People a witness,
004:041 and **We** brought thee as a witness
004:046 and say: "**We** hear and **we** disobey";
004:046 If only they had said: "**We** hear and **we** obey";
004:046 and say: "**We** hear and **we** disobey";
004:047 as **We** cursed the Sabbath-breakers:
004:047 believe in what **We** have (now) revealed, confirming
004:047 before **We** change the face and fame of some
004:054 But **We** had already given the people of Abraham
004:056 **We** shall soon cast into the Fire:
004:056 **We** shall change them for fresh skins, that they
004:057 **We** shall soon admit to Gardens, with rivers
004:057 **We** shall admit them to shades, cool
004:062 "**We** meant no more than good-will and conciliation!"
004:064 **We** sent not a Messenger, but to be obeyed,
004:066 If **We** had ordered them to sacrifice their lives
004:067 And **We** should then have given them from
004:068 And **We** should have shown them the Straight Way.
004:072 in that **we** were not present among them."
004:074 soon shall **We** give him a reward of great (value).
004:079 is from thyself and **We** have sent thee as
004:080 **We** have not sent thee to watch over them.
004:091 in their case **We** have provided you with a clear
004:097 "Weak and oppressed were **we** in the earth."
004:105 **We** have sent down to thee the Book in truth,
004:114 **We** shall soon give a reward of the highest (value).
004:115 **We** shall leave him in the path he has chosen,
004:122 **We** shall soon admit them to Gardens, with rivers
004:131 Verily **We** have directed the people
004:141 they say: "Were **we** not with you?"
004:141 And did **we** not guard you from the Believers?"
004:141 "Did **we** not gain an advantage over you.
004:150 saying: "**We** believe in some but reject others":
004:151 and **We** have prepared for Unbelievers
004:152 **We** shall soon give their (due) rewards: for Allah
004:153 even so **We** forgave them; and gave Moses
004:154 and (once again) **We** commanded them: "Transgress
004:154 **We** said: "Enter the gate with humility";
004:154 **We** raised over them the Mount (Sinai);
004:154 And **We** took from them a solemn Covenant.
004:157 "**We** killed Christ Jesus the son of Mary,

WE (continued)

004:160 **We** made unlawful for them certain (foods)
004:161 **We** have prepared for those among them who reject
004:162 to them shall **We** soon give a great reward.
004:163 **We** have sent thee inspiration,
004:163 as **We** sent it to Noah and the Messengers after
004:163 **We** sent inspiration to Abraham.
004:163 and to David **We** gave the Psalms.
004:164 told thee the story; of others **We** have not;
004:164 Of some messengers **We** have already told thee
004:174 from your Lord for **We** have sent unto you
005:007 when ye said: "**We** hear and **we** obey":
005:012 and **We** appointed twelve chieftains among them, and
005:013 **We** cursed them, and made their hearts grow hard:
005:014 **We** did take a Covenant, but they forgot a good
005:014 that was sent them: so **We** stirred up enmity and
005:018 "**We** are sons of Allah, and His beloved."
005:022 (once) they leave, then shall **we** enter."
005:022 never shall **we** enter it until they leave it:
005:024 and fight ye two, while **we** sit here.
005:024 They said: O "Moses! **we** shall never enter it
005:032 **We** ordained for the Children of Israel that if
005:041 "**We** believe" with their lips but whose
005:044 It was **We** who revealed the Torah (to Moses):
005:045 **We** ordained therein for them: "Life for life,
005:046 **We** sent him the Gospel: therein was
005:046 **We** sent Jesus the son of Mary, confirming the Torah
005:048 have **We** prescribed a Law and an Open Way.
005:048 To thee **We** sent the Scripture in truth, confirming
005:052 saying: "**We** do fear lest a change
005:059 no other reason than that **we** believer in Allah,
005:061 "**We** believe": but in fact they enter
005:064 Amongst them **We** have placed enmity and hatred
005:065 **We** should indeed have blotted out their
005:070 **We** took the Covenant of the Children
005:082 who say, "**We** are Christians:" because amongst
005:083 they pray: "Our Lord! **we** believe; write us
005:084 **we** long for our Lord to admit us to
005:084 "What cause can **we** have not to believe in Allah
005:104 the ways **we** found our fathers following."
005:106 if **we** do, then behold! **we** shall be sinners.
005:106 **we** shall hide not the evidence **we** owe to Allah if
005:106 "**We** will not take for it a price even though
005:107 "**We** affirm that our witness is truer than that
005:107 and that **we** have not trespassed (beyond the truth):
005:107 if **we** did, behold! **we** will be wrong-doers."
005:109 They will say: "**We** have no knowledge: it is
005:111 **we** bow to Allah as Muslims'."
005:111 they said, '**We** have faith, and do thou
005:113 They said: "**We** only wish to eat thereof
005:113 and that **we** ourselves may be witnesses
006:006 for whom **We** poured out rain from the
006:006 in strength such as **We** have not given to you-
006:006 yet for their sins **We** destroyed them, and raised
006:006 Generations **We** had established on the earth,
006:006 how many of those before them **We** did destroy?-
006:007 If **We** had sent unto thee a written (Message)
006:008 If **We** did send down an angel, the matter
006:009 **We** should have sent him as a man.
006:009 If **We** had made it an angel,
006:009 And **We** should certainly have caused them confusion
006:020 Those to whom **We** have given the Book know this
006:022 On the day shall **We** gather them all together:

WE (continued)

006:022 **We** shall say to those who ascribed partners
006:023 "By Allah Our Lord, **we** were not those who joined gods
006:025 but **We** have thrown veils on their hearts,
006:027 "Would that **we** were but sent back!
006:027 Then would **we** not reject the Signs of our Lord,
006:029 and never shall **we** be raised up again."
006:031 and they say: "Ah! woe unto us that **we** neglected;
006:033 **We** know indeed the grief which their words
006:038 Nothing have **We** omitted from the Book, and they
006:042 and **We** afflicted the nations with suffering and
006:042 Before thee **We** sent (Messengers)
006:044 **We** opened to them the gates of all (good)
006:044 on a sudden, **We** called them to account, when lo!
006:046 See how **We** explain the Signs by various
006:048 **We** send the Messengers only to give
006:053 Thus did **We** test some of them by other,
006:055 Thus do **We** explain the Signs in detail: that
006:063 (**we** vow) **we** shall truly show our gratitude.'?"
006:065 See how **We** explain the Signs in diverse ways;
006:071 and **we** have been directed to submit ourselves
006:071 Say: "Shall **we** call on others besides Allah,-
006:072 that **we** shall be gathered together."
006:075 So also did **We** show Abraham the kingdom
006:083 **We** raise whom **We** will, degree after degree:
006:083 which **We** gave to Abraham (to use)
006:084 **We** gave him Isaac and Jacob:
006:084 thus do **We** reward those who do good:
006:084 all (three) **We** guided:
006:084 and before him, **We** guided Noah, and among
006:086 and to all **We** gave favour above the nations:
006:087 **We** chose them, and **We** guided them to a straight Way.
006:089 These were the men to whom **We** gave the Book,
006:089 behold! **We** shall entrust their charge to a new
006:092 And this is a Book which **We** have sent down,
006:094 all (the favours) which **We** bestowed on you:
006:094 and alone as **We** created you for the first time:
006:094 **We** see not with you your intercessors whom ye
006:097 **We** detail Our Signs for people who know.
006:098 **We** detail Our signs for people who understand.
006:099 from some **We** produce green (crops), out of
006:099 with it **We** produce vegetation of all kinds:
006:099 out of which **We** produce, close-compounded
006:105 Thus do **We** explain the Signs
006:105 **We** may make the matter clear to those who know.
006:107 but **We** made thee not one to watch over their doings
006:108 Thus have **We** made alluring to each people
006:110 **We** (too) shall turn to (confusion) their hearts
006:110 **We** shall leave them in their trespasses,
006:111 and **We** gathered together all things
006:111 Even if **We** did send unto them angels, and the
006:112 Likewise did **We** make for every Messenger
006:114 to whom **We** have given the Book, that it
006:122 to whom **We** gave life, and a light
006:123 Thus have **We** placed leaders in every town,
006:124 "**We** shall not believe until **we** receive (exactly) like
006:126 **We** have detailed the Signs for those who receive
006:128 but (alas!) **we** reached our term-which Thou
006:128 "Our Lord! **we** made profit from each other:
006:129 Thus do **We** make the wrong-doers turn to
006:130 "**We** bear witness against ourselves." It was
006:138 except those whom-so they say-**We** wish; further,
006:146 for **We** are True (in Our ordinances).

WE (continued)

006:146 and **We** forbade them the fat of the ox
006:146 **We** forbade every (animal) with undivided hoof,
006:148 nor should **we** have had any forbidden thing."
006:148 **we** should not have given partners to Him, nor
006:151 **We** provide sustenance for and for them;-
006:152 no burden do **We** place on any soul, but that
006:154 Moreover, **We** gave Moses the Book, completing
006:155 which **We** have revealed as a blessing: so follow
006:156 **we** remained unacquainted with all that they
006:157 In good time shall **We** requite those who
006:157 **we** should have followed its guidance
006:158 Say: "Wait ye: **we** too are waiting."
007:004 **We** destroyed (for their sins)?
007:005 "Indeed **we** did wrong."
007:006 Then shall **We** question those to whom
007:006 and those by whom **We** sent it.
007:007 for **We** were never absent (at any time or place).
007:007 And verily **We** shall recount their whole
007:010 It is **We** who have placed you
007:011 then **We** bade the angels prostrate to Adam,
007:011 It is **We** who created you and gave
007:023 **we** have wronged our own souls: if Thou
007:023 **we** shall certainly be lost."
007:026 **We** have bestowed raiment upon you to
007:027 **We** made the Satans friends (only) to
007:028 they say: "**We** found our fathers doing so";
007:032 Thus do **We** explain the Signs in detail
007:042 no burden do **We** place on any soul, but that
007:043 And **We** shall remove from their hearts
007:043 never could **we** have found guidance, had it not
007:044 "**We** have indeed found the promises
007:051 That day shall **We** forget them as they
007:052 based on knowledge, Which **We** explained in detail,-
007:052 For **We** had certainly sent unto them a Book, based
007:053 Have **we** no intercessors now to
007:053 Or could **we** be sent back?
007:053 Then should **we** behave differently from our
007:057 thus shall **We** raise up the dead:
007:057 **We** drive them to a land that is dead, make rain
007:058 thus do **We** explain the Signs by various
007:059 **We** sent Noah to his people. He said: "O
007:060 "Ah! **we** see thee evident error."
007:064 and **We** delivered him, and those
007:064 But **We** overwhelmed in the flood those who
007:065 To the 'Ad people, (**We** sent) Hud, one of
007:066 "Ah! **we** see thou art in folly!"
007:066 and "**We** think thou art a liar!"
007:070 that **we** may worship Allah alone, and give up
007:072 by Our Mercy and **We** cut off the roots
007:072 **We** saved him and those who adhered to him, by Our
007:073 To the Thamud people (**We** sent) Salih, one of
007:075 They said: "**We** do indeed believe in the
007:076 **we** reject what ye believe in."
007:080 **We** also (sent) Lut: he said to his people: "Do ye
007:083 But **We** saved him and his family, except
007:084 And **We** rained down on them
007:085 To the Madyan people **We** sent Shu'aib, one of
007:088 said: "O Shu'aib! **we** shall certainly drive thee
007:088 He said: "What! even though **we** do detest (them)?
007:089 "**We** should indeed forge a lie against Allah,
007:089 if **we** returned to your religion after Allah
007:089 nor could **we** by any manner of means return

WE (continued)

007:094 Whenever **We** sent a prophet to a town,
007:094 **We** took up its people in suffering
007:095 Behold! **We** called them to account of a sudden,
007:095 Then **We** changed their suffering
007:096 and **We** brought them to book for their misdeeds.
007:096 **We** should indeed have opened out to them
007:100 **We** could punish them (too) for their sins,
007:100 if **We** so willed,
007:101 **We** (thus) relate unto thee: there came
007:102 Most of them **We** found not men (true)
007:102 **We** found rebellious and disobedient.
007:103 Then after them **We** sent Moses with Our Signs
007:113 they said, "Of course **we** shall have a (suitable)
007:113 a (suitable) reward if **we** win!"
007:115 or shall **we** have the (first) throw?"
007:117 **We** revealed to Moses "Throw thy rod": and behold!
007:121 Saying: "**We** believe in the Lord of the Worlds.
007:125 "For us, **we** are but sent back unto our Lord."
007:126 on us simply because **we** believed in the Signs
007:127 and **we** have over them (power) irresistible.
007:127 (only) their females will **we** save alive;
007:127 He said: "Their male children will **we** slay;
007:129 They said: "**We** have had (nothing but) trouble,
007:130 **We** punished the people of Pharaoh with years
007:132 **we** shall never believe in thee."
007:133 So **We** sent on them: Wholesale Death,
007:134 and **we** shall send away the Children
007:134 **we** shall truly believe in thee,
007:135 But when **We** removed the Plague from them
007:136 So **We** exacted retribution from them:
007:136 **We** drowned them in the sea, because they
007:137 And **We** made a people, considered weak
007:137 lands whereon **We** sent down our blessings.
007:137 and **We** levelled to the ground the great
007:138 **We** took the Children of Israel (with safety)
007:141 And remember, **We** rescued you from
007:142 **We** appointed for Moses thirty nights,
007:145 And **We** ordained for him in the
007:149 **we** shall indeed be among the Losers.
007:152 thus do **We** recompense those who invent
007:156 for **we** have turned unto Thee."
007:160 **We** gave them the shade of clouds, and sent
007:160 **We** have provided for you": (but they rebelled);
007:160 **We** directed Moses by inspiration, when his
007:160 **We** divided them into twelve tribes or nations.
007:161 **We** shall forgive you your faults;
007:161 **We** shall increase (the portion of)
007:162 so **We** sent on them a plague from heaven.
007:163 thus did **We** make a trial of them,
007:165 **We** rescued those who forbade evil;
007:165 but **We** visited the wrong-doers with a
007:166 **We** said to them: "Be ye apes,
007:168 **We** have tried them with both prosperity
007:168 **We** broke them up into sections
007:170 never shall **We** suffer the reward of the
007:171 When **We** raised the mount over them, as if
007:171 "Hold firmly to what **We** have given you, and bring
007:171 to fall on them (**We** said): "Hold firmly
007:172 They said: "Yea! **we** do testify! (This), lest ye
007:172 "Of this **we** were never mindful":
007:173 but **we** are (their) descendants after them:
007:174 Thus do **We** explain the Signs in detail;

WE (continued)

007:175 to whom **We** sent Our Signs, but he
007:176 **We** should have elevated him with Our Signs;
007:179 **We** have made for Hell: They have
007:181 Of those **We** have created are people who direct
007:182 **We** will lead them step by step to ruin
007:189 **we** vow **we** shall (ever) be grateful."
008:003 **We** have given them for sustenance:
008:019 if ye return (to the attack) so shall **We**.
008:021 "**We** hear," but listen not:
008:031 if **we** wished, **we** could say (words) like these:
008:031 they say: "**We** have heard this (before):
008:041 the revelation **We** sent down to our Servant
008:054 and **We** drowned the people of Pharaoh: for they
008:054 the Signs of their Lord so **We** destroyed them
009:011 (thus) do **We** explain Signs in detail, for those
009:042 "If **we** only could, **we** should certainly have come
009:050 they say, "**We** took indeed our precautions
009:052 But **we** can expect for you either that Allah
009:052 So wait (expectant); **we** too will wait with you."
009:059 to Allah do **we** turn our hopes!"
009:065 "**We** were only talking idly and in play."
009:066 If **We** pardon some of you,
009:066 **We** will punish other amongst you, for that
009:086 **we** would be with those who sit (at home)."
009:094 **we** shall not believe you: Allah hath
009:101 thou knowest them not: **We** know them:
009:101 twice shall **We** punish them: and in
010:002 that **We** have set Our inspiration to a man
010:011 But **We** leave those who rest not their hope
010:012 But when **We** have removed his affliction,
010:013 Generations before you **We** destroyed when they
010:013 Thus do **We** requite those who sin!
010:014 Then **We** made you heirs in the land after them,
010:021 When **We** make mankind taste of some mercy
010:022 from this, **we** shall truly show our gratitude!
010:023 and **We** shall show you the truth of all that ye did.
010:024 is as the rain which **We** send down from the skies:
010:024 Thus do **We** explain the Signs in detail for those who
010:024 and **We** make it like a harvest clean-mown,
010:028 **We** shall separate them, and their
010:028 One Day shall **We** gather them all together.
010:028 Then shall **We** say to those who joined gods
010:029 **we** certainly knew nothing of your worship of us!"
010:046 Whether **We** show thee (realized in thy lifetime)
010:046 **We** promise them,-or **We** take thy soul (before that),-
010:061 **We** are Witnesses thereof when ye are deeply engrossed
010:070 Then shall **We** make them taste the severest
010:073 while **We** drowned in the Flood those who
010:073 They rejected him, but **We** delivered him, and those
010:073 and **We** made them inherit (the earth),
010:074 Thus do **We** seal the hearts of the transgressors.
010:074 Then after him **We** sent (many) messengers
010:075 Then after them sent **We** Moses and Aaron
010:078 **We** found our fathers following,-in order
010:078 But not **we** shall believe in you!"
010:085 They said: "In Allah do **we** put our trust.
010:087 **We** inspired Moses and his brother with this
010:090 **We** took the Children of Israel across the sea:
010:092 "This day shall **We** save thee in thy body,
010:093 **We** settled the Children of Israel in a
010:094 **We** have revealed unto thee, then ask
010:098 When they believed, **We** removed from them

WE (continued)

010:098   a single township (among those **We** warmed), which
010:103   that **We** should deliver those who believe!
010:103   In the end **We** deliver Our messengers
011:008   If **We** delay the chastisement for them
011:009   If **We** give man a taste of mercy from Ourselves,
011:010   But if **We** give him a taste of (Our) favours
011:015   to them **We** shall pay (the price of) their deeds
011:025   **We** sent Noah to his People (with a mission);
011:027   apparently nor do **we** see in you (all) any
011:027   among his people said: "**We** see (in) thee
011:027   in fact **we** think ye are liars!"
011:027   nor do **we** see that any follow thee but the
011:028   Shall **we** compel you to accept it when ye
011:038   **we** (in our turn) can look down on you with
011:040   **We** said: "Embark therein, of each kind two,
011:048   Peoples to whom **We** shall grant their pleasures
011:049   of the Unseen, which **We** have revealed unto thee:
011:050   To the 'Ad People (**We** sent) Hud, one of
011:053   and **we** are not the ones to desert our gods on thy word!
011:053   Nor shall **we** believe in thee!
011:054   "**We** say nothing but that (perhaps) some of
011:058   **We** saved them from a severe chastisement.
011:058   **We** saved Hud and those who believed with him,
011:061   To the Thamud People (**We** sent) Salih, one of
011:062   But **we** are really in suspicious (disquieting)
011:066   **We** saved Salih and those who believed with him,
011:070   They said: "Fear not: **we** have been sent
011:071   and she laughed: but **We** gave her Glad tidings
011:079   indeed thou knowest quite well what **we** want!"
011:079   They said: "Well dost thou know **we** have no need
011:081   **we** are Messengers from thy Lord! By no means
011:082   When Our decree issued, **We** turned (the cities)
011:084   To the Madyan people (**We** sent) Shu'aib, one of
011:087   that **we** leave off doing what **we** like with our property?
011:087   Does thy prayer command thee that **we** leave off
011:091   thou sayest **we** do not understand! In fact
011:091   **we** should certainly have stoned thee!
011:091   In fact among us **we** see that thou hast no strength!
011:094   **We** saved Shu'aib and those who believed with him,
011:096   And **We** sent Moses, with Our Clear (Signs) and an
011:100   of communities which **We** relate unto thee: of them
011:101   It was not **We** that wronged them: they wronged
011:104   Nor shall **We** delay it but for a term appointed.
011:109   but verily **We** shall pay them back (in full) their portion
011:110   **We** certainly gave the Book to Moses,
011:116   them whom **We** saved (from harm)?
011:120   with it **We** make firm they heart:
011:120   All that **We** relate to thee of the stories
011:121   "Do whatever ye can: **we** shall do our part;
011:122   "And wait ye! **we** too shall wait."
012:002   **We** have sent it down as an Arabic Qur'an, in order
012:003   **We** do relate unto thee the most beautiful
012:003   in that **We** reveal to thee this (portion of the) Qur'an:
012:008   are loved more by our father than **we**:
012:008   but **we** are a goodly body!
012:011   seeing **we** are indeed his sincere well-wishers?
012:012   and **we** shall take every care of him."
012:014   then should **we** be the losers!
012:014   devour him while **we** are (so large) a party,
012:015   and **We** put into his heart (this Message):
012:017   even though **we** tell the truth."
012:017   **we** went racing with one another, and left

WE (continued)

012:021   Thus did **We** establish Joseph in the land,
012:021   much good, or **we** shall adopt him as a son."
012:021   that **We** might teach him the interpretation
012:022   **We** gave him power and knowledge:
012:022   thus do **We** reward those who do right.
012:024   thus (did **We** order) that **We** might turn away from him
012:030   **we** see she is evidently going astray."
012:036   for **we** see thou art one that doth good (to all)."
012:038   and never could **we** attribute any partners
012:044   and **we** are not skilled in the interpretation
012:051   no evil know **we** against him!"
012:056   **We** bestow of Our mercy on whom **We** please,
012:056   Thus did **We** give established power to Joseph
012:056   and **We** suffer not, to be lost, the reward
012:061   indeed **we** shall do it."
012:061   They said: "**We** shall try to win him from his father:
012:063   No more measure of grain shall **we** get
012:063   that **we** may get our measure;
012:063   and **we** will indeed take every care of him."
012:063   (unless **we** take our brother): so send our
012:065   What (more) can **we** desire?
012:065   so **we** shall get (more) food for our family;
012:065   **we** shall take care of out brother;
012:066   he said: "Over all that **we** say, be Allah
012:072   They said: "**We** miss the great beaker of the king;
012:073   know that **we** came not to make mischief in the land,
012:073   and **we** are no thieves!"
012:075   Thus it is **We** punish the wrong-doers!
012:076   Thus did **We** plan for Joseph.
012:076   **We** raise to degrees (of wisdom) whom **We** please:
012:078   for **we** see that thou art (gracious) in doing good."
012:079   He said: "Allah forbid that **we** take other than
012:079   indeed (if **we** did so), **we** should be acting wrongfully."
012:079   other than him with whom **we** found our property:
012:081   **we** bear witness only to what **we** know,
012:081   and **we** could not well guard against the unseen!
012:082   and the caravan in which **we** returned,
012:082   and (you will find) **we** are indeed telling the truth."
012:082   Ask at the town where **we** have been and the
012:088   **we** have (now) brought but scanty capital:
012:088   so pay us full measure, (**we** pray thee), and treat
012:091   and **we** certainly have been guilty of sin!"
012:097   for **we** were truly at fault."
012:102   which **We** reveal by inspiration unto thee:
012:109   Nor did **We** send before thee (as Messengers)
012:109   (as Messengers) any but men, whom **We** did inspire,-
012:110   and those whom **We** will are delivered into safety.
013:004   yet some of them **We** make more excellent
013:005   shall **we** indeed then be in a creation renewed?"
013:005   "When **we** are (actually) dust,
013:022   **We** have bestowed for their sustenance, secretly
013:030   **We** send down unto thee by inspiration; yet do
013:030   Thus have **We** sent thee amongst a People
013:036   Those to whom **We** have given the Book rejoice at
013:037   Thus have **We** revealed it to be a judgment
013:038   **We** did send messengers before thee, and appointed
013:040   **We** promised them or take to Us thy soul
013:040   Whether **We** shall show thee (within thy lifetime)
013:041   See they not that **We** gradually reduce the land
014:001   A Book which **We** have revealed unto thee, in order
014:004   **We** sent not a messenger except (to teach) in the
014:005   **We** sent Moses with Our Signs (and the command),

WE (continued)

014:009   and **we** are really in suspicious (disquieting) doubt
014:009   "**We** do deny (the mission) on which ye have
014:011   "True, **we** are human like yourselves, but Allah
014:012   Why **we** should not put our trust on Allah.
014:012   **We** shall certainly bear with patience all the
014:012   indeed He has guided us to the Ways **we** (follow).
014:013   "Be sure **we** shall drive you out of our land,
014:013   "Verily **We** shall cause the wrong-doers to perish!
014:014   "And verily **We** shall cause you to abide
014:021   (now) whether **we** rage, or bear (these torments)
014:021   "For us, **we** but followed you; can ye
014:021   **we** should have given it to you:
014:021   They will reply, "If **we** had received the
014:031   the Sustenance **We** have given them, secretly and
014:038   what **we** conceal and what **we** reveal:
014:044   **we** will answer Thy Call, and follow
014:045   and **We** put forth (many) Parables in your behoof!"
014:045   ye were clearly shown how **We** dealt with them;
015:004   Never did **We** destroy a population that had not
015:008   **We** send not the angels down except for just cause:
015:009   **We** have, without doubt, sent down the Message;
015:009   and **We** will assuredly guard it (from corruption).
015:010   **We** did send messengers before thee amongst
015:012   Even so do **We** let it creep into the
015:014   Even if **We** opened out to them a gate
015:015   nay, **we** have been bewitched by sorcery."
015:016   It is **We** who have set out constellations in
015:017   And (moreover) **we** have guarded them from every
015:019   And the earth **We** have spread out (like a carpet);
015:020   And **We** have provided therein means of subsistence,-
015:021   but **We** only send down thereof in due and ascertainable
015:022   And **We** send the fecundating winds, then cause
015:023   And verily, it is **We** Who give life, and Who
015:023   it is **We** Who remain Inheritors
015:026   **We** created man from sounding clay, from mud
015:027   And the Jinn race, **We** had created before, from the
015:047   And **We** shall remove from their hearts any lurking
015:052   "**We** feel afraid of you!"
015:053   They said: "Fear not! **we** give thee glad tidings
015:055   They said: "**We** give thee glad tidings in truth;
015:058   They said: "**We** have been sent to a people
015:059   them **we** are certainly (charged) to save
015:060   "Except his wife, who, **we** have ascertained,
015:063   They said: "Yea, **we** have come to thee
015:064   "**We** have come to thee with the Truth
015:064   and assuredly **we** tell the truth.
015:066   And **We** made known this decree to him, that the
015:070   They said: "Did **we** not forbid thee (to speak)
015:074   And **We** turned (the Cities) upside down,
015:079   So **We** exacted retribution from them.
015:081   **We** sent them Our Signs, but they
015:085   **We** created not the heavens, the earth, and all
015:087   And **We** have bestowed upon thee the Seven Oft-
015:088   (Wistfully) at what **We** have bestowed on certain
015:090   (Of just such wrath) as **We** sent down
015:092   Therefore, by the Lord, **We** will, of a surety
015:095   For sufficient are **We** unto thee
015:097   **We** do indeed know how thy heart is distressed
016:028   "**We** did no evil (knowingly)."
016:035   nor should **we** have prescribed prohibitions other
016:035   neither **we** nor our fathers,-nor should
016:035   "If Allah had so willed, **we** should not have

WE (continued)

016:036   For **We** assuredly sent amongst every People
016:040   For to anything which **We** have willed,
016:040   **We** but say the Word, "Be," and it is.
016:041   **We** will assuredly give a goodly home in this
016:043   And before thee **We** sent were but men,
016:043   to whom **We** granted inspiration:
016:044   and Scriptures and **We** have sent down unto thee
016:044   (**We** sent them) with Clear Signs and Scriptures
016:055   the favours **We** have bestowed on them!
016:056   **We** have bestowed for their sustenance! By Allah,
016:063   By Allah, **We** (also) sent (our prophets) to
016:064   And **We** sent down the Book to thee so that
016:066   **We** produce, for your drink, milk, pure and
016:075   on whom **We** have bestowed goodly favours from
016:084   On the Day **We** shall raise from all Peoples
016:086   our 'partners', those whom **we** used to invoke
016:088   will **We** add Chastisement to Chastisement;
016:089   and **We** have sent down to thee the Book explaining
016:089   On the day **We** shall raise from all peoples
016:089   and **We** shall bring thee as a witness against these
016:096   And **We** will certainly bestow, on those
016:097   and **We** will bestow on such their reward
016:097   to him will **We** give a life that is
016:101   When **We** substitute one revelation for another,-
016:103   **We** know indeed that they say, "It is
016:118   **We** did them no wrong, but they
016:118   as **We** have mentioned to thee before:
016:118   To the Jews **We** prohibited such things as
016:122   And **We** gave him Good in this world, and he
016:123   Then **We** revealed to thee "Follow the ways
017:001   **We** did Bless,-in order that **We** might show him
017:002   **We** gave Moses the Book, and made
017:003   whom **We** carried (in the Ark) with Noah!
017:004   And **We** decreed for the Children of Israel
017:005   **We** sent against you Our servants given to terrible
017:006   Then did **We** grant you victory over them:
017:006   **We** gave you increase in resources
017:007   (**We** permitted your enemies) to disfigure your faces,
017:008   **We** shall revert (to Our punishments):
017:008   and **We** have made Hell a prison for those who reject
017:010   that **We** have prepared for them a Chastisement
017:012   **We** have made the Night and the Day as two
017:012   the Sign of the Night have **We** made dark
017:012   all things have **We** explained in detail.
017:012   **We** have made bright that ye may seek bounty from
017:013   **We** shall bring out for him a scroll, which he
017:013   Every man's fate **We** have fastened on his
017:015   nor would **We** punish until,
017:015   **We** had sent a messenger (to give warning).
017:016   then **We** destroy them utterly.
017:016   **We** command those among them who are given
017:016   When **We** decide to destroy a town,
017:017   How many generations have **We** destroyed after Noah?
017:018   to such persons as **We** will:
017:018   **We** readily grant them-such things as **We** will,
017:018   in the end have **We** provided Hell for them:
017:020   **We** bestow freely on all-these as well as those:
017:021   See how **We** have bestowed more on some than on
017:031   **We** shall provide, sustenance for them
017:033   **We** have given his heir authority
017:041   **We** have explained (things) in various (ways)
017:045   **We** put, between thee and those who believe not

WE (continued)

017:046   And **We** put coverings over their hearts
017:047   **We** know best what it is they listen, when they
017:049   They say: "What! when **we** are reduced to bones
017:049   should **we** really be raised up (to be) a new creation?
017:054   **We** have not sent thee to be a disposer
017:055   and **We** gave to David the Psalms.
017:055   and **We** made some of the Prophets to excel others
017:058   There is not a population but **We** shall destroy
017:059   **We** sent the She-camel to the Thamud-
017:059   **We** only sent the Signs by way of frightening
017:059   And **We** refrain from sending the Signs,
017:060   **We** put fear (and warning) into them, but it
017:060   Behold! **We** told thee that thy Lord doth
017:060   **We** granted the Vision which **We** showed thee,
017:061   Behold! **We** said to the angels: "Prostrate unto
017:070   **We** have honoured the sons of Adam; provided them
017:071   On the day **We** shall call together all human
017:073   away from that which **We** had revealed unto thee,
017:074   And had **We** not given thee strength, thou wouldst
017:075   In that case **We** should have made thee taste
017:077   way with the messengers **We** sent before thee:
017:082   **We** send down (stage by stage) of the Qur'an
017:083   Yet when **We** bestow Our favours on man, he turns
017:086   **We** could take away that which **We** have sent thee
017:089   And **We** have explained to man, in this Qur'an,
017:090   They say: "**We** shall not believe in thee,
017:093   until thou send to us a book that **we** could read."
017:093   No, **we** shall not even believe in thy mounting until
017:095   **We** should certainly have sent them down from the
017:097   **We** shall increase for them the fierceness
017:097   On the Day of Judgment **We** shall gather them
017:098   should **we** really be raised up (to be) a new creation?"
017:098   "When **we** are reduced to bones and broken dust,
017:101   To Moses **We** did give nine Clear Signs:
017:103   but **We** did drown him and all who were with him.
017:104   And **We** said thereafter to the Children of Israel,
017:104   **We** gathered you together in a mingled crowd
017:105   **We** sent down the (Qur'an) in Truth, and in
017:105   and **We** sent thee but to give Glad Tidings
017:106   **We** have revealed it by stages.
017:106   (It is) a Qur'an which **We** have divided
018:007   in order that **We** may test them-as to which
018:007   That which is on earth **We** have made but as
018:008   Verily what is on earth **We** shall make but as
018:011   Then **We** drew (a veil) over their ears, for a
018:012   Then **We** roused them, in order to test which of
018:013   **We** relate to thee their story in truth: they were
018:013   in their Lord, and **We** increased them in guidance:
018:014   **We** gave strength to their hearts: behold, they
018:014   if **we** did; **we** should indeed have uttered an enormity!
018:014   never shall **we** call upon any god other than Him:
018:018   and **We** turned them on their right and their
018:019   They said, "**We** have stayed (perhaps) a day,
018:019   **We** raised them up (from sleep), that they
018:021   Thus did **We** make their case known to the people,
018:028   nor obey any whose heart **We** have permitted to
018:029   for the wrong-doers **We** have prepared a Fire
018:030   and work righteousness, verily **We** shall not
018:032   the two **We** placed tillage.
018:032   **We** provided two gardens of grape-vines and
018:033   **We** caused a river to flow.
018:045   **We** send down from the skies: the earth's

WE (continued)

018:047   nor shall **We** leave out any one of them.
018:047   a level stretch, and **We** shall gather them,
018:047   On the Day **We** shall remove the mountains, and thou
018:048   **We** shall not fulfil the appointment made to you
018:048   come to Us (bare) as **We** created you first:
018:050   Behold! **We** said to the angels, "Prostrate to Adam":
018:052   and **We** shall make for them a place
018:054   **We** have explained in detail in this Qur'an, for the
018:056   **We** only send the Messengers to give glad tidings
018:057   Verily **We** have set veils over their hearts
018:059   but **We** fixed an appointed time for their
018:059   Such were the towns **We** destroyed when they
018:062   truly **we** have suffered much fatigue at this
018:063   when **we** betook ourselves to the rock?
018:064   Moses said: "That was what **we** were seeking after":
018:065   On whom **We** had bestowed Mercy from Ourselves
018:065   from Ourselves and whom **We** had taught knowledge
018:080   and **we** feared that he would grieve them by
018:081   "So **we** desired that their Lord would give them
018:084   and **We** gave him the ways and the means to all ends.
018:084   Verily **We** established his power on earth,
018:086   **We** said: "O Zul-Qarnain! (thou hast authority),
018:087   He said: "Whoever doth wrong, him shall **we** punish;
018:088   as **We** order it by our command."
018:090   for whom **We** had provided no covering protection
018:091   **We** completely understood what was before him.
018:094   shall **we** then render thee tribute in order that
018:099   and **We** shall collect them all together.
018:099   On that day **We** shall leave them to surge
018:100   And **We** shall present Hell that day for Unbelievers
018:102   Verily **We** have prepared Hell for the Unbelievers
018:103   Say: "Shall **we** tell you of those who lose most
018:105   nor shall **We**, on the Day of Judgement, give them any
018:109   my Lord, even if **we** added another ocean like it,
019:007   **We** give thee good news of a son: his name
019:007   that name have **We** conferred distinction before."
019:012   and **We** gave him Wisdom even as a youth,
019:017   then **We** sent to her Our angel, and he
019:021   and (**We** wish) to appoint him as a Sign unto men
019:029   They said: "How can **we** talk to one who is
019:040   It is **We** Who will inherit the earth, and all
019:049   **We** made a prophet.
019:049   **We** bestowed on him Isaac and Jacob,
019:050   And **We** bestowed of Our Mercy on them,
019:050   and **We** granted them lofty honour on the tongue
019:052   And **We** called him from the right side
019:053   And, out of Our Mercy, **We** gave him his brother
019:057   And **We** raised him to a lofty station.
019:058   and Israel-of those whom **We** guided and chose.
019:058   and of those whom **We** carried (in the Ark)
019:063   Such is the Garden which **We** give as an
019:064   (The angels say:) "**We** descend not but by
019:067   that **We** created him before out of nothing?
019:068   then shall **We** bring them forth on their
019:068   **We** shall gather them together, and (also)
019:069   Then shall **We** certainly drag out from every
019:070   And certainly **We** know best those who are most
019:072   and **We** shall leave the wrong-doers therein,
019:072   But **We** shall save those who guarded against evil,
019:074   before them have **We** destroyed, who were
019:079   Nay! **We** shall record what he says,
019:079   and **We** Shall add and add to his punishment.

019:083 Seest thou not that **We** have set Satans
019:084 for **We** but count out to them a (limited)
019:085 The day **We** shall gather the righteous to (Allah)
019:086 And **We** shall drive the sinners to Hell,
019:097 So have **We** made the (Qur'an) easy in thine
019:098 (countless) generations before them have **We** destroyed?
020:002 **We** have not sent down the Qur'an to thee to be
020:021 **We** shall return it at once to its
020:023 "In order that **We** may show thee of
020:033 "That **we** may celebrate Thy praise without stint,
020:037 "And indeed **We** conferred a favour on thee
020:038 "Behold! **We** sent to thy mother, by inspiration,
020:040 but **We** saved thee from trouble,
020:040 and **We** tired thee in various ways.
020:040 So **We** brought thee back to thy mother, that her
020:045 "Our Lord! **we** fear lest He hasten with insolence
020:047 'Verily **we** are Messengers sent by thy Lord:
020:047 indeed, have **we** come from thy Lord!
020:053 With it have **We** produced divers pairs of plants
020:055 From the (earth) did **We** create you, and into
020:055 and from it shall **We** bring you out once again.
020:055 and into it shall **We** return you, and from
020:056 And **We** showed Pharaoh all Our Signs, but he
020:058 "But **we** can surely produce magic to match thine!
020:058 between us and thee, which **we** shall not fail
020:058 not fail to keep-neither **we** nor thou-in a place
020:065 thou throw (first) or that **we** be the first
020:068 **We** said: "Fear not! for thou hast indeed
020:070 "**We** believe in the Lord of Aaron and Moses."
020:072 They said: "Never shall **we** prefer thee to what
020:073 For us, **we** have believed in our Lord: may He
020:077 **We** sent an inspiration to Moses: "Travel by
020:080 **We** delivered you from your enemy,
020:080 and **We** made a Covenant with you on the
020:080 and **We** sent down to you Manna and quails:
020:081 **We** have provided for your sustenance, but commit
020:085 (Allah) said: "**We** have tested thy people in thy
020:087 and **we** threw them (into the fire), and that
020:087 They said: "**We** broke not the promise to thee,
020:087 but **we** were made to carry the weight of the
020:091 They had said: "**We** will not cease to worship it,
020:097 **we** will certainly burn it in a blazing fire
020:099 for **We** have sent thee a reminder from Us.
020:099 Thus do **We** relate to thee some stories
020:102 that Day, **We** shall gather the sinful, blear-eyed
020:104 **We** know best what they will say, when the
020:113 Thus have **we** sent this down-an Arabic Qur'an-
020:115 and **We** found on his part no firm resolve.
020:115 **We** had already, beforehand, taken the
020:116 When **We** said to the angels, "Prostrate yourselves
020:117 Then **We** said: "O Adam! verily, this is
020:124 a life narrowed down, and **We** shall raise him up
020:127 And thus do **We** recompense him who transgresses
020:128 generations before them **We** destroyed, in whose
020:131 for the things **We** have given for enjoyment
020:131 of this world, through which **We** test them:
020:132 **We** ask thee not to provide sustenance:
020:132 **We** provide it for thee.
020:134 **we** should certainly have followed thy Signs before
020:134 before **we** were humbled and put to shame."
020:134 Had **We** destroyed them a punishment before this,
021:006 the towns which **We** destroyed believed:

021:007 to whom **We** granted inspiration: if ye
021:007 Before thee, also, the messengers **We** sent were but men,
021:008 Nor did **We** give them bodies that ate no food,
021:009 Then **We** fulfilled to them Our promise,
021:009 but **We** destroyed those who transgressed beyond
021:009 and **We** saved them and those whom **We** willed,
021:010 **We** have revealed for you (O men!) a book
021:011 **We** utterly destroyed because of their iniquities,
021:014 **we** were indeed wrong-doers!"
021:015 till **We** made them as a field that is mown,
021:016 Not for (idle) sport did **We** create the heavens
021:017 **We** should surely have taken it from the things nearest
021:017 if **We** would do (such a thing)!
021:018 Nay, **We** hurl the Truth against falsehood, and it
021:025 Not a messenger did **We** send before thee
021:029 thus do **We** reward those who do wrong.
021:029 such a one **We** should reward with Hell:
021:030 before **We** clove them asunder?
021:030 **We** made from water every living thing.
021:031 and **We** have made therein broad highways
021:031 And **We** have set on the earth mountains standing
021:032 And **We** have made the heavens as a
021:034 **We** granted not to any man before thee
021:035 and **We** test you by evil and by good
021:044 see they not that **We** gradually reduce the land
021:044 Nay, **We** gave the good things of this life
021:046 **we** did wrong indeed!"
021:047 and enough are **We** to take account.
021:047 **We** will bring it (to account):
021:047 **We** shall set up scales of justice for the
021:048 In the past **We** granted to Moses and Aaron
021:050 this is a blessed message which **We** have sent down:
021:051 and well were **We** acquainted with him.
021:051 **We** bestowed aforetime on Abraham his rectitude
021:053 They said, "**We** found our father worshipping them."
021:060 They said, "**We** heard a youth talk of them:
021:069 **We** said, "O Fire! be thou cool, and (a means of)
021:070 but **We** made them the Greater losers.
021:071 But **We** delivered him and (his nephew)
021:071 to the land which **We** have blessed for the nations.
021:072 Jacob, and **We** made righteous men of every
021:072 And **We** bestowed on him Isaac and, as an
021:073 and **We** sent them inspiration to do good deeds,
021:073 And **We** made them leaders, guiding (men)
021:074 **We** gave Judgment and Knowledge,
021:074 and **We** saved him from the town which
021:075 And **We** admitted him to Our Mercy:
021:076 **We** listened to his (prayer) and delivered him and his
021:077 so **We** drowned them (in the Flood) all together.
021:077 **We** helped him against people who rejected
021:078 **We** did witness their judgment.
021:079 To Solomon **We** inspired the (right)
021:079 it was **We** Who did (all these things).
021:079 to each (of them) **We** gave Judgment and Knowledge;
021:080 It was **We** Who taught him the making of
021:081 for **We** do know all things.
021:081 to the land which **We** had blessed:
021:082 and it was **We** Who guarded them.
021:084 So **We** listened to him:
021:084 and **We** restored his people to him, and doubled
021:084 **We** removed the distress that was on him,
021:086 **We** admitted them to Our Mercy:

WE (continued)

021:087 he imagined that **We** had no power over him!
021:088 So **We** listened to him: and delivered
021:088 and thus do **We** deliver those who have faith.
021:090 **We** cured his wife's (barrenness) for him.
021:090 So **We** listened to him: and **We** granted him Yahya:
021:091 and **We** made her and her son a Sign for all peoples.
021:091 **We** breathed into her from Our spirit,
021:094 **We** shall record it in his favour.
021:095 is a ban on any population which **We** have destroyed:
021:097 "Ah! woe to us! **we** were indeed heedless of this;
021:097 nay, **we** truly did wrong!"
021:104 so shall **We** produce a new one:
021:104 **We** produced the first Creation,
021:104 The Day that **we** roll up the heavens like a scroll
021:104 a promise **We** have undertaken: truly shall **We** fulfil it.
021:105 Before this **We** wrote in the Psalms, after the
021:107 **We** sent thee not, but as a mercy for all creatures.
022:005 (consider) that **We** created you out of dust,
022:005 in order that **We** may manifest (Our Power) to you;
022:005 and **We** cause whom **We** will to rest in the womb
022:005 then do **We** bring you out as babes,
022:005 barren and lifeless, but when **We** pour down rain
022:009 and on the Day of Judgment **We** shall make him
022:016 Thus have **We** sent down Clear Signs; and verily
022:025 which **We** have made (open) to (all) men-
022:025 **We** cause to taste of a most grievous chastisement.
022:026 Behold! **We** pointed the site, to Abraham, of the
022:034 To every people did **We** appoint rites (of sacrifice),
022:035 **We** have bestowed upon them.
022:036 The sacrificial camels **We** have made for you
022:036 thus have **we** made animals subject to you,
022:041 if **We** establish them in the land,
022:045 How many populations have **We** destroyed, which were
022:052 Never did **We** send a messenger or a prophet
022:067 To every People have **We** appointed rites
023:012 Man **We** did create from a quintessence (of clay);
023:013 Then **We** placed him as (a drop of) sperm in a
023:014 then of that clot **We** made a (foetus) lump;
023:014 then **We** developed out of it another creature:
023:014 Then **We** made the sperm into a clot of
023:014 then **We** made out of that lump bones and clothed
023:017 and **We** are never unmindful of (Our) Creation.
023:017 And **We** have made, above you, seven tracts;
023:018 And **We** send down water from the sky according
023:018 and **We** caused it to soak in the soil;
023:018 and **We** certainly are able to drain it off (with ease).
023:019 With it **We** grow for you gardens of date-palms
023:021 **We** produce (milk) for you to drink; there are,
023:023 and certainly **We** sent Noah to his people:
023:024 never did **we** hear such a thing (as he says),
023:027 So **We** inspired him (with this message);
023:030 (for men to understand); lo! **We** put (men) to test.
023:031 Then **We** raised after them another generation.
023:032 And **We** sent to them a messenger from among
023:033 in the Hereafter, and on whom **We** had bestowed
023:037 **We** shall die and **we** live!
023:037 But **we** shall never be raised up again!
023:038 but **we** are not the ones to believe in him!
023:041 and **We** made them as rubbish of dead leaves
023:042 Then **We** raised after them other generations.
023:044 Then sent **We** Our messengers in succession:
023:044 **We** made them as a tale (that is told):

WE (continued)

023:044 so **We** made them follow each other (in punishment):
023:045 Then **We** sent Moses and his brother Aaron,
023:047 They said: "Shall **we** believe in two men
023:049 And **We** gave Moses the Book, in order
023:050 **We** gave them both shelter on high ground,
023:050 And **We** made the son of Mary and his mother
023:055 Do they think that because **We** have granted them
023:056 **We** would hasten them on in every good?
023:062 On no soul do **We** place a burden greater than
023:064 Until, when **We** seize in Punishment those of
023:071 Nay, **We** have sent them their admonition, but they
023:075 If **We** had mercy on them and removed
023:076 **We** inflicted Punishment on them, but they
023:077 Until **We** open on them a gate leading to
023:082 They say: "What! when **we** die and become
023:082 could **we** really be raised up again?
023:090 **We** have sent them the Truth:
023:095 And **We** are certainly able to show thee
023:096 **We** are well acquainted with the things they say.
023:106 and **we** became a people astray!
023:107 then shall **we** be wrong-doers indeed!"
023:107 if ever **we** return (to evil), then shall
023:109 'Our Lord! **we** believe; then do Thou forgive us,
023:113 They will say: "**We** stayed a day or part
023:115 "Did ye then think that **We** had created you
024:001 in it have **We** sent down Clear Signs, in order
024:001 A Sura which **We** have sent down and which
024:001 and which **We** have ordained:
024:034 **We** have already sent down to you verses making
024:046 **We** have indeed sent down Signs that make
024:047 They say, "**We** believe in Allah and in the
024:047 and in the Messenger, and **we** obey":
024:051 "**We** hear and **we** obey":
025:011 but **We** have prepared a Blazing Fire for such as deny
025:018 not meant was it for us that **we** should take
025:019 him shall **We** cause to taste of a grievous Chastisement
025:020 **We** have made some of you as a trail for others:
025:020 And the messengers whom **We** sent before thee
025:021 to us, or (why) do **we** not see Our Lord?"
025:023 And **We** shall turn to whatever deeds they did
025:023 and **We** shall make such deeds as floating dust scattered
025:031 Thus have **We** made for every prophet an enemy
025:032 and **We** have rehearsed it to thee in slow,
025:032 that **We** may strengthen thy heart thereby,
025:033 but **We** reveal to thee the truth and the best
025:035 (Before this), **We** sent Moses the Book,
025:036 And **We** commanded: "Go ye both, to the
025:036 **We** destroyed with utter destruction.
025:037 and **We** have prepared for (all) wrong-doers
025:037 **We** drowned them, and **We** made them as a Sign
025:039 each one **We** broke to utter annihilation (for their sins).
025:039 To teach one **We** set forth parables and examples;
025:042 had it not been that **we** were constant to them!"-
025:045 Then do **We** make the sun its guide;
025:046 Then **We** draw it in towards Ourselves,-
025:048 and **We** send down pure water from the sky,-
025:049 of things **We** have created,-cattle and
025:049 That with it **We** may give life to a dead land,
025:050 And **We** have distributed the (water) amongst them,
025:051 **We** could have sent a warner to every town.
025:056 But thee **We** only sent to give to give glad tidings
025:060 Shall **we** adore that which thou commandest us?"

WE (continued)

026:004 **We** could send down to them from the sky a Sign,
026:007 noble things of all kinds **we** have produced therein?
026:015 **We** are with you, and will listen (to your call).
026:016 to Pharaoh, and say: '**We** have been sent by the
026:018 (Pharaoh) said: "Did **we** not cherish thee as a
026:040 "That **we** may follow the sorcerers if they win?"
026:041 shall **we** have a (suitable) reward if **we** win?"
026:044 it is **we** who will certainly win!"
026:047 Saying: "**We** believe in the Lord of the Worlds.
026:050 **we** shall but return to our Lord!
026:051 since **we** are the first to believe."
026:052 By inspiration **We** told Moses: "Travel by
026:056 "But **we** are a multitude amply fore-warned."
026:057 So **We** expelled them from gardens, springs,
026:059 Thus it was, but **We** made the Children of Israel
026:061 "**We** are sure to be overtaken."
026:063 Then **We** told Moses by inspiration: "Strike the
026:064 And **We** made the other party approach thither.
026:065 **We** delivered Moses and all who were with him;
026:066 But **We** drowned the others.
026:071 They said: "**We** worship idols,
026:071 and **we** remain constantly in attendance on them."
026:074 our fathers doing thus (what **we** do)."
026:074 They said: "Nay, but **we** found our fathers
026:097 "'By Allah, **we** were truly in an error manifest,
026:098 "'When **we** held you as equals with the
026:100 "'Now, then, **we** have none to intercede (for us),
026:102 **we** shall truly be of those who believe!'"
026:102 "'Now if **we** only had a chance of return,
026:111 They said: "Shall **we** believe in thee when it
026:119 So **we** delivered him and those with him.
026:120 Thereafter **We** drowned those who remained behind.
026:138 "And **we** are not the ones to receive Pains and
026:139 So they rejected him, and **We** destroyed them.
026:170 So **We** delivered him and his family,-all
026:172 Then the rest **We** destroyed utterly.
026:173 **We** rained down on them a shower (of brimstone):
026:186 like us, and indeed **we** think thou art a liar!
026:198 Had **We** revealed it to any of the non-Arabs,
026:200 Thus have **We** caused it to enter the hearts
026:203 Then they will say: "Shall **we** be respited?"
026:205 If **we** do let them enjoy (this life) for a few years,
026:208 Never did **We** destroy a town but had its warners-
026:209 and **We** never are unjust.
027:004 **We** have made their deeds pleasing in their eyes;
027:015 **We** gave knowledge to David and Solomon: and they
027:016 and **we** have been given of everything, this is
027:016 He said: "O ye people! **we** have been taught
027:027 (Solomon) said: "Soon shall **we** see whether thou
027:033 They said: "**We** are endued with strength,
027:037 **we** shall expel them from there in disgrace,
027:037 **we** shall come to them with such hosts as they
027:042 and **we** have submitted to Allah (in Islam)."
027:045 **We** sent (aforetime), to the Thamud, their brother
027:047 They said: "Ill omen do **we** augur from thee
027:049 and that **we** shall then say to his heir
027:049 that **we** shall make a secret night attack on him
027:049 '**We** were not present at the slaughter of his
027:049 and **we** are positively telling the truth.'"
027:050 but **We** too planned, even while
027:051 of their plot!-this, that **We** destroyed them
027:053 And **We** saved those who believed and practiced

WE (continued)

027:054 (**We** also sent) Lut (as a Messenger): behold, he
027:057 her **We** destined to be of those who lagged behind.
027:057 But **We** saved him and his family, except his wife:
027:058 And **We** rained down on them a shower (of brimstone):
027:060 Yea, with it **We** cause to grow well-planted
027:067 The Unbelievers say:" What! when **we** become dust,-
027:067 become dust,-**we** and our fathers,-shall
027:067 shall **we** really be raised (from the dead)?
027:068 "It is true **we** were promised this,
027:068 **we** and our fathers before (us):
027:082 **We** shall bring forth from the earth a beast
027:083 The Day **We** shall gather together from every
027:086 See they not that **We** have made the Night
028:003 **We** rehearse to thee some of the story
028:005 And **We** wished to be gracious to those who
028:007 and **We** shall make him one of Our messengers."
028:007 So **We** sent this inspiration to the mother of Moses:
028:007 for **We** shall restore him to thee,
028:009 or **we** may adopt him as a son."
028:010 had **We** not strengthened her heart (with faith),
028:012 And **We** ordained that he refused suck at first,
028:013 Thus did **We** restore him to his mother, that her
028:014 for thus do **We** reward those who do good.
028:014 **We** bestowed on him wisdom and knowledge:
028:023 They said: "**We** cannot water (our flocks) until the
028:028 Be Allah a witness to what **we** say."
028:035 He said: "**We** will certainly strengthen thy arm
028:036 never did **we** hear the like among our
028:040 and **We** flung them into the sea:
028:040 So **We** seized him and his hosts,
028:041 And **We** made them (but) leaders inviting
028:042 In this world **We** made a Curse to follow them:
028:043 after **We** had destroyed the earlier generations,
028:043 **We** did reveal to Moses the Book
028:044 when **We** decreed the commission to Moses, nor wast
028:045 but it is **We** Who send messengers (with) inspiration).
028:045 But **We** raised up (new) generations, and long
028:046 (the Mountain of) Tur when **We** called (to Moses).
028:047 **We** should then have followed the Signs and been amongst
028:047 If (**We** had) not (sent thee to the Quraish),
028:048 And they say: "For us, **we** reject all (such things)!"
028:051 Now have **We** brought them the word in order
028:052 Those to whom **We** sent the Book before this,-
028:053 indeed **we** have been Muslims (bowing to Allah's Will)
028:053 they say: "**We** believe therein, for it is
028:054 out of what **We** have given them.
028:055 peace be to you: **we** seek not the ignorant."
028:057 Have **We** not established for them a secure sanctuary,
028:057 They say: "If **we** were to follow the guidance
028:057 **we** should be snatched away from our land."
028:058 and **We** are their heirs!
028:058 And how many towns **We** destroyed, which exulted
028:059 nor are **We** going to destroy a population except
028:061 and one to whom **We** have given the good
028:061 one to whom **We** have made a goodly promise,
028:063 these are the ones whom **we** led astray:
028:063 **we** led them astray, as **we** were astray ourselves:
028:063 **we** free ourselves (from them) to you.
028:075 and **We** shall say: "Produce your proof":
028:075 And from each people shall **We** draw a witness,
028:076 **We** had bestowed on him, that their
028:079 "Oh! that **we** had the like of what Qurun has got!

WE (continued)

028:081   Then **We** caused the earth to swallow up him
028:083   That Home of the Hereafter **We** shall give to
029:002   left alone on saying, "**We** believe", and that
029:003   **We** did test those before them, and Allah
029:007   righteous deeds,-from them shall **We** blot out
029:007   have committed, and **We** shall reward them according
029:008   **We** have enjoined on man kindness to parents:
029:009   righteous deeds,-them shall **We** admit to the
029:010   "**We** believe in Allah"; but when they suffer
029:010   to say, "**We** have (always) been with you!"
029:012   and **we** will bear (the consequences) of your
029:014   **We** did sent Noah to his people, and he
029:015   and **We** made the (Ark) a Sign for all Peoples!
029:015   But **We** saved him and the Companions of the Ark,
029:016   And (**We** also saved) Abraham: behold, he said
029:027   And **We** gave (Abraham) Isaac and Jacob,
029:027   and **We** granted him his reward in this life;
029:031   "**We** are indeed going to destroy the people
029:032   They said: "**We** know well who is there:
029:032   **we** will certainly save him and his following,-
029:033   **we** are (here) to save thee and thy following,
029:034   "For **we** are going to bring down on the
029:035   And **We** have left thereof an evident Sign,
029:036   (**We** sent) their brother Shu'aib.
029:040   **We** sent a violent tornado (with showers
029:040   some **We** caused the earth to swallow up;
029:040   Each one of them **We** seized for his crime:
029:040   and some **We** drowned (in the waters):
029:043   And such are the Parables **We** set forth for
029:046   who do wrong but say, "**We** believe in the Revelation
029:046   and it is to Him **we** submit (in Islam)."
029:047   And thus (it is) that **We** have sent down
029:051   **We** have sent down to thee the Book
029:058   to them shall **We** give a Home in Heaven,-
029:067   **We** have made a Sanctuary secure, and that
029:069   **We** will certainly guide them to Our Paths:
030:027   (**We** can think of) in the heavens and the earth:
030:028   Thus do **We** explain the Signs in detail to a
030:028   as equals in the wealth **We** have bestowed on you?
030:034   for the (favours) **We** have bestowed on them!
030:035   Or have **We** sent down authority to them,
030:036   When **We** give men a taste of Mercy, they exult
030:047   **We** did indeed send, before thee, messengers to
030:047   **We** meted out Retribution:
030:051   And if **We** (but) send a Wind from which they see
030:058   Verily **We** have propounded for men, in this
031:010   **We** send down rain from the sky, and produce
031:012   **We** bestowed (in the past) wisdom on Luqman:
031:014   And **We** have enjoined on man (to be good) to his
031:021   "Nay, **we** shall follow the ways that **we** found our fathers
031:023   and **We** shall tell them the truth of their deeds:
031:024   **We** grant them their pleasure for a little while:
031:024   in the end shall **We** drive them to a chastisement
032:010   And they say: "What! when **we** lie, hidden and
032:010   shall **we** indeed be in a Creation renewed?"
032:012   for **we** do indeed (now) believe."
032:012   "Our Lord! **We** have seen and **we** have heard:
032:012   (to the world): **we** will work righteousness:
032:013   **We** could certainly have brought every soul
032:013   If **We** had so willed,
032:014   and **We** too will forget you-taste ye
032:016   **We** have bestowed on them.

WE (continued)

032:021   And indeed **We** will make them taste of the
032:022   who transgress **We** shall exact (Due) Retribution.
032:023   and **We** made it a guide to the Children of Israel.
032:023   **We** did indeed aforetime give the Book to Moses:
032:024   And **We** appointed, from among them, Leaders, giving
032:026   how many generations **We** destroyed before them,
032:027   And do they not see that **We** do drive Rain
033:007   **We** took from them a solemn Covenant:
033:007   And remember **We** took from the Prophets
033:009   but **We** sent against them a hurricane and forces
033:031   and **We** have prepared for her
033:031   to her shall **We** grant her reward twice:
033:037   **We** joined her in marriage to thee: in order
033:045   O Prophet! Truly **We** have sent thee as a Witness,
033:050   O prophet! **We** have made lawful to thee
033:050   **We** know what **We** have appointed for them
033:060   **We** shall certainly stir thee up against them:
033:066   **we** had obeyed Allah and obeyed the Messenger!"
033:067   And they would say: "Our Lord! **We** obeyed
033:072   **We** did indeed offer the Trust to the Heavens
034:007   "Shall **we** point out to you a man that will
034:009   If **We** wished, **We** could cause the earth to swallow them
034:010   and **We** made the iron soft for Him;-
034:010   **We** bestowed Grace aforetime on David
034:012   and **We** made a Font of molten brass to flow for him;
034:012   **We** made him taste of the Chastisement of the Blazing
034:012   And to Solomon (**We** made) the Wind (obedient):
034:014   Then, when **We** decreed (Solomon's) death,
034:016   and **We** sent against them the flood (released)
034:016   and **We** converted their two Garden (rows) into
034:017   and never do **We** give (such) requital except to such as
034:017   That was the Requital **We** gave them because
034:018   **We** had poured Our blessings,
034:018   **We** had placed Cities in prominent positions,
034:018   **We** had appointed stages of journey in due
034:019   and **We** dispersed them all in scattered fragments.
034:019   At length **We** made them as a tale (that is told),
034:021   except that **We** might test the man who believes
034:024   it is that either **we** or ye are on right guidance
034:025   nor shall **we** be questioned as to what ye do."
034:028   **We** have not sent thee but as a (Messenger)
034:031   for you, **we** should certainly have been believers!"
034:031   The Unbelievers say: "**We** shall neither believe
034:032   "Was it **we** who kept you back from Guidance
034:033   **We** shall put yokes on the necks of the Unbelievers:
034:034   Never did **We** send a Warner to a population,
034:034   "**We** believe not in the (message) with which
034:035   and in sons, and **we** cannot be chastised."
034:035   They said: "**We** have more in wealth and in sons,
034:042   and **We** shall say to the wrong-doers, "Taste ye
034:044   But **We** had not given them Books which they
034:045   a tenth of what **We** had granted to those: yet when
034:052   "**We** do believe (now) in the (truth)";
035:009   and **We** drive them to a land that is dead,
035:024   Verily **We** have sent thee with truth, as a
035:027   With it **We** then bring out produce of various
035:029   **We** have provided for them, secretly and
035:031   That which **We** have revealed to thee of the Book
035:032   to such of Our servants as **We** have chosen:
035:032   Then **We** have given the Book for inheritance to such
035:036   Thus do **We** reward every ungrateful one!
035:037   "Did **we** not give you long enough life so that

WE (continued)

035:037 Bring us out: **we** shall work righteousness,
035:037 not the (deeds) **we** used to do!"-
035:040 Or have **We** given them a Book from which
036:008 **We** have put yokes round their necks right up
036:009 And **We** have put a bar in front of them and a
036:009 **We** have covered them up: so that
036:012 Verily **We** shall give life to the dead,
036:012 and of all things have **We** taken account.
036:012 and **We** record that which they sent before and that
036:014 When **We** (first) sent to them two messengers,
036:014 but **We** strengthened them with a third:
036:014 they said, "Truly, **we** have been sent on a
036:016 **we** have been sent on a mission to you:
036:018 desist not, **we** will certainly stone you,
036:018 The (people) said: "For us, **We** augur an evil
036:028 And **We** sent not down against his People,
036:031 how many generations before them **We** destroyed?
036:033 **We** do give it life, and produce grain therefrom,
036:034 and **We** cause springs to gush forth therein.
036:034 And **We** produce therein orchards with date-palms
036:037 **We** withdraw therefrom the Day, and behold
036:039 And the Moon,-**We** have measured for her stations
036:041 And a Sign for them is that **We** bore their race
036:042 And **We** have created for them similar (vessels)
036:043 If it were Our Will, **We** could drown them;
036:047 who believe: "Shall **we** then feed those whom,
036:065 That Day shall **We** set a seal on their mouths.
036:066 **We** could surely have blotted out their eyes;
036:067 **We** could have transformed them in their places;
036:068 If **We** grant long life to any,
036:068 **We** cause him to be reversed in nature:
036:069 **We** have not instructed the (Prophet) in Poetry,
036:071 See they not that it is **We** Who have created
036:072 And that **We** have subjected them to their (use)?
036:076 Verily **We** know what they hide as well as what they
036:077 **We** Who created Him from sperm?
037:006 **We** have indeed decked the lower heaven
037:011 or (other) beings **We** have created?
037:011 Them have **We** created out of a sticky clay!
037:016 "What! when **we** die, and become dust and bones,
037:016 shall **we** (then) be raised up (again)?
037:030 "Nor had **we** any authority over you.
037:031 of our Lord that **we** shall indeed (have to) taste
037:032 "We led you astray: for truly **we** were ourselves astray."
037:034 Verily that is how **We** shall deal with Sinners.
037:036 And say: "What! Shall **we** give up our gods
037:053 "`When **we** die and become dust and bones,
037:053 shall **we** indeed receive rewards and punishments.?'"
037:058 "Is it (the case) that **we** shall not die,
037:059 and that **we** shall not be punished?"
037:063 For **We** have truly made it (as) a trial
037:072 But **We** sent aforetime, among them, warners.
037:075 and **We** are the Best to hear prayer.
037:076 And **We** delivered him and his people from the
037:078 And **We** left (this blessing) for him
037:080 Thus indeed do **We** reward those who do right.
037:082 Then the rest **We** overwhelmed in the Flood.
037:098 but **We** made them the ones must humiliated!
037:101 So **We** gave him the good news of a forbearing son.
037:104 **We** called out to him, "O Abraham!
037:105 thus indeed do **We** reward those who do right.
037:107 And **We** ransomed him with a momentous sacrifice:

WE (continued)

037:108 And **We** left for him among generations (to come)
037:110 Thus indeed do **We** reward those who do right.
037:112 And **We** gave him the good news of Isaac-
037:113 **We** blessed him and Isaac: but of their
037:114 **We** bestowed Our favour on Moses and Aaron,
037:115 And **We** delivered them and their people
037:116 And **We** helped them, so they were victorious;
037:117 And **We** gave them the Book which helps
037:118 And **We** guided them to the Straight Way.
037:119 And **We** left for them among generations (to come)
037:121 Thus indeed do **We** reward those who do right.
037:129 And **We** left for him among generations (to come)
037:131 Thus indeed do **We** reward those who do right.
037:134 Behold, **We** delivered him and his adherents,
037:136 Then **We** destroyed the rest.
037:145 But **We** cast him forth on the naked shore
037:146 And **We** caused to grow over him, a spreading
037:147 And **We** sent him (on a mission) to a
037:148 so **We** permitted them to enjoy (their life) for a while.
037:150 Or that **We** created the angels female, and they
037:165 "And **we** are verily ranged in ranks (for service);
037:166 "And **we** are verily those who declare
037:168 "If only **we** had before us a message
037:169 "**We** should certainly have been Servants of Allah,
038:003 How many before them did **We** destroy?
038:007 "**We** never heard (the like) of this in the
038:018 It was **We** that made the hills declare, in unison
038:020 **We** strengthened his kingdom, and gave
038:022 they said: "Fear not: **We** are two disputants,
038:024 **We** had tried him: he asked forgiveness of his Lord,
038:025 So **We** forgave him this (lapse): he enjoyed,
038:026 O David! **We** did indeed make thee a vicegerent
038:027 **We** create heaven and earth and all between!
038:028 Shall **We** treat those who guard against evil,
038:028 Shall **We** treat those who believe and work
038:029 (Here is) a Book which **We** have sent down
038:030 To David **We** gave Solomon (for a son),-
038:034 And **We** did try Solomon: **We** placed on his throne
038:036 Then **We** subjected the Wind to his power, to flow
038:043 And **We** gave him (back) his people and double
038:044 Truly **We** found him full of patience and constancy.
038:046 Verily **We** did chose them for a special (purpose)-
038:062 that **we** see not men who **we** used to number
038:063 "Did **we** treat them (as such) in ridicule, or have
039:002 Verily it is **We** Who have revealed the Book
039:003 "**We** only serve them in order that they may
039:027 **We** have put forth for men, in the
039:041 Verily **We** have revealed the Book to thee in Truth,
039:049 but when **We** bestow a favour upon him as from Us,
039:074 **We** can dwell in the Garden as **we** will:
040:011 Now have **we** recognized our sins:
040:023 Of old **We** sent Moses, with Our Signs
040:047 "**We** but followed you: can ye
040:048 "**We** are all in this (Fire)! Truly, Allah has
040:051 **We** will, without doubt, help Our
040:053 and **We** gave the Book in inheritance to the Children
040:053 **We** did aforetime give Moses the Guidance,
040:070 **We** sent Our messengers: but soon
040:074 nay, **we** invoked not, of old, anything
040:077 and whether **We** show thee (in this life) some part
040:077 or **We** take thy soul (to Our Mercy) (before that),
040:077 some part of what **We** promise them,-

WE (continued)

040:078 **We** did aforetime send messengers before thee:
040:078 and some whose story **We** have not related to thee.
040:078 whose story **We** have related to thee, and some
040:084 and **we** reject the partners we used to join with Him."
040:084 they said: "**We** believe in Allah,-the One God,
041:005 for us, **we** shall do (what **we** will!)"
041:011 "**We** do come (together), in willing obedience."
041:012 And **We** adorned the lower heaven with lights,
041:014 so **we** disbelieve in the Message you were sent with.
041:016 So **We** sent against them a furious Wind
041:016 that **We** might give them a taste of a Chastisement
041:017 As to the Thamud, **We** gave them guidance, but they
041:018 But **We** delivered those who believed
041:025 And **We** have destined for them intimate companions
041:027 and **We** will requite them for the worst
041:027 But **We** will certainly give the Unbelievers a taste
041:029 **we** shall crush them beneath our feet, so that
041:031 "**We** are your protectors in this life and in
041:039 but when **We** send down rain to it, it is
041:044 Had **We** sent this as a Qur'an (in a language)
041:045 **We** certainly gave Moses the book aforetime:
041:047 "**We** do assure Thee not one of us can bear witness!"
041:050 When **We** give him a taste of some mercy from Us,
041:050 But **We** will show the Unbelievers the truth of all
041:050 and **We** shall give them the taste of a sever chastisement.
041:051 When **We** bestow favours on man, he turns
041:053 Soon will **We** show them Our Signs in the (furthest)
042:007 Thus have **We** sent by inspiration to thee
042:013 the which **We** have sent by inspiration to thee-
042:013 and that which **We** enjoined on Abraham,
042:020 **We** grant somewhat thereof, but he
042:020 of the Hereafter, **We** give increase in his tilth;
042:023 **We** shall give Him an increase of good
042:038 of what **We** bestow on them for Sustenance;
042:048 And truly, when **We** give man a taste of Mercy
042:048 **We** have not sent thee as a guard over them.
042:052 but **We** have made the (Qur'an) a Light,
042:052 And thus have **We**, by Our command,
042:052 wherewith **We** guide such of Our servants as **We** will;
043:003 **We** have made it a Qur'an in Arabic, that ye
043:005 Shall **We** then take away the Reminder from you
043:006 **We** sent amongst the peoples of old?
043:008 So **We** destroyed men-stronger in power than these;-
043:011 and **We** raise to life therewith a land that is dead;
043:013 for **we** could never be able to do it.
043:014 "And to Our Lord, surely, Must **We** turn back!"
043:020 **we** should not have worshipped such (deities)!"
043:021 What! have **We** given them a Book before this,
043:022 Nay! they say: "**We** found Our fathers following
043:022 and **we** do guide ourselves by their footsteps."
043:023 Just in the same way, whenever **We** sent a Warner
043:023 "**We** found Our fathers following a certain religion,
043:023 and **we** will certainly follow in their footsteps."
043:024 They said: "For us, **We** deny that ye (prophets)
043:025 So **We** exacted retribution from them:
043:030 they said: "This is sorcery, and **we** do reject it."
043:032 It is **We** Who portion out between them their
043:032 and **We** raise some of them above others in ranks,
043:033 might become of one community **We** would provide,
043:036 **We** appoint for him a Satan, to be
043:041 Even if **We** take thee away,
043:041 **We** shall be sure to exact retribution from them,

WE (continued)

043:042 which **We** have promised them:
043:042 Or **We** shall show thee that (accomplished)
043:042 for verily **We** shall prevail over them.
043:045 whom **We** sent before thee;
043:045 did **We** appoint any deities other than
043:046 **We** did send Moses aforetime, with Our Signs,
043:048 **We** showed them Sign after Sign, each greater
043:048 and **We** seized them with Punishment, in order
043:049 for **We** shall truly accept guidance."
043:050 But when **We** removed the Chastisement from them,
043:055 and **We** drowned them all.
043:055 **We** exacted retribution from them,
043:056 And **We** made them (a people) of the Past and an
043:059 and **We** made him an example to the
043:059 **We** granted Our favour to him,
043:060 **We** could make angels from amongst you,
043:076 Nowise shall **We** be unjust to them:
043:078 Verily **We** have brought the truth to you: but most
043:079 But it is **We** Who settle things.
043:080 Or do they think that **We** hear not their secrets
043:080 Indeed (**We** do), and Our Messengers are by them,
044:003 for **We** (ever) wish to warn (against Evil).
044:003 **We** sent it down during a blessed night:
044:005 For **We** (ever) send (revelations),
044:012 for **We** do really believe!"
044:015 **We** shall indeed remove the Chastisement for a
044:016 The day **We** shall seize you with a mighty onslaught:
044:016 **We** will indeed (then) exact Retribution!
044:017 **We** did, before them, try the people of Pharaoh:
044:028 And **We** made other people inherit (those things)!
044:030 **We** did deliver aforetime the Children of Israel
044:032 And **We** chose them aforetime above the
044:035 and **we** shall not be raised again.
044:037 **We** destroyed them because they were guilty of sin.
044:038 **We** created not the heavens, the earth,
044:039 **We** created them not except for just ends:
044:054 and **We** shall wed them to maidens
044:058 Verily, **We** have made this (Qur'an) easy, in thy
045:006 which **We** rehearse to thee in truth:
045:016 **We** gave them, for Sustenance, things good and pure;
045:016 and **We** favoured them above the nations.
045:016 **We** did aforetime grant to the Children of Israel
045:017 And **We** granted them clear Signs in affairs
045:018 Then **We** put thee on the (right) Way of Religion:
045:021 think that **We** shall hold them as equal with those
045:024 **We** shall die and **we** live, and nothing
045:029 for **We** were wont to put on record all that they did.""
045:032 and **we** have no firm assurance.'"
045:032 ye used to say, '**We** know not what is the Hour:
045:032 **we** only think it a conjecture,
045:034 **We** will forget you as ye forgot the meeting
046:003 **We** created not the heavens and the earth and all
046:015 **We** have enjoined on man kindness to his parents:
046:016 Such are they from whom **We** shall accept the best
046:025 Thus do **We** recompense those given to sin!
046:026 and **We** had endowed them with (faculties of)
046:026 **We** have not given to you (ye Quraish)!
046:026 And **We** had firmly established them in a
046:027 and **We** have shown the Signs in various ways,
046:027 **We** destroyed aforetime towns round about you;
046:029 Behold, **We** turned towards thee a company of Jinns
046:030 **We** have heard a Book revealed after Moses,

WE (continued)

047:013 have **We** destroyed (for their sins)?
047:026 "**We** will obey you in part of (this) matter";
047:030 Had **We** so willed, **We** could have shown them up to
047:031 And **We** shall try you until **We** test those among you
047:031 and **We** shall try your reported (mettle).
048:001 Verily **We** have granted thee a manifest Victory:
048:008 **We** have truly sent thee as a witness,
048:011 will say to thee: "**We** were engaged in (looking after)
048:013 His Messenger, **We** have prepared, for those
048:025 **We** should certainly have punished the Unbelievers
049:013 O mankind! **We** created you from a single (pair)
049:014 but ye (only) say, '**We** have submitted our wills
049:014 The desert Arabs say, "**We** believe."
050:003 "What! when **we** die and become dust,
050:003 (shall **we** live again?)
050:004 **We** already know how much of them the earth
050:006 How **We** have made it and adorned it,
050:007 And the earth-**We** have spread it out, and set
050:009 and **We** produce therewith Gardens and Grain
050:009 And **We** send down from the sky Rain charged
050:011 and **We** give (new) life therewith to land
050:015 Were **We** then weary with the first Creation,
050:016 It was **We** who created man,
050:016 for **We** are nearer to him than (his) jugular vein.
050:016 and **We** know what suggestions his soul makes to him:
050:022 now have **We** removed thy veil, and sharp
050:030 The Day **We** will ask Hell, "Art thou Filled to the full?"
050:036 generations before them did **We** destroy (for their Sins),-
050:038 **We** created the heavens and the earth and all
050:043 Verily it is **We** Who give Life and Death;
050:045 **We** know best what they say; and thou
051:032 They said, "**We** have been sent to a people
051:035 Then **We** evacuated those of the Believers
051:036 But **We** found not there any except one
051:037 And **We** left there a Signs for such as fear
051:038 Behold, **We** sent him to Pharaoh, with authority
051:040 So **We** took him and his forces, and threw
051:041 behold, **We** sent against them the devastating Wind:
051:047 and **We** indeed have vast power.
051:047 **We** have built the Firmament with might:
051:048 how excellently **We** do spread out!
051:048 And **We** have spread out the (spacious) earth:
051:049 And of every thing **We** have created pairs:
052:020 and **We** shall wed them to maidens, with beautiful,
052:021 to them shall **We** join their families:
052:021 nor shall **We** deprive them (of the fruit)
052:022 And **We** shall bestow on them, of fruit
052:026 They will say: "Aforetime, **We** were not without
052:028 "Truly **we** did call unto Him from of old:
052:030 Or do they say:-" A Poet! **we** await for him
054:011 So **We** opened the gates of heaven, with water
054:012 And **We** caused the earth to gush forth with springs,
054:013 But **We** bore him on an (Ark) made of
054:015 And **We** have left this as a Sign (for all time):
054:017 And **We** have indeed made the Qur'an easy to
054:019 For **We** sent against them a furious wind, on a
054:022 But **We** have indeed made the Qur'an easy to
054:024 Truly should **we** then be in error and madness.
054:024 Shall **we** follow such a one?
054:027 For **We** will send the she-camel by way
054:031 For **We** sent against them a single Mighty Blast,
054:032 And **We** have indeed made the Qur'an easy to

WE (continued)

054:034 **We** sent against them a violent tornado with
054:034 Lut's household: them **We** delivered by early Dawn,-
054:035 Thus do **We** reward those who give thanks.
054:037 but **We** blinded their eyes.
054:040 And **We** have indeed made the Qur'an easy to
054:042 but **We** seized them with the Seizure of a Mighty,
054:044 "**We** acting together can defend ourselves"?
054:049 **We** created in proportion and measure.
054:051 have **We** destroyed gangs like unto you:
055:031 Soon shall **We** settle your affairs, O both
056:035 **We** have created them of special creation.
056:047 "What! when **we** die and become dust and bones,
056:047 shall **we** then indeed be raised up again?-
056:048 "(**We**) and our fathers of old?"
056:057 It is **We** Who have created you:
056:059 Is it ye who create it, or are **We** the Creators?
056:060 **We** have decreed Death to be your common lot,
056:060 and **We** are not to be frustrated
056:064 Is it ye that cause it to grow, or are **We** the Cause?
056:065 Were it Our Will, **we** could make it broken orts.
056:066 (Saying), "**We** are indeed left with debts
056:067 "Indeed **we** are deprived."
056:069 Do ye bring it Down (in rain) from the Cloud, or do **We**?
056:070 Were it Our Will, **We** could make it saltish
056:072 which feeds the fire, or do **We** grow it?
056:073 **We** have made it a reminder and an article
056:085 But **We** are nearer to him than ye, and yet see not,-
057:014 (Those without) will call out, "Were **we** not with you?"
057:017 Already have **We** shown the Signs plainly to you,
057:022 a Book before **We** bring it into existence:
057:025 and **We** sent down Iron, in which
057:025 **We** sent aforetime our messengers with Clear
057:026 And **We** sent Noah and Abraham, and established
057:027 Then, in their wake, **We** followed them up with
057:027 **We** did not prescribe for them:
057:027 (**We** commanded) only the seeking for the Good
057:027 Yet **We** bestowed, on those among them who believed,
057:027 **We** sent after them Jesus the son of Mary,
057:027 and **We** ordained in the hearts of those followed him
058:005 for **We** have already sent down Clear Signs.
059:011 and if ye are attacked (in fight) **we** will help you."
059:011 "If ye are expelled, **We** too will go out with you,
059:011 and **we** will never hearken to any one in your affair;
059:021 Had **We** sent down this Qur'an on a mountain,
059:021 such are the similitudes which **We** propound to men,
060:004 "Our Lord! in Thee do **we** trust,
060:004 and to Thee do **we** turn in repentance:
060:004 **we** have rejected you, and there has arisen,
060:004 "**We** are clear of you and of whatever ye worship
061:014 but **We** gave power to those who believed against their
061:014 Said the Disciples, "**We** are Allah's helpers!"
063:001 they say, "**We** bear witness that thou art indeed
063:008 They say, "If **we** return to Madinah, surely the
063:010 **We** have bestowed on you, before Death
064:008 and in the Light which **We** have sent down.
065:008 did **We** not then call to account,-to severe account?-
065:008 and **We** chastised them with a horrible Chastisement.
066:012 and **We** breathed into her (body) of Our spirit;
067:005 and **We** have made such (Lamps) (as) missiles
067:005 And **We** have, (from of old), adorned the
067:009 but **we** rejected him and said, 'Allah never sent
067:010 "Had **we** but listened or used our intelligence,

WE (continued)

067:010	we should not (now) be among the Companions
067:029	we have believed in Him,
067:029	and on Him have we put our trust:
068:016	Soon shall We brand (the beast) on the snout!
068:017	Verily We have tried them as We tried the People
068:026	they said: "We have surely lost our way:
068:027	"Indeed we are deprived (of the fruits of our labour)!"
068:029	Verily we have been doing wrong!"
068:031	We have indeed transgressed!
068:032	for we do turn to Him (in repentance)!"
068:035	Shall We then treat the People of Faith
068:044	We draw them on little by little from directions
069:011	We, when the water (of Noah's flood) overflowed
069:012	That We might make it a Reminder unto you,
069:045	We should certainly seize him by his right hand
069:046	And We should certainly then cut off the artery
069:049	And We certainly know that there are amongst you
070:007	But We see it (quite) near.
070:039	By no means! for We have created them out of
070:040	in the East and the West that We can certainly-
070:041	and We are not to be defeated (in Our Plan).
071:001	We sent Noah to his People (with the Command):
072:001	'We have really heard a wonderful Recital!
072:002	we shall not join (in worship) any (gods) with our Lord,
072:002	and we have believed therein:
072:005	'But we do think that no man or Jinn
072:008	'And we pried into the (secrets of) heaven;
072:008	but we found it filled with stern guards and flaming fires.
072:009	'We used, indeed, to sit there in (hidden)
072:010	'And we understand not whether ill is intended
072:011	we follow divergent paths.
072:012	nor can we escape Him by flight.
072:012	'But we think that we can by no means frustrate
072:013	'And as for us, since we have listened to the Guidance,
072:013	we have accepted it:
072:016	We should certainly have bestowed on them
072:017	"That We might try them by that (means).
073:005	Soon shall We send down to thee a weighty Word.
073:015	even as We sent a messenger to Pharaoh.
073:015	We have sent to you, (O men!) a Messenger,
073:016	so We seized him with a heavy Punishment.
074:031	And We have set none but angels as guardians
074:031	and We have fixed their number only as trial
074:043	They will say: "We were not of those who prayed;
074:044	"Nor were we of those who fed the indigent;
074:045	"But we used to talk vanities with vain talkers;
074:046	"And we used to deny the Day of Judgment,
075:003	Does man think that We cannot assemble his bones?
075:004	Nay, We are able to put together in perfect order
075:018	But when We have recited it, follow thou
076:002	so We gave him (the gifts), of Hearing and Sight.
076:002	Verily We created Man from a drop of mingled sperm,
076:003	We showed him the Way:
076:004	For the Rejecters We have prepared Chains, Yokes,
076:009	(Saying), "We feed you for the sake of Allah alone:
076:009	no reward do we desire from you,
076:010	"We only fear a Day of frowning and distress
076:023	It is We Who have sent down the Qur'an
076:028	and We have made their frame strong;
076:028	but, when We will, We shall exchange their likes.
076:028	It is We Who created them,
077:016	Did We not destroy the men of old (for their evil)?

WE (continued)

077:017	So shall We make later (generations) follow them.
077:018	Thus do We deal with men of sin.
077:020	Have We not created you from a fluid
077:021	The which We placed in a place of rest,
077:023	For We do determine for We are the Best
077:025	Have We not made the earth (as a place)
077:038	We shall Gather you together and those before (you)!
077:044	Thus do We certainly reward the Doers of Good.
078:006	Have We not made the earth as a wide expanse,
078:008	And (have We not) created you in pairs,
078:012	And (have We not) built over you
078:014	And do We not send down from the clouds
078:015	That We may produce therewith grain and vegetables,
078:029	And all things have We preserved on record.
078:030	for no increase shall We grant you, except in
078:040	Verily, We have warned you of a Chastisement near,-
079:010	They say (now): "What! shall we indeed be returned
079:011	"What!-when we shall have become rotten bones?"
080:024	Then let man look at his Food, (and how We provide it):
080:025	For that We pour forth water in abundance,
080:026	And We split the earth in fragments,
087:006	By degrees shall We teach thee (the Message),
087:008	And We will make it easy for thee (to follow)
090:004	Verily We have created Man into toil and struggle.
090:008	Have We not made for him a pair of eyes?-
092:007	We will indeed make smooth for him
092:010	We will indeed make smooth for him
092:012	Verily We take upon Us to guide,
094:001	Have We not expanded thee thy breast?-
095:004	We have indeed created man in the best of molds,
095:005	Then do We abase him (to be) the lowest of the low,
096:015	We will drag him by the forelock,-
096:018	We will call on the angels of punishment
097:001	We have indeed revealed this (Message)
108:001	To thee have We granted the Abundance.

WEAK

002:282	If the party liable is mentally deficient, or weak,
004:005	To those weak of understanding give not
004:028	for man was created weak in (resolution).
004:075	being weak, are ill-treated (and oppressed)?
004:097	"Weak and oppressed were we in the earth."
004:098	weak and oppressed, men, women, and children who
004:127	the children who are weak and oppressed
007:137	considered weak (and of no account), inheritors
008:026	a small (band), deemed weak through the land, and
008:066	for He knoweth that there is a weak spot in you:
014:021	the weak say to those who were arrogant, "For us
034:031	deemed weak will say to the arrogant ones:
034:032	who had been deemed weak: "Was it we
034:033	Those who had been deemed weak will say to
040:047	The weak ones (who followed) will say to those

WEAKEN

003:146	nor did they weaken (in will) nor give in.
018:056	to weaken the truth, and they treat My Signs

WEAKEST

019:075	and (who) weakest in forces!
072:024	who it is that is weakest in (his) helper

WEAKNESS

030:054	after strength, give (you) weakness and a hoary head:
030:054	then gave (you) strength after weakness,
030:054	Allah Who created you in a state of (helpless) weakness,

WEALTH

002:215 Say: Whatever **wealth** ye spend that is good,
002:247 gifted with **wealth** in abundance?"
002:261 spend their **wealth** in the way of Allah
002:262 their **wealth** in the cause of Allah,
002:264 spend their **wealth** to be seen of men,
002:265 those who spend their **wealth** seeking to please
003:014 and (**wealth** of) cattle and well-tilled land.
004:161 and that they devoured men's **wealth** wrongfully;
008:036 The Unbelievers spend their **wealth** to hinder
009:024 or your kindred: the **wealth** that ye have gained;
009:034 who in falsehood devour the **wealth** of men
009:055 Let not their **wealth** nor their children
009:069 and more flourishing in **wealth** and children.
009:085 Nor let their **wealth** nor their children
009:086 those with **wealth** and influence among them
009:088 fight with their **wealth** and their persons:
009:103 Of their **wealth** take alms, that so
010:058 the (**wealth**) they hoard.
010:088 the features of their **wealth**, and send
010:088 and his Chiefs splendor and **wealth** in the life
011:029 I ask you for no **wealth** in return: my reward
017:026 but squander not (your **wealth**) in the manner
017:064 mutually share with them **wealth** and children;
018:034 "More **wealth** have I than you, and more honour
018:039 less than thee in **wealth** and sons,
018:046 **Wealth** and sons are allurements of the
019:077 "I shall certainly be given **wealth** and children"?
023:055 granted them abundance of **wealth** and sons,
026:088 "The Day whereon neither **wealth** nor sons will avail,
027:036 he said: "Will ye given me abundance in **wealth**?
028:077 "But seek, with the (**wealth**) which Allah
030:028 to share as equals in the **wealth** We have
034:035 They said: "We have more in **wealth** and in sons,
034:037 It is not your **wealth** nor your sons, that will
038:032 And he said, "Truly do I prefer **wealth** to the
043:032 is better than the (**wealth**) which they amass.
051:019 And in their **wealth** there is a due share
053:048 That it is He Who giveth **wealth** and satisfaction,
061:011 Cause of Allah, with your **wealth** and your persons:
068:014 Because he possesses **wealth** and (numerous) sons.
069:028 "Of no profit to me has been my **wealth**!
070:018 And collect (**wealth**) and hide it (from use)!
070:024 And those in whose **wealth** is a recognized right
071:012 "Give you increase in **wealth** and sons;
071:021 whose **wealth** and children give them no Increase
089:020 And ye love **wealth** with inordinate love!
090:006 "**Wealth** have I squandered in abundance!"
092:011 Nor will his **wealth** profit him when he falls
092:018 Those who spend their **wealth** for increase
100:008 And violent is he in his love of **wealth**.
104:002 Who pileth up **wealth** and layeth it by,
104:003 Thinking that his **wealth** would make him
111:002 No profit to him from all his **wealth**, and all

WEALTHY

002:236 the **wealthy** according to his means,
034:034 to a population, but the **wealthy** ones among
043:023 the **wealthy** ones among them said: "We found
059:007 make a circuit between the **wealthy** among you.

WEANING

002:233 If they both decide on **weaning**,
031:014 And in years twain was his **weaning**:
046:015 to his **weaning** is (a period of) thirty months.

WEAR

007:031 O Children of Adam! **wear** your beautiful apparel
016:014 and that ye may extract therefrom ornaments to **wear**;
018:031 of gold, and they will **wear** green garments
035:012 and ye extract ornaments to **wear**;

WEARIED

046:033 and never **wearied** with their creation, is able

WEARINESS

035:035 no toil nor sense of **weariness** shall touch
050:038 nor did any sense of **weariness** touch Us.

WEARISOME

016:076 a **wearisome** burden is he to his master;

WEARY

021:019 nor are they (ever) **weary** (of His service):
041:049 Man does not **weary** of asking for good (things),
047:035 Be not **weary** and faint-hearted crying for peace,
050:015 Were We then **weary** with the first Creation,
088:003 Laboring (hard), **weary**,-

WEAVING

012:102 in the process of **weaving** their plots.

WED

004:025 they may **wed** believing girls from among those
004:025 the means wherewith to **wed** free believing women,
004:025 **wed** them with the leave of their owners,
028:027 He said: "I intended to **wed** one of these
033:050 the Prophet wishes to **wed** her;-this only
044:054 and We shall **wed** them to maidens with beautiful
052:020 and We shall **wed** them to maidens, with beautiful,

WEDLOCK

004:023 and two sisters in **wedlock** at one and the same time,
004:025 when they are taken in **wedlock**,
033:037 and thy favour: "Retain thou (in **wedlock**) thy wife

WEEP

009:082 Let them laugh a little: much will they **weep**:
053:060 And will ye laugh and not **weep**,-

WEEPING

012:016 in the early part of the night, **weeping**.

WEIGH

017:035 and **weigh** with a balance that is straight:
026:182 And **weigh** with scales true and upright.

WEIGHED

009:042 but the distance was long, (and **weighed**) on them.

WEIGHT

006:152 give measure and **weight** with (full) justice;-
007:085 Give just measure and **weight**, nor withhold
010:061 (so much as) the **weight** of an atom on the
011:084 And give not short measure or **weight**: I see you
011:085 "And O my people! give just measure and **weight**,
018:105 on the Day of Judgment, give them any **Weight**.
020:087 but we were made to carry the **weight** of the
021:047 (no more than) the **weight** of a mustard seed, We will
026:148 with spathes near breaking (with the **weight** of fruit)?
031:016 "If there be (but) the **weight** of a mustard-seed
034:022 they have no power,-not the **weight** of an atom,-
055:009 So establish **weight** with justice and fall
083:003 or **weight** to men, give less than due.
099:007 an atom's **weight** of good, see it!
099:008 an atom's **weight** of evil, shall see it.

WEIGHTS

051:002 And those that lift and bear away heavy **weights**;

WEIGHTY

006:019 Say: "What thing is most **weighty** in evidence?"
073:005 Soon shall We send down to thee a **weighty** Word.

WELCOME

038:059 No **welcome** for them! Truly, they
038:060 No **welcome** for you! It is ye

WELL

002:026 even of a gnat as **well** as anything above it.
002:065 And **well** ye knew those amongst you
002:095 And Allah is **well** acquainted with
002:096 for Allah sees **well** all that they do.
002:110 for Allah sees **well** all that ye do.
002:144 The people of the book know **well** that
002:197 For Hajj are the months **well** known.
002:215 Allah knoweth it **well**.
002:229 such persons wrong (themselves as **well** as others).
002:231 **well** acquainted with all things.
002:233 that Allah sees **well** what ye do.
002:234 And Allah is **well** acquainted with what ye do.
002:237 For Allah sees **well** all that ye do.
002:265 Allah seeth **well** whatever ye do.
002:271 If ye disclose (acts of) charity, even so it is **well**,
002:271 And Allah is **well** acquainted with what ye do.
002:273 be assured Allah knoweth it **well**.
002:282 And Allah is **well** acquainted with all things.
003:075 and (**well**) they know it.
003:078 and (**well**) they know it!
003:092 and whatever ye give, Allah knoweth it **well**.
003:115 for Allah knoweth **well** those that do right.
003:119 Allah knoweth **well** all the secrets of the heart."
003:153 For Allah is **well** aware of all that ye do.
003:154 for Allah knoweth **well** the secrets of your hearts.
003:156 and Allah sees **well** all that ye do.
003:163 and Allah sees **well** all that they do.
003:180 and Allah is **well** acquainted with all that ye do.
004:091 secure from you as **well** as that of their people:
004:094 for Allah is **well** aware of all that ye do.
004:165 Messengers who gave good news as **well** as warning,
005:007 for Allah knoweth **well** the secrets of your hearts.
005:029 thee draw on thyself my sin as **well** as thine,
005:071 But Allah sees **well** all that they do.
005:094 of game **well** within reach of your hands and
005:097 and that Allah is **well** acquainted with all things.
006:073 He knoweth the Unseen as **well** as that which is open.
006:073 For He is the Wise, **well** acquainted (with all things).
006:114 They know full **well**, to whom
007:026 as **well** as to be an adornment to you, but the
007:185 may **well** be that their term is nigh drawing
008:043 **well** the (secrets) of (all) hearts.
008:072 as **well** as those who gave (them)
008:074 as **well** as those who give (them) asylum and aid,-
009:044 And Allah knoweth **well** those who do their duty.
009:047 But Allah knoweth **well** those who do wrong.
009:078 and that Allah knoweth **well** all things unseen?
009:079 as **well** as those who give according to their means,-
009:101 as **well** as among the Madinah folk:
010:036 Verily Allah is **well** aware of all that they do.
010:079 Said Pharaoh: "Bring me every sorcerer **well** versed."
011:005 knoweth **well** the (inmost secrets) of the hearts.
011:024 and those who can see and hear **well**.
011:079 They said: "**Well** dost thou know we have no need
011:079 indeed thou knowest quite **well** what we want!"
011:111 For He knoweth **well** all that they do.

WELL (continued)

011:112 (from the Path): for He seeth **well** all that ye do.
011:120 as **well** as an exhortation and a message of
012:010 throw him down to the bottom of the **well**: he will
012:015 to the bottom of the **well**: and We
012:019 and he let down his bucket (into the **well**)...
012:019 But Allah knoweth **well** all that they do!
012:050 For my Lord is certainly **well** aware of their snare."
012:073 (The brothers) said: "By Allah! **well** ye know that
012:081 and we could not **well** guard against the unseen!
013:023 they shall enter there, as **well** as the righteous
014:046 but their plots were (**well**) within the sight of Allah,
017:007 If ye did **well**, ye did **well** for yourselves;
017:020 We bestow freely on all-these as **well** as those:
017:031 sustenance for them for them as **well** as for you.
017:096 **well** acquainted with His servants, and He
017:102 Moses said, "Thou knowest **well** that these things
017:110 by whatever name ye call upon Him, (it is **well**):
020:059 be assembled when the sun is **well** up."
021:032 We have made the heavens as a canopy **well** guarded:
021:051 and **well** were We acquainted with him.
021:065 (they said), "Thou knowest full **well** that these
022:011 if good befalls them, they are, therewith, **well** content;
022:020 within their bodies, as **well** as (their) skins.
022:059 to a place they with they shall be **well** pleased:
023:022 And on them, as **well** as in ships, ye ride.
023:096 We are **well** acquainted with the things they say.
024:012 though **well** of their people and say, "This (charge) is
024:028 and Allah knows **well** all that ye do.
024:030 and Allah is **well** acquainted with all that they do.
024:041 And Allah knows **well** all that they do.
024:053 Allah is **well** acquainted with all that ye do."
024:064 **Well** doth He know what ye are intent upon:
025:015 a reward as **well** as a final abode.
025:017 as **well** as those whom they worship besides Allah,
025:024 The Companions of the Garden will be **well**, that Day,
027:074 as **well** as all that they reveal.
027:088 for He is **well** acquainted with all that ye do.
028:025 (**well**) hast thou escaped from unjust people."
028:035 you two as **well** as those who follow you."
029:032 They said: "We know **well** who is there: we will
031:023 of their deeds: for Allah knows **well** all that
031:029 is **well** acquainted with all that ye do?
033:002 for Allah is **well** acquainted with (all)
034:011 balancing **well** the rings of chain armour,
035:008 for Allah knows **well** all that they do!
035:031 to His servants-**well** acquainted and fully Observant.
036:036 as **well** as their own (human) kind and (other) things
036:076 what they hide as **well** as what they disclose.
037:158 but the Jinns know (quite **well**) that they
039:007 For He knoweth **well** all that is in (men's) hearts.
039:073 **Well** have ye done! Enter ye here,
041:043 (all) Forgiveness as **well** as a most
042:012   for He knows full **well** all things.
042:024 For He knows **well** the secrets of all hearts.
048:011 But Allah is **well** acquainted with all that ye do.
048:024 And Allah sees **well** all that ye do.
048:026 and **well** were they entitled to it
049:013 and is **well** acquainted (with all things).
049:018 and Allah sees **well** all that ye do."
053:032 He knows you **well** when He brings you out
057:004 And Allah sees **well** all that ye do.
057:010 And Allah is **well** acquainted with all that ye do.

WELL (continued)

057:025   as **well** as many benefits for mankind, that Allah
058:022   Allah will be **well** pleased with them, and they
060:001   for I know full **well** all that ye conceal
060:003   between you: for Allah sees **well** all that ye do.
062:007   And Allah knows **well** those that do wrong!
064:002   are Believers: and Allah see **well** all that ye do.
064:004   yes, Allah knows **well** the (secrets) of (all) hearts.
064:008   And Allah is **well**-acquainted with all that ye do.
089:028   **well** pleased (thyself), and **well**-pleasing unto Him!
098:008   Allah **well** pleased with them, and they

WELL-ACQUAINTED

004:127   but Allah is **well-acquainted** therewith.
004:128   Allah is **well-acquainted** with all that ye do.
004:135   verily Allah is **well-acquainted** with all that ye do.
005:008   For Allah is **well-acquainted** with all that ye do.
008:075   Verily Allah is **well-acquainted** with all things.
009:016   And Allah is **well-acquainted** with (all)
011:001   and **Well-Acquainted** (with all things):
023:051   for I am **well-acquainted** with (all) that you do.
042:027   For He is with His Servants **well-acquainted**, Watchful.
058:003   And Allah is **well-acquainted** with (all) that ye do.
058:011   and Allah is **well-acquainted** with all ye do.
058:013   and Allah is **well-acquainted** with all that ye do.
059:018   for Allah is **well-acquainted** with (all) that ye do.
063:011   and Allah is **well acquainted** with (all) that ye do.
100:011   **well-acquainted** with them, (Even to) that Day?

WELL-ARRANGED

025:032   rehearsed it to thee in slow, **well-arranged** stages,

WELL-AWARE

006:103   He is subtle **well-aware**.

WELL-BUILT

022:045   and neglected, and castles lofty and **well-built**?

WELL-DOERS

033:029   prepared for the **well-doers** amongst you

WELL-GROUNDED

004:162   **well-grounded** in knowledge, and the Believers,

WELL-GUARDED

052:024   as Pearls **well-guarded**.
056:023   Like unto Pearls **well-guarded**.
056:078   In a Book **well-guarded**,

WELL-KNOWN

026:038   for the appointment of a day **well-known**,
056:050   for the meeting appointed for a Day **Well-known**.

WELL-NIGH

024:035   whose Oil is **well-nigh** luminous, though fire
024:043   The vivid flash of its lightning **well-nigh** blinds the sight.
025:042   "He indeed would **well-nigh** have misled us

WELL-OFF

004:006   If the guardian is **well-off**, let him

WELL-PLANTED

027:060   **well-planted** orchards full of beauty and delight:

WELL-PLEASED

005:119   Allah **well-pleased** with them, and they
009:100   **well-pleased** is Allah with them,
019:006   one with whom Thou art **well-pleased**!"
021:028   **well-pleased** and they stand in awe and reverence
093:005   thou shalt be **well-pleased**.

WELL-PLEASING

089:028   well pleased (thyself), and **well-pleasing** unto Him!

WELL-TILLED

003:014   and (wealth of) cattle and **well-tilled** land.

WELL-VERSED

007:109   "This is indeed a sorcerer **well-versed**.
007:112   And bring up to thee all (our) sorcerers **well-versed**."
026:034   a sorcerer **well-versed**:
026:037   (our) sorcerers **well-versed**."

WELL-WISHERS

012:011   seeing we are indeed his sincere **well-wishers**?

WELLS

022:045   And how many **wells** are lying idle and neglected,
034:013   Basins as large as **wells**, and (cooking)

WENT

002:061   rebelled and **went** on transgressing.
002:061   This because they **went** on rejecting
002:097   a confirmation of what **went** before,
002:198   even though, before this, ye **went** astray.
003:003   confirming what **went** before it;
005:077   of people who **went** wrong in times gone by,-
007:038   it curses its sister-People (that **went** before),
007:142   his brother Aaron (before he **went** up): "Act for me
007:150   and **went** near to slaying me!
007:175   so Satan followed him up, and he **went** astray.
010:019   for a word that **went** forth before from thy Lord,
010:037   it is a confirmation of (revelations) that **went** before it,
011:044   rested on Mount Judi and the word **went** forth:
011:044   Then the word **went** forth: "O earth! swallow up
012:017   we **went** racing with one another, and left
012:111   of what **went** before it,-a detailed
014:009   (O people!), of those who (**went**) before you?
015:013   of those **went** before them.
016:033   So did those who **went** before them. But Allah
016:035   So did those who **went** before them. But what
018:035   He **went** into his garden while he wronged himself:
018:064   so they **went** back on their footsteps,
020:129   been for a word that **went** forth before from thy Lord,
028:079   So he **went** forth among his people in the
037:071   many of the ancients **went** astray;-
041:045   for a Word that **went** forth before from thy Lord,
042:014   been for a Word that **went** forth before from thy Lord,
046:026   when they **went** on rejecting the Signs of Allah:
061:005   Then when they **went** wrong, Allah let

WENTEST

018:039   "Why didst thou not, as thou **wentest** into thy

WERE

002:014   we (**were**) only jesting."
002:025   we **were** fed with before,"
002:028   Seeing that ye **were** without life,
002:061   They **were** covered with humiliation and misery:
002:074   Thenceforth **were** your hearts hardened:
002:084   and to this ye **were** witness.
002:093   and their hearts **were** filled
002:133   **Were** ye witnesses when Death appeared
002:140   and the Tribes **were** Jews or Christians?
002:142   the Qiblah to which they **were** used?"
002:170   fathers **were** void of wisdom and guidance?.
002:171   is as if one **were** to shout like a goat-herd,
002:214   those of faith who **were** with him cried:
002:214   and **were** so shaken in spirit that even the Messenger
002:243   though they **were** thousands (in number),
002:246   if ye **were** commanded to fight,
002:246   seeing that we **were** turned out of our homes
002:246   But when they **were** commanded to fight,
002:249   But those who **were** convinced
003:030   it will wish there **were** a great distance between

WERE (continued)

003:049	in that I make for you out of clay, as it **were**,
003:065	the Torah and the Gospel **were** not revealed till after him?
003:099	while ye **were** yourselves witnesses
003:103	for ye **were** enemies and He joined your hearts
003:103	and ye **were** on the brink of the Pit of Fire,
003:110	it **were** best for them:
003:123	when ye **were** helpless:
003:144	many **were** the Messengers that passed away before Him.
003:144	If he died or **were** slain,
003:152	His permission **were** about to annihilate your enemy,
003:153	Behold! ye **were** climbing up the high ground,
003:167	these **were** told: "Come, fight in the way of Allah
003:167	They **were** that day nearer to Unbelief than of Faith,
003:184	so **were** rejected messengers before thee,
003:195	and fought and **were** slain, verily,
003:195	and **were** drive out therefrom, or suffered harm
004:039	And what burden **were** it on them if they had faith
004:042	wish that the earth **were** made one with them:
004:044	to those who **were** given a portion of the Book?
004:051	to those who **were** given a portion of the Book?
004:060	though they **were** ordered to reject him.
004:064	when they **were** unjust to themselves,
004:066	what they **were** (actually) told, it would
004:072	in that we **were** not present among them."
004:077	to those who **were** told to hold back their hands
004:083	**Were** it not for the Grace
004:094	Even thus **were** ye yourselves before, till Allah
004:097	They say: "In what (plight) **were** ye?"
004:097	"Weak and oppressed **were** we in the earth."
004:102	if ye **were** negligent of your arms and your baggage,
004:129	(as it **were**) hanging (in the air).
004:133	If it **were** His will, He could destroy you,
004:141	they say: "**Were** we not with you?"
004:153	but they **were** seized for their presumption,
004:161	That they took usury, though they **were** forbidden;
005:017	if His Will **were** to destroy Christ the son of Mary,
005:023	**were** two on whom Allah had bestowed His Grace:
005:044	and they **were** witnesses thereto:
005:053	That they **were** with you?"
005:075	many **were** the Messengers that passed
005:078	Curses **were** pronounced on those among
005:079	evil indeed **were** the deeds which they did.
005:104	their fathers **were** void of knowledge and guidance?.
005:107	known that these two **were** guilty of the sin (of perjury),
005:110	And behold! thou makest out of clay as it **were**,
006:010	Mocked **were** (many) Messengers before thee;
006:010	but the scoffers **were** hemmed in by the thing
006:023	"By Allah Our Lord, we **were** not those
006:027	"Would that we **were** but sent back!
006:028	to the things they **were** forbidden, for they
006:028	But if they **were** returned, they would
006:034	Rejected **were** the Messengers before thee:
006:035	If it **were** Allah's will, He could gather
006:044	when lo! they **were** plunged in despair!
006:058	Say: "If what ye would see hastened **were** in my power,
006:088	If they **were** to join other gods with Him,
006:089	These **were** the men to whom We gave the Book,
006:090	Those **were** the (prophets) who received Allah's
006:091	therein **were** ye taught that which ye knew not-
006:121	if ye **were** to obey them, ye would
006:131	(The messengers **were** sent) thus, for thy Lord
006:131	their occupants **were** unwarned.

WERE (continued)

006:133	if it **were** His Will, He could destroy you,
006:144	**Were** ye present when Allah ordered
007:007	for We **were** never absent (at any time or place).
007:045	they **were** those who denied the Hereafter."
007:048	"Of what profit **were** your hoards and your arrogant ways?
007:051	and **were** deceived by the life of the world."
007:051	and as they **were** wont to reject Our Signs.
007:064	they **were** indeed a blind people!
007:075	who **were** reckoned powerless-those among
007:086	but remember how ye **were** little, and He
007:092	it was they who **were** ruined!
007:095	"Our fathers (too) **were** touched by suffering
007:097	Our wrath by night while they **were** asleep?
007:101	Such **were** the towns whose story We (thus)
007:119	So they **were** vanquished there and then,
007:133	but they **were** steeped in arrogance, a people
007:155	when they **were** seized with violent quaking,
007:163	for they **were** given to transgression.
007:165	because they **were** given to transgression.
007:172	"Of this we **were** never mindful":
007:187	Heavy **were** its burden through the heavens
008:006	as if they **were** being driven to death
008:019	even if they **were** multiplied:
008:026	Call to mind when ye **were** a small (band),
008:042	Remember ye **were** on the hither side of the valley,
008:054	for they **were** all oppressors and wrong-doers.
009:003	If, then, ye repent, it **were** best for you; but if
009:031	yet they **were** commanded to worship but One God:
009:040	the two they **were** in the Cave, and he
009:043	who told the truth **were** seen by thee in a clear
009:046	they **were** told, "Sit ye among those who sit (inactive)."
009:065	"We **were** only talking idly and in play."
009:065	and His Messenger, that ye **were** mocking?"
009:069	they **were** mightier than you in power and more
009:074	which they **were** enable to carry out:
009:081	Those who **were** left behind (in the Tabuk expedition)
009:090	and those who **were** false to Allah and His Messenger
009:090	And there **were**, among the desert Arabs (also),
009:118	(He turned in mercy also) to the three who **were** left
010:011	If Allah **were** to hasten for men the ill
010:015	if I **were** to disobey my Lord, I should myself
010:027	as it **were**, with pieces from the depth of the
010:073	those who **were** warned (but heeded not)!
010:075	But they **were** arrogant: they **were** a wicked people.
011:019	"These **were** they who denied the Hereafter!"
011:035	Say: "If I had forged it, on me **were** my sin!
011:043	those who **were** drowned.
011:059	Such **were** the 'Ad People: they rejected
011:060	And they **were** pursued by a Curse in this Life,-
011:063	can help me against Allah if I **were** to disobey Him?
011:091	**Were** it not for the family, we should certainly
011:095	So away with Madyan as **were** Thamud gone away.
011:116	(but there **were** none) except a few among them whom
011:116	of the good things of life which **were** given them,
012:014	They said: "If the wolf **were** to devour him
012:089	not knowing (what ye **were** doing)?"
012:097	for we **were** truly at fault."
012:110	think that they **were** treated as liars,
013:014	if they **were** to stretch forth their hands
013:031	If there **were** a Qur'an with which mountains
013:031	or the earth **were** cloven asunder,
013:031	or the dead **were** made to speak,

WERE (continued)

013:031 with which mountains **were** moved,
013:032 Mocked **were** (many) messengers before thee:
014:021 the weak say to those who **were** arrogant, "For us
014:044 "What! **were** ye not wont to swear aforetime
014:045 ye **were** clearly shown how We dealt with them;
014:046 but their plots **were** (well) within the sight of Allah,
014:046 Mighty indeed **were** the plots which they made,
014:046 even though they **were** such as to shake the hills!
015:014 and they **were** to continue (all day) ascending therein,
015:076 And the (cities **were**) right on the high-road.
015:078 the Wood **were** also wrong-doers;
015:079 They **were** both on an open highway, plain to see.
016:036 of the people **were** some whom Allah guided,
016:039 may realize that they **were** liars.
016:061 It Allah **were** to punish men for their wrong-doing,
016:118 but they **were** used to doing wrong to themselves.
017:072 But those who **were** blind in this world, will be
017:086 If it **were** Our Will, We could
017:088 "If the whole of mankind and Jinn **were** to gather
017:095 Say, "If there **were** settled, on earth,
017:103 but We did drown him and all who **were** with him.
017:107 it is true that those who **were** given knowledge
018:009 and of the Inscription **were** wonders among
018:013 they **were** youths who believed in their Lord,
018:018 whilst they **were** asleep, and We
018:022 (yet others) say they **were** seven, the dog
018:022 (others) say they **were** five, the dog
018:022 (Some) say they **were** three, the dog
018:042 So his fruits **were** encompassed (with ruin),
018:058 If He **were** to call them (at once) to account for what they
018:059 Such **were** the towns We destroyed when they
018:064 Moses said: "That was what we **were** seeking after":
018:071 when they **were** in the boat, he scuttled it.
018:080 his parents **were** people of Faith, and we
018:082 to which they **were** entitled;
018:091 (He left them) as they **were**: We completely
018:097 Thus **were** they made powerless to scale it
018:104 they **were** acquiring good by their works?"
018:109 Say: "If the ocean **were** ink (wherewith to write out)
019:058 Those **were** some of the prophets on whom
019:058 (Allah) Most Gracious **were** rehearsed to them,
019:069 from every sect all those who **were** worst in
019:074 who **were** even better in equipment and in
020:070 So the magicians **were** thrown down to prostration:
020:087 but we **were** made to carry the weight of the
020:134 we **were** humbled and put to shame."
021:005 the ones that **were** sent to (prophets) of old!"
021:007 the messengers We sent **were** but men, to whom
021:008 ate no food, nor **were** they immortals.
021:011 How many **were** the towns. We utterly
021:013 the good things of this life which **were** given you,
021:014 we **were** indeed wrong-doers!"
021:022 If there **were**, in the heavens and the earth,
021:030 the heavens and the earth **were** joined together
021:041 Mocked **were** (many) Messengers before thee;
021:041 but their scoffers **were** hemmed in by the thing that they
021:051 and well **were** We acquainted with him.
021:065 Then **were** they confounded with shame:
021:074 truly they **were** a people given to Evil,
021:077 truly they **were** a people given to Evil:
021:082 And of Satans **were** some who dived for him,
021:086 for they **were** of the Righteous ones.

WERE (continued)

021:090 These (three) **were** quick in doing in good works:
021:097 "Ah! woe to us! we **were** indeed heedless of this;
021:103 (the Day) that ye **were** promised."
022:011 There are among men some who serve Allah, as it **were**,
022:045 which **were** given to wrong-doing?
022:048 give respite, which **were** given to wrong-doing?
023:046 they **were** an arrogant people.
023:048 of those who **were** destroyed.
023:091 (if there **were** many gods), behold, each god
023:105 "**Were** not My Signs rehearsed to you, and ye
023:110 while ye **were** laughing at them!
024:010 If it **were** not for God's grace and mercy on you,
024:014 **Were** it not for the grace and mercy
024:020 **Were** it not for the grace and mercy of Allah
024:021 and **were** it not for the grace and mercy of Allah on you,
024:035 the glass as it **were** a brilliant star:
024:035 is as if there **were** a Niche and within it a Lamp:
025:010 Blessed is He Who, if that **were** His Will,
025:018 for they **were** a people destroyed."
025:020 before thee **were** all (men) who ate food
025:042 had it not been that we **were** constant to them!"-
025:047 and makes the Day (as it **were**) a Resurrection.
025:073 droop not down at them as if they **were** deaf or blind;
026:004 If (such) **were** Our Will, We could
026:038 So the sorcerers **were** got together for the appointment
026:039 And the people **were** told: "Are ye (now) assembled?"-
026:065 We delivered Moses and all who **were** with him;
026:097 "By Allah, we **were** truly in an error manifest,
026:099 those who **were** steeped in guilt.
026:099 "And our seducers **were** only those who
026:173 on those who **were** admonished (but heeded not)!
026:206 the (Punishment) which they **were** promised!
026:207 the enjoyment they **were** given
027:017 and they **were** all kept in order and ranks.
027:017 And before Solomon **were** marshalled his hosts,-
027:048 There **were** in the City nine men, who made
027:049 'We **were** not present at the slaughter of his
027:052 Now such **were** their houses,-in utter
027:058 on those who **were** admonished (but heeded not)!
027:068 "It is true we **were** promised this,-we and
028:005 those who **were** being depressed in the land,
028:006 what they **were** dreading from them.
028:008 their hosts **were** men of sin.
028:009 And they perceived not (what they **were** doing)!
028:015 when its people **were** not watching:
028:023 who **were** keeping back (their flocks).
028:045 and long **were** the ages that passed over them;
028:048 which **were** formerly sent to Moses?
028:048 like those which **were** sent to Moses?"
028:057 They say: "If we **were** to follow the guidance
028:063 we led them astray, as we **were** astray ourselves:
028:071 Say: See ye? If Allah **were** to make the night
028:072 Say: see ye? If Allah **were** to make the Day
028:076 such **were** the treasures We had bestowed on him,
028:078 which **were** superior to him in strength and greater
029:010 men's oppression as if it **were** the Wrath of Allah!
029:038 from the Path, though they **were** keen-sighted.
029:040 some **were** caught by a (mighty) Blast;
030:009 They **were** superior to them in strength:
030:042 before (you): most of them **were** idolaters.
030:049 they **were** dumb with despair!
030:055 thus **were** they used to being deluded!

WERE (continued)

031:007 as if there **were** deafness in both his ears:
031:016 a mustard-seed and it **were** (hidden) in a rock,
031:027 And if all the trees on earth **were** pens and the
031:027 and the Ocean (**were** ink), with seven
032:020 of the Fire, the which ye **were** wont to reject as false."
033:011 they **were** shaken as by a tremendous shaking.
033:011 In that situation **were** the Believers tried:
033:013 though they **were** not exposed:
033:020 they would wish they **were** in the deserts
033:020 and if they **were** in your midst, they would
033:030 of you **were** guilty of evident unseemly conduct,
033:051 This **were** nigher to the cooling of their eyes,
034:012 and there **were** Jinns that worked in front of him,
034:031 Those who **were** deemed weak will say to the arrogant
034:042 the which ye **were** wont to deny!"
034:054 for they **were** indeed in suspicious (disquieting) doubt.
035:004 so **were** messengers rejected before thee:
035:014 and if they **were** to listen, they cannot answer your
035:043 the way the ancients **were** dealt with?
035:044 before them,-though they **were** superior to them
035:045 If Allah **were** to punish men according to what
036:006 whose fathers **were** not warned,
036:029 and behold! they **were** (like ashes) quenched and silent
036:043 If it **were** Our Will, We could drown them;
036:063 "This is the Hell of which ye **were** promised!
037:030 Nay, it was ye who **were** a people in
037:032 for truly we **were** ourselves astray."
037:035 For they, when they **were** told that there is
037:049 As if they **were** (delicate) eggs closely guarded.
037:070 So they (too) **were** rushed down on their footsteps!
037:073 Then see what was the End of those who **were** warned,
037:122 For they **were** two of Our believing Servants.
037:167 And there **were** those who said,
037:177 the morning for those who **were** warned (and heeded not)!
038:012 Before them (**were** many who) rejected messengers,-
038:013 such **were** the Confederates.
038:027 That **were** the thought of Unbelievers!
038:031 Behold, there **were** brought before him, at eventide,
038:047 They **were**, in Our sight, truly, of the
040:005 But (there **were** people) before them, who denied
040:010 seeing that ye **were** called to the Faith
040:012 partners **were** joined to Him, ye believed!
040:021 They **were** even superior to them
040:075 and that ye **were** wont to be insolent.
040:075 "That was because ye **were** wont to rejoice on the
040:082 They **were** more numerous than these
040:083 they **were** wont to scoff hemmed them in.
041:014 so we disbelieve in the Message you **were** sent with.
041:021 the first time, and unto Him **were** ye to return.
041:028 for that they **were** wont to reject Our Signs.
041:030 the which ye **were** promised!
041:034 become as it **were** thy friend and intimate!
041:044 they are (as it **were**) being called from a place far
042:027 If Allah **were** to enlarge the provision
043:006 But how many **were** the prophets We sent
043:009 they would be sure to reply, 'They **were** created by (Him),
043:033 And **were** it not that (all) men might become
043:038 "Would that between me and thee **were** the distance
043:054 truly **were** they a people rebellious (against Allah).
043:060 And if it **were** Our Will, We could
044:022 (But they **were** aggressive): then he cried
044:025 How many **were** the gardens and springs

WERE (continued)

044:029 nor **were** they given a respite (again).
044:037 they **were** guilty of sin.
044:037 of Tubba and those who **were** before them?
045:029 for We **were** wont to put on record all that ye did."
045:031 "**Were** not Our Signs rehearsed to you?
045:031 But ye **were** arrogant, and **were** a people given to sin!
046:011 who believe: "If (this Message) **were** a good thing,
046:020 for that ye **were** arrogant on earth
046:024 "Nay, it is the (calamity) ye **were** asking to be hastened!-
046:026 and they **were** (completely) encircled by that which
046:026 to them **were** there (faculties of) hearing, sight,
046:034 for that ye **were** wont to deny (Truth)!"
047:021 it **were** best for them if they **were** true to Allah.
047:021 **Were** it to obey and say what is just, and when
047:022 if ye **were** put in authority, that ye
047:037 If He **were** to ask you for all of them,
048:011 will say to thee: "We **were** engaged in (looking after)
048:025 ye did not know that ye **were** trampling down
048:026 and well **were** they entitled to it
049:007 Allah's Messenger: **were** he, in many matters,
050:015 **Were** We then weary with the first Creation,
051:017 They **were** in the habit of sleeping but little
051:018 they (**were** found) praying for Forgiveness;
051:035 the Believers who **were** there,
051:043 Behold, they **were** told "Enjoy (your brief day)
051:046 So **were** the people of Noah before them: for they
052:014 "Is the Fire,-which ye **were** wont to deny!
052:026 They will say: "Aforetime, We **were** not without
052:035 **Were** they created of nothing,
052:035 or **were** they themselves the creators?
052:044 **Were** they to see a piece of the sky falling
053:052 for that they **were** (all) most unjust and most
054:020 Plucking out men as if they **were** roots of
056:045 For that they **were** wont to be indulged,
056:065 **Were** it Our Will, we could make it broken orts.
056:070 **Were** it Our Will, We could make it saltish
057:014 (Those without) will call out, "Were we not with you?"
057:026 and some of them **were** on right guidance, but many
058:005 as **were** those before them:
058:008 Seest thou not those who **were** forbidden secret
058:008 to that which they **were** forbidden (to do)?
058:022 even though they **were** their fathers or their sons,
059:008 those who **were** expelled from their homes and their
059:014 thou wouldst think they **were** united, but their
061:004 as if they **were** a solid cemented structure.
062:005 The similitude of those who **were** entrusted with
066:010 but **were** told: "Enter ye the fire along with (others)
066:010 they **were** (respectively) under two of Our
067:021 with Sustenance if He **were** to withhold His provision?
067:027 is (the promise fulfilled), which ye **were** calling for!"
067:028 Say: "See ye?-if Allah **were** to destroy me,
068:019 (which swept away) all around, while they **were** sleep.
068:043 while they **were** whole, (and had refused).
069:005 But the Thamud,-they **were** destroyed by a terrible
069:006 And the 'Ad,-they **were** destroyed by a furious
069:044 And if the messenger **were** to invent any sayings
070:043 as if they **were** rushing to a goal-post
071:025 and **were** made to enter the Fire and they found-
071:025 Because of their sins they **were** drowned (in the flood),
072:004 'There **were** some foolish ones among us, who used
072:006 'True, there **were** persons among mankind who took
072:022 could deliver me from Allah (if I **were** to disobey Him),

WERE (continued)

074:043	They will say: "We **were** not of those who prayed;
074:044	"Nor **were** we of those who fed the indigent;
074:050	As if they **were** affrighted asses,
075:015	Even though he **were** to put up his excuses.
076:012	And because they **were** patient and constant, He will
077:033	"As if there **were** (a string of) yellow camels
078:019	as if there **were** doors,
078:020	as if they **were** a mirage.
078:040	"Woe unto me! Would that I **were** (mere) dust!"
085:007	(all) that they **were** doing against the Believers.
089:008	The like of which **were** not produced
098:001	**were** not going to depart (from their ways) until
102:005	Nay, **were** ye to know with certainty of mind,

WERT

002:120	**Wert** thou to follow their desires after the knowledge
002:145	**wert** to follow their (vain) desires,-
002:145	Even if thou **wert** to bring to the people all the Signs
002:145	then **wert** thou indeed (clearly) in the wrong.
003:159	**Wert** thou severe or harsh-hearted, they would
006:035	yet if thou **wert** able to seek a tunnel
006:116	**Wert** thou to follow the common run
007:187	They ask thee as it thou **wert** eager in search thereof:
010:094	If thou **wert** in doubt as to what We have
011:007	But if thou **wert** to say to them, "Ye shall
013:037	**Wert** thou to follow their (vain) desires
039:065	"If thou **wert** to join (gods with Allah),
043:009	If thou **wert** to question them, 'Who created

WEST

002:115	To Allah belong the East and the **West**;
002:142	Say: To Allah belong both East and **West**:
002:177	ye turn your faces toward East or **West**;
002:258	do thou then cause it to rise from the **West**."
007:137	inheritors of lands in both East and **West**,-
024:035	neither of the East nor of the **West**, whose Oil
026:028	the East and the **West**, and all between!
043:038	the distance of East and **West**!"
070:040	of all points in the East and the **West** that We
073:009	(He is) Lord of the East and the **West**: there is

WESTERN

028:044	Thou wast not on the **Western** Side when We

WESTS

055:017	and Lord of the two **Wests**:

WHAT

002:003	and spend out of **what** We have provided
002:023	in doubt as to **what** We have revealed
002:025	they say: "Why this is **what** we were fed
002:026	"**What** means Allah by this similitude?"
002:027	and who sunder **what** Allah has ordered
002:030	He said: "I know **what** ye know not."
002:032	save **what** Thou hast taught Us:
002:033	and I know **what** ye reveal and **what** ye conceal?"
002:041	And believe in **what** I reveal,
002:042	when ye know (**what** it is).
002:061	to produce for us of **what** the earth groweth,
002:061	and ye shall find **what** ye want!"
002:063	(saying): "Hold firmly to **what** We have
002:063	(ever) to remembrance **what** is therein,
002:068	to make plain to us **what** heifer it is!"
002:068	now do **what** ye are commanded!"
002:070	to make plain to us **what** she is:
002:072	but Allah was to bring forth **what** ye did hide.

WHAT (continued)

002:074	And Allah is not unmindful of **what** ye do.
002:076	**what** Allah hath revealed to you,
002:077	**what** they conceal and **what** they reveal?
002:079	Woe to them for **what** their hands do write,
002:080	ye say of Allah **what** ye do not know?"
002:085	But **what** is the reward for those
002:085	For Allah is not unmindful of **what** ye do.
002:087	with **what** ye yourselves desire not,
002:089	confirming **what** is with them,
002:091	"We believe in **what** was sent down to us":
002:091	confirming **what** is with them.
002:091	"Believe in **what** Allah hath sent down,"
002:093	(saying): "Hold firmly to **what** We given you,
002:097	a confirmation of **what** went before,
002:101	confirming **what** was with them,
002:102	They followed **what** the Satans recited
002:102	And they learned **what** harmed them,
002:102	Not **what** profited them.
002:113	like unto their word is **what** those say who know not,
002:133	"**What** will ye worship after me?"
002:134	ye shall not be asked about **what** they did.
002:134	and ye of **what** ye do!
002:134	They shall reap the fruit of **what** they did,
002:140	But Allah is not unmindful of **what** ye do!
002:141	They shall reap the fruit of **what** they did,
002:141	About **what** they did!
002:141	and ye of **what** ye do!
002:142	"**What** hath turned them from the Qiblah
002:144	nor is Allah unmindful of **what** they do.
002:149	And Allah is not unmindful of **what** ye do.
002:168	O ye people! eat of **what** is on earth,
002:169	For he commands you **what** is evil and shameful,
002:170	"Follow **what** Allah hath revealed,"
002:170	**What**! even though their fathers were
002:175	Ah! **what** boldness (they show) for the Fire!
002:187	and seek **what** Allah hath ordained for you,
002:187	Allah knoweth **what** ye used to do secretly
002:202	To these will be allotted **what** they have earned.
002:204	to witness about **what** is in his heart;
002:215	They ask thee **what** they should spend (in charity).
002:219	say: "**What** is beyond your needs."
002:220	to do is **what** is for their good;
002:228	according to **what** is equitable;
002:228	to hide **what** Allah hath created in their wombs,
002:233	(the foster mother) **what** ye offered,
002:233	that Allah sees well **what** ye do.
002:234	And Allah is well acquainted with **what** ye do.
002:235	Allah knoweth **what** is in your hearts,
002:240	for **what** they do with themselves,
002:253	but Allah does **what** He wills.
002:255	He knoweth **what** (appeareth to his creatures as)
002:271	And Allah is well acquainted with **what** ye do.
002:278	and give up **what** remains of your demand
002:281	Then shall every soul be paid **what** it earned,
002:282	and not diminish aught of **what** he owes.
002:284	Whether ye show **what** is in your minds
002:285	The Messenger believeth in **what** hath been
003:003	confirming **what** went before it;
003:025	and each soul will be paid out just **what** it has earned,
003:029	Say: "Whether ye hide **what** is in your hearts
003:029	He knows **what** is in the heavens,
003:029	in the heavens, and **what** is on earth.

WHAT (continued)

003:035   **what** is in my womb for Thy special service:
003:036   And Allah knew best **what** she brought forth-
003:040   "Doth Allah accomplish **what** He willeth."
003:047   He said: "Even so; Allah createth **what** He willeth:
003:049   and I declare to you **what** ye eat,
003:049   and **what** ye store in your houses.
003:050   part of **what** was (before) forbidden to you;
003:053   "Our Lord! we believe in **what** thou hast revealed,
003:058   "This is **what** we rehearse unto thee of the Signs
003:072   "Believe in the morning **what** is revealed to the
003:080   **What**! would he bid you to unbelief after ye have
003:081   confirming **what** is with you;
003:084   and in **what** has been revealed to us and
003:084   and **what** was revealed to Abraham, Isma'il;
003:093   except **what** Israel made unlawful for himself
003:104   enjoining **what** is right, and forbidding **what** is wrong:
003:110   Enjoining **what** is right, forbidding **what** is wrong,
003:114   they enjoin **what** is right, and forbid **what** is wrong;
003:117   **What** they spend in the life of this
003:118   **what** their hearts conceal is far worse.
003:137   **what** was the end of those who rejected Truth.
003:154   test **what** is in your breasts and purge
003:154   **what** they dare not reveal to thee.
003:154   and purge **what** is in your hearts.
003:161   restore **what** he misappropriated;
003:165   **What**! when a single disaster smites you,
003:166   **What** ye suffered on the day the two armies met,
003:167   saying with their lips **what** was not in their hearts.
003:179   until He separates **what** is evil from **what** is good.
003:183   with Clear Signs and even with **what** ye ask for:
003:188   who exult in **what** they have brought about,
003:188   and love to be praised for **what** they have not done,
003:194   "Our Lord! grant us **what** Thou didst promise
003:197   **what** an evil bed (to lie on)!
004:006   let him have for himself **what** is just and reasonable.
004:007   From **what** is left by parents and those nearest
004:012   In **what** ye leave, their share
004:012   In **what** your wives leave, your share
004:022   your fathers married, except **what** is past:
004:023   except for **what** is past;
004:025   according to **what** is reasonable:
004:032   to men is allotted **what** they earn,
004:032   and to women **what** they earn:
004:034   **what** Allah would have them guard.
004:036   and **what** your right hands possess:
004:038   **what** a dreadful intimate he is!
004:039   **what** Allah hath given them for sustenance?
004:039   And **what** burden were it on them if they had faith
004:047   believe in **what** We have (now) revealed,
004:047   confirming **what** was (already) with you,
004:054   for **what** Allah hath given them of His bounty?
004:061   "Come to **what** Allah hath revealed,
004:063   Those men, Allah knows **what** is in their hearts;
004:066   but if they had done **what** they were (actually) told,
004:078   But **what** hath come to these people.
004:081   on things very different from **what** thou tellest them.
004:089   the way of Allah (from **what** is forbidden).
004:097   **What** an evil refuge!
004:097   They say: "In **what** (plight) were ye?"
004:104   but you hope from Allah, **what** they have not.
004:113   taught thee **what** thou knewest not (before):
004:115   and land him in Hell, **what** an evil refuge!

WHAT (continued)

004:127   and (remember) **what** hath been rehearsed unto you
004:147   **What** can Allah gain by your punishment.
004:162   believe in **what** hath been revealed to thee and
004:162   and **what** was revealed before thee:
004:166   But Allah beareth witness that **what** He hath
005:004   eat **what** they catch for you, but pronounce
005:004   and **what** ye have taught the beasts
005:004   They ask thee **what** is lawful to them (as food).
005:014   show them **what** it is they have done.
005:017   He createth **what** He pleaseth.
005:020   He had not given to any other among the peoples.
005:044   by **what** Allah hath revealed, they are Unbelievers.
005:045   by **what** Allah hath revealed, they are wrong-doers.
005:047   by **what** Allah hath revealed therein.
005:047   by **what** Allah hath revealed, they are indeed rebel.
005:048   so judge between them by **what** Allah hath revealed,
005:048   (but His Plan is) to test in **what** He hath given you:
005:049   between them by **what** Allah hath revealed,
005:070   a Messenger with **what** they themselves desired not
005:075   yet see in **what** ways they are deluded
005:077   the bounds (of **what** is proper),
005:081   and in **what** hath been revealed to him,
005:084   "**What** cause can we have not to believe in Allah
005:089   to account for **what** is void in your oaths,
005:093   there is no blame for **what** they ate
005:095   Allah forgives **what** is past: for repetition Allah
005:097   of **what** is in the heavens and on earth and that
005:104   "Come to **what** Allah hath revealed; come to
005:104   **What**! even though their fathers were void
005:109   and ask: "**What** was the response ye received
005:116   never could I say **what** I had no right (to say).
005:116   though I know not **what** is in Thine.
005:116   Thou knowest **what** is in my heart, though I
005:117   except **what** Thou didst command me to say, to wit,
006:003   He knoweth **what** ye hide, and **what** ye reveal,
006:005   the news of **what** they used to mock at.
006:011   **what** was the end of those who rejected Truth."
006:019   Say: "**What** thing is most weighty in evidence?"
006:028   will become manifest **what** before they concealed.
006:035   and bring them a Sign,-(**what** good?).
006:050   nor do I know **what** is hidden.
006:050   I but follow **what** is revealed to me."
006:057   **What** ye would see hastened, is not in my power.
006:058   Say: "If **what** ye would see hastened
006:093   reveal the like of **what** Allah hath revealed?"
006:100   (for He is) above **what** they attribute to Him!
006:106   Follow **what** thou art taught by inspiration
006:109   but **what** will make you (Muslims) realize
006:112   so leave them and **what** they forge.
006:113   and let them earn from it **what** they may.
006:119   in detail **what** is forbidden to you-except
006:129   turn to each other, because of **what** they earn.
006:136   Out of **what** Allah hath produced in abundance
006:137   but leave alone them and **what** they forged.
006:139   They say: "**What** is in the wombs of such and such
006:142   eat **what** Allah hath provided for you,
006:145   for it is an abomination,-or **what** is impious,
006:146   except **what** adheres to their backs or their entrails,
006:151   Say: "Come, I will rehearse **what** Allah hath
007:012   (Allah) said: "**What** prevented thee from
007:028   do ye say of Allah **what** ye know not?"
007:028   say: "Nay Allah never commands **what** is Indecent:

WHAT (continued)

007:048	saying: "Of **what** profit to you were your hoards
007:070	Bring us **what** thou threatenest us with,
007:076	we reject **what** ye believe in."
007:084	then see **what** was the end of those who
007:086	And see **what** was the end of those who did mischief.
007:088	He said: "**What**! even though we do detest (them)?
007:101	they would not believe **what** they had rejected before.
007:103	so see **what** was the end of those
007:110	then **what** is it ye counsel?"
007:157	**what** is good (and pure) and prohibits them from
007:157	for he commands them **what** is just and Forbids
007:157	and Forbids them **what** is evil:
007:157	and prohibits them from **what** is bad (and impure):
007:169	And they study **what** is in the Book.
007:171	"Hold firmly to **what** We have given you, and bring
007:171	and bring (ever) to remembrance **what** is therein;
007:180	for **what** they do, they will soon be requited.
007:185	In **what** message after this will they then believe?
007:199	Hold to forgiveness; command **what** is right;
007:203	Say: "I but follow **what** is revealed
008:034	But **what** plea have they that Allah
008:048	lo! I see **what** ye see not; lo! I
008:053	on a people until they change **what** is in their
008:069	But (now) enjoy **what** ye took in war, lawful
008:070	something better than **what** has been taken from you,
009:030	they but imitate **what** the Unbelievers of old
009:038	O ye who believe! **what** is the matter with you,
009:051	except **what** Allah has decreed for us:
009:059	content with **what** Allah and His Messenger gave them,
009:061	Say, "He listens to **what** is best for you;
009:064	showing them **what** is (really passing) in their
009:067	they enjoin evil, and forbid **what** in just,
009:071	they enjoin **what** is just, and forbid **what** is evil:
009:094	to Him Who knoweth **what** is hidden and **what** is open:
009:105	of **what** is hidden and **what** is open: then will He
009:115	makes clear to them as to **what** they should avoid,
010:015	I follow naught but **what** is revealed unto me:
010:018	besides Allah, **what** can hurt them not nor profit them,
010:032	apart from the Truth, **what** (remains) but error?
010:035	**What** then is the matter with you? How judge ye?
010:039	but see **what** was the end of those who did wrong!
010:041	Ye are free from responsibility for **what** I do,
010:041	and I for **what** ye do!"
010:046	thy lifetime) some part of **what** We promise them,-
010:050	**what** portion of it would the Sinners wish to hasten?
010:052	the recompense of **what** ye earned!'"
010:059	Say: "See ye **what** things Allah hath sent down
010:060	And **what** think those who forge lies against Allah,
010:066	**What** do they follow who worship as His "partners"
010:068	Say ye about Allah **what** ye know not?
010:073	Then see **what** was the end of those who
010:074	but they would not believe **what** they had
010:080	Moses said to them: "Throw ye **what** ye (wish)
010:081	Moses said: "**What** ye have brought is sorcery:
010:094	If thou wert in doubt as to **what** We have
010:102	but (**what** happened in) the days of the men who
010:104	(behold!) I worship not **what** ye worship
011:005	He knoweth **what** they conceal, and **what** they reveal:
011:008	they are sure to say, "**What** keeps it back?"
011:012	(feel the inclination) to give up of **what** is revealed unto
011:031	nor do I know **what** is hidden, nor claim
011:031	Allah knoweth best **what** is in their souls:

WHAT (continued)

011:032	now bring upon us **what** thou threatenest us with,
011:062	forbid us the worship of **what** our fathers worshipped?
011:063	**What** then would ye add to my (portion)
011:079	indeed thou knowest quite well **what** we want!"
011:081	to her will happen **what** happens to the people.
011:087	off doing **what** we like with our property?
011:091	They said: "O Shu'aib! much of **what** thou sayest
011:107	Accomplisher of **what** He planneth.
011:109	Be not then in doubt as to **what** these men worship.
011:109	but **what** their fathers worshipped before (them):
012:025	She said: "**What** is the (fitting) punishment for
012:032	and (**what** is more) be in the company of the vilest!"
012:048	which will devour **what** ye shall have laid
012:050	and ask him, '**What** was the matter with the ladies who
012:051	"**What** was your affair when ye did seek to seduce
012:065	**What** (more) can we desire?
012:071	"**What** is it that ye miss?"
012:074	(The Egyptians) said: "**What** then shall be
012:077	and Allah knoweth best the truth of **what** ye assert!"
012:081	we bear witness only to **what** we know,
012:089	not knowing (**what** ye were doing)?"
012:102	Such is one of the stories of **what** happened unseen,
012:109	through the earth, and see **what** was the end of
012:111	but a confirmation of **what** went before it,-
013:008	Allah doth know **what** every female (womb)
013:011	until they change **what** is in themselves but when
013:018	**what** a bed of misery!
013:030	mightest rehearse unto them **what** We send down
013:036	rejoice at **what** hath been revealed unto thee:
013:039	Allah doth blot out or confirm **what** He pleaseth:
013:040	(within thy lifetime) part of **what** We promised
014:010	Ye wish to turn us away from **what** our fathers
014:027	Allah doeth **what** He willeth.
014:038	Thou dost know **what** we conceal and **what** we reveal:
014:044	"**What**! were ye not wont to swear aforetime
015:032	(Allah) said: "O Iblis! **what** is your reason for
015:054	Of **what**, then, is your good news?"
015:057	Abraham said: "**What** then is the business on which ye
015:088	(Wistfully) at **what** We have bestowed on certain
015:094	Therefore expound openly **what** thou art commanded,
015:097	is distressed at **what** they say.
016:019	And Allah doth know **what** ye conceal,
016:019	and **what** ye reveal.
016:023	Undoubtedly Allah doth know **what** they conceal,
016:023	and **what** they reveal:
016:024	"**What** is it that your Lord has revealed?"
016:030	"**What** is it that your Lord has revealed?" they say
016:035	But **what** is the mission of messengers but to
016:036	**what** was the end of those who denied (the Truth).
016:044	thou mayest explain clearly to men **what** is sent for them,
016:057	Glory be to Him!-and for themselves **what** they desire!
016:059	Ah! **what** an evil (choice) they decide on!
016:062	They attribute to Allah **what** they hate
016:066	From **what** is within their bodies,
016:096	**What** is with you must vanish:
016:096	**what** is with Allah will endure.
016:101	and Allah knows best **what** He reveals (in stages),-
017:025	Your Lord knoweth best **what** is in your hearts:
017:047	We know best **what** it is they listen, when they
017:048	See **what** similes thy strike for thee: but they
017:049	They say: "**What**! when we are reduced to bones

WHAT (continued)

017:094	**What** kept men back from Belief when Guidance
018:005	**What** they say in nothing but falsehood!
018:008	Verily **what** is on earth We shall make but as
018:015	an authority clear (and convincing) for **what** they do?
018:027	And recite (and teach) **what** has been revealed
018:042	over **what** he had spent on his property,
018:049	in great terror because of **what** is (recorded)
018:049	"Ah! woe to us! **what** a book is this! It leaves
018:055	And **what** is there to keep back men from believing,
018:058	(at once) to account for **what** they have earned,
018:063	He replied: "Sawest thou (**what** happened) when we
018:064	Moses said: "That was **what** we were seeking after":
018:091	We completely understood **what** was before him.
019:005	"Now I fear (**what**) my relatives (and colleagues)
019:054	he was (strictly) true to **what** he promised,
019:064	to Him belongeth **what** is before us
019:064	and **what** is behind us, and **what** is between:
019:066	Man says: "**What**! when I am dead, shall I
019:079	Nay! We shall record **what** he says, and We
020:006	To Him belongs **what** is in the heavens
020:007	knoweth **what** is secret and **what** is yet more hidden.
020:017	And **what** is that in thy right hand, O Moses?"
020:028	"So they may understand **what** I say:
020:051	(Pharaoh) said: "**What** then is the condition of
020:069	**What** they have faked is but a magician's trick:
020:072	to **what** has come to us of the Clear Signs
020:083	"**What** made thee hasten in advance of thy people,
020:087	and that was **what** the Samiri suggested.
020:092	(Moses) said: "O Aaron! **what** kept thee back,
020:095	(Moses) said: "**What** then is thy case, O Samiri?"
020:096	He replied: "I saw **what** they saw not: so I
020:099	We relate some stories of **what** happened before:
020:104	We know best **what** they will say, when the
020:110	He knows **what** is before or after or behind them:
020:112	nor of any curtailment (of **what** is his due).
020:130	Therefore be patient with **what** they say,
021:022	(high is He) above **what** they attribute to Him!
021:028	He knows **what** is before them,
021:028	and **what** is behind them, and they
021:052	"**What** are these images, to which ye are
021:102	**what** their souls desired, in that
021:108	Say: "**What** has come to me by inspiration
021:110	"It is He Who knows **what** is open in speech
021:110	in speech and **what** ye hide (in your hearts).
022:020	With it will be melted **what** is within their bodies
022:035	and spend (in charity) out of **what** We have
022:068	say, "Allah knows best **what** it is ye are doing."
022:076	and **what** is behind them:
022:076	He knows **what** is before them and
023:033	he eats and drinks of **what** ye drink.
023:081	similar to **what** the ancients said.
023:082	They say: "**What**! when we die and become
023:091	each god would have taken away **what** he had created,
023:092	He knows **what** is hidden and **what** is open:
023:112	He will say: "**What** number of years did ye
024:021	he will (but) command **what** is indecent and wrong:
024:026	these are not affected by **what** people say:
024:027	in order that ye may heed (**what** is seemly).
024:029	has knowledge of **what** ye reveal and **what** ye conceal.
024:031	and ornaments except **what** (ordinarily) appear thereof;
024:045	Allah creates **what** He wills; for verily
024:064	Well doth He know **what** ye are intent upon:

WHAT (continued)

024:064	He will tell them the truth of **what** they did:
025:007	And they say: "**What** sort of a messenger is this,
025:009	See **what** kinds of companions they make for thee!
025:019	"Now have they proved you liars in **what** ye say:
025:060	They say, "And **what** is (Allah) Most Gracious?
026:006	the truth of **what** they mocked at!
026:023	Pharaoh said: "And **what** is the Lord and Cherisher
026:025	"Do ye not listen (to **what** he says)?"
026:035	then **what** is it ye counsel?"
026:070	he said to his father and his people: "**What** worship ye?"
026:074	"Nay, but we found our fathers doing thus (**what** we do)."
026:112	He said: "And **what** do I know as to **what** they do?
026:188	He said: "My Lord knows best **what** ye do."
026:216	"I am free (of responsibility) for **what** ye do!"
026:226	And that they say **what** they practice not?-
026:227	know **what** vicissitudes their affairs will take!
027:014	so see **what** was the end of those who acted corruptly!
027:025	and knows **what** ye hide and **what** ye reveal.
027:025	brings forth **what** is hidden in the heavens
027:028	and (wait to) see **what** answer they return"...
027:033	so consider **what** thou wilt command."
027:035	**what** (answer) return (my) ambassadors."
027:051	Then see **what** was the end of their plot!-
027:054	"Do ye do **what** is indecent though ye see
027:063	High is Allah above **what** they associate with Him!
027:065	except Allah, knows **what** is hidden:
027:067	The Unbelievers say:" **What**! when we become dust,-
027:069	and see **what** has been the end of those guilty (of sin)."
027:084	them not in knowledge, or **what** was it ye did?"
028:006	**what** they were dreading from them.
028:009	And they perceived not (**what** they were doing)!
028:023	He said: "**What** is the matter with you?" They said:
028:028	Be Allah a witness to **what** we say."
028:040	now behold **what** was the End of those
028:054	out of **what** We have given them.
028:065	and say: "**What** was the answer ye gave to the
028:071	**what** god is there other than Allah, who can
028:072	**what** god is there other than Allah, who can
028:079	"Oh! that we had the like of **what** Qarun has got!
029:045	Recite **what** is sent of the Book by inspiration
029:052	He knows **what** is in the heavens and on earth.
029:064	**What** is the life of this world but amusement
030:009	and see **what** was the End of those before them?
030:036	evil afflicts them become of **what** their (own)
030:038	So give **what** is due to kindred, the needy
030:042	and see **what** was the End of those before (you):
031:011	now show Me **what** is there that others besides Him
031:017	enjoin **what** is just, and forbid **what** is wrong:
031:021	**What**! even if it is Satan beckoning them to the
031:034	and He Who knows **what** is in the wombs.
031:034	nor does anyone know in **what** land he is to die.
031:034	Nor does any one know **what** it is that he will earn
032:010	And they say: "**What**! when we lie, hidden and
032:017	Now no person knows **what** delights of the eye
033:005	(**what** counts is) the intention of your hearts:
033:006	nevertheless do ye **what** is just to your closest friends:
033:022	"This is **what** Allah and His Messenger had promised
033:022	and Allah and His Messenger told us **what** was true."
033:034	And recite **what** is rehearsed to you
033:038	no difficulty to the Prophet in **what** Allah has indicated
033:050	We know **what** We have appointed for them
033:063	and **what** will make thee understand?-

WHAT (continued)

034:009	See they not **what** is before them and behind
034:023	will they say, '**What** is it that your Lord commanded?'
034:025	nor shall they be questioned as to **what** ye do."
034:045	a tenth of **what** We had granted to those:
035:002	**What** Allah out of His Mercy doth bestow
035:002	**what** He doth withhold, none can
035:029	and spend (in Charity) out of **what** We have
035:031	confirming **what** was (revealed) before it:
035:040	Show me **what** it is they have created
035:044	and see **what** was the End of those before them,-
035:045	were to punish man according to **what** they deserve,
036:026	my People knew (**what** I know)!-
036:048	if **what** ye say is true?"
036:052	"This is **what** The Most Gracious had promised.
036:076	We know **what** they hide
036:076	We know **what** they hide as well as **what** they disclose.
037:016	"**What**! when we die, and become dust and bones,
037:025	"'**What** is the matter with you that ye help not each other?"
037:036	And say: "**What**! Shall we give up our gods
037:039	And you are requited naught save **what** ye did.
037:073	Then see **what** was the end of those
037:085	father and his people, "**What** is that which ye worship?
037:087	"Then **what** is your idea about the Lord of the Worlds?"
037:092	"**What** is the matter with you that ye speak not?"
037:102	I offer thee in sacrifice: now see **what** is thy view!"
037:154	**What** is the matter with you? How judge ye?
037:180	(He is free) from **what** they ascribe (to Him)!
038:008	"**What**! Has the Message been sent to him-
038:017	Have patience at **what** they say, and remember
038:075	(Allah) said: "O Iblis! **what** prevents thee from
039:008	(man) doth forget **what** he cried and prayed for before,
039:015	"Serve ye **what** ye will besides Him."
039:024	"Taste ye (the fruits of) **what** ye earned!"
039:035	to the best of **what** they have done.
039:043	**What**! Do they take for intercessors others
040:017	That day will every soul be requited for **what** it earned;
040:021	and see **what** was the End of those before them?
040:026	**What** I fear is lest he should change your religion,
040:044	"Soon will ye remember **what** I say to you (now).
040:077	thee (in this life) some part of **what** We promise them,-
040:082	and see **what** was the end of those before them?
041:005	so do thou (**what** thou wilt); for us,
041:005	for us, we shall do (**what** we will!)"
041:015	**What**! did they not see that Allah,
041:017	seized them, because of **what** they had earned.
041:025	who made alluring to them **what** was before them
041:034	Repel (Evil) with **what** is better:
041:040	Do **what** ye will: Verily He seeth (clearly)
041:044	**What**! a foreign (tongue) and (a Messenger) an Arab?"
042:009	**What**! Have they taken (for worship)
042:017	and the Balance and **what** will make thee realize
042:021	**What**! have they partners (in godhead), who have
042:022	in fear on account of **what** they have earned,
042:024	**What**! Do they say, "He has forged a falsehood
042:038	of **what** We bestow on them for Sustenance;
042:049	He creates **what** He wills.
042:051	with Allah's permission, **what** Allah wills:
042:052	not (before) **what** was revelation, and **what** was Faith;
043:016	**What**! Has He taken Daughters out of
043:016	out of **what** He Himself creates, and granted
043:017	(the birth of) **what** he sets up as a likeness to (Allah)
043:021	**What**! have We given them a Book before this,

WHAT (continued)

043:024	He said: "**What**! even if I brought you better
043:025	now see **what** was the end of those who
043:026	"I do indeed clear myself of **what** ye worship:
043:051	**What**! see ye not then?
043:079	**What**! have they settled some Plan
044:036	if **what** ye say is true!"
044:037	**What**! are they better than the people of Tubba
044:050	"Truly this is **what** ye used to doubt!"
045:006	then in **what** exposition will they believe after
045:014	each People according to **what** they have earned.
045:021	**What**! do those who do evil deeds think that
045:022	soul may find the recompense of **what** it has earned,
045:024	And they say: "**What** is there but our life in this world?
045:025	"Bring (back) our forefathers, if **what** ye say is true!"
045:032	ye used to say, 'We know not **what** is the Hour:
045:033	will appear to them the evil (fruits) of **what** they did,
046:004	Show me **what** it is they have created on earth,
046:004	Say: "Do ye see **what** it is ye invoke beside Allah?
046:009	nor do I know **what** will be done with me or with you.
046:030	revealed after Moses, confirming **what** came before it:
047:010	and see **what** was the End of those before them
047:016	"**What** is it he said just then?"
047:021	Were it to obey and say **what** is just, and when
047:026	who hate **what** Allah has revealed,
048:010	one who fulfills **what** he has covenanted with Allah,-
048:011	They say with their tongues **what** is not in their hearts.
048:018	He knew **what** was in their hearts, and He
048:027	For He knew **what** ye knew not,
049:006	become full of repentance for **what** ye have done.
049:016	Say: "**What**! Will ye tell Allah about your Religion?"
050:003	"**What**! when we die and become dust,
050:016	and We know **what** suggestions his soul makes to him:
050:025	"Who forbade **what** was good, transgressed all
050:032	"This is **what** was promised for you,-
050:045	We know best **what** they say; and thou
051:014	this is **what** ye used to ask to be hastened!"
051:031	(Abraham) said: "And **what**, O ye Messengers,
053:010	to His Servant-(conveyed) **what** He (meant) to convey.
053:012	Will ye then dispute with him concerning **what** he saw?
053:016	Behold, the Lote-tree was shrouded with **what** shrouds.
053:021	**What**! for you the male sex, and for
053:023	nothing but conjecture and **what** their own souls desire!-
053:031	and he rewards those who do good, with **what** is best.
053:035	**What**! Has he knowledge of the Unseen so that
053:036	is he not acquainted with **what** is in the books of Moses-
053:039	That man can have nothing but **what** he strives for;
054:024	For they said: "**What**! a man! a solitary from among
056:008	**what** will be the Companions of the Right Hand?
056:009	**what** will be the Companions of the Left Hand?
056:027	**what** will be the Companions of the Right Hand!
056:041	**what** will be the Companions of the Left Hand!
056:047	"**What**! when we die and become dust and bones,
057:004	He knows **what** enters within the earth
057:004	within the earth and **what** comes forth out of it,
057:004	**what** comes down from heaven and **what** mounts up to
057:020	And **what** is the life of this world,
058:007	will He tell them **what** they did on the Day of Judgment.
059:006	**What** Allah has bestowed on His Messenger
059:007	So take **what** the Messenger gives you,
059:007	**What** Allah has bestowed on His Messenger
059:007	and refrain from **what** He prohibits you.
059:018	and let every soul look to **what** (provision) he has

WHAT (continued)

060:010	ask for **what** ye have spent on their dowers,
060:010	the Unbelievers **what** they have spent (on their dower).
060:010	and let the (Unbelievers) ask for **what** they have spent
060:011	wives have deserted the equivalent of **what** they had spent
064:004	He knows **what** is in the heavens and on earth;
064:004	and He knows **what** ye conceal and **what** ye reveal:
064:018	Knower of **what** is hidden and **what** is open,
065:006	according to **what** is just and reasonable.
065:007	on any person beyond **what** He has given him.
065:007	spend according to **what** Allah has given him.
066:006	but do (precisely) **what** they are commanded.
068:036	**What** is the matter with you? How judge ye?
069:002	**What** is the Sure Reality?
069:003	**what** will make thee realize **what** the Sure Reality is?
069:038	So I do call to witness **what** ye see
069:039	And **what** ye see not,
070:036	Now **what** is the matter with the Unbelievers
071:013	"**What** is the matter with you, the ye
072:023	"Unless I deliver **what** I receive from Allah
073:010	And have patience with **what** they say, and leave
074:027	And **what** will explain to thee **what** Hell-Fire is?
074:031	Unbelievers may say, "**What** doth Allah intend by this?"
074:042	"**What** led you into Hell-Fire?"
074:049	Then **what** is the matter with them that they
077:007	Assuredly, **what** ye are promised must come to pass.
077:012	For **what** Day are these (Portents) deferred?
077:014	**what** will explain to thee **what** is the Day of Sorting out?
077:050	Then **what** Message, after that, will they believe in?
078:001	Concerning **what** are they disputing?
078:038	and he will say **what** is right.
079:010	They say (now): "**What**! shall we indeed be returned
079:011	"**What**!-when we shall have become rotten bones?"
079:027	**What**! Are ye the more difficult to create or the
080:003	But **what** could tell thee but that perchance
080:017	Woe to man! **what** hath made him reject Allah?
080:018	From **what** stuff Hath He created him?
080:023	**what** Allah Hath commanded him.
081:009	For **what** crime she was killed;
081:014	(Then) shall each soul know **what** it has put forward.
082:005	it hath sent forward and (**what** it hath) kept back.
082:005	(Then) shall each soul know **what** it hath sent
082:006	O man! **what** has seduced thee from thy Lord
082:017	**what** will explain to thee **what** the Day of Judgment is?
082:018	**what** will explain to thee **what** the Day of Judgment is?
083:008	And **what** will explain to thee **what** Sijjin is?
083:019	And **what** will explain to thee **what** 'Illiyin is?
083:036	the Unbelievers have been paid back for **what** they did?
084:004	And casts forth **what** is within it and becomes
084:020	**What** then is the matter with them, that they
084:023	full knowledge of **what** they secrete (in their breasts).
086:002	**what** will explain to thee **what** the Night-Visitant is?-
086:005	Now let man but think from **what** he is created!
087:007	for He knoweth **what** is manifest and **what** is hidden.
090:012	And **what** will explain to thee the path that is steep?-
095:007	**What** then, can after this make you deny the last
097:002	**what** will explain to thee **what** the Night of Power is?
099:003	'**What** is the matter with her?'-
101:002	**What** is the (Day) of Clamour?
101:003	**what** will explain to thee **what** the (Day) of Noise
101:010	And **what** will explain to Thee **what** this is?
104:005	**what** will explain to thee That which Breaks to Pieces?

WHATEVER

002:110	and **whatever** good ye send forth
002:197	And **whatever** good ye do,
002:215	Say: **Whatever** wealth ye spend that is good,
002:215	And **whatever** ye do that is good,
002:251	and taught him **whatever** (else) He willed.
002:265	Allah seeth well **whatever** ye do.
002:270	And **whatever** ye spend in charity or
002:270	or **whatever** you vow to make,
002:272	**Whatever** of good ye give benefits your own soul,
002:272	**Whatever** good ye give, shall be rendered
002:273	And **whatever** of good ye give,
003:092	and **whatever** ye give, Allah knoweth it well.
003:161	shall every soul receive its due **whatever** it earned,
004:079	but **whatever** evil happens to thee, is from
004:079	**Whatever** good, (O man!) happens to thee,
006:012	there is no doubt **whatever**, it is they
006:059	He knoweth **whatever** there is on the earth
006:135	Say: "O my people! do **whatever** ye can: I will
007:132	"**Whatever** be the Signs thou bringest, to work
008:060	**Whatever** ye shall spend in the cause of Allah,
010:055	to Allah belongeth **whatever** is in the heavens
010:061	In **whatever** business thou mayest be,
010:061	and **whatever** portion thou mayest be reciting
010:061	and **whatever** deed ye (mankind) may be doing,-
011:093	"And O my people! do **whatever** ye can: I will
011:121	"Do **whatever** ye can: we shall do our part;
012:038	could we attribute any partners **whatever** to Allah:
012:040	**Whatever** ye worship apart from Him is nothing
013:015	**Whatever** beings there are in the heavens
014:038	for nothing **whatever** is hidden from Allah,
016:052	To Him belongs **whatever** is in the heavens
017:110	by **whatever** name ye call upon Him, (it is well):
020:072	So decree **whatever** thou desirest to degree:
024:064	doth belong **whatever** is in the heavens and on
025:023	And We shall turn to **whatever** deeds they did
029:042	of (everything) **whatever** that they call upon
030:054	He creates **whatever** He wills, and it
031:017	and bear with patient constancy **whatever** betide thee;
031:030	and because **whatever** else they invoke besides
034:047	Say: "**Whatever** reward do I ask of you:
035:044	to be frustrated by anything **whatever** in the
036:023	of no use **whatever** will be their intercession
036:057	they shall have **whatever** they call for;
039:039	Say: "O my people! Do **whatever** ye can: I will
039:043	no power **whatever** and no intelligence?"
042:010	**Whatever** it be wherein ye differ, the decision
042:011	there is nothing **whatever** like unto Him, and He
042:015	"I believe in **whatever** Book Allah has sent down;
042:030	**Whatever** misfortune happens to you, is because
042:036	**Whatever** ye are given (here) is (but)
042:053	**whatever** is in the heavens and **whatever** is on earth.
051:042	It left nothing **whatever** that it came up against,
053:023	for which Allah has sent down no authority (**whatever**).
057:001	**Whatever** is in the heavens and on earth,-
057:029	that they have no power **whatever** over the Grace
058:017	Of no profit **whatever** to them, against Allah,
059:001	**Whatever** is in the heavens and on earth,
059:005	**Whatever** ye cut down (O ye Muslims!) of the tender
059:024	**whatever** is in the heavens and on earth,
060:004	"We are clear of you and of **whatever** ye worship
060:012	any other thing **whatever** with Allah, that they
064:001	**Whatever** is in the heavens and on earth,

WHATEVER (continued)

068:038 That ye shall have, through it **whatever** ye choose?
068:039 shall have **whatever** ye shall demand?
073:020 And **whatever** good ye send forth for yourselves,
082:008 In **whatever** Form He wills, does He

WHATSOEVER

018:026 with any person **whatsoever**.

WHEN

002:011 **When** it is said to them: "Make not mischief
002:013 **When** it is said to them: "Believe as the others
002:014 but **when** they are alone with their evil ones,
002:014 **When** they meet those who believe.
002:017 **when** it lighted all around him,
002:020 and **when** the darkness grows on them,
002:022 unto Allah **when** ye know (the truth).
002:033 "**When** he had told them their names,
002:035 things therein as (where and **when**) ye will;
002:042 nor conceal the Truth **when** ye know (what it is).
002:048 a day **when** one soul shall not avail another
002:074 which **when** split asunder send fort water;
002:076 Behold! **when** they meet the men of Faith,
002:076 but **when** they meet each other in private,
002:089 And **when** there comes; to them a Book
002:089 **when** there comes to them that which they (should)
002:091 **When** it is said to them, "Believe in what Allah
002:101 And **when** came to them a Messenger
002:117 **when** He decreeth a matter He saith to it: "Be,"
002:123 a day **when** one soul shall not avail another,
002:133 **when** Death appeared before Jacob?
002:156 Who say, **when** afflicted with calamity:
002:170 **When** it is said to them: "Follow what Allah
002:180 It is prescribed, **when** death approaches
002:186 of every suppliant **when** he calleth on Me:
002:186 **When** My servants ask thee concerning Me,
002:196 and **when** ye are in peaceful conditions (again),
002:198 Then **when** ye pour down from (Mount) 'Arafat,
002:200 So **when** ye have accomplished your rites,
002:205 **When** he turns his back,
002:206 **When** it is said to him, "Fear God,"
002:214 "**When** (will come) the help of Allah"
002:222 But **when** they have purified themselves,
002:223 so approach your tilth **when** or how ye will;
002:229 except **when** both parties fear that
002:231 **When** ye divorce women, and they (are about to)
002:232 **When** ye divorce women,
002:234 **when** they have fulfilled their term,
002:239 but **when** ye are in security,
002:246 But **when** they were commanded to fight,
002:247 authority over us **when** we are better fitted
002:249 **When** they crossed the river,
002:249 **When** Talut set forth with the armies,
002:250 **When** they advanced to meet Goliath
002:254 **when** no bargaining (will avail),
002:259 **When** this was shown clearly to him,
002:267 **when** ye yourselves would not receive it
002:281 **when** ye shall be brought back to Allah.
002:282 O ye who believe! **when** ye deal with each other,
002:282 refuse **when** they are called on (for evidence).
003:025 But how (will they fare) **when** We gather them
003:030 "On the day **when** every soul will be confronted
003:036 **When** she was delivered, she said: "O my Lord!
003:044 **when** they dispute (the point).
003:044 **when** they cast lots with pens,

WHEN (continued)

003:047 how shall I have a son **when** man hath touched Me?"
003:047 **when** He hath decreed a matter,
003:052 **When** Jesus found unbelief on their part
003:065 **when** the Torah and the Gospel were not revealed
003:098 **when** Allah is Himself witness to all ye do?
003:106 On the day **when** some faces will be
003:112 except **when** under a covenant (of protection)
003:119 but **when** they are alone,
003:119 **when** they meet you, they say, "We believe";
003:123 **when** ye were helpless:
003:152 His promise to you **when** we with His permission
003:156 **when** they are travelling through the earth
003:159 Then, **when** thou hast taken a decision,
003:164 on the Believers **when** He sent among them
003:165 What! **when** a single disaster smites you,
004:002 their property (**when** they reach their age),
004:006 **When** ye release their property to them,
004:021 **when** ye have gone in unto each other,
004:025 **when** they are taken in wedlock,
004:043 except **when** you are passing by (through the mosque),
004:058 and **when** ye judge between people that ye
004:061 **When** it is said to them: "Come to what
004:062 How then, **when** they are seized by misfortune.
004:064 If they had only, **when** they were unjust
004:077 **When** (at length) the order for fighting
004:081 but **when** they leave thee, a section
004:083 **When** there comes to them some matter
004:086 **When** a (courteous) greeting is offered you,
004:094 O ye who believe! **when** ye go out in the cause
004:097 **When** angels take the souls of those who die
004:101 **When** ye travel through the earth, there is
004:102 **when** they finish their prostrations, let them
004:102 **When** thou (O Messenger) art with them,
004:103 **When** ye have performed the prayers, remember
004:103 but **when** ye are free from danger, set up
004:108 while He is with them **when** they plot by night.
004:140 that **when** ye hear the Message of Allah
004:142 **When** they stand up to prayer, they stand
005:002 But **when** ye are clear of the Sacred Precincts
005:005 **when** ye give them their due dowers, and desire
005:006 O ye who believe! **when** ye prepare for prayer, wash
005:007 **when** ye said: "We hear and we obey":
005:011 unto you **when** certain men formed the design to
005:020 **when** He produced prophets among you, made you
005:023 **when** once ye are in, victory will be yours;
005:043 **when** they have (their own) Torah before them?
005:058 **When** ye proclaim your call to prayer, they take
005:061 **When** they come to thee, they say: "We believe":
005:083 And **when** they listen to the revelation
005:093 **when** they guard themselves from evil, and believe,-
005:101 **when** the Qur'an is being revealed, they will
005:104 **When** it is said to them: "Come to what Allah
005:106 O ye who believe! **when** death approaches any of you,
005:106 witnesses among yourselves **when** making bequests,-
005:109 On the day **when** Allah will gather the
005:110 (violence to) thee **when** thou didst show them
005:117 **when** Thou didst take me up thou wast the Watcher
006:005 And now they rejected the truth **when** it reaches them:
006:025 in so much that **when** they come to thee,
006:027 **when** they shall be made to stand by the Fire!
006:030 **when** they shall be made to stand before
006:043 **When** the suffering reached them from Us,

WHEN (continued)

006:044 But **when** they forget the warning
006:044 **when** lo! they were plunged in despair!
006:054 **When** those come to thee who believe
006:061 At length, **when** death approaches one of you.
006:063 **when** ye call upon Him in humility
006:068 **When** thou seest men engaged in vain
006:076 But **when** it set, he said: "I love not
006:076 **When** the night covered him over, he saw
006:077 **When** he saw the moon rising in splendor, He said:
006:077 But **when** the moon set, he said: "Unless my
006:078 But **when** the sun set, he said: "O my people!
006:078 **When** he saw the sun rising (in splendor),
006:080 about Allah, **when** He (Himself) hath guided me?
006:081 **when** ye fear not to give partners to Allah without
006:091 do they make **when** they say: "Nothing doth Allah send
006:093 **when** he hath received none, or (again)
006:099 **when** they begin to bear fruit, feast your
006:101 **when** He hath no consort? He
006:114 **When** He it is Who hath sent
006:119 **when** He hath explained to you in detail
006:124 **When** there comes to them a Sign
006:128 On the day **when** He will gather them
006:144 Were ye present **when** Allah ordered
006:164 **When** He is the Cherisher of all
007:005 **When** (thus) Our punishment took them, no cry
007:012 thee from prostrating **when** I commanded thee?"
007:022 **when** they tasted of the tree, their shameful
007:028 **When** they commit an indecency, they say: "We
007:034 Appointed: **when** their term is reached, not an hour
007:037 until, **when** Our messengers (of death) arrive
007:047 **When** their eyes shall be turned towards
007:053 On the day **when** it is fulfilled those who
007:057 **when** they have carried the heavy-laden clouds.
007:116 So **when** they threw, they bewitched
007:126 in the Signs of our Lord **when** they reached us!
007:131 But **when** good (times) came, they said,
007:131 **when** gripped by calamity, they ascribed it
007:134 And **when** the Plague fell on them, they said:
007:135 But **when** We removed the Plague from them
007:140 **when** it is He who hath endowed you with
007:143 **When** his Lord manifested Himself to the mount,
007:143 **When** he recovered his senses he said: "Glory be
007:143 **When** Moses came to the place appointed by Us,
007:149 **When** they repented, and saw that
007:150 **When** Moses came back to his people, angry and
007:154 **When** the anger of Moses was appeased, he took
007:155 **when** they were seized with violent quaking,
007:160 **when** his (thirsty) people asked him for Water:
007:164 **When** some of them said: "Why do ye preach to a
007:165 **When** they disregarded the warnings that had
007:166 **When** in their insolence they transgressed
007:171 **When** We raised the mount over them, as if
007:172 **When** thy Lord drew forth from the
007:187 None be He can reveal as to **when** it will occur.
007:187 the final Hour-**when** will be its appointed time?
007:189 **When** they are united, she bears
007:189 **When** she grows heavy, they both
007:190 But **when** He giveth them a goodly child,
007:201 bring Allah to remembrance **when** lo! they see (aright)
007:201 **when** a thought of evil from Satan
007:204 **When** the Qur'an is read, listen to
008:002 **when** Allah is mentioned, fell a tremor

WHEN (continued)

008:002 and **when** they hear His revelations rehearsed,
008:015 O ye who believe! **when** ye meet the Unbelievers
008:017 **when** thou threwest (a handful of dust) ,
008:020 from him **when** ye hear (him speak).
008:024 **when** He calleth you to that which will give you life;
008:026 Call to mind **when** ye were a small (band),
008:031 **When** Our Signs are rehearsed to them, they say:
008:034 **when** they keep out (men) from the Sacred Mosque-
008:044 And remember **when** ye met, He showed
008:045 **when** ye meet a force, be firm, and call
008:048 but **when** the two forces came in sight
008:050 **when** the angels take the souls of the
009:005 But **when** the forbidden months are past, then fight
009:035 On the Day **when** it will be heated in the fire of Hell,
009:038 that, **when** ye are asked to go forth in the Cause of Allah,
009:040 help him, **when** the Unbelievers drove him out:
009:076 But **when** He did bestow of His bounty, they became
009:086 **When** a Sura comes down, enjoining them to believe
009:092 and **when** thou saidst, "I can find no mounts for you,"
009:094 present their excuses to you **when** ye return to them.
009:095 **when** ye return to them, that ye
009:114 But **when** it became clear to him that he was
009:122 and admonish the people **when** they return to them,-
010:012 **When** trouble toucheth a man, he crieth to Us
010:012 But **when** We have removed his affliction,
010:013 Generations before you We destroyed **when** they did
010:015 But **when** Our Clear Signs are rehearsed unto them,
010:021 **When** We make mankind taste of some mercy
010:022 till **when** ye even board ships;-they sail
010:023 But **when** He delivereth them, behold! they
010:045 And on the day **when** He will gather them together:
010:047 **when** their Messenger comes (before them),
010:048 They say: "**When** will this promise come to pass-
010:049 a term appointed: **when** their term is reached,
010:051 **when** it actually cometh to pass?
010:054 **when** they see the Chastisement:
010:061 **when** ye are deeply engrossed therein.
010:076 **When** the Truth did come to them from Us, they said:
010:077 **when** it hath (actually) reached you?
010:080 **When** the sorcerers came, Moses said
010:081 **When** they had had their throw, Moses said:
010:090 At length, **when** overwhelmed with the flood, he said
010:098 **When** they believed, We removed from them
011:005 Ah! even **when** they cover themselves
011:024 Are they equal **when** compared?
011:028 compel you to accept it **when** ye are averse to it?
011:058 So **when** Our decree issued, We saved Hud
011:066 **When** Our Decree issued, We saved Salih
011:070 But **when** he saw their hands not reaching
011:074 **When** fear had passed from (the mind of) Abraham
011:077 **When** Our Messengers came to Lut, he was
011:082 **When** Our decree issued, We turned (the cities)
011:094 **When** Our decree issued, We saved Shu'aib
011:101 **when** there issued the decree of thy Lord: nor did
011:102 **when** He chastises communities in the midst of
012:022 **When** Joseph attained his full manhood, We gave
012:028 So **when** he saw his shirt,-that it
012:031 **When** they saw him, they did extol him,
012:031 **When** she heard of their malicious talk, she sent
012:050 But **when** the messenger came to him, (Joseph) said:
012:051 **when** ye did seek to seduce Joseph"?
012:054 Therefore **when** he had spoken to him, he said:

WHEN (continued)

012:056 to take possession therein **as when,** or where he pleased.
012:059 And **when** he had furnished them forth
012:062 they should know it only **when** they return to their people;
012:063 Now **when** they returned to their father, they said:
012:064 with any result other than **when** I trusted you with
012:065 Then **when** they opened their baggage, they found
012:066 (and made powerless) and **when** they had sworn
012:068 And **when** they entered in the manner
012:069 Now **when** they came into Joseph's presence,
012:070 At length **when** he had furnished them forth
012:080 Now **when** they saw no hope of his (yielding),
012:094 **When** the Caravan left (Egypt), their father
012:096 Then **when** the bearer of the good news came,
012:099 Then **when** they entered the presence of Joseph,
012:100 He was indeed good to me **when** He took
012:102 **when** they concerted their plans together in the
012:110 **when** the messengers give up hope (of their people)
013:005 "**When** we are (actually) dust, shall we
013:011 but **when** (once) Allah willeth a people's
014:006 to you **when** He delivered you from the people
014:014 **when** they shall stand before My tribunal,-such
014:022 And Satan will say **when** the matter is decided:
014:042 a Day **when** the eyes will fixedly stare in horror,-
014:044 warn mankind of the day **when** the Wrath will reach them:
015:029 "**When** I have fashioned him (in due proportion)
015:052 **When** they entered his presence and said,
015:061 At length **when** the messengers arrived among
015:065 **when** a portion of the night (yet remains), and do
015:085 And the Hour is coming (**when** this will be manifest).
016:021 nor do thy know **when** they will be raised up.
016:024 **When** it is said to them, "What is it
016:030 To the righteous (**when**) it is said, "What is
016:053 and moreover, **when** ye are touched by distress,
016:054 Yet, **when** He removes the distress from you,
016:058 **When** news is brought to one of them, of (the
016:061 **when** their Term expires, they would
016:078 from the wombs of your mothers **when** ye knew nothing;
016:080 **when** ye travel and **when** ye stop (in your travels)
016:085 **When** the wrong-doers (actually) see the
016:086 **When** those who gave partners to Allah will see
016:091 Fulfil the Covenant of Allah **when** ye have
016:098 **When** thou dost read the Qur'an, seek Allah's
016:101 **When** We substitute one revelation for another,-
017:005 **When** the first of the warnings came to pass,
017:007 so **when** the second of the warnings came to pass,
017:016 **When** We decide to destroy a town, We command
017:035 Give full measure **when** ye measure, and weigh
017:045 **When** thou dost recite the Qur'an, We put,
017:046 **when** thou dost mention thy Lord-and Him
017:047 **when** they listen to thee;
017:047 and **when** they meet in private behold, the wicked
017:049 They say: "What! **when** we are reduced to bones
017:051 Then will they say: "**When** will that be?"
017:052 "It will be on a Day **when** He will call you,
017:067 But **when** He brings you back safe to land, ye turn
017:067 **When** distress seizes you at sea, those that
017:068 beneath the earth **when** ye are on land, or that
017:083 and **when** Evil seizes him he gives himself
017:083 Yet **when** We bestow Our favours on man, he turns
017:094 kept men back for Belief **when** Guidance came to them,
017:098 and said, "**When** we are reduced to bones and dust,
017:101 **when** he came to them, Pharaoh said to him:

WHEN (continued)

017:104 but **when** the second of the warnings came to pass,
017:107 **when** it is recited to them, fall down
018:016 "**When** ye turn away from them and the things
018:017 from their Cave, and **when** it set, turning away
018:017 the sun, **when** it rose, declining to the right from their
018:024 and remember thy Lord **when** thou forgettest,
018:059 **when** they committed iniquities; but We
018:061 But **when** they reached the Junction, they forgot
018:062 **When** they had passed on (some distance), Moses said
018:063 (what happen) **when** we betook ourselves to the rock?
018:071 **when** they were in the boat, he scuttled it.
018:074 until, **when** they met a young man, he slew him.
018:077 **when** they came to the inhabitants of a town,
018:086 Until, **when** he reached the setting of the sun,
018:090 Until, **when** he came to the rising of the sun,
018:093 Until, **when** he reached (a tract) between two
018:096 **when** he had made it (red) as fire, he said:
018:096 At length, **when** he had filled up the space
018:098 but **when** the promise of my Lord comes to pass,
019:008 have a son, **when** my wife is barren and I have
019:009 **when** thou hadst been nothing!'"
019:016 **when** she withdrew from her family to a place
019:035 **When** He determines a matter, He only says
019:039 **when** the matter will be determined: for (behold),
019:049 **When** he had turned away from them and from
019:066 Man says: "What! **when** I am dead, shall I
019:073 **When** Our Clear Signs are rehearsed to them,
019:075 **when** they see the warning of Allah (being fulfilled)
020:011 But **when** he came to the fire, he was call
020:049 (**When** this message was delivered), (Pharaoh) said:
020:059 be assembled **when** the sun is well up."
020:083 (**When** Moses was up on the mount, Allah said):
020:092 thee back, **when** thou sawest them going wrong.
020:102 The Day **when** the Trumpet will be sounded: that Day,
020:104 **when** the best of them in judgment will say:
020:116 **When** We said to the angels, "Prostrate yourselves
020:126 **when** Our Signs came unto thee, forgot them:
021:012 Yet, **when** they felt Our Punishment (coming),
021:036 **When** the Unbelievers see thee, they treat
021:038 They say: "**When** will this promise come to pass,
021:039 (the time) **when** they will not be able to ward
021:039 and (**when**) no help can reach them!
021:045 not hear the call, (even) **when** they are warned!
021:076 (Remember) Noah, **when** he cried (to Us) aforetime:
021:078 **when** they gave judgment in the matter of the
021:083 And (remember) Job, **when** he cried to his Lord
021:087 And remember Zun-nun, **when** he departed in wrath:
021:089 **when** he cried to his Lord: "O my Lord! leave me
022:005 but **when** We pour down rain on it,
022:035 **when** Allah is mentioned, are filled with fear,
022:036 **when** they are down on their sides (after slaughter),
022:052 **when** he framed a desire, Satan threw some (vanity)
022:072 **When** Our Clear Signs are rehearsed to them,
023:027 then **when** comes Our command, and the oven gushes
023:028 And **when** thou hast embarked on the Ark-
023:035 "Does he promise that **when** ye die and become
023:064 Until, **when** We seize in Punishment those of
023:082 They say: "What! **when** we die and become
023:099 Until, **when** death comes to one of them, he says:
023:101 Then **when** the Trumpet is blown, there will
024:012 men and women-**when** ye heard of the affair,-
024:013 **When** they have not brought the witnesses,

WHEN (continued)

024:016	**when** ye heard it, say? "It is not right for us to speak
024:024	On the Day **when** their tongues, their hands,
024:033	maids to prostitution **when** they desire chastity,
024:037	is for the Day **when** hearts and eyes will be
024:039	for water; until **when** he comes up to it,
024:048	**When** they are summoned to Allah and His
024:051	**when** summoned to Allah and His Messenger,
024:059	But **when** the children among you come of age,
024:062	**when** they are with him on a matter requiring
024:062	so **when** they ask for thy leave, for some
025:012	**When** it sees them from a place far off, they will
025:013	And **when** they are cast, bound together, into a
025:037	**when** they rejected the messengers, We drowned
025:041	**When** they see thee, they treat
025:042	Soon they will know, **when** they see the Chastisement,
025:060	**When** it is said to them, "Adore ye
025:063	and **when** the ignorant address them, they say,
025:067	Those who, **when** they spend, are not
025:073	Those who, **when** they are admonished with the
026:020	Moses: "I did it then, **when** I was in error.
026:021	"So I fled from you (all) **when** I feared you;
026:041	So **when** the sorcerers arrived, they said
026:045	**when** behold, it straightway swallows up all the
026:061	And **when** the two bodies saw each other,
026:072	He said: "Do they listen to you **when** ye call (on them),
026:080	"And **when** I am ill, it is He Who cures me;
026:087	on the Day **when** (men) will be raised up;-
026:098	"'When we held you as equals with the
026:111	**when** it is the meanest that follow thee?"
026:130	"And **when** ye strike you strike like tyrants.
027:008	But **when** he came to the (Fire), a voice
027:010	But **when** he saw it moving (of its own accord)
027:013	But **when** Our Signs came to them, visibly they
027:018	At length, **when** they came to a valley of ants,
027:034	She said: "Kings, **when** they enter a country,
027:036	Now **when** (the embassy) came to Solomon, he said:
027:040	Then **when** (Solomon) saw it placed firmly
027:042	So **when** she arrived, she was asked, "Is this
027:044	but **when** she saw it, she thought it was a lake
027:049	we shall then say to his heirs (**when** he seeks vengeance):
027:062	Or, who listens to the distressed **when** it calls on Him,
027:065	nor can they perceive **when** they shall be
027:067	The Unbelievers say:" What! **when** we become dust,-
027:071	They also say: "**When** will this promise (come to pass)?
027:080	(especially) **when** they turn back in retreat.
027:082	And **when** the Word is fulfilled against them
027:084	Until, **when** they come (before the Judgment-Seat),
028:007	but **when** thou hast fears about him, cast him
028:014	**When** he reached full age, and was
028:015	the City at a time **when** its people were not watching:
028:018	fearful and vigilant **when** behold, the man
028:019	Then, **when** he was about to lay his hands on their
028:022	Then **when** he turned his face towards (the land of)
028:023	And **when** he arrived at the watering (place)
028:025	So **when** he came to him and narrated the story,
028:029	Now **when** Moses had fulfilled the term, and was
028:030	But **when** he came to the (Fire), he was
028:031	But **when** he saw it moving (of its own accord)
028:036	**When** Moses came to them with Our Clear Signs,
028:044	**when** We decreed the commission to Moses, nor wast
028:046	(the Mountain of) Tur **when** We called (to Moses).
028:048	But (now), **when** the Truth has come to them

WHEN (continued)

028:053	And **when** it is recited to them, they say:
028:055	And **when** they hear vain talk, they turn
028:059	a population except **when** its members practice
029:010	"We believe in Allah"; but **when** they suffer
029:031	**When** Our Messengers came to Abraham with the
029:033	And **when** Our Messengers came to Lut, he was
029:065	but **when** He had delivered them safely
029:068	or rejects the Truth **when** it reaches him?
030:012	On the Day **when** the Hour will come, the guilty
030:014	On the Day **when** the Hour will come, that Day
030:017	**when** ye reach eventide and **when** ye rise in the
030:018	and **when** the day begins to decline.
030:025	then **when** He calls you, by a single call,
030:033	but **when** He gives them a taste of Mercy
030:033	**When** trouble touches men, they cry
030:036	**When** We give men a taste of Mercy, they exult
030:036	and **when** some evil afflicts them because of what their
030:048	then **when** He has made them reach such of His servants
030:052	**when** they show their backs and turn away.
031:007	**When** Our Signs are rehearsed to such a one,
031:021	**When** they are told to follow the (revelation)
031:032	**When** a wave covers them like the canopy
031:032	But **when** He has delivered them safely to land,
031:033	**when** no father can avail aught for his son, nor a
032:010	And they say: "What! **when** we lie, hidden and
032:012	If only thou couldst see **when** the guilty ones
032:015	**when** they are recited to then fall down in adoration,
032:028	They say: "**When** will this decision be, if ye
033:009	**when** there came down on you hosts (to overwhelm you):
033:019	but **when** the fear is past, they will
033:019	Then **when** fear comes, thou wilt
033:022	**When** the Believers saw the Confederate forces,
033:036	**when** a matter has been decided by Allah and His
033:037	Then **when** Zaid had dissolved (his marriage)
033:037	**when** the latter have dissolved (their marriage)
033:049	O ye who believe! **when** ye marry believing women,
033:053	but **when** ye are invited, enter;
033:053	and **when** ye have taken your meal, disperse,
033:053	And **when** ye ask (his ladies) for anything
033:059	outer garments over their person (**when** out of doors):
034:007	**when** ye are all scattered to pieces in disintegration,
034:014	Then, **when** We decreed (Solomon's) death,
034:014	so **when** he fell down, the Jinns saw plainly that
034:023	**when** terror is removed from their hearts (at the Day of
034:029	They say: "**When** will this promise (come to pass)
034:031	Couldst thou but see **when** the wrong-doers
034:033	**When** they see the Chastisement: We shall
034:043	say of the Truth **when** it comes to them, "This is nothing
034:043	**When** Our Clear Signs are rehearsed to them,
034:045	yet **when** they rejected My messengers,
034:051	If thou couldst but see **when** they will quake
035:042	but **when** a warner came to them, it has only increased
035:045	a stated Term: **when** their Term expires,
036:014	**When** We (first) sent to them two messengers,
036:045	**When** they are told, "Fear ye that which is
036:047	And **when** they are told, "Spend ye of (the bounties)
036:048	Further, they say, "**When** will this promise
036:051	**when** behold! from the sepulchers (men) will
036:053	**when** lo! they will be brought up before Us!
036:080	**when** behold! ye kindle therewith (your own fires)!
036:082	Verily, **when** He intends a thing, His Command
037:013	And, **when** they are admonished, pay no heed,-

WHEN (continued)

037:014 And, **when** they see a Sign, turn it to mockery,
037:016 "What! **when** we die, and become dust and bones,
037:035 For they, **when** they were told that there is
037:053 "'When we die and become dust and bones,
037:102 Then, **when** (the son) reached (the age of)
037:103 So **when** they had both submitted (to Allah),
037:140 **When** he ran away (like slave from captivity)
037:177 But **when** it descends upon their courtyards
038:003 **when** there was no longer time for being saved!
038:015 which (**when** it comes) will brook no delay.
038:022 **When** they entered the presence of David, and he
038:069 Exalted Chiefs, **when** they discuss (matters)
038:072 "**When** I have fashioned him and breathed
039:007 **when** He will tell you the truth of all
039:008 but **when** He bestoweth a favour upon him
039:008 **When** some trouble toucheth man he crieth
039:032 and rejects the Truth **when** it comes to him!
039:045 **When** Allah, Alone is mentioned, the hearts
039:045 but **when** (gods) other than He are mentioned, behold,
039:049 but **when** We bestow a favour upon him as from Us,
039:049 Now, **when** trouble touches man, he cries to Us;
039:058 "Or (lest) it should say **when** it (actually) sees
039:068 **when**, behold, they will be standing and looking on!
039:068 **when** all that are in the heavens and on earth will swoon,
039:071 led to Hell in groups; until, **when** they arrive there,
040:012 but **when** partners were joined with Him, ye believed!
040:012 "This is because, **when** Allah was invoked as the
040:018 **when** the Hearts will (come) right up to the throats
040:025 Now, **when** he brought them in Truth, from Us,
040:028 **when** he has indeed come to you with Clear (Signs)
040:032 a Day **when** there will be mutual calling
040:033 A day **when** ye shall turn your backs and flee:
040:034 **when** he died, ye said: 'No messenger will Allah
040:046 **when** the Hour comes to pass: "Cast ye the people of
040:051 and on the Day **when** the Witnesses will stand forth,-
040:052 The Day **when** no profit will it be to Wrong-doers
040:068 and **when** He decides upon an affair, He says
040:071 **When** the yokes (shall be) round their necks,
040:078 but **when** the Command of Allah issued, the matter
040:083 For **when** their messengers came to them
040:084 But **when** they saw Our Might, they said
040:085 **when** they (actually) saw Our Punishment was not
041:020 At length, **when** they reach the (Fire),
041:039 but **when** We send down rain to it, it is
041:041 Those who reject the Message **when** it comes to them
041:050 **When** We give him a taste of some mercy from Us,
041:051 and **when** Evil seizes him, (he comes) full
041:051 **When** We bestow favours on man, he turns
042:007 (**when**) some will be in the Garden, and some
042:029 He has power to gather them together **when** He wills.
042:037 and, **when** they are angry ever then forgive;
042:039 And those who, **when** an oppressive wrong
042:044 **when** in sight of the Chastisement, say: "Is there
042:048 And truly, **when** We give man a taste of Mercy
042:048 exult thereat, but **when** some ill happens to him,
043:013 and **when** so seated, ye may remember the (kind) favour
043:017 **When** news is brought to one of them of
043:030 But **when** the Truth came to them, they said:
043:038 At length, **when** (such a one) comes to Us, he says
043:039 **When** ye have done wrong, it will
043:047 But **when** he came to them with Our Signs, behold,
043:050 But **when** We removed the Chastisement from them,

WHEN (continued)

043:055 **When** at length they provoked Us, We exacted
043:057 **When** (Jesus) the son of Mary is held up as an
043:063 **When** Jesus came with Clear Signs, he said:
044:041 The Day **when** no protector can avail his client
045:009 And **when** he learns something of Our Signs,
045:025 And **when** Our Clear Signs are rehearsed to them,
045:032 "And **when** it was said that the promise of Allah
046:006 And **when** mankind are gathered together (at the
046:007 **When** Our Clear Signs are rehearsed to them,
046:007 of the Truth **when** it comes to them: "This is evident
046:015 At length, **when** he reaches the age of full strength and
046:023 He said: "The Knowledge (of **when** it will come)
046:024 Then, **when** they saw a could advancing towards
046:026 **when** they went on rejecting the Signs of Allah:
046:029 **when** they stood in the presence therefo, they said,
046:029 "Listen in silence!" **When** the (reading) was finished,
047:004 Therefore, **when** ye meet the Unbelievers (in fight),
047:004 at length, **when** ye have thoroughly subdued them,
047:016 to thee, till **when** they go out from thee,
047:018 some tokens thereof, and **when** it comes to them,
047:020 But **when** a Sura of decisive meaning is revealed,
047:021 and **when** a matter is resolved on, it were
047:027 But how (will it be) **when** the angels take their
047:035 crying for peace, **when** ye are the Uppermost:
048:015 **when** ye set forth to acquire booty (in war):
048:018 The Believers **when** they swore Fealty to thee
050:003 "What! **when** we die and become dust,
050:005 But they deny the truth **when** it comes to them:
050:041 And listen the Day **when** the Caller will call
050:042 The Day **when** they will hear a (mighty) Blast
050:044 The Day **when** the Earth will be rent asunder,
051:012 They ask, "**When** will be the Day of Judgement
051:013 (It will be) a Day **when** they will be tried
051:028 (**When** they did not eat), He conceived
052:009 On the Day **when** the firmament will be
052:046 The Day **when** their plotting will avail them
053:001 By the Star **when** it goes down,-
053:032 He knows you well **when** He brings you out
053:032 and **when** ye are hidden in your mother's wombs.
053:046 From a seed **when** lodged (in its place);
055:037 **When** the sky is rent asunder, and it becomes
055:046 But for such as fear the time **when** they will
056:001 **When** the Event Inevitable cometh to pass,
056:004 **When** the earth shall be shaken to its depths,
056:047 "What! **when** we die and become dust and bones,
056:083 **when** (the soul of the dying man) reaches the throat,
058:008 And **when** they come to thee, they salute thee,
058:009 O ye who believe! **when** ye hold secret counsel,
058:011 And **when** ye are told to rise up,
058:011 O ye who believe! **When** ye are told to make room
058:012 O ye who believe! **When** ye consult the Messenger
059:016 like Satan **when** he says to man, "Disbelieve":
059:016 but **when** (man) disbelieves, Satan says,
060:004 **when** they said to their people: "We are clear you
060:004 but not **when** Abraham said to his father: "I will
060:010 O ye who believe! **when** there come to you
060:012 O Prophet! **when** believing women come to thee
061:005 Then **when** they went wrong, Allah let
061:006 But **when** he came to them with Clear Signs,
062:009 O ye who believe! **when** the call is proclaimed
062:010 And **when** the Prayer is finished, then may
062:011 But **when** they see some bargain or some pastime,

WHEN (continued)

063:001 **When** the Hypocrites come to thee, they say,
063:004 **When** thou lookest at them, their bodies
063:004 and **when** they speak, thou listenest
063:005 And **when** it is said to them, "Come, the
063:011 **when** the time appointed (for it) has come;
065:001 O Prophet! **when** ye do divorce women, divorce them
065:002 Thus **when** they fulfil their term appointed,
066:003 **When** the Prophet disclosed a matter in confidence
066:003 Then **when** he told her thereof, she said,
067:016 **when** it shakes (as in an earthquake)?
067:025 They ask: **When** will this promise be (fulfilled)?
067:027 At length, **when** they see it close at hand,
068:015 **When** to him are rehearsed Our Signs, "Tales of
068:017 **when** they resolved to gather the fruits of the
068:026 But **when** they saw the (garden), they said:
068:048 **when** he cried out in agony.
068:051 thee up with their eyes **when** they hear the Message;
069:011 We, **when** the water (of Noah's flood) overflowed
069:013 Then, **when** one Blast is sounded on the Trumpet,
070:020 Fretful **when** evil touches him;
070:021 And niggardly **when** good reaches him;-
071:004 For **when** the Term given by Allah is accomplished,
072:019 "Yet **when** the Devotee of Allah stands forth
072:024 At length, **when** they see (with their own eyes)
073:006 is a time **when** impression is more keen and speech
074:008 Finally **when** the Trumpet is sounded,
075:006 He questions: "**When** is the Day of Resurrection?"
075:007 At length, **when** the Sight is dazed,
075:018 But **when** We have recited it, follow thou
075:026 Yea, **when** (the soul) reaches to the collar-bone
076:001 **when** he was nothing-(not even) mentioned?
076:020 And **when** thou lookest, it is there thou wilt see a
076:028 but, **when** We will, We shall exchange their likes.
077:008 Then **when** the stars become dim;
077:009 **When** the heaven is cleft asunder;
077:010 **When** the mountains are scattered (to the winds)
077:011 And **when** the messengers are (all) appointed
077:035 That will be a Day **when** they shall not
077:048 And **when** it is said to them, "Prostrate yourselves!"
078:040 the Day **when** man will see (the Deeds) which his hands
079:011 "What!-**when** we shall have become rotten bones?"
079:014 **When**, behold, they will be brought out to the open.
079:034 Therefore, **when** there comes the great,
079:035 The Day **when** Man shall remember (all) that
079:042 '**When** will be its appointed time?'
080:022 Then, **when** it is His will, He will
080:033 At length, **when** there comes the Deafening Noise,-
081:001 **When** the sun (with its spacious light) is folded up;
081:002 **When** the stars fall, losing their lustre;
081:003 **When** the mountains vanish (like a mirage);
081:004 **When** the she-camels, ten months with young,
081:005 **When** the wild beasts are herded together
081:006 **When** the oceans boil over with a swell;
081:007 **When** the souls are sorted out,
081:008 **When** the female (infant), Buried alive,
081:010 **When** the Scrolls are laid open;
081:011 **When** the sky is unveiled:
081:012 **When** the Blazing Fire is kindled to fierce heat;
081:013 And **when** the Garden is brought near;-
082:001 **When** the Sky is cleft asunder;
082:002 **When** the Stars are scattered;
082:003 **When** the Oceans are suffered to burst forth;

WHEN (continued)

082:004 And **when** the Graves are turned upside down;-
082:019 (It will be) the Day **when** no soul shall have
083:002 Those who, **when** they have to receive by measure
083:003 But **when** they have to give by measure or weight
083:006 A Day **when** (all) mankind will stand before
083:013 **When** Our Signs are rehearsed to him, he says,
083:031 And **when** they returned to their own people,
084:001 **When** the Sky is rent asunder,
084:003 And **when** the Earth is flattened out,
084:021 And **when** the Qur'an is read to them, they fall
089:004 And by the Night **when** it passeth away;-
089:015 Now, as for man, **when** his Lord trieth him,
089:016 But **when** He trieth him, restricting his
089:021 Nay! **When** the earth is pounded to powder,
092:011 **when** he falls headlong (into the Pit).
093:002 And by the Night **when** it is still,-
094:007 **when** thou art free (from thine immediate task),
096:010 A votary **when** he (turns) to pray?
099:001 **When** the Earth is shaken to her
100:009 Does he not know,-**when** that which is in the
110:001 **When** comes the Help of Allah, and Victory,

WHENCE

002:199 Then return from the place **whence** it is usual
003:037 He said: "O Mary! **whence** (comes) this to you?"
003:165 do ye say? "**Whence** is this?"

WHENCESOEVER

002:149 From **whencesoever** thou startest forth,
002:150 So from **whencesoever** thou startest forth,

WHENEVER

002:087 Is it that **whenever** there comes to you
002:282 **whenever** ye make a commercial contract;
006:152 **whenever** ye speak, speak justly, even if
007:035 O ye children of Adam! **whenever** there come to you
007:094 **Whenever** We sent a prophet to a town, We took
009:124 **Whenever** there cometh down a Sura, some of
009:127 **Whenever** there cometh down a Sura, they look
019:058 **Whenever** the Signs of (Allah) Most Gracious were
043:023 Just in the same way, **whenever** We sent a Warner
083:030 And **whenever** they passed by them, used to
083:032 And **whenever** they saw them, they would

WHERE

002:035 things therein as (**where** and when) ye will;
002:191 from **where** they have turned you out;
004:019 except **where** they have been guilty of open lewdness;
006:022 "**Where** are the partners whom ye
006:124 Allah knoweth best **where** to place His mission.
007:027 from a position **where** ye cannot see them:
007:037 they say: "**Where** are the things that ye
007:092 in the homes **where** they had flourished:
009:006 and then escort him to **where** he can be secure,
012:056 to take possession therein as when, or **where** he pleased.
012:082 Ask at the town **where** we have been and the
013:041 (**Where**) Allah commands, there is none to put
016:027 and say: "**Where** are My `partners' concerning whom
020:058 in a place **where** both shall have even chances."
026:092 '**Where** are the (gods) ye worshipped-
028:062 and say: "**Where** are my `partners'?-whom ye
028:074 He will say: "**Where** are My `partners' whom ye
037:116 And We helped them, so they were victorious;
040:073 "**Where** are the (deities) to which ye gave
041:047 "**Where** are the partners (ye attributed) to Me?"
057:013 Then seek a light (**where** ye can)!"

WHERE (continued)
075:010 That Day will Man say "**Where** is the refuge?"
076:006 A Fountain **where** the Devotees of Allah do drink,
088:011 **Where** they shall hear no (word) of vanity:

WHEREAS
064:015 **whereas** Allah, with Him is the highest Reward.

WHEREBY
006:122 and a Light **whereby** he can walk

WHEREIN
002:213 concerning that **wherein** they differed.
002:213 in matters **wherein** they differed;
003:055 between you of the matters **wherein** ye dispute.
006:164 of things **wherein** ye disputed."
009:021 for them, **wherein** are delights that endure:
009:063 **Wherein** they shall dwell.
010:037 **wherein** there is no doubt-from the
016:039 of that **wherein** they differ, and that
016:069 of varying colours, **wherein** is healing for men:
016:092 (the truth of) that **wherein** ye disagree.
018:003 **Wherein** they shall remain forever:
018:108 **Wherein** they shall dwell (for aye): no change
024:043 mountain masses (of clouds) **wherein** is hail:
032:025 matters **wherein** they differ (among themselves).
038:042 here is (water) **wherein** to wash, cool and
039:003 in that **wherein** they differ.
042:010 Whatever it be **wherein** ye differ, the decision
044:027 And pleasant things **wherein** they had
046:024 a wind **wherein** is a Grievous Chastisement!
052:045 **wherein** they shall be thunderstruck.
079:043 **Wherein** art thou (concerned) with the
098:003 **Wherein** are books right and straight.

WHEREOF
012:041 **whereof** ye twain do enquire."
041:003 A Book, **whereof** the verses are explained in detail;
042:023 That is (the Bounty) **whereof** Allah gives Glad
046:003 turn away from that **whereof** they are warned.
046:008 He knows best of that **whereof** ye talk (so glibly)!
050:020 that will be the Day **whereof** warning (had been given).
057:007 of the (substance) **whereof** He has made you heirs.
057:021 the width **whereof** is as the width of heaven
069:023 The Fruits **whereof** (will hang in bunches)
069:032 **whereof** the length is seventy cubits!
070:004 unto Him in a Day the measure **whereof** is (as)
083:028 from (the waters) **whereof** drink those Nearest to Allah.

WHEREON
007:137 lands **whereon** We sent down our blessings.
009:077 (to last) till the day **whereon** they shall meet Him:
026:088 "The Day **whereon** neither wealth nor sons will avail,
040:016 The Day **whereon** they will (all) come forth:
070:043 The Day **whereon** they will issue from their
073:018 **Whereon** the sky will be cleft asunder?
101:004 (It is) a Day **whereon** Men will be like

WHERESOEVER
002:148 **Wheresoever** ye are,
002:150 and **wheresoever** ye are, turn your face thither:
019:031 "And He hath made me blessed **wheresoever** I be,
057:004 And He is with you **wheresoever** ye may be.
058:007 but He is with them, **wheresoever** they be:

WHEREVER
002:144 **wherever** ye are, turn your faces in that direction.
002:191 And slay them **wherever** ye catch them,
003:112 (like a tent) **wherever** they are found,

WHEREVER (continued)
004:078 "**Wherever** ye are, death will find you out,
004:089 seize them and slay them **wherever** ye find them;
004:091 seize them and slay them **wherever** ye get them:
009:005 then fight and slay the Pagans **wherever** ye find them,
033:061 **wherever** they are found, they shall be seized and slain.

WHEREWITH
004:025 the means **wherewith** to wed free believing women,
005:016 **Wherewith** Allah guideth all who seek His good
007:179 eyes **wherewith** they see not,
007:179 They have hearts **wherewith** they understand not,
007:179 and ears **wherewith** they hear not.
009:092 no resources **wherewith** to provide the expenses.
014:032 and with it bringeth our fruits **wherewith** to feed you;
018:109 (**wherewith** to write out) the words of my Lord,
042:052 **wherewith** We guide such of Our servants as We will;
093:005 give thee (that **wherewith**) thou shalt be well-pleased.

WHEREWITHAL
024:033 the **wherewithal** for marriage keep themselves
058:012 (the **wherewithal**), Allah is Oft-Forgiving

WHETHER
002:006 **whether** thou warn them or do not warn them;
002:282 **whether** it be small or big:
002:284 **Whether** ye show what is in your minds
003:029 Say: "**Whether** ye hide what is in your hearts
003:128 **whether** He turn in mercy to them, or punish them;
003:134 **whether** in prosperity, or in adversity;
004:007 **whether** the property be small or large,
004:011 Ye know not **whether** your parents or your children
004:074 **whether** he is slain or gets victory, soon shall
004:135 and **whether** it be (against) rich or poor:
004:149 **Whether** you do openly a good deed or conceal
005:041 (**whether** it be) among those who say: "We believe"
005:057 **whether** among those who received the Scripture before
006:047 **whether** suddenly or openly,
006:151 **whether** open or secret;
007:033 indecent deeds, **whether** open or secret;
007:193 for you it is the same **whether** ye call or ye keep silent,
009:041 Go ye forth, (**whether** equipped) lightly or heavily,
009:080 **Whether** thou ask for their forgiveness, or not,
009:106 **whether** He will punish them, or turn in mercy
009:120 **whether** they suffered thirst, or fatigue,
010:046 **Whether** We show thee (realized in thy lifetime)
011:041 in the name of Allah, **whether** it move or be at rest!
011:088 He said: "O my people! see ye **whether** I have
013:010 It is the same (to Him) **whether** any of you conceal his
013:010 **whether** he lie hid by night or walk forth freely by day.
013:040 **Whether** We shall show thee (within thy lifetime)
014:021 (now) **whether** we rage, or bear (these torments)
014:038 from Allah, **whether** on earth or in heaven.
016:049 **whether** moving creatures or the angels:
017:023 **Whether** one or both of them attain old age
017:107 Say: "**Whether** ye believe in it or not, it is
020:065 They said: "O Moses! **whether** wilt thou that thou
021:109 but I know not **whether** that which ye are
022:015 then let him see **whether** his plan will remove that which
024:061 on you, **whether** ye eat in company or separately.
026:136 **whether** thou admonish us or be not
027:027 **whether** thou hast told the truth or lied!
027:040 to test me **whether** I am grateful or ungrateful!
027:041 let us see **whether** she is guided (to the truth)
033:054 **Whether** ye reveal anything or conceal it,
036:010 The same is to them **whether** thou admonish them

WHETHER (continued)

038:039 **whether** thou bestow them (on others)
040:040 **whether** man or woman-and is a believer-such will
040:043 **whether** in this world, or the Hereafter;
040:077 and **whether** We show thee (in this life) some part
052:016 to you **whether** ye bear it with patience, or not:
063:006 It is equal to them **whether** thou pray for their
067:013 And **whether** ye hide your word or make it
072:010 'And we understand not **whether** ill is intended
072:010 or **whether** their Lord (really) intends to guide
072:025 Say: "I know not **whether** the (Punishment) which ye
072:025 or **whether** my Lord will appoint for it
076:003 **whether** he be grateful or ungrateful.
077:006 **Whether** of Justification or of Warning;-

WHICH

002:024 **which** is prepared for those who reject faith.
002:025 beneath **which** rivers flow.
002:036 the state (of felicity) in **which** they had been.
002:040 favour **which** I bestowed upon you,
002:041 confirming the revelation **which** is with you,
002:047 favour **which** I bestowed upon you,
002:059 the word from that **which** had been given them;
002:074 and others **which** sink for fear of Allah.
002:074 there are some from **which** rivers gush forth;
002:074 others there are **which** when split asunder send forth
002:088 (**which** preserve Allah's word, we need no more)"
002:089 that **which** they (should) have recognized,
002:090 (the revelation) **which** Allah has sent down,
002:090 for **which** they have sold their souls,
002:095 on account of the (sins) **which** their hands
002:102 **which** they did sell their souls,
002:120 the knowledge **which** hath reached thee,
002:122 the special favour **which** I bestowed upon you,
002:124 with certain Commands, **which** he fulfilled:
002:142 the Qiblah to **which** they were used?"
002:143 the Qiblah to **which** thou wast used,
002:146 the truth **which** they themselves know.
002:148 To each is a goal to **which** Allah turns him;
002:164 and the life **which** He gives therewith
002:164 in the rain **which** Allah sends down
002:164 and the clouds **which** they trail
002:169 of Allah that of **which** ye have no knowledge.
002:173 and that on **which** any other name hath been invoked
002:177 to fulfil the contracts **which** ye have made;
002:185 in **which** was sent down the Qur'an,
002:216 ye dislike a thing **which** is good for you,
002:216 and that ye love a thing **which** is bad for you.
002:230 **which** He makes plain to those who know.
002:239 He had taught you, **which** ye knew not (before).
002:245 **which** Allah will double unto his credit
002:264 **which** leaves it (just) a bare stone.
002:264 barren rock, on **which** is a little soil;
002:267 good things **which** ye have (honorably) earned,
002:267 and do not even aim at anything **which** is bad,
002:267 **which** We have produced for you,
002:282 but if it be a transaction **which** ye carry out
002:286 like that **which** Thou didst lay on those
003:009 a Day about **which** there in no doubt;
003:025 against a Day about **which** there is no doubt,
003:044 as to **which** of them should be charged
003:044 **which** We reveal unto thee (O Prophet!)
003:050 to attest the Torah **which** was before me.
003:066 in matters of **which** ye have no knowledge?

WHICH (continued)

003:066 **which** ye had some Knowledge!
003:067 and bowed his will to Allah's (**which** is Islam).
003:070 of **which** ye are (yourselves) witnesses?
003:073 like unto that **which** was sent unto you?
003:092 unless ye give (freely) of that **which** ye love:
003:103 by the Rope **which** Allah (stretches out for you),
003:117 likened to a Wind **which** brings a nipping frost:
003:131 Fear the fire, **which** is prepared for those
003:151 for **which** He had sent no authority:
003:152 in sight (of the Victory) **which** ye covet.
003:179 the Believers in the state in **which** ye are now,
003:180 withhold of the gifts **which** Allah hath given them
003:182 **which** your hands sent on before ye:
003:198 and that **which** is from Allah is the best (bliss)
004:003 or that **which** your right hands possess.
004:005 **which** Allah has assigned to you to manage,
004:031 of the things **which** ye are forbidden to do,
004:032 in **which** Allah hath bestowed His gifts more
004:037 hide the bounties **which** Allah hath bestowed on them;
004:058 the teaching **which** He giveth you!
004:062 Because of the deeds **which** their hands
004:087 the Day of Judgment, about **which** there is no doubt.
004:102 let the other party come up **which** hath not yet prayed-
004:105 by that **which** Allah has shown thee; so be not
004:127 There is not a good deed **which** ye do, but
004:136 and the scripture **which** He hath sent
004:136 and the scripture **which** He sent
004:160 good and wholesome **which** had been lawful for them;
004:171 and His Word, **which** He bestowed on Mary,
005:003 that **which** is sacrificed on stone (altars);
005:003 that **which** hath been killed by strangling, or by
005:003 and that on **which** hath been invoked
005:003 that **which** hath been (partly) eaten
005:007 and His Covenant, **which** He ratified with you,
005:021 enter the holy land **which** Allah hath assigned unto you,
005:048 the truth of the matters in **which** ye dispute;
005:049 (teaching) **which** Allah hath sent down to thee.
005:052 **which** they secretly harboured in their hearts.
005:054 **which** He will bestow on whom He pleaseth.
005:059 come to us and that **which** came before (us),
005:067 **which** hath been sent to thee from thy Lord.
005:076 something **which** hath no power either
005:079 evil indeed were the deeds **which** they did.
005:079 the iniquities **which** they committed:
005:080 **which** their souls have sent forward before
005:084 **which** has come to us, seeing that we long for
005:087 the good things **which** Allah hath made lawful
005:088 **which** Allah hath provided for you, lawful
005:101 about things **which**, if made plain to you, may
005:119 "This is a day on **which** the truthful will profit
006:003 the (recompense) **which** ye earn (by your deeds).
006:009 caused them confusion in a matter **which** they have
006:024 but the (lie) **which** they invented will leave
006:033 it is the Signs of Allah, **which** the wicked deny.
006:033 know indeed the grief **which** their words do cause thee:
006:041 (the distress) **which** occasioned your call upon Him,
006:041 (the false gods) **which** ye join with Him!"
006:073 He knows the Unseen as well as that **which** is open.
006:081 **Which** of (us) two parties hath more
006:083 **which** We gave to Abraham (to use)
006:091 **which** ye knew not-neither ye nor your fathers."
006:091 the Book **which** Moses brought?-A light

WHICH (continued)

006:092	And this is a Book **which** We have sent down,
006:092	(the revelations) **which** came before it:
006:094	all (the favours) **which** We bestowed on you:
006:099	out of **which** We produce, close-compounded
006:118	on **which** Allah's name hath been pronounced,
006:119	on **which** Allah's name hath been pronounced,
006:121	Eat not of (meats) on **which** Allah's name
006:122	from **which** he can never come out?
006:128	**which** Thou didst appoint for us."
006:138	and cattle on **which** (at slaughter) the name
006:140	and forbid food **which** Allah hath provided
006:143	**which** the wombs of the two females enclose?
006:144	**which** the wombs of the two females enclose?-
006:145	(meat) on **which** a name has been invoked,
006:151	**which** Allah hath made sacred, except by
006:152	but that **which** it can bear;-whenever ye speak
006:155	**which** We have revealed as a blessing: so follow
007:032	(**which** He hath provided) for sustenance?
007:032	**which** He hath produced for His servants,
007:033	of **which** ye have no knowledge.
007:033	for **which** He hath given no authority;
007:042	but that **which** it can bear,-they will be
007:052	based on knowledge, **Which** We explained in detail,-
007:058	springs up nothing but that **which** is scanty,
007:070	**which** our fathers used to worship.
007:071	over names **which** ye have devised-ye and
007:075	in the revelation **which** hath been sent
007:079	convey to you the message for **which** I was
007:087	and a party **which** does not believe,
007:087	believes in the Message with **which** I have been sent,
007:093	convey to you the Messages for **which** I was
007:117	all the falsehoods **which** the fake!
007:123	Surely this is a trick **which** ye have planned
007:135	them according to a fixed term **which** they had to fulfil,-
007:137	**which** Pharaoh and his people erected (with such pride).
007:139	and vain is the (worship) **which** they practice."
007:144	take then the (revelation) **which** I give thee,
007:156	"And ordain for us that **which** is good, in this
007:157	the Light **which** is sent down with him,-it is
007:162	changed the word from that **which** had been given them
008:024	to that **which** will give you life; and know
008:025	And fear the trial **which** affecteth not in
008:051	"because of the deeds **which** your (own) hands sent forth.
008:053	the Grace **which** He hath bestowed on a people
009:024	in **which** ye delight-are dearer to you than Allah
009:024	the commerce in **which** ye fear a decline:
009:026	and sent down forces **which** ye saw not:
009:029	forbidden **which** hath been forbidden by Allah
009:035	(treasure) **which** ye hoarded for yourselves:
009:040	with forces **which** ye saw not, and humbled
009:072	men and women, Gardens under **which** rivers flow,
009:074	only return for the bounty with **which** Allah and
009:074	meditated a plot **which** they were enable to carry out:
009:089	Gardens under **which** rivers flow, to dwell therein:
009:097	of the command **which** Allah hath sent down
009:100	hath He prepared Gardens under **which** rivers flow,
009:109	**Which** then is best?-he that layeth his foundation
009:111	Then rejoice in the bargain **which** ye have concluded:
009:124	some of them say: "**Which** of you has had his faith
010:024	**which** provides food for men and animals:
010:024	is as the rain **which** We send down from the skies:
010:098	township (among those We warned) **which** believed,-

WHICH (continued)

011:007	**which** of you is best in conduct.
011:008	completely encircled by that **which** they used to mock at!
011:035	And I am free of the sins of **which** ye are guilty!
011:046	So ask not of Me that of **which** thou hast
011:047	of **which** I have no knowledge and unless Thou
011:049	of the Unseen, **which** We have revealed unto thee:
011:057	have conveyed the Message with **which** I was
011:062	to that to **which** thou invitest us."
011:086	'That **which** is left you by Allah is best for you,
011:087	leave off the worship **which** our fathers practiced,
011:088	to do that **which** I forbid you to do.
011:098	be the place to **which** they are led!
011:099	**which** shall be given (unto them)!
011:100	of communities **which** We relate unto thee:
011:103	that is a Day for **which** mankind will be gathered
011:116	of the good things of life **which** were given them,
012:018	against that **which** ye assert, it is
012:033	to my liking than that to **which** they invite me:
012:037	This is part of the (Duty) **which** my Lord hath taught me
012:040	for **which** Allah hath sent down no authority:
012:040	is nothing but names **which** ye have named, ye and
012:047	except a little, of **which** ye shall eat.
012:048	(all) except a little **which** ye shall have
012:048	**which** will devour what ye shall have laid
012:049	a year in **which** the people will have abundant water,
012:049	and in **which** the will press (wine and oil).
012:062	their stock-in-trade (with **which** they had bartered)
012:082	and the caravan in **which** we returned,
012:086	and I know from Allah that **which** ye know not.
012:096	'I know from Allah that **which** ye know not?"
012:102	happened unseen, **which** We reveal by inspiration
013:001	that **which** hath been revealed unto thee
013:009	He knoweth the Unseen and that **which** is open:
013:017	while that **which** is for the good of mankind remains
013:017	(ore) **which** they heat in the fire,
013:019	that **which** hath been revealed unto thee from
013:021	things **which** Allah hath commanded to be joined,
013:025	those things **which** Allah has commanded to be
013:026	(**which** He giveth) to whom so He pleaseth.
013:031	with **which** mountains were moved, or the earth
013:035	The parable of the Garden **which** the righteous
013:037	the knowledge **which** hath reached thee, then wouldst
014:001	A Book **which** We have revealed unto thee, in order
014:009	"We do deny (the mission) on **which** ye have
014:009	as to that to **which** ye invite us."
014:018	as ashes, on **which** the wind blows furiously
014:023	admitted to Gardens beneath **which** rivers flow,-
014:031	of a Day in **which** there will be neither mutual
014:046	Mighty indeed were the plots **which** they made,
015:057	the business on **which** ye (Have come), O ye
015:063	to thee to accomplish that of **which** they doubt.
016:010	the vegetation on **which** ye feed your cattle.
016:013	And the things on this earth **which** He has
016:031	Gardens of Eternity **which** they will enter:
016:032	(the good) **which** ye did (in the world)."
016:034	at **which** they had scoffed hemmed them in.
016:040	For to anything **which** We have willed, We but
016:056	We have bestowed for their sustenance!
016:064	to them those things in **which** they differ,
016:080	**which** ye find so light (and handy) when ye
016:092	the yarn **which** she has spun, after it
016:112	because of the (evil) **which** (its people) wrought.

WHICH (continued)

016:114   **which** Allah has provided for you, lawful and good;
016:115   and any (food) over **which** the name of other than
017:009   to that **which** is most right (or stable),
017:013   for him a scroll, **which** he will see spread open.
017:028   from thy Lord **which** thou dost expect, yet speak
017:033   Nor take life-**which** Allah has made sacred-
017:036   And pursue not that of **which** thou hast no knowledge;
017:039   (precepts of) wisdom, **which** thy Lord has revealed
017:051   "Or any created matter **which**, in your minds,
017:060   **which** We showed thee, but as a trail for men,-
017:073   away from that **which** We had revealed unto thee,
017:082   of the Qur'an that **which** is a healing and a mercy
017:086   We could take away that **which** We have sent thee
017:099   a term appointed, of **which** there is no doubt.
017:106   (It is) a Qur'an **which** We have divided (into parts
018:007   That **which** is on earth We have made but as
018:007   as to **which** of them are best in conduct.
018:012   **which** of the two parties was best at calculating
018:019   let him find out **which** is the best food
018:042   on his property, **which** had (now) tumbled to pieces
018:045   dry stubble, **which** the winds do scatter:
018:045   it is like the rain **which** We send down
018:057   forgetting the (deeds) **which** his hands have sent
018:058   beyond **which** they will find no refuge.
018:061   **which** took its course through the sea (straight)
018:066   of the (Higher) Truth **which** thou hast been taught?"
018:068   about things **which** are beyond your knowledge?"
018:078   (those things) over **which** thou was unable
018:082   a buried treasure, to **which** they were entitled;
018:082   of (those things) over **which** thou wast unable
018:095   He said: "(The power) in **which** my Lord has
019:034   about **which** they (vainly) dispute.
019:042   **which** heareth not and seeth not, and can
019:043   hath come knowledge **which** hath not reached thee:
019:061   Gardens of Eternity, those **which** (Allah) Most
019:063   Such is the Garden **which** We give as an
019:071   a Decree **which** must be accomplished.
019:073   those who believe, "**Which** of the two sides is best
020:058   **which** we shall not fail to keep-neither we nor thou-
020:069   "Throw that **which** is in thy right hand:
020:069   quickly will it swallow up that **which** they have faked:
020:071   **which** of us can give the more severe and the
020:073   and the magic to **which** thou didst compel us:
020:076   Gardens of Eternity, beneath **which** flow rivers:
020:131   of this world, through **which** We test them:
021:006   the towns **which** We destroyed believed: will these
021:010   a book **which** We give you eminence.
021:013   of this life **which** were given you, and to
021:032   the Signs **which** these things (point to)!
021:050   **which** We have sent down: will ye
021:052   to **which** ye are (so assiduously) devoted?"
021:071   to the land **which** We have blessed for the nations.
021:074   the town **which** practiced abominations:
021:078   of the field into **which** the sheep of certain
021:081   to the land **which** We had blessed:
021:095   or any population **which** We have destroyed:
021:109   but I know not whether that **which** ye are
022:010   of the deeds **which** thy hands sent forth, for verily
022:014   to Gardens, beneath **which** rivers flow:
022:015   his plan will remove that **which** enrages (him)!
022:023   to Gardens beneath **which** rivers flow: they shall
022:025   **which** We have made (open) to (all) men-

WHICH (continued)

022:028   over the cattle **which** He has provided for
022:040   in **which** the name of Allah is commemorated
022:045   We destroyed, **which** were given to wrong-doing?
022:046   but the hearts **which** are in their breasts.
022:048   give respite, **which** were given to wrong-doing?
022:059   to a place with **which** they shall be well pleased:
022:067   appointed rites **which** they must follow:
022:069   concerning the matter in **which** ye differ."
022:071   and of **which** they have (really) no knowledge:
022:071   things for **which** no authority has been sent down to them,
023:020   Mount Sinai, **which** produces oil, and relish
023:036   "Far, very far is that **which** ye are promised!
023:053   each party rejoices in that **which** is with itself.
023:062   before Us is a record **which** clearly speaks
023:063   deeds of theirs, **which** they will (continue) to do,-
023:075   and removed the distress **which** is on them,
023:093   (in my lifetime) that **which** they are warned
023:095   thee (in fulfillment) that against **which** they are warned.
023:096   Repel evil with that **which** is best:
024:001   and **which** We have ordained:
024:001   A Sura **which** We have sent down and
024:015   of your mouths things of **which** ye had no knowledge;
024:029   living in, **which** serve some (other) use for you:
024:033   out of the means **which** Allah has given to you.
024:036   **which** Allah hath permitted to be raised to honour;
024:039   **which** the man parched with thirst mistakes for water;
024:055   after the fear in **which** they (lived), to one
024:055   their religion-the one **which** He has chosen
024:061   or in houses of **which** the keys are in
025:004   "Naught is this but a lie **which** he has forged,
025:005   **which** he has caused to be written:
025:010   Gardens beneath **which** rivers flow; and He
025:040   have passed by the town on **which** was rained
025:060   Shall we adore that **which** thou commandest us?"
026:004   a Sign, to **which** they would bend their necks
026:019   a deed of thine **which** (thou knowest) thou didst,
026:022   "And this is the favour with **which** thou dost
026:043   "Throw ye-that **which** ye are about to throw!"
026:045   all the falsehoods **which** they fake!
026:206   the (Punishment) **which** they were promised!
027:019   for Thy favours, **which** Thou has bestowed on me
027:022   "I have compassed **which** thou hast not compassed,
027:036   is better than that **which** He has given you!
027:036   But that **which** Allah has given me is better
027:038   **which** of you can bring me her throne before they
027:072   the events **which** ye wish to hasten on
027:076   the matters in **which** they disagree.
027:090   that **which** ye have earned by your deeds?"
028:048   like those **which** were sent to Moses?"
028:048   reject (the Signs) **which** were formerly sent to Moses?
028:049   **which** is a better Guide than either of them,
028:057   to **which** are brought as tribute fruits of all kinds,-
028:058   **which** exulted in their life (of ease and plenty)!
028:060   but that **which** is with Allah is better
028:060   The (material) things **which** ye are given are but
028:072   who can give you a Night in **which** ye can rest?
028:075   and the (lies) **which** they invented will leave
028:077   with the (wealth) **which** Allah has bestowed on thee,
028:078   because of a certain knowledge **which** I have."
028:078   **which** were superior to him in strength and greater
029:008   anything of **which** thou hast no knowledge,
029:046   "We believe in the Revelation **which** has

WHICH (continued)

029:046   and in that **which** came do to you;
029:051   the Book **which** is rehearsed to them?
029:058   beneath **which** flow rivers,-to dwell therein
029:062   (**which** He gives) to whichever of His servants
029:067   Then, do they believe in that **which** is vain,
030:009   (Signs), (**which** they rejected, to their own destruction):
030:030   the nature in **which** Allah has made mankind:
030:032   each party rejoicing in that **which** is with itself!
030:035   authority to them, **which** speaks to them the things to
030:035   to **which** they pay part-worship?
030:039   but that **which** you give for charity, seeking the
030:039   That **which** you give in usury for increase
030:043   from Allah the Day **which** there is no chance
030:051   And if We (but) send a Wind from **which** they see
031:015   of **which** thou hast no knowledge, obey them not;
032:002   the revelation of the Book in **which** there is no doubt,-
032:005   on a Day, the measure of **which** is a thousand
032:016   (in charity) out of the sustenance **which** We have
032:020   of the Fire, the **which** ye were wont to reject as false.
033:002   But follow that **which** comes to thee by inspiration
033:027   and of a land **which** ye had not frequented (before).
033:037   that **which** Allah was about to make manifest:
033:051   with that **which** thou hast to give them:
034:014   **which** kept (slowly) gnawing away at his staff:
034:018   Between them and the Cities on **which** We had
034:023   'That **which** is true and just; and He
034:030   for a Day, **which** ye cannot put back for an hour
034:034   with **which** ye have been sent."
034:042   the **which** ye were wont to deny!"
034:043   from the (worship) **which** your fathers practiced."
034:044   We had not given them Books **which** they could study,
035:031   That **which** We have revealed to thee of the Book
035:040   from **which** they (can derive) clear (evidence)?-
036:012   and We record that **which** they sent before
036:012   sent before and that **which** they leave behind,
036:033   and produce grain therefrom, of **which** ye do eat.
036:036   of **which** they have no knowledge.
036:042   similar (vessels) on **which** they ride.
036:045   When they were told, "Fear ye that **which** is before you
036:045   before you and that **which** will be after you,
036:047   "Spend ye of (the bounties) **which** Allah has provided
036:063   "This is the Hell of **which** ye were promised!
036:071   among the things **which** Our hands have fashioned-
036:071   cattle, **which** are under their dominion?-
037:085   and to his people, "What is that **which** ye worship?
037:095   He said: "Worship ye that **which** ye have
037:117   We gave them the Book **which** helps to make things clear;
038:015   mighty Blast, **which** (when it comes) will brook
038:029   (Here is) a Book **which** We have sent down
038:035   and grant me a Kingdom, **which**, will not
038:068   "From **which** ye do turn away!
039:046   in those matters about **which** they have differed."
039:047   **which** they could never have counted upon!
039:048   encircled by that **which** they used to mock at!
039:055   "And follow the Best that **which** revealed to you
040:008   **which** Thou hast promised to them,
040:028   of the (calamity) of **which** he warns you:
040:029   "I but point out to you that **which** I see (myself);
040:034   of the (mission) for **which** he had come:
040:056   (the quest of) greatness, **which** they shall never attain to:
040:070   and the (revelations) with **which** We sent
040:073   "Where are the (deities) to **which** ye gave

WHICH (continued)

040:081   then **which** of the Signs of Allah will ye deny?
040:083   but that very (Wrath) at **which** they were
041:005   (concealed) from that to **which** thou dost invite us,
041:023   "But this thought of yours **which** ye did entertain
041:030   the **which** ye were promised!
041:040   **Which** is better?-he that is cast into the Fire, or he that
042:007   the Day of Assembly, of **which** there is no doubt:
042:013   the **which** We have sent by inspiration to thee-
042:013   and that **which** We enjoined on Abraham,
042:013   for you as that **which** He enjoined on Noah-
042:013   hard is the (way) to **which** thou callest them.
042:034   of the (evil) **which** (the men) have earned:
042:036   but that **which** is with Allah is better
042:047   before there come a Day **which** there will be
042:048   to him, on account of the deeds **which** his hands
043:012   and cattle on **which** ye ride,
043:021   before this, to **which** they are holding fast?
043:024   you better guidance than that **which** ye found
043:032   is better than the (wealth) **which** they amass.
043:033   and (silver) stair-ways on **which** to go up,
043:034   and couches (of silver) on **which** they could recline,
043:042   thee that (accomplished) **which** We have promised them:
043:063   to you some of the (points) on **which** ye dispute:
043:072   Such will be the Garden of **which** ye are made
043:073   of fruit, from **which** ye shall eat.
043:083   of theirs, **which** they have been promised.
044:033   in **which** there was a manifest trial.
045:006   **which** We rehearse to thee in truth:
045:017   matters in **which** they set up differences.
045:026   for the Day of Judgement about **which** there is
045:033   by that **which** they used to mock at!
046:009   I follow but that **which** is revealed to me
046:015   Thy favour **which** Thou hast bestowed upon me,
046:016   **which** was made to them (in this life).
046:019   according to the deeds **which** they (have done),
046:022   with **which** thou dost threaten us, if thou
046:023   I proclaim to you the mission on **which** I have
046:026   (completely) encircled by that **which** they used
046:026   in a (prosperity and) power **which** We have
047:006   And admit them to the Garden **which** He has
047:012   to Gardens beneath **which** rivers flow; while those
047:013   with more power than thy city **which** has driven thee out,
047:015   of the Garden **which** the righteous are promised:
047:015   rivers of milk of **which** the taste never changes;
047:028   This because they followed that **which** displeased Allah,
048:005   who believe, to Gardens beneath **which** rivers flow,
048:017   him to Gardens beneath **which** rivers flow;
048:021   but **which** Allah has compassed:
048:021   **which** are not within your power,
048:029   like a seed **which** sends forth its blade,
050:019   "This was the thing **which** thou wast trying to escape!"
051:005   Verily that **which** ye are promised is true;
051:009   Through **which** are deluded (away from the Truth)
051:016   Taking joy in the things **which** their Lord gives them,
051:022   as (also) that **which** ye are promised.
051:060   from the Day of theirs **which** they have
052:014   "Is the Fire,-**which** ye were wont to deny!
052:018   Enjoying the (Bliss) **which** their Lord
052:038   by **which** they can (climb up to heaven and) listen
053:011   in no way falsified that **which** he saw.
053:023   for **which** Allah has sent down no authority
053:023   These are nothing but name **which** ye have devised,-

WHICH (continued)

053:054 So that there covered it that **which** covered.
053:055 Then **which** of the favours of thy Lord, (O man),
054:026 **which** is the liar the insolent one!
054:034 (**which** destroyed them), except Lut's household:
055:013 Then **which** of the favours of your Lord
055:016 Then **which** of the favours of your Lord
055:018 Then **which** of the favours of your Lord
055:020 **which** they do not transgress:
055:021 Then **which** of the favours of your Lord
055:023 Then **which** of the favours of your Lord
055:025 Then **which** of the favours of your Lord
055:028 Then **which** of the favours of your Lord
055:030 Then **which** of the favours of your Lord
055:032 Then **which** of the favours of your Lord
055:034 Then **which** of the favours of your Lord
055:036 Then **which** of the favours of your Lord
055:038 Then **which** of the favours of your Lord
055:040 Then **which** of the favours of your Lord
055:042 Then **which** of the favours of your Lord
055:043 This is the Hell **which** the Sinners deny:
055:045 Then **which** of the favours of your Lord
055:047 Then **which** of the favours of your Lord
055:049 Then **which** of the favours of your Lord
055:051 Then **which** of the favours of your Lord
055:053 Then **which** of the favours of your Lord
055:055 Then **which** of the favours of thy Lord
055:057 Then **which** of the favours of your Lord
055:059 Then **which** of the favours of your Lord
055:061 Then **which** of the favours of your Lord
055:063 Then **which** of the favours of your Lord
055:065 Then **which** of the favours of your Lord
055:067 Then **which** of the favours of your Lord
055:069 Then **which** of the favours of your Lord
055:071 Then **which** of the favours of your Lord
055:073 Then **which** of the favours of your Lord
055:075 Then **which** of the favours of your Lord
055:077 Then **which** of the favours of your Lord
056:068 See ye the water **which** ye drink?
056:071 See ye the Fire **which** ye kindle?
056:072 It is ye who grow the trees **which** feeds the fire, or do
056:079 **Which** none shall touch but those who are clean:
057:012 Gardens beneath **which** flow rivers!
057:016 the Truth **which** has been revealed (to them),
057:020 and the growth **which** it brings forth,
057:021 **which** He bestows on whom He pleases:
057:025 And We sent down iron, in **which** is great might,
057:027 **which** they invented for themselves, We did not
057:028 by **which** ye shall walk (straight in your path),
058:006 Allah has reckoned and **which** they forgot,
058:006 and tell them of their deeds (**which**) Allah has
058:008 to that **which** they were forbidden (to do)?
058:022 beneath **which** Rivers flow, to dwell
059:002 came to them from quarters from **which** they little
059:021 such are the similitudes **which** We propound to men,
061:002 Why say ye that **which** ye do not?
061:003 of Allah that ye say that **which** ye do not.
061:006 confirming the Taurat (**which** came) before me,
061:012 and admit you to Gardens beneath **which** rivers flow,
061:013 And another (favour will He bestow), **which** ye do love,-
062:004 **which** He bestows on whom He will: and Allah
062:005 is that of a donkey **which** carries huge tomes
062:008 Say "The Death from **which** ye flee will truly

WHICH (continued)

062:011 Say: "That **which** Allah has is better than any
063:010 out of the substance **which** We have bestowed
064:008 and in the Light **which** We have sent down.
064:009 He will admit them to gardens beneath **which** rivers flow,
065:005 the Command of Allah, **which** He has sent down to you:
065:011 to Gardens beneath **which** rivers flow, to dwell
066:001 Holdest thou to be forbidden that **which** Allah has made
066:006 over **which** are (appointed) angels stern (and)
066:008 to Gardens beneath **which** rivers flow,-the Day
067:002 that He may try **which** of you is best in deed:
067:015 its tracts and enjoy of the sustenance **which** He furnishes:
067:027 is (the promise fulfilled), **which** ye were calling for!"
067:029 soon will ye know **which** (of us) it is that is in manifest
068:001 Nun. By the Pen and by the (Record) **which** (men) write,-
068:006 **Which** of you is afflicted with madness.
068:007 **which** (among men) hath strayed from His Path:
068:019 a visitation from thy Lord, (**which** swept away) all around,
068:037 Or have ye a Book through **which** ye learn-
068:040 Ask thou of them, **which** of them will stand
069:037 "**Which** none do eat but those in sin."
070:002 The Unbelievers the **which** there is none
070:042 that Day of theirs **which** they have been promised!
070:044 Such is the Day the **which** they are promised!
072:024 (with their own eyes) that **which** they are promised,-
072:025 whether the (Punishment) **which** ye are promised is near,
077:002 **Which** then blow violently in tempestuous Gusts,
077:021 The **which** We placed in a place of rest,
077:029 **which** ye used to reject as false!
077:031 "(**Which** yields) no shade of coolness, and is
078:003 About **which** they cannot agree.
078:040 man will see (the Deeds) **which** his hands have sent
082:015 **Which** they will enter on the Day of Judgment,
083:014 is the stain of the (ill) **which** they do!
083:017 "This is the (reality) **which** ye rejected as false!"
083:021 To **which** bear witness those Nearest (to Allah).
085:011 Beneath **which** Rivers flow: that is
086:011 By the Firmament **which** giveth returns rain,
086:012 And by the Earth **which** opens out (for the gushing
087:013 In **which** he will then neither die nor live.
088:007 **Which** will neither nourish nor satisfy hunger.
089:008 The like of **which** were not produced
092:019 from anyone for **which** a reward is expected
094:003 The **which** did gall thy back?-
094:004 And raised high the esteem (in **which**) thou (art held)?
096:005 Taught man that **which** he knew not.
098:008 Gardens of Eternity, Beneath **which** rivers flow;
100:009 Does he not know,-when that **which** is in the
100:010 And that **which** is (locked up) in (human)
104:004 to be thrown into that **which** Breaks to Pieces.
104:005 That **which** Breaks to Pieces?
104:007 The **which** doth mount (Right) to the Hearts:
105:005 and straw (of **which** the corn) has been eaten up.
109:002 I worship not that **which** ye worship,
109:003 Nor will ye worship that **which** I worship.
109:004 that **which** ye have been wont to worship,
109:005 Nor will ye worship that **which** I worship.

WHICHEVER

016:076 his master; **whichever** way he directs him,
028:028 **whichever** of the two terms I fulfil, let there
029:062 (which He gives) to **whichever** of His servants

WHILE

002:019 the **while** they are in terror of death.

WHILE (continued)

002:126	for a **while** will I grant them their pleasure,
002:187	**while** ye are in retreat in the mosques.
002:266	**while** he is stricken with old age,
003:039	**While** he was standing in prayer in the chamber,
003:071	**while** ye have knowledge?
003:083	**While** all creatures in the heavens and on earth have,
003:099	**while** ye were yourselves witnesses (to Allah's Covenant)?
003:101	**while** unto you are rehearsed the Signs of Allah,
003:154	**while** another band was stirred to anxiety
003:164	**while**, before that, they had been in manifest error.
003:168	**while** they themselves sit (at ease):
004:108	**while** He is with them when they plot by night.
005:001	are forbidden **while** ye are in the Sacred Precincts
005:024	and fight ye two, **while** we sit here.
005:095	**while** in the Sacred Precincts or in the state
006:091	**while** ye conceal much (of its contents):
007:004	or **while** they slept for their afternoon rest.
007:095	**while** they realized not (their peril).
007:097	Our wrath by night **while** they were asleep?
007:098	**while** they played about (care-free)?
007:111	"Keep him and his brother in suspense (for a **while**);
007:182	lead them step by step to ruin **while** they know not.
008:006	as if they were being driven to death **while** they saw it.
008:048	**while** I am near to you":
009:016	alone **while** Allah has not yet known those
009:017	of Allah **while** they witness against their own
009:085	that their souls may depart **while** they are unbelievers.
009:093	such as claim exemption **while** they are rich.
010:073	**while** We drowned in the Flood those who
010:091	"Ah now!-but a little **while** before, wast thou
010:098	enjoy (their life) for a **while**.
011:081	Now travel with thy family **while** yet a part
011:117	to destroy the towns unjustly **while** their people
012:013	devour him **while** ye attend not to him."
012:014	devour him **while** we are (so large) a party,
012:015	the truth of this affair **while** they perceive not."
012:107	(final) Hour all of a sudden **while** they perceive not?
013:013	the **while** they are disputing about Allah,
013:017	**while** that which is for the good of mankind remains
016:103	**while** this is Arabic, pure and clear.
017:012	made dark **while** the Sign of the Day We have
017:052	ye tarried but a little **while**!"
017:076	(therein) after thee, except for a little **while**.
018:017	**while** they lay in the open space in the midst
018:035	He went into his garden **while** he wronged himself:
018:104	**while** they thought that they were acquiring good
019:046	now get away from me for a good long **while**!"
020:125	**while** I had sight (before)?"
023:040	(Allah) said: "In but a little **while**, they are
023:110	**while** ye were laughing at them!
024:015	**while** it was most serious in the sight of Allah.
024:058	the **while** ye doff your clothes for the
026:036	"Keep him and his brother in suspense (for a **while**),
026:202	of a sudden, **while** they perceive it not;
027:050	even **while** they perceived it not.
029:014	them **while** they (persisted in) sin.
029:053	reach them,-of a sudden, **while** they perceive not!
031:024	We grant them their pleasure for a little **while**:
032:016	the **while** they call on their Lord, in Fear
033:018	but come to fight except for just a little **while**,
034:037	**while** secure they (reside) in the dwellings on high?
036:049	it will seize them **while** they are yet disputing

WHILE (continued)

037:012	Truly dost thou marvel, **while** they ridicule,
037:148	to enjoy (their life) for a **while**.
037:174	So turn thou away from them for a little **while**,
037:178	So turn thou away from them for a little **while**,
038:088	the truth of it (all) after a **while**."
039:008	Say, "Enjoy thy disbelief for a little **while**:
039:055	of a sudden, **while** ye perceive not!-
040:041	to call you to Salvation **while** ye call me to the Fire!
043:066	of a sudden, **while** they perceive not?
044:015	We shall indeed remove the Chastisement for a **while**,
046:010	and has believed **while** ye are arrogant,
047:003	**While** those who believe follow the Truth
047:012	**while** those who reject Allah will enjoy (this world)
048:026	**While** the Unbelievers got up in their hearts
051:043	"Enjoy (your brief day) for a little **while**!"
051:044	seized them, even **while** they were looking on.
052:048	of thy Lord the **while** thou standest forth,
053:007	**While** he was in the highest part of the horizon:
056:084	And ye the **while** (sit) looking on,-
059:008	**while** seeking Grace from Allah and (His) Good
063:010	why didst thou not give me respite for a little **while**?
066:008	**while** they say, "Our Lord! perfect our light
068:019	(which swept away) all around, **while** they were asleep.
068:043	**while** they were whole, (and had refused).
073:011	and bear with them for a little **while**.
077:046	enjoy yourselves (but) a little **while**, for that
086:017	give respite to them gently (for a **while**).
088:004	The **while** they enter the Blazing Fire,-
088:005	The **while** they are given, to drink,
100:004	And raise the dust in clouds the **while**,

WHILST

002:030	**Whilst** we do celebrate Thy praises
005:117	I was a witness over them **whilst** I dwelt amongst them;
006:131	the towns unjustly **whilst** their occupants
006:136	**whilst** the share of Allah reacheth
008:033	**whilst** they could ask for pardon.
008:033	**whilst** thou wast amongst them;
018:018	**whilst** they were asleep,

WHIRLWIND

002:266	that it should be caught in a **whirlwind**,

WHISPER

007:020	to **whisper** suggestions to them, in order
019:098	or hear (so much as) a **whisper** of them?
114:004	(of Evil), who withdraws (after his **whisper**),-

WHISPERED

020:120	But Satan **whispered** evil to him: he said,

WHISPERER

114:004	From the mischief of the **Whisperer** (of Evil),

WHISPERS

020:103	In **whispers** will they consult each other:
114:005	Who **whispers** into the hearts of Mankind,-

WHISTLING

008:035	is nothing but **whistling** and clapping of hands:

WHIT

004:049	and they will not be wronged a **whit**.
011:101	profited them no **whit** when there issued the decree

WHITE

002:187	until the **white** thread of dawn appear to you
003:106	some faces will be (lit up with) **white**,
003:107	But those whose faces will be (lit with) **white**,
007:108	and behold! it was **white** to all beholders!

WHITE (continued)

012:084   And his eyes became **white** with sorrow, and he
020:022   it shall come forth **white** (and shining),
026:033   and behold, it was **white** to all beholders!
027:012   and it will come forth **white** without stain
028:032   and it will come forth **white** without stain
035:027   the mountains are tracts **white** and red,

WHITHER

015:065   but pass on **whither** ye are ordered."
081:026   Then **whither** go ye?

WHITHERSOEVER

002:115   **whithersoever** ye turn, there is Allah's Face.
038:036   to flow gently to his order, **whithersoever** he willed,-

WHO

001:007   and **who** go not astray.
002:002   to those **who** fear Allah;
002:003   **Who** believe in the Unseen,
002:004   And **who** believe in the Revelation
002:005   and it is these **who** will prosper.
002:006   As to those **who** reject Faith,
002:008   Of the people there are some **who** say
002:009   deceive Allah and those **who** believe,
002:012   the ones **who** make mischief,
002:014   When they meet those **who** believe.
002:016   These are they **who** have bartered
002:017   a man **who** kindled a fire;
002:021   **who** created you and those **who** came before you
002:022   **who** has made the earth your couch,
002:024   which is prepared for those **who** reject faith.
002:025   **who** believe and work righteousness,
002:026   Those **who** believe know that it is the truth
002:026   except those **who** forsake (the path),
002:026   but those **who** reject Faith say: "What Means
002:027   and **who** sunder what Allah has ordered
002:027   Those **who** break Allah's Covenant
002:029   It is He **who** hath created for you
002:030   therein one **who** will make mischief
002:032   in truth it is Thou **who** art perfect
002:034   he was of those **who** reject Faith.
002:039   "But those **who** reject Faith
002:043   with those **who** bow down (in worship).
002:045   except to those **who** are humble.
002:046   **Who** bear in mind the certainty
002:058   (the portion of) those **who** do good."
002:062   Those **who** believe (in the Qur'an)
002:062   and **who** believe in Allah and the last day,
002:062   and those **who** follow the Jewish (Scriptures),
002:065   amongst you **who** transgressed in the matter
002:066   and a lesson to those **who** fear Allah.
002:078   **who** know not the Book,
002:079   Then woe to those **who** write the Book
002:081   Nay, those **who** seek gain in Evil,
002:082   But those **who** have faith
002:085   for those among you **who** behave like this
002:085   the same people, **who** slay among yourselves,
002:086   These are the people **who** buy the life of this world
002:090   Chastisement of those **who** reject Faith.
002:097   glad tidings for those **who** believe,
002:098   Allah is an enemy to those **who** reject Faith.
002:099   but those **who** are perverse.
002:113   what those say **who** know not,
002:114   And **who** is more unjust than he **who** forbids
002:118   any people **who** hold firmly to Faith (in their hearts).

WHO (continued)

002:121   those **who** reject faith therein,
002:125   My House for those **who** compass it round,
002:129   **Who** shall rehearse Thy Signs to them
002:130   And **who** turns away from the religion
002:137   it is they **who** are in schism;
002:138   and **who** can give a better hue than Allah.
002:140   **who** is more unjust than those **who** conceal the testimony
002:143   those **who** would turn on their heels (from the Faith).
002:143   to those **who** followed the Messenger from those
002:153   O ye **who** believe! seek help with
002:153   for God is with those **who** patiently persevere.
002:154   And say not of those **who** are slain
002:155   to those **who** patiently persevere,
002:156   **Who** say, when afflicted with calamity:
002:158   So if those **who** visit the House
002:158   He **Who** recognizeth and knoweth.
002:159   Those **who** conceal the clear (Signs)
002:160   Except those **who** repent and make amends
002:161   Those **who** reject Faith, and die rejecting,
002:165   Yet there are men **who** take (for worship)
002:166   clear themselves of those **who** follow (them):
002:166   Then would those **who** are followed clear
002:167   And those **who** followed would say: "If only
002:171   The parable of those **who** reject Faith
002:172   O ye **who** believe! eat of the good things
002:174   Those **who** conceal Allah's revelations in the Book,
002:175   They are the ones **who** buy Error
002:176   the Book in truth but those **who** seek causes
002:177   for the wayfarer, for those **who** ask,
002:178   O ye **who** believe! the law of equality
002:181   the guilt shall be on those **who** make the change.
002:183   O ye **who** believe! fasting is prescribed to you
002:184   For those **who** can do it (with hardship),
002:185   So every one of you **who** is present (at his home)
002:190   Fight in the cause of Allah those **who** fight you
002:191   Such is the reward of those **who** reject faith.
002:193   except to those **who** practice oppression.
002:194   Allah is with those **who** restrain themselves
002:195   for Allah loveth those **who** do good.
002:200   There are men **who** say: "Our Lord! Give us
002:201   And there are men **who** say: "Our Lord! give us
002:207   And there is the type of man **who** gives his life
002:208   O ye **who** believe! enter into Islam
002:212   The life of this world is alluring to those **who** reject faith,
002:212   and they scoff at those **who** believe.
002:214   those of faith **who** were with him cried:
002:214   came to those **who** passed away before you?
002:218   Those **who** believed and those **who** suffered exile
002:220   but Allah knows the man **who** means mischief
002:220   means mischief from the man **who** means good.
002:221   a slave woman **who** believes is better
002:221   a man slave **who** believes is better
002:222   Allah loves those **who** keep themselves pure and clean.
002:222   For Allah loves those **who** turn to Him constantly
002:223   good tidings to those **who** believe.
002:224   for Allah is One **who** heareth and knoweth
002:226   For those **who** take an oath for abstention
002:230   which He makes plain to those **who** know.
002:232   **who** believe in Allah and the Last Day.
002:233   for him **who** desires to complete the term.
002:236   is due from those **who** wish to do the right thing.
002:240   Those of you **who** die and leave widows

WHO (continued)

002:243	thy vision to those **who** abandoned their homes,
002:245	**Who** is he that will loan to Allah a beautiful loan,
002:246	knowledge of those of those **who** do wrong.
002:249	But those **who** were convinced that they must meet
002:249	Allah is with those **who** steadfastly persevere."
002:249	only those **who** taste not of it go with me;
002:254	Those **who** reject Faith-they are the wrong-doers
002:254	O ye **who** believe! spend out of (the bounties)
002:255	**Who** is thee can intercede in His presence
002:257	Of those **who** reject faith the patrons
002:257	Allah is the Protector of those **who** have faith:
002:258	"My Lord is He **Who** Giveth life and death."
002:258	was he confounded **who** (in arrogance) rejected Faith.
002:258	to one **who** disputed with Abraham about his Lord,
002:259	of one **who** passed by a hamlet,
002:261	The parable of those **who** spend their wealth
002:262	Those **who** spend their wealth in the cause
002:264	And Allah guideth not those **who** reject faith.
002:264	O ye **who** believe! cancel not your charity
002:264	like those **who** spend their wealth in the cause of Allah
002:265	those **who** spend their wealth seeking to please
002:267	O ye **who** believe! give of the good things
002:273	**who**, in Allah's cause are restricted (from travel).
002:274	Those **who** (in charity) spend of their goods by night
002:275	Those **who** after receiving admonition
002:275	but those **who** repeat (the offense)
002:275	Those **who** devour usury will not stand
002:277	Those **who** believe, and do deeds
002:278	O ye **who** believe! fear Allah,
002:282	Let him **who** incurs the liability dictate,
002:282	O ye **who** believe! when ye deal with each other,
003:003	It is He **Who** sent down to thee (step by step),
003:004	Then those **who** reject Faith in the Signs
003:006	He it is **Who** shapes you in the wombs
003:007	He it is **Who** has sent down to thee the Book:
003:007	And those **who** are firmly grounded in knowledge
003:010	Those **who** reject faith,
003:012	Say to those **who** reject Faith: "Soon
003:016	(Namely), those **who** say: "Our Lord!
003:017	and **who** pray for forgiveness in the early hours
003:017	**who** worship devoutly:
003:017	Those **who** show patience, (firmness and self-control);
003:017	**who** spend (in the way of God);
003:017	**who** are true (in word and deed);
003:020	the Book and to those **who** are unlearned:
003:020	to Allah and so have those **who** follow me."
003:021	and slay those **who** teach just dealing with mankind,
003:021	As to those **who** deny the Signs of Allah,
003:023	those **who** have been given a portion of the Book?
003:032	Allah loveth not those **who** reject Faith.
003:043	(in prayer) with those **who** bow down."
003:051	"It is Allah **who** is my Lord and your Lord;
003:052	"**Who** will be my helpers to (the work of) Allah?"
003:053	then write us down among those **who** bear witness."
003:055	**who** follow thee superior to those **who** reject faith,
003:055	(of the falsehoods) of those **who** blaspheme;
003:056	"As to those **who** reject faith,
003:057	but Allah loveth not those **who** do wrong.
003:057	"As to those **who** believe and work righteousness,
003:060	so be not of those **who** doubt
003:061	And invoke the curse of Allah on those **who** lie!
003:063	Allah hath full knowledge of those **who** do mischief.

WHO (continued)

003:066	Ah! Ye are those **who** fell to disputing (even)
003:066	It is Allah **Who** knows, and ye **who** know not!
003:068	and Allah is the Protector of those **who** have faith.
003:068	as are also this Prophet and those **who** believe:
003:068	are those **who** follow him,
003:075	others, **who**, if entrusted with a single silver coin,
003:075	Among the People of the Book are some **who**,
003:076	verily Allah loves those **who** act aright.
003:077	As for those **who** sell the faith they owe to Allah
003:078	it is they **who** tell a lie against Allah,
003:078	a section **who** distort the Book with their tongues;
003:079	Him (**Who** is truly the Cherisher of all)
003:085	in the ranks of those **who** have lost.
003:086	**who** reject faith after they accepted it and bore
003:090	for they are those **who** have gone astray.
003:090	But those **who** reject faith after they accepted it.
003:091	As to those **who** reject faith, and die rejecting,
003:097	those **who** can afford the journey;
003:099	Why obstruct those **who** believe, from the path of Allah,
003:100	O ye **who** believe! if ye listen to a faction
003:102	O ye **who** believe! fear Allah as He should be feared,
003:105	Be not like those **who** are divided amongst themselves
003:110	among them are some **who** have faith,
003:116	Those **who** reject faith, neither their
003:117	harvest of men **who** have wronged their own souls:
003:118	O ye **who** believe! take not into your intimacy
003:119	Ah! ye are those **who** love them,
003:130	O ye **who** believe! devour not usury,
003:131	prepared for those **who** reject Faith.
003:134	Those **who** spend (freely), whether in prosperity,
003:134	for Allah loves those **who** do good:
003:134	**who** restrain anger, and pardon (all) men;
003:135	and **who** can forgive sins except Allah?
003:135	And those **who**, having done an act of indecency
003:136	for those **who** work (and strive)!
003:137	what was the end of those **who** rejected Truth.
003:138	a guidance and instruction to those **who** fear Allah!
003:142	**who** fought hard (in His Cause) and remained steadfast
003:144	those **who** (serve him) with gratitude.
003:146	And Allah loves those **who** are firm and steadfast.
003:148	For Allah loveth those **who** do good.
003:149	O ye **who** believe! If ye obey the Unbelievers,
003:152	for Allah is full of grace to those **who** believe.
003:155	it was Satan **who** caused them to fail,
003:155	Those of you **who** turned back on the day the two
003:156	**who** say of their brethren, when they travelling
003:156	O ye **who** believe! Be not like the Unbelievers,
003:159	For Allah loves those **who** put their trust (in Him).
003:160	if He forsakes you, **who** is there, after that,
003:162	the man **who** draws on Himself the wrath of Allah,
003:162	Is the man **who** follows the good pleasure of Allah
003:169	Think not those **who** are slain in Allah's way as dead.
003:170	**who** have not yet joined them (in their bliss),
003:172	Of those **who** answered the call of Allah
003:172	those **who** do right and refrain from wrong
003:176	not those grieve thee **who** rush headlong into Unbelief:
003:177	Those **who** purchase Unbelief at the price of Faith,
003:180	And let not those **who** covetously withhold of the
003:181	Allah hath heard the taunt of those **who** say:
003:182	for Allah never do injustice those **who** serve Him."
003:184	**who** came with Clear Signs, and the Scriptures.
003:185	Only he **who** is saved far from the fire and

WHO (continued)

003:186   from those **who** received the Book before you
003:186   and from those **who** worship parties besides Allah.
003:188   **who** exult in what they have brought about,
003:191   Men **who** remember Allah, standing, sitting,
003:195   those **who** have left their homes, and were driven
003:198   On the other hand, for those **who** fear their Lord,
003:199   those **who** believe in Allah, in the revelation to you,
003:200   O ye **who** believe! Persevere in patience
004:001   **Who** created you from a single person,
004:010   Those **who** unjustly eat up the property of orphans,
004:013   those **who** obey Allah and His Messenger will be
004:014   But those **who** disobey Allah and His Messenger
004:017   **who** do evil in ignorance and repent soon afterwards;
004:018   nor of those **who** die rejecting faith:
004:018   of those **who** continue to do evil, until death
004:019   O ye **who** believe! ye are forbidden to inherit
004:023   (those **who** have been) wives of your son
004:023   foster-mothers (**who** gave you suck),
004:025   for those among you **who** fear sin;
004:027   **who** follow their lusts is that ye should turn
004:029   O ye **who** believe! eat not up your property
004:036   those in need, neighbors **who** are of kin,
004:036   neighbors **who** are strangers, the Companion
004:037   for We have prepared, for those **who** resist Faith,
004:037   (Nor) those **who** are niggardly,
004:038   (Nor) those **who** spend of their substance, to be
004:042   On that day those **who** reject Faith and
004:043   O ye **who** believe! approach not prayers in a state
004:044   to those **who** were given a portion of the Book?
004:046   those **who** displace words from their (right) places,
004:049   to those **who** claim purity for themselves?
004:051   to those **who** were given a portion of the Book?
004:056   Those **who** reject Our Signs, We shall soon
004:057   But those **who** believe and do
004:058   For Allah is He **Who** heareth and seeth all things.
004:059   O ye **who** believe! obey Allah, and obey
004:060   to those **who** declare that they believe in
004:069   the martyres, and the Righteous (**who** do good):
004:069   All **who** obey Allah and the Messenger are in the
004:069   of the Prophets (**who** teach), the Sincere
004:071   O ye **who** believe! take your precautions.
004:072   men **who** would tarry behind:
004:074   **who** sell the life of this world for the Hereafter.
004:074   To him **who** fighteth in the cause of Allah, whether
004:075   and raise for us from Thee one **who** will help!"
004:075   the cause of Allah and of those **who**, being
004:075   and raise for us from Thee one **who** will protect;
004:076   Those **who** believe fight in the cause of Allah,
004:076   and those **who** reject Faith fight in the cause
004:077   to those **who** were told to hold back their hands
004:077   the Hereafter is the best for those **who** do right:
004:080   He **who** obeys the Messenger, obeys Allah:
004:090   Except those **who** join a group between whom
004:090   or those **who** approach you with hearts restraining
004:092   For those **who** find this beyond their means,
004:094   and say not to anyone **who** offers you a salutation:
004:094   O ye **who** believe! when ye go out in the cause
004:095   to those **who** strive and fight with their goods
004:095   And those **who** strive and fight in the cause
004:095   except those **who** are disabled.
004:095   but those **who** strive and fight hath He
004:095   Not equal are those Believers **who** sit (at home),

WHO (continued)

004:095   those **who** sit (at home).
004:095   those **who** sit at home by a great reward.
004:097   those **who** die in sin against their soul.
004:098   Except those **who** are (really) weak and oppressed,
004:098   and children **who** have no means in their power,
004:100   He **who** forsakes his home in the cause of Allah,
004:105   those **who** betray their trust;
004:109   but **who** will contend with Allah on their behalf
004:109   or **who** will carry their affairs through?
004:114   to him **who** does this, seeking the good-pleasure
004:116   one **who** joins other gods with Allah,
004:122   But those **who** believe and do deeds
004:125   than one **who** submits his whole self to Allah,
004:125   **Who** can be better in religion than one
004:127   the children **who** are weak and oppressed:
004:135   O ye **who** believe! stand out firmly for justice,
004:136   And **who** denieth Allah, His angels, His Books,
004:136   O ye **who** believe! believe in Allah
004:137   Those **who** believe, then reject Faith,
004:139   Those **who** take for friends Unbelievers rather
004:140   and those **who** defy Faith-all in Hell;
004:141   (These are) the ones **who** wait and watch about you:
004:142   but it is Allah **who** deceive them.
004:144   O ye **who** believe! take not for friends
004:146   Except for those **who** repent, mend (their life),
004:148   except by one **who** has been wronged,
004:148   for Allah is He **who** heareth and knoweth all things.
004:150   Those **who** deny Allah and his Messenger,
004:152   To those **who** believe in Allah and His messengers
004:157   And those **who** differ therein are full of doubts,
004:161   among them **who** reject faith a grievous chastisement.
004:162   and (especially) those **who** establish regular prayer
004:162   But those among them **who** are well-grounded
004:165   Messengers **who** gave good news as well
004:167   Those **who** reject Faith and keep off
004:168   Those **who** reject Faith and do wrong,-Allah will
004:172   those **who** disdain His worship and are arrogant,
004:173   but those **who** are disdainful and arrogant, He will
004:173   But those **who** believe and do deeds
004:175   Then those **who** believe in Allah, and hold
004:176   those **who** leave no descendants or ascendants
004:176   if (such a deceased was) a woman, **who** left no child,
005:001   O ye **who** believe! fulfil (all) obligations.
005:002   O ye **who** believe! violate not the sanctity
005:003   This day have those **who** reject Faith given up
005:005   those **who** have lost (all spiritual good).
005:005   are (not only) chaste women **who** are believers,
005:006   O ye **who** believe! when ye prepare for prayer, wash
005:008   O ye **who** believe! stand out firmly for Allah,
005:009   To those **who** believe and do deeds of righteousness
005:010   Those **who** reject faith and deny Our Signs will be
005:011   O ye **who** believe! call in remembrance
005:013   for Allah loveth those **who** are kind.
005:014   From those, too, **who** call themselves Christians,
005:016   Wherewith Allah guideth all **who** seek His good
005:017   Say: "**Who** then hath the least power against Allah,
005:027   the sacrifice of those **who** are righteous.
005:029   and that is the reward of those **who** do wrong."
005:031   **who** scratched the ground, to show him how
005:033   **who** wage war against Allah and His Messenger,
005:034   Except for those **who** repent before they
005:035   O ye **who** believe! do your duty to Allah,

WHO (continued)

005:036   As to those **who** reject Faith,-if they had
005:041   **who** race each other into Unbelief:
005:041   to others **who** have never so much as come to thee.
005:041   men **who** will listen to any lie,-will listen even
005:041   (whether it be) among those **who** say: "We believe"
005:042   For Allah loveth those **who** judge in equity.
005:044   by the Prophets **who** bowed (as in Islam)
005:044   It was We **who** revealed the Torah (to Moses):
005:046   an admonition to those **who** fear Allah.
005:047   by what Allah hath revealed, they are indeed rebel.
005:050   But **who**, for a people whose faith is assured,
005:051   O ye **who** believe! take not the Jews and the
005:053   **who** swore their strongest oaths by Allah,
005:053   And those **who** believe will say: "Are these the men
005:054   O ye **who** believe! if any from among you turn
005:055   those **who** establish regular prayers and pay
005:056   As to those **who** turn (for friendship)
005:057   or among those **who** reject Faith:
005:057   those **who** take your religion for a mockery
005:057   those **who** received the Scripture before you,
005:057   O ye **who** believe! take not for friends
005:060   those **who** worshipped Evil (Tagut)-these are
005:060   Those **who** incurred the curse of Allah
005:064   And Allah loveth not those **who** do mischief.
005:067   Allah will defend thee from men (**who** mean mischief).
005:067   For Allah guideth not those **who** reject Faith.
005:069   Those **who** follow the Jewish (Scriptures),
005:069   Those **who** believe (in the Qur'an).
005:069   any **who** believe in Allah and the Last Day
005:072   Certainly they disbelieve **who** say: "Allah is Christ
005:073   They disbelieve **who** say: Allah is one
005:077   of people **who** went wrong in times gone by,-
005:077   **who** misled many, and strayed themselves
005:078   **who** rejected Faith, by the tongue
005:082   And men **who** have renounced the world, and they
005:082   **who** say, "We are Christians:" because amongst
005:085   Such is the recompense of those **who** do good.
005:086   But those **who** reject Faith and belie
005:087   O ye **who** believe! make not unlawful the good
005:090   O ye **who** believe! intoxicants and
005:093   For Allah loveth those **who** do good.
005:093   On those **who** believe and do deeds
005:094   O ye **who** believe! Allah doth but make a trial
005:094   that He may test **who** feareth Him unseen:
005:094   any **who** transgress thereafter will have
005:095   O ye **who** believe! kill not game, while in
005:096   for the benefit of yourselves and those **who** travel;
005:101   O ye **who** believe! ask not questions about things
005:103   it is the disbelievers **who** invent a lie against Allah
005:103   **Who** instituted (superstitions like those of) a
005:105   no hurt can come to you from those **who** stray.
005:105   O ye **who** believe! guard your own souls: if ye
005:106   O ye **who** believe! when death approaches any of you,
005:107   nearest in kin from among those **who** claim a lawful right:
005:109   it is Thou **who** knowest in full all that is hidden.
005:120   and it is He **who** hath power over all things.
006:001   Yet those **who** reject Faith hold (others)
006:001   Praise be to Allah, **Who** created the heavens
006:002   He it is **Who** created you from clay, and then
006:011   what was the end of those **who** rejected Truth."
006:012   It is they **who** have lost their own souls,
006:013   **Who** heareth and knoweth all things.

WHO (continued)

006:014   of those **who** join gods with Allah."
006:014   the first of those **who** bow to Allah (in Islam),
006:020   Those **who** have lost their own souls refuse
006:021   **Who** doth more wrong than he **who** inventeth a lie
006:022   We shall say to those **who** ascribed partners (to Us):
006:023   not those **who** joined gods with Allah."
006:025   Of them there are some **who** (pretend to) listen to thee;
006:027   but would be amongst those **who** believe!"
006:031   Lost indeed are they **who** treat it as a falsehood
006:032   for those **who** are righteous.
006:035   **who** are swayed by ignorance (and impatience)!
006:036   Those **who** listen (in truth), be sure,
006:039   Those **who** reject Our Signs are deaf and dumb,-
006:046   **who**-a god other than Allah-could restore them to you?"
006:047   will any be destroyed except those **who** do wrong?"
006:048   so those **who** believe and mend (their lives),-
006:049   But those **who** reject Our Signs,-them shall
006:052   Send not away those **who** call on their Lord
006:053   Doth not Allah know best those **who** are grateful?.
006:054   **who** believe in Our Signs, say: "Peace be on you:
006:056   the company of those **who** receive guidance."
006:058   But Allah knoweth best those **who** do wrong."
006:059   a Record Clear (to those **who** can read).
006:060   It is He **Who** doth take your souls by night,
006:063   Say: "**Who** is it that delivereth you from the dark
006:068   sit not thou in the company of those **who** do wrong.
006:070   such is (the end of) those **who** deliver themselves
006:070   Leave alone those **who** take their religion
006:073   It is He **Who** created the heavens and
006:077   I shall surely be among those **who** go astray."
006:079   toward Him **Who** created the heavens and the
006:082   "It is those **who** believe and mix not
006:084   thus do We reward those **who** do good:
006:089   to a new People **who** reject them not.
006:090   were the (prophets) **who** received Allah's guidance.
006:091   Say: "**Who** then sent down the Book
006:092   Those **who** believe in the Hereafter believe in
006:093   or (again) **who** saith, "I can reveal the like of what Allah
006:093   one **who** inventeth a lie against Allah, or saith,
006:093   **Who** can be more wicked than one **who**
006:095   It is Allah **Who** causeth the seed-grain and the
006:097   It is He **Who** maketh the stars
006:097   We detail Our Signs for people **who** know.
006:098   It is He **who** hath produced you from a single soul:
006:098   We detail Our signs for people **who** understand.
006:099   It is He **who** sendeth down rain from the skies:
006:099   in these things there are signs for people **who** believe.
006:105   We may make the matter clear to those **who** know.
006:106   those **who** join gods with Allah.
006:113   **who** have no faith in the Hereafter:
006:114   Never be then of those **who** doubt.
006:114   **Who** hath sent unto you the Book, explained
006:115   for He is the one **Who** heareth and knoweth all.
006:117   He knoweth best those **who** are rightly guided.
006:117   Thy Lord knoweth best **who** strayeth from His Way:
006:119   Thy Lord knoweth best those **who** transgress.
006:120   those **who** earn sin will get due recompense
006:122   be like him **who** is in the depths of darkness,
006:122   Can he **who** was dead, to whom We give life,
006:125   lay abomination on those **who** refuse to believe.
006:126   the Signs for those **who** receive admonition.
006:135   soon will ye know **who** it is whose end

WHO (continued)

006:140   Lost are those **who** slay their children,
006:141   It is He **who** produceth gardens,
006:144   But **who** doth more wrong than one
006:144   than one **who** invents a lie against Allah, to lead
006:145   For Allah guideth not people **who** do wrong.
006:145   by one **who** wishes to eat it, unless it
006:146   For those **who** followed the Jewish Law, We
006:148   Those **who** give partners (to Allah) will say:
006:154   those **who** would do right, and explaining
006:157   those **who** turn away from Our Signs, with
006:157   then **who** could do more wrong than one
006:157   than one **who** rejecteth Allah's Signs, and turneth
006:159   As for those **who** divide their religion and
006:163   those **who** submit to His Will.
006:165   It is He **Who** hath made you the inheritors
007:010   It is We **who** have placed you with authority on earth,
007:011   It is We **who** created you and gave you shape:
007:011   he refused to be of those **who** prostrate.
007:015   "Be thou among those **who** have respite."
007:032   Say: **Who** hath forbidden the beautiful
007:032   in detail for those **who** know.
007:032   for those **who** believe, (and) purely for
007:035   those **who** are righteous and mend (their lives),
007:036   But those **who** reject Our Signs and treat
007:037   **Who** is more unjust than one **who** forges a lie against
007:038   of the Peoples **who** passed away before you-men
007:040   To those **who** reject Our Signs and treat
007:041   such is Our requital of those **who** do wrong.
007:042   But those **who** believe and work righteousness,-
007:043   **Who** hath guided us to this (felicity):
007:045   "Those **who** would hinder (men) from the
007:045   they were those **who** denied the Hereafter."
007:046   **who** would know every one by his marks:
007:050   hath Allah forbidden to those **who** rejected Him;
007:052   a guide and a mercy to all **who** believe.
007:053   those **who** have forgotten it before will say: "The
007:054   **Who** created the heavens and the earth
007:055   those **who** trespass beyond bounds.
007:056   is (always) near to those **who** do good.
007:057   It is He **Who** sendeth the Winds
007:058   by various (symbols) to those **who** are grateful.
007:064   those **who** rejected Our Signs, they were
007:072   the roots of those **who** rejected Our Signs and
007:072   We saved him and those **who** adhered to him, by Our
007:075   those among them **who** believe: "Know ye
007:075   his people said to those **who** were reckoned powerless-
007:082   these are indeed men **who** want to be clean and pure!"
007:083   she was of those **who** lagged behind.
007:084   those **who** indulged in sin and crime!
007:086   the path of Allah those **who** believe in Him, and
007:086   And see what was the end of those **who** did mischief.
007:087   **who** believes in the message with which
007:088   (thee) and those **who** believe with thee; or else
007:092   the men **who** rejected Shu'aib-
007:092   The men **who** rejected Shu'aib became as if
007:092   it was they **who** were ruined!
007:093   a people **who** refuse to believe!"
007:100   To those **who** inherit the earth in succession
007:101   the heart of those **who** reject Faith.
007:103   of those **who** made mischief.
007:126   as Muslims (**who** bow to Thy Will)"!
007:140   when it is He **who** hath endowed you with

WHO (continued)

007:141   of punishment **who** slew your male children and
007:141   **who** afflicted you with the worst of punishment
007:142   the way of those **who** do mischief."
007:144   and be of those **who** give thanks."
007:146   Those **who** behave arrogantly on the earth
007:147   Those **who** reject Our Signs and the Meeting
007:151   of those **who** sow mercy!"
007:152   Those **who** took the calf (for worship) will
007:152   those **who** invent (falsehoods).
007:153   But those **who** do wrong but repent
007:155   for Thou art the best of those **who** forgive.
007:156   That (Mercy) I shall ordain for those **who** do right,
007:156   and pay Zakat and those **who** believe in Our Signs;
007:157   it is they **who** will prosper."
007:157   So it is those **who** believe in him, honor him,
007:157   "Those **who** follow the Messenger, the unlettered
007:158   **who** believed in Allah and His Words:
007:159   there is a section **who** guide and do justice
007:161   (the portion of) those **who** do good."
007:165   We rescued those **who** forbade evil; but We
007:167   those **who** would afflict them with grievous chastisement.
007:170   As to those **who** hold fast by the Book
007:172   "Am I not your Lord (**who** cherishes and sustains you)?"-
007:173   the deeds of men **who** followed falsehood?"
007:176   of those **who** reject Our Signs; so relate
007:177   **who** reject Our signs and wrong their own souls.
007:178   such are the persons **who** lose.
007:181   are people **who** direct (others) with truth,
007:182   Those **who** reject Our signs, We shall
007:188   to those **who** have faith."
007:189   It is He **Who** created you from a single person.
007:196   **Who** revealed the Book, (from time to time),
007:201   Those **who** fear Allah, when a thought
007:203   and Guidance, and Mercy, for any **who** have Faith."
007:205   and be not thou of those **who** are unheedful.
007:206   Those **who** are near to thy Lord, disdain not
008:002   For, Believers are those **who**, when Allah
008:003   **Who** establish regular prayers and spend
008:014   for those **who** reject is the chastisement
008:015   O ye **who** believe! when ye meet the Unbelievers
008:017   It is not ye **who** slew them; it was Allah:
008:017   He **who** heareth and knoweth (all things).
008:018   He **Who** makes feeble the Plans and stratagems
008:019   for verily Allah is with those **who** believe!
008:020   O ye **who** believe! obey Allah and His Messenger,
008:021   Nor be like those **who** say, "We hear,"
008:022   and the dumb,-those **who** understand not.
008:024   O ye **who** believe! give your response
008:025   not in particular (only) those of you **who** do wrong:
008:029   O ye **who** believe! if ye fear Allah, He will
008:042   and those **who** lived might live after a Clear Sign
008:042   **who** died might die after a clear Sign (had been
008:042   is He **Who** heareth and knoweth (all things).
008:045   O ye **who** believe! when ye meet a force,
008:046   for Allah is with those **who** patiently persevere.
008:047   And be not like those **who** started from their homes
008:053   and verily Allah is He **Who** heareth and knoweth
008:055   beasts in the sight of Allah are those **who** reject Him:
008:057   those **who** follow them, that they may remember.
008:064   and unto those **who** follow thee among the Believers.
008:066   for Allah is with those **who** patiently persevere.
008:070   O Prophet! say to those **who** are captives in your hands:

WHO (continued)

008:071   **who** hath (full) knowledge and wisdom.
008:072   Those **who** believed, and emigrated and fought
008:072   as well as those **who** gave (them) asylum and aid,-
008:072   **who** believed but did not emigrate ye owe no duty
008:074   Those **who** believe, and emigrate, and fight
008:074   as well as those **who** give (them) asylum and aid,-
008:075   And those **who** accept Faith subsequently, and
009:002   with shame those **who** reject Him.
009:003   a grievous chastisement to those **who** reject Faith.
009:004   ye have entered into alliance and **who** have not
009:010   It is they **who** have transgressed all bounds.
009:011   for those **who** understand.
009:013   Will you not fight people **who** violated their oaths,
009:016   known those among you **who** strive with might and main,
009:018   It is they **who** are expected to be on true guidance.
009:019   (the pious service of) those **who** believe in Allah
009:019   and Allah guides not those **who** do wrong.
009:020   Those **who** believe, and emigrate and strive
009:020   They are the people **who** will achieve (salvation).
009:023   O ye **who** believe! Take not for protectors
009:028   O ye **who** believe! Truly the Pagans are unclean;
009:029   Fight those **who** believe not in Allah nor the
009:033   It is He **who** hath sent His Messenger
009:034   those **who** hoard gold and silver and spend
009:034   **who** in falsehood devour the wealth of men
009:034   O ye **who** believe! There are indeed many among
009:036   with those **who** restrain themselves.
009:037   not those **who** reject Faith.
009:038   O ye **who** believe! what is the matter with you,
009:043   **who** told the truth were seen by thee in a clear
009:044   Those **who** believe in Allah and the Last Day
009:044   And Allah knoweth well those **who** do their duty.
009:045   **who** believe not in Allah and the Last Day,
009:046   were told, "Sit ye among those **who** sit (inactive)."
009:047   But Allah knoweth well those **who** do wrong.
009:047   among you **who** would have listened to them.
009:049   Among them is (many) a man **who** says: "Grant me
009:058   **who** slander thee in the matter of (the distribution of)
009:061   But those **who** molest the Prophet will have
009:061   Among them are men **who** molest the Prophet and say,
009:061   and is a Mercy to those of you **who** believe."
009:063   that for those **who** oppose Allah and His Messenger,
009:070   **Who** wrongs them, but they wrong their own souls.
009:075   Amongst them are men **who** made a Covenant
009:075   and be truly amongst those **who** are righteous.
009:079   as well as those **who** give according to their means,-
009:079   **who** slander such of the Believers as give themselves
009:080   Allah guideth not those **who** are perversely rebellious.
009:081   Those **who** were left behind (in the tabuk expedition)
009:083   then sit ye (now) with those **who** stay behind."
009:086   we would be with those **who** sit (at home)."
009:087   **who** remain behind (at home):
009:088   and it is they **who** will prosper.
009:088   But the Messenger, and those **who** believe with him,
009:090   Men **who** made excuses and came to claim
009:090   and those **who** were false to Allah and His Messenger
009:091   or **who** find no resources to spend (on the Cause),
009:091   There is no blame on those **who** are infirm, or ill,
009:092   Nor (is there blame) on those **who** came to thee to be
009:093   prefer to stay with the (women) **who** remain behind:
009:094   to Him **Who** knoweth what is hidden and what
009:096   Allah is not pleased with those **who** disobey.

WHO (continued)

009:100   the first of those **who** forsook (their homes)
009:100   and (also) those **who** follow them in (all) good deeds,
009:100   and of those **who** gave them aid,
009:102   Others (there are **who**) have acknowledged
009:103   and Allah is one **who** heareth and knoweth.
009:107   And there are those **who** put up a mosque by way
009:107   and in preparation for one **who** warred against
009:108   In it are men **who** love to be purified;
009:108   and Allah loveth those **who** make themselves pure.
009:110   The foundation of those **who** so build is never free
009:111   and **who** is more faithful to his Covenant than Allah?
009:113   for the Prophet and those **who** believe,
009:117   **who** followed Him in a time of distress,
009:118   turned in mercy also) to the three **who** were left Behind;
009:119   O ye **who** Believe! Fear Allah and be
009:119   and be with those **who** are truthful.
009:120   the reward to be lost of those **who** do good;-
009:123   Fight the Unbelievers **who** are near to you,
009:123   O ye **who** believe! Fight the Unbelievers
009:123   and know that Allah is with those **who** fear Him.
009:124   Yea, those **who** believe, their faith is increased,
010:003   **Who** created the heavens and the earth in six
010:004   It is He **Who** beginneth the process of Creation,
010:004   those **who** believe and work righteousness,
010:004   but those **who** reject Him will have draughts of
010:005   doth He explain His Signs in detail, for those **who** know.
010:005   It is He **Who** made the sun to be a shining glory
010:006   are Signs for those **who** fear Him.
010:007   Those **who** rest not their hope on their
010:007   and those **who** heed not Our Signs,-
010:009   Those **who** believe, and work righteousness,
010:011   But We leave those **who** rest not their hope
010:013   Thus do We requite those **who** sin!
010:015   those **who** rest not their hope on their meeting with Us,
010:017   **Who** doth more wrong than such as forge a lie against
010:017   But never will prosper those **who** sin.
010:022   He it is **Who** enableth you to traverse through
010:024   the Signs in detail for those **who** reflect.
010:026   To those **who** do right is a goodly (reward)-yea,
010:027   But those **who** have earned evil will have
010:028   Then shall We say to those **who** joined gods
010:031   Or **who** is it that has power over hearing and sight?
010:031   And **who** is it that brings out the living from the dead
010:031   Say: "**Who** is it that sustains you (in life) from the sky
010:031   And **who** is it that rules and regulates all affairs?"
010:033   proved true against those **who** rebel:
010:034   Say: "It is Allah **Who** originates Creation
010:035   Say: "It is Allah **Who** gives guidance towards Truth.
010:035   **who** finds not guidance (himself) unless he is guided?
010:035   Is then He **Who** gives guidance to Truth more worthy
010:039   but see what was the end of those **who** did wrong!
010:040   those **who** are out for mischief.
010:040   Of them there are some **who** believe therein,
010:040   believe therein, and some **who** do not:
010:042   Among them are some **who** (pretend to)
010:043   And among them are some **who** look at thee:
010:045   **who** denied the meeting with Allah and refused
010:056   Is it He **who** giveth life and **who** taketh it, and to
010:057   and for those **who** believe, a Guidance and a Mercy.
010:060   And what think those **who** forge lies against Allah,
010:063   Those **who** believe and (constantly) guard against evil;-
010:065   it is He **Who** heareth and knoweth (all things).

WHO (continued)

010:066	What do they follow **who** worship as His "partners"
010:067	for those **who** listen (to His Message).
010:069	Say: "Those **who** forge a lie against Allah
010:072	of those **who** submit to Allah's Will (in Islam)."
010:073	those **who** rejected Our Signs.
010:073	those **who** were warned (but heeded not)!
010:081	the work of those **who** make mischief.
010:083	and one **who** transgressed all bounds.
010:085	for those **who** practice oppression;
010:086	from those **who** reject (Thee)."
010:087	and give Glad Tidings to those **who** believe!"
010:089	and follow not the path of those **who** know not."
010:090	I am of those **who** submit (to Allah in Islam)."
010:092	a Sign to those **who** come after thee!
010:094	then ask those **who** have been reading the Book
010:095	or thou shalt be of those **who** perish.
010:095	Nor be of those **who** reject the Signs of Allah,
010:099	all **who** are on earth!
010:100	place abomination on those **who** will not understand.
010:101	neither Signs nor Warners profit those **who** believe not.
010:102	of the men **who** passed away before them?
010:103	that We should deliver those **who** believe!
010:103	Our messengers and those **who** believe:
010:104	But I worship Allah-**who** will take your souls
010:106	thou shalt certainly be of those **who** do wrong."
010:108	Those, **who** receive guidance, do so for their own souls;
010:108	those **who** stray, do so to their own loss:
011:001	in detail, from One **Who** is Wise and Well-
011:003	and His abounding grace on all **who** abound in merit!
011:007	He it is **Who** created the heavens and the earth
011:011	Not so do those **who** show patience and constancy,
011:015	Those **who** desire the life of the Present
011:017	Can they be (like) those **who** accept a Clear
011:018	"These are the ones **who** lied against their Lord!
011:018	**Who** doth more wrong than those **who** forge a lie
011:018	the Curse of Allah is on those **who** do wrong!-
011:019	"Those **who** would hinder (men) from the path of
011:019	"These were they **who** denied the Hereafter!"
011:021	They are the ones **who** have lost their own souls:
011:022	ones **who** will lose most in the Hereafter!
011:023	But those **who** believe and work righteousness,
011:024	and those **who** can see and hear well.
011:029	I will not drive away (in contempt) those **who** believe:
011:030	"And O my People! **who** would help me
011:036	except those **who** have believed already!
011:037	on behalf of those **who** are in sin: for they
011:039	"But soon will ye know **who** it is on whom
011:042	**who** had separated himself (from the rest):
011:043	those **who** were drowned.
011:044	"Away with those **who** do wrong!"
011:048	the Peoples (**who** will spring) from those with thee:
011:049	for the End is for those **who** are righteous.
011:051	My reward is from none but Him **Who** created Me:
011:058	We saved Hud and those **who** believed with him,
011:061	It is He **Who** hath produced you from the earth
011:063	**who** then can help me against Allah if i were to disobey
011:066	We saved Salih and those **who** believed with him,
011:083	ever far from those **who** do wrong!
011:093	soon will ye know **who** it is on whom descends the
011:093	and **who** is a liar!
011:094	We saved Shu'aib and those **who** believed with him,
011:103	for those **who** fear the Chastisement of the Hereafter:

WHO (continued)

011:106	Those **who** are wretched shall be in the Fire:
011:108	And those **who** are blessed shall be in the Garden:
011:112	thou and those **who** with thee turn (unto Allah);
011:113	And incline not to those **who** do wrong, or the
011:116	men of righteousness **who** prohibited men from
011:120	a message of remembrance to those **who** believe.
011:121	Say to those **who** do not believe: "Do whatever
012:003	among those **who** knew it not.
012:021	The man in Egypt **who** bought him, said to his wife:
012:022	thus do We reward those **who** do right.
012:023	Truly to no good come those **who** do wrong!"
012:025	punishment for one **who** formed an evil
012:045	But the man **who** had been released,
012:045	and **who** now remembered him after (so long)
012:045	one of the two (**who** had been in prison) and
012:050	'What was the matter with the ladies **who** cut their hands?'
012:051	he is indeed of those **who** are (ever) true
012:051	it was I **who** sought to seduce him he is indeed
012:056	the reward of those **who** do good.
012:057	for those **who** believe, and are constant in righteousness.
012:064	of those **who** show mercy!"
012:072	for him **who** produces it. Is (the reward of) a camel load:
012:077	a brother of his **who** did steal before (him)."
012:078	aged and venerable, (**who** will grieve for him):
012:087	except those **who** have no faith."
012:090	to be lost, of those **who** do right."
012:092	of those **who** show mercy?
012:109	for those **who** do right.
012:110	Our punishment from those **who** are in sin.
013:002	Allah is He **Who** raised the heavens without any
013:003	in these things are Signs for those **who** consider!
013:003	And it is He **Who** spread out the earth, and set
013:004	there are Signs for those **who** understand!
013:005	those **who** deny their Lord!
013:012	it is He **Who** doth raise up the clouds,
013:012	It is He **Who** doth show you the lightning, by way
013:016	"Are the blind equal with those **who** see?
013:016	to Allah partners **who** have created (anything) as He
013:016	Say: "**Who** is the Lord and Sustainer of the heavens and
013:018	For those **who** respond to their Lord, are (all)
013:018	But those **who** respond no to Him,-even if
013:019	Is then one **who** doth know that that which hath been
013:019	like one **who** is blind?
013:019	those **who** are endued with understanding that receive
013:020	Those **who** fulfil the Covenant of Allah and fail
013:021	Those **who** join together those things which
013:022	Those **who** patiently persevere, seeking the
013:025	But those **who** break the Covenant of Allah,
013:027	to himself those **who** turn to Him in penitence,-
013:028	"Those **who** believe, and whose hearts find
013:029	"For those **who** believe and work righteousness,
013:033	Nay! to those **who** believe not, their devising
013:033	Is then He **Who** standeth over every soul
013:036	those **who** reject a part thereof.
013:042	**who** gets home in the End.
014:003	Those **who** prefer the life of this world to the Hereafter,
014:003	**who** hinder (men) from the Path of Allah and seek
014:009	(O people!), of those **who** (went) before you?
014:009	And those **who** (came) after them?
014:010	It is He **Who** invites you, in order
014:012	For those **who** put their trust should put

WHO (continued)

014:018   The parable of those **who** reject their Lord
014:021   the weak say to those **who** were arrogant, "For us
014:022   "It was Allah **Who** gave you a promise of Truth:
014:023   But those **who** believe and work righteousness
014:027   Allah will establish in strength those **who** believe,
014:027   but Allah will leave to stray, those **who** do wrong:
014:028   to those **who** have exchanged the favour of Allah.
014:031   Speak to My servants **who** have believed, that they
014:032   It is Allah **Who** hath created the heavens
014:032   it is He **Who** hath made the ships subject to you,
014:036   he then **who** follows my (ways) is of me, and he
014:039   "Praise be to Allah, **who** hath granted unto me
014:040   make me one **who** establishes regular Prayer,
014:042   the deeds of those **who** do wrong.
014:045   dwelt in the dwellings of men **who** wronged themselves
015:002   Often will those **who** disbelieve, wish that
015:013   such has been the way of those **who** went before them.
015:016   It is We **who** have set out constellations in
015:023   and **Who** it is We
015:023   And verily, it is We **Who** give life, and **Who** give death:
015:023   it is We **Who** remain inheritors (after al else passes away).
015:024   To Us are known those of you **who** hasten forward,
015:024   and those **who** lag behind.
015:025   Assuredly it is thy Lord **who** will gather them
015:031   among those **who** prostrated themselves.
015:032   those **who** prostrated themselves?"
015:056   He said: "And **who** despairs of the mercy
015:060   those **who** will lag behind."
015:060   "Except his wife, **who**, we have ascertained,
015:075   for those **who** by tokens do understand.
015:077   Behold! in this is a Sign for those **who** believe!
015:086   For verily it is thy Lord **Who** is the All-Creator,
015:090   as We sent down on those **who** divided (Scripture into
015:091   (So also on such) **who** have made Qur'an into shreds
015:094   those **who** join false gods with Allah.
015:095   unto thee against those **who** scoff.-
015:096   Those **who** adopt, with Allah, another god:
015:098   and be of those **who** prostrate themselves in adoration.
016:010   It is He **Who** sends down rain from the sky:
016:011   is a Sign for those **who** give thought.
016:012   for men **who** are wise.
016:013   is a Sign for men **who** are mindful.
016:014   It is He **Who** has made the sea subject, that ye
016:017   Is then He **Who** creates like one that creates not?
016:022   as to those **who** believe not in the Hereafter,
016:030   To those **who** do good, there is good in this world,
016:035   So did those **who** went before them.
016:036   what was the end of those **who** denied (the Truth).
016:038   that Allah will not raise up those **who** die:
016:041   To those **who** leave their homes in the cause of Allah,
016:042   (They are) those **who** persevere in patience,
016:043   ask of those **who** possess the Message.
016:045   Do then those **who** devise evil (plots) feel
016:060   To those **who** believe not in the Hereafter,
016:064   a guide and a mercy to those **who** believe.
016:065   verily in this is a Sign for those **who** listen.
016:066   pure and agreeable to those **who** drink it.
016:067   in this also is a Sign for those **who** are wise.
016:069   for those **who** give thought.
016:070   It is Allah **who** creates you and takes your souls
016:070   of you there are some **who** are sent back to a feeble age,
016:076   is such a man equal with one **who** commands justice,

WHO (continued)

016:078   It is He **Who** brought you forth from the wombs
016:079   are Signs for those **who** believe.
016:080   It is Allah **who** made your habitations homes of rest
016:081   It is Allah **who** made out of the things He created,
016:086   When those **who** gave partners to Allah will see
016:088   Those **who** reject Allah and hinder (men) from
016:092   And be not like the woman **who** breaks into untwisted
016:096   on those **who** patiently persevere, their reward
016:099   **who** believe and put their trust in their Lord.
016:100   **who** join partners with Allah.
016:100   **who** take him as patron and
016:102   in order to strengthen those **who** believe,
016:104   Those **who** believe not in the Signs of Allah,-
016:105   it is they **who** lie!
016:105   It is those **who** believe not in the Signs of
016:106   Any one **who**, after accepting Faith in Allah,
016:107   and Allah will not guide those **who** reject Faith.
016:110   and **who** thereafter strive and fight for the Faith
016:110   But verily thy Lord,-to those **who** leave their
016:116   For those **who** ascribe false things to Allah,
016:119   to those **who** do wrong in ignorance,
016:119   but **who** thereafter repent and make amends,-
016:121   **Who** chose him, and guided him to a Straight Way.
016:124   for those **who** disagreed (as to its observance);
016:125   **who** have strayed from His Path,
016:125   and **who** receive guidance.
016:126   for those **who** are patient.
016:128   and those **who** do good.
016:128   For Allah is with those **who** restrain themselves,
017:001   Glory to (Allah) **Who** did take His Servant
017:001   **Who** heareth and seeth (all things).
017:008   made Hell a prison for those **who** reject (all Faith).
017:009   to the Believers **who** work deeds of righteousness,
017:010   And to those **who** believe not in the Hereafter,
017:015   **Who** receiveth guidance, receiveth it
017:015   **who** goeth astray doth so to his own loss:
017:016   We command those among them **who** are given the good
017:019   Those **who** do wish for the (things of) the Hereafter,
017:025   Most Forgiving to those **who** turn to Him
017:045   We put, between thee and those **who** believe not
017:051   Say: "He **Who** created you first!"
017:051   Then will they say: "**Who** will cause us to return?"
017:057   means of access to their Lord,-as to **who** are nearest:
017:071   those **who** are given their record in their right hand
017:072   But those **who** were blind in this world, will be
017:082   and a mercy to those **who** believe:
017:084   knows best **who** it is that is best guided on the Way.
017:099   **Who** created the heavens and the earth, has power
017:103   but We did drown him and all **who** were with him.
017:107   it is true that those **who** were given knowledge
017:111   Say: "Praise be to Allah **Who** begets no son,
018:001   Praise be to Allah, **Who** hath sent to His Servant the
018:002   to the Believers **who** work righteous deeds,
018:004   warn those (also) **who** say, "Allah hath begotten a son":
018:013   they were youths **who** believed in their Lord,
018:015   **Who** doth more wrong than such as invent
018:021   those **who** prevailed over their affair said, "Let us
018:028   one **who** follows his own desires, and his affair
018:028   those **who** call on their Lord morning and evening,
018:029   "The Truth is form your Lord" let him **who** will, believe,
018:029   and let him **who** will, reject (it):
018:030   of any **who** do a (single) righteous deed.

WHO (continued)

018:030   As to those **who** believe and work righteousness,
018:037   "Dost thou deny Him **Who** created thee out of dust,
018:045   it is (only) Allah **Who** prevails over all things.
018:057   And **who** doth more wrong than one **who** is reminded
018:057   **who** is reminded of the Signs of his Lord but turns
018:074   "Hast thou slain an innocent person **who** had slain none?
018:079   was after them a king **who** seized on every boat by force.
018:093   a people **who** scarcely understood a word.
018:101   and **who** had been unable even to hear.
018:103   Say: "Shall we tell you of those **who** lose most
018:105   They are those **who** deny the Signs of their Lord
018:107   As to those **who** believe and work righteous deeds,
019:029   "How can we talk to one **who** is a child in the cradle?"
019:040   It is We **Who** will inherit the earth, and all
019:059   a posterity **who** missed prayers and followed
019:060   Except those **who** repent and believe, and work
019:063   Our Servants **who** guard against evil.
019:065   knowest thou of any **who** is worthy of the same Name
019:069   from every sect all those **who** were worst in obstinate
019:070   And certainly We know best those **who** are most worthy
019:072   But We shall save those **who** guarded against evil,
019:073   Unbelievers say to those **who** believe, "Which of the
019:074   **who** were even better in equipment and in glitter to the
019:075   **who** is worst in position, and **who** weakest in forces!
019:076   doth increase in guidance those **who** seek guidance:
019:077   man **who** rejects Our Signs, yet says: "I shall
019:096   On those **who** believe and work deeds of righteousness,
020:003   But only as an admonition to those **who** fear (Allah),-
020:004   A revelation from Him **Who** created the earth
020:039   and he will be taken up by one **who** is an enemy
020:040   'Shall I show you one **who** will nurse and rear the (child)?'
020:047   And peace to all **who** follow guidance!
020:048   those **who** reject and turn away.'"
020:049   (Pharaoh) said: "**Who**, then, O Moses, is the
020:050   He said: "Our Lord is He **Who** gave to each (created)
020:053   "He **Who** has made for you the earth like a carpet
020:064   he wins (all along) to-day **who** gains the upper hand."
020:071   **who** has taught you magic!
020:072   has come to us of the Clear Signs Him **Who** created us!
020:074   Verily he **who** comes to his Lord as a sinner
020:075   to Him as believers **who** have worked righteous deeds,-
020:076   is the reward of those **who** purify themselves (from evil).
020:082   He that forgives again and again to those **who** repent,
020:082   believe, and do right,-**who**, in fine, are on true guidance."
020:112   But he **who** works deeds of righteousness, and has
020:127   him **who** transgresses beyond bounds and believes
020:135   ye know **who** it is that is on the straight and even Way,
020:135   and **who** it is that has received guidance."
021:007   ask of those **who** possess the Message.
021:009   those **who** transgressed beyond bounds.
021:019   those **who** are with Him are not too proud to serve Him,
021:021   gods from the earth **who** can raise (the dead)?
021:029   thus do We reward those **who** do wrong.
021:033   It is He **Who** created the Night and the Day,
021:036   "The one **who** talks of your gods?"
021:042   Say, "**Who** can keep you safe by night and by day
021:044   Is it then they **who** will win?
021:048   for those **who** would do right,-
021:049   and **who** hold the Hour (of judgment) in awe.
021:049   Those **who** fear their Lord in their
021:055   or are you one of those **who** jest?"
021:056   He **Who** created them (from nothing):

WHO (continued)

021:059   They said, "**Who** has done this to our gods?
021:077   We helped him against people **who** rejected Our Signs:
021:079   with David: it was We **Who** did (all these things).
021:080   It was We **Who** taught him the making of coats of mail
021:082   and it was We **Who** guarded them.
021:082   And of Satans were some **who** dived for him,
021:084   for all **who** serve Us.
021:088   and thus do We deliver those **who** have faith.
021:091   And (remember) her **who** guarded her chastity:
021:106   for people **who** would (truly) worship Allah.
021:110   "It is He **Who** knows what is open in speech
022:006   and it is He **Who** has power over all things.
022:006   it is He **Who** gives life to the dead,
022:007   Allah will raise up all **who** are in the graves.
022:011   There are among men some **who** serve Allah,
022:014   **who** believe and work righteous deeds, to Gardens,
022:017   Those **who** believe (in the Qur'an),
022:017   those **who** follow the Jewish (scriptures), and the
022:019   but those **who** deny (their Lord),-for them
022:023   Allah will admit those **who** believe and work
022:024   to the path of Him **Who** is Worthy of (all) Praise.
022:025   As to those **who** have rejected (Allah), and would
022:026   for those **who** compass it round, or stand up,
022:034   the Good News to those **who** humble themselves,
022:035   **who** show patient perseverance over their afflictions,
022:037   the Good News to all **who** do good.
022:038   Verily Allah will defend (from ill) those **who** believe:
022:040   (They are) those **who** have been expelled from their homes
022:040   Allah will certainly aid those **who** aid His (cause);-
022:041   (They are) those **who**, if We establish them in the land,
022:050   "Those **who** believe and work righteousness,
022:051   "But those **who** strive against Our Signs,
022:053   is a disease and **who** are hardened of heart:
022:054   Allah is the Guide of those **who** believe,
022:055   Those **who** reject Faith will not cease to be in doubt
022:056   so those **who** believe and work righteous deeds will be
022:057   And for those **who** reject Faith and deny Our Signs,
022:058   Those **who** leave their homes in the cause of Allah,
022:058   He **Who** bestows the best Provision.
022:061   **Who** hears and sees (all things).
022:066   It is He **Who** gave you life,
022:072   with violence those **who** rehearse Our Signs to them.
022:073   feeble are those **who** petition and those whom they
022:075   He **Who** hears and sees (all things).
022:077   O ye **who** believe! bow down, prostrate yourselves,
022:078   It is He **Who** has named you Muslims, both before
023:002   Those **who** humble themselves in their prayers;
023:003   **Who** avoid vain talk;
023:004   **Who** are active in giving zakat;
023:005   **Who** guard their modesty,
023:008   Those **who** faithfully observe their trust
023:009   And **who** (strictly) guard their prayer;-
023:011   **Who** will inherit Paradise: they will
023:020   and relish for those **who** use it for food.
023:028   **Who** has saved us from the people **who** do wrong."
023:033   **who** disbelieved and denied the Meeting in the
023:038   "He is only a man **who** invents a lie against Allah,
023:041   So away with the people **who** do wrong!
023:048   and they became of those **who** were destroyed.
023:057   Verily those **who** live in awe for fear of their Lord;
023:058   Those **who** believe in the Signs of their Lord;
023:059   Those **who** join not (in worship) partners with their Lord;

WHO (continued)

023:060	And those **who** dispense their charity with their hearts
023:061	It is these **who** hasten in every good work,
023:061	good work, and these **who** are foremost in them.
023:064	those of them **who** received the good things
023:072	He is the Best of those **who** give sustenance.
023:074	And verily those **who** believe not in the Hereafter
023:078	It is He **Who** has created for you (the faculties of)
023:080	It is He **Who** gives life and death,
023:086	Say: "**Who** is the Lord of the seven heavens,
023:088	**Who** protects (all), but is not protected (of any)?
023:088	Say: "**Who** is it in whose hands is the sovereignty of
023:094	out me not amongst the people **who** do wrong!"
023:103	will be those **who** have lost their souls;
023:109	for Thou art the best of those **Who** show mercy!'
023:109	**who** used to pray, 'Our Lord! we believe;
023:113	but ask those **who** keep account."
023:118	for Thou art the Best of those **Who** show mercy!"
024:004	And those **who** launch a charge against chaste women,
024:005	Except those **who** repent thereafter and mend their
024:006	by Allah that he is of those **who** speak the Truth.
024:006	And for those **who** launch a charge against their waives.
024:011	Those **who** brought forward the lie are a body among
024:011	and to him **who** took on himself the lead among them,
024:019	Those **who** love (to see) scandal circulate among the
024:021	and Allah is One **Who** hears and knows (all things).
024:021	O ye **who** believe! follow not Satan's footsteps:
024:022	Let not those among you **who** are endued with grace
024:022	and those **who** have left their homes in Allah's cause":
024:023	Those **who** slander chaste women,
024:027	O ye **who** believe! enter not houses other than your own,
024:031	small children **who** have no carnal knowledge of women;
024:032	Marry those among you **who** are single,
024:033	Let those **who** find not the wherewithal for marriage
024:034	and an admonition for those **who** fear (Allah).
024:034	people **who** passed away before you,
024:044	It is Allah **Who** alternates the Night and the Day:
024:044	is an instructive example those **who** have vision!
024:050	Nay, it is they themselves **who** do wrong.
024:055	those among you **who** believe and work righteous deeds,
024:058	O ye **who** believe! let those whom your right possess,
024:058	and the (children) among you **who** have not come of age
024:060	and Allah is One **Who** sees and knows all things.
024:062	Only those are Believers **who** believe in Allah and
024:062	those **who** ask for the leave are those **who** believe in
024:062	are those **who** believe in Allah and His Messenger;
024:063	Allah doth know those of you **who** slip away under
024:063	let those beware **who** withstand the Messenger's order,
025:001	Blessed is He **Who** sent down the Criterion
025:002	it is He **Who** created all things, and ordered
025:004	In truth it is they **who** have put forward an iniquity
025:006	by Him **Who** knows the secret (that is) in the heavens
025:007	"What sort of messenger is this, **who** eats food, and walks
025:010	Blessed is He **Who**, if that were His Will,
025:017	"Was it ye **who** led these my servants astray,
025:020	For Allah is One **Who** sees (all things).
025:020	**who** ate food and walked through the markets.
025:021	Those **who** do not hope to meet Us (for Judgment)
025:032	Those **who** reject Faith say: "Why is not the Qur'an
025:034	Those **who** will be gathered to Hell (prone) on their
025:036	to the people **who** have rejected Our Signs":
025:042	**who** it is that is most misled in Path!
025:047	And He it is **Who** makes the Night as a Robe

WHO (continued)

025:048	And He it is **Who** sends the Winds as heralds
025:053	It is He **Who** has let free the two bodies of flowing
025:054	It is He **Who** has created man from water:
025:057	that each one **who** will may take a (straight) Path to his
025:058	And put thy trust in Him **Who** lives and dies not;
025:059	He **Who** created the heavens and the earth
025:061	Blessed is He **Who** made Constellations in the skies,
025:062	And it is He **Who** made the Night and the Day
025:063	are those **who** walk on the earth in humility,
025:064	Those **who** spend the night in adoration
025:065	Those **who** say, "Our Lord! avert from us the Wrath
025:067	Those **who**, when they spend, are not extravagant
025:068	Those **who** invoke not, with Allah, any other god,
025:072	Those **who** witness no falsehood, and, if
025:073	Those **who**, when they are admonished with the Signs
025:074	And those **who** pray, "Our Lord! Grant unto us wives
025:074	and offspring **who** will be the comfort of our eyes,
025:075	Those are the ones **who** will be rewarded with the
026:027	**who** has been sent to you is a veritable madman!"
026:044	"By the might of Pharaoh it is we **who** will certainly win!"
026:049	**who** has taught you sorcery!
026:065	We delivered Moses and all **who** were with him;
026:078	"**Who** created me, and it is He **Who** guides me;
026:079	"**Who** gives me food and drink,
026:080	"And when I am ill, it is He **Who** cures me;
026:081	"**Who** will cause me to die, and then
026:082	"And **Who**, I hope, will forgive
026:099	our seducers were only those **who** were steeped in guilt.
026:102	we shall truly be of those **who** believe!'"
026:114	"I am not one to drive away those **who** believe.
026:118	the Believers **who** are with me."
026:120	Thereafter We drowned those **who** remained behind.
026:132	"Yea, fear Him **Who** has bestowed on you freely all that
026:151	follow not the bidding of those **who** are extravagant,-
026:152	"**Who** make mischief in the land, and mend
026:171	Except an old woman **who** lingered behind.
026:173	on those **who** were admonished (but heeded not)!
026:184	and (**Who** created) the generations before (you)."
026:184	"And fear Him **Who** created you and
026:213	or thou wilt be among those **who** will be punished.
026:215	And lower thy wing to the Believers **who** follow thee.
026:218	**Who** seeth thee standing forth (in prayer),
026:219	those **who** prostrate themselves.
026:220	For it is He **Who** heareth and knoweth all things.
026:224	it is those straying in Evil, **who** follow them:
026:227	Except those **who** believe, work righteousness,
027:003	Those **who** establish regular prayers and give
027:004	As to those **who** believe not in the Hereafter,
027:014	so see what was the end of those **who** acted corruptly!
027:015	of His servants **who** believe!"
027:015	**Who** has favoured us above many of His servants
027:025	So that they worship not Allah **Who** brings forth
027:036	Nay it is ye **who** rejoice in your gift!
027:040	Said one **who** had knowledge of the Book: "I will
027:041	those **who** are not rightly guided."
027:048	**who** made mischief in the land, and would not reform.
027:053	And We saved those **who** believed and practiced
027:056	men **who** want to be clean and pure!"
027:057	to be of those **who** lagged behind.
027:058	on those **who** were admonished (but heeded not)!
027:059	(**Who**) is better?- Allah or the false gods they associate
027:060	Or, **who** has created the heaven and the earth,

WHO (continued)

027:060   and **who** sends you down rain from the sky?
027:060   Nay, they are a people **who** swerve from justice.
027:061   Or, **who** has made the earth firm to live in;
027:062   and **Who** relieves his suffering, and makes
027:062   Or, **Who** listens to the distressed when he calls
027:063   and **who** sends the winds as heralds of glad tidings,
027:063   Or, **Who** guides you through the depths of darkness
027:064   Or, **Who** originates Creation, then repeats it,
027:064   and **Who** gives you sustenance
027:077   and a Mercy to those **who** believe.
027:081   to listen **who** believe in Our Signs, so they
027:083   those **who** reject Our Signs, and they
027:087   in the heavens, and those **who** are on earth,
027:087   with terror those **who** are in the heavens,
027:088   **Who** disposes of all things in perfect order:
027:091   Him **Who** has sanctified it and to Whom (belong) all
027:091   **who** bow in Islam to Allah's Will,-
027:093   **Who** will soon show you His Signs, so that
028:003   in Truth, for people **who** believe.
028:005   those **who** were being depressed in the land,
028:014   for thus do We reward those **who** do good.
028:017   never shall I be a help to those **who** sin!"
028:018   the man **who** had, the day before, sought his
028:019   and not to be one **who** sets things right!"
028:023   **who** were keeping back (their flocks).
028:026   to employ is the (man) **who** is strong and trusty."
028:031   and fear not: for thou art of those **who** are secure.
028:035   you two as well as those **who** follow you."
028:037   **who** it is that comes with guidance from Him
028:040   of those **who** did wrong!
028:045   **Who** send messengers (with inspiration).
028:047   amongst those **who** believe!"
028:050   and **who** is more astray than one **who** follows his own
028:056   and He knows best those **who** receive guidance.
028:061   but **who**, on the Day of judgment, is to be among
028:061   and **who** is going to reach its (fulfillment),
028:071   **who** can give you light?
028:072   **who** can give you a Night in which ye can rest?
028:076   for Allah loveth not those **who** exult (in riches).
028:077   for Allah loves not those **who** do mischief."
028:080   is best for those **who** believe and work
028:080   save those **who** steadfastly persevere (in good)."
028:080   But those **who** had been granted (true) knowledge
028:082   those **who** reject Allah will assuredly never prosper."
028:082   **Who** enlarges the provision or restricts it,
028:082   And those **who** had envied his position the day before
028:083   give to those **who** intend not high-handedness
028:085   and **who** is in manifest error."
028:085   Say: "My Lord knows best **who** it is that brings
028:085   Verily He **Who** ordained the Qur'an for thee,
028:086   in any way to those **who** reject (Allah's Message).
028:087   these **who** join gods with Allah.
029:003   **who** are true from those **who** are false.
029:007   Those **who** believe and work righteous deeds,-
029:009   And those **who** believe and work righteous deeds,-
029:011   And Allah most certainly knows those **who** believe,
029:011   and as certainly those **who** are Hypocrites.
029:012   And the Unbelievers say to those **who** believe: "Follow
029:023   it is they **who** shall despair of My mercy:
029:023   they **who** will (suffer) a most grievous Chastisement.
029:023   Those **who** reject the Signs of Allah and the
029:024   Verily in this are Signs for people **who** believe.

WHO (continued)

029:030   Help Thou me against people **who** do mischief!"
029:032   They said: "We know well **who** is there:
029:032   she is of those **who** lag behind!"
029:033   she is of those **who** lag behind.
029:035   for any people **who** (care to) understand.
029:040   it was not Allah **Who** wronged them: they wronged
029:041   is that of the Spider, **who** builds (to itself) a house;
029:041   The parable of those **who** take protectors other than
029:043   but only those understand them **who** have Knowledge.
029:044   verily in that is a Sign for those **who** believe.
029:046   unless it be with those of them **who** do wrong
029:051   to those **who** believe.
029:052   those **who** believe in vanities and reject Allah,
029:056   O My servants **who** believe! truly, spacious
029:058   But those **who** believe and work deeds
029:058   an excellent reward for those **who** do (good)!-
029:059   Those **who** persevere in patience, and put
029:060   It is Allah **Who** feeds (both) them and you:
029:061   **who** has created the heavens and the earth
029:063   And if indeed thou ask them **who** it is that sends
029:068   And **who** does more wrong than he **who** invents
029:068   a home in Hell for those **who** reject Faith?
029:068   **who** invents a lie against Allah or rejects
029:069   for verily Allah is with those **who** do right.
029:069   And those **who** strive in Our (Cause),-We will
030:008   **who** deny the meeting with their Lord
030:009   it was not Allah **Who** wronged them, but they
030:010   In the long run evil will be the End of those **who** do evil;
030:011   It is Allah **Who** begins the creation; then repeats
030:015   Then those **who** have believed and worked
030:016   And those **who** have rejected Faith and falsely
030:019   and **Who** gives life to the earth after it is dead:
030:019   It is He **Who** brings out the living from the dead,
030:021   verily in that are Signs for those **who** reflect.
030:022   are Signs for those **who** know.
030:023   verily in that are Signs for those **who** hearken.
030:024   are Signs for those **who** are wise.
030:027   It is He **Who** begins (the process of) creation;
030:029   But **who** will guide those whom Allah leaves astray?
030:031   and be not ye among those **who** join gods with Allah,-
030:032   Those **who** split up their Religion, and become
030:037   are Signs for those **who** believe.
030:038   and it is they **who** will prosper.
030:038   that is best for those **who** seek the Countenance,
030:039   it is those **who** will get a recompense multiplied.
030:040   your (false) "Partners" **who** can do any single
030:040   It is Allah **Who** has created you: further, He
030:044   Those **who** reject Faith will suffer from that
030:044   and those **who** work righteousness will make
030:045   That He may reward those **who** believe and work
030:045   those **who** reject Faith.
030:047   then, to those **who** transgressed, We meted
030:047   incumbent upon Us to aid those **who** believed.
030:048   It is Allah **Who** sends the Winds, and they
030:050   verily the Same will give life to the men **who** are dead:
030:053   **who** believe in Our Signs and submit (their wills in
030:054   and it is He **Who** has all knowledge and power.
030:054   It is Allah **Who** created you in a state of (helpless)
030:059   Allah seal up the hearts of those **who** understand not.
030:060   **who** have (themselves) no certainty of faith.
031:004   Those **who** establish regular Prayer, and give zakat
031:005   and these are the ones **who** will prosper.

WHO (continued)

031:006	those **who** purchase idle tales, without knowledge
031:008	For those **who** believe and work righteous deeds,
031:012	Any **who** is (so) grateful does so to the profit of his own
031:015	and follow the way of those **who** turn to Me:
031:020	Yet these are among men those **who** dispute about Allah,
031:025	**who** it is that created the heavens and the earth.
031:028	for Allah is He **Who** hears and sees (all things).
031:031	**who** constantly persevere and give thanks.
031:034	It is He **Who** sends down rain,
031:034	and He **Who** knows what is in the wombs.
032:004	It is Allah **Who** has created the heavens and the
032:007	He **Who** has created all things in the best way
032:015	Only those believe in Our Signs **who**, when they
032:018	than the man **who** is rebellious and wicked?
032:018	Is then the man **who** believes no better than the
032:019	For those **who** believe and do righteous deeds,
032:020	As to those **who** are rebellious and wicked,
032:022	**who** transgress We shall exact (Due) Retribution.
032:022	and **who** then turns away therefrom?
032:022	And **who** does more wrong than one to whom are recited
033:009	O ye **who** believe! Remember the Grace of Allah,
033:017	Say: "**Who** is it that can screen you from Allah
033:018	**who** keep back (men) and those **who** say to their
033:019	like one **who** faints from death:
033:021	**who** hope in Allah and the Final Day,
033:021	and **who** remember Allah much.
033:023	Among the Believers are men **who** have been true
033:026	And those of the people of the Book **who** aided them-
033:035	and women **who** engage much in Allah's remembrance,
033:035	for men and women **who** guard their chastity,
033:035	for men and women **who** humble themselves,
033:035	for men and women **who** fast,
033:035	for men and women **who** are patient and constant,
033:035	for men and women **who** give in charity,
033:037	Behold! thou didst say to one **who** had received the grace
033:039	(It is the practice of those) **who** preach the Messages of
033:041	O ye **who** believe! remember Allah, with much
033:043	He it is **Who** sends blessings on you, as do
033:046	And as one **who** invites to Allah's (Grace)
033:049	O ye **who** believe! when ye marry believing women,
033:050	of thy maternal uncles and aunts, **who** migrated with thee;
033:050	and any believing woman **who** gives herself to the Prophet
033:053	O ye **who** Believe! enter not the Prophet's houses,-
033:057	Those **who** annoy Allah and his Messenger-
033:058	And those **who** annoy believing men and women
033:060	and those **who** stir up sedition in the City,
033:062	(approved) of Allah among those **who** lived aforetime:
033:069	O ye **who** believe! be ye not like those **who** hurt Moses,
033:070	O ye **who** believe! fear Allah, and make
034:003	it will come upon you;-by Him **Who** knows the unseen,
034:004	That He may reward those **who** believe and work
034:005	But those **who** strive against Our Signs,
034:008	Nay, it is those **who** believe not in the Hereafter,
034:021	from him **who** is in doubt concerning it:
034:021	We might test the man **who** believes in the Hereafter,
034:024	Say: "**Who** gives you sustenance, from the
034:026	the One **Who** knows all."
034:031	Those **who** were deemed weak will say to the arrogant
034:032	say to those **who** had been deemed weak: "Was it we
034:032	Nay, rather it was ye **who** transgressed."
034:032	"Was it we **who** kept you back from Guidance
034:033	Those **who** had been deemed weak will say to

WHO (continued)

034:037	but only those **who** believe and work righteousness-
034:038	Those **who** strive against Our Signs, to frustrate
034:039	for He is the Best of those **Who** grant Sustenance.
034:043	a man **who** wishes to hinder you from the (worship)
034:050	of my Lord to me: it is He **Who** hears all things,
035:001	**Who** made the angels messengers with wings,-
035:007	For those **who** reject Allah, is a terrible Chastisement
035:007	but for those **who** believe and work righteous deeds,
035:008	upon is as good, (equal to one **who** is rightly guided)?
035:009	It is Allah **Who** sends forth the Winds, so that
035:010	it is He **Who** exalts each Deed of Righteousness.
035:014	(O man) can inform you like Him **who** is All-Aware.
035:022	make those to hear **who** are (buried) in graves.
035:026	In the end did I punish those **who** rejected Faith:
035:028	among His Servants **who** have knowledge:
035:029	Those **who** rehearse the Book of Allah,
035:032	and some **who** are, by Allah's leave, foremost in good
035:032	own souls; some **who** follow a middle course:
035:032	among them some **who** wrong their own souls;
035:034	**Who** has removed from us (all) sorrow:
035:035	"**Who** has, out of His bounty, settled us
035:036	But those **who** reject (Allah)-for them
035:039	he **who** disbelieves his disbelief be on his own self
035:041	It is Allah **Who** sustains the heavens and the earth,
036:006	**who** therefore remain heedless (of the Signs of Allah).
036:021	"Obey those **who** ask no reward of you (for themselves),
036:021	and **who** are themselves guided.
036:022	"Why should not I serve Him **Who** created me,
036:036	**Who** created in pairs all things that the earth produces,
036:047	the Unbelievers say to those **who** believe: "Shall we then
036:052	**Who** hath raised us up from our beds of repose?...
036:070	That it may give abomination to any (**who** are) alive,
036:070	may be proved true against those **who** reject (Truth).
036:071	See they not that it is We **Who** have created for them-
036:077	We **Who** created Him from sperm?
036:078	"**Who** can give life to (dry) bones and decomposed
036:079	**Who** created them for the first time!
036:080	"The same **Who** produces for you fire out of
036:081	"Is not He **Who** created the heavens and the earth
037:001	By those **who** range themselves in ranks,
037:003	Those **who** thus proclaim the message (of Allah)!
037:028	They will say: "It was ye **who** used to come to us from
037:030	Nay, it was ye **who** were a people in obstinate rebellion!
037:046	of a taste delicious to those **who** drink (thereof),
037:052	"**Who** used to say, Do you really believe?
037:061	For the like of this let all strive, **who** wish to strive.
037:073	Then see what was the End of those **who** were warned,
037:080	Thus indeed do We reward those **who** do right.
037:105	thus indeed do We reward those **who** do right.
037:110	Thus indeed do We reward those **who** do right.
037:121	Thus indeed do We reward those **who** do right.
037:131	Thus indeed do We reward those **who** do right.
037:135	among those **who** lagged behind:
037:135	Except an old woman **who** was among those
037:166	"And we are verily those **who** declare (Allah's) glory!"
037:167	And there were those **who** said,
037:177	the morning for **who** were warned (and heeded not)!
038:012	Before them (were many **who**) rejected messengers,-
038:024	the Partners (in business) **who** wrong each other:
038:024	**who** believe and work deeds of righteousness,
038:026	for those **who** wander astray from the Path of Allah,
038:028	Shall We treat those **who** believe and work deeds of

WHO (continued)

038:028   the same as those **who** turn aside from the right?
038:028   the same as those **who** do mischief on earth?
038:028   Shall We treat those **who** guard against evil, the same
038:043   for all **who** have Understanding.
038:060   It is ye **who** have brought this upon us!
038:074   and became one of those **who** reject Faith.
039:002   Verily it is We **Who** have revealed the Book
039:003   But those **who** take for protectors others than Allah
039:005   He **Who** forgives again and again?
039:009   one **who** worships devoutly during the hours of the night
039:009   those **who** know and those **who** do not know?
039:009   It is those **who** are endued with understanding that
039:009   and **who** places his hope in the Mercy of his Lord-
039:009   **who** takes heed of the Hereafter,
039:009   (like one **who** does Not)?
039:010   Say: "O ye my servants **who** believe! Fear your
039:010   Good is the reward for those **who** do good in this world.
039:010   **who** patiently persevere will truly receive a reward
039:012   of those **who** submit to Allah in Islam."
039:015   those in loss are those **who** lose their own souls
039:017   Those **who** eschew Taghut and fall not into its worship,-
039:018   Those **who** listen to the Word, and follow
039:019   Punishment is justly due (equal to one **who** eschews evil)?
039:019   Wouldst thou, then, deliver one (**who** is) in the Fire?
039:020   But it is for those **who** fear their Lord,
039:023   the skins of those **who** fear their Lord tremble thereat;
039:024   Is, then, one **who** has to ward off the brunt of the
039:032   **Who**, then, doth more wrong than one
039:032   one **who** utters a lie concerning Allah and rejects
039:033   And he **who** brings the Truth and he
039:033   and he **who** confirms (and supports) it-
039:033   such are the men **who** do right.
039:034   such is the reward of those **who** do good:
039:038   indeed thou ask them **who** it is that created the heavens
039:038   In Him trust those **who** put their trust."
039:040   "**Who** it is to whom comes a Chastisement or ignominy,
039:042   Verily in this are Signs for those **who** reflect.
039:045   the hearts of those **who** believe not in the Hereafter
039:052   Verily, in this are signs for those **who** believe!
039:053   Say: "O my Servants **who** have transgressed against
039:056   and was but among those **who** mocked!'
039:058   I should certainly be among those **who** do good!'
039:059   and became one of those **who** reject Faith!'"
039:060   see those **who** told lies against Allah;-their faces
039:063   and those **who** reject the Signs of Allah,-
039:063   it is they **who** will be in loss.
039:066   Nay, but worship Allah, and be of those **who** give thanks.
039:073   those **who** feared their Lord will be led to the Garden
039:074   **Who** has truly fulfilled His promise to us,
039:074   for those **who** work (righteousness)!"
040:003   **Who** forgiveth Sin, accepteth Repentance, is Severe
040:005   **who** denied (the Signs),-the People of Noah,
040:007   and implore Forgiveness for those **who** believe:
040:007   Those **who** bear the Throne (of Allah) and those
040:007   Forgive, then, those **who** turn in repentance,
040:013   but only those receive admonition **who** turn (to Allah).
040:013   He it is **Who** showeth you His Signs, and sendeth
040:018   will the wrong-doers have, **who** could be listened to.
040:020   Verily it is Allah (alone) **Who** hears and sees (all things).
040:025   "Slay the sons of those **who** believe with him,
040:027   one **who** believes not in the Day of Account!"
040:028   Truly Allah guides not one **who** transgresses and lies!

WHO (continued)

040:028   **who** had concealed his faith, said: "Will ye slay a man
040:029   but **who** will help us from the Punishment of Allah,
040:030   Then said the man **who** believed: "O my People!
040:031   and the Thamud, and those **who** came after them:
040:038   The man **who** believed said further: "O my People!
040:042   **Who** forgives again and again!
040:043   ye do call me to one **who** has no claim to be called to,
040:047   The weak ones (**who** followed) will say to those
040:047   will say to those **who** had been arrogant, "We but
040:048   Those **who** had been arrogant will say: "We are
040:051   help Our messengers and those **who** believe,
040:056   it is He **Who** hears and sees (all things).
040:056   Those **who** dispute about the Signs of Allah
040:058   nor are (equal) those **who** believe and work deeds of
040:058   Not equal are the blind and those **who** (clearly) see:
040:058   and those **who** do evil.
040:060   but those **who** are too arrogant to serve Me will surely
040:061   It is Allah **Who** has made the Night for you,
040:063   Thus are deluded those **who** are wont to reject the Signs
040:064   It is Allah **Who** has made for you the earth as a resting
040:067   though of you there are some **who** die before;-
040:067   It is He **Who** has created you from dust, then from
040:068   It is He **Who** gives Life and Death;
040:070   Those **who** reject the Book and the (revelations)
040:078   there and then, those **who** stood on Falsehoods.
040:079   It is Allah **Who** made cattle for you, that ye
041:003   a Qur'an in Arabic, for people **who** understand;-
041:006   And woe to those **who** join gods with Allah,-
041:007   Those **who** pay not zakat,
041:007   and **who** even deny the Hereafter.
041:008   For those **who** believe and work deeds of
041:009   Say: Is it that ye Deny Him **Who** created the earth
041:010   alike for (all) **who** ask.
041:015   **Who** created them, was superior to them in strength?
041:015   and said: "**Who** is superior to us in strength?"
041:018   **who** believed and practiced righteousness.
041:021   (He) **Who** giveth speech to everything:
041:025   **who** have passed away, is proved against them;
041:025   **who** made alluring to them what was before them and
041:029   among Jinns and men, **who** misled us:
041:030   In the case of those **who** say, "Our Lord is Allah",
041:033   And says, "I am of those **who** bow in Islam"?
041:033   **Who** is better in speech than one **who** calls (men)
041:035   will be goodness except those **who** exercise patience
041:036   He is the One **Who** hears and knows all things.
041:037   but prostrate to Allah, **Who** created them,
041:038   **who** celebrate His praises by night and by day.
041:039   Truly, He **Who** gives life to the (dead) earth
041:039   can surely give life to (men) **who** are dead.
041:040   Those **who** pervert the Truth in Our Signs are not
041:041   Those **who** reject the Message when it comes to them
041:044   "It is a guide and a healing to those **who** believe;
041:044   and for those **who** believe not, there is a deafness in
041:052   **Who** is more astray than one **who** is in schism far
042:006   And those **who** take as protectors others besides Him,-
042:009   and it is He **Who** gives life to the dead:
042:009   it is He **Who** has power over all things.
042:013   and guides to Himself those **who** turn (to Him).
042:013   to those **who** worship other things than Allah,
042:014   **who** have inherited the Book after them are in
042:016   But those **who** dispute concerning Allah after He
042:017   It is Allah **Who** has sent down the Book in truth,

WHO (continued)

042:018	Only those wish to hasten it **who** believe not in it:
042:018	those **who** believe hold it in awe, and know
042:021	**who** have established for them some religion without
042:022	But those **who** believe and work righteous deeds
042:023	to His Servants **who** believe and do righteous deeds.
042:026	And He listens to those **who** believe and do deeds of
042:033	everyone **who** patiently perseveres and is grateful.
042:035	But let those know, **who** dispute about Our Signs,
042:036	(it is) for those **who** believe and put their trust in their
042:037	Those **who** avoid the greater sins and indecencies
042:038	Those **who** respond to their Lord, and establish
042:038	**who** spend out of what We bestow on them for
042:038	**who** (conduct) their affairs by mutual Consultation;
042:039	And those **who**, when an oppressive wrong is inflicted
042:040	for (Allah) loveth not those **who** do wrong.
042:042	The blame is only against those **who** oppress men
042:045	indeed in loss **who** lose themselves and their families.
043:009	'Who created the heavens and the earth?'
043:013	**Who** has subjected these to Our (use), for we
043:019	make into females angels **who** themselves serve Allah.
043:025	now see what was the end of those **who** rejected (Truth)!
043:027	"(I worship) only Him **Who** made me, and He
043:028	among those **who** came after him, that they
043:032	It is We **Who** portion out between them their
043:032	Is it they **who** would portion out the Mercy
043:052	**who** is a contemptible wretch and can scarcely express
043:069	Those **who** have believed in Our Signs and submitted
043:076	but it is they **who** have been unjust themselves.
043:079	But it is We **Who** settle things.
043:084	It is He **Who** is God in heaven and God on earth;
043:086	only he **who** bears witness to the Truth,
043:087	If thou ask them, **Who** Created them, they will
043:088	Truly these are a people **who** believe not!"
044:008	it is He **Who** gives life and gives death,-
044:037	the people of Tubba and those **who** were before them?
045:003	are Signs for those **who** believe.
045:011	and for those **who** reject the Signs of their Lord,
045:012	It is Allah **Who** has subjected the sea to you,
045:013	are Signs indeed for those **who** reflect.
045:014	to forgive those **who** do not hope for the Day of Allah;
045:014	Tell those **who** believe, to forgive
045:018	and follow not the desires of those **who** know not.
045:021	with those **who** believe and do righteous deeds,-
045:021	What! do those **who** do evil deeds think that We shall
045:023	**Who**, then, will guide him after Allah (has withdrawn
045:026	Say: "It is Allah **Who** gives you life, then gives you
045:030	Then, as to those **who** believed and did righteous deeds,
045:031	But as to those **who** reject Allah, (to them will be said):
046:003	but those **who** reject Faith turn away from that whereof
046:005	And **who** is more astray than one **who** invokes,
046:005	and **who** (in fact) are unconscious of their call (to them)?
046:011	Unbelievers say of those **who** believe: "If (this Message)
046:012	and as Glad Tidings to those **who** do right.
046:013	Verily those **who** say, "Our Lord is Allah,"
046:017	But (there is one) **who** says to his parents,
046:031	**who** invites (you) to Allah, and believe in him:
046:032	**who** invites (Us) to Allah, he cannot
046:033	**Who** created the heavens and the earth, and never
046:035	destroyed except those **who** transgress?
047:001	Those **who** reject Allah and hinder (men) from the
047:002	But those **who** believe and work deeds
047:003	This because those **who** reject Allah

WHO (continued)

047:003	While those **who** believe follow the Truth
047:004	But those **who** are slain in the way of Allah,
047:007	O ye **who** believe! if ye will help (the cause of) Allah,
047:008	But those **who** reject (Allah),- for them
047:010	and similar (fates await) those **who** reject Allah.
047:010	what was the End of those before them (**who** did evil)?
047:011	Allah is the Protector of those **who** believe,
047:011	but those **who** reject Allah have no protector.
047:012	while those **who** reject Allah will enjoy (this world)
047:012	Verily Allah will admit those **who** believe and do
047:014	Is then one **who** is on a clear (Path) from his Lord,
047:015	rivers of wine, a joy to those **who** drink;
047:016	and **who** follow their own lusts.
047:016	they say to those **who** have received Knowledge, "What
047:016	And among them are men **who** listen to thee,
047:017	But to those **who** receive Guidance, He increases
047:019	and for the men and women **who** believe:
047:020	Those **who** believe say, "Why is not a Sura sent down
047:025	Those **who** turn back as apostates after Guidance
047:026	they said to those **who** hate what Allah has revealed,
047:031	among you **who** strive their utmost and persevere
047:032	Those **who** disbelieve, hinder (men) from the Path of
047:033	O ye **who** believe! obey Allah, and obey
047:034	Those **who** disbelieve, and hinder (men) from the
047:038	But any **who** are niggardly are so at the expense of
048:004	It is He **who** sent down Tranquillity into the hearts of
048:005	That He may admit the men and women **who** believe,
048:006	men and women, **who** think an evil thought of Allah.
048:010	then any one **who** violates His oath,
048:010	any one **who** fulfils what he has covenanted with Allah,-
048:010	Verily those **who** plight their fealty to thee plight their
048:011	Say: "**Who** then has any power at all (to intervene)
048:011	The desert Arabs **who** lagged behind will say
048:013	for those **who** reject Allah, a Blazing fire!
048:015	Those **who** lagged behind (will say), when ye
048:016	Say to the desert Arabs **who** lagged behind:
048:017	and he **who** turns back, (Allah) will punish him with
048:024	And it is He **who** has restrained their hands
048:025	They are the ones **who** disbelieved and hindered
048:028	It is He **who** has sent His Messenger with Guidance
048:029	and those **who** are with him are strong against the
048:029	those among them **who** believe and do righteous deeds
049:001	for Allah is He **who** hears and knows all things.
049:001	O ye **who** believe! put not yourselves forward before
049:002	O ye **who** believe! raise not your voices above the voice
049:004	Those **who** shout out to thee from without the Inner
049:006	O ye **who** believe! if a sinner comes to you with any news
049:007	those **who** walk in righteousness;-
049:009	for Allah loves those **who** are fair (and just).
049:011	and those **who** do not desist are (indeed) doing wrong.
049:011	O ye **who** believe! let not some men among you laugh at
049:012	O ye **who** believe! avoid suspicion as much (as possible):
049:013	in the sight of Allah is (he **who** is) the most righteous
049:015	**who** have believed in Allah and His Messenger,
050:016	It was We **who** created man, and We
050:025	"Who forbade what was good, transgressed all bounds,
050:026	"Who set up another god besides Allah: throw him
050:033	"Who feared The Most Gracious unseen, and brought
050:037	or **who** gives ear and earnestly witnesses.
050:043	Verily it is We **Who** give Life and Death;
051:011	Those **who** (flounder) heedless in a flood of confusion:
051:034	from thy Lord for those **who** trespass beyond bounds."

WHO (continued)

051:035 Then We evacuated those of the Believers **who** were there,
051:058 For Allah is He **Who** gives (all) Sustenance,-
052:021 And those **who** believe and whose seeds follow them
052:042 those **who** disbelieve are themselves ensnared in a Plot.
052:047 And verily, for those **who** do wrong, there is
053:027 Those **who** believe not in the Hereafter,
053:029 Therefore shun those **who** turn away from
053:030 and He knoweth best those **who** receive guidance.
053:030 those **who** stray from His path,
053:031 and He rewards those **who** do good, with what
053:031 so that He rewards those **who** do evil,
053:032 He knows best **who** it is that guards against evil.
053:032 Those **who** avoid great sins and indecent deeds,
053:033 Seest thou one **who** turns back,
053:037 And of Abraham **who** fulfilled his (commandments)
053:043 That it is He **who** Granteth Laughter and Tears;
053:044 That it is He **who** Granteth Death and Life;
053:048 That it is He **Who** giveth wealth and satisfaction,
053:050 And that it is He **Who** destroyed the (powerful) ancient
054:014 a recompense to one **who** had been rejected (with scorn)!
054:031 the dry stubble used by one **who** pens cattle.
054:035 Thus do We reward those **who** give thanks.
055:002 It is He **Who** has taught the Qur'an.
055:010 It is He **Who** has spread out the earth for (His) creatures:
056:057 It is We **Who** have created you:
056:059 Is it ye **who** create it, or are We the Creators?
056:072 Is it ye **who** grow the tree which feeds the fire,
056:079 Which none shall touch but those **who** are clean:
056:092 he be of those **who** deny (the truth) **who** go wrong,
057:002 it is He **Who** gives life and Death;
057:004 He it is **Who** created the heavens and the earth
057:007 those of you **who** believe and spend (in charity),-
057:009 He is the One **Who** Sends to His Servants manifest Signs,
057:010 before the Victory, (with those **who** did so later).
057:010 than those **who** spent (freely) and fought afterwards.
057:010 among you are those **who** spent (freely) and fought,
057:011 **Who** is he that will loan to Allah a beautiful Loan?
057:015 nor of those **who** rejected Allah.
057:018 For those **who** give in Charity, men and women,
057:019 And those **who** believe in Allah and His messengers-
057:019 but those **who** reject Allah and deny Our Signs,-
057:021 prepared for those **who** believe in Allah and His
057:025 that Allah may test **who** it is that will help,
057:027 of those **who** followed him Compassion and Mercy.
057:027 on those among them **who** believed, their (due) reward,
058:001 woman **who** pleads with thee concerning her husband
058:002 can be their mothers except those **who** gave them birth.
058:003 But those **who** pronounce the word "Zihar" to their wives
058:004 For those **who** Reject (Him) , there is a grievous
058:005 Those **who** oppose (the commands of) Allah and His
058:008 Seest thou not those **who** were forbidden secret
058:009 O ye **who** believe! when ye hold secret counsel,
058:011 those of you **who** believe and **who** have been granted
058:011 O ye **who** believe! When ye are told to make room in the
058:012 O ye **who** believe! When ye consult the Messenger
058:014 Seest thou not those **who** turn (in friendship) to such
058:020 Those **who** oppose (the commands of) Allah and
058:021 "It is I and My messengers **who** must prevail":
058:022 loving those **who** oppose Allah and His Messenger,
058:022 **who** believe in Allah and the Last Day,
059:002 It is He **who** got out the Unbelievers among the
059:008 those **who** were expelled from their homes and their

WHO (continued)

059:009 And those **who** before them, had homes
059:010 **who** came before us into the Faith and leave not,
059:010 (or sense of injury) against those **who** have believed.
059:010 And those **who** came after them say: "Our Lord!
059:015 Like those **who** lately preceded them, they have
059:018 O ye **who** believe! Fear Allah, and let
059:019 And be ye not like those **who** forgot Allah;
059:022 **Who** knows (all things) both secret and open;
060:001 O ye **who** believe! take not My enemies and yours
060:008 to those **who** fight you not for (your) Faith
060:008 for Allah loveth those **who** are just.
060:009 to those **who** fight you for (your) Faith, and drive
060:010 (on their dowers of women **who** came over to you).
060:010 O ye **who** believe! when there come to you believing
060:013 O ye **who** believe! turn not (for friendship) to people on
061:002 O ye **who** believe! why say ye that which ye do not?
061:004 Truly Allah loves those **who** fight in His Cause
061:005 For Allah guides not those **who** are rebellious
061:007 And Allah guides not those **who** do wrong.
061:007 **Who** doth greater wrong than one **who** forges falsehood
061:009 It is He **Who** has sent His Messenger with Guidance
061:010 O ye **who** believe! shall I lead you to a bargain
061:014 O ye **who** believe! be ye helpers of Allah:
061:014 "**Who** will be my helpers to (the work of) Allah"?
061:014 power to those **who** believed against their enemies,
062:002 It is He **Who** has sent amongst the Unlettered
062:003 Along with others of them, **who** have not already
062:005 and Allah guides not people **who** do wrong.
062:005 but **who** subsequently failed in those (obligations),
062:005 The similitude of those **who** were entrusted with
062:005 similitude of the people **who** falsify the Signs of Allah:
062:009 O ye **who** believe! when the call is proclaimed
063:007 They are the ones **who** say, "Spend nothing
063:007 "Spend nothing on those **who** are with Allah's
063:009 O ye **who** believe! let not your riches or your
064:002 It is He **Who** has created you;
064:005 of those **who** rejected Faith aforetime?
064:009 those **who** believe in Allah and work righteousness,-
064:010 But those **who** reject Faith and treat Our Signs as
064:014 O ye **who** believe! truly, among your wives and your
065:001 and any **who** transgresses the limits of Allah,
065:002 **who** believes in Allah and the Last Day.
065:002 And for those **who** fear Allah,
065:004 and for those **who** fear Allah, He will
065:004 and for those **who** have no courses (it is the same):
065:004 for those **who** are pregnant, their period is until they
065:010 O ye men of understanding **who** have believed!-
065:011 And those **who** believe in Allah and work righteousness
065:011 lead forth those **who** believe and do righteous deeds from
065:011 A Messenger, **who** rehearses to you the Signs of Allah
065:012 Allah is He **Who** created seven Firmaments and of
066:003 she said, "**Who** told thee this?"
066:003 He said, "He told me **Who** is the Knower, The Aware."
066:004 one among those **who** believe,-and furthermore,
066:005 **who** submit (their wills), **who** believe, **who** are devout;
066:005 **who** worship (in humility), **who** fast,-
066:005 **who** turn to Allah in repentance,
066:006 **who** flinch not (from executing) the Commands they
066:006 O ye **who** believe! save yourselves and your families
066:008 O ye **who** believe! turn to Allah with sincere repentance:
066:008 humiliated the Prophet and those **who** believe with him.
066:011 as an example to those **who** believe, the wife of Pharaoh:

WHO (continued)

066:012	Mary the daughter of 'Imran, **who** guarded her chastity;
067:002	He **Who** created Death and Life, that He
067:003	He **Who** created the seven heavens one above another:
067:006	For those **who** reject their Lord (and Cherisher)
067:012	As for those **who** fear their Lord unseen, for them
067:015	It is He **Who** has made the earth manageable for you,
067:016	Do ye feel secure that He **Who** is in Heaven will not
067:017	Or do ye feel secure that He **Who** is in Heaven will not
067:020	Nay, **who** is there that can help you, (even as)
067:021	Or **who** is there that can provide you with Sustenance
067:022	or one **who** walks evenly on a Straight Way?
067:022	Is then one **who** walks headlong, with his
067:023	Say: "It is He **Who** has created you, and made
067:024	Say: "It is He **Who** has multiplied you through
067:028	yet **who** can deliver the Unbelievers from a grievous
067:030	**who** then can supply you with clear-flowing water?"
068:007	And He knows best **who** receive (True) Guidance.
068:008	So obey not to those **who** deny (the Truth).
070:013	His kindred **who** sheltered him.
070:023	Those **who** remain steadfast to their prayer;
070:025	For the (needy) **who** asks and him **who** is deprived
070:026	And those **who** hold to the truth of the Day of Judgment;
070:027	And those **who** fear the punishment of their Lord,-
070:029	And those **who** guard their chastity,
070:031	But those **who** trespass beyond this are transgressors;-
070:032	And those **who** respect their trusts and covenants;
070:033	And those **who** stand firm in their testimonies;
070:034	And those **who** (strictly) guard their worship;-
071:028	Forgive me, my parents, all **who** enter my house in Faith,
072:004	**who** used to utter extravagant lies against Allah;
072:006	**who** took shelter with persons among the Jinns,
072:009	any **who** listens now will find a flaming fire watching
072:013	and any **who** believes in his Lord has no fear,
072:014	Now those **who** submit their wills-they have
072:015	'But those **who** swerve,-they are
072:024	Then will they know **who** it is that is weakest in (his)
073:011	the good things of life, (**who** yet) deny the Truth);
074:043	They will say: "We were not of those **who** prayed;
074:044	"Nor were we of those **who** fed the indigent;
074:055	Let any **who** will, keep it in remembrance!
075:027	"**Who** is a magician (to restore him)?"
076:023	It is We **Who** have sent down the Qur'an
076:028	It is We **Who** created them, and We have
078:038	none shall speak except any **who** permitted by the Most
079:001	By the (angels) **who** tear out (the souls of the wicked)
079:002	By those **who** gently draw out (the souls of the blessed)
079:003	And by those **who** glide along (on errands of mercy),
079:036	Hell-fire shall be placed in full view for him **who** sees.-
080:005	As to one **who** regards himself as self-sufficient,
080:008	But as to him **who** came to thee striving earnestly,
080:012	Therefore let **who** will, keep it in remembrance.
082:007	Him **Who** created thee, fashioned thee
083:002	Those **who**, when they have to receive by measure
083:026	and for this let those aspire, **who** have aspirations:
083:029	Those in sin used to laugh at those **who** believed,
084:007	Then he **who** is given his Record in his Right hand,
084:010	But he **who** is given his Record behind his back,-
084:025	Except to those **who** believe and work righteous deeds:
085:010	Those **who** persecute the Believers, men and women,
085:011	For those **who** believe and do righteous deeds,
085:013	It is He **Who** Creates from the very beginning,
087:002	**Who** hath created, and further, given order

WHO (continued)

087:003	**Who** hath measured. And granted guidance;
087:004	And **Who** bringeth out the (green and luscious) pasture,
087:010	He will heed **who** fears:
087:012	**Who** will enter the Great Fire,
087:014	But he will prosper **who** purify himself.
089:005	(or evidence) for those **who** understand?
089:009	**who** cut out (huge) rocks in the valley?-
090:017	Then will he be of those **who** believe, and enjoin
090:019	But those **who** reject Our Signs, they are
092:005	So he **who** gives (in charity) and fears (Allah),
092:008	But he **who** is a greedy miser and thinks himself
092:016	**Who** give the lie to Truth and turn their backs.
092:018	Those **who** spend their wealth for increase in self-
093:010	Nor repulse him **who** asks;
096:001	in the name of thy Lord and Cherisher, **Who** created-
096:004	He **Who** taught (the use of) the Pen,-
096:009	Seest thou one **who** forbids-
098:001	Those **who** disbelieve, among the People of the Book
098:006	Those **who** disbelieve, among the People of the Book
098:007	Those **who** have faith and do righteous deeds,-
099:007	Then shall anyone **who** has done an atom's weight of
099:008	And anyone **who** has done an atom's weight of evil,
104:002	**Who** pileth up wealth and layeth it by,
106:004	**Who** provides them with food against hunger,
107:001	Seest thou one **who** denies the Judgment (to come)?
107:002	Then such is the one **who** repulses the orphan,
107:005	**Who** are neglectful of their Prayers,
107:006	Those **who** (want but) to be seen,
108:003	For he **who** hateth thee,-he will
113:004	From the mischief of those **who** blow on knots;
114:004	(of Evil), **who** withdraws (after his whisper),-
114:005	**Who** whispers into the hearts of Mankind,-

WHOEVER

002:097	Say: **Whoever** is an enemy to Gabriel -
002:098	**Whoever** is an enemy to Allah and His angels and
002:108	But **whoever** changeth from Faith to Unbelief,
002:112	Nay, **whoever** submits his whole self to Allah and is
002:178	After this **whoever** exceeds the limits shall be in grave
002:256	**whoever** rejects Tagut and believes in Allah
002:283	Conceal not evidence; for **whoever** conceals it,
003:097	**whoever** enters it attains security;
003:101	**Whoever** holds firmly to Allah will be shown
004:085	and **whoever** recommends and helps an evil cause,
004:085	**Whoever** intercedes in a good cause becomes
004:092	and **whoever** kills a Believer by mistake it is
004:119	**Whoever**, forsaking Allah, takes Satan for a friend,
004:123	**whoever** works evil, will be requited accordingly.
005:072	**Whoever** joins other gods with Allah,-Allah will
012:108	with a certain knowledge I and **whoever** follows me.
016:097	**Whoever** works righteousness, man or woman,
018:087	He said: "**Whoever** doth wrong, him shall we punish;
018:088	"But **whoever** believes, and works righteousness
018:110	**whoever** expects to meet his Lord, let him
021:094	**Whoever** works any act of righteousness and has
022:004	that **whoever** turns to him for friendship,
022:030	**whoever** honours the sacred rites of Allah,
022:032	and **whoever** holds in honour the Rites of Allah,
025:019	And **whoever** among you does wrong, him shall
025:071	And **whoever** repents and does good has truly
031:022	**Whoever** submits his whole self to Allah, and is
035:018	And **whoever** purifies himself does so for the
038:061	**Whoever** brought this upon us,-add to

WHOEVER (continued)

041:046   **whoever** works evil, it is against his own soul:
041:046   **Whoever** works righteousness benefits his own soul;
081:028   (With profit) to **whoever** among you wills to go straight:

WHOLE

002:112   submits his **whole** self to Allah and is a doer of good,
002:233   suck to their offspring for two **whole** years,
003:007   the **whole** of it is from our Lord:"
003:020   say: "I have submitted my **whole** self to Allah
003:119   though ye believe in the **whole** of the Book,
003:133   (of the **whole**) of the heavens and of the earth,
004:020   Even if ye had given the latter a **whole** treasure for dower,
004:043   until after washing your **whole** body if ye are ill,
004:125   than one who submits his **whole** self to Allah,
005:006   bathe your **whole** body.
005:032   it would be as if he slew the **whole** people:
005:032   he saved the life of the **whole** people.
007:007   We shall recount their **whole** story with knowledge,
007:029   and that ye set your **whole** selves (to Him)
010:016   A **whole** lifetime before this have I tarried
017:088   Say: "If the **whole** of mankind and Jinns were to
020:087   of the ornaments of the (**whole**) people, and we
026:095   "And the **whole** hosts of Iblis together.
028:078   Allah had destroyed, before him, (**whole**) generations,-
031:022   Whoever submits his **whole** self to Allah,
033:071   That He may make your conduct **whole** and sound
039:067   on the Day of Judgement the **whole** of the earth
068:043   while they were **whole**, (and had refused).
069:007   the (**whole**) people lying overthrown in its (path),

WHOLE-HEARTEDLY

002:208   enter into Islam **whole-heartedly**;
073:008   the Lord and devote thyself to Him **wholeheartedly**.

WHOLESALE

007:133   **Wholesale** Death, Locusts, lice, Frogs, and

WHOLESOME

004:160   (foods) good and **wholesome** which had been lawful
016:067   strong drink, and **wholesome** food: behold, in this
077:027   and provided for you water sweet (and **wholesome**)?

WHOLLY

003:154   Say thou: "Indeed, this affair is **wholly** Allah's."
025:026   shall be (**wholly**) for The Most Gracious:
082:019   will be (**wholly**) with Allah.

WHOM

001:007   The way of those on **whom** thou hast bestowed Thy
002:105   Allah will choose for His special Mercy **whom** He will -
002:121   Those to **whom** We have given the Book
002:138   and it is He. **Whom** we worship.
002:142   He guideth **whom** He will to a Way that is straight.
002:157   They are those on **whom** (descend) blessings from their
002:212   His abundance without measures on **whom** He will.
002:213   For Allah guides **whom** He will to a path that is straight.
002:247   Allah granteth His authority to **whom** He pleaseth;
002:261   Allah giveth manifold increase to **whom** He pleaseth:
002:269   He granteth wisdom to **whom** He pleaseth;
002:269   and he to **whom** wisdom is granted receiveth
002:272   the right path **whom** He pleaseth.
002:275   not stand except as stands one **whom** the Satan
002:284   and punisheth **whom** He pleaseth.
002:284   He forgiveth **whom** He pleaseth,
003:013   with His aid **whom** He pleaseth.
003:026   Thou enduest with honour **whom** Thou pleasest,
003:026   thou givest power to **whom** Thou pleasest,

WHOM (continued)

003:026   and thou bringest low **whom** Thou pleasest:
003:026   Thou strippest off Power from **whom** Thou pleasest:
003:027   to **whom** Thou pleasest, without measure."
003:037   to **whom** He pleases, without measure."
003:073   He granteth them to **whom** He pleaseth:
003:074   specially chooseth **whom** He pleaseth:
003:079   that a man, to **whom** is given the Book, and Wisdom.
003:129   and punisheth **whom** He pleaseth;
003:129   He forgiveth **whom** He pleaseth and punisheth
003:154   those for **whom** death was decreed would certainly
003:172   Those to **whom** men said: "A great army
003:179   but He chooses of his Messengers **whom** He pleases.
003:192   "Our Lord! any **whom** Thou dost admit to the Fire,
004:001   through **Whom** ye demand your mutual (rights),
004:022   And marry not women **whom** your fathers married,
004:023   born of your wives to **whom** ye have gone in,
004:024   except those **whom** your right hands possess:
004:025   from among those **whom** your right hand possess:
004:033   To those also, to **whom** your right hand was pledged,
004:048   but He forgiveth anything, to **whom** He pleaseth;
004:049   Nay-but Allah doth purify **whom** He pleaseth.
004:052   and those **whom** Allah hath cursed, thou wilt find,
004:052   They are (men) **whom** Allah hath cursed:
004:058   your trusts to those to **whom** they are due;
004:069   those on **whom** is the Grace of Allah,
004:088   **whom** Allah hath thrown out of the Way?
004:088   For those **whom** Allah hath thrown out of the Way,
004:090   between **whom** and you there is a treaty (of peace),
004:092   with **whom** ye have a treaty of mutual alliance,
004:116   but He forgiveth **whom** He pleaseth
004:127   to **whom** ye give not the portions prescribed,
004:127   and yet **whom** ye desire to marry,
004:143   **Whom** Allah leaves straying, never wilt
005:018   He forgiveth **whom** He pleaseth, and He
005:018   and He punisheth **whom** He Pleaseth: and to Allah
005:023   were two on **whom** Allah had bestowed His Grace:
005:040   and He forgiveth **whom** he pleaseth:
005:040   He punisheth **whom** He pleaseth,
005:054   **whom** He will love as they will love him,
005:054   which He will bestow on **whom** He pleaseth.
005:060   those of **whom** some He transformed into apes
005:088   but fear Allah, in **Whom** ye believe.
005:096   and fear Allah, to **Whom** ye shall be gathered back.
006:006   for **whom** We poured out rain from the skies
006:012   Say: "To **whom** belongeth all that is in the heavens
006:019   that I may warn you and all **whom** it reaches.
006:020   Those to **whom** We have given the Book know this
006:022   **whom** ye (invented and) talked about?"
006:039   **whom** He willeth, He placeth on the Way that is 'Straight.
006:039   **whom** Allah willeth, He leaveth to wander:
006:056   other than Allah, **whom** ye call upon."
006:071   like one **whom** the Satans have made into a fool,
006:083   We raise **whom** We will, degree after degree:
006:088   He giveth that guidance to **whom** He pleaseth,
006:089   These were the men to **whom** We gave the Book,
006:094   **whom** ye thought to be partners in your affairs:
006:108   Revile not ye those **whom** they call upon besides Allah,
006:114   to **whom** We have given the Book,
006:122   to **whom** We gave life, and a light whereby he can walk
006:125   Those **whom** Allah willeth to guide,- He openeth
006:125   those **whom** He willeth to leave straying,
006:133   in your place appoint **whom** He will as your successors,

WHOM (continued)

006:138 except those **whom**-so they say-We wish;
007:006 and those by **whom** We sent it.
007:006 to **whom** Our Message was sent and those
007:048 call to certain men **whom** they will know by their marks,
007:049 the men **whom** you swore that Allah with His Mercy
007:105 One for **whom** it is right to say nothing but truth about
007:155 and Thou leadest **whom** Thou wilt
007:155 by it Thou causest **whom** Thou wilt to stray,
007:156 He said: "I afflict My Punishment on **whom** I will;
007:157 **whom** they find mentioned in their own (Scriptures),-
007:158 to **Whom** belongeth the dominion of the heavens
007:164 preach to a people **whom** Allah will destroy or
007:175 the story of the man to **whom** We sent Our Signs,
007:178 **whom** He rejects from His guidance.
007:178 **Whom** Allah doth guide,-he is on the right path:
007:194 Verily those **whom** ye call upon besides Allah
008:024 and that it is He to **Whom** ye shall (all) be gathered.
008:028 and that it is Allah with **whom** lies your highest reward.
008:056 They are those with **whom** thou didst make a covenant,
008:060 and others besides, **whom** ye may not know,
008:060 but **whom** Allah doth know.
008:072 except against a people with **whom** ye have a treaty
009:001 to those of the Pagans with **whom** ye have contracted
009:004 those Pagans with **whom** ye have entered into alliance
009:007 **whom** ye made a treaty near the sacred mosque?
009:013 Nay, it is Allah **whom** ye should more justly fear,
009:015 For Allah will turn (in mercy) to **whom** He will:
009:027 turn (in mercy) to **whom** He will:
010:024 people to **whom** it belongs think they have all powers
010:025 He doth guide **whom** He pleaseth to a way that is straight.
010:090 no god except Him **Whom** the Children of Israel believe
010:096 Those against **whom** the Word of thy Lord hath been
011:016 are those for **whom** there is nothing in the Hereafter
011:031 Nor yet do I say, of those **whom** your eyes do despise
011:039 on **whom** will descend a Chastisement that will
011:039 on **whom** will be unloosed a Chastisement lasting."
011:040 against **whom** the Word has already gone forth,-
011:043 any but those on **whom** He hath mercy!"-
011:048 (there will be other) Peoples to **whom** We shall grant
011:093 soon will ye know who it is on **whom** descends the
011:101 other than Allah **whom** they invoked,
011:116 Except a few among them **whom** We saved (from harm)?
011:119 Except those on **whom** thy Lord hath bestowed His Mercy:
012:032 the man about **whom** ye did blame me!
012:042 to that one **whom** he considered about to be saved,
012:043 **whom** seven lean ones devour,-
012:046 of seven fat kine **whom** seven lean ones devour,
012:056 We bestow of Our mercy on **whom** We please,
012:076 We raise to degrees (of wisdom) **whom** We please:
012:079 other than him with **whom** we found our property:
012:100 Verily my Lord is gracious to **whom** He wills
012:109 (as Messengers) any but men, **whom** We did inspire,-
012:110 and those **whom** We will are delivered into safety.
013:026 (which He giveth) to **whom** so He pleaseth.
013:027 Say: "Truly Allah leaveth, to stray **whom** He will;
013:030 a People before **whom** (long since) have (other) Peoples
013:033 And those **whom** Allah leads astray, no one can guide.
013:036 Those to **whom** We have given the Book rejoice at
014:002 to **Whom** do belong all things in the heavens and on earth!
014:004 So Allah leads astray those **whom** He pleases and guides
014:004 and guides **whom** He pleases and He is Exalted in power,
015:006 They say: "O thou to **whom** the Message is being

WHOM (continued)

015:033 **Whom** Thou didst create from sounding clay,
016:020 Those **whom** they invoke besides Allah create nothing
016:025 of those without knowledge, **whom** they misled.
016:027 concerning **whom** ye used to dispute (with the godly)/"
016:036 of the people were some **whom** Allah guided,
016:036 and some on **whom** Error became inevitably (established).
016:043 to **whom** We granted inspiration:
016:071 to those **whom** their right hands possess,
016:075 on **whom** We have bestowed goodly favours from
016:086 our 'partners', those **whom** we used to invoke
016:093 and He guides **whom** He pleases:
016:093 but he leaves straying **whom** He pleases,
016:114 if it is He **whom** ye serve.
017:003 **whom** We carried (in the Ark) with Noah!
017:030 provide sustenance in abundance for **whom** He pleaseth,
017:056 Say: "Call on those-besides Him-**whom** ye fancy:
017:057 Those **whom** they call upon do seek (for themselves)
017:061 "Shall I prostrate to one **whom** Thou didst create from
017:062 one **whom** thou hast honoured above me!
017:064 And Arouse those **whom** thou canst among them,
017:097 It is he **whom** Allah guides,
017:097 but he **whom** He leaves astray-for such wilt thou
018:017 but he **whom** Allah leaves to stray,-for him
018:017 he **whom** Allah guides is rightly guided;
018:052 "Call on those **whom** ye thought to be My partners,"
018:065 from Ourselves and **whom** We had taught knowledge
018:065 On **whom** We had bestowed Mercy from Ourselves
018:090 for **whom** We had provided no covering protection
019:006 one with **whom** Thou art well-pleased!"
019:048 and from those **whom** ye invoke besides Allah:
019:049 and from those **whom** they worshipped besides Allah,
019:058 and of those **whom** We carried (in the Ark)
019:058 and Israel-of those **whom** We guided and chose.
019:058 on **whom** Allah did bestow His Grace,-
020:081 and those on **whom** descends My Wrath
020:097 now look at thy god, of **whom** thou hast become a
020:109 except for those for **whom** permission has been
021:007 to **whom** We granted inspiration:
021:009 and We saved them and those **whom** We willed,
021:028 except for those who with **whom** He is well-pleased
021:101 Those for **whom** the Good (Record) from Us
022:004 About the (Satan) it is decreed that whoever
022:005 to you; and We cause **whom** We will to rest in
022:016 and verily Allah doth guide **whom** He will!
022:018 are (also) such as unto **whom** the chastisement
022:039 To those against **whom** war is made, permission is
022:054 And that those on **whom** knowledge has been
022:062 and those besides Him **whom** they invoke,-
022:073 feeble are those who petition and those **whom** they
022:073 Those on **whom**, besides Allah ye call,
023:006 or (the captives) **whom** their right hands possess,-
023:027 of them against **whom** the Word has already gone forth:
023:033 on **whom** We had bestowed the good things of this life,
023:084 Say: "To **whom** belong the earth and all beings therein?
024:021 but Allah doth purify **whom** He pleases:
024:031 or the slaves **whom** their right hands possess,
024:035 Allah doth guide **whom** He will to His Light:
024:037 By men **whom** neither trade nor sale can divert
024:038 for those **whom** He will, without measure.
024:040 for any to **whom** Allah giveth not light,
024:043 and He turns it away from **whom** He pleases.
024:043 He strikes therewith **whom** He pleases

WHOM (continued)

024:046	and Allah guides **whom** He wills to a Way that is straight.
024:058	Let those **whom** your right hands possess,
024:062	give leave to those of them **whom** thou wilt,
025:002	He to **Whom** belongs the dominion of the heavens
025:017	as well as those **whom** they worship besides Allah,
025:020	And the messengers **whom** We sent before thee
025:041	in mockery: "Is this the one **whom** Allah has sent
026:075	"Did ye then see **whom** ye have been worshipping,-
026:166	"And leave those **whom** Allah has created for you
026:221	on **whom** it is that the Satans descend?
027:005	Such are they for **whom** a grievous Chastisement
027:059	and Peace on His servants **whom** He has chosen
027:091	Who has sanctified it and to **Whom** (belong) all things:
028:046	to give warning to a people to **whom** no warner had come
028:052	Those to **whom** We sent the Book before this,-
028:056	but Allah guides those **whom** He will and He best those
028:056	wilt not be able to guide everyone **whom** thou lovest:
028:061	and one to **whom** We have given the good things
028:061	one to **whom** We have made a goodly promise,
028:062	My 'parthners'?-**whom** ye imagined (to be such)?"
028:063	these are the ones **whom** we led astray:
028:063	Those against **whom** the charge will be proved,
028:074	**whom** ye imagined (to be such)?"
029:021	"He punishes **whom** He pleases,
029:021	and He grants mercy to **whom** He pleases,
030:005	He gives victory to **whom** He will, and He
030:028	partners among those **whom** your right hands possess,
030:029	But who will guide those **whom** Allah leaves astray?
032:003	to **whom** no warner has come before thee:
032:022	to **whom** are recited the Signs of his Lord,
033:004	nor has He made your wives **whom** ye divorce by Zihar
033:050	the captives **whom** their right hands possess;-
033:050	the captives of war **whom** Allah has assigned to thee;
033:050	and those **whom** thy right possess out of the captives
033:050	to thee thy wives to **whom** thou hast paid their dowers;
033:055	or the (slaves) **whom** their right hands possess.
034:001	Praise be to Allah, to **Whom** belong all things
034:003	from **Whom** is not hidden the least little atom in the
034:006	And those to **whom** knowledge has come see that
034:022	Say: "Call upon other (gods) **whom** ye fancy,
034:023	except for those for **whom** He has granted permission.
034:027	Say: "Show me those **whom** ye have joined with Him
034:036	to **whom** He pleases, but most men know not."
034:037	are the ones for **whom** there is a multiplied Reward
035:008	then, to **whom** the evil of his conduct is made alluring,
035:008	For Allah leaves to stray **whom** He wills,
035:008	and guides **whom** He wills.
035:013	And those **whom** ye invoke besides Him
035:025	to **whom** came their messengers with Clear Signs,
035:040	of yours **whom** ye call upon besides Allah?
036:022	and to **Whom** ye shall (all) be brought back,
036:047	"Shall we then feed those **whom**, if Allah had so willed,
038:022	two disputants, one of **whom** has wronged the other:
038:075	**whom** I have created with My hands?
039:004	He pleased out of those **whom** He doth create:
039:004	He could have chosen **whom** He pleased
039:018	those are the ones **whom** Allah has guided,
039:019	Is, then, one against **whom** the decree of Punishment
039:023	He guides therewith **whom** He pleases, but such
039:040	and on **whom** descends a Chastisement that abides."
039:040	"Who it is to **whom** comes a Chastisement
039:042	those on **whom** He has passed the degree of death,

WHOM (continued)

040:009	and any **whom** Thou dost preserve from ills
040:020	but those **whom** (men) invoke besides Him,
040:033	any **whom** Allah leaves to stray,
040:042	join with Him partners of **whom** I have no knowledge;
040:066	those **whom** ye invoke besides Allah,-seeing that
041:034	then will he between **whom** and thee was hatred become
042:008	but He admits **whom** He will to His Mercy;
042:012	and restricts the Sustenance to **whom** He will:
042:013	Allah chooses to Himself those **whom** He pleases,
042:019	He gives Sustenance to **whom** He pleases:
042:044	For any **whom** Allah leaves astray, there is
042:046	and for any **whom** Allah leaves to stray, there is
042:050	and He leaves barren **whom** He will:
042:053	The Way of Allah, to **whom** belongs whatever is
043:045	and question thou our messengers **whom** We sent
043:085	And blessed is He to **Whom** belongs the dominion
043:086	And those **whom** they invoke besides Allah have no
046:016	Such are they from **whom** We shall accept the best
046:018	Such are they against **whom** is the word true among
046:028	to them from those **whom** they worshipped as gods,
047:014	no better than one to **whom** the evil of his conduct
047:023	Such are the men **whom** Allah has cursed
048:014	and He punishes **whom** He wills:
048:014	He forgives **whom** He wills,
048:025	that He may admit to His Mercy **whom** He will.
048:025	believing men and believing women **whom** ye did not
053:026	has given leave for **whom** He pleases and that
055:056	**whom** no man or Jinn before them has touched;-
055:074	**Whom** no man or Jinn before them has touched;-
057:016	not become like those to **whom** was given The Book
057:021	which He bestows on **whom** He pleases:
058:009	and fear Allah, to **whom** ye shall be brought back.
059:022	Allah is He, than **Whom** there is no other god;-
059:023	Allah is He, than **Whom** there is no other god;-
060:007	between you and those **whom** ye (now) hold as enemies.
060:011	and fear Allah, in **Whom** ye believe.
060:013	(for friendship) to people on **whom** is the Wrath
062:004	Bounty of Allah, which He bestows on **whom** He will:
070:030	and the (captives) **whom** their right hands possess,-
072:027	"Except an apostle **whom** He has chosen:
074:011	the (creature) **whom** I created (bare and) alone!-
074:012	To **whom** I granted resources in abundance,
074:014	To **whom** I made (life) smooth and comfortable!
074:031	**whom** He pleaseth, and guide **whom** He pleaseth;
076:031	He will admit to His Mercy **Whom** He will;
085:009	Him to **Whom** belongs the dominion of the heavens

WHOMSOEVER

010:107	He causeth it to reach **whomsoever** of His servants
011:013	and call (to your aid) **whomsoever** ye can,
013:013	and therewith He striketh **whomsoever** He will.
030:037	the provision and restricts it to **whomsoever** He pleases?
057:029	His Hand, to bestow it on **whomsoever** He wills.

WHOSE

001:007	Those **whose** (portion) is not wrath,
002:024	**whose** fuel is Men and Stones,
002:114	**whose** zeal is (in fact) to ruin them?
002:196	This is for those **whose** household is not in (the precincts
002:204	**whose** speech about this world's life may dazzle thee,
002:237	by him in **whose** hands is the marriage tie;
003:007	But those in **whose** hearts is perversity follow
003:022	They are those **whose** works will bear no fruit
003:106	to those **whose** faces will be black,

WHOSE (continued)

003:107   But those **whose** faces will be (lit with) white,
003:133   and for a Garden **whose** width is that (of the whole)
003:162   and **whose** abode is in Hell? A woeful refuse!
004:012   If the man or woman **whose** inheritance is in question,
004:034   **whose** part ye fear disloyalty and ill-conduct,
004:075   **Whose** people are oppressors; and raise for us
004:075   Men, women, and children, **whose** cry is: "Our Lord!
004:087   And **whose** word can be truer than Allah's?
004:109   of men on **whose** behalf ye may contend in this world;
004:122   and **whose** word can be truer than Allah's?
005:041   but **whose** hearts have no faith;
005:050   But who, for a people **whose** faith is assured,
005:052   Those in **whose** heart is a disease-thou seest how
006:051   in **whose** (hearts) is the fear that they will be brought
006:135   will ye know **whose** end will be (best) in the Hereafter:
007:008   those **whose** scale (of good) will be heavy,
007:009   Those **whose** scale will be light, will find
007:101   Such were the towns **whose** story We (thus)
008:049   Lo! the Hypocrites in **whose** hearts is a disease:
009:045   and the Last Day, and **whose** hearts are in doubt,
009:060   for those **whose** hearts have been (recently) reconciled
009:108   There is a mosque **whose** foundation was laid from the
009:125   But those in **whose** hearts is a disease,-it will
010:039   that **whose** knowledge they cannot compass,
012:018   it is Allah (alone) **whose** help can be sought."
012:023   But she, in **whose** house he was, sought to
012:075   in **whose** saddle-bag it is found, should be
013:005   They are those round **whose** necks will be
013:028   and **whose** hearts find satisfaction in the remembrance
014:024   a goodly tree, **whose** root is firmly fixed, and its
015:020   for **whose** sustenance ye are not responsible.
016:028   "(Namely) those **whose** lives the angels take in
016:032   (Namely) those **whose** lives the angels take in
016:108   Those are they **whose** hearts, ears, and eyes
017:001   Farthest Mosque **whose** precincts We did Bless,-
017:019   the ones **whose** striving will be thanked (by Allah).
018:028   nor obey any **whose** heart We have permitted to neglect
018:029   We have prepared Fire **whose** (smoke and flames),
018:101   (Unbelievers) **whose** eyes had been under a veil
018:104   "Those **whose** efforts have been wasted in this life,
020:109   and **whose** word is acceptable to Him.
020:128   in **whose** haunts they (now) move?
021:112   the One **Whose** assistance should be sought against
022:013   (Perhaps) they call on one **whose** hurt is nearer
022:025   and any **whose** purpose therein is profanity
022:035   To those **whose** hearts, when Allah is mentioned,
022:053   but a trial for those in **whose** hearts is a disease
023:007   But those **whose** desires exceed those limits are
023:088   Say: "Who is it in **whose** hands is the sovereignty
023:102   Then those **whose** balance (of good deeds)
023:103   But those **whose** balance is light, will be
024:035   **whose** Oil is well-nigh luminous,
024:041   **Whose** praises all beings in the heavens and on
028:037   from Him and **whose** End will be best in the Hereafter:
028:079   Said those **whose** aim is the Life of this World:
029:005   For those **whose** hopes are in the meeting with Allah,
032:026   in **whose** dwellings they (now) go to and fro?
033:012   The Hypocrites and those in **whose** hearts is a disease
033:032   lest one in **whose** heart is a disease should be moved
033:051   if thou invite one **whose** (turn) thou hadst set aside.
033:060   Truly, it the Hypocrites, in **whose** hearts is a disease,
036:006   warn a people, **whose** fathers were not warned,

WHOSE (continued)

036:083   So glory to Him in **Whose** hands is the dominion
037:021   the Day of sorting Out, **whose** truth ye (once) denied!"
038:050   Gardens of Eternity, **whose** doors will (ever) be open
039:022   Is one **whose** heart Allah has opened to Islam,
039:022   Woe to those **whose** hearts are hardened against
040:016   **Whose** will be the Dominion that Day?
040:078   and some **whose** story We have not related to thee.
040:078   **whose** story We have related to thee, and some
047:016   Such are men **whose** hearts Allah has sealed,
047:020   thou wilt see those in **whose** hearts is a disease
047:029   Or do those in **whose** hearts is a disease,
048:025   trampling down and on **whose** account a guilt
052:021   and **whose** seeds follow them in Faith,-to them
055:054   **whose** inner linings will be of rich brocade:
056:033   **Whose** season is not limited, nor (supply)
060:006   for those **whose** hope is in Allah and in the last Day.
060:011   Then pay to those **whose** wives have deserted
061:006   to come after after me, **whose** name shall be Ahmad.
065:007   and the man **whose** resources are restricted,
066:006   your families from a fire **whose** fuel is Men and Stones,
067:001   Blessed be He in **Whose** hands is Dominion;
068:020   dark and desolate spot, (**whose** fruit had been gathered).
070:024   And those in **whose** wealth is a recognized right
071:021   **whose** wealth and children give them no Increase
074:031   in **whose** hearts is a disease and the Unbelievers
076:007   and they fear a Day **whose** evil flies far and wide.
101:006   Then, he **whose** balance (of good deeds) will be
101:008   But he **whose** balance (of good deeds) will be

WHOSO

073:019   Therefore, **whoso** will, let him take a (straight)
078:039   **whoso** will, let him take a (straight) Return to his Lord!

WHOSOEVER

002:038   **whosoever** follows My guidance,
020:123   **whosoever** follows My guidance, will not
020:124   "But **whosoever** turns away from My Message,
076:029   **whosoever** will, let him take a (straight) Path to his Lord.
079:026   for **whosoever** feareth (Allah).

WHY

002:025   they say: "**Why,** this is what we were fed with before,"
002:091   Say: **Why** then have ye slain the prophets
002:118   Or **why** cometh not unto us a Sign?"
002:118   "**Why** speaketh not Allah unto us?
003:065   Ye people of the Book! **why** dispute ye about Abraham,
003:066   but **why** dispute ye in matters of which ye have no
003:070   **Why** reject ye the Signs of Allah,
003:071   **Why** do ye clothe truth with falsehood,
003:098   **why** reject ye the Signs of Allah,
003:099   **why** obstruct ye those who believe,
003:183   **why** then did ye slay them, if ye speak the truth?.
004:075   And **why** should ye not fight in the cause
004:077   **why** hast Thou ordered us to fight?
004:088   **Why** should ye be divided into two parties
005:018   Say: "**Why** then doth He punish you for your sins?
005:043   But **why** do they come to thee for decision,
005:063   **Why** do not the Rabbis and the doctors of laws
005:074   **Why** turn they not to Allah, and seek
006:008   They say: "**Why** is not an angel sent down to him?"
006:037   They say: "**Why** is not a Sign sent down to him
006:043   **why** then did they not call (Allah) in humility?
006:119   **Why** should ye not eat of (meats) on which Allah's
007:164   When some of them said: "**Why** do ye preach to a
007:203   they say: "**Why** hast thou not got it together?"

WHY (continued)

009:043 **Why** didst thou grant them exemption until those who
009:054 The only reasons **why** their contributions are not
010:020 They say: "**Why** is not a Sign sent down to him
011:012 lest they say, "**Why** is not a treasure sent down unto him,
011:012 or **why** does not an angel come down with him?"
012:011 **why** dost thou not trust us with Joseph,-seeing we
013:007 And the Unbelievers say: "**Why** is not a Sign
013:027 The Unbelievers say: "**Why** is not a Sign
014:012 **Why** we should not put our trust on Allah.
015:007 "**Why** bringest thou not angels to us if it be
018:015 **why** do they not bring forward an authority
018:039 "**Why** didst thou not, as thou wentest into thy
019:042 "O my father! **why** worship that which heareth not
020:125 **why** hast thou raised me up blind, while I
020:133 They say: "**Why** does he not bring us a Sign
024:012 **Why** did not the Believers-men and women-
024:013 **Why** did they not bring four witnesses to prove it?
024:016 And **why** did ye not, when ye heard it,
025:007 **Why** has not an angel been sent down to him
025:008 "Or (**why**) has not a treasure been bestowed
025:008 or **why** has he (not) a garden for enjoyment?"
025:021 or (**why**) do we not see Our Lord?"
025:021 "**Why** are not the angels sent down to us,
025:032 "**Why** is not the Qur'an revealed to him
027:020 and he said: "**Why** is it I see not the Hoopoe?
027:046 He said: "O my people! **why** ask ye to hasten
028:047 **why** didst Thou not send us a messenger?
028:048 "**Why** are not (Signs) sent to him, like those
029:050 Yet they say: "**Why** are not Signs sent down
036:022 "**Why** should not I serve Him Who created me,
041:021 "**Why** bear ye witness against us?"
041:044 "**Why** are not its verses explained in detail?
043:031 Also, they say: "**Why** is not this Qur'an sent down
043:053 or (**why**) come (not) with him angels accompanying him
043:053 "Then **why** are not gold bracelets bestowed on him,
046:028 **Why** then was no help forthcoming to them
047:020 "**Why** is not a Sura sent down (for us)?"
056:057 **why** will ye not admit the Truth?
056:062 **why** then do ye not take heed?
056:070 then **why** do ye not give thanks?
056:083 Then **why** do ye not (intervene) when (the soul of
056:086 Then **why** do you not,-if you are exempt from (future)
058:008 "**Why** does not Allah Punish us for our words?
061:002 O ye who believe! **why** say ye that which ye do not?
061:005 "O my people! **why** do ye vex and insult me,
063:010 **Why** didst thou not give me respite for a little while?
066:001 O Prophet! **why** holdest thou to be forbidden
068:028 "Did I not say to you, '**Why** not glorify (Allah)?'"

WICKED

006:033 it is the Signs of Allah, which the **wicked** deny.
006:093 Who can be more **wicked** than one who
006:093 the **wicked** (do fare) in the agonies of death!-
006:123 its **wicked** men, to plot (and burrow) therein:
006:124 Soon will the **wicked** be overtaken by humiliation
007:145 soon shall I show you the homes of the **wicked**,
009:008 and most of them are rebellious and **wicked**.
009:053 a people rebellious and **wicked**."
010:075 But they were arrogant: they were a **wicked** people.
016:063 but Satan made, (to the **wicked**), their own
017:047 behold, the **wicked** say, "Ye follow none other than
024:004 for such men are **wicked** transgressors;-
024:055 they are rebellious and **wicked**.

WICKED (continued)

025:008 The **wicked** say: "Ye follow none other than a man
026:222 They descend on every lying, **wicked** person,
028:032 for truly they are a people rebellious and **wicked**."
028:078 But the **wicked** are not called (immediately)
029:031 for truly they are **wicked** men."
032:018 no better than the man who is rebellious and **wicked**?
032:020 As to those who are rebellious and **wicked**, their abode
071:027 and they will breed none but **wicked** ungrateful ones.
079:001 who tear out (the souls of the **wicked**) with violence;
082:014 And the **Wicked**-they will be in the Fire,
083:007 Nay! Surely the Record of the **Wicked** is (preserved)
091:012 Behold, the most **wicked** man among them

WICKEDLY

016:103 The tongue of him they **wickedly** point to
029:034 because they have been **wickedly** rebellious."
051:046 for they **wickedly** transgressed.

WICKEDNESS

002:150 Except those of them that are bent on **wickedness**;
002:197 let there be no obscenity, nor **wickedness**,
002:282 it would be **wickedness** in you.
029:029 And practice **wickedness** (even) in your councils?"
049:011 ill-seeming is a name connoting **wickedness**,
056:046 And persisted obstinately in **wickedness** supreme!

WIDE

009:025 For all that it is **wide**, did constrain
030:020 behold, ye are men scattered (far and **wide**)!
035:040 Show me what it is they have created in the (**wide**) earth.
042:028 and scatters His Mercy (far and **wide**).
076:007 and they fear a Day whose evil flies far and **wide**.
077:003 And scatter (things) far and **wide**;
078:006 Have We not made the earth as a **wide** expanse,
079:030 moreover, hath He extended (to a **wide** expanse);
091:006 By the Earth and its (**wide**) expanse;

WIDELY

005:064 Nay, both His hands are **widely** outstretched:

WIDOWS

002:234 If any of you die and leave **widows** behind;
002:240 should bequeath for their **widows** a year's maintenance
002:240 Those of you who die and leave **widows** should
033:053 or that ye should marry his **widows** after him

WIDTH

003:133 and for a Garden whose **width** is that (of the whole)
057:021 the **width** whereof is as the **width** of heaven

WIFE

002:035 dwell thou and thy **wife** in the Garden;
002:102 the means to sow discord between man and **wife**.
002:230 So if a husband divorces his **wife** (irrevocably),
003:035 Behold! **wife** of 'Imran said: "O my Lord!
003:040 seeing I am very old, and my **wife** is barren?"
004:020 But if ye decide to take one **wife** in place of another,
004:128 If a **wife** fears cruelty or desertion
007:019 "O Adam! dwell thou and thy **wife** in the Garden,
007:083 But We saved him and his family, except His **wife**:
011:071 And his **wife** was standing (there), and she
011:081 but thy **wife** (will remain behind):
012:021 said to his **wife**: "Make his stay (among us)
012:025 an evil design against thy **wife**, but prison
012:029 (O **wife**), ask forgiveness for thy sin, for truly
012:030 Ladies said in the City: "The **wife** of the great
012:051 Said the 'Aziz's **wife**: "Now is the truth manifest
015:060 "Except his **wife**, who, we have ascertained,

WIFE (continued)

019:005   but my **wife** is barren: so give me an heir

019:008   when my **wife** is barren and I have grown quite decrepit

020:117   this is an enemy to thee and thy **wife**:

024:008   But it would avert the punishment from the **wife**,

027:057   But We saved him and his family, except his **wife**:

028:009   The **wife** of Pharaoh said: "(Here is) a joy of the eye,

029:032   and his following,-except his **wife**: she is

029:033   and thy following, except thy **wife**: she is

033:037   "Retain thou (in wedlock) thy **wife**, and fear Allah."

051:029   But his **wife** came forward clamouring: she smote

066:010   to the Unbelievers, the **wife** of Noah and the **wife** of Lut:

066:011   to those who believe, the **wife** of Pharaoh: behold

070:012   His **wife** and his brother,

072:003   He has taken neither a **wife** nor a son.

080:036   And from his **wife** and his children.

111:004   His **wife** shall carry the (crackling) wood-as fuel!

WIFE'S

021:090   We cured his **wife's** (barrenness) for him.

WIVES

024:006   a charge against their **wives**, and have

WILD

005:003   (partly) eaten by a **wild** animal; unless

015:072   in their **wild** intoxication, they wander

081:005   When the **wild** beasts are herded together

WILFUL

002:173   without **wilful** disobedience,

006:145   without **wilful** disobedience, nor transgressing

006:146   this in recompense for their **wilful** disobedience:

016:115   without **wilful** disobedience, nor transgressing

WILL

002:005   and it is these who **will** prosper.

002:006   or do not warn them; they **will** not believe.

002:015   so they **will** wander like blind ones (to and fro).

002:015   Allah **will** throw back their mockery on them,

002:018   they **will** not return (to the path).

002:028   then **will** He cause you to die,

002:028   and **will** again bring you to life;

002:028   and again to Him **will** ye return.

002:030   therein one who **will** make mischief

002:030   "I **will** create a vicegerent on earth."

002:035   things therein as (where and when) ye **will**;

002:036   On earth **will** be your dwelling place

002:044   **Will** ye not understand?

002:054   that **will** be better for you in the sight of your Maker."

002:061   He said: "**Will** ye exchange the better for the worse?

002:075   entertain the hope that they **will** believe in you?

002:096   **will** not save him from (due) chastisement

002:097   (revelation) to they heart by Allah's **will**,

002:105   But Allah **will** choose for His

002:105   for His special Mercy whom He **will**

002:112   he **will** get his reward with his Lord;

002:113   but Allah **will** judge between them

002:120   Never **will** the Jews or the Christians

002:124   He said: "I **will** make thee an Imam

002:126   but **will** soon drive them to the torment

002:126   for a while **will** I grant them their pleasure,

002:128   bowing to Thy (**Will**),

002:128   bowing to Thy (**will**),

002:130   and he **will** be in the Hereafter

002:131   He said: "I submit (my **will**) to the Lord

002:131   "Submit (thy **will** to Me):"

002:133   "What **will** ye worship after me?"

WILL (continued)

002:137   but Allah **will** suffice thee as against them,

002:139   Say: **Will** ye dispute with us about Allah,

002:142   He guideth whom He **will** to a Way

002:142   The Fools among the people **will** say:

002:145   nor indeed **will** they follow each other's Qibla.

002:148   Allah **will** bring you together.

002:152   Then do ye remember Me; I **will** remember you.

002:162   Their penalty **will** not be lightened,

002:162   nor **will** respite be their (lot).

002:162   They **will** abide therein:

002:165   and Allah **will** strongly enforce the Punishment:

002:167   Thus **will** Allah show them (the fruits of) their deeds

002:167   Nor **will** there be a way for them out of the Fire.

002:174   grievous **will** be their Chastisement.

002:174   Allah **will** not address them on the Day

002:184   But he that **will** give more, of his own free **will**,

002:186   let them also, with a **will**, listen to my call,

002:200   But they **will** have no portion in the Hereafter.

002:202   To these **will** be allotted what they have earned.

002:203   ye **will** surely be gathered unto Him.

002:210   **Will** they wait until Allah comes to them

002:212   His abundance without measures on whom He **will**.

002:212   But the righteous **will** be above them

002:213   For Allah guides whom He **will** to a path

002:214   "When (**will** come) the help of Allah"

002:217   their works **will** bear no fruit in this life

002:217   of the Fire and **will** abide therein.

002:217   they **will** be Companions of the Fire

002:217   Nor **will** they cease fighting you until

002:223   so approach your tilth when or how ye **will**;

002:225   Allah **will** not call you to account

002:245   which Allah **will** double unto his credit

002:245   Who is he that **will** loan to Allah a beautiful loan,

002:246   that ye **will** not fight?"

002:249   he said: "Allah **will** test you at the stream;

002:249   said: "How oft, by Allah's **will**, hath a small force

002:251   By Allah's **will** they routed them:

002:254   when no bargaining (**will** avail),

002:257   from light they **will** lead them forth

002:257   They **will** be Companions of the fire,

002:260   they **will** come to thee (flying) with speed.

002:264   They **will** be able to do nothing with aught they have

002:269   none **will** receive admonition but men of understanding

002:271   it **will** remove from you some of your (stains of) evil.

002:275   Those who devour usury will not stand except as stands

002:275   they **will** abide therein (for ever).

002:276   but **will** give increase for deeds of charity:

002:276   Allah **will** deprive usury of all blessing,

002:277   **will** have their reward with their Lord:

003:004   reject faith in the Sings of Allah **will** suffer the

003:007   and none **will** grasp the Message except men of

003:009   "Our Lord! Thou art He that **will** gather mankind

003:010   progeny **will** avail them aught against Allah:

003:011   (Their plight **will** be) no better than that of the people

003:012   "Soon **will** ye be vanquished and gather together

003:019   Allah is Islam (submission to His **Will**):

003:022   nor **will** they have anyone to help.

003:022   They are those whose works **will** bear no fruit

003:025   and each soul **will** be paid out just what it has earned,

003:025   But how (**will** they fare) when We gather them

003:030   "On the day when every soul **will** be confronted

003:030   it **will** wish there were a great distance between

WILL (continued)

003:031 Allah **will** love you and forgive you your sins:
003:045 his name **will** be Christ Jesus, the son of Mary,
003:048 "And Allah **will** teach him the Book and Wisdom,
003:052 "Who **will** be my helpers to (the work of) Allah?"
003:055 and I **will** judge between you of the matters wherein
003:055 I **will** make those who follow thee superior
003:055 "O Jesus! I **will** take thee and raise thee to Myself
003:056 I **will** punish them with severe chastisement
003:056 nor **will** they have anyone to help.
003:057 Allah **will** pay them (in full) their reward;
003:064 are Muslims (bowing to Allah's **Will**)."
003:067 and bowed his **will** to Allah's (which is Islam).
003:075 **will** not repay it unless thou constantly stoodest
003:075 **will** (readily) pay it back;
003:077 nor **will** He cleanse them (of sin):
003:077 nor **will** Allah (deign to) speak to them
003:080 after ye have bowed your **will** (to Allah in Islam)?
003:083 bowed to His **Will** (accepted Islam),
003:084 and to Allah do we bow our **will** (in Islam)."
003:085 and in the Hereafter he **will** be in the ranks
003:085 never **will** it be accepted of him;
003:088 In that **will** they dwell; nor **will** their punishment
003:090 never **will** their repentance be accepted;
003:091 and they **will** find on helpers.
003:101 firmly to Allah **will** be shown a way that is straight.
003:106 to those whose faces **will** be black, (**will** be said):
003:106 and some faces **will** be (in the gloom of) black:
003:106 some faces **will** be (lit up with) white,
003:107 they **will** be in (the light of) Allah's Mercy;
003:107 But those whose faces **will** be (lit with) white,
003:111 They **will** do you no harm, barring a trifling
003:111 they **will** show you their backs, and no help
003:115 nothing **will** be rejected of them;
003:116 they **will** be companions of the Fire,
003:116 (numerous) progeny **will** avail them aught against Allah:
003:118 they **will** not fail to corrupt you.
003:120 not the least harm **will** their cunning do to you;
003:144 not the least harm **will** he do to Allah;
003:144 **will** ye then turn back on your heels?
003:144 **will** swiftly reward those who (serve him) with
003:146 nor did they weaken (in **will**) nor give in.
003:149 and ye **will** turn back (from Faith)
003:149 they **will** drive you back on your heels,
003:151 their abode **will** be the Fire:
003:176 not the least harm **will** they do to Allah:
003:176 Allah's Plan is that He **will** give them no portion
003:177 but they **will** have a grievous punishment.
003:177 not the least harm **will** they do to Allah,
003:178 but they **will** have a shameful punishment.
003:179 Nor **will** He disclose to you the secrets
003:179 Allah **will** not leave the Believers in a state in which
003:180 soon it **will** be tied to their necks like a twisted collar,
003:180 Nay, it **will** be the worse of them:
003:185 and admitted to the Garden **will** have succeeded:
003:186 certainly hear much that **will** grieve you,
003:192 and never **will** wrong-doers find any helpers!
003:195 verily, I **will** blot out from them their iniquities,
003:195 "Never will I suffer to be lost the work of any of you,
003:199 they **will** not sell the Signs of Allah
004:003 That **will** be more suitable, to prevent you
004:010 they **will** soon be enduring a blazing Fire!
004:013 **will** be admitted to Gardens with rivers flowing

WILL (continued)

004:013 and that **will** be the Supreme achievement.
004:014 and transgress His limits **will** be admitted to a Fire,
004:017 to them **will** Allah turn in mercy;
004:019 forbidden to inherit women against their **will**.
004:035 Allah **will** cause their reconciliation:
004:042 and disobey the Messenger **will** wish that
004:042 but never **will** they hide a single fact from Allah!
004:046 and but few of them **will** believe.
004:049 and they **will** not be wronged a whit.
004:075 and raise for us from Thee one who **will** help!"
004:075 and raise for us from Thee one who **will** protect;
004:077 never **will** ye be dealt unjustly in the very least!
004:078 "Wherever ye are, death **will** find you out,
004:084 be that Allah **will** restrain the fury of the Unbelievers;
004:087 of a surety He **will** gather you together
004:091 Others you **will** find that wish to be secure from
004:097 Such men **will** find their abode in Hell.
004:099 For these, there is hope that Allah **will** forgive:
004:109 or who **will** carry their affairs through?
004:109 but who **will** contend with Allah on their behalf
004:110 he **will** find Allah Oft-Forgiving, Most Merciful.
004:113 But (in fact) they **will** only lead their own souls astray,
004:118 "I **will** take of Thy servants a portion marked off:
004:119 "I **will** mislead them, and I **will** create in them false
004:119 I **will** order them to slit the ears of cattle,
004:121 and from it they **will** find no way of escape.
004:121 They (his dupes) **will** have their dwelling in hell,
004:123 Nor **will** he find, besides Allah,
004:123 whoever works evil, **will** be requited accordingly.
004:124 they **will** enter Heaven, and not the least
004:124 and not the least injustice **will** be done to them.
004:130 Allah **will** provide abundance for each of them
004:133 If it were His **will**, He could destroy you,
004:137 Allah **will** not forgive them nor guide them
004:140 For Allah **will** collect the Hypocrites and those
004:141 But Allah **will** judge betwixt you on the Day of
004:141 And never **will** Allah grant to the Unbelievers
004:145 The hypocrites **will** be in the lowest depths of the Fire:
004:146 And soon **will** Allah grant to the Believers
004:146 if so they **will** be (numbered) with the Believers.
004:159 He **will** be a witness against them;
004:168 Allah **will** not forgive them nor guide them
004:171 desist: it **will** be better for you:
004:172 He **will** gather them all together unto Himself
004:173 He **will** punish with a grievous chastisement:
004:173 He **will** give their (due) rewards,-and more,
004:173 nor **will** they find, besides Allah, any to
004:175 soon **will** He admit them to Mercy and Grace
005:001 according to His **Will** and Plan.
005:005 and in the Hereafter he **will** be in the ranks
005:010 and deny Our Signs **will** be Companions of Hell-fire.
005:012 verily I **will** wipe out from you your evils,
005:014 And soon **will** Allah show them what it is they have done.
005:016 by His **Will**, unto the light,-guideth them
005:017 if His **Will** were to destroy Christ the son of Mary,
005:021 for then **will** ye be overthrown, to your own ruin."
005:023 when once ye are in, victory **will** be yours;
005:026 in distraction **will** they wander through the land:
005:026 Allah said: "Therefore **will** the land be out of their reach
005:027 Said the latter: "Be sure I **will** slay thee."
005:037 their Chastisement **will** be one that endures.
005:037 but never **will** they get out therefrom:

WILL (continued)

005:037 Their wish **will** be to get out of the Fire,
005:041 **will** listen even to others who have never so much
005:041 men who **will** listen to any lie,-
005:041 Allah's **will** to purify their hearts.
005:044 by the Prophets who bowed (as in Islam) to Allah's **will**,
005:048 it is He that **will** show you the truth of the matters
005:052 Ah! perhaps Allah **will** give (thee) victory,
005:052 or a decision from Him then **will** they regret of
005:053 And those who believe **will** say: "Are these
005:053 All that they do **will** be in vain,
005:053 and they **will** fall into (nothing but) ruin.
005:054 which He **will** bestow on whom He pleaseth.
005:054 whom He **will** love as they **will** love him,
005:054 soon **will** Allah produce a people whom He
005:067 And Allah **will** defend thee from men (who mean
005:072 and the Fire **will** be his abode.
005:072 Allah **will** forbid him the Garden,
005:072 There **will** for the wrong-doers be no one to help.
005:073 a grievous chastisement **will** befall the disbelievers.
005:076 Say: **Will** ye worship, besides Allah, something
005:080 and in torment **will** they abide.
005:089 but He **will** call you to account for your deliberate Oaths:
005:089 Allah **will** not call you to account for what is void in your
005:091 and from prayer: **will** ye not then abstain?
005:094 **will** have a grievous chastisement.
005:095 for repetition Allah **will** punish him for Allah
005:101 Allah **will** forgive those: for Allah
005:101 they **will** be made plain to you:
005:105 it is He that **will** inform you of all that ye do.
005:106 "We **will** not take for it a price even though
005:107 if we did, behold! we **will** be wrong-doers."
005:109 They **will** say: "We have no knowledge:
005:109 On the day when Allah **will** gather the Messengers
005:110 Then **will** Allah say: "O Jesus the son of Mary!
005:115 I **will** punish him with a chastisement such as I
005:115 Allah said: "I **will** send it down unto you: but
005:116 And behold! Allah **will** say "O Jesus the son of Mary!
005:116 He **will** say: "Glory to Thee! never could
005:119 Allah **will** say: "This is a day on which the truthful **will**
006:012 who have lost their own souls, that **will** not believer.
006:012 That He **will** gather you together for
006:023 There **will** then be (left) no excuse for them
006:024 (lie) which they invented **will** leave them in the lurch.
006:025 they **will** not believe in them;
006:027 They **will** say: "Would that we were but sent back!
006:028 **will** become manifest what before they concealed.
006:030 He **will** say: "Is not this the truth?"
006:030 They **will** say: "Yea, by our Lord!"
006:030 He **will** say: "Taste ye then the Chastisement,
006:032 **Will** ye not then understand?
006:035 If it were Allah's **will**, He could gather them unto true
006:036 then **will** they be turned unto Him.
006:036 as to the dead, Allah **will** raise them up:
006:036 Those who listen (in truth), be sure, **will** accept:
006:041 and if it be His **Will**, He would remove (the distress)
006:047 **will** any be destroyed except those who do wrong?"
006:050 **Will** ye then consider not?
006:051 that they **will** be brought (to judgment) before their Lord
006:051 except from Him they **will** have no protector
006:056 Say: "I **will** not follow your vain desires:
006:060 in the end unto Him **will** be your return,
006:060 then **will** He show you the truth of all that ye did.

WILL (continued)

006:070 they **will** have for drink (only) boiling water,
006:070 (or reparation) none **will** be accepted:
006:070 it **will** find for itself no protector or intercessor
006:073 His **will** be the dominion the day
006:073 the day the trumpet **will** be blown.
006:080 **Will** ye not (yourselves) be admonished?
006:083 We raise whom We **will**, degree after degree:
006:104 Lord proofs (to open your eyes): if any **will** see,
006:104 it **will** be for (the good of) his own soul:
006:104 if any **will** be blind, it **will** be to his own (harm):
006:107 If it had been Allah's **Will**, they would
006:108 In the end **will** they return to their Lord and He
006:109 but what **will** make you (Muslims) realize
006:109 they **will** not believe."?
006:116 they **will** lead thee away from the Way of Allah.
006:120 those who earn sin **will** get due recompense
006:124 Soon **will** the wicked be overtaken
006:127 For them **will** be a Home of Peace
006:127 He **will** be their Friend, because they
006:128 Their friends amongst men **will** say: "Our Lord!
006:128 you **will** dwell therein for ever,
006:128 He **will** say: "The Fire be your dwelling-place:
006:128 On the day when He **will** gather them all together,
006:130 So against themselves **will** they bear witness
006:130 They **will** say: "We bear witness against ourselves."
006:133 if it were His **Will**, He could destroy you,
006:133 in your place appoint whom He **will** as your successors,
006:134 All that hath been promised unto you **will** come to pass:
006:135 the wrong-doers **will** not prosper."
006:135 whose end **will** be (best) in the Hereafter:
006:135 soon **will** ye know who it is whose end
006:135 I **will** do (my part):
006:138 soon **will** He requite them for what they forged.
006:139 He **will** soon punish them:
006:147 never **will** His wrath be turned back.
006:148 give partners (to Allah) **will** say: "If Allah had wished,
006:149 if it had been His **Will**.
006:151 Say: "Come, I **will** rehearse what Allah hath
006:153 they **will** scatter you about from His (great) path:
006:158 no good **will** it do to a soul to believe then,
006:159 He **will** in the end tell them the truth
006:163 those who submit to His **Will**.
006:164 He **will** tell you the truth of things
007:008 whose scale (of good) **will** be heavy, **will** prosper:
007:008 The balance that day **will** be true (to a nicety):
007:009 **will** find their souls in perdition,
007:009 Those whose scale **will** be light,
007:016 lo! I **will** lie in wait for them on Thy Straight Way:
007:017 "Then **will** I assault them from before them
007:018 Hell **will** I fill with you all.
007:024 On earth **will** be your dwelling-place and your
007:037 and they **will** bear witness against themselves,
007:037 They **will** reply, "They have left us in the lurch,"
007:038 He **will** say: "Enter ye in the company of the Peoples
007:038 He **will** say: "Doubled for all": but this
007:039 Then the first **will** say to the last: "See then!
007:040 nor **will** they enter the Garden, until the
007:040 no opening **will** there be of the gates of heaven,
007:042 they **will** be Companions of the Garden,
007:043 beneath them **will** be rivers flowing;-and they
007:044 **will** call out to the Companions of the Fire: "We have
007:046 they **will** call out to the Companions of the Garden,

WILL (continued)

007:046   and on the Heights **will** be men who would know
007:047   they **will** say: "Our Lord! send us not to the company
007:048   The men on the Heights **will** call to certain men whom
007:048   whom they **will** know from their marks,
007:050   They **will** say: "Both these things hath Allah
007:050   of the Fire **will** call to the Companions of the Garden:
007:053   In fact they **will** have lost their souls,
007:053   and the things they forged **will** leave them in the lurch.
007:053   who have forgotten it before **will** say: "The Messengers
007:058   by the **Will** of its Cherisher, springs up
007:065   **Will** ye not fear (Allah)?"
007:085   that **will** be best for you, if ye have Faith.
007:089   thereto unless it be as in the **will** of Allah, our Lord.
007:124   "Be sure I **will** cut off your hands and your feet
007:124   and I **will** crucify you all."
007:126   our souls unto Thee as Muslims (who bow to Thy **Will**)"!
007:127   (only) their females **will** we save alive;
007:127   He said: "Their male children **will** we slay;
007:129   "It may be that your Lord **will** destroy your enemy
007:146   they **will** not adopt it as the Way;
007:146   they **will** not believe in them;
007:146   them **will** I turn away from My Signs:
007:146   that is the Way they **will** adopt.
007:152   Those who took the calf (for worship) **will** indeed be
007:155   If it had been Thy **will** thou couldst have destroyed,
007:156   "I afflict My Punishment on whom I **will**; but My Mercy
007:157   it is they who **will** prosper."
007:164   preach to a people whom Allah **will** destroy or
007:169   **Will** ye not understand?
007:169   saying (for excuse): "(Everything) **will** be forgiven us."
007:176   If it had been Our **Will**, We should have elevated him
007:180   for what they do, they **will** soon be requited.
007:182   We **will** lead them step by step to ruin
007:183   Respite **will** I grant unto them:
007:185   In what message after this **will** they then believe?
007:186   He **will** leave them in their trespasses, wandering
007:187   the (final) Hour-when **will** be its appointed time?
007:187   Only, all of a sudden, **will** it come to you."
007:187   none be He can reveal as to when it **will** occur.
007:193   If ye call them to guidance, they **will** not obey:
007:196   and He **will** befriend the righteous.
008:009   "I **will** assist you with a thousand of the angels,
008:012   I **will** instill terror into the hearts of the Unbelievers:
008:014   Thus (**will** it be said): "Taste ye then of the (punishment)
008:019   Not the least good **will** your forces be to you even if
008:019   it ye desist (from wrong), it **will** be best for you:
008:024   when He calleth you to that which **will** give you life;
008:029   He **will** grant you a Criterion (to judge between right and
008:036   but in the end they **will** have (only) regrets and sighs:
008:036   at length they **will** be overcome:
008:036   and the Unbelievers **will** be gathered together to Hell;-
008:036   and so **will** they continue to spend;
008:037   They **will** be the ones to have lost.
008:053   "Because Allah **will** never change the Grace
008:055   they **will** not believe.
008:059   they **will** never frustrate (them).
008:065   they **will** vanquish two hundred:
008:065   if a hundred. They **will** vanquish a thousand
008:066   and if a thousand, they **will** vanquish two thousand,
008:066   they **will** vanquish two hundred, and if a thousand,
008:070   and He **will** forgive you: for Allah is Oft-forgiving,
008:070   He **will** give you something better than what has been

WILL (continued)

009:002   Go ye, then for four mouths, (as ye **will**),
009:002   but that Allah **will** cover with shame those who reject
009:013   **Will** ye not fight people who violated their oaths
009:014   Fight them, and Allah **will** punish them
009:015   For Allah **will** turn (in mercy) to whom He **will**:
009:020   They are the people who **will** achieve (salvation).
009:022   They **will** dwell therein for ever.
009:027   Again **will** Allah, after this, turn (in mercy)
009:027   turn (in mercy) to whom He **will**: for Allah
009:028   And if ye fear poverty, soon **will** Allah enrich you,
009:032   but Allah **will** not allow but that His light should be
009:035   On the Day when it **will** be heated in the fire of Hell,
009:035   and with it **will** be branded their foreheads,
009:039   He **will** punish you with a grievous penalty,
009:051   Say: "Nothing **will** happen to us except what
009:052   that Allah **will** send His punishment from Him
009:052   So wait (expectant); we too **will** wait with you."
009:053   not from you **will** it be accepted:
009:059   Allah and His Messenger **will** soon give us of His bounty:
009:061   But those who molest the Prophet **will** have a grievous.
009:064   But verily Allah **will** bring to light all that ye fear
009:066   We **will** punish other amongst you, for that
009:071   On them **will** Allah pour His mercy:
009:074   Allah **will** punish them with a grievous chastisement
009:074   If they repent, it **will** be best for them:
009:079   Allah **will** throw back their ridicule on them:
009:080   their forgiveness, Allah **will** not forgive them:
009:082   Let them laugh a little: much **will** they weep:
009:088   and it is they who **will** prosper.
009:090   Soon **will** a grievous chastisement seize the
009:094   in the end **will** ye be brought back to Him
009:094   then **will** He show you the truth of all that ye did."
009:094   your actions that Allah and His Messenger **will** observe:
009:094   They **will** present their excuses to you when ye return to
009:095   They **will** swear to you by Allah, when ye return to them,
009:096   They **will** swear unto you, that ye maybe pleased with
009:099   soon **will** Allah admit them to His Mercy:
009:102   Perhaps Allah **will** turn unto them (in mercy):
009:105   soon **will** ye be brought back to the Knower of what
009:105   soon **will** Allah observe your work,
009:105   then **will** He show you the truth of all that ye did."
009:106   whether He **will** punish them, or turn in mercy
009:107   They **will** indeed swear that their intention
009:115   And Allah **will** not mislead a people after He
009:125   it **will** add doubt to their doubt,
009:125   and they **will** die in a state of Unbelief.
010:003   **will** ye not receive admonition?
010:004   To Him **will** be your return-of all of you.
010:004   but those who reject Him **will** have draughts of boiling
010:009   beneath them **will** flow rivers in Gardens of Bliss.
010:009   their Lord **will** guide them because of their Faith:
010:010   and the end of their prayer **will** be: "Praise be to Allah,
010:010   (This **will** be) their prayer therein: "Glory to Thee,
010:010   O Allah!" and "Praise" **will** be their greeting therein
010:016   I tarried amongst you: **will** ye not then understand?"
010:017   But never **will** prosper those who sin.
010:020   I too **will** wait with you."
010:026   they **will** abide therein (for aye)!
010:027   ignominy **will** cover their (faces):
010:027   their faces **will** be covered, as it were,
010:027   who have earned evil **will** have a reward of like evil:
010:027   they **will** abide therein (for aye)!

WILL (continued)

010:027 no defender **will** they have from (the wrath of)
010:030 they **will** be brought back to Allah their rightful
010:030 invented falsehoods **will** leave them in the lurch.
010:030 There **will** every soul see (the fruits of)
010:031 They **will** soon say: "Allah".
010:031 Say, "**Will** ye not then show piety (to Him)?"
010:033 verily they **will** not believe.
010:043 the blind,-even though they **will** not see?
010:044 Verily Allah **will** not deal unjustly with man
010:045 And on the day when He **will** gather them together:
010:045 they **will** recognize each other:
010:045 assuredly those **will** be lost who denied the meeting
010:045 (it **will** be) as if they had tarried but an hour of a day:
010:047 (before them), the matter **will** be judged between
010:047 and they **will** not be wronged.
010:048 They say: "When **will** this promise come to pass-
010:051 (It **will** then be said): 'Ah! now? and ye wanted
010:052 "At length **will** be said to the wrong-doers: 'Taste ye
010:054 and no wrong **will** be done unto them.
010:054 but the judgment between them **will** be with justice,
010:069 "Those who forge a lie against Allah **will** never prosper."
010:070 and, then, to Us **will** be their return.
010:072 of those who submit to Allah's **Will** (in Islam)."
010:077 But sorcerers **will** not prosper."
010:081 Allah **will** surely make it of no effect:
010:084 if ye submit (your **will** to His)."
010:088 so they **will** not believe until they see the grievous
010:093 Verily Allah **will** judge between them as to the schisms
010:099 Wilt thou then compel mankind against their **will**,
010:099 If it had been the Lord's **Will**, they would all have
010:100 and He **will** place abomination on those who
010:100 No soul can believe, except by the **Will** of Allah,
010:100 on those who **will** not understand.
010:102 for I too, **will** wait with you."
010:104 But I worship Allah-who **will** take your souls
011:008 and they **will** be completely encircled by that which
011:008 nothing **will** turn it away from them,
011:014 **Will** ye even then submit (to Islam)?"
011:017 the Fire **will** be their promised meeting place.
011:018 They **will** be brought before their Lord,
011:018 and the witnesses **will** say. "These are the
011:020 They **will** not escape in earth, nor have
011:020 Their chastisement **will** be doubled!
011:022 are the very ones who **will** lose most in the Hereafter!
011:023 they **will** be Companions of the Garden, to dwell
011:024 **Will** ye not them take heed?
011:029 but I **will** not drive away (in contempt) those who
011:030 **Will** ye not then take heed?
011:031 **will** not grant them (all) that is good:
011:033 ye **will** not be able to frustrate it!
011:033 He said: "Truly, Allah **will** bring it on you
011:034 "Of no profit **will** be my counsel to you, much as
011:034 He is your Lord! and to Him **will** ye return!
011:036 "None of thy People **will** believe except those
011:039 on whom **will** descend a Chastisement that
011:039 that **will** cover them with shame,-
011:039 "But soon **will** ye know who it is on whom
011:039 on whom **will** be unloosed a Chastisement lasting."
011:043 The son replied: "I **will** be take myself to some
011:043 to some mountain: it **will** save me from the water."
011:048 but in the end **will** a grievous Chastisement
011:048 but (there **will** be other) Peoples to whom We shall

WILL (continued)

011:048 the Peoples (who **will** spring) from those with thee:
011:051 **will** ye not then understand?
011:052 He **will** send you the skies pouring abundant rain,
011:057 My Lord **will** make another People to succeed you,
011:057 and you **will** not harm Him in the least.
011:064 or a swift Punishment **will** seize you!
011:065 in your homes for three days (then **will** be your ruin):
011:081 but thy wife (**will** remain behind):
011:081 to her **will** happen what happens to the people.
011:084 that **will** compass (you) all round.
011:093 I **will** do (my part): soon **will** ye know who it is on
011:098 but woeful indeed **will** be the place to which the are led!
011:098 He **will** go before his people on The Day of Judgment,
011:103 a Day for which mankind **will** be gathered together:
011:103 that **will** be a Day of Testimony.
011:105 of those (gathered) some **will** be wretched
011:105 be wretched and some **will** be blessed.
011:106 there **will** be for them therein (nothing but) the heaving
011:107 They **will** dwell therein so long as the heavens and the
011:108 they **will** dwell therein so long as the heavens and the
011:111 And, of a surety, to all **will** your Lord pay back
011:113 or the Fire **will** touch you; and ye have no protectors
011:115 For verily Allah **will** not suffer the reward of the
011:118 but they **will** not cease to differ,
011:119 "I **will** fill Hell with jinns and men all together."
012:006 "Thus **will** thy Lord choose thee and teach thee
012:009 (there **will** be time enough) for you to be righteous after
012:010 he **will** be picked up by some caravan of travellers."
012:021 may be he **will** bring us much good,
012:037 I **will** surely reveal to you the truth and meaning
012:041 and the birds **will** eat from off his head.
012:041 as for the other, he **will** hang from the cross,
012:041 As to one of you, he **will** pour out the wine for his Lord
012:045 said: "I **will** tell you the truth of its interpretation:
012:048 which **will** devour what ye shall have laid by in advance
012:048 "Then **will** come after that (period) seven dreadful (years),
012:049 a year in which the people **will** have abundant water,
012:049 "Then **will** come after that (period) a year
012:049 and in which they **will** press (wine and oil)."
012:052 that Allah **will** never guide the snare of the false ones
012:054 I **will** take him specially to serve about my own person."
012:063 and we **will** indeed take every care of him."
012:066 that ye **will** be sure to bring him back to me unless ye are
012:066 (Jacob) said: "Never **will** I send him with you until ye
012:072 I **will** be bound by it."
012:078 aged and venerable, (who **will** grieve for him):
012:080 Therefore **will** I not leave this land until my father
012:082 and (you **will** find) we are indeed telling the truth."
012:083 May be Allah **will** bring them (back) all to me
012:090 never **will** Allah suffer the reward to be lost,
012:092 Allah **will** forgive you, and He is the Most Merciful
012:093 he **will** come to see (clearly).
012:098 He said: "Soon **will** I ask my Lord for forgiveness
012:101 as one submitting to Thy **Will** (as a Muslim),
012:103 Yet no faith **will** the greater part of mankind have,
012:108 Glory to Allah! and never **will** I join gods with Allah!"
012:109 **Will** ye not then understand?
012:110 (Respite **will** be granted) until, when the messengers
012:110 But never **will** be warded off Our punishment from them
012:110 and those whom We **will** are delivered into safety.
013:005 are those round whose necks **will** be yokes (of servitude):
013:005 they **will** be Companions of the Fire, to dwell

WILL (continued)

013:011 nor **will** they find, besides Him, any to protect
013:011 Verily never **will** Allah change the condition of a people
013:013 and therewith He striketh whomsoever He **will**...
013:018 For them **will** the reckoning be terrible:
013:018 their abode **will** be Hell,-what a
013:027 Say: "Truly Allah leaveth, to stray, whom He **will**;
013:031 verily, Allah **will** not fail in His promise.
013:031 never **will** disaster cease to seize them for their (ill)
013:033' Is it that ye **will** inform Him of something He knoweth
013:042 and soon **will** the Unbelievers know who gets
014:002 a terrible Chastisement (their Unfaith **will** bring them)!-
014:007 "If ye are grateful, I **will** add more (favours)
014:017 and in front of him **will** be a chastisement unrelenting.
014:017 come to him from every quarter, yet **will** he not die;
014:017 death **will** come to him from every quarter,
014:017 In gulps **will** he sip it, but never **will** he be near
014:019 If He so **will**, He can remove you and put (in your place)
014:021 They **will** reply, "If we had received the guidance of
014:021 They **will** all be marshalled before Allah together:
014:021 **will** the weak say to those who were arrogant, "For us,
014:022 And Satan **will** say when the matter is decided:
014:023 their greeting therein **will** be: "Peace!"
014:023 and work righteousness **will** be admitted to Gardens
014:027 but Allah **will** leave, to stray, those who do wrong:
014:027 Allah **will** establish in strength those who believe,
014:029 They **will** burn therein,-an evil place to stay in!
014:031 of a Day in which there **will** be neither mutual
014:034 never **will** ye be able to number them.
014:041 on the Day that the Reckoning **will** be established!"
014:042 a Day when the eyes **will** fixedly stare in horror,-
014:044 then **will** the wrong-doers say: "Our Lord!
014:044 of the Day when the Wrath **will** reach them:
014:044 we **will** answer Thy Call, and follow the messengers!"
014:048 to a different Earth, and so **will** be the Heavens,
014:048 One day the Earth **will** be changed to a different Earth,
014:048 and (men) **will** be marshalled forth,
015:002 Often **will** those who disbelieve, wish that
015:003 soon for they **will** soon know.
015:009 and We **will** assuredly guard it (from corruption).
015:025 Assuredly it is thy Lord who **will** gather them
015:039 I **will** make (wrong) fair-seeming to them on
015:039 and I **will** put them all in the wrong,-
015:045 The righteous (**will** be) amid Gardens and fountains
015:046 (Their greeting **will** be): "Enter ye here in Peace and
015:047 (they **will** be) brothers (joyfully) facing each other on
015:050 **will** be indeed the most grievous Chastisement.
015:060 **will** be among those who **will** lag behind."
015:085 the Hour is surely coming (when this **will** be manifest).
015:092 Therefore, by the Lord, We **will**, of a surety
015:096 another god: but soon **will** they come to know.
016:017 **Will** ye not receive admonition?
016:021 nor do thy know when they **will** be raised up.
016:025 how grievous the burdens they **will** bear!
016:027 Those endued with knowledge **will** say: "This Day,
016:027 He **will** cover them with shame, and say:
016:028 (The angels **will** reply), "Nay, but verily Allah knoweth
016:031 Gardens of Eternity which they **will** enter:
016:031 they **will** have therein all that they wish:
016:038 that Allah **will** not raise up those who die:
016:041 but truly the reward of the Hereafter **will** be greater,
016:041 We **will** assuredly give a goodly home in this world;
016:045 or that the Wrath **will** not seize them from directions

WILL (continued)

016:045 **will** not cause the earth to swallow them up,
016:052 then **will** ye fear other than Allah?
016:055 but soon **will** ye know (your folly)!
016:062 and they **will** be the first to be hastened on into it!
016:066 And verily in cattle (too) **will** ye find an instructive Sign.
016:071 **Will** they then deny the favour of Allah?
016:072 **will** they then believe in vain things,
016:081 that ye may surrender to His **will** (in Islam).
016:084 nor **will** they be allowed to make amends.
016:084 then **will** no excuse be accepted from Unbelievers,
016:085 nor **will** they then receive respite.
016:085 see the Chastisement then **will** it in no way be mitigated,
016:086 But they **will** throw back their word at them
016:086 who gave partners to Allah **will** see their "partners,"
016:086 they **will** say: "Our Lord! these are our `partners',
016:088 for them **will** We add Chastisement to Chastisement;
016:092 for Allah **will** test you by this;
016:092 He **will** certainly make clear to you (the truth of) that
016:096 what is with Allah **will** endure.
016:096 And We **will** certainly bestow, on those who patiently
016:097 and We **will** bestow on such their reward
016:097 to him **will** We give a life that is that is good and pure,
016:104 and theirs **will** be a grievous Chastisement.
016:104 Allah **will** not guide them, and theirs
016:106 and theirs **will** be a dreadful Chastisement.
016:107 and Allah **will** not guide those who reject Faith.
016:109 in the Hereafter they **will** be the losers.
016:111 On the Day every soul **will** come up pleading
016:111 and every soul **will** be recompensed (fully) for
016:111 and none **will** be unjustly dealt with.
016:116 who ascribe false things to Allah, **will** never prosper.
016:117 but they **will** have a most grievous Chastisement.
016:122 And We gave him Good in this world, and he **will** be,
016:124 but Allah **will** judge between on the Day of Judgment,
017:013 which he **will** see spread open.
017:014 (It **will** be said to him:) "Read thine (own) record:
017:018 Hell for them: they **will** burn therein:
017:018 such things as We **will**, to such persons as We **will**:
017:019 the ones whose striving **will** be thanked (by Allah).
017:034 **will** be enquired into (on the Day of Reckoning).
017:051 Then **will** they say: "Who **will** cause us to return?"
017:051 and say "When **will** that be?"
017:051 Then **will** they wag their heads towards thee,
017:051 Say, "Maybe it **will** be quite soon!
017:052 and ye **will** think that ye tarried but a little while!
017:052 "It **will** be on a Day when He **will** call you,
017:052 and ye **will** answer (His call) with (words of) His praise,
017:062 I **will** surely bring his descendants under my sway-
017:063 verily Hell **will** be the recompense of you (all)-
017:068 or that He **will** not send against you a violent tornado
017:068 Do ye then feel secure that He **will** not cause you to be
017:069 or do you feel secure that He **will** not send you back
017:071 and they **will** not be dealt with unjustly in the least.
017:071 record in their right hand **will** read it (with pleasure),
017:072 **will** be blind in the Hereafter,
017:079 soon **will** thy Lord raise thee to a Station of Praise and
017:086 If it were Our **Will**, We could take away that which We
017:092 as thou sayest (**will** happen), against us;
017:097 their abode **will** be Hell:
018:016 your Lord **will** shower His mercies on you and dispose
018:024 "I hope that my Lord **will** guide me ever closer
018:029 like the walls and roof of a tent, **will** hem them in:

WILL (continued)

018:029 if they implore relief they **will** be granted water like
018:029 him who **will**, believe, and let him who **will**, reject (it):
018:029 like melted brass, that **will** scald their faces,
018:031 beneath them rivers **will** flow;
018:031   they **will** be adorned therein with bracelets of gold,
018:031 For them **will** be Gardens of Eternity;
018:031 and they **will** wear green garments of fine silk and heavy
018:031 they **will** recline therein on raised thrones.
018:035 "I deem not that this **will** ever perish,"
018:036 do I deem that the Hour (of Judgment) **will** (ever) come:
018:039 say: Allah's **Will** (be done)!
018:040 and that He **will** send on thy garden thunderbolts
018:040 "It may be that my Lord **will** give me something
018:041 "Or the water of the garden **will** run off underground
018:048 And they **will** be marshalled before thy Lord
018:049 and not one **will** thy Lord treat with injustice.
018:049 they **will** say, "Ah! woe to us! What a book is this!
018:049 And the Book (of Deeds) **will** be placed (before you);
018:049 They **will** find all that they did, placed before
018:050 **Will** ye then take him and his progeny as protectors
018:052 On the Day He **will** say, "Call on those whom ye thought
018:052 My partners," and they **will** call on them,
018:052 but they **will** not listen to them;
018:053 no means **will** they find to turn away therefrom.
018:057 even then **will** they never accept guidance.
018:058 beyond which they **will** find no refuge.
018:060 "I **will** not give up until I reach the junction
018:069 "Thou wilt find me if Allah so **will**, (truly) patient:
018:078 now I **will** tell thee the interpretation of (those things)
018:083 Say, "I **will** rehearse to you something of his story.""
018:087 and He **will** punish him with a punishment unheard-of
018:088 and easy **will** be his task as we it by our command.
018:095 I **will** erect a strong barrier between you and them:
018:098 my Lord comes to pass, He **will** make it into dust;
018:099 the trumpet **will** be blown, and We
018:105 vain **will** be their works, nor shall We, on the Day
018:108 no change **will** they wish for from them.
019:005 my relatives (and colleagues) (**will** do) after me:
019:006 "(One that) **will** (truly) inherit me, and inherit
019:009 He said: "So (it **will** be): thy Lord saith,
019:015 he **will** be raised up to life (again)!
019:021 He said: "So (it **will** be): thy Lord saith,
019:025 it **will** let fall fresh ripe dates upon thee.
019:026 and this day **will** I enter into no talk with any human
019:038 How plainly **will** they see and hear,
019:038 the Day that they **will** appear before Us!
019:039 when the matter **will** be determined: for (behold),
019:040 It is We Who **will** inherit the earth,
019:040 to Us **will** they all be returned.
019:043 so follow me: I **will** guide thee to a Way that
019:046 I **will** indeed stone thee:
019:047 I **will** pray to my Lord for thy forgiveness:
019:048 "And I **will** turn away from you (all) and from
019:048 I **will** call on my Lord perhaps,
019:059 then, **will** they face Destruction,-
019:060 for these **will** enter the Garden
019:060 and **will** not be wronged in the least,-
019:062 They **will** not there hear any vain discourse,
019:062 and they **will** have therein their sustenance,
019:071 Not one of you but **will** pass over it:
019:075 they **will** at length realize who is worst
019:095 And every one of them **will** come to him singly

WILL (continued)

019:096 **will** The Most Gracious bestow Love.
020:039 and he **will** be taken up by one who is an enemy
020:039 the river **will** cast him up on the bank,
020:040 who **will** nurse and rear the (child)?"
020:069 quickly **will** it swallow up that which they have faked
020:071 and I **will** have you crucified on trunks
020:071 Be sure I **will** cut off your hands and feet
020:076   they **will** dwell therein for aye:
020:091 They had said: "We **will** not cease to worship it,
020:091 **will** devote ourselves to it until Moses returns
020:097 but thy (punishment) in this life **will** be that
020:097 we **will** certainly burn it in a blazing fire
020:097 thou hast a promise that **will** not fail:
020:100 verily they **will** bear a burden on the Day
020:101 and grievous **will** the burden be to them on the Day,-
020:101 They **will** abide in this (state):
020:102 The Day when the Trumpet **will** be sounded: that Day,
020:103 In whispers **will** they consult each other:
020:104 in judgment **will** say: "Ye tarried not longer than a day!"
020:104 We know best what they **will** say, when the
020:105 say, "My Lord **will** uproot them and scatter them as dust;
020:106 "He **will** leave them as plains smooth and level;
020:108 On that Day **will** they follow the caller
020:108 and the voices **will** be hushed to The Most Gracious:
020:111 The Sustainer, helpless indeed **will** be the man
020:112 **will** have no fear of harm nor of any curtailment
020:123 **will** not lose his way, nor fall into misery.
020:125 He **will** say: "O my Lord! why hast thou raised me up
020:126 (Allah) **will** say: "Thus didst thou, when Our
021:003 **Will** ye go to witchcraft with your eyes open?"
021:006 **will** these believe?
021:010 **Will** ye not then understand?
021:010 a book which We give you eminence.
021:023 but they **will** be questioned (for theirs).
021:030 **Will** they not then believe?
021:037 soon (enough) **will** I show you My Signs;
021:038 They say: "When **will** this promise come to pass,
021:039 (the time) when they **will** not be able to ward off the Fire
021:040 no power **will** they have then to avert it,
021:040 to avert it, nor **will** they (then) get respite.
021:044 Is it then they who **will** win?
021:045 but the deaf **will** not hear the call,
021:046 they **will** then say, "Woe to us! we did wrong indeed!"
021:047 so that not a soul **will** be dealt with unjustly in the least.
021:047 We **will** bring it (to account):
021:050 **will** ye then reject it?
021:057 "And by Allah, I **will** certainly plan against
021:080 **will** ye then be grateful?
021:093   (yet) **will** they all return to Us.
021:094 and has Faith,-his endeavour **will** not be rejected:
021:097 Then **will** the True Promise draw nigh (of fulfillment):
021:097 the eyes of the Unbelievers **will** fixedly stare in horror:
021:098 To it **will** ye (surely) come!
021:099 But each one **will** abide therein.
021:100 nor **will** they there hear (aught else).
021:100 There, sobbing **will** be their lot,
021:101 **will** be removed far therefrom.
021:102 in that **will** they dwell.
021:102 Not the slightest sound **will** they hear of Hell:
021:103 The Great Terror **will** bring them no grief:
021:103 but the angels **will** meet them (with mutual greetings):
021:108 **will** ye therefore bow to His **Will** (in Islam)?"

WILL (continued)

022:001 the Hour (of judgment) **will** be a thing terrible!
022:002 but dreadful **will** be the Chastisement of Allah.
022:004 turns to him for friendship, him **will** he lead astray,
022:004 and he **will** guide him to the Chastisement
022:005 and We cause whom We **will** to rest in the womb
022:007 And verily the Hour **will** come:
022:007 or about (the fact) that Allah **will** raise up all who are in
022:010 (It **will** be said): "This is because of the deeds
022:014 Verily Allah **will** admit those who believe
022:015 his plan **will** remove that which enrages (him)!
022:015 If any think that Allah **will** not help him
022:016 and verily Allah doth guide whom He **will**!
022:017 Allah **will** judge between them on the Day of
022:019 over their heads **will** be poured out boiling water.
022:019 for them **will** be cut out a garment of Fire:
022:020 With it **will** be melted what is within their bodies,
022:021 In addition there **will** be maces of iron
022:022 and (it **will** be said), "Taste ye the chastisement of
022:022 they **will** be forced back therein,
022:023 Allah **will** admit those who believe and work
022:023 and their garments there **will** be of silk.
022:025 them **will** We cause to taste of a most grievous
022:027 they **will** come to thee on foot and (mounted)
022:038 Verily Allah **will** defend (from ill) those who believe
022:040 Allah **will** certainly aid those who aid His (cause);-
022:040 Exalted in Might, (Able to enforce His **Will**).
022:047 But Allah **will** not fail in His promise.
022:051 they **will** be Companions of the Fire."
022:052 but Allah **will** cancel anything (vain) that Satan throws
022:052 and Allah **will** confirm (and establish) His Signs:
022:055 Those who reject Faith **will** not cease to be
022:056 and work righteous deeds **will** be in Gardens of Delight.
022:056 On that Day the Dominion **will** be that of Allah:
022:056 He **will** judge between them: so those
022:057 there **will** be a humiliating Punishment.
022:058 on them **will** Allah bestow verily a goodly Provision.
022:059 Verily He **will** admit them to a place with which they
022:060 Allah **will** help him: for Allah is One that blots our (sins)
022:066 **will** cause you to die, and **will** again give you life:
022:069 "Allah **will** judge between you on the Day of Judgment
023:010 Those **will** be the heirs,
023:011 Who **will** inherit Paradise: they **will** dwell therein
023:015 After that, at length, ye **will** die.
023:016 Again, on the Day of Judgment, **will** ye be raised up.
023:023 Ye have no other god but Him. **Will** ye not fear (Him)?"
023:032 Ye have no other god but Him. **Will** ye not fear (Him)?"
023:034 behold, it is certain ye **will** be lost.
023:044 a people that **will** not believe!
023:060 because they **will** return to their Lord;-
023:062 They **will** never be wronged.
023:063 which they **will** (continue) to do,-
023:064 behold, they **will** groan in supplication!
023:065 (It **will** be said): "Groan not in supplication this day;
023:077 then Lo! they **will** be plunged in despair therein!
023:080 of Night and Day: **will** ye not then understand?
023:085 They **will** say, "To Allah!"
023:085 Say: "Yet **will** ye not receive admonition?"
023:087 They **will** say, "(They belong) to Allah."
023:087 Say: "**Will** ye not then fear?"
023:089 They **will** say, "(It belongs) to Allah."
023:101 there **will** be no more relationships between
023:101 nor **will** one ask after another!

WILL (continued)

023:102 (of good deeds) is heavy,-they **will** be successful.
023:103 their souls; in Hell **will** they abide.
023:103 **will** be those who have lost their souls;
023:104 and they **will** therein grin, with their lips displaced.
023:104 The Fire **will** burn their faces, and they
023:106 They **will** say: "Our Lord! our misfortune
023:108 He **will** say: "Be ye driven into it (with ignominy)!
023:112 He **will** say: "What number of years did ye stay on earth?"
023:113 They **will** say: "We stayed a day or part of a day:
023:114 He **will** say: "Ye stayed not but a little,-
023:117 and his reckoning **will** be only with his Lord!
024:011 to every man among them (**will** come the punishment)
024:011 among them, **will** be a Chastisement grievous.
024:019 **will** have a grievous Chastisement in this life
024:021 of any **will** follow the footsteps of Satan,
024:021 he **will** (but) command what is indecent and wrong:
024:024 their hands, and their feet **will** bear witness
024:025 and they **will** realize that Allah is the (very) Truth,
024:025 On that Day Allah **will** pay them back (all) their
024:030 that **will** make for greater purity for them:
024:032 Allah **will** give them means out of His grace:
024:035 Allah doth guide whom He **will** to His Light:
024:037 for the Day when hearts and eyes **will** be turn about,-
024:038 for Allah doth provide for those whom He **will**,
024:039 and Allah **will** pay him his account:
024:050 Allah and His Messenger **will** deal unjustly with them?
024:051 it is such as these that **will** prosper.
024:052 and fear Allah and do right, that **will** triumph.
024:055 'They **will** worship Me (along) and not associate aught
024:055 that He **will**, of a surety, grant them in the land,
024:055 and that He **will** change (their state),
024:055 that He **will** establish in authority their religion
024:064 and one day they **will** be brought back to Him,
024:064 He **will** tell them the truth of what they did:
025:009 and never a way **will** they be able to find!
025:010 if that were His **Will**, could give thee better (things) than
025:012 they **will** hear its fury and its raging sigh.
025:013 they **will** plead for destruction there and then!
025:016 "For them there **will** be therein all that they wish for:
025:016 they **will** dwell (there) for aye:
025:017 He **will** ask: "Was it ye led these My servants astray.
025:017 The Day He **will** gather them together as well
025:018 They **will** say: "Glory to Thee! not meant
025:019 (Allah **will** say): "Now have they proved you liars
025:020 **will** ye have patience?
025:022 no joy **will** there be to the sinners that Day:
025:022 the (angels) **will** say: "There is a barrier forbidden
025:024 The Companions of the Garden **will** be well,
025:026 it **will** be a Day of dire difficulty for the Misbelievers.
025:027 The Day that the wrong-doers **will** bite at his hands,
025:027 he **will** say, "Oh! would that i had taken a (straight) path
025:030 Then the Messenger **will** say: "O my Lord, Truly
025:034 they **will** be in an evil plight,
025:034 Those who **will** be gathered to Hell
025:042 Soon **will** they know, when they see the Chastisement,
025:051 Had it been Our **Will**, We could
025:057 that each one who **will** may take a (straight) Path
025:069 the Day of Judgment **will** be doubled to him,
025:069 and he **will** dwell therein in ignominy,-
025:070 for Allah **will** change the evil of such persons
025:074 and offspring who **will** be the comfort of our eye,
025:075 Those are the ones who **will** be rewarded with the

WILL (continued)

025:077 and soon **will** come the inevitable (punishment)!"
026:003 It may be thou **will** kill thy self with grief,
026:004 If (such) were Our **Will**, We could
026:006 so they **will** know soon (enough) the truth of what
026:011 "The people of Pharaoh: **will** they not fear Allah?"
026:012 I do fear that they **will** charge me with falsehood:
026:013 "My breast **will** be straitened.
026:013 And my tongue **will** not speak (plainly):
026:015 We are with you, and **will** listen (to your call).
026:029 I **will** certainly put thee in prison!"
026:044 it is we who **will** certainly win!"
026:049 and I **will** crucify you all"
026:049 Be sure I **will** cut off your hands and your feet
026:051 our Lord **will** forgive us our faults,
026:062 Soon **will** He guide me!
026:081 "Who **will** cause me to die, and then
026:082 **will** forgive me my faults on the Day of Judgment.
026:087 on the Day when (men) **will** be raised up;-
026:088 "The Day whereon neither wealth nor sons **will** avail,
026:089 "But only he (**will** prosper) that brings to Allah a sound
026:090 the Garden **will** be brought near,
026:091 the Fire **will** be placed in full view;
026:094 "Then they **will** be thrown headlong into the (Fire),-
026:096 "They **will** say there in their mutual bickerings:
026:106 "**Will** ye not fear (Allah)?
026:124 "**Will** ye not fear (Allah)?
026:142 said to them: "**Will** you not fear (Allah)?
026:146 "**Will** ye be left secure, in (the enjoyment of) all
026:161 "**Will** ye not fear (Allah)?
026:165 **will** ye approach males,
026:177 "**Will** ye not fear (Allah)?
026:201 They **will** not believe in it until they see the grievous
026:202 But the (Penalty) **will** come to them of a sudden,
026:203 Then they **will** say: "Shall we be respited?"
026:207 It **will** profit them not the enjoyment they were given.
026:213 or thou wilt be among those who **will** be punished.
026:227 And soon **will** the unjust know what vicissitudes their
026:227 what vicissitudes their affairs **will** take!
026:005 and in the Hereafter theirs **will** be the greatest loss.
027:007 or I **will** bring you a burning brand (to light our fuel),
027:007 soon **will** I bring you from there some information,
027:012 and it **will** come forth white without stain (or harm):
027:019 that I may work the righteousness that **will** please Thee:
027:021 "I **will** certainly punish him with a severe punishment,
027:036 he said: "**Will** ye give me abundance in wealth?
027:037 in disgrace, and they **will** feel humbled (indeed)."
027:037 with such hosts as they **will** never be able to meet:
027:039 "I **will** bring it to thee before thou rise from thy council:
027:040 "I **will** bring it to thee before even thy glance returns
027:071 They also say: "When **will** this promise (come to pass)?
027:078 Verily thy Lord **will** decide between them by His Decree:
027:084 (Allah) **will** say; "Did ye reject My Signs, though ye
027:085 And the Word **will** be fulfilled against them,
027:085 and they **will** be unable to speak (in plea).
027:087 And the Day that the Trumpet **will** be sounded-
027:087 except such as Allah **will** please (to exempt):
027:087 **will** be smitten with terror those who are in the heavens
027:089 And they **will** be secure from terror that Day.
027:089 If any do good, he **will** have better than it.
027:090 their faces **will** be thrown headlong into the Fire:
027:091 who bow in Islam to Allah's **Will**,-
027:093 Who **will** soon show you His Signs, so that

WILL (continued)

028:009 It may be that he **will** be of use to us,
028:012 the people of a house that **will** nourish and bring
028:022 that my Lord **will** show me the smooth and straight Path."
028:027 if thou complete ten years, it **will** be (grace) from thee.
028:032 and it **will** come forth white without stain (or harm),
028:035 He said: "We **will** certainly strengthen thy arm
028:037 from Him and whose End **will** be best in the Hereafter:
028:037 that the wrong-doers **will** not prosper."
028:042 Day of Judgment they **will** be among the loathed
028:053 (bowing to Allah's **Will**) from before this."
028:054 Twice **will** they be given their reward, for that
028:056 but Allah guides those whom He **will** and He
028:060 **will** ye not then be wise?
028:062 That Day (Allah) **will** call to them, and say:
028:063 **will** say: "Our Lord! these are whom we led astray:
028:063 Those against whom the charge **will** be proved,
028:064 It **will** be said (to them): "Call upon your 'partners'
028:064 (how they wish) 'If only they had been open to guidance!'
028:064 they **will** call upon them, but they **will** not listen to them;
028:064 and they **will** see the Chastisement (before them);
028:065 That Day (Allah) **will** call to them, and say: "What was
028:066 and they **will** not be able (even) to question each other.
028:066 Then the arguments that day **will** be obscure to them
028:071 **Will** ye not then hearken?
028:072 **Will** ye not then see?
028:074 The Day that He **will** call on them,
028:074 He **will** say: "Where are My `partners' whom ye
028:075 which they invented **will** leave them in the lurch.
028:082 those who reject Allah **will** assuredly never prosper."
028:085 **will** bring thee back to the Place of return.
028:088 Everything (that exists) **will** perish except His Face.
028:088 and to Him **will** ye (all) be brought back.
029:002 Do men think that they **will** be left alone
029:002 and that they **will** not be tested?
029:003 and Allah **will** certainly know those who are true
029:004 who practise evil think that they **will** get the better of us?
029:008 and I **will** tell you (the truth) of all that ye did.
029:012 and we **will** bear (the consequences) of your faults:
029:012 Never in the least **will** they bear their faults:
029:013 They **will** bear their own burdens,
029:013 they **will** be called to account for their falsehoods.
029:016 that **will** be best for you-if ye understand!
029:017 to Him **will** be your return.
029:020 so **will** Allah produce a later creation:
029:022 "Not on earth nor in heaven **will** ye be able (fleeing)
029:023 they who **will** (suffer) a most grievous Chastisement.
029:025 curse each other: and your abode **will** be the Fire,
029:026 "I **will** leave home for the sake of my Lord:
029:027 and he **will** be in the Hereafter of the Righteous.
029:032 we **will** certainly save him and his following,-
029:038 clearly **will** appear to you from (the traces) of their
029:053 and it **will** certainly reach them,-of a sudden,
029:054 Hell **will** encompass the rejecters of Faith!-
029:061 (to His Law) , they **will** certainly reply, "Allah."
029:063 earth after its death they **will** certainly reply, "Allah!"
029:066 But soon **will** they know.
029:069 We **will** certainly guide them to Our Paths:
030:003 **will** soon be victorious-
030:005 He gives victory to whom He **will**,
030:010 In the long run evil **will** be the End of those who
030:012 On the Day that the Hour **will** come,
030:012 the guilty **will** be struck dumb with despair.

WILL (continued)

030:013   No intercessor **will** they have among their "Partners",
030:013   and they **will** (themselves) reject their "Partners."
030:014   On the Day that the Hour **will** come, that Day
030:029   To them there **will** be no helpers.
030:029   But who **will** guide those whom Allah leaves astray?
030:034   but soon **will** ye know (your folly).
030:038   and it is they who **will** prosper.
030:039   who **will** get a recompense multiplied.
030:039   **will** have no increase with Allah:
030:039   seeking the Countenance of Allah, (**will** increase):
030:039   it is these who **will** get a recompense multiplied.
030:040   then He **will** cause you to die;
030:040   and again He **will** give you life.
030:044   Those who reject Faith **will** suffer from that rejection:
030:044   **will** make provision for themselves (in heaven):
030:050   verily the Same **will** give life to the men who ate dead:
030:055   the transgressors **will** swear that tarried not but an hour.
030:055   the day that the Hour (of reckoning) **will** be established,
030:056   and faith **will** say: "Indeed ye did tarry,
030:057   nor **will** they be allowed to make amends.
030:057   that Day on excuse of theirs **will** avail the Transgressors,
031:005   and those are the ones who **will** prosper.
031:006   for such there **will** be a humiliating Chastisement.
031:008   there **will** be Gardens of Bliss,-
031:015   is to Me, and I **will** tell you all that ye did."
031:016   in the heavens or on earth, Allah **will** bring it forth:
031:025   They **will** certainly say, "Allah."
031:034   know what it is that he **will** earn on the morrow:
032:004   **Will** ye not then receive admonition?
032:011   put in charge of you, **will** (duly) take your souls:
032:012   the guilty ones **will** bend low their heads before
032:012   us back (to the world): we **will** work righteousness:
032:013   but the Word from Me **will** come true,
032:013   "I **will** fill Hell with Jinns and men all together."
032:014   and We too **will** forget you-taste ye the chastisement
032:020   and it **will** be said to them: "Taste ye the Chastisement
032:020   and wicked, their abode **will** be the Fire:
032:020   get away therefrom, they **will** be forced thereinto,
032:021   And indeed We **will** make them taste of the lighter
032:025   Verily thy Lord **will** judge between them on the Day
032:028   They say: "When **will** this decision be, if ye
032:029   Nor **will** they be granted a respite."
032:029   no profit **will** it be to Unbelievers if they
033:016   a brief (respite) **will** ye be allowed to enjoy!"
033:016   Say: "Running away **will** not profit you if ye
033:017   Nor **will** they find for themselves,
033:019   they **will** smite you with sharp tongues,
033:024   and punish the Hypocrites if that be His **Will**,
033:028   I **will** provide for your enjoyment and set you free
033:044   salutation on the Day they meet Him **will** be "peace!";
033:060   then **will** they not be able to stay in it as thy neighbours
033:063   and what **will** make thee understand?
033:065   no protector **will** they find, nor helper.
033:066   they **will** say: "Woe to us! would that we had
033:066   The Day that their faces **will** be turned over
034:003   "Never to us **will** come the Hour": say, "Nay!
034:003   it **will** come upon you;-by Him Who knows the unseen,
034:005   for such **will** be a Chastisement of Painful wrath.
034:007   "Shall we point out to you a man that **will** tell you,
034:023   They **will** say, 'That which is true and just;
034:023   **will** they say, 'What is it that your Lord commanded?'
034:026   and **will** in the end decide the matter between us

WILL (continued)

034:026   Say: "Our Lord **will** gather us together
034:029   They say: "When **will** this promise (come to pass)
034:031   the wrong-doers **will** be made to stand before their Lord,
034:031   Those who were deemed weak **will** say to the arrogant
034:032   The arrogant ones **will** say to those who had been deemed
034:033   **will** say to the arrogant ones: Nay! it was a plot (of yours)
034:037   that **will** bring you nearer to Us in degree:
034:038   **will** be given over into the Chastisement.
034:040   On the day He **will** gather them all together,
034:041   They **will** say, "Glory to thee! Thou art
034:049   and Falsehood showeth not its face and **will** not return."
034:051   If thou couldst but see when they **will** quake with terror:
034:051   and they **will** be seized from a position (quite) near.
034:051   but then there **will** be no escape (for them),
034:052   And they **will** say, "We do believe (now) in the (Truth)";
035:009   even so (**will** be) the Resurrection!
035:010   and the plotting of such **will** be void (of result).
035:014   they **will** reject your "Partnership."
035:014   they **will** not listen to your call, and if
035:029   hope for a Commerce that **will** never fail:
035:030   For He **will** pay them their meed,
035:030   nay, He **will** give them (even) more out of His Bounty:
035:033   Gardens of Eternity **will** they enter:
035:033   therein **will** they be adorned with bracelets of gold
035:033   and their garments there **will** be of silk.
035:034   And they **will** say: "Praise be to Allah, Who has
035:035   settled us in a Home that **will** last:
035:036   for them **will** be the Fire of Hell:
035:037   Therein **will** they cry aloud (for assistance):
035:043   evil plotting of Evil **will** hem in only the authors thereof.
036:010   whether thou admonish them: they **will** not believe.
036:018   punishment indeed **will** be inflicted on you by us."
036:018   if ye desist not, we **will** certainly stone you,
036:023   of no use whatever **will** be their intercession
036:031   Not to them **will** they return:
036:032   **will** be brought before Us (for judgment).
036:035   **will** they not then give thanks?
036:043   If it were Our **Will**, We could drown them;
036:045   which is before you and that which **will** be after you,
036:048   Further, they say, "When **will** this promise
036:049   They **will** not (have to) wait for aught but a single
036:049   it **will** seize them while they are yet disputing
036:050   No (chance) **will** they then have, by **will**, to dispose
036:051   (men) **will** rush forth to their Lord.
036:052   They **will** say: "Ah! woe unto us! Who hath
036:052   (A voice **will** say): "This is what The Most Gracious
036:053   It **will** be no more than a single Blast,
036:053   they **will** all be brought up before Us!
036:054   Then, on that Day, not a soul **will** be wronged
036:056   They and their associates **will** be in pleasant shade,
036:057   (Every) fruit **will** be there for them;
036:065   But their hands **will** speak to Us,
036:066   If it had been Our **Will**, We could surely have
036:067   And if it had been Our **Will**, We could have transformed
036:068   **will** they not then understand?
036:073   **Will** they not then be grateful?
036:079   Say, "He **will** give them life Who created
036:083   and to Him **will** ye be all brought back.
037:019   and behold, they **will** begin to see!
037:019   Then it **will** be a single (compelling) cry;
037:020   They **will** say, "Ah! woe to us! this is the Day
037:021   (A voice **will** say,) "This is the Day of sorting Out,

WILL (continued)

037:027 And they **will** turn to one another, and question
037:028 They **will** say: "It was ye who used to come to us
037:029 They **will** reply: "Nay, ye yourselves had no Faith!
037:033 Truly, that day, they **will** (all) share in the Chastisement.
037:045 Round **will** be passed to them a Cup from a clear-flowing
037:047 nor **will** they suffer intoxication therefrom.
037:048 And beside them **will** be chaste women;
037:050 Then they **will** turn to one another and question
037:051 One of them **will** say: "I had an intimate companion
037:066 Truly they **will** eat thereof and fill their bellies
037:067 Then on top of that they **will** be given a mixture made of
037:091 and said, "**Will** ye not eat (of the offerings before you)?
037:099 He said: "I **will** go to my Lord! He **will** surely guide me!
037:102 thou **will** find me, if Allah so wills one of the steadfast."'
037:124 "**Will** ye not fear (Allah)?
037:125 "**Will** ye call upon Baal and forsake the Best of
037:127 and they **will** certainly be called up (for punishment),
037:138 And by night: **will** ye not understand?
037:155 **Will** ye not then receive admonition?
037:158 that they **will** be brought before Him.
037:170 they reject it: but soon **will** they know!
037:177 Evil **will** be the morning for those who were
038:011 and they **will** be put to flight.
038:015 which (when it comes) **will** brook no delay.
038:026 for it **will** mislead thee from the Path of Allah:
038:035 **will** not belong to another after me:
038:039 no account **will** be asked."
038:050 whose doors will (ever) **will** (ever) be open to them;
038:051 Therein **will** they recline (at ease);
038:052 And beside them **will** be chaste women
038:054 it **will** never fail;-
038:054 Truly such **will** be Our Bounty (to you);
038:055 **will** be an evil place of (final) Return!-
038:056 Hell!-they **will** burn therein-an evil bed
038:061 They **will** say: "Our Lord! Whoever brought
038:062 And they **will** say: "How is it with us that we
038:082 I **will** lead them all astray.
038:085 "That I **will** certainly fill Hell with thee
039:003 Truly Allah **will** judge between them in that
039:007 when He **will** tell you the truth of all that ye did
039:010 **will** truly receive a reward without measure!"
039:015 "Serve ye what ye **will** besides Him."
039:024 It **will** be said to the wrong-doers: "Taste ye
039:030 and truly they (too) **will** die (one day).
039:031 In the End **will** ye (all) dispute on the Day of Judgment,
039:035 So that Allah **will** remit from them (even) the
039:039 I **will** do (my part): but soon **will** ye know-
039:047 but something **will** confront them from Allah,
039:048 For the evils of their Deeds **will** confront them,
039:048 and they **will** be (completely) encircled by the which
039:051 of their deeds **will** soon overtake them (too),
039:059 "(The reply **will** be) `Nay, but there came to thee
039:060 their faces **will** be turned black;
039:061 But Allah **will** deliver the righteous for they
039:063 it is they who **will** be in loss.
039:065 truly fruitless **will** be thy work (in life),
039:067 the whole of the earth **will** be but His handful,
039:067 and the heavens **will** be rolled up in His right hand:
039:068 they **will** be standing and looking on!
039:068 when all that are in heaven and on earth **will** swoon,
039:068 Then **will** a second one be sounded,
039:068 except such as it **will** please Allah (to exempt).

WILL (continued)

039:068 The Trumpet **will** (just) be sounded,
039:069 and they **will** no be wronged (in the least).
039:069 And the Earth **will** shine with the light of its Lord:
039:069 the Record (of Deeds) **will** be placed (open);
039:069 and the witnesses **will** be brought forward;
039:070 And to every soul **will** be paid in full (the fruit)
039:071 when they arrive there, its gates **will** be opened.
039:071 And its Keepers **will** say, "Did not messengers
039:071 The Unbelievers **will** be led to Hell in groups;
039:071 The answer **will** be: "True: but the Decree of
039:072 (To them) **will** be said: "Enter ye the gates of Hell.
039:073 behold, they arrive there; its gates **will** be opened;
039:073 And those feared their Lord **will** be led to the Garden
039:073 and its Keepers **will** say: "Peace be upon you!
039:074 We can dwell in the Garden as we **will**:
039:074 They **will** say: "Praise be to Allah, Who has
039:075 between them (at Judgment) **will** be in (perfect)
039:075 and the cry (on all sides) **will** be, "Praise be to Allah,
040:009 and that **will** be truly the highest Achievement.
040:010 The Unbelievers **will** be addressed: "Greater was
040:011 They **will** say:" Our Lord! twice hast Thou made us
040:012 (The answer **will** be): "This is because,
040:016 The Day whereon they **will** (all) come forth:
040:016 Whose **will** be the Dominion that Day?
040:017 no injustice **will** there be that Day, for Allah
040:017 That Day **will** every soul be requited for what
040:018 when the hearts **will** (come) right up to the Throats
040:018 nor intercessors **will** the wrong-doers have,
040:020 And Allah **will** judge with (Justice and) Truth:
040:020 **will** not (be in a position) to judge at all.
040:028 then **will** fall on you something of the (calamity)
040:028 said: "**Will** ye slay a man because he says,
040:029 but who **will** help us from the Punishment of Allah,
040:032 a Day when there **will** be mutual calling (and warning),-
040:034 ye said: 'No messenger **will** Allah send after him.'
040:038 I **will** lead you to the Path of Right.
040:039 it is the Hereafter that is the Home that **will** last.
040:040 such **will** enter the Garden (of Bliss):
040:040 therein **will** they have abundance without measure.
040:040 "He that works evil **will** not be requited but by the like
040:043 or the Hereafter; our Return **will** be to Allah;
040:043 and the Transgressors **will** be Companions of the Fire!
040:044 "Soon **will** ye remember what I say to you (now).
040:046 and (the Sentence **will** be) on the Day when the
040:046 In front of the Fire **will** they be brought,
040:047 **will** say to those who had been arrogant, "We but
040:047 Behold, they **will** dispute with each other
040:048 Those who had been arrogant **will** say: "We are
040:049 Those in the Fire **will** say to the Keepers of Hell:
040:050 Clear Signs?" They **will** say: "Yes."
040:050 They **will** say: "Did there not come to you
040:050 They **will** reply, "Then pray (as ye like)!
040:051 and on the Day when the Witnesses **will** stand forth,-
040:051 We **will**, without doubt, help Our messengers
040:052 but they **will** (only) have the Curse and the Home
040:052 The Day when no profit **will** it be to Wrong-doers
040:059 The Hour **will** certainly come:
040:060 to serve Me **will** surely enter Hell abased."
040:060 I **will** answer your (Prayer):
040:074 They **will** reply: "They have left us in the lurch:
040:081 then which of the Signs of Allah **will** ye deny?
041:005 for us, we shall do (what we **will**!)"

WILL (continued)

041:008 deeds of righteousness is a reward that **will** never fail.
041:016 more humiliating still: and they **will** find no help.
041:016 of the Hereafter **will** be more humiliating still:
041:019 they **will** be marched in ranks.
041:019 the enemies Allah **will** be gathered together to the Fire,
041:020 and their skins **will** bear witness against them,
041:021 They **will** say to their skins: "Why bear ye
041:021 They **will** say: "Allah hath given us speech,-
041:024 the Fire **will** be a Home for them!
041:027 But We **will** certainly give the Unbelievers a taste
041:027 and We **will** requite them for the worst of their deeds.
041:028 therein **will** be for them the Eternal Home:
041:029 And the Unbelievers **will** say: "Our Lord! Show us those,
041:034 then **will** he between whom and thee was hatred become
041:035 And no one **will** be granted such goodness except
041:040 Do what ye **will**: Verily He seeth (clearly)
041:047 They **will** say, "We do assure Thee not one of us can
041:047 The Day that (Allah) **will** propound to them
041:048 to invoke aforetime **will** leave them in the lurch,
041:048 and they **will** perceive that they have no way of escape.
041:050 that the Hour (of Judgment) **will** (ever) be established;
041:050 But We **will** show the Unbelievers the truth of all
041:053 Soon **will** We show them Our Signs in the (furthest)
042:007 (when) some **will** be in the Garden, and some in the
042:008 and the wrong-doers **will** have no protector
042:008 but He admits whom He **will** to His Mercy;
042:012 He enlarges and restricts the Sustenance to who He **will**:
042:015 Allah **will** bring us together,
042:016 and for them **will** be a Chastisement Terrible.
042:017 **will** make thee realize that perhaps the Hour
042:021 the wrong-doers **will** have a grievous Chastisement.
042:022 righteous deeds **will** be in the Meadows of the Gardens:
042:022 That **will** indeed be the magnificent Bounty (of Allah).
042:033 If it be His **Will**, He can still the Wind:
042:042 for such there **will** be a Chastisement grievous.
042:045 **will** say: "Those are indeed in loss who lose
042:047 of refuge nor **will** there be for you any room
042:047 there come a Day which there **will** be no putting back,
042:047 That Day there **will** be for you no place of refuge
042:049 bestows (children) male and female according to His **Will**,
042:050 and He leaves barren whom He **will**:
042:052 wherewith We guide such of Our servants as We **will**;
043:011 even so **will** ye be raised (from the dead);-
043:019 Their evidence **will** be recorded,
043:019 and they **will** be called to account!
043:020 "If it had been the **will** of (Allah) Most Gracious,
043:023 and we **will** certainly follow in their footsteps."
043:027 and He **will** certainly guide me."
043:039 it **will** avail you nothing, that day,
043:060 And if it were Our **Will**, We could make angels
043:067 Friends on that Day **will** be foes, one to another
043:071 there **will** be there all that the souls could desire,
043:071 To them **will** be passed round, dishes and goblets
043:072 Such **will** be the Garden of which ye are made
043:074 The Sinners **will** be in the Punishment of Hell,
043:075 and in despair **will** they be there overwhelmed.
043:075 Nowise **will** the (punishment) be lightened for them,
043:077 He **will** say, "Nay, but ye shall abide!"
043:077 They **will** cry: "O Malik! would that thy Lord put an end
043:087 Who created them, they **will** certainly say, Allah:
043:088 Truly these are a people who believe not!"
044:010 for the Day hat the sky **will** bring forth a kind of smoke

WILL (continued)

044:011 this **will** be a Chastisement Grievous.
044:012 (They **will** say:) "Our Lord! remove the
044:015 (but) truly ye **will** revert (to your ways).
044:016 We **will** indeed (then) exact Retribution!
044:044 **Will** be the food of the Sinful,-
044:045 Like molten brass; it **will** boil in their insides,
044:047 (A voice **will** cry:) "Seize ye him and drag him
044:051 As to the Righteous (they **will** be) in a
044:053 and in rich brocade, they **will** face each other;
044:056 and He **will** preserve them from the Chastisement
044:056 Nor **will** they there taste Death, except the first death,
044:057 That **will** be the supreme achievement!
045:006 then in what exposition **will** they believe after
045:009 for such there **will** be a humiliating Chastisement.
045:015 In the end **will** ye (all) be brought back to your Lord.
045:017 Verily thy Lord **will** judge between them on the
045:019 They **will** be of no use to thee in the sight of Allah:
045:021 that equal **will** be their Life and their death.
045:023 Who, then, **will** guide him after Allah
045:023 **Will** ye not then receive admonition?
045:026 then He **will** gather you together for the Day
045:027 that Day **will** the followers of Falsehood perish!
045:028 every nation **will** be called to its Record:
045:030 to His Mercy: that **will** be the manifest triumph.
045:030 their Lord **will** admit them to His Mercy:
045:031 (to them **will** be said): "Were not Our Signs rehearsed
045:033 and they **will** be completely encircled by that which
045:033 Then **will** appear to them the evil (fruits) of what they
045:034 It **will** also be said: "This Day We **will** forget you as ye
046:005 such as **will** not answer him to the Day of Judgment,
046:006 they **will** be hostile to them and deny that (men) had
046:009 nor do I know what **will** be done with me or with you.
046:011 themselves thereby, they **will** say, "This is an (old),
046:018 for they **will** be (utterly) lost.
046:019 and no injustice **will** be done to them.
046:020 And on the Day that the Unbelievers **will** be placed
046:020 (it **will** be said to them): "Ye squandered your good
046:023 the Knowledge (of when it **will** come) is only with Allah:
046:024 they said, "This cloud **will** give us rain!"
046:025 "Everything **will** it destroy by the command
046:031 He **will** forgive you your faults.
046:034 "Yea, by our Lord!" (He **will** say): "Then taste ye the
046:034 (they **will** be asked), "Is this not the Truth?"
046:034 Day that the Unbelievers **will** be placed before the Fire,
046:034 They **will** say, "Yea, by our Lord"
046:035 (it **will** be) as if they had not tarried more than an hour
047:001 their deeds **will** Allah bring to naught.
047:002 He **will** remove from them their ills and improve their
047:004 He **will** never let their deeds be lost.
047:004 but if it had been Allah's **Will**, He could certainly have
047:005 Soon **will** He guide them and improve their condition,
047:007 He **will** help you, and plant your feet firmly.
047:007 if ye **will** help (the cause of) Allah,
047:008 and (Allah) **will** bring their deeds to naught.
047:012 Verily Allah **will** admit those who believe and do
047:012 and the Fire **will** be their abode.
047:012 while those who reject Allah **will** enjoy (this world)
047:022 that ye **will** do mischief in the land, and break
047:026 "We **will** obey you in part of (this) matter";
047:027 But how (**will** it be) when the angels take their
047:029 think that Allah **will** not bring to light all their rancor?
047:032 **will** not harm Allah in the least,

WILL (continued)

047:032 but He **will** make their deeds of no effect.
047:034 then die disbelieving,- Allah **will** not forgive them.
047:035 and **will** never put you in loss for your (good) deeds.
047:036 He **will** grant you your recompense,
047:036 and **will** not ask you (to give up) your possession.
047:038 He **will** substitute in your stead another people;
048:010 Allah **will** soon grant him a great Reward.
048:011 if His **Will** is to give you some loss or to give you
048:011 the desert Arabs who lagged behind **will** say to thee:
048:015 then they **will** say, "But ye are jealous of us.
048:015 Those who lagged behind (**will** say), when ye
048:015 Say: "Not thus **will** ye follow us:
048:016 Allah **will** grant you a goodly reward,
048:016 He **will** punish you with a grievous Chastisement."
048:017 (Allah) **will** admit him to Gardens beneath which rivers
048:017 (Allah) **will** punish him with a grievous Chastisement.
048:019 And many gains **will** they acquire (besides):
048:025 that He may admit to His mercy whom He **will**.
049:014 He **will** not belittle aught of your deeds:
049:016 Say: "What! **Will** ye tell Allah about your Religion?"
050:011 thus **will** be the Resurrection.
050:020 that **will** be the Day whereof Warning (had been given).
050:021 with each **will** be an (angel) to drive,
050:021 And there **will** come forth every soul:
050:022 (It **will** be said:) "Thou wast heedless of this;
050:023 And his companion **will** say: "Here is (his Record)
050:024 (The sentence **will** be:) "Throw, both of you, into Hell
050:027 His companion **will** say: "Our Lord! I did not make
050:028 He **will** say: "Dispute not with each other
050:030 It **will** say, "Are there any more (to come)?"
050:030 The Day We **will** ask Hell, "Art thou filled to the full?"
050:031 And the Garden **will** be brought nigh to the
050:032 (A voice **will** say:) "This is what was promised for you,-
050:035 There **will** be for them therein all that they wish,-
050:041 Day when the Caller **will** call out from a place quite near,-
050:042 that **will** be the day of Resurrection.
050:042 The Day when they **will** hear a (mighty) Blast
050:044 that **will** be a gathering together,-
050:044 The Day when the Earth **will** be rent asunder,
051:006 verily Judgment and Justice **will** surely come to pass.
051:012 They ask, "When **will** be the Day of Judgement and
051:013 (It **will** be) a Day when they **will** be tried (and tested)
051:015 they **will** be in the midst of Gardens and Springs,
051:021 As also in your own selves: **will** ye not then see?
051:027 He said, "**Will** ye not eat?"
052:007 Chastisement of the Lord **will** indeed come to pass;-
052:009 Day when the firmament **will** be in dreadful commotion.
052:010 And the mountains **will** move.
052:014 "This," it **will** be said, "Is the Fire,-
052:017 they **will** be in Gardens, and in Happiness,-
052:019 (To them **will** be said:) "Eat and drink ye,
052:020 They **will** recline (with ease) upon couches arranged
052:024 Round about them **will** serve, (devoted) to them,
052:025 They **will** advance to each other, engaging in
052:026 They **will** say: "Aforetime, We were not without
052:031 I too **will** wait along with you!"
052:046 The Day when their plotting **will** avail them nothing
053:012 **Will** ye then dispute with him concerning what he saw?
053:026 their intercession **will** avail nothing except after Allah
053:040 That (the fruit of) his striving **will** soon come in sight;
053:041 Then **will** he be rewarded with a reward complete;
053:060 And **will** ye laugh and not weep,-

WILL (continued)

054:006 Day that the Caller **will** call (them) to a terrible affair,
054:007 They **will** come forth,-their eyes humbled-from
054:008 "Hard is this Day!" The Unbelievers **will** say.
054:015 then is there any that **will** receive admonition?
054:022 then is there any that **will** receive admonition?
054:026 Ah! they **will** know on the morrow, which is
054:027 For We **will** send the she-camel by way
054:032 then is there any that **will** receive admonition?
054:040 then is there any that **will** receive admonition?
054:045 Soon **will** their multitude be put to flight,
054:045 and they **will** show their backs.
054:046 and that Hour **will** be most grievous and most bitter.
054:048 (they **will** hear): "Tastes ye the touch of Hell!"
054:048 The Day they **will** be dragged through the Fire
054:051 then is there any that **will** receive admonition?
054:054 they **will** be in the midst of Gardens and Rivers.
055:013 which of the favours of your Lord **will** ye deny?
055:016 which of the favours of your Lord **will** ye deny?
055:018 which of the favours of your Lord **will** ye deny?
055:021 which of the favours of your Lord **will** ye deny?
055:023 which of the favours of your Lord **will** ye deny?
055:025 which of the favours of your Lord **will** ye deny?
055:026 All that is on earth **will** perish:
055:027 But **will** abide (for ever) the Face of thy Lord,-
055:028 which of the favours of your Lord **will** ye deny?
055:030 which of the favours of your Lord **will** ye deny?
055:032 which of the favours of your Lord **will** ye deny?
055:034 which of the favours of your Lord **will** ye deny?
055:035 On you **will** be sent (O ye evil ones twain)!
055:035 No defense **will** ye have:
055:036 which of the favours of your Lord **will** ye deny?
055:038 which of the favours of your Lord **will** ye deny?
055:039 **will** be asked of man or Jinn as to his sin,
055:040 which of the favours of your Lord **will** ye deny?
055:041 and they **will** be seized by their forelocks and feet.
055:041 (For) the sinners **will** be known by their Marks:
055:042 which of the favours of your Lord **will** ye deny?
055:044 of boiling hot water **will** they wander round!
055:045 which of the favours of your Lord **will** ye deny?
055:046 there **will** be two Gardens-
055:046 they **will** stand before (the Judgment Seat of)
055:047 which of the favours of your Lord **will** ye deny?-
055:049 which of the favours of your Lord **will** ye deny?-
055:050 In them (each) **will** be two Springs flowing (free);
055:051 which of the favours of your Lord **will** ye deny?-
055:052 In them **will** be Fruits of every kind, two and two.
055:053 which of the favours of your Lord **will** ye deny?
055:054 whose inner linings **will** be of rich brocade:
055:054 They **will** recline on Carpets,
055:054 the Fruit of the Gardens **will** be Near (and easy of reach).
055:055 which of the favours of your Lord **will** ye deny?
055:056 In them **will** be (Maidens), Chaste, restraining
055:057 which of the favours of your Lord **will** ye deny?
055:059 which of the favours of your Lord **will** ye deny?
055:061 which of the favours of your Lord **will** ye deny?
055:063 which of the favours of your Lord **will** ye deny?
055:065 which of the favours of your Lord **will** ye deny?
055:066 In them (each) **will** be two springs pouring forth
055:067 which of the favours of your Lord **will** ye deny?
055:068 In them **will** be Fruits, and dates and pomegranates:
055:069 which of the favours of your Lord **will** ye deny?
055:070 In them **will** be fair (Maidens), good, beautiful;-

WILL (continued)

055:071 which of the favours of your Lord **will** ye deny?
055:073 which of the favours of your Lord **will** ye deny?
055:075 which of the favours of your Lord **will** ye deny?
055:077 which of the favours of your Lord **will** ye deny?
056:002 Then **will** no (soul) deny its coming.
056:003 (Many) **will** it bring low; (many) **will** it exalt;
056:008 what **will** be the Companions of the Right Hand?
056:008 Then (there **will** be) the Companions of the Right Hand,-
056:009 what **will** be the Companions of the Left Hand?
056:010 Foremost (in faith) **will** be Foremost (in the Hereafter).
056:011 These **will** be those Nearest to Allah:
056:015 (They **will** be) on couches encrusted (with gold and
056:017 Round about them **will** (serve) youths of perpetual
056:019 No after-ache **will** they receive therefrom,
056:019 nor **will** they suffer intoxication:
056:022 And (there **will** be) Companions with beautiful,
056:025 No frivolity **will** they hear therein, nor any
056:027 what **will** be the Companions of the Right Hand!
056:028 (They **will** be) among lote-trees without thorns,
056:041 what **will** be the Companions of the Left Hand!
056:042 (They **will** be) in the midst of a fierce Blast of Fire
056:050 "All **will** certainly be gathered together for the
056:051 "Then **will** ye truly,-O ye that go wrong,
056:052 "Ye **will** surely taste of the Tree of Zaqqum.
056:053 "Then **will** ye fill your insides therewith,
056:056 Such **will** be their entertainment on the Day
056:057 why **will** ye not admit the Truth?
056:065 Were it Our **Will**, we could make it broken orts.
056:070 Were it Our **Will**, We could make it saltish
057:011 For (Allah) **will** increase it manifold to his credit,
057:011 and he **will** have (besides) a generous reward.
057:011 Who is he that **will** loan to Allah a beautiful Loan?
057:012 (Their greeting **will** be): "Good News for you this Day!
057:013 It **will** be said: "Turn Ye back to your rear!
057:013 So a wall **will** be put up betwixt them,
057:013 all alongside, **will** be (wrath and) Punishment!
057:013 Within it **will** be Mercy throughout, and without it,
057:013 The day **will** the Hypocrites-men and women-say to
057:014 (Those without) **will** call out, "Were we not with you?"
057:014 (The others) **will** reply, "True! but ye led yourselves
057:025 that Allah may test who is that **will** help,
057:028 and He **will** bestow on you a double portion
057:028 and He **will** forgive you (your past):
057:028 He **will** provide for you a light by which ye shall walk
058:005 and His Messenger **will** be humbled to dust,
058:005 the Unbelievers (**will** have) a humiliating Chastisement,
058:006 On that Day Allah **will** raise them all up (again) and tell
058:007 in the end **will** He tell them what they did on the Day
058:008 Enough for them is Hell: in it **will** they burn,
058:011 (Ample) room **will** Allah provide for you.
058:011 Allah **will** raise up, to (suitable) ranks (and degrees)
058:012 That **will** be best for you, and most conducive
058:017 they **will** be Companions of the Fire,
058:017 **will** be their riches nor their sons:
058:018 then **will** they swear to Him as they swear to you:
058:018 The Day **will** Allah raise them all up
058:019 Truly, it is the Party of Satan that **will** lose.
058:020 Allah and His Messenger **will** be among those
058:022 Truly it is the Party of Allah that **will** achieve Success.
058:022 And He **will** admit them to Gardens beneath which
058:022 Allah **will** be well pleased with them, and they
059:011 and if ye are attacked (in fight) we **will** help you."

WILL (continued)

059:011 and we **will** never hearken to any one in your affair;
059:011 "If ye are expelled, We too **will** go out with you,
059:012 and if they do help them, they **will** turn their backs;
059:012 and if they are attacked (in fight), they **will** never help
059:012 so they **will** receive no help.
059:012 If they are expelled, never **will** they go out with them;
059:014 They **will** not fight you (even) together, except in
059:017 The end of both **will** be that they will go into the Fire,
059:020 that **will** achieve Felicity.
060:003 on the Day of Judgment: He **will** judge between you:
060:003 Of no profit to you **will** be your relatives
060:004 said to his father: "I **will** pray for forgiveness
060:007 It may be that Allah **will** Establish friendship
060:010 And there **will** be no blame on you if ye marry
060:012 and that they **will** not disobey thee in any just matter,-
060:012 that they **will** not commit adultery (or fornication),
060:012 that they **will** not utter slander,
060:012 that they **will** not steal,
060:012 that they **will** not kill their children,
060:012 that they **will** not associate in worship and other thing
061:008 but Allah **will** complete His Light,
061:010 to a bargain that **will** save you
061:011 and your persons: that **will** be best for you,
061:012 He **will** forgive you your sins, and admit
061:013 And another (favour **will** He bestow),
061:014 to the Disciples, "Who **will** be my helpers to
062:004 which He bestows on whom He **will**:
062:007 But never **will** they express their desire (for Death),
062:008 "The Death from which ye flee **will** truly overtake you:
062:008 and He **will** tell you the things that ye did!"
062:008 then **will** ye be sent back to the Knower of things secret
063:005 "Come, the Messenger of Allah **will** pray for your
063:006 honourable (element) **will** expel therefrom the meaner."
063:011 But to no soul **will** Allah grant respite when the
064:007 think that they **will** not be raised up (for Judgment).
064:009 and He **will** admit them to gardens beneath which
064:009 that **will** be a day of mutual loss and gain (among you).
064:009 He **will** remove from them their ills,
064:009 that **will** be the Supreme Triumph.
064:010 they **will** be Companions of the Fire,
064:017 He **will** double it to your (credit),
064:017 and He **will** grant you Forgiveness:
065:001 perchance Allah **will** bring about thereafter
065:003 For Allah **will** surely accomplish His purpose:
065:004 He **will** make things easy for them.
065:005 from him and **will** enlarge his reward.
065:005 He **will** remove his evil deeds from him
065:007 After a difficulty, Allah **will** soon grant relief.
065:011 He **will** admit to Gardens beneath which rivers flow,
066:004 and furthermore, the angels,-**will** back (him) up.
066:005 that Allah **will** give him in exchange Consorts
066:007 (It **will** be said), "O ye Unbelievers! make no
066:008 Their Light **will** run forward before them and by
066:008 the Day that Allah **will** not permit to be humiliated
066:008 that your Lord **will** remove from you your evil deeds,
067:004 (thy) vision **will** come back to thee dull and discomfited
067:007 they **will** hear the (terrible) drawing in of its breath
067:008 its Keepers **will** ask, "Did no Warner come to you?"
067:009 They **will** say: "Yes indeed: a Warner came to us,
067:010 They **will** further say: "Had we but listened or used our
067:011 They **will** then confess their sins:
067:016 is in heaven **will** not cause you to be swallowed

WILL (continued)

067:017 is in Heaven will not send against you a violent
067:025 They ask: When will this promise be (fulfilled)?
067:027 grieved will be the faces of the of the Unbelievers
067:027 of the Unbelievers, and it will be said (to them):
067:029 so soon will ye know which (of us) it is that is in
068:005 Soon wilt thou see and they will see,
068:018 But made no reservation, ("If it be Allah's **Will**").
068:032 "It may be that our Lord will give us in exchange
068:040 which of them will stand surety of that!
068:043 Their eyes will be cast down,-ignominy will cover them;
068:045 A (long) respite will I grant them: truly powerful
069:003 what will make thee realize what the Sure Reality is?
069:016 for it will that Day be flimsy,
069:016 And the sky will be rent asunder,
069:017 And the angels will be on its sides,
069:017 and eight will, that Day, bear the Throne
069:018 not an act of yours that ye hide will be hidden.
069:019 Then He that will be given his Record in his
069:019 in his right hand will say: "Ah here! read ye my Record!
069:021 And he will be in a life of Bliss,
069:023 The Fruits whereof (will hang in bunches)
069:025 And he that will be given his Record in his
069:025 will say: "Ah! would that my record had not been given
069:030 (The stern command will say): "Seize ye him,
070:008 The Day that the sky will be like molten brass,
070:009 And the mountains will be like wool,
070:010 And no friend will ask after a friend,
070:011 the sinner's desire will be: would that he could redeem
070:011 Though they will be put in sight of each other,-
070:035 Such will be the honoured ones in the in the Gardens
070:043 The Day whereon they will issue from their from their
071:011 "`He will send rain to you in abundance;
071:018 "`And in the End He will return you into the (earth),
071:027 and they will breed none but wicked ungrateful ones.
071:027 they will but mislead Thy devotees,
072:009 but any who listens now will find a flaming fire
072:017 He will cause him to undergo ever-growing
072:024 then will they know who it is that is weakest in (his)
072:025 or whether my Lord will appoint for it a distant term.
073:014 and the mountains will be in violent commotion.
073:014 And the mountains will be as a heap of sand
073:017 a Day that will make children hoary-headed?-
073:018 Whereon the sky will be cleft asunder?
073:019 Therefore, whoso will, let him take a (straight)
074:009 That will be-that Day-a Day of Distress,-
074:017 Soon will I visit him with a mount of calamities!
074:026 Soon will cast him into Hell-Fire!
074:027 And what will explain to thee what Hell-Fire is?
074:038 Every soul will be (held) in pledge for its deeds.
074:040 they will question each other,
074:040 (They will be) in Gardens (of Delight);
074:043 They will say: "We were not of those who prayed;
074:048 Then will no intercession of (any) intercessors profit them.
074:055 Let any who will, keep it in remembrance!
074:056 But none will keep it in remembrance except as
075:010 That Day will Man say "Where is the refuge?"
075:012 that Day will be the place of rest.
075:013 That Day will Man be told (all) that he put forward,
075:014 Nay, man will be evidence against himself,
075:022 Some faces, that Day, will beam (in brightness and
075:024 And some faces, that Day, will be sad and dismal,
075:027 And there will be a cry, "Who is a magician

WILL (continued)

075:028 And he will think that it was (the Time)
075:029 And one leg will be joined with another:
075:030 That Day the Drive will be (all) to thy Lord!
075:036 Does Man think that he will be left uncontrolled,
076:011 and will shed over them brightness and a (blissful) Joy.
076:011 But Allah will deliver them from the evil of that Day,
076:012 He will reward them with a Garden and (garments
076:013 they will see there neither the sun's (excessive heat)
076:014 And the shades of the (Garden) will come low over them,
076:014 there will hang low easy to reach.
076:015 And amongst them will be passed round vessels of silver
076:016 they will determine the measure thereof (according to
076:017 And they will be given to drink there of a Cup mixed
076:019 And round about them will (serve) youths of perpetual
076:021 and their Lord will give to them to drink a pure drink.
076:021 and they will be adorned with Bracelets of silver;
076:021 Upon them will be green Garments of fine silk
076:027 and put away behind them a Day (that will be) hard.
076:028 but, when We will, We shall exchange their likes.
076:029 This is an admonition: whosoever will, let him take
076:030 But ye will not, except as Allah wills;
076:031 He will admit to His Mercy Whom He will;
077:014 And what will explain to thee what is the day of Sorting
077:029 (It will be said:) "Depart ye to that which ye used to
077:035 That will be a Day when they shall not be able to speak,
077:036 Nor will it be open to them to put forth pleas.
077:038 That will be a Day of Sorting out!
077:050 Then what Message, after that, will they believe in?
078:023 They will dwell therein for ages.
078:031 Verily the Righteous there will be an Achievement,
078:038 Day that the Spirit and the angels will stand forth in ranks,
078:038 and he will say what is right.
078:039 therefore, whoso will, let him take a (straight) Return
078:040 and the Unbeliever will say, "Woe unto me! Would that
078:040 man will see (the Deeds) which his hands have sent forth,
079:006 can be in commotion will be in violent commotion,
079:008 Hearts that Day will be in agitation;
079:009 Cast down will be (their owners') eyes.
079:013 But verily, it will be but a single (compelling) Cry,
079:014 When, behold, they will be brought out to the open.
079:039 The Abode will be Hell-Fire;
079:041 Their abode will be the Garden.
079:042 'When will be its appointed time?'
079:046 (it will be) as if they had tarried but a single evening,
080:012 Therefore let whose will, keep it in remembrance.
080:022 Then, when it is His will, He will raise him up (again).
080:037 will have enough concern (of his own) to make him
080:038 Some Faces that Day will be beaming.
080:040 And other faces that Day will be dust-stained;
080:041 Blackness will cover them:
080:042 Such will be the Rejecters of Allah, the Doers
081:029 But ye shall not will Except as Allah wills,-
082:013 As for the Righteous, they will be in Bliss;
082:014 And the Wicked-they will be in the Fire,
082:015 Which they will enter on the Day of Judgment,
082:016 And they will not be able to keep away therefrom.
082:017 And what will explain to thee what the Day of Judgment
082:018 what will explain to thee what the Day of Judgment is?
082:019 will be (wholly) with Allah.
082:019 (It will be) the Day when no soul shall have no power
083:004 Do they not think that they will be raised up?-
083:006 will stand before the Lord of the Worlds?

WILL (continued)

083:008 And what **will** explain to thee what Sijjin is?
083:015 form (the Light of) their Lord that Day, **will** they be veiled.
083:016 Further, they **will** enter the Fire of Hell.
083:017 Further, it **will** be said to them: "This is the (reality) which
083:019 And what **will** explain to thee what 'Illiyin is?
083:022 Truly the Righteous **will** be in Bliss.
083:023 On raised couches **will** they command a sight
083:025 Their thirst **will** be slaked with Pure Wine sealed;
083:026 The seal thereof **will** be Musk: and for this
083:027 With it **will** be (given) a mixture of Tasnim:
083:034 this Day the Believers **will** laugh at the Unbelievers:
083:035 On raised couches they **will** command (a sight)
083:036 **Will** not the Unbelievers have been paid back for what
084:005 (then **will** come Home the full Reality).
084:008 Soon **will** his account be taken by an easy reckoning,
084:009 And he **will** turn to his people, rejoicing!
084:011 Soon **will** he cry for Perdition,
084:012 And he **will** enter a Blazing Fire.
084:025 for them is a Reward that **will** never fail.
085:010 they **will** have the Chastisement of the of the Burning
085:010 not turn in repentance, **will** have the Chastisement Hell:
085:011 who believe and do righteous deeds, **will** be Gardens.
086:002 And what **will** explain to thee what the Night-Visitant
086:009 The Day that (all) things secret **will** be tested,
086:010 (Man) **will** have no power, and no helper.
087:008 And We **will** make it easy for thee (to follow)
087:010 He **will** heed who fears:
087:011 But it **will** be avoided by the most unfortunate one,
087:012 Who **will** enter the Great Fire,
087:013 In which he **will** then neither die nor live.
087:014 But he **will** prosper who purify himself.
088:002 Some faces, that Day, **will** be humiliated,
088:006 No food **will** there be for them but a bitter Dhari
088:007 Which **will** neither nourish nor satisfy hunger.
088:008 (Other) faces that Day **will** be joyful,
088:012 Therein **will** be a bubbling spring:
088:013 Therein **will** be couches (of dignity),
088:024 Allah **will** chastise him with a mighty Chastisement.
088:025 For to Us **will** be their Return;
088:026 Then it **will** be for Us to call them to account.
089:023 (face to face),-on that Day **will** man remember,
089:023 but how **will** that remembrance profit him?
089:024 He **will** say: "Ah! would that I had sent forth
089:025 For, that Day, His Chastisement **will** be such as
089:026 And His bonds **will** be such as none (other) can bind.
089:027 (To the righteous soul **will** be said:) "O (thou) soul,
090:012 And what **will** explain to thee the path that is steep.
090:017 Then **will** he be of those who believe, and enjoin
090:020 On them **will** be Fire Vaulted over (all round).
092:007 We **will** indeed make smooth for him the path to Ease.
092:010 We **will** indeed make smooth for him the Path to Misery;
092:011 Nor **will** his wealth profit him when he falls
092:021 And soon **will** they attain (complete) satisfaction.
093:004 And verily the hereafter **will** be better for thee
093:005 And soon **will** thy Guardian-Lord give thee
096:015 We **will** drag him by the forelock,-
096:018 We **will** call on the angels of punishment
097:002 And what **will** explain to thee what the Night of Power
098:006 the Book and among the Polytheists, **will** be in hell-fire,
098:008 They **will** dwell therein for ever; Allah well pleased
099:004 On that Day **will** she declare her tidings:
099:005 For that thy Lord **will** have given her inspiration.

WILL (continued)

099:006 On that Day **will** men proceed in groups sorted out,
101:003 And what **will** explain to thee what the (Day) of Clamour
101:004 a Day whereon men **will** be like moths Scattered about,
101:005 And the mountains **will** be like carded wool.
101:006 he whose balance (of good deeds) **will** be (found) heavy,
101:007 **Will** be in a life of good pleasure and satisfaction.
101:008 he whose balance (of good deeds) **will** be (found) light,-
101:009 **Will** have his home in a (bottomless) pit.
101:010 And what **will** explain to Thee what this is?
104:004 He **will** be sure to be thrown into that which Breaks
104:005 And what **will** explain to thee That which Breaks to
108:003 he **will** be cut off (from Future Hope).
109:003 Nor **will** ye worship that which I worship.
109:004 And I **will** not worship that which ye have been wont
109:005 Nor **will** ye worship that which I worship.
111:003 Burnt soon **will** he be in a Fire of blazing Flame!

WILLED

002:020 And if Allah **willed**,
002:251 and taught him whatever (else) He **willed**.
002:253 If Allah had so **willed**, succeeding generations
002:253 If Allah had so **willed**, they would not have fought
005:048 If Allah had so **willed**, He would have made you a single
006:112 If thy Lord had so **willed**, they would not have done it:
006:137 If Allah had **willed**, they would not have done so:
007:100 if We so **willed**, We could punish them (too) for their
008:007 but Allah **willed** to establish the Truth according to His
010:016 Say: "If Allah had so **willed**, I should not have rehearsed
011:118 If thy Lord had so **willed**, He could have made mankind
012:076 by the law of the king except that Allah **willed** it (so).
013:031 Do not the Believers know, that had Allah (so) **willed**,
016:009 if Allah had **willed**, He could guided all of you.
016:035 "If Allah had so **willed**, we should not have worshipped
016:040 For to anything which We have **willed**, We but
016:093 If Allah so **willed**, He could make you all one People:
021:009 and We saved them and those whom We **willed**,
025:045 If He **willed**, He could make it stationary!
032:013 If We had so **willed**, We could have certainly have brought
036:047 if Allah had so **willed**, He could have fed, (Himself)?-
038:036 whithersoever he **willed**,-
042:008 If Allah had so **willed**, He could have made them a single
042:024 But is Allah **willed**, He could seal up thy heart.
047:030 Had We so **willed**, We could have shown them up to thee,

WILLETH

002:255 aught of his knowledge except as He **willeth**.
003:040 "Doth Allah accomplish what He **willeth**."
003:047 He said: "Even so; Allah createth what He **willeth**:
006:039 whom Allah **willeth**, He leaveth to wander:
006:039 whom He **willeth**, He placeth on the Way that is Straight.
006:080 unless my Lord **willeth**, (nothing can happen),
006:125 those whom He **willeth** to leave straying,
006:125 Those whom Allah **willeth** to guide,-
006:128 you will dwell therein for ever, except as Allah **willeth**."
007:188 or harm to myself except as Allah **willeth**.
010:049 no power over any harm or profit to myself Allah **willeth**.
011:034 if it be that Allah **willeth** to leave you astray:
011:107 heavens and the earth endure, except as thy Lord **willeth**:
011:108 the heavens and the earth endure, except thy Lord **willeth**:
013:011 but when (once) Allah **willeth** a people's punishment,
014:027 Allah doeth what He **willeth**.

WILLING

003:083 **willing** or unwilling, bowed to His Will (accepted
009:029 until they pay the Jizya with **willing** submission,

WILLING (continued)

041:011   "We do come (together), in **willing** obedience."

WILLINGLY

009:053   Say: "Spend (for the Cause) **willingly** or unwillingly:

041:011   "Come ye together, **willingly** or unwillingly."

WILLS

002:070   we wish indeed for guidance if Allah **wills**."

002:253   but Allah does what He **wills**.

009:028   enrich you, if He **wills**, out of His bounty,

011:033   He said: "Truly, Allah will bring it on you if He **wills**-

012:100   Verily my Lord is gracious to whom He **wills** for verily

018:024   Except "If Allah so **wills**" and remember thy Lord when

022:018   for Allah carries out all that He **wills**.

022:034   submit then your **wills** to Him (in Islam):

024:045   Allah creates what He **wills**; for verily

024:046   and Allah guides whom He **wills** to a way

028:027   indeed, if Allah **wills**, one of the righteous."

030:048   as He **wills**, behold, they do rejoice!-

030:048   as He **wills**, and break them into fragments,

030:053   in Our Signs and submit (their **wills** in Islam).

030:054   He creates whatever He **wills**,

035:008   to stray whom He **wills**, and guides whom He **wills**.

035:022   Allah can make any that He **wills** to hear;

037:102   if Allah so **wills** one of the steadfast."

039:038   if Allah **wills** some affliction for me,

039:038   remove His affliction or if He **wills** some Mercy

042:029   He has power to gather them together when He **wills**.

042:049   He creates what He **wills**. He bestows (children)

042:051   with Allah's permission, what Allah **wills**:

048:014   He forgives whom He **wills**, and He punishes

048:014   and He punishes whom He **wills**:

048:027   ye shall center the Sacred Mosque, if Allah **wills**,

049:014   ye (only) say, "We have submitted our **wills** to Allah,'

057:029   to bestow it on whomsoever He **wills**.

066:005   who submit (their **wills**), who believe, who are

072:014   'Amongst us are some that submit their **wills** (to Allah),

072:014   Now those who submit their **wills**-they have

074:056   none will keep it in remembrance except as Allah **wills**:

076:030   But ye will not, except as Allah **wills**;

081:028   (With profit) to whoever among you **wills** to go straight:

081:029   But ye shall not will except as Allah **wills**,

082:008   In whatever Form He **wills**, does He put thee together.

087:007   Except as Allah **wills**: for He knoweth what is manifest

WILT

002:030   They said, "**Wilt** thou place therein one who will make

002:096   Thou **wilt** indeed find them,

004:052   thou **wilt** find, have no one to help.

004:143   never **wilt** thou find for him the Way.

004:145   no helper **wilt** thou find for them;

005:013   nor **wilt** thou cease to find them-barring a few,

005:029   for thou **wilt** be among the companions of the Fire,

005:082   to the Believers **wilt** thou find those who say,

005:082   to the Believers **wilt** thou find the Jews and Pagans;

005:083   thou **wilt** see their eyes overflowing with tears,

007:017   nor **wilt** Thou find, in most of them, gratitude

007:115   They said: "O Moses! **wilt** thou throw (first),

007:127   "**Wilt** thou leave Moses and his people,

007:134   if thou **wilt** remove the Plague from us,

007:155   by it Thou causest whom Thou **wilt** to stray,

007:155   and Thou leadest whom Thou **wilt** into the right path.

007:173   **wilt** Thou then destroy us because of the deeds

007:198   Thou **wilt** see them looking at thee, but they see not.

010:099   **Wilt** thou then compel mankind, against their will,

WILT (continued)

012:017   But thou **wilt** never believe us even though we tell the

012:085   said: "By Allah! (never) **wilt** thou cease to remember

014:049   And thou **wilt** see the Sinners that day bound together

017:022   or thou (O man!) **wilt** sit in disgrace and destitution.

017:062   If Thou **wilt** but respite me to the Day of Judgment,

017:077   thou **wilt** find no change in Our ways.

017:097   for such **wilt** thou find no protector besides Him.

018:017   for him **wilt** thou find no protector to lead him to the

018:027   and none **wilt** thou find as a refuge other than Him.

018:041   so that thou **wilt** never be able to find it."

018:047   and thou **wilt** see the earth as a level stretch,

018:049   and thou **wilt** see the sinful in great terror

018:067   (The other) said: "Verily thou **wilt** not be able

018:069   Moses said: "Thou **wilt** find me, if Allah

020:065   They said: "O Moses! whether **wilt** thou that thou

020:097   be that thou **wilt** say, 'Touch me not';

020:107   Nothing crooked or curved **wilt** thou see in their place."

020:126   so **wilt** thou, this day, be forgotten.

022:072   thou **wilt** notice a denial on the faces of the Unbelievers!

023:093   Say: "O my Lord! if Thou **wilt** show me (in my lifetime)

024:043   Then **wilt** thou see rain issue forth from their midst.

024:062   give leave to those of them whom thou **wilt**,

026:167   O Lut! thou **wilt** assuredly be cast out!"

026:213   or thou **wilt** be among those who will be punished.

027:012   (thou **wilt** take) to Pharaoh and his people:

027:033   so consider what thou **wilt** command."

027:081   only those **wilt** thou get to listen who believe in our Signs,

028:027   thou **wilt** find me, indeed, if Allah wills, one of the

028:056   It is true thou **wilt** not be able to guide everyone whom

030:053   only those **wilt** thou make to hear, who believe

033:019   thou **wilt** see them looking to thee, their eyes

033:062   no change **wilt** thou find in the practice (approved) of

035:043   But no change **wilt** thou find in Allah's way

035:043   no turning off **wilt** thou find in Allah's way

039:021   then it withers; thou **wilt** see it grow yellow;

039:030   Truly thou **wilt** die (one day) and truly

039:046   it is Thou that **wilt** judge between Thy Servants in those

039:060   On the Day of Judgement **wilt** thou see those who told

039:065   and thou **wilt** surely be among the losers.

039:075   And thou **wilt** see the angels surrounding the

040:009   on them **wilt** Thou have bestowed Mercy indeed:

041:005   so do thou (what thou **wilt**); for us, we shall do (what we

042:022   Thou **wilt** see the wrong-doers in fear on account

042:044   And thou **wilt** see the wrong-doers, when in

042:045   And thou **wilt** see them brought forward to the

045:028   And thou **wilt** see every nation bowing the knee:

047:020   thou **wilt** see those in whose hearts is a disease

047:030   but surely thou **wilt** know them by the tone of their

048:023   no change **wilt** thou find in the practice of Allah.

048:029   Thou **wilt** see them bow and prostrate themselves

053:055   (O man), **wilt** thou dispute about?

057:020   thou **wilt** see it grow yellow; then it becomes

058:022   Thou **wilt** not find any people who believe

067:003   **wilt** thou see in the Creation of The Most Gracious.

068:005   Soon **wilt** thou see and they will see,

076:020   it is there thou **wilt** see a Bliss and Realm Magnificent.

083:024   Thou **wilt** recognize in their Faces the beaming

WIN

007:113   a (suitable) reward if we **win**!"

012:061   They said: "We shall try to **win** him from his father:

021:044   Is it they who will **win**?

026:040   "That we may follow the sorcerers if they **win**?"

WIN (continued)

026:041 shall we have a (suitable) reward if we **win**?"
026:044 it is we who will certainly **win**!"

WIND

003:117 likened to a **Wind** which brings a nipping frost:
010:022 they sail with them with a favourable **wind**,
010:022 then comes a stormy **wind** and the waves
014:018 on which the **wind** blows furiously on a tempestuous day:
015:027 from the fire of a scorching **wind**.
021:081 the violent (unruly) **wind** flow (tamely) for Solomon,
022:031 or the **wind** had swooped (like a bird on its prey)
030:051 And if We (but) send a **Wind** from which they see
034:012 And to Solomon (We made) the **Wind** (obedient):
038:036 Then We subjected the **Wind** to his power, to flow
041:016 against them a furious **Wind** through days of disaster,
042:033 If it be His Will, He can still the **Wind**:
046:024 a **wind** wherein is a Grievous Chastisement!
051:041 We sent against them the devastating **Wind**:
052:027 us from the Chastisement of the Scorching **Wind**.
054:019 For We sent against them a furious **wind**,
069:006 were destroyed by a furious **wind**, exceedingly violent;

WINDING

046:021 his people beside the **winding** Sand-tracts:

WINDS

002:164 in the change of the **winds**, and the clouds which
007:057 the **Winds** like heralds of glad tidings,
015:022 And We send the fecundating **winds**,
018:045 but it becomes day stubble, which the **winds** do scatter:
025:048 And He it is Who sends the **Winds** as heralds
027:063 and who sends the **winds** as heralds of glad tidings,
030:046 that He sends the **Winds**, as heralds of glad tidings,
030:048 It is Allah Who sends the **Winds**,
035:009 It is Allah Who sends forth the **Winds**,
045:005 and in the change of the **winds**,- are Signs for those
051:001 By the (**Winds**) that scatter broadcast;
077:001 By the (**Winds**) Sent Forth one after another
077:010 the mountains are scattered (to the **winds**) as dust;

WINE

002:219 They ask thee concerning **wine** and gambling.
012:036 "I see myself (in a dream) pressing **wine**."
012:041 he will pour our out the **wine** for his lord to drink:
012:049 and in which they will press (**wine** and oil)."
047:015 rivers of **wine**, a joy to those who drink;
083:025 Their thirst will be slaked with Pure **Wine** sealed;

WING

015:088 but lower thy **wing** (in gentleness) to the Believers.
017:024 out of kindness, lower to them the **wing** of humility,
026:215 And lower thy **wing** to the Believers who follow thee.

WINGS

006:038 nor a being that flies on its **wings**,
024:041 and the birds (of the air) **wings** outspread?
035:001 the angels messengers with **wings**,-two, or three
067:019 spreading their **wings** and folding them in?

WINK

083:030 used to **wink** at each other (in mockery);

WINS

020:064 he **wins** (all along) to-day who gains the upper hand."

WINTER

106:002 journeys by **winter** and summer,-

WIPE

005:012 verily I will **wipe** out from you your evils,

WISDOM

002:032 perfect in knowledge and **wisdom**."
002:129 and instruct them in Scripture and **Wisdom**,
002:151 and instructing you in Scripture and **Wisdom**,
002:170 fathers were void of **wisdom** and guidance?.
002:171 they are void of **wisdom**.
002:231 the Book and **Wisdom**, for your instruction.
002:251 and Allah gave him power and **wisdom**
002:269 and he to whom **wisdom** is granted receiveth
002:269 He granteth **wisdom** to whom He pleaseth;
003:048 the Book and **Wisdom**, the Torah and the Gospel.
003:058 of the Signs and the Message of **Wisdom**."
003:079 that a man, to whom is given the Book, and **Wisdom**.
003:081 saying: "I give you a Book and **Wisdom**:
003:118 to you the Signs, if ye have **wisdom**.
003:164 and instructing them in Scripture and **Wisdom**,
004:017 for Allah is full of knowledge and **wisdom**.
004:054 the people of Abraham the Book and **Wisdom**,
004:092 for Allah hath all knowledge and all **wisdom**.
004:104 And Allah is full of knowledge and **wisdom**.
004:111 for Allah is full of knowledge and **wisdom**.
004:113 sent down to thee the Book and **wisdom** and taught
005:038 and Allah is Exalted in Power full of **Wisdom**.
005:103 but most of them lack **wisdom**.
005:110 Behold! I taught thee the Book and **Wisdom**,
006:083 for thy Lord is full of **wisdom** and knowledge.
006:128 For thy Lord is full of **wisdom** and knowledge.
006:139 for He is full of **Wisdom** and Knowledge.
006:151 thus doth He command you, that ye may learn **wisdom**.
008:071 who hath (full) knowledge and **wisdom**.
009:060 and Allah is full of knowledge and **wisdom**.
010:001 These are the Ayats of the Book of **Wisdom**.
012:002 in order that ye may learn **wisdom**.
012:006 For thy Lord is full of knowledge and **wisdom**."
012:076 We raise to degrees (of **wisdom**) whom We please:
012:083 For He is indeed full of knowledge and **wisdom**."
012:100 He is full of knowledge and **wisdom**.
014:004 and He is Exalted in power, Full of **Wisdom**.
015:025 for He is Perfect in **Wisdom** and Knowledge.
016:060 for He is the Exalted in Power, Full of **Wisdom**.
016:125 Way of thy Lord with **wisdom** and beautiful preaching;
017:039 These are among the (precepts of) **wisdom**,
019:012 and We gave him **Wisdom** even as a youth,
022:046 so that their hearts (and minds) may thus learn **wisdom**
022:052 for Allah is full of knowledge and **wisdom**:
024:010 Full of **Wisdom**,-(ye would be ruined indeed).
024:018 for Allah is full of knowledge and **wisdom**.
024:058 for Allah is full of knowledge and **wisdom**.
024:059 for Allah is full of knowledge and **wisdom**.
026:021 has (since) invested me with judgment (and **wisdom**)
026:083 "O my Lord! bestow **wisdom** on me,
028:014 We bestowed on him **wisdom** and knowledge:
030:027 for He is Exalted in Might, Full of **Wisdom**.
031:012 We bestowed (in the past) **wisdom** on Luqman:
031:027 for Allah is Exalted in power, Full of **Wisdom**.
033:001 verily Allah is full of knowledge and **wisdom**.
033:034 of the Signs of Allah and His **Wisdom**:
035:002 and He is the Exalted in Power, Full of **Wisdom**.
036:002 By the Qur'an, full of **Wisdom**,-
038:020 and gave him **wisdom** and sound judgment
039:001 from Allah, the Exalted in Power, Full of **Wisdom**.
040:008 the Exalted in Might, Full of **Wisdom**.
041:042 by One Full of **Wisdom**, Worthy of all Praise.

WISDOM (continued)

042:003   Allah, Exalted in Power, Full of **Wisdom**.
043:004   high (in dignity), full of **wisdom**.
043:063   "Now have I come to you with **Wisdom**,
043:084   Full of **Wisdom** and Knowledge.
044:004   In that (night) is made distinct every affair of **wisdom**,
045:002   is from Allah the Exalted in Power, Full of **Wisdom**.
045:037   and He is Exalted in Power, Full of **Wisdom**!
046:002   is from Allah the Exalted in Power, Full of **Wisdom**.
048:004   and Allah is full of Knowledge and **Wisdom**;-
048:007   and Allah is Exalted in Power, Full of **Wisdom**.
048:019   Exalted in Power, Full of **Wisdom**.
049:008   and Allah is full of Knowledge and **Wisdom**.
051:030   and He is full of **Wisdom** and Knowledge."
053:006   Endued with **Wisdom**:
054:005   A **wisdom** far-reaching:-but (the preaching
059:014   that is because they are a people devoid of **wisdom**.
060:010   and Allah is Full Knowledge and **Wisdom**.
062:002   and to instruct them in The Book and **Wisdom**,-
064:018   is open, Exalted in Might, Full of **Wisdom**.
066:002   Full of Knowledge and **Wisdom**.
076:030   for Allah is full of Knowledge and **Wisdom**.

WISE

002:129   for Thou art the Exalted in Might, the **Wise**."
002:164   Signs for a people that are **wise**.
002:197   So fear Me, O ye that are **wise**.
002:209   then know that Allah is Exalted in Power, **Wise**.
002:220   He is indeed Exalted in Power, **Wise**."
002:228   and Allah is Exalted in Power, **Wise**.
002:240   And Allah is Exalted in Power, **Wise**.
002:260   Then know that Allah is Exalted in Power, **Wise**."
003:006   the Exalted and Might, the **Wise**.
003:018   the Exalted in Power, the **Wise**.
003:062   the Exalted in Power, the **Wise**.
003:126   the Exalted, the **Wise**:
004:032   And in no **wise** covet those things in which
004:056   for Allah is Exalted in Power, **Wise**.
004:130   for Allah is He that careth for all and is **Wise**.
004:158   and Allah is Exalted in Power, **Wise**;
004:165   for Allah is Exalted in Power, **Wise**.
005:118   Thou art the Exalted, the **Wise**.
006:018   and He is the **Wise**, acquainted with all things."
006:073   For He is the **Wise**, well acquainted
008:010   Exalted in Power, Wide.
008:049   behold! Allah is Exalted in might, **Wise**.
008:063   for He is Exalted in might, **Wise**.
008:067   and Allah is Exalted in might, **Wise**.
009:040   for Allah is Exalted in might, **Wise**.
009:071   for Allah is Exalted in power, **Wise**.
009:106   and Allah is All-Knowing, **Wise**.
009:110   And Allah is All-Knowing, **Wise**.
010:094   thy Lord: so be in no **wise** of those in doubt.
010:105   and never in any **wise** be of the Unbelievers;
011:001   from One Who is **Wise** and Well-Acquainted
016:012   verily in this are Signs for men who are **wise**.
016:067   in this also is a Sign for those who are **wise**.
027:009   the Exalted in Might, the **Wise**!...
028:060   will ye not then be **wise**?
029:026   my Lord: for He is Exalted in Might, and **Wise**."
029:042   and He is Exalted (in power), **Wise**.
030:024   are Signs for those who are **wise**.
031:002   These are Verses of the **Wise** Book,-
031:009   and He is Exalted in power, **Wise**.

WISE (continued)

031:028   your resurrection is in no **wise** but as an individual soul:
034:027   Nay, He is Allah, the Exalted in Power, the **Wise**."
042:051   what Allah wills: for He is Most High, Most **Wise**.
045:005   the winds,- are Signs for those that are **wise**.
057:001   for He is the Exalted in Might, the **Wise**.
059:001   for He is the Exalted in Might, the **Wise**.
059:024   and He is the Exalted in Might, the **Wise**.
060:005   the Exalted in Might, the **Wise**."
061:001   the Exalted in Might, the **Wise**.
062:001   the Holy One, the Exalted in Might, the **Wise**.
062:003   is Exalted in Might, **Wise**.

WISEST

095:008   Is not Allah the **wisest** of Judges?

WISH

002:058   and eat of the plenty therein as ye **wish**;
002:070   we **wish** indeed for guidance if Allah wills."
002:105   It is never the **wish** of those without Faith among the
002:109   People of the Book **wish** they could turn you (people)
002:228   if they **wish** for reconciliation.
002:236   is due from those who **wish** to do the right thing.
002:266   Does any of you **wish** that he should have a garden
003:030   it will **wish** there were a great distance between
003:069   It is the **wish** of a section of the People
003:143   Ye did indeed **wish** for Death before ye
004:026   and (He doth **wish** to) turn to you (in Mercy):
004:026   Allah doth **wish** to make clear to you and to guide you
004:027   Allah doth **wish** to turn to you,
004:027   but the **wish** of those who follow their lusts is that ye
004:028   Allah doth **wish** to lighten your (burdens):
004:042   **wish** that the earth were made one with them:
004:044   and **wish** that ye should lose the right path.
004:060   But Satan's **wish** is to lead them astray far away
004:060   Their (real) **wish** is to resort together for judgment
004:073   "Oh! I **wish** I had been with them:
004:089   They but **wish** that ye should reject Faith.
004:091   Others you will find that **wish** to be secure from
004:102   the Unbelievers **wish**, if ye were negligent of
004:144   do ye **wish** to offer Allah an open proof against
004:150   and **wish** to separate between Allah and His
004:150   and **wish** to take a course midway,
005:006   Allah doth not **wish** to place you in a difficulty,
005:037   Their **wish** will be to get out of the Fire,
005:113   They said: "We only **wish** to eat thereof and satisfy
006:138   except those whom-so they say-We **wish**; further,
007:019   and enjoy (its good things) as ye **wish**:
007:161   "Dwell in this town and eat therein as ye **wish**,
009:055   in reality Allah's **Wish** is to punish them with these
009:085   Allah's **Wish** is to punish them with these things
010:050   what portion of it would the Sinners **wish** to hasten?
010:080   "Throw ye what ye (**wish**) to throw!"
011:019   path of Allah and **wish** it to be crooked:
011:088   I **wish** not, in opposition to you, to do
014:010   Ye **wish** to turn us away from what our fathers
015:002   who disbelieve, **wish** that they had been Muslims.
016:031   they will have therein all that they **wish**:
017:018   If any do **wish** for the transitory things
017:019   Those who do **wish** for the (things of) the Hereafter,
018:108   no change will they **wish** for from them.
019:021   and (We **wish**) to appoint him as a Sign unto men
021:017   If it had been Our **wish** to take (just) a pastime,
022:022   Every time they **wish** to get away therefrom,
023:024   his **wish** is to assert his superiority over you:

WISH (continued)

024:022 do you not **wish** that Allah should forgive you?
025:016 "For them there will be therein all that they **wish** for:
027:072 some of the events which ye **wish** to hasten on may
028:064 If only they had been open to guidance!'
032:020 every time they **wish** to get away therefrom,
033:017 can screen you from Allah if it be His **wish** to give you
033:020 they would **wish** they were in the deserts
037:061 For the like of this let all strive, who **wish** to strive.
037:176 Do they **wish** (indeed) to hurry on Our Punishment?
039:034 They shall have all that they **wish** for,
041:037 if it is Him ye **wish** to serve.
042:018 Only those **wish** to hasten it who believe not in it:
042:022 before their Lord, all that they **wish** for.
044:003 for We (ever) **wish** to warn (against Evil).
048:015 They **wish** to change Allah's word: Say: "Not thus
050:035 There will be for them therein all that they **wish**,-
058:003 to their wives then **wish** to go back on the words

WISHED

002:220 And if Allah had **wished**,
006:148 will say: "If Allah had **wished**, we should
008:007 ye **wished** that the one unarmed should be yours,
008:031 if we **wished**, we could say (words) like these:
018:077 (Moses) said: "If thou hadst **wished**, surely thou
018:079 I but **wished** to render it unserviceable, for there
023:024 if Allah had **wished** (to send messengers),
028:005 And We **wished** to be gracious to those who
034:009 If We **wished**, We could cause the earth to swallow them
039:004 Had Allah **wished** to take to Himself a son,

WISHES

002:096 each one of them **wishes** he could be given a life of a
002:196 if any one **wishes** to continue the 'umra on the hajj,
006:145 (meat) forbidden to be eaten by one who **wishes** to eat it,
033:033 And Allah only **wishes** to remove all abomination
033:050 herself to the Prophet is the Prophet **wishes** to wed her;
034:043 a man who **wishes** to hinder you from the (worship)
040:031 but Allah never **wishes** injustice to His Servants.
049:007 were he, in many matters to follow your (**wishes**),
075:005 But man **wishes** to do wrong (even) in the time in front
076:016 determine the measure thereof (according to their **wishes**).

WISTFULLY

015:088 (**Wistfully**) at what We have bestowed on certain

WIT

005:117 didst command me to say, to say, to **wit**, 'Worship Allah,

WITCHCRAFT

021:003 Will ye go to **witchcraft** with your eyes open?"

WITH

002:014 but when they are alone **with** their evil ones,
002:014 they say: "We are really **with** you,
002:025 "Why, this is what we were fed **with** before,"
002:025 Every time they are fed **with** fruits therefrom,
002:036 **with** enmity between yourselves.
002:040 and fulfil your Covenant **with** Me
002:040 and I shall fulfil My Covenant **with** you,
002:041 confirming the revelation which is **with** you,
002:042 And cover not Truth **with** falsehood,
002:043 **with** those who bow down (in worship).
002:045 **with** patient perseverance and prayer:
002:060 We said "strike the rock **with** thy staff."
002:061 They were covered **with** humiliation and misery:
002:062 shall have their reward **with** their Lord
002:073 "Strike the (body) **with** a piece of the (heifer)."

WITH (continued)

002:079 those who write the Book **with** their own hands,
002:079 to traffic **with** it for a miserable price!
002:083 treat **with** kindness your parents and kindred,
002:087 a Messenger **with** what ye yourselves desire not,
002:087 and strengthened him **with** the holy spirit.
002:087 and followed him up **with** a succession of Messengers;
002:087 ye are puffed up **with** pride?
002:089 confirming what is **with** them,
002:091 confirming what is **with** them.
002:092 There came to you Moses **with** clear (Signs);
002:093 and their hearts were filled (**with** the love) of the Calf
002:094 Say: "If the last Home, **with** Allah,
002:095 acquainted **with** the wrong-doers.
002:101 confirming what was **with** them,
002:110 ye shall find it **with** Allah:
002:112 he will get his reward **with** his Lord;
002:120 the Christians be satisfied **with** thee unless thou follow
002:124 was tried by his lord **with** certain Commands,
002:125 and We covenanted **with** Abraham and Isma'il,
002:126 and feed its People **with** fruits,
002:127 raised the foundations the House (**with** this prayer):
002:130 as debase their souls **with** folly?
002:135 and he joined not gods **with** Allah."
002:139 Say: Will ye dispute **with** us about Allah,
002:153 for God is **with** those who patiently persevere.
002:153 **with** patient Perseverance and Prayer:
002:155 We shall test you **with** something of fear and hunger,
002:156 Who say, when afflicted **with** calamity:
002:165 (for worship) other besides Allah, as equal (**with** Allah):
002:178 and compensate him **with** handsome gratitude.
002:184 For those who can do it (**with** hardship),
002:186 let them also, **with** a will, listen to My call,
002:187 so now associate **with** them,
002:187 but do not associate **with** your wives while
002:188 **with** intent that ye may eat up wrongfully and
002:194 Allah is **with** those who restrain themselves
002:197 And take a provision (**with** you) for the journey,
002:200 yea, **with** far more heart and soul.
002:210 **with** angels (in His train) and the question is (thus)
002:213 Allah sent Messengers **with** glad tidings and warnings;
002:213 and **with** them He sent the Book in truth,
002:214 those of faith who were **with** him cried:
002:220 if ye mix their affairs **with** yours,
002:229 or separate **with** kindness.
002:231 well acquainted **with** all things.
002:234 And Allah is well acquainted **with** what ye do.
002:235 but do not make a secret contract **with** them except
002:240 for what they do **with** themselves,
002:247 gifted **with** wealth in abundance?"
002:247 abundantly **with** knowledge and bodily prowess:
002:248 **with** (an assurance) therein of security from your Lord,
002:249 Allah is **with** those who steadfastly persevere."
002:249 only those who taste not of it go **with** me;
002:249 he and the faithful ones **with** him,
002:249 he goes not **with** my army;
002:249 When Talut set forth **with** the armies,
002:249 "This day we cannot cope **with** Goliath and his forces."
002:253 Those Messengers We endowed **with** gifts, some above
002:253 and strengthened him **with** the Holy Spirit.
002:258 to one who disputed **with** Abraham about his Lord,
002:259 and clothe them **with** flesh."
002:260 they will come to thee (flying) **with** speed.

WITH (continued)

002:262 for them their reward is **with** their Lord;
002:262 **with** reminders of their generosity or **with** injury,
002:264 do nothing **with** aught they have earned.
002:266 in a whirlwind, **with** fire therein, and be burnt up?
002:266 while he is stricken **with** old age,
002:266 should have a garden **with** date-palms and vines
002:267 yourselves would not receive it except **with** closed eyes.
002:268 Satan threatens you **with** poverty and bids
002:271 And Allah is well acquainted **with** what ye do.
002:272 and ye shall not be dealt **with** unjustly.
002:274 have their reward **with** their Lord:
002:277 will have their reward **with** their Lord:
002:279 and ye shall not be dealt **with** unjustly.
002:281 and none shall be dealt **with** unjustly.
002:282 O ye who believe! when ye deal **with** each other,
002:282 And Allah is well acquainted **with** all things.
002:283 his heart is tainted **with** sin.
002:283 deposits a thing on trust **with** another,
002:283 a pledge **with** possession (may serve the purpose).
003:013 these saw **with** their own eyes twice their number.
003:013 But Allah doth support **with** His aid whom He pleaseth.
003:014 but **with** Allah is the best of the goals (to return to).
003:015 nearness to their Lord **with** rivers flowing beneath;
003:015 **with** spouses purified and the good pleasure
003:018 and those endued **with** knowledge,
003:020 So if they dispute **with** thee,
003:021 and slay those who teach just dealing **with** mankind,
003:026 Thou enduest **with** honour whom Thou pleasest,
003:028 no relation left **with** Allah except by way of precaution,
003:030 be confronted **with** all the good it has done,
003:037 he found her supplied **with** sustenance.
003:041 thou shalt speak no man for three days but **with** signals.
003:043 (in prayer) **with** those who bow down."
003:044 nor wast thou **with** them when they dispute (the point).
003:044 thou wast not **with** them when they cast lots **with** pens,
003:044 should be charged **with** the care of Mary:
003:049 the Children of Israel, (**with** this message):
003:049 I have come to you, **with** a Sign from your Lord,
003:050 I have come to you **with** a Sign from your Lord.
003:056 I will punish them **with** severe chastisement
003:061 If any one disputes in this manner **with** thee,
003:064 that we associate no partners **with** Him;
003:067 And he joined not gods **with** Allah.
003:071 Why do ye clothe truth **with** falsehood,
003:075 others, who, if entrusted **with** a single silver coin,
003:075 if entrusted **with** a hoard of gold,
003:078 a section who distort the Book **with** their tongues;
003:081 confirming what is **with** you;
003:081 and I am **with** you among the witnesses."
003:103 and remember **with** gratitude Allah's favour on you;
003:106 some faces will be (lit up **with**) white,
003:107 But those whose faces will be (lit **with**) white,
003:124 should help you **with** three thousand angels
003:125 **with** five thousand angels clearly marked.
003:136 and Gardens **with** rivers flowing underneath,
003:143 now ye have seen it **with** your own eyes (and flinch!).
003:144 those who (serve him) **with** gratitude.
003:145 those that (serve us **with**) gratitude.
003:146 and **with** them (fought) large bands of godly men?
003:146 if they met **with** disaster in Allah's way,
003:151 for that they joined partners **with** Allah,
003:152 His promise to you when we **with** His permission

WITH (continued)

003:154 a band of you overcome **with** slumber,
003:154 "If we had had anything to do **with** this affair,
003:156 "If they had stayed **with** us, they would
003:159 that thou dost deal gently **with** them.
003:161 and none shall be dealt **with** unjustly.
003:165 smote (your enemies) **with** one twice as great,
003:166 was **with** the leave of Allah, in order that He might test
003:167 saying **with** their lips what was not in their hearts.
003:170 and **with** regard to those left behind, who have
003:174 And they returned **with** Grace and Bounty from Allah:
003:180 and Allah is well acquainted **with** all that ye do.
003:183 **with** Clear Signs and even **with** what ye ask for:
003:184 who came **with** Clear Signs, and the Scriptures.
003:187 and purchased **with** it some miserable gain!
003:191 (**with** the saying): "Our Lord not for naught
003:192 truly Thou coverest **with** shame,
003:195 into Gardens **with** rivers flowing beneath;
003:198 are Gardens, **with** rivers flowing beneath;
003:199 For them is a reward **with** their Lord,
004:002 not their substance (by mixing it up) **with** your own.
004:003 be able to deal justly (**with** them),
004:003 be able to deal justly **with** the orphans,
004:005 take it and enjoy it **with** right good cheer.
004:013 will be admitted to Gardens **with** rivers flowing
004:019 Nor should ye treat them **with** harshness,
004:019 **with** them on a footing of kindness and equity
004:024 ye seek (them in marriage) **with** gifts from your property,
004:025 wed them **with** the leave of their owners,
004:035 and is acquainted **with** all things.
004:036 Serve Allah, and join not any partners **with** Him;
004:042 wish that the earth were made one **with** them:
004:043 or ye have been in contact **with** women,
004:046 and "Ra'ina" **with** a twist of their tongues
004:047 confirming what was (already) **with** you,
004:048 to set up partners **with** Allah is to devise a sin
004:048 that partners should be set up **with** him;
004:057 **with** rivers flowing beneath, their eternal home:
004:058 ye judge between people that ye judge **with** justice:
004:059 and those charged **with** authority among you.
004:064 in accordance **with** the leave of Allah.
004:065 but accept them **with** the fullest conviction.
004:073 "Oh! I wish I had been **with** them:
004:077 never will ye be dealt unjustly in the very least!
004:083 or to those charged **with** authority among them,
004:086 meet it **with** a greeting still more courteous,
004:090 or those who approach you **with** hearts restraining their
004:091 We have provided you **with** a clear argument against them.
004:092 **with** whom ye have a treaty of mutual alliance,
004:092 to a people at war **with** you, and he was Believer,
004:094 **with** Allah are profits and spoils abundant.
004:095 in the cause of Allah **with** their goods and their persons.
004:095 who strive and fight **with** their goods and persons than to
004:100 his reward becomes due and sure **with** Allah:
004:102 Taking their arms **with** them:
004:102 let them pray **with** thee, taking all precautions,
004:102 When thou (O Messenger) art **with** them,
004:102 let one party of them stand up (in prayer) **with** thee.
004:108 while He is **with** them when they plot by night.
004:109 but who will contend **with** Allah on their behalf
004:115 If anyone contends **with** the Messenger even after
004:116 (the sin of) joining other gods **with** Him:
004:116 one who joins other gods **with** Allah,

WITH (continued)

004:122 soon admit them to Gardens ,**with** rivers flowing beneath,
004:128 Allah is well-acquainted **with** all that ye do.
004:135 verily Allah is well-acquainted **with** all that ye do.
004:139 Nay, all honor is **with** Allah.
004:140 ye are not to sit **with** them unless they turn to a different
004:141 they say: "Were we not **with** you?"
004:146 if so they will be (numbered) **with** the Believers.
004:149 or conceal it or cover evil **with** pardon,
004:154 We said: "Enter the gate **with** humility";
004:157 are full of doubts, **with** no (certain) knowledge.
004:166 He hath sent from His (Own) knowledge,
004:173 He will punish **with** a grievous chastisement:
005:001 are all beasts of cattle **with** the exception named:
005:003 also is the division (of meat) by raffling **with** arrows:
005:003 **with** no inclination to transgression,
005:006 or ye have been in contact **with** women, and you
005:006 rub your heads (**with** water); and wash your feet to the
005:007 and His Covenant, which He ratified **with** you,
005:008 For Allah is well-acquainted **with** all that ye do.
005:012 and Allah said: "I am **with** you: if ye (but)
005:012 and admit you to Gardens **with** rivers flowing beneath;
005:032 Our Messengers **with** Clear Signs, yet, even after
005:033 and strive **with** might and main for mischief
005:035 and strive **with** might and main in His cause:
005:041 those who say "We believe" **with** their lips but whose
005:053 That they were **with** you?"
005:054 lowly **with** the Believers, mighty against the Rejecters.
005:061 and they go out **with** the same.
005:061 say: "We believe but in fact they enter **with** a disbelief,
005:070 a Messenger **with** what they themselves desired not
005:072 Whoever joins other gods **with** Allah,-Allah will
005:080 souls have sent forward before them (**with** the result),
005:085 their prayer hath Allah rewarded them **with** Gardens
005:085 **with** rivers flowing underneath, their eternal home.
005:091 and hatred between you, **with** intoxicants and gambling,
005:097 and that Allah is well acquainted **with** all things.
005:110 Behold! I strengthened thee **with** the Holy Spirit.
005:112 a Table set (**with** viands) from heaven?"
005:114 a table set (**with** viands), that there may
005:115 I will punish him **with** a chastisement such as I
005:119 Allah well-pleased **with** them, and they **with** Allah:
005:119 **with** rivers flowing beneath, their eternal home:
006:001 (others) as equal **with** their Guardian Lord.
006:002 And there is **with** Him another determined term;
006:007 so that they could touch it **with** their hands,
006:009 they have already covered **with** confusion.
006:014 of those who join gods **with** Allah."
006:017 if He touch thee **with** happiness, He hath power over
006:017 "If Allah touch thee **with** affliction, none can
006:018 and He is the Wise, acquainted **with** all things."
006:019 (your blasphemy of) joining others **with** Him."
006:023 not those who joined gods **with** Allah."
006:025 they (but) dispute **with** thee;
006:034 **with** patience and constancy they bore their
006:041 (the false gods) which ye join **with** Him!"
006:042 and We afflicted the nations **with** suffering and
006:050 "I tell you not that **with** me are the treasures of Allah,
006:057 The Command rests **with** none but Allah:
006:059 **With** Him are the keys of the Unseen,
006:059 Not a leaf doth fall but **with** His knowledge:
006:065 or to cover you **with** confusion in party strife,
006:070 **with** it (Al-Qur-an) lest a soul is caught in its

WITH (continued)

006:073 He Who created the heavens and the earth **with** truth:
006:073 for He is the Wise, well acquainted (**with** all things).
006:080 His people disputed **with** him.
006:080 I fear not (the beings) ye associate **with** Allah:
006:080 He said: "(Come) ye to dispute **with** me,
006:081 (the beings) ye associate **with** Allah, when ye
006:082 and mix not their beliefs **with** wrong-that are
006:088 If they were to join other gods **with** Him,
006:094 We see not **with** you your intercessors whom ye
006:097 that ye may guide yourselves, **with** their help,
006:099 **with** it We produce vegetation of all kinds:
006:099 feast your eyes **with** the fruit and the ripeness thereof.
006:100 Yet they make the Jinns equals **with** Allah,
006:106 those who join gods **with** Allah.
006:112 inspiring each other **with** flowery discourses
006:121 their friends to contend **with** you if ye were to obey them,
006:127 a Home of Peace **with** their Lord:
006:141 and dates, and tilth **with** produce of all kinds, and olives
006:141 is He who produceth Gardens **with** trellises and without,
006:143 Tell me **with** knowledge if ye are truthful:
006:146 We forbade every (animal) **with** undivided hoof,
006:146 or their entrails, or is mixed up **with** a bone:
006:149 Say: "**With** Allah is the argument that reaches home:
006:150 as equal **with** their Guardian Lord.
006:151 join not anything **with** Him:
006:152 give measure and weight **with** (full) justice;-
006:154 that they might believe in the meeting **with** their Lord.
006:156 we remained unacquainted **with** all that they
006:157 **with** a dreadful chastisement for their turning away.
006:159 their affair is **with** Allah:
006:161 and he (certainly) joined not gods **with** Allah."
007:002 that **with** it thou mightest warn (the erring) and a
007:007 We shall recount their whole story **with** knowledge,
007:010 We Who created you placed you **with** authority on earth,
007:010 and provided you therein **with** means for the fulfillment
007:018 Hell will I fill **with** you all.
007:024 "Get ye down, **with** enmity between yourselves.
007:036 who reject Our Signs and treat them **with** arrogance,-
007:040 who reject Our Signs and treat them **with** arrogance,
007:049 that Allah **with** His Mercy would never bless?
007:055 Call on your Lord **with** humility and in private:
007:056 but call on Him **with** fear and longing
007:064 and those **with** him, in the Ark:
007:070 Bring us what thou threatenest us **with**,
007:071 dispute ye **with** me over names which ye have devised-
007:073 or ye shall be seized **with** a grievous punishment."
007:087 in the Message **with** which I have been sent,
007:088 (thee) and those who believe **with** thee;
007:101 their Messengers **with** clear (Signs);
007:103 We sent Moses **with** Our Signs to Pharaoh and his chiefs.
007:105 from your Lord **with** a clear (Sign):
007:105 so let the children of Israel depart along **with** me."
007:106 "If indeed thou hast come **with** a Sign,
007:130 people of Pharaoh **with** years (of drought) and shortness
007:131 connected **with** Moses and those **with** Him!
007:134 and we shall send away the Children of Israel **with** thee."
007:137 and his people erected (**with** such pride).
007:138 took the Children of Israel (**with** safety) across the sea.
007:140 He Who hath endowed you **with** gifts above the nations?"
007:141 who afflicted you **with** the worst of punishment
007:142 thus was completed the term **with** his Lord,
007:142 and completed (the period) **with** ten (more):

WITH (continued)

007:145 (and said): "Take and hold these **with** firmness,
007:152 and **with** shame in this life:
007:152 will indeed be overwhelmed **with** wrath from their Lord,
007:155 when they were seized **with** violent quaking,
007:157 the Light which is sent down **with** him,-it is
007:160 asked him for Water: "Strike the rock **with** thy staff":
007:164 destroy or visit **with** a terrible punishment?"-
007:165 We visited the wrong-doers **with** a grievous punishment,
007:167 who would afflict them **with** grievous Chastisement.
007:168 We have tried them **with** both prosperity and adversity:
007:176 We should have elevated him **with** Our Signs;
007:181 who direct (others) **with** truth, and dispense
007:184 Their Companion is not seized **with** madness:
007:187 Say: "The knowledge thereof is **with** Allah (alone),
007:187 Say: "The knowledge thereof is **with** my Lord (alone):
007:189 in order that he might dwell **with** her (in love).
007:195 Have they feet to walk **with**? Or hands to lay hold **with**?
007:195 Or eyes to see **with**? Or ears to hear **with**?
007:200 from Satan assail thy (mind), seek refuge **with** Allah;
007:204 When the Qur'an is read, listen to it **with** attention,
007:205 **with** humility and remember without loudness in words,
008:004 they have grades of dignity **with** their Lord,
008:006 Disputing **with** thee concerning the truth after it was made
008:009 "I will assist you **with** a thousand of the angels,
008:011 Remember He covered you **with** drowsiness,
008:012 thy Lord inspired the angels (**with** the message):
008:012 "I am **with** you: give firmness to the Believers:
008:019 for verily Allah is **with** those who believe!
008:026 strengthened you **with** His aid,
008:028 and that it is Allah **with** whom lies your highest reward.
008:046 for Allah is **with** those who patiently persevere.
008:056 They are those **with** whom thou didst make a covenant
008:057 gain the mastery over them in war, disperse, **with** them,
008:062 He it is that hath strengthened thee **with** His aid and
008:062 His aid and **with** (the company of) the Believers,
008:066 will vanquish two thousand, **with** the leave of Allah:
008:066 for Allah is **with** those who patiently persevere.
008:072 except against a people **with** whom ye have
008:072 **with** their property and their persons,
008:075 Verily Allah is well-acquainted **with** all things.
009:001 to those of the Pagans **with** whom ye have
009:002 that Allah will cover **with** shame those who reject Him.
009:003 dissolve (treaty) obligations **with** the Pagans.
009:004 (But the treaties are) not dissolved **with** those Pagans
009:004 those Pagans **with** whom ye have entered into alliance
009:004 So fulfil your engagements **with** them to the
009:007 before Allah and His Messenger, **with** the Pagans,
009:007 those **with** whom ye made a treaty near the Sacred
009:008 **With** (fair words from) their mouths they please you,
009:016 those among you who strive **with** might and main,
009:016 And Allah is well-acquainted **with** (all) that ye do.
009:017 It is not for such as join gods **with** Allah,
009:019 and strive **with** might and main in the cause of Allah?
009:020 and strive **with** might and main, in Allah's cause,
009:020 **with** their goods and their persons,
009:022 Verily **with** Allah is a reward, the greatest (of all).
009:029 until they pay the Jizya **with** willing submission,
009:031 from having the partners they associate (**with** Him).
009:032 would they extinguish Allah's light **with** their mouths,
009:033 His Messenger **with** Guidance and the and the Religion
009:035 and **with** it will be branded their foreheads,
009:036 know that Allah is **with** those who restrain themselves.

009:037 in order to agree **with** the number of months forbidden
009:038 as compared **with** the Hereafter.
009:038 O ye who believe! what is the matter **with** you,
009:039 He will punish you **with** a grievous penalty,
009:040 "Have no fear, for Allah is **with** us":
009:040 and strengthened him **with** forces which ye saw not,
009:041 and struggle, **with** your goods and your person,
009:042 we should certainly have come out **with** you,"
009:044 exemption from fighting **with** their goods and persons.
009:047 If they had come out **with** you, they would not have added
009:052 So wait (expectant); we too will wait **with** you."
009:055 punish them **with** these things in this life,
009:057 would turn straightway thereto **with** an obstinate rush.
009:059 If only they had been content **with** what Allah
009:065 they declare (**with** emphasis): "We were only
009:070 To them came their messengers **with** Clear Signs.
009:074 for the bounty **with** which Allah and His Messenger
009:074 Allah will punish them **with** a grievous chastisement
009:075 them are men who made a Covenant **with** Allah,
009:077 because they broke their Covenant **with** Allah,
009:081 **with** their goods and their persons,
009:083 say: "Never shall ye come out **with** me, nor fight
009:083 and they ask permission to come out (**with** thee),
009:083 then sit ye (now) **with** those who stay behind."
009:083 nor fight an enemy **with** me:
009:085 Allah's Wish is to punish them **with** these things
009:086 we would be **with** those who sit (at home)."
009:086 those **with** wealth and influence among them ask thee
009:086 and fight along **with** His Messenger, those **with**
009:087 They prefer to be **with** (the women), who remain
009:088 strive fight **with** their wealth and their persons:
009:088 But the Messenger, and those who believe **with** him,
009:092 their eyes streaming **with** tears of grief that they had no
009:092 on those who came to thee to be provided **with** mount.
009:093 prefer to stay **with** the (women) who remain behind:
009:096 that ye may be pleased **with** them.
009:096 But if ye are pleased **with** them.
009:096 Allah is not pleased **with** those who disobey.
009:100 well-pleased is Allah **with** them, as are they **with** him:
009:102 mixed an act that was good **with** another that was evil.
009:109 And it doth crumble to pieces **with** him,
009:117 Allah turned **with** favour to the Prophet,
009:119 and be **with** those who are truthful.
009:121 requite them **with** the best (possible reward).
009:123 and know that Allah is **with** those who fear Him.
010:003 No intercessor (can plead **with** Him) except after
010:004 that He may reward **with** justice those who believe
010:007 Those who rest not their hope on their meeting **with** Us,
010:007 but are pleased and satisfied **with** the life of the Present,
010:011 those who rest not their hope on their meeting **with** Us,
010:013 their Messengers came to them **with** Clear Signs,
010:015 those who rest not their hope on their meeting **with** Us,
010:018 and they say; "These are our intercessors **with** Allah."
010:020 Then ye wait: I too will wait **with** you."
010:022 they sail **with** them **with** a favourable wind,
010:024 (it grows) till the earth is clad **with** its golden
010:027 **with** pieces from the depth of the darkness of Night:
010:028 Then shall We say to those who joined gods (**with** Us):
010:035 What then is the matter **with** you? How judge ye?
010:039 Nay, they charge **with** falsehood that whose
010:041 If they charge thee **with** falsehood, say: "My work
010:044 Verily Allah will not deal unjustly **with** man in aught:

WITH (continued)

010:045 who denied the meeting **with** Allah and refused
010:047 the matter will be judged between them **with** justice,
010:054 but the judgment between them will be **with** justice,
010:071 that I should stay (**with** you) and remind (you) the Signs
010:073 and those **with** him, in the Ark, and We made
010:075 and Aaron to Pharaoh and his chiefs **with** Our Signs.
010:087 We inspired Moses and his brother **with** this message:
010:090 At length, when overwhelmed **with** the flood
010:102 Say: "Wait ye then: for I too, will wait **with** you."
010:105 set thy face towards Religion **with** true piety,
010:107 If Allah do touch thee **with** hurt, there is
011:001 and Well-Acquainted (**with** all things):
011:001 **with** verses fundamental (of established meaning),
011:005 Ah! even when they cover themselves **with** their garments,
011:012 or why does not an angel come down **with** Him?
011:014 Revelation is sent down (replete) **with** the knowledge
011:025 We sent Noah to his people (**with** a mission): "I have
011:031 "I tell you not that **with** me are the Treasures of Allah,
011:032 They said: "O Noah! thou hast disputed **with** us,
011:032 now bring upon us what thou threatenest us **with**,
011:032 and how much hast thou prolonged the dispute **with** us:
011:038 can look down on you **with** ridicule likewise!
011:039 descend a Chastisement that will cover them **with** shame,-
011:040 But only a few believed **with** him.
011:042 So the Ark floated **with** them on the waves (towering)
011:042 and be not **with** the Unbelievers!"
011:042 "O my son! embark **with** us, and be not
011:044 the word went forth: "Away **with** those who do wrong!"
011:047 Noah said: "O my Lord! i do seek refuge **with** Thee,
011:048 of the People who will spring) from those **with** thee:
011:048 "O Noah come down (from the Ark) **with** Peace from Us,
011:054 some of our gods may have seized thee **with** evil."
011:057 conveyed the Message **with** which I was sent to you.
011:058 We saved Hud and those who believed **with** him,
011:060 Away **with** the 'Ad the People of Hud!
011:066 We saved Salih and those who believed **with** him,
011:068 So away **with** the Thamud!
011:069 and hastened to entertain them **with** roasted calf.
011:069 came Our Messengers to Abraham **with** glad tidings.
011:074 he began to plead **with** Us for Lut's people.
011:078 and cover me not **with** shame about my guests!
011:081 Now travel **with** thy family while yet a part of the night
011:085 commit not evil in the land **with** intent to do mischief.
011:087 forbeareth **with** faults and is right-minded!
011:087 off doing what we like **with** our property?
011:092 For ye cast Him away your backs (**with** contempt).
011:092 my family of more consideration **with** you than Allah?
011:093 for I too am watching **with** you!"
011:094 believed **with** him, by (special) Mercy from Us:
011:095 So away **with** Madyan as were Thamud gone away.
011:096 And We sent Moses, **with** Our Clear (Signs) and an
011:112 thou and those who **with** thee turn (unto Allah);
011:119 "I will fill Hell **with** Jinns and men all together."
011:120 **with** it We make firm they heart:
012:011 why dost thou not trust us **with** Joseph,-
012:012 "Send him **with** us to-morrow to enjoy himself
012:017 "O our father! we went racing **with** one another,
012:017 and left Joseph **with** our things:
012:018 minds have made up a tale (that may pass) **with** you,
012:018 They stained his shirt **with** false blood.
012:024 And (**with** passion) did she desire him,
012:030 her slave truly hath he inspired her **with** violent love:

WITH (continued)

012:036 Now **with** him there came into the prison two young men.
012:050 'What was the matter **with** the ladies who cut their hands?
012:054 thou art of high standing **with** us, invested **with** all trust."
012:059 them forth **with** provisions (suitable) for them,
012:062 their stock-in-trade (**with** which they had bartered)
012:063 so send our brother **with** us, that we
012:064 He said: "Shall I trust you **with** him **with** any result other
012:064 other than when I trusted you **with** his brother aforetime?
012:066 "Never will I send him **with** you until ye swear a
012:067 can profit you aught against Allah (**with** my advice):
012:069 he received his (full) brother to stay **with** him.
012:070 them forth **with** provisions (suitable) for them,
012:076 all endued **with** knowledge is One, the All-Knowing.
012:076 So he began (the search) **with** their baggage,
012:079 other than him **with** whom we found our property:
012:080 ye did fail in your duty **with** Joseph?
012:084 And his eyes became white **with** sorrow,
012:084 and he was suppressed **with** silent sorrow.
012:089 He said: "Know ye how ye dealt **with** Joseph,
012:093 "Go **with** this my shirt, and cast it the face of my father:
012:093 come ye (here) to me together **with** all your family."
012:099 a home for his parents **with** himself,
012:101 (as a Muslim), and unite me **with** the righteous."
012:102 nor wast thou (present) **with** them when they concerted
012:106 Allah without associating (others as partners) **with** Him!
012:108 Glory to Allah! and never will I join gods **with** Allah!"
012:108 **with** a certain knowledge I and whoever follows me.
012:111 instruction for men endued **with** understanding.
013:002 that ye may believe **with** certainty in the meeting
013:002 in the meeting **with** your Lord.
013:004 watered **with** the same water,
013:004 and gardens of vines and fields sown **with** corn,
013:008 Every single thing is **with** Him in (due) proportion.
013:012 the clouds, heavy **with** (fertilizing) rain!
013:013 and so do the angels, **with** awe:
013:015 to Allah **with** good-will or in spite of themselves:
013:016 Or the depths of darkness equal **with** Light?
013:016 Say: "Are the blind equal **with** those who see?
013:019 are endued **with** understanding that receive admonition;-
013:022 and turn off Evil **with** good: for such there is the final
013:023 enter unto them from every gate (**with** the salutation)
013:031 If there were a Qur'an **with** which mountains were moved,
013:031 but, truly, the Command is **with** Allah in things!
013:036 and not to join partners **with** Him.
013:039 **with** Him is the Mother of the Book.
014:005 We sent Moses **with** Our Signs (and the command).
014:009 To them came Messengers **with** Clear (Signs);
014:012 We shall certainly bear **with** patience all the
014:021 or bear (these torments) **with** patience:
014:022 I reject your former act in associating me **with** Allah.
014:023 to dwell therein for aye **with** the leave of their Lord.
014:027 those who believe, **with** the Word that stands firm,
014:028 **With** ingratitude and caused their people to descend to
014:032 and **with** it bringeth out fruits wherewith to feed you.
014:037 and feed them **with** Fruits:
014:037 so fill the hearts of some among men **with** love towards
014:041 "O our Lord! cover (us) **with** Thy Forgiveness-me,
014:043 They running forward **with** necks outstretched,
014:045 ye were clearly shown how We dealt **with** them;
014:050 and their faces covered **with** Fire;
015:021 its (sources and) treasures (inexhaustible) are **with** Us;
015:022 therewith providing you **with** water (in abundance),

WITH (continued)

015:053   glad tidings of a son endowed **with** knowledge."
015:064   "We have come to thee **with** the Truth and assuredly
015:065   "Then travel by night **with** thy household,
015:084   to them was all that they did (**with** such art and care)!
015:085   overlook (any human faults) **with** gracious forgiveness.
015:094   those who join false gods **with** Allah.
015:096   Those who adopt, **with** Allah, another god:
016:002   send down His angels **with** inspiration of His Command,
016:003   created the heavens and the earth **with** truth far is he
016:007   not (otherwise) reach except **with** souls distressed:
016:011   **With** it He produces for you corn, olives, date-palms,
016:015   mountains standing firm, least it should shake **with** you;
016:027   concerning whom ye used to dispute (**with** the godly)?"
016:027   He will cover them **with** shame, and say: "Where are
016:027   Those endued **with** knowledge will say: "This Day,
016:027   are the Unbelievers covered **with** Shame and Misery,-
016:028   Then would they offer submission (**with** the pretense)
016:036   (**with** the Command), "Serve Allah and eschew Evil":
016:044   (We sent them) **with** Clear Signs and Scriptures
016:053   unto Him ye cry **with** groans;
016:054   Some of you turn to other gods to join **with** their Lord-
016:058   and he is filled **with** inward grief!
016:059   **With** shame does he hide himself from his people,
016:073   for sustenance, **with** anything in heavens or earth,
016:076   is such a man equal **with** one who commands justice,
016:076   one of them dumb, **with** no power of any sort;
016:094   **With** the result that someone's foot may slip after it was
016:095   for **with** Allah is (a prize) far better for you,
016:096   what is **with** Allah will endure.
016:096   What is **with** you must vanish:
016:100   who join partners **with** Allah.
016:111   and none will be unjustly dealt **with**.
016:112   abundantly supplied **with** sustenance from every
016:120   in faith, and he joined not gods **with** Allah.
016:123   in Faith, and he joined not gods **with** Allah."
016:125   and argue **with** them in ways that are best
016:125   Way of thy Lord **with** wisdom and beautiful preaching;
016:127   for thy patience is but **with** the help from Allah;
016:128   For Allah is **with** those who restrain themselves,
017:003   whom We carried (in the Ark) **with** Noah!
017:004   on the earth and be elated **with** mighty arrogance
017:007   and to visit **with** destruction all that fell into their power.
017:019   and strive therefor **with** all due striving,
017:022   Take not **with** Allah another god;
017:035   and weigh **with** a balance that is straight:
017:037   Nor walk on the earth **with** insolence:
017:039   Take not, **with** Allah, another object of worship,
017:042   Say: if there had been (other) gods **with** Him,-
017:052   (His call) **with** (words of) His praise,
017:058   the Day of Judgment or punish it **with** a dreadful
017:064   among them, **with** thy (seductive) voice;
017:064   them **with** thy cavalry and thy infantry;
017:064   mutually share **with** them wealth and children;
017:068   a violent tornado (**with** showers of stones) so that
017:070   provided them **with** transport on land and sea;
017:071   will not be dealt **with** unjustly in the least.
017:071   all human beings **with** their (respective) Imams:
017:071   record in their right hand will read it (**with** pleasure),
017:077   (This was Our) way **with** the messengers We sent
017:088   even if they backed up each other **with** help and support.
017:089   men refuse (to receive it) except **with** ingratitude!
017:093   "Or thou have a house adorned **with** gold,

WITH (continued)

017:096   for He is well acquainted **with** His servants,
017:099   the unjust refuse (to receive it) except **with** ingratitude.
017:103   but We did drown him and all who were **with** him.
018:018   and wouldst certainly have been filled **with** terror of them.
018:019   and let him behave **with** care and courtesy,
018:019   ye then one of you **with** this money of yours to the town:
018:026   **with** Him is (the knowledge of) the secrets of the
018:026   He share His Command **with** any person whatsoever.
018:028   And keep yourself content **with** those who call on their
018:031   be adorned therein **with** bracelets of gold,
018:032   of grape-vines and surrounded them **with** date-palms;
018:037   in the course of the argument **with** him:
018:038   and none shall I associate **with** my Lord.
018:042   So his fruits were encompassed (**with** ruin),
018:048   before thy Lord in ranks (**with** the announcement),
018:049   and not one will thy Lord treat **with** injustice.
018:056   but the Unbelievers dispute **with** vain argument,
018:067   be able to have patience **with** me!
018:072   thou canst have no patience **with** me?"
018:075   thou canst have no patience **with** me?"
018:086   to punish them, or to treat them **with** kindness."
018:087   him **with** a punishment unheard-of (before).
018:095   help me therefore **with** strength (and labour):
018:096   "Blow (**with** your bellows)" then, when he
019:004   and the hair of my head doth glisten **with** grey:
019:006   one **with** whom Thou art well-pleased!"
019:012   "O Yahay! take hold of the Book **with** might":
019:022   and she retired **with** him to a remote place.
019:026   will I enter into no talk **with** any human being.'"
019:058   those whom We carried (in the Ark) **with** Noah,
019:068   shall gather them together and (also) Satans (**with** them);
019:071   **with** thy Lord, a Decree which must be accomplished.
019:078   or has he taken a promise **with** the Most Gracious?
019:083   to incite them **with** fury?
019:092   For it is not consonant **with** the majesty of The Most
019:097   that **with** it thou mayest give glad tidings to the
020:018   on it I lean; **with** it I beat down fodder for my flocks;
020:039   but I endued thee **with** love from Me:
020:040   thou tarry a number of years **with** the people of Midian.
020:042   Go, thou and they brother **with** My Signs,
020:045   We fear lest he hasten **with** insolence against us,
020:046   He said: "Fear not: for I am **with** you:
020:047   **with** a Sign, indeed, have we come from they Lord!
020:047   the Children of Israel **with** us, and afflict them not:
020:052   "The knowledge of that is **with** my Lord, duly recorded:
020:053   **With** it have We produced divers pairs of plants
020:054   Signs for men endued **with** understanding.
020:057   to drive us out of our land **with** thy magic, O Moses?
020:062   So they disputed, one **with** another, over their affair,
020:063   and to do away **with** your most cherished way.
020:063   is to drive you out from your land **with** their magic,
020:077   "Travel by night **with** my servants,
020:078   Then Pharaoh pursued them **with** his forces,
020:080   and We made a Covenant **with** you on the right side
020:102   We shall gather the sinful, blear-eyed (**with** terror).
020:114   Be not in haste **with** the Qur'an before its revelation
020:123   from the Garden, **with** enmity one to another;
020:128   for men endued **with** understanding.
020:130   Therefore be patient **with** what they say,
020:134   Had We destroyed them with a punishment before this,
021:003   Will ye go to witchcraft **with** your eyes open?"
021:003   Their hearts toying as **with** trifles.

WITH (continued)

021:019 even those who are **with** Him are not too proud to serve
021:024 this is the Message of those **with** me and the Message
021:028 except for those who **with** whom He is well-pleased
021:029 such a one We should reward **with** Hell:
021:031 mountains standing firm, lest it should shake **with** them,
021:036 they treat thee not except **with** ridicule.
021:047 so that not a soul will be dealt **with** unjustly in the least.
021:051 and well were We acquainted **with** him.
021:062 "Art thou the one that did this **with** our gods,
021:065 Then were they confounded **with** shame:
021:079 the hills and the birds celebrate Our praises, **with** David:
021:103 but the angels will meet them (**with** mutual greetings):
022:019 These two antagonists dispute **with** each other
022:020 **With** it will be melted what is within their bodies,
022:023 be adorned therein **with** bracelets of gold and pearls;
022:026 (Saying): "Associate not anything (in worship) **with** Me;
022:035 when Allah is mentioned, are filled **with** fear,
022:036 and such as beg **with** due humility:
022:041 **with** Allah rests the end (and decision) of all affairs.
022:042 the Peoples before them (**with** their prophets),-
022:059 to a place **with** which they shall be well pleased:
022:063 and forthwith the earth becomes clothed **with** green?
022:067 let them not then dispute **with** thee on the matter,
022:068 If they do wrangle **with** thee,
022:072 They nearly attack **with** violence those who rehearse
022:078 to strive, (**with** sincerity and under discipline):
023:006 Except **with** those joined to them in the marriage bond,
023:014 of that lump bones and clothed the bones **with** flesh;
023:018 and We certainly are able to drain it off (**with** ease).
023:019 **With** it We grow for you gardens of date-palms
023:025 wait (and have patience) **with** him for a time."
023:027 So We inspired him (**with** this message);
023:028 on the Ark-thou and those **with** thee,-say: "Praise
023:029 enable me to disembark **with** Thy blessing:
023:041 Then the Blast overtook them **with** justice,
023:041 So away **with** the people who do wrong!
023:044 so away **with** a people that will not believe!
023:045 his brother Aaron, **with** Our Signs and authority
023:050 and security and furnished **with** springs.
023:051 for I am well-acquainted **with** (all) that you do.
023:053 each party rejoices in that which is **with** itself.
023:059 Those who join not (in worship) partners **with** their Lord;
023:060 who dispense their charity **with** their hearts full of fear,
023:071 If the Truth had been in accord **with** their desires,
023:091 nor is there any god along **with** Him:
023:096 Repel evil **with** that which is best:
023:096 We are well acquainted **with** the things they say.
023:097 seek refuse **with** Thee from the suggestions of the Satans.
023:098 "And I seek refuge **with** Thee, O my Lord!
023:104 and they will therein grin, **with** their lips displaced.
023:108 He will day: "Be ye driven into it (**with** ignominy)!
023:110 "But ye treated them **with** ridicule,
023:117 and his reckoning will be only **with** his Lord!
024:002 of fornication,-flog each of them **with** a hundred stripes;
024:003 sexual relations **with** any but an adulteress
024:003 none can have sexual relations **with** her but an
024:004 flog them **with** eighty stripes;
024:008 four times (**with** an oath) by Allah,
024:022 **with** grace and amplitude of means resolve by oath
024:030 and Allah is well acquainted **with** all that they do.
024:039 parched **with** thirst mistakes for water;
024:040 overwhelmed **with** billow topped by billow,

WITH (continued)

024:041 and the birds (of the air) **with** wings outspread?
024:049 they come to him **with** all submission.
024:050 Allah and His Messenger will deal unjustly **with** them?
024:053 Allah is well acquainted **with** all that ye do."
024:055 and not associate aught **with** Me.'
024:061 nor in one afflicted **with** illness, nor in yourselves,
024:062 when they are **with** him on a matter requiring
025:007 been sent down to him to give admonition **with** him?
025:025 The Day the heaven shall be rent asunder **with** clouds,
025:027 that I had taken a (straight) path **with** the Messenger!
025:030 Truly my people treated this Qur'an **with** neglect."
025:035 his brother Aaron **with** him as Minister;
025:036 We destroyed **with** utter destruction.
025:040 did they not then see it (**with** their own eyes)?
025:049 That **with** it We may give life to a dead land,
025:052 them **with** the utmost strenuousness, **with** the (Qur'an).
025:058 to be acquainted **with** the faults of His servants;-
025:059 about Him of any acquainted (**with** such things).
025:068 Those who invoke not, **with** Allah, any other god,
025:072 they pass by it **with** honourable (avoidance);
025:073 when they are admonished **with** the Signs of their Lord,
025:075 be rewarded **with** the highest place in heaven,
025:075 be met **with** salutations and peace,
025:077 not concern Himself **with** you but for your call on Him:
026:003 It may be thou will kill thy self **with** grief,
026:012 I do fear that they will charge me **with** falsehood:
026:015 We are **with** you, and will listen (to your call).
026:015 "By no means! proceed then, both of you, **with** Our Signs;
026:017 "'Send thou **with** us the Children of Israel.'"
026:021 invested me **with** judgment (and wisdom) and
026:022 "And this is the favour **with** which thou dost
026:052 "Travel by night **with** My servants; for surely
026:062 (Moses) said: "By no means! my Lord is **with** me!
026:063 "Strike the sea **with** thy rod."
026:065 We delivered Moses and all who were **with** him;
026:083 and join me **with** the righteous;
026:098 we held you as equal **with** the Lord of the Worlds;
026:113 "Their account is only **with** my Lord, if ye
026:118 the Believers who are **with** me."
026:119 in the Ark filled (**with** all creatures).
026:119 So we delivered him and those **with** him.
026:148 spathes near breaking (**with** the weight of fruit)?
026:148 "And corn-fields and date palms **with** spathes near
026:149 carve house out of (rocky) mountains **with** great skill.
026:156 "Touch her not **with** harm, lest the
026:182 And weigh **with** scales true and upright.
026:193 **With** it came down the Truthful spirit
026:213 So call not on any other god **with** Allah,
027:021 "I will certainly punish him **with** a severe punishment,
027:022 and I have come to thee from Saba **with** tidings true.
027:023 a woman ruling over them and provided every requisite;
027:028 Go thou, **with** this letter of mine, and deliver
027:033 but the command is **with** thee; so consider what thou
027:033 They said: "We are endued **with** strength,
027:035 and (wait) to see **with** what (answer) return (my)
027:037 we shall come to them **with** such hosts as they will never
027:044 "This is but a palace paved smooth **with** slabs of glass."
027:044 (in Islam), **with** Solomon, to the Lord of the Worlds."
027:045 they became two factions quarreling **with** each other.
027:047 omen do we augur from thee and those that are **with** thee."
027:047 He said: "Your ill omen is **with** Allah;
027:059 or the false gods they associate (**with** Him)?

WITH (continued)

027:060   Yea, **with** it We cause to grow well-planted
027:063   High is Allah above what they associate **with** Him!
027:087   will be smitten **with** terror those who are in the heavens,
027:088   for He is well acquainted **with** all that ye do.
028:010   had We not strengthened her heart (**with** faith),
028:015   and Moses struck him **with** his fist and killed him.
028:023   He said: "What is the matter **with** you?"
028:029   and was travelling **with** his family, he perceived a fire
028:034   so send him **with** me as a helper,
028:035   **with** Our Signs shall ye triumph,-
028:035   and invest you both **with** authority, so they
028:036   When Moses came to them **with** Our Clear Signs,
028:037   who it is that comes **with** guidance from Him
028:045   Who send messengers (**with** inspiration).
028:054   that they avert Evil **with** Good, and that
028:057   They say: "If we were to follow the guidance **with** thee,
028:060   but that which is **with** Allah is better and more enduring:
028:077   "But seek, **with** the (wealth) which Allah has bestowed
028:087   these who join gods **with** Allah.
029:005   For those whose hopes are in the meeting **with** Allah
029:006   And if any strive (**with** might and main), they do
029:008   to join **with** Me (in worship) anything of which
029:010   "We have (always) been **with** you!"
029:013   and (other) burdens along **with** their own,
029:023   and the Meeting, **with** Him (in the Hereafter),-
029:031   Our Messengers came to Abraham **with** the good news,
029:036   nor commit evil on the earth, **with** intent to do mischief."
029:039   there came to them Moses **with** Clear Signs,
029:039   but they behaved **with** insolence on the earth;
029:040   We sent a violent tornado (**with** showers of stones),
029:046   And dispute ye not **with** the People of the Book,
029:046   unless it be **with** those of them who do wrong
029:048   (able) to transcribe it **with** thy right hand: in that case,
029:049   evident in the hearts of those endowed **with** knowledge:
029:050   Say: "The Signs are indeed **with** Allah: and I
029:069   for verily Allah is **with** those who do right.
030:004   **with** Allah is the Command in the Past and in
030:005   **With** the help of Allah.
030:008   deny the meeting **with** their Lord (at the Resurrection)!
030:009   there came to them their messengers **with** Clear (Signs),
030:012   the guilty will be struck dumb **with** despair.
030:021   that ye may dwell in tranquillity **with** them,
030:024   and **with** it gives life to the earth after it is dead:
030:031   and be not ye among those who join gods **with** Allah,-
030:032   each party rejoicing in that which is **with** itself!
030:039   will have no increase **with** Allah:
030:047   and they came to them **with** Clear Signs:
030:049   just before this-they were dumb **with** despair!
030:056   But those endued **with** knowledge and faith
031:010   standing firm, lest it should shake **with** you;
031:013   "O my son! join not in worship (others) **with** Allah:
031:015   in this life **with** justice (and consideration),
031:015   join in worship **with** Me things of which thou
031:017   and bear **with** patient constancy whatever betide
031:027   **with** seven Oceans behind it to add to its (supply),
031:029   and that Allah is well acquainted **with** all that ye do?
031:034   Verily the knowledge of the Hour is **with** Allah (alone).
031:034   and He is acquainted (**with** all things).
031:034   Verily **with** Allah is full knowledge and He
032:010   Nay, they deny the meeting **with** their Lord!
032:013   "I will fill Hell **with** Jinns and men all together."
032:015   nor are they (ever) puffed up **with** pride.

WITH (continued)

032:024   so long as they persevered **with** patience and continued
033:002   for Allah is well acquainted **with** (all) that ye do.
033:014   have brought it to pass, **with** none but a brief delay!
033:015   already covenanted **with** Allah not to turn their backs,
033:015   and a covenant **with** Allah must (surely) be answered
033:019   they will smite you **with** sharp tongues,
033:023   been true to their Covenant **with** Allah:
033:032   in whose heart is a disease should be moved **with** desire:
033:037   Then when Zaid had dissolved (his marriage) **with** her,
033:037   to the Believers in (the matter of) marriage **with** the wives
033:037   when the latter have dissolved (their marriage) **with** them.
033:041   O ye who believe! remember **with** much remembrance;
033:050   of thy maternal uncles and aunts, who migrated **with** thee;
033:051   **with** that which thou hast to give them.
033:056   and salute him **with** all respect.
033:063   say, "The knowledge thereof is **with** Allah (alone)":
033:068   Chastisement and curse them **with** a very great Curse!"
033:073   (**With** the result) that Allah has to punish the Hypocrites,
034:008   falsehood against Allah, or is he afflicted **with** madness."
034:010   echo ye back the Praises of Allah **with** him!
034:023   "No intercession can avail **with** Him, except for
034:027   me those whom ye have joined **with** Him as partners:
034:033   They are filled **with** remorse.
034:034   "We believe not in the (Message) **with** which ye have
034:051   If thou couldst but see when they will quake **with** terror:
034:053   **with** regard to the Unseen from a position far off?
034:054   as was in the past **with** their partisans:
035:001   the angels messengers **with** wings,-two, or three
035:011   or lays down (her load), but **with** His knowledge.
035:024   Verily We have sent thee **with** truth,
035:025   to whom came their messengers **with** Clear Signs,
035:027   **With** it We then bring out produce of various
035:031   **with** respect to His servants-well acquainted and Fully
035:033   will they be adorned **with** bracelets of gold and pearls;
035:043   but looking the way the ancients were dealt **with**?
036:014   but We strengthened them **with** a third:
036:019   They said: "Your evil omens are **with** yourselves:
036:034   We produce therein orchards **with** date-palms and Vines,
036:047   "Spend ye of (the bounties) **with** which Allah has
037:006   the lower heaven **with** beauty (in) the stars,-
037:025   "What is the matter **with** you that ye help not each other/
037:034   Verily that is how We shall deal **with** Sinners.
037:035   would puff themselves up **with** Pride,
037:037   Nay! he has come **with** the (very) Truth,
037:048   **with** big eyes (of wonder and beauty).
037:084   Behold, He approached his Lord **with** a sound heart.
037:092   "What is the matter **with** you that ye speak not?"
037:093   striking (them) **with** the right hand.
037:094   Then came (the worshippers) **with** hurried steps, to him.
037:102   (the son) reached (the age of) (serious) work **with** him,
037:107   And We ransomed him **with** a momentous sacrifice:
037:154   What is the matter **with** you? How judge ye?
038:010   mount up **with** the ropes and means (to reach that end)!
038:018   in unison **with** him, Our Praises, at eventide and a break
038:019   all **with** him did turn (to Allah).
038:022   now between us **with** truth,
038:022   decide and treat us not **with** injustice,
038:041   "Satan has afflicted me **with** distress and suffering"!
038:042   "Strike **with** thy foot: here is (water) wherein to wish,
038:059   Here is a troop rushing headlong **with** you!
038:062   they will say: "How is it **with** us that we see not men
038:075   thyself to one whom I have created **with** My hands?

WITH (continued)

038:085   fill Hell **with** thee and those that follow thee,-every one."
039:007   If ye are grateful, He is pleased **with** you.
039:009   endued **with** understanding that receive admonition.
039:011   to serve Allah **with** sincere devotion;
039:014   Allah I serve, **with** my sincere (and exclusive) devotion:
039:016   **with** this doth Allah warn off His servants: "O my
039:018   and those are the ones endued **with** understanding.
039:023   in the form of a Book, consistent **with** itself,
039:029   belonging to many partners at variance **with** each other,
039:036   to frighten thee **with** other (gods) besides Him!
039:045   who believe not in the Hereafter are filled **with** disgust,
039:045   behold, they are filled **with** joy!
039:065   "If thou wert to join (gods **with** Allah), truly fruitless
039:069   And the earth will shine **with** the light of its Lord:
040:012   ye believe! the command is **with** Allah, Most High,
040:014   Call ye, then, upon Allah **with** sincere devotion to Him,
040:020   And Allah will judge **with** (Justice and) Truth:
040:022   there came to them their messengers **with** Clear (Signs),
040:023   We sent Moses, **with** Our Signs and Authority manifest,
040:025   "Slay the sons of those who believe **with** him,
040:028   indeed come to you **with** Clear (Signs) from your Lord?
040:034   there came Joseph in times gone by, **with** Clear Signs,
040:042   and to join **with** Him partners of whom I have no
040:047   Behold, they will dispute **with** each other
040:050   to you your messengers **with** Clear Signs?"
040:070   and the (revelations) **with** which We sent
040:083   when their messengers came to them **with** Clear Signs,
040:084   and we reject the partners we used to join **with** Him."
040:085   **with** His servants (from the most ancient times).
041:006   And woe to those who join gods **with** Allah,-
041:009   And do ye join equals **with** Him?
041:012   and We adorned the lower heaven **with** lights,
041:012   and (provided it) **with** guard.
041:014   so we disbelieve in the Message you were sent **with**.
041:034   Repel (Evil) **with** what is better:
041:054   doubt concerning the Meeting **with** their Lord?
042:010   the decision thereof is **with** Allah:
042:027   for He is **with** His Servants well-acquainted,
042:036   but that which is **with** Allah is better
042:042   oppress men **with** wrong-doing and insolently
042:045   humbleness (and) looking **with** a stealthy glance.
042:051   to reveal, **with** Allah's permission, what Allah
043:004   of the Book, **with** Us, high (in dignity),
043:015   to some of His servants a share **with** Him, truly is man
043:017   and he is filled **with** inward grief!
043:018   in a dispute (to be associated **with** Allah)?
043:024   we deny that which ye (prophets) are sent **with**."
043:046   **with** Our Signs, to Pharaoh and his Chiefs:
043:047   But when he came to them **with** Our Signs, behold,
043:048   and We seized them **with** Punishment, in order
043:049   they Lord for us according to his covenant **with** thee;
043:053   **with** him angels accompanying him in procession?"
043:063   When Jesus came **with** Clear Signs,
043:063   "Now have I come to you **with** Wisdom,
043:083   and play (**with** vanities) until they meet that Day of theirs,
043:085   **with** Him is the knowledge of the Hour
043:086   bears witness to the Truth, and **with** full knowledge.
044:016   The day We shall seize you **with** a mighty onslaught:
044:019   for I come to you **with** authority manifest.
044:020   "For me, I have sought Safety **with** my Lord
044:023   "March forth **with** My servants by night: for ye
044:054   to maidens **with** beautiful, big, and lustrous eyes.

045:021   as equal **with** those who believe and do righteous deeds,-
045:029   "This Our Record speaks about you **with** truth:
046:009   nor do I know what will be **with** me or **with** you.
046:010   of Israel testifies to its similarity (**with** earlier scriptures),
046:020   ye be recompensed **with** a Chastisement of humiliation:
046:022   upon us the (calamity) **with** which thou dost threaten us,
046:023   knowledge (of when it will come) is only **with** Allah:
046:026   and We had endowed them **with** (faculties of) hearing,
046:033   and never wearied **with** their creation,
047:004   (He lets you find) in other to test you, some **with** others.
047:013   **with** more power than thy city which has driven thee out,
047:020   is a disease looking at thee **with** a look of one in at swoon
047:025   and buoyed them up **with** false hopes.
047:035   when ye are the Uppermost: for Allah is **with** you,
048:003   And that Allah may help thee **with** powerful help.
048:010   what he has covenanted **with** Allah,-
048:011   They say **with** their tongues what is not
048:011   acquainted **with** all that ye do.
048:011   power at all (to intervene) on your behalf **with** Allah,
048:016   He will punish you **with** a grievous Chastisement."
048:017   (Allah) will punish him **with** a grievous Chastisement.
048:018   and He rewarded them **with** a speedy Victory;
048:025   the Unbelievers among them **with** a grievous punishment.
048:027   if Allah wills, **with** minds secure, heads shaved,
048:028   His Messenger **with** Guidance and the Religion
048:029   it fills the Unbelievers **with** rage at him.
048:029   and those who are **with** him are strong
048:029   (filling) the sowers **with** wonder and delight.
049:006   if a sinner comes to you **with** any news,
049:009   then make peace between them **with** justice, and be fair:
049:009   until it complies **with** the command of Allah;
049:013   and is well acquainted (**with** all things).
049:015   but have striven **with** their belongings and their persons
050:004   **with** Us is a Record guarding (the full account).
050:009   Rain charged **with** blessing, and We
050:010   tall (and stately) palm-trees, **with** shoots of fruit-stalks,
050:015   Were We then weary **with** the first Creation,
050:021   **with** each will be an (angel) to drive,
050:023   "Here is (his record) ready **with** me!"
050:028   "Dispute not **with** each other in My Presence:
050:029   "The Word changes not with Me, and I do not
050:035   all that they wish,-and there is more **with** Us.
050:039   Bear, then **with** patience, all that they say,
050:045   So admonish **with** the Qur'an such as fear My Warning!
051:003   And those that flow **with** ease and gentleness;
051:007   By the Sky **with** (its) numerous Paths,
051:028   gave him glad tidings a son endowed **with** knowledge.
051:038   We sent him to Pharaoh, **with** authority manifest.
051:047   We have built the Firmament **with** might:
051:051   And make not another an object of worship **with** Allah:
052:006   And by the Ocean filled **with** Swell;-
052:016   to you whether ye bear it **with** patience, or not:
052:019   "Eat and drink ye, **with** profit and health,
052:020   **with** beautiful, big and lustrous eyes.
052:020   They will recline (**with** ease) on couches
052:023   one **with** another, a cup free of frivolity,
052:031   I too will wait along **with** you!"
052:037   Or are the Treasures of they Lord **with** them,
052:040   so that they are burdened **with** a load of debt?-
052:043   the things they associate **with** Him!
053:006   Endued **with** Wisdom: for he appeared (in stately form)
053:012   **Will ye them dispute with** him concerning what he saw?

WITH (continued)

053:016 Behold, the Lote-tree was shrouded **with** what shrouds.
053:027 name the angels **with** female names.
053:031 and He rewards those who do good, **with** what is best.
053:036 Nay, is he not acquainted **with** what is in the books
053:041 Then will he be rewarded **with** a reward complete;
054:008 Hastening, **with** eyes transfixed, towards the
054:011 We opened the gates of heaven, **with** water pouring forth.
054:012 And We caused the earth to gush forth **with** springs,
054:013 made of broad planks and caulked **with** palm-fibre:
054:014 a recompense to one who had been rejected (**with** scorn)!
054:034 against them a violent tornado **with** showers of stones,
054:042 but We seized them **with** the Seizure of a Mighty,
054:055 In a sure abode **with** a Sovereign Omnipotent.
055:009 So establish weight **with** justice and fall not short
055:012 Also corn **with** (its) leaves and stalk for fodder,
056:015 on couches encrusted (**with** gold and precious stones),
056:018 **With** goblets, (shining) beakers, and cups
056:020 And **with** fruits, any that they may select;
056:022 **with** beautiful, big, and lustrous eyes,-
056:029 Among Talh trees **with** flowers (or fruits)
056:055 diseased camels raging **with** thirst!
056:066 (Saying), "We indeed left **with** debts (for nothing):
056:093 For him is Entertainment **with** Boiling Water,
057:004 And He is **with** you wheresoever ye may be.
057:008 How is it **with** you that you not believe in Allah?-
057:010 And Allah is well acquainted **with** all that you do.
057:010 How is it **with** you that you spend not in the cause
057:010 before the Victory, (**with** those who did so later).
057:013 So a wall will be put up betwixt them, **with** a gate therein.
057:014 (Those without) will call out, "Were we not **with** you?"
057:025 We sent aforetime our messengers **with** Clear Signs and
057:025 and sent down **with** them the Book and the Balance
057:027 We followed them up **with** (others of) Our messengers:
058:001 of the woman who pleads **with** thee concerning her
058:003 well-acquainted **with** (all) that ye do.
058:007 but He is **with** them, wheresoever they be:
058:011 and Allah is well-acquainted **with** all ye do.
058:013 your private consultation (**with** him)?
058:013 and Allah is well-acquainted **with** all that ye do.
058:022 Allah will be well pleased **with** them, and they **with** Him
058:022 and strengthened them **with** a spirit from Himself.
059:002 take warning, then, O ye **with** eyes (to see)!
059:005 cover **with** shame the rebellious transgressors.
059:006 ye made no expedition **with** either cavalry or camelry:
059:011 "If ye are expelled, We too will go out **with** you,
059:012 If they are expelled, never will they go out **with** them;
059:018 for Allah is well-acquainted **with** (all) that ye do.
060:004 example (to follow) in Abraham and those **with** him,
060:008 **with** regard to those who fight you not for (your) Faith
060:008 from dealing kindly and justly **with** them:
060:009 **with** regard to those who fight you not for (your), Faith,
060:010 He judges (**with** justice) between you.
060:012 in worship any other thing whatever **with** Allah,
061:006 But when he came to them **with** Clear Signs,
061:008 Allah's Light (by blowing) **with** their mouths:
061:009 He Who has sent His Messenger **with** Guidance and the
061:011 Cause of Allah, **with** your wealth and your persons:
062:005 entrusted **with** the (obligations of) Taurat,
063:007 nothing on those who are **with** Allah's Messenger,
063:011 and Allah is well acquainted **with** (all) that ye do.
064:003 He has created the heavens and the earth **with** the truth,
064:006 because there came to them messengers **with** Clear Signs,

WITH (continued)

064:008 And Allah is well-acquainted **with** all that ye do.
064:015 Whereas Allah, **with** Him is the highest Reward.
065:002 two persons from among you, endued **with** justice,
065:002 on equitable terms or part **with** them on equitable terms;
065:008 and We chastised them **with** a horrible Chastisement.
066:003 He said, "He told me Who is the Knower, The Aware."
066:008 O ye who believe! turn to Allah **with** sincere repentance:
066:008 humiliated the Prophet and those who believe **with** him.
066:009 Unbelievers and the Hypocrites, and be harsh **with** them.
066:010 "Enter ye the Fire along **with** (others) that enter!"
067:005 adorned the lowest heaven **with** Lamps,
067:008 Almost bursting **with** fury:
067:017 against you a violent tornado (**with** showers of stones),
067:021 provide you **with** Sustenance if He were to
067:022 one who walks headlong **with** his face grovelling,
067:026 "As to the knowledge of the time it is **with** Allah alone:
067:028 See ye?- if Allah were to destroy me, and those **with** me,
067:030 who the can supply you **with** clear-flowing water?"
068:006 Which of you is afflicted **with** madness.
068:011 A slanderer, going about **with** calumnies,
068:013 Violent (and cruel),-**with** all that, of a doubtful birth,-
068:034 for the Righteous are Gardens of Delight, **with** their Lord.
068:036 What is the matter **with** you? How judge ye?
068:039 Or have ye Covenants **with** Us on oath,
068:044 Then leave Me alone **with** such as reject this Message:
068:046 so that they are burdened **with** a load of debt?-
068:048 So wait **with** patience for the command of thy Lord,
068:051 thee up **with** their eyes when they hear the Message;
069:010 so He punished them **with** an abundant Penalty.
069:024 "Eat ye and drink ye, **with** full satisfaction;
070:030 Except **with** their wives and the (captives)
070:036 Now what is the matter **with** the Unbelievers
071:001 (**with** the Command): "Do thou warn thy People
071:007 covered themselves **with** their garments, grown
071:013 "`What is the matter **with** you, that ye are not conscious
072:002 We shall not join (in worship) any (gods) **with** our Lord,
072:006 who took shelter **with** persons among the Jinns,
072:008 filled **with** stern guards and flaming fires.
072:018 so invoke not any one along **with** Allah;
072:020 and I join not **with** Him any (false god)."
072:024 (**with** their own eyes) that which they are promised,-
072:026 nor does He make any one acquainted **with** His Secrets.-
072:028 and He encompasses all that is **with** them, and takes
073:007 prolonged occupation **with** ordinary duties:
073:010 And have patience **with** what they say, and leave
073:010 and leave them **with** noble (dignity).
073:011 and bear **with** them for a little while.
073:011 And leave Me (alone to deal **with**) those in
073:012 **With** Us are Fetters (to bind them), and a Fire
073:016 so We seized him **with** a heavy Punishment.
073:020 ye send forth for yourselves ye shall find it **with** Allah.
073:020 and so doth a party of those **with** thee.
074:011 Leave Me alone, (to deal) **with** the (creature)
074:017 Soon will I visit him **with** a mount of calamities!
074:045 "But we used to talk vanities **with** vain talkers;
074:049 Then what is the matter **with** them that they turn away
075:029 And one leg will be joined **with** another:
076:005 of a Cup (of Wine) mixed **with** Kafur,-
076:012 He will reward them **with** a Garden and (garments
076:017 of a Cup mixed **with** Zanjabil,-
076:021 and they will be adorned **with** Bracelets of silver;
076:024 Therefore be patient **with** constancy to the Command

WITH (continued)

077:018 Thus do We deal **with** men of sin.
078:037 none shall have power to argue **with** Him.
079:001 (the souls of the wicked) **with** violence;
079:012 They say: "It would, in that case, be a return **with** loss!"
079:029 Its night doth He endow **with** darkness,
079:029 and its splendor doth He bring out (**with** light).
079:043 Wherein art thou (concerned) **with** the declaration
079:044 **With** they Lord is the final end of it.
080:009 And **with** fear (in his heart),
080:030 And enclosed Gardens, dense **with** lofty trees,
081:001 When the sun (**with** its spacious light) is folded up;
081:004 When the she-camels, ten months **with** young,
081:006 When the oceans boil over **with** a swell;
081:007 the souls are sorted out, (Being joined, like **with** like);
081:020 Endued **with** Power, held in honour by the Lord
081:021 **With** authority there, (and) faithful of his trust.
081:028 (**With** profit) to whoever among you wills to go straight:
082:019 will be (wholly) **with** Allah.
083:025 Their thirst will be slaked **with** Pure Wine sealed;
083:027 **With** it will be (given) a mixture of Tasnim:
084:020 What then is the matter **with** them, that they
085:001 By the Sky, **with** its constellations;
085:005 Fire supplied (abundantly) **with** Fuel:
088:009 Pleased **with** their Striving,-
088:024 Allah will chastise him **with** a mighty Chastisement.
089:006 how they Lord dealt **with** the 'Ad (people),-
089:007 Of the (city of) Iram, **with** lofty pillars,
089:009 And **with** the Thamud (people), who cut
089:010 And **with** Pharaoh, lord of Stakes?
089:019 And ye devour inheritance-all **with** greed,
089:020 And ye love wealth **with** inordinate love!
090:015 To the orphan **with** claims of relationship,
093:009 Therefore, treat not the orphan **with** harshness,
094:005 So, verily, **with** every difficulty, there is relief:
094:006 Verily, **with** every difficulty there is relief.
096:018 will call on the angels of punishment (to deal **with** him)!
098:008 Allah well pleased **with** them, and they **with** Him:
098:008 Their reward is **with** Allah:
099:003 'What is the matter **with** her?'-
100:001 By the (Steeds) that run, **with** panting (breath),
100:011 well-acquainted **with** them, (Even to) that Day?
102:005 Nay, were ye to know **with** certainty of mind,
102:007 Again, ye shall see it **with** certainty of sight!
105:001 how thy Lord dealt with the Companions of the Elephant?
105:004 Striking them **with** stones of baked clay.
106:002 familiarity **with** the journeys by winter and summer,-
106:004 Who provides them **with** food against hunger,
106:004 and **with** security against fear (of danger).
113:001 Say: I seek refuge **with** the Lord of the Dawn,
114:001 I seek refuge **with** the Lord and Cherisher of Mankind,

WITHDRAW

004:090 therefore if they **withdraw** from you but fight you not,
004:091 if they **withdraw** not from you nor give you (guarantees)
011:009 from Ourselves, and then **withdraw** it from him,
036:037 We **withdraw** therefrom the Day, and behold

WITHDRAWN

033:020 They think that the Confederates have not **withdrawn**;
045:023 after Allah (has **withdrawn** Guidance)?

WITHDRAWS

043:036 If anyone **withdraws** himself from remembrance
114:004 (of Evil), who **withdraws** (after his whisper),-

WITHDREW

019:016 when she **withdrew** from her family to a place
020:060 So Pharaoh **withdrew**: he concerted his plan,

WITHERED

006:059 nor anything fresh or dry (green or **withered**),
012:043 seven green ears of corn, and seven (others) **withered**.
012:046 of corn and (seven) others **withered**:
036:039 like the old (and **withered**) lower part of date-stalk.

WITHERS

039:021 then it **withers**; thou wilt see it grow yellow;
057:020 delight (the hearts of) the tillers; soon it **withers**;

WITHHOLD

003:180 **withhold** of the gifts which Allah hath given them
007:085 nor **withhold** from the people the things that are their
011:044 and O shy! **withhold** (thy rain)!"
011:085 nor **withhold** from the people the things that are their
026:183 And **withhold** not things justly due to men,
035:002 His Mercy doth bestow no mankind none can **withhold**:
035:002 what He doth **withhold**, none can grant,
038:039 whether thou bestow them (on others) or **withhold** them,
047:037 and press you, ye would covetously **withhold**,
067:021 with Sustenance is he were to **withhold** His provision?
069:047 Nor could any of you **withhold** him (from Our wrath).
081:024 Neither doth he **withhold** Grudgingly a knowledge

WITHHOLDS

022:065 He **withholds** the sky from falling on the earth

WITHIN

002:050 drowned Pharaoh's people **within** your very sight.
002:124 is not **within** the reach of evil-doers."
005:094 of game well **within** reach of your hands and
006:002 yet ye doubt **within** yourselves!
013:040 (**within** thy lifetime) part of what We promised
014:046 (well) **within** the sight of Allah, even though
016:066 From what is **within** their bodies, between
016:069 from **within** their bodies a drink of varying
022:020 With it will be melted what is **within** their bodies,
023:021 from **within** their bodies We produce (milk)
023:027 "Construct the Ark **within** Our sight and under Our
024:035 is as if there were a Niche and **within** it a Lamp:
030:004 **Within** a few years, with Allah is the Command in
030:056 "Indeed ye did tarry, **within** Allah's Decree,
034:046 or (it may be) singly,-and reflect (**within** yourselves):
041:047 (**within** her womb) nor bring forth (young),
048:021 which are not **within** your power, but which Allah has
057:004 **within** the earth and what comes forth out of it,
057:013 **Within** it will be Mercy throughout, and without
084:004 And casts forth what is **within** it and becomes
099:002 And the Earth throws up her burden (from **within**),

WITHOUT

002:002 in it is guidance sure; **without** doubt,
002:028 Seeing that ye were **without** life,
002:061 and slaying His Messengers **without** just cause.
002:071 or water the fields; sound and **without** blemish."
002:089 they had prayed for victory against those **without** Faith.
002:089 but the curse of Allah is on those **without** Faith,
002:102 taught anyone (such things) **without** saying: "We are
002:104 to those **without** Faith is a grievous punishment.
002:105 **without** Faith among the people of the Book
002:108 hath strayed **without** doubt from the even way.
002:118 Say those **without** knowledge: "Why speaketh not
002:173 one is forced by necessity **without** wilful disobedience,
002:212 His abundance **without** measures on whom He will.

WITHOUT (continued)

002:214 ye shall enter the Garden (of Bliss) **without** such (trials)
002:240 a year's maintenance **without** expulsion;
003:008 Grantor of bounties **without** measure.
003:025 just what it has earned, **without** (favour or) injustice?
003:027 to whom Thou pleasest, **without** measure."
003:037 to whom He pleases, **without** measure."
003:068 **Without** doubt, among men, the nearest of kin
003:142 enter Heaven **without** Allah testing those
003:153 **without** even casting a side glance at anyone,
003:179 ye have a reward great **without** measure.
004:142 they stand **without** earnestness, to be seen
005:058 a people **without** understanding.
005:068 over (these) people **without** Faith.
006:081 **without** any warrant having been given to you?
006:119 do mislead (men) by low desires **without** knowledge.
006:122 Thus to those **without** Faith their own deeds seem
006:140 from folly, **without** knowledge, and forbid food which
006:141 with trellises and **without**, and dates, and tilth
006:144 to lead astray men **without** knowledge? For
006:145 is forced by necessity, **without** wilful disobedience,
007:027 (only) to those **without** Faith.
007:071 ye and your fathers,-**without** authority from Allah?
007:138 He said: "Surely ye are a people **without** knowledge."
007:205 and remember **without** loudness in words, in the
008:065 for these are a people **without** understanding.
009:006 are men **without** knowledge.
009:026 thus doth He reward those **without** Faith.
009:042 they would (all) **without** doubt have followed thee,
010:042 even though they are **without** understanding.
011:015 their deeds therein,-**without** diminution.
011:022 **Without** a doubt, these are the very ones who
011:075 For Abraham was, **without** doubt, forbearing
011:108 thy Lord willeth: a gift **without** break.
011:109 their portion **without** (the least) abatement.
012:070 ye are thieves, **without** doubt!"
012:106 not in Allah **without** associating (others as partners)
013:002 He Who raised the heavens **without** any pillars that ye
013:014 for the prayer of those **without** Faith is nothing
013:028 for **without** doubt in the remembrance of Allah
014:037 in a valley **without** cultivation, but Thy
015:009 We have, **without** doubt, sent down the Message;
015:089 warneth openly and **without** ambiguity,"-
016:025 burdens of those **without** knowledge, whom they
016:046 to and fro, **without** a chance of their frustrating Him?-
016:062 **without** doubt for them is the Fire,
016:109 **Without** doubt, in the Hereafter they will be the losers.
016:115 one is forced by necessity, **without** wilful disobedience,
018:008 but as dust and dry soil (**without** growth or herbage).
019:068 So, by thy Lord, **without** doubt, We shall
020:022 (and shining), **without** harm (or stain),-
020:033 "That we may celebrate Thy praise **without** stint,
020:034 "And remember Thee **without** stint:
020:077 and **without** (any other) fear."
020:077 **without** fear of being overtaken (by Pharaoh)
020:082 "But, **without** doubt, I am (also) He that forgives again
021:025 We send before thee **without** this inspiration sent by Us
021:089 "O my Lord! leave me not **without** offspring,
022:003 are such as dispute about Allah, **without** knowledge,
022:008 such as one as disputes about Allah **without** knowledge,
022:008 **without** guidance, and **without** a Book of Enlightenment,-
024:038 doth provide for those whom He will, **without** measure.
026:196 **Without** doubt it is (announced) in the revealed Books

WITHOUT (continued)

027:012 his hosts crush you (under foot) **without** knowing it."
028:032 and it will come forth white **without** stain (or harm),
029:045 of Allah is the greatest (thing in life) **without** doubt.
031:006 purchase idle tales, **without** knowledge (or meaning),
031:010 He created the heavens **without** any pillars
031:019 harshest of sounds **without** doubt is the braying of the
031:020 **without** guidance, and **without** a Book to enlighten them!
031:020 those who dispute about Allah, **without** knowledge
033:053 taken your meal, disperse, **without** seeking familiar talk.
035:024 **without** a warner having lived among them (in the past).
038:009 the Grantor of Bounties **without** measure?
038:027 Not **without** purpose did We create heaven and earth and
038:035 for thou art the Grantor of Bounties (**without** measure)."
039:010 will truly receive a reward **without** measure!"
039:028 a Qur'an in Arabic, **without** any crookedness (therein):
040:035 **without** any authority that hath reached them.
040:040 therein will they have abundance **without** measure.
040:043 "**Without** doubt ye do call me to one who has no claim
040:050 But the Prayer of those **without** Faith is nothing
040:051 We will, **without** doubt, help Our messengers
040:056 of Allah **without** any authority bestowed on them,-
042:021 some religion **without** the permission of Allah?
046:017 have passed before me (**without** rising again)?"
046:020 for that ye were arrogant on earth **without** just cause,
048:025 guilt would have accrued to you **without** (your)
048:027 heads shaved, hair cur short, and **without** fear.
049:004 from **without** the Inner Apartments-most of
052:026 not **without** fear for the sake of our people.
055:033 pass ye! not **without** authority shall ye be able to pass!
056:028 (They will be) among lote-trees **without** thorns,
057:013 Within it will be Mercy throughout, and **without** it,
057:014 (Those **without**) will call out, "Were we not with you?"
064:006 But Allah can do **without** (them):
074:010 Far from easy for those **without** Faith.
075:036 be left uncontrolled, (**without** purpose)?
081:023 And **without** doubt he saw him in the clear horizon.
085:016 Doer (**without** let) of all that He intends.

WITHSTAND

024:063 who **withstand** the Messenger's order, lest some

WITNESS

002:084 And to this ye were **witness**.
002:143 and the Messenger a **witness** over yourselves;
002:204 to **witness** about what is in his heart;
002:282 and let neither scribe nor **witness** suffer harm.
003:018 that is the **witness** of Allah, His angels,
003:052 and do thou bear **witness** that we are Muslims.
003:053 then write us down among those who bear **witness**."
003:064 say ye: "Bear **witness** that we (at least) are Muslims
003:081 He said: "Then bear **witness**, and I am with you
003:086 and bore **witness** that the Messenger was true
003:098 when Allah is Himself **witness** to all ye do?
004:033 For truly Allah is **witness** to all things.
004:041 How then if We brought from each People a **witness**,
004:041 a **witness** against these People!
004:079 and enough is Allah for a **witness**.
004:159 He will be a **witness** against them;
004:166 But Allah beareth **witness** that what He hath sent
004:166 and the angels bear **witness**:
004:166 but enough is Allah for a **Witness**.
005:107 "We affirm that our **witness** is truer than that
005:111 and do thou bear **witness** that we bow to Allah
005:117 and Thou art a **Witness** to all things.

WITNESS (continued)

005:117 and I was a **witness** over them whilst I
006:019 Can ye possibly bear **witness** that besides Allah there
006:019 Say: "Allah is **Witness** between me and you:
006:019 Say: "Nay! I cannot bear **witness!**"
006:130 they bear **witness** that they rejected Faith.
006:130 "We bear **witness** against ourselves."
007:037 and they will bear **witness** against themselves,
009:017 of Allah while they **witness** against their owns souls
010:029 "Enough is Allah for a **witness** between us and you:
010:046 ultimately Allah is **witness** to all that they do.
011:017 and followed by a **witness** from Him and before
011:054 He said; "Call Allah to **witness**, and do ye bear **witness**,
012:026 And one of her household saw (this) and bore **witness**,
012:066 be Allah the **Witness** and Guardian!"
012:081 we bear **witness** only to what we know,
013:043 "Enough for a **witness** between me and you is Allah,
016:084 the Day We shall raise from all Peoples a **Witness**:
016:089 bring thee as a **witness** against these (thy people):
016:089 We shall raise all peoples a **witness** against them,
017:096 Say: "Enough is Allah for a **witness** between me
018:051 I called them not to **witness** the creation
021:056 and I am a **witness** to this (truth).
021:061 the eyes of the people, that they may bear **witness:**"
021:078 We did **witness** their judgment.
022:017 for Allah is **witness** of all things.
022:028 "That they may **witness** the benefits (provided)
022:078 that the Messenger may be a **witness** for you,
024:002 the Believers **witness** their punishment.
024:008 the wife, if she bears **witness** four times
024:024 bear **witness** against them as to their actions.
025:072 Those who **witness** no falsehood, and, if
028:028 Be Allah a **witness** to what we say."
028:044 nor wast thou a **witness** (of those events).
028:075 And form each people shall We draw a **witness**,
029:052 "Enough is Allah for a **Witness** between me and you:
033:045 O Prophet! Truly We have sent thee as a **Witness**,
033:055 for Allah is **Witness** to all things.
034:047 and He is **Witness** to all things."
036:065 and their feet bear **witness**, to all that they did.
041:020 and their skins will bear **witness** against them,
041:021 "Why bear ye **witness** against us?"
041:022 and your skins should bear **witness** against you!
041:047 "We do assure Thee not one of us can bear **witness!**"
041:053 enough that thy Lord doth **witness** all things?
043:019 Did they **witness** their creation?
043:051 (**witness**) these streams flowing underneath my (palace)?
043:086 only he who bears **witness** to the Truth,
046:008 Enough is He for a **witness** between me and you!
046:010 and a **witness** from among the Children of Israel
048:008 We have truly sent thee as a **witness**,
048:028 and enough is Allah for a **Witness**.
050:021 and an (angel) to bear **witness**.
058:006 for Allah is **Witness** to all things.
059:011 But Allah is **witness** that they are indeed liars.
063:001 they say, "We bear **witness** that thou art indeed the
063:001 And Allah beareth **witness** that the Hypocrites
065:002 for **witness** two persons from among you, endued with
069:038 So I do call to **witness** what ye see
070:040 Now I do call to **witness** the Lord of all points
073:015 a Messenger, to be a **witness** concerning you,
081:015 So verily I call to **witness** the Planets-that recede,
083:021 To which bear **witness** those Nearest (to Allah).

WITNESS (continued)

084:016 So I do call to **witness** the ruddy glow of Sunset;
085:003 and the subject of the **witness;**-
085:009 And Allah is **Witness** to all things.
100:007 And to that (fact) he bears **witness** (by his deeds);

WITNESSED

017:078 in the morning prayer for the recital of dawn is **witnessed**.
085:007 And they **witnessed** (all) that they were doing

WITNESSES

002:023 and call your **witnesses** or helpers
002:133 Were ye **witnesses** when Death appeared
002:143 That ye might be **witnesses** over the nations,
002:282 But take **witnesses** whenever ye make a commercial
002:282 And get two **witnesses**, out or your own men.
002:282 a man and two women, such as ye choose, for **witnesses**,
002:282 The **witnesses** should not refuse when they are called on
003:070 of which ye are (yourselves) **witnesses**?
003:081 and I am with you among the **witnesses**."
003:099 yourselves **witnesses** (to Allah's Covenant)?
004:006 take **witnesses** in their presence:
004:015 **witnesses** from amongst you against them;
004:135 stand out firmly for justice, as **witnesses** to Allah,
005:008 as **witnesses** to fair dealing, and let not the hatred
005:044 and they were **witnesses** thereto:
005:083 write us down among the **witnesses**.
005:106 (take) **witnesses** among yourselves when making
005:113 be **witnesses** to the miracle.
006:150 If they bring such **witnesses**, be not
006:150 Say: "Bring forward your **witnesses** to prove
010:061 We are **Witnesses** thereof when ye are deeply engrossed
011:018 and the **witnesses** will say. "These are the ones who lied
022:078 and ye be **witnesses** for mankind!
024:004 and produce not four **witnesses**,
024:013 Why did they not bring four **witnesses** to prove it?
024:013 When they have not brought the **witnesses**, such men,
037:150 and they are **witnesses** (thereto)?
039:069 and the **witnesses** will be brought forward;
040:051 and on the Day when the **Witnesses** will stand forth,-
050:037 or who gives ear and earnestly **witnesses**.
085:003 By one that **witnesses**, and the subject of the witness;-

WIVES

002:187 night of the fasts, is the approach to your **wives**.
002:187 do not associate with your **wives** while ye are in retreat
002:223 Your **wives** are as a tilth unto you so approach
002:226 an oath for abstention from their **wives**,
002:229 to take back any of your gifts from (your **wives**),
004:012 In what your **wives** leave, your share
004:023 (those who have been) **wives** of your son
004:023 foster-sisters; your **wives**, mothers;
004:023 born of your **wives** to whom ye have gone in,
004:129 between **wives** even if it is your ardent desire:
013:038 and appointed for them **wives** and children:
025:074 "Our Lord! Grant unto us **wives** and offspring
033:004 nor has He made your **wives** whom ye divorce
033:006 and his **wives** are their mothers.
033:037 with the **wives** of their adopted sons,
033:050 for them as to their **wives** and the captives
033:050 to thee thy **wives** to whom thou hast paid their
033:052 nor to change them for (other) **wives**, even though
033:059 O prophet! Tell thy **wives** and daughters, and the
037:022 "The wrong-doers and their **wives**, and the
040:008 their fathers, their **wives**, and their posterity!
043:070 ye and your **wives**, in (beauty and) rejoicing.

WIVES (continued)

058:002 If any men among you divorce their **wives** by Zihar
058:003 to their **wives** then wish to go back on the words
060:010 They are not lawful (**wives**) for the Unbelievers,
060:011 And if any of your **wives** deserts you to the
060:011 Then pay to those whose **wives** have deserted
064:014 among your **wives** and your children are (some
070:030 Except with their **wives** and the (captives)

WOE

002:079 Then **woe** to those who write the Book
002:079 **Woe** to them for what their hands do write,
005:031 "**Woe** is me!" said he: "Was I not even able
006:031 and they say: "Ah! **woe** unto us that we neglected;
018:042 and he could only say, "**Woe** is me! Would I had
018:049 "Ah! **woe** to us! what a book is this! It leaves
019:037 and **woe** to the Unbelievers because of the (coming)
020:061 Moses said to them: "**Woe** to you! Forge not ye a lie
021:014 "Ah! **woe** to us! we were indeed wrong-doers!"
021:018 Ah! **woe** be to you for the (false) things ye ascribe
021:046 they will then say, "**Woe** to us! we did wrong indeed!"
021:097 "Ah! **woe** to us! we were indeed heedless of this;
025:028 "Ah! **woe** is me! would that I had never taken
033:066 they will say: "**Woe** to us! would that we had
036:052 They will say: "Ah! **woe** unto us! Who hath
037:020 They will say, "Ah! **woe** to us! this is the Day of
038:027 But **woe** to the Unbelievers because of the Fire (of Hell!)
039:022 **Woe** to those whose hearts are hardened against
039:056 say: 'Ah! **woe** is me!-in that I neglected (my Duty)
041:006 And **woe** to those who join gods with Allah,-
043:065 then **woe** to the wrong-doers, from the Chastisement
045:007 **Woe** to each sinful imposter.
046:017 (and rebuke the son): "**Woe** to thee! have Faith!
051:060 **Woe**, then, to the Unbelievers, from the Day
052:011 Then **woe** that Day to the rejecters (of Truth);-
074:019 And **woe** to him! How he determined!-
074:020 Yea, **woe** to him: how he determined!-
075:034 **Woe** to thee, (O man!) yea, **woe**!
075:035 Again, **woe** to thee, (O man!), yea **woe**!
077:015 Ah **woe**, that Day, to the Rejecters of Truth!
077:019 Ah **woe**, that Day, to the Rejecters of Truth!
077:024 Ah **woe**, that Day, to the Rejecters of Truth!
077:028 Ah **woe**, that Day, to the Rejecters of Truth!
077:034 Ah **woe**, that Day, to the Rejecters of Truth!
077:037 Ah **woe**, that Day, to the Rejecters of Truth!
077:040 Ah **woe**, that Day, to the Rejecters of Truth!
077:045 Ah **woe**, that Day, to the Rejecters of Truth!
077:047 Ah **woe**, that Day, to the Rejecters of Truth!
077:049 Ah **woe**, that Day, to the Rejecters of Truth!
078:040 will say, "**Woe** unto me! Would that I were (mere) dust!
080:017 **Woe** to man! what hath made him reject Allah?
083:001 **Woe** to those that deal in fraud,-
083:010 **Woe**, that Day, to those that deny-
085:004 **Woe** to the makers of the pit (of Fire),
104:001 **Woe** to every (kind of) scandal-monger and backbiter,
107:004 So **woe** to the worshippers

WOEFUL

003:162 and whose abode is in Hell? A **woeful** refuge!
011:098 into the Fire but **woeful** indeed will be the place to which
011:099 and **woeful** is the gift which shall be given (Unto them)!

WOLF

012:013 I fear lest the **wolf** should devour him
012:014 They said: "If the **wolf** were to devour him
012:017 and the **wolf** devoured him.

WOMAN

002:178 the **woman** for the **woman**.
002:221 Do not marry Unbelieving **woman** until they believe:
002:221 a slave **woman** who believes is better than
002:221 is better than an unbelieving **woman**.
004:012 If the man or **woman** whose inheritance is in question,
004:129 but turn not away (from a **woman**) altogether,
004:176 if (such a deceased was) a **woman**, who left no child,
005:075 His mother was a **woman** of truth.
011:072 a child, seeing I am an old **woman**, and my husband
016:092 And be not like a **woman** who breaks into untwisted
016:097 man or **woman**, and has Faith, verily, to him
019:028 a man of evil, nor thy mother a **woman** unchaste!"
024:002 The **woman** and the man guilty of fornication,-
026:171 Except an old **woman** who lingered behind.
027:023 "I found (there) a **woman** ruling over them
033:036 It is not fitting for a Believer, man or **woman**,
033:050 and any believing **woman** who gives herself
037:135 Except an old **woman** who was among those who
040:040 whether man or **woman**-and is a believer-such will
051:029 "A barren old **woman**!"
058:001 of the **woman** who pleads with thee concerning her
060:011 (by the coming over of a **woman** from the other side).
065:006 let another **woman** suckle (the child)

WOMB

003:035 what is in my **womb** for Thy special service:
013:008 Allah doth know what every female (**womb**) doth bear,
041:047 (within her **womb**) nor bring forth (young),

WOMBS

002:228 to hide what Allah hath created in their **wombs**,
003:006 shapes you in the **wombs** as He pleases.
004:001 and be heedful the **wombs** (that bore you):
006:139 the **wombs** of such and such cattle is specially
006:143 which the **wombs** of the two females enclose?
006:144 which the **wombs** of the two females enclose?-
013:008 how much the **wombs** fall short (of their time or number)
016:078 from the **wombs** of your mothers when ye knew nothing:
022:005 to rest in the **wombs** for an appointed term,
031:034 and He Who knows what is in the **wombs**.
039:006 He creates you, in the **wombs** of your mothers,
053:032 and when ye are hidden in your mother's **wombs**.

WOMEN

002:221 Do not marry unbelieving **women** (idolaters),
002:222 so keep away from **women** in their courses,
002:228 And **women** shall have rights similar to the rights
002:228 Divorced **women** shall wait concerning themselves
002:231 When ye divorce **women**, and they (are about to)
002:232 When ye divorce **women**,
002:236 ye divorce **women** before consummation
002:241 For divorced **women** is a suitable Gift
002:282 not two men, then a man and two **women**,
003:014 the love of things they covet: **women** and sons;
003:042 chosen thee above the **women** of all nations.
003:061 our sons and your sons, our **women** and your **women**,
004:001 scattered (like seeds) countless men and **women**;
004:003 marry **women** of your choice, two, or three, or four;
004:005 And give the **women** (on marriage) their dower
004:007 a share for men and a share for **women**,
004:015 If any of your **women** are guilty of lewdness,
004:019 forbidden to inherit **women** against their will.
004:022 And marry not **women** whom your fathers married,
004:024 Also (prohibited are) **women** already married,
004:025 the means wherewith to wed free believing **women**,

WOMEN (continued)

004:025 their punishment is half that for free **women**.
004:032 and to **women** what they earn:
004:034 Therefore the righteous **women** are devoutly
004:034 As to those **women** on whose part ye fear
004:034 Men are the protectors and maintainers of **women**,
004:043 or ye have been in contact with **women**,
004:075 Men, **women**, and children, whose cry is: "Our Lord!
004:098 weak and oppressed, men, **women**, and children who
004:127 concerning the orphaned **women** to whom ye give
004:127 They ask thy instruction concerning the **Women**.
005:005 are (not only) chaste **women** who are believers,
005:005 but chaste **women** among the People of the Book,
005:006 or ye have been in contact with **women**,
006:139 and forbidden to our **women**;
007:081 on men in preference to **women**:
009:067 The Hypocrites, men and **women**, are alike:
009:068 men and **women**, and the rejecters of Faith,
009:071 The Believers, men and **women**, are protectors,
009:072 Allah has promised to Believers, men and **women**,
009:087 They prefer to be with (the **women**), who remain
009:093 to stay with the (**women**) who remain behind:
012:028 (her husband said): "Behold! it is a snare of you **women**!
024:004 And those who launch charge against chaste **women**,
024:012 men and **women**-when ye heard of the affair,-
024:023 indiscreet and believing **women** are cursed
024:026 **Women** impure are for men impure,
024:026 and men impure are for **women** impure,
024:026 and **women** of purity are for men of purity,
024:026 and men of purity are for **women** of purity:
024:031 And say to the believing **women** that they should
024:031 who have no carnal knowledge of **women**;
024:031 or their sisters' sons, or their **women**,
024:060 Such elderly **women** as are past the prospect
027:055 really approach men in your lusts rather than **women**?
028:023 and besides them he found two **women** who were
033:032 ye are not like any of the (other) **women**:
033:035 for men and **women** who guard their chastity,
033:035 for men and **women** who give in charity,
033:035 for men and **women** who are patient and constant,
033:035 for men and **women** who fast,
033:035 for men and **women** who humble themselves,
033:035 and for men and **women** who engage much in Allah's
033:035 for believing men and **women**,
033:035 For Muslim men and **women**,-
033:035 for devout men and **women**, for true men and **women**,
033:049 When ye marry believing **women**,
033:052 is not lawful for thee (to marry more) **women** after this,
033:055 sisters' sons, or their **women**,
033:058 those who annoy Believing and **women** undeservedly,
033:059 and the believing **women**, that they should cast
033:073 Allah has to punish the Hypocrites, men and **women**,
033:073 and the Unbelievers, men and **women**,
033:073 Allah turns in Mercy to the Believers, men and **women**:
037:048 And besides them will be chaste **women**;
038:052 chaste **women** restraining their glances,
047:019 and for the men and **women** who believe:
048:005 That He may admit the men and **women** who believe,
048:006 the Hypocrites, men and **women**,
048:006 and the Polytheists, men and **women**, who think
048:025 believing men and believing **women** whom ye did
049:011 nor let some **women** laugh at others:
057:012 and the believing **women**-how their Light

WOMEN (continued)

057:013 The day will the Hypocrites-men and **women**-say to
057:018 For those who give in charity, men and **women**,
060:010 (on their dowers of **women** who came over to you).
060:010 when they come to you believing **women** refugees,
060:010 to the ties (marriage contract) of unbelieving **women**:
060:012 O Prophet! when believing **women** come to thee
065:001 O Prophet! when ye do divorce **women**, divorce them
065:004 Such of your **women** as have passed the age
065:006 Let the **women** live (in 'Iddat) in the same style as you
071:028 and (all) believing and believing **women**:
085:010 Those who persecute the Believers, men and **women**,

WOMEN'S

002:222 They ask thee concerning **women's** courses.

WOMEN-FOLK

002:049 slaughtered your sons and let your **women-folk** live;
014:006 slaughtered your sons, and let your **women-folk** live:

WONDER

007:063 "Do ye **wonder** that there hath come to you a reminder
007:069 "Do ye **wonder** that there hath come to you a message
011:073 They said: "Dost thou **wonder** at Allah's decree?
037:048 with big eyes (of **wonder** and beauty).
038:004 So they **wonder** that a Warner has come to them
048:029 (filling) the sowers with **wonder** and delight.
050:002 But they **wonder** that there has come to them
053:059 Do ye then **wonder** at this recital?

WONDERFUL

006:101 **Wonderful** Originator of the heavens
011:072 That would indeed be a **wonderful** thing!"
050:002 "This is a **wonderful** thing!
072:001 'We have really heard a **wonderful** Recital!
091:005 By the Firmament and its (**wonderful**) structure;

WONDERMENT

010:002 Is it a matter of **wonderment** to men that We
056:065 And ye would be left in **wonderment**,

WONDERS

003:191 and contemplate the (**wonders** of) creation
018:009 the Inscription were **wonders** among Our Signs?

WONT

007:051 and as they were **wont** to reject Our Signs.
012:047 shall ye diligently sow as is your **wont**:
014:044 "What! were ye not **wont** to swear aforetime
032:020 the which ye were **wont** to reject as false."
034:042 the which ye were **wont** to deny!"
040:063 Thus are deluded those who are **wont** to reject
040:075 "That was because ye were **wont** to rejoice on the
040:075 the Truth, and that ye were **wont** to be insolent.
040:083 they were **wont** to scoff hemmed them in.
041:028 for that they were **wont** to reject Our Signs.
045:029 for We were **wont** to put on record all that ye did."
046:034 for that ye were **wont** to deny (Truth)!"
052:014 "Is the Fire,-which ye were **wont** to deny!
056:045 For that they were **wont** to be indulged,
109:004 that which ye have been **wont** to worship,

WOOD

015:078 the Companion of the **Wood** were also wrong-doers;
026:176 The Companions of the **Wood** rejected the messengers.
038:013 and the Companions! of the **Wood**;-such were
050:014 The Companions of the **Wood**, and the
111:004 His wife shall carry the (crackling) **wood**-as fuel!

WOOL

016:080 and out of their **wool**,

WOOL (continued)

016:080 and their soft fibers (between **wool** and hair),
070:009 And the mountains will be like **wool**,
101:005 And the mountains will be like carded **wool**.

WORD

002:059 But the transgressors changed the **word**
002:075 seeing a party of them heard the **Word** of Allah,
002:088 (which preserve Allah's **word**, we need no more)"
002:113 Like unto their **word** is what those say who know not;
003:017 who are true (in **word** and deed);
003:039 confirming the truth of a **Word** from Allah,
003:045 glad tidings of a **Word** from Him:
003:077 solemn plighted **word** for a small price,
003:181 their **word** and (their act) of slaying the Prophets
004:063 and speak to them a **word** to reach their very souls.
004:087 And whose **word** can be truer than Allah's?
004:122 and whose **word** can be truer than Allah's?
004:171 and His **Word**, which He bestowed on Mary,
005:073 If they desist not from their **word** (of blasphemy),
006:073 His **Word** is the Truth.
006:115 The **Word** of thy Lord doth find its fulfillment
007:135 Behold! they broke their **word**!
007:162 changed the **word** from that which had been given them
009:006 so that he may hear the **Word** of Allah;
009:040 But the **word** of Allah is exalted to the heights:
009:040 and humbled to the depths the **word** of the Unbelievers.
010:019 for a **word** that went forth before from thy Lord,
010:033 Thus is the **Word** of thy Lord proved true
010:096 Those against whom the **Word** of thy Lord
011:040 against whom the **Word** has already gone forth,-
011:044 Then the **word** went forth: "O earth! swallow up
011:044 rested on Mount Judi and the **word** went forth:
011:048 The **word** came: "O Noah! come down (from the
011:053 we are not the ones to desert our gods on thy **word**!
011:110 had it not been that a **Word** had gone forth
011:119 and the **Word** of thy Lord shall be fulfilled:
013:020 and fail not in their plighted **word**;
013:025 their **word** thereto and cut asunder those things
014:024 a parable?-a goodly **Word** like a goodly tree,
014:026 And the parable of an evil **Word** is that
014:027 those who believe, with the **Word** that stands firm,
016:040 We but say the **Word**, "Be," and it is.
016:086 But they will throw back their **word** at them
017:016 the **word** is proved true against them;
017:023 say not to then a **word** of contempt,
017:028 yet speak to them a **word** of easy kindness.
018:093 who scarcely understood a **word**.
020:007 If thou pronounce the **word** aloud, (it is no matter):
020:089 see that it could not return them a **word** (for answer),
020:094 and thou didst not observe my **word**!'"
020:109 and whose **word** is acceptable to Him.
020:129 Had it not been for a **Word** that went forth
021:004 **word** (spoken) in the heavens and the earth:
022:030 and shun the **word** that is false,-
023:027 of them against whom the **Word** has already gone forth:
023:068 Do they not ponder over the **Word** (of Allah),
023:100 "By no means! it is but a **word** he says."-
027:082 And when the **Word** is fulfilled against them
027:085 And the **Word** will be fulfilled against them,
028:051 Now have We brought them the **word** in order that they
032:013 but the **Word** from Me will come true, "I Will
034:031 throwing back the **word** (of blame) on one another!
036:007 The **Word** is proved true against the greater

WORD (continued)

036:052 And true was the **word** of the messengers!"
036:058 "Peace!"-a **Word** (of salutation) from a Lord Most
036:070 and that the **word** may be proved true against those
037:031 the **Word** of our Lord that we shall indeed (have to)
037:171 Already has Our **Word** been passed before (this)
039:018 Those who listen to the **Word**, and follow
040:006 Thus was the **Word** of thy Lord proved true
041:025 and the **word** among the previous generations of
041:045 for a **Word** that went forth before from thy Lord,
042:014 Had it not been for a **Word** that went forth before
043:028 And he left it as a **Word** to endure among those
043:050 from them, behold, they broke their **word**.
046:018 the **word** proved true among the previous generations
048:015 They wish to change Allah's **word**: Say: "Not thus
050:018 Not a **word** does he utter but there is a vigilant Guardian.
050:029 "The **Word** changes not before Me, and I
054:050 And Our Command is but a single **Word**,-like the
058:003 But those who pronounce the **word** "Zihar" to their
067:013 And whether ye hide your **word** or make it known,
069:040 That this is verily the **word** of a honoured messenger;
069:041 It is not the **word** of a poet:
069:042 Nor is it the **word** of a soothsayer:
073:005 Soon shall We send down to thee a weighty **Word**.
074:025 "This is nothing but the **word** of a mortal!"
081:019 Verily this is the **word** of a most honourable Messenger,
081:025 Nor is it the **word** of a Satan accursed.
086:013 Behold this is the **Word** that distinguishes
088:011 Where they shall hear no (**word**) of vanity:

WORDS

002:037 Then learnt Adam from his Lord certain **words**
002:118 before them **words** of similar import.
002:263 Kind **words** and the covering of faults
004:005 and speak to them **words** of kindness and justice.
004:008 and speak to them **words** of kindness and justice.
004:009 let them fear Allah, and speak appropriate **words**.
004:046 those who displace **words** from their (right) places,
004:108 In **words** that He cannot approve:
004:148 shouting of evil **words** in public speech,
005:013 they change the **words** from their (right) places
005:041 They change the **words** from their (right) places;
005:063 sinful **words** and eating things forbidden?
006:033 the grief which their **words** do cause thee:
006:034 the **Words** (and Decrees) of Allah.
006:115 none can change His **Words**:
007:144 and the **words** I (have spoken to thee);
007:158 who believed in Allah and His **Words**:
007:205 and remember without loudness in **words**,
008:007 to establish the Truth according to His **words**,
008:031 if we wished, we could say (**words**) like these:
009:008 With (fair **words** from) their mouths they please
009:009 The **Words** of Allah have they sold for a miserable
010:064 no change can there be in the **Words** of Allah.
010:082 "And Allah by His **Words** doth prove and establish
013:033 or is it (just) a show of **words**?"
017:052 (His call) with (**words** of) His praise,
018:027 none can change His **Words**,
018:109 were ink (wherewith to write out) the **words** of my Lord,
018:109 be exhausted than would the **words** of my Lord,
031:027 yet would not the **Words** of Allah be exhausted
035:010 To Him mount up (all) **Words** of Purity:
042:024 and proves the Truth by His **Words**.
058:002 And in fact they use **words** (both) iniquitous

WORDS (continued)

058:003 then wish to go back on the **words** they uttered,-
058:008 "Why does not Allah punish us for our **words**.?"
063:004 and when they speak; thou listenest to their **words**.
066:012 to the truth of the **words** of her Lord and of His

WORK

002:025 who believe and **work** righteousness,
002:062 and **work** righteousness, shall have their reward
002:082 have faith and **work** righteousness,
002:273 seeking (for trade or **work**):
003:052 "Who will be my helpers to (the **work** of) Allah?"
003:057 "As to those who believe and **work** righteousness,
003:136 for those who **work** (and strive)!
003:195 I suffer to be lost the **work** of any of you,
005:005 If anyone rejects faith, fruitless is his **work**,
005:069 and **work** righteousness,-on them shall be no fear,
005:103 or stallion-camels freed from **work**:
007:042 But those who believe and **work** righteousness,-
007:132 to **work** therewith the sorcery on us,
009:105 soon will Allah observe your **work**,
009:105 And say: "**Work** (righteousness): soon will
010:004 those who believe and **work** righteousness, but those
010:009 Those who believe, and **work** righteousness,
010:041 say: "My **work** to me, and yours to you!
010:081 the **work** of those who make mischief.
011:011 show patience and constancy, and **work** righteousness;
011:023 But those who believe and **work** righteousness,
013:025 to be joined, and **work** mischief in the land;
013:029 "For those who believe and **work** righteousness,
014:023 who believe and **work** righteousness will be admitted
017:009 to the Believers who **work** deeds of righteousness,
018:002 to the Believers who **work** righteous deeds,
018:030 As for those who believe and **work** righteousness,
018:107 As to those who believe and **work** righteous deeds,
018:110 let him **work** righteousness, and in the worship of his
019:060 those who repent and believe, and **work** righteousness:
019:096 On those who believe and **work** deeds of righteousness,
021:082 some who dived for him, and did other **work** besides;
022:014 who believe and **work** righteous deeds, to Gardens,
022:023 will admit those who believe and **work** righteous deeds,
022:050 "Those who believe and **work** righteousness, for them is
022:056 so those who believe and **work** righteous deeds
023:051 good and pure, and **work** righteousness:
023:061 It is those who hasten in every good **work**,
023:100 "In order that I may **work** righteousness in the things
024:055 who believe and **work** righteous deeds, that He
026:227 Except those who believe, **work** righteousness,
027:019 and that I may **work** the righteousness that will please
028:015 He said: "This is a **work** of Satan:
028:080 is best for those who believe and **work** righteousness:
029:007 Those who believe and **work** righteous deeds,-
029:009 And those who believe and **work** righteous deeds,-
029:058 But those who believe and **work** deeds of righteousness-
030:030 no change (there is) in the **work** (wrought) by Allah:
030:044 and those who **work** righteousness will make provision
030:045 and **work** righteous deeds, out of His Bounty.
031:008 For those who believe and **work** righteous deeds,
032:012 will **work** righteousness: for we do indeed (now)
034:004 those who believe and **work** deeds of righteousness:
034:011 of chain armour, and **work** ye righteousness;
034:037 but only those who believe and **work** Righteousness-
035:007 but for those who believe and **work** righteous deeds,
035:037 Bring us out: we shall **work** righteousness,

WORK (continued)

037:102 (the age of) (serious) **work** with him, he said:
038:024 who believe and **work** deeds of righteousness,
038:028 those who Believe and **work** deeds of righteousness,
039:065 truly fruitless will be thy **work** (in life),
039:074 for those who **work** (righteousness)!"
040:058 those who believe and **work** deeds of righteousness,
041:008 For those who believe and **work** deeds of
042:022 But those who believe and **work** righteous deeds
043:032 so that some may command **work** from others.
046:015 and that I may **work** righteousness such as Thou
047:002 But those who believe **and work** deeds of righteousness,
061:014 "Who will be my helpers to (the **work** of) Allah?"
064:009 And those who believe in Allah and **work** righteousness,-
065:011 and **work** righteousness, He will admit to Gardens
084:025 Except to thsoe who believe and **work** righteous deeds:

WORKED

017:101 to have been **worked** upon by sorcery!"
020:075 who have **worked** righteous deeds,-for them
028:067 and **worked** righteousness, haply he shall be one
030:015 and **worked** righteous deeds, shall be
034:012 and there were Jinns that **worked** in front of him,
034:013 They **worked** for him as he desired,
077:043 heart's content: for that ye **worked** (Righteousness).

WORKING

026:183 in the land, **working** mischief.

WORKS

002:217 their **works** will bear no fruit in this life
003:022 They are those whose **works** will bear no fruit
003:114 and they hasten (in emulation) in (all) good **works**;
004:123 whoever **works** evil, will be requited accordingly.
005:063 Evil indeed are their **works**.
005:080 Evil indeed are (the **works**) which their souls
007:137 the great **works** and fine Buildings which Pharaoh
009:017 The **works** of such bear no fruit:
009:069 They!-their **works** are fruitless in this world
014:018 their Lord is that their **works** are as ashes,
016:097 Whoever **works** righteousness, man or woman
018:088 "But whoever believes, and **works** righteousness-
018:104 they were acquiring good by their **works**?"
018:105 vain will be their **works**, nor shall We,
020:112 But he who **works** deeds of righteousness,
021:090 these (three) were ever quick in doing in good **works**:
021:094 Whoever **works** any act of righteousness and has
025:070 and **works** righteous deeds, for Allah
033:031 and work righteousness,-to her shall We grant her
040:040 and he that **works** a righteous deed-whether man
040:040 "He that **works** evil will not be requited but by
041:033 than one who calls (men) to Allah, **works** righteousness,
041:046 Whoever **works** righteousness benefits his own soul;
041:046 whoever **works** evil, it is against his own soul;
045:015 if he does evil, it **works** against (His own soul).
052:021 (of the fruit) of aught of their **works**:

WORLD

002:086 buy the life of this **world** at the price
002:114 and in the **world** to come,
002:114 but disgrace in this **world**,
002:130 Him We chose and rendered pure in this **world**:
002:200 "Our Lord! Give us (thy bounties) in this **world**!"
002:201 in this **world** and good in the Hereafter.
002:212 The life of this **world** is alluring
003:022 no fruit in this **world** and in the Hereafter,
003:045 held in honour in this **world** and the Hereafter

WORLD (continued)

003:056 severe chastisement in this **world** and the Hereafter
003:117 life of this (material) **world** may be likened
003:148 And Allah gave them a reward in this **world**,
003:152 Among you are some that hanker after this **world**
003:185 for the life of this **world** is but goods and chattels
004:074 who sell the life of this **world** for the Hereafter.
004:077 Say: "Short is the enjoyment of this **world**:
004:109 whose behalf ye may contend in this **world**;
005:033 that is their disgrace in this **world**, and a heavy
005:041 For them there is disgrace in this **world**, and in
005:082 And men who have renounced the **world**, and they
006:032 Nothing is the life of this **world** but play
006:070 and are deceived by the life of this **world**.
006:130 It was the life of this **world** that deceived them.
007:032 Say: they are, in the life of this **world**,
007:051 and were deceived by the life of the **world**."
007:169 they chose (for themselves) the vanities of this **world**,
008:067 Ye look for the temporal goods of this **world**;
009:038 Do ye prefer the life of this **world** to the Hereafter?
009:069 are fruitless in this **world** and in the Hereafter,
009:085 to punish them with these things in this **world**,
010:070 A little enjoyment in this **world**!-
012:101 Thou art my Protector in this **world** and in the Hereafter.
013:026 (The worldly) rejoice in the life of this **world**:
013:026 but the life of this **world** is but little comfort
013:034 For them is a Penalty in the life of this **world**,
014:003 Those who prefer the life of this **world** to the Hereafter,
014:027 stands firm, in this **world** and in the Hereafter:
016:030 there is good in this **world**, and the Home of the
016:032 (the good) which ye did (in the **world**)."
016:041 We will assuredly give a goodly home in this **world**;
016:107 they love the life of this **world** better than the Hereafter:
016:122 And We gave him Good in this **world**,
017:072 But those who were blind in this **world**,
018:045 forth to them the similitude of the life of this **world**:
018:046 sons are allurements of the life of this **world**:
020:072 decree (touching) the life of this **world**.
020:131 the splendour of the life of this **world**,
022:011 they lose both this **world** and the Hereafter:
022:015 help him (His Messenger) in this **world** and the
023:037 "There is nothing but our life in this **world**!
023:064 the good things of this **world**, behold, they
024:014 in this **world** and the Hereafter, a grievous
026:165 "Of all the creatures in the **world**,
028:042 In this **world** We made a Curse to follow them:
028:077 nor forget thy portion in this **world**:
028:079 Said to those whose aim is the life of this **World**: "Oh!
029:064 What is the life of this **world** but amusement
030:007 they know but the outer (things) in the life of this **world**:
032:012 now then send us back (to the **world**):
033:028 "If it be that ye desire the life of this **world**,
033:057 Allah has cursed them in this **world** and in the
039:010 for those who do good in this **world**.
040:043 whether in this **world**, or the Hereafter;
042:020 and to any that desires the tilth of this **world**,
043:032 between them their livelihood in the life of this **world**:
045:024 "What is there but our life in this **world**?
045:035 and the life of this **world** deceived you."
046:020 "Ye squandered your good things in the life of the **world**,
047:012 enjoy (this **world**) and eat as cattle eat; and the
047:036 The life of this **world** is but play and amusement:
053:029 nothing but the life of this **world**.

WORLD (continued)

057:020 of this **world**, but goods and chattels of deception?
057:020 Know ye (all), that the life of this **world** is but play
059:003 He would certainly have punished them in this **world**:
079:038 And had preferred the life of this **world**,
087:016 Nay (behold), ye prefer the life of this **world**;
102:001 (the good things of this **world**) diverts you

WORLD'S

002:204 whose speech about this **world's** life may
003:014 Such are the possessions of this **world's** life;
040:051 who believe, (both) in this **world's** life and on

WORLDLY

013:026 (The **worldly**) rejoice in the life of this world:
021:111 and a grant of (**worldly**) livelihood (to you) for time."
028:079 in the (pride of his **worldly**) glitter.
029:066 and giving themselves up to (**worldly**) enjoyment!
036:044 and by way of (**worldly**) convenience (to serve them)

WORLDS

001:002 the Cherisher and Sustainer of the **Worlds**:
002:251 but Allah is full of bounty to all the **worlds**.
003:096 full of blessings and of guidance for all the **worlds**.
005:028 for I do fear Allah, the Cherisher of the **worlds**.
006:045 Praise be to Allah, the Cherisher of the **Worlds**.
006:071 to submit ourselves to the Lord of the **worlds**;
006:162 the Cherisher of the **Worlds**:
007:054 the Cherisher and Sustainer of the **Worlds**!
007:061 from the Lord and Cherisher of the **Worlds**!"
007:067 from the Lord and Cherisher of the **Worlds**!
007:104 I am a messenger from the Lord of the **worlds**,-
007:121 Saying: "We believe in the Lord of the **Worlds**.
010:010 the Cherisher and Sustainer of the **Worlds**!"
010:037 from the Lord of the **Worlds**.
026:016 by the Lord and Cherisher of all the **Worlds**;
026:023 and Cherisher of the **Worlds**?"
026:047 Saying: "We believe in the Lord of the **Worlds**.
026:077 not so the Lord and Cherisher of the **Worlds**;
026:098 with the Lord of the **Worlds**;
026:109 my reward is only from the Lord of the **Worlds**:
026:127 my reward is only from the Lord of the **Worlds**.
026:145 my reward is only from the Lord of the **Worlds**.
026:164 my reward is only from the Lord of the **Worlds**.
026:180 my reward is only from the Lord of the **Worlds**.
026:192 from the Lord of the **Worlds**:
027:008 the Lord of the **Worlds**!
027:044 with Solomon, to the Lord of the **Worlds**."
028:030 Verily I am Allah, the Lord of the **Worlds**...
032:002 from the Lord of the **Worlds**.
037:087 about the Lord of the **Worlds**?"
037:182 the Lord and Cherisher of the **Worlds**.
038:087 a Reminder to (all) the **Worlds**.
039:075 to Allah, the Lord of the **Worlds**!"
040:064 So Glory to Allah, the Lord of the **Worlds**!
040:065 Lord of the **Worlds**!
040:066 (in Islam) to the Lord of the **Worlds**."
041:009 He is the Lord of (all) the **Worlds**.
043:046 "I am a messenger of the Lord of the **Worlds**."
045:036 the earth, Lord and Cherisher of all the **worlds**!
055:031 O both ye **worlds**!
056:080 A Revelation from the Lord of the **Worlds**.
059:016 I do fear Allah, the Lord of the **Worlds**!"
068:052 a Message to all the **worlds**.
069:043 from the Lord of the **Worlds**.
081:027 a Message to (all) the **Worlds**:

WORLDS (continued)

083:006   will stand before the Lord of the **Worlds**?

WORM

034:014   his death except a little **worm** of the earth,

WORN

067:004   to thee dull and discomfited, in a state **worn** out.

WORSE

002:061   exchange the better for the **worse**?
002:074   and even **worse** in hardness.
002:191   for Persecution is **worse** than slaughter;
002:217   Tumult and oppression are **worse** than slaughter.
003:118   what their hearts conceal is far **worse**.
003:180   Nay, it will be the **worse** of them:
005:060   these are (many times) **worse** in rank, and far
005:060   something much **worse** than this, (as judged)
012:077   he (simply) said (to himself): "Ye are the **worse** situated:
022:072   Say, "Shall I tell you of something (far) **worse** than

WORSHIP

001:005   Thee do we **worship**, and Thine aid we seek.
002:021   O ye people! **worship** your Guardian-Lord,
002:043   with those who bow down (in **worship**).
002:051   ye took the calf (for **worship**),
002:054   wronged yourselves by your **worship** of the calf:
002:083   **worship** none but Allah;
002:114   that in places for the **worship** of Allah,
002:116   everything renders **worship** to Him.
002:133   "What will ye **worship** after me?"
002:133   **worship** thy God and the God of thy fathers,
002:138   It is He. Whom we **worship**.
002:165   Yet there are men who take (for **worship**) others besides
002:172   and be grateful to Allah if it is Him ye **worship**.
003:017   who **worship** devoutly: who spend (in the way of Allah);
003:043   "O Mary! **worship** thy Lord devoutly;
003:051   then **worship** Him. This is a Way that is straight."
003:064   that we **worship** none but Allah;
003:096   The first House (of **worship**) appointed for men
003:186   and from those who **worship** parties besides Allah.
004:172   Christ disdaineth not to serve and **worship** Allah,
004:172   those who disdain His **worship** and are arrogant,
005:055   they bow down humbly (in **worship**).
005:072   "O children of Israel! **worship** Allah, my Lord
005:076   Say: Will ye **worship**, besides Allah, something
005:117   to wit, '**Worship** Allah, my Lord and your Lord':
006:056   Say: "I am forbidden to **worship** those-other
006:064   and yet ye **worship** false gods!"
006:102   the Creator of all things: then **worship** ye Him:
007:059   **worship** Allah! ye have not other god but Him.
007:065   He said: "O my people! **worship** Allah! ye have
007:070   that we may **worship** Allah alone,
007:070   and give up that which our fathers used to **worship**.
007:073   he said: "O my people! **worship** Allah; ye have
007:085   he said: "O my people! **worship** Allah; ye have
007:139   and vain is the (**worship**) which they practice."
007:148   They took it for **worship** and they did wrong.
007:148   the body of a calf, (for **worship**):
007:152   Those who took the calf (for **worship**) will
007:206   who are near to they Lord, disdain not to **worship** Him:
009:031   yet they were commanded to **worship** but One God:
010:029   knew nothing of your **worship** of us!"
010:066   What do they follow who **worship** as His "partners"
010:087   make your dwellings into places of **worship**,
010:104   But I **worship** Allah-who will take your souls
010:104   I **worship** not what ye **worship** other than Allah!

WORSHIP (continued)

011:002   (It teacheth) that ye should **worship** none but Allah.
011:050   He said: "O my people! **worship** Allah! ye have
011:061   He said: "O my people! **worship** Allah: ye have
011:062   Dost thou (now) forbid us the **worship** of what
011:084   he said: "O my people! **worship** Allah: ye have
011:087   leave off the **worship** which our fathers practiced,
011:109   Be not then in doubt as to what these men **worship**.
011:109   They **worship** nothing but what their fathers worshipped
011:123   so **worship** Him, and put thy trust in Him:
012:040   Whatever ye **worship** apart from Him is nothing
012:040   He hath commanded that ye **worship** none but Him:
013:016   (for **worship**) protectors other than Him,
013:036   Say: "I am commanded to **worship** Allah,
014:010   to turn us away from what our fathers used to **worship**;
016:051   Allah has said: "Take not (for **worship**) two gods:
016:073   And **worship** others than Allah,-such as
017:023   Thy Lord hath decreed that ye **worship** none but Him,
017:039   with Allah, another object of **worship**, lest thou
018:015   for **worship** gods other than Him:
018:016   and the things they **worship** other than Allah,
018:021   "Let us surely build a place of **worship** over them."
018:110   and in the **worship** of his Lord, admit no one
019:042   "O my father! why **worship** that which heareth not
019:065   and of al that is in between: so **worship** Him,
019:065   and be constant and patient in His **worship**:
019:081   And they have taken (for **worship**) gods other
019:082   Instead, they shall reject their **worship**,
020:091   they had said "We will not cease to **worship** it,
021:021   Or have they taken (for **worship**) gods from
021:024   Or have they taken for **worship** (other) gods
021:025   therefore **worship** and serve Me.
021:066   (Abraham) said, "Do ye then **worship**, besides Allah,
021:067   and upon the things that ye **worship** besides Allah!
021:098   and the (false) gods that ye **worship** besides Allah,
021:106   for people who would (truly) **worship** Allah.
022:026   "Associate not anything (in **worship**) with Me;
022:071   Yet they **worship**, besides Allah,
023:023   "O my people! **worship** Allah! Ye have
023:032   (saying), "**Worship** Allah! ye have no other god
023:059   Those who join not (in **worship**) partners with
024:055   'They will **worship** Me (along) and not
025:017   as well as those whom they **worship** besides Allah,
025:055   Yet do they **worship**, besides Allah, things that
026:070   he said to his father and his people: "What **worship** ye?"
026:071   They said: "We **worship** idols, and we
027:025   So that they **worship** not Allah Who brings forth
027:043   the **worship** of others besides Allah:
029:008   to join with Me (in **worship**) anything of which
029:017   "For ye do **worship** idols besides Allah, and ye
029:017   The things that ye **worship** besides Allah have no
029:025   (for **worship**) idols besides Allah, out of
029:065   they give a share (of their **worship** to others)!-
031:013   join not in **worship** (others) with Allah:
031:013   for false **worship** is indeed the highest wrong-doing."
031:015   join in **worship** with Me things of which thou
034:040   "Was it you that these men used to **worship**?"
034:043   from the (**worship**) which your fathers practiced."
036:060   that ye should not **worship** Satan;
036:061   "And that ye should **worship** Me, (for that)
036:074   Yet they take (for **worship**) gods other than Allah,
037:085   his people, "What is that which ye **worship**?
037:095   He said: "**Worship** ye that which ye have

WORSHIP (continued)

037:161 For, verily, neither ye nor those ye **worship**
039:017 Those who eschew Taghut and fall not into its **worship**,-
039:064 some one other than Allah that ye order me to **worship**,
039:066 Nay, but **worship** Allah, and be of those who give thanks.
040:012 as the Only (object of **worship**) ye did
042:009 (for **worship**) protectors besides Him?
042:013 to those who **worship** other things than Allah,
043:026 "I do indeed clear myself of what ye **worship**:
043:027 "(I **worship**) only Him Who made me, and He
043:064 "For Allah, He is my and your Lord: so **worship** ye Him:
043:081 I would be the first to **worship**."
046:021 "**Worship** ye none other than Allah:
051:051 And make not another object of **worship** with Allah:
060:004 clear of you and of whatever ye **worship** besides Allah:
060:012 not associate in **worship** any other thing
066:005 in repentance, who **worship** (in humility),
070:034 And those who (strictly) guard their **worship**;-
071:003 "That ye should **worship** Allah, fear Him,
072:002 We shall not join (in **worship**) any (gods)
072:018 "And the places of **worship** are for Allah (alone):
098:005 been commanded no more than this: to **worship** Allah,
106:003 Let them **worship** the Lord of this House,
109:002 I **worship** not that which ye **worship**,
109:003 Nor will ye **worship** that which I **worship**.
109:004 that which ye have been wont to **worship**,
109:004 And I will not **worship** that which
109:005 Nor will ye **worship** that which I **worship**.

WORSHIPPED

002:092 yet ye **worshipped** the Calf (even) after that,
004:153 Yet they **worshipped** the calf even after
005:060 those who **worshipped** Evil (Tagut)-these are
010:028 "It was not us that ye **worshipped**!"
011:062 of what our fathers **worshipped**?
011:109 but what their fathers **worshipped** before (them):
016:035 not have **worshipped** aught but Him-neither we
019:049 and from those whom they **worshipped** besides Allah,
026:092 'Where are the (gods) ye **worshipped**-
028:063 It was not us they **worshipped**."
034:041 Nay, but they **worshipped** the Jinns:
037:022 and the things they **worshipped**-
043:020 we should not have **worshipped** such (deities)!"
043:045 other than The Most Gracious, to be **worshipped**?
046:006 to them and deny that (men) had **worshipped** them.
046:028 to them from those whom they **worshipped** as gods,

WORSHIPPER

020:097 of whom thou hast become a devoted **worshipper**:

WORSHIPPERS

003:079 "Be ye my **worshippers** rather than Allah's":
003:079 "Be ye **worshippers** of Him (Who is truly the Cherisher
016:035 The **worshippers** of false gods say: "If Allah
037:094 Then came (the **worshippers**) with hurried steps,
107:004 So woe to the **worshippers**

WORSHIPPING

014:035 and preserve me and my sons from **worshipping** idols.
021:053 They said, "We found our father **worshipping** them."
026:075 whom ye have been **worshipping**,-
027:024 **worshipping** the sun besides Allah:

WORSHIPS

039:009 Is one who **worships** devoutly during the hours

WORST

007:141 who afflicted you with the **worst** of punishment

WORST (continued)

007:195 scheme (your **worst**) against me,
008:022 For the **worst** of beasts in the sight of Allah
008:055 For the **worst** of beasts in the sight of Allah
009:097 The Bedouin Arabs are the **worst** in unbelief
011:055 So scheme (your **worst**) against me, all of you,
019:069 who were **worst** in obstinate rebellion against (Allah)
019:075 they will at length realize who is **worst** in position,
039:035 (even) the **worst** in their deeds and give them their
041:027 for the **worst** of their deeds.
098:006 They are the **worst** of creatures.

WORTHLESS

004:002 nor substitute (your) **worthless** things for (their) good
063:004 They are as (**worthless** as hollow) pieces of timber

WORTHY

002:267 and **Worthy** of all praise.
004:131 And Allah is free of wants, **worthy** of all praise.
009:108 it is more **worthy** of thy standing forth (for prayer)
010:035 gives guidance to Truth more **worthy** to be followed,
011:073 For He is indeed **worthy** of all praise,
014:001 in Power, **Worthy** of all Praise!-
014:008 **Worthy** of all praise.
019:065 knowest thou of any who is **worthy** of the same name
019:070 are most **worthy** of being burned therein.
022:024 to the path of Him Who is **Worthy** of (all) Praise.
022:064 all wants, **worthy** of all praise.
026:125 "I am to you a messenger **worthy** of all trust.
026:143 I am to you a messenger **worthy** of all trust.
026:162 "I am to you a messenger **worthy** of all trust.
026:178 "I am to you a messenger **worthy** of all trust.
027:029 a letter **worthy** of respect.
031:012 **worthy** of all praise.
031:026 **worthy** of all praise.
034:006 of the Exalted (in Might), **Worthy** of all praise.
035:015 the One Free of all wants, **worthy** of all praise.
037:142 and he had done acts **worthy** of blame.
041:042 **Worthy** of all Praise.
042:028 **Worthy** of all Praise.
044:018 I am to you a messenger **worthy** of all trust;
048:026 and well were they entitled to it and **worthy** of it.
057:024 free of all needs, **worthy** of all praise.
060:006 of all Wants, **Worthy**, of all Praise.
064:006 of all needs, **worthy** of all praise.
085:008 Exalted in Power, **worthy** of all Praise!

WOULD

002:009 Fain **would** they deceive Allah
002:102 the buyers of (magic) **would** have no share in the
002:108 **Would** ye question your Messenger
002:135 if ye **would** be guided (to salvation)."
002:135 Say thou: "Nay! (I **would** rather) the Religion
002:143 who **would** turn on their heels (from the Faith).
002:143 And never **would** Allah make your faith of no effect.
002:145 they **would** not follow thy Qiblah;
002:165 Behold, they **would** see the Punishment:
002:166 and all relations between them **would** be cut off.
002:166 they **would** see the Chastisement and all
002:166 Then **would** those who are followed clear them only
002:167 we **would** clear ourselves of them,
002:229 If ye (judges) do indeed fear that they **would** be unable
002:229 both parties fear that they **would** be unable to keep
002:251 the earth **would** indeed be full of mischief,
002:253 succeeding generations **would** not have fought
002:253 they **would** not have fought each other;

WOULD (continued)

002:267   when ye yourselves **would** not receive it
002:282   it **would** be wickedness in you.
003:078   you **would** think it is a part of the Book,
003:079   on the contrary (he **would** say): "Be ye worshippers
003:080   Nor **would** he instruct you to take angels
003:080   What! **would** he bid you to unbelief after ye have
003:091   never **would** be accepted from any such as much
003:100   they **would** (indeed) render you apostates
003:101   And how **would** ye deny Faith while unto you
003:125   your Lord **would** help you with five thousand angels
003:142   Did ye think that ye **would** enter Heaven
003:154   **would** certainly have gone forth to the place
003:156   they **would** not have died, or been slain."
003:159   they **would** have broken away from about thee:
003:167   They said: "Had we known there **would** be a fight,
003:168   they **would** not have been slain."
004:009   as they **would** have for their own if they had left
004:020   **would** ye take it by slander and a manifest sin?
004:034   what Allah **would** have them guard.
004:046   it **would** have been better for them, and more proper;
004:064   they **would** have found Allah indeed Oft-returning,
004:066   very few of them **would** have done it:
004:066   it **would** have been best for them,
004:066   and **would** have gone farthest to strengthen
004:072   are certainly among you men who **would** tarry behind:
004:073   they **would** be sure to say-as it there had never
004:082   they **would** surely have found therein much discrepancy.
004:083   all but a few of you **would** have followed Satan.
004:083   **would** have known it from them (direct).
004:088   **Would** ye guide those whom Allah hath thrown out
004:090   and they **would** have fought you:
004:113   a party of them **would** certainly have plotted
004:140   if ye did, ye **would** be like them.
005:032   it **would** be as if he slew the whole people:
005:032   it **would** be as if he saved the life of the whole people.
005:036   Theirs **would** be a grievous Chastisement.
005:036   it **would** never be accepted of them.
005:043   yet even after that, they **would** turn away.
005:048   He **would** have made you a single People,
005:066   they **would** have eaten both from above them
005:071   They thought there **would** be no trial
005:081   never **would** they have taken them for friends
005:108   or else they **would** fear that other oaths
005:108   that other oaths **would** be taken after their oaths.
006:007   the Unbelievers **would** have been sure to say: "This
006:008   the matter **would** be settled at once,
006:008   and no respite **would** be granted them.
006:015   Say: "I **would**, if I disobeyed my Lord, indeed
006:016   and that **would** be a Mighty Triumph.
006:027   "**Would** that we were but sent back!
006:027   but **would** be amongst those who believe!"
006:027   Then **would** we not reject the Signs of our Lord,
006:028   they **would** certainly relapse to the things they were
006:040   **would** ye then call upon other than Allah?-
006:041   "Nay,-On Him **would** ye call, and if
006:041   and ye **would** forget (the false gods)
006:041   He **would** remove (the distress) which occasioned
006:056   if I did, I **would** stray from the path, and be
006:057   What ye **would** see hastened is not in my power.
006:058   Say: "If what ye **would** see hastened wee in my power,
006:058   the matter **would** be settled at once between you and me.
006:088   all that they did **would** be vain for them.

WOULD (continued)

006:107   they **would** not have taken false gods:
006:109   a (special) Sign came to them, by it they **would** believe.
006:112   If they Lord had so willed, they **would** not have done it:
006:121   ye **would** indeed be Pagans.
006:121   that **would** be impiety.
006:131   for thy Lord **would** not destroy the towns unjustly
006:137   if Allah had willed, they **would** not have done so:
006:148   given partners to Him, nor **would** our fathers;
006:154   completing (Our favour) to those who **would** do right,
007:045   "Those who **would** hinder (men) from the of Allah
007:046   who **would** know every one by his marks:
007:049   that Allah with His Mercy **would** never bless?
007:101   but they **would** not believe what they had rejected
007:167   thy Lord did declare that He **would** send against them,
007:167   those who **would** afflict them with grievous chastisement.
007:169   that they **would** not ascribe to Allah anything but the
007:169   came their way, they **would** (again) seize them.
008:023   they **would** but have turned back and declined (faith).
008:023   He **would** indeed have made them listen:
008:038   their past **would** be forgiven them;
008:042   ye **would** certainly have failed in the appointment:
008:043   and ye **would** surely have disputed in (your) decision:
008:043   ye **would** surely have been discouraged,
008:068   a severe punishment **would** have reached you
008:073   there **would** be tumult and oppression on earth,
009:016   Do you think that you **would** be left alone while
009:032   Fain **would** they extinguish Allah's light
009:039   but Him ye **would** not harm in the least,
009:042   they **would** (all) without doubt have followed thee,
009:042   they **would** destroy their own souls;
009:042   They **would** indeed swear by Allah, "If we only
009:046   they **would** certainly have made some preparation
009:047   they **would** not have added to your (strength)
009:047   and there **would** have been some among you
009:047   among you who **would** have listened to them.
009:057   they **would** turn straightway thereto with an obstinate
009:059   (That **would** been the right course).
009:075   they **would** give (largely) in charity,
009:086   we **would** be with those who sit (at home)."
010:011   as they **would** fain hasten on the good,-
010:011   then **would** their respite be settled at once.
010:013   with Clear Signs, but they **would** not believe!
010:014   after them, to see how ye **would** behave!
010:019   their differences **would** have been settle between
010:050   what portion of it **would** the Sinners wish to hasten?
010:051   "**Would** ye then believe in it at last, when it
010:054   they **would** declare (their) repentance when they
010:054   **would** fain give it in ransom:
010:074   but they **would** not believe what they had already
010:096   of thy Lord hath been verified **would** not believe-
010:099   they **would** all have believed,-
011:007   after death, the Unbelievers **would** be sure to say,
011:030   "And O my People! who **would** help me against Allah
011:063   What then **would** ye add to my (portion)
011:072   That **would** indeed be a wonderful thing!"
011:080   He said: "**Would** that I had power to suppress you
011:110   the matter **would** have been decided between them:
011:117   Nor **would** thy Lord be the One to destroy
012:024   did she desire him, and he **would** have desired her,
013:018   **would** they offer it for ransom.
013:031   or the dead were made to speak, (this **would** be the one!)
014:047   Never think that Allah **would** fail His messengers

WOULD (continued)

015:008   behold! no respite **would** they have!
015:015   They **would** only say: "Our eyes have been intoxicated:
016:018   never **would** ye be able to number them:
016:018   If ye **would** count up the favours of Allah,
016:028   Then **would** they offer submission (with the pretence),
016:061   just as they **would** not be able to anticipate it
016:061   they **would** not be able to delay (the punishment)
016:061   He **would** not leave, on the on the (earth),
017:004   mighty arrogance (and twice **would** they be punished)!
017:004   that twice **would** they do mischief on the earth
017:015   nor **would** We punish until, We had sent
017:042   behold, they **would** certainly have sought out
017:073   they **would** certainly have made thee (their) friend!
017:076   but in that case they **would** not have stayed
017:100   behold, ye **would** keep them back, for fear
018:020   they **would** stone you or force you to return
018:020   and in that case ye **would** never attain prosperity."
018:042   **Would** I had never ascribed partners to my Lord
018:050   Evil **would** be the exchange for the wrong-doers!
018:058   then surely He **would** have hastened their Punishment:
018:080   and we feared that he **would** grieve them by obstinate
018:081   "So we desired that their Lord **would** give them in
018:109   be exhausted than **would** the words of my Lord,
018:109   sooner **would** the ocean be exhausted than
019:023   **would** that I had been a thing forgotten."
019:023   "Ah! **would** that I had died before this!
019:058   they **would** fall down in prostrate adoration and in tears.
020:134   they **would** have said: "Our Lord ! If only thou hadst
021:017   if We **would** do (such a thing)!
021:022   besides Allah, there **would** have been ruin in both!
021:034   if then thou shouldst die, **would** they live permanently?
021:048   a Light and a Message for those who **would** do right,-
021:099   If these had been gods, they **would** not have got there!
021:106   for people who **would** (truly) worship Allah.
022:025   and **would** keep back (men) from the Way of Allah,
022:040   there **would** surely have been pulled down monasteries,
022:073   they **would** have no power to release it from the fly:
023:056   We **would** hasten them on in every good? Nay, they
023:071   and all beings therein **would** have been in ruin.
023:075   they **would** obstinately persist in their transgression,
023:091   each god **would** have taken away what he had created,
023:091   and some **would** have lorded it over others!
023:115   and that ye **would** not be brought back to Us
024:008   But it **would** avert the punishment from the wife,
024:010   Full of Wisdom,-(ye **would** be ruined indeed).
024:014   a grievous chastisement **would** have seized you
024:020   kindness and mercy, (ye **would** be ruined indeed).
024:021   not one of you **would** ever have been pure:
024:053   command them, they **would** leave (their homes).
025:027   "Oh! **would** that I had taken a (straight) path
025:028   "Ah! woe is me! **would** that I had never taken
025:042   "He indeed **would** well-nigh have misled us
026:004   to which they **would** bend their necks in humility.
026:199   recited it to them they **would** not have believed in it.
027:048   who made mischief in the land, and **would** not reform.
027:055   "**Would** ye really approach men in your lusts
028:039   they **would** not have to return to Us!"
028:076   that their very keys **would** have been a burden
028:086   that the Book **would** be sent to thee except as
029:048   indeed, **would** the talkers of vanities have doubt.
029:053   the Punishment **would** certainly have come to them:
031:027   yet **would** not the Words of Allah be exhausted

WOULD (continued)

033:014   They **would** certainly have brought it to pass,
033:020   they **would** fight but little.
033:020   they **would** wish they were in the deserts (wandering)
033:030   the Punishment **would** be doubled to her,
033:066   they will say: "Woe to us! **would** that we had
033:067   And they **would** say: "Our Lord! We obeyed
034:014   they **would** not have tarried in the humiliating
034:033   it **would** only be a requital for their (ill) Deeds.
035:037   so that he that **would** should receive admonition?
035:042   they **would** be more rightly guided than anyone
035:045   He **would** not leave on the back of the (earth)
036:024   "I **would** indeed, then be in manifest Error.
036:026   He said: "Ah me! **would** that my People knew
036:043   then **would** there be no helper (to hear their cry),
036:047   He **would** have fed, (himself)?-
037:035   **would** puff themselves up with Pride,
037:054   He said: "**Would** ye like to look down?"
037:144   He **would** certainly have remained inside the Fish
037:172   That they **would** certainly be assisted,
039:013   Say: "I **would**, if I disobeyed my Lord,
039:038   they **would** be sure to say, "Allah."
039:047   (in vain) **would** they offer it for ransom from the
041:014   He **would** certainly have sent down angels:
041:044   they **would** have said: "Why are not its verses
041:045   (their differences) **would** have been settled between
042:014   the matter **would** have been settled between them:
042:021   the matter **would** have been decided between them
042:027   they **would** indeed transgress beyond all bounds
042:033   then **would** they become motionless on the back
042:043   that **would** truly be an affair of great resolution.
043:009   They **would** be sure to reply, 'They were created by
043:032   Is it they who **would** portion out the Mercy
043:033   (all) men might become one community **would** provide,
043:038   "**Would** that between me and thee were the distance
043:077   They will cry: "O Malik! **would** that thy Lord
043:081   I **would** be the first to worship."
046:011   (such men) **would** not have gone to it first,
047:037   and press you, ye **would** covetously withhold,
047:037   and He **would** bring out all your ill-feeling.
047:038   then they **would** not be like you!
048:012   and the Believers **would** never return to their families;
048:022   they **would** certainly turn their backs;
048:022   then **would** they find neither protector nor helper.
048:025   a guilt **would** have accrued to you without (your)
048:025   (Allah **would** have allowed you to force your way,
049:005   it **would** be best for them: but Allah is Oft-Forgiving,
049:007   your (wishes), ye **would** certainly suffer:
049:012   Nay, ye **would** abhor it... But fear Allah;
049:012   **Would** any of you like to eat the flesh of his dead
051:009   (away from the Truth) such as **would** be deluded.
052:044   they **would** (only) say: "Clouds gathered in heaps!"
053:022   Behold, such **would** be indeed a division most unfair!
056:065   And ye **would** be left in wonderment,
056:081   Is it such a Message that ye **would** hold in light esteem?
059:002   Little did ye think that they **would** get out:
059:002   that their fortresses **would** defend them from Allah!
059:003   He **would** certainly have punished them in this world:
060:002   If they overcome you they **would** behave to you
068:009   thou shouldst be pliant: so **would** thy be pliant.
068:022   in the morning, if ye **would** gather the fruits."
068:049   he **would** indeed have been cast off on the naked shore,
068:051   And the Unbelievers **would** almost trip thee up

WOULD (continued)

069:020 that my Account **would** (one Day) reach me!"
069:025 "Ah! **would** that my record had not been given to me!
069:027 "Ah! **would** that (Death) had made an end of me!
069:033 "This was he that **would** not believe in Allah Most High,
069:034 "And **would** not encourage the feeding of the indigent!
070:011 **would** that he could redeem himself from the
070:015 By no means! for it **would** be the Blazing Fire-
072:007 ye thought, that Allah **would** not raise up any one
078:040 "Woe unto me! **Would** that I were (mere) dust!"
079:012 They say: "It **would**, in that case, be a return with lost!"
083:031 to their own people, they **would** return jesting;
083:032 they **would** say, "Behold! These are the people truly
084:014 did he think that he **would** not have to return (to Us)!
089:024 He will say: "Ah! **would** that I had sent forth (Good
102:005 with certainty of mind, (ye **would** beware)!
104:003 Thinking that his wealth **would** make him last for ever!

WOULDST

002:120 then **wouldst** thou find neither Protector
004:077 **Wouldst** Thou not grant us respite to our
005:067 thou **wouldst** not have fulfilled and proclaimed
005:116 Thou **wouldst** indeed have known it.
007:155 **wouldst** Thou destroy us for the deeds of the foolish
013:037 then **wouldst** thou find neither protector nor
017:074 thou **wouldst** nearly have inclined to them a little.
017:075 and moreover thou **wouldst** have found none to help
017:086 then **wouldst** thou find none to plead thy affair
018:006 Thou **wouldst** only, perchance, fret thyself
018:017 Thou **wouldst** have seen the sun, when it rose,
018:018 Thou **wouldst** have thought awake, whilst they
018:018 thou **wouldst** have certainly turned back from their flight,
018:018 and **wouldst** certainly have been filled with terror of them.
018:070 The other said: "If then thou **wouldst** follow me,
018:076 then **wouldst** thou have received (full) excuse from my
024:053 if only thou **wouldst** command them, they would
039:019 **Wouldst** thou, then, deliver one (who is)
059:014 thou **wouldst** think they were united,
059:021 verily, thou **wouldst** have seen it humble itself
063:005 and though **wouldst** see them turning away their faces
076:019 thou **wouldst** think them scattered Pearls.
079:018 "And say to him, `**Wouldst** thou that thou shouldst

WOUND

003:140 If a **wound** hath touched you, be sure a similar
003:140 be sure a similar **wound** hath touched the others.

WOUNDED

003:172 even after being **wounded**, those who do right
005:045 tooth for tooth, and **wounded** equal for equal."

WOUNDS

069:036 the foul pus from the washing of **wounds**,

WRANGLE

002:253 but they (chose) to **wrangle**,
022:068 If they do **wrangle** with thee,

WRANGLING

002:197 nor **wrangling** in the Hajj.

WRAPPED

074:001 O thou **wrapped** up (in a mantle)!

WRAPPINGS

002:088 They say, "Our hearts are the **wrappings**
004:155 that they said, "Our hearts are the **Wrappings**; nay,

WRATH

001:007 Those whose (portion) is not **wrath**,
002:061 they drew on themselves the **wrath** of Allah.

WRATH (continued)

002:090 have they drawn on themselves **Wrath** upon **Wrath**.
003:112 they draw on themselves **wrath** from Allah.
003:162 the man who draws on Himself the **wrath** of Allah,
004:093 and the **wrath** and the curse of Allah are upon him,
005:060 Those who incurred the curse of Allah and His **wrath**,
005:080 that Allah's **wrath** is on them,
006:147 never will His **wrath** be turned back.
006:148 until they tasted of Our **wrath**.
007:071 He said: "Punishment and **wrath** have already
007:097 Our **wrath** by night while they were asleep?
007:152 will indeed be overwhelmed with **wrath** from their Lord
008:016 he draws on himself the **wrath** of Allah,
010:027 no defender will they have from (the **wrath** of) Allah:
012:107 against them covering veil of the **wrath** of Allah.
014:021 then avail us at all against the **wrath** of Allah?"
014:044 when the **Wrath** will reach them:
015:090 (Of just such **wrath**) as We sent down on those
016:026 and the **Wrath** seized them from directions
016:034 and that every (**Wrath**) at which they had scoffed
016:045 or that the **Wrath** will not seize them from directions
016:094 and a mighty **Wrath** descend on you.
016:106 to Unbelief,-on them is **Wrath** from Allah,
016:113 falsely rejected him; so the **Wrath** seized them
017:057 they hope foe His Mercy and fear His **Wrath**:
017:057 for the **Wrath** of thy Lord is something to take heed of.
018:055 or the **Wrath** be brought to them face to face?
020:081 My **Wrath** do perish indeed!
020:081 lest My **Wrath** should descend on you:
020:086 that **Wrath** should descend from your Lord on you,
021:042 and by day from (the **Wrath** of) The Most Gracious?"
021:046 If but a breath of the **Wrath** of thy Lord do touch them
021:087 And remember Zun-nun, when he departed in **wrath**:
024:009 she solemnly invokes the **wrath** of Allah on herself
025:065 for its **Wrath** is indeed an affliction grievous,-
025:065 avert from us the **Wrath** of Hell,
029:010 treat men's oppression as if it were the **Wrath** of Allah!
029:029 "Bring us the **Wrath** of Allah if thou tellest the truth."
034:005 for such will be a Chastisement of Painful **wrath**.
040:083 but that very (**Wrath**) at which they were wont to scoff
042:016 on them is **Wrath**, and for them will be a Chastisement
048:006 the **Wrath** of Allah is on them:
054:037 My **Wrath** and My Warning."
057:013 all alongside will be (**wrath** and) Punishment!
058:014 to such a have the **Wrath** of Allah upon them?
059:002 But the (**wrath** of) Allah came to them
060:013 to the people on whom is the **Wrath** of Allah.
069:047 Nor could any of you withhold him (from Our **wrath**).

WREAK

007:126 "But thou dost **wreak** thy vengeance on us

WRETCH

031:032 except only a perfidious ungrateful (**wretch**)!
043:052 who is a contemptible **wretch** and can scarcely express

WRETCHED

011:105 some will be **wretched** and some will be blessed.
011:106 Those who are **wretched** shall be in the Fire:

WRITE

002:079 Woe to them for what their hands do **write**,
002:079 Then woe to those who **write** the Book
002:282 as Allah has taught him, so let him **write**.
002:282 let not the scribe refuse to **write**:
002:282 let a scribe **write** down faithfully as between the parties:
003:053 then **write** us down among those who bear witness."

WRITE (continued)

005:083 we believe, **write** us down among the witnesses.
018:109 ocean were ink (wherewith to **write** out) the words
052:041 is in their hands and they **write** it down?
068:001 By the Pen and by the (Record) which (men) **write**,-
068:047 is in their hands, so that they can **write** it down?

WRITING

002:282 reduce to **writing** (your contract) for a future period,
002:282 reduce them to **writing**
002:282 there is no blame on you if ye reduce it not to **writing**.
003:145 the term being fixed as by **writing**.
007:154 in the **writing** thereon was Guidance and Mercy
024:033 ask for a deed in **writing** (for emancipation)
031:027 of Allah be exhausted (in the **writing**):
033:006 such is the **writing** in the Book (of Allah).
082:011 Kind and honorable, **writing** down (your deeds):

WRITTEN

006:007 had sent unto thee a **written** (Message) on parchment,
017:058 That is **written** in the (eternal) Record.
025:005 which he has caused to be **written**:
058:022 For such He has **written** Faith in their hearts,
080:015 (**Written**) by the hands of scribes-

WRONG

002:051 and ye did grievous **wrong**.
002:053 and the criterion (between right and **wrong**),
002:145 then wert thou indeed (clearly) in the **wrong**.
002:182 there is no **wrong** in Him;
002:185 guidance and judgment (between right and **wrong**).
002:229 such persons **wrong** (themselves as well as others).
002:246 knowledge of those of those who do **wrong**.
003:003 Criterion (of judgement between right and **wrong**).
003:057 but Allah loveth not those who do **wrong**.
003:104 and forbidding what is **wrong**:
003:110 Enjoining what is right, forbidding what is **wrong**,
003:114 and forbid what is **wrong**;
003:117 but they **wrong** themselves.
003:135 persisting knowingly in (the **wrong**) they have done.
003:140 And Allah loveth not those that do **wrong**.
003:154 moved by **wrong** suspicions of Allah-suspicions
003:172 and refrain from **wrong** have a great reward;
004:168 Those who reject Faith and do **wrong**,-Allah will
005:008 to you make you swerve to **wrong** and depart form
005:029 and that is the reward of those who do **wrong**."
005:077 of people who went **wrong** in times gone by,-
006:021 Who doth more **wrong** than he who inventeth
006:047 will any be destroyed except those who do **wrong**?"
006:058 But Allah knoweth best those who do **wrong**."
006:068 sit not thou in the company of those who do **wrong**.
006:082 and mix not their beliefs with **wrong**-that are
006:144 But who doth more **wrong** than one who invents a lie
006:145 For Allah guideth not people who do **wrong**.
006:157 then who could do more **wrong** than one who rejecteth
006:160 No **wrong** shall be done unto them.
007:005 on cry did they utter but this: "Indeed we did **wrong**."
007:041 such is Our requital of those who do **wrong**.
007:148 They took it for worship and they did **wrong**.
007:153 But those who do **wrong** but repent thereafter and
007:177 who reject Our signs and **wrong** their own souls.
008:019 if ye desist (from **wrong**), it will be best for you:
008:025 not in particular (only) those of you who do **wrong**:
008:029 you a Criterion (to judge between right and **wrong**),
009:019 and Allah guides not those who do **wrong**.
009:023 above faith: if any of you do so, they do **wrong**.

WRONG (continued)

009:036 that is the right religion so **wrong** not yourselves
009:037 the Unbelievers are led to **wrong** thereby:
009:047 But Allah knoweth well those who do **wrong**.
009:070 Who wrongs them, but they **wrong** their own souls.
009:109 And Allah guideth not people that do **wrong**.
010:013 before you We destroyed when they did **wrong**:
010:017 Who doth more **wrong** than such as forge a lie
010:039 but see what was the end of those who did **wrong**!
010:054 and no **wrong** will be done unto them.
010:106 thou shalt certainly be of those who do **wrong**."
011:018 the Curse of Allah is on those who do **wrong**!-
011:018 Who doth more **wrong** than those who forge a lie
011:044 the word went forth: "Away with those who do **wrong**!"
011:083 ever far from those who do **wrong**!
011:102 He chastises communities in the midst of their **wrong**:
011:113 And incline not to those who do **wrong**,
012:023 Truly to no good come those who do **wrong**!"
014:027 But Allah will leave, to stray, those who do **wrong**:
014:042 the deeds of those who do **wrong**.
015:039 and I will put them all in the **wrong**,-
015:039 because Thou hast put me in the **wrong**,
015:039 I will make (**wrong**) fair-seeming to them on
015:042 put themselves in the **wrong** and follow thee."
016:118 We did them no **wrong**, but they
016:118 but they were used to doing **wrong** to themselves.
016:119 to those who do **wrong** in ignorance,
016:126 to the **wrong** that has been done to you:
018:015 Who doth more **wrong** than such as invent
018:057 And who doth more **wrong** than one who is reminded
018:087 He said: "Whoever doth **wrong**, him shall we punish;
020:092 thee back, when thou sawest them going **wrong**,
021:029 thus do We reward those who do **wrong**.
021:046 "Woe to us! we did **wrong** indeed!"
021:064 and said, "Surely ye are the ones in the **wrong**."
021:087 Glory to Thee: I was indeed **wrong**!"
021:097 we were indeed heedless of this; nay, we truly did **wrong**!"
022:041 enjoin the right and forbid **wrong**:
022:071 for those that do **wrong** there is no helper.
023:028 Who has saved us from the people who do **wrong**."
023:041 So away with the people who do **wrong**!
023:094 amongst the people who do **wrong**!"
024:021 he will (but) command what is indecent and **wrong**:
024:050 Nay, it is they themselves who do **wrong**.
024:058 it is not **wrong** for you or for them to move about
025:019 And whoever among you does **wrong**, him shall
027:011 "But if any have done **wrong** and have thereafter
028:040 now behold! what was the End of those who did **wrong**!
029:046 who do **wrong** but say, "We believe in the Revelation
029:068 And who does more **wrong** than he who invents
031:017 enjoin what is just, and forbid what is **wrong**:
031:032 among them those that falter between (right and **wrong**).
032:022 And who does more **wrong** than one to whom
033:036 he is indeed on a clearly **wrong** Path.
035:032 among them some who **wrong** their own souls;
037:069 Truly they found their fathers on the **wrong** Path;
037:113 and (some) that obviously do **wrong**, to themselves.
038:024 the Partners (in business) who **wrong** each other:
039:032 Who, then, doth more **wrong** than one who
042:039 when an oppressive **wrong** is inflicted on them,
042:040 for (Allah) loveth not those who do **wrong**.
042:041 defend themselves after a **wrong** (done) to him,
043:039 When ye have done **wrong**, it will avail you nothing,

WRONG (continued)

049:011   and those who do not desist are (indeed) doing **wrong**.
052:047   And verily, for those who do **wrong**, there is
053:017   (His) sight never swerved, nor did it go **wrong**!
056:051   O ye that go **wrong**, and deny (the truth);
056:092   of those who deny (the truth) who go **wrong**,
057:020   is a Chastisement sever (for the devotees of **wrong**).
057:025   the Book and the Balance (of Right and **Wrong**),
060:009   (in these circumstances), that do **wrong**.
061:005   Then when they went **wrong**, Allah let
061:005   Allah let their hearts go **wrong**.
061:007   And Allah guides not those who do **wrong**.
061:007   Who doth greater **wrong** than one who forges
062:005   and Allah guides not people who do **wrong**.
062:007   And Allah knows well those that do **wrong**!
065:001   does verily **wrong** his (own) soul:
066:011   and save me from those that do **wrong**";
068:029   Verily we have been doing **wrong**!"
075:005   But man wishes to do **wrong** (even) in the time
091:008   And its inspiration as to its **wrong** and its right;

WRONG-DOER

011:031   I should, if I did, indeed be a **wrong-doer**."
025:027   The Day that the **wrong-doer** will bite

WRONG-DOERS

002:054   and slay yourselves (the **wrong-doers**);
002:095   And Allah is well-acquainted with the **wrong-doers**.
002:254   Those who reject Faith-they are the **wrong-doers**
002:270   But the **wrong-doers** have no helpers.
003:094   they are indeed unjust **wrong-doers**.
003:128   for they are indeed **wrong-doers**.
003:151   and evil is the home of the **wrong-doers**!
003:192   and never will **wrong-doers** find any helpers!
005:045   by what Allah hath revealed, they are **wrong-doers**.
005:072   There will for the **wrong-doers** be no one to help.
005:081   but most of them are rebellious **wrong-doers**.
005:107   if we did, behold! we will be **wrong-doers**."
006:021   But verily the **wrong-doers** never shall prosper.
006:045   Of the **wrong-doers** the last remnant was cut off
006:129   Thus do We make the **wrong-doers** turn to each other,
006:135   the **wrong-doers** will not prosper."
007:044   "The curse of Allah is on the **wrong-doers**;
007:047   send us not to the company of the **wrong-doers**."
007:165   but We visited the **wrong-doers** with a grievous
008:054   for they were all oppressors and **wrong-doers**.
010:052   "At length will be said to the **wrong-doers**: 'Taste ye the
011:067   The (mighty) Blast overtook the **wrong-doers**,
011:094   but the (mighty Blast did seize the **wrong-doers**,
011:116   But the **wrong-doers** pursued the enjoyment of the
012:075   Thus it is We punish the **wrong-doers**!
014:013   "Verily We shall cause the **wrong-doers** to perish!
014:022   For **wrong-doers** there must be a grievous Chastisement.
014:044   then will the **wrong-doers** say: "Our Lord! respite us
015:078   the Companions of the Wood were also **wrong-doers**;
016:085   When the **wrong-doers** (actually) see the Chastisement
018:029   for the **wrong-doers** We have prepared a Fire
018:050   Evil would be the exchange for the **wrong-doers**!
019:072   the **wrong-doers** therein, (humbled) to their knees.
021:003   The **wrong-doers** conceal their private counsels,
021:014   "Ah! woe to us! we were indeed **wrong-doers**!"
022:053   verily the **wrong-doers** are in a schism far (from the
023:027   and address me not in favour of the **wrong-doers**:
023:107   then shall we be **wrong-doers** indeed!"
025:037   for (all) **wrong-doers** a grievous Chastisement:

WRONG-DOERS (continued)

028:037   that the **wrong-doers** will not prosper."
030:029   Nay, the **wrong-doers** (merely) fellow their
034:031   the **wrong-doers** will be made to stand before
034:042   and We shall say to the **wrong-doers**, "Taste ye
035:037   for the **Wrong-doers** there is no helper."
035:040   the **wrong-doers** promise each other nothing but
037:022   "The **wrong-doers** and their wives, and the
037:063   We have truly made it (as) a trial for the **wrong-doers**.
038:055   Yea, such! But-for the **wrong-doers** will be
039:024   It will be said to the **wrong-doers**: "Taste ye
039:047   Even if the **wrong-doers** had all that there is
039:051   And the **wrong-doers** of this (generation)-
040:018   intimate friend nor intercessors will **wrong-doers** have,
040:052   will it be to **Wrong-doers** to present their excuses,
042:008   and the **wrong-doers** will have no protector
042:021   the **wrong-doers** will have a grievous Chastisement.
042:022   Thou wilt see the **wrong-doers** in fear on account
042:044   And thou wilt see the **wrong-doers**, when in
042:045   Behold! Truly the **wrong-doers** are in a lasting
043:065   then woe to the **wrong-doers**, from the Chastisement
045:019   it is only **wrong-doers** (that stand as) Protectors,
051:059   For the **wrong-doers**, their portion is like
059:017   Such is the reward of **wrong-doers**.
071:024   the **wrong-doers** but in straying (from their mark)."
071:028   **wrong-doers** grant Thou no increase but in
076:031   but the **wrong-doers**,-for them has He prepared

WRONG-DOING

002:182   partiality or **wrong-doing** on the part of the testator.
013:006   full of forgiveness for mankind for their **wrong-doing**.
016:028   take in a state of **wrong-doing** to their own souls.
016:061   If Allah were to punish men for their **wrong-doing**,
022:045   We destroyed, which were given to **wrong-doing**?
022:048   did I give respite, which were given to **wrong-doing**?
027:052   in utter ruin,-because they practised **wrong-doing**.
027:085   be fulfilled against them, because of their **wrong-doing**,
028:021   save me from people given to **wrong-doing**."
028:050   For Allah guides not people given to **wrong-doing**.
031:013   for false worship is indeed the highest **wrong-doing**."
042:042   oppress men with **wrong-doing** and insolently
091:011   (their prophet) through their inordinate **wrong-doing**.

WRONG-DOINGS

009:102   (there are who) have acknowledged their **wrong-doings**:

WRONGDOING

049:007   to you unbelief, **wrongdoing**, and rebellion:

WRONGED

002:054   **wronged** yourselves by your worship of the calf:
003:117   harvest of men who have **wronged** their own souls:
003:117   it is not Allah that hath **wronged** them,
003:135   an act of indecency or **wronged** their own souls.
004:049   and they will not be **wronged** a whit.
004:148   except by one who has been **wronged**, for Allah
007:023   they said: "Our Lord we have **wronged** our own souls:
010:047   and they will not be **wronged**.
011:101   It was not We that **wronged** them:
011:101   they **wronged** their own souls:
014:045   of men who **wronged** themselves ye were clearly shown
016:033   nay, they **wronged** their own souls.
016:033   But Allah **wronged** them not: nay,
018:035   He went into his garden while he **wronged** himself:
019:060   and will not be **wronged** in the least,-
022:039   permission is given (to fight), because they are **wronged**;-
023:062   They will never be **wronged**.

WRONGED (continued)

027:044   I have indeed **wronged** my soul:
028:016   I have indeed **wronged** by soul! Do Thou
029:040   it was not Allah Who **wronged** them:
029:040   they **wronged** themselves.
030:009   but they **wronged** their own souls.
030:009   it was not Allah Who **wronged** them, but they
034:019   but they **wronged** themselves (therein).
036:054   on that Day, not a soul will be **wronged** in the least,
038:022   two disputants, one of whom has **wronged** the other:
038:024   "He has undoubtedly **wronged** thee in demanding thy
039:069   and they will not be **wronged** (in the least).
045:022   it has earned, and none of them shall be **wronged**.

WRONGFULLY

002:092   and ye did behave **wrongfully**.
002:188   intent that ye may eat up **wrongfully** and knowingly
004:161   and that they devoured men's wealth **wrongfully**;
007:009   for that they **wrongfully** treated Our Signs.
007:103   But they **wrongfully** rejected them: so see
012:079   indeed (if we did so), we should be acting **wrongfully**."
017:033   And if anyone is slain **wrongfully**, We have
017:059   a visible Sign-but they treated her **wrongfully**:
022:025   whose purpose therein is profanity **wrongfully** them will
027:014   souls acknowledged them **wrongfully** and out of pride:

WRONGS

002:231   if anyone does that, He **wrongs** his own soul.
004:110   If anyone does evil or **wrongs** his own soul but
009:070   Who **wrongs** them, but they wrong their own souls.
010:044   it is man that **wrongs** his own soul.

WROTE

021:105   Before this We **wrote** in the Psalms, after the

WROUGHT

007:147   rewarded except as they have **wrought**?
016:112   because of the (evil) which (its people) **wrought**.
030:030   on change (there is) in the work (**wrought**) by Allah:
042:030   is because of the things your hands have **wrought**,

Y

YA
019:001   Kaf. Ha. **Ya**. 'Ain. Sad.
036:001   **Ya** - Sin.

YAGUTH
071:023   Wadd nor Suwa, neither **Yaguth** nor Yauq, nor Nasr';-

YAHYA
003:039   "Allah doth give thee glad tidings of **Yahya**,
019:007   good news of a son: his name shall be **Yahya**:
019:012   "O **Yahya**! take hold of the Book with might":
021:090   So We listened to him: and We granted him **Yahya**:

YARN
016:092   into untwisted strands the **yarn** which she has spun,

YATHRIB
033:013   "Ye men of **Yathrib**! Ye cannot

YAUQ
071:023   Wadd nor Suwa, neither Yaguth nor **Yauq**, nor Nasr';-

YE
002:021   that **ye** may become righteous,
002:021   O **ye** people! worship your Guardian-Lord,
002:022   unto Allah when **ye** know (the truth).
002:023   if **ye** are truthful.
002:023   And if **ye** are in doubt
002:024   But if **ye** cannot-and of a surety **ye** cannot
002:028   How can **ye** reject the faith in Allah?
002:028   and again to Him will **ye** return.
002:028   Seeing that **ye** were without life,
002:030   He said: "I know what **ye** know not."
002:031   names of these if **ye** are right."
002:033   and I know what **ye** reveal and what **ye** conceal?"
002:035   things therein as (where and when) **ye** will;
002:035   or **ye** run into harm and transgression."
002:036   And We said: "Get **ye** down, (all you people),
002:038   We said: "Get **ye** down all from here;
002:042   when **ye** know (what it is).
002:044   Do **ye** enjoin right conduct on the people,
002:044   and yet **ye** study the Scripture?
002:044   Will **ye** not understand?
002:051   and **ye** did grievous wrong.
002:051   **ye** took the calf (for worship),
002:054   "O my people! **Ye** have indeed wronged yourselves
002:055   And remember **ye** said: "O Moses!
002:056   **ye** had the chance to be grateful.
002:058   and eat of the plenty therein as **ye** wish;
002:061   and **ye** shall find what **ye** want!"
002:061   He said: "Will **ye** exchange the better
002:061   Go **ye** down to any town,
002:061   And remember **ye** said: "O Moses!
002:063   perchance **ye** may fear Allah."
002:064   But **ye** turned back thereafter:
002:064   **ye** had surely been among the lost.
002:065   "Be **ye** apes, despised and rejected."
002:065   And well **ye** knew those amongst you
002:067   "Allah commands that **ye** sacrifice a heifer.
002:068   now do what **ye** are commanded!"
002:072   but Allah was to bring forth what **ye** did hide.
002:072   Remember **ye** slew a man and fell into a dispute

002:073   perchance **ye** may understand.
002:074   And Allah is not unmindful of what **ye** do.
002:075   Can **ye** (O **ye** men of Faith) entertain
002:076   Do **ye** not understand (their aim)?
002:080   Say: "Have **ye** taken a promise from Allah,
002:080   **ye** say of Allah what **ye** do not know?"
002:083   Then did **ye** turn back,
002:083   and **ye** backslide (even now).
002:084   and this **ye** solemnly ratified.
002:084   and to this **ye** were witness.
002:085   a part of the Book that **ye** believe in,
002:085   they come to you as captives, **ye** ransom them,
002:085   and do **ye** reject the rest?
002:085   After this it is **ye**, the same people,
002:085   For Allah is not unmindful of what **ye** do.
002:087   **ye** are puffed up with pride?
002:087   Some **ye** called impostors, and others **ye** slay!
002:087   a Messenger with what **ye** yourselves desire not,
002:091   if **ye** did indeed believe?"
002:091   Say: Why then have **ye** slain the prophets
002:092   yet **ye** worshipped the Calf (even) after that,
002:092   and **ye** did behave wrongfully.
002:093   behests of your Faith if ye have any faith!"
002:094   then seek **ye** for death, if **ye** are sincere."
002:104   O **ye** of Faith! say not (to the Prophet)
002:107   And besides Him **ye** have neither patron nor helper.
002:108   Would **ye** question your Messenger
002:109   back to infidelity after **ye** have believed,
002:110   **ye** shall find it with Allah:
002:110   and whatever good **ye** send forth
002:110   for Allah sees well all that **ye** do.
002:111   Say: "Produce your proof if **ye** are truthful."
002:115   whithersoever **ye** turn, there is Allah's 'Face.
002:125   and take **ye** the Station of Abraham
002:133   "What will **ye** worship after me?"
002:133   Were **ye** witnesses when Death appeared
002:134   and **ye** of what **ye** do!
002:134   **ye** shall not be asked about what they did.
002:135   if **ye** would be guided (to salvation)."
002:136   Say ye: "We believer in Allah,
002:137   So if they believe as **ye** believe,
002:139   for our doings and **ye** for yours;
002:139   Say: Will **ye** dispute with us about Allah,
002:140   Say: Do **ye** know better than Allah?
002:140   But Allah is not unmindful of what **ye** do!
002:140   Or do **ye** say that Abraham,
002:141   and **ye** of what **ye** do! **Ye** shall not be asked!-
002:143   That **ye** might be witnesses over the nations,
002:144   wherever **ye** are, turn your faces in that direction.
002:148   Wheresoever **ye** are, Allah will bring you together.
002:149   And Allah is not unmindful of what **ye** do.
002:150   and **ye** may (consent to) be guided.
002:150   and wheresoever **ye** are, turn your face thither:
002:151   A similar (favour have **ye** already received)
002:152   Then do **ye** remember Me; I will remember you.
002:153   O **ye** who believe! seek help with
002:154   though **ye** perceive (it) not.
002:168   O **ye** people! eat of what is on earth,
002:169   of Allah that of which **ye** have no knowledge.
002:169   and that **ye** should say of Allah
002:172   if it is Him **ye** worship.
002:172   O **ye** who believe! eat of the good things

1055

YE (continued)

002:177 **ye** turn your faces toward East or West;
002:177 to fulfil the contracts which **ye** have made;
002:178 O **ye** who believe! the law of equality
002:179 O **ye** men of understanding;
002:179 that **ye** may restrain yourselves.
002:183 that **ye** may (learn) self-restraint.
002:183 O **ye** who believe! fasting is prescribed to you
002:184 And it is better for you that **ye** fast, if **ye** only knew.
002:185 and perchance **ye** shall be grateful.
002:187 while **ye** are in retreat in the mosques.
002:187 They are your garments and **ye** are their garments.
002:187 Allah knoweth what **ye** used to do secretly
002:188 with intent that **ye** may eat up wrongfully
002:189 it is virtue if **ye** fear Allah.
002:189 and fear Allah: that **ye** may prosper.
002:189 **ye** enter your houses from the back:
002:191 And slay them wherever **ye** catch them,
002:194 transgress **ye** likewise against him.
002:196 send and offering for sacrifice, such as **ye** may find,
002:196 but if **ye** are prevented (from completing it),
002:196 and when **ye** are in peaceful conditions (again),
002:197 So fear Me, O **ye** that are wise.
002:197 And whatever good **ye** do,
002:198 even though, before this, **ye** went astray.
002:198 It is no crime in you if **ye** seek of the bounty
002:198 Then when **ye** pour down from (Mount) 'Arafat,
002:200 So when **ye** have accomplished your rites,
002:200 as **ye** used to celebrate the praises of your fathers,-
002:203 **ye** will surely be gathered unto Him.
002:208 O **ye** who believe! enter into Islam
002:209 If **ye** backslide after the clear (Signs)
002:214 Or do **ye** think that **ye** shall enter Garden (of Bliss)
002:215 Say: Whatever wealth **ye** spend that is good,
002:215 And whatever **ye** do that is good,
002:216 and that **ye** love a thing which is bad for you.
002:216 But Allah knoweth, and **ye** know not.
002:216 **ye** dislike a thing which is good for you,
002:216 Fighting is prescribed upon you, and **ye** dislike it.
002:219 His Signs: in order that **ye** may consider-
002:220 if **ye** mix their affairs with yours,
002:222 **ye** may approach them as ordained for you
002:223 so approach your tilth when or how **ye** will;
002:223 and know that **ye** are to meet Him
002:229 If **ye** (judges) do indeed fear that they would be
002:231 When **ye** divorce women, and they (are about to)
002:232 When **ye** divorce women,
002:232 and Allah knows, and **ye** knows not.
002:233 that Allah sees well what **ye** do.
002:233 (the foster mother) what **ye** offered,
002:233 if **ye** decide on a foster-mother for your offspring
002:233 provided **ye** pay (the foster mother)
002:234 And Allah is well acquainted with what **ye** do.
002:235 Allah knows that **ye** cherish them in your hearts:
002:235 There is no blame on you if **ye** make an indirect
002:236 **ye** divorce women before consummation
002:237 And if **ye** divorce them before consummation,
002:237 For Allah sees well all that **ye** do.
002:239 If **ye** fear (an enemy), pray on foot,
002:239 but when **ye** are in security,
002:239 which **ye** knew not (before).
002:242 in order that **ye** may understand.
002:246 if **ye** were commanded to fight,

YE (continued)

002:246 that **ye** will not fight?"
002:248 Symbol for you if **ye** indeed have faith."
002:254 O **ye** who believe! spend out of (the bounties)
002:264 O **ye** who believe! cancel not your charity
002:265 Allah seeth well whatever **ye** do.
002:266 clear to you (His) Signs; that **ye** may consider.
002:267 good things which **ye** have (honorably) earned,
002:267 out of it **ye** may give away something,
002:267 when **ye** yourselves would not receive it
002:267 O **ye** who believe! give of the good things
002:270 And whatever **ye** spend in charity or whatever
002:271 but if **ye** conceal them,
002:271 And Allah is well acquainted with what **ye** do.
002:271 If **ye** disclose (acts of) charity,
002:272 and **ye** shall only do so seeking
002:272 and **ye** shall not be dealt with unjustly.
002:272 Whatever good **ye** give, shall be
002:272 **ye** give benefits your own souls,
002:273 And whatever of good **ye** give,
002:278 O **ye** who believe! fear Allah,
002:278 if **ye** are indeed believers.
002:279 but if **ye** repent **ye** shall have your capital sums:
002:279 If **ye** do it not, take notice of war
002:279 and **ye** shall no be dealt with unjustly.
002:280 that is best for you if **ye** only knew.
002:280 But if **ye** remit it by way of charity,
002:281 when **ye** shall be brought back to Allah.
002:282 if **ye** reduce it no to writing.
002:282 such as **ye** choose, for witnesses,
002:282 **ye** carry out on the spot among yourselves,
002:282 If **ye** do (such harm), it would be
002:282 whenever **ye** make a commercial contract;
002:282 O **ye** who believe! when **ye** deal with each other,
002:283 If **ye** are on a journey, and cannot find a scribe,
002:283 And Allah knoweth all that **ye** do.
002:284 Whether **ye** show what is in your minds
003:012 "Soon will **ye** be vanquished
003:020 "Do **ye** (also) submit yourselves?"
003:028 that **ye** may guard yourselves from them.
003:029 Say: "Whether **ye** hide what is in your hearts
003:031 Say: "If **ye** do love Allah, follow me:
003:049 Surely therein is a Sign for you if **ye** did believe.
003:049 and what **ye** store in your houses.
003:049 and I declare to you what **ye** eat,
003:055 between you of the matters wherein **ye** dispute.
003:055 then shall **ye** all return to Me,
003:064 say **ye**: "Bear witness that we (at least) are Muslims
003:065 **Ye** people of the Book! why dispute **ye** about Abraham,
003:065 Have **ye** no understanding?
003:066 Ah! **Ye** are those who fell to disputing (even)
003:066 in matters of which **ye** have no knowledge?
003:066 but why dispute **ye** in matters of which
003:066 It is Allah Who knows, and **ye** who know not!
003:066 which **ye** had some Knowledge!
003:070 of which **ye** are (yourselves) witnesses?
003:070 **Ye** People of the Book!
003:070 Why reject **ye** the Signs of Allah,
003:071 **Ye** People of the Book!
003:071 Why do **ye** clothe truth with falsehood,
003:071 while **ye** have knowledge?
003:073 (fear **ye**) lest a revelation be sent to someone
003:079 for **ye** have taught the Book and **ye** have

YE (continued)

003:079	"Be **ye** worshippers of Him (Who is truly
003:079	"Be **ye** my worshippers rather than Allah's":
003:079	and **ye** have studied it earnestly."
003:080	after **ye** have bowed your will (to Allah in Islam)?
003:081	do **ye** believe him and render him help."
003:081	Allah said: "Do **ye** agree, and take My covenant
003:092	and whatever **ye** give, Allah knoweth it well.
003:092	unless **ye** give (freely) of that which **ye** love:
003:092	By no means shall **ye** attain righteousness unless
003:093	Say: "Bring **ye** the Torah and study it,
003:093	if **ye** be men of truth."
003:098	why reject **ye** the Signs of Allah,
003:098	when Allah is Himself witness to all **ye** do?
003:099	why obstruct **ye** those who believe,
003:099	while **ye** were yourselves witnesses
003:099	But Allah is not unmindful of all that **ye** do."
003:099	Say: "O **ye** People of the Book!
003:100	render you apostates after **ye** have believed!
003:100	O **ye** who believe! if **ye** listen to a faction
003:101	And how would **ye** deny Faith while unto you
003:102	O **ye** who believe! fear Allah as He should be feared,
003:103	so that by His Grace, **Ye** became brethren;
003:103	and **ye** were on the brink of the Pit of Fire,
003:103	that **ye** may be guided.
003:103	for **ye** were enemies and He joined your hearts
003:106	"Did **ye** reject Faith after accepting it?
003:110	**Ye** are the best of Peoples, evolved for mankind.
003:118	the Signs, if **ye** have wisdom.
003:118	O **ye** who believe! take not into your intimacy
003:119	though **ye** believe in the whole of the Book,
003:119	Ah! **ye** are those who love them,
003:120	But if **ye** are patient and do right,
003:123	Allah had helped you at Badr, when **ye** were helpless:
003:123	then fear Allah; thus may **ye** show your gratitude.
003:125	"Yea,-if **ye** remain firm, and act aright,
003:130	that **ye** may (really) prosper.
003:130	O **ye** who believe! devour not usury,
003:132	that **ye** may obtain mercy.
003:139	for **ye** must gain mastery if **ye** are true in Faith.
003:142	Did **ye** think that **ye** would enter Heaven
003:143	**Ye** did indeed wish for Death before **ye** encountered
003:143	now **ye** have seen it with your own eyes (and **ye** flinch!).
003:144	will **ye** then turn back on your heels?
003:149	O **ye** who believe! If **ye** obey the Unbelievers,
003:149	and **ye** will turn back (from Faith) to your own loss.
003:152	until **ye** flinched and fell to disputing about the order,
003:152	in sight (of the Victory) which **ye** covet.
003:153	Behold! **ye** were climbing up the high ground,
003:153	For Allah is well aware of all that **ye** do.
003:156	and Allah sees well all that **ye** do.
003:156	O **ye** who believe! Be not like the Unbelievers,
003:157	And if **ye** are slain, or die, in the way of Allah,
003:158	Lo! it is unto Allah that **ye** are brought together.
003:158	And if **ye** die, or are slain,
003:165	although **ye** smote (your enemies) with one twice
003:165	do **ye** say? "Whence is this?"
003:166	What **ye** suffered on the day the two armies met,
003:168	from your own selves, if **ye** speak the truth."
003:175	be **ye** not afraid of them, but fear Me, if **ye** have Faith.
003:179	**ye** have a reward great without measure.
003:179	and if **ye** believe and do right,
003:179	the Believers in the state in which **ye** are now,

YE (continued)

003:180	and Allah is well acquainted with all that **ye** do.
003:181	"Taste **ye** the Chastisement of the scorching Fire!
003:182	which your hands sent on before **ye**:
003:183	why then did **ye** slay them, if **ye** speak the truth?.
003:183	with Clear Signs and even with what **ye** ask for:
003:186	But if **ye** persevere patiently,
003:186	**Ye** shall certainly be tried and tested in your possessions
003:186	and **ye** shall certainly hear much that will grieve you,
003:193	'Believe **ye** in the Lord', and we have believed.
003:195	**ye** are members, one of another;
003:200	and fear Allah; that **ye** may prosper.
003:200	O **ye** who believe! Persevere in patience
004:001	through Whom **ye** demand your mutual (rights),
004:003	If **ye** fear that **ye** shall not be able to deal justly
004:003	but if **ye** fear that **ye** shall not be able deal justly with
004:006	When **ye** release their property to them,
004:006	if then **ye** find sound judgment in them,
004:011	**Ye** know not whether your parents or your children
004:012	but if they leave a child, **ye** get a fourth;
004:012	their share is a fourth, if **ye** leave no child;
004:012	but if **ye** leave a child, they get an eighth;
004:012	In what **ye** leave; their share is a fourth,
004:019	kindness and equity if **ye** take a dislike to them it may
004:019	it may be that **ye** dislike a thing,
004:019	Nor should **ye** treat them with harshness,
004:019	that **ye** may take away part of the dower **ye** have given
004:019	O **ye** who believe! **ye** are forbidden to inherit women
004:020	even if **ye** had given the latter a whole treasure for dower,
004:020	But if **ye** decide to take one wife in the place of another,
004:020	would **ye** take it by slander and a manifest sin?
004:021	when **ye** have gone in unto each other,
004:021	And how could **ye** take it when
004:023	born of your wives to whom **ye** have gone in,
004:023	no prohibition if **ye** have not gone in;
004:024	a dower is prescribed, **ye** agree mutually (to vary it),
004:024	provided **ye** seek (them in marriage) with gifts from your
004:025	**Ye** are one from another: wed them with their leave
004:025	but it is better for you that **ye** practice self-restraint.
004:027	follow their lust is that **ye** should turn away (from Him),
004:029	O **ye** who believe! eat not up your property
004:031	of the things which **ye** are forbidden to do,
004:031	If **ye** (but) eschew the most heinous of the things
004:034	whose part **ye** fear disloyalty and ill-conduct,
004:035	If **ye** fear a breach between them twain,
004:036	the Companion by your side, the way-farer (**ye** meet),
004:043	O **ye** who believe! approach not prayers in a state
004:043	until after washing your whole body if **ye** are ill,
004:043	or **ye** have been in contact with women,
004:043	until **ye** can understand all that **ye** say,
004:043	and **ye** find no water, then take for yourselves clean sand
004:044	and wish that **ye** should lose the right path.
004:047	O **ye** people of the Book! believe in what We have (now)
004:058	when **ye** judge between people that **ye** judge with justice:
004:059	O **ye** who believe! obey Allah, and obey
004:059	if **ye** do believe in Allah and the Last Day:
004:059	If **ye** differ in anything among yourselves,
004:071	O **ye** who believe! take your precautions.
004:075	And why should **ye** not fight in the cause
004:076	so fight **ye** against the friends, of Satan:
004:077	never will **ye** be dealt unjustly in the very least!
004:078	"Wherever **ye** are, death will find you out,
004:078	even if **ye** are in towers built up strong and high!"

004:088 Why should **ye** be divided into two parties
004:088 Would **ye** guide those whom Allah hath thrown out
004:089 seize them and slay them wherever **ye** find them;
004:089 They but wish that **ye** should reject Faith.
004:092 with whom **ye** have a treaty of mutual alliance,
004:094 O **ye** who believe! when **ye** go out in the cause
004:094 for Allah is well aware of all that **ye** do.
004:094 Even thus were **ye** yourselves before, till Allah
004:097 They say: "In what (plight) were **ye**?"
004:101 there is no blame on you if **ye** shorten your prayers,
004:101 When **ye** travel through the earth, there is
004:102 the inconvenience of rain or because **ye** are ill;
004:102 But there is no blame on you if **ye** put away
004:102 the Unbelievers wish, if **ye** were negligent of
004:103 When **ye** have performed the prayers, remember
004:103 but when **ye** are free from danger, set up
004:104 if **ye** are suffering hardships,
004:109 whose behalf **ye** may contend in this world;
004:127 that **ye** stand firm for justice to orphans.
004:127 There is not a good deed which **ye** do,
004:127 and yet whom **ye** desire to marry,
004:127 to whom **ye** give not the portions prescribed,
004:128 But if **ye** do good and practice self-restraint,
004:128 Allah is well-acquainted with all that **ye** do.
004:129 **Ye** are never able to do justice between wives
004:129 If **ye** come to a friendly understanding,
004:131 But if **ye** deny Him, lo! unto Allah belong all
004:135 follow not the lusts (of your hearts), lest **ye** swerve,
004:135 and if **ye** distort (Justice) or decline to do justice,
004:135 O **ye** who believe! stand out firmly for justice,
004:135 verily Allah is well-acquainted with all that **ye** do.
004:136 O **ye** who believe! believe in Allah
004:140 to a different theme: if **ye** did, **ye** would be like them.
004:140 that when **ye** hear the Message of Allah held in
004:140 **ye** are not to sit with them unless they turn to a
004:141 if **ye** do gain a victory from Allah, they say:
004:144 do **ye** wish to offer Allah an open proof against
004:144 O **ye** who believe! take not for friends
004:147 If **ye** are grateful and **ye** believe?
004:170 But if **ye** reject Faith, to Allah belong
004:176 thus doth Allah make clear to you (His law), lest **ye** err.
005:001 O **ye** who believe! fulfil (all) obligations.
005:001 are forbidden while **ye** are in the Sacred Precincts
005:002 but help **ye** not one another in sin and rancor:
005:002 Help **ye** one another in righteousness and piety,
005:002 But when **ye** are clear of the Sacred Precincts
005:002 and of the state of pilgrimage, **ye** may hunt and let not
005:002 O **ye** who believe! violate not the sanctity
005:003 unless **ye** are able to slaughter it (in due form);
005:004 and what **ye** have taught the beasts and birds of prey,
005:005 when **ye** give them their due dowers, and desire chastity,
005:006 to complete His favour to you, that **ye** may be grateful.
005:006 O **ye** who believe! when **ye** prepare for prayer,
005:006 or **ye** have been in contact with women,
005:006 and you find no water, then take clean sand or earth,
005:006 If **ye** are in a state of ceremonial impurity, bathe
005:006 But if **ye** are ill, or on a journey, or one of you cometh
005:007 when **ye** said: "We hear and we obey":
005:008 For Allah is well-acquainted with all that **ye** do.
005:008 O **ye** who believe! stand out firmly for Allah,
005:011 O **ye** who believe! call in remembrance
005:012 if **ye** (but) establish regular Prayers, pay Zakat

005:015 revealing to you much that **ye** used to hide in the Book,
005:018 Nay, **ye** are but men, of the men He hath created:
005:019 lest **ye** should say: "There came unto us no bringer
005:021 for then will **ye** be overthrown, to your own ruin."
005:023 But on Allah put your trust if **ye** have faith."
005:023 when once **ye** are in, victory will be yours;
005:024 and thy Lord, and fight **ye** two, while we sit here.
005:035 O **ye** who believe! do your duty to Allah,
005:035 and main in His cause: that **ye** may prosper.
005:041 they say, "If **ye** are given this, take it, but if
005:048 the truth of the matters in which **ye** dispute;
005:051 O **ye** who believe! take not the Jews and the
005:054 O **ye** who believe! if any from among you turn
005:057 O **ye** who believe! take not for friends
005:057 but fear **ye** Allah, if **ye** have Faith (indeed).
005:058 When **ye** proclaim your call to prayer, they take
005:059 do **ye** disapprove of us for no other reason than that
005:068 Say: "O People of the Book, **ye** have no ground to stand
005:068 to stand upon unless **ye** stand fast by the Torah.
005:076 Say: Will **ye** worship, besides Allah, something
005:087 O **ye** who believe! make not unlawful the good
005:088 but fear Allah, in Whom **ye** believe.
005:089 That is the expiation for the oaths **ye** have sworn.
005:089 make clear to you His Signs, that **ye** may be grateful.
005:090 O **ye** who believe! intoxicants and gambling,
005:090 eschew such (abomination), that **ye** may prosper.
005:091 of Allah and from prayer: will **ye** not then abstain?
005:094 O **ye** who believe! Allah doth but make a trial
005:095 O **ye** who believe! kill not game, while in
005:095 know **ye** that it is Our Messenger's duty to
005:095 and beware (of evil): if **ye** do turn back, know
005:096 and fear Allah, to Whom **ye** shall be gathered back.
005:096 as long as **ye** are in the Sacred Precincts or in
005:097 that **ye** may know that Allah hath knowledge of what
005:098 Know **ye** that Allah is strict in punishment and
005:099 but Allah knoweth all that **ye** reveal and **ye** conceal.
005:100 O **ye** that understand that (so) **ye** may prosper."
005:101 O **ye** who believe! ask not questions about things
005:101 But if **ye** ask about things when the Qur'an
005:105 O **ye** who believe! guard your own souls:
005:105 it is He that will inform you of all that **ye** do.
005:105 if **ye** follow (right) guidance.
005:106 from outside if **ye** are journeying through the earth,
005:106 O **ye** who believe! when death approaches any of you,
005:106 If **ye** doubt (their truth), detain them
005:109 the response **ye** received (from men to your teaching)?"
005:112 Said Jesus: "Fear Allah, if **ye** have faith."
006:002 yet **ye** doubt within yourselves!
006:003 the (recompense) which **ye** earn (by your deeds).
006:003 He knoweth what **ye** hide, and what **ye** reveal,
006:019 Can **ye** possibly bear witness that besides Allah
006:022 whom **ye** (invented and) talked about?"
006:030 He will say: "Taste **ye** then the Chastisement,
006:030 the Chastisement, because **ye** rejected Faith."
006:032 Will **ye** not then understand?
006:040 Say: "Think **ye** to yourselves, if there come
006:040 would **ye** then call upon other than Allah?-
006:040 (Reply) if **ye** are truthful!
006:040 or the Hour (that **ye** dread),
006:041 "Nay,-On Him would **ye** call, and if
006:041 and **ye** would forget (the false gods)
006:041 (the false gods) which **ye** join with Him!"

006:046 Say: "Think **ye**, if Allah took away your hearing
006:047 Say: "Think **ye**, if the Punishment of Allah
006:050 Will **ye** then consider not?
006:056 other than Allah, whom **ye** call upon."
006:057 on a clear Sign from my Lord, but **ye** reject Him.
006:057 What **ye** would see hastened is not in my power.
006:058 Say: "If what **ye** would see hastened
006:060 then will He show you the truth of all that **ye** did.
006:060 and hath knowledge of all that **ye** have done by day:
006:063 when **ye** call upon Him in humility
006:064 and yet **ye** worship false gods!"
006:067 and soon shall **ye** know it."
006:080 He said: "(Come) **ye** to dispute with me,
006:080 I fear not (the beings) **ye** associate with Allah:
006:080 Will **ye** not (yourselves) be admonished?
006:081 "How should I fear (the beings) **ye** associate with Allah,
006:081 when **ye** fear not to give partners to Allah without
006:081 (Tell me) if **ye** know.
006:091 while **ye** conceal much (of its contents):
006:091 which **ye** knew not-neither **ye** nor your fathers."
006:091 but **ye** make it into (separate) sheets for show,
006:091 therein were **ye** taught that which **ye** knew not-
006:093 This day shall **ye** receive your reward,-
006:093 for that **ye** used to tell lies against Allah,
006:094 **Ye** have left behind you all (the favours)
006:094 whom **ye** thought to be partners in your affairs:
006:094 "And behold! **ye** come to Us bare and alone
006:095 then how are **ye** deluded away from the truth?
006:097 that **ye** may guide yourselves, with their help,
006:102 the Created of all things: then worship **ye** Him:
006:108 Revile not **ye** those whom they call upon besides
006:118 if **ye** have faith in His Signs.
006:119 Why should **ye** not eat of (meats) on which Allah's
006:121 if **ye** were to obey them, **ye** would indeed be Pagans.
006:128 "O **ye** assembly of Jinns much (toll) did **ye** take of men."
006:130 "O **ye** assembly of Jinns and men!
006:134 nor can **ye** frustrate it (in the least bit).
006:135 soon will **ye** know who it is whose end will be (best)
006:135 Say: "O my people! do whatever **ye** can:
006:143 Tell me with knowledge if **ye** are truthful:
006:144 Were **ye** present when Allah ordered you such a thing?
006:148 Say: "Have **ye** any (certain) Knowledge?
006:148 **Ye** follow nothing but conjecture: **Ye** do nothing but lie."
006:151 thus doth He command you, that **ye** may learn wisdom.
006:152 whenever **ye** speak, speak justly, even if a near relative
006:152 thus doth He command you, that **ye** may remember.
006:153 thus doth He command you, that **ye** may be righteous.
006:155 so follow it and be righteous, that **ye** may receive mercy:
006:156 Lest **ye** should say: "The Book was sent down to two
006:157 Or lest **ye** should say: "If the Book had only been sent
006:158 Say: "Wait **ye**: we too are waiting."
006:164 tell you the truth of things wherein **ye** disputed."
007:003 Little it is **ye** remember of admonition.
007:010 small are the thanks that **ye** give!
007:019 and enjoy (its good things) as **ye** wish:
007:020 lest **ye** should become angels or such beings as live
007:024 (Allah) said: "Get **ye** down, with enmity between
007:025 He said: "Therein shall **ye** live, and therein shall **ye** die:
007:025 but from it shall **ye** be taken out (at last)."
007:026 O **ye** children of Adam! We have bestowed
007:027 O **ye** children of Adam! Let not Satan seduce you,
007:027 from a position where **ye** cannot see them:

007:028 do **ye** say of Allah what **ye** know not?"
007:029 and that **ye** set your whole selves (to Him)
007:029 He created you in the beginning, so shall **ye** return."
007:033 of which **ye** have no knowledge.
007:035 O **ye** children of Adam! whenever there come to you
007:037 the things that **ye** used to invoke besides Allah?"
007:038 "Doubled for all": but this **ye** do not know.
007:038 He will say: "Enter **ye** in the company of the Peoples
007:039 the Chastisement for all that **ye** did!"
007:039 "See then! no advantage have **ye** over us;
007:039 so taste **ye** of the Chastisement
007:043 **Ye** have been made its inheritors,
007:049 Enter **ye** the Garden: no fear shall be on you,
007:049 nor shall **ye** grieve."
007:057 perchance **ye** may remember.
007:059 Worship Allah! **ye** have not other god but Him.
007:062 and I know from Allah something that **ye** know not.
007:063 "Do **ye** wonder that there hath come to you a reminder
007:063 to warn you,-so that **ye** may fear Allah
007:065 "O my people! Worship Allah! **ye** have no other god
007:065 Will **ye** not fear (Allah)?"
007:069 that so **ye** may prosper."
007:069 the benefits (**ye** have received) from Allah:
007:069 "Do **ye** wonder that there hath come a message
007:071 **ye** and your fathers, without authority from Allah?
007:071 dispute **ye** with me over names which **ye** have devised-
007:073 or **ye** shall be seized with a grievous punishment."
007:073 Worship Allah! **ye** have no other god but Him.
007:074 **ye** build for yourselves palaces and castles
007:074 the benefits (**ye** have received) from Allah,
007:075 "Know **ye** indeed that Salih is a messenger
007:076 "For our part, we reject what **ye** believe in."
007:079 but **ye** love not good counsellors!"
007:080 "Do **ye** commit lewdness such as no people in creation
007:081 **ye** are indeed a people transgressing beyond bounds."
007:081 "For **ye** practice your lusts on men in preference
007:085 worship Allah; **ye** have no other god but Him.
007:085 that will be best for you, if **ye** have Faith.
007:086 but remember how **ye** were little, and He gave you
007:088 or else **ye** (thou and they) shall have to return to our
007:090 said: "If **ye** follow Shu'aib, be sure then **ye** are ruined!
007:110 then what is it **ye** counsel?"
007:114 for **ye** shall in that case be (raised to posts)
007:116 Said Moses: "Throw **ye** (first)."
007:123 Surely this is a trick which **ye** have planned
007:123 but soon shall **ye** know (the consequences).
007:123 Said Pharaoh: "Believe **ye** in him before I
007:129 that so He may see how **ye** act."
007:138 He said: "Surely **ye** are a people without knowledge."
007:150 did **ye** make haste to bring on the judgment of your
007:150 that **ye** have done in my place in my absence:
007:158 follow him that (so) **ye** may be guided."
007:161 "Dwell in this town and eat therein as **ye** wish,
007:164 When some of them said: "Why do **ye** preach to a
007:166 "Be **ye** apes, despised and rejected."
007:169 Will **ye** not understand?
007:171 what is therein; perchance **ye** may fear Allah".
007:172 lest **ye** should say on the Day of Judgment: "Of
007:173 Or lest **ye** should say: "Our fathers before us took
007:193 it is the same whether **ye** call them or **ye** keep silent.
007:193 If **ye** call them to guidance, they will not obey:
007:194 Verily those whom **ye** call upon besides Allah

YE (continued)

007:194 listen to your prayer, if **ye** are (indeed) truthful!
007:197 "But those **ye** call upon besides Him, are unable
007:204 and hold your peace: that **ye** may receive Mercy.
008:001 obey Allah and His Messenger, if **ye** do believe."
008:007 **ye** wished that the one unarmed should be yours,
008:009 Remember **ye** implored the assistance of your Lord,
008:012 smite **ye** above their necks and smite all their finger-tips
008:014 "Taste **ye** then of the (punishment): for those
008:015 O **ye** who believe! when **ye** meet the Unbelievers
008:017 It is not **ye** who slew them; it was Allah:
008:019 if **ye** desist (from wrong), it will be best for you:
008:019 if **ye** return (to the attack), so shall We.
008:019 (O Unbelievers!) if **ye** prayed for victory and judgment
008:020 turn not away from him when **ye** hear (him speak).
008:020 O **ye** who believe! obey Allah and His Messenger,
008:024 and that it is He to Whom **ye** shall (all) be gathered.
008:024 O **ye** who believe! give your response to Allah and
008:026 that **ye** might be grateful.
008:026 Call to mind when **ye** were a small (band),
008:027 O **ye** that believe! betray not the trust
008:028 And know **ye** that your possessions and your
008:029 O **ye** who believe! if **ye** fear Allah, He will
008:035 "Taste **ye** the Chastisement because **ye** blasphemed."
008:041 if **ye** do believe in Allah and in the revelation
008:041 that **ye** may acquire (in war), a fifth share
008:042 **ye** would certainly have failed in the in the appointment:
008:042 Remember **ye** were on the hither side of the valley,
008:042 and the caravan on lower ground than **ye**.
008:042 but (thus **ye** met), that Allah might accomplish
008:042 Even if **ye** had made a mutual appointment to meet,
008:043 and **ye** would surely have disputed in (your) decision:
008:043 **ye** would surely have been discouraged,
008:044 And remember when **ye** met, He showed
008:045 O **ye** who believe! when **ye** meet a force, be firm,
008:045 in remembrance much (and often); that **ye** may prosper.
008:046 lest **ye** lose heart and your power depart;
008:048 lo! I see what **ye** see not;
008:057 If **ye** gain the mastery over them in war,
008:060 and others besides, whom **ye** may not know,
008:060 Whatever **ye** shall spend in the cause of Allah,
008:060 and **ye** shall not be treated unjustly.
008:067 **Ye** look for the temporal goods of this world;
008:068 reached you for the (ransom) that **ye** took.
008:069 But (now) enjoy what **ye** took in war,
008:072 did not emigrate **ye** owe no duty of protection
008:072 against a people **ye** have a treaty of mutual alliance.
008:072 and (remember) Allah seeth all that **ye** do.
008:073 unless **ye** do this, (protect each other),
009:001 with whom **ye** have contracted mutual alliances:-
009:002 Go **ye**, then, for four months, (as you will),
009:002 but know **ye** that **ye** cannot frustrate Allah
009:003 If, then, **ye** repent, it were best for you;
009:003 know **ye** that **ye** cannot frustrate Allah,
009:003 but if **ye** turn away,
009:004 Pagans with whom **ye** have entered into alliance
009:005 then fight and slay them wherever **ye** find them,
009:007 whom **ye** made a treaty near the sacred mosque?
009:007 stand true to you, stand **ye** true to them:
009:012 fight **ye** the chiefs of Unfaith: for their oaths or nothing
009:013 Nay, it is Allah whom **ye** should more justly fear,
009:013 Will **ye** not fight people who violated their oaths,
009:013 Do **ye** fear them?

YE (continued)

009:013 justly fear, if **ye** believe!
009:016 And Allah is well-acquainted with (all) that **ye** do.
009:019 Do **ye** make the giving of drink to pilgrims,
009:023 O **ye** who believe! Take not for protectors
009:024 the commerce in which **ye** fear a decline:
009:024 or the dwellings in which **ye** delight-are dearer to you
009:024 the wealth that **ye** have gained;
009:025 did constrain you, and **ye** turned back in retreat.
009:026 and sent down forces which **ye** saw not:
009:028 O **ye** who believe! Truly the Pagans are unclean;
009:028 And if **ye** fear poverty, soon will Allah enrich you,
009:034 O **ye** who believe! There are indeed many among
009:035 taste **ye**, then, the (treasures) **ye** hoarded!"
009:035 (treasure) which **ye** hoarded for yourselves:
009:038 Do **ye** prefer the life of this world to the Hereafter
009:038 **ye** cling heavily to the earth?
009:038 O **ye** who believe! what is the matter with you,
009:038 hat when **ye** are asked to go forth in the Cause of Allah,
009:039 but Him **ye** would not harm in the least,
009:039 Unless **ye** go forth, He will punish you
009:040 and strengthened you with forces which **ye** saw not,
009:040 If **ye** help not (the Prophet), (it is no matter):
009:041 Go **ye** forth, (whether equipped) lightly
009:041 That is best for you, if **ye** (but) knew.
009:046 were told, "Sit **ye** among those who sit (inactive)."
009:053 for **ye** are indeed a people rebellious and wicked."
009:064 all that **ye** fear (should be revealed)."
009:064 Say: "Mock **ye**! But verily Allah will bring to light
009:065 and His Messenger, that **ye** were mocking?"
009:066 Make **ye** no excuses:
009:066 **ye** have rejected Faith after **ye** had accepted it.
009:069 their enjoyment of their portion: and **ye** have of yours,
009:069 and **ye** indulge in idle talk as they did.
009:083 say: "Never shall **ye** come out with me, nor fight
009:083 for **ye** preferred to sit inactive on the first occasion:
009:083 then sit **ye** (now) with those who stay behind."
009:094 will present their excuses to you when **ye** return to them.
009:094 He show you the truth of all that **ye** did."
009:094 in the end will **ye** be brought back to Him
009:095 They will swear to you by Allah, when **ye** return to them,
009:095 that **ye** may leave them alone.
009:096 that **ye** may be pleased with them.
009:096 But if **ye** are pleased with them.
009:105 then will He show you the truth of all that **ye** did."
009:105 soon will **ye** be brought back to the Knower of what
009:111 Then rejoice in the bargain which **ye** have concluded:
009:116 Except for Him **ye** have no protector nor helper.
009:119 O **ye** who Believe! Fear Allah and be
009:123 O **ye** who believe! Fight the Unbelievers who are
009:128 it grieves him that **ye** should suffer,
010:003 will ye not receive admonition?
010:003 This is Allah your Lord; Him therefore serve **ye**:
010:005 that **ye** might know the number of years and the
010:014 after them, to see how **ye** would behave!
010:016 I tarried amongst you: will **ye** not then understand?"
010:018 Say: "Do **ye** indeed inform Allah of something
010:020 Then wait **ye**: I too will wait with you".
010:021 Our messengers record all the plots that **ye** make!"
010:022 till when **ye** even board ships;-
010:023 and We shall show you the truth of all that **ye** did.
010:028 "To your place! **ye** and those **ye** joined as 'partners'."
010:028 "It was not us that **ye** worshipped!"

YE (continued)

010:031	Say, "Will **ye** not then show piety (to Him)?"
010:032	How then are **ye** turned away?
010:034	then how are **ye** deluded away (from the truth)?"
010:035	What then is the matter with you? How judge **ye**?
010:038	besides Allah, if it be **ye** speak the truth!"
010:041	and I for what **ye** do!"
010:041	**Ye** are free from responsibility for what I do,
010:048	will this promise come to pass-if **ye** speak the truth?"
010:050	Say: "Do **ye** see-if His punishment should come
010:051	"Would **ye** then believe in it at last,
010:051	and **ye** wanted (aforetime) to hasten it on!"
010:052	**Ye** get but the recompense of what **ye** earned!'"
010:052	the wrong-doers: 'Taste **ye** the enduring punishment!
010:053	And **ye** cannot frustrate it!"
010:056	and to Him shall **ye** all be brought back.
010:059	Say: "See **ye** what things Allah hath sent down
010:059	or do **ye** forge (things) to attribute to Allah?"
010:059	Yet **ye** hold forbidden some things thereof and (some
010:061	and whatever deed **ye** (mankind) may be doing,-
010:061	Witnesses thereof when **ye** are deeply engrossed therein.
010:067	the Night that **ye** may rest therein, and the Day
010:068	Say **ye** about Allah what **ye** know not?
010:068	No warrant have **ye** for this!
010:071	get **ye** then an agreement about your plan
010:072	"But if **ye** turn back, (consider): no reward
010:077	Said Moses: "Say **ye** (this) about the Truth when it
010:080	Moses said to them: "Throw **ye** what **ye** (wish)
010:081	Moses said: "What **ye** have brought is sorcery:
010:084	said: "O my People! if **ye** do (really) believe in Allah,
010:084	then in Him put your trust if **ye** submit (your will to His)."
010:089	(O Moses and Aaron)! So stand **ye** straight,
010:102	Say: "Wait **ye** then: for I too,
010:104	Say: "O **ye** men! if **ye** are in doubt as to my religion,
010:104	I worship not what **ye** worship other than Allah!
010:108	Say: "O **ye** men! now Truth hath reached you
011:002	(It teacheth) that **ye** should worship none
011:003	But if **ye** turn away, then I fear for you
011:003	"(And to preach thus), `Seek **ye** the forgiveness
011:007	"**Ye** shall indeed be raised up after death,
011:013	Say, "Bring **ye** then ten Suras forged, like unto it,
011:013	other than Allah!-if **ye** speak the truth!
011:013	and call (to your aid) whomsoever **ye** can,
011:014	know **ye** that this Revelation is sent down
011:014	Will **ye** even then submit (to Islam)?"
011:024	Will **ye** not them take heed?
011:026	"That **ye** serve none but Allah:
011:027	in fact we think **ye** are liars!"
011:028	Shall we compel you to accept it when **ye** are averse to it?
011:028	said: "O my people! see **ye** if (it be that) I have a Clear
011:029	and **ye** I see are the ignorant ones!
011:030	Will **ye** not then take heed?
011:033	**ye** will not be able to frustrate it!
011:034	He is your Lord! and to Him will **ye** return!
011:035	And i am free of the sins of which **ye** are guilty!
011:038	He said: "If **ye** ridicule us now, we (in our turn)
011:039	"But soon will **ye** know who it is on whom will
011:041	So he said: "Embark **ye** on the Ark,
011:050	**ye** have no other god but Him.
011:051	Him who created Me: will **ye** not then understand?
011:052	so turn **ye** not back in sin!"
011:054	and do **ye** bear witness, that I am free from the sin
011:057	"If **ye** turn away,-I (at least) have conveyed

YE (continued)

011:061	**ye** have not other god but Him.
011:063	What then would **ye** add to my (portion)
011:063	He said: "O my people! Do **ye** see?-If I have
011:073	O **ye** people of the house! For He is indeed
011:078	they are purer for you (if **ye** marry)!
011:084	**ye** have no other god but Him.
011:086	left you by Allah is best for you, if **ye** (but) believed!
011:088	He said: "O my people! see **ye** whether I have a Clear
011:089	lest **ye** suffer a fate similar to that of the people of
011:092	But verily my Lord encompasseth all that **ye** do!
011:092	For **ye** cast Him away behind your backs
011:093	And watch **ye**! for I too am watching with you!"
011:093	"And O my people! do whatever **ye** can: I will
011:093	soon will **ye** know who it is on whom descends the
011:112	for He seeth well all that **ye** do.
011:113	and **ye** have no protectors other than Allah,
011:113	nor shall **ye** be helped.
011:121	"Do whatever **ye** can: we shall do our part;
011:122	"And wait **ye**! we too shall wait."
011:123	and thy Lord is not unmindful of aught that **ye** do.
012:002	in order that **ye** may learn wisdom.
012:009	"Slay **ye** Joseph or cast him out to some (unknown) land,
012:010	"Slay no Joseph, but if **ye** must do something,
012:013	devour him while **ye** attend not to him."
012:013	"Really it saddens me that **ye** should take him away:
012:018	patience is most fitting: against that which **ye** assert,
012:032	the man about whom **ye** did blame me!
012:040	**ye** and your fathers,-for which Allah hath sent
012:040	He hath commanded that **ye** worship none but Him:
012:040	Whatever **ye** worship apart from Him is nothing
012:040	is nothing but names which **ye** have named,
012:041	been decreed that matter whereof **ye** twain do enquire."
012:043	O **ye** chiefs! expound to me my vision if it be
012:043	if it be that **ye** can interpret visions."
012:045	of its interpretation: send **ye** me (therefore)."
012:047	except a little, of which **ye** shall eat.
012:047	shall **ye** diligently sow as is your wont:
012:047	**ye** shall leave them in the ear,-except a little,
012:047	and the harvests that **ye** reap,
012:048	which will devour what **ye** shall have laid by in advance
012:048	(all) except a little which **ye** shall have (specially)
012:050	So the king said: "Bring **ye** him unto me."
012:051	when **ye** did seek to seduce Joseph"?
012:059	"Bring unto me a brother **ye** have, of the same father
012:059	see **ye** not that I pay put full measure,
012:060	**ye** shall have no measure (of corn) from me,
012:060	nor shall **ye** (even) come near me."
012:060	"Now if **ye** bring him not to me, **ye** shall have no
012:066	in Allah's name, that **ye** will be sure to bring him back
012:066	unless **ye** are yourselves hemmed in (and made
012:066	I send him with you until **ye** swear a solemn oath to me,
012:067	enter not all by one gates: enter **ye** by different gates.
012:070	Then shouted out a Crier: "O **ye** (in) the Caravan!
012:070	Behold! **ye** are thieves, without doubt!"
012:071	"What is it that **ye** miss?"
012:073	(The brothers) said: "By Allah! well **ye** know that
012:074	if **ye** are (proved) to have lied?"
012:077	"**Ye** are the worse situated:
012:077	and Allah knoweth best the truth of what **ye** assert!"
012:080	"Know **ye** not that your father did take an oath
012:080	before this, **ye** did fail in your duty with Joseph?
012:081	"Turn **ye** back to your father, and say, 'O our father!

012:083 Jacob said: "Nay, but **ye** have yourselves contrived
012:086 and I know from Allah that which **ye** know not.
012:087 "O my sons! go **ye** and enquire about Joseph
012:089 He said: "Know **ye** how **ye** dealt with Joseph,
012:089 not knowing (what **ye** were doing)?"
012:093 Then come **ye** (here) to me together with all your family."
012:096 'I know from Allah that which **ye** know not?"
012:099 and said: "Enter **ye** Egypt (all) in safety
012:109 Will **ye** not then understand?
013:002 without any pillars that **ye** can see;
013:002 that **ye** may believe with certainty in the
013:016 Say: "Do **ye** then take (for worship) protectors
013:024 "Peace unto you for that **ye** persevered in patience!
013:033 Say: "But name them! is it that **ye** will inform
014:007 "If **ye** are grateful, I will add more (favours)
014:007 but if **ye** show ingratitude, truly My punishment
014:008 And Moses said: "If **ye** show ingratitude,
014:008 **ye** and all on earth together,-yet is Allah
014:009 (disquieting) doubt as to that to which **ye** invite us."
014:009 "We do deny (the mission) on which **ye** have been sent,
014:010 They said: "Ah! **ye** are no more then human,
014:010 **Ye** wish to turn us away from what our fathers
014:013 or **ye** shall return to our religion."
014:021 can **ye** then avail us at all against the Wrath of Allah
014:022 authority over you except call you, but **ye** listened to me;
014:022 I cannot listen to your cries, nor can **ye** listen to mine.
014:030 But verily **ye** are making straightway for Hell!"
014:034 But if **ye** count the favours of Allah,
014:034 never will **ye** be able to number them.
014:034 And He giveth you of all that **ye** ask for.
014:044 "What! were **ye** not wont to swear aforetime
014:044 to swear aforetime that **ye** suffer no decline?
014:045 **ye** were clearly shown how We dealt with them;
014:045 "And **ye** dwelt in the dwellings of men
015:020 for whose sustenance **ye** are not responsible.
015:022 though **ye** are not the guardians of its stores.
015:029 fall **ye** down in obeisance unto him."
015:046 "Enter **ye** here in Peace and Security."
015:054 He said: "Do **ye** give me such glad tidings
015:057 O **ye** messengers (of Allah)?"
015:057 "What then is the business on which **ye** (Have come),
015:062 He said: "**Ye** appear to be uncommon folk."
015:065 but pass on whither **ye** are ordered."
015:071 (to marry), if **ye** must act (so)."
016:001 seek **ye** not then to hasten it:
016:005 and numerous benefits, and of their (meat) **ye** eat.
016:005 from them **ye** derive warmth,
016:006 and as **ye** lead them froth to pasture in the morning.
016:006 And **ye** have a sense of pride and beauty in them
016:006 in them as **ye** drive them home in the evening,
016:007 loads to lands that **ye** could not (otherwise) reach
016:008 created (other) things of which **ye** have no knowledge.
016:010 out (grows) the vegetation on which **ye** feed your cattle.
016:010 is He Who sends down rain from the sky from it **ye** drink,
016:014 and that **ye** may extract therefrom ornaments
016:014 and that **ye** may be grateful.
016:014 that **ye** may eat thereof flesh that is fresh and tender,
016:014 that **ye** may seek (thus) of the bounty of Allah
016:015 that **ye** may guide yourselves;
016:017 Will **ye** not receive admonition?
016:018 never would **ye** be able to number them:
016:018 If **ye** would count up the favours of Allah,

016:019 and what **ye** reveal.
016:019 And Allah doth know what **ye** conceal,
016:027 concerning whom **ye** used to dispute (with the godly)?"
016:028 verily Allah knoweth all that **ye** did;
016:032 because of (the good) which **ye** did (in the world)."
016:032 enter **ye** the Garden,
016:043 if **ye** realize this not, ask of those who possess the
016:052 then will **ye** fear other than Allah?
016:053 And **ye** have no good thing but is from Allah:
016:053 and moreover, when **ye** are touched by distress,
016:053 unto Him **ye** cry with groans;
016:055 but soon will **ye** know (your folly)!
016:056 By Allah, **ye** shall certainly be called to account
016:066 And verily in cattle (too) will **ye** find an instructive
016:067 and the vine, **ye** get out strong drink,
016:074 for Allah knoweth, and **ye** know not.
016:078 from the wombs of your mothers when **ye** knew nothing;
016:078 that **ye** may give thanks (to Allah).
016:080 when **ye** travel and when **ye** stop (in your travels),
016:080 which **ye** find so light (and handy)
016:081 that **ye** may surrender to His Will (in Islam).
016:086 back their words at them (and say): "Indeed **ye** are liars!"
016:090 that **ye** may receive admonition.
016:091 and break not your oaths after **ye** have confirmed them;
016:091 indeed **ye** have made Allah your surety;
016:091 Fulfil the Covenant of Allah when **ye** have entered into
016:091 for Allah knoweth all that **ye** do.
016:092 (the truth of) that wherein **ye** disagree.
016:093 but **ye** shall certainly be called to account
016:094 and **ye** may have to taste the evil (consequences)
016:095 (a prize) far better for you, if **ye** only knew.
016:114 if it is He whom **ye** serve.
016:126 but if **ye** show patience, that is indeed the best (course)
016:126 And if **ye** punish, let your punishment be proportionate
017:003 O **ye** that are sprung from those whom We carried in the
017:007 If **ye** did well, **ye** did well for yourselves;
017:007 if **ye** did evil (**ye** did it) against yourselves.
017:008 show Mercy unto you; but it **ye** revert (to your sins),
017:012 We have made bright that **ye** may seek bounty from
017:012 Bounty from your Lord and that **ye** may know the
017:023 Thy Lord hath decreed that **ye** worship none but Him,
017:023 and that **ye** be kind to parents.
017:025 in your hearts: if **ye** do deeds of righteousness,
017:035 Give full measure when **ye** measure, and weigh
017:040 Truly **ye** utter a most dreadful saying!
017:044 and yet **ye** understand not how they declare His glory:
017:047 "**Ye** follow none other than a man bewitched!"
017:050 Say: "(Nay!) be **ye** stones or iron,
017:051 is hardest (to be raised up)-(yet shall **ye** be raised up)!"
017:052 and **ye** will answer (His call) with (words of) His praise,
017:052 and **ye** will think that **ye** tarried but a little while!"
017:056 Say: "Call on those-besides Him-whom **ye** fancy:
017:066 in order that **ye** may seek of His Bounty.
017:067 **ye** turn away (from Him). Most ungrateful is man!
017:067 those that **ye** call upon-besides Himself-leave you
017:068 so that **ye** shall find no protector?
017:068 be swallowed up beneath the earth when **ye** are on land,
017:068 Do **ye** then feel secure that He will not cause you to be
017:069 so that **ye** find no helper therein against Us?
017:069 Or do **ye** feel secure that He will not send you back
017:100 Say: "If **ye** had control of the Treasures of the Mercy
017:100 behold, **ye** would keep them back, for fear

017:107 Say: "Whether **ye** believe in it or not,
017:110 by whatever name **ye** call upon Him, (it is well):
018:016 "When **ye** turn away from them and the things
018:019 "How long have **ye** stayed (here)?"
018:019 "Allah (alone) knows best how long **ye** have stayed here...
018:019 some to you, (that **ye** may satisfy your hunger therewith)
018:019 Now send **ye** then one of you with this money of yours
018:020 and in that case **ye** would never attain prosperity."
018:048 aye, **ye** thought We shall not fulfil the appointment made
018:048 (with the announcement), "Now have **ye** come to Us
018:050 Will **ye** then take him and his progeny as protectors
018:052 "Call on those whom **ye** thought to be My partners,"
019:036 Him therefore serve **ye**: this is a Way that is straight.
019:048 and from those whom **ye** invoke besides Allah:
019:089 Indeed **ye** have put forth a thing most monstrous!
020:010 "Tarry **ye**; I perceive a fire; perhaps I can
020:047 "So go **ye** both to him, and say, `Verily we
020:061 Forge not **ye** a lie against Allah, lest He destroy you
020:066 He said, "Nay, throw **ye** first!" Then behold
020:071 (Pharaoh) said: "Believe **ye** in Him before I give you
020:071 So shall **ye** know for certain, which of us can give
020:080 O **ye** Children of Israel! We delivered you from your
020:086 Or did **ye** desire that Wrath should descend from
020:086 and so **ye** broke your promise to me?"
020:090 said to them: "O my people! **ye** are being tested
020:103 "**Ye** tarried not longer than ten (days);"
020:104 will say: "**Ye** tarried not longer than a day!"
020:123 He said: "Get **ye** down, both of you,-all together,
020:135 and soon shall **ye** know who it is that is on the straight
020:135 Say: "Each one (of us) is waiting: wait **ye**, therefore,
021:003 Will **ye** go to witchcraft with your eyes open?"
021:007 if **ye** know this not, ask of those who possess the
021:010 Will **ye** not then understand?
021:013 in order that **ye** may be called to account.
021:018 woe be to you for (false) things **ye** ascribe (to Us).
021:035 to Us must **ye** return.
021:038 come to pass, if **ye** are telling the truth?"
021:050 will **ye** then reject it?
021:052 to which **ye** are (so assiduously) devoted?"
021:054 in manifest error-**ye** and your fathers."
021:054 He said, "Indeed **ye** have been in manifest error-
021:057 after **ye** go away and turn your backs"...
021:064 and said, "Surely **ye** are the ones in the wrong."
021:066 (Abraham) said, "Do **ye** then worship, besides Allah,
021:067 that **ye** worship besides Allah! Have **ye** no sense?"
021:068 and protect your gods, if **ye** do (anything at all)!"
021:080 will **ye** then be grateful?
021:098 and the (false) gods that **ye** worship besides Allah,
021:098 To it will **ye** (surely) come!
021:098 Verily **ye**, (Unbelievers), and the false
021:103 (the Day) that **ye** were promised."
021:108 will **ye** therefore bow to His Will (in Islam)?"
021:109 whether that which **ye** are promised is near or far.
021:110 in speech and what **ye** hide (in your hearts).
021:112 sought against the blasphemies **ye** utter!
022:002 The Day **ye** shall see it, every mother
022:005 O mankind! if **ye** have a doubt about the Resurrection,
022:005 then (foster you) that **ye** may reach your age of full
022:022 "Taste **ye** the Chastisement of Burning!"
022:028 then eat **ye** thereof and feed the distressed
022:033 In them **ye** have benefits for a term appointed:
022:036 eat **ye** thereof, and feed such as (beg not but)

022:036 made animals subject to you, that **ye** may be grateful.
022:037 that **ye** may glorify Allah for His guidance to you:
022:068 say, "Allah knows best what it is **ye** are doing."
022:069 concerning the matter in which **ye** differ."
022:073 Those on whom, besides Allah **ye** call,
022:077 O **ye** who believe! bow down, prostrate yourselves,
022:077 and do good; that **ye** may prosper.
022:078 and **ye** be witnesses for mankind!
022:078 And strive in His cause as **ye** ought to strive,
023:015 After that, at length, **ye** will die.
023:016 will **ye** be raised up.
023:019 and of them **ye** eat (and have enjoyment),-
023:019 in them have **ye** abundant fruits:
023:021 and of their (meat) **ye** eat;
023:021 And in cattle (too) **ye** have an instructive example:
023:022 And on them, as well as in ships, **ye** ride.
023:023 Will **ye** not fear (Him)?"
023:023 **Ye** have no other god but Him.
023:032 (saying), "Worship Allah! **ye** have no other god
023:032 Will **ye** not fear (Him)?"
023:033 he eats and drinks of what **ye** drink.
023:034 "If **ye** obey a man like yourselves, behold,
023:034 behold, it is certain **ye** will be lost.
023:035 "Does he promise that when **ye** die and become dust
023:035 **ye** shall be brought forth (again)?
023:036 "Far, very far is that which **ye** are promised!
023:051 O **ye** messenger! enjoy (all) things good and pure,
023:051 for I am well-acquainted with (all) that you do.
023:065 for **ye** shall certainly not be helped by Us.
023:066 but **ye** used to turn back on your heels-
023:078 little thanks it is **ye** give!
023:079 and to Him shall **ye** be gathered back.
023:080 of Night and Day: will **ye** not then understand?
023:084 the earth and all beings therein? (Say) if **ye** know!"
023:085 Say: "Yet will **ye** not receive admonition?"
023:087 Say: "Will **ye** not then fear?"
023:088 but is not protected (of any)? (Say) if **ye** know."
023:089 Say: "Then how are **ye** deluded?"
023:105 and **ye** did but treat them as falsehoods?"
023:108 He will say: "Be **ye** driven into it (with ignominy)!
023:108 and speak **ye** not to Me!
023:110 "But **ye** treated them with ridicule,
023:110 you forgot My Message while **ye** were laughing at them!
023:112 "What number of years did **ye** stay on earth?"
023:114 if **ye** had only known!
023:114 He will say: "**Ye** stayed not but a little,-
023:115 "Did **ye** then think that We had created you
023:115 and that **ye** would not be brought back
024:001 in order that **ye** may receive admonition.
024:002 if **ye** believe in Allah and the Last Day:
024:010 Full of Wisdom,-(**ye** would be ruined indeed).
024:012 men and women-when **ye** heard of the affair,-
024:014 seized you in that **ye** rushed glibly into this affair.
024:015 and **ye** thought it to be a light matter,
024:015 of your mouths things of which **ye** had no knowledge;
024:015 Behold, **ye** received it on your tongues,
024:016 And why did **ye** not, when **ye** heard it, say? "It is not
024:017 if **ye** are (true) Believers.
024:017 that **ye** may never repeat such (conduct),
024:019 Allah knows, and **ye** know not.
024:020 full of kindness and mercy, (**ye** would be ruined indeed).
024:021 O **ye** who believe! follow not Satan's footsteps:

YE (continued)

024:027   in order that **ye** may heed (what is seemly).
024:027   O **ye** who believe! enter not houses
024:027   until **ye** have asked permission and saluted
024:028   and Allah knows well all that **ye** do.
024:028   if **ye** are asked to go back, go back
024:028   If **ye** find no one in the house, enter not
024:029   of what **ye** reveal and what **ye** conceal.
024:031   And O **ye** Believers! turn **ye** all together towards
024:031   towards Allah in repentance that **ye** may be successful.
024:033   in order that **ye** may make a gain in the goods of this life,
024:033   give them such a deed if **ye** know any good in them;
024:053   Say: "Swear **ye** not; obedience is (more) reasonable;
024:053   Allah is well acquainted with all that **ye** do."
024:054   If **ye** obey him, **ye** shall be on right guidance.
024:054   but if **ye** turn away, he is only responsible for the duty
024:054   the duty placed on him and **ye** for that placed on you.
024:056   that **ye** may receive mercy.
024:058   O **ye** who believe! let those whom your right hands
024:058   the while **ye** doff your clothes for the noonday heat;
024:061   But if **ye** enter houses, salute each other
024:061   that **ye** should eat in your own houses,
024:061   whether **ye** eat in company or separately.
024:061   make clear the Signs to you: that **ye** may understand.
024:064   Well doth He know what **ye** are intent upon:
025:008   "**Ye** follow none other than a man bewitched."
025:017   "Was it **ye** who led these my servants astray,
025:019   "Now have they proved you liars in what **ye** say:
025:019   so **ye** cannot avert (your penalty) nor (get) help."
025:020   will **ye** have patience?
025:036   And We commanded: "Go **ye** both, to the people who
025:060   When it is said to them, "Adore **ye** The Most Gracious!",
025:077   but **ye** have indeed rejected (Him),
026:024   and all between,- if **ye** had but sure belief."
026:025   "Do **ye** not listen (to what he says)?"
026:028   If **ye** only had sense!"
026:035   then what is it **ye** counsel?"
026:039   "Are **ye** (now) assembled?"-
026:042   for **ye** shall in that case be (raised to posts) nearest
026:043   "Throw **ye**-that which **ye** are about to throw!"
026:049   Said (Pharaoh): "Believe **ye** in Him before I give
026:049   But soon shall **ye** know!
026:052   for surely **ye** shall be pursued."
026:070   he said to his father and his people: "What worship **ye**?"
026:072   "Do they listen to you when **ye** call (on them),
026:075   said: "Do **ye** then see whom **ye** have been worshipping,-
026:076   "**Ye** and your fathers before you?-
026:092   'Where are the (gods) **ye** worshipped-
026:106   "Will **ye** not fear (Allah)?
026:113   if **ye** could (but) understand.
026:124   "Will **ye** not fear (Allah)?
026:128   "Do **ye** build a landmark on every high place
026:129   "And do **ye** get for yourselves fine buildings
026:130   "And when **ye** strike you strike like tyrants.
026:132   Him Who has bestowed on you freely all that **ye** know.
026:146   in (the enjoyment of) all that **ye** have here?-
026:146   "Will **ye** be left secure,
026:149   "And **ye** carve house out of (rocky) mountains
026:155   and **ye** have a right of watering,
026:161   "Will **ye** not fear (Allah)?
026:165   will **ye** approach males,
026:166   Nay, **ye** are a people transgressing (all limits)!"
026:177   "Will **ye** not fear (Allah)?

YE (continued)

026:188   He said: "My Lord knows best what **ye** do."
026:216   "I am free (of responsibility) for what **ye** do!"
027:007   that **ye** may warm yourselves."
027:016   He said: "O **ye** people! we have been taught
027:018   "O **ye** ants, get into your habitations,
027:025   and knows what **ye** hide and what **ye** reveal.
027:029   (The Queen) said: "**Ye** chiefs! here is-delivered to me-
027:031   "'Be **ye** not arrogant against me,
027:032   She said: "**Ye** chiefs! advise me in (this) my affair:
027:036   Nay it is **ye** who rejoice in your gift!
027:036   he said: "Will **ye** give me abundance in wealth?
027:038   He said (to his own men): "**Ye** Chiefs! which of
027:046   If only **ye** ask Allah for forgiveness,
027:046   **ye** may hope to receive mercy."
027:046   He said: "O my people! why ask **ye** to hasten
027:047   yea, **ye** are a people under trial."
027:054   "Do **ye** do what is indecent though **ye** see (its iniquity)?
027:055   Nay, **ye** are a people (grossly) ignorant!"
027:055   "Would **ye** really approach men in your lust
027:062   Little it is that **ye** heed!
027:064   if **ye** are telling the truth!"
027:069   Say: "Go **ye** through the earth and see what has
027:071   If **ye** are truthful."
027:072   the events which **ye** wish to hasten on may be (close)
027:084   not in knowledge, or what was it **ye** did?"
027:084   though **ye** comprehended them not in knowledge,
027:084   "Did **ye** reject My signs,
027:088   for He is well acquainted with all that **ye** do.
027:090   "Do **ye** receive a reward other than that which
027:090   that which **ye** have earned by your deeds?"
027:093   and thy Lord is not unmindful of all that **ye** do.
027:093   so that **ye** shall know them":
028:029   burning firebrand, that **ye** may warm yourselves."
028:029   "Tarry **ye**; I perceive a fire;
028:035   with Our Signs shall **ye** triumph,-
028:049   (Do), if **ye** are truthful!"
028:049   Say: "Then bring **ye** a Book from Allah,
028:060   The (material) things which **ye** are given are but
028:060   will **ye** not then be wise?
028:062   whom **ye** imagined (to be such)?"
028:065   "What was the answer **ye** gave to the messengers?"
028:070   and to Him shall **ye** (all) be brought back.
028:071   Say: See **ye**? If Allah were to make the night
028:071   Will **ye** not then hearken?
028:072   Who can give you a Night in which **ye** can rest?
028:072   Will **ye** not then see?
028:072   Say: see **ye**? If Allah were to make the Day perpetual
028:073   that **ye** may rest therein,
028:073   and in order that **ye** may be grateful.
028:073   and that **ye** may seek of His Grace;-
028:074   whom **ye** imagined (to be such)?"
028:088   and to Him will **ye** (all) be brought back.
029:008   **Ye** have (all) to return to Me,
029:008   and I will tell you (the truth) of all that **ye** did.
029:016   that will be best for you-if **ye** understand!
029:017   "For **ye** do worship idols besides Allah,
029:017   and **ye** invent falsehood.
029:017   The things that **ye** worship besides Allah have no
029:017   then seek **ye** sustenance from Allah, serve Him,
029:018   "And if **ye** reject (the Message),
029:021   He pleases, and towards Him are **ye** turned.
029:022   "Not on earth nor in heaven will **ye** be able (fleeing)

029:022 (His Plan), nor have **ye**, beside Allah, any protector

029:025 **ye** shall disown each other and curse each other:

029:025 And He said: "For you, **ye** have taken (for worship)

029:025 aboe will be the Fire, and **ye** shall have none to help."

029:028 he said to his people: "**Ye** do commit lewdness,

029:029 "Do **ye** indeed approach men, and cut off the highway?-

029:045 And Allah knows the (deeds) that **ye** do.

029:046 And dispute **ye** not with the People of the Book,

029:055 "Taste **ye** (the fruits) of your deeds!"

029:056 therefore serve **ye** Me-(and Me alone)!

029:057 in the end to Us shall **ye** be brought back.

030:011 then shall **ye** be brought back to Him.

030:017 and when **ye** rise in the morning;

030:017 So glory be to Allah, when **ye** reach eventide and when

030:019 and thus shall **ye** be brought out (from the dead).

030:020 behold, **ye** are men scattered (far and wide)!

030:021 that **ye** may dwell in tranquillity with them,

030:023 and the quest that **ye** (make for livelihood) out of His

030:023 His Signs is the sleep that **ye** take by night and by day,

030:025 behold, **ye** (straightway) come forth.

030:028 Do **ye** fear them as **ye** fear each other?

030:028 do **ye** have partners among those whom your right

030:031 and be not **ye** among those who join gods with Allah,-

030:031 Turn **ye** in repentance to Him, and fear

030:034 but soon will **ye** know (your folly).

030:046 in order that **ye** may be grateful.

030:046 and that **ye** may seek of His Bounty:

030:056 the Day of Resurrection: but **ye-ye** did not know!"

030:056 "Indeed **ye** did tarry, within Allah's Decree,

030:058 "**Ye** do nothing but talk vanities."

031:010 the heavens without any pillars that **ye** can see;

031:015 is to Me, and I will tell you all that **ye** did."

031:020 Do **ye** not see that Allah has subjected to your

031:029 is well acquainted with all that **ye** do?

032:004 will **ye** not then receive admonition?

032:004 on the Throne: **ye** have none, besides Him,

032:009 and sight and understanding little thanks do **ye** give!

032:011 then shall **ye** be brought back to your Lord."

032:014 "Taste **ye** then-for **ye** forgot the Meeting of this Day

032:014 taste **ye** the Chastisement of Eternity for your (evil)

032:020 said to them: "Taste **ye** the Chastisement of the Fire,

032:020 of the fire, the which **ye** were wont to reject as false."

032:028 if **ye** are telling the truth?"

033:002 for Allah is well acquainted with (all) that **ye** do.

033:004 your wives whom **ye** divorce by Zihar your mothers:

033:005 But if **ye** know not their father's names,

033:005 there is no blame on you if **ye** make a mistake therein:

033:006 nevertheless do **ye** what is just to your closest friends:

033:009 against them a hurricane and forces that **ye** saw not:

033:009 O **ye** who believe! Remember the Grace of Allah,

033:009 but Allah sees (clearly) all that **ye** do.

033:010 and **ye** imagined various (vain) thoughts about Allah!

033:013 "**Ye** men of Yathrib! **Ye** cannot stand (the attack)!

033:016 if **ye** are running away from death or slaughter;

033:016 and even if (**ye** do escape),

033:016 more than a brief (respite) will **ye** be allowed to enjoy!"

033:021 **Ye** have indeed in the Messenger of Allah

033:026 (so that) some **ye** slew, and some **ye** made captives.

033:027 and of a land which **ye** had not frequented (before).

033:028 "If it be that **ye** desire the life of this world,

033:029 But if **ye** seek Allah and His Messenger,

033:032 if **ye** do fear (Allah), be not too complaisant of speech,

033:032 O Consorts of the Prophet! **ye** are not like any of the

033:032 but speak **ye** a speech (that is) just.

033:033 all abomination from you, **ye** Members of the Family,

033:041 O **ye** who believe! remember Allah, with much

033:049 O **ye** who believe! when **ye** marry believing women,

033:049 and then divorce them before **ye** have touched them,

033:049 no period of 'Iddat have **ye** to count in respect

033:053 but when **ye** are invited, enter;

033:053 and when **ye** have taken your meal, disperse,

033:053 And when **ye** ask (his ladies) for anything **ye** want,

033:053 O **ye** who Believe! enter not the Prophet's houses,-

033:053 or that **ye** should marry his widows after him

033:053 right for you that **ye** should annoy Allah's Messenger,

033:054 Whether **ye** reveal anything or conceal it,

033:056 O **ye** that believe! send **ye** blessings on him,

033:069 O **ye** who believe! be **ye** not like those who hurt Moses,

033:070 O **ye** who believe! fear Allah, and make your utterance

034:007 that **ye** shall (then be raised) in a New Creation?

034:007 when **ye** are all scattered to pieces in desintegration,

034:010 "O **ye** Mountains! echo **ye** back the Praises of Allah

034:010 Praises of Allah with him! and **ye** birds (also)!

034:011 for be sure I see (clearly) all that **ye** do."

034:011 the rings of chain armour, and work **ye** righteousness;

034:022 Say: "Call upon other (gods) whom **ye** fancy,

034:024 and certain it is that either we or **ye** are on right guidance

034:025 Say: "**Ye** shall not be questioned as to our sins,

034:025 nor shall we be questioned as to what **ye** do."

034:027 joined with Him as partners: by no means (can **ye**).

034:027 Say: "Show me those whom **ye** have joined with

034:029 (come to pass) if **ye** are telling the truth?"

034:030 which **ye** cannot put back for an hour nor put forward."

034:032 Nay, rather it was **ye** who transgressed."

034:033 Behold! **ye** (constantly) ordered us to be ungratefull

034:034 not in the (Message) with which **ye** have been sent."

034:039 and nothing do **ye** spend in the least (in His Cause)

034:042 the which **ye** were wont to deny!"

034:042 "Taste **ye** the Chastisement of the Fire,-

034:046 that **ye** do stand up before Allah,-(it may be)

035:003 how then are **ye** perverted?

035:012 of Allah that **ye** may be grateful.

035:012 that **ye** may seek (thus) of the Bounty of Allah

035:012 and **ye** extract ornaments to wear;

035:012 (kind of water) do **ye** eat flesh fresh and tender,

035:013 And those whom **ye** invoke besides Him

035:014 If **ye** invoke them, they will not listen to your call,

035:015 O **ye** men! it is **ye** that have need of Allah:

035:037 So taste **ye** (the fruit of your deeds):

035:040 Say: "Have **ye** seen (these) `partners' of yours

035:040 of yours whom **ye** call upon besides Allah?

036:015 The (people) said: "**Ye** are only men like ourselves;

036:015 **Ye** do nothing but lie."

036:018 an evil omen from you: if **ye** desist not,

036:019 (deem **ye** this an evil omen), if **ye** are admonished?

036:019 Nay, but **ye** are a people transgressing all bounds!"

036:022 Who created me, and to Whom **ye** shall (all) be

036:033 and produce grain therefrom, of which **ye** do eat.

036:045 in order that **ye** may receive Mercy," (they turn back).

036:045 When they are told, "Fear **ye** that which is before you

036:047 **Ye** are in nothing but manifest error."

036:047 "Spend **ye** of (the bounties) with which Allah

036:048 if what **ye** say is true?"

036:054 and **ye** shall but be repaid the meeds of your past

YE (continued)

YE (continued)

036:059 And O ye in sin! get ye apart this Day!
036:060 that ye should not worship Satan;
036:060 "Did I not enjoin on you, O ye children of Adam,
036:061 "And that ye should worship Me, (for that) this
036:062 Did ye not, then understand?
036:063 "This is the Hell of which ye were promised!
036:064 "Embrace ye the (Fire) this Day,
036:064 for that ye (persistently) rejected (Truth)."
036:080 when behold! ye kindle therewith (your own fires)!
036:083 and to Him will ye be all brought back.
037:018 Say thou: "Yea, and ye shall then be humiliated
037:021 whose truth ye (once) denied!"
037:022 "Bring ye up," it shall be said, "The wrong-doers
037:025 "What is the matter with you that ye help not each other?'"
037:028 They will say: "It was ye who used to come to us
037:029 They will reply: "Nay, ye yourselves had no Faith!
037:030 Nay, it was ye who were a people in obstinate rebellion!
037:038 Ye shall indeed taste of the Grievous Chastisement;-
037:039 And you are requited naught save what ye did.
037:054 He said: "Would ye like to look down?"
037:085 his people, "What is that which ye worship?
037:086 "Is it a Falsehood- gods other than Allah that ye desire?
037:091 and said, "Will ye not eat (of the offerings before you)?
037:092 "What is the matter with you that ye speak not?"
037:095 "Worship ye that which ye have (yourselves) carved?
037:124 Behold, he said to his people, "Will ye not fear (Allah)?
037:125 "Will ye call upon Baal and forsake the Best of Creators,-
037:137 Verily, ye pass by their (sites), by day-
037:138 And by night: will ye not understand?
037:154 What is the matter with you? How judge ye?
037:155 Will ye not then receive admonition?
037:156 Or have ye an authority manifest?
037:157 Then bring ye your Book (of authority)
037:157 (of authority) if ye be truthful!
037:161 For, verily, neither ye nor those ye worship
038:006 "Walk ye away, and remain constant to your gods!
038:060 "Nay, ye (too)! No welcome for you!
038:060 It is ye who have brought this upon us!
038:068 "From which ye do turn away!
038:072 fall ye down in prostrated unto him."
038:088 "And ye shall certainly know the truth of it (all) after
039:006 then how are ye turned away (from your true Lord)?
039:007 If ye reject (Allah), truly Allah hath no need of you:
039:007 if ye are grateful, He is pleased with you.
039:007 He will tell you the truth of all that ye did (in this life).
039:010 Say: "O ye my servants who believe! Fear your Lord.
039:015 "Serve ye what ye will besides Him."
039:016 "O my servants! Then fear ye Me!"
039:024 "Taste ye (the fruits of) what ye earned!"
039:031 In the End will ye (all) dispute on the Day
039:038 Say: "See ye then? The things ye invoke besides
039:039 Say: "O my people! Do whatever ye can:
039:039 I will do (my part): but soon will ye know-
039:044 it is to Him that ye shall be brought back."
039:054 comes on you: after that ye shall not be helped.
039:054 "Turn ye to your Lord (in repentance) and submit
039:055 comes on you-of a sudden, while ye perceive not!-
039:064 that ye order me to worship, O ye ignorant ones?"
039:072 "Enter ye the gates of Hell, to dwell therein:
039:073 Well have ye done! Enter ye here, to dwell therein."
040:010 seeing that ye were called to the Faith
040:010 to the Faith and ye used to refuse."

040:012 the Only (object of worship), ye did reject Faith,
040:012 but when partners were joined to Him, ye believed!
040:014 Call ye, then, upon Allah with sincere devotion
040:028 said: "Will ye slay a man because he says,
040:029 this day: ye have the upper hand in the land:
040:033 no defender shall ye have from Allah:
040:033 A day when ye shall turn your backs and flee:
040:034 but ye ceased not to doubt of the (mission)
040:034 ye said: 'No messenger will Allah send after him.'
040:041 to call you to Salvation while ye call me to the Fire!
040:042 "Ye do call upon me to blaspheme against Allah,
040:043 "Without doubt ye do call me to one who has no claim
040:044 "Soon will ye remember what I say to you (now).
040:046 "Cast ye the People of Pharaoh into the severest Penalty"
040:047 can ye then take (on yourselves) from us some share of
040:050 They will reply, "Then pray (as ye like)!
040:058 Little do ye learn by admonition!
040:061 made the Night or you, that ye may rest therein,
040:062 then how ye are deluded away from the Truth!
040:066 to invoke those whom ye invoke besides Allah,-
040:067 a Term appointed: in order that ye may understand.
040:073 "Where are the (deities) to which ye gave part-worship-
040:075 "That was because ye were wont to rejoice on the
040:075 than the Truth, and that ye were wont to be insolent.
040:076 "Enter ye the gates of Hell, to dwell therein:
040:079 that ye may use some for riding and some for food;
040:080 and on them and on ships ye are carried.
040:080 that ye may through them attain to any need
040:081 then which of the Signs of Allah will ye deny?
041:009 Say: Is it that ye Deny Him Who created the earth
041:009 And do ye join equals with Him?
041:011 "Come ye together, willingly or unwillingly."
041:021 "Why bear ye witness against us?"
041:021 the first time, and unto Him were ye to return.
041:022 Allah knew not many of the things that ye used to do!
041:022 "Ye did not seek to hide yourselves, lest your hearing
041:022 But ye did think that Allah knew not many
041:023 and (now) have ye become of those utterly lost!"
041:023 "But this thought of yours which ye did entertain
041:026 that ye may gain the upper hand!"
041:030 the Garden (of Bliss), the which ye were promised!
041:030 "Fear ye not!" (they suggest), "nor grieve!
041:031 therein shall ye have all that you shall desire;
041:031 therein shall ye have all that ye ask for!-
041:037 if it is Him ye wish to serve.
041:040 Do what ye will: Verily He seeth (clearly) all that ye do.
041:047 "Where are the partners (ye attributed) to Me?"
041:052 from Allah, and yet do ye reject it?
041:052 Say: "See ye if the (Revelation) is (really) from Allah,
042:010 Whatever it be wherein ye differ, the decision
042:013 Namely, that ye should remain steadfast in Religion,
042:025 and He knows all that ye do.
042:031 nor have ye, besides Allah, anyone to protect or to help.
042:031 Nor can ye escape through the earth;
042:036 Whatever ye are given (here) is (but) the enjoyment
042:047 Respond ye to your Lord, before there come a Day
043:003 that ye may be able to understand.
043:005 for that ye are a people transgressing beyond bounds?
043:010 in order that ye may find guidance (on the way);
043:011 even so will ye be raised (from the dead);-
043:012 and has made the ships and cattle on which ye ride,
043:013 In order that ye may sit firm and square on their backs,

YE (continued)

043:013	ye may remember the (kind) favour of your Lord,
043:024	than that **which ye** found your fathers following?"
043:024	we deny that which **ye** (prophets) are sent with."
043:026	"I do indeed clear myself of what **ye** worship:
043:039	When **ye** have done wrong, it will avail you nothing,
043:039	that day, that **ye** shall be partners in punishment!
043:044	and soon shall **ye** (all) be brought to account.
043:051	What! see **ye** not then?
043:061	have no doubt about the (Hour), but follow **ye** Me:
043:063	clear to you some of the (points) on which **ye** dispute:
043:064	He is my Lord and your Lord: so worship **ye** Him:
043:068	No fear shall be on you today, nor shall **ye** grieve,-
043:070	Enter **ye** the Garden, **ye** and your wives,
043:071	and **ye** shall abide therein (for aye).
043:072	**ye** are made heirs for your (good) deeds (in life).
043:073	**Ye** shall have therein abundance of fruit,
043:073	of fruit, from which **ye** shall eat.
043:077	"Nay, but **ye** shall abide!"
043:085	And to Him shall **ye** be brought back.
044:007	if **ye** (but) have an assured faith.
044:015	(but) truly **ye** will revert (to your ways).
044:021	"If **ye** believe me not, at least keep yourselves away
044:023	for **ye** are sure to be pursued.
044:036	(back) our forefathers, if what **ye** say is true!"
044:047	(A voice will cry:) "Seize **ye** him and drag him
044:050	"Truly this is what **ye** used to doubt!"
045:012	and that **ye** may be grateful.
045:012	it by His command, that **ye** may seek of His Bounty,
045:015	In the end will **ye** (all) be brought to your Lord.
045:023	Will **ye** not then receive admonition?
045:025	"Bring back our forefathers, if what **ye** say is true!"
045:028	"This Day shall **ye** be recompensed for all that **ye** did!
045:029	for We were wont to put on record all that **ye** did."
045:031	But **ye** were arrogant, and were a people given to sin!
045:032	**ye** used to say, 'We know not what is the Hour:
045:034	"This Day We will forget you as **ye** forgot the meeting
045:034	and your abode is the Fire, and no helpers have **ye**!
045:035	"This, because **ye** used to take the Signs of Allah in jest,
046:004	Say: "Do **ye** see what it is **ye** invoke beside Allah?
046:004	or any remnant of knowledge (**ye** may have),
046:004	if **ye** are telling the truth!"
046:008	He knows best of that whereof **ye** talk (so glibly)!
046:008	then can **ye** have no power to help me against Allah.
046:010	and **ye** reject it, and a witness from among the Children
046:010	Say: "See **ye**? If (this teaching) be from Allah,
046:010	believed while **ye** are arrogant, (how unjust **ye** are!)
046:017	Do **ye** hold out the promise to me that I shall be raised
046:020	and **ye** took your pleasure out of them:
046:020	"**Ye** squandered your good things in the life of the world,
046:020	but to-day shall **ye** be recompensed with a Chastisement
046:020	for that **ye** were arrogant on earth without just cause,
046:020	and that **ye** (ever) transgressed."
046:021	"Worship **ye** none other than Allah: truly I fear
046:023	but I see that **ye** are a people in ignorance!"...
046:024	"Nay, is the (calamity) **ye** were asking to be hastened!-
046:026	power which We have not given to you (**ye** Quraish)!
046:034	for that **ye** were wont to deny (Truth)!"
046:034	"Then taste **ye** the Chastisement, for that
047:004	Therefore, when **ye** meet the Unbelievers (in fight),
047:004	Thus (are **ye** commanded): but if it had been Allah's 'Will,
047:004	at length, when **ye** have thoroughly subdued them,
047:007	O **ye** who believe! if **ye** will help (the cause of) Allah,

YE (continued)

047:019	for Allah knows how **ye** move about and how
047:019	and how **ye** dwell in your homes.
047:022	if **ye** were put in authority,
047:022	that **ye** will do mischief in the land,
047:030	And Allah knows all that **ye** do.
047:033	O **ye** who believe! obey Allah, and obey the Messenger,
047:035	crying for peace, when **ye** are the Uppermost:
047:036	and if **ye** believe and guard against evil,
047:037	and press you, **ye** would covetously withhold,
047:038	But Allah is free of all wants, and it is **ye** that are needy.
047:038	If **ye** turn back (from the Path),
047:038	Behold, **ye** are those invited to spend (of your substance)
048:009	that **ye** may assist and honor him, and celebrate
048:009	In order that **ye** (O men) may believe in Allah
048:011	But Allah is well acquainted with all that **ye** do.
048:012	in your hearts, and **ye** conceived an evil thought,
048:012	"Nay, **ye** thought that the Messenger and the Believers
048:012	for **ye** are a people doomed to perish."
048:015	"But **ye** are jealous of us." Nay, but little do they
048:015	when **ye** set forth to acquire booty (in war):
048:015	Say: "Not thus will **ye** follow us: Allah has already
048:016	Then if **ye** show obedience, Allah will grant you
048:016	but if **ye** turn back as **ye** did before, He will punish
048:016	"**Ye** shall be summoned (to fight) against a people
048:016	then shall **ye** fight, or they shall submit.
048:020	Allah has promised you many gains that **ye** shall acquire,
048:024	And Allah sees well all that **ye** do.
048:025	women whom **ye** did not know that **ye** were trampling
048:027	**ye** shall enter the Sacred Mosque, if Allah wills,
048:027	For He knows what **ye** knew not, and He granted,
049:001	O **ye** who believe! put not yourselves forward
049:002	lest your deeds become vain and **ye** perceive not.
049:002	as **ye** may speak aloud to one another,
049:002	O **ye** who believe! raise not your voices above the voice
049:006	become full of repentance for what **ye** have done.
049:006	ascertain the truth, lest **ye** harm people unwittingly,
049:006	O **ye** who believe! if a sinner comes to you with any news,
049:007	to follow your (wishes), **ye** would certainly suffer:
049:009	fall into a fight, make **ye** peace between them:
049:009	then fight **ye** (all) against the one that transgresses
049:010	And fear Allah, that **ye** may receive Mercy.
049:011	O **ye** who believe! let not some men among you
049:012	Nay, **ye** would abhor it... But fear Allah:
049:012	O **ye** who believe! avoid suspicion as much (as possible):
049:013	that **ye** may know each other (not that **ye** may despise
049:014	But if **ye** obey Allah and His Messenger, He will
049:014	Say, "**Ye** have no faith; but **ye** (only) say, 'We have
049:016	Say: "What! Will **ye** tell Allah about your Religion?"
049:017	if **ye** be true and sincere.
049:018	and Allah sees well all that **ye** do."
050:034	"Enter **ye** therein in Peace and Security;
051:005	Verily that which **ye** are promised is true;
051:008	Truly **ye** are of varying opinion.
051:014	"Taste **ye** your trial! this is what **ye** used to ask to be
051:021	As also in your own selves: will **ye** not then see?
051:022	as (also) that which **ye** are promised.
051:023	as the fact that **ye** can speak intelligently to each other.
051:027	He said, "Will **ye** not eat?"
051:031	O **ye** Messengers, is your errand (now)?"
051:049	We have created pairs: that **ye** may reflect.
052:014	"Is the Fire,-which **ye** were wont to deny!
052:015	"Is this then a magic, or is it **ye** that do not see?

YE (continued)

052:016 "Burn **ye** therein: the same is it to you whether **ye** bear it
052:016 **ye** but receive the recompense of your (own) deeds."
052:019 "Eat and drink **ye**, with profit and health,
052:031 Say thou: "Await **ye**!-I too will wait along with you!"
052:039 Or has He only daughters and **ye** have sons?
053:012 Will **ye** then dispute with him concerning what he saw?
053:019 Have **ye** seen Lat, an 'Uzza,
053:023 **ye** and your fathers,-for which Allah has sent down no
053:023 These are nothing but names which **ye** have devised,-
053:032 and when **ye** are hidden in your mother's wombs.
053:059 Do **ye** then wonder at this recital?
053:060 And will **ye** laugh and not weep,-
053:062 But fall **ye** down in prostration to Allah,
054:037 "Now taste **ye** My Wrath and My Warning."
054:039 "So taste **ye** My Chastisement and My Warning."
054:043 Or have **ye** an immunity in the Sacred Books?
054:048 (they will hear): "Tastes **ye** the touch of Hell!"
055:008 In order that **ye** may not transgress (due) balance.
055:013 Then which of the favours of your Lord will **ye** deny?
055:016 Then which of the favours of your Lord will **ye** deny?
055:018 Then which of the favours of your Lord will **ye** deny?
055:021 Then which of the favours of your Lord will **ye** deny?
055:023 Then which of the favours of your Lord will **ye** deny?
055:025 Then which of the favours of your Lord will **ye** deny?
055:028 Then which of the favours of your Lord will **ye** deny?
055:030 Then which of the favours of your Lord will **ye** deny?
055:031 Soon shall We settle your affairs, O both **ye** worlds!
055:032 Then which of the favours of your Lord will **ye** deny?
055:033 O **ye** assembly of Jinns and men!
055:033 not without authority shall **ye** be able to pass!
055:033 If it be **ye** can pass beyond the zones of the heavens
055:034 Then which of the favours of your Lord will **ye** deny?
055:035 On you will be sent (O **ye** evil ones twain)!
055:035 molten brass. No defense will **ye** have:
055:036 Then which of the favours of your Lord will **ye** deny?
055:038 Then which of the favours of your Lord will **ye** deny?
055:040 Then which of the favours of your Lord will **ye** deny?
055:042 Then which of the favours of your Lord will **ye** deny?
055:045 Then which of the favours of your Lord will **ye** deny?
055:047 Then which of the favours of your Lord will **ye** deny?-
055:049 Then which of the favours of your Lord will **ye** deny?-
055:051 Then which of the favours of your Lord will **ye** deny?-
055:053 Then which of the favours of your Lord will **ye** deny?
055:055 Then which of the favours of your Lord will **ye** deny?
055:057 Then which of the favours of your Lord will **ye** deny?
055:059 Then which of the favours of your Lord will **ye** deny?
055:061 Then which of the favours of your Lord will **ye** deny?
055:063 Then which of the favours of your Lord will **ye** deny?
055:065 Then which of the favours of your Lord will **ye** deny?
055:067 Then which of the favours of your Lord will **ye** deny?
055:069 Then which of the favours of your Lord will **ye** deny?
055:071 Then which of the favours of your Lord will **ye** deny?
055:073 Then which of the favours of your Lord will **ye** deny?
055:075 Then which of the favours of your Lord will **ye** deny?
055:077 Then which of the favours of your Lord will **ye** deny?
056:007 And **ye** shall be sorted out into three classes.
056:051 "Then will **ye** truly,-O **ye** that go wrong,
056:052 "**Ye** will surely taste of the Tree of Zaqqum.
056:053 "Then will **ye** fill your insides therewith,
056:055 "Indeed **ye** shall drink like diseased camels
056:057 why will **ye** not admit the Truth?
056:058 Do **ye** then see? The (human Seed) that **ye** emit,-

YE (continued)

056:059 Is it **ye** who create it, or are We the Creators?
056:061 creating you (again) in (Forms) that **ye** know not.
056:062 And **ye** certainly know already the first form
056:062 why then do **ye** not take heed?
056:063 See **ye** the seed that **ye** sow in the ground?
056:064 Is it **ye** that cause it to grow, or are We the Cause?
056:065 And **ye** would be left in wonderment,
056:068 See **ye** the water which **ye** drink?
056:069 Do **ye** bring it Down (in rain) from the Cloud,
056:070 then why do **ye** not give thanks?
056:071 See **ye** the Fire which **ye** kindle?
056:072 Is it **ye** who grow the tree which feeds the fire,
056:076 And that is indeed a mighty adjuration if **ye** but knew,-
056:081 Is it such a Message that **ye** would hold in light esteem?
056:082 that **ye** should declare it false?
056:082 And have **ye** made it your livelihood that
056:083 Then why do **ye** not (intervene) when (the soul of
056:084 And **ye** the while (sit) looking on,-
056:085 But We are nearer to him than **ye**, and yet see not,-
056:086 Then why do **ye** not,-if you are exempt from (future)
056:087 if **ye** are true (in your claim of Independence)?
057:004 And He is with you wheresoever **ye** may be.
057:004 And Allah sees well all that **ye** do.
057:008 if **ye** are men of faith.
057:010 And Allah is well acquainted with all that **ye** do.
057:013 "Turn **ye** back to your rear!
057:013 Then seek a light (where **ye** can)!"
057:014 **ye** waited (to our ruin); **ye** doubted (Allah's promise);
057:014 "True! but **ye** led yourselves into temptation;
057:017 shown the Signs plainly to you, that **ye** may understand.
057:017 Know **ye** (all) that Allah giveth life to the earth after
057:020 Know **ye** (all), that the life of this world is but play
057:021 Be **ye** foremost (in seeking) forgiveness from your
057:023 In order that **ye** may not despair over matters
057:028 O **ye** that believe! fear Allah, and believe
057:028 by which **ye** shall walk (straight in your path),
058:003 this are **ye** admonished to perform:
058:003 and Allah is well-acquainted with (all) that **ye** do.
058:004 This, that **ye** may show your faith in Allah and His
058:009 O **ye** who believe! when **ye** hold secret counsel,
058:009 and fear Allah, to whom **ye** shall be brought back.
058:011 and Allah is well-acquainted with all **ye** do.
058:011 And when **ye** are told to rise up,
058:011 O **ye** who believe! When **ye** are told to make room
058:012 O **ye** who believe! When **ye** consult the Messenger
058:012 But if **ye** find not (the wherewithal),
058:013 Is it that **ye** are afraid of spending sums in charity
058:013 and Allah is well-acquainted with all that **ye** do.
058:013 If, then, **ye** do not so, and Allah forgives you,
059:002 Little did **ye** think that they would get out:
059:002 O **ye** with eyes (to see)!
059:005 Whether **ye** cut down (O **ye** Muslims!) of the tender
059:005 of the tender palm-trees, Or **ye** left them standing
059:006 for this **ye** made no expedition with either cavalry or
059:011 "If **ye** are expelled, We too will go out with you,
059:011 and if **ye** are attacked (in fight) We will help you."
059:013 Of a truth **ye** arouse greater fear in their hearts,
059:018 O **ye** who believe! Fear Allah, and let every soul look
059:018 for Allah is well-acquainted with (all) that **ye** do.
059:019 And be **ye** not like those who forgot Allah;
060:001 If **ye** have come out to strive in My Way and seek
060:001 (simply) **ye** believe in Allah your Lord!

YE (continued)

060:001 I know full well all that **ye** conceal and all that **ye** reveal.
060:001 O **ye** who believe! take not My enemies and yours
060:002 and they desire that **ye** should reject the Truth.
060:003 for Allah sees well all that **ye** do.
060:004 and of whatever **ye** worship besides Allah:
060:004 unless **ye** believe in Allah and Him alone":
060:007 those whom **ye** (now) hold as enemies.
060:010 if **ye** marry them on payment of their dower to them.
060:010 O **ye** who believe! when there come to you believing
060:010 if **ye** ascertain that they are Believers,
060:010 ask for what **ye** have spent on their dowers,
060:011 and fear Allah, in Whom **ye** believe.
060:011 and **ye** have your turn (by the coming over of a woman
060:013 O **ye** who believe! turn not (for friendship) to people
061:002 O **ye** who believe! why say **ye** that which **ye** do not?
061:003 in the sight of Allah that **ye** say that which **ye** do not.
061:005 though **ye** know that I am the messenger of Allah (sent)
061:005 "O my people! why do **ye** vex and insult me,
061:010 O **ye** who believe! shall I lead you to a bargain that will
061:011 that will be best for you, if **ye** but knew!
061:011 and that **ye** strive (your utmost) in the Cause of Allah,
061:011 That **ye** believe in Allah and His Messenger,
061:013 And another (favour will He bestow), which **ye** do love,-
061:014 O **ye** who believe! be **ye** helpers of Allah:
062:006 then express your desire for Death, if **ye** are truthful!"
062:006 "O **ye** of Jewry! if **ye** think that **ye** are friends to Allah,
062:008 "The Death from which **ye** flee will truly overtake you:
062:008 then will **ye** be sent to the Knower of things secret and
062:008 and He will tell you the things that **ye** did!"
062:009 that is best for you if **ye** but knew!
062:009 O **ye** who believe! when the call is proclaimed
062:010 and remember Allah frequently that **ye** may prosper.
062:010 then may **ye** disperse through the land, and seek
063:009 O **ye** who believe! let not your riches or your children
063:011 and Allah is well acquainted with (all) that **ye** do.
064:002 and Allah see well all that **ye** do.
064:004 and He knows what **ye** conceal and what **ye** reveal:
064:007 then shall **ye** be told (the truth) of all that **ye** did.
064:007 Say: Yea, by my Lord, **ye** shall surely be raised up:
064:008 And Allah is well-acquainted with all that **ye** do.
064:012 but if **ye** turn back, the duty of Our Messenger is but
064:014 But if **ye** forgive and overlook, and cover up (their faults),
064:014 O **ye** who believe! truly, among your wives and your
064:016 So fear Allah as much as **ye** can;
064:017 If **ye** loan to Allah a beautiful loan, He will
065:001 O Prophet! when **ye** do divorce women, divorce them
065:004 prescribed period, if **ye** have any doubt, is three months,
065:006 And if **ye** find yourselves in difficulties,
065:006 Let the women live (in 'iddat) in the same style as **ye** live,
065:010 O **ye** men of understanding-who have believed!-
065:012 that **ye** may know that Allah has power over all things,
066:004 but if **ye** back up each other against him,
066:004 If **ye** two turn in repentance to Allah,
066:006 O **ye** who believe! save yourselves and your families
066:007 (It will be said), "O **ye** Unbelievers! make no excuses
066:007 **Ye** are being but requited for all that **ye** did!"
066:008 O **ye** who believe! turn to Allah with sincere repentance:
066:010 "Enter **ye** the Fire along with (others) that enter!"
067:009 **ye** are in nothing but a grave error!'"
067:013 And whether **ye** hide your word or make it known,
067:015 so traverse **ye** through its tracts and enjoy of the
067:016 Do **ye** feel secure that He Who is in Heaven will not

YE (continued)

067:017 so that **ye** shall know how (terrible) was My warning?
067:017 Or do **ye** feel secure that He Who is in Heaven will not
067:023 seeing and understanding: little thanks it is **ye** give.
067:024 and to Him shall **ye** be gathered together."
067:025 If **ye** are telling the truth.
067:027 is (the promise fulfilled), which **ye** were calling for!"
067:028 Say: "See **ye**?-if Allah were to destroy me,
067:029 so soon will **ye** know which (of us) it is that is in
067:030 Say: "See **ye**?-if your stream be some morning lost
068:022 "Go **ye** to your tilth (betimes) in the morning,
068:022 if **ye** would gather the fruits."
068:036 What is the matter with you? How judge **ye**?
068:037 Or have **ye** a Book through which **ye** learn-
068:038 That **ye** shall have, through it whatever **ye** choose?
068:039 (providing) that **ye** hall have whatever **ye** shall demand?
068:039 Or have **ye** Covenants with Us on oath,
069:018 not an act of yours that **ye** hide will be hidden.
069:018 That Day shall **ye** be brought to Judgment:
069:019 "Ah here! read **ye** my Record!
069:024 "Eat **ye** and drink **ye**, with full satisfaction;
069:024 because of the (good) that **ye** sent before you,
069:030 "Seize **ye** him, and bind **ye** him,
069:031 "And burn **ye** him in the Blazing Fire.
069:038 So I do call to witness what **ye** see
069:039 And what **ye** see not,
069:041 little it is **ye** believe!
069:042 of a soothsayer: little admonition it is **ye** receive.
071:003 "That **ye** should worship Allah, fear Him,
071:004 it cannot be put forward: if **ye** only knew."
071:013 that **ye** are not conscious of Allah's majesty,-
071:015 "'See **ye** not how Allah has created the seven
071:020 That **ye** may go about therein, in spacious roads."
072:007 'And they (came to) think as **ye** thought,
072:025 whether the (Punishment) which **ye** are promised is near,
073:017 Then how shall **ye**, if **ye** deny (Allah),
073:020 read **ye**, therefore, of the Qur'an as much as may be easy
073:020 He knoweth that **ye** are unable to keep count thereof.
073:020 Read **ye**, therefore, as much of the Qur'an as may be
073:020 And whatever good **ye** send forth for yourself,
073:020 for yourself, **ye** shall find it with Allah.
073:020 and seek **ye** the Grace of Allah:
075:020 Nay, (**ye** men!) but **ye** love the fleeting life,
076:030 But **ye** will not, except as Allah wills;
077:007 Assuredly, what **ye** are promised must come to pass.
077:029 (It will be said:) "Depart **ye** to that which **ye** used to
077:030 "Depart **ye** to a Shadow (of smoke ascending)
077:039 Now, if **ye** have a trick (or plot),
077:043 "Eat **ye** and drink **ye** to your heart's content:
077:043 for that **ye** worked (Righteousness).
077:046 (O **ye** Unjust!) Eat **ye** and enjoy yourselves (but)
077:046 for that **ye** are Sinners.
078:018 and **ye** shall come forth in crowds;
078:030 "So taste **ye** (the fruits of your deeds);
079:027 What! Are **ye** the more difficult to create or the
081:026 Then whither go **ye**?
081:029 But **ye** shall not will Except as Allah wills,-
082:009 Nay! but **ye** do Reject The Judgment!
082:012 They know all that **ye** do.
083:017 "This is the (reality) which **ye** rejected as false!"
084:019 **Ye** shall surely travel from stage to stage.
087:016 Nay (behold), **ye** prefer the life of this world;
089:017 Nay, nay! But **ye** honour not the orphans!

YE (continued)

089:018 Nor do **ye** encourage one another to feed the poor!-
089:019 And **ye** devour inheritance-all with greed,
089:020 And **ye** love wealth with inordinate love!
092:004 Verily, (the ends) **ye** strive for are diverse.
102:002 Until **ye** visit the graves.
102:003 But nay, **ye** soon shall know (the reality).
102:004 Again, **ye** soon shall know!
102:005 Nay, were **ye** to know with certainty of mind,
102:005 with certainty of mind, (**ye** would beware)!
102:006 **Ye** shall certainly see Hell-fire!
102:007 Again, **ye** shall see it with certainty of sight!
102:008 about the joy (**ye** indulged in)!
102:008 Then, shall **ye** be Questioned that Day about the
109:001 Say: O **ye** that reject Faith!
109:002 I worship not that which **ye** worship,
109:003 Nor will **ye** worship that which I worship.
109:004 that which **ye** have been wont to worship,
109:005 Nor will **ye** worship that which I worship.

YEA

002:126 He said: "(**Yea**), and such as reject Faith,
002:200 **yea**, with far more heart and soul.
002:260 He said: "**Yea**! but to satisfy my own heart."
003:125 "**Yea**,-if ye remain firm, and act aright,
004:132 **Yea**, unto Allah belong all things in the heavens
006:028 **Yea**, in their own (eyes) will become manifest
006:030 They will say: "**Yea**, by our Lord!" He will say:
007:114 He said: "**Yea**, (and more),-for ye shall in that case
007:172 They said: "**Yea**! we do testify! (This),
009:124 **Yea**, those who believe, their faith is increased,
010:026 is a goodly (reward)-**yea**, more (than in measure)!
015:063 They said: "**Yea**, we have come to thee to accomplish
017:111 **Yea**, magnify Him for His greatness and glory!"
020:130 **yea**, celebrate them for part of the hours of the night,
024:033 **yea**, give them something yourselves out of the means
024:042 **Yea**, to Allah belongs the dominion of the heavens
026:042 He said: "**Yea**, (and more),-for ye shall in that case be
026:132 "**Yea**, fear Him Who has bestowed on you freely
027:047 **yea**, ye are a people under trial."
027:060 **Yea**, with it We cause to grow well-planted orchards
030:018 **Yea**, To Him be praise, in the heavens and on earth;
036:081 **Yea**, indeed! for He is the Creator Supreme,
037:018 Say thou: "**Yea**, and ye shall then be humiliated
038:055 **Yea**, such! But-for the wrong-doers will be
038:057 **Yea**, such!-Then shall they taste it,-a boiling
043:010 (**Yea**, the same that) has made for you the earth
043:029 **Yea**, I have given the good things of this life
043:058 **yea**, they are a contentious people.
046:033 **Yea**, verily He has power over all things.
046:034 "Is this not the Truth?" they will say, "**Yea**, by our Lord!"
053:031 **Yea**, to Allah belongs all that is in the heavens
054:021 **Yea**, how (terrible) was my Chastisement and my
056:049 Say: "**Yea**, those of old and those of later times,
059:018 **Yea**, fear Allah: for Allah is well-acquainted with
063:001 **Yea**, Allah knoweth that thou art indeed His Messenger.
064:004 **yea**, Allah knows well the (secrets) of (all) hearts.
064:007 Say: "**Yea**, by my Lord, ye shall surely be raised up:
073:020 **Yea**, better and greater, in Reward, and seek ye
074:020 **Yea**, woe to him: how he determined!-
075:026 **Yea**, when (the soul) reaches to the collar-bone
075:034 Woe to thee, (O man!) **yea**, woe!
075:035 Again, woe to thee, (O man!), **yea** woe!
089:030 "**Yea**, enter thou My Heaven!"

YEAR

009:028 after this **year** of theirs, approach the Sacred Mosque.
009:036 the number months sight of Allah is twelve (in a **year**)-
009:037 they make it lawful one **year**, and forbidden another **year**,
009:126 are tried every **year** once or twice?
012:049 a **year** in which the people will have abundant

YEAR'S

002:240 their widows a **year's** maintenance without expulsion;

YEARNING

021:090 they used to call on Us in **yearning** and awe.

YEARS

002:096 be given a life of a thousand **years**:
002:233 suck to their offspring for two whole **years**,
002:259 But Allah caused him to die for a hundred **years**,
002:259 hast tarried thus a hundred **years**:
005:026 the land be out of their reach for forty **years**:
007:130 punished the people of Pharaoh with **years** (of drought)
010:005 that ye might know the number of **years** and the
012:042 and (Joseph) lingered in prison a few (more) **years**.
012:047 (Joseph) said: "For seven **years** shall ye diligently sow
012:048 will come after that (period) seven dreadful (**years**),
017:012 and that ye may know the number and count of the **years**:
018:011 (a veil) over their ears, for a number of **years**,
018:012 at calculating the term of **years** they had tarried!
018:025 stayed in their Cave three hundred **years**, and nine (more).
018:060 or (until) I spend **years** and **years** in travel."
020:040 Then didst thou tarry a number of **years** with the
022:047 the sight of thy Lord a thousand **years** of your reckoning.
023:112 He will say: "What number of **years** did ye stay on earth?
026:018 didst thou not stay in our midst many **years** of thy life?
026:205 If We do let them enjoy (this life) for a few **years**,
028:027 serve me for eight **years**, but if thou complete ten **years**,
029:014 and he tarried among them a thousand **years** less fifty:
030:004 Within a few **years**, with Allah is the Command in the
031:014 And in **years** twain was his weaning:
032:005 measure of which is a thousand **years** of your reckoning.
046:015 he reaches the age of full strength and attains forty **years**,
070:004 the measure whereof is (as) fifty thousand **years**:

YELLOW

030:051 a Wind from which they see (their tilth) turn **yellow**,-
039:021 then it withers; thou wilt see it grow **yellow**;
057:020 soon it withers; thou wilt see it grow **yellow**;
077:033 (A string of) **yellow** camels (marching swiftly)."

YES

007:044 They shall say, "**Yes**"; but a Crier shall proclaim
040:050 your messengers with Clear Signs?" They will say: "**Yes**."
067:009 They will say: "**Yes** indeed: a Warner did come to us,

YESTERDAY

028:019 intention to slay me as thou slewest a man **yesterday**?

YET

002:044 and **yet** ye study the Scripture?
002:091 **yet** they reject all besides,
002:092 **yet** ye worshipped the Calf (even) after that,
002:113 **Yet** they (profess) to study the (same) Book.
002:165 **Yet** there are men who take (for worship)
002:204 **yet** is he the most contentious of enemies.
003:067 Abraham was not a Jew nor **yet** a Christian;
003:170 who have not **yet** joined them (in their bliss),
004:102 the other party come up which hath not **yet** prayed
004:127 and **yet** whom ye desire to marry,
004:153 **Yet** they worshipped the calf even after
005:003 **yet** fear them not but fear Me.

YET (continued)

005:032   **yet**, even after that, many of them continued
005:043   **yet** even after that, they would turn away.
005:071   **yet** again many of them became blind and deaf.
005:071   **yet** Allah (in mercy) turned to them:
005:075   **yet** see in what ways they are deluded
006:001   **Yet** those who reject Faith hold (others) as equal with
006:002   **yet** ye doubt within yourselves!
006:006   **yet** for their sins We destroyed them,
006:035   **yet** if thou wert able to seek a tunnel in the ground
006:046   by various (symbols): **Yet** they turn aside.
006:064   and **yet** ye worship false gods!"
006:099   each similar (in kind) **yet** different (in variety):
006:100   **Yet** they make the Jinns equals with Allah,
006:165   **yet** He is indeed Oft-Forgiving, Most Merciful.
009:002   but know **yet** that ye cannot frustrate Allah
009:016   alone while Allah has not **yet** known those among you
009:031   **yet** they were commanded to worship but One God:
009:056   **yet** they are afraid (of you).
009:106   There are (**yet**) others, held in suspense for the
009:126   **Yet** they turn not in repentance,
010:055   **Yet** most of them do not understand.
010:059   **Yet** ye hold forbidden some things thereof and (some
010:071   **yet** I put my trust in Allah get ye then an agreement
011:017   **yet** many among men do not believe!
011:031   Nor **yet** do I say, of those whom your eyes
011:081   Now travel with thy family while **yet** a part of the night
012:038   **yet** most men are not grateful.
012:053   "**Yet** I do not absolve my own self (of blame):
012:103   **Yet** no faith will the greater part of mankind have,
012:105   **Yet** they turn (their faces) away from them!
013:004   **yet** some of them We make more excellent than others
013:006   **yet** have come to pass, before them, (many) exemplary
013:013   **Yet** these (are the men) the while they are disputing
013:030   **yet** do they reject (Him), the Most Gracious!
013:033   And **yet** they ascribe partners to Allah,
014:008   **yet** is Allah Free of all wants, Worthy of
014:017   from every quarter, **yet** will he not die;
015:065   when a portion of the night (**yet** remains),
016:037   **yet** Allah guideth not such as He leaves to stray,
016:054   **Yet**, when He removes the distress from you,
016:112   **yet** was it ungrateful for the favours of Allah:
017:008   It may be that your Lord may (**yet**) show Mercy
017:028   **yet** speak to them a word of easy kindness.
017:044   and **yet** ye understand not how they declare His
017:051   (to be raised up)-(**yet** shall ye be raised up)!"
017:083   **Yet** when We bestow Our favours on man, he turns
017:089   **yet** the greater part of men refuse (to receive it)
018:022   (**yet** others) say they were seven, the dog being the
019:077   man who rejects Our Signs, **yet** says: "I shall certainly
020:007   knoweth what is secret and what is **yet** more hidden.
021:001   **yet** they heel not and they turn away.
021:012   **Yet**, when they felt Our Punishment (coming),
021:032   **Yet** do they turn away from the Signs
021:039   not **yet** from their backs, and (when) no help can reach
021:042   **Yet** they turn away from the remembrance
021:093   (**yet**) will they all return to Us.
022:002   thou shalt see mankind as in a drunken riot, **yet** not drunk:
022:003   And **yet** among men there are such as dispute
022:008   **Yet** there is among men such a one as disputes
022:047   **Yet** they ask thee to hasten on the Punishment!
022:071   **Yet** they worship, besides Allah,
023:085   Say: "**Yet** will ye not receive admonition?"

YET (continued)

024:033   but if anyone compels them, **yet**, after such compulsion,
025:003   **Yet** have they taken, besides Him, gods that
025:053   **yet** has He made a barrier between them,
025:055   **Yet** do they worship, besides Allah, things that
026:206   **Yet** there comes to them at length the (Punishment)
027:073   **yet** most of them are ungrateful.
028:046   **Yet** (art thou sent) as a Mercy from thy Lord,
029:039   **yet** they cold not overreach (Us).
029:050   **Yet** they say: "Why are not Signs sent down
030:008   **yet** are there truly many among men who deny
031:015   **yet** bear them company in this life with justice
031:020   **Yet** there are among men those who dispute
031:027   **yet** would not the Words of Allah be exhausted
033:015   And **yet** they had already covenanted with Allah
034:045   **yet** when they rejected My messengers,
035:012   **Yet** from each (kind of water) do ye eat flesh fresh
036:049   It will seize them while they are **yet** disputing among
036:074   **Yet** they take (for worship) gods other than Allah,
036:077   **Yet** behold! he (stands forth) as an open adversary!
038:008   Nay, they have not **yet** tasted My Punishment!
038:023   **yet** he says, 'Commit her to my care,' and he overcame
039:023   (**yet**) repeating (its teaching in various aspects):
040:057   than the creation of men: **yet** most men know not.
040:059   therein is no doubt: **yet** most men believe not.
040:061   **yet** most men give no thanks.
040:082   **yet** all that they accomplished was of no profit to them.
041:004   **yet** most of them turn away,
041:052   (Revelation) is (really) from Allah, and **yet** do ye reject
043:015   **Yet** they attribute to some of His servants
044:009   **Yet** they play about in doubt.
044:014   **Yet** they turn away from him and say: "Tutored (by
045:008   **yet** is obstinate and lofty, as if he had not heard them:
049:014   for not **yet** has Faith entered your hearts.
052:021   (**Yet**) is each individual in pledge for his deeds.
056:085   But We are nearer to him than ye, and **yet** see not,-
057:027   **Yet** We bestowed, on those among them who believed,
058:008   forbidden secret counsels **yet** revert to that which they
067:028   **yet** who can deliver the Unbelievers from a grievous
072:019   "**Yet** when the Devotee of Allah stands forth
073:011   the good things of life, (who (**yet**) deny the Truth);
073:020   **yet** others fighting in Allah's Cause.
074:015   **Yet** is he greedy-that I should add (**yet** more);
085:019   And **yet** the Unbelievers (persist) in rejecting

YIELD

002:265   but makes it **yield** a double increase of harvest,
006:093   stretch forth their hands (saying), "**Yield** up your souls.

YIELDING

012:080   Now when they saw no hope of his (**yielding**),

YIELDS

041:039   it is stirred to life and **yields** increase.
077:031   "(Which **yields**) no shade of coolness,

YOKE

006:138   there are cattle forbidden to **yoke** or burden,

YOKES

007:157   and from the **yokes** that are upon them.
013:005   those round whose necks will be **yokes** (of servitude):
034:033   We shall put **yokes** on the necks of the Unbelievers:
036:008   We have put **yokes** round their necks right up
040:071   When the **yokes** (shall be) round their necks,
076:004   prepared Chains, **Yokes**, and a Blazing Fire.

YOU

002:014 they say: "We are really with **you**,
002:021 Who created **you** and those who came before
002:021 came before **you** that ye may become righteous,
002:028 and will again bring **you** to life;
002:028 and He gave **you** life;
002:028 then will He cause **you** to die,
002:029 He Who hath created for **you** all things that are on earth;
002:033 Allah said: "Did I not tell **you** that I know the secrets of
002:038 there comes to **you** guidance from Me,
002:040 and I shall fulfil My Covenant with **you**,
002:040 favour which I bestowed upon **you**,
002:041 confirming the revelation which is with **you**,
002:047 and that I preferred **you** to all others.
002:047 favour which I bestowed upon **you**,
002:049 they set **you** hard tasks and chastisement,
002:049 delivered **you** from the people of Pharaoh:
002:050 and saved **you** and drowned Pharaoh's people
002:050 And remember We divided the sea for **you**
002:052 Even then We did forgive **you**,
002:052 there was a chance for **you** to be grateful.
002:053 there was a chance for **you** to be guided aright.
002:054 for **you** in the sight of your Maker.
002:054 Then He turned towards **you** (in forgiveness):
002:055 thereupon, thunderbolt seized **you**.
002:056 Then We raised **you** up after your death;
002:057 and sent down to **you** manna and quails,
002:057 And We gave **you** the shade of clouds
002:057 the good things We have provided for **you**:"
002:058 forgive **you** your faults and increase (the portion of)
002:063 We have given **you** and bring (ever) to remembrance
002:063 and We raised above **you** the Mount (Sinai)
002:064 the Grace and Mercy of Allah to **you** ye had surely
002:065 amongst **you** who transgressed in the matter
002:073 and showeth **you** His Signs,
002:075 entertain the hope that they will believe in **you**?
002:076 they say: "Shall **you** tell them what Allah
002:076 what Allah hath revealed to **you**,
002:076 that they may engage **you** in argument about it
002:083 except a few among **you**, and ye backside (even now).
002:084 shed no blood amongst **you**,
002:085 and if they come to **you** as captives,
002:085 not lawful for **you** to banish them.
002:085 for those among **you** who behave like this
002:085 and banish a party of **you** from their homes;
002:087 comes to **you** an Messenger with what ye yourselves
002:092 There came to **you** Moses with clear (Signs);
002:093 (saying): "Hold firmly to what We given **you**,
002:093 and We raised above **you** the mount (Sinai):
002:094 Say: "If the last Home with Allah, be for **you** specially,
002:105 good should come down to **you** from your Lord.
002:109 wish they could turn **you** (people) back to infidelity
002:110 send forth for your souls before **you**,
002:122 and that I preferred **you** to all others.
002:122 the special favour which I bestowed upon **you**,
002:132 "O my sons! Allah hath chosen the Faith for **you**;
002:143 Thus have We made of **you** an Ummah
002:148 Allah will bring **you** together.
002:150 and that I may complete My favours on **you**,
002:150 be no ground of dispute against **you** among the people,
002:151 in that We have sent among **you** a Messenger
002:151 rehearsing to **you** Our Signs, and purifying **you**,
002:151 and instructing **you** in Scripture and Wisdom,

YOU (continued)

002:152 Then do ye remember Me; I will remember **you**.
002:155 Be sure We shall test **you** with something
002:168 for he is to **you** an avowed enemy.
002:169 For he commands **you** what is evil and shameful,
002:172 the good things that We have provided for **you**.
002:173 He hath only forbidden **you** dead meat,
002:178 prescribed to **you** in cases of murder:
002:179 there is (saving of) Life to **you**.
002:180 when death approaches any of **you**,
002:183 O ye who believe! fasting is prescribed to **you**
002:183 as it was prescribed to those before **you**,
002:184 And it is better for **you** that ye fast,
002:184 but if any of **you** is ill, or on a journey,
002:185 He does not want to put **you** to difficulties.
002:185 So every one of **you** who is present (at his home)
002:185 (He wants **you**) to complete the prescribed period,
002:185 Allah intends every facility for **you**;
002:185 and to glorify Him in that He has guided **you**;
002:187 and seek what Allah hath ordained for **you**,
002:187 but He turned to **you** and forgave **you**:
002:187 appear to **you** distinct from its black thread;
002:187 Permitted to **you** on the night of the fasts,
002:187 but He turned to **you** and forgave **you**:
002:190 Fight in the cause of Allah those who fight **you**
002:191 unless they (first) fight **you** there;
002:191 but if they fight **you**, slay them.
002:191 from where they have turned **you** out;
002:194 transgresses the prohibition against **you**,
002:196 And if any of **you** is ill,
002:197 And take a provision (with **you**) for the journey,
002:198 and celebrate His praises as He has directed **you**,
002:198 It is no crime in **you** if ye seek of the bounty
002:208 the Satan for he is to **you** an avowed enemy.
002:209 the clear (signs) have come to **you**,
002:214 came to those who passed away before **you**?
002:216 Fighting is prescribed for **you**,
002:216 and that ye love a thing which is bad for **you**.
002:216 ye dislike a thing which is good for **you**,
002:217 And if any of **you** turn back from their faith
002:217 Nor will they cease fighting **you** until
002:217 until they turn **you** back from your faith
002:219 Thus doth Allah make clear to **you** His Signs:
002:220 He could have put **you** into difficulties:
002:221 even though he allure **you**.
002:221 Unbelievers do (but) beckon **you** to the Fire.
002:221 Even though she allure **you**.
002:222 ye may approach them as ordained for **you** by Allah
002:223 Your wives are as a tilth unto **you** so approach your
002:225 Allah will not call **you** to account for thoughtlessness
002:229 It is not lawful for **you**, (men),
002:231 but solemnly rehearse Allah's favours on **you**,
002:231 He sent down to **you** the Book and Wisdom,
002:232 This instruction is for all amongst **you**,
002:232 most virtue and purity amongst **you**,
002:233 for your offspring there is no blame on **you**,
002:234 there is no blame on **you** if they dispose of themselves
002:234 If any of **you** die and leave widows behind;
002:235 There is no blame on **you** if ye make an indirect offer
002:235 a secret contract with them except that **you** speak to them
002:236 There is no blame on **you** if ye divorce women
002:239 in the manner He has taught **you**,
002:240 there is no blame on **you** for what they do

YOU (continued)

002:240	Those of **you** who die and leave widows
002:242	Thus doth Allah make clear His Signs to **you**:
002:245	It is Allah that giveth (**you**) want or Plenty,
002:247	"Allah hath appointed Talut as king over **you**."
002:247	He said: "Allah hath chosen him above **you**.
002:248	shall come to **you** the Ark of the Covenant,
002:248	Symbol for **you** if ye indeed have faith."
002:249	he said: "Allah will test **you** at the stream;
002:254	(the bounties) We have provided for **you**,
002:266	Does any of **you** wish that he should have a garden
002:266	clear to **you** (His) Signs; that ye may consider.
002:267	the fruits of the earth which We have produced for **you**,
002:268	and bids **you** to conduct unseemly.
002:268	Allah promiseth **you** His forgiveness and bounties.
002:268	Satan threatens **you** with poverty and bids
002:270	or whatever **you** vow to make,
002:271	it will remove from **you** some of your (stains of) evil.
002:271	that is best for **you**:
002:272	shall be rendered back to **you**,
002:272	It is not for **you** to guide them to the right path.
002:280	that is best for **you** if ye only knew.
002:282	for it is Allah that teaches **you**.
002:282	there is no blame on **you** if ye reduce it not to writing.
002:282	it would be wickedness in **you**.
002:283	And if one of **you** deposits a thing on trust with another,
002:284	Allah calleth **you** to account for it.
003:006	shapes **you** in the wombs as He pleases.
003:013	"There has already been for **you** a Sign
003:015	Say: shall I give **you** glad tidings of things
003:028	But Allah cautions **you** (to fear) Himself;
003:030	But Allah cautions **you** (to fear) Him
003:031	Allah will love **you** and forgive **you** your sins:
003:037	He said: "O Mary! whence (comes) this to **you**?"
003:049	Surely therein is a Sign for **you** if ye did believe.
003:049	I have come to **you**, with a Sign from your Lord,
003:049	in that I make for **you** out of clay, as it were,
003:049	and I declare to **you** what ye eat,
003:050	And to make lawful to **you** part of what was (before)
003:050	"(I have come to **you**), to attest the Torah
003:050	I have come to **you** with a Sign from your Lord.
003:050	part of what was (before) forbidden to **you**;
003:055	between **you** of the matters wherein ye dispute.
003:064	come to common terms as between us and **you**:
003:069	But they shall lead astray (not **you**),
003:069	the People of the Book to lead **you** astray.
003:073	should engage **you** in argument before your Lord?
003:073	like unto that which was sent unto **you**?
003:078	so that **you** would think it is a part of the Book,
003:080	What! would he bid **you** to unbelief after ye have
003:080	Nor would he instruct **you** to take angels
003:081	and take My covenant as binding on **you**?"
003:081	then comes to **you** an Messenger, confirming
003:081	and I am with **you** among the witnesses."
003:081	confirming what is with **you**;
003:081	saying: "I give **you** a Book and Wisdom:
003:100	indeed render **you** apostates after ye have believed!
003:101	and among **you** lives the Messenger?
003:101	while unto **you** are rehearsed the Signs of Allah,
003:103	and He saved **you** from it.
003:103	Thus doth Allah make His Signs clear to **you**:
003:103	by the Rope which Allah (stretches out for **you**),
003:103	and remember with gratitude Allah's favour on **you**;

YOU (continued)

003:104	Let there arise out of **you** a band of people
003:111	They will do **you** no harm, barring a trifling
003:111	if they come out to fight **you**, they will show
003:111	they will show **you** their backs, and no help
003:118	We have made plain to **you** the Signs,
003:118	they will not fail to corrupt **you**.
003:118	They only desire for **you** to suffer:
003:119	when they meet **you**, they say, "We believe";
003:119	bite off the very tips of their fingers at **you** in their rage.
003:119	but they love **you** not,
003:120	not the least harm will their cunning do to **you**;
003:120	If aught that is good befalls **you**, it grieves them;
003:120	but if some misfortune overtakes **you**,
003:123	Allah had helped **you** at Badr, when ye
003:124	Is it not enough for **you** that Allah should help
003:124	should help **you** with three thousand angels
003:125	your Lord would help **you** with five thousand angels
003:125	even if the enemy should rush here on **you** in hot haste,
003:126	Allah made it but a message of hope for **you**,
003:137	that have passed away before **you**:
003:140	If a wound hath touched **you**, be sure a similar
003:142	without Allah testing those of **you** who fought hard
003:149	they will drive **you** back on your heels,
003:152	Among **you** are some that hanker after this world
003:152	Then did He divert **you** from your foes
003:152	and disobeyed it after He brought **you** in sight
003:152	from your foes in order to test **you**.
003:152	But He forgave **you**:
003:152	His promise to **you** when we with His permission
003:153	(the booty) that had escaped **you** and for (the ill)
003:153	and for (the ill) that had befallen **you**.
003:153	There did Allah give **you** one distress after another
003:153	to teach **you** not to grieve for (the booty)
003:153	and the Messenger in your rear was calling **you** back.
003:154	Say: "Even if **you** had remained in your homes,
003:154	a band of **you** overcome with slumber,
003:155	Those of **you** who turned back on the day the two hosts
003:160	if He forsakes **you**, who is there, after that,
003:160	after that, that can help **you**?
003:160	If Allah helps **you**, none can overcome **you**:
003:165	What! when a single disaster smites **you**,
003:167	we should certainly have followed **you**."
003:173	"A great army is gathering against **you**,
003:175	the Satan that suggests to **you** the fear of his votaries:
003:179	nor will Allah disclose to **you** the secrets of the Unseen,
003:183	Say: "There came to **you** Messengers before me,
003:185	Day of Judgement shall **you** be paid your full recompense.
003:186	and ye shall certainly hear much that will grieve **you**,
003:186	from those who received the Book before **you**
003:195	I suffer to be lost the work of any of **you**,
003:199	those who believe in Allah, in the revelation to **you**,
004:001	for Allah ever watches over **you**.
004:001	Who created **you** from a single person,
004:003	to prevent **you** from doing injustice.
004:005	which Allah has assigned to **you** to manage,
004:005	remit any part of it to **you**, take it and enjoy it
004:011	Allah (thus) directs **you** as regards your children's
004:011	or your children are nearest to **you** in benefit.
004:015	witnesses from amongst **you** against them;
004:016	If two persons among **you** are guilty of lewdness,
004:021	and they have taken from **you** a solemn covenant?
004:023	foster-mothers (who gave **you** suck),

YOU (continued)

004:023	Prohibited to **you** (for marriage) are: your mother,
004:024	ye agree mutually (to vary it), there is no blame on **you**,
004:024	Thus hath Allah ordained (prohibitions) against **you**:
004:024	the enjoyment **you** have of them as a duty; but if,
004:025	but it is better for **you** that ye practise self-restraint.
004:025	If any of **you** have not the means wherewith to wed
004:025	for those among **you** who fear sin;
004:026	and to guide **you** into the ways of those before **you**;
004:026	and (He doth wish to) turn to **you** (in Mercy):
004:026	Allah doth wish to make clear to **you** and
004:027	Allah doth wish to turn to **you**,
004:029	for verily Allah hath been to **you** Most Merciful.
004:029	be amongst **you** traffic and trade by mutual good-will:
004:031	and admit **you** to the Gate of great honor.
004:032	gifts more freely on some of **you** than on others:
004:034	for Allah is Most High, Great (above **you** all).
004:043	except when **you** are passing by (through the mosque),
004:043	or one of **you** cometh from the privy,
004:046	and "Here may **you** not heard"; and "Ra'ina"
004:047	confirming what was (already) with **you**,
004:047	fame of some (of **you**) beyond all recognition,
004:058	the teaching which He giveth **you**!
004:058	Allah doth command **you** to render back your trusts
004:059	and those charged with authority among **you**.
004:072	if a misfortune befalls **you**, they say: "Allah did
004:072	There are certainly among **you** men who would tarry
004:073	had never been ties of affection between **you** and them,
004:073	But if good fortune comes to **you** from Allah,
004:078	"Wherever ye are, death will find **you** out,
004:083	the Grace and Mercy of Allah unto **you**,
004:083	all but a few of **you** would have followed Satan.
004:086	When a (courteous) greeting is offered **you**,
004:087	gather **you** together on the Day of Judgement,
004:090	withdraw from **you** but fight **you** not,
004:090	and (instead) send **you** (guarantees of) peace,
004:090	no way for **you** (to war against them).
004:090	or those who approach **you** with hearts restraining
004:090	them from fighting **you** or fighting their own people.
004:090	He could have given them power over **you**,
004:090	and they would have fought **you**:
004:090	between whom and **you** there is a treaty (of peace),
004:091	Others **you** will find that wish to be secure from
004:091	if they withdraw not from **you** nor give
004:091	nor give **you** (guarantees) of peace besides restraining
004:091	their case We have provided **you** with a clear argument
004:092	to a people at war with **you**, and he was a Believer,
004:094	and say not to any one who offers **you** a salutation:
004:094	till Allah conferred on **you** His favours:
004:097	spacious enough for **you** to move yourselves
004:101	for the Unbelievers are unto **you** open enemies.
004:101	for fear the Unbelievers may attack **you**:
004:101	there is no blame on **you** if ye shorten your prayers,
004:102	to assault **you** in a single rush.
004:102	But there is no blame on **you** if ye put away your arms
004:104	but **you** hope from Allah, what they have not.
004:127	been rehearsed unto **you** in the Book, concerning
004:127	Say: Allah doth instruct **you** about them:
004:131	and **you** (O Muslims) to fear Allah,
004:131	We have directed the people of the Book before **you**,
004:133	If it were His will, He could destroy **you**,
004:140	Already has He sent **you** word in the Book,
004:141	"Did we not gain an advantage over **you**.

YOU (continued)

004:141	they say: "Were we not with **you**?"
004:141	And did we not guard **you** from the Believers?"
004:141	(These are) the ones who wait and watch about **you**:
004:141	betwixt **you** on the Day of Judgment.
004:149	Whether **you** do openly a good deed or conceal
004:170	believe in him: it is best for **you**.
004:170	the Messenger hath come to **you** in truth from Allah:
004:171	"Three": desist: it will be better for **you**:
004:174	come to **you** a convincing proof from your Lord
004:174	sent unto **you** a light (that is) manifest.
004:176	thus doth Allah make clear to **you** (His law),
005:001	Lawful unto **you** (for food) are all beasts of cattle
005:002	lead **you** to transgression (and hostility on your part).
005:002	In (once) shutting **you** out of the Sacred Mosque
005:003	This day have I perfected your religion for **you**,
005:003	and have chosen for **you** Islam as your religion.
005:003	completed my favour upon **you**,
005:003	Forbidden to **you** (for food) are: dead meat, blood,
005:004	Say: Lawful unto **you** are (all) things good and pure:
005:004	in the manner directed to **you** by Allah:
005:004	eat what they catch for **you**, but pronounce
005:005	things good and pure made lawful unto **you**.
005:005	is lawful unto **you** and yours is lawful unto them.
005:005	(Lawful unto **you** in marriage) are (not only)
005:006	Allah doth not wish to place **you** in a difficulty,
005:006	to make **you** clean, and to complete His favour to **you**,
005:006	or one of **you** cometh from the privy or ye have
005:007	And call in remembrance the favour of Allah unto **you**,
005:007	and His Covenant, which He ratified with **you**,
005:008	the hatred of others to **you** make **you** swerve to wrong
005:011	remembrance the favour of Allah unto **you** when certain
005:011	formed the design to stretch out their hands against **you**,
005:011	but (Allah) held back their hands from **you**:
005:012	Allah said: "I am with **you**: if ye (but) establish regular
005:012	but if any of **you**, after this, resisteth faith,
005:012	and admit **you** to Gardens with rivers flowing beneath;
005:012	verily I will wipe out from **you** your evils,
005:015	there hath come to **you** Our Messenger,
005:015	There hath come to **you** from Allah a (new) light
005:015	revealing to **you** much that ye used to hide in the Book,
005:018	Say: "Why then doth He punish **you** for your sins?
005:019	O People of the Book! now hath come unto **you**,
005:019	but now hath come unto **you** a bringer of glad tidings
005:019	making (things) clear unto **you**, Our Messenger,
005:020	made **you** kings, and gave **you** what He had not given to
005:020	when He produced prophets among **you**,
005:020	Call in remembrance the favour of Allah unto **you**,
005:021	the holy land which Allah hath assigned unto **you**,
005:048	but (His Plan is) to test **you** in what He hath given **you**:
005:048	it is He that will show **you** the truth of the matters
005:048	To each among **you** have We prescribed a Law and an
005:048	He would have made **you** a single People,
005:048	The goal of **you** all is to Allah;
005:051	And he amongst **you** that turns to them
005:053	That they were with **you**?"
005:054	if any from among **you** turn back from his Faith,
005:057	those who received the Scripture before **you**,
005:059	and (perhaps) that most of **you** are rebellious
005:060	Say: "Shall I point out to **you** something much worse
005:068	all the revelation that has come to **you** from your Lord."
005:076	no power either to harm or benefit **you**?
005:087	made lawful for **you**, but commit no excess:

YOU (continued)

005:088 the things which Allah hath provided for **you**,
005:089 Allah will not call **you** to account for what is void
005:089 but He will call **you** to account for your deliberate oaths:
005:089 Thus doth Allah make clear to **you** His Signs,
005:091 to excite enmity and hatred between **you**,
005:091 and hinder **you** from the remembrance of Allah,
005:094 make a trial of **you** in a little matter of game
005:095 As adjudged by two just men among **you**;
005:095 If any of **you** doth so intentionally,
005:096 Lawful to **you** is the pursuit of water-game and
005:101 they will be made plain to **you**: Allah will
005:101 may cause **you** trouble.
005:101 about things which, if made plain to **you**,
005:102 Some people before **you** did ask such questions,
005:105 The return of **you** all is to Allah:
005:105 no hurt can come to **you** from those who stray.
005:105 it is He that will inform **you** of all that ye do.
005:106 when death approaches any of **you**,
005:106 and the chance of death befalls **you** (thus).
005:115 but if any of **you** after that resisteth faith,
005:115 Allah said: "I will send it down unto **you**:
006:002 He it is Who created **you** from clay,
006:002 and then decreed a stated term (for **you**).
006:006 in strength such as We have not given to **you**-
006:012 He will gather **you** together for the Day of Judgment,
006:019 that I may warn **you** and all whom it reaches.
006:019 Say: "Allah is Witness between me and **you**:
006:038 but (forms part of) communities like **you**.
006:040 if there come upon **you** the Punishment of Allah,
006:046 other than Allah-could restore them to **you**?"
006:047 if the Punishment of Allah comes to **you**,
006:050 Say: "I tell **you** not that with me are the Treasures
006:050 Nor do I tell **you** I am an angel.
006:054 "Peace be on **you**: your Lord hath inscribed for
006:054 verily, if any of **you** did evil in ignorance,
006:058 the matter would be settled at once between **you** and me.
006:060 by day doth He raise **you** up again;
006:060 then will He show **you** the truth of all that ye did.
006:061 and He sets guardians over **you**.
006:061 At length, when death approaches one of **you**.
006:063 Say: "Who is it that delivereth **you** from the dark
006:064 Say: "It is Allah that delivereth **you** from these
006:065 send calamities on **you**, from above and below,
006:065 giving **you** a taste of mutual vengeance-
006:065 or to cover **you** with confusion in party strife,
006:081 without any warrant having been given to **you**?
006:090 Say: "No reward for this do I ask of **you**:
006:094 and alone as We created **you** for the first time:
006:094 and your (pet) fancies have left **you** in the lurch!"
006:094 Ye have left behind **you** all (the favours)
006:094 We see not with **you** your intercessors whom ye
006:094 so now all relations between **you** have been cut off,
006:094 all (the favours) which We bestowed on **you**:
006:097 It is He Who maketh the stars (as beacons) for **you**,
006:098 It is He Who hath produced **you** from a single soul:
006:104 "Now have come to **you**, from your Lord proofs
006:109 but what will make **you** (Muslims) realize
006:114 Who hath sent unto **you** the Book, explained
006:119 when He hath explained to **you** in detail
006:119 in detail what is forbidden to **you**-except
006:121 inspire their friends to contend with **you** if ye were
006:128 your dwelling-place you will dwell therein for ever,

YOU (continued)

006:130 setting forth unto **you** My Signs and warning **you**
006:130 there not unto **you** messengers from amongst **you**,
006:133 He raised **you** up from the posterity of other people.
006:133 if it were His Will, He could destroy **you**,
006:134 All that hath been promised unto **you** will come to pass:
006:142 for he is to **you** an avowed enemy.
006:142 eat what Allah hath provided for **you**,
006:144 Were ye present when Allah ordered **you** such a thing?
006:149 He could indeed have guided **you** all."
006:151 what Allah hath (really) prohibited **you** from":
006:151 We provide sustenance for **you** and for them;-
006:151 thus doth He command **you**, that ye may learn wisdom.
006:152 thus doth He command **you**, that ye may remember.
006:153 they will scatter **you** about from His (great) path:
006:153 thus doth He command **you**, that ye may be righteous.
006:157 Now then hath come unto **you** a Clear (Sign)
006:164 He will tell **you** the truth of things wherein ye disputed."
006:165 that He may try **you** in the gifts He hath given **you**:
006:165 It is He Who hath made **you** the inheritors of the earth:
006:165 He hath raised **you** in ranks, some above others:
007:003 (O men!) the revelation given unto **you** from your Lord,
007:010 It is He Who placed **you** with authority on earth,
007:010 and provided **you** therein with means for the fulfillment
007:011 It is We who created **you** and gave **you** shape;
007:018 Hell will I fill with **you** all.
007:019 approach not this tree, lest **you** become of the unjust."
007:020 "Your Lord only forbade **you** this tree,
007:022 and tell **you** that Satan was an avowed enemy unto **you**?"
007:022 "Did I not forbid **you** that tree, and tell
007:026 We Have bestowed raiment upon **you** to cover your shame,
007:026 as well as to be an adornment to **you**,
007:027 Let not Satan seduce **you**, in the same manner
007:027 for he and his tribe see **you** from a position
007:029 such as He created **you** in the beginning,
007:035 rehearsing My Signs unto **you**,-
007:035 come to **you** messengers from amongst **you**,
007:038 of the Peoples who passed away before **you**-men
007:043 "Behold! the Garden before **you**! Ye have
007:044 have **you** also found your Lord's promises true?"
007:046 "Peace be upon **you**": they have not entered it,
007:048 saying: "Of what profit to **you** were your hoards
007:049 the men whom **you** swore that Allah with His Mercy
007:049 Enter ye the Garden: no fear shall be on **you**,
007:059 I fear for **you** the Punishment of a dreadful Day!"
007:062 "I but I convey to **you**" the Message
007:062 Sincere is my advice to **you**,
007:063 through a man of your own people, to warn **you**,-
007:063 come to **you** a reminder from your Lord,
007:068 "I but convey to **you** the messages of my Lord:
007:068 I am to **you** a sincere and trustworthy adviser".
007:069 He made **you** inheritors after the people of Noah,
007:069 and gave **you** a stature tall among the nations.
007:069 There hath come to **you** a message from your Lord
007:069 through a man of your own people, to warn **you**?
007:071 Then wait: I am amongst **you**, also waiting."
007:071 have already come upon **you** from your Lord:
007:073 This she-camel of Allah is a Sign unto **you**:
007:073 Now hath come unto **you** a clear (Sign) from your Lord!
007:074 and gave **you** habitations in the land:
007:074 "And remember how He made **you** inheritors
007:079 I gave **you** good counsel, but ye love not good
007:079 convey to **you** the message for which I was sent by

YOU (continued)

007:080 no people in creation (ever) committed before **you**?
007:085 that will be best for **you**, if ye have Faith.
007:085 Now hath come unto **you** a clear (Sign) from your Lord!
007:086 remember how ye were little, and He gave **you** increase.
007:087 "And if there is a party among **you** who believes
007:093 I gave **you** good counsel, but how
007:093 convey to **you** the Messages for which I was
007:105 Now have I come unto **you** (people), from your
007:110 "His plan is to get **you** out of your land:
007:123 "Believe in him before I give **you** permission?
007:124 and I will crucify **you** all."
007:129 and make **you** inheritors in the earth;
007:140 it is He Who endowed **you** with gifts above the nations?"
007:140 He said: "Shall I seek for **you** a god other than Allah,
007:141 who afflicted **you** with the worst of punishment
007:141 And remember We rescued **you** from Pharaoh's people,
007:145 soon shall I show **you** the homes of the wicked,-
007:158 Say: "O men! I am sent unto **you** all, as the Messenger
007:160 We have provided for **you**": (but they rebelled);
007:161 We shall forgive **you** your faults;
007:171 "Hold firmly to what We have given **you**, and bring
007:172 "Am I not your Lord (who cherishes and sustains **you**)?"-
007:176 or if **you** leave him alone, he (still) lolls out his tongue,
007:176 if **you** attack him, he lolls out his tongue,
007:187 Only, all of a sudden, will it come to **you**."
007:189 It is He Who created **you** from a single person,
007:193 for **you** it is the same whether ye call them or ye keep
007:194 ye call besides Allah are servants like unto **you**:
007:197 are unable to help **you**, and indeed to help themselves."
008:007 Behold! Allah promised **you** one of the two parties,
008:009 And He answered **you**: "I will assist **you** with a thousand
008:011 to give **you** calm as from Himself,
008:011 from heaven, to clean **you** therewith,
008:011 Remember He covered **you** with drowsiness,
008:011 and He caused rain to descend on **you** from heaven,
008:011 to remove from **you** the stain of Satan,
008:012 "I am with **you**: give firmness to the Believers:
008:019 now hath the judgment come to **you**:
008:019 if ye desist (from wrong), it will be best for **you**:
008:019 Not the least good will your forces be to **you** even if
008:024 when He calleth **you** to that which will give **you** life;
008:025 not in particular (only) those of **you** who do wrong:
008:026 and gave **you** good things for sustenance:
008:026 and afraid that men might despoil and kidnap **you**;
008:026 but He provided a safe asylum for **you**,
008:026 strengthened **you** with His aid,
008:027 nor misappropriate knowingly things entrusted to **you**.
008:029 grant **you** a Criterion (to judge between right and wrong),
008:029 remove from **you** (all) evil deeds and forgive **you**:
008:043 but Allah saved (**you**): for He knoweth well the (secrets)
008:044 and He made **you** appear as contemptible in their eyes.
008:044 He showed them to **you** as few in your eyes,
008:048 "No one among men can overcome **you** this day,
008:048 and said: "Lo! I am clear of **you**; lo! I see what ye see not:
008:048 while I am near to **you**":
008:060 spend in the Cause of Allah, shall be repaid unto **you**,
008:065 there are twenty amongst **you**, patient and persevering,
008:066 if there are a hundred of **you**, patient and persevering,
008:066 for He knoweth that there is a weak spot in **you**:
008:068 would have reached **you** for the (ransom) that ye took.
008:070 He will give **you** something better than what has been
008:070 what has been taken from **you**, and He will forgive **you**:

YOU (continued)

008:075 and fight for the Faith in your company,-they are of **you**.
009:003 If, then, ye repent, it were best for **you**;
009:004 have not subsequently failed **you** in aught,
009:004 nor aided any one against **you**.
009:007 stand true to **you**, stand ye true to them:
009:008 seeing that if they get an advantage over **you**,
009:008 they respect not in **you** the ties either of kinship or
009:008 With (fair words from) their mouths they please **you**,
009:008 but their hearts are averse from **you**;
009:013 plotted to expel the Messenger, and attack **you** first?
009:014 and disgrace them, help **you** (to victory) over them,
009:016 Do **you** think that **you** would be left alone while
009:016 known those among **you** who strive with might and main,
009:023 if any of **you** do so, they do wrong.
009:024 in which ye delight-are dearer to **you** than Allah
009:025 but they availed **you** naught: the land.
009:025 behold! your great numbers elated **you**,
009:025 Assuredly Allah did help **you** in many battle-fields
009:025 all that is wide, did constrain **you**, and ye turned back
009:028 soon will Allah enrich **you**, if He wills, out of His bounty,
009:036 fight the Pagans all together as they fight **you** all together.
009:038 O ye who believe! what is the matter with **you**,
009:039 He will punish **you** with a grievous penalty,
009:041 That is best for **you**, if ye (but) knew.
009:042 we should certainly have come out with **you**,"
009:047 some among **you** who would have listened to them.
009:047 If they had come out with **you**, they would not have
009:047 to and fro in your midst and sowing sedition among **you**,
009:052 Say: "Can **you** expect for us (any fate) other than
009:052 So wait (expectant); we too will wait with **you**."
009:052 But we can expect for **you** either that Allah
009:053 not from **you** will it be accepted:
009:056 but they are not of **you**: yet they are afraid (of **you**).
009:056 They swear by Allah that they are indeed of **you**;
009:061 Say, "He listens to what is best for **you**;
009:061 and is a Mercy to those of **you** who believe."
009:062 To **you** they swear by Allah. In order to please **you**:
009:066 If We pardon some of **you**,
009:066 We will punish other amongst **you**,
009:069 they were mightier than **you** in power and more
009:069 As in the case of those before **you**:
009:069 and ye have of yours, as did those before **you**;
009:092 "I can find no mounts for **you**," they turned
009:094 "Present on excuses: we shall not believe **you**:
009:094 They will present their excuses to **you** when ye return
009:094 informed us of the true state of matters concerning **you**:
009:094 them will He show **you** the truth of all that ye did."
009:095 They will swear to **you** by Allah, when ye return
009:096 They will swear unto **you**, that ye may be pleased
009:098 and watch for disasters for **you**:
009:101 of the desert Arabs round about **you** are Hypocrites,
009:105 then will He show **you** the truth of all that ye did."
009:123 and let them find harshness in **you**:
009:123 Fight the Unbelievers who are near to **you**,
009:124 "Which of **you** has had his faith increased by it?"
009:127 (saying), "Doth anyone see **you**?" then they turn away:
009:128 should suffer, ardently anxious is he over **you**:
009:128 Now hath come unto **you** a Messenger
010:004 To Him will be your return-of all of **you**.
010:013 Generations before **you** We destroyed when they
010:014 Then We made **you** heirs in the land after them,
010:016 nor should He have made it known to **you**.

010:016 I should not have rehearsed it to **you**, nor should
010:016 I tarried amongst **you**: will ye not then understand?"
010:020 I too will wait with **you**."
010:022 He it is Who enableth **you** to traverse through
010:023 and We shall show **you** the truth of all that ye did.
010:029 "Enough is Allah for a witness between us and **you**:
010:031 Say: "Who is it that sustains **you** (in life)
010:035 What then is the matter with **you**? How judge ye?
010:038 and call (to your aid) anyone **you** can, besides
010:041 say: "My work to me, and yours to **you**!
010:050 His punishment should come to **you** by night or by day,-
010:057 there hath come to **you** an admonition from your Lord
010:059 what things Allah hath sent down to **you** for sustenance?
010:059 Say: "Hath Allah indeed permitted **you**, or do ye forge
010:067 and the Day to make things visible (to **you**).
010:067 He it is that hath made **you** the Night
010:071 so your plan be not to **you** dark and dubious.
010:071 that I should stay (with **you**) and remind
010:071 and remind (**you**) the Signs of Allah,-
010:072 no reward have I asked of **you**: my reward
010:077 about the Truth when it hath (actually) reached **you**?
010:078 But not we shall believe in **you**!"
010:102 for I too, will wait with **you**."
010:108 "O ye men! Now Truth hath reached **you** from your Lord!
010:108 and I am not (set) over **you** to arrange your affairs."
011:002 (Say:) "Verily I am (sent) unto **you** from Him
011:003 that He may grant **you** enjoyment, good (and
011:003 for **you** the Chastisement of a Great Day:
011:007 that He might try **you**, which of **you** is best in conduct.
011:025 "I have come to **you** as a clear warner.
011:026 Verily I do fear for **you** the punishment
011:027 apparently nor do we see in **you** (all) any
011:028 Shall we compel **you** to accept it when ye
011:029 I ask **you** for no wealth in return: my reward
011:031 "I tell **you** not that with me are the Treasures of Allah,
011:033 He said: "Truly, Allah will bring it on **you** if He wills-
011:034 "Of no profit will be my counsel to **you**,
011:034 much as I desire to give **you** (good) counsel,
011:034 if it be that Allah willeth to leave **you** astray:
011:038 can look down on **you** with ridicule likewise!
011:050 **You** are only forgers.
011:051 "O my people! I ask of **you** no reward
011:052 He will send **you** the skies pouring abundant rain,
011:055 all of **you**, and give me no respite.
011:057 conveyed the Message with which I was sent to **you**.
011:057 My Lord will make another People to succeed **you**,
011:057 and **you** will not harm Him in the least.
011:061 from the earth and settled **you** therein:
011:061 It is He Who hath produced **you** from the earth
011:064 or a swift Punishment will seize **you**!
011:064 This she-camel of Allah is a sign to **you**:
011:073 The grace of Allah and His blessings on **you**,
011:078 Is there not among **you** a single right-minded man?"'
011:078 they are purer for **you** (if ye marry)!
011:080 to suppress **you** or that I could betake myself to
011:081 and let not any of **you** look back:
011:084 I see **you** in prosperity, but I fear for **you** the
011:084 the Chastisement of a Day that will compass (**you**) all
011:086 'That which is left **you** by Allah is best for **you**,
011:086 But I am not set over **you** to keep watch!"
011:088 I wish not, in opposition to **you**,
011:088 to do that which I forbid **you** to do.

011:089 Let not my dissent (from **you**) cause **you** to sin,
011:089 nor the people of Lut far off from **you**!
011:092 Is then my family of more consideration with **you** than
011:093 for I too am watching with **you**!"
011:113 those who do wrong or the Fire will touch **you**;
011:116 If only there had been the generations before **you**,
012:009 (there will be time enough) for **you** to be righteous after
012:009 the favour of your father may be given to **you** alone:
012:018 minds have made up a tale (that may pass) with **you**,
012:028 "Behold! It is a snare of **you** women!
012:032 She said: "There before **you** is the man about whom ye
012:037 any food comes (in due course) to feed either of **you**
012:037 and meaning of this ere it befall **you**.
012:037 (I assure **you**) abandoned the ways of a people
012:037 I will surely reveal to **you** the truth and meaning
012:039 "O my two companions. Of the prison! (I ask **you**):
012:041 As to one of **you**, he will pour out the wine
012:045 said: "I will tell **you** the truth of its interpretation:
012:064 He said: "Shall I trust **you** with him with any result other
012:064 other than when I trusted **you** with his brother aforetime?
012:066 I send him with **you** until ye swear a solemn oath to me,
012:067 Not that I can profit **you** aught against Allah
012:080 your father did take an oath from **you** in Allah's name,
012:082 and (**you** will find) we are indeed telling the truth."
012:083 have yourselves contrived a story (good enough) for **you**.
012:092 "This day let no reproach be (cast) on **you**:
012:092 Allah will forgive **you**, and He is the Most Merciful
012:096 He said: "did I not say to **you**, 'I know from Allah that
012:098 "Soon will I ask my Lord for forgiveness for **you**:
012:100 and brought **you** (all here) out of the desert,
013:010 whether any of **you** conceal his speech or declare it openly;
013:012 It is He Who doth show **you** the lightning, by way
013:024 "Peace unto **you** for that ye persevered in patience!
013:043 "Enough for a witness between me and **you** is Allah,
014:006 "Call to mind the favour of Allah to **you** when He
014:006 when He delivered **you** from the people of Pharaoh:
014:006 they set **you** hard task and punishments,
014:007 I will add more (favours) unto **you**;
014:009 Has not the story reached **you**, (O people!),
014:009 of those who (went) before **you**?-
014:010 in order that He may forgive **you** your sins
014:010 It is He Who invites **you**, in order
014:010 your sins and give **you** respite for a term
014:011 It is not for us to bring **you** an authority
014:012 bear with patience all the hurt **you** may cause us.
014:013 "Be sure We shall drive **you** out of our land,
014:014 "And verily We shall cause **you** to abide in the
014:019 remove **you** and put (in your place) a new Creation?
014:021 "For us, we but followed **you**;
014:021 we should have given it to **you**:
014:022 I had no authority over **you** except to call **you**,
014:022 but I failed in my promise to **you**.
014:022 "It was Allah Who gave **you** a promise of Truth:
014:032 Who hath made to ships subject to **you**,
014:032 and with it bringeth out fruits wherewith to feed **you**;
014:032 and the rivers (also) hath He made subject to **you**.
014:033 And He hath made subject to **you** the sun
014:033 Night and the Day hath He (also) made subject **you**.
014:034 And He giveth **you** of all that ye ask for.
015:020 for **you** and for those for whose sustenance ye are not
015:022 therewith providing **you** with water (in abundance),
015:024 To Us are known those of **you** who hasten forward,

YOU (continued)

015:052 "We feel afraid of **you**!"
015:065 let no one amongst **you** look back, but pass on
016:005 And cattle He has created for **you** (men):
016:008 and donkeys, for **you** to ride and as an adornment;
016:009 He could have guided all of **you**.
016:011 With it He produces for **you** corn, olives, date-palm
016:012 He has made subject to **you** the Night and the Day;
016:015 mountains standing firm, lest it should shake with **you**;
016:032 saying (to them), "Peace be on **you**; enter ye
016:054 Yet, when He removes the distress from **you**,
016:054 behold! some of **you** turn to other gods
016:070 and of **you** there are some who are sent back
016:070 It is Allah who creates **you** and takes yours souls
016:071 sustenance more freely on some of **you** than on others;
016:072 and made for **you**, out of them, sons and daughters
016:072 And Allah has made for **you** mates of your own nature,
016:072 and provided for **you** sustenance of the best:
016:078 and He gave **you** hearing and sight and intelligence
016:078 It is He Who brought **you** forth from the wombs
016:080 made your habitations homes of rest and quiet for **you**;
016:080 and made for **you** out of the skins of animals,
016:080 and articles of convenience (to serve **you**) for a time.
016:081 Thus does He complete His favours on **you**,
016:081 He created, some things to give **you** shade;
016:081 He made **you** garments to protect **you** from heat,
016:081 and coats of mail to protect **you** from your (mutual)
016:090 He instructs **you**, that ye may receive admonition.
016:092 for Allah will test **you** by this;
016:092 will certainly make clear to **you** (the truth of) that
016:093 He could make **you** all one People:
016:094 and a mighty Wrath descend on **you**.
016:095 (a prize) far better for **you**, if ye only knew.
016:096 What is with **you** must vanish:
016:114 which Allah has provided for **you**, lawful and good;
016:115 He has only forbidden **you** dead meat, and blood,
016:126 to the wrong that has been done to **you**:
017:005 We sent against **you** Our servants given to terrible
017:006 Then did We grant **you** victory over them:
017:006 and made **you** the more numerous in man power.
017:006 We gave **you** increase in resources and sons,
017:008 that your Lord may (yet) show Mercy unto **you**;
017:031 shall provide, sustenance for them as well as for **you**.
017:040 then your Lord, (O Pagans!) preferred for **you** sons,
017:051 Say: "He Who created **you** first!"
017:052 "It will be on the Day when He will call **you**,
017:054 if He please, He granteth **you** mercy,
017:054 It is your Lord that knoweth **you** best:
017:056 to remove your troubles from **you** nor to change them."
017:063 verily Hell will be the recompense **you** (all)-
017:066 For He is unto **you** Most Merciful.
017:066 go smoothly for **you** through the sea, in order
017:067 leave **you** in the lurch!
017:067 But when He brings **you** back safe to land,
017:067 When distress seizes **you** at sea, those that
017:068 or that He will not send against **you** a violent
017:068 not cause **you** to be swallowed up beneath the
017:069 to drown **you** because of your ingratitude,
017:069 and send against **you** a heavy gale to drown
017:069 not send **you** back a second time to sea and send
017:085 a little that is communicated to **you**, (O men!)"
017:096 "Enough is Allah for a witness between me and **you**:
017:104 We gathered **you** together in a mingled crowd

YOU (continued)

018:016 His mercies on **you** and dispose of your affair
018:019 Now send ye then one of **you** with this money
018:019 the best food (to be had) and bring some to **you**,
018:019 and let him not inform anyone about **you**.
018:020 they would stone **you** or force **you** to return
018:020 "For if thy should come upon **you**, they would
018:034 "More wealth have I than **you**, and more honour
018:048 not fulfil the appointment made to **you** to meet (Us)!":
018:048 "Now have ye come to Us (bare) as We created **you** first:
018:049 Adn the Book (of Deeds) will be placed (before **you**);
018:050 And they are enemies to **you**!
018:063 none but Satan made me forget to tell (**you**) about it:
018:083 Say, "I will rehearse to **you** something of his story."
018:095 a strong barrier between **you** and them:
018:103 Say: "Shall we tell **you** of those who lose most
019:048 "And I will turn away from **you** (all) and from
019:071 Not one of **you** but will pass over it:
020:010 perhaps I can bring **you** some burning brand
020:040 and saith, 'Shall I show **you** one who will nurse
020:042 either of **you**, in keeping Me in remembrance.
020:043 "Go, both of **you**, to Pharaoh, for he
020:046 He said: "Fear not: for I am with **you**:
020:049 "Who then, O Moses, is the Lord of **you** two?"
020:053 "He Who has made for **you** the earth
020:053 has enabled **you** to go about therein by roads
020:055 and from it shall We bring **you** out once again.
020:055 and into it shall We return **you**,
020:055 From the (earth) did We create **you**,
020:061 Moses said to them: "Woe to **you**! Forge not
020:061 lest He destroy **you** (at once) utterly by
020:063 their object is to drive **you** out from your land
020:071 "Believe ye in Him before I give **you** permission?
020:071 and I will have **you** crucified on trunks of palm-trees
020:071 Who has taught **you** magic!
020:080 and We made a Covenant with **you** on the
020:080 and We sent down to **you** Manna and quails:
020:080 We delivered **you** from your enemy,
020:081 lest My Wrath should descend on **you**:
020:086 did not your Lord make a handsome promise to **you**?
020:086 that Wrath should descend from your Lord on **you**,
020:086 Did then the promise seem to **you** long (in coming)?
020:098 But the God of **you** all is Allah:
020:117 so let him not get **you** both out of the Garden,
020:123 there comes to **you** guidance from Me,
020:123 He said: "Get ye down, both of **you**,-all together,
021:010 a book which We give **you** eminence.
021:010 We have revealed for **you** (O men!) a book
021:013 the good things of this life which were given **you**,
021:018 Ah! woe be to **you** for the (false) things
021:035 and We test **you** by evil and by good
021:037 soon (enough) will I show **you** My Signs;
021:042 Say, "Who can keep **you** safe by night and by day
021:045 Say, "I do but warn **you** according to revelation":
021:055 or are **you** one of those who jest?"
021:055 They said, "Have **you** brought us the Truth,
021:066 be of any good to **you** nor do **you** harm?
021:067 "Fie upon **you**, and upon the things that ye
021:080 to guard **you** from each other's violence:
021:109 proclaimed the Message to **you** all alike and in truth;
021:111 "I know not but that it may be a trial for **you**,
021:111 a grant of (worldly) livelihood (to **you**) for a time.
022:005 in order that We may manifest (Our power) to **you**;

YOU (continued)

022:005 then (foster **you**) that ye may reach your age of full
022:005 then do We bring **you** out as babes,
022:005 (consider) that We created **you** out of dust,
022:005 and some of **you** are called to die, and some
022:030 except those mentioned to **you** (as exceptions):
022:030 Lawful to **you** (for food in pilgrimage) are cattle
022:036 in them is (much) good for **you**:
022:036 for **you** as among the Signs from Allah:
022:036 We made animals subject to **you**, that ye may be
022:037 He has thus made them subject to **you**, that ye
022:037 that ye may glorify Allah for His guidance to **you**:
022:042 If they disbelieve **you** so did the Peoples
022:049 Say: "O men! I am (sent) to **you** only to give a clear
022:065 made subject to **you** (men) all that is on the earth
022:066 will cause **you** to die, and will again give you life:
022:066 It is He Who gave **you** life,
022:069 "Allah will judge between **you** on the Day of Judgment
022:072 Say, "Shall I tell **you** of something (far) worse than
022:078 He has chosen **you**, and has imposed no difficulties
022:078 imposed no difficulties on **you** in religion;
022:078 It is He Who has named **you** Muslims, both before
022:078 that the Messenger may be a witness for **you**,
023:017 And We have made, above **you**, seven tracts;
023:019 With it We grow for **you** gardens of date-palms
023:021 We produce (milk) for **you** to drink; there are,
023:021 numerous (other) benefits for **you**;
023:024 his wish is to assert his superiority over **you**:
023:066 "My Signs used to be rehearsed to **you**,
023:078 It is He Who has created for **you** (the faculties
023:079 And He has multiplied **you** through the earth,
023:105 "Were not My Signs rehearsed to **you**,
023:110 made **you** forget My Message while ye were
023:115 "Did ye then think that We had created **you** in jest,
024:002 let not compassion move **you** in their case,
024:010 If it were not for Allah's grace and mercy on **you**,
024:011 on the contrary it is good for **you**:
024:011 think it not to be an evil to **you**;
024:014 Were it not for the grace and mercy of Allah on **you**,
024:014 seized **you** in that ye rushed glibly into this affair.
024:017 Allah doth admonish **you**, that ye may never repeat
024:018 And Allah makes the Signs plain to **you**:
024:020 were in not for the grace and mercy of Allah on **you**,
024:021 for the grace and mercy of Allah on **you**,
024:021 not one of **you** would ever have been pure:
024:022 Let not those among **you** who are endued with grace
024:022 do **you** not wish that Allah should forgive **you**?
024:027 that is best for **you**, in order that ye may heed
024:028 enter not until permission is given to **you**:
024:029 for living in, which serve some (other) use for **you**:
024:032 Marry those among **you** who are single,
024:033 out of the means which Allah has given to **you**.
024:034 We have already sent down to **you** verses making
024:034 people who passed away before **you**,
024:054 the duty placed on him and ye for that placed on **you**.
024:055 Allah has promised, to those among **you** who believe
024:058 and the (children) among **you** who have not come
024:058 it is not wrong for **you** or for them to move about
024:058 thus does Allah make clear the Signs to **you**:
024:059 But when the children among **you** come of age,
024:059 thus does Allah make clear His Signs to **you**:
024:061 there is no blame on **you**, whether ye eat in company
024:061 thus does Allah make clear the Signs to **you**:

YOU (continued)

024:063 yourselves like the summons of one **you** to another:
024:063 Allah doth know those of **you** who slip away under
025:019 And whoever among **you** does wrong, him shall
025:019 "Now have they proved **you** liars in what ye say:
025:020 We have made some of **you** as a trail for others:
025:022 "There is a barrier forbidden (to **you**) altogether!"
025:047 And He it is Who makes the Night as a Robe for **you**,
025:057 Say: "No reward do I ask of **you** for it but this:
025:077 not concern Himself with **you** but for your call on Him:
026:015 We are with **you**, and will listen (to your call).
026:015 "By no means! proceed then both of **you**, with Our Signs;
026:016 "So go forth, both of **you**, to Pharaoh,
026:021 "So I fled from **you** (all) when I feared **you**;
026:022 that **you** hast enslaved the Children of Israel!"
026:027 who has been sent to **you** is a veritable madman!"
026:030 "Even if I showed **you** something clear (and) convincing?"
026:035 "His plan is to get **you** out of your land
026:049 "Believe ye in Him before I give **you** permission?
026:049 Surely he is your leader, who has taught **you** sorcery!
026:049 and I will crucify **you** all"
026:072 He said: "Do they listen to **you** when ye call (on them),
026:073 "Or do **you** good or harm?"
026:076 "Ye and your fathers before **you**?-
026:093 "'Besides Allah? Can they help **you** or help themselves?'
026:098 "'When we held **you** as equals with the Lord of the Worlds;
026:107 "I am to **you** a trustworthy messenger.
026:109 "No reward do I ask of **you** for it: my reward
026:125 "I am to **you** a messenger worthy of all trust.
026:127 "No reward do I ask of **you** for it: my reward
026:130 "And when ye strike **you** strike like tyrants.
026:132 Him Who has bestowed on **you** freely all that ye know.
026:133 "Freely has He bestowed on **you** cattle and sons,-
026:135 "Truly I fear for **you** the Chastisement
026:142 said to them: "Will **you** not fear (Allah)?
026:143 I am to **you** a messenger worthy of all trust.
026:145 No reward do I ask of **you** for it: my reward
026:156 lest the Chastisement of a Great Day seize **you**."
026:162 "I am to **you** a messenger worthy of all trust.
026:164 "No reward do I ask of **you** for it: my reward
026:166 those whom Allah has created for **you** to be your mates?
026:178 "I am to **you** a messenger worthy of all trust.
026:180 "No reward do I ask of **you** for it: my reward
026:184 and (Who created) the generations before (**you**)."
026:184 "And fear Him Who created **you** and (Who created)
026:221 Shall I inform **you**, (O people!), on whom
027:007 soon will I bring **you** from there some information,
027:007 or I will bring **you** a burning brand (to light our fuel),
027:018 and his host crush **you** (under foot) without knowing it."
027:036 given me is better than that which He has given **you**!
027:038 which of **you** can bring me her throne before they
027:060 and who sends **you** down rain from the sky?
027:062 and makes **you** (mankind) inheritors of the earth?
027:063 Or, Who guides **you** through the depths of darkness
027:064 and who gives **you** sustenance from heaven and earth?
027:093 Who will soon show **you** His Signs, so that
028:012 and bring him up for **you** and take care of him."
028:012 "Shall I point out to **you** the people of the house
028:023 He said: "What is the matter with **you**?"
028:029 I hope to bring **you** from there some information,
028:035 ye triumph,- **you** two as well as those who follow **you**."
028:035 so they shall not be able to touch **you**:
028:035 and invest **you** both with authority,

YOU (continued)

028:038 I know for **you** but myself: therefore O Haman!
028:055 "To us our deeds, and to **you** yours; peace be to **you**:
028:063 we free ourselves (from them) to **you**.
028:071 is there other than Allah, who can give **you** light?
028:071 were to make the Night perpetual over **you** to the Day
028:072 who can give **you** a Night in which ye can rest?
028:072 the Day perpetual over **you** to the Day of Judgment,
028:073 has made for **you** Night and Day,-that ye
028:080 (true) knowledge said: "Alas for **you**! The reward
028:087 Let no one turn **you** away from Allah's revelations
029:008 and I will tell **you** (the truth) of all that ye did.
029:010 "We have (always) been with **you**!"
029:016 that will be best for **you**-if ye understand!
029:017 have no power to give **you** sustenance:
029:018 reject (the Message), so did generations before **you**:
029:025 And He said: "For **you**, ye have taken (for worship)
029:028 as no people in Creation (ever) committed before **you**.
029:038 clearly will appear to **you** from (the traces) of their
029:046 and in that which came down to **you**;
029:052 "'Enough is Allah for a Witness between me and **you**:
029:060 It is Allah Who feed (both) them and **you**:
030:020 that He created **you** from dust; and then,-behold,
030:021 that He created for **you** mates from among yourselves,
030:024 He shows **you** the lightning, by way both of fear
030:025 then when He calls **you**, by a single call,
030:028 He does propound to **you** a similitude from yourselves:
030:028 in the wealth We have bestowed on **you**?
030:039 That which **you** give in usury for increase
030:039 but that which **you** give for charity, seeking the
030:040 then He will cause **you** to die;
030:040 and again He will give **you** life.
030:040 It is Allah Who has created **you**: further,
030:042 and see what was the End of those before (**you**):
030:046 giving **you** a taste of His Mercy,
030:054 It is Allah Who created **you** in a state of (helpless)
030:054 then gave (**you**) strength after weakness,
030:054 give (**you**) weakness and a hoary head:
031:010 mountains standing firm, lest it should shake with **you**;
031:015 in the End the return of **you** all is to Me,
031:015 and I will tell **you** all that ye did."
031:020 made His bounties flow to **you** in exceeding measure,
031:031 that He may show **you** of His Signs?
031:033 let not the present life deceive **you**,
031:033 nor let the Chief Deceiver deceive **you** about Allah.
032:004 besides Him, to protect or intercede (for **you**):
032:009 And He gave **you** (the faculties of) hearing and sight
032:011 Say: "The Angel of Death, put in charge of **you**, will (duly)
032:014 and We too will forget **you**-taste ye the chastisement
033:004 But Allah tells (**you**) the Truth,
033:005 there is no blame on **you** if ye make a mistake therein:
033:009 when there came down on **you** hosts (to overwhelm **you**):
033:009 remember the Grace of Allah, (bestowed) on **you**,
033:010 above **you** and from below **you**, and behold,
033:010 Behold! they came on **you** from above **you**
033:016 Say: "Running away will not profit **you** if ye
033:017 to give **you** punishment or to give **you** Mercy?"
033:017 Say: "Who is it that can screen **you** from Allah
033:018 Verily Allah knows those among **you** who keep
033:019 Covetous over **you**. Then when fear comes,
033:019 they will smite **you** with sharp tongues,
033:020 and seeking news about **you** (from a safe distance);
033:027 And He made **you** heirs of their lands,

YOU (continued)

033:028 enjoyment and set **you** free in a handsome manner.
033:029 for the well-doers amongst **you** a great reward.
033:030 any of **you** were guilty of evident unseemly conduct,
033:031 But any of **you** that is devout in the service
033:033 Allah only wishes to remove all abomination from **you**,
033:033 and to make **you** pure and spotless.
033:034 And recite what is rehearsed to **you** in your homes,
033:043 He it is Who sends blessings on **you**,
033:043 that He may bring **you** out from the depths of darkness
033:053 Nor is it right for **you** that ye should annoy Allah's
033:053 the Prophet: he is shy to dismiss **you**, but Allah
033:053 until leave is given **you**,- for a meal, (and then)
033:053 but Allah is not shy (to tell **you**) the truth.
033:071 conduct whole and sound and forgive **you** your sins:
034:003 by my Lord, it will come upon **you**;
034:007 "Shall we point out to **you** a man that will tell **you**,
034:024 Say: "Who gives **you** sustenance, from the heavens
034:026 decide the matter between us (and **you**) in truth
034:030 Say: "The appointment to **you** is for a Day,
034:031 "Had it not been for **you**, we should certainly have
034:032 "Was it we who kept **you** back from Guidance
034:032 from Guidance after it reached **you**? Nay, rather,
034:037 that will bring **you** nearer to Us in degree:
034:040 "Was it **you** that these men used to worship?"
034:043 a man who wishes to hinder **you** from the (worship)
034:046 Say: "I do admonish **you** on one point: that ye
034:046 he is no less than a Warner to **you**, in face
034:047 Say: "Whatever reward do I ask of **you**: it is
035:003 O men! Remember the grace of Allah unto **you**!
035:003 to give **you** Sustenance from heaven or earth?
035:005 nor let the Chief Deceiver deceive **you** about Allah.
035:005 let not then this present life deceive **you**,
035:006 Verily Satan is an enemy to **you**: so treat him
035:011 then from a sperm-drop; then He made **you** in pairs.
035:011 And Allah did create **you** from dust;
035:014 And none, (O man!) can inform **you** like Him
035:016 He could blot **you** out and bring in a New Creation:
035:037 Did we not give **you** long enough life so that
035:037 And (moreover) the warner came to **you**.
035:039 He it is that has made **you** inheritors in the earth:
036:014 "Truly, we have been sent on a mission to **you**."
036:016 doth know that we have been sent on a mission to **you**:
036:018 punishment indeed will be inflicted on **you** by us."
036:018 "For us, we augur an evil omen from **you**: if ye desist not,
036:018 we will certainly stone **you**,
036:021 "Obey those who ask no reward of **you** (for themselves),
036:025 "'For me, I have faith in the Lord of **you** (all):
036:045 which is before **you** and that which will be after **you**,
036:047 ye of the (bounties) which Allah has provided **you**,"
036:060 for that he was to **you** an enemy avowed?-.
036:060 "Did I not enjoin on **you**, O ye children of Adam,
036:062 "But he did lead astray a great multitude of **you**.
036:080 "The same Who produces for **you** fire out of the green
037:025 "'What is the matter with **you** that ye help not each other?'"
037:030 "Nor had we any authority over **you**.
037:032 "We led **you** astray: for truly we were ourselves astray."
037:039 And **you** are requited naught save what ye did.
037:052 "Who used to say, Do **you** really believe?
037:091 "Will ye not eat (of the offerings before **you**)?
037:092 "What is the matter with **you** that ye speak not?"
037:096 "But Allah has created **you** and your handiwork!"
037:154 What is the matter with **you**? How judge ye?

YOU (continued)

038:006 For this is truly a thing designed (against **you**)!
038:053 Such is the Promise made to **you** for the Day of Account!
038:054 Truly such will be Our Bounty (to **you**);
038:059 Here is a troop rushing headlong with **you**!
038:060 "Nay, ye (too) No welcome for **you**! It is ye who have
038:086 Say: "No reward do I ask of **you** for this (Qur'an),
039:006 He creates **you**, in the wombs of your mothers,
039:006 and He sent down for **you** eight head of cattle in pairs:
039:006 He created **you** (all) from a single person:
039:007 when He will tell **you** the truth of all that ye did
039:007 He is pleased with **you**.
039:007 If ye reject (Allah), truly Allah hath no need of **you**;
039:054 before the Chastisement comes on **you**:
039:055 the Best that which was revealed to **you** from your Lord,
039:055 before the Chastisement comes on **you**-of a sudden,
039:071 and warning **you** of the Meeting of this Day
039:071 from among yourselves, rehearsing to **you** the Signs
039:071 "Did not messengers come to **you** from among
039:073 "Peace be upon **you**! Well have ye done!
040:010 to Allah to **you** than (is) your aversion to yourselves,
040:013 He it is Who showeth **you** His Signs, and sendeth
040:013 and sendeth down sustenance for **you** from the sky:
040:028 the (calamity) of which he warns **you**:
040:028 when he has indeed come to **you** with Clear (Signs)
040:028 then will fall on **you** something of the (calamity)
040:029 "I but point out to **you** that which I see (myself);
040:029 nor do I guide **you** but to the Path of Right!"
040:030 I do fear for **you** something like the Day (of disaster)
040:032 "And, O my People! I fear for **you** a Day when there
040:034 "And to **you** there came Joseph in times gone by,
040:038 I will lead **you** to the Path of Right.
040:041 for me to call **you** to Salvation while ye call
040:042 and I call **you** to the Exalted in Power,
040:044 "Soon will ye remember what I say to **you** (now).
040:047 "We but followed **you**: can ye then take (on yourselves)
040:050 not come to **you** your messengers with Clear Signs?"
040:061 and the Day, as to give **you** light.
040:061 Is Allah Who has made the Night for **you**,
040:064 and has provided for **you** Sustenance, of things
040:064 It is Allah Who has made for **you** the earth
040:064 and has given **you** shape-and made your shapes beautiful,-
040:067 then lets **you** (grow and) reach your age of full strength;
040:067 It is He Who has created **you** from dust, then from
040:067 and lets **you** reach a Term appointed;
040:067 then lets **you** become old,
040:067 though of **you** there are some who die before;-
040:067 then does He get **you** out (into the light) as a child:
040:079 It is Allah Who made cattle for **you**, that ye
040:080 there are (other) advantages in them for **you** (besides);
040:081 And He shows **you** (always) His Signs;
041:006 Say thou: "I am but a man like **you**:
041:013 "I have warned **you** of a thunderbolt like the
041:014 so we disbelieve in the Message **you** were sent with.
041:021 He created **you** for the first time,
041:022 And your skins should bear against **you**!
041:023 concerning your Lord, hath brought **you** to destruction,
041:031 therein shall ye have all that **you** shall desire;
042:011 by this means does He multiply **you**:
042:011 He had made for **you** pairs from among yourselves,
042:013 for **you** as that which He enjoined on Noah-
042:015 There is no contention between us and **you**.
042:015 Our deeds, and for **you** for your deeds.

YOU (continued)

042:015 and I am commanded to judge justly between **you**.
042:023 Say: "No reward do I ask of **you** for this except
042:030 Whatever misfortune happens to **you**, is because
042:047 nor will there be for **you** any room for denial
042:047 That Day there will be for **you** no place of refuge
043:005 We then turn away the Reminder from **you** altogether,
043:010 (Yea, the same that) has made for **you** the earth
043:010 and has made for **you** roads (and channels)
043:012 and has made for **you** ships and cattle
043:016 and granted to **you** sons for choice?
043:024 Even if I brought **you** better guidance than that which
043:039 it will avail **you** nothing, that day,
043:060 We could make angels amongst **you**,
043:062 for he is to **you** an enemy avowed.
043:062 Let not the Satan hinder **you**:
043:063 he said: "Now have I come to **you** with Wisdom,
043:063 clear to **you** some of the (points) on which ye dispute:
043:068 No fear shall be on **you** today, nor shall ye grieve,-
043:078 but most of **you** have a hatred for Truth.
043:078 Verily We have brought the truth to **you**:
044:008 the Lord and Cherisher to **you** and your earliest ancestors.
044:016 The day We shall seize **you** with a mighty onslaught:
044:018 I am to **you** a messenger worthy of all trust;
044:019 for I come to **you** with authority manifest.
045:012 It is Allah Who has subjected the sea to **you**,
045:013 And He has subjected to **you**, as from Him,
045:026 Say: "It is Allah Who gives **you** life,
045:026 then gives **you** death;
045:026 then He will gather **you** together for the Day
045:029 "This Our Record speaks about **you** with truth:
045:031 "Were not Our Signs rehearsed to **you**?
045:034 We will forget **you** as ye forgot the meeting
045:035 and the life of the world deceived **you**."
046:008 Enough is He for a witness between me and **you**!
046:009 nor do I know what will be done with me or with **you**.
046:017 But (there is one) who says to his parents, "Fie on **you**!
046:021 truly I fear for **you** the Chastisement
046:023 I proclaim to **you** the mission on which I have
046:026 power which We have not given to **you** (ye Quraish)!
046:027 We destroyed aforetime towns round about **you**;
046:031 and deliver **you** from a Chastisement Grievous.
046:031 He will forgive **you** your faults.
046:031 hearken to the one who invites (**you**) to Allah,
047:004 (He lets **you** fight) in order to test **you**, some with others.
047:007 He will help **you**, and plant your feet firmly.
047:022 Then, is it to be expected of **you**, if ye put in
047:026 "We will obey **you** in part of (this) matter";
047:031 And We shall try **you** until We test those among
047:031 among **you** who strive their utmost and persevere
047:035 for Allah is with **you**, and will never put **you** in loss
047:036 and will not ask **you** (to give up) your possession.
047:036 He will grant **you** your recompense,
047:037 If He were to ask **you** for all of them,
047:037 and press **you**, ye would covetously withhold,
047:038 but among **you** are some that are niggardly.
048:011 His Will is to give **you** some loss or to give **you** some
048:015 to acquire booty (in war): "Permit us to follow **you**."
048:016 He will punish **you** with a grievous Chastisement."
048:016 Allah will grant **you** a goodly reward,
048:020 and that He may guide **you** to a Straight Path;
048:020 and He has given **you** these beforehand;
048:020 Allah has promised **you** many gains that ye shall acquire,

YOU (continued)

048:020 and He has restrained the hands of men from **you**;
048:022 If the Unbelievers should fight **you**, they would
048:024 after that He gave **you** the victory over them.
048:024 their hands from **you** and your hand from them
048:025 a guilt would have accrued to **you** without (your)
048:025 (Allah would have allowed **you** to force your way,
048:025 and hindered **you** from the Sacred Mosque and the
049:006 If a sinner comes to **you** with any news, ascertain the
049:007 but Allah has endeared the Faith to **you**,
049:007 And know that among **you** is Allah's Messenger:
049:007 and He has made hateful to **you** unbelief, wrongdoing,
049:011 Let not some men among **you** laugh at others:
049:012 Would any of **you** like to eat the flesh of his dead
049:013 of Allah is (he who is) the most righteous of **you**.
049:013 Verily the most honoured of **you** in the sight
049:013 and made **you** into nations and tribes, that ye
049:013 O mankind! We created **you** from a single (pair) of a
049:017 a favour upon **you** that He has guided **you** to the Faith,
050:024 "Throw, both of **you**, into Hell every contumacious
050:028 I had already in advance sent **you** Warning.
050:032 "This is what was promised for **you**,-for every
051:051 I am from Him a Warner to **you**, clear and open!
052:016 the same is it to **you** whether ye bear it with patience,
052:031 I too will wait along with **you**!"
053:021 What! for **you** the male sex, and for Him, the female?
053:032 He knows **you** well when He brings **you** out of the earth,
054:051 have We destroyed gangs like unto **you**:
055:035 On **you** will be sent (O ye evil ones twain)!
056:057 It is We Who have created **you**:
056:061 creating **you** (again) in (Forms) that ye know not.
056:086 if **you** are exempt from (future) account,-
057:004 And He is with **you** wheresoever ye may be.
057:007 out of the (substance) whereof He has made **you** heirs.
057:007 For, those of **you** who believe and spend (in charity)
057:008 How is it with **you** that **you** not believe in Allah?-
057:008 And the Messenger invites **you** to believe in your Lord
057:009 that He may lead **you** from the depths of Darkness
057:009 And verily, Allah is to **you** Most Kind and Merciful.
057:010 How is it with **you** that **you** spend not in the cause
057:010 Not equal among **you** are those who spent (freely)
057:012 (Their greeting will be): "Good News for **you** this Day!
057:014 (Those without) will call out, "Were we not with **you**?"
057:014 and (your false) desires deceived **you**;
057:014 And the Deceiver deceived **you** in respect of Allah.
057:015 that is the proper place to claim **you**: and an evil refuge
057:015 "This Day shall no ransom be accepted of **you**,
057:017 Already have We shown the Signs plainly to **you**,
057:023 not exult over favours bestowed upon **you**.
057:023 that ye may not despair over matters that pass **you** by,
057:028 and He will bestow on **you** a double portion
057:028 He will provide for **you** a light by which ye shall walk
057:028 and He will forgive **you** (your past):
058:001 Allah (always) hears the arguments between both of **you**:
058:002 If any men among **you** divorce their wives by Zihar
058:011 those of **you** who believe and who have been granted
058:011 (ample) room will Allah provide for **you**.
058:012 That will be best for **you**, and most conducive to purity
058:013 If, then, ye do not so, and Allah forgives **you**,
058:014 They are neither of **you** nor of them, and they
058:018 then will they swear to Him as they swear to **you**:
059:007 So take what the Messenger gives **you**,
059:007 and refrain from what He prohibits **you**.

YOU (continued)

059:007 (merely) make a circuit between the wealthy among **you**.
059:011 "If ye are expelled, we too will go out with **you**,
059:011 and if ye are attacked (in fight) we will help **you**."
059:014 They will not fight **you** (even) together, except in
060:001 And any of **you** that does this has strayed from the
060:001 though they have rejected the truth that has come to **you**,
060:002 their hands and their tongues against **you** for evil;
060:002 they overcome **you** they would behave to **you** as enemies,
060:003 Of no profit to **you** will be your relatives
060:003 He will judge between **you**: for Allah sees well all that
060:004 "We are clear of **you** and of whatever ye worship
060:004 we have rejected **you**, and there us and **you**, enmity and
060:004 There is for **you** an excellent example (to follow)
060:006 indeed in them an excellent example for **you** to follow,
060:007 Establish friendship between **you** and those whom
060:008 Allah forbids **you** not, with regard to those who
060:008 to those who fight **you** not for (your) Faith
060:008 (your) Faith nor drive **you** out of your homes,
060:009 and drive **you** out of your homes,
060:009 and support (others) in driving **you** out,
060:009 to those who fight **you** for (your) Faith,
060:009 Allah only forbids **you**, with regard to those who
060:010 He judges (with justice) between **you**.
060:010 And there will be no blame on **you** if ye marry
060:010 (on the dowers of women who came over to **you**).
060:010 when there come to **you** believing women refugees,
060:011 And if any of your wives deserts **you** to the Unbelievers,
061:005 ye know that I am the messenger Allah (sent) to **you**?"
061:006 I am the messenger of Allah (sent) to **you**,
061:010 that will save **you** from a grievous Chastisement?-
061:010 O ye who believe! shall I lead **you** to a bargain
061:011 that will be best for **you**, if ye but knew!
061:012 and admit **you** to Gardens beneath which rivers flow,
061:012 He will forgive **you** your sins,
062:008 "The Death form which ye flee will truly overtake **you**:
062:008 and He will tell **you** the things that ye did!"
062:009 that is best for **you** if ye but knew!
063:009 your children divert **you** from the remembrance of Allah.
063:010 out to the substance We have bestowed on **you**,
063:010 Death should come to any of **you** and he should say,
064:002 and of **you** are some that are Unbelievers,
064:002 It is He Who has created **you**;
064:003 and has given **you** shape, and made your shapes beautiful:
064:005 Has not the story reached **you**, of those who rejected
064:009 that will be a day of mutual loss and gain (among **you**).
064:009 The Day that He assembles **you** (all) for a Day
064:017 and He will grant **you** Forgiveness:
065:002 for witness two persons from among **you**, endued with
065:005 the Command of Allah, which He has sent down to **you**:
065:010 For Allah hath indeed sent down to **you** a Message,-
065:011 A Messenger, who rehearses to **you** the Signs
066:002 Allah has already ordained for **you**, the expiation
066:005 It may be, if he divorced **you** (all), that Allah
066:005 in exchange Consorts better than **you**,-who submit
066:008 that your Lord will remove from **you** your evil deeds,
066:008 and admit **you** to Gardens beneath which Rivers flow,-
067:002 that He may try which of **you** is best in deed:
067:008 its Keepers will ask, "Did no Warner come to **you**?"
067:015 He Who has made the earth manageable for **you**,
067:016 He Who is in heaven will not cause **you** to be swallowed
067:017 He Who is in Heaven will not send against **you** a violent
067:020 Nay, who is there that can help **you**,

YOU (continued)

067:021 Or who is there that can provide **you** with Sustenance
067:023 and made for **you** the faculties of hearing
067:023 Say: "It is He Who has created **you**,
067:024 Say: "It is He Who has multiplied **you** through the earth,
067:030 who then can supply **you** with clear-flowing water?"
068:006 Which of **you** is afflicted with madness.
068:024 person break in upon **you** into the (garden) this day."
068:028 "Did I not say to **you**, 'Why not glorify (Allah)?'"
068:036 What is the matter with **you**? How judge ye?
069:011 carried **you** (mankind), in the floating (Ark),
069:012 That We might make it a Reminder unto **you**,
069:024 because of the good that ye sent before **you**,
069:047 Nor could any of **you** withhold him (from Our wrath).
069:049 know that there are amongst **you** those that reject (it).
071:002 He said: "O my People! I am to **you** a Warner,
071:004 and give **you** respite for a stated Term:
071:004 "So He may forgive **you** your sins and give
071:011 "He will send rain to **you** in abundance;
071:012 and bestow on **you** Rivers (of flowing water).
071:012 "Give **you** increase in wealth and sons;
071:012 and bestow on **you** Gardens and bestow
071:013 "What is the matter with **you**, the ye are not
071:014 that it is He that has created **you** in diverse stages?
071:017 "And Allah has produced **you** from the earth,
071:018 "And in the End He will return **you** into the (earth),
071:018 and raise **you** forth (again at the Resurrection)?
071:019 "And Allah has made the earth for **you** as a carpet
072:021 Say: "It is not in my power to cause **you** harm,
072:021 or to bring **you** to right conduct."
073:015 to be a witness concerning **you**,
073:015 We have sent to **you**, (O men!) a Messenger,
073:020 knoweth that there may be (some) among **you** in ill-health;
073:020 of the Qur'an as much as may be easy for **you**.
073:020 of the Qur'an as much as may be easy (for **you**);
073:020 So He hath turned to **you** (in mercy):
074:037 To any of **you** that chooses to press forward,
074:042 "What led **you** into Hell-Fire?"
076:009 (Saying), "We feed **you** for the sake of Allah alone:
076:009 no reward do we desire from **you**, nor thanks.
076:022 "Verily this is a Reward for **you**, and your
077:020 Have We not created **you** from a fluid
077:027 and provided for **you** water sweet (and wholesome)?
077:038 We shall Gather **you** together and those before (**you**)!
078:008 And (have We not) created **you** in pairs,
078:012 And (have We not) built over **you** the seven firmaments,
078:030 for no increase shall We grant **you**, except in
078:040 Verily, We have warned **you** of a Chastisement near,-
079:033 A provision for **you** and your cattle.
080:032 A provision for **you** and your cattle.
081:028 (With profit) to whoever among **you** wills to
082:010 (are appointed angels) to protect **you**,-
082:010 But verily over **you** (are appointed angels)
092:014 Therefore do I warn **you** of a Fire blazing fiercely;
095:007 can after this make **you** deny the Last Judgment?
102:001 diverts **you** (from the more serious things),
109:006 To **you** be your Way, and to me mine.

YOUNG

002:068 should be neither too old nor too **young**,
006:143 or (the **young**) which the wombs of the two females
006:144 or (the **young**) which the wombs of the two females
012:019 Good news! Here is a (fine) **young** man!
012:036 Now with him there came into the prison two **young** men.

YOUNG (continued)

015:067 came in (mad) joy (at news of the **young** men).
018:074 when they met a **young** man, he slew him
041:047 (within her womb) nor bring forth (**young**),
081:004 When the she-camels, ten months with **young**,

YOUR

002:021 O ye people! worship **your** Guardian-Lord,
002:022 who has made the earth **your** couch,
002:022 and the heaven **your** canopy;
002:022 and brought forth therewith fruits for **your** sustenance;
002:023 and call **your** witnesses or helpers
002:036 and **your** means of livelihood for a time."
002:036 On earth will be **your** dwelling place
002:040 and fulfil **your** Covenant with Me and I shall
002:043 and bow down **your** heads with those who bow down
002:049 therein was a tremendous trial from **your** Lord.
002:049 slaughtered **your** sons and let **your** women-folk live;
002:050 drowned Pharaoh's people within **your** very sight.
002:054 so turn (in repentance) to **your** Maker,
002:054 that will be better for you in the sight of **your** Maker.
002:054 wronged yourselves by **your** worship of the calf:
002:056 Then We raised you up after **your** death;
002:058 forgive you **your** faults and increase (the portion of)
002:063 And remember We took **your** Covenant
002:074 Thenceforth were **your** hearts hardened:
002:076 engage you in argument about it before **your** Lord?"
002:083 treat with kindness **your** parents and kindred,
002:084 And remember We took **your** Covenant (to this effect):
002:084 nor turn out **your** own people from **your** homes:
002:093 And remember We took **your** Covenant and raised
002:093 behests of **your** Faith if you have any faith!"
002:105 That any good should come down to you from **your** Lord.
002:108 Would ye question **your** Messenger as Moses was
002:110 whatever good ye send forth for **your** souls before you,
002:111 Say: "Produce **your** proof if ye are truthful."
002:139 seeing that He is our Lord and **your** Lord;
002:143 and never would Allah make **your** faith of no effect.
002:144 wherever ye are, turn **your** faces in that direction.
002:150 And wheresoever ye are, turn **your** face thither:
002:151 We have sent among you a Messenger of **your** own,
002:155 lives and the fruits (of **your** toil),
002:163 And **your** God is One God:
002:177 to spend of **your** substance,
002:177 for **your** kin, for orphans,
002:177 ye turn **your** faces toward East or West;
002:178 This is a concession and a Mercy from **your** Lord.
002:187 then complete **your** fast till the night appears;
002:187 but do not associate with **your** wives while
002:187 is the approach to **your** wives.
002:187 They are **your** garments and ye are their garments.
002:188 And do not eat up **your** property among yourselves
002:189 ye enter **your** houses from the back:
002:195 not **your** own hands contribute to (**your**) destruction;
002:195 And spend or **your** substance in the cause of Allah,
002:196 and do not shave **your** heads until the offering reaches
002:198 the bounty of **your** Lord (during pilgrimage).
002:200 So when ye have accomplished **your** rites,
002:200 as ye used to celebrate the praises of **your** fathers,
002:217 fighting you until they turn you back from **your** faith
002:219 say: "What is beyond **your** needs."
002:220 they are **your** brethren;
002:221 Nor marry (**your** girls) to unbelievers
002:223 **Your** wives are as a tilth unto you

YOUR (continued)

002:223	so approach **your** tilth when or how ye will;
002:223	But do some good act for **your** souls beforehand;
002:224	an excuse in **your** oaths against doing good,
002:225	to account for thoughtlessness in **your** oaths,
002:225	but for the intention in **your** hearts;
002:229	to take back any of **your** gifts from (**your** wives),
002:231	the Book and Wisdom, for **your** instruction.
002:233	for **your** offspring there is no blame on you,
002:235	betrothal or hold it in **your** hearts.
002:235	Allah knoweth what is in **your** hearts,
002:235	Allah knows that ye cherish them in **your** hearts:
002:238	Guard strictly **your** (habit of) prayers.
002:245	and to Him shall be **your** return.
002:248	of security from **your** Lord,
002:264	Cancel not **your** charity by reminders of **your** generosity
002:271	it will remove from you some of **your** (stains of) evil.
002:272	Whatever of good ye give benefits **your** own souls,
002:278	remains of **your** demand for usury,
002:279	ye shall have **your** capital sums:
002:282	And get two witnesses, out or **your** own men.
002:282	to writing (**your** contract) for a future period,
002:284	Whether ye show what is in **your** minds or conceal it,
003:029	Say: "Whether ye hide what is in **your** hearts or reveal it,
003:031	Allah will love you and forgive you **your** sins:
003:049	and what ye store in **your** houses.
003:049	I have come to you, with a Sign from **your** Lord,
003:050	I have come to you with a Sign from **your** Lord.
003:051	"It is Allah who is my Lord and **your** Lord;
003:061	our sons and **your** sons, our women and **your** women,
003:073	"And believe no one unless he follows **your** religion."
003:073	should engage you in argument before **your** Lord?
003:080	after ye have bowed **your** will (to Allah in Islam)?
003:103	He joined **your** hearts in love,
003:118	into **your** intimacy those outside **your** ranks:
003:119	Say: "Perish in **your** rage; Allah knoweth
003:122	Remember two of **your** parties meditated cowardice;
003:123	then fear Allah; thus may ye show **your** gratitude.
003:125	**your** Lord would help you with five thousand angels
003:126	and an assurance to **your** hearts:
003:133	for forgiveness from **your** Lord and for a Garden
003:140	from **your** ranks Martyr-witnesses (to Truth).
003:143	with **your** own eyes (and flinch!).
003:144	will ye then turn back on **your** heels?
003:149	they will drive you back on **your** heels,
003:149	and ye will turn back (from Faith) to **your** own loss.
003:150	Nay, Allah is **your** Protector, and He
003:152	His permission were about to annihilate **your** enemy,
003:152	from **your** foes in order to test you.
003:153	and the Messenger in **your** rear was calling you back.
003:154	for Allah knoweth well the secrets of **your** hearts.
003:154	and purge what is in **your** hearts.
003:154	test what is in **your** breasts and purge
003:154	Say: "Even if you had remained in **your** homes,
003:165	smote (**your** enemies) with one twice as great,
003:167	or (at least) drive (the foe from **your** city)."
003:168	Say: "Avert death from **your** own selves,
003:182	which **your** hands sent on before ye:
003:185	shall you be paid **your** full recompense.
003:186	and tested in **your** possessions and in yourselves;
004:001	through Whom ye demand **your** mutual (rights),
004:001	O mankind! fear **your** Guardian Lord, Who created
004:002	their substance (by mixing it up) with **your** own.

YOUR (continued)

004:002	nor substitute (**your**) worthless things for (their)
004:003	marry women of **your** choice, two, or three, or four;
004:003	or that which **your** right hands possess.
004:005	give not **your** property which Allah has assigned
004:011	directs you as regards **your** children's (inheritance):
004:011	or **your** children are nearest to you in benefit.
004:011	Ye know not whether **your** parents or
004:012	In what **your** wives leave, **your** share is a half,
004:015	If any of **your** women are guilty of lewdness,
004:022	and marry not women whom **your** fathers married,
004:023	foster-sisters; **your** wives, mothers;
004:023	**your** step-daughters under **your** guardianship,
004:023	**your** son proceeding from **your** loins;
004:023	**your** mother, daughters, sisters, father's sisters,
004:024	ye seek (them in marriage) with gifts from **your** property,
004:024	except those whom **your** right hands possess:
004:025	from among those whom **your** right hand possess:
004:025	and Allah hath full knowledge about **your** faith.
004:028	Allah doth wish to lighten **your** (burdens):
004:029	Eat not up **your** property among yourselves in vanities:
004:031	We shall remit **your** evil deeds, and admit
004:033	To those also, to whom **your** right hand was pledged,
004:036	the Companion by **your** side, the way-farer (ye meet),
004:036	and what **your** right hands possess:
004:043	and rub therewith **your** faces and hands.
004:043	until after washing **your** whole body if ye are ill,
004:045	But Allah hath full knowledge of **your** enemies:
004:058	to render **your** trusts to those to whom they are due;
004:071	O ye who believe! take **your** precautions.
004:101	if ye shorten **your** prayers, for fear
004:102	negligent of **your** arms and **your** baggage,
004:102	put away **your** arms because of the inconvenience
004:103	standing, sitting down, or lying down on **your** sides;
004:123	Not **your** desires, nor those of the People of the Book
004:129	between wives even if it is **your** ardent desire:
004:135	even as against yourselves, or **your** parents, or **your** kin,
004:135	Follow not the lusts (of **your** hearts),
004:147	What can Allah gain by **your** punishment.
004:171	commit no excesses in **your** religion:
004:174	hath come to you a convincing proof from **your** Lord
005:002	transgression (and hostility on **your** part).
005:003	those who reject Faith given up all hope of **your** religion:
005:003	This day have I perfected **your** religion for you,
005:003	and have chosen for you Islam as **your** religion.
005:005	the People of the Book, revealed before **your** time,
005:006	wash **your** faces, and **your** hands (and arms) to the
005:006	and (wash) **your** feet to the ankles.
005:006	bathe **your** whole body.
005:006	rub **your** heads (with water);
005:006	and rub therewith **your** faces and hands.
005:007	for Allah knoweth well the secrets of **your** hearts.
005:012	verily I will wipe out from you **your** evils,
005:018	Say: "Why then doth He punish you for **your** sins?
005:021	for then will ye be overthrown, to **your** own ruin."
005:023	But on Allah put **your** trust if ye have faith."
005:034	for those who repent before they fall into **your** power:
005:035	O ye who believe! do **your** duty to Allah,
005:051	and the Christians for **your** friends and protectors:
005:055	**Your** (real) friends are (no less than) Allah,
005:057	those who take **your** religion for a mockery
005:058	When ye proclaim **your** call to prayer, they take
005:068	all the revelation that has come to you from **your** Lord."

YOUR (continued)

005:072 of Israel! Worship Allah, my Lord and **your** Lord."
005:077 exceed not in **your** religion the bounds
005:089 to account for what is void in **your** oaths,
005:089 to account for **your** deliberate oaths:
005:089 But keep to **your** oaths.
005:089 on a scale of the average for the food of **your** families;
005:089 If that is beyond **your** means, fast for three days.
005:094 well within reach of **your** hands and **your** lances,
005:105 O ye who believe! guard **your** own souls:
005:106 of **your** own (brotherhood) or others from outside
005:109 ye received (from men to **your** teaching)?"
005:117 to wit, 'Worship Allah, my Lord and **your** Lord':
006:003 the (recompense) which ye earn (by **your** deeds).
006:019 (**your** blasphemy of) joining others with Him."
006:041 (the distress) which occasioned **your** call upon Him,
006:046 and sealed up **your** hearts,
006:046 took away **your** hearing and **your** sight,
006:054 **your** Lord hath inscribed for Himself (the rule of)
006:056 Say: "I will not follow **your** vain desires:
006:060 It is He Who doth take **your** souls by night,
006:060 in the end unto Him will be **your** return,
006:066 the responsibility for arranging **your** affairs;
006:078 from **your** (guilt) of giving partners to Allah.
006:091 which ye knew not-neither ye nor **your** fathers."
006:093 This day shall ye receive **your** reward,-
006:093 (saying), "Yield up **your** souls.
006:094 whom ye thought to be partners in **your** affairs:
006:094 We see not with you **your** intercessors whom ye
006:094 and **your** (pet) fancies have left you in the lurch!"
006:099 feast **your** eyes with the fruit and the ripeness therefo.
006:102 That is Allah, **your** Lord! There is no
006:104 I am not (here) to watch over **your** doings."
006:104 from **your** Lord proofs (to open **your** eyes):
006:128 He will say: "The Fire be **your** dwelling-place:
006:133 and in **your** place appoint whom He will
006:133 whom He will as **your** successors,
006:147 say: "**Your** Lord is full of Mercy All-embracing;
006:150 Say: "Bring forward **your** witnesses to prove
006:151 kill not **your** children on a plea of want;-
006:151 be good to **your** parents;
006:157 then hath come to you a Clear (Sign) from **your** Lord,-
006:164 **Your** return in the end is toward Allah:
007:003 the revelation given unto you from **your** Lord,
007:010 you therein with means for the fulfillment of **your** life:
007:020 he said: "**Your** Lord only forbade you this tree,
007:024 On earth will be **your** dwelling-place and
007:024 and **your** means of livelihood,-for a time."
007:026 bestowed raiment upon you to cover **your** shame,
007:027 he got **your** parents out of the Garden,
007:029 making **your** devotion sincere such as He created
007:029 and that ye set **your** whole selves (to Him)
007:031 wear **your** beautiful apparel at every time and place
007:043 for **your** deeds (of righteousness)."
007:044 have you also found **your** Lord's promises true?"
007:048 were **your** hoards and **your** arrogant ways?
007:050 that Allah doth provide for **your** sustenance."
007:054 **Your** Guardian Lord is Allah, Who created
007:055 Call on **your** Lord with humility and in private:
007:056 but call, on Him with fear and longing (in **your** hearts):
007:063 through a man of **your** own people, to warn you,
007:063 come to you a reminder from **your** Lord,
007:069 through a man of **your** own people, to warn you?

YOUR (continued)

007:069 there hath come to you a message from **your** Lord
007:071 have already come upon you from **your** Lord:
007:071 names which ye have devised- ye and **your** fathers,-
007:073 Now hath come unto you a clear (Sign) from **your** Lord!
007:081 "For ye practice **your** lusts on men in preference
007:082 they said, "Drive them out of **your** city: these are
007:085 Now hath come unto you a clear (Sign) from **your** Lord!
007:089 if we returned to **your** religion after Allah hath
007:105 from **your** Lord with a clear (Sign):
007:110 "His plan is to get you out of **your** land:
007:124 "Be sure I will cut off **your** hands and
007:124 and **your** feet on opposite sides,
007:129 He said: "It may be that **your** Lord will destroy
007:129 will destroy **your** enemy and make you inheritors
007:141 in that was a momentous trial from **your** Lord.
007:141 of punishment who slew **your** male children and
007:141 and saved alive **your** females:
007:150 make haste to bring on the judgment of **your** Lord?"
007:161 We shall forgive you **your** faults;
007:164 "To discharge our duty to **your** Lord and perchance
007:172 "Am I not **your** Lord (who cherishes and sustains you)?"
007:194 and let them listen to **your** prayer,
007:195 Say: "Call **your** `god-partners', scheme (**your** worst)
007:203 This is (nothing but) lights from **your** Lord,
007:204 listen to it with attention, and hold **your** peace:
008:009 Remember ye implored the assistance of **your** Lord.
008:010 and an assurance to **your** heart: (in any case)
008:011 and to plant **your** feet firmly therewith.
008:011 the stain of Satan, to strengthen **your** hearts,
008:015 never turn **your** backs to them.
008:019 good will **your** forces be to you even if they
008:024 give **your** response to Allah and His Messenger,
008:028 and that it is Allah with whom lies **your** highest reward.
008:028 and **your** progeny are but a trial:
008:028 And know ye that **your** possessions and
008:040 be sure that Allah is **your** Protector-
008:043 and ye would surely have disputed in (**your**) decision:
008:044 He showed them to you as few in **your** eyes,
008:046 lest ye lose heart and **your** power depart;
008:051 "because of (the deeds) which **your** (own) hands sent
008:060 Against them make ready **your** strength to the
008:060 to the utmost of **your** power,
008:060 the enemies, of Allah and **your** enemies, and others
008:066 For the present, Allah hath lightened **your** (burden),
008:070 "If Allah findeth any good in **your** hearts, He will
008:070 say to those who are captives in **your** hands:
008:072 it is **your** duty to help them, except against
008:072 but if they seek **your** aid in religion,
008:075 and fight for the Faith in **your** company,-they are of you.
009:002 that ye cannot frustrate Allah (by **your** falsehood),
009:004 So fulfil **your** engagements with them to the
009:011 they are **your** brethren in Faith:
009:012 their oaths after their covenant, and attack **your** Faith,-
009:014 and Allah will punish them by **your** hands, and disgrace
009:023 Take not for protectors **your** fathers
009:023 and **your** brothers if they love infidelity above Faith:
009:024 Say: If it be that **your** fathers, **your** sons,
009:024 **your** brothers, **your** mates, or **your** kindred:
009:025 behold! **your** great numbers elated you,
009:039 and put others in **your** place;
009:041 and struggle, with **your** goods and **your** person,
009:047 added to **your** (strength) but only (made for) disorder,

YOUR (continued)

009:047	hurrying to and fro in **your** midst and
009:094	it is **your** action that Allah and His Messenger
009:105	soon will Allah observe **your** work,
010:003	Verily **your** Lord is Allah, Who created
010:003	This is Allah **your** Lord; Him therefore serve ye:
010:004	To Him will be **your** return-of all of you
010:023	O mankind! your insolence is against **your** own souls,
010:023	in the end, to Us is **your** return,
010:028	"To **your** place! ye and those ye joined as 'partners'."
010:029	knew nothing of **your** worship of us!"
010:032	Such is Allah, **your** true Lord: apart from
010:034	Say: "Of **your** `partners,' can any originate
010:035	Say: "Of **your** 'partners' is there any that
010:038	and call (to **your** aid) anyone you can,
010:057	there hath come to you an admonition from **your** Lord
010:057	and a healing for the (diseases) in **your** hearts,-
010:071	"O my People, if it be hard on **your** (mind) that I
010:071	about **your** plan and among **your** Partners,
010:071	Then pass **your** sentence on me,
010:071	in Him put **your** trust if ye submit (**your** will to His)."
010:087	"Provide dwellings for **your** People in Egypt,
010:087	make **your** dwellings into places of worship,
010:089	Allah said: "Accepted is **your** prayer (O Moses and Aaron)!
010:104	Who will take **your** souls (at death):
010:108	Now Truth hath reached you from **your** Lord!
010:108	and I am not (set) over you to arrange **your** affairs."
011:003	'Seek ye the forgiveness of **your** Lord,
011:004	"To Allah is **your** return, and He
011:013	and call (to **your** aid) whomsoever ye can,
011:014	"If then they (**your** false gods) answer not **your** (call),
011:028	but that the Mercy hath been obscured from **your** sight?
011:031	**of those your** eyes do despise that Allah will not
011:034	He is **your** Lord! and to Him will ye return!
011:040	of each kind two, male and female and **your** family-
011:052	Ask forgiveness of **your** Lord,
011:052	and add strength to **your** strength:
011:055	So scheme (**your** worst) against me, all of you,
011:056	my Lord and **your** Lord!
011:065	"Enjoy yourselves in **your** homes for three days:
011:065	(then will be **your** ruin): (behold) there a promise not
011:088	I only desire (**your**) betterment to the best or my power;
011:090	"But ask forgiveness of you Lord, and turn
011:092	For ye cast Him away behind **your** backs (with contempt).
011:111	to all will **your** Lord pay back (in full the recompense)
012:009	that so the favour of **your** father may be given to you
012:018	He said: "Nay, but **your** minds have made up
012:028	a snare of you women! Truly, mighty is **your** snare!
012:040	names which ye have named, ye and **your** fathers,-
012:047	shall ye diligently sow as is **your** wont:
012:051	"What was **your** affair when ye did seek to seduce
012:080	ye did fail in **your** duty with Joseph?
012:080	"Know ye not that **your** father did take an oath from you
012:081	"Turn ye back to **your** father, and say,
012:093	Then come Ye (here) to me together with all **your** family."
013:002	may believe with certainty in the meeting with **your** Lord.
014:006	a tremendous trial from **your** Lord."
014:006	slaughtered **your** sons, and let **your** women-folk
014:007	And remember! **your** Lord caused to be declared
014:010	in order that He may forgive you **your** sins
014:019	can remove you and put (in **your** place) a new Creation?
014:022	I cannot listen to **your** cries, nor can
014:022	I reject **your** former act in associating Me with Allah:

YOUR (continued)

014:022	but reproach **your** own souls.
014:030	Say: "Enjoy (**your** brief power)! But verily
014:045	and We put forth (many) Parables in **your** behoof!"
015:032	(Allah) said: "O Iblis! what is **your** reason for not being
015:054	Of what, then, is **your** good news?"
016:002	so do **your** duty unto Me."
016:007	And they carry **your** heavy loads to lands that ye
016:007	for **your** Lord is indeed Most Kind, Most Merciful.
016:010	the vegetation on which ye feed **your** cattle.
016:022	**Your** God is One God: as to those
016:024	"What is it that **your** Lord has revealed?"
016:030	"What is it that **your** Lord has revealed?" they say
016:055	Then enjoy (**your** brief day); but soon
016:055	but soon will ye know (**your** folly)!
016:056	certainly be called to account for **your** false inventions.
016:066	We produce, for **your** drink, milk,
016:070	It is Allah Who creates you and takes **your** souls at death;
016:072	And Allah has made for you mates of **your** own nature,
016:078	from the wombs of **your** mothers when ye
016:080	when ye travel and when ye stop (in **your** travels);
016:080	It is Allah who made **your** habitations homes of
016:081	to protect you from **your** (mutual) violence.
016:081	of the hills He made some for **your** shelter;
016:091	indeed ye have made Allah **your** surety;
016:091	and break not **your** oaths after ye have confirmed them;
016:092	Using **your** oaths to deceive one another,
016:093	but ye shall certainly be to account for all **your** actions.
016:094	And take not **your** oaths, to practice
016:116	for any false thing that **your** tongues may put forth,
016:126	let **your** punishment be proportionate to the
017:002	"'Take not other than Me as Disposer of (**your**) affairs."
017:005	they entered very inmost parts of **your** homes;
017:007	and to enter **your** Temple as they had entered it before,
017:007	(We permitted **your** enemies) to disfigure **your** faces,
017:008	but if ye revert (to **your** sins),
017:008	It may be that **your** Lord may (yet) show Mercy
017:012	Bounty from **your** Lord and that ye may know
017:025	**Your** Lord knoweth best what is in **your** hearts:
017:026	but squander not (**your** wealth) in the manner
017:031	Kill not **your** children for fear of want:
017:040	Has then **your** Lord, (O Pagans!) preferred for
017:051	"Or any created matter which, in **your** minds,
017:054	It is **your** Lord that knoweth you best:
017:055	And it is **your** Lord that knoweth best all beings
017:056	the power to remove **your** troubles from you
017:066	**Your** Lord is He that maketh the Ship go smoothly
017:069	to drown you because of **your** ingratitude,
017:084	but **your** Lord knows best who it is that is best guided
018:016	and dispose of **your** affair towards comfort and ease."
018:016	**your** Lord will shower His mercies on you
018:019	**your** hunger therewith) and let him behave with
018:029	Say, "The Truth is from **your** Lord"
018:058	But **your** Lord is Most Forgiving, Full of Mercy.
018:068	about things which are beyond **your** knowledge?"
018:096	"Blow (with **your** bellows)" then, when he
018:110	that **your** God is one God:
019:036	Verily Allah is my Lord and **your** Lord:
020:054	Eat (for yourselves) and pasture **your** cattle:
020:059	Moses said: "**Your** tryst is the Day of the Festival,
020:063	object is to drive you out from **your** land with their magic,
020:063	and to do away with **your** most cherished way.
020:064	"Therefore concert **your** plan, and then

YOUR (continued)

020:071	Be sure I will cut off **your** hands and feet
020:071	Surely this must be **your** leader.
020:080	We delivered you from **your** enemy,
020:081	We have provided for **your** sustenance, but commit
020:086	that Wrath should descend from **your** Lord on you,
020:086	and so ye broke **your** promise to me?"
020:086	He said: "O my people! did not **your** Lord make a
020:088	"This is **your** god, and the god of Moses,
020:090	for verily **your** Lord is (Allah) Most Gracious:
021:003	Will ye go to witchcraft with **your** eyes open?"
021:013	and to **your** homes, in order that ye may be called
021:024	"Bring **your** convincing proof:
021:036	"The one who talks of **your** gods?"
021:054	in manifest error-ye and **your** fathers."
021:056	He said, "Nay, **your** Lord is the Lord of the
021:057	after ye go away and turn **your** backs"...
021:057	I will certainly plan against **your** idols-
021:068	"Burn him and protect **your** gods, if ye do
021:080	the making of coats of mail for **your** benefit,
021:092	is a single Ummah and I am **your** Lord and Cherisher:
021:103	"This is **your** Day,-(the Day) that ye were promised."
021:108	by inspiration is that **your** God is one God:
021:110	in speech and what ye hide (in **your** hearts).
022:001	O mankind! Fear **your** Lord! For the convulsion
022:005	that ye may reach **your** age of full strength;
022:034	But **your** God is One God:
022:034	submit then **your** wills to Him (in Islam):
022:037	it is **your** piety that reaches Him:
022:047	of thy Lord is like a thousand years of **your** reckoning.
022:077	and adore **your** Lord; and do good;
022:078	it is the religion of **your** father Abraham.
022:078	He is **your** Protector-the best to protect
023:052	is a single Ummah and I am **your** Lord and Cherisher:
023:066	but ye used to turn back on **your** heels-
024:015	and said out of **your** mouths things of which ye
024:015	Behold, ye received it on **your** tongues,
024:027	enter not houses other than **your** own, until ye
024:029	It is no fault on **your** part to enter houses
024:032	and the virtuous ones among **your** slaves,
024:033	And if any of **your** slaves ask for a deed in writing
024:033	But force not **your** maids to prostitution
024:058	the while ye doff **your** clothes for the noonday heat;
024:058	permission (before they come to **your** presence),
024:058	these are **your** three times of undress:
024:058	Let those whom **your** right hands possess,
024:061	houses of which the keys are in **your** possession,
024:061	or **your** mother's brothers, or **your** mother's sisters,
024:061	that ye should eat in **your** own houses,
024:061	or **your** brothers, or **your** sisters,
024:061	or **your** father's brothers, or **your** fathers's sisters,
024:061	or those of **your** fathers, or **your** mothers,
025:019	so ye cannot avert (**your** penalty) nor (get) help."
025:077	not concern Himself with you but for **your** call on Him:
026:015	We are with you, and will listen (to **your** call).
026:026	of **your** fathers from the beginning!"
026:026	(Moses) said: "**Your** Lord and the Lord of
026:027	(Pharaoh) said: "Truly **your** messenger who has
026:035	is to get you out of **your** land by his sorcery;
026:049	Surely he is **your** leader, who has taught you sorcery!
026:049	Be sure I will cut off **your** hands and **your** feet on
026:076	"Ye and **your** fathers before you?-
026:166	has created for you to be **your** mates?

YOUR (continued)

026:168	He said: "I do detest **your** doings."
027:018	"O ye ants, get into **your** habitations,
027:032	no affair have I decided except in **your** presence."
027:036	Nay it is ye who rejoice in **your** gift!
027:047	He said: "**Your** ill omen is with Allah;
027:055	ye really approach men in **your** lusts rather than women?
027:056	"Drive out the followers of Lut from **your** city:
027:060	it is not in **your** power to cause the growth of the trees
027:064	Say, "Bring forth **your** argument, if ye
027:072	ye wish to hasten on may be (close) in **your** pursuit!
027:090	that which ye have earned by **your** deeds?"
028:064	"Call upon **your** `partners' (for help)": l
028:075	and We shall say: "Produce **your** Proof":
029:012	and we will bear (the consequences) of **your** faults."
029:017	to Him will be **your** return.
029:025	and **your** abode will be the Fire,
029:029	And practise wickedness (even) in **your** councils?"
029:046	Our God and **your** God is one;
029:055	"Taste ye (the fruits) of **your** deeds!"
030:021	and mercy between **your** (hearts):
030:022	and the variations in **your** languages and **your** colours:
030:028	partners among those whom **your** right hands possess,
030:034	but soon will ye know (**your** folly).
030:034	Then enjoy (**your** brief day); but soon
030:040	further, He has provided for **your** sustenance;
030:040	Are there any of **your** (false) "Partners" who can do
031:020	that Allah has subjected to **your** (use) all things
031:028	And **your** creation or **your** resurrection is in no wise
031:033	O mankind! do **your** duty to **your** Lord and fear
032:005	a thousand years of **your** reckoning.
032:011	will (duly) take **your** souls:
032:011	then shall ye be brought back to **your** Lord."
032:014	the chastisement of Eternity for **your** (evil) deeds!"
033:004	nor has He made **your** adopted sons **your** sons.
033:004	Such is (only) **your** (manner of) speech by **your** mouths.
033:004	He made **your** wives whom ye divorce by
033:004	ye divorce by Zihar **your** mothers:
033:005	(what counts is) the intention **your** hearts:
033:005	(then they are) **your** Brothers in faith, or **your** friends.
033:006	do ye what is just to **your** closest friends:
033:020	and if they were in **your** midst, they would fight
033:028	I will provide for **your** enjoyment and set you free
033:033	And stay quietly in **your** houses,
033:034	what is rehearsed to you in **your** homes,
033:040	Muhammad is not the father of any of **your** men,
033:051	and Allah knows (all) that is in **your** hearts:
033:053	and when ye have taken **your** meal, disperse,
033:053	that makes for greater purity for **your** hearts and for theirs.
033:070	and make **your** utterance straight forward:
033:071	and sound and forgive you **your** sins: he that
033:071	That He may make **your** conduct whole and sound
034:015	"Eat of the Sustenance (provided) by **your** Lord,
034:023	'What is it that **your** Lord commanded?'
034:037	It is not **your** wealth nor **your** sons, that will
034:043	from the (worship) which **your** fathers practiced."
034:046	**your** Companion is not possessed:
035:013	Such is Allah **your** Lord: to Him belongs all Dominion.
035:014	if they were to listen, they cannot answer **your** (prayer).
035:014	the Day of Judgment they will reject **your** "Partnership."
035:014	they will not listen to **your** call,
035:037	So taste ye (the fruit of **your** deeds):
036:019	They said: "**Your** evil omens are with yourselves:

YOUR (continued)

036:054	but be repaid the meeds of **your** past Deeds.
036:080	when behold! ye kindle therewith (**your** own fires)!
037:004	Verily, verily, **your** God is One!-
037:018	be humiliated (on account of **your** evil)."
037:087	"Then what is **your** idea about the Lord of the worlds?"
037:096	"But Allah has created you and **your** handiwork!"
037:126	"Allah, **your** Lord and Cherisher and the
037:126	and the Lord and Cherisher of **your** fathers of old?"
037:157	Then bring ye **your** Book (of authority)
038:006	"Walk ye away, and remain constant to **your** gods!
039:006	then how are ye turned away (from **your** true Lord)?
039:006	He creates you, in the wombs of **your** mothers,
039:006	Such is Allah, **your** Lord and Cherisher:
039:007	In the End, to **your** Lord is **your** return,
039:010	Fear **your** Lord: good is (the reward) for those
039:031	on the Day of Judgment, in the presence of **your** Lord.
039:054	"Turn ye to **your** Lord (in repentance) and submit
039:055	the Best that which was revealed to you from **your** Lord,
039:071	rehearsing to you the Signs of **your** Lord, and warning
040:010	to you than (is) **your** aversion to yourselves,
040:026	What I fear is lest he should change **your** religion,
040:027	my Lord and **your** Lord (for protection)
040:028	indeed come to you with Clear (Signs) from **your** Lord?
040:033	A day when ye shall turn **your** backs and flee:
040:049	"Pray to **your** Lord to lighten us the Chastisement
040:050	not come to you **your** messengers with Clear Signs?"
040:060	And **your** Lord says: "Call on Me; I will
040:060	I will answer **your** (Prayer):
040:062	Such is Allah, **your** Lord, the Creator
040:064	such is Allah **your** Lord.
040:064	and made **your** shapes beautiful,-
040:067	then lets you (grow and) reach **your** age of full strength;
040:080	to any need (there may be) in **your** hearts;
041:006	that **your** God is One God:
041:022	and **your** skins should bear witness against you!
041:022	seek to hide yourselves, lest **your** hearing, **your** sight,
041:023	yours which ye did entertain concerning **your** Lord,
041:031	"We are **your** protectors in this life and in
042:015	Allah is Our Lord and **your** Lord!
042:015	Our deeds, and for you for **your** deeds.
042:030	is because of the things **your** hands have wrought,
042:047	Respond ye to **your** Lord, before there come a Day
042:047	will there be for you any room for denial (of **your** sins)!
043:013	ye may remember the (kind) favour of **your** Lord,
043:024	than that which ye found **your** fathers following?"
043:064	"For Allah, He is my Lord and **your** Lord:
043:070	ye and **your** wives, in (beauty and) rejoicing.
043:072	ye are made heirs for **your** (good) deeds (in life).
044:008	the Lord and Cherisher to you and **your** earliest ancestors.
044:015	(but) truly ye will revert (to **your** ways).
044:020	my Lord and **your** Lord, against **your** injuring me.
045:015	be brought back to **your** Lord.
045:034	And **your** abode is the Fire,
046:020	and ye took **your** pleasure out of them:
046:020	"Ye squandered **your** good things in the life
046:031	He will forgive you **your** faults,
047:007	He will help you, and plant **your** feet firmly.
047:019	and how ye dwell in **your** homes.
047:022	and break **your** ties of kith and kin?
047:031	and We shall try **your** reported (mettle).
047:033	and make not vain **your** deeds!
047:035	and will never put you in loss for **your** (good) deeds.

YOUR (continued)

047:036	He will grant you **your** recompense, and will
047:036	and will not ask you (to give up) **your** possession.
047:037	and He would bring out all **your** ill-feeling.
047:038	to spend (of **your** substance) in the Way of Allah:
047:038	he will substitute in **your** stead another people;
048:011	(to intervene) on **your** behalf with Allah,
048:012	this seemed pleasing in **your** hearts, and ye conceived,
048:021	other gains (there are), which are not within **your** power,
048:024	their hands from you and **your** hand from them
048:025	would have accrued to you without (**your**) knowledge,
048:025	(Allah would have allowed you to force **your** way,
048:025	but He held back **your** hands) that He may admit to His
049:002	lest **your** deeds become vain and ye perceive not.
049:002	Raise not **your** voices above the voice of the Prophet,
049:007	and has made it beautiful in **your** hearts,
049:007	to follow **your** (wishes), ye would certainly suffer:
049:010	reconciliation between **your** two (contending) brothers;
049:014	He will not belittle aught of **your** deeds:
049:014	for not yet has Faith entered **your** hearts.
049:016	Say: "What Will ye tell Allah about **your** Religion?"
049:017	Say, "Count not **your** Islam as a favour upon me:
051:014	"Taste ye **your** trial! this is what ye used to ask to be
051:021	As also in **your** own selves: will ye not then see?
051:022	And in heaven is **your** Sustenance,
051:031	O ye Messengers, is **your** errand (now)?"
051:043	"Enjoy (**your** brief day) for a little while!"
052:016	ye but receive the recompense of **your** (own) deeds."
052:019	with profit and health, because of **your** (good) deeds."
053:002	**Your** Companion is neither astray nor being misled,
053:023	but names which ye have devised,-ye and **your** fathers,-
053:032	and when ye are hidden in **your** mother's wombs.
053:061	Wasting **your** time in vanities?
054:043	Are **your** Unbelievers, (O Quraish),
055:013	Then which of the favours of **your** Lord will ye deny?
055:016	Then which of the favours of **your** Lord will ye deny?
055:018	Then which of the favours of **your** Lord will ye deny?
055:021	Then which of the favours of **your** Lord will ye deny?
055:023	Then which of the favours of **your** Lord will ye deny?
055:025	Then which of the favours of **your** Lord will ye deny?
055:028	Then which of the favours of **your** Lord will ye deny?
055:030	Then which of the favours of **your** Lord will ye deny?
055:031	Soon shall We settle **your** affairs, O both
055:032	Then which of the favours of **your** Lord will ye deny?
055:034	Then which of the favours of **your** Lord will ye deny?
055:036	Then which of the favours of **your** Lord will ye deny?
055:038	Then which of the favours of **your** Lord will ye deny?
055:040	Then which of the favours of **your** Lord will ye deny?
055:042	Then which of the favours of **your** Lord will ye deny?
055:045	Then which of the favours of **your** Lord will ye deny?
055:047	Then which of the favours of **your** Lord will ye deny?-
055:049	Then which of the favours of **your** Lord will ye deny?-
055:051	Then which of the favours of **your** Lord will ye deny?-
055:053	Then which of the favours of **your** Lord will ye deny?
055:055	Then which of the favours of **your** Lord will ye deny?
055:057	Then which of the favours of **your** Lord will ye deny?
055:059	Then which of the favours of **your** Lord will ye deny?
055:061	Then which of the favours of **your** Lord will ye deny?
055:063	Then which of the favours of **your** Lord will ye deny?
055:065	Then which of the favours of **your** Lord will ye deny?
055:067	Then which of the favours of **your** Lord will ye deny?
055:069	Then which of the favours of **your** Lord will ye deny?
055:071	Then which of the favours of **your** Lord will ye deny?

YOUR (continued)

055:073	Then which of the favours of **your** Lord will ye deny?
055:075	Then which of the favours of **your** Lord will ye deny?
055:077	Then which of the favours of **your** Lord will ye deny?
056:053	"Then will ye fill **your** insides therewith,
056:060	We have decreed Death to be **your** common lot,
056:061	From changing **your** Forms and creating you
056:082	And have ye made it **your** livelihood that ye
056:087	if ye are true (in **your** claim of Independence)?
057:008	believe in **your** Lord and has indeed taken **your** Convenant,
057:013	Let us borrow (a light) from **your** Light!"
057:013	"Turn ye back to **your** rear!
057:014	and (**your** false) desires deceived you;
057:015	who rejected Allah. **Your** abode is the Fire:
057:021	forgiveness from **your** Lord, and a Garden (of Bliss),
057:022	or in **your** souls but is recorded in a Book before
057:028	A Light by which ye shall walk (straight in **your** path),
057:028	and He will forgive you (**your** past):
058:004	show **your** faith in Allah and His Messenger.
058:012	something in charity before **your** private consultation.
058:013	spending sums in charity before **your** private consultation
059:011	and we will never hearken to any one in **your** affair;
060:001	(Simply) because ye believe in Allah **your** Lord!
060:001	offering them (**your**) love,
060:001	the Messenger and yourselves (from **your** homes),
060:003	of no profit to you will be your relatives **your** relatives
060:003	and **your** children on the Day of Judgment:
060:008	nor drive you out of **your** homes,
060:008	with regard to those who fight you not for (**your**) Faith
060:009	with regard to those who fight you for (**your**) Faith,
060:009	and drive you out of **your** homes, and support
060:011	And if any of **your** wives deserts you to the Unbelievers,
060:011	and ye have **your** turn (by the coming over of a woman
061:011	ye strive (**your** utmost) in the Cause of Allah,
061:011	Cause of Allah, with **your** wealth and **your** persons:
061:012	He will forgive you **your** sins, and admit
062:006	then express **your** desire for Death,
063:005	the Messenger of Allah will pray for **your** forgiveness,"
063:009	O ye who believe! let not **your** riches or **your** children
064:003	and made **your** shapes beautiful:
064:014	among **your** wives and **your** children are (some
064:015	**Your** riches and **your** children may be but a trial:
064:016	and spend in charity for the benefit of **your** own souls:
064:017	He will double it to **your** (credit),
065:001	and fear Allah **your** Lord:
065:004	Such of **your** women as have passed the age of monthly
065:006	then spend (**your** substance) on them until they
065:006	and if they suckle **your** (offspring), give them
065:006	in the same style as ye live, according to **your** means:
066:002	the expiration of **your** oaths (in some cases):
066:002	and Allah is **your** Protector, and He is Full of Knowledge
066:004	repentance to Allah, **your** hearts are indeed so inclined;
066:006	Save yourselves and **your** families from a Fire
066:008	that **your** Lord will remove from you **your** evil deeds,
067:013	And whether ye hide **your** word or make it
067:030	Say: "See ye?-if **your** stream be some morning lost
068:022	"Go ye to **your** tilth (betimes) in the morning,
071:004	"So He may forgive you **your** sins and give you
071:010	"Saying, `Ask forgiveness from **your** Lord, for He
071:023	'Abandon not **your** gods: abandon neither Wadd nor
076:022	and **your** Endeavour is accepted and recognized."
077:043	"Eat ye and drink ye to **your** heart's content:
078:009	And made **your** sleep for rest,

YOUR (continued)

078:030	"So taste ye (the fruits of **your** deeds);
079:024	Saying, "I am **your** Lord, Most High."
079:033	A provision for you and **your** cattle.
080:032	A provision for you and **your** cattle.
081:022	And (O people!) **your** Companion is not one possessed;
082:011	Kind and honorable, writing down (**your** deeds):
109:006	To you be **your** Way, and to me mine.

YOURS

002:139	for our doings and ye for **yours**;
005:005	is lawful unto you and **yours** is lawful unto them.
005:023	when once ye are in, victory will be **yours**; but
006:130	and warning you of the meeting of this Day of **yours**?"
008:007	you one of the two parties, that it should be **yours**:
008:007	ye wished that the one unarmed should be **yours**,
009:069	their enjoyment of their portion: and ye have of **yours**,
010:041	say: "My work to me, and **yours** to you!
018:019	one of you with this money of **yours** to the town:
021:092	Verily, this Ummah of **yours** is a single Ummah,
023:052	And verily this Ummah of **yours** is a single
024:061	or in the house of a sincere friend of **yours**:
028:055	"To us our deeds, and to you **yours**;
032:014	for ye forgot the Meeting of this day of **yours**,
034:033	"Nay! it was a plot (of **yours**) by day and by night:
034:047	"Whatever reward do I ask of you: it is **yours**:
035:040	'Partners' of **yours** whom ye call upon besides Allah?
039:071	and warning you of the Meeting of this Day of **yours**?"
040:029	"O my people! **yours** is the dominion this day:
041:023	"But this thought of **yours** which ye did entertain
045:034	forget you as ye forgot the meeting of this Day of **yours**!
060:001	not My enemies and **yours** as friends (or protectors),
069:018	not an act of **yours** that ye hide will be hidden.
'02:220	if ye mix their affairs with **yours**,

YOURSELF

018:028	And keep **yourself** content with those who call

YOURSELVES

002:036	with enmity between **yourselves**.
002:044	and forget to practice it **yourselves**,
002:048	Then guard **yourselves** against a day when one soul
002:054	and slay **yourselves** (the wrong-doers);
002:054	wronged **yourselves** by your worship of the calf:
002:072	a dispute among **yourselves** as to the crime:
002:085	who slay among **yourselves**,
002:087	with what ye **yourselves** desire not,
002:123	Then guard **yourselves** against a day
002:143	and the Messenger a witness over **yourselves**;
002:179	that ye may restrain **yourselves**.
002:187	used to do secretly among **yourselves**:
002:188	your property among **yourselves** for vanities,
002:237	And do not forget liberality between **yourselves**.
002:267	when ye **yourselves** would not receive it
002:282	ye carry out on the spot among **yourselves**,
002:282	to prevent doubts among **yourselves**
003:020	"Do ye (also) submit **yourselves**?"
003:028	that ye may guard **yourselves** from them.
003:061	our women and your women, ourselves and **yourselves**:
003:070	of which ye are (**yourselves**) witnesses?
003:099	**yourselves** witnesses (to Allah's Covenant)?
003:103	and be not divided among **yourselves**;
003:165	Say (to them): "It is from **yourselves**:
003:186	and tested in your possessions and in **yourselves**;
004:029	nor kill (or destroy) **yourselves**:
004:029	your property among **yourselves** in vanities:

YOURSELVES (continued)

004:043   then take for **yourselves** clean sand (or earth),
004:059   If ye differ in anything among **yourselves**,
004:094   Even thus were ye **yourselves** before, till Allah
004:097   to move **yourselves** away (form evil)?"
004:102   but take (every) precaution for **yourselves**.
004:135   as witnesses to Allah, even as against **yourselves**,
004:144   an open proof against **yourselves**?
005:006   then take for **yourselves** clean sand or earth,
005:096   for the benefit of **yourselves** and those who
005:106   (take) witnesses among **yourselves** when making
006:002   yet ye doubt within **yourselves**!
006:040   Say: "Think ye to **yourselves**, if there come
006:080   Will ye not (**yourselves**) be admonished?
006:097   that ye may guide **yourselves**,
007:024   "Get ye down, with enmity between **yourselves**.
007:074   ye build for **yourselves** palaces and castles in (open)
007:087   hold **yourselves** in patience until Allah doth decide
008:001   and keep straight the relations between **yourselves**:
009:035   (treasure) which ye hoarded for **yourselves**:
009:036   the right religion so wrong not not **yourselves** therein,
009:128   a Messenger from amongst **yourselves**:
011:065   So he said: "Enjoy **yourselves** in your homes
012:059   of the same father as **yourselves**,
012:066   ye are **yourselves** hemmed in (and made powerless).
012:083   but ye have **yourselves** contrived a story (good enough)
014:011   "True, we are human like **yourselves**,
016:015   and rivers and ways: that ye may guide **yourselves**;
016:094   to practice deception between **yourselves**.
017:007   If ye did well, ye did well for **yourselves**;
017:007   if ye did evil (ye did it) against **yourselves**.
018:016   betake **yourselves** to the Cave:
018:110   Say: "I am but a man like **yourselves**,
020:054   Eat (for **yourselves**) and pasture your cattle:
020:116   "Prostrate **yourselves** to Adam," they prostrated
021:003   "Is this (one) more than a man like **yourselves**?
022:077   O ye who believe! Bow down, prostrate **yourselves**,
023:024   "He is no more than a man like **yourselves**:
023:033   "He is no more than a man like **yourselves**;
023:034   "If ye obey a man like **yourselves**, behold,
024:011   who brought forward the lie are a body among **yourselves**:
024:028   that makes for greater purity for **yourselves**:
024:033   yea, give them something **yourselves** out of
024:061   nor in one afflicted with illness, nor in **yourselves**, that ye
024:063   of the Messenger among **yourselves** like the
026:128   a landmark on every high place to amuse **yourselves**?
026:129   "And do ye get for **yourselves** fine buildings
027:007   (to light our fuel), that ye may warm **yourselves**."
028:029   burning firebrand, that ye may warm **yourselves**."
029:025   and regard between **yourselves** in this life;
030:021   that He created for yu mates from among **yourselves**,
034:046   and reflect (within **yourselves**):
036:019   They said: "Your evil omens are with **yourselves**:
037:029   They will reply: "Nay, ye **yourselves** had no Faith!
037:095   "Worship ye that which ye have (**yourselves**) carved?
039:071   "Did not messengers come to you from among **yourselves**,s
040:010   than (is) your aversion to **yourselves**,
040:047   can ye then take (on **yourselves**) from us
041:022   "Ye did not seek to hide **yourselves**,
042:011   He has made for you pairs from among **yourselves**,
044:021   at least keep **yourselves** away from me."
045:004   And in the creation of **yourselves** and the fact
049:001   not **yourselves** forward before Allah and His Messenger;

YOURSELVES (continued)

053:032   Therefore hold not **yourselves** purified:
057:014   "True! But ye led **yourselves** into temptation;
057:020   boasting and muliplying, (in rivalry) among **yourselves**,
060:001   out the Messenger and **yourselves** (from your homes),
064:014   your children are (some that are) enemies to **yourselves**:
065:006   And if ye find **yourselves** in difficulties,
066:006   O ye who believe! save **yourselves** and your families
073:017   guard **yourselves** against a Day that will make children
073:020   And whatever good ye send forth for **yourselves**,
077:046   enjoy **yourselves** (but) a little while,
077:048   And when it is said to them "Prostrate **yourselves**!"

YOUTH

018:080   "As for the **youth**, his parents were people of Faith,
019:012   and We gave him Wisdom even as a **youth**,
021:060   They said, "We heard a **youth** talk of them:

YOUTHS

018:010   Behold, the **youths** betook themselves to the
018:013   they were **youths** who believed in their Lord,
018:082   "As for the wall, it belonged to two **youths**, orphans,
052:024   (devoted) to them, **youths** (handsome) as Pearls
056:017   about them will (serve) **youths** of perpetual (freshness),
076:019   about them will (serve) **youths** of perpetual (freshness):

Z

ZAID
033:037   Then when **Zaid** had dissolved (his marriage)

ZAKARIYA
003:037   to the care of **Zakariya** was she assigned.
003:038   There did **Zakariya** pray to his Lord,
006:085   And **Zakariya** and John, and Jesus and Elias:
019:002   the Mercy of thy Lord to His Servant **Zakariya**.
019:007   (His prayer was answered): "O **Zakariya**! We give
019:010   (**Zakariya**) said "O my Lord! give me a Sign."
019:011   So **Zakariya** came out to his people from his chamber:
021:089   And (remember) **Zakariya**,

ZAKAT
002:043   And be steadfast in prayer: give **Zakat**,
002:083   be steadfast in prayer; and Give **Zakat**,
002:110   And be steadfast in prayer: give **Zakat**,
002:177   to be steadfast in prayer, and give **Zakat**,
002:277   and establish regular prayers and give **Zakat**,
004:077   but establish regular prayers and spend in regular **Zakat**?
005:012   pay **Zakat**, believe in My Messengers,
005:055   those who establish regular prayers and pay **Zakat**
007:156   and pay **zakat** and those who believe in the Our Signs;-
009:005   and pay **Zakat** then open the way for them:
009:011   and pay **Zakat** they are your brethren in Faith:
009:018   and pay **Zakat**, and fear none (at all) except Allah
009:071   they observe regular prayers, pay **zakat** an obey
019:055   to enjoin on his people Prayer and **zakat** and he was
021:073   and to Give **zakat** and they constantly served Us
022:041   establish regular prayer, and
022:044   establish regular prayers and give **zakat**,
022:078   give **zakat** and hold fast to Allah!
023:004   Who are active in giving **zakat**;
024:037   nor from paying **zakat** their (only) fear is for the Day
024:056   So establish regular Prayer and give **zakat** and obey
027:003   Those who establish regular prayers and give **zakat**,
031:004   and give **zakat** and have sure faith in the Hereafter.
033:033   and give **Zakat** and obey Allah and His Messenger.
041:007   Those who pay not **zakat** and who even deny the
058:013   give **Zakat** and obey Allah and His Messenger.
073:020   and establish regular prayers and give **zakat**,
098:005   and to give **zakat**;

ZANJABIL
076:017   drink there of a Cup (of Wine) mixed with **Zanjabil**,-

ZAQQUM
037:062   Is that the better entertainment or the Tree of **Zaqqum**?
044:043   Verily the tree of **Zaqqum**
056:052   "Ye will surely taste of the Tree of **Zaqqum**.

ZEAL
002:114   Whose **zeal** is (in fact) to ruin them?
033:022   only added to their faith and their **zeal** in obedience.

ZIHAR
033:004   your wives whom ye divorce by **Zihar** your mothers:
058:002   If any men among you divorce their wives by **Zihar**
058:003   But those who divorce their wives by **Zihar**,

ZODIACAL
015:016   It is We who have set out the **Zodiacal** Signs in the

085:001   By the Sky, (displaying) the **Zodiacal** Signs;

ZONES
002:019   in it are **zones** of darkness, and thunder and lightning:
055:033   If it be ye can pass beyond the **zones** of the heavens

ZUL-KIFL
021:085   And (remember) Isma`il, Idris, and **Zul-kifl**,
038:048   And commemorate Isma`il, Elisha, and **Zul-Kifl**:

ZUL-QARNAIN
018:086   We said: "O **Zul-qarnain**! (thou hast authority),
018:083   They ask thee concerning **Zul-qarnain**.
018:094   They said: "O **Zul-qarnain**! the Gog and Magog

ZULAIKHA
012:031   When (**Zulaikha**) heard of their malicious talk,

ZUN-NUN
021:087   And remember **Zun-nun**,

APPENDIX I

EXPLANATION

The appendix to the main concordance is a listing by Surah and Ayat only, of eleven words:

A,	An,	And,	Are,	As,	For,
In,	Is,	Of,	The,	&	To.

These words were chosen because although others words may fit the same category, these words are least likely to be used to search for a specific text and at the same time they represented the greatest reduction in pages thereby reducing the overall cost of printing this book.

Note:

Only one listing of surah and ayat is listed no matter how many times the word may appear in a particular ayat.

A								
Surah 2	002:176	003:069	004:019	004:153	006:007	007:064	008:033	**Surah 10**
002:007	002:178	003:072	004:020	004:154	006:009	007:066	008:038	010:002
002:010	002:180	003:073	004:021	004:156	006:015	007:067	008:041	010:004
002:012	002:182	003:075	004:024	004:157	006:016	007:068	008:042	010:005
002:013	002:184	003:077	004:031	004:159	006:021	007:069	008:044	010:012
002:017	002:185	003:078	004:035	004:161	006:031	007:073	008:045	010:015
002:019	002:186	003:079	004:037	004:162	006:035	007:075	008:049	010:016
002:023	002:188	003:081	004:038	004:166	006:037	007:077	008:053	010:017
002:024	002:197	003:085	004:040	004:171	006:038	007:081	008:056	010:019
002:026	002:213	003:086	004:041	004:173	006:044	007:084	008:065	010:020
002:030	002:216	003:091	004:042	004:174	006:046	007:085	008:066	010:022
002:036	002:217	003:094	004:043	004:175	006:057	007:087	008:067	010:024
002:041	002:221	003:097	004:044	004:176	006:059	007:089	008:068	010:025
002:048	002:222	003:100	004:045	**Surah 5**	006:060	007:093	008:072	010:026
002:049	002:223	003:101	004:046	005:003	006:065	007:094	008:074	010:027
002:052	002:226	003:102	004:048	005:006	006:067	007:095	**Surah 9**	010:029
002:053	002:228	003:104	004:049	005:009	006:068	007:100	009:001	010:037
002:059	002:229	003:105	004:050	005:012	006:070	007:104	009:003	010:038
002:066	002:230	003:111	004:051	005:013	006:071	007:105	009:007	010:045
002:067	002:231	003:112	004:053	005:014	006:076	007:106	009:008	010:047
002:069	002:234	003:113	004:054	005:015	006:087	007:107	009:009	010:049
002:071	002:235	003:117	004:055	005:016	006:089	007:109	009:010	010:057
002:072	002:236	003:126	004:063	005:019	006:090	007:111	009:021	010:061
002:073	002:237	003:127	004:064	005:022	006:091	007:113	009:022	010:068
002:074	002:238	003:133	004:067	005:027	006:092	007:116	009:024	010:069
002:075	002:240	003:136	004:072	005:031	006:093	007:123	009:030	010:070
002:079	002:241	003:138	004:073	005:032	006:098	007:128	009:034	010:075
002:080	002:245	003:140	004:074	005:033	006:101	007:133	009:036	010:085
002:083	002:246	003:144	004:077	005:036	006:109	007:135	009:037	010:091
002:085	002:248	003:145	004:078	005:038	006:122	007:137	009:039	010:092
002:087	002:249	003:148	004:079	005:041	006:124	007:138	009:043	010:098
002:089	002:258	003:153	004:081	005:044	006:127	007:140	009:049	**Surah 11**
002:096	002:259	003:154	004:083	005:046	006:136	007:141	009:050	011:001
002:097	002:260	003:156	004:085	005:048	006:138	007:143	009:053	011:003
002:100	002:261	003:159	004:086	005:050	006:143	007:148	009:057	011:006
002:101	002:264	003:162	004:087	005:051	006:144	007:159	009:061	011:008
002:104	002:265	003:164	004:090	005:052	006:145	007:161	009:064	011:009
002:109	002:266	003:165	004:091	005:054	006:146	007:162	009:074	011:010
002:111	002:269	003:167	004:092	005:057	006:151	007:163	009:075	011:011
002:112	002:280	003:172	004:093	005:058	006:152	007:164	009:077	011:012
002:116	002:282	003:173	004:094	005:061	006:154	007:165	009:079	011:017
002:117	002:283	003:176	004:095	005:066	006:155	007:171	009:082	011:018
002:118	002:286	003:177	004:098	005:070	006:157	007:176	009:084	011:022
002:119	**Surah 3**	003:178	004:100	005:073	006:158	007:184	009:086	011:025
002:123	003:003	003:179	004:102	005:075	006:161	007:187	009:090	011:026
002:125	003:009	003:180	004:112	005:089	**Surah 7**	007:188	009:095	011:027
002:126	003:013	003:183	004:113	005:094	007:002	007:189	009:098	011:028
002:128	003:021	003:185	004:114	005:095	007:004	007:190	009:101	011:031
002:129	003:023	003:186	004:115	005:097	007:008	007:200	009:103	011:039
002:134	003:024	003:187	004:118	005:103	007:024	007:201	009:107	011:040
002:138	003:025	003:188	004:119	005:106	007:027	007:203	009:108	011:048
002:141	003:030	003:195	004:125	005:107	007:034	**Surah 8**	009:111	011:056
002:142	003:036	003:199	004:127	005:108	007:037	008:002	009:114	011:058
002:143	003:038	**Surah 4**	004:128	005:110	007:038	008:005	009:115	011:060
002:144	003:039	004:001	004:129	005:112	007:041	008:009	009:117	011:062
002:148	003:040	004:002	004:134	005:114	007:044	008:010	009:118	011:063
002:151	003:041	004:007	004:138	005:115	007:046	008:016	009:120	011:064
002:164	003:045	004:009	004:140	005:116	007:052	008:017	009:121	011:065
002:167	003:047	004:010	004:141	005:117	007:054	008:024	009:122	011:069
002:171	003:049	004:011	004:146	005:119	007:057	008:026	009:124	011:070
002:174	003:050	004:012	004:149	**Surah 6**	007:059	008:028	009:125	011:072
	003:051	004:014	004:150	006:002	007:061	008:029	009:127	011:076
	003:067	004:018	004:151	006:004	007:063	008:032	009:128	011:077

011:078	013:027	016:064	017:085	019:024	**Surah 21**	023:020	025:026	026:197
011:081	013:029	016:065	017:091	019:026	021:002	023:024	025:027	026:202
011:084	013:030	016:067	017:093	019:027	021:003	023:025	025:028	026:205
011:088	013:031	016:069	017:094	019:028	021:005	023:032	025:029	026:208
011:089	013:033	016:070	017:095	019:029	021:010	023:033	025:037	**Surah 27**
011:093	013:034	016:075	017:096	019:030	021:015	023:034	025:038	027:001
011:099	013:036	016:076	017:098	019:034	021:017	023:038	025:040	027:002
011:103	013:037	016:080	017:099	019:035	021:025	023:040	025:041	027:005
011:104	013:038	016:084	017:104	019:036	021:026	023:044	025:043	027:007
011:108	013:043	016:089	017:106	019:041	021:029	023:050	025:046	027:008
011:110	**Surah 14**	016:092	017:110	019:043	021:032	023:052	025:047	027:010
011:111	014:001	016:094	**Surah 18**	019:044	021:035	023:054	025:049	027:012
011:114	014:002	016:095	018:002	019:045	021:037	023:062	025:051	027:018
011:116	014:003	016:097	018:004	019:046	021:040	023:077	025:053	027:020
011:120	014:004	016:101	018:005	019:049	021:046	023:100	025:055	027:021
Surah 12	014:006	016:102	018:007	019:051	021:047	023:106	025:057	027:023
012:005	014:010	016:103	018:011	019:053	021:048	023:109	025:061	027:029
012:008	014:016	016:104	018:015	019:054	021:050	023:113	025:066	027:034
012:014	014:017	016:106	018:019	019:056	021:056	023:114	025:067	027:035
012:015	014:018	016:112	018:021	019:057	021:060	**Surah 24**	**Surah 26**	027:039
012:018	014:019	016:113	018:022	019:059	021:069	024:001	026:004	027:040
012:019	014:022	016:117	018:027	019:071	021:072	024:002	026:005	027:043
012:020	014:024	016:120	018:029	019:078	021:074	024:003	026:008	027:044
012:021	014:031	016:121	018:030	019:084	021:077	024:004	026:014	027:047
012:025	014:037	**Surah 17**	018:031	019:085	021:084	024:006	026:018	027:049
012:026	014:042	017:001	018:033	019:087	021:084	024:007	026:019	027:052
012:028	014:043	017:002	018:034	019:088	021:091	024:008	026:027	027:054
012:031	014:044	017:003	018:037	019:089	021:092	024:011	026:032	027:055
012:035	014:048	017:005	018:047	019:091	021:095	024:014	026:034	027:058
012:036	014:052	017:008	018:049	019:092	021:104	024:015	026:036	027:060
012:037	**Surah 15**	017:009	018:052	019:093	021:106	024:016	026:038	027:061
012:042	015:001	017:010	018:056	019:098	021:107	024:019	026:041	027:075
012:043	015:004	017:013	018:061	**Surah 20**	021:111	024:023	026:054	027:077
012:044	015:005	017:015	018:063	020:004	**Surah 22**	024:026	026:056	027:081
012:045	015:011	017:016	018:071	020:010	022:001	024:033	026:063	027:082
012:047	015:014	017:023	018:074	020:020	022:002	024:035	026:067	027:083
012:048	015:018	017:026	018:077	020:029	022:005	024:036	026:089	027:090
012:049	015:019	017:028	018:079	020:037	022:008	024:039	026:101	027:092
012:055	015:021	017:029	018:081	020:040	022:011	024:040	026:102	**Surah 28**
012:059	015:027	017:031	018:082	020:047	022:015	024:043	026:103	028:004
012:065	015:041	017:032	018:086	020:053	022:018	024:046	026:107	028:006
012:066	015:053	017:035	018:087	020:058	022:019	024:050	026:115	028:008
012:070	015:058	017:040	018:088	020:061	022:025	024:055	026:121	028:009
012:072	015:065	017:042	018:090	020:067	022:031	024:060	026:125	028:010
012:077	015:077	017:044	018:093	020:069	022:033	024:061	026:128	028:011
012:078	015:083	017:045	018:094	020:074	022:047	024:062	026:135	028:012
012:080	015:092	017:047	018:095	020:077	022:049	024:063	026:137	028:015
012:083	**Surah 16**	017:048	018:098	020:080	022:050	**Surah 25**	026:139	028:017
012:094	016:004	017:049	018:101	020:086	022:052	025:002	026:143	028:019
012:099	016:006	017:052	018:110	020:088	022:053	025:004	026:154	028:020
012:101	016:011	017:054	**Surah 19**	020:089	022:055	025:007	026:155	028:021
012:104	016:013	017:058	019:002	020:094	022:057	025:008	026:156	028:023
012:107	016:028	017:059	019:007	020:096	022:058	025:009	026:158	028:027
012:108	016:032	017:060	019:008	020:097	022:059	025:011	026:162	028:028
012:111	016:036	017:062	019:010	020:099	022:066	025:012	026:166	028:029
Surah 13	016:038	017:065	019:012	020:100	022:070	025:013	026:173	028:030
013:002	016:041	017:068	019:016	020:104	022:072	025:014	026:174	028:031
013:003	016:046	017:069	019:017	020:120	022:073	025:015	026:178	028:032
013:005	016:047	017:070	019:019	020:124	022:078	025:016	026:186	028:033
013:007	016:056	017:074	019:020	020:128	**Surah 23**	025:018	026:187	028:034
013:011	016:058	017:076	019:021	020:129	023:012	025:019	026:189	028:038
013:017	016:061	017:079	019:022	020:133	023:013	025:020	026:190	028:042
013:018	016:063	017:082	019:023	020:134	023:014	025:022	026:192	028:044

028:045	**Surah 32**	034:046	037:045	039:040	043:007	046:014	**Surah 51**	056:039
028:046	032:003	034:051	037:046	039:041	043:011	046:015	051:011	056:040
028:047	032:005	034:052	037:063	039:042	043:015	046:016	051:013	056:042
028:049	032:008	034:053	037:064	039:049	043:017	046:020	051:019	056:050
028:057	032:010	034:054	037:067	039:055	043:018	046:021	051:026	056:073
028:058	032:017	**Surah 35**	037:084	039:068	043:021	046:023	051:028	056:076
028:059	032:023	035:003	037:086	039:069	043:022	046:024	051:029	056:077
028:061	032:026	035:007	037:088	039:074	043:023	046:026	051:032	056:078
028:072	032:029	035:009	037:097	**Surah 40**	043:028	046:028	051:033	056:080
028:075	**Surah 33**	035:010	037:100	040:016	043:029	046:029	051:037	056:081
028:076	033:003	035:011	037:101	040:020	043:036	046:030	051:039	056:089
028:078	033:005	035:013	037:102	040:024	043:038	046:031	051:043	**Surah 57**
028:079	033:007	035:016	037:106	040:028	043:043	046:035	051:050	057:007
028:086	033:008	035:018	037:107	040:032	043:044	**Surah 47**	051:051	057:010
Surah 29	033:009	035:023	037:112	040:033	043:046	047:014	051:052	057:011
029:014	033:011	035:024	037:145	040:036	043:052	047:015	051:053	057:013
029:015	033:012	035:029	037:146	040:037	043:054	047:018	**Surah 52**	057:018
029:020	033:013	035:032	037:147	040:040	043:056	047:020	052:002	057:020
029:023	033:014	035:035	037:148	040:049	043:057	047:021	052:003	057:020
029:034	033:015	035:040	037:158	040:054	043:058	047:029	052:015	057:021
029:040	033:016	035:042	037:164	040:057	043:059	**Surah 48**	052:023	057:022
029:041	033:018	035:045	037:168	040:064	043:061	048:001	052:030	057:028
029:044	033:020	**Surah 36**	037:174	040:067	043:064	048:006	052:032	**Surah 58**
029:048	033:027	036:004	037:178	040:078	043:065	048:008	052:034	058:003
029:050	033:028	036:005	**Surah 38**	**Surah 41**	043:066	048:010	052:038	058:004
029:052	033:029	036:006	038:004	041:002	043:078	048:012	052:040	058:005
029:053	033:031	036:009	038:005	041:003	043:081	048:013	052:042	058:007
029:054	033:032	036:011	038:006	041:005	043:088	048:016	052:043	058:015
029:055	033:033	036:012	038:007	041:006	**Surah 44**	048:017	052:044	058:016
029:057	033:036	036:013	038:011	041:008	044:003	048:018	**Surah 53**	058:022
029:058	033:038	036:014	038:015	041:013	044:006	048:020	053:009	**Surah 59**
029:065	033:044	036:016	038:025	041:016	044:010	048:025	053:013	059:007
029:067	033:045	036:018	038:026	041:024	044:011	048:027	053:022	059:013
029:068	033:046	036:019	038:029	041:027	044:013	048:028	053:034	059:014
Surah 30	033:047	036:020	038:030	041:028	044:014	048:029	053:041	059:015
030:003	033:048	036:029	038:034	041:032	044:015	**Surah 49**	053:046	059:021
030:004	033:049	036:030	038:035	041:041	044:016	049:003	053:047	**Surah 60**
030:008	033:053	036:033	038:040	041:043	044:017	049:006	053:056	060:005
030:015	033:057	036:037	038:043	041:044	044:018	049:008	**Surah 54**	060:011
030:025	033:058	036:038	038:044	041:045	044:022	049:009	054:002	**Surah 61**
030:028	033:060	036:041	038:046	041:047	044:024	049:010	054:004	061:004
030:033	033:061	036:044	038:049	041:050	044:029	049:011	054:005	061:006
030:036	033:064	036:046	038:057	**Surah 42**	044:033	049:012	054:006	061:010
030:039	033:068	036:049	038:058	042:008	044:047	049:013	054:014	061:013
030:041	**Surah 34**	036:052	038:059	042:014	044:051	049:017	054:015	061:014
030:046	034:004	036:053	038:061	042:016	044:057	**Surah 50**	054:019	**Surah 62**
030:047	034:005	036:054	038:065	042:021	**Surah 45**	050:002	054:024	062:005
030:051	034:007	036:058	038:086	042:024	045:008	050:003	054:025	**Surah 63**
030:054	034:008	036:062	038:087	042:026	045:009	050:004	054:029	063:002
Surah 31	034:009	036:065	038:088	042:030	045:010	050:005	054:031	063:003
031:003	034:012	036:069	**Surah 39**	042:040	045:011	050:015	054:034	063:010
031:006	034:014	036:075	039:004	042:041	045:015	050:018	054:035	**Surah 64**
031:007	034:015	036:082	039:005	042:042	045:020	050:026	054:042	064:005
031:016	034:019	**Surah 37**	039:006	042:044	045:023	050:031	054:050	064:009
031:016	034:020	037:009	039:008	042:045	045:031	050:032	054:055	064:015
031:020	034:022	037:010	039:010	042:047	**Surah 46**	050:033	**Surah 55**	064:017
031:022	034:028	037:011	039:013	042:048	046:003	050:034	055:020	**Surah 65**
031:024	034:030	037:014	039:021	042:051	046:004	050:037	055:035	065:002
031:029	034:033	037:019	039:023	042:052	046:008	050:041	**Surah 56**	065:003
031:032	034:034	037:021	039:026	**Surah 43**	046:009	050:042	056:013	065:007
031:033	034:037	037:030	039:028	043:003	046:010	050:044	056:014	065:008
	034:043	037:036	039:029	043:005	046:011		056:024	065:010
	034:045	037:041	039:032		046:012			

065:011
065:012
Surah 66
066:003
066:006
066:011
Surah 67
067:004
067:008
067:009
067:012
067:017
067:022
067:026
067:028
Surah 68
068:003
068:011
068:013
068:019
068:020
068:024
068:032
068:037
068:045
068:046
068:052
Surah 69
069:005
069:006
069:012
069:021
069:022
069:032
069:041
069:042
069:043
069:048
069:050
Surah 70
070:001
070:003
070:004
070:005
070:006
070:010
070:024
070:028
070:043
Surah 71
071:001
071:002
071:004
071:016
071:019
071:022
071:026
Surah 72
072:001
072:003
072:009
072:013

072:019
072:025
072:027
Surah 73
073:003
073:004
073:005
073:006
073:011
073:012
073:013
073:014
073:015
073:016
073:017
073:019
073:020
Surah 74
074:001
074:009
074:017
074:025
074:031
074:036
074:051
Surah 75
075:027
075:037
075:038
Surah 76
076:001
076:002
076:004
076:005
076:006
076:007
076:010
076:011
076:012
076:017
076:018
076:020
076:021
076:022
076:026
076:027
076:029
076:031
Surah 77
077:005
077:011
077:020
077:021
077:022
077:025
077:030
077:033
077:035
077:038
077:039
077:046

Surah 78
078:006
078:010
078:011
078:013
078:017
078:020
078:021
078:022
078:025
078:026
078:034
078:036
078:039
078:040
Surah 79
079:004
079:012
079:013
079:023
079:026
079:030
079:033
079:045
079:046
Surah 80
080:011
080:019
080:032
080:034
Surah 81
081:003
081:006
081:019
081:024
081:025
081:027
Surah 82
082:007
Surah 83
083:005
083:006
083:009
083:020
083:023
083:027
083:028
083:035
Surah 84
084:012
084:024
084:025
Surah 85
085:021
085:022
Surah 86
086:004
086:006
086:014
086:015
086:016
086:017

Surah 88
088:005
088:006
088:010
088:012
088:024
Surah 89
089:013
Surah 90
090:008
090:009
090:014
Surah 91
091:013
091:014
Surah 92
092:008
092:014
092:019
Surah 95
095:006
Surah 96
096:002
096:010
096:016
Surah 97
097:003
Surah 101
101:004
101:007
101:009
101:011
Surah 104
104:006
104:008
Surah 111
111:003
111:005

AN

Surah 2
002:066
002:067
002:097
002:098
002:114
002:124
002:126
002:143
002:164
002:168
002:196
002:206
002:208
002:221
002:224
002:226
002:233
002:235
002:239
002:248

Surah 3
003:012
003:126
003:135
003:136
003:197
003:198
Surah 4
004:005
004:009
004:012
004:022
004:085
004:097
004:105
004:115
004:128
004:141
004:144
004:153
Surah 5
005:045
005:046
005:048
005:090
005:095
Surah 6
006:008
006:009
006:038
006:050
006:112
006:142
006:145
Surah 7
007:022
007:026
007:028
007:034
007:169
007:185
Surah 8
008:010
Surah 9
009:003
009:008
009:037
009:057
009:068
009:073
009:083
009:095
009:102
009:109
009:114
009:120
Surah 10
010:002
010:023
010:045
010:049
010:057

010:061
010:071
010:093
Surah 11
011:012
011:031
011:037
011:072
011:096
011:120
Surah 12
012:002
012:005
012:025
012:080
Surah 13
013:038
Surah 14
014:011
014:026
014:029
Surah 15
015:079
Surah 16
016:004
016:008
016:059
016:066
016:077
Surah 17
017:014
017:032
017:053
017:063
017:075
017:079
017:080
017:095
Surah 18
018:014
018:015
018:059
018:074
Surah 19
019:005
019:037
019:063
Surah 20
020:002
020:003
020:039
020:077
020:113
020:117
Surah 21
021:072
Surah 22
022:005
Surah 23
023:021
023:046

Surah 24
024:003
024:008
024:011
024:012
024:034
024:035
024:044
024:057
Surah 25
025:001
025:004
025:007
025:021
025:031
025:034
025:065
025:066
025:076
Surah 26
026:019
026:097
026:171
Surah 28
028:004
028:008
028:015
Surah 29
029:035
029:058
Surah 30
030:055
Surah 31
031:028
Surah 33
033:014
033:053
Surah 34
034:022
034:030
Surah 35
035:006
Surah 36
036:018
036:019
036:060
036:077
Surah 37
037:051
037:135
037:156
Surah 38
038:055
038:056
Surah 39
039:032
039:060
Surah 40
040:023
040:068

Surah 41
041:036
041:044
Surah 42
042:007
042:023
042:039
042:040
042:043
Surah 43
043:036
043:056
043:057
043:059
043:062
Surah 44
044:007
Surah 46
046:009
046:011
046:035
Surah 48
048:006
048:012
Surah 50
050:008
050:021
Surah 51
051:051
Surah 54
054:013
054:025
054:038
054:043
054:050
Surah 55
055:004
Surah 56
056:073
Surah 57
057:015
Surah 60
060:004
060:006
Surah 66
066:009
066:010
066:011
Surah 67
067:016
067:020
Surah 68
068:025
Surah 69
069:010
069:018
069:027
069:040
Surah 72
072:027

Surah 73
073:019
Surah 74
074:054
Surah 75
075:027
Surah 76
076:029
Surah 78
078:031
Surah 79
079:025
Surah 84
084:008
Surah 90
090:002
Surah 93
093:006
Surah 99
099:007
099:008
Surah 105
105:005

AND

Surah 1
001:002
001:005
001:007
Surah 2
002:003
002:004
002:005
002:007
002:008
002:009
002:010
002:015
002:016
002:017
002:018
002:019
002:020
002:021
002:022
002:023
002:024
002:025
002:026
002:027
002:028
002:029
002:030
002:031
002:032
002:033
002:034
002:035
002:036
002:037

002:038	002:116	002:194	002:269	003:062	003:147	004:025	004:099	005:006
002:039	002:117	002:195	002:270	003:064	003:148	004:026	004:100	005:007
002:040	002:119	002:196	002:271	003:065	003:149	004:029	004:102	005:008
002:041	002:122	002:197	002:272	003:066	003:150	004:030	004:104	005:009
002:042	002:124	002:198	002:273	003:067	003:151	004:031	004:107	005:010
002:043	002:125	002:199	002:274	003:068	003:152	004:032	004:108	005:011
002:044	002:126	002:200	002:275	003:069	003:153	004:032	004:111	005:012
002:045	002:127	002:201	002:277	003:071	003:154	004:033	004:112	005:013
002:046	002:128	002:202	002:278	003:073	003:156	004:034	004:113	005:014
002:047	002:129	002:203	002:279	003:075	003:157	004:035	004:115	005:015
002:049	002:130	002:204	002:281	003:076	003:158	004:036	004:119	005:016
002:050	002:131	002:205	002:282	003:077	003:159	004:038	004:120	005:017
002:051	002:132	002:207	002:283	003:078	003:161	004:039	004:121	005:018
002:053	002:133	002:208	002:284	003:079	003:162	004:040	004:122	005:019
002:054	002:134	002:210	002:286	003:080	003:163	004:041	004:124	005:020
002:055	002:135	002:212	**Surah 3**	003:081	003:164	004:042	004:125	005:021
002:057	002:136	002:213	003:003	003:083	003:167	004:043	004:126	005:024
002:058	002:137	002:214	003:004	003:084	003:170	004:044	004:127	005:024
002:060	002:138	002:215	003:007	003:085	003:171	004:045	004:128	005:025
002:061	002:139	002:216	003:011	003:086	003:172	004:046	004:129	005:029
002:062	002:140	002:217	003:012	003:087	003:173	004:047	004:130	005:030
002:063	002:141	002:218	003:014	003:089	003:174	004:049	004:131	005:031
002:064	002:142	002:219	003:015	003:090	003:179	004:051	04:132	005:032
002:065	002:143	002:220	003:016	003:091	003:180	004:052	004:133	005:035
002:066	002:149	002:221	003:017	003:092	003:181	004:054	004:134	005:036
002:067	002:150	002:222	003:018	003:093	003:183	004:055	004:136	005:038
002:069	002:151	002:223	003:020	003:094	003:184	004:057	004:137	005:039
002:071	002:152	002:224	003:021	003:096	003:185	004:058	004:140	005:040
002:072	002:153	002:225	003:022	003:101	003:186	004:059	004:141	005:041
002:073	002:154	002:227	003:023	003:102	003:187	004:060	004:143	005:044
002:074	002:155	002:228	003:025	003:103	003:188	004:061	004:146	005:045
002:075	002:156	002:230	003:026	003:104	003:189	004:062	004:147	005:046
002:077	002:157	002:231	003:027	003:105	003:190	004:063	004:148	005:048
002:078	002:158	002:232	003:029	003:106	003:191	004:064	004:150	005:049
002:079	002:159	002:233	003:030	003:108	003:192	004:065	004:151	005:051
002:080	002:160	002:234	003:031	003:109	003:193	004:066	004:152	005:053
002:081	002:161	002:235	003:032	003:110	003:194	004:067	004:153	005:054
002:082	002:163	002:236	003:033	003:111	003:195	004:068	004:154	005:055
002:083	002:164	002:237	003:034	003:112	003:198	004:069	004:155	005:056
002:084	002:165	002:238	003:035	003:113	003:199	004:070	004:157	005:057
002:085	002:166	002:240	003:036	003:114	003:200	004:071	004:158	005:058
002:087	002:167	002:244	003:037	003:117	**Surah 4**	004:073	004:159	005:059
002:089	002:168	002:245	003:039	003:120	004:001	004:075	004:160	005:060
002:090	002:169	002:246	003:040	003:121	004:002	004:076	004:161	005:061
002:092	002:170	002:247	003:041	003:122	004:005	004:077	004:162	005:062
002:093	002:171	002:248	003:042	003:125	004:006	004:078	004:163	005:063
002:094	002:172	002:249	003:043	003:126	004:007	004:079	004:164	005:064
002:095	002:173	002:250	003:045	003:127	004:008	004:081	004:166	005:065
002:097	002:174	002:251	003:046	003:129	004:009	004:083	004:167	005:066
002:098	002:175	002:253	003:047	003:130	004:011	004:084	004:168	005:067
002:099	002:177	002:255	003:048	003:132	004:012	004:084	004:169	005:068
002:101	002:178	002:256	003:049	003:133	004:013	004:085	004:170	005:069
002:102	002:180	002:258	003:050	003:134	004:014	004:087	004:171	005:070
002:103	002:181	002:259	003:051	003:135	004:015	004:089	004:172	005:071
002:104	002:182	002:260	003:052	003:136	004:016	004:090	004:173	005:072
002:107	002:184	002:261	003:053	003:137	004:017	004:091	004:175	005:074
002:109	002:185	002:262	003:054	003:138	004:018	004:092	004:176	005:076
002:110	002:186	002:263	003:055	003:140	004:019	004:093	**Surah 5**	005:077
002:111	002:187	002:264	003:056	003:141	004:020	004:094	005:001	005:078
002:112	002:188	002:265	003:057	003:142	004:021	004:095	005:002	005:080
002:113	002:189	002:266	003:058	003:143	004:022	004:096	005:003	005:081
002:114	002:191	002:267	003:059	003:145	004:023	004:097	005:004	005:082
002:115	002:193	002:268	003:061	003:146	004:024	004:098	005:005	005:083

005:084	006:057	006:154	007:078	007:169	008:047	009:047	009:120	010:098
005:085	006:058	006:155	007:082	007:170	008:048	009:048	009:122	010:100
005:086	006:059	006:156	007:083	007:171	008:049	009:049	009:123	010:101
005:088	006:060	006:157	007:084	007:172	008:050	009:050	009:124	010:103
005:090	006:061	006:159	007:085	007:174	008:052	009:051	009:125	010:105
005:091	006:062	006:161	007:086	007:175	008:053	009:053	009:126	010:107
005:092	006:063	006:162	007:087	007:176	008:054	009:054	009:128	010:108
005:093	006:064	006:163	007:088	007:177	008:056	009:055	**Surah 10**	010:109
005:094	006:065	**Surah 7**	007:089	007:179	008:060	009:058	010:002	**Surah 11**
005:095	006:067	007:002	007:091	007:181	008:061	009:059	010:003	011:001
005:096	006:070	007:003	007:094	007:183	008:062	009:060	010:004	011:002
005:097	006:071	007:006	007:095	007:185	008:063	009:061	010:005	011:004
005:098	006:072	007:007	007:096	007:187	008:064	009:062	010:006	011:005
005:099	006:073	007:010	007:100	007:188	008:065	009:063	010:007	011:006
005:100	006:074	007:011	007:102	007:189	008:066	009:065	010:009	011:007
005:102	006:075	007:012	007:103	007:194	008:067	009:067	010:010	011:008
005:104	006:079	007:017	007:107	007:195	008:069	009:068	010:018	011:010
005:106	006:082	007:018	007:108	007:196	008:070	009:069	010:022	011:011
005:107	006:083	007:019	007:108	007:197	008:071	009:070	010:023	011:012
005:108	006:084	007:021	007:111	007:200	008:072	009:071	010:024	011:013
005:109	006:085	007:022	007:112	007:202	008:073	009:072	010:028	011:014
005:110	006:086	007:023	007:114	007:203	008:074	009:073	010:029	011:015
005:111	006:087	007:024	007:116	007:204	008:075	009:074	010:030	011:016
005:113	006:089	007:025	007:117	007:205	**Surah 9**	009:075	010:031	011:017
005:114	006:091	007:027	007:118	007:206	009:001	009:076	010:034	011:018
005:116	006:092	007:028	007:119	**Surah 8**	009:003	009:077	010:037	011:019
005:117	006:093	007:029	007:122	008:001	009:004	009:078	010:038	011:021
005:119	006:094	007:030	007:124	008:002	009:005	009:079	010:040	011:023
005:120	006:095	007:031	007:126	008:003	009:006	009:080	010:041	011:024
Surah 6	006:096	007:032	007:127	008:004	009:007	009:081	010:043	011:028
006:001	006:097	007:033	007:128	008:007	009:008	009:083	010:045	011:029
006:002	006:098	007:035	007:129	008:008	009:009	009:084	010:047	011:030
006:003	006:099	007:036	007:130	008:009	009:011	009:085	010:051	011:032
006:005	006:100	007:037	007:131	008:010	009:012	009:086	010:053	011:033
006:006	006:102	007:038	007:133	008:011	009:013	009:087	010:054	011:034
006:008	006:105	007:040	007:134	008:012	009:014	009:088	010:055	011:035
006:009	006:106	007:041	007:136	008:013	009:015	009:090	010:056	011:037
006:011	006:108	007:042	007:137	008:016	009:016	009:091	010:057	011:040
006:012	006:110	007:043	007:139	008:017	009:018	009:092	010:058	011:042
006:013	006:111	007:046	007:141	008:018	009:019	009:094	010:059	011:043
006:014	006:112	007:048	007:142	008:019	009:020	009:095	010:060	011:044
006:016	006:113	007:051	007:143	008:020	009:021	009:097	010:061	011:045
006:018	006:115	007:052	007:144	008:022	009:023	009:098	010:063	011:047
006:019	006:122	007:053	007:145	008:023	009:024	009:100	010:064	011:048
006:022	006:123	007:054	007:146	008:024	009:025	009:103	010:065	011:052
006:025	006:124	007:055	007:147	008:025	009:026	009:104	010:066	011:053
006:026	006:125	007:056	007:148	008:026	009:028	009:105	010:067	011:054
006:029	006:128	007:057	007:149	008:027	009:029	009:106	010:068	011:055
006:029	006:130	007:058	007:150	008:028	009:030	009:107	010:070	011:056
006:031	006:133	007:061	007:151	008:029	009:031	009:108	010:071	011:057
006:032	006:136	007:062	007:152	008:030	009:033	009:109	010:072	011:058
006:034	006:137	007:063	007:153	008:034	009:034	009:109	010:073	011:059
006:035	006:138	007:064	007:154	008:035	009:035	009:109	010:075	011:060
006:038	006:139	007:066	007:155	008:036	009:036	009:110	010:078	011:061
006:039	006:140	007:067	007:156	008:037	009:037	009:111	010:082	011:063
006:041	006:141	007:068	007:157	008:039	009:039	009:112	010:083	011:064
006:042	006:142	007:069	007:158	008:040	009:040	009:113	010:086	011:066
006:043	006:143	007:070	007:159	008:041	009:041	009:114	010:087	011:067
006:046	006:144	007:071	007:160	008:042	009:042	009:115	010:088	011:068
006:048	006:146	007:072	007:161	008:043	009:043	009:116	010:089	011:069
006:052	006:150	007:073	007:164	008:044	009:044	009:117	010:090	011:070
006:054	006:151	007:074	007:166	008:045	009:045	009:118	010:091	011:071
006:056	006:152	007:077	007:168	008:046	009:046	009:119	010:093	011:072

011:073	012:043	013:023	015:017	016:040	016:119	017:080	018:060	019:065
011:074	012:044	013:025	015:019	016:042	016:120	017:081	018:065	019:068
011:075	012:045	013:028	015:020	016:043	016:121	017:082	018:078	019:070
011:077	012:047	013:029	015:021	016:044	016:122	017:083	018:080	019:072
011:078	012:049	013:030	015:022	016:046	016:123	017:088	018:081	019:073
011:081	012:050	013:032	015:023	016:047	016:125	017:089	018:082	019:074
011:082	012:051	013:033	015:024	016:048	016:126	017:091	018:084	019:075
011:084	012:052	013:034	015:025	016:049	016:127	017:092	018:087	019:076
011:085	012:056	013:035	015:027	016:050	016:128	017:095	018:088	019:077
011:087	012:057	013:036	015:029	016:051	**Surah 17**	017:096	018:094	019:079
011:088	012:058	013:038	015:035	016:052	017:001	017:097	018:095	019:080
011:089	012:059	013:041	015:039	016:053	017:002	017:098	018:098	019:081
011:090	012:062	013:042	015:042	016:056	017:004	017:099	018:099	019:082
011:093	012:063	013:043	015:043	016:057	017:005	017:102	018:100	019:086
011:094	012:064	**Surah 14**	015:045	016:058	017:006	017:103	018:101	019:090
011:095	012:065	014:002	015:046	016:059	017:007	017:104	018:105	019:093
011:096	012:066	014:003	015:047	016:062	017:008	017:105	018:106	019:094
011:097	012:067	014:004	015:050	016:064	017:009	017:108	018:107	019:095
011:098	012:068	014:005	015:052	016:065	017:010	017:109	018:110	019:096
011:099	012:073	014:006	015:056	016:066	017:012	017:111	**Surah 19**	019:097
011:100	012:077	014:007	015:064	016:067	017:017	**Surah 18**	019:004	**Surah 20**
011:102	012:078	014:008	015:065	016:068	017:018	018:001	019:005	020:004
011:105	012:080	014:009	015:066	016:069	017:019	018:002	019:006	020:006
011:106	012:081	014:010	015:069	016:070	017:021	018:008	019:008	020:007
011:107	012:082	014:011	015:070	016:072	017:022	018:009	019:011	020:014
011:108	012:083	014:013	015:072	016:073	017:023	018:010	019:012	020:017
011:111	012:084	014:014	015:074	016:074	017:024	018:013	019:013	020:018
011:112	012:086	014:015	015:076	016:075	017:025	018:014	019:014	020:020
011:113	012:087	014:016	015:078	016:076	017:026	018:015	019:015	020:021
011:114	012:088	014:017	015:084	016:077	017:027	018:016	019:017	020:022
011:115	012:089	014:019	015:085	016:078	017:028	018:017	019:020	020:027
011:116	012:090	014:022	015:087	016:079	017:029	018:018	019:021	020:029
011:119	012:091	014:023	015:089	016:080	017:030	018:019	019:022	020:032
011:120	012:092	014:024	015:094	016:080	017:032	018:020	019:023	020:034
011:122	012:093	014:026	015:098	016:081	017:033	018:021	019:025	020:037
011:123	012:096	014:027	015:099	016:083	017:034	018:023	019:026	020:039
Surah 12	012:099	014:028	**Surah 16**	016:086	017:035	018:024	019:030	020:040
012:004	012:100	014:030	016:001	016:087	017:036	018:025	019:031	020:041
012:006	012:101	014:031	016:003	016:088	017:039	018:026	019:032	020:042
012:007	012:104	014:032	016:004	016:089	017:040	018:027	019:033	020:045
012:008	012:105	014:033	016:005	016:090	017:043	018:028	019:035	020:046
012:012	012:106	014:034	016:006	016:091	017:044	018:029	019:036	020:047
012:015	012:108	014:035	016:007	016:092	017:045	018:030	019:037	020:048
012:017	012:109	014:036	016:008	016:093	017:046	018:031	019:038	020:053
012:019	012:110	014:037	016:010	016:094	017:047	018:032	019:039	020:054
012:021	012:111	014:038	016:011	016:096	017:048	018:033	019:040	020:055
012:022	**Surah 13**	014:039	016:012	016:097	017:049	018:034	019:042	020:056
012:023	013:002	014:040	016:013	016:099	017:051	018:038	019:043	020:058
012:024	013:003	014:041	016:014	016:100	017:052	018:039	019:048	020:059
012:025	013:004	014:043	016:015	016:101	017:055	018:040	019:049	020:060
012:026	013:006	014:044	016:016	016:102	017:057	018:042	019:050	020:063
012:027	013:007	014:045	016:019	016:103	017:059	018:044	019:051	020:064
012:031	013:009	014:048	016:020	016:104	017:060	018:046	019:052	020:066
012:032	013:011	014:049	016:022	016:106	017:064	018:047	019:053	020:069
012:033	013:012	014:050	016:023	016:107	017:069	018:048	019:054	020:070
012:034	013:013	014:051	016:025	016:108	017:070	018:049	019:055	020:071
012:036	013:015	014:052	016:026	016:110	017:071	018:050	019:056	020:073
012:037	013:016	**Surah 15**	016:027	016:111	017:072	018:051	019:057	020:077
012:038	013:017	015:003	016:030	016:112	017:073	018:052	019:058	020:078
012:039	013:018	015:004	016:034	016:113	017:074	018:053	019:059	020:080
012:040	013:020	015:009	016:036	016:114	017:075	018:055	019:060	020:081
012:041	013:021	015:014	016:037	016:115	017:078	018:056	019:062	020:082
012:042	013:022	015:016	016:039	016:116	017:079	018:057	019:064	020:086

020:087	021:067	022:045	023:080	024:047	025:071	026:129	027:030	028:024
020:088	021:068	022:046	023:082	024:048	025:072	026:130	027:033	028:025
020:089	021:069	022:048	023:083	024:050	025:074	026:131	027:034	028:026
020:090	021:071	022:050	023:084	024:051	025:075	026:133	027:035	028:028
020:094	021:072	022:052	023:086	024:052	025:076	026:134	027:037	028:029
020:096	021:073	022:053	023:091	024:054	025:077	026:138	027:039	028:031
020:097	021:074	022:054	023:092	024:055	**Surah 26**	026:139	027:040	028:032
020:101	021:075	022:056	023:095	024:055	026:009	026:140	027:042	028:033
020:105	021:076	022:057	023:097	024:056	026:013	026:144	027:043	028:034
020:106	021:078	022:058	023:098	024:057	026:014	026:147	027:044	028:035
020:108	021:079	022:060	023:104	024:058	026:015	026:148	027:047	028:037
020:109	021:082	022:061	023:105	024:059	026:016	026:149	027:048	028:038
020:112	021:083	022:062	023:106	024:060	026:018	026:150	027:049	028:039
020:113	021:084	022:063	023:108	024:061	026:019	026:151	027:050	028:040
020:115	021:085	022:064	023:109	024:062	026:021	026:152	027:051	028:041
020:117	021:087	022:065	023:111	024:064	026:022	026:155	027:053	028:042
020:120	021:088	022:066	023:115	**Surah 25**	026:023	026:159	027:056	028:043
020:121	021:089	022:070	023:117	025:002	026:024	026:163	027:057	028:045
020:122	021:090	022:071	023:118	025:004	026:026	026:166	027:058	028:047
020:124	021:091	022:072	**Surah 24**	025:005	026:028	026:169	027:059	028:048
020:127	021:092	022:073	024:001	025:006	026:030	026:170	027:060	028:050
020:130	021:094	022:074	024:002	025:007	026:032	026:173	027:061	028:053
020:131	021:096	022:075	024:003	025:009	026:033	026:175	027:062	028:054
020:132	021:098	022:076	024:004	025:010	026:036	026:179	027:063	028:055
020:134	021:109	022:077	024:005	025:012	026:037	026:181	027:064	028:056
020:135	021:110	022:078	024:006	025:013	026:039	026:182	027:066	028:058
Surah 21	021:111	022:078	024:007	025:018	026:042	026:183	027:067	028:060
021:001	**Surah 22**	**Surah 23**	024:009	025:019	026:044	026:184	027:068	028:061
021:004	022:002	023:008	024:010	025:020	026:048	026:186	027:069	028:062
021:009	022:003	023:009	024:011	025:021	026:049	026:189	027:074	028:064
021:013	022:004	023:014	024:012	025:023	026:055	026:191	027:075	028:065
021:015	022:005	023:017	024:014	025:024	026:056	026:199	027:077	028:066
021:016	022:006	023:018	024:015	025:025	026:058	026:209	027:078	028:067
021:018	022:007	023:019	024:016	025:031	026:061	026:214	027:082	028:068
021:019	022:008	023:020	024:018	025:032	026:063	026:215	027:083	028:069
021:020	022:009	023:021	024:019	025:033	026:064	026:217	027:085	028:070
021:022	022:011	023:022	024:020	025:034	026:065	026:219	027:086	028:073
021:024	022:013	023:023	024:021	025:035	026:068	026:220	027:087	028:075
021:025	022:014	023:025	024:022	025:036	026:069	026:223	027:088	028:077
021:026	022:015	023:027	024:023	025:037	026:070	026:224	027:089	028:078
021:027	022:016	023:028	024:024	025:038	026:071	026:226	027:090	028:080
021:028	022:017	023:029	024:025	025:039	026:076	026:227	027:091	028:081
021:030	022:018	023:032	024:026	025:040	026:077	**Surah 27**	027:092	028:082
021:031	022:022	023:033	024:027	025:047	026:078	027:002	027:093	028:083
021:032	022:023	023:037	024:028	025:048	026:079	027:003	**Surah 28**	028:085
021:033	022:025	023:041	024:029	025:049	026:080	027:004	028:003	028:086
021:035	022:026	023:045	024:030	025:050	026:081	027:005	028:004	028:087
021:036	022:027	023:046	024:031	025:053	026:082	027:008	028:005	028:088
021:039	022:028	023:047	024:031	025:054	026:083	027:010	028:006	**Surah 29**
021:040	022:029	023:048	024:032	025:055	026:087	027:011	028:007	029:002
021:042	022:030	023:049	024:033	025:056	026:091	027:012	028:008	029:003
021:044	022:031	023:050	024:034	025:058	026:092	027:014	028:009	029:005
021:047	022:032	023:051	024:035	025:059	026:094	027:015	028:010	029:006
021:048	022:034	023:052	024:036	025:060	026:095	027:016	028:011	029:007
021:049	022:035	023:055	024:037	025:061	026:099	027:017	028:012	029:008
021:050	022:036	023:060	024:038	025:062	026:104	027:018	028:013	029:009
021:051	022:037	023:061	024:039	025:063	026:108	027:019	028:014	029:010
021:052	022:039	023:063	024:041	025:064	026:110	027:020	028:015	029:011
021:054	022:040	023:071	024:042	025:066	026:112	027:022	028:018	029:012
021:056	022:041	023:074	024:043	025:067	026:118	027:023	028:019	029:013
021:057	022:042	023:075	024:044	025:068	026:119	027:024	028:020	029:014
021:058	022:043	023:078	024:045	025:069	026:122	027:025	028:022	029:015
021:064	022:044	023:079	024:046	025:070	026:126	027:028	028:023	029:016

029:017	030:027	032:023	033:066	035:021	037:013	037:167	**Surah 39**	040:026
029:018	030:031	032:024	033:067	035:022	037:014	037:169	039:003	040:027
029:020	030:032	032:026	033:068	035:024	037:015	037:173	039:005	040:028
029:021	030:036	032:027	033:069	035:025	037:016	037:175	039:006	040:031
029:023	030:037	032:030	033:070	035:026	037:017	037:175	039:008	040:032
029:025	030:038	**Surah 33**	033:071	035:027	037:018	037:177	039:009	040:034
029:026	030:040	033:001	033:072	035:028	037:019	037:179	039:012	040:035
029:027	030:041	033:003	033:073	035:029	037:022	037:180	039:014	040:036
029:028	030:042	033:004	**Surah 34**	035:031	037:023	037:181	039:015	040:037
029:029	030:044	033:005	034:001	035:032	037:027	037:182	039:016	040:040
029:032	030:045	033:006	034:002	035:033	037:036	**Surah 38**	039:017	040:041
029:033	030:046	033:007	034:004	035:034	037:037	038:002	039:018	040:042
029:035	030:047	033:008	034:006	035:037	037:039	038:004	039:021	040:043
029:036	030:048	033:009	034:008	035:038	037:042	038:006	039:023	040:046
029:037	030:051	033:010	034:009	035:041	037:048	038:010	039:024	040:051
029:038	030:052	033:012	034:010	035:043	037:050	038:011	039:025	040:052
029:039	030:053	033:013	034:011	035:044	037:053	038:012	039:029	040:053
029:040	030:054	033:014	034:012	**Surah 36**	037:055	038:013	039:030	040:054
029:042	030:056	033:014	034:013	036:006	037:059	038:014	039:032	040:055
029:043	**Surah 31**	033:015	034:015	036:009	037:066	038:017	039:033	040:056
029:044	031:003	033:016	034:016	036:011	037:071	038:018	039:035	040:057
029:045	031:004	033:018	034:017	036:012	037:075	038:019	039:037	040:058
029:046	031:005	033:019	034:018	036:015	037:076	038:020	039:038	040:060
029:047	031:006	033:020	034:019	036:017	037:077	038:022	039:040	040:061
029:048	031:008	033:021	034:020	036:018	037:078	038:023	039:042	040:064
029:049	031:009	033:022	034:021	036:021	037:079	038:024	039:043	040:066
029:050	031:010	033:023	034:023	036:022	037:085	038:025	039:044	040:067
029:051	031:014	033:024	034:024	036:027	037:089	038:026	039:046	040:068
029:052	031:015	033:025	034:026	036:028	037:090	038:027	039:047	040:070
029:053	031:016	033:026	034:028	036:029	037:091	038:028	039:048	040:071
029:055	031:017	033:027	034:033	036:033	037:096	038:029	039:051	040:075
029:056	031:018	033:028	034:035	036:034	037:097	038:031	039:054	040:076
029:058	031:019	033:029	034:036	036:036	037:103	038:032	039:055	040:077
029:059	031:020	033:030	034:037	036:037	037:107	038:033	039:056	040:078
029:060	031:022	033:031	034:039	036:038	037:108	038:034	039:059	040:079
029:061	031:023	033:033	034:040	036:039	037:109	038:035	039:062	040:080
029:062	031:025	033:034	034:042	036:041	037:112	038:037	039:063	040:081
029:063	031:026	033:035	034:043	036:042	037:113	038:040	039:065	040:082
029:064	031:027	033:036	034:045	036:044	037:114	038:041	039:066	040:083
029:065	031:028	033:037	034:046	036:045	037:115	038:042	039:067	040:084
029:066	031:029	033:038	034:047	036:047	037:116	038:043	039:068	040:085
029:067	031:030	033:039	034:049	036:052	037:117	038:044	039:069	**Surah 41**
029:068	031:031	033:040	034:050	036:054	037:118	038:045	039:070	041:004
029:069	031:032	033:042	034:051	036:056	037:119	038:047	039:071	041:005
Surah 30	031:033	033:043	034:052	036:059	037:120	038:048	039:072	041:006
030:004	031:034	033:044	034:053	036:061	037:125	038:049	039:073	041:007
030:005	**Surah 32**	033:045	034:054	036:065	037:126	038:051	039:074	041:008
030:008	032:004	033:046	**Surah 35**	036:067	037:127	038:052	039:075	041:009
030:009	032:006	033:048	035:001	036:069	037:129	038:057	**Surah 40**	041:010
030:010	032:007	033:049	035:002	036:070	037:130	038:058	040:003	041:011
030:013	032:008	033:050	035:004	036:072	037:134	038:062	040:005	041:012
030:015	032:009	033:051	035:007	036:073	037:138	038:065	040:007	041:013
030:016	032:010	033:052	035:008	036:075	037:141	038:066	040:008	041:014
030:017	032:012	033:053	035:009	036:078	037:142	038:070	040:009	041:015
030:018	032:013	033:055	035:010	036:081	037:143	038:072	040:010	041:016
030:019	032:014	033:056	035:011	036:082	037:146	038:074	040:011	041:018
030:020	032:015	033:057	035:012	036:083	037:147	038:075	040:013	041:020
030:021	032:016	033:058	035:013	**Surah 37**	037:148	038:076	040:019	041:021
030:022	032:018	033:059	035:014	037:005	037:149	038:078	040:020	041:022
030:023	032:019	033:060	035:016	037:007	037:150	038:083	040:021	041:023
030:024	032:020	033:061	035:018	037:008	037:158	038:084	040:023	041:024
030:025	032:021	033:063	035:019	037:009	037:165	038:085	040:024	041:025
030:026	032:022	033:064	035:020	037:010	037:166	038:088	040:025	041:027

041:029	**Surah 43**	044:026	046:021	048:026	051:025	053:062	056:010	058:003
041:030	043:004	044:027	046:026	048:027	051:027	**Surah 54**	056:014	058:004
041:031	043:007	044:028	046:027	048:028	051:028	054:001	056:015	058:005
041:033	043:008	044:029	046:028	048:029	051:029	054:002	056:018	058:006
041:034	043:009	044:032	046:030	**Surah 49**	051:030	054:003	056:020	058:007
041:035	043:010	044:033	046:031	049:001	051:031	054:006	056:021	058:008
041:036	043:011	044:035	046:032	049:002	051:037	054:009	056:022	058:009
041:037	043:012	044:037	046:033	049:003	051:038	054:012	056:032	058:010
041:038	043:013	044:038	046:034	049:006	051:039	054:013	056:034	058:011
041:039	043:014	044:041	046:035	049:007	051:040	054:014	056:036	058:012
041:041	043:016	044:047	**Surah 47**	049:008	051:041	054:015	056:040	058:013
041:044	043:017	044:052	047:001	049:009	051:042	054:016	056:042	058:014
041:048	043:018	044:053	047:002	049:010	051:043	054:017	056:043	058:018
041:049	043:019	044:054	047:005	049:011	051:047	054:021	056:046	058:020
041:050	043:022	044:055	047:006	049:012	051:048	054:022	056:047	058:021
041:051	043:023	044:056	047:007	049:013	051:049	054:024	056:048	058:022
041:052	043:026	044:059	047:008	049:014	051:050	054:027	056:049	**Surah 59**
041:053	043:027	**Surah 45**	047:010	049:015	051:051	054:028	056:051	059:001
Surah 42	043:028	045:003	047:012	049:015	051:056	054:029	056:054	059:002
042:004	043:029	045:004	047:013	049:016	**Surah 52**	054:030	056:060	059:003
042:005	043:030	045:005	047:014	049:017	052:006	054:031	056:061	059:004
042:006	043:032	045:006	047:015	049:018	052:010	054:032	056:062	059:005
042:007	043:033	045:008	047:016	**Surah 50**	052:012	054:036	056:065	059:006
042:008	043:034	045:009	047:017	050:003	052:017	054:037	056:070	059:007
042:009	043:035	045:010	047:018	050:006	052:018	054:039	056:073	059:008
042:010	043:038	045:011	047:019	050:007	052:019	054:040	056:076	059:009
042:011	043:044	045:012	047:020	050:008	052:020	054:045	056:082	059:010
042:012	043:045	045:013	047:021	050:009	052:021	054:046	056:084	059:011
042:013	043:046	045:016	047:022	050:010	052:022	054:047	056:085	059:012
042:014	043:048	045:017	047:023	050:011	052:027	054:049	056:089	059:012
042:015	043:049	045:018	047:025	050:014	052:036	054:050	056:089	059:015
042:016	043:051	045:020	047:027	050:016	052:038	054:051	056:090	059:018
042:017	043:052	045:021	047:028	050:017	052:039	054:053	056:092	059:019
042:018	043:054	045:022	047:030	050:019	052:041	054:054	056:094	059:020
042:019	043:055	045:023	047:031	050:020	052:046	**Surah 55**	**Surah 57**	059:021
042:020	043:056	045:024	047:032	050:021	052:047	055:005	057:001	059:022
042:022	043:058	045:025	047:033	050:022	052:048	055:006	057:002	059:023
042:023	043:059	045:027	047:034	050:023	052:049	055:007	057:003	059:024
042:024	043:060	045:028	047:035	050:025	**Surah 53**	055:009	057:004	**Surah 60**
042:025	043:061	045:030	047:036	050:029	053:008	055:011	057:005	060:001
042:026	043:063	045:031	047:037	050:031	053:009	055:012	057:006	060:002
042:028	043:064	045:032	047:038	050:033	053:011	055:015	057:007	060:003
042:029	043:069	045:033	**Surah 48**	050:034	053:019	055:017	057:008	060:004
042:030	043:070	045:034	048:002	050:035	053:020	055:022	057:009	060:004
042:032	043:071	045:035	048:003	050:037	053:021	055:024	057:010	060:005
042:033	043:075	045:036	048:004	050:038	053:023	055:027	057:011	060:006
042:036	043:077	045:037	048:005	050:039	053:025	055:029	057:012	060:007
042:037	043:080	**Surah 46**	048:006	050:040	053:026	055:033	057:013	060:008
042:038	043:082	046:003	048:007	050:041	053:028	055:035	057:014	060:009
042:039	043:083	046:005	048:008	050:043	053:029	055:037	057:015	060:010
042:040	043:084	046:006	048:009	050:045	053:030	055:041	057:016	060:011
042:041	043:085	046:008	048:010	**Surah 51**	053:031	055:044	057:018	060:012
042:042	043:086	046:009	048:011	051:002	053:032	055:052	057:019	**Surah 61**
042:043	043:089	046:010	048:012	051:003	053:037	055:054	057:020	061:001
042:044	**Surah 44**	046:011	048:013	051:004	053:043	055:058	057:021	061:005
042:045	044:006	046:012	048:014	051:006	053:044	055:062	057:024	061:006
042:046	044:007	046:013	048:017	051:012	053:045	055:068	057:025	061:007
042:048	044:008	046:015	048:018	051:013	053:048	055:076	057:026	061:009
042:049	044:014	046:016	048:019	051:015	053:050	055:078	057:027	061:011
042:050	044:019	046:017	048:020	051:018	053:051	**Surah 56**	057:028	061:012
042:052	044:020	046:018	048:021	051:019	053:052	056:005	**Surah 58**	061:013
042:053	044:024	046:019	048:024	051:022	053:053	056:007	058:001	061:014
	044:025	046:020	048:025	051:023	053:060	056:009	058:002	

Surah 62	067:002	070:024	074:003	077:027	080:040	087:018	094:008	110:003
062:001	067:004	070:025	074:004	077:031	**Surah 81**	087:019	**Surah 95**	**Surah 111**
062:002	067:005	070:026	074:005	077:038	081:013	**Surah 88**	095:001	111:002
062:003	067:006	070:027	074:007	077:041	081:017	088:015	095:002	112:004
062:004	067:009	070:029	074:011	077:042	081:018	088:016	095:003	**Surah 113**
062:005	067:012	070:030	074:013	077:043	081:021	088:018	095:006	113:005
062:007	067:013	070:032	074:014	077:046	081:022	088:019	**Surah 96**	**Surah 114**
062:008	067:014	070:033	074:018	077:048	081:023	088:020	096:001	114:001
062:009	067:015	070:034	074:019	**Surah 78**	**Surah 82**	088:023	096:003	114:006
062:010	067:019	070:037	074:022	078:007	082:004	**Surah 89**	096:013	
062:011	067:021	070:040	074:023	078:008	082:005	089:003	096:019	**<u>ARE</u>**
Surah 63	067:023	070:041	074:027	078:009	082:007	089:004	**Surah 97**	
063:001	067:024	070:042	074:028	078:010	082:011	089:009	097:002	**Surah 2**
063:004	067:027	**Surah 71**	074:029	078:011	082:014	089:010	097:004	002:003
063:005	067:028	071:002	074:031	078:012	082:016	089:012	**Surah 98**	002:005
063:007	067:029	071:003	074:033	078:013	082:017	089:015	098:001	002:008
063:008	**Surah 68**	071:004	074:034	078:014	**Surah 83**	089:019	098:002	002:011
063:010	068:001	071:005	074:041	078:015	083:008	089:020	098:003	002:012
063:011	068:004	071:007	074:046	078:016	083:012	089:022	098:005	002:013
Surah 64	068:005	071:009	074:056	078:018	083:019	089:023	098:006	002:014
064:001	068:007	071:012	**Surah 75**	078:019	083:026	089:026	098:007	002:016
064:002	068:013	071:016	075:002	078:020	083:030	089:027	098:008	002:019
064:003	068:014	071:017	075:008	078:025	083:031	089:028	**Surah 99**	002:023
064:004	068:020	071:018	075:009	078:029	083:032	**Surah 90**	099:002	002:025
064:005	068:025	071:019	075:013	078:032	**Surah 84**	090:002	099:003	002:029
064:006	068:042	071:021	075:017	078:034	084:002	090:003	099:008	002:031
064:007	068:043	071:022	075:019	078:037	084:003	090:004	**Surah 100**	002:045
064:008	068:048	071:023	075:021	078:038	084:004	090:009	100:002	002:046
064:009	068:050	071:024	075:022	078:040	084:005	090:010	100:003	002:068
064:010	068:051	071:025	075:024	**Surah 79**	084:009	090:012	100:004	002:070
064:011	**Surah 69**	071:026	075:027	079:003	084:012	090:017	100:005	002:074
064:012	069:003	071:027	075:028	079:018	084:017	**Surah 91**	100:007	002:078
064:013	069:004	071:028	075:029	079:019	084:018	091:001	100:008	002:081
064:014	069:005	**Surah 72**	075:032	079:021	084:021	091:005	100:010	002:082
064:015	069:006	072:002	075:038	079:023	084:025	091:006	**Surah 101**	002:086
064:016	069:007	072:003	075:039	079:025	**Surah 85**	091:007	101:003	002:087
064:017	069:009	072:007	**Surah 76**	079:028	085:003	091:008	101:005	002:088
064:018	069:010	072:008	076:002	079:029	085:007	091:010	101:007	002:093
Surah 65	069:012	072:010	076:004	079:030	085:008	091:013	101:010	002:094
065:001	069:014	072:011	076:007	079:031	085:009	091:014	**Surah 103**	002:099
065:002	069:016	072:013	076:008	079:032	085:010	091:015	103:003	002:100
065:003	069:017	072:014	076:008	079:033	085:011	**Surah 92**	**Surah 104**	002:102
065:004	069:021	072:016	076:010	079:036	085:013	092:003	104:001	002:111
065:005	069:023	072:018	076:011	079:038	085:014	092:005	104:002	002:118
065:006	069:024	072:020	076:012	079:040	085:018	092:006	104:005	002:121
065:007	069:025	072:023	076:014	**Surah 80**	085:019	092:008	**Surah 105**	002:137
065:008	069:026	072:024	076:015	080:001	**Surah 86**	092:009	105:003	002:139
065:009	069:030	072:027	076:017	080:004	086:001	092:013	105:005	002:144
065:011	069:031	072:028	076:019	080:009	086:002	092:016	**Surah 106**	002:148
065:012	069:034	**Surah 73**	076:020	080:014	086:007	092:019	106:002	002:150
Surah 66	069:039	073:004	076:021	080:016	086:010	092:021	106:004	002:154
066:002	069:044	073:006	076:022	080:019	086:012	**Surah 93**	**Surah 107**	002:157
066:003	069:046	073:008	076:024	080:021	086:016	093:002	107:003	002:158
066:004	069:049	073:009	076:025	080:024	**Surah 87**	093:004	**Surah 108**	002:164
066:006	**Surah 70**	073:010	076:026	080:026	087:002	093:005	108:002	002:165
066:008	070:004	073:011	076:027	080:027	087:003	093:006	**Surah 109**	002:166
066:009	070:009	073:012	076:028	080:028	087:004	093:007	109:004	002:171
066:010	070:010	073:013	076:030	080:029	087:005	093:008	109:006	002:175
066:011	070:012	073:014	**Surah 77**	080:030	087:007	093:011	**Surah 110**	002:176
066:012	070:014	073:020	077:003	080:031	087:008	**Surah 94**	110:001	002:177
Surah 67	070:017	**Surah 74**	077:011	080:032	087:015	094:002	110:002	002:187
067:001	070:018	074:002	077:014	080:035	087:017	094:004		002:189
	070:021		077:026	080:036				

002:196	003:156	**Surah 5**	006:132	**Surah 9**	010:022	012:077	016:125	022:036
002:197	003:157	005:001	006:138	009:004	010:026	012:082	016:126	022:039
002:200	003:158	005:002	006:140	009:005	010:027	012:110	**Surah 17**	022:040
002:201	003:163	005:003	006:141	009:006	010:032	**Surah 13**	017:003	022:041
002:217	003:168	005:004	006:142	009:008	010:034	013:001	017:016	022:045
002:219	003:169	005:005	006:143	009:009	010:040	013:003	017:019	022:046
002:220	003:179	005:006	006:146	009:011	010:041	013:004	017:020	022:053
002:222	003:181	005:013	006:158	009:012	010:042	013:005	017:027	022:058
002:223	003:190	005:018	006:162	009:018	010:043	013:011	017:039	022:062
002:229	003:195	005:022	**Surah 7**	009:019	010:060	013:013	017:049	022:068
002:230	003:198	005:023	007:010	009:020	010:061	013:015	017:053	022:072
002:231	003:199	005:024	007:014	009:021	010:064	013:016	017:055	022:073
002:239	**Surah 4**	005:027	007:026	009:024	010:067	013:018	017:057	**Surah 23**
002:243	004:008	005:041	007:032	009:028	010:068	013:019	017:068	023:001
002:247	004:011	005:042	007:033	009:030	010:092	013:033	017:071	023:004
002:252	004:013	005:043	007:035	009:034	010:099	013:035	017:098	023:006
002:254	004:015	005:044	007:036	009:036	010:104	013:036	**Surah 18**	023:007
002:255	004:016	005:045	007:037	009:037	**Surah 11**	**Surah 14**	018:007	023:017
002:257	004:019	005:047	007:049	009:038	011:008	014:003	018:017	023:018
002:263	004:023	005:049	007:053	009:042	011:016	014:005	018:046	023:021
002:264	004:024	005:051	007:054	009:045	011:018	014:007	018:050	023:030
002:266	004:025	005:053	007:058	009:053	011:021	014:009	018:068	023:036
002:273	004:031	005:055	007:081	009:054	011:022	014:010	018:105	023:038
002:275	004:034	005:058	007:082	009:056	011:024	014:011	**Surah 19**	023:040
002:278	004:036	005:059	007:085	009:058	011:027	014:018	019:004	023:047
002:282	004:037	005:060	007:090	009:060	011:028	014:030	019:038	023:061
002:283	004:043	005:062	007:125	009:061	011:029	**Surah 15**	019:039	023:063
Surah 3	004:046	005:063	007:131	009:062	011:031	015:001	019:070	023:074
003:007	004:051	005:064	007:138	009:064	011:035	015:020	019:073	023:083
003:010	004:052	005:075	007:139	009:066	011:037	015:021	019:076	023:089
003:014	004:056	005:080	007:147	009:067	011:049	015:022	019:090	023:090
003:015	004:058	005:081	007:157	009:069	011:050	015:024	**Surah 20**	023:093
003:017	004:062	005:082	007:168	009:071	011:053	015:036	020:047	023:095
003:020	004:069	005:090	007:173	009:075	011:062	015:044	020:054	023:096
003:022	004:072	005:096	007:177	009:080	011:078	015:059	020:063	023:100
003:023	004:075	005:100	007:178	009:085	011:081	015:065	020:075	023:111
003:052	004:078	005:104	007:179	009:087	011:083	015:068	020:082	**Surah 24**
003:064	004:091	005:106	007:181	009:088	011:085	015:071	020:084	024:004
003:066	004:093	005:118	007:189	009:091	011:089	015:075	020:090	024:011
003:068	004:094	005:119	007:191	009:093	011:098	015:095	020:128	024:017
003:070	004:095	**Surah 6**	007:194	009:095	011:099	**Surah 16**	**Surah 21**	024:022
003:073	004:098	006:019	007:197	009:096	011:100	016:009	021:005	024:023
003:075	004:101	006:022	007:205	009:097	011:106	016:012	021:019	024:026
003:082	004:102	006:025	007:206	009:100	011:108	016:013	021:026	024:028
003:090	004:103	006:028	**Surah 8**	009:101	011:110	016:020	021:038	024:032
003:094	004:104	006:031	008:001	009:102	011:114	016:021	021:045	024:039
003:097	004:109	006:032	008:002	009:103	011:117	016:022	021:047	024:045
003:101	004:120	006:035	008:004	009:106	**Surah 12**	016:027	021:052	024:047
003:104	004:127	006:039	008:022	009:107	012:001	016:027	021:055	024:048
003:105	004:128	006:040	008:028	009:108	012:007	016:042	021:064	024:050
003:108	004:129	006:050	008:031	009:110	012:008	016:049	021:083	024:055
003:110	004:140	006:052	008:034	009:111	012:011	016:050	021:096	024:058
003:112	004:141	006:053	008:044	009:113	012:014	016:053	021:098	024:060
003:113	004:143	006:059	008:055	009:119	012:036	016:067	021:109	024:061
003:114	004:147	006:062	008:056	009:123	012:038	016:070	**Surah 22**	024:062
003:119	004:151	006:070	008:065	009:126	012:039	016:071	022:003	024:064
003:120	004:155	006:082	008:066	009:127	012:044	016:075	022:005	**Surah 25**
003:128	004:157	006:092	008:070	**Surah 10**	012:051	016:079	022:007	025:003
003:135	004:162	006:095	008:072	010:001	012:057	016:083	022:011	025:005
003:139	004:172	006:099	008:073	010:006	012:066	016:086	022:018	025:013
003:141	004:173	006:109	008:074	010:007	012:070	016:086	022:030	025:021
003:146	004:176	006:111	008:075	010:015	012:073	016:108	022:035	025:044
003:152		006:117		010:018	012:074			025:050

025:063	029:011	034:019	039:052	**Surah 46**	056:066	066:006	**Surah 83**	002:275
025:067	029:012	034:024	039:068	046:003	056:067	**Surah 67**	083:013	002:282
025:073	029:021	034:029	**Surah 40**	046:004	056:079	067:007	083:032	002:285
025:075	029:031	034:033	040:006	046:005	056:085	067:009	**Surah 86**	**Surah 3**
Surah 26	029:033	034:037	040:048	046:006	056:086	067:011	086:015	003:003
026:002	029:034	034:043	040:058	046:007	056:087	067:020	**Surah 88**	003:006
026:015	029:043	**Surah 35**	040:060	046:010	**Surah 57**	067:025	088:005	003:013
026:039	029:049	035:003	040:062	046:016	057:008	**Surah 68**	088:017	003:021
026:043	029:050	035:004	040:063	046:018	057:010	068:015	088:019	003:024
026:051	029:052	035:012	040:067	046:019	057:016	068:027	**Surah 90**	003:044
026:054	029:060	035:019	040:069	046:023	057:019	068:034	090:018	003:049
026:056	029:061	035:020	040:073	046:032	057:019	068:041	090:019	003:056
026:061	029:067	035:021	040:078	**Surah 47**	057:024	068:046	**Surah 92**	003:057
026:077	**Surah 30**	035:022	040:080	047:004	**Surah 58**	**Surah 69**	092:004	003:059
026:092	030:007	035:027	**Surah 41**	047:015	058:003	069:014	**Surah 98**	003:064
026:118	030:008	035:028	041:003	047:016	058:004	069:024	098:003	003:068
026:138	030:020	035:032	041:005	047:023	058:010	069:049	098:006	003:077
026:151	030:021	035:043	041:025	047:024	058:011	**Surah 70**	098:007	003:078
026:166	030:022	**Surah 36**	041:031	047:035	058:013	070:030	**Surah 107**	003:081
026:209	030:023	036:015	041:037	047:038	058:014	070:031	107:005	003:091
026:212	030:024	036:019	041:038	**Surah 48**	058:015	070:041		003:102
026:223	030:026	036:021	041:039	048:012	058:018	070:044		003:145
026:227	030:036	036:037	041:040	048:015	058:019	**Surah 71**	**AS**	003:165
Surah 27	030:037	036:045	041:041	048:021	058:022	071:013		003:169
027:001	030:040	036:047	041:044	048:025	**Surah 59**	**Surah 72**	**Surah 2**	**Surah 4**
027:005	030:050	036:049	041:047	048:029	059:008	072:011	002:006	004:005
027:008	030:058	036:070	041:054	**Surah 49**	059:009	072:014	002:013	004:009
027:012	**Surah 31**	036:071	**Surah 42**	049:007	059:011	072:015	002:023	004:011
027:033	031:002	**Surah 37**	042:005	049:009	059:012	072:018	002:026	004:024
027:041	031:005	037:002	042:014	049:010	059:012	072:024	002:035	004:034
027:047	031:006	037:008	042:018	049:011	059:013	072:025	002:038	004:041
027:049	031:007	037:010	042:032	049:015	059:014	**Surah 73**	002:058	004:047
027:055	031:011	037:011	042:033	**Surah 50**	059:019	073:012	002:072	004:056
027:056	031:020	037:013	042:036	050:005	059:020	073:020	002:085	004:073
027:060	031:021	037:039	042:037	050:006	059:021	**Surah 74**	002:101	004:077
027:064	031:031	037:065	042:039	050:016	**Surah 60**	074:030	002:102	004:079
027:066	031:032	037:075	042:045	050:030	060:004	**Surah 75**	002:108	004:081
027:068	**Surah 32**	037:113	**Surah 43**	**Surah 51**	060:008	075:004	002:119	004:089
027:071	032:015	037:150	043:005	051:005	060:010	075:009	002:121	004:091
027:073	032:017	037:152	043:021	051:008	060:013	**Surah 77**	002:125	004:100
027:086	032:018	037:163	043:024	051:009	**Surah 61**	077:007	002:126	004:107
027:087	032:019	037:165	043:037	051:020	061:005	077:010	002:130	004:127
Surah 28	032:020	037:166	043:053	051:022	061:014	077:011	002:137	004:135
028:002	032:022	**Surah 38**	043:058	051:053	**Surah 62**	077:012	002:146	004:163
028:020	032:026	038:002	043:072	**Surah 52**	062:006	077:023	002:148	004:165
028:031	032:028	038:008	043:080	052:032	**Surah 63**	077:046	002:165	004:171
028:032	032:030	038:011	043:087	052:037	063:002	**Surah 78**	002:167	004:176
028:048	**Surah 33**	038:022	043:088	052:040	063:004	078:001	002:171	**Surah 5**
028:049	033:005	038:024	**Surah 44**	052:042	063:007	**Surah 79**	002:183	005:003
028:057	033:006	038:039	044:022	**Surah 53**	063:009	079:027	002:185	005:004
028:058	033:013	038:079	044:023	053:023	**Surah 64**	**Surah 81**	002:188	005:005
028:059	033:016	**Surah 39**	044:024	053:032	064:002	081:004	002:196	005:008
028:060	033:023	039:003	044:037	**Surah 54**	064:014	081:005	002:198	005:024
028:061	033:032	039:006	044:059	054:043	064:016	081:007	002:200	005:029
028:062	033:035	039:007	**Surah 45**	054:047	**Surah 65**	081:010	002:214	005:031
028:063	033:053	039:009	045:003	**Surah 55**	065:001	**Surah 82**	002:222	005:032
028:074	033:061	039:015	045:004	055:024	065:004	082:002	002:223	005:036
028:078	**Surah 34**	039:018	045:005	055:062	065:006	082:003	002:229	005:038
Surah 29	034:007	039:022	045:006	**Surah 56**	065:007	082:004	002:231	005:041
029:003	034:008	039:029	045:013	056:059	**Surah 66**	082:010	002:239	005:044
029:005	034:013	039:042	045:020	056:060	066:004		002:247	005:048
029:010	034:017	039:045	045:025	056:064	066:005		002:255	005:054
							002:265	005:056

005:058	008:011	012:047	017:060	021:032	026:197	034:017	**Surah 42**	**Surah 52**
005:060	008:023	012:056	017:065	021:072	**Surah 27**	034:019	042:003	052:017
005:064	008:043	012:059	017:079	021:084	027:004	034:025	042:006	052:024
005:095	008:044	012:075	017:086	021:104	027:006	034:027	042:013	**Surah 54**
005:096	008:054	012:088	017:092	021:107	027:010	034:028	042:015	054:004
005:097	008:058	012:101	017:102	**Surah 22**	027:030	034:039	042:027	054:015
005:110	008:072	012:106	**Surah 18**	022:002	027:037	034:044	042:032	054:020
005:111	008:074	012:109	018:005	022:003	027:054	034:054	042:048	054:035
005:115	**Surah 9**	012:110	018:007	022:005	027:063	**Surah 35**	042:052	054:054
Surah 6	009:002	012:111	018:008	022:008	027:066	035:001	**Surah 43**	**Surah 55**
006:001	009:007	**Surah 13**	018:015	022:011	027:074	035:006	043:017	055:024
006:006	009:017	013:003	018:021	022:012	027:087	035:008	043:028	055:039
006:009	009:018	013:016	018:027	022:018	027:088	035:018	043:040	055:046
006:020	009:031	013:018	018:030	022:020	**Surah 28**	035:024	043:057	055:072
006:031	009:036	013:023	018:038	022:025	028:009	035:032	**Surah 44**	**Surah 57**
006:036	009:038	013:038	018:039	022:030	028:019	**Surah 36**	044:006	057:021
006:073	009:069	013:043	018:046	022:031	028:031	036:011	044:019	057:024
006:094	009:077	**Surah 14**	018:047	022:036	028:034	036:036	044:024	057:025
006:097	009:079	014:005	018:048	022:078	028:035	036:076	044:034	**Surah 58**
006:110	009:091	014:009	018:050	**Surah 23**	028:038	036:077	044:042	058:005
006:125	009:093	014:011	018:051	023:013	028:046	**Surah 37**	044:051	058:008
006:128	009:098	014:014	018:056	023:022	028:057	037:010	044:057	058:010
006:133	009:099	014:018	018:061	023:024	028:063	037:049	**Surah 45**	058:014
006:150	009:100	014:030	018:079	023:041	028:068	037:063	045:008	058:018
006:155	009:101	014:046	018:080	023:044	028:077	037:102	045:013	**Surah 59**
006:159	009:115	**Surah 15**	018:082	023:050	028:086	037:130	045:017	059:009
006:160	009:120	015:042	018:088	023:105	**Surah 29**	037:163	045:019	**Surah 60**
Surah 7	**Surah 10**	015:056	018:091	**Surah 24**	029:010	**Surah 38**	045:021	060:001
007:003	010:011	015:074	018:096	024:013	029:011	038:028	045:023	060:002
007:019	010:012	015:090	018:102	024:024	029:028	038:037	045:030	060:007
007:020	010:017	015:091	018:107	024:035	029:047	038:038	045:034	060:009
007:026	010:024	**Surah 16**	018:110	024:051	029:062	038:043	**Surah 46**	060:010
007:027	010:027	016:002	**Surah 19**	024:052	**Surah 30**	038:063	046:005	060:013
007:029	010:028	016:006	019:005	024:055	030:028	**Surah 39**	046:012	**Surah 61**
007:041	010:037	016:008	019:012	024:059	030:034	039:003	046:015	061:004
007:051	010:045	016:022	019:013	024:060	030:046	039:008	046:028	061:007
007:054	010:049	016:037	019:017	024:061	030:048	039:023	046:035	061:014
007:080	010:061	016:061	019:021	**Surah 25**	**Surah 31**	039:036	**Surah 47**	**Surah 63**
007:089	010:066	016:071	019:031	025:011	031:007	039:037	047:012	063:004
007:092	010:093	016:073	019:063	025:015	031:028	039:047	047:014	**Surah 64**
007:126	010:094	016:077	019:065	025:017	**Surah 32**	039:049	047:015	064:010
007:128	010:104	016:089	019:076	025:020	032:006	039:065	047:025	064:016
007:139	**Surah 11**	016:100	019:087	025:023	032:017	039:067	**Surah 48**	**Surah 65**
007:143	011:034	016:102	019:093	025:034	032:019	039:068	048:008	065:004
007:146	011:055	016:106	019:098	025:035	032:020	039:074	048:016	065:006
007:147	011:062	016:116	**Surah 20**	025:037	032:024	**Surah 40**	048:029	065:006
007:150	011:068	016:118	020:003	025:038	**Surah 33**	040:012	**Surah 49**	**Surah 66**
007:154	011:082	016:124	020:016	025:041	033:003	040:034	049:002	066:011
007:157	011:088	016:124	020:022	025:043	033:011	040:035	049:012	**Surah 67**
007:158	011:095	**Surah 17**	020:040	025:047	033:038	040:050	049:017	067:005
007:161	011:095	017:002	020:074	025:048	033:043	040:064	**Surah 50**	067:007
007:170	011:107	017:007	020:075	025:062	033:045	040:067	050:011	067:012
007:171	011:108	017:011	020:087	025:066	033:046	040:083	050:045	067:016
007:177	011:109	017:012	020:105	025:068	033:048	**Surah 41**	**Surah 51**	067:020
007:180	011:112	017:018	020:106	025:073	033:050	041:011	051:009	067:026
007:186	011:120	017:020	020:123	**Surah 26**	033:052	041:012	051:015	**Surah 68**
007:187	**Surah 12**	017:024	**Surah 21**	026:018	033:053	041:017	051:021	068:017
007:188	012:002	017:026	021:002	026:021	033:059	041:020	051:022	068:021
007:191	012:006	017:031	021:003	026:098	033:060	041:034	051:023	068:044
Surah 8	012:019	017:042	021:006	026:112	033:067	041:043	051:034	**Surah 69**
008:001	012:021	017:057	021:015	026:115	**Surah 34**	041:044	051:037	069:007
008:005	012:041	017:059	021:030	026:169	034:013			
008:006								

Surah 70	083:033	002:085	002:224	003:105	004:034	004:155	005:106	006:162
070:004	**Surah 86**	002:088	002:225	003:106	004:035	004:157	005:108	006:164
070:006	086:015	002:089	002:226	003:107	004:036	004:160	005:114	006:165
070:017	**Surah 87**	002:090	002:227	003:110	004:037	004:161	005:116	**Surah 7**
070:043	087:007	002:094	002:228	003:113	004:038	004:165	**Surah 6**	007:004
Surah 71	**Surah 89**	002:095	002:229	003:115	004:039	004:166	006:002	007:007
071:016	089:015	002:096	002:231	003:116	004:043	004:169	006:006	007:009
071:019	089:025	002:097	002:232	003:118	004:045	004:170	006:012	007:010
Surah 72	089:026	002:102	002:233	003:120	004:046	004:171	006:013	007:013
072:007	**Surah 91**	002:105	002:237	003:121	004:047	004:174	006:014	007:016
072:013	091:002	002:109	002:240	003:124	004:049	004:176	006:023	007:017
Surah 73	091:003	002:110	002:241	003:126	004:054	**Surah 5**	006:028	007:020
073:014	091:004	002:114	002:243	003:128	004:055	005:001	006:031	007:024
073:015	091:008	002:115	002:246	003:131	004:056	005:002	006:032	007:027
073:020	091:014	002:125	002:248	003:133	004:058	005:003	006:049	007:030
Surah 74	**Surah 92**	002:126	002:254	003:134	004:059	005:004	006:051	007:031
074:031	092:001	002:127	002:255	003:135	004:060	005:006	006:052	007:032
074:033	092:002	002:128	002:257	003:136	004:064	005:007	006:054	007:033
074:034	**Surah 95**	002:129	002:259	003:139	004:066	005:008	006:057	007:036
074:050	095:006	002:132	002:261	003:143	004:074	005:013	006:066	007:037
074:056	**Surah 96**	002:139	002:262	003:148	004:075	005:017	006:067	007:038
Surah 75	096:007	002:143	002:267	003:151	004:077	005:018	006:070	007:039
075:018	**Surah 98**	002:144	002:268	003:152	004:079	005:021	006:072	007:040
Surah 76	098:008	002:148	002:271	003:153	004:083	005:026	006:073	007:041
076:005	**Surah 103**	002:153	002:272	003:154	004:084	005:028	006:074	007:042
076:027	103:003	002:159	002:273	003:155	004:088	005:029	006:079	007:043
076:030	**Surah 111**	002:160	002:275	003:159	004:090	005:032	006:082	007:050
Surah 77	111:004	002:164	002:276	003:165	004:092	005:033	006:083	007:052
077:010	**Surah 113**	002:165	002:278	003:173	004:093	005:034	006:088	007:053
077:025	113:003	002:167	002:280	003:174	004:094	005:036	006:090	007:055
077:029	113:005	002:168	002:282	003:178	004:096	005:038	006:091	007:056
077:032		002:169	002:283	003:180	004:097	005:039	006:093	007:059
077:033		002:172	002:284	003:182	004:099	005:041	006:094	007:074
077:041	**FOR**	002:173	**Surah 3**	003:183	004:100	005:042	006:096	007:076
Surah 78	**Surah 2**	002:174	003:007	003:185	004:101	005:043	006:097	007:079
078:006	002:003	002:175	003:008	003:188	004:102	005:044	006:098	007:081
078:007	002:016	002:177	003:009	003:190	004:103	005:045	006:099	007:085
078:010	002:020	002:178	003:010	003:191	004:105	005:049	006:100	007:087
078:011	002:022	002:181	003:011	003:194	004:106	005:050	006:104	007:089
078:019	002:024	002:182	003:013	003:197	004:107	005:051	006:112	007:093
078:020	002:025	002:184	003:014	003:198	004:111	005:056	006:114	007:096
078:021	002:029	002:185	003:015	003:199	004:113	005:057	006:115	007:100
078:028	002:036	002:187	003:017	**Surah 4**	004:119	005:059	006:120	007:105
Surah 79	002:037	002:188	003:024	004:001	004:122	005:064	006:124	007:107
079:004	002:041	002:189	003:028	004:002	004:125	005:067	006:126	007:111
079:025	002:048	002:190	003:031	004:006	004:127	005:072	006:127	007:114
079:037	002:050	002:191	003:035	004:007	004:130	005:073	006:128	007:125
079:040	002:051	002:194	003:037	004:009	004:130	005:074	006:131	007:128
079:045	002:052	002:195	003:038	004:011	004:133	005:081	006:132	007:137
079:046	002:053	002:196	003:041	004:013	004:134	005:083	006:136	007:138
Surah 80	002:054	002:197	003:049	004:015	004:135	005:084	006:138	007:140
080:005	002:057	002:199	003:073	004:016	004:138	005:085	006:139	007:142
080:008	002:059	002:206	003:074	004:017	004:139	005:087	006:140	007:145
Surah 81	002:060	002:208	003:077	004:018	004:140	005:088	006:141	007:146
081:017	002:061	002:210	003:079	004:020	004:143	005:089	006:142	007:148
081:018	002:064	002:212	003:080	004:023	004:144	005:089	006:144	007:151
081:029	002:070	002:213	003:083	004:024	004:145	005:093	006:145	007:152
Surah 82	002:074	002:215	003:089	004:025	004:146	005:095	006:146	007:154
082:013	002:079	002:216	003:090	004:028	004:148	005:096	006:150	007:155
Surah 83	002:080	002:219	003:091	004:029	004:151	005:097	006:151	007:155
083:017	002:081	002:220	003:093	004:030	004:152	005:101	006:156	007:156
	002:082	002:222	003:096	004:032	004:153	005:103	006:157	007:157
		002:223	003:103	004:033	004:154	005:104	006:159	007:160

007:162	009:039	010:065	012:009	014:020	016:081	018:020	020:076	022:036
007:163	009:040	010:067	012:018	014:021	016:088	018:029	020:077	022:037
007:169	009:041	010:068	012:019	014:022	016:091	018:031	020:081	022:039
007:179	009:042	010:070	012:020	014:023	016:092	018:032	020:089	022:040
007:180	009:044	010:081	012:024	014:025	016:093	018:038	020:090	022:050
007:183	009:045	010:085	012:025	014:030	016:095	018:046	020:097	022:052
007:193	009:047	010:087	012:029	014:034	016:101	018:050	020:099	022:053
007:196	009:048	010:093	012:031	014:038	016:110	018:051	020:109	022:054
007:200	009:051	010:097	012:035	014:039	016:111	018:052	020:118	022:057
007:203	009:052	010:098	012:036	014:044	016:112	018:054	020:121	022:059
Surah 8	009:053	010:102	012:040	014:047	016:114	018:055	020:122	022:060
008:002	009:060	010:107	012:041	014:052	016:116	018:058	020:124	022:063
008:003	009:061	010:108	012:047	**Surah 15**	016:121	018:059	020:128	022:064
008:014	009:063	010:109	012:048	015:003	016:124	018:068	020:129	022:065
008:017	009:066	**Surah 11**	012:050	015:008	016:125	018:073	020:130	022:067
008:019	009:068	011:003	012:057	015:020	016:126	018:077	020:131	022:070
008:022	009:071	011:005	012:059	015:025	016:127	018:079	020:132	022:071
008:026	009:074	011:008	012:065	015:032	016:128	018:080	**Surah 21**	022:073
008:029	009:080	011:011	012:068	015:034	**Surah 17**	018:082	021:010	022:074
008:033	009:082	011:016	012:070	015:041	017:001	018:090	021:016	022:075
008:038	009:083	011:017	012:072	015:042	017:004	018:100	021:018	022:076
008:041	009:084	011:023	012:075	015:043	017:007	018:102	021:021	022:078
008:043	009:086	011:026	012:076	015:044	017:008	018:107	021:023	**Surah 23**
008:046	009:088	011:029	012:078	015:070	017:010	018:108	021:024	023:006
008:047	009:089	011:037	012:080	015:075	017:011	018:109	021:028	023:011
008:048	009:092	011:041	012:083	015:077	017:013	**Surah 19**	021:031	023:019
008:051	009:095	011:046	012:084	015:085	017:015	019:009	021:044	023:020
008:052	009:098	011:047	012:088	015:086	017:018	019:010	021:047	023:021
008:054	009:099	011:048	012:097	015:093	017:019	019:013	021:048	023:025
008:055	009:100	011:049	012:098	015:095	017:030	019:021	021:069	023:026
008:058	009:102	011:051	012:099	**Surah 16**	017:031	019:024	021:071	023:027
008:061	009:103	011:057	012:100	016:005	017:032	019:039	021:075	023:029
008:063	009:106	011:060	012:104	016:007	017:033	019:044	021:080	023:030
008:065	009:107	011:061	012:109	016:008	017:034	019:046	021:081	023:039
008:066	009:108	011:065	012:111	016:011	017:036	019:047	021:082	023:051
008:067	009:111	011:066	**Surah 13**	016:012	017:037	019:051	021:084	023:054
008:068	009:113	011:068	013:002	016:013	017:040	019:052	021:086	023:057
008:069	009:114	011:072	013:003	016:018	017:048	019:060	021:090	023:065
008:070	009:115	011:073	013:004	016:033	017:053	019:061	021:091	023:072
008:072	009:116	011:074	013:005	016:036	017:054	019:081	021:098	023:078
008:074	009:117	011:075	013:006	016:037	017:057	019:084	021:101	023:092
008:075	009:118	011:076	013:011	016:040	017:060	019:085	021:104	023:109
Surah 9	009:120	011:078	013:014	016:044	017:065	019:092	021:106	023:111
009:002	009:121	011:084	013:016	016:047	017:066	**Surah 20**	021:107	023:115
009:003	009:122	011:086	013:017	016:049	017:070	020:002	021:111	023:118
009:004	009:127	011:090	013:018	016:051	017:076	020:007	**Surah 22**	**Surah 24**
009:005	**Surah 10**	011:091	013:022	016:055	017:078	020:014	022:001	024:004
009:006	010:005	011:092	013:024	016:056	017:079	020:015	022:004	024:005
009:007	010:006	011:093	013:025	016:057	017:081	020:018	022:005	024:006
009:009	010:011	011:103	013:028	016:060	017:087	020:024	022:009	024:010
009:011	010:012	011:104	013:029	016:061	017:090	020:026	022:010	024:011
009:012	010:015	011:106	013:031	016:062	017:095	020:035	022:013	024:014
009:015	010:019	011:107	013:034	016:065	017:096	020:041	022:014	024:018
009:016	010:020	011:111	013:038	016:066	017:097	020:043	022:017	024:020
009:017	010:024	011:112	013:043	016:067	017:100	020:046	022:018	024:021
009:021	010:026	011:114	**Surah 14**	016:069	017:110	020:053	022:019	024:022
009:022	010:027	011:115	014:002	016:070	017:111	020:054	022:024	024:023
009:023	010:029	011:119	014:005	016:072	**Surah 18**	020:068	022:026	024:026
009:025	010:040	011:123	014:010	016:073	018:007	020:071	022:028	024:027
009:027	010:041	**Surah 12**	014:011	016:074	018:010	020:072	022:029	024:028
009:028	010:057	012:005	014:012	016:077	018:011	020:073	022:030	024:029
009:035	010:059	012:006	014:014	016:079	018:015	020:074	022:033	024:030
009:037	010:064	012:007	014:016	016:080	018:017	020:075	022:034	024:032

024:033
024:034
024:035
024:036
024:037
024:038
024:039
024:040
024:044
024:045
024:054
024:055
024:058
024:059
024:060
024:062
024:064
Surah 25
025:008
025:009
025:011
025:013
025:014
025:015
025:016
025:018
025:020
025:021
025:024
025:026
025:028
025:031
025:037
025:039
025:043
025:047
025:054
025:057
025:062
025:065
025:068
025:070
025:077
Surah 26
026:032
026:036
026:038
026:042
026:050
026:052
026:077
026:086
026:100
026:109
026:127
026:129
026:135
026:145
026:164
026:166
026:180
026:204
026:205

026:211
026:220
Surah 27
027:002
027:005
027:006
027:012
027:019
027:021
027:039
027:040
027:043
027:046
027:052
027:059
027:065
027:079
027:086
027:088
027:091
027:092
Surah 28
028:003
028:004
028:006
028:007
028:008
028:009
028:012
028:014
028:015
028:016
028:017
028:018
028:020
028:024
028:025
028:026
028:027
028:031
028:032
028:034
028:038
028:047
028:048
028:050
028:053
028:054
028:057
028:061
028:064
028:070
028:073
028:076
028:077
028:078
028:079
028:080
028:083
028:085
Surah 29
029:005
029:006

029:013
029:015
029:016
029:017
029:019
029:020
029:024
029:025
029:026
029:026
029:031
029:034
029:035
029:040
029:043
029:044
029:045
029:051
029:052
029:053
029:058
029:060
029:062
029:068
029:069
Surah 30
030:008
030:010
030:021
030:022
030:023
030:024
030:027
030:034
030:037
030:038
030:039
030:040
030:044
030:045
030:050
030:058
030:060
Surah 31
031:006
031:008
031:013
031:016
031:017
031:018
031:019
031:023
031:024
031:027
031:028
031:029
031:031
031:033
Surah 32
032:004
032:012
032:014
032:017

032:019
032:027
Surah 33
033:002
033:004
033:008
033:013
033:015
033:017
033:018
033:019
033:021
033:024
033:025
033:028
033:029
033:030
033:031
033:034
033:035
033:036
033:044
033:048
033:050
033:052
033:053
033:055
033:057
033:060
033:064
033:065
033:073
Surah 34
034:004
034:005
034:009
034:010
034:011
034:012
034:013
034:015
034:019
034:023
034:030
034:031
034:033
034:037
034:039
034:042
034:051
034:054
Surah 35
035:001
035:007
035:008
035:010
035:013
035:017
035:018
035:028
035:029
035:030
035:031

035:032
035:034
035:036
035:037
035:039
035:043
035:044
035:045
Surah 36
036:007
036:018
036:021
036:023
036:025
036:027
036:028
036:030
036:032
036:033
036:037
036:038
036:039
036:041
036:042
036:044
036:049
036:057
036:060
036:061
036:064
036:069
036:071
036:074
036:078
036:079
036:079
036:080
036:081
Surah 37
037:007
037:009
037:024
037:032
037:035
037:036
037:041
037:057
037:061
037:063
037:064
037:078
037:081
037:103
037:106
037:108
037:111
037:119
037:122
037:127
037:129
037:132
037:148
037:161

037:165
037:174
037:177
037:178
Surah 38
038:003
038:006
038:015
038:017
038:026
038:030
038:035
038:043
038:046
038:049
038:051
038:053
038:055
038:059
038:060
038:077
038:086
Surah 39
039:003
039:005
039:006
039:007
039:008
039:010
039:017
039:020
039:027
039:032
039:034
039:036
039:038
039:041
039:042
039:043
039:047
039:048
039:052
039:053
039:060
039:061
039:074
Surah 40
040:007
040:008
040:013
040:017
040:021
040:022
040:027
040:030
040:032
040:034
040:037
040:041
040:044
040:049
040:055
040:061

040:064
040:077
040:078
040:079
040:080
040:083
Surah 41
041:003
041:005
041:006
041:008
041:010
041:021
041:024
041:025
041:027
041:028
041:031
041:038
041:039
041:044
041:045
041:049
Surah 42
042:005
042:009
042:011
042:012
042:013
042:014
042:015
042:016
042:021
042:022
042:023
042:024
042:026
042:027
042:030
042:033
042:035
042:036
042:038
042:040
042:042
042:044
042:046
042:047
042:050
042:051
Surah 43
043:005
043:010
043:012
043:013
043:016
043:024
043:033
043:035
043:036
043:042
043:044
043:049

043:049
043:061
043:062
043:064
043:066
043:071
043:072
043:074
043:075
043:078
Surah 44
044:003
044:005
044:006
044:010
044:012
044:015
044:019
044:020
044:023
044:024
044:031
044:039
044:040
044:042
044:055
044:059
Surah 45
045:003
045:004
045:005
045:009
045:010
045:011
045:013
045:014
045:016
045:022
045:026
045:028
045:029
Surah 46
046:003
046:008
046:014
046:015
046:017
046:018
046:020
046:021
046:034
Surah 47
047:002
047:003
047:004
047:008
047:013
047:015
047:018
047:019
047:019
047:020

047:021
047:023
047:035
047:037
Surah 48
048:004
048:005
048:006
048:007
048:011
048:012
048:013
048:020
048:027
048:028
Surah 49
049:001
049:003
049:005
049:006
049:009
049:012
049:014
Surah 50
050:008
050:009
050:011
050:016
050:032
050:035
050:036
050:037
050:044
Surah 51
051:018
051:019
051:020
051:034
051:037
051:043
051:046
051:055
051:058
051:059
Surah 52
052:021
052:026
052:029
052:030
052:040
052:047
052:048
052:049
Surah 53
053:006
053:013
053:018
053:021
053:023
053:026
053:039
053:052

004:084	005:024	006:036	007:009	007:152	009:008	**Surah 10**	011:031	012:073
004:085	005:026	006:038	007:016	007:154	009:010	010:000	011:037	012:075
004:089	005:032	006:039	007:017	007:156	009:011	010:003	011:038	012:077
004:091	005:033	006:042	007:019	007:157	009:015	010:005	011:041	012:078
004:094	005:034	006:043	007:020	007:158	009:017	010:006	011:048	012:080
004:095	005:035	006:044	007:027	007:159	009:018	010:009	011:052	012:082
004:097	005:038	006:051	007:029	007:161	009:019	010:011	011:053	012:083
004:098	005:039	006:052	007:030	007:163	009:020	010:012	011:056	012:095
004:100	005:041	006:054	007:032	007:166	009:024	010:014	011:057	012:099
004:102	005:042	006:055	007:034	007:167	009:025	010:018	011:060	012:100
004:104	005:044	006:057	007:037	007:168	009:027	010:023	011:061	012:101
004:105	005:046	006:058	007:038	007:169	009:029	010:024	011:062	012:102
004:108	005:048	006:059	007:040	007:174	009:030	010:026	011:065	012:105
004:109	005:052	006:060	007:052	007:185	009:034	010:030	011:067	012:106
004:113	005:053	006:061	007:053	007:186	009:035	010:031	011:078	012:110
004:114	005:054	006:062	007:054	007:187	009:036	010:044	011:084	012:111
004:115	005:055	006:063	007:055	007:189	009:037	010:046	011:085	**Surah 13**
004:119	005:059	006:065	007:056	007:190	009:038	010:049	011:088	013:000
004:120	005:060	006:068	007:060	007:205	009:039	010:051	011:090	013:002
004:121	005:061	006:070	007:061	**Surah 8**	009:040	010:054	011:091	013:003
004:125	005:062	006:074	007:064	008:000	009:041	010:055	011:094	013:004
004:126	005:064	006:077	007:067	008:002	009:042	010:057	011:099	013:005
004:127	005:068	006:078	007:069	008:004	009:043	010:058	011:102	013:006
004:129	005:069	006:080	007:073	008:005	009:044	010:061	011:103	013:008
004:131	005:071	006:082	007:074	008:008	009:045	010:064	011:106	013:011
004:132	005:073	006:085	007:075	008:010	009:047	010:066	011:108	013:015
004:134	005:075	006:091	007:076	008:013	009:055	010:067	011:109	013:017
004:136	005:077	006:092	007:078	008:015	009:058	010:068	011:110	013:018
004:137	005:080	006:093	007:080	008:016	009:060	010:070	011:111	013:020
004:140	005:081	006:094	007:081	008:017	009:061	010:071	011:112	013:021
004:142	005:082	006:096	007:084	008:022	009:062	010:072	011:115	013:024
004:145	005:084	006:099	007:085	008:023	009:064	010:073	011:116	013:025
004:148	005:088	006:108	007:086	008:024	009:065	010:078	011:120	013:026
004:150	005:089	006:109	007:087	008:025	009:067	010:083	011:123	013:027
004:151	005:093	006:110	007:089	008:030	009:069	010:084	**Surah 12**	013:028
004:152	005:094	006:111	007:091	008:036	009:071	010:085	012:000	013:030
004:153	005:095	006:113	007:092	008:037	009:072	010:087	012:002	013:031
004:154	005:096	006:114	007:094	008:039	009:074	010:088	012:003	013:034
004:155	005:097	006:115	007:098	008:041	009:075	010:090	012:007	013:037
004:157	005:098	006:118	007:100	008:042	009:081	010:091	012:008	013:041
004:158	005:103	006:119	007:111	008:043	009:084	010:092	012:016	013:042
004:159	005:107	006:122	007:114	008:044	009:085	010:093	012:020	**Surah 14**
004:162	005:108	006:123	007:120	008:045	009:086	010:094	012:021	014:000
004:165	005:109	006:133	007:121	008:048	009:091	010:098	012:023	014:001
004:170	005:110	006:134	007:123	008:049	009:094	010:101	012:030	014:002
004:171	005:111	006:135	007:126	008:052	009:097	010:102	012:031	014:004
004:175	005:116	006:136	007:127	008:053	009:099	010:103	012:034	014:005
Surah 5	005:118	006:137	007:128	008:055	009:100	010:104	012:036	014:009
005:000	**Surah 6**	006:139	007:129	008:057	009:101	010:105	012:037	014:010
005:001	006:000	006:141	007:131	008:060	009:102	**Surah 11**	012:042	014:014
005:002	006:003	006:143	007:132	008:061	009:106	011:000	012:043	014:016
005:003	006:006	006:145	007:133	008:063	009:107	011:001	012:044	014:017
005:004	006:009	006:146	007:134	008:066	009:108	011:003	012:045	014:019
005:005	006:010	006:147	007:136	008:067	009:110	011:006	012:047	014:022
005:006	006:012	006:150	007:137	008:069	009:111	011:007	012:048	014:025
005:007	006:013	006:154	007:139	008:070	009:112	011:009	012:049	014:027
005:011	006:014	006:157	007:141	008:071	009:117	011:016	012:052	014:029
005:012	006:019	006:159	007:143	008:072	009:118	011:017	012:056	014:031
005:015	006:024	006:161	007:145	008:074	009:120	011:020	012:057	014:037
005:019	006:025	006:164	007:146	008:075	009:122	011:021	012:062	014:038
005:020	006:028	006:165	007:147	**Surah 9**	009:123	011:022	012:066	014:039
005:022	006:032	**Surah 7**	007:148	009:004	009:125	011:027	012:068	014:042
005:023	006:035	007:000	007:150	009:005	009:126	011:029	012:070	014:045

Col 1	Col 2	Col 3	Col 4	Col 5	Col 6	Col 7	Col 8	Col 9
029:064	032:002	034:021	037:008	039:029	040:082	043:013	046:028	051:015
029:067	032:003	034:022	037:030	039:031	040:083	043:018	046:029	051:016
029:068	032:004	034:024	037:033	039:032	040:084	043:023	046:031	051:017
029:069	032:006	034:026	037:043	039:035	**Surah 41**	043:031	046:032	051:018
Surah 30	032:007	034:027	037:055	039:037	041:000	043:032	046:035	051:019
030:000	032:009	034:031	037:075	039:038	041:003	043:035	**Surah 47**	051:021
030:003	032:010	034:034	037:078	039:041	041:005	043:039	047:000	051:022
030:004	032:011	034:035	037:082	039:042	041:009	043:040	047:002	051:032
030:005	032:015	034:037	037:102	039:044	041:010	043:048	047:004	051:038
030:007	032:016	034:039	037:108	039:045	041:011	043:053	047:015	051:041
030:008	032:017	034:041	037:119	039:046	041:012	043:057	047:019	051:043
030:009	032:021	034:046	037:129	039:047	041:014	043:063	047:020	051:052
030:010	032:023	034:052	037:145	039:052	041:015	043:069	047:022	**Surah 52**
030:015	032:024	034:054	037:165	039:054	041:016	043:070	047:026	052:000
030:017	032:025	**Surah 35**	**Surah 38**	039:056	041:019	043:071	047:029	052:003
030:018	032:026	035:000	038:000	039:060	041:026	043:072	047:031	052:009
030:021	**Surah 33**	035:002	038:002	039:063	041:030	043:074	047:032	052:012
030:022	033:000	035:008	038:003	039:065	041:031	043:075	047:035	052:017
030:023	033:003	035:011	038:007	039:067	041:033	043:084	047:038	052:020
030:024	033:004	035:016	038:008	039:068	041:036	**Surah 44**	**Surah 48**	052:021
030:026	033:005	035:022	038:009	039:069	041:038	044:000	048:000	052:025
030:027	033:006	035:024	038:017	039:070	041:040	044:004	048:005	052:041
030:028	033:011	035:026	038:018	039:071	041:044	044:009	048:007	052:042
030:030	033:012	035:027	038:019	039:073	041:045	044:033	048:009	052:044
030:031	033:020	035:028	038:020	039:074	041:046	044:038	048:010	052:048
030:032	033:021	035:029	038:023	**Surah 40**	041:048	044:041	048:011	**Surah 53**
030:033	033:022	035:032	038:024	040:000	041:049	044:042	048:012	053:000
030:036	033:023	035:035	038:026	040:002	041:050	044:045	048:013	053:005
030:037	033:024	035:038	038:030	040:003	041:052	044:051	048:015	053:006
030:039	033:025	035:039	038:032	040:007	041:053	044:053	048:018	053:007
030:041	033:028	035:040	038:034	040:008	041:054	044:055	048:019	053:011
030:043	033:031	035:043	038:038	040:015	**Surah 42**	044:058	048:023	053:026
030:044	033:032	035:044	038:044	040:017	042:000	**Surah 45**	048:024	053:027
030:046	033:033	035:045	038:047	040:020	042:003	045:000	048:026	053:031
030:048	033:034	**Surah 36**	038:051	040:021	042:004	045:002	048:029	053:032
030:053	033:035	036:000	038:059	040:022	042:007	045:003	**Surah 49**	053:036
030:054	033:037	036:005	038:060	040:025	042:010	045:004	049:000	053:040
030:058	033:038	036:006	038:061	040:026	042:013	045:005	049:002	053:045
Surah 31	033:048	036:009	038:063	040:027	042:014	045:006	049:003	053:046
031:000	033:049	036:012	038:066	040:029	042:015	045:009	049:007	053:061
031:004	033:050	036:024	038:072	040:030	042:016	045:010	049:012	053:062
031:007	033:051	036:025	**Surah 39**	040:034	042:017	045:013	049:013	**Surah 54**
031:009	033:053	036:027	039:000	040:035	042:018	045:015	049:015	054:000
031:010	033:057	036:036	039:001	040:037	042:020	045:017	049:016	054:024
031:011	033:060	036:037	039:002	040:042	042:021	045:019	**Surah 50**	054:027
031:012	033:062	036:038	039:003	040:043	042:022	045:022	050:000	054:029
031:013	033:066	036:040	039:005	040:046	042:023	045:024	050:005	054:043
031:014	033:069	036:041	039:006	040:047	042:027	045:035	050:006	054:047
031:015	033:073	036:045	039:007	040:048	042:033	045:037	050:007	054:049
031:016	**Surah 34**	036:047	039:008	040:049	042:036	**Surah 46**	050:014	054:051
031:017	034:000	036:054	039:009	040:050	042:040	046:000	050:015	054:052
031:018	034:001	036:055	039:010	040:051	042:044	046:002	050:019	054:054
031:019	034:003	036:056	039:012	040:053	042:045	046:004	050:028	054:055
031:020	034:006	036:059	039:015	040:055	042:053	046:005	050:033	**Surah 55**
031:023	034:007	036:067	039:017	040:056	**Surah 43**	046:012	050:034	055:000
031:024	034:008	036:068	039:019	040:066	043:000	046:015	050:036	055:006
031:026	034:009	036:069	039:020	040:067	043:003	046:016	050:037	055:008
031:027	034:012	036:083	039:021	040:072	043:004	046:019	050:038	055:009
031:028	034:013	**Surah 37**	039:022	040:074	043:008	046:020	050:042	055:029
031:031	034:014	037:000	039:023	040:075	043:009	046:022	**Surah 51**	055:044
031:034	034:015	037:001	039:026	040:077	043:010	046:023	051:000	055:048
Surah 32	034:018	037:002	039:027	040:078	043:011	046:026	051:011	055:050
032:000	034:019	037:006	039:028	040:080	043:012	046:027		

002:262	003:098	004:025	004:147	005:103	006:102	007:146	008:075	009:117
002:263	003:099	004:026	004:148	005:104	006:103	007:150	**Surah 9**	009:118
002:264	003:101	004:027	004:149	005:105	006:106	007:153	009:005	009:121
002:265	003:104	004:030	004:152	005:107	006:111	007:155	009:006	009:122
002:266	003:105	004:032	004:155	005:108	006:114	007:156	009:010	009:123
002:267	003:109	004:033	004:158	005:109	006:115	007:157	009:013	009:124
002:269	003:110	004:034	004:159	005:110	006:119	007:158	009:015	009:125
002:271	003:112	004:035	004:165	005:116	006:122	007:159	009:016	009:128
002:273	003:114	004:038	004:166	005:119	006:126	007:167	009:017	009:129
002:275	003:117	004:040	004:169	005:120	006:128	007:169	009:018	**Surah 10**
002:280	003:118	004:045	004:170	**Surah 6**	006:132	007:171	009:022	010:002
002:282	003:120	004:048	004:171	006:002	006:133	007:176	009:025	010:003
002:283	003:124	004:050	004:174	006:003	006:135	007:178	009:027	010:004
002:284	003:126	004:055	004:176	006:007	006:136	007:183	009:028	010:005
002:285	003:128	004:056	**Surah 5**	006:008	006:138	007:184	009:030	010:008
Surah 3	003:129	004:058	005:002	006:012	006:139	007:185	009:031	010:015
003:002	003:131	004:059	005:003	006:013	006:141	007:187	009:033	010:018
003:003	003:133	004:060	005:004	006:014	006:142	007:189	009:035	010:020
003:004	003:136	004:061	005:005	006:016	006:145	007:190	009:036	010:021
003:005	003:138	004:063	005:008	006:018	006:146	007:193	009:037	010:022
003:006	003:141	004:069	005:008	006:019	006:147	007:196	009:038	010:023
003:007	003:144	004:070	005:014	006:029	006:149	007:199	009:040	010:024
003:009	003:150	004:074	005:015	006:030	006:152	007:203	009:041	010:025
003:011	003:151	004:075	005:016	006:031	006:153	007:204	009:049	010:026
003:013	003:152	004:076	005:017	006:032	006:155	**Surah 8**	009:051	010:029
003:014	003:153	004:077	005:018	006:033	006:159	008:002	009:055	010:031
003:015	003:154	004:078	005:028	006:034	006:161	008:010	009:059	010:032
003:018	003:155	004:079	005:029	006:035	006:164	008:013	009:060	010:033
003:019	003:156	004:081	005:031	006:037	006:165	008:014	009:061	010:034
003:020	003:158	004:084	005:033	006:038	**Surah 7**	008:016	009:062	010:035
003:025	003:159	004:086	005:034	006:039	007:003	008:017	009:063	010:036
003:026	003:160	004:087	005:038	006:050	007:010	008:018	009:064	010:037
003:028	003:162	004:089	005:039	006:051	007:011	008:019	009:068	010:044
003:029	003:165	004:090	005:041	006:053	007:013	008:023	009:070	010:046
003:030	003:170	004:092	005:043	006:054	007:026	008:024	009:071	010:049
003:031	003:173	004:093	005:045	006:057	007:028	008:025	009:072	010:053
003:035	003:174	004:094	005:048	006:059	007:034	008:028	009:073	010:054
003:036	003:175	004:096	005:049	006:060	007:037	008:029	009:080	010:055
003:038	003:176	004:099	005:050	006:061	007:038	008:030	009:081	010:056
003:040	003:178	004:100	005:051	006:062	007:040	008:032	009:085	010:058
003:044	003:179	004:101	005:052	006:063	007:041	008:035	009:088	010:060
003:047	003:180	004:102	005:054	006:064	007:044	008:038	009:089	010:061
003:049	003:181	004:104	005:056	006:066	007:053	008:039	009:091	010:062
003:051	003:182	004:106	005:058	006:067	007:054	008:040	009:092	010:064
003:054	003:185	004:108	005:064	006:069	007:056	008:041	009:093	010:065
003:058	003:186	004:111	005:066	006:070	007:057	008:042	009:094	010:067
003:059	003:188	004:112	005:068	006:071	007:058	008:046	009:095	010:068
003:062	003:195	004:113	005:072	006:072	007:061	008:048	009:096	010:072
003:066	003:197	004:114	005:073	006:073	007:062	008:049	009:097	010:076
003:067	003:198	004:119	005:074	006:076	007:067	008:051	009:098	010:077
003:068	003:199	004:122	005:076	006:077	007:073	008:052	009:099	010:081
003:069	**Surah 4**	004:126	005:077	006:078	007:075	008:053	009:100	010:089
003:072	004:002	004:127	005:080	006:082	007:087	008:061	009:102	010:090
003:073	004:006	004:128	005:085	006:083	007:089	008:062	009:103	010:101
003:074	004:007	004:129	005:089	006:088	007:100	008:063	009:104	010:103
003:075	004:011	004:130	005:091	006:090	007:105	008:064	009:105	010:107
003:078	004:012	004:131	005:093	006:092	007:109	008:066	009:106	010:109
003:079	004:016	004:132	005:095	006:095	007:110	008:067	009:107	**Surah 11**
003:081	004:017	004:134	005:096	006:096	007:123	008:069	009:108	011:001
003:087	004:018	004:135	005:097	006:097	007:128	008:070	009:109	011:004
003:089	004:022	004:138	005:098	006:098	007:131	008:071	009:110	011:006
003:091	004:023	004:139	005:099	006:099	007:139	008:072	009:111	011:007
003:097	004:024	004:142	005:101	006:100	007:140	008:074	009:113	011:009

011:010	012:076	014:036	016:082	018:008	020:063	022:025	023:101	025:031
011:011	012:080	014:038	016:095	018:014	020:069	022:030	023:102	025:032
011:012	012:083	014:039	016:096	018:017	020:073	022:031	023:103	025:041
011:014	012:084	014:047	016:097	018:019	020:074	022:032	023:116	025:042
011:016	012:090	014:051	016:100	018:021	020:076	022:033	**Surah 24**	025:047
011:017	012:092	014:052	016:103	018:022	020:088	022:034	024:003	025:048
011:018	012:098	**Surah 15**	016:104	018:026	020:090	022:035	024:005	025:053
011:029	012:100	015:006	016:105	018:029	020:095	022:036	024:006	025:054
011:031	012:102	015:016	016:106	018:038	020:098	022:037	024:008	025:055
011:034	012:104	015:018	016:110	018:039	020:109	022:038	024:009	025:058
011:039	012:109	015:021	016:114	018:042	020:110	022:039	024:010	025:059
011:041	012:111	015:023	016:115	018:044	020:112	022:039	024:011	025:060
011:045	**Surah 13**	015:025	016:116	018:045	020:114	022:040	024:012	025:061
011:046	013:001	015:032	016:117	018:049	020:117	022:046	024:016	025:062
011:049	013:002	015:037	016:119	018:051	020:118	022:047	024:018	025:065
011:051	013:003	015:041	016:126	018:054	020:123	022:048	024:020	025:066
011:056	013:005	015:043	016:127	018:055	020:124	022:050	024:021	025:070
011:061	013:006	015:044	016:128	018:057	020:127	022:052	024:022	**Surah 26**
011:064	013:007	015:054	**Surah 17**	018:058	020:128	022:053	024:023	026:008
011:066	013:008	015:057	017:001	018:078	020:129	022:054	024:025	026:009
011:072	013:009	015:077	017:009	018:082	020:131	022:058	024:026	026:022
011:073	013:010	015:085	017:011	018:095	020:132	022:059	024:027	026:023
011:077	013:011	015:086	017:014	018:098	020:135	022:060	024:028	026:027
011:078	013:012	015:097	017:016	018:106	**Surah 21**	022:061	024:029	026:034
011:081	013:013	015:099	017:017	018:110	021:003	022:062	024:030	026:035
011:086	013:014	**Surah 16**	017:021	**Surah 19**	021:004	022:063	024:032	026:044
011:087	013:016	016:001	017:025	019:002	021:005	022:064	024:033	026:049
011:090	013:017	016:002	017:027	019:005	021:015	022:065	024:035	026:051
011:092	013:018	016:003	017:031	019:008	021:016	022:066	024:036	026:062
011:093	013:019	016:007	017:032	019:009	021:022	022:068	024:037	026:067
011:099	013:022	016:010	017:033	019:021	021:024	022:070	024:039	026:068
011:102	013:024	016:011	017:035	019:029	021:025	022:071	024:040	026:078
011:103	013:025	016:013	017:038	019:033	021:028	022:072	024:041	026:080
011:107	013:026	016:014	017:043	019:034	021:033	022:073	024:042	026:086
011:114	013:027	016:017	017:044	019:035	021:036	022:074	024:043	026:103
011:123	013:029	016:018	017:047	019:036	021:037	022:075	024:044	026:104
Surah 12	013:030	016:022	017:051	019:040	021:044	022:076	024:046	026:111
012:005	013:031	016:024	017:053	019:043	021:050	022:078	024:049	026:113
012:006	013:033	016:029	017:054	019:044	021:056	**Surah 23**	024:050	026:121
012:008	013:034	016:030	017:055	019:047	021:060	023:024	024:051	026:122
012:018	013:035	016:035	017:057	019:063	021:087	023:025	024:052	026:127
012:019	013:036	016:037	017:058	019:064	021:092	023:033	024:053	026:136
012:023	013:038	016:038	017:062	019:065	021:095	023:034	024:054	026:137
012:025	013:039	016:040	017:065	019:071	021:103	023:036	024:057	026:139
012:026	013:040	016:044	017:066	019:073	021:106	023:037	024:058	026:140
012:027	013:041	016:047	017:067	019:075	021:108	023:038	024:059	026:145
012:028	013:042	016:049	017:078	019:092	021:109	023:044	024:060	026:155
012:030	013:043	016:051	017:081	**Surah 20**	021:110	023:052	024:061	026:158
012:031	**Surah 14**	016:052	017:082	020:005	021:112	023:053	024:062	026:159
012:032	014:004	016:053	017:084	020:006	**Surah 22**	023:061	024:064	026:164
012:033	014:007	016:058	017:085	020:007	022:004	023:062	**Surah 25**	026:174
012:037	014:008	016:060	017:087	020:008	022:005	023:070	025:001	026:175
012:040	014:010	016:062	017:096	020:014	022:006	023:072	025:002	026:180
012:047	014:011	016:063	017:097	020:015	022:008	023:075	025:004	026:190
012:050	014:016	016:065	017:098	020:017	022:009	023:078	025:006	026:191
012:051	014:018	016:066	017:099	020:018	022:010	023:078	025:007	026:192
012:053	014:020	016:067	017:100	020:036	022:011	023:080	025:010	026:196
012:057	014:021	016:069	017:106	020:039	022:012	023:086	025:015	026:197
012:064	014:022	016:076	017:107	020:049	022:013	023:088	025:020	026:211
012:065	014:024	016:077	017:110	020:050	022:017	023:091	025:021	026:220
012:071	014:026	016:078	**Surah 18**	020:051	022:018	023:092	025:022	026:221
012:072	014:032	016:080	018:005	020:052	022:020	023:096	025:028	026:224
012:075	014:034	016:081	018:007	020:059	022:024	023:100	025:029	

Surah 27	Surah 29	031:023	034:027	037:035	039:038	041:034	043:061	047:024
027:005	029:004	031:025	034:030	037:041	039:040	041:036	043:062	047:029
027:013	029:005	031:026	034:037	037:058	039:042	041:037	043:064	047:035
027:016	029:006	031:027	034:039	037:060	039:044	041:039	043:076	047:036
027:020	029:010	031:028	034:043	037:062	039:045	041:040	043:079	047:038
027:025	029:018	031:029	034:046	037:064	039:046	041:041	043:082	Surah 48
027:026	029:019	031:030	034:047	037:085	039:047	041:042	043:084	048:004
027:029	029:023	031:033	034:048	037:086	039:049	041:043	043:085	048:005
027:030	029:026	031:034	034:050	037:087	039:053	041:044	Surah 44	048:006
027:033	029:032	Surah 32	034:054	037:092	039:056	041:046	044:004	048:007
027:036	029:033	032:002	Surah 35	037:102	039:060	041:047	044:008	048:010
027:040	029:041	032:003	035:002	037:149	039:062	041:049	044:035	048:011
027:041	029:042	032:004	035:003	037:154	039:063	041:050	044:036	048:014
027:042	029:044	032:005	035:005	037:159	039:064	041:052	044:040	048:017
027:044	029:045	032:018	035:006	037:180	039:067	041:053	044:042	048:019
027:047	029:046	Surah 33	035:007	Surah 38	039:072	041:054	044:050	048:024
027:052	029:047	033:001	035:008	038:001	Surah 40	Surah 42	Surah 45	048:028
027:054	029:051	033:002	035:009	038:004	040:002	042:004	045:002	048:029
027:059	029:052	033:003	035:010	038:005	040:003	042:005	045:008	Surah 49
027:060	029:056	033:004	035:011	038:006	040:010	042:007	045:010	049:001
027:062	029:060	033:005	035:013	038:007	040:011	042:009	045:011	049:003
027:063	029:063	033:006	035:014	038:023	040:012	042:010	045:012	049:005
027:065	029:064	033:012	035:015	038:026	040:013	042:011	045:013	049:007
027:068	029:067	033:017	035:017	038:029	040:015	042:013	045:014	049:008
027:073	029:068	033:019	035:018	038:030	040:016	042:015	045:015	049:011
027:075	029:069	033:022	035:028	038:042	040:017	042:016	045:019	049:012
027:077	Surah 30	033:024	035:030	038:044	040:018	042:017	045:021	049:013
027:078	030:004	033:025	035:031	038:049	040:020	042:018	045:024	049:014
027:082	030:005	033:030	035:032	038:053	040:022	042:019	045:025	049:016
027:088	030:006	033:031	035:034	038:059	040:026	042:023	045:026	Surah 50
027:093	030:011	033:032	035:037	038:060	040:028	042:025	045:027	050:002
Surah 28	030:019	033:034	035:038	038:062	040:029	042:026	045:032	050:003
028:009	030:020	033:036	035:039	038:064	040:033	042:027	045:034	050:004
028:013	030:021	033:037	035:040	038:065	040:035	042:028	045:037	050:011
028:015	030:022	033:038	035:041	038:067	040:037	042:029	Surah 46	050:018
028:016	030:023	033:039	035:044	038:080	040:039	042:030	046:002	050:022
028:019	030:024	033:040	Surah 36	038:084	040:040	042:033	046:004	050:023
028:023	030:025	033:043	036:005	038:087	040:041	042:035	046:005	050:032
028:026	030:026	033:048	036:007	Surah 39	040:050	042:036	046:007	050:034
028:034	030:027	033:050	036:010	039:001	040:055	042:039	046:008	050:035
028:036	030:030	033:051	036:017	039:002	040:056	042:040	046:009	050:037
028:037	030:032	033:052	036:033	039:003	040:057	042:041	046:011	050:043
028:038	030:038	033:053	036:037	039:004	040:059	042:042	046:013	Surah 51
028:045	030:039	033:055	036:038	039:005	040:061	042:044	046:015	051:005
028:049	030:040	033:059	036:040	039:006	040:062	042:046	046:017	051:014
028:050	030:043	033:060	036:041	039:007	040:064	042:048	046:023	051:019
028:053	030:046	033:063	036:045	039:009	040:065	042:050	046:024	051:022
028:056	030:048	033:073	036:048	039:010	040:067	042:051	046:033	051:023
028:060	030:054	Surah 34	036:052	039:014	040:068	042:053	046:034	051:030
028:061	030:056	034:001	036:063	039:015	040:076	Surah 43	Surah 47	051:031
028:068	030:060	034:002	036:069	039:017	040:077	043:004	047:002	051:053
028:070	Surah 31	034:003	036:077	039:019	040:079	043:011	047:004	051:054
028:071	031:009	034:004	036:081	039:020	Surah 41	043:015	047:008	051:058
028:072	031:011	034:006	036:082	039:021	041:005	043:017	047:009	051:059
028:073	031:012	034:008	036:083	039:022	041:006	043:018	047:011	Surah 52
028:075	031:013	034:009	Surah 37	039:023	041:008	043:030	047:014	052:008
028:079	031:014	034:019	037:004	039:024	041:009	043:031	047:015	052:014
028:080	031:015	034:019	037:009	039:026	041:012	043:032	047:016	052:015
028:082	031:016	034:021	037:015	039:028	041:015	043:035	047:019	052:016
028:083	031:017	034:022	037:020	039:032	041:025	043:038	047:020	052:021
028:084	031:019	034:023	037:021	039:034	041:028	043:044	047:021	052:028
028:085	031:021	034:024	037:025	039:036	041:030	043:052	047:022	052:032
028:088	031:022	034:026	037:034	039:037	041:033	043:057		

052:040	**Surah 57**	061:009	067:026	074:027	083:020	097:003	002:058	002:149
052:041	057:001	061:012	067:027	074:031	**Surah 84**	**Surah 98**	002:060	002:150
052:043	057:002	**Surah 62**	067:029	074:035	084:001	098:005	002:061	002:151
052:047	057:003	062:001	**Surah 68**	074:047	084:003	098:008	002:064	002:154
Surah 53	057:004	062:002	068:003	074:049	084:004	**Surah 99**	002:065	002:155
053:002	057:007	062:003	068:006	074:054	084:007	099:001	002:067	002:158
053:004	057:008	062:004	068:007	074:056	084:010	099:003	002:068	002:159
053:015	057:009	062:005	068:009	**Surah 75**	084:020	**Surah 100**	002:069	002:161
053:026	057:010	062:009	068:033	075:006	084:021	100:006	002:073	002:164
053:030	057:011	062:010	068:036	075:007	084:025	100:008	002:074	002:165
053:031	057:012	062:011	068:046	075:008	**Surah 85**	100:009	002:075	002:166
053:032	057:015	**Surah 63**	068:047	075:010	085:009	100:010	002:076	002:167
053:036	057:020	063:003	068:051	075:017	085:011	**Surah 101**	002:080	002:168
053:042	057:021	063:004	068:052	075:019	085:012	101:002	002:081	002:169
053:043	057:022	063:005	**Surah 69**	075:027	085:013	101:003	002:082	002:170
053:044	057:024	063:006	069:002	**Surah 76**	085:014	101:004	002:083	002:171
053:048	057:025	063:011	069:003	076:020	085:021	101:010	002:085	002:172
053:049	057:028	**Surah 64**	069:013	076:022	**Surah 86**	101:011	002:086	002:173
053:050	057:029	064:001	069:014	076:023	086:002	**Surah 103**	002:087	002:174
053:056	**Surah 58**	064:002	069:032	076:028	086:003	103:002	002:089	002:175
Surah 54	058:002	064:003	069:040	076:029	086:004	**Surah 104**	002:090	002:176
054:001	058:003	064:004	069:041	076:030	086:005	104:006	002:090	002:177
054:002	058:004	064:006	069:042	**Surah 77**	086:006	**Surah 107**	002:091	002:178
054:008	058:006	064:007	069:043	077:009	086:008	107:002	002:093	002:179
054:009	058:007	064:008	069:048	077:014	086:013	**Surah 110**	002:095	002:180
054:015	058:008	064:010	069:050	077:031	086:014	110:003	002:096	002:182
054:017	058:011	064:012	069:051	077:048	**Surah 87**	**Surah 112**	002:097	002:184
054:022	058:012	064:013	**Surah 70**	**Surah 78**	087:007	112:001	002:100	002:185
054:025	058:013	064:014	070:002	078:017	087:017	112:003	002:101	002:186
054:026	058:019	064:015	070:004	078:021	**Surah 88**		002:102	002:187
054:028	058:021	064:017	070:014	078:038	088:018		002:104	002:188
054:032	058:022	064:018	070:024	078:039	088:020	**OF**	002:105	002:189
054:040	**Surah 59**	**Surah 65**	070:025	**Surah 79**	**Surah 89**	**Surah 1**	002:106	002:190
054:046	059:001	065:002	070:028	079:026	089:005	001:001	002:107	002:191
054:050	059:002	065:003	070:036	079:044	089:014	001:002	002:108	002:194
054:051	059:004	065:004	070:044	**Surah 80**	089:021	001:004	002:109	002:195
054:052	059:007	065:005	**Surah 71**	080:007	089:023	001:007	002:112	002:196
054:053	059:008	065:006	071:004	080:011	**Surah 90**	**Surah 2**	002:113	002:197
Surah 55	059:011	065:012	071:010	080:013	090:011	002:000	002:114	002:198
055:002	059:013	**Surah 66**	071:013	080:022	090:012	002:003	002:117	002:200
055:010	059:014	066:001	071:014	**Surah 81**	090:013	002:004	002:118	002:204
055:011	059:015	066:002	**Surah 72**	081:001	**Surah 91**	002:008	002:119	002:204
055:017	059:017	066:003	072:003	081:008	091:013	002:012	002:120	002:207
055:020	059:018	066:004	072:005	081:011	091:015	002:013	002:122	002:208
055:026	059:020	066:006	072:010	081:012	**Surah 92**	002:017	002:124	002:210
055:037	059:022	066:009	072:016	081:013	092:008	002:019	002:125	002:211
055:043	059:023	**Surah 67**	072:021	081:019	092:019	002:020	002:126	002:212
055:060	059:024	067:001	072:023	081:022	**Surah 93**	002:024	002:127	002:213
Surah 56	**Surah 60**	067:002	072:024	081:025	093:002	002:026	002:128	002:214
056:033	060:004	067:006	072:025	081:027	093:003	002:029	002:129	002:217
056:057	060:006	067:008	072:028	**Surah 82**	**Surah 94**	002:031	002:130	002:218
056:059	060:007	067:012	**Surah 73**	082:001	094:005	002:032	002:131	002:221
056:064	060:009	067:014	073:006	082:017	094:006	002:033	002:132	002:229
056:072	060:010	067:015	073:007	082:018	**Surah 95**	002:034	002:133	002:230
056:076	060:012	067:016	073:009	**Surah 83**	095:008	002:035	002:134	002:231
056:077	060:013	067:017	073:019	083:007	**Surah 96**	002:036	002:135	002:232
056:081	**Surah 61**	067:019	073:020	083:008	096:003	002:039	002:136	002:233
056:089	061:001	067:020	**Surah 74**	083:009	096:008	002:040	002:140	002:234
056:091	061:003	067:021	074:008	083:014	096:011	002:047	002:141	002:235
056:093	061:006	067:022	074:015	083:017	**Surah 97**	002:049	002:143	002:236
056:095	061:007	067:023	074:024	083:018	097:002	002:054	002:144	002:237
	061:008	067:024	074:025	083:019		002:057	002:145	002:238
							002:146	002:240

002:243	003:039	003:135	004:023	004:131	005:045	006:025	006:133	007:057
002:244	003:041	003:137	004:024	004:134	005:046	006:027	006:136	007:058
002:246	003:042	003:140	004:025	004:135	005:047	006:032	006:137	007:059
002:248	003:044	003:141	004:026	004:136	005:048	006:033	006:138	007:060
002:248	003:045	003:142	004:027	004:140	005:049	006:034	006:139	007:061
002:249	003:046	003:146	004:031	004:141	005:050	006:037	006:141	007:062
002:251	003:049	003:148	004:032	004:142	005:051	006:038	006:142	007:063
002:252	003:050	003:150	004:034	004:145	005:052	006:039	006:143	007:065
002:253	003:052	003:151	004:036	004:146	005:054	006:040	006:144	007:066
002:254	003:054	003:152	004:038	004:148	005:056	006:044	006:145	007:067
002:255	003:055	003:153	004:039	004:152	005:059	006:045	006:146	007:068
002:257	003:058	003:154	004:043	004:153	005:060	006:047	006:147	007:069
002:259	003:059	003:155	004:044	004:154	005:062	006:050	006:148	007:072
002:260	003:060	003:156	004:045	004:155	005:063	006:052	006:150	007:073
002:261	003:061	003:157	004:046	004:157	005:064	006:053	006:151	007:075
002:262	003:063	003:159	004:047	004:159	005:065	006:054	006:152	007:077
002:263	003:064	003:161	004:051	004:160	005:066	006:055	006:158	007:082
002:263	003:065	003:162	004:054	004:164	005:068	006:056	006:159	007:083
002:264	003:066	003:163	004:055	004:165	005:070	006:057	006:161	007:084
002:265	003:068	003:164	004:057	004:167	005:071	006:059	006:162	007:085
002:266	003:069	003:166	004:062	004:169	005:072	006:060	006:163	007:086
002:267	003:070	003:167	004:063	004:171	005:073	006:061	006:164	007:089
002:269	003:071	003:168	004:064	004:173	005:075	006:063	006:165	007:095
002:271	003:072	003:169	004:066	004:176	005:077	006:065	**Surah 7**	007:096
002:272	003:073	003:171	004:069	**Surah 5**	005:078	006:067	007:000	007:097
002:273	003:074	003:172	004:073	005:000	005:080	006:068	007:003	007:099
002:274	003:075	003:174	004:074	005:001	005:081	006:070	007:008	007:101
002:275	003:077	003:175	004:075	005:002	005:084	006:071	007:010	007:102
002:276	003:078	003:177	004:076	005:003	005:085	006:075	007:011	007:103
002:277	003:078	003:179	004:077	005:004	005:086	006:078	007:013	007:104
002:278	003:079	003:180	004:081	005:005	005:088	006:081	007:016	007:105
002:279	003:081	003:181	004:083	005:006	005:089	006:083	007:017	007:109
002:280	003:083	003:181	004:084	005:007	005:090	006:085	007:018	007:110
002:282	003:085	003:182	004:086	005:008	005:091	006:088	007:019	007:113
002:283	003:087	003:184	004:087	005:009	005:092	006:090	007:022	007:116
002:285	003:090	003:185	004:088	005:010	005:093	006:091	007:024	007:118
Surah 3	003:092	003:186	004:089	005:011	005:094	006:092	007:026	007:121
003:000	003:093	003:187	004:090	005:012	005:095	006:093	007:027	007:122
003:003	003:095	003:189	004:091	005:013	005:096	006:096	007:028	007:126
003:004	003:096	003:190	004:092	005:014	005:097	006:097	007:029	007:127
003:007	003:097	003:191	004:093	005:015	005:100	006:099	007:030	007:128
003:008	003:098	003:193	004:094	005:016	005:103	006:101	007:031	007:130
003:011	003:099	003:194	004:095	005:017	005:104	006:102	007:032	007:131
003:013	003:100	003:195	004:097	005:018	005:105	006:104	007:033	007:134
003:014	003:101	003:196	004:100	005:019	005:106	006:107	007:035	007:137
003:015	003:102	003:199	004:102	005:020	005:107	006:108	007:036	007:138
003:015	003:103	**Surah 4**	004:104	005:022	005:110	006:109	007:037	007:141
003:016	003:104	004:000	004:106	005:026	005:112	006:111	007:038	007:142
003:017	003:106	004:001	004:107	005:027	005:114	006:112	007:039	007:144
003:018	003:107	004:003	004:109	005:028	005:115	006:113	007:040	007:145
003:019	003:108	004:005	004:111	005:029	005:116	006:114	007:041	007:146
003:020	003:110	004:006	004:113	005:030	005:119	006:115	007:042	007:148
003:021	003:112	004:008	004:114	005:031	005:120	006:116	007:043	007:150
003:023	003:113	004:009	004:115	005:032	**Surah 6**	006:118	007:044	007:151
003:026	003:114	004:010	004:116	005:033	006:000	006:119	007:045	007:154
003:027	003:115	004:011	004:118	005:035	006:004	006:121	007:046	007:155
003:028	003:116	004:012	004:119	005:036	006:005	006:122	007:047	007:158
003:030	003:117	004:015	004:121	005:037	006:006	006:126	007:048	007:159
003:033	003:119	004:016	004:122	005:038	006:011	006:127	007:050	007:160
003:034	003:122	004:017	004:123	005:040	006:012	006:128	007:051	007:161
003:035	003:126	004:018	004:124	005:042	006:014	006:129	007:053	007:163
003:036	003:127	004:019	004:125	005:043	006:015	006:130	007:054	007:164
003:037	003:133	004:020	004:130	005:044	006:019	006:132	007:056	007:167

007:169	009:004	009:103	010:087	011:070	012:050	013:028	015:038	016:071
007:170	009:005	009:104	010:088	011:071	012:051	013:029	015:044	016:072
007:172	009:006	009:105	010:089	011:073	012:052	013:031	015:045	016:073
007:173	009:008	009:106	010:090	011:074	012:053	013:033	015:047	016:075
007:175	009:009	009:107	010:092	011:075	012:054	013:034	015:048	016:076
007:176	009:010	009:108	010:093	011:076	012:055	013:035	015:051	016:077
007:179	009:012	009:109	010:094	011:078	012:056	013:037	015:052	016:078
007:181	009:014	009:110	010:095	011:079	012:057	013:038	015:053	016:079
007:185	009:015	009:111	010:096	011:081	012:059	013:039	015:054	016:080
007:187	009:016	009:112	010:098	011:084	012:060	013:040	015:056	016:081
007:188	009:017	009:113	010:100	011:088	012:063	013:042	015:057	016:081
007:189	009:018	009:115	010:102	011:089	012:064	013:043	015:059	016:083
007:201	009:019	009:116	010:104	011:090	012:065	**Surah 14**	015:061	016:088
007:205	009:020	009:117	010:105	011:091	012:068	014:000	015:063	016:090
Surah 8	009:021	009:120	010:106	011:092	012:069	014:001	015:065	016:091
008:000	009:022	009:124	010:107	011:093	012:072	014:002	015:066	016:092
008:001	009:023	009:125	010:108	011:097	012:074	014:003	015:067	016:094
008:003	009:025	009:129	**Surah 11**	011:098	012:076	014:004	015:078	016:095
008:004	009:028	**Surah 10**	011:000	011:099	012:077	014:005	015:080	016:096
008:005	009:029	010:000	011:001	011:100	012:078	014:006	015:082	016:097
008:007	009:030	010:001	011:003	011:101	012:080	014:008	015:083	016:101
008:009	009:031	010:002	011:005	011:102	012:083	014:009	015:084	016:103
008:010	009:033	010:004	011:007	011:103	012:085	014:009	015:088	016:104
008:011	009:034	010:005	011:009	011:105	012:086	014:010	015:090	016:105
008:012	009:035	010:006	011:010	011:106	012:087	014:011	015:092	016:107
008:014	009:036	010:007	011:011	011:107	012:090	014:013	015:098	016:112
008:016	009:037	010:008	011:012	011:111	012:091	014:015	**Surah 16**	016:113
008:017	009:038	010:009	011:014	011:114	012:092	014:016	016:000	016:114
008:018	009:040	010:010	011:015	011:115	012:093	014:017	016:001	016:115
008:022	009:041	010:012	011:016	011:116	012:094	014:018	016:002	016:121
008:025	009:048	010:015	011:017	011:119	012:096	014:021	016:005	016:122
008:027	009:052	010:018	011:018	011:120	012:099	014:022	016:006	016:123
008:029	009:055	010:021	011:019	011:123	012:100	014:023	016:008	016:124
008:030	009:056	010:023	011:023	**Surah 12**	012:101	014:025	016:009	016:125
008:031	009:056	010:024	011:024	012:000	012:102	014:026	016:010	016:127
008:032	009:057	010:025	011:026	012:001	012:102	014:028	016:011	**Surah 17**
008:034	009:058	010:026	011:027	012:003	012:103	014:031	016:014	017:000
008:035	009:059	010:027	011:031	012:006	012:104	014:034	016:018	017:001
008:036	009:060	010:029	011:034	012:009	012:106	014:035	016:024	017:002
008:038	009:061	010:030	011:035	012:010	012:107	014:036	016:025	017:004
008:041	009:063	010:033	011:036	012:012	012:109	014:037	016:027	017:005
008:042	009:066	010:034	011:037	012:015	012:110	014:039	016:028	017:007
008:043	009:068	010:035	011:038	012:016	012:111	014:042	016:029	017:009
008:047	009:069	010:036	011:040	012:019	**Surah 13**	014:044	016:030	017:012
008:048	009:070	010:037	011:041	012:021	013:000	014:045	016:031	017:013
008:050	009:071	010:039	011:043	012:024	013:001	014:046	016:032	017:015
008:051	009:072	010:040	011:045	012:026	013:003	014:047	016:033	017:016
008:052	009:074	010:045	011:046	012:028	013:004	014:050	016:034	017:017
008:054	009:075	010:046	011:047	012:030	013:005	014:052	016:035	017:018
008:055	009:076	010:050	011:048	012:031	013:008	**Surah 15**	016:036	017:019
008:056	009:079	010:052	011:049	012:032	013:010	015:000	016:039	017:020
008:060	009:081	010:055	011:050	012:033	013:011	015:001	016:041	017:023
008:062	009:083	010:058	011:051	012:036	013:012	015:010	016:043	017:024
008:065	009:084	010:060	011:052	012:037	013:014	015:012	016:046	017:025
008:066	009:091	010:061	011:054	012:038	013:015	015:013	016:047	017:026
008:067	009:092	010:062	011:055	012:039	013:016	015:019	016:054	017:027
008:072	009:093	010:064	011:056	012:041	013:017	015:020	016:056	017:028
008:073	009:094	010:071	011:059	012:042	013:018	015:022	016:058	017:031
008:074	009:097	010:072	011:060	012:043	013:020	015:024	016:059	017:033
008:075	009:098	010:073	011:061	012:044	013:022	015:027	016:060	017:034
Surah 9	009:099	010:074	011:062	012:045	013:023	015:029	016:067	017:036
009:001	009:100	010:081	011:064	012:046	013:025	015:030	016:069	017:038
009:003	009:101	010:083	011:066	012:047	013:026	015:035	016:070	017:039

017:042	018:046	019:067	020:132	022:019	023:070	**Surah 25**	026:059	027:014
017:052	018:047	019:070	020:133	022:021	023:072	025:000	026:061	027:015
017:054	018:049	019:071	020:135	022:022	023:078	025:002	026:063	027:016
017:055	018:050	019:073	**Surah 21**	022:023	023:080	025:003	026:067	027:017
017:057	018:051	019:075	021:000	022:024	023:083	025:005	026:069	027:018
017:058	018:052	019:076	021:002	022:025	023:086	025:007	026:077	027:019
017:059	018:054	019:077	021:005	022:026	023:088	025:009	026:082	027:020
017:062	018:055	019:080	021:006	022:027	023:091	025:011	026:084	027:026
017:063	018:057	019:084	021:007	022:028	023:097	025:019	026:085	027:028
017:065	018:058	019:087	021:011	022:030	023:099	025:020	026:095	027:029
017:066	018:060	019:092	021:013	022:032	023:102	025:021	026:098	027:030
017:068	018:062	019:093	021:015	022:033	023:107	025:024	026:102	027:034
017:069	018:065	019:094	021:019	022:034	023:109	025:026	026:103	027:038
017:070	018:066	019:095	021:022	022:035	023:109	025:029	026:105	027:039
017:075	018:077	019:096	021:024	022:036	023:110	025:037	026:109	027:040
017:078	018:078	019:098	021:028	022:040	023:112	025:038	026:118	027:041
017:079	018:080	**Surah 20**	021:029	022:041	023:113	025:040	026:121	027:042
017:080	018:081	020:000	021:030	022:042	023:116	025:043	026:125	027:043
017:082	018:082	020:009	021:035	022:043	023:118	025:044	026:127	027:044
017:083	018:083	020:015	021:036	022:044	**Surah 24**	025:048	026:129	027:049
017:085	018:086	020:023	021:037	022:047	024:000	025:049	026:135	027:051
017:088	018:090	020:040	021:040	022:048	024:002	025:053	026:137	027:052
017:089	018:096	020:042	021:042	022:051	024:006	025:054	026:139	027:056
017:091	018:098	020:043	021:044	022:052	024:007	025:055	026:143	027:057
017:097	018:101	020:047	021:046	022:053	024:009	025:057	026:145	027:058
017:099	018:103	020:049	021:047	022:054	024:010	025:058	026:146	027:060
017:100	018:105	020:051	021:049	022:055	024:011	025:059	026:148	027:061
017:101	018:106	020:052	021:051	022:056	024:012	025:063	026:149	027:062
017:102	018:107	020:053	021:055	022:058	024:013	025:064	026:151	027:063
017:103	018:109	020:057	021:056	022:064	024:014	025:065	026:153	027:068
017:104	018:110	020:059	021:058	022:069	024:015	025:069	026:155	027:069
017:108	**Surah 19**	020:066	021:059	022:071	024:016	025:070	026:156	027:070
Surah 18	019:000	020:067	021:060	022:072	024:018	025:073	026:157	027:072
018:000	019:002	020:070	021:061	022:074	024:020	025:074	026:158	027:073
018:002	019:004	020:071	021:066	022:078	024:021	025:075	026:160	027:076
018:005	019:006	020:072	021:069	**Surah 23**	024:022	025:076	026:162	027:079
018:007	019:007	020:076	021:072	023:000	024:026	**Surah 26**	026:164	027:083
018:009	019:012	020:077	021:075	023:012	024:029	026:000	026:165	027:085
018:010	019:016	020:079	021:078	023:013	024:031	026:002	026:173	027:088
018:011	019:019	020:080	021:079	023:014	024:032	026:006	026:174	027:091
018:012	019:023	020:081	021:080	023:016	024:033	026:007	026:176	027:092
018:014	019:025	020:083	021:082	023:017	024:034	026:008	026:178	027:093
018:016	019:028	020:086	021:083	023:019	024:035	026:010	026:180	**Surah 28**
018:017	019:030	020:087	021:085	023:020	024:035	026:011	026:185	028:000
018:018	019:034	020:088	021:086	023:021	024:036	026:014	026:187	028:002
018:019	019:035	020:094	021:087	023:024	024:037	026:015	026:189	028:003
018:021	019:037	020:096	021:089	023:026	024:038	026:016	026:190	028:007
018:022	019:039	020:097	021:092	023:027	024:040	026:017	026:192	028:008
018:023	019:041	020:098	021:093	023:033	024:041	026:018	026:196	028:009
018:026	019:049	020:099	021:094	023:039	024:042	026:019	026:197	028:010
018:027	019:050	020:100	021:097	023:041	024:043	026:021	026:198	028:011
018:028	019:051	020:104	021:102	023:044	024:045	026:022	026:200	028:012
018:029	019:052	020:112	021:111	023:048	024:047	026:023	026:202	028:013
018:030	019:053	020:113	**Surah 22**	023:050	024:048	026:024	026:209	028:015
018:031	019:054	020:115	022:000	023:052	024:051	026:026	026:216	028:020
018:032	019:055	020:117	022:001	023:053	024:055	026:028	026:223	028:021
018:033	019:056	020:120	022:002	023:055	024:058	026:035	026:227	028:022
018:034	019:058	020:121	022:004	023:057	024:059	026:038	**Surah 27**	028:023
018:036	019:061	020:123	022:005	023:058	024:060	026:041	027:000	028:024
018:037	019:062	020:124	022:008	023:060	024:061	026:044	027:001	028:025
018:040	019:063	020:127	022:009	023:063	024:062	026:047	027:008	028:026
018:041	019:064	020:130	022:010	023:064	024:063	026:048	027:010	028:027
018:045	019:065	020:131	022:017	023:068	024:064	026:058	027:011	028:028

028:029	029:049	031:026	033:060	**Surah 36**	037:067	038:049	039:072	**Surah 41**
028:030	029:053	031:027	033:062	036:000	037:071	038:050	039:075	041:000
028:031	029:054	031:031	033:069	036:002	037:073	038:052	**Surah 40**	041:004
028:034	029:055	031:032	**Surah 34**	036:003	037:074	038:053	040:000	041:008
028:036	029:057	031:033	034:000	036:006	037:075	038:055	040:002	041:009
028:038	029:058	031:034	034:004	036:007	037:081	038:058	040:004	041:012
028:040	029:062	**Surah 32**	034:005	036:009	037:087	038:064	040:005	041:013
028:041	029:063	032:000	034:006	036:011	037:091	038:066	040:006	041:016
028:042	029:064	032:002	034:009	036:012	037:101	038:069	040:007	041:017
028:044	029:065	032:005	034:010	036:013	037:102	038:072	040:008	041:019
028:045	029:067	032:006	034:011	036:015	037:112	038:073	040:010	041:022
028:046	**Surah 30**	032:007	034:012	036:020	037:113	038:074	040:011	041:023
028:048	030:000	032:008	034:013	036:021	037:114	038:075	040:012	041:025
028:049	030:003	032:009	034:014	036:023	037:122	038:078	040:015	041:026
028:050	030:005	032:011	034:015	036:025	037:125	038:081	040:016	041:027
028:054	030:006	032:014	034:018	036:032	037:126	038:086	040:018	041:028
028:057	030:007	032:015	034:022	036:033	037:128	038:088	040:019	041:030
028:058	030:009	032:016	034:022	036:035	037:132	**Surah 39**	040:021	041:033
028:060	030:010	032:017	034:023	036:036	037:141	039:000	040:022	041:035
028:061	030:015	032:020	034:031	036:038	037:142	039:001	040:023	041:038
028:067	030:016	032:021	034:033	036:039	037:144	039:004	040:025	041:040
028:071	030:022	032:022	034:039	036:044	037:145	039:007	040:025	041:041
028:072	030:023	032:023	034:041	036:046	037:146	039:008	040:027	041:042
028:073	030:024	032:025	034:042	036:047	037:151	039:009	040:028	041:047
028:076	030:027	032:027	034:043	036:050	037:157	039:012	040:029	041:048
028:077	030:029	032:029	034:045	036:052	037:160	039:013	040:030	041:049
028:078	030:033	**Surah 33**	034:046	036:054	037:164	039:015	040:031	041:050
028:079	030:036	033:000	034:047	036:055	037:168	039:016	040:034	041:051
028:080	030:038	033:001	034:048	036:058	037:169	039:018	040:035	041:053
028:082	030:039	033:003	034:050	036:060	037:180	039:019	040:037	**Surah 42**
028:083	030:040	033:004	**Surah 35**	036:062	037:182	039:020	040:038	042:000
028:084	030:041	033:005	035:000	036:063	**Surah 38**	039:021	040:039	042:003
028:085	030:042	033:006	035:001	036:072	038:000	039:022	040:040	042:005
028:087	030:043	033:007	035:002	036:080	038:001	039:023	040:042	042:006
Surah 29	030:045	033:009	035:005	036:081	038:007	039:024	040:043	042:007
029:000	030:046	033:013	035:006	036:083	038:008	039:026	040:045	042:011
029:006	030:048	033:014	035:008	**Surah 37**	038:009	039:027	040:046	042:012
029:007	030:050	033:019	035:010	037:000	038:010	039:029	040:047	042:016
029:008	030:054	033:021	035:011	037:003	038:011	039:031	040:049	042:020
029:009	030:055	033:023	035:012	037:005	038:012	039:034	040:050	042:021
029:010	030:056	033:024	035:014	037:008	038:013	039:035	040:052	042:022
029:012	030:057	033:025	035:015	037:010	038:014	039:037	040:053	042:023
029:013	030:058	033:026	035:018	037:011	038:016	039:040	040:054	042:024
029:015	030:059	033:027	035:018	037:017	038:017	039:042	040:055	042:026
029:018	030:060	033:028	035:020	037:018	038:018	039:044	040:056	042:028
029:023	**Surah 31**	033:029	035:021	037:020	038:021	039:045	040:057	042:029
029:024	031:000	033:030	035:024	037:021	038:022	039:046	040:058	042:030
029:025	031:002	033:031	035:027	037:031	038:024	039:047	040:061	042:033
029:026	031:003	033:032	035:028	037:036	038:025	039:048	040:062	042:034
029:027	031:006	033:033	035:029	037:037	038:026	039:049	040:063	042:035
029:029	031:008	033:034	035:030	037:038	038:027	039:050	040:064	042:036
029:031	031:009	033:037	035:031	037:040	038:028	039:051	040:065	042:038
029:033	031:010	033:038	035:032	037:043	038:029	039:053	040:066	042:041
029:034	031:011	033:039	035:033	037:046	038:031	039:055	040:067	042:043
029:038	031:012	033:040	035:035	037:048	038:032	039:059	040:069	042:044
029:040	031:015	033:043	035:036	037:051	038:035	039:060	040:074	042:045
029:041	031:016	033:045	035:037	037:055	038:037	039:062	040:076	042:047
029:042	031:017	033:048	035:039	037:056	038:040	039:063	040:077	042:048
029:045	031:019	033:049	035:040	037:057	038:044	039:066	040:078	042:049
029:046	031:021	033:050	035:042	037:061	038:045	039:067	040:081	042:050
029:047	031:022	033:051	035:043	037:062	038:046	039:069	040:082	042:051
029:047	031:023	033:054	035:044	037:064	038:047	039:070	040:085	042:052
029:048	031:025	033:059	035:045	037:065	038:048	039:071		042:053

Surah 43	045:002	047:028	**Surah 51**	053:038	055:054	057:008	061:001	067:003
043:000	045:004	047:030	051:000	053:040	055:055	057:009	061:003	067:005
043:004	045:005	047:032	051:008	053:047	055:057	057:010	061:005	067:006
043:006	045:006	047:034	051:011	053:049	055:059	057:014	061:006	067:007
043:008	045:008	047:036	051:012	053:051	055:061	057:015	061:009	067:010
043:009	045:009	047:037	051:015	053:052	055:063	057:016	061:011	067:011
043:013	045:010	047:038	051:017	053:053	055:065	057:019	061:012	067:013
043:015	045:011	**Surah 48**	051:018	053:055	055:067	057:020	061:014	067:015
043:016	045:012	048:000	051:020	053:056	055:069	057:021	**Surah 62**	067:017
043:017	045:014	048:002	051:023	**Surah 54**	055:071	057:024	062:000	067:018
043:020	045:016	048:004	051:024	054:000	055:073	057:025	062:001	067:023
043:025	045:017	048:004	051:028	054:001	055:075	057:026	062:003	067:026
043:026	045:018	048:004	051:030	054:005	055:076	057:027	062:004	067:027
043:029	045:019	048:005	051:033	054:009	055:077	057:028	062:005	067:029
043:031	045:020	048:006	051:035	054:011	055:078	057:029	062:006	**Surah 68**
043:032	045:022	048:007	051:039	054:013	**Surah 56**	**Surah 58**	062:007	068:000
043:034	045:024	048:008	051:044	054:019	056:000	058:000	062:008	068:002
043:035	045:026	048:010	051:046	054:020	056:008	058:001	062:009	068:006
043:036	045:027	048:014	051:049	054:025	056:009	058:005	062:010	068:013
043:038	045:032	048:015	051:051	054:027	056:012	058:006	**Surah 63**	068:015
043:046	045:033	048:019	051:052	054:033	056:013	058:007	063:000	068:017
043:051	045:034	048:020	051:057	054:034	056:014	058:011	063:001	068:027
043:054	045:035	048:023	051:058	054:036	056:017	058:012	063:002	068:028
043:056	045:036	048:025	051:059	054:041	056:018	058:013	063:005	068:034
043:057	045:037	048:026	051:060	054:042	056:021	058:014	063:007	068:035
043:058	**Surah 46**	048:028	**Surah 52**	054:046	056:024	058:016	063:009	068:039
043:059	046:000	048:029	052:000	054:048	056:027	058:017	**Surah 64**	068:040
043:061	046:002	048:029	052:001	054:050	056:035	058:019	064:000	068:046
043:063	046:004	**Surah 49**	052:007	054:052	056:037	058:020	064:001	068:048
043:065	046:005	049:000	052:013	054:054	056:038	058:022	064:002	068:050
043:066	046:007	049:002	052:016	**Surah 55**	056:039	**Surah 59**	064:004	**Surah 69**
043:071	046:008	049:003	052:018	055:000	056:040	059:000	064:005	069:000
043:072	046:010	049:004	052:019	055:007	056:041	059:001	064:006	069:004
043:073	046:011	049:006	052:021	055:013	056:042	059:002	064:007	069:005
043:074	046:012	049:008	052:022	055:015	056:043	059:003	064:009	069:007
043:078	046:014	049:009	052:023	055:016	056:048	059:005	064:010	069:008
043:082	046:015	049:011	052:026	055:017	056:049	059:007	064:011	069:010
043:083	046:016	049:012	052:027	055:018	056:052	059:009	064:012	069:011
043:084	046:017	049:013	052:028	055:021	056:054	059:010	064:014	069:017
043:085	046:018	049:013	052:029	055:022	056:056	059:011	064:016	069:018
043:086	046:020	049:014	052:035	055:023	056:062	059:013	064:018	069:021
043:088	046:021	049:015	052:037	055:025	056:073	059:014	**Surah 65**	069:024
Surah 44	046:023	049:016	052:038	055:027	056:074	059:015	065:000	069:027
044:004	046:025	049:018	052:040	055:028	056:075	059:016	065:001	069:028
044:007	046:026	**Surah 50**	052:044	055:029	056:080	059:017	065:004	069:034
044:010	046:028	050:000	052:045	055:030	056:083	059:020	065:005	069:036
044:017	046:029	050:003	052:047	055:032	056:087	059:021	065:007	069:040
044:018	046:035	050:004	052:048	055:033	056:088	059:023	065:008	069:041
044:030	**Surah 47**	050:007	052:049	055:034	056:089	**Surah 60**	065:009	069:042
044:037	047:000	050:010	**Surah 53**	055:035	056:090	060:000	065:010	069:043
044:039	047:001	050:012	053:000	055:036	056:091	060:001	065:011	069:046
044:040	047:002	050:013	053:003	055:038	056:092	060:003	065:012	069:047
044:043	047:004	050:014	053:007	055:039	056:095	060:004	**Surah 66**	069:050
044:044	047:007	050:019	053:009	055:040	056:096	060:006	066:000	069:051
044:046	047:009	050:022	053:014	055:042	**Surah 57**	060:008	066:002	069:052
044:047	047:010	050:024	053:015	055:044	057:000	060:009	066:003	**Surah 70**
044:048	047:011	050:034	053:018	055:045	057:001	060:010	066:010	070:000
044:049	047:014	050:036	053:029	055:046	057:002	060:011	066:011	070:003
044:051	047:015	050:038	053:030	055:047	057:003	060:012	066:012	070:005
044:055	047:018	050:039	053:032	055:049	057:004	060:013	**Surah 67**	070:011
044:056	047:020	050:040	053:035	055:051	057:005	**Surah 61**	067:000	070:026
Surah 45	047:022	050:042	053:036	055:052	057:006	061:000	067:002	070:027
045:000	047:026		053:037	055:053	057:007			070:035

070:038	**Surah 76**	079:005	**Surah 86**	096:018	**Surah 109**	002:039	002:119	002:194
070:039	076:000	079:015	086:000	**Surah 97**	109:000	002:040	002:120	002:195
070:040	076:001	079:025	086:003	097:000	**Surah 110**	002:041	002:121	002:196
070:042	076:002	079:038	086:012	097:001	110:000	002:042	002:122	002:197
Surah 71	076:005	079:040	**Surah 87**	097:002	110:001	002:044	002:124	002:198
071:000	076:006	079:044	087:000	097:003	110:003	002:046	002:125	002:199
071:012	076:008	**Surah 80**	087:001	097:005	**Surah 111**	002:047	002:126	002:200
071:013	076:009	080:000	087:015	**Surah 98**	111:000	002:049	002:127	002:201
071:025	076:010	080:010	087:016	098:000	111:001	002:050	002:128	002:203
071:026	076:011	080:011	087:018	098:001	111:003	002:051	002:129	002:204
071:027	076:012	080:015	087:019	098:004	111:005	002:053	002:130	002:205
Surah 72	076:014	080:037	**Surah 88**	098:006	**Surah 112**	002:054	002:131	002:207
072:000	076:015	080:042	088:000	098:007	112:000	002:056	002:132	002:208
072:001	076:016	**Surah 81**	088:001	098:008	**Surah 113**	002:057	002:133	002:209
072:003	076:017	081:000	088:005	**Surah 99**	113:000	002:058	002:134	002:210
072:008	076:019	081:019	088:011	099:000	113:001	002:059	002:135	002:211
072:013	076:021	081:020	088:013	099:007	113:002	002:060	002:136	002:212
072:014	076:024	081:021	**Surah 89**	099:008	113:003	002:061	002:137	002:213
072:017	076:025	081:024	089:000	**Surah 100**	113:004	002:062	002:140	002:214
072:018	076:026	081:025	089:007	100:000	113:005	002:063	002:141	002:217
072:019	076:030	081:029	089:008	100:002	**Surah 114**	002:064	002:142	002:218
072:024	**Surah 77**	**Surah 82**	089:010	100:005	114:000	002:065	002:143	002:219
072:027	077:000	082:000	089:013	100:008	114:001	002:068	002:144	002:220
072:028	077:006	082:015	**Surah 90**	**Surah 101**	114:002	002:069	002:145	002:221
Surah 73	077:013	082:017	090:000	101:000	114:003	002:071	002:146	002:223
073:000	077:014	082:018	090:002	101:001	114:004	002:072	002:147	002:225
073:003	077:015	**Surah 83**	090:008	101:002	114:005	002:073	002:149	002:228
073:008	077:016	083:000	090:009	101:003		002:075	002:150	002:229
073:009	077:018	083:006	090:014	101:006		002:076	002:154	002:230
073:011	077:019	083:007	090:015	101:007	# THE	002:078	002:155	002:231
073:014	077:021	083:011	090:017	101:008		002:079	002:157	002:232
073:020	077:022	083:013	090:018	**Surah 102**	**Surah 1**	002:080	002:158	002:233
Surah 74	077:024	083:014	090:019	102:000	001:001	002:081	002:159	002:235
074:000	077:028	083:015	**Surah 91**	102:001	001:002	002:082	002:160	002:236
074:009	077:030	083:016	091:000	102:005	001:004	002:083	002:161	002:236
074:017	077:031	083:018	091:013	102:007	001:006	002:085	002:164	002:237
074:024	077:033	083:023	091:015	**Surah 103**	001:007	002:086	002:165	002:238
074:025	077:034	083:024	**Surah 92**	103:000	**Surah 2**	002:087	002:166	002:239
074:029	077:037	083:027	092:000	103:003	002:000	002:088	002:167	002:240
074:031	077:038	083:035	092:003	**Surah 104**	002:002	002:089	002:168	002:241
074:035	077:040	**Surah 84**	092:014	104:000	002:003	002:090	002:170	002:244
074:037	077:041	084:000	092:020	104:001	002:004	002:091	002:171	002:246
074:039	077:044	084:002	**Surah 93**	104:006	002:006	002:092	002:172	002:248
074:040	077:045	084:005	093:000	**Surah 105**	002:007	002:093	002:173	002:249
074:041	077:047	084:015	093:011	105:000	002:008	002:094	002:174	002:251
074:043	077:049	084:016	**Surah 94**	105:001	002:010	002:095	002:175	002:252
074:044	**Surah 78**	084:023	094:000	105:003	002:011	002:096	002:176	002:253
074:046	078:000	**Surah 85**	**Surah 95**	105:004	002:012	002:097	002:177	002:254
074:048	078:011	085:000	095:000	105:005	002:013	002:100	002:178	002:255
074:052	078:016	085:002	095:002	**Surah 106**	002:018	002:101	002:179	002:256
074:056	078:017	085:003	095:003	106:000	002:019	002:102	002:180	002:257
Surah 75	078:021	085:004	095:004	106:001	002:020	002:103	002:181	002:258
075:000	078:022	085:008	095:005	106:003	002:022	002:104	002:182	002:259
075:004	078:030	085:009	095:008	106:004	002:024	002:105	002:184	002:260
075:005	078:033	085:010	**Surah 96**	**Surah 107**	002:026	002:107	002:185	002:261
075:006	078:037	085:012	096:000	107:000	002:028	002:108	002:185	002:262
075:011	078:040	085:014	096:001	107:003	002:029	002:109	002:186	002:263
075:012	**Surah 79**	085:015	096:002	107:005	002:030	002:113	002:187	002:264
075:028	079:000	085:016	096:004	**Surah 108**	002:031	002:114	002:188	002:265
075:037	079:001	085:017	096:008	108:000	002:033	002:115	002:189	002:267
075:039	079:002	085:018	096:011		002:034	002:116	002:190	002:270
	079:003		096:017		002:035	002:117	002:191	002:272
					002:036	002:118	002:193	002:273

002:275	003:070	003:153	004:026	004:125	005:031	005:108	006:058	006:143
002:280	003:071	003:154	004:027	004:126	005:032	005:109	006:059	006:144
002:281	003:072	003:155	004:030	004:127	005:033	005:110	006:060	006:145
002:282	003:073	003:156	004:031	004:129	005:035	005:111	006:061	006:146
002:283	003:074	003:157	004:034	004:131	005:036	005:112	006:062	006:149
002:284	003:075	003:159	004:035	004:132	005:037	005:113	006:063	006:150
002:285	003:077	003:161	004:036	004:134	005:038	005:114	006:065	006:152
002:286	003:078	003:162	004:037	004:135	005:039	005:115	006:066	006:154
Surah 3	003:079	003:163	004:038	004:136	005:040	005:116	006:068	006:156
003:000	003:081	003:164	004:039	004:137	005:041	005:117	006:069	006:157
003:002	003:083	003:166	004:040	004:138	005:042	005:118	006:070	006:158
003:003	003:084	003:167	004:042	004:140	005:043	005:119	006:071	006:159
003:004	003:085	003:168	004:043	004:141	005:044	005:120	006:075	006:161
003:005	003:086	003:170	004:044	004:142	005:045	**Surah 6**	006:076	006:162
003:006	003:087	003:171	004:046	004:143	005:046	006:000	006:077	006:163
003:007	003:091	003:172	004:047	004:145	005:047	006:001	006:078	006:164
003:008	003:093	003:173	004:051	004:146	005:048	006:003	006:079	006:165
003:010	003:095	003:174	004:054	004:148	005:050	006:004	006:080	**Surah 7**
003:011	003:096	003:175	004:056	004:152	005:051	006:005	006:081	007:000
003:013	003:097	003:176	004:058	004:153	005:052	006:006	006:085	007:002
003:014	003:098	003:177	004:059	004:154	005:053	006:007	006:086	007:003
003:015	003:099	003:178	004:060	004:155	005:054	006:008	006:088	007:008
003:016	003:100	003:179	004:061	004:157	005:055	006:010	006:089	007:010
003:017	003:101	003:180	004:062	004:159	005:056	006:011	006:090	007:011
003:018	003:103	003:181	004:064	004:160	005:057	006:012	006:091	007:013
003:019	003:104	003:182	004:065	004:162	005:059	006:013	006:092	007:014
003:020	003:106	003:183	004:068	004:163	005:060	006:014	006:093	007:016
003:021	003:107	003:184	004:069	004:164	005:061	006:015	006:094	007:019
003:022	003:108	003:185	004:070	004:165	005:062	006:016	006:095	007:022
003:023	003:109	003:186	004:074	004:166	005:063	006:018	006:096	007:026
003:024	003:110	003:187	004:075	004:167	005:064	006:019	006:097	007:027
003:027	003:112	003:188	004:076	004:169	005:065	006:020	006:099	007:029
003:028	003:113	003:189	004:077	004:170	005:066	006:021	006:100	007:030
003:029	003:114	003:190	004:080	004:171	005:067	006:022	006:101	007:031
003:030	003:115	003:191	004:082	004:172	005:068	006:024	006:102	007:032
003:033	003:116	003:192	004:083	004:176	005:069	006:025	006:104	007:033
003:034	003:117	003:193	004:084	**Surah 5**	005:070	006:027	006:105	007:036
003:036	003:118	003:194	004:087	005:000	005:072	006:028	006:108	007:037
003:037	003:119	003:195	004:088	005:001	005:073	006:030	006:109	007:038
003:039	003:120	003:196	004:089	005:002	005:075	006:031	006:110	007:039
003:040	003:121	003:198	004:092	005:003	005:077	006:032	006:111	007:040
003:041	003:122	003:199	004:093	005:004	005:079	006:033	006:113	007:042
003:042	003:124	**Surah 4**	004:094	005:005	005:080	006:034	006:114	007:043
003:044	003:125	004:000	004:095	005:006	005:081	006:035	006:115	007:044
003:045	003:126	004:001	004:097	005:007	005:083	006:036	006:116	007:045
003:046	003:127	004:003	004:100	005:008	005:085	006:038	006:121	007:046
003:048	003:128	004:005	004:101	005:011	005:087	006:039	006:122	007:049
003:049	003:129	004:006	004:102	005:012	005:088	006:040	006:124	007:050
003:050	003:131	004:007	004:103	005:013	005:089	006:041	006:125	007:051
003:052	003:132	004:008	004:104	005:014	005:091	006:042	006:126	007:053
003:053	003:133	004:009	004:105	005:015	005:092	006:043	006:128	007:054
003:054	003:135	004:010	004:106	005:016	005:093	006:044	006:129	007:056
003:055	003:136	004:011	004:108	005:017	005:095	006:045	006:130	007:057
003:056	003:137	004:012	004:109	005:018	005:096	006:046	006:131	007:058
003:058	003:140	004:013	004:113	005:019	005:097	006:047	006:133	007:059
003:059	003:144	004:015	004:114	005:020	005:099	006:048	006:134	007:060
003:060	003:145	004:017	004:115	005:021	005:100	006:050	006:135	007:061
003:061	003:146	004:018	004:116	005:023	005:101	006:051	006:136	007:062
003:062	003:148	004:019	004:117	005:026	005:103	006:052	006:137	007:064
003:064	003:149	004:020	004:119	005:027	005:104	006:054	006:138	007:065
003:065	003:150	004:023	004:122	005:028	005:105	006:055	006:139	007:066
003:068	003:151	004:024	004:123	005:029	005:106	006:056	006:141	007:067
003:069	003:152	004:025	004:124	005:030	005:107	006:057	006:142	007:068

007:069	007:152	008:036	009:034	009:120	010:076	011:050	012:020	012:109
007:072	007:154	008:037	009:035	009:121	010:077	011:052	012:021	012:110
007:073	007:155	008:038	009:036	009:122	010:078	011:053	**Surah 13**
007:074	007:156	008:040	009:037	009:123	010:080	011:054	012:023	013:000
007:075	007:157	008:041	009:038	009:127	010:081	011:057	012:024	013:001
007:076	007:158	008:042	009:039	009:128	010:082	011:059	012:025	013:002
007:077	007:159	008:043	009:040	009:129	010:083	011:060	012:026	013:003
007:078	007:160	008:047	009:041	**Surah 10**	010:088	011:061	012:027	013:004
007:079	007:161	008:048	009:042	010:000	010:089	011:062	012:028	013:005
007:084	007:162	008:049	009:043	010:001	010:090	011:066	012:030	013:006
007:085	007:163	008:050	009:044	010:002	010:090	011:067	012:032	013:007
007:086	007:164	008:051	009:045	010:003	010:093	011:068	012:033	013:008
007:087	007:165	008:052	009:048	010:004	010:094	011:070	012:035	013:009
007:088	007:167	008:053	009:049	010:005	010:095	011:073	012:036	013:010
007:089	007:168	008:054	009:051	010:006	010:096	011:074	012:037	013:011
007:090	007:169	008:055	009:053	010:007	010:097	011:076	012:038	013:012
007:091	007:170	008:056	009:054	010:008	010:098	011:078	012:039	013:013
007:092	007:171	008:057	009:058	010:010	010:100	011:081	012:040	013:014
007:093	007:172	008:058	009:059	010:011	010:101	011:082	012:041	013:015
007:096	007:173	008:059	009:060	010:012	010:102	011:084	012:042	013:016
007:097	007:174	008:060	009:061	010:014	010:103	011:085	012:043	013:017
007:099	007:175	008:061	009:063	010:015	010:104	011:087	012:044	013:018
007:100	007:176	008:062	009:064	010:018	010:105	011:088	012:045	013:019
007:101	007:178	008:063	009:067	010:020	010:107	011:089	012:046	013:020
007:103	007:179	008:064	009:068	010:021	010:108	011:093	012:047	013:021
007:104	007:180	008:065	009:069	010:022	010:109	011:094	012:049	013:022
007:105	007:185	008:066	009:070	010:023	**Surah 11**	011:097	012:050	013:023
007:106	007:187	008:067	009:071	010:024	011:000	011:098	012:051	013:024
007:109	007:188	008:068	009:072	010:025	011:003	011:099	012:052	013:025
007:111	007:190	008:072	009:073	010:026	011:005	011:100	012:053	013:026
007:113	007:193	008:073	009:074	010:027	011:007	011:101	012:054	013:027
007:115	007:196	008:074	009:077	010:030	011:008	011:102	012:055	013:028
007:116	007:199	008:075	009:079	010:031	011:012	011:103	012:056	013:030
007:117	007:202	**Surah 9**	009:081	010:032	011:013	011:105	012:057	013:031
007:120	007:204	009:001	009:082	010:033	011:014	011:106	012:059	013:032
007:121	007:205	009:002	009:083	010:034	011:015	011:107	012:064	013:033
007:122	**Surah 8**	009:003	009:087	010:035	011:016	011:108	012:065	013:034
007:123	008:000	009:004	009:088	010:037	011:017	011:109	012:066	013:035
007:126	008:001	009:005	009:089	010:038	011:018	011:110	012:068	013:036
007:127	008:003	009:006	009:090	010:039	011:019	011:111	012:070	013:037
007:128	008:004	009:007	009:091	010:042	011:021	011:112	012:072	013:038
007:129	008:005	009:008	009:092	010:043	011:022	011:113	012:073	013:039
007:130	008:006	009:009	009:093	010:045	011:023	011:114	012:074	013:040
007:131	008:007	009:010	009:094	010:047	011:024	011:115	012:075	013:041
007:132	008:009	009:012	009:095	010:048	011:026	011:116	012:076	013:042
007:134	008:011	009:013	009:097	010:050	011:027	011:117	012:077	013:043
007:135	008:012	009:014	009:098	010:052	011:028	011:119	012:080	**Surah 14**
007:136	008:014	009:015	009:099	010:053	011:029	011:120	012:081	014:000
007:137	008:015	009:016	009:100	010:054	011:031	011:123	012:082	014:001
007:138	008:016	009:017	009:101	010:055	011:032	**Surah 12**	012:083	014:002
007:139	008:017	009:018	009:104	010:057	011:035	012:000	012:085	014:003
007:140	008:018	009:019	009:105	010:058	011:037	012:001	012:088	014:004
007:141	008:019	009:020	009:106	010:060	011:038	012:003	012:090	014:005
007:142	008:022	009:022	009:107	010:061	011:040	012:004	012:092	014:006
007:143	008:025	009:024	009:108	010:062	011:041	012:006	012:093	014:009
007:144	008:026	009:025	009:109	.010:064	011:042	012:009	012:094	014:009
007:145	008:027	009:026	009:110	010:066	011:043	012:010	012:096	014:010
007:146	008:029	009:028	009:111	010:067	011:044	012:013	012:099	014:012
007:147	008:030	009:029	009:112	010:068	011:045	012:014	012:100	014:013
007:148	008:031	009:030	009:113	010:070	011:046	012:015	012:101	014:014
007:149	008:032	009:031	009:116	010:071	011:047	012:016	012:102	014:015
007:150	008:034	009:032	009:117	010:073	011:048	012:017	012:103	014:018
007:151	008:035	009:033	009:118	010:074	011:049	012:019	012:107	014:019

014:021	015:085	016:082	017:038	018:026	019:019	020:048	021:017	022:006
014:022	015:086	016:083	017:039	018:027	019:023	020:049	021:018	022:007
014:023	015:087	016:084	017:040	018:028	019:024	020:051	021:019	022:009
014:024	015:098	016:085	017:041	018:029	019:025	020:052	021:021	022:010
014:025	015:099	016:087	017:042	018:030	019:027	020:053	021:022	022:011
014:026	**Surah 16**	016:088	017:044	018:031	019:029	020:055	021:024	022:012
014:027	016:000	016:089	017:045	018:032	019:033	020:059	021:026	022:013
014:028	016:001	016:090	017:046	018:033	019:034	020:061	021:030	022:015
014:031	016:003	016:091	017:047	018:034	019:035	020:065	021:031	022:017
014:032	016:006	016:092	017:055	018:036	019:037	020:068	021:032	022:018
014:033	016:009	016:094	017:056	018:037	019:038	020:069	021:033	022:022
014:034	016:010	016:095	017:057	018:041	019:039	020:070	021:036	022:024
014:037	016:012	016:097	017:058	018:044	019:040	020:071	021:038	022:025
014:039	016:013	016:098	017:060	018:045	019:041	020:072	021:039	022:026
014:041	016:014	016:102	017:061	018:046	019:046	020:073	021:041	022:027
014:042	016:015	016:103	017:062	018:047	019:050	020:076	021:042	022:028
014:044	016:016	016:104	017:063	018:048	019:051	020:077	021:044	022:029
014:045	016:018	016:105	017:066	018:049	019:052	020:078	021:045	022:030
014:046	016:022	016:107	017:067	018:050	019:054	020:080	021:046	022:031
014:047	016:023	016:109	017:068	018:051	019:055	020:081	021:047	022:032
014:048	016:024	016:110	017:070	018:052	019:056	020:083	021:048	022:033
014:049	016:025	016:112	017:071	018:053	019:058	020:085	021:049	022:034
Surah 15	016:026	016:113	017:072	018:054	019:060	020:086	021:055	022:036
015:000	016:027	016:114	017:076	018:055	019:061	020:087	021:056	022:037
015:001	016:028	016:115	017:077	018:056	019:063	020:088	021:058	022:040
015:006	016:029	016:118	017:078	018:057	019:064	020:094	021:059	022:041
015:007	016:030	016:121	017:079	018:059	019:065	020:096	021:061	022:042
015:008	016:031	016:122	017:080	018:060	019:072	020:097	021:062	022:044
015:009	016:032	016:123	017:082	018:061	019:073	020:098	021:063	022:046
015:010	016:033	016:124	017:084	018:063	019:074	020:100	021:064	022:047
015:012	016:034	016:125	017:085	018:064	019:075	020:101	021:067	022:048
015:013	016:035	016:126	017:088	018:066	019:076	020:102	021:070	022:051
015:016	016:036	016:127	017:089	018:067	019:078	020:104	021:071	022:053
015:019	016:039	**Surah 17**	017:090	018:070	019:083	020:105	021:074	022:054
015:022	016:041	017:000	017:092	018:071	019:085	020:108	021:075	022:055
015:027	016:043	017:001	017:093	018:077	019:086	020:109	021:077	022:056
015:028	016:044	017:002	017:095	018:078	019:087	020:111	021:078	022:058
015:030	016:045	017:003	017:097	018:079	019:090	020:113	021:079	022:060
015:035	016:046	017:004	017:099	018:080	019:091	020:114	021:080	022:062
015:036	016:048	017:005	017:100	018:082	019:092	020:115	021:081	022:063
015:038	016:049	017:006	017:101	018:084	019:093	020:116	021:083	022:064
015:039	016:052	017:007	017:102	018:086	019:095	020:117	021:084	022:065
015:042	016:054	017:009	017:103	018:090	019:096	020:119	021:086	022:067
015:043	016:055	017:010	017:104	018:094	019:097	020:120	021:087	022:069
015:045	016:058	017:012	017:105	018:095	**Surah 20**	020:121	021:089	022:072
015:049	016:059	017:013	017:108	018:096	020:000	020:123	021:096	022:073
015:050	016:060	017:015	017:110	018:098	020:002	020:124	021:097	022:078
015:051	016:061	017:016	**Surah 18**	018:099	020:004	020:127	021:097	**Surah 23**
015:056	016:062	017:017	018:000	018:102	020:005	020:130	021:098	023:000
015:057	016:063	017:018	018:001	018:105	020:006	020:131	021:101	023:001
015:059	016:064	017:019	018:002	018:107	020:007	020:132	021:102	023:006
015:061	016:065	017:020	018:009	018:109	020:008	020:133	021:103	023:010
015:064	016:067	017:021	018:010	018:110	020:009	020:135	021:104	023:014
015:065	016:068	017:024	018:011	**Surah 19**	020:010	**Surah 21**	021:105	023:016
015:066	016:069	017:026	018:012	019:000	020:011	021:000	021:106	023:018
015:067	016:071	017:027	018:014	019:002	020:012	021:003	021:109	023:024
015:073	016:072	017:028	018:016	019:004	020:013	021:004	021:112	023:027
015:074	016:075	017:031	018:017	019:006	020:015	021:005	**Surah 22**	023:028
015:076	016:077	017:033	018:018	019:010	020:027	021:006	022:000	023:029
015:078	016:078	017:034	018:019	019:011	020:038	021:007	022:001	023:033
015:080	016:079	017:035	018:021	019:012	020:039	021:011	022:002	023:038
015:082	016:080	017:036	018:022	019:015	020:040	021:013	022:004	023:039
015:083	016:081	017:037	018:024	019:016	020:047	021:016	022:005	023:041

023:049	024:036	025:058	026:095	027:005	028:002	028:080	030:006	031:024
023:050	024:037	025:059	026:098	027:006	028:003	028:081	030:007	031:025
023:058	024:038	025:060	026:104	027:008	028:004	028:082	030:008	031:027
023:062	024:039	025:061	026:105	027:009	028:005	028:083	030:009	031:029
023:064	024:040	025:062	026:109	027:011	028:006	028:084	030:010	031:030
023:067	024:041	025:063	026:111	027:012	028:007	028:085	030:011	031:031
023:068	024:042	025:064	026:118	027:014	028:008	028:086	030:012	031:032
023:070	024:043	025:065	026:119	027:016	028:009	028:087	030:014	031:033
023:071	024:044	025:069	026:122	027:018	028:010	028:088	030:016	031:034
023:072	024:047	025:070	026:123	027:019	028:011	**Surah 29**	030:017	**Surah 32**
023:073	024:049	025:073	026:127	027:020	028:012	029:000	030:018	032:000
023:074	024:051	025:074	026:129	027:022	028:013	029:005	030:019	032:002
023:075	024:054	025:075	026:135	027:024	028:015	029:007	030:022	032:003
023:078	024:055	025:077	026:136	027:025	028:016	029:008	030:023	032:004
023:079	024:056	**Surah 26**	026:137	027:026	028:018	029:009	030:024	032:005
023:080	024:057	026:000	026:138	027:027	028:019	029:010	030:025	032:006
023:081	024:058	026:002	026:140	027:029	028:020	029:012	030:026	032:007
023:083	024:059	026:004	026:141	027:030	028:022	029:013	030:028	032:009
023:084	024:060	026:005	026:145	027:031	028:023	029:014	030:029	032:010
023:086	024:061	026:006	026:146	027:033	028:024	029:015	030:030	032:011
023:088	024:063	026:007	026:148	027:034	028:025	029:017	030:034	032:012
023:090	024:064	026:009	026:151	027:036	028:026	029:018	030:035	032:013
023:091	**Surah 25**	026:010	026:152	027:039	028:027	029:020	030:037	032:014
023:092	025:000	026:011	026:153	027:040	028:028	029:023	030:038	032:015
023:094	025:001	026:016	026:154	027:041	028:029	029:024	030:039	032:016
023:096	025:002	026:017	026:156	027:042	028:030	029:025	030:040	032:017
023:097	025:004	026:021	026:158	027:043	028:032	029:026	030:041	032:018
023:100	025:005	026:022	026:159	027:044	028:036	029:027	030:042	032:020
023:100	025:006	026:023	026:160	027:045	028:037	029:029	030:043	032:021
023:101	025:007	026:024	026:164	027:046	028:038	029:031	030:046	032:022
023:104	025:008	026:026	026:165	027:048	028:039	029:034	030:048	032:023
023:109	025:011	026:028	026:172	027:049	028:040	029:036	030:049	032:025
023:111	025:015	026:031	026:173	027:051	028:041	029:037	030:050	032:027
023:116	025:017	026:034	026:175	027:056	028:042	029:038	030:052	032:028
023:117	025:018	026:036	026:176	027:058	028:043	029:039	030:053	032:029
023:118	025:020	026:038	026:180	027:059	028:044	029:040	030:055	**Surah 33**
Surah 24	025:021	026:039	026:183	027:060	028:045	029:041	030:056	033:000
024:000	025:022	026:040	026:184	027:061	028:046	029:043	030:057	033:001
024:002	025:024	026:041	026:187	027:062	028:047	029:044	030:058	033:004
024:003	025:025	026:044	026:189	027:063	028:048	029:045	030:059	033:005
024:006	025:026	026:045	026:191	027:064	028:051	029:046	030:060	033:006
024:007	025:027	026:046	026:192	027:065	028:052	029:047	**Surah 31**	033:007
024:008	025:029	026:047	026:193	027:066	028:053	029:048	031:000	033:008
024:009	025:030	026:048	026:195	027:067	028:055	029:049	031:002	033:009
024:011	025:031	026:051	026:196	027:068	028:057	029:050	031:003	033:010
024:012	025:032	026:053	026:197	027:069	028:059	029:051	031:004	033:011
024:013	025:033	026:059	026:198	027:072	028:060	029:052	031:005	033:012
024:014	025:035	026:061	026:200	027:076	028:061	029:053	031:006	033:013
024:015	025:036	026:063	026:201	027:079	028:063	029:054	031:009	033:014
024:018	025:037	026:064	026:206	027:080	028:064	029:055	031:010	033:018
024:019	025:038	026:066	026:207	027:081	028:065	029:057	031:011	033:019
024:020	025:040	026:068	026:210	027:082	028:066	029:060	031:012	033:020
024:021	025:041	026:077	026:215	027:083	028:067	029:061	031:013	033:021
024:023	025:042	026:082	026:217	027:084	028:068	029:062	031:014	033:022
024:024	025:044	026:083	026:221	027:085	028:070	029:063	031:015	033:023
024:025	025:045	026:084	026:224	027:086	028:071	029:064	031:016	033:024
024:028	025:047	026:085	026:227	027:087	028:072	029:067	031:017	033:025
024:030	025:048	026:087	**Surah 27**	027:088	028:074	029:068	031:018	033:026
024:031	025:049	026:088	027:000	027:090	028:075	**Surah 30**	031:019	033:028
024:032	025:050	026:090	027:001	027:091	028:076	030:000	031:020	033:029
024:033	025:052	026:091	027:002	027:092	028:077	030:002	031:021	033:030
024:034	025:053	026:092	027:003	**Surah 28**	028:078	030:004	031:022	033:031
024:035	025:055	026:094	027:004	028:000	028:079	030:005	031:023	033:032

033:033	034:043	036:036	037:088	038:032	039:046	040:045	041:037	043:002
033:034	034:045	036:037	037:091	038:035	039:047	040:046	041:038	043:004
033:037	034:048	036:038	037:092	038:036	039:048	040:047	041:039	043:005
033:038	034:049	036:039	037:093	038:037	039:050	040:049	041:040	043:006
033:039	034:050	036:040	037:094	038:044	039:051	040:050	041:042	043:008
033:040	034:052	036:041	037:097	038:046	039:052	040:051	041:043	043:009
033:043	034:053	036:046	037:098	038:047	039:053	040:052	041:045	043:010
033:044	034:054	036:047	037:101	038:048	039:054	040:053	041:046	043:011
033:047	**Surah 35**	036:051	037:102	038:049	039:055	040:055	041:047	043:013
033:048	035:000	036:052	037:105	038:053	039:056	040:056	041:048	043:017
033:050	035:001	036:054	037:112	038:055	039:057	040:057	041:050	043:020
033:051	035:002	036:055	037:117	038:059	039:058	040:058	041:052	043:023
033:053	035:003	036:061	037:118	038:060	039:059	040:059	041:053	043:025
033:055	035:005	036:063	037:125	038:061	039:060	040:061	041:054	043:029
033:056	035:006	036:064	037:126	038:062	039:061	040:062	**Surah 42**	043:030
033:057	035:008	036:066	037:128	038:064	039:062	040:063	042:000	043:031
033:059	035:009	036:069	037:136	038:065	039:063	040:064	042:004	043:032
033:060	035:010	036:070	037:140	038:066	039:065	040:065	042:005	043:033
033:062	035:012	036:071	037:141	038:069	039:067	040:066	042:006	043:035
033:063	035:013	036:075	037:142	038:071	039:068	040:067	042:007	043:036
033:064	035:014	036:079	037:144	038:073	039:069	040:069	042:008	043:037
033:066	035:015	036:080	037:145	038:075	039:070	040:070	042:009	043:038
033:066	035:018	036:081	037:146	038:078	039:071	040:071	042:010	043:040
033:067	035:019	036:083	037:150	038:079	039:072	040:072	042:011	043:043
033:069	035:020	**Surah 37**	037:154	038:081	039:073	040:073	042:012	043:044
033:071	035:021	037:000	037:158	038:084	039:074	040:074	042:013	043:045
033:072	035:024	037:003	037:159	038:087	039:075	040:075	042:014	043:046
033:073	035:025	037:005	037:160	038:088	**Surah 40**	040:076	042:015	043:050
Surah 34	035:026	037:006	037:163	**Surah 39**	040:000	040:077	042:016	043:051
034:000	035:027	037:008	037:164	039:000	040:002	040:078	042:017	043:056
034:001	035:029	037:011	037:170	039:001	040:003	040:081	042:018	043:057
034:002	035:031	037:020	037:177	039:002	040:004	040:082	042:019	043:059
034:003	035:032	037:021	037:180	039:004	040:005	040:084	042:020	043:060
034:006	035:036	037:022	037:181	039:005	040:006	040:085	042:021	043:061
034:007	035:037	037:023	037:182	039:006	040:007	**Surah 41**	042:021	043:063
034:008	035:039	037:025	**Surah 38**	039:007	040:008	041:000	042:022	043:065
034:009	035:040	037:028	038:000	039:008	040:009	041:002	042:023	043:066
034:010	035:041	037:031	038:001	039:009	040:010	041:003	042:024	043:067
034:011	035:042	037:033	038:002	039:010	040:012	041:006	042:025	043:070
034:012	035:043	037:036	038:003	039:012	040:013	041:007	042:026	043:071
034:014	035:044	037:037	038:004	039:013	040:014	041:009	042:027	043:072
034:015	035:045	037:038	038:006	039:015	040:015	041:010	042:028	043:074
034:016	**Surah 36**	037:040	038:007	039:017	040:016	041:011	042:029	043:075
034:017	036:000	037:051	038:008	039:018	040:018	041:012	042:030	043:078
034:018	036:002	037:055	038:009	039:019	040:019	041:013	042:031	043:081
034:021	036:003	037:057	038:010	039:020	040:021	041:014	042:032	043:082
034:022	036:005	037:058	038:012	039:021	040:025	041:015	042:033	043:085
034:023	036:006	037:060	038:013	039:022	040:026	041:016	042:034	043:086
034:024	036:007	037:061	038:013	039:023	040:027	041:017	042:036	043:087
034:026	036:010	037:062	038:014	039:024	040:028	041:019	042:037	043:088
034:027	036:011	037:063	038:016	039:025	040:029	041:020	042:040	**Surah 44**
034:029	036:012	037:064	038:017	039:026	040:030	041:021	042:042	044:000
034:030	036:013	037:065	038:018	039:027	040:031	041:022	042:044	044:002
034:031	036:015	037:068	038:019	039:031	040:034	041:024	042:045	044:007
034:032	036:017	037:069	038:021	039:032	040:035	041:025	042:046	044:008
034:033	036:018	037:071	038:022	039:033	040:036	041:026	042:047	044:010
034:034	036:020	037:073	038:023	039:034	040:037	041:027	042:048	044:011
034:036	036:023	037:074	038:024	039:035	040:038	041:028	042:049	044:012
034:037	036:025	037:075	038:026	039:038	040:039	041:029	042:051	044:013
034:039	036:026	037:076	038:027	039:041	040:040	041:030	042:052	044:015
034:040	036:030	037:079	038:028	039:042	040:041	041:031	042:053	044:016
034:041	036:033	037:082	038:030	039:044	040:042	041:035	**Surah 43**	044:017
034:042	036:035	037:087	038:031	039:045	040:043	041:036	043:000	044:018

044:023	046:019	048:025	051:016	053:020	055:007	056:050	058:016	**Surah 63**
044:024	046:020	048:026	051:017	053:021	055:009	056:051	058:017	063:000
044:025	046:021	048:027	051:018	053:023	055:010	056:052	058:018	063:001
044:030	046:022	048:028	051:019	053:025	055:013	056:056	058:019	063:002
044:032	046:023	048:029	051:020	053:026	055:016	056:057	058:020	063:004
044:037	046:024	**Surah 49**	051:023	053:027	055:017	056:058	058:022	063:005
044:038	046:025	049:000	051:024	053:029	055:018	056:059	**Surah 59**	063:007
044:040	046:026	049:002	051:035	053:031	055:019	056:062	059:000	063:008
044:041	046:027	049:003	051:037	053:032	055:021	056:063	059:001	063:009
044:043	046:028	049:004	051:040	053:035	055:023	056:064	059:002	063:010
044:044	046:029	049:006	051:041	053:036	055:024	056:068	059:003	063:011
044:046	046:030	049:007	051:043	053:038	055:025	056:069	059:005	**Surah 64**
044:047	046:031	049:009	051:044	053:040	055:027	056:071	059:007	064:000
044:048	046:032	049:010	051:046	053:042	055:028	056:072	059:008	064:001
044:051	046:033	049:011	051:047	053:047	055:029	056:073	059:009	064:003
044:056	046:034	049:012	051:048	053:049	055:030	056:074	059:010	064:004
044:057	046:035	049:013	051:052	053:050	055:032	056:080	059:011	064:005
Surah 45	**Surah 47**	049:014	051:053	053:051	055:033	056:083	059:015	064:006
045:000	047:000	049:015	051:054	053:052	055:034	056:084	059:016	064:007
045:002	047:001	049:016	051:055	053:053	055:036	056:087	059:017	064:008
045:003	047:002	049:017	051:059	053:055	055:037	056:090	059:018	064:009
045:004	047:003	049:018	051:060	053:056	055:038	056:091	059:019	064:010
045:005	047:004	**Surah 50**	**Surah 52**	053:057	055:040	056:092	059:020	064:011
045:006	047:006	050:000	052:000	**Surah 54**	055:041	056:095	059:021	064:012
045:008	047:007	050:001	052:001	054:000	055:042	056:096	059:023	064:013
045:011	047:009	050:002	052:004	054:001	055:043	**Surah 57**	059:024	064:015
045:012	047:010	050:004	052:005	054:003	055:044	057:000	**Surah 60**	064:016
045:013	047:011	050:005	052:006	054:005	055:045	057:001	060:000	**Surah 65**
045:014	047:012	050:006	052:007	054:006	055:046	057:002	060:001	065:000
045:015	047:014	050:007	052:009	054:008	055:047	057:003	060:002	065:001
045:016	047:015	050:009	052:010	054:009	055:049	057:004	060:003	065:002
045:017	047:018	050:011	052:011	054:011	055:051	057:005	060:005	065:002
045:018	047:019	050:012	052:013	054:012	055:053	057:006	060:006	065:004
045:019	047:020	050:013	052:014	054:017	055:054	057:007	060:010	065:005
045:021	047:022	050:014	052:016	054:018	055:055	057:008	060:011	065:006
045:022	047:023	050:015	052:017	054:020	055:057	057:009	060:012	065:007
045:026	047:024	050:017	052:018	054:022	055:059	057:010	060:013	065:008
045:027	047:027	050:019	052:021	054:023	055:061	057:012	**Surah 61**	065:009
045:028	047:030	050:020	052:026	054:025	055:063	057:013	061:000	065:010
045:030	047:032	050:024	052:027	054:026	055:065	057:014	061:001	065:011
045:032	047:033	050:029	052:028	054:027	055:067	057:015	061:003	065:012
045:033	047:034	050:030	052:029	054:028	055:069	057:016	061:005	**Surah 66**
045:034	047:035	050:031	052:033	054:031	055:071	057:017	061:006	066:000
045:035	047:036	050:033	052:034	054:032	055:073	057:019	061:008	066:002
045:036	047:038	050:036	052:035	054:033	055:075	057:020	061:009	066:003
045:037	**Surah 48**	050:038	052:036	054:036	055:077	057:021	061:011	066:004
Surah 46	048:000	050:039	052:037	054:038	055:078	057:025	061:012	066:006
046:000	048:002	050:040	052:041	054:040	**Surah 56**	057:027	061:013	066:008
046:002	048:004	050:041	052:043	054:041	056:000	057:029	061:014	066:009
046:003	048:005	050:042	052:044	054:042	056:001	**Surah 58**	**Surah 62**	066:010
046:004	048:006	050:043	052:046	054:043	056:004	058:000	062:000	066:011
046:005	048:007	050:044	052:048	054:046	056:005	058:001	062:001	066:012
046:006	048:010	050:045	052:049	054:047	056:008	058:003	062:002	**Surah 67**
046:007	048:011	**Surah 51**	**Surah 53**	054:048	056:009	058:004	062:004	067:000
046:009	048:012	051:000	053:000	054:050	056:010	058:005	062:005	067:002
046:010	048:014	051:001	053:001	054:051	056:021	058:006	062:006	067:003
046:011	048:016	051:004	053:007	054:054	056:024	058:007	062:007	067:005
046:012	048:017	051:007	053:010	**Surah 55**	056:026	058:008	062:008	067:006
046:014	048:018	051:009	053:011	055:000	056:027	058:009	062:009	067:007
046:015	048:020	051:010	053:014	055:001	056:038	058:010	062:010	067:010
046:016	048:022	051:012	053:015	055:002	056:041	058:011	062:011	067:011
046:017	048:023	051:013	053:016	055:005	056:042	058:012		067:013
046:018	048:024	051:015	053:018	055:006	056:043	058:014		

067:014	069:030	072:014	076:004	**Surah 79**	082:002	086:001	091:004	098:006
067:015	069:031	072:016	076:005	079:000	082:003	086:002	091:005	098:007
067:016	069:032	072:017	076:008	079:001	082:004	086:003	091:006	**Surah 99**
067:019	069:034	072:018	076:009	079:002	082:009	086:007	091:007	099:000
067:020	069:036	072:019	076:010	079:005	082:013	086:009	091:011	099:001
067:021	069:040	072:025	076:011	079:006	082:014	086:011	091:012	099:002
067:023	069:041	072:026	076:013	079:014	082:015	086:012	091:013	099:003
067:024	069:042	072:028	076:014	079:015	082:017	086:013	**Surah 92**	099:006
067:025	069:043	**Surah 73**	076:016	079:016	082:018	086:017	092:000	**Surah 100**
067:026	069:044	073:000	076:023	079:020	082:019	**Surah 87**	092:001	100:000
067:027	069:046	073:004	076:024	079:025	**Surah 83**	087:000	092:002	100:001
067:028	069:048	073:006	076:025	079:027	083:000	087:001	092:003	100:003
067:029	069:050	073:008	076:026	079:030	083:006	087:004	092:004	100:004
067:030	069:052	073:009	076:027	079:032	083:007	087:006	092:006	100:005
Surah 68	**Surah 70**	073:011	076:031	079:034	083:011	087:008	092:007	100:009
068:000	070:000	073:014	**Surah 77**	079:035	083:012	087:009	092:009	**Surah 101**
068:001	070:002	073:016	077:000	079:038	083:013	087:011	092:010	101:000
068:002	070:003	073:018	077:001	079:039	083:014	087:012	092:011	101:001
068:008	070:004	073:020	077:008	079:040	083:015	087:015	092:013	101:002
068:015	070:006	**Surah 74**	077:009	079:041	083:016	087:016	092:016	101:003
068:016	070:008	074:000	077:010	079:042	083:017	087:017	092:020	101:005
068:017	070:009	074:008	077:011	079:043	083:018	087:018	**Surah 93**	**Surah 102**
068:019	070:011	074:011	077:013	079:044	083:022	087:019	093:000	102:000
068:020	070:015	074:025	077:014	079:046	083:024	**Surah 88**	093:001	102:001
068:021	070:016	074:029	077:015	**Surah 80**	083:026	088:000	093:002	102:002
068:022	070:017	074:031	077:016	080:000	083:028	088:001	093:003	102:003
068:024	070:025	074:032	077:021	080:001	083:032	088:004	093:004	102:008
068:025	070:026	074:033	077:023	080:002	083:034	088:005	093:009	**Surah 103**
068:026	070:027	074:034	077:024	080:004	083:036	088:017	093:011	103:000
068:027	070:030	074:035	077:025	080:015	**Surah 84**	088:018	**Surah 94**	103:001
068:028	070:035	074:039	077:026	080:026	084:000	088:019	094:000	103:003
068:033	070:036	074:041	077:028	080:028	084:001	088:020	094:003	**Surah 104**
068:034	070:037	074:044	077:031	080:033	084:002	**Surah 89**	094:004	104:000
068:035	070:038	074:046	077:034	080:037	084:003	089:000	**Surah 95**	104:006
068:036	070:039	074:047	077:037	080:042	084:005	089:001	095:000	104:007
068:039	070:040	074:049	077:040	**Surah 81**	084:006	089:002	095:001	**Surah 105**
068:042	070:043	074:053	077:041	081:000	084:016	089:003	095:002	105:000
068:047	070:044	074:056	077:044	081:001	084:017	089:004	095:004	105:001
068:048	**Surah 71**	**Surah 75**	077:045	081:002	084:018	089:006	095:005	105:005
068:049	071:000	075:000	077:047	081:003	084:020	089:007	095:007	**Surah 106**
068:050	071:001	075:001	077:049	081:004	084:021	089:008	095:008	106:000
068:051	071:004	075:002	**Surah 78**	081:005	084:022	089:009	**Surah 96**	106:001
068:052	071:006	075:004	078:000	081:006	**Surah 85**	089:011	096:000	106:002
Surah 69	071:013	075:005	078:002	081:007	085:000	089:017	096:001	106:003
069:000	071:015	075:006	078:006	081:008	085:001	089:018	096:004	**Surah 107**
069:001	071:016	075:007	078:007	081:010	085:002	089:021	096:008	107:000
069:002	071:017	075:008	078:010	081:011	085:003	089:027	096:011	107:001
069:003	071:018	075:009	078:011	081:012	085:004	**Surah 90**	096:015	107:002
069:004	071:019	075:010	078:012	081:013	085:006	090:000	096:018	107:003
069:005	071:024	075:012	078:014	081:015	085:007	090:003	096:019	107:004
069:006	071:025	075:020	078:017	081:017	085:009	090:010	**Surah 97**	**Surah 108**
069:007	071:026	075:021	078:018	081:018	085:010	090:011	097:000	108:000
069:009	071:028	075:025	078:019	081:019	085:011	090:012	097:001	108:001
069:010	**Surah 72**	075:026	078:020	081:020	085:012	090:013	097:002	**Surah 109**
069:011	072:000	075:028	078:022	081:023	085:013	090:014	097:003	109:000
069:012	072:001	075:030	078:030	081:024	085:014	090:015	097:004	**Surah 110**
069:013	072:002	075:032	078:031	081:025	085:015	090:016	097:005	110:000
069:014	072:003	075:040	078:034	081:027	085:017	090:018	**Surah 98**	110:001
069:015	072:006	**Surah 76**	078:037	081:029	085:018	090:019	098:000	110:002
069:016	072:008	076:000	078:038	**Surah 82**	085:019	**Surah 91**	098:001	110:003
069:017	072:011	076:002	078:039	082:000	**Surah 86**	091:002	098:004	
069:023	072:012	076:003	078:040	082:001	086:000	091:003	098:005	
069:024	072:013							

006:122	007:065	007:164	008:067	009:110	010:078	011:101	012:085	014:037
006:123	007:068	007:165	008:070	009:111	010:080	011:109	012:086	014:039
006:124	007:069	007:166	008:072	009:112	010:084	011:110	012:088	014:044
006:125	007:070	007:167	**Surah 9**	009:113	010:087	011:111	012:090	014:046
006:129	007:072	007:168	009:001	009:114	010:088	011:113	012:093	014:048
006:132	007:073	007:169	009:003	009:115	010:090	011:115	012:096	014:051
006:134	007:074	007:170	009:004	009:117	010:091	011:117	012:100	**Surah 15**
006:136	007:075	007:171	009:006	009:118	010:092	011:118	012:101	015:003
006:137	007:079	007:175	009:007	009:120	010:093	011:120	012:108	015:006
006:138	007:080	007:176	009:012	009:121	010:094	011:121	012:110	015:007
006:139	007:081	007:180	009:013	009:122	010:098	011:123	012:111	015:008
006:142	007:082	007:182	009:014	009:123	010:099	**Surah 12**	**Surah 13**	015:011
006:144	007:085	007:185	009:015	009:125	010:104	012:003	013:004	015:014
006:145	007:086	007:186	009:017	009:128	010:107	012:004	013:006	015:016
006:146	007:087	007:187	009:018	**Surah 10**	010:108	012:005	013:007	015:018
006:148	007:088	007:188	009:019	010:002	010:109	012:006	013:010	015:022
006:150	007:089	007:189	009:024	010:004	**Surah 11**	012:009	013:011	015:024
006:151	007:093	007:190	009:027	010:005	011:002	012:010	013:014	015:028
006:152	007:094	007:191	009:030	010:010	011:003	012:012	013:015	015:031
006:154	007:095	007:193	009:031	010:011	011:004	012:013	013:016	015:033
006:156	007:096	007:194	009:033	010:012	011:007	012:014	013:017	015:039
006:157	007:099	007:195	009:037	010:013	011:008	012:015	013:018	015:044
006:158	007:100	007:196	009:038	010:014	011:010	012:016	013:021	015:048
006:160	007:101	007:197	009:040	010:015	011:012	012:021	013:025	015:058
006:161	007:102	007:198	009:045	010:016	011:013	012:023	013:026	015:059
006:163	007:103	007:199	009:046	010:018	011:014	012:025	013:027	015:062
Surah 7	007:105	007:201	009:047	010:020	011:015	012:026	013:030	015:063
007:002	007:107	007:203	009:048	010:021	011:019	012:030	013:031	015:064
007:006	007:108	007:204	009:051	010:022	011:023	012:031	013:031	015:066
007:008	007:110	007:205	009:054	010:023	011:024	012:032	013:032	015:070
007:011	007:111	007:206	009:055	010:024	011:025	012:033	013:033	015:071
007:013	007:112	**Surah 8**	009:057	010:025	011:028	012:034	013:036	015:072
007:020	007:113	008:006	009:059	010:026	011:029	012:035	013:037	015:079
007:021	007:114	008:007	009:060	010:028	011:031	012:036	013:038	015:084
007:022	007:117	008:008	009:061	010:030	011:033	012:037	013:040	015:088
007:026	007:123	008:010	009:062	010:031	011:034	012:038	013:041	015:092
007:027	007:126	008:011	009:064	010:035	011:036	012:041	**Surah 14**	015:096
007:029	007:127	008:012	009:070	010:038	011:037	012:042	014:001	**Surah 16**
007:030	007:128	008:015	009:072	010:041	011:042	012:042	014:002	016:001
007:033	007:129	008:016	009:074	010:042	011:043	012:043	014:003	016:002
007:034	007:131	008:019	009:077	010:045	011:048	012:046	014:004	016:003
007:035	007:132	008:024	009:079	010:046	011:050	012:050	014:006	016:006
007:036	007:133	008:026	009:081	010:047	011:052	012:051	014:007	016:007
007:037	007:134	008:027	009:083	010:048	011:053	012:052	014:009	016:008
007:039	007:135	008:029	009:085	010:049	011:054	012:054	014:010	016:012
007:040	007:136	008:030	009:086	010:050	011:057	012:056	014:011	016:014
007:042	007:137	008:031	009:087	010:051	011:061	012:060	014:012	016:018
007:043	007:138	008:033	009:089	010:053	011:062	012:061	014:013	016:022
007:044	007:139	008:036	009:090	010:055	011:063	012:062	014:014	016:024
007:045	007:143	008:037	009:091	010:056	011:064	012:063	014:017	016:027
007:046	007:144	008:038	009:092	010:057	011:065	012:065	014:021	016:028
007:047	007:145	008:040	009:093	010:059	011:069	012:065	014:022	016:029
007:048	007:146	008:041	009:094	010:060	011:074	012:066	014:023	016:030
007:050	007:147	008:042	009:095	010:065	011:075	012:068	014:024	016:032
007:051	007:148	008:043	009:097	010:066	011:077	012:069	014:027	016:033
007:052	007:150	008:044	009:099	010:067	011:080	012:073	014:028	016:035
007:053	007:151	008:047	009:100	010:068	011:081	012:074	014:029	016:037
007:056	007:155	008:048	009:101	010:070	011:084	012:075	014:030	016:039
007:057	007:156	008:051	009:105	010:071	011:085	012:076	014:031	016:040
007:058	007:158	008:058	009:106	010:072	011:086	012:077	014:032	016:041
007:059	007:160	008:060	009:107	010:074	011:088	012:080	014:033	016:043
007:062	007:161	008:062	009:108	010:075	011:089	012:081	014:034	016:044
007:063	007:163	008:065	009:109	010:076	011:098	012:083	014:034	016:045

016:046	017:016	017:111	018:100	**Surah 20**	**Surah 21**	022:006	023:075	025:011
016:047	017:017	**Surah 18**	018:101	020:002	021:001	022:009	023:076	025:015
016:048	017:018	018:001	018:105	020:003	021:002	022:010	023:077	025:018
016:049	017:020	018:002	018:107	020:006	021:003	022:011	023:079	025:019
016:052	017:023	018:006	018:109	020:008	021:005	022:014	023:080	025:021
016:054	017:024	018:007	018:110	020:010	021:006	022:015	023:081	025:022
016:055	017:025	018:010	**Surah 19**	020:011	021:007	022:018	023:083	025:023
016:056	017:026	018:012	019:002	020:013	021:009	022:021	023:084	025:029
016:057	017:027	018:013	019:003	020:015	021:012	022:022	023:085	025:031
016:058	017:028	018:014	019:004	020:021	021:013	022:023	023:087	025:032
016:060	017:029	018:016	019:010	020:022	021:014	022:024	023:089	025:033
016:061	017:032	018:017	019:011	020:024	021:017	022:025	023:091	025:034
016:062	017:033	018:017	019:012	020:031	021:018	022:026	023:092	025:036
016:063	017:034	018:019	019:014	020:038	021:019	022:027	023:095	025:039
016:064	017:039	018:020	019:015	020:039	021:022	022:030	023:099	025:040
016:065	017:042	018:021	019:016	020:040	021:025	022:031	023:105	025:042
016:066	017:043	018:023	019:017	020:043	021:026	022:034	023:107	025:049
016:068	017:047	018:024	019:018	020:044	021:031	022:035	023:108	025:050
016:069	017:049	018:027	019:019	020:047	021:032	022:036	023:109	025:051
016:070	017:051	018:028	019:021	020:048	021:034	022:037	023:115	025:052
016:071	017:053	018:029	019:022	020:050	021:035	022:039	**Surah 24**	025:053
016:075	017:054	018:030	019:023	020:053	021:037	022:040	024:003	025:056
016:076	017:055	018:031	019:024	020:057	021:038	022:044	024:004	025:057
016:077	017:056	018:032	019:026	020:058	021:039	022:045	024:011	025:058
016:078	017:057	018:033	019:027	020:061	021:040	022:046	024:013	025:060
016:080	017:059	018:034	019:029	020:063	021:043	022:047	024:015	025:062
016:081	017:061	018:036	019:032	020:065	021:044	022:048	024:016	025:066
016:082	017:062	018:037	019:033	020:066	021:045	022:049	024:018	025:069
016:084	017:064	018:041	019:035	020:070	021:046	022:051	024:019	025:071
016:086	017:067	018:042	019:037	020:072	021:047	022:054	024:024	025:074
016:087	017:068	018:043	019:040	020:073	021:048	022:055	024:028	025:077
016:088	017:069	018:044	019:042	020:074	021:052	022:059	024:029	**Surah 26**
016:089	017:073	018:045	019:043	020:075	021:056	022:060	024:030	026:004
016:090	017:074	018:048	019:045	020:077	021:058	022:064	024:031	026:005
016:092	017:075	018:049	019:047	020:080	021:059	022:065	024:033	026:010
016:093	017:076	018:050	019:048	020:082	021:064	022:066	024:034	026:015
016:094	017:079	018:051	019:052	020:084	021:066	022:067	024:035	026:016
016:097	017:080	018:052	019:054	020:086	021:071	022:071	024:036	026:025
016:102	017:081	018:053	019:055	020:087	021:073	022:072	024:038	026:027
016:103	017:082	018:055	019:057	020:088	021:074	022:073	024:039	026:032
016:106	017:083	018:056	019:058	020:089	021:075	022:076	024:040	026:033
016:110	017:084	018:057	019:061	020:090	021:076	022:078	024:042	026:034
016:113	017:085	018:058	019:063	020:091	021:077	**Surah 23**	024:046	026:035
016:116	017:086	018:060	019:064	020:096	021:079	023:006	024:048	026:036
016:118	017:087	018:062	019:067	020:099	021:080	023:014	024:049	026:037
016:119	017:088	018:063	019:072	020:101	021:081	023:018	024:051	026:041
016:120	017:089	018:066	019:073	020:108	021:083	023:021	024:054	026:042
016:121	017:090	018:067	019:074	020:109	021:084	023:023	024:055	026:043
016:123	017:091	018:070	019:075	020:114	021:086	023:024	024:058	026:050
016:124	017:092	018:071	019:078	020:116	021:087	023:028	024:059	026:051
016:125	017:093	018:077	019:079	020:117	021:088	023:029	024:060	026:053
016:126	017:094	018:078	019:080	020:118	021:089	023:030	024:061	026:061
Surah 17	017:098	018:079	019:081	020:119	021:090	023:032	024:062	026:069
017:001	017:099	018:080	019:083	020:120	021:093	023:038	024:063	026:070
017:002	017:101	018:082	019:084	020:121	021:097	023:040	024:064	026:072
017:005	017:102	018:083	019:085	020:122	021:098	023:044	**Surah 25**	026:077
017:007	017:103	018:084	019:086	020:123	021:105	023:046	025:001	026:081
017:008	017:104	018:086	019:090	020:128	021:108	023:047	025:002	026:089
017:009	017:105	018:087	019:091	020:131	021:109	023:060	025:003	026:090
017:010	017:106	018:090	019:093	020:132	021:111	023:063	025:005	026:091
017:011	017:107	018:097	019:095	020:133	**Surah 22**	023:066	025:007	026:092
017:014	017:108	018:098	019:097	020:134	022:004	023:068	025:009	026:100
017:015	017:110	018:099			022:005	023:073	025:010	026:106

026:107	027:066	028:063	030:010	**Surah 33**	034:038	036:065	038:008	039:049
026:112	027:071	028:064	030:011	033:001	034:039	036:066	038:010	039:050
026:114	027:072	028:065	030:016	033:002	034:040	036:067	038:011	039:054
026:116	027:073	028:066	030:017	033:006	034:041	036:068	038:016	039:055
026:124	027:076	028:068	030:018	033:009	034:042	036:070	038:017	039:059
026:125	027:077	028:070	030:019	033:010	034:043	036:072	038:019	039:063
026:128	027:080	028:071	030:024	033:013	034:044	036:073	038:022	039:064
026:136	027:081	028:072	030:026	033:014	034:045	036:075	038:023	039:065
026:138	027:082	028:074	030:027	033:015	034:046	036:078	038:024	039:067
026:142	027:085	028:076	030:028	033:016	034:047	036:081	038:025	039:068
026:143	027:086	028:077	030:029	033:017	034:050	036:083	038:027	039:070
026:161	027:087	028:078	030:030	033:018	034:053	**Surah 37**	038:030	039:071
026:162	027:091	028:081	030:031	033:019	**Surah 35**	037:011	038:032	039:072
026:166	027:092	028:082	030:033	033:022	035:001	037:014	038:033	039:073
026:177	027:093	028:083	030:034	033:023	035:003	037:019	038:034	039:074
026:178	**Surah 28**	028:084	030:035	033:024	035:004	037:020	038:035	039:075
026:181	028:003	028:085	030:037	033:028	035:006	037:023	038:036	**Surah 40**
026:183	028:005	028:086	030:038	033:030	035:008	037:026	038:040	040:003
026:187	028:006	028:087	030:040	033:031	035:009	037:027	038:041	040:005
026:194	028:007	028:088	030:043	033:033	035:010	037:028	038:042	040:007
026:197	028:008	**Surah 29**	030:047	033:034	035:011	037:031	038:044	040:008
026:198	028:009	029:007	030:052	033:036	035:012	037:045	038:050	040:010
026:199	028:010	029:008	030:053	033:037	035:013	037:046	038:053	040:011
026:200	028:011	029:009	030:055	033:038	035:014	037:050	038:054	040:012
026:202	028:012	029:010	030:056	033:039	035:018	037:052	038:056	040:013
026:204	028:013	029:012	030:057	033:043	035:022	037:054	038:058	040:014
026:206	028:015	029:013	030:058	033:046	035:025	037:056	038:060	040:015
026:215	028:017	029:014	**Surah 31**	033:047	035:030	037:061	038:061	040:018
Surah 27	028:018	029:016	031:003	033:049	035:031	037:068	038:062	040:020
027:004	028:019	029:017	031:006	033:050	035:032	037:075	038:063	040:021
027:007	028:020	029:018	031:007	033:051	035:034	037:077	038:070	040:022
027:008	028:021	029:021	031:009	033:052	035:037	037:078	038:071	040:024
027:011	028:024	029:022	031:012	033:052	035:039	037:079	038:075	040:026
027:012	028:025	029:025	031:013	033:053	035:041	037:085	038:087	040:028
027:013	028:026	029:028	031:014	033:055	035:042	037:091	**Surah 39**	040:029
027:015	028:027	029:031	031:015	033:060	035:044	037:094	039:002	040:031
027:018	028:028	029:033	031:020	033:065	035:045	037:099	039:003	040:033
027:019	028:029	029:034	031:021	033:066	**Surah 36**	037:103	039:004	040:034
027:022	028:030	029:035	031:022	033:067	036:008	037:104	039:005	040:037
027:028	028:032	029:036	031:023	033:072	036:010	037:108	039:006	040:038
027:029	028:034	029:038	031:024	033:073	036:012	037:109	039:007	040:041
027:031	028:035	029:039	031:025	**Surah 34**	036:013	037:113	039:008	040:042
027:033	028:036	029:040	031:026	034:001	036:014	037:117	039:011	040:043
027:035	028:038	029:041	031:027	034:003	036:016	037:118	039:012	040:044
027:036	028:039	029:045	031:029	034:005	036:017	037:119	039:017	040:046
027:037	028:041	029:046	031:032	034:006	036:022	037:120	039:018	040:047
027:037	028:042	029:047	031:033	034:007	036:025	037:124	039:019	040:049
027:038	028:043	029:048	031:034	034:009	036:028	037:129	039:021	040:050
027:039	028:044	029:050	**Surah 32**	034:012	036:030	037:130	039:022	040:052
027:040	028:045	029:051	032:003	034:015	036:031	037:140	039:023	040:053
027:041	028:046	029:053	032:004	034:017	036:034	037:141	039:024	040:054
027:042	028:047	029:054	032:005	034:022	036:036	037:146	039:025	040:056
027:044	028:048	029:057	032:011	034:025	036:039	037:147	039:029	040:060
027:045	028:048	029:058	032:012	034:026	036:040	037:148	039:032	040:061
027:046	028:050	029:061	032:015	034:028	036:043	037:159	039:035	040:063
027:049	028:052	029:062	032:020	034:029	036:044	037:163	039:036	040:064
027:054	028:053	029:063	032:022	034:030	036:046	037:171	039:037	040:065
027:056	028:055	029:065	032:023	034:031	036:047	037:176	039:038	040:066
027:057	028:056	029:066	032:024	034:032	036:048	037:180	039:040	040:068
027:059	028:057	029:069	032:026	034:033	036:049	037:182	039:041	040:073
027:060	028:059	**Surah 30**	032:027	034:034	036:050	**Surah 38**	039:042	040:074
027:061	028:061	030:005	032:029	034:036	036:051	038:004	039:044	040:075
027:062	028:062	030:009		034:037	036:060	038:006	039:048	040:076

040:077	042:046	044:015	**Surah 47**	050:030	**Surah 55**	060:002	**Surah 67**	072:009
040:078	042:047	044:017	047:001	050:031	055:033	060:003	067:004	072:010
040:080	042:048	044:018	047:002	050:033	055:035	060:004	067:005	072:013
040:082	042:049	044:019	047:004	050:043	055:039	060:006	067:008	072:014
040:083	042:051	044:022	047:006	050:045	055:072	060:008	067:009	072:017
040:084	042:052	044:023	047:008	**Surah 51**	**Surah 56**	060:009	067:016	072:019
040:085	042:053	044:024	047:012	051:006	056:001	060:010	067:021	072:021
Surah 41	**Surah 43**	044:034	047:013	051:014	056:004	060:011	067:024	072:022
041:005	043:003	044:050	047:014	051:015	056:005	060:012	067:026	**Surah 73**
041:006	043:007	044:051	047:015	051:023	056:011	060:013	067:027	073:002
041:011	043:009	044:054	047:016	051:026	056:045	**Surah 61**	067:028	073:005
041:012	043:011	**Surah 45**	047:017	051:032	056:047	061:005	**Surah 68**	073:008
041:014	043:013	045:006	047:018	051:033	056:060	061:006	068:008	073:011
041:015	043:014	045:007	047:021	051:038	056:064	061:006	068:015	073:012
041:015	043:015	045:008	047:022	051:042	056:085	061:007	068:017	073:015
041:017	043:016	045:010	047:024	051:051	056:088	061:008	068:021	073:019
041:019	043:017	045:012	047:025	051:052	**Surah 57**	061:010	068:022	073:020
041:020	043:018	045:013	047:026	051:053	057:002	061:012	068:028	**Surah 74**
041:021	043:019	045:014	047:029	051:059	057:004	061:013	068:029	074:011
041:022	043:021	045:015	047:030	051:060	057:005	061:014	068:032	074:012
041:023	043:023	045:016	**Surah 52**	**Surah 52**	057:008	**Surah 62**	068:039	074:013
041:025	043:026	045:017	052:007		057:009	062:002	068:042	074:014
041:026	043:028	045:019	052:011		057:010	062:006	068:043	074:016
041:028	043:029	045:020	052:013		057:011	062:008	068:052	074:019
041:030	043:030	045:025	**Surah 48**	052:014	057:012	062:009	**Surah 69**	074:020
041:033	043:031	045:027	048:002	052:016	057:013	062:011	069:015	074:027
041:036	043:033	045:028	048:004	052:017	057:014	**Surah 63**	069:018	074:028
041:037	043:034	045:029	048:005	052:019	057:015	063:001	069:025	074:031
041:039	043:036	045:030	048:007	052:020	057:016	063:004	069:028	074:036
041:041	043:038	045:031	048:010	052:021	057:017	063:005	069:038	074:037
041:043	043:040	045:032	048:011	052:024	057:018	063:006	069:044	074:045
041:044	043:041	045:033	048:012	052:025	057:024	063:007	**Surah 70**	074:046
041:046	043:043	045:035	048:014	052:027	057:029	063:008	070:001	074:047
041:047	043:044	045:036	048:015	052:032	**Surah 58**	063:010	070:002	074:052
041:048	043:045	**Surah 46**	048:016	052:038	058:001	063:011	070:016	**Surah 75**
041:050	043:046	046:005	048:017	052:044	058:003	**Surah 64**	070:022	075:004
041:051	043:047	046:006	048:018	**Surah 53**	058:004	064:001	070:023	075:005
041:053	043:048	046:007	048:020	053:004	058:005	064:003	070:026	075:015
Surah 42	043:049	046:008	048:025	053:010	058:006	064:006	070:028	075:016
042:003	043:051	046:009	048:026	053:023	058:008	064:009	070:030	075:017
042:004	043:056	046:010	048:028	053:025	058:009	064:010	070:038	075:019
042:007	043:058	046:011	049:002	053:026	058:010	064:012	070:040	075:025
042:008	043:059	046:012	**Surah 49**	053:031	058:011	064:014	070:041	075:026
042:009	043:062	046:015	049:002	053:042	058:012	064:017	070:042	075:027
042:010	043:063	046:016	049:004	053:062	058:014	**Surah 65**	070:043	075:030
042:012	043:065	046:017	049:005	**Surah 54**	058:017	065:002	**Surah 71**	075:033
042:013	043:067	046:019	049:006	054:004	058:018	065:005	071:001	075:034
042:014	043:069	046:020	049:007	054:006	058:022	065:006	071:002	075:035
042:015	043:071	046:022	049:011	054:012	**Surah 59**	065:007	071:005	075:040
042:018	043:074	046:023	049:012	054:014	059:002	065:008	071:007	**Surah 76**
042:019	043:076	046:024	049:014	054:017	059:006	065:010	071:008	076:002
042:020	043:077	046:025	049:017	054:022	059:007	065:011	071:009	076:005
042:023	043:078	046:026	**Surah 50**	054:025	059:008	**Surah 66**	071:011	076:014
042:026	043:080	046:027	050:002	054:028	059:009	066:001	071:023	076:016
042:027	043:081	046:028	050:005	054:029	059:011	066:003	071:024	076:017
042:029	043:082	046:029	050:008	054:032	059:016	066:004	071:025	076:021
042:030	043:083	046:030	050:011	054:037	059:018	066:005	071:028	076:023
042:031	043:085	046:031	050:016	054:040	059:021	066:008	**Surah 72**	076:024
042:034	043:086	046:032	050:017	054:041	059:023	066:010	072:001	076:026
042:038	**Surah 44**	046:033	050:019	054:045	059:024	066:011	072:002	076:027
042:041	044:003	046:034	050:021	054:054	**Surah 60**	066:012	072:004	076:029
042:044	044:008	046:035	050:029		060:001		072:007	076:031
042:045	044:013							

Surah 77	082:019	Surah 94
077:001	**Surah 83**	094:008
077:007	083:001	**Surah 95**
077:010	083:002	095:005
077:011	083:003	**Surah 96**
077:014	083:008	096:008
077:015	083:010	096:010
077:019	083:013	096:017
077:023	083:017	096:018
077:024	083:019	096:019
077:025	083:021	**Surah 97**
077:028	083:028	097:002
077:029	083:029	**Surah 98**
077:030	083:030	098:001
077:034	083:031	098:004
077:035	**Surah 84**	098:005
077:036	084:002	098:005
077:037	084:009	098:006
077:040	084:014	**Surah 99**
077:041	084:016	099:001
077:043	084:019	099:006
077:045	084:021	**Surah 100**
077:047	084:024	100:006
077:048	084:025	100:007
077:049	**Surah 85**	100:011
Surah 78	085:004	**Surah 101**
078:004	085:009	101:003
078:005	**Surah 86**	101:010
078:027	086:002	**Surah 102**
078:034	086:008	102:005
078:037	086:017	**Surah 104**
078:039	**Surah 87**	104:001
Surah 79	087:008	104:004
079:005	**Surah 88**	104:005
079:010	088:005	104:006
079:014	088:021	104:007
079:016	088:022	**Surah 107**
079:017	088:025	107:001
079:018	088:026	107:004
079:019	**Surah 89**	107:006
079:027	089:018	107:007
079:030	089:021	**Surah 108**
Surah 80	089:023	108:001
080:002	089:027	108:002
080:005	089:028	**Surah 109**
080:006	**Surah 90**	109:004
080:007	090:012	109:006
080:008	090:015	**Surah 111**
080:017	090:016	111:002
080:021	**Surah 91**	
080:037	091:007	
Surah 81	091:008	
081:012	091:013	
081:015	**Surah 92**	
081:027	092:006	
081:028	092:007	
Surah 82	092:009	
082:003	092:010	
082:010	092:012	
082:016	092:016	
082:017	092:017	
082:018	092:020	